Comment utiliser le dictionnaire

vogue; **out of f.,** passé de mode; démodé; **in the** f., à la dernière mode; **to set the f.,** (i) faire écc fixer, mener, la mode; **to become the f., come** devenir la mode; **it's all the f.,** c'est la grande *Com:* **f. house,** maison *f* de haute couture; f présentation *f* de collections; **f. magazine,** jou de modes.

fashion² *v.tr.* (*a*) façonner, former; confectionner (une robe, etc.); (*b*) **fully fashioned,** (entièrement) diminué, proportionné.

fashionable ['fæʃ(ə)nəbl] *a.* à la mode, en vogue; **blue is very f. this year,** le bleu se porte beaucoup cette année. **-ably** *adv.* (habillé) à la mode.

fast¹ [fɑːst] *n.* jeûne *m*; *Ecc:* **f. day,** jour *m* de jeûne; **to break one's f.,** rompre le jeûne.

fast² *v.i.* (*a*) jeûner; (*b*) *Med:* être à la diète. **fasting** *n.* (*a*) jeûne *m*; (*b*) *Med:* diète (absolue).

fast³ **I.** *a.* **1.** (*a*) (*of stake, etc.*) ferme, fixe, solide; (*of grip, etc.*) tenace; *Nau: etc:* **to make a rope f.,** amarrer un cordage; (*b*) *Nau:* **to make f. (to a buoy),** prendre le corps-mort; **to make f. (alongside),** s'amarrer; (*c*) (*of door, lid, etc.*) bien fermé; (*d*) (*of colour*) solide, résistant; **these colours are not f.,** ces couleurs ne résistent pas. **2.** (*a*) rapide; **you're a f. walker,** vous marchez vite; *Rail:* **f. train,** rapide *m;* express *m*; (*b*) *Games:* (billard, court) qui rend bien; (*c*) *Phot:* (pellicule) rapide; (*d*) *F:* **he pulled a f. one on me,** il m'a joué un mauvais tour. **3.** (*of clock, watch*) en avance; **my watch is five minutes f.,** ma montre avance de cinq minutes. **4.** *F: O:* (*of pers.*) (trop) émancipé; **to lead a f. life,** mener une vie dissolue. **II.** *adv.* **1.** ferme, solidement; **to hold f.,** tenir ferme; tenir bon; **to stand f.,** tenir bon; ne pas bouger; **to stick f.,** (i) bien tenir; (ii) rester pris, rester collé; *Tex:* **f. dyed,** grand teint *inv*; **to be f. asleep,** dormir d'un profond sommeil; *F:* **to play f. and loose,** jouer double jeu (**with s.o.,** avec qn). **2.** vite, rapidement; **to run f.,** courir vite; **not so f.!** pas si vite! doucement! **bad news travels f.,** les mauvaises nouvelles courent vite.

fastback ['fɑːstbæk] *a.* & *n. Aut:* (à) arrière profilé.

fasten ['fɑːs(ə)n] **1.** *v.tr.* (*a*) (*attach*) attacher (**to, on,** à); **to f. papers together with a clip,** attacher des papiers (ensemble) avec une agrafe; **to f. one's eyes on s.o.,** fixer le regard sur qn; (*b*) (*hold securely*) fixer, assurer; **to f. a door with a bolt,** fermer une porte au verrou. **2.** *v.i.* s'attacher, se fixer; (*a*) (*with passive force*) (*of garment*) s'agrafer, se boutonner (*at the back,* par derrière); (*of door, etc.*) se fermer; **door that fastens with a bolt,** porte qui se ferme au verrou; (*b*) **the crab fastened on to his leg,** le crabe s'accrocha à sa jambe. **fasten down** *v.tr.* fixer (qch.) à terre ou en place. **fastening** *n.* **1.** action *f* d'attacher; fixage *m*, fixation *f* (de qch. sur qch.); (*with bolts*) boulonnage *m*; agrafage *m* (d'un vêtement). **2.** (*a*) = FASTENER; (*b*) **fastenings,** attaches *fpl.* **fasten up** *v.tr.* agrafer, boutonner (sa robe, etc.).

fastener ['fɑːsnər] *n.* **1.** attache *f*; (*of garment*) agrafe *f*; (*of purse*) fermoir *m*; (*of window, etc.*) fermeture *f*; (*of French window*) espagnolette *f*; **zip f.,** fermeture à glissière, *R.t.m:* fermeture éclair; **snap f.,** bouton (fermoir) à pression.

fastidious [fæ'stidiəs] *a.* difficile, délicat (**about sth.,** sur qch.); **to be f.,** être difficile à contenter; faire le difficile. **-ly** *adv.* avec une délicatesse exagérée.

fastidiousness [fæs'tidiəsnis] *n.* goût *m* difficile.

fast-moving ['fɑːst'muːviŋ] *a.* rapide.

fastness ['fɑːstnis] *n.* (*a*) solidité *f* (d'une couleur, etc.); (*b*) rapidité *f*, vitesse *f*; (*c*) **mountain f.,** repaire *m* (de brigands).

fat¹ [fæt] *a.* (**fatter; fattest**) **1.** (*a*) (*of pers.*) gros, *f.* grosse; gras, *f.* grasse; corpulent; (*of meat*) gras; (*of tissue*) adipeux; **to get f.,** engraisser; **to grow f. at**

headword in bold sans serif	
superior numbers to distinguish between parts of speech	chiffres supérieurs distinguant les catégories grammaticales
main division **I.** adjective	division principale **I.** pour l'adjectif
subdivision **1., 2., 3.** etc. showing different uses of adjective second subdivision (*a*), (*b*), (*c*) etc. showing further uses of adjective	subdivision **1., 2., 3.** etc. montrant les différents usages de l'adjectif seconde subdivision (*a*), (*b*), (*c*) etc. montrant d'autres usages de l'adjectif
obsolescent word or expression	emploi vieilli
main division **II.** adverb	division principale **II.** pour l'adverbe
colloquial or idiomatic expression	expression familière ou idiomatique
phonetics in IPA	transcription phonétique selon l'API
transitive verb	verbe transitif
intransitive verb	verbe intransitif
compound verb in sans serif	verbe à particule en Linéales grasses
derivative in sans serif	dérivé en Linéales grasses
cross reference	renvoi
explanations in italics	gloses en italiques
comparative and superlative of adjective	comparatif et superlatif de l'adjectif

HARRAP'S

SHORTER

French-English

DICTIONARY

DICTIONNAIRE

Anglais-Français

HARRAP'S
SHORTER
French-English
DICTIONARY
DICTIONNAIRE
Anglais-Français

Edited by

Peter Collin
Helen Knox
Margaret Ledésert
René Ledésert

HARRAP

First published in Great Britain 1982
by Harrap Limited
19–23 Ludgate Hill, London EC4M 7PD

ISBN 0 245–53926–3

Reprinted 1984, 1985 (with corrections), 1986
Printed in new format 1987
Reprinted 1987 (twice)

Photoset on Monotype Lasercomp
by Richard Clay (The Chaucer Press) Limited,
Bungay, Suffolk, England.
Printed in Great Britain
at The Bath Press, Avon

Dépôt légal, 2e trimestre, 1982
Bibliothèque nationale du Québec

Preface

This dictionary is an entirely new work – a condensed version of *Harrap's New Standard French and English Dictionary* with a certain number of modifications and additions to bring the text fully up to date.

Content

The selection of the material to be included was no easy task. A dictionary such as this must be geared to meet the needs of the student, the translator, the businessman, the traveller and the general reader. While highly specialized scientific and technical terms are not required in a dictionary of this scope, those widely used, in particular those which appear frequently in the media, have been listed. A large range of colloquialisms has been included, together with a reasonable selection of widely used slang.

French is the language not only of France but also of parts of Canada, Belgium and Switzerland, so words and expressions used in these countries are listed and marked *Fr.C:*, *Belg:* and *Sw.Fr:* respectively. As far as the English word list is concerned, words and expressions used in North America, Australia and New Zealand have been included. For Americanisms, a distinction is made between usage in North America generally (*NAm:*) and that confined to the United States (*U.S:*) or to Canada (*Can:*). American orthography differs in some respects from that used in the British Isles, and a new feature of this dictionary is the inclusion of alternative spellings in the main text rather than referring the user to the preface for a list of the major differences.

Layout

The section **'How to use the dictionary'** gives a detailed guide to the layout (see endpapers).

In the longer articles subdivisions are used to distinguish between the different meanings or functions of a word. The major divisions **I.**, **II.**, etc. indicate different parts of speech, e.g. adjective (*a.*), noun (*n.*), adverb (*adv.*), or the transitive (*v.tr.*) or intransitive (*v.i.*) use of a verb; **1.**, **2.**, etc. and (*a*), (*b*), etc. are used mainly to show the different meanings of a word, **1.** and **2.** a greater difference than that implied by (*a*) and (*b*), though in shorter articles. **1.** and **2.** divide transitive uses of a verb; and the principal use of (i) and (ii) is to separate two distinct meanings of an idiomatic phrase.

The principal parts of irregular verbs are given after the infinitive. Irregular plural or feminine forms of nouns and French adjectives are also shown, as is the gender of French nouns.

Owing to the different systems of administration, etc. in the different countries, it is not always possible to give true translations for functions or offices. In such cases the sign = has been used to indicate the nearest equivalent.

In order to keep the work within a reasonable compass, a number of space-saving devices have been adopted. When in an example a word is used in exactly the same form as the headword it is represented by the initial letter, though plural nouns or verb conjugations in which the form differs from the infinitive are written in full. In the English–French part, derivative adverbs are listed under the adjective, and compound verbs (e.g. **to come down**) and participial adjectives or nouns under the verb.

Economies have also been made by the reduction in the number of words deriving from prefixes such as **auto-**, **anti-**, **psycho-**, **sub-**, etc. A broad representative selection has been made of those most widely used and those which present difficulties in translation. Moreover, most proper names do not appear if the English and French forms are identical, unless they are used attributively or appear in some idiomatic phrase or traditional saying.

In English there are no definite rules for the use of the hyphen; we have used it only when its absence would cause ambiguity or would be confusing or unpleasing to the eye because of the juxtaposition of two vowels or two consonants, e.g. **de-icing, book-keeping**. Many dictionaries include long lists of 'two-word headwords'; many of these cannot really be considered as words in their own right, and have been listed mainly under the first element.

Phonetics

The phonetics of each headword are given, using the symbols of the International Phonetic Association. It should, however, be emphasized that this is not primarily a phonetic dictionary and that the phonetics are intended merely as a general guide to the pronunciation used by cultured people in English or French. For English, received pronunciation (RP) has been taken as the norm; this is generally described as the English of Southern England, though it would perhaps be more accurate to call it the English of the speaker who has no particular regional inflexions, an English that is readily understood everywhere, even though it sounds foreign, partly because of variations of rhythm, to an American. American pronunciations have been given alongside the British where there is a marked difference (e.g. **tomato** *Eng.* [tə'mɑːtou], *NAm:* [tə'meitou]); but it would be impossible to list the various shades of pronunciation and length of vowel sounds. One outstanding example: the vowel sound in words such as **glass** or **castle** is generally intermediate between [ɑː] and [æ], nearing [ɑː] in Southern England and [æ] in Northern England, Scotland and North America; in this dictionary it is transcribed [ɑː] throughout.

Editorial methods

The compilation of the manuscript was undertaken by a team of eight, working to pre-determined criteria. The text was checked letter by letter by one of the editorial team to ensure accuracy and reasonable uniformity in layout and style. The manuscript was then sent letter by letter to the printers, who supplied us with galley proofs, which were read by several proof readers, the corrections collated, each letter checked for inconsistencies and the galleys returned to the printers for setting in page. We would like to thank them for the extremely efficient way in which they coped with an often difficult manuscript.

The work of the present team would not have been possible without the efforts of those who preceded it. We naturally owe a great debt to the author of the original *Harrap's Standard French and English Dictionary,* the late J. E. Mansion, and all those who worked with him. Two of them, H. R. Elphick and his wife Flora, are still working with us, giving continuity through their personal experience of the principles underlying the conception of the original work. Then there is the large number of helpers, working both in the Harrap offices and outside, who since 1946 have contributed to the research work for *Harrap's New Standard French and English Dictionary*. They are too numerous to mention individually, but without their research the production of this dictionary could not have been achieved.

The Editors
London, 1982

Préface

Ce dictionnaire est complètement nouveau: c'est un abrégé du *Harrap's New Standard French and English Dictionary* présenté avec un certain nombre de modifications et d'additions afin de le mettre à jour.

Contenu

Choisir ce qu'il fallait conserver et ce qu'il fallait omettre n'a pas été facile, car un dictionnaire de cette importance doit satisfaire aux besoins de l'étudiant, du traducteur, de l'homme d'affaires, du voyageur et de tous ceux qui lisent des romans, des revues ou des journaux dans une langue étrangère. Les mots scientifiques ou techniques utilisés uniquement par des spécialistes n'ont pas droit de cité, mais il faut garder ceux qui appartiennent à la langue de tous les jours, surtout ceux que le public connaît par la télévision ou la presse. Il faut également y mettre des mots familiers et des idiotismes, aussi bien qu'un choix de mots et d'expressions argotiques d'usage courant.

Le français est la langue maternelle non seulement des Français mais aussi des habitants de certaines parties du Canada, de la Belgique et de la Suisse; nous avons donc mis dans ce dictionnaire des mots et des expressions employés dans ces pays en les marquant *Fr.C:*, *Belg:* et *Sw.Fr:* selon le cas. L'anglais, langue principale des Îles Britanniques, de l'Amérique de Nord, de l'Australie et de la Nouvelle-Zélande, présente des complications supplémentaires; il n'est pas difficile de signaler par *Austr:* et *N.Z:* les expressions australiennes ou néo-zélandaises mais, pour l'Amérique du Nord, il faut distinguer entre les mots utilisés partout dans le continent (*NAm:*) et ceux qu'on rencontre seulement aux États-Unis (*U.S:*) ou seulement au Canada (*Can:*). En outre, nous avons indiqué dans le texte même du dictionnaire les différences orthographiques entre l'anglais britannique et l'anglais américain.

Disposition typographique

La rubrique **'Comment utiliser le dictionnaire'** (voir pages de garde) donne une explication détaillée de la disposition typographique.

Dans les articles plus importants des sous-titres **I.**, **II.**, etc. séparent les différents sens ou fonctions grammaticales d'un mot, ou indiquent les différentes parties du discours, par exemple adjectif (*a.*), nom commun (*n.*), adverbe (*adv.*), ou encore séparent un verbe transitif (*v.tr.*) d'un verbe intransitif (*v.i.*); les différences importantes du sens ou de l'usage d'un mot sont indiquées par les numéros **1.**, **2.**, etc., tandis que (*a*), (*b*), etc. montrent des différences moindres; et (i), (ii), etc. marquent les différents sens d'une locution.

La conjugaison des verbes irréguliers, les pluriels irréguliers et les formes féminines irrégulières des adjectifs français sont tous indiqués.

Étant données les différences dans les structures administratives et autres de différents pays, il n'est pas toujours possible de traduire exactement les diverses charges, fonctions, etc. Dans de tels cas, le signe = a été utilisé pour indiquer l'équivalent le plus proche.

Le but de tout lexicographe est de présenter un nombre maximum de mots et d'expressions sans accroître démesurément le volume de son dictionnaire. À cette fin nous avons représenté les mots-clefs dans les articles par leur lettre initiale lorsque leur orthographe ne comporte pas de variantes. Dans la partie anglais-français les adverbes suivent l'adjectif dont ils dérivent et les verbes sont suivis par les verbes à postposition (*p.ex.* **to come down**) et par les formes participiales du verbe simple (*p.ex.* **coming**).

Nous avons également limité la liste des mots qui dérivent des préfixes tels que **auto-**, **anti-**, **psycho-**, **sous-**, etc., en citant seulement ceux qui sont le plus fréquemment utilisés et ceux dont la traduction présente des difficultés. De plus, dans la plupart des cas, un nom propre dont l'orthographe est exactement la même en français et en anglais ne paraît que quand il s'emploie comme attributif ou dans une locution.

Il n'existe pas en anglais de règle absolue pour l'emploi du trait d'union: nous l'avons donc employé seulement quand son absence pouvait mener à l'ambiguïté, ce qui est le cas pour certains adjectifs, *p.ex.* **a white-coated man**, **a little-used car** (qui est une voiture qui a peu roulé, tandis que **a little used car** est une petite voiture qui a fait déjà beaucoup de kilomètres); ou bien pour éviter la juxtaposition de deux voyelles ou de deux consonnes, *p.ex.* **de-icing**, **book-keeping**. Dans certains dictionnaires anglais-anglais on trouve des séries de mots-clefs composés de deux mots avec ou sans trait d'union (*p.ex.* **two-seater**, **rock bottom**); quand nous considérons qu'ils ne constituent pas de vrais mots nous les avons classés sous le mot-clef qui forme leur premier élément, là où ils sont employés dans un sens attributif.

Phonétique

Quoique cet ouvrage ne soit pas un dictionnaire de phonétique, nous avons donné la notation phonétique de chaque mot-clef selon les principes de *l'Association phonétique internationale*, dans l'intention de fournir un guide général à la prononciation de l'homme cultivé qui, en parlant, ne trahit pas ses origines régionales. Comme la notation phonétique des mots anglais est destinée principalement à ceux dont la langue maternelle n'est pas l'anglais, nous avons donné la prononciation soignée du mot, car son usage ne peut jamais constituer une faute véritable. Mais il ne faut toutefois pas oublier qu'un mot prononcé séparément ne peut pas tenir compte du rythme de la phrase qui est très important en anglais et qui parfois constitue une différence entre l'anglais britannique et l'anglais américain. Quand il y a une vraie différence entre l'usage britannique et l'usage américain, nous avons donné les deux prononciations (*p.ex.* **tomato** *Eng.* [tə'mɑːtou], *NAm:* [tə'meitou]). Mais, surtout en ce qui concerne les voyelles, il y a de légères différences de prononciation qui indiquent des différences régionales ou de milieu; il faut donc comprendre que certains symboles peuvent varier dans leur prononciation. Par exemple, dans des mots tels que **glass** ou **castle**, la prononciation est généralement intermédiaire entre [ɑː] et [æ], plus près de [ɑː] dans l'Angleterre du

Sud, approchant [æ] dans l'Angleterre du Nord, l'Écosse et l'Amérique; pour ce dictionnaire nous avons choisi [ɑː].

Méthodes de travail

Le manuscrit a été préparé par une équipe de huit rédacteurs. Avant de l'envoyer chez l'imprimeur, le texte a été relu, lettre par lettre, afin d'arriver à un maximum d'exactitude et d'uniformité. Plusieurs lecteurs ont corrigé les épreuves en placard qui ont été ensuite mises en page. Nous remercions tous ceux qui ont d'une manière si efficace contribué à l'impression d'un manuscrit parfois difficile à suivre.

Nous n'aurions pas pu accomplir cette tâche sans le travail de ceux qui nous ont précédé, surtout de feu J. E. Mansion, auteur du premier *Harrap's Standard French and English Dictionary*, et de tous ses collaborateurs. Nous sommes particulièrement heureux d'avoir comme membres de notre équipe actuelle Monsieur et Madame H. R. Elphick, qui l'un et l'autre ont travaillé à la compilation du dictionnaire original; leur connaissance personnelle des méthodes utilisées dans cet ouvrage a été un apport précieux. Nous remercions également tous les collaborateurs qui, travaillant dans les bureaux de la maison Harrap et ailleurs ont, depuis 1946, contribué par leurs recherches à la compilation du *Harrap's New Standard French and English Dictionary*. Ils sont trop nombreux pour en citer les noms, mais sans leur collaboration ce dictionnaire-ci n'aurait jamais vu le jour.

Les rédacteurs
Londres, 1982

Abbreviations used in the dictionary

Abréviations utilisées dans le dictionnaire

A:	*archaism; ancient; in former use*	désuet
a., adj.	*adjective*	adjectif
abbr.	*abbreviation*	abréviation
abs.	*absolutely; absolute use*	emploi absolu
Ac:	*acoustics*	acoustique
acc.	*accusative*	accusatif
Adm:	*administration; civil service*	administration
adv.	*adverb*	adverbe
adv.phr.	*adverbial phrase*	locution adverbiale
Aer:	*aeronautics*	aéronautique
Agr:	*agriculture*	agriculture
A.Hist:	*ancient history*	histoire ancienne
Algae:	*algae*	algues
Amph:	*Amphibia*	amphibiens
Anat:	*anatomy*	anatomie
Ann:	*Annelida, worms*	annelés
Ant:	*antiquity, antiquities*	antiquité
Anthr:	*anthropology*	anthropologie
Ap:	*apiculture*	apiculture
approx.	*approximately*	sens approché
Arach:	*Arachnida*	arachnides
Arb:	*arboriculture*	arboriculture; sylviculture
Arch:	*architecture*	architecture
Archeol:	*archaeology*	archéologie
Arms:	*arms; armaments*	armes; armements
Art:	*art*	beaux-arts
Artil:	*artillery*	artillerie
Astr:	*astronomy*	astronomie
Astrol:	*astrology*	astrologie
Atom.Ph:	*atomic, nuclear, physics*	sciences atomiques
attrib.	*attributive*	attributif
Austr:	*Australia; Australian(ism)*	Australie; australien; expression australienne
Aut:	*motoring; automobile industry*	automobilisme; industrie automobile
aux:	*auxiliary*	auxiliaire
Av:	*aviation; aircraft*	aviation; avions
B:	*Bible; biblical*	Bible; biblique
Bac:	*bacteriology*	bactériologie
Bak:	*baking*	boulangerie
Ball:	*ballistics*	ballistique
Bank:	*banking*	opérations de banque
Belg:	*Belgium; Belgian*	Belgique; belge
B.Hist:	*Bible history*	histoire sainte
Bib:	*bibliography*	bibliographie

Bill:	*billiards*	jeu de billard
Bio-Ch:	*biochemistry*	biochimie
Biol:	*biology*	biologie
Bookb:	*bookbinding*	reliure
Book-k:	*book-keeping*	comptabilité
Bootm:	*boot and shoe industry*	cordonnerie; industrie de la chaussure
Bot:	*botany*	botanique
Box:	*boxing*	boxe
Breed:	*breeding*	élevage
Brew:	*brewing*	brasserie
Brickm:	*brickmaking*	briqueterie
Can:	*Canada, Canadian(ism)*	Canada; canadien; expression canadienne
Cards:	*card games*	jeux de cartes
Carp:	*carpentry*	charpenterie; menuiserie du bâtiment
Cer:	*ceramics*	céramique
cf.	*refer to*	conferatur
Ch:	*chemistry*	chimie
Chess:	*chess*	jeu d'échecs
Ch. of Eng:	*Church of England*	Église anglicane
Cin:	*cinema*	cinéma
Civ.E:	*civil engineering*	génie civil
Clockm:	*clock and watch making*	horlogerie
Cmptr:	*computers; data processing*	ordinateurs; informatique
Coel:	*Coelenterata*	cœlentérés
cogn.acc.	*cognate accusative*	accusatif de l'objet interne
coll.	*collective*	collectif
Com:	*commerce; business term*	(terme du) commerce
comb.fm.	*combining form*	forme de combinaison
Comest:	*comestibles, food*	comestibles
comp.	*comparative*	comparatif
Conch:	*conchology*	conchyliologie
conj.	*conjunction*	conjonction
Const:	*construction, building industry*	industrie du bâtiment
Coop:	*cooperage*	tonnellerie
Corr:	*correspondence, letters*	correspondance, lettres
Cost:	*costume; clothing*	costume; habillement
cp.	*compare*	comparer
Cr:	*cricket*	cricket
Crust:	*Crustacea*	crustacés
Cryst:	*crystallography*	cristallographie
Cu:	*cullinary; cooking*	cullinaire; cuisine

Cust:	*customs*	douane
Cy:	*bicycles; cycling*	bicyclettes; cyclisme
Danc:	*dancing*	danse
dat.	*dative*	datif
def.	(i) *definite;* (ii) *defective* (*verb*)	(i) défini; (ii) (verbe) défectif
dem.	*demonstrative*	démonstratif
Dent:	*dentistry*	art dentaire
Dial:	*dialectal*	dialectal
dim.	*diminutive*	diminutif
Dipl:	*diplomacy; diplomatic*	diplomatie; diplomatique
Dist:	*distilling*	distillation
Dom.Ec:	*domestic economy: household equipment*	économie domestique; ménage
Draw:	*drawing*	dessin
Dressm:	*dressmaking*	couture (mode)
Dy:	*dyeing*	teinture
E.	*east*	est
Ecc:	*ecclesiastical*	église et clergé
Echin:	*Echinodermata*	échinodermes
e.g.	*for example*	par exemple
El:	*electricity: electrical engineering*	électricité; électrique; électrotechnique
Elcs:	*electronics*	électronique
Eng.	*England; English*	Angleterre; anglais, britannique
Engr:	*engraving*	gravure
Ent:	*entomology*	entomologie
Equit:	*equitation*	équitation
esp.	*especially*	surtout
etc.	*et cetera*	et cætera
Eth:	*ethics*	morale
Ethn:	*ethnology*	ethnologie
Exp:	*explosives*	explosifs
f.	*feminine*	féminin
F:	*colloquial*(*ism*)	familier; style de la conversation
Farr:	*farriery*	maréchalerie
Fb:	(*Association*) *football*	football
Fenc:	*fencing*	escrime
Fig:	*figurative*	sens figuré
Fin:	*finance*	finances
Fish:	*fishing*	pêche
For:	*forestry*	forêts
Fort:	*fortification*	fortification
Fr.	*France; French*	France; français
Fr.C:	*French Canadian*	canadien français
Fung:	*fungi*	champignons
Furn:	*furniture*	mobilier
Games:	*games*	jeux
Gasm:	*gasmaking*	industrie du gaz
Geog:	*geography*	géographie
Geol:	*geology*	géologie
Glassm:	*glassmaking*	verrerie
Golf:	*golf*	golf
Gr.	*Greek*	grec
Gr.Ant:	*Greek antiquity*	antiquité grecque
Gr.Civ:	*Greek civilization*	civilisation grecque
Gram:	*grammar*	grammaire
Gym:	*gymnastics*	gymnastique
Hairdr:	*hairdressing*	coiffure
Harn:	*harness; saddlery*	sellerie; harnais
Her:	*heraldry*	blason
Hist:	*history; historical*	histoire; historique
Hort:	*horticulture*	horticulture
Hum:	*humorous*	humoristique
Husb:	*animal husbandry*	élevage
Hyd.E:	*hydraulic engineering*	hydromécanique
Hyg:	*hygiene; sanitation*	hygiène; installations sanitaires
I.C.E:	*internal combustion engines*	moteurs à combustion interne
Ich:	*ichthyology; fish*	ichtyologie; poissons
imp.	*imperative*	impératif
impf.	*imperfect tense*	imparfait
impers.	*impersonal*	impersonnel
ind.	*indicative*	indicatif
Ind:	*industry; industrial*	industrie; industriel
indef.	*indefinite*	indéfini
ind.tr.	*indirectly transitive*	transitif avec régime indirect
inf.	*infinitive*	infinitif
Ins:	*insurance*	assurance
int.	*interjection*	interjection
interr.	*interrogative*	interrogatif
inv.	*invariable*	invariable
Iron:	*ironic*(*ally*)	ironique(ment)
Jew:	*Jewish*	juif, juive
Jewel:	*jewellery*	bijouterie
Join:	*joinery*	menuiserie
Journ:	*journalism; journalistic*	journalisme; style journalistique
Jur:	*jurisprudence; legal term*	droit; terme de palais
Knit:	*knitting*	tricot
Lacem:	*lacemaking*	dentellerie
Lap:	*lapidary arts*	arts lapidaires; taillerie
Laund:	*laundering*	blanchissage
Leath:	*leatherwork*	travail du cuir
Ling:	*linguistics; language*	linguistique; langue
Lit:	*literary use; literature; literary*	forme littéraire; littérature; littéraire
Lith:	*lithography*	lithographie
Locksm:	*locksmithery*	serrurerie
Log:	*logic*	logique
Lt.	*Latin*	latin
m.	*masculine*	masculin
Magn:	*magnetism*	magnétisme
Mapm:	*mapmaking*	cartographie
Mch:	*machines; machinery*	machines; machines à vapeur
Mch.Tls:	*machine tools*	machines-outils
Meas:	*weights and measures*	poids et mesures
Mec:	*mechanics*	mécanique
Mec.E:	*mechanical engineering*	industries mécaniques
Med:	*medicine; illnesses; medical*	médecine; maladies; médical
Metall:	*metallurgy*	métallurgie
Metalw:	*metalworking*	travail des métaux

Meteor:	*meteorology*	météorologie
Mil:	*military; army*	militaire; armée de terre
Mill:	*milling*	meunerie
Min:	*mining and quarrying*	exploitation des mines et carrières
Miner:	*mineralogy*	minéralogie
M.Ins:	*marine insurance*	assurance maritime
Moll:	*molluscs*	mollusques
Moss:	*mosses and lichens*	muscinées
Mount:	*mountaineering*	alpinisme
Mth:	*mathematics*	mathématiques
Mus:	*music*	musique
Myr:	*Myriapoda*	myriapodes
Myth:	*mythology*	mythologie
n.	*noun*	nom commun
N.	*north*	nord
NAm:	*North American*	de l'Amérique du Nord
N.Arch:	*naval architecture*	architecture navale
Nat.Hist:	*natural history*	histoire naturelle
Nau:	*nautical*	terme de marine
Nav:	*navigation*	navigation
Navy:	*Navy*	marine militaire
Needlew:	*needlework*	couture (travaux d'aiguille)
neg.	*negative*	négatif
Num:	*numismatics*	numismatique
num.a.	*numeral adjective*	adjectif numéral
N.Z:	*New Zealand*	(de la) Nouvelle-Zélande
O:	*obsolescent*	vieilli
Obst:	*obstetrics*	obstétrique
Oc:	*oceanography*	océanographie
occ.	*occasionally*	parfois
onomat.	*onomatopoeia*	onomatopée
Opt:	*optics*	optique
Orn:	*ornithology; birds*	ornithologie; oiseaux
p.	(i) *past;* (ii) *participle*	(i) passé; (ii) participe
P:	*uneducated speech; slang*	expression populaire; argot
Paint:	*painting trade*	peinture en bâtiment
Pal:	*paleography*	paléographie
Paleont:	*paleontology*	paléontologie
Paperm:	*papermaking*	fabrication du papier
Parl:	*parliament*	parlement
Pej:	*pejorative*	péjoratif
pers.	*person(s); personal*	personne(s); personnel
Petr:	*petroleum industry*	industrie pétrolière
p.h.	*past historic*	passé historique
Ph:	*physics*	physique
Pharm:	*pharmacy*	pharmacie
Phil:	*philosophy*	philosophie
Phot:	*photography*	photographie
Phot.Engr:	*photo-engraving; process work*	procédés photo-mécaniques; photogravure
phr.	*phrase*	locution
Physiol:	*physiology*	physiologie
Pisc:	*pisciculture*	pisciculture
pl.	*plural*	pluriel
Plumb:	*plumbing*	plomberie
P.N:	*public notice*	affichage; avis au public

Poet:	*poetical*	poétique
Pol:	*politics; political*	politique
Pol.Ec:	*political econony, economics*	économie politique
poss.	*possessive*	possessif
Post:	*postal services*	postes et télécommunications
p.p.	*past participle*	participe passé
pr.	*present (tense)*	présent (de l'indicatif)
pref.	*prefix*	préfixe
Prehist:	*prehistory*	préhistoire
prep.	*preposition*	préposition
prep.phr.	*prepositional phrase*	locution prépositive
Pr.n.	*proper name*	nom propre
pron.	*pronoun*	pronom
Pros:	*prosody*	prosodie; métrique
Prov:	*proverb*	proverbe
pr.p.	*present participle*	participe présent
Psy:	*psychology*	psychologie
Psychics:	*psychics*	métapsychisme
p.t.	*past tense*	passé défini
Publ:	*publishing*	édition
Pyr:	*pyrotechnics*	pyrotechnie
qch.	(*something*)	quelque chose
qn	(*someone*)	quelqu'un
q.v.	*which see*	se reporter à ce mot
Rac:	*racing*	courses
Rad:	*radar*	radar
Rail:	*railways, railroads*	chemins de fer
R.C.Ch:	*Roman Catholic Church*	Église catholique
Rec:	*tape recorders; record players*	magnétophones; tourne-disques
rel.	*relative*	relatif
Rel:	*religion(s)*	religion(s)
Rel.H:	*religious history*	histoire des religions
Rept:	*reptiles*	reptiles
Rh:	*rhetoric*	rhétorique
Ropem:	*ropemaking*	corderie
Row:	*rowing*	aviron
R.t.m:	*registered trademark*	marque déposée
Rugby Fb:	*Rubgy (football)*	rugby
S.	*south*	sud
s.a.	*see also*	voir
Sch:	*schools and universities; students (slang, etc.)*	écoles; universités; (argot, etc.) scolaire
Scot:	*Scotland; Scottish*	Écosse; écossais
Scout:	*Scout and Guide Movements*	scoutisme
Sculp:	*sculpture*	sculpture
Ser:	*sericulture*	sériciculture
sg., sing.	*singular*	singulier
Ski:	*skiing*	ski
Sm.a:	*small arms*	armes portatives
s.o.	*someone*	(quelqu'un)
Soapm:	*soapmaking*	savonnerie
Sp:	*sport*	sport
Space:	*astronautics; space travel*	astronautique; voyages interplanétaires
Spong:	*sponges*	spongiaires
Stat:	*statistics*	statistique
St.Exch:	*Stock Exchange*	terme de Bourse
sth.	*something*	(quelque chose)
Stonew:	*stoneworking*	taille de la pierre
suff.	*suffix*	suffixe
Sug.-R:	*sugar refining*	raffinerie du sucre

Surg:	*surgery*	chirurgie
Surv:	*surveying*	géodésie et levé de plans
Sw.Fr:	*Swiss French*	mot utilisé en Suisse
Swim:	*swimming*	natation
Tail:	*tailoring*	mode masculine
Tan:	*tanning*	tannage des cuirs
Tchn:	*technical*	terme technique, terme de métier
Telecom:	*telecommunications*	télécommunications
Ten:	*tennis*	tennis
Tex:	*textiles; textile industry*	industries textiles
Tg:	*telegraphy*	télégraphie
Th:	*theatre; theatrical*	théâtre
Theol:	*theology*	théologie
thg.	*thing(s)*	(chose(s))
Tls:	*tools*	outils
Toil:	*toilet; makeup*	toilette; maquillage
Town P:	*town planning*	urbanisme
Toys:	*toys*	jouets
Tp:	*telephony*	téléphonie
Trans:	*transport*	transports
Turf:	*turf, horse racing*	turf
T.V:	*television*	télévision
Typ:	*typography*	typographie
Typew(r):	*typing; typewriters*	dactylographie; machines à écrire
U.S:	*United States; American*	États-Unis; américain
usu.	*usually*	d'ordinaire
usu. with sg. const.	*usually with singular construction*	verbe généralement au singulier
v.	*verb*	verbe
V:	*vulgar; not in polite use*	trivial

var.	*variable*	variable
Veh:	*vehicles*	véhicules
Ven:	*venery; hunting*	chasse
Vet:	*veterinary science*	art vétérinaire
v.i.	*intransitive verb*	verbe intransitif
v.ind.tr.	*indirectly transitive verb*	verbe transitif indirect
Vit:	*viticulture*	viticulture
v.pr.	*pronominal verb*	verbe pronominal
v.tr.	*transitive verb*	verbe transitif
W.	*west*	ouest
Wine-m:	*wine making*	industrie du vin
with sg. or pl.	*with singular or plural construction*	verbe au singulier ou au pluriel
Wr:	*wrestling*	lutte
W.Tel:	*wireless telegraphy and telephony; radio*	téléphonie et télégraphie sans fil; radio
W.Tg:	*wireless telegraphy*	télégraphie sans fil
W.Tp:	*wireless telephony*	téléphonie sans fil
X-Rays:	*X Rays*	rayons X
Y:	*yachting*	yachting
Z:	*zoology; mammals*	zoologie; mammifères
=	*nearest equivalent (of an institution, an office, etc., when systems vary in the different countries)*	équivalent le plus proche (d'un terme désignant une institution, une charge, etc., dans les cas où les systèmes varient dans les différents pays)

50 famous English proverbs

chosen by Anthony Burgess

all's well that ends well
tout est bien qui finit bien

all's fair in love and war
en amour, la ruse est de bonne guerre

all that glitters is not gold
tout ce qui brille n'est pas or

as well be hanged for a sheep as for a lamb
autant vaut être pendu pour un mouton que pour un agneau

beggars can't be choosers
ne choisit pas qui emprunte

better late than never
mieux vaut tard que jamais

a bird in the hand is worth two in the bush
un tiens vaut mieux que deux tu l'auras

birds of a feather flock together
qui se ressemble s'assemble

blood is thicker than water
nous sommes unis par la voix, la force, du sang

charity begins at home
charité bien ordonnée commence par soi(-même)

discretion is the better part of valour
l'essentiel du courage, c'est la prudence

don't count your chickens before they are hatched
il ne faut pas vendre la peau de l'ours avant de l'avoir tué

don't put all your eggs in one basket
il ne faut pas mettre tous ses œufs dans le même panier

don't wash your dirty linen in public
il faut laver son linge sale en famille

an Englishman's home is his castle
charbonnier est maître chez soi

enough is as good as a feast
assez vaut (un) festin

every cloud has a silver lining
dans toute chose il y a un bon côté

every little helps
on fait feu de tout bois

familiarity breeds contempt
la familiarité engendre, fait naître, le mépris

first come first served
les premiers vont devant

forgive and forget
il faut oublier et pardonner

God helps him who helps himself
aide-toi, le ciel t'aidera

half a loaf is better than no bread
faute de grives, on mange des merles

he who pays the piper calls the tune
qui paye a bien le droit de choisir

if the cap fits, wear it!
qui se sent morveux se mouche!

it is an ill wind that blows nobody any good
à quelque chose malheur est bon

it's no use crying over spilt milk
à chose faite point de remède
least said soonest mended
moins on en parle, mieux cela vaut
live and let live
il faut que tout le monde vive
look before you leap
il faut réfléchir avant d'agir
many hands make light work
à plusieurs mains, l'ouvrage avance
more haste less speed
plus on se hâte moins on avance
necessity is the mother of invention
nécessité est mère de l'invention
never look a gift horse in the mouth
à cheval donné on ne regarde pas à la bride
no news is good news
point de nouvelles, bonnes nouvelles
once bitten twice shy
chat échaudé craint l'eau froide
one man's meat is another man's poison
ce qui guérit l'un tue l'autre
people who live in glass houses shouldn't throw stones
il faut être sans défauts pour critiquer autrui
the proof of the pudding is in the eating
à l'œuvre on connaît l'artisan
the road to hell is paved with good intentions
l'enfer est pavé de bonnes intentions
there are none so deaf as those that will not hear
il n'est pire sourd que celui qui ne veut pas entendre
too many cooks spoil the broth
trop de cuisinières gâtent la sauce
two's company, three's a crowd
deux s'amusent, trois s'embêtent
when in Rome do as the Romans do
il faut hurler avec les loups
while the cat's away the mice (will) play
quand le chat n'est pas là, les souris dansent
you cannot make a silk purse out of a sow's ear
on ne saurait faire d'une buse un épervier
you can't have your cake and eat it
on ne peut pas avoir le drap et l'argent
one swallow doesn't make a summer
une hirondelle ne fait pas le printemps
a stitch in time saves nine
un point à temps en épargne cent
it never rains but it pours
un malheur, un bonheur, ne vient jamais seul

50 famous French proverbs

chosen by Pierre Daninos ("Major Thompson")

à l'impossible nul n'est tenu
one can't do the impossible

après la pluie, le beau temps
every cloud has a silver lining

à quelque chose malheur est bon
it's an ill wind that blows nobody any good

à tout péché miséricorde
there is mercy for everything

aux innocents les mains pleines
fortune favours fools; beginners have all the luck

c'est dans le malheur qu'on connaît ses vrais amis
a friend in need is a friend indeed

c'est en forgeant qu'on devient forgeron
practice makes perfect

charité bien ordonnée commence par soi-même
charity begins at home

chat échaudé craint l'eau froide
once bitten twice shy

comme on fait son lit on se couche
as we make our bed, so must we lie

dans le doute, abstiens-toi
when in doubt, don't

de deux maux il faut choisir le moindre
one must choose the lesser of two evils

deux avis valent mieux qu'un
two heads are better than one

faute de grives, on mange des merles
beggars can't be choosers; half a loaf is better than no bread

honni soit qui mal y pense
evil be to him who evil thinks

il faut battre le fer pendant qu'il est chaud
strike while the iron is hot

il ne faut pas vendre la peau de l'ours avant de l'avoir tué
don't count your chickens before they are hatched

il n'y a pas de fumée sans feu
there's no smoke without fire

il y a loin de la coupe aux lèvres
there's many a slip 'twixt (the) cup and (the) lip

la caque sent toujours le hareng
what's bred in the bone will come out in the flesh

la fin justifie les moyens
the end justifies the means

la nuit, tous les chats sont gris
by night all cats are grey

l'appétit vient en mangeant
the more you get the more you want

le malheur des uns fait le bonheur des autres
one man's joy is another man's sorrow

l'enfer est pavé de bonnes intentions
the road to hell is paved with good intentions
les absents ont toujours tort
the absent are always in the wrong
les loups ne se mangent pas entre eux
there is honour among thieves
les murs ont des oreilles
walls have ears
l'habit ne fait pas le moine
it is not the cowl that makes the monk
l'habitude est une seconde nature
use is second nature
l'homme propose, Dieu dispose
man proposes, God disposes
loin des yeux, loin du cœur
out of sight, out of mind
mieux vaut tard que jamais
better late than never
ne réveillez pas le chat qui dort
let sleeping dogs lie
on ne fait pas d'omelette sans casser d'œufs
you can't make an omelette without breaking eggs
petit à petit, l'oiseau fait son nid
little strokes fell great oaks
pierre qui roule n'amasse pas mousse
a rolling stone gathers no moss
plus on se hâte, moins on avanee
more haste less speed
prudence est mère de sûreté
discretion is the better part of valour
quand on parle du loup, on en voit la queue
talk of the devil and he will appear
qui aime bien châtie bien
spare the rod and spoil the child
qui dort dîne
he who sleeps forgets his hunger
qui se ressemble s'assemble
birds of a feather flock together
qui trop embrasse mal étreint
grasp all, lose all
qui veut noyer son chien l'accuse de la rage
give a dog a bad name (and hang him)
tel est pris qui croyait prendre
it's a case of the biter bit
tel père, tel fils
like father like son
tout ce qui brille n'est pas or
all that glitters is not gold
une hirondelle ne fait pas le printemps
one swallow doesn't make a summer
un malheur n'arrive jamais seul
misfortunes never come singly

PART ONE

ENGLISH–FRENCH

Table of Phonetic Symbols

Consonants and semiconsonants

[p]	pat [pæt]; top [tɔp]
[b]	but [bʌt]; tab [tæb]
[m]	mat [mæt]; ram [ræm]; prism [ˈpriz(ə)m]
[f]	fat [fæt]; laugh [lɑːf]; ruff, rough [rʌf]; elephant [ˈelifənt]
[v]	vat [væt]; avail [əˈveil]; rave [reiv]
[t]	tap [tæp]; pat [pæt]; patter [ˈpætə*r*]; trap [træp]
[d]	dab [dæb]; madder [ˈmædə*r*]; build [bild]
[n]	no, know [nou]; ban [bæn]; banner [ˈbænə*r*]; pancake [ˈpænkeik]; nab [næb]; gnat [næt]
[s]	sat [sæt]; scene [siːn]; mouse [maus]; ice [ais]; psychology [saiˈkɔlədʒi]
[θ]	thatch [θætʃ]; ether [ˈiːθə*r*]; faith [feiθ]; breath [breθ]
[z]	zinc [ziŋk]; buzz [bʌz]; houses [ˈhauziz]; business [ˈbiznis]
[ð]	that [ðæt]; there [ðεə*r*]; mother [ˈmʌðə*r*]; breathe [briːð]
[l]	lad [læd], all [ɔːl]; table [ˈteibl]; chisel [ˈtʃiz(ə)l]
[ʃ]	sham [ʃæm]; dish [diʃ]; sugar [ˈʃugə*r*]; ocean [ˈouʃ(ə)n]; nation [ˈneiʃ(ə)n]; machine [məˈʃiːn]
[tʃ]	chat [tʃæt]; search [səːtʃ]; chisel [ˈtʃiz(ə)l]; thatch [θætʃ]; rich [ritʃ]
[ʒ]	pleasure [ˈpleʒə*r*]; vision [ˈviʒ(ə)n]; beige [beiʒ]
[dʒ]	jam [dʒæm]; jail, gaol [dʒeil]; gem [dʒem]; gin [dʒin]; rage [reidʒ]; edge [edʒ]; badger [ˈbædʒə*r*]
[k]	cat [kæt]; kitten [ˈkit(ə)n]; choir, quire [ˈkwaiə*r*]; cue, queue [kjuː]; arctic [ˈɑːktik]; pique [piːk]; exercise [ˈeksəsaiz]
[g]	go [gou]; ghost [goust]; guard [gɑːd]; again [əˈgen]; egg [eg]; exist [egˈzist]; hungry [ˈhʌŋgri]
[h]	hat [hæt]; cohere [kouˈhiə*r*]
[χ]	loch [lɔχ]
[ŋ]	bang [bæŋ]; sing [siŋ]; singer [ˈsiŋə*r*]; anchor [ˈæŋkə*r*]; anger [ˈæŋgə*r*]; link [liŋk]
[r]	rat [ræt]; arise [əˈraiz]; barring [ˈbɑːriŋ]
[*r*]	(*sounded only when a final* **r** *is carried on to the next word*) far [fɑː*r*]; sailor [ˈseilə*r*]; finger [ˈfiŋgə*r*]
[j]	yam [jæm]; yet [jet]; youth [juːθ]
[w]	wall [wɔːl]; await [əˈweit]; quite [kwait]
[(h)w]	what [(h)wɔt]; why [(h)wai]

Vowels and vowel combinations

[iː]	bee [biː]; fever [ˈfiːvə*r*]; see, sea [siː]; release [riˈliːs]
[iə]	beer, bier [biə*r*]; appear [əˈpiə*r*]; really [ˈriəli]
[i]	bit [bit]; added [ˈædid]; drastic [ˈdræstik]; sieve [siv]
[e]	bet [bet]; leopard [ˈlepəd]; menace [ˈmenəs]; said [sed]
[ei]	date [deit]; day [dei]; rain, rein, reign [rein]
[εə]	bear, bare [bεə*r*], there, their [ðεə*r*]; airy [ˈεəri]
[æ]	bat [bæt]; add [æd]
[ai]	aisle, isle [ail]; height [hait]; life [laif]; fly [flai]; beside [biˈsaid]
[ɑː]	art [ɑːt]; ask [ɑːsk]; car [kɑː*r*]; father [ˈfɑːðə*r*]
[au]	fowl, foul [faul]; house [haus]; cow [kau]
[ɔ]	wad [wɔd]; wash [wɔʃ]; lot [lɔt]; what [(h)wɔt]
[ɔː]	all [ɔːl]; haul [hɔːl]; saw [sɔː]; caught, court [kɔːt]; short [ʃɔːt]; wart [wɔːt]; thought [θɔːt]
[ɔi]	boil [bɔil]; toy [tɔi]; oyster [ˈɔistə*r*]; loyal [ˈlɔiəl]
[ou]	low [lou]; soap [soup]; rope [roup]; road, rode, rowed [roud]; sew, so, sow (*verb*) [sou]
[uː]	shoe [ʃuː]; prove [pruːv]; threw, through [θruː]; frugal [ˈfruːg(ə)l]; (*slightly shorter*) room [ru(ː)m]
[juː]	few [fjuː]; huge [hjuːdʒ]; humour [ˈhjuːmə*r*]
[(j)uː]	suit [s(j)uːt], suicide [ˈs(j)uːisaid]
[(j)uə]	lurid [ˈl(j)uərid]; lure [l(j)uə*r*]
[u]	put [put]; wool [wul]; wood, would [wud]; full [ful]
[ju]	incubate [ˈinkjubeit]; duplicity [djuˈplisiti]
[uə]	poor [puə*r*]; sure [ʃuə*r*]
[ʌ]	cut [kʌt]; sun, son [sʌn]; cover [ˈkʌvə*r*]; rough [rʌf]
[əː]	curl [kəːl]; herb [həːb]; learn [ləːn] myrrh [məː*r*]
[ə]	decency [ˈdiːsənsi]; obey [əˈbəi] amend [əˈmend]; delicate [ˈdelikət]

A

A, a¹ [ei] **1.** (*a*) (la lettre) A, a. *m*; **it's spelt with two a's,** cela s'écrit avec deux a; **he knows the case from A to Z,** il connaît l'affaire à fond; **A 1** ['ei'wʌn], *NAm: also* **A number 1,** de première qualité; (*house number*) **51 A,** 51 bis; (*b*) *Sch:* **A stream** = classe *f* de type 1; **A levels** = baccalauréat *m*, F: bac *m*; (*c*) **A road** = route nationale. **2.** *Mus:* la *m*; **in A flat,** en la bémol. **3.** *Cin:* **A film,** film interdit aux moins de 14 ans. **4. A bomb,** bombe *f* A.

a², *before vowel* an [ə, ən; *stressed* ei, æn] *indef. art.* **1.** un, une; (*a*) **a man,** un homme; **an old man,** un vieillard; **a history,** une histoire; **a hotel** [əhou'tel], **an hotel** [ənou'tel], un hôtel; **an hour** [ən'auər], une heure; **a unit** [ə'ju:nit], une unité; **an M.P.** [ən'em-'pi:], un député; **a man and (a) woman,** un homme et une femme; **a wife and mother,** une épouse et mère; (*b*) **such a stupid man,** un homme si stupide; **so, too, high a price,** un prix si, trop, élevé. **2.** (*def. art. in Fr.*) (*a*) **to have a red nose,** avoir le nez rouge; **I have a sore throat,** j'ai mal à la gorge; (*b*) **to have a taste for sth.,** avoir le goût de qch.; *Iron:* **a fine excuse!** la belle excuse! (*c*) (*generalizing*) **a woman takes life too seriously,** les femmes prennent la vie trop au sérieux. **3.** (*distributive*) (*a*) **apples at thirty pence a kilo,** pommes à trente pence le kilo; **five francs a head,** cinq francs par tête; (*b*) (*time*) **three times a week, a year,** trois fois par semaine, par an; **fifty kilometres an hour,** cinquante kilomètres à l'heure. **4.** (*partitive in Fr.*) **it has given me an appetite,** cela m'a donné de l'appétit. **5.** (*a*) (= **a certain**) **I know a doctor who . . .,** je connais un certain médecin qui . . .; **in a sense,** dans un certain sens; (*b*) (= **the same**) **to come in two at a time,** entrer deux par deux; **all of a size,** tous de la même grandeur, taille; (*c*) (= **a single**) **I haven't understood a word,** je n'ai pas compris un seul mot. **6.** (*omitted in Fr.*) (*a*) **he is an Englishman, a father, a barrister,** il est anglais, père, avocat; (*b*) (*before nouns in apposition*) **Caen, a large town in Normandy,** Caen, ville importante de Normandie; (*c*) **to put an end to sth.,** mettre fin à qch.; **to make a fortune,** faire fortune; (*d*) **what a man!** quel homme! **what a pity!** quel dommage! (*e*) **as a rule,** en règle générale; **to live like a prince,** vivre en prince; **to sell sth. at a loss,** vendre qch. à perte; **within a short time,** à bref délai.

Aachen ['ɑ:χən, 'ɑ:kən] *Pr.n. Geog:* Aix-la-Chapelle.

aback [ə'bæk] *adv.* **to be taken a.,** être, rester, déconcerté, interdit.

abacus, *pl.* **-ci, -cuses** ['æbəkəs, -sai, -si:; -kəsiz] *n.* **1.** *Mth*: abaque *m*; boulier *m* compteur. **2.** *Arch:* abaque, tailloir *m* (de chapiteau).

abaft [ə'bɑ:ft] *Nau:* **1.** *adv.* sur l'arrière; vers l'arrière. **2.** *prep.* **a. the mast,** sur l'arrière, du mât.

abalone [æbə'louni] *n. Moll:* ormeau *m*.

abandon¹ [ə'bændən] *n.* désinvolture *f*, entrain *m*.

abandon² *v.tr.* abandonner; délaisser (sa famille, etc.); renoncer à (un projet); *Nau:* **to a. ship,** abandonner, évacuer, le bâtiment; **to a. all hope,** abandonner tout espoir. **abandoned** *a.* **1.** abandonné; délaissé. **2.** *O:* dévergondé; (femme) perdue.

abandonment [ə'bændənmənt] *n.* abandonnement *m*.

abase [ə'beis] *v.tr. Lit:* abaisser, humilier (qn); **to a. oneself,** s'abaisser, s'humilier.

abasement [ə'beismənt] *n. Lit:* humiliation *f*.

abash [ə'bæʃ] *v.tr.* confondre, décontenancer (qn); **to be abashed at sth.,** être tout interdit de qch.

abate [ə'beit] *v.i.* (*of storm, etc.*) diminuer, faiblir; (*of storm, fear, pain*) se calmer, s'apaiser; (*of flood*) baisser; **the wind abated,** le vent tomba.

abatement [ə'beitmənt] *n.* (*a*) diminution *f*, affaiblissement *m*; apaisement *m* (d'une tempête); abaissement *m* (des eaux); (*b*) **noise a. campaign,** campagne *f* contre le bruit.

abattoir ['æbətwɑ:r] *n.* abattoir *m*.

abbess ['æbes, -is] *n.* abbesse *f*; supérieure *f* (de couvent).

abbey ['æbi] *n.* (*a*) abbaye *f*; (*b*) **a. (church),** (église) abbatiale (*f*).

abbot ['æbət] *n.* abbé *m* (d'un monastère); (père) supérieur *m*.

abbreviate [ə'bri:vieit] *v.tr.* abréger (un mot, etc.).

abbreviation [əbri:vi'eiʃ(ə)n] *n.* abréviation *f*.

ABC, abc ['eibi:'si:] *n.* (*a*) ABC, abc *m*; (*b*) *Sch:* abécédaire *m*; (*c*) ABC (d'un art, d'une science).

abdicate ['æbdikeit] **1.** *v.tr.* abdiquer (un trône); renoncer à (un droit, une charge). **2.** *v.i.* abdiquer.

abdication [æbdi'keiʃ(ə)n] *n.* abdication *f* (d'un trône); renonciation *f* (à un droit).

abdomen ['æbdəmən] *n.* abdomen *m*.

abdominal [əb'dɔmin(ə)l] *a.* abdominal, -aux.

abduct [əb'dʌkt] *v.tr. Jur:* enlever (qn); détourner (un(e) mineur(e)).

abduction [əb'dʌkʃ(ə)n] *n. Jur:* enlèvement *m*; détournement *m* (de mineur(e)); **a. by force,** rapt *m*.

abductor [əb'dʌktər] **1.** *n. Jur:* ravisseur *m*; auteur *m* d'enlèvement; détourneur *m* (de mineur(e)). **2.** *a.* & *n. Anat:* **a. (muscle),** (muscle) abducteur (*m*).

abeam [ə'bi:m] *adv. Nau: Av:* par le travers; en belle.

aberrant [ə'berənt] *a.* aberrant, anormal.

aberration [æbər'eiʃ(ə)n] *n.* **1.** aberration *f*, déviation *f* (de qn, d'un navire). **2.** (*a*) égarement *m* (des passions, etc.); **mental a.,** égarement de l'esprit; aberration; confusion mentale; (*b*) écart *m* (de conduite). **3.** *Astr: Mth: Opt: etc:* aberration. **4.** *Biol:* aberration; anomalie *f*.

abet [ə'bet] *v.tr.* **(abetted) 1. to a. s.o. in a crime,** encourager qn à un crime; *Jur:* **to aid and a. s.o.,** être le complice de qn. **2.** encourager (le crime). **abetting** *n. Jur:* **(aiding and) a.,** complicité *f*.

abeyance [ə'beiəns] *n.* suspension *f* (d'une loi); **the matter is still in a.,** la question est toujours pendante, en suspens; **law in a.,** loi inappliquée; **to fall into a.,** tomber en désuétude; *Jur:* **estate in a.,** succession vacante.

abhor [əb'hɔ:r] *v.tr.* **(abhorred)** abhorrer, avoir (qn, qch.) en horreur.

abhorrence [əb'hɔrəns] *n.* horreur *f* (**of,** de).

abhorrent [əb'hɔrənt] *a.* odieux, répugnant (**to,** à).

abide [ə'baid] *v.* (*p.t.* & *p.p.* **abided**) **1.** *v.i.* (*a*) *A:* & *Lit:* rester, demeurer (**with s.o.,** avec qn); (*b*) **to a. by (sth.),** rester fidèle à, tenir (une promesse); se conformer à, se soumettre à, respecter (une règle, une décision, une loi); **I a. by my decision, by what I said,** je maintiens ma décision, mon dire; (*c*) (*of thg*) durer; demeurer. **2.** *v.tr.* **I can't a. him,** je ne peux pas le sentir. **abiding** *a.* permanent; durable.

ability [ə'biliti] *n.* **1.** (*a*) capacité *f*, pouvoir *m* (**to do sth.,** de faire qch.); (*b*) *Jur:* habilité *f* (à succéder, à tester); capacité légale. **2.** habileté *f*, capacité, compétence *f*; **man of great a.,** homme très doué; **to do sth. to the best of one's a.,** faire qch. dans la mesure de ses moyens; faire qch. de son mieux.

abject ['æbdʒekt] *a.* **1.** abject, misérable; **a. poverty,** misère *f*. **2.** (*a*) bas, vil; (*b*) servile (**to,** envers). **-ly** *adv.* **1.** abjectement, misérablement. **2.** (*a*) bassement; (*b*) avec servilité.

abjuration [æbdʒu'reiʃ(ə)n] *n.* abjuration *f* (**of,** de); reniement *m* (de sa foi).

abjure [əb'dʒuər] *v.tr.* abjurer (sa foi, ses erreurs); renier (sa religion).

ablation [æb'leiʃ(ə)n] *n. Geol: Surg:* ablation *f*.

ablative ['æblətiv] *a. & n. Gram:* **a. (case),** (cas) ablatif (*m*); **in the a.,** à l'ablatif; **a. absolute,** ablatif absolu.

ablaze [ə'bleiz] *adv. & a.* en feu, en flammes; **to be a.,** flamber; **a. with light,** resplendissant de lumière; **a. with anger,** enflammé de colère.

able ['eibl] *a.* **1.** (*a*) capable, compétent; habile; **a very a. man,** un homme de haute capacité; *Jur:* **a. in body and mind,** sain de corps et d'esprit; (*b*) **to be a. to do sth.,** (i) savoir, être capable de, faire qch.; (ii) pouvoir, être en mesure de, être à même de, faire qch.; **I shan't be a. to come,** je ne pourrai pas venir; **better a. to do sth.,** plus capable de faire qch.; **I'll do it if I'm a.,** je la ferai si possible; **a. to pay,** en mesure de payer; (*c*) *Jur:* apte, habile (à léguer, à succéder). **2. a. piece of work,** travail compétent; travail bien fait; **your a. assistance,** votre aide efficace. **ably** *adv.* habilement; avec compétence.

able-bodied ['eibl'bɔdid] *a.* fort, robuste; *Mil:* (i) valide; (ii) bon pour le service.

ablution [ə'bluːʃ(ə)n] *n.* ablution *f*; *F:* **to perform one's ablutions,** faire ses ablutions.

abnegate ['æbnigeit] *v.tr.* renoncer à (une croyance, un privilège, etc.).

abnegation [æbni'geiʃ(ə)n] *n.* renoncement *m*; **self-a.,** renoncement à, abnégation *f* de, soi-même.

abnormal [æb'nɔːm(ə)l] *a.* anormal, -aux. **-ally** *adv.* anormalement.

abnormality [æbnɔː'mæliti] *n.* **1.** caractère anormal (de qch.). **2.** anomalie *f*, aberration *f*.

aboard [ə'bɔːd] **1.** *adv.* à bord; **to go a.,** aller, monter, à bord; s'embarquer; **to take sth. a.,** embarquer qch.; **all a.!** *Nau:* embarquez! *Rail: etc:* en voiture! **2.** *prep.* **a. ship.** à bord (d'un navire); **a. a train, a bus, an aircraft,** dans un train, un autobus, un avion.

abode [ə'boud] *n.* **1.** *Lit:* demeure *f*, habitation *f*. **2.** (*a*) *Lit:* (lieu *m* de) séjour *m*; (*b*) *Jur:* **place of a.,** domicile *m*; **of, with, no fixed a.,** sans domicile fixe.

abolish [ə'bɔliʃ] *v.tr.* abolir, supprimer (un usage, un abus); abroger (une loi).

abolition [æbə'liʃ(ə)n] *n.* abolition *f*; suppression *f*; abrogation *f* (d'une loi).

abolitionism [æbə'liʃənizm] *n. Hist:* abolitionnisme *m*.

abolitionist [æbə'liʃənist] *n. & a. Hist:* abolitionniste (*mf*).

abominable [ə'bɔminəbl] *a.* abominable; **the a. snowman,** l'abominable homme des neiges. **-ably** *adv.* abominablement.

abominate [ə'bɔmineit] *v.tr.* abominer, détester; avoir (qch.) en abomination.

abomination [əbɔmin'eiʃ(ə)n] *n.* **1.** abomination *f*. **2.** *F:* **this coffee's an a.,** ce café est abominable.

aboriginal [æbə'ridʒin(ə)l] *a. & n.* aborigène (*m*), indigène (*mf*).

aborigine [æbə'ridʒiniː] *n.* aborigène *m*.

abort¹ [ə'bɔːt] *n.* (*a*) *Mil.Av: etc:* mission non accomplie; **launch a.,** termination prématurée d'un lancement; (*b*) *Cmptr:* suspension *f* d'exécution (d'un programme).

abort² **1.** *v.i.* (*a*) *Biol:* avorter; (*b*) (*of project*) avorter. **2.** *v.tr.* (*a*) faire avorter (une femme); (*b*) faire avorter (un projet); *Cmptr:* suspendre l'exécution d'(un programme).

abortion [ə'bɔːʃ(ə)n] *n.* **1.** (*a*) *Obst:* avortement *m*; **to procure an a.,** faire avorter (qn); (*b*) avortement (d'un projet). **2.** *F:* (*a*) avorton *m*, monstre *m*; (*b*) œuvre manquée; **what an a.!** quelle horreur!

abortionist [ə'bɔːʃənist] *n.* médecin avorteur; avorteuse *f*.

abortive [ə'bɔːtiv] *a.* (*of plan, etc.*) avorté, manqué; **a. attempt,** essai qui n'aboutit à rien; coup manqué; *Mil: etc:* **a. attack,** attaque avortée; **a. mission,** mission non accomplie. **-ly** *adv.* sans succès.

abound [ə'baund] *v.i.* (*a*) abonder, foisonner; (*b*) abonder (**in, with,** en). **abounding** *a. Lit:* abondant.

about [ə'baut] *adv. & prep.* **1.** (*a*) autour (de); **the hills (round) a. the town,** les collines à l'entour de la ville; **the people a. us,** les gens auprès de nous, qui nous entourent; (*b*) de côté et d'autre; **to stroll a.,** se promener de ci, de là, de côté et d'autre; **to follow s.o. a.,** suivre qn partout; **don't leave those papers lying a.,** ne laissez pas traîner ces papiers; **there's a great deal of flu a. at present,** il y a beaucoup de grippe actuellement; (*c*) **there was nobody a.,** il n'y avait personne (de visible); (*after illness*) **to be up and a., out and a., again,** être de nouveau sur pied; **to be a. early,** être matinal; (*d*) **there is something unusual a. him,** il y a dans sa personne quelque chose de pas ordinaire; **there's something a. a horse that . . .,** il y a chez le cheval un je ne sais quoi qui . . .. **2.** (*a*) **to do sth. turn and turn a.,** faire qch. à tour de rôle, tour à tour; (*b*) **the other way a.,** en sens inverse; **to turn a.,** faire demi-tour; se retourner; *Mil:* **a. turn!** *U.S:* **a. face!** demi-tour! **3.** environ, presque; **there are a. thirty,** il y en a environ trente; il y en a une trentaine; **he's a. my age,** il a à peu près mon âge; **it will cost a. a hundred francs,** ça coûtera dans les cent francs; **that's a. right,** c'est à peu près cela; **it's a. time,** (i) il est presque temps; (ii) *Iron:* il est grand temps; **a. one o'clock,** vers une heure. **4.** au sujet de; **to enquire a. sth.,** se renseigner sur, au sujet de, qch.; **to speak a. sth.,** parler de qch.; **to quarrel a. nothing,** se quereller à propos de rien; **what's it all a.?** de quoi s'agit-il? **I know what it's all a.,** je sais de quoi il s'agit; **how, what, a. a game of bridge?** si on faisait un bridge? **what a. my bath?** et mon bain? **5.** (*a*) **to be a. to do sth.,** être sur le point de faire qch.; **what were you a. to say?** qu'est-ce que vous alliez dire? **he is a. to leave,** il est sur son départ; (*b*) **to go a. one's work, one's business,** faire sa besogne; vaquer à ses affaires; **while you are a. it,** pendant que vous y êtes; **be quick a. it!** dépêchez-vous!

about-face, about-turn [ə'baut'feis,-'təːn] *n.* (i) demi-tour *m*; (ii) revirement *m* (d'opinion); **to do an a.-f., a.-t.,** (i) faire demi-tour; (ii) changer complètement d'avis, d'opinion.

above [əb'ʌv] I. *adv. & prep.* **1.** au-dessus (de); (*a*) **the water reached a. their knees,** l'eau leur montait jusqu'au-dessus des genoux; (*b*) **the tenants of the flat a.,** les locataires du dessus; **heavens a.!** juste ciel! **a voice from a.,** une voix d'en haut; **view from a.,** vue plongeante; **policy imposed from a.,** politique qui vient d'en haut; (*c*) **a mountain rises a. the lake,** une montagne s'élève au-dessus du lac, domine le lac; **his voice was heard a. the din,** on entendait sa voix par-dessus le tumulte; **the Seine a. Paris,** la Seine en amont de Paris; **a. ground,** sur terre; *Min:* au jour, à la surface; (*d*) **he is a. me in rank,** il est mon supérieur (hiérarchique); **a. one's station,** au-dessus de sa condition; **to live a. one's means,** vivre au-dessus de ses moyens; **temperature a. normal,** température supérieure à la normale; **a. criticism,** hors de l'atteinte de la critique; **that's a. me,** cela me dépasse; **a. all ...,** surtout ..., par-dessus tout ...; (*e*) *F:* **to get a. oneself,** s'en faire accroire. **2.** (*in book, etc.*) ci-dessus; **the paragraph a.,** le paragraphe ci-dessus; **as a.,** comme ci-dessus. **3.** (*of pers.*) **to be a. suspicion,** être au-dessus de tout soupçon; **I am a. doing that,** je me respecte trop pour faire cela. **4. a. twenty,** plus de vingt; **she is a. forty,** elle a passé la quarantaine; **over and a. that,** en plus de cela. **II.** *a.* (*in book, etc.*) **the a. quotation,** le citation ci-dessus. **III.** *n.* **the a. is a quotation from** *Hamlet*, le passage ci-dessus est une citation de *Hamlet*; **the a. was the driver of the vehicle,** le susdit était le conducteur du véhicule.

aboveboard [əˈbʌvbɔːd] **1.** *adv.* **to play fair and a.,** jouer cartes sur table. **2.** *a.* franc; **everything is a.,** tout est franc et loyal; **his conduct was completely a.,** il a agi en tout bien (et) tout honneur.

above-mentioned, above-named [əˈbʌv-ˈmenʃənd,-ˈneimd] *a.* susmentionné; susdit.

abracadabra [æbrəkəˈdæbrə] *n.* abracadabra *m.*

abrade [əˈbreid] **1.** *v.tr.* user (qch.) par le frottement, par abrasion; abraser; écorcher (la peau). **2.** *v.i.* s'user par le frottement.

abrasion [əˈbreiʒ(ə)n] *n.* **1.** (usure par le) frottement; abrasion *f*; *Cin:* (*on film*) **abrasions,** éraflures *fpl.* **2.** *Med:* écorchure *f*, éraflure (de la peau).

abrasive [əˈbreisiv] *a. & n.* abrasif (*m*).

abreast [əˈbrest] *adv.* (*a*) (*of horses, etc.*) de front; *Navy:* **line a.,** en ligne de front; **to come a. of a car,** arriver à la hauteur d'une voiture; **three, four, a.,** trois, quatre, de front; **to march two, four, a.,** marcher par deux, par rangs de quatre; (*b*) **to keep a. of a science,** suivre les progrès d'une science; **to keep, be, a. of the times,** suivre, être de, son temps.

abridge [əˈbridʒ] *v.tr.* abréger (un ouvrage, etc.); raccourcir (un livre, un chapitre). **abridged** *a.* (édition) abrégée; **a. version,** abrégé *m*, résumé *m.*

abridg(e)ment [əˈbridʒmənt] *n.* **1.** abrégement *m* (d'un ouvrage, etc.). **2.** abrégé *m*, résumé *m.*

abroad [əˈbrɔːd] *adv.* **1.** (*a*) à l'étranger; en voyage; **to live a.,** vivre à l'étranger; **our colleagues from a.,** nos collègues étrangers; **capital invested a.,** capitaux placés dehors; (*b*) *A:* (*of pers.*) **to venture a.,** sortir (de la maison). **2.** de tous côtés; **scattered a.,** éparpillé de tous côtés; **the news got a.,** la nouvelle s'est répandue.

abrogate [ˈæbrəgeit] *v.tr.* abroger (une loi).

abrogation [æbrəˈgeiʃ(ə)n] *n.* abrogation *f.*

abrupt [əˈbrʌpt] *a.* **1.** abrupt; (départ, personne) brusque; (départ) brusqué, précipité; (ton) cassant; (style) heurté, saccadé; **the evening came to an a. end,** la soirée s'acheva brusquement. **2.** (pente) abrupte, raide; (cap) escarpé, à pic; (montée) ardue, raide. **-ly** *adv.* **1.** abruptement; brusquement. **2.** abruptement; à pic; en pente raide.

abruptness [əˈbrʌptnis] *n.* **1.** brusquerie *f*, manière brusque; précipitation *f* (d'un départ); caractère heurté, saccadé (du style). **2.** raideur *f* (d'une pente).

abscess [ˈæbses] *n.* abcès *m.*

abscond [æbˈskɔnd] *v.i.* se soustraire à la justice; s'enfuir, s'évader (**from,** de); *F:* décamper, filer. **absconding 1.** *a.* en fuite. **2.** *n.* évasion *f*, fuite *f.*

absconder [æbˈskɔndər] *n.* fugitif, -ive; évadé, -ée.

abseiling [æbˈsailiŋ] *n. Mount:* rappel *m.*

absence [ˈæbsəns] *n.* **1.** absence *f*, éloignement *m* (**from,** de); **to be conspicuous by one's a.,** briller par son absence; *Jur:* **sentenced in one's a.,** condamné(e) par contumace; **leave of a.,** congé *m*; *Mil: etc:* **a. without leave,** absence illégale. **2.** manque *m* (de franchise, etc.); **in the a. of definite information,** faute de, à défaut de, renseignements précis. **3. a. of mind,** distraction *f*, préoccupation *f.*

absent[1] [ˈæbsənt] *a.* **1.** (*a*) absent (**from,** de); *Mil: etc:* **a. without leave,** porté manquant; (*b*) manquant; **in this animal the teeth are a.,** chez cet animal les dents sont absentes, manquent. **-ly** *adv.* distraitement; d'un air distrait.

absent[2] [æbˈsent] *v.pr.* **to a. oneself,** s'absenter (**from,** de).

absentee [æbsənˈtiː] *n.* **1.** (*a*) absent, -ente; manquant, -ante (à l'appel); (*b*) *Ind: etc:* absentéiste *mf.* **2.** *Hist:* **a. landlord,** absentéiste.

absenteeism [æbsənˈtiːizm] *n.* absentéisme *m.*

absentminded [ˈæbsəntˈmaindid] *a.* distrait, préoccupé. **-ly** *adv.* distraitement; d'un air distrait.

absentmindedness [ˈæbsəntmaindidnis] *n.* distraction *f*, préoccupation *f.*

absinth(e) [ˈæbsinθ, -ɛ̃t] *n.* absinthe *f.*

absolute [ˈæbsəluːt] **1.** *a.* (*a*) absolu; **case of a. necessity,** cas de nécessité absolue, de force majeure; **a. power,** pouvoir absolu; *Pol:* **a. majority,** majorité absolue; (*b*) *Gram:* (construction) absolue; **ablative a.,** ablatif absolu; (*c*) (humidité, température) absolue; **a. zero,** zéro absolu; *Mth:* **a. value,** valeur absolue; *Cmptr:* **a. code,** code réel, langage *m* machine; (*d*) **it's an a. scandal,** c'est un véritable scandale; *F:* **he's an a. fool,** c'est un parfait imbécile. **2.** *n. Phil:* **the a.,** l'absolu *m.* **-ly** *adv.* (*a*) absolument; **you're a. right,** vous avez entièrement, tout à fait, raison; **it is a. forbidden,** il est formellement interdit; (*b*) *Gram:* **verb used a.,** verbe employé absolument.

absolution [æbsəˈluːʃ(ə)n] *n. Ecc:* absolution *f.*

absolutism [ˈæbsəluːtizm] *n. Pol:* absolutisme *m.*

absolve [əbˈzɔlv, -ˈsɔlv] *v.tr.* **1.** absoudre (qn) (**of a sin,** d'un péché); **he was absolved from all blame,** il fut reconnu qu'il n'était aucunement responsable. **2.** affranchir, dégager, délier (qn) (**from an obligation, a vow,** d'une obligation, d'un vœu).

absorb [əbˈsɔːb, -ˈzɔːb] *v.tr.* **1.** (*a*) absorber (un liquide, la chaleur, etc.); (*b*) amortir (un choc, un son). **2.** (*a*) **his business absorbs him,** ses affaires l'absorbent; (*b*) **to become absorbed in sth.,** s'absorber dans qch.; **to listen with absorbed interest,** écouter avec un intérêt profond. **absorbing** *a.* **1.** (matière) absorbante. **2.** (sujet) absorbant, passionnant.

absorbency [əbˈsɔːbənsi, -ˈzɔːb-] *n.* capacité *f* d'absorption.

absorbent [əbˈsɔːbənt, -ˈzɔːb-] *a. & n.* absorbant (*m*).

absorber [əbˈsɔːbər, -ˈzɔːb-] *n. Aut: etc:* amortisseur *m* (de choc, etc.).

absorption [əbˈsɔːpʃ(ə)n, -zɔːb-] *n.* **1.** (*a*) absorption *f*; (*b*) amortissement *m* (de sons, de chocs, etc.). **2.** absorption (de l'esprit).

abstain [əbˈstein] *v.i.* **1.** s'abstenir (**from (doing) sth.,** de (faire) qch.); **to a. from meat,** faire maigre. **2.** (*a*) s'abstenir de boissons alcooliques; (*b*) s'abstenir, ne pas voter.

abstainer [əbˈsteinər] *n.* **to be a total a.,** ne pas boire d'alcool.

abstemious [əbˈstiːmiəs] *a.* sobre, tempérant, abstinent; (repas) frugal. **-ly** *adv.* sobrement; (manger) frugalement.

abstemiousness [əbˈstiːmiəsnis] *n.* sobriété *f*, tempérance *f*; abstinence *f.*

abstention [əbˈstenʃ(ə)n] *n.* **1.** abstention *f*, abstinence *f* (**from** de). **2.** *Pol:* abstention.

abstentionist [abˈstenʃənist] *n. Pol:* abstentionniste *mf.*

abstinence [ˈæbstinəns] *n.* (*a*) abstinence *f* (**from,** de); *Ecc:* **day of a.,** jour *m* d'abstinence; (*b*) **(total)**

a., abstinence (complète) de boissons alcooliques.

abstract[1] ['æbstrækt] **1.** *a.* (*a*) (nombre, nom, art) abstrait; **a. science,** science abstraite; **a. artist,** abstrait *m*; (*b*) abstrait, abstrus. **2.** *n.* (*a*) **the a.,** l'abstrait *m*; **in the a.,** dans l'abstrait; (*b*) peinture, sculpture, abstraite. **-ly** *adv.* abstraitement.

abstract[2] ['æbstrækt] *n.* résumé *m*, abrégé *m*.

abstract[3] [æb'strækt] *v.tr.* **1.** (*a*) soustraire, dérober (**sth. from s.o.,** qch. à qn); détourner (de l'argent); (*b*) détourner (l'attention de qn); (*c*) *Ch:* extraire (par distillation). **2.** abstraire, faire abstraction d'(une qualité, une conception). **3.** résumer, abréger (un texte); dépouiller (un livre); relever (un compte). **abstracted** *a.* distrait. **abstractedly** *adv.* distraitement; d'un air distrait.

abstraction [æb'strækʃ(ə)n] *n.* **1.** (*a*) soustraction *f* (de papiers, etc.); détournement *m* (d'argent); (*b*) *Ch: Ind:* extraction *f* (par distillation). **2.** (*a*) *Phil:* abstraction *f*; (*b*) idée abstraite; **to lose oneself in abstractions,** se perdre dans les abstractions. **3.** distraction; préoccupation *f* (d'esprit); **in a moment of a.,** dans un moment d'inattention. **4.** *Art:* peinture, sculpture, abstraite.

abstruse [æb'stru:s] *a.* abstrus.

abstruseness [æb'stru:snis] *n.* caractère abstrus.

absurd [əb'sə:d] **1.** *a.* absurde; **it's a.!** c'est ridicule! **2.** *n.* **the a.,** l'absurde. **-ly** *adv.* (*a*) absurdement; (*b*) *F:* **she's a. rich,** elle est ridiculement riche.

absurdity [əb'sə:diti] *n.* absurdité *f*; **speech full of absurdities,** discours plein d'absurdités.

abundance [ə'bʌndəns] *n.* **1.** (*a*) abondance *f*; **in a.,** en abondance, à profusion; (*b*) **to live in a.,** vivre dans l'abondance. **2.** *Biol: etc:* abondance (d'une espèce, etc.). **3.** *Cards:* (*in solo whist*) (*also* **abondance** [abɔ̃'dɑ̃:s]) abondance.

abundant [ə'bʌndənt] *a.* abondant (**in,** en); fertile (en blé, etc.); **there is a. evidence that . . .,** il a été amplement démontré que . . . . **-ly** *adv.* abondamment; en abondance; à foison.

abuse[1] [ə'bju:s] *n.* **1.** (*a*) abus *m* (**of,** de); *Jur:* **a. of authority,** abus d'autorité, de pouvoir; **a. of trust,** prévarication *f*; (*b*) abus; **to remedy an a.,** redresser un abus; (*c*) emploi abusif (d'un terme, etc.). **2.** insultes *fpl*, injures *fpl*; **term of a.,** injure; **to shower a., on s.o.,** accabler qn d'injures.

abuse[2] [ə'bju:z] *v.tr.* **1.** abuser de (son autorité, la confiance de qn, etc.); mésuser de (son pouvoir); faire abus de (qch.); **a much abused word,** mot employé abusivement. **2.** (*a*) maltraiter, houspiller (qn); (*b*) *Jur:* violer (une femme). **3.** (*a*) médire de (qn); dénigrer (qn); (*b*) injurier, dire des injures à (qn).

abusive [ə'bju:siv] *a.* **1.** (emploi) abusif (d'un mot). **2.** (propos) injurieux; (homme) grossier. **-ly** *adv.* (parler) injurieusement, grossièrement.

abut [ə'bʌt] *v.i.* **(abutted, abutting) to a. on, against (sth.),** aboutir, confiner, à (un champ, une rivière, etc.); *Const:* s'appuyer, buter, contre (une paroi); s'arc-bouter contre (un mur).

abutment [ə'bʌtmənt] *n. Arch: Civ.E:* (*a*) arc-boutant *m*, *pl.* arcs-boutants (d'une muraille); contrefort *m*; (*b*) butée *f*, culée *f* (d'un pont); piédroit *m* (d'une voûte).

abysmal [ə'bizm(ə)l] *a.* (*a*) sans fond; **a. ignorance,** ignorance profonde; (*b*) *F:* atroce. **-ally** *adv.* atrocement; **a. ignorant,** d'une ignorance profonde.

abyss [ə'bis] *n.* **1.** abîme *m*, gouffre *m*. **2.** *Oc:* abysse *m*, zone abyssale.

abyssal [ə'bis(ə)l] *a. Oc:* abyssal.

Abyssinia [æbi'siniə] *Pr.n. Geog:* Abyssinie *f*.

Abyssinian [æbi'siniən] **1.** *a. Geog:* abyssinien, abyssin; *Z:* **A. cat,** chat abyssin. **2.** *n.* (*a*) Abyssinien, -ienne; (*b*) *Ling:* abyssinien *m*.

acacia [ə'keiʃə] *n. Bot:* acacia *m*; **false a.,** faux acacia; robinier *m*.

academic [ækə'demik] **1.** *a.* (*a*) *Phil:* académique; (*b*) **a. discussion,** discussion abstraite; **of purely a. interest,** qui n'est intéressant qu'au point de vue théorique; (*c*) (carrière, costume, année, etc.) universitaire; (*d*) *Art:* (peinture, etc.) académique. **2.** *n.* universitaire *mf*. **-ally** *adv.* académiquement.

academicals [ækə'demik(ə)lz] *n.pl.* **(full) a.,** toge *f*, épitoge *f* et bonnet *m* universitaires.

academician [əkædə'miʃ(ə)n] *n.* académicien *m*; *esp.* **Royal A.,** membre de la *Royal Academy* (des Beaux-Arts).

academicism [æka'demisizm], **academism** [ə'kædəmizm] *n.* académisme *m*.

academy [ə'kædəmi] *n.* **1.** *Gr.Phil:* l'Académie *f* (de Platon). **2.** (*a*) académie; **the Royal A. (of Arts),** (i) l'Académie royale des Beaux-Arts; (ii) le Salon (de Londres); **a. of music,** conservatoire *m*; **fencing a.,** salle *f* d'escrime; (*b*) **military a.,** école *f* militaire. **3.** *Scot:* = lycée *m*; *U.S:* collège (privé).

acanthus [ə'kænθəs] *n.* **1.** *Bot:* acanthe *f*. **2.** *Arch:* (feuille *f* d')acanthe.

accede [æk'si:d] *v.i.* **1. to a. to the throne,** monter sur le trône. **2. to a. to (sth.),** donner son adhésion à (un traité); donner suite à (une demande, une prière).

accelerate [ək'seləreit] **1.** (*a*) *v.tr.* accélérer (la marche, le pouls, un travail); presser (un mouvement, un travail); précipiter (les événements); (*b*) *v.i. Aut:* accélérer. **2.** *v.i.* (*of motion, etc.*) s'accélérer. **accelerated** *a.* (mouvement, etc.) accéléré; *Cin:* **a. motion,** accéléré *m*.

acceleration [əkselə'reiʃ(ə)n] *n.* accélération *f*; **negative a.,** accélération retardatrice, négative; **uniform a.,** vitesse uniformément accélérée.

accelerator [ək'seləreitər] **1.** *a.* & *n.* accélérateur, -trice. **2.** *n. Aut: Atom.Ph: etc:* accélérateur *m*; **to step on the a.,** accélérer.

accent[1] ['æks(ə)nt] *n.* **1.** (*a*) accent *m*; **to have a German a.,** avoir l'accent allemand; **to speak with an a.,** parler avec un accent; (*b*) **in broken accents,** d'une voix brisée, entrecoupée. **2.** (*a*) *Pros:* accent, temps marqué; (*b*) *Mus:* (i) temps fort; (ii) accent (mélodique); (*c*) **fashion with the a. on youth,** mode qui met l'accent sur la jeunesse. **3. acute, grave, a.,** accent aigu, accent grave.

accent[2] [æk'sent] *v.tr.* accentuer (une syllabe, etc.). **accented** *a.* accentué; *Ling:* accentuel.

accentuate [æk'sentjueit] *v.tr.* accentuer, faire ressortir (un détail, etc.); accuser (un contraste). **accentuated** *a.* fortement marqué; accentué.

accentuation [æksentju'eiʃ(ə)n] *n.* accentuation *f* (d'une voyelle, d'un détail, etc.).

accept [ək'sept] *v.tr.* (*a*) accepter (un cadeau, une invitation, une offre); agréer (les salutations, les prières, de qn); admettre (les raisons, les excuses, de qn); agréer (un prétendant); donner son adhésion à (un traité); **to be accepted,** être accepté; **contrary to accepted opinion,** à l'encontre des idées reçues; **the accepted custom,** l'usage admis; *Com:* **to a. a bill,** accepter un effet; **to a. (delivery of) goods,** prendre des marchandises en recette; (*b*) **to a. the inevitable,** se soumettre au destin.

acceptability [əkseptə'biliti] *n.* acceptabilité *f*.

acceptable [ək'septəbl] *a.* (*a*) acceptable, agréable; **sacrifice a. to God,** sacrifice *m* agréable à Dieu; **your cheque was most a.,** votre chèque est arrivé fort à propos; (*b*) admissible, acceptable; possible; *F:* **just about a.,** tolérable, supportable.

acceptance [ək'septəns] *n.* (*a*) acceptation *f*; accueil *m* favorable (de qch.); (*of story, etc.*) **to find a.,** trouver créance; *Com:* **to present a bill for a.,** présenter une traite à l'acceptation; **a. bank, house,**

banque *f* d'escompte d'effets étrangers; (*b*) *Com: Ind:* réception (d'un article commandé); **a. test, trial,** essai *m* de réception, de recette.

acceptation [æksep'teiʃ(ə)n] *n.* acception *f*; **in the full a. of the word,** dans toute l'acception du mot.

acceptor [ək'septər] *n.* (*a*) *Com:* accepteur *m*; tiré *m*; (*b*) *Ch: etc:* accepteur.

access ['ækses] *n.* **1.** accès *m*, abord *m*; **means of a.,** moyens *mpl* d'accès; **difficult of a.,** d'un accès, d'une approche, difficile; **door that gives a. to a room,** porte qui donne accès à une pièce; *P.N: Aut:* **a. only,** entrée interdite (sauf aux riverains); **a. road,** route *f* d'accès; *Cmptr:* **random a. storage,** mémoire *m* à accès sélectif; **to have a. to s.o.,** avoir accès chez, auprès de, qn. **2.** accès (de colère, etc.).

accessary [ək'sesəri] *n.* = ACCESSORY 3.

accessibility [æksesi'biliti] *n.* accessibilité *f.*

accessible [ək'sesəbl] *a.* (endroit, personne, etc.) accessible, abordable; **knowledge a. to everyone,** connaissances *fpl* à la portée de tout le monde.

accession [æk'seʃ(ə)n] *n.* **1.** admission *f* (de lumière, d'air). **2.** (*a*) accroissement *m* (par addition); **accession(s) book,** registre *m* des additions (à une bibliothèque); **a. number,** numéro *m* matricule; (*b*) adhésion *f* (**to a party,** à un parti); (*c*) accession *f*, assentiment *m*, adhésion (**to a treaty,** à un traité). **3.** (*a*) **a. to manhood,** arrivée *f* à l'âge d'homme; (*b*) accession (**to power,** au pouvoir); avènement *m*, accession *f* (**to the throne,** au trône).

accessory [ək'sesəri] **1.** *a.* accessoire, (**to,** à); (matériel) annexe; *Bot:* **a. bud, shoot,** prompt-bourgeon *m*, *pl.* prompts-bourgeons. **2.** *n.* accessoire *m*; **car, toilet, accessories,** accessoires d'automobile, de toilette; *Cost:* **accessories,** accessoires. **3.** *n.* **a. to a crime,** complice *m*, d'un crime; **a. before the fact,** complice par instigation, par assistance; **a. after the fact,** complice par aide après coup.

accident [æksid(ə)nt] *n.* (*a*) accident *m*; *Jur:* cas fortuit; **by a.,** accidentellement; par hasard; (*b*) **serious, fatal, a.,** accident grave, mortel; **to have an a.,** (i) être, se trouver, victime d'un accident; (ii) *F:* (*esp. of child*) faire pipi dans sa culotte; **car a.,** accident d'automobile; **the victims of the a.,** les victimes de l'accident, les accidentés *mpl*; **accidents will happen,** on ne peut pas parer à tout.

accidental [æksi'dent(ə)l] **1.** *a.* (*a*) accidentel, fortuit; **a. meeting,** rencontre *f* de hasard; (*b*) accessoire, subsidiaire. **2.** *n. Mus:* accident *m*; signe accidentel. **-ally** *adv.* (*a*) accidentellement, par hasard; (*b*) accidentellement, par mégarde; *Hum:* **a. on purpose,** comme par hasard; exprès.

accident-prone ['æksid(ə)ntproun] *a.* prédisposé aux accidents.

acclaim [ə'kleim] *v.tr.* (*a*) acclamer; accueillir (qn) par des acclamations; (*b*) **Charlemagne was acclaimed emperor,** Charlemagne fut acclamé, proclamé, empereur.

acclamation [æklə'meiʃ(ə)n] *n.* acclamation *f*; **carried by a.,** adopté par acclamation.

acclimate [ə'klaimeit, 'æklimeit] *v.tr.* *NAm:* = ACCLIMATIZE.

acclimation [ækli'meiʃ(ə)n] *n.* *NAm:* = ACCLIMATIZATION.

acclimatization [əklaimətai'zeiʃ(ə)n] *n.* **1.** acclimatement *m* (**to,** à). **2.** acclimatation *f.*

acclimatize [ə'klaimətaiz] *v.tr.* acclimater; naturaliser (une plante, etc.); **to become acclimatized,** *v.i.* **to a.,** s'acclimater.

accolade ['ækəleid] *n.* accolade *f.*

accommodate [ə'kɔmədeit] *v.tr.* **1.** (*a*) accommoder (ses goûts à ceux d'un autre); **to a. oneself to circumstances,** s'adapter aux circonstances; (*b*) arranger (une querelle); concilier (des opinions). **2.** (*a*) **to do sth. to a. s.o.,** faire qch. pour arranger qn; (*b*) **to a. s.o. with sth.,** donner, fournir, qch. à qn; fournir qn de qch; **to a. s.o. with a loan,** faire un prêt à qn. **3.** loger, recevoir (tant de personnes); **restaurant that can a. 50 people,** restaurant où il y a de la place pour 50 personnes. **accommodating** *a.* complaisant, obligeant.

accommodation [əkɔmə'deiʃ(ə)n] *n.* **1.** (*a*) ajustement *m*, adaptation *f* (**to,** à); *Physiol:* accommodation (de l'œil); (*b*) arrangement *m* (d'une dispute); **to come to an a.,** arriver à un compromis; s'arranger (à l'amiable). **2.** (*of pers.*) complaisance *f*, accommodement. **3.** (*a*) commodité *f*, facilitiés *fpl*; *Nau:* **a. ladder,** échelle *f* de commandement, de coupée; *Rail: U.S:* **a. (train),** (train *m*) omnibus (*m*); **a. address,** adresse *f* de convention; (*b*) (*NAm: usu.* **accommodations**) logement *m*; chambre(s) *f*(*pl*) (d'hôtel); **furnished a.,** chambres garnies; **there is a. in this hotel for 50 people,** cet hôtel peut loger 50 personnes; (*c*) avance *f*, prêt *m* (d'argent).

accompaniment [ə'kʌmp(ə)nimənt] *n.* (*a*) accompagnement *m*; *Cu:* **roast pork with an a. of apple sauce,** rôti de porc avec accompagnement de compote de pommes; (*b*) *Mus:* accompagnement (**on the piano,** au piano).

accompanist [ə'kʌmp(ə)nist] *n.* *Mus:* accompagnateur, -trice.

accompany [ə'kʌmp(ə)ni] *v.tr.* **1.** accompagner (qn); **to be accompanied by s.o.,** être accompagné de qn. **2.** (*a*) **he accompanied these words with a smile,** il accompagna ces mots d'un sourire; (*b*) **fever accompanied by, with, delirium,** fièvre accompagnée de délire. **3.** *Mus:* accompagner (qn) (**on the piano,** au piano).

accomplice [ə'kɔmplis, -'kʌm-] *n.* complice *mf*; **his accomplices in crime,** les complices de ses crimes.

accomplish [ə'kɔmpliʃ -'kʌm-] *v.tr.* accomplir, achever, venir à bout de (qch.); mener à bonne fin (une tâche); effectuer (un voyage, une traversée); **to a. one's object,** atteindre son but; **mission accomplished,** mission accomplie. **accomplished** *a.* **1.** achevé; **a. fact,** fait accompli. **2.** (danseur, pianiste) accompli; **to be very a.,** être très accompli.

accomplishment [ə'kɔmpliʃmənt, -'kʌm-] *n.* **1.** (*a*) accomplissement *m*, achèvement *m* (d'une tâche, etc.); réalisation *f* (d'un projet); (*b*) chose accomplie, réalisée. **2.** art *m* d'agrément, talent *m* (d'agrément); **she has many accomplishments,** elle est très accomplie; elle possède de nombreux talents.

accord[1] [ə'kɔːd] *n.* **1.** (*a*) accord *m*, consentement *m*; **with one a.,** d'un commun accord; (*b*) *Lit: & NAm:* pacte *m*. **2. to do sth. of one's own a.,** faire qch. de son plein gré, de sa propre volonté.

accord[2] **1.** *v.i.* s'accorder, être d'accord, concorder (**with,** avec). **2.** *v.tr.* accorder, concéder (qch.) (**to,** à). **according** *adv. used in:* **1.** *conj. phrs.* **a. to how it is done,** suivant la façon dont on le fait; **a. to whether one is rich or poor,** selon qu'on est riche ou pauvre. **2.** *prep. phr.* (*a*) **a. to instructions,** selon, suivant, d'après, les ordres; **a. to age,** par rang d'âge; **a. to plan,** conformément au plan; (*b*) **a. to him,** d'après lui; à ce qu'il dit; **a. to that,** d'après cela; **the Gospel a. to St Luke,** l'Evangile selon saint Luc; **a. to our means,** selon nos moyens. **accordingly** *adv.* **1.** (*a*) **to act a.,** agir en conséquence. **2.** donc; **a. I wrote to him,** je lui ai donc écrit; en conséquence je lui ai écrit.

accordance [ə'kɔːdəns] *n.* **1.** accord *m*, conformité; **in a. with our instructions,** conformément à nos ordres. **2.** octroi *m*, concession *f* (d'un privilège).

accordant [ə'kɔːd(ə)nt] *a.* **1.** concordant; d'accord. **2.** d'accord (**to, with,** avec); conforme (**to, with,** à).

accordion [ə'kɔːdiən] *n.* accordéon *m*; **piano a.,**

accordéon à touches; **a. player,** accordéoniste *mf*; *Dressm: etc:* **a. pleats,** plis *mpl* en accordéon; **a. door,** porte *f* repliable, *F:* porte accordéon.

accordionist [ə'kɔːdiənist] *n.* accordéoniste *mf*.

accost [ə'kɔst] *v.tr.* (*a*) accoster, aborder (qn, un navire); (*b*) (*of prostitute*) racoler (qn).

account[1] [ə'kaunt] *n.* **1. to be quick at accounts,** être un calculateur rapide. **2.** (*a*) *Com:* compte *m*; **have an a.,** *U.S:* **a charge a., with s.o.,** avoir un compte chez qn; **put it on, charge it to, my a.,** inscrivez-le, mettez-le, à mon compte; **to pay a sum on a.,** payer une somme en acompte, à compte, à valoir; **to settle an a.,** (i) régler une note, un compte; (ii) *Fig:* régler ses comptes (**with s.o.,** avec qn); (*b*) **the accounts,** la comptabilité (d'une entreprise, etc.); **accounts department,** (service *m* de) la comptabilité; **profit and loss a.,** compte des profits et pertes; **to keep the accounts,** tenir les livres, les écritures, les comptes; (*c*) *Bank:* **bank a.,** compte en banque; **current, deposit, joint, a;** compte courant, de dépôt, joint; **to open an a.,** ouvrir un compte; **statement of a.,** relevé *m* de compte; (*d*) *St. Exch:* **the A.,** la liquidation (mensuelle); **a. day,** (jour *m* de) liquidation; (jour de) réglement *m*; **dealings for the a.,** négociations *fpl* à terme; (*e*) état *m*, note *f* (de dépenses); exposé *m* (de ses opérations); (*f*) (*in advertising*) budget *m* (publicitaire); **we were pleased to get X & Co.'s a.,** nous étions contents d'avoir X et Cie comme clients; (*g*) **to turn sth. to a.,** tirer parti, avantage, de qch.; mettre qch. à profit; **to turn sth. to good a.,** tirer un bon parti de qch.; (*h*) **to call s.o. to a. (for sth.),** demander une explication de qn, demander compte à qn (de qch.); **to bring s.o. to a.,** faire payer ses méfaits à qn; **to give a good a. of oneself,** (i) justifier de sa bonne conduite; (ii) s'acquitter bien. **3.** (*a*) **of no a.,** (homme) insignifiant, de peu d'importance; **to take sth. into a., to take a. of sth.,** tenir compte de qch.; faire entrer qch. en ligne de compte; **taking everything into a.,** tout calcul fait, tout bien calculé; **to leave (sth.) out of a., to take no a. of (sth.),** ne pas tenir compte de (qch.); ne pas compter (qch.); négliger (une circonstance); (*b*) **I did it on a. of you,** je l'ai fait à cause de vous; **on a. of sth.,** à, pour, cause de qch.; en raison de, qch.; **on no a., not on any a.,** dans aucun cas; (*c*) **to act on one's own a.,** agir de sa propre initiative, de soi-même; **to set up in business on one's own a.,** s'établir à son compte. **4.** récit *m*, relation *f*, narration *f* (d'un fait); exposé *m* (de la situation); compte *m* rendu (dans un journal); **to give an a. of sth.,** faire le récit, la relation, de qch.; **by all accounts,** au dire de tout le monde.

account[2] *v.tr. & ind.tr.* **1. to a. s.o. guilty,** tenir qn pour coupable. **2.** (*a*) **to a. for (sth.),** rendre compte de (sa conduite, une dépense); rendre raison de (sa conduite); justifier (sa conduite, une dépense); expliquer (une circonstance); **I can't a. for it,** je ne me l'explique pas; (*after accident, etc.*) **three people have still not been accounted for,** trois personnes n'ont pas encore été retrouvées; **there is no accounting for tastes,** chacun (à) son goût; (*b*) *F:* (= **kill**) **to a. for s.o.,** faire son affaire à qn. **accounting** *n.* comptabilité *f*; **cost a.,** comptabilité de prix de revient; **a. machine,** machine *f* comptable.

accountable [ə'kauntəbl] *a.* **to be a. to s.o. for sth.,** être responsable de qch. envers qn; être comptable à qn de qch.; **to be a. for a sum of money,** être redevable d'une somme d'argent; **I am a. to no one,** je ne dois rendre compte à personne.

accountancy [ə'kauntənsi] *n.* comptabilité *f*; expertise *f* comptable.

accountant [ə'kauntənt] *n.* (*a*) (agent *m*) comptable (*m*); **chief a.,** chef *m* de (la) comptabilité; (*b*) **chartered a.,** *U.S:* **certified public a.,** = (i) expert *m* comptable; (ii) conseiller fiscal; (*c*) **turf a.,** bookmaker *m*.

accoutrements, *NAm:* **accouterments** [ə'kuːtrəmənts, ə'kuːtəmənts] *n.pl.* équipement *m* (du soldat).

accredit [ə'kredit] *v.tr.* accréditer (un ambassadeur) (**to a government,** auprès d'un gouvernement). **accredited** *a.* (*of pers.*) accrédité, autorisé.

accretion [ə'kriːʃ(ə)n] *n.* (*a*) accroissement *m* organique; (*b*) accrétion *f*; accroissement par alluvion, par addition.

accrue [ə'kruː] *v.i.* **1.** (*a*) provenir, dériver (**from,** de); (*b*) (*of moneys, land, etc.*) **to a. to s.o.,** revenir à qn. **2.** *Fin:* (*of interest*) s'accumuler; **accrued interest,** intérêt couru; intérêts (ac)cumulés.

accumulate [ə'kjuːmjuleit] **1.** *v.tr.* (*a*) accumuler, amasser (une fortune, etc.); amonceler, entasser (des objets); emmagasiner (de l'électricité, etc.); (*b*) *Cmptr:* (ac)cumuler, totaliser (dans un registre, etc.). **2.** *v.i.* s'accumuler, s'amonceler, s'amasser. **accumulated** *a.* accumulé; **a. dividends,** dividendes accumulées; *Cmptr:* **a. error,** erreur cumulée.

accumulation [əkjuːmju'leiʃ(ə)n] *n.* **1.** (*a*) accumulation *f*; amoncellement *m*, entassement *m*; emmagasinage *m* (de la chaleur, de l'électricité); (*b*) *Cmptr:* accumulation, cumul *m*. **2.** amas *m*, tas *m* (d'objets, de sable, etc.); accumulation (de faits).

accumulative [ə'kjuːmjulətiv] *a.* qui s'accumule; *Fin:* cumulatif.

accumulator [ə'kjuːmjuleitər] *n.* **1.** (*pers.*) accumulateur, -trice (de richesses, etc.). **2.** (*a*) *Mec.E: Civ.E:* accumulateur *m* (d'énergie, de vapeur, etc.); (*b*) *El:* accumulateur; (*c*) *Cmptr:* accumulateur. **3.** *Turf:* **a. (bet),** pari *m* avec report.

accuracy ['ækjurəsi] *n.* (*a*) exactitude *f;* justesse *f*, précision *f*; (*b*) fidélité *f* (de mémoire); exactitude (d'une citation); (*c*) *Cmptr:* **a. control character, system,** caractère *m*, système *m*, de contrôle de précision.

accurate ['ækjurət] *a.* (*a*) exact, juste, précis; **a. scales,** balance *f* juste; **he is a. at figures,** c'est un bon calculateur; **to be (strictly) a. . . .,** pour être tout à fait exact . . .; **to take a. aim,** viser juste; (*b*) (mémoire, traduction, dessin) fidèle; (citation) exacte. **-ly** *adv.* (*a*) exactement; avec précision; (*b*) (traduire) fidèlement; (dessiner qch.) correctement.

accurateness ['ækjurətnis] *n.* exactitude *f*; précision *f*.

accursed [ə'kəːsid] *a. Lit:* maudit.

accusation [ækju'zeiʃ(ə)n] *n.* **1.** accusation *f*; *Jur:* incrimination *f*. **2.** *Jur:* acte *m* d'accusation.

accusative [ə'kjuːzətiv] *a. & n. Gram:* **a. (case),** (cas) accusatif (*m*); **in the a.,** à l'accusatif.

accuse [ə'kjuːz] *v.tr.* accuser (**s.o. of sth., of doing sth.,** qn de qch., de faire qch.); *Jur:* incriminer (qn). **accused** *n. Jur:* **the a.,** l'inculpé(e); le, la, prévenu(e) (d'un délit); l'accusé(e) (d)un crime). **accusing** *a.* accusateur, -trice. **accusingly** *adv.* d'une manière accusatrice.

accuser [ə'kjuːzər] *n.* accusateur, -trice.

accustom [ə'kʌstəm] *v.tr.* accoutumer, habituer (**s.o. to sth., to do sth.,** qn à qch., à faire qch.); **to a. oneself,** s'accoutumer, s'habituer (**to sth.,** à qch.); se faire (à la discipline, etc.). **accustomed** *a.* **1.** accoutumé, habitué (**to,** à); **to be a. to . . .,** (i) avoir coutume de . . .; (ii) être accoutumé à . . .; **I am a. to getting up early,** j'ai l'habitude de me lever de bonne heure; **to get a. to sth.,** s'accoutumer à qch. **2.** habituel, coutumier.

ace [eis] *n.* **1.** (*a*) (*at dice, dominoes, cards*) as *m*; *F:* **to have an a. up one's sleeve,** avoir un as dans sa manche; (*b*) *Ten:* **(service) a.,** ace *m.* **2.** (*pers.*) as; **flying a.,** as de l'aviation; **a. reporter,** journaliste d'élite. **3. within an a. of sth.,** à deux doigts de qch.

acerb(ic) [ə'sə:b(ik] *a.* (*of fruit*) aigre; (*of pers.*) acerbe, mordant.

acerbity [ə'sə:biti] *n.* aigreur *f*; acerbité *f.*

acetate ['æsiteit] *n. Ch:* acétate *m.*

acetic [æ'si:tik, -'set-] *a. Ch:* (acide, etc.) acétique.

acetone ['æsitoun] *n. Ch:* acétone *f.*

acetylene [æ'setili:n] *n. Ch:* acétylène *m*; **a. lamp** lanterne *f* à acétylène; **a. welding,** soudure *f* autogène.

ache[1] [eik] *n.* mal *m,* douleur *f*; **stomach a.,** mal de ventre; **to have (a) stomach a.,** avoir mal au ventre; *F:* **I'm all aches and pains,** j'ai mal partout.

ache[2] *v.i.* **my head aches,** j'ai mal à la tête; **it makes my head a.,** cela me donne mal à la tête; **I'm aching all over,** j'ai mal partout; **it makes my heart a.,** cela me serre le cœur; *F:* **he was aching to join in the fight,** il brûlait de prendre part au combat. **aching** *a.* (dent, tête, etc.) qui (vous) fait mal; (*of leg, Lit: of heart*) endolori; *F:* **to have an a. void,** avoir l'estomac creux.

achieve [ə'tʃi:v] *v.tr.* **1.** accomplir (un exploit); exécuter, réaliser (une entreprise). **2.** acquérir (une honneur); se faire (une réputation). **3.** atteindre (à), arriver à (un but); **to a. one's purpose, one's ends,** parvenir, en venir, à ses fins; **to a. the impossible,** faire l'impossible; **he will never a. anything,** il n'arrivera jamais à rien.

achievement [ə'tʃi:vmənt] *n.* **1.** accomplissement *m,* réalisation *f,* exécution *f* (d'un projet, etc.). **2.** (*a*) exploit *m,* (haut) fait; (*b*) **when we consider his a.,** lorsque nous considérons (i) son œuvre, (ii) l'effort qu'il a accompli.

Achilles [ə'kili:z] *Pr.n.m.* Achille; **Achilles' tendon,** tendon *m* d'Achille; **gambling is his Achilles' heel,** le jeu est son point faible.

achromatic [ækrou'mætik] *a. Opt:* achromatique.

achy ['eiki] *a.* courbaturé; *F:* **I feel rather a.,** j'ai mal un peu partout.

acid[1] ['æsid] *a.* (*a*) acide; *Comest:* **a. drop,** bonbon acidulé; *Ch:* **a. solution,** solution *f* acide; (*b*) (ton, réponse) acide. **-ly** *adv.* aigrement, avec aigreur.

acid[2] *n.* (*a*) acide *m*; **a. bath,** bain *m* acide; **a. test,** (i) épreuve à la pierre de touche; (ii) épreuve décisive, concluante; (*b*) *F:* **(= L.S.D.)** acide *m.*

acidic [ə'sidik] *a.* acide; **a. rocks,** roches acides.

acidify [ə'sidifai] **1.** *v.tr.* acidifier.

acidity [ə'siditi] *n.* **1.** (*a*) acidité *f*; (*b*) *Med:* aigreurs *fpl.* **2.** aigreur (d'une réponse).

acidosis [əsi'dousis] *n. Med:* acidose *f.*

acidulate [ə'sidjuleit] *v.tr.* aciduler.

acidulous [ə'sidjuləs] *n.* acidulé.

ack-ack ['æk'æk] *n. Mil:* (i) artillerie anti-aérienne; (ii) Défense contre avions (D.C.A.); **a.-a. fire,** tir anti-aérien.

acknowledge [ək'nɔlidʒ] *v.tr.* **1.** (*a*) reconnaître, avouer (une erreur, une dette, etc.); **he was acknowledged as king,** il fut reconnu pour roi; **to a. sth. as a fact,** faire la constatation de qch.; **to a. oneself beaten, to a. defeat,** s'avouer, se reconnaître, vaincu; (*b*) reconnaître (un service); se montrer reconnaissant, exprimer sa reconnaissance, d'(un service). **2.** répondre à (une courtoisie, un salut, etc.); **to a. (receipt of) a letter,** accuser réception d'une lettre; *Nau:* **to a. a signal,** faire l'aperçu. **acknowledged** *a.* **1.** (*a*) (fait) reconnu, avéré; (*b*) **an a. thief,** un voleur reconnu. **2.** (expert, etc.) qui fait autorité.

acknowledg(e)ment [ək'nɔlidʒmənt] *n.* **1.** (*a*) reconnaissance *f* (d'une erreur, etc.); aveu *m* (d'une faute); constatation *f* (d'un fait); (*b*) reconnaissance (d'un service); **in a. of,** pour témoigner ma, sa, reconnaissance de (ce service). **2.** reçu *m,* quittance *f* (d'un paiement); **a. (of receipt),** accusé de réception (d'une lettre). **3. acknowledgements,** remerciements *mpl.*

acme ['ækmi] *n. Lit:* comble *m* (de la perfection); sommet *m* (de la gloire); apogée *m* (de la puissance).

acne ['ækni] *n. Med:* acné *f.*

acolyte ['ækəlait] *n.* acolyte *m.*

aconite ['ækənait] *n. Bot: Pharm:* aconit *m.*

acorn ['eikɔ:n] *n. Bot:* gland *m* (de chêne).

acotyledon [eikɔti'li:d(ə)n] *n.* plante *f* acotylédone.

acoustic [ə'ku:stik] *a.* (*a*) acoustique; (signal, etc.) sonore; *Anat:* **a. nerve,** nerf acoustique, auditif; (*b*) **a. tile,** carreau *m,* panneau *m,* insonorisant. **-ally** *adv.* acoustiquement.

acoustics [ə'ku:stiks] *n.pl.* (*with sg. or pl. const.*) acoustique *f*; **the a. of this hall are excellent,** cette salle a une bonne acoustique.

acquaint [ə'kweint] *v.tr.* **1. to a. s.o. with (sth.),** informer, avertir, qn de (qch.); faire savoir (qch.) à qn; apprendre (un fait) à qn; mettre qn au courant de (ses fonctions, la situation). **2. to be acquainted with s.o., sth.,** connaître qn, qch.; être au fait, au courant, de qch.; **to become acquainted,** (i) (*of two people*) faire connaissance; (ii) (*of pers.*) faire, lier, connaissance (**with s.o.,** avec qn); faire la connaissance (**with s.o.,** de qn); prendre connaissance (**with the facts,** des faits); s'initier (**with one's duties,** à ses fonctions).

acquaintance [ə'kweintəns] *n.* **1.** (*a*) **a. with,** connaissance *f* d'(un fait, une langue); (*b*) **a. with s.o.,** connaissance de qn; **to make s.o.'s a.,** faire la connaissance de qn. **2.** (*pers.*) connaissance; **he is an a. (of mine),** je le connais; **to have a wide circle of acquaintances,** avoir des relations très étendues.

acquiesce [ækwi'es] *v.i.* acquiescer, donner son assentiment (**in a request,** à une demande); accepter (**in an arrangement**, un arrangement).

acquiescence [ækwi'es(ə)ns] *n.* acquiescement *m* (**in,** à); assentiment *m,* consentement *m.*

acquiescent [ækwi'es(ə)nt] *a.* consentant.

acquire [ə'kwaiər] *v.tr.* acquérir (qch.); prendre, contracter (une habitude); **to a. a taste for sth.,** prendre goût à qch.; **acquired taste,** goût acquis.

acquirement [ə'kwaiəmənt] *n.* **1.** acquisition *f* (**of,** de). **2.** (*a*) talent (acquis); (*b*) connaissance *f.*

acquisition [ækwi'ziʃ(ə)n] *n.* **1.** acquisition *f* (**of,** de); *Cmptr:* **data a.,** saisie *f,* collecte *f,* rassemblement *m,* de données. **2.** acquisition; **my new acquisitions,** mes nouvelles acquisitions.

acquisitive [ə'kwizitiv] *a.* thésauriseur, -euse.

acquit [ə'kwit] *v.tr.* **(acquitting, acquitted) 1.** acquitter, s'acquitter d'(une dette); régler (une dette). **2.** acquitter (un accusé); **to a. s.o. of (sth.),** absoudre qn d'(une faute); décharger qn d'(une accusation). **3. to a. oneself well,** bien s'en tirer.

acquittal [ə'kwit(ə)l] *n.* **1.** *Jur:* acquittement *m* (d'un accusé, d'un débiteur); décharge *f* (d'un accusé). **2.** exécution *f,* accomplissement *m* (d'un devoir).

acquittance [ə'kwitəns] *n. Com: Jur:* acquit *m,* acquittement *m* (d'une dette).

acre ['eikər] *n. Meas:* acre *f* (0·4 hectare); (*approx.* =) arpent *m,* demi-hectare *m*; **vast acres,** des terres étendues.

acreage ['eikəridʒ] *n.* superficie *f* (en mesures agraires).

acrid ['ækrid] *a.* **1.** (goût, fumée) âcre. **2.** (style) mordant; (critique) acerbe; (humeur) âcre.

acrimonious [ækri'mouniəs] *a.* acrimonieux; (*of woman*) acariâtre; **the discussion became a.,** la discussion s'envenimait. **-ly** *adv.* avec acrimonie.

acrimony ['ækriməni], **acrimoniousness** [ækri'mouniəsnis] *n.* acrimonie *f*; aigreur *f* (de ton, de caractère).

acrobat ['ækrəbæt] *n.* acrobate *mf.*
acrobatic [ækrə'bætik] **1.** *a.* acrobatique; **a. feat,** acrobatie *f*; tour *m* d'acrobate, d'acrobatie. **2.** *n.pl.* **acrobatics,** acrobatie *f.*
acronym ['ækrənim] *n.* sigle *m.*
acropolis [ə'krɔpəlis] *n.* acropole *f.*
across [ə'krɔs] *adv. & prep.* **1.** en travers (de); **with his arms folded a. his chest,** les bras croisés sur la poitrine; **line drawn a. the page,** ligne tirée en travers de la page. **2.** (*a*) **to walk a. (a street),** traverser (une rue); **a. country,** à travers champs; **to swim a. a river,** traverser une rivière à la nage; **to go a. a bridge,** passer (sur) un pont; franchir un pont; (*of play*) **to get, come, a.,** passer la rampe; plaire à l'assistance; **to get sth. a. to s.o.,** faire comprendre qch. à qn; (*b*) **to come a. a passage in a book,** rencontrer (par hasard) un passage dans un livre; **we ran a. each other,** nous nous sommes rencontrés; (*c*) *F:* **to come a. with the money,** payer; **the police persuaded him to come a.,** la police l'a persuadé de parler. **3.** (*a*) **the distance a.,** (i) la distance en largeur; (ii) la longueur de la traversée; **2 km a.,** 2 km de large; **he is broad a. the shoulders,** il est large d'épaules; (*b*) **a. the street,** de l'autre côté de la rue; **the countries a. the seas,** les pays d'outremer; **they talked to each other a. the table,** ils se parlaient d'un côté de la table à l'autre; (*c*) (*in crossword*) horizontalement.
across-the-board [ə'krɔsðə'bɔːd] *a.* général; **an a.-t.-b. wage increase,** une augmentation générale des salaires; **a.-t.-b. cuts,** réduction linéaire générale (des droits de douane, etc.).
acrostic [ə'krɔstik] *a. & n.* acrostiche (*m*).
acrylic [ə'krilik] *Ch:* **1.** *a.* acrylique. **2.** *n.* (*a*) résine *f* acrylique; (*b*) fibre *f* acrylique.
act¹ [ækt] *n.* **1.** (*a*) acte *m* (de justice, de bonté, etc.); **a. of grace,** measure *f* de grâce; **a. of war,** acte de guerre; (*b*) *Theol:* **a. of faith,** acte de foi; (*c*) **A. of Parliament,** loi *f*, décret *m*; **Companies A.,** loi sur les sociétés; **factory a.,** législation industrielle; loi sur les accidents du travail; **land a.,** loi agraire; (*d*) **the Acts of the Apostles,** les Actes des Apôtres. **2.** action *f*; **an a. of folly,** une folie; **to catch s.o. in the (very) a.,** prendre qn sur le fait, en flagrant délit, *F:* la main dans le sac; *Jur: Ins:* **a. of God,** (i) (cas de) force majeure; (ii) cas fortuit; cause naturelle. **3.** *Th: etc:* (*a*) acte (d'une pièce); (*b*) numéro *m* (d'un artiste); **circus a.,** numéro de cirque; **to put on an a.,** jouer la comédie; **it's all an a.,** c'est du cinéma; **to get in on the a.,** se mettre dans le mouvement; **to be, to let s.o., in on the a.,** être, mettre qn, dans le coup.
act² **1.** *v.tr.* (*a*) jouer, représenter (une pièce, un personnage); remplir (un rôle); **to a. Hamlet,** jouer, faire, Hamlet; **to a. the fool, the goat,** faire l'imbécile, *F:* le zigoto; (*b*) **to a. a part,** feindre; faire, jouer, la comédie; **he was only acting,** il faisait semblant; (*c*) **to a. the part of an honest man,** se conduire, agir, en honnête homme. **2.** *v.i.* (*a*) agir; prendre des mesures; **it is time to a.,** il est temps d'agir; **he did not know how to a.,** il ne savait (i) quoi faire, comment se conduire, (ii) quel parti prendre; **to a. prudently, promptly,** agir prudemment, promptement; **I acted for the best,** j'ai fait pour le mieux; **to a. for s.o.,** agir au nom de qn; représenter qn; **to a. as secretary, etc.,** exercer les fonctions de secrétaire, etc.; **to a. on (sth.),** agir d'après (un conseil), suivre (un conseil); exécuter (un ordre); donner suite à (une lettre); (*b*) **the police refused to a.,** la police refusa d'intervenir; **the brake refuses to a.,** le frein ne fonctionne pas; **the engine acts as a brake,** le moteur fait fonction de frein; (*c*) (*of remedy*) faire son effet; **to a. on the brain, the bowels,** agir, exercer une action, sur le cerveau, sur l'intestin; **acid that acts on metals,** acide qui mord sur les métaux, qui entame les métaux; (*d*) *Th: Cin:* jouer; **he can't a.,** c'est un mauvais acteur; **to a. in a film,** tourner dans un film; (*e*) **to a. up,** (i) (*of pers.*) se conduire mal; (ii) (*of machine*) marcher mal; **the car's acting up again,** la voiture recommence à faire des siennes. **acting 1.** *a.* suppléant; intérimaire; **a. manager,** (i) directeur gérant; (ii) directeur intérimaire; gérant *m* provisoire. **2.** *n.* (*a*) action *f*; (*b*) *Th:* jeu *m*, interprétation *f* (d'un acteur); (*c*) **she's done some a.,** elle a fait du théâtre; *F:* **it's just a.,** c'est de la comédie.
action ['ækʃ(ə)n] *n.* **1.** action *f* (d'une personne, d'un remède, etc.); **the a. of water,** le travail des eaux, l'action de l'eau (sur la berge d'une rivière, etc.); **to take a.,** agir; intervenir; **industrial a.,** grève *f*; **line of a.,** ligne *f* de conduite; **man of a.,** homme d'action; **sphere of a.,** sphère *f* d'activité; **to put a plan into a.,** mettre un projet à exécution; **to come into a.,** entrer en action, en jeu; (*of machine*) **in a.,** en marche; **to bring the law into a.,** faire intervenir la loi; **out of a.,** hors de service; en panne; **to put a machine out of a.,** détraquer une machine; *Cmptr:* **a. switch,** touche *f*, bouton *m*, de service; *Art:* **a. painting,** peinture gestuelle. **2.** action, acte *m*, fait *m*; **impulsive a.,** action irréfléchie; coup *m* de tête. **3.** *Th:* action (d'une pièce); **the a. takes place in . . .,** la scène se passe à . . . **4.** (*a*) action, gestes *mpl* (d'un joueur); train *m*, allure *f*, action (d'un cheval); (*b*) mécanisme *m* (d'une montre, etc.); jeu *m* (d'une pompe, d'une serrure); mécanique *f* (d'un piano, d'un orgue). **5.** *Jur:* **a. at law, legal a.,** action en justice; procès *m*; **a. for libel,** procès, plainte *f*, en diffamation; **a. for damages,** action en dommages et intérêts; **to bring an a. against s.o.,** intenter une action, un procès, à, contre, qn. **6.** (*a*) *Mil: etc:* combat *m*, engagement *m*; **naval a.,** engagement naval, opération navale; **to go into a.,** entrer en action, engager le combat; **ready for a.,** prêt(s) à combattre; **to send troops into a.,** faire intervenir, faire donner, des troupes; **out of a.,** (i) hors de combat; (ii) hors de service, *F:* de cause; **killed in a.,** tué à l'ennemi; **his illness will put, keep, him out of a. for a month,** sa maladie le mettra hors de combat pendant un mois; (*b*) activité *f*; **let's have a bit of a.!** un peu d'activité! *F:* grouillez-vous!
actionable ['ækʃənəbl] *a. Jur:* (mot, action) qui expose à des poursuites; actionnable.
activate ['æktiveit] *v.tr.* **1.** (*a*) *Ch: Biol: etc:* activer; **activated carbon,** carbon actif, activé; (b) *Cmptr:* lancer (un programme). **2.** *Ph:* rendre (un corps) radio-actif.
activation [ækti'veiʃ(ə)n] *n.* (*a*) activation *f*; (*b*) *Cmptr:* déclenchement *m*; commande *f.*
active ['æktiv] **1.** *a.* (*a*) (homme, etc.) actif; (cerveau) éveillé; (imagination) vive; **a. life,** vie active; **to be still a.,** être encore alerte, allant, actif; (*of volcano*) **to become a.,** entrer en activité; (*b*) *Cmptr:* (compte, fichier) mouvementé; (programme) en cours d'exécution; **a. store,** mémoire active; (*c*) *Ph:* radio-actif; (*d*) **a. charcoal,** charbon actif; (*e*) *Mec:* (pression) effective; *El:* **a. cell,** élément (d'accu) chargé. **2.** *a. & n. Gram:* **verb in the a. (voice),** verbe *m* à l'actif *m*. **3.** *a.* (*a*) (rôle, etc.) actif; **to take an a. part in sth.,** prendre une part active, effective, à qch.; (*b*) *Mil: etc:* (service) actif; **to be on the a. list,** (i) être sur l'annuaire de l'armée active; (ii) être en service actif, en activité de service; **to see a. service for the first time,** (i) faire sa première campagne; (ii) recevoir le baptême du feu. **-ly** *adv.* activement.
activist ['æktivist] *n. Pol:* activiste *mf.*
activity [æk'tiviti] *n.* **1.** activité *f*; **in full a.,** en pleine activité; **economic a.,** activité économique. **2.** activité, action *f*; **his numerous activities leave him little leisure,** ses nombreuses occupations lui laissent peu de loisirs. **3.** *Ph:* (*a*) radioactivité *f*; (*b*) (*of a source*)

activité. **4.** *Cmptr:* mouvement *m* (portant sur un fichier).

actor ['æktər] *n.* acteur *m*; comédien *m*; **film a.,** acteur de cinéma; **to be an a., a film a.,** faire du théâtre, du cinéma.

actress ['æktris] *n.* actrice *f*; comédienne *f*; **film a.,** actrice de cinéma.

actual ['æktjuəl] *a.* **1.** réel, véritable; (fait) positif; (cas) concret; **a. size,** grandeur réelle, vraie grandeur; **to give the a. figures,** donner les chiffres mêmes; **in a. fact,** effectivement, en fait; *Com:* **a. cost,** prix *m* (i) d'achat, (ii) de revient. **2.** actuel, présent; **the a. state of affairs,** l'état de choses actuel. **-ally** *adv.* **1.** (*a*) réellement, effectivement; en fait, en réalité; **a., I rather like it,** à vrai dire, ça me plaît beaucoup; (*b*) **he a. swore,** il est allé (même) jusqu'à lâcher un juron; **he a. said good morning to me,** à mon grand étonnement il m'a dit bonjour. **2.** *occ.* actuellement, à présent.

actuality [æktju'æliti] *n.* (*a*) réalité *f*; (*b*) actualité *f*; le temps présent; **play that lacks a.,** pièce qui n'a aucun rapport avec la vie d'aujourd'hui.

actuarial [æktju'ɛəriəl] *a.* actuariel.

actuary ['æktjuəri] *n.* *Ins:* actuaire *m*; **actuaries' tables,** tables *fpl* de mortalité.

actuate ['æktjueit] *v.tr.* **1.** mettre en action, faire marcher (une machine, etc.). **2.** faire agir (qn); **actuated by jealousy,** poussé par la jalousie.

actuation [æktju'eiʃ(ə)n] *n.* mise *f* en action (d'une machine, etc.).

acuity [ə'kju(:)iti] *n.* acuité *f* (d'une pointe, de l'esprit, de la douleur, etc.); **visual a.,** acuité visuelle.

acumen ['ækjumən] *n.* pénétration *f*, finesse *f* (d'esprit); perspicacité *f*; **he's got plenty of business a.,** il est très commerçant.

acupressure ['ækjupreʃər] *n.* digitopuncture *f*.

acupuncture ['ækjupʌŋktjər] *n.* acupuncture *f*.

acupuncturist [ækju'pʌŋktjərist] *n.* *Med:* acupuncteur *m*.

acute [ə'kju:t] *a.* **1.** (*a*) (angle) aigu; (pointe) aiguë; (*b*) *Gram:* (accent) aigu. **2.** (*a*) (son) aigu; (douleur) aiguë, intense; vive (douleur); **a. remorse,** remords cruels; (*of anxiety, etc.*) **to become more a.,** s'aviver; (*b*) *Med: etc:* (maladie, période) aiguë; **operation for a. appendicitis,** opération à chaud pour l'appendicite; **the present a. crisis,** la crise qui sévit actuellement. **3.** (*a*) (ouïe) fine; (vue) perçante; (*b*) (esprit) fin, perspicace; **an a. observer,** un observateur pénétrant; **an a. businessman,** un homme d'affaires avisé, perspicace. **-ly** *adv.* **1.** vivement; intensément. **2.** finement; avec perspicacité.

acute-angled [ə'kju:tæŋgld] *a.* à angle(s) aigu(s).

acuteness [ə'kju:tnis] *n.* **1.** aiguïté *f* (d'un angle). **2.** (*a*) acuité *f* (d'une douleur, d'un son); intensité *f* (d'une douleur, d'un remords); (*b*) caractère aigu (d'une maladie, d'un accès). **3.** (*a*) finesse *f* (d'ouïe); acuité (de la vision); vivacité *f* (d'un sentiment); (*b*) pénétration *f*, perspicacité *f* (de l'esprit).

ad [æd] *n.* *F:* annonce *f*; **small ads,** petites annonces.

adage ['ædidʒ] *n.* adage *m*; maxime *f*.

adagio [ə'dɑ(d)ʒiou] *adv.* & *n.* adagio (*m*).

Adam ['ædəm] *Pr.n.m.* Adam; **Adam's apple,** pomme *f* d'Adam; **not to know s.o. from A.,** ne connaître qn ni d'Ève ni d'Adam.

adamant ['ædəmənt] *a.* dur; inflexible, intransigeant; **he is a. on this point,** sur ce point il ne transige pas. **-ly** *adv.* inflexiblement; d'une manière intransigeante.

adapt [ə'dæpt] **1.** *v.tr.* adapter, ajuster (**sth. to sth.,** qch. à qch.); remanier (une œuvre); **to a. a novel for the stage,** adapter un roman à la scène; **text adapted from Cicero,** texte d'après Cicéron; **to a. oneself,** s'adapter, s'accommoder (**to circumstances, new surroundings,** aux circonstances, etc.). **2.** *v.i.* s'adapter; **to a. to a new environment,** s'adapter à un nouveau milieu; **failure to a.,** refus *m* de s'adapter. **adapted** *a.* (*a*) **a. to sth.,** approprié à, fait pour, qch.; (*b*) (roman, etc.) adapté (**for the stage,** à la scène).

adaptability [ədæptə'biliti] *n.* faculté *f* d'adaptation; **a. to environment,** adaptabilité *f* au milieu.

adaptable [ə'dæptəbl] *a.* **1.** (*a*) adaptable, ajustable (**to,** à); (*b*) susceptible d'être utilisé (**for,** pour; **to an end,** dans un but). **2.** (personne) qui s'arrange de tout, qui s'accommode à toutes les circonstances.

adaptation [ædæp'teiʃ(ə)n] *n.* **1.** (*a*) adaptation *f*, appropriation *f* (**of sth. to sth.,** de qch. à qch.); **a. for the stage,** adaptation à la scène; (*b*) *Biol:* adaptation, finalité *f*; (*c*) *Opt:* **dark, light, a.,** adaptation à l'obscurité, à la lumière. **2.** (*novel, play*) adaptation.

adapter, adaptor [ə'dæptər] *n.* **1.** adaptateur *m*, auteur *m* d'une adaptation. **2.** intermédiaire *m* de raccord; (*a*) *El:* adaptateur; raccord *m* (de lampe); (*b*) *Phot:* parquet *m* d'adaptation (de l'appareil); **lens a.,** bague *f* porte-objectif; (*c*) *Rec:* centreur *m*.

adaptive [ə'dæptiv] *a.* *Biol:* (mécanisme) adaptif.

add [æd] *v.tr.* & *v.ind.tr.* **1.** (*a*) ajouter (**to,** à); **to a. to (sth.),** faire une addition à, agrandir (un bâtiment); augmenter, ajouter à (une difficulté, etc.); rehausser (la beauté de qn, qch.); accentuer (une difficulté, une crise); **to a. water to (sth.),** ajouter de l'eau à (qch.); **to a. sth. in,** ajouter, inclure, qch.; *Mth:* **to a. a zero,** apposer un zéro; **added reason,** raison de plus; **to a. to my work,** par surcroît de besogne; **to a. to my misfortune,** pour mettre le comble à mon malheur; (*b*) ajouter; **he added that . . .,** il ajouta que . . .. **2.** *Mth:* (*a*) **to a. six to eight,** additionner six avec huit; ajouter six à huit; **to a. (up, together) ten numbers,** additionner dix nombres; faire l'addition de dix nombres; **to a. up a column of figures,** totaliser une colonne de chiffres; **to a. up correctly,** additionner correctement; (*b*) **to a. up to (sth.),** (i) donner un total de (tant); (ii) *Fig:* signifier (qch.); **the accounts won't a. up,** je n'arrive pas à faire accorder les comptes; **it just doesn't a. up,** cela n'a ni rime ni raison. **3.** *Carp: Needlew:* raccorder (une pièce à une autre). **adding** *n.* addition *f*; **a. machine,** machine *f* à calculer; calculatrice *f*; *Cmptr:* **a. circuit,** circuit additionneur, d'addition.

addendum, *pl.* **-a** [æ'dendəm, -ə] *n.* (*a*) addenda *m*; (*b*) addition *f* (à un livre, etc.); supplément *m*.

adder[1] ['ædər] *n.* **1.** (*pers.*) additionneur, -euse. **2.** (*a*) machine *f* à additionner; additionneuse *f*; (*b*) *Cmptr:* additionneur.

adder[2] *n.* vipère *f*.

addict[1] ['ædikt] *n.* (*a*) personne adonnée à (l'opium, etc.); *Med:* intoxiqué, -ée; **drug a.,** toxicomane *mf*; drogué(e) *mf*; **morphine a.,** morphinomane *mf*; (*b*) *F:* fanatique *mf* (de football, de la danse, etc.).

addict[2] [ə'dikt] *v.tr.* **to be addicted to (sth.),** s'adonner à, être adonné à (l'alcool, l'opium, etc.); **to become addicted to drugs, to morphine,** devenir toxicomane, morphinomane.

addiction [ə'dikʃ(ə)n] *n.* (*a*) inclination *f* (**for,** à); (*b*) *Med:* assuétude *f*; **drug a.,** toxicomanie *f*; **a. to morphia,** morphinomanie *f*.

addictive [ə'diktiv] *a.* *Med:* (drogue) qui cause le phénomène de dépendance.

addition [ə'diʃ(ə)n] *n.* **1.** (*a*) addition *f*; **he has just had an a. to his family,** sa famille vient d'augmenter; **additions to the staff,** adjonction *f* de personnel; **in a.,** en outre, de plus; par surcroît; **in a. to sth.,** en plus de qch.; **in a. to that sum,** outre cette somme; **in a. to these misfortunes,** pour surcroît de malheur; **to pay sth. in a.,** payer un supplément; (*b*) *Const:* rajout *m*, extension *f* (à un bâtiment); (*c*) *Cmptr:*

addition; **a. circuit,** circuit *m* d'addition. **2.** *Mth:* addition.

additional [ə'diʃən(ə)l] *a.* additionnel, supplémentaire; **a. postage,** surtaxe *f*; *Post:* **for each a. 50 gr.,** au-dessus, par 50 gr.; *Adm:* **a. tax,** impôt additionnel; supplément *m* d'imposition; *Fin: Com: etc:* **a. payment,** supplément; *Ins:* **a. clause,** avenant *m*; **a. security,** contre-caution *f*. **-ally** *adv.* en outre (**to,** de); en sus; par addition; en supplément (**to,** de).

additive ['æditiv] *n.* additif *m.*

addled ['ædl(ə)d] *a.* (*a*) (œuf) pourri, gâté, couvi; (*b*) *F:* (cerveau) trouble, brouillé.

address[1] [ə'dres] *n.* **1.** (*a*) adresse *f* (d'une personne, d'une lettre); **of no (known) a.,** sans domicile connu; **home, private, a.,** adresse privée, personnelle; **a. book,** carnet *m* d'adresses; (*b*) *Cmptr:* **base a.,** adresse de base. **2.** *A: & Lit: pl.* **to pay one's addresses to a lady,** faire la cour à une femme. **3.** discours *m*, allocution *f*. **4. form of a.,** titre *m* (à donner en s'adressant à qn).

address[2] *v.tr.* **1.** (*a*) **to a. a letter to s.o.,** adresser une lettre à qn.; (*b*) **to a. a letter,** mettre, écrire, l'adresse sur une lettre; **a stamped, addressed, envelope,** une enveloppe timbrée avec son adresse. **2.** (*a*) **to a. reproaches, criticisms, to s.o.,** adresser des reproches, des critiques, à qn; (*b*) **to a. s.o.,** (i) aborder, accoster, qn; (ii) adresser la parole à qn; **he addressed me as 'Colonel',** il m'a appelé "Colonel"; (*c*) **to a. a crowd,** haranguer une foule; **to a. a meeting,** prendre la parole à une réunion; (*d*) *Cmptr:* adresser, accéder à. **3.** *Golf:* viser (la balle). **4.** *O:* **to a. oneself to a task,** se mettre à une tâche.

addressee [ædre'si:] *n.* destinataire *mf*; receveur *m* (d'un télégramme, etc.).

adduce [ə'dju:s] *v.tr.* alléguer, apporter (des raisons, des preuves, etc.); invoquer, citer (une autorité).

adduct [æ'dʌkt] *v.tr. Physiol:* déterminer l'adduction (d'un muscle, etc.).

adduction [æ'dʌkʃ(ə)n] *n.* **1.** allégation *f* (d'une raison); citation *f*, invocation *f* (d'une autorité). **2.** *Physiol:* adduction *f*.

adenoidal [ædi'nɔid(ə)l] *a.* adénoïdien.

adenoids ['ædinɔidz] *n.pl. Med:* végétations *fpl* (adénoïdes).

adept ['ædept] **1.** *a.* **to be a. in sth., at doing sth.,** être expert, habile, à qch., à faire qch. **2.** *n.* adepte *mf*; expert *m* (**in,** en).

adequacy ['ædikwəsi] *n.* adéquation *f*; suffisance *f*.

adequate ['ædikwət] *a.* (*a*) adéquat, suffisant (**to,** à); compétent; **a. supply,** quantité suffisante (de viande, etc.); **a. reward,** récompense adéquate, suffisante; **room of a. size,** pièce *f* d'une grandeur raisonnable; (*b*) proportionné (**to,** à); **a. remuneration for the work carried out,** rémunération proportionnée, correspondant, au travail accompli; (*c*) **this material is scarcely a. for a winter coat,** ce tissu n'est guère approprié à un manteau d'hiver. **-ly** *adv.* suffisamment, convenablement.

adhere [əd'hiər] *v.i.* **1.** (*of thg*) adhérer, se coller (**to,** à); **the scab adheres to the wound,** la croûte tient à la plaie. **2.** (*of pers.*) (*a*) **to a. to a party,** adhérer, donner son adhésion, à un parti; (*b*) **to a. to (sth.),** observer (une promesse, une règle, etc.); persister dans (sa décision); s'en tenir à, maintenir (sa décision).

adherence [əd'hiərəns] *n.* **1.** (*of thg*) adhérence *f* (**to,** à). **2.** (*of pers.*) adhésion *f* (à un parti).

adherent [əd'hiərənt] **1.** *a.* (*a*) adhérent (**to,** à); collé, attaché (**to,** à); (*b*) *Nat.Hist:* connexe (**to,** avec); adhérent. **2.** *n.* adhérent, -ente; partisan *m.*

adhesion [əd'hi:ʒ(ə)n] *n.* **1.** adhésion *f* (**to,** à); accession *f* (à un parti). **2.** *Mec: Med: Surg: Bot:* adhérence *f*.

adhesive [əd'hi:siv] **1.** *a.* (ruban, etc.) adhésif; (enveloppe) gommée; **a. stamp,** timbre adhésif, mobile; *Med:* **a. plaster,** *NAm:* **a. tape,** sparadrap *m.* **2.** *a.* adhérent; *Mec:* **a. capacity,** pouvoir adhérent. **3.** *n.* colle *f*, adhésif *m.*

ad hoc ['æd'hɔk] *Lt. adv. & adj. phr.* ad hoc; **ad h. committee,** comité spécial, ad hoc.

adieu [ə'dju:] *A. & Lit:* **1.** *int.* adieu! **2.** *n.* **to bid s.o. a.,** dire adieu *m*, faire ses adieux, à qn.

ad infinitum ['ædinfi'naitəm] *Lt. adv. phr.* à l'infini; *F:* **he went on talking ad i.,** il parlait à n'en plus finir.

adipose ['ædipous] *a.* (tissu) adipeux.

adiposity [ædi'pɔsiti] *n.* adiposité *f*.

adjacent [ə'dʒeisənt] *a.* (angle, terrain) adjacent; contigu, -uë, attenant (**to,** à); avoisinant; (pays) limitrophe (**to,** de); **a. rooms,** chambres contiguës; **to be a. to sth.,** être contigu à qch.; avoisiner qch.; *Jur:* **a. owner,** riverain *m.*

adjectival [ædʒik'taivl] *a. Gram:* adjectif, adjectival; **a. clause,** proposition adjective. **-ally** *adv.* adjectivement; **present participle used a.,** participe présent adjectivé.

adjective ['ædʒiktiv] *a. & n. Gram:* adjectif (*m*).

adjoin [ə'dʒɔin] **1.** *v.tr.* avoisiner (un lieu); être contigu à (qch.); toucher à, attenir à (qch.). **2.** *v.i.* **the two houses a.,** les deux maisons sont contiguës. **adjoining** *a.* (*a*) contigu, -uë; **garden a. mine,** jardin attenant au mien; (*b*) **the a. room,** la pièce voisine, à côté.

adjourn [ə'dʒə:n] **1.** *v.tr.* **to a. sth. to, until, the next day, for a week,** ajourner, différer, remettre, renvoyer, qch. au lendemain, à huitaine. **2.** *v.i.* (*a*) lever la séance, clore les débats; (*of meeting, etc.*) (i) s'ajourner (**until,** à); (ii) être levé; **the meeting adjourned at 3 o'clock,** la séance a été levée à trois heures; (*b*) (*of persons*) **to a. to the drawing room,** passer au salon.

adjournment [ə'dʒə:nmənt] *n.* (*a*) ajournement *m*, suspension *f* (d'une séance, etc.); (*b*) renvoi *m*, remise *f* (d'une affaire, etc.); **a. for a week,** remise à huitaine.

adjudge [ə'dʒʌdʒ] *v.tr.* **1. to a. s.o. guilty,** déclarer qn coupable. **2.** adjuger, décerner (un prix, une récompense) (**to s.o.,** à qn); **to a. damages,** adjuger, accorder, des dommages-intérêts.

adjudicate [ə'dʒu:dikeit] *v.tr. & i.* juger, décider (une affaire); prononcer sur (une affaire); adjuger, décerner (un prix); **to a. s.o. bankrupt,** déclarer, mettre, qn en faillite.

adjudication [ədʒu:di'keiʃ(ə)n] *n.* jugement *m*, décision *f*, arrêt *m*; **a. of bankruptcy,** jugement déclaratif de faillite.

adjudicator [ə'dʒu:dikeitər] *n.* (*a*) arbitre *m*; juge *m*; (*b*) (*in musical competitions, etc.*) membre *m* du jury.

adjunct ['ædʒʌŋkt] *n.* **1.** (*a*) (*pers.*) adjoint, -ointe, (**to,** de); auxiliaire *mf*; (*b*) (*thg*) accessoire *m* (**of,** de). **2.** *Gram:* complément *m* (du verbe, etc.).

adjust [ə'dʒʌst] **1.** *v.tr.* arranger (une affaire, une querelle); concilier, régler (un différend); arrêter, redresser (un compte); *M.Ins:* **to a. an average,** répartir une avarie. **2.** *v.tr.* (*a*) ajuster (qch. à qch.); **to a. oneself to sth.,** s'adapter à qch.; (*b*) régler, ajuster (une balance, les freins, une montre, un compas, etc.); étalonner (un instrument); rectifier, centrer (un outil); tarer (une soupape); mettre (un microscope, un moteur) au point; égaliser (la pression, etc.); *Nau:* compenser, corriger (les compas); *Fin:* **to a. prices,** ajuster les prix; (*c*) ajuster, arranger (son chapeau, ses vêtements, etc.). **3.** *v.i.* s'adapter (**to sth.,** à qch.). **adjusted** *a. Psy:* **(well) a.,** (bien) équilibré. **adjusting** *n.* mise *f* au point; réglage *m*, tarage *m*; centrage *m*; **a. screw,** vis *f* de réglage, de rappel; *Fin:* **a. of prices,** ajustement *m* des prix.

adjustable [ə'dʒʌstəbl] *a.* **1.** (différend) susceptible d'accommodement. **2.** *Mec.E: Cmptr: etc:* ajustable, réglable; *Aut:* **a. front seats,** sièges *mpl* avant réglables; **a. spanner,** clef anglaise, clef à molette.

adjuster [ə'dʒʌstər] *n.* **1.** (*pers.*) (*a*) ajusteur *m*; régleur *m*; metteur *m* au point; (*b*) *M.Ins:* **average a.,** dispacheur *m*. **2.** appareil *m*, de réglage.

adjustment [ə'dʒʌstmənt] *n.* **1.** ajustement *m* (d'un différend, etc.); arrangement *m* (d'une affaire); règlement *m* (d'un compte, etc.); *M.Ins:* **average a.,** répartition *f* d'avaries; dispache *f*. **2.** (*a*) adaptation *f*; **period of a.,** période *f* d'adaptation; (*b*) ajustement (d'une balance); rectification *f* (d'un outil, d'un instrument); réglage *m* (d'un mécanisme); tarage *m* (d'une soupape); mise *f* au point (d'un microscope, etc.); *Nau:* compensation *f*, correction *f* (des compas); **fine a.,** réglage de précision; **out of a.,** déréglé, décalé.

adjutant ['ædʒətənt] *n.* **1.** *Mil:* (i) capitaine *m* adjudant major; (ii) officier adjoint; **a. general,** adjudant général. **2.** *Orn:* **a. (bird),** marabout *m* des Indes, *F:* adjudant *m*.

ad lib ['æd'lib] *adv.phr. F:* à volonté; (*of food, drink*) à discrétion.

ad-lib[1] ['æd'lib] *v.i. & tr.* **(ad-libbed, ad-libbing)** *F:* improviser. **ad-libbing** *n.* improvisation *f*.

ad-lib[2] *a. F:* improvisé.

adman, *pl.* **-men** ['ædmæn, -men] *n. F:* publicitaire *m*.

admass ['ædmæs] *n. F:* le grand public.

admin [əd'min] *n. F:* administration *f*.

administer [əd'ministər] *v.tr.* (*a*) administrer, régir (un pays); administrer, gérer (des affaires, des biens); appliquer (les lois); **to a. justice,** dispenser, rendre, la justice; (*b*) administrer (les derniers sacrements, un médicament (**to s.o.,** à qn); faire, adresser (une réprimande) (**to s.o.,** à qn); **to a. an, the, oath to s.o.,** faire prêter serment à qn; assermenter qn.

administration [ədmini'streiʃ(ə)n] *n.* **1.** (*a*) administration *f*, gestion *f* (des affaires, d'une fortune, etc.); régie *f* (d'une succession, etc.); (*b*) *Jur:* **letters of a.,** lettres *fpl* d'administration; (*c*) administration (de la justice, des sacrements, d'un remède); prestation *f* (de serment). **2.** *coll. esp. U.S:* **the A.,** l'administration, le gouvernement.

administrative [əd'ministrətiv] *a.* administratif; *Ind:* **a. expenses,** frais *mpl* d'administration; (*in civil service*) **the a. grade,** les fonctionnaires supérieurs. **-ly** *adv.* administrativement.

administrator [əd'ministreitər] *n.* **1.** administrateur *m*; gérant *m* (d'une entreprise); gestionnaire *m*. **2.** *Jur:* curateur *m* (des biens d'un mineur, etc.); administrateur (d'une succession).

admirable ['ædmərəbl] *a.* admirable. **-ably** *adv.* admirablement; **he succeeded a.,** il a réussi à merveille.

admiral ['ædmərəl] *n.* **1.** (i) amiral *m*; (ii) vice-amiral *m* d'escadre. **2.** *Ent:* **red a.,** vulcain *m*.

admiralty ['ædm(ə)rəlti] *n.* **1.** (*a*) *Hist:* **the A.** = le Ministère de la Marine; **First Lord of the A.** = Ministre *m* de la Marine; (*b*) **A. Board** = division navale du ministère de la Défense; **court of A.,** tribunal *m* maritime. **2.** *Geog:* **the A. Islands,** les îles de l'Amirauté.

admiration [ædmə'reiʃ(ə)n] *n.* admiration *f* (**of, for,** pour); **to fill s.o. with a.,** remplir qn d'admiration, émerveiller qn.

admire [əd'maiər] *v.tr.* **1.** admirer; **to a. oneself in a glass,** se mirer dans une glace. **2.** exprimer son admiration de (qch.); s'extasier devant (un bébé). **admiring** *a.* (regard, ton, etc.) admiratif. **admiringly** *adv.* avec admiration.

admirer [əd'maiərər] *n.* (*a*) admirateur, -trice; (*b*) *O:* soupirant *m* (d'une femme).

admissibility [ədmisi'biliti] *n.* admissibilité *f* (d'une preuve, etc.); *Jur:* recevabilité *f* (d'un pourvoi, d'un témoignage).

admissible [əd'misibl] *a.* (*a*) (idée, projet) admissible; *Jur:* (pourvoi) recevable; (*b*) *Mec.E: etc:* **a. play,** jeu permis, admis.

admission [əd'miʃ(ə)n] *n.* **1.** (*a*) admission *f*, accès *m* (à une école, à un emploi, etc.); **to gain a.,** se faire recevoir (dans une société); trouver accès (auprès de qn); se faire admettre (dans un endroit); **a. free,** entrée gratuite; (*b*) prix d'entrée; (*c*) *Cust:* **free, temporary, a.,** admission en franchise, temporaire. **2.** (*a*) admission, acceptation *f* (d'un argument, d'une preuve); (*b*) *Jur:* reconnaissance *f* (d'un fait allégué); confession *f* (d'un crime, etc.); aveu *m*; **by, on, his own a.,** de son propre aveu. **3.** *Mch: I.C.E:* admission, adduction *f*, introduction *f*, entrée *f* (de la vapeur, des gaz, etc.); injection *f* (de l'eau); *I.C.E:* **a. stroke,** course aspirante.

admit [əd'mit] *v.* **(admitted; admitting) 1.** *v.tr.* (*a*) admettre (qn à qch., dans un endroit); laisser entrer (qn); livrer passage à (qn); **children not admitted,** les enfants ne sont pas admis; **he was admitted to hospital,** il a été admis à l'hôpital; (*b*) **the windows do not a. enough air,** les fenêtres ne laissent pas entrer assez d'air; (*c*) admettre (une vérité, des excuses); consentir (un fait); reconnaître (un principe, sa faute); convenir de (ses torts); concéder (qu'on a tort); **it must be admitted that . . .,** il faut reconnaître que + *ind*; **to a. one's guilt,** se reconnaître, s'avouer, coupable; **I a. I was wrong,** j'ai eu tort, j'en conviens; **I had to a. to myself that . . .,** j'ai dû m'avouer à moi-même que . . . . **2.** *v.ind.tr.* **his conduct admits of no excuse, of no explanation,** sa conduite est sans excuse, est inexplicable. **admitted** *a.* **1.** (usage, etc.) admis. **2.** (vérité) reconnue, avouée; **an a. thief,** un voleur avéré. **admittedly** *adv.* de l'aveu général; **a. he's right, but . . .,** il faut reconnaître qu'il a raison, mais . . . .

admittance [əd'mitəns] *n.* **1.** permission *f* d'entrer; entrée *f* (**to,** dans); accès *m* (à un endroit, auprès de qn); **to gain a. to a place,** parvenir à entrer dans un lieu; **to refuse s.o. a.,** refuser de laisser entrer qn; **no a.,** entrée interdite, défense *f* d'entrer. **2.** *El:* admittance *f*.

admixture [əd'mikstjər] *n.* **1.** mélange *m*; dosage *m*. **2.** *Pharm:* (ad)mixtion *f*; **water with an a. of alcohol,** eau additionnée d'alcool.

admonish [əd'mɔniʃ] *v.tr.* (*a*) admonester, reprendre (qn); faire des remontrances à (qn); (*b*) *A:* **to a. s.o. to do sth.,** exhorter qn à faire qch.

admonition [ædmə'niʃ(ə)n] *n.* remontrance *f*, réprimande *f*; *Ecc:* admonition *f*, exhortation *f*.

ad nauseam [æd'nɔːsiæm] *Lt.adv.phr.* jusqu'à la nausée; *F:* à n'en plus finir.

ado [ə'duː] *n.* agitation *f*, bruit *m*, embarras *m*; **without (any) more a., without further a.,** sans plus de façons, de cérémonie, d'embarras; **to make much a. about nothing,** faire beaucoup de bruit pour rien.

adobe [ə'doubi] *n.* (*brick or house*) adobe *m*.

adolescence [ædə'lesəns] *n.* adolescence *f*.

adolescent [ædə'lesənt] *a. & n.* adolescent, -ente.

Adonis [ə'dounis] **1.** (*a*) *Pr.n.m. Myth:* Adonis; (*b*) *n.m.* Adonis. **2.** *n. Ent: Bot:* adonis *f*.

adopt [ə'dɔpt] *v.tr.* **1.** adopter (un enfant, une coutume). **2.** (*a*) adopter (une ligne de conduite, un plan); choisir, embrasser (une carrière); instaurer (des mesures, une méthode); se rallier à (une opinion); suivre (un conseil); *Pol:* choisir (qn comme candidat à un siège); **to a. a patronizing tone,** prendre un ton protecteur; (*b*) approuver (les minutes d'un conseil d'administration). **adopted** *a.* (enfant, mot) adopté; **a. son,** fils adoptif; **my a. country,** mon pays d'adoption.

adoption [ə'dɔpʃ(ə)n] *n.* **1.** adoption *f* (d'un enfant, d'une coutume, d'un pays); **I am an American by a.,** je suis américain d'adoption. **2.** adoption (d'une loi, d'un plan); choix *m* (d'une carrière); instauration *f* (des mesures, d'une méthode); *Pol:* choix (de qn comme candidat).

adoptive [ə'dɔptiv] *a.* (enfant, père) adoptif.

adorable [ə'dɔːrəbl] *a.* adorable. **-ably** *adv.* adorablement; à ravir.

adoration [ædə'reiʃ(ə)n] *n.* adoration *f.*

adore [ə'dɔːr] *v.tr.* adorer (qn, qch.); aimer (qn) à l'adoration. **adoring** *a.* (*a*) adorant; **a. eyes,** yeux adorants; (*b*) (*of pers.*) adorateur, -trice. **adoringly** *adv.* avec adoration.

adorer [ə'dɔːrer] *n.* adorateur, -trice.

adorn [ə'dɔːn] *v.tr.* orner, parer, embellir (**with,** de).

adornment [ə'dɔːnmənt] *n.* **1.** ornementation *f.* **2.** ornement *m,* parure *f.*

adrenal [æ'driːn(ə)l] **1.** *a.* surrénal, -aux. **2.** *n.* (capsule) surrénale (*f*).

adrenalin(e) [ə'drenəlin] *n.* adrénaline *f.*

Adriatic [eidri'ætik] *a. Geog:* **the A. Sea,** *n.* **the Adriatic,** la mer Adriatique, l'Adriatique *f.*

adrift [ə'drift] *adv. Nau:* à la dérive; (*of ship*) **to run, go, a.,** aller à la dérive; dériver; **to break a.,** rompre ses amarres; partir en dérive; **to turn a vessel a.,** abandonner, laisser aller, un navire à la dérive; *Fig:* **to turn s.o. a.,** abandonner qn; **to cut oneself a. from s.o.,** rompre avec qn; *F:* **to come a.,** (*of rope, etc.*) se détacher; se défaire; (*of plan, etc.*) tomber à l'eau.

adroit [ə'drɔit] *a.* (discours) adroit; (politique, personne) adroite, habile. **-ly** *adv.* adroitement, habilement.

adroitness [ə'drɔitnis] *n.* adresse *f,* dextérité *f.*

adulation [ædju'leiʃ(ə)n] *n. Lit:* adulation *f,* flatterie *f.*

adult ['ædʌlt, ə'dʌlt] *a.* & *n.* adulte (*mf*); **a. education,** enseignement *m* des adultes; **an a. lion,** un lion adulte.

adulterate [ə'dʌltəreit] *v.tr.* adultérer (une substance); frelater (du vin, etc.); corrompre (une langue); **adulterated milk,** lait additionné d'eau.

adulteration [ədʌltə'reiʃ(ə)n] *n.* adultération *f* (des médicaments); frelatage *m* (des boissons).

adulterator [ə'dʌltəreitər] *n.* adultérateur *m;* frelateur *m* (d'aliments, etc.).

adulterer, adulteress [ə'dʌltərər, ə'dʌltərəs] *n.* (*pers.*) adultère *m f.*

adulterous [ə'dʌlt(ə)rəs] *a.* adultère. **-ly** *adv.* par adultère; (vivre) en état d'adultère.

adultery [ə'dʌltəri] *n.* adultère *m.*

ad valorem ['ædvæ'lɔːrem] *Lt.phr. Com: Ind:* **ad v. duty,** droit *m* sur la valeur; droit ad valorem.

advance¹ [əd'vaːns] *n.* **1.** (*a*) avance *f;* marche *f* en avant; **a. towards sth.,** acheminement *m* à, vers, qch.; *Mil:* **a. party,** (i) détachement *m* d'avant-garde; (ii) détachement précurseur; **a. guard,** avant-garde *f; adv.phr.* **in a.,** (i) en avant; (ii) en avance; (iii) d'avance, à l'avance; **in a. of the others,** avant les autres, en avant des autres; **to be in a. of one's time,** être en avance sur son temps; devancer son époque; **to pay in a.,** payer d'avance; **to pay a sum in a.,** verser une provision, des provisions; avancer un paiement; *Corr:* **thanking you in a.,** en vous remerciant d'avance; avec mes remerciements anticipés; *Th: etc:* **to book in a.,** louer à l'avance; (*b*) **a. notice,** préavis *m;* **a. payment,** paiement par anticipation. **2.** avancement *m,* progrès *m,* développement *m* (des sciences, etc.); **great advances in medicine,** de grands pas en avant dans le domaine de la médecine. **3. to make an a., advances, to s.o.,** faire une avance, des avances, à, auprès de, qn. **4.** *Com: Fin:* (*a*) avance (de fonds); à-valoir *m inv.*; **a. on a contract,** acompte *m* sur contrat; (*b*) augmentation *f* (de prix); hausse *f;* (*at auction*) **any a.?** qui dit mieux?

advance² **I.** *v.tr.* **1.** (*a*) avancer (le pied, *Chess:* un pion, etc.); (*b*) avancer (la date d'une conférence, l'heure d'un paiement, etc.); (*c*) avancer (une idée, une opinion); présenter, mettre en avant (une opinion, une observation); alléguer (un prétexte). **2.** (*a*) faire progresser, faire avancer (les sciences, etc.); faire avancer (des troupes); (*b*) *Cmptr:* faire progresser (le compteur); faire défiler (la bande magnétique); faire avancer (le papier sur l'imprimante, la carte dans la piste); (*c*) élever, porter, faire avancer (qn à un grade supérieur); (*d*) accélérer (la croissance, le développement, etc.). **3.** augmenter, hausser (le prix de qch.). **4. to a. s.o. money,** avancer de l'argent à qn; **sums advanced,** avances *f,* provisions *f.* **II.** *v.i.* **1.** s'avancer (**towards,** vers); (*of troops*) se porter en avant; **the season is advancing,** la saison s'avance; **to a. two steps, two paces,** faire deux pas en avant. **2.** (*a*) avancer (en âge, dans ses études); *Biol: etc:* évoluer; **the work is advancing,** l'ouvrage avance, fait des progrès; (*b*) (*of officer, etc.*) recevoir de l'avancement; monter (en grade). **3.** *Fin:* (*of shares, etc.*) augmenter de prix, hausser; **prices are advancing,** les prix sont à la hausse. **advanced** *a.* **1.** (*a*) (poste) avancé; (études, opinions) avancées; (civilisation) évoluée; (économie) développée; (pays) développé, industrialisé; **to hold very a. ideas,** avoir des idées très avancées; (*b*) (cours) supérieur; (étudiant) avancé; **a. mathematics,** mathématiques supérieures; (*c*) *Tchn:* perfectionné; (technique) d'avant-garde. **2.** (*a*) **the night is far a.,** il est tard dans la nuit; **the season is a.,** c'est la fin de saison; (*b*) **he died at an a. age,** il est mort très vieux. **advancing** *a.* qui s'avance; **a. storm,** orage qui s'avance.

advancement [əd'vaːnsmənt] *n.* (*a*) avancement *m* (d'une personne, des sciences); progrès *m* (des sciences); **economic a.,** le essor *m* économique; (*b*) *Cmptr:* progression *f* (du compteur); avancement, défilement *m* (du papier, de la bande).

advantage¹ [əd'vaːntidʒ] *n.* (*a*) avantage *m;* **to have, gain, the a. over s.o.,** avoir, remporter, l'avantage sur qn; **this article has the a. of cheapness,** cet article se recommande par son bon marché; **you will find it an a. to . . .,** vous aurez avantage à . . .; **to take a. of sth.,** profiter de qch.; tirer avantage, profit, de qch.; **to take a. of s.o.,** abuser de la crédulité, de la bonne volonté, de qn; **he took a. of the fact that . . .,** il profita du fait que . . .; **to turn sth. to a.,** tirer parti de qch.; mettre qch. à profit; (*of event*) **to turn out to s.o.'s a.,** tourner à l'avantage de qn; profiter à qn; **to show off sth. to a.,** faire valoir qch.; (*b*) *Ten:* avantage.

advantage² *v.tr.* avantager, favoriser (qn, qch.).

advantageous [ædvən'teidʒəs] *a.* avantageux (**to,** pour); profitable, utile (**to,** à). **-ly** *adv.* avantageusement; utilement.

advent ['ædvənt] *n.* **1.** *Ecc:* (*a*) **Advent,** l'Avent *m;* **A. Sunday,** le premier dimanche de l'Avent; (*b*) **the second A.,** le second Avènement. **2.** arrivée *f* (d'une chose importante); venue *f,* avènement *m* (de qch., d'un personnage).

Adventist ['ædvəntist] *n. Rel.H:* Adventiste *mf;* **Seventh-day A.,** adventiste du septième jour.

adventitious [ædven'tiʃəs] *a.* **1.** adventice; (*a*) (fait) accessoire; (*b*) accidentel, fortuit. **2.** *Bot:* **a. roots,** racines adventives.

adventure¹ [əd'ventjər] *n.* (*a*) aventure *f;* **life of a.,** vie *f* d'aventure, aventureuse; **a. story,** roman d'aventure(s); (*b*) aventure (qui arrive à qn); **after many adventures,** après bien des péripéties.

adventure² 1. *v.tr.* aventurer, hasarder, risquer (sa fortune, sa vie, etc.). 2. *v.i.* s'aventurer, se hasarder (dans un endroit, dans une entreprise).
adventurer [əd'ventjərər] *n.* aventurier *m.*
adventuresome [əd'ventjəsəm], *a.* aventureux; téméraire.
adventuress [əd'ventjəris] *n.f.* *Pej:* aventurière; intrigante.
adventurous [əd'ventjərəs], *a.* aventureux; audacieux; **a. man,** homme *m* d'aventures; homme entreprenant. **-ly** *adv.* aventureusement.
adventurousness [əd'ventjərəsnis] *n.* hardiesse *f,* audace *f;* esprit *m* d'aventures.
adverb ['ædvə:b] *n.* *Gram:* adverbe *m.*
adverbial [əd'və:biəl] *a.* *Gram:* adverbial; **a. phrase,** locution adverbiale. **-ally** *adv.* adverbialement; **adjective used a.,** adjectif employé comme adverbe.
adversary ['ædvəs(ə)ri] *n.* adversaire *mf.*
adverse ['ædvə:s] *a.* adverse; (*a*) contraire, opposé (**to,** à); **a. wind,** vent *m* contraire; (*b*) ennemi (**to,** de); hostile (**to,** à, envers); **a. fortune,** fortune *f* adverse; (*c*) (rapport, influence) défavorable; (balance) déficitaire. **-ly** *adv.* **to influence s.o. a.,** exercer une influence défavorable sur qn; **to report a. (on s.o., sth.),** faire un rapport défavorable (sur qn, qch.).
adversity [əd'və:siti] *n.* adversité *f.*
advert ['ædvə:t] *n.* *F:* réclame *f;* annonce *f.*
advertise ['ædvətaiz] *v.tr.* & *i.* (*a*) (i) (faire) annoncer, faire savoir (un événement dans les journaux); (ii) afficher (une vente, etc.); **to a. in a paper,** (faire) insérer une annonce dans un journal; **to a. for s.o., sth.,** chercher qn, qch., par voie d'annonce; **house advertised for sale,** maison *f* dont la mise en vente est (i) annoncée, (ii) affichée; (*b*) faire de la réclame, de la publicité (pour un produit); **it pays to a.,** la publicité fait gagner de l'argent; **as advertised,** conforme à la spécification publicitaire; *F:* **you needn't a. the fact,** vous n'avez pas besoin de le crier sur les toits; (*c*) *Rail: etc:* **the advertised time of departure,** l'heure prévue pour le départ. **advertising** *n.* publicité *f,* réclame *f;* annonces *fpl;* **a. medium,** organe *m* de publicité; **a. agency,** bureau *m,* agence *f,* de publicité; **a. agent,** agent *m* de publicité; annoncier *m;* **a. space,** emplacement réservé à la publicité.
advertisement [əd'və:tismənt] *n.* 1. publicité *f,* réclame *f;* *T.V: etc:* spot *m* publicitaire; **bad a.,** contrepublicité *f.* 2. (*a*) (*in newspaper*) annonce *f;* **classified advertisements,** petites annonces; (*b*) (*on wall, etc.*) affiche *f.*
advertiser ['ædvətaizər] *n.* 1. (*a*) annonceur *m;* (*b*) faiseur *m* de réclame. 2. journal *m* d'annonces.
advice [əd'vais] *n.* 1. conseil(s) *m* (*pl*), avis *m;* **piece of a.,** conseil; **to ask, seek, s.o.'s a.,** demander conseil à qn; **to take s.o.'s a.,** suivre le conseil de qn; **to take medical, legal, a.,** consulter un médecin, un homme de loi; **on s.o.'s a.,** sur l'avis, le conseil, de qn. 2. avis; *Com:* **a. note,** lettre *f,* note *f,* d'avis; **as per a.,** suivant avis; **until further a.,** jusqu'à nouvel avis.
advisability [ədvaizə'biliti] *n.* opportunité *f;* **a. of doing sth.,** utilité *f* qu'il y aurait à faire qch.
advisable [əd'vaizəbl] *n.* 1. (démarche) recommandable, recommandée, judicieuse; **it would be a. to . . .,** il serait prudent de . . . . 2. opportun, à propos; convenable (**for,** pour); **it might be a. to . . .,** peut-être conviendrait-il de . . .; **if you consider, think, it a.,** si bon vous semble.
advise [əd'vaiz] *v.tr.* 1. (*a*) **to a. s.o.,** conseiller qn; **to a. s.o. against sth.,** déconseiller qch. à qn; **to a. s.o. to do sth., against doing sth.,** conseiller, déconseiller, à qn de faire qch.; **I strongly a. you to . . .,** je vous recommande instamment de . . .; **what do you a. me to do?** que me conseillez-vous? (*b*) recommander, conseiller (qch., une ligne de conduite) (**to s.o.,** à qn). 2. **to a. s.o. on a question,** renseigner qn sur une question; **to a. on a question,** servir de conseil pour une question. 3. **to a. s.o. of sth.,** avertir, prévenir, instruire, qn de qch.; **to a. s.o. that . . .,** avertir, prévenir, qn que . . . **advisedly** [æd'vaizidli] *adv.* (*a*) de propos délibéré; (*b*) en connaissance de cause.
adviser, advisor [əd'vaizer] *n.* conseiller, -ère; **legal a.,** conseiller juridique; **spiritual a.,** directeur *m* de conscience.
advisory [əd'vaizəri] *a.* (conseil) consultatif; **in an a. capacity,** à titre consultatif.
advocacy ['ædvəkəsi] *n.* plaidoyer *m* (en faveur d'une cause).
advocate¹ ['ædvəkət, -eit] *n.* 1. *Jur:* *Scot:* avocat *m;* **the Lord A.** = le Procureur général. 2. avocat; défenseur *m* (d'une cause, d'une doctrine, etc.); **the advocates of free trade,** les partisans du libre-échange; *Ecc:* & *F:* **Devil's a.,** avocat du diable.
advocate² ['ædvəkeit] *v.tr.* (*a*) plaider en faveur de (qch.); soutenir (une cause); (*b*) préconiser (l'emploi de qch.); conseiller (une ligne de conduite).
adze, *NAm:* *also* **adz** [ædz] *n.* *Tls:* (*a*) (h)erminette *f;* (*b*) sape *f* (d'un piolet).
Aegean [i'dʒi:ən] *a.* 1. *Geog:* **the A. sea,** *n.* **the Aegean,** la mer Égée. 2. *A.Hist:* égéen, -enne.
aegis, *NAm:* *also* **egis** ['i:dʒis] *n.* égide *f;* protection *f;* **under the a. of . . .,** sous l'égide de . . .
aeolian [i:'ouliən] *a.* éolien; *Mus:* **a. harp,** harpe éolienne.
aeon, *NAm:* *also* **eon** ['i:ən] *n.* période *f* de temps sans mesure; éternité *f;* **for aeons upon aeons,** pendant des siècles, des éternités.
aerate ['ɛəreit] *v.tr.* 1. (*a*) aérer; (*b*) *Physiol:* artérialiser (le sang). 2. gazéifier (de l'eau, une eau minérale). **aerated** *a.* (*a*) aéré; (*b*) (*of water*) gazeux.
aeration [ɛə'reiʃ(ə)n] *n.* (*a*) aération *f;* (*b*) *Physiol:* artérialisation *f* (du sang).
aerial ['ɛəriəl] 1. *a.* aérien; (orchidée, etc.) aéricole; *Bot:* **a. root,** racine aérienne; **a. photography,** photographie aérienne. 2. *n.* antenne *f;* **transmitting, receiving, a.,** antenne d'émission, réceptrice.
aerie ['eəri, 'iəri] *n.* (*esp. NAm.*) aire *f* (d'un aigle).
aerobatics [ɛərou'bætiks] *n.pl.* (*usu. with sg. const.*) *Av:* acrobaties aériennes; voltige *f.*
aerodrome ['ɛəroudroum] *n.* aérodrome *m.*
aerodynamic [ɛəroudai'næmik] *a.* aérodynamique; **a. centre,** *Ph:* *Mec:* centre *m* aérodynamique; *Ph:* centre de poussée; *Av:* foyer *m* (de profile d'aile).
aerodynamics [ɛəroudai'næmiks] *n.pl.* (*usu. with sg. const.*) aérodynamique *f.*
aerodyne ['ɛəroudain] *n.* *Aer:* aérodyne *m.*
aero-engine ['ɛərouendʒin] *n.* moteur *m* d'avion.
aerofoil ['ɛəroufɔil] *n.* *Av:* plan *m* à profil d'aile; surface portante, sustentrice.
aeromodeller ['ɛərou'mɔdlər] *n.* aéromodéliste *m.*
aeromodelling ['ɛərou'mɔdliŋ] *n.* aéromodélisme *m.*
aeronaut ['ɛərounɔ:t] *n.* aéronaute *mf.*
aeronautic(al) [ɛərou'nɔ:tik(l)] *a.* aéronautique.
aeronautics [ɛərou'nɔ:tiks] *n.pl.* (*usu. with sg. const.*) (*a*) aéronautique *f;* (*b*) navigation aérienne.
aeroplane ['ɛərəplein] *n.* avion *m.*
aerosol ['ɛərəsɔl] *n.* aérosol *m;* *Com:* bombe *f.*
aerospace ['ɛərouspeis] *n.* (*a*) l'espace aérien et interplanétaire; (*b*) l'aérospatiale *f;* **a. industries,** industries aérospatiales.
aerostat ['ɛəroustæt] *n.* *Av:* aérostat *m.*
aerostatic [ɛərou'stætik] 1. *a.* aérostatique.
aerostatics [ɛərou'stætiks] *n.pl.* (*usu. with sg. const.*) aérostatique *f.*
aesthete, *NAm:* *also* **esthete** ['i:sθi:t] *n.* esthète *mf.*

aesthetic, *NAm: also* **esthetic** [iːsˈθetik] *a.* esthétique. **-ally** *adv.* esthétiquement.

aesthetics, *NAm: also* **esthetics** [iːsˈθetiks] *n.pl.* (*usu. with sg. const.*) esthétique *f.*

aetiology, *NAm:* **etiology** [iːtiˈɔlədʒi], *n.* étiologie *f.*

afar [əˈfaːr] *adv. chiefly Lit:* **from a.,** de loin.

affability [æfəˈbiliti] *n.* affabilité *f* (**towards,** envers, avec); courtoisie *f.*

affable [ˈæfəbl] *a.* affable, courtois (**to, with,** envers, avec). **-ably** *adv.* avec affabilité, avec courtoisie.

affair [ɛˈfɛər] *n.* (*a*) affaire *f*; **that's my a.,** ça, c'est mon affaire; ça ne vous regarde pas; **to put one's affairs in order,** mettre de l'ordre dans ses affaires; **in the present state of affairs,** du train où vont les choses; *F:* **that's a nice, fine, state of affairs!** en voilà du propre! (*b*) **affairs of state,** les affaires de l'État; **foreign affairs,** les affaires étrangères; (*c*) **(love) a.,** affaire (de cœur); intrigue *f*; aventure *f*; *A:* **a. of honour,** affaire d'honneur, duel *m.*

affect¹ [əˈfekt] *v.tr.* faire parade de, simuler (l'indifférence, la douleur). **affected** *a.* (*a*) (*of pers., manners*) affecté, maniéré, affété; (*style*) maniéré, (re)cherché, apprêté; (*b*) (indifférence, etc.) simulée; **a. cheerfulness,** gaieté *f* d'emprunt. **affectedly** *adv.* avec affectation; d'une manière affectée.

affect² *v.tr.* **1.** atteindre, toucher (qn); affecter (un organe, etc.); influer sur (qch.); altérer (la santé); **the economic crisis which is affecting the country at present,** la crise économique qui frappe le pays en ce moment; **it affects me personally,** cela me touche personnellement; **those most directly affected,** les premiers intéressés. **2.** affecter, affliger, toucher (qn); **to be much affected by sth.,** être très affecté, affligé, de qch. **affected** *a.* (*a*) **to be a. with a disease,** être atteint d'une maladie; **the lung is a.,** le poumon est atteint, attaqué, touché; (*b*) ému, touché. **affecting** *a.* (spectacle, etc.) touchant, attendrissant.

affectation [æfekˈteiʃ(ə)n] *n.* **1.** affectation *f,* simulation *f* (d'intérêt, d'indifférence, etc.). **2.** affectation; manque *m* de naturel; afféterie *f,* apprêt *m* (de langage).

affectedness [əˈfektidnis] *n.* affectation *f*; manque *m* de naturel; afféterie *f,* apprêt *m* (de langage, etc.)

affection [əˈfekʃ(ə)n] *n.* **1.** affection *f,* tendresse *f*; attachement *m*; **to have an a. for s.o.,** ressentir de l'affection pour qn; **he is held in great a.,** il est très aimé; **to gain, win, s.o.'s a.,** se faire aimer de qn. **2.** *Med:* affection (de poitrine, de la peau, etc.).

affectionate [əˈfekʃ(ə)nət] *a.* affectueux. **-ly** *adv.* affectueusement; *Corr:* **yours a.,** bien affectueusement.

affective [əˈfektiv] *a.* affectif.

affidavit [ˌæfiˈdeivit] *n. Jur:* déclaration *f* par écrit et sous serment; **to swear an a.,** certifier sous serment une déclaration (écrite).

affiliate [əˈfilieit] *v.tr.* (*a*) (*of society, etc.*) s'affilier (des membres, etc.); (*b*) *v.tr. & i.* **to a. (oneself) to with, a society,** s'affilier à une société; **affiliated company,** filiale *f.*

affiliation [əfiliˈeiʃ(ə)n] *n.* **1.** (*a*) affiliation *f* (à une société); (*b*) **political affiliations,** attaches *fpl* politiques. **2.** *Jur:* procédure *f* en recherche de paternité; **a. order,** assignation *f* d'enfant à un père putatif.

affinity [əˈfiniti] *n.* (*a*) affinité *f* (**with, to,** avec; **between,** entre); (*b*) conformité *f* de caractère; (*c*) *Mth: Biol:* affinité; *Ch:* **a. for a body,** affinité pour un corps; (*d*) parenté *f* par alliance; *Jur:* affinité *f.*

affirm [əˈfəːm] *v.tr.* **1.** affirmer, soutenir (**that,** que); **to a. sth. to s.o.,** affirmer qch. à qn. **2.** *Jur:* confirmer, homologuer (un jugement).

affirmation [æfəˈmeiʃ(ə)n] *n.* **1.** (*a*) affirmation *f,* assertion *f*; (*b*) *Jur:* déclaration solennelle (tenant lieu de serment). **2.** *Jur:* confirmation *f,* homologation *f* (d'un jugement).

affirmative [əˈfəːmətiv] **1.** *a.* affirmatif; **to make an a. sign,** faire un signe affirmatif; faire signe que oui. **2.** *n.* **in the a.,** affirmativement; **the answer is in the a.,** la réponse est oui. **-ly** *adv.* affirmativement.

affix¹ [ˈæfiks] *n.* **1.** addition *f* (à un mémoire). **2.** *Ling:* affixe *m.*

affix² [əˈfiks] *v.tr.* attacher (**sth. to sth.,** qch. à qch.); apposer (un sceau, un timbre) (**to a document,** à, sur, un document).

afflict [əˈflikt] *v.tr.* affliger; **to be afflicted with rheumatism,** être affligé de rhumatismes; **to be afflicted at, by a piece of news,** être affligé, s'affliger, d'une nouvelle. **afflicted 1.** *a.* affligé. **2.** *n.pl.* **the a.,** les affligés.

affliction [əˈflikʃ(ə)n] *n.* **1.** affliction *f*; **deafness is a great a.,** la surdité est une grande affliction. **2.** calamité *f,* revers *m.* **3. the afflictions of old age,** les infirmités *fpl* de la vieillesse.

affluence [ˈæfluəns] *n.* **1.** affluence *f*; foule *f* (de gens, etc.). **2.** abondance *f,* richesse *f*; **to live in a.,** vivre dans l'abondance.

affluent [ˈæfluənt] *a.* **1.** abondant, riche (**in,** en). **2.** riche; **a. society,** société *f* d'abondance. **-ly** *adv.* (vivre) dans l'abondance *f.*

afford [əˈfɔːd] *v.tr.* **1.** (*usu. with* **can**) (*a*) avoir les moyens (pécuniaires) (de faire qch.); être en mesure (de faire qch.); **an extravagance I could ill a.,** une extravagance qui n'était guère dans mes moyens; **I can't a. it,** mes moyens ne le permettent pas; (*b*) **I can a. to wait,** je peux attendre; **can you a. the time?** disposez-vous du temps (nécessaire)? **I cannot a. to create a bad impression,** cela me nuirait de faire une mauvaise impression. **2.** (*a*) *Lit:* (*of pers.*) donner, accorder (qch. à qn); **kind heaven a. him everlasting rest,** que Dieu dans sa miséricorde lui donne le repos éternel; (*b*) (*of thg*) fournir, offrir; **the trees afforded us very little shelter,** les arbres ne nous fournissaient qu'un piètre abri; *Lit:* **it affords me great pleasure,** cela me fait grand plaisir.

afforest [əˈfɔrist, ə-] *v.tr.* boiser (une terre).

afforestation [əfɔrisˈteiʃ(ə)n] *n.* boisement *m,* afforestation *f.*

affranchise [əˈfræn(t)ʃaiz] *v.tr.* affranchir (un serf, un esclave).

affranchisement [əˈfræn(t)ʃizmənt] *n.* affranchissement *m* (d'un serf, d'un esclave).

affray [əˈfrei] *n. Jur:* bagarre *f,* échauffourée *f.*

affront¹ [əˈfrʌnt] *n.* affront *m,* offense *f.*

affront² *v.tr.* offenser; faire (un) affront à (qn).

Afghan [ˈæfgæn] **1.** *a. Geog:* afghan; *Z:* **A. hound,** lévrier afghan. **2.** *n.* **1.** (*a*) Afghan, -ane; (*b*) *Ling:* afghan *m.* **3.** *NAm:* **a.,** couverture *f* de laine tricotée (au crochet).

Afghanistan [æfˈgænistɑːn] *Pr.n. Geog:* Afghanistan *m.*

afield [əˈfiːld] *adv.* **to go far a., farther a.,** aller très loin, plus loin.

afire [əˈfaiər] *adv. & a. A. & Lit:* en feu; enflammé.

aflame [əˈfleim] *adv. & a. Lit:* en flammes, embrasé; **to be a. with colour,** briller de vives couleurs; rutiler.

afloat [əˈflout] *adv. & a.* **1.** (*a*) à flot, sur l'eau; à la mer; (*of ship, F: of pers.*) **to be a.,** être à flot; **to keep a ship a.,** maintenir un navire à flot; *F:* (*of pers.*) **to keep a.,** se maintenir à flot; surnager; **to keep s.o. a. (financially),** renflouer qn; (*b*) **service a.,** service *m* à bord; **to serve a.,** servir sur mer; (*c*) **to be a. in space,** planer dans l'espace. **2.** (*of rumour, etc.*) **to be a.,** courir, circuler.

afoot [əˈfut] *adv.* **a plan is a. to . . .,** on envisage, on a formé, un projet pour . . .; **there's something a.,** il se prépare, se trame, quelque chose.

aforementioned, aforesaid [ə'fɔ:menʃənd, -sed] *a. Jur:* susmentionné, susnommé, susdit; mentionné ci-dessus.

aforethought [ə'fɔ:θɔ:t] *a. Jur:* **with malice a.,** avec préméditation, avec intention criminelle.

afraid [ə'freid] *a.* pris de peur; **to be a. of s.o., sth.,** avoir peur de qn, qch.; craindre qn, qch.; **don't be a.,** n'ayez pas peur; ne craignez rien; **to make s.o. a.,** faire peur à qn; effrayer qn; **to be a. to do, of doing, sth.,** ne pas oser faire qch.; avoir peur, craindre, de faire qch.; **I am afraid he will die,** je crains qu'il ne meure; **I'm a. we shall be very late,** j'ai bien peur que nous allions arriver très en retard; **I'm a. so, not,** j'ai bien peur que oui, que non; **I'm a. he's out,** je regrette, mais il est sorti.

afresh [ə'freʃ] *adv.* de nouveau, à nouveau; **to start (sth.) a.,** recommencer (qch.).

Africa ['æfrikə] *Pr.n. Geog:* Afrique *f*; **in A.,** en Afrique.

African ['æfrik(ə)n] **1.** *a. Geog:* africain; *Bot:* **A. violet,** saintpaulia *m*; Z: **A. elephant,** éléphant *m* d'Afrique. **2.** *n.* Africain, -aine.

Afrikaans [æfri'kɑ:ns] *n. Ling:* afrika(a)ns *m.*

Afrikaaner [æfri'kɑ:nər] **1.** *a.* afrikander. **2.** *n.* Afrikander *mf.*

Afro ['æfrou] *a.* (coiffure) afro.

Afro-American ['æfrouə'merik(ə)n] **1.** *a.* afro-américain. **2.** *n.* Afro-américain, -aine.

Afro-Asian ['æfrou'eiʃən] *a.* afro-asiatique.

aft [ɑ:ft] *adv. Nau: Av:* sur, à, vers, l'arrière; **to go a.,** aller à l'arrière; **a. of the mast,** sur l'arrière du mât; **to have the wind dead a.,** avoir le vent en poupe.

after ['ɑ:ftər] **I.** *adv.* après. **1.** (*order*) **to come a.,** venir après, à la suite. **2.** (*time*) **he was ill for months a.,** il en est resté malade pendant des mois; **soon, long, a.,** bientôt, longtemps, après; **the night, the week, a.,** la nuit, la semaine, d'après; **a year a.,** un an après, plus tard; **the day a.,** le lendemain; **the morning a.,** (i) le lendemain matin; (ii) *F:* la gueule de bois. **II.** *prep.* après. **1.** (*place*) **to run a. s.o.,** courir après qn; **close the door a. you,** fermez la porte après vous; *F:* **to be a. s.o., sth.,** être en quête de qn, de qch.; **the police are a. you,** la police est à vos trousses; **what's he a.?** (i) qu'est-ce qu'il a en tête? (ii) qu'est-ce qu'il cherche? **2.** (*time*) (*a*) **to reign a. s.o.,** régner après qn; **a. three days,** trois jours après, plus tard; **a. dinner,** après dîner; **a. this date,** passé cette date; **a. all's said and done,** au bout du compte, à fin (des fins); **a. all,** après tout; **the day a. the battle,** le lendemain de la bataille; **the day a. tomorrow,** après-demain; **it is a. five (o'clock),** il est cinq heures passées; *U.S:* **twenty a. four,** quatre heures vingt; **one a. the other,** l'un après l'autre; les uns après les autres; (entrer) à la file; **he read page a. page,** il lut page sur page; **time a. time,** maintes (et maintes) fois; **day a. day,** jour après jour; **year a. year,** une année après l'autre, tous les ans; (*b*) (*in compounds forming adjs.*) **a.-dinner speech,** discours *m* d'après dîner; **the a.-war years,** les années d'après-guerre. **3.** (*order*) (*a*) **after you,** après vous; (*at a meal*) servez-vous d'abord; (*b*) **I put Milton a. Dante,** je mets Milton au-dessous de Dante. **4.** (*manner*) **a man a. my own heart,** un homme qui m'est sympathique; **landscape a. Turner,** paysage d'après Turner, à la (manière de) Turner; *F:* **a. a fashion,** tant bien que mal. **5.** *Dial:* (*Irish*) **to be a. doing sth.,** (i) être en train de faire qch; (ii) être disposé à faire qch. **III.** *conj.* (*a*) après que + *ind.*; **I came a. he had gone,** je suis venu après qu'il fut parti; (*b*) après + *infin.*; **a. I had seen him I went out,** après l'avoir vu, je suis sorti. **IV.** *a.* (*a*) à venir; **in a. years,** plus tard (dans la vie); (*b*) *Nau:* arrière; **a. cabin,** cabine *f* sur l'arrière; **a. hold,** cale *f* arrière.

afterbirth ['ɑ:ftəbə:θ] *n. Obst:* arrière-faix *m*, délivre *m;* placenta *m.*

afterburner ['ɑ:ftəbə:nər] *n.* dispositif *m* de post-combustion.

aftercare ['ɑ:ftəkɛər] *n.* postaire *f*; soins post-natals, post-opératoires, etc.; surveillance *f* (de convalescents, de délinquents, etc.).

afterglow ['ɑ:ftəglou] *n.* dernières lueurs, derniers reflets (du soleil couchant).

afterlife ['ɑ:ftəlaif] *n.* **1.** la vie après la mort. **2.** suite *f* de la vie; **in a.,** plus tard dans la vie.

aftermath ['ɑ:ftəmæθ, -mɑ:θ] *n.* **1.** *Agr:* regain *m* (de foin); arrière-foin *m.* **2.** suites *fpl* (d'un événement); **the a. of war,** (i) les répercussions *fpl* de la guerre; (ii) l'après-guerre *m.*

aftermost ['ɑ:ftəmoust] *a. Nau:* (partie) la plus en arrière, la plus à l'arrière.

afternoon [ɑ:ftə'nu:n] **1.** *n.* après-midi *m or f inv.*; **this a.,** cet(te) après-midi; **in the a.,** (pendant) l'après-midi; **Tuesday a.,** mardi après-midi; **good a.!** bonjour!; **a. tea,** thé *m*, goûter *m.* **2.** *adv. esp. NAm:* **afternoons,** (pendant) l'après-midi.

afters ['ɑ:ftəz] *n.pl. F:* dessert *m.*

after-sales ['ɑ:ftəseilz] *a. Com:* (service) après-vente.

aftershave ['ɑ:ftəʃeiv] *a. & n.* **a. (lotion),** lotion *f* après-rasage.

aftershock ['ɑ:ftəʃɔk] *n. Geol:* réplique *f* (d'un séisme).

aftertaste ['ɑ:ftəteist] *n.* arrière-goût *m.*

afterthought ['ɑ:ftəθɔ:t] *n.* réflexion *f* après coup; **to add sth. as an a.,** ajouter qch. après coup.

after-treatment ['ɑ:ftətri:tmənt] *n.* soins ultérieurs (à donner à un convalescent); traitement ultérieur (d'un produit).

afterwards ['ɑ:ftəwədz] *adv.* après, plus tard, ensuite; **a long time a.,** longtemps après.

again [ə'gen, *occ.* ə'gein] *adv.* **1.** (*a*) de nouveau, encore; **once a.,** encore une fois, une fois de plus; *F:* **not you a.!** (c'est) toi encore! **don't do it a.!** ne recommencez pas, plus! **never a.,** (ne . . .) jamais plus; plus jamais (. . . ne); **a. and a., time and (time) a.,** maintes et maintes fois; **I have told you so a. and a.,** je vous l'ai dit vingt fois, cent fois; **now and a.,** de temps en temps; de temps à autre; **as much a.,** deux fois autant; **half as much a.,** de moitié plus; **half as long a.,** de moitié plus long; (*b*) **to begin a.,** recommencer; **to come a.,** revenir; **I've seen him a.,** je l'ai revu; **I hope I shall find it a.,** j'espère bien le retrouver; (*c*) **what was your name a.?** rappelez-moi votre nom. **2.** (*a*) de plus, d'ailleurs, en outre; **a. I am not sure that . . .,** d'ailleurs je ne suis pas sûr que . . .; (*b*) **(then) a., (and) a.,** d'autre part; d'un autre côté.

against [ə'genst, *occ.* ə'geinst] *prep.* contre. **1.** (*a*) **to fight a. s.o.,** se battre contre qn; **to march a. the enemy,** marcher à l'ennemi; **to argue a. sth.,** plaider à contrepied de qch.; **she was a. the idea,** elle s'opposait à l'idée; **a. my will,** contre mon gré; **to act a. the law,** agir contrairement à la loi; **a. the rules,** contraire aux règlements; **conditions are a. us,** les conditions nous sont défavorables; **there is no law a. it,** il n'y a pas de loi qui s'y oppose; **a. the nap,** à contre-poil, à rebours, à rebrousse-poil; **a. the grain,** contre le fil, à contre-fil, à rebours; **a. the light,** à contre-jour; **a. the tide,** au contre-sens de la marée; **to go a. nature,** aller à l'encontre de la nature; **it was a race a. time,** on n'avait guère le temps de le faire; (*b*) **to warn s.o. a. s.o., sth.,** mettre qn en garde contre qn, qch.; **protected a. the cold,** protégé contre le froid; (*c*) **to come up a. (sth.),** se heurter contre (qch.); rencontrer (des difficultés); (*d*) **leaning a. the wall,** appuyé contre le mur; **to place sth. a. a wall,**

adosser qch. à un mur; (*e*) **to check sth. a. a list,** vérifier qch. d'après une liste; (*f*) **a cross is placed a. each name,** une croix est placée à côté de chaque nom. **2. my rights (as) a. the government,** mes droits vis-à-vis du gouvernement. **3. to show up a. a background,** se détacher sur un fond. **4. three deaths this year as a. thirty in 1970,** trois morts cette année contre trente en 1970.

agape [ə'geip] *adv. & a.* bouche bée; **to stand a.,** rester bouche bée.

agar-agar ['eigə'eigər] *n.* agar-agar *m*, gélose *f.*

agaric ['ægərik] *n. Fung:* agaric *m*; **fly a.,** (amanite *f*) tue-mouches (*m*); fausse oronge.

agate ['ægət] *n. Miner:* agate *f.*

Agatha ['ægəθə] *Pr.n.f.* Agathe.

agave ['ægeiv, ə'geivi] *n. Bot:* agave *m.*

age[1] [eidʒ] *n.* **1.** (*a*) âge *m*; **to be past middle a.,** être sur le retour; **twenty years of a.,** âgé de vingt ans; **what a. is he?** quel âge a-t-il? **when I was your a.,** quand j'avais votre âge; **he doesn't look his age.,** il ne porte pas son âge; *F:* **be your a.!** voyons, tu n'es plus un enfant! **to be under a.,** être mineur; **full a.,** âge légal; (état *m* de) majorité (*f*); **to be of a.,** être majeur; **to come of a.,** atteindre sa majorité; **coming of a.,** entrée *f* en majorité; **to be over a. to do sth.,** être trop âgé pour faire qch.; **to be of an a. to marry,** être en âge de se marier; **a. of discretion,** âge de raison, de discrétion; **mental a.,** âge mental; *Adm: Mil:* **a. group,** classe *f*; **he comes into the 15 to 20 a. group,** il fait partie du groupe, de la classe, des 15 à 20 ans; **pensionable a., retirement a.,** âge de (la mise à) la retraite; *Bot:* **a. ring,** cerne *m* (d'un arbre); (*b*) **(old) a.,** vieillesse *f*; **the house is falling to pieces with a.,** la maison tombe de vieillesse, de vétusté. **2.** (*a*) âge, époque *f*, siècle *m*; **the a. we live in,** notre siècle, le siècle où nous vivons; **in our a.,** à notre époque; **the atomic a.,** l'âge, l'ère *f*, atomique; *Hist: Prehist:* **the Stone A.,** l'âge de pierre; **the Bronze A.,** l'âge du bronze; (*b*) *F:* **it's ages, an a., since I saw him, I haven't seen him for ages,** il y a une éternité que je ne l'ai vu.

age[2] *v.* **(aged** [eidʒd], **ageing,** *NAm: also* **aging** ['eidʒiŋ]) **1.** *v.i.* vieillir, prendre de l'âge; **he had aged beyond recognition,** il avait vieilli à ne plus le reconnaître. **2.** *v.tr.* (*a*) vieillir; rendre (qn) vieux; (*b*) *Ind: etc:* mûrir (un produit); vieillir (un métal). **aged** *a.* **1.** ['eidʒid] âgé; vieux; **an a. man,** un vieillard; *n.pl.* **the a.,** les vieillards, les vieux. **2.** [eidʒd] (*a*) **a. twenty,** âgé de vingt ans; (*b*) **I found him greatly a.,** je l'ai trouvé bien vieilli. **ageing** *NAm: also* **aging 1.** *a.* (*a*) vieillissant; qui fait vieux; **a. population,** population vieillissante. **2.** *n.* vieillissement *m* (d'une personne, d'un vin, etc.).

ageless ['eidʒlis] *a.* **1.** toujours jeune. **2.** éternel.

agency ['eidʒənsi] *n.* **1.** (*a*) action *f*, opération *f*; **the a. of water,** l'action de l'eau; (*b*) **through s.o.'s a.,** par l'entremise, l'intermédiaire *m*, de qn. **2.** (*a*) *Com:* agence *f*, bureau *m*; **sole a. for a firm,** représentation exclusive d'une maison; **advertising a.,** agence de publicité; **news, press, a.,** agence de presse; **employment a.,** agence de placement; **estate a.,** agence immobilière; **travel a.,** agence de tourisme; (*b*) *Bank: etc:* succursale *f.*

agenda [ə'dʒendə] *n.* ordre *m* du jour, programme *m* (d'une réunion); **question on the a.,** question à l'ordre du jour.

agent ['eidʒənt] *n.* **1.** (*a*) agent, -ente; **to be a free a.,** avoir (le droit d'agir selon) son libre arbitre; (*b*) *Com: etc:* agent, représentant *m*; **a. for the firm of . . .,** représentant de la maison . . .; **sole a.,** agent exclusif; **forwarding a., transit a.,** transitaire *m*; **advertising a.,** agent de publicité; **insurance a.,** agent d'assurances; **(real-)estate a.,** agent immobilier; (*c*) **secret a.,** agent secret; **double a.,** agent double; (*d*) *Jur:* mandataire *mf*; fondé(e) de pouvoir. **2.** agent (chimique, thérapeutique, etc.).

age-old ['eidʒould] *a.* (coutume, etc.) séculaire.

agglomerate[1] [ə'glɔmərət] **1.** *a.* aggloméré. **2.** *n. Geol:* agglomérat *m.*

agglomerate[2] [ə'glɔməreit] **1.** *v.tr.* agglomérer. **2.** *v.i.* s'agglomérer.

agglomeration [əglɔmə'reiʃ(ə)n] *n.* agglomération *f.*

agglutinate [ə'glu:tineit] **1.** *v.tr.* agglutiner. **2.** *v.i.* s'agglutiner.

agglutination [əglu:ti'neiʃ(ə)n] *n.* agglutination *f.*

aggrandize [ə'grændaiz] *v.tr.* agrandir (un État, l'importance de qn).

aggrandizement [ə'grændizmənt] *n.* agrandissement *m* (d'un État, etc.).

aggravate ['ægrəveit] *v.tr.* **1.** (*a*) aggraver (une faute, une difficulté, un crime); empirer (un mal); envenimer (une plaie, une querelle); *Jur:* **aggravated larceny,** vol qualifié; (*b*) augmenter (l'indignation, la douleur). **2.** *F:* agacer, exaspérer (qn). **aggravating** *a.* **1.** (circonstance) aggravante. **2.** *F:* exaspérant; **a. child,** enfant insupportable.

aggravation [ægrə'veiʃ(ə)n] *n.* **1.** (*a*) aggravation *f* (d'un crime, d'une maladie); envenimement *m* (d'une plaie, d'une querelle); (*b*) *F:* exaspération *f*, agacement *m*. **2.** circonstance aggravante.

aggregate[1] ['ægrigət] **1.** *a.* (*a*) collectif; *Pol.Ec:* global, -aux; **for an a. period of three years,** pendant trois ans en tout; **a. output,** production globale; (*b*) *Bot: Geol: Z:* agrégé. **2.** *n.* (*a*) ensemble *m*, total *m*; **world aggregates,** totaux mondiaux; **in the a.,** en somme, dans l'ensemble; (*b*) masse *f*, assemblage *m*, agrégation *f*; *Ch: Miner:* agrégat; (*c*) *Civ.E:* granulat *m.*

aggregate[2] ['ægrigeit] **1.** *v.tr.* (*a*) *Ph:* agréger; (*b*) s'élever à (un nombre); monter à (un total). **2.** *v.i. Ph:* s'agréger.

aggregation [ægri'geiʃ(ə)n] *n.* **1.** (*a*) *Ph:* agrégation *f*, agglomération *f*; (*b*) *Pol.Ec:* **a. of production functions,** agrégation de fonctions de production. **2.** agrégat *m.*

aggression [ə'greʃ(ə)n] *n.* agression *f*; **war of a.,** guerre *f* d'agression.

aggressive [ə'gresiv] *a.* agressif; (regard, air) cassant; (politique) militante; *Psy:* **a. impulse,** impulsion agressive. **-ly** *adv.* d'une manière agressive; d'un ton agressif.

aggressiveness [ə'gresivnis] *n.* caractère agressif; agressivité *f.*

aggressor [ə'gresər] *n.* agresseur *m*; **a. nation,** pays *m* agresseur.

aggrieved [ə'gri:vd] *a.* **to be, feel, a. at, by, sth.,** être chagriné, blessé, de qch.; se sentir lésé; *Jur:* **the a. party,** la partie lésée.

aggro ['ægrou] *n. F:* (*a*) provocation *f*; incitation *f* à la bagarre; (*b*) bagarre(s); grabuge *m.*

aghast [ə'gɑ:st] *a.* consterné **(at,** de); pantois; **to stand a.,** en être tout pantois.

agile ['ædʒail] *a.* agile; leste. **-ly** *adv.* agilement.

agility [ə'dʒiliti] *n.* agilité *f.*

aging ['eidʒiŋ] *a. & n. NAm:* = AGEING; *see* AGE[2].

agio ['ædʒiou] *n. Fin:* **1.** agio *m*; prix *m* du change. **2.** commerce *m* du change.

agitate ['ædʒiteit] **1.** *v.tr.* (*a*) agiter, remuer (qch.); tourmenter (la surface de l'eau); (*b*) agiter, troubler (qn, l'esprit de qn). **2.** *v.i.* **to a. for, against, sth.,** faire de l'agitation, mener une campagne, en faveur de, contre, qch. **agitated** *a.* agité; ému; troublé.

agitation [ædʒi'teiʃ(ə)n] *n.* **1.** agitation *f* (de l'air, de la mer); mouvement *m*. **2.** (*a*) agitation, émotion *f*, trouble *m*; **in a state of a.,** agité; (*b*) agitation (ouvrière, etc.); troubles.

agitator ['ædʒiteitər] *n.* **1.** (*pers.*) agitateur, -trice; contestataire *m.* **2.** *Ind:* agitateur *m.*

aglow [ə'glou] *a.* **1.** (*of thg*) enflammé, embrasé; **to be a. with colour,** briller de vives couleurs. **2.** (*of pers.*) **face a. with delight,** visage rayonnant de joie, tout épanoui; **a. with health,** resplendissant de santé.

agnostic [æg'nɔstik] *a.* & *n.* agnostique (*mf*).

agnosticism [æg'nɔstisizm] *n.* agnosticisme *m.*

ago [ə'gou] *adv.* (*a*) **ten years a.,** il y a dix ans; **he arrived an hour a.,** il est arrivé il y a une heure; il est là depuis une heure; **a little while a.,** tout à l'heure; tantôt; (*b*) **long a.,** il y a longtemps; **not long a.,** il n'y a pas longtemps; **not so long ago,** il n'y a pas si longtemps; **how long a. is it since . . .?** combien de temps y a-t-il que . . .? depuis combien de temps . . .? **as long a. as 1840,** déjà en 1840; dès 1840; **I knew him long a.,** je l'ai connu dans le temps.

agog [ə'gɔg] *adv.* & *a.* **to be all a. (with excitement),** être en l'air, en émoi (**about sth.,** à cause de qch.).

agonize ['ægənaiz] *v.i.* *Lit:* être au supplice, au martyre. **agonized** *a.* (cri) d'angoisse; **with an a. expression (on her face),** d'un regard plein d'angoisse. **agonizing** *a.* (douleur, peur) atroce; (spectacle) navrant, angoissant; (*of situation, decision, dilemma, etc.*) angoissant. **agonizingly** *adv.* avec angoisse; **a. slow,** d'une lenteur insupportable.

agony ['ægəni] *n.* **1.** angoisse *f*; **in an a. of pain,** en proie à des douleurs atroces; **to suffer agonies, to be in a.,** être au supplice, au martyre; *Journ:* **a. column,** courrier *m* du cœur; *F:* **to pile on the a.,** forcer la dose. **2. (death) a.,** agonie *f.* **3. in an a. of fear,** saisi d'une peur atroce.

agoraphobia [ægərə'foubiə] *n.* *Psy:* agoraphobie *f.*

agrarian [ə'grɛəriən] **1.** *a.* (loi, mesure) agraire. **2.** *a.* & *n.* *Pol:* agrarien (*m*).

agree [ə'gri:] **1.** *v.i.* & *tr.* consentir, donner son adhésion (**to a proposal,** à une proposition); faire droit (à une requête); convenir de (qch.); accepter (une condition); **to a. to do sth.,** accepter, convenir, de faire qch.; consentir à faire qch.; **I a. that he was mistaken,** j'admets qu'il s'est trompé; *Jur:* **conditions agreed upon,** conditions acceptées d'un commun accord; **let's a. to differ,** différons à l'amiable; **to a. to sth. being done,** accepter que qch. se fasse; **unless otherwise agreed,** sauf arrangement contraire; **agreed!** entendu! soit! d'accord! **2.** *v.i.* (*a*) (*of two or more people*) s'accorder; être d'accord; tomber d'accord; **we shall never a.,** jamais nous ne nous mettrons d'accord; (*b*) **to a. with (s.o., sth.),** (i) donner raison à (qn); être du même avis que (qn); s'accorder, être d'accord, avec (qn); (ii) accepter (une théorie); approuver (une décision); partager, se ranger à (l'opinion de qn); **I quite a.,** bon, d'accord! **he entirely agrees with you,** il est entièrement de votre avis; *F:* **I couldn't a. (with you) more!** tu l'as bien dit! **everyone agrees, it is generally agreed, that . . .,** tout le monde accepte que . . .; (*c*) **'you're right!' he agreed,** 'vous avez raison', acquiesça-t-il. **3.** *v.i.* (*of thgs*) (*a*) s'accorder, être d'accord, concorder (ensemble); (*of ideas, opinions*) se rencontrer; **that does not a. with what he said,** cela ne s'accorde pas, n'est pas d'accord, avec ce qu'il a dit; (*b*) *Gram:* s'accorder; **the verb agrees with the subject in number,** le verbe s'accorde en nombre avec le sujet; (*c*) convenir (**with,** à); réussir; **the climate doesn't a. with him,** le climat ne lui convient pas, ne lui va pas; **lobster doesn't a. with me,** le homard ne me réussit pas. **4.** *v.tr.* s'accorder, se mettre d'accord, sur (les prix, les conditions, etc.). **agreed** *a.* (prix, etc.) convenu.

agreeable [ə'griəbl] *a.* **1.** agréable (**to,** à); (*of pers.*) aimable (**to,** envers); **if that is a. to you,** si cela vous convient. **2.** (*of pers.*) **to be a. to sth., to doing sth.,** consentir à qch., à faire qch.; accepter qch., de faire qch.; **I am (quite) a.,** je veux bien. **-ably** *adv.* agréablement.

agreement [ə'gri:mənt] *n.* **1.** *Com: Jur: etc:* convention *f*, acte *m*, contrat *m*; **written a.,** convention par écrit; **collective wage a.,** convention collective des salaires; **to enter into, conclude, an a. with s.o.,** passer un traité, un contrat, avec qn. **2.** (*a*) accord *m* (**on, about,** sur); **to be in a. with s.o.,** être d'accord avec qn; **to be in a. with a decision,** approuver une décision; **to come to an a.,** tomber d'accord; **to come to, arrive at, reach, an a. with s.o.,** se mettre d'accord avec qn; s'accommoder, s'arranger, avec qn; *Com:* **as per a.,** comme (il a été) convenu; **by mutual a.,** de gré à gré; d'un commun accord; (*b*) *Com: Ind:* entente *f* (entre producteurs, etc.); **marketing a.,** accord de commercialisation; (*c*) **to have an a. with s.o.,** avoir une entente, un arrangement, avec qn. **3.** (*a*) conformité *f*, concordance *f* (de différentes choses); (*b*) *Gram:* accord (**with,** avec); **a. of adjectives,** concordance des adjectifs.

agricultural [ægri'kʌltʃər(ə)l] *a.* (produit, machine, etc.) agricole; (peuple) agriculteur; (instrument) aratoire; **a. engineer,** ingénieur *m* agronome; **a. labourer, worker,** ouvrier *m* agricole; **a. college,** école *f* d'agriculture.

agricultur(al)ist [ægri'kʌltʃər(əl)ist] *n.* agriculteur *m.*

agriculture ['ægrikʌltʃər] *n.* agriculture *f.*

agronomic [ægrə'nɔmik] *a.* agronomique.

agronomist [ə'grɔnəmist] *n.* agronome *m.*

agronomy [ə'grɔnəmi] *n.* agronomie *f.*

aground [ə'graund] *adv.* *Nau:* échoué; au sec; (*of ship*) **to run a.,** (s')échouer.

ague ['eigju:] *n.* *Med: A:* fièvre (paludéenne) intermittente.

ah [ɑ:] *int.* ah! ha!

aha [ə'hɑ:] *int.* haha!

ahead [ə'hed] *adv.* **1.** *Nau:* (*a*) **to be a.,** être sur l'avant, en avant (du navire); **the ship was right a.,** le navire était droit devant; **to go a.,** aller de l'avant; **full speed a.!** en avant toute! (*b*) **wind a.,** vent debout; (*c*) *Navy:* **line a.,** en ligne de file, en colonne; **single line a.,** ligne de file. **2.** (*a*) **to get a.,** (i) (*of pers., car, etc.*) prendre de l'avance; (ii) *Fig:* (*of pers.*) avancer (dans sa carrière); (*of runner, cyclist, etc.*) **to draw a.,** se décoller; **to be a. of the bunch,** mener le peloton; **to go on a.,** prendre les devants; **a. of s.o.,** en avant de qn; **to get a. of s.o.,** dépasser qn; **to be two hours a. of s.o.,** avoir deux heures d'avance sur qn; **he is a. of his form,** il est en avance sur sa classe; **to be a. of one's time,** être en avance sur son temps; **to be a. of time,** (i) être, arriver, avoir fini, avant l'heure; (ii) (*of clock*) avancer; **you've got your best years a. of you,** vous avez vos meilleures années devant vous; **to look a.,** penser à l'avenir; **how far a. should one book?** combien de temps faut-il retenir d'avance? (*b*) **they went straight a.,** ils allaient (tout) droit devant eux; **go a.!** (i) allez! (ii) vas-y! allez-y!

ahoy [ə'hɔi] *int.* *Nau:* **boat, ship, a.!** oh(é) du canot! du navire!

aid[1] [eid] *n.* **1.** aide *f*, assistance *f*, secours *m*; **with, by, the a. of s.o., sth.,** avec l'aide de qn; à l'aide de qch.; **to go to s.o.'s a.,** aller, se porter, au secours de qn; **collection in a. of . . .,** quête *f* au profit de . . .; *F:* **what's (all) this in a. of?** c'est en quel honneur? **mutual a.,** entraide *f*; **mutual-a. society,** société *f* de secours mutuels, d'assistance mutuelle; **legal a.,** assistance judiciaire; **medical a.,** soins médicaux; **first a.,** premiers secours (aux blessés); soins d'urgence. **2. beauty aids,** produits *mpl* de beauté; **hearing a., deaf a.,** audiophone *m; Sch:* **audio-visual aids,** matériel audio-visuel.

aid[2] *v.tr.* **1.** aider, assister, secourir (qn); donner aide à (qn); venir en aide à (qn); venir à l'aide de (qn); prêter son concours, son appui, à (qn); **to a. one another,** s'aider les uns les autres, s'entraider; *Jur:* **to a. and abet s.o.,** être le complice de qn. **2.** soutenir, venir en aide à (une entreprise); (*of treatment, etc.*) contribuer à (la guérison de qn). **aiding** *n. Jur:* **a. and abetting,** complicité *f.*

aide [eid] *n.* aide *mf*; assistant(e).

aide-de-camp ['eid(d)əkɑ̃] *n.* (*pl.* **aides-de-camp** ['eid(d)əkɑ̃]) *Mil:* aide *m* de camp.

aide-mémoire ['eidmemwɑːr] *n. Dipl:* aide-mémoire *m inv.*

ail [eil] **1.** *v.tr. A:* **what ails you?** qu'est-ce que vous avez? **2.** *v.i.* être souffrant. **ailing** *a.* souffrant.

aileron ['eilərɔn] *n. Av:* aileron *m.*

ailment ['eilmənt] *n.* mal *m*; maladie (légère); **childish ailments,** maladies d'enfants.

aim[1] [eim] *n.* **1.** (*a*) action *f* de viser; **to miss one's a.,** (i) (*with firearm*) manquer le but, manquer son coup; (ii) frapper à faux; **to take a. at s.o., sth.,** viser qn, qch.; **to take a.,** mettre en joue; prendre sa visée; (*b*) but *m*; **missiles that fall short of their a.,** projectiles *mpl* qui n'atteignent pas le but. **2.** but, dessein *m*; visées *fpl*; **his a. was to . . .,** il avait pour but de . . .; il visait à . . .; **he has one a. in life,** sa vie n'a qu'un (seul) but; **with the a. of doing sth.,** dans le dessein de faire qch.

aim[2] **1.** *v.tr.* (*a*) **to a. a stone, a blow, at s.o.,** lancer une pierre à qn; porter, allonger, un coup à qn; (*b*) ajuster (un fusil, etc.); *Mil:* pointer; **to a. a gun, a pistol, at s.o.,** coucher qn en joue avec un fusil, un pistolet; (*c*) **remark aimed at s.o.,** remarque adressée à qn; **to a. a criticism at s.o.,** porter une critique sur qn. **2.** *v.i.* (*a*) **to a. at s.o. (with a gun),** ajuster, viser, qn; mettre, coucher, qn en joue; (*b*) **to a. at becoming sth., to a. to become sth.,** aspirer, viser, à devenir qch; **what are you aiming at?** quel but poursuivez-vous? où voulez-vous en venir? *F:* **I a. to go,** j'ai l'intention d'y aller. **aiming** *n.* visée *f*; *Mil:* pointage *m.*

aimless ['eimlis] *a.* sans but, sans objet; **an a. sort of life,** une vie désœuvrée. **-ly** *adv.* sans but, sans objet; **to wander about a.,** aller, errer, à l'aventure.

aimlessness ['eimlisnis] *n.* manque *m* de but à atteindre; manque d'ambition.

ain't [eint] *A: & P:* = **am not, is not, are not;** *see* BE.

air[1] [ɛər] *n.* **1.** (*a*) air *m*; **breath of a.,** souffle *m* d'air; **fresh a.,** air frais; **to go out for a breath of (fresh) a.,** sortir prendre l'air, le frais; **fresh-a. fiend,** pleinairiste *mf*; **in the open a.,** en plein air, au grand air, à ciel ouvert; **a. temperature,** température ambiante; *F:* **I can't live on a.,** je ne vis pas de l'air du temps; **to walk on a.,** être aux anges; **to be in the a.,** (*of rumour*) circuler; (*of idea*) être dans l'air; (*of project*) être encore vague; **there's something in the a.,** il y a quelque chose dans l'air; il se prépare quelque chose; *F:* **it's all hot a.,** ce sont des discours en l'air; **castles in the a.,** châteaux *mpl* en Espagne; **to melt, vanish, into thin a.,** s'évanouir, disparaître (aux yeux de qn); (*b*) *Lit: Nau:* brise *f*, vent *m*; (*c*) *Tchn:* **compressed a.,** air comprimé; *Ch: Ind:* **liquid a.,** air liquide; *Mec.E:* **a. filter,** filtre *m* à air; **a. compressor,** compresseur *m* d'air; **a. duct,** conduite *f* d'air, amenée *f* d'air; *El:* **a. gap,** entrefer *m*; **a. pocket,** (i) *Av:* trou *m* d'air; (ii) *Hyd.E: etc:* cantonnement *m* d'air, poche *f* d'air; (*d*) *attrib.* à air comprimé, pneumatique; **a. gun,** fusil *m* à air comprimé; **a. gauge,** micromètre *m* pneumatique. **2.** (*a*) **high up in the a.,** très haut au-dessus de nous, très haut dans le ciel; **in the a.,** en l'air, dans les airs; **to throw sth. (up) in the a.,** jeter qch. en l'air; *F:* **to go up in the a.** exploser (de colère); (*b*) *Meteor:* **upper a.,** haute atmosphère, couches supérieures de l'atmosphère; (*c*) *Av:* **by a.,** par avion, par air; **a. traffic,** circulation aérienne, trafic aérien; **a. traffic controller,** contrôleur *m* de la circulation aérienne, aiguilleur *m* du ciel; **a. transport,** transports aériens, par avion; **a. letter,** aérogramme *m*; **a. travel,** voyages *mpl* par avion; **a. hostess,** hôtesse *f* de l'air; **a. terminal,** aérogare *f*; **a. show,** salon *m* de l'aéronautique, de l'aviation; (*d*) *Adm:* **the Air Ministry** = le Ministère de l'Air; *Mil.Av:* **the Air Force,** l'Aviation *f*; **a. base,** base aérienne; **a. officer,** officier *m* d'aviation; **a. attack,** attaque aérienne; **a. defence, reconnaissance,** défense, reconnaissance, aérienne; **a. cover,** couverture aérienne, (force de) protection aérienne. **3.** *W.Tel: F:* **to be on the a.,** (i) (*of pers.*) parler à la radio; (ii) (*of programme*) être radiodiffusé; (*of station*) émettre; faire des émissions; **to put a play on the a.,** mettre une pièce en ondes. **4.** *Mus:* air. **5.** air, mine *f*, apparence *f*; **he has an a. about him,** il s'impose; **to carry sth. off with an a.,** faire qch. avec aplomb; **to give oneself, to put on, airs,** se donner des airs; faire le suffisant, la suffisante.

air[2] **1.** *v.tr.* (*a*) aérer (une pièce, du linge, etc.); éventer (des vêtements); mettre (des vêtements) à l'air, à l'évent; bassiner (un lit); (*b*) **to a. one's grievances,** exposer des griefs (personnels); (*c*) faire parade de, faire étalage de (ses opinions, son savoir); donner libre cours à (ses sentiments). **2.** *v.i.* s'aérer; s'éventer. **airing** *n.* **1.** (*a*) ventilation *f* (d'une salle, etc.); aérage *m*, aération *f*; (*b*) séchage *m* (de vêtements); **a. cupboard,** armoire chauffante. **2.** (*a*) (petite) promenade; **to take an a.,** prendre l'air; (*b*) **to give a project an a.,** lancer un ballon d'essai.

airbed ['ɛəbed] *n.* matelas *m* pneumatique.

airborne ['ɛəbɔːn] *a.* **1.** (matière, poussière, etc.) en suspension dans l'air. **2.** (*a*) (*of aircraft*) en vol, sustenté; (*of balloon*) en l'air; (*of aircraft*) **to become a.,** décoller; (*b*) *Mil:* (troupes, unités) aéroportées; **a. attack,** attaque exécutée par des troupes aéroportées, assaut vertical; (*c*) *Av:* (équipement, radar) de bord.

airbrush ['ɛəbrʌʃ] *n. Paint:* aérographe *m*; pinceau *m* à air; pistolet vaporisateur.

airbus ['ɛəbʌs] *n.* aérobus *m*, airbus *m.*

air-commodore ['ɛə'kɔmədɔər] *n. Mil.Av:* = général *m* de brigade (aérienne).

air-conditioned ['ɛəkən'diʃ(ə)nd] *a.* climatisé, à air conditionné.

air-conditioning ['ɛəkə'diʃ(ə)niŋ] *n.* climatisation *f*, conditionnement *m* (de l'air).

air-cooled ['ɛəkuːld] *a.* refroidi par l'air; *I.C.E:* **a.-c. engine,** moteur *m* à refroidissement par air.

air-cooling ['ɛəkuːliŋ] *n.* refroidissement *m* par l'air.

aircraft ['ɛəkrɑːft] *n.* (*pl.* **aircraft**) (*a*) appareil *m* (d'aviation); (*b*) avion *m*; **short-take-off-and-landing a.,** avion à décollage et à atterrissage court; **vertical-take-off-and-landing a.,** avion à décollage et à atterrissage vertical; (*c*) **single-seat(er) a.,** avion à une place, (avion) monoplace (*m*); **two-seat(er) a.,** avion à deux places, (avion) biplace (*m*); (*d*) **jet(-propelled) a.,** avion à réaction; **twin-engine a.,** (avion) bimoteur (*m*); (*e*) **civil a.,** avion civil; **charter a.,** (i) avion charter; (ii) avion-taxi *m*, *pl.* avions-taxis; **transport a.,** avion de transport; **passenger a.,** avion (de transport) de passagers; (*f*) **military a.,** avion, appareil, militaire; **reconnaissance a.,** avion de reconnaissance; **training a., trainer a.,** avion-école *m*, *pl.* avions-écoles; (*g*) **naval a., fleet a.,** appareil de l'aéronavale; **a. carrier,** porte-avions *m inv*; (*h*) **a. factory,** usine d'aviation; **a. manufacturer,** constructeur *m* d'avions, avionneur *m*; **a. engineering,** ingénierie *f* aéronautique.

aircraftman, *pl.* **-men** ['ɛəkrɑːftmən] **aircraftwoman,** *pl.* **-women** ['ɛəkrɑːftwumən, - wimen]

n. (femme) soldat de la WRAF; **leading aircraftman, aircraftwoman,** (femme) caporal de la WRAF.
aircrew ['ɛəkru:] *n. Av:* équipage *m.*
airdrome ['ɛədroum] *n. NAm:* aérodrome *m.*
airdrop ['ɛədrɔp] *n. Av:* largage *m* (de charges).
Airedale ['ɛədeil] *n.* chien *m* airedale; airedale *m.*
airer ['ɛərər] *n.* chevalet *m* (pour linge).
airfield ['ɛəfi:ld] *n.* champ *m* d'aviation, terrain *m* d'aviation, aérodrome *m.*
airflow ['ɛəflou] *n.* (*a*) écoulement *m* d'air; **smooth, turbulent, a.,** écoulement régulier, turbulent; (*b*) *U.S: Aut:* **a. body,** carrosserie *f* aérodynamique.
airfoil ['ɛəfɔil] *n. NAm:* = AEROFOIL.
airframe ['ɛəfreim] *n.* cellule *f* d'avion, fuselage *m.*
airiness ['ɛərinis] *n.* **1.** (*a*) situation aérée (d'un bâtiment); (*b*) bonne ventilation (d'une pièce). **2.** légèreté *f* (d'esprit); insouciance *f*; désinvolture *f.*
airless ['ɛəlis] *a.* **1.** privé d'air, renfermé. **2.** sans air. **3.** (temps, soirée) sans vent, lourd(e).
airlessness ['ɛəlisnis] *n.* **1.** manque *m* d'air (d'une pièce). **2.** lourdeur *f* (du temps, etc.).
airlift¹ ['ɛəlift] *n. Av:* pont aérien; transport aérien.
airlift² *v.tr.* transporter par avion.
airline ['ɛəlain] *n.* ligne, compagnie, aérienne.
airliner ['ɛəlainər] *n.* avion *m* de ligne.
airlock ['ɛəlɔk] *n.* **1.** (*a*) *Civ.E:* écluse *f*, sas *m* pneumatique, à air (d'un caisson); (*b*) *Nau:* sas (de la chaufferie); (*c*) *Space:* sas (d'entrée, de sortie). **2.** *Mch: etc:* (*in pipe*) bouchon *m* d'air; poche *f* d'air.
airmail¹ ['ɛəmeil] *n.* (*a*) poste aérienne; service postal aérien; **by a.,** par avion; (*b*) courrier *m* par avion; **a. letter,** lettre (envoyée) par avion.
airmail² *v.tr.* envoyer (une lettre, etc.) par avion.
airman, *pl.* **-men** ['ɛəmən] *n.m.* (*a*) aviateur; (*b*) *Mil.Av: U.S:* **a. (basic),** soldat.
airplane ['ɛəplein] *n. NAm:* avion *m.*
airport ['ɛəpɔ:t] *n. Av:* aéroport *m*; **London A.,** l'aéroport de Londres.
air-raid ['ɛəreid] *n.* raid aérien; attaque, incursion, aérienne; **a.-r. precautions,** défense passive; **a.-r. warning,** alerte aérienne.
airscrew ['ɛəskru:] *n. Av: O:* hélice *f.*
air-sea ['ɛə'si] *a.* **a.-s. rescue,** sauvetage *m* aéromaritime, sauvetage aérien en mer.
airship ['ɛəʃip] *n.* dirigeable *m*; aéronef *m.*
airsick ['ɛəsik] *a.* **to be a.,** avoir le mal de l'air.
airsickness ['ɛəsiknis] *n.* mal *m* de l'air.
airspace ['ɛəspeis] *n. Av: etc:* espace aérien.
airspeed ['ɛəspi:d] *n. Av:* vitesse *f* (d'un avion).
airstrip ['ɛəstrip] *n. Av:* bande *f*, piste *f*, d'atterrissage.
airtight ['ɛətait] *a.* (clôture) hermétique; (récipient, etc.) à clôture hermétique; étanche (à l'air).
air-to-air ['ɛətu'ɛər] *a. Mil:* (engin) air-air *inv.*
air-to-ground ['ɛətə'graund] *a. Mil:* air-sol *inv.*, air-terre *inv.*
air-to-surface ['ɛətə'sə:fəs] *a.* (engin) (i) *Mil:* air-sol *inv*; (ii) *Navy:* air-surface *inv.*
airway ['ɛəwei] *n.* **1.** *Min:* voie *f* d'air, d'aérage; galerie *f* d'aérage. **2.** *Av:* (*a*) route, ligne, voie, aérienne; **a. marker,** balise *f* d'entrée de piste; (*b*) radioalignement *m*; **flying airways,** radio-balisage *m.* **3.** *W.Tel: T.V: U.S:* chaîne *f.*
airwoman, *pl.* **-women** ['ɛəwumən, -wimin] *n.f.* aviatrice.
airworthiness ['ɛəwə:ðinis] *n. Av:* tenue *f* en l'air, navigabilité *f*; **certificate of a.,** certificat *m* de navigabilité.
airworthy ['ɛəwə:ði] *a. Av:* (i) en état de prendre l'air, en bon état de vol, de navigabilité; (ii) muni d'un certificat de navigabilité; **to be a.,** tenir l'air.
airy ['ɛəri] *a.* **1.** bien aéré, ouvert à l'air; **a. room,** pièce bien aérée. **2.** léger, impalpable. **3.** (*a*) (*of conduct, etc.*) léger, insouciant, désinvolte, cavalier; (*b*) (promesses) vaines, illusoires. **-ily** *adv.* légèrement; d'un ton dégagé, cavalier; avec désinvolture.
airy-fairy ['ɛəri'fɛəri] *a. F:* (*of pers.*) farfelu; (*of ideas, etc.*) impraticable, irréalisable.
aisle [ail] *n.* **1.** *Ecc.Arch:* bas-côté *m*, *pl.* bas-côtés; nef (col)latérale; collatéral *m*, *pl.* -aux. **2.** (*a*) **to walk up the a.,** se marier (à l'église); (*b*) passage *m* (entre bancs); couloir central (d'un autobus, etc.); allée (de cinéma, etc.); *Th: F:* **to have them rolling in the aisles,** avoir un succès fou.
aitch [eitʃ] *n.* (la lettre) h *m*; **to drop one's aitches,** ne pas aspirer les h.
aitchbone ['eitʃboun] *n. Cu:* culotte *f* (de bœuf).
ajar [ə'dʒɑ:r] *adv. & a.* (*of door, window*) entrouvert, entrebâillé; **to leave the door a.,** entrebâiller la porte.
akimbo [ə'kimbou] *adv.* **with arms a.,** les (deux) poings sur les hanches; **to stand with arms a.,** faire le pot à deux anses.
akin [ə'kin] *adv. & a.* **1. a. to s.o., sth.,** apparenté à qn, qch. **2. feeling a. to fear,** sentiment voisin de l'effroi.
alabaster ['æləbæstər, -bɑ:-] *n.* albâtre *m.*
à la carte [ælə'kɑ:t] *a. & adv.* à la carte.
alacrity [ə'lækriti] *n.* empressement *m*, promptitude *f*; **he accepted with a.,** il a accepté avec enthousiasme.
Aladdin [ə'lædin] *Pr.n.m. Myth:* Aladin.
Alan ['ælən] *Pr.n.m.* Alain.
alarm¹ [ə'lɑ:m] *n.* **1.** alarme *f*, alerte *f*; **false a.,** fausse alerte; **state of a.,** état d'alerte; **to raise, give, the a.,** donner l'éveil, l'alerte, l'alarme; **a. signal,** signal d'alarme. **2.** alarme, frayeur *f*; s'alarmer; **he ran and hid in a.,** effrayé, il s'est caché; *Orn: etc:* **a. call,** cri *m* d'alarme. **3.** (*a*) avertisseur *m*; sonnette *f* d'alarme; **burglar a.,** signalisateur *m* antivol; **fire a.,** avertisseur d'incendie; (*b*) sonnerie *f* (du réveil); **a. (clock),** réveille-matin *m inv*, réveil *m*; **to wind up the a.,** remonter la sonnerie; **to set the a. for six o'clock,** mettre le réveil à six heures.
alarm² *v.tr.* **1.** (*a*) alarmer, donner l'alarme à (qn); (*b*) alerter (des troupes). **2.** effrayer; **to be alarmed at sth.,** s'alarmer, s'effrayer, de qch.; être alarmé de qch.; **don't be alarmed,** ne vous effrayez pas. **alarming** *a.* alarmant; effrayant. **alarmingly** *adv.* d'une mannière alarmante, effrayante.
alarmist [ə'lɑ:mist] *a. & n.* alarmiste (*mf*).
alas [ə'læs, ə'lɑ:s] *int.* hélas!
Alaska [ə'læskə] *Pr.n. Geog:* Alaska *m*; *Cu:* **baked A.,** omelette norvégienne.
alb [ælb] *n. Ecc.Cost:* aube *f.*
Albania [æl'beiniə] *Pr.n.Geog:* Albanie *f.*
Albanian [æl'beiniən]. **1.** *a. Geog:* albanais. **2.** *n.* (*a*) Albanais, -aise; (*b*) *Ling:* albanais *m.*
albatross ['ælbətrɔs] *n. Orn:* albatros *m.*
albeit [ɔ:l'bi:it] *conj. Lit:* quoique, bien que, + *sub*; **a brilliant, a. slipshod, writer,** écrivain brilliant, bien que négligeant.
albinism ['ælbinizm] *n.* albinisme *m.*
albino, *pl.* **-os** [æl'bi:nou, -ouz] *a. & n.* albinos (*mf*); **a. rabbit,** lapin *m* russe.
Albion ['ælbiən] *Pr.n.A. Geog: Lit:* Albion *f*; **perfidious A.,** la perfide Albion.
album ['ælbəm] *n.* **1.** album *m*; **loose-leaf a.,** album à feuilles mobiles. **2.** *Rec:* album *m.*
albumen ['ælbjumin, æl'bju:min] *n.* **1.** albumen *m*, blanc *m* d'œuf. **2.** albumine *f* (du sérum du sang). **3.** *Bot:* albumen (de l'embryon).
albumin ['ælbjumin, æl'bju:min] *n. Ch:* albumine *f.*
alchemist ['ælkəmist] *n.* alchimiste *m.*
alchemy ['ælkəmi] *n.* alchimie *f.*
alcohol ['ælkəhɔl] *n.* alcool *m*; **wood a.,** méthanol *m*;

a. content, teneur *m* en alcool, pourcentage *m* d'alcool; *Med: U.S:* **rubbing a.** = alcool à 90°.

alcoholic [ælkə'hɔlik] **1.** *a.* alcoolique; **a. drink,** boisson alcoolisée. **2.** *n.* (*pers.*) alcoolique *mf.*

alcoholism ['ælkəhɔlizm] *n.* alcoolisme *m.*

alcove ['ælkouv] *n.* alcôve *f*; niche *f* (dans un mur); **dining a.,** coin *m* des repas, coin salle à manger.

aldehyde ['ældihaid] *n. Ch:* aldéhyde *f.*

alder ['ɔːldər] *n. Bot:* aune *m*, aulne *m.*

alderman, *pl.* **-men** ['ɔːldəmən] *n.m. Adm:* (i) = conseiller municipal; (ii) = conseiller général.

Alderney ['ɔːldəni] *Pr.n. Geog:* Aurigny *m.*

ale [eil] *n.* **1.** bière anglaise (légère); ale *f*; **pale a., brown a.,** bière blonde, brune. **2. ginger a.,** boisson gazeuse au gingembre.

Alec(k) ['ælik] *Pr.n.m.* (*dim. of* **Alexander**) Alexandre; *F:* **a smart A.,** (i) un combinard; (ii) un je-sais-tout.

alehouse ['eilhaus] *n. A:* cabaret *m.*

alert[1] [ə'ləːt] **1.** *a.* (*a*) alerte, vigilant, éveillé; (*b*) actif, vif, preste; **a. mind,** esprit présent, vif, éveillé. **2.** *n.* alerte *f*; **to be on the a.,** être sur le qui-vive, être en état d'alerte; **to be on the a. against an attack,** veiller en prévision d'une attaque.

alert[2] *v.tr.* alerter; **troops have been alerted,** les troupes sont en état d'alerte; **to a. s.o. to a danger,** avertir qn d'un danger.

alertness [ə'ləːtnis] *n.* **1.** (*a*) vigilance *f*; (*b*) promptitude *f* (**in doing sth.,** à faire qch.). **2.** vivacité *f.*

Alexander [ælig'zɑːndər] *Pr.n.m.* Alexandre.

Alexandria [ælig'zɑːndriə] *Pr.n. Geog:* Alexandrie *f.*

alexandrine [ælig'zɑːndrain] *a. & n. Pros:* alexandrin (*m*).

alfalfa [æl'fælfə] *n. Bot:* luzerne *f.*

alfresco [æl'freskou] *a. & adv.* en plein air; **a. meal,** repas *m* en plein air.

alga, *pl.* **-ae** ['ælgə, 'ældʒiː] *n. Bot:* algue *f.*

algal ['ælgl] *a.* **1.** des algues. **2.** *Fung:* (*of cells in lichen*) gonidial, -aux; gonimique.

algebra ['ældʒibrə] *n.* algèbre *f.*

algebraic(al) [ældʒi'breiik(l)] *a.* (signe, somme, etc.) algébrique.

Algeria [æl'dʒiəriə] *Pr.n. Geog:* Algérie *f.*

Algerian [æl'dʒiəriən] **1.** (*of Algeria*) (*a*) *a.* algérien; (*b*) *n.* Algérien, -ienne. **2.** (*of Algiers*) (*a*) *a.* algérois; (*b*) *n.* Algérois, -oise.

Algiers [æl'dʒiəz] *Pr.n.Geog:* Alger *m.*

algol ['ælgɔl] *n. Cmptr:* algol *m.*

alias ['eiliəs] **1.** *adv.* alias, autrement dit, autrement nommé; **John X, a. Y,** John X, connu sous le nom de Y, dit Y. **2.** *n.* (*pl.* **aliases** ['eiliəsiz]) nom emprunté, nom d'emprunt, faux nom; **to travel under an a.,** voyager sous un faux nom.

alibi ['ælibai] *n. Jur:* alibi *m*; **to produce an a.,** produire, fournir, un alibi; **to establish an a.,** prouver, établir, son alibi.

alien ['eiliən] **1.** *a. & n. Jur:* étranger, -ère (non naturalisé(e)); **undesirable a.,** étranger indésirable. **2.** *a.* étranger (à qch.); contraire, opposé (à qch.); qui répugne (à qch.); **an action entirely a. to her nature,** une action entièrement contraire à sa nature.

alienable ['eiliənəbl] *a. Jur:* (bien) aliénable.

alienate ['eiliəneit] *v.tr.* **1.** *Jur:* aliéner (des biens, etc.). **2.** détacher, éloigner, désaffectionner (qn, les esprits); **to a. s.o. from his friends,** détacher qn de ses amis. **3.** détourner (une somme).

alienation [eiliə'neiʃ(ə)n] *n.* **1.** *Jur:* aliénation *f* (de biens). **2.** aliénation (de cœurs); désaffection *f.* **3. mental a.,** aliénation mentale.

alienist ['eiliənist] *n. Med:* aliéniste *mf.*

alight[1] [ə'lait] *v.i.* **1.** descendre (de cheval, de voiture). **2.** (*a*) (*of bird*) s'abattre, se poser; (*b*) (*of falling object*) se poser (**on,** sur).

alight[2] *a.* allumé, en feu; **to catch a.,** s'allumer; prendre feu; **to set sth. a.,** mettre le feu à qch.; mettre qch. en feu.

align [ə'lain] **1.** *v.tr.* (*a*) aligner (des soldats, etc.); mettre (des objets) en ligne; *Cmptr:* aligner, cadrer (des cartes); (*b*) *Mec.E:* dresser (des arbres, etc.); faire coïncider (les axes); dégauchir, redresser (des organes faussés ou gauchis); *Elcs:* aligner, redresser, régler; *Aut:* régler le parallélisme (des roues); (*c*) *Fin:* (*of country*) aligner (sa monnaie) (**on,** sur). **2.** *v.i.* (*a*) s'aligner, se mettre en ligne; prendre position; (*b*) (*of shafts, etc.*) coïncider.

alignment [ə'lainmənt] *n.* (*a*) alignement *m*; tracé *m* (d'une voie ferrée, etc.); *Cmptr:* alignement, cadrage *m*; **out of a.,** (i) désaligné; (ii) *Const:* hors d'œuvre; (ii) *Typ:* (ligne) sortante; (*b*) redressage *m*, dégauchissement *m* (d'organes faussés, etc.); centrage *m*, équerrage *m*; (*c*) *Elcs:* alignement, redressage, réglage *m*; (*d*) *Aut:* parallélisme *m* (des roues); **front wheel a.,** parallélisme des roues avant; (*e*) *Fin:* **a. of currencies,** alignement des monnaies.

alike [ə'laik] **1.** *a.* semblable, pareil, ressemblant; **they are very much a.,** ils se ressemblent beaucoup; **no two are a.,** il n'y en a pas deux de pareils; **you are all a.!** vous êtes tous les mêmes! **2.** *adv.* pareillement; de même; **to treat everybody a.,** traiter tout le monde de la même manière, de la même façon; **dressed a.,** habillés de même; vêtus uniformément; **every day, summer and winter a.,** tous les jours, été comme hiver.

aliment ['ælimənt] *n.* **1.** aliment *m.* **2.** *Scot: Jur:* = ALIMONY.

alimentary [æli'mentəri] *a.* **1.** *Anat:* **a. canal,** tube digestif. **2. a. substances,** substances *fpl* alimentaires.

alimentation [ælimen'teiʃ(ə)n] *n.* alimentation *f.*

alimony ['æliməni] *n. Jur:* pension *f* alimentaire (faite à l'épouse après séparation de corps); **to pay one's wife a.,** fournir des aliments à son épouse.

aline [ə'lain] *v.,* **alinement** [ə'lainm(ə)nt] *n. esp. U.S:* = ALIGN, ALIGNMENT.

alive [ə'laiv] *a.* **1.** (*a*) (*of pers.*) **to be (still) a.,** être (encore) vivant, en vie; vivre (encore); **to keep s.o. a.,** maintenir qn en vie; **to come a. again,** revenir à la vie; ressusciter; **to be burnt, buried, a.,** être brûlé, enterré, vif; *F:* **to be a. and kicking,** être plein de vie; **dead or a.,** mort ou vif; **more dead than a.,** plus mort que vif; **when your father was a.,** du vivant de votre père; **no man a.,** personne, aucun homme, au monde; (*b*) **to keep (sth.) a.,** garder, entretenir (un souvenir); entretenir, ne pas laisser languir (la conversation). **2. to be fully a. to (sth.),** avoir pleinement conscience de (qch); se rendre compte de, comprendre bien (l'importance de qch.); **I am a. to the fact that . . .,** je n'ignore pas que. . . **3. he is very much a.,** (i) il est très remuant; (ii) il a l'esprit très éveillé; **look a.!** remuez-vous (donc)! **4. the cheese was a. with maggots,** le fromage grouillait de vers; **the street was a. with people,** la rue fourmillait de monde. **5.** *El: esp. U.S:* **the wire was a.,** le fil était sous tension.

alkali ['ælkəlai] *n. Ch:* alcali *m*; **a. metal,** métal alcalin.

alkaline ['ælkəlain] *a. Ch:* alcalin.

alkaloid ['ælkəlɔid] *a. & n. Ch:* alcaloïde (*m*).

all [ɔːl] **1.** *a. & pron.* tout, tous; (*a*) *a.* **a. France,** toute la France; **a. men,** tous les hommes; **a. the others,** tous les autres; **to be a. things to a. men,** être tout à tous; **a. day,** toute la journée; **a. his life,** toute sa vie; **a. the way,** (i) tout le long du chemin; (ii) jusqu'au bout; **is that a. the luggage you're taking?** c'est tout ce que vous emportez de bagages? **for a. his wealth,** en dépit de, malgré, sa fortune; **with a. speed,** au plus vite, à toute vitesse; **beyond a. doubt,** sans le moindre doute; **at a. hours,** à toute heure; **in a. sorts**

of ways, de toutes les façons; **a. that's nonsense,** tout ça, c'est des bêtises; **and a. that,** et tout cela, et tout le reste; **you're not as ill as a. that,** vous n'êtes pas (aus)si malade que ça; (*b*) *pron.* **a. are agreed that . . .,** tous, toutes, sont d'accord que . . .; **a. of us,** nous tous; **a. together,** tous, toutes, à la fois, ensemble; **a. but he, him,** tous sauf, excepté, lui; **a. and sundry,** tous sans exception; *F:* **he must be a. of sixty,** il doit avoir au moins soixante ans; (*c*) *pron.* **we a. love him,** nous l'aimons tous; **I know it a.,** (i) je sais tout cela; (ii) (*of poem, etc.*) je le sais en entier; **take it a.,** prenez le tout; **in the middle of it a.,** au milieu de tout cela; (*d*) *adv. Games:* **five a.,** *Fb: etc:* cinq à cinq; (*at dominoes*) cinq partout; *Ten:* **four (games) a.,** quatre (jeux) partout; **fifteen a.,** quinze à quinze; (*e*) *pron.* **almost a.,** presque tout; **a. that glitters is not gold,** tout ce qui brille n'est pas or; **a. that happens,** tout ce qui arrive; **for a. he may say,** en dépit de ce qu'il dit; quoi qu'il en dise; **that's a.,** c'est tout; voilà tout; **is that a.?** (i) est-ce tout? (ii) *Iron:* n'est-ce que cela? ce n'est que ça? **if that's a.,** si ce n'est que cela; **all's well,** tout va bien; **I think that's about a.,** je crois que c'est tout; **it was a. I could do not to laugh,** je me tenais à quatre pour ne pas rire; **when all's said and done,** somme toute, en fin de compte; **after a.,** après tout. **2.** (*a*) *pron.* **once and for a.,** une fois pour toutes; **for a. I know,** autant que je sache; **for a. I care,** pour (tout) ce que cela me fait; **thirty men in a.,** trente hommes en tout; **above a.,** surtout; **most of a.,** surtout, le plus; **when I was busiest of a.,** au moment où j'étais le plus occupé; (*b*) *adv.phr.* **do you know him at a.?** le connaissez-vous aucunement? **I didn't speak at a.,** je n'ai pas parlé du tout; **I'm not at a. astonished,** je n'en suis aucunement étonné; **not at a.,** (i) pas du tout, *F:* du tout; (ii) (*when thanked*) je vous en prie; **nothing at a.,** rien du tout; **if he comes at a.,** s'il lui arrive de venir; **if it is at a. cold,** s'il fait le moindre froid; **why do it at a.?** pourquoi se donner la peine de le faire? (*c*) *adv.phr.* **a. but impossible,** presque impossible; **it's a. but done,** c'est pour ainsi dire fini, fait; c'est comme fait; (*d*) *adv. or adj.phr.* **(taking it) a. in a.,** à tout prendre; (*e*) *pron.* **and a.,** et (tout) le reste; **I'll sell you the house, the furniture, the carpets and a.,** je vous vends la maison, y compris les meubles, les tapis et tout le bataclan; (*f*) *pron. P:* **damn a.,** rien du tout, rien de rien; **I've done damn a. today,** je n'ai rien fichu aujourd'hui. **3.** *adv.* tout; **she is a. alone,** elle est toute seule; **to be (dressed) a. in black,** être habillé(e) tout en noir, tout de noir; **she is a. ears, a. impatience,** elle est tout oreilles, tout impatience; **a. in one piece,** tout d'une pièce; **she is a. for accepting this offer,** elle est tout en faveur d'accepter cette offre; **my wife was a. for calling in a doctor,** ma femme voulait à toute force, à tout prix, appeler un médecin; **he's not a. bad,** il n'est pas entièrement mauvais; **a. the better, a. the worse (for me),** tant mieux, tant pis (pour moi); **you will be a. the better for it,** vous vous en trouverez (d'autant) mieux; **the time came a. too soon,** l'heure n'arriva que trop tôt; **a. at once,** (i) tout à coup, subitement; (ii) tout d'un coup, tous à la fois; **that's a. nonsense,** tout cela est absurde; **that's a. very well, but . . .,** tout cela est bel et bien mais . . .; *F:* **he's not a. there,** il est un peu simple d'esprit. **4.** *n.* tout *m*, totalité *f*; **to stake one's a.,** risquer le tout pour le tout; **I would give my a. to see her,** je donnerais tout ce que j'ai pour la voir.

all-absorbing ['ɔːləb'sɔːbiŋ] *a.* absorbant, passionnant.

Allah ['ælə] *Pr.n.m.* Allah.

all-American ['ɔːlə'merikən] *a.* cent pour cent américain.

Allan ['ælən] *Pr.n.m.* Alain.

all-around ['ɔːlə'raund] *a. NAm:* (athlète) complet; (homme) universel.

allay [ə'lei] *v.tr.* (*a*) apaiser, calmer (une tempête, une colère); (*b*) calmer (la frayeur); endormir, dissiper (les soupçons); (*c*) alléger, calmer, soulager (la douleur); apaiser (la soif, la faim, la fièvre).

all-clear ['ɔːl'kliər] *n.* (signal *m* de) fin *f* d'alerte.

all-conquering ['ɔːl'kɔnk(ə)riŋ] *a.* (amour, etc.) qui triomphe de tout.

allegation [æli'geiʃ(ə)n] *n.* allégation *f*; **to make an a.,** alléguer qch.

allege [ə'ledʒ] *v.tr.* alléguer, prétendre (**that,** que + *ind.*); **the words alleged to have been spoken by . . .,** les propos qui auraient été tenus par . . .; **he was alleged to be dead,** on le prétendait, disait, mort. **alleged** *a.* (motif) allégué; **the a. thief,** le voleur présumé. **allegedly** [ə'ledʒidei] *adv.* prétendument.

allegiance [ə'liːdʒəns] *n.* **1.** fidélité *f*, obéissance *f* (**to,** à); **to owe a. to (s.o.),** devoir fidélité et obéissance à (un roi); **to renounce one's a. to a party,** se détacher d'un parti. **2. to take the oath of a.,** prêter serment *m* d'allégeance.

allegoric(al) [æli'gɔrik(l)] *a.* allégorique. **-ally** *adv.* allégoriquement, sous forme d'allégorie.

allegory ['æligəri] *n.* allégorie *f*.

allegretto [æli'gretou] *adv. & n.* allegretto (*m*).

allegro [ə'legrou, -'lei-] *adv. & n.* allegro (*m*).

alleluia, -luja [æli'luːjə] *int. & n.* alléluia (*m*).

all-embracing [ɔːlim'breisiŋ] *a.* (amour) qui embrasse tout; **a.- e. knowledge,** vaste érudition.

allergen ['ælədʒen] *n. Med:* allergène *m*.

allergic [ə'ləːdʒik] *a. Med:* allergique (**to,** à); **I'm a. to him,** je ne peux pas le sentir.

allergy ['ælədʒi] *n. Med:* allergie *f*.

alleviate [ə'liːvieit] *v.tr.* alléger, soulager (la douleur); adoucir (le chagrin); apaiser (la soif); **pain-alleviating medicine,** potion anodine.

alleviation [əliːvi'eiʃ(ə)n] *n.* allègement *m*, soulagement *m*; adoucissement *m*.

alley ['æli] *n.* (*a*) (*in park, etc.*) allée *f*; (*b*) ruelle *f*; **blind a.,** impasse *m*; **blind-a. job,** situation *f* sans avenir; *F:* **a. cat,** chat *m* de gouttière; (*c*) **bowling a.,** bowling *m*.

alleyway ['æliwei] *n.* **1.** ruelle *f*; passage étroit. **2.** *N.Arch:* coursive *f*.

alliance [ə'laiəns] *n.* **1.** alliance *f*. *Hist:* **the Triple A.,** la Triple Alliance; la Triplice; **to enter into an a.,** s'allier (**with,** avec); **political a.,** apparentement *m*; **to make a political a. with a party,** s'apparenter avec un parti. **2. a. by marriage,** alliance; apparentage *m*.

allied *see* ALLY[2].

alligator ['æligeitər] *n.* **1.** (*a*) *Rept:* alligator *m*; (*b*) *Leath:* crocodile *m*. **2.** *Bot: esp. NAm:* **a. pear,** (poire *f* d')avocat (*m*).

all-important ['ɔːlim'pɔːt(ə)nt] *a.* de la plus haute importance.

all-in ['ɔːlin] **1.** *Com:* (*a*) *a.* **a.-in price,** prix *m* tout compris; prix forfaitaire; *Ins:* **a.-in policy,** police *f* tous risques; (*b*) *adv.* tout compris. **2.** *Sp:* **a.-in wrestling,** catch *m*.

all-inclusive ['ɔːlin'kluːsiv] *a.* (prix) tout compris.

alliteration [əlitə'reiʃ(ə)n] *n.* allitération *f*.

alliterative [ə'litərətiv, -reit-] *a.* allitératif.

all-night ['ɔːlnait] *a.* (veillée, etc.) de la nuit entière; *Adm: etc:* **a.-n. service,** permanence *f* de nuit; *Mil: etc:* **a.-n. pass,** permission *f* de la nuit.

allocate ['æləkeit] *v.tr.* (*a*) allouer, assigner (qch. à qn, à qch.); **to a. a sum to sth.,** affecter, assigner, une somme à qch.; (*b*) **to a. duties,** attribuer, distribuer, des fonctions (**to,** à).

allocation [ælə'keiʃ(ə)n] *n.* **1.** (*a*) allocation *f*, affectation *f* (d'une somme); **a. of capital,** affectation des investissements; (*b*) répartition *f* (de dépenses, de moyens, etc.); attribution *f* (de fonctions); (*c*) **a. of contract,** adjudication *f;* **a. to lowest tender,** adjudication au mieux-disant. **2.** part assignée; somme assignée.

allot [ə'lɔt] *v.tr.* **(allotted) 1. to a. sth. to s.o.,** attribuer, assigner, qch. à qn; **to a. sth. to, for, an object,** affecter, destiner, qch. à un but. **2.** répartir, distribuer (des fonctions, des sièges, *Fin:* des actions).

allotment [ə'lɔtmənt] *n.* **1.** (*a*) attribution *f* (de qch. à qn); affectation *f* (d'une somme à un but); (*b*) partage *m*, répartition *f*; distribution *f* (des chambres, de fonctions, etc.); lotissement *m* (de parts, d'une propriété); *Fin:* **a. of shares,** attribution d'actions; **letter of a.,** (lettre *f* d')avis (*m*) de répartition; lettre d'allocation. **2.** (*a*) portion *f*, part *f*, lot *m*; (*b*) jardin ouvrier.

all-out ['ɔːl'aut] *F:* **1.** *a.* (effort) suprême, maximum; (attaque) à fond; **a.-o. strike, war,** grève, guerre, totale. **2.** *adv.* (*without hyphen*) complètement, entièrement; **to go a. o.,** ne pas s'épargner.

all-over ['ɔːl'ouvər] *a.* **with an a.-o. pattern,** dont le dessin couvre toute la surface.

allow [ə'lau] *v.tr.* **1.** (*a*) faire droit à (une demande, une réclamation); admettre (une requête); (*b*) *NAm: F:* juger, opiner, affirmer **(that,** que). **2.** (*a*) permettre (qch.); **to a. s.o. sth.,** permettre qch. à qn; **to a. s.o. to do sth.,** permettre à qn de, autoriser qn à, faire qch.; **to be allowed to compete,** etre admis à concourir; **I am allowed to do it,** on me permet, il m'est permis, de le faire; **a. me!** permettez (-moi)!; **a. me to . . .,** permettez-moi de . . .; **passengers are not allowed on the bridge,** la passerelle est interdite aux voyageurs; **as soon as circumstances a.,** dès que les circonstances le permettront; (*b*) **to a. oneself to be led, deceived,** se laisser mener, tromper; **I will not a. you to be ill-treated,** je ne vous laisserai pas maltraiter; (*c*) *ind.tr. O:* **his condition would not a. of his going out,** son état ne lui permettait pas de sortir. **3.** (*a*) **to a. s.o. £1000 a year,** faire, accorder, allouer, à qn une rente de £1000; **to a. a debtor time to pay,** accorder un délai à un débiteur; **at the end of the six months allowed,** à l'expiration du délai de six mois; **we must a. one hour for dressing,** il faut compter une heure pour nous habiller; (*b*) *Com: Fin:* **to a. s.o. a discount,** consentir, accorder, faire, un escompte, une remise, à qn; (*c*) *v.i.* **to a. for sth.,** tenir compte de qch.; faire la part de qch.; avoir égard à qch.; prévoir (des difficultés, des retards, etc.); **after allowing for . . .,** déduction faite de . . .; **to a. so much for carriage,** (i) ajouter, (ii) déduire, tant pour le port; **you must a. for his being ill,** il faut tenir compte de ce qu'il est malade.

allowable [ə'lauəbl] *a.* (*a*) admissible; légitime; (*b*) *Com: etc:* (dépense) déductible.

allowance [ə'lauəns] *n.* **1.** (*a*) pension *f* alimentaire (donnée volontairement); rente *f*; **to make one's mother an a. of £1000 a year,** faire à sa mère une rente de £1000 par an; **to stop, cut off, s.o.'s a.,** couper les vivres à qn; (*b*) *Adm: etc:* allocation *f*; dégrèvement *m* (pour charges de famille, etc.); **cost-of-living a.,** indemnité *f* de vie chère; **family allowances,** allocations familiales; **supplementary allowances,** majorations *fpl* de pension; *Fin:* **personal a.,** abattement personnel (sur l'impôt); *Adm: Com:* **entertainment a.,** frais *mpl* de représentation; **travel, travelling, a.,** indemnité de déplacement; (*c*) *Trans:* **(free) luggage a.,** bagages *mpl* en franchise; (*d*) *Rac:* **time a.,** rendement *m* de temps; *Turf:* **weight a.,** décharge *f*. **3.** *Com: Fin:* remise *f*, rabais *m*, déduction *f*; **to make an a. on an article,** faire un rabais sur un article. **4.** (*a*) *MecE: etc:* tolérance; (*in minting coins*) faiblage *m*; (*b*) **to make allowance(s) for sth.,** tenir compte de qch.; **to make allowances for s.o.,** avoir de l'indulgence pour qn.

alloy[1] ['ælɔi] *n.* alliage *m*; **a. steel,** acier allié.

alloy[2] [ə'lɔi] **1.** *v.tr.* allier (l'or avec l'argent, etc.). **2.** *v.i.* (*of metals*) s'allier (l'un avec l'autre). **alloyed** *a.* (*of metal, etc.*) allié **(with,** à, avec).

all-powerful ['ɔːl'pauəful] *a.* tout-puissant, toute-puissante, *pl.* tout-puissants, toutes-puissantes.

all-purpose ['ɔːl'pəːpəs] *a.* universel; à tout faire; **a.-p. computer,** calculateur universel.

all-round ['ɔːl'raund] *a.* (*a*) (athlète, etc.) complet; **an a.-r. man,** un homme universel; **a.-r. improvement,** amélioration générale, sur toute la ligne; (*b*) **car with a.-r. vision,** voiture *f* à carrosserie panoramique.

all-rounder ['ɔːl'raundər] *n.* homme universel; athlète complet.

allspice ['ɔːlspais] *n. Bot:* poivre *m* de la Jamaïque.

all-star ['ɔːl'stɑːr] *a. Th: etc:* **a.-s. performance,** spectacle joué exclusivement par des vedettes.

all-time ['ɔːltaim] *a. F:* (record) sans précédent, inouï; **a.-t. high, low,** record le plus élevé, le plus bas.

allude [ə'l(j)uːd] *v.ind.tr.* **to a. to sth., to s.o.,** (*of pers.*) faire allusion à qch., à qn; (*of phrase*) avoir trait à, se rapporter à, qch., qn; **I am not alluding to anybody in particular,** je ne vise personne.

allure [ə'l(j)u(ə)r] *v.tr.* attirer, séduire (qn). **alluring** *a.* attrayant, attirant, séduisant.

allusion [ə'l(j)uːʒ(ə)n] *n.* allusion *f*; **to make an a. to sth.,** faire allusion à qch.; **in a. to sth.,** par allusion à qch.

alluvial [ə'luːviəl] **1.** *a. Geol:* (*terrain*) alluvial; (dépôt) alluvien; **a. plain,** plaine alluviale; **a. deposits,** alluvions *fpl.* **2.** *n. Austr:* alluvions aurifères.

alluvium [ə'luːviəm] *n. Geol:* (*a*) alluvions *fpl*; (*b*) (*in restricted sense*) limon *m*.

all-weather ['ɔːlweðər] *a. Av: etc:* (avion, atterrissage) tous temps.

ally[1] ['ælai] *n.* (*a*) allié, -ée; coallié, -ée; *Hist:* (*World War I, II*) **the Allies,** les Alliés; **to become allies,** s'allier (ensemble); se coaliser; (*b*) partisan, -ane; **he found plenty of allies in his campaign against . . .,** il a trouvé beaucoup de partisans, d'adhérents, pour sa campagne contre . . ..

ally[2] [ə'lai] *v.tr.* (*a*) allier (qn, qch.) **(to, with,** à, avec); (*b*) **this newspaper is allied with another,** ce journal est associé avec un autre. **allied** ['ælaid] *a.* **1.** allié **(to, with,** à, avec); **the A. Powers,** les Puissances alliées; **closely a. industries,** industries connexes. **2.** *Biol: Med: etc:* du même ordre, de la même nature; *Nat.Hist:* (espèce) voisine.

alma mater ['ælmə'meitər, -'mɑːtər] *n.* l'université *f*, l'école *f*, où l'on a fait ses études.

almanac ['ɔlːmənæk, 'æl-] *n.* almanach *m*.

almighty [ɔːl'maiti] **1.** *a. & n.* tout-puissant, toute-puissante; **the A.,** le Tout-Puissant, le Très-Haut. **2.** *F:* (*a*) *a.* **an a. row, din,** un fracas de tous les diables; (*b*) *adv. NAm:* très; **he's a. stubborn,** il est têtu comme une mule.

almond ['ɑːmənd] *n.* (*a*) amande *f*; **sweet, bitter, a.,** amande douce, amère; **burnt almonds,** amandes grillées; pralines *fpl*; **ground almonds,** amandes pilées; **a. oil,** huile *f* d'amande; **a. paste,** pâte *f* d'amandes; **a.(-shaped) eyes,** yeux *m* en amande; (*b*) **a. tree,** amandier *m*; **a. grove,** amandaie *f*.

almoner ['ɑːmənər, 'æl-] *n.* **1.** aumônier *m*. **2.** *A:* assistant(e) social(e) (d'un hôpital).

almost ['ɔːlmoust] *adv.* presque; à peu près, quasi; **a. blind,** quasi aveugle; **a. nothing,** presque rien; **it's a. six (o'clock),** il est presque six heures; **he a. fell,** il a failli tomber.

alms [ɑːmz] *n.sg. or pl.* aumône *f*; **to give a. to s.o.,** donner, faire, l'aumône à qn; faire la charité à qn; **a. box,** tronc *m* pour les pauvres.

almshouse ['ɑːmzhaus] *n.* hospice *m.*

aloe ['ælou] *n.* **1.** *Bot:* aloès *m.* **2.** *pl.* (*usu. with sg. const.*) *Pharm:* **aloes,** aloès; **bitter aloes,** amer *m* d'aloès.

aloft [ə'lɔft] *adv.* (*a*) *Nau:* dans la mâture; **a. there!** oh(é) de la hune! (*b*) en haut, en l'air.

alone [ə'loun] *a.* (*not used before noun*) **1.** seul; **he lives (all) a.,** il demeure (tout) seul; **I like being a.,** j'aime la solitude; **a. at last!** enfin seul(s)! **we are not a. in thinking that . . .,** nous ne sommes pas seuls à trouver que . . .; **I did it a.,** je l'ai fait tout seul, à moi seul; *B:* **man does not live by bread a.,** l'homme ne vit pas que de pain; **I want to speak to you a.,** je voudrais vous parler seul à seul; **with that charm which is his a.,** avec ce charme qui lui est propre; *F:* **to go it a.,** faire cavalier seul. **2.** (*a*) **to let, leave, s.o., sth., a.,** (i) laisser qn tranquille, en paix; (ii) laisser (qn) faire; (iii) ne pas se mêler de qch.; **leave these things a.,** ne touchez pas à tout ça; **leave me a.!** laissez-moi donc! *F:* fichez-moi la paix! **a subject better left a.,** un sujet qu'il ne faut toucher que du bout du doigt; **your work is all right, leave it a.,** votre travail est bien, n'y retouchez pas; *Prov:* **let well a., leave well a.,** le mieux est (souvent) l'ennemi du bien; (*b*) *conj.* **let a . . .,** sans parler de . . ., sans compter . . .; **they were six in the car, let a. the dogs,** ils étaient six dans l'auto, sans compter les chiens, sans parler des chiens. **3.** *adv.* seulement **you a. can help me,** vous êtes le seul qui puissiez m'aider.

along [ə'lɔŋ] **1.** *prep.* le long de; (*a*) **to walk a. the shore,** longer la plage, se promener (tout) le long de la plage; **to go a. a street,** suivre une rue; passer par une rue; **to sail a. the coast,** longer, suivre, la côte; côtoyer le rivage; **to crawl a. the ground,** ramper à la surface du sol; **victorious all a. the line,** victorieux sur toute la ligne; (*b*) **trees a. the river,** arbres qui bordent la rivière, sur le bord de la rivière. **2.** *adv.* (*a*) **to move a.,** avancer; **to walk, stride, a.,** avancer à grandes enjambées; **come a. with me,** venez-vous-en avec moi; **come a.!** arrivez donc! venez donc! *F:* **come a. now!** sois, soyez, raisonnable! **he'll be a. in ten minutes,** il va arriver dans dix minutes; **bring a tent a. with you,** apportez une tente; *P:* **get a. (with you)!** (i) allez! filez! (ii) *Iron:* allons donc! (*b*) *NAm:* **a. about four o'clock,** vers quatre heures; **the afternoon was well a.,** l'après-midi tirait à sa fin; (*c*) **I knew that all a.,** je le savais dès, depuis, le commencement; **I said so all a.,** c'est ce que j'ai toujours dit; (*d*) *F:* **to get a.,** s'en tirer tant bien que mal; **to get a. with s.o.,** s'accorder bien avec qn.

alongshore [ə'lɔŋ'ʃɔːr] *adv.* le long de la côte.

alongside [ə'lɔŋ'said] *adv. & prep. Nau:* **a. (a ship, a quay),** accosté (le long d'un navire, d'un quai); **to come a. (of) a ship,** accoster, aborder, un navire; **to walk a. s.o.,** marcher côte à côte avec qn.

aloof [ə'luːf] **1.** *adv.* **to keep a. (from sth.),** se tenir à l'écart, à distance, éloigné (de qch.); **to stand a. from a cause,** se tenir en dehors d'une cause. **2.** *a.* (*of pers.*) distant; **she was reserved and a.,** elle était réservée et distante.

aloofness [ə'luːfnis] *n.* attitude distante; réserve *f.*

alopecia [ælou'piːʃə] *n. Med:* alopécie *f.*

aloud [ə'laud] *adv.* à haute voix; (tout) haut; **to read a.,** lire à haute voix.

alp [ælp] *n. Geog:* (*a*) alpe *f*; pâturage *m* de montagne; (*b*) **the Alps,** les Alpes; **the Swiss, French, Alps,** les Alpes suisses, françaises.

alpaca [æl'pækə] *n.* **1.** *Z:* alpaca *m*, alpaga *m.* **2.** *Tex:* alpaga *m*; **a. wool,** laine *f* d'alpaga.

alpenhorn ['ælpənhɔːn] *n. Mus:* cor *m* des Alpes.

alpha ['ælfə] *n.* (*a*) *Gr.Alph:* alpha *m*; *Fig:* **a. and omega,** l'alpha et l'oméga, le commencement et la fin; (*b*) *Ph:* **a. rays,** rayons *mpl* alpha.

alphabet ['ælfəbet] *n.* alphabet *m.*

alphabetic(al) [ælfə'betik(l)] *a.* (ordre, etc.) alphabétique. **-ally** *adv.* alphabétiquement; par ordre alphabétique.

alphabetize ['ælfəbetaiz] *v.tr.* classer par ordre alphabétique.

alpine ['ælpain] *a.* (club, chasseur) alpin; (site, paysage, climat) alpestre; **a. range,** chaîne de montagnes alpine; *Bot:* **a. plant,** *n.* **alpine,** plante alpine, alpicole.

alpinist ['ælpinist] *n.* alpiniste *mf.*

already [ɔːl'redi] *adv.* déjà; dès à présent: **ten o'clock a.!** déjà dix heures!

alright [ɔːl'rait] *adv.* (*incorrect spelling*) = **all right.** *see* RIGHT[1] 4.

Alsatian [æl'seiʃ(ə)n] **1.** *a.* alsacien; (vin) d'Alsace; (littérature) alsatique. **2.** *n.* (*a*) Alsacien, -ienne; (*b*) (*dog*) berger allemand.

also ['ɔːlsou] *adv.* aussi; **he a. saw it,** il l'a vu également; lui aussi l'a vu; **not only . . . but a. . . .,** non seulement . . . mais encore . . ., mais aussi . . .; *Turf:* **a. ran,** non classés, ont couru aussi; *F:* **an a. ran,** (i) concurrent qui n'a pas été classé; (ii) une non-valeur.

altar ['ɔːltər] *n.* autel *m*; **high a.,** maître-autel *m*, *pl.* maîtres-autels; **a. cloth,** nappe *f* d'autel; **a. screen,** retable *m;* **a. boy,** enfant *m* de chœur; **to lead s.o. to the a.,** conduire qn à l'autel.

altarpiece ['ɔːltəpiːs] *n.* tableau *m* d'autel; retable *m.*

alter ['ɔːltər] **1.** *v.tr.* (*a*) changer (qch.); modifier (un dessin, etc.); remanier (un texte, etc.); retoucher (un vêtement, etc.); **that alters the case, the situation,** voilà qui change les choses, la situation; **the time of the train has been altered,** on a changé l'heure du train; **I shall have to a. this dress before I can wear it,** il me faudra faire des retouches à cette robe avant de la porter; *Nau:* **to a. course,** changer de route; (*b*) *NAm: Austr:* châtrer. **2.** *v.i.* changer; **he has greatly altered,** il a bien changé; **her whole outlook has altered,** elle a complètement changé d'horizon.

alteration ['ɔːltə'reiʃ(ə)n] *n.* (*a*) remaniement *m* (de qch.); retouche *f* (à qch.); modification (apportée à qch.); changement *m;* **slight a.,** petite modification; **timetable subject to a.,** (i) horaire *m* susceptible de révisions; (ii) programme *m* sauf modifications; *Tail: Dressm:* **alterations in three days,** retouches (aux vêtements) dans un délai de trois jours; (*b*) *Cmptr:* modification; **a. switch,** inverseur *m*; (*c*) **marginal alterations,** corrections *fpl* en marge.

altercation [ɔːltə'keiʃ(ə)n] *n* altercation *f*, dispute *f*, querelle *f*; **to have an a.,** se disputer.

alter ego ['æltər'egou] *Lt.phr. used as n.* alter ego *m.*

alternate[1] [ɔːl'təːnət] **1.** *a.* (*a*) alternatif, alterné, alternant; **to come on a. days,** venir tous les deux jours; **a. layers of stone and timber,** couches alternantes, alternées, de pierre et de bois; (*b*) *Av: etc:* **a. route,** parcours *m* de rechange; **a. airfield,** aérodrome *m* de dégagement; (*c*) *Cmptr:* **a. action switch,** bouton *m* à double effet; **a. operation,** travail *m* en bascule; (*d*) *U.S.* = ALTERNATIVE **1.** (*a*). **2.** *a. Mth: Bot:* (angles, feuilles) alternes. **3.** *a. Pros:* (rimes) croisées. **4.** *n. esp. NAm:* remplaçant, -ante. **-ly** *adv.* **1.** alternativement; tour à tour; en alternance. **2.** *Bot:* **leaves placed a.,** feuilles alternes.

alternate[2] ['ɔːltəneit] **1.** *v.tr.* (*a*) faire alterner (deux choses); employer (deux choses) tour à tour, alternativement; (*b*) *Agr:* **to a. crops,** alterner des récoltes; (*c*) *Cmptr:* utiliser en bascule. **2.** *v.i.* alterner (**with,** avec); se succéder (tour à tour). **alternating** *a.* **1.** alternant, alterné. **2.** (*a*) (courant) alternatif; (*b*) *Mec.E:* (mouvement) alternatif, de va-et-vient; (*c*) *Cmptr:* **a. operation,** travail *m* en bascule.

alternation [ɔːltəˈneiʃ(ə)n] *n.* **1.** alternation *f* (d'un mouvement). **2.** alternance *f* (du jour et de la nuit, *Biol:* de générations, *Geol:* des couches). **3.** (*a*) *El:* alternance; (*b*) *Cmptr:* alternance; bascule *f* de tampons.

alternative [ɔːlˈtəːnətiv] **1.** *a.* (*a*) alternatif; autre; **an a. proposal,** une contre-proposition; (*b*) (route) d'emprunt; (aérodrome) de dégagement. **2.** *n.* (*a*) alternative *f*; **the a. of a fine or a month's imprisonment,** l'alternative d'une amende ou d'un mois de prison; (*b*) **the a. would be to . . .,** une autre solution serait de . . .; **to have no a.,** ne pas avoir le choix; **he had no a. but to obey,** il n'a pu faire autrement que d'obéir; **there is no a.,** il n'y a pas d'alternative. **-ly** *adv.* avec l'alternative de . . .; ou bien.

alternator [ˈɔːltəneitər] *n. El:* alternateur *m.*

although [ɔːlˈðou] *conj.* (*a*) quoique, bien que + *sub*; **a. I have never seen him I often write to him,** quoique je ne l'aie jamais vu je lui écris souvent; (*b*) **a. I am a father,** tout père que je suis; **a. not beautiful, she was attractive,** sans être belle elle plaisait.

altimeter [ˈæltimiːtər] *n. Av:* altimètre *m*; **radio a.,** radiosonde *f.*

altitude [ˈæltitjuːd] *n.* (*a*) altitude *f*, élévation *f* (au-dessus du niveau de la mer); **at these altitudes,** à cette altitude; *Av:* **cruising a.,** altitude de croisière; **a. recorder,** enregistreur *m* d'altitude; **a. sickness,** mal *m* d'altitude; mal des aviateurs; (*b*) hauteur *f* (d'un astre, d'un triangle).

alto [ˈæltou] *n. Mus:* **1.** alto *m*; **a. clef,** clef *f* d'ut troisième ligne; **to sing a.,** chanter la partie alto. **2.** (*a*) (*male voice*) haute-contre *f, pl.* hautes-contre; (*b*) (*female voice*) contralto *m.* **3.** (*a*) alto (à cordes); (*b*) **a. trombone, saxophone,** trombone *m*, saxophone *m*, alto.

altogether [ɔːltəˈgeðər] **1.** *adv.* (*a*) entièrement, tout à fait; **to change sth. a.,** changer qch. de fond en comble, radicalement; **it's a. out of the question,** c'est absolument impossible; (*b*) somme toute . . .; **taking things a.,** à tout prendre. **2.** *n. F:* **in the a.,** complètement nu, dans le costume d'Adam.

altruism [ˈæltruizm] *n.* altruisme *m.*

altruist [ˈæltruist] *n.* altruiste *mf.*

altruistic [æltruˈistik] *a.* altruiste.

alum [ˈæləm] *n.* alun *m*; *Phot:* **a. bath,** bain aluné.

alumina [əˈl(j)uːminə] *n. Miner:* alumine *f.*

aluminium [æljuˈminiəm] *NAm:* **aluminum** [əˈluːminəm] *n.* aluminium *m*; **a. oxide,** alumine *f.*

aluminize [əˈl(j)uːminaiz] *v.tr.* **1.** *Metall:* combiner avec de l'aluminium; **aluminized steel,** acier *m* à l'aluminium. **2.** *Tchn:* aluminiser; aluminer (un miroir). **3.** (*a*) *Ch:* aluminer; (*b*) *Dy:* aluner.

alumna, *pl.* **-ae** [əˈlʌmnə,-iː] *n.f. NAm:* ancienne élève (d'un collège); ancienne étudiante (d'une université).

alumnus, *pl.* **-i** [əˈlʌmnəs, -ai] *n.m. NAm:* ancien élève (d'un collège); ancien étudiant (d'une université).

always [ˈɔːlwəz, -wiz, (*stressed* -weiz)] *adv.* (*a*) toujours; **nearly, almost, a.,** presque toujours; **a. smiling,** toujours riant; **the office is a. open,** le bureau est ouvert en permanence; **he is a. complaining,** il se plaint tout le temps; (*b*) **I can a. try,** je puis toujours, quand même, essayer; **there's a. the old age pension,** en tout cas on aura la retraite de vieillesse.

alyssum [ˈælis(ə)m] *n. Bot:* alysson *m*, alysse *m.*

am. *see* BE.

a.m. [ˈei ˈem] *abbr. for* **ante meridiem,** avant midi; **five a.m.,** cinq heures du matin.

amalgam [əˈmælgəm] *n* amalgame *m.*

amalgamate [əˈmælgəmeit] **1.** *v.tr.* (*a*) amalgamer (l'or, l'étain); (*b*) amalgamer (des idées); fusionner (des sociétés, *Fin:* des actions, etc.); unifier (les industries). **2.** *v.i.* (*of metals, ideas*) s'amalgamer; (*of companies*) fusionner.

amalgamation [əmælgəˈmeiʃ(ə)n] *n.* **1.** amalgamation *f* (des métaux). **2.** fusionnement *m* (de deux sociétés, *Fin:* d'actions); mélange *m* (de races, etc.); **a. of industries,** unification industrielle.

amaryllis [æməˈrilis] *n. Bot:* amaryllis *f* (belle-dame); lis *m* de Saint-Jacques.

amass [əˈmæs] *v.tr.* amasser; accumuler.

amateur [ˈæmətəːr, æməˈtəːr, ˈæmətjuər] *n.* (*a*) amateur *m* (de peintures, etc.); (*b*) amateur, dilettante *m*; **he paints as an a.,** il peint en amateur; *Pej:* **he's an a. at painting,** il peint en amateur, *F:* il barbouille; (*c*) *Sp:* amateur; (*d*) **a. painter,** peintre *m* amateur; **a. championship,** championnat *m* d'amateur; *Turf:* **a. rider,** gentleman rider *m.*

amateurish [æməˈtəːriʃ] *a. Pej:* (travail, etc.) d'amateur. **-ly** *adv.* en amateur.

amateurism [ˈæmətərizm] *n.* **1.** dilettantisme *m.* **2.** *Sp:* amateurisme *m.*

amatory [ˈæmət(ə)ri] *a.* (sentiment) amoureux; (lettre) d'amour; (poème) érotique.

amaze [əˈmeiz] *v.tr.* confondre, stupéfier, étonner; **his courage amazed me,** son courage m'a stupéfié; **it amazes me that he could have done such a thing,** je m'étonne qu'il ait pu faire une telle chose; *Iron:* **you a. me!** voilà qui m'étonne! vraiment? **amazing** *a.* stupéfiant, étonnant; (dextérité) prestigieuse; **it's a.!** je n'en reviens pas! **amazingly** *adv.* étonnamment; **he's doing a. well,** il réussit à merveille.

amazement [əˈmeizmənt] *n.* stupéfaction *f*; stupeur *f*; (grand) étonnement; **to listen in a.,** écouter avec stupeur; **I heard with a. that . . .,** j'ai été stupéfait d'apprendre que . . ..

Amazon [ˈæməz(ə)n] **1.** *n.f.* (*a*) *Myth:* Amazone, (femme) guerrière; (*b*) femme forte et athlétique. **2.** *Pr.n. Geog:* **the (river) A.,** l'Amazone *f*; **the A. basin,** le bassin amazonien.

Amazonian [æməˈzouniən) *a.* **1.** (*a*) d'Amazone; (*b*) (*of woman*) forte et athlétique. **2.** *Geog:* de l'Amazone, amazonien.

ambassador [æmˈbæsədər] *n.* (*a*) ambassadeur *m*, (*woman*) ambassadrice *f*; **the British A. to Japan,** l'ambassadeur d'Angleterre auprès du Japon; (*b*) ambassadeur, -drice (de l'art, du goût, etc.).

ambassadorial [æmbæsəˈdɔːriəl] *a.* d'ambassadeur.

ambassadress [æmˈbæsədris] *n.f.* ambassadrice.

amber [ˈæmbər] *n.* **1.** ambre *m*; **yellow a.,** ambre jaune; succin *m.* **2.** *a.* (*a*) d'ambre, en ambre; **a. varnish,** vernis *m* au succin; (*b*) **a. (-coloured),** ambré; *Adm:* **a. light,** feu *m* orange.

ambergris [ˈæmbəgriːs] *n.* ambre gris.

ambidextrous [ˈæmbiˈdekstrəs] *a.* ambidextre.

ambience [ˈæmbiəns] *n.* ambiance *f.*

ambient [ˈæmbiənt] *a.* ambiant.

ambiguity [ˈæmbiˈgjuːiti] *n.* **1.** ambiguïté *f.* **2.** équivoque *f.*

ambiguous [æmˈbigjuəs] *a.* **1.** ambigu, -uë, équivoque. **2.** incertain; **an a. conflict,** un conflit d'issue douteuse. **3.** obscur; difficile à comprendre; **a. style,** style confus. **-ly** *adv.* d'une manière ambiguë, équivoque.

ambiguousness [æmˈbigjuəsnis] *n.* ambiguïté *f.*

ambition [æmˈbiʃ(ə)n] *n.* ambition *f*; **the a. to succeed,** l'ambition de réussir; **eaten up with a.,** devoré d'ambition; **to have great ambitions,** avoir de hautes visées.

ambitious [æmˈbiʃəs] *a.* **1.** ambitieux; **to be a. to do sth.,** ambitionner de faire qch. **2.** (projet, etc.) ambitieux. **-ly** *adv.* ambitieusement.

ambitiousness [æmbiʃəsnis] *n.* caractère ambitieux.

ambivalence [æm'bivələns] *n.* ambivalence *f.*
ambivalent [æm'bivələnt] *a.* ambivalent.
amble[1] ['æmbl] *n.* **1.** *Equit:* amble *m*, entre-pas *m.* **2.** (*of pers.*) pas *m* tranquille; allure *f* tranquille.
amble[2] *v.i.* **1.** *Equit:* aller (à) l'amble; **to a. along,** chevaucher à l'amble; **to make a horse a.,** mettre un cheval à l'amble. **2.** *F:* (*of pers.*) **to a. along,** aller, marcher, d'un pas tranquille; flâner. **ambling** *a.* (cheval) ambleur, qui va (à) l'amble; **a. mare,** haquenée *f.*
ambrosia [æm'brouziə] *n.* ambroisie *f.*
ambrosial [æm'brouziəl] *a.* ambrosiaque.
ambulance ['æmbjuləns] *n.* ambulance *f*; **a. train,** train *m* sanitaire; **a. ship,** navire *m* hôpital; **flying a., a. plane,** avion *m* sanitaire; **a. post,** poste *m* d'ambulance; **a. man,** ambulancier(-brancardier) *m*; infirmier *m.*
ambulatory[1] ['æmbjulət(ə)ri, -leit-] *a.* **1.** ambulant, mobile; *Jur:* (tribunal) ambulatoire. **2.** *Med:* (traitement) ambulatoire; (malade) ambulant, sur pied.
ambulatory[2] *n.* promenoir *m*, préau *m*; *Ecc.Arch:* déambulatoire *m.*
ambush[1] ['æmbuʃ] *n.* embuscade *f*; guet-apens *m*, *pl.* guets-apens; **to be, lie, in a.,** être, se tenir, en embuscade; être à l'affût; **troops in a.,** troupes embusquées.
ambush[2] **1.** *v.tr.* attirer (l'ennemi) dans un piège, dans un traquenard; **to be ambushed,** tomber dans une embuscade. **2.** *v.i.* s'embusquer; se tenir en embuscade.
ameba [ə'mi:bə] *n.*, **amebic** [ə'mi:bik] *a.* *NAm:* = AMOEBA, AMOEBIC.
ameliorate [ə'mi:liəreit] **1.** *v.tr.* améliorer. **2.** *v.i.* s'améliorer, s'amender.
amelioration [əmi:liə'reiʃ(ə)n] *n.* amélioration *f.*
amen ['ɑ:'men, 'ei'men] *int.* amen; ainsi soit-il; **and we all say a. to that,** c'est ce que nous souhaitons tous.
amenable [ə'mi:nəbl] *a.* **1.** sujet (**to,** à); **the case is not a. to ordinary rules,** ce cas n'est pas sujet aux règles ordinaires. **2.** (*a*) **a. (to sth.),** soumis (à la loi, la discipline); docile (aux conseils), sensible (à la bonté); **a. to reason,** raisonnable; disposé à entendre raison; (*b*) (enfant) soumis, docile.
amend [ə'mend] **1.** *v.tr.* (*a*) amender, modifier (un projet de loi); apporter, faire, une modification à (un projet); rectifier (un compte); corriger (un texte); (*b*) réformer (sa vie). **2.** *v.i.* s'amender, se corriger.
amendment [ə'mendmənt] *n.* (*a*) modification *f* (d'un projet de loi); rectification *f* (d'un compte); correction *f* (d'un texte); redressement *m* (d'une erreur); (*b*) *Pol: etc:* amendement *m*; **to move an a.,** proposer un amendement (**to a bill,** à un projet de loi).
amends [ə'mendz] *n.pl.* réparation *f*, dédommagement *m*, compensation *f*; **to make a.,** faire amende honorable; **to make a. to s.o. for sth.,** dédommager qn de qch.; faire réparation à qn de qch.
amenity [ə'mi:niti] *n.* **1.** agrément *m* (d'un lieu). **2. amenities** (*a*) aménités *fpl*, civilités *fpl*; (*b*) agréments (d'un lieu); aménagements *mpl* (d'un hôtel); *Jur:* **compensation for loss of amenities,** dommages-intérêts *mpl* pour atteinte portée à l'agrément (d'une propriété); (*c*) (*in hospital*) **a. bed,** chambre privée (payante).
America [ə'merikə] *Pr.n. Geog:* Amérique *f*; **North, South, A.,** Amérique du Nord, du Sud; **Latin A.,** Amérique latine; **in A.,** en Amérique.
American [ə'merik(ə)n] **1.** *a.* (*a*) *Geog:* américain; **A. Indian,** Amérindien, -ienne; (*b*) *Ling:* **A. English,** américain *m*; (*c*) **A. cloth,** toile cirée; **A. organ,** harmonium *m.* **2.** *n.* (*a*) Américain, -aine; **North A.,** Nord-Américain, -aine; **South A.,** Sud-Américain, -aine; (*b*) *Ling:* américain *m.*
Americanism [ə'merikənizm] *n.* *Ling: etc:* américanisme *m.*
Americanize [ə'merikənaiz] *v.tr.* américaniser.
Amerind ['æmərind], **Amerindian** [æmər'indiən] **1.** *a.* amérindien. **2.** *n.* Amérindien, -ienne.
amethyst ['æmiθist] *n.* améthyste *f.*
amiability [eimiə'biliti] *n.* amabilité *f* (**to,** envers).
amiable ['eimiəbl] *a.* aimable (**to,** envers); **to be most a.,** être d'une grande amabilité; **to make oneself a. to s.o.,** faire l'aimable auprès de qn. **-ably** *adv.* aimablement; avec amabilité.
amicability [æmikə'biliti] *n.* **1.** nature, disposition, amicale. **2.** concorde *f.*
amicable ['æmikəbl] *a.* **1.** (*of manner, etc.*) amical; (*of pers.*) bien disposé; **a. designs,** desseins *mpl* pacifiques; **a. relations,** relations amicales. **2.** amiable; *Jur:* **a. settlement,** arrangement *m* à l'amiable. **-ably** *adv* **1.** amicalement; **to live a. together,** vivre en harmonie. **2. to settle a matter a.,** s'arranger à l'amiable.
amid [ə'mid] *prep. Lit:* au milieu de; parmi; entre.
amide ['æmaid] *n. Ch:* amide *f.*
amidships [ə'midʃips] *adv. Nau:* **1.** au milieu du navire; **cabin a.,** cabine *f* par le travers. **2. to put the helm a.,** mettre la barre droite; **helm a.!** barre à zéro! zéro (la barre)!
amidst [ə'midst] *prep.* = AMID.
amino-acid [æ'mi:nou'æsid] *n. Ch:* aminoacide *m.*
amiss [ə'mis] *adv. & a.* **1. to take sth. a.,** prendre qch. de travers, en mal, en mauvaise part; **he took it very much a.,** il a très mal pris la chose. **2.** mal à propos; **that would not come a.,** cela n'arriverait pas mal (à propos); **something is a.,** il y a quelque chose qui cloche.
amity ['æmiti] *n.* amitié *f*, concorde *f*; bons rapports (entre deux pays); **to live in a. with s.o.,** vivre en amitié, en bonne intelligence, avec qn.
ammeter ['æmitər] *n.* ampèremètre *m.*
ammo ['æmou] *n. F:* = AMMUNITION.
ammonia [ə'mouniə] *n. Ch:* ammoniaque *f*, gaz ammoniac; **a. water,** eau ammoniacale.
ammoniac [ə'mouniæk] **1.** *a.* ammoniac, -aque; **sal a.,** sel ammoniac. **2.** *n.* **(gum) a.,** gomme ammoniaque.
ammoniated [ə'mounieitid] *a. Pharm: etc:* ammoniacé, ammoniaqué.
ammonite ['æmənait] *n. Paleont:* ammonite *f.*
ammonium [ə'mouniəm] *n. Ch:* ammonium *m*; **a. carbonate, sulphate,** carbonate *m*, sulfate *m*, d'ammonium.
ammunition [æmju'niʃ(ə)n] *n. Mil:* **1.** (*a*) munitions *fpl*; **live a.,** munitions réelles, pour tir réel; **blank a.,** munitions à blanc; **dummy a.,** fausses munitions; (*b*) projectile *m*, cartouche *f.* **2.** *attrib.* (*a*) **a. box,** coffre *m* à munitions; **a. train,** (i) *Artil: etc:* train *m* de combat; (ii) *Rail:* train de munitions; **a. depot, a. dump,** dépôt *m* de munitions; (*b*) réglementaire; de l'intendance.
amnesia [æm'ni:ziə] *n. Med:* amnésie *f.*
amnesic [æm'ni:zik] *a.* amnésique.
amnesty[1] ['æmnisti] *n.* amnistie *f*; pardon collectif.
amnesty[2] *v.tr.* amnistier.
amoeba, *NAm: also* **ameba,** *pl.* **-as, -ae** [ə'mi:bə, -əz, -i:] *n. Prot:* amibe *f.*
amoebic, *NAm: also* **amebic** [ə'mi:bik] *a. Med:* amibien; **a. dysentery,** dysenterie amibienne.
amok [ə'mʌk] *adv.* **to run a.,** (i) tomber dans une folie furieuse; (ii) *F:* devenir fou furieux.
among [ə'mʌŋ], **amongst** [ə'mʌŋst] *prep.* parmi, entre; (*a*) **house standing a. trees,** maison située au milieu des arbres, environnée d'arbres; **to wander a. the ruins,** errer dans les ruines; **I caught sight of him**

a. the crowd, je l'aperçus au milieu de la foule, parmi la foule; (*b*) **to live a. savages,** vivre au milieu des sauvages; **we are a. friends,** nous sommes entre amis; **this expression is current a. young people,** cette expression est courante chez les jeunes; (*c*) **a. the guests were . . .,** au nombre des invités se trouvaient . . .; **not one a. them,** pas un d'entre eux, parmi eux; **a. other things he said that . . .,** il a dit entre autres que . . .; (*d*) **they quarrel a. themselves,** ils se disputent entre eux.

amoral [ei'mɔrəl] *a.* amoral, -aux.

amorous ['æmərəs] *a.* **1.** amoureux (**of s.o.,** de qn); **a. verse,** poésie *f* érotique. **2. to be of an a. disposition,** être d'un tempérament amoureux; avoir un tempérament amoureux. **-ly** *adv.* amoureusement.

amorphous [ə'mɔ:fəs] *a.* **1.** *Biol: Ch:* amorphe. **2.** (opinions) sans forme; (projet) vague, amorphe.

amortization [əmɔ:ti'zeiʃ(ə)n] *n.* **1.** *Com: Fin:* amortissement *m* (d'une dette, etc.). **2.** *Jur:* aliénation *f* en mainmorte.

amortize [ə'mɔ:taiz] *v.tr.* **1.** *Com: Fin:* amortir (une dette). **2.** *Jur:* aliéner (une terre) en mainmorte.

amount¹ [ə'maunt] *n.* **1.** *Com:* somme *f*, montant *m*, total *m* (d'une facture, etc.); (*on bus, etc.*) **please tender the exact a.,** on est prié de faire l'appoint; **(up) to the a. of . . .,** jusqu'à concurrence de . . .; *Book-k:* **a. carried forward,** report à nouveau. **2.** (*a*) quantité *f*; **a. of work that an engine will do,** somme de travail que peut rendre, fournir, une machine; **in small amounts,** par petites quantités; (*b*) *F:* **he has any a. of money,** il a de l'argent tant et plus.

amount² *v.i.* **1.** (*of money, etc.*) s'elever, (se) monter (**to,** à); **transactions amounting to several million pounds,** opérations qui se chiffrent par plusieurs millions de livres; **I don't know what my debts a. to,** j'ignore le montant de mes dettes. **2.** équivaloir, se réduire, revenir (**to,** à); **these conditions a. to a refusal,** ces conditions équivalent à un refus; **it amounts to the same thing,** cela revient au même; **all that amounts to very little, to nothing,** tout cela ne signifie pas grand-chose, se réduit à rien; *F:* **he'll never a. to much,** il ne sera, fera, jamais grand-chose.

amour [ə'muər] *n.* intrigue amoureuse, liaison *f.*

amp [æmp] *n. El.Meas: F:* ampère *m*; **a 13-a. plug,** une fiche de 13 ampères.

ampere ['æmpɛər] *n. El.Meas:* ampère *m.*

ampersand ['æmpəsænd] *n. Typ:* et commercial.

amphetamine [æm'fetəmin] *n Pharm:* amphétamine *f.*

amphibia [æm'fibiə] *n.pl. Z:* amphibiens *mpl.*

amphibian [æm'fibiən] *a. & n.* **1.** *Z:* amphibie (*m*). **2.** *Trans:* (char *m*, canon *m*, etc.) amphibie.

amphibious [æm'fibiəs] *a.* (animal, avion, etc.) amphibie.

amphitheatre, *NAm:* **amphitheater** ['æmfiθiətər] *n. Arch: Th: etc:* amphithéâtre *m.*

amphora, *pl.* **-ae** ['æmfərə, -i:] *n.* amphore *f.*

ample ['æmpl] *a.* (*a*) (vêtement, sac) ample, large; **man of a. proportions,** homme corpulent; (*b*) abondant; **a. resources,** d'abondantes ressources; **to have a. means,** avoir de la fortune; **an a. supply of coal for the winter,** largement assez de charbon pour l'hiver; **a. proof,** preuve évidente; (*c*) **to have a. time (to do sth.),** avoir largement le temps (de faire qch.). **amply** *adv.* amplement, grandement; **a. rewarded,** largement recompensé.

ampleness ['æmplnis] *n.* ampleur *f*, abondance *f* (de ressources).

amplification [æmplifi'keiʃ(ə)n] *n.* **1.** augmentation *f*, extension *f*; **he added some details in a. of his report,** il ajouta des détails supplémentaires à son compte rendu. **2.** *Opt:* grossissement *m* (d'une lentille, etc.). **3.** *Ph: El:* amplification *f* (de puissance, de tension, de son, etc.).

amplifier ['æmplifaiər] *n.* **1.** (*a*) *Phot:* (lentille) amplificatrice *f*; (*b*) *Artil:* **torque a.,** amplificateur *m* de couple. **2.** *Ph: El:* amplificateur ; **a. circuit,** circuit *m* d'amplification.

amplify ['æmplifai] *v.tr.* **1.** amplifier (un exposé, etc.); ajouter des détails à (un rapport, etc.). **2.** *Ph: El:* amplifier (le courant, la puissance, le son, etc.).

amplitude ['æmplitju:d] *n.* (*a*) amplitude *f*; étendue *f* (de l'espace); ampleur *f* (des dimensions, des ressources, etc.); (*b*) *Astr:* amplitude (d'un astre); (*c*) *Ph:* amplitude (des oscillations, des vibrations); **magnetic a.,** déclinaison *f* magnétique.

ampoule ['æmpu:l] *n. Med:* ampoule *f* (pour une injection hypodermique).

amputate ['æmpjuteit] *v.tr.* amputer, faire l'amputation de (la jambe, etc.); **his right leg was amputated,** il a été amputé de la jambe droite.

amputation [æmpju'teiʃ(ə)n] *n. Surg:* amputation *f.*

amputee [æmpju'ti:] *n.* amputé, -ée.

amuck [ə'mʌk] *adv.* = AMOK.

amulet ['æmjulet] *n.* amulette *f.*

amuse [ə'mju:z] *v.tr.* amuser, divertir, faire rire (qn); **to a. oneself,** s'amuser, se divertir; **to a. oneself by, with, doing sth.,** s'amuser, se récréer, à faire qch., en faisant qch.; **to a. oneself with sth.,** s'amuser avec qch.; **to keep s.o. amused,** (i) amuser qn; (ii) occuper qn; **that'll keep them amused,** ça les occupera. **amused** *a.* amusé, diverti; **to be a. at, by, sth.,** être amusé de qch.; s'amuser de qch. **amusing** *a.* amusant, divertissant; *Iron:* **how a.!** comme c'est amusant! **amusingly** *adv.* d'une manière amusante.

amusement [ə'mju:zmənt] *n.* amusement *m*; (*a*) divertissement *m*; **place of a.,** lieu *m* de divertissement; **smile of a.,** sourire amusé; **to the great a. of the children,** au grand amusement des enfants; (*b*) distraction *f*; **we have few amusements here,** nous avons ici peu de distractions; **a. park,** parc *m* d'attractions.

an. *see* A².

anabaptist [ænə'bæptist] *a. & n. Rel.H:* anabaptiste (*mf*).

anachronism [ə'nækrənizm] *n.* anachronisme *m.*

anachronistic [ənækrə'nistik] *a.* anachronique.

anaconda [ænə'kɔndə] *n. Rept:* anaconda *m.*

anaemia, *NAm:* **anemia** [ə'ni:miə] *n.* anémie *f.*

anaemic, *NAm:* **anemic** [ə'ni:mik] *a.* (*a*) *Med:* anémique; **to become a.,** s'anémier; (*b*) faible, sans énergie.

anaesthesia, *NAm:* **anesthesia** [ænəs'θi:ziə] *n.* anesthésie *f*; **general, local, a.,** anesthésie générale, locale; **spinal a.,** anesthésie rachidienne.

anaesthetic, *NAm:* **anesthetic** [ænəs'θetik] *a. & n.* anesthésique (*m*); **under the a.,** sous l'effet *m* de l'anasthésique.

anaesthetist, *NAm:* **anesthetist** [ə'ni:sθətist] *n.* anesthésiste *mf.*

anaesthetize, *NAm:* **anesthetize** [ə'ni:sθətaiz] *v.tr. Med:* anesthésier.

anagram ['ænəgræm] *n.* anagramme *f.*

anal ['ein(ə)l] *a. Anat: Z:* anal, -aux.

analgesia [ænæl'dʒi:ziə] *n. Med:* analgésie *f.*

analgesic [ænæl'dʒi:sik, -zik] *a. & n. Med:* analgésique (*m*).

analog ['ænəlɔg] *n.* (*a*) *NAm:* = ANALOGUE; (*b*) *Cmptr:* **a. computer,** calculateur *m* analogique.

analogical [ænə'lɔdʒikl] *a.* analogique. **-ally** *adv.* analogiquement, par analogie.

analogize [ə'nælədʒaiz] **1.** *v.tr.* représenter, expliquer (qch.) par analogie. **2.** *v.i.* raisonner par analogie.

analogous [ə'næləgəs] *a.* analogue (**to, with,** à). **-ly** *adv.* d'une manière analogue (**to, with,** à).

analogue, *NAm:* **analog** ['ænəlɔg] *n.* analogue *m.*

analogy [ə'nælədʒi] *n.* analogie *f* (**to, with,** avec; **between,** entre); **by a. with ...,** par analogie avec. . . .

analyse, *NAm:* **analyze** ['ænəlaiz] *v.tr.* **1.** *esp. Ch: Mth: etc:* analyser; faire l'analyse de (qch.); *Com:* dépouiller, décomposer (un compte); *Gram:* analyser (une phrase, un texte, etc.); faire l'analyse logique (d'une phrase). **2.** *Psy:* psychanalyser.

analysis, *pl.* **-es** [ə'næləsis, -i:z] *n.* **1.** analyse *f*; (*a*) *Ch:* **qualitative a.,** analyse qualitative; **quantitative a.,** analyse quantitative; dosage *m*; **wet, dry, a.,** analyse par voie humide, sèche; *Ph:* **spectral, spectrum, a.,** analyse spectrale; *Mth:* **differential a.,** analyse différentielle; *Cmptr: etc:* **systems a.,** analyse fonctionnelle; **operations a.,** recherche opérationnelle; (*b*) analyse (d'un texte, etc.); *Gram:* analyse logique (d'une phrase). **2.** psychanalyse *f.*

analyst ['ænəlist] *n.* **1.** *Ch: Mth: etc:* analyste *mf*; *Pol.Ec:* économiste-statisticien *m, pl.* économistes-statisticiens; *Cmptr:* **systems a.,** analyste de systèmes, analyste fonctionnel(le). **2.** *Psy:* (psych-) analyste *mf.*

analytic(al) [ænə'litik(l)] *a.* analytique; **analytical mind,** esprit *m* d'analyse; **analytic psychology,** psychologie introspective.

analyze ['ænəlaiz] *v.tr.* = ANALYSE.

anaphrodisiac [ænæfrə'di:ziæk] *a. & n. Pharm:* anaphrodisiaque (*m*).

anarchist ['ænəkist] *a. & n.* anarchiste (*mf*).

anarchy ['ænəki] *n.* anarchie *f.*

anastigmat [æ'næstigmæt] *a. & n. Opt: Phot:* **a. (lens),** objectif *m* anastigmat(ique); anastigmat *m.*

anastigmatic [ænæstig'mætik] *a. Opt:* anastigmat(ique).

anathema [ə'næθəmə] *n.* anathème *m*; **his name is a.,** son nom est maudit; **it's, he's, a. to me,** c'est ma bête noire.

anathematize [ə'næθəmətaiz] *v.tr.* frapper (qn) d'anathème.

anatomical [ænə'tɔmikl] *a.* anatomique; **a. specimen,** pièce *f* d'anatomie; préparation *f* anatomique. **-ally** *adv.* anatomiquement.

anatomist [ə'nætəmist] *n.* anatomiste *mf.*

anatomy [ə'nætəmi] *n.* **1.** structure *f* anatomique; (d'un homme, d'un animal). **2.** (*a*) (*science*) anatomie *f*; **human a.,** anatomie humaine; (*b*) (*textbook*) cours *m* d'anatomie. **3.** (*a*) anatomie, dissection *f*; (*b*) *Fig:* analyse *f.*

ancestor ['ænsestər] *n.* ancêtre *m*; aïeul *m, pl.* aïeux; **our ancestors,** nos ancêtres, nos aïeux; **a. worship,** culte *m* des ancêtres; nécrolâtrie *f.*

ancestral [æn'sestr(ə)l] *a.* (*a*) héréditaire, de famille; **his a. home,** la demeure de ses ancêtres; (*b*) *Biol:* ancestral, -aux.

ancestress ['ænsestris] *n.f.* aïeule.

ancestry ['ænsestri] *n.* **1.** ascendance *f*; race *f*; lignée *f*, lignage *m*; **both families were of French a.,** l'une et l'autre famille avaient une ascendance française. **2.** *coll:* ancêtres *mpl*; ascendants *mpl*; aïeux *mpl.*

anchor[1] ['æŋkər] *n.* (*a*) *Nau: etc:* ancre *f*; **sheet a.,** (i) ancre de veille; (ii) *Fig:* ancre, planche *f*, de salut; **buoy,** bouée *f* de mouillage, d'ancre; **stand by to a.!** pare à mouiller! **to let go, drop, the a.,** jeter, mouiller, l'ancre; **to weigh a.,** lever l'ancre; appareiller; **to lie, ride, at a.,** être à l'ancre; mouiller; **at a.,** au mouillage; **to slip the a.,** filer (sa chaîne) par le bout; (*of ship*) **to drag her a.,** chasser sur son ancre, sur ses ancres; (*b*) *Const:* **a. iron, tie,** grappin *m*; **a. plate, stay,** plaque *f*, câble *m*, d'ancrage.

anchor[2] **1.** *v.tr.* (*a*) *Nau:* ancrer, mouiller (un navire); (*b*) *Nau: etc:* hauban(n)er (un mât, etc.); *Const:* affermir (qch.) par des ancres; *Mil:* abattre (une pièce). **2.** *v.i.* (*a*) *Nau:* jeter l'ancre; mouiller, prendre son mouillage; (*b*) *F:* s'ancrer (dans un lieu). **anchored** *a.* **1.** (*a*) *Nau:* ancré, mouillé; à l'ancre; (*b*) **firmly a. faith,** foi solidement ancrée. **2.** en forme d'ancre. **anchoring** *n.* ancrage *m*, mouillage *m.*

anchorage ['æŋkəridʒ] *n.* **1.** *Nau:* (*a*) ancrage *m*, mouillage *m*; **to leave the a.,** dérader; (*b*) droits *mpl* d'ancrage, de stationnement. **2.** *Civ.E: Const:* ancrage; point *m* d'attache (d'un tirant, etc.).

anchorite ['æŋkərait] *n.* anachorète *m.*

anchorman ['æŋkəmən] *n.m.* (*a*) *Sp.* dernier coureur (d'une équipe); *Rugby Fb:* pilier *m*; (*b*) *W.Tel: T.V:* présentateur (coordinateur) d'émissions en multiplex.

anchovy ['æntʃəvi, æn'tʃouvi] *n. Ich: Cu:* anchois *m*; **a. butter, paste,** beurre *m*, pâte *f*, d'anchois.

ancient ['einʃ(ə)nt] *a.* (*a*) ancien; (monument) historique; (chêne) centenaire; **family of a. descent,** famille ancienne, de longue lignée; *Jur:* **a. lights,** servitude *f* de vue; (*b*) **A. Rome,** la Rome antique; **the a. world,** le monde antique; **a. history,** l'histoire ancienne; (*of pers.*) très vieux; (*of thg*) antique, antédiluvien; *F:* (*d*) *n.pl.* **the Ancients,** les anciens *mpl.*

ancillary [æn'siləri] *a.* subordonné (**to,** à); auxiliaire; **a. equipment,** matériel *m* annexe, d'appoint; accessoires *mpl*; (*in hospital*) **a. staff, a. workers,** personnel hospitalier non médical.

and [ænd, *unstressed* ənd, ən, n] *conj.* et. **1.** (*a*) (*connecting words*) **a knife a. fork,** un couteau et une fourchette; **(my) father a. mother are out,** mon père et ma mère sont sortis; **four a. five make(s) nine,** quatre plus cinq font neuf; (*b*) (*with numerals*) (i) *A: & Lit:* **five a. twenty,** vingt-cinq; (ii) **two hundred a. two,** deux cent deux; **four and a half,** quatre et demi; **four a. three quarters,** quatre trois quarts; **an hour and twenty minutes,** une heure vingt minutes; *A:* **three (shillings) a. six(pence),** trois shillings six pence; (*c*) **ham a. eggs,** des œufs au jambon; **now a. then,** de temps en temps; (*d*) (*after* **without**) ni; **he came without pencils a. paper,** il est venu sans crayons ni papier; (*e*) **he speaks English, a. very well too,** il parle anglais et même très bien; **a. what about the invalids?** et les malades? (*f*) (*repetition*) **for miles a. miles,** pendant des milles et des milles; **better a. better,** de mieux en mieux; **smaller a. smaller,** de plus en plus petit; **I knocked a. knocked again,** je frappai tant et plus; **over a. over again,** maintes et maintes fois; (*g*) **a. so on, a. so forth,** et ainsi de suite. **2.** (*connecting clauses*) (*a*) **he could read a. write,** il savait lire et écrire; (*b*) **move (an inch) a. you're a dead man,** un pas et vous êtes mort; (*c*) **go a. look for it,** allez le chercher; **come a. see me,** venez me voir; **wait a. see,** attendez voir; **try a. help me,** tâchez de m'aider; (*d*) **a. not,** sans (que); **to look for sth. a. not see it,** chercher qch. sans le voir; **I can listen to that record all day a. not get tired of it,** je peux écouter ce disque toute la journée sans m'en lasser. **3.** *n.* (*a*) **without ifs a. ands,** sans si ni mais; (*b*) *Cmptr:* (*usu. written* AND) **a. circuit, element,** circuit *m* ET, élément *m* ET.

Andalusia [ændə'lu:siə, -ziə] *Pr.n. Geog:* Andalousie *f.*

andante [æn'dænti] *adv. & n. Mus:* andante *m.*

andantino [ændæn'ti:nou] *adv. & n. Mus:* andantino *m.*

Andean ['ændiən] *a. Geog:* andin; des Andes.

Andes ['ændi:z] *Pr.n. pl. Geog:* **the A.,** les Andes *fpl,* la Cordillère des Andes.

andiron ['ændaiən] *n.* (*a*) landier *m;* (*b*) chenet *m.*

Andorra [æn'dɔrə] *Pr.n. Geog:* (la république d')Andorre *f;* **A. (City),** Andorre la Vieille.

Andrew ['ændru:] *Pr.n.m.* André.

androgen ['ændroudʒən] *n.m. Biol:* androgène.

anecdotal [ænik'doutl] *a.* anecdotique.

anecdote ['ænikdout] *n.* anecdote *f.*

anemia [ə'ni:miə] *n., etc.* = ANAEMIA, etc.

anemometer [æne'mɔmitər] *n. Meteor:* anémomètre *m.*

anemone [ə'neməni] *n.* **1.** *Bot:* anémone *f.* **2.** *Coel:* **sea a.,** anémone de mer.

aneroid ['ænərɔid] *a. Ph:* (baromètre) anéroïde.

anesthesia [ænes'θi:ziə] *n., etc.* = ANAESTHESIA, *etc.*

aneurism, aneurysm ['ænjurizm] *n. Med:* anévrisme *m.*

anew [ə'nju:] *adv. O: & NAm:* **1.** de nouveau; **to begin a.,** commencer de nouveau, recommencer. **2.** à nouveau; **to create sth. a.,** créer qch. à nouveau.

angel ['eindʒ(ə)l] *n.* **1.** (a) ange *m;* **the a. of death,** l'ange de la mort; **guardian a.,** ange gardien; **fallen a.,** ange déchu; *F:* **an a. passes,** un ange passe; *F:* **you a.! you're an a.!** tu es un amour! **be an a. and do up my dress,** sois gentil et agrafe-moi ma robe; (*b*) *Th: etc: F:* bailleur *m* de fonds; commanditaire *m;* (*c*) *Av: F:* écho radar non identifié. **2. a. face,** visage *m* d'ange, visage angélique; *Cu:* **a. cake, a. food (cake),** (variété de) gâteau *m* de Savoie.

Angela ['ændʒələ] *Pr.n.f.* Angèle.

angelfish ['eindʒəlfiʃ] *n. Ich:* ange *m* de mer, angelot *m.*

angelic [æn'dʒelik] *a.* angélique; (sourire) d'ange. **-ally** *adv.* angéliquement.

Angelica [æn'dʒelika] **1.** *Pr.n.f.* Angélique. **2.** *n. Bot: Cu: etc:* angélique *f.*

angelus ['ændʒələs] *n. Ecc:* angélus *m.*

anger¹ ['æŋgər] *n.* colère *f;* emportement *m;* **in a fit, moment, of a.,** dans un accès de colère; **to speak in a.,** parler sous le coup de la colère.

anger² *v.tr.* irriter (qn); mettre (qn) en colère; **he is easily angered,** il se met facilement en colère; il est irascible. **angered** *a.* irrité, furieux.

angina [æn'dʒainə] *n Med:* (*a*) angine *f;* (*b*) **a. pectoris** ['pektəris] angine de poitrine.

angle¹ ['æŋgl] *n.* **1.** (*a*) *Mth:* angle *m;* **acute, obtuse, a.,** angle aigu, obtus; **right a.,** angle droit, angle de 90°; **at right angles to . . .,** à angle droit avec . . ., perpendiculaire à . . .; **at an a. of . . .,** sous un angle de . . .; **at an a.,** de biais; **the house stands at an a. to the street,** la maison fait angle sur la rue; (*b*) *Astr:* **hour a.,** angle horaire; **meridian a.,** angle méridien; (*c*) *Opt:* **a. of incidence,** angle d'incidence; **a. of vision, visual, viewing, a.,** angle de vision, angle visuel; *Phot:* **a. of view,** angle de champ; **wide a.,** grand angle; **wide-a. lens,** objectif grand angulaire; *Cin:* **a. shot,** prise *f* de vue oblique; (*d*) angle, point *m* de vue; **to study a problem from every a., from all angles,** étudier un problème sur toutes ses faces, sous tous les angles; *F:* **what's your a. on this?** qu'est-ce que vous pensez de ça? **2.** (*a*) *Artil: Ball:* **a. of deflection,** angle de dérive; **a. of elevation, of altitude,** angle de hausse, de tir positif; **a. of sight,** angle de mire, de visée; (*b*) *Mil.Av:* **dropping a.,** angle de visée (de bombardement). **3.** *Av: etc:* **a. of attack, of incidence,** (i) *Av: etc:* angle d'attaque, d'incidence (d'un plan dans l'atmosphère); (ii) *Nau:* (angle d') incidence *f* du vent sur une voile; **critical a. (of attack), stalling a.,** angle critique; **a. of ascent, of climb,** angle de montée (d'un avion, d'un projectile); **helm, steering, a.,** angle de braquage. **4.** *Nau:* **a. of heel, of list, listing a.,** angle de gîte. **5.** (*a*) *Civ.E:* **a. of gradient, of slope,** angle de déclivité; (*b*) *Const:* coin *m,* encoignure *f,* angle (d'une pièce); (*c*) *MecE:* **a. of torque,** angle de torsion; (*d*) *Mch.Tls:* **a. of clearance, relief a.,** angle d'incidence, de dépouille; **cutting a.,** angle de coupe; (*e*) *Const:* **a. bar, a. iron, a. piece, a. plate,** cornière *f,* équerre *f;* **a. bracket,** équerre; **a. brace,** (i) *Tls:* foret *m* à angle; (ii) *Const:* aisselier *m,* contrefiche *f* (de ferme de toit); *Surv:* **a. gauge,** goniomètre *m.* **6.** *El: Elcs:* **a. of loss, loss a.,** angle de pertes; **phase a.,** angle de phase.

angle² **1.** *v.i.* (*a*) obliquer; faire des angles; (*b*) *Ten:* jouer la diagonale. **2.** *v.tr.* (*a*) *Tchn:* angler (une moulure, etc.); (*b*) orienter (un compte-rendu); présenter (des faits) d'une façon tendancieuse, d'un point de vue préjugé. **angled** *a.* (*a*) à angle, aux angles; **acute-a.,** acutangle, aux angles aigus; (*b*) *Sp:* **a. shot,** coup *m* en diagonale; (*c*) (*of report, etc.*) partial; tendancieux.

angle³ *v.i.* (*a*) pêcher à la ligne; **to a. for trout,** pêcher la truite; (*b*) *F:* **to a. for compliments, for an invitation,** quêter des compliments, une invitation. **angling** *n.* pêche *f* à la ligne.

Angle⁴ *n. Hist:* Angle *mf;* **the Angles and Saxons,** les Angles et les Saxons.

angler ['æŋglər] *n.* **1.** pêcheur *m* à la ligne. **2.** *Ich:* **a. (fish),** poisson grenouille *m, pl.* poissons-grenouilles.

Anglican ['æŋglikən] *Ecc:* **1.** *a.* anglican; **the A. Church,** l'Église anglicane. **2.** *n.* Anglican, -ane.

Anglicanism ['æŋglikənizm] *n.* **1.** *Ecc:* anglicanisme *m.* **2.** *U.S:* anglomanie *f.*

Anglicism ['æŋglisizm] *n.* anglicisme *m.*

Anglicist ['æŋglisist] *n.* angliciste *mf.*

Anglicize ['æŋglisaiz] *v.tr.* angliciser.

Anglo-American ['æŋglouə'merikən] **1.** *a.* anglo-américain. **2.** *n.* Anglo-Américain, -aine, *pl.* Anglo-Américains, -aines.

Anglo-Arab ['æŋglou'ærəb] *a. & n.* anglo-arabe (*m*), *pl.* anglo-arabes.

Anglo-Catholic ['æŋglou'kæθ(ə)lik] *a. & n. Ecc:* anglo-catholique (*mf*).

Anglo-French ['æŋglou'frenʃ] **1.** *a.* franco-britannique, *pl.* franco-britanniques; *Hist:* **the A.-F. wars,** les guerres avec la France; les guerres de France. **2.** *n. Ling:* anglo-normand *m.*

Anglo-Indian ['æŋglou'indiən] **1.** *a.* anglo-indien, *pl.* anglo-indiens. **2.** *n.* (*a*) *Adm:* Eurasien, -ienne (qui a du sang indien); (*b*) Anglo-Indien, -ienne.

Anglo-Irish ['æəglou'airiʃ] **1.** *a.* anglo-irlandais. **2.** *n.pl.* **the A.-I.,** les Anglo-Irlandais *mpl.*

Anglophile ['æŋgloufail] *n.* anglophile *mf.*

Anglophobe ['æŋgloufoub] *a. & n.* anglophobe (*mf*).

Anglophobia ['æŋglou'foubiə] *n.* anglophobie *f.*

Anglo-Saxon ['æŋglou'sæks(ə)n] **1.** *a.* anglo-saxon. **2.** *n.* Anglo-Saxon, -onne, *pl.* Anglo-Saxons, -onnes. **3.** *n. Ling:* anglo-saxon *m.*

Angola [æŋ'goulə] *Pr.n. Geog:* Angola *m.*

angora [æŋ'gɔ:rə] *n.* (*a*) **a. (goat, cat, rabbit),** (chèvre *f,* chat *m,* lapin *m*) angora *m;* (*b*) *Tex:* angora; **a. wool,** laine *f* angora; **an a. jumper,** un pull en angora.

angostura [æŋgəs'tjuərə] *n. Pharm: etc:* angusture *f; R.t.m.* **a. bitters,** bitters *m* à base d'angusture.

angry ['æŋgri] *a.* (*a*) fâché, irrité, courroucé (**with,** *NAm:* **at, s.o. about sth.,** contre qn de qch.); **he is very a.,** il est très fâché; **to be a. about sth.,** être fâché de qch.; **he was a. at being kept waiting,** il était irrité qu'on le fît attendre; **to be a. with oneself,** être mécontent de soi; s'en vouloir; **to get a.,** se mettre en colère; se fâcher, s'irriter; **to get a. with s.o.,** se fâcher contre qn; **to make s.o. a.,** fâcher, exaspérer, qn; mettre qn en colère; (*b*) (voix) irritée; (paroles) violentes; **he sent me an a. letter,** il m'a envoyé une lettre furieuse; **an a. young man,** un contestataire; *Lit:* **the a. sea,** la mer courroucée, en courroux; **a. sky,** ciel *m* sombre; ciel à l'orage; (*c*) *Med:* **a. sore,** plaie irritée, enflammée. **-ily** *adv.* en colère; avec colère.

angstrom ['æŋstrəm] *n. Ph.Meas:* angström *m.*

anguish ['æŋgwiʃ] *n.* **1.** angoisse *f*; douleur *f*; **to be in a.,** être dans l'angoisse; être au supplice; **to cause s.o. a.,** angoisser qn. **2.** *Med:* angoisse.

anguished ['æŋgwiʃt] *a.* angoissé, tourmenté.

angular ['æŋgjulər] *a.* **1.** (vitesse, etc.) angulaire. **2.** (*a*) (rocher, visage) anguleux; (corps) décharné, osseux; (*b*) (mouvement) saccadé.

anhydride [æn'haidraid] *n. Ch:* anhydride *m.*

anhydrous [æn'haidrəs] *a. Ch:* anhydre.

aniline ['ænilain] *n. Ch:* aniline *f*; **a. dyes,** colorants *mpl* azoïques.

animal ['ænim(ə)l] **1.** *n.* animal *m*, *pl.* -aux; **draught a.,** bête *f* de trait; **a. husbandry,** élevage *m*; *Art:* **a. painter,** animalier *m.* **2.** *a.* **the a. kingdom,** le règne animal; **a. life,** vie animale; **food of a. origin,** aliments d'origine animale.

animalcule, *pl.* **-cula, -cules** [æni'mælkju:l, -kjulə, -kju:lz] *n. Prot:* animalcule *m.*

animalism ['æniməlizm] *n.* **1.** *Biol:* animalisme *m.* **2.** activité animale. **3.** animalité *f*, sensualité *f.*

animate¹ [ænimət] *a.* animé; doué de vie; **to become a.,** s'animer.

animate² ['ænimeit] *v.tr.* animer; encourager, stimuler (qn); mouvementer (la conversation). **animated** *a.* (discussion) animée; **to become a.,** s'animer; (*of discussion*) s'échauffer; *Cin:* **a. cartoon,** dessins animés. **animatedly** *adv.* d'un ton animé; avec vivacité; avec entrain.

animation [æni'meiʃ(ə)n] *n.* **1.** animation *f*; vivacité *f*; chaleur *f* (du style); feu *m*, entrain *m*, verve *f* (d'un orateur). **2.** stimulation *f.* **3.** *Cin:* animation.

animator ['ænimeitər] *n.* animateur, -trice.

animism ['ænimizm] *n.* **1.** *Phil:* animisme *m*; attribution d'une âme aux objects inanimés. **2.** *Phil: Theol:* spiritualisme *m.*

animist ['ænimist] *a. & n. Phil:* animiste (*mf*).

animosity [æni'mɔsiti] *n.* animosité *f*; **to feel a. against s.o.,** ressentir de l'animosité contre qn.

animus ['æniməs] *n.* **1.** stimulation *f.* **2.** animosité *f.*

anion ['ænaiən] *n. Ph: El:* anion *m.*

anise ['ænis] *n. Bot:* anis *m*; **star a.,** anis étoilé; **to flavour sth. with a.,** aniser qch.

aniseed ['ænisi:d] *n.* (graine *f* d')anis *m*; *Cu:* **a. cake,** gâteau *m* à l'anis.

anisette [æni'zet] *n.* (*liqueur*) anisette *f.*

ankle ['æŋk(ə)l] *n.* cheville *f* (du pied); **a. bone,** astragale *m*; **a. joint,** cheville *f*, attache *f* du pied; **a. boot,** chaussure montante; bottine *f*; (*furlined*) bottillon *m*; **a. socks,** socquettes *fpl*: **a. strap,** barrette *f* (de chaussure); **a. support,** chevillière *f*; **a.-length dress,** robe *f* qui descend jusqu'à la cheville.

anklet ['æŋklət] *n.* **1.** (*a*) manille *f* (de forçat); (*b*) bracelet *m*, anneau *m*, de cheville. **2.** *NAm.:* socquette *f.*

ankylose ['æŋkilouz] *Med:* **1.** *v.tr.* ankyloser. **2.** *v.i.* s'ankyloser.

ankylosis [æŋki'lousis] *n. Med:* ankylose *f.*

Ann [æn] *Pr.n.f.* Anne.

annalist ['ænəlist] *n.* annaliste *m.*

annals ['æn(ə)lz] *n.pl.* annales *fpl.*

Anne [æn] *Pr.n.f.* (*a*) Anne; *Hist:* **A. of Austria,** Anne d'Autriche; (*b*) *F:* **Queen Anne's dead,** (i) c'est de l'histoire ancienne; (ii) ta combinaison passe, tu cherches une belle-mère.

anneal [ə'ni:l] *v.tr. Metall:* recuire, adoucir (un métal, le verre); détremper (un métal). **annealing** *n.* recuit *m*, recuite *f* (d'un métal, du verre); *Metall:* adoucissement *m*; **box a., close a.,** recuit en vase clos; **a. furnace,** four *m* (i) à recuire, (ii) à cloche.

annelid ['ænəlid] *n. Nat.Hist:* annélide *f.*

annex¹ [ə'neks] *v.tr.* **1.** annexer (**sth. to sth.,** qch. à qch.); ajouter, joindre (une pièce à un mémoire). **2.** annexer (une province).

annex² *n.* = ANNEXE.

annexation [æneks'eiʃ(ə)n] *n.* annexion *f* (**of,** de), mainmise *f* (**of,** sur).

annexe ['æneks] *n.* annexe *f*; dépendance *f.*

annihilate [ə'naiəleit] *v.tr.* anéantir, réduire à néant (une flotte, une armée); *Fig:* annihiler, supprimer (le temps, l'espace).

annihilation [ənaiə'leiʃ(ə)n] *n.* (*a*) anéantissement *m* (d'une flotte, d'un peuple); annihilation *f*; (*b*) *Atom.Ph:* annihilation; dématérialisation *f.*

anniversary [æni'və:s(ə)ri] *n.* anniversaire *m*; **it's our wedding a.,** c'est l'anniversaire de notre mariage; **on the a. of . . .,** le jour (de l')anniversaire de . . ..

Anno Domini ['ænou'dɔminai, -ni:] **1.** *Lt.phr.* (*abbr.* **A.D.** ['ei'di:]) en l'an du Seigneur, de grâce; **in 1066 A.D.,** en 1066 apr. J.-C. (après Jésus-Christ). **2.** *n.* *F:* vieillesse *f*; **I'm not ill, it's just anno domini,** je ne suis pas souffrant, je me fais vieux.

annotate ['ænəteit] *v.tr.* annoter (un livre, etc.); commenter (un texte); **annotated text,** texte avec commentaire.

annotation [ænə'teiʃ(ə)n] *n.* annotation *f.*

annotator ['ænəteitər] *n.* annotateur, -trice; commentateur, -trice.

announce [ə'nauns] *v.tr.* annoncer (qn. qch.); faire l'annonce de (qch.); **the Prime Minister has announced his cabinet,** le premier ministre a fait connaître la composition de son ministère.

announcement [ə'naunsmənt] *n.* **1.** annonce *f*, avis *m*; (*of birth, marriage, etc.*) faire-part *m inv.*; *Journ:* **a. of death,** avis mortuaire. **2.** *Jur:* affiche *f* judiciaire.

announcer [ə'naunsər] *n.* **1.** annonceur *m.* **2.** *W.Tel: T.V:* annonceur; speaker *m*, speakerine *f.*

annoy [ə'nɔi] *v.tr.* (*a*) contrarier, chagriner (qn); (*b*) gêner, fâcher, *F:* embêter (qn); **he annoys me,** il me fâche, il m'exaspère; **stop annoying your little sister,** cesse de taquiner ta petite sœur; **it annoys me to have to work on Sundays,** cela me fâche d'être obligé de travailler le dimanche. **annoyed** *a.* contrarié, ennuyé; fâché; **to get a.,** se fâcher (**at sth.,** de qch.; **with s.o.,** contre qn). **annoying** *a.* contrariant, fâcheux, ennuyeux, *F:* embêtant; **the a. thing about it is that . . .,** le fâcheux de l'affaire c'est que . . .; **how a.!** que c'est embêtant! **annoyingly** *adv.* d'une façon agaçante, *F:* embêtante.

annoyance [ə'nɔiəns] *n.* **1.** contrariété *f*, chagrin *m*; **look of a.,** air contrarié, fâché. **2.** désagrément *m*, ennui *m*, *F:* embêtement *m*; **source of a.,** désagrément, cause *f* d'ennuis; **petty annoyances,** petits ennuis.

annual ['ænjuəl] **1.** *a.* (congé, paiement, etc.) annuel; **a. instalment,** annuité *f*; **a. report,** rapport *m* de gestion (d'une compagnie); **he has an a. salary of £5000,** il gagne £5000 par an; *Bot:* **a. ring,** couche annuelle (d'un arbre). **2.** *n.* (*a*) *Bot:* plante annuelle; (*b*) *Publ:* annuaire *m*; publication annuelle. **-ally** *adv.* annuellement; tous les ans.

annuity [ə'nju:iti] *n.* **1. a. in redemption of debt,** annuité *f.* **2.** rente (annuelle); **government a.,** rente sur l'État; **perpetual a.,** rente perpétuelle; rente en perpétuel; **life a.,** rente viagère, pension viagère; **to buy an a.,** placer son argent en viager, à fonds perdu; **to pay s.o. an a.,** servir, faire, une rente à qn.

annul [ə'nʌl] *v.tr.* (**annulled**) annuler, résilier, résoudre (un contrat, un acte); annihiler (un testament); dénoncer (un traité); dissoudre (un mariage); abroger (une loi); casser, infirmer (une décision); **his**

marriage was annulled, son mariage a été déclaré nul.

annular ['ænjulər] *a.* (éclipse, doigt, espace) annulaire.

annulment [ə'nʌlmənt] *n.* annulation *f,* résiliation *f,* résolution *f* (d'un contrat, d'un acte, etc.); cassation *f* (d'un testament); dissolution *f* (d'un mariage); abrogation *f* (d'une loi); abolition *f* (d'un décret); **decree of a.,** décret abolitif.

annunciation [ənʌnsi'eiʃ(ə)n] *n.* **1.** *Ecc:* **the A.,** l'Annonciation *f.* **2.** proclamation *f,* annonce *f.*

anode ['ænoud] *n. El:* anode *f;* électrode positive; plaque *f;* **a. voltage,** tension *f* de plaque; **a. current,** courant *m* anodique.

anodyne ['ænoudain] *a. & n.* (*a*) *Med: etc:* anodin (*m*); calmant (*m*); antalgique (*m*); (*b*) *a.* (remarque) qui ne peut blesser personne.

anoint [ə'nɔint] *v.tr.* oindre; **to a. s.o. with oil,** oindre qn d'huile; **to a. s.o. king, bishop,** sacrer qn roi, évêque; **the Lord's Anointed,** l'Oint *m* du Seigneur. **anointing** *n.* **1.** onction *f.* **2.** sacre *m* (d'un roi, d'un évêque).

anomalous [ə'nɔmələs] *a.* **1.** *Bot: Med: etc:* anomal, -aux; *Gram:* **a. verb,** verbe anomal. **2.** exceptionnel, irrégulier; anormal, -aux.

anomaly [ə'nɔməli] *n.* (*a*) *Ph: etc:* anomalie *f;* (*b*) *Biol: etc:* anomalie, irrégularité *f,* aberration *f.*

anon[1] [ə'nɔn] *adv. A:& Hum:* **1.** tout à l'heure, bientôt. **2.** plus tard; **more of this a.,** je reviendrai sur cela.

anon[2] *a.* anonyme.

anonymity [ænə'nimiti] *n.* anonyme *m,* anonymat *m.*

anonymous [ə'nɔniməs] *a.* (don, lettre, etc.) anonyme; **a. writer,** anonyme *m;* **to remain a.,** garder l'anonyme, l'anonymat. **-ly** *adv.* anonymement; **to write a.,** écrire sous (le couvert de) l'anonymat.

anorak ['ænəræk] *n. Cost:* anorak *m.*

anorexia [ænə'reksiə] *n. Med:* anorexie *f;* **a. nervosa** [nəː'vouzə] anorexie mentale.

another [ə'nʌðər] *a. & pron.* **1.** encore (un); **a. cup of tea,** encore une tasse de thé; **a. fifty years,** encore cinquante ans; **in a. ten years,** dans dix ans d'ici; **without a. word,** sans (un mot de) plus. **2.** un(e) autre, un(e) second(e); *F:* **have a. (drink)!** encore un(e)? **3.** (*a*) un(e) autre; **take this cup away and bring me a. (one),** enlevez cette tasse et apportez-m'en une autre; **that's (quite) a. matter,** c'est (tout) autre chose; **I feel a. man,** je me sens tout autre, tout rajeuni; **a. time,** une autre fois; **let's do it a. way,** faisons autrement; *F:* **tell me a.!** ce n'est pas vrai! (*b*) **she now has a. husband,** elle a maintenant un nouveau mari. **4.** (*a*) **science is one thing, art is a.,** la science est une chose, l'art en est une autre; (*b*) **one way or a.,** d'une façon ou d'une autre; **taking one thing with a., we just manage,** l'un dans l'autre, on arrive à joindre les deux bouts; (*c*) (*reciprocal*) **one a.,** l'un l'autre, les uns les autres; **love one a.,** aimez-vous les uns les autres; **he and his wife adore one a.,** lui et sa femme s'adorent (l'un l'autre); **they give one a. presents,** ils se donnent des cadeaux (l'un à l'autre); **to help one a.,** s'entraider.

Ansaphone ['ɑːnsəfoun] *n. R.t.m: Tp:* répondeur(-)enregistreur *m.*

answer[1] ['ɑːnsər] *n.* **1.** (*a*) réponse *f* (à une question, à une lettre); réplique *f* (à une critique); **she made no a.,** elle n'a pas répondu; **he has an a. to everything,** il a réponse à tout; *F:* **to know all the answers,** (i) être au courant de tout; être à la page; (ii) se vanter de son savoir; (iii) savoir se tirer d'affaire; connaître les trucs; **her only a. was to burst into tears,** pour toute réponse elle a fondu en larmes; *F:* **it's the a. to a maiden's prayer,** c'est exactement ce qu'il nous faut; *Corr:* **in a. to your letter,** en réponse à votre lettre; (*b*) *Jur: etc:* **a. to a charge,** réfutation *f* à une accusation; **I have a complete a. to the charge,** je suis prêt à réfuter entièrement cette accusation; (*c*) *Cmptr:* **a. mode,** mode *f* réponse; (*d*) *Mus:* (*in counterpoint*) réplique; (*e*) *Fenc:* riposte *f.* **2.** *Mth: etc:* solution *f* (d'un problème).

answer[2] *v.tr. & i.* **1.** (*a*) répondre, faire réponse, à (qn); **to a. back,** répliquer; répondre; **don't a. back!** pas de réplique! (*of dog*) **answers to the name of Rover,** répond au nom de Rover; (*b*) répondre à (une question, une lettre); **letters to be answered,** lettres à répondre; **letters answered,** lettres répondues; **the question is not easy to a.,** c'est une question à laquelle il n'est pas facile de répondre; (*c*) **to a. the bell, the telephone,** répondre à un coup de sonnette, au téléphone; **to a. the door,** aller ouvrir; venir ouvir; (*d*) (*of ship*) **to a. the helm,** obéir à la barre; (*e*) *Jur:* **to a. a charge,** répondre à, réfuter, une accusation; (*f*) **to a. (to) a description,** répondre à un signalement; (*g*) **to a. a prayer,** exaucer une prière. **2. to a. the purpose,** remplir le but; **that will a. my purpose,** cela fera mon affaire. **3. to a. for s.o., for s.o.'s honesty,** répondre de qn; se porter garant de qn, de l'intégrité de qn; **to a. for one's actions,** prendre la responsabilité de ses propres actes; **he has a lot to a. for,** il est responsable de bien des choses. **answering** *a.* **1. an a. cry,** un cri jeté en réponse. **2.** qui répond, correspond (**to,** à); **someone a. to your description,** quelqu'un qui répondait à votre description. **3.** *Tp:* **a. service,** répondeur *m* téléphonique.

answerable ['ɑːns(ə)rəbl] *a.* **1.** (*a*) garant, responsable (**to s.o. for sth.,** envers qn de qch.); (*b*) **to be a. to an authority,** relever d'une autorité; **he is a. to nobody,** il ne doit de comptes à personne. **2.** (accusation) réfutable.

ant [ænt] *n.* fourmi *f;* **soldier a.,** soldat *m* des bois; **white a.,** fourmi blanche; termite *m;* *F:* **to have ants in one's pants,** avoir la bougeotte; (*b*) *Z:* **a. bear,** tamanoir *m;* *Ent:* **a. lion,** fourmi-lion *m.*

antacid [ænt'æsid] **1.** *a. & n. Med:* antiacide (*m*); alcalin (*m*). **2.** *a.* résistant aux acides.

antagonism [æn'tægənizm] *n.* (*a*) antagonisme *m,* opposition *f;* (*b*) *Bio-Ch:* **bacterial a.,** antagonisme microbien.

antagonist [æn'tægənist] *n.* **1.** antagoniste *mf,* adversaire *m.* **2.** *Bio-Ch:* antagoniste *m.*

antagonistic [æntægə'nistik] *a.* (*a*) opposé, contraire (**to,** à); (milieu), antagonique; *Anat:* (muscle) antagoniste; (*b*) hostile (**to,** à).

antagonize [æn'tægənaiz] *v.tr.* **1.** (*of a force*) s'opposer à (une autre force); contrarier (une force). **2.** éveiller l'antagonisme, l'hostilité, de (qn); éloigner (qn); **to a. the public,** ranger l'opinion contre soi.

antarctic [æn'tɑːktik] **1.** *a.* (pôle, faune, etc.) antarctique. **2.** *n.* **the A.,** l'Antarctique *m.*

Antarctica [æn'tɑːktikə] *Pr.n. Geog:* Antarctique *m.*

ante ['ænti] *n. Cards:* (*at poker*) **1.** première mise. **2.** ouvreur (primitif).

anteater ['æntiːtər] *n. Z:* fourmilier *m;* **great a.,** tamanoir *m;* **scaly a.,** pangolin *m;* **spiny a.,** échidné *m.*

antebellum [ænti'beləm] *a. U.S:* qui existait avant la guerre Civile.

antecedence [ænti'siːd(ə)ns] *n.* **1.** (*a*) antériorité *f;* (*b*) priorité *f.* **2.** *Astr:* antécédence *f.*

antecedent [ænti'siːd(ə)nt] **1.** *a.* antécédent, antérieur (**to,** à); *Geog:* **a. river, stream,** antécédent *m.* **2.** *n.* (*a*) *Gram: Log: Mth:* antécédent *m;* (*b*) *Mus:* thème *m* (d'une fugue); (*c*) **his antecedents,** (i) ses antécédents; son passé; (ii) ses ancêtres.

antechamber ['æntitʃeimbər] *n.* **1.** antichambre *f.* **2.** *I.C.E:* préchambre *f;* **Diesel engine with a.,** moteur *m* Diesel à chambre de précombustion.

antedate [ænti'deit] *v.tr.* **1.** (*a*) antidater (une

nomination, un document); (*b*) faire remonter (un événement) trop loin dans le passé. **2.** précéder; venir avant (un événement).
antediluvian [æntidi'lu:viən] *a.* antédiluvien.
antelope ['æntiloup] *n.* (*pl.* **antelopes,** *occ.* **antelope**) *Z:* antilope *f*; **sable a.,** antilope noire géante.
antenatal [ænti'neitl] *a.* prénatal, -als.
antenna [æn'tenə] *n.* **1.** (*pl.* **-ae** [-i:]) *Ent: Crust:* antenne *f*; *Moll:* tentacule *m*; corne *f* (de limaçon). **2.** (*pl. usu.* **-as** [-əz]) *NAm: W.Tel: T.V:* antenne.
antepenult(imate) [æntipe'nʌlt(imət)] *a.* & *n.* antépénultième (*f*).
anterior [æn'tiəriər] *a.* (*a*) antérieur, -eure (**to,** à); *Gram:* **past a.,** passé antérieur; (*b*) *Anat:* (muscle, etc.) antérieur.
anteroom ['æntiru(:)m] *n.* antichambre *f*, vestibule *m.*
anthem ['ænθəm] *n.* **1.** *Ecc.Mus:* motet *m.* **2.** (*a*) **national a.,** hymne national; (*b*) *Lit:* chant *m* d'allégresse.
anther ['ænθər] *n. Bot:* anthère *f.*
anthill ['ænthil] *n.* fourmilière *f.*
anthologist [æn'θɔlədʒist] *n.* anthologue *m.*
anthology [æn'θɔlədʒi] *n.* anthologie *f.*
Anthony ['æntəni] *Pr.n.m.* Antoine.
anthracite ['ænθrəsait] *n. Min:* anthracite *m.*
anthrax ['ænθræks] *n.* **1.** *Vet: Med:* (*a*) anthrax *m*; pustule charbonneuse; (*b*) charbon *m*; **a. bacillus,** bacille charbonneux. **2.** *Ent:* anthrax.
anthropoid ['ænθrəpɔid] *a.* & *n.* (*a*) anthropoïde (*m*); (*b*) *Z:* (singe *m*) anthropomorphe (*m*); anthropoïde (*m*).
anthropological ['ænθrəpə'lɔdʒikl] *a.* anthropologique.
anthropologist [ænθrə'pɔlədʒist] *n.* anthropologiste *mf*, anthropologue *mf.*
anthropology [ænθrə'pɔlədʒi] *n.* anthropologie *f.*
anthropometry [ænθrə'pɔmitri] *n.* anthropométrie *f.*
anthropomorphism [ænθrəpou'mɔ:fizm] *n. Phil:* anthropomorphisme *m.*
anthropophagous [ænθrə'pɔfəgəs] *a.* anthropophage.
anthropophagy [ænθrə'pɔfədʒi] *n.* anthropophagie *f.*
anti ['ænti] **1.** *a. F:* **he's just a.,** c'est un contestataire. **2.** *n.* opposant *m.*
anti- *pref.* anti-.
anti-aircraft ['ænti'ɛəkrɑ:ft] *a.* (canon, etc.) antiaérien; **a.-a. defence,** défense contre avions.
antibacterial [æntibæk'tiəriəl] *a. Med:* antibactérien.
antiballistic [æntibə'listik] *a.* antiballistique, antimissile; **a. missile,** engin *m*, fusée *f*, antimissile.
antibiotic [æntibai'ɔtik] *a.* & *n.* antibiotique (*m*).
antibody ['æntibɔdi] *n. Physiol:* anticorps *m.*
Antichrist ['æntikraist] Antéchrist *m.*
antichristian [ænti'kristjən] *a.* antichrétien.
anticipate [æn'tisipeit] *v.tr.* **1.** (*a*) anticiper sur (les événements, etc.); savourer (un plaisir) d'avance; (*b*) escompter (un résultat, un vote, etc.). **2.** prévenir, devancer (qn); prévenir (les ordres de qn); devancer (les désirs de qn); aller au-devant de (qch.). **3.** prévoir, envisager, s'attendre à (une difficulté, un plaisir, etc.); se promettre (un plaisir); **to a. the worst,** s'attendre au pire.
anticipation [æntisi'peiʃ(ə)n] *n* **1.** anticipation *f*; attente *f*; *Corr:* **thanking you in a.,** en vous remerciant d'avance. **2.** prévision *f.*
anticlerical [ænti'klerikl] *a.* & *n.* anticlérical, -aux.
anticlericalism [ænti'klerikəlizm] *n.* anticléricalisme *m.*
anticlimax [ænti'klaimæks] *n.* **1.** *Rh:* anticlimax *m.* **2.** (i) retour *m* à l'ordinaire; (ii) déception *f*; **the fifth act forms an a.,** avec le cinquième acte nous retombons dans l'ordinaire, sur terre.
anticline ['æntiklain] *n. Geol:* anticlinal, -aux *m.*
anticlockwise [ænti'klɔkwaiz] *adv.* & *a.* en sens inverse des aiguilles d'une montre.
anticoagulant [æntikou'ægjulənt] *a.* & *n. Med:* anticoagulant (*m*).
anticolonialism [æntikə'louniəlizm] *n.* anticolonialisme *m.*
anticonstitutional [æntikɔnsti'tju:ʃn(ə)l] *a.* anticonstitutionnel.
antics [æntiks] *s.pl.* (*a*) bouffonneries *fpl*, singeries *fpl*; **he's up to his a. again,** le voilà de nouveau qui fait le bouffon, qui fait des farces; (*b*) gambades *fpl*, cabrioles *fpl.*
anticyclone [ænti'saikloun] *n.* anticyclone *m.*
anti-dazzle [ænti'dæzl] *a.* anti-aveuglant, *pl.* anti-aveuglants; anti-éblouissant, *pl.* anti-éblouissants.
antidepressant [æntidi'presənt] *a.* & *n. Pharm:* euphorisant (*m*).
antidote ['æntidout] *n.* antidote *m*, contrepoison *m.*
anti-Establishment ['æntiis'tæbliʃmənt] *a.* anticonformiste.
antifascism [ænti'fæʃizm] *n. Pol:* antifascisme *m.*
antifascist [ænti'fæʃist] *a.* & *n.* antifasciste (*mf*).
antifreeze ['æntifri:z] *a.* & *n. Aut:* antigel (*m*).
antigen ['æntidʒen] *n. Med:* antigène *m.*
anti-glare [ænti'glɛər] *a.* = ANTI-DAZZLE.
Antigua [æn'ti:gə] *Pr.n. Geog:* Antigua *m.*
anti-hero, anti-heroine ['ænti'hiərou, -'herouin] *n. Lit:* anti-héros *m*, *pl.* anti-héros; antihéroïne *f*, *pl.* anti-héroïnes.
antihistamine [ænti'histəmin] *a.* & *n. Med:* antihistaminique (*m*).
anti-icing [ænti'aisiŋ] **1.** *n.* antigivrage *m.* **2.** *a.* antigivre *inv.*
anti-knock [ænti'nɔk] *a.* & *n. I.C.E:* antidétonnant (*m*).
antilog ['æntilɔg] *n. Mth: F:* antilog *m.*
antilogarithm [ænti'lɔgəriθm] *n. Mth:* antilogarithme *m.*
antimacassar [æntimə'kæsər] *n.* têtière *f* (de fauteuil, etc.).
antimatter ['æntimætər] *n.* antimatière *f.*
antimilitarism [ænti'militərizm] *n.* antimilitarisme *m.*
anti-missile [ænti'misail] *a.* (missile) antimissile.
antimony [æntiməni] *n.* antimoine *m.*
antinazi [ænti'na:tsi] *a.* & *n. Pol:* antinazi, -ie.
anti-novel ['æntinɔv(ə)l] *n. Lit:* antiroman *m.*
antiparticle ['ænti'pɑ:tikl] *n. Atom.Ph:* antiparticule *f.*
antipathetic(al) [æntipə'θetik(l)] *a.* antipathique (**to,** à).
antipathy [æn'tipəθi] *n.* antipathie *f*; **to feel a. for s.o.,** avoir de l'antipathie pour, contre, qn.
antipersonnel [æntipə:sə'nel] *a.* (*of bomb*) antipersonnel.
antiperspirant [ænti'pə:spirənt] *a.&n. Hyg:* antiperspirant (*m*).
antiphon ['æntifɔn] *n. Ecc.Mus:* (*a*) antienne *f*; (*b*) antiphon *m.*
antipodean [æntipə'di(:)ən] *a.* **1.** *Geog:* antipode; antipodal, -aux. **2.** diamétralement opposé (**to,** à).
antipodes [æn'tipədi:z] *n.pl. Geog:* **the a.,** les antipodes *mpl*; **at the a.,** aux antipodes.
antiproton [ænti'proutɔn] *n. Ph:* antiproton *m.*
antiquarian [ænti'kwɛəriən] **1.** *a.* ancien; **a. collection,** collection *f* d'antiquités; **a. bookshop,** librairie spécialisée dans les vieilles éditions. **2.** *n.* antiquaire *mf.*
antiquary ['æntikwəri] *n.* amateur *m* d'antiquités; antiquaire *m.*

antiquated ['æntikweitid] *a.* vieilli; désuet; suranné; **an a. kitchen range,** une cuisinière (à charbon) d'autrefois.

antique [æn'ti:k] **1.** *a.* antique, ancien; **a. statue,** statue ancienne; **a. furniture,** meubles *mpl* d'époque. **2.** *n.* (*a*) *Art:* **the a.,** l'antique *m*; (*b*) antiquité *f*; **a. shop,** magasin *m* d'antiquités; **a. dealer,** antiquaire *mf*; **antiques,** (i) antiquités; (ii) meubles d'époque.

antiquity [æn'tikwiti] *n.* (*a*) ancienneté *f* (d'un usage, etc.); (*b*) l'antiquité (grecque, romaine); **the works of art of classical a.,** les antiquités; **women in a.,** la femme dans le monde ancien; (*c*) **Roman antiquities in Provence,** les monuments romains en Provence.

antiracialism [ænti'reiʃəlizm], **antiracism** [ænti'reisizm] *n.* antiracisme *m.*

antirrhinum [ænti'rainəm] *n. Bot:* muflier *m*; *F:* gueule-de-loup *f*, *pl.* gueules-de-loup.

anti-rust [ænti'rʌst] *a. & n.* **a.-r. (composition),** (enduit *m*) antirouille (*m inv*).

anti-Semite [ænti'si:mait] *n.* antisémite *mf.*

anti-Semitic [æntisi'mitik] *a.* antisémitique.

anti-Semitism [ænti'semitizm] *n.* antisémitisme *m.*

antisepsis [ænti'sepsis] *n. Med:* antisepsie *f.*

antiseptic [ænti'septik] *a. & n. Med:* antiseptique (*m*).

antiserum [ænti'siərəm] *n. Med:* antisérum *m.*

antisocial [ænti'souʃl] *a.* antisocial, -aux.

antistatic [ænti'stætik] *a.* antistatique.

anti-submarine [ænti'sʌbməri:n] *a.* anti-sous-marin.

anti-tank [ænti'tæŋk] *a. Mil:* (défense, roquette, etc.) antichar(s).

anti-theft [ænti'θeft] *a.* (serrure, etc.) antivol *inv*; **a.-t. device,** antivol *m inv.*

antithesis, *pl.* **-es** [æn'tiθisis, -i:z] *n.* **1.** antithèse *f* **(between,** entre; **to, of,** de). **2.** opposé *m*, contraire *m* **(of,** de).

antitoxin [ænti'tɔksin] *n. Med:* antitoxine *f.*

antivivisectionist [æntivivi'sekʃənist] *n.* antivivisection(n)iste *mf.*

antler ['æntlər] *n.* andouiller *m* (d'un cerf, etc.); **the antlers,** les bois *mpl.*

Antony ['æntəni] *Pr.n.m.* Antoine.

antonym ['æntənim] *n.* antonyme *m.*

Antwerp ['æntwə:p] *Pr.n. Geog:* Anvers *m.*

anus ['einəs] *n. Anat:* anus *m.*

anvil ['ænvil] *n.* **1.** *Metalw:* enclume *f.* **2.** *Anat:* enclume (de l'oreille).

anxiety [æŋ'zaiəti] *n.* **1.** (*a*) inquiétude *f*; **deep a.,** anxiété *f*, angoisse *f*; **to cause s.o. great a.,** donner de grandes inquiétudes, bien des soucis, à qn; **to be full of a.,** être anxieux; (*b*) sollicitude *f* (pour la sûreté de qn); (*c*) désir *m* (d'aider qn, de plaire à qn). **2.** *Med:* anxiété.

anxious ['æŋkʃəs] *a.* **1.** (*a*) (*of pers.*) inquiet, -ète, soucieux, ennuyé **(about,** sur, de; au sujet de); **very, extremely, a.,** tourmenté, angoissé; **to be a. for s.o., for s.o.'s safety,** (i) être plein de sollicitude pour qn, pour la sûreté de qn; (ii) craindre pour qn; **I am a. about his health,** sa santé me préoccupe; (*b*) (*of thg*) inquiétant; **an a. moment,** un moment d'anxiété. **2.** désireux; **to be a. to do sth.,** tenir à faire qch.; être désireux, soucieux, de faire qch.; **why are you so a. to go?** (i) pourquoi êtes-vous si impatient de partir? (ii) pourquoi tenez-vous tant à y aller? **3.** *Med:* anxieux. **-ly** *adv.* **1.** (*a*) avec inquiétude; (*b*) anxieusement, avec anxiété. **2.** avec sollicitude. **3.** avec impatience.

any ['eni] *a. pron. & adv.* **I.** *a. qualifying phrs.* **1.** (*some; one*) (*a*) **have you a. milk, a. books?** avez-vous du lait, des livres? **have you a. more milk?** avez-vous encore du lait? **is there a. hope?** y a-t-il de l'espoir? (*stressed*) y a-t-il aucun espoir? (*b*) **he knows French if a. man does,** il sait le français comme pas un. **2.** (*a*) **not a.,** ne . . . aucun, nul; **he hasn't a. reason to complain,** il n'a aucune raison de se plaindre; **he hasn't a. more money,** il n'a plus d'argent; **I don't think a. of the guests have arrived yet,** je ne pense pas qu'aucun des invités soit encore arrivé; (*b*) (*with implied negation*) **he is forbidden to do a. work,** tout travail lui est interdit; **it is difficult to find a. explanation for it,** il est difficile d'en trouver aucune explication. **3.** (*a*) n'importe (le)quel; **come a. day (you like),** venez n'importe quel jour; **a. of us,** n'importe qui d'entre nous; **a. man, woman, or child,** qui que ce soit, homme, femme, ou enfant; **under a. pretext,** sous n'importe quel prétexte; **a. doctor will tell you that,** n'importe quel médecin vous le dira; **that may happen at a. time,** cela peut arriver n'importe quand; **I expect him a. moment now,** je l'attends d'un instant à l'autre; **take a. two cards,** prenez deux cartes quelconques; *F:* **a. old thing,** n'importe quoi; **a. old book,** un livre quelconque; (*b*) (*every*) **a. pupil who forgets his books will be punished,** tout élève qui oubliera ses livres sera puni; **at a. rate, in a. case,** en tout cas. **II.** *pron.* (*a*) **he has no money and no prospect of a.,** il est sans argent et sans l'espoir d'en avoir; (*b*) **I need some ink; have you a.?** il me faut de l'encre; en avez-vous? **is there a. more?** y en a-t-il encore? **I needn't say a. more,** pas besoin d'en dire davantage. **III.** *adv.* (*a*) **I'm not a. better,** je ne vais pas mieux; **I can't speak a. more plainly,** je ne peux pas parler plus clairement; **I can't go a. further,** je ne puis pas aller plus loin; **I don't see him a. longer, a. more,** je ne le vois plus; *F:* **a. old how,** n'importe comment; (*b*) *NAm: F:* **that didn't help us a.,** cela ne nous a été d'aucun secours; (*c*) *conj phr.* **I didn't do it a. more than you did,** je ne l'ai pas fait plus que vous.

anybody ['enibɔdi] *pron & n.,* **anyone** ['eniwʌn], *pron.* (*no pl.*) NOTE: *in examples where one of the forms is preferred, the word has been printed in full.* **1.** (*indeterminate*) quelqu'un; (*with implied negation*) personne; **can you see a. over there?** voyez-vous quelqu'un là-bas? **does a. dare to say so?** y a-t-il personne qui ose le dire? **2.** (*in neg. sentences*) **not a.,** ne . . . personne; **you needn't disturb a.,** il est inutile que vous dérangiez personne; **there was hardly a.,** il n'y avait presque personne; **I won't speak to a.,** je ne parlerai (pas) à qui que ce soit. **3.** n'importe qui; tout le monde; **a. will tell you so,** le premier venu vous le dira; **a. would think he was mad,** on le croirait fou; **a. but me,** tout autre que moi; **bring along a. you like,** amenez qui vous voudrez; **I challenge a. to . . .,** je défie qui que ce soit de . . .; **I haven't met a. else,** je n'ai rencontré personne d'autre; *Sp:* **it's anybody's match, game, race, etc.,** n'importe qui, n'importe quelle équipe, peut gagner, peut remporter la victoire; **it's a.'s guess!** qui sait? **4.** *F:* **is he anybody?** est-il quelqu'un? **he never will be anybody,** ce sera toujours une nullité.

anyhow ['enihau] *adv.* **1.** *F:* **to do sth. (all) a.,** (i) faire qch. d'une manière quelconque; (ii) faire qch. n'importe comment, tant bien que mal; **the room looks all a.,** la pièce est en désordre, en pagaille. **2.** en tout cas, de toute façon; **a. it's too late now,** en tout cas il est trop tard maintenant; **a. you can always try,** vous pouvez toujours essayer.

anyplace ['enipleis] *adv. NAm: F:* n'importe où; (*in neg. sentences*) nulle part; **a. else,** n'importe où ailleurs; (*in neg. sentences*) nulle part ailleurs.

anything ['eniθiŋ] *pron.* **1.** quelque chose; (*with implied negation*) rien; **can I do a. for you?** est-ce que je puis vous aider? **have you a. to write with?** avez-vous de quoi écrire? **is there a. more pleasant than . . .?** est-il rien de plus agréable que . . .? (*in shop*) **a. else, madam?** et avec cela, madame? **if a. should happen to him,** (i) s'il lui arrivait quelque malheur; (ii) s'il mourait; **do you see a. of your friend?** voyez-vous quelquefois votre ami? **is (there) a. the matter?** y a-t-il quelque chose qui ne marche pas? **2.** (*in neg. sentences*) **not a.,** ne . . . rien; **he doesn't do a.,** il ne fait rien; **I shan't give you a. at all,** je ne vous donnerai rien du tout; **hardly a.,** presque rien; **it doesn't mean a.,** cela ne veut rien dire. **3.** n'importe quoi; tout; **he eats a.,** il mange de tout; **a. you like,** tout ce que vous voudrez; **a. will do,** n'importe quoi fera l'affaire; **I love a. French,** j'aime tout ce qui est français; **he would do a. for me,** il ferait tout pour moi; **I would have given a. not to go,** j'aurais tout donné pour ne pas y aller; **he's a. but mad,** il est loin d'être fou; **he's not mad, a. but,** il n'est pas fou, loin de là. **4.** *adv.phr.* (*intensive*) *F:* **to work like a.,** travailler comme un fou; **it's raining like a.,** il pleut à torrents; **as easy as a.,** facile comme tout.

anyway ['eniwei] *adv.* = ANYHOW 2.

anywhere ['eni(h)wɛər] *adv.* **1.** n'importe où; **put it a.,** mettez-le n'importe où; **can you see it a.?** pouvez-vous le voir quelque part? **I'd know him a.,** je le reconnaîtrais entre mille; **it's miles from a.,** c'est au bout du monde, en plein bled; **a. else,** partout ailleurs; **has he a. near finished?** est-il près d'avoir fini? **2. not a.,** nulle part; en aucun endroit, en aucun lieu; **I can't find it a.,** je ne le trouve nulle part.

aorta [ei'ɔːtə] *n. Anat:* aorte *f.*

aortic [ei'ɔːtik] *a. Anat: Med:* (insuffisance, etc.) aortique.

apace [ə'peis] *adv. A. & Lit:* à grands pas; vite, rapidement.

Apache [ə'pætʃi] *n.* Apache *mf.*

apart [ə'pɑːt] *adv.* **1.** (*a*) **the garage stands a. from the house,** le garage est séparé de la maison; **he stood a. from the others,** il se tenait à l'écart des autres; (*b*) **they consider themselves in a class a.,** ils se considèrent au-dessus des autres; **place set a. for worship,** endroit destiné au culte. **2.** (*separated*) (*a*) **they are a mile a.,** ils sont à un mille l'un de l'autre; **lines 10 centimetres a.,** lignes espacées de 10 centimètres; **to stand with one's feet wide a.,** se tenir les jambes écartées; **towns as far a. as New York and Tokyo,** des villes aussi éloignées que New York et Tokyo; (*b*) (*time*) **children born two years a.,** des enfants nés à un intervalle de deux ans; (*c*) **the boys and girls were kept a.,** on tenait séparés les garçons et les filles; **it is difficult to tell them a.,** il est difficile de les distinguer l'un de l'autre; **this problem cannot be treated a.,** c'est un problème qu'on ne peut pas considérer séparément. **3. to take a machine a.,** démonter, désassembler, une machine; **my dress is coming a. at the seams,** ma robe commence à se découdre; *F:* **to take a room a.,** fouiller une pièce à fond. **4.** (*without considering*) (*a*) **joking a.,** plaisanterie à part; (*b*) **a. from,** à part; sauf; **a. from the fact that . . .,** indépendamment du fait que . . .; outre que . . .; **a. from a few mistakes,** à part, sauf, quelques erreurs; **a. from him there is nobody who can do it,** à part lui personne ne peut le faire.

apartheid [ə'pɑːtait, -eit] *n.* apartheid *m.*

apartment [ə'pɑːtmənt] *n.* **1.** (*a*) salle *f*; pièce *f*; **state apartments,** grands appartements; salons *mpl* d'apparat; (*b*) (*usu. pl.*) *A:* logement *m*; appartement *m*; **(furnished) apartments to let,** chambres (meublées) à louer. **2.** *NAm:* (= *flat*) appartement; **a. block, building,** immeuble divisé, maison divisée, en appartements.

apathetic [æpə'θetik] *a.* apathique, indifférent. **-ally** *adv.* avec indifférence.

apathy ['æpəθi] *n.* apathie *f*; indifférence *f.*

ape[1] [eip] *n.* (*a*) *Z:* (grand) singe (sans queue); **the higher apes,** les primates *mpl*; (*b*) *F:* **he's a big a.,** c'est une grande brute.

ape[2] *v.tr.* singer.

apelike ['eiplaik] *a.* comme un singe; (visage) simiesque.

Apennines (the) [ðiː'æpinainz] *Pr.n.pl. Geog:* les Apennins *mpl.*

aperient [ə'piəriənt] *a. & n. Med:* laxatif (*m*).

aperitif [ə'peritif] *n.* apéritif *m.*

aperture ['æpətjuər] *n.* (*a*) ouverture *f*, orifice *f*; lumière *f* (d'une pinnule, etc.); regard *m*, fenêtrelle *f* (de fourneau, etc.); (*b*) *Phot:* ouverture (d'un objectif, du diaphragme).

apex, *pl.* **apexes, apices** ['eipeks, -iz, 'eipisiːz] *n.* **1.** (*a*) sommet *m* (d'un triangle, d'un édifice, d'une montagne); point culminant, apogée *m* (d'une carrière) (*b*) *Nat.Hist:* pointe *f*, extrémité *f*; sommet (d'un organe, etc.). **2.** *Astr:* (*a*) **a. of the sun's motion,** apex *m* de la sphère céleste; (*b*) *Anat:* apex (du cœur), sommet (du poumon).

aphasia [ə'feiziə] *n. Med:* aphasie *f.*

aphid ['eifid, 'æfid] *n. Ent:* aphis *m*, puceron *m.*

aphis, *pl.* **-ides** ['eifis, 'æfis; -idiːz] *n. Ent:* aphis *m*, puceron *m*; **woolly a.,** puceron lanigère.

aphorism ['æfərizm] *n.* aphorisme *m.*

aphrodisiac [æfrou'diziæk] *a. & n.* aphrodisiaque (*m*).

apiarist ['eipiərist] *n.* apiculteur *m.*

apiary ['eipiəri] *n.* rucher *m.*

apiculture ['eipikʌltjər] *n.* apiculture *f.*

apiculturist [eipi'kʌltʃərist] *n.* apiculteur *m.*

apiece [ə'piːs] *adv.* chacun; (*of thg*) **to cost ten pence a.,** coûter dix pence (la) pièce; (*of pers.*) **he gave them five francs a.,** il leur donna cinq francs chacun.

aplenty [ə'plenti] *adv. NAm: F:* en abondance.

aplomb [ə'plɔm] *n.* aplomb *m*; confiance *f* en soi.

apocalypse [ə'pɔkəlips] *n.* apocalypse *f*; **the A. (of St John),** les Révélations *fpl* de saint Jean, l'Apocalypse; **the four horsemen of the A.,** les quatre cavaliers de l'Apocalypse.

apocalyptic [əpɔkə'liptik] *a.* apocalyptique.

Apocrypha (the) [ðiə'pɔkrifə] *n.pl. B.Lit:* **1.** les livres *mpl* deutérocanoniques. **2.** les apocryphes *mpl.*

apocryphal [ə'pɔkrifəl] *a.* apocryphe.

apogee ['æpə(d)ʒiː] *n.* apogée *m.*

apolitical [eipə'litik(ə)l] *a.* apolitique.

Apollo [ə'pɔlou] *Pr.n.m. Myth:* Apollon.

apologetic [əpɔlə'dʒetik] *a.* **1.** (ton, etc.) d'excuse; **to be very a.,** se confondre en excuses; **he was quite a. about it,** il s'en est excusé vivement. **2.** (livre, etc.) apologétique. **-ally** *adv.* **1.** pour s'excuser; en s'excusant. **2.** sous forme d'apologie, de justification.

apologize [ə'pɔlədʒaiz] *v.i.* **to a. to s.o. for sth.,** s'excuser de qch. auprès de qn; faire, présenter, des excuses, ses excuses, à qn pour qch.; **to a for doing sth.,** s'excuser de faire qch.; **I a. for having kept you waiting,** excusez-moi de vous avoir fait attendre.

apology [ə'pɔlədʒi] *n.* **1.** (*a*) excuses *fpl*; **letter of a.,** lettre *f* d'excuses; **to make, offer, an a.,** faire, présenter, des excuses; **to demand an a.,** exiger des excuses; (*b*) *F:* **an a. for a dinner,** un semblant de dîner. **2.** *Lit:* apologie *f*, justification *f* (de sa vie).

apoplectic [æpə'plektik] *a.* (personne) apoplectique; (attaque) d'apoplexie; **he had an a. fit, stroke,** il fut frappé d'apoplexie.

apoplexy ['æpəpleksi] *n. Med:* apoplexie *f.*

apostasy [ə'pɔstəsi] *n.* apostasie *f.*

apostate [ə'pɔstət] *a. & n.* apostat, -ate; relaps, -se.

apostatize [ə'pɔstətaiz] *v.i.* apostasier (**from one's faith,** sa foi).

apostle [əˈpɔsl] *n.* apôtre *m*; **the Apostles' Creed,** le Symbole des Apôtres; **a. spoon,** cuiller *f* avec figurine d'apôtre.

apostolic(al) [æpɔsˈtɔlik(l)] *a. Ecc:* (bénédiction, etc.) apostolique; **a. succession,** succession *f* apostolique.

apostrophe [əˈpɔstrəfi] *n. Rh: Gram:* apostrophe *f.*

apostrophize [əˈpɔstrəfaiz] *v.tr.* **1.** *Lit:* apostropher (qn). **2.** mettre un apostrophe à (un mot).

apothecary [əˈpɔθik(ə)ri] *n. A:* apothicaire *m*, pharmacien *m*; **apothecaries' weights and measures,** poids et mesures employés en pharmacie.

apotheosis, *pl.* **-oses** [əpɔθiˈousis, -ˈousi:z] *n.* apothéose *f.*

appal, *NAm: also* **appall** [əˈpɔ:l] *v.tr.* **(appalling; appalled)** consterner; mettre (qn) au désespoir; **to be appalled,** être au désespoir. **appalling** *a.* épouvantable, effroyable; *F:* **to make an a. row,** faire un bruit de tous les diables. **appallingly** *adv.* épouvantablement, effroyablement; **he's a. stupid,** il est d'une stupidité extraordinaire.

Appalachian [æpəˈlætʃən, -ˈleitʃ-] *a. Geog:* **the A. Mountains,** *n.* **the Appalachians,** les (monts *mpl*) Appalaches (*mpl*).

apparatus, *pl.* **-us, -uses** [æpəˈreitəs, -əsiz] *n.* (*often coll.*) **1.** appareil *m*, dispositif *m*, mécanisme *m*; **laboratory a.,** appareils de laboratoire; *Gym:* **a. work,** gymnastique *f* aux agrès; *Physiol:* **the digestive a.,** l'appareil digestif. **2.** *Lit:* **critical a., a. criticus** [ˈkritikəs], appareil, apparat *m*, critique (d'un texte).

apparel [əˈpær(ə)l] *n. A: & Lit: NAm:* (*a*) vêtement(s) *m(pl)*; (*b*) parure *f.*

apparent [əˈpærənt] *a.* (*a*) (qui est, qui semble être) apparent, manifeste, évident; **the truth became a. to him,** la vérité lui apparut; **as will soon become a.,** comme on le verra bientôt; **in spite of his a. indifference,** malgré son air d'indifférence; (*b*) *Pol.Ec:* **a. consumption,** consommation apparente; *Astr:* **a. diameter,** diamètre apparent; *Jur:* **heir a.,** héritier présomptif. **-ly** *adv.* apparemment; à ce qu'il semble; **he is a. going to Venice,** il paraît qu'il va aller à Venise.

apparition [æpəˈriʃ(ə)n] *n.* **1.** apparition *f.* **2.** fantôme *m*, revenant *m*, apparition.

appeal[1] [əˈpi:l] *n.* **1.** (*a*) appel *m* (au calme, au secours, etc.); recours *m* (à l'arbitrage, etc.); **a. to arms,** recours aux armes; (*b*) *Jur:* **a. at law,** appel; **a. against a sentence,** appel d'une condamnation; **Court of A.,** cour *f* d'appel; **Supreme Court of A.,** cour de cassation; **without a.,** sans appel; **notice of a.,** intimation *f* (d'appel); **to lodge an a.,** se pourvoir en appel; **acquitted on a.,** acquitté en seconde instance; **military a. court.,** conseil de révision. **2.** (*a*) appel (en faveur d'une cause, etc.); **to make an a. to s.o.'s generosity,** faire appel à la générosité de qn; (*b*) attrait *m*, attraction *f*; **this painting has great a.,** cette peinture est très attrayante; **she has great a.,** elle a beaucoup de charme; **sex a.,** sex-appeal *m*; **emotional a.,** attrait sentimental; *Com:* **sales a.,** attraction commerciale. **3.** prière *f*, supplication *f*; **with a look of a.,** d'un air suppliant.

appeal[2] *v.i.* **1.** *Jur: etc:* interjeter appel; **to a. from a judgment,** appeler d'un jugement; **to a. to another court,** en appeler à un autre tribunal; introduire un recours devant un autre tribunal; **to a. against a decision,** réclamer contre une décision; *Jur:* faire opposition à une décision; faire appel (à un tribunal) d'une décision. **2. to a. to s.o. for help,** demander des secours à qn; faire appel à qn; **to a. to s.o.'s generosity,** faire appel à la générosité de qn; **I a. to you to . . .,** je vous supplie de. . . . **3. to a. to s.o., to s.o.'s imagination,** s'adresser à qn, à l'imagination de qn; (*of thg*) attirer, séduire, charmer, l'imagination; **the plan appeals to me,** le projet me sourit; **it doesn't a. to me,** cela ne me dit rien; **the idea did not a. to him,** l'idée ne l'enchantait guère; **to a. to the emotions,** faire appel aux sentiments; *Com:* **styles that a. to the young,** modes *fpl* qui s'adressent aux jeunes. **appealing** *a.* **1.** (regard, ton, etc.) suppliant. **2.** (ton) émouvant. **3.** (personnalité) sympathique. **appealingly** *adv.* **1.** d'un ton, d'un regard, suppliant; **to look at s.o. a.,** regarder qn d'un air suppliant. **2. she smiles so a.,** elle a le sourire si sympathique, si attrayant.

appear [əˈpiər] *v.i.* **1.** paraître, apparaître; devenir visible; se montrer; **a head appeared at the window,** un visage s'est montré à la fenêtre; **a huge lorry suddenly appeared out of the fog,** un gros camion a surgi tout à coup dans le brouillard. **2.** (*a*) se présenter; *Jur:* comparaître, paraître; **to a. before a court,** comparaître devant un tribunal; **to fail to a.,** faire défaut; **failure to a.,** défaut *m* de comparution; **to a. for s.o.,** répondre pour qn; représenter qn; (*of counsel*) plaider pour qn; (*b*) (*of actor*) **to a. on the stage,** (i) entrer en scène; (ii) faire du théâtre; *F:* **that was when I appeared on the scene,** c'est à ce moment que je suis arrivé; (*c*) (*of book*) paraître; **a new daily will a. in March,** un nouveau quotidien sortira au mois de mars. **3.** (*a*) **to a. sad,** paraître, sembler avoir l'air, triste; **he appeared to hesitate,** il paraissait hésiter, il avait l'air d'hésiter; **he appears to have a lot of friends,** il semble avoir beaucoup d'amis; **there appears to be a mistake,** il semble(rait) qu'il y ait erreur; **it appears not,** il paraît que non; **to make it a. that . . .,** prétendre que . . .; (*b*) **it appeared later that . . .,** on a vu par la suite, plus tard, que . . .; **as appears from these records,** comme il ressort de ces pièces.

appearance [əˈpiərəns] *n.* **1.** (*a*) apparition *f*; entrée *f*; **to put in an a.,** (i) paraître (chez qn); (ii) faire acte de présence; **he failed to put in an a.,** il ne s'est pas montré (à la cérémonie); *Th:* **first a. of Miss X,** début *m* de Mlle X; **to make one's first a.,** débuter; faire ses débuts; (*b*) *Jur:* comparution *f* (devant un tribunal); (*c*) *Publ:* parution *f* (d'un livre). **2.** (*a*) apparence *f*, aspect *m*, air *m;* **from his a. one would say . . .,** à son air, à son extérieur, on dirait . . .; **one should not judge by appearances,** il ne faut pas juger selon les apparences; **an a. of gaiety,** un air de gaieté; **at first a.,** à première vue; au premier coup d'œil; (*b*) apparence; **appearances are against him,** les apparences sont contre lui; **to, by, all appearance(s),** selon toute apparence; apparemment; **to keep up appearances,** sauver, garder, les apparences.

appease [əˈpi:z] *v.tr.* (*a*) apaiser, calmer, tranquilliser (qn); (*b*) apaiser, assouvir (la faim, une passion).

appeasement [əˈpi:zmənt] *n.* (*a*) apaisement *m*, adoucissement *m*; (*b*) assouvissement *m*; (*c*) **policy of a.,** politique *f* d'apaisement, de conciliation.

appellant [əˈpelənt] *a. & n. Jur:* appelant, -ante.

appellate [əˈpelət, -leit] *a. Jur:* (juridiction) d'appel.

appellation [æpeˈleiʃ(ə)n] *n.* appellation *f*, nom *m.*

append [əˈpend] *v.tr.* (*a*) attacher, joindre (qch. à qch.); (*b*) apposer (sa signature), ajouter (des notes marginales); **to a. a document to a dossier,** annexer un document à un dossier.

appendage [əˈpendidʒ] *n.* **1.** accessoire *m*, apanage *m* **(to,** de). **2.** *Anat: Nat.Hist:* appendice *m*; annexe *f* (d'un organe).

appendectomy [æpenˈdektəmi], **appendicectomy** [əpendiˈsektəmi] *n. Surg:* appendicectomie *f.*

appendicitis [əpendiˈsaitis] *n. Med:* appendicite *f.*

appendix, *pl.* **-ixes, -ices** [ə'pendiks, -iksiz, -isi:z] *n.* **1.** *Anat:* appendice *m*; **vermiform a.,** appendice vermiculaire; *Med:* **grumbling a.,** appendicite *f* chronique. **2.** annexe *f* (d'un rapport, etc.); appendice (d'un livre).

appertain [æpə'tein] *v.i. Adm: & Lit:* **1.** appartenir **(to,** à); **lands appertaining to the Crown,** terres dépendantes de la Couronne. **2. duties appertaining to my office,** devoirs qui incombent à mes fonctions.

appetite ['æpitait] *n.* (*a*) appétit *m*; **to have a good a.,** avoir bon appétit; **to have a small, poor, a.,** avoir peu d'appétit; **to spoil, take away, s.o.'s a.,** couper l'appétit, la faim, à qn; **to give s.o. an a., to whet s.o.'s a.,** mettre qn en appétit, donner de l'appétit à qn; **loss of a.,** manque *m* d'appétit, *Med:* inappétence *f*, anorexie *f*; (*b*) **a. for revenge,** soif *f* de vengeance.

appetizer ['æpitaizər] *n.* (*a*) *O:* apéritif *m*; (*b*) *Comest:* (i) amuse-gueule *m*, *pl.* amuse-gueule(s); (ii) *O:* hors-d'œuvre *m inv.*

appetizing ['æpitaiziŋ] *a.* appétissant, alléchant. **-ly** *adv.* d'une façon appétissante.

applaud [ə'plɔ:d] *v.tr. & i.* **1.** applaudir (qn); battre, claquer, des mains; **to be applauded,** être applaudi; soulever les applaudissements. **2.** approuver (une décision, etc.); **to a. s.o.'s efforts,** applaudir aux efforts de qn.

applause [ə'plɔ:z] *n.* **1.** applaudissements *mpl*; **to meet, be greeted, with a.,** être applaudi; soulever les applaudissements; **to win a.,** se faire applaudir **(from,** par, de). **2.** approbation *f*.

apple ['æpl] *n.* **1.** (*a*) pomme *f*; **eating, dessert, a.,** pomme à couteau, pomme à dessert; **cooking a.,** pomme à cuire; **a. core,** trognon *m* de pomme; *Cu:* **baked a.,** pomme cuite (au four); **stewed apples,** compote *f* de pommes; pommes en compote; **a. sauce,** compote de pommes; **a. tart,** tarte *f* aux pommes; **a. pie** = tarte, tourte *f*, aux pommes; **in a.-pie order,** admirablement rangé, en ordre parfait; *F:* **a.-pie bed,** lit *m* en portefeuille; **a. brandy,** eau-de-vie *f* de cidre; = calvados *m*; (*b*) **a. (tree),** pommier *m*; **a. orchard,** pommeraie *f*; (*c*) **crab a.,** pomme sauvage; **crab a. tree,** pommier sauvage. **2. a. of the eye,** prunelle *f* de l'œil; **he's, she's, it's, the a. of his eye,** il en prend soin comme de la prunelle de ses yeux.

applecart ['æplkɑ:t] *n.* voiture *f* à bras (de marchand des quatre saisons); *F:* **to upset the a.,** brouiller les cartes.

applejack ['æpldʒæk] *n.* eau-de-vie *f* de cidre; = calvados *m.*

appliance [ə'plaiəns] *n.* (*a*) appareil *m*, dispositif *m*; **mechanical a.,** engin *m* mécanique; **electrical appliances,** appareils électriques; **household appliances,** appareils ménagers; (*b*) autopompe *f*, pompe *f* à incendie; (*c*) accessoire *m* (d'une machine, etc.).

applicable [ə'plikəbl, 'æplikəbl] *a.* applicable **(to,** à); approprié **(to,** à).

applicant ['æplikənt] *n.* **1.** candidat, -ate (à un emploi), demandeur *m* (d'un brevet); *Fin:* **a. for shares,** souscripteur d'actions. **2.** *Jur:* demandeur, -deresse; requérant, -ante.

application [æpli'keiʃ(ə)n] *n.* **1.** (*a*) application *f*, applicage *m* **(of sth. to sth.,** de qch. à, sur, qch.); apposition *f* (d'une couche de vernis, etc.); *Mec.E:* **gradual a. of power,** entraînement progressif; **a. of the brake,** freinage *m*; serrage *m* du frein; (*b*) (*thing applied*) application; enduit *m*; (*c*) application (d'une théorie, d'un principe, d'une découverte, etc.); **practical applications of a process,** réalisations *fpl* d'un procédé. **2.** assiduité *f*, application (à l'étude, etc.); esprit de suite. **3.** (*a*) demande *f* (d'emploi, de secours, de brevet); **to make an a. for sth.,** formuler une demande pour obtenir qch.; **samples are sent on a.,** on envoie des échantillons sur demande; **a. form,** bulletin *m* de demande; (*b*) *Fin:* **a. for shares,** demande de titres en souscription; **to make a. for shares,** souscrire (à) des actions; **a. form,** bulletin *m* de souscription.

applicator ['æplikeitər] *n. Pharm: etc:* applicateur *m*; dispositif *m* pour l'application (de médicaments, etc.).

appliqué [æ'pli:kei] *n. Needlew:* **1.** broderie *f* d'application *f*. **2.** applique *f*.

apply [ə'plai] *v.tr. & i.* **1.** (*a*) appliquer **(sth. to sth.,** qch. sur qch.); **to a. the brake,** freiner; serrer le frein; (*b*) appliquer (un système, une théorie, etc.); mettre (un système, une théorie, etc.) en pratique; **this rule applies to all cases,** cette règle est applicable, s'applique, à tous les cas. **2. to a. one's mind to sth.,** appliquer son esprit à qch.; s'appliquer à qch.; **to a. oneself to one's work,** travailler avec application; s'attacher à son travail. **3.** (*a*) **to a. to s.o. for sth.,** s'adresser, recourir, avoir recours, à qn pour obtenir qch.; **to a. for a job,** poser sa candidature à un emploi; solliciter, postuler, un emploi; **a. within,** s'adresser ici; (*b*) *Fin:* **to a. for shares,** souscrire (à) des actions. **applied** *a.* (mathématiques, etc.) appliquées; (sciences) expérimentales; **a. psychology,** psychotechnique *f*.

appoint [ə'pɔint] *v.tr.* **1.** (*a*) **to a. s.o. (to be) manager,** nommer qn directeur; (*b*) nommer (un directeur, un comité, etc.); constituer (un comité); désigner (un expert); instituer (un héritier); **to a. s.o. to sth., to do sth.,** nommer qn à qch.; désigner qn pour faire qch.; **to a. s.o. to a post,** désigner qn pour, à, un poste; **newly appointed officials,** fonctionnaires entrants, nouvellement nommés. **2.** fixer, désigner (l'heure, l'endroit); arrêter (un jour). **3.** *Jur:* léguer, transmettre, (des biens) avec faculté de distribution. **appointed** *a.* **1.** (agent) attitré. **2.** (l'heure) convenue, fixée; **on the a. day,** le jour convenu. **3. well a. house,** maison bien montée, bien agencée, bien installée.

appointment [ə'pɔintmənt] *n.* **1.** rendez-vous *m*; (*for business*) entrevue *f*; *Adm:* convocation *f*; **to make, fix, an a. with s.o.,** fixer un rendez-vous, donner rendez-vous, à qn; **to make an a. with s.o. for three o'clock, for Monday,** prendre rendez-vous pour trois heures, pour lundi; **to meet s.o. by a.,** se rencontrer avec qn sur rendez-vous; **have you an a.?** avez-vous un rendez-vous? *Adm:* êtes-vous convoqué? **2.** *Jur:* **power of a.,** faculté *f* de distribution (de biens) (accordée à un légataire). **3.** (*a*) nomination *f* (de qn à un emploi); *Adm:* désignation *f* (de qn pour un emploi); *Mil: Navy:* affectation *f* (de qn à un navire, une unité); (*of shop, etc.*) **by a. to His, Her, Majesty,** fournisseur breveté, attitré, de sa Majesté; *Journ:* **appointments vacant,** offres *fpl* d'emploi; **appointments board,** (i) bureau *m* de placement; (ii) *Sch:* département *m* d'information et de prospective; (*b*) place *f*, charge *f*, emploi *m*. **4. appointments,** aménagement *m*, installation *f* (d'une maison).

apportion [ə'pɔ:ʃ(ə)n] *v.tr.* répartir (les frais); lotir (une propriété); **to a. sth. to s.o.,** assigner qch. à qn; **to a. (out) a sum among several people,** partager, distribuer, une somme entre plusieurs personnes.

apportionment [ɛ'pɔ:ʃ(ə)nmənt] *n.* partage *m*, répartition *f* (d'impôts, de dépenses, etc.); allocation *f* (de vivres, etc.); distribution *f* (de parts, d'une propriété).

apposite ['æpəzit] *a.* juste; approprié **(to,** à); (remarque) faite à propos; (observation) juste.

apposition [æpə'ziʃ(ə)n] *n.* **1.** *Gram: etc:* apposition *f*; **words in a.,** mots appositifs, en apposition. **2.** *Bot: etc:* apposition.

appraisal [ə'preiz(ə)l] *n.* évaluation *f*, estimation *f*, appréciation *f*; (*before auction*) prisée *f*; **official a.,** expertise *f*; **self a.,** autocritique *f*.

appraise [ə'preiz] *v.tr.* priser, estimer, évaluer (qch.) (**at so much,** à tant); apprécier la valeur de (qch.); faire l'expertise (des dégâts).

appreciable [ə'pri:ʃiəbl] *a.* (différence, etc.) appréciable; (changement, etc.) sensible; (variation) notable. **-ably** *adv.* à un degré appréciable; sensiblement.

appreciate [ə'pri:ʃieit, -sieit] **1.** *v.tr.* (*a*) évaluer (des marchandises); estimer la valeur de (qch.); **he was never appreciated at his true worth,** il n'a jamais été apprécié à sa juste valeur; (*b*) apprécier; faire cas de (qch.); **I fully a. (the fact) that . . .,** je me rends clairement compte que . . .; **I greatly a. your kindness,** je suis très sensible à votre gentillesse; **I a. your having done this,** je vous suis reconnaissant d'avoir fait cela. **2.** *Fin:* (*a*) *v.tr.* hausser la valeur de (qch.); (*b*) *v.i.* (*of goods, etc.*) augmenter de valeur; hausser de prix; monter; **the franc has appreciated in terms of other currencies,** le franc s'est apprécié par rapport aux autres monnaies. **3.** *v.i.* s'améliorer.

appreciation [əpri:ʃi'eiʃ(ə)n, əpri:si-] *n.* **1.** (*a*) appréciation *f* ((i) du prix, de la valeur, de qch.; (ii) d'un service, de la situation, etc.); estimation *f* (de la valeur de qch.); (*b*) **to give, write, an a. of a new play,** faire la critique d'une nouvelle pièce; *Sch:* **literary a.,** explication *f* de texte, explication littéraire; **musical a.,** appréciation musicale; **I should like to express my a. of your kindness,** j'aimerais bien vous dire combien je suis sensible à votre gentillesse. **2.** accroissement *m*, hausse *f*, de valeur; amélioration *f*, valorisation *f*, plus-value *f*, *pl.* plus-values; **a. of assets,** plus-value d'actif; **a. in prices,** amélioration des prix.

appreciative [ə'pri:ʃiətiv, -siətiv] *a.* **1.** élogieux; **a few a. words,** quelques paroles élogieuses. **2.** appréciateur, -trice; **to be a. of music,** apprécier la musique. **-ly** *adv.* (*a*) favorablement; (*b*) **the audience listened a.,** les auditeurs ont écouté avec appréciation.

apprehend [æpri'hend] *v.tr.* **1.** *Jur:* arrêter (qn). **2.** comprendre; percevoir. **3.** *A: & Lit:* appréhender, craindre (un danger, etc.).

apprehension [æpri'henʃ(ə)n] *n.* **1.** *Jur:* arrestation *f*. **2.** (*a*) perception *f* (d'un son, etc.); compréhension *f* (des faits); (*b*) *Psy:* entendement *m*, appréhension *f*; **to be slow of a.,** avoir l'intelligence, la conception, lente. **3.** appréhension, crainte *f*; **to give cause for a.,** motiver des craintes.

apprehensive [æpri'hensiv] *a.* timide, craintif; **to be a. for s.o., for s.o.'s safety,** craindre pour qn, pour la sûreté de qn. **-ly** *adv.* avec appréhension.

apprentice¹ [ə'prentis] (*a*) apprenti, -ie; **carpenter's a.,** apprenti menuisier; (*b*) débutant, -ante.

apprentice² *v.tr.* **to a. s.o. to s.o.,** placer, mettre, qn en apprentissage chez qn. **apprenticed** *a.* en apprentissage (**to s.o.,** chez qn).

apprenticeship [ə'prenti(s)ʃip] *n.* apprentissage *m*.

apprise [ə'praiz] *v.tr. Lit:* **to a. s.o. of sth.,** apprendre qch. à qn; prévenir, informer, qn de qch.

appro ['æprou] *n. Com: F:* **on a.,** à l'essai.

approach¹ [ə'proutʃ] *n.* **1.** (*a*) approche *f*; venue *f* (du printemps); approche, approches (de la mort); (*b*) *Lit:* **man easy of a.,** homme qui est d'un abord facile; (*c*) **his a. to the problem,** sa méthode d'attaque du problème, la façon dont il aborde le problème; **I don't like his a.,** je n'aime pas sa façon de s'y prendre; (*d*) **to make approaches to s.o.,** faire des avances *fpl* à qn. **2.** voie *f* d'accès; **the a. to a town,** les abords, les approches, d'une ville; **a. to a harbour,** atterrage *m*, accès, d'un port. **3.** rapprochement *m*; **it is the nearest a. to perfection,** cela approche le plus près de la perfection. **4.** *Golf:* **a. shot,** coup *m* d'approche. **5.** *Av:* **a. aids,** moyens *mpl* d'approche; **a. end of runway,** entrée *f* de piste, seuil *m* de la piste.

approach² **1.** *v.i.* approcher, s'approcher; *Golf:* jouer le coup d'approche; **Christmas is approaching,** Noël approche. **2.** *v.tr.* (*a*) approcher; **we are approaching London,** nous approchons de Londres; **the wind was approaching gale force,** le vent soufflait presque en tempête; **something approaching a feeling of relief,** un sentiment presque de soulagement; (*b*) s'approcher de (qn); aborder, approcher (qn); **to a. s.o. on the subject of . . .,** approcher qn au sujet de . . .; **to be easy, difficult, to a.,** avoir l'abord facile, difficile; (*c*) tâter, pressentir (qn); (*d*) aborder, s'attaquer à, (une question). **approaching** *a.* approchant; **his a. death,** sa mort prochaine; **the a. car,** la voiture qui vient, venait, en sens inverse; **an a. storm,** une tempête qui arrive.

approachable [ə'proutʃəbl] *a.* (personne, endroit) accessible, approchable; (personne, côte) abordable.

approbation [æprə'beiʃ(ə)n] *n.* approbation *f*: jugement *m* favorable; **smile of a.,** sourire approbateur.

appropriate¹ [ə'proupriət] *a.* **1.** approprié (**to,** à); **salary a. to an office,** traitement *m* que comporte une fonction. **2.** propre, convenable, (**to, for,** à); juste, à propos; (nom) bien choisi; (musique, etc.) de circonstance; **to take a. action,** prendre les mesures indiquées. **-ly** *adv.* convenablement, proprement; à propos; **a. dressed,** en tenue convenable.

appropriate² [ə'prouprieit] *v.tr.* **1.** (*a*) s'approprier (qch.); s'emparer de (qch.); **to a. s.o.'s ideas,** prendre, dérober, ses idées à qn; (*b*) s'attribuer, se destiner, se réserver (qch.). **2.** approprier, appliquer, affecter, consacrer (**sth. to, for, a purpose,** qch. à une destination).

appropriateness [ə'proupriətnis] *n.* convenance *f*, justesse *f*, à-propos *m*.

appropriation [əproupri'eiʃ(ə)n] *n.* **1.** appropriation *f*, prise *f* de possession (**of,** de). **2.** (*a*) appropriation, application *f*, affectation *f* (de qch. à un usage); (*b*) affectation de fonds; *Fin:* attribution *f* (d'une somme). **3.** *Pol:* crédit *m* (budgétaire).

approval [ə'pru:v(ə)l] *n.* **1.** approbation *f*, agrément *m*; **for a.,** pour approbation; **to meet with s.o.'s a.,** recevoir, obtenir, l'approbation de qn; **gesture, sign, of a.,** geste, signe, approbatif; **to nod a.,** approuver de la tête. **2.** *Adm:* ratification *f*, homologation *f* (d'un document) **3.** *Com:* (*a*) **on a.,** à condition, à l'essai; **book sent on a.,** livre envoyé à l'examen; (*b*) *NAm:* **approvals,** marchandises envoyées à titre d'essai.

approve [ə'pru:v] **1.** *v.tr.* approuver, sanctionner (une action); ratifier, homologuer (une décision); agréer (un contrat); **read and approved,** lu et approuvé; **approved by the government,** agréé par l'État. **2.** *v.i.* **to a. of sth.,** approuver qch.; **I don't a. of your friends,** vos amis ne me plaisent pas; **to a. of s.o.'s choice,** applaudir au choix de qn; **I don't a. of the plan,** je ne suis pas d'accord avec ce projet. **approved** *a.* approuvé, agréé; réglementaire; *Adm:* (**officially**) **a.,** homologué; *Breed:* **a. stallion,** étalon autorisé; *Sch: A:* **a. school,** école *f* pour les délinquants juvéniles. **approving** *a.* approbateur, -trice. **approvingly** *adv.* avec approbation; d'un air, d'un ton, approbateur.

approximate¹ [ə'prɔks(i)mət] *a.* **1.** *Biol: Ph:* rapproché, proche, voisin. **2.** (calcul, etc.) approximatif, approché; **a. value,** valeur approximative; **-ly** *adv.* approximativement; à peu près; **five miles are a.**

eight kilometres, cinq milles valent à peu près huit kilomètres; **his income is a. £5000,** son revenu est d'environ cinq mille livres.

approximate² [ə'prɔksimeit] **1.** *v.tr.* **to a. a case to another,** rapprocher un cas d'un autre. **2.** *v.i.* **to a. to the truth,** se rapprocher de la vérité.

approximation [əprɔksi'meiʃ(ə)n] **1.** rapprochement *m* (d'opinions, etc.). **2.** approximation *f*; **this figure is only an a.,** ceci n'est qu'un chiffre approximatif.

appurtenance [ə'pəːtinəns] *n.* **1.** *Jur:* **house with all its appurtenances,** immeuble avec ses appartenances et dépendances. **2. appurtenances,** accessoires *mpl.*

apricot ['eiprikɔt] *n.* (*a*) *Hort:* abricot *m*; **a. (tree),** abricotier *m*; (*b*) (*colour*) abricot *m inv.*

April ['eipril] *n.* avril *m*; **in A.,** en avril, au mois d'avril; **A. showers** = giboulées *fpl* de mars; **A. Fool's Day,** le premier avril; **to make an A. fool of s.o.,** donner, faire, un poisson d'avril à qn; **A. fool!** poisson d'avril!

a priori ['eiprai'ɔːrai, æpri'ɔːri] *adv. & a.* a priori; **a p. reasoning,** raisonnement *m* a priori.

apron ['eiprən] *n.* **1.** *Cost:* tablier *m*; *F:* **to be tied to one's mother's a. strings,** être pendu(e) aux jupons de sa mère. **2.** (*a*) *Hyd.E:* radier *m* (d'un bassin); *Av:* aire *f* de manœuvre, de stationnement; tablier, aire en dur (pour révision et réparation des avions); (*c*) *Tls:* **a. lathe,** tour *m* à tablier; (*d*) *Th:* **a. (stage),** avant-scène *f, pl.* avant-scènes.

apropos ['æprəpou] **1.** *a.* **a very a. remark,** une observation très à propos, très opportune. **2.** *prep. phr.* **it was mentioned a. of the holidays,** on en a parlé à propos des vacances.

apse [æps] *n. Ecc.Arch:* abside *f.*

apsidal ['æpsid(ə)l] *a. Ecc.Arch:* absidal, -aux.

apt [æpt] *a.* **1.** (mot) juste, fin; (expression) heureuse, qui convient. **2. a. to do sth.** (*a*) (*of pers.*) enclin, porté, sujet, à faire qch.; **he is a. to forget,** il a une tendance à oublier; (*b*) (*of thg*) sujet à, susceptible de, faire qch. **3.** (élève, etc.) intelligent, habile. **-ly** *adv.* avec justesse; à propos; **a. chosen name,** nom bien choisi.

aptitude ['æptitjuːd] *n.* **a. for sth.,** aptitude *f* à, pour, qch.; **to have an a. for learning,** être apte à apprendre; **to show great a.,** montrer de grandes dispositions; **a. test,** test *m* d'aptitude, d'intelligence pratique.

aptness ['æptnis] *n.* **1.** justesse *f*, à-propos *m* (d'une expression, d'une citation, etc.). **2.** (*of pers., thg*) tendance *f* (**to do sth.,** à faire qch.).

aqualung ['ækwəlʌŋ] *n.* scaphandre *m* autonome.

aquamarine [ækwəmə'riːn] *n. Miner:* aigue-marine *f, pl.* aigues-marines.

aquanaut ['ækwənɔːt] *n.* aquanaute *mf*; plongeur, -euse.

aquaplane¹ ['ækwəplein] *n. Sp:* aquaplane *m.*

aquaplane² *v.i.* **1.** *Sp:* faire de l'aquaplane. **2.** *Aut:* faire de l'aquaplaning. **aquaplaning** *n.* **1.** *Sp:* l'aquaplane *m.* **2.** *Aut:* aquaplaning *m*, effet *m* d'hydroglisseur.

aquarelle [ækwə'rel] *n. Art:* aquarelle *f.*

aquarium, *pl.* **-iums, -ia** [ə'kwɛəriəm, -iəmz, -iə] *n.* aquarium *m.*

Aquarius [ə'kwɛəriəs] *Pr.n. Astr:* le Verseau.

aquatic [ə'kwætik] *a.* **1.** (plante, etc.) aquatique. **2. a. sports,** *n.pl.* **aquatics,** sports *mpl* nautiques.

aquatint ['ækwətint] *n. Engr:* aquatinte *f.*

aqueduct ['ækwidʌkt] *n.* aqueduc *m.*

aqueous ['eikwiəs] *a.* **1.** aqueux; **a. humour,** humeur aqueuse (de l'œil); *Pharm:* **a. solution,** solluté *m.*

aquilegia [ækwi'liːdʒiə] *n. Bot:* aquilégie *f.*

aquiline ['ækwilain] *a.* aquilin; **a. nose,** nez aquilin, busqué, en bec d'aigle.

Aquinas [ə'kwainæs] *a.* **Saint Thomas A.,** saint Thomas d'Aquin.

Arab ['ærəb] **1.** *Ethn:* (*a*) *a.* arabe; **the A. world,** le monde arabe; *Pol:* **the A. League,** la Ligue arabe; (*b*) *n.* Arabe *mf.* **2.** *a. & n.* (cheval *m*) arabe (*m*). **3.** *n. F: O:* **street a.,** gamin *m* des rues.

arabesque [ærə'besk] **1.** *a. Arch:* (décoration) arabesque, dans le style arabe. **2.** *n.* (*a*) *usu. pl. Arch:* arabesque(s) *f(pl)*; (*b*) *Danc:* arabesque.

Arabia [ə'reibiə] *Pr.n.Geog:* Arabie *f*; **Saudi A.,** Arabie Saoudite, Séoudite.

Arabian [ə'reibiən] **1.** *a.* (*a*) arabique, arabe; **the A. Gulf,** le golfe Arabique; **the A. Peninsula,** la péninsule d'Arabie; **A. camel,** dromadaire *m*; (*b*) *Lit:* **The A. Nights,** les Mille et une Nuits. **2.** Arabe *mf* (d'Arabie).

Arabic ['ærəbik] **1.** *a.* (*a*) (langue, littérature) arabe; **A. scholar,** arabisant *m*; **A. numerals,** chiffres *mpl* arabes; (*b*) **gum a.,** gomme *f* arabique. **2.** *n. Ling:* arabe *m.*

Arabist ['ærəbist] *n.* arabisant *m.*

arable ['ærəbl] *a.* (terre) arable.

arachnid [ə'ræknid] *n. Z:* arachnide *m.*

Aramaic [ærə'meiik] *a. & n. Ling:* araméen (*m*).

arbiter ['ɑːbitər] *n.* arbitre *m* (de la mode, etc.); **a. of taste,** arbitre des élégances.

arbitrage ['ɑːbitridʒ] *n. Fin: St.Exch:* arbitrage *m.*

arbitrariness ['ɑːbitrərinis] *n.* arbitraire *m* (d'une décision, etc.).

arbitrary ['ɑːbitrəri] *a.* (décision, etc.) arbitraire. **-ily,** *adv.* arbitrairement.

arbitrate ['ɑːbitreit] **1.** *v.tr.* arbitrer, juger, trancher (un différend). **2.** *v.i.* décider en qualité d'arbitre; arbitrer.

arbitration [ɑːbi'treiʃ(ə)n] *n.* arbitrage *m*; **to refer a question to a.,** soumettre une question à un arbitrage; **a. court, court of a.,** tribunal arbitral; **a. clause,** clause *f* d'arbitrage.

arbitrator ['ɑːbitreitər] *n. Jur:* arbitre *m*; médiateur, -trice.

arbor¹ ['ɑːbər] *n. Mec.E:* (*a*) arbre *m* (de roue, de meule); **a. shaft,** joint *m* de cardan; (*b*) mandrin *m* (de tour); **cutter, milling, a.,** mandrin de fraisage.

arbor² *n. NAm:* = ARBOUR.

arboreal [ɑː'bɔːriəl] *a.* **1.** d'arbre(s). **2.** (animal) arboricole; (existence) sur les arbres.

arboriculture ['ɑːbərikʌltjər] *n.* arboriculture *f.*

arbour, *NAm:* **arbor** ['ɑːbər] *n. Hort:* berceau *m* de verdure; tonnelle *f*, charmille *f*; **vine a.,** treille *f.*

arbutus [ɑː'bjuːtəs] *n.* arbousier *m; NAm:* **(trailing) a.,** épigée rampante.

arc¹ [ɑːk] *n.* **1.** (*a*) *Mth: etc:* arc *m* (de cercle, etc.); **to describe an a.,** décrire un arc; *Artil:* **a. of fire,** champ *m* de tir (d'un canon, etc.); (*b*) *Mec:* secteur *m.* **2.** *El:* **electric a.,** arc électrique; **a. lamp, a. light,** lampe *f* à arc.

arc² *v.i.* **(arcing** ['ɑːkiŋ]; **arced** [ɑːkt]) *El:* faire jaillir un arc, amorcer l'arc; (*of dynamo, commutator*) **to a. (over),** cracher; projeter des étincelles. **arcing** ['ɑːkiŋ] *n. El:* amorçage (d'arc); crachement *m.*

arcade [ɑː'keid] *n.* **1.** (*a*) arcade(s) *f* (*pl*) (en bord de rue); (*b*) galerie *f* (marchande); passage (couvert). **2.** *Arch:* **(blind) a.,** arcature *f.* **3.** *Anat:* arcade *f.*

arcaded [ɑː'keidid] *a.* bordé d'arcades.

Arcadia [ɑː'keidiə] *Pr.n.A.Geog. & Lit:* Arcadie *f.*

Arcadian [ɑː'keidiən] **1.** *a.* arcadien. **2.** *n.* Arcadien, -ienne.

arch¹ [ɑːtʃ] *n.* **1.** *Arch: Const:* voûte *f*; arc *m*; **a. of a vault,** arceau *m*; **semicircular a.,** arc en plein cintre; **pointed, gothic, a.,** arc brisé; **Tudor a.,** arc en carène; **a. stone,** voussoir *m.* **2.** (*a*) *Civ.E:* arche *f* (d'un pont, d'un viaduc); (*b*) *Min:* estau *m*; (*c*) voûte (d'un fourneau). **2.** (*a*) arcade *f* (d'une selle); (*b*) *Anat:* arc (des sourcils, etc.); arcade (orbitaire); crosse *f* (de l'aorte); cambrure *f* (du pied); **a. support,** cambrure (pour chaussures); **to suffer from fallen arches,** avoir les pieds plats.

arch² **1.** *v.tr.* (*a*) voûter (une porte, un passage); (*b*) arquer, cintrer; cambrer; **the cat arches its back,** le chat fait le dos rond. **2.** *v.i.* se voûter, former voûte, bomber. **arched** *a.* (*a*) à arc, en voûte; voûté; voussé; **a. window,** fenêtre (i) cintrée, (ii) en arc brisé; (*b*) (nez, etc.) arqué, busqué; (pied, cou de pied) cambré; **a. neck,** encolure rouée (d'un cheval).

arch³ *a.* (*of women and children*) espiègle; malicieux; coquin. **-ly** *adv.* d'un air espiègle; d'un air malicieux.

arch⁴ *a. & pref.* archi-; grand; insigne; **a. enemy,** adversaire, ennemi, numéro un; **a. traitor,** traître *m* insigne; architraître.

archaeological, *NAm: also* **archeological** [ɑːkiə'lɔdʒik(ə)l] *a.* archéologique. **-ally** *adv.* archéologiquement.

archaeologist, *NAm: also* **archeologist** [ɑːki'ɔlədʒist] *n.* archéologue *mf.*

archaeology, *NAm: also* **archeology** [ɑːki'ɔlədʒi] *a.* archéologie *f.*

archaic [ɑː'keiik] *a.* archaïque.

archaism ['ɑːkeiizm] *n.* archaïsme *m.*

archangel ['ɑːkeindʒ(ə)l] *n.* archange *m.*

archbishop [ɑːtʃ'biʃəp] *n.m.* archevêque; **archbishop's palace,** palais *m* archiépiscopal.

archdeacon [ɑːtʃ'diːk(ə)n] *n.m.* archidiacre.

archdiocese [ɑːtʃ'daiəsiːz, -sis] *n. Ecc:* archidiocèse *m*, archevêché *m.*

archduchess [ɑːtʃ'dʌtʃis] *n.f.* archiduchesse.

archduchy [ɑːtʃ'dʌtʃi] *n.* archiduché *m.*

archduke [ɑːtʃ'djuːk] *n.m.* archiduc.

archer ['ɑːtʃər] *n.* **1.** archer *m.* **2.** *Astr:* **the A.,** le Sagittaire.

archery ['ɑːtʃəri] *n.* tir *m* à l'arc.

archetypal [ɑːki'taipl] *a.* archétypal, -aux.

archetype ['ɑːkitaip] *n.* archétype *m.*

archiepiscopal [ɑːkii'piskəp(ə)l] *a.* archiépiscopal, -aux.

Archimedes [ɑːki'miːdiːz] *Pr.n.m. Gr.Hist:* Archimède; *Ph:* **Archimedes' principle,** le principe d'Archimède; **Archimedes' screw,** vis *f* d'Archimède.

archipelago, *pl.* **-o(e)s** [ɑːki'peləgou, -ouz] *n. Geog:* archipel *m.*

architect ['ɑːkitekt] *n.* architecte *m*; **naval a.,** ingénieur *m* des constructions navales, du génie maritime; *Lit:* **to be the a. of one's fortunes,** être l'artisan de sa fortune.

architectural [ɑːki'tektjərəl] *a.* architectural, -aux. **-ally** *adv.* au point de vue architecture.

architecture ['ɑːkitektjər] *n.* architecture *f.*

architrave ['ɑːkitreiv] *n.* **1.** *Arch:* architrave *f.* **2.** *Const:* encadrement *m* (d'une porte, d'une fenêtre).

archives ['ɑːkaivz] *n.pl.* archives *fpl.*

archivist ['ɑːkivist] *n.* archiviste *mf.*

archness ['ɑːtʃnis] *n.* espièglerie *f*, malice *f.*

archway ['ɑːtʃwei] *n.* passage voûté; porte cintrée, voûte *f* d'entrée; arcade *f.*

arctic ['ɑːktik] **1.** *a.* (territoire, cercle, etc.) arctique. **2.** *n.* **the A.,** l'Arctique *m.*

arc-weld [ɑːk'weld] *v.tr. Metalw:* souder à l'arc (électrique). **arc-welding** *n.* soudure *f* à l'arc.

ardent ['ɑːd(ə)nt] *a.* **1.** (*of heat, etc.*) ardent. **2.** (désir, amour) passionné. **-ly** *adv.* ardemment; avec ardeur.

ardour, *NAm:* **ardor** ['ɑːdər] *n.* ardeur *f.*

arduous ['ɑːdjuəs] *a.* (sentier, travail) ardu, pénible. **-ly** *adv.* péniblement.

arduousness ['ɑːdjuəsnis] *n.* difficulté *f*, dureté *f.*

are *see* BE.

area ['ɛəriə] *n.* **1.** (*a*) aire *f*, superficie *f* (d'un cercle, d'un champ, d'une pièce, etc.); (*b*) surface *f*; *Mec.E: etc:* **bearing a.,** surface de contact; *Av:* **wing a.,** surface d'ailes, des plans de sustentation; *Nau:* **sail a.,** surface de voilure; *Typ:* **type a.,** justification *f*; *Med: etc:* **the affected a.,** la partie atteinte; (*c*) *Civ.E: etc:* **hard surfaced a.,** aire en dur; *Av:* **landing, servicing, a.,** aire d'atterrissage, d'entretien; *Aut:* **parking a.,** parking *m*; (*on motorway*) **service a.,** relais *m* d'autoroute; (*in park*) **play a.,** aire de jeu; **dining a.,** coin *m* salle à manger; (*d*) *Opt:* **light, dark, a.,** plage lumineuse, sombre. **2.** (*a*) étendue *f* (de pays), territoire *m*, région *f*; zone *f*; périmètre *m* (d'influence, etc.); **mining a.,** région minière; **cotton (growing) a.,** région du coton; *Geog:* **drainage, catchment, a.,** aire de drainage; (*in town*) **residential a.,** quartier résidentiel; **industrial a.,** zone industrielle; **customs a.,** territoire douanier; **currency a.,** zone monétaire; **suburban a.,** zone suburbaine; **the Greater London a.,** l'agglomération londonienne; le grand Londres; (*b*) *Pol.Ec: etc:* **economic a.,** secteur *m* économique; **growth a.,** secteur de croissance; **problem a.,** domaine *m* problématique; **an a. of agreement,** un terrain d'entente; (*c*) *Mil: etc:* **forward a.,** zone de l'avant, zone avancée; **prohibited, restricted, a.,** zone prohibée; **a. bombing,** bombardement *m* sur zone; (*d*) *Cmptr:* **storage a.,** zone de mémoire; **input, output, a.,** zone d'entrée, de sortie; (*e*) *Rad:* **interference a., mush a.,** zone de brouillage; (*f*) *Anat:* **areas of the brain,** territoires cérébraux. **3.** *Const:* (*also NAm:* **areaway** ['ɛəriəwei]) cour *f* d'entrée en sous-sol (sur la rue); **a. steps,** escalier *m* de service (du sous-sol).

areca ['ærikə] *n. Bot:* **a. nut,** noix *f* d'arec *m*; **a. palm (tree),** aréquier *m.*

arena, *pl.* **-as** [ə'riːnə, -əz] *n.* **1.** (*a*) arène *f*; (*b*) champ *m* (d'une activité, etc.); **the political a.,** la scène politique.

aren't [ɑːnt] (*a*) = **are not;** (*b*) **a. I?** = **am I not?** *see* BE.

Argentina [ɑːdʒ(ə)n'tiːnə] *Pr.n. Geog:* Argentine *f.*

Argentine ['ɑːdʒəntain] *a.&n. Geog:* **the A. Republic,** *n.* **the A.,** la République Argentine, l'Argentine *f.*

Argentinian [ɑːdʒən'tiniən] **1.** *a. Geog:* argentin. **2.** *n.* Argentin, -ine.

argon ['ɑːgɔn] *n. Ch:* argon *m.*

Argonaut ['ɑːgənɔːt] *n.* **1.** *Gr.Myth:* Argonaute *m.* **2.** *Moll:* **a.,** voilier *m*, argonaute.

arguable ['ɑːgjuəbl] *a.* (opinion) discutable, soutenable, défendable. **-ably** *adv.* indubitablement; sans doute.

argue ['ɑːgju(ː)] **1.** *v.tr.* (*a*) discuter, débattre, (une question); (*b*) **to a. that,** soutenir, maintenir, que (qch. est impossible, etc.). **2.** *v.i.* (*a*) argumenter **(for, against, sth.,** en faveur de, contre, qch,); plaider **(for, against, sth.,** pour, contre, qch.); **all this argues in his favour,** tout ceci témoigne en sa faveur; (*b*) (i) discuter, raisonner **(with s.o. about sth.,** avec qn sur qch.); (ii) se disputer **(about sth.,** à propos de qch.); **to a. about politics,** discuter (de) politique; **he's always arguing,** c'est un argumentataire; **don't a.!** pas de discussion! **arguing** *n.* argumentation *f*; *F:* **and no a.!** pas de discussion!

argument ['ɑːgjumənt] *n.* **1.** argument *m* **(for, against,** en faveur de, contre); **to follow s.o.'s (line of) a.,** suivre le raisonnement de qn; **that is another a. for dismissing him,** c'est une raison de plus pour le congédier; **let us suppose for argument's sake that . . .,** supposons à titre d'exemple que . . .. **2.** (i) discussion *f*, débat *m*; (ii) dispute *f*; **to have an a. about sth.,** (i) discuter de, sur, qch.; (ii) se disputer à propos de qch.; **to get the best of an a.,** l'emporter dans une discussion; **to obey without a.,** obéir sans argument. **3.** *Lit:* argument (d'un ouvrage); sommaire *m.*

argumentative [ɑːgju'mentətiv] *a.* (*of pers.*) raisonneur; disposé à argumenter, à disputailler.

argy-bargy[1] ['ɑːdʒi'bɑːdʒi] *n. F:* chamaillerie *f.*

argy-bargy[2] *v.i. F:* argumenter, raisonner; disputailler.

aria ['ɑːriə) *n. Mus:* aria *f.*

Arian ['ɛəriən] *Rel.H:* **1.** *a.* arien. **2.** *n.* Arien, -ienne.

arid ['ærid] *a.* (terre, sujet) aride.

aridity [æ'riditi], **aridness** ['æridnis] *n.* aridité *f.*

Aries ['ɛəriːz] *Pr.n.Astr:* le Bélier.

aright [ə'rait] *adv. A: & Lit:* bien, juste.

arise [e'raiz] *v.i.* **(arose** [ə'rouz]; **arisen** [ə'riz(ə)n]) **1.** (*a*) *Lit:* s'élever; **a prophet arose,** un prophète surgit, se révéla; (*b*) *B: Ecc:* **to a. from the dead,** ressusciter (des morts). **2.** (*of thg*) (*a*) s'élever, surgir, survenir, se produire; **a storm arose,** il survint une tempête; **if complications a.,** s'il survient des complications; **if the need arises,** si besoin est; **the question has not yet arisen,** la question ne s'est pas encore posée; **should the occasion a. ...,** le cas échéant ...; (*b*) émaner, provenir, résulter **(from,** de); **obligations that a. from a clause,** obligations qui émanent d'une clause.

aristocracy [æris'tɔkrəsi] *n.* **1.** aristocratie *f.* **2.** (i) gouvernement *m,* (ii) état gouverné, par une aristocratie.

aristocrat ['æristəkræt, ə'ris-] *n.* aristocrate *mf.*

aristocratic [æristə'krætik] *a.* aristocratique. **-ally** *adv.* aristocratiquement.

Aristotelian [æristɔ'tiːliən] *a.* aristotélicien.

Aristotle ['æristɔtl] *Pr.n.m. Gr.Phil:* Aristote.

arithmetic [ə'riθmətik] *n.* arithmétique *f;* calcul *m;* **mental a.,** calcul mental, calcul de tête; **a. (book),** arithmétique.

arithmetic(al) [æriθ'metik(l)] *a.* arithmétique. **-ally** *adv.* arithmétiquement.

ark [ɑːk] *n.* **1.** arche *f;* **Noah's a.,** l'arche de Noé. **2. the A. of the Covenant,** l'Arche d'alliance.

arm[1] [ɑːm] *n.* **1.** (*a*) bras *m* (de personne, de vertébré, de brachiopode); **upper a.,** haut *m* du bras, arrière-bras *m inv;* **to carry a child in one's arms,** porter un enfant dans ses bras; **child, infant, in arms,** enfant *m* au berceau; **to carry sth. under one's a.,** porter qch. sous le bras; **to carry a basket over, on, one's a.,** porter un panier au bras; **to walk a. in a.,** marcher bras dessus bras dessous; **to receive s.o. with open arms,** recevoir qn à bras ouverts; **to keep s.o. at arms' length,** tenir qn à distance; (*b*) **the secular a.,** le bras séculier; (*c*) **a. of the law,** (i) l'autorité de la loi; (ii) *F:* représentant *m* de la loi. **2.** manche *f* (de robe, etc.); bras (de mer, d'un fleuve, de fauteuil, de levier); fléau *m* (de balance); bras, patte *f* (d'ancre); branche *f* (d'arbre, de tenailles); accoudoir *m* (de fauteuil); potence *f* (d'enseigne de boutique, etc.); *Nau:* **yard a.,** fusée *f,* bout *m,* de vergue; *Rec:* **(pick-up) a.,** bras de lecture.

arm[2] *n.* **1.** (*a*) *usu.pl.* armes *fpl;* **side arms,** armes blanches; **small arms,** armes portatives; **the arms race,** la course aux armements; **arms manufacturer,** armurier *m,* fabricant *m* d'armes; **arms trade,** commerce *m* des armes, d'armes; **call to arms,** appel *m* aux armes; **nation in arms,** nation *f* en armes; **to take up arms,** prendre les armes, s'armer **(against,** contre); **to rise up in arms,** se dresser en armes **(against s.o., sth.,** contre qn, qch.); *Fig:* **to be up in arms against s.o., about sth.,** être en révolte, en rébellion ouverte, contre qn, qch.; (*b*) *Mil:* **the profession of arms,** le métier, la carrière, des armes; le métier militaire; (*c*) *Mil:* (*branch*) arme; **the Fleet Air Arm,** l'aéronavale *f.* **2.** *Her:* **arms,** armoiries *fpl,* armes.

arm[3] **1.** *v.tr.* (*a*) armer (qn, un régiment, une place forte, etc.); **to a. oneself with an umbrella,** s'armer, se nantir, d'un parapluie; *Lit:* **to a. oneself with patience,** s'armer de patience; (*b*) armer (une bombe, une fusée, une torpille, une mine); (*c*) *Tchn:* armer (un aimant, une poutre, etc.); renforcer (une poutre, etc.). **2.** *v.i.* s'armer **(against s.o.,** contre qn); prendre les armes. **armed** *a.* **1.** armé **(with a gun,** d'un fusil); **a. to the teeth,** armé jusqu'aux dents; **a. man,** homme armé; *Mil:* **a. forces,** forces armées. **2.** (*a*) **a. conflict,** conflit armé; **a. warfare,** guerre *f* par les armes; **to offer a. resistance,** résister par les armes, se défendre les armes à la main; (*b*) (neutralité, paix) armée; **a. truce,** suspension *f* d'armes. **3.** (*of bomb, fuse, torpedo, mine, etc.*) armé. **4.** *Tchn:* (*of beam, magnet, etc.*) armé.

armada [ɑː'mɑːdə] *n.* (*a*) *Hist:* armada *f;* **the invincible A.,** l'Invincible Armada; (*b*) grande flotte de guerre; (*c*) **air a.,** flotte aérienne.

armadillo [ɑːmə'dilou] *n.* **1.** *Z:* tatou *m;* **giant a.,** tatou géant. **2.** *Crust:* armadille *m or f.*

armament ['ɑːməmənt] *n.* **1.** armement *m* (d'une troupe, etc.). **2.** (*equipment*) armement; (*of ship*) artillerie *f,* munitions *fpl* de guerre; **naval armaments,** armements navals. **3.** (*force*) forces *fpl;* armée *f,* flotte navale.

armature ['ɑːmətjər] *n.* **1.** *Biol: etc:* armure *f.* **2.** *El:* induit *m* (d'un condensateur, d'une dynamo); armature *f* (d'une magnéto, d'une petite dynamo). **3.** *Const:* armature (d'un édifice en ciment, etc.).

armband ['ɑːmbænd] *n.* brassard *m* (de deuil).

armchair ['ɑːmtʃɛər] *n.* fauteuil *m;* **a. strategist, politician,** stratège *m,* politicien *m,* en chambre.

Armenia [ɑː'miːniə] *Pr.n. Geog:* Arménie *f.*

Armenian [ɑː'miːniən] **1.** *a.* arménien. **2.** *n.* (*a*) Arménien, -ienne; (*b*) *Ling:* arménien *m.*

armful ['ɑːmful] *n.* brassée *f;* **to bring armfuls of flowers, flowers by the a.,** apporter des fleurs à pleins bras, plein les bras.

armhole ['ɑːmhoul] *n.* emmanchure *f.*

armistice ['ɑːmistis] *n.* armistice *m;* **A. day,** l'anniversaire *m* de l'Armistice (de 1918).

armless ['ɑːmlis] *a.* sans bras.

armlet ['ɑːmlit] *n.* **1.** bracelet (porté au-dessus du coude). **2.** brassard *m.*

armorial [ɑː'mɔːriəl] *a.* armorial, -aux; héraldique; **a. bearings,** armoiries *fpl.*

armory ['ɑːməri] *n.* **1.** (science *f* du) blason *m;* l'art *m* héraldique. **2.** *NAm:* = ARMOURY.

armour[1], *NAm:* **armor**[1] ['ɑːmər] *n.* **1.** *Hist:* armure *f* (de chevalier, etc.); **suit of a.,** armure complète; **in full a.,** armé de pied en cap. **2.** (*a*) *N.Arch:* cuirasse *f,* cuirassement *m,* blindage *m* (d'un bâtiment); *Mil:* blindage (d'un véhicule, d'un char de combat, etc.); **a.-plated,** cuirassé; blindé; **a.-piercing,** (obus) perforant, de rupture; (*b*) *Mil: coll.* l'arme blindée, les blindés *mpl.* **3.** *Tp:* armure *f,* armature *f* (de câble); *El:* blindage (d'un transformateur, etc.).

armour[2], *NAm:* **armor**[2] *v.tr.* **1.** cuirasser (un navire); blinder (un train, etc.). **2.** *El:* armer (un câble); blinder (un transformateur). **armoured,** *NAm:* **armored** *a.* **1.** *Navy:* (croiseur, pont) cuirassé; *Mil:* (véhicule, train) blindé; **a. troops,** *U.S:* **a. corps,** les blindés *mpl;* **a. car,** (i) engin blindé de reconnaissance; (ii) voiture blindée (de police); (iii) fourgon *m* bancaire. **2.** *Tchn: Tp:* (câble, tuyau) armé; *El:* (transformateur) blindé.

armourer, *NAm:* **armorer** ['ɑːmərər] *n. Ind: Mil: Navy:* armurier *m.*

armoury, *NAm:* **armory** ['ɑːməri] *n.* **1.** (*a*) magasin *m* d'armes; (*in barracks*) armurerie *f;* (*b*) (*in museum, etc.*) salle *f* d'armes. **2.** *U.S:* (*a*) fabrique *f* d'armes; (*b*) (*workshop*) armurerie.

armpit ['ɑːmpit] *n. Anat:* aisselle *f.*

armrest [ˈɑːmrest] *n. Aut: etc:* accoudoir *m*, appuie-bras *m*.

army [ˈɑːmi] *n.* **1.** (*a*) armée *f* (de terre); **to be in the a.,** être dans l'armée, au régiment; être soldat, militaire; **to go into, join, the a.,** (i) s'engager, s'enrôler, se faire soldat; (ii) (*conscription*) partir au régiment, entrer au service; **standing, regular, a.,** armée permanente, active; **professional a.,** armée de métier; **a. corps,** corps *m* d'armée; **A. list,** annuaire *m* militaire; cadres *mpl* de l'armée; **a. lorry,** camion *m* militaire; (*b*) **the Salvation A.,** l'Armée du Salut. **2.** (*a*) armée (de fourmis, sauterelles, etc.); (*b*) foule *f*, multitude *f* (d'hommes, etc.); armée (de fonctionnaires, de serviteurs). **3.** *NAm: Ent:* **a. worm,** ver *m* militaire.

arnica [ˈɑːnikə] *n.* **1.** *Bot:* arnica *f*, arnique *f*. **2.** *Pharm:* (teinture *f* d')arnica.

aroma [əˈroumə] *n.* arôme *m*.

aromatic [ærouˈmætik] **1.** *a.* (*a*) aromatique; (parfum) balsamique; (*b*) *Ch:* (série, composé) aromatique. **2.** *n.* (*a*) aromate *m*; (*b*) *Ch:* **aromatics,** carbures *mpl* aromatiques, à noyau.

around [əˈraund] **1.** *adv.* (*a*) autour, à l'entour; **all a.,** tout autour, de tous côtés; **the woods (all) a.,** les bois d'alentour; (*b*) **to wander a.,** rôder; (*c*) *F:* **he's now able to get a. again,** il est de nouveau sur pied; (*d*) **this product has been a. for a long time,** ce produit est en circulation depuis longtemps; *F:* **she's been a.,** elle est avertie. **2.** *prep.* (*a*) autour de; **his arms were a. her neck,** il avait les bras autour de son cou; **the people a. him,** les gens qui l'entourent; (*b*) **to travel a. the country,** parcourir le pays; (*c*) environ; **at a. four o'clock,** sur les quatre heures.

arouse [əˈrauz] *v.tr.* **1.** (*a*) réveiller, éveiller (qn); **to a. s.o. from his sleep,** tirer qn de son sommeil; (*b*) secouer (qn) (de sa paresse, de sa torpeur); stimuler (qn). **2.** exciter, éveiller (un sentiment); soulever (des passions); piquer, éveiller, provoquer (la jalousie); chatouiller (la curiosité); éveiller (des soupçons).

arpeggio [ɑːˈpedʒiou] *n. Mus:* arpège *m*.

arrack [ˈærək] *n. Dist:* arac(k) *m*.

arraign [əˈrein] *v.tr.* **1.** (*a*) *Jur:* poursuivre (qn) en justice; traduire (qn) devant un tribunal; (*b*) accuser, mettre en cause. **2.** *Lit:* attaquer (qn, une opinion).

arraignment [əˈreinmənt] *n. Jur:* (*a*) mise *f* en accusation; mise en jugement; (*b*) acte *m* d'accusation.

arrange [əˈrein(d)ʒ] *v.tr.* **1.** (*a*) disposer, mettre en ordre, ranger, arranger (les meubles, etc.); ordonner (un cortège, etc.); disposer (des fleurs); **to a. books in alphabetical order,** ranger des livres par ordre alphabétique; (*b*) *Mus:* **piece arranged for the piano,** morceau adapté, arrangé, pour piano. **2.** arranger (un mariage, etc.); organiser (un concert, etc.); **to a. to do sth.,** (i) s'arranger, prendre ses dispositions, pour faire qch.; (ii) s'arranger avec qn pour faire qch.; convenir de faire qch.; **to a. for sth. to be done,** prendre des dispositions, des mesures, pour que qch. se fasse; **everything is arranged,** tout est en ordre; **it was arranged that . . .,** il fut convenu que . . .; **try to a. it,** tâchez d'arranger la chose; **a. it among yourselves,** arrangez cela entre vous; entendez-vous là-dessus; **the meeting arranged for tomorrow,** la réunion prévue pour demain. **3.** accommoder, ajuster, arranger (un différend).

arrangement [əˈrein(d)ʒmənt] *n.* **1.** (*a*) arrangement *m*, disposition *f*, aménagement *m*, mise *f* en ordre (**of,** de); **to make arrangements for sth., to do sth., for sth. to be done,** prendre des dispositions, des mesures, faire des préparatifs, pour qch., pour faire qch., pour que qch. se fasse; **to make arrangements for a journey,** faire ses préparatifs pour un voyage; (*b*) **flower a.,** (i) l'art *m* de disposer les fleurs; (ii) composition florale; (*c*) *Mus:* **a. for piano,** arrangement, adaptation *f*, pour piano. **2.** accommodement *m* (d'un différend); accord *m*, entente *f*; *Jur:* transaction *f*; *Com: etc:* **to make an a., to come to an a., with s.o.,** faire un arrangement, prendre un arrangement, avec qn; **to come to an a. with one's creditors,** parvenir à un accord avec ses créanciers; **price by a.,** prix à débattre.

arranger [əˈrein(d)ʒər] *n. esp. Mus:* arrangeur, -euse.

arrant [ˈærənt] *a.* insigne; (menteur, etc.) achevé.

array¹ [əˈrei] *n.* **1.** (*a*) rangs *mpl*; **in close a.,** en rangs serrés; **in battle a.,** en ordre de bataille; (*b*) étalage *m*; **an imposing a. of tools,** un imposant déploiement d'outils; (*c*) *Mth:* rangée *f*, tableau *m* (de chiffres). **2.** *Lit:* parure *f*, appareil *m*; **in rich a.,** paré de ses plus beaux atours.

array² *v.tr.* **1.** ranger, mettre en ordre; disposer, déployer (des troupes, etc.) (en ordre de bataille). **2.** *Lit:* revêtir, orner, parer (**s.o. in sth.,** qn de qch.).

arrears [əˈriəz] *n.pl.* **1.** arriéré *m*, arrérages *mpl*; **rent a.,** arriéré de loyer; **work in a.,** travail *m* en retard; **let one's rent fall into a.,** être en retard pour payer son loyer.

arrest¹ [əˈrest] *n.* **1.** (*a*) arrestation *f* (d'un malfaiteur); *Jur:* prise *f* de corps; **under a.,** en état d'arrestation; **warrant of a., a. warrant,** mandat *m* d'arrêt; (*b*) *Mil: Navy:* arrêts *mpl*; **open a.,** arrêts simples; **close a.,** arrêts forcés, de rigueur; **house a.,** (i) *Mil: Navy:* arrêts à la chambre; (ii) *Pol: etc:* résidence surveillée; **under a.,** aux arrêts. **2.** (*a*) arrêt *m*, suspension *f* (d'un mouvement, du progrès, etc.); **cardiac a.,** arrêt du cœur; (*b*) *Jur:* **a. of judgment,** sursis *m*, surséance *f*, à l'exécution d'un jugement.

arrest² *v.tr.* **1.** (*a*) arrêter (le mouvement, le progrès, de qn, de qch.); **arrested growth, development (of s.o., of sth.),** arrêt *m* dans la croissance (de qn), dans le développement (de qch.); (*b*) *Jur:* **to a. judgment,** suspendre l'exécution d'un jugement. **2.** (*a*) arrêter (un malfaiteur); mettre (qn) en état d'arrestation; appréhender (qn) au corps; (*b*) *Scot: & Nau:* saisir (des biens mobiliers, un navire). **3.** arrêter, fixer, retenir (l'attention, les regards). **arresting 1.** *a.* (spectacle, etc.) frappant; qui arrête l'attention. **2.** *n.* (*a*) *Jur:* arrestation *f*; prise *f*, appréhension *f*, de corps; (*b*) *Mec.E: etc:* arrêt *m*; **a. device,** dispositif *m* d'arrêt.

arrester [əˈrestər] **1.** (*a*) celui qui arrête (un malfaiteur); (*b*) *Scot: Jur:* saisissant *m* (de biens mobiliers). **2.** *Tchn:* (*a*) intercepteur *m*, séparateur *m*; **lightning a.,** parafoudre *m*; **spark a.,** pare-étincelles *m inv*; (*b*) *Av:* **a. gear,** (*on runway*) dispositif *m* d'arrêt; (*on carrier deck*) dispositif d'appontage.

arris [ˈæris] *n.* arête vive (d'un prisme, d'une cannelure).

arrival [əˈraiv(ə)l] *n.* **1.** (*a*) arrivée *f*; **on a.,** à l'arrivée (de qn, de qch.); *Post:* **to await a.,** ne pas faire suivre; (*b*) *Com:* arrivage *m* (de marchandises); (*c*) *Nau:* entrée *f* (d'un navire); **port of a.,** port *m* d'arrivée; (*d*) *Trans:* débarquement *m* (de voyageurs); **on a.,** au débarquement; **arrivals and departures,** arrivées et départs. **2.** (*pers.*) arrivant, -ante; **a new a.,** (i) un nouveau venu, une nouvelle venue; (ii) un nouveau-né; **late arrivals,** retardataires *mpl*.

arrive [əˈraiv] *v.i.* **1.** (*a*) arriver (**at, in,** à, dans); **he has just arrived,** il arrive à l'instant; **he is expected to a. next week,** on attend son arrivée pour la semaine prochaine; **as soon as he arrived,** dès son arrivée; **to a. on the scene, to a. unexpectedly,** survenir; (*b*) (*of day, moment, new baby*) arriver; (*c*) **to a. at the age of sixty,** atteindre, parvenir à, arriver à, l'âge de soixante ans; **to a. at a decision,** arriver, en venir, aboutir, à une décision; **to a. at a price,** calculer, fixer, un prix; convenir d'un prix. **2.** réussir, arriver.

arrogance ['ærəgəns] *n.* arrogance *f.*

arrogant ['ærəgənt] *a.* arrogant. **-ly** *adv.* avec arrogance.

arrogate ['ærougeit] *v.tr. Lit: & Jur:* **1. to a. sth. to oneself,** s'arroger qch. **2.** attribuer injustement (qch.) **(to s.o.,** à qn).

arrow¹ ['ærou] *n.* **1.** (*a*) flèche *f*; **to shoot, let fly, an a.,** lancer, décocher, une flèche; **to fly straight as an a.,** voler droit comme une flèche; **as swift as an a.,** vif comme l'éclair; *Arch:* **a. slit,** arch(i)ère *f*; (*b*) flèche (indicatrice, de direction). **2.** *Surv:* fiche *f* (d'arpenteur); zéro *m* (d'un vernier).

arrow² *v.tr.* marquer (qch.) d'une flèche; flécher (une route, une direction).

arrowhead ['ærouhed] *n.* **1.** tête *f*, fer *m*, pointe *f*, de flèche. **2.** flèche (indicatrice, de direction). **3.** *Bot:* fléchière *f*, sagittaire *f*, flèche *f* d'eau.

arrowroot ['ærouru:t] *n.* **1.** *Bot:* marante *f.* **2.** *Cu:* arrowroot *m.*

arse¹ [ɑ:s] *n. P:* (*not in polite use*) cul *m*, derrière *m*; **a. over tip,** à la renverse; cul par-dessus tête.

arse² *v.i. P:* (*not in polite use*) **to a. about,** faire l'imbécile, l'idiot.

arsenal ['ɑ:sən(ə)l] *n.* arsenal *m*, -aux.

arsenic ['ɑ:s(ə)nik] *n.* arsenic *m.*

arson ['ɑ:s(ə)n] *n.* incendie *m* volontaire; *Jur:* crime *m* d'incendie; **to commit a.,** provoquer (volontairement) un incendie.

arsonist ['ɑ:sənist] *n.* incendiaire *mf.*

art¹ [ɑ:t] *n.* **1.** art *m*; (*a*) **the (fine) arts,** les beaux-arts *mpl.*; **a. school,** école *f* des beaux-arts; **a. student,** élève *mf*, étudiant, -ante, d'une école des beaux-arts; **a. exhibition,** exposition *f* d'art; **a. gallery,** galerie *f*; **work of a.,** œuvre *m* d'art; **a. for art's sake,** l'art pour l'art; (*b*) *Sch:* **faculty of arts,** faculté des lettres; **arts student,** étudiant, -ante, en lettres; **bachelor of arts** = licencié, -ée, ès lettres; (*c*) **arts and crafts,** (i) artisanat *m* d'expression; (ii) *Sch:* travaux manuels; (*d*) **the a. of war,** l'art militaire; l'art de la guerre; **the black a.,** la magie noire; **the noble a.,** le noble art, la boxe. **2.** artifice *m*; stratagème *m*; ruse *f.*

art² *A: & B: see* BE; **thou a. good,** tu es bon.

artefact ['ɑ:tifækt] *n.* produit œuvré; *Archeol:* objet façonné.

arterial [ɑ:'tiəriəl] *a.* **1.** *Anat: Med: etc:* (sang, etc.) artériel. **2. a. road,** grande voie de communication.

arteriosclerosis [ɑ:'tiəriousklə'rousis] *n.* artériosclérose *f.*

artery ['ɑ:təri] *n.* **1.** *Anat:* artère *f.* **2. main arteries,** grandes voies de communication, grandes artères.

artesian [ɑ:'ti:ziən, -'ti:ʒən] *a.* **a. well,** puits artésien.

artful ['ɑ:tful] *a.* **1.** (*of pers.*) rusé, astucieux; malin, -igne; **a. as a monkey,** malin comme un singe. **2.** (*of thg*) ingénieux; **an a. dodge,** un truc ingénieux. **-fully** *adv.* astucieusement.

artfulness ['ɑ:tfulnis] *n.* **1.** astuce *f* (de qn). **2.** ingéniosité *f* (de qch.).

arthritic [ɑ:'θritik] *a. & n. Med:* arthritique (*mf*).

arthritis [ɑ:'θraitis] *n. Med:* arthrite *f*; **rheumatoid a.,** rhumatisme articulaire.

arthropod ['ɑ:θroupɔd] *n. Z:* arthropode *m.*

arthrosis [ɑ:'θrousis] *n. Med:* arthrose *f.*

Arthurian [ɑ:'θjuəriən] *a. Lit. Hist:* (cycle, etc.) d'Arthur; (roman) arthurien.

artichoke ['ɑ:titʃouk] *n.* **1. globe a.,** artichaut *m*; *Cu:* **a. hearts,** fonds *mpl*, cœurs *mpl*, d'artichaut. **2. Jerusalem a.,** topinambour *m.*

article¹ ['ɑ:tikl] *n.* **1.** (*a*) *Com: Jur:* article *m*, clause *f* (d'une convention, d'un traité); **articles of apprenticeship,** contrat *m* d'apprentissage; **articles of war,** *Mil:* code *m* (de justice) militaire; *Navy:* code de justice maritime; *Nau:* **ship's articles,** (i) contrat *m* d'engagement, conditions *fpl* d'embarquement; (ii) rôle *m* de l'équipage; (*b*) **a. of faith,** article de foi; (*c*) *Jur:* chef *m* d'accusation. **2.** *Journ: etc:* article (de journal, de revue, d'encyclopédie); **feature a.,** article d'intérêt général; **leading a.,** éditorial *m*, -aux. **3.** article, objet *m*; **a. of clothing,** vêtement *m*; **toilet articles,** produits *mpl* de toilette. **4.** *Gram:* **definite, indefinite, a.,** article défini, indéfini.

article² *v.tr.* **to a. s.o. to an attorney, an architect,** placer qn (comme élève) chez un avoué, un architecte; **articled clerk,** clerc d'avoué lié par un contrat d'apprentissage.

articulate¹ [ɑ:'tikjulət] **1.** *a. & n. Z:* articulé (*m*). **2.** *a.* **a. speech,** (i) langage articulé; (ii) langage net, distinct; (*of pers.*) **to be a.,** s'exprimer facilement, avec facilité. **-ly** *adv.* (parler) (i) d'une voix articulée, (ii) distinctement, nettement, (iii) avec facilité.

articulate² [ɑ:'tikjuleit] *v.tr. & i.* **1.** *Anat:* articuler (un squelette, etc.); (*passive*) s'articuler; **bone that articulates, is articulated, with another,** os qui s'articule, est articulé, avec un autre. **2.** articuler (un mot, etc.); **he doesn't a. his words,** son énonciation est mauvaise. **articulated** *a. Nat.Hist: Ling: etc:* articulé; *Veh:* **a. vehicle,** semi-remorque *f*, *pl.* semi-remorques.

articulateness [ɑ:'tikjulətnis] *n.* **1.** caractère articulé (d'un langage). **2.** articulation nette; netteté *f* d'énonciation. **3.** facilité *f* d'expression.

articulation [ɑ:tikju'leiʃ(ə)n] *n. Nat.Hist: Mec.E: Ling: etc:* articulation *f*; *Ling:* **faulty a.,** défaut *m* de prononciation.

artifact ['ɑ:tifækt] *n.* = ARTEFACT.

artifice ['ɑ:tifis] *n.* **1.** artifice *m*, ruse *f*; combinaison *f*; **a. of war,** ruse de guerre, artifice de guerre; stratagème *m.* **2.** art *m*, habileté *f*, adresse *f.*

artificial [ɑ:ti'fiʃ(ə)l] *a.* **1.** artificiel; **a. wood,** similibois *m*; **a. respiration,** respiration artificielle; **a. limb,** prothèse *f* orthopédique; **a. manure,** engrais *mpl* chimiques; *Astr: etc:* **a. horizon,** horizon artificiel; *Cmptr:* **a. language,** langage artificiel. **2.** (sourire, etc.) affecté; (style) factice, recherché; **she is very a.,** elle manque de naturel. **-ally** *adv.* artificiellement.

artificiality [ɑ:tifiʃi'æliti] **1.** artificialité *f*; nature artificielle (d'un produit, etc.) **2.** caractère artificiel, manque *m* de naturel (d'une personne).

artillery [ɑ:'tiləri] *n.* artillerie *f*; **field a.,** (i) *Mil:* artillerie de campagne; (ii) *Navy:* artillerie de débarquement; **heavy, light, a.,** artillerie lourde, légère; **naval a.,** artillerie navale; **anti-aircraft, anti-tank, a.,** artillerie anti-aérienne, anti-chars; **a. fire,** tir *m* d'artillerie.

artilleryman, *pl.* **-men** [ɑ:'tilərimən, -men] *n.m.* artilleur *m.*

artisan [ɑ:ti'zæn] *n.* artisan *m*, ouvrier *m.*

artist ['ɑ:tist] *n.* (*a*) artiste *mf* (peintre); **he is an a.,** il est artiste, il est peintre; **pavement a.,** barbouilleur, -euse, de trottoir; (*b*) **this dancer is really an a.,** ce danseur est un vrai artiste.

artiste [ɑ:'ti:st] *n. Th:* artiste *mf.*

artistic [ɑ:'tistik] *a.* (arrangement) artistique; (style, goût, tempérament) artiste; (toilette) de bon goût. **-ally** *adv.* (*a*) artistement, avec art, artistiquement; (*b*) du point de vue artistique.

artistry ['ɑ:tistri] *n.* art *m* (avec lequel qch. a été ordonné, truqué, etc.).

artless ['ɑ:tlis] *a.* **1.** sans art, dénué d'art. **2.** naturel, simple; sans artifice. **3.** naïf, ingénu. **-ly** *adv.* **1.** sans art. **2.** naturellement, simplement; sans artifice. **3.** naïvement, ingénument.

artlessness ['ɑ:tlisnis] *n.* **1.** naturel *m*, simplicité *f.* **2.** naïveté *f*, ingénuité *f.*

art nouveau ['ɑ:nu:'vou] *a. & n. Art:* modern style (*m*).

arty ['ɑːti] *a. Pej:* (mobilier, etc.) qui affiche des goûts artistiques; prétentieux.
arty-crafty ['ɑːti'krɑːfti] *a. F:* bohême, artiste.
arum ['ɛərəm] *n. Bot:* arum *m*; **a. lily,** calla *f.*
Aryan ['ɛəriən] *Ethn: Ling: etc:* **1.** *a.* aryen. **2.** *n.* Aryen, -enne.
as [əz, *stressed* æz] **I.** *adv.* **1.** aussi, si; **I am as tall as you,** je suis aussi grand que vous; **I can do that as well as you,** je peux faire cela (tout) aussi bien que vous; **is it as high as that?** est-ce si haut que ça? *F:* **he was as deaf as a post,** il était sourd comme un pot. **2. I worked as hard as I could,** j'ai travaillé tant que j'ai pu; **as much for your sake as for mine,** tant pour vous que pour moi; **as soon, as much, as possible,** aussitôt, autant, que possible. **3. as for that, as to that,** quant à cela, pour cela; **as for you,** quant à vous; **to question s.o. as to his motives, interroger qn** sur ses motifs. **II.** *conj. & adv.* **1.** (*degree*) (*a*) que; **you are as tall as he is,** vous êtes aussi grand que lui; **I came down as fast as I could,** je suis descendu aussi vite que possible; **you are not as, not so, tall as he is,** vous n'êtes pas si, aussi, grand que lui; **he's not such a fool as he looks,** il n'est pas si bête qu'il en a l'air; **a house twice as large as this,** une maison deux fois plus grande que celle-ci; **she was as good as she was pretty,** elle était aussi sage que jolie; **to be as good as one's word,** tenir ses promesses; **by day as well as by night,** le jour comme la nuit, de jour comme de nuit; (*b*) (*in similes*) comme; **as pale as death,** pâle comme un mort; **as white as a sheet,** blanc comme un linge; **it's as easy as anything,** c'est simple comme bonjour; c'est facile comme tout. **2.** (*a*) (*concessive*) **ignorant as he is,** tout ignorant qu'il est; **much as I like him,** quelle que soit mon affection pour lui; **be that as it may,** quoi qu'il en soit; (*b*) **covered with dust as he was, he didn't want to come in,** couvert qu'il était de poussière, il ne voulait pas entrer. **3.** (*manner*) (*a*) comme; **do as you like,** faites comme vous voulez, comme vous voudrez; **it happened as I told you,** cela s'est passé comme je vous l'ai dit; **as often happens,** comme il arrive souvent; ainsi qu'il arrive souvent; **leave it as it is,** laissez-le tel quel, tel qu'il est; **as it is, we must . . .,** les choses étant ainsi, comme il en est, il nous faut . . .; *Mil: Gym:* **as you were!** revenez! au temps! (*b*) **as a man lives, so he dies,** comme on a vécu, ainsi l'on meurt; (*c*) **they rose as one man,** ils se levèrent comme un seul homme; (*d*) (*introducing a complement*) **to consider s.o. as a friend,** considérer qn comme un ami; **to treat s.o. as a stranger,** traiter qn en étranger; **to recognize s.o. as one's son,** reconnaître qn pour son fils; **he was often ill as a child,** enfant il fut souvent malade; il fut souvent malade dans son enfance; **to use sth. as a flag,** se servir de qch. comme drapeau, en guise de drapeau; **to send sth. as a present,** envoyer qch. en, comme, cadeau; *Th:* **X as Hamlet,** X dans le rôle de Hamlet; **to act as interpreter,** servir d'interprète; **I acted in my capacity as a magistrate,** j'ai agi en ma qualité de magistrat; **to be dressed as a boy,** être habillé(e) en garçon; **as a very old friend of your father's,** en tant que vieil ami de votre père; **my rights as a father,** mes droits de père; **as one doctor to another,** soit dit entre médecins; **as a revenge for . . .,** pour se venger de . . .. **4.** (*time*) (*a*) **as I was opening the door,** comme j'ouvrais la porte; au moment où j'ouvrais la porte; **he went out (just) as I came in,** il est sorti comme, au moment (même) où, j'entrais; **one day as I was sitting . . .,** un jour que j'étais assis . . .; (*b*) **he drew back as I advanced,** à mesure que j'avançais, il reculait; **as and when required,** à discrétion; **as and when I want,** à mon bon plaisir. **5.** (*reason*) **as you are not ready, we cannot go,** comme vous n'êtes pas prêt, nous ne pouvons pas partir; **as I am going that way, I shall fetch them,** puisque j'y passe, je les rapporterai. **6.** (*result*) **he is not so foolish as to believe it,** il n'est pas assez stupide pour le croire; **put on your gloves so as to be ready,** mettez vos gants pour être prêt, de manière à être prêt. **7. mother is well, as are the children,** maman va bien, de même que les enfants. **III.** *rel.pron.* **beasts of prey, (such) as the lion or tiger,** les bêtes fauves, telles que, comme, le lion ou le tigre; **he was a foreigner, as they noticed from his pronunciation,** il était étranger, ce qui se remarquait à sa prononciation.
asbestos [æz'bestəs] *n. Miner:* amiante *m.*
asbestosis [æzbes'tousis] *n. Med:* asbestose *f.*
ascend [ə'send] **1.** *v.i.* monter; **the balloon was ascending,** le ballon montait; *Ecc:* **He ascended into Heaven,** Il monta aux Cieux. **2.** *v.tr.* (*a*) monter sur (le trône); (*b*) remonter (un fleuve). **ascending** *a.* **1.** *Astr: Mth: etc:* ascendant; **a. series,** progression croissante; **in a. order,** en ordre croissant; *Mus:* **a. scale,** gamme ascendante, montante. **2.** (*a*) *Meteor:* (courant) ascendant; (*b*) **steeply a. path,** sentier *m* raide; (*c*) *Bot:* (tige) montante. **3.** *Jur:* **a. line,** ascendance *f*; ligne ascendante (de parenté).
ascendancy, -ency [ə'sendənsi] *n. Lit:* ascendant *m* (**over s.o.,** sur qn); **to gain the a. over s.o.,** prendre de l'ascendant sur qn.
ascendant, -ent [ə'sendənt] **1.** *a.* (*a*) *Astrol: Mth: etc:* ascendant; **a. star,** astre ascendant; (*b*) *Bot:* (tige) montante. **2.** *n.* (*a*) *Astrol:* ascendant *m*; **to be in the a.,** (i) être à l'ascendant; (ii) *Fig:* avoir le dessus, s'affirmer; **his star is in the a.,** son étoile est à l'ascendant; son étoile grandit; (*b*) *Jur:* ascendant; **our ascendants and our descendants,** nos ascendants et nos descendants.
ascension [ə'senʃ(ə)n] **1.** *n.* ascension *f*; *esp. Ecc:* **A. Day,** jour *m*, fête *f*, de l'Ascension. **2.** *Pr.n. Geog:* **A. (Island),** (l'île *f* de l')Ascension.
ascent [ə'sent] *n.* **1.** (*a*) ascension *f* (d'une montagne); **first a.,** première *f*; **balloon a.,** ascension en ballon; **to make an a.,** faire une ascension; (*b*) *Fig:* **the a. of Napoleon,** l'ascension, l'essor *m*, de Napoléon; (*c*) montée *f*, remontée *f* (d'un piston, etc.). **2.** montée, pente *f*; **steep a.,** montée raide. **3.** *Jur:* **line of a.,** ascendance *f.*
ascertain [æsə'tein] *v.tr.* constater (un fait); s'assurer, s'informer, de (la vérité de qch.); se rendre compte de (sa position); **to a. sth. from s.o.,** s'informer de qch. auprès de qn; **to a. that all danger is over,** s'assurer qu'il n'y a plus de danger.
ascertainment [æsə'teinmənt] *n.* **1.** constatation *f* (d'un fait). **2.** vérification *f.*
ascetic [ə'setik] **1.** *a.* (vie, etc.) ascétique. **2.** *n.* ascète *mf*, ascétique *mf.* **-ally** *adv.* ascétiquement; (vivre) en ascète.
asceticism [ə'setisizm] *n.* ascétisme *m*; ascétique *f.*
ascorbic [əs'kɔːbik] *a.* (acide, etc.) ascorbique.
ascribable [ə'skraibəbl] *a.* attribuable, imputable (**to,** à).
ascribe [ə'skraib] *v.tr.* **1.** attribuer, imputer (**to,** à). **2. to a. a characteristic to s.o., a meaning to a word,** attribuer, prêter, un trait à qn, un sens à un mot.
ascription [ə'skripʃ(ə)n] *n.* attribution *f*, imputation *f* (**of sth. to sth.,** de qch. à qch.).
asdic ['æzdik] *n. Nav:* asdic *m.*
asepsis [ei'sepsis] *n. Med:* asepsie *f.*
aseptic [ei'septik] *a. & n. Med:* aseptique (*m*).
asexual [ei'seksjuəl] *a. Biol:* asexué, asexuel; *Bot:* (fleur) neutre; **a. reproduction,** reproduction asexuée.
ash[1] [æʃ] *n. Bot:* **a. (tree),** frêne *m*; **mountain a.,** sorbier commun, sauvage, des oiseaux, des oiseleurs.
ash[2] *n.* **1.** (*a*) cendre(s) *f* (*pl*); **cigar a.,** cendre de cigare; **to reduce, burn, sth. to ashes,** réduire qch. en

cendres; **volcanic a.,** cendres volcaniques; **a. cloud,** nuée *f* de cendres (au-dessus d'un volcan); *Lit:* **to rake over the ashes of the past,** tisonner les cendres du passé; **to rise from the ashes,** renaître de ses cendres; *Ecc:* **A. Wednesday,** le mercredi des Cendres; (*b*) *Mch: etc:* **ashes,** escarbilles *fpl*; **a. heap,** crassier *m*; (*c*) *a. & n.* (*colour*) cendré (*m*), gris cendré (*m*) *inv*. **2. ashes,** (*a*) cendres (des morts); dépouille mortelle; (*b*) *Cr:* **the Ashes,** le trophée que les équipes anglaises et australiennes se disputent.

ashamed [ə'ʃeimd] *a.* **1.** honteux, confus; **to be a. of s.o., of sth.,** avoir honte de qn, de qch.; **I am a. of you,** vous me faites honte; **to feel a.,** être couvert de confusion; **you make me feel a.,** (i) vous me rendez confus; (ii) vous me faites honte; **I am a. to say that . . .,** j'avoue à ma confusion que . . .; **you ought to be a. of yourself,** vous devriez avoir honte, être honteux; **there is nothing to be a. of,** il n'y a pas de quoi avoir honte. **2. a. to beg,** trop fier pour mendier.

ash-blond(e) ['æʃ'blond] *a.* blond cendré *inv*; *n.* **she's an a. -b.,** elle a les cheveux blond cendré.

ashcan ['æʃkæn] *n. NAm:* boîte *f* à ordures; poubelle *f*.

ashen[1] ['æʃn] *a.* de frêne, en frêne.

ashen[2] *a. Lit:* **1.** (pluie, etc.) de cendres. **2.** (*of colour*) cendré; (*of face*) pâle comme la mort; **his face turned a.,** il devint blême; son visage blémit.

ashlar ['æʃlər] *n. Const: Arch:* (*a*) pierre *f* de taille; (*b*) parements *mpl*, revêtement *m* (des murs d'un édifice).

ashore [ə'ʃɔːr] *adv. Nau:* **1.** à terre; **to be a.,** être à terre; **to go a.,** aller, descendre, à terre; débarquer; **to set, put, s.o. a.,** débarquer qn. **2.** (*of ship*) échoué; **to be driven a.,** être jeté à la côte; **to run a.,** s'échouer; faire côte.

ashpan ['æʃpæn] *n.* cendrier *m* (de poêle); garde-cendres *m inv*.

ashtray ['æʃtrei] *n.* cendrier *m*.

ashy ['æʃi] *a.* **1.** cendreux, couvert de cendres. **2.** cendré, couleur de la cendre.

Asia ['eiʃə] *Pr.n. Geog:* Asie *f*; **A. Minor,** Asie Mineure.

Asian ['eiʃ(ə)n] **1.** *a.* asiatique, asiate; *Med:* **A. flu,** grippe *f* asiatique. **2.** *n.* Asiatique *mf*.

Asiatic [eisi'ætik] **1.** *a.* asiatique. **2.** *n.* Asiatique *mf*.

aside [ə'said] **1.** *adv.* de côté; à l'écart; à part; **to pull a.,** écarter (un rideau, etc.); **to lay, put, sth. a.,** mettre qch. de côté; **to stand a.,** (i) se tenir à l'écart, à part; (ii) se ranger; **to turn a.,** se détourner (**from,** de); **I took, drew, him a.,** je le pris à part, à l'écart, en particulier; **leaving politics a., I think . . .,** la politique à part, je pense . . .; *Th:* **(words spoken) a.,** (paroles dites) en aparté. **2.** *prep.phr. NAm:* **aside from,** (*a*) à part; **a. from my own interest,** mon propre intérêt à part; (*b*) excepté, sauf; **a. from being frightened I was unhurt,** j'en ai été quitte pour la peur. **3.** *n.* remarque faite à l'écart; à-côté *m*, *pl.* à-côtés; *Th:* aparté *m*.

asinine ['æsinain] *a.* (*a*) asinien; (*b*) stupide, sot.

ask [ɑːsk] *v.tr. & i.* (**asked** [ɑːskt]) demander. **1. to a. s.o. sth.,** demander qch. à qn; **a. him his name, how old he is,** demandez-lui son nom, son âge; **to a. the time,** demander l'heure; **to ask s.o. the way,** demander son chemin à qn; **to a. s.o. a question,** poser une question à qn; **a. any questions you like,** posez toutes les questions que vous voulez; **it may be asked whether . . .,** on peut se demander si . . .; **I've often asked myself whether . . .,** je me suis souvent demandé, je me suis souvent posé la question, si . . .; *F:* **if you a. me,** à mon avis. **2.** (*a*) **to a. a favour of s.o., to a. s.o. a favour,** demander une faveur à qn; **if it isn't asking too much,** si ce n'est pas une trop grande faveur à vous demander; **to a. s.o.'s permission to do sth.,** demander à qn la permission de faire qch.; (*b*) **to a. 600 francs for sth.,** demander 600 francs pour, de, qch.; **how much are you asking for it?** combien en voulez-vous? **3.** (*a*) **to a. to do sth.,** demander à faire qch.; demander la permission, l'autorisation, de faire qch.; **to a. to be excused,** (i) s'excuser de partir; (ii) *Sch:* demander la permission de sortir; (*b*) **to a. s.o. to do sth.,** demander à qn, prier qn, solliciter qn, de faire qch.; **ask him to wait, to come in,** priez-le d'attendre, d'entrer. **4.** (*a*) **to a. about sth.,** se renseigner sur qch.; **to ask s.o. about sth.,** interroger qn sur qch.; **he asked me all about my work,** il m'a interrogé longuement sur mon travail; (*b*) **to a. after, about, s.o., s.o.'s health,** demander des nouvelles de qn, de la santé de qn. **5.** (*a*) **to a. for s.o.,** demander à voir qn; **I asked for the manager,** je demandai à parler au gérant; (*b*) **to a. for sth.,** demander qch.; solliciter qch.; **to a. s.o. for sth.,** demander qch. à qn; **we were asked for our passports,** on nous demanda nos passeports; **to a. for work,** demander du travail; **to a. for sth. to eat, to drink,** demander à manger, à boire; **to a. for more,** en redemander; **to a. for sth. back,** redemander (un objet prêté, etc.); **to be asking for trouble,** aller au-devant des ennuis; *F:* **he's been asking for it!** il l'a bien cherché! il ne l'a pas volé! **6.** inviter; **to a. s.o. to lunch,** inviter qn à déjeuner; **to a. s.o. back,** rendre une invitation; rendre la politesse; **to a. s.o. in,** demander à qn, prier qn, d'entrer; inviter qn à entrer; **I have asked him to come for the weekend,** je l'ai invité à passer le week-end chez nous. **asking** *n.* **1. it's yours for the a.,** il n'y a qu'à (le) demander. **2. a. price,** prix demandé.

askance [ə'skæns, -ɑːns] *adv.* de côté, du coin de l'œil, obliquement; **to look a. at s.o., at sth.,** regarder qn, qch., de travers, avec méfiance.

askew [ə'skjuː] *adv.* (*a*) de biais, de travers; (mettre son chapeau) de guingois; (*b*) **to cut (a plank, etc.) a.,** couper (une planche, etc.) à fausse équerre.

aslant [ə'slɑːnt] **1.** *adv.* obliquement, de travers, de biais. **2.** *prep.* en travers de (qch.).

asleep [ə'sliːp] *adv. & a.* **1.** endormi; **to be a.,** dormir; **to be fast, sound, a.,** être profondément endormi, plongé dans le sommeil; **to fall a.,** s'endormir. **2. my foot is a.,** j'ai le pied engourdi, endormi.

asocial [ei'souʃ(ə)l] *a.* asocial, -aux.

asp [æsp] *n. Rept:* (vipère *f*) aspic (*m*).

asparagus [əs'pærəgəs] *n. coll. Hort: Cu:* asperges *fpl*; **a stick of a.,** une asperge; *Bot:* **a. fern,** asparagus *m*.

aspect ['æspekt] *n.* **1.** exposition *f*; orientation *f*; (*of house*) **to have a northern a.,** être exposé au nord; **flats with southern a.,** appartements *m* côté midi. **2.** (*a*) air *m* (de qn, qch.); **man of serious a.,** homme d'un air sérieux; (*b*) aspect *m* (d'un problème, etc.); **to examine the different aspects of a subject,** examiner les différents aspects d'un sujet; (*c*) *Astrol:* aspect (des planètes). **3.** *Ling: Gram:* aspect (du verbe).

aspen ['æspən] *n. Bot:* (peuplier *m*) tremble (*m*); **a. leaf,** feuille *f* de tremble.

asperges [æs'pəːdʒiːz], **aspergillum** [æspə'dʒiləm] *n. Ecc:* aspergès *m*, goupillon *m*.

asperity [æs'periti] *n.* **1.** (*a*) âpreté *f* (d'un reproche, de la voix); (*b*) rigueur *f*, sévérité *f* (du climat); (*c*) rudesse *f* (de caractère); aspérité *f* (de style). **2.** (*excrescence*) aspérité.

aspersion ['əspəːʃ(ə)n] *n.* **1.** (*sprinkling*) aspersion *f*. **2.** calomnie *f*; **to cast aspersions,** répandre des calomnies (**on s.o.,** sur qn); porter atteinte (**on s.o.'s honour,** à l'honneur de qn).

asphalt[1] ['æsfælt] *n. Miner: Civ.E:* asphalte *m*; (*loosely*) bitume *m*; **a. roadway,** chaussée asphaltée.

asphalt² *v.tr. Civ.E:* asphalter, bitumer (une route, etc.). **asphalting** *n.* asphaltage *m*, bituminage *m*.
asphyxia [æs'fiksiə] *n.* asphyxie *f*.
asphyxiate [æs'fiksieit] **1.** *v.tr.* asphyxier. **2.** *v.i.* s'asphyxier.
asphyxiation [æsfiksi'eiʃ(ə)n] *n.* asphyxie *f*.
aspic ['æspik] *n. Cu:* aspic *m*.
aspidistra [æspi'distrə] *n. Bot:* aspidistra *m*.
aspirant ['æspirənt] *n.* aspirant, -ante (**to, after,** à); candidat, -ate.
aspirate¹ ['æspirət] *Ling:* **1.** *a.* aspiré. **2.** *n.* (*a*) (lettre) aspirée (*f*); (*b*) (la lettre) h.
aspirate² ['æspireit] *v.tr.* **1.** aspirer (une voyelle, l'h). **2.** aspirer (un gaz, un liquide); **aspirating filter,** filtre *m* à vide.
aspiration [æspi'reiʃ(ə)n] *n.* **1.** *Ling: Med: etc:* aspiration *f*. **2.** aspiration; désir *m*.
aspirator ['æspireitər] *n. Ph: Med:* aspirateur *m*.
aspire [ə'spaiər] *v.i.* aspirer; **to a. to, after, sth.,** aspirer, prétendre, viser, à qch.; ambitionner qch.; **to a. to do sth.,** aspirer à, ambitionner de, faire qch. **aspiring** *a.* futur (docteur, danseur, champion, etc.); (docteur, etc.) en herbe; **to be an a. artist, etc.,** avoir l'ambition de devenir artiste, etc.
aspirin ['æsp(i)rin] *n. Pharm:* **1.** aspirine *f*. **2.** comprimé *m* d'aspirine.
ass¹ *n.* **1.** [æs] âne *m*; **she a.,** ânesse *f*; **ass's milk,** lait *m* d'ânesse; **wild a.,** hémione *m*; onagre *m*. **2.** [æs, *occ.* ɑːs] âne; idiot, -ote; **don't be a silly a.,** ne fais pas l'imbécile, l'idiot; **to make an a. of oneself,** (i) faire l'idiot, l'imbécile; (ii) se donner en spectacle.
ass² [æs, ɑːs] *v.i. F:* **to a. about,** faire l'imbécile, l'idiot; faire des bêtises.
ass³ [æs] *n. U.S: P:* (*not in polite use*) cul *m*.
assail [ə'seil] *v.tr. A: & Lit:* (*a*) assaillir, attaquer (l'ennemi); (*b*) **to a. s.o. with questions,** accabler qn de questions; **assailed with doubts,** saisi de doutes.
assailant [ə'seilənt] *n.* assaillant, -ante; agresseur *m*.
assassin [ə'sæsin] *n.* **1.** assassin *m* (d'un homme d'État, etc.). **2.** *Hist:* **Assassins,** Assassins, Ismaïliens *mpl*.
assassinate [ə'sæsineit] *v.tr.* assassiner.
assassination [əsæsi'neiʃ(ə)n] *n.* assassinat *m*.
assault [ə'sɔːlt] *n.* **1.** assaut *m*; attaque (brusquée); **to take, carry, a town by a.,** prendre une ville d'assaut; **a. craft,** engin *m* d'assaut; **a. course,** (i) parcours *m* du combattant; (ii) piste *f* d'assaut. **2.** (*a*) *Jur:* tentative *f* de voie de fait; **unprovoked a.,** agression *f*; **a. and battery,** (menaces *fpl* et) voies *fpl* de fait; coups *mpl* et blessures *fpl*; **criminal a.,** (i) tentative de viol; (ii) viol *m*; **indecent a.,** attentat *m* à la pudeur; outrage *m* aux mœurs.
assault² *v.tr.* **1.** attaquer, assaillir (une position); donner l'assaut à (une ville, etc.). **2.** (i) attaquer (qn); (ii) (*sexually*) violenter (une femme); **charged with assaulting s.o.,** accusé de s'être porté, livré, à des voies de fait sur qn; **to be assaulted,** être victime (i) d'une agression, (ii) d'un attentat à la pudeur.
assay¹ [ə'sei] *n. Metall: etc:* essai *m* (d'un métal précieux, d'un minerai); *Ch:* dosage *m*; *Adm:* **a. office,** bureau *m* de garantie (des métaux précieux).
assay² *v.tr.* essayer, titrer, analyser (un métal précieux, un minerai); faire l'essai d'(un métal); coupeller (l'or, etc.). **assaying** *n.* essai *m*, titrage *m*, analyse *f* (d'un minerai, etc.); coupellation *f* (de l'or, etc.).
assemblage [ə'semblidʒ] *n.* **1.** assemblage *m* (de pièces de menuiserie, etc.). **2.** (*a*) assemblage, réunion *f* (de personnes); rassemblement *m*; (*b*) collection *f* (d'objets).
assemble [ə'sembl] **1.** *v.tr.* (*a*) assembler (des personnes); ameuter (des révoltés, etc.); convoquer (un parlement); *Mil:* rassembler (des troupes); (*b*) *Tchn:* assembler (des pièces de menuiserie, etc.); *Mec.E:* ajuster, assembler, monter, (une machine); habiller (une montre, etc.). **2.** *v.i.* s'assembler; se rassembler; (*of insurgents, etc.*) s'ameuter.
assembler [ə'semblər] *n. Ind:* monteur, -euse.
assembly [ə'sembli] *n.* **1.** réunion *f*; (*a*) **place of a.,** lieu *m* de réunion; *Jur:* **unlawful a.,** attroupement *m*; (*b*) **a. rooms,** salle *f* des fêtes, salle de danse; (*c*) *Sch: etc:* rassemblement *m*; *Mil:* **a. area,** zone *f* d'attente. **2.** *Pol: etc:* assemblée *f*; **the National A.,** l'Assemblée nationale. **3.** *Ind: etc:* montage *m*; **a. shop, hall,** salle, atelier *m*, de montage; **a. line,** chaîne *f* de montage; **work on the a. line,** travail *m* à la chaîne.
assent¹ [ə'sent] *n.* assentiment *m*, consentement *m*; *Jur:* agrément *m*; **the royal a.,** le consentement du souverain: **by common a.,** du consentement de tous.
assent² *v.i.* (*a*) accéder, acquiescer, donner son assentiment (**to,** à); (*b*) (*of sovereign, etc.*) sanctionner (une loi, etc.).
assert [ə'səːt] *v.tr.* **1.** (*a*) revendiquer (ses droits, etc.); **to a. one's claims to . . .,** faire valoir ses droits à . . .; (*b*) **to a. oneself,** s'imposer; s'affirmer; **you must a. your authority,** il vous faut imposer votre autorité. **2.** protester de (son innocence, etc.); affirmer, prétendre, soutenir (**that,** que).
assertion [ə'səːʃ(ə)n] *n.* **1.** revendication *f*. **2.** assertion *f*, affirmation *f*; **to make an a.,** affirmer qch.
assertive [ə'səːtiv] *a.* (*of tone, manner, etc.*) autoritaire.
assess [ə'ses] *v.tr.* **1.** (*a*) répartir, établir (un impôt); (*b*) estimer (la valeur de qch.); **to a. the damage,** évaluer les dégâts; *Nau:* évaluer l'avarie; *Jur:* **to a. the damages,** fixer les dommages et intérêts; (*c*) juger de (la qualité d'un produit). **2.** *Adm:* **to a. s.o. in, at, so much,** coter, imposer, taxer, qn à tant. **4.** (*a*) **to a. a property (for taxation),** évaluer une propriété; (*b*) **if we a. this speech at its true worth,** si nous estimons ce discours à sa juste valeur.
assessment [ə'sesmənt] *n.* **1.** (*a*) répartition *f*, assiette *f* (d'un impôt); (*b*) estimation *f* (de la valeur de qch.); evaluation *f* (de dégâts, *Nau:* d'avarie, *Adm:* d'une propriété); *Jur:* **a. of damages,** fixation *f* de dommages et intérêts; (*c*) imposition *f* (d'une commune, d'un immeuble); (*d*) cotisation *f* (du contribuable); **basis of a.,** assiette *f* des impôts; **notice of a.,** avertissement *m* des contributions; **year of a.,** année *f* d'imposition. **2.** (*amount*) cote *f*, taxe officielle; **a. on landed property,** cote foncière; **a. on income,** cote mobilière; impôt *m* sur le revenu.
assessor [ə'sesər] *n.* **1.** *Jur:* assesseur (adjoint à un juge); juge assesseur. **2.** répartiteur *m* (d'un impôt, etc.).
asset ['æset] *n.* **1.** chose *f* dont on peut tirer avantage; possession *f*; avoir *m*; **his knowledge of French is a great a. to him,** sa connaissance du français lui est un avantage précieux. **2.** *Fin: etc:* **assets,** actif *m*, avoir(s) *m(pl)*; *Jur:* masse *f* (d'une succession, d'une société); masse active (d'une liquidation après faillite); **capital assets,** actif immobilisé; **frozen assets,** fonds bloqués, non liquides.
asseverate [a'sevəreit] *v.tr.* affirmer (solennellement) (**that,** que + *ind.*); protester de (son innocence).
assiduity [æsi'djuiti] *n.* assiduité *f*, diligence *f* (**in doing sth.,** à faire qch.).
assiduous [ə'sidjuəs] *a.* **1.** (*of pers.*) assidu; diligent. **2.** (travail) assidu. **-ly** *adv.* assidûment.
assign [ə'sain] *v.tr.* **1.** (*a*) assigner (**to,** à); donner (qch.) en partage (à qn); (*b*) **to a. a reason for sth.,** donner la raison de qch; **to a. a meaning to a word,** attribuer un sens à un mot; (*c*) fixer, assigner, (une

heure, un lieu); (*d*) assigner, attribuer (une tâche, une fonction (**to s.o.,** à qn). **2.** *Jur:* céder, transférer (une propriété) (**to s.o.,** à qn); transmettre (des actions, un brevet) (**to s.o.,** à qn).

assignation [æsig'neiʃ(ə)n] *n.* **1.** distribution *f,* répartition *f,* attribution *f* (de biens). **2.** *Jur:* cession *f,* transfert *m* (de biens, de dettes, etc.); transmission *f* (d'actions, de brevet). **3.** (*a*) fixation *f* (d'une heure, d'un lieu de rendez-vous); (*b*) rendez-vous *m;* (*c*) rendez-vous galant.

assignment [ə'sainmənt] *n.* **1.** (*a*) distribution *f,* répartition *f,* attribution *f* (de biens); (*b*) affectation *f,* allocation *f* (de qch. à qn); **a. of s.o. to a post,** affectation de qn à un poste; (*c*) *Jur: etc:* cession *f,* transfert *m* (de biens, de dettes, etc.); **deed of a.,** acte attributif, acte de transfert. **2.** *Sch: etc:* tâche assignée; *Journ:* reportage assigné (à un tel); **a dangerous a.,** (i) une tâche dangereuse; (ii) un poste dangereux.

assimilate [ə'simileit] **1.** *v.tr.* (*a*) (*make alike*) **to a. the laws of two countries,** assimiler les lois de deux pays; (*b*) assimiler (des aliments); (*c*) assimiler (des idées, des immigrants). **2.** *v.i.* (*a*) **to a. to, with, sth.,** s'assimiler à qch.; (*b*) *Ling:* (*of consonants*) s'assimiler; (*c*) **in this country foreigners find it difficult to a.,** dans ce pays les étrangers s'adaptent difficilement.

assimilation [əsimi'leiʃ(ə)n] *n.* **1.** assimilation *f* (**to, with,** à); *Ling:* assimilation (de consonnes). **2.** assimilation (**to,** à); comparaison *f* (**to,** avec). **3.** (*a*) *Physiol:* assimilation (des aliments); (*b*) *Bot:* photo-synthèse *f;* (*c*) assimilation (d'idées).

Assisi [ə'si:zi, ə'si:si] *Pr.n. Geog:* Assise *f;* **St. Francis of A.,** Saint François d'Assise.

assist [ə'sist] **1.** *v.tr.* aider (qn); prêter son concours, son assistance, à (qn); seconder (qn) (dans son travail); **to a. s.o. in (doing) sth.,** aider qn à faire qch. **2.** *v.i.* prendre part (**at a ceremony, etc.,** à une cérémonie, etc.).

assistance [ə'sistəns] *n.* aide *f,* secours *m,* assistance *f;* **to give s.o. a.,** prêter aide, assistance, (son) concours, à qn; **to come to s.o.'s a.,** venir à l'aide de, en aide à, qn; **with the a. of sth., of s.o.,** à l'aide de qch., avec l'aide de qn; **to be of a. to s.o.,** aider qn, être utile à qn; *Adm: A:* **National A.** = aide sociale.

assistant [ə'sistənt] **1.** *a.* qui aide; auxiliaire; adjoint; **a. manager,** sous-directeur *m, pl.* sous-directeurs; **a. lecturer,** *esp. NAm:* **a. professor** = maître assistant (à une université). **2.** *n.* aide *mf;* adjoint, -ointe; **(shop) a.,** vendeur, -euse; **laboratory a.,** laborantin, -ine.

assize [ə'saiz] *n.* **1.** *Jur:* (*a*) (*usu. pl.*) **(court of) assizes, a. court,** (cour *f* d')assises *fpl;* **to be brought before the assizes,** être traduit en cour d'assises; (*b*) *Scot:* (i) jugement *m* par jury; (ii) **the a.,** le jury.

associate[1] [ə'souʃiət] **1.** *a.* associé; *Ind: etc:* (société) affiliée, apparentée; *esp. NAm:* **a. professor** = professeur *m* de faculté. **2.** *n.* (*a*) associé, -ée; adjoint, -ointe; membre correspondant, associé(e) (d'une académie); (*b*) compagnon *m,* camarade *mf;* **I don't like his associates,** je n'aime pas ses fréquentations; (*c*) (*of thg*) accessoire *m* (de qch.).

associate[2] [ə'souʃieit] **1.** *v.tr.* associer (qn, qch.) (**with,** avec qn, à qch.); **to a. oneself,** s'associer (**with,** avec qn, à qch.); **to be associated with s.o. in an undertaking,** s'associer avec qn pour une entreprise. **2.** *v.i.* (*a*) **to a. with s.o. in sth., in doing sth.,** s'associer, s'unir, avec qn pour qch., pour faire qch.; (*b*) **to a. with s.o.,** fréquenter qn; **to a. with undesirable companions,** faire de mauvaises fréquentations. **associated** *a.* (sujet, *Adm:* territoire) associé.

association [əsousi'eiʃ(ə)n] *n.* **1.** (*a*) association *f;* **a. of ideas,** association d'idées; **land full of historic associations,** pays *m* fertile en souvenirs historiques; *Jur:* **deed of a.,** acte *m* d'association; (*b*) fréquentation *f* (**with s.o.,** de qn); **through long a. with . . .,** à force de fréquenter . . .; **in a. with . . .,** associé à . . .. **2.** (*a*) association, société *f;* amicale *f* (de professeurs, etc.); **to form an a.,** constituer une société; **trade a.,** association professionnelle; **Young Men's, Young Women's, Christian A.,** Union chrétienne de jeunes gens, de jeunes femmes; (*b*) **a. football,** football *m* association.

assonance ['æsənəns] *n. Ling:* assonance *f.*

assorted [ə'sɔ:tid] *a.* (*a*) assorti; **well a. couple,** époux (bien) assortis; (*b*) (bonbons, etc.) assortis; (couleurs) variées; **box of a. screws,** boîte *f* de vis assorties.

assortment [ə'sɔ:tmənt] *n.* assortiment *m* de bonbons, d'outils, etc.); jeu *m* (d'outils).

assuage [ə'sweidʒ] *v.tr. Lit:* apaiser (la douleur).

assume [ə'sju:m] *v.tr.* **1.** prendre, se donner (un air, une mine, un ton); affecter, revêtir (une forme, un caractère). **2.** (*a*) prendre sur soi, assumer (une charge, une responsabilité); se charger (d'un devoir); (*b*) prendre (le pouvoir, le commandement); prendre en main (la conduite des affaires). **3.** s'attribuer, s'arroger, s'approprier (un droit, un titre, etc.); adopter, emprunter (un nom); *Jur:* **to a. ownership,** faire acte de propriétaire. **4.** simuler, affecter; **to a. a virtue,** se parer d'une vertu; affecter une vertu. **5.** présumer, supposer (qch.); tenir (qch.) comme établi; **I a. that he will come,** je présume qu'il viendra; **he was assumed to be rich,** on le supposait riche; **in the absence of proof he must be assumed to be innocent,** en l'absence de preuves, il doit être présumé innocent; **let us a. that . . .,** prenons, mettons, supposons, que . . .; **assuming that the story is true,** en supposant, en admettant, que l'histoire soit vraie; **to a. the worst,** mettre les choses au pis. **assumed** *a.* **1.** supposé, feint, faux ; **with a. nonchalance,** avec une affectation d'indifférence; **a. name,** pseudonyme *m;* nom supposé, nom d'emprunt, nom de guerre. **2. a. load (on a bridge, etc.),** surcharge *f* hypothétique; **a. rate of increase,** taux *m* d'accroissement présumé.

assumption [ə'sʌm(p)ʃ(ə)n] *n.* **1.** *Ecc:* assomption *f* (de la Vierge); **Feast of the A.,** fête *f* de l'Assomption. **2.** (*a*) action *f* de prendre (une forme, un caractère); *Jur:* **unauthorized a. of a right,** usurpation *f* d'un droit; (*b*) **a. of office,** entrée *f* en fonctions. **3.** (*a*) affectation *f* (de vertu); **he turned away with an a. of indifference,** il se détourna en feignant l'indifférence; (*b*) arrogance *f,* prétention(s) *f(pl),* présomption *f.* **4.** supposition *f,* hypothèse *f; Phil:* postulat *m;* **I am going on the a. that . . .,** je me fonde sur l'hypothèse que . . . .

assurance [ə'ʃuerəns] *n.* **1.** (*a*) assurance *f;* **I have every a. that he will help us,** j'ai la ferme assurance qu'il nous aidera; (*b*) promesse (formelle); (*c*) affirmation *f;* **a. to the contrary,** affirmation contraire; **I can give you the a. that . . .,** je peux vous assurer, vous affirmer, que . . . . **2.** *Ins:* **life a.,** assurance sur la vie; assurance-vie, *pl.* assurances-vie; **a. company,** compagnie *f* d'assurances. **3.** (i) assurance, fermeté *f,* confiance *f;* aplomb *m;* (ii) hardiesse *f,* présomption *f;* **to answer with a.,** répondre (i) d'un ton assuré, avec assurance; (ii) d'un ton hardi, hardiment.

assure [ə'ʃuər] *v.tr.* (*a*) *Ins:* assurer (la vie de qn); **to a. one's life,** s'assurer (sur la vie); (*b*) assurer (la paix, le bonheur, de qn). (*c*) **to a. s.o. of the truth of sth.,** assurer qn de la vérité de qch.; **to a. s.o. of a fact,** assurer, affirmer, un fait à qn; **he assures me that it is true,** il me certifie que c'est vrai; **he will do it, I can a. you!** il le fera, je vous assure! **assured** **1.** *a.* (succès, etc.) assuré. **2.** *n. Ins:* assuré, -e. **assuredly** [ə'ʃuəridli] *adv.* assurément, sans aucun doute.

Assyria [ə'siriə] *Pr.n. A.Geog:* Assyrie *f.*
Assyrian [ə'siriən] *A. Hist:* **1.** *a.* assyrien. **2.** *n.* (*a*) Assyrien, -ienne; (*b*) *Ling:* assyrien *m.*
aster ['æstər] *n.* **1.** *Bot:* aster *m*; **China a.,** aster de Chine; reine-marguerite *f, pl.* reines-marguerites. **2.** *Biol:* aster.
asterisk ['æst(ə)risk] *n.* astérisque *m.*
astern [ə'stə:n] *Nau: Av:* **1.** *adv.* (*a*) à l'arrière, sur l'arrière; **two guns a.,** deux canons à l'arrière, en poupe; (*b*) **to go, come, a.,** culer; aller de l'arrière; faire machine, marche, arrière; **full speed a.!** en arrière à toute vitesse! en arrière toute! (*c*) **to make a boat fast a.,** amarrer un canot derrière; **to fall, drop, a.,** rester en arrière (d'un autre navire); **ship right a.,** navire droit derrière. **2.** *prep.phr.* **a. of a ship,** derrière un navire; sur l'arrière d'un navire; à la traîne; **to pass a. of a ship,** passer sur l'arrière d'un navire.
asteroid ['æstərɔid] **1.** *a.* en forme d'étoile. **2.** *n.* *Astr:* astéroïde *m.*
asthma ['æs(θ)mə] *n.* asthme *m.*
asthmatic [æs(θ)'mætik] *a.* & *n.* asthmatique (*mf*).
astigmatic [æstig'mætik] *Opt: a.* & *n.* astigmate (*mf*).
astigmatism [æ'stigmətizm] *n. Opt:* astigmatisme *m.*
astir [ə'stə:r] *adv.* & *a.* *O:* **1.** actif; en mouvement; animé. **2.** debout, levé; **to be a. at six o'clock,** être debout à six heures. **3.** en émoi, agité; **the whole town was a.,** toute la ville était en émoi.
astonish [ə'stɔniʃ] *v.tr.* étonner, surprendre; jeter (qn) dans l'étonnement; **you a. me,** vous m'étonnez; **to be astonished at seeing sth.,** être étonné, s'étonner, de voir qch.; **I am astonished that . . .,** cela m'étonne que + *sub.*; **to look astonished,** avoir l'air étonné. **astonishing** *a.* étonnant, surprenant; **it is a. to me that . . .,** je m'étonne que . . . . **astonishingly** *adv.* étonnamment; **a. enough, he arrived,** chose étonnante, il est arrivé.
astonishment [ə'stɔniʃmənt] *n.* étonnement *m*; (grande) surprise; **to my great a.,** à mon grand étonnement, à ma grande surprise; **look of a.,** regard étonné; **I fell back in a.,** j'ai eu un sursaut d'étonnement.
astound [ə'staund] *v.tr.* confondre; frapper de stupeur; stupéfier; **I was astounded by it,** j'en demeurai (i) stupéfait, (ii) atterré. **astounding** *a.* abasourdissant, renversant.
Astrakhan [æstrə'kæn] **1.** *Pr.n. Geog:* astrak(h)an. **2.** *n.* (*fur*) astrakan *m.*
astral ['æstr(ə)l] *a.* astral.
astray [ə'strei] *adv.* & *a.* (i) égaré; (ii) *Pej:* dévoyé; **to go a.,** (i) (*of pers., letter, etc.*) s'égarer; (ii) *Pej:* se dévoyer; se débaucher; **to lead s.o. a.,** (i) égarer qn; induire qn en erreur; (ii) dévoyer qn; détourner qn de la bonne voie.
astride [ə'straid] *adv.* & *prep.* **1.** à califourchon; **to ride a.,** monter à califourchon (sur un cheval, etc.); **to sit a. sth.,** être à cheval, chevaucher, être à califourchon, sur qch. **2. to stand a.,** se tenir (debout) les jambes écartées.
astringent [ə'strin(d)ʒənt] *a.* & *n.* astringent (*m*); styptique (*m*).
astrologer [ə'strɔlədʒər] *n.* astrologue *m.*
astrological [æstrə'lɔdʒikl] *a.* astrologique.
astrology [ə'strɔlədʒi] *n.* astrologie *f.*
astronaut ['æstrənɔ:t] *n.* astronaute *m.*
astronautics [æstrə'nɔ:tiks] *n.pl.* astronautique *f.*
astronomer [ə'strɔnəmər] *n.* astronome *m.*
astronomic(al) [æstrə'nɔmik(l)] *a.* (année, unité, etc.) astronomique; *F:* (*of sale, etc.*) **to reach astronomical figures,** atteindre des chiffres astronomiques. **-ally** *adv.* astronomiquement.
astronomy [ə'strɔnəmi] *n.* astronomie *f.*
astrophysics [æstrou'fiziks] *n.pl.* (*usu. with sg.const.*) astrophysique *f.*
astute [əs'tju:t] *a.* **1.** fin, avisé, pénétrant. **2.** *Pej:* astucieux, rusé. **-ly** *adv.* **1.** avec finesse; avec une grande pénétration. **2.** *Pej:* astucieusement.
astuteness [əs'tju:tnis] *n.* **1.** finesse *f*, sagacité *f.* **2.** *Pej:* astuce *f.*
asunder [ə'sʌndər] *adv. A:* & *Lit:* **1.** éloignés, écartés (l'un de l'autre). **2. to tear sth. a.,** déchirer qch. en deux; **to break a.,** se casser en deux.
asylum [ə'sailəm] *n.* **1.** (*a*) *Hist:* asile *m* (inviolable); (*b*) asile, (lieu *m* de) refuge (*m*); **political a.,** asile politique. **2.** *A:* hospice *m*; **(lunatic) a.,** asile d'aliénés; **orphan a.,** orphelinat *m.*
asymmetric(al) [eisi'metrik(l)] *a.* asymétrique.
asymmetry [ei'simitri] *n.* asymétrie *f.*
at [æt, *unstressed* ət] *prep.* à. **1.** (*a*) **at the centre, at the top,** au centre, au sommet; **at table, at church, at school, at the station,** à table, à l'église, à l'école, à la gare; **at my side,** à mes côtés, à côté de moi; **at hand,** sous la main; **at Oxford,** à Oxford; **at sea,** en mer; (*b*) **at home,** à la maison, chez soi; **at my uncle's, at the tailor's,** chez mon oncle, chez le tailleur; (*c*) **to sit at the window,** se tenir (au)près de la fenêtre; (*d*) *U.S: F:* **where are we at?** où en sommes-nous? **2. at six o'clock,** à six heures; **at present,** à présent; **at that time,** à cette époque, en ce temps-là; **at the weekend,** pendant, durant, le weekend; **at a time when . . .,** dans un moment où . . .; **two at a time,** deux par deux, deux à la fois; **at the beginning of the year,** au commencement de l'année; **at the beginning,** au début; **at night,** la nuit, le soir; **at first,** d'abord; **at last,** enfin, à la fin; **at once,** immédiatement. **3. at two francs a pound,** à deux francs la livre; **apples at 30p a pound,** des pommes à 30 pence la livre. **4. at my request,** sur ma demande; **boys at play,** élèves en récréation; **at all events,** en tout cas. **5. quick at repartee,** prompt à la repartie; **to be good, bad, at mathematics,** être fort, faible, en mathématiques; **to be good at games,** être sportif. **6.** (*a*) **to look at s.o., sth.,** regarder qn, qch.; **to be surprised, delighted at sth.,** être étonné, enchanté, de qch.; **to aim at s.o.,** viser qn; (*b*) **to laugh at s.o.,** se moquer de qn; **to swear at s.o.,** jurer contre qn; **what are you driving at?** où voulez-vous en venir? (*c*) **to be at work,** être au travail; **to be at sth.,** être occupé à faire qch., s'occuper de qch.; **to keep s.o. at it,** faire trimer qn; **she's at it again,** voilà qu'elle recommence! la voilà qui recommence! **while we are at it,** pendant que nous y sommes; **he's a writer and a poor one at that!** il est écrivain et encore assez médiocre; (*d*) *F:* **she is always at him,** elle ne peut pas le laisser tranquille; elle lui casse tout le temps les pieds; **she's always on at me,** elle s'en prend toujours à moi; (*to dog*) **at him!** pille! pille!
atavism ['ætəvizm] *n.* atavisme *m.*
atavistic [ætə'vistik] *a.* atavique.
ataxia [ə'tæksiə], **ataxy** [ə'tæksi] *n. Med:* ataxie *f*; **locomotor a.,** ataxie locomotrice progressive; tabes *m* dorsalis.
ate. *see* EAT.
atheism ['eiθiizm] *n.* athéisme *m.*
atheist ['eiθiist] *n.* athée *mf.*
atheistic(al) [eiθi'istik(l)] *a.* **1.** (doctrine) athéistique. **2.** (personne) athée.
Athenian [ə'θi:niən] *Geog:* **1.** *a.* athénien; d'Athènes. **2.** *n.* Athénien, -ienne.
Athens ['æθənz] *Pr.n. Geog:* Athènes *f.*
athlete ['æθli:t] *n.* athlète *mf*; *Med:* **athlete's foot,** pied *m* d'athlète, mycose *f.*
athletic [æθ'letik] *a.* (*a*) athlétique; **a. club,** société *f* d'athlétisme; (*b*) **he's very a.,** c'est un sportif.

athletics [æθ'letiks] *n.pl.* (*usu. with sg.const.*) athlétisme *m.*

at-home [ət'houm] *n.* réception *f*; (*evening*) soirée *f.*

athwart [ə'θwɔːt] *Nau:* **1.** *adv.* en travers; par le travers. **2.** *prep.* en travers de.

atishoo [ə'tiʃuː] *int.* (*sneeze*) atchoum!

Atlantic [ət'læntik] *a. & n. Geog:* **the A. (Ocean),** l'(océan) Atlantique *m*; **A. liner,** transatlantique *m.*

Atlas ['ætləs] **1.** *Pr.n.m. Gr.Myth:* Atlas. **2.** *Pr.n. Geog:* **the A. Mountains,** l'Atlas *m.* **3.** *n.* **a.,** (*a*) *Anat:* atlas; (*b*) *Paperm:* atlas; **an a. folio,** un in-folio format atlas, format atlantique; (*c*) *Geog: etc:* atlas. **4.** *n.* **a.,** *Arch:* (*pl.* **atlantes** [ət'læntiːz]) atlante *m*, télamon *m.*

atmosphere ['ætməsfiər] *n.* **1.** atmosphère *f* (terrestre, planétaire etc.). **2.** atmosphère, ambiance *f*; *F:* **I don't like atmospheres,** je n'aime pas les milieux où l'on se dispute. **3.** *Ph. Meas:* atmosphère.

atmospheric [ætməs'ferik] **1.** *a.* (pression, condition, etc.) atmosphérique. **2.** *W.Tel: etc:* **atmospherics,** (parasites *mpl*) atmosphériques (*fpl*).

atoll ['ætɔl] *n. Geog:* atoll *m.*

atom ['ætəm] *n.* (*a*) *Ph:* atome *m*; **a. bomb,** bombe *f* atomique; (*b*) **not an a. of common sense,** pas l'ombre, pas un grain, de bon sens; **smashed to atoms,** réduit en miettes, en poudre.

atomic [ə'tɔmik] *a.* (énergie, guerre, *Ph:* poids, nombre, etc.) atomique; **a. reactor,** pile *f* atomique; **a. physicist,** atomiste *m*; **the a. age,** l'ère *f*, l'âge *m*, atomique.

atomics [ə'tɔmiks] *n.pl.* (*usu. with sg.const.*) sciences *fpl* atomiques.

atomize ['ætəmaiz] *v.tr.* atomiser; pulvériser; vaporiser.

atomizer ['ætəmaizər] *n.* atomiseur *m*; pulvérisateur *m*; vaporisateur *m*; *I.C.E:* gicleur *m.*

atonal [ei'toun(ə)l] *a. Mus:* atonal, -aux.

atone [ə'toun] *v.i.* **to a. for,** expier, racheter, réparer (une faute, un péché).

atonement [ə'tounmənt] *n.* expiation *f*, réparation *f* (**for,** de); **in a. for a wrong,** en réparation d'un tort; *Theol:* **to make a.,** satisfaire; *Jew.Rel:* **Day of A.,** Fête *f* du Grand Pardon.

atrocious [ə'trouʃəs] *a.* **1.** (crime) atroce; **a. act,** atrocité *f.* **2.** *F:* (jeu de mots, etc.) exécrable; (chapeau) affreux. **-ly** *adv.* **1.** atrocement. **2.** *F:* exécrablement; **a. bad,** exécrable.

atrocity [ə'trɔsiti] *n.* **1.** atrocité *f* (d'un crime, *F:* d'un calembour). **2.** atrocité *f*; **to witness atrocities,** assister à des atrocités.

atrophy¹ ['ætrəfi] *n.* atrophie *f.*

atrophy² ['ætrəfi, -fai] **1.** *v.tr.* atrophier. **2.** *v.i.* s'atrophier. **atrophied** *a.* atrophié.

attaboy ['ætəbɔi] *int. esp. U.S: F:* bravo! à la bonne heure!

attach [ə'tætʃ] *v.tr. & i.* (*a*) attacher, lier, fixer, accrocher, connecter (**sth. to sth.,** qch. à qch.); interconnecter (deux choses); annexer (un document); **house with garage attached,** maison avec garage attenant; **to be attached to s.o., to a party,** être attaché à qn, à un parti; (*of ship*) **to be attached to a squadron,** faire partie d'une escadre; **official temporarily attached to another department,** fonctionnaire détaché à un autre service; (*b*) *Jur:* mettre une saisie-arrêt sur (des biens mobiliers, un salaire); (*c*) **I a. no importance to it,** je n'y prête, n'y attache, aucune importance; **one cannot a. any blame to him,** on ne peut lui imputer aucune responsabilité (de l'accident).

attaché [ə'tæʃei] *n.* **1.** *Dipl:* attaché *m*; **military a.,** attaché militaire. **2.** **a. case,** mallette *f* (pour documents).

attachment [ə'tætʃmənt] *n.* **1.** (*a*) action *f* d'attacher (qch. à qch.); attachement *m*; (*b*) attache *f*, lien *m*; **attachments of a muscle,** attaches d'un muscle. **2.** accessoire *m* (d'un tour, d'une machine à coudre, etc.); **lathe with drilling a.,** tour avec accessoire pour foret. **3.** *Mil:* rattachement *m*, stage *m*; **to serve an a. with the French army,** faire un stage dans l'armée française. **4.** attachement *m* (**of s.o. for s.o., to sth.,** de qn pour qn, à qch.); affection *f* (**for,** pour); **to form an a. for s.o.,** s'attacher à qn; se prendre d'affection pour qn. **5.** *Jur:* arrêt *m*, saisie *f*, saisie-arrêt *f*; **a. of real property,** saisie immobilière.

attack¹ [ə'tæk] *n.* **1.** (*a*) *Mil: etc:* attaque *f*, assaut *m*; **combined a.,** attaque combinée; **night a.,** attaque de nuit; **to launch an a.,** lancer une attaque; (*b*) attaque (**on s.o., a project, etc,** de qn, d'un projet, etc.); *Jur:* atteinte *f* (à l'honneur). **2.** (*a*) attaque, crise *f* (de goutte, etc.); poussée *f* (de fière); **liver a.,** crise de foie; **a. of nerves,** crise de nerfs; (*b*) attentat *m* (sur la vie, la personne, de qn). **3.** *Mus:* attaque (d'une note).

attack² *v.tr.* **1.** (*a*) *Mil:* attaquer, assaillir (l'ennemi); **to be attacked,** subir une attaque; être attaqué; (*b*) attaquer (qn, les droits de qn, un projet, etc.); s'attaquer à (qn, un abus, etc.); (*c*) s'attaquer à (un travail, un problème, etc.). **2.** (*a*) (*of disease*) s'attaquer à, atteindre (qn, un organe, etc.); (*b*) (*of rust*) attaquer, ronger (le fer). **attacking** *a.* attaquant, assaillant; **a. party,** corps *m* d'attaque.

attacker [ə'tækər] *n.* attaquant, -ante, agresseur *m*, assaillant, -ante.

attain [ə'tein] *v.tr. & i.* atteindre, parvenir à, arriver à (un grand âge, ses fins, etc.); s'élever jusqu'à (un haut rang); acquérir (des connaissances); **to a. one's majority,** arriver à, atteindre, sa majorité; **to a. happiness,** atteindre au bonheur; **to a. (to) perfection, power, honours,** atteindre à la perfection, arriver au pouvoir.

attainable [ə'teinəbl] *a.* accessible; réalisable.

attainment [ə'teinmənt] *n.* **1.** (*no pl.*) arrivée *f* (à ses fins); obtention *f*, réalisation *f*; **for the a. of his purpose,** pour atteindre, arriver, à ses fins. **2.** (*usu. pl.*) acquisition(s) *f*(*pl*) de l'esprit; connaissance(s) *f*(*pl*); savoir *m*; **man of considerable attainments,** homme qui a beaucoup d'instruction, d'acquis; **his linguistic attainments,** sa connaissance des langues.

attempt¹ [ə'tempt] *n.* **1.** tentative *f*, essai *m*, effort *m*; **an a. at a smile,** l'ébauche *f* d'un sourire; **without (making) any a. at concealment,** sans chercher à se cacher; **a. to escape,** tentative d'évasion; **to make an a. at (doing) sth., to do sth.,** essayer, tâcher, de faire qch.; s'essayer à faire qch.; **first a.,** coup *m* d'essai; première tentative; **at the first a.,** du premier coup; **to make another a.,** renouveler ses tentatives; revenir à la charge; **to give up the a.,** y renoncer; **he failed in the a.,** il n'a pas réussi. **2.** (*a*) attentat *m* (**on s.o.'s life,** contre la vie de qn); **to make an a. on s.o.'s life,** attenter à la vie de qn; **to make an a. to beat a record,** essayer de battre un record.

attempt² *v.tr.* (*a*) **to a. to do sth.,** essayer, tenter, tâcher, de faire qch.; chercher à faire qch.; **he attempted to get up,** il essaya de se lever; (*b*) **he attempted a smile,** il essaya un sourire; il s'efforça de sourire; **to a. a piece of work,** entreprendre un travail; s'attaquer à un travail; **to a. the impossible,** tenter l'impossible; **attempted murder, theft,** tentative *f* d'assassinat, de vol.

attend [ə'tend] **1.** *v.i.* (*a*) **to a. to sth.,** faire, prêter, attention à qch.; (*b*) **to a. to (sth.),** s'occuper, se charger d'(une affaire); vaquer à (ses occupations, etc.); veiller à (ses intérêts, sa santé, etc.); soigner (sa santé, son style, etc.); *Com:* exécuter (une commande); **I shall a. to it,** je m'en occuperai, je m'en chargerai; (*c*) **to a. to s.o.,** s'occuper de qn; servir (un client); **are you being attended to?** est-ce qu'on vous sert? **2.** *v.tr.* (*of doctor*) soigner, donner des soins à (un malade); **the attending physician,** le médecin traitant. **3.** *v.tr. & i.* (*a*) **we were attended by three waiters,** nous étions servis par trois garçons; **to a. (on) a prince,** suivre, accompagner, un prince; (*b*) *Lit:* **success attended my efforts,** mes efforts furent couronnés de succès. **4.** *v.tr.* aller à (l'église, l'école); assister à (une conférence, une réunion); suivre (un cours); **the lectures are well attended,** les cours sont très suivis.

attendance [ə'tendəns] *n.* **1. to be in a. on (s.o.),** (i) (*of doctor*) donner des soins à (un malade); (ii) (*of courtier*) être de service auprès d'(un roi, etc.); *F:* **to dance a. on s.o.,** faire l'empressé auprès de qn. **2.** présence *f* (à une réunion, etc.); **regular a.,** assiduité *f*; **school a.,** fréquentation *f* scolaire; **a. register,** registre *m* de présence; **non a.,** absence *f*. **3.** assistance *f*; **there was a good a. at the meeting,** il y avait une assistance nombreuse à la réunion.

attendant [ə'tendənt] **1.** *a. Lit:* **a. on s.o., sth.,** qui accompagne qn, qch.; *Jur:* **a. circumstances,** circonstances concomitantes (d'un crime, etc.). **2.** *n.* (*a*) surveillant, -ante; *Adm:* préposé, -ée; (*in museum, etc.*) gardien *m*, gardienne *f*; (*in theatre*) ouvreuse *f*; (*in laboratory*) préparateur, - trice; (*b*) (*usu.pl.*) suivants *mpl*, gens *mpl* (d'un roi, etc.); **the prince and his attendants,** le prince et sa suite; (*c*) *A:* **(medical) a.,** médecin *m*.

attention [ə'tenʃ(ə)n] *n.* **1.** (*a*) attention *f* **(to,** à); **a. to truth, to detail,** préoccupation *f* de la vérité, des détails; **to give one's a. to sth.,** se préoccuper de qch; *Com:* **your orders shall have our best a.,** vos ordres seront exécutés avec le plus grand soin; *Adm: Com:* **for the a. of Mr X,** à l'attention de M. X; **to turn one's a. to sth.,** diriger son attention vers qch.; porter son attention sur qch.; **to pay a. to sth.,** faire attention à qch.; avoir égard à qch.; **to pay a. to s.o., to give one's a. to s.o.,** prêter (son) attention à qn; **pay a.!** faites attention! **to call, attract, draw, (s.o.'s) a. to sth.,** appeler, attirer, l'attention (de qn) sur qch.; faire remarquer qch. (à qn); **to catch s.o.'s a.,** attirer, fixer, l'attention de qn; **to attract everybody's a.,** fixer tous les regards; **to hold, engage, s.o.'s a.,** retenir l'attention de qn; **to be all a.,** être (tout yeux et) tout oreilles; (*b*) soins *mpl*, entretien *m*; **the batteries require daily, monthly, a.,** les accus exigent un entretien journalier, des soins mensuels. **2.** (*often in pl.*) attention(s), soins *mpl*, prévenance(s) *f(pl)*; *O:* **to pay one's attentions to a lady,** faire la cour à une dame. **3.** *Mil:* **a.!** garde-à-vous! **to come to a.,** se mettre au garde-à-vous; **to stand at a.,** être, se tenir, au garde-à-vous.

attentive [ə'tentiv] *a.* **1.** attentif **(to,** à); soigneux **(to,** de). **2. to be very a. to s.o.,** être aux petits soins pour qn; être très attentioné pour qn; être très empressé auprès de qn; se montrer galant (auprès d'une femme). **-ly** *adv.* attentivement; (écouter) avec attention.

attentiveness [ə'tentivnis] *n.* **1.** attention *f*. **2.** prévenances *fpl*, soins *mpl* **(to, for, s.o.,** pour qn).

attenuate [ə'tenjueit] **1.** *v.tr.* (*a*) amincir; (*b*) raréfier (un gaz, etc.); (*c*) atténuer, diminuer (la gravité de qch., etc.). **2.** *v.i.* s'atténuer; diminuer.

attenuation [ətenju'eiʃ(ə)n] *n.* atténuation *f*, diminution *f* (de qch).

attest [ə'test] *v.tr.* **1.** (*a*) attester, certifier (un fait); **to a. that . . .,** attester, certifier, que + *ind.*; **the document attests the fact that . . .,** le document démontre que . . .; *Husb:* **attested herd,** troupeau tuberculiné; (*b*) affirmer (qch.) sous serment; légaliser (une signature); **attested copy,** copie certifiée; (*c*) *v.i.* **to a. to sth.,** (i) témoigner de qch.; (ii) attester qch., se porter garant, témoin, de qch. **2.** *Jur:* assermenter (qn).

attestation [ætes'teiʃ(ə)n] *n.* **1.** *Jur:* (*a*) déposition *f* (d'un témoin); témoignage *m*; (*b*) attestation *f*; (*c*) légalisation *f* (d'une signature). **2.** prestation *f* de serment.

attic ['ætik] *n.* grenier *m*; **a. room,** mansarde; *f*; **a. window,** (i) fenêtre *f* en mansarde; (ii) lucarne *f*.

Attica ['ætikə] *Pr.n. Geog: Hist:* Attique *f*.

attire[1] [ə'taiər] *n.* **1.** vêtements *mpl*; costume *m*; **night a.,** vêtements de nuit. **2.** ramure *f* (d'un cerf).

attire[2] *v.tr.* **1.** *A: & Lit:* (*usu. passive or reflexive*) vêtir; parer. **2.** *Ven:* **stag attired,** cerf ramé.

attitude ['ætitju:d] *n.* **1.** (*a*) attitude *f*, pose *f*; **to strike an a.,** prendre une attitude dramatique; poser; (*b*) **a. of mind,** manière *f* de penser, de voir; disposition *f* d'esprit; état *m* d'esprit; **to maintain a firm a.,** (i) rester ferme; (ii) garder bonne contenance. **2.** (*of horse*) station *f*. **3.** *Av: etc:* attitude (d'un avion, d'un missile, etc., sur sa trajectoire).

attorney [ə'tə:ni] *n. Jur:* (*a*) *A: & NAm:* **a. (at law)** = avoué *m*; *U.S:* **District A.** = procureur *m* de la République; (*b*) **A. General** = (i) *Eng:* Procureur général; (ii) *U.S:* Procureur général d'un État; (iii) *Can:* Ministre *m* de la Justice; (*c*) procureur *m*, fondé *m* de pouvoir(s); **power of a.,** procuration *f*, mandat *m*, pouvoirs *mpl*; **full power of a.,** procuration générale.

attract [ə'trækt] *v.tr.* **1.** (*a*) attirer **(to,** à, vers); **a magnet attracts iron,** l'aimant attire le fer; (*b*) attirer (une foule, l'attention de qn). **2.** séduire, attirer; exercer une attraction sur (qn); avoir de l'attrait pour (qn); **he is not attracted to her,** elle ne lui plaît pas; *F:* elle ne lui dit rien.

attraction [ə'trækʃ(ə)n] *n.* **1.** attraction *f*, *Lit:* attirance *f* **(to,** vers); *Ph:* **molecular a.,** attraction moléculaire. **2.** (*usu. pl.*) attractions *fpl*, charme *m*, attraits *mpl*; **physical attractions,** charmes physiques. **3. the chief a.,** le clou (de la fête, du spectacle, etc.); **the great a. of the day,** la grande attraction du jour.

attractive [ə'træktiv] *a.* **1.** (*of magnet, etc.*) attractif, attirant. **2.** (*of pers., offer, manner*) attrayant, attirant, séduisant; (appartement, village) coquet; **this prospect was a.,** cette perspective me souriait, m'attirait; *Com:* **a. prices,** prix intéressants. **-ly** *adv.* d'une manière attrayante, séduisante.

attractiveness [ə'træktivnis] *n.* attrait *m*.

attributable [ə'tribjutəbl] *a.* attribuable, imputable **(to,** à).

attribute[1] ['ætribju:t] *n.* **1.** attribut *m*, qualité *f*. **2.** symbole *m*, attribut. **3.** *Gram:* épithète *f*.

attribute[2] [ə'tribju(:)t] *v.tr.* attribuer, imputer, référer **(to,** à); **comedy attributed to Shakespeare,** comédie attribuée à Shakespeare; **you a. to him qualities that he does not possess,** vous lui prêtez des qualités qu'il n'a pas.

attribution [ætri'bju:ʃ(ə)n] *n.* attribution *f*, imputation *f* **(to,** à).

attributive [ə'tribjutiv] *Gram:* **1.** *a.* **a. adjective,** épithète *f*; adjectif qualificatif. **2.** *n.* épithète. **-ly** *adv.* (mot employé) avec force qualificative.

attrition [ə'triʃ(ə)n] *n.* **1.** usure *f* par le frottement; **war of a.,** guerre *f* d'usure. **2.** *Theol:* attrition.

attune [ə'tju:n] *v.tr. Lit:* accorder, harmoniser **(to,** avec); **ear attuned to every sound,** oreille exercée à saisir tous les sons.

atypic(al) [ei'tipik(l)] *a. Med: etc:* atypique.

aubergine ['oubə(d)ʒi:n] *n. Bot: Cu:* aubergine *f*.

auburn ['ɔ:bən] *a.* (cheveux) châtain roux.

auction[1] ['ɔ:kʃ(ə)n] *n.* **(sale by) a., a. sale,** vente *f* à l'enchère, aux enchères; (vente à la) criée *f*; **Dutch a.,** vente à la baisse, enchère *f* au rabais; **to sell goods by a.,** *U.S:* **at a.,** vendre des marchandises aux enchères; (*of fish, etc.*) vendre à la criée; **to put sth. up for a.,** mettre qch. aux enchères; **a. room,**

salle *f* des ventes; (*for fish, vegetables, etc.*) chambre *f* des criées.

auction² *v.tr.* vendre (qch.) aux enchères; mettre (qch.) aux enchères; vendre (des denrées, un immeuble par autorité de justice) à la criée.

auctioneer [ɔːkʃə'niər] *n.* **1.** commissaire-priseur *m*, *pl.* commissaires-priseurs. **2.** (*at a sale*) directeur *m* de la vente; (*at fish, vegetable, market etc.*) crieur *m*.

audacious [ɔː'deiʃəs] *a.* **1.** audacieux, hardi, intrépide. **2.** *Pej:* effronté, hardi. **-ly** *adv.* **1.** audacieusement, avec audace. **2.** *Pej:* effrontément.

audacity [ɔː'dæsiti] *n.* **1.** audace *f*; intrépidité *f*, hardiesse *f*. **2.** *Pej:* effronterie *f*; **the lies which he had the a. to spread,** les mensonges qu'il a osé répandre.

audibility [ɔːdi'biliti] *n.* perceptibilité *f*, audibilité *f* (d'un son).

audible ['ɔːdibl] *a.* (*of sound*) perceptible (à l'oreille); (*of speech, voice*) audible; distinct; **he was scarcely a.,** on l'entendait à peine; *Ph:* **a. frequency,** fréquence *f* audible. **-ibly** *adv.* distinctement; **to speak a.,** parler de façon à être entendu.

audience ['ɔːdjəns] *n.* **1.** audience *f*; **to grant s.o. an a.,** accorder audience à qn; **to hold an a.,** tenir une audience; **a. chamber,** salle *f* d'audience. **2.** assistance *f*, assistants *mpl*; *Th:* spectateurs *mpl*, auditoire *m*, public *m*; (*at concert*) auditeurs *mpl*; **the whole a. applauded,** toute la salle applaudit; **to perform before a large a.,** jouer, chanter, etc., devant un nombreux public.

audio ['ɔːdiou] **1.** *a.* sonore; **a. typist,** dactylo *f* audiomagnéto. **2.** *n.* (reproduction *f* du) son *m*.

audiofrequency [ɔːdiou'friːkwənsi] *n.* *W.Tel: etc:* audiofréquence *f*; fréquence *f* acoustique.

audio-visual ['ɔːdiou'vizjuəl] *a.* audiovisuel.

audit¹ ['ɔːdit] *n.* (*a*) vérification *f*, apurement *m*, censure *f* (de comptes); vérification(s) comptable(s); *Adm:* **A. office** = la Cour des comptes; (*b*) *Pol.Ec:* **internal a.,** contrôle *m* interne.

audit² *v.tr.* vérifier, apurer, examiner (des comptes); **to a. the accounts of a company,** vérifier et certifier la comptabilité d'une société. **auditing** *n.* vérification *f* et certification *f* des écritures; apurement *m*.

audition¹ [ɔː'diʃ(ə)n] *n.* **1.** ouïe *f*; faculté *f* d'entendre. **2.** audition *f*, séance *f* d'essai.

audition² *v.tr.* & *i.* auditionner.

auditive ['ɔːditiv] *a.* auditif.

auditor ['ɔːditər] *n.* **1.** auditeur *m* (d'une conférence, etc.). **2.** (*a*) *Adm:* commissaire *m* aux comptes; vérificateur *m* des comptes; (*b*) *Com: Fin:* expert-comptable *m*; commissaire aux comptes (d'une société); censeur *m* (d'une compagnie d'assurances).

auditorium [ɔːdi'tɔːriəm] *n.* salle *f* (de théâtre, de concerts, de conférences, etc.).

auditory ['ɔːdit(ə)ri] *a.* (nerf, etc.) auditif; **the a. organ,** l'organe *m* de l'ouïe.

auger ['ɔːgər] *n.* **1.** *Tls:* tarière *f*; foret *m*. **2.** *Min: Civ.E:* tarière (de sondage).

aught [ɔːt] *n. A: & Lit:* quelque chose *m*, quoi que ce soit; **for a. I know,** (pour) autant que je sache.

augment¹ ['ɔːgmənt] *n. Gram:* augment *m*.

augment² [ɔːg'ment] **1.** *v.tr.* (*a*) augmenter, accroître (qch.) (**with, by,** de); (*b*) *Mus:* **augmented interval,** intervalle augmenté. **2.** *v.i.* augmenter, s'accroître.

augmentation [ɔːgmen'teiʃ(ə)n] *n.* augmentation *f*, accroissement *m* (de fortune, etc.).

augur¹ ['ɔːgər] *n. Rom. Ant:* (*pers.*) augure *m*.

augur² *v.tr.* & *i.* *Lit:* (*a*) augurer, présager, prédire; (*b*) (*of thg*) **it augurs no good,** cela ne présage, n'annonce, rien de bon; **it augurs well, ill,** cela est de bon, de mauvais, augure (**for,** pour).

augury ['ɔːgjuri] *n.* **1.** augure *m*; présage *m*. **2.** science *f* des augures; science augurale.

august¹ [ɔː'gʌst] *a.* (assemblée) auguste; (maintien) imposant, majestueux.

August² ['ɔːgəst] *n.* août *m*; **in A.,** au mois d'août, en août; **(on) the first of A.,** le premier août.

Augustinian [ɔːgəs'tiniən] *Rel.H:* **1.** *a.* augustinien; de Saint-Augustin; **A. monk, friar,** Augustin *m*. **2.** *n.* Augustin(e).

Augustus [ɔː'gʌstəs] *Pr.n.m.* Auguste.

auk [ɔːk] *n. Orn:* alque *f*; **great a.,** grand pingouin.

auld [ɔːld] *a. Scot:* vieux; **a. lang syne,** le temps jadis; le bon vieux temps.

aunt [ɑːnt] *n.f.* **1.** (*a*) tante; (*b*) *F:* tante (à la mode de Bretagne). **2.** *F:* (*a*) **A. Sally,** (i) = jeu *m* de massacre; (ii) objet *m* de dérision.

auntie, aunty ['ɑːnti] *n.f. F:* tatie, tata.

au pair ['ou'pɛər] **1.** *a.* & *n.* **au p. (girl),** étudiante au pair. **2.** *adv.* **she's staying with them au p.,** elle est chez eux au pair.

aura ['ɔːrə] *n.* **1.** *Med:* aura *f*; **epileptic a.,** aura épileptique. **2.** *Lit:* aura (de sainteté, etc.).

aural ['ɔːrəl, aurəl] *a.* auditif, sonore; **a. surgeon, specialist,** auriste *m*; *W.Tel: etc:* **a. reception,** réception *f* du son.

aureola [ɔː'riələ], **aureole** ['ɔːrioul] *n.* **1.** *Art:* auréole le *f*, gloire *f* (d'un saint). **2.** *Astr:* auréole (du soleil).

auricular [ɔː'rikjulər] **1.** *a.* (*a*) *Anat:* (conduit, etc.) auriculaire; (*b*) (témoin, etc.) auriculaire; *Ecc:* **a. confession,** confession *f* auriculaire. **2.** *n.* (doigt *m*) auriculaire (*m*).

aurochs ['ɔːrɔks] *n. Z:* aurochs *m*.

Aurora [ɔː'rɔːrə] **1.** *Pr.n.f. Myth:* Aurore. **2. a.,** aurore *f*; **a. borealis, australis,** aurore boréale, australe.

auscultation [ɔːsk(ə)l'teiʃ(ə)n] *n. Med:* auscultation *f*; **to examine by a.,** ausculter (un malade).

auspices ['ɔːspisiz] *n.pl.* auspices *mpl*; (*a*) **favourable a.,** d'heureux auspices; (*b*) **under the a. of the United Nations,** sous les auspices des Nations Unies.

auspicious [ɔːs'piʃəs] *a.* **1.** (*a*) (vent, etc.) propice, favorable; (*b*) (signe) de bon augure. **2.** (âge) heureux, prospère; **on this a. occasion,** en ce jour mémorable. **-ly** *adv.* (*a*) sous d'heureux auspices; (*b*) favorablement; **to begin a.,** commencer heureusement.

auspiciousness [ɔːs'piʃəsnis] *n.* heureux auspices; aspect *m* favorable, propice (d'une entreprise, etc.).

Aussie ['ɔzi] *F:* **1.** *a.* australien. **2.** *n.* (*a*) Australien, -ienne; **the Aussies,** les Australiens; (*b*) l'Australie *f*; (*c*) *Ling:* l'anglais australien.

austere [ɔːs'tiər] *a.* (vie, style, etc.) austère; (appartement) sans luxe, d'un goût sévère; **to lead an a. life,** vivre en ascète. **-ly** *adv.* austèrement; avec austérité.

austerity [ɔːs'teriti] *n.* austérité *f*; sévérité *f* de goût; **a. measures,** mesures *fpl* d'austérité.

Australasia [ɔstrə'leiʒə, -'leiʃə] *Pr.n. Geog:* Australasie *f*.

Australasian [ɔstrə'leiʒ(ə)n, -'leiʃ(ə)n] **1.** *a.* australasien. **2.** *n.* Australasien, -ienne.

Australia [ɔ'streiliə] *Pr.n. Geog:* Australie *f*; **South A.,** Australie méridionale; **Western A.,** Australie occidentale.

Australian [ɔs'treiliən] **1.** *a.* australien. **2.** *n.* (*a*) Australien, -ienne; (*b*) l'anglais australien.

Austria ['ɔstriə] *Pr.n. Geog:* Autriche *f*.

Austrian ['ɔstriən] **1.** *a.* autrichien. **2.** *n.* Autrichien, -ienne.

Austro-Hungarian ['ɔstrouhʌŋ'gɛəriən] *a. Hist:* austro-hongrois; **the A.-H. Empire,** l'empire d'Autriche-Hongrie.

autarchy ['ɔːtɑːki] *n.* autarchie *f*.

autarky ['ɔːtɑːki] *n.* autarcie *f*.

authentic [ɔː'θentik] *a.* (*a*) (document, fait, his-

toire, etc.) authentique; (*b*) *Ecc.Mus:* (mode, cadence) authentique. **-ally** *adv.* authentiquement.
authenticate [ɔː'θentikeit] *v.tr.* **1.** certifier, homologuer, légaliser, valider (un acte, etc.). **2.** (*a*) établir l'authenticité de (qch.); (*b*) *Mil:* (*signals*) identifier (un correspondant).
authentication [ɔːθenti'keiʃ(ə)n] *n.* **1.** authentication *f*; certification *f* (d'une signature, etc.); homologation *f*, législation *f*, validation *f*. **2.** (*a*) preuve *f* de l'authenticité (d'un document, etc.); (*b*) *Mil: W.Tel: etc:* identification *f* (d'un correspondant).
authenticity [ɔːθen'tisiti] *n.* authenticité *f*.
author ['ɔːθər] *n.* (*a*) auteur *m* (d'un livre); **she is the a. of several novels,** elle est l'auteur de plusieurs romans; (*b*) auteur (d'une théorie, etc.); **to be the a. of one's own misfortunes,** être l'auteur de sa ruine.
authoress [ɔːθər'es] *n.f.* femme *f* auteur, écrivain.
authoritarian [ɔːθɔri'tɛəriən] *a. & n.* autoritaire (*m*).
authoritative [ɔː'θɔritətiv] *a.* **1.** (caractère) autoritaire; (ton) d'autorité. **2.** (*a*) revêtu d'autorité; (document) qui fait foi, qui fait autorité; (*b*) **to have sth. from an a. source,** avoir qch. de source autorisée, de bonne source. **-ly** *adv.* **1.** autoritairement. **2. I can state it a.,** je puis l'affirmer de bonne source.
authority [ɔː'θɔriti] *n.* autorité *f*. **1. to have, exercise, a. over s.o.,** (i) avoir, exercer une, autorité sur qn; (ii) avoir de l'ascendant sur qn. **2.** autorisation *f*, mandat *m*; **to have a. to act,** avoir qualité *f* pour agir; **to give s.o. a. to do sth.,** autoriser qn à faire qch.; **to act on s.o.'s a.,** agir sur l'autorité de qn; **to do sth. on one's own a.,** faire qch. de sa propre autorité. **3.** (*a*) (*of pers., book*) **to be an a. on sth.,** faire autorité en matière de qch.; être expert dans la matière; (*b*) **to have sth. on good a.,** tenir, savoir, qch. de bonne part, de bonne source, de source autorisée; **to quote s.o. as one's a.,** se réclamer de qn; **to quote one's authorities,** citer ses sources, ses auteurs. **4.** *Adm:* **administrative a.,** service administratif; **the authorities,** l'administration *f*; les autorités; **the health authorities,** les services d'hygiène; **the military authorities,** les autorités militaires.
authorization [ɔːθ(ə)rai'zeiʃ(ə)n] *n.* autorisation *f* (**to do sth.,** de faire qch.); pouvoir *m*; mandat *m*.
authorize ['ɔːθəraiz] *v.tr.* autoriser (qn, qch.) (**to do sth.,** à faire qch.) **to be authorized to act,** avoir qualité pour agir. **authorized** *a.* (*a*) autorisé; *Ecc:* **the A. Version,** la traduction anglaise de la Bible de 1611; *Adm:* **a. charges,** prix homologués; (*b*) *Mil: etc:* réglementaire.
authorship ['ɔːθəʃip] *n.* **1.** profession *f*, qualité *f*, d'auteur. **2. to establish the a. of a book,** identifier l'auteur d'un livre.
autism ['ɔːtizm] *n. Med:* autisme *m*.
autistic [ɔː'tistik] *a. Med:* autistique.
auto ['ɔːtou] *n. NAm: F:* automobile *f*, voiture *f*.
autobiographic(al) [ɔːtoubaiə'græfik(l)] *a.* autobiographique.
autobiography [ɔːtoubai'ɔgrəfi] *n.* autobiogra phie *f*.
autocade ['ɔːtoukeid] *n. U.S:* cortège *m* de voitures.
autocracy [ɔː'tɔkrəsi] *n.* autocratie *f*.
autocrat ['ɔːtəkræt] *n.* autocrate *m*.
autocratic(al) [ɔːtə'krætik(l)] *a.* autocratique; (*of pers.*) autocrate; (caractère) absolu. **-ally** *adv.* autocratiquement.
autocue ['ɔːtoukjuː] *n. TV:* téléprompteur *m*.
auto-cycle ['ɔːtousaikl] *n.* cyclomoteur *m*.
autodidact [ɔːtou'daidækt] *n.* autodidacte *mf*.
autogenous [ɔː'tɔdʒinəs] *a.* autogène; **a. welding,** soudure *f* autogène.
autogiro [ɔːtou'dʒairou] *n. Av:* autogyre *m*.
autograph¹ ['ɔːtəgrɑːf, -græf] **1.** *n.* autographe *m*; **a. album,** album *m* de signatures. **2.** *a.* **a. letter of Byron,** lettre *f* autographe de Byron.
autograph² *v.tr.* **1.** écrire (une lettre, etc.) de sa propre main. **2.** écrire son autographe dans (un livre); signer, dédicacer (un exemplaire); mettre son autographe à (un document). **3.** *Lith:* autographier (un manuscrit, etc.).
autographic(al) [ɔːtə'græfik(l)] *a.* **1.** (lettre) autographe. **2.** *Lith:* (encre, papier) autographique.
autogyro [ɔːtou'dʒairou] *n. Av:* autogyre *m*.
automat ['ɔːtəmæt] *n. NAm:* restaurant *m* à distributeurs automatiques.
automate ['ɔːtəmeit] *v.tr.* automatiser, rendre automatique. **automated** *a.* automatisé.
automatic [ɔːtə'mætik] *a.* (*a*) automatique; **a. vending machine,** distributeur *m* automatique; *Sm.a:* **a. pistol,** *n.* **automatic,** automatique *m*; *Cmptr:* **a. coding,** codage *m* automatique; *Av:* **a. pilot,** pilote *m* automatique; *I.C.E:* **a. transmission,** transmission *f* automatique; **a Renault a.,** une Renault (avec boîte de vitesses) automatique; (*b*) (mouvement) automatique, inconscient, machinal. **-ally** *adv.* automatiquement.
automation [ɔːtə'meiʃ(ə)] *n.* **1.** automatisation *f*. **2.** l'automatique *f*.
automatization [ɔːtɔmətai'zeiʃ(ə)n] *n.* automatisation *f*.
automaton, *pl.* **-ons, -a** [ɔː'tɔmətən, -ənz, -ə] *n.* automate *m*.
automobile ['ɔːtəmoubiːl] *n.* (*a*) *NAm:* automobile *f*, voiture *f*; (*b*) **a. club,** club *m* automobile.
automotive [ɔːtou'moutiv] *a.* **1.** automoteur, -trice. **2.** *esp. NAm:* automobile; **a. engineering,** technique *f* automobile.
autonomous [ɔː'tɔnəməs] *a.* autonome.
autonomy [ɔː'tɔnəmi] *n.* autonomie *f*.
autopilot ['ɔːtoupailət] *n. Av:* pilote *m* automatique.
autopsy ['ɔːtɔpsi, ɔː'tɔpsi] *n.* autopsie *f*.
autosuggestion [ɔːtousə'dʒestʃ(ə)n] *n.* autosuggestion *f*.
autotype ['ɔːtoutaip] *n.* **1.** *Typ:* (*process or image*) phototypographie *f*. **2.** reproduction *f*, copie *f* (de tableau, sculpture, etc.).
autumn ['ɔːtəm] *n.* automne *m*; **in a.,** en automne; **an a. evening,** une soirée d'automne; **a. plants,** plantes automnales. *Bot:* **a. crocus,** colchique *m* d'automne.
autumnal [ɔː'tʌmn(ə)l] *a.* automnal; d'automne; **a. equinox,** équinoxe *m* d'automne.
auxiliary [ɔːg'ziliəri] *a. & n.* auxiliaire (*mf*); subsidiaire (**to,** à); supplémentaire; (machine, etc.) de secours; (chauffage, éclairage) d'appoint; *Gram:* **a. verb,** *n.* **a.,** verbe *m* auxiliaire; *Tchn:* **a. engine,** machine *f* auxiliaire; *Mil:* **a. troops,** *n.pl.* **auxiliaries,** (troupes *fpl*) auxiliaires (*mpl*).
avail¹ [ə'veil] *n. Lit:* avantage *m*, utilité *f*; **of no a., without a.,** sans effet; **to be of little a.,** être peu utile, peu avantageux; **to work to little, to no, a.,** travailler sans (grand) résultat.
avail² *v.tr. & i.* **1.** *Lit:* profiter, servir, être utile, à (qn); **nothing availed against the storm,** contre la tempête nous ne pouvions rien. **2. to a. oneself of (sth.),** se servir, s'aider, de (qch.); profiter de (qch.); user, faire usage, d'(un droit); **to a. oneself of the opportunity to do sth.,** saisir l'occasion de faire qch.
availability [əveilə'biliti] *n.* **1.** disponibilité *f* (de matériaux, d'hommes, etc.). **2.** *Rail: etc:* validité *f* (d'un billet).
available [ə'veiləbl] *a.* **1.** (*a*) disponible; (*of pers.*) libre; *Bank:* réalisable; **to try every a. means,** essayer de tous les moyens possibles; **a. time,** temps *m* disponible; **a. funds,** fonds *mpl* liquides, disponibles; disponibilités *fpl*; **capital that can be made a.,** capitaux *mpl* mobilisables; (*b*) accessible; *Com:* **a. in all**

bookshops, se trouve, s'achète, chez tous les libraires. **2.** (*of rail ticket, etc.*) valable, bon, valide (pour deux mois, etc.); utilisable (par tous les trains); **period for which a ticket is a.,** durée *f* de validité d'un billet.

avalanche ['ævəlɑːnʃ] *n.* avalanche *f* (de neige, *Fig:* de félicitations, etc.); **mud a.,** coulée *f* de boue.

avant-garde ['ævɑ̃'gɑːd] *Lit: etc:* **1.** *n.* l'avant-garde *f.* **2.** *a.* d'avant-garde, avant-gardiste; **an a.-g. film,** un film d'avant-garde.

avarice ['ævəris] *n.* avarice *f.*

avaricious [ævə'riʃəs] *a.* avare, avaricieux. **-ly** *adv.* avaricieusement.

avast [ə'vɑːst] *int. Nau:* tiens bon! tenez bon! baste!

Ave (Maria) ['ɑːvi(mə'riə] *n.* avé (Maria) *m inv.*

avenge [ə'ven(d)ʒ] *v.tr.* venger (qn, une injure); **to a. oneself for an insult,** se venger d'une injure; **his death will be avenged,** sa mort trouvera des vengeurs. **avenging** *a.* (ange, etc.) vengeur.

avenger [ə'ven(d)ʒər] *n.* vengeur *m*, vengeresse *f.*

avens ['ævənz] *n. Bot:* **1. wood a.,** benoîte *f.* **2. mountain a.,** chêneau *m.*

avenue ['ævinjuː] *n.* (*a*) avenue *f*; (*b*) *esp. U.S:* (belle) rue; boulevard *m*; (*c*) chemin *m* d'accès; *Fig:* **to explore every a. that might lead to an agreement,** explorer toutes les voies *f* pouvant amener à un accord; (*d*) promenade plantée d'arbres.

aver [ə'vəːr] *v.tr.* **(averring; averred)** *Lit:* avérer, déclarer, affirmer (que).

average[1] ['ævəridʒ] *n.* **1.** (*a*) moyenne *f*; **rough a.,** moyenne approximative; **on an a.,** en moyenne; **above the a.,** au-dessus de la moyenne; (*b*) *Fb: etc:* **goal a.,** goal-average *m*, avérage *m.* **2.** *M.Ins:* avarie(s) *f* (*pl*); **a. adjustment,** dispache *f.*

average[2] *a.* (prix, temps, poids, etc.) moyen; **the a. Englishman,** l'Anglais moyen; **of a. height,** de taille moyenne; **a. speed,** vitesse moyenne; **the a. reader,** le lecteur moyen; **of good a. quality,** de bonne qualité moyenne.

average[3] *v.tr. & i.* **1.** prendre, établir, faire, la moyenne (des résultats, des ventes, etc.). **2.** (*a*) **to a. so much,** donner, atteindre, rendre, une moyenne de tant; **the sales a. a thousand copies a year,** la vente moyenne, la moyenne des ventes, est de mille exemplaires par an; (*b*) **to a. eight hours' work a day,** travailler en moyenne huit heures par jour.

averse [ə'vəːs] *a.* opposé; **to be a. to, from, sth.,** répugner à qch.; **he is not a. to a glass of beer,** il prend volontiers un verre de bière.

aversion [ə'vəːʃ(ə)n] *n.* **1.** aversion *f*, répugnance *f*; **to feel, have, an a. to, for, s.o.,** se sentir de l'aversion pour, envers, qn; **to feel, have, a great a. to sth., to doing sth.,** se sentir une grande répugnance pour qch., à faire qch. **2.** objet *m* d'aversion; **my pet a.,** ma bête noire.

avert [ə'vəːt] *v.tr.* **1.** détourner (les yeux, son regard, ses pensées) **(from,** de). **2.** écarter, éloigner, prévenir (des soupçons, un danger, un malheur); conjurer (une catastrophe); détourner (un coup); parer à (un accident).

aviary ['eiviəri] *n.* volière *f.*

aviation [eivi'eiʃ(ə)n] *n.* aviation *f*; **civil, military, a.,** aviation civile, militaire.

aviator ['eivieitər] *n.* aviateur, -trice.

aviculture ['eivikʌltjər] *n.* aviculture *f.*

avid ['ævid] *a.* avide **(of, for,** de). **-ly** *adv.* avidement; avec avidité.

avidity [ə'viditi] *n.* avidité *f* **(for,** de, pour).

avocado [ævə'kɑːdou] *n. Bot:* **1.** avocatier *m.* **2. a. (pear),** avocat *m.*

avoid [ə'vɔid] *v.tr.* **1.** éviter (qn, qch.); **to a. doing sth.,** éviter de faire qch.; **I could not a. speaking to him,** je ne pouvais faire autrement que de lui parler; **to a. paying tax,** se soustraire à l'impôt. **2.** se soustraire (au châtiment, etc.); esquiver (les attentions de qn, un coup, une difficulté); **to a. a collision,** parer à, éviter, une collision; **to a. s.o.'s eye,** fuir le regard de qn; **to a. the issue,** contourner les difficultés.

avoidable [ə'vɔidəbl] *a.* évitable.

avoidance [ə'vɔidəns] *n.* **1.** action *f* d'éviter; **tax a.,** évasion fiscale. **2.** *Jur:* **a. of an agreement,** résolution *f*, résiliation *f*, résiliement *m*, d'un contrat; (*in contract*) **condition of a.,** condition *f* résolutoire.

avoirdupois [ævədə'pɔiz] *n.* **1.** poids *m* du commerce; **ounce a.,** once *f* avoirdupois. **2.** *NAm:* (*of pers.*) excès *m* de poids; embonpoint *m.*

avow [ə'vau] *v.tr.* **1.** (*a*) **to a. oneself a socialist,** se déclarer, s'avérer, socialiste. **2.** avouer, admettre (une faute); **to a. oneself beaten,** s'avouer vaincu. **avowed** *a.* (ennemi, etc.) déclaré; **an a. atheist,** un athée avoué.

avuncular [ə'vʌŋkjulər] *a.* avunculaire.

await [ə'weit] *v.tr.* **1.** (*a*) *Lit:* (*of pers.*) attendre (qch., *occ.* qn); *Com:* **awaiting your instructions,** dans l'attente de vos instructions; (*b*) **soldiers awaiting discharge,** soldats *m* en instance de réforme; *Com:* **parcels awaiting delivery,** colis *m* en souffrance. **2.** (*of thg*) attendre (qn); **there was a surprise awaiting us,** une surprise nous attendait.

awake[1] [ə'weik] *v.* (*p.t.* **awoke** [ə'wouk]; *p.p.* **awoken** [ə'woukən]) **1.** *v.i.* (*a*) s'éveiller, se réveiller; (*b*) **to a. to (sth.),** se rendre compte d'(un danger, un fait, etc.); prendre conscience d'(un danger, etc.); **to a. from (sth.),** revenir d'(une illusion, un rêve, etc.). **2.** *v.tr.* éveiller, réveiller (qn, les remords de qn); éveiller (la curiosité, les soupçons); faire naître (un espoir, une passion).

awake[2] *a.* **1.** éveillé; **to lie a., to keep a.,** rester éveillé; **I was a.,** je ne dormais pas; **to keep s.o. a.,** tenir qn éveillé; **wide a.,** (i) bien éveillé, tout éveillé; (ii) *F:* averti. **2.** attentif; **to be a. to (sth.),** (i) avoir conscience d'(un danger); se rendre compte d'(un danger, un fait, etc.); (ii) veiller à, sur (ses intérêts).

awaken [ə'weik(ə)n] *v.tr. & i.* = AWAKE[1]. **awakening** *n.* (*a*) réveil *m*; (*b*) **a rude a.,** une amère désillusion.

award[1] [ə'wɔːd] *n.* **1.** *Jur:* arbitrage *m*; sentence arbitrale; décision (arbitrale), adjudication *f*; **to make an a.,** rendre un jugement (arbitral). **2.** (*a*) *Jur:* dommages-intérêts *mpl*; (*b*) *Mil: etc:* distinction *f* honorifique; *Sch: etc:* récompense *f*; **to make an a.,** (i) décerner un prix, une récompense; (ii) juger un candidat (à un examen).

award[2] *v.tr.* adjuger, décerner (un prix, une récompense); adjuger (un marché, un contrat); conférer (un bénéfice, une dignité); accorder (une augmentation de salaire); **to a. s.o. a sum as damages,** allouer, attribuer, à qn une somme à titre de dommages-intérêts. **awarding** *n.* décernement *m* (d'un prix, etc.); adjudication *f* (d'un prix, d'un marché, etc.); attribution *f* (de courses, etc.).

aware [ə'wɛər] *a.* **to be a. of sth.,** avoir connaissance, avoir conscience, être au courant, de qch.; savoir, ne pas ignorer, qch.; **I wasn't a. of him,** je ne m'étais pas aperçu qu'il était là; **I am a. of all the circumstances,** je connais tous les détails; **I am well, fully, a. that . . .,** je n'ignore pas que . . .; **not that I am a. of,** pas que je sache; **to become a. of sth.,** prendre connaissance (d'un fait); **I became a. of a smell of burning,** j'ai perçu une odeur de brûlé.

awareness [ə'wɛənis] *n.* conscience *f* (de qch.); **a sudden a.,** une prise de conscience.

awash [ə'wɔʃ] *a.* **1.** *Nau:* (*of submarine, etc.*) à fleur d'eau; **rocks a. at high tide,** roches *fpl* couvertes d'eau à marée haute. **2.** inondé; **the street was a.,** la rue était inondée.

away [ə'wei] *adv.* **1.** (*in compound verbs*) (*a*) **to go a.,** partir, s'en aller; **to walk, drive, a.,** partir à pied, en voiture; **to run, fly, a.,** s'enfuir, s'envoler; **to take sth. a.,** emporter qch.; **put that knife a.!** pose ce couteau! (*b*) (*of snow*) **to melt a.,** fondre; (*of sound*) **to fade, die, a.,** s'éteindre; **to fritter a.,** gaspiller (son argent, son temps); (*c*) **to do a. with,** abolir (qch.); tuer (qn). **2.** (*elliptical*) **a. with you!** allez-vous-en! filez! **a. with him!** emmenez-le! *A: & Lit:* **we must a.,** il nous faut partir; *F:* **well a.,** (i) bien en train; (ii) ivre, soûl. **3.** (*continuity*) **to work a.,** travailler toujours; continuer à travailler; **to slave a. at sth.,** s'éreinter à qch. **4.** (*without delay*) **to do sth. right, straight, a.,** faire qch. tout de suite, sur-le-champ. **5.** (*a*) loin; **far a.,** dans le lointain, au loin; **a. in the distance,** tout au loin; **the town is five miles a.,** la ville est à (une distance de) cinq milles; **please stand a little farther a.,** voudriez-vous vous éloigner un peu; **this is far and a. the best,** c'est de beaucoup, sans comparaison, le meilleur; (*b*) **to hold sth. a. from sth.,** tenir qch. éloigné, loin, de qch.; **to turn (one's face) a. from sth.,** détourner la tête de qch.; **the signpost pointed a. from the village,** le bras du poteau indiquait une direction opposée à celle du village; (*c*) **a. from home,** absent (de chez soi); **he is a.,** il est absent; **to stay a.,** rester absent; ne pas venir; **to keep a.,** se tenir à l'écart; éviter (un endroit, etc.); (*d*) *a. Sp:* **a. ground,** terrain *m* adverse; **a. match,** match *m* à l'extérieur, sur terrain adverse; *adv.* **to play a.,** jouer à l'extérieur. **6.** (*time*) **a. back,** dès; **I knew him a. back in 1950,** je l'ai connu dès 1950.

awe¹ [ɔ:] *n.* (i) crainte *f*; (ii) respect *m*; révérence *f*; **to strike s.o. with a.,** (*of pers.*) imposer à qn un respect mêlé de crainte; (*of object, phenomenon*) frapper qn d'une terreur mystérieuse; **to stand in a. of s.o.,** (i) craindre, redouter, qn; (ii) avoir une crainte respectueuse de qn.

awe² *v.tr.* remplir de crainte; intimider (qn); inspirer un respect mêlé de crainte à (qn).

aweigh [ə'wei] *adv. Nau:* **with anchor a.,** l'ancre dérapée; **anchors a.!** levez l'ancre!

awe-inspiring ['ɔ:inspaiəriŋ], **awesome** ['ɔ:səm] *a.* d'une majesté émotionnante; imposant, impressionnant; (spectacle) grandiose; **an awesome silence,** un silence qui inspire un effroi religieux.

awe-struck ['ɔ:strʌk] *a.* **1.** frappé d'une terreur mystérieuse. **2.** intimidé.

awful ['ɔ:ful] *a.* **1.** terrible, effroyable; **to die an a. death,** mourir d'une mort terrible; **that's the a. part of it,** c'est cela le plus terrible. **2.** (*a*) terrifiant; (*b*) imposant, solennel. **3.** *F:* terrible, affreux, abominable; **it's simply a.,** c'est affreux; **he's an a. fool,** il est bien bête; **what a. weather!** quel temps abominable! **4.** *adv. P:* terriblement; **I'm a. glad to see you,** je suis rudement content de vous voir. **-fully** *adv.* **1.** terriblement, effroyablement. **2.** solennellement. **3.** *F:* **I'm a. sorry,** je regrette infiniment, énormément; **I'm a. glad,** je suis joliment content; **a. funny,** amusant, drôle, comme tout; **she's a. nice,** elle est gentille comme tout; **thanks a.!** merci mille fois!

awfulness ['ɔ:fulnis] *n.* **1.** caractère imposant, solennité *f* (d'un lieu). **2.** caractère terrible (d'une situation).

awhile [ə'(h)wail] *adv. Lit:* pendant quelque temps; un peu; **wait a.,** attendez un peu.

awkward ['ɔ:kwəd] *a.* **1.** gauche, maladroit, disgracieux, balourd; **the a. age,** l'âge ingrat; **to be a. with one's hands,** avoir la main maladroite; **a. sentence,** phrase gauche, mal venue. **2.** embarrassé, gêné; **I felt very a.,** je me suis senti très gêné, embarrassé. **3.** fâcheux, embarrassant, gênant; **it would be a. if we met,** une rencontre serait embarrassante; **an a. silence,** un silence gêné; **to arrive at an a. moment,** arriver mal à propos; **to ask a. questions,** poser des questions embarrassantes. **4.** incommode, peu commode; (outil) peu maniable; (virage) difficile, dangereux; *F:* **he's an a. customer,** c'est un homme difficile; il n'est pas commode. **-ly** *adv.* **1.** gauchement, maladroitement, disgracieusement. **2.** d'une manière embarrassée, d'un ton embarrassé, gêné. **3.** d'une façon gênante, embarrassante; **to be a. placed,** se trouver dans une situation embarrassante, dans une une fausse position. **4. the lever is a. placed,** le levier est mal placé.

awkwardness ['ɔ:kwədnis] *n.* **1.** (i) gaucherie *f*; maladresse *f*; (ii) manque *m* de grâce; balourdise *f*. **2.** embarras *m*, gêne *f*; **a moment of a.,** un moment de gêne. **3.** inconvénient *m*, difficulté *f*, incommodité *f* (d'une situation, etc.).

awl [ɔ:l] *n. Tls:* alêne *f*; poinçon *m*, perçoir *m*.

awn [ɔ:n] *n. Bot:* barbe *f* (de l'orge, etc.).

awning ['ɔ:niŋ] *n* (*a*) tente *f*, vélum *m*; banne *f* (de boutique, etc.); bâche *f* (de charrette); **a. (blind),** store *m* à l'italienne; (*b*) *Nau:* tente, tendelet *m*; cabane *f* (de canot); **rain a.,** taud *m*, taude *f*; **a. deck,** pont-abri *m*, *pl.* ponts-abris; (*c*) marquise *f* (de théâtre, d'hôtel, etc.).

awry [ə'rai] *adv. & a. O:* de travers; de guingois; (*of plans, etc.*) **to go all a.,** aller tout de travers.

axe¹, *NAm: also* **ax**, *pl.* **axes** [æks, 'æksiz] *n.* **1.** hache *f*; **broad a.,** doloire *m*; **ice a.,** piolet *m*; **a. head,** fer *m* de hache; *Fig:* **to have an a. to grind,** agir dans un but intéressé. **2.** *Adm: F:* **the a.,** coupe *f* dans les prévisions budgétaires; réductions *fpl* sur les traitements; diminutions *fpl* de personnel.

axe², *NAm: also* **ax** *v.tr.* **1.** mettre la cognée à (un arbre); tailler, dresser, dégrossir (du bois). **2.** *Adm: F:* renvoyer (qn); abandonner (un projet) (pour des raisons d'économie); **to a. public expenditure,** porter la hache dans les dépenses publiques.

axial ['æksiəl] *a.* axial, -aux.

axil ['æksil] *n. Bot:* aisselle *f* (d'une feuille).

axiom ['æksiəm] *n.* axiome *m*.

axiomatic [æksiə'mætik] *a.* (*a*) axiomatique; (*b*) évident.

axis, *pl.* **axes** ['æksis, 'æksi:z] *n.* **1.** axe *m* (d'une sphère, d'une plante, d'un cristal, *Geol:* d'un plissement); **a. of the earth,** axe de la terre; **a. of revolution,** axe de révolution. **2.** *Anat:* axis *m* (du cou).

axle ['æksl] *n.* **1.** *Veh:* **a. (tree),** essieu *m*; *Rail:* **driving a.,** essieu moteur; *Aut:* **front, rear, a.,** essieu, pont *m*, avant, arrière; **a. box,** boîte *f* de l'essieu. **2.** tourillon *m*, arbre *m*, axe *m* (d'une roue, etc.).

ay(e) [ai] **1.** *adv. & int.* (*a*) (*esp. Scot.*) oui; mais oui; (*b*) *Nau:* **a., a., sir!** (i) oui, mon commandant! (ii) paré! **2.** *n.* (*in voting*) **ayes and noes,** voix *fpl* pour et contre; **the ayes have it,** les voix pour l'emportent.

azalea [ə'zeiliə] *n. Bot:* azalée *f*.

azimuth ['æziməθ] *n. Astr: Surv: etc:* azimut *m*.

Azores (the) [ði:ə'zɔ:z] *Pr.n.pl. Geog:* les Açores *fpl*.

Aztec ['æztek] *Ethn: Hist:* **1.** *a.* aztèque. **2.** *n.* (*a*) Aztèque *mf*; (*b*) *Ling:* aztèque *m*.

azure ['æʒər, 'eiʒer] **1.** *n. Lit:* azur *m*. **2.** *a. Lit:* d'azur, azuré; **an a. sky,** un ciel d'azur.

B

B, b [biː] *n.* **1.** (*a*) (la lettre) B, b *m*; (*b*) (*in numbering*) **51B,** 51 (i) bis, (ii) ter; *Mil:* **B company,** deuxième compagnie *f*; (*c*) **B road** route *f* secondaire; (*d*) *Sch:* = assez bien. **2.** *Mus:* si *m*; **B flat,** si bémol.

baa¹ [bɑː] *n.* bêlement *m*; **baa!** bê! (*child's language*) **b.-lamb,** petit agneau.

baa² *v.i.* **(baaed, baa'd** [bɑːd]) bêler.

baba ['bɑːbə] *n. Cu:* **rum b.,** baba *m* au rhum.

babbitt ['bæbit] *n.* **b. (metal),** métal *m* antifriction.

babble¹ ['bæb(ə)l] *n.* **1.** babillage *m.* **2.** bavardage *m.* **3.** murmure *m* (d'un ruisseau).

babble² *v.i.* (*a*) babiller; (*b*) bavarder, jaser; **to b. on,** parler sans s'arrêter; (*c*) (*of stream*) murmurer, gazouiller. **babbling 1.** *a.* (*a*) babillard, bavard, jaseur; (*b*) (*of stream*) murmurant. **2.** *n.* = BABBLE¹.

babbler ['bæblər] *n.* (*a*) babillard, -arde; (*b*) bavard, -arde; jaseur, -euse (qui laisse échapper des secrets).

babe [beib] *n.* **1.** *Lit: etc:* petit enfant, bambin *m*; **a b. in arms,** (i) un enfant porté au bras; (ii) *Fig:* un naïf, une naïve. **2.** *NAm: F:* jolie fille; **hi, b.!** bonjour, ma jolie!

Babel ['beibəl] **1.** *Pr.n.* **the Tower of B.,** la Tour de Babel. **2.** *n.* **b. of voices,** brouhaha *m.*

baboon [bə'buːn] *n. Z:* babouin *m.*

baby¹ ['beibi] *n.* **1.** (*a*) bébé *m*; **she has had a b. boy, girl,** elle a eu un petit garçon, une petite fille; **the b. of the family,** le benjamin; **to behave like a b.,** faire le bébé; *F:* **to leave s.o. holding the b.,** laisser payer les pots cassés à qn; (*b*) *F:* **the dictionary is his b.,** le dictionnaire est (i) sa création, (ii) sa marotte, (iii) sa responsabilité; (*c*) *U.S: F:* (i) jeune fille *f*, nana *f*; (*as address*) chéri(e); (ii) type *m*; (iii) machin *m*; **I've been driving this b. for a year,** je conduis cette bagnole depuis un an. **2.** (*a*) **b. scales,** pèse-bébé *m*, *pl.* pèse-bébés; *NAm:* **b. carriage,** voiture *f* d'enfant; **b. walker,** trotteuse *f*; **b. talk,** babil enfantin; **b. minder,** gardeuse *f* d'enfants; *F:* **b. face,** visage poupin; (*b*) **b. elephant,** bébé éléphant; (*c*) **b. carrots,** de toutes petites carottes; *Mus:* **b. grand,** (piano *m*) demi-queue *m.*

baby² *v.tr.* **(babied)** *F:* traiter (qn) en bébé; dorloter (qn).

baby-faced ['beibifeist] *a.* à visage poupin.

babyhood ['beibihud] *n.* première enfance; bas âge.

babyish ['beibiiʃ] *a.* de petit enfant; bébête; puéril.

Babylon ['bæbilən] *Pr.n. A.Geog:* Babylone *f.*

Babylonia [bæbi'louniə] *Pr.n. A.Geog:* Babylonie *f.*

Babylonian [bæbi'louniən] **1.** *a. B.Hist:* babylonien. **2.** *n.* Babylonien, -ienne.

baby-sit ['beibisit] *v.i.* **(-sat, -sitting)** garder les bébés; *F:* faire du baby-sitting. **baby-sitting** *n.* garde *f* des bébés; *F:* baby-sitting *m.*

baby-sitter ['beibisitər] *n.* garde-bébé *mf*, *pl.* gardes-bébés.

baby-snatcher ['beibisnætʃər] *n.* (*a*) kidnappeur, -euse; (*b*) *F:* (i) vieux barbeau; (ii) femme qui épouse un garçon beaucoup plus jeune qu'elle.

baby-snatching ['beibisnætʃiŋ] *n.* (*a*) enlèvement *m*, rapt *m*, d'enfant, kidnapping *m*; (*b*) *F:* **I don't go in for b.-s.,** moi je ne les prends pas au berceau.

baccalaureate [bækə'lɔːriət] *n. NAm: Sch:* = licence *f*; *Fr.C:* baccalauréat *m.*

baccara(t) ['bækərɑː] *n. Cards:* baccara *m.*

bacchanal ['bækən(ə)l] **1.** *a.* bachique. **2.** *n.* bacchanale *f*; débauche *m* bachique.

bacchanalia [bækə'neiliə] *n.pl.* bacchanales *fpl.*

bacchanalian [bækə'neiliən] *a.* bachique.

baccy ['bæki] *n. F: O:* tabac *m*, *P:* perlot *m.*

bachelor ['bætʃələr] *n.m.* **1.** *Hist:* bachelier (aspirant à la chevalerie); **knight b.,** chevalier. **2.** célibataire, garçon; **b. flat,** appartement *m* pour célibataire; **b. uncle,** oncle non marié. **3.** *Sch:* = licencié, -ée; **B. of Arts, of Science,** *approx.* = licencié, -ée, ès lettres, ès sciences; **B. of laws** = licencié, -ée, en droit.

bachelorhood ['bætʃələhuːd] *n.* célibat *m*; vie *f*, état *m*, de garçon.

bacillary [bə'siləri] *a. Biol:* bacillaire.

bacillus, *pl.* **-i** [bə'siləs, -ɑi] *n. Biol: Med:* bacille *m.*

back¹ [bæk] **I.** *n.* **1.** (*a*) dos *m* (de qn, d'un animal); **to fall on one's b.,** tomber à la renverse; **mind your backs!** attention, s'il vous plaît! **to be at the b. of s.o., of sth.,** (i) être derrière qn, qch.; (ii) soutenir qn, qch.; **to do sth. behind s.o.'s b.,** faire qch. à l'insu de qn; **he laughs at you behind your b.,** il se moque de vous quand vous avez le dos tourné; **to turn one's b. on s.o.,** (i) tourner le dos à qn; (ii) abandonner qn; **to sit, stand, with one's b. to s.o.,** tourner le dos à qn; **sitting with one's b. to the light,** assis à contre-jour; **to be glad to see the b. of s.o.,** être content d'être débarrassé de qn; **I saw him only from the b.,** je ne l'ai vu que de dos; **to be on one's b.,** (i) être étendu sur le dos; (ii) être alité; *F:* **get off my b.!** fiche-moi la paix! **the cat arches its b.,** le chat fait le gros dos; **to put, get, s.o.'s b. up,** mettre qn en colère; **b. to b.,** dos à dos; adossés; **b. to front,** sens devant derrière; **with one's b. to the wall,** (i) adossé au mur; (ii) poussé au pied du mur; **to put one's b. into it,** s'y mettre énergiquement; **b patting,** félicitations *pl*; **p. slapping,** cordialité exubérante; (*b*) les reins *mpl*; **to break one's b.,** se casser les reins; *F:* **he won't break his b. working,** il ne se casse pas, au travail; **to break the b. of the work,** faire le plus dur, le plus gros, du travail; (*c*) (*of ship*) **to break her b.,** se briser en deux; se casser. **2.** (*a*) dos (d'un couteau, d'un outil, d'un livre); envers *m* (d'un tissu); verso *m* (d'une page); dos, verso (d'un chèque); (*b*) dossier *m* (d'une chaise, etc.); **adjustable b.,** dossier inclinable; (*c*) revers *m* (d'une médaille); revers, dessus *m* (de la main); **he knows London like the b. of his hand,** il connaît Londres comme le fond de sa poche; (*d*) derrière *m* (d'une maison); arrière *m* (d'une maison, d'une voiture); dos (de la langue); **b. of the mouth,** arrière-bouche *f*; **b. of the throat,** arrière-gorge *f*; **carriage at the b. of the train,** voiture *f* en queue de, du, train; **the vocabulary is at the b. of the book,** le vocabulaire est à la fin du livre; **the dress fastens at the b.,** *U.S:* **in b.,** la robe s'agrafe dans le dos; **idea at the b. of one's mind,** idée *f* derrière la tête. **3.** (*a*) *Arch:* extrados *m* (d'une voûte); fond *m* (d'une armoire, d'une salle); **the b. of the stage,** le fond de la scène; *F:* **to live at the b. of beyond,** habiter un trou perdu; (*b*) table *f* du fond (d'un violon, etc.). **4.** *Sp:* (*a*) (*pers.*) **(full) b.**, arrière *m*; **right, left, b.**, arrière droit, gauche; (*b*) position *f* d'arrière. **II.** *a.* (*a*) (partie, roue, etc.) arrière; (porte, jardin, etc.) de derrière; **b. room,** pièce *f* qui donne sur l'arrière; *F:* **b.-room boy,** savant *m* qui travaille (i) à l'arrière-plan, (ii) à des recherches secrètes; **the b. streets of a town,** les bas quartiers d'une ville; **the b. page,** la dernière page; **b. axle,** essieu *m* arrière; **b. seat,** siège *m* arrière; **to take a b. seat,** passer au second plan; s'effacer; *Aut: F:* **b.-seat driver,** personne qui donne des conseils au conducteur; (*b*) (*in opposite direction*) (mouvement) inverse; *Ling:* **b. formation,** dérivation régressive; (*c*) (*time*) *Com:* **b. orders,** commandes *fpl* en attente; **b. interest,** arrérages *mpl*; **b. rent,** arriéré(s) *m(pl)* de loyer; *Adm:* **b. pay,** rappel *m* de traitement; *Journ:* **b. number,** vieux numéro (d'un journal); (*d*) *NAm:* **b. road,** petite route. **III.** *adv.* **1.** (*of place*) (*a*) en arrière; **stand b.!** rangez-vous! **to step b. a pace,** faire un pas en arrière; **far b.,** loin derrière (les autres, etc.); dans les derniers rangs; **house standing b. from the road,** maison écartée du chemin; maison en retrait; *NAm:* **b. of sth.,** derrière qch.; (*b*) **to hit, strike, b.,** rendre coup pour coup; **to get one's own b.,** prendre sa revanche; **to call s.o. b.,** rappeler qn; *Tp:* **ring, call, me b. in an hour,** rappelez-moi dans une heure; **to come b.,** revenir; **to go, walk, turn, b.,** (i) retourner (**to,** à); (ii) rebrousser chemin; **to make one's way b.,** s'en retourner; (*c*) de retour; **to arrive, come, b.,** rentrer; **when will he be b.?** quand sera-t-il de retour? **I'll be b.,** (i) je serais de retour; (ii) *F:* vous aurez de mes nouvelles; **I expect him b. tomorrow,** j'attends son retour pour demain; **as soon as I am, get, b.,** dès mon retour; **he's just b. from a trip,** il arrive de voyage; (*d*) **a few pages b.,** quelques pages plus haut; **he left him three miles b.,** il l'a laissé à trois milles d'ici; (*e*) **b. home,** chez nous. **2.** (*time*) **a few years b.,** il y a (déjà) quelques années; **way b. in the Middle Ages,** à une période reculée du moyen âge; **as far b. as 1914,** déjà en 1914, dès 1914.

back² **1.** *v.tr.* (*a*) renforcer (un mur, une carte, etc.); épauler (une route, un accotement); endosser (un livre); rentoiler (un tableau); maroufler (une toile); (*b*) (i) soutenir, appuyer, seconder (qn); (ii) *Com: etc:* financer (qn, un projet, etc.); avaliser, endosser (un effet); **to b. s.o. in an argument,** donner raison à qn; (*c*) *Sp: etc:* parier, miser, sur (un cheval, une équipe, etc.); jouer (un cheval); **well-backed horse,** cheval très coté; *Turf: & Fig:* **to b. the wrong horse,** parier, miser, sur le mauvais cheval; (*d*) reculer (une charrette); faire reculer (un cheval); *Mch:* mettre (une machine) en arrière; refouler (un train); **to b. one's car into the garage,** entrer en marche arrière dans le garage; *Nau:* **to b. the oars, to b. water,** ramer à rebours, déramer; (*e*) *Nau:* masquer, coiffer (une voile); (*f*) servir de fond à (qch.). **2.** *v.i.* (*a*) aller en arrière; marcher à reculons; (*of horse*) reculer; *Aut: etc:* faire marche arrière; reculer; (*of train*) **to b. into the station,** reculer dans la gare; (*b*) **the house backs on (to) our garden,** la maison donne par derrière sur notre jardin. **back away** *v.i.* reculer. **back down** *v.i.* (*a*) descendre (une échelle, etc.) à reculons; (*b*) avouer qu'on est dans son tort; (*c*) reculer; **backed** *a.* **1. b. on to sth.,** adossé à qch. **2.** (*a*) à dos, à dossier; (*b*) **broad-b.,** à large dos, qui a le dos large; **high-b. chair,** chaise *f* à grand dossier. **3.** *Com:* **b. bills,** papier fait. **backing** *n.* **1.** (*a*) renforcement *m* (d'un mur, d'une carte, etc.); *Const: Civ.E:* remplage *m*; *Bookb:* endossement *m* (d'un livre); *Art: etc:* marouflage *m* (d'une toile); rentoilage *m* (d'un tableau); argenture *f* (d'un miroir); (*b*) *Turf:* paris *mpl* (pour un cheval); (*c*) (i) **b. (up),** soutien *m*, appui *m* (de qn); (ii) **financial b.,** financement *m* (de qn, d'un projet, etc.); *Fin:* **b. of the currency,** garantie *f* de la circulation; (*d*) *Mus:* accompagnement *m*. **2.** renfort *m*, support *m*, soutien *m* (d'un mur); *Furn:* dossier *m* (d'un tapis); *Art: etc:* **cloth b.,** marouflage. **3.** recul *m*, reculement *m* (d'un cheval, d'une charrette); refoulement *m* (d'un train); marche *f* (en) arrière (d'une voiture, etc.). **back off** *v.i.* reculer. **back out** *v.i.* (*a*) (*of pers. etc.*) sortir à reculons; *Aut:* sortir en marche arrière; (*b*) *F:* retirer sa promesse, se dédire; **to b.out of an undertaking,** se retirer d'une entreprise; **he's trying to b.out of it,** il voudrait se dédire; (*c*) *F:* se défiler. **back up 1.** *v.tr.* (*a*) soutenir, appuyer (qn, qch.); prêter son appui à (qn); seconder (qn); **to b. s.o. up in an argument,** donner raison à qn; (*b*) faire reculer (une voiture, etc.). **2.** *v.i.* reculer; faire marche arrière.

backache ['bækeik] *n.* mal *m* de reins.

backbench ['bæk'ben(t)ʃ] *n. Pol: usu.pl.* banquettes *fpl* des députés sans portefeuille.

backbencher ['bæk'ben(t)ʃər] *n. Pol:* député *m* sans portefeuille.

backbite ['bækbait] *v.tr.* médire de (qn). **backbiting** *n.* médisance *f*.

backboiler ['bæk'bɔilər] *n.* chauffe-eau *m inv* derrière un foyer domestique.

backbone ['bækboun] *n.* (i) épine dorsale, colonne vertébrale; (ii) grande arête (de poisson); **English to the b.,** anglais jusqu'au bout des ongles; **he's got no b.,** il n'a pas de moelle dans les os; **he is the b. of the movement,** c'est lui qui mène le mouvement.

backbreaking ['bækbreikiŋ] *a.* (travail, etc.) éreintant.

backchat ['bæktʃæt] *n. F:* (*a*) impertinence *f*; **none of your b.!** pas de réplique! (*b*) reparties *fpl*.

backcloth ['bæ(k)klɔθ] *n. Th:* toile *f* de fond; arrière-scène *f*, *pl.* arrière-scènes.

back-comb ['bæk'koum] *v.tr. Hairdr:* crêper.

backdate ['bæk'deit] *v.tr.* antidater; **increase backdated to July 1st,** augmentation avec effet rétroactif au 1er juillet.

backdrop ['bækdrɔp] *n.* (*a*) *Th:* toile *f* de fond; arrière-scène *f*, *pl.* arrière-scènes; (*b*) arrière-plan *m*, *pl.* arrière-plans.

backer ['bækər] *n.* **1.** *Turf:* parieur, -euse. **2.** *Com:* (*a*) **b. of a bill,** donneur *m* d'aval; (*b*) commanditaire *m*; (*c*) **financial b.,** bailleur, -euse, de fonds. **3.** *Pol: etc:* partisan *m*.

backfire¹ ['bæk'faiər] *n.* **1.** *I.C.E:* (*a*) allumage prématuré; (*b*) retour de flamme (au carburateur); pétarade *f*. **2.** *U.S:* contre-feu (d'incendie de forêt, etc.).

backfire² *v.i.* **1.** *I.C.E:* (*a*) s'allumer prématurément; pétarader; (*b*) avoir des retours; pétarader. **2.** *Fig:* **the plan backfired,** le projet leur est retombé sur le dos.

backgammon ['bækgæmən] *n.* (jeu *m* de) trictrac (*m*); (jeu de) jacquet (*m*); **b. board,** trictrac, jacquet.

background ['bækgraund] *n.* **1.** fond *m*, arrière-plan *m*, *pl.* arrière-plans; arrière-corps *m inv* (d'un bas-relief); **b. of mountains,** fond de montagnes; **in the b.,** dans le fond, à l'arrière-plan; **against a dark b.,** sur (un) fond sombre; **to keep (oneself), to stay, in the b.,** s'effacer; **to push s.o. into the b.,** (i) mettre, reléguer, qn au second plan; (ii) prendre le pas sur qn; **b. music,** (i) *Th: Cin:* fond sonore; (ii) musique *f* d'ambiance; musique de fond; **b. noise,** bruit *m* de fond. **2.** (*a*) (*of pers.*) (i) origines *fpl*; (ii) formation *f*, éducation *f*; (iii) *Med:* antécédents *mpl* (d'un malade); **cultural b.,** fonds *m* de culture; culture générale; **young man of good b.,** garçon *m* de bonne famille; **to be brought up in a middle-class b.,** être élevé dans un milieu bourgeois; (*b*) contexte *m* historique (d'un événement); données *fpl* de base (d'un problème); **b. reading,** lectures générales (autour d'un sujet).

backhand ['bækhænd] *n.* **1.** *Ten:* revers *m*; **b. stroke,** coup *m* de revers; **to have a good b.,** être bon pour les revers. **2.** écriture renversée, penchée à gauche.
backhanded ['bæk'hændid] *a.* coup (i) de revers, (ii) inattendu, déloyal; (compliment) équivoque; **in a b. way,** déloyalement.
backhander [bæk'hændər] *n. F:* **1.** coup *m* de revers; coup du revers de la main. **2.** riposte inattendue; attaque déloyale. **3.** pot-de-vin *m.*
backlash ['bæklæʃ] *n.* **1.** *Mec.E:* retour *m* (de dents, de la denture). **2.** contrecoup *m* (d'un événement); effet *m* de boumerang *m*; coutre-courant *m* (politique, etc.).
backless ['bæklis] *a.* (robe, etc.) sans dos; (banc, etc.) sans dossier.
backlog ['bæklɔg] *n.*(*a*) arriéré *m* (de travail); *Com:* **b. of orders,** commandes non exécutées; (*b*) *NAm:* réserve *f.*
backpack ['bækpæk] *n.* sac *m* à dos.
backpacking ['bækpækiŋ] *n. NAm:* **to go b.,** faire du tourisme à pied.
back-pedal ['bæk'pedəl] *v.i.* **(back-pedalled,** *NAm:* **-pedaled)** (*a*) rétropédaler; (*b*) en rabattre; faire marche arrière. **back pedalling,** *NAm* **pedaling** *n.* rétropédalage *m.*
backrest ['bækrest] *n.* **1.** *Tchn:* lunette *f* (de tour). **2.** *Furn:* (*a*) dossier-lit *m*, *pl.* dossiers-lits; (*b*) dossier *m* (de siège).
backsheesh, backshish [bæk'ʃi:ʃ] *n.* = BAKSHEESH.
backside ['bæk'said] *n. F:* derrière *m*, postérieur *m*, *P:* cul *m.*
backsight ['bæksait] *n. Sm.a:* hausse *f.*
backslide ['bækslaid] *v.i.* **(backslid)** retomber dans l'erreur, dans le vice; rechuter. **backsliding** *n.* rechute *f*, dans le vice; récidive *f.*
backspace ['bækspeis] *v.i. Typew:* rappeler le chariot.
backspacer ['bæk'speisər] *n.* (*also* **backspace key**) *Typew:* rappel *m* de chariot; rappel arrière.
backstage ['bæk'steidʒ] *adv.* (*a*) derrière la scène; dans les coulisses; (*b*) à l'arrière-plan.
backstairs ['bæk'stɛəz] *n.* (i) escalier *m* de service; (ii) escalier dérobé; **b. influence,** protections *fpl* en haut lieu; *F:* pistonnage *m*, piston *m.*
backstitch ['bækstitʃ] *n. Needlew:* point *m* arrière.
backstroke ['bækstrouk] *n.* **1.** (*a*) coup *m* de revers; (*b*) contre-coup *m*, *pl.* contre-coups. **2.** course *f* arrière, course de retour (d'un piston, etc.). **3.** *Swim:* nage *f* sur le dos; **100 metres b.,** 100 mètres dos.
backtrack ['bæktræk] *v.i.* (*a*) revenir sur ses pas; (*b*) en rabattre; faire marche arrière.
back-up ['bækʌp] *n.* soutien *m*, appui *m*; *Mil: etc:* renforcement *m*; *Med:* soins *mpl* supplémentaires.
backward ['bækwəd] **1.** *a.* (*a*) (mouvement, etc.) rétrograde; (regard, etc.) en arrière; **b. and forward motion,** mouvement de va-et-vient; (*b*) (fruits) tardifs; (enfant) (i) arriéré; (élève) retardataire, en retard; (race) moins évoluée; **the b. state of the country,** le retard dont souffre le pays; (*c*) **to be b. in doing sth.,** être lent à faire qch.; *F:* **he isn't b. in coming forward,** il ne fait pas le modeste. **2.** *adv.* = BACKWARDS.
backwardness ['bækwədnis] *n.* **1.** retard *m* (d'un enfant, de la moisson); tardiveté *f* (des fruits); arriération mentale. **2. b. in doing sth.,** hésitation *f* à faire qch.
backwards ['bækwədz] *adv.* (sauter, se pencher) en arrière; (aller, marcher) à reculons; (tomber) à la renverse; **to look b.,** (i) jeter un coup d'œil en arrière; (ii) (*in time*) remonter dans le passé; (*of water*) **to flow b.,** couler à contre-courant; **to say the alphabet b.,** réciter l'alphabet à rebours; **to know sth. b.,** connaître qch. parfaitement; **b. and forwards,** d'avant en arrière et d'arrière en avant; **to walk b. and forwards,** aller et venir; **movement b. and forwards,** mouvement *m* de va-et-vient; **to go b. and forwards,** faire la navette (entre deux endroits).
backwash ['bækwɔʃ] *n.* remous *m.*
backwater ['bækwɔ:tər] *n.* **1.** *Hyd.E:* eau arrêtée (par un bief, etc.). **2.** (i) bras *m* de décharge (d'une rivière); (ii) accul *m* (de la mer); **to live in a b.,** habiter un trou perdu.
backwoods ['bækwudz] *n pl.* (*a*) forêts *fpl* de l'intérieur (*b*) *F:* **to live in the b.,** habiter un trou perdu, un bled.
backwoodsman, *pl.* **-men** [bæk'wudzmən] *n.m.* (*a*) colon des forêts (de l'Amérique du Nord); (*b*) *F:* rustre, rustaud.
backyard ['bæk'jɑ:d] *n.* arrière-cour *f*, *pl.* arrière-cours.
bacon ['beik(ə)n] *n.* lard *m*; porc salé et fumé; bacon *m*; **streaky b.,** = petit salé; *F:* **to save one's b.,** sauver sa peau.
bacterial [bæk'tiəriəl] *a.* bactérien.
bacteriological [bæktiəriə'lɔdʒik(ə)l] *a.* bactériologique.
bacteriologist [bæktiəri'ɔlədʒist] *n.* bactériologiste *mf*, bactériologue *mf.*
bacteriology [bæktiəri'ɔlədʒi] *n.* bactériologie *f.*
bacterium, *pl.* **-ia** [bæk'tiəriəm, -iə] *n.* bactérie *f.*
bad [bæd] **I.** *a.* **(worse** [wə:s]; **worst** [wə:st]) mauvais. **1.** (*a*) de mauvaise qualité; *F:* **he's always turning up like a b. penny,** il revient à tout bout de champ; **b. debt,** mauvaise créance; **it's not b.,** ce n'est pas mal du tout; ce n'est pas si mal; **he's not b. loooking,** il n'est pas mal; (*of food, etc.*) **to go b.,** se gâter, s'avarier; (*b*) (*incorrect*) **b. translation,** mauvaise traduction; **he speaks b. French,** il parle mal le français; **b. at maths,** nul en maths; **to get into b. habits, ways,** prendre de mauvaises habitudes; (*c*) (*unfortunate*) **it's a b. business!** c'est une mauvaise affaire! **to be in a b. way,** être en mauvais état; **he'll come to a b. end,** il finira mal; **to have a b. name,** avoir une mauvaise réputation; **it wouldn't be a b. thing, plan, to . . .,** on ne ferait pas mal de . . .; **things are going from b. to worse,** les choses vont de mal en pis; **that looks b.,** c'est (un) mauvais signe; (*d*) **to feel b. about sth.,** avoir du remords au sujet de qch.; (*e*) **b. blood,** ressentiment *m*, rancune *f.* **2.** (*a*) (*wicked*) **b. man,** méchant homme; **b. language,** gros mots *mpl*; *F:* **he's a b. lot,** c'est un vaurien; (*b*) (*unpleasant*) mauvaise (nouvelle, odeur, humeur, etc.); gros (rhume); violent (mal de tête); (accident, faute, etc.) grave; **b. weather,** mauvais temps; *Nau:* gros temps; **to be on b. terms with s.o.,** être mal avec qn, en mauvais termes avec qn; **it's (really) too b.! that's too b.!** c'est (par) trop fort! c'est bien dommage! **it's too b. of him!** ce n'est vraiment pas bien de sa part! (*c*) **to be b. for s.o., for sth.,** ne rien valoir à qn, pour qch.; **all that whisky is b. for him,** tout ce whisky ne lui vaut rien; (*d*) *F:* (*ill*) **I feel b.,** je ne me sens pas bien; **my b. leg,** ma jambe malade; **I'm not so b.,** je ne vais pas trop mal; **how's business?—not so b.,** comment vont les affaires?—pas si mal. **II.** *n.* (*a*) **to take the b. with the good,** accepter la mauvaise fortune aussi bien que la bonne; (*b*) **to go to the b.,** (i) (*of pers.*) mal tourner; (ii) (*of business*) être en mauvaise passe; (*c*) **to be 500 francs to the b.,** être en perte de 500 francs. **badly** *adv.* **(worse** [wə:s]; **worst** [wə:st]) **1.** mal; **b. dressed,** mal habillé; **to do, come off, b.,** mal réussir; **to be very b. off,** être dans la gêne; **things are going b.,** les choses vont mal; **he speaks English b.,** il parle mal l'anglais; **to behave b.,** se mal conduire, se conduire mal; **he took it very b.,** il a très mal pris la chose; (*of machine, etc.*) **to work b.,** mal fonctionner.

2. **b. wounded,** gravement, grièvement, blessé; **the b. disabled,** les grands infirmes, les grands mutilés; *Sp: etc:* **b. beaten,** battu à plate(s) couture(s). 3. **to want sth. b.,** avoir grande envie de qch.; **I need it b.,** j'en ai grand besoin.

baddie ['bædi] *n. F:* méchant *m.*

bade *see* BID².

badge [bædʒ] *n.* 1. (*a*) insigne *m* (d'un membre d'une société); médaille *f* (de porteur, etc.); *Mil:* écusson *m* (d'un régiment, etc.); (*b*) *Scout:* brevet *m*; badge *m.* 2. symbole *m*, signe distinctif.

badger¹ ['bædʒər] *n. Z:* blaireau *m.*

badger² *v.tr.* harceler, tourmenter, importuner (qn); **to b. s.o. into granting a favour, to b. a favour out of s.o.,** obtenir une faveur de qn à force d'importunités.

badminton ['bædmintən] *n. Games:* badminton *m.*

badness ['bædnis] *n.* 1. mauvaise qualité. 2. (*of pers.*) méchanceté *f.*

bad-tempered ['bæd'tempəd] *a.* grincheux; acariâtre; **to be b.-t.,** avoir le caractère mal fait; **he is a b.-t. man,** il a mauvais caractère.

baffle¹ ['bæfl] *n.* 1. *Tchn:* chicane *f*; déflecteur *m*; **b. plate,** plaque-chicane *f*, *pl.* plaques-chicanes. 2. *W.Tel:* **b. (board),** écran *m* (de haut-parleur).

baffle² *v.tr.* 1. (*a*) confondre, déconcerter, dérouter (qn); (*b*) confondre (l'imagination, etc.); **to b. definition,** échapper à toute définition; **mystery that has baffled all investigators,** mystère *m* qui a déjoué toutes les recherches. 2. *Tchn:* décaler (des ouvertures, etc.); établir des chicanes dans (un conduit, etc.). **baffling** *a.* déconcertant; (mystère, etc.) inexplicable.

bag¹ [bæg] *n.* 1. sac *m*; **travel(ling) b.,** sac de voyage; **paper b.,** sac en papier; *F:* **there's bags of room,** la place ne manque pas. 2. (*a*) *Nat. Hist:* sac, poche *f*; (*b*) *Husb:* pis *m*, mamelle *f* (de vache); (*c*) *Obst:* **b. of waters,** poche des eaux; (*d*) *F:* **bags under the eyes,** poches sous les yeux. 3. *Ven:* **the b.,** le tableau; **to make a good b.,** faire un grand abattis de gibier; (*of fighter pilot, etc.*) avoir un beau tableau de chasse; *F:* **in the b.,** dans le sac; **it's in the b.,** c'est du tout cuit. 4. *F:* **bags,** pantalon *m.* 5. *P:* **old b.,** vieille chipie.

bag² *v.* **(bagged; bagging)** 1. *v.tr.* (*a*) **to b. sth.,** mettre qch. en sac; (*b*) *Ven:* abattre, tuer (du gibier); *Av: F:* abattre (des avions); (*c*) *F:* empocher; s'emparer de (qch.); mettre la main sur (qch.); accaparer (les meilleures places); **bags I go first!** c'est moi le premier! 2. *v.i.* (se) gonfler, s'enfler; (*of garment, etc.*) bouffer, avoir trop d'ampleur; **trousers that b. at the knees,** pantalon qui fait des poches aux genoux.

bagatelle [bægə'tel] *n.* 1. (*a*) bagatelle *f*; (*b*) *Mus:* petite pièce; divertissement *m.* 2. *Games:* billard anglais.

baggage ['bægidʒ] *n.* 1. *Mil:* bagage *m*; **b. waggon,** fourgon *m* à bagages. 2. *esp. NAm:* bagages; *Rail:* **b. car,** fourgon *m* à bagages; *Av: etc:* **b. handler,** bagagiste *m.*

baggy ['bægi] *a.* (vêtement) trop ample; (pantalon) flottant, bouffant.

bagpipe(s) ['bægpaip(s)] *n.* (*pl.*) cornemuse *f.*

bah [bɑ:] *int.* bah!

Bahama [bə'hɑ:mə] *Pr.n. Geog:* **the B. Islands, the Bahamas,** les Lucayes *fpl*, les îles *fpl* Bahamas, l'archipel *m* des Bahamas.

bail¹ [beil] *n. Jur:* (*a*) cautionnement *m*; (*b*) (*pers.*) caution *f*, garant *m*; (*c*) somme fournie à titre de cautionnement; **to go, stand, b., for s.o.,** se porter garant de qn; fournir caution pour qn (pour sa libération provisoire); **to be on b.,** être en liberté provisoire (sous caution); **to surrender to one's b.,** comparaître en jugement; *F:* **to jump (one's) b.,** se dérober à la justice (alors qu'on jouit de la liberté provisoire).

bail² *v.tr. Jur:* (*a*) accorder la liberté provisoire à (qn) sous caution; (*b*) **to b. s.o. (out),** (i) se porter caution pour qn; (ii) *F:* tirer qn d'affaire.

bail³ *n. Cr:* **bails,** barrettes *fpl*, bâtonnets *mpl.*

bail⁴ *n. Nau:* écope *f.*

bail⁵ 1. *v.tr.* **to b. (out),** écoper, vider (un canot, l'eau d'une embarcation). 2. *v.i. Av:* = BALE⁴ 2.

bailer ['beilər] *n. Nau:* écope *f.*

Bailey¹ [beili] *Pr.n.* **the Old B.** (= *the Central Criminal Court*), le tribunal principal de Londres en matière criminelle; la cour d'assises de Londres.

Bailey² *Pr.n.* **B. bridge,** pont *m* Bailey.

bailiff ['beilif] *n.* 1. *Jur:* **sheriff's b.,** agent *m* de poursuites; huissier *m.* 2. régisseur *m* (d'un domaine, d'une ferme); **water b.,** garde-pêche *m*, *pl.* gardes-pêche. 3. *Hist:* bailli *m.*

bairn [bɛə(r)n] *n. Scot:* enfant *mf.*

bait¹ [beit] *n.* (*a*) *Fish:* amorce *f*, appât *m*; **live b.,** appât vivant; **ground b.,** amorce de fond; (*b*) *F:* appât, leurre *m*; **to rise to, swallow, the b.,** mordre à l'hameçon; *F:* gober le morceau.

bait² *v.tr.* 1. harceler (un animal); harceler, tourmenter (qn) 2. amorcer (un hameçon, un piège, etc.) (**with,** avec); mettre l'appât à (la ligne). **baiting** *n.* 1. harcèlement *m* (des animaux); **badger b.,** déterrage *m* du blaireau. 2. amorçage *m* (d'un hameçon, d'un piège, etc.).

baize [beiz] *n.* feutrine *f*; **green b.,** tapis vert; **green b. door,** porte feutrée.

bake [beik] 1. *v.tr.* (*a*) (faire), cuire (qch.) au four; **to b. bread,** faire cuire le pain; **baked potatoes,** pommes *fpl* de terre au four, en robe de chambre, en robe des champs; (*b*) cuire (des briques, la porcelaine, etc.); **earth baked by the sun,** sol durci, desséché, par le soleil; (*c*) *Metall:* étuver (un moule). 2. *v.i.* (*of bread, etc.*) cuire (au four); *F:* **I'm baking, I'm baked,** je crève de chaleur **baking** 1. (*a*) *F:* **b. hot,** excessivement chaud; (journée) torride. 2. *n.* (*a*) cuisson *f* (du pain, etc.); **b. sheet,** tôle *f* (à gâteaux); plaque *f*; **b. tin,** (i) plat *m* à rôtir; (ii) moule *m* à gâteaux; **b. powder,** levure chimique, artificielle; (*b*) cuisson, cuite *f* (des briques, etc.); (*c*) *Metall:* étuvage *m*, étuvement *m* (des moules); (*d*) (*batch*) fournée *f* (de pain); cuite (de briques, etc.).

baker ['beikər] *n.* boulanger *m*, boulangère *f*; **baker's shop,** boulangerie *f*; **baker's dozen,** treize douze, treize à la douzaine, une treizaine.

bakery ['beikəri] *n.* (*a*) boulangerie *f*; (*b*) *Mil: etc:* manutention *f.*

baksheesh, bakshish ['bækʃi:ʃ] *n.* bakchich *m.*

Balaclava [bælə'klɑ:və] *Pr.n. Geog:* Balaklava; **B. helmet,** *n.* **b.,** passe-montagne *m*, *pl.* passe-montagnes.

balalaika [bælə'laikə] *n. Mus:* balalaïka *f.*

balance¹ ['bæləns] *n.* 1. (*a*) balance *f*; *Astr:* **the B.,** la Balance; **Roman b.,** balance romaine; **spring b.,** peson *m*; **b. beam,** (i) fléau *m* de balance; (ii) *Hyd.E:* balancier *m*, flèche *f* (d'une porte d'écluse); **to turn the b.,** faire pencher la balance; **to be, hang, in the b.,** être, rester, en balance; (*b*) *Clockm:* **b. (wheel),** balancier (de montre); roue *f* de rencontre (d'une horloge); régulateur *m*; **b. spring,** ressort *m*; (*c*) *Mec.E: etc:* **b. (weight),** contrepoids *m*; masse *f* d'équilibrage. 2. équilibre *m*; **to keep one's b.,** se tenir en équilibre; **to lose one's b.,** perdre l'équilibre; **to throw s.o. off (his) b.,** (i) faire perdre l'équilibre à qn; (ii) *F:* interloquer qn; **off b.,** (esprit) désaxé, déséquilibré; *Hist:* **the b. of power,** la balance politique. 3. *Com: Fin:* (*a*) solde *m*, reliquat *m* (d'un compte); **credit, debit, b.,** solde créditeur, débiteur; **b. carried forward,** report *m* à nouveau; (*b*) balance, bilan *m*; **b. sheet,** bilan *m* (d'inventaire); **to strike a**

b., (i) établir une balance; arrêter un compte; (ii) dresser, établir, le bilan; **b. of trade,** balance du commerce; **b. of payments,** balance des paiements; **on b.,** tout bien considéré.

balance² **1.** *v.tr.* (*a*) balancer, peser (les conséquences de qch., etc.); (*b*) mettre, maintenir, (un objet) en équilibre; équilibrer (une embarcation); faire contrepoids à (qch.); *Aut:* équilibrer (les roues); (*c*) **one thing balances another,** une chose compense l'autre; (*d*) *Com: Fin:* balancer, solder, aligner (un compte); compenser (une dette); équilibrer (le budget); **to b. the books,** régler les livres. **2.** *v.i.* (*a*) se faire contrepoids; (*of scales*) se faire équilibre; **the two things b.,** les deux choses se balancent, se font équilibre; (*b*) *Com: Fin:* (*of accounts*) se balancer, s'équilibrer, se solder; **account that balances,** compte en balance; (*c*) osciller, balancer; (*of pers.*) hésiter; balancer (entre deux partis); (*d*) *Danc:* balancer. **balanced** *a.* **1.** équilibré, compensé; (jugement, esprit) pondéré; **to have a well b. mind,** avoir l'esprit bien équilibré; **(well) b. diet,** régime *m* (alimentaire) bien équilibré; **2.** en nombre égal; de force, de valeur, égale; **the two parties are pretty well b.,** les deux partis sont à peu près en nombre égal. **balancing** *n.* **1.** (*a*) mise *f* en équilibre; *W.Tel:* neutralisation *f*; *Aut:* équilibrage (des roues); **b. pole,** contrepoids *m* (de danseur de corde); *Th:* **b. act,** tours *m* d'équilibre; **a political b. act,** des acrobaties politiques; (*b*) **b. of accounts,** règlement *m*, solde *m*, alignement *m*, des comptes; (*c*) *Art:* balancement (des figures dans un tableau). **2.** ajustement *m* (de deux choses); compensation *f* (de qch. par qch.).

balcony ['bælkəni] *n.* **1.** balcon *m.* **2.** *Th:* fauteuils *mpl* de première ou deuxième galerie.

bald [bɔːld] *a.* **1.** (*a*) **b. (headed),** chauve; **b. patch,** commencement *m* de tonsure; **he is going b.,** il commence à perdre ses cheveux; *F:* **b. as a coot,** chauve comme un œuf: (*b*) *Aut:* (pneu) lisse. **2.** (*of style, etc.*) décharné; plat; **b. statement of (the) facts,** simple exposition *f* des faits; exposition des faits sans glose. **-ly** *adv.* platement; sèchement.

balderdash ['bɔːldədæʃ] *n.* bêtises *fpl*, balivernes *fpl.*

balding ['bɔːldiŋ] *a.* qui devient chauve.

baldness ['bɔːldnis] *n.* **1.** calvitie *f*, alopécie *f.* **2.** maigreur *f* (du style, etc.).

bale¹ [beil] *n.* *Com:* balle *f*, ballot *m* (de marchandises); **b. of paper,** ballot de dix rames de papier.

bale² *v.tr.* emballotter, paqueter (des marchandises). **baling** *n.* mise *f* en balles; paquetage *m.*

bale³ *n.* = BAIL⁴.

bale⁴ **1.** *v.tr.* = BAIL⁵ 1. **2.** *v.i.* *Av:* **to b. out,** sauter (en parachute) d'un avion en perdition. **baling** *n.* **b. out,** saut *m* en parachute.

Balearic [bæli'ærik] *a.* *Geog:* **the B. Islands,** les îles *fpl* Baléares.

baleful ['beilful] *a.* *Lit:* sinistre, maléfique. **-fully** *adv.* sinistrement.

baler¹ [beilər] *n.* **1.** presse *f* à balles, à emballer; *Agr:* **pick-up b.,** ramasseuse-presse *f*, *pl.* ramasseuses-presses. **2.** *Com:* (*pers.*) emballeur, -euse.

baler² *n.* = BAILER.

balk¹ [bɔːk] *n* **1.** *Agr:* billon *m.* **2.** pierre *f* d'achoppement; obstacle *m.* **3.** *Const:* (grosse) poutre, solive *f.*

balk² **1.** *v.tr.* (*a*) déjouer, frustrer, contrarier (les desseins de qn); (*b*) entraver (qn). **2.** *v.i.* (*of horse*) refuser; se dérober; **to b. at (sth.),** s'arrêter, reculer, hésiter, devant (une difficulté, une dépense).

Balkan ['bɔːlkən] *Geog:* **1.** *a.* **the B. States,** les États *mpl* balkaniques; **the B. Peninsula,** la péninsule des Balkans. **2.** *Pr.n.pl.* **the Balkans,** (i) les (monts) Balkans; (ii) les États balkaniques.

ball¹ [bɔːl] n. **1.** (*a*) boule *f* (de croquet, de neige); balle *f* (de cricket, de tennis, etc.); ballon *m* (d'enfant, de football); bille *f* (de billard); balle (de fusil); boulet *m* (de canon); pelote *f* (de laine, de ficelle); *U.S:* **b. game,** base-ball *m*; **b. park,** terrain *m* de base-ball; **to wind wool into a b.,** mettre de la laine en pelote; **black b. (for voting),** boule noire; **b. lightning,** éclair *m* en boule; **to knock the balls about,** *Ten: etc:* peloter; *Bill:* caramboler les billes; *Fb:* **to kick the b. about,** s'amuser avec le ballon; *Cr:* **no b.,** balle nulle; **to play b.,** (i) jouer à la balle; (ii) *Fig:* coopérer, jouer le jeu; *F:* **to be on the b.,** (i) avoir de la présence d'esprit; (ii) connaître son affaire; **to keep the b. rolling,** soutenir la conversation; **to start the b. rolling,** mettre le bal en train; **the b. is in your court,** c'est votre tour; c'est à vous; **to have the b. at one's feet,** avoir la balle, la partie, belle; (*b*) *Mec.E:* bille (de roulement); **b. cage,** cage *f* à billes; **b. race,** (i) chemin *m*, voie *f*, de roulement (pour billes); (ii) cage à billes; **b. valve,** (i) soupape *f* à boulet; (ii) robinet *m* à flotteur; (*c*) **b.(-and-socket) joint,** (i) *Anat:* énarthrose *f*; (ii) *Mec.E:* joint *m* à rotule articulation *f* à genouillère; *Civ.E:* **b. mill,** moulin *m* à boulets; (*d*) *V:* **balls,** couilles *fpl*; **balls!** quelles conneries! **2.** (*a*) lentille *f* (de pendule); (*b*) éminence métatarsienne (du pied); **b. of the thumb,** (éminence *f*) thénar (*m*); (*c*) globe *m* (de l'œil); (*d*) (*Hort:* **b. of earth,** motte *f*; (*e*) *Metall:* loupe *f* (de fer fondu). **3.** *Vet:* (*bolus*) boulette *f.*

ball² **1.** *v.tr.* (*a*) agglomérer; *Metall:* baller (le fer); (*b*) *Tex:* mettre (la laine) en pelote; (*c*) *P:* **balled up** (*also* **ballsed up**), (i) embrouillé; (ii) foutu. **2.** *v.tr.* *Vet:* administrer une boulette à (un cheval). **3.** *v.i.* s'agglomérer.

ball³ *n.* (*a*) *Danc:* bal *m*, *pl.* bals; **to open the b.,** ouvrir le bal; **b. dress,** robe *f* de bal; (*b*) *P:* **to have a b.,** *U.S:* **to have (oneself) a b.,** se paillarder.

ballad ['bæləd] *n.* **1.** *Mus:* romance *f.* **2.** *Lit:* ballade *f.*

ballast¹ ['bæləst] *n.* **1.** *Nau: Aer:* lest *m*; **ship in b. (-trim),** navire *m* sur lest; **to take in b.,** faire son lest; **to discharge b.,** se délester; jeter du lest; **b. tank,** ballast *m* (de sous-marin). **2.** *Civ.E:* pierraille *f*, cailloutage *m*; *Rail:* ballast, empierrement *m*; **b. bed,** (i) *Rail: etc:* coffre *m*, empierrement (de la voie); (ii) encaissement *m* (d'une route); *Rail:* **b. truck, car,** wagon *m* de terrassement.

ballast² *v.tr.* **1.** *Nau: Aer:* lester. **2.** *Civ.E:* empierrer, ensabler; caillouter; *Rail:* ballaster.

ballboy ['bɔːlbɔi] *n.m.* *Ten: etc:* ramasseur de balles.

ballcock ['bɔːlkɔk] *n.* robinet *m*, soupape *f*, à flotteur.

ballerina [bælə'riːnə] *n.* *Danc:* ballerine *f.*

ballet ['bælei] *n.* ballet *m*; **b. dancer,** danseur, -euse, de ballet; *f.* ballerine; **b. shoe,** chausson *m* de danse.

ballistic [bə'listik] *a.* balistique.

ballistics [bə'listiks] *n.pl.* (*usu. with sg. const.*) balistique *f.*

balloon [bə'luːn] *n.* **1.** (*a*) *Aer:* ballon *m*; aérostat *m*; **captive b.,** (ballon) captif (*m*); **dirigible b.,** (ballon) dirigeable (*m*); **hot air b.,** montgolfière *f*, ballon à air chaud; **barrage b.,** ballon de protection; **b. barrage,** barrage *m* de ballons; *Meteor:* **sounding b.,** ballon-sonde *m*, *pl.* ballons-sondes; (*b*) (*toy*) ballon d'enfant. **2.** (*a*) *Ch:* **b. (flask),** ballon; (*b*) **b. glass,** verre *m* ballon. **3.** (*in cartoons, comic strips*) banderole *f.*

ballooning [bə'luːniŋ] *n.* **1.** aérostation *f.* **2.** ballonnement *m* (d'un vêtement, d'une voile, etc.).

balloonist [bə'luːnist] *n.* aéronaute *m*, aérostier *m.*

ballot¹ ['bælət] *n.* **1.** **b. (ball),** boule *f* de scrutin. **2.** (*a*) tour *m* de scrutin; **to vote by b.,** voter au scrutin; **second b.,** ballottage *m*, deuxième tour de scrutin; (*b*) scrutin *m*, vote *m*; **b. paper,** bulletin *m* de vote; **b. box,** urne *f* de scrutin.

ballot² *v.i.* (*a*) voter au scrutin; **to b. for s.o.,** voter pour qn; **to b. against s.o.,** voter contre qn; (*b*) tirer au sort; **to b. for a place, etc.,** tirer une place, etc., au sort. **balloting** *n.* **1.** élection *f* au scrutin. **2.** tirage *m* au sort.

ballpoint ['bɔl:pɔint] *n.* **b. (pen),** stylo *m* (à) bille.

ballroom ['bɔ:lru:m] *n.* salle *f* de bal; salle de danse; **b. dancing,** danses *fpl* de bal, de salon.

balls-up ['bɔ:lzup] *n. P:* **to make a (right) b.-up,** faire une connerie, une couillonade.

bally ['bæli] *a. F: O:* sacré; satané.

ballyhoo [bæli'hu:] *n. P:* **1.** grosse réclame; battage *m.* **2.** barat(t)in *m.*

balm [bɑ:m], *n. Pharm: etc:* baume *m.*

balminess ['bɑ:minis] *n.* **1. the b. of the evening air,** l'air embaumé du soir. **2.** *F:* loufoquerie *f.*

balmy ['bɑ:mi] *a.* **1.** balsamique. **2.** (*a*) (air, temps) embaumé, parfumé; (*b*) *Lit:* doux; calmant, adoucissant. **3.** *F:* toqué, loufoque.

baloney [bə'louni] *n. F:* **it's all b.,** (i) c'est des histoires, de la fantaisie; (ii) c'est du chiqué, du boniment.

balsa ['bɔ(:)lsə] *n.* **b. (wood),** balsa *m.*

balsam ['bɔ:lsəm] **1.** baume *m*; *Pharm: etc:* **friar's b.,** baume de benjoin. **2.** *Bot:* **garden b.,** balsamine *f.* **3.** *Arb:* **b. fir,** sapin baumier.

Baltic ['bɔ:ltik] *a. Geog:* balte, baltique; **the B. Sea,** *n.* **the Baltic,** la (mer) Baltique; **B. port,** port *m* balte; *Com:* **the B. Exchange,** bourse *f* du commerce étranger des houilles, des bois, des huiles, et des céréales.

baluster ['bæləstər] *n.* **1.** balustre *m.* **2. balusters,** rampe *f* d'escalier.

balustrade [bæləs'treid] *n.* balustrade *f.*

bamboo [bæm'bu:] *n.* bambou *m*; **b. cane,** bambou, bamboche *f*; *Cu:* **b. shoots,** pousses *fpl* de bambou; *Pol:* **b. curtain,** rideau *m* de bambou.

bamboozle [bæm'bu:zl] *v.tr. F:* mystifier, enjôler, embobeliner (qn); **you've been bamboozled,** on vous a refait; **to b. s.o. out of sth.,** (i) frauder qn de qch.; (ii) soutirer qch. à qn.

ban¹ [bæn] *n.* (*a*) *Hist:* ban *m*, bannissement *m*, proscription *f*; (*b*) *Ecc:* interdit *m*; anathème *m*; (*c*) **driving b.,** suspension *f* du permis de conduire; **atomic test b.,** interdiction *f* des essais atomiques.

ban² *v.tr.* **(banned)** interdire (qn, qch.); mettre (un livre) à l'index; **play banned by the censor,** pièce interdite par la censure; **b. the bomb!** non à la bombe atomique! **to be banned from driving,** se voir retirer son permis de conduire.

banal [bæ'næl] *a.* banal; ordinaire.

banality [bə'næliti] *n.* banalité *f.*

banana [bə'nɑ:nə] *n.* **1.** banane *f*; **b. boat,** bananier *m*; *F:* **b. republic,** petit pays qui dépend de capitaux étrangers. **2. b. (tree),** bananier; **b. plantation,** bananeraie *f.*

band¹ [bænd] *n.* **1.** (*a*) lien *m* (de fer); frette *f*; cercle *m* (d'un tonneau); bandage *m* (d'une roue); **steel b.,** ruban *m* d'acier; (*b*) bande *f* (de papier, de toile); ruban (d'un chapeau); *Bookb:* nerf *m*; (*raised*) nervure *f*; bague *f* (de cigare); (*round arm*) **crêpe b.,** brassard *m* de crêpe, de deuil; **rubber, elastic, b.,** élastique *m*; (*c*) bande, raie *f* (de couleur, etc.); **bands of the spectrum,** bandes du spectre; (*d*) *W.Tel: Elcs:* **frequency b.,** bande de fréquence; (*e*) *Cmptr:* piste *f*, bande de fréquence; **calling b.,** bande d'appel; (*f*) *Rec:* plage *f* (d'un disque). **2.** *Mec.E: etc:* bande, courroie *f* (de transmission); **canvas b. (of conveyor),** bâche *f*; *Ind:* **b. conveyor,** tapis roulant. **3.** *Ecc.Cost: etc:* **bands,** rabat *m.*

band² *v.tr.* **1.** bander (un ballot); mettre (un journal, etc.) sous bande. **2.** rayer; zébrer de rayures. **banded** *a.* à bandes; rayé; *Nat.Hist:* fascié.

band³ *n.* **1.** (*a*) bande *f*, troupe *f*; (*b*) compagnie *f*; *Pej:* clique *f* (de personnes). **2.** *Mus:* orchestre *m*; **regimental b.,** la musique du régiment; **brass b.,** fanfare *f*; **jazz b.,** jazz-band *m*, *pl.* jazz-bands; **steel b.,** steel-band *m pl.* steel-bands; *F:* **one-man b.,** homme-orchestre *m*, *pl.* hommes-orchestres.

band⁴ *v.i. & pr.* **to b. (together),** (i) se liguer; se réunir en bande; (ii) s'ameuter.

bandage¹ ['bændidʒ] *n.* (*a*) *esp. Med:* bandage *m*, bande *f*; (*for blindfolding*) bandeau *m*; **crêpe b.,** bande Velpeau; *F:* velpeau *m*; **to put a b. on s.o., sth.,** bander qn, qch.

bandage² *v.tr.* bander; mettre un pansement sur (une plaie). **bandaging** *n.* bandage *m*; pansement *m.*

bandan(n)a [bæn'dænə] *n.* (i) foulard *m*, (ii) mouchoir *m* (à pois ou en couleurs).

bandbox ['bændbɔks] *n.* carton *m* à chapeau(x).

banderol(e) ['bændərɔl] *n.* banderole *f.*

bandit ['bændit] *n.* bandit *m*; **one-armed b.,** machine *f* à sous; *F:* tire-pognon *m*, *pl.* tire-pognons.

banditry ['bænditri] *n.* brigandage *m.*

bandmaster ['bændmɑ:stər] *n. Mil: etc:* chef de musique, de fanfare.

bandoleer, bandolier [bændə'liər] *n.* cartouchière *f* (portée en bandoulière).

bandsaw ['bændsɔ:] *n.* scie *f* à ruban; scie sans fin.

bandsman, *pl.* **-men** ['bændzmən] *n.m.* musicien (d'un orchestre, d'une harmonie); (*of brass band*) fanfariste.

bandstand ['bændstænd] *n.* kiosque *m* à musique.

bandwagon ['bændwæg(ə)n] *n.* (*a*) char *m* des musiciens (en tête de la cavalcade); (*b*) *F:* **to climb, jump, on the b.,** se mettre dans le mouvement; prendre le train en marche.

bandy¹ ['bændi] *v.tr.* (se) renvoyer (des paroles); échanger (des plaisanteries, des coups); **to b. words,** se chamailler; **her name was being bandied about,** on faisait du bruit à son sujet.

bandy² *a.* **1. b. legs,** jambes arquées, bancales. **2. b.(-legged),** bancal, aux jambes arquées.

bane [bein] *n. Lit:* peste *f*; *F:* **he's the b. of my life,** il m'empoisonne l'existence.

baneful ['beinful] *a. Lit:* funeste; (influence) néfaste. **-fully** *adv.* funestement.

bang¹ [bæŋ] *n.* coup (violent); détonation *f* (de fusil, etc.); claquement *m* (de porte); *Av:* **sonic b.,** bang *m*; (*of firework, etc.*) **to go off with a b.,** détoner; faire pétard; *F:* **to go (off, over) with a b.,** faire réussite.

bang² **1.** *v.i.* (*a*) **to b. at, on, the door,** donner de grands coups dans la porte; **to b. on the table with one's fist,** frapper la table du poing; (*b*) (*of door*) claquer, battre; **the door banged shut,** la porte a claqué. **2.** *v.tr.* (*a*) frapper (violemment); **he banged his head on a low beam,** il s'est cogné la tête sur une poutre basse; (*b*) **to b. the door,** (faire) claquer la porte. **bang down** *v.tr.* **to b. down the lid.,** abattre violemment le couvercle; **he banged it down on the table,** il l'a posé avec violence sur la table. **banging** (*a*) *n.* coups violents; claquement *m* (de porte); (*b*) *a.* (porte) qui claque.

bang³ **1.** *int.* pan! v'lan! boum! *F:* **b. went a fiver!** j'ai dépensé cinq livres d'un seul coup! **2.** *adv.* **to go b.,** éclater; **he crashed b. into the tree,** il est rentré pile dans l'arbre; **to fall b. in the middle,** tomber en plein milieu; *F:* **b. on time,** exactement à l'heure; **it's b. on,** c'est au poil.

bang⁴ *n. esp. NAm:* frange *f.*

banger ['bæŋər] *n. F:* **1.** saucisse *f.* **2.** *Pyr:* pétard *m.* **3.** (*car*) **old b.,** vieux tacot, vieille guimbarde.

Bangladesh [bæŋglə'deʃ] *Pr.n. Geog:* Bangladesh *m*, Bangla Desh *m.*

bangle ['bæŋgl] *n.* **1.** bracelet *m*; **slave b.,** bracelet esclave. **2.** anneau attaché autour de la cheville.

banish [ˈbæniʃ] *v.tr.* **1.** bannir, exiler (qn); proscrire (qn). **2.** bannir, chasser (la crainte, les soucis).

banishment [ˈbæniʃmənt] *n.* bannissement *m*, proscription *f*, exil *m*; **to go into b.,** partir pour l'exil.

banisters [ˈbænistəz] *n.pl.* **1.** balustres *mpl* (d'escalier). **2.** rampe *f* (d'escalier).

banjo, *pl.* **-os, -oes** [ˈbændʒou, -ouz] *n. Mus:* banjo *m*.

banjoist [ˈbændʒouist] *n.* joueur, -euse, de banjo.

bank¹ [bæŋk] *n.* **1.** (*a*) talus *m*; terrasse *f*; levée *f* de terre; (*in garden*) glacis *m*; *Civ.E:* banquette *f*, remblai *m*; *Rail:* rampe *f*; *Turf:* banquette (irlandaise); **b. of flowers,** tertre *m* de fleurs; (*b*) *Geog:* banc *m* (de sable, de coquillages, de roches); **the Banks of Newfoundland,** le Banc de Terre-Neuve; (*c*) digue *f*; (*d*) panne *f* (de nuages); banc (de brouillard). **2.** berge *f*, accotement *m*, banquette *f* (d'une rivière, d'un canal, etc.); bord *m*, rive *f* (d'une rivière, d'un lac); **the banks,** le rivage. **3.** *Av:* inclinaison *f*; virage *m* incliné.

bank² **1.** *v.tr.* (*a*) contenir (une rivière) par des berges; (*b*) **to b. up,** remblayer, terrasser, amonceler (de la terre, etc.); *Civ.E:* **to b. a road** surhausser, relever, un virage; **banked corner,** dévers *m*; (*c*) **to b. up the fire,** recharger le feu; *Mch:* **to b. (up) fires,** couvrir les feux. **2.** *v.i.* (*of snow, clouds, mist, etc.*) s'entasser, s'accumuler. **3.** *v.i. Av:* s'incliner sur l'aile; virer (sur l'aile). **banking** *n.* **1.** (*a*) remblayage *m*; surhaussement *m*, relèvement *m* (d'un virage); (*b*) **b. up,** haussement *m* du niveau (d'une rivière). **2.** remblai *m*. **3.** *Av:* inclinaison *f*; virage incliné.

bank³ *n.* **1.** *Com: Fin:* (*a*) banque *f*; **merchant b.,** banque d'affaires; **savings b.,** caisse d'épargne; **the B. of England,** la Banque d'Angleterre; **b. account,** compte *m* en banque; **b. clerk,** employé, -ée, de banque; **b. holiday,** (jour *m* de) fête légale (où les banques n'ouvrent pas); (*b*) (bureau *m* de) banque. **2.** (*gaming*) banque (de celui qui tient le jeu); **to break the b.,** faire sauter la banque. **3.** (*a*) *Cmptr:* **data b.,** fichier central; (*b*) *Med:* **blood, eye, b.,** banque du sang, des yeux.

bank⁴ *v.tr. & i.* **1.** mettre, déposer, (de l'argent) en banque; **to b. with s.o.,** avoir un compte en banque chez qn. **2.** (*gaming*) tenir la banque. **3. to b. on sth.,** compter sur qch.; caver, miser, sur (un événement); **to b. on success,** escompter un succès. **banking** *n.* **1.** affaires *fpl*, opérations *fpl*, de banque; établissement *m* bancaire; **b. hours,** heures *fpl* de la banque. **2.** profession *f* de banquier; la banque.

bank⁵ *n.* **1.** *Nau:* (*a*) banc *m* (de rameurs); (*b*) rang *m* d'avirons); (*c*) travée *f* (de sièges). **2.** (*a*) *Typewr:* rang *m* (de touches); (*b*) *Cin:* rampe *f* (de projecteurs); (*c*) *Mus:* clavier *m* (d'un orgue). **3.** *Ind:* groupe *m*, batterie *f* (de chaudières, de transformateurs, etc.); *I.C.E:* rangée *f* (de cylindres); *Tp:* groupe (de broches, de contacts).

bankable [ˈbæŋkəbl] *a. Fin:* (effet, etc.) bancable.

banker [ˈbæŋkər] *n.* **1.** *Fin:* banquier *m*; **banker's draft,** chèque *m* bancaire, de banque; **banker's order,** ordre *m* de transfert permanent. **2.** (*gaming*) banquier, tailleur *m*.

banknote [ˈbæŋknout] *n.* billet *m* de banque.

bankrupt¹ [ˈbæŋkrʌpt] *a. & n.* **1.** (commerçant) failli (*m*); **fraudulent b.,** banqueroutier *m*; **to go b.,** (i) faire faillite; (*fraudulently*) faire banqueroute; (ii) (*of business*) *F:* sauter; **to be b.,** être en faillite; **to adjudge, adjudicate, s.o. b.,** déclarer, mettre, qn en faillite; *n. Jur:* **undischarged b.,** failli non réhabilité. **2.** (*a*) *F:* (homme) (i) criblé de dettes; (ii) fauché.

bankrupt² *v.tr.* **1.** mettre (qn) en faillite. **2.** ruiner (qn).

bankruptcy [ˈbæŋkrəp(t)si] *n.* **1.** faillite *f*; **fraudulent b.,** banqueroute *f*. **2.** ruine *f*.

banner [ˈbænər] *n.* **1.** (*a*) bannière *f*, étendard *m*; **to enlist under s.o.'s b.,** se ranger sous la bannière de qn; *U.S:* **the Star-Spangled B.,** la bannière étoilée; (*b*) *Ecc:* bannière. **2.** (*a*) *NAm:* excellent; (*b*) *Journ:* **b. heading,** manchette *f*.

bannisters [ˈbænistəz] *n.pl.* = BANISTERS.

banns [bænz] *n.pl.* bans *mpl* (de mariage); **to put up, publish, the b.,** (faire) publier les bans.

banquet¹ [ˈbæŋkwit] *n.* banquet *m*; dîner *m* de gala.

banquet² **1.** *v.tr.* offrir un banquet. à (qn). **2.** *v.i.* banqueter; festoyer. **banqueting** *n.* **b. hall,** salle *f* de banquet.

banshee [bænˈʃiː] *n. Myth:* = dame blanche.

bantam [ˈbæntəm] *n.* **1.** *Husb:* coq *m*, poule *f*, (de) bantam; coq nain. **2.** *Box:* **b. weight,** poids *m* coq, poids bantam.

banter [ˈbæntər] *n.* (*a*) badinage *m*; (*b*) raillerie *f*.

bantering [ˈbæntəriŋ] *a.* (ton, etc.) railleur.

Bantu [ˈbænˈtuː] **1.** *a. Ethn:* bantou. **2.** *n.* (*a*) *Ethn:* Bantou, -oue; (*b*) *Ling:* bantou *m*.

bap [bæp] *n.* petit pain rond au lait.

baptism [ˈbæptizm] *n.* baptême *m*; **b. of fire,** baptême du feu.

baptismal [bæpˈtizm(ə)l] *a.* (registre) baptistaire; (nom) de batême; **b. font,** fonts *mpl* baptismaux.

baptist [ˈbæptist] *n.* **1.** **(St.) John the Baptist,** saint Jean-Baptiste. **2.** *Ecc:* baptiste *mf*; **the B. doctrine,** baptisme *m*.

baptist(e)ry [ˈbæptistri] *n.* baptistère *m*.

baptize [bæpˈtaiz] *v.tr.* baptiser (qn, un navire, etc.); **to be baptized,** recevoir le baptême; **to be baptized (in the name of) John,** être baptisé du nom de Jean.

bar¹ [bɑːr] *n.* **1.** (*a*) barre *f* (de fer, de bois, de chocolat, etc.); tablette *f* (de chocolat); barre (de savon); lingot *m* (d'or); élément *m* (d'un feu électrique); *Cmptr:* barre, barreau *m*; barre (d'une porte); raie *f* (de couleur); barrette *f* (d'une médaille); **with b.** = avec palme *f*; *Gym:* **parallel bars,** barres parallèles; **horizontal b.,** barre fixe; *Cmptr:* **b. code,** code-bar *m*; (*b*) **bars,** barreaux *mpl* (d'une fenêtre, d'une cage, d'une prison); **to be behind (prison) bars,** être derrière les barreaux, sous les verrous; (*c*) **bars,** barres (de la bouche d'un cheval); (*d*) (*in river, harbour*) barre (de sable), traverse *f*. **2.** (*a*) empêchement *m*, obstacle *m*; **to be a b. to sth.,** être un empêchement, faire obstacle, à qch.; **the colour b.,** racisme *m*; ségrégation raciale; (*b*) *Jur:* exception *f*; fin *f* de non-recevoir. **3.** *Jur:* (*a*) barre (des accusés); **the prisoner at the b.,** l'accusé; (*b*) barreau (des avocats); **to read for the b.,** faire son droit; **to be called to the b.,** être reçu au barreau, être reçu avocat; (*c*) *coll.* **the B.,** l'Ordre *m* des avocats. **4.** (*a*) bar *m*; café *m*; *F:* bistro *m*; **refreshment b.,** buvette *f* (de gare, etc.); **snack b.,** snack(-bar) *m*; **coffee b.,** café *m*; **milk b.,** milk-bar *m*; **wine b.,** bar où l'on sert surtout du vin; **lounge b.,** bar salon; (*b*) comptoir *m* (d'un café); *F:* **he's always propping up the b.,** c'est un vrai pilier de café, de bar; (*c*) (*in store, etc.*) **key b.,** clef-minute *m inv.*; **heel b.,** talon-minute *m inv.* **5.** (*a*) barre, ligne *f*, trait *m*; (*b*) *Mus:* **b. (line),** barre; **double b.,** double barre; (*c*) *Mus:* mesure *f*. **6.** *Meteor: Meas:* bar.

bar² *v.tr.* **(barred; barring)** **1.** barrer (une porte, etc.); griller (une fenêtre); **to b. the door against s.o.,** barrer la porte à qn. **2.** (*a*) barrer (un chemin); **to b. s.o.'s way,** barrer la route à qn; couper (le) chemin à qn; (*b*) **to b. s.o. from sth.,** exclure qn de qch; interdire qch. à qn; **to b. s.o. from doing sth.,** défendre à qn de faire qch. **3.** (*a*) défendre, prohiber, interdire (une action); exclure (un sujet de conversation); (*b*) *Jur:* opposer une fin de non-recevoir à (une action). **barred** *a.* **1.** barré; muni d'une grille, de barreaux; **b. window,** fenêtre grillée. **2.** *Jur:* **b. by limitation,**

(droit) périmé. **barring 1.** *n.* (*a*) barrage *m* (d'une porte, etc.); (*b*) interdiction *f* (d'une action, etc.). **2.** *prep.* excepté, sauf, à part; **b. accidents,** sauf accident, sauf imprévu.

bar³ *prep.* excepté, sauf; à part; à l'exception de; **b. one,** sauf un, sauf une; **b. none,** sans exception.

bar⁴ *n. Ich:* maigre *m.*

barb¹ [bɑːb] *n.* **1.** (*a*) barbillon *m*, dardillon *m* (d'un hameçon); barbelure *f* (d'une flèche); ardillon *m* (d'un crochet); (*b*) picot *m* (de fil de fer barbelé); (*c*) *Engr: Metalw:* barbe *f*, bavure *f* (de métal). **2. barbs,** (*a*) *Ich: Vet:* barbillons; *Bot:* arêtes *fpl*; (*b*) barbes (d'une plume).

barb² *v.tr.* garnir de barbelures, de barbillons; **to b. a hook,** relever le barbillon d'un hameçon. **barbed** *a.* **1.** *Bot:* aristé; hameçonné. **2.** barbelé; **b. arrow,** flèche barbelée; **b. wire,** fil de fer barbelé; barbelé *m*; **b.-wire fence,** haie de barbelé; **b.-wire entanglements,** barbelés *mpl.* **3.** *Fig:* **b. words,** paroles *fpl* acerbes.

Barbados [bɑː'beidɔs] *Pr.n. Geog:* Barbade *f.*

barbarian [bɑː'bɛəriən] *a. & n.* barbare (*mf*).

barbaric [bɑː'bærik] *a.* barbare; rude, primitif.

barbarism ['bɑːbərizm] *n.* **1.** *Gram: Ling:* barbarisme *m.* **2.** barbarie *f*, rudesse *f.*

barbarity [bɑː'bæriti] *n.* **1.** barbarie *f*, cruauté *f.* **2.** acte *m* de barbarie; cruauté *f.*

barbarous ['bɑːbərəs] *a.* **1.** barbare. **2.** cruel, barbare. **-ly** *adv.* cruellement.

Barbary ['bɑːbəri] *Pr.n. Geog:* **the B. States,** la Barbarie, les États *mpl* barbaresques; **B. horse,** cheval *m* barbe; **B. ape,** magot *m.*

barbecue ['bɑːbikjuː] *n.* **1.** (*a*) barbecue *m*; gril *m*; (*b*) bœuf, porc, rôti tout entier, à la broche. **2.** grillade *f* en plein air; barbecue.

barbecue² *v.tr.* (*a*) rôtir (un animal entier) à la broche; (*b*) griller (de la viande) sur un barbecue.

barbel ['bɑːb(ə)l] *n.* **1.** *Ich:* barbeau (commun). **2.** barbillon *m* (d'un poisson).

bar(-)bell ['bɑː'bel] *n. Gym:* barre *f* (i) à disques, (ii) à sphères.

barber ['bɑːbər] *n.* barbier *m*; coiffeur *m.*

barbershop ['bɑːbəʃɔp] *n. NAm:* **1.** salon *m* de coiffure (pour hommes). **2.** *Mus:* **b. harmony,** chants *mpl* à quatre voix d'hommes.

barbican ['bɑːbikən] *n. Fort:* barbacane *f.*

barbitone ['bɑːbitoun] *n. Pharm:* véronal *m.*

barbiturate [bɑː'bitjuəreit] *n. Ch:* barbiturique *m.*

barbituric [bɑːbi'tjuːrik] *a.* barbiturique.

barcarol(l)e ['bɑːkəroul] *n. Mus:* barcarolle *f.*

Barcelona [bɑːsi'lounə] *Pr.n. Geog:* Barcelone *f.*

bard [bɑːd] *n.* **1.** (*Celtic*) barde *m.* **2.** poète *m*; *Lit:* **the B.,** Shakespeare.

bardic ['bɑːdik] *a.* (poésie) des bardes.

bare¹ ['bɛər] *a.* **1.** (pays) nu, dénudé; (tête, jambe, etc.) nue; (arbre) dénudé, dépouillé; (poi trine) découverte; (placard, rayon) vide; *El:* (fil) dénudé; **to fight with b. hands,** se battre à mains nues; **to lie, sleep, on the b. boards,** coucher sur la dure; **the b. facts,** le fait brutal; **to lay b.,** mettre à nu, exposer (une surface, des fautes, son cœur); dévoiler (un secret, une fraude); déchausser (des fondations, des racines, etc.). **2. to earn a b. living,** gagner tout juste, à peine, de quoi vivre; **the b. minimum,** le strict minimum; **the b. necessities (of life),** juste ce qu'il faut pour vivre; **b. majority,** faible majorité *f*; *Sch:* **he got a b. pass,** il a été reçu sans mention. **-ly** *adv.* **1. room b. furnished,** pièce (i) à peine, (ii) pauvrement, meublée. **2.** à peine, tout juste; **I b. know him,** je le connais à peine; **he can b. read and write,** c'est tout juste s'il sait lire et écrire.

bare² *v.tr.* mettre (qch.) à nu; se découvrir (la tête); déchausser (des racines, etc.); **to b. one's teeth,** montrer ses dents.

bareback ['bɛəbæk] *adv.* **to ride b.,** monter (un cheval) à nu, à cru.

barefaced ['bɛəfeist] *a. F:* (mensonge, etc.) éhonté, effronté.

barefoot(ed) ['bɛə'fut(id)] **1.** *a.* aux pieds nus; les pieds nus. **2.** *adv.* nu-pieds; (à) pied nus.

bare-headed ['bɛə'hedid] *a. & adv.* nu-tête, (la) tête nue.

bare-legged ['bɛə'leg(i)d] *a. & adv.* nu-jambes, (les) jambes nues; aux jambes nues.

bareness ['bɛənis] *n.* **1.** dénuement *m* (d'une chambre, etc.). **2.** pauvreté *f* (de style, etc.).

bargain ['bɑːgin] *n.* (*a*) marché *m*, affaire *f*; **a good, bad, b.,** une bonne, une mauvaise, affaire; **to strike a b. with s.o.,** conclure, faire, un marché avec qn; **to drive a hard b.,** chercher à gagner le dernier centime; **into the b.,** par-dessus le marché, en plus; **it's a b.!** c'est entendu! (*b*) *Com:* **b. sale,** (vente *f* de) soldes *mpl*; **b. price,** prix exceptionnel; **a real b.,** une véritable occasion; **b. offer,** offre avantageuse; occasion *f*; **b. counter,** rayon *m* des soldes; **b. hunter,** chercheur, -euse, d'occasions.

bargain² *v.i.* (*a*) entrer en négociations, négocier (**with s.o.,** avec qn); **to b. with s.o. for sth.,** traiter, faire marché, de qch. avec qn; **I didn't b. for that,** je ne m'attendais pas à cela; **he got more than he bargained for,** il a eu du fil à retordre; (*b*) **to b. with s.o.,** marchander qn. **bargaining** *n.* marchandage *m*; *Ind:* **collective b.** = convention collective.

barge¹ [bɑːdʒ] *n.* (*a*) chaland *m*, péniche *f*; **motor b.,** chaland à moteur; (*b*) (*with sails*) gabare *f*, barge *f*; (*c*) *Navy:* deuxième canot *m* (d'un navire de guerre); (*d*) **state b.,** barque *f* de cérémonie.

barge² *v.i. F:* **to b. into, against, s.o., sth.,** venir se heurter contre qn, qch.; se cogner sur qn, contre qch.; **to b. in,** intervenir mal à propos; **to b. into a room,** faire irruption dans une pièce.

bargee [bɑː'dʒiː] *n.* (*a*) chalandier *m*; (*b*) marinier *m.*

bargeman ['bɑːdʒmən] *n. U.S:* = BARGEE.

bargepole ['bɑːdʒpoul] *n.* gaffe *f*; *F:* **I wouldn't touch it with a b.,** (i) ça me dégoûterait d'y toucher; (ii) je ne veux rien avoir à faire avec ça.

baritone ['bæritoun] *n. Mus:* (*voice, singer, instrument*), baryton *m.*

barium ['bɛəriəm] *n. Ch:* baryum *m*; *Med:* **b. meal,** sulfate *m* de baryum.

bark¹ [bɑːk] *n.* **1.** écorce *f* (d'arbre); **to strip the b. off a tree,** écorcer un arbre. **2. (tanner's) b.,** tan *m.*

bark² *v.tr.* (*a*) écorcer (un arbre); (*b*) **to b. one's shins,** s'écorcher, s'érafler, les tibias.

bark³ *n.* **1.** aboiement *m*, aboi *m*; glapissement *m* (du renard); **his b. is worse than his bite,** il aboie plus qu'il ne mord. **2.** *F:* toux sèche.

bark⁴ **1.** *v.i.* aboyer (**at,** après, contre, à); (*of fox*) glapir; **to b. up the wrong tree,** suivre une fausse piste. **2.** *v.tr.* dire (qch.) d'un ton sec, cassant; **to b. out an order,** donner un ordre d'un ton sec. **barking 1.** *a.* (*a*) (chien) aboyeur; (renard) glapissant; (*b*) *F:* (toux) sèche. **2.** *n.* aboiement *m* (d'un chien); glapissement *m* (d'un renard).

bark⁵ *n.* **1.** *Nau:* trois-mâts *m.* **2.** *Poet:* barque *f.*

barkeep(er) ['bɑːkiːp(ə)r] *n.m. NAm:* garçon de comptoir; barman.

barker ['bɑːkər] *n. A: & NAm:* **fairground b.,** aboyeur *m.*

barley ['bɑːli] *n.* (*a*) orge *f*, **pearl b.,** orge *m* perlé; (*b*) **b. meal, sugar,** farine *f*, sucre *m*, d'orge; **b. water,** tisane *f* d'orge.

barleycorn ['bɑːlikɔːn] *n.* grain *m* d'orge.

barm [bɑːm] *n.* levure *f* (de bière); levain *m* de bière.

barmaid ['bɑːmeid] *n.f.* serveuse (dans un bar); barmaid.

barman, -men ['bɑːmən] *n.m.* garçon de comptoir; barman.
barminess ['bɑːminis] *n. F:* loufoquerie *f.*
barmy ['bɑːmi] *a.* **1.** contenant de la levure; écumeux; en fermentation. **2.** *F:* toqué, loufoque.
barn [bɑːn] *n.* (*a*) grange *f*; **b. dance,** danses folkloriques; (*b*) *NAm:* étable *f*; écurie *f*; (*c*) *NAm:* dépôt *m* de tramways.
barnacle ['bɑːnəkl] *n.* **1.** *Orn:* **b. (goose),** bernacle *f*, bernache *f* (nonnette). **2.** (*a*) *Crust:* (i) **(stalked, ship, goose) b.,** anatif(e) *m*, *F:* bernacle; (ii) **(acorn) b.,** balane *m*, gland *m* de mer.
barnstorm ['bɑːnstɔːm] *v.i.* faire une tournée théâtrale, électorale, etc.
barnstormer ['bɑːnstɔːmər] *n.* (*a*) acteur, -trice, ambulant(e); (*b*) orateur électoral
barnyard ['bɑːnjɑːd] *n.* basse-cour *f*, *pl.* basses-cours.
barometer [bə'rɔmitər] *n.* baromètre *m*; **b. reading,** hauteur *f* barométrique; **the b. is at fair,** le baromètre est au beau fixe.
barometric [bærə'metrik] *a.* (pression, etc.) barométrique.
baron ['bærən] *n.* **1.** (*a*) baron *m*; (*b*) *F:* grand manitou (industriel). **2.** *Cu:* **b. of beef,** double aloyau *m.*
baroness ['bærənes] *n.f.* baronne.
baronet ['bærənet] *n.m.* baronnet.
baronetcy ['bærənitsi] *n.* dignité *f* de baronnet; **to be given a b.,** être élevé au rang de, être créé, baronnet.
baronial [bə'rouniəl] *a.* baronnial; **b. hall,** demeure seigneuriale.
barony ['bærəni] *n.* **1.** baronnie *f.* **2.** (*in Ireland*) subdivision *f* d'un comté. **3.** *Scot:* grande propriété terrienne.
baroque [bə'rɔk] *a. & n. Hist. of Art:* baroque (*m*).
barque [bɑːk] *n. Nau:* trois-mâts *m* barque.
barrack¹ ['bærək] *n.* **1.** (*a*) *Mil:* *usu. pl.* **barracks** (*with sg. or pl. const.*) caserne *f*; quartier *m*; **detention barracks,** locaux *mpl* disciplinaires; **to be confined to barracks,** être consigné; **b. square,** cour *f* du quartier; (*b*) *Can:* = gendarmerie *f.* **2.** *Pej: F:* (*large ugly building*) caserne.
barrack² *v.tr. Mil:* caserner (des troupes).
barrackroom ['bærəkruːm *n.* chambrée *f*; **b. language,** langage *m* de corps de garde, de caserne.
barracuda [bærə'kjuːdə] *n. Ich:* barracuda *m*, bécune *f.*
barrage ['bærɑːʒ, bæ·rɑːʒ] *n.* **1.** *Hyd.E:* barrage *m* (d'un fleuve). **2.** *Mil: Artil:* barrage. **3.** torrent *m* (de questions, d'injures).
barrel ['bær(ə)l] *n.* **1.** (*a*) tonneau *m*, barrique *f*, fût *m* (de vin, etc.); baril *m* (de pétrole); caque *f*, baril (de harengs, etc.); *F:* **to scrape the bottom of the b.,** gratter le fonds du panier; (*b*) **biscuit b.,** *NAm:* **cracker b.,** boîte *f*, seau *m*, à biscuits; (*c*) *NAm: F:* grande quantité (**of,** de). **2.** cylindre *m*, partie *f* cylindrique; caisse *f* (d'un tambour); canon *m* (de fusil, de serrure, de clef); corps *m*, barillet *m* (de pompe); cylindre, barillet (de serrure); fusée *f*, mèche *f*, tambour *m* (de cabestan, de treuil); *Artil:* tube *m* de canon); **b. organ,** (i) orgue mécanique; (ii) orgue de Barbarie; piano *m* mécanique (à cylindre); *Av:* **b. roll,** tonneau *m*; *Arch:* **b. vault,** voûte *f* en berceau.
barren ['bær(ə)n] *a.* (*a*) stérile; (terrain) aride; **b. lands,** *n.pl. NAm:* **barrens,** terrains infertiles; lande(s) *f* (*pl*); (*b*) (sujet) maigre; **mind b. of ideas,** esprit dépourvu d'idées.
barrenness ['bærənnis] *n.* stérilité *f.*
barricade¹ ['bærikeid, bæri'keid] *n.* barricade *f.*
barricade² *v.tr.* barricader.
barrier ['bæriər] *n.* (*a*) barrière *f*; *Mil: etc:* barrage *m* (d'obstacles); *Av:* **sound, sonic, b.,** mur *m* du son; *Rail:* **ticket b.,** portillon *m* d'accès; *Geog:* **ice b.,** muraille *f*, falaise *f*, de glace; **b. ice,** banquise *f*; **b. reef,** récif *m* en barrière; **the Great B. Reef,** la Grande Barrière; (*b*) **the language b.,** le mur des langues; **b. to progress,** obstacle *m* au progrès.
barrister ['bæristər] *n. Jur:* **b.(-at-law)** = avocat *m.*
barrow¹ ['bærou] *n.* (*a*) brouette *f*; (*b*) baladeuse *f*, voiture *f* à bras; charrette *f* à bras; **b. boy,** marchand *m* des quatre saisons; (*c*) *Rail:* diable *m.*
barrow² *n. Archeol:* tumulus *m*; tertre *m* (funéraire).
bartender ['bɑːtendər] *n.* garçon *m* de comptoir; barman *m.*
barter¹ ['bɑːtər] *n.* échange *m*; troc *m.*
barter² **1.** *v.tr.* **to b. sth. for sth.,** échanger, troquer, qch. contre qch. **2.** *v.i.* faire le commerce d'échange; faire le troc.
Bartholomew [bɑː'θɔləmjuː] *Pr.n.m.* Barthélemy; *Hist:* **the Massacre of St. B.,** le Massacre de la Saint-Barthélemy.
barytone ['bæritoun] *n.* = BARITONE.
basal ['beisəl] *a.* basal; fondamental.
basalt ['bæsɔːlt] *n.* basalte *m.*
basaltic [bə'sɔːltik] *a.* basaltique.
bascule ['bæskjuːl] *n. Civ.E:* bascule *f*; **b. bridge,** pont(-levis) *m* à bascule (*pl.* ponts-levis).
base¹ [beis] *n.* **1.** (*a*) base *f* (de triangle; (*b*) *Mth: Cmptr:* base; (*c*) *Ling:* base, racine *f*; (*d*) *Ch:* base (d'un sel); (*e*) *Surv:* base; **b. line,** (i) *Ten:* ligne *f* de fond; (ii) *Art:* ligne de fuite. **2.** (*a*) fondement *m*; base; *Const:* soubassement *m*; socle *m*, pied *m*, assise *f*; sole *f*, embase (de machine-outil, etc.); *Fig:* base (d'un raisonnement, d'une proposition); (*b*) *Phot:* support *m* (du film, de l'émulsion); (*c*) *El:* culot *m* (d'une lampe); (*d*) *Rail:* patin *m* (de rail). **3.** (*a*) *Mil: etc:* base (d'opérations, de ravitaillement); **naval b.,** base navale; **submarine b.,** nid *m* de sous-marins; **air b.,** base aérienne; (*b*) **rocket b.,** base de lancement (de fusées); (*c*) (*baseball*) base, piquet *m*; *Fig:* **to get to first b.,** faire les premiers pas (vers un objectif); **to be off b.,** (i) se tromper; (ii) *NAm: F:* être fou, cinglé.
base² *v.tr.* **1.** baser, fonder (un calcul, un espoir) **(on,** sur); asseoir, fonder, appuyer (une opinion) **(on,** sur); **to b. oneself on sth.,** se baser sur qch.; **this novel is based on the events of 1939,** ce roman est basé sur les événements de 1939. **2.** (*of firm, etc.*) **to be based at X,** être basé à X.
base³ *a.* (*a*) (homme) vil; (motif) bas, indigne; (action) ignoble, indigne; (*b*) **b. metals,** métaux vils; (*c*) **b. coin(age),** (i) pièce *f*, monnaie *f*, de mauvais aloi; (ii) fausse monnaie.
baseball ['beisbɔːl] *n. Sp:* base-ball *m*; **b. player,** baseballeur *m*, joueur *m* de base-ball.
baseboard ['beisbɔːd] *NAm:* plinthe *f.*
Basel ['bɑːz(ə)l] *Pr.n. Geog:* Bâle *f.*
baseless ['beislis] *a.* sans base, sans fondement.
basement ['beismənt] *n.* **1.** soubassement *m* (d'une construction). **2.** sous-sol *m*; **b. flat,** (appartement *m* de) sous-sol.
baseness ['beisnis] *n.* bassesse *f* (d'une action, etc.).
bash¹ [bæʃ] *n. F:* (*a*) coup *m*, enfoncement *m*; **the saucepan has had a b.,** la casserole est bosselée, cabossée; (*b*) coup (sur la figure); coup de poing violent; **to have a b. at sth.,** s'attaquer à qch., *F:* tenter le coup.
bash² *v.tr. F:* **to b. one's head,** se cogner la tête; **to b. (in) a hat,** aplatir, cabosser, un chapeau (d'un coup de poing); **to b. s.o. up,** tabasser qn. **bashing** *n. F:* volée *f* de coups; rossée *f*; *Mil: etc:* **to take, get, a b.,** prendre quelque chose; **union b.,** mesures anti-syndicales.
bashful ['bæʃf(u)l] *a.* (*a*) modeste, timide; **b. lover,**

amoureux transi; (*b*) modeste, pudique. **-fully** *adv.* (*a*) modestement; timidement; (*b*) pudiquement.
bashfulness [ˈbæʃf(u)lnis] *n.* modestie *f*; timidité *f*.
basic [ˈbeisik] *a.* **1.** (*a*) (principe, etc.) fondamental; (vérité) première; *Ling:* (vocabulaire) de base; **to learn some b. French,** apprendre des éléments de français; (*b*) **b. pay,** salaire *m* de base; *Pol.Ec:* **b. commodity,** denrée *f* témoin. **2. b. slag,** scorie *f* basique. **3.** *n.pl.* **basics,** choses essentielles; éléments *mpl.* **-ally** *adv.* fondamentalement; à la base; au fond.
basil¹ [ˈbæz(ə)l] *n. Bot:* basilic *m*.
basilica [bəˈzilikə] *n. Ecc.Arch:* basilique *f*.
basilisk [ˈbæzilisk] *n. Myth: Rept:* basilic *m*.
basin [ˈbeis(ə)n] *n.* **1.** (*a*) bassin *m*; (*for soup, etc.*) écuelle *f*, bol *m*; (*for milk*) jatte *f*; vasque *f*, coupe *f* (d'une fontaine); **sugar b.,** sucrier *m*; (*b*) (*for washing up, etc.*) bassine *f*; cuvette *f*; **hand b.,** lavabo *m*. **2.** *Geog:* (*a*) bassin; **catchment b.,** bassin hydrographique; **the Paris B.,** le Bassin parisien; (*b*) **coal b.,** bassin houiller. **3.** (*a*) *Geog:* port naturel; rade fermée; (*b*) *Nau:* bassin; **tidal b.,** bassin à flot; (*c*) (*in canal, river*) garage *m*; **dry b.,** garage à sec.
basinful [ˈbeis(ə)nful] *n.* **1.** plein bol, bolée *f*, écuellée *f*. **2.** pleine cuvette. **3.** *P:* **to have had a b.,** (i) en avoir tout son soûl; (ii) en avoir ras le bol; en avoir marre.
basis, *pl.* **bases** [ˈbeisis, -iːz] *n.* **1.** base *f* (de négociations, etc.); fondement *m* (d'une opinion, etc.); assiette *f* (d'un impôt); **on the b. of . . .,** à partir de . . . . **2.** *Mth:* matrice *f* de base.
bask [bɑːsk] *v.i.* (*a*) **to b. in the sun,** se chauffer (au soleil); *F:* faire le lézard, lézarder; **to b. in s.o.'s favour,** jouir de la faveur de qn; (*b*) *Ich:* **basking shark,** pèlerin *m*.
basket [ˈbɑːskit] *n.* **1.** (*a*) corbeille *f*; panier *m*; (*carried on back*) hotte *f*; (*for coal, etc.*) banne *f*, manne *f*; (*plaited shopping basket*) cabas *m*; couffin *m*; (*in basketball*) panier; **vegetable b.,** calais *m*; **oyster b.,** cloyère *f*; **laundry b.,** corbeille à linge; **linen b.,** panier à linge; **waste paper b.,** corbeille *f* à papier; **picnic b.,** (i) panier; (ii) mallette *f*, de pique-nique; (*b*) *F:* **(you) silly b.!** espèce d'idiot! **2.** (*a*) **b. making,** vannerie *f*; **b. maker,** vannier *m*; (*b*) *Furn: etc:* (chaise, etc.) en rotin, en osier; (*c*) (*of sword*) **b. hilt,** (garde *f* en) coquille (*f*). **3.** *Ent:* **pollen b.,** corbeille (d'abeille).
basketball [ˈbɑːskitbɔːl] *n. Games:* basket-ball *m*, *F:* basket *m*; **b. player,** basket(t)eur, -euse.
basketful [ˈbɑːskitful] *n.* plein panier; panerée *f*.
basketry [ˈbɑːskitri] *n.* vannerie *f*.
basketwork [ˈbɑːskitwəːk] *n.* **1.** vannerie *f*. **2.** *Const: etc:* clayonnage *m*; entrelacement *m*.
Basle [bɑːl] *Pr.n. Geog:* Bâle.
Basque [bɑːsk] **1.** *a. Ethn:* basque; **the B. Country,** le Pays basque. **2.** *n.* (*a*) *Ethn:* Basque *mf*; (*b*) *Ling:* basque *m*. **3.** *n. Cost:* **b.,** basque *f*.
bass¹ [bæs] *n. Ich:* **1.** (*a*) perche commune; (*b*) **sea b.,** serran *m*. **2.** bar *m*; **striped b.,** bar rayé.
bass² [bæs] *n.* (*a*) *Bot:* liber *m*; (*b*) tille *f*, filasse *f*; **b. rope,** bastin *m*.
bass³ [beis] **1.** *n.* (*a*) (*voice or singer*) basse *f*; **deep b.,** basse profonde; (*b*) (*instrument*) (i) basse; (ii) contrebasse *f*; (*c*) **figured b.,** basse chiffrée, figurée. **2.** *a.* (*a*) *Mus:* **b. voice,** voix *f* de basse; **b. part,** partie *f* de basse; **b. clef,** clef *f* de fa; (*b*) **b. tones,** sons *mpl* graves.
basset [ˈbæsit] *n.* **b. (hound),** basset *m*.
bassinet(te) [bæsiˈnet] *n.* **1.** moïse *m*. **2.** voiture *f* d'enfant (en osier).
bassist [ˈbæsist] *n. Mus:* bassiste *m*.
bassoon [bəˈsuːn] *n. Mus:* basson *m*; **double b.,** contrebasson *m*.
bassoonist [bəˈsuːnist] *n. Mus:* basson *m*, bassoniste *m*.
basso-profondo, -profundo [ˈbæsouprəˈfʌndou] *n.* (voix *f* de) basse profonde.
bast [bæst] *n.* = BASS².
bastard [ˈbæstəd, ˈbɑːstəd] **1.** *a.* & *n.* bâtard, -arde; *Jur:* enfant naturel, -elle. **2.** *a.* corrompu; bâtard; **b. file,** lime bâtarde; (*of paper, book, etc.*) **b. size,** format bâtard; *Typ:* **b. title,** faux titre; **b. hand,** (écriture) bâtarde. **3.** *n. P:* salaud; **you b.!** espèce de salaud! **a b. of a job,** un chien de travail; (*of work, problem*) **it's a b.,** c'est vachement difficile.
bastardy [ˈbæstədi] *n.* bâtardise *f*; *Jur:* **b. case,** action *f* en désaveu de paternité.
baste¹ [beist] *v.tr. Needlew:* bâtir, faufiler (un corsage, etc.); **to b. on a lining,** glacer une doublure. **basting** *n.* bâti *m*, faufilure *f*; glacis *m* (de doublure); **b. thread,** faufil *m*, bâti *m*.
baste² *v.tr. Cu:* arroser (de sa graisse, de son jus) (un rôti). **basting** *n.* arrosement *m*, arrosage *m* (d'un rôti).
bastion [ˈbæstiən] *n. Fort:* bastion *m*.
bat¹ [bæt] *n.* (*a*) *Z:* chauve-souris *f*, *pl.* chauves-souris; *F:* **he went down the road like a b. out of hell,** il a descendu la rue comme un bolide; **to have bats in the belfry,** avoir une araignée au plafond.
bat² *n.* **1.** batte *f* (de cricket, de base-ball, etc.); **he's a good b.,** il manie bien la batte; **to do sth. off one's own b.,** faire qch. de sa propre initiative. **2.** raquette *f* (de ping-pong).
bat³ *v.i.* **(batted; batting)** manier la batte (au cricket, au base-ball); *Cr:* être au guichet. **batting** *n. Cr: etc:* maniement *m* de la batte.
bat⁴ *v.tr.* battre (des paupières); **he didn't b. an eyelid,** il n'a pas sourcillé, tiqué.
batch [bætʃ] *n.* **1.** fournée *f* (de pain, *F:* de prisonniers); tas *m*, paquet *m*, (de lettres). **2.** lot *m* (de marchandises, *etc.*, *Cmptr:* de données). **3.** gâchée *f* (de ciment, de béton).
bated [ˈbeitid] *a.* **with b. breath,** (parler) à voix basse; (attendre) en retenant son haleine.
bath¹, *pl.* **baths** [bɑːθ, bɑːðz] *n.* **1.** bain *m*; **cold b.,** bain froid; **to take, have, a b.,** prendre un bain, se baigner; **to give a child a b.,** baigner un enfant; **b. salts,** sels *mpl* de bain; **b. towel,** serviette *f* de bain; **b. wrap,** sortie *f* de bain; **public baths,** (i) bains publics; (ii) (*swimming*) piscine *f*; **Turkish b.,** bain turc; **steam b.,** (i) *Med:* bain de vapeur; (ii) étuve *f* humide (de hammam); *Min:* **pithead baths,** lavabo *m*; **the Order of the Bath,** l'Ordre *m* du Bain. **2.** (*a*) baignoire *f*; **hip b., sitz b.,** bain de siège; (*b*) *Phot: etc:* cuvette *f*. **3.** (*liquid*) **acid, alkaline, b.,** bain acide, alcalin; *Phot:* **fixing b.,** bain de fixage, fixateur *m*.
bath² **1.** *v.tr.* baigner, donner un bain à (qn). **2.** *v.i.* prendre un bain.
bathe¹ [beið] *n.* bain *m* (de rivière, de mer); baignade *f*; **to go for a b.,** (aller) se baigner.
bathe² **1.** *v.tr.* (*a*) baigner; **to b. one's face,** se baigner la figure; **face bathed in tears,** visage baigné de larmes; **bathed in perspiration,** trempé de sueur, en nage; (*b*) *NAm:* baigner (un enfant); (*c*) laver, lotionner (une plaie). **2.** *v.i.* (*a*) se baigner, prendre un bain (de mer, de rivière); (*b*) *U.S:* prendre un bain (dans la baignoire). **bathing** *n.* (*a*) bains *mpl* de mer, baignades *fpl*; **b. place,** baignade; **b. resort,** station *f* balnéaire; plage *f*; **b. costume, suit,** costume *m*, maillot *m*, de bain; **b. trunks,** caleçon *m*, slip *m*, de bain; **b. cap,** bonnet *m* de bain; (*b*) lotion *f* (d'une plaie, etc.).
bather [ˈbeiðər] *n.* baigneur, -euse.
bathmat [ˈbɑːθmæt] *n.* descente *f*, tapis *m*, de bain.
bathos [ˈbeiθɔs] *n.* chute *f* du sublime au ridicule.
bathrobe [ˈbɑːθroub] *n.* peignoir *m*.

bathroom ['bɑːθruːm] *n.* salle *f* de bain(s); **b. scales,** pèse-personne *m*, *pl.* pèse-personnes.
bathtub ['bɑːθtʌb] *n.* baignoire *f*; tub *m*.
bathwater ['bɑːθwːɔtər] *n.* bain *m*; **my bathwater's too hot,** mon bain est trop chaud; *F:* **to throw the baby out with the b.,** se montrer plus zélé que prudent.
batman, *pl.* **-men** ['bætmən] *n.m. Mil:* (*pers.*) ordonnance *m or f*.
baton ['bætən] *n.* **1.** (*a*) bâton *m* (de maréchal, etc.); **conductor's b.,** baguette *f*, bâton, de chef d'orchestre; (*b*) *Sp:* (*in relay race*) témoin *m*. **2.** bâton (d'agent de police); **b. charge,** charge à la matraque.
bats [bæts] *a. F:* loufoque, toqué.
batsman, *pl.* **-men** ['bætsmən] *n.m. Cr:* batteur.
battalion [bə'tæljən] *n. Mil:* (*a*) bataillon *m*; **b. commander,** commandant *m* de bataillon; **tank b., armoured b.,** bataillon de chars; (*b*) *U.S:* groupe *m* (d'artillerie).
batten[1] ['bæt(ə)n] *n.* **1.** (*a*) *Carp: etc:* (i) couvre-joint *m*, *pl.* couvre-joints; (ii) latte *f*, liteau *m*; **half-round b.,** baguette demi-ronde; (*b*) *Nau:* barre *f*, latte, tringle *f*. **2.** *Th:* **the battens,** les herses *fpl* (d'éclairage). **3.** *Carp:* planche *f* (de parquet).
batten[2] *v.tr.* (*a*) *Carp:* latter, voliger; (*b*) *Nau:* **to b. down the hatches,** condamner les panneaux.
batten[3] *v.i. Lit:* s'engraisser, se bourrer, se repaître (**on,** de); **to b. on s.o.,** s'enrichir aux dépens de qn.
batter[1] ['bætər] *n. Cr:* batteur *m*.
batter[2] *n.* **1.** *Cu:* pâte *f* lisse; pâte à frire; **pancake b.,** pâte à crêpes. **2.** *Typ:* caractère endommagé, écrasé.
batter[3] *v.tr.* (*a*) battre; *Artil:* battre en brèche, canonner (une ville); (*b*) *Typ:* endommager (des caractères); (*c*) bossuer (une casserole, un chapeau, etc.); (*d*) maltraiter (un enfant, etc.). **batter down** *v.tr.* abattre, démolir (une porte, etc.); battre (un mur) en brèche. **battered** *a.* (*a*) (mobilier, etc.) délabré; (chapeau) cabossé; (casserole, etc.) bossuée, bosselée; **a b. old car,** une vieille voiture délabrée; (*b*) (visage) meurtri; **b. wives,** femmes battues; **b. child, baby,** enfant maltraité; enfant martyr. **batter in** *v.tr.* enfoncer (une porte, etc.); **the skull of the victim was battered in,** la victime a eu le crâne défoncé. **battering** *n.* (*a*) *A.Mil:* **b. ram,** bélier *m*; (*b*) **child, wife, b.,** maltraitement *m* d'enfants, de femmes.
battery ['bæt(ə)ri] *n.* **1.** *Jur:* voie *f* de fait; **assault and b.,** voies de fait; coups *mpl* et blessures *fpl*. **2.** *Artil:* (*a*) groupe *m* (d'artillerie); (*b*) batterie *f*; **field b.,** batterie de campagne. **3.** (*a*) batterie (de fours à coke, etc.); (*b*) *El:* pile *f*, batterie; **dry b.,** (batterie de) piles sèches; (*c*) *El:* **(storage) b.,** accumulateur *m*, *F:* accu *m*; (*d*) *Husb:* batterie (d'élevage); **b. farming,** élevage *m* en batterie(s); **b. hen,** poulet *m* de batterie; (*e*) *Psy:* batterie (de tests). **4.** *Sp:* (*baseball*) **the b.,** le lanceur et le receveur. **5.** (*set*) batterie (de cuisine, etc.).
battle[1] ['bætl] *n.* bataille *f*, combat *m*; **pitched b.,** bataille rangée; *Navy:* **b. cruiser,** croiseur *m* de combat; **b. fleet,** flotte *f* de ligne, de combat; **b. area,** zone *f* de bataille, d'engagement; **to fight, win, a b.,** livrer, gagner, une bataille; **killed in b.,** tué à l'ennemi; **b. cry,** cri *m* de guerre; **b. dress,** tenue *f* de campagne, de combat; **to join b. with s.o.,** entrer en lutte avec qn, livrer bataille à qn; **that's half the b.,** c'est bataille à moitié gagnée; **the first blow is half the b.,** le premier coup en vaut deux; **b. royal,** mêlée générale; bagarre *f*.
battle[2] **1.** *v.i.* se battre, lutter **(with s.o. for sth.,** avec qn pour qch.); **to b. with, against, a fire,** combattre, lutter, contre un incendie; **to b. one's way through difficulties,** se frayer un chemin à travers les difficultés. **2.** *v.tr. U.S:* combattre (une doctrine, etc.).
battleaxe ['bætlæks] *n.* **1.** *A.Mil:* hache *f* d'armes. **2.** *n.f.F:* virago, mégère.
battledore ['bætldɔːr] *n. Sp:* raquette *f*; **to play at b. and shuttlecock,** jouer au volant.
battledress ['bætldres] *n. Mil:* tenue *f* de campagne.
battlefield ['bætlfiːld] *n.* champ *m* de bataille.
battlements ['bætlmənts] *n.pl.* (*a*) *Arch:* créneaux *mpl*; (*b*) parapet *m*, rempart *m*.
battleship ['bætlʃip] *n. Navy: Hist:* bâtiment *m* de ligne; cuirassé *m*; **pocket b.,** cuirassé de poche.
batty ['bæti] *a. F:* toqué, timbré; cinglé.
batwing ['bætwiŋ] *a.* en forme d'aile de chauve-souris; **b. sleeves,** manches *fpl* kimono.
bauble ['bɔːbl] *n.* **1.** babiole *f*, colifichet *m*. **2. jester's b.,** marotte.
baulk [bɔːk] *n.* & *v.* = BALK [1], [2].
bauxite ['bɔːksait] *n. Miner:* bauxite *f*.
Bavaria [bə'vɛəriə] *Pr.n. Geog:* Bavière *f*.
Bavarian [bə'vɛəriən] **1.** *a. Geog:* bavarois. **2.** *n. Geog:* Bavarois, -oise.
bawdiness ['bɔːdinis] *n.* obscénité *f*; impudeur *f*.
bawdy ['bɔːdi] *a.* obscène, paillard, impudique; **b. talk,** propos orduriers; **b. house,** maison *f* de prostitution.
bawl [bɔːl] *v.tr.* & *i* (*a*) brailler; crier à tue-tête, *F:* beugler; *P:* gueuler (**at s.o.,** contre qn); **to b. out an order,** gueuler un ordre; (*b*) pleurer bruyamment; brailler; (*c*) *P:* **to b. s.o. out,** engueuler qn.
bay[1] [bei] *n. Bot:* **sweet b., b. laurel,** laurier commun, laurier des poètes; *Cu:* **b. leaf,** feuille *f* de laurier; **b. tree,** laurier *m*; **b. wreath, bays,** couronne *f* de laurier(s).
bay[2] *n. Geog:* baie *f*; (*small*) anse *f*; **Hudson B.,** la Baie d'Hudson; **the B. of Biscay,** le golfe de Gascogne.
bay[3] *n.* **1.** (*a*) (*of bridge, roof, etc.*) travée *f*; (*b*) (*of joists*) claire-voie *f*, *pl.* claires-voies. **2.** (*a*) enfoncement *m*; baie *f* (d'une porte, etc.); *Mil:* (*in trench*) niche *f*; *Av:* **bomb b.,** soute *f* à bombes; (*b*) *Rail:* quai *m* subsidiaire; quai en cul-de-sac; (*c*) **sick b.,** infirmerie *f*; **parking b.,** place *f* de stationnement; **loading b.,** quai *m* de chargement; **b. window,** fenêtre *f* en baie, en saillie; baie.
bay[4] *n.* **to bring a stag to b.,** mettre un cerf aux abois; forcer, acculer, un cerf; **to be at b.,** être aux abois, à l'accul; **to keep, hold, the enemy at b.,** tenir l'ennemi en échec.
bay[5] *v.i.* (*a*) (*of hound*) aboyer; donner de la voix; (*b*) **to b. (at) the moon,** hurler, aboyer, à la lune. **baying** *n.* aboiement *m*.
bay[6] *a.* & *n.* (cheval) bai (*m*).
bayberry ['beibəri] *n. Bot:* **1.** baie *f* de laurier. **2.** piment *m* de la Jamaïque. **3.** *NAm:* cirier *m*.
bayonet[1]['beiənit] *n. Mil:* baïonnette *f*; **with fixed bayonets,** baïonnette au canon; **b. charge,** charge *f* à la baïonnette; *Mec.E: etc:* **b. joint,** joint *m* en baïonnette; *El:* **b. holder, socket,** douille *f* à baïonnette (de lampe électrique).
bayonet[2] *v.tr.* **(bayoneted)** percer (qn) d'un coup de baïonnette.
bazaar [bə'zɑːr] *n.* **1.** bazar *m*. **2.** vente *f* de charité.
bazooka [bə'zuːkə] *n.* **1.** *Artil:* bazooka *m*.
be [biː] *v.i.* (*pr.ind.* **am** [æm], **are** [ɑːr], **is** [iz], *pl.* **are;** *past ind.* **was** [wɔːz], **were** [wɛər], **was,** *pl.* **were;** *pr. sub.* **be;** *past sub.* **were;** *pr.p.* **being** ['biːiŋ], *p.p.* **been** [biːn]; *imp.* **be;** *I am, he is, she is, it is, we are, you are, they are, can be shortened into:* **I'm, he's, she's, it's, we're, you're, they're;** *is not, are not, was not, were not, into:* **isn't, aren't, wasn't, weren't)** être. **1.** (*a*) **Mary is pretty,** Marie est jolie; **the weather was fine,** le temps était beau; **time is money,** le temps, c'est de l'argent; **he's a bit odd, is Bob,** c'est un drôle

de garçon que Bob; (*b*) **his father is a doctor,** son père est médecin; **he is an Englishman,** il est anglais, c'est un Anglais; **are they English?—yes, they are,** sont-ils anglais?—oui, ils le sont; **if I were you,** à votre place, si j'étais vous; **as it is, we must go,** les choses étant ainsi il nous faut partir; (*c*) **unity is strength,** l'union fait la force; **three and two are five,** trois et deux font cinq; **money isn't everything,** l'argent ne fait pas tout. **2.** (*a*) **the books are on the table,** les livres sont, se trouvent, sur la table; **I was at the meeting,** j'ai assisté à la réunion; **I don't know where I am,** (i) je ne sais pas où je suis; (ii) je ne sais pas où j'en suis; **where was I?** où en étais-je? **you never know where you are with him,** avec lui on ne sait jamais à quoi s'en tenir; **here I am,** me voici; **ah, there you are!** vous voilà donc! (*b*) (*health*) **how are you?** comment allez-vous? comment vous portez-vous? **I am better,** je vais mieux, je me sens mieux; (*c*) (*measure*) **how much is that?** combien cela coûte-t-il? c'est combien? **how far is it to London?** combien y a-t-il d'ici à Londres? (*d*) (*time*) **when is the concert?** quand le concert aura-t-il lieu? **today is the tenth,** nous sommes (aujourd'hui) le dix (du mois); **tomorrow is Friday,** c'est demain vendredi. **3.** (*a*) **to be cold, hot,** (i) (*of water, etc.*) être froid, chaud; (ii) (*of pers.*) avoir froid, chaud; **to be ashamed of s.o., of sth.,** avoir honte de qn, de qch.; **to be hungry, thirsty,** avoir faim, soif; **to be right, wrong,** avoir raison, avoir tort; **my hands are cold,** j'ai froid aux mains; (*b*) **to be twenty (years old),** avoir vingt ans, être âgé de vingt ans; **the wall is six metres high,** le mur a six mètres de haut; (*c*) **he was so foolish as to . . .,** il a eu la sottise de . . .. **4.** (*exist, remain*) (*a*) **to be or not to be,** être ou ne pas être; **business is not what it was,** les affaires ne sont plus ce qu'elles étaient; **that may be,** cela se peut; **to see things as they are,** voir les choses comme elles sont; **however that may be,** quoi qu'il en soit; **let me be!** laissez-moi tranquille! (*b*) *impers.* **there is, there are,** il y a; **there is a man in the garden,** il y a un homme dans le jardin; **what is there to see?** qu'est-ce qu'il y a à voir? **there will be dancing,** on dansera; **there were a dozen of us,** nous étions une douzaine. **5.** (*go or come*) **I have been to see David,** j'ai été voir David; **I have been to the museum,** j'ai visité le musée; **I have never been to Venice,** je n'ai jamais été à Venise; **he was into the room like a flash,** il est entré dans la pièce en coup de foudre; **where have you been?** d'où venez-vous? **has anyone been?** est-il venu quelqu'un? **has the postman been?** est-ce que le facteur est passé? *P:* **(now) you've been and gone and done it!** vous en avez fait une belle! **be off (with you)!** partez! *F:* filez! **6.** *impers.* (*a*) **it is six o'clock,** il est six heures; **it is late,** il est tard; **it is a fortnight since I saw him,** il y a quinze jours que je ne l'ai vu; (*b*) **it is fine, cold,** il fait beau (temps), il fait froid; (*c*) **it is easy to do it,** il est facile de le faire; **it is right that . . .,** il est juste que + *sub*; **it is said that . . .,** on dit que . . .; **it is for you to decide,** c'est à vous de décider; **what is it?** (i) que voulez-vous? (ii) qu'est-ce qu'il y a? **as it were,** pour ainsi dire, en quelque sorte; *F:* **what's it to be?** (i) qu'est-ce que vous prenez? (ii) décidez donc! **7.** (*auxiliary*) (*a*) (*forming continuous tenses*) **I am, was, doing sth.,** je fais, je faisais, qch.; je suis, j'étais, en train de faire qch.; **they are always laughing,** ils sont toujours à rire; **the house is being built,** la maison est en construction; **I have (just) been writing,** je viens d'écrire; **I have been waiting for a long time,** il y a longtemps que j'attends, j'attends depuis longtemps; (*b*) (*with a few intr. verbs as aux. of perfect*) **the sun is set,** le soleil est couché; **the guests were all gone,** les invités étaient tous partis; (*c*) (*forming passive*) (i) **he was killed,** il a été tué; **he is respected by all,** il est respecté de tous; **he was always being laughed at,** on se moquait toujours de lui; **he is to be pitied,** il est à plaindre; **what's to be done?** que faire? (*d*) (*denoting future*) **I am to see him tomorrow,** je dois le voir demain; **he was never to see them again,** il ne devait plus les revoir; **is the house going to be sold?** est-ce qu'on va vendre la maison? (*e*) (*necessity, duty*) **am I to do it or not?** faut-il que je le fasse ou non? **8.** (*a*) **the bride to be,** la mariée; *F:* **a has-been,** un homme fini; **the be-all and end-all,** le but suprême la fin des fins; (*b*) **what are you at?** que faites-vous? **while we are at it,** pendant que nous y sommes; **she is always at him,** (i) elle ne peut pas le laisser tranquille; (ii) elle l'embête tout le temps; (*c*) **I am all for reform,** je suis pour, je suis partisan de, la réforme; **I'm all for staying here,** je ne demande qu'à rester ici. **9.** (*elliptical*) **is your book published?—it is,** est-ce que votre livre est sorti?—oui; **are you happy?—yes, I am,** êtes-vous heureux?—(mais) oui! **wasn't he listening?—no, he wasn't,** est-ce qu'il n'écoutait pas?—non; **so, you're back, are you?** alors, vous voilà de retour? **she is beautiful, isn't she?** elle est belle, n'est-ce pas? **being** ['bi:iŋ] **1.** *a.* **for the time b.,** pour le moment; temporairement; **this is my home for the time b.,** voici où j'habite provisoirement. **2.** *n.* (*a*) existence *f*, être *m*; **those to whom I owe my b.,** ceux qui m'ont donné le jour; (*b*) **to come into b.,** prendre forme, prendre naissance; **the company is still in b.,** la société existe toujours; (*c*) être; **all my b. rebels at the idea,** tout mon être se révolte à cette idée; (*d*) **a human b.,** un être humain; **human beings,** le genre humain, les humains *mpl*; **the Supreme B.,** l'Être Supreme.

beach[1] [bi:tʃ] *n.* **1.** (*a*) plage *f*; grève *f*; rivage *m*; **sandy b.,** plage de sable; **you're not the only pebble on the b.,** il n'y a pas que vous sur terre; (*b*) **b. ball,** ballon *m* de plage; **b. hut,** cabine *f* (de bains, de plage).

beach[2] *v.tr.* (*a*) échouer (un navire); (*b*) tirer (une embarcation) à sec.

beachcomber ['bi:tʃkoumər] *n.* **1.** vague déferlante. **2.** (*pers.*) batteur *m* de grève.

beachhead ['bi:tʃhed] *n. Mil:* tête *f* de pont (de débarquement).

beachwear ['bi:tʃwɛər] *n.* vêtements *mpl* de plage.

beacon ['bi:k(ə)n] *n.* **1.** (*a*) *A:* feu *m* d'alarme; (*b*) (i) tour *f*, (ii) colline *f*, du feu d'alarme. **2.** feu de joie. **3.** (*a*) *Nau: Av:* phare *m*; balise *f*; feu; **b. light,** feu de balisage; (*b*) *Nau: Av:* **radio b.,** radiophare *m*; **marker b.,** radiobalise *f*; **radar b.,** balise radar; radar *m* de radionavigation; (*c*) *Adm: Aut:* **Belisha b.,** sphère orange lumineuse (indiquant un passage clouté).

bead[1] [bi:d] *n.* **1.** (*for prayers*) grain *m*; **(string of) beads,** chapelet *m*; **to tell one's beads,** égrener, dire, son chapelet; *Arch:* **b. moulding,** patenôtre *f*. **2.** (*a*) (*ornament*) perle *f* (de verroterie, d'émail, etc.); **(string of) beads,** collier *m*; (*b*) goutte *f*, perle; *Metall:* goutte (de matière en fusion); **beads of dew,** perles de rosée; **there were beads of perspiration on his forehead,** la sueur perlait sur son front; (*c*) bulle *f* (sur le vin); (*d*) *Arch: Join:* perle, baguette *f*. **3.** *Sm.a:* guidon *m*, mire *f* (de fusil). **4.** *Metalw:* cordon *m* de soudure.

bead[2] **1.** *v.tr.* (*a*) couvrir, orner (qch.) de perles; (*b*) *Arch: Join:* appliquer une baguette sur (qch.). **2.** *v.i.*(*of liquid*) perler, faire la perle, faire chapelet. **beaded** *a.* **1.** (*a*) *Tex:* (*of material*) perlé; (*b*) (éclair, etc.) en chapelet. **2.** *Arch: Join:* **b. strip,** chapelet *m*. **beading** *n.* **1.** garniture *f* de perles. **2.** (*a*) *Arch: Join:* baguette *f*; (*b*) (*of tyre*) talon *m*, bourrelet *m*.

beady ['bi:di] *a.* (yeux) en vrille; **b. eyed,** aux yeux en vrille.

beagle ['bi:gl] *n.* (*dog*) beagle *m*, briquet *m*.

beagling ['bi:gliŋ] *n.* chasse *f* au briquet.
beak [bi:k] *n.* **1.** bec *m* (d'oiseau, de tortue, de cruche, de vase, etc.); *F:* nez crochu (d'une personne). **2. b. iron,** (i) bec (d'enclume); (ii) bigorne *f.*
beaked [bi:kt] *a.* **1.** (*a*) (animal *m*) à bec; *Bot:* rostré; *Her:* becqué; *Z:* **b. whale,** hyperoodon *m*; (*b*) (nez) crochu. **2. b. anvil,** bigorne *f.*
beaker ['bi:kər] *n.* **1.** (*a*) *Lit:* gobelet *m*; coupe *f*; (*b*) timbale *f*; gobelet. **2.** *Ch:* vase à bec.
beam¹ [bi:m] *n.* **1.** (*a*) *Const:* poutre *f* (en bois), solive *f*, madrier *m*; (*small*) poutrelle *f*; **b. and joists,** solivure *f*; **ceiling b.,** doubleau *m*; **cross b.,** sommier *m*, traverse *f*; (*b*) *Gym:* **(balance) b.,** poutre horizontale; **cross b.,** portique *m*; (*c*) fléau *m* (d'une balance); (*d*) **b. engine,** machine *f* à balancier; (*e*) *Nau:* verge (d'une ancre); (*f*) *Tex:* rouleau *m* (d'un métier); (*g*) *Leath:* chevalet *m* (de corroyeur). **2.** *Nau: N.Arch:* (*a*) bau *m*, *pl.* baux; (*of ship*) **to be on her b. ends,** être accoté, sur le côté; *F:* **to be on one's b. ends,** être, se trouver, à bout de ressources; (*b*) travers *m* (d'un navire); **on the port, starboard, b.,** par le travers bâbord, tribord; (*c*) **(breadth of) b.,** largeur *f* (d'un navire); **broad in the b.,** (i) (navire) à larges baux; (ii) *F:* (femme) aux larges hanches. **3.** (*a*) rayon *m* (de lumière, de soleil); grand, large, sourire (de joie); (*b*) faisceau *m* (d'un phare); **4.** *El:* faisceau *m*; **electronic, radar, b.,** faisceau électronique, radar; **radio b.,** faisceau hertzien; *Av:* **radio landing b.,** axe balisé d'atterrissage; *F:* **you are completely off b.,** tu dérailles.
beam² **1.** *v.tr.* (*a*) (*b*) *W.Tg:* transmettre (un message) par ondes dirigées; (*b*) *Av:* (*of aircraft*) **to be beamed in on Orly,** être dirigé vers Orly. **2.** *v.i.* (*a*) (*of the sun*) rayonner; (*b*) (*of pers.*) rayonner (de joie); **beaming with health,** resplendissant de santé. **beaming** *a.* (soleil, visage) rayonnant, radieux; **b. smile,** sourire radieux; large sourire.
bean [bi:n] *n.* **1.** (*a*) **broad b.,** fève *f*; **French b.,** *NAm:* **string b.,** haricot vert, *Fr.C:* fève verte; **runner b.,** haricot d'Espagne; **wax b.,** haricot beurre; **butter b.,** (i) (*also NAm:* **Lima b.**) haricot de Lima; (ii) haricot beurre; *U.S:* **bush b.,** haricot (blanc); **kidney b., haricot b.,** haricot Soissons *m*; **soya b.,** soya *m*, soja *m*, pois chinois; *Cu:* **dried beans, haricot beans,** haricots secs; **baked beans,** haricots blancs (en conserve) à la sauce tomate; *Fr.C.:* fèves au lard; (*b*) *F:* **to be full of beans,** être plein de verve, plein d'entrain; **it isn't worth a b.,** ça ne vaut pas un radis; **he hasn't a b.,** il n'a pas le sou, *P:* pas un radis; **to spill the beans,** vendre la mèche; *O:* **old b.,** mon vieux. **2.** grain *m* (de café); graine *f*, fève (de cacao). **3.** *U.S:* *P:* tête *f*, *F:* boule *f.*
beanery ['bi:nəri] *n.* *U.S.:* petit restaurant pas cher.
beanfeast ['bi:nfi:st], **beano** ['bi:nou] *n.* *F: O:* régal *m*; bombe *f.*
beanpole ['bi:npoul] *n.* (*a*) rame *f* pour haricots; (*b*) *F:* (*pers.*) manche *m* à balai, échalas *m.*
beanstalk ['bi:nstɔ:k] *n.* tige *f* de fève, de haricot.
bear¹ ['bɛər] *n.* **1.** (*a*) ours *m*; **she b.,** ourse *f*; **b. cub,** ourson *m*; **brown b.,** ours brun; **polar b.,** ours blanc; **b. pit,** fosse *f* aux ours; *F:* **b. hug,** forte étreinte; **to be like a b. with a sore head,** être d'une humeur massacrante; *Geog:* **the Great B. Lake,** le grand lac de l'Ours; (*b*) *Astr:* **the Great, Little, B.,** la Grande, Petite, Ourse. **2.** *St.Exch:* baissier *m*, joueur *m* à la baisse; **to go a b.,** spéculer à la baisse; **to sell a b.,** vendre à découvert. **3.** *Metall:* loup *m.*
bear² *v.* **(beared)** *St.Exch:* **1.** *v.tr.* **to b. the market,** chercher à faire baisser les cours. **2.** *v.i.* spéculer à la baisse.
bear³ *v.tr. & i.* (*p.t.* **bore** [bɔ:r] *p.p.* **borne** [bɔ:n]) **1.** (*a*) porter (un fardeau, des armes, un nom, une date, etc.); **the document bears your signature,** le document porte votre signature; **to b. s.o. a grudge,** garder rancune à qn; **to b. sth. in mind,** (i) se souvenir de qch.; (ii) tenir compte de qch.; **it bears no relation, no resemblance, to . . .,** cela n'a aucun rapport, aucune ressemblance, avec . . .; **to b. witness to sth.,** rendre, porter, témoignage de qch.; témoigner de qch.; (*b*) supporter, soutenir (un poids); supporter, (la souffrance); supporter (les conséquences); souffrir (la douleur, etc.); **to b. the responsibility of sth.,** avoir la responsabilité de qch.; **his language does not b. repeating,** son langage n'est pas à répéter; **he could b. it no longer,** il ne pouvait plus y tenir; **to grin and b. it,** faire bonne mine à mauvais jeu; **I can't b. him, b. the sight of him,** je ne peux pas le souffrir, le sentir; **I can't b. the idea of it,** je ne peux pas en souffrir, en supporter, l'idée; **it doesn't b. thinking about,** l'idée en est insupportable; (*c*) *v.i.* **I don't know how she bears with his bad temper,** je ne sais pas comment elle supporte sa mauvaise humeur; **2.** (*a*) **to be borne backwards, along, away,** être refoulé, emporté; (*b*) **it was gradually borne in upon him that . . .,** peu à peu il s'est rendu compte que . . .; (*c*) **to b. on sth.,** buter, appuyer, sur qch.; **beam bearing upon two uprights,** poutre *f* qui s'appuie sur deux montants; (*d*) **to bring all one's strength to b. on a lever,** s'appuyer de toutes ses forces sur un levier; **to bring all one's energies to b. on sth.,** apporter, consacrer, toute son énergie à qch.; **to bring one's mind to b. on sth.,** porter son attention sur qch.; **to bring influence, pressure, to b. on s.o.,** exercer une influence, une pression, sur qn. **3.** (*a*) *Nau:* **the cape bears north-north-west,** on relève le cap au nord-nord-ouest; (*b*) (*of pers., road*) **to b. to the right, left,** tourner à droite, à gauche; prendre à droite, à gauche; (*of ship*) **to b. round,** arriver en grand. **4.** (*a*) donner naissance à (un enfant); **she has borne him three sons,** elle lui a donné trois fils; *see also* BORN; (*b*) **capital that bears interest,** capital *m* qui porte intérêt; **to b. fruit,** (i) (*of tree*) porter fruit; (ii) (*of work, etc.*) porter fruit, fructifier; **my enquiries bore fruit,** mes recherches ont été couronnées de succès. **bear away** **1.** *v.tr.* emporter, enlever (qch.). **2.** *v.i.* *Nau:* **to b. a. (for a point),** laisser arriver, laisser porter (sur une pointe, sur un cap). **bear down** *v.i.* *Nau:* **to b. down (up)on sth.,** courir sur qch.; **to b. d. on the enemy,** foncer, laisser porter, fondre, sur l'ennemi; *F:* **to b. down on s.o.,** fondre sur qn. **bearing** **1.** *a.* (*a*) (essieu, etc.) porteur; **b. wall,** mur *m* d'appui; **b. surface,** surface *f* d'appui; tablette *f* (d'une solive); *Mec.E:* surface portante, de portage; (*b*) (*in compounds*) **fruit-b.,** fructifère, qui porte des fruits; **interest-b. capital,** capital qui rapporte; **silver-b.,** argentifère; **wool-b.,** lanifère. **2.** *n.* (*a*) port *m* (d'armes, de nouvelles); (*b*) (*of pers.*) port, maintien *m*; conduite *f*; (*c*) *Her:* **(armorial) bearings,** armoiries *fpl*, blason *m*; (*d*) *Civ.E: Const: etc:* (appareil *m* d')appui (*m*) (d'un pont métallique); surface *f* d'appui (d'une poutre); portée *f* (de poutres); chape *f* (d'une balance); *Arch:* dé *m*; (*e*) *Mec.E:* palier *m*; roulement *m*; coussinet *m*; **self-lubricating b.,** palier graisseur; **ball, roller, needle, b.,** roulement à billes, à rouleaux, à aiguilles;, (*f*) *Surv: etc:* gisement *m*, azimut *m*; orientation *f*; direction *f*; *esp. Nau: Av:* relèvement *m*; position *f*; **true b.,** azimut, gisement, géographique; relèvement vrai; **compass b.,** relèvement au compas; **to take the ship's bearings,** faire le point; **to take one's bearings,** s'orienter; se repérer; **to lose one's bearings,** perdre sa direction, sa route; *F:* perdre le nord; **to get one's bearings,** retrouver sa direction, sa route; (*g*) portée (d'une question, d'un argument); rapport *m* (**on a question,** avec une question); (*of fact, etc.*) **it has no b. on the matter,** cela n'a aucun rapport avec l'affaire; (*h*) **(child) b.,** mise *f*

au monde (d'un enfant). **bear out** *v.tr.* (*a*) emporter (un cadavre, etc.); (*b*) **to b. out a statement,** confirmer, justifier, une assertion; **to b. s.o. out, to b. out what s.o. has said,** corroborer ce que qn a dit. **bear up 1.** *v.tr.* soutenir (qn, qch.). **2.** *v.i.* **to b. up against, under, misfortune,** faire face, tenir tête, au malheur; **b. up!** tenez bon! du courage! *F:* **how are you?—(oh, I'm) bearing up,** comment ça va?—(eh bien,) ça va; je me défends.

bearable ['bɛərəbl] *a.* supportable; **the situation is no longer b.,** la situation n'est plus tenable. **-ably** *adv.* d'une façon supportable.

bearbaiting ['bɛəbeitiŋ] *n.* combats *mpl* d'ours et de chiens.

beard¹ [biəd] *n.* (*a*) barbe *f*; **to have a b.,** porter la barbe; **a week's b.,** une barbe de huit jours; (*b*) *Nat. Hist:* barbe; (*c*) *Bot:* arête *f* (d'épi); (*d*) barbelure *f* (d'une flèche, d'un hameçon); (*e*) *Metalw:* barbe (d'une pièce de fonte, etc.); (*f*) *Typ:* talus *m* (d'un caractère); (*g*) *Woodw:* arête.

beard² *v.tr.* **1.** braver, défier, narguer (qn); *F:* **to b. the lion in his den,** affronter la colère de qn. **2.** *Metalw:* **to b. off,** ébarber (une pièce de fonte). **bearded** *a.* (homme, blé, poisson) barbu; (flèche) barbelée; **black-b. man,** homme *m* à barbe noire.

beardless ['biədlis] *a.* imberbe, sans barbe.

bearer ['bɛərər] *n.* **1.** (*pers.*) (*a*) porteur *m* (de nouvelles, de brancard, *Mount: etc:* de bagages, etc.); **the b. of this letter,** le porteur de cette lettre; (*at funeral*) **the bearers,** les porteurs; (*b*) porteur (d'un chèque); titulaire *mf* (d'un passeport); *Fin:* **b. bond, cheque,** titre *m*, chèque, au porteur. **2.** (*of tree*) **to be a good b.,** être de bon rapport. **3.** *Const: Mec.E:* support *m*; **b. joist,** lambourde *f* (de parquet).

beargarden ['bɛəgɑːd(ə)n] *n.* **1.** fosse *f* aux ours. **2.** pétaudière *f*; **to turn the place into a b.,** mettre le désordre partout.

bearish ['bɛəriʃ] *a.* **1.** (manières) d'ours; (*of pers.*) bourru; peu sociable. **2.** *St.Exch:* *F:* **b. tendency,** tendance *f* à la baisse.

bearskin ['bɛəskin] *n.* **1.** peau d'ours (garnie de son poil); oursin *m.* **2.** *Mil.Cost:* bonnet *m* à poil.

beast [biːst] *n.* **1.** (*a*) bête f; **wild b.,** (i) bête sauvage; (ii) bête féroce; **the king of the beasts,** le roi des animaux; **b. of prey,** carnassier *m*; **b. of burden,** bête de somme; (*b*) *B:* **the B.,** l'Antéchrist *m*; (*c*) *Husb:* **beasts,** bétail *m*, bestiaux *mpl*; cheptel *m.* **2.** (*a*) *Fig:* animal *m*, brute *f*, abruti *m*; **to sink to the level of a b.,** s'avilir; (*b*) *F:* rosse *f*; goujat *m*; **the little b.,** le petit diable; **he's a perfect b.!** c'est une rosse! **it was a perfect b. of a day,** il a fait un temps abominable, un temps de chien; **a b. of a job,** (i) un chien de métier; (ii) un travail de chien.

beastliness ['biːstlinis] *n.* bestialité *f*, brutalité *f.*

beastly ['biːstli] **1.** *a.* (*a*) bestial; brutal; (*b*) *F:* sale, dégoûtant; **a b. job,** (i) un chien de métier; (ii) un travail de chien; **what b. weather!** quel sale temps! **2.** *adv.* *F:* terriblement; **it's b. cold,** il fait bigrement froid.

beat¹ [biːt] *n.* **1.** (*a*) battement *m* (du cœur, etc.); batterie *f* (de tambour); son *m* (du tambour); *Hor:* battement (d'un mouvement); (*b*) *Mus:* (i) mesure *f*, temps *m*; (ii) mouvement de la main en battant la mesure. **2.** *Ph:* battement (d'ondes sonores). **3.** *Cmptr:* battement. **4.** (*a*) ronde *f* (d'un agent de police); **policeman on the b.,** agent qui fait sa ronde; *F:* **it's off my b. altogether,** ce n'est pas de ma compétence; (*b*) *U.S:* circonscription électorale. **5.** *Ven:* (terrain *m* de) battue *f.*

beat² *v.tr. & i.* (*p.t.* **beat;** *p.p.* **beaten** ['biːtn]) **1.** (*a*) battre (qn, qch.); **to b. s.o. with a stick,** donner des coups de bâton à qn; **to b. s.o. black and blue,** meurtrir, rouer, qn de coups; **to b. s.o. to death,** assommer qn (à coups de trique, etc.); **to b. sth. flat,** aplatir qch. à coups de marteau, etc.; **to b. one's breast,** se frapper la poitrine; **to b. a carpet,** battre un tapis; **to b. eggs,** battre des œufs; **the rain was beating against the window panes,** la pluie battait contre les vitres; **the waves b. against the shore,** les vagues déferlent sur le rivage; (*b*) **to b. a drum,** battre du tambour; **to b. to arms,** battre la générale; **to b. the retreat,** battre la retraite; **to b. a retreat,** (i) *Mil:* battre en retraite; (ii) *Fig:* se retirer, se dérober; se dédire; **to b. time (to music),** battre la mesure; **his heart is beating with joy,** son cœur bat de joie; (*c*) *Ven:* **to b. a wood (for game),** battre, traquer, un bois; *F:* **to b. about the bush,** tourner autour du pot; **not to b. about the bush,** (i) aller droit au but; ne pas y aller par quatre chemins; (ii) répondre sans ambages, carrément; (*d*) *Nau:* **to b. to windward,** louvoyer; *F:* **go on, b. it!** allons, file! fiche le camp! (*e*) (*of bird*) **to b. its wings,** battre des ailes. **2.** (*conquer*) (*a*) battre, vaincre, (l'ennemi); **to b. s.o. at chess,** battre qn aux échecs; **they were beaten,** ils ont été vaincus; *F:* **that beats me!** ça me dépasse! **that beats everything!** ça c'est le comble, le bouquet! (*b*) (*get ahead of*) devancer (qn); *F:* **he b. me to it,** il m'a fauché ma place; (*c*) battre (un record); (*d*) *U.S:* *P:* rouler, refaire (qn); **to b. the customs,** frauder la douane. **beat back** *v.tr.* repousser (qn, l'ennemi); rabattre (les flammes). **beat down 1.** *v.tr.* (*a*) (r)abattre (qch.); damer (la terre); (*b*) **to b. down the price of sth.,** marchander sur le prix de qch.; **to b. s.o. down,** faire baisser le prix à qn; marchander (avec) qn. **2.** *v.i.* **the sun is beating down on our heads,** le soleil nous tape sur la tête. **beaten** *a.* **1. the b. track,** le chemin battu; **house off the b. track,** maison écartée. **2.** (or, fer) battu, martelé; **b. earth,** terre battue. **3.** (ennemi) battu, vaincu. **beat in** *v.tr.* enfoncer, défoncer (une porte, etc.). **beating 1.** *a.* (*a*) (cœur) palpitant; (*b*) (pluie) battante. **2.** *n.* (*a*) battement *m* (d'ailes, du cœur, etc.); (*b*) *Tchn:* battage *m*; (*c*) *Ven:* rabattage *m*, rabat *m* (du gibier); traque *f*; (*d*) *Nau:* louvoyage *m*; (*e*) coups *mpl*; raclée *f*, rossée *f*; **to give s.o. a b.,** rosser qn; (*f*) défaite *f* (dans un match, etc.); **to get a good b.,** être battu à plate(s) couture(s); **beat off** *v.tr.* repousser (qn, un assaut). **beat out** *v.tr.* (*a*) frayer (un chemin); (*b*) battre, aplatir (le fer); marteler, écolleter (l'or, etc.); (*c*) **to b. out a rhythm,** *F:* **to b. it out,** marquer un rythme; (*d*) **to b. s.o.'s brains out,** assommer qn, décerveler qn; (*e*) **to b. the dust out of sth.,** battre qch. pour en faire sortir la poussière. **beat up 1.** *v.tr.* (*a*) *Ven:* rabattre, traquer (le gibier); (*b*) *F:* **to b. s.o. up,** assommer qn; tabasser qn. **2.** *v.i.* *Nau:* louvoyer vers la terre; gagner vers la terre.

beat³ *a.* *F:* (*a*) **you have me b.,** je ne suis pas de force, j'y renonce; (*b*) **dead b.,** mort de fatigue; éreinté.

beat⁴ *n.* *F:* beatnik *m.*

beater ['biːtər] *n.* **1.** (*pers.*) (*a*) batteur, -euse; **gold b.,** batteur d'or; (*b*) *Ven:* rabatteur *m*, traqueur *m.* **2.** (*a*) batte *f*; *Mus:* tringle *f* (de triangle); **(egg) b.,** fouet *m*; *For:* **fire b.,** batte à feu; (*b*) *Paperm:* pilon *m*; (*c*) *Tex:* volant *m.*

beatific [bi(ː)ə'tifik] *a.* (vision, etc.) béatifique; (sourire) béat. **-ally** *adv.* d'un air, béatifique.

beatification [bi(ː)ætifi'keiʃ(ə)n] *n.* *Ecc:* béatification *f.*

beatify [bi(ː)'ætifai] *v.tr.* *Ecc:* béatifier.

beatitude [bi(ː)'ætitjuːd] *n.* béatitude *f.*

beatnik ['biːtnik] *n.* beatnik *m.*

beau, *pl.* **beaus, beaux** [bou, bouz] *n.* **1.** élégant *m*, dandy *m.* **2.** *A:* & *U.S:* prétendant *m* (d'une jeune fille); galant *m.*

beaut [bjuːt] *n.* *U.S. Austr:* *F:* **what a b.!** quelle merveille!

beautician [bju(:)ˈtiʃ(ə)n] *n.* (i) esthéticien, -ienne; (ii) visagiste *mf.*

beautiful [ˈbju:tif(u)l] **1.** (très) beau, (très) belle; **a b. face,** un très beau visage; **at twenty she was b.,** à vingt ans c'était une beauté. **2.** (dîner, temps, etc.) magnifique. **3.** *n.* **the b.,** le beau. **-fully** *adv.* admirablement; à merveille; **that will do b.,** cela fera l'affaire parfaitement, à merveille.

beautify [ˈbju:tifai] *v.tr.* embellir, enjoliver.

beauty [ˈbju:ti] *n.* beauté *f.* **1.** (*a*) **to be in the flower of one's b.,** être dans toute sa beauté; **the beauties of nature,** les beautés de la nature; **b. spot,** (i) site *m*, coin *m*, pittoresque; (ii) (*on skin*) grain *m* de beauté; (*artificial*) mouche *f*; **b. aids, preparations,** produits *mpl* de beauté; **b. parlour, salon,** institut *m* de beauté; **b. competition,** concours *m* de beauté; **b. queen,** reine *f* d'un concours de beauté; (*b*) **that's the b. of it,** (i) voilà ce qui en fait le charme; (ii) c'est là le plus beau de l'affaire; (iii) c'est là le plaisant de l'affaire. **2.** (*a*) **she was a b. in her day,** elle a été une beauté dans son temps; **B. and the Beast,** la Belle et la Bête; **the Sleeping B.,** la Belle au bois dormant; (*b*) *F:* **isn't it a b.?** (*of flower, etc.*) n'est-ce pas qu'elle est jolie? (*of car, etc.*) n'est-ce pas qu'elle est chic? **it's a b.,** c'est un rêve; *P:* **he fetched him a b. on the chin,** il lui a flanqué un coup magnifique, formidable, au menton.

beaver [ˈbi:vər] *n.* **1.** *Z:* (*a*) castor *m*; *F:* **to work like a b.,** travailler comme quatre; **an eager b.,** un(e) zélé(e); (*b*) **b. rat,** rat musqué. **2.** (*fur*) castor; **b. lamb,** mouton doré. **3.** *Tex:* castorine *f.*

becalmed [biˈkɑ:md] *a.* (*of ship*) accalminé, encalminé.

because [biˈkɔ(:)z] **1.** *conj.* (*a*) parce que; **I eat b. I'm hungry,** je mange parce que j'ai faim; (*b*) **I was all the more astonished b. I had been told . . .,** j'en fus d'autant plus étonné qu'on m'avait assuré . . .; **b. he dashed off a sonnet he thinks himself a poet,** pour avoir bâclé un sonnet il se croit poète. **2.** *prep.phr.* **b. of sth.,** à cause de qch.; **he has been retired b. of his illness,** on l'a mis à la retraite vu, en raison de, sa maladie; **I said nothing b. of the children,** je n'ai rien dit à cause de la présence des enfants.

béchamel [ˈbeʃəmel] *n. Cu:* **b. sauce,** béchamel *f*, sauce *f* (à la) béchamel.

beck¹ [bek] *n. Dial:* ruisseau *m.*

beck² *n.* signe *m* (de tête, de la main); **to have s.o. at one's b. and call,** avoir qn à ses ordres, à sa disposition; **to be at s.o.'s b. and call,** obéir aux moindres volontés de qn; être aux ordres de qn.

beckon [ˈbek(ə)n] *v.tr. & i.* faire signe (**to s.o.,** à qn); appeler (qn) du doigt, de la main; **to b. s.o. in,** faire signe à qn d'entrer.

become [biˈkʌm] *v.* (*p.t.* **became** [biˈkeim]; *p.p.* **become**) **1.** *v.i.* (*a*) devenir, se faire (prêtre, médecin, etc.); devenir (grand, roi, l'ennemi de qn, etc.); **to b. old, thin,** vieillir, maigrir; **to b. suspicious of s.o.,** concevoir des soupçons contre qn; **the murmurs became louder,** les murmures se faisaient plus forts; **custom that has become law,** usage *m* qui a passé en loi; (*b*) **to b. accustomed, attached, interested,** s'accoutumer, s'attacher, s'intéresser; (*of pers.*) **to b. known,** commencer à être connu; se faire connaître; (*c*) **what has b. of X?** qu'est devenu X? **what will b. of him?** que va-t-il devenir? **I don't know what has b. of him,** je ne sais pas ce qu'il est devenu. **2.** *v.tr.* convenir à, être propre à (qn, qch.); (*of clothes, etc.*) aller bien à (qn). **becoming** *a.* (*a*) convenable, bienséant; (*b*) (*of dress, etc.*) seyant (**to,** à); qui sied (à); qui va bien (à); **b. dress,** robe avantageuse.

bed¹ [bed] *n.* **1.** (*a*) lit *m*; **single b.,** lit pour une personne; **double b.,** lit de, pour, deux personnes; grand lit; **twin beds,** lits jumeaux; **camp b.,** lit de camp; **spare b.,** lit d'ami; **b. of state,** lit de parade; **the marriage b.,** le lit conjugal; **b. settee,** canapé-lit *m*, *pl.* canapés-lits; **to sleep in separate beds,** faire lit à part; **to be in b.,** (i) être couché; (ii) (*through illness*) être alité, être au lit; garder le lit; **to go to b.,** se coucher; **to take, keep, to one's b.,** prendre, garder, le lit; **to keep s.o. in b.,** garder qn au lit; **I'm going home to b.,** je vais rentrer me coucher; **to put a child to b.,** coucher un enfant, mettre un enfant au lit; **to make the beds,** faire les lits; (*at hotel*) **b. and breakfast,** chambre *f* et petit déjeuner; *F:* **he got out of b. the wrong side,** il s'est levé du pied gauche; *Cost:* **b. jacket,** liseuse *f*; **b. linen,** literie *f*; *Med:* **b. wetting,** incontinence *f* nocturne; (*b*) **feather b.,** lit de plume; **air b.,** matelas *m* pneumatique; **water b.,** matelas à eau; (*c*) *F:* **to go to b. with a woman,** coucher avec une femme. **2.** (*a*) lit (d'une rivière, de la mer); fond *m* (de billard, d'une voiture, etc.); *Hyd.E:* **filter b.,** lit de filtrage; (*b*) *Hort:* planche *f*, carré *m* (de fleurs, de légumes); **flower b.,** parterre *m*; (*round*) corbeille *f*; **oyster b.,** huîtrière *f*; (i) banc *m* d'huîtres; (ii) parc *m* à huîtres; (*c*) *Geol:* assise *f*, couche *f*; *Miner:* gisement *m*; (*d*) *Civ.E:* *Rail:* infrastructure *f*; *Const:* *Civ.E:* *etc:* assise, lit (de béton); assise (de pierres); *Mill:* **b. stone,** meule *f* de dessous; (meule) gisante (*f*); (*e*) *Mec.E:* banc (de tour); sommier *m* (d'une machine); table (de raboteuse); **(engine) b.,** support *m*, bâti *m*; *Av:* berceau *m* (de moteur), carlingue *f*; (*f*) *Typ:* marbre *m* (de la presse); *Journ:* **the paper has gone to b.,** le journal est tombé.

bed² *v.* **(bedded) 1.** *v.tr.* (*a*) **to b. (down) horses,** faire la litière aux chevaux; (*b*) *Hort:* **to b. (out) plants,** dépoter des plantes; **to b. (in) seedlings,** repiquer des plants; (*c*) parquer (des huîtres); (*d*) *Civ.E:* enrocher (un bâtardeau); (*e*) *Const:* sceller (une poutre dans un mur, etc.); asseoir (une pierre, les fondations); (*f*) *Metall:* **to b. (in) a mould,** enterrer un modèle (dans le sable). **2.** *v.i.* (*a*) (*of animal*) se gîter; *F:* (*of pers.*) **to b. down,** se coucher; (*b*) (*of foundations, bridge, etc.*) **to b. (down),** prendre son assiette; se tasser (dans la terre, etc.). **bedding** *n.* **1.** (*a*) parcage *m* (des huîtres); (*b*) *Civ.E:* enrochement *m* (d'un bâtardeau, etc.); *Nau:* engravement *m* (d'un navire); (*c*) *Const:* scellement *m* (d'une poutre dans un mur, etc.); assiette *f* (d'une pierre); (*d*) *Metall:* enterrage *m* (d'un modèle); (*e*) *Husb:* préparation *f* de la litière; (*f*) *Hort:* **b. out,** dépotage *m*, dépotement *m* (de plantes); **b. (-out) plants,** plants *mpl* à repiquer; **b. roses,** roses *fpl* pour massifs, pour corbeilles; (*g*) *Metall:* mise *f* en lit, étalement *m* (du minerai). **2.** (*a*) literie *f*; (*b*) *Mil:* *Navy:* (matériel *m* de) couchage (*m*). **3.** (*a*) *Husb:* litière *f*; (*b*) *Civ.E:* matériau *m* d'enrochement, d'assise. **4.** *Geol:* stratification *f.* **5.** lit (d'une chaudière, etc.).

bedbug [ˈbedbʌg] *n.* punaise *f* des lits.

bedchamber [ˈbedtʃeimbər] *n. Lit:* chambre *f* à coucher; (*at court*) **Lady of the B.,** dame *f* du lit.

bedclothes [ˈbedklouðz] *n.pl.* couvertures *fpl* et draps *mpl* de lit; **to turn down the b.,** faire la couverture (de lit).

bedcover [ˈbedkʌvər] *n.* dessus *m* de lit.

bedevil [biˈdev(ə)l] *v.tr.* **1.** ensorceler (qn). **2.** taquiner, tourmenter (qn). **3.** gâcher (qch.); **industrial relations bedevilled by politics,** rapports entre patrons et ouvriers envenimés par la politique.

bedfellow [ˈbedfelou] *n.* camarade *mf* de lit; **they make strange bedfellows,** c'est une association inattendue; c'est un couple disparate.

bedhead [ˈbedhed] *n.* chevet *m*; tête *f* (de lit).

bedlam [ˈbedləm] *n.* (*a*) *A:* maison *f* de fous, d'aliénés; (*b*) *F:* charivari *m*, tohu-bohu *m.*

Bedouin [ˈbeduin] **1.** *a.* bédouin. **2.** *n.* (*pl.* **Bedouin(s)**) Bédouin, -ine.

bedpan ['bedpæn] *n. Hyg:* bassin *m* de lit.
bedpost ['bedpoust] *n.* colonne *f* de lit.
bedraggled [bi'dræg(ə)ld] *a.* (*a*) crotté, taché de boue; (*b*) trempé (d'eau); (*c*) (vêtement) dépenaillé.
bedridden ['bedrid(ə)n] *a.* cloué au lit.
bedrock ['bedrɔk] *n.* (*a*) *Geol:* roche *f* de fond; (*b*) fondement *m* (de sa croyance, etc.); **to get down to b.,** voir au fond des choses.
bedroll ['bedroul] *n. U.S: Mil:* rouleau *m* de (matériel de) couchage.
bedroom ['bedru(:)m] *n.* chambre *f* à coucher; **spare b.,** chambre d'ami; **b. slippers,** pantoufles *fpl*; *Th:* **b. farce,** comédie *f* leste.
bedside ['bedsaid] *n.* chevet *m*; bord *m* du lit; **b. rug,** descente *f* de lit; **b. lamp,** lampe *f* de chevet; veilleuse *f*; **b. table,** table *f* de nuit, de chevet; (*of doctor*) **to have a good b. manner,** avoir un comportement agréable au chevet du malade.
bed-sittingroom ['bedsitiŋru:m] *n., F:* **bed-sit(ter)** ['bed'sit(ər)] *n.* studio *m*; chambre meublée.
bedsock ['bedsɔk] *n.* chausson *m* de nuit.
bedsore ['bedsɔ:r] *n.* escarre (produite par le séjour au lit); *Med:* décubitus *m.*
bedspread ['bedspred] *n.* dessus *m* de lit.
bedstead ['bedsted] *n.* châlit *m*, bois *m* de lit.
bedstraw ['bedstrɔ:] *n. Bot:* gaillet *m.*
bedtick[1] ['bedtik] *n. U.S:* punaise *f* des lits.
bedtick[2], **bedticking** ['bedtikiŋ] *n.* toile *f* à matelas.
bedtime ['bedtaim] *n.* heure *f* du coucher; **what is your b.?** à quelle heure vous couchez-vous? **it's past your b.,** vous devriez être déjà couché; **b. stories,** histoires *fpl* pour l'heure du coucher, pour endormir.
bee [bi:] *n.* **1.** abeille *f*; **queen b.,** reine *f* des abeilles; **honey b.,** abeille domestique; **working b.,** abeille ouvrière; **bees' nest,** nid *m* d'abeilles; **to keep bees,** élever des abeilles; *F:* **to be a busy b.,** faire la mouche du coche; **to have a b. in one's bonnet,** avoir une idée fixe. **2.** *Bot:* **b. balm,** monarde *f* d'Amérique; **b. orchis,** ophrys *f* abeille; *Orn:* **b. eater,** guêpier *m* (d'Europe). **3.** (*a*) réunion *f* (pour travaux en commun); (*b*) concours *m*; **spelling b.,** concours (oral) d'orthographe.
beech [bi:tʃ] *n.* **1.** hêtre *m*; **copper b.,** hêtre rouge, pourpre. **2.** *Com:* **b. (wood),** bois *m* de hêtre; **b. furniture,** meubles *mpl* en hêtre.
beechmast ['bi:tʃmɑ:st] *n.* faînes *fpl* (comme nourriture de pourceaux).
beechnut ['bi:tʃnʌt] *n.* faîne *f.*
beef[1] [bi:f] *n.* **1.** (*no pl.*) (*a*) *Cu:* bœuf *m*; **roast b.,** rôti *m* de bœuf, rosbif *m*; **salt b.,** bœuf salé; **corned b.,** corned beef *m*, conserve *f* de bœuf, *F:* singe *m*; **stewed b.,** ragoût *m* de bœuf, bœuf (à la) mode; **b. cattle,** bœufs de boucherie; (*b*) *F:* **to have plenty of b.,** avoir du muscle; être costaud. **2.** (*pl.* **beeves** [bi:vs], **beefs** [bi:fs]) *U.S:* (*a*) **a b.,** un bœuf, une vache; (*b*) bœuf(s), à l'engrais. **3.** (*pl.* **beefs**) *F:* plainte *f*, grief *m*; **he enjoys a good b.,** il aime ronchonner, rouspéter.
beef[2] *F:* **1.** *v.i.* ronchonner, rouspéter. **2.** *v.tr.* **to b. up,** gonfler l'importance de (qch.); renforcer (l'armée). **beefing** *n. F:* ronchonnement *m*, rouspétance *f.*
beefburger ['bi:fbə:gər] *n.* boulette de bœuf hâché fourrée dans un petit pain; hamburger *m.*
beefcake ['bi:fkeik] *n. F:* poitrine (d'homme) nue.
beefeater ['bi:fi:tər] *n. F:* hallebardier *m* (i) de la garde du corps, (ii) de service à la Tour de Londres.
beefsteak ['bi:f'steik] *n. Cu:* bifteck *m*; *Fung:* **b. fungus,** langue-de-bœuf *f*, *pl.* langues-de-bœuf.
beeftea [bi:f'ti:] *n.* bouillon *m* de bœuf.
beefy ['bi:fi] *a. F:* (homme) musclé, costaud.
beehive ['bi:haiv] *n. Ap:* ruche *f.*
beekeeper ['bi:ki:pər] *n.* apiculteur *m.*
beekeeping ['bi:ki:piŋ] *n.* apiculture *f.*
beeline ['bi:lain] *n.* ligne *f* à vol d'abeille, à vol d'oiseau; *F:* **to make a b. for sth.,** aller droit, directement, vers qch.; s'avancer en droite ligne vers qch.
Beelzebub [bi'elzibʌb] *Pr.n.m.* **1.** *B.Hist:* Belzébuth. **2.** le Diable.
been. *see* BE.
beep[1] [bi:p] *n.* bip-bip *m* (d'un satellite, etc.).
beep[2] *v.i.* (*of satellite, etc.*) faire bip-bip. **beeping** *n.* bip-bip *m* (d'un satellite, etc.).
beeper ['bi:pər] *n. NAm:* récepteur *m* d'appel, récepteur de poche.
beer [bi:ər] *n.* **1.** bière *f*; (*a*) **draught b.,** bière au tonneau, à la pompe, sous pression; **bottled b.,** bière en bouteille; **small b.,** petite bière; *F:* **to think no small b. of oneself,** ne pas se prendre pour de la petite bière; **b. barrel, bottle,** tonneau *m*, bouteille *f*, à bière; **b. garden,** café *m* en plein air; **b. glass,** verre *m* à bière; chope *f*; **b. mat,** sous-bock *m inv.*; *Can:* **b. parlour,** bar *m*; (*b*) **to order a b.,** demander une bière. **2. ginger b.,** boisson gazeuse au gingembre.
beery ['biəri] *a.* **1.** (atmosphère, etc.) qui sent la bière. **2.** un peu gris; **b. voice,** voix avinée.
beeswax ['bi:zwæks] *n.* (*a*) cire *f* d'abeilles; (*b*) cire à parquet.
beet [bi:t] *n. NAm:* = BEETROOT; *Bot:* betterave *f*; **fodder b.,** betterave fourragère; **sugar b.,** betterave à sucre; **b. sugar,** sucre *m* de betterave; **b. industry,** industrie betteravière.
beetle[1] ['bi:tl] *n.* masse *f* (en bois); maillet *m*; (*for paving*) hie *f*, demoiselle *f*; (*for quarrying*) batterand *m*; *Civ.E:* **b. head,** mouton *m.*
beetle[2] *n. Ent:* coléoptère *m*; scarabée *m.*
beetle[3] *v.i. F:* **to b. off, away,** décamper; s'en aller.
beetle[4] *a.* **b. brows,** sourcils (i) proéminents, (ii) touffus; **b. browed,** aux sourcils (i) proéminents, (ii) touffus.
beetlecrushers ['bi:tlkrʌʃəz] *n.pl. P:* **1.** (*feet*) arpions *mpl*, ripatons *mpl.* **2.** (*boots*) godillots *m pl.*
beetling ['bi:tliŋ] *a.* **1.** (*of rock, etc.*) surplombant, en surplomb. **2.** = BEETLE[4].
beetroot ['bi:tru:t] *n.* betterave (potagère).
befall [bi'fɔ:l] *v.tr. & i.* (*conj. like* FALL; *used only in 3rd pers.*) *Lit:* arriver, survenir (à qn).
befit [bi'fit] *Lit: v.tr.* **(befitted)** (*used only in 3rd pers.*) convenir à (qn, qch.); **it does not b. a man to . . .,** ce n'est pas le fait d'un homme de . . .. **befitting** *a.* convenable, seyant **(for s.o., sth.,** à qn, qch.).
before [bi'fɔ:r] **1.** *adv.* (*a*) (*space*) en avant, devant; **to go on b.,** marcher en avant; **this page and the one b.,** cette page et la précédente; (*b*) (*time*) auparavant, avant; **two days b.,** deux jours avant, deux jours auparavant; **the day b.,** la veille; **the year b.,** l'année d'avant; un an auparavant; **she had come two years b.,** elle était venue il y a deux ans; **a moment b.,** un moment auparavant, plus tôt; **I have seen him b.,** je l'ai déjà vu; **I have never seen him b.,** je ne l'ai jamais vu (de ma vie); **to go on as b.,** faire comme par le passé; **you should have told me so b.,** vous auriez dû me le dire plus tôt. **2.** *prep.* (*a*) (*place*) devant; **b. my (very) eyes,** sous mes (propres) yeux; **b. God and man,** devant Dieu et les hommes; **to appear b. the judge,** comparaître par-devant le juge; **that is the task b. us,** c'est là la tâche qui nous incombe; (*b*) (*time*) avant; **b. long,** avant longtemps, sous peu; **not b. Easter,** pas avant Pâques; **it ought to have been done b. now,** ce devrait être déjà fait; **to arrive an hour b. time,** arriver avec une heure d'avance; *F:* **it's not b. time,** ce n'est pas trop tôt; **I got here b. you,** je vous ai devancé; **the day b. the battle,** la veille de la bataille; **two days b. Christmas,** l'avant-veille de

Noël; **b. answering,** avant de répondre; (*c*) (*order*) **b. anything (else) I must have . . .,** il me faut avant tout . . .; **death b. dishonour,** plutôt la mort que le déshonneur; **ladies b. gentlemen,** les dames d'abord; **the welfare of the country comes b. everything,** le bien de la patrie prime tout. **3.** *conj.* avant que (ne) + *sub.*; (*a*) **come and see me b. you leave,** venez me voir avant de partir, avant votre départ; **don't come in b. I call you,** n'entrez pas avant que, sans que, je vous appelle; **it was long b. he came,** il fut longtemps à venir; **you'll be ruined b. you know where you are,** vous allez vous ruiner en moins de rien; (*b*) **I will die b. I yield,** je préfère mourir plutôt que de céder; (*c*) **b. I forget, they expect you this evening,** j'oubliais de vous dire qu'on vous attend ce soir.

beforehand [bi'fɔːhænd] *adv.* au préalable, à l'avance, d'avance; **to come an hour b.,** venir une heure d'avance; **I must tell you b. that . . .,** il faut vous dire d'avance, au préalable, que . . .; **if I come I shall let you know b.,** si je viens je vous préviendrai.

befriend [bi'frend] *v.tr.* se montrer l'ami de (qn).

befuddle [bi'fʌdl] *v.tr.* (*a*) griser (qn); **befuddled (with drink),** éméché; (*b*) brouiller les idées de (qn).

beg [beg] *v.tr. & i.* **(begged; begging) 1.** (*a*) mendier; (*with passive force*) **these jobs go begging,** ce sont des emplois qui trouvent peu d'amateurs; (*b*) (*of dog*) **to sit up and b.,** faire le beau. **2.** (*a*) **to b. a favour of s.o.,** solliciter une faveur de qn; demander une faveur à qn; **to b. (of) s.o. to do sth.,** prier, supplier, qn de faire qch.; **I b. to inform you that . . .,** j'ai l'honneur de vous faire savoir que . . .; **to b. for mercy,** demander grâce; **I b. your pardon,** je vous demande pardon; **I b. (of) you!** je vous en prie! (*b*) **to b. the question,** faire une pétition de principe. **begging 1.** *a.* (frère, ordre) mendiant; **b. letter,** lettre quémandant une contribution, *esp.* de l'argent. **2.** *n.* (*a*) mendicité *f*; **to live by b.,** vivre d'aumône; **b. bowl,** sébile *f* (de mendiant); (*b*) **b. the question,** pétition *f* de principe.

beget [bi'get] *v.tr.* (*p.t.* **begot** (bi'gɔt], *B:* **begat** [bi'gæt]; *p.p.* **begotten** [bi'gɔtn]) **1.** *B.Lit:* engendrer, procréer; **Abraham begat Isaac,** Abraham engendra Isaac; *B:* **the only begotten son of the Father,** le Fils unique du Père. **2.** *Lit:* causer, susciter; **discord begets crime,** la discorde enfante le crime.

beggar[1] ['begər] *n.* **1. b.(-man, -woman),** mendiant, -e, gueux, -euse; *Prov:* **beggars can't be choosers,** ne choisit pas qui emprunte; faute de souliers on va nu-pieds. **2.** *F:* individu *m*; **poor b.!** pauvre diable! **lucky b.!** chançard! veinard! **you little b.!** petit coquin! petit espiègle!

beggar[2] *v.tr.* **(beggared** ['begəd]**) 1. to b. s.o.,** réduire qn à la mendicité. **2. to b. description,** défier toute description; être indescriptible.

beggarly ['begəli] *a.* minable, misérable; mesquin; (salaire) dérisoire; **for a b. few hundred francs!** pour quelques malheureux cent francs!

beggar-my-neighbour ['begəmi'neibər] *n. Cards:* bataille *f.*

begin [bi'gin] *v.tr. & i.* (*p.t.* **began** [bi'gæn]; *p.p.* **begun** [bi'gʌn]) commencer (un discours, une tâche, etc.); entamer, amorcer (une conversation, etc.); attaquer (un repas, etc.); **to b. at the beginning,** commencer par le commencement; **before winter begins,** avant le début de l'hiver; **the day began well, badly,** la journée s'annonça bien, mal; **to b. a fresh chapter,** entamer un nouveau chapitre; **to b. to do sth., to b. doing sth.,** commencer à faire qch.; se mettre à faire qch.; **to b. to laugh, to cry, to b. laughing, crying,** se mettre à rire, à pleurer; **to b. to boil, to melt,** entrer en ébullition, en fusion; **he soon began to complain,** il ne tarda pas à se plaindre; **we began, we were beginning, to get hungry,** nous commencions à avoir faim; **it doesn't b. to compare with . . .,** cela est loin d'être comparable à . . .; **to b. by doing sth.,** débuter, commencer, par faire qch.; **b. with me,** commencez par moi; **the play begins with a prologue,** la pièce débute par un prologue; **to b. with, I thought he was wrong,** pour commencer je pensais qu'il avait tort; **to b. again,** recommencer. **beginning** *n.* commencement *m*; début *m* (d'un discours, d'une carrière, etc.); origine *f*, naissance *f* (du monde, etc.); **in the b.,** au commencement, au début; **from the b.,** dès le commencement; **from b. to end,** depuis le commencement jusqu'à la fin; **at the b. of term,** à la rentrée (des classes); **the first beginnings of civilization,** les rudiments *mpl* de la civilisation; **to make a b.,** commencer, débuter.

beginner [bi'ginər] *n.* **1.** premier *m* à agir; *Th:* **beginners please!** en scène pour le un! **2.** commençant, -ante; débutant, -ante; novice *mf*; **beginner's luck,** aux innocents les mains pleines.

begone [bi'gɔn] *p.p. A: & Lit:* (*used as imp.*) va-t'en! allez-vous-en!

begonia [bi'gouniə] *n. Bot:* bégonia *m.*

begrime [bi'graim] *v.tr. Lit:* noircir, salir.

begrudge [bi'grʌdʒ] *v.tr.* **1.** donner (qch.) à contrecœur; **to b. doing sth.,** faire qch. à contrecœur. **2. to b. s.o. sth.,** envier qch. à qn; **they b. him his food,** on lui mesure, on lui reproche, sa nourriture.

beguile [bi'gail] *v.tr. Lit:* **1.** enjôler, séduire (qn); **to b. s.o. with promises,** bercer qn de promesses. **2. to b. the time,** faire passer le temps; tromper son ennui. **beguiling** *a.* (sourire) enjôleur, séduisant.

begum ['beigəm] *n.f.* bégum.

behalf [bi'hɑːf] *n.* **on b. of s.o.,** au nom de qn; de la part de qn; *Com:* au compte, à l'acquit, de qn; **he is acting on my b.,** il agit pour moi, pour mon compte; **don't be uneasy on my b.,** ne vous inquiétez pas à mon sujet.

behave [bi'heiv] *v.i.* **1. to b. well, badly, wisely,** se comporter, se conduire, bien, mal, prudemment; **to b. well towards, to, s.o.,** bien agir envers qn; **what a way to b.!** quelles manières! **2. to know how to b.,** savoir vivre; **I'll teach him how to b.!** je lui apprendrai la politesse! (*to child, etc.*) **b. yourself!** tiens-toi (comme il faut)! sois sage! **3.** réagir. **behaved** *a.* (*with adv. prefixed*) **well b.,** sage; qui se conduit bien; **badly b.,** qui se conduit, qui se tient, mal.

behaviour, *NAm:* **behavior** [bi'heivjər] *n.* **1.** comportement *m*; maintien *m*; conduit *f* **(to, towards, s.o.,** avec, envers, qn); **good b.,** bonne conduite; **to be on one's best b.,** se surveiller. **2.** fonctionnement *m* (d'une machine); tenue *f* (d'une voiture).

behaviourism, *NAm:* **behaviorism** [bi'heivjərizm] *n.* behavio(u)risme *m.*

behead [bi'hed] *v.tr.* décapiter. **beheading** *n.* décapitation *f.*

behest [bi'hest] *n. Lit:* commandement *m*, ordre *m.*

behind [bi'haind] **1.** *adv.* (*a*) derrière, par derrière; **to attack s.o. from b.,** attaquer qn par derrière; **to come b.,** venir derrière; suivre; **to fall, lag, b.,** s'attarder; **to stay, remain, b.,** (i) rester, demeurer, en arrière; (ii) ne pas partir (avec les autres); (*b*) **to be b. with one's work,** être en retard dans son travail; *Sp:* **they are only three points b.,** ils ne sont qu'à trois points. **2.** *prep.* (*a*) derrière; **he hid b. it,** il s'est caché derrière; **look b. you,** regardez derrière vous; **garden b. the house,** jardin derrière la maison; **to walk, follow, close b. s.o.,** marcher sur les talons de qn; **what's b. all this?** qu'y a-t-il derrière tout cela? *Th: etc:* **b. the scenes,** dans la coulisse; (*b*) **to be b. s.o.,** soutenir qn; donner son appui à qn; **he has the minister b. him,** il a le ministre derrière, avec, lui; il est protégé par le ministre; (*c*) **to put sth. b. one,** rejeter le souvenir de (qch); rejeter (une pensée); **it's all b. me now,** c'est passé pour moi; (*d*) en arrière de, en retard sur (qn, qch.); **b. the times,** arriéré, attardé. **3.** *n. F:* derrière *m, P:* cul *m*; *F:* **to kick s.o.'s b.,** botter le derrière de, à, qn.

behindhand [bi'haindhænd] *adv. & a.* en arrière, en retard; **to be b. with the rent,** être en retard pour, avec, le loyer; **I am b. with my work,** mon travail est en retard.

behold [bi'hould] *v.t.r.* (*p.t. & p.p.* **beheld** [bi'held]) *Lit:* **1.** voir; apercevoir. **2.** *imp.* **b.!** voyez!

beholden [bi'hould(ə)n] *a.* **to be b. to s.o.,** être redevable à qn (**for,** de); être obligé à, envers, qn (**for,** de).

beholder [bi'houldər] *n.* spectateur, -trice; témoin *m*; **beauty is in the eye of the b.,** il n'y a point de laides amours.

behove [bi'houv], *NAm:* **behoove** [bi'hu:v] *v.tr. impers. Lit:* incomber à; **it behoves him to . . .,** il lui appartient de . . ..

beige [beiʒ] *a. & n.* (*colour*) beige (*m*); blond (*m*).

Beirut [bei'ru:t] *Pr.n. Geog:* Beyrouth *m.*

bejewelled, *NAm:* **bejeweled** [bi'dʒu(:)əld] *a.* paré de bijoux.

belabour, *NAm:* **belabor** [bi'leibər] *v.tr.* (*a*) rouer (qn) de coups; (*b*) accabler (qn) d'injures.

belated [bi'leitid] *a.* **1.** (voyageur, etc.) attardé. **2.** renseignement, etc.) tardif; (invité, etc.) en retard.

belay [bi'lei] *v.tr.* (*a*) *Nau:* tourner, amarrer (une manœuvre); (*b*) *Mount:* assurer (la corde). **belaying** *n.* (*a*) *Nau:* tournage *m*, amarrage *m*; **b. pin, cleat,** cabillot *m*, taquet *m*; (*b*) *Mount:* assurance *f* (de la corde).

belch[1] [bel(t)ʃ] *n.* **1.** éructation *f*, renvoi *m*; *P:* rot *m.* **2.** vomissement *m* (de flammes, etc.).

belch[2] **1.** *v.i.* avoir un renvoi; éructer; *F:* roter. **2.** *v.tr.* **to b. forth, out,** vomir (des flammes, de la fumée, etc.).

beleaguered [bi'li:gəd] *a.* (*of city, etc.*) assiégé.

belfry ['belfri] *n.* beffroi *m*, clocher *m.*

Belgian ['beldʒən] **1.** *a.* (*a*) belge; de Belgique. **2.** *n.* Belge *mf.*

Belgium ['beldʒəm] *Pr.n. Geog:* Belgique *f.*

belie [bi'lai] *v.tr.* (*pr.p.* **belying** [bi'laiiŋ]) démentir (une promesse, etc.); **his appearance belies him,** on le méjugerait sur sa mine.

belief [bi'li:f] *n.* **1.** croyance *f*; conviction *f*; **b. in ghosts,** croyance aux revenants; **b. in God,** croyance en Dieu; **it is beyond b.,** c'est incroyable; **to the best of my b.,** à ce que je crois; **it is my b. that . . .,** je suis convaincu que . . .; j'ai la conviction que . . .. **2.** foi *f*, confiance *f* (en qn, en qch).

believable [bi'li:vəbl] *a.* croyable.

believe [bi'li:v] **1.** *v.tr.* (*a*) croire (une nouvelle, etc.); ajouter foi à (une rumeur); **I b. that it is true,** je crois que c'est vrai; **I b. (that) I am right,** je crois avoir raison; **I b. him to be alive,** je le crois vivant; **he is believed to be in Paris,** on le croit à Paris; **the house was believed to be haunted,** la maison passait pour être hantée; **he believes himself to have been unfairly treated,** il se croit (la) victime d'une injustice; **I b. not,** je crois que non; je ne le crois pas; **I b. so,** je crois que oui; je le crois; **I don't b. a word of it,** je n'en crois rien, pas un mot; **I don't know what to b.,** je ne sais que croire; **I could scarcely b. my eyes,** j'en croyais à peine mes yeux; **seeing is believing,** voir c'est croire; **to make s.o. b. that . . .,** faire croire à qn que . . .; *F:* **don't you b. it!** n'en croyez rien! **I can well b. it,** je suis prêt à le croire; **b. it or not, he fell for her!** il s'est épris d'elle, figure-toi! (*b*) **to b. s.o.,** croire qn, accorder créance au dire de qn; **if he is to be believed,** à l'en croire; s'il faut l'en croire; *F:* **he's a smart one, b. me** [bili:v'mi:]! *F:* **b. you me!** c'est un malin croyez-moi! **2.** *v.i.* (*a*) **to b. in (one) God,** croire en (un seul) Dieu; **to b. in ghosts,** croire aux revenants; **to b. in (s.o., sth.),** avoir confiance en (qn); croire à (la parole de qn); être partisan d'(une méthode); **I don't b. in doctors,** je n'ai pas confiance dans les médecins. **3.** **to make b. to do sth.,** faire semblant de faire qch.

believer [bi'li:vər] *n.* **1.** *Rel:* croyant, -ante. **2.** **to be a b. in sth.,** (i) croire à qch.; (ii) être partisan *m* de qch.; **I am not a b. in patent medicines,** je ne crois pas à l'efficacité des spécialites pharmaceutiques.

Belisha [bə'li:ʃə] *Pr.n. Adm: Aut:* **B. beacon,** sphère orange lumineuse (indiquant un passage clouté).

belittle [bi'litl] *v.tr.* rabaisser, déprécier, amoindrir (qn, le mérite de qn); décrier (qn); **to b. oneself,** (i) se déprécier; (ii) se déconsidérer (aux yeux de qn, auprès de qn).

bell[1] [bel] *n.* **1.** (*a*) cloche *f*; (*small*) clochette *f*; (*in house*) sonnette *f*; (*fixed*) timbre *m*; (*for cattle, etc.*) clochette, clarine *f*; **sleigh b.,** grelot *m*; **electric b.,** sonnerie *f* (électrique); *Tp:* timbre d'appel; **call b.,** sonnerie d'appel; avertisseuse *f*; **set of bells,** sonnerie (d'une église); (*of a church*) **great b.,** bourdon *m*; **chime of bells,** carillon *m*; *Mus:* **tubular bells,** carillon (d'orchestre); **there's a ring at the b., there's the b.,** on sonne; **to ring the b.,** (i) sonner; (ii) (*handbell*) agiter la sonnette; **that rings a b.,** cela me rappelle, dit, quelque chose; (*b*) **the dinner b.,** la cloche du dîner; **passing b.,** glas *m*; (*c*) *Nau:* **to strike the bells,** piquer l'heure; **six bells,** six coups (de cloche). **2.** calice *m* (d'une fleur); pavillon *m* (d'une trompette, etc.); campane *f* (d'une colonne); vase *m* (de chapiteau); *Hort:* cloche; *Metall:* cône *m*, cloche (d'un haut fourneau); **diving b.,** cloche à, de, plongeurs. **3.** (*a*) **b. founder,** fondeur *m* de cloches; **b. foundry,** fonderie *f* de cloches; **b. ringing,** (i) carillonnement *m*; (ii) art *m* campanaire; **b. tower,** clocher *m*, campanile *m*; (*b*) *O:* **b.-bottomed trousers, b. bottoms,** pantalon *m* à pattes d'éléphant; *Ch:* **b. jar,** cloche; **b. tent,** tente *f* conique; (*c*) **b. buoy,** bouée *f* à cloche. **4.** *Bot:* **Canterbury b.,** campanule *f* à grosses fleurs.

bell[2] **1.** *v.tr.* attacher une clochette autour du cou (d'une vache). **2.** *v.i.* (*a*) (*of skirt, etc.*) faire cloche; ballonner; (*b*) (*of tube, etc.*) **to b. out,** s'évaser, renfler.

bell[3] *n.* bramement *m* (du cerf).

bell[4] *v.i.* (*of deer*) bramer.

belladonna [belə'dɔnə] *n. Bot: Pharm:* belladone *f.*

bellboy ['belbɔi] *n.m. NAm:* groom (d'hôtel); chasseur.

belle [bel] *n.f.* (*pers.*) beauté; **the b. of the ball,** la reine, la beauté, du bal.

bellflower ['belflauər] *n. Bot:* campanule *f.*

bellhop ['belhɔp] *n. NAm: F:* = BELLBOY.

bellicose ['belikous] *a.* belliqueux.

bellicosity [beli'kɔsiti] *n.* humeur belliqueuse; caractère belliqueux; agressivité *f.*

belligerence [be'lidʒərəns] *n.* belligérence *f.*

belligerent [be'lidʒərənt] (*a*) *a. & n.* belligérant (*m*); (*b*) *a.* belliqueux, agressif, belligérant.

bellow[1] ['belou] *n.* (*a*) beuglement *m*, mugissement *m*; (*b*) hurlement *m* (de douleur, etc.).

bellow[2] **1.** *v.i.* (*of bull*) beugler, mugir; (*of pers., ocean*) mugir, hurler. **2.** *v.tr.* **to b. (out),** hurler (un ordre); *F:* beugler (une chanson). **bellowing** *n.* **1.** beuglement *m*, mugissement *m* (d'un animal). **2.** hurlements *mpl* (d'une personne).

bellows ['belouz] *n.pl.* **1.** (*a*) **(a pair of) b.,** un soufflet (pour le feu); (*b*) *F:* les poumons *mpl.* **2.** soufflerie *f* (d'un orgue).

bellpull ['belpul] *n.* **1.** cordon *m* de sonnette. **2.** poignée *f* de sonnette.

bellpush ['belpuʃ] *n.* bouton *m* (de sonnerie); bouton d'appel.
bell-shaped ['belʃeipt] *a.* en forme de cloche.
bellwether ['belweðər] *n.m. Husb:* sonnailler; bélier.
belly¹ ['beli] *n.* **1.** (*a*) ventre *m* (de l'homme, d'un animal); *P:* panse *f*, bedaine *f*; *Cu:* **b. of pork,** poitrine *f* de porc; **to have an empty b.,** avoir l'estomac creux; **his eyes are bigger than his b.,** il a les yeux plus grands que le ventre; *Anat: F:* **b. button,** nombril *m*; **b. dance,** danse *f* du ventre; **b. laugh,** rire rabelaisien, énorme; (*b*) *Leath:* flanc *m*. **2.** (*a*) ventre (d'une cruche, d'un avion, d'un navire, etc.); panse (d'une cruche); *Av:* **b. tank,** réservoir ventral; **b. landing,** atterrissage *m* sur le ventre; (*b*) *Mus:* table *f* d'harmonie (d'un violon, etc.). **3.** *Nau:* creux *m*, renflement *m* (d'une voile).
belly² *Nau:* **1.** *v.tr.* (*of wind*) **to b. (out) the sails,** enfler, gc fler, les voiles. **2.** *v.i.* (*of sail*) faire (le) sac; s'enfler, se gonfler.
bellyache¹ ['belieik] *n. F:* mal *m* de ventre.
bellyache² *v.i. P:* ronchonner, rouspéter; *P:* râler.
bellyband ['belibænd] *n. Harn:* sous-ventrière *m*, *pl.* sous-ventrières.
bellyflop¹ ['beliflɔp] *n. Swim: F:* **to do a b.,** faire un plat.
bellyflop² *v.i. F:* **1.** *Swim:* faire un plat. **2.** *Can:* aller en traîneau à plat ventre.
bellyful ['beliful] *n.* plein ventre, *F:* ventrée *f*; *F:* **to have had a b.,** (i) en avoir tout son soûl; (ii) en avoir ras le bol; en avoir marre.
bellyland ['belilænd] *v.i. Av:* atterrir sur le ventre.
belong [bi'lɔŋ] *v.i.* **1.** (*a*) appartenir, être (**to,** à); **that book belongs to me,** ce livre m'appartient, est à moi; *Jur:* **to b. to s.o. by right,** compéter à qn; (*of land, etc.*) **to b. to the Crown,** dépendre de la Couronne. **2.** être propre (à qch.); **to what category do they b.?** à quelle catégorie appartiennent-ils? **things that b. together,** choses *fpl* qui vont ensemble. **3.** (*a*) **to b. to a society,** faire partie d'une société; **do you b. to this club?** êtes-vous membre de ce cercle? **I b. here,** (i) je suis d'ici; (ii) je me sens chez moi ici; **to feel that one doesn't b.,** se sentir isolé, intrus; (*b*) **this is where the spoons b.,** c'est ici qu'on range les cuillers; **to put things back where they b.,** remettre les choses à leur place. **belongings** *n.pl.* affaires *fpl*, effets *mpl* (appartenant à qn); **personal b.,** objets personnels.
beloved 1. *a.* [bi'lʌvd], aimé; **b. by all,** aimé de tous, par tout le monde. **2.** *a. & n.* [bi'lʌvid] bien-aimé(e), chéri(e); **the b. wife of . . .,** l'épouse bien-aimée de . . .; **my b.,** mon, ma, bien-aimé(e); *Ecc:* **dearly b. (brethren),** mes bien chers frères.
below [bi'lou] **1.** *adv.* (*a*) en bas, (au-)dessous; **remain b.,** restez en bas; **voices from b.,** des voix qui venaient d'en bas; **the tenants (of the flat) b.,** les locataires du dessous; **here b. (on earth),** ici-bas; *Nau:* **all hands b.!** tout le monde en bas! (*b*) **the passage quoted b.,** le passage cité (i) ci-dessous, (ii) plus loin, ci-après. **2.** *prep.* au-dessous de; (*a*) **b. the knee,** au-dessous du genou; (*b*) **b. (the) average,** au-dessous de la moyenne; *F:* **I'm feeling a bit b. par,** je ne suis pas dans mon assiette; **temperature b. normal,** température inférieure à la normale; **ten degrees b. zero,** *F:* **ten degrees b.,** dix degrés au-dessous de zéro; moins dix; **b. sea level,** au-dessous du niveau de la mer; (*c*) **b. the surface,** sous la surface; *Th:* **b. stage,** les dessous *mpl*; (*d*) **b. the bridge,** en aval du pont.
belt¹ [belt] *n.* **1. (waist) b.,** ceinture *f*; *Mil:* ceinturon *m*; **to tighten one's b.,** (i) serrer sa ceinture; (ii) *Fig:* se boucler, se serrer, la ceinture; **shoulder b.,** baudrier *m*, banderole *f*; **(ladies') suspender b.,** porte-jarretelles *m inv*; *Aut: Av:* **seat b., safety b.,** ceinture de sécurité; (*judo*) **to be a brown b.,** être ceinture marron; *Box:* **to hold the b.,** être le champion; **blow below the b.,** coup bas; *Fig:* **to hit s.o. below the b.,** donner à qn un coup en traître, un coup bas; frapper qn déloyalement. **2.** (*a*) *Mec.E: etc:* courroie *f* (de transmission); corde plate; **V(-shaped) b.,** courroie en (forme de) coin, courroie trapézoïdale; **chain b.,** courroie articulée; *Civ.E: etc:* **b. conveyor,** transporteur *m* à courroie, à ruban, à bande; **conveyor b.,** bande transporteuse, courroie de transport, ruban, tapis, roulant; *Ind:* **endless b.,** courroie sans fin; **assembly b.,** chaîne *f* de montage; (*b*) *Mil:* (*of machine gun*) **feed b., loading b.,** bande-chargeur *f* (souple), *pl.* bandes-chargeurs. **3.** (*a*) *Town P:* **green b.,** ceinture, zone, verte; *NAm:* **b. line,** ligne *f* (de chemin de fer) de ceinture; (*b*) *Arch: Astr:* bande; **the belts of Jupiter,** les zones, bandes, de Jupiter; (*c*) **trade-wind b.,** zone des (vents) alizes; **standard time b.,** fuseau *m* horaire; **corn, cotton, b.,** région *f* du maïs, du coton; **coal b.,** zone houillère.
belt² *v.tr.* **1.** ceinturer, ceindre (qn, qch.). **2.** entourer (qch.) d'une ceinture; former une ceinture autour de (qch.). **3.** *Mec.E:* relier (deux machines, etc.) par une courroie. **4.** *F:* donner des coups de courroie à (qn); fustiger (qn). **belt along** *v.i. F:* courir, aller, conduire, à toute vitesse. **belted** *a.* ceinturé; **b. overcoat,** pardessus *m* avec ceinture. **belting** *n.* **1.** (*a*) ceinture(s) *f(pl)*, courroie(s) *f(pl)*; (*b*) matière *f* à courroies. **2.** *Mec.E:* transmission *f*. **3.** *F:* **to give s.o. a (good) b.,** administrer une correction à qn (avec une courroie). **belt out** *v.tr. F:* vociférer, gueuler (un ordre, etc.). **belt up** *v.i. P:* se taire; **b. up!** ta gueule!
belvedere ['belvidiər] *n. Arch:* belvédère *m*, mirador(e) *m*.
bemoan [bi'moun] *v.tr.* pleurer (qch.); **to b. the loss of sth.,** se lamenter de, pleurer, la perte de qch.
bemuse [bi'mju:z] *v.tr. Lit:* stupéfier; ahurir.
ben [ben] *n. Geog: Scot:* sommet *m*, pic *m*; **B. Nevis,** le mont Nevis.
bench [ben(t)ʃ] *n.* **1.** (*a*) banc *m*, banquette *f*; gradin *m* (d'amphithéâtre); *Jur:* siège *m* (du juge); banc (des magistrats, des témoins); *Aut:* **b. seat,** banquette *f*; *Parl:* **the Treasury B., Front B.,** le banc ministériel; *Jur:* **the B.,** (i) la magistrature; le pouvoir judiciaire; (ii) la Cour; **to be on the B.,** (i) être magistrat; (ii) siéger au tribunal; **to be raised to the B.,** être nommé (i) juge, (ii) évêque; (*b*) *Fb: etc:* banc (pour les joueurs qui ne sont pas sur le terrain); **to be on the b.,** (i) attendre son tour; (ii) avoir été retiré du jeu, renvoyé du terrain. **2.** (*a*) établi *m* (de menuisier); banc, marbre *m* (d'ajusteur); selle *f* (de tonnelier); *Hort:* tablette *f* (de serre); **b. holdfast, b. hook,** valet *m* d'établi; (*b*) **optical b.,** banc optique; *Mec.E:* **testing b.,** banc d'essai, d'épreuve; **b. test,** essai *m* au banc; *Ch: etc:* **laboratory b.,** paillasse *f*; table de manipulation. **3.** banc; estrade *f* (sur laquelle on exhibe un chien, etc., à une exposition); *U.S:* **b. show,** exposition canine. **4.** (*a*) banquette (de terre); *Const:* gradin; redan *m*; (*b*) *Civ.E:* accotement *m*, berme *f* (d'un chemin).
benchmark ['ben(t)ʃmɑ:k] *n.* **1.** *Surv:* repère *m* (de nivellement). **2.** *Cmptr: etc:* point *m* de référence.
bend¹ [bend] *n. Nau:* nœud *m*; **fisherman's b.,** nœud de grappin; **sheet b.,** nœud d'écoute.
bend² *n. Her:* bande *f*; **b. sinister,** barre *f*.
bend³ *n.* **1. forward, backward, b.,** inclination *f* (du corps) en avant, en arrière. **2.** courbure *f*; courbe *f*; (*of road, pipe*) coude *m*; (*of road*) tournant *m*, angle *m*, virage *m*; (*of river*) boucle *f*; *Anat:* saignée *f* (du bras); *Tchn:* **return b., U b.,** (i) courbe de retour; (ii) tube *m* en U, coude en U; *P.N:* **bends for 3 kilometres,** virages sur 3 kilomètres; *Aut:* **to take a b. at**

speed, prendre, un virage à toute vitesse; *F:* **to be round the b.,** être fou, cinglé. **3.** *Med: F:* **the bends,** la maladie des caissons.

bend[4] *v.* (*p.t.* **bent** [bent]; *p.p.* **bent,** *A:* **bended**) **I.** *v.tr.* **1.** (*a*) courber (un osier, le corps); plier (le coude, etc.); ployer, fléchir (le genou); baisser (la tête); arquer (le dos); cambrer, cintrer (un tuyau, un rail); cambrer, arquer (du bois, du fer); dévirer (du bois); *Ph:* réfracter (la lumière); infléchir (un rayon); **to b. one's head over a book,** pencher la tête sur un livre; **to b. s.o. to one's will,** plier qn à sa volonté; (*b*) tendre, bander (un arc, un ressort); (*c*) **to b. a rod, a key (out of shape),** forcer, fausser, une barre de fer, une clef; (*d*) forcer, donner une entorse à (la loi, une règle, etc.); *Sp:* **to b. a match,** arranger d'avance le résultat d'un match. **2.** *Nau:* (*a*) étalinguer (un câble); frapper (une manœuvre); enverguer (une voile); **to b. on a signal,** frapper un signal; (*b*) abouter (deux cordages). **II.** *v.i.* (*of rod, branch, etc.*) plier, ployer; (*of branch, pers.*) se courber; (*of pers.*) se pencher; (*of road, river*) tourner, faire un tournant; **to bend under a strain,** (*of wood, iron*) arquer; (*of steel plate, etc.*) s'envoiler; (*of rod, wheel*) se voiler; (*of pers.*) **to b. to s.o.'s will,** se plier à, fléchir devant, la volonté de qn; **old man bending under a heavy load,** vieillard courbé sous un pesant fardeau; **she was bending over him,** elle se penchait sur lui; **the road bends to the right,** la route tourne, fait un tournant, à droite. **bend back 1.** *v.tr.* replier; recourber (une lame, etc.); réfléchir (la lumière). **2.** *v.i.* se recourber; se réfléchir; (*of pers.*) se pencher en arrière. **bend down 1.** *v.tr.* courber, ployer (une branche); **the tree was bent down by the weight of the fruit,** l'arbre penchait sous le poids des fruits. **2.** *v.i.* se courber, se baisser. **bended** ['bendid] *a. Lit:* **on one's b. knees,** (demander qch.) à genoux. **bend forward,** *v.i.* se pencher en avant. **bending** *n.* **1.** (*a*) cintrage *m*; (*b*) *Mec.E: etc:* arcure *f*, arqûre *f* (d'une partie métallique); envoilure *f* (de l'acier à la trempe, etc.); voilure *f* (d'une roue); (*c*) flexion *f*; *Mec:* **b. strength,** résistance *f* à la flexion; **b. test,** essai *m*, épreuve *f*, de ployage, de flexion; **b. moment,** moment *m* de flexion; moment fléchissant; (*d*) bandage *m* (d'un arc). **2.** (*of pers.*) penchement *m*. **3.** *Nau:* aboutage *m* (de deux cordages). **bend over 1.** *v.i.* (*of pers.*) se pencher; *F:* **he bent over backwards to help me,** il s'est mis en quatre pour m'aider. **2.** *v.tr.* replier (une tôle, etc.). **bent** *a.* **1.** (*a*) (i) courbé, plié, arqué; (essieu, levier) coudé; (dos, vieillard) voûté; (ii) faussé, fléchi, gauchi; **to become b.,** (i) s'arquer, se courber; (*with age*) se voûter, s'affaisser; (ii) (*of rod, spring*) fléchir, gauchir; **b. chassis,** châssis tordu; (*b*) *P:* (i) malhonnête, déshonnête; (fonctionnaire, politicien, etc.) corrompu, vénal; (match de boxe, etc.) truqué; (ii) homosexuel, inverti. **2.** déterminé, résolu **(on doing sth.,** à faire qch.); **he is b. on seeing me,** il veut absolument me voir; **b. on self destruction,** obstiné à se perdre.

bender ['bendər] *n. P:* soûlerie *f*; **to go on a b.,** se soûler.

beneath [bi'ni:θ] **1.** *adv.* dessous, au-dessous; en bas; **from b.,** de dessous. **2.** *prep.* (*a*) **to marry b. one,** faire une mésalliance; **b. contempt,** complètement méprisable, indigne d'attention; **he would consider it b. him to complain,** il dédaignerait de se plaindre; (*b*) **the plank gave way b. me,** la planche a cédé sous mon poids.

Benedictine [beni'diktin] **1.** *Ecc:* (*a*) *a.* bénédictin; (*b*) *n.* Bénédictin, -ine. **2.** *n. R.t.m:* (*also* [-ti:n] (*liqueur*) Bénédictine *f*.

benediction [beni'dikʃ(ə)n] *n.* bénédiction *f;* (*at meals*) bénédicité *m.*

benefaction [beni'fakʃ(ə)n, 'beni-] *n.* **1.** *Lit:* bienfaisance *f.* **2.** (*a*) *Lit:* bienfait *m*; (*b*) œuvre *f* de bienfaisance, de charité; legs *m* charitable.

benefactor, -tress ['benifæktər, -tris] *n.* **1.** bienfaiteur, -trice. **2.** donateur, -trice.

benefice ['benifis] *n. Ecc: Hist:* bénéfice *m.*

beneficence [bi'nefis(ə)ns] *n.* **1.** bienfaisance *f.* **2.** œuvre *f* de bienfaisance.

beneficent [bi'nefisənt] *a.* **1.** bienfaisant. **2.** salutaire.

beneficial [beni'fiʃ(ə)l] *a.* **1.** salutaire, avantageux; **b. to the health,** salutaire pour la santé; **b. to business,** avantageux pour les affaires, aux affaires. **2.** *Jur:* **b. owner, occupant,** usufruitier, -ière.

beneficiary [beni'fiʃəri] *a. & n.* (*a*) *Ecc:* bénéficier, -ière; (*b*) *Jur:* bénéficiaire (*m*); ayant droit *m*, *pl.* a yants droit.

benefit[1] ['benifit] *n.* **1.** avantage *m*, profit *m*; **to derive b. from sth.,** profiter de qch.; **I get, gain, no b. from it,** il ne m'en revient aucun avantage; **fringe benefits,** avantages accessoires; (*for employees*) compléments *mpl* de salaire en nature; **performance for the b. of the blind,** représentation *f* au profit des aveugles; **let me add for your b. that . . .,** j'ajouterai à votre intention que . . .; **for the b. of one's health,** dans l'intérêt de sa santé; *Jur:* **b. of the doubt,** bénéfice *m* du doute; **to give s.o. the b. of the doubt,** faire bénéficier qn du doute; *F:* **to live with s.o. without b. of clergy,** se marier avec qn de la main gauche. **2.** *Th: Sp:* **b. (performance, match),** représentation *f*, match *m*, au bénéfice de qn. **3.** *Adm: Ins:* indemnité *f*, allocation *f*; **social security benefits,** prestations sociales; **unemployment b.,** indemnité de chômage; **sickness b.,** indemnité de maladie, secours médical; **maternity b.,** allocation de maternité.

benefit[2] **1.** *v.tr.* faire du bien, être avantageux, profiter, à (qn, qch.); **a steady exchange rate benefits trade,** un change stable est avantageux au commerce, favorise le commerce. **2.** *v.i.* **to b. by, from, sth.,** profiter de qch.; tirer avantage de qch.; **you will b. by a holiday,** un congé vous fera du bien; **to b. from a rise in prices,** profiter, tirer profit, d'une hausse de prix.

Benelux ['benilʌks] *n. Geog:* Bénélux *m.*

benevolence [bi'nevələns] *n.* **1.** bienveillance *f*, bonté *f.* **2. act of b.,** bienfait *m*; don *m* charitable.

benevolent [bi'nevələnt] *a.* **1.** bienveillant **(to,** envers). **2.** bienfaisant, charitable **(to,** envers); **b. society,** association *f* de bienfaisance.

Bengal [beŋ'gɔ:l] **1.** *Pr.n. Geog:* Bengale *m.* **2.** *a.* **B. light,** feu *m* de Bengale.

Bengali [beŋ'gɔ:li], **Bengalese** [beŋgə'li:z] **1.** *a. Geog:* bengali *inv*, bengalais. **2.** *n.* (*a*) Bengali *mf inv.*; Bengalais, -aise; (*b*) *Ling:* bengali *m.*

benighted [bi'naitid] *n. o:* **1.** (voyageur, etc.) surpris par la nuit. **2.** plongé dans (les ténèbres de) l'ignorance.

benign [bi'nain] *a.* (*a*) bénin, *f* bénigne; favorable; (climat) doux; (*b*) *Med:* **b. tumour,** tumeur bénigne.

Benjamin ['ben(d)ʒ(ə)min] *Pr.n.m.* Benjamin; *F:* **the B. of the family,** le benjamin de la famille.

bent[1] [bent] *n.* penchant *m*, inclination *f*, disposition *f* **(for,** pour); **to follow one's b.,** suivre son penchant, son inclination; **to have a natural b. for music,** avoir des dispositions naturelles pour la musique.

bent[2]. *See* BEND[4].

bent[3] *n. Bot:* **b. (grass),** (i) jonc *m*; (ii) agrostide *f.*

bentwood ['bentwud] *a.* (chaise) en bois courbé.

benumb [bi'nʌm] *v.tr.* (*a*) engourdir.

benzene ['benzi:n] *n. Ch:* benzène *m.*

benzine ['benzi:n, ben'zi:n] *n. Ch: Ind:* benzine *f.*

benzol ['benzɔl] *n. Ch: Com:* benzol *m.*

bequeath [bi'kwi:ð] *v.tr.* léguer **(to,** à).

bequest [bi'kwest] *n.* legs *m.*

berate [bi'reit] *v.tr.* gronder, réprimander (qn).

Berber ['bə:bər] **1.** *a.* berbère. **2.** *n.* (*a*) Berbère *mf*; (*b*) *Ling:* berbère *m.*

bereave [bi'ri:v] *v.tr.* (*p.t. & p.p. usu.* **bereft** [bi'reft]) priver, déposséder **(s.o. of sth.,** qn de qch.); **bereft of all hope,** privé de tout espoir; ayant perdu tout espoir. **bereaved** *a.* affligé (d'un deuil); **the b. family,** *n.pl.* **the b.,** la famille du mort, de la morte.

bereavement [bi'ri:vmənt] *n.* perte *f* (d'un parent); deuil *m*; **owing to a recent b.,** en raison d'un deuil récent.

beret ['berei, 'beri] *n. Cost:* béret *m*; *Mil:* **the red berets,** les bérets rouges, les parachutistes *mpl.*

Bergamo ['bə:gəmou] *Pr.n. Geog:* Bergame *f.*

bergamot ['bə:gəmɔt] *n. Bot:* bergamote *f.*

beriberi ['beri'beri] *n. Med:* béribéri *m.*

Berlin [bə:'lin] *Pr.n. Geog:* Berlin; **East, West, B.,** Berlin Est, Berlin Ouest.

Berliner [bə:'linər] *n. Geog:* Berlinois, -oise.

berm [bə:m] *n. Fort:* berme *f* (d'un rempart); *Civ.E:* berme, banquette *f* (d'un canal).

Bermuda [bə:'mju:də] *Pr.n. Geog:* **the B. Islands,** *n.pl.* **the Bermudas,** les Bermudes *fpl*; *Cost:* **B. shorts,** *n.pl.* **bermudas,** bermuda *m*; *Y:* **B. rig,** gréement *m* Marconi.

Bern(e) [bə:n] *Pr.n. Geog:* Berne *f.*

Bernese [bə:'ni:z, 'bə:-] *Geog:* **1.** *a.* bernois; **the B. Alps,** les Alpes bernoises. **2.** *n.* Bernois, -oise.

berried ['berid] *a.* **1.** *Bot:* à baies, couvert de baies. **2.** (crustacé) œuvé.

berry¹ ['beri] *n.* **1.** *Bot:* baie *f*; **coffee b.,** fruit *m* du caféier, cerise *f* de caféier; **holly b.,** cenelle *f.* **2.** frai *m* (de poisson); œufs *mpl* (de crustacé); **lobster in b.,** homard œuvé.

berry² *v.i.* **to go berrying,** aller à la cueillette des baies.

berserk [bə(:)'zə:k] **1.** *a.* (personne, rage) furieuse; **to go b.,** devenir fou furieux. **2.** *n.* (*also* **berserker** [bə(:)'zə:kər]) berserk *m.*

berth¹ [bə:θ] *n.* **1.** *Nau:* (*a*) évitée *f*, évitage *m*; **to give a ship a wide b.,** éviter, parer, un navire; passer au large d'un navire; *F:* **to give s.o. a wide b.,** éviter qn; (*b*) **(anchoring) b.,** poste *m* de mouillage, d'amarrage; (*c*) poste *m* à quai; emplacement *m*; **loading b.,** emplacement de chargement. **2.** (*a*) *Nau: Rail:* couchette *f* (de passager, de voyageur); (*b*) *Nau:* cadre *m* (d'officier, d'homme d'équipage). **3.** (*a*) emplacement (de qch.); (*b*) *F:* emploi *m*; **to find a soft b.,** trouver un emploi pépère.

berth² **1.** *v.tr.* (*a*) donner, assigner, un poste à (un navire); (*b*) accoster (un navire) le long du quai; amener, amarrer, (un navire) à quai. **2.** *v.i.* (*a*) (*of ship*) (i) mouiller; (ii) aborder à quai; se ranger à quai; (*b*) (*of passengers or crew*) **to b. forward, aft,** coucher à l'avant, à l'arrière. **berthing** *n.* **1.** (*a*) mouillage *m*; (*b*) abordage *m* à quai. **2.** aménagements *mpl* (à bord); postes *mpl* de couchage.

beryl ['beril] *n. Miner:* béryl *m.*

beryllium [be'riliəm] *n. Ch:* béryllium *m.*

beseech [bi'si:tʃ] *v.tr.* (*p.t. & p.p.* **besought** [bi'sɔ:t]) *Lit:* supplier, implorer **(s.o. to do sth.,** qn de faire qch.); **help me, I b. you,** aidez-moi, je vous en supplie. **beseeching** *a.* (air, ton) suppliant.

beset [bi'set] *v.tr.* **(beset; besetting)** *Lit:* **1.** cerner (des troupes); assaillir, obséder (qn); **b. with dangers, with difficulties,** environné, entouré, de dangers, de difficultés. **2.** (*of misfortunes, temptations, etc.*) assaillir (qn); **to be b. by doubts,** être assailli de doutes. **besetting** *a.* (*of idea, thought, etc.*) obsédant; **it's his b. sin,** c'est son grand défaut, son péché mignon.

beside [bi'said] *prep.* **1.** (*a*) à côté, auprès, de (qn, qch.); **seated b. me,** assis à côté de moi, à mes côtés; (*b*) (*comparison*) à côté de, auprès de (qn, qch.); **b. him everyone else appears slow,** à côté de lui tous les autres paraissent lents; (*c*) en dehors de; **other people b. ourselves,** d'autres (personnes) que nous. **2.** (*a*) **b. the question, the point, the mark,** à côté de la question, hors de propos, en dehors du sujet; **that is b. the point,** cela n'a rien à voir à l'affaire; (*b*) **b. oneself with joy, with anger,** fou de joie, de colère.

besides [bi'saidz] **1.** *adv.* (*a*) en outre, en plus; **many more b.,** encore bien d'autres; **nothing b.,** rien de plus; (*b*) **it is too late; b., I am tired,** il est trop tard; d'ailleurs, du reste, et en outre, je suis fatigué. **2.** *prep.* excepté, hormis; sans compter; **there are others b. him,** il y en a d'autres que lui; **b. which, he was unwell,** sans compter qu'il était indisposé.

besiege [bi'si:dʒ] *v.tr.* assiéger (une ville, *Fig:* qn); faire le siège (d'une ville).

besieger [bi'si:dʒər] *n.* assiégeant *m.*

besmirch [bi'smə:tʃ] *v.tr. Lit:* salir, tacher (qch.); salir, ternir (la mémoire de qn, etc.).

besom ['bi:zəm] *n.* balai *m* (de jonc).

besotted [bi'sɔtid] *a.* **1.** abruti (par l'opium, la boisson). **2.** affolé, entiché **(with s.o.,** de qn).

bespatter [bi'spætər] *v.tr.* éclabousser; **bespattered with mud,** tout couvert de boue.

bespectacled [bi'spektək(ə)ld] *a.* qui porte des lunettes; portant lunettes; à lunettes.

bespoke [bi'spouk] *a.* (*a*) (vêtement) (fait) sur commande, sur mesure; (*b*) **b. tailor, shoemaker,** tailleur *m*, cordonnier *m*, à façon.

Bess [bes] *Pr.n.f.* (*dim. of Elizabeth*) Lisette, Babette.

best¹ [best] **1.** *a. & n.* (le) meilleur, (la) meilleure; (*neuter*) le mieux; **the b. man on earth,** le meilleur homme du monde; **may the b. man win,** que le meilleur gagne; (*at wedding*) **b. man,** garçon *m* d'honneur; **my b. dress,** ma plus belle robe; **I am acting in your b. interests,** j'agis au mieux de vos intérêts; **with the b. will in the world,** avec la meilleure volonté du monde; **he can sing with the b.,** il chante comme pas un; **we are the b. of friends,** nous sommes les meilleurs amis du monde; **b. friend,** ami(e) intime, de cœur; **I am in the b. of health,** je me porte à merveille; je suis en excellente santé; **the b. of it is that . . .,** le plus beau de l'affaire c'est que . . .; **the b. part of the year,** la plus grande partie de l'année; **I waited for the b. part of an hour,** j'ai attendu une petite heure; **this is the b. there is,** voici ce qu'il y a de meilleur, de mieux; *F:* **the b. of luck! all the b.!** bonne chance! meilleurs souhaits! *U.S:* **my brother sends his b.,** bien des choses de la part de mon frère; **to know what is b. for s.o.,** savoir ce qui va, convient, le mieux à qn; **it is b. to . . .,** le mieux c'est de . . .; **the b. thing you can do, the b. course to take, the b. way, is to . . .,** ce qu'il y a de mieux à faire c'est de . . .; **it would be b., the b. plan would be, to . . .,** le mieux serait de . . .; **I thought it (would be) b. to stay,** j'ai pensé qu'il valait mieux rester; **to do one's b., the b. one can, to . . .,** faire ce qu'on peut, faire de son mieux, pour . . .; **I did my b. to comfort her,** je la consolai de mon mieux; **he did his b. to smile,** il s'efforça de sourire; **I am doing my (level) b., the b. I can, for you,** je fais tout ce que je peux pour vous; **do the b. you can,** (i) arrangez-vous; (ii) faites pour le mieux; **to look one's b.,** être, paraître, à son avantage; **she looks her b. in the morning,** elle est à son avantage le matin; **to be at one's b.,** être en train, en forme; **that is Dickens at his b.,** voilà du meilleur Dickens; **to get the b. out of s.o.,** encourager qn à faire de son mieux; **to get, have, the b. of it, of the bargain, to come off b.,** l'emporter, avoir l'avantage; avoir le dessus; **to have the b. of an argument,** l'emporter dans une discussion; **to hope for the b.,** ne pas désespérer, avoir bon espoir; **to make the b. of sth.,** s'accommoder de qch.; **to make the b. of a bad job,** faire bonne mine à mauvais jeu; **to make the b. of the circumstances,** s'adapter aux circonstances; **to play the b. of three games,** jouer en parties liées; jouer au meilleur de trois; *F:* **six of the b.,** une fessée magistrale. **2.** *a. & n.* (*a*) **at (the) b.,** au mieux; *St.Exch:* **to sell at b.,** vendre au mieux; **at b. he will get 2000 votes,** au mieux, il aura 2000 suffrages; **he was undemonstrative at the b. of times,** même dans ses meilleurs moments il était peu démonstratif; (*b*) **to act for the b.,** agir pour le mieux; **I did it for the b.,** j'ai fait pour le mieux; **it's all for the b.,** (i) tout est pour le mieux; (ii) c'est dans la meilleure intention; (*c*) **to do sth. to the b. of one's ability,** faire qch. de son mieux; **to the b. of my belief, knowledge,** à ce que je crois, autant que je sache; **to the b. of my judgment,** autant que je peux en juger. **3.** *adv.* (*a*) **he does it (the) b.,** c'est lui qui le fait le mieux; **I comforted her as b. I could,** je la consolai de mon mieux; **I came, got, down as b. I could,** je suis descendu comme j'ai pu; **you know b.,** c'est vous (qui êtes) le mieux placé pour en juger; **do as you think b.,** faites comme bon vous semble(ra); (*b*) **the b. dressed man,** l'homme le mieux habillé; **the b. known book,** le livre le mieux, le plus, connu; **the b. looking women,** les femmes les plus jolies.

best² *v.tr. F:* l'emporter sur (qn); *F:* enfoncer (qn).

bestial ['bestiəl] *a.* bestial. **-ally** *adv.* bestialement.

bestiality [besti'æliti] *n.* bestialité *f.*

bestir [bi'stəːr] *v.pr.* **(bestirred) to b. oneself,** se remuer, se démener, s'activer; *F:* se grouiller.

bestow [bi'stou] *v.tr. Lit:* accorder, donner (**sth. upon s.o.,** qch. à qn); **to b. a favour on s.o.,** accorder une faveur à qn.

bestride [bi'straid] *v.tr.* (*p.t.* **bestrode** [bi'stroud]; *p.p.* **bestridden** [bi'stridn]) **1.** être à cheval, à califourchon, sur (qch.). **2.** enjamber (un fossé, etc.).

bestseller ['best'selər] *n.* **1.** (*a*) livre *m* à succès; best-seller *m*, *pl.* best-sellers; (*b*) auteur *m* d'un livre à succès. **2.** article *m* de grosse vente.

bestselling [best'seliŋ] *a.* (livre, auteur) à grand succès; (livre, article, etc.) de grosse vente.

bet¹ [bet] *n.* pari *m*; **to make, lay, a b.,** parier, faire un pari; **your best b. would be to . . .,** ce que vous avez de mieux à faire c'est . . .; **it's my b. that he'll come,** je parie qu'il viendra.

bet² *v.tr. & i.* (*p.t.* **bet;** *p.p.* **bet,** *occ.* **betted**) (*a*) parier (une somme); **to b. on a horse,** miser sur, jouer, un cheval; **to b. ten to one that . . .,** parier à dix contre un que . . .; (*b*) **to b. with s.o.,** parier avec qn; **I'll b. you that . . .,** je vous parierais que . . ., parions que . . .; **to b. on sth.,** parier sur qch.; *F:* **you b.!** pour sûr! **I'll b. you anything (you like) that . . .,** j'en donnerais ma tête à couper que . . .; **I b. you don't!** chiche (que tu ne le feras pas)! **b. you I will!** chiche (que je le fais)! **betting** *n.* (*a*) les paris; **the b. ran high,** on a parié gros; (*b*) cote *f*; **the b. is twenty to one,** la cote est à vingt contre un; **the b. is that . . .,** il y a fort à parier que . . .; (*c*) **b. book,** carnet *m* de paris; **b. shop,** (i) bureau *m*, agence *f*, de bookmaker; (ii) = bureau du pari mutuel.

betel ['biːt(ə)l] *n.* **1.** (*masticatory*) bétel *m.* **2.** *Bot:* (*a*) bétel; (*b*) **b. nut,** (noix *f* d')arec (*m*); **b. (nut) palm,** arec, aréquier *m.*

Bethlehem ['beθlihem, -liəm] *Pr.n. B.Hist:* Bethléem *m*; *Bot:* **star of B.,** ornithogale *m* (à ombelle); *F:* dame *f*, belle *f*, d'onze-heures.

betide [bi'taid] *v.tr. A: & Lit:* (*used only in*) **woe b. him, you, etc., if ever . . .,** malheur à lui, à toi, etc., gare à lui, à toi, etc., si jamais . . ..

betimes [bi'taimz] *adv. Lit:* de bonne heure.

betray [bi'trei] *v.tr.* **1.** trahir (qn, sa patrie, sa foi, etc.). **2.** (*a*) révéler, laisser voir, trahir (son ignorance, son émotion); (*b*) trahir, livrer, révéler (un secret).

betrayal [bi'treiəl] *n.* **1.** trahison *f.* **2** révélation *f* (de son ignorance, etc.).

betrayer [bi'treiər] *n.* (*a*) traître, -esse; (*b*) révélateur, -trice (d'un secret).

betrothal [bi'trouðəl] *n. Lit:* fiançailles *fpl.*

betrothed [bi'trouðd] *a. & n. Lit:* fiancé(e).

better¹ ['betər] **1.** *a. & n.* meilleur; **they have seen b. days,** ils ont connu des jours meilleurs; **you will find no b. hotel,** vous ne trouverez pas mieux comme hôtel; **he's a b. man than you,** il est votre supérieur; **you are b. than I am,** vous êtes plus fort que moi; **he is no b. than his brother,** il ne vaut pas mieux que son frère; **to appeal to s.o.'s b. feelings,** faire appel aux bons sentiments de qn; **I had hoped for b. things,** j'avais espéré mieux; **for the b. part of the day,** pendant la plus grande partie du jour; *P:* **my b. half,** ma (chère) moitié, ma légitime. **2.** *adv. & a.* mieux; (*a*) **that's b.,** voilà qui est mieux; **nothing could be b., it couldn't be b.,** c'est on ne peut mieux; **so much the b.,** tant mieux; (*in marriage ceremony*) **to take s.o. for b. or for worse,** prendre qn pour les bons comme pour les mauvais jours; **to get b.,** (i) (*of thgs*) s'améliorer; (*of wine, etc.*) rabonnir; se bonifier; (ii) (*of pers.*) se remettre, se rétablir; **the weather is b.,** il fait meilleur; **to be b. (in health),** aller, se porter, mieux; **I hope you will soon be b.,** j'espère que vous serez bientôt rétabli; **change for the b.,** amélioration *f*; changement *m* en bien; **he has changed for the b.,** il a changé à son avantage; **things are taking a turn for the b.,** les choses prennent meilleure tournure; **to get the b. of s.o.,** (i) l'emporter sur qn; prendre le dessus sur qn; (ii) (*cheat*) refaire qn, mettre qn dedans; **to get the b. of (sth.),** surmonter, vaincre (un obstacle, etc.); maîtriser (sa colère, etc.); **his shyness got the b. of him,** sa timidité l'a repris; **to be (all) the b. for doing sth.,** se trouver mieux d'avoir fait qch.; **I think all the b. of you for it,** je vous en estime d'autant plus; **you will be all the b. for it,** vous vous en trouverez (d'autant) mieux; **all the b. (for me)!** tant mieux (pour moi)! **to go one b. than s.o.,** (r)enchérir, surenchérir, faire une surenchère, sur qn; (*b*) **it is b. that it should be so,** il vaut mieux qu'il en soit ainsi; **it is b. to do without it,** il vaut mieux, mieux vaut, s'en passer; **it would be b. for you to go,** il vaudrait mieux que vous y alliez. **3.** *adv.* (*a*) mieux; **b. and b.,** de mieux en mieux; **I know that b. than you,** je sais cela mieux que vous; **to know s.o. b.,** mieux connaître qn; **the more I know him the b. I like him,** plus je le connais plus je l'aime; **I can understand it all the b. because . . .,** je le conçois d'autant mieux que . . .; **you had b. stay,** il vaut mieux que vous restiez; **I had b. begin by . . .,** je ferai bien de commencer par . . .; **we'd b. be going back,** il est temps de rebrousser chemin; **you had b. not,** ne vous en avisez pas; **to think b. of it,** changer d'opinion, se raviser; **you'll think b. of it,** vous en reviendrez; **to think b. of s.o. for doing sth.,** estimer qn davantage d'avoir, pour avoir, fait qch.; **b. still,** (i) mieux encore; (ii) qui mieux est; (iii) ce qui serait mieux; (*b*) **b. dressed,** mieux habillé; **b. known,** plus connu; **b. looking,** (i) de meilleure mine; (ii) plus jolie; **b. tempered,** d'une humeur plus égale; **to be b. off,** (i) être plus à son aise (matériellement); (ii) se trouver dans de meilleures conditions; **he is b. off where he is,** il est bien mieux où il est; **the children of b.-off parents,** les enfants de parents aisés.

better² **1.** *v.tr.* (*a*) améliorer (qch.); rendre (qch.) meilleur; rabonnir (le vin, etc.); **to b. oneself,** améliorer sa condition; (*b*) surpasser (un exploit, un ouvrage); **can you b. that?** pouvez-vous faire mieux que cela? **2.** *v.i.* (*of thg*) s'améliorer, devenir meilleur; (*of wine, etc.*) se bonifier, (se) rabonnir.

better³, bettor ['betər] *n.* parieur, -euse.

betterment ['betəmənt] *n.* **1.** amélioration *f.* **2.** plus-value foncière, *pl.* plus-values.

between [bi'twi:n] **1.** *prep.* entre; (*a*) entre (deux maisons, etc.); **a table stood b. him and the door,** une table le séparait de la porte; **to stand b. two opponents,** s'interposer, intervenir, entre deux adversaires; **no one can come b. us,** personne ne peut nous séparer; **to be b. life and death,** être entre la vie et la mort; **the truth is b. the two,** la vérité est entre les deux, dans l'entre-deux; **to be something b. . . . and . . .,** tenir le milieu entre . . . et . . .; (*b*) **b. eight and nine o'clock,** entre huit et neuf heures; **b. now and Monday,** d'ici (à) lundi; **b. twenty and thirty,** de vingt à trente; (*c*) **you must choose b. them,** il faut choisir entre les deux; **to distinguish b. A, B, and C,** distinguer entre A, B, et C; (*d*) **we bought it b. us,** nous l'avons acheté à nous deux, à nous trois, etc.; **b. the two, the three, of them,** à eux deux, à eux trois; **they scored 1500 b. them,** ils ont marqué 1500 à eux (i) deux; (ii) tous; (*e*) **they shared the loot b. them,** ils se sont partagé le butin; **b. ourselves . . .,** entre nous; **this is strictly b. ourselves, b. you and me,** que cela reste entre nous; *F:* **b. you (and) me and the gatepost,** (soit dit) entre nous; **there is no love lost b. them,** ils ne peuvent pas se souffrir, se sentir. **2.** *adv.* **(in) b.,** (i) entre les deux; (ii) dans l'intervalle; **we attended two meetings and had lunch (in) b.,** nous avons assisté à deux séances et avons déjeuné dans l'intervalle.

between-decks [bi'twi:n'deks] *Nau:* **1.** *adv.* dans l'entrepont. **2.** *n.* l'entrepont *m.*

between-season [bi'twi:n'si:zn] *n.* demi-saison *f*, *pl.* demi-saisons.

betweentime(s), betweenwhile(s) [bi'twi:ntaim(z), -wail(z)] *adv.* dans l'intervalle *m*, dans les intervalles; entre-temps.

betwixt [bi'twikst] *adv. F:* **it's b. and between,** c'est entre les deux.

bevel[1] ['bev(ə)l] *n.* **1.** (*a*) biseau *m*; **b. edge,** bord biseauté, en chanfrein; **b. cut,** fausse coupe; (*b*) conicité *f* (d'un engrenage, etc.); **b. gear,** engrenage à biseau; **b. drive,** transmission *f* par pignons. **2. b. rule, b. square,** fausse équerre.

bevel[2] *v.* **(bevelled,** *NAm:* **beveled) 1.** *v.tr.* biseauter, chanfreiner; tailler (qch.) en biseau; **to b. off a corner,** dégraisser un coin. **2.** *v.i.* (*of thg*) biaiser; aller de biais; aller en biseau. **bevelled,** *NAm:* **beveled** *a.* (bord) biseauté, en biseau, en chanfrein. **bevelling,** *NAm:* **beveling** *n.* biseautage *m*, équerrage *m*, chaufreinage *m.*

beverage ['bevəridʒ] *n.* boisson *f*; **alcoholic b.,** boisson alcoolisée; *Can:* **b. room,** bar *m.*

bevy ['bevi] *n.* **1.** bande *f*, troupe *f*; **b. of girls,** bande de jeunes filles. **2.** *Ven:* volée *f* (d'alouettes, de cailles); harde *f*, troupe (de chevreuils).

bewail [bi'weil] *v.tr.* pleurer (qch.); se lamenter sur (son sort).

beware [bi'wɛər] *v.ind.tr. & Poet: v.tr.* (*used only in inf. and imp.*) se méfier, se défier (**of s.o.,** de qn); se garder (**of sth.,** de qch.); prendre garde (**of sth.,** à qch.); **b.!** prenez garde! **b. of pickpockets,** attention aux pickpockets; **b. of the dog** = chien méchant; **to b. of doing sth.,** se garder de faire qch.

bewilder [bi'wildər] *v.tr.* (*a*) désorienter, dérouter (qn); troubler (qn); (*b*) abasourdir (qn). **bewildered** *a.* (*a*) désorienté; ahuri; (air) hébété; (*b*) abasourdi, confondu. **bewildering** *a.* déroutant; ahurissant.

bewilderment [bi'wildəmənt] *n.* (*a*) désorientation *f*; trouble *m*, confusion *f*; (*b*) abasourdissement *m.*

bewitch [bi'witʃ] *v.tr.* ensorceler; (*a*) jeter un sort sur (qn); (*b*) enchanter (qn). **bewitching** *a.* (sourire) ravissant.

bey [bei] *n.* bey *m.*

beyond [bi'jɔnd] **1.** *adv.* au-delà, par-delà, plus loin; **the ocean and the lands b.,** l'océan *m* et les terres au-delà. **2.** *prep.* au-delà de, par-delà; (*a*) (*place*) **the house is b. the church,** la maison est au-delà de, plus loin que, l'église; **b. the seas,** par-delà les mers; au-delà des mers; **to be b. the pale,** être au ban de la société; (*b*) (*time*) **b. a certain date,** passé une certaine date; **b. the usual hour,** plus tard que d'ordinaire; (*c*) (*surpassing*) **b. all praise,** au-dessus de tout éloge; **to live b. one's means,** vivre au-delà, de ses moyens; **it's b. me,** cela me dépasse; je n'y comprends rien; **circumstances b. our control,** circonstances indépendantes de notre volonté; **it's b. my power,** cela passe ma capacité; **it's b. my power to save him,** je suis impuissant à le sauver; **I will not go b. what I said,** je m'en tiens à ce que j'ai dit; **b. doubt,** hors de doute, sans le moindre doute; **b. question,** indiscutablement; incontestablement; **fact b. doubt, question,** fait avéré; **b. belief,** incroyable(ment); à ne pas y croire; **b. measure,** outre mesure, sans mesure; **that's (going) b. a joke,** cela dépasse les bornes (de la plaisanterie); **b. repair,** irréparable; (*of sick pers.*) **he is b. recovery,** il n'est plus possible de le sauver; (*d*) (*except*) **he has nothing b. his wages,** il n'a rien que son salaire. **3.** *n.* **the b.,** l'au-delà *m*; **at the back of b.,** tout au bout du monde; **he lives at the back of b.,** il habite un trou perdu.

bezel ['bezəl] *n.* **1.** biseau *m*, bezel *m* (d'une pierre taillée). **2.** chaton *m.* (de bague).

bi-annual [bai'ænjuəl] *a.* semestriel. **-ally** *adv.* deux fois par an.

bias[1] ['baiəs] *n.* **1.** *Dressm:* biais *m*; **material cut on the b.,** étoffe coupée en biais, de biais; **b. binding,** ruban *m* en biais. **2.** *Sp:* (*bowls*) (*a*) décentrement *m*; (*b*) déviation (due au décentrement). **3. to have a b. towards s.o., sth.,** avoir un parti pris pour qn, pour qch.; pencher vers (une opinion, etc,). **4.** *Elcs:* **grid b.,** polarisation *f* de la grille; **b. winding,** enroulement *m* de polarisation.

bias[2] *v.tr.* (*p.t. & p.p.* **bias(s)ed) 1.** *Sp:* (*bowls*) altérer le centre de gravité de (la boule). **2.** rendre (qn) partial; prédisposer; prévenir (qn) (**towards, in favour of,** en faveur de; **against,** contre); influencer (qn). **3.** *Elcs:* polariser (la grille). **bias(s)ed** *a.* **1.** *Sp:* (*bowls*) (boule) décentrée. **2.** *Tex:* (tissu) en fil biais. **3.** partial; **b. opinion,** opinion préconçue. **4.** *Stat:* **b. sample,** échantillon biaisé, avec erreur systématique; **b. error,** erreur *f* systématique.

bib [bib] *n.* **1.** bavette *f*, bavoir *m* (d'enfant). **2.** bavette (de tablier); *F:* **in one's best b. and tucker,** sur son trente-et-un.

bible ['baibl] *n.* Bible *f*; **a B.,** une Bible; **B. class,** classe *f* d'instruction religieuse; **B. stories,** histoires tirées de la Bible; **this dictionary is his b.,** il fait de ce dictionnaire sa bible.

biblical ['biblik(ə)l] *a.* biblique.

bibliographer [bibli'ɔgrəfər] *n.* bibliographe mf.

bibliographic(al) [bibliə'græfik(ə)l] *n.* bibliographique; (*at end of book*) **b. note,** souscription *f.*

bibliography [bibli'ɔgrəfi] *n.* **1.** (*study*) bibliographie *f.* **2.** liste *f* bibliographique; bibliographie.

bibliophile ['bibliəfail] *n.* bibliophile *mf.*

bibulous ['bibjuləs] *a.* (*pers.*) adonné à la boisson.

bicameral (bai'kæmərəl] *a.* bicaméral; **b. system,** bicamérisme.

bicarb [bai'kɑ:b] *n. F:* bicarbonate *m* de soude.

bicarbonate [bai'kɑ:bəneit] *n.* bicarbonate *m* (de soude, etc.).

bicentenary ['baisen'ti:nəri], **bicentennial** ['baisen'teniəl] *a. & n.* bicentenaire (*m*).

biceps ['baiseps] *n. Anat:* biceps *m.*

bicker ['bikər] *v.i.* se quereller, se chamailler. **bickering** *n.* querelles *fpl*; chamailleries *fpl.*

bicolour(ed), *NAm:* **colour(ed)** ['bai'kʌlər, -'əd] *a. Bot: etc:* bicolore.

biconcave ['bai'kɔŋkeiv] *a.* biconcave.
biconvex ['bai'kɔnveks] *a.* biconvexe.
bicycle¹ ['baisikl] *n.* bicyclette *f*; vélo *m*; **to ride a b.,** faire de la bicyclette, du vélo; **b. track,** piste *f* cyclable.
bicycle² *v.i.* faire de la bicyclette; aller à bicyclette.
bid¹ [bid] *n.* **1.** (*a*) enchère *f*, offre *f*, mise *f*; **higher, further, b.,** offre supérieure; surenchère *f*; **closing, last, b.,** dernière mise, dernière enchère; **takeover b.,** offre publique d'achat; (*b*) **to make a b. for power,** (i) viser au pouvoir; (ii) tenter un coup d'état; (*c*) *Cards:* (*bridge*) appel *m*; (*solo whist, boston*) demande *f*; **b. of two diamonds,** appel de deux carreaux; **no b.!** passe! **2.** *U.S:* soumission *f* (dans une adjudication).
bid² *v.tr. & i.* (*p.t.* **bade** [bæd, beid] **bid;** *p.p.* **bidden** [bidn], **bid**) **1.** *A. & Lit:* commander, ordonner (**s.o. do sth.,** à qn de faire qch.); **to b. s.o. (to) be silent,** ordonner à qn de se taire; commander le silence à qn. **2.** (*a*) (*b*) **to b. s.o. welcome,** souhaiter la bienvenue á qn; **to b. s.o. goodbye,** dire au revoir, faire ses adieux, à qn; (*c*) **the weather bids fair to be fine, to improve,** le temps s'annonce beau. **3.** (*p.t. & p.p.* **bid**) (*a*) (*at auction*) **to b. for sth.,** (i) faire une offre pour qch.; (ii) mettre une enchère sur qch.; **to b. ten pounds,** faire une offre de dix livres; (*b*) *Cards:* **to b. three diamonds,** demander, appeler, trois carreaux; (*c*) *U.S:* faire une soumission (**on sth.,** pour qch.).
bidding *n.* **1.** commandement *m*, ordre *m*; **to do s.o.'s b.,** exécuter les ordres de qn. **2.** enchères *fpl*, mises *fpl*; **to start the b. at £5000,** commencer les enchères à £5000.
bidder ['bidər] *n.* **1.** (*at sale*) enchérisseur *m*; **there were no bidders,** il n'y a pas eu de prenants; **the highest b.,** le plus offrant; le dernier enchérisseur. **2.** *Cards:* demandeur, -euse; déclarant, -ante.
bide [baid] *v.tr.* **(bided) to b. one's time,** attendre l'heure, son heure; attendre le bon moment.
bidet ['bi:dei] *n. Hyg:* bidet *m* (de toilette).
biennial [bai'enjəl] **1.** *a.* biennal. **2.** *a. & n. Bot:* **b. (plant),** plante bisannuelle. **-ally** *adv.* tous les deux ans.
bier [biər] *n.* civière *f* (pour un cercueil, un mort).
biff¹ [bif] **1.** *n. P:* baffe *f*. **2.** *int.* v'lan! pan!
biff² *v.tr. P:* flanquer une baffe à (qn).
bifocal [bai'fouk(ə)l] *a. Opt:* bifocal; *n.pl.* **bifocals,** verres bifocaux, à double foyer.
bifurcate ['baifə:keit] *v.tr. & i.* bifurquer.
bifurcation [baifə:'keiʃ(ə)n] *n.* bifurcation *f*.
big [big] **1.** *a.* **(bigger** ['bigər]; **biggest** ['bigist]) (*a*) grand; (*bulky*) gros; **b. hotel,** grand hôtel; **b. man,** (i) homme de grande taille; (ii) gros homme; (iii) homme important; **b. enough to defend oneself,** de taille à se défendre; **to earn b. money,** gagner gros; **b. drop in prices,** forte baisse de prix; **to be doing a b. trade,** faire de grosses affaires; **he had b. ideas,** il voyait grand; **that's b. of you,** (i) c'est généreux, magnanime, de votre part; (ii) *Iron:* grand merci! **the b. names in the theatre world,** les gens importants du théâtre; *F:* **b. pot, shot, noise, gun,** gros bonnet, *P:* grosse légume; *Th:* **the b. scene,** la grande scène; *Sp:* **b. field (of starters),** champ fourni; **to grow big(ger),** (i) grandir; (ii) grossir; *F:* **he's getting too b. for his boots,** il se croit important; **you're the biggest fool of the lot!** c'est vous le plus bête de tous! **he's not a b. eater,** il n'est pas gros mangeur; **the b. toe,** le gros orteil; **b. drum,** grosse caisse; *F:* **a b. A,** un A majuscule; **my b. brother,** mon frère aîné; **B. Brother,** (i) chef *m* d'un État autoritaire; (ii) État qui exerce un paternalisme autoritaire; **to be in the b. time,** (i) être en haut de l'échelle; (ii) être le dessus du panier; **b.-time actor,** acteur *m* de premier rang; (*of circus*) **b. top,** chapiteau *m*; *I.C.E:* **b. end,** tête *f* de bielle; *Ven:* **b. game,** (i) gros gibier; (ii) les grands fauves; (*b*) **b. with child,** grosse (d'enfant); enceinte; **b. with consequences,** gros, lourd, de conséquences. **2.** *adv.* **to talk b.,** (i) se vanter; faire l'important; (ii) le prendre de haut; **to think b.,** avoir des idées larges, voir grand; *F:* **to go over, go down, b.,** décrocher le grand succès.
bigamist ['bigəmist] *n.* bigame *mf*.
bigamous ['bigəməs] *a.* bigame; **b. marriage,** bigamie *f*.
bigamy ['bigəmi] *n.* bigamie *f*.
big-bellied ['big'belid] *a.* ventru, pansu.
big-boned ['big'bound] *a.* fortement charpenté.
biggish ['bigiʃ] *a.* (*a*) assez grand; (*b*) assez gros.
bighead ['bighed] *n. F:* (*a*) crâneur,-euse (*b*) *NAm:* suffisance *f*, prétention *f*.
bigheaded ['big'hedid] *a. F:* crâneur.
bigheadedness ['big'hedidnis] *n. F:* suffisance *f*, prétention *f*.
big-hearted ['big'hɑ:tid] *a.* **to be b.-h.,** avoir du cœur.
bight [bait] *n.* **1.** *Nau:* double *m*, bal(l)ant *m*, anse *f* (d'un cordage). **2.** *Geog:* enfoncement *m* (d'une côte); crique *f*, anse (peu profonde et assez étendue); **the Great Australian B.,** la Grande Baie Australienne; le Grand Golfe Australien, de l'Australie.
bigmouth ['bigmauθ] *n. P:* gueulard, -arde.
bigness ['bignis] *n.* **1.** grandeur *f*. **2.** grosseur *f*.
bigot ['bigət] *n.* **1.** fanatique *mf* (en politique, etc.); sectaire *mf*. **2.** (*religious*) bigot, -ote.
bigoted ['bigətid] *a.* **1.** fanatique; à l'esprit étroit. **2.** (*in religion*) bigot.
bigotry ['bigətri] *n.* **1.** fanatisme *m*; étroitesse *f* d'esprit. **2.** (*in religion*) bigotisme *m*, bigoterie *f*.
bigwig ['bigwig] *n. F:* personnage important; gros bonnet, *P:* grosse légume.
bijou ['bi:ʒu:] *n.* bijou, -oux *m*; objet *m* d'art de facture délicate; **b. flat,** petit appartement coquet.
bike¹ [baik] *n. F:* (*a*) vélo *m*; bécane *f*; (*b*) moto *f*.
bike² *v.i. F:* (*a*) faire (i) du vélo, (ii) de la moto; (*b*) aller (i) à, en, vélo, (ii) à, en, moto (**to,** à).
bikini [bi'ki:ni] *n. Cost:* bikini *m*; deux-pièces *m. inv.*
bilabial [bai'leibiəl] *a. & n. Ling:* (consonne) bilabiale (*f*).
bilateral [bai'lætər(ə)l] *a.* (accord, etc.) bilatéral; *Med:* **b. paralysis,** diplégie *f*. **-ally** *adv.* bilatéralement.
bilberry ['bilbəri] *n. Bot:* airelle *f*, myrtille *f*.
bile [bail] *n. Physiol:* bile *f*; **b. duct,** canal *m* biliaire; **b. stones,** calculs *mpl* biliaires.
bilge [bildʒ] *n.* **1.** *Nau:* (*a*) fond *m* de cale; **b. pump,** pompe *f* de drain, de cale; (*b*) **b. (water),** eau *f* de cale; *F:* **to talk a lot of b.,** dire des bêtises *fpl*; bafouiller. **2.** bouge *m* (d'une barrique).
bilharzia [bil'hɑ:ziə] *n. Med:* **1.** bilharzia *f*, bilharzie *f*. **2.** bilharziose *f*.
biliary ['biliəri] *a. Physiol:* biliaire.
bilingual [bai'liŋgw(ə)l] *a.* bilingue.
bilingualism [bai'liŋgwəlizm] *n.* bilinguisme *m*.
bilious ['biliəs] *a.* **1.** bilieux; (tempérament) cholérique; **b. attack,** crise *f* de foie. **2.** *F:* colérique.
biliousness ['biliəsnis] *n.* affection bilieuse.
bilk [bilk] *v.tr.* **1.** tromper (qn); payer (qn) en monnaie de singe. **2.** laisser (qn) en plan; filouter qn).
bilker ['bilkər] *n.* escroc *m* (*esp.* qui s'enfuit sans payer qn).
bill¹ [bil] *n.* **1.** bec *m* (d'oiseau, d'ancre). **2.** *Geog:* bec, promontoire *m*.
bill² *v.i.* (*of birds*) se becqueter; *F:* (*of couple*) **to b. and coo,** faire les tourtereaux; se faire des mamours.
bill³ *n.* **1.** *Com:* note *f*, facture *f*, mémoire *m*; (*in restaurant*) addition *f*; **to make out a b.,** rédiger une facture; **to foot the b.,** payer la note. **2.** *Com: Fin:*

(*a*) effet *m* (de commerce); billet *m*; **bills,** valeurs *fpl*; papier *m* (bancable); **long(-dated), short(-dated) bills,** papier, effets, à longue, courte, échéance; **day b.,** effet à date fixe; **b. of exchange,** lettre *f* de change; **b. book,** carnet *m* d'échéances; **b. broker,** courtier *m*, agent *m*, de change; (*b*) *NAm:* billet de banque; **five-dollar b.,** billet de cinq dollars; (*c*) *Adm:* bon *m* (de l'Amirauté, etc.); **exchequer b.,** bon du Trésor britannique. **3.** *Th: etc:* affiche *f*; placard *m*; *P.N:* **stick no bills!** défense d'afficher; (*of actor*) **to head, top, the b.,** être en vedette sur l'affiche; faire tête d'affiche; (*of play*) **to fill the b.,** tenir l'affiche; *F:* **that will fill, fit, the b.,** cela fera l'affaire; **double b.,** programme de deux pièces, films, etc. **4.** (*a*) **b. of fare,** carte *f* du jour, menu *m*; (*b*) *Nau:* **b. of health,** patente *f* de santé; **b. of lading,** (i) connaissement *m*; police *f* de chargement; (ii) *Rail: U.S:* feuille *f* d'expédition; *Cust:* **b. of entry,** déclaration *f* d'entrée (en douane); (*c*) **b. of sale,** acte *m*, contrat *m*, de vente; facture; (*d*) **wages b.,** masse globale des salaires; *Civ.E:* **b. of quantities,** devis *m*. **5.** *Pol:* (*a*) projet *m* de loi; (*private*) proposition *f* de loi; **to pass, reject, a b.,** adopter, repousser, un projet de loi; (*b*) *Hist:* **B. of Rights,** (i) la Loi de 1689 déterminant les droits du citoyen anglais; (ii) *U.S:* les amendements de 1791 à la Constitution de 1787. **6.** *Jur:* résumé des chefs d'accusation (présenté au jury); *U.S:* (*of Grand Jury*) **to find a true b. against s.o.,** déclarer fondés les chefs d'accusation.

bill⁴ *v.tr.* **1.** (*a*) facturer (des marchandises); (*b*) **to b. s.o. for sth.,** envoyer une facture à qn pour qch. **2.** afficher (une vente, un spectacle, etc.); annoncer (une vente) par voie d'affiches; mettre (une pièce) à l'affiche; (*of event*) **billed as the greatest show on earth,** annoncé, affiché, comme le plus grand spectacle du monde. **billing** *n. Th: etc:* affichage *m*; (*of actor*) **to get top b.,** faire tête d'affiche.

billboard ['bilbɔːd] *n.* panneau *m* d'affichage.

billet¹ ['bilit] *n.* **1.** *Mil:* (*a*) billet *m* de logement; (*b*) (i) logement *m* (chez l'habitant); (ii) cantonnement *m*. **2.** logement (d'un évacué). **3.** *F: O:* situation *f*, emploi *m*.

billet² *v.* **(billeted) 1.** *v.tr.* (*a*) *Mil:* **to b. troops on s.o., on, in, a town,** loger des troupes chez qn; cantonner des troupes dans une ville; (*b*) loger (un évacué; **on,** chez). **2.** *v.i.* loger (**with,** chez). **billeting** *n.* cantonnement *m*; logement *m* chez l'habitant; **b. officer,** officier de cantonnement.

billet³ *n.* **1.** rondin *m*, bille *f*, billette *f* (de bois de chauffage, etc.); bois *m* de quartier. **2.** *Metall:* billette, larget *m* (d'acier); lopin *m*.

billfold ['bilfould] *n. NAm:* portefeuille *m*.

billhook ['bilhuk] *n. Tls:* vouge *m*; serpe *f*; croissant *m* (à élaguer); serpette *f*; courbet *m*.

billiard ['biliəd] *n.* **1.** (*a*) *pl. usu. with sg. const.* (jeu *m* de) billard (*m*); **bar billiards,** billard russe; **to play billiards,** jouer au billard; (*b*) **b. ball, cue,** bille *f*, queue *f*, de billard; **b. room,** (salle *f* de) billard; **b. table,** billard. **2.** *NAm:* carambolage *m*.

billion ['biliən] *n.* **1.** billion *m* (10^{12}). **2.** *NAm:* milliard *m* (10^9).

billow¹ ['bilou] *n.* grande vague; lame *f* (de mer); *Lit:* **the billows,** les flots *mpl*.

billow² *v.i.* (*of the sea*) se soulever en vagues; (*of crowds, flames, etc.*) ondoyer.

billowy ['biloui] *a.* (flot) houleux; (mer) houleuse.

billposter, billsticker ['bilpoustər, -stikər] *n.* afficheur *m*; colleur *m* d'affiches; placardeur *m*.

billposting, billsticking ['bilpoustiŋ, -stikiŋ] *n.* affichage *m*, placardage *m*.

Billy ['bili] **1.** *Pr.n.m.* (*dim. of William*) Guillaume. **2.** *n.* **billy,** *pl.* **billies** ['biliz]; (*a*) *Austr: N.Z:* gamelle *f*; bouilloire *f* (à thé); (*b*) **b. (club),** (i) *P:* gourdin *m*; (ii) *NAm:* matraque *f*.

billycan ['bilikæn] *n.* = BILLY 2 (*a*).

billy-goat ['biligout] *n.* bouc *m*.

billy-o(h) ['biliou] *adv.phr. F: O:* **it's raining like b.-o.,** il pleut à verse.

bimetallic [baimi'tælik] *a.* **1.** *Pol.Ec:* (système) bimétallique. **2.** *Tchn:* **b. strip,** bilame *f*.

bimetallism [bai'metəlizm] *n. Pol.Ec:* bimétallisme *m*.

bimonthly [bai'mʌnθli] **1.** *a. & n.* (*a*) bimensuel (*m*); semi-mestriel; (*b*) bimestriel; *n.* revue, publication, bimestrielle. **2.** *adv.* (*a*) bimensuellement, deux fois par mois; (*b*) tous les deux mois.

bin [bin] *n.* **1.** (*a*) coffre *m*, huche *f*, bac *m*; **litter b.,** boîte *f* à ordures; (*b*) compartiment *m*, casier *m*; **wine b.,** casier à bouteilles; porte-bouteilles *m inv.*; (*c*) **cement b.,** silo *m* à ciment; *Min:* **ore b.,** réservoir *m*, caisson *m*, à minerai. **2.** *P:* **loony b.,** maison *f* de fous.

binary ['bainəri] **1.** *a. Mth: etc:* binaire. **2.** *a. & n. Astr:* **b. (star),** binaire (*f*.)

bind¹ [baind] *n.* **1.** *Mus:* ligature *f*, liaison *f*. **2.** *Hort:* sarment *m*, tige *f*, liane *f* (de houblon, etc.). **3.** *Min:* couche *f* d'argile dure (entre deux couches de houille). **4.** *F:* (*a*) (*thg*) scie *f*; **what an awful b.!** quelle barbe! (*b*) *U.S:* **to be in a b.,** être en mauvaise passe.

bind² *v.* (*p.t. & p.p.* **bound** [baund]) **I.** *v.tr.* **1.** (*a*) attacher, lier (qch.); lier, attacher, ligoter (un prisonnier); **to b. s.o. hand and foot,** lier pieds et poings à qn; **they are bound together by a close friendship,** ils sont liés d'une étroite amitié; (*b*) **they are very much bound up in each other,** ils sont très attachés l'un à l'autre; **the present is bound up with the past,** le présent se relie au passé; (*c*) **to b. sth. (down) to, on, sth.,** attacher qch. à qch.; **to b. (on) one's skis,** fixer ses skis. **2.** (*a*) **to b. (up),** bander, panser (une blessure); (*b*) border (un manteau, un chapeau); brider (une boutonnière); (*c*) fretter (une roue, une poutre, etc.). **3.** (*a*) **to b. (up) a sheaf,** lier une gerbe; **to b. (up) one's hair,** se faire un chignon; (*b*) relier (un livre); **bound in boards,** cartonné; **bound in cloth,** relié toile; (*with passive force*) **your book is binding,** votre livre est à la reliure; (*c*) lier, agglutiner (du sable, etc.); cohérer, fixer (la poussière d'une route); **stones bound together with cement,** pierres liées avec du ciment. **4.** (*a*) (*of pers., obligation, promise, etc.*) lier, engager (qn); **to b. s.o. to pay a debt,** astreindre, obliger, qn à payer une dette; **to b. oneself to do sth.,** s'engager à faire qch.; *Jur:* **to b. s.o. over to keep the peace,** exiger de qn sous caution qu'il ne se livrera à aucune voie de fait; **to be bound over,** être sommé par un magistrat d'observer une bonne conduite; (*b*) **to be bound to do sth.,** être obligé, tenu, de faire qch.; devoir faire qch.; **you are in duty bound to do it,** votre devoir vous y oblige; **to be in honour bound to do sth.,** être engagé d'honneur à faire qch.; **to be bound by an oath,** être engagé sous serment, lié par un serment; (*c*) **he's bound to come,** il ne peut pas manquer de venir; **it's bound to rain tomorrow,** il pleuvra sûrement demain; **it's bound to happen,** c'est fatal; (*d*) *F:* **he'll come, I'll be bound,** il viendra, j'en suis sûr, je vous le promets; (*e*) *NAm:* **he's bound to come and see you,** il veut absolument venir vous voir. **II.** *v.i.* **1.** (*of gravel, etc.*) se lier, s'agglomérer, s'agglutiner; (*of cement*) durcir, prendre. **2.** *F:* se plaindre; ronchonner. **binding 1.** *a.* (*a*) (agent) agglomérant, agglutinant; (*b*) obligatoire (**upon s.o.,** pour qn); **b. agreement,** obligation *f* irrévocable; **agreement b. (up)on s.o.,** contrat *m* qui lie qn; **decision b. on all parties,** décision *f* obligatoire pour tous; (*c*) *Med:* astringent, constipant. **2.** *n.* (*a*) agglutination *f*; agrégation *f*; **b. material,** matière agglomérante, d'agrégation; liant *m*, agglomérant *m* (d'une route); (*b*) fixation *f*; serrage *m*; cerclage *m* (d'une roue); (*c*) *Mec.E: etc:* coincement *m*, blocage *m*; (*d*) lien *m*, ligature *f*; bandage *m* (d'une poutre, etc.); (*e*) *Sp:* fixation (de ski); **safety (release) bindings,** fixations de sécurité; (*f*) reliure *f* (d'un livre); **quarter b.,** demi-reliure *f*; **cloth b.,** reliure en toile; **limp b.,** cartonnage *m* souple; **perfect b.,** reliure arraphique, sans couture; (*g*) bordure *f*, liséré *m* (d'une robe, etc.); *Furn:* **upholstery b.,** galon *m* de finition.

binder [ˈbaindər] *n.* **1.** (*pers.*) (*a*) *Agr:* lieur, -euse; (*b*) (*bookbinder*) relieur, -euse. **2.** (*a*) *Agr:* (*machine*) lieuse *f* (de gerbes); (*for hay*) botteleuse *f*; **b. twine,** ficelle *f* à lier; (*b*) *Needlew:* ourleur *m* (d'une machine à coudre). **3.** lien *m* (de gerbe, fagot) **4. (spring-back) b.,** biblorhapte *m* (pour papiers); relieur *m*. **5.** (*a*) *Cu:* liant *m* (d'une sauce); (*b*) *Civ.E:* liant; agglomérant *m*; matériau *m* d'agrégation. **6.** (*a*) *Carp:* entrait *m*; sommier *m* (de plancher); (*b*) *Const:* parpaing *m*. **7.** (*binding clip*) étrier *m* de serrage, de pression. **8.** *Com:* convention *f* liant le vendeur.

bindery [ˈbaind(ə)ri] *n.* atelier *m* de reliure.

bindweed [ˈbaindwiːd] *n. Bot:* liseron *m*.

binge [bin(d)ʒ] *n. F:* bombe *f*; **to go on a b.,** faire la bombe, la noce.

bingo [ˈbiŋgou] **1.** *n.* (sorte de) loto (joué collectivement). **2.** *int.* et voilà!

binnacle [ˈbinəkl] *n. Nau:* habitacle *m*.

binocular [biˈnɔkjulər, bai-] **1.** *a.* (vision, etc.) binoculaire. **2.** *n.pl.* **binoculars,** jumelles *fpl*.

binomial [baiˈnoumiəl] **1.** *a.* (*a*) *Mth:* (facteur, etc.) binôme; **the b. theorem,** le binôme de Newton; le théoreme de Newton. **2.** *n.* binôme *m*.

biochemic(al) [ˈbaiouˈkemik(əl)] *a.* biochimique.

biochemist [ˈbaiouˈkemist] *n.* biochimiste *mf*.

biochemistry [ˈbaiouˈkemistri] *n.* biochimie *f*.

biodegradable [baioudiˈgreidəbl] *a.* biodégradable.

biogenesis [baiouˈdʒenisis] *n. Biol:* biogénèse *f*.

biographer [baiˈɔgrəfər] *n.* biographe *m*, auteur *m* d'une biographie.

biographic(al) [baiəˈgræfik(l)] *a.* biographique; **b. novel,** vie, biographie, romancée.

biography [baiˈɔgrəfi] *n.* biographie *f*.

biologic(al) [baiəˈlɔdʒik(l)] *a.* biologique; **b. warfare,** guerre *f* bactériologique. **-ally** *adv.* biologiquement.

biologist [baiˈɔlədʒist] *n.* biologiste *mf*.

biology [baiˈɔlədʒi] *n.* biologie *f*.

bionics [baiˈɔniks] *n.pl.* (*usu. with sg. const.*) bionique *f*.

biophysics [baiouˈfiziks] *n.* (*usu. with sg. const.*) biophysique *f*.

biopsy [ˈbaiɔpsi, baiˈɔpsi] *n. Surg:* biopsie *f*.

bioscope [ˈbaiəskoup] *n.* **1.** bioscope *m*. **2.** (*in S. Africa*) cinéma *m*.

biosynthesis [baiouˈsinθəsis] *n.* biosynthèse *f*.

biotechnology [baioutekˈnɔlədʒi] *n.* ergonomie *f*.

biotope [ˈbaiətoup] *n. Nat.Hist:* biotope *m*, habitat *m*.

bipartisan [baipɑːtiˈzæn] *a. Pol: etc:* biparti(te).

bipartite [baiˈpɑːtait] *a.* **1.** *Nat.Hist:* biparti(te). **2.** *Jur:* (document) rédigé en double.

biped [ˈbaiped] *a. & n.* bipède (*m*).

biplane [ˈbaiplein] *n. Av:* (avion) biplan (*m*).

bipolar [baiˈpoulər] *a. El: Physiol: etc:* bipolaire.

birch¹ [bəːtʃ] *n.* **1.** *Bot:* (*a*) bouleau *m*; **silver b.,** bouleau blanc; (*b*) **b. (wood),** (bois *m* de) bouleau. **2. b. (rod),** verge *f*; **to give s.o. the b.,** donner les verges, le fouet, à qn; fouetter qn.

birch² *v.tr.* donner les verges, le fouet, à (qn); fouetter (qn). **birching** *n.* fouettée *f*.

bird [bəːd] *n.* **1.** (*a*) oiseau *m*; **song b.,** oiseau chanteur; **cage b.,** oiseau d'appartement; *F:* **a little bird told me,** mon petit doigt me l'a dit; **night b.,** (i) oiseau de nuit, nocturne; (ii) (*pers.*) coureur, -euse, de nuit; noctambule *mf*; **b. of passage,** oiseau de passage, passager; **I'm just a b. of passage,** je ne suis que de passage; **b. of prey,** oiseau de proie; rapace *m*; **b. of paradise,** oiseau de paradis; paradisier *m*; *F:* **to give s.o. the b.,** (i) envoyer promener qn; (ii) *Th: etc:* huer, siffler, qn; chahuter qn; *Prov:* **the early b. catches the worm,** heure du matin, heure du gain; **to be an early b.,** être matinal; *Prov:* **a b. in the hand is worth two in the bush,** un 'tiens' vaut mieux que deux 'tu l'auras'; mieux vaut tenir que courir; *U.S: F:* **it's (strictly) for the birds,** c'est de la roupie de sansonnet; **b. shot,** cendrée *f*; **b. house,** volière *f*; **b. fancier,** (i) oiselier *m*; aviculteur *m*; (ii) connaisseur *m* en oiseaux; **b. table,** mangeoire *f* pour les oiseaux (dans un jardin); **bird's nest,** (i) nid *m* d'oiseau; (ii) *Cu:* nid d'hirondelle; **to go b. nesting,** aller dénicher des oiseaux; *F:* **to be b. brained,** avoir une cervelle de moineau; (*b*) **(farmyard) b.,** volaille *f*; (*c*) *Ven:* **the birds are shy this year,** le gibier est timide cette année. **2.** (*a*) *F:* type *m*, individu *m*; **he's a queer b.,** c'est un drôle d'individu; **a home b.,** un casanier, une casanière; (*b*) *P:* (*woman*) nana *f*. **3.** (*a*) volant *m* (de jeu de badminton); (*b*) *Sp:* pigeon artificiel. **4.** *Mil: F:* engin téléguidé. **5.** *P:* prison *f*; **to do b.,** faire de la taule.

birdbath [ˈbəːdbɑːθ] *n.* bain *m* pour les oiseaux.

birdcage [ˈbəːdkeidʒ] *n.* cage *f* (d'oiseau); (*large*) volière *f*.

birdcall [ˈbəːdkɔːl] *n.* **1.** cri *m* d'oiseau. **2.** *Ven:* appeau *m*, pipeau *m*, chanterelle *f*.

birdcatcher [ˈbəːdkætʃər] *n.* oiseleur *m*.

birdie [ˈbəːdi] *n. F:* **1.** gentil petit oiseau. **2.** *Golf:* (trou "fait" en) un coup de moins que la normale.

birdlike [ˈbəːdlaik] *a.* avien; comme (d')un oiseau.

birdlime [ˈbəːdlaim] *n.* glu *f*.

birdseed [ˈbəːdsiːd] *n.* millet *m*; graines *fpl* pour oiseaux.

bird's-eye [ˈbəːdzai] *n.* **1.** (*a*) *Bot:* véronique *f*; (*b*) **b.-e. mahogany,** acajou moucheté; **b.-e. maple,** érable madré, à broussin; (*c*) *Tex:* œil-de-perdrix *m*, *pl.* œils-de-perdrix. **2.** (*a*) **b.-e. view,** vue *f* à vol d'oiseau; photographie aérienne oblique; *Cin:* prise *f* de vues en plongeon; *Fig:* **b.-e. view of the situation,** résumé *m* de la situation.

bird's-foot [ˈbəːdzfut] *n. Bot:* pied-d'oiseau *m*, *pl.* pieds-d'oiseau; **b.-f. trefoil,** lotier *m*, corne *f* du diable.

birdwatcher [ˈbəːdwɔtʃər] *n.* observateur, -trice, d'oiseaux.

birdwatching [ˈbəːdwɔtʃiŋ] *n.* observation *f* des oiseaux (dans leur milieu naturel).

biretta [biˈretə] *n. Ecc.Cost:* barrette *f*.

biro [ˈbairou] *n.* (*R.t.m*) (marque de) stylo *m* (à) bille.

birth [bəːθ] *n.* **1.** (*a*) naissance *f*; **to give b. to a child,** mettre au monde, donner naissance à, un enfant; **Irish by b.,** Irlandais de naissance; **from b.,** (aveugle, etc.) de naissance; (délicat) dès, depuis, sa naissance; **b. certificate,** (i) acte *m*, (ii) extrait *m*, de naissance; **b. control,** contrôle *m*, limitation *f*, des naissances; **b. rate,** (taux *m* de) natalité (*f*); (*b*) genèse *f* (d'une idée, etc.); naissance (d'une nouvelle industrie, etc.); (*c*) enfantement *m*, couches *fpl*, accouchement *m*; **premature b.,** accouchement prématuré, avant terme; **b. pangs,** (i) douleurs *fpl* d'accouchement; (ii) *Fig:* l'accouchement difficile (d'un nouveau système, etc.). **2.** mise *f* bas (d'un animal); **to give b. to a litter,** mettre bas une portée.

birthday [ˈbəːθdei] *n.* anniversaire *m*; jour *m* de

naissance; date *f* de naissance; **happy b.!** bon, joyeux anniversaire! **b. present,** cadeau *m* d'anniversaire; **B. Honours,** distinctions honorifiques accordées à l'occasion de l'anniversaire du souverain; *F:* **to be in one's b. suit,** être dans le, en, costume d'Adam.

birthmark ['bəːθmɑːk] *n.* envie *f*; tache *f* de vin.

birthplace ['bəːθpleis] *n.* (*a*) lieu *m* de naissance; (*b*) berceau *m* (d'une religion, etc.).

birthright ['bəːθrait] *n.* **1.** droit *m* d'aînesse. **2.** droit de naissance, droit du sang; patrimoine *m*.

birthstone ['bəːθstoun] *n. Astrol: etc:* pierre *f* porte-bonheur.

Biscay ['biskei] *Pr.n. Geog:* **the Bay of B.,** le golfe de Gascogne.

biscuit ['biskit] *n.* **1.** (*a*) biscuit *m*; **(sweet) biscuits,** gâteaux secs; **ship's b.,** biscuits de mer; **dog b.,** biscuit, gâteau, de chien; **b. factory,** biscuiterie *f*; *F: O:* **that takes the b.!** ça, c'est le bouquet! (*b*) *NAm:* petit gâteau (feuilleté). **2.** *Cer:* **b. ware,** biscuit. **3.** *a. & n.* (*colour*) biscuit (*m*).

bisect [bai'sekt] **1.** *v.tr. Mth: etc:* couper, diviser, (une ligne, un angle) en deux parties égales; bissecter (un angle, etc.). **2.** *v.i.* (*of road, etc.*) bifurquer.

bisection [bai'sekʃ(ə)n] *n.* bissection *f*.

bisector [bai'sektər] *n.* ligne *f* de bissection, bissectrice *f*.

bisexual [bai'seksjuəl] *a. Bot: Psy:* bis(s)exué, bis(s)exuel.

bishop ['biʃəp] *n.* **1.** *Ecc:* évêque *m*; **bishop's palace,** palais épiscopal; évêché *m*. **2.** *Chess:* fou *m*. **3.** (*mulled wine*) bi(s)chof *m*.

bishopric ['biʃəprik] *n.* (*office or diocese*) évêché *m*.

bisk [bisk] *n.* = BISQUE³.

bismuth ['bizməθ] *n. Miner: Pharm:* bismuth *m*.

bison ['baisən] *n.* bison *m* (de l'Amérique septentrionale).

bisque¹ [bisk] *n. Golf: Ten:* bisque *f*.

bisque² *n. Cer:* (*a*) biscuit *m*; (*b*) porcelaine blanche sans couverte.

bisque³ **1.** *Cu:* bisque *f* (de homard, etc.). **2.** *NAm:* glace *f* (i) aux noix, (ii) aux macarons.

bistre ['bistər] *a. & n.* bistre (*m*).

bisulphite [bai'sʌlfait] *n. Ch:* bisulfite *m*; **sodium b.,** sulfite *m* acide de sodium, de soude.

bit [bit] *n.* **1.** *Harn:* mors *m* (d'une bride); **to champ the b.,** (i) (*of horse*) mâcher son mors; (ii) (*of pers.*) ronger son frein; (*of horse, pers.*) **to take the b. between its, one's, teeth,** prendre le mors aux dents; s'emballer. **2.** *Tls:* (*a*) mèche *f* (de vilebrequin); foret *m*; (*b*) mors (d'une tenaille, d'un étau); ciseau *m* (d'un rabot); (*c*) **copper b., soldering b.,** fer *m* à souder, soudoir *m*.

bit² *n.* **1.** (*a*) morceau *m* (de pain, etc); **he has eaten every b.,** il a tout mangé; *F:* **she's a nice little b.,** c'est une jolie fille; **made of bits and pieces,** *F:* **bits and bobs,** fait de pièces et de morceaux, *F:* de bric et de broc; *F:* **my bits and pieces,** mes affaires *fpl*; *Th:* **b. part,** rôle *m* de figurant; (*b*) bout *m* (de papier, de ficelle, etc.); brin *m* (de paille, etc.); **a (little) b. of** hope, un petit brin d'espoir; **to do one's b.,** y aller de sa personne, y mettre du sien; *F:* **to make a b.,** faire sa pelote; **to make a b. on the side,** faire de la gratte; (*c*) *F:* (*coin*) pièce *f*; *A:* **threepenny b.,** pièce de trois pence; *NAm:* **two bits,** vingt-cinq cents. **2.** (*a*) **a b.,** un peu (**of,** de); **a tiny, little, b.,** un tout petit peu; **I'm a b. late,** je suis un peu en retard; **he's a b. jealous,** il est quelque peu jaloux; **he's a b. of an artist,** il est un peu artiste; *F:* **he's a b. of a lad,** il aime (i) faire la bombe, (ii) courir les jupes; **wait a b.!** attendez un peu! **that takes a b. of doing,** ça c'est bien compliqué; **a good b. older,** sensiblement plus âgé; *F:* **it's a b. much!** ça c'est vraiment trop fort! **b. by b.,** peu à peu, petit à petit; **not a b. (of it)!** pas du tout! **I don't care a b.,** cela m'est bien égal; **it's not a b. of use,** cela ne sert absolument à rien; (*b*) **a b. of news,** une nouvelle; **a b. of luck,** une chance; une aubaine; (*c*) **to tear sth. to bits,** déchirer qch. en morceaux; **smashed to bits,** brisé (en mille morceaux); **to take sth. to bits,** démonter qch.; **in bits,** en morceaux.

bit³ *n. Cmptr:* bit *m*.

bitch¹ [bitʃ] *n.f.* **1.** (*a*) chienne; **terrier b.,** terrier *m* femelle; (*b*) femelle (de renard, etc.); **wolf b., b. wolf,** louve. **2.** *P:* garce; (vieille) chipie; **she's a little b.,** c'est une petite rosse.

bitch² *P:* **1.** *v.tr.* gâcher (un travail); **he bitched up the whole business for us,** il nous a tout bousillé. **2.** *v.i.* rouspéter.

bitchy ['bitʃi] *a. P:* garce; vache; **that was a b. thing to do!** quel tour de vache!

bite¹ [bait] *n.* **1.** (*a*) coup *m* de dent: *Dent:* articulé *m* dentaire; (*b*) *Fish:* touche *f*; **I haven't had a b. all day,** je n'ai pas eu une seule touche de toute la journée; (*c*) *esp. U.S:* **to put the b. on s.o.,** toucher qn (pour 100 dollars, etc.). **2.** (*a*) (*wound*) morsure *f*; (*b*) piqûre *f*, morsure (d'un insecte). **3.** *F:* bouchée *f*, morceau *m*; **would you like a b. (to eat)?** voulez-vous manger quelque chose? **I haven't had a b. all day,** je n'ai rien mangé de la journée; **to take a big b. out of sth.,** mordre dans qch. à pleine bouche. **4.** (*a*) *Tchn:* mordant *m* (de lime, etc.); (*b*) piquant *m* (d'une sauce, d'un vin); (*c*) adhérence *f* (des roues à la surface, etc.); (*d*) *Engr:* corrosion *f* (d'une plaque par l'acide).

bite² *v.tr. & i.* (*p.t.* **bit** [bit]; *p.p.* **bitten** [bitn]) **1.** (*a*) mordre; donner un coup de dent à (qn, qch.); (*of insect*) piquer; **the dog bit him in the leg,** le chien l'a mordu à la jambe; **to b. one's lips, one's nails,** se mordre les lèvres, se ronger les ongles; **to b. the dust,** mordre la poussière; **the fish is biting,** le poisson mord (à l'hameçon); **does the dog b.?** est-ce que le chien est méchant? *Prov:* **once bitten twice shy,** chat échaudé craint l'eau froide; **to get bitten,** se faire mordre; se faire piquer; *F:* **what's bitten him?** quel chien l'a mordu? quelle mouche le pique? (*b*) *Austr: F:* **to b. s.o.,** toucher qn (pour 10 dollars, etc.). **2.** (*of wind, cold*) couper (le visage, etc.); (*of pepper*) piquer (la langue); **acid bites (into) metal,** l'acide mord, attaque, le métal. **3.** *v.i.* (*of screw, file*) mordre (**on,** sur); (*of tool*) mordre, s'engager; (*of anchor*) mordre, prendre fond; **screw that won't b.,** vis *f* qui foire. **bite back** *v.tr.* ravaler (une réplique). **bite off** *v.tr.* enlever, détacher, (qch.) d'un coup de dent(s); *F:* **to b. s.o.'s head off,** rembarrer qn; **to b. off more than one can chew,** tenter qch. au-dessus de ses forces. **biting** *a.* (*of cold*) cuisant, âpre, perçant; (*of wind*) cinglant, piquant; (*of style, wit,*) mordant, caustique; **b. irony,** ironie amère.

bitter ['bitər] **1.** *a.* (goût) amer; (vin) acerbe; (vent) aigre, piquant; (ennemi) implacable; (conflit) aigu; (temps) rigoureux; (ton) aigre, âpre; (froid, vent) glacial, cinglant; (bière) amère; **b. hatred,** haine acharnée; **b. tears,** larmes amères; **b. disappointment,** cruelle déception; **b. experience,** amère déception; expérience cruelle; **to feel, be, b. about sth.,** ressentir de l'amertume de qch.; *Fig:* **to go on, to resist, to the b. end,** aller, résister, jusqu'au bout. **2.** *n.* (*a*) bière amère; (*b*) **bitters,** (*n*) bitter(s) *m(pl)*, amer(s) *m(pl)*. **-ly** *adv.* amèrement; avec amertume; **it was b. cold,** il faisait un froid de loup; **to cry b.,** pleurer amèrement; **b. disappointed,** cruellement déçu.

bittern ['bitə(ː)n] *n. Orn:* butor *m*.

bitterness ['bitənis] *n.* **1.** (*a*) amertume *f* (d'une boisson, etc.); (*b*) rigueur *f*, âpreté *f* (du temps); amertume (de la douleur); aigreur *f*, acrimonie *f* (de paroles, d'une querelle); l'âpreté (des reproches). **2.** rancune *f*, rancœur *f*.

bittersweet [ˈbitəswiːt] **1.** *a.* aigre-doux, -douce. **2.** *n. Bot:* douce-amère *f*, *pl.* douces-amères.

bitty [ˈbiti] *a. F:* (livre, etc.) d'un style décousu.

bitumen [ˈbitjumin] *n.* (*a*) *Ch: Miner:* bitume *m*; goudron minéral; asphalte minéral; (*b*) *Austr: F:* route goudronnée.

bituminous [biˈtjuːminəs] *a.* bitumineux; **b. coal,** houille grasse, collante.

bivalent [ˈbaiˈveilənt] *a. Ch:* bivalent.

bivalve [ˈbaivælv] *a. & n. Moll:* bivalve (*m*).

bivouac¹ [ˈbivuæk] *n. Mil: etc:* bivouac *m*.

bivouac² *v.i.* **(bivouacked; bivouacking)** bivouaquer.

bi-weekly [ˈbaiˈwiːkli] **1.** *a.* (*a*) de tous les quinze jours; (*b*) semi-hebdomadaire. **2.** *adv.* (*a*) tous les quinze jours; (*b*) deux fois par semaine.

bizarre [biˈzɑːr] *a.* bizarre. **-ly** *adv.* bizarrement.

bizarreness [biˈzɑːnis] *n.* bizarrerie *f*.

blab¹ [blæb] **blabber** [ˈblæbər] *esp U.S:* **blabbermouth** [ˈblæbəmauθ] *n. F:* jaseur, -euse; bavard, -e.

blab² *v.* **(blabbed; blabbing)** *F:* **1.** *v.i.* jaser, bavarder; causer (indiscrètement); *F:* vendre la mèche. **2.** *v.tr.* **to b. out,** divulguer, laisser échapper (un secret).

black¹ [blæk] **I.** *a.* **1.** noir; (*a*) **b. dress,** robe noire; **b. hair,** cheveux noirs; **(jet-)b. horse,** cheval moreau; **b. and tan (dog),** (chien) noir et feu *inv.* **b. coffee,** café noir; *esp. SW.Fr:* café nature; **b. spot,** (i) (*on furniture, etc.*) noircissure *f*; (ii) *Aut: etc:* point noir; endroit *m* à accidents; *Hist:* **the B. Death,** la Peste Noire; *Jur:* **the B. cap,** le bonnet noir (que coiffait le juge en prononçant une condamnation à mort); *Av:* **b. box,** boîte noire; **to be in s.o.'s b. books,** être mal vu de qn; *Meteor:* **b. ice,** verglas *m*; *Can:* **b. blizzard,** tourbillon *m* de poussière; *Geog:* **the B. Sea,** la Mer noire; **the B. Forest,** la Forêt noire; *Cu:* **b. pudding,** boudin *m*; (*in balloting*) **b. ball,** noire *f*; *Ind:* **to declare a ship, a firm, b.,** mettre un navire, une entreprise, à l'index; **b. with age,** noirci par le temps; **it, the night, was pitch b.,** il faisait noir comme dans un four; **to look as b. as thunder,** avoir l'air furieux; **to give s.o. a b. look,** regarder qn d'un air furieux; **things are looking b.,** les affaires prennent une mauvaise tournure; **to paint things blacker than they are,** noircir la situation; **to beat s.o. b. and blue,** meurtrir, rosser, qn de coups; **to be b. and blue all over,** être tout meurtri (de coups); **b. eye,** œil poché, *F:* œil au beurre noir; (*b*) **the b. races,** les races noires; **a b. man, woman,** un noir, une noire; (*c*) (visage, etc.) sale, noir; **his hands were b.,** il avait les mains sales, toutes noires; *Geog:* **the B. Country,** le Pays Noir (de l'Angleterre). **2.** (*a*) (nuage, ciel, etc.) sombre; (*b*) **he's in one of his b. moods,** il est dans ses mauvais jours; (*c*) **the b. art, b. magic,** la magie noire; **b. mass,** messe noire; (*d*) (humour, plaisanterie, comédie) macabre; (*e*) **b. market,** marché noir; **b. marketeer,** profiteur *m* du marché noir. **II.** *n.* noir *m*. **1. animal b.,** noir animal; **carbon b.,** noir de fumée, de pétrole. **2.** (*a*) **she always wears b.,** elle porte toujours le noir; elle est toujours en noir; (*b*) *F:* **in the b.,** solvable; sans dettes; (*c*) **to work in b. and white,** faire du dessin à l'encre, au crayon noir; **b.-and-white postcard,** carte *f* en noir; **b. and white television,** télévision *f* en noir et blanc; **I have his consent in b. and white,** j'ai son consentement par écrit; **I should like to have it in b. and white,** je voudrais avoir cela dans les formes; (*d*) *Gaming:* **the b.,** le noir. **3.** (*a*) (*pers.*) Noir, -e; (*b*) cheval noir; (*c*) (*in snooker*) la bille noire. **4.** (*smut*) (*a*) noiré *m*, flocon *m* de suie; (*b*) *Agr:* charbon *m*, suie *f*, brûlure *f*, nielle *f* (des céréales).

black² **1.** *v.tr.* noicir (qch.); **to b. one's face,** se charbonner le visage; **to b. s.o.'s eye,** pocher l'œil à qn; donner à qn un œil au beurre noir. **2.** *v.tr. Ind:* refuser de travailler avec (une compagnie, un homme non syndiqué); mettre (un navire, une entreprise) à l'index. **3.** *v.i. Nau:* **to b. down,** galipoter. **blacking** *n.* **1.** (*a*) noircissement *m*; (*b*) *Ind:* mise *f* à l'index (d'un navire, d'une entreprise). **2.** (*a*) *Nau:* galipot *m*; (*b*) *A:* cirage *m* (à chaussures). **black out** **1.** *v.i.* (*a*) devenir obscur; s'éteindre; (*b*) occulter, voiler, masquer, les lumières; faire le black-out; *Th:* éteindre la rampe, couper la lumière; *Cin:* fermer en fondu; (*c*) (i) perdre connaissance, s'évanouir; (ii) avoir un trou de mémoire. **2.** *v.tr.* (*a*) effacer, rayer (qch.) (d'un gros trait noir); (*b*) (i) éteindre, (ii) voiler, masquer, les lumières dans (une maison, etc.); faire le black-out dans (une maison).

blackball [ˈblækbɔːl] *v.tr.* blackbouler (qn). **blackballing** *n.* blackboulage *m*.

blackbeetle [ˈblækbiːtl] *n. Ent: F:* (*a*) blatte *f*, cafard *m*, cancrelat *m*; (*b*) escarbot *m*.

blackberry [ˈblækb(ə)ri] *n.* mûre *f* (de ronce); mûre sauvage; **b. bush,** ronce *f*, mûrier *m*, des haies.

blackberrying [ˈblækberiiŋ] *n.* **to go b.,** aller cueillir des mûres; aller à la cueillette des mûres.

blackbird [ˈblækbəːd] *n. Orn:* (*a*) merle (noir); (*b*) *NAm:* (variété d')étourneau *m*.

blackboard [ˈblækbɔːd] *n.* tableau noir.

black-bordered [ˈblækˈbɔːdəd] *a.* à bordure noire.

blackcap [ˈblækkæp] *n. Orn:* fauvette *f* à tête noire.

blackcock [ˈblækkɔk] *n. Orn:* tétras *m* lyre; coq des bouleaux.

blackcurrant [ˈblækkʌrənt] *n.* (*bush or fruit*) cassis *m*.

blacken [ˈblæk(ə)n] **1.** *v.tr.* noircir (un mur, la réputation de qn); obscurcir (le ciel); (*with smoke*) enfumer (du papier, du verre); **to b. s.o.'s character,** calomnier qn. **2.** *v.i.* (se) noircir; devenir noir; s'assombrir; (*of painting, portrait*) **to b. with age,** pousser, tirer, au noir. **blackening** *n.* noircissement *m*.

black-faced [ˈblækfeist] *a.* **1.** à la figure noire. **2.** *Typ:* (caractère) gras.

blackfly [ˈblækflai] *n. Ent: F:* mouche noire.

blackguard [ˈblægɑːd] *n. A:* fripouille *f*; canaille *f*.

blackhead [ˈblækhed] *n.* comédon *m*; point noir (sur le visage, etc.).

blackheart [ˈblækhɑːt] *a. & n.* **b. (cherry),** guigne noire.

blackish [ˈblækiʃ] *a.* noirâtre, tirant sur le noir.

blackjack [ˈblækdʒæk] *n.* **1.** *U.S:* nerf *m* de bœuf. **2.** outre *f* en cuir vernie de noir. **3.** *Cards:* vingt-et-un *m*.

blacklead¹ [ˈblækled] *n.* mine *f* de plomb; plombagine *f*, graphite *m*.

blacklead² *v.tr. O:* passer (un poêle, etc.) à la mine de plomb.

blackleg¹ [ˈblækleg] *n. Ind: F:* renard *m*; jaune *m*.

blackleg² *v.* **(blacklegged; blacklegging)** *Ind:* **1.** *v.tr.* prendre la place (des grévistes, etc.). **2.** *v.i.* trahir ses camarades.

blacklist¹ [ˈblæklist] *n.* liste noire; **to be on the b.,** être noté, suspect.

blacklist² *v.tr.* inscrire, mettre (qn, une entreprise, etc.) sur la liste noire.

blackmail¹ [ˈblækmeil] *n.* chantage *m*; extorsion *f* (sous menace de scandale).

blackmail² **1.** *v.tr.* soumettre (qn) à un chantage; *F:* faire chanter (qn); **to be blackmailed,** être victime d'un chantage. **2.** *v.i.* faire du chantage.

blackmailer [ˈblækmeilər] *n.* maître-chanteur *m*, *pl.* maîtres-chanteurs.

blackness [ˈblæknis] *n.* **1.** noirceur *f*. **2.** obscurité *f*.

blackout [ˈblækaut] *n.* **1.** (*a*) occultation *f*; black-out *m*; (i) extinction *f*, (ii) camouflage *m*, des lumières; (*b*) panne *f* d'électricité; (*c*) *Cin:* fermeture *f* en fondu. **2.** (i) évanouissement *m*; (ii) trou *m* de mémoire.

Blackshirt [ˈblækʃəːt] *n. Pol:* fasciste *m*; chemise noire.

blacksmith ['blæksmiθ] *n.* forgeron *m*; maréchal ferrant.

blackthorn ['blækθɔːn] *n.* **1.** *Bot:* épine noire, prunier épineux, prunellier *m.* **2.** gourdin *m* (d'épine).

blackwater ['blækwɔːtər] *a. Med:* **b. fever,** hématurie *f.*

bladder ['blædər] *n.* (*a*) vessie *f*; (*b*) vésicule *f*; **gall b.,** vésicule biliaire; **air b.,** (i) *Ich:* vésicule aérienne; (ii) *Algae:* vésicule aérocyste *f*; (*c*) vessie (de ballon).

bladderworm ['blædəwəːm] *n. Vet:* cysticerque *m.*

bladderwort ['blædəwəːt] *n. Bot:* utriculaire *f.*

bladder-wrack ['blædəræk] *n. Algae:* goémon jaune vésiculeux.

blade [bleid] *n.* **1.** brin *m* (d'herbe); pampe *f* (de blé); *Bot:* limbe *m.* **2.** (*a*) lame *f* (de couteau, d'épée, *Bot:* de feuille); couperet *m* (de la guillotine); feuille *f*, lame (d'une scie); **razor b.,** lame de rasoir; (*b*) sabre *m* ou épée *f.* **3.** pale *f* (d'aviron, d'hélice); pelle *f* (d'aviron); ailette *f* (de ventilateur, de turbine); aube *f* (de roue hydraulique); fer *m* (de bêche); *Rail:* aiguille *f* (de croisement); *Aut:* balai *m* (d'un essuie-glace); *Cin:* **blades of a shutter,** pales, secteurs *mpl*, d'un obturateur. **4.** *Anat:* **shoulder b.,** omoplate *f.*

bladebone ['bleidboun] *n.* **1.** *Anat:* omoplate *f.* **2.** *Cu:* paleron *m*; macreuse *f.*

bladed ['bleidid] *a.* à lame(s), à aile(s), à pales; **three-b.,** (canif) à trois lames; (hélice) à trois ailes.

blah(-blah) ['blɑː(blɑː)] *n. F:* bla-bla-bla *m*, baratin *m*; **it's all b.(-b.),** tout ça c'est de la blague.

blame¹ [bleim] *n.* **1.** reproches *mpl*; condamnation *f*; **to deserve b.,** mériter des reproches; **to be free from b.,** être au-dessus de tout reproche. **2.** responsabilité *f*; faute *f*; **to lay, put, the b. (for sth.) on s.o., to lay the b. (for sth.) at s.o.'s door,** rejeter, faire retomber, le blâme, la faute (de qch.) sur qn; **to bear, take, the b.,** supporter le blâme; endosser la faute; **to shift the b. on to s.o. else,** s'excuser sur qn; se décharger d'une faute sur qn.

blame² *v.tr.* **1.** blâmer, condamner (qn); **to b. s.o. for sth.,** blâmer qn de qch.; reprocher qch. à qn; attribuer (un malheur, etc.) à qn; **he can't be blamed for it,** on ne peut pas l'en blâmer; **I have nothing to b. myself for,** je n'ai rien à me reprocher; **to have only oneself to b., to have nobody to b. but oneself,** n'avoir à s'en prendre qu'à soi-même; **he is to b.,** c'est de sa faute. **2.** (*a*) **to b. sth. for an accident,** attribuer un accident à qch.; (*b*) **to b. sth. on s.o.,** rejeter la faute, la responsabilité, de qch. sur qn.

blameless ['bleimlis] *a.* innocent, irréprochable, irrépréhensible; (vie) sans reproche, irréprochable. **-ly** *adv.* irréprochablement.

blanch [blɑːn(t)ʃ] **1.** *v.tr.* blanchir. **2.** *v.i.* (*a*) (*of hair, etc.*) blanchir; (*b*) (*of pers.*) blêmir, pâlir.

blancmange [blə'mɔnʒ] *n. Cu:* blanc-manger *m*, *pl.* blanc-mangers.

bland [blænd] *a.* **1.** (*of pers., speech*) (*a*) doux, *f* douce; affable; (*b*) *Pej:* doucereux, mielleux; (sourire) narquois. **2.** (*of air, food, drink*) doux. **-ly** *adv.* avec affabilité; *Pej:* mielleusement.

blandish ['blændiʃ] *v.tr.* cajoler, caresser, flatter.

blandishments ['blændiʃmənts] *n.pl.* cajoleries *fpl*, câlineries *fpl*, flatterie *f.*

blank¹ [blæŋk] *a.* **1.** (*a*) (papier) blanc; (page) vierge, blanche; *Geog:* (carte) muette; **b. voting paper,** bulletin blanc; **b. space,** espace *m* vide; blanc *m*; (*b*) *Com: Fin:* **b. credit,** crédit *m* en blanc; **b. cheque,** (i) formule *f* de chèque; (ii) chèque *m* en blanc; (iii) *Fig:* carte blanche; (*c*) **to be, come, up against a b. wall,** se trouver devant l'impossible; se trouver coincé; (*d*) **b. verse,** vers blancs, non rimés; (*e*) (porte, fenêtre) feinte, aveugle; (cartouche) à blanc; (*f*) *Cards:* **to be b. in clubs,** ne pas avoir de trèfles dans son jeu. **2.** (*a*) (existence) vide; (regard) sans expression; **he gave me a b. look,** il m'a regardé d'un air incompréhensif; **my mind went b.,** je me sentais la tête vide; (*b*) **to look b.,** avoir l'air confondu, déconcerté, ahuri; **a look of b. astonishment,** un air ébahi, confondu; (*c*) profond (découragement); (impossibilité) absolue; **b. refusal,** refus absolu. **-ly** *adv.* (regarder qn) (i) sans expression, d'un air incompréhensif, (ii) d'un air déconcerté.

blank² *n.* **1.** (*a*) (*in document, etc.*) blanc *m*, vide *m*; (*in memory*) trou *m*, lacune *f*, vide; **to leave blanks,** laisser des blancs; **his mind is a b.,** (i) il ne se souvient de rien; (ii) il a, se sent, la tête vide; *Cards:* **to have a b. in clubs,** ne pas avoir de trèfles dans son jeu; (*b*) *NAm:* formulaire *m*, formule *f* (de télégramme, etc.); (*c*) cartouche *f* à blanc; **to fire blanks,** tirer à blanc; (*d*) blanc (de cible); (*e*) (*domino*) blanc; (*f*) (*in lottery*) billet blanc, perdant; **to draw a b.,** échouer; éprouver une déception. **2.** (*a*) (*in minting coins*) flan *m* (de métal); (*b*) *Metalw: Mec.E:* flan; masselotte *f*; galette *f.* **3.** (*a*) *Typ:* tiret *m* (remplaçant un mot grossier, etc.); (*b*) *Typ:* blocage *m*; (*c*) **Mr, Mrs, B.,** M., Mme, Trois-Étoiles, M. X., Mme X.

blank³ *NAm:* **1.** *v.tr.* (*a*) **to b. (out),** cacher; obscurcir; (*b*) **to b. (off),** obturer (un orifice); (*c*) *Typ:* **to b. (out),** faire le blocage. **2.** *v.i.* **to b. (out),** (i) (*of sound*) s'éteindre; (ii) (*of pers.*) avoir un trou de mémoire.

blanket¹ ['blæŋkit] *n.* **1.** couverture *f* (de lit, de cheval); manteau *m* (de brouillard, etc.); couche (de neige); **electric b.,** couverture chauffante (électrique); *Needlw:* **b. stitch,** point *m* de languette; *F:* (*pers*) **wet b.,** rabat-joie *m inv.* **2.** *attrib. Com: etc:* (terme, etc.) général.

blanket² *v.tr.* **1.** (*a*) mettre une couverture à (qch.); **the mountain was blanketed in fog,** la montagne était couverte d'un manteau de brouillard; (*b*) **to b. (out),** étouffer (un incendie, des flammes). **2.** *Nau: esp. Y:* déventer (un navire, un yacht).

blankness ['blæŋknis] *n.* **1.** air confus, décontenancé. **2.** vide *m*, néant *m* (de la pensée, etc.); vacuité *f* (d'un regard).

blare¹ ['blɛər] *n.* sonnerie *f*, son *m*, accents cuivrés (de la trompette); **the b. of the brass band,** le son éclatant de la fanfare.

blare² **1.** *v.i.* (*of trumpet*) sonner; **the band blared (out, forth),** la fanfare éclata; **the radio was blaring away,** la radio marchait à fond, à casser les oreilles. **2.** *v.tr.* **the band blared (out) a march,** la fanfare fit retentir une marche.

Blarney¹ ['blɑːni] **1.** *Pr.n.* **B. Castle,** le château de Blarney (en Irlande); **the B. Stone,** pierre située dans la muraille du château; *F:* **to have kissed the B. Stone,** avoir le don de la flatterie, de la cajolerie. **2.** *n.* **b.,** cajolerie *f*, boniments *mpl*, flatterie séduisante.

blarney² *v.tr.* cajoler (qn); séduire (qn) par des propos flatteurs.

blasé ['blɑːzei] *a.* blasé.

blaspheme [blæs'fiːm] *v.i.* blasphémer. **2.** *v.tr.* **to b. the name of God,** blasphémer le saint nom de Dieu.

blasphemer [blæs'fiːmər] *n.* blasphémateur, -trice.

blasphemous ['blæsfəməs] *a.* (*of pers.*) blasphémateur, -trice; (*of words, etc.*) blasphématoire, impie. **-ly** *adv.* avec blasphème; avec impiété; **to speak b.,** blasphémer.

blasphemy ['blæsfəmi] *n.* blasphème *m.*

blast¹ [blɑːst] *n.* **1.** bouffée *f* de vent, coup *m* de vent; rafale *f* (de vent); **b. of steam,** jet *m* de vapeur. **2.** *Nau: etc:* **b. on the whistle, on the siren,** coup *m* de sifflet, de sirène; *Mil:* **whistle b.,** commandement *m* au sifflet; **b. on the trumpet,** sonnerie *f* de trompette. **3.** *Metall:* air *m*, vent *m* (de la soufflerie); soufflerie *f*, soufflage *m* (d'un haut fourneau); **b. furnace,** haut fourneau *m*; (*of furnace*) **to be in b.,** être allumé, en marche; **out of b.,** hors feu; **to be in full b.,** être en pleine activité, travailler à plein rendement; *F:* **to turn the radio on full b.,** faire gueuler, brailler, la radio. **4.** (*a*) souffle (d'une bombe, d'une explosion, etc.); (*b*) *Min:* (i) explosion *f*, coup de mine; (ii) charge *f* d'explosif; **to fire a b.,** faire jouer une mine, faire partir un pétard; **b. hole,** (i) *Min:* pétard, trou *m* de mine; (ii) *Mil:* fourneau de mine.

blast² **1.** *v.tr.* (*a*) *Min:* faire sauter (à la dynamite, etc.); (*b*) brûler, flétrir (une plante); ruiner, briser (l'avenir de qn); détruire (le bonheur); (*of lightning*) foudroyer (un arbre, etc.); (*c*) *F:* envoyer (qn) au diable; *int.* **b. (it)!** zut! **b. you, him!** que le diable t'emporte, l'emporte! **2.** *v.i.* (*a*) (*of brass instrument*) sonner; (*b*) (*of radio, etc.*) **to b. (away),** hurler, brailler. **blasted** *a.* **1.** (lande) désolée; (chêne) foudroyé. **2.** *F:* sacré; **you b. idiot!** espèce d'idiot! **blasting** *n.* (*a*) travail *m* aux explosifs; exploitation *f* à la mine; **beware of b.!** attention aux coups de mine! (*b*) destruction *f*, anéantissement *m* (d'un espoir, etc.); ruine *f* (d'une carrière); foudroiement *m* (d'un arbre). **blast off** *v.i.* (*of rocket, missiles*) décoller.

blastoderm ['blæstoudə:m] *n. Biol:* blastoderme *m.*

blastoff ['blɑ:stɔf] *n.* décollage *m* (d'une fusée).

blatancy ['bleitənsi] *n.* **1.** vulgarité criarde. **2.** caractère flagrant (d'une injustice, etc.).

blatant ['bleitənt] *a.* **1.** (*of pers., manners*) qui s'impose désagréablement à l'oreille, à la vue; d'une vulgarité criarde. **2.** (injustice) criante; (mensonge) flagrant. **-ly** *adv.* **1.** avec une vulgarité criarde. **2.** d'une manière flagrante.

blather¹ ['blæðər] *n. F:* paroles *fpl* en l'air, bêtises *fpl.*

blather² *v.i. F:* parler à tort et à travers; dire des bêtises.

blaze¹ [bleiz] *n.* **1.** (*a*) flamme(s) *f*(*pl*), feu *m*; flambée *f*; **in a b.,** en feu, en flammes; (*b*) **b. of anger,** éclat *m* de colère; **in a b. of anger,** enflammé de colère. **2.** flamboiement *m* (du soleil); éclat (des couleurs, des diamants, etc.); **the garden was a b. of colour,** le jardin était resplendissant de couleur; **in the full b. of publicity,** sous les feux de la rampe. **3.** *F:* (*a*) **go to blazes!** allez au diable! (*b*) **what the blazes does he want?** que diable veut-il? **to work like blazes,** travailler furieusement; **to run like blazes,** courir comme un dératé.

blaze² *v.i.* (*a*) (*of fire, etc.*) flamber; (*of sun, colours*) flamboyer; **a fire was blazing in the grate,** un feu flambait au foyer; **when the firemen arrived the fire, the house, was blazing,** lorsque les pompiers sont arrivés l'incendie faisait rage, la maison était embrasée; **the sun was blazing down on the beach,** le soleil dardait, déversait, ses rayons sur la plage; (*b*) (*of pers.*) **to b. with anger,** être enflammé de colère; **his eyes were blazing with anger,** ses yeux lançaient des flammes de colère. **blazing** *a.* **1.** (*a*) en feu, enflammé; (navire) embrasé; (*b*) (feu, soleil) flambant, ardent; **b. star,** (i) *Her:* comète *f*; (ii) *Bot:* alétris *m.* (*c*) **2.** *F:* (mensonge) éclatant; **a b. row,** une dispute violente. **blaze up** *v.i.* (*a*) (*of thg*) s'embraser; s'enflammer; (*b*) *F:* (*of pers.*) s'emporter (de colère).

blaze³ *n.* **1.** (*on face of horse, ox*) marque allongée blanche. **2.** (*on tree*) **b. (mark),** blanchis *m*, griffe *f.*

blaze⁴ *v.tr.* griffer, blanchir, marteler (un arbre); **to b. a trail,** tracer un chemin; faire œuvre de pionnier; poser des jalons (dans une science, etc.). **blazing** *n.* martelage *m*, griffage *m* (des arbres).

blazer ['bleizər] *n. Cost:* blazer *m*; veston *m* de sport.

blazon¹ ['bleizən] *n. Her:* (*a*) blason *m* (composant un écu); (*b*) armoiries *fpl*; (*c*) étendard armorié.

blazon² *v.tr.* **1.** *Her:* blasonner; marquer (qch.) aux armoiries de qn. **2.** embellir, orner (de dessins héraldiques). **3.** **to b. out sth.,** publier, proclamer, qch.; **to b. news abroad,** publier une nouvelle à son de trompe.

bleach¹ [bli:tʃ] *n.* décolorant *m*; eau oxygénée; **(household) b.,** eau de Javel.

bleach² **1.** *v.tr. Tex: etc:* blanchir; *Ch: etc:* décolorer; *Hairdr:* oxygéner. **2.** *v.i.* blanchir; se décolorer. **bleaching** *n. Tex: etc:* blanchiment *m*; *Ch:* décoloration *f*; **b. agent,** produit blanchissant; décolorant *m.*

bleachers ['bli:tʃəz] *n.pl. NAm:* gradins *mpl.*

bleak¹ [bli:k] *n. Ich:* ablette *f.*

bleak² *a.* **1.** (temps) morne, triste; (terrain) exposé au vent; (vent) froid. **2.** (avenir) morne; (sourire) pâle; **the prospects are b.,** les perspectives sont peu encourageantes. **-ly** *adv.* d'un air morne; tristement.

bleakness ['bli:knis] *n.* aspect *m* morne; tristesse *f.*

bleary ['bliəri] *a.* **1.** **b.-eyed,** aux yeux troubles. **2.** (*of outline*) vague, imprécis.

bleat¹ [bli:t] *n.* (*a*) bêlement *m*; (*b*) *F:* plainte *f.*

bleat² *v.i.* (*a*) bêler; (*of ram*) blatérer; (*of goat, old man, etc.*) chevroter; (*b*) *F:* (i) se plaindre; (ii) dire des bêtises; **what's he bleating about?** de quoi se plaint-il? **bleating** **1.** *a.* (*a*) bêlant; (*b*) **b. voice,** voix chevrotante. **2.** *n.* (*a*) bêlement *m*; (*b*) plaintes *fpl.*

bleed [bli:d] *v.* (*p.t. & p.p.* **bled** [bled]) **1.** *v.tr.* (*a*) *Med:* saigner (qn); *F:* **to b. s.o. (for money),** saigner qn; extorquer de l'argent à qn; **to b. s.o. white,** saigner qn à blanc; (*b*) *Mec.E:* purger (une canalisation, etc.); (*c*) *Bookb:* trop rogner (un livre); **bled(-off) illustrations,** illustrations *fpl* à marges perdues, à fond perdu. **2.** *v.i.* (*a*) saigner; perdre du sang; **his nose is bleeding,** il saigne du nez; **to b. to death,** mourir d'effusion de sang; (*b*) (*of tree, etc.*) pleurer, perdre sa sève; (*c*) *Civ.E: etc:* (*of riveted joints; of water, gas, etc.*) fuir; (*d*) (*of colour*) s'étendre, couler (au lavage); déteindre. **bleeding** **1.** *a.* (*a*) saignant; **with a b. heart,** le cœur navré de douleur; (*b*) *Bot:* **b. heart,** cœur-de-Marie *m*, *pl.* cœurs-de-Marie; cœur-de-Jeannette *m*, *pl.* cœurs-de-Jeannette; (*c*) *P:* sacré; **you b. liar!** sacré menteur! **2.** *n.* (*a*) écoulement *m* de sang; *Bot:* écoulement de sève; (*of vine, etc.*) pleurs *mpl*; **b. at the nose,** saignement *m* de nez; **I can't stop the b.,** je n'arrive pas à arrêter le sang; (*b*) *Med:* saignée *f*; (*c*) *Civ.E: etc:* fuite *f* (d'eau, de gaz, etc.,).

bleeder ['bli:dər] *n.* **1.** *Med: F:* hémophilique *mf.* **2.** *P:* (*a*) salaud *m*; (*b*) **poor b.,** pauvre type *m.* **3.** *Tchn:* dispositif *m* de drainage.

bleep [bli:p] *v.i.* (*of satellite, radio signal*) faire bip-bip. **bleeping** *n.* bip-bip *m* (d'un satellite, etc.).

bleep(-bleep) *n.* bip-bip *m* (d'un satellite, etc.).

bleeper ['bli:pər] *n.* récepteur *m* d'appel, de poche.

blemish¹ ['blemiʃ] *n.* **1.** défaut *m*; imperfection *f* (physique ou morale). **2.** tache *f*, tare *f.*

blemish² *v.tr.* **1.** tacher, entacher, ternir (une réputation, etc.). **2.** abîmer, gâter (une œuvre d'art, etc.).

blench¹ [blen(t)ʃ] *v.i.* sourciller, broncher; **without blenching,** sans sourciller.

blench² *v.i.* blêmir; **to b. with terror,** pâlir de terreur.

blend¹ [blend] *n.* mélange *m* (de thés, de whiskys, de tabacs; *F:* de races, etc.).

blend² **1.** *v.tr.* (*a*) **to b. sth. with sth.,** mêler qch. à, avec, qch.; joindre, unir, qch. à qch.; **to b. one colour with another,** (i) mélanger une couleur avec une autre; (ii) fondre deux couleurs; (iii) allier, marier, deux couleurs; (*b*) (re)couper (des vins, des whiskys); mélanger (des thés, des cafés); **our teas are carefully blended,** nos thés sont mélangés avec soin. **2.** *v.i.* se mêler, se mélanger, se confondre (**into,** en); (*of voices, etc.*) se marier harmonieusement; (*of colours*) s'allier, se marier; se raccorder; (*of ideas, etc.*)

fusionner; **the colours b. well,** les couleurs sont bien agencées, vont bien ensemble. **blending** *n.* mélange *m* (de thés, de tabacs, etc.); alliance *f* (de deux qualités); *Winem:* assemblage *m*, coupage *m*; *Ch: Metall:* alliage *m* (de métaux); fusion *f* (d'idées, etc.).

blender ['blendər] *n. Dom.Ec:* mixer *m*, mixeur *m*.

bless [bles] *v.tr.* (*p.t. & p.p.* **blessed** [blest]; *p.p. occ.* **blest** [blest]) bénir. **1. to b. God,** bénir, adorer, Dieu. **2.** (*of God, priest*) bénir (le peuple); consacrer, bénir (une cloche); **God b. (you)!** que (le bon) Dieu vous bénisse! *F:* (*when s.o. sneezes*) **(God) b. you!** à vos souhaits! que Dieu vous bénisse! **3. to be blessed, blest, with sth.,** jouir de qch.; avoir le bonheur de posséder qch.; **to be blessed with a cheerful disposition,** être doué d'un heureux caractère; *F:* **he hasn't a penny to b. himself with,** il n'a pas le sou. **4. I b. my lucky stars, that . . .,** je bénis mon étoile de ce que . . .; **b. me! b. my soul!** *O:* **b. my heart!** mon Dieu! **well, I'm blest!** par exemple! **I'm blest if I know,** que le diable m'emporte si je le sais. **blessed** ['blesid] *a.* (*a*) **the B. Virgin,** la Sainte Vierge; (*b*) *R.C.Ch: etc:* bienheureux; **the late king, of b. memory,** le feu roi, d'heureuse mémoire; **b. are the poor in spirit,** heureux les pauvres en esprit; (*c*) *F:* **every b. day,** tous les jours que Dieu fait; **the whole b. day,** toute la sainte journée; **the whole b. lot,** tout le bazar, tout le bataclan. **blessing** *n.* bénédiction *f*; **to give, pronounce, the b.,** donner la bénédiction; (*at meal*) **to ask, say, a b.,** dire le bénédicité; **the blessings of God,** les grâces *fpl* de Dieu; **the blessings of civilization,** les avantages *mpl*, bienfaits *mpl*, de la civilisation; **it turned out to be a b. in disguise,** à la longue nous avons pu nous en féliciter; **to count one's blessings,** s'estimer heureux avec ce qu'on a; **he gave the plan his b.,** il a donné sa bénédiction au projet. **blest** *a.* bienheureux; *n.pl.* **the B.,** les Bienheureux *mpl*; les saints *mpl* au Paradis.

blessedness ['blesidnis] *n.* béatitude *f*; félicité *f*.

blether¹ ['bleðər] *n. F:* paroles *fpl* en l'air; bêtises *fpl*.

blether² *v.i. F:* parler à tort et à travers; dire des bêtises; **blethering idiot,** espèce d'idiot.

blight¹ [blait] *n.* **1.** rouille *f* (des céréales); brunissure *f* (des pommes de terre); cloque *f* (des pêches, etc.). **2.** (*a*) influence *f* néfaste; (*b*) **his arrival cast a b. over the company,** son arrivée a jeté un froid sur la compagnie.

blight² *v.tr.* rouiller (le blé); (*of sun*) brouir; (*of wind*) flétrir; **blighted leaf,** feuille cloquée; **to b. s.o.'s hopes,** flétrir les espérances de qn.

blighter ['blaitər] *n. F:* (*a*) salaud *m*; **the little b.,** le petit coquin; (*b*) individu *m*, type *m*; **poor b.,** pauvre type; **(you) lucky b.!** veinard!

Blighty ['blaiti] *n. Mil: F: A:* l'Angleterre *f*; le pays.

blimey ['blaimi] *int. P:* mince alors!

blimp [blimp] *n.* **1.** *Aer:* (petit) dirigeable de reconnaissance. **2.** réactionnaire endurci; **a real Colonel B.,** une vraie culotte de peau, un scro(n)gneugneu.

blind¹ [blaind] *a.* **1.** (*a*) aveugle; **b. from birth,** aveugle-né(e), *pl.* aveugles-né(e)s; aveugle de naissance; **b. in one eye,** borgne; **a b. man, woman,** un, une, aveugle; *n.pl.* **the b.,** les aveugles; **it is a case of the b. leading the b.,** c'est un aveugle qui en conduit un autre; **to be struck b.,** être frappé de cécité; **he's as b. as a bat,** il est myope comme une taupe; **b. with anger,** aveuglé par la colère; **b. obedience,** soumission *f* aveugle; **to turn a b. eye on, to, sth.,** fermer les yeux sur qch., refuser de voir qch.; *Av:* **b. flying,** vol *m* sans visibilité, vol en P.S.V. (pilotage sans visibilité); (*b*) **to be b. to s.o.'s faults,** ne pas voir les défauts de qn; être aveugle aux défauts de qn; **in a b. stupor,** *F:* **b. drunk,** complètement soûl; bourré; (*b*) **b. spot,** (i) *Anat:* papille *f* optique; (ii) côté faible (de qn); (iii) angle mort; **that's his b. spot,** c'est là où où il montre des préjugés. **2.** (*a*) (virage) masqué, sans visibilité; **b. ditch,** saut *m* de loup; (*b*) *Med:* **double b. test,** épreuve pratiquée à l'insu du malade et du médecin; *F:* **b. date,** (i) rendez-vous (avec qn qu'on ne connaît pas); (ii) inconnu(e) (avec qui on a rendez-vous). **3.** (trou, fistule) borgne; (chemin, tunnel) sans issue; *Arch:* fausse (porte); (fenêtre, porte) feinte, aveugle; **b. alley,** impasse *f*; cul-de-sac *m*, *pl.* culs-de-sac; **b.-alley job,** occupation *f*, situation *f*, sans avenir; *Rail:* **b. siding,** cul-de-sac. **4.** *F:* **he didn't take a b. bit of notice,** il n'a pas fait la moindre attention. **5.** *adv.* **to fire b.,** tirer au jugé; *Av:* **to fly b.,** voler à l'aveuglette; *F:* **to go at a thing b.,** se lancer à l'aveugle dans une entreprise; **b. drunk,** complètement ivre, soûl. **-ly** *adv.* (*a*) sans y voir; à l'aveugle(tte); (obéir) aveuglément; (*b*) à l'aveugle; sans réflexion.

blind² *v.tr.* **1.** (*a*) aveugler (qn); frapper (qn) de cécité; **blinded ex-service men,** aveugles *mpl* de guerre; (*b*) aveugler, éblouir (qn); **the sun is blinding him,** le soleil l'aveugle, l'éblouit; **blinded by passion,** aveuglé par la passion; **to b. s.o., oneself, to facts,** aveugler qn, s'aveugler, sur les faits. **2.** (*a*) *Civ.E:* ensabler (une chaussée, une voie ferrée); (*b*) *Mil: Min:* blinder (une galerie, etc.). **blinding 1.** *a.* aveuglant; **b. headache,** mal de tête fou; *Aut:* **b. headlights,** phares éblouissants, aveuglants. **2.** *n.* (*a*) éblouissement *m* (par des phares, etc.); (*b*) *Civ.E:* ensablement *m*; *Mil:* blindage *m*; (*c*) *Civ.E:* couche *f* de sable (sur une route).

blind³ *n.* **1.** store *m* (à l'italienne); abat-jour *m inv*; **roller b.,** store à, sur, rouleau; **Venetian b.,** jalousie *f* (à lames mobiles); (*over pavement*) **shop b.,** banne *f*. **2.** (*a*) *Mil: Fort:* blinde *f*; (*b*) *NAm:* œillère *f* (de cheval). **3.** (*a*) prétexte *m*, masque *m*; **his attitude was only a b.,** son attitude n'était qu'un prétexte; (*b*) organisation camouflée.

blinder ['blaindər] *n.pl. NAm: Harn:* œillère *f*.

blindfold¹ ['blaindfould] **1.** *a.* les yeux bandés; *Chess:* **b. player,** joueur *m* qui joue sans voir l'échiquier. **2.** *adv.* (*recklessly*) aveuglément. **3.** *n.* bandeau *m* sur les yeux.

blindfold² *v.tr.* bander les yeux à, de (qn); couvrir les yeux de (qn) avec un bandeau.

blindman's buff ['blaindmænz'bʌf] *n. Games:* colin-maillard *m*.

blindness ['blaindnis] *n.* **1.** cécité *f*. **2.** aveuglement *m*; **b. to the facts,** refus *m* d'envisager les faits.

blindstitch¹ ['blaindstitʃ] *n. Needlew:* point perdu.

blindstitch² *v.tr. Needlew:* coudre (qch.) à points perdus.

blindworm ['blaindwəːm] *n. Rept:* orvet *m*.

blink¹ [bliŋk] *n.* **1.** battement *m*, clignotement *m*, clignement *m*, de paupières. **2.** lueur momentanée; vision momentanée. **3.** *P:* (*of television set, etc.*) **on the b.,** en panne, qui fait des siennes.

blink² **1.** *v.i.* (*a*) battre, cligner, des paupières; clignoter; ciller (les paupières); (*b*) (*of light*) papilloter; vaciller. **2.** *v.tr.* (*a*) **to b. away a tear,** refouler une larme d'un battement de paupières; (*b*) **to b. the facts,** fermer les yeux sur la vérité. **blinking 1.** *a.* (*a*) clignotant; (*b*) (feu) papillotant, clignotant; (*c*) *F: O:* **what a b. nuisance!** quelle barbe! **b. idiot!** espèce d'idiot! **2.** *n.* (*a*) clignotement *m*; (*b*) papillotage *m*.

blinker ['bliŋkər] *n.* **1.** (*a*) *Harn:* œillère *f*; (*b*) *F:* (*of pers.*) **he goes about in blinkers,** il a, il porte, des œillères. **2.** (*a*) phare *m* à éclats (sur un aérodrome); (*b*) *Aut:* clignotant *m*.

blintz(e) [blints] *n. NAm: Cu:* crêpe fourrée (au fromage, aux fruits, etc.).

blip [blip] *n. Rad:* spot *m* (sur l'écran); top *m* d'écho.

bliss [blis] *n.* béatitude *f*, félicité *f*.

blissful ['blisful] *a.* (bien)heureux; **b. days,** jours sereins. **-fully** *adv.* heureusement; **b. happy,** au comble du bonheur; **to be b. unaware that . . .,** n'avoir aucun soupçon que . . ..

blister¹ ['blistər] *n.* **1.** (*a*) (*on skin*) ampoule *f*, cloque *f*; (*b*) (*on paint*) boursouflure *f*; *Glassm:* bulle *f*; cloche *f*; *Metall:* soufflure *f*; (*c*) *Com:* **b. pack,** emballage-bulle *m inv;* (*d*) *Med:* vesicatoire *m.*

blister² **1.** *v.tr.* (*a*) faire venir les ampoules *fpl* à (la main, etc.); **blistered heel,** ampoule au talon; (*b*) *Med:* appliquer un vésicatoire sur (la peau). **2.** *v.i.* se couvrir d'ampoules; (*of paint*) cloquer; se boursoufler, gondoler. **blistering 1.** *a.* (*a*) *Med:* (emplâtre) vésicant; (*b*) (*of sun, heat*) brûlant, ardent; (*c*) (*of remark, etc.*) cinglant, mordant, caustique; (attaque) foudroyante. **2.** *n.* (*a*) *Med:* vésication *f*; (*b*) formation *f* d'ampoules (à la peau); (*c*) cloquage *m*, gondolage *m* (de la peinture).

blithe [blaið] *a.* joyeux, folâtre. **-ly** *adv.* joyeusement, allègrement.

blithering ['bliðəriŋ] *a. F:* sacré; **b. idiot!** espèce d'idiot!

blitz¹[blits] *n.* (*a*) blitz *m*; bombardement aérien; (*b*) *F:* **to have a b. on sth.,** s'attaquer à qch.

blitz² *v.tr.* bombarder; **the house was blitzed,** la maison a été endommagée, détruite, par un bombardement.

blizzard ['blizəd] *n.* blizzard *m*, tempête *f* de neige.

bloat¹ [blout] **1.** *v.tr.* boursoufler; gonfler; bouffir. **2.** *v.i.* se gonfler; se bouffir. **bloated** *a.* gonflé; bouffi; boursouflé.

bloat² *v.tr.* bouffir (des harengs).

bloater ['bloutər] *n. Com:* hareng bouffi.

blob [blɔb] *n.* **1.** tache *f* (de couleur); pâté *m* (d'encre). **2.** *Cr: F:* zéro *m*; **to make a b.,** remporter une veste.

bloc [blɔk] *n. Pol: etc:* bloc *m.*

block¹ [blɔk] *n.* **1.** (*a*) bloc *m* (de marbre, etc.); tronçon *m* (de bois); quartier *m* (de roche); carreau *m* (de pierre taillée); brique *f* (de verre); tête *f* à perruque (de coiffeur); forme *f* (pour chapeaux); sellette *f* (de décrotteur); *Aut:* **engine b.,** bloc moteur; *Toys:* **building blocks,** (jeu *m* de) cubes *mpl*; (*of pers.*) **like a b. of stone,** (i) immobile; (ii) dur; (iii) silencieux, muet; (*b*) **(chopping) b.,** billot *m*; **butcher's b.,** billot de boucher; hachoir *m*; *Hist:* **to perish on the b.,** périr sur le billot; (*c*) *Equit:* **mounting b.,** montoir *m*; *Sp:* **starting b.,** bloc de départ; (*d*) (*chock*) tin *m*, cale *f*; **angle blocks,** coins *mpl*; **to put a car up on blocks,** mettre une voiture sur cales; (*e*) sabot *m* (de frein); (*f*) *P:* tête *f*, caboche *f*; **I'll knock your b. off!** je vais t'amocher la figure! **2.** (*a*) bloc, pâté *m*, de maisons (entre quatre rues); **b. of flats,** immeuble divisé en appartements; **office b.,** immeuble de bureaux; *NAm:* **he lives two blocks from us,** il habite à deux rues de nous; **to walk round the b.,** faire le tour du pâté de maisons; (*b*) *Austr:* (i) quartier *m* (d'une ville); (ii) boulevard *m*; (*c*) *esp. Austr:* lot *m* (de terrains); (*d*) bloc (de papier, à dessin); *Fin:* **b. of shares,** tranche *f* d'actions; **b. booking,** location *f* (de places de théâtre, etc.) en bloc. **3.** (*a*) **traffic b.,** embouteillage *m*; (*b*) *Parl:* avis *m* préalable d'opposition (à un projet de loi); (*c*) **mental b.,** blocage mental. **4.** *Rail:* canton *m*, tronçon *m* (de ligne); **b. system,** bloc-système *m*; **b. section,** cantonnement. **5.** (*a*) *Engr:* (*wood*) planche *f*; bois *m*; *Typ:* (*metal*) cliché *m*; (*b*) *Phot.Engr:* **b. process,** phototypographie *f*; (*c*) *Typ:* **b. letter,** lettre moulée; **b. letters,** le moulé; **to write sth. in b. capitals,** écrire qch. en majuscules d'imprimerie. (*d*) *Carp:* **sandpaper b.,** cale; **mitre b.,** boîte *f* à onglets. **6.** *Nau: etc:* (i) chape *f*; (ii) poulie *f*; **b. and tackle,** moufle *f*; palan *m.*

block² *v.tr.* **1.** bloquer, obstruer (un passage, etc.); bloquer, enrayer (une roue); entraver, gêner (la circulation); arrêter (le progrès); **to b. s.o.'s way,** barrer le passage à qn; bloquer le chemin à qn; *Parl:* **to b. a bill,** faire de l'obstruction à un projet de loi. **2.** *Games:* (*a*) *Cr:* arrêter (la balle) sans la relancer; bloquer (la balle); (*b*) (*dominoes*) fermer (le jeu); (*c*) *Fb: etc:* gêner (un adversaire); (*d*) *Cards:* **to b. (a suit),** faire une impasse. **3.** (*a*) *Bookb:* gaufrer, frapper (la couverture d'un livre); (*b*) enformer (un chapeau); (*c*) *Bootm:* cambrer la forme (d'un soulier); (*d*) **to b. out, in,** ébaucher, esquisser (un projet, etc.). **4.** (*a*) **to b. (out),** cacher (la vue); (*b*) (*of censor*) **to b. out,** caviarder (un passage); **blocked-out passage,** caviar *m.* **blocking** *n.* **1.** (*a*) encombrement *m*; embouteillage *m* (d'une rue); **b. (up),** (i) obstruction *f*; (ii) murage *m* (d'une porte, etc.); (iii) bâclage *m* (d'un port); (*b*) *Rail:* **b. device,** dispositif bloqueur; (*c*) *El:* blocage *m* (du courant). **2.** *Bookb:* gaufrage *m*, frappe *f*. **3. b. out,** oblitération *f*; (*by censor*) caviardage *m.* **block up** *v.tr.* (*a*) boucher, bloquer, fermer (un trou); boucher, murer (une porte, une fenêtre); *Nau:* bâcler (un port); (*b*) obstruer, engorger (un tuyau, etc.).

blockade¹ [blɔ'keid] *n.* **1.** *Mil: Nau:* blocus *m*; **to run the b.,** forcer le blocus; **b. runner,** forceur *m* de blocus. **2.** *NAm:* arrêt de circulation des trains (dû aux neiges); encombrement *m*, embouteillage *m* (d'une rue).

blockade² *v.tr.* **1.** bloquer (une ville, un port); faire le blocus (d'une place forte). **2.** *NAm:* bloquer (la circulation); encombrer (une rue).

blockage ['blɔkidʒ] *n.* obstruction *f* (d'un tuyau, d'une artère, etc.); embouteillage *m* (d'une rue); **mental b.,** blocage mental.

blockbuster ['blɔkbʌstər] *n.* (*a*) *Mil:* bombe *f* de très grosse calibre; (*b*) F: **his speech was a real b.,** son discours (i) a eu une très grande portée, (ii) a causé beaucoup de consternation; **this show will be a b.,** ce spectacle aura un succès fou.

blockhead ['blɔkhed] *n. F:* lourdaud *m*; gros bête.

blockhouse ['blɔkhaus] *n. Mil:* blockhaus *m.*

bloke [blouk] *n. F:* (*man*) type *m.*

blond, *f.* **blonde** [blɔnd] *a. & n.* blond, *f.* blonde.

blood¹ [blʌd] *n.* **1.** sang *m*; (*a*) **b. vessel,** vaisseau sanguin; **b. group,** groupe sanguin; **b. count,** numération *f* globulaire; **b. sample,** prise *f* de sang; **b. test,** examen *m* du sang; **b. transfusion,** transfusion *f* de sang; **b. donor,** donneur, -euse, de sang; **b. bank,** banque *f* du sang; **b. poisoning,** septicémie *f*; toxémie *f*; *F:* **b. blister,** pinçon *m*; *Fig:* **to sweat b.,** suer sang et eau; (*b*) **his b. is up,** il est furieux; **it makes my b. boil, run cold,** cela me fait bouillir, me glace, le sang; **to commit a crime in cold b.,** commettre un crime de sang-froid; **there's bad b. between them,** il y a de vieilles rancunes entre eux; *Ind: etc:* **the committee needs new, fresh, b.,** le comité a besoin d'être rajeuni; (*c*) **to shed, spill, b.,** verser le sang; **b. money,** prix *m* du sang; **to draw b.,** faire saigner qn; **b. sports,** la chasse; *F:* **he's out for b.,** il cherche à se venger; *Prov:* **one cannot get b. out of a stone,** on ne saurait tirer de l'huile d'un mur. **2.** (*a*) **b. relation,** parent(e) par le sang; **it runs in his b.,** il chasse de race; **the call of b.,** la voix du sang; **b. is thicker than water,** nous sommes unis par la voix, la force, du sang; **b. brother,** compagnon par le cœur; (*b*) **prince of the b.,** prince *m* du sang; **blue b.,** sang royal; sang illustre, aristocratique; **b. horse,** (cheval) pur-sang *m inv*; *Prov:* **b. will tell,** bon sang ne peut mentir.

blood² *v.tr.* (*a*) *Ven:* donner (aux chiens) le goût du sang; initier (un chasseur débutant, en l'aspergeant du sang de la bête morte); (*b*) *Mil:* **to b. the troops,** donner aux troupes le baptême du feu. **blooded** *a.* **1.** (*of horse, etc.*) **to be b.,** avoir du sang, de la race. **2. warm-b., cold-b. animals,** animaux à sang chaud, à sang froid.

blood-and-thunder [ˈblʌdən(d)ˈθʌndər] *a.* (film, roman, etc.) sensationnel, mélodramatique.
bloodbath [ˈblʌdbɑːθ] *n.* carnage *m*, massacre *m.*
bloodcurdling [ˈblʌdkəːdliŋ] *a.* à vous tourner les sangs; qui (vous) fige, à (vous) figer, le sang.
bloodhound [ˈblʌdhaund] *n.* **1.** limier *m*; chien *m* de Saint-Hubert. **2.** *F:* (*of pers.*) limier.
bloodiness [ˈblʌdinis] *n.* état sanglant.
bloodless [ˈblʌdlis] *a.* **1.** (*a*) exsangue; pâle; (*b*) insensible, froid; (*c*) sans vitalité; (personne) qui n'a pas de sang dans les veines. **2.** (victoire, etc.) sans effusion de sang. **-ly** *adv.* sans effusion de sang.
blood-red [ˈblʌdˈred] *a.* rouge comme du sang; rouge sang.
bloodshed [ˈblʌdʃed] *n.* **1.** effusion *f* de sang; **without b.,** sans verser de sang. **2.** carnage *m.*
bloodshot [ˈblʌdʃɔt] *a.* (œil) injecté de sang; (*of eye*) **to become b.,** s'injecter.
bloodstain [ˈblʌdstein] *n.* tache *f* de sang.
bloodstained [ˈblʌdsteind] *a.* taché, souillé, de sang; ensanglanté.
bloodstock [ˈblʌdstɔk] *n.* chevaux *mpl* pur sang.
bloodstone [ˈblʌdstoun] *n. Miner:* (*a*) jaspe sanguin; (*b*) hématite *f*, sanguine *f.*
bloodstream [ˈblʌdstriːm] *n. Physiol:* le sang.
bloodsucker [ˈblʌdsʌkər] *n.* sangsue *f.*
bloodsucking [ˈblʌdsʌkiŋ] *a.* (*a*) *Ent: etc:* hématophage; (*b*) *F:* vampirique.
bloodthirsty [ˈblʌdθəːsti] *a.* sanguinaire; altéré de sang.
bloody¹ [ˈblʌdi] **1.** *a.* sanglant; ensanglanté, taché de sang; *F:* **B. Mary,** (i) la reine Mary I (d'Angleterre); (ii) mélange *m* de vodka et de jus de tomate. **2.** *a. P:* sacré; **a b. liar,** un sacré menteur; **(you) b. fool!** sacré imbécile! **3.** *adv. P:* **it's b. hot!** quelle sacrée chaleur! **he can b. well do it himself!** il n'a qu'à se démerder tout seul!
bloody² *v.tr.* **(bloodied)** ensanglanter; souiller (ses mains, etc.) de sang.
bloody-minded [ˈblʌdiˈmaindid] *a. P:* vache; **he's just b.-m.,** c'est un mauvais coucheur.
bloody-mindedness [ˈblʌdiˈmaindidnis] *n. P:* **it's sheer b.-m.,** ce n'est rien que pour emmerder le monde.
bloom¹ [bluːm] *n.* **1.** (i) fleur *f*; (ii) floraison *f*, épanouissement *m*; **to burst into b.,** fleurir; **flower in b.,** fleur éclose; **in full b.,** épanoui, en pleine floraison; **in the b. of youth,** à, dans, la fleur de l'âge, de la jeunesse. **2.** (*a*) velouté *m*, pruine *f*, duvet *m* (du raisin, d'une pêche); (*b*) efflorescence *f*, fleur (du soufre sur le caoutchouc, etc.); (*c*) bouquet *m* (du vin). **3.** *Ch:* **cobalt, zinc, b.,** fleur de cobalt, de zinc.
bloom² *v.i.* fleurir; être en fleur. **blooming 1.** *a.* (*a*) fleurissant; en fleur; (*b*) florissant; **b. with health,** resplendissant de santé. **2.** *F:* (*a*) *a.* **you b. idiot!** sacré idiot! **it's a b. lie!** ça, pour un mensonge! (*b*) *adv.* **I b. well shall go!** et moi je te dis que j'irai! **3.** *n.* floraison *f*, fleuraison *f.*
bloom³ *n. Metall:* masse *f* de fer cinglé, brame *f*; bloom *m*, loupe *f.*
bloom⁴ *v.tr. Metall:* cingler, dégrossir (une masse de fer). **blooming** *n.* dégrossissage *m* (du fer); **b. mill,** blooming *m*; train *m* à blooms.
bloomer [ˈbluːmər] *n.* **1.** *Typ:* majuscule ornée. **2.** *F:* bévue *f*, gaffe *f*; **to make a b.,** faire une gaffe.
bloomers [ˈbluːməz] *n.pl. Cost: A:* culotte bouffante (de femme).
blossom¹ [ˈblɔsəm] *n.* fleur *f* (des arbres); **tree in b.,** arbre *m* en fleur(s); **orange b.,** fleur d'oranger.
blossom² *v.t.* (*of tree*) fleurir; **she had blossomed (out) into a charming young woman,** elle était devenue une charmante jeune femme. **blossoming** *n.* fleuraison *f*, floraison *f*; épanouissement *m.*
blot¹ [blɔt] *n.* (*a*) tache *f*; (*of ink*) pâté *m*; (*b*) **a b. on s.o.'s honour,** une tache à l'honneur de qn; **this factory is a b. on the landscape,** cette usine gâche le paysage.
blot² *v.* **(blotted; blotting) 1.** *v.tr.* (*a*) tacher, souiller, ternir; *F:* **to b. one's copybook,** ternir sa réputation; (*b*) (*of ink*) faire des pâtés sur (qch.). **2.** *v.tr.* sécher l'encre (d'une lettre, etc.); passer le buvard sur (l'encre). **3.** *v.i.* (*of blotting paper*) boire l'encre. **blot out** *v.tr.* (*a*) effacer (un souvenir, etc.); (*b*) (*of fog, etc.*) cacher, masquer (l'horizon, etc.). **blotting** *n.* (*a*) séchage *m* (au papier buvard); **b. paper,** (papier *m*) buvard (*m*); **b. pad,** (bloc *m*) buvard; sous-main *m inv*; (*b*) maculage *m* (du papier).
blotch¹ [blɔtʃ] *n.* **1.** tache *f*, éclaboussure *f* (d'encre, de couleur). **2.** tache rouge (sur la peau).
blotch² *v.tr.* couvrir (la peau) de taches, de rougeurs; **cold blotches the skin,** le froid marbre la peau.
blotchy [ˈblɔtʃi] *a.* **1.** (teint) brouillé, couperosé; (peau) couverte de rougeurs. **2.** tacheté.
blotter [ˈblɔtər] *n.* **1.** (bloc *m*) buvard (*m*). **2.** (*a*) *Com:* brouillard *m*, main courante; (*b*) *NAm: Adm:* registre *m* (d'arrestations, etc.); livre *m* d'écrou.
blotto [ˈblɔtou] *a. P:* complètement ivre; bourré.
blouse [blauz] *n.* **1.** corsage *m*, chemisier *m* (de femme). **2.** *NAm:* vareuse *f* (de marin, etc.).
blow¹ [blou] *n.* **1.** coup *m* de vent. **2.** souffle *m*; (*to child*) **give your nose a good b.,** mouche-toi bien.
blow² *v.* (*p.t.* **blew** [bluː]; *p.p.* **blown** [bloun]) **1.** *v.i.* (*a*) (*of wind*) souffler; **the wind is blowing,** il fait du vent; il vente; **it's blowing hard,** le vent souffle fort, il fait grand vent; **it was blowing a gale,** le vent soufflait en tempête; **the wind was blowing down the chimney,** le vent s'engouffrait dans la cheminée; **my papers blew out of the window,** mes papiers se sont envolés par la fenêtre; **the door blew open,** le vent a ouvert la porte; **the wind's blowing from the west,** le vent souffle de l'ouest; (*b*) (*of pers., animal*) souffler; (*of whale*) rejeter l'eau par les évents; **to b. on one's fingers,** souffler dans ses doigts; (*c*) *esp. NAm: F:* se vanter; (*d*) (*of fuse*) sauter. **2.** *v.tr.* (*a*) **the wind is blowing the rain against the windows,** le vent chasse la pluie contre les vitres; (*of wind*) **to b. a ship ashore,** pousser un navire à la côte; **to be blown out to sea,** être poussé au large; **it's an ill wind that blows nobody any good,** à quelque chose malheur est bon; (*b*) (*of pers.*) **to b. the dust off sth.,** souffler sur qch, pour enlever la poussière; **to b. s.o. a kiss,** envoyer un baiser à qn; **to b. one's nose,** se moucher; (*c*) donner un coup de (sifflet); souffler (l'orgue); sonner de (la trompette); **to b. the horn,** sonner du cor; *F:* **to b. one's own trumpet,** chanter ses propres louanges; (*d*) faire (des bulles de savon); souffler (le verre); vider (un œuf); (*e*) essouffler (un cheval, etc.); (*f*) *El:* faire sauter (les plombs); **to b. (open) a safe,** faire sauter un coffre-fort; *Aut:* **to b. a gasket,** faire sauter un joint; *F:* (*of pers.*) **to b. one's top,** sortir de ses gonds; **to b. the gaff,** vendre la mèche; (*g*) *F:* gâcher, bousiller (qch.); louper (une occasion); (*h*) *F:* gaspiller (son argent); (*i*) *F: O:* **b. the expense!** je me moque de la dépense! **I'll be blowed if . . .,** que le diable m'emporte si . . .; **well, I'm blowed!** ça, par exemple! **b. it!** zut! **blow about 1.** *v.i.* (*of leaves, etc.*) voler çà et là. **2.** *v.tr.* agiter, faire voler (qch.); disperser (les feuilles, etc.). **blow away 1.** *v.tr.* (*of wind, etc.*) emporter (qch.). **2.** *v.i.* (*of papers, etc.*) s'envoler. **blow down** *v.tr.* (*of wind*) abattre, renverser (un arbre, etc.). **blow in 1.** *v.tr.* (*of wind, etc.*) enfoncer (un carreau, une porte). **2.** *v.i.* (*a*) (*of window, etc.*) s'enfoncer; (*b*) *F:* (*of pers.*) arriver à l'improviste. **blowing** *n.* **1.** soufflement *m* (du vent). **2.** soufflage *m* (du verre, etc.). **3.** *F:* **b. up,** semonce *f*, engueulade *f.* **blown** *a.* **1.** (*of pers.*) essoufflé,

hors d'haleine. **2.** (*of food*) **(fly) b.,** gâté par les mouches. **3.** *El:* **b. fuse,** fusible fondu; plomb sauté. **blow off 1.** *v.tr.* (*of wind, etc.*) emporter (un chapeau, etc.); (*of pers.*) souffler (la poussière); *Mch: etc:* lâcher (de la vapeur); vider, vidanger (la chaudière). **2.** *v.i.* (*of hat, etc.*) s'envoler. **blow out 1.** *v.tr.* (*a*) souffler (une bougie); (*b*) chasser, expulser (de l'air); gonfler (ses joues); (*c*) **to b. out one's brains,** se brûler la cervelle. **2.** *v.i.* (*a*) (*of candle*) s'éteindre; (*b*) *Min:* (*of shot*) faire canon; *Aut: etc:* (*of gasket*) sauter; (*of tyre*) éclater; *El:* (*of fuse*) sauter; (*c*) (*of storm*) **to b. itself out,** se dissiper, se calmer. **blow over 1.** *v.tr.* (*of wind*) renverser (une table, etc.). **2.** *v.i.* (*of storm*) se calmer, se dissiper; **the scandal soon blew over,** le scandale a été vite oublié. **blow up 1.** *v.i.* (*a*) (*of mine*) éclater, sauter; (*of boiler, etc.*) crever, exploser; *F:* (*of pers.*) éclater (de rage); (*b*) (*of situation*) **to b. up into a crisis,** prendre les proportions d'une crise; **there's a gale blowing up,** il se prépare une tempête. **2.** *v.tr.* (*a*) faire sauter, (faire) exploser (une mine, etc.); *F:* engueuler (qn); (*b*) gonfler (un pneu, etc.); souffler (un ballon, etc.); (*c*) *Phot:* agrandir (une photo); (*d*) *F:* exagérer (un incident, etc.).

blow³ *v.i.* (*p.t.* **blew** [bluː]; *p.p.* **blown** [bloun]) *Lit:* (*of flower*) s'épanouir; **full-blown roses,** roses fraîches écloses.

blow⁴ *n.* **1.** coup *m* (de poing, etc.); **at the first b.,** du premier coup; **at a (single) b.,** d'un (seul) coup; **to strike a b.,** porter, asséner, donner, un coup; **to come, get, to blows, to exchange blows,** en venir aux coups, aux mains; **to return b. for b.,** rendre coup pour coup; **to strike a b. for, against, sth.,** se battre pour, contre, qch.; **knockout b.,** (i) coup d'assommoir; (ii) *Box:* knock-out *m*; **b. by b. account,** compte-rendu minutieux, détaillé. **2.** (*a*) coup (du sort); **it came as a crushing b. to us,** ce fut un coup d'assommoir pour nous; **his death is a sad b. to his family,** sa mort est un rude coup pour sa famille; (*b*) **b. to s.o.'s pride,** atteinte *f* à la vanité de qn.

blowcock ['bloukɔk] *n. Mch:* robinet *m* d'extraction, de vidange.

blower ['blouər] *n.* **1.** (*pers.*) (*a*) souffleur, -euse (de verre, etc.); (*b*) **horn b.,** sonneur *m* de cor. **2.** (*a*) écran *m* à tirage, tablier *m*, rideau *m* (de cheminée); (*b*) *Ind: etc:* ventilateur soufflant; (*c*) *Agr:* ensileuse *f*; (*d*) insufflateur *m* (à poudre insecticide); (*e*) *F:* (i) téléphone *m*; (ii) porte-voix *m inv.* **3.** *Min:* échappement *m* de gaz; soufflard *m* (de grisou). **4.** *Z:* **b. (dolphin),** souffleur.

blowfly, *pl.* **-flies** ['blouflai, -flaiz] *n.* mouche *f* à viande, de la viande; lucilie *f*.

blowhard ['blouhɑːd] *n. U.S:* vantard, -arde.

blowhole ['blouhoul] *n.* **1.** *Z:* évent *m* (d'une baleine). **2.** bouche *f* d'aération (d'un tunnel).

blowlamp ['bloulæmp] *n.* **1.** chalumeau *m*, lampe *f* à souder, à braser. **2.** brûloir *m* (de peintre en bâtiments).

blowout ['blouaut] *n.* **1.** *Metall:* mise *f* hors feu (d'un haut fourneau). **2.** *Min: etc:* éruption *f* (de gaz, de pétrole, etc.) au cours d'un sondage. **3.** *El:* (*a*) soufflage *m* d'étincelles; (*b*) **magnetic b.,** souffleur *m* magnétique. **4.** *Aut: etc:* éclatement *m* (de pneu). **5.** *P:* ripaille *f*, grande bouffe.

blowpipe ['bloupaip] *n.* **1.** sarbacane *f*. **2.** (*a*) *Ch: Metall:* chalumeau *m*; (*b*) *Glassm:* canne *f*, fêle *f* (de souffleur). **3.** *Mus:* porte-vent *m inv* (de cornemuse).

blowtorch ['bloutɔːtʃ] *n.* = BLOWLAMP.

blowup ['blouʌp] *n. F:* **1.** (*a*) dispute *f*, querelle *f*; (*b*) accès *m* de fureur. **2.** *Phot:* agrandissement *m*.

blow-valve ['blouvælv] *n. Mch:* reniflard *m* (de chaudière à vapeur).

blowy ['bloui] *a.* venteux; tempétueux.

blowzy ['blauzi] *a.* (*of woman*) (*a*) ébouriffée, mal peignée; (*b*) mal soignée.

blubber¹ ['blʌbər] *n.* graisse *f*, lard *m*, de baleine.

blubber² *v.i. F:* pleurer bruyamment, pleurer comme un veau (**over,** sur).

bludgeon¹ ['blʌdʒən] *n.* gourdin *m*, matraque *f*.

bludgeon² *v.tr.* asséner un coup de matraque à (qn); matraquer (qn); **to b. s.o. into doing sth.,** forcer qn à faire qch. par des méthodes brutales.

blue¹ [bluː] **I.** *a.* **1.** (*a*) bleu; **dark b., light b.,** bleu foncé *inv.*, bleu clair *inv.*; **navy b.,** bleu marine *inv.*; **face b. with cold,** visage violacé par le froid; *Med:* **b. baby,** enfant bleu; *Comest:* **b. cheese,** fromage bleu; **to go b.,** (i) (*of thg.*) virer au bleu; (ii) (*of pers.*) prendre un teint violacé; *F:* **I've told you so until I'm b. in the face,** je me tue à vous le dire; **once in a b. moon,** en de rares ocasions; (*b*) **b. blood,** sang aristocratique; (*c*) *Pol:* conservateur, -trice. **2.** triste; sombre; déprimé; **to feel b.,** avoir le cafard. **3.** *F:* obscène, vert; **to tell b. stories,** en raconter des vertes; **b. film,** film *m* porno. **II.** *n.* **1.** (*a*) bleu *m*; **dark, light, b.,** bleu foncé, bleu clair; **navy b.,** bleu marine; **sky b.,** bleu (de) ciel *inv.*; (*b*) **a bolt from the b.,** un événement imprévu; un coup de foudre; **he arrived out of the b.,** il est arrivé à l'improviste. **2. the blues,** (i) des idées noires; le cafard; (ii) *Mus:* le blues. **3.** (*a*) *Pol:* conservateur, -trice; **a true b.,** (i) un patriote; (ii) un conservateur; (*b*) *Sp:* **(Oxford, Cambridge, etc.) b.,** sportif chevronné (de l'université d'Oxford, de Cambridge, etc.); (*c*) *Mil:* **the Blues,** (i) la Cavalerie de la Maison du Souverain; (ii) *U.S: Hist:* l'armée *f* du Nord. **4.** *Laund:* bleu (d'empois).

blue² *v.tr.* **1.** bleuir; teindre (qch.) en bleu; *Laund:* mettre, passer (le linge) au bleu. **2.** *F:* **to b. one's money,** gaspiller, manger, son argent.

Bluebeard ['bluːbiəd] *Pr.n.m.* Barbe-bleue *m*.

bluebell ['bluːbel] *n. Bot:* **1.** jacinthe *f* sauvage, des bois. **2.** *Scot:* campanule *f*.

blueberry ['bluːb(ə)ri] *n. Bot:* airelle *f*, myrtille *f*; *Fr.C:* bleuet *m*.

bluebird ['bluːbəːd] *n. NAm: Orn:* rouge-gorge bleu.

blue-black ['bluː'blæk] *a.* **1.** noir tirant sur le bleu. **2.** (encre) bleue-noire.

bluebottle ['bluːbɔtl] *n.* **1.** *Bot:* bleuet *m*. **2.** *Ent:* mouche *f* à viande. **3.** *F:* (*policeman*) flic *m*.

blue-chip ['bluːtʃip] *a. St.Exch:* **b.-c. stocks,** actions triées sur le volet.

blue-collar ['bluː'kɔlər] *a.* **b.-c. worker,** ouvrier *m*, travailleur manuel, *Fr.C:* col bleu.

blue-eyed ['bluːaid] *a.* **1.** aux yeux bleus. **2.** *F:* **b.-e. boy,** (i) le chouchou de sa maman; (ii) le favori du patron.

blueness ['bluːnis] *n.* couleur bleue; bleu *m*.

blue-pencil ['bluː'pens(ə)l] *v.tr.* censurer (un article).

blueprint ['bluːprint] *n.* (*a*) dessin négatif, photocalque *m*; (*b*) plan (détaillé), projet *m*, épure *f*.

bluestocking ['bluːstɔkiŋ] *n.* (*woman*) bas-bleu *m*, *pl.* bas-bleus.

bluff¹ [blʌf] **1.** *a.* (*a*) (*of cliff, coast*) escarpé, à pic; *Nau:* **b. (bowed),** (navire) à proue renflée, renflé de l'avant; (*b*) (*of pers.*) brusque; un peu bourru. **2.** *n.* cap *m*, falaise *f*, à pic; à-pic *m*, *pl.* à-pics.

bluff² *n.* (*a*) *Cards:* (*at poker*) bluff *m*, cassade *f*; **to call s.o.'s b.,** (i) (*at poker*) inviter l'adversaire à mettre cartes sur table; (ii) prendre qn au mot; relever le défi de qn; (*b*) bluff, battage *m*; **piece of b.,** coup *m* de bluff.

bluff³ *Cards: etc:* **1.** *v.tr.* bluffer (qn); **to b. one's way out of a tricky situation,** se tirer d'affaire par un coup de bluff. **2.** *v.i.* faire du bluff, de l'épate; *Cards:* faire cassade.

bluffer ['blʌfər] *n.* bluffeur, -euse.

blunder[1] ['blʌndər] *n.* bévue *f*; gaffe *f*.

blunder[2] *v.i.* **1.** faire une bévue, une gaffe. **2. to b. along,** s'avancer d'un pas maladroit; **to b. against, into, s.o., sth.,** se heurter contre qn, qch.; heurter qn, qch.; **he managed to b. through,** il s'en est tiré tant bien que mal. **blundering 1.** *a.* brouillon, malavisé; maladroit. **2.** *n.* maladresse *f*.

blunderbuss ['blʌndəbʌs] *n. Hist:* (*gun*) trombion *m*.

blunderer ['blʌndərər] *n.* gaffeur, -euse.

blunt[1] [blʌnt] *a.* (*a*) (*of knife, cutting edge, etc.*) (i) mousse; (ii) émoussé; (*of needle, pencil*) épointé; (instrument) contondant; (*b*) (*of pers., question, etc.*) brusque; (*of pers., reply, etc.*) carré; (fait) brutal; (refus) tranché. **-ly** *adv.* brusquement; carrément; brutalement; **to speak b.,** parler net, carrément.

blunt[2] *v.tr.* **1.** (*a*) émousser (un couteau, etc.); épointer (un crayon, etc.); (*b*) émousser (les sentiments, la colère de qn); **to b. the edge of the pain,** émousser la douleur. **2.** aplatir, abattre (un angle).

bluntness ['blʌntnis] *n.* **1.** manque *m* de tranchant. **2.** brusquerie *f*; sans-façon *m*; **b. of speech,** franc-parler *m*.

blur[1] [bləːr] *n.* **1.** tache *f*, macule *f*, barbouillage *m* (d'encre, etc.); *Typ:* frison *m*; (*offset*) graissage *m*. **2.** (*a*) apparence confuse; brouillard *m*; **b. of tears,** voile *m* de larmes; (*b*) *Phot:* flou *m*.

blur[2] *v.tr.* **(blurred; blurring) 1.** barbouiller (d'encre, etc.); *Typ:* maculer, mâchurer; (*offset*) graisser. **2.** brouiller, troubler; **eyes blurred with tears,** yeux voilés de larmes; **the haze has blurred the outline of the mountains,** la brume a estompé les contours de la montagne. **blurred** *a.* (photographie) floue; (contours) noyés, indécis, flous; (souvenirs) confus, estompés; *Med:* **b. vision,** vue trouble. **blurring** *n.* **1.** maculage *m*, barbouillage *m*. **2.** *Opt:* halo *m*, flou *m*.

blurb [bləːb] *n. F:* baratin *m* publicitaire; (*a*) **(publisher's) b.,** prière d'insérer; (*b*) annonce sur la jaquette d'un livre.

blurt ['bləːt] *v.tr.* **to b. out a secret,** lâcher (à l'étourdie), laisser échapper, un secret; **he blurted out the truth,** il a révélé, trahi la vérité.

blush[1] [blʌʃ] *n.* **1.** aspect *m*; **at (the) first b.,** à l'abord, au premier abord, au premier aspect. **2.** (*a*) rougeur *f* (de modestie, de honte); **a b. rose to her cheeks,** un flux de sang lui est monté au visage; **to hide one's blushes,** baisser le nez; (*b*) *Lit:* **the first b. of dawn,** les premières rougeurs de l'aube.

blush[2] *v.i.* (*of pers.*) rougir; **to b. for, with, shame,** rougir de honte; **to b. crimson,** devenir tout rouge; **to b. to the roots of one's hair,** rougir jusqu'au bout des oreilles. **blushing 1.** *a.* (*of pers.*) rougissant. **2.** *n.* rougissement *m*.

bluster[1] ['blʌstər] *n.* fureur *f*, fracas *m* (de l'orage).

bluster[2] *v.i.* (*a*) (*of wind*) souffler en rafales; (*b*) (*of pers.*) parler haut; faire de l'esbroufe; **he blusters to cover up his ignorance,** il parle haut pour cacher son ignorance. **blustering 1.** *a.* (*a*) (vent) violent; (*b*) (*pers.*) fanfaron. **2.** *n.* fanfaronnade(s) *f*(*pl*).

blustery ['blʌst(ə)ri] *a.* (vent) violent; (jour) venteux.

boa ['bouə] *n.* **1.** *Rept:* boa *m*; **b. constrictor,** boa constricteur, constrictor. **2.** *Cost:* **feather b.,** boa.

boar ['bɔːr] *n. Z:* verrat *m*; **wild b.,** sanglier *m*; (*young*) marcassin *m*; **b. hunting,** la chasse au sanglier; **boar's head,** *Cu:* hure *f* de sanglier.

board[1] [bɔːd] *n.* **1.** (*a*) planche *f*, (*thick*) madrier *m*; **bread b.,** planche à (couper le) pain; **ironing b.,** planche à repasser; **sleeve b.,** pied *m* à manches; *Swim:* **diving b.,** plongeoir *m*; *Mus:* **finger b.,** touche *f* (de violon); (*b*) **(notice) b.,** tableau *m* de publicité, d'affichage; écriteau *m*; **sandwichman's b.,** panneau *m*; *Aut: etc:* **instrument b.,** tableau de bord; *Sch:* **to write sth. on the b.,** écrire qch. au tableau noir; (*c*) *Cmptr:* **control b.,** tableau de commande; (*d*) *Th:* **the boards,** la scène, les planches. **2.** (*a*) carton *m*; (*b*) *Bookb:* **the boards,** les plats *mpl* (d'un livre); **in paper boards,** cartonné; **limp boards,** cartonnage *m* souple. **3.** (*a*) table *f*; **the festive b.,** la table du festin; (*b*) table, nourriture *f*; **b. and lodging, full b.,** pension (complète); **with b. and lodging,** nourri et logé; (*c*) **(gaming) b.,** table de jeu; **to sweep the b.,** faire table rase; (*d*) *Games:* tableau *m* (de jeu); (*draughts*) damier *m*; (*chess*) échiquier *m*; **4.** (*a*) *Adm: etc:* conseil *m*; comité *m*; **b. of enquiry,** commission *f* d'enquête; **disciplinary b.,** conseil de discipline; **advisory b.,** comité consultatif; **b. of trustees,** conseil de gestion (d'un musée, etc.); **b. of examiners,** jury *m* d'examen; **medical b.,** conseil de santé; **b. of directors,** conseil d'administration (d'une société); **b. meeting,** réunion *f* du conseil d'administration; (*b*) *Adm:* **B. of Trade,** (i) *Eng: A:* = Ministère *m* du Commerce; (ii) *U.S:* = chambre *f* de commerce; **National Coal B.** = administration *f* des charbonnages. **5.** *Nau:* bord *m*; **on b.,** à bord; **to take goods on b.,** embarquer des marchandises; **to go on b.,** monter à bord; s'embarquer; **to go by the b.,** (i) (*of mast, etc.*) s'en aller par-dessus bord; (ii) *Fig:* (*of plan, hopes*) être abandonné; (*of reputation*) être perdu; **to let sth. go by the b.,** abandonner qch.

board[2] **1.** *v.tr.* (*a*) planchéier, faire un plancher dans (une pièce); (*b*) *Bookb:* cartonner (un livre); (*c*) *Leath:* rebrousser (le cuir). **2.** (*a*) *v.i.* être en pension; **I b. at Mrs B.'s,** je suis en pension chez Mme B.; (*b*) *v.tr.* avoir (qn) en pension chez soi. **3.** *v.tr.* (*a*) *Nau:* aborder, accoster. *Adm:* arraisonner (un navire); (*b*) aller, monter, à bord (d'un navire, d'un avion); monter dans (un train, un autobus); (*c*) *Navy:* aborder (un navire), prendre (un navire) à l'abordage. **boarding** *n.* **1.** (*a*) *Const:* planchéiage *m*; (*b*) *Bookb:* cartonnage *m* (d'un livre); (*c*) *Leath:* rebroussement *m* (du cuir). **2.** (*a*) pension *f*; **b. house,** pension de famille; **b. school,** pensionnat *m*. **3.** (*a*) *Nau:* accostage *m*; abordage *m*; *Adm:* arraisonnement *m*; **b. party,** (i) détachement *m* de visite; (ii) détachement d'abordage; (*b*) *Nau: Av:* embarquement *m*; **b. card,** carte *f* d'embarquement. **4.** *coll.* planches *fpl*; *Const:* bardage *m*. **board out** *v.tr.* mettre (des enfants) en pension; placer (des enfants) dans une famille. **board up** *v.tr.* boucher (une fenêtre); condamner (une porte).

boarder ['bɔːdər] *n.* **1.** pensionnaire *mf*; interne *mf*. **2.** *Nau:* abordeur *m*.

boardroom ['bɔːdruːm] *n. Ind: etc:* salle *f* de réunion du conseil d'administration.

boast[1] [boust] *n.* vantardise *f*; **it is their b. that . . .,** ils se vantent que . . . .

boast[2] **1.** *v.i.* se vanter; **to b. of, about, sth.,** se vanter, se faire gloire, de qch.; **without wishing to b.,** sans vanité. **2.** *v.tr.* revendiquer (qch.); **the school boasts a fine library,** l'école est fière de posséder une belle bibliothèque. **boasting** *n.* vantardise *f*.

boaster ['boustər] *n.* vantard, -arde.

boastful ['boustful] *a.* vantard. **-fully** *adv.* avec vantardise.

boat[1] [bout] *n.* **1.** bateau *m*; canot *m*; embarcation *f*; **cargo b.,** cargo *m*; **passenger b.,** paquebot *m*; **sailing b.,** bateau à voiles; **pleasure b.,** bateau de plaisance; **fishing b.,** bateau de pêche; barque *f* de pêcheur; **ship's b.,** embarcation de bord; **b. deck,** pont *m* des embarcations; **b. stations!** chacun à son poste d'abandon! **b. race,** course *f* à l'aviron; **b. train,** train *m* du bateau; **I came by b.,** je suis venu sur, par, le bateau; **we're all in the same b.,** nous sommes tous dans le même cas; **to miss the b.,** manquer le coche. **2.** *Dom.Ec:* **sauce b.,** saucière *f.*

boat² *v.i.* se promener en bateau; canoter; faire du canotage. **boating** *n.* canotage *m*; **to go b.,** faire du canotage; **b. song,** barcarolle *f.*

boatbuilder ['boutbildər] *n.* constructeur *m* de canots, de bateaux de plaisance.

boater ['boutər] *n. Cost:* canotier *m*; **straw b.,** chapeau *m* (en paille) régate.

boathook ['bouthuk] *n. Nau:* gaffe *f.*

boathouse ['bouthaus] *n.* hangar *m* à bateaux.

boatload ['boutloud] *n.* (*a*) batelée *f* (de bois, etc.); (*b*) plein bateau (de personnes).

boatman, *pl.* **-men** ['boutmən] *n.m.* **1.** batelier. **2.** (*a*) gardien de canots; (*b*) loueur de canots. **3.** *n. Ent:* **(water) b.,** corise *f.*

boatswain ['bousn] *n. Nau:* maître *m* d'équipage, maître principal de manœuvre, *F:* bosco *m.*

boatyard ['boutjɑːd] *n.* chantier *m* de construction pour canots et bateaux de plaisance.

bob¹ [bɔb] *n.* **1.** (*a*) *Mec:* lentille *f* (d'un pendule); plomb *m* (d'un fil à plomb); poids *m* (au bout de la queue d'un cerf-volant); (*b*) *Fish:* (i) bouchon *m* (de ligne); (ii) paquet *m* de vers (pour la pêche à l'anguille). **2.** coiffure *f* à la Ninon, à la Jeanne d'Arc. **3.** *Sp:* bob(sleigh) *m.*

bob² *v.* **(bobbed) 1.** *v.tr.* (*a*) **to have one's hair bobbed,** se faire coiffer à la Ninon, à la Jeanne d'Arc. **2.** *v.i. Fish:* pêcher (les anguilles) avec un paquet de vers.

bob³ *v.i.* **1.** s'agiter; **to b. down,** se baisser subitement; **to b. up,** surgir brusquement; revenir à la surface; *F:* (*of pers.*) réapparaître d'une façon inattendue; **to b. up and down in the water,** danser sur l'eau; (*of fisherman's float*) **to b. under,** plonger. **2.** *A:* (*with cogn. acc.*) **to b. a curtsey,** faire une petite révérence.

bob⁴ *n.* **1.** petite secousse; petit coup. **2.** *A:* petite révérence. **3.** (*a*) carillon *m*; (*b*) chacune des variations du carillon.

Bob⁵ *Pr.n.m.* Robert; *F:* **and Bob's your uncle!** ça y est! et voilà!

bob⁶ *n.inv. F: A:* shilling *m.*

bobbin ['bɔbin] *n.* **1.** (*a*) *Tex:* bobine *f* (de la navette); **b. frame,** bobinoir *m*; **b. winder,** bobineuse *f*; (*b*) **lace b.,** fuseau *m*; **b. lace,** dentelle *f* au fuseau. **2.** *El:* corps *m* de bobine.

bobble ['bɔbl] *n. F:* pompon *m.*

Bobby ['bɔbi] **1.** *Pr.n.m.* (*dim*) Robert. **2.** *n. F: O:* (*policeman*) flic *m.*

bobby-pin ['bɔbipin] *n. NAm:* pince *f* (à cheveux).

bobbysocks ['bɔbisɔks] *n.pl. NAm: F:* socquettes *fpl.*

bobbysoxer ['bɔbisɔksər] *n.f. NAm: F:* adolescente (qui porte des socquettes).

bobcat ['bɔbkæt] *n. NAm: Z:* lynx *m* rufus.

bobsled¹, bobsleigh¹ ['bɔbsled, -slei] *n.* bobsleigh *m*; bob *m*; **b. race,** course de bob.

bobsled², bobsleigh² *v.i.* **(bobsledded)** faire du bob(sleigh).

bobtail ['bɔbteil] *n.* **1.** queue écourtée (d'un cheval, d'un chien). **2.** (*dog*) anglais *m* sans queue; bobtail *m.*

bock [bɔk] *n.* bière brune (allemande).

bod [bɔd] *n. F:* type *m*; **any old b.,** n'importe qui.

bode [boud] *v.tr. & i. A: & Lit:* présager; **to b. well, ill,** être de bon, de mauvais, augure.

bodice ['bɔdis] *n. Cost:* corsage *m* (d'une robe).

bodily ['bɔdili] **1.** *a.* corporel, physique; (maladie) du corps; **one's b. needs,** ses besoins matériels; **b. harm,** lésion corporelle; **to be in b. fear of s.o.,** craindre d'être attaqué par qn. **2.** *adv.* (*a*) corporellement; **he was carried b. to the door,** on l'a saisi (par le corps) et transporté jusqu'à la porte; (*b*) entièrement; en masse.

bodkin ['bɔdkin] *n.* (*a*) passe-lacet *m*, *pl.* passe-lacets; (*b*) *Needlew:* poinçon *m.*

body ['bɔdi] *n.* **1.** (*a*) corps *m* (d'une personne, d'un animal); **the human b.,** le corps humain; **to throw oneself b. and soul into sth.,** se jeter à corps perdu dans qch; **to have just enough to keep b. and soul together,** avoir tout juste de quoi vivre; *Art:* **b. colour,** gouache *f*; (*b*) **(dead) b.,** cadavre *m*, corps (mort); **the resurrection of the b.,** la résurrection des morts; **over my dead b.!** à mon corps défendant! **2.** (*a*) sève *f*, générosité *f* (d'un vin); **wine with b.,** vin généreux; (*of wine*) **to get b.,** s'enforcir; (*b*) corps, consistance *f* (d'un papier, d'une peinture, etc.); (*c*) *Mus:* **to give b. to the tone,** nourrir le son. **3.** (*a*) **legislative b.,** corps législatif; **public b.,** corporation *f*; **b. politic,** corps politique; **learned b.,** corps savant; **governing b.,** conseil *m* de direction; **electoral b.,** collège électoral; (*b*) **large b. of people,** foule nombreuse; assistance nombreuse; **b. of troops,** troupe armée; **the main b.,** le gros (de l'armée); **to come in a b.,** venir en masse; (*c*) recueil *m* (de lois); étendue *f* (d'eau). **4.** (*a*) corps (de document, de bâtiment, etc.); vaisseau *m*, nef *f* (d'église); tronc *m* (d'arbre, d'homme); coffre *m* (d'un instrument de musique); fuselage *m* (d'avion); nacelle *f* (d'une voiture d'enfant); ventre *m* (de haut fourneau); coque *f* (de chaudière); fût *m* (d'un cric, d'un tambour); *Typ:* panse *f* (d'un a, d'un d); *I.C.E:* culot *m* (de bougie); *Typ:* **b. type,** caractères *mpl* de texte; (*b*) *Aut: etc:* bâti *m*, corps, caisse *f*; carrosserie *f*; **standard b.,** carrosserie de série. **5.** *Ph: etc:* corps *m*; *Astr:* **heavenly b.,** corps céleste; astre *m.*

bodybuilder ['bɔdibildər] *n.* **1.** *Aut: etc:* (*pers.*) carrossier *m.* **2.** (*a*) aliment reconstituant; (*b*) (*pers.*) culturiste *m*; (*c*) extenseur *m.*

body-building ['bɔdibildiŋ] *n.* culture *f* physique, culturisme *m.*

bodyguard ['bɔdigɑːd] *n.* (*a*) gardes *mpl* du corps; (*b*) garde *m* du corps; *F:* gorille *m.*

bodywork ['bɔdiwəːk] *n. Aut: etc:* carrosserie *f.*

Boer ['buər, 'bouər] **1.** *a.* boer; **the B. War,** la guerre des Boers. **2.** *n.* Boer *mf.*

boffin ['bɔfin] *n. F:* savant *m.*

bog¹ [bɔg] *n.* **1.** fondrière *f*; marécage *m*; **peat b.,** tourbière *f*; *Miner:* **b. iron,** fer *m* des lacs, des marais. **2.** *P:* chiottes *fpl.*

bog² *v.tr. & i.* **(bogged) to get bogged down,** (i) (*of cart, horse, etc.*) s'embourber; s'enfoncer dans une fondrière; (ii) *F:* (*of pers., discussion, etc.*) se trouver dans une impasse.

bogey ['bougi] *n.* **1.** (*a*) *A:* diable *m*; (*b*) fantôme *m*, spectre *m*; épouvantail *m.* **2.** *Golf:* un coup au-dessus de la normale.

bogeyman, *pl.* **-men** ['bougimæn, -men] *n.* **the b.,** croque-mitaine *m*; le Père Fouettard.

boggle [bɔgl] *v.i.* **to b. at doing sth.,** rechigner à faire qch.; **the mind boggles,** cela confond l'imagination.

boggy ['bɔgi] *a.* marécageux; tourbeux.

bogie ['bougi] *n. Rail:* bog(g)ie *m.*

bogus ['bougəs] *a.* faux, *f* fausse; *Com:* **b. company,** société *f* qui n'existe pas; société fantôme; *F:* **he's completely b.,** il est faux comme un jeton.

Bohemia [bou'hiːmiə] **1.** *Pr.n. Geog:* Bohême *f.* **2.** *n.* (vie *f* de) bohème.

Bohemian [bou'hiːmiən] **1.** *Geog:* (*a*) *a.* bohémien; (*b*) *n.* Bohémien, -ienne. **2. b.,** (*a*) *a.* (vie, etc.) de bohème; (*b*) *n.* (i) (*gipsy*) bohémien, -ienne; (ii) bohème *mf.*

boil¹ [bɔil] *n. Med:* furoncle *m.*

boil² *n.* (*of water, etc.*) **to come to the b.,** commencer à bouillir; entrer en ébullition; **the water is on the b.,** l'eau bout; **to bring the water to the b.,** amener l'eau à l'ébullition; faire bouillir l'eau.

boil³ **1.** *v.i.* (*a*) (*of water, etc.*) bouillir; (*violently*) bouillonner; **to begin to b.,** entrer en ébullition; *Cu:* **allow to b. gently,** laissez mijoter; **to let the kettle b. dry,** laisser évaporer complètement l'eau de la bouilloire; *F:* **to keep the pot boiling,** faire bouillir la marmite; **it makes my blood b.!** ça me fait bouillir le sang! **to b. with rage,** bouillir de colère; *F:* **I'm boiling!** je crève de chaleur! (*b*) (*of sea, etc.*) bouillonner, tourbillonner. **2.** *v.tr.* (*a*) faire bouillir (de l'eau, etc.); *Cu:* faire cuire (qch.) à l'eau; cuire (du sucre); **to b. an egg,** faire cuire un œuf à la coque; *P:* **go and b. your head!** va te faire cuire un œuf! (*b*) *Paperm:* décreuser (des fibres végétales). **boil away** *v.i.* (*a*) continuer à bouillir; (*b*) ébouillir; (*of sauce, etc.*) se réduire. **boil down** **1.** *v.tr.* réduire (une solution); (faire) réduire (un sirop, etc.); *F:* condenser (un article, etc.). **2.** *v.i.* (*of sauce, etc.*) se réduire; *F:* se ramener, se résumer, revenir (**to,** à); **this is what it all boils down to,** voilà à quoi cela revient, se résume. **boiled** *a.* **1.** cuit à l'eau; bouilli; **b. egg,** œuf *m* à la coque; **lightly b., soft b., egg,** œuf mollet. **2.** *Paint:* **b. oil,** huile cuite. **boiling** **1.** *a.* bouillant; bouillonnant; **b. water,** eau bouillante; (*b*) (*of sea*) bouillonnant, tourbillonnant. **2.** *adv.* **b. hot,** tout bouillant; *F:* **I'm b. hot,** je crève de chaleur. **3.** *n.* **1.** (*a*) bouillonnement *m*, ébullition *f*; **b. point,** point *m* d'ébullition: (*b*) *Paperm:* décreusage *m* (des fibres végétales). **boil over** *v.i.* (*of liquid*) s'en aller, se sauver.

boiler ['bɔilər] *n.* **1.** (*pers.*) fabricant *m*, raffineur *m* (de sucre, etc.). **2.** (*a*) chaudière *f*; *Mch:* générateur *m*; (*b*) *Dom.Ec:* **double b.,** bain-marie *m*, *pl.* bains-marie; (*c*) **b. maker,** chaudronnier *m*; **b. room,** salle *f* des chaudières; *Nau:* chambre *f* de chauffe; *Cost:* **b. suit,** bleu *m* de chauffe. **3.** *Cu:* poule *f* (à la casserole).

boilerman, *pl.* **-men** ['bɔiləmən] *n.m. Mch:* chauffeur.

boisterous ['bɔist(ə)rəs] *a.* (*of pers.*) bruyant, turbulent; tapageur; (*of wind*) violent; (*of sea*) tumultueux; (*of weather*) tempétueux; **b. spirits,** gaieté débordante, tapageuse. **-ly** *adv.* bruyamment; tumultueusement.

bold [bould] *a.* **1.** hardi; (i) courageux; (ii) audacieux, téméraire; (ton, regard) assuré, confiant; **b. stroke,** (i) coup hardi; (ii) coup d'audace; **b. enterprise,** entreprise audacieuse; **if I may be so b.,** si je puis prendre une telle liberté; **to put a b. face, front, on it,** payer d'audace. **2.** impudent, effronté; **as b. as brass,** d'un air effronté. **3.** (*a*) **b. features,** traits accusés; *Typ:* **b. type,** caractères gras; *n.* **in b.,** en gras; (*b*) *Art: etc:* (style, trait, coup de pinceau) hardi; (coloris) vigoureux; **in b. relief,** en puissant relief. **-ly** *adv.* **1.** hardiment; (i) courageusement; (ii) audacieusement; **to state sth. b.,** affirmer qch. avec confiance; **to treat a subject b.,** traiter un sujet hardiment. **2.** effrontément. **3.** *Art: etc:* avec hardiesse.

boldface ['bouldfeis] *n. Typ:* caractères *mpl* gras.

boldness ['bouldnis] *n.* **1.** hardiesse *f* (de conduite, etc.); (i) courage *m*; (ii) audace *f*. **2.** effronterie *f*, impudence *f*. **3.** (*a*) escarpement *m* (d'une falaise); (*b*) *Art: Lit:* hardiesse (de style, de pinceau).

bole [boul] *n.* fût *m*, tronc *m* (d'un arbre).

bolero *n.* **1.** *Danc: Mus:* [bɔ'lɛərou] boléro *m*. **2.** *Cost:* ['bɔlərou] boléro.

boletus [bɔ'li:təs] *n. Fung:* bolet *m*; **edible b.,** cèpe *m*.

Bolivia [bə'liviə] *Pr.n. Geog:* Bolivie *f*.

Bolivian [bə'liviən] *Geog:* **1.** *a.* bolivien. **2.** *n.* Bolivien, -ienne.

boll [boul] *n. Bot:* capsule *f* (du cotonnier, du lin); *Ent:* **b. weevil,** anthonome *m* (du cotonnier).

bollard ['bɔləd] *n.* **1.** *Nau:* bitte *f* (d'amarrage, de tournage). **2.** (*on road*) borne *f*.

bollocks ['bɔləks] *n.pl. V:* couilles *fpl*; **b.!** c'est de la couille!

Bologna [bə'lɔnjə] *Pr.n. Geog:* Bologne *f*.

Bolognese [bɔlə'nji:z] *Geog:* **1.** *a.* bolonais. **2.** *n.* Bolonais, -aise.

boloney [bə'louni] *n. F:* idioties *fpl*, foutaises *fpl*.

Bolshevik ['bɔlʃivik], **Bolshevist** ['bɔlʃivist] *a.* & *n.* bolchevik (*mf*), bolcheviste (*mf*).

Bolshevism ['bɔlʃəvizm] *n.* bolchevisme *m*.

Bolshie, Bolshy ['bɔlʃi] *F:* **1.** *a.* **he's b.,** il embête tout le monde; c'est un mauvais coucheur; **he turned b.,** il a commencé à râler. **2.** *n.* rouge *mf*.

bolster¹ ['boulstər] *n.* **1.** traversin *m* (de lit). **2.** (*a*) *Mec.E:* coussinet *m*; (*b*) *Metalw:* contre-poinçon *m*, *pl.* contre-poinçons. **3.** *Const:* racinal, -aux *m*; *Civ.E: Const:* chapeau *m* (de poteau). **4.** *Nau:* coussin *m* (de capelage, de ferrure). **5.** *Veh:* lisoir *m*, traverse *f*, sommier *m*.

bolster² *v.tr.* **1. to b. up,** (i) soutenir, relever, la tête de (qn) avec des oreillers; (ii) appuyer, soutenir (qn); (iii) étayer (une théorie). **2.** rembourrer.

bolt¹ [boult] *n.* **1.** carreau *m* (d'arbalète); **he has shot his last b.,** (i) il a vidé son carquois; (ii) il a fourni son effort maximum; (iii) il a dit son dernier mot. **2.** éclair *m*; coup *m* de foudre; **it's like a b. from the blue,** c'est comme un coup de foudre. **3.** (*a*) **(sliding) b.,** verrou *m* (de porte); pêne *m* (de serrure); (*b*) *Sm.a:* culasse *f* mobile. **4.** *Mec.E:* boulon *m*; cheville *f*; goupille *f*; **nuts and bolts,** visserie *f*. **5.** (*a*) pièce *f* (de toile); **a b. of cloth,** une coupe de drap; (*b*) botte *f* (d'osier). **6.** *Bookb:* **bolts,** témoins *mpl*. **7.** *F:* fuite *f*; **to make a b. for it,** décamper, déguerpir.

bolt² **1.** *v.tr.* (*a*) verrouiller; fermer (une porte) à, au, verrou; **to b. oneself in,** s'enfermer au verrou; (*b*) *Mec.E:* boulonner, cheviller. **2.** *v.i.* (*a*) (*of horse*) s'emballer, s'emporter; prendre le mors aux dents; (*b*) *F:* (*of pers.*) décamper, déguerpir. **3.** *v.i.* (*of plant*) monter en graine. **4.** *v.tr.* gober; **to b. one's dinner,** bouffer son dîner.

bolt³ *adv.* **b. upright,** droit comme un piquet.

bolthole ['boulthoul] *n.* **1.** trou *m* de refuge (d'un animal); *Mil:* abri *m* de bombardement. **2.** échappée *f*; *F:* **to arrange a b. for oneself,** se ménager une porte de sortie.

bolus ['bouləs] *n. Pharm:* bol *m*.

bomb¹ [bɔm] *n.* (*a*) *Mil: etc:* bombe *f*; **incendiary b.,** bombe incendiaire; **atom, nuclear, b.,** bombe atomique, nucléaire; **hydrogen b.,** bombe à (l')hydrogène; **flying b.,** bombe volante; **time b.,** bombe à retardement; **plastic b.,** (bombe au) plastic (*m*); **smoke b.,** bombe fumigène; **to release, drop, a b.,** jeter, lâcher, larguer, une bombe; **b. disposal,** désamorçage *m* et enlèvement *m* des bombes non éclatées; déminage *m*; **b. crater,** entonnoir *m*, cratère *m*; *Av:* **b. bay,** soute *f* à bombes; *F:* **it goes, it's going, like a b.,** ça marche à merveille; *F:* **it costs a b.,** ça coûte les yeux de la tête; (*b*) *Med:* **cobalt b.,** bombe au cobalt.

bomb² *v.tr.* bombarder, lancer des bombes sur (une ville, etc.); **to be bombed out,** (*of factory etc.*) être détruit par un bombardement; (*of pers.*) perdre sa maison, être sinistré, dans un bombardement. **bombing** *n. Av:* bombardement *m*; **dive b.,** bombardement en piqué; **b. run,** course *f* de visée.

bombard [bɔm'bɑ:d] *v.tr. Mil: etc:* bombarder (une ville, un port); *Fig:* **to b. s.o. with questions,** assaillir qn de questions.

bombadier [bɔmbə'diər) *n.* **1.** *Artil:* brigadier *m*. **2.** *U.S: Av:* bombadier *m*.

bombardment [bɔm'bɑ:dmənt] *n. Mil: etc:* bombardement *m*.

bombasine, bombazine ['bɔmbəzi:n] *n. Tex:* bombasin *m*.

bombast ['bɔmbæst] *n.* emphase *f*, boursouflure *f* (de style).

bombastic [bɔm'bæstik] *a.* (style) ampoulé, boursouflé, emphatique. **-ally** *adv.* d'un style ampoulé, emphatique.

bomber ['bɔmər] *n.* **1.** (*pers.*) (*a*) *Mil:* grenadier *m*; (*b*) *Av:* bombadier *m*; (*c*) terroriste *mf* qui se sert de bombes. **2.** (*aircraft*) bombardier.

bombproof ['bɔmpru:f] *a.* à l'épreuve des bombes; **b. shelter,** abri blindé.

bombshell ['bɔmʃel] *n.* (*a*) obus *m*; (*b*) coup *m* de foudre; **this news came as a b. to us,** cette nouvelle nous a atterrés.

bombsight ['bɔmsait] *n.* *Av:* viseur *m*, collimateur *m*, de bombardement.

bombthrower ['bɔmθrouər] *n.* **1.** (*pers.*) lanceur *m* de bombes. **2.** lance-bombes *m.inv.*

bona fide ['bounə'faidi] (*a*) *a. & adv.* de bonne foi; sérieux; **b. f. purchaser,** acheteur *m* de bonne foi; **b. f. offer,** offre sérieuse; (*b*) *n.* **one's bona fides,** sa bonne foi, sa sincérité.

bonanza [bə'nænzə] **1.** *n.* **to strike a b.,** recontrer un filon riche. **2.** *a.* **b. year,** année *f* de prospérité, d'abondance.

Bonapartist ['bounəpɑ:tist] *n. & a.* bonapartiste (*mf*).

bonbon ['bɔnbɔn] *n.* bonbon *m.*

bond¹ [bɔnd] *n.* **1.** lien *m*; attache *f*; *Lit:* **bonds,** fers *mpl*, liens; **to break one's bonds asunder, to burst one's bonds,** rompre, briser, ses liens, ses fers. **2.** (*a*) lien (d'osier, pour fagots, etc.); *Civ.E: etc:* attache; *Fig:* **bonds of friendship,** liens d'amitié; (*b*) *Rail:* éclisse *f* (de rail conducteur); (*c*) *Const:* **(system of) b.,** appareil *m* (en liaison); (*d*) *Carp: Metalw:* assemblage *m*; (*e*) *Ch:* liaison *f*; (*f*) adhésion *f*; adhérence *f*. **3.** (*a*) engagement *m*, contrat *m*; (*b*) *Jur:* obligation *f*; engagement; **mortgage b.,** titre *m* hypothécaire; lettre *f* de gage; (*c*) *Fin:* bon *m*; *U.S:* obligation; **Treasury bonds,** bons du Trésor; **bearer b.,** bon au porteur; **registered b.,** bon nominatif; **government bonds,** (i) rentes *fpl* sur l'État; (ii) titres de rente; **premium bonds,** (i) obligations à primes; (ii) bons à lots; (*d*) *Jur:* caution *f*; **Admiralty b.,** caution en garantie de dommages-intérêts. **4.** *Com: Cust:* (*of goods*) **to be in b.,** être à l'entrepôt, en dépôt; **to take goods out of b.,** dédouaner des marchandises.

bond² *v.tr.* **1.** *Const:* (*a*) (en)lier, liaisonner (des pierres); (*b*) appareiller (un mur, des moellons). **2.** coller (des métaux, etc.). **3** *Com:* entreposer, mettre en dépôt, à l'entrepôt (des marchandises). **bonded** *a.* **1.** *Const:* (*of masonry*) en liaison. **2.** *Com:* (*of goods*) en dépôt, en entrepôt; **b. warehouse,** entrepôt *m* en douane. **3.** *Fin:* (dette) garantie par obligations. **bonding** *n.* **1.** *Const:* (*a*) liaison *f* (de pierres); (*b*) appareillage *m*. **2.** *Metalw:* collage *m* (des métaux). **3.** *Com:* entreposage *m* (de marchandises).

bondage ['bɔndidʒ] *n.* **1.** *Lit:* esclavage *m*, asservissement *m*. **2.** *Hist:* servage *m*.

bondholder ['bɔndhouldər] *n.* *Fin:* obligataire *m*; détenteur *m*, porteur *m*, de bons, d'obligations.

bondstone ['bɔndstoun] *n.* *Const:* parpaing *m*.

bone¹ [boun] *n.* **1.** (*a*) os *m*; (*of fish*) arête *f*; *F:* **he's nothing but skin and bones,** il est maigre comme un clou; il n'a que la peau et les os; **he won't make old bones,** il ne fera pas de vieux os; **frozen to the b.,** gelé jusqu'aux os; **to work one's fingers to the b.,** se tuer à travailler; **to be b. idle, b. lazy,** être paresseux comme une couleuvre; **I feel it in my bones,** j'en ai le pressentiment; **b. of contention,** sujet *m* de dispute; *F:* **to have a b. to pick with s.o.,** avoir maille à partir avec qn.; **to make no bones about doing sth.,** ne pas hésiter à faire qch.; **he made no bones about it,** il y est allé carrément; (*of joke, etc.*) **near the b.,** risqué; d'un goût douteux; (*b*) **b. ash, b. earth,** cendre *f*, poudre *f*, terre *f*, d'os; *Cer:* **b. china,** porcelaine *f* tendre anglaise. **2. bones,** (i) (*of the dead*) ossements *mpl*; (ii) *Cost:* armature *f* (d'un bustier, etc.).

bone² *v.tr.* **1.** désosser (la viande); ôter les arêtes (du poisson). **2.** garnir (un corset) de baleines. **3.** *v.ind.tr.* *NAm: P:* **to b. up on sth.,** potasser qch. **boned** *a.* **1.** (*of meat*) désossé; (*of fish*) sans arêtes. **2.** (corset) baleiné.

bonehead ['bounhed] *n.* *F:* idiot, -ote; tête *f* de bois.

boneless ['bounlis] *a.* **1.** désossé; sans os; sans arêtes. **2.** *F:* mou; sans caractère.

bonemeal ['bounmi:l] *n.* engrais *m* d'os (broyés).

boneshaker ['bounʃeikər] *n.* *F:* **1.** *A:* vélocipède *m* à bandages de fer. **2.** (*car*) vieux clou, vieille guimbarde.

bonfire ['bɔnfaiər] *n.* (*a*) feu *m* de joie; (*b*) feu de jardin.

bonhomie ['bɔnɔmi:] *n.* bonhomie *f*, jovialité *f*.

bonkers ['bɔŋkəz] *a.* *P:* cinglé.

bonnet¹ ['bɔnit] *n.* **1.** *Cost:* (*a*) bonnet, béret (écossais); (*b*) capote *f*, bonnet (de femme, d'enfant). **2.** (*a*) *Aut: Av:* capot *m*; (*b*) *Nau:* couvercle *m*, chapeau *m* (de cheminée); (*c*) chapeau, capot, couvercle (de soupape, de vanne).

bonny ['bɔni] *a.* *esp. Scot:* joli; gentil, *f.* gentille; **a b. baby,** un bébé magnifique.

bonus, *pl.* **-uses** ['bounəs, -əsiz] *n.* gratification *f*, bonification *f*; prime *f*; **to work on a b. system,** travailler à la prime; **cost-of-living b.,** indemnité *f* de vie chère, de cherté de vie; *Ins:* **no-claims b.,** bonification pour non-sinistre; bonus *m*; *Com: etc:* **Christmas b.,** gratification de fin d'année; **productivity b.,** *U.S:* **merit b.,** prime de rendement.

bony ['bouni] *a.* **1.** osseux. **2.** (*pers.*) à, aux, gros os; (corps, contours) anguleux; (doigt, visage) décharné. **3.** (*of meat*) plein d'os; (*of fish*) plein d'arêtes.

boo¹ [bu:] **1.** *int.* hou! *F:* **he can't say b. to a goose,** c'est un timide. **2.** *n.* huée *f*.

boo² *v.tr. & i.* **to b. (at) s.o.,** huer, chahuter, qn; **to be booed off the stage,** quitter la scène au milieu des huées. **booing** *n.* huées *fpl*; chahutage *m*.

boob¹ [bu:b] *n.* *P:* **1.** (*a*) idiot, -ote; crétin *m*; (*b*) gaffe *f*. **2.** (*not in polite use*) **boobs,** nénés *mpl.*

boob² *v.i.* *P:* faire une gaffe.

booby ['bu:bi] *n.* **1.** (*a*) idiot, -ote: crétin *m*, nouille *f*; **b. trap,** (i) attrape-nigaud *m*, *pl.* attrape-nigauds; (ii) *Mil:* piège *m*; mine-piège *f*, *pl.* mines-pièges; (*b*) le dernier (dans un concours, etc.); **b. prize,** prix décerné par plaisanterie à celui qui vient en dernier. **2.** *Orn:* fou *m*.

booby-trap ['bu:bitræp] *v.tr.* *Mil: etc:* piéger.

boogie-woogie ['bu:gi'wu:gi] *n.* *Mus:* boogie-woogie *m*.

book¹ [buk] *n.* **1.** (*a*) livre *m*; **old books,** (i) vieux bouquins; (ii) vieilles éditions; **the b. trade,** l'industrie *f* du livre; la librairie; **school b.,** livre scolaire; livre de classe; **not published in b. form,** inédit en librairie; **b. club,** club *m* du livre; **b. learning,** érudition *f*; savoir acquis dans les livres; **b. plate,** ex-libris *m inv*; **b. post,** service postal des imprimés; **by the b.,** selon les règles; (*of subject*) **to be a closed b. to s.o.,** être lettre close pour qn; (*b*) livret *m*, libretto *m* (d'un opéra); (*c*) *O:* **the good B.,** la Bible; **to swear on the B.,** prêter serment sur la Bible; (*d*) **blue b.,** (i) *Adm:* = livre jaune; (ii) *U.S:* registre *m* (des employés de l'État, etc.); (iii) *U.S:* = Bottin mondain; (iv) *U.S: Sch:* cahier bleu (dans lequel les candidats écrivent leurs copies d'examen); (*e*) recueil *m* (de chansons, de prières, etc.); **telephone b.,** annuaire *m* des téléphones. **2.** (*a*) *Com: Fin: etc:* registre; **account b.,** livre de comptes; **b. value,** valeur *f* comptable; **cash b.,** livre de caisse; **bank b.,** livret, carnet *m*, de banque; **cheque b.,** carnet de chèques, chéquier *m*; **to keep the books of a firm,** tenir les livres d'une maison; **to be in s.o.'s good books,** être bien vu de qn; **to be in s.o.'s bad books,** être mal vu, mal noté, de, par, qn; **to bring s.o. to b. for sth.,** forcer qn à rendre compte de qch.; *F:* **to throw the b. at s.o.,** accabler qn d'accusations; (*b*) *Nau:* **ship's books,** livres de bord; **signal b.,** tome *m* des signaux; (*c*) *Sch: etc:* **exercise b.,** cahier; **rough b.,** brouillon *m*; (*d*) *Turf:* **betting b.,** livre de paris; **to make a b.,** faire un livre; (*e*) **b. of stamps, of tickets,** carnet de timbres, de billets; **b. of needles,** sachet *m*, jeu *m*, d'aiguilles; **b. of matches,** pochette *f* d'allumettes; **b. matches,** allumettes plates.

book² 1. *v.tr.* (*a*) inscrire, enregistrer (une commande, etc.); (*b*) (*at hotel*) **to b. s.o. in,** inscrire qn au registre; (*c*) *F:* (*of policeman*) (i) dresser une contravention à (qn); (ii) *U.S:* arrêter (qn). **2.** *v.tr.* retenir, réserver (une place, une chambre); louer (une place) d'avance; *Rail: Av:* (i) réserver, (ii) prendre (un billet, une place); *Th: etc:* engager (un artiste); (*of theatre, flight, etc.*) **fully booked,** complet; **I'm booked (up) for this evening,** je suis pris ce soir. **3.** *v.i. Rail: etc:* (i) réserver, (ii) prendre, une place, un billet; **to b. through to Nice,** prendre un billet direct pour Nice. **booking** *n.* **1.** enregistrement *m*, inscription *f*. **2.** (*a*) réservation *f* (d'une chambre, d'une place, etc.); *Th: etc:* engagement *m* (d'un artiste); location *f* (de places, de billets); **block b.,** location, réservation, en bloc; **b. clerk,** employé(e) du guichet; **b. office,** guichet *m* de réservation, de location; (*b*) (*at hotel*) réservation; *Th: etc:* engagement.

bookable ['bukəbl] *a. Th: etc:* (*of seat*) qui peut être réservé, loué à l'avance.

bookbinder ['bukbaindər] *n.* relieur, -euse.

bookbinding ['bukbaindiŋ] *n.* reliure *f*.

bookcase ['bukkeis] *n. Furn:* bibliothèque *f*.

bookend ['bukend] *n.* serre-livres *m inv.*

bookie ['buki] *n. Turf: F:* bookmaker *m*, book *m*.

bookish ['bukiʃ] *a.* **1.** (*of pers.*) studieux. **2.** (*of pers., of style*) pédantesque, livresque.

book-keeper ['bukki:pər] *n. Com:* teneur *m* de livres; comptable *m*.

book-keeping ['bukki:piŋ] *n. Com:* tenue *f* de(s) livres; **single-entry b.-k.,** unigraphie *f*; **double-entry b.-k.,** tenue des livres en partie double.

booklet ['buklit] *n.* livret *m*; opuscule *m*; brochure *f*; **descriptive b.,** notice descriptive (d'une machine).

booklover ['buklʌvər] *n.* bibliophile *m*.

bookmaker ['bukmeikər] *n.* **1.** faiseur *m* de livres. **2.** *Turf:* bookmaker *m*.

bookmark(er) ['bukmɑ:k(ər)] *n.* signet *m*.

bookrest ['bukrest] *n.* appui-livre(s) *m inv*, porte-livres *m inv.*

bookroom ['bukru:m] *n.* (*a*) cabinet *m* de lecture (d'une librairie); (*b*) (*in house*) (petite) bibliothèque.

bookseller ['bukselər] *n.* libraire *m*; **secondhand b.,** bouquiniste *m*.

bookselling ['bukseliŋ] *n.* (commerce *m* de) librairie *f*.

bookshelf, *pl.* **-shelves** ['bukʃelf, -ʃelvz] *n.* rayon *m* (à livres).

bookshop ['bukʃɔp] *n.* librairie *f*.

bookstall ['bukstɔ:l] *n.* **1.** étalage *m* de livres; **secondhand b.,** étalage de bouquiniste. **2.** bibliothèque *f* de gare.

bookstore ['bukstɔ:r] *n. NAm:* librairie *f*.

bookwork ['bukwə:k] *n.* **1.** *Com:* tenue *f* des livres. **2.** *Sch: etc:* étude *f* des livres. **3.** *Typ:* labeur *m*.

bookworm ['bukwə:m] *n.* **1.** *Ent:* anobion *m*, ptine *m*. **2.** *F:* (*pers.*) dévoreur, -euse, de livres; bouquineur, -euse.

boom¹ [bu:m] *n.* **1.** (*at harbour mouth*) barrage *m* flottant; barre, estacade, flottante. **2.** *Nau:* (*a*) boutdehors *m* (de foc), *pl.* bouts-dehors; gui *m*; (*b*) **swinging b.,** tangon *m*; (*c*) **derrick b.,** mât *m* de charge; **cargo b.,** corne *f* de charge; (*d*) flèche *f* (d'une grue); (*f*) *Cin: T.V:* perche *f* (de microphone), *F:* girafe *f*.

boom² *n.* grondement *m*, retentissement *m* (du canon, du tonnerre, des vagues); mugissement *m* (du vent); tons *mpl* sonores (de la voix); ronflement *m* (de l'orgue); bourdonnement *m* (de cloches); *Av:* **sonic b.,** bang *m* (supersonique).

boom³ *v.i.* (*of wind, etc.*) retentir, gronder, mugir (sourdement); (*of guns*) gronder, tonner; (*of organ*) ronfler; (*of bells*) bourdonner; **his voice boomed,** sa voix retentissait. **booming** *a.* (vent) mugissant, (tonnerre) retentissant; **b. voice,** voix retentissante.

boom⁴ *n. Com: Fin: etc:* boom *m*, période *f* d'essor; vague *f* de prospérité; **b. town,** ville *f* champignon.

boom⁵ *v.i.* être en hausse; faire de la hausse; **trade, business, is booming,** les affaires marchent bien, sont en plein essor.

boomerang¹ ['bu:məræŋ] *n.* boomerang *m*.

boomerang² *v.i.* faire boomerang.

boon¹ [bu:n] *n.* (*a*) *Lit:* faveur *f*; (*b*) bienfait *m*, avantage *m*; **I found it a great b.,** cela m'a rendu grand service.

boon² *a.* **b. companion,** gai, bon, compagnon.

boor ['buər] *n.* rustre *m*, rustaud *m*.

boorish ['buəriʃ] *a.* rustre, rustaud, grossier. **-ly,** *adv.* grossièrement; en rustre.

boorishness ['buəriʃnis] *n.* grossièreté *f*; manque *m* de savoir-vivre.

boost¹ [bu:st] *n.* **1. to give a b. to (sth., s.o.),** faire de la réclame, du battage, pour (un produit); relancer (une industrie, la production, etc.); augmenter (le recrutement, la vente de qch., etc.); relever (le moral); *F:* pistonner (qn). **2.** (*a*) *El:* survoltage *m*; (*b*) *Av:* surpression *f*.

boost² *v.tr.* **1.** faire de la réclame, du battage, pour (un produit); relancer (une industrie, la production, etc.); augmenter (le recrutement, le nombre, etc.); relever (le moral); *F:* pistonner (qn). **2.** surélever (la vitesse, l'énergie, la pression, de qch.); *El:* survolter.

booster ['bu:stər] *n.* (*a*) *El:* survolteur *m*; (*b*) (*of missile*) propulseur *m* auxiliaire de départ; **b. rocket,** fusée de démarrage; (*c*) *Av:* démarreur *m* auxiliaire; accélérateur *m* (de décollage); (*d*) *Tchn:* surpresseur *m*; **b. station,** station *f* auxiliaire de pompage; station relais; (*e*) *Elcs:* préamplificateur *m* d'antenne; (*f*) *Ch:* renforçateur *m*; (*g*) *Med:* **b. dose, injection,** *F:* dose *f*, injection *f*, piqûre *f*, de rappel.

boot¹ [bu:t] *n.* **1.** (i) **(ankle-) b.,** (i) chaussure montante; bottine *f*; (ii) **(high) b.,** botte *f*; **laced b.,** brodequin *m*; **fur-lined b.,** bottillon *m*; **riding boots,** bottes à l'écuyère; **b. strap,** tirant *m* de botte; *F:* **the boot's on the other foot, leg,** (i) c'est tout (juste) le contraire; (ii) les rôles sont renversés; **you can bet your boots that . . .,** je te garantis que . . .; *F:* **to give s.o. the b.,** mettre, flanquer, qn à la porte; **to get the b.,** être mis à la porte; *F:* **as tough as old boots,** dur comme tout. **2.** *Ind:* hotte *f*, trémie *f* (pour alimenter une machine, etc.); **charging b.,** entonnoir *m*. **3.** *Aut:* coffre *m*.

boot² *v.tr.* **1.** chausser (qn). **2.** *F:* flanquer des coups de pied à (qn); **to b. s.o. out,** flanquer qn à la porte.

boot³ *n.* (*only in the phrase*) **to b.,** par surcroit, en sus; par-dessus le marché.

bootblack ['bu:tblæk] *n.* cireur *m* (de chaussures).

bootee [bu:'ti:] *n.* (*a*) bottillon *m*; (*b*) bottine *f* d'enfant; chausson tricoté (de bébé).

booth [bu:ð] *n.* baraque *f*, tente *f* (de marché, de forains); loge *f* (de foire); **telephone b.,** cabine *f* téléphonique; **polling b.,** isoloir *m*; bureau *m* de scrutin;

Cin: **projection b.,** cabine *f* de projection.
bootjack ['bu:tdʒæk] *n.* arrache-chaussures *m inv*, tire-botte *m*, *pl.* tire-bottes.
bootlace ['bu:tleis] *n.* lacet *m* (de botte).
bootleg[1] ['bu:tleg] *n.* produit *m* (*esp.* alcool) (i) vendu illégalement, (ii) passé en fraude.
bootleg[2] **(bootlegged) 1.** *v.tr.* (i) transporter, (ii) produire, vendre, (de l'alcool) illégalement. **2.** *v.i.* trafiquer (surtout en boissons alcooliques); faire de la contrebande. **bootlegging** *n.* contrebande *f* (*esp.* de l'alcool); bootlegging *m.*
bootlicker ['bu:tlikər] *n. F:* lèche-bottes *m inv.*
bootmaker ['bu:tmeikər] *n.* bottier *m*; cordonnier *m.*
booty ['bu:ti] *n.* butin *m.*
booze[1] [bu:z] *v.i. F:* boire (comme un trou); lever le coude; picoler.
booze[2] *n. P:* **1.** boisson *f* (*esp.* alcoolique); **there's no more b.,** il n'y a plus rien à boire. **2. to go on the b.,** se mettre à boire.
boozer ['bu:zər] *P:* **1.** ivrogne *m*, soûlard; *m.* **2.** bistrot *m.*
booze-up ['bu:zʌp] *n. P:* beuverie *f*; soûlerie *f.*
boozy ['bu:zi] *a. F:* soûlard; pompette; **a b. evening,** une soirée passée à boire.
bop [bop] *n. Mus:* bop *m.*
bo-peep [bou'pi:p] *n. F:* cache-cache *m. inv.*
boracic [bə'ræsik] *a. Ch:* (acide) borique; *Pharm:* **b. ointment,** pommade *f* boriquée.
borage ['bɔridʒ] *n. Bot: Pharm:* bourrache *f.*
borax ['bɔ:ræks] *n. Ch: etc:* borax *m.*
bordeaux [bɔ:'dou] *n.* (*wine*) bordeaux *m.*
border ['bɔ:dər] *n.* **1.** bord *m*; lisière *f*, bordure *f*; marge *f*; frontière *f* (entre deux pays); **to cross the b.,** passer la frontière; **b. town,** ville *f* frontière; **b. region,** région frontalière; **the B.,** (i) la frontière écossaise (et les comtés limitrophes); (ii) la frontière entre les États-Unis et le Mexique. **2.** (*a*) galon *m* (d'un habit); bordure (d'un tableau, d'un tapis, etc.); encadrement *m* (d'un panneau); carnèle *f* (d'une pièce de monnaie); *Typ:* **(ornamental) b.,** (i) dentelle *f*, (ii) vignette *f* (d'une page); *Th:* **the borders,** (i) les coulisses *fpl*; (ii) les frises *fpl*; (*b*) **flower b.,** plate-bande *f*, *pl.* plates-bandes; **grass b.,** cordon *m* de gazon.
border[2] **1.** *v.tr.* (*a*) border (un habit, un chemin, etc.); lisérer (un mouchoir); encadrer; (*b*) border; confiner à (un pays, etc.); **the countries that b. the Mediterranean,** les pays qui bordent la Méditerranée. **2.** *v.i.* **to b. on (sth.),** (*a*) (*of territory*) toucher, confiner, à (un autre pays); **the two countries b. on one another,** les deux pays se touchent; **his estate borders on mine,** sa terre tient à la mienne; (*b*) **to b. on (sth.),** approcher, être voisin, de (la folie, etc.); friser (le mensonge, etc.); toucher à (l'absurde); **he was bordering on sixty,** il frisait la soixantaine. **bordering** *a.* (*a*) contigu, -uë, aboutissant **(on,** à); voisin **(on,** de); limitrophe **(on,** de); **countries b. the Mediterranean,** pays *mpl* en bordure de la Méditerranée; (*b*) **emotion b. on terror,** émotion voisine de la terreur.
borderer ['bɔ:dərər] *n.* habitant, -ante, de la frontière, (*esp.* de la frontière d'Écosse); frontalier; -ière.
borderland ['bɔ:dəlænd] *n.* (*a*) pays *m* frontière, limitrophe; marche *f*; (*b*) *Fig:* frontière *f* **(between sleeping and waking,** du sommeil et du réveil).
borderline ['bɔ:dəlain] *n.* (*a*) ligne *f* de séparation (entre deux catégories, etc.); frontière *f* (entre deux états); **the b. between sanity and insanity,** la limite entre le bon sens et la folie; (*b*) **b. case,** (i) cas *m* limite; (ii) cas indéterminé.
bore[1] ['bɔ:r] *n.* **1.** (*a*) calibre *m*, alésage *m* (d'un tuyau, etc.); calibre (d'une arme à feu); (*b*) âme *f* (d'une arme à feu); **smooth, rifled, b.,** âme lisse, rayée. **2.** *Min:* trou *m* de sonde; sondage *m*, forage *m.*
bore[2] *v.tr. & i.* **1.** foncer (un puits); forer, percer (un trou); aléser (un cylindre); (*of insect*) **to b. into wood,** creuser un trou, une galerie, dans le bois; **to b. through sth.,** percer qch.; *Min:* **to b. for water, minerals,** faire un sondage, sonder, pour trouver de l'eau, des minéraux. **2.** *Equit:* (*of horse*) bourrer; **to b. on the bit,** se braquer sur le mors. **3.** *Turf:* couper un concurrent. **boring 1.** *a. Ent:* térébrant. **2.** *n.* percement *m* (d'un trou, etc.); *Mec.E:* forage *m*, perçage *m*; (*of cylinder*) alésage *m*; *Min:* sondage *m*, forage; **to make borings,** faire des sondages; **b. mill,** aléseuse fraiseuse; **b. machine,** *Mec.E:* foreuse *f*, perceuse *f*; (*for cylinders*) alésoir *m*; *Min: etc:* sondeuse *f*, sonde *f*; **b. tool,** *Mec.E:* outil *m* à aléser; alésoir *m*; *Min: etc:* outil de sondage; sonde *f.*
bore[3] *n.* (*a*) personne ennuyeuse; *F:* raseur, -euse; **what a b. (he is)!** ce qu'il est barbant, rasoir! (*b*) (*thg*) corvée *f*, *F:* scie *f*; **what a b.!** quelle corvée!
bore[4] *v.tr.* ennuyer, *F:* raser, barber (qn); **to be, get, bored,** s'ennuyer; **I'm never bored,** je ne m'ennuie jamais; *F:* **it bores me stiff, to death, to tears,** ça me fait mourir, crever, d'ennui; **he bores me stiff,** il m'ennuie à mourir. **boring** *a.* ennuyeux, *F:* barbant, rasoir.
bore[5] *n.* mascaret *m*; raz *m* de marée; barre *f* d'eau.
bore[6] *see* BEAR[3].
boredom ['bɔ:dəm] *n.* ennui *m.*
borehole ['bɔ:houl] *n. Min:* **1.** trou *m* de sonde; sondage *m.* **2.** trou de mine.
borer ['bɔ:rər] *n.* **1.** (*pers.*) foreur *m*, perceur *m*; sondeur *m* (de puits). **2.** foret *m*, tarière *f*; perçoir *m*; (*of cylinder*) alésoir *m*; *Min:* fleuret *m*, sonde. **3.** *Equit:* cheval *m* qui se braque. **4.** (*a*) *Moll:* taret *m*; (*b*) *Ent:* insecte térébrant.
boric ['bɔrik] *a. Ch:* (acide, etc.) borique.
born [bɔ:n] **1.** (*p.p. of* BEAR[3] *used in formation of passive verb*) **to be b.,** naître; **I was b. in London,** je suis né à Londres; **the house where I was b.,** ma maison natale; **he is French b.,** il est français de naissance; **when I was b.,** lors de ma naissance; **he was b. in 1930,** il est né en 1930; **to be b. deaf, blind,** être sourd, aveugle, de naissance; **to be b. lucky,** être né coiffé; *F:* **do you think I was b. yesterday?** croyez-vous que je suis né d'hier? *Fig:* **crime b. of poverty,** crime né de la misère; *Theol:* **b. again,** régénéré. **2.** *a.* **he's a b. storyteller,** c'est un conteur né; **a Londoner b. and bred,** un vrai Londonien de Londres; **in all my b. days,** de toute ma vie.
borne *see* BEAR[3].
Borneo ['bɔ:niou] *Pr.n. Geog:* Bornéo *m.*
borough ['bʌrə] *n.* (*a*) ville *f* (avec municipalité); **b. council,** conseil municipal; (*b*) circonscription électorale (urbaine).
borrow ['bɔrou] *v.tr. & i.* emprunter **(from,** à); **may I b. your pen?** pourriez-vous me prêter votre stylo? *Fin: etc:* **to b. (money) from s.o.,** faire un emprunt à qn; emprunter à qn; **to b. an idea from s.o.,** emprunter une idée à qn; **this word was borrowed from Latin,** ce mot est un emprunt au latin. **borrowed** *a.* **b. capital,** capitaux empruntés, d'emprunt; **he's living on b. time,** (i) il a déjà dépassé l'âge où la plupart des gens meurent; (ii) il ne lui reste que peu de temps à vivre. **borrowing** *n.* (*action or sth. borrowed*) emprunt *m.*
borrower ['bɔrouər] *n.* emprunteur, -euse.
borstal ['bɔ:st(ə)l] *n. Adm:* maison *f* de redressement (pour jeunes délinquants âgés de 15 à 21 ans); **b. boy,** jeune délinquant.
borzoi ['bɔ:zɔi] *n.* lévrier *m* russe; barzoï *m.*
bosh [bɔʃ] *n. & int. F:* bêtises *fpl*, blague *f.*
bos'n ['bousn] *n.* = BOATSWAIN.

bosom[1] ['buz(ə)m] **1.** *n.* (*a*) (i) poitrine *f* (d'une personne); (ii) seins *mpl* (d'une femme); (*b*) **in the b. of one's family,** au sein de sa famille; **in the b. of the Church,** dans le giron de l'Église. **2.** *a.* **b. friend,** ami(e) intime.

Bosphorus (the) [ðə'bɔsfərəs] (*U.S: also* **Bosporus** ['bɔspərəs]) *Pr.n. Geog:* le Bosphore.

boss[1] [bɔs] **1.** protubérance *f*; *Arch: Metall: Z: etc:* bosse *f*; *Furn:* capiton *m.* **2.** (*a*) *Mec.E:* mamelon *m*, portée *f*; (*of wheel, crank*) **centre b.,** tourteau *m*; (*b*) *Av:* moyeu *m* (de l'hélice).

boss[2] *F:* **1.** *n.* (*a*) **the b.,** (i) le patron, la patronne, (ii) le chef; **the trade-union bosses,** les grands chefs du syndicat; **she's the b. here,** c'est elle qui porte la culotte; (*b*) *Pol: NAm:* chef d'un parti. **2.** *a. esp. NAm:* épatant, merveilleux.

boss[3] *v.tr. F:* mener, diriger (qn, qch.); **to b. the show,** contrôler tout; faire la loi; **stop bossing me about!** j'en ai assez de vous et de vos ordres!

boss[4] *a. F:* **to make a b. shot,** rater, manquer, son coup; **b. eyed,** (i) qui louche; (ii) borgne.

boss[5] *v.tr. F:* louper (un travail, etc.); rater (son coup).

bossiness ['bɔsinis] *n. F:* autoritarisme *m*; façons *fpl* autoritaires.

bossy[1] ['bɔsi] *a. F:* autoritaire; **he's so b.,** il veut toujours faire la loi.

bosun ['bousn] *n.* = BOATSWAIN.

botanic(al) [bə'tænik(l)] *a.* botanique; **b. garden(s),** jardin *m* botanique.

botanist ['bɔtənist] *n.* botaniste *mf.*

botanize ['bɔtənaiz] *v.i.* herboriser, botaniser.

botany ['bɔtəni] *n.* botanique *f*; **b. wool,** laine très fine (importée d'Australie).

botch[1] [bɔtʃ] *n. F:* travail mal fait, bousillé; **you've made an awful b. of it,** tu l'as bien bousillé, loupé.

botch[2] *v.tr. F:* (*a*) bousiller, louper (un travail, etc.); **botched-up work,** travail mal torché, loupé; (*b*) **to b. (sth.) up,** rafistoler (qch.).

botcher ['bɔtʃər] *n. F:* bousilleur *m*; savetier *m.*

both [bouθ] **1.** *a. & pron.* tous (les) deux, toutes (les) deux; l'un(e) et l'autre; **b. brothers, b. (of) the brothers,** les deux frères; l'un et l'autre frère; **b. (of them) are dead,** ils sont morts tous (les) deux; **he has two houses, b. of which are vacant,** il a deux maisons, qui sont vides toutes les deux; **she kissed him on b. cheeks,** elle l'a embrassé sur les deux joues; **to hold sth. in b. hands,** tenir qch. à deux mains; **on b. sides,** des deux côtés; **b. alike,** l'un comme l'autre; **b. of us saw it,** nous deux l'avons vu; nous l'avons vu tous (les) deux; **you can't have it b. ways,** on ne peut pas avoir le drap et l'argent; *Nau:* **stop b. engines,** stoppez partout. **2.** *adv.* **b. you and I,** (et) vous et moi; **she is b. intelligent and beautiful,** elle est à la fois intelligente et belle.

bother[1] ['bɔðər] *n.* ennui *m*; *F:* embêtement *m*; embarras *m*; **I'm in a bit of (a) b., I'm having a bit, a spot, of b.,** j'ai des ennuis (**with,** avec); **if it's not too much b.,** si cela ne vous dérange pas trop; **it's not worth the b.,** cela ne vaut pas la peine.

bother[2] **1.** *v.tr.* (*a*) gêner (qn); ennuyer, *F:* embêter (qn); déranger (qn); **does the light b. you?** est-ce que la lumière vous gêne? **don't b. me!** laissez-moi tranquille! **I can't be bothered to do it,** je n'ai pas envie de le faire; **b. (it)!** zut! **b. the man!** qu'il aille au diable! (*b*) inquiéter (qn); tracasser (qn); **to be bothered about sth.,** s'inquiéter de qch.; se faire du mauvais sang de qch.; **don't b. yourself, your head, about me,** ne vous inquiétez pas de moi; *F:* **I'm not bothered!** cela m'est bien égal! je m'en fiche! **2.** *v.i.* s'inquiéter (**about,** de); s'occuper (**with,** de); prendre, se donner, la peine (**to do sth.,** de faire qch.); **he doesn't b. about anything,** il ne s'inquiète de rien; **he didn't even b. to apologize,** il ne s'est même pas excusé; **don't b. to ring me up,** ce n'est pas la peine de me téléphoner.

botheration [bɔðə'reiʃ(ə)n] *F: O:* **1.** *n.* ennui *m*, vexation *f.* **2.** *int.* zut!

bothersome ['bɔðəsəm] *a.* importun, gênant; embarrassant.

bottle[1] [bɔtl] *n.* (*a*) bouteille *f*; (*small*) flacon *m*; (*wide-mouthed*) bocal *m*; **stone b.,** cruchon *m*; **wine b.,** bouteille à vin: **b. of wine,** bouteille de vin; *F:* **to be fond of the b.,** aimer la bouteille; **to be on the b.,** être adonné à la boisson; lever le coude; **to hit the b.,** boire (trop); **b. brush,** goupillon *m*; hérisson *m*; **b. opener,** ouvre-bouteille(s) *m inv*; décapsuleur *m*; **b. party,** boum à laquelle chacun apporte à boire; **b. bank,** dépôt *m* de bouteilles; (*b*) flacon (de parfum, etc.); (*c*) **(feeding, baby's) b.,** biberon *m*; **brought up on the b., b.-fed,** élevé, allaité, au biberon; (*d*) **hot-water b.,** bouillotte *f*; (*e*) *Med:* urinal *m* de lit, *F:* pistolet *m*; (*f*) *Box:* **b. holder,** soigneur *m*, second *m.*

bottle[2] *v.tr.* mettre (du vin) en bouteilles; conserver (des fruits, etc.) en bocal. **bottled** *a.* (vin, bière) en bouteille(s); **b. fruit,** fruits *mpl* en bocaux. **bottle up** *v.tr.* étouffer (ses sentiments); refouler, ravaler (sa colère). **bottling** *n.* mise *f* en bouteille(s); mise en bocaux.

bottle-green ['bɔtl'gri:n] *a.* vert bouteille.

bottleneck ['bɔtlnek] *n.* **1.** goulot *m* (de bouteille). **2.** (*a*) rétrécissement *m* de la chaussée; (*b*) *Aut:* embouteillage *m*, bouchon *m.* **3.** (*in production, etc.*) goulet *m*, goulot, d'étranglement.

bottlewasher ['bɔtlwɔʃər] *n.* **1.** (*pers.*) laveur, -euse, de bouteilles; *F:* **head cook and b.,** (i) factotum *m*; (ii) homme qui mène toute l'affaire. **2.** (*machine*) rince-bouteilles *m inv.*

bottom[1] ['bɔtəm] *n.* **1.** bas *m* (d'une colline, d'un escalier, d'une page); fond *m* (d'un puits, d'une boîte, de la mer); plafond *m* (d'un canal, d'un réservoir); ballast *m*, assiette *f* (d'une chaussée, etc.); **at the b. of the garden,** au fond du jardin; **he's at the b. of the class,** il est à la queue de la classe; il est le dernier de sa classe; **at the b. of the page,** au, en, bas de la page; **b. fishing,** pêche *f* à la ligne de fond; **to send a ship to the b.,** envoyer un bâtiment au fond; (*of ship*) **to go to the b.,** couler à fond; (*of ship*) **to strike, touch, b.,** talonner; toucher le fond; **prices have reached rock b.,** les prix sont au plus bas; **from the b. of one's heart,** du fond du cœur; **to get to the b. of sth., of things,** découvrir la cause, l'origine, de qch.; aller au fond des choses; **to be at the b. of sth.,** (i) (*of pers.*) être derrière qch; être l'instigateur de qch.; (ii) être la cause de qch. **2.** bas-fond *m*, *pl.* bas-fonds (de terrain). **3.** (*a*) (i) fond, (ii) dessous *m* (d'assiette, de verre, etc.); siège *m* (d'une chaise); **to put sth. b. up(wards),** mettre qch. sens dessus dessous; **box with a false b.,** boîte *f* à double fond; **to knock the b. out of (sth.),** (i) défoncer (une boîte, etc.); (ii) démolir (un argument); **the b. has fallen out of the market,** le marché s'est effondré; *F:* **bottoms up!** (i) cul sec! (ii) à votre santé! (*b*) *Cmptr:* bas *m* (d'une gamme); (*c*) *Bill:* **to put b. on a ball,** faire de l'effet à revenir, de l'effet rétrograde. **4.** *F:* derrière *m* (d'une personne). **5.** *Nau:* (*a*) carène *f*, fond (d'un navire); (*b*) navire *m.* **6.** *attrib.* **b. half,** partie inférieure; **b. book (of a pile),** livre qui est en bas, tout en dessous; **b. end of the table,** (bas) bout de la table; **b. stair,** marche *f* du bas, première marche (de l'escalier), dernière marche (en descendant); **b. price,** prix plancher; **at rock b. prices,** aux plus bas prix; *Aut:* **in b. gear,** en première (vitesse); *F:* **you can bet your b. dollar that . . .,** vous pouvez être sûr que . . .

bottom[2] **1.** *v.tr.* (*a*) mettre un siège à (une chaise). **2.** *v.i.* (*of ship, etc.*) toucher le fond.

bottomless ['bɔtəmlis] *a.* **1.** (puits, etc.) sans fond. **2.** (réserve) inépuisable.
botulism ['bɔtjulizm] *n. Med:* botulisme *m.*
bouclé ['bu:klei] *a.* & *n. Tex:* bouclé (*m*); **b. wool,** bouclette *f.*
boudoir ['bu:dwɑ:r] *n.* boudoir *m.*
bougainvillea [bu:gən'viliə] *n. Bot:* bougainvillée *f.*
bough [bau] *n.* branche *f,* rameau *m* (d'arbre).
bought. *see* BUY[1].
bouillon ['bu:jɔn] *n. Cu:* bouillon *m,* consommé *m.*
boulder ['bouldər] *n.* gros caillou; (gros) bloc de pierre roulé; *Geol:* **b. clay,** argile *f* à blocaux.
boulevard ['bu:ləvɑ:d] *n. NAm:* **1.** boulevard *m.* **2.** terre-plein (central), *pl.* terre-pleins.
bounce[1] [bauns] *n.* **1.** (*a*) (*of ball*) rebond *m,* rebondissement *m;* **to catch the ball on the b.,** prendre la balle au bond; (*b*) *NAm:* **b. back,** (i) écho *m;* (ii) *Th: etc:* retour *m,* rentrée *f* (d'un artiste, etc.). **2.** *F:* (*of pers.*) (i) vantardise *f;* (ii) vitalité *f;* **he's as full of b. as ever,** il est toujours aussi plein d'énergie.
bounce[2] **1.** *v.i.* (*a*) (*of ball, etc.*) rebondir; (*b*) (*of pers.*) **to b. into, out of, a room,** entrer dans une pièce, sortir d'une pièce, en coup de vent, en trombe; (*of actor, etc.*) **to b. back,** faire son retour (après un échec); (*c*) (*of pers.*) faire l'important; se vanter; **cheque that bounces,** chèque *m* sans provision. **2.** *v.tr.* (*a*) faire rebondir (une balle); (*b*) *NAm: F:* donner son congé à (qn); flanquer (qn) à la porte (du cabaret, etc.). **bouncing** *a.* **1.** rebondissant. **2. b. baby,** bébé plein de vie et de santé.
bouncer ['baunsər] *n. F:* **1.** videur *m* (dans une boîte de nuit, etc.). **2.** *Cr:* balle *f* qui rebondit en hauteur. **3.** chèque *m* sans provision.
bouncy ['baunsi] *a.* (*a*) rebondissant; élastique; (*b*) *F:* (*of pers.*) dynamique.
bound[1] [baund] *n.* (*usu. pl.*) limite(s) *f(pl),* bornes *fpl;* **to beat the bounds,** constater solennellement (en procession) les limites d'une paroisse; **out of bounds,** (i) défendu; *Mil: etc:* consigné; (ii) *Golf: Fb: etc:* hors des limites, hors du jeu; **to go beyond the bounds of reason,** dépasser les bornes de la raison; **my fury knew no bounds,** je n'ai pu contenir ma fureur; **to keep within bounds,** rester dans la juste mesure; user de modération.
bound[2] *n.* bond *m,* saut *m;* **at one b.,** d'un (seul) bond, d'un saut, d'un seul élan; **to advance by leaps and bounds,** avancer à pas de géant.
bound[3] *v.i.* bondir, sauter; (*of ball, etc.*) rebondir; **to b. forward,** bondir en avant.
bound[4] *a. Nau:* **ship b. for America,** navire *m* en partance pour, en route pour, l'Amérique; **homeward b.,** (i) (navire) retournant au port, au pays; (cargaison) de retour; (ii) *F:* (*of pers.*) en route pour la maison; **outward b.,** (navire) (i) sur son départ, en partance, (ii) en route pour l'étranger, etc.; **where are you b. for?** où allez-vous?
boundary ['baund(ə)ri] *n.* **1.** limite *f,* bornes *fpl;* frontière *f;* **b. adjustment,** rectification *f* de frontière; **b. line,** ligne frontière, ligne de démarcation; *Sp:* ligne du jeu; **b. stone,** borne, pierre *f* de bornage. **2.** *Cr:* **to hit, score, a b.,** envoyer la balle jusqu'aux limites du terrain.
bounden ['baundən] *a. Lit:* **b. duty,** devoir impérieux.
bounder ['baundər] *n. F: O:* goujat *m.*
boundless ['baundlis] *a.* sans bornes, illimité, infini.
bounteous ['bauntiəs] *a. Lit:* **1.** (*of pers.*) libéral, généreux. **2. b. harvest,** moisson abondante.
bounteousness ['bauntiəsnis] *n. Lit:* **1.** bonté *f.* générosité *f.* **2.** abondance *f* (des moissons, etc.).
bountiful ['bauntiful] *a. Lit:* **1.** bienfaisant; **b. rains,** pluies fécondes. **2.** généreux, libéral.
bounty ['baunti] *n.* **1.** *Lit:* bonté *f,* générosité *f,* libéralité *f.* **2.** (*a*) gratification *f* (à un employé, etc.); (*b*) *Adm: Ind:* indemnité *f;* prime *f* (à l'exportation, etc.); subvention *f;* (*c*) *Mil: Nau:* prime (d'engagement).
bouquet *n.* **1.** [bu'kei] bouquet *m* (de fleurs, de feu d'artifice). **2.** ['bukei] bouquet (du vin).
Bourbon *n.* **1.** ['buəbɔn] *Hist:* Bourbon. **2.** *NAm:* ['bɔ:b(ə)n] whisky *m* de maïs.
bourdon ['buəd(ə)n] *n. Mus:* (*of organ, bagpipes*) bourdon *m.*
bourgeois ['buəʒwɑ:] *a.* & *n. usu. Pej:* bourgeois, -oise.
bourgeoisie [buəʒwɑ:'zi:] *n.* bourgeoisie *f.*
bout [baut] *n.* **1.** (*at games, etc.*) tour *m,* reprise *f;* **fencing b.,** passe *f* d'armes; assaut *m* d'armes; **wrestling b.,** assaut de lutte; **boxing b.,** combat *m* de boxe. **2.** (*a*) accès *m,* poussée *f* (de fièvre); quinte *f* (de toux); (*b*) **drinking b.,** soûlerie *f.*
boutique [bu:'ti:k] *n.* (*a*) petit magasin de modes; (*b*) (*in department store*) boutique *f.*
bovine ['bouvain] **1.** *a.* (*a*) *Z:* bovin; (*b*) (esprit) lourd. **2.** *n.pl. Z:* les bovins *m.*
bow[1] [bou] *n.* **1.** arc *m;* **to draw a b.,** bander, tendre, un arc; **to have two strings, more than one string, to one's b.,** avoir deux cordes, plus d'une corde, à son arc; **I have still one, another, string to my b.,** il me reste encore une ressource. **2.** (*a*) *Mus:* archet *m* (de violon, etc); (*b*) *Mus:* coup *m* d'archet; (*c*) *Tls:* **b. saw,** scie *f* à archet, à arc. **3.** *Const:* **b. window,** fenêtre *f* en saillie (courbe), en rotonde. **4.** nœud *m* (de ruban); **b. tie,** nœud (de) papillon. **5.** *Harn:* **(saddle) b.,** arçon *m.* **6.** *Tchn:* (*a*) arceau *m,* anse *f* (de cadenas); anneau *m* (de clef); collier *m* (d'éperon); (*b*) **b. compass,** compas *m* à balustre.
bow[2] [bou] *v.tr.* **1.** courber (qch.). **2.** *Mus:* gouverner l'archet dans (un passage); **bowed instrument,** instrument à archet.
bow[3] [bau] *n.* salut *m;* (i) révérence *f;* (ii) inclination *f* de tête; **to take a b.,** saluer; **to make a deep, low, b. to s.o.,** saluer qn profondément.
bow[4] [bau] **1.** *v.i.* (*a*) (i) s'incliner; baisser la tête; (ii) faire une génuflexion; **to b. to s.o.,** s'incliner devant qn; saluer qn; **to b. and scrape,** faire des salamalecs, des courbettes; **to b. down before s.o.,** (i) se prosterner devant qn; (ii) faire des courbettes devant qn; (*b*) **to b. to (sth.),** se soumettre à (la volonté de qn, une décision, etc.); **to b. to the inevitable,** s'incliner devant les faits. **2.** *v.tr.* (*a*) incliner, baisser (la tête); fléchir (le genou); (*b*) courber, voûter (le dos, les épaules, de qn); **to become bowed,** se voûter. **bowed** *a.* **with b. head,** (i) la tête inclinée; (ii) la tête baissée (de honte, etc.); **b. with age,** courbé par le fardeau des ans; **b. (down) with grief,** accablé de douleur. **bowing** *n.* saluts *mpl;* **b. and scraping,** courbettes *fpl,* salamalecs *mpl.* **bow out** *v.i.* se retirer.
bow[5] [bau] *n.* **1.** *Nau:* (*often pl.*) avant *m,* étrave *f,* bossoir *m;* **b. rope,** amarre *f* de bout, de l'avant; **on the port, starboard, b.,** par le bossoir bâbord, tribord; **to cross the bows of a ship,** couper la route d'un navire; **b. wave,** lame d'étrave. **2.** *Row:* nageur *m* de tête, de l'avant; **b. oar,** aviron *m* de l'avant.
bowdlerize ['baudləraiz) *v.tr.* expurger, émasculer, châtrer (une œuvre littéraire).
bowel ['bauəl] *n.* (*a*) *Anat:* intestin *m;* **the bowels,** les intestins; **b. complaint,** affection intestinale; (*b*) *Lit:* **the bowels of the earth,** les entrailles *fpl,* le sein, de la terre.
bower[1] ['bauər] *n.* **1.** berceau *m* de verdure; charmille *f,* tonnelle *f.* **2.** *Poet: A:* appartement *m* (d'une dame); boudoir *m.*
bower[2] *n. Nau:* **b. (anchor),** ancre *f* de bossoir.
bowfronted ['bou'frʌntid] *a. Furn:* à devant bombé; (*of house*) à fenêtres en saillie.

bowl[1] [boul] *n.* **1.** (*a*) bol *m*; jatte *f*; coupe *f* (de cristal, etc.); cuvette *f*; bassin *m*; bassine *f*; plonge *f* (d'évier); cuvette (de W.C.); **finger b.,** rince-doigts *m inv*; *Cu:* **mixing b.,** bol à mélanger; **salad b.,** saladier *m*; **washing-up b.,** bassine à vaisselle; **goldfish b.,** bocal *m* à poissons rouges; (*b*) (*contents*) **a b. of milk,** un bol, une jatte, de lait. **2.** fourneau *m*, godet *m* (de pipe à tabac); cuilleron *m* (de cuiller); coupe *f* (de verre à pied); culot *m* (de lampe); plateau *m* (de balance); *Nau:* cuvette (du compas). **3.** *NAm:* (*a*) *Geog:* cuvette, bassin; (*b*) amphithéâtre *m*.

bowl[2] *n.* boule *f*; **(game of) bowls,** (i) (jeu *m* de) boules; (ii) *U.S:* (jeu de) quilles *fpl*; **to play (at) bowls,** jouer (i) aux boules, (ii) *U.S:* aux quilles.

bowl[3] **1.** *v.tr.* rouler, faire courir (un cerceau). **2.** (*at bowls*) (*a*) *v.tr.* lancer, rouler (la boule); (*b*) *v.i.* jouer aux boules. **3.** *Cr:* (*a*) *v.tr. & i.* lancer, servir (la balle); (*b*) *v.tr.* **to b. s.o. (out),** renverser le guichet à qn. **bowl along** *v.i.* rouler rapidement; filer. **bowling** *n.* (*a*) jeu *m* de boules; **b. match,** match *m* de boules; **b. green,** (pelouse *f* pour) jeu de boules; (*b*) **(tenpin) b.,** bowling *m*; **b. alley,** bowling; (*c*) lancement *m* de la boule, *Cr:* de la balle. **bowl over** *v.tr.* (*a*) renverser (les quilles, etc.); (*b*) *F:* déconcerter, renverser (qn).

bow-legged ['bou'leg(i)d] *a.* bancal, -als.

bowlegs ['bou'legz] *n.pl.* jambes arquées, torses.

bowler[1] ['boulər] *n.* **1.** joueur *m* de boules; bouliste *m*. **2.** *Cr:* bôleur *m*, lanceur *m*, serveur *m*.

bowler[2] *n.* **b. (hat),** (chapeau) melon (*m*).

bowlful ['boulful] *n.* plein bol (de qch.); jatte *f*, jattée *f* (de lait, etc.); cuvette *f*, bassinée *f* (d'eau, etc.).

bowline ['boulin] *n.* *Nau:* (*a*) bouline *f*; (*b*) **b. (knot),** nœud *m* de chaise, nœud d'agui.

bowser ['bauzər] *n.* *Petr:* camion-citerne *m*, *pl.* camions-citernes.

bowsprit ['bousprit] *n.* *Nau:* beaupré *m*.

bowstring ['boustriŋ] *n.* **1.** corde *f* d'arc. **2.** (*for execution*) lacet *m*, cordon *m*.

bow-wow ['bau'wau] **1.** *int.* oua-oua! **2.** *n.* *F:* (*child's word*) toutou *m*.

box[1] [bɔks] *n.* (*a*) *Bot:* **b. (tree),** buis *m*; (*b*) *Com:* (bois *m* de) buis.

box[2] *n.* **1.** (*a*) boîte *f*; coffret *m*; (*large*) coffre *m*; caisse *f*; (*for food, etc.*) bac *m*; **cardboard b.,** carton *m*; **jewel b.,** coffret à bijoux; **tool b.,** coffre à outils; **window b.,** caisse, bac, à fleurs (pour fenêtres, balcons); **post, letter, b.,** boîte à, aux, lettres; **post office b., P.O. Box,** boîte postale, B.P.; (*in newspaper advertisement*) **Box number 12,** Référence 12; *Gym:* **(vaulting) b.,** cheval *m* de bois; *Mil:* **ammunition b.,** coffre à munitions; *Av: etc:* **black b.,** boîte noire; (*b*) **strong b., safe-deposit b.,** coffre-fort *m*, *pl.* coffres-forts; **deed b.,** coffret à documents; **cash b.,** caisse; (*c*) *Ecc:* **alms b.,** tronc *m*; (*d*) **b. camera,** appareil *m* rigide, en box; **b. kite,** cerf-volant *m* cellulaire, *pl.* cerfs-volants; *Tls:* **b. spanner, wrench,** clef *f*, dé *m*, en douille, en tube; *Dressm:* **b. pleat,** pli creux, double pli; (*e*) (*contents*) boîte (de chocolats, d'allumettes, etc.); caisse (de marchandises, etc.); **Christmas b.** = étrennes *fpl*; (*f*) *F:* **the b.,** la télé. **2.** *A.Veh:* siège *m* (du cocher). **3.** (*a*) *Th:* loge *f*; (*on ground floor*) baignoire *f*; **stage b.,** loge d'avant-scène; **prompt b.,** trou *m* du souffleur; (*b*) stalle *f* (d'écurie); **loose b.,** box *m*, *pl.* boxes; **horse b.,** (i) *Aut:* van *m*; (ii) *Rail:* wagon *m* à chevaux; (*c*) *Jur:* **jury b.,** banc(s) *m*(*pl*) du jury; **witness b.** = barre *f* des témoins; (*d*) **sentry b.,** guérite *f*; *Rail:* **signal b.,** cabine *f*, poste *m*, d'aiguillage; *Tp:* **call, telephone, b.,** cabine téléphonique; **shooting b.,** pavillon *m* de chasse. **4.** *Tchn:* boîte (d'essieu, de frein); moyeu *m* (de roue); palâtre *m*, palastre *m* (d'une serrure); *Typ:* cassetin *m*; *Aut:* **gear b.,** boîte de vitesses; carter *m* de transmission. **5.** (*a*) case *f* (à remplir sur une formule, etc.); encadré *m* (dans un journal); (*b*) *Aut:* **b. junction,** zone quadrillée. **6.** *Cmptr:* case, pavé *m* (d'organigramme).

box[3] *v.tr.* emboîter, encaisser, encartonner (qch.); mettre (qch.) en boîte; coffrer. **boxed** *a.* **1.** *Com: etc:* en boîte; en étui. **2. b. in,** encaissé; enfermé; **b. up,** enfermé; à l'étroit. **box in** *v.tr.* encaisser, enfermer; *Typ:* encadrer (un texte). **boxing** *n.* **1.** emboîtement *m*; encaissement *m*. **2. B. Day,** la Saint-Étienne, le lendemain de Noël.

box[4] *n.* **b. (on the ear),** gifle *f*, claque *f*, taloche, *f*.

box[5] **1.** *v.tr.* **to b. s.o.'s ears,** gifler qn; flanquer une claque, une taloche, à qn. **2.** *v.i.* *Sp:* boxer; faire la boxe; (*of two opponents*) se boxer. **boxing** *n.* la boxe; **b. glove,** gant *m* de boxe; **b. match,** match *m* de boxe.

box-calf ['bɔks'kɑːf] *n.* box-calf *m*; *F:* box *m*.

boxcar ['bɔkskɑːr] *n.* *Rail:* wagon (couvert); fourgon *m*.

boxer[1] ['bɔksər] *n.* boxeur *m*, pugiliste *m*. **2.** (*dog*) boxer *m*.

Boxer[2] *n.* *Hist:* Boxer *m* (chinois).

boxful ['bɔksful] *n.* pleine boîte, plein coffre, pleine caisse (de qch.).

box-office ['bɔksɔfis] *n.* *Th:* bureau *m* de location; caisse *f*, guichet *m*; (*of play, etc.*) **a b.-o. success,** un succès populaire.

boxroom ['bɔksruːm] *n.* débarras *m*.

boxwood ['bɔkswud] *n.* (bois *m* de) buis (*m*).

boy [bɔi] *n.m.* **1.** (*a*) garçon; **boys will be boys,** on ne peut pas empêcher les garçons de se conduire en garçons; **she ought to have been a b.,** c'est un garçon manqué; (*b*) **he has two boys and a girl,** il a deux garçons et une fille; (*c*) *Sch:* élève *m*; **day b.,** externe; **an old b.,** un ancien élève; *F:* **the old b. network,** le réseau des relations entre anciens camarades d'école, de collège; (*d*) *F:* **her b. friend,** son petit ami, son ami; **b.-meets-girl story,** roman d'amour (conventionnel); (*e*) *F:* **a nice old b.,** un vieillard sympathique; **one of the boys,** un joyeux vivant; **come on boys!** allons-y les gars! *esp. NAm:* **oh b.!** ben alors! dis donc! *O:* **I say old b.!** dis, mon vieux! (*f*) *P:* **the big boys,** les grosses légumes. **2.** (*a*) (*in Africa, etc.*) **(house) b.,** domestique *m*; boy *m*; (*b*) **stable b.,** garçon d'écurie; **telegraph b.,** porteur de télégrammes; **ship's b.,** mousse *m*; **errand b.,** (i) garçon de courses, (ii) garçon livreur; **office b.,** garçon de bureau.

boycott[1] ['bɔikɔt] *n.* boycottage *m*; **to put (s.o., sth.) under a b., to put a b. on (s.o., sth.)** boycotter (qn, une entreprise, etc.).

boycott[2] *v.tr.* boycotter (qn, une entreprise, etc.).

boyhood ['bɔihud] *n.* (i) enfance *f*, première jeunesse, (ii) adolescence *f* (d'un garçon).

boyish ['bɔiiʃ] *a.* **1.** puéril, enfantin; gamin. **2.** (nature, apparence) jeune. **3.** (manières) de garçon.

boyishness ['bɔiiʃnis] *n.* manières, air, de garçon, de jeune homme.

bra [brɑː] *n.* soutien-gorge *m*, *pl.* soutiens-gorge; (*strapless*) bustier *m*..

brace[1] [breis] *n.* **1.** (*a*) *Const: etc:* (*in tension*) attache *f*, lien *m*; entretoise *f*, étrésillon *m*; (*in compression*) contrefiche *f*, moise *f*; **anchor b.,** ancre *f*, ancrure *f*; **cross, diagonal, b.,** écharpe *f*, diagonale *f*; *Aut:* croisillon (du châssis); (*b*) *Dent:* appareil *m* dentaire; (*c*) *Med:* **(surgical) b.,** armature *f* orthopédique. **2.** *Cost:* **braces,** bretelles *fpl* (de pantalon). **3.** *inv.* couple *f* (de perdrix); laisse *f* (de lévriers); paire *f* (de pistolets, etc.); **two b. of partridges,** deux couples de perdrix. **4.** *Tls:* **b. (and bit),** vilebrequin *m* (à main); **ratchet b.,** (i) *Mec.E:* perçoir *m*, foret *m*, à rochet; (ii) *Carp:* vilebrequin à cliquet; *Aut:* **wheel b.,** vilebrequin (à roues). **5.** *Nau:* bras *m* (de vergue); **main b.,** grand bras. **6.** *Mus: Typ:* accolade *f.*

brace² *v.tr.* **1.** *Const: etc:* ancrer (une construction); armer (une poutre); entretoiser, étrésillonner (une charpente); moiser (des étais); affermir (un mur) par des ancres; *Av:* croisillonner (une aile). **2.** fortifier (le corps); tonifier (les nerfs); **to b. s.o. up,** (re)donner de la vigueur, du courage, à qn; remonter qn; **to b. oneself to do sth.,** raidir ses forces, se raidir, pour faire qch.; s'armer de (tout son) courage pour faire qch; **b. yourself!** (i) tiens ferme! (ii) du courage! **3.** (*a*) **to b. (the skin of) a drum,** tendre la peau d'un tambour; bander un tambour; (*b*) **to b. the knees,** tendre les jarrets; (*c*) tendre, bander (l'arc). **4.** *Typ:* accolader, accoler (des mots). **5.** *Nau:* brasser (les vergues); **to b. round,** contrebrasser. **bracing 1.** *a.* (air, climate, etc.) fortifiant, vivifiant, tonifiant. **2.** *n.* (*a*) *Const: etc:* ancrage *m*; entretoisement *m*; armement *m* (d'une poutre); renforcement *m* (d'un mur); *Av:* croisillonnage *m*; **b. strut,** jambe *f* de force; (*b*) retrempe *f* (du corps); tonification *f* (des nerfs); (*c*) *Nau:* brassage *m* (des vergues).

bracelet ['breislit] *n.* **1.** bracelet *m*; **chain b.,** gourmette *f*; **b. watch,** montre-bracelet *f*, *pl.* montres-bracelets. **2.** *F:* **bracelets,** menottes *fpl*, bracelets.

bracer ['breisər] *n. F:* (*a*) petit verre (de spiritueux); (*b*) **to go out for a b.,** sortir prendre un peu d'air.

brachial ['brækiəl, 'breik-] *a. Anat:* brachial, -aux.

brachiopod ['brækiəpɔd] *n. Moll:* brachiopode *m.*

brachycephalic [brækise'fælik] *a.* brachycéphale.

bracken ['bræk(ə)n] *n. Bot:* fougère à l'aigle.

bracket¹ ['brækit] *n.* **1.** (*a*) *Const: etc:* console *f*; potence *f*; *Arch:* corbeau *m*; **angle b.,** console à équerre; (*b*) *Const: Mec.E:* tasseau *m*, patte *f* (de fixation, de sustentation); **bearing b.,** chaise (suspendue, pendante); (*c*) applique *f* (pour lampe); **b. lamp,** (lampe *f* d')applique; **wall b.,** console murale. **2.** (*a*) *Typ: etc:* (i) **square b.,** crochet *m*; **round b.,** parenthèse *f*; **in brackets,** entre parenthèses; entre crochets; (ii) accolade *f*; (*b*) *Adm:* tranche *f* (de revenus); fourchette *f* (de salaires); cédule *f* (d'impôts); **the 15 to 20 age b.,** le groupe, la classe, des 15 à 20 ans.

bracket² *v.tr.* **(bracketed)** (*a*) mettre (des mots, etc.) (i) entre crochets, (ii) entre parenthèses; (*b*) réunir (des mots) par une accolade; accolader, accoler (deux mots, etc.); accoupler les noms de (deux personnes); associer (deux idées); placer (deux candidats) ex æquo; **bracketed together,** classés ex æquo. **bracketing** *n.* (*a*) mise *f* entre parenthèses; (*b*) accolement *m.*

brackish ['brækiʃ] *a.* (eau) saumâtre.

brad [bræd] *n.* pointe *f*; clou à tête perdue, étêté.

bradawl ['brædɔ:l] *n. Tls:* alêne plate; poinçon *m.*

brae [brei] *n. Scot:* pente *f*, côte *f*, colline *f.*

brag¹ [bræg] *n.* vantardise *f*, hâblerie *f.*

brag² *v.i.* **(bragged),** hâbler, se vanter; **to b. of, about, sth.,** se vanter de qch. **bragging 1.** *a.* vantard. **2.** *n.* vantardise *f.*

braggart ['brægət] *a.* & *n.* vantard (*m*).

Brahman ['brɑ:mən] *n.m.* brahmane.

Brahmanism ['brɑ:mənizm] *n.* brahmanisme *m.*

Brahmin ['brɑ:min] **1.** *n.m.* brahmane. **2.** *n. U.S: F:* intellectuel, -elle.

braid¹ [breid] *n.* **1.** tresse *f* (de cheveux). **2.** (*a*) *Cost: Dressm: Furn:* galon *m*, ganse *f*; cordonnet *m*, lacet *m* (de bordure); passepoil *m*, soutache *f*, passement *m*; (*of officers*) **gold b.,** galon; (*b*) *El:* guipage *m* (de fils conducteurs).

braid² *v.tr.* **1.** *O:* tresser (ses cheveux, de la paille). **2.** galonner, soutacher; passementer (le bord d'une chaise, etc.). **braiding** *n.* **1.** *O:* tressage *m.* **2.** (garniture *f* de) galon; soutache *f*, passement *m.*

Braille [breil] *n.* Braille *m*; **B. alphabet,** alphabet *m* Braille; **in B.,** en Braille.

brain¹ [brein] *n.* **1.** cerveau *m*; **electronic b.,** cerveau électronique; **b. death,** mort *f* du cerveau; **b. fever,** fièvre cérébrale; **b. disease,** maladie cérébrale; **he has money on the b.,** il est obsédé par l'argent; **to have a tune on the b.,** être hanté, obsédé, par un air. **2. brains,** (i) *Cu:* cervelle *f* (de veau, etc.); (ii) (*of pers.*) intelligence *f*; **he has brains, a good b.,** il est intelligent; **he's the brains of the family, of the business,** c'est lui le plus intelligent de la famille; c'est lui qui dirige la maison; **to rack one's brains,** se creuser la cervelle, le cerveau; se casser la tête. **2.** *F:* personne intelligente; cerveau; **to call in the best brains,** faire appel à tous les talents; **brains trust,** *NAm:* **b. trust,** brain-trust *m*, *pl.* brain-trusts; groupe *m* d'experts; *F:* **the b. drain,** le drainage des cerveaux.

brain² *v.tr.* défoncer le crâne à (qn); assommer (qn).

brainchild ['breintʃaild] *n.* idée originale (de qn).

brainless ['breinlis] *a.* sans cervelle; stupide.

brainpower ['breinpauər] *n.* intelligence *f.*

brainstorm ['breinstɔ:m] *n.* **1.** transport *m* au cerveau. **2.** *NAm: F:* (*a*) idée *f* de génie; (*b*) idée insensée.

brainwash ['breinwɔʃ] *v.tr.* soumettre (qn) à un lavage de cerveau. **brainwashing** *n.* lavage *m* de cerveau.

brainwave ['breinweiv] *n. F:* inspiration *f*; idée *f*, trait *m*, de génie; idée lumineuse.

brainwork ['breinwɔ:k] *n.* travail intellectuel, travail de tête.

brainworker ['breinwɔ:kər] *n.* intellectuel, -elle; travailleur intellectuel.

brainy ['breini] *a. F:* intelligent, calé.

braise [breiz] *v.tr. Cu:* braiser; cuire (qch.) à l'étouffée; **braised beef,** = ragoût *m* de bœuf; **braised chicken,** poulet *m* en cocotte. **braising** *n.* cuisson *f* à l'étouffée.

brake¹ [breik] *n.* fourré *m*, hallier *m.*

brake² *n.* **1.** *Tex:* (*for flax, hemp*) brisoir *m*, broie *f.* **2.** *Agr:* **b. (harrow),** brise-mottes *m inv.*

brake³ *v. tr. Tex:* briser, broyer, macquer (du lin, du chanvre).

brake⁴ *n. Veh: etc:* frein *m*; **hand b.,** frein à main; frein à levier; **foot b.,** frein à pédale, au pied; **air b.,** (i) *Veh:* frein pneumatique, à air comprimé; (ii) *Av:* frein aérodynamique, aérofrein *m*; **emergency b.,** frein de secours; **disc b.,** frein à disque; **b. horsepower,** puissance *f* au frein; **b. block,** sabot *m* de frein; patin *m*; **b. lining,** garniture *f* de frein; **b. fluid,** liquide *m* pour freins (hydrauliques); *Rail:* **b. van,** wagon-frein *m*, *pl.* wagons-freins; fourgon *m*; **to apply, put on, the brake(s),** freiner; mettre, serrer, le frein; **to slam on the brakes,** bloquer les freins; **to release the brake(s),** desserrer le frein; **to put a b. on a project,** donner un coup de frein à un projet.

brake⁵ *v.i.* freiner; serrer, mettre, le frein; **to b. hard,** bloquer les freins. **braking** *n.* freinage *m*; serrage *m* des freins; coup *m* de frein; **b. distance,** distance *f* d'arrêt, de freinage.

brake⁶ *n.* = BREAK³.

brakesman, *NAm:* **brakeman,** *pl.* **-men** ['breik(s)mən] *n.m. Rail: etc:* garde-frein(s), *pl.* gardes-frein(s).

bramble ['bræmbl] *n. Bot:* (*a*) ronce *f*, mûrier *m*, des haies; (*b*) mûre *f* (de ronce), mûre sauvage; mûron *m*; (*c*) **brambles,** ronces.

brambly ['bræmbli] *a.* plein, couvert, de ronces.

bran [bræn] *n. Mill:* son *m*; *Husb:* **b. mash,** son mouillé; **b. tub,** baquet rempli de son où l'on plonge la main pour en retirer une surprise.

branch¹ [brɑ:n(t)ʃ] *n.* **1.** branche *f*, rameau *m* (d'un arbre); **the branches,** le branchage, les branches. **2.**

(*a*) *Min:* rameau (d'une galerie); branche, embranchement *m* (d'une route, d'un chemin de fer); branche, bras *m* (d'un fleuve); *Rail:* **b. line,** (ligne *f* d')embranchement; (*b*) branche (de chandelier, *Anat:* d'artère, *Mth:* d'une courbe); (*c*) branche (d'une famille, d'une science, d'une industrie, etc.); **the different branches of industry,** les différentes branches de l'industrie; (*d*) *Adm: Com:* branche, succursale *f*, filiale *f* (d'une société, d'une maison de commerce); succursale (d'une banque); **b. office,** (i) agence *f*; (ii) bureau *m* de quartier; (*e*) *Mil:* arme *f* (du service); service *m*, direction *f* (de l'administration); bureau (d'état-major); (*f*) *Cmptr:* branchement *m*.

branch² *v.i.* **1.** *Bot:* pousser des branches; **to b. out,** se ramifier; (*of organization, etc.*) étendre au loin ses ramifications; (*of pers.*) **to b. out into . . .,** étendre ses activités, son commerce, à . . . . **2.** (*of road, etc.*) bifurquer; **at the point where the road branches,** à la bifurcation des routes. **branched** *a.* **1.** *Bot:* branchu, rameux. **2. b. candlestick,** chandelier *m* à (plusieurs) branches.

branchia, branchiae ['bræŋkiə, -kii:] *n.pl.* (*of aquatic animals*) branchies *fpl*; *Ich:* ouïes *fpl*.

branchiate ['bræŋkiət] *a.* branchié.

branchiopod, *pl.* **-s** ['bræŋkiəpɔd, -z] *n. Crust:* branchiopode *m*.

brand¹ [brænd] *n.* **1.** brandon *m*, tison *m*. **2.** *Poet:* flambeau *m*. **3.** (*a*) fer chaud; (*b*) *Husb: etc:* marque (faite avec un fer chaud); *Hist:* flétrissure *f*, stigmate *m* (sur l'épaule). **4.** *Com:* (*a*) marque (de fabrique); **a good b. of cigars,** une bonne marque de cigares; (*b*) sorte *f*, qualité *f* (d'une marchandise); **b. new,** tout neuf, flambant neuf. **5.** *Agr:* brûlure *f*, brouissure *f*; rouille *f* (des plantes).

brand² *v.tr.* **1. to b. with a hot iron,** marquer (qn, un animal, une marchandise) au fer chaud; *Hist:* flétrir (un criminel); estamper (un esclave). **2. to be branded on s.o.'s memory,** être gravé dans la mémoire de qn. **3. to b. s.o. with infamy,** flétrir, stigmatiser, qn; **to be branded as a swindler,** être noté (d'infamie) comme escroc. **branded** *a.* **1.** marqué à chaud; **to be b.,** porter la marque. **2.** (produit) de marque. **branding** *n. Husb: etc:* marquage *m* au fer chaud.

brandish ['brændiʃ] *v.tr.* brandir (une arme, etc.).

brandy ['brændi] *n.* (*a*) cognac *m*; **liqueur b.,** fine *f*; **b. and soda** = fine à l'eau; (*b*) **cherry b.,** cherry (-brandy) *m*; **plum b.,** eau-de-vie *f* de prunes; (*c*) **b. snap,** galette *f* au gingembre.

brash [bræʃ] *a.* effronté, présomptueux, impudent; exubérant; impétueux; (*of colour*) cru. **-ly** *adv.* effrontément.

brashness ['bræʃnis] *n.* effronterie *f*, impudence *f*; exubérance *f*; impétuosité *f*.

brass [brɑ:s] *n.* **1.** (*c*) cuivre *m* jaune; laiton *m*; **b. foundry,** fonderie *f* de cuivre; robinetterie *f*; **b. plate,** plaque *f* de cuivre; plaque à la porte d'un médecin, etc.; *Mus:* **b. instrument,** instrument *m* de cuivre; **as bold as b.,** d'un air effronté; **to get down to b. tacks,** en venir au fait; *F:* **b. hat,** officier *m* d'état-major; **the top b.,** *U.S:* **high b.,** les gros bonnets, *P:* les grosses légumes; (*b*) *Bookb:* fer *m*. **2.** (*a*) les cuivres (du ménage, etc.); **to do the b., the brasses,** faire les cuivres; (*b*) *Mec.E:* coussinet *m* de bielle, de palier; coquille *f* (de coussinets); (*c*) *coll.* (*in band, orchestra*) **the b.,** les cuivres; **b. band,** fanfare *f*; (*d*) (*in church*) plaque tombale en cuivre; **b. rubbing,** frottis *m* d'une plaque tombale en cuivre; (*e*) **horse b.,** médaillon *m* de cuivre (fixé sur l'harnachement du cheval). **3.** *F:* argent *m*, galette *f*.

brassière ['bræsiɛr] *n. Cost:* soutien-gorge *m*, *pl.* soutiens-gorge; (*strapless*) bustier *m*.

brassiness ['brɑ:sinis] *n.* **1.** apparence 'toc' (d'un bijou censé être en or, etc.). **2.** sons cuivrés (d'une musique). **3.** *F:* effronterie *f*.

brassware ['brɑ:swɛər] *n.* dinanderie *f*.

brasswork ['brɑ:swək] *n.* **1.** les cuivres *mpl*. **2.** *Ind:* cuivrerie *f*.

brassy¹ ['brɑ:si] *n. Golf:* brassie *m*.

brassy² *a.* **1.** (*a*) (*of colour, etc.*) qui ressemble au cuivre; (*b*) (son) cuivré, claironnant. **2.** *F:* (*of pers.*) effronté.

brat [bræt] *n. usu. Pej:* gosse *mf*, môme *mf*.

bravado [brə'vɑ:dou] *n.* bravade *f*.

brave¹ [breiv] **1.** *a.* courageux, brave, vaillant; **as b. as a lion,** courageux comme un lion; **to put a b. face on it,** faire bonne contenance. **2.** *n.* (*Am. Indian warrior*) brave *m*. **-ly** *adv.* courageusement, vaillamment.

brave² *v.tr.* braver, défier (qn); braver, affronter (un danger, etc.); **to b. it out,** ne pas se laisser démonter.

bravery ['breivəri] *n.* bravoure *f*, courage *m*; vaillance *f*.

bravo ['brɑ:vou] *int.* bravo!

bravura [bræ'v(j)u:rə] *n. Mus:* air *m*, morceau *m*, de bravoure.

brawl¹ [brɔ:l] *n.* rixe *f*, bagarre *f*; **drunken b.,** querelle *f* d'ivrognes.

brawl² *v.i.* (*of pers.*) se bagarrer. **brawling** *n.* rixe *f*; bagarre *f*.

brawler ['brɔ:lər] *n.* bagarreur, -euse.

brawn [brɔ:n] *n.* **1.** muscles *mpl*; *F:* **to have plenty of b.,** être bien musclé, *F:* avoir du biceps. **2.** *Cu:* fromage *m* de tête.

brawny ['brɔ:ni] *a.* charnu, musculeux; (*of pers.*) musclé, bien bâti.

bray¹ [brei] *n.* braiment *m* (d'un âne).

bray² *v.i.* (*of donkey*) braire.

braze [breiz] *v.tr. Tchn:* braser; souder (qch.) au laiton. **brazing** *n.* brasage *m*, brasure *f*; soudure *f* au laiton; **b. lamp,** lampe *f* à braser.

brazen¹ ['breiz(ə)n] *a.* **1.** (*a*) *Lit:* d'airain; **b. vessel,** vase *m* d'airain; (*b*) **the b. notes of the trumpet,** les sons d'airain de la trompette. **2.** effronté, impudent, cynique; **b. lie,** mensonge audacieux, effronté. **-ly** *adv.* effrontément; cyniquement; sans honte.

brazen² *v.tr.* **to b. it out,** payer d'effronterie, payer de toupet.

brazier ['brɑiziər] brasero *m* (à charbon de bois).

Brazil [brə'zil] **1.** *Pr.n. Geog:* Brésil *m*. **2.** (*a*) **b. nut,** noix *f* d'Amérique, du Brésil.

Brazilian [brə'ziliən] *Geog:* **1.** *a.* brésilien. **2.** *n.* Brésilien, -ienne.

breach¹ [bri:tʃ] *n.* **1.** infraction *f*, contravention *f* (aux règles, au devoir, etc.); violation *f* (de la loi, etc.); manquement *m* (au devoir, à l'honneur, à la discipline, etc.); rupture *f* (de contrat); **b. of faith,** manque *m* de foi; **b. of trust,** (i) abus *m* de confiance; malversation *f*; (*of official*) fait *m* de charge; prévarication *f*; (ii) violation d'un des devoirs d'un mandataire; **b. of good manners,** manque de savoir-vivre; **to commit a b. of etiquette,** manquer au protocole; **b. of professional secrecy,** violation du secret professionnel; **b. of privilege,** atteinte portée aux privilèges; **b. of the peace,** attentat *m* contre l'ordre public; **b. of promise,** (i) manque de parole; (ii) *Jur:* rupture de promesse de mariage. **2.** brouille *f*, rupture (entre deux amis, etc.). **3.** trou *m*, brèche *f* (dans un mur, etc.); *Mil:* **to stand in the b.,** monter sur la brèche; **to make a b. in the enemy's lines,** percer les lignes de l'ennemi.

breach² *v.tr.* ouvrir une brèche dans (une digue, un mur); battre (un mur) en brèche; *Mil:* percer (les lignes ennemies).

bread [bred] *n.* (*a*) pain *m*; **brown b.,** pain bis; **black**

b., pain de seigle; **French b.**, pain croustillant (à la française); **a loaf of b.**, un pain; une miche; **b. and butter,** pain beurré; **a slice of b. and butter,** une tartine de beurre, une tartine beurrée; **to be on b. and water,** être au pain (sec) et à l'eau; **to take the b. out of s.o.'s mouth,** prendre le pain dans la bouche de qn; **to earn one's daily b.**, gagner sa vie, son pain; **poetry doesn't earn one one's b. and butter,** la poésie ne nourrit pas son homme; *F:* **b.-and-butter letter,** lettre *f* de château; **he knows on which side his b. is buttered,** il sait où est son avantage, son intérêt; *Ecc:* **give us this day our daily b.**, donne-nous aujourd'hui notre pain de ce jour; (*b*) **b. bin,** (i) boîte *f* à pain; (ii) huche *f* à pain; **b. knife,** couteau *m* à pain; **b. slicer, cutter,** tranche-pain *m inv*; taille-pain *m inv*; *Cu:* **b. pudding,** gâteau *m* de pain; **b. sauce,** sauce *f* à la mie de pain; (*c*) *P:* argent *m*, galette *f*.

breadbasket ['bredbɑːskit] *n.* **1.** (*a*) corbeille *f* à pain; (*b*) *NAm:* région productrice de céréales panifiables. **2.** *P:* estomac *m*, bedaine *f*.

breadboard ['bredbɔːd] *n.* **1.** planche *f* à pain. **2.** *Elcs: etc:* montage expérimental.

breadcrumb ['bredkrʌm] *n.* miette *f* (de pain); *Cu:* **breadcrumbs,** chapelure *f*; **fried in breadcrumbs,** pané.

breadfruit ['bredfruːt] *n. Bot:* fruit *m* à pain; **b. tree,** artocarpe *m*, arbre *m* à pain; jaquier *m*.

breadline ['bredlain] *n.* (*a*) *Hist: NAm:* queue *f* (du public) pour toucher les bons de pain, pour recevoir de la nourriture gratuite; (*b*) **on the b.**, indigent; sans ressources.

breadth [bredθ] *n.* **1.** largeur *f*; (*of material*) lé *m*, laize *f*; **finger's b.**, travers *m* de doigt. **2.** largeur *f* (d'expression, de pensée, d'esprit, de vues); facture *f* large (d'un tableau); ampleur *f* (de style, de son).

breadwinner ['bredwinər] *n.* soutien *m* de famille.

break[1] [breik] *n.* **1.** (*a*) brisure *f*, cassure *f* (dans une assiette, etc.); trouée *f*, percée *f*, brèche *f* (dans une haie); éclaircie *f* (à travers les nuages); *El:* rupture *f* (du circuit); *Typ:* **b. line,** dernière ligne (d'un alinéa); (*b*) lacune *f* (dans une succession); *W.Tel: T.V:* (i) coupure *f* (dans un programme, pour y introduire une publicité); (ii) interruption *f* (en cas de panne); **b. of continuity,** solution *f* de continuité; **b. in a journey,** arrêt *m* en cours de route; **without a b.**, sans discontinuer; (*c*) rupture (entre deux amis, deux pays); **b. with a tradition,** rupture avec une tradition. **2.** (*a*) **b. in the weather,** changement *m* du temps; **b. in the voice,** (i) *Physiol:* mue *f* (à la puberté); (ii) altération *f* de la voix (par l'émotion); (iii) *Mus:* passage *m* d'un registre à l'autre; (*b*) brisure (d'une ligne); *Constr:* brisis *m* (d'un comble); angle *m* (d'un mur); (*c*) *Games:* effet *m* (de la balle). **3.** (*a*) (moment *m* de) repos (*m*), répit (*m*); pause *f*, arrêt *m* (dans un travail, une conversation, etc.); **an hour's b. for lunch,** une heure de battement pour le déjeuner; **coffee b.**, pause-café *f*; **a weekend in the country makes a pleasant b.**, un week-end à la campagne offre un repos agréable; (*b*) *Sch:* (i) intervalle *m* (entre les classes); récréation *f* (d'interclasse); (ii) vacances *fpl*; (*c*) *Mus:* pause *f*; (*in jazz*) break *m*. **4.** *Lit:* **b. of day,** point *m* du jour. **5. prison b., gaol b.**, évasion *f* de prison; **to make a b. for it,** s'évader. **6.** chance *f*; (*a*) **a good, bad, b.**, une bonne, mauvaise, chance; **we had a lucky b.**, nous avons eu de la veine; (*b*) **give him a b.**, donnez-lui (i) une chance, (ii) une seconde chance. **7.** (*a*) *Bill: etc:* (i) l'acquit *m*; (ii) série *f*, suite *f* (de coups gagnants); (*b*) *Ten:* rupture (du service de l'adversaire).

break[2] *v.* (*p.t.* **broke** [brouk]; *p.p.* **broken** ['brouk(ə)n]) **I.** *v.tr.* **1.** (*a*) casser (un verre, un œuf, un bâton, un jouet, etc.); briser (un verre, un carreau, les liens d'amitié, etc.); rompre (un bâton, une corde, *Nau:* les amarres, etc.); entamer (la peau); *Jur:* (i) briser, (ii) lever (les scellés); *Tex:* battre, teiller (le lin); *Min:* concasser (le minerai); *El:* interrompre (le courant); couper (un circuit); *Av:* franchir (le mur du son); **to b. sth. into pieces,** mettre qch. en morceaux; **to b. one's arm, one's neck,** se casser le bras, le cou; *Fig:* **to b. the ice,** rompre la glace; (*b*) **to b. a branch from a tree,** détacher une branche d'un arbre; (*c*) **to b. ground,** (i) *Agr:* défricher un terrain; (ii) *Civ.E: etc:* donner les premiers coups de pioche; (iii) entamer le travail; **to b. new, fresh, ground,** faire œuvre de pionnier; (*d*) **to b. a ten pound note,** entamer un billet de dix livres; **to b. a dinner set,** dépareiller un service de table. **2.** (*a*) rompre (le silence, le jeûne, etc.); **to b. step,** rompre le pas; **to b. ranks,** rompre les rangs; **to b. the thread of a story,** interrompre, couper, le fil d'une narration; **to b. one's journey,** s'arrêter en route; faire étape; *Nau: etc:* faire escale; (*b*) amortir (une chute, la force de qch.); arrêter (le vent); rompre (le courant); **to b. the force of a blow,** amortir, rompre, un coup. **3.** (*a*) dresser, entraîner (un cheval); corriger (une mauvaise habitude); **to b. s.o. into the work,** rompre qn à un travail; **to b. s.o., oneself, of a habit,** corriger, guérir, qn; se corriger, se défaire, d'une habitude; (*b*) briser (un alibi, une grève, etc.); battre (un record); *Mil:* casser (un officier); *Gaming:* **to b. the bank,** faire sauter la banque; *Ten:* **to b. one's opponent's service,** gagner le service de son adversaire; (*c*) briser (la résistance de qn); abattre, dompter (l'orgueil de qn); ruiner (la santé de qn); **to b. s.o.'s heart,** briser le cœur à qn; **to b. s.o.'s spirit,** briser le courage de qn; **to b. s.o.**, (i) ruiner qn; (ii) (*of grief, etc.*) briser qn. **4.** (*a*) violer, enfreindre, ne pas observer (une loi, une règle, une trêve, etc.); manquer à (sa parole, un rendez-vous, etc.); rompre (un contrat, etc.); **to b. the peace,** troubler l'ordre public; **to b. one's word to s.o.**, manquer de parole, fausser parole, à qn; (*b*) **to b. gaol,** s'évader du prison; *Ven:* (*of animal*) **to b. cover,** débucher; *Mil: Sch:* **to b. bounds,** violer la consigne; **insolence that has broken all bounds,** insolence qui ne connaît plus de bornes. **5.** (*a*) **to b. the news of sth. to s.o.**, apprendre qch. à qn; **to b. bad news gently to s.o.**, apprendre une mauvaise nouvelle doucement à qn; (*b*) *Physiol:* **to b. wind,** lâcher un vent; (*c*) *Nau:* déferler (un drapeau, un signal). **II.** *v.i.* **1.** (*a*) se casser; se briser; se rompre; (*of limb*) se fracturer, se casser; (*of bubble, abscess*) crever; (*of wave*) se briser; déferler; (*of troops*) se débander; **to b. in two, into pieces,** se casser en deux, en morceaux; **the sea breaks against the rocks,** la mer (se) brise sur les rochers; (*b*) (*of heart*) se briser, se fendre; (*of health*) s'altérer; (*of pers.*) **to b. under torture,** s'effondrer sous la torture; (*c*) **to b. with s.o., with a tradition,** rompre avec qn, avec une tradition. **2.** (*a*) (*of weather*) changer; se gâter; (*of heatwave*) passer, prendre fin; (*of voice*) (i) *Physiol:* muer; (ii) (*with emotion*) s'altérer, s'étrangler; (*b*) *Games:* (*of ball*) avoir de l'effet; dévier. **3.** (*a*) (*of storm*) éclater, se déchaîner; (*of news, scandal*) éclater; **day was beginning to b.**, le jour commençait à se lever; (*b*) **to b. free from one's bonds,** briser ses liens. **4.** *Bill: etc:* donner l'acquit. **break away 1.** *v.tr.* détacher (qch.) (**from,** de). **2.** *v.i.* (*of thg*) se détacher (**from,** de); (*of pers.*) se dégager, se détacher (**from,** de); (*of prisoner*) s'évader; (*of province*) se séparer (d'un État); **to b. away from a party,** lâcher, abandonner, un parti. **break down 1.** *v.tr.* (*a*) abattre, démolir (un mur, etc.); enfoncer (une porte); briser (la résistance); vaincre, surmonter (des préjugés); **to b. down all opposition,** vaincre toute opposition; (*b*) concasser, broyer, *Ch:* décomposer (une substance); *Ch:* dissocier (des molécules); (*c*) *Fin: etc:* décomposer (un compte); analyser (un compte, une statistique). **2.** *v.i.* (*a*) (*of health*) s'altérer, se détraquer; (*of the mind*) s'ébranler, sombrer; (*of plan, negotiations*) échouer; (*of argument, resistance, hopes*) s'effondrer; (*of pers.*) (i) faire une dépression nerveuse; (ii) éclater en sanglots, fondre en larmes; (iii) faire des aveux complets; (*b*) (*of car, machinery, etc.*) tomber, rester, en panne; (*of ship*) subir une avarie. **break even** *v.i.* (*a*) équilibrer son budget; rentrer dans ses frais; (*b*) *Cards:* cesser la partie à jeu égal. **break in 1.** *v.tr.* (*a*) enfoncer (une porte, etc.); (*b*) dresser (un cheval); culotter (une pipe); briser (des souliers neufs); *NAm:* roder (une voiture); **to b. s.o., oneself, in to sth.,** rompre qn, se rompre, à qch. **2.** *v.i.* (*a*) intervenir, s'interposer; faire irruption (**on s.o.,** chez qn); **to b. in on a conversation,** interrompre une conversation; (*b*) (*of burglar*) s'introduire par effraction. **breaking** *n.* (*a*) brisement *m* (d'un carreau, etc.); rupture *f* (du silence, etc.); interruption *f* (d'un voyage); *Jur:* (i) bris *m*, (ii) levée *f* (des scellés); *Tex:* battage *m*, teillage *m* (du lin); *Min:* concassage *m* (du minerai); *El:* interruption *f* (du courant); rupture (du circuit); *Av:* franchissement *m* (du mur du son); *Jur:* **b. and entering,** entrée *f* par effraction (dans une maison); **b. of new ground,** (i) *Agr:* défrichage *m*; (ii) œuvre *f* de pionnier; (*b*) brisement (des flots); *Med:* aboutissement *m* (d'un abscès); fracture *f* (d'un os, etc.); **b. of the voice,** (i) *Physiol:* mue *f*; (ii) (*with emotion*) altération *f* de la voix; *Mec.E:* **b. strain,** tension *f* de rupture; **b. point,** (i) *Mec.E:* limite *f* critique (de la résistance); point *m* de rupture; (ii) limite (des forces, etc.); **to try s.o.'s patience to b. point,** pousser à bout la patience de qn; (*c*) dressage *m* (d'un cheval); (*d*) amortissement *m* (d'une chute, de la force de qch.); (*e*) brisement *m* d'une grève, du cœur de qn); destruction (de la puissance de qn); (*f*) violation *f* (de la loi, etc.); rupture (d'un traité, etc.); **b. of one's word,** manque *f* de parole. **break into** *v.i.* (*a*) entrer de force, s'introduire par effraction, dans (une maison, etc.); (*of burglar*) cambrioler (une maison); **to b. into the till,** forcer la caisse; (*b*) **to b. into laughter,** éclater de rire; **to b. into a tune,** entonner un air; **to b. into a trot,** prendre le trot, se mettre, passer, au trot; **her face broke into a smile,** son visage s'épanouit en un sourire; (*c*) entamer (des provisions, un billet d'une livre, etc.). **break loose** *v.i.* se dégager de ses liens; s'évader (**from,** de); (*of ship*) partir en dérive; **all hell has broken loose,** les diables sont déchaînés. **break off 1.** *v.tr.* (*a*) casser, rompre (qch.); détacher (qch.) (**from,** de); (*b*) abandonner (un travail, etc.); rompre (des négociations, etc.); **to b. off relations with s.o.,** rompre avec qn. **2.** *v.i.* (*a*) se casser net; se détacher net; se détacher (**from,** de); (*b*) discontinuer; **to b. off in the middle of a speech,** s'arrêter au milieu d'un discours; **to b. off for ten minutes,** prendre dix minutes de repos; **to b. off for lunch,** s'arrêter pour déjeuner. **break open 1.** *v.tr.* enfoncer (une porte); forcer (une serrure, un coffre-fort); éventrer (une caisse), etc.). **2.** *v.i.* (*of box, etc.*) s'ouvrir; se casser. **break out 1.** *v.i.* (*a*) s'échapper, s'évader (d'une prison, etc.); (*b*) (*of fire, war, disease, etc.*) éclater, se déclarer; **a quarrel broke out between them,** ils se sont mis à se quereller; (*c*) **to b. out into a sweat,** se mettre à transpirer; (*of face, etc.*) **to b. out in spots,** se couvrir de boutons. **2.** *v.tr. NAm:* (*a*) ouvrir (une bouteille, une boîte, etc.); sortir (qch.) de sa cachette; (*b*) déferler (un drapeau). **break through** *v.tr.* enfoncer (une barrière, etc.); se frayer un chemin à travers (une barrière, une foule, etc.); faire une brèche dans (un mur, etc.); (*of sun*) percer (les nuages); *Av:* franchir (le mur du son). **break up 1.** *v.tr.* mettre, briser, (qch.) en morceaux; démolir (un bâtiment, un navire, etc.); morceler (une propriété); démembrer (un empire); répartir (le travail); disperser (une foule, une famille); détruire (un mariage); dissoudre (une assemblée); (inter)rompre (une conférence); rompre (une coalition); *Ch:* résoudre (un composé); *Agr:* ameublir (le sol); **to b. up a word into syllables,** décomposer un mot en syllabes; **to b. up a fight,** séparer des combattants; *F:* **b. it up!** la paix! **2.** *v.i.* (*a*) (*of ship, empire, etc.*) se démembrer; (*of road surface*) se désagréger; (*of ice*) débâcler; **ship breaking up,** navire en perdition; (*b*) (*of company, meeting*) se séparer; (*of group*) se disjoindre; (*of crowd, etc.*) se disperser; (*of clouds*) se dissiper, se disperser; *F:* (*of pers.*) se casser; décliner; **their marriage has broken up,** leur mariage est en ruine; **the meeting broke up in confusion,** la séance fut levée dans le tumulte; (*c*) *Sch:* entrer en vacances; **we b. up on 4th,** nos vacances commencent le 4; (*d*) (*of weather*) se gâter. **broken** *a.* **1.** (*a*) cassé; brisé; rompu; (*of limb*) fracturé, cassé; **a b. toy,** un jouet cassé; (*b*) (coke, gravier) concassé; (pierres) (con)cassées; (*c*) *Com:* **b. lots,** articles dépareillés. **2.** (*a*) (terrain) accidenté; (chemin) raboteux, défoncé; (rivage) tourmenté; (contour) anfractueux; **forest b. by large clearings,** forêt trouée de larges clairières; (*b*) (sommeil) interrompu; (paroles) entrecoupées; **voice b. with sobs,** voix entrecoupée de sanglots; **in a b. voice,** d'une voix entrecoupée, altérée; **to speak b. English,** estropier l'anglais. **3.** (*a*) (mariage) en ruine; (cœur) brisé; **b. home,** foyer détruit; **a b. man,** (i) un homme ruiné; (ii) un homme au cœur brisé; (iii) un homme abattu, découragé; (*b*) (promesse) violée, manquée. **brokenly** *adv.* sans suite; par saccades; (parler) à voix entrecoupée.

break³ *n.* **1.** (*a*) *A. Veh:* break *m*; (*b*) voiture *f* de dressage (des chevaux). **2.** *Aut:* **shooting b.,** break (de chasse).

break⁴ *v.tr.* = BRAKE³.

breakable ['breikəbl] **1.** *a.* cassable; cassant, fragile. **2.** *n.pl.* **breakables,** objets *mpl* fragiles.

breakage ['breikidʒ] **1.** rupture *f* (d'une chaîne, d'un arbre d'hélice, etc.); bris *m*, fracture *f* (de verre, etc.). **2. to pay for breakages,** payer la casse.

breakaway ['breikəwei] *n.* **1.** sécession *f*, désertion *f* (**from,** de). **2.** *Sp:* (*a*) *Box:* séparation *f* (de deux boxeurs); (*b*) *Fb:* échappée *f* (de l'ailier, etc.); (*c*) *Rac:* faux départ. **3.** (*a*) *Rail:* dérive *f* (de wagons); (*b*) *Austr:* ruée *f* (d'un troupeau). **3.** *attrib.* (*a*) **b. union,** syndicat dissident; (*b*) (jeune homme, etc.) rebelle.

breakdown ['breikdaun] *n.* **1.** (*a*) insuccès *m*, échec *m* (d'une tentative); rupture *f* (des négociations); écroulement *m* (d'un système); arrêt complet (dans un service); (*b*) écroulement (de la santé); **nervous b.,** épuisement nerveux; dépression nerveuse; **mental b.,** effondrement *m* de la raison; (*c*) panne *f*; *Trans:* avarie *f* de route; **b. service,** service *m* de dépannage; **b. gang,** équipe *f* de dépannage; **b. van,** *NAm:* **truck,** camion *m* de dépannage; dépanneuse *f*. **2.** *El:* claquage *m*; **b. voltage,** tension *f* claque. **3.** *Ch:* dissociation *f*. **4.** analyse *f* (statistique, etc.); décomposition *f* (d'un compte, etc.; répartition *f*, classement *m* (de la population, par classes, âges, etc.).

breaker ['breikər] *n.* **1.** (*pers.*) (*a*) casseur, -euse; briseur, -euse; **stone b.,** casseur de pierres; **breaker's yard,** chantier de démolition (de voitures, navires, etc.); **strike b.,** briseur de grève; *F:* jaune *m*; (*b*) dresseur, -euse (de chevaux, etc.); (*c*) violateur, -trice, infracteur, - trice (d'une loi, etc.). **2.** (*apparatus*) (*a*) brisoir *m*; *Civ.E: etc:* concasseur *m*; casse-pierre(s) *m inv*; *Nau:* **ice b.,** brise-glace(s) *m inv*; (*b*) *El:* **circuit b.,** coupe-circuit *m inv*, disjoncteur *m*. **3.** *Nau:* vague déferlante, brisante.

break-even ['breik'i:v(ə)n] *a.* à budget équilibré; **b.-e. point,** seuil *m* de rentabilité.

breakfast¹ ['brekfəst] *n.* petit déjeuner; **to have (one's) b.,** déjeuner; prendre le, son, (petit) déjeuner; **b. cup (and saucer),** déjeuner; **b. cereals,** céréales *fpl* (en flocons); **wedding b.,** repas *m* de noces.

breakfast² *v.i.* déjeuner (le matin).

break-in ['breikin] *n.* **1.** (*by burglar, etc.*) effraction *f*; **2.** *NAm: Mec.E: etc:* rodage *m.*

breakneck ['breiknek] *a.* **b. speed,** vitesse, allure, folle, vertigineuse.

break-out ['breikaut] *n.* évasion *f* (de prison, etc.).

breakthrough ['breikθru:] *n.* (*a*) *Mil:* percée *f* (des lignes ennemies); (*b*) percée (technologique); bond *m* en avant; invention *f* révolutionnaire.

breakup ['breikʌp] *n.* **1.** dissolution *f* (d'une empire, d'une assemblée); destruction *f* (d'un mariage, etc.); affaissement *m* (des forces physiques); bris *m* (d'un navire, etc.). **2.** changement *m* (du temps); débâcle *f* (des glaces).

breakwater ['breikwɔ:tər] *n.* **1.** brise-lames *m inv*; môle *m*; jetée *f*; estacade *f*. **2.** éperon *m* (d'un pont).

bream [bri:m] *n. Ich:* brème *f*; **sea b.,** pagre *m*; dorade *f*, brème de mer.

breast¹ [brest] *n.* **1.** sein *m*, mamelle *f*; **b. feeding,** allaitement *m* (naturel); **child at the b.,** enfant au sein. **2.** (*a*) poitrine *f* (de personne, d'animal); poitrail *m* (de cheval); devant *m* (d'une chemise, etc.); **to make a clean b. of it,** tout avouer; (*of water, etc.*) **b. high, b. deep,** jusqu'à la poitrine; *Cost:* **b. pocket,** poche *f* de poitrine; **inside b. pocket,** poche intérieure, (à) portefeuille; *Swim:* **b. stroke,** brasse *f*; (*b*) *Cu:* blanc *m* (de volaille). **3.** (*a*) *Metall:* ventre *m* (de haut fourneau); (*b*) *Const:* **chimney b.,** manteau *m* de cheminée; **b. wall,** (i) mur *m* de soutènement; (ii) allège *f* de fenêtre; mur à hauteur d'appui; (*c*) *Nau:* **b. rail,** lisse *f* d'appui; lisse de fronteau; (*d*) *Hyd. E:* **b. wheel,** roue *f* de côté. **4.** *Min:* front *m* de taille, d'abattage.

breast² *v.tr.* **1.** *Lit:* affronter, faire front à (un danger); affronter, gravir (une colline); (*of swimmer*) **to b. the waves,** fendre la lame. **2.** *Sp:* **to b. the tape,** arriver le premier.

breastbone ['brestboun] *n. Anat: Z:* sternum *m*; *Orn:* bréchet *m.*

breastfeed ['brestfi:d] *v.tr.* (*p.t. & p.p.* **-fed** [-fed]) élever (un enfant) au sein, allaiter (un enfant).

breastplate ['brestpleit] *n. Arm:* plastron *m*; cuirasse *f*.

breastwork ['brestwə:k] *n.* parapet *m.*

breath [breθ] *n.* (*a*) haleine *f*, souffle *m*; **to draw b.,** respirer; **give me time to take b.,** donnez-moi le temps de souffler; **to draw, take, a deep, long, b.,** respirer profondément, à pleins poumons; **to draw one's last b.,** rendre le dernier soupir; **to have bad b.,** avoir mauvaise haleine; **the b. of life,** le souffle vital; le souffle de la vie; **music is the very b. of life to me,** je ne pourrais pas vivre sans musique; **all in the same b.,** tout d'une haleine; **they are not to be mentioned in the same b.,** on ne saurait les comparer; **to hold one's b.,** retenir son souffle; **to gasp for b.,** haleter; **to waste one's b.,** perdre son temps en discours inutiles; perdre ses paroles; **I'm wasting my b.,** c'est comme si je chantais; **to be short of b.,** être essoufflé; avoir la respiration coupée; **out of b.,** hors d'haleine, à bout de souffle; essoufflé; **to get out of b.,** perdre haleine; **to take s.o.'s b. away,** couper la respiration, le souffle, à qn; ébahir, interloquer, qn; **to get one's b. (back), to recover one's b.,** reprendre haleine; **under one's b.,** (parler) d'une voix très basse, à voix basse; (jurer) en sourdine; **the first b. of spring,** les premiers effluves du printemps; **a b. of wind, of air,** un souffle de vent, d'air; (*b*) *Ling:* **b. consonant,** consonne soufflante; (*c*) *Adm:* **b. test,** alcoo(l)test *m.*

breathalyse ['breθəlaiz] *v.tr.* donner l'alcoo(l)test *m* à (qn).

breathalyser, *NAm:* **breathalizer** ['breθəlaizər] *n. Adm:* **b. test,** alcoo(l)test *m.*

breathe [bri:ð] **1.** *v.i.* (*a*) respirer, souffler; **to b. hard,** haleter; **to b. heavily,** (i) respirer bruyamment; (ii) respirer péniblement; **to b. again,** respirer de nouveau; **to b. on one's fingers,** souffler dans ses doigts; *F:* **to b. down s.o.'s neck,** talonner qn; (*b*) (*of voice, instrument, wind*) soupirer, souffler doucement. **2.** *v.tr.* (*a*) respirer (l'air); (*b*) exhaler, laisser échapper (un soupir); murmurer (une prière); **he breathed a sigh of relief,** il poussa un soupir de soulagement; *Lit:* **to b. one's last,** rendre le dernier soupir; rendre l'âme; **don't b. a word (of it)!** n'en soufflez (pas un) mot! (*c*) *Ling:* aspirer (un son). **breathed** *a. Ling:* (consonne) sourde, forte; (voyelle) aspirée. **breathing** *n.* **1.** (*of pers.*) respiration *f*; souffle *m*; **heavy b.,** (i) respiration bruyante; (ii) respiration pénible; oppression *f*; *Min: etc:* **b. apparatus,** appareil *m* respiratoire, masque *m* de protection; **b. space,** (i) le temps de souffler, de respirer; répit *m*, relâche *f*; (ii) place *f*, espace *m*, pour respirer. **2.** aspiration *f* (d'un son).

breather ['bri:ðər] *n. F:* moment *m* de repos (pour souffler); **to give s.o. a b.,** laisser souffler qn; laisser un moment de répit à qn; **to go for a b.,** aller respirer un peu d'air; sortir prendre l'air, un brin d'air.

breathless [breθlis] *a.* **1.** hors d'haleine, essoufflé, haletant; **b. with running,** hors d'haleine, essoufflé, d'avoir couru; **b. chase,** poursuite *f* à perte d'haleine. **2. b. suspense,** attente fiévreuse; (*of film, etc.*) **to hold s.o. b.,** tenir qn en haleine, en suspens. **-ly** *adv.* **1.** en haletant; (courir) à perte d'haleine. **2.** (attendre, écouter) en retenant son haleine.

breathlessness ['breθlisnis] *n.* essoufflement *m*; respiration essoufflée; (*of patient*) manque *m* de souffle; oppression *f*.

breathtaking ['breθteikiŋ] *a.* **it's b.,** c'est à vous couper le souffle.

breathy ['breθi] *a.* (*a*) **b. voice,** voix haletante; (*b*) *Mus:* (voix) qui manque d'attaque.

breech [bri:tʃ] *n.* **1.** (*a*) *Obst:* **b. presentation,** présentation *f* par le siège; **b. (delivery, birth),** accouchement *m* par le siège; (*b*) *Harn:* **b. band,** avaloire *f*. **2.** (*a*) **(pair of) breeches** ['britʃiz], culotte *f*; **knee breeches,** culotte; **riding breeches,** culotte de cheval. **3.** *Artil: Sm.a:* culasse *f*, tonnerre *m*; **b. action, mechanism,** mécanisme *m* de culasse. **4.** *Nau:* **breeches buoy,** bouée *f* culotte.

breed¹ [bri:d] *n.* race *f* (d'hommes, d'animaux).

breed² *v.* (*p.t. & p.p.* **bred** [bred]) **1.** *v.tr.* (*a*) produire, procréer (des enfants, des petits); (*b*) faire naître; **dirt breeds disease,** la malpropreté engendre la maladie; (*c*) élever (du bétail, des lapins, etc.); (*d*) (*of pers.*) **to be town bred, country bred,** avoir été élevé à la ville, à la campagne; *Prov:* **what's bred in the bone will come out in the flesh,** bon chien chasse de race. **2.** *v.i.* (*a*) (i) (*of animals, people*) multiplier; se reproduire; (ii) (*of opinions, etc.*) se propager; (*b*) (*of pers.*) faire de l'élevage *m.* **breeding** *n.* **1.** (*a*) reproduction *f*, multiplication *f* (des êtres); **b. ground,** endroit fréquenté par certains animaux à l'époque de la reproduction; **b. ground of anarchists,** pépinière *f* d'anarchistes; (*b*) élevage *m* (d'animaux domestiques, etc.); **animal kept for b. purposes,** (animal) reproducteur (*m*); **b. stock,** animaux élevés en vue de la reproduction; **sheep b.,** élevage des moutons; **silkworm b.,** sériciculture *f*. **2.** (*a*) éducation (d'un enfant, etc.); (*b*) **(good) b.,** bonne éducation, bonnes manières; savoir-vivre *m*; l'usage du monde; **to lack b.,** manquer de savoir-vivre.

breeder ['bri:dər] *n.* **1.** reproducteur, -trice. **2.** éleveur, -euse (d'animaux); **poultry b.,** aviculteur, -trice; **silkworm b.,** séricliculteur *m.*

breeze¹ [bri:z] *n.* brise *f*; **gentle, light, b.,** petite, légère, brise; **land b.,** brise de terre; vent *m* d'amont; **sea b.,** brise de mer, du large; *Nau:* **strong, stiff, b.,** vent frais, grosse brise; **fresh b.,** bonne brise.

breeze² *v.i.* (*a*) *Nau:* (*of wind*) **to b. up,** fraîchir; (*b*) *F:* **to b. in, out,** entrer, sortir, (i) en coup de vent, (ii) d'une façon désinvolte; **to b. along,** passer vite.

breeze³ *n.* (*a*) braise *f* de houille; charbonnaille *f*; **coke b.,** grésillon *m* de coke, poussier *m* de coke; (*b*) **b. concrete,** ciment *m* de laitier; **b. block, brick,** parpaing *m.*

breezeway ['bri:zwei] *n.* *U.S:* passage couvert (souvent entre la maison et le garage).

breezy ['bri:zi] *a.* **1.** (jour, endroit, etc.) venteux. **2.** *F:* jovial; désinvolte; (*of speech*) plein de verve; **b. welcome,** accueil cordial (et bruyant). **-ily** *adv.* avec verve; avec désinvolture.

Bremen ['breimən] *Pr.n. Geog:* Brême.

Bren ['bren] *n. Mil:* **B. (gun),** fusil-mitrailleur; **B. carrier,** chenillette *f* porte-fusil-mitrailleur, *pl.* chenillettes porte-fusil(s)-mitrailleur(s).

brent ['brent] *n. Orn:* **b. (goose),** bernache *f* cravant.

brethren *n.pl. see* BROTHER 2 (*b*).

Breton ['bretən]. **1.** *a. Geog:* breton. **2.** *n.* (*a*) Breton, -onne; (*b*) *Ling:* breton *m.*

breve [bri:v] *n.* **1.** *Hist:* bref *m* (du pape). **2.** *Pros:* brève *f.* **3.** *Mus:* (*a*) *A:* brève, carrée *f*; (*b*) **b. rest,** demi-bâton *m*, *pl.* demi-bâtons.

brevet ['brevit, *esp. NAm:* brə'vet] *n. Mil:* brevet *m* d'honorariat.

breviary ['bri:viəri] *n. Ecc:* bréviaire *m.*

brevity ['breviti] *n.* **1.** brièveté *f*, concision *f* (de style); laconisme *m* (d'expression). **2.** brièveté, courte durée (de la vie, etc.).

brew¹ [bru:] *n.* (*a*) brassin *m*, cuvée *f*; (*b*) infusion *f* (de thé); (*c*) **home b.,** bière, cidre, de ménage.

brew² **1.** *v.tr.* (*a*) brasser (de la bière); **home brewed,** (*of beer*) brassé à la maison; (*of cider*) de ménage; (*b*) faire infuser (du thé); préparer (un bol de punch). **2.** *v.i.* (*a*) (*of tea, etc.*) infuser; (*b*) *F:* **there's a storm brewing,** (i) un orage couve, se prépare; (ii) *F:* c'est un bain, un bouillon, qui chauffe; **there's something brewing,** il y a quelque chose dans l'air. **brewing** *n.* (*a*) brassage *m* (de la bière); (*b*) infusion *f* (du thé); préparation *f* (d'un bol de punch). **brew up** *v.i. F:* faire infuser le thé.

brewer ['bru(:)ər] *n.* brasseur *m.*

brewery ['bru(:)əri] *n.* brasserie *f.*

briar¹ ['braiər] *n.* (*a*) *Bot:* **wild b.,** églantier commun, rosier *m* sauvage; **sweet b.,** églantier odorant; **b. rose,** églantine *f*; (*b*) **briars,** ronces *fpl.*

briar² *n.* = BRIER¹.

bribable ['braibəbl] *a.* corruptible.

bribe¹ [braib] *n.* paiement *m* illicite; *F:* pot-de-vin *m*, *pl.* pots-de-vin; **to take a b., bribes,** se laisser corrompre.

bribe² *v.tr.* corrompre, soudoyer; *F:* graisser la patte à (qn); **to b. s.o. to silence,** acheter le silence de qn. **bribing** *n.* corruption *f*; subornation *f* (de témoins); *F:* graissage *m* de patte.

bribery ['braibəri] *n.* corruption *f*; **open, not open, to b.,** corruptible, incorruptible.

bric-a-brac ['brikəbræk] *n.* (*no pl.*) bric-à-brac *m.*

brick¹ [brik] *n.* **1.** (*a*) brique *f*; **air b.,** brique perforée; **fire b.,** brique réfractaire; **b. kiln,** four *m* à briques; **one cannot make bricks without straw,** on ne peut pas faire un miracle; *F:* **to come down on s.o. like a ton of bricks,** tomber sur le dos à qn; **to drop a b.,** faire une bourde, une gaffe; **b. (red),** rouge brique *inv*; (*b*) (*toy*) **box of (building) bricks,** jeu *m* de cubes, de construction; (*c*) **b. wall,** mur *m* en briques; *F:* **to run one's head against a b. wall,** donner de la tête contre un mur; se buter à l'impossible; **b. partition,** cloison *f* de briques. **2.** *F: O:* **he's a b.,** c'est un chic type. **3.** bloc *m* (de thé, etc.); pain *m* (de savon, de glace, etc.).

brick² *v.tr.* briqueter; garnir (qch.) en briques; **to b. up,** murer, maçonner (une fenêtre).

brickbat ['brikbæt] *n. NAm:* (i) fragment *m* de brique; (ii) *F:* insulte *f.*

bricklayer ['brikleiər] *n.* maçon *m* en briques; briqueteur *m.*

bricklaying ['brikleiiŋ] *n.* maçonnerie *f* en briques; briquetage *m.*

brickmaker ['brikmeikər] *n.* briquetier *m.*

brickwork ['brikwə:k] *n.* briquetage *m*; maçonnerie *f* de brique; **brickworks,** briqueterie *f.*

bridal ['braid(ə)l] *a.* nuptial, de noce(s); **b. veil,** voile *m* de mariée; (*in hotel*) **b. suite,** appartement *m* pour jeunes mariés.

bride [braid] *n.f.* (i) fiancée (sur le point de se marier); (ii) (nouvelle) mariée; **the b. and bridegroom,** (i) les futurs conjoints; (ii) les nouveaux mariés.

bridegroom ['braidgrum] *n.m.* (i) fiancé (sur le point de se marier); (ii) (nouveau) marié.

bridesmaid ['braidzmeid] *n.f.* demoiselle *f* d'honneur (de la mariée).

bridge¹ [bridʒ] *n.* **1.** (*a*) pont *m*; **stone b.,** pont en pierre; **swing b.,** pont tournant; **suspension b.,** pont suspendu; **cantilever b.,** pont cantilever; **pontoon b.,** pont de bateaux; **Bailey b.,** pont Bailey; **loading b.,** pont de chargement; **road, railway, b.,** pont routier, de chemin de fer; **b. building,** construction *f* de ponts; pontage *m*; *Mil:* **b. train,** (i) train *m* de pontons; (ii) corps *m* des pontonniers; **to cross a b.,** traverser un pont; *Fig:* **that's a b. we'll cross when we get, come, to it,** chaque chose en son temps; (*b*) *Wr:* pont; **to make a b.,** ponter; (*c*) (*in billiards, etc.*) chevalet *m.* **2.** *Nau:* passerelle *f*; **fore b.,** passerelle de commandement; **b. house,** rouf-passerelle *m.* **3.** *El: etc:* (*a*) **measuring b.,** pont de mesure; **induction b.,** balance *f* d'induction; (*b*) **b. piece,** pont polaire (d'accus); **b. connection,** couplage *m* en pont. **4.** (*a*) dos *m*, arête *f* (du nez); chevalet *m* (d'un violon); arcade *f* (d'une paire de lunettes); autel *m* (d'une chaudière); (*b*) *Dent:* bridge *m.*

bridge² *v.tr.* construire un pont sur (un cours d'eau); **to b. a gap,** relier les bords d'une brèche; combler une lacune; (*esp. for supplies*) faire la soudure; **that will b. (over) the difficulty,** cela nous aidera à surmonter la difficulté. **bridging** *n.* **1.** construction *f* d'un pont (sur un fleuve); pontage *m*; **b. party,** équipe *f* de pontonniers. **2.** (*a*) comblement *m* (d'une lacune); soudure *f*; **b. loan,** crédit *m* de relais, provisoire; (*b*) *Cin:* **b. title,** titre *m* de liaison; (*c*) *Const: Carp:* **b. piece,** entretoise *f*; (*d*) *El: Elcs:* **b. connection,** montage *m* en pont.

bridge³ *n. Cards:* bridge *m*; **game of b.,** (partie *f* de) bridge; **auction b.,** bridge aux enchères; **contract b.,** bridge contrat; **to play b.,** jouer au bridge; bridger; **b. player,** bridgeur, -euse; *Cu:* **b. roll,** petit pain (au lait).

bridgehead ['bridʒhed] *n. Mil:* tête *f* de pont.

bridgework ['bridʒwə:k] *n.* **1.** construction *f* de ponts. **2.** *Dent:* bridge *m.*

bridle¹ ['braidl] *n.* **1.** (*a*) *Harn:* bride *f*; **b. bit,** mors *m* de bride; **b. rein,** rênes *fpl* de bride; **b. path,** route cavalière; (*in forest, etc.*) piste cavalière; (*b*) frein *m.* **2.** *Nau:* branche *f.*

bridle² **1.** *v.tr.* (*a*) brider (un cheval); (*b*) maîtriser, mettre un frein à (ses passions). **2.** *v.i.* **to b. (up),** (i) redresser la tête; se rengorger; (ii) se rebiffer.

brief¹ [bri:f] **1.** *a.* (of *letter, interval, etc.*) court; (*of discussion, explanation, etc.*) bref, succinct, concis; (exposé) sommaire; (séjour, etc.) passager, de courte durée; **for a b. period,** pendant peu de temps; **in b.,** en raccourci, en résumé; **to be b.,** pour vous dire la chose en deux mots; bref. **2.** *n.pl. Cost:* **briefs,** slip *m*; **bikini briefs,** slip bikini. **-ly** *adv.* (*a*) brièvement; en peu de mots; en raccourci; (*b*) (pendant) un instant.

brief² *n.* **1.** *Ecc:* bref *m*; **apostolic b.,** bref apostolique. **2.** (*a*) *Jur:* dossier *m* (d'une procédure); **to take a b.,** accepter un dossier; **to hold a b.,** être chargé d'une cause; **to hold a b. for s.o.,** représenter qn en justice; **to hold a watching b. for s.o.,** veiller (en justice) aux intérêts de qn; *Fig:* **I don't hold any b. for him,** ce n'est pas mon affaire de plaider sa cause; (*b*) *U.S: Jur:* **b. (of argument),** conclusions (présentées à la cour avant l'audience). **3.** *Av: Com: etc:* instructions *fpl.*

brief³ *v.tr.* **1. to b. a barrister,** confier une cause à un avocat. **2.** (*a*) *Av: Com: etc:* donner une mission à (qn); munir (qn) d'instructions, fournir des directives à (qn); (*b*) **to b. s.o. on sth.,** donner des informations *fpl* de qch. à qn; faire l'exposé *m* de qch. à qn. **briefing** *n.* **1. b. of a barrister** = constitution *f* d'avoué. **2.** instructions *fpl*, directives *fpl* (de mission); réunion *f* d'information; *Av:* briefing *m.*

briefcase ['bri:fceis] *n.* serviette *f* (en cuir); porte-documents *m inv.*

briefness ['bri:fnis] *n.* brièveté *f*; concision *f.*

brier¹ ['braiər] *n.* **1.** *Bot:* bruyère (arborescente). **2. b. root, b. wood,** racine *f* de bruyère.

brier² *n.* = BRIAR¹.

brig [brig] *n.* **1.** *Nau:* brick *m.* **2.** *NAm: Navy:* prison *f*, cellule *f* (à bord d'un navire).

brigade [bri'geid] *n.* **1.** *Mil:* (*a*) brigade *f*; (*b*) *O:* **infantry b.,** régiment d'infanterie; (*c*) *U.S:* **artillery b.,** brigade d'artillerie; (*e*) *F:* **one of the old b.,** un vieux de la vieille. **2.** corps organisé (pour un service public, etc.).

brigadier [brigə'diər] *n. Mil:* **b.(-general),** général *m* de brigade.

brigand ['brigənd] *n.* brigand *m*, bandit *m.*

brigandage ['brigəndidʒ] *n.* brigandage *m.*

bright [brait] **I.** *a.* **1.** (*a*) (*of star, metal, gem, etc.*) brillant; (*of sun*) éclatant; (*of fire, light, etc.*) vif; **b. eyes,** yeux brillants, lumineux; (*b*) (*of day, weather, etc.*) clair; **b. intervals,** éclaircies *f*; **to become brighter,** s'éclaircir; (*c*) (*of colour*) vif, *f.* vive; éclatant; **b. red,** rouge vif; (*d*) (*of sound*) clair; éclatant; (*e*) **b. future,** avenir brillant, qui promet; **brighter days,** des jours plus heureux; **to look on the b. side of things,** prendre les choses par le bon côté. **2.** (*a*) vif, animé, sémillant; (*of face, smile*) gai; (*b*) *F:* éveillé, intelligent; (idée) lumineuse; **he's not very b.,** ce n'est pas un as. **II** *adv.* **to get up b. and early,** se lever de bonne heure. **brightly** *adv.* **1.** brillamment; avec éclat; **the sun was shining b.,** le soleil brillait avec éclat; **b. polished,** reluisant d'éclat. **2.** d'un ton vif; gaiement.

brighten ['brait(ə)n] **1.** *v.tr.* **to b. (up),** faire briller, faire reluire (qch.); fourbir (le métal); aviver (une couleur); égayer (une salle, qn). **2.** *v.i.* **to b. (up),** (*of pers., face*) s'épanouir; se dérider; (*of weather*) s'éclaircir; (*of the future*) s'éclaircir, devenir moins sombre; **his eyes brightened,** ses yeux s'allumèrent, brillèrent. **brightening** *n.* (*a*) **b. (up),** éclaircissement *m* (du ciel, du temps); (*b*) avivage *m* (de couleurs).

brightness ['braitnis] *n.* éclat *m* (du soleil, d'une lampe, d'un son); intensité *f* (d'éclairage); luminosité *f* (d'une surface); brillant *m* (de l'acier); clarté *f* (du jour, d'un son); vivacité *f* (de l'intelligence, d'une couleur); *F:* intelligence *f* (d'un enfant, etc.); *Opt:* brillance *f*; *T.V:* **b. (control),** (dispositif *m* de réglage de la) luminosité.

brill [bril] *n. Ich:* barbue *f.*

brilliance ['briliəns], **brilliancy** ['briliənsi] *n.* **1.** (*a*) éclat *m*, brillant *m*, lustre *m*; (*b*) *Ac:* netteté *f* (du son); (*c*) *Opt: etc:* luminance *f.* **2. brilliance,** intelligence *f* remarquable (de qn.); brillant (d'esprit, de style, etc.); habileté *f* remarquable (d'un chirurgien, etc.).

brilliant¹ ['briliənt] *a.* (*a*) (éclairage) intense, brillant; (soleil) brillant, éclatant; (*b*) (*of pers.*) très intelligent, très doué; (idée) lumineuse; (succès) éclatant; **he's not b.,** il n'est pas brillant; (*c*) *F:* **I'm not feeling very b.,** je ne suis pas dans mon assiette. **-ly** *adv.* brillamment; (*a*) avec éclat; **the sun was shining b.,** le soleil brillait avec éclat; **b. lit,** vivement éclairé; (*b*) **b. intelligent,** d'une intelligence brillante; *Mus:* **to play b.,** jouer avec brio.

brilliant² *n.* **1.** *Lap:* brillant *m.* **2.** *Typ:* corps *m* $3\frac{1}{2}$.

brilliantine ['briliənti:n] *n. Toil:* brillantine *f.*

brim¹ [brim] *n.* bord *m* (de verre, de chapeau, etc.); **to fill a glass to the b.,** remplir un verre à ras bord.

brim² *v.i.* **(brimmed)** (*of vessel*) être plein jusqu'au bord; **to b. over,** déborder, regorger (**with sth.,** de qch.); **eyes brimming with tears,** yeux noyés de larmes; **brimming over with health, with life,** débordant de santé, de vie.

brimful ['brimful] *a.* (*a*) (*of glass, etc.*) plein jusqu'au bord; plein à déborder; débordant; **to fill a glass b.,** remplir un verre à ras bord; (*b*) **b. of health, of life,** débordant de santé, de vie.

brimless ['brimlis] *a.* (chapeau) sans bord(s).

brimstone ['brimstən] *n.* **1.** *A:* soufre (brut). **2.** *Ent:* **b. (butterfly),** citron *m.*

brindle(d) ['brindl(d)] *a.* moucheté, tacheté; à rayures.

brine [brain] *n.* eau salée; saumure *f.*

bring [briŋ] *v.* (*p.t. & p.p.* **brought** [brɔ:t]) **I.** *v.tr.* **1.** (*a*) amener (qn, un animal); apporter (qch., une lettre, une nouvelle, etc.) **b. your friend (along),** amenez votre ami; **she brought a lot of luggage (with her),** elle a apporté beaucoup de bagages; **what brings you to London?** qu'est-ce qui vous amène à Londres? (*b*) **to b. a child into the world,** mettre au monde un enfant; (*c*) **to b. (s.o.) before a court,** faire comparaître (qn) devant un tribunal; soumettre, déférer (un litige) à un tribunal; (*d*) **to b. an action against s.o.,** intenter un procès contre, à, qn; **to b. an accusation, a charge, against s.o.,** porter une accusation contre qn. **2.** (*a*) **to b. s.o. (good) luck, bad luck,** porter bonheur, malheur, à qn; **to b. new hope to s.o.,** redonner de l'espoir à qn; **you've brought it on yourself,** vous l'avez voulu; **to b. tears to s.o.'s eyes,** faire venir les larmes aux yeux de qn; **to b. discord into a family,** semer la discorde dans une famille; **it has brought me great happiness,** cela m'a apporté un grand bonheur; (*b*) **to b. s.o. to his senses,** ramener qn à la raison; **to b. s.o. into the conversation,** mêler qn à la conversation; **to b. sth. into question,** mettre qch. en question; **to b. sth. into disrepute,** discréditer qch.; **to b. sth. to s.o.'s attention,** appeler, attirer, l'attention de qn sur qch.; **to b. sth. to mind,** rappeler qch.; **to b. sth. to light,** déterrer (des objets anciens, des manuscrits); révéler (un crime, un secret); **to b. sth. to an end,** mettre fin à qch; **to b. sth. to a successful conclusion,** faire aboutir qch.; **to b. sth. home to s.o.,** faire sentir qch. à qn. **3. to b. oneself to do sth.,** se résoudre, se décider, à faire qch.; **he cannot b. himself to speak about it,** il lui est trop pénible d'en parler. **bring about** *v.tr.* (*a*) amener, causer, occasionner (qch.); amener, ménager (une réconciliation); entraîner (la ruine de qn); provoquer (un accident, etc.); (*b*) effectuer, accomplir (qch.); opérer (un changement, un miracle); (*c*) *Nau:* retourner, faire virer (un navire). **bring back** *v.tr.* (*a*) rapporter (qch.); ramener (qn); (*b*) (*of letter, etc.*) rappeler (des souvenirs); **it brings back my childhood to me,** cela me rappelle mon enfance; (*c*) rétablir (la liberté, la discipline, la monarchie, etc.); ramener (la confiance); **to b. s.o. back to health,** rétablir la santé de qn; **to b. s.o. back to life,** ramener qn à la vie; (*d*) **to b. a case back before the court,** ressaisir le tribunal d'un différend. **bring down** *v.tr.* (*a*) abattre (un arbre, du gibier, un avion); descendre (une perdrix, un avion); mettre à bas, faire crouler, faire effondrer (un mur, une maison); terrasser (un adversaire); faire tomber (un gouvernement); *Th: F:* **to b. d. the house,** faire crouler la salle (sous les applaudissements); (*b*) faire descendre (qn); descendre (un objet du grenier, etc.); (*c*) abaisser, faire baisser (le prix); avilir (la monnaie, les prix); abaisser, réduire (la natalité); (*d*) réduire (une enflure); faire baisser (la fièvre d'un malade). **bring forth** *v.tr. A: & Lit:* mettre au monde (des enfants); (*of animal*) mettre bas (des petits); (*of plant*) produire (des fruits). **bring forward** *v.tr.* (*a*) avancer (une chaise, etc.); amener, faire avancer, faire approcher (qn); produire (un témoin); avancer, présenter, (un argument); alléguer (une preuve); (*b*) avancer (une réunion, etc.); **the meeting has been brought forward from 14th to 7th,** la séance a été avancée du 14 au 7; (*c*) *Com:* reporter (une somme); **brought forward,** à reporter; report *m*. **bring in** *v.tr.* (*a*) introduire, faire entrer (qn); apporter, rentrer (qch.); introduire, lancer (une mode, etc.); faire intervenir (qn); **b. him in,** faites-le entrer; **to b. in the harvest,** rentrer la moisson; (*b*) (*of capital, investment*) **to b. in interest,** rapporter; porter intérêt; **investment that brings in 10%,** placement *m* qui rend 10%; **this land brings him in an income of £5000,** cette terre lui vaut £5000 de rente; (*c*) déposer, présenter (un projet de loi); (*d*) *Jur:* (*of jury*) **to b. in a verdict,** rendre un verdict. **bring off** *v.tr.* réussir (un coup, etc.). **bring on** *v.tr.* (*a*) produire, occasionner (une maladie, etc.); provoquer (une crise d'asthme, etc.); (*b*) (*of sun, etc.*) faire pousser (les plantes); (*of teacher, trainer*) faire faire des progrès à (qn); (*c*) *Th:* amener, apporter, sur la scène; **in the second act an elephant is brought on,** au second acte on fait paraître en scène un éléphant. **bring out** *v.tr.* (*a*) sortir (qch.); faire sortir (qn); (*b*) révéler, faire ressortir (le sens de qch.); faire valoir (une couleur, un détail, etc.); **to b. out the best, the worst, in s.o.,** faire ressortir les bonnes, les mauvaises, qualités de qn; (*c*) publier, sortir (un livre); (*d*) **the sun has brought out the roses,** le soleil a fait épanouir les roses; *Fig:* **to b. s.o. out,** faire sortir qn de sa réserve. **bring over** *v.tr.* amener, apporter (qch.). **bring round** *v.tr.* (*a*) faire reprendre connaissance à (qn); ranimer (qn); (*b*) remettre (qn) de bonne humeur; (*c*) convertir (qn) (**to an opinion,** à une opinion); (*d*) (r)amener (la conversation) (**to a subject,** à un sujet); (*e*) *Nau: etc:* faire virer (un navire, etc.). **bring to 1.** *Nau: v.tr.* mettre (un navire) en panne; couper l'erre à (un navire). **2.** *v.tr.* **to b. s.o. to,** faire reprendre connaissance à qn; ranimer qn. **bring together** *v.tr.* réunir; mettre (des personnes) en contact; rassembler (des documents); **he brought them together again,** il les a (i) réunis, (ii) réconciliés; *Jur:* **to b. the parties together,** mettre les parties en présence. **bring up 1.** *v.tr.* (*a*) monter (qch.); faire monter (qn); (*b*) **to b. up one's food,** vomir; (*c*) apporter, approcher, avancer (qch.); amener, faire approcher (qn); faire avancer (des troupes); amener (des renforts); (*d*) élever (des enfants); **I was brought up by an aunt,** j'ai été élevé par une tante; **I was brought up to be polite,** j'ai été élevé dans la politesse; **well, badly, brought up child,** enfant bien, mal, élevé; (*e*) *Nau:* mouiller, arrêter (un navire); (*of pers.*) **to be brought up short by sth.,** buter contre qch.; se heurter à qch.; (*f*) soulever (une question); mettre (une question) sur le tapis; **to b. sth. up (against s.o.),** objecter qch. (à qn); *Jur:* faire état de qch. (contre un accusé); (*g*) **to be brought up before the magistrate,** comparaître devant le tribunal. **2.** *v.i. Nau:* (*of ship*) mouiller.

brink [briŋk] *n.* bord *m* (d'un précipice, d'un fleuve); *Fig:* **to stand shivering on the b.,** hésiter à faire le plongeon; *Fig:* **on the b. of . . .,** tout près de . . .; **to be on the b. (of sth.),** être au bord (des larmes); être à la veille (d'une découverte, de la ruine); être à deux doigts (de la ruine, de la mort).

brinkmanship ['briŋkmənʃip] *n.* acrobatie *f* politique; politique *f* du bord de l'abîme.

briny ['braini] **1.** *a.* saumâtre, salé. **2.** *n. F:* **the b.,** la mer, la grande tasse.

briquette [bri'ket] *n. Fuel:* briquette *f*.

brisk [brisk] *a.* **1.** (*a*) (*of pers., movement*) vif, actif, animé; *Nau:* (vent) rond; **at a b. pace,** à vive allure; **to take a b. walk,** se promener à bon pas; (*b*) *Com:* (commerce) actif; (demande) animée; **business is b.,** les affaires marchent. **2.** (air) vivifiant; (temps) frais. **-ly** *adv.* vivement, activement; avec entrain; **to step out b.,** marcher d'un pas accéléré.

brisket ['briskit] *n. Cu:* poitrine *f*, avant-cœur *m* (de bœuf).

briskness ['brisknis] *n.* **1.** (*a*) vivacité *f*, activité *f*, animation *f*, entrain *m*; (*b*) activité (des affaires, du marché). **2.** fraîcheur *f* (de l'air, etc.).

bristle¹ ['brisl] *n.* **1.** soie *f* (de porc, de chenille); soie, poil *m* (de brosse); poil raide (de la barbe). **2.** *Bot:* soie, poil.

bristle² **1.** *v.tr.* (*of animal*) hérisser (ses poils, ses soies). **2.** *v.i.* (*of animal, hair, etc.*) **to b. (up),** se hérisser; *F:* (*of pers.*) se rebiffer, se hérisser.

bristly ['brisli] *a.* (*a*) couvert de soies, de poils raides; (moustache) hérissée, raide; (*b*) *Bot:* poilu; garni de soies.

Bristol ['brist(ə)l] *Pr.n.* **B. board,** carton *m* Bristol; bristol *m*; *Nau:* **(shipshape and) B. fashion,** en bon ordre.

Britain ['brit(ə)n] *Pr.n. Geog:* **(Great) B.,** la Grande-Bretagne.

Britannia [bri'tæniə] *Pr.n.* (nom symbolique de) la Grande-Bretagne; *Com:* **B. metal,** métal anglais.

Britannic [bri'tænik] *a.* **His, Her, B. Majesty,** Sa Majesté britannique.

Briticism ['britisizm] *n. NAm: Ling:* anglicisme *m*.

British ['britiʃ] *a.* britannique, de la Grande-Bretagne; (*in Fr. usu.*) anglais, d'Angleterre; **the B. Isles,** les Iles Britanniques; **the B. consul,** le consul d'Angleterre; **B. goods,** produits anglais, marchandises anglaises; *NAm:* **B. English,** l'anglais britannique; *n.pl.* **the B.,** les Britanniques, les Anglais.

Britisher ['britiʃər] *n. NAm:* natif, -ive, de (la) Grande-Bretagne; Britannique *mf*, *F:* Anglais, -aise.

Briton ['brit(ə)n] *n.* **1.** *Hist:* Breton, -onne (de la Grande-Bretagne). **2.** Britannique, Anglais, -aise.

Brittany ['britəni] *Pr.n. Geog:* Bretagne *f*.

brittle ['britl] *a.* fragile, cassant; **in a b. voice,** d'une voix crispée.

broach¹ [broutʃ] *n.* **1.** *Cu:* broche *f* (à rôtir). **2.** *Tls:* (*a*) équarrissoir *m*; mèche *f* de foret; (*b*) *Coop:* perçoir *m*.

broach² *v.tr.* (*a*) *Metalw:* équarrir, brocher; (*b*) *Coop:* percer (un fût); (*c*) entamer, aborder (une question, etc.); **to b. the subject,** entrer en matière.

broad [brɔːd] **1.** *a.* (*a*) large; **the road is 15 metres b.,** la route a 15 mètres de large; **a b. smile,** un large sourire; *Sp: NAm:* **b. jump,** saut *m* en longueur; **to have a b. back,** (i) avoir une forte carrure; (ii) *Fig:* avoir bon dos; **in b. daylight,** (i) en plein jour; (ii) *Fig:* à la lumière du grand jour; devant tout le monde; *Ling:* **b. vowel,** voyelle large; **it's as b. as it is long,** cela revient au même; c'est tout un; (*b*) (règle) générale; (règle) de principe; (distinction) sommaire; **b. outline,** aperçu *m* (d'un projet, etc.); **term used in its broadest sense,** terme employé dans un sens (très) large; (*c*) (accent) prononcé; **to speak b. Yorkshire,** parler avec un accent prononcé; (*d*) **b. humour,** humour de mauvais goût, peu délicat; **b. joke,** grosse plaisanterie; plaisanterie risquée; (*e*) **b. views, ideas, outlook,** idées larges, tolérantes. **2.** *n.* (*a*) **the b. of the back,** toute la largeur du dos; le milieu du dos; (*b*) *Geog:* **the Norfolk Broads,** la région de lacs du Norfolk; (*c*) *esp. U.S: P:* femme *f*, nana *f*. **-ly** *adv.* **1.** (*a*) largement; **smiling b.,** avec un large sourire; (*b*) généralement; **b. speaking,** généralement parlant; d'une façon générale. **2.** (parler) (i) avec un accent prononcé, (ii) grossièrement.

broad-brimmed [ˈbrɔːdˈbrimd] *a.* (chapeau) à large bord.

broadcast [ˈbrɔːdkɑːst] **I.** *v.* (*p.t. & p.p.* **broadcast**) **1.** *v.tr.* (*a*) *Agr:* semer (du grain) à la volée; (*b*) répandre (une nouvelle). **2.** *W.Tel: TV:* (*a*) *v.tr.* transmettre, (radio)diffuser, téléviser (un programme, etc.); **commentary b. from X,** radio reportage *m* depuis X; (*b*) *v.i.* parler, chanter, etc., à la radio; paraître à la télévision. **II.** *n. W.Tel: TV:* émission *f*; programme radiodiffusé, télévisé; **simultaneous, recorded, live, b.,** émission simultanée, en différé, en direct. **III. 1.** *a.* (*a*) *Agr:* semé à la volée; **b. sowing,** semis *m* à la volée; (*b*) *W.Tel: TV:* (radio)diffusé; télévisé; **b. announcement,** annonce *f* (i) par radio, (ii) télévisée; **b. account,** radioreportage *m* (d'un match, etc.). **2.** *adv. Agr:* **to sow b.,** semer à la volée. **broadcasting** *n.* **1.** *Agr:* semis *m* à la volée. **2.** *W.Tel: TV:* radio-émission *f*; radiodiffusion *f*; **(television) b.,** télévision *f*; **news b.,** radioreportage *m*; téléreportage *m*; **b. station,** station *f* de radiodiffusion, de télévision; **the British B. Corporation, the BBC** [biːbiːˈsiː] la Corporation Britannique de radiodiffusion; **this is the end of today's b.,** voici la fin de nos émissions pour aujourd'hui. **broadcaster** [ˈbrɔːdkɑːstər] *n.* radioreporter *m*; speaker, speakerine.

broadcloth [ˈbrɔːdklɔθ] *n. Tex:* **1.** drap noir fin (pour vêtements d'hommes). **2.** *NAm:* popeline *f*.

broaden [ˈbrɔːd(ə)n] **1.** *v.tr.* élargir; **to b. s.o.'s outlook,** élargir l'horizon de qn. **2.** *v.i.* s'élargir.

broad-leaved [ˈbrɔːdˈliːvd] *a. Bot:* à larges feuilles; latifolié.

broadloom [ˈbrɔːdluːm] *a.* (tapis) grande largeur.

broadminded [ˈbrɔːdˈmaindid] *a.* **to be b.** avoir l'esprit large, être tolérant, large d'esprit.

broad-mindedness [ˈbrɔːdˈmaindidnis] *n.* largeur *f* d'esprit; tolérance *f*.

broadness [ˈbrɔːdnis] *n.* largeur *f*.

broadsheet [ˈbrɔːdʃiːt] *n.* **1.** *Typ:* in-plano *m inv.* **2.** feuille imprimée; prospectus *m*.

broad-shouldered [ˈbrɔːdˈʃouldəd] *a.* large d'épaules, aux larges épaules.

broadside [ˈbrɔːdsaid] *n. Nau:* (*a*) flanc *m*, travers *m* (du navire); **collision b. on,** abordage *m* par le travers; (*b*) bordée *f*; **to fire a b.,** tirer une bordée.

broadways, broadwise [ˈbrɔːdweiz, -waiz] *adv.* en large; dans le sens de la largeur.

brocade[1] [brəˈkeid] *n. Tex:* brocart *m*.

brocade[2] *v.tr. Tex:* brocher; **brocaded gown,** robe *f* de brocart.

broccoli [ˈbrɔkəli] *n. Hort:* brocoli *m*.

brochure [brouˈʃjuəːr, ˈbrouʃəːr] *n.* brochure *f*, dépliant *m*; prospectus *m* publicitaire.

brogue[1] [broug] *n.* chaussure *f* de marche, de golf.

brogue[2] *n.* accent irlandais.

broil[1] [brɔil] *n.* querelle *f*; échauffourée *f*; rixe *f*.

broil[2] *v.tr. & i.* (*a*) *NAm: Cu:* griller; (faire) cuire sur le gril; (*b*) *F:* **we were broiling (hot),** on grillait.

broiler [ˈbrɔilər] *n.* **1.** *NAm:* gril *m*, rôtissoire *f*. **2. b. (fowl),** poulet *m* de chair (à rôtir); **b. house,** batterie *f* (pour l'élevage des poulets de chair).

broke[1] [brouk] *a. F:* (*a*) **to be (stony, dead) b.,** être sans le sou; être fauché; être à sec; (*b*) *Austr:* **to be b. for a feed,** avoir faim.

brokendown [ˈbrouk(ə)nˈdaun] *a.* (*of horse*) fourbu; (*of house, furniture*) délabré; (*of car, etc.*) en panne; (*of mechanism*) détraqué.

brokenhearted [ˈbrouk(ə)nˈhɑːtid] *a.* navré de douleur; au cœur brisé; **to die b.-h.,** mourir de douleur, de chagrin.

broken-winded [ˈbrouk(ə)nˈwindid] *a. Vet:* (cheval) poussif.

broker [ˈbroukər] *n.* **1.** (*a*) *Com:* courtier *m* (de commerce); **bill b.,** courtier de change; **insurance b.,** courtier d'assurances; (*b*) *St.Exch:* agent *m* de change; courtier de bourse; **outside b.,** coulissier *m*; courtier marron, libre. **2.** (*secondhand*) brocanteur, -euse. **3.** *Jur:* (i) = *approx.* commissaire-priseur *m*; (ii) = *approx.* huissier *m*.

brokerage [ˈbroukəridʒ] *n. Fin:* (frais *mpl* de) courtage (*m*).

brolly [ˈbrɔli] *n. F:* parapluie *m*, pépin *m*, riflard *m*.

bromide [ˈbroumaid] *n.* **1.** *Ch:* bromure *m*; **potassium b.,** bromure de potassium; *Phot:* **b. (paper),** papier *m* au gélatinobromure (d'argent). **2.** *P:* (*a*) homme ennuyeux; raseur *m*; (*b*) banalité *f*.

bronchial [ˈbrɔŋkiəl] *a. Anat:* (artère, asthme, etc.) bronchique; **the b. tubes,** les bronches *fpl*; *Med:* **b. pneumonia,** broncho-pneumonie *f*.

bronchitic [brɔŋˈkitik] *a. & n. Med:* bronchitique (*mf*).

bronchitis [brɔŋˈkaitis] *n. Med:* bronchite *f*.

bronchopneumonia [ˈbrɔŋkounjuːˈmouniə] *n. Med:* broncho-pneumonie *f*.

bronco [ˈbrɔŋkou] *n.* cheval sauvage, non dressé, de l'Amérique; **b. buster,** dresseur *m* de chevaux.

brontosaur(us) [ˈbrɔntəsɔːr, brɔntəˈsɔːrəs] *n. Paleont:* brontosaure *m*.

bronze[1] [brɔnz] **1.** *n.* (*a*) *Metall:* bronze *m*; *Prehist:* **the B. Age,** l'âge *m* du bronze; (*b*) *Art:* (objet *m* en) bronze. **2.** *attrib.* (statue) de, en, bronze; *Sp: etc:* **b. medal,** médaille *f* de bronze.

bronze[2] **1.** *v.tr.* (*a*) bronzer (le fer, etc.); (*b*) mordorer (le cuir, des souliers). **2.** *v.i.* se bronzer; brunir; *Phot:* se métalliser. **bronzed** *a.* (teint) bronzé, basané. **bronzing** *n.* bronzage *m*.

brooch [broutʃ] *n. Cost:* broche *f* (de diamants, etc.).

brood[1] [bruːd] *n.* **1.** (*a*) couvée *f* (de poussins); volée *f* (de pigeons); naissain *m* (d'huîtres, de moules); (*b*) *Breed:* **b. hen,** (poule) couveuse (*f*); **b. mare,** (jument) poulinière (*f*); (*c*) *Ap:* **b. cell,** cellule *f* d'incubation. **2.** *F:* (*a*) enfants *mpl*; marmaille *f*; (*b*) *Pej:* race *f* (de scélérats, etc.).

brood[2] *v.i.* **1.** (*of hen*) couver, accouver. **2.** *Fig:* (*a*) broyer du noir; **to b. on, over, sth.,** remâcher (le passé); rêver à qch.; ruminer (une idée); **to b. over things,** remuer, repasser, des idées dans sa tête; (*b*) *Lit:* **night broods over the scene,** la nuit plane sur la scène.

brooder [ˈbruːdər] *n.* **1.** (poule) couveuse (*f*). **2.** couveuse (artificielle).

broody [ˈbruːdi] *a.* (*a*) (poule) couveuse, qui demande à couver; (*b*) *F:* (*of pers.*) pensif; rêveur.

brook¹ [bruk] *n.* **1.** ruisseau *m.* **2.** *Ich:* **b. trout,** saumon *m* de fontaine.

brook² *v.tr.* (*used only in neg. sentences*) *Lit:* (ne pas) souffrir; (ne pas) endurer; **the matter brooks no delay,** l'affaire n'admet aucun retard; **he will b. no insolence,** il ne supporte pas d'impertinence.

broom [bru:m] *n.* **1.** *Bot:* genêt m (à balai). **2.** balai *m.*

broomstick ['bru(:)mstik] *n.* manche *m* à balai.

broth [brɔθ] *n. Cu:* (*a*) bouillon *m*, potage *m*; (*b*) **Scotch b.,** soupe *f* (de mouton) avec orge et légumes.

brothel ['brɔθ(ə)l] *n.* maison *f* de prostitution, bordel *m*; *Jur:* maison de débauche.

brother ['brʌðər] *n.m.* **1.** frère; **half b.,** demi-frère; **older b.,** frère aîné; **younger b.,** (frère) cadet (*m*); *Com:* **Thomas Brothers, Thomas Bros.,** maison *f* Thomas frères. **2.** (*a*) *Ecc:* frère (d'une communauté); **lay b.,** frère lai; (*b*) (*fellow member, pl. usu.* **brethren** ['breðrin] (i) frère (d'une société religieuse); (ii) confrère *m* (d'un corps de métier); (*c*) **brothers in arms,** frères d'armes; **b. officers,** officiers *mpl* du même régiment.

brotherhood ['brʌðəhud] *n.* **1.** fraternité *f.* **2.** (*a*) confraternité *f*, société *f*; (*religious*) confrérie *f*; (*b*) *esp. U.S.:* syndicat ouvrier.

brother-in-law ['brʌðərinlɔ:], *n.m.* (*pl.* **brothers-in-law**) beau-frère, *pl.* beaux-frères.

brotherliness ['brʌðəlinis] *n.* **1.** amour fraternel. **2.** confraternité *f.*

brotherly ['brʌðəli] *a.* (amour, etc.) fraternel.

brouhaha [bru:'hɑ:hɑ:] *n.* brouhaha *m.*

brow [brau] *n.* **1.** (*a*) arcade sourcilière; (*b*) sourcil *m*; **to knit one's brows,** froncer les sourcils. **2.** (*a*) *Anat:* front *m*; (*b*) *Ven:* **b. antler,** maître andouiller *m.* **3.** front (de colline); bord *m* (de précipice, etc.); (*on road*) **the b. of a hill,** le haut d'une côte.

browbeat ['braubi:t] *v.tr.* intimider, rudoyer (qn); **to b. s.o. into doing sth.,** rabrouer qn pour lui faire faire qch. **browbeating** *n.* intimidation *f.*

brown¹ [braun] **1.** *a.* (*a*) brun; marron *inv*; **b. hair,** cheveux bruns, châtains; **light b. hair,** cheveux châtain clair; **b. shoes,** chaussures *fpl* marron; **b. paper,** papier *m* d'emballage, papier kraft; **b. bread,** pain bis; **b. sugar,** cassonade *f*; **b. ale** = bière brune; (*of pers.*) **to be b.** être hâlé, bronzé (*b*) *Z:* **b. bear,** ours brun; *Ich:* **b. trout,** truite saumonée. **2.** *n.* brun *m*; marron *m.*

brown² **1.** *v.tr.* (*a*) brunir; bronzer; **face browned by the sun,** teint bruni, hâlé, au solel!; (*b*) *Cu:* rissoler (la viande); faire dorer (le poisson); faire roussir (du beurre, une sauce); praliner (des amandes). **2.** *v.i.* (*a*) (se) brunir; **his face browns easily,** son visage (se) brunit facilement (*b*) *Cu:* prendre couleur; se rissoler; roussir. **browning** *n.* **1.** (*a*) brunissement *m*; bronzage *m*; pralinage *m* (des amandes). **2.** *Cu:* colorant brun (pour les sauces). **brown off** *v.tr.* *F:* décourager (qn); **to be browned off,** être découragé.

brown-eyed ['braunaid] *a.* aux yeux bruns.

brown-haired ['braun'hɛəd] *a.* châtain, aux cheveux châtains.

brownie ['brauni] *n.* **1.** lutin *m* (bienfaisant); farfadet *m.* **2.** *Scout:* jeannette *f.* **3.** *NAm: Cu:* petit gâteau *m* au chocolat et aux noisettes.

browning ['brauniŋ] *n. Sm.a:* browning *m.*

brownish ['brauniʃ] *a.* brunâtre.

browse [brauz] *v.tr. & i.* (*a*) brouter (l'herbe); paître; **to b. (on) leaves,** brouter des feuilles; (*b*) **to b. (among books),** feuilleter des livres; bouquiner. **browsing** *n.* **1.** broutement *m* (des animaux). **2.** flânerie *f* (*esp.* parmi les livres).

brucellosis [bru:si'lousis] *n. Med: Vet:* brucellose *f.*

bruise¹ [bru:z] *n.* meurtrissure *f*; contusion *f*; bleu *m*; (*on fruit*) talure *f*, meurtrissure.

bruise² *v.* **1.** (*a*) *v.tr.* meurtrir, contusionner (une partie du corps); meurtrir, taler (un fruit); **to b. one's arm,** se meurtrir au bras, le bras; (*b*) *v.i.* (*of fruit, etc.*) se meurtrir. **2.** *v.tr.* broyer, écraser, concasser (une substance); égruger (le blé). **bruising** *n.* **1.** contusion *f.* **2.** broyage *m*, écrasement, concassage *m*; égrugeage *m.*

bruiser ['bru:zər] *n. Box: F:* boxeur *m*; cogneur *m.*

brumbie, brumby ['brʌmbi] *n. Austr: F:* cheval sauvage, non dressé.

brunch [brʌnʃ] *n. F:* repas *m* tenant lieu de *breakfast* et de *lunch.*

brunette [bru:'net] *a. & n.* brune (*f*), brunette (*f*).

brunt [brʌnt] *n.* choc *m*; **to bear the b. of (sth.),** soutenir le plus fort de (l'attaque, la tempête, etc.); soutenir le poids de (la colère de qn); **to bear the b. of the expense,** faire tous les frais.

brush¹ [brʌʃ] *n.* **1.** (*a*) broussailles *fpl*; **b. harrow,** herse *f* d'épines; (*b*) *U.S: Austr: etc:* brousse *f*; **b. fire,** incendie *m* de forêt. **2.** (*a*) brosse *f*; balai *m*; **hard b.,** (i) (*for shoes, etc.*) brosse à décrotter; (ii) (*for pans, etc.*) brosse à récurer; **scrubbing b.,** brosse dure; **dustpan and b.,** balayette *f* et ramasse-poussière *m inv*; **bottle b.,** goupillon *m*; **washing-up b.,** lavette *f*; (*b*) **clothes b.,** brosse à habits; **hat b.,** brosse à chapeau; **shaving b.,** blaireau *m*; (*c*) **(paint) b.,** pinceau *m*, brosse; **flat b.,** queue-de-morue *f*, *pl.* queues-de-morue; **paste b.,** pinceau à colle; (*d*) *Art:* touche *f* (de peintre); **to paint with a full b.,** peindre dans la pâte; (*e*) *Type:* **b. proof,** épreuve *f* à la brosse; morasse *f*; (*f*) queue *f* (de renard). **3.** *El:* (*a*) balai (de commutateur, de génératrice); **(contact) b.,** frotteur *m*; **carbon b.,** balai en charbon; **b. holder,** porte-balai(s) *m inv*; (*b*) faisceau *m* de rayons électriques. **4.** (*a*) **to give (sth.) a b.,** donner un coup *m* de brosse à (des vêtements, etc.); (*b*) rencontre *f*, échauffourée *f* (avec l'ennemi); **at the first b.,** au premier abord; *F:* **to have a b. with the police,** avoir des ennuis avec la police.

brush² **1.** *v.tr.* (*a*) brosser (un habit, les cheveux); balayer (un tapis); **to b. one's hair,** se brosser les cheveux; **to b. one's teeth,** se brosser, se laver, les dents; (*b*) effleurer, raser, frôler, érafler (une surface); (*c*) gratter (la laine, le nylon); (*d*) **to b. the dust off sth.,** enlever la poussière de qch. (à la brosse, en brossant); **to b. sth. clean,** nettoyer qch. avec une brosse, à la brosse. **2.** *v.i.* **to b. against, past, s.o.,** frôler, friser, qn en passant; **to b. against sth.,** frôler, érafler, qch. **brush aside** *v.tr.* écarter (qn, une difficulté). **brush away** *v.tr.* enlever (de la boue, etc.) d'un coup de brosse, de balai; essuyer furtivement (une larme); écarter (une difficulté, etc.). **brush down** *v.tr.* donner un coup de brosse à (qn); brosser (un cheval). **brushed** *a. Tex:* **b. wool,** laine grattée; **b. nylon,** nylon gratté. **brushing** *n.* coup *m* de brosse; brossage *m*; balayage *m.* **brush off** *v.tr.* (*a*) enlever (de la boue, etc.) d'un coup de brosse, de balai; (*b*) (*with passive force*) **the dirt will b. off when it's dry,** la boue s'enlèvera à la brosse quand elle sera sèche; (*c*) *F:* envoyer promener (qn). **brush over** *v.tr.* enduire (une surface) à la brosse; badigeonner (une surface) (**with,** de). **brush up** *v.tr.* (*a*) brosser, donner un coup de brosse à (un chapeau, etc.); *F:* se remettre à (un sujet); repasser (un sujet); **to b. up one's French,** dérouiller son français; (*b*) gratter (la laine); (*c*) **to b. up the crumbs,** ramasser les miettes (avec la brosse).

brushdown ['brʌʃdaun] *n.* **to give s.o. a b.,** donner un coup de brosse à qn; **to give a horse a b.,** brosser, panser, un cheval.

brushoff ['brʌʃɔf] *n. F:* **to give s.o. the b.,** envoyer promener qn.
brushup ['brʌʃʌp] *n.* coup *m* de brosse; **to have a wash and b.,** faire un brin, un bout, de toilette.
brushwood ['brʌʃwud] n. (a) broussailles *fpl*; (*b*) mort-bois *m*; menu bois; brindilles *fpl*; (*c*) *Civ. E: etc:* fascines *fpl.*
brushwork ['brʌʃwɔ:k] *n.* **1.** travail *m* au pinceau. **2.** *Art:* touche *f* (du peintre); facture *f.*
brusque [bru:sk] *a.* brusque; (ton) rude, bourru. **-ly** *adv.* brusquement.
brusqueness ['bru:sknis] *n.* brusquerie *f*; rudesse *f.*
Brussels ['brʌs(ə)lz] *Pr.n. Geog:* Bruxelles; **B. sprouts,** choux *mpl* de Bruxelles.
brutal ['bru:t(ə)l] *a.* brutal, -aux; **the b. truth,** la vérité brutale. **-ally** *adv.* brutalement.
brutality [bru:'tæliti] **1.** brutalité *f* (**to,** envers). **2.** *Jur:* sévices *mpl* (**to,** envers).
brutalize ['bru:təlaiz] *v.tr.* **1.** abrutir (qn). **2.** brutaliser, maltraiter (qn).
brute [bru:t] **1.** *n.* (*a*) brute *f*; bête *f* brute; (*b*) *F:* (*of pers.*) brute; **you b.!** espèce d'animal! **what a b.!** quel animal! (*c*) *F:* **a b. of a job,** un travail de chien. **2.** *a.* (*a*) **b. beast,** bête brute; (*b*) **b. force,** la force brutale; **by b. force,** de vive force; (*c*) **b. matter,** matière *f* brute.
brutish ['bru:tiʃ] *a.* **1.** de brute; bestial, -aux. **2.** abruti; brutal, -aux. **-ly** *adv.* en brute; comme une brute.
bryony ['braiəni] *n. Bot:* bryone *f*, couleuvrée *f.*
bubble[1] ['bʌbl] *n.* **1.** (*a*) bulle *f* (d'air, de savon); (*in boiling liquid*) bouillon *m*; **b. bath,** bain *m* de mousse; (*b*) *Glassm:* soufflure *f*; *Cer:* cloche *f*; *Metall:* boursouflement *m*; poche *f* d'air; (*c*) bouillonnement *m*; *Ch: etc:* barbotage *m.* **2.** *Cu: F:* **b. and squeak,** réchauffé *m* en friture de pommes de terres et de choux. **3.** projet *m* chimérique; **to prick the b. of s.o.'s expectations,** réduire à néant les espérances de qn.
bubble[2] *v.i.* (*a*) (*of boiling liquid, etc.*) bouillonner; dégager des bulles; (*of wine*) pétiller; *Ch: Ind:* (*of gas through liquid*) barboter; (*b*) (*of liquid poured*) faire glouglou, glouglouter. **bubble over** *v.i.* déborder (en bouillonnant, en moussant); **to b. over with vitality, with high spirits,** déborder de vie, de gaîté; **to b. over with joy,** pétiller de joie; **he was bubbling over with laughter,** il ne se tenait pas de rire. **bubbling 1.** *a.* bouillonnant; (*of wine*) pétillant. **2.** *n.* (*a*) bouillonnement *m*; pétillement *m*; (*b*) *Ch: etc:* barbotage *m.*
bubbly ['bʌbli] **1.** *a.* plein de bulles; pétillant. **2.** *n. F:* champagne *m*; vin mousseux.
bubonic [bju(:)'bɔnik] *a. Med:* (peste) bubonique.
buccaneer[1] [bʌkə'niər] *n.* (*a*) *Hist:* flibustier *m*; (*b*) boucanier *m*, flibustier; pirate *m.*
buccaneer[2] *v.i.* faire le boucanier; faire le métier de pirate; flibuster.
buck[1] [bʌk] *n.* **1.** (*a*) daim *m*, chevreuil *m* (mâle); (*b*) mâle *m* (du renne, du chamois, etc.); **b. rabbit,** lapin *m* (mâle); *F:* **b. teeth,** dents *fpl* de lièvre; (*c*) = BUCKSKIN. **2.** *NAm:* (*a*) *usu. Pej:* (jeune) Indien *m* (d'Amérique); (*b*) *F:* homme, type *m.* **3.** (*a*) chevalet *m*, chèvre *f* (de sciage); (*b*) *Gym:* mouton *m.* **4.** *Equit:* **b. (jump),** saut *m* de mouton. **5.** *NAm: F:* dollar *m*; **to make a fast b.,** faire un coup de fric.
buck[2] **1.** *v.i.* (*a*) (*of horse*) faire le gros dos; faire un haut-de-corps; **to b. (jump),** faire le saut de mouton; (*b*) *Av:* (*of aircraft*) se cabrer; (*c*) *esp. U.S:* résister; se regimber; s'opposer (**against,** à). **2.** *v.tr.* (*of horse, etc.*) **to b. s.o. off,** désarçonner qn; *NAm:* **to b. the question,** renvoyer la balle. **bucked** *a. F:* (i) ragaillardi; (ii) enchanté; **I was really b. to hear the news,** (i) ça m'a remonté le cœur, (ii) j'ai été enchanté, d'apprendre la nouvelle. **bucking** *n.* sauts *mpl* de mouton (d'un cheval, etc.). **buck up** *F:* **1.** *v.tr.* **to b. s.o. up,** remonter le courage de (qn); ragaillardir (qn); donner du cœur à (qn); **that will b. you up,** ça vous remontera, vous retapera. **2.** *v.i.,* (i) reprendre courage; (ii) se hâter, se remuer; **b. up!** (i) courage! (ii) dépêche-toi! *F:* grouille-toi!
buck[3] *n. U.S.: Cards:* objet *m* que l'on place devant un joueur pour marquer que c'est à lui de donner; *F:* **to pass the b. to s.o.,** (i) (*at poker*) passer la parole au suivant; (ii) *Fig:* mettre l'affaire sur le dos de qn; passer la décision à qn.
bucket[1] ['bʌkit] *n.* **1.** (*a*) seau *m*; *F:* **it's coming down in buckets,** il pleut à verse, à seaux; *P:* **to kick the b.,** mourir, casser sa pipe; **b. chain,** chaîne *f* de personnes qui se passent des seaux d'eau (en cas d'incendie); (*b*) *Min: Ind:* baluchon *m*, baquet *m*; benne *f* (d'une grue); (*c*) piston *m* (à clapet); (*d*) auget *m*, auge *f* (d'une roue hydraulique); **b. wheel,** roue *f* à augets; **b. elevator,** élévateur *m* à godets; (*e*) godet *m*, louchet *m* (d'une drague); **b. dredger,** drague à godets; (*f*) bassicot *m* (de téléphérage); (*g*) *Aut:* **b. seat,** baquet; (*h*) *Cmptr:* compartiment *m* (en mémoire). **2.** *Fin: F:* **b. shop,** bureau *m* d'un courtier marron.
bucket[2] *v.i.* **it's bucketing down,** il pleut à verse, à seaux.
bucketful ['bʌkitful] *n.* (*pl.* **bucketsful, bucketfuls**) plein seau.
buckle[1] ['bʌkl] *n.* **1.** boucle *f*, agrafe *f* (d'une courroie, d'une ceinture, etc.). **2.** *Tchn:* gauchissement *m*, voile *m* (d'une roue, etc.).
buckle[2] **1.** *v.tr.* (*a*) boucler (une valise, etc.); agrafer (une ceinture, etc.); (*b*) *Tchn:* déjeter; gauchir; voiler (une roue); tordre (une plaque d'accumulateur, etc.). **2.** *v.i.* (*a*) *F:* (*of pers.*) **to b. to a task,** s'appliquer à un travail; **to b. to,** s'y atteler; s'y mettre. **3.** *v.i.* **to b. (up),** (*of metal, etc.*) se déjeter, gauchir; (*of wheel, sheet iron*) se voiler. **buckled** *a.* **1.** bouclé; agrafé. **2.** déjeté; gauchi; voilé; tordu. **buckling** *n.* **1.** agrafage *m.* **2.** (*of metal, etc.*) déformation *f*, gauchissement *m*; voilure *f.*
buckler ['bʌklər] *n.* (*a*) *Arm:* écu *m*, bouclier *m*; targe *f*; (*b*) *Fig:* bouclier.
buckling ['bʌkliŋ] *n.* hareng cuit et fumé.
buckram ['bʌkram] *n. Tex:* bougran *m.*
bucksaw ['bʌksɔ:] *n. Tls:* scie *f* à bûches.
buckshee ['bʌk'ʃi:] *F:* **1.** *a. & adv. F:* gratis *inv;* **we got in b.,** on est entré gratis, sans payer. **2.** *n. esp. Mil:* (*extra ration*) **a bit of b.,** du rabiot.
buckshot ['bʌkʃɔt] *n. Ven:* chevrotines *fpl.*
buckskin ['bʌkskin] *n.* peau *f* de daim; **b. breeches,** *n.pl.* **buckskins,** culotte *f* de peau (de daim).
buckthorn ['bʌkθɔ:n] *n. Bot:* nerprun *m.*
buckwheat ['bʌk(h)wi:t] *n. Agr:* sarrasin *m*; **b. cake,** galette *f* de blé noir.
bucolic [bju(:)'kɔlik] **1.** *a.* (vie, poésie, poète) bucolique. **2.** *n.pl.* **bucolics,** bucoliques *fpl.*
bud[1] [bʌd] *n.* (*a*) *Bot:* bourgeon *m*; bouton *m* (de fleur); (*of tree*) **to be in b.,** bourgeonner; (*b*) *Anat:* **taste b.,** papille gustative, bouton gustatif.
bud[2] *v.* **(budded) 1.** *v.i.* (*a*) (*of tree, plant*) bourgeonner; (*of flower*) boutonner. **2.** *v.tr. Hort:* greffer (un arbre fruitier) par œil détaché; écussonner (un arbre). **budding 1.** *a.* (*a*) (plante, arbre) bourgeonnant; **a b. rose,** une rose en bouton; (*b*) (artiste, avocat, etc.) en herbe; (passion) naissante. **2.** *n.* (i) bourgeonnement *m*, boutonnement *m*; (ii) poussée *f* des boutons.
Buddha ['budə] *Pr.n.m.* (le) Bouddha.
Buddhism ['budizm] *n.* bouddhisme *m.*
Buddhist ['budist] **1.** *n.* bouddhiste *mf.* **2.** *a.* bouddhique, bouddhiste.
buddleia ['bʌdliə] *n. Bot:* buddleia *f.*

buddy ['bʌdi] *n. F:* ami *m*, copain *m*.

budge [bʌdʒ] **1.** *v.i.* (*a*) bouger, céder; reculer; **to refuse to b.,** refuser de bouger; **I won't b. an inch,** je ne reculerai pas d'un centimètre; (*b*) bouger, remuer; **if you (so much as) b.,** si vous faites le moindre mouvement. **2.** *v.tr.* (*in neg. sentences*) **I couldn't b. him,** il est resté inébranlable; **he couldn't b. it,** il ne pouvait pas le bouger.

budgerigar ['bʌdʒərigɑːr] *n. Orn:* perruche *f*.

budget[1] ['bʌdʒit] *n.* (*a*) *Fin: etc:* budget *m*; **to balance the b.,** équilibrer le budget; **family, household, b.,** budget familial, du ménage; *Parl:* **to pass the b.,** voter le budget; (*b*) *Com:* **b. prices,** prix raisonnables, avantageux; **b. account** = (i) compte permanent; (ii) (*in bank*) compte crédit.

budget[2] *v.i. Fin: etc:* budgétiser; **to b. for (sth.),** porter, inscrire (qch.) au budget; budgétiser (des dépenses); prévoir (une dépense, une difficulté, etc.). **budgeting** *n.* budgétisation *f*.

budgetary ['bʌdʒitəri] *a. Fin: etc:* budgétaire.

budgie ['bʌdʒi] *n. Orn: F:* perruche *f*.

buff[1] [bʌf] *n.* **1.** (peau *f* de) buffle (*m*); *Metalw:* **b. stick,** polissoir *m*. **2.** (*a*) couleur *f* chamois; jaune clair *inv*; (*b*) *a.* de couleur chamois. **3.** *F:* **in the b.,** tout nu. **4.** *U.S:* enthousiaste *mf*; **he is a film b.,** c'est un passionné du cinéma.

buff[2] *v.tr.* **1.** *Metalw: etc:* polir, émeuler (un métal, etc.) (au buffle); **to b. one's nails,** se polir les ongles. **2.** *Leath:* effleurer (les peaux). **buffing** *n.* **1.** *Metalw: etc:* polissage *m*, émeulage *m*; bufflage *m*; **b. wheel,** meule *f* à polir, à buffler; disque *m* en buffle. **2.** *Leath:* effleurage *m*.

buffalo, *pl.* **-oes** ['bʌfəlou, -ouz] *n.* **1.** *Z:* (*a*) buffle *m*; **water b.,** karbau *m*; **young b.,** bufflon *m*; (*b*) *U.S:* bison *m*.

buffer[1] ['bʌfər] *n.* (*a*) appareil *m* de choc; amortisseur *m*; *Rail:* (i) tampon *m* (de choc); (ii) (*at end of line*) butoir *m*, heurtoir *m*; (*b*) *El: Elcs:* (circuit *m*) tampon; *W.Tel:* **b. stage,** étage *m* tampon, intermédiaire; (*d*) *Artil:* **recoil b.,** frein *m*, amortisseur de recul; (*e*) *Pol:* **b. state,** état *m* tampon; *Pol.Ec:* **b. stocks,** stocks régulateurs, tampon, de régularisation; (*of pers.*) **to act as a b.,** servir de tampon.

buffer[2] *n. F:* **old b.,** vieille ganache, vieux bonze.

buffer[3] *n.* polissoir *m*.

buffet[1] ['bʌfit] *n.* coup *m* (de poing); gifle *f*.

buffet[2] *v.tr.* (*a*) bourrer (qn) de coups; tomber sur (qn) à coups de poing; (*b*) (*of ship*) **buffeted by the waves, the wind,** battu, ballotté, par les vagues; secoué par le vent. **buffeting** *n.* succession *f* de coups, de chocs.

buffet[3] *n.* **1.** ['bʌfit] *Furn:* buffet *m*. **2.** ['bufei] (*a*) (*refreshment bar*) buffet; *Rail:* **b. car,** voiture-buffet, *pl.* voitures-buffets; (*b*) (*on menu*) **cold b.,** viandes froides; assiette anglaise; (*c*) **b. lunch, b. meal,** lunch *m*; repas *m* à la fourchette; **cold b.,** buffet froid.

buffoon [bə'fuːn] *n.* bouffon *m*, paillasse *m*, clown *m*; **to act, play, the b.,** faire le bouffon.

buffoonery [bə'fuːnəri] *n.* bouffonneries *fpl*; baladinage *m*.

bug[1] [bʌg] *n.* **1.** (*a*) **(bed) b.,** punaise *f* (des lits); (*b*) *esp. U.S:* insecte *m*; *U.S:* **potato b.,** doryphore *m*; (*c*) *F:* virus *m*, microbe *m*; **to catch a b.,** attraper un microbe; *F:* **to have the skiing b.,** avoir la passion, la folie, du ski. **2.** *esp. U.S:* erreur *f*, mauvais fonctionnement. **3.** micro clandestin.

bug[2] *v.tr.* (*a*) camoufler des micros clandestins dans (une pièce); brancher (un téléphone) sur la table d'écoute; intercepter (une conversation); (*b*) taper sur les nerfs à (qn); emmerder (qn). **bugging** *n.* installation *f* des micros clandestins; **b. device,** micro clandestin.

bugaboo ['bʌgəbuː] *n.* = BUGBEAR.

bugbear ['bʌgbɛər] *n. F:* (*a*) croquemitaine *m*; épouvantail *m*; (*b*) cauchemar *m*; **maths is my b.,** les math, c'est mon cauchemar.

bugger[1] ['bʌgər] *n.* **1.** *Jur:* pédéraste *m*. **2.** *P:* (*not in polite use*) (*a*) bougre *m*, salaud *m*; **silly b.!** espèce d'idiot! **poor b.,** pauvre type; (*b*) **a b. of a job,** un travail de chien.

bugger[2] **1.** *v.tr.* (*a*) sodomiser; (*b*) *P:* **b. (it)!** merde! (*c*) *P:* **to b. sth. up,** bousiller qch. **2.** *v.i. P:* **to b. about,** lambiner; **to b. off,** foutre le camp; **b. off!** (i) fous le camp! (ii) fous-moi la paix!

buggery ['bʌgəri] *n.* sodomie *f*.

buggy *n. Veh:* (*a*) boghei *m*, buggy *m*; **(American) b.,** américaine *f*; (*b*) *NAm:* **baby b.,** poussette *f* d'enfant; (*c*) **beach, dune, b.,** (dune) buggy *m*; *Space:* **moon b.,** jeep *f* lunaire.

bugle[1] ['bjuːgl] *n. Mil:* clairon *m*; **key(ed) b.,** bugle *m*; **b. call,** coup *m*, sonnerie *f*, de clairon.

bugle[2] *n. Bot:* bugle *f*.

bugler ['bjuːglər] *n.* clairon *m*; sonneur *m* de clairon.

build[1] [bild] *n.* **1.** construction *f*; façons *fpl* (d'un navire, etc.); style *m* (d'un édifice). **2.** carrure *f*, taille *f*, conformation *f* (d'une personne); **man of powerful b.,** homme à forte membrure; **of slight b.,** fluet.

build[2] *v.tr.* (*p.t. & p.p.* **built** [bilt]) **1.** bâtir (une maison, etc.); construire (un navire, un pont, une route, etc.); édifier (un temple); faire (son nid, etc.) (**with,** avec); **the walls were built of granite,** les murs étaient (bâtis) en granit; **to b. on a piece of land,** bâtir un terrain; **the stables are built on to the house,** les écuries tiennent à la maison; **to b. on sand,** bâtir sur le sable; **the house is being built,** la maison est en construction. **2.** (*a*) **to b. one's hopes on sth.,** fonder, baser, ses espoirs sur qch.; **to b. on a promise,** miser, faire fond, sur une promesse: **I'm building my hopes on you,** je compte sur vous; (*b*) *esp. NAm: Com:* **to b. (certain characteristics) into a product,** incorporer (certaines charactéristiques) dans un produit; (*c*) *Med: etc:* **to b. in an immunity,** créer une immunité. **build up 1.** *v.tr.* (*a*) (i) rehausser, (ii) réparer (un mur, etc.); **this area has been very much built up,** on a beaucoup construit par ici; (*b*) affermir (la santé); reconstituer (ses forces); (*c*) bâtir, échafauder, construire (une théorie, un système); développer (un commerce); se faire (une réputation); (*d*) accumuler (une collection, une bibliothèque); (*e*) *Mil: etc:* constituer (des réserves); mettre sur pied (des unités, des renforts, etc.); (*f*) faire de la publicité pour (qn, un produit, etc.); (*g*) *El:* amorcer (un champ électrique). **2.** *v.i.* (*a*) (*of pressure, tension, etc.*) s'accumuler, augmenter; (*of traffic*) devenir dense; (*of snow*) s'amonceler; (*b*) *El:* (*of magnetic field*) s'amorcer. **built** *a.* **1.** bâti; **British b.,** de construction anglaise; **solidly b.,** (*of house, etc.*) solidement bâti, construit; (*of pers.*) qui a la charpente solide; **a powerfully b. man,** un homme à forte membrure. **2. b.-in,** (*a*) (placard) incorporé; (poutre) encastrée; **b.-in resistance,** opposition congénitale; (*b*) (énergie) inhérente (d'un atome). **3. b.-up,** (*a*) **b.-up area,** agglomération (urbaine); (*b*) (poutre) composée, rapportée; (*c*) *Cost:* (épaules) surhaussées; (talons) compensés.

builder ['bildər] *n.* entrepreneur *m* en bâtiments; constructeur *m* (de navires, etc.); créateur *m*, fondateur *m* (d'un empire, etc.).

building ['bildiŋ] *n.* **1.** (*a*) construction *f*; **b. plot,** terrain à bâtir; **b. site,** (i) terrain à bâtir; (ii) chantier *m* (de construction); **b. estate,** lotissement *m*; **b. materials,** matériaux *mpl* de construction); **b. contractor,** entrepreneur *m* de bâtiments; **b. workers,** ouvriers *mpl* du bâtiment; **the b. trade,** le bâtiment; **b. society** = coopérative *f*, société *f*, immobilière; *N.Arch:* **b. slip,** cale *f* de construction; (*b*) **b. up,** (i) rehaussement *m* (d'un mur, etc.); (ii) reconstruction *f* (de ses forces); (iii) accumulation *f* (d'un système, etc.); (v) *El:* amorçage *m* d'un champ); (vi) accumulation (de la pression, de la tension, etc.). **2.** bâtiment; immeuble *m;* maison *f;* édifice *m;* **public b.,** (i) édifice public; (ii) monument *m;* **farm buildings,** bâtiments, dépendances *fpl,* d'une ferme.

build-up ['bildʌp] *n.* **1.** élaboration *f,* développement *m* (d'un système, etc.). **2.** *Mil:* mise *f* sur pied (d'unités, de renforts, etc.); constitution *f* (de réserves en hommes, de matériel, etc.). **3.** (*a*) *Ph:* manifestation croissante (d'un phénomène); *Mec:* montée *f* en accélération; (*b*) accumulation *f,* augmentation *f* (de la pression, de la tension). **4.** publicité *f;* campagne *f* publicitaire. **5. traffic b.-up,** bouchon *m* de circulation.

bulb¹ [bʌlb] *n.* **1.** *Bot:* bulbe *m,* oignon *m* (de tulipe, etc.), **2.** *Anat:* bulbe (pileux aortique, etc.). **3.** *El:* ampoule *f,* lampe *f.* **4.** (*a*) *Ph:* boule *f,* cuvette *f,* ampoule, réservoir *m* (de thermomètre); (*b*) *Ch:* (*flask*) ballon *m;* (*c*) poire *f* (en caoutchouc).

bulbous ['bʌlbəs] *a.* bulbeux; *Bot:* **b. root,** racine bulbeuse; (*of pers.*) **b. nose,** gros nez.

Bulgaria [bʌl'gɛəriə] *Pr.n. Geog:* Bulgarie *f.*

Bulgarian [bʌl'gɛəriən] **1.** *a. Geog:* bulgare. **2.** *n.* (*a*) Bulgare *mf;* (*b*) *Ling:* bulgare *m.*

bulge¹ [bʌldʒ] *n.* (*a*) bombement *m,* ventre *m,* renflement *m;* protubérance *f;* (*of bottle, vase*) panse *f;* *Arch:* jarret *m;* (*in tyre*) soufflure *f;* *Mil:* saillant *m* (du front); *Pol.Ec:* *F:* poussée *f;* (*b*) *N.Arch:* caisson *m* pare-torpilles.

bulge² *v.i.* **to b. (out),** bomber, ballonner; faire saillie; (*of wall, etc.*) se déjeter; *Arch:* jarreter; **sack bulging with potatoes,** sac bourré de pommes de terre. **bulging 1.** *a.* (front, etc.) bombé; (ventre) ballonnant; (yeux) protubérants; (joues) bouffies; (sac, etc.) bourré, plein à craquer; (mur) qui fait ventre. **2.** *n.* bombement *m,* renflement *m* (d'un mur, etc.); ballonnement *m.*

bulk¹ [bʌlk] *n.* **1.** (*a*) *Nau:* charge *f;* chargement arrimé; **to break b.,** (i) désarrimer; rompre charge; commencer le déchargement; (ii) disposer d'une partie des marchandises; (*b*) *Com: etc:* **in b.,** en bloc, globalement; en gros; **to buy in b.,** acheter par grosses quantités; **b. buying,** achat massif, en gros; **to sell in b.,** vendre en vrac; **b. concrete,** béton *m* en masse; *Nau:* **b. carrier,** navire *m* pour le transport en vrac (du pétrole, etc.); *Post:* **b. rate,** affranchissement *m* à forfait; (*c*) *Cmptr:* volume *m,* masse *f* (d'informations). **2.** (*a*) grandeur *f,* grosseur *f,* masse, volume *m;* encombrement *m* (d'un colis); (*b*) *Paperm:* bouffant *m* (du papier). **3. the b.,** la masse, la plupart (des hommes); le gros (de l'armée); la plus grosse partie (de ses biens, etc.).

bulk² **1.** *v.i.* (*a*) (*of material, wood, etc.*) (se) gonfler (par l'humidité); (*b*) **to b. large,** occuper une place importante (**in s.o.'s eyes,** aux yeux de qn). **2.** *v.tr.* (*a*) réunir, grouper, (plusieurs colis) en un seul; entasser (des marchandises) en vrac; (*b*) *Cust:* mesurer le contenu (d'une caisse de thé, etc.); (*c*) *Publ:* **to b. up a book,** imprimer un livre sur du papier bouffant.

bulkhead ['bʌlkhed] *n. N.Arch: etc:* cloison *f;* **watertight b.,** cloison étanche; **collision b.,** cloison de choc, d'abordage.

bulkiness ['bʌlkinis] *n.* **1.** volume excessif; encombrement *m.* **2.** grosseur *f.*

bulky ['bʌlki] *a.* **1.** volumineux, encombrant; (livre) épais; *Nau:* **b. cargo,** chargement volumineux. **2.** gros, *f.* grosse.

bull¹ [bul] *n.* **1.** (*a*) taureau *m;* **b. calf,** jeune taureau, taurillon *m;* **to take the b. by the horns,** prendre le taureau par les cornes; **like a b. in a china shop,** comme un éléphant dans un magasin de porcelaine; (*b*) mâle *m* (de l'éléphant, de la baleine, etc.); **b. elephant,** éléphant *m* mâle; (*c*) *Astr:* **the B.,** le Taureau; (*d*) *P:* agent *m* de police, flic *m;* (*e*) *Mil:* *P:* fourbissage *m;* (*f*) *P:* foutaise *f.* **2.** *St.Exch:* spéculateur *m* à la hausse; haussier *m;* **b. transaction,** opération *f* à la hausse. **3.** noir *m,* blanc *m,* mouche *f* (d'une cible); **he made six bulls,** il a fait mouche six fois. **4.** (*a*) **b. bitch, pup,** chienne *f,* chiot *m,* de bouledogue; (*b*) **b. terrier,** bull-terrier *m, pl.* bull-terriers; (*c*) **b. mastiff,** molosse *m.*

bull² *St.Exch:* **1.** *v.tr.* **to b. the market,** chercher à faire hausser les cours. **2.** *v.i.* spéculer à la hausse.

bull³ *n. Ecc:* bulle *f;* **Papal b.,** bulle du Pape.

bulldog ['buldɔg] *n.* **1.** bouledogue *m;* **2. b. clip,** pince *f* à dessin. **3.** *F:* (i) personne d'un courage obstiné; (ii) appariteur *m* du censeur (aux universités d'Oxford et de Cambridge).

bulldoze ['buldouz] **1.** *v.tr.* (*a*) dégager, déblayer (un terrain) (au bulldozer); démolir (une maison, etc.) (au bulldozer); (*b*) *F:* menacer, intimider, brutaliser (qn).

bulldozer ['buldouzər] *n. Civ.E:* bulldozer *m;* bouteur *m.*

bullet ['bulit] *n. Sm.a:* balle *f;* (de fusil, de revolver); **b. hole,** trou *m* de balle **riddled with bullets,** criblé de balles; *F:* **to stop a b.,** recevoir une balle.

bullet-headed ['bulit'hedid] *a.* **1.** à tête ronde. **2.** *esp. U.S:* *F:* entêté.

bulletin ['bulitin] *n.* bulletin *m,* communiqué *m;* **news b.,** bulletin d'actualités; *W.Tel: etc:* radio journal *m;* informations *fpl;* **b. board,** tableau *m* d'affichage.

bulletproof ['bulitpru:f] *a.* à l'épreuve des balles; (gilet, etc.) antiballes, pare-balles *inv.*

bullfight ['bulfait] *n.* course *f,* combat *m,* de taureaux; corrida *f.*

bullfighter ['bulfaitər] *n.* matador *m.*

bullfighting ['bulfaitiŋ] *n.* combats *mpl* de taureaux, courses *fpl* de taureaux; tauromachie *f.*

bullfinch ['bulfin(t)ʃ] *n.* **1.** *Orn:* bouvreuil *m* (pivoine).

bullfrog ['bulfrɔg] *n. Amph:* grenouille *f* taureau.

bullheaded ['bul'hedid] *a. F:* d'une impétuosité de taureau.

bullion¹ ['buliən] *n.* or *m* en barres; or, argent *m,* en lingot(s); valeurs *fpl* en espèces; *Fin:* métal *m;* *Veh:* **b. van,** fourgon *m* bancaire.

bull-necked ['bul'nekt] *a.* au cou de taureau.

bullock ['bulək] *n. Husb:* bœuf *m;* **young b.,** bouvillon *m;* **b. cart,** char *m* à bœufs.

bullring ['bulriŋ] *n.* arène *f* (pour les courses de taureaux).

bull's-eye ['bulzai] *n.* **1.** *Glassm:* boudine *f;* **b.-e. panes,** carreaux *mpl* à boudines, en culs-de-bouteille. **2.** *Nau:* verre mort; lentille *f.* **3.** noir *m;* blanc *m,* mouche *f* (d'une cible); **to hit the, make a, b.-e.,** faire mouche; mettre dans le noir, dans le blanc, (*at darts*) dans le mille. **4.** *Comest:* gros bonbon (en boule) à la menthe.

bullshit ['bulʃit] *n. P:* (*not in polite use*) foutaise *f.*

bully¹ ['buli] *n.* (*a*) tyran *m,* brutal *m;* *Sch:* brimeur *m;* (*b*) homme *m* de main (d'un aventurier politique, etc.); (*c*) **b. boy,** voyou *m,* dur *m.*

bully² *v.tr.* brutaliser, rudoyer, (qn); **to b. s.o. into doing sth.,** faire faire qch. à qn à force de menaces; **he bullies his wife,** il brutalise sa femme. **bullying 1.** *a.* brutal, -aux. **2.** *n.* (*a*) intimidation *f;* (*b*) *Sch:* brimades *fpl.*

bully³ *int. F: O:* **b. for you!** (i) vous avez de la chance! (ii) bravo pour vous!

bully⁴ *n. Sp:* (*hockey*) engagement *m* (du jeu).

bully⁵ *v.i.* (*in hockey*) **to b. (off),** engager (le jeu); mettre la balle en jeu.

bully[6] *a. F:* **b. beef,** bœuf *m* de conserve, *F:* singe *m.*
bulrush ['bulrʌʃ] *n. Bot:* jonc *m* des marais.
bulwark ['bulwɔːk] *n.* **1.** *A.Fort:* rempart *m.* **2.** *Nau:* **bulwarks,** pavois *m*, bastingage *m.*
bum[1] (bʌm] *n. F:* derrière *m*, *P:* cul *m.*
bum[2] *esp. NAm: P:* **1.** *a.* moche, minable; **b. check,** chèque *m* sans provision. **2.** *n.* (*pers.*) fainéant *m*; clochard *m*; trimardeur *m.* **3.** *n.* **to be on the b.,** (i) vivre aux dépens des autres; (ii) trimarder; lambiner.
bum[3] *v.* **(bummed)** *NAm: P:* **1.** *v.i.* **to b. (around),** flâner; fainéanter. **2.** *v.tr.* **to b. a cigarette from, off, s.o.,** taper qn d'une cigarette; **to b. a ride,** faire de l'auto-stop.
bumblebee ['bʌmblbiː] *n. Ent: F:* bourdon *m.*
bumbler ['bʌmblər] *n. F:* **an old b.,** un vieux maladroit.
bumboat ['bʌmbout] *n. Nau:* bateau *m* à provisions.
bumf [bʌmf] *n.* **1.** *P:* papier *m* hygiénique, papier cul. **2.** *F:* paperasserie *f.*
bummaree [bʌmə'riː] *n.* (*a*) courtier *m* en poisson (au marché de Billingsgate); (*b*) courtier en viande (au marché de Smithfield).
bump[1] [bʌmp] *n.* **1.** (*a*) choc (sourd); secousse *f*, heurt *m*, coup *m*; cahot *m* (d'une voiture); **to sit down with a b.,** faire un casse-cul; (*b*) *Row:* heurt d'un canot par le poursuivant (dans une *bumping race*). **2.** (*a*) inégalité *f*, rugosité *f* (d'un chemin, d'une surface, etc.); (*b*) bosse *f*, enflure *f*; (*in phrenology*) protubérance *f*, *F:* bosse (du crâne). **3.** *Av:* trou *m* d'air.
bump[2] **1.** *v.tr.* (*a*) cogner, frapper; **to b. one's head on, against, sth.,** se cogner la tête contre qch.; (*b*) *Row:* heurter (le canot qu'on poursuit, dans une *bumping race*). **2.** *v.i.* se cogner, se heurter, buter **(into, against, sth.,** contre qch.); entrer en collision (avec qch.); (*of car, etc.*) tamponner **(into another car,** une autre voiture); **to b. along** (*in cart, etc.*), cahoter; **I bumped into him in the street,** je l'ai rencontré par hasard dans la rue. **bumping** *n.* heurtement *m*; cahotement *m*; *Row:* **b. race,** course-poursuite *f* (dans laquelle chaque bateau doit rattraper le précédent et de son avant en heurter l'arrière). **bump off** *v.tr. F:* assassiner, supprimer (qn). **bump up** *v.tr. F:* **to b. up the prices,** faire monter les prix (d'une façon exagérée).
bump[3] *adv. & int.* pan! boum! *F:* **things that go b. in the night,** des bruits étranges qui se font entendre pendant la nuit.
bumper ['bʌmpər] *n.* **1.** (*a*) rasade *f* (de champagne, etc.); (*b*) *attrib.* **b. crop, harvest,** récolte *f* magnifique, exceptionnelle. **2.** *Aut:* pare-choc(s) *m*; **front, rear, b.,** pare-choc(s) avant, arrière; **the cars were b. to b.,** les voitures se suivaient pare-choc(s) contre pare-choc(s).
bumpety-bump ['bʌmpiti'bʌmp] *adv. F:* en cahotant; **my heart went b.-b.,** mon cœur battait la chamade.
bumph [bʌmf] *n.* = BUMF.
bumpkin ['bʌm(p)kin] *n.* **country b.,** rustre *m*, rustaud *m.*
bumptious ['bʌm(p)ʃəs] *a.* orgueilleux, suffisant, outrecuidant; **to be b.,** faire l'important.
bumpy ['bʌmpi] *a.* **1.** (chemin, etc.) cahoteux, défoncé, inégal; *Av:* (vol) chahuté. **2.** (*of forehead, etc.*) couvert de bosses.
bun [bʌn] *n.* **1.** *Cu:* petit pain au lait; **Bath b.,** *bun* saupoudré de sucre; **hot cross b.,** *bun* à la cannelle (qu'on mange le vendredi saint). **2.** *Hairdr:* chignon *m.*
bunch[1] [bʌn(t)ʃ] *n.* (*a*) botte *f* (de radis, etc.); bouquet *m* (de fleurs); grappe *f* (de raisin); touffe *f* (d'herbes); houppe *f* (de plumes); trousseau *m* (de clefs); régime *m* (de bananes); (*b*) groupe *m* (de personnes); *U.S:* troupeau *m* (de bestiaux); **he's the best, the pick, of the b.,** c'est lui le meilleur (de la bande); *Rac:* **the b.,** le peloton.
bunch[2] **2.** *v.tr.* botteler (des radis, etc.); lier (des fleurs, etc.) en bouquet. **2.** *v.i.* **to b. (together),** se presser en foule, se serrer, se tasser; se pelotonner.
bundle[1] ['bʌndl] *n.* (*a*) paquet *m* (de linge, etc.); ballot *m* (de marchandises, d'effets); baluchon *m* (d'effets); botte *f* (d'asperges, etc.); faisceau *m* (de cannes, de nerfs, de fils, etc.); liasse *f* (de billets de banque, de papiers); fagot *m* (de bois); tas *m* (de choses diverses); *Nat.Hist:* **vascular b.,** faisceau vasculaire; *F:* **she's a b. of nerves,** c'est un paquet de nerfs; (*b*) *U.S: F:* **to make a b.,** faire un paquet, faire sa pelote.
bundle[2] *v.tr.* (*a*) **to b. (sth.) (up),** empaqueter (qch.); mettre, lier, (qch.) en paquet; botteler (du foin); mettre (des documents) en liasse; (*b*) *F:* **to b. papers into a drawer,** fourrer des papiers dans un tiroir; **to b. s.o. out,** faire sortir (qn) à la hâte; **to b. s.o. off,** se débarrasser de qn (sans cérémonie).
bunfight ['bʌnfait] *n. F:* thé *m* (où tout le monde s'écrase).
bung[1] [bʌŋ] *n.* bonde *f*, bondon *m* (de fût).
bung[2] *v.tr.* **1. to b. (up),** bondonner (un fût); boucher (un orifice); (*of nose, pipe, etc.*) **to be bunged up,** être bouché. **2.** *F:* mettre, fourrer (qch.); **b. it in a drawer,** fourre-le dans un tiroir.
bungalow ['bʌŋgəlou] *n.* bungalow *m.*
bunghole ['bʌŋhoul] *n.* (*trou*) bonde *f* (de fût).
bungle[1] ['bʌŋgl] *n.* gâchis *m*, maladresse *f*, bousillage *m*; **to make a b. of sth.,** bousiller, gâcher, qch.
bungle[2] **1.** *v.tr.* bousiller, gâcher, *F:* louper (un travail). **2.** *v.i.* s'y prendre maladroitement. **bungling** **1.** *a.* maladroit. **2.** *n.* bousillage *m*, gâchis *m.*
bungler ['bʌŋglər] *n.* (*a*) bousilleur, -euse (de travail); gâcheur, -euse; (*b*) maladroit, -e.
bunion ['bʌniən] *n. Med:* inflammation *f* de la base du gros orteil, *F:* oignon *m.*
bunk[1] [bʌŋk] *n.* (*a*) *Nau: Rail: etc:* couchette *f*; *Furn:* **b. beds,** lits superposés; (*b*) *NAm: F:* logement *m.*
bunk[2] *v.i.* (*a*) *Nau:* être logé **(forward,** à l'avant); (*b*) *F:* **to b. down,** (aller) se coucher; (*c*) *NAm: F:* passer la nuit **(with friends,** chez des amis).
bunk[3] *n. F:* **to do a b.,** déguerpir, décamper.
bunk[4] *n. F:* bêtises *fpl.*
bunker[1] ['bʌŋkər] *n.* **1.** *Nau:* soute *f* (à charbon, mazout, etc.); réservoir *m*, caisse *f* (à huile); (*b*) *Dom.Ec:* **coal b.,** coffre *m* à charbon. **2.** *Golf:* banquette *f*, bunker *m.* **3.** *Mil:* blockhaus *m*; abri bétonné.
bunker[2] *v.tr.* **1.** *Nau:* (*a*) mettre (du combustible) en soute; (*b*) *v.i.* se ravitailler en charbon; charbonner. **2.** *Golf:* **to be bunkered,** se trouver dans le sable.
bunkhouse ['bʌŋkhaus] *n. NAm:* baraquement pourvu de couchettes (pour bûcherons etc.).
bunkum ['bʌnkəm] *n. F:* bêtises *fpl*, foutaise *f.*
bunny ['bʌni] *n. F:* **1. b. (rabbit),** Jeannot lapin *m*; petit lapin. **2. b. (girl),** employée de boîte de nuit (habillée en lapin).
Bunsen ['bʌns(ə)n] *Pr.n. Ch: etc:* **B. burner,** bec *m* Bunsen.
bunting[1] ['bʌntiŋ] *n. Orn:* bruant *m*; **corn b.,** (bruant) proyer (*m*); **reed b.,** bruant des roseaux; **snow b.,** bruant des neiges.
bunting[2] *n.* **1.** *Tex:* étamine *f* (à pavillon); molleton *m* à drapeaux; draperie *f.* **2.** *coll: F:* drapeaux *mpl*, pavillons *mpl;* pavoisement *m*; **decorated with b.,** pavoisé.
buoy[1] [bɔi] *n. Nau:* bouée *f*; balise flottante; **wreck b.,** bouée d'épave; **mooring, anchor, b.,** (bouée de) corps-mort (*m*), *pl.* corps-morts; coffre *m* d'amar-

rage; **bell b.,** bouée à cloche; **light b.,** bouée lumineuse.

buoy² *v.tr.* **1.** (*a*) *Nau:* **to b. up,** faire flotter (un objet); (*b*) **to b. s.o. up,** soutenir, appuyer, qn; **buoyed up with new hope,** animé, soutenu, par un nouvel espoir. **2.** marquer (une épave) d'une bouée; baliser (un chenal).

buoyancy [ˈbɔiənsi] *n.* **1.** (*a*) *Nau: Aer:* flottabilité *f* (d'un objet); **b. bag, chamber, tank,** ballonnet *m*, chambre *f*, réservoir *m*, de flottabilité; (*b*) **centre of b.,** centre *m* de poussée; **b. chamber,** flotteur *m* (d'une torpille). **2.** (*a*) entrain *m*, allant *m*, optimisme *m*; **man full of b.,** homme *m* qui a du ressort; (*b*) *Com:* fermeté (du marché).

buoyant [ˈbɔiənt] *a.* **1.** (*a*) flottable; (*b*) **salt water is more b. than fresh,** l'eau salée porte mieux que l'eau douce; (*c*) *Civ.E:* **b. foundation,** radier *m* en béton. **2.** (*a*) (*of pers.*) optimiste, plein d'entrain, allègre; **b. step,** pas *m* élastique; (*b*) *Com:* (marché) soutenu; **the market is b.,** le marché reste ferme. **-ly** *adv.* avec entrain; avec optimisme.

bur [bəːr] *n.* = BURR¹ 1.

burble [ˈbəːbl] *v.i.* **1.** (*a*) murmurer (des sons inarticulés); (*b*) *F:* débiter des inepties. **2.** glousser (**with laughter,** de rire).

burbot [ˈbəːbət] *n. Ich:* lotte *f*, barbot *m*, barbot(t)e *f*.

burden¹ [ˈbəːdn] *n.* **1.** (*a*) fardeau *m*, charge *f*; *Lit:* **tax b., b. of taxation,** poids de la fiscalité, des impôts; *Jur:* **b. of proof,** charge, fardeau, de la preuve; obligation *f* de faire la preuve; **the b. of proof rests with him,** c'est à lui que la preuve incombe; **to be a b. to s.o.,** être à charge à qn; **to make s.o.'s life a b.,** rendre la vie dure à qn; **beast of b.,** bête *f* de somme, de charge; (*b*) *Nau:* charge, contenance *f* d'un navire. **2.** *O:* (*a*) refrain *m* (d'une chanson); (*b*) substance *f* (d'un discours, d'une plainte).

burden² *v.tr.* (*a*) charger, alourdir, accabler (**s.o. with sth.,** qn de qch.); **to b. one's memory with useless facts,** se charger la mémoire de faits inutiles; **burdened estate,** domaine grevé d'hypothèques; domaine hypothéqué; (*b*) être un fardeau pour (qn).

burdensome [ˈbəːd(ə)nsəm] *a.* onéreux (**to,** à).

burdock [ˈbəːdɔk] *n. Bot:* bardane *f*, glouteron *m*.

bureau, *pl.* **-eaux** [ˈbjuərou, -ouz] *n.* **1.** *Furn:* (*a*) bureau *m*; secrétaire *m*; (*b*) *U.S:* commode *f*. **2.** (*a*) bureau; **employment b.,** bureau de placement; **information b.,** (i) office *m* de renseignements; (ii) syndicat *m* d'initiative; (*b*) *U.S:* (*government department*) bureau; service *m*; **Census B.,** Bureau des statistiques.

bureaucracy [bjuəˈrɔkrəsi] *n.* bureaucratie *f*.

bureaucrat [ˈbjuərəkræt] *n.* bureaucrate *m*.

bureaucratic [bjuərəˈkrætik] *a.* bureaucratique.

burette [bjuəˈret] *n. Ch:* éprouvette graduée, burette *f*.

burg [bəːg] *n. NAm: F:* bourg *m*; municipalité *f*, ville *f*.

burgeon [ˈbəːdʒən] *v.i. Lit:* bourgeonner.

burgess [ˈbəːdʒis] *n.* **1.** *Hist:* citoyen *m*. **2.** (*a*) député *m* (représentant une ville); (*b*) *U.S:* = conseiller municipal.

burglar [ˈbəːglər] *n.* cambrioleur *m*; **b. alarm,** signalisateur *m* anti-vol.

burglarize [ˈbəːgləraiz] *v.tr. & i. NAm:* cambrioler.

burglarproof [ˈbəːgləpruːf] *a.* (serrure, coffre-fort) incrochetable, inviolable.

burglary [ˈbəːgləri] *n.* vol *m* avec effraction; cambriolage *m*.

burgle [ˈbəːgl] *v.tr. & i.* cambrioler, dévaliser (une maison); faire du cambriolage.

Burgundian [bəːˈgʌndiən] **1.** *a.* bourguignon. **2.** *n.* Bourguignon, -onne.

Burgundy [ˈbəːgəndi] **1.** *Pr.n.Geog:* Bourgogne *f*. **2.** *n.* **b.,** bourgogne *m*, vin *m* de Bourgogne.

burial [ˈberiəl] *n.* (*a*) enterrement *m*, inhumation *f*; (*b*) **b. ground,** cimetière *m*; **b. place.** (lieu *m* de) sépulture; **b. service,** office *m* des morts; *Prehist:* **b. mound,** tumulus *m*.

burin [ˈbjuərin] *n. Tls:* burin *m*.

burk [bəːk] *n. P:* **you (great) b!** espèce d'idiot!

burlap [ˈbəːlæp] *n. Tex:* gros canevas; toile *f* d'emballage.

burlesque¹ [bəːˈlesk] **1.** *a.* burlesque. **2.** *n.* (*a*) burlesque *m*; (*b*) parodie *f*; (*c*) *U.S:* revue *f* vulgaire, *esp.* striptease *m*.

burlesque² *v.tr.* parodier; tourner (qn, qch.) en ridicule.

burliness [ˈbəːlinis] *n.* (*a*) forte carrure; (*b*) *NAm:* brusquerie *f*.

burly [ˈbəːli] *a.* (*of pers.*) (*a*) solidement bâti; robuste; de forte carrure; (*b*) *NAm:* brusque; bourru.

Burma [ˈbəːmə] *Pr.n. Geog:* Birmanie *f*.

Burmese [bəːˈmiːz] **1.** *a. Geog:* birman; *Z:* **Burmese cat,** (i) chat burmese; (ii) chat birman ganté. **2.** *n.* (*a*) Birman, -ane; (*b*) *Ling:* birman *m*.

burn¹ [bəːn] *n.* **1.** *Med: etc:* brûlure *f*. **2.** *Space:* allumage *m*; poussée *f* (d'une fusée).

burn² *v.* (*p.t. & p.p.* **burnt** [bəːnt] *occ.* **burned) 1.** *v.tr.* (*a*) brûler; (*of boiler*) **to b. coal, oil, gas,** chauffer au charbon, au mazout, au gaz; *Fig:* **to b. one's boats, one's bridges,** brûler ses vaisseaux; **to b. the candle at both ends,** brûler la chandelle par les deux bouts; **to b. the midnight oil,** travailler, veiller, fort avant dans la nuit; **to b. sth. to ashes,** réduire qch. en cendres; **to be burnt alive, to be burnt to death,** être brûlé vif; **to b. one's fingers,** se brûler les doigts; *Fig:* **he burnt his fingers over it,** il s'est fait échauder (dans cette affaire); **money burns a hole in his pocket,** l'argent lui brûle les doigts, la poche; **to have money to b.,** avoir de l'argent à n'en savoir que faire; **acids b. into metal,** les acides rongent le métal; **mustard burns the tongue,** la moutarde brûle la langue; (*b*) *Ind:* cuire (des briques, du charbon de bois); vulcaniser, cuire (le caoutchouc); (*c*) *Cu:* brûler (le rôti, une casserole); *Metalw:* surchauffer le fer. **2.** *v.i.* (*a*) brûler; (*of house, etc.*) être en feu; (*of wound, eyes*) cuire; **to make the fire b.,** faire flamber, faire marcher, le feu; **his cheeks were burning with shame,** il avait les joues rouges de honte; **to b. with impatience,** griller d'impatience; *F:* **his ears must have been burning,** les oreilles ont dû lui tinter; **magnesium burns white,** le magnésium brûle avec une flamme blanche; (*b*) *I.C.E:* (*of mixture*) exploser; (*c*) *Cu:* (*of meat, toast, etc.*) brûler; (*of sauce, milk, etc.*) attacher. **burn down 1.** *v.tr.* brûler, incendier (une ville, etc.); détruire (une maison) par le feu. **2.** *v.i.* (*a*) (*of building, etc.*) être détruit par le feu, par un incendie; (*b*) (*of fire*) baisser; **the fire had burned down,** le feu était bas. **burning 1.** *a.* (*a*) (*of fever, thirst, desire, etc.*) brûlant, ardent; **b. question,** question brûlante; (*b*) (charbon) embrasé, allumé; (ville, maison) incendiée, enflammée, en feu; (*c*) (chaleur) brûlante, torride; *F:* **I'm b. (hot),** je brûle de chaleur; (*d*) **b. bush,** (i) *B:* buisson ardent; (ii) *Bot:* fraxinelle *f*; (*e*) (bois, etc.) à brûler. **2.** *n.* (*a*) incendie *m* (d'une maison, etc.); *Ch: etc:* combustion *f*; *Hist:* **b. (at the stake),** supplice *m* du bûcher; **there's a smell of b.,** cela sent le brûlé; **b. sensation,** (i) sensation *f* de chaleur (excessive); (ii) douleur cuisante; (*b*) *Cu:* coup *m* de feu; *Metalw:* brûlure *f* (de l'acier); (*c*) cuite *f*, cuisson *f* (de briques, de tuiles, etc.); **lime b.,** chaufournerie *f*, cuisson de la chaux; (*b*) (*batch*) fournée *f* (de briques, etc.). **burn off** *v.tr.* brûler (la peinture, etc.); décaper (la peinture) à la lampe à brûler; enlever (de la rouille, etc.) au feu. **burn out 1.** *v.tr.* (*a*) cautériser (une plaie); (*b*) *Aut: etc:* brûler (la garniture des freins); *El:* brûler, court-circuiter (une bobine); griller (une lampe); (*c*) **the building was**

burnt out, le feu a complètement détruit l'intérieur de la maison; (*d*) **to b. itself out,** (*of fire*) s'éteindre; (*of pers*) **to b. oneself out,** se ruiner la santé, s'épuiser (par excès de travail). **2.** *v.i.* (*of fire, oil lamp, candle, etc.*) s'éteindre; (*of candle*) brûler jusqu'au bout; (*of electric lamp*) claquer, griller. **burnt** *a.* **1.** (*a*) (*of pers., thg*) brûlé; **to be b. beyond recognition,** être carbonisé; **a b. child dreads the fire,** chat échaudé craint l'eau froide; *Cu:* **b. almonds,** amandes grillées; **b. sugar,** caramel *m*; (*b*) (odeur, goût) de brûlé, de roussi. **2.** (*of earth, clay*) cuit. **3. b. out,** (*a*) (volcan) éteint; *Fig.* **b.-out case,** homme, femme, qui a épuisé son talent; (*b*) (maison, voiture, etc.) réduite en carcasse par le feu; (*c*) *Mch: etc:* (tube) brûlé; (roulement) grippé; *El:* (bobine) grillée; (lampe) claquée. **burn up 1.** *v.tr.* (*a*) brûler (entièrement); consumer; (*b*) (*of sun*) griller, flétrir (les feuilles, etc.). **2.** *v.i.* (*a*) (*of fire*) se ranimer; flamber; *F:* (*of pers*) s'emporter, s'enflammer de colère; (*b*) (*of rocket*) brûler, se consumer.

burn³ *n. Scot:* ruisseau *m.*

burner ['bəːnər] *n.* **1.** (*pers.*) brûleur, -euse; **charcoal b.,** charbonnier *m*; **lime b.,** chaufournier *m.* **2.** (*a*) (*of gas cooker*) brûleur; feu *m*; (*b*) bec *m* (de gaz, pour acétylène, etc.); brûleur (à gaz); **oxyacetylene b.,** chalumeau *m* (oxyacétylénique).

burnish¹ ['bəːniʃ] *n.* éclat *m*; poli *m*, brillant *m*; bruni *m.*

burnish² 1. *v.tr.* (*a*) brunir; polir, lisser; (*b*) *Phot:* satiner (une épreuve). **2.** *v.i.* se polir; prendre de l'éclat. **burnishing** *n.* brunissage *m*; polissage *m*, lissage *m.*

burnisher ['bəːniʃər] *n.* **1.** (*pers.*) brunisseur, -euse. **2.** *Tls:* brunissoir *m*; polissoir *m.*

burnous(e) [bəː'nuːs] *n.* burnous *m* (d'Arabe).

burp¹ [bəːp] *n.* éructation *f*, *F:* rot *m.*

burp² 1. *v.i.* éructer, *F:* roter. **2.** *v.tr.* faire roter (un bébé).

burr¹ [bəːr] *n.* **1.** *Bot:* teigne *f* (de bardane); **chestnut b.,** bogue *f*; *F:* (*of pers.*) **to stick to s.o. like a b.,** se cramponner, s'accrocher, à qn. **2.** (*a*) (*on tree*) broussin *m*; (*b*) **b. walnut,** (plaqué *m* en) ronce *f* de noyer. **3.** *Engr: Metalw:* barbe *f*, bavure *f*; **to take the burrs off metal,** ébarber le métal. **4.** *Tls: Dent:* fraise *f.*

burr² *n.* (*a*) *Ling:* r de la gorge; **to speak with a b.,** grasseyer; (*b*) ronflement *m* (d'une machine).

burr³ *v.* (**burred**) **1.** *v.tr.* **to b. one's r's,** prononcer l'r de la gorge; grasseyer. **2.** *v.i.* (*of machine, etc.*) ronfler.

burro ['bʌrou] *n. U.S:* âne *m.*

burrow¹ ['bʌrou] *n.* terrier *m*; renardière *f* (de renard); clapier *m* (de lapin).

burrow² 1. *v.i.* (*of rabbits, etc.*) (i) fouir la terre; (ii) (se) terrer; (*of moles*) tracer; **to b. into the archives,** fouiller, fouiner, dans les archives. **2.** *v.tr.* (*a*) creuser, pratiquer (un trou, un terrier); **to b. one's way underground,** creuser (un chemin) sous terre; (*b*) (*of rabbits*) **to b. the ground,** percer la terre. **burrowing** *a.* (animal) fouisseur; (insecte) fossoyeur, mineur.

bursar ['bəːsər] *n. Sch:* **1.** économe *mf*, intendant *m.* **2.** *esp. Scot:* boursier, -ière.

bursary ['bəːsəri] *n.* **1.** bureau *m* de l'économe; économat *m*; intendance *f.* **2.** *esp. Scot:* bourse *f* (d'études).

bursitis [bə'saitis] *n. Med:* bursite *f.*

burst¹ [bəːst] *n.* **1.** éclatement *m*, explosion *f* (d'une bombe, d'une chaudière, etc.). **2.** jaillissement *m*, jet *m* (de flamme); coup *m* (de tonnerre); (*of gunfire*) rafale *f*; (*of machine gun*) giclée *f*; éclat *m* (de rire, etc.); explosion (de colère); élan *m* (d'éloquence); salve *f* (d'applaudissements); poussée *f* (d'activité); accès *m* (d'enthousiasme); *Sp:* **b. of speed,** emballage *m*; **final b.,** finish *m.*

burst² *v.* (*p.t. & p.p.* **burst**) **1.** *v.i.* (*a*) (*of boiler, bomb, etc.*) éclater, exploser, faire explosion; (*of boiler*) sauter; (*of abscess*) crever, percer; (*of bubble, cloud*) crever; (*of bud*) éclore; **to b. in pieces,** voler en éclats; **her heart was ready to b.,** son cœur se brisait; (*b*) **to be bursting at the seams,** (i) (*of dress, etc.*) se découdre; (ii) *F:* (*of building, etc.*) être plein à éclater; (*c*) **to be bursting with pride,** crever d'orgueil; **to be bursting with health,** déborder de santé; **to be bursting with impatience,** bouillir d'impatience; **I was bursting to tell him so,** je mourais d'envie de le lui dire; (*d*) **to b. into flame(s),** s'enflammer brusquement; **to b. into song,** entonner une chanson; (*of tree*) **to b. into blossom,** commencer à fleurir; **to b. into laughter, into tears, to b. out laughing, crying,** éclater de rire; fondre en larmes; (*e*) **to b. into a room,** entrer dans une pièce en coup de vent, en trombe; **the crowd b. through the police cordon,** la foule a enfoncé le cordon de police; (*of sun*) **to b. through a cloud,** percer un nuage; **a cry b. from his lips,** un cri s'échappa de ses lèvres; (*f*) **to b. upon s.o.'s sight,** se présenter aux yeux de qn; (*of sound*) **to b. upon s.o.'s ears,** venir (subitement) frapper les oreilles de qn; **the truth b. upon me,** soudain la vérité m'apparut. **2.** *v.tr.* faire éclater (qch.); crever, éclater (un ballon, un pneu); faire sauter (une chaudière); rompre (ses liens); **to b. a blood vessel,** se rompre un vaisseau sanguin; (*of river*) **to b. its banks,** crever, rompre, ses berges. **burst in 1.** *v.tr.* enfoncer (une porte). **2.** *v.i.* faire irruption; (*of pers.*) entrer en trombe, en coup de vent; **to b. in on a conversation,** interrompre brusquement une conversation. **bursting 1.** *a.* sur le point (i) d'éclater, (ii) de crever, (iii) d'éclore. **2.** *n.* éclatement *m*, explosion *f* (d'une bombe, etc.); crevaison *f* (d'un pneu); rupture *f* (de barrage). **burst open 1.** *v.tr.* ouvrir (une porte) subitement; enfoncer, briser (une porte, etc.); faire sauter (le couvercle, la serrure). **2.** *v.i.* (*of door, etc.*) s'ouvrir tout d'un coup.

Burton ['bəːtn] *n. P:* **to have gone for a B.,** (*of soldier*) être (i) mort, (ii) manquant; *Av:* avoir fait un trou dans l'eau; (*of plate, etc.*) être cassé; (*of ball, etc.*) être perdu pour de bon.

bury ['beri] *v.tr.* (*p.t. & p.p.* **buried**) (*a*) enterrer, inhumer, ensevelir (un mort); (*at sea*) immerger (un mort); **to b. s.o. alive,** enterrer qn vif; (*b*) enterrer (qch.); enfouir (qch., un animal); (*of snow, earthquake*) ensevelir (une ville, une maison); **buried treasure,** trésor enterré, enfoui; *El:* **buried cable,** câble souterrain; **I found the letter buried under my papers,** j'ai trouvé la lettre enfouie sous mes papiers; *F:* **to b. the hatchet,** enterrer la hache de guerre; faire la paix; se réconcilier; (*c*) (*of animal*) **to b. itself,** se terrer, s'enfouir; (*of pers.*) **to b. oneself in the country,** s'enterrer, s'enfouir, s'ensevelir, dans la campagne; **to b. oneself in one's work,** se plonger, s'enfoncer, s'absorber, dans son travail; (*d*) **to b. one's face in one's hands,** se cacher la figure dans les mains; **to b. one's hands in one's pockets,** fourrer les, ses, mains dans ses poches. **burying 1.** *a.* (insecte) enfouisseur; **b. beetle,** nécrophore *m.* **2.** *n.* enterrement *m*, ensevelissement *m*; **b. ground,** cimetière *m.*

bus¹, *pl.* **buses**, *U.S:* **busses** [bʌs, 'bʌsiz] *n.* **1.** autobus *m*; (*on country services*) car *m*; **double-decker b.,** autobus à impériale; **to go by b.,** aller en autobus; **to miss the b.,** (i) manquer, rater, l'autobus; (ii) *F:* laisser échapper l'occasion; manquer le coche; **b. stop,** arrêt *m* d'autobus; **b. station,** gare routière. **2.** *F:* **old b.,** (*car*) vieille bagnole; (*aircraft*) coucou *m.* **3.** *esp: NAm:* table desserte roulante (dans un restaurant).

bus² 1. *v.i.* (*a*) voyager par autobus; (*b*) *esp. NAm:*

travailler comme aide-serveur, aide-serveuse. **2.** *v.tr.* transporter (qn, qch.) par autobus, en car.

busboy ['bʌsbɔi] *n. esp. NAm:* aide-serveur *m, pl.* aides-serveurs.

busby ['bʌzbi] *n. Mil:* bonnet *m* de hussard.

bush¹ [buʃ] *n.* **1.** (*a*) buisson *m;* (*of lilac, etc.*) arbrisseau *m;* (*small*) arbuste *m;* **rose b.,** rosier *m;* **redcurrant b.,** groseillier *m;* (*b*) (*clump of bushes*) fourré *m,* taillis *m;* (*c*) queue *f* (du renard). **2.** (*esp. in Africa, Austr.*) **the b.,** la brousse; **to take to the b.,** prendre la brousse; **b. shirt, b. jacket** = saharienne *f;* **b. hat,** chapeau *m* de brousse; *F:* **b. telegraph,** téléphone *m* arabe; *Av:* **b. pilot,** pilote *m* de ligne opérant sur une région peu habitée, sur la brousse, *Can:* sur le Grand Nord.

bush² *n. Mec.E:* bague *f;* coussinet *m.*

bush³ *v.tr. Mec.E:* baguer, manchonner; mettre un coussinet à (un palier, etc.). **bushing** *n.* **1.** manchonnage *m.* **2.** manchon *m;* coussinet *m* métallique.

bushbaby ['buʃbeibi] *n. Z:* galago *m.*

bushbuck ['buʃbʌk] *n. Z:* guib *m.*

bushed [buʃt] *a.* (*a*) *Austr:* perdu, égaré, dans la brousse; (*b*) *F:* (i) désorienté; (ii) fatigué, éreinté.

bushel ['buʃəl] *n.* boisseau *m* (= *approx.* 36 litres); **to hide one's light under a b.,** cacher son talent.

bushfire ['buʃfaiər] *n.* feu *m* de brousse.

bushman, *pl.* **-men** ['buʃmən] *n.* **1.** *Ethn:* **Bushman,** (*a*) *a.* boschiman; (*b*) *n.* Boschiman, -ane; (*c*) *Ling:* boschiman *m.* **2.** (*a*) colon *m* (de la brousse australienne); (*b*) personne *f* qui connaît la brousse; broussard *m.*

bushw(h)acker ['buʃ(h)wækər] *n. esp. NAm:* **1.** (*a*) (i) colon *m,* habitant, -ante, de la brousse; (ii) bûcheron *m;* (*b*) bandit *m* (de la brousse). **2.** *Tls:* serpe *f.*

bushy ['buʃi] *a.* **1.** (*a*) touffu, épais, -aisse; buissonneux, broussailleux; (*b*) (sourcils) broussailleux; (barbe) fournie; (cheveux) épais, touffus, embroussaillés. **2.** (*of shrub*) bouissonnant.

business ['biznis] *n.* **1.** (*a*) affaire *f;* besogne *f;* **to have b. with s.o.,** avoir affaire avec qn; **what's your b. (with him)?** que (lui) voulez-vous? **it is, it is not, my b. to . . .,** c'est, ce n'est pas, à moi de . . .; **it's not your b., it's none of your b.,** ce n'est pas votre affaire; cela ne vous regarde pas; **mind your own b.,** occupez-vous de ce qui vous regarde; **to make it one's b. to do sth.,** prendre sur soi de faire qch.; **to go about one's b.,** vaquer à ses affaires; **let's get down to b.!** maintenant, allons-y! **we got through a lot of b.,** nous avons abattu de la besogne; **to mean b.,** avoir des intentions sérieuses; (*b*) **the b. before a meeting,** l'agenda *m;* l'ordre *m* du jour; (*c*) affaire; **it's a bad, sad, sorry, b.,** c'est une malheureuse, triste, affaire; **I'm sick of the whole b.,** j'en ai assez de toute cette affaire. **2.** (i) métier *m;* (ii) commerce *m;* (iii) les affaires; **to carry on a b.,** exercer un métier, un commerce; **to go into, to set up in, b. as a grocer,** s'établir épicier; **what's his line of b.?** qu'est-ce qu'il fait (comme métier)? (*of firm*) **to go out of b.,** faire faillite; **to go to London on b.,** aller à Londres pour affaires; **a profitable piece of b.,** une affaire profitable; **to lose b.,** perdre de la clientèle; **to do b. with s.o.,** faire des affaires avec qn; **shop with a thriving b.,** commerce qui marche bien; **it's good for b.,** c'est bon pour les affaires; **how's b.?** comment vont les affaires? **b. is slow,** les affaires ne vont pas; **to talk b.,** parler affaires; **the tourist trade is big b. today,** le tourisme est une affaire de grande importance aujourd'hui; (*b*) entreprise *f;* (fonds *m* de) commerce (*m*); **he is the owner of a small b.,** il est propriétaire (i) d'une petite entreprise, (ii) d'un petit commerce; **he worked up a small firm into a big b.,** à partir d'une petite maison il a créé une grosse entreprise; (*c*) **b. hours,** heures *fpl* de bureau, de travail, d'ouverture; **b. lunch, trip,** déjeuner *m,* voyage *m,* d'affaires; **b. manager,** directeur commercial; **b. career,** carrière *f* d'affaires; **b. card,** carte *f* (de visite) d'affaires; **b. studies,** études commerciales. **3.** *Th:* jeux *mpl* de scène.

businesslike ['biznislaik] *a.* **1.** (*of pers.*) capable; méthodique; (*of transaction*) régulier, sérieux; (*of thg*) pratique. **2.** (*of style*) net, précis; (*of manner*) sérieux, avisé.

businessman, *pl.* **-men** ['biznismæn, -men] *n.m.,* **businesswoman,** *pl.* **women** ['bizniswumən, -wimin] *n.f.* (i) homme, femme, d'affaires; (ii) commerçant, -ante; **to be a good b.,** s'entendre aux affaires; **big businessman,** brasseur *m* d'affaires.

busker ['bʌskər] *n.* musicien ambulant, des rues.

busman, *pl.* **-men** ['bʌsmən] *n.m.* (i) conducteur, (ii) receveur, d'autobus; *F:* **to take a busman's holiday,** faire du métier en guise de congé ou de loisirs.

bust¹ [bʌst] *n.* **1.** *Sculp:* buste *m.* **2.** poitrine *f* (de femme).

bust² *a. F:* (*a*) (*of thg*) cassé; (*of balloon, etc.*) crevé; (*b*) **to go b.,** faire faillite; perdre tout son argent.

bust³ *F:* **1.** *v.i.* éclater; (se) casser, crever. **2.** *v.tr.* (*a*) casser (qch.); crever (un ballon, etc.); (*b*) **to b. up,** rompre, briser (un mariage, une amitié, etc.); (*c*) *U.S:* dresser (des chevaux sauvages); (*d*) arrêter (un voleur, etc.); écraser (une bande de trafiquants, etc.).

bustard ['bʌstəd] *n. Orn:* outarde *f.*

buster ['bʌstər] *n.* **1.** *NAm: F:* (i) (petit) garçon; (ii) homme *m,* type *m;* (*as address*) **hi, b.!** *P:* alors, mon pote! **2.** *NAm:* **bronco b.,** dresseur *m* de chevaux.

bustle¹ ['bʌsl] *n.* mouvement *m;* remue-ménage *m;* **the b. in the streets,** l'animation *f* des rues.

bustle² **1.** *v.i.* **to b. (about),** se remuer, s'activer, s'affairer. **2.** *v.tr.* faire dépêcher (qn); **to b. s.o. out of the house,** pousser qn dehors. **bustling** *a.* (*of pers.*) affairé; (rue, vie) animée; (rue) (i) mouvementée, (ii) affairée.

bustle³ *n. A. Cost:* tournure *f* (de derrière de jupe).

bust-up ['bʌstʌp] *n. F:* **1.** faillite *f;* destruction *f* (d'un mariage). **2.** querelle *f;* brouille *f;* **to have a b.-up,** se brouiller.

busty ['bʌsti] *a. F:* (femme) à la poitrine plantureuse.

busy¹ ['bizi] **1.** *a.* **(busier, busiest)** (*a*) (i) affairé; occupé; (ii) actif, allant; **a b. man,** un homme (i) occupé, (ii) actif; **my work keeps me b. all the morning,** mon travail m'occupe toute la matinée; **to keep (oneself) b.,** s'occuper; bien employer son temps; **to be b. with sth., b. doing sth.,** être occupé à, de, qch., à, de, faire qch.; **to get b.,** se mettre à la tâche, au travail; *F:* **get b.!** grouille-toi! (*b*) (jour, etc.) chargé; (route) à grande circulation; *Rail:* (ligne) à grand trafic; **b. street,** rue (i) mouvementée, animée, passante, (ii) très affairée, très commerçante; **the hotel industry is at its busiest in August,** l'industrie hôtelière est au plus haut de son activité au mois d'août; (*of business, etc.*) **we're not b. at the moment,** nous travaillons au ralenti en ce moment; (*c*) *Tp: NAm:* **line b.,** ligne occupée; **b. tone,** tonalité *f* d'occupation. **-ily** *adv.* activement; avec empressement; d'un air affairé.

busy² *v.tr.* **to b. oneself with sth.,** s'occuper à, de, qch.; **to b. oneself (with) doing sth.,** s'occuper à, de, faire qch.

busybody ['bizibɔdi] *n.* officieux, -euse; **he's an awful b.,** il se mêle des affaires de tout le monde.

but [bʌt] **1.** *conj.* (*a*) (*coordinating*) mais; **he is small b. strong,** il est petit mais fort; **b. I tell you I saw it!** (mais) puisque je vous dis que je l'ai vu! (*b*) (*subordinating*) *A: & Lit:* **I cannot b. believe that . . .,** il m'est impossible de ne pas croire que . . .; (*c*) (*intensive*) **not merely once, b. twice,** pas une fois, mais deux; **nobody, b. nobody personne,** mais absolument personne. **2.** *adv.* ne . . . que; seulement; **it's nothing b. laziness,** c'est de la pure paresse; **had I b. known!** si j'avais su! **one can b. try,** on peut toujours essayer; **it seems b. yesterday,** cela me semble pas plus tard qu'hier; **if I could b. see him!** si je pouvais seulement le voir! **3.** *conj. or prep.* (*a*) **any day b. tomorrow,** n'importe quel jour excepté, sauf, demain; **all b. he, b. him,** tous excepté lui; tous sauf lui; **none b. he,** personne d'autre que lui; **anyone b. me,** tout autre que moi; **anything b. that,** n'importe quoi plutôt que cela; **it never rains b. it pours,** un malheur ne vient jamais seul; **he is anything b. a hero,** il n'est rien moins qu'un héros; **there is nothing for it b. to obey,** il n'y a qu'à obéir; **what could I do b. invite him?** que pouvais-je faire d'autre que de l'inviter? **he is anything b. happy,** il n'est pas du tout heureux; (*b*) **the last b. one,** l'avant-dernier; **the next house b. one,** la deuxième maison (à partir d'ici); (*c*) **b. for,** sans; **b. for the rain I should have gone out,** sans la pluie je serais sorti. **4.** *n.* **there is a b.,** il y a un mais.

butane [ˈbjuːtein] *n. Ch:* butane *m.*

butch [butʃ] *F:* **1.** *a.* (*of man, woman*) costaud. **2.** *n.* (*a*) (*man*) costaud m, dur *m*; (*b*) lesbienne *f*, gouine *f* (d'apparence masculine).

butcher¹ [ˈbutʃər] *n.* (*a*) boucher, bouchère; **butcher's boy,** garçon boucher; **pork b.** = charcutier *m*; **butcher's shop, trade,** boucherie *f*; (*b*) *Pej:* boucher, massacreur *m*; (*c*) *F:* (*surgeon*) boucher, charcutier.

butcher² *v.tr.* **1.** (*a*) abattre (un animal); (*b*) *U.S:* dépecer (une bête); (*c*) *Pej:* massacrer, égorger (qn). **2.** *F:* (*of surgeon*) charcuter (un patient).

butchery [ˈbutʃəri] *n.* **1.** (*trade*) boucherie *f.* **2.** *Pej:* boucherie, massacre *m.*

butler [ˈbʌtlər] *n.* maître *m* d'hôtel (d'une maison privée); **butler's pantry,** office *f.*

butt¹ [bʌt] *n.* (*a*) barrique *f*, futaille *f*; (*b*) tonneau *m* (pour l'eau de pluie, etc.).

butt² *n.* **1.** (*a*) souche *f* (d'arbre, etc.); billot *m* (d'arbre); bout *m* (de cigare, etc.); (*b*) *Bookb:* onglet *m* (d'une feuille isolée); (*c*) *NAm: F:* (*of pers.*) derrière *m.* **2. b. (end),** (i) gros bout, talon *m*, pommeau *m*, (ii) gros brin (d'une canne à pêche). **3.** *Bill:* masse *f*, talon (de la queue). **4. b. (end),** crosse *f* (de fusil). **5.** *Carp:* **b. (end),** about *m*; **b. joint,** joint *m* bout à bout; **b. hinge,** charnière *f; Metalw:* **b. welding,** soudure *f* bout à bout. **6.** *Leath:* croupon *m.*

butt³ 1. *v.tr.* (*a*) *Carp: etc:* (r)abouter, raboutir (deux pièces); (*b*) étayer, buter (une poutre, etc.) (**against,** contre). **2.** *v.i.* (*of prop, etc.*) s'étayer, buter (**against,** contre).

butt⁴ *n.* **1.** *Mil:* butte *f* (de tir); **the butts,** le champ de tir. **2.** but *m*; (*of pers.*) souffre-douleur *m inv.*

butt⁵ *n* (*a*) coup *m* de (la) tête; coup de corne (d'un bélier, etc.); (*b*) *Wr:* **head b.,** coup de tête.

butt⁶ 1. *v.i.* **to b. into, against, s.o., sth.,** donner du front, buter, contre qn, qch.; **to b. into the conversation, to b. in,** intervenir sans façon dans la conversation. **2.** *v.tr.* donner contre (qn, qch.) de la tête; (*of ram*) donner un coup de corne à (qn). **butting** *n.* coups *mpl* de tête, de cornes.

butter¹ [ˈbʌtər] *n.* (*a*) beurre *m*; **unsalted b.,** beurre frais; **salt(ed) b.,** beurre salé; **dairy b.,** beurre laitier; *Cu:* **melted b.,** beurre fondu; *F:* **b. wouldn't melt in her mouth,** elle fait la sainte nitouche; **b. dish,** beurrier *m*; **b. knife,** couteau *m* à beurre; (*b*) **cocoa b., peanut b.,** beurre de cacao, d'arachide.

butter² *v.tr.* (*a*) beurrer (du pain); *F:* **to b. s.o. up,** flatter, pateliner, qn; (*b*) *Cu:* accommoder (des légumes, etc.) au beurre.

butterball [ˈbʌtəbɔːl) *n. U.S: F:* obèse *mf*; personne boulotte.

buttercup [ˈbʌtəkʌp] *n. Bot:* renoncule *f* des champs; *F:* bouton *m* d'or, bassinet *m* des champs.

butterfat [ˈbʌtəfæt] *n.* matière grasse (contenue dans le lait).

butterfingered [ˈbʌtəfiŋgəd] *a. F:* maladroit, empoté; **he's b.,** tout lui glisse des mains, des doigts.

butterfingers [ˈbʌtəfiŋgəz] *n. F:* maladroit, -e; empoté, -ée.

butterfly [ˈbʌtəflai] *n.* **1.** *Ent:* papillon *m* (diurne); **b. net,** filet *m* à papillons; *F:* **to have butterflies (in one's stomach),** avoir l'estomac serré. **2.** (*a*) *Cost:* **b. bow,** nœud *m* (de) papillon; (*b*) *Tchn:* **b. nut,** écrou *m* à oreilles, à ailettes; écrou ailé; (écrou) papillon; **b. valve,** (soupape *f* à) papillon; vanne *f*; (*c*) *Swim:* **b. (stroke),** (nage, brasse *f*) papillon. **3.** *F:* personne *f* frivole; papillon.

buttermilk [ˈbʌtəmilk] *n.* babeurre *m.*

butterscotch [ˈbʌtəskɔtʃ] *n.* caramel *m* (dur) au beurre.

buttery¹ [ˈbʌtəri] *n.* (*a*) dépense *f*, office *f* (*esp.* dans les universités anglaises); **b. hatch,** passe-plats *m inv*; (*b*) buffet *m* (où l'on sert des repas légers).

buttery² *a:* (*a*) de beurre; (*b*) (*like butter*) butyreux; (*c*) graisseux, onctueux.

buttock [ˈbʌtək] *n.* (*a*) fesse *f*; **the buttocks,** le derrière, les fesses; (*b*) *Wr:* **cross b.,** ceinture *f* arrière, à rebours; tour *m* de hanche.

button¹ [ˈbʌtən] *n.* **1.** (*a*) bouton *m*; **as bright as a b.,** (i) brillant comme un sou neuf; (ii) (*of child*) vif, éveillé; (*b*) **buttons,** chasseur *m* (d'hôtel, de club, etc.); groom *m.* **2.** (*a*) bouton, pressoir *m* (de sonnerie électrique, etc.); poussoir *m* (d'une montre à répétition); (*b*) bouton (de fleuret, de queue de violon); mouche *f* (de fleuret); (*c*) *Row:* taquet *m* (d'aviron); (*d*) *Comest:* **chocolate buttons,** pastilles *fpl* de chocolat; (*e*) *Ch:* culot *m* (au fond du creuset); (*f*) Bot: **b. rose,** bouton de rose; **b. mushroom,** champignon *m* en bouton.

button² *v.tr.* **1.** (*a*) **to b. sth. (up),** boutonner qch.; (*of pers.*) **buttoned up,** (i) boutonné jusqu'au menton; (ii) *F:* silencieux, renfermé; (*b*) (*with passive force*) (*of garment*) (se) boutonner; **dress that buttons behind,** robe *f* qui (se) boutonne par derrière. **2.** (*a*) *Fenc:* moucheter (une épée).

buttonhole¹ [ˈbʌtənhoul] *n.* **1.** boutonnière *f*; *Needlew:* **b. stitch,** point de boutonnière. **2.** *Surg:* boutonnière; petite incision. **3.** (fleur portée à la) boutonnière.

buttonhole² *v.tr.* **1.** *F:* **to b. s.o.,** attraper, retenir, qn par le revers de l'habit; agrafer, cueillir, qn (au passage). **2.** *Needlew:* (*a*) festonner; (*b*) *v.i.* faire une boutonnière.

buttress¹ [ˈbʌtris] *n. Arch:* contrefort *m*; **flying b.,** arc-boutant *m*, *pl.* arcs-boutants.

buttress² *v.tr. Const:* arc-bouter; étayer.

butty *n.* **1.** [ˈbʌti, ˈbu(ː)ti] *F:* copain *m.* **2.** [ˈbu(ː)ti] *Dial:* sandwich *m.*

buxom [ˈbʌksəm] *a.* (femme) à la forte poitrine; (femme) aux formes rebondies, plantureuses.

buy¹ [bai] *v.tr.* (*p.t. & p.p.* **bought** [bɔːt]) **1.** (*a*) acheter (**sth. from s.o.,** qch. à qn); **to b. sth. cheap,** acheter qch. (à) bon marché; **money cannot b. it,** cela ne se paie pas; **a dearly bought advantage,** un avantage chèrement payé; (*b*) **to b. s.o. sth.,** acheter qch. à qn; **my father had bought me a bicycle,** mon père m'avait acheté une bicyclette. **2.** (*a*) corrompre, suborner (un témoin, etc.); (*b*) *F:* croire; gober; **I won't b. that!** tu ne me feras pas gober ça! **I'll b. it!** je te crois. **buy back** *v.tr.* racheter (qch.). **buy in** *v.tr.* (*a*) (*at auction*) racheter (pour le compte du vendeur); (*b*) s'approvisionner de (denrées, etc.). **buying** *n.*

achat(s) *m(pl)*; **b. and selling,** achat et vente *f*; **b. back,** rachat *m*; **b. out,** (i) désintéressement *m* (d'un associé); (ii) *Mil:* rachat (de qn); **b. up,** accaparement *m* (de denrées). **buy off** *v.tr.* se débarrasser de (qn) en lui payant une somme d'argent; *F:* acheter (qn). **buy out** *v.tr.* (*a*) *Com:* désintéresser (un associé, etc.); **he was bought out for £50,000,** on lui a acheté sa part pour £50,000; (*b*) *Mil:* racheter (qn); **to b. oneself out,** se racheter. **buy up** *v.tr. Com:* acheter (qch.) en masse; rafler, accaparer (des denrées, etc.).

buy² *n.* achat *m*; affaire *f*; **a good b.,** une occasion, une affaire; **a bad b.,** un mauvais achat.

buyer ['baiər] *n.* **1.** acheteur, -euse; acquéreur *m*; **prospective b.,** acheteur potentiel, éventuel; *Fin:* **buyers' market,** marché demandeur; marché orienté à la hausse. **2.** (*for shop*) acheteur; **head b.,** acheteur principal.

buzz¹ [bʌz] *n.* bourdonnement *m* (d'un insecte, etc.); bruissement *m* (d'abeilles); bruit confus, brouhaha *m* (de conversation); vrombissement (d'un avion); *W.Tel:* ronflement *m*; *F:* **to give s.o. a b.,** donner un coup de fil à qn.

buzz² **1.** *v.i.* (*a*) (*of insect, etc.*) bourdonner; (*of aircraft, etc.*) vrombir; **the whole town was buzzing with excitement,** la ville était en pleine agitation; (*b*) *F:* **to b. about, around,** s'activer. **2.** *v.tr. NAm: F:* donner un coup de téléphone à (qn); *Av: etc: F:* frôler, harceler (un avion). **buzzing** *n.* bourdonnement *m* (d'un insecte, *Med:* des oreilles). **buzz off** *v.i. F:* s'en aller, décamper; **b. off!** va-t-en! file!

buzzard ['bʌzəd] *n. Orn:* buse *f*, busard *m*.

buzzer ['bʌzər] *n.* (*a*) *Nau: Ind:* sirène *f*; (*b*) *Tp: etc:* vibreur *m*; sonnerie ronflante; (*c*) *El:* trembleur *m*.

by¹ [bai] **I.** *prep.* **1.** (*near*) (*a*) (au)près de, à côté de (qn, qch.); **sitting by the fire,** assis près du feu; **by the sea,** au bord de la mer; (*in place names*) **X-by-Y,** X-lès-Y, X-lez-Y; **X-by-Sea,** X-sur-Mer; **by oneself,** seul; à l'écart; (*b*) quart *m*; **north by east,** nord quart nord-est; **north-east by north,** nord nord-est quart-nord; **north-east by east,** nord-est quart-est; **east by north,** est quart nord-est; (*c*) *Nau:* **by the head, by the stern,** sur nez, sur cul. **2.** (*via*) par; **to go by the same road,** aller par la même route; **by land and sea,** par terre et par mer. **3.** (*agency, means*) (*a*) par, de; **to be punished by s.o.,** être puni par qn; **to be loved by s.o.,** être aimé, se faire aimer, de qn; **to have a child by s.o.,** avoir un enfant de qn; **to die by one's own hand,** mourir de ses propres mains; **he took me by the arm, hand,** il m'a pris par le bras, la main; **made by hand,** fait à la main; **to call s.o. by his name,** appeler qn par son nom; **to live by one's work,** vivre de son travail; **what do you mean by that?** qu'entendez-vous par là? **by force,** de force; **by way of a joke,** par plaisanterie; **by chance,** par hasard; **cheerful by nature,** gai de caractère; gai par nature; **to do sth. (all) by oneself,** faire qch. (tout) seul; **by heart,** par cœur; **to divide by three,** diviser par trois; **three metres by two,** trois mètres sur deux; **by land, by sea,** par (voie de) terre, mer; **to travel by rail,** voyager par le, en, chemin de fer; **to come by car, by motorcycle,** venir en voiture, à motocyclette; (*b*) **to earn one's living by teaching,** gagner sa vie en enseignant; **I shall gain, lose, by (doing) it,** j'y gagnerai, j'y perdrai; **to begin, end, by laughing,** commencer, finir, par rire; **we shall lose nothing by waiting,** nous ne perdrons rien pour attendre. **4.** (*according to*) **by my watch,** à ma montre; **to set one's watch by the time signal,** régler sa montre sur le signal horaire; **to judge by appearances,** juger sur l'apparence; **I can tell it by your face,** on le voit à votre visage; **to sell sth. by the pound, by the dozen,** vendre qch. à la livre, à la douzaine; **to rent a house by the year,** louer une maison à l'année. **5. by degrees,** par degrés; **by turn(s),** tour à tour; **one by one,** un à un; **to come in by twos, two by two,** entrer deux par deux; **by twos and threes,** par deux ou trois; **little by little,** peu à peu, petit à petit; **day by day,** jour par jour, de jour en jour. **6.** (*during*) **by day,** de jour, le jour; **by night,** de nuit, la nuit; **by daylight,** au jour. **7.** (*time*) **he will be here by three o'clock,** il sera ici avant, pour, trois heures; **you will hear from us by Monday,** vous aurez de nos nouvelles d'ici lundi; **he ought to be here by now, by this time,** il doit, il devrait, être déjà ici; **by the time (that) you have finished, I shall be gone,** quand vous aurez fini je serai parti; **you shall have it by tomorrow,** vous l'aurez pour demain; **they were tired by the end of the day,** ils étaient fatigués à la fin de la journée; **by 1970,** dès 1970. **8.** (*to the extent of*) **longer by two metres,** plus long de deux mètres; **by far,** de beaucoup. **9. I know him by name, by sight,** je le connais de nom, de vue; **to do one's duty by s.o.,** faire son devoir envers qn; *F:* **it's all right by me!** ça (me) va! d'accord! **10.** (*in oaths*) **by God,** au nom de Dieu; **to swear by all one holds sacred,** jurer par tout ce qu'on a de plus sacré. **11.** *Mil:* **by the right!** guide à droite! **II.** *adv.* **1.** (*near*) près; **close by,** tout près, ici près, tout à côté; **taking it by and large,** à tout prendre; généralement. **2.** (*aside*) **to lay, set, put, sth. by,** mettre qch. de côté; **to put, lay, money by,** mettre de l'argent de côté. **3. to go, pass, by,** passer; **the time goes by,** le temps passe. **4.** *adv.phrs.* **by and by,** tout à l'heure; bientôt, tantôt; **by the by(e), by the way,** à propos.

bye¹ [bai] *n.* **1.** *Cr:* balle passée. **2.** *Sp:* (*of player*) **to have a b.,** être exempt (d'une épreuve, d'un match dans un tournoi). **3. by the b . . .,** à propos . . ..

bye² *int. F:* au revoir! **b. for now!** à bientôt!

bye-bye ['bai 'bai] *F:* **1.** *int.* adieu! au revoir! **2.** *n.* (*child's language*) **to go to b.-b., to go b.-byes,** aller faire dodo.

by(e)-law ['bailɔː] *n.* arrêté municipal.

by-election ['baii'lekʃən] *n. Pol:* élection partielle.

bygone ['baigɔn] **1.** *a.* passé, ancien, d'autrefois; **in b. days,** autrefois; dans l'ancien temps. **2.** *n.pl.* **bygones,** (*a*) le passé; **let bygones be bygones,** oublions le passé; passons l'éponge (là-dessus); (*b*) antiquités *f*; objets *m* folkloriques.

bypass¹ ['baipɑːs] *n.* **1.** (*a*) *Mch: etc:* (conduit *m* de) dérivation (*f*); **b. valve,** soupape *f* de dérivation; (*b*) *Av:* **b. ratio,** taux *m* de dilution. **2.** *El:* dérivation. **3.** *Civ.E:* route *f* d'évitement.

bypass² *v.tr.* **1.** *Mch:* amener (la vapeur, etc.) en dérivation. **2.** *El:* mettre hors circuit. **3.** (*a*) (*of road, pers.*) contourner, éviter (une ville, etc.); dévier (la circulation); (*b*) laisser (qn) de côté; court-circuiter (un intermédiaire, etc.).

by-play ['baiplei] *n. Th: etc:* (i) jeu *m* accessoire; jeu de second plan; (ii) aparté mimé; jeu muet.

by-product ['baiprɔdʌkt] *n. Ind:* sous-produit *m*, *pl.* sous-produits; produit dérivé.

byre ['baiər] *n. esp. Scot:* étable *f* à vaches.

byroad ['bairoud] *n.* (*a*) chemin détourné; embranchement *m*; (*b*) chemin vicinal; route vicinale, cantonale.

bystander ['baistændər] *n.* spectateur, -trice.

byway ['baiwei] *n.* chemin détourné, voie indirecte; **byways of history,** à-côtés *mpl* de l'histoire.

byword ['baiwəːd] *n.* **1.** *A:* proverbe *m*, dicton *m*; **to have become a b.,** être passé en proverbe. **2.** (*of pers.*) **the b. of the village,** la fable, la risée, du village.

Byzantine [bai'zæntain] *Hist:* **1.** *a.* byzantin; **the B. Empire,** l'Empire byzantin, l'Empire romain d'Orient. **2.** *n.* Byzantin, -ine.

Byzantium [b(a)i'zæntiuin] *Pr.n. A.Geog:* Byzance *f*.

C

C, c [siː] *n.* **1.** (la lettre) C, c *m;* **2.** *Mus:* ut *m*, do *m*, **3.** *Sch:* **to get a C,** avoir une note médiocre (pour un devoir). **4.** *U.S: F:* **C note,** billet *m* de cent dollars.

cab [kæb] *n.* **1.** (*a*) *A:* fiacre *m*; **hansom c.,** cab *m*; (*b*) taxi *m*; **to call, hail, a c.,** appeler, héler, un taxi; **c. driver,** chauffeur *m* de taxi; **c. rank,** station *f* de taxis. **2.** cabine *f* (de locomotive, de grue, etc.).

cabal [kə'bæl] *n.* **1.** cabale *f*, brigue *f*. **2.** coterie *f*.

cabaret ['kæbərei] *n.* **1.** cabaret *m* (genre montmartrois). **2. c. (show),** concert *m* genre music-hall (donné dans un restaurant, etc.); attractions *fpl.*

cabbage ['kæbidʒ] *n.* (*a*) chou *m*, *pl.* choux; **red c.,** chou rouge; (*b*) **c. lettuce,** laitue pommée; **c. palm,** palmiste *m*; **c. rose,** rose *f* chou, *pl.* roses chou; (*c*) *Ent:* **c. butterfly, c. white,** piéride *f* du chou.

cab(b)alistic [kæbə'listik] *a.* cabalistique.

cabby ['kæbi] *n. F:* chauffeur *m* de taxi.

caber ['keibər] *n. Scot:* tronc *m* (de mélèze, de pin, etc.); *Sp:* **tossing the c.,** concours *m* de lancement d'un tronc de mélèze.

cabin ['kæbin] *n.* **1.** (*a*) cabane *f*, case *f;* (*b*) *Rail:* poste *m*, cabine *f*, d'aiguillage; **driver's c.,** cabine *f*, poste de conduite; (*c*) (*on barge, etc.*) cabane. **2.** (*a*) *Nau:* cabine; *Navy:* chambre *f*; **c. boy,** mousse *m*; **c. trunk,** malle *f* de cabine; (*b*) *Nau:* **c. cruiser,** yacht *m* de croisière (à moteur); (*c*) *Av:* cabine; habitacle *m*.

cabinet ['kæbinit] *n.* **1.** *Furn:* (*a*) meuble *m* à tiroirs; (*antique*) cabinet *m*; **filing c.,** fichier *m*, classeur *m*; **bathroom c.,** armoire *f* à pharmacie; (*b*) coffret *m* (de poste de radio, etc.); (*c*) **c. maker,** ébéniste *m*; menuisier *m* en meubles. **2.** (*a*) petite chambre; cabinet; (*b*) *Pol:* cabinet, ministère *m*; **shadow c.,** conseil *m* de ministres fantôme; **C. minister,** ministre *m* (d'État), membre du cabinet (ministériel); **to form a c.,** former un ministère. **3.** *Phot:* **c. size,** format *m* album.

cable¹ ['keibl] *n.* **1.** *Nau: etc:* câble *m*; **anchor c.,** câble d'ancre; **c. ship,** câblier *m*; **c. locker,** puits *m* aux chaînes; *Meas:* **cable('s) length,** encâblure *f*. **2.** *El: etc:* (*a*) câble, fil *m*; (fil) conducteur *m*; **overhead, underground, submarine, c.,** câble aérien, souterrain, sous-marin; **twin c.,** câble à deux conducteurs; **telegraph c.,** câble télégraphique; **to lay a c.,** poser un câble; (*b*) *Telecom:* câble, câblogramme *m*; **c. address,** adresse *f* télégraphique; (*c*) **c. railway,** (chemin *m* de fer) funiculaire (*m*); **c. car,** (i) funiculaire; (ii) (cabine *f* de) téléphérique *m*; (*d*) *Phot:* **c. release,** déclencheur *m*; (*e*) *Knit:* **c. stitch,** point natté.

cable² *v.tr.* (*a*) câbler (un message); (*b*) *v.tr. & i.* **to c. (to) s.o.,** câbler à qn; aviser qn par câble. **cabling** *n.* **1.** envoi *m* d'un câblogramme. **2.** *coll.* câbles *mpl*; **a hundred metres of c.,** cent mètres de câble.

cablegram ['keiblgræm] *n.* câblogramme *m*.

cableway [keiblwei] *n.* transporteur aérien à câbles; blondin *m*.

cabman, *pl.* **-men** ['kæbmən] *n.* chauffeur *m* de taxi.

cabochon ['kæbəʃɔn] *n. Lap:* cabochon *m*.

caboodle [kə'buːdl] *n. F:* **the whole (kit and) c.,** tout le bazar; tout le bataclan.

caboose [kə'buːs] *n.* **1.** *Nau:* cuisine *f*, coquerie *f*. **2.** (*a*) *NAm: Rail:* fourgon *m* de queue (d'un train de marchandises); (*b*) *Can:* baraquement *m* mobile (pour bûcherons, etc.).

cacao [kə'kɑːou, kə'keiou] *n. Bot:* **1. c. (bean),** (graine *f*, fève *f*, de) cacao (*m*); **c. pod,** cabosse *f*. **2. c. (tree),** cacaotier *m*, cacaoyer *m*.

cache [kæʃ] *n.* **1.** cache *f*, cachette *f* (d'explorateur). **2. arms, drugs, c.,** dépôt caché d'armes, de drogues.

cachet ['kæʃei] *n.* **1. to have a certain c.,** avoir un certain cachet. **2.** *Pharm:* cachet (d'aspirine, etc.).

cackle¹ ['kækl] *n.* **1.** (*of hen*) caquet *m*. **2.** *F:* (*of pers.*) (*a*) caquet; **cut the c.!** la ferme! (*b*) rire saccadé.

cackle² *v.i.* (*a*) (*of hen*) caqueter; (*of goose*) cacarder; (*b*) (*of pers.*) (i) caqueter, cailleter; (ii) faire entendre un rire saccadé.

cacophony [kæ'kɔfəni] *n.* cacophonie *f*.

cactus, *pl.* **-ti** ['kæktəs; -tiː, -tai], *n. Bot:* cactus *m*.

cad [kæd] *n.m.* salaud *m*; canaille *f*.

cadastral [kə'dæstrəl] *a. Surv:* (registre, etc.) cadastral, -aux.

cadaver [kə'dævər] *n. esp. NAm:* cadavre *m*.

cadaverous [kə'dævərəs] *a.* (*a*) (teint, etc.) cadavéreux; (*b*) émacié, décharné.

caddie¹ ['kædi] *n. Golf:* caddie *m*; **c. car(t),** poussette *f* (pour crosses de golf).

caddie² *v.i. Golf:* **to c. for s.o.,** servir de caddie à qn.

caddy¹ ['kædi] *n.* **tea c.,** boîte *f* à thé.

caddy² *n. & v.i.* = CADDIE [1, 2].

cadence ['keidəns] *n.* **1.** cadence *f*, rythme *m*. **2.** *Mus:* cadence; **perfect, imperfect, c.,** cadence parfaite, imparfaite.

cadenza [kə'denzə] *n. Mus:* cadence *f* (d'un concerto).

cadet [kə'det] *n. Mil: etc:* (*a*) élève *m* d'une école militaire; élève officier; (*b*) *Sch:* élève de la préparation militaire; **c. corps,** peloton *m* de préparation militaire.

cadge [kædʒ] *v.tr.* mendier, quémander; écornifler (un repas); **to c. sth. from s.o.,** taper qn de qch.

cadger ['kædʒər] *n.* quémandeur, -euse; tapeur, -euse; écornifleur *m*.

Cadiz [kə'diz] *Pr.n. Geog:* Cadix.

cadmium ['kædmiəm] *n. Miner:* cadmium *m*.

caecum, *NAm:* **cecum,** *pl.* **-a** ['siːkəm, -ə] *n. Anat:* cæcum *m*.

Caesar ['siːzər] *Pr.n.m.* César; **Julius C.,** Jules César.

Caesarean, Caesarian [si(ː)'zɛəriən] *a. & n.* **1.** *Hist: Pol:* Césarien, -ienne. **2.** *Obst:* **C. (operation, section),** (opération) césarienne (*f*).

café ['kæfei] *n.* = café-restaurant *m*, *pl.* cafés-restaurants; **transport c.** = restaurant *m* de routiers.

cafeteria [kæfi'tiəriə] *n.* caféteria *f*, (restaurant *m*) libre-service (*m*), *pl.* libres-services.

caffeine ['kæfiːn] *n.* caféine *f*; **c. free,** (i) sans caféine; (ii) décaféiné.

caftan ['kæftæn] *n. Cost:* caf(e)tan *m*.

cage¹ [keidʒ] *n.* **1.** cage *f* (à oiseaux, etc.); **c. bird,** oiseau *m* de volière, d'appartement; *Mil:* **prisoners' c.,** parc *m*, cage, à prisonniers (de guerre). **2.** (*a*) (i) cage, (ii) cabine *f* (d'ascenseur); (*b*) *Min:* cage d'extraction. **3.** *Anat:* **rib c.,** cage thoracique. **4.** *Mec.E:* cage, lanterne *f* (de roulement à billes); corbeille *f* (de soupape).

cage² *v.t.r.* (*a*) encager; mettre (un oiseau, etc.) en cage; (*b*) emprisonner, encager (qn).
cagey ['keidʒi] *a. F:* prudent, circonspect; cachottier; **to be c. about one's age,** ne pas vouloir avouer son âge.
cahoots [kə'hu:ts] *n.pl. F:* **to be in c. with s.o.,** être d'intelligence avec qn; être de mèche avec qn.
caiman ['keimən] *n. Rept:* caïman *m.*
Cain [kein] *Pr.n.m. B:* Caïn; *F:* **to raise C.,** (i) faire un bruit, un fracas, de tous les diables; (ii) faire une scène monumentale.
cairn ['kɛən] *n.* **1.** cairn *m*, tumulus *m* de pierres. **2.** (*dog*) **c. (terrier),** terrier *m* cairn.
cairngorm [kɛən'gɔ:m] *n. Lap:* pierre *f* de cairngorm.
Cairo ['kaiərou] *Pr.n.m. Geog:* le Caire.
caisson ['keis(ə)n] *n.* **1.** *Hyd.E:* caisson *m*, *Med:* **c. disease,** maladie *f* des caissons. **2.** *Nau:* bateau-porte *m* (de bassin de radoub), *pl.* bateaux-portes.
cajole [kə'dʒoul] *v.tr.* cajoler; enjôler; *F:* embobiner; **to c. s.o. into doing sth.,** persuader qn de faire qch.
cajolery [kə'dʒouləri] *n.* cajolerie(s) *f(pl).*
cake¹ [keik] *n.* **1.** (*a*) gâteau *m*; pâtisserie *f*; **(small) cakes,** (petits) gâteaux, pâtisseries; **fruit c.,** cake *m*; **sponge c.,** (i) = gâteau de Savoie, gâteau mousseline; (ii) (*small*) = biscuit *m* de Savoie; *Iron:* **that takes the c.!** ça c'est le comble, le bouquet! **it's a piece of c.,** c'est simple comme bonjour; c'est du gâteau! **they're going, selling, like hot cakes,** ça se vend comme des petits pains; *Prov:* **you can't have your c. and eat it,** on ne peut pas avoir le drap et l'argent; (*b*) croquette *f*; boulette *f*. **2.** (*a*) pain *m* (de savon, etc.); tablette *f* (de chocolat, de couleur); (*b*) *Husb:* **cattle c.,** tourteau *m*; **oil, linseed, c.,** (i) tourteau de lin; (ii) tourte *f* (pour engrais).
cake² *v.i.* (*a*) former une croûte; faire croûte; (*b*) s'agglutiner; s'agglomérer; (*of blood, etc.*) se cailler. **caked** *a.* **1.** (*a*) qui forme une croûte; (*b*) agglutiné. **2. c. with mud, with blood,** plaqué de boue, de sang.
cakeshop ['keikʃɔp] *n.* pâtisserie *f*.
calabash ['kæləbæʃ] *n.* **1. c. (gourd),** calebasse *f*, gourde *f*; **c. tree,** calebassier *m*. **2.** (*a*) (*bottle*) calebasse, gourde *f*; (*b*) pipe *f* en (forme de) calebasse.
calamitous [kə'læmitəs] *a.* calamiteux; désastreux.
calamity [kə'læmiti] *n.* **1.** calamité *f*, infortune *f*, malheur *m*; *U.S: F:* **a C. Jane,** une pessimiste; une rabat-joie *inv.* **2.** désastre *m*; sinistre *m.*
calcareous [kæl'kɛəriəs] *a. Geol: etc:* calcaire.
calceolaria [kælsiə'lɛəriə] *n. Bot:* calcéolaire *f*.
calcification [kælsifi'keiʃ(ə)n] *n.* calcification *f* (des tissus organiques).
calcify ['kælsifai] *Ch: etc:* **1.** *v.tr.* calcifier; pétrifier (le bois, etc.). **2.** *v.i.* se calcifier.
calcination [kælsi'neiʃ(ə)n] *n. Ch: Ind:* calcination *f*; frittage *m*; cuisson *f*; grillage *m.*
calcine ['kælsain] **1.** *v.tr. Ch: Ind:* calciner; fritter (des carbonates, etc.); cuire (le gypse, etc.); *Metall:* griller (le minerai). **2.** *v.i.* se calciner.
calcium ['kælsiəm] *n. Ch:* calcium *m*; **c. carbide, chloride,** carbure *m*, chlorure *m*, de calcium.
calculable ['kælkjuləbl] *a.* calculable; chiffrable.
calculate ['kælkjuleit] *v.tr. & i.* **1.** (*a*) calculer, évaluer; estimer (une distance); calculer, mesurer (ses paroles); faire le compte de (sa fortune); (*b*) *esp. NAm:* **to c. on sth., on doing sth.,** compter sur qch., compter faire qch. **2.** *NAm: F:* croire, supposer **(that,** que). **calculated** *a.* (*a*) (insolence, etc.) délibérée, calculée; **c. risk,** risque calculé; (*b*) **c. to do sth.,** fait pour, propre à, faire qch.; **words c. to reassure us,** paroles propres à nous rassurer. **calculating 1.** *a.* (*of pers.*) calculateur, -trice. **2.** *n.* calcul *m*; estimation *f*; **c. machine,** machine *f* à calculer.
calculation [kælkju'leiʃ(ə)n] *n.* calcul *m*; **to make a c.,** effectuer un calcul; **to upset s.o.'s calculations,** déjouer les calculs de qn.
calculator ['kælkjuleitər] *n.* **1.** (*pers.*) calculateur, -trice; chiffreur, -euse. **2.** machine *f* à calculer; calculatrice *f*. **3.** barème *m.*
calculus ['kælkjuləs] *n.* **1.** *Med:* (*pl.* **calculi** ['kælkjulai]) calcul (vésical, etc.); **urinary c.,** urolithe *m*. **2.** *Mth:* **(infinitesimal) c.,** calcul infinitésimal; **differential, integral, c.,** calcul différentiel, intégral.
Calcutta [kæl'kʌtə] *Pr.n. Geog:* Calcutta.
Caledonia [kæli'douniə] *Pr.n.Lit:* Calédonie *f*.
Caledonian [kæli'douniən] **1.** *a.* calédonien. **2.** *n.* Calédonien, -ienne.
calendar ['kælindər] *n.* **1.** calendrier *m*; (*a*) **Julian, Gregorian, c.,** calendrier julien, grégorien; **c. month,** mois civil; **c. year,** année civile; (*b*) **tear-off c.,** calendrier bloc; calendrier à effeuiller. **2.** (*a*) *Ecc:* calendrier (des saints); (*b*) annuaire *m* (d'une université, d'une institution, etc.); (*c*) *Jur:* rôle *m* des causes; rôle des assises; (*d*) *U.S:* ordre *m* du jour (du Congrès).
calends ['kælindz] *n.pl. Rom.Ant:* calendes *fpl.*
calf¹, *pl.* **calves** [kɑ:f, kɑ:vz] *n.* **1.** (*a*) veau *m*; **cow in, with c.,** vache pleine; (*b*) *Leath:* veau; vachette *f*; *Bookb:* **c. binding,** reliure *f* en veau. **2.** (*a*) **buffalo c.,** buffletin *m*; **whale c.,** baleineau *m*; **elephant c.,** éléphanteau *m*; (*b*) **sea c.,** phoque commun; (*c*) glaçon (détaché d'un iceberg); veau. **3.** *F:* **c. love,** les premières amours.
calf², *pl.* **calves** *n.* mollet *m* (de la jambe); **c.-length boots,** demi-bottes *fpl.*
calfskin ['kɑ:fskin] *n.* (cuir *m* de) veau (*m*).
caliber ['kælibər] *n. NAm:* = CALIBRE.
calibrate ['kælibreit] *v.tr.* étalonner (un compteur, etc.); calibrer (un tube); graduer (un thermomètre); tarer (un ressort); vérifier le calibre d'(un canon).
calibration [kæli'breiʃ(ə)n] *n.* étalonnage *m* (d'un compteur, etc.); calibrage *m* (d'un tube); tarage *m* (d'un ressort).
calibre, *NAm:* **caliber** ['kælibər] *n.* (*a*) calibre *m*, alésage *m* (d'un canon, d'un tube); (*b*) calibre (d'une personne); **a man of your c.,** un homme de votre calibre.
calico ['kælikou] **1.** *n. Tex:* (*a*) calicot *m*; *Com:* blanc *m* de coton; **printed c.,** calicot imprimé; indienne *f*; (*b*) *NAm:* calicot imprimé; indienne *f*; (*c*) *Dressm:* percaline *f* (pour doublures). **2.** *a.* (*a*) de calicot; (*b*) *NAm:* varié, bigarré, (*of material*) à pois.
California [kæli'fɔ:niə] *Pr.n. Geog:* Californie *f*.
Californian [kæli'fɔ:niən] **1.** *a.* californien. **2.** *n.* Californien, -ienne.
caliper ['kælipər] *n.* = CALLIPER.
caliph ['keilif] *n.* calife *m.*
calisthenics [kælis'θeniks] *n.pl.* (*usu. with sg. const.*) callisthénie *f*.
calk¹ [kɔ:k] *n.* **1.** *Farr:* crampon *m* (de fer à cheval). **2.** *Bootm:* crampon à glace.
calk² [kɔ:k, kælk] *v.tr. Art: etc:* décalquer.
calk³ [kɔ:k] *v.tr.* = CAULK.
call¹ [kɔ:l] *n.* **1.** (*a*) (*shout*) appel *m*, cri *m*; (*b*) (i) cri (d'un oiseau); (ii) (*instrument*) **bird c.,** pipeau *m*. **2.** (*summons*) (*a*) appel; **c. for help,** appel au secours; **to come at, to answer, s.o.'s c.,** venir, répondre, à l'appel de qn; **on c.,** de garde; **to be within c.,** être à portée de voix; **to give s.o. a c.,** (i) appeler qn; (ii) réveiller qn; *F:* **to obey a c. of nature,** faire ses besoins; *F:* **to have a close c.,** l'échapper belle; **c. button,** bouton *m* d'appel; (*b*) sonnerie *f* (de clairon); batterie *f* (de tambour); *Nau:* coup *m* de sifflet; **bugle, trumpet, c.,** coup, appel, de clairon, de trompette; (*c*) **roll c.,** appel nominal; (*d*) vocation *f*; **he felt a c. (to the ministry),** il se sentait la vocation (pour l'Église); (*e*)

Tp: **telephone c.,** appel téléphonique; coup de téléphone; **local c.,** communication urbaine, locale; **personal c.,** *esp. U.S:* **person to person c.,** appel avec préavis, de personne à personne; **reversed charge c.,** *NAm:* **collect c.,** communication avec P.C.V.; **to give s.o. a c.,** téléphoner à qn; appeler qn (au téléphone); **to put a c. through,** donner la communication; *W.Tel: Navy:* **c. letters, sign,** lettres *fpl*, indicatif *m*, d'appel; *Tg:* **c. key,** touche *f* d'appel; **c. girl,** prostituée *f* sur rendez-vous téléphonique: call-girl *f*; (*f*) invitation *f*; (*g*) *Cards:* (*at bridge*) appel; (*at solo whist, boston*) demande *f*; **c. for trumps,** invite *f* d'atout; **a c. of three diamonds,** une annonce de trois carreaux; (*h*) *Th:* **curtain c.,** rappel *m* (d'un acteur); **to take a curtain c.,** paraître devant le rideau. **3.** visite *f*; *Com:* passage *m* (d'un représentant); **official c.,** visite officielle; **to pay, make, a c. on s.o.,** faire (une) visite à qn; **to return s.o.'s c.,** rendre la visite de qn; *F:* **to pay a c.,** aller faire une petite commission; *Nau:* **port of c.,** port *m* d'escale. **4.** (*a*) demande *f* (d'argent); *Fin:* appel de fonds, de versement; **payable at c.,** remboursable sur demande, à vue; **money at, on, c., c. money,** prêts *mpl* au jour le jour; argent *m* à court terme; (*b*) *St.Exch:* **c. (option),** option *f* d'achat; prime *f*.

call[2] **1.** *v.tr.* (*a*) appeler (qn); crier (qch.); **to c. the banns,** publier les bans; **to c. a halt,** (i) crier, dire, halte (**to sth.,** à qch.); (ii) faire halte; **to c. the roll,** faire l'appel; (*b*) appeler (qn); héler (un taxi); convoquer (une assemblée); appeler (les pompiers, un ascenseur); *Jur:* appeler (une cause); *Th:* rappeler (un acteur); **to c. the doctor,** faire venir, appeler, le médecin; **to be called away,** être appelé dehors; **c. me at six o'clock,** réveillez-moi à six heures; **duty calls (me),** le devoir m'appelle; *Mil:* **to c. to arms,** battre la générale; **to c. s.o.'s attention to sth.,** attirer l'attention de qn sur qch.; (*c*) *Tp:* téléphoner à (qn), appeler (qn); **who's calling, please?** c'est de la part de qui? (*d*) appeler; **he is called Martin,** (i) il s'appelle Martin; (ii) on l'appelle Martin; **to c. s.o. after s.o.,** donner le nom de qn à qn; **to c. oneself a colonel,** se qualifier de colonel; s'attribuer le titre de colonel; **c. me by my Christian, first, name,** appelez-moi par mon prénom; **to c. s.o. names,** injurier, invectiver, qn; **to c. s.o. a liar, a child,** traiter, qualifier, qn de menteur, d'enfant; **we'll c. it £3,** (i) mettons £3; (ii) va pour £3; **I c. that a dirty trick,** voilà ce que j'appelle un sale tour; (*e*) *Cards:* appeler, déclarer (deux carreaux, etc.); **to c. spades,** déclarer pique; *abs.* **to c.,** (i) appeler (l'atout); (ii) (*at poker*) forcer l'adversaire à déclarer son jeu; (*f*) décréter, ordonner (une grève). **2.** *v.i.* (*a*) (i) appeler; (*of bird, etc.*) crier; (ii) *Ven:* frouer; (*b*) **to c. (on s.o.),** (i) faire une visite (chez qn); (ii) passer, se rendre, se présenter (chez qn); **has anyone called?** est-il venu quelqu'un? **I must c. at the grocer's,** il faut que je passe chez l'épicier; **to c. again,** repasser (chez qn); (*c*) **the train calls at every station,** le train s'arrête, fait halte, à toutes les gares; *Nau:* (*of ship*) **to c. at a port,** faire escale à un port. **call back 1.** *v.tr.* (*a*) rappeler (qn); (*b*) *Tp:* **c. me back later,** rappelez-moi plus tard. **2.** *v.i.* **I shall c. back for it,** je repasserai le prendre. **call down** *v.tr.* faire descendre (qn); descendre demander (à qn) de. **call for** *v.ind.tr.* (*a*) appeler, faire venir (qn); faire apporter (qch.); commander (une consommation, etc.); **to c. for help,** crier au secours; appeler à l'aide; (*b*) venir prendre, venir chercher (qn, qch.); **I will c. for you at nine,** je viendrai vous chercher à neuf heures; **to be (left till) called for,** à remettre au messager; *Post:* pour attendre l'arrivée; (*on envelope*) poste restante; colis restant; *Rail:* en gare; (*c*) demander, exiger (une explication, des excuses); **to c. for volunteers,** demander des volontaires; *Cards:* **to c. for trumps,** inviter l'atout; (*d*) demander, comporter, réclamer, exiger (l'attention, des réformes); **situation that calls for tactful handling,** situation qui demande à être maniée avec tact; *F:* **this calls for a celebration, a drink!** il faut fêter, arroser, ça! **call in 1.** *v.tr.* (*a*) faire entrer (qn); demander à (qn) d'entrer; (*b*) (i) retirer (une monnaie, un livre) de la circulation; (ii) **to c. in one's money,** faire rentrer ses fonds; (*c*) faire appel, avoir recours, à (un spécialiste). **2.** *v.i.* **to c. in (at s.o.'s house, at the grocer's),** passer (chez qn, chez l'épicier); **to c. in to see s.o.,** (i) aller, (ii) venir, voir qn. **calling** *n.* **1.** (*a*) appel *m*, cri(s) *m(pl)*; (*b*) **c. (together),** convocation *f* (d'une assemblée, etc.). **2.** visite *f* (**on,** à). **3.** (*a*) vocation *f* (**for,** pour); (*b*) vocation, profession *f*, métier *m*. **4. c. in,** retrait *m* (de monnaies). **5. c. off,** (*a*) rappel *m* (des chiens); (*b*) rupture *f* (d'un marché); **c. off of a strike,** retrait *m* d'un ordre de grève. **6. c. up,** (*a*) (i) évocation *f* (d'une idée, d'un souvenir); (ii) évocation (d'un esprit); (*b*) appel *m* au téléphone; (*c*) appel sous les drapeaux, sous les armes. **call off** *v.tr.* (*a*) rappeler (un chien); décommander (une grève); rompre, annuler (un marché). **call on** *v.tr.* (*a*) invoquer (le nom de Dieu); (*b*) **to c. on s.o. for sth.,** demander qch. à qn; réclamer qch. à qn; (*c*) **to c. on s.o. to do sth.,** sommer, requérir, qn de faire qch., appeler qn à faire qch.; **I now c. on Mr S.,** la parole est à M. S.; (*d*) rendre visite à (qn); aller, passer, se rendre, chez (qn); aller voir (qn). **call out 1.** *v.tr.* faire sortir (qn); prier (qn) de sortir; appeler (les pompiers); **to c. out workers (on strike),** donner l'ordre de grève à des ouvriers. **2.** *v.i.* appeler; **to c. out for sth.,** appeler pour demander qch. **call up** *v.tr.* (*a*) faire monter (qn); (*b*) (i) évoquer (une idée, un souvenir); (ii) évoquer (un esprit); (*c*) appeler (qn) au téléphone; (*d*) *Mil: Navy:* mobiliser (un réserviste); appeler (un réserviste) sous les drapeaux, sous les armes; **to be called up,** être mobilisé; (*e*) *Fin:* **called-up capital,** capital appelé.

callbox ['kɔːlbɔks] *n.* cabine *f* téléphonique.

callboy ['kɔːlbɔi] *n. Th: etc:* avertisseur *m*.

caller [kɔːlər] *n.* **1.** visiteur, -euse; **to be a frequent c. at s.o.'s house,** fréquenter chez qn. **2.** *Tp:* demandeur, -euse (de la communication).

calligrapher [kə'ligrəfər] *n.* calligraphe *m*.

calligraphy [kə'ligrəfi] *n.* calligraphie *f*.

calliper ['kælipər] *n.* **1. c. compasses, (pair of) callipers,** compas *m* de calibre, à calibrer. **2. c. (splint),** attelle-étrier *f*, *pl.* attelles-étriers.

callisthenics [kælis'θeniks] *n.pl.* (*usu. with sg. const.*) callisthénie *f*.

callosity [kæ'lɔsiti] *n.* callosité *f*.

callous ['kæləs] *a.* **1.** (*of skin, feet, hands*) calleux. **2.** (homme, cœur) insensible, endurci; (homme) dur, sans cœur. **-ly** *adv.* sans pitié; sans cœur.

calloused ['kæləst] *a.* **c. hands,** mains calleuses.

callousness ['kæləsnis] *n.* insensibilité *f* (**to,** à); dureté *f*; manque *m* de cœur, de pitié.

callow ['kælou] *a.* (*a*) (*of fledgling*) sans plumes; (*b*) **c. youth,** jeune homme imberbe, sans expérience.

callowness ['kælounis] *n.* jeunesse *f*; manque *m* de maturité.

call-up ['kɔːlʌp] *n. Mil: etc:* appel *m* sous les drapeaux; **c.-up papers,** fascicule *m* de mobilisation.

callus ['kæləs] *n.* cal *m*, *pl.* cals; durillon *m*.

calm[1] [kɑːm] *n.* (*a*) calme *m*; tranquillité *f*, sérénité *f* (d'esprit); (*b*) *Nau:* calme; **dead, flat, c.,** calme plat; **period of c.,** accalmie *f*; **c. before a storm,** bonace *f*; calme avant la tempête.

calm[2] *a.* (*a*) calme, tranquille; (esprit) rassis, posé; **to remain, keep, c.,** rester calme; ne pas perdre la tête; **to grow calmer,** se calmer; (*b*) *Nau:* (mer) calme, molle; (journée) sans vent; **a sea as c. as a millpond,**

une mer d'huile. **-ly** *adv.* avec calme; tranquillement.

calm³ **1.** *v.tr.* calmer, apaiser (la tempête, la colère, etc.); remettre, détendre, tranquilliser (l'esprit); atténuer, adoucir (la douleur); **c. yourself,** remettez-vous! calmez-vous! **to c. s.o. down,** pacifier qn. **2.** *v.i.* **to c. down,** (*of storm, grief, etc.*) se calmer, s'apaiser, se modérer; se pacifier; (*of grief*) s'adoucir; (*of the mind*) se tranquilliser; *Nau:* (*of sea*) calmir. **calming** **1.** *a.* (effet, etc.) tranquillisant, calmant. **2.** *n.* apaisement *m* (des flots, de la colère, etc.); adoucissement *m* (de la douleur).

calmness ['kɑːmnis] *n.* tranquillité *f*, calme *m.*

caloric [kə'lɔrik] *n. Ph:* calorique *m.*

calorie ['kæləri] *n. Ph:* calorie *f*; **low-c. diet,** régime de basses calories, hypocalorique.

calorific [kælə'rifik] *a. Ph:* (valeur, etc.) calorifique.

calumniate [kə'lʌmnieit] *v.tr.* calomnier.

calumny ['kæləmni] *n.* calomnie *f.*

Calvary ['kælvəri] **1.** *Pr.n.* **(Mount) C.,** le Calvaire. **2.** *n.* calvaire *m.*

calve [kɑːv] *v.i.* (*of cow, iceberg, etc.*) vêler. **calving** *n.* vêlage *m*, vêlement *m.*

Calvinism ['kælvinizm] *n. Rel.H:* calvinisme *m.*

Calvinist ['kælvinist] *n. & a. Rel.H:* calviniste (*mf*).

calypso [kə'lipsou] *n. Poet: Danc: Mus:* calypso *m.*

calyx, *pl.* **-yxes, -yces** ['keiliks, -iksiːz, -isiːz] *n. Bot:* calice *m.*

cam [kæm] *n. Mec.E: etc:* came *f*; excentrique *m.*

camber¹ ['kæmbər] *n.* cambrure *f* (d'une poutre, etc.); courbure *f*; bombement *m* (d'une chaussée); *N.Arch:* tonture *f* (du pont); *Av:* flèche *f* (d'aile).

camber² **1.** *v.tr.* bomber (une chaussée); cambrer (une poutre). **2.** *v.i.* (*a*) se bomber, se cambrer; (*b*) avoir de la cambrure; bomber.

Cambodia [kæm'boudiə] *Pr.n. A.Geog:* Cambodge *m.*

Cambodian [kæm'boudiən] *A:* **1.** *Geog: a.* cambodgien. **2.** *n.* Cambodgien, -ienne.

cambric ['kæmbrik, 'keim] *n. Tex:* batiste *f* (de lin).

camel ['kæm(ə)l] *n.* (*a*) *Z:* chameau *m*; **she c.,** chamelle *f*; **Bactrian c.,** chameau (bactrien); **Arabian c.,** dromadaire *m*; **c. driver,** chamelier *m*; *Mil:* **c. corps,** compagnies *fpl* de méharistes; (*b*) (*colour*) chameau *inv.*

camelhair ['kæməlhɛər] *n.* poil *m* de chameau; **c. brush,** pinceau *m* en petit-gris (pour l'aquarelle); **c. coat,** manteau *m* en poil de chameau.

camellia [kə'miːliə] *n. Bot:* camélia *m.*

cameo ['kæmiou] *n.* **1.** camée *m.* **2.** *Th: Cin:* petit rôle (joué par un acteur connu).

camera ['kæm(ə)rə] *n.* **1.** (*a*) *Phot:* appareil *m* (photographique); **reflex c.,** appareil reflex; **film,** *NAm:* **movie, c.,** caméra *f*; **television c.,** caméra de télévision; **on c.,** en champ, à l'écran; (*b*) *Opt:* **c. obscura** [ɔb'skjuːrə] chambre noire. **2.** *Jur:* **in c.,** à huis clos.

cameraman, *pl.* **-men** ['kæm(ə)rəmən] *n.m. Cin: TV:* cameraman, opérateur.

Cameroun [kæmə'ruːn] *Pr.n.* **the Republic of C.,** la République fédérale du Cameroun.

camomile ['kæməmail] *n. Bot:* camomille *f*; **c. tea,** (tisane *f* de) camomille.

camouflage¹ ['kæmuflɑːʒ] *n.* camouflage *m*; *Mil:* **c. painting, net(ting),** peinture *f*, filet *m*, de camouflage.

camouflage² *v.tr.* camoufler.

camp¹ [kæmp] *n.* (*a*) camp *m*; campement *m*; **holiday c.,** camp de vacances; (*for children*) = colonie *f* de vacances; **gipsy c.,** camp, campement, de gitans; *Pol:* **concentration c.,** camp de concentration; **to pitch c.,** établir un camp; **to strike, break, c.,** lever le camp; **c. bed,** lit *m* de camp; **c. stool, chair,** pliant *m*; chaise pliante; **c. site,** emplacement *m* du camp; (terrain *m* de) camping; **to go over to the other c.,** passer dans l'autre camp; **to have a foot in both camps,** manger à deux râteliers.

camp² **1.** *v.i.* **to c. (out),** camper. **2.** *v.tr. & i. Th: F:* **to c. (it up),** outrer (le mauvais goût). **camping** *n.* camping *m*; *esp. Mil:* campement *m*; **c. site,** (terrain *m* de) camping; **to go c.,** faire du camping.

camp³ *a.* **1.** *Th: F:* affecté, poseur. **2.** *P:* homosexuel, tapette.

campaign¹ [kæm'pein] *n.* (*a*) campagne *f* (militaire); **c. medal,** médaille commémorative; (*b*) **election c.,** campagne électorale; **to lead, conduct, a c. against s.o.,** mener (une) campagne contre qn; (*c*) *Com:* campagne de vente, publicitaire, etc.; **press c.,** campagne de presse.

campaign² *v.i.* faire (une) campagne; faire des campagnes.

campaigner [kæm'peinər] *n.* **1. old c.,** vieux soldat; vieux troupier. **2.** militant, -ante (pour, contre, qch.).

campanologist [kæmpə'nɔlədʒist] *n.* spécialiste *mf* de l'art campanaire; carillonneur *m.*

campanology [kæmpə'nɔlədʒi] *n.* art *m* campanaire; art du carillon.

campanula [kəm'pænjulə] *n. Bot:* campanule *f.*

camper ['kæmpər] *n.* **1.** campeur, -euse. **2.** voiture-camping *f.*

campfire ['kæmp'faiər] *n.* feu *m* de camp.

camphor ['kæmfər] *n.* camphre *m*; **c. oil,** essence *f* de camphre; **c. tree,** camphrier *m.*

camphorated ['kæmfəreitid] *a.* camphré; **c. oil,** huile camphrée.

campion ['kæmpiən] *n. Bot:* lychnide *f*, lychnis *m*; **white c.,** compagnon blanc.

campus ['kæmpəs] *n.* campus *m* (universitaire).

camshaft ['kæmʃɑːft] *n. Mec.E:* arbre *m* à came(s), à excentrique; *I.C.E:* arbre de distribution.

can¹ [kæn] *n.* **1.** bidon *m*, broc m, pot *m* (pour liquides); boîte *f* (à lait, d'un film); **watering c.,** arrosoir *m*; *NAm:* **trash, garbage, c.,** poubelle *f*; *F:* **to carry the c.,** payer les pots cassés; *Cin: TV: F:* (*of film*) **in the c.,** prêt à montrer, à téléviser. **2.** boîte (de conserve); **c. opener,** ouvre-boîte(s) *m*, *pl.* ouvre-boîtes. **3.** *U.S: P:* (*a*) prison *f*, *F:* taule *f*; (*b*) **the c.,** les cabinets *mpl*, les toilettes.

can² *v.tr.* **(canned) 1.** mettre, conserver (de la viande, etc.) en boîte. **2.** *NAm: F:* (*a*) congédier, renvoyer (qn); (*b*) **c. it!** la ferme! **3.** *W.Tel:T.V:* enregistrer; transcrire; *F:* **canned music,** musique enregistrée, *F:* de conserve. **4.** *F:* **to get canned,** se soûler. **canning** *n.* mise *f* en conserve, en boîte; **c. industry,** industrie *f* de conserves alimentaires.

can³ [*stressed form* kæn; *unstressed* k(ə)n] *modal aux. v.* (*pr.* **can**; *neg.* **cannot** ['kænɔt] (*U.S:* **can not** ['kæn'nɔt]); *p.t. & condit.* **could** [kud]; *no inf., pr.p. & p.p.; defective parts are supplied from "to be able to"*; **cannot** *and* **could not** *are often contracted into* **can't** [kɑːnt], **couldn't** ['kudnt]) **1.** (*a*) pouvoir; **I c. do it,** je peux le faire; **we cannot,** *U.S:* **c. not, possibly do it,** nous ne pouvons absolument pas le faire; **I will come as soon, as often, as I c.,** je viendrai aussitôt, aussi souvent, que possible; **he will do what he c.,** il fera ce qu'il pourra; **I will help you all I c.,** je vous aiderai de mon mieux; **I can't very well accept,** il m'est difficile d'accepter; *F:* **c. do!** ça va! bien sûr! **(it) can't be helped!** tant pis! (*b*) **it can't be done,** il est impossible de le faire; **how could he say that?** comment a-t-il pu dire cela? **what c. it be?** qu'est-ce que cela peut bien être? **c. it be true?** serait-ce vrai? **(it) could be,** c'est possible; (*c*) (*emphatic*) **I never** *could* **understand maths,** je n'ai jamais été capable de comprendre les maths; **what** *can* **he want?** qu'est-ce qu'il peut bien me vouloir? (*d*) (*intensive*) **how** *could*

you! à quoi pensez-vous? **he could not have been kinder,** il n'aurait pu être plus aimable. **2.** savoir; **I c. swim,** je sais nager; **a man who c. cook,** un homme qui sait faire la cuisine; **he c. play the violin,** il joue du violon. **3.** (*a*) **you don't know how silly a girl c. be,** vous ne savez pas à quel point les jeunes filles sont parfois sottes; **the crossing c. be rough,** il arrive que la traversée soit mauvaise; (*b*) (*permission*) **when c. I move in?** quand pourrai-je emménager? **you c. go,** vous pouvez vous retirer; **c. I ask you something?** est-ce que je peux vous demander quelque chose? **you can't smoke in here,** il est défendu de fumer ici. **4. I c. see nothing,** je ne vois rien; **I could hear them talking,** je les entendais parler; **I c. see you don't believe me,** je vois bien que vous ne me croyez pas; **how c. you tell?** comment le savez-vous? **5.** (*a*) **he could have done it,** il aurait pu le faire; (*b*) **I could not have asked for anything better,** je n'aurais pas désiré mieux; (*c*) **I could weep, could have wept,** j'ai envie, j'avais envie, de pleurer. **I could have smacked his face!** je l'aurais giflé! **6.** (*elliptically*) **I cannot but believe him,** je suis bien forcé de le croire; **you c. but try,** vous pouvez toujours essayer.

Canada ['kænədə] *Pr.n. Geog:* (*a*) Canada *m*; **in C.,** au Canada; (*b*) *Orn:* **C. goose,** bernache *f* du Canada.

Canadian [kə'neidiən] **1.** *a.* canadien; *Ling:* **C. French, English,** le français, l'anglais, du Canada. **2.** *n.* Canadien, -ienne.

Canadianism [kə'neidiənizm] *n.* mot canadien, expression canadienne.

canal [kə'næl] *n.* **1.** *Hyd.E:* canal, -aux; **slip c.,** canal maritime; **c. boat, barge,** péniche *f*; *Geog:* **the C. zone,** la zone du Canal de Panama. **2.** *Anat: etc:* canal; aqueduc *m* (de Fallope, etc.); **alimentary c.,** canal alimentaire; **auditory c.,** conduit auditif.

canalization [kænəlai'zeiʃ(ə)n] *n.* canalisation *f.*

canalize ['kænəlaiz] *v.tr.* (*a*) canaliser (une rivière, etc.); (*b*) canaliser (une ville); poser les conduites *fpl* dans (une ville).

canapé ['kænəpei] *n. Comest:* canapé *m.*

canard ['kænɑːd, kə'nɑːd] *n.* canard *m*, fausse nouvelle.

Canary [kə'nɛəri] **1.** *Pr.n. Geog:* **the C. Islands, the Canaries,** les îles Canaries. **2.** *n.* (*a*) *Orn:* serin *m*, canari *m*; (*b*) *Bot:* **c. grass,** alpiste *m*; *Com:* **c. seed,** (grains *mpl* de) millet *m*; (*c*) **c. yellow,** jaune canari.

canasta [kə'næstə] *n. Cards:* canasta *f.*

cancan ['kænkæn] *n. Danc:* (French) cancan *m.*

cancel ['kæns(ə)l] *v.tr.* **(cancelled,** *NAm:* **canceled)** (*a*) annuler (un chèque, une dette, une commande); annuler, résilier, résoudre (un marché, un contrat); révoquer (un acte, un testament); rappeler (un message); révoquer, contremander (un ordre); supprimer (un train); décommander (une réunion, une invitation, une réservation, etc.); oblitérer (un timbre); *Mil:* lever (une consigne); *Book-k:* (*of two entries*) **to c. each other,** s'annuler, se contrepasser; (*b*) *Mth:* éliminer (des facteurs équivalents d'une fraction). **cancel out** *v.i.* **1.** *U.S:* **he cancelled out of the meeting,** il a annulé sa participation à la réunion. **2.** *Mth:* (*of terms*) s'annuler, s'éliminer.

cancellation [kænsə'leiʃ(ə)n] *n.* annulation *f*; résiliation *f* (d'une commande, d'une vente, d'un contrat); *Post:* oblitération *f*; **c. of an order,** révocation *f* d'un ordre; contrordre *m*; **there have been several cancellations,** il y a plusieurs réservations qui ont été annulées.

cancer ['kænsər] **1.** *n.* (*a*) *Med:* cancer *m*; **c. of the lung, lung c.,** cancer du poumon; **c. patient,** cancéreux, -euse; **c. specialist,** cancérologue *mf*; **c. research,** cancérologie *f.* **2.** *Pr.n. Astr:* **C.,** le Cancer; *Geog:* **the Tropic of C.,** le tropique du Cancer.

cancerous ['kæns(ə)rəs] *a. Med:* cancéreux.

candelabra, *pl.* **-as** [kændi'lɑːbrə, -əz], **candelabrum,** *pl.* **-a** [kændi'lɑːbrəm, -ə] *n.* candélabre *m.*

candid ['kændid] *a.* franc, *f* franche; sincère; **c. camera,** caméra *f* invisible. **-ly** *adv.* franchement; sincèrement.

candidacy ['kændidəsi] *n. NAm:* candidature *f.*

candidate ['kændideit] *n.* candidat *m*, aspirant *m*, prétendant *m* **(for sth.,** à qch.); **to stand as c. for sth.,** se présenter comme candidat à qch.; poser sa candidature à qch.

candidature ['kændidətjər] *n.* candidature *f.*

candidness ['kændidnis] *n.* franchise *f*, sincérité *f.*

candle[1] ['kænd(ə)l] *n.* **1. wax c.,** bougie *f*; **tallow c.,** chandelle *f*; **church c.,** cierge *m*; **c. grease,** suif *m*; **to burn the c. at both ends,** brûler la chandelle par les deux bouts; **he cannot, is not fit to, hold a c. to you,** il n'est rien à côté de vous. **2.** *Pyr:* **Roman c.,** chandelle romaine.

candle[2] *v.tr.* mirer (des œufs).

candlelight ['kændllait] *n.* lumière *f* de chandelle, de bougie; **by c.,** à la chandelle, à la bougie.

Candlemas ['kændlmæs] *n. Ecc:* la Chandeleur.

candlestick ['kændlstik] *n.* chandelier *m*, bougeoir *m.*

candlewick ['kændlwik] *n.* **1.** mèche *f* de bougie, de chandelle. **2.** *Tex:* candlewick *m*, chenille *f* de coton.

candour, *NAm:* **candor** ['kændər] *n.* franchise *f*; sincérité *f.*

candy[1] ['kændi] *n.* **1. (sugar) c.,** sucre candi; **stick of (sugar) c.,** sucre *m* de pomme; sucre d'orge. **2.** *NAm:* bonbon *m*; **c. store,** confiserie *f*; *F:* **it's like taking c. from a baby,** c'est simple comme bonjour.

candy[2] **1.** *v.tr.* (*a*) faire candir (le sucre); (*b*) glacer (des fruits). **2.** *v.i.* (*of sugar*) se cristalliser. **candied** *a.* candi; glacé, confit (au sucre); **c. peel,** zeste confit.

candyfloss ['kændiflɔs] *n. Comest:* barbe *f* à papa.

candy-striped ['kændistraipt] *a. Tex:* pékiné.

cane[1] [kein] *n.* **1.** *Bot: etc:* (*a*) canne *f*, jonc *m*; (canne de) bambou *m*; rotin *m*; **c. chair, furniture,** siège *m*, meubles *mpl*, en rotin; **c.-seated chair,** chaise cannée; (*b*) **sugar c.,** canne à sucre; **c. sugar,** sucre *m* de canne; (*c*) **raspberry c.,** tige *f* de framboisier. **2.** (*a*) (*walking stick*) canne; (*b*) (*switch*) badine *f*; (*for punishment*) canne; **to get the c.,** être fouetté.

cane[2] *v.tr.* **1.** battre, frapper (qn) à coups de canne; donner des coups de canne à (qn). **2.** canner (une chaise). **caning** *n.* **1.** (volée *f* de) coups *mpl* de canne. **2.** cannage *m* (de chaises).

canine ['keinain, 'kæ-] **1.** (*a*) *a.* canin; de chien; **c. devotion,** dévotion *f* de chien; (*b*) *n.pl.* **canines,** canidés *mpl.* **2.** *a.* & *n.* **c. (tooth),** (dent) canine (*f*), (dent) œillère (*f*).

canister ['kænistər] *n.* boîte *f* (en fer blanc) (à thé, etc.).

canker[1] ['kæŋkər] *n.* (*a*) *Med:* ulcère rongeur; (*b*) *Vet:* (i) crapaud *m* (au sabot); (ii) gale *f* de l'oreille (du chien, etc.); (*c*) *Bot:* chancre *m*; (*in wood*) nécrose *f*; (*d*) *Fig:* chancre.

cankerworm ['kæŋkəwəːm] *n.* ver rongeur (des plantes).

cannabis ['kænəbis] *n.* cannabis *m*; **c. resin,** cannabine *f.*

cannery ['kænəri] *n.* conserverie *f.*

cannibal ['kænib(ə)l] *n.* & *a.* cannibale (*mf*).

cannibalism ['kænibəlizm] *n.* cannibalisme *m.*

cannibalize ['kænibəlaiz] *v.tr. Mec.E: etc:* démonter (une machine, etc.) pour en réutiliser les pièces.

cannon[1] ['kænən] *n.* **1.** (*usu. inv.*) *Artil:* canon *m*; **c. shot,** (i) boulet *m* de canon; (ii) coup *m* de canon; **c.**

fodder, chair *f* à canon. **2.** *Bill:* carambolage *m*; **c. off the cushion,** bricole *f*.

cannon² *v.i.* **(cannoned) 1.** *Bill:* faire un carambolage; caramboler; **to c. off the cushion,** jouer la bricole. **2. to c. into s.o.,** se heurter contre qn.

cannonade [kænə'neid] *n.* canonnade *f*.

cannonball ['kænənbɔːl] *n. Artil:* boulet *m* de canon.

canny ['kæni] *a. esp. Scot:* (*a*) prudent, circonspect; avisé; rusé; **c. answer,** réponse *f* de Normand; (*b*) économe. **-ily** *adv.* prudemment.

canoe¹ [kə'nuː] *n.* (i) canoë *m*; (ii) périssoire *f*; **dugout c.,** pirogue *f*; **to paddle one's own c.,** conduire seul sa barque.

canoe² *v.i.* **(canoed; canoeing)** faire du canoë, de la périssoire. **canoeing** *n.* canoë *m*.

canoeist [kə'nu(ː)ist] *n.* canoéiste *mf*.

canon¹ ['kænən] *n.* **1.** (*a*) *Ecc:* canon *m* de la messe, etc.); **c. law,** droit *m* canon; (*b*) *Lit:* règle *f*, critère *m*; canon. **2.** *Mus:* canon.

canon² *n. Ecc:* chanoine *m*.

cañon ['kænjən] *n. Geog:* cañon *m*, canyon *m*.

canonical [kə'nɔnikl] *a. Ecc:* **1.** (devoir, etc.) canonical; (droit, épître, résidence, etc.) canonique; **c. hours,** (i) heures canoniales; (ii) *Jur:* heures pendant lesquelles il est permis de célébrer les mariages. **2. c. dress,** *n.pl.* **canonicals,** vêtements sacerdotaux. **3.** *Fig:* autorisé, accepté. **4.** *Mus:* (passage) en forme de canon.

canonization [kænənai'zeiʃ(ə)n] *n. Ecc:* canonisation *f*.

canonize ['kænənaiz] *v.tr.* **1.** *Ecc:* canoniser (qn). **2.** sanctionner (un usage).

canoodle [kə'nuːdl] *v.i. P:* se faire des mamours.

canopy ['kænəpi] *n.* **1.** dais *m* (d'un trône); baldaquin *m* (de lit); *Ecc:* ciel *m* (d'autel, etc.); hotte *f* (de foyer); (*over doorway*) auvent *m*, marquise *f*; calotte *f* (de parachute); *Av:* verrière *f* (d'habitacle); **c. of leaves,** voûte *f* de feuillage, de verdure. **2.** *Arch:* gable *m*, gâble *m* (de comble, de fenêtre).

cant¹ [kænt] *n.* **1.** (*a*) *Arch: Carp: etc:* chanfrein *m*; biseau *m*; *Mec.E:* arête *f* (de boulon). **2.** (*a*) *Carp: Civ.E: etc:* inclinaison *f*, dévers *m*; *Rail:* surélévation *f*, dévers (du rail extérieur); (*b*) **to give sth. a c.,** incliner qch.; **to have a c.,** pencher.

cant² **1.** *v.tr.* (*a*) *Carp: etc:* biseauter, écorner; (*b*) dévoyer, incliner (une poutre, un montant); incliner, pencher (un fût); *Rail:* surhausser (le rail extérieur); (*c*) renverser, retourner (qch.); *Nau:* chavirer (un canot pour le réparer); (*d*) jeter, lancer, (qch.) de côté, de biais. **2.** *v.i.* (*a*) *Carp: Civ.E: etc:* s'incliner; (*b*) se trouver incliné; pencher; (*c*) *Nau:* (*of ship*) éviter.

cant³ *n.* (*a*) argot *m* (des voleurs, des mendiants, etc.); (*b*) langage *m* hypocrite; **c. phrase,** cliché *m*.

cant⁴ *v.i.* **1.** faire l'hypocrite. **2.** parler en argot.

cantaloup(e) ['kæntəluːp] *n. Hort:* cantaloup *m*.

cantankerous [kæn'tæŋk(ə)rəs] *a.* (*a*) revêche, acariâtre; (*b*) querelleur, -euse.

cantata [kæn'tɑːtə] *n. Mus:* cantate *f*.

canteen [kæn'tiːn] *n.* **1.** (*a*) cantine *f* (dans une usine, une caserne, etc.); (*b*) magasin *m* à l'usage des soldats (dans une caserne, etc.). **2.** *Mil:* (*a*) bidon *m*; (*b*) gamelle *f*; (*c*) cantine à vivres. **3. c. of cutlery,** ménagère *f*.

canter¹ ['kæntər] *n. Equit:* petit galop.

canter² **1.** *v.i.* aller au petit galop. **2.** *v.tr.* faire aller (un cheval) au petit galop.

Canterbury ['kæntəb(ə)ri] *Pr.n. Geog:* Cantorbéry *m*; *Bot:* **C. bell(s),** campanule *f*.

canticle ['kæntikl] *n.* cantique *m*.

cantilever ['kæntiliːvər] *n. Arch:* encorbellement *m*; *Civ.E: etc:* **c. beam,** poutre *f* en porte-à-faux; **c. bridge,** pont *m* cantilever.

canto ['kæntou] *n. Lit:* chant *m* (d'un poème).

Cantonese [kæntə'niːz] **1.** *Geog: a.* cantonais. **2.** *n.* (*a*) Cantonais, -aise; (*b*) *Ling:* cantonais *m*.

cantor ['kæntɔːr] *n. Ecc:* chantre *m*.

Canuck [kə'nʌk, kə'nuk] *n. U.S: F:* Canadien(ne) français(e).

canvas ['kænvəs] *n.* **1.** (*a*) *Tex:* canevas *m*; (grosse) toile; toile de tente: **c. bucket,** seau *m* en toile; **c. shoes,** chaussures *fpl* de toile; espadrilles *fpl*; **under c.,** (i) *Mil: etc:* sous la tente; (ii) *Nau:* sous voile; (*b*) *Needlew:* **c. work,** tapisserie *f*, broderie *f*, sur canevas, sur toile. **2.** *Art:* tableau *m*, toile *f*. **3.** *Box: Wr:* tapis *m*.

canvass¹ ['kænvəs] *n.* = CANVASSING.

canvass² *v.tr. & i.* **1.** (*a*) discuter (une affaire); examiner minutieusement (une question); (*b*) *NAm: Pol:* pointer, vérifier (des suffrages). **2.** *Pol: Com:* solliciter (des suffrages, des commandes); **to c. s.o.,** solliciter (i) la voix, (ii) la clientèle, de qn; *Pol:* **to c. (a district),** faire une tournée électorale (dans une région); *Com:* **to c. for customers,** prospecter la clientèle.

canvasser ['kænvəsər] *n. Pol: etc:* solliciteur, -euse; prospecteur, -trice.

canvassing ['kævəsiŋ] *n.* **1.** discussion *f*; *NAm:* pointage *m*, vérification *f* (des suffrages). **2.** sollicitation *f* (de suffrages, de commandes); *Pol:* propagande électorale.

canyon ['kænjən] *n. Geog:* canyon *m*, cañon *m*.

cap¹ [kæp] *n.* **1.** (*a*) *Cost:* bonnet *m*; (*with peak*) casquette *f*; toque *f* (universitaire, de jockey); képi *m* (de militaire); bonnet, béret *m* (de marin); **skull c.,** calotte *f*; **bathing, swimming, c.,** bonnet de bain, baigneuse *f*; *Sp:* **football c.,** cape *f*; **to win one's c.,** gagner sa cape; *Sch:* **in c. and gown,** en costume académique; **to come c. in hand,** se présenter chapeau bas; **if the c. fits, wear it!** qui se sent morveux se mouche! **to put on one's thinking c.,** méditer une question; *Min:* **c. lamp,** photophore *m*; (*b*) *Orn:* capuchon *m*, chapeau *m* (d'un oiseau). **2.** (*a*) chapiteau *m* (de colonne); chapeau (de champignon); comble *m* en dôme, lanterne *f* (de bâtiment); (*b*) *Tchn:* chapeau (de protection); capuchon (d'un stylo, de valve à pneu); calotte (d'une pompe); capsule *f* (de bouteille); *Mec.E:* chapeau, couvercle *m* (de palier, de soupape); *Phot:* **lens c.,** bouchon *m* d'objectif; *Hyg: F:* **(Dutch) c.,** diaphragme (contraceptif). **3.** *Exp:* amorce *f*, capsule; *Sm.a:* **percussion c.,** amorce.

cap² *v.tr.* **(capped** [kæpt]) **1.** (*a*) coiffer (qn) d'un bonnet, d'une casquette; (*b*) *Scot: N.Z: Sch:* conférer un diplôme à (un candidat); (*c*) *Sp:* donner sa cape à (un joueur). **2.** coiffer, couronner, recouvrir (**sth. with sth.,** qch. de qch.); coiffer (une fusée, un pieu); capsuler (une bouteille); (*over cork*) surboucher (une bouteille). **3.** surpasser (qch.); **to c. a quotation,** renchérir sur une citation; **that caps everything, the lot!** ça c'est le comble! le bouquet! **capping** *n.* **1.** (*a*) capsulage *m* (d'une bouteille); amorçage *m* (d'un obus); (*b*) *Scot: N.Z: Sch:* présentation *f* des diplômes. **2.** chapeau *m*, chape *f* (d'une charpente, d'un pieu, etc.).

cap³ *n. Typ: F:* majuscule *f*.

capability [keipə'biliti] *n.* **1.** (*a*) capacité *f* (**of doing sth.,** pour faire qch.); faculté *f* (**to do sth.,** de faire qch.); (*b*) susceptibilité *f* (d'amélioration, etc.). **2. to have capabilities,** (*of pers.*) être doué; promettre; avoir des moyens.

capable ['keipəbl] *a.* **1.** (*a*) capable (**of sth., of doing sth.,** de qch., de faire qch.); **to show what one is c. of,** montrer ce dont on est capable; (*b*) (*of pers.*) capable, compétent; **the business is in c. hands,** l'affaire est en bonnes mains. **2.** susceptible (d'amélioration, etc.). **-ably** *adv.* avec compétence; d'une manière compétente.

capacious [kə'peiʃəs] *a.* vaste, spacieux; ample.

capacitate [kə'pæsiteit] *v.tr. Jur:* donner pouvoir, qualité, à (qn) (**to act,** pour agir).

capacity [kə'pæsiti] *n.* **1.** (*a*) capacité *f* (d'un cylindre, etc., d'un accumulateur, d'un condensateur); contenance *f* (d'un tonneau, etc.); **cubic c.,** volume *m*; (*b*) *Trans: Ind: etc:* rendement *m*; débit *m*; **production c.,** capacité de production; **to work at full c.,** travailler à plein rendement; (*of vehicle*) **carrying c.,** charge *f* utile; (*of crane*) **lifting c.,** puissance de levage; (*c*) **seating c.,** nombre *m* de places (dans un autobus, un théâtre, etc.); **to play to c.,** (i) *Th: etc:* jouer à bureaux fermés; (ii) *Sp:* jouer à guichets fermés; **storage c.,** (i) *Ind: etc:* capacité de stockage; (ii) *Cmptr:* capacité de mémoire; *F:* **he has a remarkable c. for whisky,** il peut absorber des quantités extraordinaires de whisky. **2.** capacité (**for,** pour, de); aptitude *f* (à faire qch.); **c. for work, for love,** capacité de travailler, d'aimer; **to the utmost of my c.,** dans toute la mesure de mes moyens. **3. to have c., no c., to act,** avoir, ne pas avoir, qualité pour agir; **in the c. of . . .,** en qualité de . . .; **to act in one's official c.,** agir dans l'exercice de ses fonctions.

cape¹ [keip] *n. Cost:* (*a*) pèlerine *f*, cape *f*; (*small*) collet *m*; (*b*) *Ecc:* camail *m*, *pl.* camails.

cape² *n.* cap *m*, promontoire *m*; **the C. (of Good Hope),** le Cap (de Bonne-Espérance); **C. Town,** le Cap; *Ethn:* **C. Coloured,** métis *m* (de l'Afrique du Sud).

caper¹ ['keipər] *n. Bot:* **1.** câprier *m*. **2.** *Cu:* câpre *f*.

caper² *n.* (*a*) cabriole *f*, gambade *f*; (*b*) *F:* farce *f*; **to cut capers,** faire des farces, des sottises.

caper³ *v.i.* **to c. (about),** faire des cabrioles; cabrioler; gambader.

capercaillie, capercailzie [kæpə'keil(j)i] *n. Orn:* grand tétras; (grand) coq *m* de bruyère.

capful ['kæpful] *n.* pleine capsule (d'un liquide).

capillary [kə'piləri] *a.* (tube, pression, etc.) capillaire; *Anat:* **the c. vessels,** *n.pl.* **the capillaries,** les vaisseaux capillaires; les capillaires *mpl.*

capital¹ ['kæpit(ə)l] *n. Arch:* chapiteau *m*.

capital² **I.** *a.* **1.** (*a*) capital, -aux; **c. letter,** (lettre) capitale (*f*), (lettre) majuscule (*f*); **a c. A,** un grand A; (*b*) **c. city,** (ville) capitale (*f*). **2.** (*a*) *Jur:* **c. crime, offence,** crime capital, puni de mort; **c. punishment,** peine capitale, peine de mort; (*b*) **c. sin,** péché capital; **c. error,** erreur fatale; *Navy:* **c. ship,** bâtiment *m* de ligne; **of c. importance,** d'une importance capitale. **3.** *F:* excellent. **II.** *n.* **1.** (*a*) *Typ:* capitale *f*, majuscule *f*; (*on form*) **(write in) block capitals,** écrire en capitales d'imprimerie; (*b*) capitale (d'un pays). **2.** *Fin:* capital *m*, capitaux *mpl*, fonds *m*(*pl*); **working c.,** fonds, capital, d'exploitation; **to live on one's c.,** vivre sur son capital; **to make c. out of sth.,** profiter, tirer parti, de qch.; **c. assets,** actif immobilisé; **c. goods,** moyens *mpl* de production; **c. expenditure,** dépenses *fpl* en immobilisations; frais *mpl* d'équipement; **c. investment,** investissement *m* de capitaux; **c. gains tax,** impôt *m* sur les plus-values (en capital). **capitally** *adv. F:* admirablement (bien); à merveille.

capitalism ['kæpitəlizm] *n.* capitalisme *m*.

capitalist ['kæpitəlist] *n.* capitaliste *mf.*

capitalist(ic) [kæpitə'list(ik)] *a.* capitaliste.

capitalization [kæpitəlai'zeiʃ(ə)n] *n.* **1.** capitalisation *f* (des intérêts, etc.). **2.** emploi *m* des majuscules.

capitalize ['kæpitəlaiz] *v.tr.* **1.** capitaliser (une rente, etc.). **2.** écrire (un mot) avec une majuscule. **3.** *v.tr. & i.* **to c. (on) sth.,** tourner qch. à son avantage.

capitation [kæpi'teiʃ(ə)n] *n. Pol.Ec:* capitation *f*; *Adm:* **c. grant,** allocation *f* (de tant) par tête.

Capitol (the) [ðə'kæpitəl] *n.* le Capitole (de Rome, de Washington, etc.).

capitulate [kə'pitjuleit] *v.i.* capituler (**to,** devant).

capitulation [kəpitju'leiʃ(ə)n] *n.* **1.** (*a*) énumération *f* des chapitres, des articles (d'un traité, etc.). **2.** capitulation *f* (d'une place forte).

capon ['keipən] *n. Cu:* chapon *m*.

caprice [kə'pri:s] *n.* **1.** caprice *m*, lubie *f*. **2.** *Mus:* caprice.

capricious [kə'priʃəs] *a.* capricieux. **-ly** *adv.* capricieusement.

Capricorn ['kæprikɔ:n] *n. Astr:* le Capricorne; *Geog:* **the Tropic of C.,** le tropique du Capricorne.

capsicum ['kæpsikəm] *n.* **1.** *Bot:* piment *m*. **2.** *Cu:* piment, poivron *m*.

capsize [kæp'saiz] **1.** *v.i.* (*of boat*) chavirer. **2.** *v.tr.* faire chavirer (une embarcation).

capstan ['kæpst(ə)n] *n.* **1.** *Nau: etc:* cabestan *m*; poupée *f* de halage. **2.** *Mec.E:* revolver *m* (de tour); **c. lathe,** tour *f* à revolver.

capsular ['kæpsjulər] *a. Biol: etc:* capsulaire.

capsule ['kæpsju:l] *n.* capsule *f*; **space c.,** cabine, capsule, spatiale.

captain¹ ['kæptin] *n.* **1.** (*a*) chef *m*, capitaine *m*; **the great captains of industry,** les grands capitaines, les chefs, de l'industrie; (*b*) *Sp:* capitaine, chef, d'équipe; (*c*) *Scout:* chef(e)taine *f* (de guides); (*d*) *Nau:* capitaine, commandant *m* (d'un navire); (*e*) *Av:* commandant de bord; (*f*) capitaine (des pompiers). **2.** (*rank*) (*a*) *Mil:* capitaine; (*W.R.A.C.*) première classe; (*b*) *Navy:* capitaine de vaisseau; **c. of the fleet,** capitaine de pavillon; (*c*) *Mil.Av:* **group c.,** colonel *m* (d'aviation).

captain² *v.tr.* **1.** commander (une compagnie, etc.). **2.** conduire, mener (une expédition, etc.); *Sp:* être capitaine, chef, (d'une équipe).

captaincy ['kæptinsi] *n.* **1.** grade *m* de capitaine. **2.** *Sp:* commandement *m* de l'équipe.

caption¹ ['kæpʃ(ə)n] *n.* (*a*) (*in newspaper, book*) en-tête *m*, *pl.* en-têtes; chapeau *m*; (*b*) (*of illustration*) légende *f*; (*c*) *Cin:* sous-titre *m*, *pl.* sous-titres (d'un film muet); (*d*) *Journ:* rubrique *f*.

caption² *v.tr.* écrire la légende (d'une illustration).

captious ['kæpʃəs] *a.* **1.** (raisonnement) captieux, sophistique. **2.** (*of pers.*) pointilleux, chicaneur.

captivate ['kæptiveit] *v.tr.* charmer, captiver, séduire (tous les cœurs, etc.). **captivating** *a.* séduisant; captivant; enchanteur, -eresse.

captivation [kæpti'veiʃ(ə)n] *n.* séduction *f*; ensorcellement *m*.

captive ['kæptiv] **1.** *a.* (*a*) captif; **he was taken c.,** on l'a fait prisonnier; **c. balloon,** ballon captif; (*b*) **c. state,** état *m* de captivité. **2.** *n.* captif, -ive; prisonnier, -ière.

captivity [kæp'tiviti] *n.* captivité *f*; **animals in c.,** animaux *mpl* en captivité.

captor ['kæptər] *n.* (*a*) celui qui fait qn prisonnier; (*b*) ravisseur *m*.

capture¹ ['kæptjər] *n.* **1.** capture *f*, prise *f* (d'un navire, d'un prisonnier, d'un animal, etc.). **2.** (*thg or pers. taken*) prise.

capture² *v.tr.* **1.** capturer (un navire, un malfaiteur, un animal, etc.); prendre (une ville) (**from,** sur); s'emparer d'(un malfaiteur); captiver (l'attention, l'imagination, de qn); (*of artist, painting*) saisir (une ressemblance); *Com:* **to c. the market,** accaparer la vente. **2.** *W.Tel: etc:* capter (des ondes, une émission).

capuchin ['kæpu(t)ʃin] *n.* **1.** *Ecc:* **C.,** capucin, -ine. **2.** *Cost:* mante *f* à capuchon; capeline *f*.

car [kɑːr] *n.* **1.** *Lit:* char *m*; **triumphal c.,** char de triomphe. **2. (motor) c.,** automobile *f*, voiture *f*; **sports c.,** voiture (de) sport; **racing c.,** voiture de course; **c. park,** parc *m* de stationnement; *F:* parking *m*; **to go by c.,** aller en voiture. **3.** *Rail:* (*a*) *NAm:* voiture, wagon *m*; **freight c.,** wagon à, de, marchandises; **dump c.,** wagon à bascule; (*b*) **dining, restaurant, c.,** wagon-restaurant *m*, *pl.* wagons-restaurants; **buffet, refreshment, c.,** voiture-bar *f*, *pl.* voitures-bars; **sleeping c.,** wagon-lit *m*, *pl.* wagons-lits. **4.** (*a*) nacelle *f* (d'un pont transbordeur, *Aer:* d'un ballon); (*b*) *NAm:* cabine *f* (d'un ascenseur).

carafe [kə'ræf, -'rɑːf] *n.* carafe *f*; carafon *m*.

caramel ['kærəmel] *n.* **1.** caramel *m*; **c. cream, cream c.,** crème caramel; **c. custard,** crème (renversée) au caramel. **2.** bonbon *m* au caramel. **3.** (couleur *f*) caramel *inv*.

caramelize ['kærəməlaiz] **1.** *v.tr.* caraméliser. **2.** *v.i.* se caraméliser.

carapace ['kærəpeis] *n.* *Crust:* carapace *f*.

carat ['kærət] *n.* *Meas:* **1.** (*for diamonds*) **metric c.,** carat *m* (de 200 milligrammes). **2.** (*for gold*) carat (de fin); **eighteen-c. gold,** or à dix-huit carats.

caravan ['kærəvæn] *n.* **1.** caravane *f*; convoi *m* des déserts; **to travel in c.,** voyager en convoi. **2.** roulotte *f* (de romanichel, de forains); remorque *f*, roulotte, de camping; caravane; **c. site,** camping *m* (pour caravanes).

caravan(n)ing [kærə'væniŋ] *n.* camping *m* (en caravane).

caraway ['kærəwei] *n.* *Bot:* carvi *m*, cumin *m* des prés; **c. seeds,** graines *fpl* de carvi.

carbide ['kɑːbaid] *n.* *Ch:* *Ind:* carbure *m*.

carbine ['kɑːbain] *n.* **1.** (*a*) carabine *f*. **2.** *U.S:* mitraillette *f*.

carbohydrate [kɑːbou'haidreit] *n.* *Ch:* hydrate *m* de carbone; *pl.* (*in dieting*) les glucides.

carbolic [kɑː'bɔlik] *a.* *Ch:* phénique; **c. acid,** acide *m* phénique, phénol *m*.

carbon ['kɑːbən] *n.* **1.** *Ch:* carbone *m*; **c. dioxide,** gaz *m* carbonique; **c. monoxide,** oxyde *m* de carbone; *Prehist:* **c. dating,** datation *f* au carbone 14. **2.** (*a*) *Metall:* **powdered c.,** charbon *m* en poudre; **c. electrode,** électrode *f* de charbon; (*b*) *Typew:* **c. (paper),** (papier *m*) carbone; **c. (copy),** double *m* (au carbone).

carbonaceous [kɑːbə'neiʃəs] *a.* **1.** *Ch:* carboné. **2.** *Geol:* carbonifère.

carbonate ['kɑːbəneit] *n.* *Ch:* carbonate *m*.

carbonic [kɑː'bɔnik] *a.* *Ch:* carbonique.

carboniferous [kɑːbə'nifərəs] *a.* & *n.* carbonifère (*m*).

carbonization [kɑːbən(a)i'zeiʃ(ə)n] *n.* **1.** carbonisation *f* (du bois, etc.). **2.** *I.C.E:* *etc:* encrassement *m*, calaminage *m*.

carbonize ['kɑːbənaiz] **1.** *v.tr.* (*a*) *Ch:* carboniser, *I.C.E:* carburer; (*b*) *Ind:* carboniser, charbonner (du bois, etc.). **2.** *v.i.* *I.C.E:* *etc:* s'encrasser, se calaminer.

carborundum [kɑːbə'rʌndəm] *n.* carborundum *m*.

carboy ['kɑːbɔi] *n.* bonbonne *f*, ballon *m*.

carbuncle ['kɑːbʌŋkl] *n.* **1.** *Lap:* escarboucle *f*. **2.** *Med:* furoncle *m*.

carburetter, carburettor, *NAm:* **carburetor** [kɑːbju'retər] *n.* *I.C.E:* carburateur *m*.

carcass, *occ.* **carcase** ['kɑːkəs] *n.* **1.** cadavre *m*, carcasse *f* (d'un animal). **3.** carcasse (d'une maison, d'un navire); charpente *f* (d'une maison).

carcinogen [kɑː'sinoudʒen] *n.* *Med:* substance *f* cancérigène, cancérogène.

carcinogenic [kɑːsinou'dʒenik] *a.* *Med:* cancérigène.

carcinoma [kɑːsi'noumə] *n.* *Med:* carcinome *m*.

card¹ [kɑːd] *n.* **1. playing c.,** carte *f* à jouer; **court c.,** *NAm:* **face c.,** figure *f*; **pack,** *NAm:* **deck, of cards,** jeu *m* de cartes; **to play one's cards well,** (i) bien jouer ses cartes; (ii) *Fig:* bien jouer son jeu; **to play one's last c.,** jouer sa dernière carte, son va-tout; **to hold all the winning cards,** avoir tous les atouts dans son jeu, en main; **c. player,** joueur, -euse, de cartes; **to show one's cards,** (i) montrer, découvrir, son jeu; (ii) jouer cartes sur table; (iii) dévoiler ses batteries; **to put one's cards on the table,** mettre cartes sur table; **to have a c. up one's sleeve,** avoir encore une ressource; **it is on,** *NAm:* **in, the cards that . . .,** il est bien possible, il se pourrait fort bien, que . . .; *F:* **he's a (great) c.,** c'est un original. **2.** (*a*) **visiting c.,** carte de visite; **business c.,** carte d'adresse, d'affaires; (*b*) **invitation c.,** carte d'invitation; **correspondence c.,** carte correspondance; **Christmas c.,** carte de Noël; **cigarette c.,** image *f* offerte avec un paquet de cigarettes; **identity c.,** carte d'identité; **banker's c., cheque c.,** carte bancaire; (*c*) (*for card index*) fiche *f*; **c. index,** fichier *m*; *Cmptr:* *etc:* **punched c.,** carte perforée; (*d*) *Golf:* carte du parcours; *Rac:* programme *m* des courses; **score c.,** carton *m*; (*e*) carte (de sécurité sociale); *F:* **to get one's cards,** être renvoyé; (*f*) *O:* **dance c.,** carnet *m* de bal; (*g*) carte (de laine, de boutons).

card² *v.tr.* **1.** mettre (des notes, etc.) sur fiche. **2.** encarter (des boutons, etc.).

card³ *n.* *Tex:* carde *f*, peigne *m*.

card⁴ *v.tr.* *Tex:* carder, peigner (la laine, etc.). **carding** *n.* cardage *m*, peignage *m*; **c. machine,** cardeuse *f*.

cardamom ['kɑːdəməm] *n.* **1.** *Bot:* cardamome *m*. **2.** *Com:* graine *f* de cardamome.

cardboard ['kɑːdbɔːd] *n.* carton *m*, cartonnage *m*; **corrugated c.,** carton ondulé.

cardiac ['kɑːdiæk] *a.* (*a*) *Anat:* (muscle, etc.) cardiaque; (*b*) *Med:* cardiaque; (arrêt) du cœur.

cardigan ['kɑːdigən] *n.* cardigan *m*; gilet *m* (de laine).

cardinal [kɑːdin(ə)l] **I.** *a.* **1.** cardinal, -aux; **c. numbers,** nombres cardinaux; **the four c. points,** les quatre points cardinaux; **c. virtues,** vertus cardinales. **2.** (*a*) (*colour*) pourpre, cardinal *inv*; (*b*) *Bot:* **c. flower,** cardinale *f*. **II.** *n.* *Ecc:* cardinal *m*, *pl.* cardinaux.

cardiogram ['kɑːdiougræm] *n.* *Med:* cardiogramme *m*.

cardiograph ['kɑːdiougræf] *n.* *Med:* cardiographe *m*.

cardiologist [kɑːdi'ɔlədʒist] *n.* *Med:* cardiologue *mf*.

cardiology [kɑːdi'ɔlədʒi] *n.* *Med:* cardiologie *f*.

cardiovascular ['kɑːdiou'væskjulər] *a.* *Med:* cardio-vasculaire, *pl.* cardio-vasculaires.

cardsharp(er) ['kɑːdʃɑːp(ər)] *n.* tricheur *m*; fileur *m* de cartes.

care¹ ['kɛər] *n.* **1.** souci *m*, inquiétude *f*; **to be full of cares,** être plein de soucis; **life of c.,** vie pleine de soucis. **2.** soin(s) *m*(*pl*), attention *f*; précaution(s) *f*(*pl*); **constant c.,** soins continuels, assidus; **to do sth. with great c.,** faire qch. avec beaucoup de soin; **c. for details,** attention aux détails; **to drive without due c.,** conduire avec négligence; **to take c. of s.o., of sth.,** (i) prendre, avoir, soin de qn, de qch.; (ii) s'occuper de qn, de qch.; (iii) *U.S:* *F:* écarter (un obstacle, etc.); **to take c. to do sth.,** avoir (bien) soin, prendre (bien) garde, de faire qch.; **take c.!** faites attention! prenez garde! **take c. of yourself,** (i) soignez-vous bien; (ii) prenez des précautions; **to take c. of one's health,** ménager sa santé; (*on parcel, etc.*) **glass, with c.,** fragile. **3.** soin(s), charge *f*; entretien *m* d'une machine, etc.); *Adm* **children in c.,** enfants assistés; **to put s.o., sth., in s.o.'s c.,**

confier qn, qch., aux soins de qn; **write to me c. of Mrs X, c/o Mrs X,** *U.S:* **in c. of Mrs X,** écrivez-moi aux bons soins de Mme X, chez Mme X; **to be in, under, s.o.'s c.,** être confié aux soins de qn. **4. cares of State,** responsabilités *fpl* d'État.

care² *v.i.* **1.** se soucier, s'occuper, se préoccuper (**about,** de); **people who c.,** des gens compatissants; **that's all he cares about,** il n'y a que cela qui l'intéresse; **I don't c. what he says,** peu m'importe ce qu'il dit; **what do I c.?** que m'importe? qu'est-ce que cela me fait? **who cares?** qu'est-ce que ça fait? **I don't c. whether he likes it or not,** que cela lui plaise ou non, ça m'est parfaitement égal; **for all I c.,** pour (tout) ce que ça me fait; **I don't c.! as if I cared!** ça m'est égal! je m'en fiche! **I couldn't c. less,** *F:* **I don't c. a damn, two hoots,** je m'en fiche éperdument; je m'en fous; **couldn't-c.-less attitude,** je-m'en-foutisme *m.* **2. to c. for invalids, children,** soigner des malades, des enfants; **to look well cared for,** avoir un air soigné, une apparence soignée. **3.** (*a*) **to c. for s.o.,** aimer qn; avoir un penchant pour qn; **he doesn't c. for her,** elle ne lui plaît pas; (*b*) **I don't c. for this music,** cette musique ne me dit rien; **would you c. to come with me?** voulez-vous m'accompagner? aimeriez-vous m'accompagner? **if you c. to join us,** si cela vous plaît de venir avec nous, d'être des nôtres. **caring** *a.* (*of pers., society, etc.*) compatissant; humain; humanitaire.

careen [kə'riːn] *Nau:* **1.** *v.tr.* (*a*) abattre, mettre, (un navire) en carène; (*b*) caréner (un navire). **2.** *v.i.* (*a*) (*of ship*) se coucher; (*b*) *NAm:* (*of car, etc.*) pencher sur le côté. **careening** *n. Nau:* carénage *m.*

career¹ [kə'riər] *n.* **1.** course (précipitée). **2.** carrière *f*; *Sch:* **careers master,** orienteur professionnel; **c. diplomat,** diplomate *m* de carrière; **c. girl,** femme qui veut faire une carrière.

career² *v.i.* courir rapidement, follement; **to c. along,** aller à toute vitesse.

careerist [kə'riərist] *n.* arriviste *mf*; carriériste *mf.*

carefree ['kɛəfriː] *a.* libre de soucis; insouciant; sans souci; **c. childhood,** enfance insouciante.

careful ['kɛəful] *a.* **1.** soigneux (**of,** de); attentif (**of,** à); **to be c. of one's reputation,** être soucieux, jaloux, de sa réputation; **to be c. with one's money,** regarder à ses sous; **to be c. to do sth.,** avoir soin de faire qch.; veiller à faire qch.; **be c. you don't fall, not to fall,** faites attention à, de, ne pas tomber; **be c. what you say,** faites attention à ce que vous dites; **(be) c.!** faites attention! **c. English speech,** l'anglais parlé surveillé; **c. consideration of a question,** examen attentif, approfondi, d'une question. **2.** prudent, circonspect; **c. answer,** une réponse bien pesée, réfléchie. **-fully** *adv.* **1.** soigneusement, avec soin; attentivement. **2.** prudemment; **to live c.,** (i) soigner sa santé; (ii) vivre avec économie.

carefulness ['kɛəfulnis] *n.* **1.** soin *m*, attention *f.* **2.** prudence *f.*

careless ['kɛəlis] *a.* **1.** (*a*) insouciant, peu soucieux (**of, about,** de); nonchalant; étourdi; **a c. person,** un, une, sans-souci *inv*; (*b*) (observation) inconsidérée, irréfléchie, faite à la légère; (faute) d'inattention. **2.** négligent, sans soin; **accused of c. driving,** accusé de négligence au volant; **to be c. about one's appearance,** être négligé de sa personne. **-ly** *adv.* **1.** avec insouciance, nonchalamment; étourdiment. **2.** négligemment, sans soin.

carelessness ['kɛəlisnis] *n.* **1.** (*a*) insouciance *f*; (*b*) inattention *f*, étourderie *f.* **2.** manque *m* de soin; négligence *f.*

caress¹ [kə'res] *n.* caresse *f.*

caress² *v.tr.* caresser.

caret ['kærət] *n. Typ:* signe *m* d'omission.

caretaker ['kɛəteikər] *n.* **1.** concierge *mf* (d'un immeuble, etc.); gardien *m* (d'un musée, etc.). **2.** *Pol:* **c. cabinet,** cabinet *m* intérimaire.

careworn ['kɛəwɔːn] *a.* (visage, etc.) rongé, usé, par les soucis.

cargo, pl. **-oes** ['kɑːgou, -ouz] *n. Nau: Av:* (*a*) cargaison *f*, chargement *m*; **full c.,** plein chargement; **general, mixed, c.,** cargaison mixte; **c. boat, ship,** cargo *m*; **c. plane,** avion-cargo *m*, *pl.* avions-cargos; cargo aérien.

Caribbean [kæri'bi(ː)ən] *a. & n. Geog:* **the C. (Sea),** la Mer des Caraïbes, des Antilles; **the C. islands,** les Antilles *fpl.*

caribou [kæri'buː] *n. Z:* caribou *m*, *pl.* -ous.

caricature¹ ['kærikətjər] *n.* caricature *f.*

caricature² *v.tr.* caricaturer.

caricaturist [kærikə'tjuːrist] *n.* caricaturiste *m.*

caries ['kɛəriiːz] *n. Med: Dent:* carie *f.*

carillon [kə'riljən] *n. Mus:* carillon *m.*

carless ['kɑːlis] *a.* sans voiture.

carload ['kɑːloud] *n.* **1.** pleine voiture. **2.** *NAm: Rail:* (*a*) plein wagon (de marchardises); (*b*) quantité *f* (de marchandises) nécessaire pour remplir un wagon.

Carmelite ['kɑːməlait] *n.* **C. (nun),** carmélite *f.*

carmine ['kɑːm(a)in] **1.** *n.* carmin *m.* **2.** *a.* carminé; carmin *inv*; (lèvres) de carmin.

carnage ['kɑːnidʒ] *n.* carnage *m.*

carnal ['kɑːn(ə)l] *a.* charnel; (i) sensuel; (ii) sexuel; **c. sins,** péchés *mpl* de la chair; **c. knowledge,** connaissance charnelle. **-ally** *adv.* charnellement.

carnation¹ [kɑː'neiʃ(ə)n] **1.** *n.* carnation *f*; incarnat *m.* **2.** *a.* (teint) incarnat, incarnadin.

carnation² *n. Bot:* œillet *m.*

carnival ['kɑːniv(ə)l] *n.* **1.** carnaval *m*, *pl.* -als (avant le carême). **2.** réjouissances *fpl*; fête *f.*

carnivora [kɑː'nivərə] *n.pl. Z:* carnivores *mpl.*

carnivore ['kɑːnivɔːr] *n.* **1.** *Z:* carnivore *m.* **2.** *Bot:* plante *f* carnivore.

carnivorous [kɑː'niv(ə)rəs] *a.* **1.** (*of animal*) carnivore, carnassier. **2.** (*of pers., plant*) carnivore.

carol¹ ['kær(ə)l] *n.* chant *m*, chanson *f*; *esp.* **Christmas c.,** noël *m*; **c. singer,** chanteur, -euse, de noëls.

carol² *v.i. & tr.* **(carolled,** *NAm: also* **caroled)** *Poet:* (*a*) chanter (joyeusement); (*b*) (*of lark*) tire-lirer; grisoller.

Carolina [kærə'lainə] *Pr.n. Geog:* Caroline *f*; **South, North, C.,** Caroline du Sud, du Nord; **the Carolinas,** la Caroline du Sud et la Caroline du Nord.

Carolingian [kærou'lin(d)ʒiən] *Hist:* **1.** *a.* carolingien. **2.** *n.* Carolingien *m.*

carom ['kærəm] *n. NAm: Bill:* carambolage *m.*

carotid [kə'rɔtid] *a. & n. Anat:* (artère) carotide (*f*).

carouse [kə'rauz] *v.i.* faire la fête, *F:* la bombe.

carp¹ [kɑːp] *n. Ich:* (*pl.* **carp**) carpe *f.*

carp² *v.i.* épiloguer, gloser; **to c. at s.o.,** censurer qn; **to c. at sth.,** trouver à redire à qch. **carping 1.** *a.* (critique) pointilleuse, malveillante. **2.** *n.* censure *f.*

Carpathian [kɑː'peiθiən] *a. & n.pl. Geog:* **the C. (Mountains),** les (Monts) Carpates *mpl.*

carpel ['kɑːpel] *n. Bot:* carpelle *m*, carpophylle *m.*

carpenter¹ ['kɑːpintər] *n.* charpentier *m*; menuisier *m* en bâtiments; *Nau:* **ship's c.,** matelot *m* charpentier.

carpenter² **1.** *v.i.* faire de la charpenterie. **2.** *v.tr.* charpenter (qch.).

carpentry ['kɑːpintri] *n.* **1.** (*a*) charpenterie *f*; (*b*) grosse menuiserie. **2.** charpente *f*; les bois *mpl* (d'un édifice, etc.).

carpet¹ ['kɑːpit] *n.* (*a*) tapis *m*; **fitted c.,** tapis ajusté; moquette *f*; **c. sweeper,** balai *m* mécanique; **c. tack,** fixe-tapis *m inv*; **c. slippers,** pantoufles *fpl;* **to lay a c.,** poser un tapis; *F:* **to lay down the red c. for s.o., to give s.o. the red-c. treatment,** recevoir qn la croix et la bannière; **to sweep (sth.) under the c.,**

enterrer (une question); **to be on the c.,** (i) (*of question*) être sur le tapis; (ii) (*of pers.*) être sur la sellette; **to have, put, s.o. on the c.,** réprimander qn; (*b*) tapis (de verdure, de fleurs, etc.).

carpet² *v.tr.* **1.** recouvrir (le plancher) d'un tapis, d'une moquette; moquetter. **2.** *F: O:* réprimander (qn). **carpeting** *n.* (*a*) pose *f* de tapis, de moquette; (*b*) *coll.* moquette.

carpetbagger ['kɑːpitbægər] *n. esp. U.S: F:* **1.** candidat (au parlement) étranger à la circonscription. **2.** aventurier *m* politique.

carport ['kɑːpɔːt] *n. Aut:* abri-garage *m, pl.* abris-garages.

carriage ['kæridʒ] *n.* **1.** (i) port *m,* transport *m;* (ii) *Com:* (frais *mpl* de) port; *Com:* **c. free,** franc de port; franco; **c. paid,** (en) port payé; **c. forward,** (en) port dû. **2.** port, maintien *m,* tenue *f* (d'une personne); **free, easy, c.,** allure dégagée. **3.** (*a*) *Veh:* voiture *f;* équipage *m,* attelage *m;* **open, closed, c.,** voiture découverte, fermée; **c. and pair,** voiture à deux chevaux; **c. drive,** avenue *f* pour voitures; **c. entrance,** porte cochère; (*b*) **baby c.,** voiture d'enfant; **invalid c.,** voiture d'infirme; (*c*) *Rail:* voiture, wagon *m* (de chemin de fer). **4.** *Tchn:* (*a*) *Artil:* **gun c.,** affût *m; Navy:* **launching c.,** chariot *m* (de torpille); (*b*) *Veh:* train *m* (de la voiture); (*c*) *Mec.E:* chariot (d'un tour, d'une machine à écrire, etc.).

carriageway ['kæridʒwei] *n.* chaussée *f;* **dual c.,** route à quatre voies.

carrier ['kæriər] *n.* **1.** (*a*) *Med: etc:* porteur, -euse (d'une maladie, de germes, de bacilles); (*b*) *Com:* (i) camionneur *m;* (ii) commissionnaire *m* expéditeur; transporteur *m;* (iii) voiturier *m,* messager *m; Jur:* **common c.,** (i) voiturier public; (ii) entrepreneur *m* de messageries maritimes. **2.** (*a*) support *m;* (*b*) **luggage c.,** porte-bagages *m inv* (de bicyclette, etc.); **c. bag,** (grand) sac (en papier, en plastique); (*c*) cartouche *f* (pour pigeon voyageur, etc.); (*d*) *Ind:* transporteur *m;* **overhead c.,** transporteur aérien. **3.** (*a*) *Navy:* **aircraft c.,** porte-avions *m inv; Av:* **troop c.,** (avion *m* de) transport (*m*) de troupes; *Mil:* **armoured personnel c.,** véhicule blindé de transport de troupes; (*b*) *Nau:* **bulk c.,** navire pour le transport en vrac (du grain, etc.). **4.** *Orn:* **c. pigeon,** pigeon voyageur.

carrier-based ['kæriə'beist] *a. Av: Navy:* embarqué; **c.-b. aircraft,** l'aviation embarquée.

carrion ['kæriən] *n.* charogne *f; Orn:* **c. crow,** corneille noire, corbine *f.*

carrot ['kærət] *n. Hort:* carotte *f; F:* **carrots, c. top,** (i) cheveux *mpl* rouges; (ii) (*pers.*) rouquin *m;* poil *m* de carotte.

carroty ['kærəti] *a. F:* (*of pers., hair*) roux, *f* rousse.

car(r)ousel [kærə'zel] *n.* (*a*) *NAm:* chevaux *mpl* de bois; (*b*) (*at airport*) carrousel *m* (pour bagages).

carry ['kæri] *v.tr.* **(carried) 1.** porter (un enfant, un fardeau, etc.); transporter (des marchandises, etc.); camionner (des marchandises); **I don't c. much money about, on, me,** je ne porte jamais beaucoup d'argent sur moi; **the bus carried us to our destination,** l'autobus nous a conduits, transportés, à notre destination; **a memory that he will c. with him to the grave,** un souvenir qu'il emportera dans la tombe; *Nau:* **we were carrying livestock,** nous avions du bétail à bord. **2.** (*of wires, etc.*) conduire, transmettre (le son, etc.); (*of pipes*) amener (l'eau, etc.). **3. to c. death and destruction everywhere,** porter partout le carnage; **to c. sth. in one's head,** retenir qch. dans sa tête. **4.** enlever (une forteresse); emporter (une position) d'assaut; **to c. all before one,** (i) remporter tous les prix; (ii) vaincre toutes les résistances; triompher sur toute la ligne; **to c. one's point,** établir la validité d'un argument. **5.** (i) adopter, (ii) faire adopter, faire passer (une proposition); **the bill was carried,** le project a été adopté. **6.** (*a*) porter (un revolver, une montre) sur soi; (*of pers., opinion*) **to c. weight, authority,** avoir du poids, de l'autorité; (*of money*) **to c. interest,** porter intérêt; (*b*) *Com:* tenir (un article); avoir (des marchandises) en magasin, en dépôt. **7.** (*of woman*) **to c. a child,** être enceinte. **8. to c. one's head high,** porter la tête haute; **to c. oneself well, badly,** se tenir bien, mal. **9.** *Arch: Const:* porter, supporter (une poutre, une voûte). **10.** *Mth:* **to c. a figure,** retenir un chiffre; **c. two and seven are nine,** deux de retenue et sept font neuf. **11.** *v.i.* (*a*) (*of gun, sound, etc.*) porter; **his voice carries well,** il a une voix qui porte bien; (*b*) *U.S:* (*of resolution, etc.*) passer. **carry along** *v.tr.* emporter, entraîner (qn, qch.); **mud carried along by the stream,** vase charriée par le ruisseau. **carry away** *v.tr.* (*a*) emporter, enlever (qch.); entraîner, emmener (qn); (*b*) **to be carried away,** être emporté, enlevé, entraîné (par une émotion, l'enthousiasme, etc.). **carry back** *v.tr.* (*a*) rapporter (qch.); ramener (qn); (*b*) reporter (qch.); remmener (qn); (*c*) **that carries me back to my youth,** cela me rappelle ma jeunesse. **carry forward** *v.tr.* (*a*) avancer (qch.); (*b*) *Book-k:* **to c. an item forward,** reporter un article; **carried forward,** report *m;* à reporter. **carrying 1.** *a.* (*a*) **c. party,** équipe *f* de porteurs; (*b*) *Mch:* (*of locomotive*) **c. axle,** essieu porteur. **2.** *n.* (*a*) port *m,* transport *m;* (*of vehicle*) **c. capacity,** charge *f* utile; (*b*) adoption *f,* vote *m* (d'un projet de loi, etc.); *F:* **carrying(s) on,** scène *f.* **carry off** *v.tr.* (*a*) emporter (qch.); emmener (qn); enlever, emporter (qn); (*b*) remporter (le prix); (*c*) faire passer, faire accepter (qch. d'insolite); *F:* **to c. it off,** (i) faire passer la chose; (ii) réussir le coup. **carry on 1.** *v.tr.* poursuivre, continuer (un travail); continuer (une tradition); exercer (un commerce, un métier); entretenir (une correspondance); soutenir (une conversation). **2.** *v.i.* (*a*) **to c. on during s.o.'s absence,** continuer le travail, diriger les affaires, pendant l'absence de qn; *Adm:* assurer l'intérim; **c. on!** continuez! (*b*) persévérer, persister; **I shall c. on to the end,** j'irai jusqu'au bout; (*c*) *F:* se comporter; **I don't like the way she carries on,** je n'aime pas ses façons; (*d*) *F:* faire des scènes; s'emporter; **don't c. on like that!** ne vous emballez pas comme ça! (*e*) *P:* **to c. on with s.o.,** avoir une liaison avec qn. **carry out** *v.tr.* (*a*) porter (qch.) dehors, hors de la salle, etc.; transporter (qn) au grand air; (*b*) mettre à exécution (un projet, une menace, une décision); effectuer (une expérience, *Av:* un vol); remplir (les instructions de qn); mettre en pratique (une théorie); exécuter (un programme); exercer (un mandat); donner suite à (une idée, *Com:* une commande); satisfaire à (une obligation, un désir); se décharger (d'une commission); mener à bonne fin (un travail); s'acquitter (d'une tâche, d'une fonction); appliquer (la loi, un principe); **to c. out a procedure,** suivre un mode de procédure. **carry over** *v.tr.* (*a*) transporter (qch.) de l'autre côté; (faire) passer (qn) (dans le bac, etc.); (*b*) *Book-k:* reporter (une somme) d'une page à une autre; **to c. over a balance,** transporter un solde; (*c*) *Typ:* **lines carried over,** report *m.* **carry through** *v.tr.* (*a*) mener (une entreprise) à bien, à bonne fin, à bon terme; exécuter (un travail, un calcul); (*b*) **his strong constitution carried him through his illness,** sa forte santé l'aida à surmonter cette maladie.

carryall ['kæriɔːl] *n.* **1.** *U.S: Veh:* cariole *f.* **2.** (sac *m*) fourre-tout (*m*) *inv.*

carrycot ['kærikɔt] *n.* moïse *m;* porte-bébé *m inv.*

carry-on ['kæri'ɔn] *n. F:* (i) scène *f;* (ii) affaire scandaleuse; **what a c.-on!** quelle histoire!

carsick ['kɑːsik] *a.* **to be c.,** avoir le mal de voiture, de la route.

carsickness ['kɑːsiknis] *n.* mal *m* de voiture, de la route.

cart[1] [kɑːt] *n.* charrette *f* (à deux roues); (*with springs*) carriole *f*; **bullock, ox, c.,** char *m* à bœufs; **tip c.,** tombereau *m*; **c. track,** chemin charretier; *Fig:* **to put the c. before the horse,** mettre la charrue devant les bœufs.

cart[2] *v.tr.* charrier, voiturer (qch.); **they carted the rubbish away, off,** ils ont enlevé, emporté, les ordures; *F:* **I'm tired of carting these huge parcels (around, about),** j'en ai assez de (trans)porter ces gros colis.

cartage ['kɑːtidʒ] *n.* **1.** charroi *m*, charriage *m*; camionnage *m*. **2.** (prix *m* de) camionnage *m*.

cartel [kɑː'tel] *n. Ind: etc:* cartel *m*.

carter ['kɑːtər] *n.* (*a*) charretier *m*; (*b*) camionneur *m*.

Cartesian [kɑː'tiːziən] *a. Phil:* cartésien.

carthorse ['kɑːthɔːs] *n.* cheval *m* de charrette.

Carthusian [kɑː'θjuːziən] *a.* & *n.* **1.** chartreux, -euse. **2.** (élève ou ancien élève) de l'école de *Charterhouse*.

cartilage ['kɑːtilidʒ] *n.* cartilage *m*.

cartload ['kɑːtloud] *n.* charretée *f*, voiturée *f* (**of,** de); tombereau *m* (de charbon, de fumier).

cartographer [kɑː'tɔgrəfər] *n.* cartographe *m*.

cartography [kɑː'tɔgrəfi] *n.* cartographie *f*.

cartomancy ['kɑːtəmænsi] *n.* cartomancie *f*.

carton ['kɑːtən] *n.* (*a*) (boîte *f* en) carton (*m*); (*b*) pot *m* (en carton, en plastique) (de crème, etc.); carton (de lait, etc.).

cartoon [kɑː'tuːn] *n.* **1.** *Art:* carton *m*. **2.** (*a*) dessin *m* (humoristique ou satirique); **strip c.,** bande dessinée; (*b*) portrait caricaturé; caricature *f*; (*c*) *Cin:* **(animated) c.,** dessin animé.

cartoonist [kɑː'tuːnist] *n.* caricaturiste *m*; dessinateur, -trice (de dessins humoristiques, satiriques).

cartridge ['kɑːtridʒ] *n.* **1.** (*a*) cartouche *f* (d'arme à feu); **blank c.,** cartouche à blanc; **c. clip,** chargeur *m*; **c. belt,** (i) ceinture-cartouchière *f*, *pl.* ceintures-cartouchières; (ii) bande-chargeur souple, articulée (*pl.* bandes-chargeurs) (de mitraillette); (*b*) *Artil:* gargousse *f* (de grosse pièce). **2.** cartouche (à film, à encre, *El:* de fusible, etc.). **3.** *Rec: etc:* (i) robot *m*; (ii) cassette *f*; *Rec:* cellule *f*. **4.** *Ind: Art:* **c. paper,** papier *m* à cartouches, papier-cartouche *m*.

cartwheel ['kɑːt(h)wiːl] *n.* **1.** roue *f* de charrette. **2.** *Gym:* **to turn cartwheels,** faire la roue.

cartwright ['kɑːtrait] *n.* charron *m*.

carve [kɑːv] *v.tr.* **1.** (*a*) sculpter (du marbre, etc.); graver, ciseler (un dessin, un nom, etc., sur le marbre, etc.); **to c. a statue in, out of, marble,** sculpter une statue dans le marbre; **carved lion,** lion sculpté; **to c. out a career for oneself,** se faire une carrière; (*b*) *v.i.* **to c. in marble, wood,** sculpter dans le marbre, le bois; (*c*) (*with pass. force*) **wood that carves well, badly,** bois *m*, qui se prête bien, mal, à la sculpture. **2.** (*a*) découper (de la viande); dépecer (une volaille); (*b*) **to c. s.o. up,** (i) attaquer qn avec un couteau; (ii) critiquer qn brutalement. **carving** *n.* **1.** (*a*) sculptage *m*; (*b*) *Art:* sculpture *f*; gravure *f*; ciselure *f*; **wood c.,** sculpture sur bois. **2.** découpage *m* (de la viande); **c. knife, fork,** couteau *m*, fourchette *f*, à découper.

carver ['kɑːvər] *n.* **1.** sculpteur *m* (sur bois); ciseleur *m*. **2.** (*a*) (*pers.*) découpeur, -euse; (*b*) couteau *m* à découper. **3.** fauteuil *m* de table (qu'occupe le chef de famille).

carwash ['kɑːwɔʃ] *n.* (*a*) lavage *m* de voitures; (*b*) lave-auto *m*.

caryatid, *pl.* **-ides, -ids** [kæri'ætid, -idiːz, -idz] *n. Arch:* cariatide *f*.

cascade[1] [kæs'keid] *n.* chute *f* d'eau; cascade *f*.

cascade[2] *v.i.* tomber en cascade; cascader.

case[1] [keis] **1.** cas *m*; *Jur:* **a c. in point,** un cas d'espèce; **to put the c. clearly,** exposer clairement le cas, la situation; **if that is the c.,** s'il en est ainsi; **should that be the c.,** le cas échéant; **that would meet the c.,** cela ferait (bien) l'affaire; **it's a c. of now or never,** il s'agit de saisir l'occasion, de faire vite; **in c. of emergency, accident, need,** en cas d'urgence, d'accident, de besoin; **in c. he isn't there,** au cas, dans le cas, où il n'y serait pas; **in any c.,** en tout cas; de toute façon; **in that c.,** en ce cas; **in such a c., in such cases,** en pareil cas; en pareille circonstance; **in his c.,** dans son cas; **just in c.,** à titre de précaution; **as the c. may be,** selon le cas; selon les circonstances; **in most cases,** dans la plupart des cas. **2.** (*a*) *Med:* cas (de jaunisse, de scarlatine, etc.); **c. history,** antécédents *mpl*; histoire *f* de la maladie; **c. load,** (nombre *m* de) dossiers (d'un médecin, d'une assistante sociale, etc.); (*b*) malade *mf*; **heart c.,** cardiaque *mf*; (*c*) *F:* **he's a c.,** c'est un drôle de type. **3.** *Jur: etc:* (*a*) cause *f*; affaire *f*; **civil, criminal, c.,** affaire civile, criminelle; **divorce c.,** procès *m* en divorce; **famous cases,** causes célèbres; **test c.,** cas dont la solution fait jurisprudence; précédent *m*; **c. law,** jurisprudence *f*; **to state the c.,** faire l'exposé des faits; (*b*) **to put the c. for the prisoner,** présenter la défense du prévenu; (*in criminal trial*) **the c. for the Crown,** l'accusation *f*; **there is no c. against you,** vous êtes hors de cause; **the c. for s.o., sth.,** les arguments *mpl* en faveur de qn, qch.; **to put up a strong c. for s.o.,** (i) prendre le parti de qn, défendre qn; (ii) recommander qn très chaudement. **4.** *Gram:* cas; **c. endings,** flexions casuelles.

case[2] *n.* **1. (packing) c.,** caisse *f*, boîte *f* (d'emballage); **c. of wine,** caisse (de 12 bouteilles) de vin. **2.** (*a*) étui *m* (à lunettes, à cigarettes, etc.); coffret *m*, écrin *m* (pour bijoux); trousse *f* (d'instruments); boite *f* (de violon); gaine *f* (de poignard, de pistolet, de momie); **record c.,** mallette *f* porte-disques; **dressing c.,** nécessaire *m*, trousse, de toilette; **card c.,** porte-cartes *m inv*; (*b*) **(display) c.,** vitrine *f*. **3.** (*a*) coffre *m*, caisse (de piano); buffet *m* (d'orgue); caisse (d'horloge); (*b*) boîtier *m* (de montre, etc.); palastre *m*, coffre (de serrure); *Sm.a:* douille *f*, étui (de cartouche); (*c*) chemise *f*, enveloppe *f* (de cylindre de moteur); bâche *f* (de turbine); *Aut:* carter *m* (du différentiel, etc.); *I.C.E:* **crank c.,** carter (du moteur). **4.** (*a*) *Bookb:* couverture *f*; (*b*) **filling c.,** carton *m*. **5.** *Typ:* casse *f*; **lower c.,** bas *m* de casse; **lower-c. letter,** minuscule *f*; **upper c.,** haut *m* de casse; **upper-c. letter,** majuscule *f*, capitale *f*.

case[3] *v.tr.* **1.** encaisser, emballer (des marchandises), mettre (des marchandises) en caisse(s). **2.** (*a*) envelopper (**with,** de); chemiser (une chaudière, un cylindre); bâcher (une turbine); (*b*) *Bookb:* cartonner (un livre). **3.** *P:* **to c. a joint,** prospecter, examiner les lieux (avant un cambriolage). **casing** *n.* **1.** (*a*) encaissage *m* (de marchandises); clissage *m* (d'une bouteille); *Bookb:* cartonnage *m* (d'un livre); (*b*) tubage *m*, cuvelage *m* (d'un puits de mine, etc.). **2.** enveloppe *f*, garniture *f* (d'une pompe, etc.); blindage *m*, chemise *f* (d'un cylindre); huche *f*, bâche fermée (d'une turbine); cage *f*, coquille *f* (d'une machine); boîte *f*, caisse *f* (de l'embrayage); revêtement *m* (d'une maçonnerie); *Min:* boisage (d'un puits, d'une galerie, etc.); *N.Arch:* entourage plein; cadre *m* (d'une hélice); manchon *m* (de gouvernail); *Civ.E:* coffrage (pour béton armé); *Mec.E: etc:* gainage *m*; *Metall:* manteau *m* (d'un moule); *Aut:* carter *m* (du différentiel, d'embrayage); **tyre c.,** enveloppe (extérieure) de pneu.

casebook ['keisbuk] *n.* **1.** recueil *m* de jurisprudence. **2.** dossier médical.

case-harden ['keishɑ:d(ə)n] *v.tr. Metall:* cémenter, aciérer (le fer); tremper, durcir (l'acier) à la surface. **case-hardened** *a.* **1.** cémenté, aciéré, trempé à la surface; (moulé) en coquille. **2.** *F:* (*of pers.*) endurci (dans le crime).
casein ['keisiin] *n. Ch: Ind:* caséine *f.*
casement ['keismənt] *n.* **1.** châssis *m* de fenêtre à deux battants; **c. window,** fenêtre *f* à deux battants; croisée *f.* **2.** *Poet:* fenêtre.
casework ['keiswə:k] *n. Med: etc:* traitement individuel; assistance individuelle.
caseworker ['keiswə:kər] *n.* assistant(e) social(e).
cash¹ [kæʃ] *n.* (*no pl.*) espèces *fpl*; numéraire *m*; argent comptant; *Com:* **c. balance,** solde actif, solde de caisse; **c. price,** prix *m* au comptant; **to pay c.,** payer comptant; **c. payment,** paiement *m* (au) comptant; **c. transaction, sale,** transaction *f*, vente *f*, au comptant; **c. discount,** escompte *m* de caisse; **c. on delivery,** paiement à la livraison; (livraison) contre remboursement; **c. and carry,** emporter-comptant *m*; *Book-k:* **c. in hand,** fonds *mpl,* espèces, en caisse; **petty c.,** petite caisse; *Fin:* **c. flow,** cash-flow *m*; **to keep the c.,** tenir la caisse; **c. box,** caisse, cassette *f*; **c. desk,** caisse; **c. register,** caisse enregistreuse; *F:* **I'm short of c.,** je suis à sec.
cash² *v.tr.* **1.** toucher (un chèque, un mandat-poste, etc.); encaisser (un effet, un coupon); escompter (un effet); changer (un billet de banque). **2. to c. a cheque for s.o.,** verser à qn le montant d'un chèque. **cash in. 1.** *v.i. F:* **to c. in on sth.,** tirer profit de qch. **2.** *v.tr. P:* **to c. in one's chips, checks,** mourir, casser sa pipe.
cashbook ['kæʃbuk] *n.* livre *m* de caisse; sommier *m.*
cashew [kæ'ʃu:] *n. Bot:* **c. (nut tree),** acajou *m* à pommes, anacardier *m*; **c. nut,** (noix *f* de) cajou *m.*
cashier¹ [kæ'ʃiər] *n.* caissier, -ière.
cashier² *v.tr. Mil: Navy:* casser (un sous-officier); réformer (un officier, par mesure disciplinaire).
cashmere ['kæʃmiər] *n. Tex:* cachemire *m*; **c. shawl,** (châle *m* de) cachemire.
casino [kə'si:nou] *n.* casino *m.*
cask [kɑ:sk] *n.* (*a*) barrique *f*, fût *m*, futaille *f*, tonneau *m*; *Com:* **wine in the c.,** vin en fût, en cercles; vin en pièce; (*b*) (*for dry goods*) boucaut *m.*
casket ['kɑ:skit] *n.* **1.** coffret *m* (à bijoux); cassette *f* (pour bijoux ou argent). **2.** (*a*) *NAm:* cercueil *m*; (*b*) (*for ashes*) urne *f.*
Caspian ['kæspiən] *a. Geog:* caspien; **the C. Sea,** la mer Caspienne.
Cassandra [kə'sændrə] **1.** *Pr.n.f. Gr.Myth:* Cassandre. **2.** *n.* oiseau *m* de malheur.
cassata [kə'sɑ:tə] *n. Comest:* cassate *f.*
cassava [kə'sɑ:və] *n.* (*a*) *Bot:* cassave *f*, manioc *m*; **c. (flour),** farine *f* de cassave; manioc *m.*
casserole¹ ['kæsəroul] *n. Cu:* **1.** cocotte *f.* **2.** ragoût *m* en cocotte.
casserole² *v.tr.* cuire (de la viande, etc.) en cocotte.
cassette [kæ'set] *n.* (*a*) *Phot:* chargeur *m*; (*b*) *Rec: Cmptr: etc:* cassette *f*; **c. recorder,** enregistreur *m* à cassette.
cassock ['kæsək] *n. Ecc:* soutane *f.*
cassowary ['kæsəwɛəri] *n. Orn:* casoar *m.*
cast¹ [kɑ:st] *n.* **1.** (*a*) jet *m* (d'une pierre); coup *m* (de dés, de filet); **at a single c.,** d'un seul coup; (*b*) *Fish:* lancer *m* (de la ligne, de la mouche, du filet). **2.** (*a*) dépouille *f* (d'insecte, de serpent, etc.); (*b*) déjections *fpl* (de ver de terre); (*c*) pelote regurgitée (par les hiboux, les faucons). **3.** (*a*) jet (d'abeilles); rejet *m* (d'essaim); (*b*) couple *m* (de faucons). **4.** (*a*) *Metall:* coulée *f*; (jet de) fonte *f*; (*b*) (i) pièce moulée; plâtre *m*; (ii) moule *m* en creux; (iii) *Med:* appareil plâtré; **plaster c.,** moulage *m* au plâtre; **to take a c. of sth.,** mouler qch.; tirer un plâtre de qch.; (*c*) *Typ:* cliché *m.* **5.** *Lit:* **a man of his c.,** un homme de sa trempe; **c. of features,** physionomie *f.* **6.** (*a*) voilure *f* (d'une poutre, etc.); (*b*) **to have a c. in one's eye,** avoir une tendance à loucher. **7.** *Th:* distribution *f* (des rôles); la troupe; **with the following c.,** avec la distribution suivante; avec le concours de . . .; **all-star c.,** interprétation confiée entièrement à des vedettes.
cast² **I.** *v.tr.* (*p.t. & p.p.* **cast**) **1.** (*a*) jeter, lancer (une pierre, etc.); porter, projeter (une ombre); **the die is c.,** le dé, le sort, en est jeté; **to c. one's one's mind back to sth.,** faire un retour sur le passé; **to c. sth. aside,** se défaire de qch.; *Nau:* **to c. the lead,** donner un coup de sonde; (*b*) (*of reptile*) jeter bas; **to c. its slough,** jeter sa dépouille; (*of horse*) **to c. a shoe,** perdre un fer. **2.** (*a*) *Fish:* (i) lancer (un filet, la ligne); (ii) **to c. a stream,** *v.i.* **to c. for fish,** pêcher au lancer; (*b*) *Pol: etc:* donner (une voix); **to c. a vote for X,** voter pour X; (*c*) *Astrol:* tirer, faire, dresser (un horoscope); (*d*) *Metall:* fondre (du métal); mouler, couler (un cylindre, etc.); sabler (une médaille); couler (une statue) **c. in one piece,** coulé en bloc; (*e*) virer (un navire); (*f*) *Th:* distribuer les rôles (d'une pièce); **to c. s.o. for a part,** assigner, attribuer, un rôle à qn. **II.** *a.* (*a*) *Metall:* coulé, fondu; **c. steel,** fonte *f* d'acier, acier fondu; **c. iron,** (fer *m* de) fonte; fonte de fer; *Fig:* **c. iron alibi,** alibi *m* irréfutable; *F:* **c. iron stomach,** estomac *m* d'autruche; (*b*) *Cer:* **c. ware,** pièces coulées. **cast away** *v.tr. Nau:* **to be c. a.,** faire naufrage. **cast down** *v.tr.* (*a*) baisser (les yeux); (*b*) *Lit:* **to be c. d.,** être abattu, découragé, déprimé. **casting 1.** *a.* **c. vote,** voix prépondérante (accordée au président d'une assemblée, d'un conseil, quand les avis sont également partagés); **the chairman has the c. vote,** la voix du président est prépondérante. **2.** *n.* (*a*) jet *m* (d'une pierre, etc.); *Fish:* (pêche *f* au) lancer (*m*); **c. net,** épervier *m*; (*b*) *Metall: Glassm: etc:* coulée *f*, coulage *m*, moulage *m*, fonte *f*; **sand c.,** coulée en sable; (*c*) *Th:* distribution *f* des rôles; (*d*) *Metall: Glassm:* pièce coulée, pièce de fonte; **heavy castings,** grosses pièces; **die c.,** pièce moulée sous pression; (*e*) *Knit:* **c. on,** montage *m* (de mailles); **c. off,** fermeture *f* (de mailles). **cast off. 1.** *v.tr.* (*a*) rejeter, repousser (qn); **c.-off clothing,** *n. pl.* **c.-offs,** vêtements de rebut; vieilles frusques; (*b*) se dépouiller de (sa réserve); (*c*) *Nau:* larguer (les amarres); (*d*) *Ven:* lâcher (les chiens); (*e*) *Knit:* fermer (des mailles). **2.** *v.i.* (*a*) *Nau:* (*of ship*) démarrer; larguer les amarres; (*b*) *Knit:* fermer les mailles. **cast on,** *v.tr. & i. Knit:* monter les mailles. **cast out,** *v.tr.* chasser, exorciser (des démons). **cast up,** *v.tr.* **flotsam c. up on the shore,** épaves rejetées sur la plage.
castanets [kæstə'nets] *n.pl.* **(pair of) c.,** (paire *f* de) castagnettes *fpl.*
castaway ['kɑ:stəwei] *n.* naufragé, -ée.
caste [kɑ:st] *n.* caste *f*; **high-c., low-c., Indian,** Indien *m* de haute, basse, caste; *Fig:* **to lose c.,** déroger (à son rang); déchoir (de son rang).
casteless ['ka:stlis] *a.* sans caste.
castellated ['kæstileitid] *a. Fort: etc:* crénelé.
caster ['kɑ:stər] *n.* **1.** (*pers.*) (*a*) jeteur, -euse; (*b*) *Metall:* fondeur *m*; mouleur, -euse (de plâtre, etc.). **2.** (*machine*) fondeuse *f.*
castigate ['kæstigeit] *v.tr.* (*a*) châtier, corriger (qn); (*b*) critiquer sévèrement (qn, un ouvrage).
castigation [kæsti'geiʃ(ə)n] *n.* (*a*) châtiment *m*, correction *f*; (*b*) critique *f* sévère.
Castilian [kæs'tiliən] **1.** *a. Geog:* castillan. **2.** *n.* (*a*) Castillan, -ane, (*b*) *Ling:* castillan *m.*
castle¹ ['kɑ:s(ə)l] *n.* **1.** (*a*) château fort; (*b*) château (royal ou seigneurial); **to build castles in the air,** bâtir des châteaux en Espagne; *Prov:* **an Englishman's**

home is his c., charbonnier est maître chez lui. **2.** *Chess:* tour *f.*

castle² *v.tr. & i. Chess:* roquer. **castling,** *n.* roque *f.*

castor ['kɑːstər] *n.* **1.** poivrière *f*; saupoudroir *m* (à sucre, etc.). **2.** *Furn:* roulette *f* (de fauteuil, etc.). **3.** *Pharm:* **c. oil,** huile *f* de ricin.

castrate [kæs'treit] *v.tr.* châtrer (une bête); castrer, émasculer (un homme).

castration [kæs'treiʃ(ə)n] *n.* castration *f*; (*of a man*) émasculation *f.*

castrato, *pl.* **-ti** [kæ'strɑːtou, -ti] *n. Mus:* castrat *m.*

casual ['kæʒju(ə)l, 'kæz-] **1.** *a.* (*a*) fortuit, accidentel; (bourgeon, plante, sujet) adventice; **to engage in c. conversation,** parler de choses et d'autres, de la pluie et du beau temps; **to throw out a c. suggestion,** suggérer qch. en passant; **c. labour,** main-d'œuvre occasionnelle, temporaire; (*b*) *Cost:* **c. clothes, clothes for c. wear,** tenue *f* de loisirs; (*c*) (*of pers.*) imprévoyant, insouciant, sans méthode; **he is really too c.,** il en prend trop à son aise. **2.** *n.pl.* **casuals,** mocassins *mpl.* **-ally,** *adv.* (*a*) fortuitement, par hasard, en passant; (*b*) **to reply c.,** répondre d'un air indifférent, négligemment.

casualty ['kæʒjuəlti, kæz-] *n.* (*a*) accident *m* (de personne); désastre *m*; **c. department,** service *m* des urgences (d'un hôpital); **c. ward,** salle *f* des accidentés; (*b*) victime *f* (d'un accident); blessé, -ée; accidenté, -ée; **there were no casualties,** il n'y a pas eu de victimes; (*c*) *Mil:* **casualties,** pertes *fpl*; **c. list, return,** état *m* des pertes; (*d*) *Pol:* **the party had many casualties in the last election,** le parti a perdu beaucoup de députés aux dernières élections.

casuist ['kæzjuist] *n.* casuiste *m.*

casuistry ['kæzjuistri] *n.* casuistique *f.*

cat [kæt] *n.* **1.** (*a*) chat, *f.* chatte; **Siamese c.,** chat siamois; **tabby c.,** chat tigré; **tom c.,** matou *m*; *F:* **ginger, marmalade, c.,** chat roux tigré; **alley c.,** chat de gouttière; **c. show,** exposition féline; **c. door,** chattière *f*; *P:* **that looks like something the cat's brought in,** ça, c'est dégoûtant; **to quarrel like c. and dog,** s'entendre comme chien et chat; *F:* **he thinks he's the cat's whiskers,** il se croit quelqu'un; *Fig:* **to see which way the c. jumps,** voir d'où vient le vent; **to play a c.-and-mouse game with s.o.,** jouer avec qn comme un chat avec une souris; *Prov:* **while the cat's away the mice (will) play,** quand le chat n'est pas là, les souris dansent; *F:* **to be like a c. on hot bricks,** être sur des épines; **to put the c. among the pigeons,** mettre le loup dans la bergerie; **there's not room to swing a c.,** il n'y a pas de place pour se retourner; (*b*) *F:* (*pers.*) (i) **(old) c.,** vieille chipie; (ii) *U.S: P:* type *m*, individu *m*; (*c*) *F:* **c. burglar,** cambrioleur *m* par escalade; **2.** *Z:* **wild c.,** chat sauvage; **civet c., musk c.,** civette *f*; **the big cats,** les grands félins. **3.** *Nau:* (*a*) (i) **c. (purchase, tackle),** capon *m*; (ii) bossoir *m* (d'ancre); (*b*) **c.(-o'-nine-tails),** martinet *m* à neuf cordes. **4.** (*a*) **cat's cradle,** jeu du berceau (joué avec une ficelle); (*b*) **cat's eye,** (i) *Lap:* œil-de-chat *m*; (ii) catadioptre *m*, cataphote *m* (*R.t.m.*) (au milieu de la route).

cataclysm ['kætəklizm] *n.* cataclysme *m.*

cataclysmic [kætə'klizmik] *a.* cataclysmique.

catacomb ['kætəkoum] *n.* (*usu.pl.*) catacombe *f.*

catafalque ['kætəfælk] *n.* **1.** catafalque *m.* **2.** char *m* funèbre.

Catalan ['kætəlæn] **1.** *a. Geog:* catalan. **2.** *n.* (*a*) Catalan, -ane; (*b*) *Ling:* catalan *m.*

catalepsy ['kætəlepsi] *n. Med:* catalepsie *f.*

cataleptic [kætə'leptik] *a. & n. Med:* cataleptique (*mf*).

catalogue¹, *NAm:* **catalog** ['kætəlɔg] *n.* **1.** catalogue *m*, liste *f*, répertoire *m*; **subject c.,** catalogue méthodique. **2.** *Com:* catalogue; **trade c.,** album(-tarif) *m*, tarif-album *m.*

catalogue², *NAm:* **catalog** *v.tr.* cataloguer. **cataloguing,** *NAm:* **cataloging** *n.* catalogage *m.*

Catalonia [kætə'louniə] *Pr.n. Geog:* Catalogne *f.*

catalysis [kə'tælisis] *n. Ch:* catalyse *f.*

catalyst ['kætəlist] *n. Ch:* catalyseur *m.*

catamaran [kætəmə'ræn] *n. Nau:* catamaran *m.*

cataplasm ['kætəplæzm] *n. Med:* cataplasme *m.*

catapult¹ ['kætəpʌlt] *n.* **1.** fronde *f.* **2.** *Av:* catapulte (de lancement).

catapult² **1.** *v.tr.* (*a*) *Av:* catapulter (un avion); (*b*) catapulter, projeter (qn, qch., au loin). **2.** *v.i.* entrer en trombe **(into a room,** dans une pièce). **catapulting** *n. Av:* catapultage *m.*

cataract ['kætərækt] *n.* **1.** cataracte *f* (d'un fleuve). **2.** *Med:* cataracte (de l'œil).

catarrh [kə'tɑːr] *n. Med:* catarrhe *m*; **bronchial c.,** bronchite *f.*

catarrhal [kə'tɑːr(ə)l] *a.* catarrhal, -aux; catarrheux.

catastrophe [kə'tæstrəfi] *n.* catastrophe *f*; désastre *m*; **the victims of the c.,** les sinistrés *mpl.*

catastrophic [kætə'strɔfik] *a.* catastrophique, désastreux. **-ally** *adv.* d'une façon catastrophique.

catcall¹ ['kætkɔːl] *n. Th: etc:* (coup *m* de) sifflet (*m*) (dirigé contre un acteur, etc.)

catcall² *v.tr. & i.* siffler (un acteur).

catch¹ [kætʃ] *n.* **1.** (*a*) prise *f* au vol (d'une balle, d'un ballon); (*of children*) **to play c.,** jouer au ballon; (*b*) *Row:* attaque *f* (au commencement du coup de nage); (*c*) **with a c. in one's voice,** d'une voix entrecoupée. **2.** (*a*) *Fish:* prise, pêche *f*; **to have a good c.,** faire (une) bonne pêche; (*b*) *F:* bon parti (à épouser); **he's, she's, no great c.,** c'est un médiocre parti. **3.** (*a*) (*on door, etc.*) loquet *m*, loqueteau *m*; (*of window*) loqueteau; (*of buckle*) ardillon *m*; (*of clasp knife*) mouche *f*; (*on garment*) agrafe *f*; *Mec.E:* crochet *m* d'arrêt; (*of wheel, winch shaft, etc.*) cliquet *m*; **safety c.,** fermoir *m* de sûreté; cran *m* de sûreté; (*b*) tenon *m* d'accrochage. **4.** attrape *f*; **there's a c. in it,** c'est une attrape; **that's, there's, the c.,** voilà le hic; *Sch: etc:* **c. question,** colle *f.* **5.** *Mus:* chanson *f* à reprises; canon *m.* **6.** (*a*) *Agr:* **c. crop,** culture dérobée; (*b*) **c. phrase,** scie *f*; *Th:* phrase comique (répétée).

catch² *v.* (*p.t. & p.p.* **caught** [kɔːt]) **1.** *v.tr.* (*a*) attraper, prendre (un poisson, un voleur, etc.); attraper, saisir (une balle, etc.); pêcher (un poisson); saisir (un voleur); attraper, ne pas manquer (un train, etc.); attirer (l'attention de qn); (*when throwing sth. to s.o.*) **c!** attrape! *Nau:* (*of sail, etc.*) **to c. the wind,** prendre le vent; **I caught him as he fell,** je l'ai retenu, attrapé, au moment où il allait tomber; **to c. s.o. doing sth., in the act, red-handed,** prendre qn en flagrant délit; *F:* **c. me!** pas de danger! pas si bête! **you won't c. me doing that again,** on ne m'y reprendra plus; **to be caught,** être pris (dans un brouillard), être surpris (par une averse); (*b*) saisir, percevoir (des sons); rencontrer (le regard de qn); (*of thg*) frapper (la vue, l'oreille); (*at meeting, etc.*) **to c. the chairman's eye,** attirer l'attention du président; **I didn't c. what you were saying,** je n'ai pas entendu ce que vous disiez; **I caught my dress on a nail,** j'ai accroché ma robe à un clou; **he caught his foot on a root and fell,** il s'est pris le pied dans une racine et il est tombé; (*c*) attraper (une maladie); contracter (une habitude); prendre (l'accent du pays); **to c. (a) cold,** (i) s'enrhumer, attraper un rhume; (ii) *Fin: F:* boire un bouillon; **to c. fire,** *U.S:* **on fire,** prendre feu; (*d*) *Box:* **he caught him with a left to the chin,** il lui a porté un gauche au menton; *F:* **you'll c. it!** tu vas écoper quelque chose! (*e*) *F:* attraper (qn); mettre (qn) dedans; tromper (qn); **you won't c. me!**

ça ne prend pas (avec moi)! **2.** *v.i.* (*a*) **to c. at sth.,** essayer de saisir qch.; s'accrocher à qch.; **a drowning man catches at a straw,** un homme qui se noie se raccroche à n'importe quoi; (*b*) (*of cog wheel*) raccroche à n'importe quoi; (*of fire*) prendre; s'allumer; (*c*) *Cu:* (*of stew, etc.*) attacher. **catching 1.** *a.* (*of disease*) contagieux, -euse; infectieux, -euse; (*of laughter*) communicatif. **2.** *n.* (*a*) prise *f*; capture *f*; (*b*) (*of toothed wheel*) engrenure *f*; (*of gearing*) quottement *m*. **catch on** *v.i. F:* (*a*) (*of fashion, play, etc.*) réussir; avoir du succès; (*of tune*) accrocher; (*b*) comprendre, saisir, piger; **he still hasn't caught on,** il n'y est pas. **catch out** *v.tr. F:* attraper (qn); prendre (qn) sur le fait, en faute; **to c. s.o. out in a lie,** surprendre qn à mentir. **catch up** *v.tr. & i.* (*a*) saisir (qch.); **to be caught up in a wave of enthusiasm,** se trouver gagné par une vague d'enthousiasme; (*b*) **to c. s.o. up, to c. up with s.o.,** rattraper qn; **our competitors are catching up with us,** nos concurrents gagnent le pas sur nous; **to c. up (with) arrears,** se remettre au courant; **to c. up on some sleep,** rattraper du sommeil; *F:* **it will c. up with you (one of these days),** ça va vous retomber sur le nez.

catchall ['kætʃɔːl] *n. NAm: F:* fourre-tout *m*.

catch-as-catch-can ['kætʃəz'kætʃ'kæn] *n. Wr:* catch *m*, lutte *f* libre.

catcher ['kætʃər] *n.* (*a*) attrapeur, -euse; preneur, -euse; **rat c.,** preneur de rats; **mole c.,** taupier *m*; (*b*) *Games:* (*baseball*) attrapeur, receveur *m*.

catchment ['kætʃmənt] *n.* **1.** *Geog: Hyd.E:* prise *f* d'eau; captation *f*, captage *m* (d'eaux); **c. area, basin,** bassin *m* hydrographique. **2.** *Adm:* **c. area of a school,** réseau *m* de ramassage des écoliers.

catchpenny ['kætʃpeni] *n.* (*thg*) attrape-sou *m*, attrape-nigaud *m*; **c. scheme, show,** attrape-nigaud.

catchword ['kætʃwəːd] *n.* **1.** (*a*) *Pol: etc:* mot *m* de ralliement; (*b*) scie *f*, rengaine *f*. **2.** *Th:* réplique *f*.

catchy ['kætʃi] *a.* (*of tune, etc.*) entraînant; facile à retenir.

catechism ['kætəkizm] *n.* catéchisme *m*.

catechize ['kætəkaiz] *v.tr.* **1.** catéchiser. **2.** interroger, questionner (qn).

catechumen [kæti'kjuːmən] *n.* catéchumène *mf*.

categoric(al) [kæti'gɔrik(l)] *a.* (réponse, refus, etc.) catégorique. **-ally** *adv.* catégoriquement.

categorize ['kætigəraiz] *v.tr.* classer par catégories.

category ['kætigəri] *n.* **1.** *Phil:* catégorie *f*. **2.** catégorie; **these facts fall into another c.,** ces faits se classent sous une autre catégorie.

cater ['keitər] *v.i.* **to c. for s.o.,** (i) approvisionner qn; pourvoir à la nourriture de qn; (ii) pourvoir aux plaisirs de qn; *P.N:* (*at restaurant*) **parties catered for** = banquets, noces, etc.; **hotel that caters for English visitors,** hôtel *m* qui s'adresse surtout à la clientèle anglaise; **to c. for all tastes,** pourvoir à tous les goûts. **catering** *n.* (*a*) **c., the c. industry,** restauration *f*; (*b*) *Av:* service traiteur; traitance *f*.

catercorner(ed) ['keitəkɔːnə(d)] *a. & adv. NAm:* diagonalement opposé(s).

caterer ['keitərər] *n.* restaurateur *m*; traiteur *m*.

caterpillar ['kætəpilər] *n.* **1.** *Ent:* chenille *f*. **2.** *Veh:* **c. (tread, track),** chenille, caterpillar *m*; **c. tractor,** tracteur *m* à chenilles.

caterwaul ['kætəwɔːl] *v.i.* **1.** (*of cat*) miauler. **2.** *F:* crier (comme les chats la nuit); faire du vacarme. **caterwauling** *n.* miaulements *mpl* (de chats).

catfish ['kætfiʃ] *n. Ich:* **1.** blennie *m* or *f*. **2.** silure *m*, poisson-chat *m*, *pl.* poissons-chats.

catgut ['kætgʌt] *n.* (*a*) corde *f* de boyau; **c. strings,** cordes en boyau (pour violon); (*b*) *Med:* catgut *m*.

cathedral [kə'θiːdrəl] *a. & n.* cathédrale *f*; **c. town,** ville épiscopale; évêché *m*.

Catherine ['kæθ(ə)rin] *Pr.n.f.* Catherine; *Hist:* **C. the Great,** la Grande Catherine; *Pyr:* **c. wheel,** soleil *m*; roue *f* à feu; tourniquet *m*; *Gym:* **to turn c. wheels,** faire la roue.

catheter ['kæθitər] *n. Med:* sonde (creuse); cathéter *m*; **indwelling c.,** sonde intérieure, à demeure.

cathode ['kæθoud] *n. El:* cathode *f*; **photo(electric) c.,** cathode photoélectrique; **c. ray,** rayon *m* cathodique; **c. ray tube,** tube *f* cathodique.

catholic ['kæθ(ə)lik] **1.** *a.* (*a*) universel; (*b*) tolérant; à l'esprit large; éclectique; **c. tastes,** goûts *mpl* éclectiques. **2.** *a. & n. Ecc:* (*a*) orthodoxe (*mf*), catholique (*mf*); (*b*) *R.C.Ch:* catholique *mf*; **I believe in one holy, c. and apostolic Church,** je crois en l'Église, une, sainte, catholique et apostolique.

catholicism [kə'θɔlisizm] *n. Ecc:* catholicisme *m*.

catkin ['kætkin] *n. Bot:* chaton *m*.

catlick ['kætlik] *n. F:* **to have, give oneself, a c.,** se laver le bout du nez.

catmint ['kætmint] *n. Bot:* cataire *f*, herbe *f* aux chats.

catnap¹ ['kætnæp] *n. F:* sieste *f*, somme *m* (de courte durée).

catnap² *v.i. F:* faire la sieste; sommeiller.

catspaw, cat's paw ['kætspɔː] *n.* **to be s.o.'s c., to be made a c. of,** tirer les marrons du feu (pour qn); être la dupe de qn.

catsup ['kætsəp] *n. U.S: Comest:* ketchup *m*.

cattery ['kætəri] *n.* chatterie *f*; pension *f* pour chats.

cattiness ['kætinis] *n. F:* méchanceté *f*; rosserie *f*.

cattle ['kætl] *n. coll.* bétail *m*; bestiaux *mpl*; **horned c.,** bêtes *fpl* à cornes; bovins *mpl*; **c. breeding,** élevage *m* du bétail; **c. market,** marché *m* aux bestiaux; **c. truck,** fourgon *m* à bestiaux; **c. show,** comice *m* agricole; *P.N:* **c. crossing,** passage *m* de troupeaux.

catty ['kæti] *a. F:* **1. there's a c. smell,** ça sent la pisse de chat. **2.** (*esp. of woman*) méchant(e), sournois(e); **c. remark,** rosserie *f*, vacherie *f*.

catty-corner(ed) ['kæti'kɔːnə(d)] *a. & adv. NAm:* diagonalement opposé(s).

catwalk ['kætwɔːk] *n.* passerelle *f* de visite; passavant *m*; *Nau:* coursive *f*.

Caucasian [kɔː'keiʒ(ə)n, -'keiziən] **1.** *a. Geog: Ethn: Ling:* caucasien; **2.** *n.* (*a*) *Ethn: Geog:* Caucasien, -ienne; (*b*) membre *m* de la race blanche.

Caucasus (the) [ðə'kɔːkəsəs] *Pr.n. Geog:* le Caucase.

caucus ['kɔːkəs] *n. Pol:* comité électoral; clique *f* politique.

caudal ['kɔːdl] *a. Z:* caudal, -aux; **c. fin,** caudale *f*.

caul [kɔːl] *n.* coiffe *f* (de nouveau-né); **born with a c.,** né coiffé.

cauldron ['kɔːldrən] *n.* chaudron *m*.

cauliflower ['kɔliflauər] *n.* **1.** chou-fleur *m*, *pl.* choux-fleurs; *Cu:* **c. cheese,** chou-fleur au gratin. **2.** *Box: etc:* **c. ear,** oreille *f* en chou-fleur.

caulk [kɔːk] *v.tr.* calfater, étouper (un navire). **caulking** *n.* calfatage *m*; **c. iron,** calfait *m*, burin *m*.

causal ['kɔːz(ə)l] *a.* causal (*no mpl*).

causative ['kɔːzətiv] *a. Gram:* (verbe) causatif.

cause¹ [kɔːz] *n.* **1.** cause *f*; **c. and effect,** la cause et l'effet; **no effect without a c.,** point d'effet sans cause; **to be the c. of an accident,** être (la) cause d'un accident. **2.** raison *f*, motif *m*, sujet *m*; **c. for litigation,** matière *f* à procès; **I have c. to be thankful,** j'ai lieu d'être reconnaissant; **to have good c. for doing sth.,** être justifié à faire qch.; avoir de bonnes raisons pour faire qch.; **to give serious c. for complaint,** donner de grands sujets de plainte; **and with good c.,** et pour cause. **3.** (*a*) *Jur:* cause; procès *m*; **to plead s.o.'s c.,** plaider la cause de qn; (*b*) **to win s.o. over to one's c.,** gagner qn à sa cause; **in the c. of justice,** pour (la cause de) la justice; **to work for a good c.,**

travailler pour une bonne cause; *F:* **it's all in a good c.,** ce n'est pas du temps perdu.

cause[2] *v.tr.* **1.** causer, occasionner (un malheur, du retard, etc.); faire arriver (un accident); provoquer (la gaîté, un accident); faire naître (une querelle); susciter (de l'étonnement); **to c. a fire,** provoquer un incendie; **to c. a sensation,** faire sensation. **2. to c. s.o. to do sth.,** faire faire qch. à qn; **to c. s.o. to be punished,** faire punir qn.

causeway ['kɔːzwei] *n.* chaussée *f*, levée *f*, digue *f* (coupant à travers des marécages).

caustic ['kɔ(ː)stik] **1.** *a.* caustique; **c. soda,** soude *f* caustique; hydrate *m* de soude; **c. wit,** esprit mordant. **2.** *n.* (*a*) *Ch: Med:* caustique *m*.

cauterization [kɔːtərai'zeiʃ(ə)n] *Med:* cautérisation *f*.

cauterize ['kɔːtəraiz] *v.tr. Med:* cautériser.

cautery ['kɔːtəri] *n.* cautère *m*.

caution[1] ['kɔːʃ(ə)n] *n.* **1.** précaution *f*, prévoyance *f*, prudence *f*; **with great c.,** avec beaucoup de circonspection. **2.** (*a*) avis *m*, avertissement *m*; **c.! steep gradient,** attention! descente rapide; (*b*) *Mil:* commandement *m* préparatoire; (*c*) réprimande *f*; **he was let off with a c.,** il s'en est tiré avec une réprimande.

caution[2] *v.tr.* **1.** (*a*) avertir (qn); mettre (qn) sur ses gardes; **to c. s.o. against sth.,** prémunir, prévenir, qn contre qch.; (*b*) *Jur:* prévenir (un suspect) que ce qu'il dira peut être utilisé contre lui au cours des poursuites, du procès. **2.** menacer (qn) de poursuites à la prochaine occasion; réprimander (qn).

cautious ['kɔːʃəs] *a.* circonspect, prudent; **to be c. in doing sth.,** faire qch. avec circonspection; **to play a c. game,** jouer serré. **-ly** *adv.* avec précaution, avec circonspection; prudemment.

cautiousness ['kɔːʃəsnis] *n.* prudence *f*.

cavalcade [kævəl'keid] *n.* cavalcade *f*; cortège *m*.

cavalier [kævə'liər] **1.** *n.m.* (*a*) *Hist:* cavalier; gentilhomme; (*b*) *Eng.Hist:* royaliste; **the Cavaliers and the Roundheads,** les Cavaliers et les Têtes rondes. **2.** *a.* cavalier, désinvolte; **with a c. air,** avec désinvolture.

cavalry ['kævəlri] *n.* cavalerie *f*.

cavalryman, *pl.* **-men** ['kævəlrimən] *n.m. Mil:* cavalier; soldat de cavalerie.

cave[1] [keiv] *n.* caverne *f*; grotte *f*; **c. art,** art *m* rupestre; **c. dweller,** troglodyte *mf*; homme *m*, femme *f*, des cavernes; **c. dwelling,** maison *f* troglodyte; *Paleont:* **c. bear,** ours *m* des cavernes.

cave[2] [keiv] *v.i.* faire de la spéléologie. **cave in** *v.i.* (i) (*of ground, structure, etc.*) céder, s'affaisser, s'effondrer; (*of structure, beam*) s'infléchir; (ii) (*of pers.*) céder, se soumettre. **caving** *n.* **1.** spéléologie *f*. **2. c. in,** effondrement *m*, affaissement *m*.

cave[3] ['keivi, 'kɑːvei] *int. Sch: F: A:* attention! pet!

caveat ['kæviæt] *n. Jur:* opposition *f* (**to,** à); avertissement *m* (**against,** contre).

caveman, *pl.* **-men** ['keivmæn, -mən] *n. Prehist:* troglodyte *mf*; homme *m* des cavernes.

caver ['keivər] *n.* spéléologue *mf*.

cavern ['kævə(ː)n] *n.* caverne *f*; souterrain *m*.

cavernous ['kævənəs] *a.* caverneux.

caviar(e) ['kæviɑːr] *n.* caviar *m*.

cavil ['kævil] *v.i.* (**cavilled,** *NAm:* **caviled**) chicaner, ergoter; **to c. at, about, sth.,** chicaner, ergoter, sur qch.

cavity ['kæviti] *n.* cavité *f*; creux *m*; alvéole *m*; *Const:* **c. wall,** mur *m* double; *Dent:* **dental c.,** cavité dentaire.

cavort [kə'vɔːt] *v.i.* faire des cabrioles; cabrioler.

cavy ['keivi] *n. Z:* cobaye *m*, cochon *m* d'Inde.

caw [kɔː] *v.i.* (*of crow, etc.*) croasser. **cawing** *n.* croassement *m*.

cayenne [kei'en] *n.* **c. (pepper),** (poivre *m* de) cayenne *m*.

cayman ['keimən] *n. Rept:* caïman *m*; *Geog:* **C. Islands,** îles Cayman.

cease [siːs] *v.tr. & i.* **1.** cesser (**doing sth.,** de faire qch.); **they have ceased to exist,** ils n'existent plus. **2.** cesser (ses efforts, etc.); *Mil:* **to c. fire,** cesser le feu; **without ceasing,** sans arrêt.

ceasefire [siːs'faiər] *n.* cessez-le-feu *m inv*.

ceaseless ['siːslis] *a.* incessant; continuel; sans fin. **-ly,** *adv.* sans cesse; sans arrêt; continuellement.

cecum ['siːkəm] *n. NAm:* = CAECUM.

cedar ['siːdər] *n. Bot:* **c. (tree),** cèdre *m*; **c. of Lebanon,** cèdre du Liban.

cede [siːd] *v.tr.esp. Jur:* céder (un bien immobilier, une province, une dette) (**to,** à).

cedilla [si'dilə] *n.* cédille *f*.

ceiling ['siːliŋ] *n.* **1.** (*a*) plafond *m* (d'une pièce, d'une voiture, etc.); **c. light,** plafonnier *m*; *F:* **to hit the c.,** entrer dans une colère bleue. **2.** (*a*) *Av:* (i) plafond; (ii) vol *m* en plafond; **to fly at the c.,** plafonner; (*b*) *Meteor:* plafond (nuageux); (*c*) *Pol.Ec: etc:* plafond; **c. price,** prix plafond.

celandine ['seləndain] *n. Bot:* (*a*) **greater c.,** chélidoine *f*; grande éclaire; (*b*) **lesser c.,** ficaire *f*; petite éclaire.

celebrant ['selibrənt] *n. Ecc:* célébrant *m*; officiant *m*.

celebrate ['selibreit] *v.tr.* **1.** *Ecc:* (*a*) célébrer (la messe, un mariage, une fête); (*b*) *abs.* célébrer la messe. **2.** (*a*) célébrer, commémorer (un événement); (*b*) *F:* fêter (qch.). **celebrated** *a.* célèbre (**for sth.,** par qch.); renommé (**for,** pour).

celebration [seli'breiʃ(ə)n] *n.* **1.** *Ecc:* célébration *f* (de la communion, d'une fête). **2.** réunion *f*, dîner *m* (pour fêter qch.); *F:* **this calls for a c.!** il faut fêter ça! ça s'arrose!

celebrity [si'lebriti] *n.* **1.** célébrité *f*, renommée *f*. **2.** (*pers.*) célébrité.

celeriac [si'leriæk] *n. Hort:* céleri-rave *m*, *pl.* céleris-raves.

celerity [si'leriti] *n.* célérité *f*.

celery ['seləri] *n. Hort:* céleri *m*; **head of c.,** pied *m* de céleri.

celestial [si'lestiəl] *a.* (sphère, etc.) céleste.

celibacy ['selibəsi] *n.* célibat *m*.

celibate ['selibət] **1.** *a.* (personne) célibataire; (vie) de célibataire. **2.** *n.* célibataire *mf*.

cell [sel] *n.* **1.** (*a*) cellule *f* (de moine, d'ermite); (*b*) (*in prison*) cellule, cachot *m*; **the cells,** les locaux *mpl* disciplinaires (d'un poste de police); (*c*) *Arch:* canton *m* (d'une voûte); (*d*) *Ap:* cellule, alvéole *m* (de ruche); (*e*) *Av:* cellule. **2.** *El: Elcs: etc:* (*a*) élément *m* (de pile); **dry c.,** pile sèche; **wet c.,** pile à liquide; **storage c.,** (i) élément d'accumulateur; (ii) *Cmptr:* cellule de mémoire; (*b*) **photoelectric c.,** cellule photoélectrique. **3.** *Biol:* cellule; **c. wall,** paroi *f* cellulaire; *Anat:* **blood c.,** globule *m*. **4.** *Pol:* **communist c.,** cellule, noyau *m*, communiste.

cellar ['selər] *n.* (*a*) cave *f*; **wine c.,** cave à vin; **to keep a good c.,** avoir une bonne cave; (*b*) chai *m* (de négociant en vins).

cellist ['tʃelist] *n. Mus:* violoncelliste *mf*.

cello ['tʃelou] *n. Mus:* violoncelle *m*.

cellular ['seljulər] *a.* **1.** *Biol:* (structure, etc.) cellulaire. **2.** cellulaire, alvéolaire; *Tex:* **c. blanket,** couverture *f* (de lit) en maille aérée.

celluloid ['seljulɔid] *n.* celluloïd(e) *m*.

cellulose ['seljulous] **1.** *a.* celluleux. **2.** *n.* cellulose *f*.

Celsius ['selsiəs] *Pr.n.m. Ph:* **C. thermometer,** thermomètre *m* de Celsius.

Celt [kelt] *n. Ethn:* Celte *mf*.

Celtic ['keltik] **1.** *a. Ethn:* celtique; celte. **2.** *n. Ling:* le celtique; les langues *fpl* celtiques.

cement¹ [si'ment] *n.* **1.** *Const: Civ.E:* ciment *m*; **quick-setting c.,** ciment à prise rapide; **c. mixer,** bétonnière *f.* **2.** (*binding element*) ciment; mastic *m.*

cement² *v.tr.* **1.** (*a*) cimenter (des pierres, des briques); cimenter, consolider (la paix, une amitié); (*b*) cimenter, enduire d'une couche de ciment (une paroi, etc.). **2.** lier au ciment. **3.** *Dent:* mastiquer, obturer (une dent). **4.** *Metall:* cémenter (le fer).

cementation [siːmen'teiʃ(ə)n] *n.* **1.** cimentation *f.* **2.** *Metall:* cémentation *f.*

cemetery ['semətri] *n.* cimetière *m.*

cenotaph ['senətæf] *n.* cénotaphe *m.*

censer ['sensər] *n. Ecc:* encensoir *m.*

censor¹ ['sensər] *n.* (*a*) *Rom.Ant:* censeur *m*; (*b*) *Adm: Mil:* censeur; **the film c.,** la censure cinématographique.

censor² *v.tr.* **1.** (*a*) interdire, censurer (une pièce de théâtre); (*b*) soumettre (une pièce, etc.) à des coupures; caviarder (un article); censurer (un film). **2. to be censored,** (i) être interdit, supprimé, par la censure; (ii) être expurgé; être soumis à des coupures. **censoring** *n.* censure *f* (des journaux, etc.).

censorious [sen'sɔːriəs] *a.* porté à censurer; sévère (**of, upon,** pour).

censorship ['sensəʃip] *n. Adm:* (*a*) la censure *f;* (*b*) **postal c.,** contrôle postal; **c. of the press,** régime préventif.

censurable ['senʃərəbl] *a.* censurable, blâmable.

censure¹ ['senʃər] *n.* censure *f,* blâme *m,* condamnation *f; Jur:* réprimande *f;* **he deserves c.,** il mérite des reproches; *Pol:* **vote of c.,** motion *f* de censure.

censure² *v.tr.* censurer; (i) blâmer, condamner; (ii) critiquer.

census ['sensəs] *n.* recensement *m.*

cent [sent] *n.* **1.** *Num:* cent *m*; *F:* sou *m*; **to pay to the last c.,** payer jusqu'au dernier sou. **2. per c.,** pour cent; **ten per c.,** dix pour cent; *Ch: etc:* **thirty per c. solution,** solution *f* à trente pour cent; **a hundred per c. efficient,** cent pour cent efficace.

centaur ['sentɔːr] *n.m. Myth:* centaure.

centenarian [senti'nɛəriən] *a.* & *n.* (*pers.*) centenaire (*mf*).

centenary [sen'tiːnəri] *a.* & *n.* (anniversaire *m*) centenaire (*m*).

centennial [sen'teniəl] **1.** *a.* centennal, -aux; séculaire. **2.** *n. NAm: N.Z:* = CENTENARY.

center ['sentər] *n.* & *v. NAm:* = CENTRE¹,².

centigrade ['sentigreid] *a. Meas:* centigrade; **c. thermometer,** thermomètre *m* centigrade.

centimetre, *NAm:* **centimeter** ['sentimiːtər] *n. Meas:* centimètre *m*; **square, cubic, c.,** centimètre carré, cube.

centipede ['sentipiːd] *n.* scolopendre *f, F:* mille-pattes *m inv.*

central ['sentr(ə)l] **1.** *a.* central, -aux; **c. point,** centre *m*; **in a c. position,** situé au centre; **c. heating,** chauffage central; **c. bank,** banque centrale; **C. America,** Amérique Centrale. **2.** *n. NAm: Tp:* central *m* (téléphonique). **-ally** *adv.* centralement; **c. situated,** central; **c. heated,** avec chauffage central.

centralize ['sentrəlaiz] **1.** *v.tr.* centraliser; **centralized planning,** planification centralisée. **2.** *v.i.* se centraliser.

centre¹, *NAm:* **center¹** ['sentər] *n.* **1.** (*a*) centre *m* (d'un cercle, de la terre, d'une ville, etc.); milieu *m* (d'une table, etc.); corps *m,* centre (d'une roue); *Med:* foyer *m* (d'infection); **in the c.,** au centre, au milieu; **the great urban centres,** les grandes agglomérations urbaines; **commercial, industrial, c.,** centre commercial, industriel; **civic, community, c.,** centre civique, social; *Ph:* **c. of gravity,** centre de gravité; **c. of attraction,** (i) *Ph:* centre d'attraction, de gravitation; (ii) *Fig:* clou *m* (d'une fête, etc.); *N.Arch:* **c. board,** dérive (centrale); **out of c.,** décentré; (*b*) *Const:* cintre *m* (d'une voûte); (*c*) *Mec.E:* pointe *f* (d'un tour); *Tls:* **c. punch,** pointeau *m*; (*d*) *Fb: etc:* **c. forward,** avant-centre *m*; **c. half,** demi-centre *m*; (*e*) *attrib.* central, -aux; du centre; *Pol:* **the c. party,** les membres *mpl* du Centre; **the c. right, left,** le centre droit, gauche. **2.** *Rec: etc:* **music c.,** combiné *m* stéréo.

centre², *NAm:* **center²** *v.tr.* & *i.* (*a*) placer (qch.) au centre; axer (qch.) sur; **to c., to be centred on s.o., sth.,** se concentrer sur qn, qch.; s'appuyer, reposer, sur qn; **all his thoughts were centred on . . .,** toutes ses pensées convergeaient vers . . .; **the whole debate centres, is centred, on . . .,** tout le débat se circonscrit autour de . . .; (*b*) centrer (une roue, une pièce sur le tour, etc.); (*c*) *Cin: Phot:* centrer, cadrer (une photo); (*d*) *Fb: etc:* centrer (le ballon, etc.); (*e*) *Const:* cintrer (une voûte). **centring** *n.* **1.** centrage *m,* guidage *m* (d'une pièce sur le tour, etc.); *Mec.E:* **c. tool,** centreur *m.* **2.** *Const:* (*a*) cintrage *m* (d'une voûte); (*b*) cintre *m* (d'une voûte).

centrepiece, *NAm:* **centerpiece** ['sentəpiːs] *n.* (pièce *f* de) milieu (*m*); surtout *m,* girandole *f.*

centrifugal [sentri'fjuːg(ə)l] *a.* (force, pompe, etc.) centrifuge.

centrifuge¹ ['sentrifjuːdʒ] *v.tr.* centrifuger (un liquide).

centrifuge² *n.* centrifugeur *m,* centrifugeuse *f.*

centripetal [sen'tripitəl] *a.* (force, etc.) centripète.

century ['sentjuri] *n.* **1.** siècle *m*; **in the nineteenth c.,** au dix-neuvième siècle; **trees centuries old,** arbres *mpl* séculaires. **2.** *Cr:* centaine, série *f* de cent.

cephalic [se'fælik] *a.* (veine, index, etc.) céphalique.

ceramic [sə'ræmik] **1.** *a.* céramique. **2.** *n.pl.* **ceramics,** la céramique.

cereal ['siəriəl] **1.** *a.* & *n.* céréale (*f*); **c. crops,** céréales. **2.** *n.pl.* **(breakfast) cereals,** céréales (en flocons).

cerebellum [seri'beləm] *n. Anat:* cervelet *m.*

cerebral ['serəbrəl] *a.* cérébral, -aux.

cerebrum ['seribrəm] *n. Anat:* cerveau *m.*

ceremonial [seri'mouniəl] **1.** *a.* de cérémonie; **c. visit,** visite *f* de cérémonie. **2.** *n.* cérémonial *m.* **-ally** *adv.* en grande cérémonie.

ceremonious [seri'mouniəs] *a.* cérémonieux. **-ly** *adv.* cérémonieusement; avec cérémonie.

ceremony ['seriməni] *n.* **1.** cérémonie *f*; **with c.,** avec cérémonie; solennellement; **without c.,** sans formalités; **to stand on c.,** faire des cérémonies; **master of ceremonies,** maître *m* des cérémonies. **2.** (*event*) cérémonie; **the marriage c.,** la cérémonie du mariage.

cert [sɔːt] *n. F:* (= CERTAINTY) **a dead c.,** une certitude (absolue); un coup sûr, une affaire sûre; *Turf:* un gagnant sûr; **it's a c.,** c'est couru.

certain ['sɔːt(ə)n] *a.* certain. **1.** (*a*) (succès, etc.) infaillible, assuré; **it's absolutely c.,** c'est sûr et certain; **he is c. to come,** il viendra sûrement; **to my c. knowledge, they are . . .,** je sais pertinemment qu'ils sont . . .; (*b*) (*of pers.*) **to be c. of sth.,** être certain, sûr, de qch.; **I am almost c.,** j'en suis presque sûr; **I am c. that he will come,** je suis certain, sûr, qu'il viendra; (*c*) **to know sth. for c.,** savoir qch. pour certain; être bien sûr de qch.; **I cannot say for c.,** je ne saurais dire avec certitude; **you shall have it tomorrow for c.,** vous l'aurez demain sans faute; (*d*) **to make c. of sth.,** (i) s'assurer de qch.; (ii) s'assurer qch.; **to make c. of a seat,** s'assurer une place. **2.** (*a*) **there are c. things that . . .,** il y a certaines choses que . . .; **women of a c. age,** les femmes d'un certain âge; **a c. person,** (une) certaine personne; **c. people,** (de) certaines gens; certains *mpl*; **a c. Mr Thomas,** un certain M. Thomas; (*b*) **he used to write to me on a c. day,** il m'écrivait à jour fixe. **-ly** *adv.* (*a*) certainement; certes; à coup sûr; (*b*) assurément; parfaitement; **you shall c. have it tomorrow,** vous l'aurez demain sans faute; **may I?—c.!** vous permettez?—je vous en prie! **c. not!** bien sûr que non!

certainty ['sə:tənti] *n.* (*a*) certitude *f* (d'un fait à venir); (*b*) chose certaine; **I know it for a c.,** je le sais à coup sûr; **it's a dead c.,** c'est une certitude absolue; (*c*) certitude (morale), conviction *f.*

certifiable ['sə:tifaiəbl] *a.* que l'on peut certifier; **c. lunatic,** aliéné interdit; *F:* **he's c.,** il est fou à lier.

certificate [sə'tifikət] *n.* **1.** certificat *m*; (*a*) **medical c.,** certificat médical; **health c.,** billet *m* de santé; (*b*) *Fin: etc:* **bearer c.,** titre au porteur; **share, stock, c.,** certificat d'action(s); **(government) savings c.,** bon *m* d'épargne; *Com:* **c. of origin,** certificat d'origine; (*c*) *Av:* **c. of airworthiness,** certificat de navigabilité; *Aut:* **test c.** = certificat d'aptitude à rouler. **2.** (*a*) certificat (d'aptitude); diplôme *m*, brevet *m*; *Nau:* **master's c.,** brevet de capitaine; (*b*) *Sch:* **C. of Secondary Education** = certificat de fin d'études secondaires. **3.** *Adm:* acte; **birth, marriage, c.,** acte de naissance, de mariage; (*when applying for passport, etc.*) extrait *m* de naissance, d'actes de l'état civil; **death c.,** (i) acte de (constat de) décès; (ii) extrait mortuaire; **registration c., c. of registration,** (i) matricule *f*; (ii) (*for alien*) permis *m* de séjour.

certificated [sə'tifikeitid] *a.* diplômé, titré.

certification [sətifi'keiʃ(ə)n] *n.* certification *f.*

certify ['sə:tifai] *v.tr.* **1.** (*a*) certifier, déclarer, attester (qch.); constater (un décès); **to c. that sth. is true,** attester, porter témoignage, que qch. est vrai; *A:* (*of doctor*) **to c. a lunatic,** déclarer qn atteint d'aliénation mentale; *F:* **you ought to be certified,** tu es complètement fou; (*b*) authentiquer, homologuer, légaliser (un document); *Com:* **certified cheque,** chèque visé pour provision; *U.S:* **certified letter,** lettre recommandée; (*c*) diplômer, breveter (qn); *U.S: Sch:* **certified teacher,** instituteur diplômé. **2.** *v.ind.tr.* **to c. to sth.,** attester qch.

certitude ['sə:titju:d] *n.* certitude *f.*

cervical ['sə:vik(ə)l, sə:'vaik(ə)l] *a.* *Anat:* cervical, -aux; *Med:* **c. smear,** frottis *m* cervical.

cervix, *pl.* **-vices** ['sə:viks, -visi:z] *n.* *Anat:* (*a*) cou *m*; (*b*) **c. uteri** ['ju:təri] col *m* de l'utérus.

cesium ['si:ziəm] *n.* *NAm:* = CAESIUM.

cessation [se'seiʃ(ə)n] *n.* cessation *f*, arrêt *m*; **c. from work,** suspension *f*, interruption *f*, du travail.

cession ['seʃ(ə)n] *n.* **1.** cession *f*; abandon *m.* **2.** (*a*) *Jur:* cession de biens (aux créanciers); (*b*) *Pol: etc:* cession (d'un territoire).

cesspit ['sespit] *n.* **1.** *Agr:* fosse *f* à fumier et à purin. **2.** = CESSPOOL.

cesspool ['sespu:l] *n.* **1.** fosse *f* d'aisances; puits absorbant. **2.** fosse de curage (d'un égout).

Ceylon [si'lɔn] *Pr.n.* *Geog: Hist:* Ceylan *m.*

chafe [tʃeif] **1.** *v.tr.* (*a*) frictionner (les membres de qn); (*b*) user, échauffer (qch.) par le frottement; écorcher (la peau); érailler (un cordage); (*c*) irriter, énerver (qn). **2.** *v.i.* (*a*) s'user par le frottement; (*of skin*) s'irriter, s'écorcher; (*of rope*) s'érailler; (*b*) (*of pers.*) **to c. at, under, sth.,** s'irriter de, contre, qch.; s'énerver de qch.; **to c. under restraint,** ronger son frein. **chafing** *n.* **1.** friction *f* (des membres). **2.** (*a*) écorchement *m* (de la peau); (*b*) usure *f*, friction, frottement *m* (d'une courroie, d'un pneu, etc.). **3.** *Dom.Ec:* **c. dish,** réchaud *m* de table.

chaff¹ [tʃa:f] *n.* **1.** (*a*) balle(s) *f* (du grain); (*b*) *Agr:* (i) menue paille; (ii) paille hachée. **2.** raillerie *f*, taquinerie *f.* **3.** *Elcs: U.S:* ruban *m* métallique antiradar.

chaff² *v.tr.* **1.** *Agr:* hacher (la paille). **2.** railler, taquiner (qn); *F:* chiner (qn).

chaffinch ['tʃæfin(t)ʃ] *n.* *Orn:* pinson *m.*

chagrin¹ ['ʃægrin] *n.* chagrin *m*, dépit *m.*

chagrin² *v.tr.* *esp. Lit:* chagriner (qn); **to be chagrined at sth.,** être vexé de, par, qch.

chain¹ [tʃein] *n.* **1.** (*a*) chaîne *f*; (*small*) chaînette *f*; *Jewel:* chaînette (pour pendentif); **watch c.,** chaîne de montre; **safety c.,** (i) (*for door*) chaîne de sûreté; (ii) (*for bracelet, etc.*) chaînette de sûreté; **to put a dog on the c.,** mettre un chien à la chaîne; **prisoner in chains,** prisonnier enchaîné; **c. gang,** chaîne de forçats; *Fig:* **to break, burst, one's chains,** rompre ses chaînes; **c. link,** chaînon *m*, maillon *m* de chaîne: **c. armour, c. mail,** (i) mailles *fpl*; (ii) cotte *f* de mailles; **bicycle c.,** chaîne de bicyclette; *Cy: etc:* **c. guard,** carter *m*; *Aut:* **snow chains,** chaînes (à neige); *Tls:* **c. saw,** tronçonneuse *f*; *Agr:* **c. harrow,** herse *f* à chaînons; (*in W.C.*) **to pull the c.,** tirer la chasse d'eau; (*b*) *Nau:* **anchor c.,** chaîne d'ancrage; **c. well,** puits *m* à chaînes, aux chaînes; (*c*) *Tchn: Mec.E:* **drive, driving, transmission, c.,** chaîne de transmission; **c. conveyor,** transporteur *m* à chaîne; *Hyd.E:* **bucket c.,** chaîne à augets, à godets; (*d*) *Geog:* chaîne (de montagnes); (*small*) chaînon: *Ind:* **c. work,** travail *m* à la chaîne; *Com:* **c. store,** (i) magasin *m* à succursales (multiples); (ii) succursale *f* (de grand magasin); (*of people*) **to form a c.,** former, faire, la chaîne (pour passer des seaux, etc.); **c. letter,** chaîne; **c. of events,** suite *f*, série *f*, d'événements; **to c. smoke,** fumer des cigarettes à la file; **c. smoker,** fumeur, -euse, invétéré(e); (*e*) *Ph: Ch: etc:* chaîne (de désintégration, etc.); **c. reaction,** réaction *f* en chaîne. **2.** *Surv: Meas:* longueur *f* de 20 m 116; **surveyor's c., measuring c.,** chaîne d'arpenteur, d'arpentage.

chain² *v.tr.* **1. to c. s.o., sth., to sth.,** attacher qn, qch., à qch. par une chaîne. **2. to c. sth. down,** retenir qch. par une chaîne; **to c. s.o. (down),** enchaîner qn; **chained to one's desk,** cloué à son bureau; **to c. up a dog,** mettre un chien à la chaîne. **3.** fermer (une porte, etc.) avec des chaînes.

chainstitch ['tʃeinstitʃ] *n.* *Needlew:* point *m* de chaînette.

chair¹ [tʃɛər] *n.* **1.** (*a*) chaise *f*; siège *m*; **folding c.,** chaise pliante; pliant *m*; **easy c.,** fauteuil *m*; **grandfather c.,** fauteuil à oreillettes; **rocking c.,** fauteuil à bascule; **deck c.,** chaise longue; transatlantique *m*, *F:* transat *m*; **high c.,** chaise haute (pour enfants); **Bath c., invalid c.,** voiture *f* de malade; fauteuil roulant; *Games:* **musical chairs,** jeu *m*, polka *f*, des chaises; **c. attendant,** loueur, -euse, de chaises, chaisière *f* (dans un parc, etc.); *Ski:* **c. lift,** télésiège *m*; (*b*) *Jur:* **electric c.,** chaise électrique; (*c*) *Sch:* chaire *f* (de professeur de faculté); (*d*) siège (de juge); fauteuil (de président); **to be in the c.,** occuper le fauteuil présidentiel; présider (la séance); (*e*) *Jur: U.S:* banc *m* des témoins. **2.** *Rail:* coussinet *m*, chaise (de rail).

chair² *v.tr.* **1.** présider (une réunion). **2.** porter (qn) en triomphe.

chairback ['tʃɛəbæk] *n.* dossier *m* de chaise.

chairman, *pl.* **-men** ['tʃɛəmən] *n.* (*a*) président, -ente; **to act as c.,** présider (la séance); **Mr C., Madam C.,** Monsieur le Président, Madame la Présidente; (*b*) *Com:* président-directeur général (d'une maison).

chairmanship ['tʃɛəmənʃip] *n.* présidence *f*; **under the c. of Mr X,** sous la présidence de M. X.

chairperson ['tʃɛəpə:sən] *n.* président, -ente.

chalet ['ʃælei] *n.* chalet *m.*

chalice ['tʃælis] *n.* (*a*) *A: & Lit:* coupe *f* (à boire); (*b*) *Ecc:* calice *m.*

chalk¹ [tʃɔ:k] *n.* **1.** (*a*) craie *f*; **c. hills, cliffs,** collines, falaises, crayeuses; (*b*) (*for writing, etc.*) craie; *Art:*

(crayon) pastel (*m*); *Bill:* blanc *m*; **c. drawing,** pastel; **c. line, mark,** (i) trait *m* à la craie; (ii) *Carp: etc:* cordeau (blanchi à la craie); (iii) ligne faite au cordeau; tringle *f*; **they are as different as c. and cheese,** c'est le jour et la nuit; (*c*) **French c.,** craie de tailleur. **2.** trait *m* à la craie (pour marquer les points dans certains jeux); *F:* **not by a long c.,** tant s'en faut; pas du tout; **by a long c.,** de beaucoup.

chalk² *v.tr.* **1.** (*a*) marquer (qch.) à la craie; *Carp: etc:* **to c. a line,** tringler une ligne (au cordeau); (*b*) *Bill:* **to c. one's cue,** frotter sa queue de blanc; (*c*) talquer; saupoudrer de talc. **2.** (*a*) **to c. (up) sth.,** écrire qch. à la craie; (*b*) **to c. up a win, a success,** remporter une victoire, un succès.

chalkpit ['tʃɔːkpit] *n.* carrière *f* de craie; crayère *f*.

chalky ['tʃɔːki] *a.* **1.** (terrain) crayeux; (sol, eau) calcaire; (dépot) calcique. **2.** (teint) pâle, terreux.

challenge¹ ['tʃælin(d)ʒ] *n.* **1.** (*a*) défi *m*; **to accept, take up, a c.,** relever un défi; **this work is a real c. to me,** ce travail est une vraie gageure pour moi; (*b*) *Sp:* défi, challenge *m*; **c. match,** challenge; **c. cup,** coupe-challenge *f*, *pl.* coupes-challenge; (*c*) *Mil:* interpellation *f* (par une sentinelle). **2.** *Jur:* récusation *f* (du jury).

challenge² *v.tr.* **1.** (*a*) **to c. s.o.,** (i) provoquer qn (au combat); (ii) *Sp:* challenger qn; **to c. s.o. to do sth.,** (i) défier qn de faire qch.; (ii) sommer qn de faire qch.; **to c. s.o. to a game of chess,** défier qn aux échecs; (*b*) *Mil:* (*of sentry*) interpeller (qn); faire une sommation à (qn). **2.** (*a*) protester contre, disputer (une affirmation); mettre en question, en doute (la parole de qn); contester (les titres de qn); **to c. s.o.'s right to do sth.,** contester à qn le droit de faire qch.; (*b*) *Jur:* récuser (un juré). **challenging** *a.* (*of look, remark, etc.*) provocateur, -trice; (air) de défi.

challenger ['tʃælin(d)ʒər] *n.* **1.** (*a*) provocateur, -trice; (*b*) *Sp:* challenger *m*; **the holder and the c.,** le détenteur et le challenger. **2.** *Jur:* récusant, -ante.

chamber ['tʃeimbər] *n.* **1.** (*a*) *A: & Lit:* salle *f*; **audience c.,** salle d'audience; **council c.,** salle du conseil; **c. music,** musique *f* de chambre; (*b*) *Lit:* **(bed-)c.,** chambre *f* (à coucher); (*c*) **c. pot,** pot *m* de chambre. **2.** (*a*) chambre (de commerce, de métiers); (*b*) *Pol:* Chambre (haute, basse); **double c. system,** système bicaméral **3.** *Jur:* **chambers,** cabinet *m* de consultation (d'un avocat); étude *f* (d'un avoué); **in chambers,** en chambre du conseil; **to hear a case in chambers,** juger une cause en référé. **4.** *Tchn:* (*a*) *Ind:* **lead c.,** chambre de plomb; (*b*) *Metall:* laboratoire *m* (de fourneau); *I.C.E: etc:* **compression c.,** chambre de compression; (*c*) chambre (d'une arme à feu); **the chambers of a revolver,** les alvéoles *mpl* d'un revolver; (*d*) **air c.,** chambre à air (d'une pompe); (*e*) *Ph:* chambre (d'ionisation, à détente); (*f*) *Nat.Hist: etc:* cavité *f*; alvéole.

chamberlain ['tʃeimbəlin] *n.* chambellan *m*.

chambermaid ['tʃeimbəmeid] *n.f.* femme de chambre (d'hôtel).

chameleon [kə'miːliən] *n. Rept:* caméléon *m*.

chamfer¹ ['ʃæmfər] *n.* **1.** biseau *m*, chanfrein *m*; arête *f* (de moulure). **2. hollow c.,** cannelure *f*.

chamfer² *v.tr.* **1.** *Carp: etc:* biseauter, chanfreiner (une planche, etc.); abattre (une arête). **2.** canneler (une colonne, etc.).

chamois ['ʃæmwɑː] *n.* (*a*) *Z:* chamois *m*; (*b*) **c.** (*also* ['ʃæmi]) **leather,** (i) (cuir *m* de) chamois; (ii) peau *f* de chamois.

champ¹ [tʃæmp] *v.tr.* (*of horse, etc.*) mâcher bruyamment (le fourrage); ronger, mâcher, mâchonner (le mors); *F:* (*of pers.*) **to c. the bit,** ronger son frein.

champ² *n. Sp: F:* champion *m*.

Champagne [ʃæm'pein] **1.** *Pr.n. Geog:* Champagne *f*. **2.** *n.* **c.,** (*a*) vin *m* de Champagne; champagne *m*; (*b*) (*colour*) champagne.

champion¹ ['tʃæmpiən] **1.** *n.* (*a*) champion, -ionne; partisan, -ane (*b*) *Sp:* champion, -ionne; **world c.,** champion du monde. **2.** (*a*) *attrib.* **a c. footballer,** un champion du football; (*b*) *a. Dial:* **that's c.!** à la bonne heure! bravo!

champion² *v.tr.* soutenir, défendre (une cause); se faire le champion (d'une cause).

championship ['tʃæmpiənʃip] *n.* **1.** *Sp: etc:* championnat *m*. **2.** défense *f* (d'une cause).

chance¹ [tʃɑːns] *n.* **1.** (*a*) chance *f*, hasard *m*; sort *m*; **game of c.,** jeu *m* de hasard; **by c.,** par hasard; **somebody I met by c.,** une connaissance de rencontre; **do you by any c. know his address?** sauriez-vous son adresse par hasard? **to leave nothing to c.,** ne rien laisser au hasard; **to leave everything to c.,** s'en remettre au hasard; **to do sth. on the off c.,** faire qch. à tout hasard; (*b*) **to look, have an eye, to the main c.,** veiller à ses propres intérêts. **2.** (*a*) occasion *f*; **now's your c.,** vous avez la partie belle; **it's your last c.,** c'est votre dernière chance; **it's a c. in a million,** ces chances-là n'arrivent qu'une fois; (*b*) **to have, to stand, a c.,** avoir des chances de succès; **he stands a good c. of being chosen,** il a des chances d'être choisi; **he hasn't the slightest c., an earthly c., of succeeding,** il n'a pas la moindre chance de réussir; **to have an even, a fifty-fifty, c.,** avoir des chances égales; **to give s.o. a c.,** (i) mettre qn à l'essai; (ii) donner une chance à qn; **to take one's c.,** risquer (les chances). **3.** risque *m*; **to take a c.,** courir un risque; **I'm taking no chances,** je ne veux rien risquer; **to take a sporting c.,** essayer le coup. **4.** *attrib.* fortuit, accidentel; **c. discovery,** découverte accidentelle; **c. meeting,** rencontre de hasard; rencontre fortuite.

chance² **1.** *v.i. Lit:* (*a*) **to c. to do sth.,** faire qch. par hasard; (*b*) **to c. (up)on s.o., sth.,** tomber (par hasard) sur qn, sur qch. **2.** *v.tr.* risquer; **to c. it, one's luck, one's arm,** risquer le coup, tenter sa chance.

chancel ['tʃɑːns(ə)l] *n. Ecc.Arch:* chœur *m*; **c. screen,** jubé *m*.

chancellery ['tʃɑːnsələri] *n.* chancellerie *f*.

chancellor ['tʃɑːnsələr] *n.* (*a*) chancelier *m* (d'une cathédrale, d'un ordre de chevalerie, d'une université); (*b*) **the Lord (High) C.,** le Grand Chancelier = Ministre *m* de la Justice); **C. of the Exchequer,** Chancelier de l'Échiquier, = Ministre des Finances.

chancery ['tʃɑːnsəri] *n.* **1.** (*a*) *Jur:* **(Court of) C.,** cour *f* de la chancellerie; (*b*) *Dipl:* chancellerie (d'une ambassade). **2.** *Box: Wr:* **hold in c.,** cravate *f*. **3.** *U.S:* (*a*) chancellerie *f*; (*b*) *Jur:* **(court of) c.,** cour d'équité.

chancre ['ʃæŋkər] *n. Med:* chancre *m*.

chancy ['tʃɑːnsi] *a. F:* chanceux, incertain; risqué.

chandelier [ʃændə'liər] *n.* lustre *m*.

chandler ['tʃɑːndlər] *n.* (*a*) chandelier, -ière; (*b*) = marchand *m* de couleurs; **ship('s) c.,** fournisseur *m* de navires; **corn c.,** marchand de blé, de grains.

change¹ [tʃein(d)ʒ] *n.* **1.** changement *m* (d'air, d'occupation, etc.); changement, variation *f* (du temps); altération *f* (du visage, de la voix); revirement *m* (d'opinion); **c. of address,** changement de domicile; **c. for the better, for the worse,** amélioration *f*, altération (de la santé, etc.); **sudden c. of fortune,** revirement de fortune; **you need a c.,** il vous faut un changement d'air, d'occupation; **this trip will be a bit of a c. for you,** ce voyage vous changera un peu; **for a c.,** pour changer; **it, that, makes a c.,** ça change toujours les idées; **c. of life,** *F:* **the c.,** retour *m* d'âge; *Aut: etc:* **oil c.,** vidange *f*. **2. c. of clothes,** vêtements *mpl* de rechange. **3.** change *m*; **to gain by the c.,** gagner au change. **4.** monnaie *f*; **small c.,** petite monnaie; **to get c.,** faire de la monnaie; **to get c. for £5,** faire la monnaie de £5; **you may keep the c.,** vous pouvez garder le reste; *F:* **he won't get much c. out of me,** il perdra ses peines avec moi **5. to ring the changes,** carillonner avec variation, avec permutations; **to ring the changes on (sth.),** ressasser, rabâcher (un sujet, etc.); broder des variations sur (un sujet); varier, donner de la variété à (un menu, un programme, etc.).

change² **1.** *v.tr.* (*a*) changer, modifier (ses projets, son genre de vie, etc.); **to c. one thing into another,** changer une chose en une autre; **to c. one's ways, one's habits,** se refaire; **to c. one's mind, one's opinion,** changer d'avis; **to c. the subject,** changer de sujet; parler d'autre chose; (*b*) changer (les draps); **to c. one's clothes,** se changer; **to c. one's dress, one's shoes,** changer de robe, de chaussures; *F:* **to c. the baby,** changer le bébé; (*c*) *Aut: etc:* remplacer (un pneu); **to c. the oil,** faire la vidange; **to c. gear,** changer de vitesse; (*d*) **to c. one's seat,** changer de place; **to c. trains,** changer de train; *v.i.* **do we c. here?** est-ce qu'on change (de train, de car, d'avion) ici? **all c.!** tout le monde descend! **to c. colour,** changer de couleur, de visage; **to c. the guard,** relever la garde; (*e*) **to c. one thing for another,** changer, troquer, une chose pour, contre, une autre; **to c. places, seats, with s.o.,** changer de place avec qn; *Fig:* **I wouldn't (like to) c. places with him,** je ne changerais pas avec lui; **to c. dollars into francs,** changer des dollars contre des francs, en francs; (*f*) **to c. a note,** (i) changer un billet (de banque); (ii) donner la monnaie d'un billet (de banque). **2.** *v.i.* (*a*) (se) changer, se modifier, varier; (*of moon*) changer de quartier; se renouveler; (*of luck*) tourner; **to c. for the better,** changer en mieux; s'améliorer; (*of weather*) tourner au beau; **to c. for the worse,** changer en mal; **to c. into sth.,** (se) changer, se transformer, en qch.; **the lights changed from green to amber,** les feux ont passé du vert à l'orange; **to c. from one system to another,** passer d'un système à un autre; **the wind has changed,** le vent a sauté, a tourné; (*b*) (*of sentries, Nau: of watches, Ind: of shifts*) se relever; (*c*) (*of pers.*) se changer; **to c. into another dress,** changer de robe; **to c. into trousers,** mettre un pantalon. **change down** *v.i. Aut:* rétrograder, passer à une vitesse inférieure; descendre les vitesses; **to c. d. into second,** passer en seconde. **change over** *v.i.* passer (d'un système à un autre). **change up** *v.i. Aut:* passer à une vitesse supérieure; monter les vitesses. **changing** **1.** *a.* changeant; (expression, etc.) mobile. **2.** *n.* changement *m*; **the c. of the guard,** la relève de la garde; *Sp: etc:* **c. room,** vestiaire *m*.

changeability [tʃein(d)ʒə'biliti], **changeableness** ['tʃein(d)ʒəb(ə)lnis] *n.* variabilité *f* (du temps, etc.); inconstance *f* (de caractère); versatilité *f*.

changeable ['tʃein(d)ʒəbl] *a.* changeant; variable, inconstant, instable; (vent) inégal; **c. character,** caractère changeant, instable.

changeless ['tʃein(d)ʒlis] *a.* immuable, inaltérable.

changeling ['tʃein(d)ʒliŋ] *n.* enfant de fées, substitué à un enfant qu'elles ont volé.

changeover ['tʃein(d)ʒouvər] *n.* **1.** changement *m*, passage *m* (d'un système à un autre, etc.). **2.** changement radical, renversement *m* (politique, etc.). **3.** relève *f* (de factionnaires, *Nau:* du quart, etc.).

changer ['tʃein(d)ʒər] *n. Tchn:* changeur *m*; *Rec:* **record c.,** changeur de disques.

channel¹ ['tʃæn(ə)l] *n.* **1.** lit *m* (d'une rivière). **2.** (*a*) passe *f*, chenal *m* (d'un port); (*b*) *Geog:* détroit *m*, canal *m*; **the (English) C.,** la Manche; **on the other side of the C.,** outre-Manche; **the C. Islands,** les îles Anglo-Normandes; **the C. Tunnel,** le tunnel sous la Manche. **3.** canal, conduit *m* (d'un liquide, d'un gaz). **4.** *Arch: etc:* cannelure *f* (d'une colonne). **5.** rigole *f* (d'irrigation). **6.** (*a*) voie *f*; **to go through the official channels,** suivre la filière, la voie hiérarchique; **through diplomatic channels,** par voie diplomatique; **channels of communication,** artères *fpl* (d'un pays); (*b*) *El: Elcs: etc:* voie; *T.V: W.Tel:* chaîne *f*; voie, piste *f* (de bande magnétique); canal (de bande perforée).

channel² *v.tr.* **(channelled,** *NAm:* **channeled) 1.** creuser des rigoles dans (un terrain). **2.** (*a*) canaliser, diriger, orienter (des efforts, des ressources, etc.) **(towards,** vers; **into,** dans); (*b*) *Cmptr:* acheminer, canaliser (des informations).

chant¹ [tʃɑːnt] *n.* (*a*) chant *m* (monotone); *Ecc:* psalmodie *f*; **plain c.,** plain-chant *m*, *pl.* plains-chants; **Gregorian c.,** chant grégorien; (*b*) chant scandé, slogans scandés (de manifestants).

chant² *v.tr.* (*a*) *Ecc:* psalmodier; (*b*) (*of demonstrators*) scander (des slogans). **chanting 1.** *a.* (*of voice, etc.*) monotone, traînant; (*of accent*) chantant. **2.** *n.* (*a*) psalmodie *f*; (*b*) chant scandé, slogans scandés (de manifestants).

chantey ['ʃænti] *n. NAm:* chanson *f* de marin.

chantry ['tʃɑːntri] *n. A. Ecc:* fondation *f* de messes pour le repos de l'âme du fondateur; **c. priest,** prêtre *m* de la fondation.

chaos ['keiɔs] *n.* chaos *m*; **in a state of c.,** dans le chaos, dans la confusion.

chaotic [kei'ɔtik] *a.* chaotique. **-ally** *adv.* chaotiquement.

chap¹ [tʃæp] *n.* gerçure *f*, crevasse *f* (sur la peau).

chap² *v.tr.* **(chapped)** gercer, crevasser (la peau); (*of hands*) **to get chapped,** *v.i.* **to c.,** se gercer, se crevasser.

chap³ *n.* (*usu. pl.*) bajoue(s) *f*(*pl*) (d'un cochon); *Cu:* **Bath c.,** joue *f* de porc fumée.

chap⁴ *n.m. F:* type; *m*; **a good c.,** un bon type; **an odd, a queer, c.,** un drôle de type; *O:* **I say, old c.!** dis, mon vieux!

chapel ['tʃæp(ə)l] *n.* **1.** (*a*) chapelle *f*; oratoire (particulier); **C. royal,** chapelle d'un palais royal; (*b*) *Sch:* chapelle (d'un collège, etc.); (*c*) **c. of ease,** chapelle de secours; (église) succursale (*f*); annexe *f*; **mortuary c., c. of rest** = chapelle ardente; (*d*) chapelle latérale (d'une cathédrale, etc.); **Lady c.,** chapelle de la Vierge; (*e*) temple (protestant); *O:* **are you church or c.?** êtes-vous anglican ou dissident? **2.** *Typ: Publ:* branche *f* du syndicat (des imprimeurs, des éditeurs); **Father of the C.,** chef *m* de l'atelier.

chaperon¹ ['ʃæpəroun] *n.* chaperon *m* (d'une jeune fille); **to act as c.,** servir de chaperon.

chaperon² *v.tr.* **(chaperoned)** chaperonner (une jeune fille).

chaplain ['tʃæplin] *n. Ecc:* aumônier *m*; **army c.,** aumônier militaire.

chaplaincy ['tʃæplinsi] *n.* aumônerie *f*.

chappie ['tʃæpi] *n.m. F: O:* = CHAP⁴.

chapter ['tʃæptər] *n.* **1.** chapitre *m* (d'un livre, etc.); **to give c. and verse for sth.,** citer ses autorités à l'appui d'une affirmation; **a new c. in one's life,** un nouveau chapitre de sa vie; **a c. of accidents,** une suite de malheurs; *F:* la série noire. **2.** *Ecc:* chapitre (de chanoines, de moines); **c. house,** salle *f* capitulaire.

char¹ [tʃɑːr] *n. Ich:* ombre *m* (chevalier), omble *m* (chevalier).

char² *n.f. F:* femme de ménage.

char³ *v.i. F:* faire des ménages.

char⁴ *v.* **(charred) 1.** *v.tr.* carboniser; réduire (du bois, des os) en charbon. **2.** *v.i.* se carboniser. **charring** *n.* carbonisation *f*.

char⁵ *n. P:* thé *m*.

charabanc ['ʃærəbæŋ] *n. A:* autocar *m*.

character ['kæriktər] *n.* **1.** (*a*) *Typ: etc:* caractère *m*; lettre *f*; **in Greek characters,** en caractères grecs; (*b*) *Cmptr:* **special, binary, c.,** caractère spécial, binaire. **2.** (*a*) caractère, marque distinctive (de qn, d'une race, d'un livre, etc.); **books of this c.,** les livres de ce genre; *Biol:* **hereditary, acquired, c.,** caractère héréditaire, acquis; (*b*) **face full of c.,** physionomie *f* qui a du caractère; **region with a c. of its own,** région *f* qui a un caractère particulier. **3. man of (strong) c.,** homme *m* de caractère, de volonté; **c. building,** formation *f* du caractère. **4.** (*a*) réputation *f*; **place of a very dubious c.,** endroit mal famé; (*b*) *A:* certificat *m* (de moralité, de bonne conduite). **5.** (*a*) *Lit: Th: etc:* personnage *m*; **a c. straight out of a novel,** un vrai personnage de roman; **in c.,** (i) *Th: etc:* dans son rôle, dans la peau du personnage; (ii) (*of person's action*) qui s'accorde bien avec son caractère; **out of c.,** (i) *Th: etc:* pas dans le rôle; (rôle) interprété à contre-sens; (ii) (*of person's action*) qui ne s'accorde guère avec son caractère; **c. actor,** acteur *m* de genre; **c. part,** rôle chargé; **c. dance,** danse *f* de caractère; (*b*) **a suspicious c.,** un individu suspect, louche; **he's a c.!** c'est un original, un numéro!

characteristic [kæriktə'ristik] **1.** *a.* (signe, goût, etc.) caractéristique; **this attitude is c. of him,** cette attitude le caractérise, lui est particulière; *Adm:* **c. signs,** signalement *m*; signes particuliers. **2.** *n.* caractéristique *f*; (*a*) trait *m*, signe *m*, de caractère; trait caractéristique; particularité *f*; (*b*) *Mth:* caractéristique (d'un logarithme). **-ally** *adv.* d'une manière caractéristique.

characterization [kæriktərai'zeiʃ(ə)n] *n.* caractérisation *f*.

characterize ['kæriktəraiz] *v.tr.* caractériser (un personnage, un siècle); être caractéristique de (qn).

characterless ['kæriktəlis] *a.* (*a*) sans caractère; (*b*) insipide; sans intérêt.

charade [ʃə'rɑːd] *n.* charade *f*.

charcoal ['tʃɑːkoul] *n.* **1.** (*a*) charbon *m* (de bois); *Med:* **c. biscuit,** biscuit *m* au charbon de bois; (*b*) **animal c.,** noir animal, charbon animal. **2.** *Art:* fusain *m*; **c. drawing,** (dessin *m* au) fusain.

chard [tʃɑːd] *n. Hort: Cu:* **Swiss c.,** bette *f*, blette *f*.

charge¹ [tʃɑːdʒ] *n.* **1.** (*a*) charge *f* (d'une cartouche, d'une mine, etc.); *Artil:* **blank c.,** charge de salut; (*b*) (*of kiln, blast furnace, etc.*) fournée *f*; (*c*) *El:* charge. **2.** (*a*) frais *mpl*, prix *m*; *Adm:* droits *mpl*; **list of charges,** tarif *m*; **scale of charges,** barème *m* des prix; **extra c.,** supplément *m*; **bank charges,** frais bancaires; **c. account,** compte crédit d'achats; (*in taxi*) **minimum c.,** prise *f* en charge; (*in museum, etc.*) **no c. for admission,** entrée gratuite; **to make a c. for sth.,** compter qch.; **free of c.,** (i) *Com: Bank:* exempt de frais, sans frais; (ii) gratis, franco; (iii) à titre gratuit, gracieux; (*b*) *Jur:* privilège *m*, droit; **charges on an estate,** charges d'une succession. **3.** (*a*) commission *f*, devoir *m*; (*b*) charge; emploi *m*; fonction *f*; (*of clergy*) cure *f*. **4.** (*a*) garde *f*, soin *m*; **to take c. of s.o., of sth.,** (i) se charger, avoir soin, de qn, de qch.; (ii) prendre qn à sa charge; **to place sth. in s.o.'s c.,** confier qch. à qn, à la garde de qn, aux mains de qn; **to have c. of sth.,** avoir qch. en garde; **person in c.,** administrateur *m* (**of,** de); délégué, préposé (**of,** à); *Mil:* **the captain in c.,** le capitaine de service; **c. hand,** chef *m* d'équipe; **c. nurse,** infirmier, -ière en chef; *Jur:* **to take s.o. in c.,** arrêter qn; (*b*) personne, chose, confiée à la garde de qn. **5.** recommandation *f*, exhortation *f*; allocution *f* (du juge au jury); résumé *m* (du juge après cause entendue). **6.** *Jur:* charge; motif *m*, chef *m* d'accusation, acte *m* d'accusation; inculpation *f*; (*by public prosecutor*) réquisitoire *m*; **to bring, lay, a c. against s.o.,** porter une accusation, porter plainte, contre qn; (*in police station*) **c. sheet,** cahier *m* des délits et écrous; **c. room,** bureau *m* (de poste de police); **on a c. of having . . .,** sous l'inculpation d'avoir . . .. **7.** (*a*) *Mil:* charge, attaque *f*; **bayonet c.,** charge, assaut *m*, à la baïonnette. **8.** *Her:* meuble *m* (de l'écu).

charge² *v.tr.* **1.** (*a*) charger (un fusil, un conducteur d'électricité, un accumulateur, etc.) (**with,** de); *El:* **charged conductor,** conducteur chargé, sous tension; (*b*) *Her:* charger (une pièce de blason d'une autre). **2. to c. s.o. with a commission,** charger qn d'une commission; **to c. s.o. to do sth.,** ordonner, à qn de faire qch. **3.** (*a*) **to c. s.o. with a crime,** charger qn d'un crime; **to c. s.o. with assault and battery,** inculper qn de coups et blessures; **charged with . . .,** inculpé de . . .; (*b*) *U.S:* **to c. that . . .,** alléguer que . . .. **4.** (*a*) *Com: Fin:* charger (un compte) (**with,** de); **to c. the postage to the customer,** débiter les frais de poste au client; **commission charged by the bank,** commission prélevée par la banque; **c. it to my account, to the bill,** portez-le sur mon compte, sur la note; (*b*) compter, demander (un prix) (**for sth.,** pour qch.); **how much do you c. an hour?** combien prenez-vous de l'heure? **to c. a fee,** percevoir un droit; *Tp:* **calls charged for,** conversations taxées. **5.** *v.tr. & i. Mil:* (*a*) charger (l'ennemi); faire une charge; (*b*) *F:* se précipiter; foncer; **he charged in,** il est entré en coup de vent; **the crowd charged across the square,** la foule s'est élancée à travers la place. **charging** *n.* chargement *m*; *El:* **battery c.,** (re)charge *f* des accus.

chargeable ['tʃɑːdʒəbl] *a.* **1.** (*of pers.*) accusable, inculpable (**with,** de). **2.** *Com: etc:* (*of item, repair, etc.*) à la charge (**to,** de).

chargé d'affaires ['ʃɑːʒeidæ'fɛər] *n. Dipl:* chargé *m* d'affaires.

charger ['tʃɑːdʒər] *n.* **1.** cheval *m* de bataille. **2.** (*device*) chargeur *m* (de fusil, d'accumulateur); chargeuse *f* mécanique (de haut fourneau, etc.); *El:* **trickle c.,** chargeur à régime lent, par filtrage.

chariot ['tʃæriət] *n. Lit: Hist:* char *m*.

charioteer [tʃæriə'tiər] *n. Hist:* conducteur *m* de char.

charisma, *pl.* **charismata** [kæ'rizmə, kæ'rizmətə] *n.* charisme *m*.

charismatic [kæriz'mætik] *a.* charismatique.

charitable ['tʃæritəbl] *a.* **1.** (personne, action) charitable. **2.** (œuvre, société) de bienfaisance, de charité; *Jur:* **c. trust,** œuvre *f* de charité. **-ably** *adv.* charitablement.

charity ['tʃæriti] *n.* **1.** charité *f*; **out of c.,** par charité; *Prov:* **c. begins at home,** charité bien ordonnée commence par soi(-même). **2.** (*a*) acte *m* de charité; (*b*) charité, aumônes *fpl*, bienfaisance *f*; **to live on c.,** vivre d'aumônes; **c. organization,** société *f* de bienfaisance; **c. ball,** bal *m* de bienfaisance. **3.** œuvre *f* de bienfaisance.

charlady ['tʃɑːleidi] *n.f.* femme de ménage.

charlatan ['ʃɑːlət(ə)n] *n.* charlatan *m*.

charleston ['tʃɑːlstən] *n. Danc:* charleston *m*.

Charley, Charlie ['tʃɑːli] *Pr.n.m.* **1.** Charlot; *Cin:* **Charlie Chaplin,** Charlot. **2.** *F:* **I felt a right, a proper, C.,** je me sentais vraiment idiot.

charlotte ['ʃɑːlət] *n. Cu:* **apple c.,** charlotte *f* (aux pommes).

charm¹ [tʃɑːm] *n.* **1.** charme *m* (**against,** contre); sortilège *m*, sort *m*, enchantement *m*; **to be under a c.,** être sous (le coup d')un charme; *F:* **it works like a c.,** ça marche à merveille. **2.** (*a*) amulette *f*, fétiche *m*; (*b*) **(lucky) c.,** breloque *f*; porte-bonheur *m inv*; **c. bracelet,** bracelet *m* porte-bonheur. **3.** (*a*) charme, agrément *m*; attrait *m* (de la jeunesse, etc.); **to be devoid of c.,** manquer de charme; *F:* **to turn on the c.,** faire du charme; (*b*) (*of woman*) **(physical) charms,** attraits, appas *mpl*.

charm² *v.tr.* **1.** (*a*) (*of witch, etc.*) charmer, enchanter (qn); **he has a charmed life,** sa vie est sous un charme; (*b*) charmer (un serpent). **2.** enchanter, charmer (qn). **charming** *a.* charmant; exquis; **Prince C.,** le Prince Charmant; **c. child,** enfant adorable; **what a c. house!** quelle maison exquise! **charmingly** *adv.* d'une façon charmante.

charmer [ˈtʃɑːmər] *n.* (*a*) charmeur, -euse; **snake c.,** charmeur de serpents; (*b*) **she's a c.,** elle est adorable; **he's a c.,** il est charmant.

charnel [ˈtʃɑːn(ə)l] *n.* **c. house,** charnier *m,* ossuaire *m.*

chart¹ [tʃɑːt] *n.* **1.** carte *f* (marine, aéronautique); **c. room,** cabine *f* des cartes. **2.** (*a*) graphique *m;* diagramme *m; Med:* **temperature c.,** feuille *f* de température; (*b*) tableau; *Com:* **colour c.,** nuancier *m.* **3.** *Mus:* **(pop) charts,** palmarès *m,* hit-parade *m.*

chart² *v.tr.* **1.** *Nau:* (*a*) porter (un rocher, etc. sur une carte); (*b*) hydrographier, faire l'hydrographie (d'une mer, etc.). **2.** porter (la température d'un malade, etc.) sur la feuille; établir le graphique (d'une série de relèvements, etc.).

charter¹ [ˈtʃɑːtər] *n.* **1.** (*a*) *Hist: Jur:* charte *f* (d'une ville, d'une université, etc.); statuts *mpl* (d'une société); privilège *m; Pol:* **the Atlantic C.,** la Charte de l'Atlantique. **2.** *Nau: Av:* affrètement *m;* **c. plane,** avion-taxi *m, pl.* avions-taxis; (avion) charter *m;* **c. flight,** vol *m* d'affrètement; **on c.,** (i) affrété; (ii) loué; (iii) sous contrat.

charter² *v.tr.* **1.** accorder une charte à (une compagnie, etc.). **2.** affréter (un navire, un avion); prendre (un navire) à fret; **to c. a coach,** affréter un car. **chartered** *a.* **1.** (compagnie, banque) privilégiée; **c. accountant** = expert *m* comptable. **2.** (navire, avion) affrété. **chartering** *n.* affrètement *m.*

charterer [ˈtʃɑːtərər] *n.* *Nau:* affréteur *m.*

charwoman, *pl.* **-women** [ˈtʃɑːwumən, -wimin] *n.f.* femme de ménage.

chary [ˈtʃɛəri] *a.* **1.** prudent, circonspect; **to be c. of doing sth.,** hésiter à faire qch. **2. to be c. of praise,** être avare de compliments. **-ily** *adv.* **1.** avec précaution, avec prudence. **2.** avec parcimonie.

chase¹ [ˈtʃeis] *n.* **1.** (*a*) chasse *f,* poursuite *f;* **to give c. to s.o.,** donner la chasse à qn; **in c. of s.o.,** à la poursuite de qn; **to go on a wild goose c.,** courir après la lune; **paper c.,** rallye-paper *m, pl.* rallye-papers; (*b*) *Turf:* steeple *m;* (*c*) *Ven:* **the c.,** la chasse, *esp.* à courre. **2.** gibier chassé; proie *f.*

chase² **1.** *v.tr.* chasser, pourchasser (le cerf). **2.** *v.tr.* (*a*) poursuivre; donner la chasse à (un voleur, l'ennemi, etc.); **to c. (a dog) away,** chasser (un chien); **to c. s.o. out of the house,** chasser qn de la maison; (*b*) *F:* **to c. (s.o., sth.) up,** presser (qn); activer (une affaire, etc.). **3.** *v.i.* **to c. (off) after sth.,** partir à la poursuite de qch.

chase³ *v.tr.* **1.** (*a*) ciseler, bretteler (l'or, l'argent); (*b*) relever (le métal) en bosse; repousser (le métal); **chased silver,** argent repoussé. **2.** sertir (un diamant) **(in gold,** dans de l'or). **chasing** *n.* (*a*) ciselage *m,* ciselure *f,* brettelure *f;* **c. hammer,** marteau *m* à chasser; (*b*) repoussage *m.*

chase⁴ *n.* *Typ:* châssis *m* (de mise en pages).

chaser [ˈtʃeisər] *n.* **1.** (*a*) chasseur *m* (du cerf); (*b*) (i) jockey *m* d'obstacles; (ii) (*horse*) steeple-chaser *m;* (*c*) *F:* **woman c.,** coureur *m* de jupons. **2.** (*a*) *Navy:* (navire) chasseur; *Av:* avion *m* de chasse; chasseur. **3.** *F:* (i) verre *m* d'alcool qu'on prend après un verre de bière, etc.; (ii) verre de bière, etc., qu'on prend après un whisky, etc.

chasm [ˈkæz(ə)m] *n.* **1.** gouffre béant. **2.** abîme *m* (entre deux personnes). **3.** vide *m* énorme.

chassis [ˈʃæsi] *n.* *Aut: Av: etc:* châssis *m.*

chaste [tʃeist] *a.* **1.** (*of pers.*) chaste; pudique. **2.** *Lit:* (*of speech, taste, style*) pur, sobre, simple. **-ly** *adv.* chastement; sobrement.

chasten [ˈtʃeis(ə)n] *v.tr. esp. Lit:* **1.** (*a*) (*of providence, suffering, etc.*) châtier, éprouver (qn); (*b*) châtier (ses passions); (*c*) rabattre la présomption, l'orgueil, de (qn); assagir (qn); **he was in a chastened mood,** il était plutôt abattu. **2.** châtier (son style, etc.).

chasteness [ˈtʃeistnis] *n.* chasteté *f.*

chastise [tʃæsˈtaiz] *v.tr.* châtier; corriger (un enfant).

chastisement [tʃæsˈtaizmənt] *n.* châtiment *m;* correction *f* (d'un enfant).

chastity [ˈtʃæstiti] *n.* (*a*) chasteté *f;* pudeur *f,* pureté *f;* (*b*) célibat *m;* virginité *f.*

chasuble [ˈtʃæzjubl, ˈtʃæzəbl] *n.* *Ecc:* chasuble *f.*

chat¹ [tʃæt] *n.* causerie *f,* causette *f;* bavardage *m;* **to have a c. with s.o.,** bavarder avec qn; *T.V:* **c. show,** émission *f* de bavardages; talk-show *m.*

chat² *v.i.* **(chatted)** causer, bavarder; **to c. with s.o.,** bavarder avec qn; faire la causette avec qn; **to c. about one thing and another,** parler de choses et d'autres. **chat up** *v.tr. F:* baratiner (une fille).

chattel [ˈtʃæt(ə)l] *n.* *Jur:* (*a*) bien *m* meuble, bien mobilier; (*b*) **chattels,** objets mobiliers; meubles *mpl;* **goods and chattels,** biens et effets *mpl.*

chatter¹ [ˈtʃætər] *n.* caquet(age) *m,* jacasserie *f* (d'oiseaux); bavardage *m* (de personnes); babil *m* (de bébes, de singes).

chatter² *v.i.* **1.** (*of birds*) caqueter, jacasser; (*of pers.*) bavarder, jaser; (*of monkeys*) babiller. **2.** (*of teeth*) claquer; **my teeth were chattering,** je claquais des dents. **chattering** *n.* **1.** caquetage *m;* bavardage *m.* **2.** claquement *m* (des dents).

chatterbox [ˈtʃætəbɔks] *n.* *F:* grand(e) bavard(e); moulin *m* à paroles.

chatterer [ˈtʃætərər] *n.* bavard, -arde; jaseur, -euse;.

chatty [ˈtʃæti] *a.* (*pers.*) bavard; (*article, etc.*) écrit sur le ton de la conversation; (*letter*) plein de bavardages.

chauffeur¹ [ˈʃoufər] *n.m.* *Aut:* chauffeur (employé par un particulier); (*of car*) **c.-driven,** conduit par un chauffeur.

chauffeur² *v.tr.* conduire (une voiture).

chauvinism [ˈʃouvinizm] *n.* chauvinism *m.*

chauvinist [ˈʃouvinist] **1.** *n.* chauvin *m.* **2.** *a.* chauvin; *F:* **male c. pig,** phallocrate *m.*

chauvinistic [ʃouviˈnistic] *a.* chauvin, chauviniste.

cheap [tʃiːp] **1.** *a.* (*a*) (à) bon marché, (à) bon compte; pas cher; **it comes cheaper to take a whole bottle,** cela revient moins cher de prendre la bouteille entière; **the cheapest,** le meilleur marché, le moins cher; **dirt c.,** pour rien; **c. fare, rate,** tarif, taux, réduit; *F:* (*of shopkeeper*) **he's very c.,** il n'est pas cher; **on the c.,** (faire qch.) (i) à peu de frais, (ii) chichement; (acheter qch.) au rabais, à bas prix; (*b*) de peu de valeur; (émotion) superficielle; **its c. and nasty,** c'est de la camelote; *F:* **to feel c.,** avoir honte; **to make oneself c.,** déroger; se déprécier. **2.** *adv. F:* = CHEAPLY. **-ly** *adv.* (à) bon marché; à bas prix; à peu de frais; **he got off c.,** il s'en est tiré à bon compte.

cheapen [ˈtʃiːp(ə)n] **1.** *v.tr.* (ra)baisser, faire baisser, le prix de (qch.); diminuer la valeur de (qch.); **to c. oneself,** se déprécier. **2.** *v.i.* devenir moins cher; diminuer de prix.

cheapjack [ˈtʃiːpdʒæk] *n.* camelot *m.*

cheapness [ˈtʃiːpnis] *n.* **1.** bon marché; bas prix (de qch.). **2.** peu *m* de valeur, basse qualité (de qch.).

cheapskate [ˈtʃiːpskeit] *n.* *F:* radin *m.*

cheat¹ [tʃiːt] *n.* **1.** trompeur, -euse (par habitude); escroc *m;* imposteur *m.* **2.** (*at games*) tricheur, -euse.

cheat² *v.tr.* **1.** tromper; frauder (qn); attraper (qn); *v.i.* frauder; **to c. s.o. out of sth.,** escroquer qch. à qn. **2.** (*at games*) tricher (qn); *v.i.* tricher, truquer. **cheating** *n.* **1.** tromperie *f*; truquage *m*. **2.** *Cards:* tricherie *f*.

check¹ [tʃek] *n.* **1.** (*a*) *Chess:* échec *m*; **c.!** échec au roi! (*b*) revers *m*; obstacle *m*. **2.** arrêt *m*; pause *f*; anicroche *f*; **(sudden) c.,** à-coup *m*, aheurtement *m*. **3.** (*a*) frein *m*; **to keep, hold, the enemy in c.,** tenir l'ennemi en échec; **to keep one's feelings in c.,** se contraindre, se contenir; (*b*) *Harn:* **c. rein,** fausses rênes. **4.** butée *f*, arrêt; *Mec.E:* **c. nut,** contre-écrou *m*, *pl.* contre-écrous; **c. valve,** *Mch: etc:* soupape *f*, clapet *m*, de retenue. **5.** contrôle *m*; (*a*) vérification *f* (d'un compte, etc.); **cross c.,** recoupement *m*; *Aut: etc:* **spot c.,** (i) vérification sur place; (ii) contrôle-surprise *m*; **c. point,** contrôle; **radar speed c.,** contrôle de vitesse par radar; **c. list,** liste *f* de contrôle; **to keep a c. on sth.,** contrôler qch.; (*b*) *Comptr:* **automatic c.,** contrôle automatique; (*c*) billet *m*; ticket *m*; (*in restaurant, etc.*) note *f*; *Rail: etc:* **luggage c.,** bulletin *m* de bagages, d'enregistrement; **cloakroom c.,** bulletin de consigne; (*d*) *U.S:* jeton de présence (à une séance); (*e*) *P:* **to hand in, cash in, one's checks,** mourir, *F:* casser sa pipe. **6.** *NAm:* = CHEQUE.

check² **1.** *v.tr.* (*a*) *Chess:* mettre (le roi) en échec; faire échec (au roi); (*b*) faire échec à, arrêter net (qn, qch.); enrayer (une crise, la hausse des prix); arrêter (une attaque); (*c*) refouler, retenir (ses larmes, sa colère); modérer (sa violence); réprimer, refréner (une passion); *I.C.E:* régler (l'allumage, etc.); (*d*) réprimander (un enfant, etc.); (*e*) vérifier (un compte, la pression, etc.); collationner (des documents); compulser (un document) sur l'original; *Typ:* (i) réviser, (ii) conférer (des épreuves); **to c. (off) names on a list, etc.,** pointer, *F:* cocher, des noms sur une liste, etc.; **to c. (off, over) goods,** vérifier, recenser, des marchandises; *Com:* **to c. the books,** pointer les écritures; **checked and double checked,** vérifié et revérifié; **to c. (up) on (sth.),** vérifier, recouper (des informations, etc.); **to c. (up) on s.o.,** enquêter sur qn (du point de vue de sécurité, etc.); *v.i.* **to c. up,** faire la vérification; (*f*) contrôler (les billets); (*g*) (faire) enregistrer (ses bagages); (*at restaurant, etc.*) mettre (son chapeau, son pardessus) au vestiaire. **2.** *v.i.* hésiter, s'arrêter (**at,** devant). **check in** *v.i.* s'inscrire (à un hôtel, etc.); signer à l'arrivée; *Av:* se présenter à l'enregistrement. **checking** *n.* **1.** (*a*) répression *f*; (*b*) *Equit:* (*of horse*) parade *f*. **2.** (*a*) contrôle *m*; vérification *f*; pointage *m*; (*b*) enregistrement *m* (de bagages). **check out** **1.** (*a*) *v.tr.* retirer (des bagages, etc.); (*b*) *v.i.* (*at hotel, etc.*) régler sa note au départ. **2.** (*a*) *v.tr.* vérifier, recouper (des informations, etc.); enquêter sur (qn) (du point de vue de sécurité, etc.); (*b*) *v.i.* (*of story, information, etc.*) s'avérer exact; (*of facts, etc.*) se recouper.

check³ *n.* *Tex:* carreau *m*; **c. material,** tissu à carreaux.

checked [tʃekt] *a.* (tissu, etc.) à carreaux, quadrillé.

checker¹ ['tʃekər] *n.* (*pers.*) contrôleur *m*, -euse.

checker² *v.tr.* *NAm:* = CHEQUER.

checkerboard ['tʃekəbɔːd] *n.* *NAm:* damier *m*.

checkers ['tʃekəz] *n.pl.* *NAm:* jeu *m* de dames.

check-in ['tʃekin] *n.* *Av:* (*a*) enregistrement *m* (des passagers); (*b*) **c.-in (desk),** guichet *m* d'enregistrement.

checkmate¹ ['tʃekmeit] *n.* **1.** *Chess:* échec et mat *m*. **2.** échec complet; défaite *f*.

checkmate² *v.tr.* **1.** *Chess:* faire (le roi) échec et mat **2.** (*a*) faire échec et mat à (qn); (*b*) contrecarrer, déjouer (les projets de qn).

check-out ['tʃekaut] *n.* (*a*) **c.-o. (point, desk),** caisse *f* (dans un supermarché); (*b*) (*in hotel*) **c.-o. time is at 12 noon,** les clients doivent quitter la chambre avant midi (le jour du départ).

checkroom ['tʃekruːm] *n.* *NAm:* (*a*) consigne *f* (de bagages); (*b*) vestiaire *m*.

checkup ['tʃekʌp] *n.* (*a*) vérification *f*; inspection *f*; (*of machinery*) révision *f*; (*b*) examen médical complet; **to give s.o. a c.,** faire le bilan de santé de qn.

cheddar ['tʃedər] *n.* (fromage *m* de) cheddar *m*.

cheek¹ [tʃiːk] *n.* **1.** (*a*) *Anat:* joue *f*; **flabby cheeks,** bajoues *fpl*; **c. to c.,** joue contre joue; **c. by jowl with s.o.,** côte à côte avec qn; (*b*) *F:* fesse *f*; (*c*) *Harn:* branche *f* (de mors). **2.** *F:* impertinence *f*, toupet *m*, culot *m*; **he's got a c., a hell of a c.,** il est culotté, gonflé; **that's enough of your c.!** (ne) te fiche pas de moi! **3.** (*a*) *Techn:* mâchoire *f* (d'étau); (*b*) *Nau:* jottereau *m* (de mât); safran *m* (de gouvernail).

cheek² *v.tr.* *F:* dire des impertinences à (qn), faire l'insolent avec (qn).

cheekbone ['tʃiːkboun] *n.* pommette *f*; **high, prominent, cheekbones,** pommettes saillantes.

cheekiness ['tʃiːkinis] *n.* *F:* effronterie *f*.

cheeky ['tʃiːki] *a.* *F:* effronté, insolent. **-ily** *adv.* d'une manière impertinente; d'un air effronté.

cheep¹ [tʃiːp] *n.* (*a*) piaulement *m*, piaulis *m* (de petits oiseaux); (*b*) *F:* **one never gets a c. out of her,** elle ne dit jamais mot.

cheep² *v.i.* (*of young birds*) piauler.

cheer¹ [tʃiər] *n.* **1.** bonne disposition (d'esprit); *Lit:* **be of good c.!** prenez courage! **2.** (*a*) hourra *m*; **cheers,** acclamations *fpl*, bravos *mpl*; **to give three cheers,** pousser trois hourras; **three cheers for X!** un ban pour X! vive X! *NAm:* **c. leader,** meneur, -euse, de ban; (*b*) *F:* **cheers!** (i) (à votre) santé! (ii) (*at parting*) à bientôt! (iii) merci!

cheer² *v.tr.* (*a*) **to c. s.o. (up),** remonter, qn; relever le moral de qn; (*b*) acclamer (qn). **2.** *v.i.* (*a*) **to c. up,** reprendre sa gaieté; se ragaillardir; **c. up!** courage! (*b*) pousser des hourras, des acclamations. **cheering** **1.** *a.* encourageant; (lettre) réconfortante. **2.** *n.* hourras *mpl*, acclamations *fpl*.

cheerful ['tʃiəf(u)l] *a.* (*of pers.*) gai; de bonne humeur; allègre; (*of face, view, etc.*) riant; (*of room*) gai, d'aspect agréable; (*of conversation, music, etc.*) égayant; (*of news, etc.*) encourageant; **that's a c. thought!** (i) ça c'est encourageant! (ii) *Iron:* comme vous êtes optimiste! **-fully** *adv.* **1.** gaiement, avec entrain; allègrement. **2.** de bon cœur, volontiers.

cheerfulness ['tʃiəfulnis] *n.* (*a*) (*of pers.*) gaieté *f*, bonne humeur; (*b*) aspect riant (du paysage); aspect agréable (d'un intérieur).

cheerio [tʃiəri'ou] *int.* *F:* **1.** (*at parting*) à bientôt! **2.** (*in drinking a toast*) à la vôtre! à la tienne!

cheerless ['tʃiəlis] *a.* morne, triste, sombre.

cheery ['tʃiəri] *a.* **1.** (*of pers.*) joyeux, gai, réjoui, guilleret. **2.** encourageant; réconfortant. **-ily** *adv.* gaiement, avec gaieté; de bonne humeur.

cheese¹ [tʃiːz] *n.* **1.** (*a*) fromage *m*; **blue c.,** (fromage) bleu *m*; **cream c.,** fromage blanc; **cottage c.,** caillé *m*; *Cu:* **cauliflower c., macaroni c.,** chou-fleur *m*, macaronis *mpl*, au gratin; **toasted c.,** rôtie *f* au fromage; *Phot: F:* **say c.!** souriez! (*b*) **the c. industry,** l'industrie fromagère; **cheese maker, manufacturer,** fromager, -ère; *Comest:* **c. biscuit,** biscuit (i) sec (non sucré), (ii) au fromage. **2.** (*pl.* **cheeses**) **a c.,** un fromage (entier); meule *f* (de fromage). **3.** gelée *f* (de prunes, etc.); **quince c.,** pâte *f* de coings.

cheese² *v.tr.* *P:* **to be cheesed (off),** en avoir marre.

cheeseboard ['tʃiːzbɔːd] *n.* (*a*) plateau *m* à fromage; (*b*) plateau de fromages.

cheeseburger ['tʃiːzbəːgər] *n.* *Comest:* petit pain rond fourré de biftek haché et de fromage.

cheesecake ['tʃiːzkeik] *n.* **1.** *Cu:* tarte *f* au fromage blanc et aux raisins secs. **2.** *NAm:* *F:* pin-up *f*.

cheesecloth ['tʃiːzklɔθ] *n.* gaze *f*; étamine *f*.
cheeseparing ['tʃiːzpɛəriŋ] **1.** *a.* parcimonieux; **c. economy,** économies *fpl* de bouts de chandelle. **2.** *n.* parcimonie *f*, lésine *f*.
cheesy ['tʃiːzi] *a.* **1.** qui a un goût de fromage, qui sent le fromage. **2.** *NAm: F:* de mauvaise qualité; moche.
cheetah ['tʃiːtə] *n. Z:* guépard *m*.
chef [ʃef] *n.m.* chef (de cuisine).
chemical ['kemik(ə)l] **1.** *a.* chimique; **c. engineering,** génie *m* chimique; **c. engineer,** ingénieur *m* chimiste; **c. warfare,** guerre *f* chimique. **2.** *n.* produit *m* chimique. **-ally** *adv.* chimiquement.
chemist ['kemist] *n.* **1.** pharmacien, -ienne; **chemist's shop,** pharmacie *f*. **2.** chimiste *m*.
chemistry ['kemistri] *n.* chimie *f*; **organic, inorganic, c.,** chimie organique, minérale; **industrial, technical, c.,** chimie industrielle.
cheque, *NAm:* **check** [tʃek] *n.* chèque *m*; **c. for ten pounds,** chèque de dix livres; **crossed c.,** chèque barré; **blank c.,** chèque en blanc; **traveller's c.,** chèque de voyage; **c. without cover,** *F:* **dud c.,** chèque sans provision; **c. book,** carnet *m* de chèques; chéquier *m*; **to cash a c.,** toucher un chèque; **to stop a c.,** suspendre le paiement d'un chèque.
chequer, *NAm:* **checker** ['tʃekər] *v.tr.* **1.** quadriller (un tissu, etc.); marquer, diviser (qch.) en carreaux. **2.** (*variegate with colour*) diaprer, bigarrer. **3.** diversifier; marquer (l'existence, etc.) de vicissitudes. **chequered,** *NAm:* **checkered** *a.* **1.** quadrillé, à carreaux, en damier. **2.** diapré, bigarré. **3.** (vie) mouvementée, pleine de vicissitudes.
chequerboard, *NAm:* **checkerboard** ['tʃekəbɔːd] *n.* damier *m*.
cherish ['tʃeriʃ] *v.tr.* **1.** chérir; soigner tendrement (un enfant). **2.** bercer, caresser (un espoir); nourrir, entretenir (une idée, une opinion); **to c. illusions,** se nourrir d'illusions; **his most cherished hopes,** ses espérances les plus chères.
cheroot [ʃə'ruːt] *n.* cigare *m* à bouts coupés.
cherry ['tʃeri] *n.* (*a*) cerise *f*; **wild c.,** merise *f*; **c. brandy,** (i) cherry-brandy *m*, *F:* cherry *m*; (ii) eau-de-vie *f* de cerises; *F:* **to take two bites at the c.,** s'y prendre à deux fois, y remordre; (*b*) **c. (tree),** cerisier *m*; **wild c.,** merisier *m*; **c. orchard,** cerisaie *f*; (*c*) *a.* **c.(-red),** cerise *inv*.
cherrystone ['tʃeristoun] *n.* noyau *m* de cerise.
cherub, *pl.* **cherubs,** *B:* **cherubim** ['tʃerəb, -z, -əbim] *n.* (*a*) *B:* chérubin *m*; (*b*) *Art:* angelot *m*, ange joufflu; (*c*) (*of child*) **a little c.,** un petit ange.
cherubic [tʃi'ruːbik] *a.* (*a*) chérubique; de chérubin; (*b*) (sourire) d'ange.
chervil ['tʃəːvil] *n. Bot:* cerfeuil *m*.
Cheshire ['tʃeʃər] *Pr.n. Geog:* le comté de Cheshire; **C. cheese,** fromage *m* de Chester; chester *m*; **to grin like a C. cat,** sourire jusqu'aux oreilles.
chess [tʃes] *n.* jeu *m* d'échecs; **to play c.,** jouer aux échecs; **c. player,** joueur, -euse, d'échecs.
chessboard ['tʃesbɔːd] *n.* échiquier *m*.
chessman, *pl.* **-men** ['tʃesmən] *n.* pièce *f* (du jeu d'échecs).
chest [tʃest] *n.* **1.** coffre *m*, caisse *f*; *Furn:* **c. of drawers,** commode *f*; **tea c.,** caisse à thé; **medicine c.,** (coffret *m* de) pharmacie. **2.** *Anat:* poitrine *f*; poitrail *m* (de cheval); **cold on the c., c. cold,** rhume *m* de poitrine; **to get sth. off one's c.,** dire ce qu'on a sur le cœur.
chesterfield ['tʃestəfiːld] *n. Furn:* canapé rembourré et capitonné (à deux accoudoirs).
chestnut ['tʃes(t)nʌt] **1.** *n.* (*a*) **(sweet, Spanish) c.,** (i) châtaigne *f* (comestible); (ii) marron *m*; **horse c.,** marron d'Inde; (*b*) **(sweet) c. (tree),** châtaignier *m*, marronnier *m*; **horse c. (tree),** marronnier *m* d'Inde; (*c*) *F:* plaisanterie usée; vieille histoire. **2.** (*a*) (*wood*) châtaignier; (*b*) (*colour*) châtain, -aine; *a.* & *n.* **c. (horse),** (cheval) alezan *m*.
chesty ['tʃesti] *a. F:* **to be c.,** être bronchitique.
chevron ['ʃevrən] *n.* chevron *m*.
chew[1] [tʃuː] *n.* **1. to have a c. at sth.,** mâchonner qch. **2.** chique *f* (de tabac).
chew[2] *v.tr.* mâcher, mastiquer (des aliments, etc.); chiquer (du tabac); mâchonner (un cigare); (*of cow*) **to c. the cud,** ruminer; *F:* **to c. sth. over,** méditer sur qch.; *F:* **to c. the rag, the fat,** (i) parler, discuter, à n'en plus finir; (ii) ronchonner. **chewing** *n.* (*a*) mastication *f*, mâchement *m*, mâchonnement *m*; (*b*) **c. gum,** chewing-gum *m*; **c. tobacco,** tabac *m* à chiquer.
chewy ['tʃu(ː)i] *a.* difficile à mâcher; (bonbon) mou.
chic [ʃiːk, ʃik] **1.** *a.* élégant, chic. **2.** *n.* chic *m*.
chicanery [ʃi'keinəri] *n.* **1.** chicanerie *f*, chicane *f*. **2.** arguties *fpl*; subtilités *fpl*; sophismes *mpl*.
chichi ['ʃiːʃiː] *F:* **1.** *a.* recherché, prétentieux; précieux. **2.** *n.* prétention *f*; affectation *f*; préciosité *f*.
chick [tʃik] *n.* **1.** poussin *m*. **2.** *F: esp. U.S:* fille *f*, nana *f*.
chickadee [tʃikə'diː] *n. NAm: Orn:* mésange *f* (à tête noire).
chicken[1] ['tʃikin] *n.* (*a*) poulet *m*; **don't count your chickens before they are hatched,** il ne faut pas vendre la peau de l'ours avant de l'avoir tué; *F:* **she's no c.,** elle n'est plus dans sa première jeunesse; (*b*) *Cu:* poulet; **spring c.,** poussin *m*; **free-range c.,** poulet fermier; **c. liver,** foie *m* de volaille; (*c*) *coll.* volaille *f*; **c. farm,** élevage *m* avicole; **c. farmer,** aviculteur *m*; **c. run,** enclos, (d'un poulailler); (*d*) *Orn: NAm:* **prairie c.,** tétras *m* cupidon, cupidon *m* des prairies; *Fr.C:* poule *f* des prairies; (*e*) *NAm: P:* mineur(e), gamin(e); (*f*) *P:* lâche *m*, froussard *m*.
chicken[2] *v.i. P:* **to c. (out),** caner; flancher.
chickenfeed ['tʃikinfiːd] *n.* **1.** nourriture *f* pour les volailles. **2.** *F:* (*a*) **it's just c.,** c'est de la gnognote; (*b*) petite monnaie.
chickenhearted, chickenlivered ['tʃikin-'hɑːtid, -'livəd] *a. F:* poltron, froussard.
chickenpox ['tʃikinpɔks] *n. Med:* varicelle *f*.
chickpea ['tʃikpiː] *n. Bot:* pois *m* chiche.
chickweed ['tʃikwiːd] *n. Bot:* mouron *m* des oiseaux; morgeline *f*.
chicory ['tʃikəri] *n.* **1.** (*a*) *Bot:* chicorée *f*; *Comest:* endive *f*; *Belg:* chicon *m*; (*b*) *NAm: Comest:* chicorée (frisée). **2. (ground) c.,** (poudre *f* de) chicorée.
chide [tʃaid] *v.tr.* (*p.t.* **chided** *or* **chid**; *p.p.* **chided** *or* **chidden**] *A:* & *Lit:* réprimander, gronder (qn).
chief [tʃiːf] **I.** *n.* (*pl.* **chiefs**) (*a*) (*pers.*) chef *m* (de tribu, de bande, de service); *F:* **the c.,** le patron; *Mil:* **c. of staff,** chef d'état-major; *F:* **he's the big white c.,** c'est lui le grand patron; (*b*) **in c.,** en chef; *Mil: Navy:* **Commander-in-c.,** commandant *m* en chef. **II.** *a.* principal; premier; (en) chef; **my c. assistant,** mon principal collaborateur; **c. reason,** raison majeure. **chiefly** *adv.* **1.** surtout, avant tout. **2.** principalement.
chieftain ['tʃiːftən] *n.m.* chef (de clan).
chiffon ['ʃifɔn] *n. Tex:* mousseline *f* de soie.
chignon ['ʃiːnjɔn] *n.* chignon *m*.
chihuahua [tʃi'wɑːwɑ] *n.* (*dog*) chihuahua *m*.
chilblain ['tʃilblein] *n. Med:* engelure *f*.
child, *pl.* **children** [tʃaild, 'tʃildrən] *n.m. or f.* (*a*) enfant *mf*; **problem c.,** enfant problème; **be a good c.!** sois sage! **to treat s.o. like a c.,** traiter qn en petit garçon, en petite fille; **come here, c.!** viens ici, petit(e)! **children's literature,** littérature enfantine; **I have known him from a c.,** (i) je l'ai connu enfant; (ii) je le connais depuis mon enfance; **it's child's play,** c'est un jeu *m* d'enfant; (*b*) **c. welfare,** protection *f*

de l'enfance; **c. murder,** infanticide *m*; **c. wife,** mariée *f* qui est toujours enfant; (*c*) *Lit:* descendant, -ante; **the children of Israel,** les enfants d'Israël.

childbearing ['tʃaildbɛəriŋ] *n.* maternité *f*; accouchement *m*; **past c.,** (femme) trop âgée pour avoir des enfants.

childbirth ['tʃaildbəːθ] *n.* accouchement *m*; **to die in c.,** mourir en couches.

childhood ['tʃaildhud] *n.* (*a*) enfance *f*; (*b*) **to be in one's second c.,** être retombé en enfance.

childish ['tʃaildiʃ] *a.* **1.** enfantin, d'enfant, d'enfance; (question) naïve; **c. games,** jeux enfantins. **2.** *Pej:* enfant, puéril; **don't be so c.,** ne faites pas l'enfant; **c. remarks,** observations enfantines.

childishness ['tʃaildiʃnis] *n. Pej:* enfantillage *m*, puérilité *f*.

childless ['tʃaildlis] *a.* sans enfant(s); (mariage) stérile; **she died c.,** elle mourut sans enfants.

childlike ['tʃaildlaik] **1.** *a.* enfantin; naïf; (sourire) d'enfant. **2.** *adv.* en enfant.

childproof ['tʃaildpruf] *a.* (dispositif) de sécurité pour enfants.

Chile ['tʃili] *Pr.n. Geog:* Chili *m*.

Chilean ['tʃiliən] **1.** *a. Geog:* chilien. **2.** *n.* Chilien, -ienne.

chili ['tʃili] *n. esp. NAm:* = CHILLI.

chill¹ [tʃil] *n.* **1.** (*a*) *Med:* coup *m* de froid; **to catch a c.,** prendre froid; attraper un refroidissement; (*b*) **c. of fear,** frisson *m* de crainte. **2.** (*a*) froideur *f* (de l'eau, du marbre, etc.); froid *m*, fraîcheur *f*; **there's a c. in the air,** il fait assez frais; **to take the c. off (sth.),** (faire) tiédir (l'eau); chambrer (le vin); (*b*) **to cast a c. over the company,** jeter du froid, un froid, sur l'assemblée.

chill² *a.* froid, glacé; (vent) frais.

chill³ **1.** *v.tr.* (*a*) refroidir, glacer (qn, qch.); faire frissonner (qn); **chilled with fear,** transi de peur; **chilled to the bone,** gelé jusqu'aux os; (*b*) réfrigérer (la viande, etc.); **chilled meat,** viande réfrigérée, frigorifiée. **2.** *v.i.* se refroidir, se glacer. **chilling** **1.** *a.* (vent, accueil) glacial (*pl.*-als); (récit, etc.) qui donne la chair de poule. **2.** *n.* réfrigération *f* (des aliments); glacement *m* (du corps, etc.).

chilli ['tʃili] *n. Cu:* piment *m* (rouge); **c. con carne,** bœuf haché aux haricots rouges et aux piments.

chilliness ['tʃilinis] *n.* **1.** (*a*) froid *m*, froideur *f*; (*b*) froideur (d'un accueil). **2.** sensation *f* de froid.

chilly¹ ['tʃili] *a.* **1.** (*of pers.*) (*a*) frileux; (*b*) **to feel c.,** avoid froid. **2.** (*of weather, etc.*) frais, *f.* fraîche; **it's c. this morning,** il fait frais ce matin. **3.** (*of pers., manner, welcome*) froid; (politesse) glaciale.

chime¹ [tʃaim] *n.* carillon *m*; **to ring the chimes,** carillonner; **door chimes,** carillon de porte.

chime² **1.** *v.i.* (*of clock, bells*) carillonner; *F:* **to c. in,** placer son mot, intervenir. **2.** *v.tr.* sonner (les cloches) en carillon; (*of clock*) carillonner (l'heure). **chiming** **1.** *a.* carillonnant; (pendule, etc.) à carillon. **2.** *n.* carillonnement *m*, carillon *m*.

chimera [k(a)i'miərə] *n. Gr.Myth: & Fig:* chimère *f*.

chimney ['tʃimni] *n.* **1.** cheminée *f* (de maison, etc.); **c. breast,** manteau *m* de (la) cheminée; **c. stack,** (i) tuyau *m* de cheminée; souche *f*; (ii) cheminée d'usine; **c. pot,** pot *m* de cheminée; **c. sweep,** ramoneur *m*; **c. corner,** coin *m* du feu; *F:* (*of pers.*) **to smoke like a c.,** fumer cigarette sur cigarette. **2.** cheminée (de bateau); verre *m* (de lampe). **3.** *Mount:* cheminée.

chimneypiece ['tʃimnipiːs] *n.* (manteau *m* de) cheminée *f*.

chimpanzee, *F:* **chimp** [tʃimp(æn'ziː)] *n.* chimpanzé *m*.

chin [tʃin] *n.* menton *m*; **double c.,** double menton; **receding c.,** menton effacé; **to keep one's c. up,** tenir bon, tenir le coup; **c. strap,** jugulaire *f* (de casque, etc.).

China ['tʃainə] **1.** *Pr.n. Geog:* Chine *f*; **the C. Sea,** la mer de Chine; **C. tea,** thé *m* de Chine. **2.** *n.* (*no pl.*) (i) porcelaine *f*; faïence fine; (ii) vaisselle *f* (de porcelaine); **c. clay,** kaolin *m*; **c. doll,** poupée *f* en porcelaine.

Chinaman, *pl* **-men** ['tʃainəmən] *n.m. O:* Chinois.

Chinatown ['tʃainətaun] *n.* quartier chinois.

chinchilla [tʃin'tʃilə] *n. Z: Com:* chinchilla *m*.

chin-chin ['tʃin'tʃin] *int. P:* (*as a toast*) santé! à la vôtre! à la tienne!

chine¹ [tʃain] *n.* (*a*) *Anat:* échine *f*; (*b*) *Cu:* échinée *f* (de porc).

chine² *v.tr.* (*of butcher*) fendre (une carcasse).

Chinese [tʃai'niːz] **1.** *a.* chinois; **the C. Ambassador,** l'ambassadeur *m* de Chine; **C. white,** blanc *m* de Chine; **C. lantern,** lanterne vénitienne. **2.** *n.* (*a*) Chinois, -oise; (*b*) *Ling:* chinois *m*.

chink¹ [tʃiŋk] *n.* fente *f*, crevasse *f*, lézarde *f* (dans un mur, etc.); entrebaillement *m* (de la porte).

chink² *n.* tintement *m* (du métal, du verre).

chink³ **1.** *v.tr.* faire sonner (son argent); faire tinter (des verres, etc.). **2.** *v.i.* sonner (sec).

Chink⁴ *n. P: Pej:* Chinois, -oise; Chinetoque *m*.

chinless ['tʃinlis] *a.* au menton fuyant; *F:* **c. wonder,** jeune homme (de bonne famille) aimable mais mou.

chintz [tʃints] *n. Tex:* chintz *m*, perse *f*, indienne *f*; **c. curtains,** rideaux *mpl* de perse.

chinwag ['ʃinwæg] *n. F:* causette *f*; bavardage *m*.

chip¹ [tʃip] *n.* **1.** éclat *m*, copeau *m* (de bois); écaille *f*, éclat (de marbre); *Metalw:* paille *f* (de laminage); **diamond chips,** semence *f* de diamants; **to have a c. on one's shoulder,** être aigri; porter rancune (contre tout le monde); *F:* **he's a c. off the old block,** c'est bien le fils de son père. **2.** brisure *f*, écornure *f* (d'assiette); brèche *f* (de lame de couteau). **3.** tranche *f* mince (de légume, etc.); *Cu:* **chips,** (i) pommes (de terre) frites, *F:* frites *fpl*; (ii) *NAm:* (pommes) chips *mpl*; *Dom.Ec:* **c. cutter,** coupe-frites *m inv*; **c. basket,** panier *m* à friteuse. **4.** (*a*) *Cards: etc:* jeton *m*; **the chips are down,** les jeux sont faits; (*b*) *Fin:* **blue chips,** valeurs sûres; (*c*) *P:* pièce *f* de monnaie; (*d*) *P:* **he's had his chips,** il est cuit, fichu. **5.** *Cmptr:* **(silicon) c.,** microplaquette *f*, *F:* puce *f*, pastille *f*.

chip² *v.tr.* **(chipped)** **1.** (*a*) tailler par éclats; hacher (le bois); cliver (la pierre); enlever (du marbre) au burin, au ciseau. **2.** (*a*) ébrécher (un couteau, une assiette); écorner (un meuble); écailler (de l'émail); (*b*) (*with passive force*) **stone, china, that chips easily,** pierre *f*, porcelaine *f*, qui s'écaille, s'ébrèche, facilement; (*c*) *F:* blaguer, railler (qn). **3.** *Golf:* prendre (la balle) en dessous. **chip in** *v.i.* (*a*) *Cards:* miser; (*b*) *F:* intervenir; se mêler à la conversation; (*c*) *F:* payer sa part. **chipped** *a.* **1.** ébréché; écaillé. **2.** *Cu:* (*a*) **c. potatoes,** pommes (de terre) frites; (*b*) *NAm:* **c. beef,** bœuf séché ou fumé coupé en tranches fines. **chipping** *n.* **1.** écaillement *m* (de pierre, de métal, etc.); clivage *m* (de pierre). **2. chippings,** éclats *mpl* (de pierre); graillons *mpl* (de marbre); copeaux *mpl* (de bois); *P.N:* **loose chippings,** gravillons *mpl*, *Fr.C:* gravelle *f*.

chipboard ['tʃipbɔːd] *n.* **1.** *NAm: Paperm:* carton gris. **2.** (panneau *m* de) bois aggloméré.

chipmunk ['tʃipmʌŋk] *n. Z:* tamia rayé, chipmunk *m*, écureuil rayé, *Fr.C:* suisse rayé, barré.

chipolata [tʃipə'lɑːtə] *n. Comest:* **c. (sausage),** chipolata *f*.

chipper ['tʃipər] *a. NAm: F:* (*of pers.*) (*a*) gai, vif, en train; (*b*) en bonne forme (physique).

chiromancer ['kaiəroumænsər] *n.* chiromancien, -ienne.

chiromancy ['kaiəroumænsi] *n.* chiromancie *f*.

chiropodist [ki'rɔpədist] *n.* pédicure *mf*.

chiropody [ki'rɔpədi] *n.* pédicurie *f*.

chiropractic ['kaiərouprӕktik] *n.* chiropraxie *f.*
chiropractor ['kaiərouprӕktər] *n.* chiropracteur *m.*
chirp¹ [tʃə:p] *n.* pépiement *m*, gazouillement *m*, gazouillis *m* (d'oiseaux); piaulement *m* (d'un poussin); cri *m*, chant *m*, *grésillement m* (du grillon).
chirp² *v.i.* **1.** (*of bird*) pépier, gazouiller; (*of chicken*) piauler; (*of grasshopper*) chanter. **2.** (*of pers.*) babiller, *P:* couiner.
chirpiness ['tʃə:pinis] *n. F:* enjouement *m*; humeur gaie.
chirpy ['tʃə:pi] *a. F:* d'humeur gaie; gaillard. **-ily** *adv.* gaiement, gaillardement.
chirrup¹ ['tʃirəp] *n.* **1.** = CHIRP¹. **2.** claquement *m* de langue (pour encourager son cheval).
chirrup² *v.i.* **1.** = CHIRP². **2.** faire claquer sa langue (pour encourager son cheval).
chisel¹ ['tʃiz(ə)l] *n.* **1.** ciseau *m* (de menuisier, etc.); **hollow c.,** gouge *f.* **2.** *Engr:* burin *m.* **3.** *Metalw:* **cold c.,** ciseau à froid.
chisel² *v.tr.* **1.** ciseler (le bois, la pierre); buriner, ciseler (le métal); **to c. sth. off,** enlever qch. au ciseau; **delicately chiselled features,** visage délicatement ciselé. **2.** *P:* rouler (qn).
chit¹ [tʃit] *n. F:* (*a*) mioche *mf*; gosse *mf*; -gamin, -ine; (*b*) jeune fille, femme.
chit² *n. F:* (*a*) petit mot, billet *m*; (*b*) facture *f*, note *f.*
chitchat ['tʃittʃӕt] *n. F:* bavardage *m*, papotage *m.*
chivalrous ['ʃivəlrəs] *a.* chevaleresque; courtois. **-ly** *adv.* chevaleresquement.
chivalry ['ʃivəlri] *n.* **1.** chevalerie *f.* **2.** conduite *f* chevaleresque; courtoisie *f.*
chives [tʃaivz] *n.pl. Bot: Cu:* ciboulette *f*, civette *f.*
chiv(v)y ['tʃivi] *v.tr. F:* poursuivre, chasser; **to c. s.o. about,** harceler, ennuyer, qn.
chloral ['klɔ:r(ə)l] *n. Ch:* chloral *m.*
chlorate ['klɔ:reit] *n. Ch:* chlorate *m.*
chloric ['klɔ:rik] *a. Ch:* (acide, etc.) chlorique.
chloride ['klɔ:raid] *n. Ch:* chlorure *m.*
chlorinate ['klɔrineit] *v.tr.* chlo(ru)rer; javelliser.
chlorination [klɔri'neiʃ(ə)n] *n.* javellisation.
chlorine ['klɔ:ri:n] *n. Ch:* chlore *m.*
chloroform¹ ['klɔrəfɔ:m] *n. Ch:* chloroforme *m.*
chloroform² *v.tr.* chloroformer.
chlorophyl(l) ['klɔrəfil] *n. Ch: Bot:* chlorophylle *f.*
choc-ice ['tʃɔkais] *n. F: Comest:* esquimau *m.*
chock [tʃɔk] *n.* cale *f*; accotoir *m*; support *m* (d'ancre, etc.); *Av: etc:* **to remove the chocks,** enlever les cales.
chock² *v.tr.* **1. to c. (up),** caler, accorer, accoter (un tonneau, etc.); accoter, caler (une roue). **2.** *Mec.E: etc:* coincer (une pièce).
chock(-)a(-)block ['tʃɔkə'blɔk] *a. F:* bondé (**with,** de); bourré (**with,** de); plein à craquer.
chock-full ['tʃɔk'ful] *a. F:* plein à craquer; bourré; **room c.-f. of people,** salle bondée de gens.
chocolate ['tʃɔklət] **1.** *n.* (*a*) chocolat *m*; **slab, bar, of c.,** tablette *f* de chocolat; **milk c.,** chocolat au lait; **plain c.,** chocolat à croquer; **cooking c.,** chocolat à cuire; **drinking c.,** chocolat (chaud); **c. biscuit,** biscuit enrobé de chocolat; **c. factory,** chocolaterie *f*; (*b*) **a c.,** un chocolat; **box of chocolates,** boîte *f* de chocolats. **2.** *a.* (de couleur) chocolat *inv*; **c. brown,** brun chocolat *inv.*
choice¹ [tʃɔis] *n.* **1.** choix *m*; (*a*) préférence *f*; **to make, take, one's c.,** faire son choix; choisir; **by c.,** par goût; **to do sth. of one's own c.,** faire qch. volontairement; (*b*) alternative *f*; **to have the c. of two evils,** avoir le choix entre deux maux; **you have no c. in the matter,** vous n'avez pas le choix. **2.** assortiment *m*, choix; **to have a wide c.,** trouver amplement de quoi choisir.
choice² *a.* **1.** bien choisi; **in a few c. sentences,** en quelques phrases bien choisies. **2.** *Com:* choisi, recherché; (article) de choix; (vin) fin; (liqueur) de marque.
choir ['kwaiər] *n.* **1.** *Arch:* chœur *m* (d'église); **c. stall,** stalle *f*; **c. screen,** jubé *m.* **2.** (*a*) chœur (de chanteurs); **male-voice c.,** orphéon *m*; (*b*) *Ecc:* maîtrise *f*; **c. school,** maîtrise; manécanterie *f.*
choirboy ['kwaiəbɔi] *n.m. Ecc:* jeune choriste, petit chanteur.
choirmaster ['kwaiəmɑ:stər] *n.m. Ecc:* maître de chapelle, de chœur.
choke¹ [tʃouk] *n.* **1.** (*a*) étranglement *m* (de canon de fusil); (*b*) *I.C.E:* buse *f* (du carburateur); starter *m*; (*c*) *Aer:* étouffoir *m.* **2.** foin *m* (d'artichaut). **3.** *El:* bobine *f* d'impédance; self *f.*
choke² **1.** *v.tr.* (*a*) étouffer, suffoquer (qn); **voice choked with sobs,** voix suffoquée, entrecoupée, par les sanglots; (*b*) étrangler (une cartouche, etc.); (*c*) **to c. (up),** obstruer, boucher (un tuyau, etc.) (**with,** de); *I.C.E:* (*of jet*) bouché; (*d*) (*of weeds*) étouffer (les fleurs). **2.** *v.i.* (*a*) étouffer, étrangler (**with,** de); **he was choking with anger,** il suffoquait de colère; **to c. with laughter,** s'étrangler de rire; (*b*) s'engorger, s'obstruer, se boucher (**with,** de); (*of filter, etc.*) se colmater; **choke back** *v.tr.* refouler, ravaler (ses larmes); refouler (ses paroles). **choke off** *v.tr. F:* (i) décourager, (ii) se débarrasser de (qn). **choking** **1.** *a.* étouffant, suffocant. **2.** *n.* (*a*) étouffement *m*, suffocation *f*; (*b*) (*c*) *El:* **c. coil,** bobine *f* d'impédance; self *f.*
choker ['tʃoukər] *n.* (*a*) foulard *m*; (*b*) cravate *f*; tour *m* de cou; (*c*) (*necklace*) collier *m* (de chien).
cholera ['kɔlərə] *n. Med: Vet:* choléra *m.*
choleric ['kɔlərik, kə'lerik] *a.* colérique, coléreux.
cholesterol [kə'lestərɔl] *n. Ch:* cholestérol *m.*
choose [tʃu:z] *v.tr.* (*p.t.*) **chose** [tʃouz]; *p.p.* **chosen** ['tʃouz(ə)n]) **1.** (*a*) choisir; porter son choix sur (qch.); **c. for yourself,** je vous laisse le choix; (*b*) **to c. from, between, several people,** choisir entre, parmi, plusieurs personnes; **there is nothing to c. between them,** l'un vaut l'autre; ils se valent; **to pick and c.,** se montrer difficile, faire le difficile. **2. I didn't c. to go there,** je n'ai pas choisi d'y aller; **I'll do as I c.,** je ferai comme il me plaît, comme bon me semble. **choosing** *n.* choix *m*; **it was none of my c.,** ce n'est pas moi qui l'ai choisi. **chosen** *a.* choisi; **the c. people,** *n.pl.* **the c.,** les élus.
choos(e)y ['tʃu:zi] *a. F:* difficile; **I'm not c.,** ça m'est égal; **don't be so c.,** ne fait pas le difficile.
chop¹ [tʃɔp] *n.* **1.** (*a*) coup *m* de hache, de couperet; (*b*) *F:* **to get the c.,** se faire saquer, être mis à la porte. **2.** *Cu:* (*a*) côtelette *f* (de mouton, de porc); **loin c.,** côte première; (*b*) **c. suey,** chopsouy *m.* **3.** (*a*) *Ten:* **c. (stroke),** volée coupée-arrêtée; *Bill:* **c. (shot),** coup piqué; (*b*) (*in karate, etc.*) coup *m* de poing porté avec le tranchant de la main.
chop² *v.* **(chopped) 1.** *v.tr.* (*a*) couper, fendre (du bois); hacher (de la viande); casser; **to c. sth. in pieces,** couper qch. en morceaux; hacher qch.; (*b*) *Ten:* couper (la balle). **2.** *v.i.* **to c. at sth.,** (i) donner des coups de hache à qch.; (ii) tenter de porter un coup à qch.; (*c*) *F:* **c., c.!** vite, vite! **chop down** *v.tr.* abattre (un arbre). **chop off** *v.tr.* trancher, couper (qch.); trancher (la tête à qn). **chopping** *n.* coupe *f* (du bois); **c. block,** billot *m*; **c. board,** hachoir *m*; **c. knife,** couperet *m*; hachoir *m.* **chop up** *v.tr.* couper (qch.) en morceaux; hacher (qch.) menu.
chop³ *n.* **chops,** bajoues *fpl*; **to lick one's chops,** se lécher les babines.
chop⁴ *v.i.* (*a*) *A:* faire le troc; **to c. and change,** tergiverser; **he's always chopping and changing,** il change d'opinion à tout bout de champ; (*b*) *Nau:* (*of wind*) **to c. (round),** changer, sauter.
chophouse ['tʃɔphaus] *n.* restaurant où on sert surtout des côtelettes et des steaks.

chopper[1] [ˈtʃɔpər] *n.* **1.** (*pers.*) fendeur, -euse (de bois). **2.** *Tls:* (*a*) couperet *m*, hachoir *m*; **meat c.,** feuille *f* de boucher. **3.** *F:* hélicoptère *m.*
chopper[2] *v.i. U.S: F:* se rendre en hélicoptère.
choppy[1] [ˈtʃɔpi] *a. Nau:* clapoteux; (mer) agitée; (vent) changeant, variable.
chopsticks [ˈtʃɔpstiks] *n.pl.* baguettes *fpl.*
choral [ˈkɔːr(ə)l] *a. Mus:* **1.** choral, -als; **c. society,** société chorale; chorale *f.* **2.** chanté en chœur; *Ecc:* (office); (symphonie) avec chœur.
choral(e) [kəˈrɑːl] *n. Mus:* choral *m,* -als.
chord[1] [kɔːd] *n.* **1.** *Poet:* corde *f* (d'une harpe); *Fig:* **to touch the right c.,** faire vibrer la corde sensible. **2.** corde (d'un arc).
chord[2] *n. Mus:* accord *m*; **broken c.,** arpège *m.*
chore [tʃɔːr] *n.* **1.** corvée *f.* **2.** *usu. pl.* travail *m* quotidien (d'un ménage); occupations *fpl.* du ménage; **the daily chores,** les corvées quotidiennes; **to do the chores,** faire le ménage.
choreographer [kɔriˈɔgrəfər] *n.* chorégraphe *mf.*
choreographic [kɔriouˈgræfik] *a.* chorégraphique.
choreography [kɔriˈɔgrəfi] *n.* chorégraphie *f.*
chorister [ˈkɔristər] *n.m.* **1.** choriste. **2.** *U.S:* chef de chœur.
chortle[1] [tʃɔːtl] *n. F:* gloussement *m* (de gaieté).
chortle[2] *v.i. F:* glousser (de joie).
chorus[1], *pl.* **-uses** [ˈkɔːrəs, -əsiz] *n.* **1.** (*a*) chœur *m*; **to sing in c.,** chanter en chœur; **c. of praise,** concert *m* de louanges; (*b*) *Th: etc:* (*singers*) chœur; **c. girl,** girl *f* (de music-hall); **c. master,** maître *m* de chant. **2.** refrain *m* (d'une chanson); **to join in the c.,** chanter le refrain en chœur.
chorus[2] *v.* **(chorused) 1.** *v.i.*faire chœur; reprendre en chœur. **2.** *v.tr.* répéter (qch.) en chœur.
chou [ʃuː] *n. Cu:* **c. pastry,** pâte *f* à choux.
chough [tʃʌf] *n. Orn:* crave *m* à bec rouge.
chow [tʃau] *n.* **1.** (*dog*) (*also* **chow chow**) chow-chow *m.* **2.** *F:* (*food*) boustifaille *f*; **c. time,** l'heure *f* du repas.
chowder [ˈtʃaudər] *n. NAm: Cu:* soupe *f* aux poissons, aux fruits de mer.
chrism [ˈkriz(ə)m] *n. Ecc:* chrême *m*; saint chrême.
Christ [kraist] *Pr.n.m.* le Christ; Jésus-Christ; **the C. Child,** l'Enfant Jésus; *int:* **C.!** bon Dieu!
christen [ˈkrisn] *v.tr.* **1.** baptiser (qn, un navire); **to c. a child George,** baptiser un enfant (sous le nom de) Georges. **2.** étrenner (qch.). **christening** *n.* baptême *m.*
Christendom [ˈkrisndəm] *n.* la chrétienté.
Christian [ˈkristjən] *a. & n.* chrétien, -ienne; **C. Scientist,** scientiste chrétien; **C. burial,** sépulture *f* en terre sainte; **C. name,** nom *m* de baptême.
Christianity [kristiˈæniti] *n.* christianisme *m*; **in a spirit of C.,** en chrétien.
christianize [ˈkristjənaiz] **1.** *v.tr.* christianiser; convertir au christianisme. **2.** *v.i.* devenir chrétien.
Christlike [ˈkraistlaik] *a.* ressemblant au Christ.
Christmas [ˈkrisməs] *n.* Noël *m*; **C. Day,** le jour de Noël; **C. Eve,** la veille de Noël; **at C.,** à (la) Noël; **merry C.!** joyeux Noël! **Father C.,** le père Noël; **C. present,** cadeau *m* de Noël; **C. stocking** = soulier *m*, sabot *m*, de Noël; **C. carol,** noël *m*; **C. pudding,** pudding *m* de Noël, plum-pudding *m*; **C. tree,** arbre *m* de Noël; *Bot:* **C. rose,** rose *f* de Noël; ellébore noir.
Christmastide [ˈkrisməstaid] *n.* époque *f*, saison *f*, de Noël; **at C.,** à la Noël.
Christopher [ˈkristəfər] *Pr.n.m.* Christophe.
chromatic [krouˈmætik] *a.* chromatique.
chrome [kroum] *n.* **1.** *Dy: Tan:* bichromate *m* de potasse. **2.** *attrib.* (*a*) **c. leather,** cuir chromé; (*b*) **c. steel,** acier chromé, au chrome; **c. nickel,** nickel-chrome *m*; (*c*) **c. yellow,** jaune de chrome.
chromium [ˈkroumiəm] *n. Ch:* chrome *m*; **c. plating,** chromage *m*; **c.-plated,** chromé.
chromosome [ˈkrouməsoum] *n. Biol:* chromosome *m.*
chronic [ˈkrɔnik] *a.* **1.** (*a*) *Med:* chronique; **c. ill health,** invalidité *f*; **a c. invalid,** un, une, chronique; (*b*) constant, continuel; (problème) chronique. **2.** *F:* insupportable; (mal de tête) fou, affreux. **-ally** *adv.* chroniquement.
chronicle[1] [ˈkrɔnikl] *n.* chronique *f*; *B.Lit:* **Chronicles,** les Chroniques.
chronicle[2] *v.tr.* **to c. events,** faire la chronique des événements; enregistrer, raconter, les faits.
chronicler [ˈkrɔniklər] *n.* chroniqueur *m.*
chronological [krɔnəˈlɔdʒik(ə)l] *a.* (ordre, etc.) chronologique. **-ally** *adv.* chronologiquement.
chronology [krəˈnɔlədʒi] *n.* chronologie *f.*
chronometer [krəˈnɔmitər] *n.* chronomètre *m.*
chronometry [krəˈnɔmitri] *n.* chronométrie *f.*
chrysalid [ˈkrisəlid] *n. Ent:* chrysalide *f.*
chrysalis, *pl.* **chrysalides, chrysalises** [ˈkrisəlis, kriˈsælidiːz, ˈkrisəlisiz] *n. Ent:* chrysalide *f.*
chrysanthemum [kriˈsænθəməm] *n. Bot:* chrysanthème *m.*
chub [tʃʌb] *n. Ich:* chevesne *m*, meunier *m.*
chubbiness [ˈtʃʌbinis] *n.* (*of pers.*) rondeur *f.*
chubby [ˈtʃʌbi] *a.* potelé, boulot, dodu, grassouillet; (*of face*) joufflu; (joues) rebondies.
chuck[1] [tʃʌk] **1.** *n.* gloussement *m* (de la volaille). **2.** *int.* (*call to fowls*) **c.! c.!** petit! petit!
chuck[2] *v.i.* (*of fowls*) glousser.
chuck[3] *n.* **1.** petite tape (sous le menton). **2.** *P:* **to give s.o. the c.,** balancer, vider, qn.
chuck[4] *v.tr.* **1. to c. s.o. under the chin,** donner une tape à qn sous le menton. **2.** (*a*) *F:* jeter, lancer (une pierre, etc.); **to c. one's money about, around,** gaspiller son argent; (*b*) *F:* lâcher, plaquer (qn, son emploi). **chuck away** *v.tr. F:* jeter (qch.) (pour s'en défaire); se débarrasser de (qch.); **that's just chucking money away,** ça c'est du gaspillage. **chuck in** *v.tr. F:* (*a*) **to c. one's hand in,** (i) jeter ses cartes sur la table; (ii) s'avouer battu; quitter la partie; (*b*) lâcher (son emploi). **chuck out** *v.tr. F:* (*a*) jeter (qch. dont on n'a plus besoin); (*b*) flanquer (qn) à la porte; balancer, vider (qn); **chucking-out time,** l'heure *f* de la fermeture (des cafés). **chuck up** *v.tr. F:* abandonner (un travail); lâcher (son emploi); **to c. everything up,** renoncer à tout.
chuck[5] *n.* **1.** *Mec.E:* mandrin *m*; c. drill, foret *m* (pour tour). **2.** *Cu:* paleron *m* (de bœuf).
chucker-out [ˈtʃʌkəˈaut] *n. F:* videur *m* (dans une boîte de nuit, etc.).
chuckhole [ˈtʃʌkhoul] *n. U.S:* nid *m* de poule (dans la route).
chuckle[1] [ˈtʃʌkl] *n.* rire étouffé; petit rire.
chuckle[2] *v.i.* rire tout bas, en soi-même (**at, over, sth.,** de qch.).
chuckwagon [ˈtʃʌkwæg(ə)n] *n. NAm: F:* (i) charrette *f*, (ii) camion *m*, qui transporte la nourriture (à des moissonneurs, des cowboys, etc.).
chuff [tʃʌf] *v.i.* (*of engine, etc.*) souffler; haleter.
chuffed [tʃʌft] *a. F:* ravi; tout content.
chug[1] [tʃʌg] *n.* souffle *m* (d'une machine à vapeur).
chug[2] *v.i.* **(chugged)** (*of engine, etc.*) souffler, haleter; **we were chugging along (in the car),** nous roulions doucement.
chum[1] [tʃʌm] *n. F:* camarade *mf*; copain *m*, copine *f.*
chum[2] *v.i.* **(chummed)** *F:* **to c. up with s.o.,** se lier d'amitié avec qn.
chummy [ˈtʃʌmi] *a. F:* amical, bon copain.
chump [tʃʌmp] *n.* **1.** (*a*) tronçon *m* (de bois); gros bout, gros morceau (de qch.); (*b*) *Cu:* **c. chop,** côtelette d'agneau (coupée dans le gigot). **2.** (*a*) *P:*

trognon *m*, caboche *f*; **off one's c.,** timbré, maboule; (*b*) *F:* **(silly) c.,** idiot, -ote.

chunk [tʃʌŋk] *n.* gros morceau (de pain, de fromage, etc.); quignon *m* (de pain); tronçon *m* (de bois).

chunky [ˈtʃʌŋki] *a.* (*a*) (*of pers.*) trapu; (*b*) gros (morceau, pullover, etc.).

Chunnel [ˈtʃʌn(ə)l] *n. F:* **the C.,** le tunnel sous la Manche.

church¹ [tʃəːtʃ] *n.* **1.** église *f*; (*protestant*) temple *m*; **c. hall,** salle paroissiale. **2.** (*a*) **the C. of England, the Anglican C.,** l'Église anglicane; **to go into the C.,** entrer dans les ordres; **High C.,** section *f* de l'Église anglicane qui se rapproche du catholicisme en matière de rituel; **the (Roman) Catholic C.,** l'Église catholique; **I believe in one holy, catholic and apostolic C.,** je crois à l'Église, une, catholique et apostolique; (*b*) **c. service,** office *m*; **c. wedding,** mariage religieux.

church² *v.tr.* (*of woman after childbirth*) **to be churched,** faire ses relevailles. **churching** *n.* relevailles *fpl*.

churchgoer [ˈtʃəːtʃgouər] *n. Ecc:* pratiquant, -ante.

churchgoing [ˈtʃəːtʃgouiŋ] *Ecc:* **1.** *a.* pratiquant. **2.** *n.* pratique *f* (de sa religion).

churchman, *pl.* **-men** [ˈtʃəːtʃmən] *n.* **1.** homme *m* d'église; ecclésiastique *m.* **2.** membre *m* d'une église, *in Eng. esp.* de l'Église anglicane.

churchwarden [ˈtʃəːtʃˈwɔd(ə)n] *n.* **1.** *Ecc:* marguillier *m*; fabricien *m*. **2. c. (pipe),** longue pipe (en terre blanche); pipe hollandaise.

churchy [ˈtʃəːtʃi] *a. F: Pej:* bigot bondieusard.

churchyard [ˈtʃəːtʃjɑːd] *n.* cimetière *m*; enclos *m* d'église.

churlish [ˈtʃəːliʃ] *a.* (*a*) mal élevé; qui n'a pas de savoir-vivre; grossier; (*b*) hargneux, grincheux.

churlishness [ˈʃəːliʃnis] *n.* (*a*) grossièreté *f*; manque *m* de savoir-vivre; (*b*) tempérament hargneux.

churn¹ [tʃəːn] *n.* **1. (butter) c.,** baratte *f*. **2. milk c.,** bidon *m* à lait.

churn² **1.** *v.tr.* (*a*) baratter (la crème); battre (le beurre); (*b*) (*of ship's screw*) **to c. up the foam,** brasser l'écume; (*c*) **to c. a thought (over) in one's mind,** agiter une pensée dans son esprit. **2.** *v.i.* (*of sea*) bouillonner. **churn out** *v.tr. F:* (*a*) pondre (des livres, etc.) en série; (*b*) débiter (des objets).

chute [ʃuːt] *n.* **1.** (*a*) *esp. NAm:* chute *f* d'eau; (*b*) *Sp:* piste *f* (pour luges, toboggans); (*c*) (*in swimming pool*) toboggan *m.* **2.** (*a*) glissière *f*; (*b*) **rubbish,** *NAm:* **garbage, c.,** vide-ordures *m.* **3.** *F:* parachute *m.*

chutney [ˈtʃʌtni] *n. Cu:* condiment *m* (à la pomme, etc.).

ciborium, *pl.* **-ia** [siˈbɔːriəm, -iə] *n. Ecc:* (*a*) ciboire *m*; (*b*) tabernacle *m* (du ciboire).

cicada [siˈkɑːdə, -ˈkeidə] *n. Ent:* cigale *f*.

cicely [ˈsis(i)li] *n. Bot:* **(sweet) c.,** myrrhe *f*.

Cicero [ˈsisərou] *Pr.n.m.* Cicéron.

cider [ˈsaidər] *n.* cidre *m*; **c. apples,** pommes *fpl* à cidre; **c. vinegar,** vinaigre *m* de cidre.

cigar [siˈgɑːr] *n.* cigare *m*; **c. case,** étui *m* à cigares; **c. cutter,** coupe-cigares *m inv*; **c. holder,** fume-cigare *m*, *pl.* fume-cigare(s).

cigarette [sigəˈret] *n.* cigarette *f*; **c. card,** image *f* offerte avec un paquet de cigarettes; **c. case,** étui *m* à cigarettes; porte-cigarettes *m inv*; **c. end,** bout *m* de cigarette, *P:* mégot *m*; **c. holder,** fume-cigarette *m*, *m, pl.* fume-cigarette(s); **c. lighter,** briquet *m*; **c. machine,** (i) machine *f*, moule *m*, à cigarettes; rouleuse *f*; (ii) distributeur *m* automatique de cigarettes; **c. paper,** papier *m* à cigarettes.

cinch [sin(t)ʃ] *n.* **1.** *NAm: Harn:* sangle *f*; sous-ventrière *f*, *pl.* sous-ventrières. **2.** *F:* certitude *f*; **it's a c.,** (i) c'est certain; c'est couru; (ii) c'est facile à faire.

cinder [ˈsindər] *n.* **1.** (*a*) cendre *f*; **burnt to a c.,** réduit en cendres; (*b*) **cinders,** cendres; (*c*) *Sp:* **c. track,** (piste) cendrée (*f*). **2. cinders,** *Ind: Mch: etc:* escarbilles *fpl*; *Geol:* **c. cone,** cône *m* de scories.

Cinderella [sindəˈrelə] *Pr.n.f.* Cendrillon.

cinecamera [ˈsiniˈkæm(ə)rə] *n.* caméra *f*.

cinefilm [ˈsinifilm] *n.* film *m* cinématographique.

cinema [ˈsinəmə] *n.* cinéma *m.*

cinematograph [sinəˈmætəgræf] *n.* cinématographe *m.*

cine-projector [ˈsiniprəˈdʒektər] *n.* projecteur *m* cinématographique, cinéprojecteur *m.*

cineraria [sinəˈrɛəriə] *n. Bot:* cinéraire *f*.

cinnabar [ˈsinəbɑːr] *n.* (*a*) *Miner:* cinabre *m*; (*b*) *Ind:* vermillon.

cinnamon [ˈsinəmən] *n.* **1.** *Cu:* cannelle *f*. **2.** *Bot:* **c. (tree),** cannelier *m.* **3.** (*colour*) cannelle *inv.*

cinq(ue)foil [ˈsiŋkfɔil] *n.* **1.** *Bot:* potentille rampante; quintefeuille *f*. **2.** *Arch:* quintefeuille *m.*

cipher¹ [ˈsaifər] *n.* **1.** *Mth:* zéro *m*; *Fig:* **he's a mere c.,** c'est un homme nul, un zéro, une nullité. **2.** (*a*) (*secret writing*) chiffre *m*; *Com:* marque *f*; **to write a message in c.,** transmettre une dépêche en chiffre, en écriture chiffrée; **c. key,** clef *f* de chiffre; **c. clerk,** chiffreur, -euse; **c. machine,** machine *f* (i) à chiffrer, (ii) à déchiffrer; (*b*) (i) message chiffré; (ii) signal chiffré; (*c*) clef (d'un chiffre). **3.** (*monogram*) chiffre, monogramme *m.*

cipher *v.tr.* chiffrer (une dépêche); transmettre en chiffre. **ciphering** *n.* chiffrage *m*, chiffrement *m.*

circle¹ [ˈsəːk(ə)l] *n.* **1.** (*a*) cercle *m*; (*of persons*) **to stand in a c.,** se tenir en cercle; faire cercle; **to go round in circles,** tourner en rond; **to have circles round one's eyes,** avoir les yeux cernés; *Aut:* **turning c.,** cercle de braquage; (*b*) **polar c.,** cercle polaire; **Arctic, Antarctic, C.,** cercle (polaire) arctique, antarctique; (*c*) *Gym:* **to do the grand c. (on the horizontal bar),** faire le grand soleil; (*d*) **vicious c.,** cercle vicieux; (*e*) *NAm:* **traffic c.,** rond-point *m*, *pl.* ronds-points; carrefour *m.* **2.** révolution *f*, orbite *mf* (d'une planète); **to come full c.,** (i) compléter son orbite; (ii) (*of pers.*) revenir à son point de départ. **3.** *Th:* **dress c.,** (premier) balcon, corbeille *f*; **upper c.,** seconde galerie. **4.** cercle, groupe *m*; **the family c.,** le sein de la famille; **in certain circles,** dans certains milieux; **in theatrical circles,** dans le monde des théâtres; **the inner c.,** le cercle intime (d'amis).

circle² **1.** *v.tr.* (*a*) *Poet:* ceindre, entourer (**with,** de); (*b*) faire le tour de (qch.); (*c*) *Gym:* **to c. the bar,** faire le grand soleil. **2.** *v.i.* (*a*) **to c. round sth.,** tourner, tournoyer, autour de qch.; **the planes are circling overhead,** les avions *mpl* décrivent des cercles au-dessus de nos têtes; (*b*) *Mil:* se rabattre (**round,** sur).

circuit [ˈsəːkit] *n.* **1.** (*a*) enceinte *f* (de murailles); (*b*) *Sp:* circuit *m*, parcours *m.* **2.** (*a*) révolution *f* (du soleil); (*b*) **to make the c. of the town,** faire le tour de la ville; (*c*) tournée *f* (de juge d'assises, etc.); *Th:* tournée dramatique; (*of judge*) **to go on c.,** aller en tournée; (*d*) circonscription *f* de tournée, ressort *m* (d'un juge d'assises). **3.** détour *m*; **to make a wide c.,** faire un grand détour. **4.** (*a*) *El:* circuit; **in, out of, c.,** en, hors de, circuit; **c. breaker,** coupe-circuit *m inv*, disjoncteur *m*, interrupteur *m*; **short c.,** court-circuit *m*, *pl.* courts-circuits; (*b*) *Elcs:* **anode c.,** circuit anodique; **grid c.,** circuit de grille; (*c*) *Tp:* **trunk c.,** circuit interurbain; (*d*) *TV:* **closed-c. television,** télévision *f* à circuit fermé.

circuitous [səːˈkju(ː)itəs] *a.* (chemin) détourné, indirect; **by c. means,** par des moyens détournés. **-ly** *adv.* (agir) par des moyens indirects, détournés.

circular [ˈsəːkjulər] **1.** *a.* circulaire; (*a*) **c. arc,** arc *m* de cercle; (*b*) (mouvement) circulaire; **c. letter,** lettre *f* circulaire; circulaire *f*; lettre collective; *Trans:* **c. tour,** tour *m* circulaire. **2.** *n.* (*a*) (lettre) circulaire (*f*); (*b*) prospectus (envoyé à tous les clients); (*c*) *Journ:* **the Court c.,** la Cour au jour le jour.

circularization [səːkjulərai'zeiʃ(ə)n] *n.* expédition *f*, envoi *m*, de circulaires, de prospectus.

circularize [ˈsəːkjuləraiz] *v.tr.* envoyer des circulaires, des prospectus, à (ses clients, etc.).

circulate [ˈsəːkjuleit] **1.** *v.i.* (*of thg, of pers.*) circuler; (*of money*) **to c. freely,** circuler librement; rouler. **2.** *v.tr.* (*a*) faire circuler (l'air, le vin, etc.); (*b*) mettre en circulation (de l'argent, des nouvelles, etc.); répandre, faire circuler (une nouvelle, etc.). **circulating 1.** *a.* circulant; **c. library,** bibliothèque circulante; *Mth:* **c. fraction,** fraction *f* périodique. **2.** *n.* circulation *f*.

circulation [səːkju'leiʃ(ə)n] *n.* (*a*) circulation *f* (de l'air, d'un liquide, de nouvelles, etc.); *Fin:* roulement *m* (de fonds); **to put a book into c.,** mettre un livre en circulation; *F:* (*of pers.*) **to be out of c.,** (i) garder la maison (à cause de maladie); (ii) être en retraite; (iii) être en prison; *Publ:* **for private c.,** hors commerce; **newspaper with a large c.,** journal à grand tirage; (*b*) *Physiol:* circulation (du sang, etc.); **to restore the c. in one's legs,** se dégourdir les jambes; (*c*) cours *m* (de la monnaie); **to put forged notes into c.,** écouler de faux billets; **notes in c.,** billets circulants.

circulatory [səːkju'leit(ə)ri, 'səːkjulət(ə)ri] *a.* *Anat: etc:* circulatoire; de la circulation.

circumcise [ˈsəːkəmsaiz] *v.tr.* circoncire (un enfant).

circumcision [səːkəm'siʒ(ə)n] *n.* **1.** circoncision *f*. **2.** *Ecc:* **the C.,** la (fête de la) Circoncision.

circumference [sə'kʌmfərəns] *n.* circonférence *f*; périphérie *f*; **thirty metres in c.,** trente mètres de circonférence.

circumflex [ˈsəːkəmfleks] *a. & n. Gram:* **c. (accent),** (accent *m*) circonflexe (*m*).

circumlocution [səːkəmlə'kjuːʃ(ə)n] *n.* circonlocution *f*; **without c.,** sans ambages.

circumnavigate [səːkəm'nævigeit] *v.tr.* faire (par mer) le tour de (qch.); doubler, contourner.

circumnavigation [səːkəmnævi'geiʃ(ə)n] *n.* circumnavigation *f*.

circumscribe [ˈsəːkəmskraib] *v.tr.* **1.** circonscrire. **2.** limiter, restreindre, (un champ d'opérations, des pouvoirs). **circumscribed** *a.* **1.** *Mth:* (cercle, etc.) circonscrit. **2.** restreint, limité.

circumscription [səːkəm'skripʃ(ə)n] *n.* **1.** restriction *f*, limitation *f* (de l'action de qn, etc.). **2.** région, circonscription (administrative).

circumspect [ˈsəːkəmspekt] *a.* circonspect; (*of pers.*) avisé; (*of conduct*) prudent; (*of speech*) mesuré. **-ly** *adv.* prudemment; avec circonspection.

circumspection [səːkem'spekʃ(ə)n] *n.* circonspection *f*.

circumstance [ˈsəːkəmstəns] *n.* **1.** *pl.* (*a*) circonstances *fpl*; **extenuating circumstances,** circonstances atténuantes; **in, under, the circumstances,** dans ces circonstances; en de telles circonstances; **in, under, no circumstances,** en aucun cas; sous aucun prétexte; **that depends on circumstances,** c'est selon; **he was the victim of circumstances,** il a été la victime des circonstances; **by force of circumstances,** par la force des choses; (*b*) conditions *fpl*; **if his circumstances allowed,** si ses moyens le permettaient; (*of pers.*) **in easy circumstances,** à l'aise. **2.** *sg. Lit:* circonstance, détail *m*. **3.** pompe *f*, appareil *m*; **with pomp and c.,** en grande cérémonie, en grand apparat.

circumstantial [səːkəm'stænʃ(ə)l] *a.* **1.** circonstanciel; **c. evidence,** preuves indirectes. **2.** accessoire, secondaire. **3.** circonstancié, détaillé.

circumstantiate [səːkəm'stænʃieit] *v.tr.* donner des détails circonstanciés sur (un rapport).

circumvent [səːkəm'vent] *v.tr.* circonvenir (qn, une manœuvre); **to c. the law,** tourner la loi.

circumvention [səːkəm'venʃ(ə)n] *n.* circonvention *f* (de la loi, etc.).

circumvolution [ˈsəːkəmvə'l(j)uːʃ(ə)n] *n.* circonvolution *f*.

circus, *pl.* **-uses** [ˈsəːkəs, -əsiz] *n.* **1.** (*a*) *Rom.Ant:* cirque *m*; (*b*) (*of roads, as Pr.n.*) rond-point *m*, *pl.* ronds-points. **2.** (*a*) cirque; **travelling c.,** cirque forain; (*b*) troupe *f*, équipe *f* (de pilotes d'automobiles de course, etc.).

cirrhosis [si'rousis] *n. Med:* cirrhose *f*.

cirrus, *pl.* **-ri** [ˈsirəs, -rai] *n.* **1.** *Nat.Hist:* cirr(he) *m*; *Bot:* vrille *f*. **2.** *Meteor:* cirrus *m*.

cissy [ˈsisi] *F:* **1.** *n.m.* mollasson *m*; poule mouillée. **2.** *a.* (*of pers., action*) mollasse, mollasson.

Cistercian [si'stəːʃ(ə)n] *a. & n. Ecc:* cistercien, -ienne; **the C. Order,** l'ordre *m* de Cîteaux.

cistern [ˈsistən] *n.* (*a*) réservoir *m* à eau (sous les combles); réservoir de chasse d'eau; (*b*) (*underground*) citerne *f*; réservoir (d'une pompe).

citadel [ˈsitədl, -del] *n.* (*a*) citadelle *f*; (*b*) lieu *m* de refuge; (*c*) temple *m* (de l'Armée de Salut).

citation [sai'teiʃ(ə)n] *n.* **1.** *Jur:* citation *f* à comparaître. **2.** citation (i) d'un auteur, d'une autorité, (ii) empruntée à un auteur. **3.** *Mil:* citation (à l'ordre du jour).

cite [sait] *v.tr.* **1.** *Jur:* (*a*) **to c. s.o. before a court,** citer qn devant un tribunal; (*b*) assigner (un témoin). **2.** (*a*) citer (un passage, un auteur); (*b*) alléguer (un auteur, une autorité). **3.** *Mil:* citer (un militaire pour son héroïsme).

citizen [ˈsitizən] *n.m. & f.* **1.** (*a*) citoyen, -enne; citadin *m*; **private c.,** simple particulier *m*; **fellow c.,** concitoyens; **citizen's band (radio),** (radio *f* de la) citizen band; (*b*) **c. of the world,** citoyen du monde, de l'univers; (*c*) *NAm:* civil *m* (par opposition à l'armée, la marine); **c. rights,** droits *mpl* civiques.

citizenship [ˈsitiznʃip] *n.* **1.** droit *m* de cité, de bourgeoisie. **2. good c.,** civisme *m*. **3. French c.,** citoyenneté française.

citrate [ˈsitreit] *n. Ch:* citrate *m*.

citric [ˈsitrik] *a. Ch:* (acide, etc.) citrique.

citron [ˈsitrən] *n.* (*a*) cédrat *m*; (*b*) **c. (tree),** cédratier *m*.

citrus [ˈsitrəs] *n.* **c. fruit,** agrume *m*.

city [ˈsiti] *n.* **1.** (*a*) *Lit:* cité *f*; **the Holy C.,** la Cité sainte; **the Celestial C.,** la Cité céleste; **the Eternal C.,** la Ville éternelle; **c. state,** état-cité *m*, *pl.* états-cités; (*b*) grande ville; **(cathedral) c.,** ville épiscopale; **the c. of Manchester,** la ville de Manchester; **c. hall,** hôtel *m* de ville; (*c*) *NAm:* ville. **2. garden c.,** cité-jardin *f*, *pl.* cités-jardins. **3.** (*a*) centre *m* (d'une grande ville); (*b*) **the C.,** (i) la Cité de Londres; (ii) la Bourse; **C. editor,** (i) rédacteur *m* de la rubrique financière; (ii) *U.S:* rédacteur de la chronique du jour; **he's in the C.,** il est dans la finance.

civet [ˈsivit] *n.* **1.** *Z:* **c. (cat),** civette *f*. **2.** (*scent*) civette.

civic [ˈsivik] *a.* civique; **the c. authorities,** les autorités municipales; **c. rights,** droits civils; *Town P:* **c. centre,** centre civique, social.

civics [ˈsiviks] *n.pl.* (*usu. with sg.const.*) *Sch:* instruction *f* civique.

civies [ˈsiviz] *n.pl.* = CIVVY 2 (*b*).

civil [ˈsiv(i)l] *a.* **1.** (*a*) (*of society, law, year, etc.*) civil; **c. war,** guerre civile; **c. defence,** protection civile; **c. rights,** (i) droits *mpl* civiques; (ii) *Jur:* droits civils; *Jur:* **c. death,** mort civile; **c. marriage,** marriage civil;

c. law, (i) droit romain; (ii) droit civil, = le code civil; **c. action, proceedings,** action civile; **c. servant,** fonctionnaire *m* (de l'État); **the C Service,** l'Administration (civile); **to be in the c. service,** être fonctionnaire; (*b*) **in c. life,** dans le civil; (*c*) *Adm:* **the C. List,** la liste civile (du souverain); **C. List pension,** pension *f* sur les fonds de la Couronne; (*d*) **c. engineer,** ingénieur constructeur; ingénieur des travaux publics. **2.** poli, civil; **he was very c. to me,** il s'est montré très aimable; **keep a c. tongue in your head!** soyez plus poli! **-illy** *adv.* civilement, poliment.

civilian [si'viljən] **I.** *n.* **1.** *Jur:* civiliste *mf.* **2.** civil *m* (par opposition à l'armée et la marine). **II.** *a.* civil; **c. clothes,** tenue civile; **in c. life,** dans le civil.

civility [si'viliti] *n.* civilité *f;* courtoisie *f,* politesse *f;* **exchange of civilities,** échange *m* d'amabilités.

civilization [sivilai'zeiʃ(ə)n] *n.* civilisation *f.*

civilize ['sivilaiz] *v.tr.* civiliser. **civilized** *a.* civilisé. (homme) cultivé.

civvy, *pl.* **-ies** ['sivi, -iz] *P:* **1.** *a.* civil; **to get back to c. street,** rentrer dans le civil. **2.** *n.* **civvies,** vêtements civils.

clack¹ ['klæk] *n.* **1.** bruit sec; claquement *m;* **click-c.,** clic-clac *m.* **2.** *Tchn:* (*a*) **c. (valve),** (soupape *f* à) clapet (*m*); (*b*) **(mill) c.,** traquet *m.* **3.** *F:* (*of pers.*) caquet *m,* jacasserie *f.*

clack² *v.i.* **1.** (*of thg*) claquer, faire clic-clac. **2.** (*of pers.*) jacasser.

clad¹ [klæd] *see* CLOTHE.

clad² *v.tr.* **(cladded)** revêtir (un pan de mur, une tôle, etc.) **(with,** de). **cladding** *n.* revêtement *m.*

claim¹ [kleim] *n.* **1.** demande *f* (de secours, etc.); revendication *f,* réclamation *f;* **wage, pay, claims,** revendications de salaire; *Av: etc:* **baggage c.,** livraison *f* de bagages consignés. **2.** droit *m,* titre *m,* prétention *f* **(to sth.,** à qch.); **to have a c. to sth.,** avoir droit à qch.; **to lay c. to sth.,** (i) prétendre à qch.; revendiquer son droit à qch.; (ii) s'attribuer qch.; **legal c. to sth.,** titre juridique à qch.; **to put in a c.,** faire valoir ses droits. **3.** *Jur:* créance *f;* **preferential c.,** créance privilégiée; privilège *m* du créancier. **4.** (*a*) *Jur:* réclamation; **to make, put in, a c. for damages,** demander une indemnité; réclamer des dommages-intérêts; **to have no c. whatever on s.o.,** n'avoir aucun recours contre qn; *Ins:* **to put in a c.,** réclamer l'indemnité (d'assurance); s'adresser à l'assurance; (*b*) **to have a c. on s.o.,** avoir prise sur qn; **I have many claims on my time,** mon temps est entièrement pris. **5.** *esp. NAm: Austr:* concession (minière).

claim² *v.tr.* (*a*) réclamer (un droit, les soins de qn); revendiquer (un droit); exiger, demander (du respect, de l'attention); *Jur:* requérir; **to c. sth. from s.o.,** réclamer qch. à qn; **to c. a privilege,** prétendre à un privilège; **to c. the right to do sth.,** (i) revendiquer, (ii) prétendre avoir, le droit de faire qch.; **the sea claims many victims,** la mer fait de nombreuses victimes; (*b*) **to c. that . . .,** prétendre, avancer, affirmer, soutenir, que . . .; **to c. to be an expert,** se faire passer pour expert; **to c. acquaintance with s.o.,** prétendre connaître qn. **claiming** *n.* réclamation *f,* revendication *f* (d'un droit, etc.).

claimant ['kleimənt] *n.* prétendant, -ante; revendicateur, -trice; *Jur:* réclamant, -ante; demandeur, -eresse; **rightful c.,** ayant droit *m, pl.* ayants droit.

clairvoyance [klɛə'vɔiəns] *n.* **1.** voyance *f;* don *m* de seconde vue. **2.** (*shrewdness*) clairvoyance *f.*

clairvoyant [klɛə'vɔiənt] **1.** *a.* (*a*) doué de seconde vue; (*b*) (*shrewd*) clairvoyant. **2.** *n.* voyant, -ante; (somnambule *mf*) extra-lucide (*mf*).

clam¹ [klæm] *n.* **1.** *Moll:* palourde *f;* clam *m; NAm:* **c. chowder,** soupe *f* aux palourdes. **2.** *F:* personne taciturne.

clam² *v.i.* **(clammed)** *P:* **to c. up,** se taire.

clambake ['klæmbeik] *n. NAm:* **1.** pique-nique *m* (*pl.* pique-niques) où l'on mange des fruits de mer. **2.** (*a*) grande réunion tapageuse; (*b*) grand rassemblement politique.

clamber ['klæmbər] *v.i.* grimper (des pieds et des mains); **to c. up a wall,** escalader un mur.

clamminess ['klæminis] *n.* moiteur froide (de la peau); humidité froide (de l'air).

clammy ['klæmi] *a.* (*of hands, skin*) (froid et) moite; (*of atmosphere*) (froid et) humide.

clamorous ['klæmərəs] *a.* bruyant, braillard; (foule) vociférante. **-ly** *adv.* bruyamment; à grands cris.

clamour¹, *NAm:* **clamor¹** ['klæmər] *n.* clameur *f;* cris *mpl;* vociférations *fpl.*

clamour², *NAm:* **clamor²** *v.i.* vociférer, crier; pousser des clameurs *fpl;* **to c. for sth.,** réclamer, demander, qch. à grands cris.

clamp¹ [klæmp] *n.* (*a*) crampon *m,* presse *f;* (*b*) *Const:* agrafe *f;* (*c*) collier *m* (de tuyau); (*d*) *Carp: etc:* (i) serre-joint *m, pl.* serre-joints; (ii) valet *m* (d'établi); mâchoire *f* de serrage; (*e*) mordache *f* (d'étau); (*f*) pince *f;* (*g*) pince (pour fils); (*h*) *Surg:* clamp *m.*

clamp² *v.tr.* **1.** cramponner, serrer; mettre (qch.) sous presse. **2.** (*a*) *Const: etc:* agrafer (deux pierres); brider (un tuyau); (*b*) bloquer (un instrument de précision); caler (un télescope); (*c*) *Surg:* clamper. **clamp down 1.** *v.tr.* fixer (qch.) par un crampon. **2.** *v.i. F:* **to c. down on s.o.,** serrer les pouces, la vis, à qn; **to c. down on (sth.),** mettre fin à (qch.). **clamping** *n.* (*a*) agrafage *m,* serrage *m;* fixation *f* (d'un outil); (*b*) *Surg:* clampage *m.*

clamp³ *n.* (*a*) silo *m* (temporaire) (de pommes de terre); (*b*) meule *f* (de briques en cuisson).

clamp⁴ *v.tr.* (*a*) mettre (des pommes de terre) en silo; (*b*) mettre (des briques) en meule.

clan¹ [klæn] *n.* **1.** *Scot:* clan *m;* **the head of the c.,** le chef de clan. **2.** *Anthr:* clan (d'une tribu); **c. name,** nom clanique. **3.** coterie *f,* clique *f;* clan; **gathering of the clans,** réunion *f* d'adhérents, de partisans.

clan² *v.i. F:* **(clanned) to c. together,** se soutenir mutuellement; faire preuve (i) d'esprit de corps, (ii) *Pej:* d'esprit de clan.

clandestine [klæn'destin] *a.* clandestin, subreptice. **-ly** *adv.* clandestinement, subrepticement; en cachette.

clang¹ [klæŋ] *n.* son, bruit, métallique; bruit retentissant.

clang² **1.** *v.i.* retentir, résonner; rendre un son métallique. **2.** *v.tr.* faire résonner (une cloche, etc.).

clanger ['klæŋər] *n. F:* **to drop a c.,** faire une gaffe, une boulette; gaffer.

clank¹ ['klæŋk] *n.* bruit sec (de chaînes, de fers).

clank² **1.** *v.i.* (*of chain, bucket*) rendre un bruit métallique; cliqueter. **2.** *v.tr.* faire cliqueter (des chaînes etc.).

clannish ['klæniʃ] *a. Pej:* qui a l'esprit de clan; (groupe, etc.) fermé.

clansman, *pl.* **-men, clanswoman,** *pl.* **-women** ['klænzmən, -mən, -wumən, -wimin] *n.* membre *m* d'un clan.

clap¹ [klæp] *n.* **1.** (*a*) battement *m* (de mains); **to give s.o. a c.,** applaudir qn; (*b*) tape *f* (de la main). **2. c. of thunder,** coup *m* de tonnerre.

clap² *v.* **(clapped) 1.** *v.tr.* (*a*) **to c. one's hands,** battre des mains; **to c. s.o. on the back,** donner à qn une tape sur le dos; **to c. a performer,** applaudir un artiste; (*b*) mettre, *F:* coller; **to c. s.o. in prison,** fourrer qn en prison; **he clapped his hat on,** il a enfoncé son chapeau sur la tête; *F:* **to c. eyes on s.o.,** voir qn (tout à coup); apercevoir qn. **2.** *v.i.* (*a*) battre des mains; frapper des, dans ses, mains; applaudir; (*b*) (*of wings*) battre. **clap on** *v.tr. Nau:* **to c. on more**

sail, augmenter de toile. **clapped** *a. P:* **c. (out),** éreinté, fourbu. **clapping** *n.* (*a*) battement *m* (des mains); (*b*) applaudissements *mpl.*

clap³ *n. P:* chaude-pisse *f.*

clapboard ['klæpbɔːrd] *n. NAm: Const:* planche *f* à clin.

clapometer [klæ'pɔmitər] *n. T.V: etc:* applaudimètre *m.*

clapper ['klæpər] *n.* **1.** battant *m* (de cloche, de moulin à blé); claquet *m* (de moulin); clapet *m* (de pompe); **c. ring,** bélière *f* (de cloche); *Mec.E:* **c. valve,** (soupape *f* à) clapet. **2.** (*a*) claquette *f*, claquoir *m*; *Cin:* **c. board,** claquette (de synchronisation); (*b*) crécelle *f* (de crieur public); (*c*) *Agr:* moulin *m* à claquet (pour effrayer les oiseaux). **3.** (*pers.*) applaudisseur, -euse. **4.** *adv.phr. P:* **like the clappers,** (travailler) comme un enragé; (courir) comme un dératé.

claptrap ['klæptræp] **1.** *n.* verbiage *m*; baratin *m*; **to talk c.,** parler pour ne rien dire. **2.** *a.* (discours) creux, sans sincérité.

claque [klæk] *n. Th:* claque *f.*

claret ['klærət] **1.** *n.* bordeaux *m* rouge. **2.** *a.* **c. (-coloured),** bordeaux *inv.*

clarification [klærifi'keiʃ(ə)n] *n.* **1.** clarification *f* (d'un liquide); soutirage *m*, collage *m* (du vin). **2.** clarification; éclaircissement *m*, élucidation *f* (d'une question, etc.).

clarify ['klærifai] **1.** *v.tr.* (*a*) clarifier (le beurre, un sirop); coller (le vin); (*b*) clarifier (sa pensée, etc.); éclaircir (l'esprit, la vision, etc.); élucider (une question). **2.** *v.i.* (*of liquid, one's thoughts*) se clarifier, s'éclaircir.

clarinet [klæri'net] *n. Mus:* clarinette *f.*

clarinettist [klæri'netist] *n.* clarinettiste *mf.*

clarion ['klæriən] *n. Poet:* clairon *m.*

clarity ['klæriti] *n.* clarté *f.*

clash¹ [klæʃ] *n.* **1.** fracas *m*; résonnement *m* (de cloches, etc.); cliquetis *m* (d'épées, etc.); son strident (de cymbales); tumulte *m* (d'armes). **2.** (*a*) conflit *m*, choc (d'opinions); (*between mobs*) échauffourée *f*; désaccord *m*, opposition *f* (d'intérêts, de doctrines); (*b*) discordance *f* (des couleurs).

clash² **1.** *v.i.* (*a*) (*of cymbals, bells, etc.*) résonner (bruyamment); (*of arms*) s'entrechoquer; (*b*) (i) (*of colours*) jurer; détonner (**with,** avec); (ii) (*of opinions, etc.*) s'opposer (**with,** à); être en conflit, en désaccord (**with,** avec); **the two dates c.,** les deux réunions, etc., tombent le même jour. **2.** *v.tr.* faire résonner (des cymbales, etc.); sonner ensemble (les cloches). **clashing** **1.** *a.* (*a*) bruyant, retentissant; (*b*) (couleurs) discordantes; (*c*) (opinions) opposées. **2.** *n.* = CLASH¹.

clasp¹ [klɑːsp] *n.* **1.** agrafe *f* (de broche, de médaille, d'album, etc.); fermeture *f* (de collier, etc.); fermoir *m*, fermail *m* (de livre, de porte-monnaie). **2.** étreinte *f*; enlacement *m*; serrement *m* (de mains).

clasp² *v.tr.* **1.** agrafer (un bracelet, etc.). **2.** (*a*) serrer, étreindre, enlacer (qn); embrasser (qch., les genoux de qn); prendre (qch.) dans ses bras; **to be clasped in each other's arms,** se tenir étroitement embrassés; (*b*) **to c. s.o.'s hand,** serrer la main à qn; **to c. one's hands,** joindre les mains.

clasp-knife, *pl.* **-knives** ['klɑːspnaif, -naivz] *n.* couteau pliant, fermant (*esp.* à cran d'arrêt).

class¹ [klɑs] *n.* classe *f.* **1.** (*a*) **the upper classes,** la haute société; **the middle class(es),** la classe moyenne; **the working classes,** la classe ouvrière; **working-c. family,** famille ouvrière; **c. consciousness,** (i) esprit *m* de caste; (ii) conscience *f* de classe; **c. war,** lutte *f* de classes; **to have c.,** avoir de la classe; (*b*) **first-c. player, hotel, etc.** joueur, -euse, hôtel *m*, etc., de premier ordre; **in the Olympic c.,** digne de participer aux Jeux olympiques; (*c*) **first-c.,** (route, billet) de première classe; *Nau: etc:* **tourist, cabin, economy, c.,** classe touriste, cabine, économique. **2.** *Sch:* (*a*) **the French c.,** la classe de français; **evening c.,** cours *m* du soir; **day release classes,** la scolarité à temps partiel; **dancing classes,** cours de danse; **in c.,** en classe; (*b*) *NAm:* promotion *f.* **3.** (*a*) catégorie *f*, sorte *f*, genre *m*; **in a c. by itself,** (article) unique; (*b*) *Nat.Hist:* les classes; (*c*) *Ins:* cote *f* (d'un navire) (au Lloyd); (*d*) *Sch:* **first c., second c., degree** = licence *f* avec mention bien, avec mention; (*e*) *Mil: U.S:* **private first c.,** soldat *m* de première classe.

class² *v.tr.* (*a*) classer; assimiler (qn, qch.) (**with,** à); **classed first,** classé premier; (*b*) *Ins:* coter (un navire); **ship classed A1,** navire classé suivant cote A1.

classic ['klæsik] **1.** *a.* (*a*) (auteur, littérature, beauté) classique; *Turf: a. & n.* **c. (race),** course *f* classique; (*b*) *F:* **a c. example,** un exemple classique, typique. **2.** *n.* (*a*) (*author, book*) classique *m*; (*b*) (*pers.*) humaniste *m*; (*c*) *pl.* (*usu. with sg.const.*) **classics,** les humanités *fpl*; le latin et le grec.

classical ['klæsik(ə)l] *a.* (*a*) (langue, théâtre, etc.) classique; **c. scholar,** humaniste *m*; (*b*) (musique) classique; (*c*) traditionnel; *Cost:* (coupe) classique. **-ally** *adv.* classiquement.

classicism ['klæsisizm] **1.** *Lit: Art:* classicisme *m.* **2.** tour *m* ou locution *f* emprunté(e) aux langues classiques.

classicist ['klæsisist] *n.* **1.** *Lit:* classique *m.* **2.** *Sch:* humaniste *m.* **3.** partisan, -ane, des études classiques.

classification [klæsifi'keiʃ(ə)n] *n.* **1.** classification *f* (des plantes, des animaux); classement *m* (de papiers, de concurrents, etc.). **2.** classification; classe *f*; *Ins:* cote *f* (d'un navire).

classifier ['klæsifaiər] *n.* (*pers.*) classificateur, -trice.

classify ['klæsifai] *v.tr.* **1.** classifier, classer; ranger par classes. **2.** classer secret (un document, etc.). **classified** *a.* **1.** classifié; classé; *Journ:* **c. advertisements,** petites annonces; **c. results,** résultats *mpl* et classements *mpl.* **2.** (*of document*) secret.

classless ['klɑːslis] *a.* (société) sans classes.

classmate ['klɑːsmeit] *n.* **1.** camarade *mf* de classe; condisciple *m.* **2.** *NAm:* camarade de promotion.

classroom ['klɑːsruːm] *n. Sch:* (salle *f* de) classe (*f*).

classy ['klɑːsi] *a. F:* bon genre; (restaurant, etc.) chic.

clatter¹ ['klætər] *n.* bruit *m*, vacarme *m*, fracas *m*; bruit (de vaisselle); clic-clac *m* (de sabots); ferraillement *m* (d'une machine).

clatter² **1.** *v.i.* faire du bruit; se choquer avec fracas; **to c. along, by,** passer avec bruit; **to come clattering down,** dégringoler; faire un bruit de dégringolade. **2.** *v.tr.* faire résonner; **don't c. your spoons!** ne faites pas de bruit avec vos cuillers!

Claudius ['klɔːdiəs] *Pr.n.m. Rom.Hist:* Claude.

clause [klɔːz] *n.* **1.** clause *f*, article *m* (d'un traité); disposition *f* (testamentaire, d'une loi); **penalty c.,** clause pénale; **arbitration c.,** clause compromissoire; **(restrictive) clauses,** modalités *fpl.* **2.** *Gram:* membre *m* de phrase; **main, subordinate, c.,** proposition principale, subordonnée.

claustrophobia [klɔːstrə'foubiə] *n. Med:* claustrophobie *f.*

claustrophobic [klɔːstrə'foubik] *a. & n. Med:* claustrophobe (*mf*).

clavichord ['klævikɔːd] *n. Mus:* clavicorde *m.*

clavicle ['klævikl] *n. Anat:* clavicule *f.*

claw¹ [klɔː] *n.* **1.** (*a*) griffe *f* (de chat, etc.); serre *f* (d'oiseau de proie); pince *f* (d'une écrevisse); (*of cat*) to sharpen its claws, se faire les griffes; **to draw in its claws,** faire patte de velours; *Furn:* **c.-footed,** (table, etc.) à pied de griffon; (*b*) *P:* (*hand*) pince, patte *f*; **to get one's claws on sth.,** mettre le grappin sur qch. **2.** *Tchn:* (*a*) (*of bench*) valet *m*; (*of vice*) mordache *f*; (*of winch shaft, etc.*) cliquet *m*; (*b*) patte (d'un grappin); (*c*) **nail c.,** arrache-clou(s) *m inv*; (*d*) panne fendue (de marteau); **c. hammer,** marteau *m* à panne fendue.

claw² **1.** *v.tr.* (*a*) griffer, égratigner; donner un coup de griffe à (qn); (*b*) agripper (qch.); (*c*) *F:* **to c. back,** regagner (qch.) péniblement; récupérer (une dépense). **2.** *v.i.* **to c. at sth.,** s'accrocher à qch.; saisir qch. avec ses griffes; agriffer, agripper, qch.

clay [klei] *n.* **1.** (*a*) argile *f*, (terre-)glaise *f*; **boulder c.,** argile à blocaux; *Cer: etc:* **china c.,** terre *f* à porcelaine, kaolin *m*; **modelling c.,** pâte *f* à modeler; **potter's c.,** terre à, de, potier, (terre-)glaise; *Lit:* **idol with feet of c.,** idole *f* aux pieds d'argile; *Sp:* **c. pigeon,** pigeon artificiel; **c. soil,** sol argileux, glaiseux; (*b*) *Lit:* **mortal c.,** le corps humain. **2. c. (pipe),** pipe *f* de, en, terre.

clayey ['kleii] *a.* argileux, glaiseux.

clean¹ [kli:n] **I.** *a.* **1.** (*a*) propre, net; (eau) pure, claire; (papier) blanc; (cassure) franche, nette; (saut) franc; **c. timber,** bois uni, sans malandres; *Typ:* **c. proof,** (i) épreuve non chargée, peu chargée; (ii) épreuve pour bon à tirer; **c. driving licence,** permis *m* de conduire vierge; *Nau:* **c. bill of health,** patente nette; *F:* **the doctor gave me a c. bill of health,** le docteur m'a trouvé en pleine forme; *Fin:* **c. bill,** effet *m* libre; **c. hands,** (i) mains *fpl* propres; (ii) (*from crime*) mains nettes; **c. living,** vie réglée; **good c. fun,** amusement innocent; **to keep sth. c.,** tenir qch. propre; *F:* **keep the party, it, c.!** pas de grossièretés! *Atom.Ph:* **c. bomb,** bombe *f* propre; (*b*) (*of animal*) propre, aux habitudes propres. **2. c. (out)lines,** contours nets; formes fines; **car with c. lines,** voiture *f* qui a de la ligne. **3.** (joueur, boxeur) impeccable. **II.** *adv.* **1.** *F:* absolument, tout à fait; **I c. forgot,** j'ai complètement oublié; **they got c. away,** ils se sont échappés sans laisser de traces. **2.** (*a*) **to cut c. through sth.,** couper, traverser, qch. de part en part; (*b*) (*of horse*) **to jump c.,** sauter franchement. **3.** *F:* **to come c.,** avouer; dire toute la vérité. **cleanly** *adv.* proprement; nettement.

clean² *n.* nettoyage *m*; **to give sth. a c.,** nettoyer qch.

clean³ **1.** *v.tr.* nettoyer (qch.); récurer (des casseroles); balayer (les rues); curer (un puits); *Cu:* vider (le poisson); *Mch:* lessiver, décrasser (une chaudière); ramoner (les tubes); *Med:* déterger (une plaie, un ulcère); *Tchn:* nettoyer, dessabler (une pièce coulée); **to c. one's teeth, one's nails,** se laver les dents; se curer les ongles; **to c. one's plate,** faire assiette nette. **2.** *v.i.* faire le nettoyage; **to go out cleaning,** faire des ménages. **cleaning** *n.* **1.** nettoyage *m*, nettoiement *m*; décrottage *m*; dégraissage *m*; purification *f*; lessivage *m*; curage *m* (d'un puits); décrassage *m* (des chaudières); ramonage *m* (des tubes); décapage *m* (d'une surface à repeindre); *Cu:* vidage *m* (du poisson); **c. woman,** femme de ménage; **(household) c. materials,** produits *mpl* d'entretien. **2. c. up,** nettoyage (d'une salle, d'un quartier criminel, etc.). **clean out** *v.tr.* (*a*) nettoyer (une armoire, etc.); curer, décrasser (un fourneau); vidanger, décombler (une fosse, etc.); ébouer (une chaudière); déboucher (un tuyau); (*b*) *F:* **cleaned out,** nettoyé (à sec); fauché; (*c*) *U.S: P:* nettoyer (un endroit de gangsters, etc.). **clean up** **1.** *v.tr.* (*a*) enlever, ramasser (des saletés, etc.); nettoyer (une salle, etc.); **to c. oneself up,** se débarbouiller; (*b*) balayer (l'ennemi); **to c. up a town,** nettoyer une ville (d'ennemis, de gangsters, etc.); (*c*) *U.S: P:* **to c. up a thousand dollars,** gagner, ramasser, mille dollars. **2.** *v.i.* (*a*) faire le nettoyage; (*b*) se nettoyer; se débarbouiller; (*c*) mettre tout en ordre; réparer le désordre; (*d*) *U.S: P:* taper dans le mille.

clean-cut ['kli:n'kʌt] *a.* (*a*) (contours, lignes) d'une grande netteté; (*b*) (*of opinion*) net, bien défini; (*of order*) précis; (*c*) (*of division*) net; brutal, -aux.

cleaner ['kli:nər] *n.* **1.** (*pers.*) (*a*) nettoyeur, -euse; **window c.,** laveur *m* de carreaux, de vitres; **dry, c.,** nettoyeur à sec; *U.S: P:* **to take s.o. to the cleaners,** (i) nettoyer, plumer, qn; (ii) démolir, éreinter (un adversaire); (*b*) femme de ménage. **2.** (*a*) appareil *m* à nettoyer; nettoyeuse *f*; **air c.,** épurateur *m* d'air; **window c.,** lave-vitres *m inv*; **pipe c.,** cure-pipe *m*, *pl.* cure-pipes; (*b*) (i) pâte *f*, (ii) liquide *m*, à nettoyer; (*for clothes*) détachant *m*.

cleanliness ['klenlinis] *n.* propreté *f*; netteté *f*; **c. of habit,** habitudes *fpl* de propreté.

clean-living ['kli:n'liviŋ] *a.* (jeune homme) réglé, qui mène une vie réglée.

cleanly ['klenli] *a.* (*of pers.*) propre (par habitude); **c. habits,** habitudes *fpl* de propreté.

cleanness ['kli:nnis] *n.* **1.** propreté *f* (des habits, de langage, d'un appartement, etc.); pureté *f* (de l'eau). **2.** netteté *f*, pureté (de lignes).

clean-out ['kli:naut] *n.* **to give a room a c.-o.,** nettoyer une chambre.

cleanse [klenz] *v.tr.* **1.** assainir, curer, débourber (un égout, etc.). **2.** purifier, dépurer (le sang); épurer (l'air, etc.); *Toil:* démaquiller (le visage); *Med:* déterger, désenvenimer (une plaie); *A: & Lit:* purifier (le cœur, l'âme, etc.). **cleansing** *n.* **1.** assainissement *m*, curage *m* (d'un chenal, d'un égout). **2.** purification *f* (du sang, de l'âme); épuration *f* (d'un gaz); *Toil:* **c. cream, milk, lotion,** crème *f*, lait *m*, de démaquillage; démaquillant *m*; **c. pads,** disques-lotion *mpl*.

cleanser ['klenzər] *n.* poudre *f*, liquide *m*, à nettoyer (la vaisselle, etc.); *Toil:* démaquillant *m*.

cleanshaven ['kli:n'ʃeivn] *a.* (*a*) sans barbe ni moustache; (visage) entièrement rasé; (*b*) rasé de frais.

cleanup ['kli:nʌp] *n.* (*a*) nettoyage *m*; **to give sth. a c.,** nettoyer qch.; (*b*) nettoyage (d'une ville capturée).

clear¹ [kliər] **I.** *a.* **1.** (*a*) (ciel, teint, œil, etc.) clair; (teint, etc.) net; (temps) clair, dégagé; **c. water,** eau claire, limpide; **on a c. day,** par temps clair; **as c. as daylight, crystal,** clair comme le jour, comme de l'eau de roche; *F:* **as c. as mud,** pas clair du tout; (*b*) **c. conscience,** conscience nette, pure; (*c*) (son, etc.) clair; **c. voice,** voix claire, nette. **2.** (*manifest*) clair, net; (signe) évident; **c. case of bribery,** cas *m* de corruption manifeste; **to make one's meaning, oneself, c.,** se faire comprendre; **to make it c. to s.o. that . . .,** faire bien comprendre à qn que . . .; **it is c. that . . .,** il est clair, évident, que . . .. **3. c. idea,** idée claire, nette; **c. thinker, c. mind,** esprit *m* lucide. **4. to be c. about sth.,** être convaincu, certain, de qch.; **I want to be quite c. on this point,** je tiens à ce qu'il n'y ait aucun malentendu sur ce point. **5.** (*a*) **c. profit,** bénéfice clair et net; **a c. ten thousand a year,** un revenu (clair et) net de dix mille livres; **c. majority,** majorité absolue (**of,** de); *Sp:* **c. winner,** vainqueur détaché; (*b*) *Jur:* **three c. days,** trois jours francs. **6.** (espace, etc.) libre; (vue, etc.) dégagée; (*of pers.*) **to be c. of sth., of s.o.,** être débarrassé de qch., de qn; **the sea is c. of ice,** la mer est libre; *Av:* **you are c. to take off,** vous êtes autorisé à, vous pouvez, décoller; *Rail:* **c. road, road c., line c.,** voie libre, signal effacé; **all c.!** (i) vous pouvez y aller, c'est libre; (ii) *Mil:* fin *f* d'alerte; (iii) *Nau:* paré! **II.** *a. or adv.* **to jump five centimetres c. of the bar,** franchir la barre avec cinq centimètres de reste; **to hang c. of the ground,** être suspendu de manière à ne pas toucher le sol; *Nau:* **to steer c. of a rock,** passer au large d'un écueil; **to stand c.,** s'écarter, se garer (pour éviter un danger); **to keep, steer, stand, c. of sth.,** rester, se tenir, à distance de qch.; éviter qch.; **stand c. of the doorway!** dégagez la porte! **stand c. of the doors!** attention aux portes! *Rail:* = attention au départ! **to pull s.o. c.,** dégager qn (**of,** de); **to get c. of s.o.,** échapper à qn; **to get c.,** se tirer d'embarras; se tirer d'affaire. **III.** *n.* **1.** espace *m* libre. **2.** (*of pers.*) **to be in the c.,** (i) être libre de tout soupçon; (ii) ne pas avoir de dettes. **3.** *Mil: etc:* **despatch sent in c.,** dépêche *f* en clair. **clearly** *adv.* **1.** (voir, parler) clair; (distinguer) clairement, nettement; (expliquer) clairement, d'une manière claire; **you must c. understand that...,** il vous faut bien comprendre que.... **2.** évidemment; sans aucun doute; **he is c. wrong,** il est évident qu'il a tort.

clear² **I.** *v.tr.* **1.** (*a*) éclaircir (le brouillard, etc.); **to c. the air,** (i) (*of thunderstorm*) rafraîchir l'air; (ii) (*of discussion, etc.*) mettre les choses au point; **to c. one's throat,** se racler la gorge; (*b*) clarifier (un liquide); purifier (le sang). **2.** justifier, innocenter (qn) **(of a charge,** d'une accusation); disculper (qn) (d'un soupçon); **to c. oneself,** se justifier. **3.** (*a*) dégager (une route, un terrain, une entrée); désencombrer (une salle, etc.); défricher (un terrain); faire évacuer (les rues, une salle); *W.Tel: etc:* éliminer (l'interférence); déboucher, dégorger (un tuyau); *Jur:* **to c. the court,** faire évacuer la salle; **to c. one's conscience,** décharger sa conscience; **to c. a way, a passage, for s.o.,** ouvrir un passage à qn; **to c. a way for oneself,** se frayer un passage; **to c. the table,** (i) débarrasser la table; (ii) défaire, enlever, le couvert; desservir; *Navy:* **to c. the decks for action,** faire le branle-bas de combat; *F:* **to c. the decks,** (i) déblayer le terrain; (ii) (tout) ranger; **the rain had cleared the streets,** la pluie avait dépeuplé les rues; **to c. slums,** supprimer des taudis; *Mil:* **to c. an area of mines,** déminer un terrain; **fresh air clears the head,** un peu d'air frais vous éclaircit les idées; *Com:* **to c. goods,** solder, liquider, des marchandises; *Rail:* **to c. the line,** (i) dégager la voie; (ii) (*after an accident*) déblayer la voie; (*b*) **c. all this out of here,** débarrassez-moi de tout cela. **4. to c. one's plate,** faire assiette nette; **to c. the letterbox,** lever le courrier; **to c. the bowels,** nettoyer, purger, dégager, les intestins. **5.** (*a*) **to c. a barrier (by 10 centimetres),** franchir une barrière (avec 10 centimètres de reste); **to c. a ditch,** sauter, franchir, un fossé; (*b*) *Nau:* **to c. the harbour,** sortir du port; quitter le port; **to c. the land,** parer la terre. **6.** (*a*) acquitter (une dette); affranchir (une propriété); purger (une hypothèque); solder, liquider, arrêter (un compte); **to c. one's property of debt,** purger son bien de dettes; (*b*) *Nau:* expédier (un navire); dédouaner (des marchandises); (*c*) **to c. an article for publication,** (i) demander l'autorisation de publier un article; (ii) autoriser la publication d'un article; *Adm: Mil:* **to c. s.o. for security,** soumettre qn à un contrôle de sécurité; attribuer à qn un certificat de sécurité. **7. to c. 10%** gagner, réaliser 10% faire un bénéfice net de 10%; **I cleared a hundred pounds,** j'ai touché, cela m'a rapporté, cent livres net. **8.** *Fin:* compenser, virer (un chèque). **II.** *v.i.* **1.** (*a*) (*of the weather*) s'éclaircir, se découvrir, se rasséréner; se (re)mettre au beau; (*of mist*) se dissiper; (*of sky*) se dégager; (*b*) (*of liquid*) se clarifier. **2.** (*of ship*) prendre la mer. **clear away** **1.** (*a*) *v.tr. & i.* enlever, ôter (qch.); écarter (un obstacle); ranger (ses affaires); (*b*) *v.i.* desservir. **2.** *v.i.* (*of mist*) se dissiper. **clearing** *n.* **1.** clarification *f* (d'un liquide). **2.** (*a*) dégagement *m*, déblaiement *m* (d'une voie); enlèvement *m* (de débris); défrichement *m* (d'un terrain); curage *m* (des fossés); éclaircissement *m* (d'une forêt); (*b*) évacuation *f* (d'une salle); levée *f* (du courrier); *Mil:* **c. station,** centre *m* de triage, d'évacuation (de blessés); (*c*) liquidation *f*, solde *m* (de marchandises). **4.** franchissement *m* (d'une barrière). **5.** (*a*) expédition *f* (d'un navire); dédouanement *m* (des marchandises); (*b*) acquittement (de dettes); liquidation (d'un compte); affranchissement *m* (d'un bien); (*c*) *Fin:* compensation *f* (de chèques); clearing *m*; **c. bank,** banque *f* de virement, de clearing; **c. house,** comptoir général de virement; clearing (house) *m*. **6.** (*in forest*) éclaircie, clairière *f*. **7. c. away,** enlèvement *m* (de débris, des couverts, etc.). **8. c. out the attic took us 2 days,** il nous a fallu 2 jours pour débarrasser, nettoyer, le grenier. **9. c. up,** (*a*) remise *f* en ordre (d'une maison, etc.); (*b*) éclaircissement *m* (d'un mystère, d'un doute, etc.). **clear off** **1.** *v.tr.* purger (une hypothèque); s'acquitter (de ses dettes); *Com:* solder (des marchandises). **2.** *v.i.* *F:* s'en aller, filer, décamper. **clear out** **1.** *v.tr.* vider (une armoire); débarrasser (un grenier); décombler (un puits); déblayer (des débris); liquider, placer (des stocks); *F:* mettre (qn) à sec. **2.** *v.i.* *F:* filer, déguerpir, se sauver; vider les lieux; **c. out!** filez! hors d'ici! **clear up** **1.** *v.tr.* (*a*) (re)mettre (une pièce) en ordre; ranger (ses affaires); (*b*) éclaircir, dissiper (un malentendu); éclaircir (un mystère, un doute); dénouer, démêler (une situation, une intrigue); résoudre (une difficulté); tirer (une affaire) au clair; (*c*) guérir (un rhume, etc.). **2.** *v.i.* (*a*) (*of the weather*) s'éclaircir; se (re)mettre au beau; (*of mystery, etc.*) s'éclaircir, s'élucider; (*b*) (*of rash, headache, etc.*) disparaître.

clearance ['kliərəns] *n.* **1.** (*a*) **slum c.,** élimination *f* des taudis; **c. area,** quartier *m* (insalubre) à démolir; *Com:* **c. sale,** vente *f* de soldes; liquidation *f*; (*b*) *For:* défrichement *m*. **2.** (*a*) *Cust: Nau:* acquit(tement) *m* (de marchandises); dédouanage *m*, dédouanement *m*; (*b*) affranchissement *m* (d'un domaine grevé); (*c*) *Mil: etc:* congé, libération *f* (d'un officier, d'un fonctionnaire); (*d*) *Nau:* départ *m* (du port); (*e*) *Av:* **flight c.,** autorisation *f* de vol; (*f*) *Adm: Mil:* **security c.,** (i) contrôle *m* de sécurité (sur qn); (ii) certificat *m* de sécurité. **3.** *Bank:* (i) compensation *f*; (ii) présentation *f* à l'encaissement (d'un chèque). **4.** *Tchn:* espace *m* libre; jeu *m* (d'un piston, etc.); jour *m*, écartement *m* (entre barreaux); entrefer *m* (entre tôles, etc.); débattement *m* (de parties qui pourraient se heurter); *Civ.E:* hauteur *f* libre; tirant *m* d'air; *Tls:* **c. angle,** angle *m* d'incidence.

clear-cut ['kliə'kʌt] *a.* (*a*) (contours, traits) nettement dessinés; (*b*) (opinion) bien définie, tranchée; (ordres) précis; (*c*) (division) nette, brutale.

clear-headed ['kliə'hedid] *a.* (*a*) qui voit juste; (*b*) perspicace; à l'esprit net.

clearness ['kliənis] n. **1.** clarté *f*, limpidité *f* (de l'eau, de l'atmosphère, etc.). **2.** netteté *f* (d'une image, de l'esprit, des idées); **c. of vision,** (i) lucidité *f* de vue; (ii) intelligence *f* lucide.

clearout ['kliəraut] *n.* action *f* de débarrasser (une chambre, un grenier, etc.).

clear-sighted ['kliə'saitid] *a.* **1.** à la vue nette. **2.** clairvoyant; qui voit juste.

clear-sightedness [kliə'saitidnis] *n.* **1.** netteté *f* de vision. **2.** clairvoyance *f*.

clearup ['kliərʌp] *n.* (*a*) remise *f* en ordre (d'une chambre); (*b*) solde *m* (d'un compte).

clearway ['kliəwei] *n.* *Adm:* grande route à stationnement interdit.

cleat [kli:t] *n.* **1.** (*a*) tasseau *m* (de bois); (*b*) attache *f* (de poutre). **2.** *Nau:* **(belaying) c.,** taquet (de tournage). **3.** *El:* serre-câble(s) *m inv*, serre-fils *m inv*.

cleavage ['kli:vidʒ] *n.* **1.** (*a*) fendage *m*; *Geol:* clivage *m*; (*b*) *Biol:* division *f* (d'une cellule); (*c*) sillon *m* mammaire; naissance des seins. **2.** fissure *f*, scission *f* (dans un parti).

cleave[1] [kli:v] *v.* (*p.t.* **cleaved, cleft** [kleft], *Lit:* **clove** [klouv]; *p.p.* **cleaved, cleft,** *Lit:* **cloven** ['klouv(ə)n]) **1.** *v.tr.* (*a*) *Lit:* fendre (le bois); (*b*) cliver (un cristal); (*c*) (*of bird, ship*) fendre (l'air, les eaux). **2.** *v.i.* (*a*) *Lit:* **to c. (asunder),** se fendre, se feuilleter; (*b*) (*of crystals*) se cliver. **cleft** *a.* fendu; **c. stick,** piquet *m* fourchu; *Fig:* **to be in a c. stick,** se trouver dans une impasse; *Med:* **c. palate,** palais fendu. **cloven,** *a.* **c. foot, hoof,** pied fourchu (d'un ruminant, du diable).

cleave[2] *v.i.* (*p.t. & p.p.* **cleaved** [kli:vd]) *Lit:* **to c. to (s.o., sth.),** être fidèle à (qn, un parti, un principe).

cleaver ['kli:vər] *n. Tls:* fendoir *m*; (*for meat*) couperet *m*; (*for wood*) merlin *m*.

clef [klef] *n. Mus:* clef *f*; **bass c.,** clef de fa; **treble c.,** clef de sol; **C c.,** clef d'ut.

cleft [kleft] *n.* fente *f*, fissure *f*, crevasse *f*.

clematis ['klemətis, klə'meitis] *n. Bot:* clématite *f*.

clemency, *pl.* **-cies** ['klemənsi, -siz] *n.* **1.** clémence *f*, indulgence *f* (**to,** envers). **2.** douceur *f* (du temps).

clement ['klemənt] *a.* **1.** (*of pers.*) clément, indulgent (to, envers, pour). **2.** (temps) doux.

clementine ['kleməntiːn, -ain] *n. Hort:* clémentine *f*.

clench[1] [klen(t)ʃ] **1.** *v.tr.* river (un clou). **2.** *v.tr.* serrer (les dents, le poing); **to c. sth. in, with, one's hand,** serrer qch. dans la main. **3.** *v.i.* (*of teeth, hands*) se serrer; (*of hands*) se crisper.

clench[2] *n.* **1.** serrage *m*, étreinte *f* (de la main). **2.** pointe abattue (d'un clou rivé).

Cleopatra [kliə'pætrə] *Pr.n.f. A.Hist:* Cléopâtre; **Cleopatra's needle,** l'Obélisque *m* de Cléopâtre.

clerestory ['kliəstəri] *n. Ecc.Arch:* fenêtres hautes (de la nef).

clergy ['klə:dʒi] *n.* (*no pl.*) **1.** *coll.* clergé *m*. **2.** (*with pl.const.*) ecclésiastiques *mpl*.

clergyman, *pl.* **-men** ['klə:dʒimən] *n.m.* ecclésiastique; pasteur (protestant); prêtre.

cleric ['klerik] *n.* ecclésiastique *m*.

clerical ['klerik(ə)l] **1.** *a.* clérical, -aux; **c. dress,** habit *m* ecclésiastique. **2.** *a.* (*a*) **c. error,** faute *f* de copiste; *Book-k:* erreur d'écritures; (*b*) **c. work,** travail *m* d'écritures, de bureau; **c. staff,** personnel *m*, employés *mpl*, de bureau.

clericalism ['klerikəlizm] *n.* cléricalisme *m*.

clerk[1] [klɑ:k, *NAm:* klə:k] *n.* **1.** (*a*) employé, -ée, de bureau; clerc *m* (d'avoué); **bank c.,** employé, -ée, de banque; **filing c.,** *U.S:* **file c.,** fichiste *m*, employé au classement; **records c.,** archiviste *m*; **shipping c.,** expéditionnaire *m*, employé de l'expédition; *Rail:* **booking c.,** employé du guichet; (*b*) *Jur:* **c. of the court,** greffier *m* (du tribunal). **2.** *Ecc:* **c. (in holy orders),** ecclésiastique *m*. **3.** (*a*) **c. of (the) works,** (i) *Const:* conducteur *m* des travaux; (ii) *Civ.E:* conducteur des ponts et chaussées; (*b*) *Rac:* **c. of the course,** commissaire *m* de la piste. **5.** *NAm:* (*a*) vendeur, -euse (de magasin); (*b*) préposé(e) à la réception (d'un hôtel).

clerk[2] *v.i.* **1.** travailler comme employé(e) de bureau. **2.** *NAm:* travailler comme vendeur, -euse (dans un magasin).

clever ['klevər] *a.* **1.** habile, adroit; **he is c. with his hands,** il est adroit, agile, de ses mains; **c. at doing sth.,** habile, ingénieux, à faire qch.; *F:* **to play it c.,** jouer serré. **2.** (*a*) intelligent; (chien, etc.) savant; *Sch:* **c. at mathematics,** fort en mathématiques; (*b*) *Pej: F:* **a c. Dick,** un je-sais-tout; **he was too c. for us,** il nous a roulés; (*c*) (ouvrage) bien fait; (plan, dispositif) ingénieux. **-ly** *adv.* **1.** habilement, adroitement. **2.** avec intelligence; bien. **3.** ingénieusement.

cleverness ['klevənis] *n.* **1.** habileté *f*, adresse *f*, dextérité *f*. **2.** intelligence *f*. **3.** ingéniosité *f* (d'une invention, etc.).

clew [klu:] *n. NAm:* = CLUE[1,2].

cliché ['kli:ʃei] *n. Typ & Fig:* cliché *m*.

click[1] ['klik] *n.* **1.** bruit sec, clic *m* (d'un pistolet qu'on arme, etc.); *Ent:* **c. beetle,** élatère *m*, *F:* taupin *m*. **2.** coup *m* de langue; *Equit:* appel *m* de langue; *Ling:* clic. **3.** *Tchn:* cliquet *m*; détente *f*; **c. and ratchet,** encliquetage *m*.

click[2]. **1.** *v.i.* cliqueter, faire tic-tac; **cameras were clicking,** partout les déclics des appareils; (*of two parts*) **to c. together,** s'assembler avec un bruit sec. **2.** *v.tr.* **to c. one's heels,** (faire) claquer les talons (en saluant); **to c. one's tongue,** claquer la langue. **3.** *v.i. F:* (*a*) (*of two pers.*) s'entendre à merveille dès l'abord; (*b*) (*of things*) aller ensemble; (*c*) **that clicks!** ça me rappelle quelque chose! **now it's clicked,** j'ai, il a, pigé; j'y suis, il y est; **clicking** *n.* cliquetis *m*.

client ['klaiənt] *n.* (*a*) client, -ente (dans les professions libérales); (*of stockbroker*) donneur *m* d'ordres; (*b*) *Com:* client, -ente (d'un magasin).

clientele [kliən'tel, kliɑ̃'tɛl] *n.* clientèle *f* (dans les professions libérales, d'un magasin, etc.).

cliff [klif] *n.* à-pic *m*, *pl.* à-pics; falaise *f*.

cliffhanger ['klifhæŋər] *n. Journ:* roman-feuilleton *m*, *pl.* romans-feuilletons dont chaque épisode se termine par un suspense; **the election, race, was a c.,** le résultat de l'élection, de la course, a été douteux jusqu'au dernier moment.

climacteric [klai'mæktərik] *n.* (*a*) **the (grand) c.,** la grande climatérique (63 ans); (*b*) climatère *f*; ménopause *f*.

climactic [klai'mæktik] *a.* arrivé à son apogée; (point) culminant.

climate ['klaimət] *n.* climat *m*; **a hostile c.,** un climat, une ambiance, hostile.

climatic [klai'mætik] *a.* (zone, influence, etc.) climatique; **c. conditions,** conditions *fpl* climatiques.

climatology [klaimə'tɔlədʒi] *n.* climatologie *f*.

climax ['klaimæks] *n.* **1.** apogée *m*, faîte *m*, point culminant (de la renommée, etc.); **to work up to a c.,** (i) procéder par gradation (ascendante); (ii) *Th: etc: F:* corser l'action; **as a c. to the entertainment . . .,** comme bouquet de la fête . . .. **2.** *Physiol:* orgasme *m*.

climb[1] [klaim] *n.* **1.** (*a*) ascension *f*, montée *f*; *Mount:* course *f* (dans les montagnes); ascension (d'une paroi abrupte); *Aut:* **hill c.,** course de côte; (*b*) *Av:* **rate of c.,** vitesse ascensionnelle, de montée. **2.** côte *f*, montée (d'une route, etc.).

climb[2] **1.** *v.i. & tr.* monter, gravir (l'escalier); grimper à (un arbre); monter à (l'échelle); escalader (une falaise); **to c. (up) a mountain,** faire l'ascension *f* d'une montagne; **to c. over the wall,** escalader le mur; **to c. on the roof,** monter, grimper, sur le toit; **to c. down a ladder,** descendre d'une échelle; **to c. out of a hole,** grimper, se hisser, en dehors d'un trou; **to c. into bed,** grimper dans son lit. **2.** *v.i.* (*a*) (*of road*) monter; (*of prices*) monter, augmenter; (*b*) (*of mountaineer*) (i) faire des ascensions; (ii) faire de la varappe; (*c*) **to c. to power,** s'élever au pouvoir; **to c. (socially, in the world),** faire son chemin; parvenir; (*d*) *Av:* prendre de l'altitude; monter. **3.** *v.i.* **to c. down,** (*a*) descendre (d'un arbre); (*b*) *F:* en rabattre; reculer. **climbing 1.** *a.* (oiseau) grimpeur; (plante) grimpante; *Av:* (vol) ascendant. **2.** *n.* (*a*) escalade *f*; montée *f*; ascension *f* (d'un arbre); *Av:* remontée *f* (après descente); **c. irons,** crampons *mpl*, grappins *mpl*; étriers *mpl* (pour l'ascension des arbres); **mountain c.,** alpinisme *m*; (*b*) **social c.,** arrivisme *m*.

climb-down ['klaim'daun] *n. F:* défaite *f*; reculade *f*.

climber ['klaimər] *n.* **1.** (*a*) alpiniste *mf*; varappeur *m*; grimpeur *m* (à un arbre); (*b*) **(social) c.**, arriviste *mf*. **2.** *Bot:* plante grimpante.

clinch¹ [klin(t)ʃ] *n.* **1.** (*a*) rivet *m*, crampon *m*; **c. nail,** clou rivé, à river; (*b*) *Nau:* étalingure *f*. **2.** (*a*) *Box:* clinch *m*; **to break a c.,** briser un corps-à-corps; **to go into a c.,** se prendre corps à corps; s'accrocher; (*b*) *F:* étreinte *f* (d'amoureux).

clinch² **1.** *v.tr.* (*a*) river (un clou); abattre, aplatir (un rivet, la pointe du clou); (*b*) *Nau:* étalinguer (une chaîne); (*c*) conclure, clore (un marché); confirmer (un argument); **that clinches it!** (i) voilà qui tranche la question! (ii) cela me décide! **2.** *v.i.* (*a*) *Box:* en venir aux prises; se prendre corps à corps; (*b*) *F:* (*of lovers*) s'étreindre.

clincher ['klin(t)ʃər] *n. F:* argument *m* irréfutable.

cling¹ [kliŋ] *v.i.* (*p.t. & p.p.* **clung** [klʌŋ]) (*a*) (*of pers.*) s'attacher, s'accrocher (**to s.o., to sth.,** à qn. à qch.); (*of burr*) s'attraper (**to,** à); **to c. close to s.o.,** se serrer, se coller, contre qn; **to c. together, to one another,** (i) rester attachés l'un à l'autre; (ii) se tenir étroitement enlacés; (*b*) **to c. to an opinion,** rester attaché à une opinion; s'obstiner dans une opinion; **to c. to a hope,** se raccrocher à un espoir; (*c*) adhérer (**to,** à); (*of plants*) s'accrocher (aux murs); (*of garment*) **to c. to the figure,** mouler le corps. **clinging** *a.* qui s'attache; qui colle; qui s'accroche; (vêtement) collant; (tissu) qui moule le corps; (parfum) tenace.

cling² *n.* **c. (peach)** = CLINGSTONE.

clingstone ['kliŋstoun] *n.* **c. (peach),** pavie *f*.

clinic ['klinik] *n.* **1.** (*centre*) dispensaire *m*. **2.** (*nursing home*) clinique *f*.

clinical ['klinik(ə)l] *a.* **1.** clinique; (thermomètre) médical; **c. death,** mort *f* clinique. **2.** impartial, objectif.

clink¹ [kliŋk] *n.* tintement *m*, choc *m* (de verres).

clink² **1.** *v.i.* (*of glasses, etc.*) tinter. **2.** *v.tr.* faire tinter; **to c. glasses,** choquer les verres; trinquer.

clink³ *n. P:* (cellule *f* de) prison *f*; *F:* taule *f*; **to be in c.,** être au bloc.

clinker ['kliŋkər] *n.* **1.** (*a*) brique hollandaise (pour carrelage); (*b*) brique vitrifiée; brique à four. **2.** mâchefer *m* (de forge, etc.); escarbilles *fpl*. **3.** *N.Arch:* **c.-built,** bordé à clin(s).

clip¹ [klip] *n.* **1.** prince *f*, serre *f*; griffe *f*; *Jewel:* clip *m*; *Hairdr:* (i) pince (pour mise en plis); (ii) (*ornament*) barrette *f*; **paper c.,** (i) agrafe *f* (pour papiers); (ii) attache métallique; (iii) (*wire*) trombone *m*; **tie c.,** pince à cravate; *Cy:* **trouser, bicycle, c.,** pince à pantalon, pince-pantalon *m inv; Surg:* **artery c.,** pince hémostatique. **2.** *El:* cosse *f* (de fil, de câble). **3.** *Rail:* serre-rail(s) *m inv.*; crapaud *m*.

clip² *v.tr.* (**clipped** [klipt]) pincer, serrer; **to c. papers together,** agrafer des papiers; **c.-on,** qui s'attache avec une agrafe; **c.-on tie,** cravate à système.

clip³ *v.tr.* **1.** tondre (un chien, le gazon); couper, tailler (une haie); rogner, cisailler (la monnaie); couper, cisailler (une tôle); **to c. the wings of a bird,** rogner les ailes à une volaille; **to c. s.o.'s wings, claws,** rogner les ongles, les griffes, à qn; **to c. ten seconds off a record,** réduire un record par dix secondes; *Ten:* **to c. the line,** mordre la ligne. **2.** poinçonner (un billet de chemin de fer). **3.** (*a*) donner un coup sec à (qch.); (*b*) *P:* **to c. s.o.'s ear,** flanquer une taloche à qn. **clipped** *a.* (prononciation) écourtée; **c. speech,** manière de parler saccadée. **clipping** *n.* **1.** (*a*) tondage *m* (de chien, etc.); (*b*) poinçonnage *m* (de billets). **2.** (*a*) coupure *f* (de journal); (*b*) **clippings,** rognures *fpl* (de papiers, d'ongles, etc.).

clip⁴ *n.* **1.** tondage *m* (de chien, etc.). **2.** *P:* **c. (on the ear),** taloche *f*. **3.** *NAm: P:* **c. joint,** boîte *f* de nuit, restaurant *m*, où l'on reçoit le coup de fusil. **4.** (*a*) *Cin:* extrait *m* de film; (*b*) *U.S: Journ:* coupure *f* (de journal).

clipboard ['klipbɔːd] *n.* tablette *f* à croquis; planchette *f* porte-papiers.

clipper¹ ['klipər] *n.* **1.** (*pers.*) tondeur, -euse. **2.** *Tls:* (*for the hair, etc.*) **clippers,** tondeuse; **hedge clippers,** taille-buissons *m inv*; **nail clippers,** coupe-ongles *m inv*. **3.** (*a*) *Nau: A:* clipper *m*.

clippie ['klipi] *n.f. F: O:* receveuse (d'autobus).

clique [kliːk] *n.* (*a*) coterie *f*; (*b*) *Pej:* clique *f*.

cliqu(e)y ['kliːki], **cliquish** ['klisːkiʃ] *a. F:* qui a l'esprit de clique.

clitoris, *pl.* **-rides** ['klitəris, -'təridiːz] *n. Anat:* clitoris *m*.

cloak¹ [klouk] *n.* **1.** (*a*) manteau *m*; **under the c. of night,** sous le couvert de la nuit; **c.-and-dagger story,** roman *m* de cape et d'épée; (*b*) *Ecc. Cost:* camail *m*, *pl.* camails.

cloak² *v.tr.* (*a*) couvrir, revêtir (qn) d'un manteau; (*b*) masquer, voiler (ses projets, ses pensées).

cloakroom ['kloukruːm] *n.* (*a*) vestiaire *m*; (*b*) toilettes *fpl*; **ladies' c.,** dames; **c. attendant,** préposé(e) (i) au vestaire, (ii) aux cabinets de toilette; (*c*) *Rail: etc:* consigne *f*.

clobber¹ ['klɔbər] *n. F:* **1.** frusques *fpl*, hardes *fpl*. **2.** effets *mpl;* **all my c.,** toutes mes affaires.

clobber² *v.tr. P:* (*a*) rosser (qn); (*b*) tancer, étriller (qn); (*c*) battre (un adversaire) à plate(s) couture(s); (*d*) persécuter (qn, un groupe). **clobbering** *n. P:* **to get a c.,** être (i) rossé, (ii) tancé, (iii) battu à plate(s) couture(s).

cloche [klɔʃ, klouʃ] *n. Hort: Cost:* cloche *f*.

clock¹ [klɔk] *n.* **1.** (*a*) horloge *f*; (*smaller*) pendule *f*; **ship's c.** horloge marine, de bord; *Aut:* **dashboard c.,** montre de bord; **grandfather c.,** horloge de parquet; **carriage, travelling, c.,** pendulette *f*; **eight-day c.,** huitaine *f*; **digital c.,** horloge digitale; *Tp:* **speaking c.,** horloge parlante; (*in factory, etc.*) **time c.,** pendule de pointage; **a full hour by the c.,** une bonne heure d'horloge; **to sleep the c. round,** faire le tour du cadran; **to work round the c.,** travailler vingt-quatre heures sur vingt-quatre; **a race against the c.,** une course contre la montre; **to beat the c.,** arriver avant temps; **to set, put, the c. back,** (i) retarder la pendule; (ii) rétrogresser; (*b*) (i) *Aut:* compteur *m* de vitesse; (ii) (*in taxi*) compteur *m* horokilométrique. **2.** *Cmptr:* (i) horloge; (ii) base *f* de temps; (iii) générateur *m* de rythme.

clock² **1.** *v.tr. F:* (*a*) chronométrer (un coureur, etc.); (*b*) atteindre, *F:* faire (une certaine vitesse) (au compteur, au chronomètre); *Aut:* **to c. ninety,** taper le 145; (*c*) **to c. up,** atteindre, parvenir à (un total); **he has clocked up 700 kilometres in two days,** il a fait 700 kilomètres en deux jours. **2.** *v.i. Ind: Com:* **to c. in, on,** pointer à l'arrivée; **to c. out, off,** pointer à la sortie. **clocking** *n.* **1.** *Sp:* chronométrage *m*. **2.** *Ind:* **c. in, on,** pointage *m* à l'arrivée; **c. off, out,** pointage à la sortie.

clocklike ['klɔklaik] *a.* (d'une régularité) d'horloge.

clockmaker ['klɔkmeikər] *n.* horloger *m*.

clock-watcher ['klɔkwɔtʃər] *n.* employé(e) qui ne pense qu'à l'heure de sortie.

clockwise ['klɔkwaiz] *adv. & a.* dans le sens des aiguilles d'une montre.

clockwork ['klɔkwəːk] *n.* rouage *m* d'horloge; mouvement *m* d'horlogerie; mécanisme *m* à ressort; *Toys:* **c. train,** chemin *m* de fer mécanique; **as regular as c.,** réglé comme une horloge; **everything is done with c. precision,** tout est réglé comme une horloge; **everything's going like c.,** tout va, marche, comme sur des roulettes.

clod [klɔd] *n.* **1.** (*a*) motte *f* (de terre); **c. breaker,**

crusher, (rouleau *m*) brise-mottes (*m inv*); *F:* **c. crushers,** gros souliers; *F:* godasses *fpl.* **2.** *F:* (*a*) rustre *m*, lourdaud *m*; (*b*) stupide *mf*.

clodhopper ['klɔdhɔpər] *n. F:* **1.** rustre *m*, lourdaud *m*. **2. clodhoppers,** gros souliers; *F:* godasses *fpl.*

clog[1] [klɔg] *n.* **1.** (*a*) entrave *f* (pour cheval); billot *m* (pour vache); (*b*) embarras *m*, entrave. **2.** gros brodequin à semelle de bois; **(wooden) c.,** sabot *m*; **c. dance,** sabotière *f*.

clog[2] *v.* **(clogged) 1.** *v.tr.* (*a*) entraver (un animal); (*b*) entraver, gêner (une entreprise, etc.); (*c*) boucher, obstruer (une artère, un tuyau, etc.); encrasser (une arme à feu, une machine); colmater (un filtre); **our boots got clogged with mud,** nos bottes se crottaient dans la boue. **2.** *v.i.* se boucher, s'obstruer, s'encrasser; (*of filter*) se colmater. **clogging** *n.* obstruction *f*; encrassement *m*; colmatage *m* (d'un filtre); empâtement *m* (d'une lime, etc.).

cloister[1] ['klɔistər] *n.* **1.** monastère *m*. **2.** (*usu. pl.*) cloître *m* (d'un couvent, d'une église, etc.).

cloister[2] *v.tr.* cloîtrer. **cloistered** *a.* (vie) de cloître.

clone[1] [kloun] *n. Bot: Biol:* clone *m*.

clone[2] *v.tr. Bot: Biol:* multiplier par clones.

close[1] [klous] **I.** *a.* **1.** (*a*) (port, etc.) fermé; *Ling:* **c. vowel,** voyelle fermée, entravée; (*b*) (air) enfermé; (odeur) de renfermé; (temps) lourd; (*c*) (secret, silence) impénétrable; (*d*) *Ven:* **c. season,** période *f* d'interdiction; chasse fermée. **2.** serré, dense; (*a*) (fourré, bois) épais, touffu; (*b*) (*of metal, stone, wood, etc.*) **c. grain,** grain fin, dense; **c. texture,** (con)texture serrée, tissu serré; (*c*) *Mil:* **in c. order,** (i) en rangs serrés; (ii) *Navy:* à distance serrée; **in c. ranks,** en rangs serrés. **3.** rapproché; (*a*) **c. intervals,** intervalles rapprochés; **c. proximity,** proximité immédiate; *F:* **that was a close thing,** nous l'avons échappé belle; il était moins cinq; **I saw him at c. quarters,** je l'ai vu de près; **in c. quarters,** à l'étroit; (*b*) *Mil:* **c. combat,** (i) (combat *m*) corps à corps (*m*); (ii) *Navy:* combat bord à bord; **c. range,** courte portée; **c.-range weapon,** arme *f* à courte portée; **to fire at c. range,** tirer à bout portant. **4.** (*a*) ajusté, serré; *Mec.E:* **c. fit,** montage, ajustage, serré; (*b*) étroit; **Italian is c. to French,** l'italien est proche du français; **c. friend,** ami intime. **5.** (*a*) minutieux, attentif; (attention) soutenue; (observateur) attentif; (étude) minutieuse; **on closer examination,** en y regardant de plus près; **after c. consideration,** après mûre considération; **to keep (a) c. watch on s.o., sth.,** surveiller qn, qch., de près; (*b*) (emprisonnement, blocus) rigoureux; (*c*) (copie, ressemblance) exacte; **c. translation,** traduction exacte, fidèle, serrée. **6.** (*a*) serré; **to cut (hair, etc.) c.,** couper (les cheveux, etc.) ras; (*b*) (*of contests*) à forces égales; **c. election,** élection vivement contestée; **c. match,** match serré; *Rac:* **c. finish,** arrivée serrée. 7. (homme) peu communicatif, réservé; **to keep sth. c.,** ne rien dire de qch.; **to play a c. game,** jouer serré. **8.** (*of pers.*) ladre, *F:* pingre. **II.** *adv.* **1. c. shut,** bien (i) fermé, (ii) bouché. **2.** près, de près, auprès; **to be, follow, c. behind s.o.,** suivre qn de près; **to stand c. against a wall,** se coller contre un mur; **houses c. together,** maisons serrées; **to sit, stand, c. together,** être, se tenir, serrés, coude à coude; **sit closer (together)!** serrez-vous! **to keep c.,** rester tout près. **3.** (*a*) **c. at hand, c. by,** tout près, tout contre; (*b*) **c. in;** *Nau:* **to stand c. in (to the land),** serrer la terre; (*c*) **c. on nine (o'clock),** tout près de neuf heures; **to be c. on fifty,** friser la cinquantaine; (*d*) **c. to, c. by s.o., sth.,** (tout) près de, à proximité de (qn, qch.); **he lives c. to here,** il demeure tout près, à deux pas (d'ici); **to come, draw, c., closer, to s.o.,** s'approcher, se rapprocher, de qn; **to keep c. to s.o.,** se tenir tout près de qn; **ship c. to the shore,** navire près de terre; **c. to the ground,** au ras du sol; **to keep c. to the text,** serrer le texte de près. **closely** *adv.* **1. c. shut,** bien (i) fermé, (ii) bouché. **2.** (*a*) **c. guarded,** étroitement gardé; **c. connected,** lié étroitement; **you are the most c. concerned,** c'est vous le premier intéressé; (*b*) **c. cut,** tondu ras; **c. contested,** vivement contesté; (*c*) (ressembler) exactement; (examiner) de près, attentivement; (suivi, observé, traduit) de près; **to watch s.o. c.,** surveiller qn de près; **to listen c.,** écouter attentivement. **3.** l'un près de l'autre; **c. packed in a box,** serrés dans une boîte; **two c. written pages,** deux pages d'une écriture serrée.

close[2] [klous] *n.* (*a*) clos *m*, enclos *m*; (*b*) enceinte *f* (de cathédrale); (*c*) *Town P:* impasse *f*; cul-de-sac *m*, *pl.* culs-de-sac.

close[3] [klouz] *n.* fin *f*, conclusion *f*, terminaison *f* (d'une action, d'un discours, etc.); fin, bout *m* (de l'année); clôture *f*, levée *f* (d'une séance); fin (du jour); *Lit:* **at c. of day,** à la chute du jour; **the year draws to a c.,** l'année tire à sa fin.

close[4] [klouz] **1.** *v.tr.* (*a*) fermer (une porte, les yeux, un livre, etc.); fermer, replier (un parapluie); barrer (une rue); *Nau:* bâcler (un port); *Rail:* bloquer (une section); **road closed to motor traffic,** route interdite à la circulation automobile; **cold closes the pores,** le froid resserre les pores; *Book-k:* **to c. the books,** régler les livres; (*b*) conclure, terminer (une série, une affaire, etc.); lever, clore (une séance); arrêter (un marché); fermer (un débat); fermer, clôturer (un compte); *St.Exch:* liquider (une opération); *Jur:* clôturer (une faillite); **to declare the discussion closed,** prononcer la clôture des débats; *v.i.* **I will now c. with a story,** pour terminer je vais vous raconter une histoire; (*c*) **to c. the ranks,** serrer les rangs. **2.** *v.i.* (*a*) (*of door, etc.*) (se) fermer; (*of wound, hole, etc.*) se refermer; **the theatre will c. for a month,** le théâtre fermera ses portes pendant un mois; **theatres c. on Good Friday,** les théâtres font relâche le vendredi saint; (*b*) finir, se terminer; *St.Exch:* **the shares closed at £1,** les actions ont terminé à £1; (*c*) **to c. round s.o.,** cerner qn, se presser autour de qn; (*d*) **to c. with s.o.,** (i) conclure le marché avec qn; (ii) en venir aux mains avec qn. **closed** *a.* **1.** (*a*) fermé; (*of pipe, etc.*) obturé, bouché; **with eyes c.,** les yeux fermés; **road c.,** rue barrée; (*b*) *P.N: Th:* **c.,** relâche; *NAm: Ven:* **c. season,** période *f* d'interdiction; chasse fermée. **2. c. professions,** professions fermées; *Ind:* **c. shop,** atelier *m*, chantier *m*, etc., qui n'admet pas de travailleurs non syndiqués; **c.-shop policy,** exclusivité syndicale. **3.** *El:* (circuit) fermé; **c.-circuit television,** télévision *f* à circuit fermé. **close down 1.** *v.tr.* fermer (une usine, etc.). **2.** *v.i.* (*a*) (*of factory, etc.*) fermer; cesser la production; chômer; (*of shop*) fermer boutique; **closing down,** cessation *f* de commerce; (*b*) *W.Tel: T.V:* terminer l'émission. **close in 1.** *v.tr.* clôturer (un terrain, etc.); entourer (un édifice, etc.) d'une clôture. **2.** *v.i.* (*a*) **the night is closing in,** la nuit tombe; **the days are closing in,** les jours (se) raccourcissent; (*b*) **to c. in on s.o.,** cerner qn de près; **darkness closed in on us,** la nuit nous enveloppa. **close up 1.** *v.tr.* (*a*) boucher, obturer (une ouverture, etc.); (*b*) *Typ:* rapprocher (les caractères); *Mil: etc:* serrer (les rangs). **2.** *v.i.* (*a*) (*of aperture*) s'obturer; (*of wound, hole, etc.*) se renfermer; (*b*) (*of people*) se serrer, se tasser; *Mil: etc:* **c. up!** serrez (les rangs)! **closing 1.** *a.* (*a*) qui (se) ferme; (*b*) dernier; final, -als; **the c. date for applications is . . .,** le registre d'inscriptions sera clos le . . .; **the c. bid,** la dernière enchère; **c. speech,** discours de fin de séance; **c. prices,** derniers cours. **2.** *n.* (*a*) fermeture *f* (des magasins, etc.); clôture *f* (d'un théâtre, etc.); barrage *m* (d'une rue); cicatrisation *f* (d'une blessure); **c.(-down),** fermeture (d'une usine); **c. time,** heure *f* de la fermeture; **early c. day,** jour *m* où les magasins sont fermés l'après-midi; (*b*) clôture (d'un compte, etc.); levée *f* (d'une séance); arrêté *m*, règlement *m* (d'un compte).

close-cropped ['klous'krɔpt] *a.* (*of hair*) coupé ras; (*of grass*) rasé, tondu, de près.

closedown ['klouzdaun] *n.* **1.** fermeture *f*, clôture *f* (d'ateliers). **2.** *W.Tel:* fin *f* d'émission.

close-fisted ['klous'fistid] *a.* avare, *F:* pingre.

close-fitting ['klous'fitiŋ] *a.* (vêtement) ajusté, collant.

close-knit ['klous'nit] *a.* (*of family, etc.*) lié, joint, étroitement.

closeness ['klousnis] *n.* **1.** rapprochement *m*, proximité *f*; intimité *f* (de contact, d'amitié). **2.** exactitude *f* (d'une description, etc.); fidélité *f*, exactitude (d'une traduction). **3.** (*a*) manque *m* d'air (d'une salle); (*b*) lourdeur *f* (du temps, de l'atmosphère). **4.** réserve *f*, caractère réservé (de qn). **5.** (*of pers.*) avarice *f*, *F:* pingrerie *f*.

close-set ['klous'set] *a.* (*of eyes, etc.*) rapprochés.

close-shaven ['klous'ʃeivn] *a.* rasé de près.

closet[1] ['klɔzit] *n.* **1.** (*a*) cabinet *m*; bureau *m*; (*b*) *A:* **(water) c.,** les cabinets. **2.** (*a*) placard *m*; armoire *f*; (*b*) **to come out of the c.,** sortir de l'anonymat.

closet[2] *v.tr.* **(closeted) to be closeted with s.o.,** être en tête-à-tête, avec qn.

close-up ['klousʌp] *n.* *Cin:* *T.V:* plan rapproché, gros plan; *T.V:* plan serré; **c.-up detail,** détail vu de près.

closure ['klouʒər] *n.* **1.** (*a*) clôture *f*, fermeture *f* (d'une séance, etc.); (*b*) *Parl:* clôture; **to move the c.,** voter la clôture. **2.** fermeture, occlusion *f*.

clot[1] [klɔt] *n.* **1.** caillot *m* (de sang, de lait). **2.** *P:* idiot, -ote, imbécile *mf*.

clot[2] *v.* **(clotted) 1.** *v.i.* se grumeler; (*of milk*) se cailler; (*of blood*) se figer, se coaguler. **2.** *v.tr.* (*a*) caillebotter (le lait, la crème); cailler (le lait); figer (le sang); (*b*) (*of blood, etc.*) coller. **clotted** *a.* (sang) coagulé; **c. cream,** crème caillée, caillebottée (par l'échaudage). **clotting** *n.* caillement *m*; coagulation *f* (du sang, etc.).

cloth, *pl.* **cloths** [klɔθ, klɔθs] *n.* **1.** (*a*) étoffe *f* de laine; drap *m*; **c. maker, manufacturer,** fabricant *m* de draps; (*b*) (*linen, cotton*) toile *f*; **c. binding,** reliure *f* en toile; **c.-bound,** relié toile; (*c*) **American c.,** molesquine *f*, moleskine *f*; (*d*) **c. of gold,** drap d'or. **2.** (*a*) linge *m*; (*for cleaning*) (i) torchon *m*; (ii) **(floor) c.,** serpillière *f*; (*b*) (*tablecloth*) nappe *f*; (*c*) tapis *m* (de billard); (*d*) *Th:* toile (de décor); (*e*) *Nau:* **ship that spreads much c.,** navire *m* qui porte une forte voilure. **3.** *F:* **the c.,** (i) l'habit *m* ecclésiastique, la soutane; (ii) le clergé.

clothe [klouð] *v.tr.* (*p.t. & p.p.* **clad** [klad] *or* **clothed** [klouðd]) vêtir, habiller **(in, with,** de); **warmly, lightly, clad,** chaudement, légèrement, vêtu. **clothing** *n.* **1.** action *f* de s'habiller; **2.** *coll.* habillement *m*, vêtements *mpl*; **dirty c.,** linge *m* sale; **articles of c.,** vêtements; **the c. trade,** l'industrie *f* du vêtement.

clothes [klouðz] *n.pl.* **1.** vêtements *mpl*, habits *mpl*; **old c.,** vieux habits; **in one's best c.,** endimanché; **to put on, take off, one's c.,** s'habiller; se déshabiller; **to go to bed with one's c. on, in one's c.,** se coucher tout habillé; **c. brush,** brosse *f* à habits; **c. hook,** patère *f* à habits. **2.** linge *m*; **dirty c.,** linge sale; **(dirty) c. basket,** panier *m* à linge; **c. horse,** séchoir *m* (a linge); **c. line,** corde *f* à (étendre le) linge; étendoir *m*; **c. peg,** pince *f* à linge; **c. prop,** *NAm:* **pole,** perche *f* de corde à linge.

clothespin ['klouðzpin] *n.* *NAm:* pince *f* à linge.

clothier ['klouðiər] *n.* **1.** fabricant *m* de draps. **2.** (*a*) marchand *m* de draps; (*b*) marchand de confections.

cloud[1] [klaud] *n.* **1.** nuage *m*; *Poet:* nuée *f*, nue *f*; **c. bank,** banc *m* de nuages; **rain c.,** nuage de pluie; *Fig:* **to have one's head in the clouds,** être dans les nuages, dans la lune; **to be on c. nine,** être aux anges; *Prov:* **every c. has a silver lining,** dans toute chose il y a un bon côté; **to be under a c.,** (i) être en défaveur; (ii) être l'objet de soupçons. **2.** (*a*) nuage, voile *m* (de fumée, de poussière); tourbillon *m* (de poussière); (*b*) *Atom.Ph:* **c. chamber,** chambre *f* de détente, d'ionisation. **3.** (*in liquid*) nuage, turbidité *f*; (*in precious stone*) nuée. **4.** nuée (de sauterelles, etc.).

cloud[2] **1.** *v.tr.* couvrir, voiler (le ciel); troubler, rendre trouble (un liquide); ternir (un miroir); troubler (le bonheur de qn); ternir (la réputation de qn); **eyes clouded with tears,** yeux voilés de larmes; **to c. the issue,** embrouiller la question. **2.** *v.i.* (*of sky*) **to c. (up, over),** se couvrir, se voiler, de nuages. **clouded** *a.* (ciel) couvert (de nuages); (liquide) trouble; **to become c.,** (*of sky*) se couvrir; (*of mind*) s'obscurcir.

cloudburst ['klaudbə:st] *n.* trombe *f*; rafale *f* de pluie.

cloud-cuckoo-land ['klaud'kuku:lænd] *n.* *Fig:* pays *m* imaginaire; pays de cocagne.

cloudiness ['klaudinis] *n.* **1.** aspect nuageux (du ciel). **2.** turbidité *f* (d'un liquide).

cloudless ['klaudlis] *a.* (ciel) sans nuages.

cloudy ['klaudi] *a.* **1.** (temps) couvert; (ciel) nuageux; **it's c.,** le temps est couvert. **2.** (liquide) trouble; (vin) louche; *Med:* (urine) chargée.

clout[1] [klaut] *n.* **1.** *A:* chiffon *m*. **2.** *F:* beigne *f*; taloche *f* (sur la tête). **3.** *F:* **to have (plenty of) c.,** (i) être puissant; (ii) avoir de l'influence, du piston.

clout[2] *v.tr.* *F:* **to c. s.o. on, over, the head,** flanquer une taloche à qn; talocher qn.

clove[1] [klouv] *n.* *Bot:* **c. of garlic,** gousse *f* d'ail.

clove[2] *n.* **1.** (*a*) clou *m* de girofle; **oil of cloves,** essence *f* de girofle; (*b*) **c. tree,** giroflier *m*. **2.** *Bot:* **c. pink,** œillet-giroflée *m*, pl. œillets-giroflées; œillet *m* des fleuristes.

clove[3]. *see* CLEAVE.[1]

clove[4] *n.* *Nau:* **c. hitch,** demi-clef *f*.

cloven-footed, -hoofed ['klouv(ə)n'futid, '-hu:t] *a.* *Z:* au pied fourchu.

clover ['klouvər] *n.* *Bot:* trèfle *m*; **c. leaf,** feuille *f* de trèfle; **four-leaved c.,** trèfle à quatre feuilles; *F:* **to be, live, in c.,** vivre comme un coq en pâte.

cloverleaf, -leafs, -leaves ['klouvəli:f, -li:fs, -li:vz] *n.* *Civ.E:* **c. (intersection),** croisement *m*, carrefour *m*, en (as de) trèfle.

clown[1] [klaun] *n.* *Th:* (*a*) bouffon *m*, pitre *m*; (*b*) clown *m* (de cirque).

clown[2] *v.i.* faire le clown, le pitre. **clowning** *n.* (i) bouffonnerie *f*, pitrerie *f*; (ii) clownerie *f* (de cirque).

cloy [klɔi] *v.tr.* (*of food, etc.*) rassasier; écœurer; *Lit:* **delights that never c.,** plaisirs dont on ne se lasse pas. **cloying** *a.* rassasiant.

club[1] [klʌb] *n.* **1.** (*a*) massue *f*, gourdin *m*; *Gym:* **Indian c.,** bouteille *f* en bois; (*b*) *Golf:* club *m*, crosse *f*. **2.** *Cards:* trèfle *m*; **ace of clubs,** as *m* de trèfle. **3.** (*a*) club *m* (politique, littéraire, etc.); **c. chair,** (fauteuil *m*) club (*m*); (*b*) cercle *m*; **literary c.,** cercle littéraire; **gambling c.,** cercle de jeu; (*c*) association *f*; société *f*; club; **youth c.,** foyer *m* des jeunes; (*associated with church*) patronage *m*; **tennis, yacht, c.,** club de tennis, de yachting; **c. tie,** cravate *f* aux couleurs d'une association sportive; (*d*) **book c.,** club du livre.

club[2] *v.* **(clubbed) 1.** *v.tr.* frapper (qn) avec une massue, avec un gourdin; **to c. s.o. to death,** tuer qn à coups de gourdin. **2.** *v.tr.* (*of several pers.*) **to c. one's resources (together),** mettre ses ressources en commun. **3.** *v.i.* **to c. together,** se cotiser, mettre son argent en commun.

clubfoot ['klʌbfut] *n.* pied *m* bot.

clubfooted ['klʌbfutid] *a.* qui a le pied bot.

clubhouse ['klʌbhaus] *n.* (local *m* du) cercle; club *m*; *Golf: Ten: etc:* pavillon *m*.

clubroom ['klʌbru:m] *n.* salle *f* de réunion (d'un cercle, etc.).

cluck¹ [klʌk] *n.* **1.** (*of hens*) gloussement *m*.

cluck² *v.i.* (*a*) (*of hen*) glousser; (*b*) *F:* (*of pers.*) faire claquer sa langue. **clucking** *n.* gloussement *m*.

clue¹ [klu:] *n.* (*a*), indication *f*, indice *m*; **to get, find, the c. to sth.,** trouver, découvrir, la clef de qch.; **to give s.o. a c.,** mettre qn sur la voie, sur la piste; (*b*) *F:* **I haven't a c.,** je n'en sais rien; je n'en ai pas la moindre idée; (*c*) *pl.* définitions *fpl* (de mots croisés).

clue² *v.tr. F:* **to c. s.o. (in, up),** renseigner qn, mettre qn à la page.

clueless ['klu:lis] *a. F:* **he's quite c.,** il ne sait rien de rien.

clump¹ [klʌmp] *n.* **1.** (*a*) bloc *m*, masse *f* (de bois, d'argile, etc.); (*b*) groupe *m*, bouquet *m* (d'arbres); massif *m* (d'arbustes, de fleurs); touffe *f* (de fleurs). **2.** (bruit *m* de) pas lourd.

clump² **1.** *v.i.* se grouper en masse compacte. **2.** *v.tr.* grouper en masse compacte; planter (des arbustes, etc.) en massif. **3.** *v.i.* **to c. (about),** marcher lourdement.

clumsiness ['klʌmzinis] *n.* **1.** maladresse *f*, gaucherie *f*. **2.** (*of shape*) grossièreté *f*, lourdeur *f*. **3.** manque *m* de tact.

clumsy ['klʌmzi] *a.* **1.** (*of pers., movement, etc.*) maladroit, gauche. **2.** (*of shape*) lourd, disgracieux; **c. boots,** godillots *mpl*. **3.** (phrase, excuse) maladroite, gauche; **c. verse,** vers mal faits; **c. forgery,** contre-façon grossière. **-ily** *adv.* **1.** maladroitement, gauchement. **2.** grossièrement; **c. built,** mal bâti. **3.** gauchement; sans tact.

clung. *see* CLING[1].

cluster¹ ['klʌstər] *n.* bouquet *m* (de fleurs, de cerises); grappe *f* (de raisins, de cerises); épi *m*, nœud *m* (de diamants); amas *m* (d'étoiles); peloton *m* (d'abeilles, etc.); groupe, rassemblement *m* (de personnes); agglomération *f* (d'îles); pâté *m* (de maisons); faisceau *m* (d'ampoules électriques).

cluster² **1.** *v.tr.* grouper (en grappes); rassembler (des objets) en groupes. **2.** *v.i.* (*a*) (*of fruit*) se former, croître, en grappes; (*b*) (*of pers.*) **to c. round s.o., sth.,** se grouper, se rassembler, autour de qn, de qch.; (*c*) (*of particles, etc.*) **to c. together,** se conglomérer.

clutch¹ [klʌtʃ] *n.* **1.** (*a*) griffe *f* (d'un animal); serre *f* (d'un oiseau de proie); **to fall into s.o.'s clutches,** tomber sous la patte de qn; **to escape from s.o.'s clutches,** se tirer des pattes de qn; (*b*) action *f* de saisir; **to make a c. at sth.,** essayer de saisir qch; (*c*) **c. bag,** *NAm:* **c. purse,** pochette *f*. **2.** *Mec.E: Aut:* embrayage *m*; **automatic c.,** embrayage automatique; autodébrayage *m*; **disc, plate, c.,** embrayage à disque, à plateau; **c. disc, plate,** disque *m*, plateau *m*, d'embrayage; **c. pedal,** pédale *f* d'embrayage, de débrayage; **to let in the c.,** embrayer; **to release, let out, the c.,** débrayer.

clutch² *v.tr. & ind.tr.* saisir, étreindre; **to c. sth. with both hands,** saisir qch. à deux mains; **to c. at sth., to c. hold of sth.,** s'agripper, se cramponner, à qch.; *Fig:* **to c. at any straw,** se raccrocher à n'importe quoi.

clutch³ *n.* couvée *f* (d'œufs, de poussins).

clutter¹ ['klʌtər] *n.* **1.** encombrement *m*, confusion *f*; entassement *m* (de mobilier, etc.); **everything's in a c.,** tout est en désordre, en pagaille.

clutter² *v.tr.* **to c. up a room,** encombrer une pièce (**with,** de); **desk cluttered with papers,** bureau encombré de papiers; **to c. up one's mind with useless facts,** charger sa mémoire de faits inutiles. **cluttered** *a.* encombré (**with,** de).

coach¹ [koutʃ] *n.* **1.** (*a*) *Veh:* carrosse *m A:* **stage c.,** diligence *m*; **c. and four,** carrosse à quatre chevaux; (*b*) car *m*; **c. station,** gare routière. **2.** *Rail:* voiture *f*, wagon *m*. **3.** (*a*) *Sch:* professeur *m* qui donne des leçons particulières; répétiteur *m*; (*b*) *Sp:* entraîneur *m*.

coach² **1.** *v.tr.* (*a*) *Sch:* donner des leçons particulières; *Th:* **to c. s.o. for a part,** faire répéter son rôle à qn; (*b*) *Sp:* entraîner (une équipe). **2.** *v.i. Sch:* donner des leçons particulières. **coaching** *n.* **1.** *A:* **c. inn,** relais *m*. **2.** (*a*) *Sch:* leçons particulières; répétitions *fpl*; (*b*) *Sp:* entraînement *m*.

coachbuilder ['koutʃbildər] *n.* carrossier *m*.

coachhouse ['koutʃhaus] *n.* remise *f* (pour voitures à chevaux).

coachman, *pl.* **-men** ['koutʃmən] *n.m.* cocher.

coachwork ['koutʃwə:k] *n.* carrosserie *f*.

coagulant [kou'ægjulənt] *n.* coagulant *m*.

coagulate [kou'ægjuleit] **1.** *v.tr.* coaguler. **2.** *v.i.* se coaguler.

coagulation [kouægju'leiʃ(ə)n] *n.* coagulation *f*.

coal¹ [koul] *n.* (*a*) charbon *m* (de terre); houille *f*; **smokeless c.,** charbon sans fumée; **coking c.,** charbon à coke; **c.-black,** noir comme du charbon; (*b*) **the c.-(-mining) industry,** l'industrie houillère; **c. mine,** mine *f* de charbon; houillère *f*; **c. mining,** exploitation *f* de la houille; **c. miner,** mineur *m*, houilleur *m*; **c. basin,** bassin houiller; **c. merchant,** (i) négociant *m* en charbon; (ii) marchand *m* de charbon; *Min:* **c. face,** front *m* de taille; **c. cutter,** (i) (*pers.*) haveur *m*; soucheur *m*; (ii) (*machine*) haveuse *f*; *Mch:* **c.-fired,** alimenté au charbon; *Dom.Ec:* **c. bunker,** coffre *m* à charbon; **c. cellar,** cave *f* au charbon; **c. scuttle,** seau *m* à charbon; charbonnière *f*; **c. shovel,** pelle *f* à charbon; (*c*) **c. gas,** gaz *m* de houille; **c. tar,** goudron *m* de houille; **c.-tar soap,** savon *m* coaltar; (*d*) **live coals,** braise *f*; charbon ardent; **to carry coals to Newcastle,** porter de l'eau à la rivière; *F:* **to haul s.o. over the coals,** réprimander, qn vertement; laver la tête à qn.

coal² *v.tr.* **1.** charbonner (du bois). **2.** approvisionner (un navire) de charbon; **to c. ship,** *v.i.* **to c.** charbonner.

coalesce [kouə'les] *v.i.* **1.** (*a*) s'unir; se fondre (ensemble); (*b*) *Ch:* se combiner. **2.** (*of parties, etc.*) fusionner.

coalescence [kouə'lesəns] *n.* (*a*) coalescence *f*, union *f*, fusion *f*; (*b*) *Ch:* combinaison *f*.

coalfield ['koulfi:ld] *n. Min:* bassin houiller.

coalition [kouə'liʃ(ə)n] *n.* coalition *f*; *Pol:* **to form a c.,** se coaliser.

coalman, *pl.* **-men** ['koulmæn, -men] *n.* (petit) marchand de charbon; charbonnier.

coaltit ['koultit] *n. Orn:* mésange noire.

coalshed ['koulʃed] *n.* hangar *m* à charbon.

coarse [kɔ:s] *a.* **1.** grossier, vulgaire; (language) grossier; **c. joke,** plaisanterie grossière. **2.** (*a*) (*of material*) gros, grossier, rude; **c. hair,** cheveux *mpl* rudes; **c. salt,** gros sel; **c. cut,** haché; (tabac) de grosse coupe; (*b*) **c. fish,** poissons d'eau douce (sauf truites et saumons); (*c*) *Mec.E:* (réglage) approximatif. **-ly** *adv.* **1.** grossièrement, vulgairement. **2.** (fait) grossièrement; (haché, etc.) gros.

coarsen ['kɔ:s(ə)n] **1.** *v.tr.* rendre plus grossier, plus rude. **2.** *v.i.* devenir plus grossier.

coarseness ['kɔ:snis] *n.* **1.** grossièreté *f*, brutalité *f* (des manières, etc.); grossièreté (d'une plaisanterie, etc.). **2.** rudesse *f* (de la peau, des cheveux); grosseur *f* de fil (d'une étoffe); gros grain (du bois).

coast¹ [koust] *n.* **1.** côte *f*, rivage *m*; (*extensive*) littoral *m*; **from c. to c.,** d'une mer à l'autre, d'un océan à l'autre; *F:* **the c. is clear,** le champ est libre. **2.** (*a*) *U.S:* (i) piste *f* (de toboggan); (ii) descente *f* (en toboggan); (*b*) *Cy: Aut:* descente en roue libre.

coast² *v.i. & tr.* **1.** *Nau:* (*a*) **to c. (along),** suivre la côte; (*b*) *Com:* caboter. **2. to c. (down),** (i) *U.S:* descendre (une côte) en toboggan; (ii) *Cy: Aut:* descendre en roue libre. **coasting** *n.* **1.** (*a*) navigation côtière; (*b*) cabotage *m*; **c. vessel,** caboteur *m*. **2.** (*a*) *U.S:* descente *f* en toboggan; (*b*) *Cy: Aut:* descente (de côte) en roue libre.

coastal ['koust(ə)l] *a.* côtier; **c. navigation,** navigation côtière; cabotage *m*; **c. trade,** commerce caboteur; cabotage *m*; **c. defence,** défense côtière.

coaster ['koustər] *n.* **1.** (*of pers., ship*) cabotier *m*, caboteur *m*. **2.** dessous *m* de bouteille, de carafe.

coastguard ['koustgɑːd] *n.* **1.** *coll.* la garde des côtes; **c. vessel, cutter,** garde-côte *m*. **2.** (*also* **coastguard(s)man** [koust'gɑːd(z)mən]) garde-côte *m*, *pl.* gardes-côte.

coastline ['koustlain] *n.* littoral *m*.

coat¹ [kout] *n.* **1.** (*a*) *Cost:* (*short*) veste *f*, veston *m*; (*long*) manteau *m*; (*for men*) pardessus *m*; **tail c.,** habit *m* à queue; **morning c.,** jaquette *f*; **car c.,** autocoat *m*; **c. hook,** patère *f*; (*b*) *Her:* **c. of arms,** armes *fpl*, armoiries *fpl*, écusson *m*. **2.** (*a*) robe (d'un chien, d'un cheval); pelage *m* (d'un fauve); (*b*) manteau, couche *f* (de neige, etc.). **3.** couche, application *f* (de peinture); pelure *f* (de vernis); enduit *m* (de goudron).

coat² *v.tr.* enduire (qch. de peinture, de goudron, etc.); enrober (qch. de chocolat, etc.); dragéifier (une pilule); revêtir, armer (un câble) (**with,** de); coucher (du papier); **to c. (sth.) with dust,** couvrir (qch.) de poussière. **coated** *a.* enduit, (re)couvert, enrobé (**with,** de); (électrode) enrobée; (langue) chargée, pâteuse; *Paperm:* (papier) couché; *Phot:* (objectif) bleuté, traité; **c. with dust,** couvert de poussière. **coating** *n.* **1.** enduisage *m*. **2.** enduit *m*, couche *f* (de peinture, etc.); pelure *f* (de vernis); pellicule *f* (de gélatine); *Tchn:* **protective c.,** couche protective.

coathanger ['kouthæŋər] *n.* cintre *m*; porte-vêtements *m inv.*

coatrack ['koutræk] *n.* portemanteau *m*.

coattails ['kout(t)eilz] *n.pl.l.* basques *f*, pan *m* d'un habit. **2.** *NAm:* **to ride on s.o.'s c.,** se faire élire dans le sillage de qn.

co-author [kou'ɔːθər] *n.* coauteur *m*.

coax [kouks] *v.tr.* cajoler, enjôler, câliner; **to c. s.o. to do sth., into doing sth.,** encourager qn à faire qch. (en le cajolant). **coaxing 1.** *a.* (ton, etc.) cajoleur. **2.** *n.* cajolerie *f*; **he took a lot of c.,** il s'est bien fait tirer l'oreille.

cob¹ [kɔb] *n.* **1.** (*horse*) cob *m*, bidet *m*. **2. c. (swan),** cygne *m* mâle. **3.** aveline *f*, grosse noisette. **4. (corn) c.,** (i) (*with grain*) épi *m* de maïs; (ii) (*without grain*) rafle *f*; *Cu:* **corn on the c.,** maïs en épi. **5.** pain rond.

cobalt ['koubɔːlt] *n.* *Ch:* cobalt *m*; **c. blue,** bleu *m* de cobalt; **c. bomb,** bombe *f* au cobalt.

cobber ['kɔbər] *n.* *Austr: F:* copain *m*, pote *m*.

cobble¹ ['kɔbl] *n.* galet *m*, caillou *m* (de chaussée).

cobble² *v.tr.* paver (une cour) de galets.

cobble³ *v.tr.* réparer (des chaussures).

cobbler ['kɔblər] *n.* cordonnier *m*.

cobblestone ['kɔblstoun] *n.* caillou *m* (de chaussée).

cobloaf ['kɔblouf] *n.* pain rond.

cobnut ['kɔbnʌt] *n.* aveline *f*, grosse noisette.

cobra ['koubrə] *n.* *Rept:* cobra *m*.

cobweb ['kɔbweb] *n.* (i) toile *f*, (ii) fil *m*, d'araignée; **to brush, sweep, away the cobwebs from sth.,** ôter les toiles d'araignées de qch.; **to go for a walk to blow away the cobwebs,** prendre l'air pour se rafraîchir les idées.

coca ['koukə] *n.* *Bot: Pharm:* coca *m or f*.

cocaine [kou'kein] *n.* *Pharm:* cocaïne *f*.

coccyx ['kɔksiks] *n.* *Anat:* coccyx *m*.

cochineal ['kɔtʃiniːl] *n.* *Dy: Ent:* cochenille *f*.

cock¹ [kɔk] *n.* **1.** (*a*) coq *m*; **fighting c.,** coq de combat; *F:* **c. of the walk, of the roost,** coq du village; *P:* **watcher c.!** salut mon vieux! (*b*) (*male*) **c. bird,** oiseau *m* mâle; **c. pheasant,** coq faisan; **c. canary,** serin *m*; **c. sparrow,** moineau *m* mâle; **c. lobster,** homard *m* mâle. **2.** (*a*) *Plumb: etc:* robinet *m*; (*b*) *Nau:* **sea c.,** robinet de prise d'eau à la mer; (*c*) *P:* pénis *m*, bit(t)e *f*. **3.** (*a*) *Sm.a:* chien *m* (de fusil); **at full c.,** au cran d'armé; *Fig:* **to go off at half c.,** mal démarrer; (*b*) (*of balance*) aiguille *f*; (*of sundial*) style *m*. **4.** *P:* bêtises *fpl*, sottises *fpl*.

cock² *v.tr.* **1.** (*a*) **to c. one's eye at s.o., sth.,** donner un coup d'œil à qn, qch.; (*b*) (*of horse, etc.*) **to c. (up) its ears,** dresser les oreilles. **2. to c. one's hat,** (i) mettre son chapeau de côté; (ii) relever, son chapeau. **3.** armer (un fusil). **cocked** *a.* (chapeau) à cornes; *F:* **to knock s.o. into a c. hat,** battre qn à plate(s) couture(s); démolir qn. **cocking** *n.* *Sm.a:* armement *m* (d'un fusil, etc.).

cock³ *n.* *Agr:* meule *f* (de foin).

cockade [kɔ'keid] *n.* cocarde *f*.

cock-a-doodle-doo ['kɔkəduːdl'duː] *int.* *F:* cocorico!

cock-a-hoop ['kɔkə'huːp] *a. & adv.* (en) jubilant; triomphant; **all c.-a-h.,** fier comme Artaban.

cock-and-bull ['kɔk(ə)nd'bul] *a.* *F:* **c.-a.-b. story,** histoire abracadabrante.

cockatoo [kɔkə'tuː] *n.* *Orn:* cacatoès *m*.

cockchafer ['kɔktʃeifər] *n.* *Ent:* hanneton *m*.

cockcrow ['kɔkkrou] *n.* chant *m* du coq; **to rise at c.,** se lever au (premier) chant du coq, à l'aube.

cocker ['kɔkər] *n.* **c. (spaniel),** (épagneul *m*) cocker (*m*).

cockerel ['kɔk(ə)r(ə)l] *n.* jeune coq *m*; coquelet *m*.

cockeyed ['kɔkaid] *a.* *F:* **1.** (*of pers.*) qui louche. **2.** (*a*) de travers, de traviole; (*b*) absurde; (histoire) qui ne tient pas debout.

cockfight ['kɔkfait] *n.* combat *m*, joute *f*, de coqs.

cockfighting ['kɔkfaitiŋ] *n.* combats *mpl*, concours *mpl*, de coqs.

cockiness ['kɔkinis] *n.* impertinence *f*; toupet *m*.

cockle¹ ['kɔkl] *n.* **1.** *Bot:* **(corn) c.,** nielle *f* des champs. **2.** *Agr:* (*disease*) nielle.

cockle² *n.* (*a*) *Moll:* coque *f*, fausse praire; (*b*) **that will warm the cockles of your heart,** voilà qui vous réchauffera.

cockleshell ['kɔklʃel] *n.* **1.** coquille *f* de coque. **2.** (*boat*) coquille de noix; coque *f*.

Cockney ['kɔkni] **1.** *a.* cockney, londonien. **2.** *n.* Londonien, -ienne, Cockney *mf* (des quartiers de l'est de Londres).

cockpit ['kɔkpit] *n.* **1.** arène *f* de combats de coqs. **2.** (*a*) *Av:* poste *m* de pilotage; cockpit *m*; (*b*) *Aut:* (*in racing car*) poste du pilote.

cockroach ['kɔkroutʃ] *n.* *Ent:* blatte *f*; cafard *m*.

cockscomb ['kɔkskoum] *n.* **1.** crête *f* de coq. **2.** *Bot:* (amarante *f*) crête-de-coq (*f*), *pl.* crêtes-de-coq.

cocksure ['kɔk'ʃuər] *a.* sûr de soi; suffisant, outrecuidant.

cocktail ['kɔkteil] *n.* (*a*) (*drink*) cocktail *m*; **c. cabinet,** bar *m* (à cocktails); **c. mixer, shaker,** shaker *m*; **c. party,** cocktail; (*b*) **fruit c.,** salade *f* de fruits (servie dans un verre); **prawn c.,** crevettes à la mayonnaise; (*c*) *Exp:* **Molotov c.,** cocktail Molotov.

cockup ['kɔkʌp] *n.* *P:* couillonnade *f*; **it was a complete c.,** ça a été un vrai bordel.

cocky ['kɔki] *a. F:* suffisant, outrecuidant; qui a du toupet; qui fait l'important.

cocoa ['koukou] *n.* (*powder or drink*) cacao *m*; **c. bean,** graine *f*, fève *f*, de cacao; **c. butter,** beurre *m* de cacao.

coconut ['koukənʌt] *n.* (noix *f* de) coco (*m*); **c. palm, tree,** cocotier *m*; **c. milk, butter,** lait *m*, beurre *m*, de coco; **c. oil,** huile *f* de coprah; **c. fibre,** fibre *f* de coco; coir *m*; **c. matting,** natte *f* en fibres de coco; **c. shy,** jeu *m* de massacre (où on essaie d'abattre des noix de coco).

cocoon[1] [kə'ku:n] *n.* cocon *m* (de ver à soie, etc.).

cocoon[2] *v.tr.* envelopper (**in,** dans).

cod[1] [kɔd] *n. Ich:* (*a*) morue *f*; **fresh c.,** morue fraîche; cabillaud *m*; **dried c.,** morue sèche; merluche *f*; **cod('s) roe,** œufs *mpl* de morue; *Pharm:* **c.-liver oil,** huile *f* de foie de morue.

coda ['koudə] *n. Mus:* coda *f*.

coddle ['kɔdl] *v.tr.* **1.** *Cu:* faire cuire (des œufs) en cocotte. **2.** choyer, dorloter (qn); **to c. oneself,** se dorloter.

code[1] [koud] *n.* **1.** code *m*; **c. of honour,** code, règles *fpl*, de l'honneur; **Highway C.** = Code de la route; **c. of criminal procedure,** code d'instruction criminelle. **2.** (*a*) *Tg: etc:* code (télégraphique, etc.); **c. letter, number,** indicatif littéral, numérique; **(dialling) c.,** indicatif (départemental); **c. word,** mot convenu; **postal, post, c.,** *U.S:* **zip c.,** code postal; (*b*) (*secret*) code, chiffre *m*; **c. letter,** lettre *f* code; **c. name,** nom conventionnel; **to write a message in c.,** chiffrer un message; **c. message,** message chiffré; **c. book,** code, carnet *m*, (i) de chiffrement, (ii) de déchiffrement; (*c*) *Cmptr:* code; **computer c.,** code machine; **c. translation,** transcodage *m*.

code[2] *v.tr.* (*a*) coder, mettre en code, en chiffre (un message, etc.); (*b*) *Cmptr:* coder, programmer, écrire (une séquence, etc.). **coded** *a.* (*a*) (*of message, etc.*) chiffré; (*b*) *Cmptr:* codé, programmé. **coding** *n.* (*a*) codification *f*; codage *m*; (*b*) *Cmptr:* codage, programmation *f*; **c. error,** erreur *f* de programmation; **c. clerk,** codeur *m*.

co-defendant ['koudi'fendənt] *n.* coaccusé, -ée; codéfendeur *m*.

codeine ['koudi:n] *n. Pharm:* codéine *f*.

coder ['koudər] *n.* (*a*) chiffreur *m*; (*b*) *Cmptr:* codeur *m*, codifieur *m*.

codex, *pl.* **-ices** ['koudeks, -isi:z] *n.* **1.** manuscrit (ancien). **2.** *Pharm:* codex *m*.

codger ['kɔdʒər] *n. F: O:* type *m*; **an old c.,** un vieux bonhomme.

codicil ['kɔdisil] *n.* codicille *m* (d'un testament).

codification [kɔdifi'keiʃ(ə)n] *n.* codification *f*.

codify ['koudifai] *v.tr.* codifier (les lois, etc.).

co-director ['koud(a)i'rektər] *n.* codirecteur, -trice.

co-driver ['kou'draivər] *n. Rac:* copilote *m*.

codswallop ['kɔdzwɔləp] *n. P:* bêtises *fpl*, tissu *m* d'âneries; **it's a load of (old) c.,** c'est du bidon.

co-ed ['kou'ed] *F:* **1.** *a. & n.* (école *f*) mixte. **2.** *n.* élève *f* d'une école mixte.

coeducation ['kouedju'keiʃ(ə)n] *n.* coéducation *f*; enseignement *m* mixte.

coeducational ['kouedju'keiʃən(əl)] *a.* coéducationnel; **c. school,** école *f* mixte.

coefficient [koui'fiʃənt] *n.* coefficient *m*.

coerce [kou'ə:s] *v.tr.* **1.** forcer, contraindre **(s.o. into doing sth.,** qn à faire qch.). **2.** réprimer par la force.

coercion [kou'ə:ʃ(ə)n] *n.* coercition *f*, contrainte *f*; *Jur:* coaction *f*; **to act under c.,** agir par contrainte.

coexist ['kouig'zist] *v.i.* coexister (**with,** avec).

coexistence ['kouig'zistəns] *n.* coexistence *f* (**with,** avec); concomitance *f*; *Pol:* **peaceful c.,** coexistence *f* pacifique.

coexistent ['kouig'zistənt] *a.* coexistant (**with,** avec).

coffee ['kɔfi] *n.* (*a*) café *m*; **c. mill,** moulin *m* à café; **ground c.,** café moulu; **c. grounds,** marc *m* de café; **instant c.,** café instantané; **black c.,** café noir; **white c.,** café crème; café au lait; (*ordering breakfast*) **c. and rolls,** café complet; **c. pot,** cafetière *f*; **c. cup,** tasse *f* à café; **c. spoon,** cuillère *f* (i) à café, (ii) (*small*) à moka; **c. bar,** café *m*; **c. table,** table *f* de salon; **c.-table book,** livre de grand format profusément illustré; **c. break,** pause-café *f*, *pl.* pauses-café; (*b*) **c. tree,** caféier *m*; **c. bean,** grain *m* de café; (*c*) **c. cream,** chocolat fourré au café; (*d*) *a.* **c.(-coloured),** (i) café *inv*; (ii) café au lait *inv*.

coffer[1] ['kɔfər] *n.* **1.** coffre *m*; **the coffers of State,** les fonds publics. **2.** *Arch:* caisson *m* (de plafond). **3.** *Hyd.E:* (*a*) chambre *f*, bassin *m*, sas *m* (d'écluse); (*b*) = COFFERDAM.

coffer[2] *v.tr.* **1.** *Min: Civ.E:* coffrer (un puits). **2.** diviser (un plafond) en caissons; **coffered ceiling,** plafond *m* à caissons. **coffering** *n. Min: etc:* coffrage *m*.

cofferdam ['kɔfədæm] *n. Hyd.E:* coffre *m*, bâtardeau *m*; caisson *m* hydraulique.

coffin ['kɔfin] *n.* **1.** cercueil *m*; bière *f*; *F:* **that's another nail in his c.,** (i) c'est (pour lui) un pas de plus vers la tombe; (ii) avec ça il va se faire renvoyer. **2.** cavité *f* du sabot (d'un cheval).

cofounder [kou'faundər] *n.* cofondateur, -trice.

cog [kɔg] *n. Mec.E:* (*a*) dent *f* (d'une roue dentée); **the cogs,** la denture; **I am only a c. in the machinery,** je ne suis qu'un rouage de la machine; (*b*) **c. rail,** crémaillère *f*; **c. railway,** *U.S:* **railroad,** chemin *m* de fer à crémaillère.

cogency ['koudʒənsi] *n.* force *f*, puissance *f*.

cogent ['koudʒənt] *a.* **1.** (argument) irrésistible; (motif) puissant; (raison) valable convaincante. **2.** (cas) urgent. **-ly** *adv.* avec force; incontestablement.

cogitate ['kɔdʒiteit] **1.** *v.i.* méditer, réfléchir (**on, over,** sur). **2.** *v.tr.* projeter, imaginer (un plan, etc.).

cogitation [kɔdʒi'teiʃ(ə)n] *n.* réflexion *f*, cogitation (**on, over,** sur).

cognac ['kɔnjæk] *n.* cognac *m*.

cognate ['kɔgneit] **1.** *n. Jur:* cognat *m*. **2.** (*a*) *a.* **c. (with sth.),** qui a du rapport (avec qch.); qui est parent (de qch.); (*b*) *a.* (mots) de même origine; (mots) congénères; *Gram:* **c. accusative,** accusatif de l'objet interne; (*c*) *n.* mot *m* de même origine.

cognition [kɔg'niʃ(ə)n] *n. Phil: Psy:* connaissance *f*, cognition *f*.

cognizance ['kɔgnizəns, *Jur:* 'kɔnizəns] *n.* **1.** (*a*) *Phil:* connaissance *f*, perception *f*; (*b*) *Jur:* connaissance; **to take c. of sth.,** prendre connaissance de qch. **2.** *Jur:* compétence *f*; **within, under, the c. of a court,** du ressort d'une cour.

cognizant ['kɔgnizənt, *Jur:* 'kɔnizənt] *a.* **1.** ayant connaissance (**of,** de); **to be c. of a fact,** être instruit d'un fait. **2.** *Jur:* **court c. of an offence,** tribunal compétent pour juger un délit.

cogwheel ['kɔg(h)wi:l] *n. Mec.E:* roue à dents, dentée; roue d'engrenage.

cohabit [kou'hæbit] *v.i.* cohabiter, vivre maritalement (**with,** avec).

cohabitation [kouhæbi'teiʃ(ə)n] *n.* cohabitation *f* (**with,** avec).

cohere [kou'hiər] **1.** *v.i.* (*a*) (*of whole, of parts*) se tenir ensemble, rester uni(s); (*b*) s'agglomérer; (*c*) (*of argument, style*) se suivre (logiquement). **2.** *v.tr.* faire tenir ensemble (des matériaux, etc.).

coherence [kou'hiərəns] *n.* **1.** cohésion *f*; adhérence *f*. **2.** (*of argument, style*) suite *f* (logique); cohérence *f*.

coherent [kou'hiər(ə)nt] *a.* **1.** (*of whole, of parts*) cohérent(s); lié(s) ensemble. **2.** (*of plan, speech, etc.*) conséquent, cohérent; (*of thinker*) qui a de la suite dans ses idées; (*of argument*) bien développé. **-ly** *adv.* (parler) d'une manière cohérente, avec cohérence.

cohesion [kou'hi:ʒ(ə)n] *n.* cohésion *f.*

cohesive [kou'hi:siv] *a.* **1.** cohésif; *Ph:* (force) de cohésion. **2.** cohésif, susceptible de cohésion.

coiffure [kwɑ:'fjuər] *n.* coiffure *f.*

coil¹ [kɔil] *n.* **1.** (*a*) rouleau *m* (de corde); *Nau:* glène *f*; cueille *f* (de filin, de câble); roue *f* (de câble); rouleau, torque *f* (de fil métallique); (*b*) *Hairdr:* rouleau (de cheveux); chignon *m*; (*c*) (*coiled tube*) serpentin *m*; (*d*) (*contraceptive*) stérilet *m*. **2.** pli *m*, repli *m* (d'un cordage); repli, nœud *m*, anneau *m* (d'un serpent). **3.** *El:* enroulement *m*; bobine *f.*

coil² **1.** *v.tr.* (en)rouler, gléner (un cordage, etc.); *El:* bobiner (des fils); (*of snake*) **to c. (itself) up,** s'enrouler, se lover; *Nau: etc:* **to c. (down) a rope,** lover un cordage. **2.** *v.i.* avancer en ondulant; serpenter. **coiled** *a.* (en)roulé, gléné; (ressort) en spirale; (serpent) lové.

coin¹ [kɔin] *n.* **1.** pièce *f* de monnaie; **gold coins,** pièces d'or. **2.** *coll.* (*no pl.*) monnaie(s) *f*(*pl*), pièces, espèces *fpl*; **small c., subsidiary c.,** monnaie divisionnaire; **c. and bullion,** métal monnayé et métal en barres; **to pay s.o. back in his own c.,** rendre la pareille à qn. **3. c.-operated,** automatique; **c.-operated laundry,** *F:* **c.-op,** laverie *f* automatique.

coin² *v.tr.* **1. to c. money,** frapper de la monnaie; *F:* **he's simply coining money, coining it,** il fait des affaires d'or. **2.** monnayer (des lingots). **3.** inventer, créer (un mot nouveau); **to c. a phrase,** (i) pour inventer un idiotisme; (ii) *Iron:* pour se servir du cliché habituel.

coinage ['kɔinidʒ] *n.* **1.** (*a*) monnayage *m*; frappe *f* (de la monnaie); (*b*) invention *f*, création *f* (d'un mot). **2.** (*a*) système *m* monétaire (d'un pays); (*b*) monnaie(s) *f*(*pl*); numéraire *m*.

coinbox ['kɔinbɔks] *n.* = taxiphone *m*.

coincide [kouin'said] *v.i.* **1.** (*in space, time*) coïncider (**with,** avec); **events that c.,** événements *mpl* qui concourent. **2.** coïncider, s'accorder, être d'accord (**with,** avec).

coincidence [kou'insidəns] *n.* **1.** (*in space, time*) coïncidence *f*; *El:* **phase c.,** concordance *f* de phase. **2.** coïncidence, rencontre *f* (d'événements); **what a c.!** quelle coïncidence!

coincidental [kouinsi'dent(ə)l] *a.* (effet) de coïncidence; (fait) de pure coïncidence.

coiner ['kɔinər] *n.* **1.** monnayeur *m*. **2.** faux monnayeur. **3.** inventeur, -trice (d'un nouveau mot, etc.).

coitus ['kouitəs] *n.* coït *m*; **c. interruptus** [intə'rʌptəs], rapport interrompu.

coke¹ [kouk] *n.* coke *m*; **c. oven,** four *m* à coke.

coke² *v.tr.* (*a*) coké(i)fier; convertir (de la houille) en coke; (*b*) (*of coal, with passive force*) se coké(i)fier, se convertir en coke. **coking 1.** *a.* (charbon, etc.) cokéfiable. **2.** *n.* cokéfaction *f*, coké(i)fication *f*.

coke³ *n. P:* (= cocaine) coco *f*, neige *f*.

coke⁴ *n. F:* Coca *m*.

col [kɔl] *n. Geog:* (*a*) col *m*; (*b*) ensellement *m*.

colander ['kʌləndər] *n. Dom.Ec:* passoire *f*.

cold¹ [kould] **I.** *a.* **1.** (*a*) (temps, bain, repas, etc.) froid; **it's c.,** il fait froid; **it's getting colder,** la température baisse; *Meteor:* **c. front,** front froid; **to get, grow, c.,** se refroidir; *Com:* **c. storage,** conservation *f* par le froid; **c. store,** chambre *f* frigorifique; *F:* **to put sth. in c. storage,** mettre (un projet) en veilleuse; **c. engine,** moteur froid; **c. meat,** viande froide; **c. meats,** *NAm:* **c. cuts,** assiette anglaise; *Toil:* **c. cream,** cold-cream *m*; *F:* **out c.,** sans connaissance, inanimé; **to knock s.o. (out) c.,** étendre qn raide (d'un coup); **to give s.o. the c. shoulder,** tourner le dos à qn; snober qn; *Pol:* **c. war,** guerre froide; (*b*) (*of pers.*) **to be, feel, c.,** avoir froid; **my hands are c.,** j'ai les mains froides, j'ai froid aux mains; **my feet are as c. as ice,** j'ai les pieds glacés; *F:* **to have c. feet,** avoir la frousse; (*c*) *Ven:* **c. scent,** piste froide; (*d*) *Atom.Ph: F:* non radioactif. **2.** (*of pers., manner, welcome, etc.*) froid; **to be c. with s.o.,** se montrer froid avec qn; *F:* **that leaves me c.,** cela me laisse froid; **he's a c. fish,** c'est un pisse-froid. **3.** *Tchn:* **c.-pressed,** embouti à froid; **c. riveting,** rivure *f* à froid. **II.** *adv.* (*a*) **the wind blows c.,** il fait un vent froid; (*b*) *U.S:* (tout) net; carrément; (*c*) *Surg:* **to operate c.,** opérer à froid. **coldly** *adv.* froidement; (regarder qn, qch.) avec froideur.

cold² *n.* **1.** froid *m*; **c. wave,** vague *f* de froid; coup *m* de froid; **I feel the c.,** je suis très frileux; **to protect oneself against the c.,** se protéger contre le froid; *F:* **to leave s.o. out in the c.,** laisser qn à l'écart; **to be left out in the c.,** rester sur le carreau; **to come in from the c.,** rentrer en faveur. **2.** *Med:* **(common) c.,** rhume *m*; **to have a c.,** être enrhumé; avoir un rhume; **bad, heavy, c.,** gros rhume; **c. in the head, head c.,** rhume de cerveau; **chest c.,** rhume de poitrine; **to catch (a) c.,** (i) s'enrhumer; (ii) *Fin: F:* boire un bouillon; **c. sore,** herpès *m*; *F:* **you'll catch your death of c.,** vous allez crever de froid.

cold-blooded ['kould'blʌdid] *a.* **1.** *Z:* (animal) à sang froid. **2.** (*of pers.*) froid, insensible; (*of action*) prémédité, délibéré; accompli de sang-froid. **-ly** *adv.* de, avec, sang-froid; avec insensibilité.

cold-bloodedness ['kould'blʌdidnis] *n.* sang-froid *m*; insensibilité *f*.

coldhearted [kould'hɑ:tid] *a.* au cœur froid; insensible; sans pitié.

coldness ['kouldnis] *n.* **1.** froideur *f*; froidure *f* (du climat, etc.) **2.** froideur (de caractère, d'un accueil); **there is a c. between them,** il y a de la froideur, du froid, entre eux.

cold-shoulder ['kould'ʃouldər] *v.tr.* battre froid à (qn); tourner le dos à (qn); snober (qn).

coleseed ['koulsi:d] *n. Bot:* (graine *f* de) colza *m*.

coleslaw ['koulslɔ:] *n. Cu:* salade *f* de chou cru.

colic ['kɔlik] *n. Med: Vet:* colique *f*.

colitis [kə'laitis] *n. Med:* colite *f*.

collaborate [kə'læbəreit] *v.i.* collaborer (**with,** avec; **on,** à).

collaboration [kəlæbə'reiʃ(ə)n] *n.* collaboration *f*.

collaborator [kə'læbəreitər] *n.* (*a*) collaborateur, -trice; coauteur *m*; (*b*) *Pol:* collaborateur, -trice (avec l'ennemi).

collage ['kɔlɑ:ʒ] *n. Art:* collage *m*.

collapse¹ [kə'læps] *n.* **1.** (*a*) écroulement *m*, effondrement *m* (d'un édifice, d'espoirs); éboulement *m* (de terre, de sable); dégonflement *m* (d'un ballon); affaissement *m* (d'un pneu); débâcle *f* (d'un établissement, d'un pays); (*b*) *Mec.E: etc:* déformation *f* (d'une plaque, etc.); (*c*) *Com:* chute subite (de prix); *Fin:* effondrement (du marché); dégringolade *f* (du franc, etc.). **2.** (*a*) *Med:* affaissement subit; collapsus *m*; (*b*) effondrement moral.

collapse² **1.** *v.i.* (*a*) (*of building, institution, etc.*) s'écrouler, s'effondrer; (*of balloon, etc.*) se dégonfler; (*of pers.*) s'effondrer; s'affaisser subitement; **he collapsed into an armchair,** il s'effondra dans un fauteuil; (*b*) *Mec.E: etc:* (*of support, wheel, etc.*) gauchir, se déformer; (*c*) (*of prices*) s'effondrer. **2.** *v.tr.* plier (une table, etc.).

collapsible [kə'læpsəbl] *a.* (*of chair, boat, etc.*) pliant, repliable; (*of handle, etc.*) rabattable; *Aut:* **c. hood,** capote pliante, rabattable.

collar¹ ['kɔlər] *n.* **1.** col *m* (de chemise, etc.); collet *m* (de manteau); tour *m* de cou (en fourrure, etc.); collier *m* (d'un ordre, etc.); **lace c.,** collerette *f* en dentelle; **detachable c.,** faux col; **Peter Pan c.,** col Claudine; **clerical c.,** col romain; **to seize,** *F:* **grab, s.o. by the c.,** prendre, saisir, qn au collet; **to get hot under the c.,** se ficher en rogne. **2. horse c.,** collier de cheval; **dog c.,** (i) collier de chien; (ii) *F:* col romain. **3.** (*a*) *Mec.E:* collier *m*, bague *f*; (*of axle, pipe*) collet; (*b*) *Nau:* collier (d'étai); (*c*) *Const:* **c. beam, tie,** entrait retroussé; (*between rafters*) traversière *f*. **4.** (*a*) *Z:* collier (d'oiseau, de quadrupède); (*b*) *Bot:* collet (de racine). **5.** *Cu:* roulade *f* (de bœuf, de veau, de poisson).

collar² *v.tr.* **1.** (*a*) colleter (qn); saisir, prendre, (qn) au collet; (*b*) *Rugby: Fb:* arrêter (l'adversaire qui détient le ballon); (*c*) *F: O:* empoigner, pincer (qn, qch.). **2.** *Mec.E:* baguer, fretter. **collared** *a. Mec.E:* (manchon) à frettes.

collarbone ['kɔləboun] *n. Anat:* clavicule *f*.

collate [kɔ'leit] *v.tr.* (*a*) rassembler (des documents, des données); *Bookb:* assembler, collationner (les feuilles); (*b*) collationner (un texte) (**with,** avec); (*c*) *Cmptr:* interclasser (des cartes). **collating** *n.* (*a*) collationnement *m*; (*b*) *Bookb:* assemblage *m*; (*c*) *Cmptr:* interclassement *m*.

collateral [kə'lætər(ə)l] *a.* **1.** (*of street, etc.*) collatéral, -aux; parallèle; *a. & n. Anat:* **c. (artery),** (artère) collatérale (*f*). **2.** *a. & n.* (*of branch of family*) collatéral, -ale. **3.** (*a*) (*of knowledge, fact*) concomitant; (*b*) (*of phenomenon*) correspondant, parallèle. **4.** (*of cause, etc.*) accessoire, subsidiaire; *Com: Jur:* **c. security,** *n.* **c.,** garantie additionnelle; nantissement *m* subsidiaire.

collation [kə'leiʃ(ə)n] *n.* **1.** (*a*) rassemblement *m* (de documents, de données); *Bookb:* assemblage *m*, collationnement *m* (des feuilles); (*b*) collation *f* (de textes); (*c*) *Cmptr:* interclassement *m* (des cartes). **2.** collation; **cold c.,** repas froid.

colleague ['kɔli:g] *n.* collègue *mf*; confrère *m*.

collect¹ ['kɔlekt] *n. Ecc:* (*prayer*) collecte *f*.

collect² [kə'lekt] **1.** *v.tr.* (*a*) rassembler (la foule, ses effets); assembler (des matériaux); réunir (des amis); recueillir (des données, des nouvelles); récolter (des documents, etc.); *Mil:* ramasser (les blessés); *Post:* lever (les lettres), faire la levée (des lettres); **I'll c. you at midday,** je passerai vous prendre à midi; (*b*) collectionner (des timbres, des livres, etc.); **I c. paintings,** je fais collection de peintures; (*c*) percevoir (les impôts); toucher (une traite); recouvrer (une créance); (*d*) aller chercher (sa valise, etc.); (*e*) recueillir, rassembler (ses idées); recueillir (ses forces); **to c. oneself,** se reprendre; se calmer; **to c. one's thoughts,** se recueillir. **2.** *v.i.* (*a*) (*of people*) s'assembler, se rassembler, se réunir; (*of thgs*) s'amasser. **collected** *a.* (*a*) recueilli; (*b*) (plein) de sang-froid. **collecting** *n.* = COLLECTION 1; **c. point,** poste *m* de ramassage, de rassemblement (du personnel, du matériel, etc.).

collect³ *a. & adv. NAm: Post:* en port dû; **to send a telegram c.,** envoyer un télégramme en port dû; *Tp:* **c. call,** communication *f* avec P.C.V.; **to call (s.o.) c.,** appeler (qn) avec P.C.V.

collection [kə'lekʃ(ə)n] *n.* **1.** (*a*) rassemblement *m*, assemblage *m* (de personne, de choses); ramassage *m* (des blessés); recouvrement *m* (d'une somme); perception *f* (des impôts); encaissement *m* (d'un billet); levée (des lettres); captation *f*, captage *m* (d'eau, de courant électrique, etc.); recueil *m* (de données); (*b*) collectionnement *m* (de timbres). **2.** *Ecc: etc:* quête *f*, collecte *f*; **to take up a c.,** faire la quête; **c. box,** tronc *m* (d'église, de quêteur); **c. plate,** plat *m* de quête. **3.** amas *m*, assemblage. **4.** collection *f* (de papillons, de timbres); recueil *m* (de chansons); **c. of plants,** collection de plantes; *Dressm: etc:* **spring c.,** collection de printemps.

collective [kə'lektiv] *a.* **1.** collectif; *Jur:* **c. ownership,** propriété collective; **c. farm,** ferme collective; *Pol.Ec:* **c. bargaining,** (négociation *f* de) convention collective; *Gram:* **c. noun,** nom collectif. **2.** *Bot:* (fruit) multiple. **-ly** *adv.* collectivement; (possédé, etc.) en commun.

collectivism [kə'lektivizm] *n. Pol.Ec:* collectivisme *m*.

collectivist [kə'lektivist] *a. & n. Pol.Ec:* collectiviste (*mf*).

collectivity [kɔlek'tiviti] *n.* **1.** collectivité *f*. **2.** propriété *f* en commun.

collectivization [kəlektivai'zeiʃ(ə)n] *n.* collectivisation *f*.

collectivize [kə'lektivaiz] *v.tr.* collectiviser.

collector [kə'lektər] *n.* **1.** (*pers.*) (*a*) quêteur, -euse (d'aumônes); collecteur, -trice (de cotisations); ramasseur *m* (de lait, etc.); *Rail:* **ticket c.,** contrôleur *m* (de billets); (*b*) encaisseur (de la Compagnie du gaz, etc.); *Adm:* percepteur *m* (des contributions directes); receveur *m* (des contributions indirectes); (*c*) collectionneur, -euse, (de peintures, de timbres-poste); **collector's piece,** pièce *f* de collection. **2.** *Mec.E: etc:* collecteur (d'huile, de vapeur, etc.); récepteur *m* (de trop-plein, etc.):

colleen ['kɔli:n] *n. Dial:* (*in Ireland*) jeune fille *f*.

college ['kɔlidʒ] *n.* **1.** colle.*fm*; *Ecc:* **the Sacred C., the C. of Cardinals,** le sacré Collège; le Collège des cardinaux; *Pol:* **electoral c.,** collège électoral. **2.** *Sch:* (*a*) collège (d'université britannique); (*b*) **military, naval, c.,** école *f* militaire, navale; (*c*) **c. of education,** *O:* **(teachers') training c.** = école normale; **agricultural c.** = institut *m* agronomique; (*d*) = lycée *m*; **technical c.** = lycée technique; (*as Pr.n.*) **Eton C.,** le collège d'Eton; (*e*) *Cu:* **c. pudding,** (variété de) pouding *m* aux raisins.

collegiate [kə'li:dʒiət] *a.* collégial, -aux; **c. church,** collégiale *f*.

collide [kə'laid] *v.i.* (*of vehicles, etc.*) se heurter, se tamponner; entrer en collision; **to c. with sth.,** rencontrer, heurter, tamponner, qch.; entrer en collision avec qch.; *Nau:* aborder (un navire); (*of pers.*) **to c. with s.o.,** (i) se heurter à, contre, qn.

collie ['kɔli] *n.* (*dog*) chien de berger écossais; colley *m*.

collier ['kɔliər] *n.* **1.** (*pers.*) houilleur *m*; mineur *m* (de charbon). **2.** *Nau:* (navire *m*) charbonnier (*m*).

colliery ['kɔliəri] *n.* houillère *f*; mine *f* de charbon.

collision [kə'liʒ(ə)n] *n.* **1.** (*a*) collision *f*; tamponnement *m* (de trains); abordage *m*, collision (de navires); **head-on c.,** collision frontale; **to come into c. with (sth.).,** tamponner (un train, une voiture), entrer en collision avec (un train, un navire, etc.), aborder (un navire); (*b*) **c. course,** cap *m* de collision; (*c*) *Atom.Ph:* choc, collision (des particules). **2.** conflit *m* (d'intérêts).

colloquial [kə'loukwiəl] *a.* familier; de (la) conversation; (langue) parlée; **c. English,** l'anglais parlé. **-ally** *adv.* familièrement; en style familier.

colloquialism [kə'loukwiəlizm] *n.* expression familière.

collusion [kə'l(j)u:ʒ(ə)n] *n.* collusion *f*; **to act in c. with s.o.,** agir de complicité, de connivence, avec qn; **to be in c. with s.o.,** être d'intelligence avec qn.

collywobbles ['kɔliwɔb(ə)lz] *n.pl. F:* **to have the c.,** avoir mal au ventre.

Colombia [kə'lʌmbiə] *Pr.n. Geog:* Colombie *f*.

Colombian [kə'lʌmbiən] *Geog:* **1.** *a.* colombien. **2.** *n.* Colombien, -ienne.

colon¹ ['koulən] *n. Anat:* côlon *m*.

colon² *n.* deux-points *m*; *Typ:* comma *m*.

colonel ['kəːn(ə)l] *n. Mil:* colonel *m*; *Mil.Av: U.S:* colonel (de l'Armée de l'air).
colonial [kə'louniəl] *a. & n.* (*a*) colonial, -aux; (*b*) *U.S: Arch: etc:* (style) du dix-huitième siècle.
colonialism [kə'louniəlizm] *n.* colonialisme *m*.
colonialist [kə'louniəlist] *a. & n.* colonialiste (*mf*).
colonist ['kɔlənist] *n.* colon *m*.
colonization [kɔlənai'zeiʃ(e)n] *n.* colonisation *f*.
colonize ['kɔlənaiz] **1.** *v.tr.* coloniser. **2.** *v.i.* former une colonie; s'établir (dans un pays nouveau).
colonizer ['kɔlənaizər] *n.* colonisateur *m*.
colonnade [kɔlə'neid] *n.* colonnade *f*.
colony ['kɔləni] *n.* colonie *f*; **to live in the colonies,** vivre aux colonies; **the English c. in Paris,** la colonie anglaise à Paris.
colophon ['kɔləfən] *n. Typ:* chiffre *m* (de l'éditeur, de l'imprimeur); marque *f* typographique.
color ['kʌlər] *n. & v. NAm:* = COLOUR[1, 2].
Colorado [kɔlə'rɑːdou] *n. Ent:* **C. beetle,** doryphore *m*.
coloration [kʌlə'reiʃ(ə)n] *n.* coloration *f*; coloris *m*; (*of textiles, etc.*) colorisation *f*.
coloratura [kɔlərə'tjuərə] *n. Mus:* (*a*) chant agrémenté de fioritures; **c. aria,** air *m* coloratur; (*b*) **c. (soprano),** coloratur *f*.
colossal [kə'lɔs(ə)l] *a.* (*a*) (*of statue, etc.*) colossal, -aux; (*b*) (succès, mensonge, etc.) colossal.
colossus, *pl.* **-i, -uses** [kə'lɔses, -ai, -əsiz] *n.* colosse *m*; **the C. of Rhodes,** le Colosse de Rhodes.
colostomy [kə'lɔstəmi] *n. Surg:* colostomie *f*.
colour[1], *NAm:* **color**[1] ['kʌlər] *n.* **1.** couleur *f*; (*a*) **what c. is it?** de quelle couleur est-ce? **the c. problem,** le problème des races de couleur; **c. bar,** *U.S:* **c. line,** discrimination, ségrégation, raciale; **local c.,** couleur locale; **to see sth. in its true colours,** voir qch. sous son vrai jour; *F:* **I've still to see the c. of his money,** je n'ai pas encore vu la couleur de son argent; **c. photography, television,** photographie *f*, télévision *f*, en couleur(s); **c. print,** reproduction *f* en couleurs; (*b*) *Art: etc:* coloris *m*; **light colours,** coloris clairs; **c. value,** valeur *f* chromatique. **2.** matière colorante; **oil c.,** couleur à l'huile; **to paint in water c.,** peindre à l'aquarelle; **box of colours,** boîte *f* de couleurs. **3.** teint *m*, couleurs; **to lose c.,** perdre ses couleurs; **indignation brought the c. to his cheeks,** l'indignation *f* colorait ses joues; **to have a fresh c.,** avoir le teint frais; *F:* **to be off c.,** être souffrant; **off-c. joke,** plaisanterie grivoise. **4.** *usu. pl.* (*a*) couleurs (d'un parti); *Nau:* pavillon *m*, couleurs; **to show, display, one's colours,** montrer son pavillon; *Mil:* **(regimental) colours,** le fanion du régiment; **c. party,** garde *f* du drapeau; **c. bearer,** porte-drapeau *m inv*; **c. sergeant,** sergent chef (de la garde du drapeau); **to serve with the colours,** servir sous les drapeaux; **with colours flying,** (à) enseignes déployées; **to pass (an examination) with flying colours,** être reçu brillamment; **to sail under false colours,** naviguer sous un faux pavillon; **to show oneself in one's true colours,** se révéler tel qu'on est; **to nail one's colours to the mast,** clouer son pavillon; *Fig:* prendre un parti irrévocable; (*b*) *Turf: Sp:* couleurs (d'un jockey, d'une équipe); (*c*) *Sp: Sch:* **to get one's colours,** recevoir une haute distinction sportive. **5.** (*a*) **the political c. of a journal,** la couleur d'un journal; (*b*) **to give, lend, c. to a story,** rendre une histoire vraisemblable; **to put a false c. on things,** mal voir les choses.
colour[2], *NAm:* **color**[2] **1.** *v.tr.* (*a*) colorer; colorier (une carte, un dessin); enluminer (une gravure); **to c. sth. blue,** colorer qch. en bleu; (*b*) donner de l'éclat à (une description); imager (son style); (*c*) présenter (un fait) sous un faux jour; **resentment will c. one's opinions,** le ressentiment agit sur, fausse, les opinions. **2.** *v.i.* (*a*) (*of thg*) se colorer; (*of fruit, etc.*) tourner; (*b*) (*of pers.*) rougir. **coloured,** *NAm:* **colored 1.** *a.* (*a*) coloré; (*of drawing*) colorié; (chemise) de couleur; **c. person,** personne *f* de couleur; **gaily c. butterfly,** papillon *m* multicolore; (*b*) **highly c. narrative,** récit coloré. **2.** *n.pl.* **coloureds,** (*a*) (*clothes*) couleurs *fpl*; (*b*) gens *mpl* de couleur. **colouring,** *NAm:* **coloring 1.** *a.* colorant. **2.** *n.* (*a*) coloration *f*; coloriage *m* (des cartes, etc.); (*b*) coloris *m* (de la peinture, du style); (*c*) teint *m* (d'une personne); (*d*) apparence *f*.
colourblind, *NAm:* **color-** ['kʌləblaind] *a.* daltonien, atteint de daltonisme.
colourblindness, *NAm:* **color-** ['kʌləblaindnis] *n.* daltonisme *m*.
colourful, *NAm:* **color-** ['kʌləful] *a.* (ciel, etc.) coloré; (style) coloré, pittoresque; **a c. character,** un original.
colourless, *NAm:* **color-** ['kʌləlis] *a.* **1.** sans couleur; incolore; **water is c.,** l'eau *f* est incolore. **2.** (*a*) terne, incolore; (visage) blême; (teint) délavé; (lumière) pâle, falote; (*b*) (style) insipide, fade; (voix), terne; (*of pers.*) sans caractère.
colourlessness, *NAm:* **color-** ['kʌləlisnis] *n.* **1.** absence *f* de couleur. **2.** (*a*) décoloration *f* (du teint); (*b*) fadeur *f* (du style); manque *m* de personnalité.
colt[1] [koult] *n.* **1.** (i) poulain *m*; (ii) jeune cheval mâle (de moins de cinq ans). **2.** débutant, -ante; novice *mf*; *Cr:* professionel *m* à ses débuts.
Colt[2] *Pr.n. Sm.a:* **C. (pistol),** pistolet *m* automatique.
coltish ['koultiʃ] *a.* **1.** sans expérience. **2.** folâtre.
coltsfoot ['koultsfut] *n. Bot:* pas-d'âne *m*.
Columbia [kə'lʌmbiə] *Pr.n. Geog:* **1. British C.,** Colombie britannique, *Fr.C:* canadienne. **2. (District of) C.,** (District fédéral de) Columbia.
columbine[1] ['kɔləmbain] *n. Bot:* ancolie *f*.
Columbine[2] *Pr.n.f. Th:* Colombine.
Columbus [kə'lʌmbəs] *Pr.n.m.* **Christopher C.,** Christophe Colomb.
column ['kɔləm] *n.* **1.** (*a*) *Arch: etc:* colonne *f*; (*b*) *Anat:* **spinal c.,** colonne vertébrale; (*c*) colonne (de mercure, de fumée); (*d*) *Aut:* **steering c.,** colonne de direction; *Av:* **control c.,** levier *m* de commande. **2.** (*a*) *Mil: Nau:* colonne; ligne *f* de file; **to march in c., in two columns,** marcher en colonne, en deux colonnes; **supply, relief, c.,** colonne de ravitaillement, de secours; (*b*) *Pol:* **fifth c.,** cinquième colonne. **3.** *Journ: Publ:* **two column page,** page de deux colonnes; **sports c.,** rubrique, chronique, sportive; **theatrical c.,** rubrique des théâtres.
columnist ['kɔləm(n)ist] *n.* **1.** *Journ:* chroniqueur *m*, courriériste *m*; **sports c.,** rubriqueur aux sports. **2.** *Pol:* **fifth c.,** membre *m* de la cinquième colonne.
colza ['kɔlzə] *n. Bot:* colza *m*; **c. oil,** huile *f* de colza.
coma ['koumə] *n. Med:* coma *m*; **to go into, be in, a c.,** entrer, être, dans le coma.
comatose ['koumətous] *a. Med:* **1.** (état) comateux. **2.** (*pers.*) dans le coma.
comb[1] [koum] *n.* **1.** *Toil:* peigne *m*; **to run a c. through one's hair,** se donner un coup de peigne; **c. maker, manufacturer,** peignier *m*. **2.** (*a*) *Tex:* peigne; (*b*) *Paint: Tchn:* peigne (à décor, à fileter). **3.** crête *f* (de coq). **4.** *Ap:* rayon *m*; **honey in the c.,** miel *m* en rayon.
comb[2] *n.* **to give one's hair a c.,** donner un coup de peigne à ses cheveux.
comb[3] **1.** *v.tr.* (*a*) peigner (les cheveux de qn); **to c. one's hair,** se peigner; **to c. down a horse,** étriller un cheval; (*b*) *Tex: etc:* peigner, carder (la laine, etc.); **combed cotton,** coton peigné; (*c*) (*of police, etc.*) ratisser; passer au peigne fin. **2.** *v.i.* (*of wave*) (i) se briser en écumant; déferler; (ii) s'ourler. **combing** *n.* **1.** (*a*) coup *m* de peigne; (*b*) *Tex:* peignage *m*,

cardage *m*; (*c*) ratissage *m* (par la police). **2. c. out,** démêlage *m* (des cheveux). **comb out** *v.tr.* **1.** (*a*) démêler (les cheveux); (*b*) carder (un matelas, etc.). **2.** *F:* (*of police*) **to c. out a district,** faire une rafle (de suspects).

combat¹ ['kɔmbæt] *n.* (*a*) combat *m*; **single c.,** combat singulier; (*b*) *Mil: etc:* **close c.,** combat rapproché; **mock c.,** combat simulé; **aerial c.,** combat aérien; **c. mission,** mission *f* tactique; **c. zone,** zone *f* de combat; **camouflaged c. clothing,** tenue *f* léopard; *U.S:* **c. fatigue,** psychose *f* traumatique.

combat² *v.* **(combated) 1.** *v.i.* combattre **(with, against,** contre). **2.** *v.tr.* lutter contre, combattre (une maladie, un préjugé).

combatant ['kɔmbətənt] *a. & n.* combattant (*m*).

combination [kɔmbi'neiʃ(ə)n] *n.* **1.** (*a*) combinaison *f*; concours *m* (de sons, de circonstances); **nitrogen in c. with oxygen,** l'azote combiné avec l'oxygène; (*b*) *Ch:* combiné *m*, combinaison; (*c*) **smokers' c.,** nettoie-pipes *m inv* (en métal). **2.** association *f* (de personnes, d'ouvriers, etc.); **to enter into a c. with ...,** s'associer avec .... **3.** *Cost: O:* **(pair of) combinations,** combinaison-culotte *f*, *pl.* combinaisons-culottes. **4. c. lock,** serrure *f* à combinaisons; serrure secrète. **5.** motocylette *f* avec sidecar.

combine¹ ['kɔmbain] *n.* **1.** *Com: Fin:* combinaison financière; cartel *m*; trust *m*. **2.** *Agr:* **c. (harvester),** moissonneuse-batteuse *f*, *pl.* moissonneuses-batteuses.

combine² [kəm'bain] **1.** *v.tr.* combiner; allier (des qualités, etc.) **(with,** à); (*of pers.*) (ré)unir, allier; **to c. forces,** joindre ses forces; **to c. strength of body with strength of mind,** allier la force du corps à celle de l'âme; **to c. business with pleasure,** joindre l'utile à l'agréable. **2.** *v.i.* (*a*) (*of pers.*) s'unir, se réunir, s'associer, s'allier; se liguer **(against,** contre); (*of workers*) se syndiquer; (*b*) *Pol:* (*of parties*) fusionner; (*c*) **everything combined to give me this impression,** tout concourait à me donner cette impression; (*d*) *Ch:* (*of elements*) se combiner. **combined** *a.* (travail) fait en collaboration; (mouvement) d'ensemble; (efforts) réunis, *Rail:* **c. rail and road ticket,** billet *m* mixte; *Mil: etc:* **c. operation,** opération combinée; opération interarmées; **c. force,** force *f* mixte; **c. fleets,** flottes combinées. **combining** *n.* combinaison *f*.

combustible [kəm'bʌstibl] **1.** *a.* combustible. **2.** *n.* (*a*) matière *f* inflammable; (*b*) (*fuel*) combustible *m*.

combustion [kəm'bʌstʃ(ə)n] *n.* combustion *f*; **spontaneous c.,** inflammation spontanée; **internal c. engine,** moteur *m* à combustion interne.

come [kʌm] *v.i.* (*p.t.* **came** [keim]; *p.p.* **come**) **1.** (*a*) venir, arriver **(to,** à); arriver **(from,** de); **he came up to me,** il est venu à moi: **here c. the children,** voici les enfants qui arrivent; **I'm coming with you,** je viens avec vous; je vous accompagne; **he comes this way every week,** il passe par ici tous les huit jours; **here he comes!** le voilà qui arrive! **c. here!** venez ici! (*to dog*) (viens) ici! **coming!** je viens! j'arrive! **I have c. to see you,** je viens vous voir; **to c. for s.o., for sth.,** venir chercher qn, qch.; **to c. to s.o. for advice,** venir demander conseil à qn; **you have c. to the wrong person,** vous vous adressez mal; **to c. to the throne,** monter sur le trône; **a crisis is coming,** une crise se prépare; **what are things coming to?** où allons-nous? **letters came pouring in,** ce fut une avalanche de lettres; **he has c. a long way,** (i) il arrive de loin; (ii) *Fig:* il a fait son chemin; **to c. and go,** aller et venir; **the idea came to me that ...,** il m'est venu à l'esprit que ..; **suddenly it came to me,** tout d'un coup (i) je m'en suis souvenu, (ii) j'ai eu une idée; **a smile came to his lips,** un sourire parut sur ses lèvres; *int.* **c. now! c., c.!** allons! voyons! *Prov:* **easy c. easy go,** ce qui vient par la flûte s'en va par le tambour; (*b*) **to c. to oneself,** (i) reprendre connaissance; (ii) recouvrer sa raison; (iii) revenir de ses erreurs; se ressaisir; (*c*) *F:* **c. summer (and) we shall meet again,** vienne l'été, on se retrouvera tous; **he will be ten c. January,** il aura dix ans en janvier. **2.** (*a*) **we must take things as they c.,** il faut prendre les choses comme elles viennent; **I've got £500 coming to me,** je vais (bientôt) toucher £500; *F:* **you've got it coming to you,** vous l'aurez bien mérité; **c. what may,** advienne que pourra; quoi qu'il arrive, advienne; (*b*) **how does the door c. to be open?** d'où vient que la porte est ouverte? *F:* **how c.?** pourquoi? **now that I c. to think of it,** maintenant que j'y songe. **3.** (*a*) **what will c. of it?** qu'en adviendra-t-il? qu'en résultera-t-il? **no good will c. of it,** cela tournera mal; **that's what comes of doing ...,** voilà ce qu'il en est de faire ...; (*b*) **word that comes from Latin,** mot *m* qui (pro)vient du latin; **to c. of a good family,** être d'une bonne famille; il descend d'une famille de paysans; **this is surprising coming from him,** cela étonne de sa part. **4.** (*a*) **the total comes to fifty francs,** la somme s'élève, à cinquante francs; **how much does it c. to?** combien cela fait-il? **it comes to this, that ...,** cela revient à ceci, que ...; (*b*) **if it comes to that ...,** à ce compte-là ...; **c. to that, what are you doing here?** pendant que j'y suis, qu'est-ce que vous faites ici? (*c*) **that doesn't c. within my duties,** cela ne rentre pas dans mes fonctions. **5.** (*a*) **that comes easy, natural, to him,** cela lui est facile, naturel; **to c. expensive, cheap,** coûter, revenir, cher; coûter peu; (*b*) **to c. apart,** se décoller; (*of seam, etc.*) **to c. apart, undone, unstitched,** se découdre; (*of tie, knot, bootlaces, etc.*) **to c. undone, untied, loose,** se dénouer, se délacer, se défaire; (*c*) **you c. first,** c'est vous le premier. **6. in the days to c.,** dans les temps à venir; à l'avenir; **that will not be for some time to c.,** cela n'arrivera pas d'ici à quelque temps. **7.** (*of butter*) prendre forme; (*of fruit, etc.*) venir; (*of teeth*) sortir. **8.** *F:* **that's coming it a bit strong,** ça, c'est un peu fort; **to c. the heavy husband,** prendre un ton de mari autoritaire. **9.** *P:* (*reach orgasm*) jouir. **come about** *v.i.* (*a*) (*of event, occurrence, etc.*) arriver, se passer, se produire; **it came about that,** il arriva, il advint, que ...; (*b*) (i) *Nau:* virer de bord; (ii) (*of the wind*) tourner. **come across** *v.i.* (*a*) trouver, rencontrer (qn, qch.) par hasard, sur son chemin; tomber sur (qn); (*b*) (*adverbial use*) *F:* (i) payer ce que l'on doit; (ii) se décider à dire la vérité; (*c*) = COME OVER (*c*). **come after** *v.i.* **1.** (*a*) suivre (qn, qch.); (*b*) poursuivre (qn, qch.). **2.** (*a*) succéder à (qn); (*b*) suivre; venir plus tard. **come along** *v.i.* (*a*) arriver, venir; **c. along!** (i) amène-toi! arrive! (ii) allons-y! (*b*) arriver; se passer; **these things c. along when you least expect them,** ces choses-là arrivent quand on s'y attend le moins. **come at** *v.i.* (*a*) (i) s'avancer vers (qn); (ii) attaquer (qn); (*b*) *O:* parvenir à (la vérité, etc.). **come away** *v.i.* (*a*) **to c. away (from a place),** partir (d'un lieu); quitter (un lieu); (*b*) se détacher; se décoller; **the handle came away (in his hand),** l'anse lui est restée dans la main. **come back** *v.i.* (*a*) revenir; **to c. back (home),** rentrer; **it's all coming back to me,** cela me revient à la mémoire; **to c. back to what I was saying ...,** pour en revenir à ce que je disais ...; (*b*) (*of fashion, etc.*) revenir en vogue; (*c*) *U.S:* *F:* répliquer; riposter. **come by** *v.i.* (*a*) (i) passer par (une maison, etc.); (ii) acquérir (qch.); obtenir (de l'argent, etc.); recevoir (une blessure, etc.); (*b*) (i) **I heard him c. by,** je l'ai entendu passer; (ii) *esp. U.S:* entrer en passant. **come down,** *v.i.* **1.** (*a*) descendre (l'échelle, l'escalier); faire la descente de (la montagne, etc.); (*of aircraft, etc.*) atterrir; **to c. down**

to breakfast, descendre déjeuner; **to c. down (in the world),** déchoir; **to c. down to earth,** descendre des nues; **prices are coming down,** les prix *mpl* baissent, sont en baisse; *F:* **to c. down on s.o.,** tomber sur le dos à qn; (*b*) (i) **to c. down in s.o.'s favour, on s.o.'s side,** se décider en faveur de qn; (ii) *F:* **to c. down generously, handsomely,** se montrer généreux. **2.** (*a*) (*of rain, etc.*) tomber; (*b*) **her hair came down to her waist,** ses cheveux lui descendaient jusqu'à la taille; (*c*) (*of tale, tradition*) venir (de nos aïeux); **the tales that have c. down to us,** les contes qui nous sont parvenus. **3.** (*a*) (*of pers., horse, tree, etc.*) s'abattre; (*of structure*) s'écrouler; **these houses are coming down soon,** on démolira bientôt ces maisons; (*b*) **to c. down with flu,** tomber malade d'une grippe. **4.** (*of problem, etc.*) se résumer, revenir (**to,** à); **the whole difficulty comes down to this question,** toute la difficulté se réduit à cette question. **come forward** *v.i.* se proposer (pour faire qch.); *Iron:* **he's not backward in coming forward,** il ne se gêne pas. **come in** *v.i.* **1.** (*a*) entrer; **to c. in again,** rentrer; **c. in!** entrez! *F:* **Mrs B. comes in twice a week,** Madame B. vient faire le ménage deux fois par semaine; *F:* **that's where I c. in,** voilà où je peux vous aider; (*b*) (*of tide*) monter; (*of ship*) arriver; (*of year*) commencer; (*of funds*) rentrer; (*of custom, etc.*) s'introduire; **this fashion is coming in again,** cette mode reprend; (*c*) (i) *Pol:* (*of party*) arriver, parvenir, au pouvoir; (ii) *Cr:* (*of batsman*) venir prendre son tour au guichet. **2.** (*a*) **to c. in useful to s.o., for sth., for doing sth.,** servir à qn, à qch., à, pour, faire qch.; (*b*) *Sp:* **to c. in first, second,** arriver premier, second. **3.** (*a*) **to c. in for a share of sth.,** avoir part à qch.; **to c. in for a scolding, for praise,** recevoir, s'attirer, une semonce, des éloges; (*b*) (i) être admis dans une affaire; (ii) avoir un rôle à jouer (dans une affaire); **to c. in with s.o.,** s'associer à qn; **and where do I c. in?** et moi, (i) qu'est-ce que j'y gagne? (ii) quel sera mon rôle? (*c*) intervenir (**between,** entre). **come into** *v.i.* (*a*) entrer dans (une chambre); **to c. into the world,** venir au monde; **to c. into power,** arriver, parvenir, au pouvoir; (*of idea*) **to c. into s.o.'s mind,** se présenter à l'esprit de qn; (*b*) entrer en possession (d'un domaine); recueillir (une succession); succéder à (une fortune). **come off** *v.i.* **1.** (*a*) descendre (d'un mur, d'une échelle, etc.); *Ind:* (*of product*) sortir (de la chaîne de fabrication); **to c. off a ship, a plane,** débarquer (d'un navire, d'un avion); **c. off it!** en voilà assez! la barbe! (*b*) **to c. off one's horse,** tomber de (son) cheval; (*c*) *Th:* (*of play*) être retiré (de l'affiche). **2.** (*a*) (*of button, etc.*) se détacher, sauter; (*of paint, stain, etc.*) s'enlever, partir; (*of fabric, etc.*) se décoller; **the colour came off on my dress,** la couleur a déteint sur ma robe; (*b*) (*of ship aground*) se déséchouer; partir. **3.** (*a*) (*of event*) avoir lieu; (*of plan, attempt, etc.*) réussir, aboutir; **did it c. off all right?** ça s'est bien passé? **my little trip abroad didn't c. off,** mon petit voyage à l'étranger ne s'est pas réalisé, *F:* est tombé à l'eau; **the experiment came off,** l'expérience a réussi; (*b*) (*of pers.*) **to c. off badly, with flying colours,** s'en mal tirer; s'acquitter brillamment; (*c*) *P:* (*reach orgasm*) jouir. **come on** *v.i.* (*a*) s'avancer; aller de l'avant; **c. on, let's have a game!** allons! faisons une partie! **c. on!** (i) en avant! (ii) arrivez! (iii) *F:* (*as challenge*) viens-y donc! (iv) *F:* (*incredulity*) allons donc! (*b*) (*of plants, children, etc.*) (bien) venir; se développer; faire des progrès; (*c*) (*of rain, illness, etc.*) survenir; (*of winter, etc.*) venir, arriver; (*of night*) tomber; **I feel a cold coming on,** je m'enrhume; (*d*) *Th:* (*of actor*) entrer en scène; (*e*) **the play, film, is coming on next week,** on va donner la pièce, le film va passer, la semaine prochaine. **come out** *v.i.* **1.** (*a*) **to c. out of a place, a room,** sortir d'un lieu, d'une pièce; (*b*) *Dent:* (*of filling*) partir; (*c*) *Ind:* **to c. out (on strike),** se mettre en grève; (*d*) **to c. badly, well, out of an affair,** se tirer mal, se bien tirer, d'une affaire; *Sch:* **to c. out first, second,** sortir premier, second, être reçu premier, second. **2.** (*a*) (*of sun, stars*) paraître; (*of buds*) éclore; *Phot:* (*of image*) se développer; (*of rash, pimples*) sortir, se montrer; (*of the truth*) se découvrir; (*of pers.*) **to c. out in a rash,** avoir une éruption (de boutons, etc.); **as soon as the news came out . . .,** dès qu'on sut la nouvelle . . .; **it came out that . . .,** il ressortit que . . .; le fait se révéla que . . .; (*b*) (*of book, journal*) paraître, sortir; (*c*) *Phot:* **he always comes out well,** il est photogénique. **3.** (*of stains*) s'enlever, s'effacer; **the colour comes out of this material,** c'est une étoffe qui se déteint. **4.** (*of problem*) se résoudre; (*of average, total, etc.*) **to c. out at . . .,** être de . . ., se monter à . . .; **her sums would never c. out right,** elle n'arrivait jamais à la solution juste; **everything will c. out (all) right in the end,** tout va s'arranger à la fin. **5.** (*a*) (*of pers.*) débuter (au théâtre); débuter, faire son entrée dans le monde; (*b*) *F:* **to c. out with a remark,** lâcher, laisser échapper, une observation; **to c. out strongly,** se prononcer avec vigueur (**for,** pour; **against,** contre). **come over** *v.i.* **1.** (*a*) traverser (la mer, les champs); **to c. over from a place,** arriver, venir, d'un lieu (situé de l'autre côté de la mer, du pont, de la montagne, etc.); (*b*) **to c. over to s.o.'s side,** passer dans le parti de qn, du côté de qn; (*c*) **how did he c. over?** quelle impression vous a-t-il faite? **he doesn't c. over well on television,** il manque de relief à la télévision; **her voice comes over well,** sa voix se reproduit bien. **2.** (*a*) (*of feeling, etc.*) envahir, gagner (qn); **a change has c. over him,** il a bien changé; **what has c. over you?** qu'est-ce qui vous est arrivé? qu'est-ce qui vous prend? (*b*) *F:* **to c. over funny,** être pris d'un malaise. **come round** *v.i.* (*a*) faire le tour; **the road is blocked, I've had to c. round by the village,** la route est bloquée, j'ai dû faire un détour par le village; (*b*) *F:* **c. round and see me one day,** venez me voir un de ces jours; (*c*) **the weekend will soon c. round,** le weekend viendra bientôt; (*d*) reprendre connaissance; revenir à soi; (*e*) **to c. round to s.o.'s way of thinking,** se convertir à l'opinion de qn; **he has c. round,** il a cédé; (*f*) *Nau:* (i) (*of ship*) venir dans le vent; (ii) (*of wind*) remonter. **come through** *v.i.* (*a*) (*of water*) pénétrer; (*of nail, etc.*) **to c. through the wood,** passer par, à travers, le bois; (*b*) (*of pers.*) **to c. through an illness,** surmonter une maladie; **he came through without a scratch,** il s'en est tiré indemne; (*c*) (*of message, etc.*) arriver; **the news has just c. through,** la nouvelle vient d'arriver. **come to** *v.i.* **1.** (*a*) = COME ROUND (*d*); (*b*) *Nau:* (*of ship*) lofer, venir dans le vent **2. to c. to power,** arriver, parvenir, au pouvoir. **come together** *v.i.* (*a*) s'assembler, se réunir; (*of troops*) opérer une jonction; (*b*) se rencontrer. **come up** *v.i.* **1.** (*a*) (i) monter (l'échelle, l'escalier, etc.); gravir (une colline); **come up to my rooms,** montez chez moi; **your coffee coming up, sir!** (voilà) votre café, monsieur! **to c. up after a dive,** revenir à la surface après un plongeon; *Nau:* (*of land, etc.*) **to c. up on the horizon,** commencer à paraître à l'horizon; (ii) **to c. up to town,** venir en ville, venir à Londres; (*b*) (*of plant*) sortir de terre; pousser; (*c*) **to c. up to s.o.,** s'approcher de qn; s'avancer vers, qn; *Ten:* **to c. up to the net,** monter au filet; (*d*) **to c. up against (sth.),** rencontrer (un obstacle, un problème, etc.); se heurter à (un refus, etc.). **2.** (*a*) *Jur:* **to c. up before the Court,** comparaître (devant le tribunal); **the case comes up (for trial) tomorrow,** la cause sera entendue demain; (*b*) (*of opportunity, question, etc.*) se présenter; (*of problem, etc.*) survenir, surgir; **to c. up**

(for discussion), venir sur le tapis; **this question had never yet come up,** cette question n'a encore jamais été soulevée; *F:* **we haven't c. up with an answer to this problem yet,** nous n'avons pas encore trouvé la solution de ce problème. **3.** (*a*) **to c. up to sth.,** atteindre jusqu'à qch; **the water came up to my knees,** l'eau me montait jusqu'aux genoux; (*b*) égaler; **to c. up to s.o.'s expectations,** répondre à l'attente de qn. **come upon** *v.i.* (*a*) *esp. Lit:* tomber, fondre, s'abattre, sur (un adversaire, etc.); (*of fear, etc.*) envahir, saisir (qn); (*b*) **to c. upon sth., s.o.,** trouver qch., rencontrer qn, par hasard; surprendre (un secret). **coming 1.** *a.* (année, semaine) qui vient; (orage) qui approche; **c. generations,** les générations futures; **it's the up-and-c. sport,** c'est le sport de l'avenir. **2.** *n.* (*a*) venue *f*, arrivée *f* (de qn); approche *f* (de la nuit); avènement *m* (du Messie); **the second C.,** le second avènement; **comings and goings,** allées *fpl* et venues; (*b*) **c. out,** (i) sortie *f* (du public d'un théâtre, etc.); (ii) apparition *f* (du soleil, etc.); éclosion *f* (des fleurs); (iii) parution *f* (d'un livre); (iv) début *m* (dans le monde).

comeback ['kʌmbæk] *n.* **1.** retour *m* (en vogue); retour au pouvoir (d'un homme politique, etc.); retour à la scène, à l'écran (d'un acteur). **2.** *esp. U.S:* revanche *f*. **3.** *F:* réplique *f*.

comedian [kə'mi:diən] *n.* **1.** *Th:* (*a*) comédien, -ienne; (*b*) comique *m* (de music-hall, etc.). **2.** auteur *m* de comédies; auteur comique.

comedienne [kəmi:di'en] *n.f. Th:* (*a*) comédienne; (*b*) actrice comique (de music-hall, etc.).

comedown ['kʌmdaun] *n. F:* humiliation *f*; déchéance *f*.

comedy ['kɔmedi] *n.* **1.** comédie *f*; le genre comique; **c. of manners,** comédie de mœurs; **musical c.,** opérette *f*; comédie musicale. **2.** (*play*) comédie; **we weren't taken in by her little c.,** sa petite comédie n'a pas pris.

come-hither [kʌm'hiðɛr] *a. F:* (regard) aguichant.

comely ['kʌmli] *a.* (*of pers.*) avenant; beau, *f.* belle.

come-on ['kʌmɔn] *n. P:* **to give s.o. the c.-o.,** encourager les avances sexuelles de qn.

comer ['kʌmər] *n.* **1.** arrivant, -ante; venant, -ante; **open to all comers,** ouvert à tout venant; **I'm ready to take on all comers,** je suis prêt à me battre avec n'importe qui. **2. first c.,** premier venu, premier arrivé.

comestible [kə'mestibl] **1.** *a. esp. NAm:* comestible. **2.** *n.pl.* **comestibles,** comestibles *mpl.*

comet ['kɔmit] *n.* comète *f*.

comeuppance [kʌm'ʌpəns] *n. F:* **she got her c.,** elle n'a que ce qu'elle mérite.

comfort¹ ['kʌmfət] *n.* **1.** consolation *f*; soulagement *m*; **to take c.,** se consoler; **that's cold c.,** c'est là une piètre consolation; **too close for c.,** plutôt dangereux; **she is a great c. to me,** elle me rend la vie douce; **it's a c. to know that . . .,** c'est une satisfaction que . . .. **2.** bien-être *m*. **3.** (*a*) confort *m*; confortable *m*; aisance *f*; **to live in c.,** vivre à l'aise; (*b*) *U.S:* **c. station,** toilettes *f pl*. **4. comforts,** commodités *fpl.*

comfort² *v.tr.* **1.** consoler, soulager; **to be comforted,** être consolé; se consoler (**by,** de). **2.** (*a*) (*of beverage, etc.*) réconforter; (*b*) redonner du courage à (qn). **comforting** *a.* réconfortant; **c. words,** paroles *fpl* de consolation, de réconfort.

comfortable ['kʌmfətəbl] *a.* **1.** (*a*) (*of bed, armchair, etc.*) confortable; (*of dress*) commode, aisé; (*of warmth, sensation*) agréable, doux, *f.* douce; **you will be more c. in this armchair,** vous serez mieux dans ce fauteuil; **to make oneself c.,** se mettre à son aise; **to be c.,** être à l'aise, à son aise; **to feel c.,** se trouver bien, à son aise; (*b*) (*of patient*) **to be c.,** ne pas souffrir; **he had a c. night,** la nuit a été bonne. **2. c. income,** revenu suffisant; ample revenu; **to be in c. circumstances,** être fort aisé, dans l'aisance. **3.** sans inquiétude; tranquille; rassuré. **-ably** *adv.* confortablement, commodément, agréablement; **to be c. off,** être à l'aise; **to live c.,** vivre à l'aise, à son aise; **we can get there c. in an hour,** une heure suffira amplement pour y aller.

comforter ['kʌmfətər] *n.* **1.** consolateur, -trice. **2.** cache-nez *m inv* (de laine). **3.** (*baby's*) tétine *f*; sucette *f*.

comfortless ['kʌmfətlis] *a.* **1.** sans confort; peu confortable. **2.** abandonné; désolé.

comfy ['kʌmfi] *a. F:* = COMFORTABLE 1 (*a*).

comic ['kɔmik] **1.** *a.* (chanson, etc.) comique; **c. opera,** opéra *m* bouffe; *Journ:* **c. strip,** bande dessinée; *F:* B.D. *f*. **2.** *n.* comédien, -ienne (de music-hall); comique *m*. **3.** *n. Journ:* (*a*) journal *m* de bandes dessinées; (*b*) *NAm: F:* **comics,** (la page des) bandes dessinées.

comical ['kɔmik(ə)l] *a.* comique, risible; drôle; **what a c. idea!** quelle drôle d'idée! **-ally** *adv.* comiquement; drôlement.

comma ['kɔmə] *n.* (*a*) virgule *f*; (*b*) **inverted commas,** guillemets *mpl*; **to put a word in inverted commas,** mettre un mot entre guillemets.

command¹ [kə'mɑ:nd] *n.* **1.** ordre *m*, commandement *m*; **to do sth. at s.o.'s c.,** agir d'après les ordres de qn; **to be at s.o.'s c.,** être aux ordres de qn; **word of c.,** commandement; *Th:* **c. performance,** représentation *f* commandée par le souverain. **2.** *Mil:* (*a*) commandement, ordre; (*b*) commandement (**of,** de; **over,** sur); gouvernement *m* (d'une place forte); commandement (d'une armée, d'une expédition); **to be in c. of a battalion,** avoir le commandement d'un bataillon, commander un bataillon; **to be first, second, in c.,** commander en premier, en second; **under (the) c. of . . .,** sous le commandement de . . .; (*c*) (*troops*) **to be responsible for one's c.,** être responsable de ses troupes; *Av:* **bomber, fighter, c.,** aviation *f* de bombardement, de chasse; (*d*) (*territory*) **Scottish c., Northern c.,** la région militaire d'Écosse, du Nord; **air, naval, c.,** région aérienne, maritime. **3.** (*a*) **to be in c. of a pass, etc.,** commander un défilé, etc.; (*b*) connaissance *f*, maîtrise *f* (d'une langue); **to have a c. of several languages,** posséder plusieurs langues; (*c*) **c. over oneself,** maîtrise de soi; (*d*) **c. of the seas,** maîtrise des mers.

command² *v.tr.* **1.** ordonner, commander (**sth.,** qch.; **s.o. to do sth.,** à qn de faire qch.); **he did what, as, I commanded him,** il a fait ce que je lui ai commandé, ordonné. **2.** (*a*) commander (un navire, un régiment); (*b*) **to c. oneself,** rester maître de soi. **3.** avoir (qch.) à sa disposition; **all the skill he could c.,** toute l'habileté qu'il possédait. **4.** (*a*) inspirer (le respect, l'admiration); forcer (l'attention); (*b*) **to c. a high price,** se vendre à un haut prix. **5.** (*of fort, etc.*) dominer (une ville, l'entrée d'un détroit, etc.); **window that commands a view over the valley,** fenêtre *f* qui qui donne sur la vallée. **commanding** *a.* **1.** *Mil:* **c. officer,** officier commandant; chef *m* de corps. **2.** (*a*) (ton) d'autorité, de commandement; (*b*) (air) imposant; (beauté) majestueuse. **3.** (lieu) éminent; (position) dominante.

commandant [kɔmən'dænt] *n.* commandant *m* (d'un camp, etc.).

commandeer [kɔmən'diər] *v.tr.* réquisitionner.

commander [kə'mɑ:ndər] *n.* **1.** (*a*) *Mil:* commandant *m* (d'armée, de compagnie, etc.); chef *m* (de section); **c.-in-chief,** commandant en chef; (*b*) *Mil.Av:* chef de bord (d'un avion, etc.); **wing c.,** lieutenant-colonel *m* (d'aviation), *pl.* lieutenants-colonels; (*c*) *Navy:* capitaine *m* de frégate; **lieutenant c.,** capitaine de corvette. **2.** (*of knights*) commandeur *m*.

commandment [kə'mɑːndmənt] *n.* commandement (divin); **the Ten Commandments,** les Dix Commandements; **to keep the commandments,** observer les commandements.

commando [kə'mɑːndou] *n.* (*a*) *Mil:* commando *m*; (*b*) soldat *m* membre d'un commando.

commemorate [kə'meməreit] *v.tr.* commémorer (qn, le souvenir de qn).

commemoration [əmemə'reiʃ(ə)n] *n.* **1.** commémoration *f*; **in c. of s.o., of sth.,** en commémoration de qn, de qch. **2.** *Ecc:* commémoraison *f.*

commemorative [kə'memərətiv] *a.* commémoratif (**of,** de); *Ecc:* **c. prayer,** commémoraison *f.*

commence [kə'mens] *v.tr.* & *i.* commencer (qch., à faire qch., par faire qch.); *Mil:* entamer (les opérations). **commencing** *a.* qui commence; **a c. salary of . . .,** des appointements *mpl* de début de . . ..

commencement [kə'mensmənt] *n.* commencement *m*, début *m.*

commend [kə'mend] *v.tr.* **1.** *Lit:* **to c. sth. to s.o.'s care,** recommander, confier, qch. aux soins de qn; **to c. one's soul to God,** recommander son âme à Dieu. **2.** (*a*) faire l'éloge de (qn); louer (qn, qch.); **to c. s.o. for bravery,** louer qn de sa bravoure; (*b*) **a course of action that did not c. itself to me,** une ligne de conduite à laquelle je ne pouvais pas donner mon approbation.

commendable [kə'mendəbl] *a.* louable; (action) digne d'éloges; **with c. promptness,** avec une louable promptitude. **-ably** *adv.* d'une manière louable.

commendation [kɔmen'deiʃ(ə)n] *n.* **1.** éloge *m* (**of,** de). **2. letters of c.,** lettres *fpl* de recommandation.

commensurable [kə'mens(j)ərəbl, -ʃər-] *a.* **1.** (*of number, etc.*) commensurable (**with, to,** avec). **2.** = COMMENSURATE 2.

commensurate [kə'mens(j)ərət, -ʃər-] *a.* **1.** coétendu (**with,** à). **2.** proportionné (**to, with,** à); **the salary offered will be c. with experience,** les appointements offerts seront en fonction de l'expérience.

comment¹ ['kɔment] *n.* observation *f*, commentaire *m*; **to make a c. on sth.,** faire des observations sur qch.; **no c.,** sans commentaire.

comment² *v.i.* **1. to c. on a text,** commenter un texte. **2. to c. on (sth.),** faire des observations sur (qch.); **nobody commented on it,** cela n'a suscité aucun commentaire.

commentary ['kɔmənt(ə)ri] *n.* **1.** commentaire *m*, glose *f.* **2. running c.,** (i) commentaire point par point; (ii) radioreportage *m* (d'un match, etc.).

commentate ['kɔmənteit] *v.i. Journ:* faire le commentaire (**on an event,** d'un événement).

commentator ['kɔmənteitər] *n.* **1.** commentateur, -trice. **2.** *W.Tel:* radioreporter *m*; *T.V:* commentateur.

commerce ['kɔməːs] *n.* commerce *m* (en gros); les affaires *fpl*; **Chamber of C.,** Chambre *f* de commerce.

commercial [kə'məːʃ(ə)l] **1.** *a.* (*a*) commercial, -aux; (port, tribunal, etc.) de commerce; (véhicule) utilitaire; (valeur) marchande; **the c. world,** le commerce; **c. bank,** banque de commerce; **c. law,** droit commercial; *O:* **c. traveller,** représentant *m*; **c. artist,** artiste *mf* en publicité; **c. radio, television,** radio, télévision, commerciale; (*b*) *usu. Pej:* (esprit) mercantile. **2.** *n. W.Tel: T.V:* émission *f* publicitaire. **-ally** *adv.* commercialement.

commercialese [kəməːʃə'liːz] *n. Pej:* (mauvais) style du commerce.

commercialism [kə'məːʃəlizm] *n.* esprit commercial; *Pej:* mercantilisme *m.*

commercialization [kəməːʃəlai'zeiʃ(ə)n] *n.* commercialisation *f.*

commercialize [kə'məːʃəlaiz] *v.tr.* commercialiser.

commie ['kɔmi] *n. F:* communiste *mf.*

commiserate [kə'mizəreit] *v.tr.* & *i.* **to c. (with) s.o.,** témoigner de la commisération à qn.

commiseration [kəmizə'reiʃ(ə)n] *n.* commisération *f*, compassion *f* (**with,** pour).

commissariat [kɔmi'sɛəriət] *n. Mil:* (*a*) intendance *f* (militaire); (*b*) les vivres *mpl.*

commissary ['kɔmisəri] *n.* **1.** commissaire *m*, délégué *m.* **2.** *Mil:* (*a*) officier *m* d'intendance; intendant *m*; (*b*) *U.S:* dépôt *m* de vivres.

commission¹ [kə'miʃ(ə)n] *n.* **1.** commission *f*; délégation *f* (de devoirs, d'autorité). **2.** (*a*) brevet *m*, titre *m*; (*b*) *Mil:* = brevet (d'officier); **to resign one's c.,** démissionner, donner sa démission; **to get a, one's, c.,** être nommé officier. **3.** ordre *m*, mandat *m*, commande *f*, mission *f*; **work done on c.,** travail fait sur commande; **to carry out a c.,** s'acquitter d'une commission. **4.** commission (parlementaire, etc.); **fact-finding c.,** commission d'enquête. **5.** *Nau: etc:* armement *m* (d'un navire); **to put a ship into c.,** armer un navire; **in c.,** (navire) en commission; (avion, usine) en service **6.** *Com:* commission; pourcentage *m*; **sale on c.,** vente *f* à la commission; **three per cent c.,** trois pour cent de commission; **c. agent,** (i) représentant *m* à la commission; (ii) *Turf:* bookmaker *m.* **7.** perpétration *f* (d'un crime).

commission² *v.tr.* **1.** (*a*) commissionner (qn); charger (qn) (**to do sth.,** de faire qch.); **to c. an artist to paint a portrait,** faire à un artiste la commande d'un portrait; **to be commissioned to do sth.,** être chargé de faire qch.; (*b*) préposer, déléguer, (qn) à une fonction; investir (qn) d'un pouvoir; nommer (un officier) à un commandement; (*c*) commander (un livre, un tableau). **2.** armer (un navire); mettre (un avion, une usine) en service. **commissioned** *a.* **1.** (navire) en commission, en armement; (navire) armé. **2.** *Mil:* **c. officer,** officier *m*; **to be c.,** être nommé officier. **commissioning** *n.* **1.** délégation *f.* **2.** nomination *f* (d'un officier) à un commandement. **3.** *Nau:* armement *m* (d'un navire).

commissionaire [kəmiʃə'nɛər] *n.* commissionnaire *m*; chasseur *m* (d'hôtel).

commissioner [kə'miʃ(ə)nər] *n.* commissaire *m*; (*a*) membre *m* d'une commission; (*b*) délégué *m* d'une commission; **c. of police** = préfet *m* de police; **c. for oaths,** officier ministériel (le plus souvent un *solicitor*) ayant qualité pour recevoir les déclarations sous serment.

commit [kə'mit] *v.tr.* **(committed) 1.** confier, remettre (**s.o., sth., to s.o.'s care,** qn, qch., aux soins, à la garde, de qn); livrer (un corps) (**to the earth,** à la terre); rendre (son âme) (**to God,** à Dieu); **to c. sth. to writing,** coucher qch. par écrit; **to c. sth. to memory,** apprendre qch. par cœur. **2.** *Jur:* **to c. s.o. to prison,** *abs.* **to c. s.o.,** (i) délivrer un mandat de dépôt contre qn; (ii) envoyer qn en prison; **to c. s.o. for trial,** (i) mettre qn en accusation; (ii) renvoyer (un prévenu) aux assises. **3.** *Pol:* renvoyer (un projet de loi) à une commission. **4.** (*a*) engager (sa parole d'honneur, etc.); **to be committed to sth., to do sth.,** être engagé à (faire) qch.; (*b*) **to c. troops,** engager des troupes à fond; (*c*) **to c. oneself,** se compromettre; **without committing myself,** sans me compromettre; sans m'engager. **5.** commettre, *Jur:* perpétrer (un crime, un délit); commettre (une erreur, une indiscrétion); **to c. suicide,** se suicider.

commitment [kə'mitmənt] *n.* **1.** (*a*) dépôt *m* (d'un document chez un notaire, etc.); (*b*) *Jur:* emprisonnement *m.* **2.** engagement *m* (financier ou autre); **I cannot do it because of other commitments,** d'autres obligations m'empêchent de le faire.

committal [kə'mit(ə)l] *n.* **1.** (*a*) mise *f* en terre (d'un cadavre); (*b*) *Jur:* emprisonnement *m*, mise en prison; **c. for trial,** détention préventive; (*c*) internement *m* (d'un aliéné) dans un hôpital psychiatrique. **2.** perpétration *f* (d'un délit, etc.).

committee [kə'miti] *n.* comité *m*; commission *f*; **to be on, sit on, a c.,** être membre, faire partie, d'un comité; **c. meeting,** réunion *f* d'un comité; *Parl:* **standing c.,** commission permanente; **select c.,** conseil, commission, d'enquête; **C. of ways and means** = Commission du budget; **c. member,** membre *m* d'un comité.

commode [kə'moud] *n.* **1.** *Furn:* commode *f.* **2. (night) c.,** chaise percée.

commodious [kə'moudiəs] *a.* spacieux.

commodity [kə'mɔditi] *n.* marchandise *f*, produit *m*; **primary, basic, c.,** produit de base; **coffee is the staple c. of Brazil,** le café est la ressource principale du Brésil; **c. market,** marché *m* de matières premières.

commodore ['kɔmədɔːr] *n.* **1.** *Navy: Nau:* (*a*) chef *m* (i) de division, (ii) de convoi; (*b*) capitaine *m* le plus ancien (d'une flotte marchande); (*c*) président *m* (d'un yacht-club). **2.** *Mil.Av:* **air c.,** général *m* de brigade.

common[1] ['kɔmən] *a.* commun. **1.** (*a*) *Sch:* **c. room,** (i) salle commune; (ii) salle des professeurs; **c. wall,** mur commun, mitoyen; **c. property,** choses communes; **c. land,** champs communs; **we have c. interests,** nous avons des intérêts communs; **to make c. cause with s.o.,** s'allier à qn; *Gram:* **c. noun,** nom commun; *Mth:* **c. divisor, factor,** commun diviseur; (*b*) public. **2.** (*a*) ordinaire; fréquent, qui arrive souvent; **c. name,** nom vulgaire (d'une plante); **in c. use,** d'usage courant; **in c. parlance,** en langage ordinaire; **it is c. (practice) to . . .,** il est d'usage de . . .; **c. or garden cabbage,** chou commun; (*b*) **the c. people,** les gens du peuple; **he lacks the c. touch,** il ne sait pas parler aux gens; (*c*) de peu de valeur. **3.** vulgaire, trivial; (accent) plébéien; **he's rather a c. little man,** il est assez vulgaire; **c. expression,** expression triviale. **-ly** *adv.* **1.** communément, ordinairement, généralement; **what is c. known as . . .,** ce qu'en langage courant on appelle . . .. **2.** vulgairement, de façon vulgaire.

common[2] *n.* **1.** (*a*) terrain, pré, communal; *Jur:* vaine pâture; **the village c.,** les communaux du village; (*b*) *Jur:* **(right of) c.,** (droits *mpl* de) servitude *f*; *esp.* droit de (vaine) pâture. **2. to have sth. in c. with s.o.,** avoir qch. en commun avec qn; **they have nothing in c.,** ils n'ont rien de commun.

commoner ['kɔmənər] *n.* **1.** bourgeois, -oise; roturier *m.* **2.** *Jur:* usager *m* d'une servitude, du droit de vaine pâture. **3.** *occ.* membre *m* de la Chambre des Communes. **4.** *Sch:* (*at Oxford*) étudiant *m* ordinaire (qui n'est pas boursier).

commonness ['kɔmənnis] *n.* **1.** fréquence *f* (d'un événement). **2.** vulgarité *f.*

commonplace ['kɔmənpleis] **1.** *n.* (*a*) lieu commun; (*b*) banalité *f*, platitude *f*; (*c*) **c. book,** mémorandum *m*; recueil *m* de faits notables. **2.** *a.* banal, -als; terre à terre.

commons ['kɔmənz] *n.pl.* **1.** (*a*) le peuple; le tiers état; (*b*) **the House of C.,** la Chambre des Communes. **2.** *Fig:* **to be on short c.,** faire maigre chère.

commonwealth ['kɔmənwelθ] *n.* **1.** état *m*; **the C.,** la chose publique. **2. the British C. (of Nations),** le Commonwealth, la Communauté britannique.

commotion [kə'mouʃ(ə)n] *n.* **1.** agitation *f*, commotion *f*; **in a state of c.,** en émoi; **to create a c.,** faire de l'éclat. **2.** troubles *mpl*; agitation (parmi le peuple).

communal ['kɔmjun(ə)l] *a.* communal, communautaire; **c. life,** la vie commune, communautaire; *Jur:* **c. estate,** communauté (conjugale). **-ally** *adv.* communalement.

commune[1] ['kɔmjuːn] *n.* (*a*) *Adm: etc:* commune *f*; (*b*) communauté *f* (de hippies, etc.).

commune[2] [kə'mjuːn] *v.i.* **1.** *Lit:* s'entretenir (**with s.o.,** avec qn). **2.** *U.S: Ecc:* communier.

communicable [kə'mjuːnikəbl] *a.* communicable.

communicant [kə'mjuːnikənt] *n.* **1.** *Ecc:* communiant, -ante.

communicate [kə'mjuːnikeit] **1.** *v.tr.* **to c. (sth.) to sth., to s.o.,** communiquer (la chaleur, etc.) à qch.; communiquer, faire parvenir (une nouvelle, etc.) à qn; donner (une maladie) à qn. **2.** *v.i.* (*a*) **to c. with s.o.,** communiquer avec qn; entrer en communication, en relations, avec qn; **to c. by letter,** communiquer par lettre; **he finds it difficult to c.,** il lui est difficile d'entrer en rapport avec les autres; (*b*) **rooms that c. with one another,** chambres qui communiquent entre elles. **3.** *Ecc:* (*a*) *v.tr.* communier (qn); (*b*) *v.i.* communier; recevoir la communion. **communicating** *a.* communicant; **c. rooms,** chambres *fpl* qui communiquent entre elles; **c. door,** porte *f* de communication.

communication [kəmjuːni'keiʃ(ə)n] *n.* **1.** (*a*) communication *f* (**of sth. to s.o.,** de qch. à qn); (*b*) communication; renseignement *m.* **2. to be in c. with . . .,** être en relation avec . . .; **to be in close c. with one another,** être en relations suivies; **to break off all c. with s.o.,** rompre toutes relations avec qn. **3.** (*a*) voie *f* d'accès; **line of c.,** voie d'intercommunication, *Mil:* ligne *f* de communication; **means of c.,** moyens *mpl* (i) de communication, (ii) de transport; *Rail:* **c. cord,** corde *f* de signal d'alarme; (*b*) *Mil:* transmissions *fpl*, liaison(s) *f*(*pl*); **radio c.,** liaison par radio.

communicative [kə'mjuːnikətiv] *a.* communicatif; expansif.

communion [kə'mjuːnjən] *n.* **1.** *usu. Lit:* communication *f* (**with s.o.,** avec qn). **2.** union *f* dans une même foi; communion *f*; **the c. of saints,** la communion des saints. **3.** *Ecc:* **the (Holy) C.,** la sainte communion; **c. wine,** (i) (*in Protestant Ch.*) vin *m* de communion; (ii) *R.C.Ch:* vin de messe; **c. cup,** calice *m*; **to administer Holy C. to s.o.,** administrer la sainte communion à qn; **to take (Holy) C.,** communier.

communiqué [kə'mjuːnikei] *n.* communiqué *m*; **joint c.,** communiqué publié conjointement.

communism ['kɔmjunizm] *n.* communisme *m.*

communist ['kɔmjunist] *a. & n.* communiste (*mf*).

community [kə'mjuːniti] *n.* **1.** communauté *f* (de biens, d'intérêts, etc.); solidarité *f* (d'intérêts). **2.** communauté, identité *f* (de goûts, etc.). **3.** *Ecc:* communauté (religieuse); ordre *m* (monastique). **4.** (*a*) **the c.,** le public; **harmful to the c.,** nuisible à la communauté; (*b*) société (de personnes); collectivité *f*; **the European c.,** la communauté européenne; (*c*) **c. singing,** chansons populaires reprises en chœur par l'assistance; (*d*) **c. centre,** centre social; *U.S:* **c. chest,** fonds *m* de secours.

commutable [kə'mjuːtəbl] *a.* **1.** permutable; interchangeable. **2.** *Jur:* (peine) commuable.

commutation [kɔmju'teiʃ(ə)n] *n.* **1.** commutation *f*; *Jur:* **c. of sentence,** commutation de peine. **2.** *U.S: Rail:* **c. ticket,** carte *f* d'abonnement.

commutator ['kɔmjuteitər] *n.* *El:* commutateur *m.*

commute [kə'mjuːt] **1.** *v.tr.* interchanger (des emplois). **2.** *v.tr.* (*a*) échanger (**for, into,** pour, contre); **to c. an annuity into, for, a lump sum,** racheter une rente par un versement global; (*b*) *Jur:* **to c. a penalty into, for, another,** commuer une peine en une autre. **3.** *v.i.* *Rail: etc:* (*a*) faire la navette entre sa résidence et son bureau; (*b*) *U.S:* s'abonner.

commuter [kə'mju:tər] *n. Rail: etc:* navetteur, -euse; personne *f* qui fait la navette entre sa résidence et son travail; **c. belt,** (grande) banlieue.

compact¹ ['kɔmpækt] *n.* convention *f*, accord *m.*

compact² [kəm'pækt] *a.* compact; serré, resserré, tassé; (terrain) liant; (style) concis. **-ly** *adv.* d'une manière compacte.

compact³ ['kɔmpækt] *n.* **1.** *Toil:* poudrier *m* (de sac à main). **2.** *NAm: Aut:* compacte *f.*

compact⁴ [kɔm'pækt] *v.tr.* (*a*) rendre (qch.) compact; tasser (de la neige); (*b*) *Civ.E:* compacter.

compactness [kəm'pæktnis] *n.* caractère compact (d'une masse, etc.); concision *f* (de style).

companion¹ [kəm'pænjən] *n.* **1.** (*a*) compagnon *m*, *f* compagne; **c. in arms,** compagnon d'armes; (*b*) **(lady) c.,** dame *f* de compagnie; (*c*) compagnon (d'un ordre). **2.** (*title of book*) manuel *m*, vade-mecum *m.* **3.** pendant *m* (à un livre, etc.).

companion² *n. Nau:* **c. (hatch),** capot *m* (de descente). **2. c. ladder,** échelle *f* de commandement; **c. way,** escalier *m* des cabines.

companionable [kəm'pænjənəbl] *a.* sociable. **-ably** *adv.* sociablement.

companionship [kəm'pænjənʃip] *n.* (*a*) compagnie *f*; (*b*) camaraderie *f.*

company ['kʌmpəni] *n.* **1.** (*a*) compagnie *f*; **to be in s.o.'s c.,** être en compagnie de qn; **to keep s.o. c.,** tenir compagnie à qn; **he's very good c.,** c'est un compagnon agréable; *Prov:* **two's c., three's a crowd,** deux s'amusent, trois s'embêtent; **to part c. with s.o.,** (i) se séparer de qn; (ii) ne plus être d'accord avec qn; (*b*) compagnie, société *f*; **a man is known by the c. he keeps,** on connaît un homme par ses fréquentations; **to get into bad c.,** faire de mauvaises fréquentations. **2.** (*a*) assemblée *f*; **present c. excepted,** les présents exceptés; (*b*) invités *mpl*; **we have c. to dinner today,** nous avons du monde à dîner aujourd'hui. **3.** *Com: Ind:* (*a*) compagnie; société; entreprise *f*; **joint stock c.,** société par actions; **limited liability c.,** société à responsabilité limitée; **public c.** = société anonyme; **insurance c.,** compagnie d'assurances; **companies' act,** loi *f* sur les sociétés; **(the firm of) Thomas and Company** (*usu.* **& Co.**), (la maison) Thomas et Compagnie (et Cie); (*b*) corporation *f* de marchands. **4.** (*a*) *Th:* troupe *f*; **touring c.,** troupe en tournée; (*b*) *Nau:* **the ship's c.,** l'équipage *m* (au complet, y compris les officiers); (*c*) *Scout:* compagnie (de guides). **5.** *Mil:* compagnie; **c. officer,** officier de compagnie.

comparable ['kɔmpərəbl] *a.* comparable (**with, to,** avec, à); assimilable (**to,** à).

comparative [kəm'pærətiv] *a.* **1.** (*a*) comparatif; *Gram:* **c. adverb,** adverbe comparatif; **c. degree,** le comparatif; *n.* **in the c.,** au comparatif; (*b*) **c. grammar, philology,** la grammaire, la philologie, comparée. **2.** (coût) comparatif; **he's a c. stranger to me,** je ne le connais guère. **-ly** *adv.* **1.** comparativement, par comparaison (**to,** à). **2.** relativement; **the next examination is c. easy,** l'examen *m* qui suit est relativement facile.

compare¹ [kəm'pεər] *n. Lit:* **beyond c.,** sans comparaison; **beauty without c.,** beauté sans pareille.

compare² **1.** *v.tr.* comparer, rapprocher (des faits, des idées); confronter (des résultats, etc.); **to c. sth. to, with, sth.,** comparer qch. à, avec, qch.; **compared with, to . . .,** en comparaison de . . ., à côté de . . ., par rapport à . . .; **to c. notes,** échanger ses impressions; (*b*) *Gram:* former les degrés de comparaison (d'un adjectif, un adverbe). **2.** *v.i.* être comparable (**with,** à); **he can't c. with you,** il ne vous est pas comparable; **to c. favourably with sth.,** ne le céder en rien à qch. **comparing** *n.* comparaison *f* (de deux personnes, de deux choses); rapprochement *m* (de faits).

comparison [kəm'pæris(ə)n] *n.* comparaison *f*; (*of documents, etc.*) collation *f*, conférence *f*; **to make, draw, a c. between sth. and sth.,** faire la comparaison de qch. avec qch.; **in, by, c.,** en comparaison; **in c. with . . .,** en comparaison de . . ., par rapport à . . ., à côté de . . .; **without c., beyond all c.,** sans comparaison; *Gram:* **degrees of c.,** degrés *mpl* de comparaison.

compartment [kəm'pɑ:tmənt] *n.* **1.** compartiment *m*; *Rail:* **smoking c.,** compartiment fumeurs; **sleeping c.,** compartiment couchette (dans un wagon-lit); *Aut:* **glove c.,** boîte *f* à gants, vide-poches *m inv*; *Trans:* **luggage c.,** soute *f* à bagages. **2.** case *f* (d'un tiroir, etc.).

compass ['kʌmpəs] *n.* **1. (a pair of) compasses,** un compas; **2.** (*a*) limite(s) *f*(*pl*), borne(s) *f*(*pl*) (d'un endroit); (*b*) *Const:* **c. brick,** brique *f* circulaire; **c. window,** fenêtre *f* en saillie ronde; *Carp:* **c. saw,** scie *f* à guichet. **3.** (*a*) étendue *f* (du savoir); espace *m* (de temps); portée *f* (de l'esprit); **beyond the c. of the human mind,** que l'esprit humain ne saurait embrasser; (*b*) *Mus:* étendue, diapason *m*, registre *m* (de la voix). **4.** *Nau: Surv: etc:* (*with moving needle*) boussole *f*; (*with moving card*) compas; **pocket c.,** boussole de poche; **mariner's c.,** compas (de mer); **steering c.,** compas de route; **c. error,** erreur *f* du compas; **the points of the c.,** les aires *fpl* de vent; **c. card,** rose *f* des vents; *Nau:* **to take a c. bearing,** prendre un relèvement au compas.

compassion [kəm'pæʃ(ə)n] *n.* compassion *f*; **to arouse c.,** faire pitié; exciter la compassion.

compassionate [kəm'pæʃənət] *a.* compatissant (**to, towards,** à, pour); **on c. grounds,** pour des raisons d'humanité; **c. leave,** permission exceptionnelle (pour raisons familiales). **-ly** *adv.* avec compassion.

compatibility [kəmpætə'biliti] *n.* compatibilité *f.*

compatible [kəm'pætəbl] *a.* compatible (**with,** avec). **-ibly** *adv.* d'une manière compatible (**with,** avec).

compatriot [kəm'pætriət, -'pei-] *n.* compatriote *mf.*

compel [kəm'pel] *v.tr.* **(compelled)** contraindre, forcer, obliger (qn) (**to do sth.,** à faire qch.); **to be compelled to do sth.,** être contraint, obligé, de faire qch.; **to c. s.o.'s admiration, respect,** commander l'admiration, le respect, de qn. **compelling** *a.* (force, curiosité, etc.) irrésistible; **a c. speaker,** un orateur *m* qui attire son auditoire; **c. need,** nécessité contraignante. **compellingly** *adv.* irrésistiblement.

compendium, *pl.* **-ums** [kəm'pendiəm(z)] *n.* **1.** abrégé *m*, précis *m*, compendium *m*; **c. of laws,** recueil *m* des lois. **2. c. of games,** malle *f* de jeux.

compensate ['kɔmpenseit] **1.** *v.tr.* (*a*) **to c. s.o. for sth.,** dédommager, indemniser, qn de qch.; (*b*) rémunérer (qn); (*c*) *Mec:* compenser (un pendule, etc.); (*of factors, etc.*) **to c. one another,** se compenser. **2.** *v.i.* **to c. for sth.,** (i) remplacer, racheter, qch.; (ii) compenser qch.; **skill may c. for lack of strength,** l'adresse *f* peut compenser, racheter, le manque de force. **compensated** *a. Mec: El: etc:* compensé. **compensating** *a.* (*a*) compensateur, -trice; **c. errors,** erreurs *fpl* qui se compensent; (*b*) *Mec.E: El: etc:* (circuit, etc.) compensateur; (soupape, bobine, etc.) de compensation.

compensation [kɔmpen'seiʃ(ə)n] *n.* **1.** compensation *f*; (*for loss, injury*) dédommagement *m*; (*for damage*) indemnité *f*, indemnisation *f*; *Jur:* réparation civile; composition *f*; **in c.,** (i) à titre de compensation; (ii) en revanche. **2.** *NAm:* rémunération *f* (des salariés).

compensator ['kɔmpenseitər] *n. El: Ph: etc:* compensateur *m*; *Aut:* palonnier *m* (du frein).

compensatory [kɔmpen'seit(ə)ri] *a.* compensateur, -trice.

compère[1] ['kɔmpɛər] *n. Th: T.V: etc:* animateur *m*, présentateur, -trice (d'un programme).
compère[2] *v.tr. Th: T.V: etc:* présenter, animer (un programme).
compete [kəm'pi:t] *v.i.* **1. to c. with s.o.,** faire concurrence à qn; concurrencer qn; **to c. with one another,** se faire concurrence. **2. to c. for a prize,** concourir pour un prix; **to c. with s.o. for a prize,** disputer un prix à qn.
competence ['kɔmpitəns] *n.* **1.** compétence *f*; aptitude *f* à (faire) qch.; capacité *f* pour (faire) qch. **2.** attributions *fpl* (d'un fonctionnaire); *Jur:* compétence; **to be within, beyond, the c. of a court,** être, ne pas être, de la compétence, du ressort, d'un tribunal.
competency ['kɔmpitənsi] *n.* = COMPETENCE.
competent ['kɔmpitənt] *a.* **1.** capable; (médecin, travail, etc.) compétent. **2.** (*a*) compétent **(in a matter,** en une matière); **c. to do sth.,** capable de faire qch.; qualifié pour faire qch.; (*b*) *Jur:* **c. to inherit,** habile à succéder. **3.** *Jur:* (tribunal) compétent. **4. c. knowledge of English,** bonne connaissance de l'anglais. **-ly** *adv.* avec compétence.
competition [kɔmpi'tiʃ(ə)n] *n.* **1.** rivalité *f*, concurrence *f*; **to enter into c. with s.o.,** concurrencer, faire concurrence à, qn. **2.** concours *m*; compétition (sportive); **c. for a prize,** concours pour un prix; **to win a prize in open c.,** remporter un prix au concours. **3.** *Com: Pol.Ec:* concurrence; **free c.,** libre concurrence; **unfair c.,** concurrence déloyale.
competitive [kəm'petitiv] *a.* **1. c. spirit,** esprit *m* de concurrence. **2. c. examination,** concours *m*. **3.** *Com: Pol.Ec:* (prix, etc.) concurrentiel, compétitif; (produits) concurrents; **in c. conditions,** en conditions de concurrence. **-ly** *adv.* **1.** en esprit de concurrence. **2. gained, obtained, c.,** obtenu au concours.
competitiveness [kəm'petitivnis] *n.* compétitivité *f*; concurrence *f* (d'un produit sur le marché).
competitor [kəm'petitər] *n.* (*a*) *Com: Sp:* concurrent, -ente; (*b*) compétiteur, -trice **(for a prize,** pour un prix).
compilation [kɔmp(a)i'leiʃ(ə)n] *n.* compilation *f* (d'un dictionnaire, etc.).
compile [kəm'pail] *v.tr.* compiler (un dictionnaire, un recueil). **compiling** *n.* = COMPILATION 1.
compiler [kəm'pailər] *n.* **1.** compilateur, -trice, rédacteur, -trice (d'un dictionnaire, etc.). **2.** *Cmptr:* compilateur.
complacency [kəm'pleisənsi] *n.* **1.** satisfaction *f*, contentement *m*. **2.** (*a*) contentement de soi-même; (*b*) (*of result, etc.*) **not to give s.o. any grounds for c.,** ne pas permettre à qn de se reposer sur ses lauriers.
complacent [kəm'pleisənt] *a.* (*of pers.*) content de soi-même; suffisant; (air) suffisant; (optimisme) béat. **-ly,** *adv.* (*a*) avec contentement, avec satisfaction; (*b*) d'un air suffisant.
complain [kəm'plein] *v.i.* **1.** se plaindre **(of,** de); **to c. that . . .,** se plaindre que + *sub. or ind.*; **I have nothing to c. of,** je n'ai pas à me plaindre; **she complained of giddiness,** elle se plaignit d'un étourdissement. **2.** adresser une réclamation **(to,** à); porter plainte **(against s.o.,** contre qn); se plaindre **(to,** à); réclamer **(against sth.,** contre qch.).
complainant [kəm'pleinənt] *n. Jur:* plaignant, -ante.
complaint [kəm'pleint] *n.* **1.** (*a*) grief *m*; sujet *m* de plainte; **I have no cause, grounds, for c.,** je n'ai aucun motif de plainte; (*b*) plainte, *f* réclamation *f*; **to lodge, make, a c. against s.o.,** porter plainte contre qn; *Adm: Com:* **complaints office,** service *m* des réclamations; (*c*) *Jur: U.S:* plainte en justice. **2.** maladie *f*; **liver c.,** maladie de, affection du, foie.
complaisance [kəm'pleizəns] *n.* complaisance *f*.
complaisant [kəm'pleiz(ə)nt] *a.* complaisant.
complement[1] ['kɔmplimənt] *n.* **1.** (*a*) plein *m* (de combustibles, etc.); (*of bus, etc.*) charge complète (de voyageurs); (*b*) *Navy: etc:* effectif *m*; **full c.,** effectif complet; (*c*) personnel *m*; **engine-room c.,** personnel des machines. **2.** complément *m* (d'un verbe, d'un angle, etc.); *Gram:* attribut *m*.
complement[2] ['kɔmpliment] *v.tr.* compléter; être, faire, le complément de (qch.).
complementary [kɔmpli'ment(ə)ri] *a.* (angle, couleur, *Cmptr:* opération, etc.) complémentaire.
complete[1] [kəm'pli:t] *a.* **1.** (*a*) complet, entier; *El:* (circuit) total; (repos) complet; **c. surprise,** surprise totale; **is the pack c.?** le jeu est-il complet? *Com:* **c. with battery,** livré avec pile; **my happiness is c.,** rien ne manque à mon bonheur; **to give a c. account,** donner tout les détails; (*b*) terminé; **my report is not yet c.,** mon rapport n'est pas encore achevé. **2.** achevé, accompli; **c. (and utter) failure,** échec total; **the operation has been a c. success,** l'opération *f* a pleinement réussi. **-ly** *adv.* complètement, totalement.
complete[2] *v.tr.* **1.** compléter (qch.); achever, terminer (un travail, etc.); mener à bien (une tâche); accomplir (son apprentissage). **2.** compléter (une collection, un nombre); rappareiller (un service à thé); *Com:* **to c. an order,** compléter une commande. **3.** remplir (une formule, un questionnaire).
completeness [kəm'pli:tnis] *n.* état complet.
completion [kəm'pli:ʃ(ə)n] *n.* achèvement *m* (d'un ouvrage); complètement *m* (d'une collection); **in process of c.,** en (cours d') achèvement; **near c.,** près d'être achevé; **to reach c.,** s'achever; (*of property*) **occupation on c. (of contract),** prise *f* de possession dès la signature du contrat.
complex ['kɔmpleks] **1.** *a.* (question, phrase) complexe. **2.** *n.* (*a*) tout (formé de parties); **industrial c.,** complexe industriel; (*b*) *Psy:* complexe; **Œdipus c.,** complexe d'Œdipe; **inferiority c.,** complexe d'infériorité.
complexion [kəm'plekʃ(ə)n] *n.* **1.** teint *m*. **2.** nature *f*, caractère *m* (de qch.); **that puts a new, a different, c. on it,** voilà qui change la situation.
complexity [kəm'pleksiti] *n.* complexité *f*.
compliance [kəm'plaiəns] *n.* (*a*) action *f* de conformer **(with,** à); **in c. with your wishes,** conformément à vos désirs; (*b*) *Pej:* soumission (abjecte).
compliant [kəm'plaiənt] *a.* complaisant, accommodant.
complicate ['kɔmplikeit] *v.tr.* compliquer **(with,** de); **that complicates matters,** cela complique la situation. **complicated** *a.* compliqué; (*of situation, etc.*) **to become c.,** se compliquer.
complication [kɔmpli'keiʃ(ə)n] *n.* complication *f*; **c. of circumstances,** engrenage *m* de circonstances; *Med:* **if no complications set in,** s'il ne survient pas de complications; **you're always making complications!** tu compliques toujours les choses!
complicity [kəm'plisiti] *n.* complicité *f* **(in,** à); connivence *f*.
compliment[1] ['kɔmplimənt] *n.* **1.** compliment *m*; **to pay a c. to s.o.,** faire, adresser, un compliment à qn; **to pay one's compliments to s.o.,** faire une visite (de politesse) à qn. **2.** (*in letter*) **to present, send, one's compliments to s.o.,** se rappeler au bon souvenir de qn; présenter ses hommages *m* à (une dame); **compliments of the season,** meilleurs souhaits (de nouvel an, Noël, etc.).
compliment[2] ['kɔmpliment] *v.tr.* complimenter, féliciter (qn); faire des compliments à (qn) **(on,** de; **on doing sth.,** d'avoir fait qch.).
complimentary [kɔmpli'ment(ə)ri] *a.* (*a*) flatteur,

-euse; **c. remarks,** compliments *mpl*; félicitations *fpl*; (*b*) gratuit; gracieux; **c. ticket,** billet *m* de faveur; *Publ:* **c. copy,** exemplaire envoyé à titre gracieux.

complin(e) ['kɔmplin] *n. Ecc:* complies *fpl*.

comply [kəm'plai] *v.i.* **to c. with (sth.),** se conformer à, accomplir (une clause d'un traité, une formalité, etc.); se soumettre à (la loi); observer, satisfaire à (une règle); accéder, répondre à (une demande); déférer à (un désir); obéir à (un ordre).

component [kəm'pounənt] **1.** *a.* **c. parts,** parties constituantes; *Ind:* pièces détachées. **2.** *n.* (*a*) composant *m*; partie composante; *Ind:* pièce détachée; (*b*) organe *m* (d'une machine).

comport [kəm'pɔːt] **1.** *v.i.* s'accorder (**with,** à). **2.** *v.pr.* **to c. oneself,** se comporter.

comportment [kəm'pɔːtment] *n.* conduite *f*, maintien *m*, comportement *m*.

compos ['kɔmpɔs] *a. Lt.phr. Jur:* **c. mentis** ['mentis], sain d'esprit.

compose [kəm'pouz] *v.tr.* **1.** (*a*) composer (un poème, une symphonie, etc.); *v.i. Mus:* composer; (*b*) *Typ:* composer (une ligne). **2.** constituer; **to be composed of sth.,** se composer, être composé, de qch. **3.** *Art:* arranger (les personnages d'un tableau). **4.** régler (un différend, etc.). **5.** (*a*) **to c. one's thoughts,** se recueillir (avant d'agir); (*b*) calmer, tranquilliser (l'esprit); **c. yourself!** calmez-vous! **composed** *a.* (*a*) calme, tranquille; (*b*) (*of manner, etc.*) composé. **composing,** *n. Mus: Typ: etc:* composition *f*.

composer ['kəm'pouzər] *n. Mus:* compositeur, -trice.

composite ['kɔmpəzit] **1.** *a.* (*a*) *Bot:* (fleur) composée; *Arch:* (chapiteau) composite; (*b*) *Cin:* **c. shot,** impression combinée. **2.** *n.* (*a*) composé *m*; (*b*) *Bot:* composée *f*.

composition [kɔmpə'ziʃ(ə)n] *n.* **1.** (*a*) action *f* de composer; composition *f* (de qch.); **a sonata of his own c.,** une sonate de sa composition; (*b*) composition (de l'air, de l'eau, etc.); (*c*) *Art:* (*distribution of elements*) composition. **2.** (*a*) mélange *m*, composé *m*; (*b*) *Const:* stuc *m*; simili marbre *m*. **3.** (*a*) **a musical c.,** une composition musicale; (*b*) *Sch:* dissertation *f*, rédaction *f*; (*c*) *Sch: O:* **prose c.,** thème *m*. **4.** *Com:* arrangement *m*, accommodement (avec des créanciers); concordat préventif (à la faillite); **to make a c.,** composer.

compositor [kəm'pɔzitər] *n. Typ:* compositeur *m*.

compost¹ ['kɔmpɔst] *n. Hort:* compost *m*; terreau *m*.

compost² *v.tr.* composter.

composure [kəm'pouʒər] *n.* calme *m*; sang-froid *m*; **to regain one's c.,** (re)trouver son sang-froid; se calmer.

compote ['kɔmpɔt] *n.* compote *f* (de fruits).

compound¹ ['kɔmpaund] **1.** *a.* (*a*) composé; combiné; *Arch:* (ordre) composite; *Gram:* (mot) composé; *Mus:* (mesure) composée; *Surg:* (fracture) compliquée; *Book-k:* **c. entry,** article composé; *Fin:* **c. interest,** intérêts composés; (*b*) *Mth:* (nombre) complexe; (*c*) *Métall: El:* (acier, enroulement) compound *inv.* **2.** *n.* (*a*) (corps *m*) composé (*m*); **chemical c.,** composé chimique; (*b*) *Tchn:* composition *f*, mastic *m*; (*c*) *Gram:* mot composé.

compound² [kəm'paund] **1.** *v.tr.* (*a*) combiner (des éléments); préparer (une drogue); (*b*) accommoder, arranger (un différend); **to c. a debt,** faire une transaction pour le règlement d'une dette; (*c*) *Jur:* **to c. a felony,** pactiser avec un crime; (*d*) aggraver (un problème, etc.). **2.** *v.i.* (*a*) s'arranger, composer (**with s.o.,** avec qn); entrer en arrangement (avec qn); transiger (avec sa conscience); (*b*) *Com:* arriver à un concordat (avec ses créanciers).

compound³ ['kɔmpaund] *n.* (*a*) enceinte *f* (d'une résidence, etc.); (*b*) cour *f* (d'une prison); (*c*) (*in S. Africa*) (i) quartier *m* des noirs (dans une mine d'or, etc.); (ii) parc *m* à bétail.

comprehend [kɔmpri'hend] *v.tr.* comprendre.

comprehensible [kɔmpri'hensəbl] *a.* compréhensible, intelligible. **-ibly** *adv.* d'une manière compréhensible, intelligible.

comprehension [kɔmpri'henʃ(ə)n] *n.* compréhension *f*. **1.** entendement *m*; **it is above, beyond, my c.,** cela me dépasse. **2.** portée *f*, étendue *f*.

comprehensive [kɔmpri'hensiv] *a.* **1.** *Phil:* **the c. faculty,** la faculté de comprendre, de concevoir. **2.** (terme, etc.) compréhensif; (étude, vue) d'ensemble; **c. knowledge,** vastes connaissances *fpl*; **c. school** = collège d'enseignement secondaire; = lycée polyvalent; **c. programme,** programme détaillé et complet.

compress¹ ['kɔmpres] *n. Med:* compresse *f*.

compress² [kəm'pres] *v.tr.* **1.** (*a*) comprimer (un gaz, l'air, etc.); bander (un ressort); (*of compressor*) refouler (l'air, etc.); (*b*) (*with passive force*) (*of gas, etc.*) se comprimer; (*of spring*) fléchir. **2.** condenser (un discours, etc.); concentrer (son style). **compressed** *a.* comprimé; **c. lips,** des lèvres serrées, pincées.

compression [kəm'preʃ(ə)n] *n.* **1.** compression *f* (d'un gaz, d'un ressort, etc.); bande *f* (d'un ressort); **force of c.,** effort *m* de compression; *I.C.E:* **c. stroke,** (temps *m* de) compression; **c. ratio,** compression volumétrique. **2.** concentration *f* (de la pensée, du style, etc.).

compressor [kəm'presər] *n.* compresseur *m* (de gaz, d'air, etc.); **air c.,** motocompresseur *m*.

comprise [kəm'praiz] *v.tr.* contenir; **the flat comprises three rooms,** l'appartement comprend trois pièces.

compromise¹ ['kɔmprəmaiz] *n.* compromis *m*, transaction *f*; **to agree to a c.,** consentir à transiger; **to make, reach, a c.,** composer (**with s.o.,** avec qn); transiger; **policy of no c.,** politique intransigeante.

compromise² **1.** *v.tr.* (*a*) compromettre (qn, son honneur, etc.); **to c. oneself with s.o.,** se compromettre avec qn; (*b*) transiger sur (un différend). **2.** *v.i.* transiger, composer; **to c. with s.o.,** s'accommoder avec qn; **if he agrees to c.,** s'il accepte un compromis. **compromising** *a.* (*of situation, etc.*) compromettant.

comptroller [kən'troulər] *n. Adm:* administrateur *m*; contrôleur *m*; vérificateur *m* (de comptes).

compulsion [kəm'pʌlʃ(ə)n] *n.* **1.** compulsion *f*; **under c.,** par contrainte; **to be under c. to do sth.,** être astreint à faire qch. **2.** *Psy:* compulsion.

compulsive [kəm'pʌlsiv] *a.* **1.** (voix, manière, etc.) qui commande l'obéissance. **2.** *Psy:* compulsif; (fumeur, joueur) invétéré. **-ly** *adv.* **1.** par force. **2.** par besoin; **to smoke c.,** ne pas pouvoir s'empêcher de fumer.

compulsory [kəm'pʌls(ə)ri] *a.* **1.** obligatoire, forcé; **c. liquidation,** liquidation forcée; **c. school attendance,** scolarité *f* obligatoire; *Sch:* **c. Latin,** latin obligatoire. **2.** coercitif; **c. powers,** pouvoirs coercitifs. **-ily** *adv.* obligatoirement; *Adm:* **to be retired c.,** être mis à la retraite d'office.

compunction [kəm'pʌŋ(k)ʃ(ə)n] *n.* componction *f*; remords *m*; **without c.,** sans (aucune) componction; sans scrupule.

computation [kɔmpju'teiʃ(ə)n] *n.* (*a*) compte *m*, calcul *m*, supputation *f*, estimation *f*; **to make a c. of sth.,** faire le calcul de qch.; calculer qch.; estimer (les dépenses, etc.); (*b*) **electronic c.,** calcul électronique.

compute¹ [kəm'pjuːt] *v.tr.* computer, calculer; **computed distance,** distance estimée. **computing** *n.* calcul *m*; estimation *f*; **c. machine,** machine *f* à calcul.

computer [kəm'pjuːtər] *n.* **1.** (*pers.*) calculateur, -trice. **2.** (*machine*) calculateur *m*; **electronic c.,** calculateur électronique; ordinateur *m*; **analog, digital, c.,** calculateur analogique, numérique; **the c. age,** l'ère *f* des ordinateurs; **c. program, language,** programme *m*, langage *m*, machine; **c. room,** salle *f* des machines, de l'ordinateur; (*pers.*) **c. expert,** informaticien, -ienne; **c. analyst,** analyste *mf* en informatique; **c. programmer,** programmeur, - euse.

computerization [kəmpjutərai'zeiʃ(ə)n] *n.* automatisation *f*, informatisation *f*.

computerize [kəm'pjuːtəraiz] *v.tr.* informatiser; équiper (une organisation) d'ordinateurs. **computerized** *a.* **c. data,** données *fpl* mécanographiques; **c. type setting,** composition *f* automatique.

comrade ['kɔmreid, -rəd] *n.* (*a*) camarade *m*, compagnon *m*; **comrades in arms,** compagnons d'armes; (*b*) (*as term of address*) camarade *mf*.

comradeship ['kɔmreidʃip, -rəd-] *n.* camaraderie *f*.

con¹ [kɔn] *v.tr.* **(conned) conning tower,** kiosque *m* (d'un sous-marin).

con² *n.* **the pros and (the) cons,** le pour et le contre.

con³ *a. F:* **c. man,** escroc *m*; **c. trick,** (i) vol *m* à l'américaine; escroquerie *f*; (ii) duperie *f*.

con⁴ *n. F:* (i) duperie *f*, supercherie *f*; (ii) escroquerie *f*.

con⁵ *v.tr.* **(conned)** *F:* (i) duper, escroquer (qn); **I've been conned,** on m'a eu; **to c. s.o. into doing sth.,** persuader qn à faire qch. par la ruse.

concave ['kɔnkeiv] *a.* concave, incurvé.

concavity [kɔn'kæviti] *n.* concavité *f*.

conceal [kən'siːl] *v.tr.* (*a*) cacher (qn, qch.); dissimuler (la vérité, etc.); masquer (ses projets, une fenêtre); voiler (ses pensées, ses desseins); **to c. oneself,** se cacher; **to c. one's intentions,** cacher, déguiser, son jeu; **to c. sth. from s.o.,** cacher qch. à qn; taire qch. à qn; (*b*) *Jur:* receler (un objet volé). **concealed** *a.* caché; dissimulé; (virage) masqué; (éclairage) indirect.

concealment [kən'siːlmənt] *n.* **1.** dissimulation *f*, déguisement *m* (de ses sentiments, etc.). **2.** *Jur:* (*a*) recèlement *m* (d'objets volés); (*b*) réticence *f*; dissimulation (de certains faits); *Fin:* **c. of assets,** dissimulation d'actif. **3.** action *f* de (se) cacher; **to keep s.o. in c.,** tenir qn caché; **a place of c.,** une cachette.

concede [kən'siːd] *v.tr.* **1.** concéder (un privilège, etc.); *Games:* rendre (des points à son adversaire); *Pol: Games: etc:* **to c. defeat,** s'avouer vaincu. **2. to c. that one is wrong,** admettre qu'on a tort.

conceit [kən'siːt] *n.* vanité *f*, suffisance *f*; **eaten up with c.,** pétri, pourri, d'amour-propre.

conceited [kən'siːtid] *a.* suffisant, vaniteux; prétentieux; **he is unbearably c.,** il est d'une suffisance insupportable. **-ly** *adv.* avec suffisance.

conceivable [kən'siːvəbl] *a.* concevable, imaginable; **it is c. that . . .,** il est concevable que + *sub.*; **by every c. means,** par tous les moyens imaginables. **-ably** *adv.* d'une façon concevable; **he could c. have done it,** il est concevable qu'il l'ait fait.

conceive [kən'siːv] *v.tr.* **1.** (*a*) concevoir (un enfant); *v.i.* concevoir; devenir enceinte; (*b*) (*of child*) **to be conceived,** être conçu. **2.** (*a*) concevoir (un projet); **to c. a dislike for s.o.,** prendre qn en aversion; (*b*) **I cannot c. why . . .,** je n'imagine pas pourquoi . . . . **3.** (*of document*) **conceived as follows,** ainsi conçu. **4.** *v.i.* **to c. of sth.,** imaginer qch.

concentrate¹ ['kɔnsəntreit] *n.* (*a*) minerai concentré; (*b*) concentré *m* (de tomates, etc.).

concentrate² **1.** *v.tr.* concentrer (des troupes, son attention, etc.); grouper (des efforts); **concentrated milk,** lait concentré; **with concentrated fury,** avec une fureur intense. **2.** *v.i.* (*a*) se concentrer; **population tends to c. in cities,** la population tend à se concentrer dans les villes; (*b*) **to c. on sth., on doing sth.,** porter toute son attention, sur qch.; s'appliquer à faire qch.

concentration [kɔnsən'treiʃ(ə)n] *n.* **1.** (*a*) concentration *f* (des troupes, etc.); **c. of effort,** convergence *f* des efforts; **c. camp,** camp *m* de concentration; (*b*) *Ch:* **(degree of) c.,** titre *m* (d'un acide, etc.). **2.** concentration, application *f* (de l'esprit); **to lose c.,** être déconcentré, perdre sa concentration. **3. the large urban concentrations,** les grandes agglomérations urbaines.

concentric [kɔn'sentrik] *a.* concentrique.

concept ['kɔnsept] *n.* concept *m*; idée générale.

conception [kən'sepʃ(ə)n] *n.* **1.** conception *f* (d'un enfant, d'une idée, etc.). **2. to have a clear c. of sth.,** se représenter clairement qch. par la pensée.

concern¹ [kən'səːn] *n.* **1.** intérêt *m* **(in,** dans); **it's no c. of mine,** cela ne me regarde pas; cela ne me concerne pas; **it's no c. of yours,** cela ne vous intéresse pas. **2.** (*a*) souci *m*; **my only c. has been to ensure . . .,** ma seule préoccupation a été d'assurer . . .; (*b*) souci, anxiété *f*, inquiétude *f*; sollicitude *f*; **to show c.,** se montrer inquiet. **3.** *Com: Ind:* entreprise *f*; maison *f* (de commerce, etc.); fonds *m* de commerce; **going c.,** affaire qui marche; (*of shop, etc.*) **to be sold as a going c.,** à vendre avec fonds.

concern² *v.tr.* **1.** (*a*) concerner, regarder, toucher, intéresser (qn, qch.); se rapporter à (qn, qch.); avoir rapport à (qch.); **this does not c. you,** (i) ceci ne vous concerne pas, ne vous touche pas; (ii) ceci n'est pas votre affaire; **matters that c. the public,** choses *fpl* qui intéressent le public; **to whom it may c.,** à qui de droit; à toutes fins utiles; (*b*) **to c. oneself with, about, in, sth.,** s'intéresser à, s'occuper de, qch. **2.** (*a*) **to be concerned in, with, sth.,** s'intéresser à, s'occuper de, qch.; **the parties concerned,** les intéressés; *Com: etc:* **the department concerned,** le service compétent; **as far as I am concerned,** en ce qui me concerne; en ce qui me regarde; quant à moi; **as far as this question is concerned,** en ce qui touche à cette question; **this book is concerned with politics,** ce livre traite de la politique; (*b*) **to be concerned about s.o., sth.,** s'inquiéter, être inquiet, de qn, de qch.; **I am concerned for his health,** l'état *m* de sa santé me donne des inquiétudes *fpl*; **I am not concerned about what they say,** je ne m'inquiète guère de ce qu'on dit. **concerning** *prep.* concernant, en ce qui concerne, au sujet de, à l'égard de (qn, qch.).

concert¹ ['kɔnsət] *n.* **1.** concert *m*; **to act in c. (with s.o.),** agir de concert, d'accord (avec qn); agir d'ensemble. **2.** *Mus:* concert; **c. performer,** concertant, - ante; concertiste *mf*; **c. hall,** salle *f* de concert; **c. grand,** piano *m* de concert.

concert² [kən'səːt] **1.** *v.tr.* concerter (des mesures, etc.). **2.** *v.i.* se concerter, tenir conseil **(with,** avec). **concerted** *a.* (plan, etc.) concerté; **c. action,** action *f* concertée, d'ensemble.

concertina¹ [kɔnsə'tiːnə] *n.* **1.** *Mus:* concertina *m*. **2.** *Rail:* **c. vestibule,** soufflet *m* (entre voitures).

concertina² *v.i.* **(concertinaed)** (*of cars, etc. in collision*) s'écraser en accordéon.

concerto [kən'tʃəːtou] *n. Mus:* concerto *m*; **piano, violin, c.,** concerto pour piano, pour violon.

concession [kən'seʃ(ə)n] *n.* (*a*) concession *f* (de terrain, d'opinion, etc.); **mining c.,** concession minière; **to make concessions,** faire des concessions; (*b*) *Com:* réduction *f*.

concession(n)aire [kənseʃə'nɛər] *n.* concessionnaire *mf*.

concessionary [kən'seʃən(ə)ri] **1.** *a.* (*a*) (compagnie, etc.) concessionnaire; (*b*) (subside, etc.) concédé; (tarif, etc.) réduit. **2.** *n.* = CONCESSION(N)AIRE.

conch [kɔŋk, kɔn(t)ʃ] *n.* **1.** *Moll:* conque *f* (de mollusque). **2.** = CONCHA.

concha, *pl.* **-ae** ['kɔŋkə, -i:] *n.* **1.** *Anat:* conque *f* (de l'oreille); oreille *f* externe. **2.** *Arch:* voûte *f* d'abside.

conciliate [kən'silieit] *v.tr.* (*a*) concilier, réconcilier (des théories contraires, des intérêts opposés); (*b*) gagner la bonne volonté de (qn).

conciliation [kənsili'eiʃ(ə)n] *n.* conciliation *f*; *Jur:* **court of c.,** bureau *m* de conciliation; (*in industrial dispute*) **c. board,** conseil *m* d'arbitrage, = conseil des prud'hommes.

conciliatory [kən'siliət(ə)ri] *a.* conciliatoire, conciliant; (esprit) de conciliation.

concise [kən'sais] *a.* concis; (style) serré; (dictionnaire) abrégé. **-ly** *adv.* brièvement, avec concision.

conciseness [kən'saisnis], **concision** [kən'siʒ(ə)n] *n.* concision *f*; **to aim at c.,** serrer son style.

conclave ['kɔnkleiv] *n.* **1.** *R.C.Ch:* conclave *m.* **2.** assemblée *f*, réunion *f* (à huis clos); **to be in c. with s.o.,** tenir conseil avec qn.

conclude [kən'klu:d] *v.tr.* **1.** conclure (la paix, un traité, etc.); arranger, régler (une affaire, un contrat). **2.** terminer, conclure, finir, achever (un discours, un ouvrage); clôturer (une session); *v.i.* (*at end of speech, etc.*) **to c.,** en conclusion; pour conclure. **3.** (*infer*) **from this I c. that . . .,** de ceci je conclus que . . . . **concluding** *a.* (mot, chapitre) final (*pl.* -als).

conclusion [kən'klu:ʒ(ə)n] **1.** conclusion *f* (de la paix, etc.). **2.** fin *f*, conclusion (d'une lettre, etc.); clôture *f* (d'une session, etc.); **in c.,** pour conclure; en conclusion; **to bring a matter to a successful c.,** mener une affaire à bonne fin. **3. without coming to a c.,** sans rien conclure; **to draw a c. from sth.,** tirer une conclusion de qch.; **to come to the c. that . . .,** conclure que . . .; **it was a foregone c.,** c'était prévu; **to jump to a c.,** arriver (i) immédiatement, (ii) prématurément, à une conclusion; **draw your own conclusions,** à vous d'en juger.

conclusive [kən'klu:siv] *a.* (*of argument*) concluant, décisif; (*of test*) probant. **-ly** *adv.* décisivement.

concoct [kən'kɔkt] *n.tr.* **1.** composer (un cocktail, etc.); confectionner (un plat). **2.** imaginer, inventer (un plan); machiner (un complot).

concoction [kən'kɔkʃ(ə)n] *n.* **1.** (*a*) confectionnement *m*, confection *f* (d'un plat, etc.); (*b*) mixtion *f*; *esp.* boisson *f*, potion *f*. **2.** (*a*) élaboration *f* (d'un plan); machination *f* (d'un complot); (*b*) **a c. of lies,** un tissu de mensonges.

concomitant [kən'kɔmitənt] **1.** *a.* concomitant (**with,** de). **2.** *n.* événement concomitant.

concord ['kɔŋkɔ:d] *n.* **1.** bonne entente, harmonie *f* (entre personnes); *Lit:* **to live in c.,** vivre en bon accord (**with,** avec). **2.** *Gram:* concordance *f*. **3.** *Mus:* accord consonant.

concordance [kən'kɔ:dəns] *n.* **1.** concordance *f*, accord *m* (**with,** avec); harmonie *f*. **2.** index *m*, concordance (de la Bible).

concordant [kən'kɔ:dənt] *a.* **1.** qui s'accorde, concordant (**with,** avec). **2.** *Mus:* harmonieux.

concordat [kɔn'kɔ:dæt] *n.* concordat *m.*

concourse ['kɔnkɔ:s] *n.* (*a*) foule *f*, rassemblement *m*, affluence *f* (de personnes); (*b*) (i) lieu *m* de rassemblement; (ii) hall *m* (de gare).

concrete¹ ['kɔnkri:t] **1.** (exemple, terme) concret; **c. music,** musique concrète; **c. suggestion, proposal,** suggestion *f*, proposition *f*, pratique, concrète. **2.** *n.* *Civ.E:* *Const:* béton *m* (de ciment); **reinforced c.,** béton armé; ciment armé; **c. mixer,** malaxeur *m* béton; bétonnière *f*; (*of new town*) **c. jungle,** forêt *f* de béton.

concrete² [kən'kri:t] **1.** *v.tr.* (*a*) concrétiser (une idée); (*b*) concréter, solidifier (une matière); (*c*) ['kɔnkri:t] *Civ.E:* *Const:* bétonner (une paroi, etc.). **2.** *v.i.* se solidifier. **concreting** *n.* *Civ.E:* bétonnage *m.*

concretion [kən'kri:ʃ(ə)n] *n.* *Med:* *Geol:* *etc:* concrétion *f*.

concubine ['kɔŋkjubain] *n.f.* **1.** concubine. **2.** seconde femme.

concur [kən'kə:r] *v.i.* **(concurred) 1.** (*a*) (*of events*) concourir, coïncider; (*b*) **to c. in a result,** concourir à un résultat. **2.** (*of pers.*) être d'accord **(with s.o.,** avec qn); être du même avis (que qn).

concurrence [kən'kʌrəns] *n.* **1.** (*a*) concours *m* (de circonstances); coopération *f* (de personnes); (*b*) simultanéité *f*. **2.** (*of pers.*) (*a*) accord *m*, concours; (*b*) assentiment *m*, consentement *m* (**in,** à).

concurrent [kən'kʌrənt] *a.* **1.** (*a*) concourant; *Mth:* **c. lines,** lignes concourantes; (*b*) (*in time*) simultané; *Jur:* **two c. sentences,** confusion *f* de deux peines; (*c*) **c. cause,** cause contribuante. **2.** concordant, d'accord; **c. views,** des opinions concordantes. **-ly** *adv.* concurremment (**with,** avec); *Jur:* **the two sentences to run c.,** avec confusion des deux peines.

concuss [kən'kʌs] *v.tr.* (*a*) ébranler, secouer (qch.); (*b*) *Med:* commotionner (le cerveau).

concussion [kən'kʌʃ(ə)n] *n.* secousse *f*, choc *m*; *Med:* commotion (cérébrale); **suffering from c.,** commotionné; *Artil:* **c. fuse,** fusée percutante.

condemn [kən'dem] *v.tr.* **1.** condamner; (*a*) **to c. s.o. to death,** condamner qn à (la) mort; (*b*) **to be condemned to sth., to do sth.,** être condamné à qch., à faire qch. **2.** déclarer (qch.) non utilisable; *Mil:* réformer (du matériel); **the bridge has been condemned as unsafe,** le pont a été fermé à la circulation à cause de son état dangereux; **these slums have been condemned (as unfit for habitation),** ces taudis ont été condamnés à être démolis. **3.** censurer, blâmer (qn, une politique, etc.); condamner (un abus, etc.). **condemned** *a.* **c. man,** condamné *m*; **c. cell,** cellule *f* des condamnés.

condemnation [kɔndem'neiʃ(ə)n] *n.* **1.** condamnation *f* (d'un coupable). **2.** censure *f*, blâme *m*. **3.** *Mil:* réforme *f* (du matériel).

condensation [kɔnden'seiʃ(ə)n] *n.* **1.** *Ph:* *Ch:* *Meteor:* *etc:* condensation *f* (d'un gaz, d'un liquide, d'un discours, etc.). **2.** liquide condensé.

condense [kən'dens] **1.** *v.tr.* (*a*) condenser (un gaz, un liquide, etc.); serrer (son style); concentrer (un produit); **to c. a chapter into a single paragraph,** condenser, un chapitre en un seul paragraphe; (*b*) concentrer (un faisceau de rayons). **2.** *v.i.* se condenser. **condensed** *a.* (lait) concentré, condensé. **condensing** *n.* condensation *f*.

condenser [kən'densər] *n.* **1.** (*a*) *Mch:* *Gasm:* *etc:* condenseur *m*; **surface c.,** condenseur par surface; (*b*) *Nau:* **freshwater c.,** distillateur *m*. **2.** *El:* condensateur *m*.

condescend [kɔndi'send] *v.i.* **1.** (*a*) condescendre (**to sth., to do sth.,** à qch., à faire qch); (*b*) s'abaisser, descendre (à, jusqu'à, faire qch.). **2.** se montrer condescendant (**to s.o.,** envers qn). **condescending** *a.* (air, sourire) condescendant. **condescendingly** *adv.* d'une manière condescendante; avec condescendance.

condescension [kɔndi'senʃ(ə)n] *n.* condescendance *f* (**to,** envers, pour).

condiment ['kɔndimənt] *n.* condiment *m*; assaisonnement *m*; **c. set,** ménagère *f*.

condisciple [kɔndi'saipl] *n.* condisciple *m.*

condition¹ [kən'diʃ(ə)n] *n.* condition *f*. **1. to impose conditions on s.o.,** (im)poser des conditions à qn; **conditions of sale,** conditions de vente; **conditions of a contract,** stipulations *fpl* d'un contrat; **on c. that**

. . ., à (la) condition que . . .; **under these conditions,** dans ces conditions. **2.** (*a*) état *m*, situation *f*; état d'entretien (du matériel, etc.); **the c. of the workers,** la situation des travailleurs; **working conditions,** conditions de travail (dans une usine); (*of machine*) **normal working conditions,** régime *m* de marche normal; **weather conditions,** conditions atmosphériques; **road conditions,** l'état des routes; **in good c.,** en bon état; **in bad c., in a poor c.,** en mauvais état; (*of person*) **to keep oneself in c.,** se maintenir en forme; **I'm out of c.,** je ne suis pas en forme; **horse in c.,** cheval *m* en chair, en condition; (*b*) état (civil). **3.** maladie *f*, affection *f* (cardiaque, etc.).

condition² *v.tr.* **1. to c. to do sth.,** stipuler qu'on fasse qch. **2.** soumettre (qch.) à une condition; conditionner (qch.); **factors that c. each other,** considérations *fpl* solidaires. **3.** *Ind: Com:* (*a*) conditionner (la soie, la laine, etc.); (*b*) vérifier l'état (d'une marchandise). **4.** *Psy:* conditionner (un sujet). **conditioned** *a.* **1. air c.,** (salle) climatisée. **2.** *Psy:* **c. reflex,** réflexe conditionné. **3.** (*of proposition, etc.*) conditionné. **conditioning** *n.* **1.** (*a*) conditionnement *m* (des textiles, etc.); (*b*) **air c.,** climatisation *f*. **2.** *Psy:* conditionnement.

conditional [kən'diʃən(ə)l] **1.** *a.* conditionnel: (*a*) **my promise was c.,** ma promesse était soumise à certaines réserves; (*b*) **c. on sth.,** dépendant de qch.; (*c*) *Gram:* (proposition) conditionnelle; **c. mood,** mode conditionnel. **2.** *n. Gram:* **in the c.,** (verbe) au conditionnel. **-ally** *adv.* conditionnellement; sous condition.

conditioner [kən'diʃənər] *n. Ind:* appareil *m* à conditionner (la soie, etc.); **air c.,** climatiseur *m*; *Toil:* **hair c.,** lotion *f* capillaire.

condole [kən'doul] *v.i.* **to c. with s.o.,** faire, exprimer, ses condoléances à qn.

condolence [kən'douləns] *n.* condoléance *f*; **to offer s.o. one's condolences,** présenter ses condoléances à qn; **letter of c.,** lettre *f* de condoléance.

condom ['kɔndəm] *n. Hyg:* condom *m*.

condominium [kɔndou'miniəm] *n.* **1.** condominium *m*. **2.** *NAm:* (*a*) copropriété *f*; (*b*) immeuble *m* en copropriété; (*c*) appartement *m* dans un immeuble en copropriété.

condone [kən'doun] *v.tr.* **1.** trouver des excuses pour (qch.); pardonner (un adultère). **2.** (*of action*) racheter (une offense).

condor ['kɔndɔːr] *n. Orn:* condor *m*.

conduce [kən'djuːs] *v.i.* (*of action or thg*) contribuer, tendre (**to,** à).

conducive [kən'djuːsiv] *a.* qui contribue (à qch.); favorable (à qch.); **this weather is not c. to work,** ce temps n'incite pas au travail.

conduct¹ ['kɔndʌkt] *n.* **1.** conduite, gestion *f*; **safe c.,** sauf-conduit *m*, *pl.* sauf-conduits. **2.** conduite (d'une personne) (**towards s.o.,** à l'égard de, avec, envers, qn); **insolent c.,** insolence *f*; **good c. certificate,** certificat *m* de moralité; *Sch:* **good c. prize,** prix *m* de sagesse; *Mil: Navy:* **c. book,** registre *m* de punitions.

conduct² [kən'dʌkt] *v.tr.* **1.** conduire, (a)mener (qn); **conducted tours,** visites guidées. **2.** (*a*) mener, gérer (des affaires); diriger (des opérations); effectuer, (une expérience); mener (une campagne) (**against s.o.,** contre qn); *Ecc:* diriger (un office); *Jur:* **to c. one's own case,** plaider soi-même sa cause; (*b*) *Mus:* diriger (un orchestre). **3. to c. oneself,** se comporter, se conduire (bien, mal). **4.** *El: Ph:* être conducteur de . . .; **substance that conducts heat, electricity,** substance conductrice de la chaleur. **conducting** *n.* **1.** conduite *f* (de touristes, etc.). **2.** conduite (d'une entreprise, etc.); art *m* de diriger (un orchestre).

conduction [kən'dʌkʃ(ə)n] *n. Ph:* conduction *f*, transmission *f* (de la chaleur, etc.); *El:* conduction.

conductivity [kɔndʌk'tiviti] *n. Ph:* conductivité *f*; **thermal c.,** conductibilité calorique.

conductor [kən'dʌktər] *n.* **1.** (*pers.*) (*a*) conducteur, -trice; (*b*) receveur *m*, (receveur-)encaisseur *m* (d'un autobus); (*c*) *Mus:* chef d'orchestre. **2.** conducteur (de l'électricité, etc.); **c. wire,** fil *m* conducteur; **lightning c.,** paratonnerre *m*; **non c.,** non-conducteur *m*; *Rail:* **c. rail,** rail *m* conducteur.

conductress [kən'dʌktris] *n.f.* receveuse (d'un autobus).

conduit ['kɔnd(w)it] *n.* (*a*) *Hyd.E:* **c. (pipe),** conduit *m*; tuyau conducteur; (*b*) *Mch: etc:* tuyau de communication; (*c*) *El:* tube *m*.

cone [koun] *n.* **1.** (*a*) *Mth:* cône *m*; **truncated c.,** cône tronqué; (*b*) *Opt:* cône (de lumière); (*c*) *Nau: etc:* **signal c.,** cône de signalisation; (*d*) *Comest:* cornet *m* (de glace). **2.** *Geol:* cône (d'un volcan). **3.** (*a*) *Mec.E:* **driving c.,** cône de commande; (*b*) *Metall:* cône de fermeture; (*c*) *Av:* **nose c.,** cône avant. **4.** *Bot:* pomme *f*, cône (de pin); **c.-bearing,** conifère. **5.** *Anat:* cône (de la rétine).

cone-shaped ['kounʃeipt] *a.* en forme de cône, conique.

coney ['kouni] *n.* lapin *m*; **c. (skin),** peau *f* de lapin.

confab ['kɔnfæb] *n. F:* (i) colloque *m*; (ii) causerie *f*; **to have a c.,** conférer; bavarder, causer.

confection [kən'fekʃ(ə)n] *n.* **1.** confectionnement *m*, confection *f* (de qch.). **2.** (*a*) *Pharm:* confection; (*b*) *A: & NAm: Cu:* (i) friandise *f*; (ii) conserve *f*.

confectioner [kən'fekʃ(ə)nər] *n. Com:* (*a*) confiseur, -euse; **confectioner's (shop),** confiserie *f*; (*b*) pâtissier, -ière.

confectionery [kən'fekʃən(ə)ri] *n.* confiserie *f*.

confederacy [kən'fed(ə)rəsi] *n.* **1.** confédération *f* (d'États). **2.** conspiration *f*.

confederate¹ [kən'fed(ə)rət] **1.** *a.* confédéré; *U.S.Hist:* **the C. States,** les États confédérés (1860–65). **2.** *n.* (*a*) confédéré *m*; (*b*) *Jur:* complice *mf*.

confederate² [kən'fedəreit] **1.** *v.tr.* confédérer (des États); **to c. oneself with . . .,** se liguer avec . . .. **2.** *v.i.* (*a*) se confédérer (**with,** avec); (*b*) conspirer (**with,** avec; **against,** contre).

confederation [kənfedə'reiʃ(ə)n] *n.* confédération *f*.

confer [kən'fəːr] *v.* **(conferred) 1.** *v.tr.* conférer (**a title on s.o.,** un titre à qn); adjuger (une récompense à qn). **2.** *v.i.* conférer, entrer en consultation (**with s.o. on sth., about sth.,** avec qn sur qch.).

conference ['kɔnfərəns] *n.* **1.** (*a*) conférence *f* **press, news, c.,** conférence de presse; **to be in c.,** être en conférence (**with,** avec); **round-table c.,** table ronde. **2.** (*a*) congrès *m*; conférence; colloque *m*; **international c.,** congrès international; (*b*) *Pol:* **Party C.,** congrès annuel du parti.

conferment [kən'fəːmənt] *n.* collation *f* (d'un titre, d'un grade).

confer(r)ee [kɔfəː'riː] *n.* participant, -ante, à une conférence.

confess [kən'fes] *v.tr.* **1.** (*a*) confesser, avouer (une faute); **to c. that . . .,** confesser que + *ind.*; **I was wrong, I c.,** j'admets que j'ai eu tort; (*b*) *v.i.* (*of criminal*) faire des aveux; (*c*) *v.ind.tr.* **to c. to a crime,** avouer un crime; **to c. to a liking for . . .,** avouer avoir un penchant, un faible, pour . . .; **to c. to (having done) sth.,** avouer qch. **2.** *Ecc:* (*a*) confesser, se confesser de (ses péchés); **to c. (oneself),** se confesser (**to s.o.,** à qn, auprès de qn); (*b*) (*of priest*) confesser (un pénitent).

confession [kən'feʃ(ə)n] *n.* **1.** confession *f*, aveu *m* (de qch.); **to make a full c.,** faire des aveux complets;

on their own c., de leur propre aveu. **2.** *Ecc:* confession; **the seal of c.**, le secret de la confession; le secret du confessionnal; **to go to c.**, aller à confesse; se confesser; **to hear s.o.'s c.**, confesser qn. **3.** confession (de foi).

confessional [kən'feʃən(ə)l] **1.** *a.* confessionnel. **2.** *n. Ecc:* confessionnal *m*; **the secrets of the c.**, les secrets *mpl* du confessionnal.

confessor [kən'fesər] *n.* **1.** *Ecc:* personne qui se confesse. **2.** *Ecc:* (*priest*) confesseur *m.* **3.** confesseur (de sa foi); *Hist:* **Edward the C.**, Édouard le Confesseur.

confetti [kən'feti(:)] *n.pl.* confetti *m.*

confidant, *f.* **confidante** [kɔnfi'dænt] *n.* confident, -ente.

confide [kən'faid] **1.** *v.tr.* (*a*) confier (un secret) (**to s.o.**, à qn); **to c. sth. to s.o.'s care,** confier qch. à la garde de qn. **2.** *v.i.* **to c. in s.o.**, se fier à qn; se confier, à qn. **confiding** *a.* **c. nature,** caractère confiant.

confidence ['kɔnfidəns] *n.* **1.** (*a*) confiance *f* (**in,** en); **to place, put, one's c. in s.o.**, placer, mettre, sa confiance en qn; faire confiance à qn; **to have every c. in s.o.**, faire toute confiance à qn; **with complete c.**, en toute assurance; *Parl:* **vote of c.**, vote *m* de confiance; **motion of no c.**, motion *f* de censure; (*b*) assurance *f*, confiance; **with c.**, (agir, etc.) avec confiance, avec assurance. **2.** confidence *f*; **to be in s.o.'s c.**, (i) partager les secrets de qn; (ii) être dans le secret; **to take s.o. into one's c.**, se confier à qn; **in c.**, confidentiellement; en confidence. **3. to make a c. to s.o.**, faire une confidence à qn. **4. c. trick,** (i) vol *m* à l'américaine; escroquerie *f*; (ii) duperie *f*; **c. trickster,** escroc *m*; voleur *m* à l'américaine.

confident ['kɔnfidənt] *a.* assuré, sûr (**of,** de); confiant; **c. of success,** sûr de réussir; **c. hope,** ferme espoir *m*; **we are c. that . . .**, nous sommes persuadés que + *ind.* **-ly** *adv.* (*a*) avec confiance; en toute confiance; (*b*) avec assurance; d'un ton assuré.

confidential [kɔnfi'denʃ(ə)l] *a.* **1.** (avis, etc.) confidentiel. **2.** (poste) de confiance; (secrétaire) particulier; **c. agent,** homme de confiance; *Pej:* affidé *m.* **-ally** adv. confidentiellement, en confidence.

confidentiality [kɔnfidenʃi'æliti] *n.* caractère confidentiel (de qch.).

configuration [kənfigju'reiʃ(ə)n] *n.* configuration *f.*

confine [kən'fain] *v.tr.* (*a*) (r)enfermer (qn dans une prison, etc.); (*b*) (re)tenir (un malade dans son lit); **to be confined to one's room,** (être obligé de) garder la chambre; **to be confined to bed,** être alité; (*c*) **to c. oneself to sth., to doing sth.,** se borner, se limiter, s'en tenir, à qch., à faire qch.; (*d*) **confined air,** air confiné; **confined space,** espace resserré; (*e*) (*of woman*) **to be confined,** accoucher.

confinement [kən'fainmənt] *n.* **1.** emprisonnement *m*; **three months' c.**, trois mois *m* de prison *f*; **solitary c.**, régime *m* cellulaire; cellule *f.* **2.** couches *fpl*, accouchement *m.* **3.** limitation *f*, restriction *f* (**to,** à).

confines ['kɔnfainz] *n.pl. Lit:* confins *mpl* (d'un lieu, etc.).

confirm [kən'fə:m] *v.tr.* (r)affermir, assurer (son pouvoir); confirmer (qn dans une opinion). **2.** confirmer (un traité, un privilège, etc.); approuver (une nomination); entériner (une décision); valider (une élection); *Jur:* homologuer (un arrêt). **3.** (a) confirmer, corroborer (une nouvelle, des soupçons; (*b*) *Av:* **flight confirmed,** vol confirmé. **4.** *Ecc:* confirmer; donner la confirmation à (qn); **to be confirmed,** recevoir la confirmation. **confirmed** *a.* (habitude) invétérée; (ivrogne) incorrigible; (célibataire) endurci.

confirmation [kɔnfə'meiʃ(ə)n] *n.* **1.** (r)affermissement *m* (de l'autorité de qn); confirmation *f* (d'un traité, etc.); corroboration *f* (d'un témoignage, etc.); *Jur:* homologation *f*; **in c. of . . .**, à l'appui de . . .; pour confirmer . . .. **2.** *Ecc:* confirmation.

confiscate ['kɔnfiskeit] *v.tr.* confisquer (**from s.o.**, à qn).

confiscation [kɔnfis'keiʃ(ə)n] *n.* confiscation *f.*

conflagration [kɔnflə'greiʃ(ə)n] *n.* (*a*) (grand) incendie; (*b*) *Fig:* conflagration *f.*

conflict¹ ['kɔnflikt] *n.* conflit *m* (de personnes); conflit, antagonisme *m* (de lois, de sentiments, d'intérêts); **armed c.**, conflit armé; **to come into, to be in, c.**, entrer, être, en conflit (**with,** avec).

conflict² [kən'flikt] *v.i.* être en conflit, en désaccord (**with sth.**, avec qch.); **duties that c. with each other,** fonctions *fpl* incompatibles. **conflicting** *a.* opposé (**with,** à); incompatible (**with,** avec); **c. evidence,** témoignages contradictoires.

confluence ['kɔnfluəns] *n. Geog:* confluent *m*, confluence *f* (de deux cours d'eau, deux glaciers).

conform [kən'fɔ:m] **1.** *v.tr.* conformer (**sth. to sth.**, qch. à qch.). **2.** *v.i.* (*a*) se conformer (**to sth.**, à qch.); **to c. to the law,** obéir aux lois; (*b*) (*of a part*) **to c. (in shape) to another part,** être identique à une autre pièce; (*c*) *Rel. Pol: etc:* **to c.**, faire acte de soumission.

conformable [kən'fɔ:məbl] *a.* **1.** (*of thg*) conforme (**to,** à). **2.** (*of pers.*) accommodant; docile (**to,** à).

conformation [kɔnfɔ:'meiʃ(ə)n] *n.* **1.** action *f* de rendre conforme (**to,** à). **2.** conformation *f*, structure *f*; configuration *f* (des montagnes, etc.); profil *m.*

conformism [kən'fɔ:mizm] *n.* (*a*) *Rel:* conformisme *m*; (*b*) conformisme.

conformist [kən'fɔ:mist] *n.* (*a*) *Rel:* conformiste *mf*; (*b*) conformiste.

conformity [kən'fɔ:miti] *n.* **1.** conformité *f* (**to, with,** à); **in c. with . . .**, conformément à . . .; **action in c. with the law,** action *f* conforme à la loi. **2.** (*a*) *U.S:* conformisme *m*; (*b*) *Rel:* conformisme.

confound [kən'faund] *v.tr.* **1.** déconcerter, renverser (les plans de qn); réduire à rien (un espoir). **2.** bouleverser, troubler (qn). **3.** *Lit:* (*a*) mettre la confusion dans (qch.); (*b*) **to c. sth. with sth.**, confondre qch. avec qch. **4.** *F:* envoyer (qn) au diable; *Lit:* **c. him!** que le diable l'emporte! **c. it!** zut alors! **confounded** *a. F:* sacré; **you c. idiot!** espèce d'idiot!

confront [kən'frʌnt] *v.tr.* **1.** être en face, se trouver en présence, de (qn, qch.); **to be confronted by, with, a difficulty,** se trouver en face d'une difficulté. **2.** affronter, faire face à (l'ennemi, un danger); tenir tête à (l'ennemi). **3. to c. s.o. with (s.o., sth.),** confronter qn avec (des témoins, etc.); mettre qn en présence, en face, de (qch.).

confrontation [kɔnfrʌn'teiʃ(ə)n] *n.* **1.** confrontation *f* (de témoins, etc.). **2.** affrontement *m.*

confuse [kən'fju:z] *v.tr.* **1.** mêler, brouiller; mettre la confusion dans (les choses). **2.** confondre (des dates, des noms, etc.); **to c. sth. with sth., s.o. with s.o.**, confondre qch. avec qch. qn avec qn. **3.** (*a*) embrouiller (qn); **to get confused,** s'embrouiller; s'y perdre; (*b*) bouleverser, ahurir (qn); (*c*) rendre (qn) confus; **to get confused,** se troubler. **confused** *a.* **1.** (*a*) embrouillé; (esprit, conscience) trouble; (souvenir) confus; (*b*) bouleversé, ahuri; (*c*) confus, honteux. **2.** (*of thg*) confus, enchevêtré; (discours) confus; **c. voices,** voix confuses. **confusing** *a.* embrouillant; **it's very c.**, on s'y perd.

confusion [kən'fju:ʒ(ə)n] *n.* **1.** (*of pers.*) confusion *f*; **in his c. he forgot his hat,** tout confus, il a oublié son chapeau. **2.** confusion, désordre *m*, désarroi *m*; **everything was in c.**, tout était en désordre; tout était pêle-mêle; **to spread c. everywhere,** jeter partout le désordre; mettre tout en confusion. **3. c. of sth. with**

sth., confusion de qch. avec qch.; **there has been a c. of names,** il y a eu confusion de noms. **4.** mélange *m.* **5.** *Med:* état confusionnel, confusion mentale.

confutation [kɔnfjuːˈteiʃ(ə)n] *n.* réfutation *f.*

confute [kənˈfjuːt] *v.tr.* **1.** convaincre (qn) d'erreur. **2.** réfuter (un argument).

congeal [kənˈdʒiːl] **1.** *v.tr.* (*a*) congeler, geler; (*b*) coaguler; cailler (le sang); figer (l'huile, le sang). **2.** *v.i.* (*a*) se congeler; geler; (*b*) (*of oil, blood*) se figer; (*of blood*) se coaguler; (*of jelly, milk*) se prendre.

congenial [kənˈdʒiːniəl] *a.* **1.** (*a*) **c. with sth.,** du même caractère, de la même nature, que qch.; **we have c. tastes,** nous avons des goûts en commun; (*b*) (esprit) sympathique, aimable; (travail) agréable. **2.** propre, qui convient (**to,** à).

congenital [kənˈdʒenit(ə)l] *a.* (*of defect, etc.*) congénital, -aux.

conger [ˈkɔŋgər] *n. Ich:* **c. (eel),** congre *m.*

congest [kənˈdʒest] **1.** *v.tr.* (*a*) *Med:* congestionner; (*b*) encombrer, embouteiller (la circulation, les rues, etc.). **2.** *v.i.* (*a*) *Med:* se congestionner; (*b*) (*of traffic, etc.*) s'accumuler. **congested** *a.* **1.** *Med:* congestionné. **2.** (*of traffic, etc.*) encombré, embouteillé; (région) surpeuplée; (rues) encombrées; **the c. state of the roads,** l'encombrement *m* des routes.

congestion [kənˈdʒestʃ(ə)n] *n.* **1.** *Med:* congestion *f* (cérébrale, pulmonaire). **2.** (*a*) encombrement *m* (de circulation, etc.); embouteillage *m*; **the new road will relieve the c. in the town,** la nouvelle route va décongestionner la ville; (*b*) (*overcrowding*) surpeuplement *m.*

conglomerate¹ [kənˈglɔmərət] *n.* (*a*) *Geol:* conglomérat *m*, aggloméré *m*; (*b*) *Pol.Ec:* conglomérat.

conglomerate² [kənˈglɔməreit] **1.** *v.tr.* conglomérer. **2.** *v.i.* se conglomérer; *Geol:* s'agglomérer.

conglomeration [kənglɔməˈreiʃ(ə)n] *n.* conglomération *f*; agrégation *f* (de roches, etc.).

Congo [ˈkɔŋgou] *Pr. n.* **1.** *Geog:* **the (River) C.,** le Congo. **2.** *Geog: Hist:* **the (Belgian) C.,** le Congo (belge).

congratulate [kənˈgrætjuleit] *v.tr.* **to c. s.o. on sth.,** féliciter qn de qch.; **I c. you,** je vous en félicite; (je vous en fais) mes compliments; **to c. oneself on sth., on having done sth.,** se féliciter de qch., d'avoir fait qch.

congratulation [kəngrætjuˈleiʃ(ə)n] *n.* félicitation *f*; **congratulations!** je vous en félicite! félicitations!

congratulatory [kənˈgrætjuleitəri] *a.* (lettre, etc.) de félicitation(s).

congregate [ˈkɔŋgrigeit] **1.** *v.tr.* rassembler, réunir. **2.** *v.i.* se rassembler, s'assembler.

congregation [kɔŋgriˈgeiʃ(ə)n] *n.* **1.** rassemblement *m.* **2.** (*a*) (*in church*) assemblée *f* des fidèles; assistance *f*; (*b*) *Sch:* (*at Oxford, Cambridge*) assemblée générale (des professeurs, etc).

congregational [kɔŋgriˈgeiʃən(ə)l] *a. Ecc:* **1.** en assemblée; **c. worship,** culte public. **2. the C. Church,** l'Église *f* congrégationaliste.

congress [ˈkɔŋgres] *n.* (*a*) congrès *m* (de l'enseignement, d'une Église, d'hommes d'État, etc.); (*b*) *Parl:* (*in Fr. & U.S.*) Congrès (du Sénat et de la Chambre); (*c*) *U.S:* session *f* du Congrès.

congressional [kɔŋˈgreʃən(ə)l] *a.* (réunion, etc.) du congrès; congressionnel.

congressman, -woman; *pl.* **-men, -women** [ˈkɔŋgresmæn, -wumən; -men, -wimin] *n. Pol: esp. U.S:* membre *m* du Congrès; congressiste *mf.*

congruent [ˈkɔŋgruənt] *a.* **1.** conforme (**with,** à). **2.** *Mth:* congruent (**with,** à); (triangles) congrus.

congruity [kɔŋˈgruiti] *n.* conformité *f* (**with,** à).

congruous [ˈkɔŋgruəs] *a.* conforme (**with,** à).

conic [ˈkɔnik] *a. Mth:* conique; **c. sections,** sections coniques.

conical [ˈkɔnik(ə)l] *a.* conique; *Mapm:* **c. projection,** projection *f* conique.

conifer [ˈkɔnifər] *n. Bot:* conifère *m.*

coniferous [kəˈnifərəs] *a. Bot:* conifère; (forêt) de conifères.

conjectural [kənˈdʒektjər(ə)l] *a.* conjectural, -aux.

conjecture¹ [kənˈdʒektjər] *n.* conjecture *f*; **to hazard a c.,** risquer une hypothèse, une supposition.

conjecture² *v.tr.* conjecturer, supposer.

conjoin [kənˈdʒɔin] **1.** *v.tr.* conjoindre. **2.** *v.i.* s'unir; se joindre ensemble; s'associer.

conjoint [ˈkɔndʒɔint] *a.* conjoint, associé. **-ly** *adv.* conjointement, ensemble.

conjugal [ˈkɔndʒug(ə)l] *a.* conjugal, -aux; **c. rights,** droits conjugaux.

conjugate¹ [ˈkɔndʒugeit] *a. Mth: Opt: Ch:* conjugué.

conjugate² **1.** *v.tr. Gram:* conjuguer (un verbe). **2.** *v.i.* (*a*) *Biol:* (*of cells*) se conjuguer; (*b*) s'unir.

conjugation [kɔndʒuˈgeiʃ(ə)n] *n.* **1.** *Gram:* conjugaison *f.* **2.** *Biol:* conjugaison, zygose *f.*

conjunct [kənˈdʒʌŋ(k)t] **1.** *a.* conjoint; associé. **2.** *n.* (*a*) associé, -ée; (*b*) chose liée (à une autre).

conjunction [kənˈdʒʌŋ(k)ʃ(ə)n] *n.* **1.** conjonction *f*; **in c. with (s.o., sth.),** conjointement, avec (qn); concurremment avec (qch.); *Astr:* **planets in c.,** planètes *fpl* en conjonction. **2.** *Gram:* conjonction.

conjunctive [kənˈdʒʌŋ(k)tiv] **1.** *a.* (tissu, etc.) conjonctif. **2.** *a. & n. Gram:* (mode) conjonctif (*m*).

conjunctivitis [kəndʒʌŋ(k)tiˈvaitis] *n. Med:* conjonctivite *f.*

conjuncture [kənˈdʒʌŋ(k)tjər] *n.* conjoncture *f*, circonstance *f.*

conjuration [kɔndʒu(ə)ˈreiʃ(ə)n] *n.* conjuration *f.*

conjure *v.* **1.** [kənˈdʒuər] *v.tr.* conjurer (**s.o. to do sth.,** qn de faire qch.). **2.** [ˈkʌndʒər] (*a*) *v.tr.* **to c. up,** évoquer (un esprit, des idées, etc.); (*b*) *v.i.* faire des tours de passe-passe. **conjuring** *n.* **1. c. up,** évocation *f* (des souvenirs, etc.). **2.** prestidigitation *f*; **c. trick,** tour *m* de passe-passe.

conjurer, conjuror [ˈkʌndʒərər] *n.* **1.** prestidigitateur *m*; illusionniste *mf.*

conk¹ [kɔŋk] *n. P:* **1.** nez *m*, blair *m*, pif *m.* **2.** tête *f*, caboche *f.* **3.** coup *m*, gnon *m.*

conk² *v.i. F:* **to c. out,** (*a*) (*of machinery, etc.*) tomber en panne; (*b*) (*of pers.*) (i) s'évanouir, (ii) mourir; (*c*) *U.S:* s'endormir.

conker [ˈkɔŋkər] *n.* marron *m* d'Inde; *Games:* **conkers,** jeu consistant à démolir le marron de son adversaire.

connect¹ [kəˈnekt] **1.** *v.tr.* (*a*) (re)lier, (ré)unir; rattacher (**sth. with, to, sth.,** qch. à qch.); mettre en communication (avec); *Mec.E: etc:* embrayer (deux arbres); joindre (des tuyaux); *El:* interconnecter (des circuits); **connected by telephone,** relié par téléphone; *Tp:* **to c. two subscribers,** mettre deux abonnés en communication; (*b*) associer (**s.o., sth., with s.o., sth.,** qn, qch., avec qn, à qch.); **to be connected with . . .,** (*of pers.*) avoir des relations, des rapports, avec . . .; (*of thg*) se rattacher, se rapporter, à . . .; **questions connected with a subject,** questions relatives à un sujet; (*c*) (*of pers.*) **to be connected with a family,** être allié à, avec, une famille. **2.** *v.i.* (*a*) se lier, se relier (**with,** à); se réunir, se raccorder; *Trans:* **to c. with a train, a flight,** faire correspondance, assurer la correspondance, avec un train, un vol; (*b*) *F:* (*of blow*) atteindre son but. **connected** *a.* **1.** (*a*) (discours) suivi, cohérent; (*b*) **closely c.,** (sciences, faits, etc.) connexes; (faits, événements) étroitement liés. **2.** (*of pers.*) **to be well c.,** être bien apparenté. **3.** *Bot: Jur:* connexe. **connecting** *a.* (*a*) **c. link,** (i) trait *m* d'union (**between . . . and,** entre . . . et); (ii) fausse maille (de chaîne); **c. wire,** fil *m* de connexion; **c. pipe,** tuyau *m* de communication, de jonction; (*b*)

Trans: **c. flight, train,** correspondance *f.*

connect² *n. Cmptr:* connexion *f*; **c. time,** durée *f* (d'établissement) de la connexion.

connection [kə'nekʃ(ə)n] *n.* **1.** rapport *m*, liaison *f* (des choses); connexion *f*, suite *f* (des idées); **close c. between two facts,** relation étroite entre deux faits; **in c. with . . .,** à propos de . . ., relatif à . . .; **in this c.,** à ce propos, à cet égard. **2. c. of s.o. with s.o.,** relations *fpl*, rapports *mpl* de qn avec qn; **to form a c. with s.o.,** établir des rapports avec qn; **I have broken off all c. with him,** j'ai cessé toutes relations avec lui; **to open up a business c. with a firm,** entrer en relations (d'affaires) avec une maison; **to have good, the right, connections,** avoir de bonnes relations. **3.** (*a*) parenté *f*; apparentage *m*; **to form a c. by marriage with a good family,** s'allier à, avec, une bonne famille; (*b*) parent, -ente; (*by marriage*) allié, -ée; **he, she, is a c. of mine,** c'est un(e) de mes parent(e)s. **4.** *Ecc:* secte *f*; **the Methodist c.,** la secte méthodiste. **5.** *Com:* clientèle *f*; **a wide c.,** une belle clientèle. **6.** *Trans:* correspondance *f*; train, avion, bateau, correspondant; **I missed my c.,** j'ai manqué, *F:* raté, ma correspondance. **7.** (*a*) *Mec.E: etc:* connexion; assemblage *m*, raccordement *m* (de tuyaux, fils, etc.); accouplement *m*, embrayage *m*, engrenage *m* (des organes d'une machine); (*b*) *El:* raccordement, connexion; branchement *m*; **wrong c.,** (i) *El:* fausse connexion; (ii) *Tp:* fausse communication; (*c*) *Cmptr:* connexion, liaison *f.* **8.** (*a*) raccord *m*, attache *f* (entre deux tuyaux, fils, etc.); **flexible c.,** raccord souple; (*b*) *El:* contact *m*; prise *f* (de courant); **earth,** *U.S:* **ground, c.,** (i) prise de terre; (ii) *Aut: etc:* mise *f* à la masse.

connexion [kə'nekʃ(ə)n] *n.* = CONNECTION.

conniption [kə'nipʃ(ə)n] *n. U.S.: F:* crise *f* de rage.

connivance [kə'naivəns] *n.* connivence *f*; **c. at, in, a crime,** complicité *f* dans un crime; **to be in c. with s.o.,** être d'intelligence avec qn.

connive [kə'naiv] *v.i.* **to c. at (sth.),** fermer les yeux sur (un abus, etc.); être de connivence dans (un crime).

connoisseur [kɔne'sɜːr] *n.* (bon) connaisseur (**of, in,** en); **to be a c.,** se connaître (**of,** en).

connotation [kɔnou'teiʃ(ə)n] *n.* (*a*) connotation *f* (d'un terme); (*b*) signification *f* (d'un mot).

connote [kɔ'nout] *v.tr.* **1.** *Log:* connoter. **2.** comporter (des conséquences, etc.). **3.** signifier.

connubial [kə'njuːbiəl] *a.* conjugal, -aux.

conquer ['kɔŋkər] *v.tr.* **1.** conquérir (un pays, l'amour de qn). **2.** vaincre, surmonter (une difficulté, sa timidité); dompter (ses passions); **Everest was conquered in 1953,** la première ascension du Mont Everest a eu lieu en 1953. **conquering** *a.* **1.** conquérant. **2.** victorieux.

conqueror ['kɔŋk(ə)rər] *n.* **1.** conquérant *m* (d'un pays); *Hist:* **(William) the C.,** Guillaume le Conquérant **2.** vainqueur *m.*

conquest ['kɔŋkwest] *n.* **1.** conquête *f*; *Hist:* **the (Norman) C.,** la conquête de l'Angleterre (1066). **2.** (pays, etc. de) conquête; **to make a c. of s.o.,** faire la conquête de qn.

consanguine [kɔn'sæŋgwin] *a.* consanguin.

consanguinity [kɔnsæŋ'gwiniti] *n.* consanguinité *f.*

conscience ['kɔnʃəns] *n.* conscience *f*; **to have an easy, a clear, c.,** avoir la conscience tranquille; **to have a guilty, bad, c.,** avoir une mauvaise conscience; **to have sth. on one's c.,** avoir qch. (qui pèse) sur la conscience; **c. money,** somme restituée par remords de conscience; **to have no c.,** n'avoir point de conscience; **a matter of c.,** une affaire de conscience; **liberty of c.,** liberté *f* de conscience; **one cannot in all c. believe that . . .,** on ne peut pas raisonnablement croire que . . ..

conscience-stricken ['kɔnʃənsstrik(ə)n] *a.* pris de remords.

conscientious [kɔnʃi'enʃəs] *a.* **1.** (travailleur, travail) consciencieux; (travail) fait en conscience. **2.** (scrupule) de conscience; **c. objector,** objecteur *m* de conscience; **c. objection,** objection *f* de conscience. **-ly** *adv.* consciencieusement.

conscious ['kɔnʃəs] *a.* **1.** (*a*) **to be c. of sth.,** avoir conscience de qch.; être conscient de qch.; **to become c. of sth.,** s'apercevoir de qch.; (*b*) (mouvement, refus, etc.) conscient; (*c*) **fashion c.,** qui suit de près la mode; **health c.,** qui se préoccupe de sa santé; (*d*) *Phil:* conscient; **man as a c. being,** l'homme en tant qu'être conscient. **2. to be c.,** avoir sa connaissance; être en pleine connaissance; **to become c.,** reprendre connaissance. **-ly** *adv.* consciemment; sciemment.

consciousness ['kɔnʃəsnis] *n.* **1.** (*a*) conscience *f*, sentiment *m* (**of,** de); (*b*) sentiment intime. **2.** *Phil:* conscience. **3.** connaissance *f*; **to lose c.,** perdre connaissance; s'évanouir; **to regain c.,** reprendre connaissance; revenir à soi.

conscript¹ ['kɔnskript] *Mil:* **1.** *a.* conscrit, appelé sous les drapeaux. **2.** *n.* conscrit *m.*

conscript² [kən'skript] *v.tr.* enrôler, engager, (des troupes) par la conscription.

conscription [kən'skripʃ(ə)n] *n. Mil:* conscription *f.*

consecrate ['kɔnsikreit] *v.tr.* **1.** *Ecc:* consacrer (une église, etc.); bénir (le pain, etc.); sacrer (un roi, un évêque). **2. to consecrate one's life to sth.,** consacrer sa vie, se vouer, à qch. **consecrated** *a.* (*of church, etc.*) consacré; (*of bread*) bénit; **in c. ground,** en terre sainte, bénite.

consecration [kɔnsi'kreiʃ(ə)n] *n.* **1.** consécration *f* (d'une église, etc.); bénédiction *f* (d'un drapeau); sacre *m* (d'un roi, d'un évêque). **2. the c. of one's life to sth.,** le dévouement de sa vie à qch.

consecutive [kən'sekjutiv] *a.* **1.** consécutif; **on three c. days,** trois jours de suite. **2.** *Gram:* **c. clause,** proposition consécutive. **-ly** *adv.* consécutivement; de suite.

consensus [kən'sensəs] *n.* consensus *m*, unanimité *f* (d'opinions, de témoignages, etc.); accord *m.*

consent¹ [kən'sent] *n.* consentement *m*, assentiment *m*; **to give one's c. to sth.,** donner son consentement à qch.; **by common c.,** de l'aveu de tout le monde; **by mutual c.,** de gré à gré; (divorce) par consentement mutuel; *Jur:* **age of c.,** âge *m* nubile.

consent² *v.i.* **to c. to sth., to do sth.,** consentir à qch., à faire qch.; **I c.,** j'y consens. **consenting** *a.* (parties) consentantes; (adulte) consentant.

consequence ['kɔnsikwəns] *n.* **1.** conséquence *f*; suites *fpl*; **the c. is that . . .,** il en résulte, il s'ensuit, que . . .; **in c.,** par conséquent; **in c. of . . .,** par suite de . . .; **to take the consequences,** accepter les conséquences; **(game of) consequences,** (jeu *m* des) petits papiers. **2.** importance *f*; conséquence; **it is of no c.,** cela n'a pas d'importance; cela ne fait rien; **he is of no c.,** il ne compte pas; **a man of c.,** un homme d'importance.

consequent *a.* **1.** (*a*) résultant; **c. upon sth.,** qui est la conséquence de qch.; qui résulte de qch. **2.** conséquent conséquent; **to be c.,** être logique. **-ly 1.** *adv. & conj.* par conséquent; donc. **2.** *adv.* logiquement.

consequential [kɔnsi'kwenʃ(ə)l] *a.* **1.** conséquent (**to,** à); dû (**to,** à); consécutif (**to,** à); *Jur:* **c. effects,** répercussions *fpl* (d'une action); **c. damages,** dommages indirects. **2.** (*of pers.*) important; plein d'importance; **to have a c. manner,** faire l'important.

conservancy [kən'sɜːvənsi] *n.* **1.** commission *f* de conservation (d'une forêt, d'un fleuve, etc.). **2.** conservation *f*, protection *f* (des forêts, etc.).

conservation [kɔnsə(:)'veiʃ(ə)n] *n.* conservation *f*; **c. of energy,** conservation de l'énergie.

conservationist [kɔnsə'veiʃənist] *n.* partisan, -ane, de la conservation (de l'environnement).

conservatism [kən'sə:vətizm] *n. Pol:* conservatisme *m.*

conservative [kən'sə:vətiv] **1.** *a.* (*a*) préservatif; conservateur, -trice; -(*b*) (evaluation) prudente; **at a c. estimate,** au minimum; au bas mot; (*c*) *Pol:* conservateur, -trice. **2.** *n. Pol:* conservateur, - trice. **-ly** *adv.* **it was c. estimated . . .,** selon des estimations modérées . . ..

conservatoire [kən'sə:vətwɑ:r] *n.* conservatoire *m* (de musique).

conservatory [kɔn'sə:vətri] *n.* (*a*) *Hort:* serre *f*; (*b*) = CONSERVATOIRE.

conserve¹ [kən'sə:v] *n. Cu:* confiture *f*, conserve *f* (de fruits).

conserve² *v.tr.* conserver, préserver (un monument ancien, etc.).

consider [kən'sidər] *v.tr.* **1.** (*a*) considérer (une question); songer à, réfléchir à (qch.); interroger (les faits); envisager (une possibilité); **I will c. it,** j'y réfléchirai; **considered opinion,** opinion réfléchie; **all things considered,** tout bien considéré; tout compte fait; (*b*) prendre (une offre) en considération; étudier (une proposition); **the jury retired to c. its verdict,** le jury se retira pour délibérer. **3.** (*a*) avoir égard à (la sensibilité de qn), regarder à (la dépense); **he is a man to be considered,** c'est un homme dont il faut tenir compte; (*b*) **when one considers that . . .,** quand on pense que . . .. **4.** (*a*) **c. it as done,** tenez cela pour fait; **c. yourself dismissed,** tenez-vous pour congédié; **to c. oneself happy,** s'estimer heureux; **I c. it my duty to . . .,** j'estime qu'il est de mon devoir de . . .; (*b*) **we c. that he ought to do it,** à notre avis il doit le faire; (*c*) **he was considering whether to go out when . . .,** il se demandait s'il sortirait quand . . .. **considering** *prep.* eu égard à (qch.); **c. his age,** étant donné son âge; **c. the circumstances,** vu les circonstances; *conj. phr.* **c. that . . .,** vu, attendu, que . . .; **c. (that) he is so young,** étant donné qu'il est si jeune; *F:* **it's not so bad c.,** ce n'est pas si mauvais après tout, malgré tout.

considerable [kən'sid(ə)rəbl] *a.* considérable. **1.** (*a*) digne d'attention; (*b*) (*of pers.*) notable, important. **2.** grand; bonne (partie); (différence) sensible; **a c. number of . . .,** un nombre considérable de. **-ably** *adv.* considérablement.

considerate [kən'sidərət] *a.* **c. (towards, to, s.o.),** prévenant, plein d'égards, (pour, envers, qn); **it's very c. of you,** c'est très aimable de votre part. **-ly** *adv.* avec considération, avec prévenance.

consideration [kənsidə'reiʃ(ə)n] *n.* **1.** considération *f*; (*a*) **to take sth. into c.,** prendre qch. en considération; tenir compte de qch.; **taking all things into c.,** tout bien considéré; **in c. of . . .,** en considération de . . .; **question under c.,** question à l'étude; **to give c. to a question,** mettre une question à l'étude; **after due c.,** après mûre réflexion; toute réflexion faite; (*b*) **there is another c.,** il y a autre chose dont il faut tenir compte; **money is always the first c.,** la question d'argent vient toujours en premier; **on no c.,** à aucun prix, **money is no c.,** l'argent n'entre pas en ligne de compte. **2.** compensation *f*, rémunération *f*; *Com: etc:* **for a c.,** moyennant paiement; **he will do it for a c.,** il le fera si vous le payez. **3.** *Jur: Fin: Com:* cause *f*, provision *f* (**for,** de). **4. to have no c. for anyone,** n'avoir de considération pour personne; **out of c. for s.o.,** par égard, pour qn; **to treat s.o. with c.,** ménager qn.

consign [kən'sain] *v.tr.* **1.** *Com:* consigner, expédier (des marchandises) (**to s.o.,** à qn); envoyer (des marchandises) en consignation (à qn). **2.** confier, remettre. (**sth. to s.o.'s care,** qch. à qn); **to c. a body to the grave,** livrer un corps à la tombe.

consignee [kɔnsai'ni:] *n.* consignataire *mf.*

consignment [kən'sainmənt] *n.* **1.** (*a*) envoi *m.* expédition *f* (de marchandises); **c. note,** (i) bordereau *m.* de consignation; (ii) *Rail:* récépissé *m*; (*b*) *Com:* **on c.,** en consignation; **to send s.o. goods on c.,** livrer à qn une marchandise en dépôt permanent. **2.** (*goods*) arrivage *m* (de marchandises); **your c. of books has duly arrived,** votre envoi de livres nous est bien parvenu.

consignor [kən'sainər] *n. Com:* consignateur, -trice, expéditeur, -trice.

consist [kən'sist] *v.i.* (*a*) **to c. of sth.,** consister en, se composer de, qch.; **inheritance consisting of a house,** héritage *m* consistant en une maison; (*b*) **to c. in sth.,** consister à qch.

consistency [kən'sistənsi] *n.* **1.** consistance *f* (d'un liquide, d'un solide). **2.** uniformité *f* (de conduite, etc.); cohérence *f* (d'un raisonnement, etc.); logique *f* (dans les idées); **to lack c.,** manquer de suite.

consistent [kən'sistənt] *a.* **1.** (*a*) (*of pers.*) conséquent; (*of conduct, etc.*) uniforme; (*of reasoning, etc.*) cohérent; (*b*) *Cmptr:* cohérent. **2.** compatible, d'accord (**with,** avec); **this action is not c. with his character,** cette action n'est pas en harmonie avec son caractère. **-ly** *adv.* **1.** logiquement; uniformément. **2. c. with,** conformément à, (des principes, etc.). **3.** régulièrement.

consistory [kən'sistəri] *n. Ecc:* **1.** consistoire (pontifical). **2. C. Court,** tribunal *m* ecclésiastique.

consolation [kɔnsə'leiʃ(ə)n] *n.* consolation *f*; **words of c.,** paroles consolatrices; **that's one c.,** c'est déjà une consolation; **c. prize,** prix *m* des perdants.

console¹ ['kɔnsoul] *n.* **1.** *Arch:* console *f* (d'un balcon, etc.); **c. table,** (table *f*) console. **2.** (*a*) console (d'orgue); (*b*) meuble *m* pour radio, télévision; (*c*) *Av:* tableau *m* de bord; (*d*) *Elcs:* console; *Cmptr:* **c. (desk), control c.,** pupitre *m* de commande.

console² [kən'soul] *v.tr.* consoler (**s.o. for a loss,** qn d'une perte). **consoling** *a.* consolateur, -trice.

consolidate [kən'sɔlideit] **1.** *v.tr.* (*a*) consolider, (r)affermir (des fondements, etc.); *Mil: etc:* consolider (une position); (*b*) consolider, unir (deux envois, deux entreprises, etc.); (*c*) *Fin:* consolider (une dette). **2.** *v.i.* se consolider. **consolidated** *a.* consolidé; *Fin:* **c. annuities,** fonds consolidés.

consolidation [kənsɔli'deiʃ(ə)n] *n.* **1.** consolidation *f*, (r)affermissement *m* (de fondements, de pouvoir, etc.); tassement *m* (de l'opinion publique). **2.** consolidation, unification *f* (des lois, de la dette publique, etc.); *Fin:* regroupement (d'actions).

consols ['kɔnsɔlz, kən'sɔlz] *n.pl. Fin:* (fonds) consolidés *mpl.*

consonance ['kɔnsənəns] *n.* **1.** *Mus: Ling:* consonance *f*. **2.** accord, conformité *f* (d'idées, etc.).

consonant ['kɔnsənənt] *n. Ling:* consonne *f.*

consort¹ ['kɔnsɔ:t] *n.* **1.** époux, -ouse; **prince c., queen c.,** prince consort, reine consort(e). **2.** *Nau:* **to sail in c.,** naviguer de conserve.

consort² [kən'sɔ:t] *v.i.* (*of pers.*) **to c. with s.o.,** s'associer avec qn; frayer avec qn; fréquenter qn.

consortium [kən'sɔ:tiəm] *n. Com: Fin:* consortium *m.*

conspicuous [kən'spikjuəs] *a.* **1.** (*a*) visible, apparent, manifeste; **in a c. position,** bien en évidence; *F:* **to be c. by one's absence,** briller par son absence; (*b*) (*of monument, landmark*) voyant. **2.** remarquable, frappant; **c. gallantry,** acte *m* de bravoure insigne; **to make oneself c.,** se faire remarquer; se signaler (**by, through,** par). **-ly** *adv.* **1.** visiblement, manifestement. **2.** remarquablement.

conspicuousness [kən'spikjuəsnis] *n.* **1.** évidence *f*, visibilité *f* (de qch.); éclat *m* (d'un uniforme, etc.). **2.** caractère *m* insigne (d'une action).
conspiracy [kən'spirəsi] *n.* **1.** conjuration *f*, complot *m*; **c. of silence,** conspiration du silence. **2.** *Jur:* entente délictueuse.
conspirator [kən'spirətər] *n.* conspirateur, -trice; conjuré, -ée.
conspiratorial [kənspirə'tɔːriəl] *a.* (air) de conspirateur.
conspire [kən'spaiər] *v.i.* (*a*) conspirer (**against,** contre); **to c. to do sth.,** comploter de faire qch.; (*b*) (*of events, etc.*) concourir, conspirer (à produire un effet); **everything conspired to make him late,** tout a contribué à le mettre en retard.
constable ['kʌŋstəbl] *n.* **(police) c.** = (i) agent *m* de police; (ii) gendarme *m*; (iii) (*in rural areas*) garde *m* champêtre; **special c.** = supplétif *m*; **chief c.** = commissaire (central) de police.
constabulary [kən'stæbjuləri] *n. coll.* la police; **the county c.** = la gendarmerie.
constancy ['kɔnstənsi] *n.* **1.** (*a*) constance *f*, fermeté *f* (de caractère); (*b*) fidélité *f* (d'un ami). **2.** (*a*) constance (de la température); (*b*) régularité *f* (du vent, etc.).
constant ['kɔnstənt] **1.** *a.* (*a*) constant; (équilibre) stable; (pression) invariable; (*b*) incessant, continuel; (soin, travail) assidu, soutenu; **through c. repetition,** à force de répéter; (*c*) (ami) fidèle. **2.** *n. Mth: Ph:* constante *f*; **time c.,** constante de temps. **-ly** *adv.* constamment; continuellement.
constellation [kɔnste'leiʃ(ə)n] *n.* constellation *f*.
consternation [kɔnstə'neiʃ(ə)n] *n.* consternation *f*; atterrement *m*; **look of c.,** air consterné; **they looked at each other in c.,** ils se regardaient atterrés.
constipate ['kɔnstipeit] *v.tr. Med:* constiper; **to be constipated,** être constipé. **constipating** *a.* constipant.
constipation [kɔnsti'peiʃ(ə)n] *n. Med:* constipation *f*.
constituency [kən'stitjuənsi] *n.* **1.** électeurs *mpl* (d'une circonscription. **2.** circonscription électorale.
constituent [kən'stitjuənt] **1.** *a.* constituant, constitutif, composant. **2.** *n.* (*a*) élément constitutif; composant *m*; (*b*) *Ling:* constituant *m*. **3.** *n.* (*pers.*) (*a*) *Jur:* commettant *m*; (*b*) *Pol:* mandant *m* (d'un député); **my constituents,** mes électeurs.
constitute ['kɔnstitjut] *v.tr.* **1.** (*a*) constituer (un tribunal); **to c. a threat to.,** constituer une menace pour . . .; (*b*) **to c. s.o. arbitrator,** constituer qn arbitre. **2.** faire (le bonheur de qn); **factors that c. an offence,** éléments constitutifs d'un délit.
constitution [kɔnsti'tjuːʃ(ə)n] *n.* **1.** constitution *f*, composition *f* (de qch.) **2.** constitution (du corps); tempérament *m*; **to have a strong, an iron, c.,** avoir une bonne constitution, une santé de fer. **3.** *Pol:* constitution (d'un État).
constitutional [kɔnsti'tjuːʃən(ə)l] **1.** *a.* (*a*) (monarque, régime) constitutionnel; (*b*) *Med:* (affection) diathésique. **2.** *n.* (petite) promenade *f*. **-ally** *adv.* **1.** *Pol:* constitutionellement. **2.** par tempérament; **c. lazy,** paresseux par tempérament.
constitutive [kən'stitjutiv] *a.* constitutif; **c. elements,** éléments constitutifs.
constrain [kən'strein] *v.tr.* **1. to c. s.o. to do sth.,** contraindre, forcer, qn à, de, faire qch.; **to find oneself constrained to do sth.,** se voir dans l'obligation de faire qch. **2.** (*a*) (*of clothing, etc.*) gêner (les mouvements); (*b*) retenir (qn) de force; contenir (qn). **constrained** *a.* (air) gêné; (voix) forcée; (sourire), embarrassé.
constraint [kən'streint] *n.* **1.** (*a*) contrainte *f*; (*b*) *Jur: etc:* coercition *f*; **to put s.o. under c.,** retenir qn de force. **2.** (*a*) (*of manner*) gêne *f*, contrainte; (*b*) retenue *f*; **without c.,** dégagé.
constrict [kən'strikt] *v.tr.* **1.** resserrer, étrangler, rétrécir (une ouverture). **2.** serrer, gêner (le corps, etc.).
constriction [kən'strikʃ(ə)n] *n.* resserrement *m*, rétrécissement *m*; *Med: Physiol:* constriction *f*.
constrictor [kən'striktər] *n.* **1.** *Anat:* (muscle) constricteur (*m*). **2.** *Rept:* **boa c.,** boa constricteur.
construct [kən'strʌkt] *v.tr.* construire (une machine, un édifice, etc.); confectionner, (un roman); **well, badly, constructed,** (phrases) bien, mal, agencées; (pièce de théâtre) bien, mal, charpentée.
construction [kən'strʌkʃ(ə)n] *n.* **1.** (*a*) construction *f* (d'un bâtiment, d'une machine, etc.); **under c.,** en (cours de) construction; **c. site,** chantier *m* de construction; (*b*) manière *f* dont une machine, etc., a été réalisée; **compact c.,** réalisation peu encombrante. **2.** (*thing constructed*) construction; édifice *m*; **all-metal c.,** construction entièrement métallique. **3.** (*a*) *Gram: etc:* construction (d'une phrase, etc.); (*b*) interprétation *f* (d'une action, etc.); **to put a good, bad, c. on s.o.'s words, actions,** interpréter en bien, en mal, les paroles, actions, de qn; **to put another c. on sth.,** interpréter qch. d'une autre façon.
constructional [kən'strʌkʃən(ə)l] *a.* (défaut) de construction; **c. engineering,** construction *f* mécanique.
constructive [kən'strʌktiv] *a.* **1.** constructif; (esprit) créateur; **c. criticism,** critique constructive. **2.** *Ind:* constructeur, -trice. **3.** *Jur:* par interprétation; par déduction. **-ly** *adv.* d'une manière constructive.
constructor [kən'strʌktər] *n.* constructeur *m*.
construe [kən'struː] *v.tr.* **1.** *O:* (*a*) *Sch:* analyser, décomposer (une phrase); (*b*) *Gram:* **preposition construed with the dative,** préposition qui gouverne le datif. **2.** interpréter (les paroles de qn).
consul ['kɔns(ə)l] *n.* **1.** *Rom. & Fr.Hist:* consul *m*. **2.** *Dipl:* consul; **c. general,** consul général.
consular ['kɔnsjulər] *a.* consulaire.
consulate ['kɔnsjulət] *n.* **1.** (*a*) *Rom.Hist:* consulat *m*; (*b*) *Fr.Hist:* **the C.,** le Consulat (1799–1804). **2.** *Dipl:* consulat; **C. General,** Consulat Général.
consult [kən'sʌlt] **1.** *v.tr.* (*a*) consulter (**s.o. on, about, sth.,** qn sur qch.); consulter (un dictionnaire); (*b*) consulter (ses intérêts); pourvoir à (son propre salut). **2.** *v.i.* consulter (avec qn); **to c. together,** se consulter. **consulting 1.** *a.* (médecin) consultant; (ingénieur) conseil. **2.** *n. Med: etc:* consultation *f*; **c. room,** cabinet *m* de consultation.
consultancy [kən'sʌltənsi] *n.* **1.** *Med:* **to be appointed to a c.,** être nommé médecin, chirurgien, consultant. **2.** *Ind:* **c. firm,** cabinet *m* d'experts-conseils.
consultant [kən'sʌltənt] *n.* (*a*), chirurgien consultant; (*b*) *Ind: etc:* expert-conseil *m*, *pl.* experts-conseils; **engineering c.,** ingénieur *m* conseil; **management c.,** conseiller *m*, ingénieur conseil, en organisation; (*c*) **beauty c.,** (i) esthéticien, (ienne; (ii) visagiste *mf*.
consultation [kɔnsəl'teiʃ(ə)n] *n.* **1.** consultation *f* (d'un dictionnaire, etc.). **2.** (*a*) consultation, délibération *f*; **to hold a c.,** délibérer, conférer; (*b*) *Jur:* consultation.
consultative [kən'sʌltətiv] *a.* consultatif.
consume [kən'sjuːm] **1.** *v.tr.* (*a*) (*of fire*) consumer, dévorer (un bâtiment, etc.); (*b*) consommer (des vivres); (*c*) **engine that consumes a ton of coal per hour,** machine *f* qui brûle une tonne de charbon par heure; (*d*) (i) perdre, (ii) passer (sa vie, son temps) (**in doing sth.,** à faire qch.); (*e*) **to be consumed with (sth.),** brûler de (désir); être rongé de (jalousie); être

miné par (l'envie); (*f*) épuiser (ses vivres, ses provisions, etc.). **2.** *v.i.* se consumer. **consuming** *a.* (*of fire, passion, etc.*) dévorant.

consumer [kən'sju:mər] *n.* consommateur, -trice (d'une denrée, etc.); **gas, electricity, consumers,** abonnés *mpl* au gaz, à l'électricité; *Pol.Ec:* **c. council,** comité (consultatif) des consommateurs; **c. goods,** biens *mpl* de consommation; **c. durables,** biens de consommation durables.

consummate¹ [kən'sʌmət] *a.* (*a*) (art) consommé, achevé; **to be a c. master of one's craft,** connaître à fond son métier; (*b*) (menteur) achevé.

consummate² ['kɔnsʌmeit] *v.tr.* consommer (un mariage, etc.).

consummation [kɔnsʌ'meiʃ(ə)n] *n.* **1.** consommation *f* (d'un mariage, etc.). **2.** achèvement *m*, fin *f*. **3.** perfection *f* (d'un art, etc.). **4.** comble *m* (des désirs).

consumption [kən'sʌm(p)ʃ(ə)n] *n.* **1.** (*a*) consommation *f* (des denrées, etc.); *Pol.Ec:* **home c.,** consommation intérieure; **for current c.,** destiné à la consommation courante; **unfit for human c.,** non comestible; (*b*) consommation, dépense *f* (de chaleur, de charbon, d'essence). **2.** (*a*) destruction *f*; (*b*) *Med: O:* c., phtisie *f*.

consumptive [kən'sʌm(p)tiv] *a. & n. Med: O:* phtisique (*mf*).

contact¹ ['kɔntækt] *n.* **1.** (*a*) contact *m*; attouchement *m*, touche *f*; **point of c.,** point *m* de contact, de tangence (de deux courbes, etc.); *Opt:* **c. lens,** verre *m*, lentille *f*, de contact; *Phot:* **c. print,** épreuve *f* par contact; (*b*) rapport *m*, contact; **preliminary contacts,** prise *f* de contact; **to be in c., to come into c., with s.o.,** être, entrer, en contact, en rapport, avec qn; *Mil:* **to establish c. with the enemy,** prendre contact avec l'ennemi; (*c*) *Med:* personne *f* ayant approché un malade contagieux; (*d*) relation *f*; **I have a c. who may be able to help you,** je connais quelqu'un qui pourrait vous aider. **2.** *El: etc:* (*a*) contact; **c. to earth,** contact avec la terre; **c. breaker,** dispositif *m* de rupture; (inter)rupteur *m*; (*b*) contact, touche; **sliding c.,** contact glissant.

contact² *v.tr.* se mettre en contact, en rapport, en relation, avec (qn); *F:* contacter (qn).

contagion [kən'teidʒ(ə)n] *n.* contagion *f*.

contagious [kən'teidʒəs] *a.* **1.** (*of disease, laughter, etc.*) contagieux; (*of laughter*) communicatif. **2.** *Vet:* **c. disease,** épizootie *f*; **c. abortion,** brucellose *f*.

contagiousness [kən'teidʒəsnis] *n.* contagiosité *f*; **the c. of laughter,** la contagion du rire.

contain [kən'tein] *v.tr.* **1.** (*a*) contenir; **a jug containing only a few drops of milk,** pot *m* qui ne contenait que quelques gouttes de lait; (*b*) contenir, renfermer; **medicine that contains arsenic,** médicament *m* où il entre de l'arsenic; **ore containing a high percentage of iron,** minerai *m* à forte teneur en fer. **2.** contenir, maîtriser (son indignation); retenir (ses sentiments); contenir (l'inflation, une attaque, etc.); **he was unable to c. his laughter,** il ne pouvait pas s'empêcher de rire; *Lit:* **to c. oneself,** se maîtriser. **3.** *Mil:* contenir (l'ennemi); **containing force,** corps de troupes destiné à arrêter l'ennemi.

container [kən'teinər] *n.* (*a*) récipient *m*; réservoir *m*; bac *m* (pour aliments); *El:* bac (d'accumulateur), (*b*) *Com: etc:* boîte *f*, récipient; coffret *m* (pour bande magnétique, etc.); (*c*) *Trans:* container *m*, conteneur *m*; **c. ship,** navire *m* porte-containers.

containerization [kənteinərai'zeiʃ(ə)n] *n. Trans:* containerisation *f*, conteneurisation *f*.

contaminate [kən'tæmineit] *v.tr.* contaminer; corrompre; souiller; **contaminated air,** air vicié.

contamination [kəntæmi'neiʃ(ə)n] *n.* contamination *f* (bactérienne, radioactive, etc.).

contango, *pl.* **-oes** [kən'tæŋgou, -ouz] *n. St.Exch:* report *m*; taux *m* du report.

contemplate ['kɔntempleit] **1.** (*a*) *v.tr.* contempler (qn, qch.); (*b*) *v.i.* se recueillir; méditer. **2.** *v.tr.* (*a*) prévoir, envisager (qch.), avoir (qch.) en vue; (*b*) **to c. doing sth.,** se proposer de, songer à, faire qch.; **to c. suicide,** songer au suicide; **that was never contemplated,** il n'a jamais été question de cela.

contemplation [kɔntem'pleiʃ(ə)n] *n.* (*a*) contemplation *f* (d'un tableau, d'une vitrine, etc.); (*b*) recueillement *m*, méditation *f*, contemplation.

contemplative [kən'templətiv] *a.* (*of character, religious life, etc.*) contemplatif.

contemporaneous [kəntempə'reiniəs] *a.* contemporain (**with,** de). **-ly** *adv.* **c. with, . . .,** au même temps que . . ..

contemporary [kən'temp(ə)rəri] *a. & n.* (*a*) contemporain, -aine (**with,** de); (*b*) (littérature) contemporaine; (meubles) contemporains; (événements) actuels; **our contemporaries,** nos contemporains.

contempt [kən'tem(p)t] *n.* **1.** mépris *m*; dédain *m*; **to hold s.o., sth., in c.,** mépriser qn, qch.; **to treat s.o., sth., with c.,** traiter qn avec dédain, avec mépris; **beneath c.,** tout ce qu'il y a de plus méprisable. **2.** *Jur:* **c. of court,** (i) outrage *m* au tribunal, offense *f* à la cour; (ii) (*non appearance*) refus *m* de comparaître.

contemptible [kən'tem(p)təbl] *a.* méprisable; (conduite) indigne.

contemptuous [kən'tem(p)tjuəs] *a.* **1. c. of sth.,** dédaigneux de qch. **2.** (air) méprisant, (geste, parole) de mépris. **-ly** *adv.* avec mépris; avec dédain.

contend [kən'tend] **1.** *v.i.* combattre, lutter (**with, against,** contre); disputer (**with s.o. about sth.,** avec qn sur qch.); **the difficulties with which I have to c.,** les difficultés avec lesquelles je suis aux prises. **2.** *v.tr.* **to c. that . . .,** prétendre, soutenir, que + *ind.* **contending** *a.* **the c. parties,** les contestants *mpl;* **the c. armies,** les armées opposées.

contender [kən'tendər] *n.* (*a*) concurrent, -ente; compétiteur, -trice; candidat, -ate; (*b*) *Sp:* challenger *m.*

content¹ ['kɔntent] *n.* **1.** (*a*) contenu *m,* volume *m* (d'un solide); capacité *f* (d'un vase); (*b*) **contents,** contenu (d'une bouteille, d'un livre, d'une lettre, etc.); (*of book*) **(table of) contents,** table *f* des matières. **2.** *Ch: Miner: etc:* teneur *f*, titre *m*; **gold, moisture, c.,** teneur en or, en humidité; **a high protein c.,** riche en protéine.

content² [kən'tent] *n.* (*a*) contentement *m*, satisfaction *f*; **to one's heart's c.,** à cœur joie; à souhait.

content³ [kən'tent] *a.* satisfait (**with,** de); **to be c. with sth.,** se contenter de qch.; **he's quite c. to stay at home,** il ne demande pas mieux que de rester à la maison. **contented** *a.* content; satisfait; (sourire) de satisfaction. **contentedly** *adv.* avec contentement; **to live c.,** vivre heureux.

content⁴ [kən'tent] *v.tr.* **1.** contenter, satisfaire (qn). **2. to c. oneself with (doing) sth.,** se contenter de (faire) qch.

contentedness [kən'tentidnis] *n.* contentement *m* (de son sort).

contention [kən'tenʃ(ə)n] *n.* **1.** lutte *f*, dispute *f*; **bone of c.,** pomme *f* de discorde. **2.** émulation *f*. **3.** affirmation *f*; **my c. is that . . .,** je soutiens que + *ind.*

contentious [kən'tenʃəs] *a.* **1.** (*of pers., humour*) querelleur, -euse. **2.** (*of issue, etc.*) contentieux.

contentment [kən'tentmənt] *n.* contentement *m.*

contest¹ ['kɔntest] *n.* (*a*) combat *m*, lutte *f* (**with,** avec, contre; **between,** entre); (*b*) concours *m*; **speed c.,** course *f* de vitesse; **beauty c.,** concours de beauté; (*c*) *U.S: Jur:* **no c.,** pas de témoins à charge.

contest² [kən'test] **1.** *v.tr.* (*a*) contester, disputer (une question) (**with, against,** avec); (*b*) **to c. s.o.'s right to do sth.,** contester à qn le droit de faire qch.; **to c. the victory with s.o.,** disputer la victoire à qn; *Sp:* **to c. a race,** se mettre sur les rangs; (*c*) disputer, se poser candidat pour (un siège au Parlement); (*d*) *Jur:* attaquer (un testament); contester (une succession). **2.** *v.i.* (*a*) se disputer (**with, against,** avec); (*b*) **to c. for a prize,** disputer un prix.

contestant [kən'testənt] *n.* **1.** contestant, -ante. **2.** compétiteur, -trice; concurrent *m*.

contestation [kɔntes'teiʃ(ə)n] *n.* (*a*) contestation *f* (d'un droit, etc.); (*b*) affirmation *f*, prétention *f*; **his c. was that . . .,** il soutenait que . . ..

context ['kɔntekst] *n.* contexte *m*; **in this c.,** à ce propos; **in, out of, c.,** en, hors de, son contexte.

contiguous [kən'tigjuəs] *a.* **1.** (*a*) contigu, -uë (**to,** à, avec); attenant (à qch.). **2.** voisin (**to,** de).

continence ['kɔntinəns] *n.* continence *f*; chasteté *f*.

continent¹ ['kɔntinənt] *a.* continent; chaste.

continent² *n. Geog:* (*a*) continent *m*; **the five continents,** les cinq parties *fpl* du monde; (*b*) **the C.,** l'Europe continentale; **on the C.,** en Europe (continentale); outre-Manche.

continental [kɔnti'nent(ə)l] **1.** *a.* (*a*) continental, -aux; (*b*) (*usu. cap.* C) de l'Europe continentale; *Dom.Ec:* **c. quilt,** couette *f*, *Sw.Fr:* duvet *m*. **2.** *n.* continental, -ale; habitant de l'Europe (continentale).

contingency [kən'tindʒənsi] *n.* **1.** contingence *f* (d'événements); éventualité *f* (d'un événement). **2.** (*a*) éventualité; imprévu *m*; **to provide for every c.,** parer à toute éventualité; **prepared for all contingencies,** préparé à toutes les éventualités; **c. plan,** plan d'urgence; **c. fund,** caisse *f* de prévoyance; (*b*) *Ind: Com:* **contingencies,** frais divers; **to allow for contingencies,** parer à l'imprévu.

contingent [kən'tindʒənt] **1.** *a.* (*a*) *Phil:* contingent; (*b*) éventuel, fortuit; aléatoire; (*c*) conditionnel; **c. on sth.,** sous (la) réserve de qch.; (*of event*) **to be c. upon sth.,** dépendre de qch. **2.** *n.* contingent *m*; *Mil:* **the annual c. (of recruits),** le contingent annuel; *F:* la classe.

continual [kən'tinjuəl] *a.* continuel; (plaintes) incessantes. **-ally** *adv.* continuellement; sans cesse.

continuance [kən'tinjuəns] *n.* **1.** continuation *f* (d'une action). **2.** (*a*) continuation, durée *f*; **c. in a place,** séjour *m* (dans un endroit).

continuation [kəntinju'eiʃ(ə)n] *n.* **1.** continuation *f* (d'une route, d'une histoire, etc.). **2.** prolongement *m* (d'un mur, etc.); suite *f* (d'un roman); **to be a c. of . . .,** faire suite à . . .. **3.** *St.Exch:* report *m*.

continue [kən'tinju:] **1.** *v.tr.* (*a*) continuer (un ouvrage, une activité, etc.); prolonger (une droite); poursuivre (un travail); continuer, reprendre (une conversation); **to c. one's studies,** (i) poursuivre, (ii) reprendre, ses études; *Journ:* **to be continued,** à suivre; **continued on page 30,** suite *f* à la page 30; (*b*) perpétuer (la race, une tradition); (*c*) **to c. one's way,** *v.i.* **to c. on one's way,** continuer son chemin; (*d*) **to c. to do sth., doing sth.,** continuer à, de, faire qch.; **after lunch we continued working,** après le déjeuner nous avons repris notre travail; (*e*) *Jur:* ajourner (un procès). **2.** *v.i.* (*a*) (se) continuer; se soutenir; (*of line*) se prolonger; (*b*) **"and then", he continued,** "et puis", continua-t-il; (*c*) **to c. in office,** garder sa charge; (*of political party*) rester au pouvoir; **his bad luck continues,** ses malheurs *mpl* se poursuivent; (*d*) *v.tr. & i.* **to c. (staying) in, at, a place,** continuer son séjour dans un endroit. **continued** *a.* (effort, intérêt) soutenu. **continuing** *a.* continu; soutenu.

continuity [kɔnti'nju:iti] *n.* **1.** continuité *f*; **to break the c. of s.o.'s ideas,** couper le fil des idées de qn. **2.** *Cin:* (*a*) scénario *m*, découpage *m*; (*b*) **c. man,** découpeur *m*; **c. girl,** script-girl *f*, *pl.* script-girls.

continuous [kən'tinjuəs] *a.* continue; **c. succession,** suite ininterrompue (de visites, etc.); *El:* **c. waves,** ondes entretenues; *Cin:* **c. performance,** spectacle permanent. **-ly** *adv.* continûment; sans interruption.

contort [kən'tɔ:t] *v.tr.* tordre (les traits, etc.); **face contorted by pain,** visage contracté, crispé, par la douleur.

contortion [kən'tɔ:ʃ(ə)n] *n.* **1.** contorsion *f* (des traits, etc.). **2. amazing contortions,** contorsions incroyables.

contortionist [kən'tɔ:ʃənist] *n.* contorsionniste *mf*.

contour ['kɔntuər] *n.* (*a*) contour *m* (d'un objet); profil *m* (du terrain); (*b*) *Surv: Mapm:* **c. (line),** courbe *f* de niveau, courbe hypsométrique; **c. map,** carte *f* en courbes de niveau.

contra ['kɔntrə] **1.** *prep.* (*abbr.* **con.**) contre. **2.** *n. Book-k:* **per c.,** par contre; **c. entry,** écriture *f* inverse.

contraband ['kɔntrəbænd] *n.* contrebande *f*; **c. goods,** marchandises *fpl* de contrebande.

contrabass ['kɔntrəbeis] *n. Mus:* contrebasse *f* (à cordes).

contra-bassoon [kɔntrəbə'su:n] *n. Mus:* contrebasson *m*.

contraception [kɔntrə'sepʃ(ə)n] *n.* contraception *f*.

contraceptive [kɔntrə'septiv] *a. & n.* contraceptif (*m*).

contract¹ ['kɔntrækt] *n.* **1.** (*a*) pacte *m*, contrat *m*; **marriage c.,** contrat de mariage; **to bind oneself by c.,** s'engager par contrat; (*b*) acte *m* de vente; **simple c.,** convention verbale; **law of c.,** droit *m* des obligations. **2.** *Ind: Com:* entreprise *f*; marché *m*; **c. work,** travail *m* à l'entreprise, à forfait; **to enter into a c.,** (i) (*of pers.*) passer (un) contrat (**with,** avec); (ii) (*of thg*) faire partie d'un contrat; **to put work out to c.,** mettre un travail à l'entreprise; **to tender for a c.,** soumissionner à une adjudication; **conditions of c.,** cahier *m* des charges; **breach of c.,** rupture *f* de contrat. **3.** *Cards:* contrat; **c. bridge,** bridge *m* contrat.

contract² [kən'trækt] **1.** *v.tr.* (*a*) contracter (une obligation, une maladie); prendre (une habitude); **to c. debts,** s'endetter; (*b*) *Com:* **to c. to do sth.,** entreprendre de faire qch. **2.** *v.i. Com:* **to c. for a supply of sth.,** entreprendre une fourniture de qch.; **to c. for work,** entreprendre des travaux à forfait; *Ind: Adm:* **to c. out, in,** renoncer, s'engager, par contrat préalable. **contracting 1.** *a.* **c. parties,** contractants *mpl*. **2.** *n.* (*a*) affermage *m* (pour annonces, etc.); (*b*) *Ind:* recours *m* à l'entreprise.

contract³ [kən'trækt] **1.** *v.tr.* (*a*) contracter (les métaux, les muscles, etc.); crisper (les traits); rétrécir (un tissu, une ouverture); resserrer (les tissus); (*b*) *Ling:* **to c.** *shall not* **into** *shan't*, contracter *shall not* en *shan't*. **2.** *v.i.* (*a*) se contracter, se rétrécir; **the pupil contracts in bright light,** la pupille se contracte à la lumière intense; (*b*) *Ling: cannot* **contracts into** *can't*, *cannot* se contracte en *can't*.

contraction [kən'trækʃ(ə)n] *n.* **1.** contraction *f*, rétrécissement *m* (de la pupille, etc.); retrait *m* (des métaux lors du refroidissement); contraction (d'un muscle). **2.** *Ling:* (*a*) contraction (de deux mots en un seul, etc.); (*b*) mot contracté. **3. c. of debts,** endettement *m*.

contractor [kən'træktər] *n.* entrepreneur *m*; **army c.,** fournisseur de l'armée; **haulage, building, c.,** entrepreneur de transports, de bâtiments.

contractual [kən'træktjuəl] *a.* contractuel.

contradict [kɔntrə'dikt] *v.tr.* contredire (qn); démentir (qn, un bruit); **to c. oneself,** se contredire; **the**

statements of the witnesses c. each other, les dépositions *fpl* des témoins se contredisent.

contradiction [kɔntrə'dikʃ(ə)n] *n.* **1.** contradiction *f*, démenti *m* (d'une nouvelle). **2.** *Phil:* contradiction, incompatibilité *f* (entre deux principes); **in c. with,** en contradiction avec; incompatible avec; **c. in terms,** contradiction dans les termes.

contradictory [kɔntrə'diktəri] *a.* **1.** (*of statement, etc.*) contradictoire; opposé (**to,** à). **2.** (*of pers.*) raisonneur, -euse.

contradistinction [kɔntrədis'tiŋ(k)ʃ(ə)n] *n.* opposition *f*, contraste *m*; **in c. to . . .,** par opposition à.

contra-indication ['kɔntrəindi'keiʃ(ə)n] *n. Med:* contre-indication *f*, *pl.* contre-indications.

contralto [kən'træltou] *a. & n. Mus:* contralto (*m*).

contraption [kən'træpʃ(ə)n] *n. F:* machin *m*, engin *m*, truc *m*.

contrapuntal [kɔntrə'pʌnt(ə)l] *a. Mus:* (morceau, accompagnement, etc.) en contrepoint.

contrariness [kən'trɛərinis] *n.* disposition *f* à tout contrarier; esprit de contradiction.

contrariwise [kɔn'treəriwaiz] *adv.* **1.** au contraire. **2.** en sens opposé. **3.** *F:* [kən'trɛəriwaiz] par esprit de contradiction.

contrary ['kɔntrəri] **1.** *a.* (*a*) contraire (**to,** à); (*of interests, etc.*) opposé (à), en opposition (avec); **c. to nature,** contre (la) nature; **c. to reason,** contraire à la raison; (*b*) (*unfavourable*) **c. winds,** vents *mpl* contraires; (*c*) *F:* [kən'trɛəri] (*of pers.*) opiniâtre; qui a l'esprit de contradiction. **2.** *n.* contraire *m*; **on the c.,** au contraire; **unless you hear to the c.,** à moins d'avis contraire. **3.** *adv.* contrairement (**to,** à); en opposition (**to,** à, avec); **to act c. to instructions,** contrevenir aux ordres reçus; **c. to my expectations,** contre mon attente. **-ily** *adv.* contrairement,

contrast¹ ['kɔntrɑːst] *n.* contraste *m* (**between,** entre); **in c. with sth.,** par contraste avec qch.; **to form a c. to . . .,** faire contraste avec . . .; **as a c. to . . .,** comme contraste à . . .

contrast² [kən'trɑːst] **1.** *v.tr.* faire contraster, mettre en contraste (**with,** avec). **2.** *v.i.* contraster (**with,** avec); **to c. strongly,** trancher (**with,** sur). **contrasting** *a.* qui fait contraste; (couleurs) opposées.

contravene [kɔntrə'viːn] *v.tr.* **1.** transgresser, enfreindre (la loi, etc.); être en contravention avec (une règle). **2.** aller à l'encontre de (qch.).

contravention [kɔntrə'venʃ(ə)n] *n.* **c. of a law,** contravention *f*, infraction *f*, à la loi; **to act in c. of a rule, a right,** agir en violation d'une règle.

contribute [kən'tribjut] *v.tr. & i.* contribuer pour (une somme); **to c. (one's share),** payer sa part; **to c. to a charity,** contribuer à une bonne œuvre; **to c. to a newspaper,** collaborer à un journal; **to c. to the success,** aider au succès; **everything contributed to make him happy,** tout contribuait à le rendre heureux.

contribution [kɔntri'bjuːʃ(ə)n] *n.* **1.** contribution *f*; cotisation *f*; **to pay one's c.,** payer sa cotisation; *Fin:* **c. of capital,** apport *m* de capitaux; (*b*) *Mil:* contribution (de guerre) **2. c. to a newspaper,** article écrit pour un journal.

contributor [kən'tribjutər] *n.* **1.** contributaire *mf*. **2.** collaborateur, -trice (**to a paper,** d'un journal).

contributory [kən'tribjutəri] *a.* contribuant; **c. causes,** causes contribuantes; *Jur: Ins:* **c. negligence,** manque *m* de précautions (de la part d'un accidenté).

contrite ['kɔntrait] *a.* contrit, pénitent, repentant. **-ly** *adv.* d'un air contrit, pénitent; avec contrition.

contrition [kən'triʃ(ə)n] *n.* contrition *f*, pénitence *f*.

contrivance [kən'traivəns] *n.* **1.** (*a*) invention *f* (d'un appareil, etc.); (*b*) ingéniosité *f*. **2.** (*a*) invention; combinaison *f*; (*b*) *Pej:* machination *f*. **3.** appareil *m*, dispositif *m*, engin *m*.

contrive [kən'traiv] *v.tr.* (*a*) inventer, concevoir (un appareil, etc.); (*b*) **to c. (a means) to do sth.,** trouver moyen de faire qch. **contrived** *a.* forcé; qui manque de naturel.

control¹ [kən'troul] *n.* **1.** autorité *f*; **state c.,** étatisme *m*; **to have c. of a business,** être à la tête d'une entreprise. **2.** contrôle *m*; maîtrise *f*; (*a*) **circumstances beyond our c.,** circonstances indépendantes de notre volonté; **these things are beyond our c.,** ces choses-là *fpl* ne se commandent pas; **to keep s.o. under strict c.,** surveiller qn de près; **she has no c. over the children,** elle n'a aucune autorité sur les enfants; **to get out of c.,** échapper à toute autorité; **to have one's horse under c.,** avoir son cheval bien en main; **self c.,** contrôle de soi-même; **to lose c. of oneself,** ne plus être maître de soi; **to regain c. of oneself,** se ressaisir; **to keep one's feelings under c.,** contenir ses sentiments; **everything is under c.,** tout est fin prêt; **to bring (sth.) under c.,** maîtriser (un incendie, etc.); enrayer (une maladie); résoudre (une difficulté); (*b*) *Pol.Ec: etc:* contrôle (des changes); contrôle, réglementation *f* (des loyers); **birth c.,** contrôle, limitation *f*, des naissances; (*c*) (*verification*) *Med:* **c. case,** cas *m* témoin; (*d*) *Tchn:* commande *f* (d'un mécanisme); manœuvre *f* (d'un train, d'un avion, d'un navire, etc.); *El: Elcs: etc:* contrôle (de fréquence, etc.); réglage *m* (de puissance, d'intensité); **temperature c.,** régulation *f* thermique; **automatic c.,** réglage automatique; **dual c.,** double commande; **remote c.,** télécommande *f*; **c. lever, mechanism,** levier *m*, appareil *m*, de commande; *Av:* **c. column,** levier de commande; **to lose c. of one's car,** perdre contrôle de sa voiture; **ship out of c.,** navire qui n'est plus maître de sa manœuvre; *Sp: Aut:* **c. point,** contrôle (du passage de voitures, etc.); *Av:* **c. tower,** tour *f* de contrôle; *Cmptr:* **data c.,** contrôle de données. **3.** *Tchn:* (organe *m* de) commande; **the controls,** les commandes; *Av:* **flying controls,** commandes de vol; *W.Tel: etc:* **volume c.,** bouton *m* de (réglage de) volume. **4.** *Psychics:* contrôleur, -euse (d'un médium).

control² *v.tr.* **1.** diriger, réglementer (des affaires, la production); régler (la dépense); commander (le mouvement d'une machine); diriger, être à la tête (d'une entreprise); *Mil:* contrôler (une région stratégique); **he cannot c. his pupils,** il ne sait pas tenir ses élèves; **to c. the traffic,** réglementer la circulation. **2.** (*a*) maîtriser (un cheval); réprimer (un soulèvement); dompter (ses passions); contrôler (ses réactions, etc.); contenir (l'inflation); enrayer (la hausse des prix); retenir (ses larmes); **to c. oneself,** se contrôler, se maîtriser; **c. yourself!** retenez-vous! **to try to c. oneself,** faire un effort sur soi-même; (*b*) *Med:* équilibrer (un diabète, etc.). **controlled** *a.* (*a*) (*of pers.*) qui sait se contenir; (bien) équilibré; (*b*) *Pol.Ec:* (économie) dirigée; (marché) réglementé; (*c*) *Adm:* (*in street*) **c. crossing,** passage réglementé (par un agent de police, etc.); (*d*) *Med:* (diabète, etc.) équilibré. **controlling** *a.* qui gouverne; (puissance) dirigeante; *Fin: Com:* **c. interest,** participation *f* majoritaire.

controller [kən'troulər] *n.* **1.** (*pers.*) contrôleur, -euse; *Av:* **air traffic c.,** contrôleur de la circulation aérienne, aiguilleur *m* du ciel. **2.** (*apparatus*) contrôleur; commande *f*; *Av:* **flight c.,** contrôleur de vol.

controversial [kɔntrə'vəːʃ(ə)l] *a.* **1.** (*of question, opinion, etc.*) controversé; (*of subject, pers., etc.*) discuté. **2.** (*of pers.*) enclin à la controverse.

controversy ['kɔntrəvəːsi, kən'trɔvəsi] *n.* polémique *f*; (*religious*) controverse *f*; **question that has given rise to much c.,** question fort controversée.

contumacy ['kɔntjuməsi, kɔn'tjuː-] *n. Jur:* contumace *f*; désobéissance *f*; rébellion *f*.

contumely ['kɔntju:mli] *n.* **1.** insolence *f*; outrage *m*; **to treat s.o. with c.,** traiter qn avec mépris. **2.** honte *f*; **to cover s.o. with c.,** couvrir qn de honte.

contusion [kən'tju:ʒ(ə)n] *n.* contusion *f*.

conundrum [kə'nʌndrəm] *n.* **1.** devinette *f*. **2.** énigme *f*.

conurbation [kɔnə:'beiʃ(ə)n] *n.* conurbation *f*.

convalesce [kɔnvə'les] *v.i.* (*a*) être en convalescence; **he is convalescing at Brighton,** il est en convalescence à Brighton; (*b*) relever de maladie.

convalescence [kɔnvə'lesəns] *n.* convalescence *f*.

convalescent [kɔnvə'lesənt] *a.* & *n.* **1.** convalescent, -ente. **2. c. home,** maison *f* de convalescence.

convection [kən'vekʃ(ə)n] *n. Ph: El: etc:* convection *f*; **c. heater,** radiateur *m* à convection.

convector [kən'vektər] *n.* appareil *m* de chauffage par convection, radiateur *m* à convection.

convene [kən'vi:n] **1.** *v.tr.* (*a*) convoquer, réunir (une assemblée); (*b*) *Jur:* **to c. s.o. before a court,** citer qn devant un tribunal. **2.** *v.i.* s'assembler.

convenience [kən'vi:niəns] *n.* **1.** commodité *f*, convenance *f*; **marriage of c.,** mariage *m* de convenance; **at your c.,** à votre bon plaisir; **at your earliest c.,** à la première occasion; dans les meilleurs délais; *Com:* **c. foods,** aliments *mpl* minute; *Nau:* **flag of c.,** pavillon *m* de complaisance. **2. (public) c.,** w.c. (publics), toilettes *fpl*. **3. rooms fitted with all modern conveniences,** chambres installées avec tout (le) confort moderne.

convenient [kən'vi:niənt] *a.* commode, pratique; (*of time*) opportun; **if it is c. to you,** si cela vous convient; si vous n'y voyez pas d'inconvénient; **to find a c. opportunity to do sth.,** trouver l'occasion *f* de faire qch. **-ly** *adv.* commodément; (*time*) opportunément, à propos.

convent ['kɔnvənt] *n.* (*a*) couvent *m*; **to enter a c.,** entrer au couvent; (*b*) **c. (school),** couvent; **she goes to the c.,** elle fait ses études au couvent, *F:* chez les bonnes sœurs.

convention [kən'venʃ(ə)n] *n.* **1.** (*a*) convention *f* (**on,** relative à); **the Hague Conventions,** les conventions de la Haye; (*b*) accord *m*, contrat *m*. **2.** (*a*) usage *m*; (*b*) (*often pl.*) convenances *fpl*; **social conventions,** les conventions sociales. **3.** assemblée *f*, convention *f*; **medical c.,** congrès médical.

conventional [kən'venʃən(ə)l] *a.* **1.** conventionnel; **c. propriety,** les convenances admises. **2.** (*a*) classique; traditionnel; *Mil:* **c. warfare, weapon,** guerre *f*, arme *f*, classique: *Const:* **c. material,** matériau traditionnel; (*b*) *Pej:* sans originalité. **-ally** *adv.* **1.** conventionnellement. **2.** (*a*) d'une manière classique; (*b*) *Pej:* sans originalité.

conventionality [kənvenʃə'næliti] *n.* **1.** (*a*) convention *f*; usage admis; (*b*) les conventions (sociales). **2.** caractère conventionnel, ordinaire (de qch.).

converge [kən'və:dʒ] **1.** *v.i.* converger (**on,** sur); **three armies were converging on Paris,** trois armées convergeaient sur Paris. **2.** *v.tr.* faire converger (des rayons lumineux, etc.).

convergence [kən'və:dʒəns] *n.* convergence *f* (de lignes, d'opinions); *Mth:* focalisation *f*.

convergent [kən'və:dʒənt] *a.* convergent.

conversant [kən'və:sənt] *a.* **c. with sth.,** versé dans, au courant de, qch.

conversation [kɔnvə'seiʃ(ə)n] *n.* (*a*) conversation *f*, entretien *m*; **to hold a c. with s.o.,** s'entretenir avec qn; **to change the c.,** changer de conversation; détourner la conversation; **he was just making c.,** il parlait pour ne rien dire; *Art:* **c. piece,** tableau *m* de genre; (*b*) *Cmptr:* dialogue *m*.

conversational [kɔnvə'seiʃən(ə)l] *a.* (*a*) de (la) conversation; **in a c. tone,** sur le ton de la conversation; **c. style,** style familier; (*b*) *Cmptr:* (mode) dialogue. **-ally** *adv.* sur le ton de la conversation.

conversationalist [kɔnvə'seiʃənəlist] *n.* **to be a good c.,** (i) bien parler; (ii) aimer la conversation.

converse¹ [kən'və:s] *v.i.* parler; **to c. with s.o. on, about, sth.,** converser avec qn sur qch.

converse² ['kɔnvə:s] *a.* & *n.* **1.** *Log:* (proposition) converse (*f*). **2.** *Mth:* (proposition) réciproque (*f*). **-ly** *adv.* réciproquement; vice versa; inversement.

conversion [kən'və:ʃ(ə)n] *n.* **1.** conversion *f* (de qn); **c. to Christianity,** conversion au christianisme. **2.** conversion (**of sth. into sth.,** de qch. en qch.); (*a*) **c. of water into steam,** conversion de l'eau en vapeur; **c. of iron into steel,** conversion du fer en acier; (*for currency, measurements, etc.*) **c. table,** table *f* de conversion; (*b*) façonnage *m* (du bois en grume); (*c*) aménagement *m*, transformation *f* (d'une maison en appartements); (*d*) *Rugby Fb:* transformation. **3.** *Jur:* **c. of funds to one's own use, improper c. of funds,** détournement *m* de fonds.

convert¹ ['kɔnvə:t] *n.* converti, -ie; **to become a c. to sth.,** se convertir à qch.; **to make a c. of s.o.,** convertir qn.

convert² [kən'və:t] *v.tr.* **1.** convertir (qn) (à une religion); **to be converted to Christianity,** se convertir au christianisme. **2.** transformer, convertir (**sth. into sth.,** qch. en qch.); (*a*) **to c. iron into steel,** convertir le fer en acier; *Rugby Fb:* **to c. a try,** transformer un essai; **converted goal,** transformation *f*; (*b*) façonner (le bois en grume); (*c*) **converted cowshed,** étable aménagée. **3. to c. funds to another purpose,** affecter des fonds à un autre usage; *Jur:* **to c. funds to one's own use,** détourner des fonds. **4.** *v.i.* (*of settee, etc.*) se transformer (**into a bed,** en lit).

converter [kən'və:tər] *n.* **1.** (*pers.*) convertisseur, -euse (des infidèles, etc.). **2.**; (*a*) *Metall:* **steel c., Bessemer c.,** convertisseur Bessemer; (*b*) *El: W.Tel: etc:* adapteur *m*; convertisseur *m*.

convertibility [kənvə:tə'biliti] *n.* convertibilité *f*.

convertible [kən'və:təbl] *a.* **1.** (*of pers.*) convertissable (**to,** a). **2.** (*a*) (*of thg*) convertible (**into,** en); (divan, etc.) transformable; (*b*) *n.* voiture *f* décapotable. **3.** *Fin:* **c. currencies,** monnaies *fpl* convertibles.

convex ['kɔnveks] *a.* **1.** convexe. **2.** *U.S:* (route, chaussée) bombée.

convexity [kən'veksiti] *n.* convexité *f*.

convey [kən'vei] *v.tr.* **1.** transporter, porter (qch., qn); (a)mener (qn). **2.** (*of air, etc.*) transmettre (le son, une odeur). **3.** transmettre (un ordre); donner (une idée); communiquer (une nouvelle) (**to,** à); **please c. my good wishes to the young couple,** veuillez transmettre tous mes vœux aux jeunes époux; **to c. one's meaning,** communiquer sa pensée. **4.** *Jur:* (*a*) faire cession (d'un bien); transférer, céder (un bien) (**to,** à); (*b*) (*of solicitor*) dresser l'acte de cession (d'une terre, etc.).

conveyance [kən'veiəns] *n.* **1.** transport *m*; moyen *m* de transport. **2.** (*a*) transmission, communication *f* (de qch. à qn); (*b*) *Ph:* transmission (du son, de la chaleur); (*c*) *Jur:* transfert *m*, cession *f*, disposition *f* (de biens). **3.** *Jur:* acte translatif de propriété; acte de cession. **4.** véhicule *m* (de transport); voiture *f*; *Jur:* **public c.,** véhicule de transport(s) en commun.

conveyancing [kən'veiənsiŋ] *n. Jur:* **1.** rédaction *f* des actes de cession, des actes translatifs de propriété. **2.** procédure translative de propriété.

conveyor, conveyer [kən'veiər] *n.* **1.** (*pers.*) (*a*) porteur, -euse (d'une lettre, d'un paquet); (*b*) voiturier *m*. **2.** *Ind:* (appareil) transporteur (*m*); transporteuse *f*; *Min:* convoyeur *m*; **roller c.,** transporteur à rouleaux; **c. belt,** convoyeur; tapis roulant; **bucket c.,** transporteur à godets. **3.** conducteur *m* (d'électricité).

convict¹ ['kɔnvikt] *n.* (*a*) détenu, -ue; (*b*) forçat *m*; bagnard *m*; **former c.,** repris *m* de justice.

convict² [kən'vikt] *v.tr.* (*a*) **to c. s.o. of a crime,** déclarer qn coupable d'un crime; **he was convicted,** il fut reconnu coupable; il fut condamné; (*b*) **you stand convicted by your own words,** vos propres paroles vous condamnent.

conviction [kən'vikʃ(ə)n] *n.* **1.** condamnation *f*; *Jur:* **previous convictions,** condamnations antérieures. **2.** conviction *f*; **to be open to c.,** être accessible à la persuasion. **3.** (*belief*) conviction; **to act from c.,** agir par conviction; **to have the courage of one's convictions,** avoir le courage de ses convictions; (*of evidence, etc.*) **to carry c.,** emporter conviction.

convince [kən'vins] *v.tr.* convaincre, persuader (**s.o. of sth., that . . .,** qn de qch., que . . .); **to allow oneself to be convinced,** se laisser convaincre. **convinced** *a.* convaincu, de conviction. **convincing** *a.* (*a*) (argument) convaincant; (langage) persuasif; (*b*) (*of performance, etc.*) qui emporte conviction. **convincingly** *adv.* d'une manière convaincante.

convivial [kən'viviəl] *a.* **1. c. evening,** soirée passée à table ou à boire. **2.** (*of pers.*) bon convive, bon vivant.

conviviality [kənvivi'æliti] *n.* franche gaieté (dans un repas); esprit *m* de société.

convocation [kɔnvə'keiʃ(ə)n] *a.* **1.** convocation *f* (d'une assemblée). **2.** *Ecc:* assemblée, synode *m*.

convoke [kən'vouk] *v.tr.* convoquer (une assemblée).

convoluted ['kɔnvəljutid] *a. Nat.Hist:* convoluté.

convolution [kɔnvə'lju:ʃ(ə)n] *n.* circonvolution *f*. **1.** repli *m*, sinuosité *f*; *Anat:* **cerebral convolutions,** circonvolutions cérébrales. **2.** enroulement *m*.

convolvulus, *pl.* **-uses** [kən'vɔlvjuləs, -əsiz] *n. Bot:* volubilis *m*, belle-de-jour *f*, *pl.* belles-de-jour.

convoy¹ ['kɔnvɔi] *n. Mil: Nau:* convoi *m*; **ship under, in, c.,** bâtiment convoyé, en convoi.

convoy² *v.tr. Mil: Nau:* convoyer, escorter.

convulse [kən'vʌls] *v.tr.* **1.** bouleverser (qn, qch., la vie de qn). **2.** *Med:* convulsionner (un muscle). **3. to be convulsed with laughter, with pain,** se tordre de rire, de douleur; **scene that convulses the audience,** scène *f* qui fait tordre de rire toute la salle.

convulsion [kən'vʌlʃ(ə)n] *n.* **1.** *Med:* (*usu. pl.*) convulsion *f*; **infantile convulsions,** convulsions des enfants. **2. to be seized with convulsions of laughter,** se tordre de rire. **3. political convulsions,** bouleversements politiques.

convulsive [kən'vʌlsiv] *a.* (mouvement, etc.) convulsif. **-ly** *adv.* convulsivement.

coo¹ [ku:] *int. P:* tiens! ça alors!

coo² *v.i.* (*of dove, F: of pers.*) roucouler; (*of baby*) gazouiller. **cooing** *n.* roucoulement *m*.

cook¹ [kuk] *n.* (*a*) cuisinier, -ère; **head c.,** chef *m* (de cuisine); *F:* **head c. and bottlewasher,** factotum *m*; *Prov:* **too many cooks spoil the broth,** trop de cuisinières gâtent la sauce; (*b*) *Nau:* cuisinier; coq *m*.

cook² **1.** *v.tr.* (*a*) (faire) cuire (de la viande, etc.); faire, préparer (un repas); **half-cooked,** demi-cuit, à moitié cuit; **ready-cooked food,** plats *mpl* cuisinés (à emporter); *F:* **to c. s.o.'s goose,** (i) renverser les projets de qn; (ii) faire son affaire à qn; (*b*) *F:* **to c. the accounts, the books,** falsifier, truquer, les comptes. **2.** *v.i.* (*a*) (*of food*) cuire; *F:* **what's cooking?** qu'est-ce qui se passe? (*b*) (*of pers.*) faire la cuisine; cuisiner. **cooking** *n.* **1.** cuisson *f* (de la viande, etc.); **c. apples,** pommes à cuire; **c. fat,** matière grasse pour la cuisine. **2.** cuisine *f*; **plain, home, c.,** cuisine bourgeoise; **to do the c.,** faire la cuisine; **c. utensils,** batterie *f* de cuisine. **3.** *F:* **c. of accounts,** falsification *f* des comptes. **cook up** *v.tr. F:* inventer, imaginer (une excuse, etc.).

cookbook ['kukbuk] *n. esp. NAm:* livre *m* de cuisine.

cooker ['kukər] *n.* **1.** (*a*) (*stove*) cuisinière *f*; **gas c.,** cuisinière à gaz; (*b*) **pressure c.,** cocotte-minute *f* (*R.t.m.*). **2.** pomme *f* à cuire.

cookery ['kukəri] *n.* (l'art de la) cuisine; **c. book,** livre *m* de cuisine.

cookie ['kuki] *n.* (*a*) *Scot:* petit pain au lait; (*b*) *esp. NAm:* (i) petit gâteau, (ii) biscuit *m*; *F:* **that's the way the c. crumbles!** c'est la vie (que veux-tu)!

cool¹ [ku:l] **1.** *a.* (*a*) (vent, temps, etc.) frais; (eau) tiède; (boisson) rafraîchissante; **it's c.,** il fait frais; **it's getting c.,** le temps se rafraîchit; *Com: etc:* **to be kept in a c. place,** tenir au frais; (*b*) calme; **to keep c. and collected,** garder son sang-froid; **as c. as a cucumber,** avec un sang-froid imperturbable; **keep c.!** du calme! (*c*) (*of pers., reception, etc.*) froid; (*d*) *F:* sans gêne; peu gêné; **I call that c.!** ça, c'est du toupet! **well, you're a c. customer!** eh bien, vous avez du culot, du toupet! (*e*) *F:* **I lost a c. thousand,** j'ai perdu mille livres bien comptées. **2.** *n.* (*a*) frais *m*, fraîcheur *f*; **in the c. of the evening,** dans la fraîcheur du soir; (*b*) *F:* **to keep, lose, one's c.,** garder, perdre, son sang-froid. **3.** *adv. F:* **to play it c.,** (i) jouer (en) décontracté; (ii) être décontracté. **coolly** *adv.* **1.** fraîchement. **2.** (agir) avec calme. **3.** (recevoir qn) froidement. **4.** *F:* effrontément.

cool² **1.** *v.tr.* rafraîchir, refroidir (l'eau, l'air); rafraîchir (le sang); refroidir (le zèle de qn); *F:* **c. it!** calme-toi! **to c. one's heels,** faire le pied de grue. **2.** *v.i.* (*of liquid*) se rafraîchir, (se) refroidir; (*of anger, friendship, etc.*) se refroidir; s'attiédir; **his anger soon cooled,** sa colère a vite passé. **cool down** **1.** *v.i.* (i) (*after exertion*) se rafraîchir; (ii) (*after anger*) s'apaiser, se calmer. **2.** *v.tr.* apaiser (qn). **cooling** **1.** *a.* (*a*) rafraîchissant; (*b*) *Ind: etc:* réfrigérant, refroidissant. **2.** *n.* rafraîchissement *m*, refroidissement *m* (de la température, etc.); *Ind:* réfrigération *f*; **air c.,** refroidissement par air; *I.C.E: etc:* **c. jacket,** chemise *f* d'eau; *Ind:* **c. tower,** tour *f* de réfrigération; refroidisseur *m*; **c. system,** système *m* de refroidissement. **cool off** **1.** (*of affection, enthusiasm*) se refroidir. **2.** *v.tr.* (*of action, etc.*) refroidir (l'enthousiasme de qn).

coolant ['ku:lənt] *n.* agent *m* de refroidissement.

cooler [ku:lər] *n.* **1.** (*a*) (appareil) rafraîchisseur (*m*); glacière; **butter c.,** beurrier refroidisseur; (*b*) *Ind:* réfrigérant *m*, refroidisseur *m*; *I.C.E:* **oil c.,** radiateur *m* d'huile. **2.** *P:* (*prison*) taule *f*.

cool-headed ['ku:l'hedid] *a.* (personne) de sang-froid, calme; imperturbable.

coolie ['ku:li] *n.* coolie *m*.

coolness ['ku:lnis] *n.* **1.** fraîcheur *f* (de l'air). **2.** (*a*) calme *m*, sang-froid *m*; (*b*) *F:* culot *m*. **3.** froideur *f* (d'un accueil).

coon [ku:n] *n.* **1.** *U.S: Z.* raton laveur. **2.** *P: Pej:* nègre *m*.

coop¹ [ku:p] *n.* (*a*) **(hen) c.,** cage *f* à poules; poulailler *m*; (*b*) **chicken c.,** poussinière *f*.

coop² *v.tr.* enfermer dans un poulailler; **to c. s.o. up,** tenir qn enfermé; **to feel cooped up,** se sentir à l'étroit.

co-op ['kou'ɔp] *n.* (*shop*) coop *f*.

cooper ['ku:pər] *n.* tonnelier *m*; barilleur *m*.

cooperage ['ku:pəridʒ] *n.* tonnellerie *f*, barillage *m*.

co-operate [kou'ɔpəreit] *v.i.* **1.** coopérer (**with s.o. in sth.,** avec qn à qch.). **2.** (*of thgs*) concourir (**in,** à).

co-operation [kouɔpə'reiʃ(ə)n] *n.* **1.** (*a*) coopération *f*; (*b*) concours *m* (**in,** à).

co-operative [kou'ɔp(ə)rətiv] *a.* **1.** (*a*) coopératif; **c. society,** société coopérative; **c. dairy,** coopérative laitière; (*b*) *n.* coopérative (agricole, vinicole, etc.). **2. to be c.,** prêter son aide; **you're not very c.,** vous ne m'aidez guère.

co-opt [kou'ɔpt] *v.tr.* coopter (qn).

co-ordinate¹ [kou'ɔːdinət] **1.** *a.* (*a*) égal, -aux (**with,** à); *Gram:* **c. clauses,** propositions coordonnées. **2.** *n.pl.* **co-ordinates,** (*a*) *Mth: Astr: etc:* coordonnées *fpl*; (*b*) *Cost: Com:* coordonnées.

co-ordinate² [kou'ɔːdineit] *v.tr.* coordonner (**with,** à, avec); **co-ordinated movement,** mouvement *m* d'ensemble. **co-ordinating** *a.* **1.** coordinateur, -trice. **2.** *Gram:* (*of conjunction*) coordonnant.

co-ordination [kouɔːdi'neiʃ(ə)n] *n.* coordination *f.*

co-ordinator [kou'ɔːdineitər] *n.* coordinateur, -trice.

coot [kuːt] *n.* **1.** *Orn:* **(common, bald) c.,** foulque *f* (macroule), *Fr.C:* foulque noire; *F:* **as bald as a c.,** chauve comme un œuf. **2.** *F:* (*pers.*) idiot, -ote.

co-ownership ['kou'ounəʃip] *n.* copropriété *f.*

cop¹ [kɔp] *n. F:* (*policeman*) flic *m*; **speed c.,** motard *m*; **to play cops and robbers,** jouer aux gendarmes et aux voleurs.

cop² *n. P:* **1. it's a fair c.!** je suis pris sur le fait. **2. it's no c., not much c.,** ça ne vaut pas grand-chose.

cop³ *v.tr. P:* attraper, pincer (qn); **to get copped,** se faire pincer (par la police, etc.); **to c. it,** (i) se faire pincer; (ii) recevoir une blessure; (iii) mourir.

cope¹ [koup] *n. Ecc:* chape *f*; pluvial *m, pl.* -aux.

cope² *v.tr.* (*a*) mettre la chape à (un évêque); (*b*) *Const:* chaperonner mettre un couronnement à (un mur). **coping** *n. Const:* chaperon *m* (d'un mur, etc.); **c. stone,** pierre *f* de couronnement.

cope³ *v.i.* (*a*) **to c. with s.o.,** s'occuper de qn; (*b*) **to c. with (sth.),** faire face à (une situation, un danger); venir à bout (d'une difficulté); **to be able to c. with a job,** être à la hauteur d'une tâche; **I just can't c.,** c'est au-dessus de mes forces; **I'll c. with it,** je m'en chargerai; **I'll c.,** je me débrouillerai.

Copenhagen [koupən'heig(ə)n] *Pr.n.* Copenhague *f.*

copier ['kɔpiər] *n.* **1.** copiste *mf.* **2.** copiste, imitateur, -trice. **3.** duplicateur *m*, copieur *m.*

co-pilot ['kou'pailət] *n. Av:* copilote *m.*

copious ['koupiəs] *a.* copieux, abondant; **c. notes,** des notes abondantes; **c. amounts,** de grandes quantités (de bière, etc.). **-ly** *adv.* copieusement.

co-plaintiff ['kou'pleintif] *n. Jur:* codemandeur, -eresse.

copper ['kɔpər] *n.* **1.** cuivre *m* (rouge). **2.** *Dom.Ec:* cuve *f* à lessive. **3.** *F:* sou *m*; **coppers,** petite monnaie; **to give a beggar a few coppers,** donner des sous à un mendiant. **4.** *attrib.* (*a*) de cuivre; en cuivre; **c. wire,** fil *m* de cuivre; (*b*) **c.(-coloured),** cuivré; *Bot:* **c. beech,** hêtre *m* rouge.

copper² *v.tr. Metalw:* cuivrer (un métal).

copper³ *n. F:* (*policeman*) flic *m.*

copperplate ['kɔpəpleit] *n.* **1.** plaque *f* de cuivre. **2.** *Engr:* taille-douce *f*; **c. printing,** impression *f* en creux, en taille-douce; **c. (writing),** écriture moulée.

coppersmith ['kɔpəsmiθ] *n.* chaudronnier *m* en, de, cuivre.

copperware ['kɔpəwɛər] *n.* dinanderie *f.*

coppery ['kɔpəri] *a.* cuivreux.

coppice ['kɔpis] *n.* taillis *m*, hallier *m.*

copra ['kɔprə] *n. Com:* copra(h) *m.*

coproduction [kouprə'dʌkʃ(ə)n] *n.* coproduction *f.*

copse [kɔps] *n.* taillis *n.*

Coptic ['kɔptik] **1.** *a.* coptique, copte. **2.** *n. Ling:* copte *m.*

copula ['kɔpjulə] *n. Gram: Log:* copule *f.*

copulate ['kɔpjuleit] *v.i.* s'accoupler.

copulation [kɔpju'leiʃ(ə)n] *n. Physiol:* copulation *f*; coït *m*; accouplement *m.*

copulative ['kɔpjulətiv] *a.* (*a*) *Gram: Log:* copulatif; (*b*) *Physiol: Anat:* copulateur, -trice.

copy¹ ['kɔpi] *n.* **1.** copie *f*; reproduction *f*; **this picture is only a c.,** ce tableau n'est qu'une copie. **2.** (*a*) copie, transcription *f* (d'une lettre, d'un texte); *Typew:* double *m*; **carbon c.,** (i) *Typew:* double (au carbone); (ii) copie exacte (de qch.); double (de qn); **rough c.,** brouillon *m*; *Jur: etc:* **fair c.,** copie (au net); (*b*) *Jur:* expédition *f* (d'un acte, d'un titre); **certified c.,** copie authentique; **true c.,** copie conforme; **file c.,** exemplaire des archives. **3.** modèle *m* (de dessin); exemple *m* (d'écriture). **4.** exemplaire *m* (d'un livre); numéro *m* (d'un journal); **500 copies of the book were printed,** le livre a été tiré à 500 exemplaires; **review, press, c.,** exemplaire de publicité, de service de presse. **5.** *Typ:* (*a*) manuscrit (destiné à l'impression); copie; (*b*) *Journ:* matière *f* à reportage; **this would make good c.,** voilà un bon sujet d'article. **6.** *Rec:* copie. **7.** *Cmptr:* **c. check,** contrôle *m* par duplication.

copy² *v.tr.* copier. **1.** (*a*) imiter, reproduire (une œuvre d'art, etc.); suivre (un dessin); (*b*) se modeler sur (qn); imiter (la démarche de qn); *Art: Lit: Mus:* copier, pasticher (le style de qn); (*c*) *v.i. Sch:* **to c.,** copier (sur un autre élève); (*d*) calquer (qch.) (**from,** sur); **expression copied from the English,** expression calquée sur l'anglais. **2. to c. (out),** copier (une lettre, etc.); **to c. out a passage from a book,** transcrire un passage d'une livre. **copying** *n.* transcription *f*, imitation *f*; *Sch:* copiage *m*; **c. machine,** duplicateur *m*; copieur *m*; **c. ink,** encre *f* à copier.

copybook ['kɔpibuk] *n.* (*a*) cahier *m* d'écriture; *F:* **to blot one's c.,** ternir sa réputation; (*b*) *attrib.* selon les règles; **a c. example,** un exemple classique.

copycat ['kɔpikæt] *n. F:* imitateur, -trice; singe *m.*

copyist ['kɔpiist] *n.* copiste *mf*; scribe *m.*

copyright¹ ['kɔpirait] *n.* droit *m* d'auteur (sur son œuvre); propriété *f* littéraire; copyright *m*; **out of c.,** (tombé) dans le domaine public; **c. reserved,** tous droits réservés; **c. notice,** mention *f* de réserve.

copyright² *v.tr. Publ:* déposer (un livre); copyrighter.

copyright³ *a.* (livre) qui est protégé par des droits d'auteur; (article) dont le droit de reproduction est réservé; (livre) qui n'est pas dans le domaine public; **c. (in all countries),** tous droits de reproduction et de traduction réservés (pour tous pays).

copywriter ['kɔpiraitər] *n.* (concepteur-) rédacteur *m* publicitaire.

coquetry ['koukitri] *n.* coquetterie *f.*

coquette [kə'ket] *n.* coquette *f.*

coquettish [kə'ketiʃ] *a.* **1.** flirteuse. **2.** (*a*) coquet; (*b*) (sourire, etc.) provocant, *F:* aguichant.

cor¹ [kɔːr] *n. Mus:* **c. anglais** [aŋ'glei], cor anglais.

cor² *int. P:* ça alors!

coral ['kɔr(ə)l] *a.* **1.** (*a*) corail *m, pl.* coraux; **c. island,** île corallienne, de corail; **c. reef,** récif corallien; **c. red,** corallin; **c. necklace,** collier *m* de corail; (*b*) *a. & n.* (*colour*) (de) corail.

corbel ['kɔːb(ə)l] *n. Arch:* corbeau *m*, console *f.*

cord¹ [kɔːd] *n.* **1.** (*a*) corde *f* (mince); cordon *m*; ficelle *f*; (*b*) *El:* cordon; (*c*) *Bookb:* nerf *m* (de dos de livre); (*d*) *Anat:* **the vocal cords,** les cordes vocales; **the spinal c.,** le cordon médullaire; **the umbilical c.,** le cordon ombilical; (*e*) *Min:* cordeau *m*, mèche *f.* **2.** (*a*) *Tex:* velours *m* à côtes; (*b*) **cords,** pantalon *m* de velours côtelé.

cord² *v.tr.* corder; attacher avec une corde; ligoter (un fagot, etc.). **corded** *a. Tex:* côtelé, à côtes.

cordage ['kɔːdidʒ] *n.* (*a*) cordage *m*; (*b*) *coll.* cordages.

cordial ['kɔːdi(ə)l] **1.** *a.* (accueil) cordial, chaleureux. **2.** *n.* cordial *m.* **-ally** *adv.* cordialement; *U.S:* (*at end of letter*) **c. yours,** bien sincèrement.

cordiality [kɔːdi'æliti] *n.* cordialité *f*; **exchange of cordialities,** échange *m* de cordialités.

cordite ['kɔːdait] *n. Exp:* cordite *f.*

cordon ['kɔːd(ə)n] *n.* **1.** (*a*) *Dressm:* cordon *m*, tresse *f*; (*b*) [kɔr'dɔ̃] cordon (d'un ordre de chevalerie); (*c*) **c. bleu** ['kɔrdɔ̃'blø] cordon(-)bleu. **2.** cordon (de police, de troupes); **sanitary c.,** cordon sanitaire. **3.** *Hort:* **c. (tree),** cordon.

cordon² *v.tr.* **the street was cordoned off by the police,** on isola la rue par un cordon de police.

corduroy ['kɔːdərɔi] *n. & a.* (*a*) *Tex:* velours à côtes, côtelé; *Cost:* **c. trousers, breeches,** *n.* **corduroys,** pantalon *m* de velours côtelé; (*b*) **c. road,** chemin *m* de rondins.

core¹ [kɔːr] *n.* centre *m*, partie centrale (d'une masse). **1.** cœur *m* (du bois, etc.); trognon *m* (d'une pomme, etc.); **hard c.,** noyau *m*; **selfish to the c.,** d'un égoïsme foncier; *F:* **he's rotten to the c.,** il est corrompu jusqu'à la moelle des os. **2.** bourbillon *m* (d'un abcès); cornillon *m* (d'un cor). **3.** (*a*) *Geol: etc:* noyau; (*of the earth*) nifé *m*; *Min:* **c. sample,** carotte *f*, témoin *m*, échantillon carotté; (*b*) *Metall:* noyau; **c. box,** boîte *f* à noyau(x); (*c*) *El:* noyau (d'un aimant); (*d*) *Civ.E: etc:* **watertight c.,** noyau d'étanchéité; (*e*) mèche *f* (d'un câble); (*f*) *Atom.Ph:* cœur (d'une pile atomique); (*g*) *Cmptr:* noyau; **c. memory,** mémoire *f* à tores (magnétiques).

core² *v.tr.* **1.** enlever le cœur (d'une pomme). **2. to c. out,** enlever le noyau (d'une pièce de fonte, etc.); noyauter, évider (un moule).

corer ['kɔːrər] *n.* (*a*) *Dom.Ec:* **apple c.,** vide-pomme *m*, *pl.* vide-pommes; (*b*) *Min: etc:* perforateur creux.

co-respondent ['kouri'spɔndənt] *n. Jur:* complice *m* de la femme (en adultère); codéfendeur *m* (en adultère).

coriander [kɔri'ændər] *n. Bot:* coriandre *f*; **c. seed,** semences *fpl* de coriandre.

Corinthian [kə'rinθiən] **1.** *a. Geog:* corinthien. **2.** *n. Geog:* Corinthien, -ienne.

cork¹ [kɔːk] *n.* **1.** *Bot:* liège *m*; **c. oak,** chêne-liège *m*, *pl.* chênes-lièges; **c. sole,** semelle *f* de, en, liège; **c.-tipped cigarettes,** cigarettes *fpl* à bouts de liège. **2.** bouchon *m* (de liège); **crown c.,** capsule *f* (métallique) de bouteille.

cork² *v.tr.* **1.** (*a*) **to c. (up) a bottle,** boucher une bouteille; (*b*) garnir (un filet, etc.) de bouchons. **2. to c. one's face,** se grimer avec un bouchon brûlé. **corked** *a.* (vin) qui sent le bouchon. **corking** *a. P: A:* épatant, fameux.

corkage ['kɔːkidʒ] *n.* (*in restaurant*) droit *m* (de débouchage) sur un vin qui a été apporté par les consommateurs.

corker ['kɔːkər] *n. P: A:* **1.** (*a*) (gros) mensonge *m.* **2.** type épatant; fille épatante.

corkscrew¹ ['kɔːkskruː] *n.* tire-bouchon *m*, *pl.* tire-bouchons; *Hairdr:* **c. curl,** tire-bouchon; boudin *m.*

corkscrew² **1.** *v.tr.* tracer (une ligne) en spirale. **2.** *v.i.* (*a*) (*of wire*) vriller; (*b*) (*of stair*) tourner en vrille.

corkwood ['kɔːkwud] *n. Bot:* bois *m* de liège.

corm [kɔːm] *n. Bot:* bulbe *m* (solide).

cormorant ['kɔːmərənt] *n. Orn:* cormoran *m.*

corn¹ [kɔːn] *n.* **1.** grain *m* (de blé, etc.). **2.** *coll.* (*a*) grains; blé(s) *m* (*pl*); céréales *fpl*; **winter c.,** semis *m* d'hiver; **C. Exchange,** halle *f* aux blés; **c. chandler, merchant,** marchand *m* de blé, de grains; (*b*) *esp. NAm:* **(Indian) c.,** maïs *m*; **c. on the cob,** maïs en épi; **c. (whiskey),** whisky *m* de maïs; (*c*) *esp. Scot:* avoine *f*; **to give one's horse a feed of c.,** donner un picotin à son cheval. **3.** *Bot:* **c. cockle,** nielle *f* des blés; **c. poppy,** coquelicot *m*; **c. salad,** mâche *f.* **4.** *F:* banalité *f.*

corn² *n.* cor *m* (à l'orteil, etc.); **c. plaster,** coricide *m*; *F:* **to tread on s.o.'s corns,** marcher sur les pieds de qn; froisser qn.

corn³ *v.tr.* saler (du bœuf); **corned beef,** bœuf de conserve, *Mil: F:* singe *m.*

cornbread ['kɔːnbred] *n. NAm: Cu:* pain *m* de farine de maïs.

corncob ['kɔːnkɔb] *n.* **1.** épi *m* de maïs. **2.** pipe *f* en épi de maïs.

corncrake ['kɔːnkreik] *n. Orn:* râle *m* des genêts; *F:* **a voice like a c.,** une voix de crécelle.

cornea ['kɔːniə] *n. Anat:* cornée *f* (de l'œil).

corneal ['kɔːniəl] *a. Anat:* cornéen; *Med:* **c. graft,** greffe *f* de la cornée.

cornelian [kɔ'niːliən] *n. Lap:* cornaline *f.*

corner¹ ['kɔːnər] *n.* **1.** coin *m*, angle *m*; **to turn down the c. of a page,** faire une corne à une page; *Const:* **c. post,** poteau *m* d'angle; borne *f*; *F:* **to rub the corners off s.o.,** dégourdir qn. **2.** (*a*) coin; encoignure *f* (d'une pièce, etc.); *Furn:* **c. cupboard,** armoire *f* de coin; **chimney c.,** coin de feu; **to put a child in the c.,** mettre un enfant au coin; **to drive s.o. into a c.,** (i) acculer qn; (ii) mettre qn au pied du mur; **driven into a c.,** au pied du mur; **in a tight c.,** en mauvaise passe; (*b*) **the four corners of the earth,** les quatre coins du monde; **to search every c. of the house,** chercher dans tous les coins et recoins de la maison; (*c*) *Fb:* **c. (kick),** coup *m* de pied de coin; corner *m*; **c. flag,** piquet *m* de coin; (*d*) commissure *f* (des lèvres, de l'œil); **to look out of the c. of one's eye,** regarder du coin de l'œil. **3.** (*a*) coin, angle (de rue); **situated at the c.,** situé au coin; **c. house,** maison *f* qui fait l'angle de la rue; **you'll find the grocer's round the c.,** vous trouverez l'épicerie en tournant le coin; **spring is just around the c.,** ce sera bientôt le printemps; **with the elections just round the c.,** avec les élections qui approchent; **to turn the c.,** (i) tourner le coin; (ii) passer le moment critique; (*of sick person*) surmonter la crise; (*b*) tournant *m*; *Aut: etc:* virage *m*; **sharp c.,** tournant brusque; *Aut: etc:* **to take a c.,** prendre un virage; virer; **to cut a c. (close),** virer court; **to cut corners,** (i) faire des économies (d'argent, de temps); (ii) contourner les règlements. **4.** *Com:* monopole *m*; corner *m.*

corner² *v.tr.* **1.** (*a*) mettre (qch.) dans un coin; (*b*) acculer, coincer (qn); (*c*) mettre (qn) au pied du mur. **2.** biseauter (le bois). **3.** *Com:* accaparer (le marché). **4.** *v.i. Aut: etc:* prendre un virage; **this car corners well,** cette voiture prend bien les virages. **cornered** *a.* acculé; coincé. **cornering** *n.* **1.** acculement *m* (d'un animal, etc.). **2.** *Com:* accaparement *m* (du marché). **3. the car is good at c.,** la voiture prend bien les virages.

cornerstone ['kɔːnəstoun] *n.* **1.** *Const:* pierre *f* angulaire; écoinçon *m*; **the c. of civilization,** la pierre angulaire de la civilisation. **2.** *Surv:* borne *f.*

cornet ['kɔːnit, *NAm:* kɔː'net] *n.* **1.** *Mus:* (*a*) cornet *m* à pistons; (*b*) (*pers.*) cornettiste *m.* **2.** cornet (en papier). **3.** (*a*) *Comest:* oublie *f* (en cornet); (*b*) **ice-cream c.,** cornet *m* de glace.

cornet(t)ist ['kɔːnitist, *NAm:* kɔː'netist] *n. Mus:* cornettiste *mf.*

cornfield ['kɔːnfiːld] *n.* champ *m* de blé, *NAm:* de maïs.

cornflakes ['kɔːnfleiks] *n.pl. Comest:* flocons *mpl* de maïs; cornflakes *mpl.*

cornflour ['kɔːnflauər] *n.* farine *f* de maïs.

cornflower ['kɔːnflauər] *n. Bot:* bleuet *m*, bluet *m*, barbeau *m*; **c. blue,** bleu barbeau *inv.*

cornice ['kɔːnis] *n.* **1.** *Arch:* corniche *f.* **2.** *Furn:* chapiteau *m* (d'armoire). **3.** *Mount:* corniche (de neige).

Cornish ['kɔːniʃ] **1.** *a.* (*a*) *Geog:* cornouaillais (*b*) *Cu:* **C. pasty,** chausson *m* de viande. **2.** *n. Ling:* cornique *m.*

Cornishman, -woman, *pl.* **-men, -women**

['kɔ:niʃmən, -wumən; -mən, -wimin] *n. Geog:* Cornouaillais, -aise (du sud-ouest de l'Angleterre).
cornmeal ['kɔ:nmi:l] *n. NAm:* farine *f* de maïs.
cornucopia, *pl.* **-as** [kɔ:nju'koupiə, -əz] *n.* corne *f* d'abondance.
Cornwall ['kɔ:nw(ə)l] *Pr.n. Geog:* Cornouailles *f.*
corny ['kɔ:ni] *a. F:* banal; **c. joke,** plaisanterie usée.
corolla [kə'rɔlə] *n. Bot:* corolle *f.*
corollary [kə'rɔləri] *n.* corollaire *m.*
corona, *pl.* **-ae** [kə'rounə, -i] *n. Astr: Bot: El: etc:* couronne *f; Astr:* **solar c.,** couronne solaire.
coronary ['kɔrənəri] (*a*) *a. & n. Anat:* **c. (artery),** artère *f* coronaire; *Med:* **c. (thrombosis),** infarctus *m* du myocarde; (*b*) *a. Med:* coronarien; (*c*) *a.* **c. cushion, ring,** bourrelet *m* (de pied de cheval).
coronation [kɔrə'neiʃ(ə)n] *n.* couronnement *m;* **c. mug,** tasse commémorative du couronnement.
coroner ['kɔrənər] *n. Jur:* coroner *m* (officier civil chargé d'instruire, assisté d'un jury, en cas de mort violente ou subite).
coronet ['kɔrənit] *n.* (*a*) (petite) couronne; cercle *m;* (*b*) (*lady's*) diadème *m.*
corporal[1] ['kɔ:pər(ə)l] *a.* corporel; (défectuosité) physique; **c. punishment,** punition corporelle.
corporal[2] *n.* (*a*) *Mil:* (*of infantry*) caporal *m,* -aux; (*of cavalry, artillery*) brigadier *m;* (*b*) *Mil.Av:* caporal-chef *m;* (*c*) (*women's services*) sixième catégorie *f.*
corporate ['kɔ:p(ə)rət] *a.* **1.** constitué (en corps); formant (un) corps; *Jur:* **body c., c. body,** corps constitué; corporation *f.* **2.** (*a*) de corporation, de corps; **c. feeling,** esprit *m* de corps; (*b*) *Com:* corporatif, de société; **c. name,** raison sociale.
corporation [kɔ:pə'reiʃ(ə)n] *n.* **1.** corporation *f.* **2.** *Com:* société enregistrée; compagnie *f;* **public c.,** entreprise publique. **3.** *Jur:* personne morale. **4. municipal c.,** conseil municipal; municipalité *f;* **the mayor and c.,** le corps municipal; *Fin:* **c. stocks,** emprunts *mpl* de ville; **c. tax,** impôt sur les sociétés. **5.** *F:* bedaine *f,* bedon *m.*
corporeal [kɔ:'pɔ:riəl] *a.* corporel, matériel.
corps [kɔ:r, *pl.* kɔ:z] *n.inv.* (*a*) corps *m;* **the diplomatic c.,** le corps diplomatique; (*b*) *Mil:* corps d'armée; **tank c.,** formation *f* de chars; **c. d'élite,** corps d'élite; (*c*) **c. de ballet** [də'bælei] corps de ballet.
corpse [kɔ:ps] *n.* cadavre *m;* corps (mort).
corpulence ['kɔ:pjuləns] *n.* corpulence *f,* obésité *f.*
corpulent ['kɔ:pjulənt] *a.* corpulent, obèse.
corpus ['kɔ:pəs] *n.* **1.** (*a*) corpus *m,* recueil *m* (d'inscriptions, etc.); (*b*) *Jur:* **c. delicti** [di'liktai], le corps du délit. **2.** *R.C.Ch:* **Corpus Christi** ['kristi], la Fête-Dieu.
corpuscle ['kɔ:pʌsl] *n.* corpuscule *m;* **red, white, blood corpuscles,** globules rouges, blancs.
corral[1] [kə'rɑ:l] *n.* corral *m, pl.* -als.
corral[2] *v.tr.* renfermer (des bestiaux, chevaux, etc.) dans un corral.
correct[1] [kə'rekt] *v.tr.* **1.** relever les fautes (d'un thème, etc.); corriger (une épreuve d'imprimerie, un thème). **2.** rectifier (une erreur); modifier (le réglage d'un instrument); *Com:* **corrected invoice,** facture rectificative. **3.** (*a*) reprendre (qn); **to c. oneself,** se reprendre; (*b*) punir, infliger une correction à (un coupable, etc.). **4.** contrebalancer (une influence, un goût).
correct[2] *a.* **1.** correct, exact; **c. answer,** réponse *f* juste; **c. to a millimetre,** exact à un millimètre près; **his prediction proved c.,** sa prédiction s'est vérifiée; **if my memory is c.,** si j'ai bonne mémoire. **2.** (*of behaviour, etc.*) bienséant, correct; (*of pers.*) comme il faut; **it's the c. thing to . . .,** la politesse veut que . . .. **-ly** *adv.* **1.** correctement; **to speak c.,** parler correctement; **or (to put it) more c.,** ou pour mieux dire. **2.** (se conduire) correctement.
correction [kə'rekʃ(ə)n] *n.* **1.** correction *f* (d'une épreuve, d'un devoir, etc.); recrificatif *m;* redressement *m* (d'un compte); **subject to c.,** sous toutes réserves. **2.** correction, punition *f.* **3.** *Ph: Artil: Mec.E: etc:* correction *Opt: etc:* **c. for astigmatism, etc.,** correction de l'astigmatisme, etc.
corrective [kə'rektiv] **1.** *n. Med:* correctif *m.* **2.** *a.* (*a*) correctif, rectifiant; (verre) correcteur; **c. exercises,** gymnastique médicale, corrective; (*b*) de correction.
correctness [kə'rektnis] *n.* correction *f,* convenance *f* (de tenue, etc.); exactitude *f,* justesse *f* (d'une description); rectitude *f* (de jugement).
corrector [kə'rektər] *n.* **1.** (*pers.*) (*a*) correcteur, -trice; (*b*) *Typ:* **press c.,** correcteur *m* (d'épreuves). **2.** *Tchn:* (appareil, dispositif) correcteur.
correlate ['kɔrileit] **1.** *v.i.* correspondre (**with, to,** à); être en corrélation (**with,** avec); *Stat:* corréler. **2.** *v.tr.* mettre (qch.) en corrélation (**with,** avec).
correlation [kɔri'leiʃ(ə)n] *n.* corrélation *f.*
correlative [kɔ'relətiv] *a. & n.* corrélatif (*m*); en corrélation (**with,** avec).
correspond [kɔris'pɔnd] *v.i.* **1.** (*a*) correspondre, être conforme (**with, to,** à); *Com:* **to c. to sample,** être conforme à l'échantillon; (*b*) correspondre (**to,** avec). **2.** correspondre (**with s.o.,** avec qn); échanger des lettres (avec qn). **corresponding** *a.* **1.** correspondant (**to,** à); conforme (**to,** à). **2. c. member,** membre correspondent (d'une société). **correspondingly** *adv.* également, à l'avenant.
correspondence [kɔris'pɔndəns] *n.* **1.** correspondance *f* (**with, to,** avec); **the c. between cause and effect,** le rapport, entre la cause et l'effet. **2.** (*a*) correspondance; **to be in c. with s.o.,** être en correspondance avec qn; *Sch:* **c. course,** cours *m* par correspondance; (*b*) courrier *m;* **to do one's c.,** faire sa correspondance.
correspondent [kɔris'pɔndənt] *n.* correspondant, -ante; **regular c.,** correspondant régulier; *Journ:* **parliamentary c.,** rédacteur *m* parlementaire; **war c.,** correspondant de guerre; **special c.,** envoyé spécial.
corridor ['kɔridɔ:r] *n.* couloir *m,* corridor *m;* **c. train,** train *m* à couloir; *Av:* **air c.,** couloir aérien.
corroborate [kə'rɔbəreit] *v.tr.* corroborer, confirmer (une déclaration); **the facts c. his statements,** les faits *mpl* viennent à l'appui de ce qu'il dit.
corroboration [kərɔbə'reiʃ(ə)n] *n.* corroboration *f,* confirmation *f;* **in c. of . . .,** à l'appui de . . ..
corroborative [kə'rɔb(ə)rətiv] *a.* qui confirme, corroborant.
corrode [kə'roud] **1.** *v.tr.* corroder, attaquer (le métal); ronger (le métal). **2.** *v.i.* se corroder.
corrosion [kə'rouʒ(ə)n] *n.* corrosion *f.*
corrosive [kə'rousiv] *a. & n.* corrosif (*m*), corrodant (*m*); **non-corrosive,** inoxydable.
corrugated ['kɔrugeitid] *a.* **c. iron,** tôle ondulée; **c. iron roof,** toit en tôle ondulée; **c. cardboard,** carton ondulé.
corrupt[1] [kə'rʌpt] *a.* (*a*) corrompu; (presse) vénale; **c. practices,** (i) tractations malhonnêtes; brigues *fpl;* (ii) trafic *m* d'influence; (*b*) (texte) corrompu, altéré. **-ly** *adv.* d'une manière corrompue; par corruption.
corrupt[2] **1.** *v.tr.* corrompre, altérer (un texte, etc.); démoraliser (qn); dépraver, (la jeunesse). **2.** *v.i.* (*a*) se corrompre; (*b*) se dépraver. **corrupting,** *a.* (*a*) corrompant; corrupteur, -trice; (*b*) dépravant.
corruptible [kə'rʌptəbl] *a.* corruptible; vénal, -aux.
corruption [kə'rʌpʃ(ə)n] *n.* **1.** (*a*) corruption *f;* (*b*) corruption, dépravation *f.* **2.** action *f* de corrompre; corruption; **bribery and c.,** corruption, subornation.
corruptive [kə'rʌptiv] *a.* corruptif.
corsage [kɔ:'sɑ:ʒ] *n.* **1.** *Cost:* corsage *m.* **2.** boutonnière (portée au corsage).

corsair ['kɔːsɛər] *n.* corsaire *m.*
corset ['kɔːsit] *n. Cost:* corset *m*; **orthopaedic, surgical, c.,** corset orthopédique.
Corsica ['kɔːsikə] *Pr.n. Geog:* Corse *f.*
Corsican ['kɔːsikən] *Geog:* **1.** *a.* corse. **2.** *n.* Corse *mf.*
cortège [kɔr'teʒ] *n.* cortège *m*; **funeral c.,** convoi *m*, cortège, funèbre.
cortex, *pl.* **-ices** ['kɔːteks, -isiːz] *n. Bot: Anat:* cortex *m.*
cortisone ['kɔːtizoun] *n. Bio-Ch: Med:* cortisone *f.*
corundum [kə'rʌndəm] *n. Miner:* corindon *m.*
corvette [kɔː'vet] *n. Nau:* corvette *f.*
cos [kɔs] *n. Hort:* **c. (lettuce),** (laitue) romaine (*f*).
cosh¹ [kɔʃ] *n. F:* matraque *f*, assommoir *m.*
cosh² *v.tr. F:* assommer, matraquer (qn).
co-signatory ['kou'signətəri] *a.* & *n.* cosignataire (*mf*).
cosine ['kousain] *n. Mth:* cosinus *m.*
cosiness ['kouzinis] *n.* confortable *m* (d'un fauteuil, d'un petit coin intime); chaleur *f* agréable (du coin du feu, etc.).
cosmetic [kɔz'metik] *a.* & *n.* cosmétique (*m*); *n.pl.* **cosmetics,** produits *mpl* de beauté; **c. surgery,** chirurgie *f* esthétique.
cosmic ['kɔzmik] *a.* (rayon, etc.) cosmique.
cosmology [kɔz'mɔlədʒi] *n.* cosmologie *f.*
cosmonaut ['kɔzmounɔːt] *n.* cosmonaute *mf.*
cosmopolitan [kɔzmə'pɔlit(ə)n] *a.* & *n.* cosmopolite (*mf*).
cosmos ['kɔzmɔs] *n.* cosmos *m*; **the c.,** l'univers *m.*
Cossack ['kɔsæk] **1.** *a.* cosaque. **2.** *n.* Cosaque *mf.*
cosset ['kɔsit] *v.tr.* dorloter, choyer, câliner (qn).
cost¹ [kɔst] *n.* **1.** coût *m*, frais *mpl*; **c. of living,** coût de la vie; **c.-of-living allowance,** indemnité *f* de cherté de vie; **at the c. of one's life,** au prix de sa vie; **at little, great, c.,** à peu de, à grands, frais; **at any c., at all costs,** à tout prix; coûte que coûte; **I learnt it to my c.,** je l'ai appris à mes dépens, pour mon malheur; *Ind: Com:* **c. price,** prix de revient; **to sell at c.,** vendre au prix coûtant; **c. accounting,** comptabilité *f* de prix de revient. **2.** *Jur:* **costs,** frais d'instance; dépens *mpl*; **they were ordered to pay costs,** ils furent condamnés aux frais.
cost² **1.** *v.i.* & *tr.* (*p.t.* & *p.p.* **cost**) coûter; **how much does it c.?** combien cela coûte-t-il? **that will c. him a great deal of money, of trouble,** cela lui coûtera beaucoup d'argent, beaucoup de peine; **to c. a fortune, the earth,** coûter un argent fou, coûter les yeux de la tête; **the attempt c. him his life,** cette tentative lui coûta la vie; **it must have c. him something to admit that,** il a dû lui en coûter de l'avouer. **2.** *v.tr.* (*p.t.* & *p.p.* **costed**) *Com: Ind:* établir le prix de revient (d'un article). **costing** *n. Ind: Com:* établissement *m* du, des, prix de revient.
co-star¹ ['koustɑːr] *n. Cin: etc:* acteur, actrice, qui partage la vedette avec un(e) autre.
co-star² *v.i. Cin: etc:* partager la vedette (**with,** avec).
Costa Rican ['kɔstə'riːkən] **1.** *a.* costaricain. **2.** *n.* Costaricain, -aine.
coster(monger) ['kɔstər, 'kɔstəmʌŋgər] *n.* marchand *m* des quatre saisons.
costive ['kɔstiv] *a.* constipé.
costliness ['kɔstlinis] *n.* **1.** richesse *f*, somptuosité *f* (de l'ameublement, etc.). **2.** haut prix, cherté *f.*
costly ['kɔstli] *a.* **1.** (*a*) précieux; (*b*) (ameublement, etc.) riche, somptueux. **2.** coûteux, cher.
costume ['kɔstjum] *n.* (*a*) costume *m*; **national c.,** costume national; **c. jewellery,** bijoux *mpl* de fantaisie; *Th:* **c. play,** pièce historique; (*b*) **bathing c.,** maillot *m* de bain; (*c*) *O:* (*woman's suit*) tailleur (*m*).
costum(i)er [kɔs'tjum(i)ər] *n.* costumier *m*; **theatrical c.,** costumier de théâtre.
cosy ['kouzi] **1.** *a.* (*of place, thg*) chaud; confortable; (*of pers.*) bien au chaud; à l'aise; **c. room,** pièce confortable; **it's c. here,** il fait bon ici; *F:* **a c. little job,** un lit de plumes. **2.** *n.* **egg c.,** couvre-œuf *m, pl.* couvre-œufs; **tea c.,** couvre-théière *m, pl.* couvre-théières. **-ily** *adv.* confortablement; douillettement.
cot [kɔt] *n.* **1.** lit *m* d'enfant. **2.** (*a*) *esp. NAm:* petit lit (pliant); lit de camp; (*b*) *Nau:* cadre *m* à l'anglaise.
cotangent ['kou'tæn(d)ʒ(ə)nt] *n. Mth:* cotangente *f.*
cote [kout] *n.* (*a*) colombier *m*; (*b*) abri *m.*
coterie ['koutəri] *n.* coterie *f.*
cottage ['kɔtidʒ] *n.* petite maison (à la campagne); cottage *m*; **thatched c.,** chaumière *f*; **c. industry,** artisanat *m*; industrie artisanale; **c. cheese,** fromage blanc; **c. hospital,** hôpital *m* de médecine générale (où on ne traite pas les cas sérieux).
cotter ['kɔtər] *n. Mec.E:* goupille *f*; clavette *f.*
cotton¹ ['kɔt(ə)n] *n.* **1.** (*a*) *Bot:* **c. (plant),** cotonnier *m*; **c. plantation,** cotonnerie *f*; (*b*) coton *m*; **c. growing,** culture *f* du coton; *U.S:* **c. belt,** région du coton; **c. mill,** filature *f* de coton; cotonnerie; *Pharm:* **c. wool,** *U.S:* **absorbent c.,** ouate *f*, coton hydrophile; **my legs feel like c. wool,** j'ai les jambes en coton; (*c*) *Bot:* **c. grass,** linaigrette *f*; lin *m* des marais. **2.** *Tex:* (*a*) **c. yarn,** coton filé; fil *m* de coton; (*b*) **c. goods,** cotonnades *fpl*; **c. (cloth),** (toile *f* de) coton; percale *f*; **coarse c.,** rouennerie *f*; **printed c.,** coton imprimé. **3.** *Dom.Ec.* **sewing c.,** fil à coudre; fil de coton; **embroidery c.,** coton à broder.
cotton² *v.i. F:* **to c. on to sth.,** piger qch.
cottonseed ['kɔtnsiːd] *n.* graine *f* de coton; **c. oil,** huile *f* de coton.
cottontail ['kɔtnteil] *n. U.S:* lapin *m* (de garenne).
cotyledon [kɔti'liːd(ə)n] *n. Bot:* cotylédon *m.*
couch¹ [kautʃ] *n. Furn:* divan *m*; **studio c.,** divan-lit *m, pl.* divans-lits.
couch² *v.tr.* **1.** (*a*) *Lit:* (*of animal*) **to be couched on the ground,** être couché par terre; (*b*) *Brew:* coucher (le grain); *Paperm:* coucher (une feuille) sur les feutres. **2.** formuler, rédiger; **their reply was couched in insulting language,** leur réponse était exprimée en termes injurieux.
couch-grass ['kautʃ-, 'kuːtʃgrɑːs] *n. Bot:* chiendent *m.*
couchette [ku'ʃet] *n. Rail: etc:* couchette *f.*
cougar ['kuːgər] *n. Z:* couguar *m*, puma *m.*
cough¹ [kɔf] *n.* toux *f*; **to have a c.,** tousser; **dry, loose, c.,** toux sèche, grasse; **whooping c.,** coqueluche *f*; **he gave a c. to warn me,** il toussa pour m'avertir; **c. mixture, c. drop, lozenge,** sirop *m* contre la toux; pastille contre, pour, la toux.
cough² **1.** *v.i.* (*of pers., of animal, F: of engine*) tousser. **2.** *v.tr.* **to c. up, out, sth.,** cracher qch. (en toussant); **to c. up phlegm, blood,** cracher des glaires, du sang; *F: v.i.* **to c. up,** payer, *P:* cracher. **coughing** *n.* toux *f*; **fit of c.,** quinte *f* de toux.
couldn't-care-less ['kud(ə)ntkɛə'les] *a.* **c.-c.-l. attitude,** je-m'en-fichisme *m*, je-m'en-foutisme *m.*
coulter ['koultər] *n. Agr:* coutre *m* (de charrue).
council ['kaunsəl] *n.* **1.** conseil *m*; *Adm:* **district c.** = conseil municipal; **county c.** = conseil départemental; **c. house** = habitation *f* à loyer modéré, H.L.M. *f*; **the Privy C.,** le Conseil privé (du souverain); **C. of Europe,** Conseil de l'Europe; **to hold a c. of war,** se réunir en conseil; *Pol.Ec:* **consumer c.,** comité (consultatif) des consommateurs. **2.** *Ecc:* concile *m* (œcuménique, etc.).
councillor ['kaunsilər] *n.* conseiller *m*; membre *m* du conseil; **county c.,** = conseiller général.
counsel¹ ['kauns(ə)l] *n.* **1.** délibération *f*; consultation *f*; **to take c. with s.o.,** consulter avec qn (**about,**

sur). **2.** conseil *m*, avis *m*. **3.** dessein *m*, intention *f*; **to keep one's (own) c.,** garder ses projets pour soi. **4.** *Jur:* (*a*) avocat *m*; conseil *m*; **to be represented by c.,** comparaître par avoué; **c. for the defence,** défenseur *m*; (*in civil law*) avocat de la défense; (*b*) **King's, Queen's, c.,** conseiller du Roi, de la Reine; conseiller de la Couronne; (*c*) *coll.* le barreau; les avocats.

counsel² *v.tr.* **(counselled,** *NAm:* **counseled) to c. s.o. to do sth.,** conseiller à qn de faire qch.

counsellor, *NAm:* **counselor** ['kauns(ə)lər] *n.* (*a*) *Dipl:* conseiller *m* d'ambassade; (*b*) conseiller *m*; **marriage guidance c.,** conseiller conjugal.

count¹ [kaunt] *n.* **1.** (*a*) compte *m*; (*of votes*) dépouillement *m*; (*of people*) dénombrement *m*; **to keep c. of . . .,** tenir le compte de . . .; **to lose c.,** perdre le compte; **to lose c. of time,** perdre la notion du temps; *Med:* **blood c.,** numération *f* globulaire; (*b*) total *m*; **this is short of the c.,** cela ne fait pas le compte; (*c*) *Cmptr:* comptage *m*. **2.** *Jur:* chef *m* (d'accusation); **not guilty on the first count,** non coupable au premier chef. **3.** *Parl:* **c. out,** ajournement *m* (quand il y a moins de quarante membres présents). **4.** *Box:* compte (de dix seconds); **to take the c.,** rester sur le plancher pour le compte; être knock-out; *F:* **to be out for the c.,** être K.O.

count² **1.** *v.tr.* (*a*) compter (des personnes, la dépense); dénombrer (des personnes, ses troupeaux, etc.); (*at election*) **to c. the votes,** dépouiller le scrutin; **without counting . . .,** sans compter . . .; (*b*) **to c. s.o. among one's friends,** compter qn parmi ses amis; **to c. s.o., sth., (to be) sth.,** tenir qn, qch., pour qch.; **to be counted as a member,** être compté au nombre des membres. **2.** *v.i.* (*a*) compter; **to c. on one's fingers,** compter sur ses doigts; **counting from tomorrow,** à compter de demain; (*b*) **to c. on doing sth.,** compter faire qch.; (*c*) **to c. on s.o., sth.,** compter sur qn, qch.; **don't c. on me,** ne comptez pas sur moi. **3.** *v.tr.* **he counted me out twenty £1 notes,** il m'a compté un à un vingt billets d'une livre; *Box:* **to be counted out,** rester sur le plancher pour le compte; être (mis) knock-out; *Pol:* **to c. out the House,** ajourner la Chambre faute d'un quorum; **(you can) c. me out,** ne comptez pas sur moi. **4.** *v.i.* (*a*) **he counts among my best friends,** il compte parmi mes meilleurs amis; *Cards:* **card that counts,** (carte) marquante (*f*); **two children c. as one adult,** deux enfants comptent comme un adulte; **he doesn't c.,** il ne compte pas; (*b*) avoir de l'importance; **every vote counts,** chaque voix a son importance; **every minute counts,** il n'y a pas une minute à perdre. **count down** *v.i.* compter à rebours. **counting** *n.* **1.** compte *m*; dépouillement *m* (du scrutin); dénombrement *m* (des personnes). **2.** *Com:* **c. house,** (service *m* de) la comptabilité.

count³ *n.m.* (*title*) comte; **the C. of Monte Cristo,** le comte de Monte Cristo.

countdown ['kauntdaun] *n.* compte *m* à rebours.

countenance¹ ['kauntinəns] *n. esp. Lit:* **1.** (i) (expression *f* du) visage; (ii) contenance *f*; **to lose c.,** se décontenancer; perdre contenance. **2.** appui *m*; **to give, lend, c. to s.o., to sth.,** appuyer qn, qch.

countenance² *v.tr.* **1.** approuver, sanctionner (une action). **2.** encourager, soutenir (qn) **(in,** dans).

counter¹ ['kauntər] *n.* **1.** (*pers.*) compteur, -euse. **2.** (*a*) *Mec.E:* compteur *m*; *Atom.Ph:* **Geiger c.,** compteur (de) Geiger; (*b*) *Cmptr:* compteur; **binary c.,** compteur binaire. **3.** *Games:* (i) (*square*) fiche *f*; (ii) (*round*) jeton *m*; *Ind:* jeton. **4.** (*a*) (*in bank, etc.*) guichets *mpl*; caisse *f*; **payable over the c.,** payable au guichet; (*b*) (*in shop*) comptoir *m*; (*in supermarket*) rayon *m*; **sold over the c.,** vendu (au) comptant; **to sell under the c.,** vendre en cachette; **c. hand,** vendeur, -euse.

counter² **1.** *n.* (*a*) *Fenc:* contre *m*; (*b*) *Box:* coup *m* d'arrêt; contre. **2.** *a.* (*a*) contraire, opposé **(to,** à); (*b*) contre-; **c. attraction,** (i) attraction opposée; (ii) attraction destinée à faire concurrence au clou de la fête, etc.; **c. declaration,** contre-déclaration *f*; *Med:* **c. indication,** contre-indication *f*; **c. reaction,** contre-réaction *f*; **c. revolution,** contre-révolution *f*. **3.** *adv.* en sens inverse; **to act c. to one's orders,** agir contrairement à ses instructions.

counter³ *v.tr.* aller à l'encontre de (qn, qch.); contrecarrer (les desseins de qn); *Box:* **to c. (a blow),** parer, bloquer (un coup) et riposter en même temps.

counteract [kauntə'rækt] *v.tr.* **1.** contrarier, contrecarrer (un projet). **2.** neutraliser (une influence); parer à (un résultat); riposter à, contrecarrer (un effet).

counterattack¹ ['kauntərətæk] *n.* *Mil:* contre-attaque *f*; retour offensif.

counterattack² *v.tr. & i.* contre-attaquer.

counterbalance¹ ['kauntəbæləns] *n.* contrepoids *m*.

counterbalance² [kauntə'bæləns] *v.tr.* contrebalancer; faire contrepoids à (qch.).

countercharge ['kauntətʃɑːdʒ] *n.* *Jur:* contre-accusation *f*; contre-plainte *f*.

countercheck ['kauntətʃek] *v.tr.* vérifier (une seconde fois).

counter-claim¹ ['kauntəkleim] *n.* *Jur:* demande reconventionnelle, reconvention *f*.

counter-claim² *v.tr.* *Jur:* faire une demande reconventionnelle (en dommages-intérêts).

counterclockwise [kauntə'klɔkwaiz] *adv.* dans le sens contraire des aiguilles d'une montre.

counterespionage [kauntər'espiənɑːʒ] *n.* contre-espionnage *m*.

counterfeit¹ ['kauntəfi(ː)t] **1.** *a.* faux; **c. coin,** fausse monnaie. **2.** *n.* contrefaçon *f*; faux *m*.

counterfeit² *v.tr.* contrefaire (la monnaie, etc.).

counterfeiting *n.* contrefaction *f*, contrefaçon *f*.

counterfeiter ['kauntəfi(ː)tər] *n.* faux monnayeur.

counterfoil ['kauntəfɔil] *n.* souche *f*, talon *m* (de chèque, de quittance).

counterintelligence ['kauntərin'telidʒəns] *n.* contre-espionnage *m*.

countermand¹ ['kauntəmɑːnd] *n.* contremandement *m*, contrordre *m*, contraviș *m*.

countermand² *v.tr.* contremander; annuler (un ordre); *Com:* **to c. the order for sth.,** décommander qch.

countermeasure ['kauntəmeʒər] *n.* contre-mesure *f*, *pl.* contre-mesures.

countermove ['kauntəmuːv] *n.* contre-mesure *f*, *pl.* contre-mesures.

counteroffensive ['kauntərə'fensiv] *n.* *Mil:* contre-offensive *f*.

counterorder ['kauntərɔːdər] *n.* contrordre *m*.

counterpane ['kauntəpein] *n.* courtepointe *f*.

counterpart ['kauntəpɑːt] *n.* **1.** (*a*) contre-partie *f*; analogue *m*; équivalent *m*; pendant *m* (d'un tableau, etc.); **to be the c. of . . .,** aller de pair avec . . .; (*b*) (*pers.*) homologue *m*. **2.** double *m* (d'un document); contre-partie.

counterplot ['kauntəplɔt] *n.* contre-ruse *f*.

counterpoint ['kauntəpɔint] *n.* *Mus:* contrepoint *m*.

counterpoise¹ ['kauntəpɔiz] *n.* **1.** contrepoids *m*; **c. bridge,** pont *m* à bascule. **2.** équilibre; **in c.,** en équilibre.

counterpoise² *v.tr.* contrebalancer; faire contrepoids à (qch.).

counterproductive ['kauntəprə'dʌktiv] *a.* qui a des effets contraires; improductif.

counterproposal ['kauntəprə'pouz(ə)l] *n.* contre-proposition *f*.

countersign¹ ['kauntəsain] *n. Mil: etc:* mot *m* d'ordre; **advance and give the c.,** avance à l'ordre.

countersign² *v.tr.* contresigner, signer en second, viser (un ordre, etc.); ratifier (un ordre).

countersignature ['kauntə'signətjər] *n.* **1.** contreseing *m.* **2.** approuvé *m.*

countersink¹ ['kauntəsiŋk] *n.* **1.** *Tls:* fraise *f.* **2.** fraisure *f* (d'un trou); noyure *f* (pour tête de vis).

countersink² *v.tr.* (*p.t. & p.p.* **countersunk**) *Carp: Mec.E: etc:* **1.** fraiser. **2.** noyer (la tête d'une vis).

counterstroke ['kauntəstrouk] *n. Mil:* retour offensif.

counter-tenor ['kauntətenər] *n. Mus:* haute-contre *f, pl.* hautes-contre; alto *m.*

counterweight ['kauntəweit] *n.* contrepoids *m.*

countess ['kauntis] *n.* (*title*) comtesse *f.*

countless ['kauntlis] *a.* innombrable, sans nombre.

countrified ['kʌntrifaid] *a.* aux allures campagnardes, provinciales; **to become c.,** se provincialiser.

country ['kʌntri] *n.* **1.** pays *m,* région *f;* **rough c.,** terrain accidenté; **open c.,** rase campagne; **flat c.,** pays, terrain, plat; **rich, fertile, c.,** pays riche, fertile; **wheat-growing c.,** région à blé. **2.** (*a*) (*political entity*) pays; **the countries of Europe,** les pays de l'Europe; *Pol:* **to go to the c.,** aller devant le pays; (*b*) **one's native c.,** sa patrie; **to love, die for, one's c.,** aimer, mourir pour, sa patrie. **3.** (*a*) (*opposed to capital*) la province; **a quiet little c. town,** une petite ville tranquille de province; **c. cousin,** cousin de province; (*b*) (*opposed to town*) campagne *f;* **in the c.,** à la campagne; **c. life,** vie de, à la, campagne; **c. gentleman,** gentilhomme campagnard; **c. house,** (i) maison *f* de campagne; (ii) manoir *m;* **to spend a day in the c.,** passer une journée à la campagne.

countryfolk ['kʌntrifouk] *n.pl.* gens *mpl* de la campagne.

countryman, -woman, *pl.* **-men, -women** ['kʌntrimən, -wumən; -men, -wimin] *n.* (*a*) campagnard, -arde; personne *f* qui habite à la campagne; (*b*) **fellow c.,** compatriote *mf.*

countryside ['kʌntrisaid] *n.* (*a*) la campagne; **beautiful c.,** beau paysage; (*b*) (*region*) pays *m.*

countrystyle ['kʌntristail] *a.* **c. cooking,** cuisine campagnarde.

county ['kaunti] *n.* comté *m;* (*a*) division territoriale et administrative (i) de la Grande-Bretagne et de l'Irlande, (ii) *U.S:* d'un *State;* **the c. of Kent,** le comté de Kent; *U.S:* **New York C.,** le comté de New York; **c. town,** chef-lieu *m* de comté, *pl.* chefs-lieux; **c. society,** l'aristocratie et la haute bourgeoisie du comté; *Cr:* **c. cricket,** les grands matches entre les équipes de comté; (*b*) les habitants *mpl* du comté.

coup [kuː] *n.* (*a*) coup (audacieux); **to bring off a c.,** réussir un coup; (*b*) **c. (d'état)** [dei'ta], coup d'état.

coupé ['kuːpei] *n. Aut:* **sports c.,** coupé *m* sport.

couple¹ ['kʌpl] *n.* **1.** deux; couple *f* (de pigeons, d'œufs, etc.); **a c. of seconds,** deux secondes; **in a c. of days,** dans deux jours. **2.** (*a*) couple *m* (de chiens de chasse); (*b*) couple *m* (d'époux, de danseurs); **the married c.,** les (deux) époux *mpl;* **the newly married c.,** les nouveaux mariés.

couple² **1.** *v.tr.* (*a*) (ac)coupler (des bœufs, deux idées); accoupler (le mâle et la femelle); associer (des noms, etc.); relier (des personnes, des objets); **common sense coupled with intelligence,** le bon sens joint à l'intelligence; (*b*) *Mec.E: etc:* engrener, embrayer (une machine); raccorder (des tuyaux); (*c*) *El:* associer, accoupler (des piles); (*d*) *Rail:* **to c. up a carriage,** atteler, accrocher, un wagon. **2.** *v.i.* (*of male and female*) s'accoupler. **coupling** *n.* **1.** accouplement *m* (de deux choses); appariement *m* (des animaux); association *f* (d'idées, de deux noms). **2.** *Tchn:* (*a*) accouplement, raccordement *m* (de deux roues, etc.); (*b*) *Rail:* attelage *m* (des wagons); (*c*) *El: etc:* couplage, association *f* (d'éléments de pile, etc.). **3.** (*device*) (*a*) (*static*) raccord, joint *m; Rail:* attelage; (*b*) (*for transmitting motion*) accouplement, embrayage *m.*

coupler ['kʌplər] *n.* **1.** (*organ*) tirant *m* à accoupler; pédale *f* d'accouplement. **2.** *Rail:* attelage *m.*

couplet ['kʌplit] *n. Pros:* distique *m.*

coupon ['kuːpɔn] *n.* coupon *m; Post:* **international reply c.,** coupon-réponse international, *pl.* coupons-réponse; *Com:* **(free) gift c.,** bon-prime *m, pl.* bons-primes; *Adm:* **petrol c.,** bon *m* d'essence; *Sp:* **football, pools, c.,** formulaire *m* de concours de pronostics de football; *Fin:* **interest c.,** coupon d'intérêts.

courage ['kʌridʒ] *n.* courage *m;* **to have the c. to do sth.,** avoir le courage de faire qch.; **to pluck up, muster up, c.,** prendre son courage à deux mains; **to restore s.o.'s c.,** rencourager qn; **c.!** du courage!

courageous [kə'reidʒəs] *a.* courageux. **-ly** *adv.* courageusement, avec courage.

courgette [kuə'ʒet] *n. Hort:* courgette *f.*

courier ['kuriər] *n.* (*a*) courrier *m,* messager *m;* (*b*) accompagnateur, -trice (de touristes).

course¹ [kɔːs] *n.* **1.** (*a*) cours *m* (d'un fleuve, du temps); courant *m* (des affaires, etc.); cours, ordre *m* (des événements); cours, trajet *m* (d'une balle, etc.); évolution *f* (d'une maladie); **in the c. of conversation,** au cours de la conversation; **in the c. of the next year,** au cours de l'année prochaine; d'ici un an; **in the c. of time,** dans la suite, le cours, des temps; **in the c. of nature, in the ordinary c. of things, events,** normalement; **in due c.,** en temps utile; **to let nature take her c.,** donner libre cours à la nature; **let things take their c.,** laissez couler l'eau; (*b*) **of c.,** bien entendu, naturellement; **of c. not!** bien sûr que non! (*c*) **that is a matter of c.,** cela va sans dire; **as a matter of c.,** tout naturellement, automatiquement. **2.** (*a*) *Sch:* cours; **to give a c. of lectures,** professer un cours; **to take, follow, a c.,** suivre un cours (de physique, etc.); **he has published a French c.,** il a publié une méthode de français; (*b*) *Med:* **c. (of treatment),** traitement *m;* **a c. of injections,** une série de piqûres. **3.** (*a*) route *f,* direction *f;* **to keep one's c.,** ne pas dévier de sa route; *Nau:* maintenir son cap; **to change one's c.,** changer de direction; *Nau:* changer le cap; **to be on c.,** suivre le cap fixé; (*of ship*) **to be driven off c.,** être drossé; (*b*) **to take a c. of action,** adopter une ligne de conduite; **it is the only c. open to me,** c'est ma seule ressource; **the right c.,** la bonne voie; (*c*) *Mch:* **upward, downward, c. of a piston,** course ascendante, descendante, d'un piston. **4.** (*of meal*) plat *m;* **four-c. dinner,** dîner *m* à quatre services; **three courses and a sweet,** trois plats et un dessert; **main c.,** plat principal. **5.** *Sp: etc:* (*a*) champ *m,* terrain *m* (de courses); *Equit:* parcours *m;* **golf c.,** terrain, de golf; *F:* golf *m.* **6.** (*a*) *Hyd.E:* canal *m;* bief *m;* (*b*) *Min:* galerie *f.* **7.** *Const:* assise *f* (de briques, de charpente); **damp c.,** couche isolante, hydrofuge, d'isolement. **8.** *Nau:* basse voile, voile basse.

course² **1.** (*a*) *v.tr. Ven:* courir (un lièvre); (*b*) *v.i.* courir le lièvre. **2.** *v.i.* (*of liquids*) courir, couler; **the blood courses through the veins,** le sang circule dans les veines. **coursing** *n.* **1.** *Ven:* chasse *f* à courre au lièvre. **2.** *Sp:* concours *m* de vitesse entre lévriers lâchés sur un lièvre en champ clos.

court¹ [kɔːt] *n.* **1.** (*a*) (*courtyard*) cour *f;* (*b*) (*in names of blocks of flats*) = résidence *f;* (*in names of palaces*) château *m;* palais *m.* **2.** (*a*) cour (royale); **c. shoe,** escarpin *m; Cards:* **c. card,** figure *f;* (*b*) **to pay c. to s.o.,** faire la cour à qn; (*of celebrity, etc.*) **to hold c.,** se faire faire la cour (par ses admirateurs). **3.** *Jur:* (*a*) (i) cour, tribunal *m;* (ii) (*courtroom*) auditoire *m* de tribunal; **law c., c. of law,** tribunal; **civil, criminal, c.,** tribunal civil, criminel; **magistrate's c.** = tribunal d'instance; **county c.,** tribunal de grande instance; **c. of appeal,** cour d'appel; **to go to c.,** aller en justice; **in open c.,** en plein tribunal; **case before the c.,** affaire *f* en cause; **to come before the c.,** comparaître devant le tribunal; **to settle a case out of c.,** arranger une affaire à l'amiable; **sale by order of the c.,** vente *f* judiciaire; (*b*) *Mil: Navy:* **c. of inquiry,** commission *f* d'enquête (sur une question de discipline). **4.** (*a*) *NAm:* **c. tennis,** jeu *m* de paume; (*b*) **tennis c.,** court *m* (de tennis), tennis *m*; **grass, hard, c.,** court sur gazon, court dur.

court² *v.tr.* **1.** (*a*) courtiser; faire la cour à (une femme); (*b*) *v.i.* **to be courting,** (i) (*of young woman, young man*) avoir un(e) petit(e) ami(e); (ii) (*of couple*) sortir ensemble; **courting couple,** couple *m* d'amoureux. **2.** rechercher (une alliance, etc.); (re)chercher, solliciter (l'amitié de qn); briguer (la faveur de qn); aller au-devant (d'un échec); braver (la mort); **to c. popularity,** chercher à se faire bien voir.

courteous ['kəːtiəs] *a.* courtois, poli **(to, towards,** envers). **-ly** *adv.* courtoisement; poliment.

courtesan [kɔːti'zæn] *n.* courtisane *f.*

courtesy ['kəːtəsi] *n.* courtoisie *f*, politesse *f*; **common c.,** la politesse la plus élémentaire; **by c. of . . .,** avec la gracieuse permission de . . .; **exchange of courtesies,** échange *m* de politesses; *F:* **c. cop,** motard *m* (de la route); *Aut:* **c. light,** plafonnier *m*; **c. title,** titre *m* de courtoisie.

courthouse ['kɔːthaus] *n.* palais *m* de justice; tribunal *m.*

courtier ['kɔːtiər] *n.* courtisan *m.*

courtly ['kɔːtli] *a.* (*a*) courtois; d'une politesse raffinée; (*b*) élégant; à l'air digne et aristocratique.

court-martial¹ ['kɔːt'mɑːʃ(ə)l] *n.* (*pl.* **courts-martial**) *Mil:* conseil *m* de guerre.

court-martial² *v.tr.* **(court-martialled,** *NAm:* **-martialed)** faire passer (qn) en conseil de guerre; **to be court-martialled,** passer en conseil de guerre.

courtroom ['kɔːtruːm] *n. Jur:* salle *f* d'audience; auditoire *m* de tribunal.

courtship ['kɔːtʃip] *n.* cour (faite à une femme); *Nat.Hist:* **c. display,** parade nuptiale.

courtyard ['kɔːtjɑːd] *n.* cour *f* (de maison, etc.).

cousin ['kʌz(ə)n] *n.* cousin, -ine; **first c., full c.,** cousin(e) germain(e); **second c.,** cousin(e) issu(e) de germain.

couture ['kuː'tjuər] *n. Dressm:* **haute c.,** haute couture.

couturier, *f.* **-ière** [kuː'tju(ə)riei, -iɛər] *n. Dressm:* (*a*) grand couturier, grande couturière; (*b*) directeur, -trice, d'une maison de haute couture.

covalent ['kou'veilənt] *a. Ch:* covalent.

cove¹ [kouv] *n. Geog:* anse *f*; petite baie; havre *m.*

cove² *n. P:O:* type *m*; **a queer c.,** un drôle de pistolet.

coven ['kʌv(ə)n] *n.* bande *f*, réunion *f*, de sorcières.

covenant¹ ['kʌvənənt] *n.* **1.** *Jur:* convention *f*, contrat *m.* **2.** *Pol:* pacte *m*, traité *m.* **3.** *Rel.H:* pacte, covenant *m.*

covenant² **1.** *v.tr.* (*a*) promettre (qch.) par contrat; (*b*) stipuler (une somme); (*c*) **to c. to do sth.,** convenir de, s'engager à, faire qch. **2.** *v.i.* **to c. with s.o. for sth.,** convenir (par contrat) de qch. avec qn.

Coventry ['kʌvəntri, 'kɔv-] *Pr.n. F:* **to send s.o. to C.,** mettre qn en quarantaine.

cover¹ ['kʌvər] *n.* **1.** (*a*) couverture *f* (de lit etc.); fourreau *m* (de parapluie); *Nau:* étui *m* (de canot); (*for chair*) **loose c.,** housse *f*; *Aut:* **car c.,** housse; (*b*) *Meteor:* **heavy cloud c.,** forte nébulosité. **2.** couvercle *m* (de marmite, etc.); cloche *f* (pour plat); capuchon *m* (de ventilateur); calotte *f* (d'une pompe); plaque *f* (d'égout); *Nau:* capot *m* (de cabestan); *Mec.E: etc:* **c. plate,** plaque de couverture. **3.** couverture (d'un livre); *Bookb:* les plats *mpl*; **to read a book from c. to c.,** lire un livre d'un bout à l'autre; **c. girl,** cover-girl *f, pl.* cover-girls. **4.** *Post:* enveloppe, pli *m*; **under separate c.,** sous pli séparé; (*for philatelists*) **first-day c.,** enveloppe (du) premier jour. **5.** *Journ:* **c. story,** article principal (illustré en couverture). **6.** (*a*) abri *m*; **to give s.o. c.,** abriter qn; **to take c.,** se mettre à l'abri; **take c.!** garez-vous! **to be under c.,** être à couvert, à l'abri; (*b*) *Ven:* (i) couvert *m*, fourré *m*; (ii) gîte *m*, remise *f*; **to take c.,** se remiser; **to break c.,** (i) sortir de son terrier; (ii) (*of pers.*) sortir de sa retraite; (*c*) *Mil: etc:* couvert, abri (contre le feu ennemi); **under c.,** à couvert, à l'abri; **to take c.,** se mettre à couvert, s'abriter; **without c.,** (à) découvert. **7.** (*a*) voile *m*, masque *m*; **under (the) c. of (sth.),** sous le couvert de (la nuit, etc.); sous le masque de (l'amitié, etc.); (*b*) *Mil.Av:* **air, radar, c.,** couverture aérienne, radar; (*c*) (*espionnage*) couverture; (*d*) *Com: Ins:* couverture, provision *f*; **with, without, c.,** (opérer) avec couverture, à découvert; *Ins:* **full c.,** garantie totale. **8.** (*in restaurant*) **c. charge,** couvert.

cover² *v.tr.* **1.** (*a*) couvrir (qn, qch.) **(with,** de); **covered with snow,** couvert de neige, par la neige; **to c. one's head,** se couvrir (la tête); **to be well covered,** (i) être chaudement vêtu; (ii) *F:* être bien en chair; (*b*) **to c. s.o. with ridicule,** couvrir qn de ridicule; **covered with shame,** couvert de honte; **to c. oneself with glory,** se couvrir de gloire. **2.** (*a*) *Mil: etc:* protéger (une frontière, etc.); couvrir (qn, etc.); (*b*) *v.i. Box: etc:* se couvrir; (*c*) *v.i.* **to c. for s.o.,** servir de couverture à qn. **3.** (*a*) couvrir, recouvrir; tapisser (un mur) **(with,** de); *Bookb:* couvrir (un livre); *El: etc:* recouvrir (un fil conducteur); (*b*) *v.i.* **paint that covers well,** peinture qui couvre bien; (*c*) *v.ind.tr.* **to c. in,** recouvrir (une canalisation sous terre, etc.); remplir (une tranchée). **4.** couvrir, parcourir (une distance); **to c. a great deal of ground,** (i) faire beaucoup de chemin; (ii) parcourir un champ très vaste. **5.** couvrir, dissimuler (son inquiétude, sa confusion, etc.); **to c. one's tracks,** dépister ses adversaires. **6. to c. s.o. with a pistol,** mettre, tenir, qn en joue; *F:* **I've got you covered,** je te tiens! **7.** comprendre, embrasser; **to c. all eventualities,** parer à toute éventualité. **8.** (*a*) couvrir (un risque); (*of creditor*) **to be covered,** être à couvert; *Ins: etc:* **to c. oneself,** se couvrir **(against a risk,** d'un risque); **the policy covers the risk of loss,** la police couvre le risque de perte; (*b*) **to c. (one's) expenses,** couvrir, faire, ses frais; **to c. a deficit,** combler un déficit; (*c*) *Journ:* couvrir (un événement sportif, etc.). **9.** *Breed:* couvrir, saillir (la femelle). **covered** *a.* (*a*) couvert; abrité; **c. market,** marché couvert; **c. way,** chemin couvert; *esp. U.S:* **c. wagon,** charette *f* à bâche; (*b*) (risque) couvert (par les assurances). **covering 1.** *a.* (*a*) **c. letter,** lettre d'introduction, de couverture; *Com:* **c. note,** garantie *f*; (*b*) *Mil:* (forces, troupes) de couverture; **c. fire,** tir *m* de soutien, de protection. **2.** *n.* (*a*) (i) action *f* de couvrir (qch.); *Breed:* action de couvrir (la femelle); (*b*) couverture *f*, enveloppe *f*, revêtement *m*, recouvrement *m*; *Furn:* housse *f*; (*c*) **c. up,** (i) recouvrement *m* (de qch.); (ii) dissimulation *f* (de la vérité); (iii) couverture *f* **(for s.o.,** de qn). **cover up 1.** *v.tr.* recouvrir; dissimuler (la vérité, des illégalités); **to c. up one's tracks,** dépister ses adversaires. **2.** *v.i.* (*a*) *v.i. Box:* se couvrir; (*b*) **to c. up for s.o.,** servir de couverture à qn.

coverage ['kʌvəridʒ] *n.* couverture *f*; champ *m* d'application (d'une activité, etc.); *Com: Ins:* couverture, provision *f*; *Journ:* **news c.,** (ensemble *m* des) informations *fpl.*

coverall(s) ['kʌvərɔːl(z)] *n.(pl.) NAm:* bleu(s) *m(pl)* (de travail).

coverlet ['kʌvəlit] *n.* dessus *m* de lit.
covert¹ ['kʌvət] *a.* (*of threat, etc.*) caché, voilé; (*of action, etc.*) clandestin. **-ly** *adv.* secrètement.
covert² *n.* **1.** *Ven:* couvert *m*; fourré *m*. **2.** *Orn:* **coverts,** plumes tectrices (de la queue, des ailes).
cover-up ['kʌvərʌp] *n.* dissimulation *f* (d'une irrégularité, etc.); **to act as a c.-up,** se prêter à une dissimulation.
covet ['kʌvit] *v.tr.* **(coveted)** (*a*) convoiter; (*b*) ambitionner (qch.), aspirer à (qch.).
covetous ['kʌvitəs] *a.* **1.** avide **(of gain,** de gain). **2.** (regard) de convoitise; **to be c. of s.o.'s property,** convoiter les biens d'autrui. **-ly** *adv.* avec convoitise.
covetousness ['kʌvitəsnis] *n.* **1.** cupidité *f*, avidité *f*. **2.** convoitise *f*.
covey ['kʌvi] *n.* compagnie *f*, vol *m* (de perdrix, etc.).
cow¹ [kau] *n.* **1.** (*a*) vache *f*; **milch, milking, c.,** vache laitière; *F:* (*of pers.*) **milch c.,** vache à lait; **c. in, with, calf,** vache pleine; **c. pat,** bouse *f* de vache; *F:* **till the cows come home,** (attendre) jusqu'à la semaine des quatre jeudis; (*b*) **sacred c.,** (i) *Rel:* vache sacrée; (ii) *F:* institution *f* intouchable; (*c*) *P:* (*woman*) **old c.,** vache, vieille bique; **silly c.,** idiote. **2.** (*of elephant, seal, etc.*) femelle *f*. **3.** *Bot:* **c. parsley,** cerfeuil *m* sauvage.
cow² *v.tr.* intimider, dompter (qn); **to look cowed,** avoir l'air d'un chien battu.
coward ['kauəd] *n.* & *a.* lâche (*mf*); poltron, -onne; **to turn c.,** perdre courage; **I'm a terrible c. in the dark,** j'ai bien peur, quand il fait noir.
cowardice ['kauədis], **cowardliness** ['kauədlinəs] *n.* lâcheté *f*; poltronnerie *f*.
cowardly ['kauədli] *a.* lâche; poltron.
cowbell ['kaubel] *n.* clochette *f* (pour bétail).
cowboy ['kaubɔi] *n.* vacher *m*; cowboy *m*.
cower ['kauər] *v.i.* **1.** se tapir (à terre); se faire tout petit. **2. to c. before s.o.,** trembler devant qn.
cowgirl ['kaugə:l] *n.* vachère *f*.
cowhand ['kauhænd] *n.* vacher *m*; cowboy *m*.
cowherd ['kauhə:d] *n.* vacher *m*; bouvier *m*.
cowhide ['kauhaid] *n.* *Leath:* (peau *f* de) vache (*f*).
cowl¹ [kaul] *n.* **1.** *Ecc:* (*a*) capuchon *m* (de moine); (*b*) têtière *f* (d'un capuchon de moine). **2.** capuchon, abat-vent *m inv; Av: Nau:* capot *m* (de moteur, de cheminée).
cowl² *v.tr.* capuchonner (une cheminée). **cowled** *a.* (en)capuchonné. **cowling** *n.* **1.** capuchonnement *m* (d'une cheminée). **2.** capot *m* (de moteur).
cowlick ['kaulik] *n.* *F:* épi *m* (de cheveux).
cowman, *pl.* **-men** ['kaumæn, -men] *n.m.* (*a*) vacher; cowboy; (*b*) *U.S:* propriétaire d'un ranch.
cowpox ['kaupɔks] *n.* *Vet:* cowpox *m*, vaccine *f*.
cowpuncher ['kaupʌn(t)ʃər] *n.m.* *U.S:* cowboy.
cowrie ['kauəri] *n.* *Moll:* porcelaine *f*; *F:* pucelage *m*.
cowshed ['kauʃed] *n.* étable *f*.
cowslip ['kauslip] *n.* *Bot:* (fleur *f* de) coucou (*m*); primevère commune.
cox¹ [kɔks] *n.* *Row:* barreur *m*.
cox² *v.tr.* & *i.* *Row:* gouverner (un canot); barrer.
coxwain ['kɔksn] *n.* **1.** *Nau:* patron *m* (d'une chaloupe, d'un canot). **2.** *Row:* barreur *m*.
coy [kɔi] *a.* (*esp. of girl*) (*a*) timide; farouche; (*b*) qui fait la sainte-nitouche. **-ly** *adv.* timidement.
coyness ['kɔinis] *n.* timidité *f*.
coyote [kɔi'jouti] *n.* *Z:* coyote *m*.
coziness ['kouzinis] *n.* *NAm:* = COSINESS.
cozy ['kouzi] *a.* *NAm:* = COSY.
crab¹ [kræb] *n.* **1.** (*a*) *Crust:* crabe *m*; cancre *m*; **fiddler c.,** crabe appelant; **c. pot,** casier *m* à crabes; (*b*) *P:* **c. (louse),** pou *m* du pubis, *P:* morpion *m*. **2.** *Astr:* **the C.,** (i) (*constellation*) le Cancer; (ii) (*nebula*) le Crabe. **3.** *Ind:* *etc:* chariot *m* (de pont roulant).
crab² *n.* **1.** *Bot:* **c. (apple),** pomme *f* sauvage; **c. (tree),** pommier *m* sauvage. **2.** *F:* personne *f* revêche.
crab³ *v.tr.* *F:* critiquer (qn, qch.); chiner (qn).
crabbed ['kræb(i)d] *a.* **1.** (*of pers.*) maussade, grincheux. **2.** (style) entortillé; (écriture) en pattes de mouche.
crabby ['kræbi] *a.* = CRABBED 1.
crack¹ [kræk] **I.** *n.* **1.** (*a*) craquement *m* (de branches, de glace, etc.); claquement *m* (de fouet); détonation *f*, claquement sec (d'une arme à feu); crépitement *m* (d'une fusillade); (*b*) *F:* **c. on the head,** coup sec sur la tête; (*c*) *F:* **to have a c. at sth.,** essayer de faire qch.; **to give s.o. a c. at sth.,** laisser qn tenter le coup. **2.** (*a*) fente *f*, fissure *f*; (*in skin, wood,*) gerçure *f*; (*in wrought steel, etc.*) tapure *f*; (*in wall, ground*) crevasse, lézarde *f*; (*in varnish, enamel*) craquelure *f*; (*in glass, pottery, bell, etc.*) fêlure *f*; *Fig:* **to paper over the cracks,** masquer les défauts; (*b*) entrebâillement *m* (d'une porte, etc.); **open the window a c.,** ouvrez la fenêtre un petit peu; (*c*) **at the c. of dawn,** à la pointe du jour. **3.** *F:* cheval *m*, joueur *m*, etc., de premier ordre; *Sp:* crack *m*. **4.** *F:* saillie *f*; **nasty c.,** plaisanterie acérée. **II.** *a.* *F:* d'élite; **c. shot,** fin tireur; tireur d'élite; **c. regiment,** régiment *m* d'élite; *Sp:* **c. player,** as *m*, crack *m*.
crack² *int.* clac! crac! pan!
crack³ **I.** *v.tr.* **1.** faire claquer (un fouet); faire craquer (ses doigts); *F:* **to c. s.o. over the head,** assommer qn. **2.** (*a*) fêler (une cloche, un verre); gercer (la peau); lézarder, crevasser (un mur, la terre); fendre (une pierre, etc.); fracturer (un os); (*b*) (i) casser (une noisette); (ii) croquer (une noisette) sous la dent; *F:* **to c. a bottle of wine (with s.o.),** vider une bouteille (avec qn); (*c*) *F:* résoudre (un problème); décrypter (un chiffre); percer (un coffre-fort); (*d*) *Ind:* fractionner (une huile lourde). **3.** faire, lâcher (une plaisanterie); **to c. jokes,** débiter des drôleries; raconter des blagues. **II.** *v.i.* **1.** craquer; (*of whip*) claquer; **a rifle cracked,** un coup de fusil partit. **2.** se fêler; (*of wall*) se lézarder; (*of skin*) se gercer; (*of steel*) s'égrener. **3.** (*a*) (*of voice*) se casser; (*at puberty*) muer; (*b*) (*of pers., health*) s'effondrer. **4.** *F:* **to get cracking,** s'y mettre; **get cracking!** grouille-toi! **crack down** *v.i.* *F:* **to c. down on s.o.,** devenir plus strict avec qn; prendre des mesures sévères avec qn. **cracked** *a.* **1.** fêlé, fendu; (*of wall*) lézardé; (*of timber*) gerçuré; (*of voice*) cassé. **2.** *F:* timbré, toqué; loufoque; **to be c.,** avoir le cerveau, le coco, fêlé. **cracking** **1.** *a.* *F:* excellent, épatant; **to be in c. (good) form,** être en pleine forme; **at a c. pace,** à fond de train. **2.** *n.* (*a*) claquement *m*, craquement *m*; (*b*) craquelure *f*, craquelage *m* (de la peinture); (*c*) fractionnement *m*, craquage *m* (d'une huile lourde). **crack up** **1.** *v.tr.* (*a*) mettre (qch.) en morceaux; (*b*) **to c. (s.o., sth.) up (to the nines),** vanter, prôner (qn, qch.); **it's not all it's cracked up to be,** ce n'est pas tout ce qu'on en dit. **2.** *v.i.* (*of empire, etc.*) se démembrer; *F:* craquer; *F:* (*of pers., health*) s'effondrer.
crackbrained ['krækbreind] *a.* *F:* au cerveau timbré, fêlé; (idée) folle.
crack-down ['krækdaun] *n.* mesure *f* énergique **(on sth.,** contre un abus); mesures sévères.
cracker ['krækər] *n.* **1. c. of jokes,** faiseur, -euse, de plaisanteries. **2.** (*a*) pétard *m*; **jumping c.,** crapaud *m*; (*b*) **(Christmas) c.,** diablotin *m*. **3. (pair of) nut crackers,** casse-noisette(s) *m inv*, casse-noix *m inv*. **4.** biscuit sec; croquet *m*; *NAm:* **c. barrel,** boîte *f* à biscuits.
crackerjack ['krækədʒæk] *NAm:* *F:* **1.** *n.* expert *m*. **2.** *a.* rupin, chouette.

crackers ['krækəz] *a. F:* **he's c.,** il est cinglé, loufoque; **to go c.,** perdre la raison, *F:* la boule.

crackle¹ ['krækl] *n.* **1.** craquement *m*; crépitement *m*, crépitation *f*; *W.Tel:* crachements *mpl.* **2.** tré-saillure *f* (de peinture, de porcelaine); *Cer:* **c. finish,** craquelage *m.* **3.** *Cer:* **c. (ware, china, glass),** craquelé *m.*

crackle² **1.** *v.i.* (*a*) (*of dried leaves, etc.*) craquer; (*of shots*) crépiter; (*of snow, something frying*) grésiller; (*of fire*) pétiller; *W.Tel:* crachoter; (*b*) se fendiller; se craqueler. **2.** *v.tr.* fendiller; *Cer:* craqueler. **crackling** **1.** *a.* pétillant, crépitant. **2.** *n.* (*a*) = CRACKLE¹ 1; (*b*) *Cer:* (*process*) craquelage *m*; (*c*) *Cu:* peau croquante (du porc rôti); couenne *f*; (*d*) *P:* **a nice bit of c.,** une belle pépée.

crackpot ['krækpɔt] *F:* **1.** *n.* cerveau fêlé; **he's a c.,** il est cinglé. **2.** *a.* (idée) folle.

crack-up ['krækʌp] *n.* débâcle *f* (d'un système, de la santé); effondrement *m* (de la raison, de la santé).

cradle¹ ['kreidl] *n.* **1.** (*a*) berceau *m* (d'un enfant, d'une civilisation); **wicker c.,** moïse *m*; **from the c.,** dès le berceau; **from the c. to the grave,** du berceau au tombeau; (*b*) *Nau:* cadre *m* (d'hôpital). **2.** *Ind:* berceau (d'une machine, etc.); cadre. **3.** (*a*) *Const: Min:* pont volant; (*b*) sellette *f* (de peintre). **4.** (*a*) *Min:* (*for gold*) **c. (rocker),** berceau; (*b*) *Cin:* **c. head,** trépied *m* à bascule (pour prise de vues). **5.** *Agr:* râteau *m*, crochets *mpl* (d'une faux). **6.** *Med:* (*a*) (*splint*) gouttière *f* (de contention); (*b*) (*over bed*) cerceau *m*, arceau *m.* **7.** *Tp:* support *m* (de combiné).

cradle² *v.tr.* **1.** (*a*) mettre, coucher, (qn) dans un berceau; **cradled in luxury,** bercé dans le luxe; (*b*) bercer (qn); **to c. a child in one's arms,** bercer un enfant dans ses bras; (*c*) tenir (qch.) délicatement.

cradlesnatcher ['kreidlsnætʃər] *n. F:* **he's, she's, a c.,** il, elle, les prend au berceau, au biberon.

cradlesnatching ['kreidlsnætʃiŋ] *n. F:* **I don't go in for c.,** je ne les prends pas au berceau, au biberon.

cradlesong ['kreidlsɔŋ] *n.* berceuse *f.*

craft [krɑft] *n.* **1.** habileté *f*, adresse *f*; (*b*) *Pej:* ruse *f*; artifice *m.* **2.** (*a*) (i) métier manuel; (ii) profession *f*; (*iii*) *Sch:* travaux manuels; **arts and crafts,** artisanat *m* d'expression; **painter who is master of his c.,** peintre *m* qui a du métier. **3.** corps *m* de métier. **4.** (*pl.* **craft**) *Nau:* embarcation *f*, petit navire; **small c.,** canots *mpl*, petits bateaux.

craftiness ['krɑːftinis] *n.* ruse *f*; *F:* roublardise *f.*

craftsman, *pl.* **-men** ['krɑːftsmən] *n.m.* **1.** artisan, ouvrier qualifié. **2.** artiste dans son métier.

craftsmanship ['krɑːftsmənʃip] *n.* **1.** dextérité manuelle; **a wonderful piece of c.,** un chef-d'œuvre merveilleux. **2.** (connaissance *f* du) métier.

crafty ['krɑːfti] *a.* astucieux, rusé, malin; *F:* roublard. **-ily** *adv.* astucieusement.

crag [kræg] *n.* rocher, flanc, de montagne escarpé; rocher à pic; **overhanging c.,** rocher en surplomb.

craggy ['krægi] *a.* **1.** rocailleux. **2.** (visage) anguleux, taillé à coups de serpe.

cram *v.* **(crammed)** **1.** *v.tr.* (*a*) fourrer **(sth. into sth.,** qch. dans qch.); **cupboards crammed with linen,** armoires bourrées de linge; (*b*) **to c. s.o. with sth.,** bourrer qn de qch.; (*c*) *Husb:* appâter, gaver (de la volaille); (*d*) **to c. food into one's mouth,** s'empiffrer, se bâfrer; (*e*) *Sch:* chauffer (un candidat pour un examen); (*of student*) **to c. maths,** potasser ferme les math. **2.** *v.i. F:* (*a*) s'entasser; **we all crammed into the car,** nous nous sommes tous entassés dans la voiture; (*b*) se gorger de nourriture; se gaver **(with,** de); (*c*) *Sch: F:* potasser; **to c. for an exam,** = bachoter. **cramming** *n.* **1.** entassement *m* (des voyageurs dans un autobus, etc.). **2.** *Husb:* gavage *m.* **3.** *Sch: F:* chauffage *m* (pour un examen).

crammer ['kræmər] *n.* **1.** *Husb:* (*pers.*) gaveur, -euse. **2.** *Sch: F:* (*a*) = bachoteur *m*; (*b*) boîte *f* à bachot.

cramp¹ [kræmp] *n. Med:* crampe *f*; **writer's c.,** crampe des écrivains; **to have c.,** être pris d'une crampe.

cramp² *n.* (*a*) *Const: etc:* **c. (iron),** crampon *m*; (*b*) *Tls:* serre-joint(s) *m inv*; (*c*) *Typ:* cornière *f.*

cramp³ *v.tr.* **1.** gêner (les mouvements, l'esprit, etc.); **to be cramped up in a small space,** être à l'étroit; *F:* **to c. s.o.'s style,** priver qn de ses moyens. **2.** (*a*) *Const:* cramponner, agrafer (des pierres, etc.); (*b*) *Carp: etc:* serrer (au serre-joint). **cramped** *a.* (pièce) étriquée; (écriture) gênée; (style) contraint; **to be c. for space,** être, se sentir, à l'étroit.

crampon ['kræmpən] *n.* crampon *m* à glace.

cranberry ['krænbəri] *n. Bot:* canneberge *f.*

crane¹ [krein] *n.* **1.** *Orn:* grue *f*; **crowned c.,** grue couronnée. **2.** *Mec.E: etc:* grue; **jib c.,** grue à volée, à flèche; *Aut:* **breakdown c.,** grue de dépannage; grue dépanneuse; **c. driver, operator,** conducteur *m* de grue; grutier *m.* **3.** *Cin:* grue de prise de vue.

crane² **1.** *v.tr.* tendre, allonger (le cou); **to c. one's neck to see sth.,** se hausser pour voir qch. **2.** *v.i.* (*a*) **to c. forward,** allonger le cou, la tête, en avant.

cranefly ['kreinflai] *n. Ent:* tipule *f.*

crane's-bill, cranesbill ['kreinzbil] *n. Bot:* bec-de-grue *m*, *pl.* becs-de-grue; géranium *m.*

cranial ['kreiniəl] *a. Anat:* (nerf, etc.) crânien.

craniology [kreini'ɔlədʒi] *n.* craniologie *f.*

cranium, *pl.* **-ia** ['kreiniəm, -iə] *n. Anat:* crâne *m.*

crank¹ [kræŋk] *n. Mec.E:* manivelle *f*; cigogne *f* (de meule à aiguiser); **c. axle,** essieu coudé.

crank² *v.tr.* **1.** *Mec.E:* couder (un essieu). **2. to c. up,** décoller (le moteur) à la manivelle; lancer (le moteur). **cranked** *a.* (essieu) coudé.

crank³ *n. F:* maniaque *mf*, excentrique *mf*; **health food c.,** fanatique *mf* des aliments naturels.

crankcase ['kræŋkkeis] *n. I.C.E:* carter *m.*

crankiness ['kræŋkinis] *n. F:* excentricité *f.*

crankshaft ['kræŋkʃɑːft] *n.* vilebrequin *m.*

cranky ['kræŋki] *a. F:* (*of pers.*) (*a*) capricieux; (*b*) excentrique; maniaque.

cranny ['kræni] *n.* (*a*) fente *f*, lézarde *f*; (*b*) niche *f*; **nooks and crannies,** coins *mpl* et recoins *mpl.*

crap¹ [kræp] *n. P:* **1.** merde *f.* **2.** (*a*) (*worthless thgs*) camelote *f*; (*b*) foutaise(s) *f* (*pl*); connerie(s) *f* (*pl*).

crap² *v.i. P:* chier.

crap³ *n. NAm:* **c. game,** jeu *m* de dés; craps *m.*

crape [kreip] *n. Tex:* **1.** crêpe noir (de deuil); **c. band,** brassard *m* de deuil. **2.** *Med:* **c. bandage,** bande *f* Velpeau; velpeau *m.*

crappy ['kræpi] *a. P:* (*a*) sale; (*b*) dégueulasse.

craps [kræps] *n.pl.* (*often with sg. const.*) *NAm:* jeu *m* de dés; craps *m*; **to shoot c.,** jouer aux dés.

crash¹ [kræʃ] *n.* **1.** fracas *m*; **to fall with a c.,** tomber avec fracas. **2.** catastrophe *f*, débâcle *f*; **financial c.,** débâcle financière; krach *m.* **3.** écrasement *m*; chute (accidentelle); *Aut: Rail: Av:* accident; *Aut: Adm:* **c. barrier,** glissière *f*; **c. helmet,** casque protecteur; **c.-proof,** antichoc *inv*; résistant aux chocs. **4.** (*a*) **c. dive,** (i) *Navy:* plongée *f* raide (d'un sous-marin); (ii) *Av:* piqué *m* catastrophique; *Av:* **c. landing,** atterrissage brutal; (*b*) *F:* **c. course,** cours (d'instruction) accéléré; *Adm:* **c. programme,** programme choc, d'urgence. **5.** *int.* patatras! **c. went the vase,** le vase tomba avec un grand fracas; **he drove c. into the wall,** il est allé s'emboutir contre le mur.

crash² **1.** *v.i.* (*a*) retentir; éclater avec fracas; **the thunder crashed,** (i) il y eut un violent coup de tonnerre; (ii) le tonnerre retentissait; (*b*) **to c. (down),** tomber avec fracas; **the vase crashed to the ground,** le vase tomba et se brisa avec fracas; **the mast came crashing**

down, le mât s'abattit; **to c. through sth.,** passer à travers qch. avec fracas; *Aut:* **to c. into a tree,** s'emboutir sur un arbre; *F:* tamponner, entrer dans, un arbre; **the two cars crashed head on,** les deux voitures se sont tamponnées de front; (*c*) *Av:* (i) (*of plane*) s'écraser sur le sol; (ii) (*of pilot*) atterrir brutalement; (*d*) (*of business, government, etc.*) sauter; (*of prices*) s'effondrer. **2.** *v.tr.* briser, fracasser; *Av:* écraser (son appareil) sur le sol; *Aut:* **to c. one's car,** avoir un accident avec sa voiture; **to c. the gears,** faire grincer la boîte de vitesses. **3.** *v.tr. & i. F:* **to c. a party,** resquiller, aller à une réunion sans être invité. **crashing** *a.* **1.** (bruit) fracassant. **2.** *F:* **a c. bore,** (i) une personne, (ii) une besogne, soirée, etc., assommante.

crash-dive ['kræʃdaiv] *v. Navy:* **1.** *v.tr.* faire plonger raide (un sous-marin). **2.** *v.i.* plonger raide.

crash-land ['kræʃ'lænd] v.i. atterrir brutalement.

crass [kræs] *a.* grossier; **c. stupidity,** stupidité grossière; **c. ignorance,** ignorance *f* crasse.

crate¹ [kreit] *n.* **1.** caisse *f* à claire-voie, en voliges; cageot *m*; (*for glass, etc.*) harasse *f*; **wicker c.,** mannequin *m.* **2.** *P:* (*aircraft*) coucou *m*; (*car*) caisse.

crate² *v.tr.* emballer (des marchandises) dans une caisse à claire-voie.

crater¹ ['kreitər] *n.* **1.** *Geol:* cratère *m* (volcanique, lunaire); **c. lake,** lac *m* de cratère. **2.** (*shell hole*) entonnoir *m*, cratère.

cravat [krə'væt] *n.* foulard *m.*

crave [kreiv] *v.tr. & i.* **1.** *Lit:* **to c. s.o.'s pardon,** demander pardon à qn; **to c. indulgence,** solliciter l'indulgence. **2. to c. (for) sth.,** désirer ardemment, réclamer, qch.; **child that craves for affection,** enfant affamé d'affection. **craving** *n.* désir ardent; appétit *m* insatiable (**for,** de); **c. for alcohol,** passion *f* de l'alcool; besoin d'alcool.

crawfish ['krɔːfiʃ] *n.* = CRAYFISH.

crawl¹ [krɔːl] *n.* **1.** rampement *m* (d'un serpent). **2.** (*a*) **to go along at a c.,** (*i*) traîner les pieds; (*ii*) *Aut:* avancer très lentement; (*b*) *F:* **pub c.,** tournée *f* des bars. **3.** *Swim:* crawl *m*; **to do the c.,** faire, nager, le crawl; crawler.

crawl² *v.i.* **1.** (*of reptile, etc.*) ramper; **to c. into a hole,** se glisser dans un trou; **to c. to the door,** gagner la porte en rampant; *F:* **to c. to s.o.,** s'aplatir devant qn; lécher les bottes à qn; **I refuse to c.,** je refuse de m'aplatir. **2.** (*a*) (*of pers.*) **to c. (along),** se traîner; **he crawled to the ditch,** il se traîna jusqu'au fossé; **to c. on one's hands and knees,** aller à quatre pattes; (*b*) avancer lentement; *Aut: F:* faire du surplace. **3. to be crawling with vermin,** grouiller de vermine; *F:* **the streets were crawling with troops,** les rues fourmillaient, grouillaient, de militaires. **4.** *Swim:* crawler; faire le crawl. **crawling 1.** *a.* (*a*) rampant; (*b*) grouillant (**with,** de); **cheese c. with maggots,** fromage *m* qui grouille de vers. **2.** *n.* (i) *Z:* reptation *f*; rampement *m*; (ii) *F:* léchage *m* de bottes.

crawler ['krɔːlər] *n.* **1.** (*a*) reptile *m*; animal *m*, bébé *m*, qui rampe; (*b*) *F:* lèche-bottes *m inv*; (*c*) *F:* **pub c.,** coureur *m* de cabarets, de bars. **2.** *Swim:* crawleur, -euse. **3.** *Aut:* **c. lane,** voie *f* pour véhicules lents.

crayfish ['kreifiʃ] *n. Crust:* **1. (freshwater) c.,** écrevisse *f.* **2.** *Com: F:* **(sea) c.,** langouste *f.*

crayon¹ ['kreiɔn, -ən] *n.* **1.** crayon *m* pastel; **coloured c.,** crayon de couleur. **2.** (dessin *m* au) pastel (*m*).

crayon² *v.tr.* **1.** dessiner (qch.) au pastel. **2.** crayonner (une esquisse).

craze¹ [kreiz] *n.* manie *f* (**for sth.,** de qch.); **discotheques are all the c.,** les discothèques font fureur.

craze² 1. *v.tr.* (*a*) rendre (qn) fou; déranger (l'esprit); (*b*) craqueler (la porcelaine). **2.** *v.i. Cer:* se craqueler. **crazed** *a.* **1.** fou, *f.* folle (**with grief,** de douleur); affolé (**with fear,** de terreur). **2.** *Cer: etc:* craquelé.

craziness ['kreizinis] *n.* (*of pers.*) folie *f*, démence *f.*

crazy ['kreizi] *a.* **1.** (*a*) (*of pers.*) fou, *f.* folle (à lier); toqué; (*of idea, etc.*) saugrenu; **c. with fear,** affolé (de terreur); *F:* **to go c.,** devenir fou (**with anger,** de colère); **to drive, send, s.o. c.,** rendre qn fou; **you're c.!** vous êtes fou! **to be c. about, over, s.o., sth.,** être fou de qn, qch.; **like c.,** comme un enragé; (*b*) *F:* (*of dress, building, angle, etc.*) bizarre. **2.** (*of building, etc.*) délabré; **c. paving,** dallage irrégulier en pierres plates. **-ily** *adv.* follement; bizarrement.

creak¹ [kriːk] *n.* cri *m*, grincement *m* (de gonds, etc.); craquement *m* (du bois, de chaussures neuves, etc.).

creak² *v.i.* (*of hinge, etc.*) grincer; (*of timber, shoes*) craquer. **creaking 1.** *a.* (gond, etc.) qui crie, qui grince; (cuir, bois) qui craque. **2.** *n.* cri(s) *m(pl)*, grincement *m*; craquement *m.*

creaky ['kriːki] *a.* (gond) qui grince; (bois) qui craque.

cream¹ [kriːm] *n.* **1.** (*a*) crème *f* (du lait); crème fraîche; **strawberries and c.,** fraises *fpl* à la crème; **clotted c.,** crème caillée; **whipped c.,** crème fouettée; **c. puff,** chou *m* à la crème; **c. jug,** pot *m* à crème; crémière *f*; (*b*) *F:* (le) meilleur; (le) dessus du panier; **the c. of society,** la crème de la société. **2.** (*a*) **coffee c.,** crème au café; (*b*) **c. of tomato, asparagus, soup,** crème de tomate, d'asperges; (*c*) **c. of tartar,** crème de tartre; (*d*) **shoe c.,** crème pour chaussures; (*e*) crème (de toilette, de beauté). **3.** *attrib.* **c.(-coloured),** (dentelles) crème *inv.*

cream² 1. *v.tr.* (*a*) **to c. (off),** écrémer (le lait); **to c. off the best part of sth.,** prélever la meilleure partie de qch.; (*b*) ajouter de la crème à (son café, etc.); (*c*) battre (du beurre) en crème. **2.** *v.i.* (*of milk*) se couvrir de crème, crémer. **creamed** *a.* **1.** (lait) écrémé. **2.** *Cu:* (poulet, etc.) à la crème; **c. potatoes,** pommes *fpl* de terre en purée.

creamery ['kriːməri] *n.* **1.** crémerie *f.* **2.** coopérative laitière; **c. butter,** beurre laitier.

creamy ['kriːmi] *a.* **1.** crémeux. **2.** (teint) velouté; **rich c. voice,** voix veloutée.

crease¹ [kriːs] *n.* **1.** (*a*) (faux) pli; **c.-resistant,** infroissable; (*b*) pli (d'un pantalon, etc.). **2.** *Sp:* ligne blanche; *Cr:* **batting c.,** ligne du batteur.

crease² 1. *v.tr.* (*a*) plisser, faire des plis à (qch.); **well-creased trousers,** pantalon avec un pli impeccable; (*b*) faire des faux plis à, froisser (une robe, etc.); (*c*) *P:* (i) assommer, (ii) épuiser, éreinter, (iii) tuer (qn). **2.** *v.i.* (*a*) se plisser; prendre un (faux) pli; (*b*) se froisser.

create [kri'eit] *v.tr.* **1.** créer (le monde, un pair, *Th:* un rôle); *pred.* **to c. s.o. an earl,** créer qn comte. **2.** (*a*) créer, susciter (une difficulté); faire, produire (une impression); **to c. a scandal,** (i) causer un scandale; (ii) faire de l'esclandre; **to c. a disturbance,** troubler l'ordre public; *v.i. P:* **to c.,** faire du tapage; faire une scène, rouspéter (**about,** à propos de); (*b*) créer (une robe, une mode, etc.).

creation [kri'eiʃ(ə)n] *n.* **1.** création *f* (du monde, d'un titre). **2.** (*thing*) création, produit *m*, œuvre *f*; **the latest creations,** les dernières modes.

creative [kri'eitiv] *a.* créateur, -trice; **c. drive,** impulsion créatrice; **a c. job,** un métier stimulant.

creativeness [kri'eitivnis], **creativity** [kriə'tiviti] *n.* faculté *f* de créer; puissance créatrice; créativité *f.*

creator [kri'eitər] *n.* créateur, -trice (d'une mode, *Th:* d'un rôle, etc.); **the C.,** le Créateur.

creature ['kriːtʃər] *n.* **1.** créature *f*, être *m* (vivant). **2.** animal *m*, bête *f*; **dumb creatures,** les bêtes. **3.** (*of pers.*) **pretty c.,** jolie créature; **poor c.!** le, la, pauvre! **4.** (*a*) **c. of the Government,** homme vendu au gouvernement; instrument *m* du gouvernement; (*b*) **man is the c. of circumstances,** l'homme dépend des circonstances; **we are creatures of habit,** nous sommes tels que nous fait l'habitude. **5.** *attrib.* **c. comforts,** aisance matérielle; **to like one's c. comforts,** aimer ses aises *fpl.*

crèche [kreiʃ, kreʃ] *n.* **1.** crèche *f.* **2.** *Ecc:* crèche.

credence ['kri:dəns] *n.* créance *f,* croyance *f,* foi *f;* **to give, attach, c. to sth.,** ajouter foi à qch; **letter of c.,** lettre *f* de créance.

credentials [kri'denʃ(ə)lz] *n.pl.* **1.** lettres *fpl* de créance (d'un diplomate, etc.). **2.** papiers *mpl* d'identité; pièces justificatives d'identité.

credibility [kredi'biliti] *n.* crédibilité *f;* **c. gap,** perte *f* de confiance (entre deux personnes, etc.).

credible ['kredibl] *a.* croyable; **it is hardly c. that . . .,** il n'est pas vraisemblable que + *sub.*

credit¹ ['kredit] *n.* **1.** croyance *f,* créance *f;* **to give c. to a report,** ajouter foi à un bruit; **facts that lend c. to a rumour,** faits *mpl* qui accréditent un bruit. **2.** crédit *m,* influence *f* (**with,** auprès de); **he has lost c. with the public,** son crédit a décliné. **3.** (*a*) mérite *m,* honneur *m;* **to take c. for an action,** s'attribuer le mérite d'une action; **with c.,** (i) (s'acquitter) honorablement; (ii) *Sch:* (être reçu à un examen) avec mention assez bien; **I gave him c. for more sense,** je lui supposais plus de jugement; **it must be said to his c. that . . .,** il faut dire à son mérite que . . .; **it does him c.,** cela lui fait (grand) honneur; **he is a c. to the school,** il fait honneur à l'école; (*b*) *Cin:* **c. titles, credits,** générique *m; Th:* crédits, remerciements *mpl.* **4.** *Com: Fin:* (*a*) crédit; **to give s.o. c.,** faire crédit à qn; **to sell on c.,** vendre à crédit; **c. bank,** banque *f* de crédit; *Bank:* **c. account,** compte créditeur; **to open c. account with s.o.,** ouvrir un crédit chez qn; **c. card,** carte *f* de crédit; **c. rating,** degré *m* de solvabilité; **to live on c.,** vivre à crédit; (*b*) *Book-k:* **debit and c.,** doit *m* et avoir *m;* **c. balance,** solde créditeur; **c. note,** note *f* de crédit; **to enter a sum to s.o.'s c.,** porter une somme au crédit, à l'actif *m,* de qn; créditer qn d'une somme; (*c*) réputation de solvabilité; crédit; **his c. is good,** on lui fait toute confiance.

credit² *v.tr.* **1.** ajouter foi à, croire (un bruit, qn); *F:* **I wouldn't have credited it,** je ne l'aurais pas cru possible; **you wouldn't c. it,** c'est à ne pas croire. **2.** (*a*) attribuer, prêter (**s.o. with a quality,** une qualité à qn); **to c. s.o. with superior intelligence,** créditer qn d'une intelligence supérieure; **I credited you with more sense,** je vous croyais, supposais, plus de jugement; **to be credited with having done sth.,** passer pour avoir fait qch.; (*b*) **to c. s.o. with a quality,** reconnaître une qualité à qn. **3.** *Com:* **to c. s.o., an account, with a sum,** créditer qn, un compte, d'une somme; porter une somme au crédit de qn, d'un compte.

creditable ['kreditəbl] *a.* (action) estimable, digne d'éloges. **-ably** *adv.* honorablement, avec honneur.

creditor ['kreditər] *n.* **1.** créancier, -ière. **2.** *attrib.* créditeur, -trice; *Pol.Ec:* **c. nation,** nation créditrice.

credo, *pl.* **-os** ['kri:dou, 'krei-, -ouz] *n. Ecc: Mus:* credo *m inv.*

credulity [kri'dju:liti] *n.* crédulité *f.*

credulous ['kredjuləs] *a.* crédule.

creed [kri:d] *n.* **1.** *Theol:* credo *m inv;* **the (Apostles') C.,** le symbole des Apôtres; le credo. **2.** croyance *f,* foi (confessionnelle). **3.** profession *f* de foi; **political c.,** credo politique.

creek [kri:k] *n.* **1.** crique *f,* anse *f.* **2.** *NAm: Austr: N.Z:* (*a*) ruisseau *m,* petit cours d'eau; (*b*) petite vallée. **3.** *P:* **to be up the c.,** être dans l'embarras; être dans le pétrin.

creel [kri:l] *n. Fish:* panier *m* de pêche; glène *f.*

creep¹ [kri:p] *n.* **1.** *F:* (*a*) **the creeps,** la chair de poule; **to give s.o. the creeps,** donner la chair de poule à qn; horripiler qn; (*b*) *P:* personnage répugnant; saligaud *m.* **2.** action *f* de ramper.

creep² *v.i.* (*p.t. & p.p.* **crept** [krept]) **1.** (*a*) (*of insect, animal, plant*) ramper; (*of roots*) tracer; (*of pers.*) se traîner; *F:* ramper (devant les grands); **to c. into bed,** se glisser dans son lit; **he crept into the room,** il entra furtivement, à pas de loup, dans la chambre; **a feeling of uneasiness crept over me,** un sentiment de gêne commençait à me gagner; (*b*) **to make s.o.'s flesh c.,** donner la chair de poule à qn. **2.** (*a*) (*of plant*) grimper; (*b*) (*of liquid, esp. of acid*) grimper. **creep along** *v.i.* s'avancer (i) en rampant, (ii) furtivement; *F:* marcher à pas de loup. **creep away** *v.i.* (*a*) s'éloigner (i) en rampant, (ii) à pas de loup. **creep by** *v.i.* **time, the hours, crept slowly by,** les heures passaient lentement. **creeping 1.** *a.* (*a*) (*of animal, plant, inflation, etc.*) rampant; *Med:* **c. paralysis,** paralysie progressive; (*b*) (homme) servile, rampant; (*c*) (*of plant*) grimpant. **2.** *n.* (*a*) rampement *m;* (*b*) = CREEP¹ **2. creep up** *v.i.* (*a*) se traîner jusqu'en haut; (*b*) s'approcher en rampant, lentement; **the speedometer crept up to 120,** l'aiguille de l'indicateur de vitesse avança lentement, monta tout doucement, jusqu'à 120; (*c*) **to c. up on s.o.,** surprendre qn, prendre qn à l'improviste; **old age has crept up on me,** j'ai vieilli sans m'en rendre compte.

creeper ['kri:pər] *n.* **1.** *Bot:* plante (i) rampante, (ii) grimpante. **2.** *NAm:* **creepers,** souliers *mpl* à semelles de crêpe; crampons *mpl* à verglas; (*b*) barboteuse *f* (d'enfant).

creepy ['kri:pi] *a. F:* **1.** rampant; **I could feel c. things on my leg,** je sentais sur ma jambe qch. qui rampait. **2. c. story,** récit *m* qui donne la chair de poule. **3.** dégoûtant; dégueulasse.

creepy-crawly ['kri:pi'krɔ:li] *F:* **1.** *a.* (*a*) **c.-c. feeling,** (i) fourmillement *m;* (ii) chair *f* de poule. **2.** *n.* insecte *m;* bestiole rampante; vermine *f.*

cremate [kri'meit] *v.tr.* incinérer (un mort).

cremation [kri'meiʃ(ə)n] *n.* incinération *f;* crémation *f.*

crematorium, *pl.* **-ia** [kremə'tɔ:riəm, -iə] crématorium *m.*

crème [kreim] *n.* crème *f;* **c. caramel** ['kærəmel], crème (renversée) au caramel; crème caramel; **c. de menthe** [də'mɑ:nt], crème de menthe.

crenel(l)ated ['krenəleitid] *a.* (*of wall, etc.*) crénelé.

Creole ['kri:oul] **1.** *Ethn: a. & n.* (*a*) créole (*mf*); (*b*) *U.S:* (descendant, -ante) des colons français ou espagnols de la Louisiane. **2.** *n. Ling:* le créole.

creosote¹ ['kri(:)əsout] *n. Ch:* créosote *f.*

creosote² *v.tr.* créosoter (le bois).

crêpe [kreip] *n.* **1.** *Tex:* crêpe *m;* **c. de Chine** [də'ʃi:n], crêpe de Chine; *Med:* **c. bandage,** bande *f* Velpeau; velpeau *m.* **2. c.-(rubber) soles,** semelles *fpl* (de) crêpe. **3. c. paper,** papier *m* crêpe. **4.** *Cu:* **c. Suzette,** crêpe Suzette.

crescendo [kri'ʃendou] *adv. & n. Mus:* crescendo (*m inv*).

crescent ['kresənt] **1.** *n.* (*a*) croissant *m* (de la lune); (*b*) *Her: etc:* croissant; (*c*) rue *f* ou côté *m* de rue en arc de cercle; (*d*) *Bak:* **c. (roll),** croissant. **2.** *a.* (*a*) croissant; **the c. moon,** le croissant de la lune; (*b*) **c.(-shaped),** en forme de croissant, de demi-lune.

cress [kres] *n. Bot:* cresson *m;* **garden c.,** cresson alénois, passerage cultivé.

crest [krest] *n.* **1.** crête *f* (de coq, reptile); huppe *f* (d'alouette); aigrette *f* (de paon). **2.** cimier *m,* crête (de casque). **3.** (*a*) crête, sommet *m* (de colline, d'une vague); (*b*) *Ph:* crête, point haut (d'une onde). **4.** *Arch:* crête, faîte *m,* faîtage *m.* **5.** *Anat:* crête, arête (d'un os). **6.** crête du cou (d'un animal). **7.** (*a*) *Her:* (*on helmet*) cimier *m;* (*on escutcheon*) timbre *m;* (*b*) (*on seal, note-paper, etc.*) armoiries *fpl;* écusson *m.*

crested ['krestid] *a.* **1.** *Orn:* à crête, à huppe; huppé;

Z: à crête, crêté; **white-c. waves,** vagues *fpl* aux crêtes blanches. **2.** (*a*) (*of helmet*) orné d'un cimier; panaché; (*b*) *F:* armorié; orné d'un écusson.

crestfallen ['krestfɔ:l(ə)n] *a.* (*of pers.*) abattu, découragé; (*of look*) déconfit; **to look c.,** baisser l'oreille.

cretaceous [kri'teiʃəs] **1.** *a.* crétacé; crayeux **2.** *a.* & *n. Geol:* **C.,** crétacé (*m*).

Cretan ['kri:t(ə)n] *Geog:* **1.** *a.* crétois. **2.** *n.* Crétois, -oise.

Crete [kri:t] *Pr.n. Geog:* Crète *f.*

cretin ['kretin] *n. Med:* crétin *m.*

cretinism ['kretinizm] *n. Med:* crétinisme *m.*

cretinous ['kretinəs] *a. Med:* crétineux.

cretonne [kre'tɔn, 'kretɔn] *n. Tex:* cretonne *f.*

crevasse [kri'væs] *n.* crevasse *f* (glaciaire).

crevice ['krevis] *n.* fente *f*; crevasse *f*, lézarde *f* (de mur); fissure *f* (de rocher).

crew¹ [kru:] *n.* **1.** *Nau:* équipage *m*; *Row: etc:* équipe *f*; *Cost:* **c. neck,** col ras le cou; *Hairdr:* **c. cut,** cheveux (coupés) en brosse. **2.** (*gang, team*) équipe; *Av:* **air, flight, c.,** équipage (d'avion); **ground c.,** équipe au sol; *Ind:* **maintenance c.,** équipe d'entretien; **c. member,** membre *m* d'équipage, d'équipe (d'avion, de char, etc.). **3.** *Pej:* bande *f*, troupe *f*; **sorry c.,** triste engeance *f.*

crew² **1.** *v.tr.* (*a*) armer (un navire d'un équipage); fournir (un avion, etc.) d'un équipage; (*b*) **yacht that can't be crewed by less than six,** yacht qui exige un équipage de six au moins. **2.** *v.i.* **to c. for s.o.,** servir d'équipier à qn.

crewel ['kru:əl] *n.* laine *f* à broder, à tapisserie.

crib¹ [krib] *n.* **1.** (*a*) *Husb:* mangeoire *f*; râtelier *m*; (*b*) *NAm:* huche *f*, coffre *m* (pour le maïs, le sel, etc.); armoire *f* (à outils). **2.** (*a*) lit *m* d'enfant; (*b*) *Ecc:* crèche *f.* **3.** *F:* (*a*) plagiat *m*; (*b*) *Sch:* traduction *f* (d'auteur), corrigé *m* (de thèmes, etc.) (employés subrepticement).

crib² *v.tr.* **(cribbed)** (*a*) reproduire, copier (un passage d'un auteur); *v.i.* **to c. from an author,** plagier un auteur; (*b*) *Sch:* (i) **to c. an exercise from another boy,** copier un devoir sur un camarade; (ii) *v.i.* se servir de traductions, de corrigés.

cribbage ['kribidʒ] *n. Cards:* cribbage *m.*

crick¹ [krik] *n.* foulure *f*; **c. in the back,** tour *m* de reins; **c. in the neck,** torticolis *m.*

crick² *v.tr.* **to c. one's neck,** se donner le torticolis.

cricket¹ ['krikit] *n. Ent:* grillon *m*; *F:* cricri *m.*

cricket² *n. Sp:* cricket *m*; **to play c.,** jouer au cricket; *Fig:* **that's not c.,** cela n'est pas de jeu, ne se fait pas; **c. field, ground,** terrain *m* de cricket.

cricketer ['krikitər] *n.* cricketeur *m*; joueur *m* de cricket.

crier ['kraiər] *n.* **town c.,** crieur public, municipal.

crikey ['kraiki] *int. P:* mince alors!

crime [kraim] *n.* (*a*) crime *m*; **capital c.,** crime capital; *Fig:* **it's a c. to cut down this tree,** c'est un crime d'abattre cet arbre; (*b*) délit *m*; faute *f*; (*c*) **to make a study of c.,** étudier le crime, la criminalité; **c. story,** roman (i) noir, (ii) policier; **c. writer,** auteur *m* de romans (i) noirs, (ii) policiers; **c. reporter,** journaliste *mf* qui fait la chronique des tribunaux; (*d*) *Mil:* **c. sheet,** feuille *f* de punitions.

Crimea (the) [ðəkrai'miə] *Pr.n. Geog:* la Crimée.

Crimean [krai'miən] *a. Hist:* **the C. War,** la guerre de Crimée.

criminal ['krimin(ə)l] **1.** *a.* criminel; (*a*) **c. act,** action criminelle; (*b*) **c. action, case,** action *f*, cas *m*, au criminel; **to take c. proceedings against s.o.,** poursuivre qn criminellement; **c. law,** droit criminel; **c. lawyer,** avocat *m* au criminel; **the C. Investigation Department, the C.I.D.** ['si:'ai:'di:] = la Police judiciaire, *F:* la P.J.; **c. record,** casier *m* judiciaire; (*c*) **it would be c. to cut down these trees,** ce serait un crime d'abattre ces arbres. **2.** *n.* (*a*) criminel, -elle; **habitual c.,** repris *m* de justice; récidiviste *mf*; (*b*) (le) coupable. **-ally** *adv.* criminellement.

criminologist [krimi'nɔlədʒist] *n.* criminologiste *mf.*

criminology [krimi'nɔlədʒi] *n.* criminologie *f.*

crimp¹ [krimp] *n.* gaufrage *m*; pli *m* (d'un drap); frisure *f* (des cheveux); sertissage *m* (d'une cartouche, etc.).

crimp² *v.tr.* (*a*) gaufrer (à la paille), plisser, crêper (de l'étoffe, etc.); (*b*) friser (les cheveux); **crimped hair,** cheveux crêpelés à gaufrures.

crimson ['krimz(ə)n] *a.* & *n.* cramoisi (*m*); **to blush c.,** devenir cramoisi; **c. with rage,** rouge de colère.

cringe [krindʒ] *v.i.* **1.** se faire tout petit; se blottir (de peur); se dérober (par crainte d'un coup); **he did not c.,** il n'a pas bronché. **2.** s'humilier, ramper, s'aplatir (**to, before, s.o.,** devant qn). **cringing** *a.* **1.** (geste) craintif. **2.** servile, obséquieux.

crinkle¹ ['kriŋkl] *n.* pli *m*, ride *f.*

crinkle² **1.** *v.tr.* froisser, chiffonner (du papier); **crinkled paper,** papier plissé, gaufré; papier crêpe, crêpé. **2.** *v.i.* (*a*) se froisser; (*b*) (*of apples, potatoes*) se rider.

crinkly ['kriŋkli] *a.* plein de rides.

crinoline ['krinəli(:)n] *n. A.Cost:* crinoline *f.*

cripple¹ ['kripl] *n.* estropié, -ée; infirme *mf*; invalide *mf.*

cripple² *v.tr.* **1.** estropier (qn); **the men who were crippled in the war,** les mutilés de guerre. **2.** disloquer (une machine, un système); désemparer (un navire); paralyser (l'industrie, la volonté). **crippled** *a.* **1.** estropié; infirme; **c. with rheumatism,** perclus de rhumatismes. **2.** (*a*) (vaisseau) désemparé; (*b*) (machine) hors de fonctionnement. **crippling** *a.* (*a*) (*of disease, etc.*) estropiant; (*b*) (*of taxation, strike, etc.*) paralysant.

crisis, *pl.* **-es** ['kraisis, -i:z] *n.* crise *f* (dans les affaires, etc.); **things are coming to a c.,** le moment décisif approche; **to go through a c.,** passer par une crise.

crisp¹ [krisp] **1.** *a.* (*a*) (*of curls*) crépu, frisé; (*b*) (biscuit, etc.) croquant, croustillant; (laitue) croquante; **the snow was c. under foot,** la neige craquait sous nos pas; (*c*) (style) nerveux; (ton) tranchant; (*d*) (air) vif. **2.** *n.* (*a*) **cooked to a c.,** rôti à point pour croquer sous la dent; (*b*) **(potato) crisps,** (pommes *fpl*) chips (*mpl*). **-ly** *adv.* (parler) d'un ton tranchant; (écrire) d'un style nerveux, net.

crisp² *v.tr.* (*a*) froncer (du crêpe); (*b*) donner du croustillant, du croquant, à (des biscuits, etc.).

crispbread ['krispbred] *n.* = biscotte *f* scandinave.

crispness ['krispnis] *n.* **1.** qualité croustillante (d'un gâteau, etc.); dureté *f* (de la neige); état parcheminé (du papier, etc.); (*of fabric, etc.*) **to lose its c.,** se défraîchir. **2.** netteté *f* (de style, etc.) **3.** froid vif (de l'air).

criss-cross¹ ['kriskrɔs] **1.** *a.* (*of pattern, etc.*) entrecroisé, treillissé. **2.** *n.* entrecroisement *m*; enchevêtrement *m.*

criss-cross² **1.** *v.tr.* entrecroiser (des fils, etc.); **brow criss-crossed with wrinkles,** front craquelé de rides. **2.** *v.i.* s'entrecroiser.

criterion, *pl.* **-ia** [krai'tiəriən, -iə] *n.* critère *m.*

critic ['kritik] *n.* (*a*) critique *m*; **music, drama, literary, c.,** critique musical, dramatique, littéraire; **film critic,** critique de cinéma; (*b*) censeur *m* (de la conduite d'autrui); critiqueur *m.*

critical ['kritik(ə)l] *a.* critique; (*a*) **a c. audience,** des auditeurs exigeants; **to be c. of s.o., sth.,** censurer qn, qch.; (*b*) (dissertation, étude) critique; (*c*) (situation, moment, âge, etc.) critique; *Med:* **in a c. state,**

dans un état critique; **c. year,** année *f* climatérique; **she is going through a c. time,** elle subit, traverse, une crise en ce moment; (*d*) *Opt:* **c. angle,** angle *m* limite, critique. **-ally** *adv.* **1.** (considérer qch.) en critique; (regarder qch.) d'un œil critique. **2. c. ill,** dangereusement malade; **the c. ill,** les grands malades.

criticism ['kritisizm] *n.* **1.** (*action, act, of criticizing*) critique *f*; **to lay oneself open to c.,** s'exposer à la critique. **2.** *Lit: Art: etc:* (*a*) critique; **textual c.,** critique des textes; (*b*) **to write a c. of a book, etc.,** faire la critique d'un livre, etc.

criticize ['kritisaiz] *v.tr.* **1.** critiquer, faire la critique de (qch.). **2.** censurer, blâmer; **to c. sth. severely,** se répandre en critiques sur qch.; **to c. the defects of a work,** relever les fautes d'un ouvrage.

critique [kri'ti:k] *n.* critique *f*; article *m* critique (sur une œuvre littéraire, etc.).

croak¹ [krouk] *n.* coassement *m* (de grenouille); croassement *m* (de corbeau).

croak² *v.i.* **1.** (*of frog*) coasser; (*of raven*) croasser. **2.** *F:* (*of pers.*) (*a*) grogner; (*b*) parler d'une voix enrouée, rauque; (*c*) *P:* crever, claquer. **croaking** *n.* coassement *m* (de grenouille); croassement *m* (de corbeau).

croaky ['krouki] *a.* (voix) enrouée, rauque.

Croat ['krouæt] **1.** *a. Geog:* croate. **2.** *n.* Croate *mf.*

Croatian [krou'eiʃən] **1.** *a. Geog:* croate. **2.** *n.* (*a*) Croate *mf*; (*b*) *Ling:* croate *m.*

crochet¹ ['krouʃei, -ʃi] *n.* **1.** (travail *m* au) crochet (*m*); **c. hook,** crochet. **2. c. work,** ouvrage *m*, travail *m*, au crochet.

crochet² *v.* **(crocheted** ['krouʃeid, -ʃid]) **1.** *v.tr.* faire (qch.) au crochet. **2.** *v.i.* faire du crochet. **crocheting** *n.* (travail *m* au) crochet (*m*).

crock¹ [krɔk] *n.* **1.** (*a*) cruche *f*; (*b*) pot *m* de terre. **2.** *Hort:* tesson *m* (pour couvrir le trou d'un pot de fleurs).

crock² *n. F:* **old c.,** (i) (*pers.*) vieux bonhomme fini, croulant *m*; (ii) (*car*) vieux clou, vieille bagnole.

crockery ['krɔkəri] *n.* (*a*) faïence *f*, poterie *f*; (*b*) *coll.* vaisselle *f* de table, de cuisine.

crocodile ['krɔkədail] *n.* (*a*) crocodile *m*; **c. tears,** larmes *fpl* de crocodile; (*b*) **c. (skin),** peau *f* de crocodile; **c. handbag,** sac *m* à main en crocodile; (*c*) *F:* élèves d'un pensionnat marchant deux à deux.

crocus, *pl.* **-uses** ['kroukəs, -əsiz] *n. Bot:* crocus *m*; **autumn c.,** safran cultivé.

croft [krɔft] *n.* **1.** petit clos. **2.** petite ferme.

crofter ['krɔftər] *n.* petit fermier.

crone [kroun] *n.* vieille (femme); commère *f.*

crony ['krouni] *n.* **(old) c.,** vieil(le) ami(e); vieux copain, vieille copine.

crook¹ [kruk] *n.* **1.** (*a*) croc *m*, crochet *m*; (*b*) houlette *f* (de berger); crosse *f* (d'évêque). **2.** angle *m*, courbure *f*; (*of river, path, etc.*) détour *m*, coude *m.* **3.** (*pers.*) escroc *m.*

crook² *v.tr.* courber, recourber. **crooked** *a.* **1.** ['krukid] (*a*) courbé (en crosse); crochu; tordu, recourbé; (*of path*) tortueux; (*of limb, tree*) contourné, déjeté; (nez) crochu, de travers; (jambes) torses; (*b*) malhonnête, déshonnête; **c. means,** moyens *mpl* obliques. **2.** [krukt] (canne, etc.) à béquille.

crook³ *a. Austr: F:* (*a*) (i) malade; (ii) furieux; **to go c.,** se mettre en colère (**at s.o.,** contre qn); (*b*) (*of machinery, etc.*) en panne; (*c*) (*of thg, place, etc.*) moche.

crookedness ['krukidnis] *n.* (*a*) irrégularité *f* (des contours, etc.); (*b*) malhonnêteté *f.*

croon [kru:n] *v.tr.* chantonner; fredonner (une chanson); chanter à demi-voix.

crooner ['kru:nər] *n.* (*a*) fredonneur, -euse; (*b*) chanteur, -euse, de charme.

crop¹ [krɔp] *n.* **1.** jabot *m.* **2.** manche *m*; **riding c.,** cravache *f*; **hunting c.,** stick *m* de chasse. **3.** (*a*) récolte *f*, moisson *f*; (*of fruit, etc.*) cueillette *f*; **second c.,** regain *m*; **cash c.,** culture commerciale; **food crops,** récoltes alimentaires; **to harvest the crops,** faire la récolte, la moisson; **a fine c. of hair,** une belle chevelure; (*b*) *For:* peuplement *m.* **4.** coupe *f* (des cheveux); **to give s.o. a close c.,** tondre les cheveux de qn.

crop² *v.* **(cropped) 1.** *v.tr.* (*a*) tondre, tailler (une haie, les cheveux, etc.); émarger (un livre); écourter, couper (les oreilles, la queue); **hair cropped close,** cheveux coupés ras; (*b*) (*of cattle*) brouter (l'herbe). **2.** (*a*) *v.i.* (*of land*) donner une récolte; (*b*) *v.tr.* cultiver (les pommes de terre, etc.); **to c. land with corn,** mettre une terre en blé. **crop up** *v.i.* (*of question, problem, etc.*) se présenter, surgir.

cropper ['krɔpər] *n.* **1.** *Agr:* (*a*) (*pers.*) cultivateur *m*; (*b*) **good, bad, c.,** plante *f* qui donne de bonnes, de mauvaises, récoltes. **2.** *F:* **to come a c.,** (i) faire une chute; ramasser une pelle; (ii) se heurter à un obstacle imprévu; (iii) *Gaming:* prendre une culotte; **to come a c. over sth.,** se casser les dents sur qch.

croquet ['kroukei, -ki] *n.* (jeu *m* de) croquet (*m*).

croquette [krɔ'ket] *n. Cu:* croquette *f.*

crosier ['krouziər] *n. Ecc:* crosse *f* (d'évêque).

cross¹ [krɔs] *n.* **1.** croix *f*; (*a*) **the stations of the C.,** le chemin de la Croix; **to bear one's c.,** porter sa croix; **to make the sign of the c.,** faire le signe de la croix; (*b*) **processional c.,** croix processionnelle; **c. bearer,** porte-croix *m inv*; **market c.,** croix de la place du marché; (*c*) **St Andrew's c.,** croix de Saint-André; **the Red C.,** la Croix rouge; **C. of the Legion of Honour,** croix de la Légion d'honneur; **Military C.,** Croix de Guerre; (*d*) **to sign with a c.,** signer d'une croix; (*e*) **c.-shaped,** en forme de croix; **c.-headed screw, screwdriver,** vis *f*, tournevis *m*, cruciforme. **2.** *Husb:* (*a*) croisement *m* (de races) (**between . . . and . . .,** entre . . . et . . .); (*b*) métis, -isse; **to be a c. between sth. and sth.,** être un mélange de qch. et de qch. **3.** (*of material*) biais *m*; **on the c.,** en biais. **4.** *Box:* cross *m*, coup croisé.

cross² **1.** *v.tr.* (*a*) croiser (deux bâtons, etc.); **to c. one's legs,** croiser les jambes; **let's keep our fingers crossed,** touchons du bois; (*b*) *Ecc:* **to c. oneself,** faire le signe de la croix; se signer; *F:* **c. my heart,** croix de bois croix de fer; (*c*) barrer (un chèque); mettre les barres à (ses t); **crossed cheque,** chèque barré; (*d*) passer (la mer, un fleuve); traverser (la rue, etc.); franchir (le seuil, la frontière); passer (sur), traverser (un pont); **the bridge that crosses the river,** le pont qui traverse la rivière; *Pol:* **to c. the floor (of the House),** changer de parti (politique); *Nau:* **to c. the line,** passer l'équateur; (*of thought*) **to c. s.o.'s mind,** se présenter à l'esprit de qn; (*e*) croiser (qn dans la rue); **to c. s.o.'s path,** (i) se trouver sur le chemin de qn; (ii) se mettre en travers de la volonté de qn; (*f*) contrarier, contrecarrer (qn, les desseins de qn); **to be crossed in love,** avoir une déception amoureuse; (*g*) *F:* tromper (qn); trahir (qn); (*h*) *Breed:* croiser, métisser (des races). **2.** *v.i.* (*a*) (*of roads, letters, breeds, etc.*) se croiser; (*of lines*) se croiser, s'entrecroiser; (*b*) passer (d'un lieu à un autre); **to c. from Dover to Calais,** faire la traversée de Douvres à Calais. **crossing** *n.* **1.** barrement *m* (d'un chèque). **2.** *Ecc:* signe *m* de croix. **3.** (*a*) traversée *f* (de la mer); passage *m* (d'un fleuve, des Alpes); *Mil:* franchissement *m* (d'un fleuve); **we had a fine, good, c.,** nous avons eu, fait, une belle traversée; (*b*) **pedestrian, zebra, c.,** passage pour piétons, passage clouté. **4.** croisement *m*, entrecroisement *m* (de lignes, de fils, etc.). **5.** (*a*) (*of roads, railway lines, etc.*) croisement, intersection *f*; carrefour *m*; jonction *f*; (*b*) *Rail:* **level,** *NAm:* **grade, c.,** passage à niveau. **6.** *Breed:*

croisement, mélange *m* (de deux espèces). **cross off** *v.tr.* rayer (un nom sur une liste, etc.). **cross out** *v.tr.* biffer, barrer, rayer (un mot, une phrase, etc.). **cross over** *v.i.* traverser une rue, la mer, etc.; **they crossed over to Cherbourg in their yacht,** ils ont fait la traversée jusqu'à Cherbourg dans leur yacht.

cross³ *a.* **1.** (*a*) transversal, -aux; oblique; mis en travers; (*b*) (entre)croisé; **c. lines,** lignes *fpl* qui se croisent; (*c*) contraire, opposé (**to,** à); **we are at c. purposes,** il y a malentendu (entre nous). **2.** (*of pers.*) maussade, de mauvaise humeur; fâché; **to get c.,** se fâcher (**with s.o.,** contre qn; **about sth.,** de qch.); **he looks c.,** il a l'air fâché; **don't be c. with me,** il ne faut pas m'en vouloir; **you never hear a c. word,** jamais on n'entend un mot vif. **-ly** *adv.* avec mauvaise humeur; d'un air, d'un ton, fâché.

crossbar ['krɔsbɑːr] *n.* (*a*) (barre *f* de) traverse (*f*), entretoise *f*; (*of window*) croisillon *m*; (*of door*) épar(t) *m*; (*b*) *Aut:* barre d'accouplement (des roues avant); (*c*) *Fb: etc:* barre transversale.

crossbeam ['krɔsbiːm] *n.* **1.** *Const:* sommier *m*, traverse *f*. **2.** (*a*) *N.Arch:* barrotin *m*; (*b*) *Civ.E:* chapeau *m* (de pilotis, etc.). **3.** *Gym:* portique *m*.

crossbencher ['krɔsben(t)ʃər] *n.* *Parl:* = député indépendant.

crossbill ['krɔsbil] *n.* *Orn:* bec-croisé *m*, *pl.* becs-croisés.

crossbones ['krɔsbounz] *n.pl.* os *mpl* en croix; **skull and c.,** tête *f* de mort et tibias croisés (du pavillon des pirates).

crossbow ['krɔsbou] *n.* arbalète *f*.

crossbred ['krɔsbred] *a.* métis, -isse.

crossbreed¹ ['krɔsbriːd] *n.* **1.** *Breed:* race croisée; produit *m* d'un croisement. **2.** *F:* métis, -isse.

crossbreed² *v.tr.* (*p.t. & p.p.* **crossbred**) croiser, métisser (des races, etc.).

cross-check¹ ['krɔs'tʃek] *n.* contre-vérification *f*, moyen *m* de recoupement.

cross-check² *v.tr.* contre-vérifier.

cross-country ['krɔs'kʌntri] *a.* (promenade) à travers champs; (véhicule) tout-terrain; *Sp:* **c.-c. running,** le cross; **c.-c. runner,** crossman *m*, *pl.* crossmen.

crosscut ['krɔskʌt] *n.* (*a*) coupe *f* en travers; **c. saw,** scie *f* passe-partout; (*b*) contre-taille *f*; **c. file,** lime *f* à taille croisée.

crosse [krɔs] *n.* *Sp:* crosse *f* (du jeu de la crosse).

cross-examination ['krɔsigzæmi'neiʃ(ə)n] *n.* (*a*) *Jur:* interrogatoire *m* contradictoire; (*b*) *F:* interrogatoire serré.

cross-examine ['krɔsig'zæmin] *v.tr.* (*a*) *Jur:* interroger (qn) contradictoirement; (*b*) *F:* soumettre (qn) à un interrogatoire serré.

cross-eyed ['krɔsaid] *a.* louche, qui louche; **to be c.-e.,** loucher.

cross-fertilization ['krɔsfəːtilai'zeiʃ(ə)n] *n.* *Bot:* (*a*) pollinisation croisée; (*b*) hybridation *f*.

crossfire ['krɔsfaiər] *n.* *Mil: etc:* feu croisé; **exposed to c.,** pris entre deux feux.

crossgrained ['krɔsgreind] *a.* **1.** (*of wood*) aux fibres irrégulières; à fibres torses. **2.** *F:* (*of pers.*) (*a*) revêche, grincheux; (*b*) bourru, ronchonneur.

crosshatch ['krɔshætʃ] *v.tr.* *Engr:* contre-hacher. **cross-hatching** *n.* (système *m* de) hachures croisées.

cross-legged ['krɔs'leg(i)d] *a.* les jambes croisées; **to sit c.-l.,** être assis en tailleur, à la Turque.

crossover ['krɔsouvər] *n.* **1.** croisement *m*; *Mec.E:* coude *m* de croisement (d'un tube); *Rail:* voie *f* de croisement. **2.** *Cost:* croisure *f* (d'un habit).

crosspiece ['krɔspiːs] *n.* (barre *f* de) traverse (*f*).

cross-question ['krɔs'kwestʃ(ə)n] *v.tr.* = CROSS-EXAMINE.

cross-reference¹ ['krɔs'ref(ə)rəns] *n.* renvoi *m*.

cross-reference² *v.tr.* numéroter (des lettres); établir les renvois (d'un livre).

crossroad ['krɔsroud] *n.* **1.** chemin *m* de traverse. **2. crossroads,** (i) carrefour *m*, croisement *m* (de routes); (ii) *U.S:* amorce *f* de bourg (à un carrefour); **we are now at the crossroads,** c'est l'heure des décisions irrévocables.

cross-section ['krɔs'sekʃ(ə)n] *n.* coupe *f* en travers; coupe, section, transversale; **a c.-s. of life,** une tranche de vie; **a c.-s. of the population,** un groupe représentant les différents étages de la société.

cross-stitch ['krɔsstitʃ] *n.* *Needlew:* point croisé.

crosstalk ['krɔstɔːk] *n.* répliques *fpl*.

crosstrees ['krɔstriːz] *n.pl.* *Nau:* barres (de hune) traversières.

crosswalk ['krɔswɔːk] *n.* *NAm:* passage clouté.

crossway ['krɔswei] *n.* *NAm:* croisement *m* (de routes).

crosswind ['krɔswind] *n.* vent *m* de travers.

crosswise ['krɔswaiz] *adv.* en travers, en croix.

crossword ['krɔswəːd] *n.* **c. (puzzle),** mots croisés.

crotch [krɔtʃ] *n.* (*a*) entrecuisse *m*; (*b*) *Tail:* fourche, fourchet *m* (du pantalon).

crotchet ['krɔtʃit] *n.* *Mus:* noire *f*.

crotchety ['krɔtʃəti] *a.* capricieux; grognon; (humeur) difficile.

crouch¹ [krautʃ] *n.* accroupissement *m*.

crouch² *v.i.* se tapir, s'accroupir; **tiger crouching for a spring,** tigre accroupi avant de sauter.

croup¹ [kruːp] *n.* croupe *f* (de cheval, etc.).

croup² *n.* *Med:* croup *m*; **false c.,** faux croup.

croupier ['kruːpiər] *n.* croupier *m*.

crow¹ [krou] *n.* *Orn:* corneille *f*; **crow's nest,** (i) nid *m* de corneille; (ii) *Nau:* nid *m* de pie; **as the c. flies,** à vol d'oiseau.

crow² *n.* **1.** chant *m* du coq; *F:* cocorico *m*. **2.** gazouillis *m* (de bébé).

crow³ *v.i.* **1.** (*of cock*) chanter; *F:* faire cocorico; *F:* **to c. over s.o.,** chanter victoire sur qn. **2.** (*of baby*) gazouiller. **crowing** *n.* **1.** chant *m* (du coq). **2.** gazouillis *m* (de bébé).

crowbar ['kroubɑːr] *n.* *Tls:* pince *f* (à levier).

crowd¹ [kraud] *n.* **1.** (*a*) foule *f*; affluence *f*; **to come in a c., in crowds,** venir en foule; **to draw crowds,** attirer la foule; (*b*) **the c.,** la foule; **to stand out from the c.,** se distinguer (de la foule). **2.** *F:* grande quantité, tas *m* (de choses). **3.** (*a*) *F:* bande *f*, clique *f*; **they're a good c.,** ce sont de bons types; **they stick to their own c.,** ils font bande à part; (*b*) *Th: Cin:* **the c.,** les figurants *mpl*; **c. scene,** scène *f* de masses.

crowd² **1.** *v.tr.* (*a*) serrer, (en)tasser (des personnes, des choses); **crowded together,** pressés, serrés, l'un contre l'autre; **we are too crowded here,** on est gêné ici; (*b*) remplir, bourrer (**with,** de); **room crowded with furniture,** pièce encombrée de meubles; **the hall was crowded with people,** la salle était bondée; **the streets were crowded,** il y avait foule dans les rues; (*c*) *Sp:* tasser (un concurrent); serrer (une autre voiture); (*d*) *U.S:* importuner (un débiteur); (*e*) forcer; **to be crowded off the pavement,** être forcé de quitter le trottoir. **2.** *v.i.* **to c. (together),** se presser en foule; se serrer; **to c. round s.o.,** se presser autour de qn; **here memories c. in on me,** ici des souvenirs m'assaillent en foule. **crowded** *a.* (pièce) (i) bondée (de gens), (ii) encombrée (de meubles); (train, etc.) bondé; (rue, profession) encombrée; (journée) chargée; **the c. events of that day,** les nombreux événements de cette journée. **crowding** *n.* encombrement *m*; entassement *m*; *Sp:* tassage *m* (d'un concurrent). **crowd out** *v.tr.* (*a*) ne pas laisser de place à (qn, qch.); (*b*) *U.S:* évincer (qn).

crowfoot ['kroufut] *n.* (*pl. usu.* **crowfoots**) *Bot:* renoncule *f* (âcre).

crown¹ [kraun] *n.* **1.** (*a*) couronne *f* (de fleurs, d'or); **the martyr's c.,** la couronne du martyre; (*b*) **royal c.,** couronne royale; **to wear the c.,** porter la couronne; (*c*) la Couronne (symbole de l'État monarchique); **C. lands, estates,** terres domaniales, appartenantes à la Couronne; **C. prince,** prince héritier; **the c. jewels,** les joyaux *mpl* de la Couronne; **C. Colony,** colonie *f* de la Couronne; *Jur:* **C. witness,** témoin *m* à charge; **C. court** = tribunal *m* de grande instance; (*d*) couronnement *m* (de la vie); comble *m* (des bonheurs, des malheurs). **2.** *Num:* couronne (de cinq shillings); *A:* **half a c.,** une demi-couronne. **3.** (*a*) sommet *m,* haut *m* (de la tête); (*b*) (i) calotte *f,* (ii) fond *m* (d'un chapeau). **4.** couronne *f* (de dent); clef *f* (d'une voûte); bombement *m* (d'un pont, d'une chaussée); cime *f* (d'un arbre); crête *f* (de colline); faîte *m* (de toit); diamant *m* (d'ancre); voûte *f* (de fourneau); *Aut:* **to drive on the c. of the road,** conduire sur l'axe de la route; *Mec.E:* **c. wheel, c. gear,** roue dentée sur une surface latérale; *Aut:* **c. wheel and pinion,** pignon *m* et couronne d'entraînement; *Com:* **c. cork,** *U.S:* **c. cap,** capsule *f* (métallique) de bouteille; **c. cork opener,** décapsulateur *m.* **5.** *Paperm:* **c. paper,** papier *m* couronne.

crown² *v.tr.* **1.** couronner (qn, la tête de qn) (**with,** de); **to c. s.o. king,** couronner qn roi; (*pers.*) **crowned head,** tête couronnée; *P:* **I'll c. you (for that)!** je vais te flanquer un de ces coups sur la tête! **2.** (*a*) récompenser (les efforts de qn); combler, couronner (le bonheur, de qn); (*b*) *F:* **to c. all,** pour comble de malheur. **3.** (*at draughts*) damer (un pion). **4.** couronner (une dent, etc.). **5.** (*a*) bomber (une route); (*b*) *v.i.* (*of road, etc.*); bomber. **crowning 1.** *a.* suprême; **as a c. folly,** pour comble de folie; **c. glory,** (i) couronnement *m* (d'une carrière, etc.); (ii) *Hum:* chevelure *f* (de qn). **2.** *n.* (*a*) couronnement *m* (d'un prince, etc.); (*b*) bombement *m* (d'une route, etc.).

crow's(-)foot, *pl.* **-feet** ['krouzfut, -fi:t] *n.* patte *f* d'oie (au coin de l'œil).

crozier ['krouziər] *n. Ecc:* crosse *f* (d'évêque).

crucial ['kru:ʃ(ə)l] *a.* (point, etc.) décisif, critique, crucial, -aux; **the c. test,** l'épreuve décisive.

crucible ['kru:sibl] *n. Metall: Ch: Ind:* creuset *m.*

crucifix ['kru:sifiks] *n.* crucifix *m,* christ *m;* **roadside c.,** calvaire *m.*

crucifixion [kru:si'fikʃ(ə)n] *n.* crucifixion *f,* crucifiement *m.*

cruciform ['kru:sifɔ:m] *a.* cruciforme; en croix.

crucify ['kru:sifai] *v.tr.* crucifier (qn, la chair, etc.); **Christ Crucified,** le Crucifié.

crude [kru:d] *a.* (*a*) (fer, pétrole, etc.) brut; (*b*) (expression) crue; (manières) grossières; (*c*) (*of method, idea, style, etc.*) informe, grossier; (outil, etc.) primitif; **c. statement of the facts,** exposition brutale des faits. **-ly** *adv.* **1.** (parler, s'exprimer) crûment, grossièrement. **2.** d'une manière fruste.

crudeness ['kru:dnis] *n.* **1.** crudité *f* (d'expression, etc.); grossièreté *f* (de manières, etc.). **2.** nature grossière, informe (du style); caractère primitif (d'un outil, etc.).

cruel ['kruəl] *a.* cruel. **-ly** *adv.* cruellement.

cruelty ['kruəlti] *n.* (*a*) cruauté *f* (**to** envers); **an act, of c.,** une cruauté; (*b*) *Jur:* sévices *mpl* (**to one's wife,** envers sa femme); **mental c.,** cruauté mentale.

cruet ['kruit] *n. Dom.Ec:* **c. (stand),** = huilier *m.*

cruise¹ [kru:z] *n.* (*a*) *Nau:* croisière *f;* **pleasure c.,** excursion *f,* voyage *m* d'agrément (en mer); (*b*) *Mil:* **c.(-type) missile,** engin *m* atmosphérique.

cruise² *v.i.* **1.** *Nau:* croiser; être en croisière. **2.** (*of taxi*) marauder; faire la maraude. **3.** *Av: Aut: etc:* **to c. at (a speed of . . .),** avoir une vitesse de croisière (de tant de km par heure). **cruising 1.** *a.* (*a*) en croisière; (*b*) (*of taxi*) en maraude. **2.** *n.* (*a*) croisière; (*b*) (*of taxi*) en maraude. **2.** *n.* (*a*) croisière(s) *f(pl);* **c. holiday,** croisière; (*b*) (*of taxi*) maraude *f;* (*c*) *Av: Aut: etc:* **c. speed,** vitesse de croisière.

cruiser ['kru:zər] *n. Nau:* **1. (battle) c.,** croiseur *m* de combat. **2. (cabin) c.,** yacht *m* de plaisance, de croisière (à moteur). **3.** *a. & n. Box:* **c. weight,** poids mi-lourd.

crumb¹ [krʌm] *n.* **1.** miette *f* (de pain); **c. of comfort,** brin *m* de consolation. **2.** (*opposed to crust*) mie *f* (de pain). **3.** *int. F:* **crumbs!** ça alors!

crumb² *v.tr. Cu:* paner (des côtelettes, etc.); couvrir de chapelure.

crumble¹ ['krʌmbl] **1.** *v.tr.* émietter (du pain); désagréger (les pierres); **to c. sth. up,** réduire qch. en miettes. **2.** *v.i.* (*of bread*) s'émietter; (*of stone, etc.*) s'effriter; (*of masonry*) s'écrouler; (*of earth*) s'ébouler; (*of empire*) s'effondrer; *St.Exch:* (*of prices*) s'effriter; **everything is crumbling to dust,** tout tombe en poussière. **crumbling 1.** *a.* qui s'écroule, qui s'effrite; (mur) croulant; (empire) qui croule. **2.** *n.* (*a*) émiettement *m;* effritement *m;* (*b*) éboulement *m,* écroulement.

crumble² *n. Cu:* **apple c.,** (genre de) charlotte *f* aux pommes.

crumbly ['krʌmbli] *a.* friable, ébouleux; (gâteau, pain) qui s'émiette trop.

crummy ['krʌmi] *a. P:* minable, moche; **what a c. joint!** quelle sale boîte!

crumpet ['krʌmpit] *n.* **1.** *Cu:* (sorte de) crêpe (servie rôtie et beurrée). **2.** *P:* **a nice bit of c.,** une belle pépée.

crumple ['krʌmpl] **1.** *v.tr.* friper, froisser (du drap, etc.); **to c. (up) paper,** (i) chiffonner, (ii) faire une boule avec, du papier. **2.** *v.i.* **to c. (up),** (*a*) se friper, se froisser; (*of leaves, parchment*) se ratatiner; (*b*) *Sp: etc:* (*of opposition,*) s'effondrer; (*c*) (*of mudguard, car*) se mettre en accordéon. **crumpling** *n.* **1.** froissement *m,* chiffonnage *m.* **2.** effondrement *m.*

crunch¹ [krʌn(t)ʃ] *n.* **1.** coup *m* de dents. **2.** bruit *m* de craquement *m;* crissement *m* (du sable). **3.** moment *m* difficile; **when it comes to the c.,** au moment critique.

crunch² **1.** *v.tr.* croquer, broyer (qch. avec les dents); écraser (la neige durcie). **2.** *v.i.* craquer, crisser; **hard snow crunches under foot,** la neige durcie craque sous les pieds. **crunching** *n.* = CRUNCH¹ 2.

crunchy ['krʌn(t)ʃi] *a.* **1.** croquant; croustillant. **2.** qui craque (sous les pas).

crupper ['krʌpər] *n.* **1.** *Harn:* croupière *f,* culière *f.* **2.** croupe *f* (de cheval).

crusade¹ [kru:'seid] *n.* **1.** *Hist:* croisade *f;* **to go on a c.,** partir en croisade. **2.** campagne *f* (contre le vice, etc.); **to start a c.,** lancer une croisade (**against,** contre).

crusade² *v.i.* **1.** *Hist:* aller ou être en croisade. **2.** mener une campagne (**against,** contre; **for,** pour).

crusader [kru:'seidər] *n.* **1.** *Hist:* croisé *m.* **2.** champion, -ionne (**for sth.,** de qch.).

crush¹ [krʌʃ] *n.* **1.** (*a*) écrasement *m;* (*b*) **c. hat,** (i) (chapeau) claque *m;* (ii) *U.S:* chapeau mou; (*c*) *Comest:* **orange, lemon, c.,** orangeade *f,* citronnade *f.* **2.** presse *f,* foule *f;* bousculade *f;* **there was a terrible c.,** il y avait un monde fou; **c. barrier,** barrière *f* pour contenir la foule; *Th:* **c. bar,** bar *m* des spectateurs. **3.** *F:* **to have a c. on s.o.,** avoir un béguin pour qn.

crush² **1.** *v.tr.* (*a*) écraser (qn, qch.); aplatir (un chapeau, etc.); exprimer le jus (des raisins, etc.); étouffer, écraser (une révolte); (*of boa constrictor*) enserrer (sa victime); (*of people*) **crushed together,** tassés, serrés; **we were nearly crushed to death,** on a failli être écrasé; (*b*) écraser (l'ennemi); **crushed,**

écrasé (**with shame,** de honte); accablé (**with grief,** de douleur); (*c*) froisser (une robe); (*d*) *Min: etc:* broyer, concasser (du minerai). **2.** *v.i.* se presser en foule, se bousculer (pour entrer dans un endroit); s'entasser (dans un endroit). **crushing 1.** *a.* (*a*) *Tchn:* (*of roller, etc.*) concasseur; (*b*) (*of news, defeat, etc.*) écrasant; (*of reply, etc.*) cinglant, humiliant; **to treat s.o. with c. contempt,** écraser qn de son mépris. **2.** *n.* aplatissage *m*, écrasement *m*; broyage *m*, concassage *m* (du minerai).

crusher ['krʌʃər] *n.* broyeur *m*, concasseur *m*.

crust[1] [krʌst] *n.* **1.** (*a*) croûte *f* (de pain, de pâté); **not a c. to eat,** pas une croûte à manger; (*b*) **piece of c.,** croûton *m*. **2.** écorce *f*, croûte (terrestre); couche *f* (de rouille); *F: O:* **the upper c.,** la fine fleur de la société. **3.** dépôt *m* (de vin en bouteille). **4.** croûte (d'une plaie).

crust[2] **1.** *v.tr.* encroûter; couvrir d'une croûte (de rouille, etc.). **2.** *v.i.* se couvrir d'une croûte; (*a*) s'incruster (de rouille, etc.); (*b*) (*of wound, etc.*) faire croûte. **crusted** *a.* **1. c. over,** couvert d'une croûte; **c. snow,** neige tôlée. **2.** (vin) qui a du dépôt.

crustacean [krʌs'teiʃən] **1.** *a.* crustacéen. **2.** *n.* crustacé *m*.

crusty ['krʌsti] *a.* **1.** *Cu:* (*a*) (pain) qui a une forte croûte; (*b*) (biscuit, etc.) croustillant. **2.** (*of pers.*) (*a*) bourru; (*b*) hargneux.

crutch [krʌtʃ] *n.* **1.** béquille *f*; **a c. to lean on,** un soutien; **to go about, walk, on crutches,** marcher avec des béquilles. **2.** (*a*) *Const: etc:* étançon *m*; (*b*) *Cy:* support *m* arrière (de motocyclette). **3.** (*a*) entrecuisse *m*; (*b*) *Tail:* fourche *f*, fourchet *m* (du pantalon).

crux, *pl.* **cruxes** [krʌks, 'krʌksiz] *n.* point capital, crucial (d'une discussion, etc.); **the c. of the matter,** le nœud de la question.

cry[1] [krai] *n.* **1.** cri *m* (d'une personne, d'un animal); **to give, utter, a c.,** pousser un cri; **it is a far c. from . . .,** il y a loin de . . .; **battle c.,** (i) cri de bataille; (ii) cri de ralliement; (*of hounds, etc.*) **to be in full c.,** être acharné à la poursuite (**after,** de). **2.** cri (de douleur); plainte *f*. **3.** action *f* de pleurer; pleurs *mpl*; **to have a good c.,** donner libre cours à ses larmes.

cry[2] *v.* (*p.t. & p.p.* **cried** [kraid]) **1.** *v.tr. & i.* (*a*) crier; pousser un cri, des cris; **to c. aloud,** pousser de grands cris; **to c. for help,** crier au secours; **to c. for mercy,** demander grâce; *F:* **for crying out loud!** nom de nom! (*b*) **to c. one's wares,** crier sa marchandise. **2.** *v.i.* s'écrier; **"that is untrue!" he cried,** "c'est faux!" s'écria-t-il. **3.** (*a*) *v.i.* pleurer; **to c. over sth.,** pleurer, verser des larmes, sur qch.; **to c. for joy,** pleurer de joie; (*b*) *v.tr.* **to c. one's eyes out,** pleurer à chaudes larmes; **she cried herself to sleep,** à force de pleurer elle s'est endormie. **cry down** *v.tr.* décrier, déprécier (qn, qch.). **crying 1.** *a.* (*a*) (*of injustice, etc.*) criant; (*of abuse, etc.*) scandaleux; **it's a c. shame that . . .,** il est scandaleux que + *sub.*; (*b*) (enfant) pleurant, qui pleure. **2.** *n.* (*a*) cri(s) *m(pl)*; clameur *f*; (*b*) pleurs *mpl*, larmes *fpl*. **cry off** *v.i.* se dédire, se faire excuser. **cry out** *v.i.* (*a*) pousser des cris; s'écrier; (*b*) **to c. out for sth.,** réclamer qch.

crybaby ['kraibeibi] *n. F:* pleurnicheur, -euse.

crypt [kript] *n. Ecc.Arch: Anat: etc:* crypte *f*.

cryptic ['kriptik] *a.* sibyllin; mystérieux; **a c. silence,** un silence énigmatique. **-ally** *adv.* énigmatiquement; (parler) à mots couverts.

cryptogram ['kriptougræm] *n.* cryptogramme *m*.

cryptographer [krip'tɔgrəfər] *n.* cryptographe *mf*.

crystal ['krist(ə)l] *n.* **1.** *Ch: Miner:* cristal *m*, -aux; **rock c.,** cristal de roche. **2.** (*a*) *a. & n.* **c. (glass),** cristal; **c. factory,** cristallerie *f*; (*b*) *a.* **c.(-clear),** clair, limpide, cristallin; *Fig:* **c.-clear,** clair comme le jour. **3.** *U.S:* verre *m* de montre. **4.** *Psychics:* **c. (ball),** boule *f* de cristal; **c. gazing,** divination *f* par la boule de cristal. **5.** *Elcs: etc:* quartz *m*, cristal; **c.-controlled,** piloté par quartz.

crystalline ['kristəlain] *a.* (*a*) cristallin; (*b*) *Anat:* (*of the eye*) **c. lens,** cristallin *m*.

crystallization [kristəlai'zeiʃ(ə)n] *n.* cristallisation *f*.

crystallize ['kristəlaiz] **1.** *v.tr.* (*a*) cristalliser; (*b*) faire candir (du sucre); **crystallized fruits,** fruits confits. **2.** *v.i.* (*a*) (se) cristalliser; *Fig:* (*of opinions, etc.*) se cristalliser; (*b*) (*of sugar*) se candir.

crystallography [kristə'lɔgrəfi] *n.* cristallographie *f*.

cub[1] [kʌb] *n.* **1.** petit *m* (d'un animal); (*of fox*) renardeau *m*; (*of bear*) ourson *m*; (*of lion*) lionceau *m*; (*of wolf*) louveteau *m*. **2.** *F:* (*a*) apprenti *m*; (*b*) jeune homme mal appris. **3.** *Scout:* louveteau.

cub[2] *v.i.* **(cubbed) 1.** (*of fox, bear, etc.*) mettre bas (des petits); (*of wolf*) louveter. **2.** *Ven:* faire la chasse au renardeau.

Cuba ['kju:bə] *Pr.n. Geog:* (l'île de) Cuba (*m*); **in C.,** à Cuba.

Cuban ['kju:bən] **1.** *a. Geog:* cubain. **2.** *n.* Cubain, -aine.

cubbyhole ['kʌbihoul] *n.* **1.** (*a*) cachette *f*, abri *m*; (*b*) (toute) petite pièce; **2.** (*a*) placard *m*; (*b*) *Aut:* vide-poche(s) *m inv*.

cube[1] [kju:b] *n.* **1.** *Mth:* cube *m*; **c. root,** racine *f* cubique. **2.** morceau *m* (de sucre); dé *m* (de pain, de viande, etc.); **stock c.,** bouillon-cube *m*.

cube[2] *v.tr.* **1.** *Mth:* cuber. **2.** (*measure*) cuber (du bois, etc.). **3.** *Cu:* couper (la viande, etc.) en dés.

cubic ['kju:bik] *a.* **1.** (*cube-shaped*) cubique. **2.** *Meas:* **c. metre,** mètre *m* cube; **c. measurement,** cubage *m*; **c. capacity,** volume *m*; *Mch:* cylindrée *f*; **c. measures,** mesures *fpl* de volume.

cubicle ['kju:bikl] *n.* (*a*) compartiment, alcôve *f* (d'un dortoir); (*b*) cabine *f* (d'une piscine); **trying-on c.,** cabine d'essayage.

cubism ['kju:bizm] *n. Art:* cubisme *m*.

cubist ['kju:bist] *a. & n. Art:* cubiste (*mf*).

cuckold ['kʌkəld] *n.* cocu *m*.

cuckoo[1] ['kuku:] *n.* **1.** (*a*) *Orn:* coucou *m*; **c. clock,** (pendule *f* à) coucou; (*b*) *int.* coucou! **2.** (*a*) *Ent:* **c.-spit,** crachat *m* de coucou; (*b*) *Bot:* **c.-pint,** pied-de-veau *m*. **3.** *F:* niais *m*; **to go c.,** devenir loufoque.

cuckoo[2] *v.i.* coucouer.

cucumber ['kju:kʌmbər] *n.* **1.** (*a*) *Hort:* concombre *m*. **2.** *Echin:* **sea c.,** concombre de mer.

cud [kʌd] *n.* bol *m* alimentaire (d'un ruminant); **to chew the c.,** (i) ruminer; (ii) *F:* (*of pers.*) ruminer une idée; méditer.

cuddle[1] ['kʌdl] *n.* étreinte *f*, embrassade *f*.

cuddle[2] **1.** *v.tr.* serrer (qn) dans ses bras. **2.** *v.i.* (*a*) se serrer (l'un l'autre); (*b*) **to c. up to s.o.,** se blottir, se pelotonner, contre qn; (*c*) (*to child*) **c. down and go to sleep,** enfonce-toi bien sous la couverture et fais dodo.

cuddly ['kʌdli] *a. F:* (enfant, etc.) qui invite aux caresses; (ours, etc.) en peluche.

cudgel[1] ['kʌdʒ(ə)l] *n.* gourdin *m*, trique *f*; **to take up the cudgels on s.o.'s behalf,** prendre fait et cause pour qn.

cudgel[2] *v.tr.* **(cudgelled,** *NAm:* **cudgeled)** donner des coups de bâton à (qn); *Fig:* **to c. one's brains,** se creuser le cerveau.

cue[1] [kju:] *n.* (*a*) *Th:* réplique *f*; **to take, miss, one's c.,** donner, manquer, la réplique; **to give s.o. his c.,** donner la réplique à qn; (*b*) *Cmptr:* caractère indicateur; (*c*) avis *m*, mot *m*; **to take one's c. from s.o.,**

prendre exemple sur qn; **(right) on c.,** au bon moment; (*d*) *Mus:* indication de rentrée (d'un instrument).

cue² *v.tr.* donner la réplique à (qn); **to c. s.o. in,** mettre qn à la page.

cue³ *n.* queue (de billard); **c. rack,** porte-queues *m inv.*

cuff¹ [kʌf] *n.* **1.** (*a*) poignet *m* (de chemise); (*starched*) manchette *f*; **double c.,** poignet mousquetaire; **c. links,** boutons (de manchette) jumelés; (*b*) (*of coat sleeve*) parement *m*; (*c*) *F:* **off the c.,** (discours, etc.) impromptu; **to do sth. off the c.,** faire qch. impromptu. **2.** *NAm:* **(trouser) cuffs,** revers *mpl* de pantalon.

cuff² *n.* taloche *f*, calotte *f*.

cuff³ *v.tr.* talocher, calotter (qn).

cuke [kju:k] *n. F:* concombre *m*.

cul-de-sac ['kʌldəsæk] *n.* (*pl.* **culs-de-sac, cul-de-sacs**) cul-de-sac *m*, *pl.* culs-de-sac; impasse *f*.

culinary ['kʌlinəri] *a.* de cuisine; culinaire.

cull¹ [kʌl] *n. Husb:* **1.** bête *f* à éliminer du troupeau. **2.** élimination *f* des sujets malsains d'un troupeau.

cull² *v.tr.* **1.** *Lit:* (*a*) cueillir (des fleurs); (*b*) choisir (**from,** dans). **2.** *Husb:* (*a*) débarrasser (un troupeau) des sujets malsains ou trop nombreux; (*b*) éliminer (les sujets malsains ou trop nombreux) d'un troupeau.

culminate ['kʌlmineit] *v.i.* **1.** *Astr:* (*of star*) culminer. **2.** atteindre son plus haut point; **to c. in sth.,** se terminer en qch.; aboutir à, dans, en, qch. **culminating** *a.* (point, moment) culminant.

culmination [kʌlmi'neiʃ(ə)n] *n.* **1.** *Astr:* culmination *f*. **2.** point culminant; apogée *m* (de la gloire, etc.).

culotte [kju(:)'lɔt] *n. Cost:* jupe-culotte *f*, *pl.* jupes-culottes.

culpability [kʌlpə'biliti] *n.* culpabilité *f*.

culpable ['kʌlpəbl] *a.* (négligence, etc.) coupable.

culprit ['kʌlprit] *n.* **1.** *Jur:* accusé, -ée; prévenu, -ue. **2.** coupable *mf*.

cult [kʌlt] *n.* (*a*) *Ecc:* culte *m* (**of,** de); (*b*) culte (de qn, qch.); **to make a c. of sth.,** avoir un culte pour qch.; **c. figure,** idole *f*.

cultivate ['kʌltiveit] *v.tr.* **1.** cultiver (la terre, un champ, des légumes, etc.). **2.** *Bac:* faire une culture (d'un bacille). **3.** (*a*) cultiver (ses amis, l'amitié de qn); (*b*) cultiver (un art); **to c. an easy manner,** arrondir ses manières. **cultivated** *a.* (*a*) (voix, etc.) qui accuse une bonne éducation; (esprit) cultivé; (*b*) **c. land,** terre cultivée.

cultivation [kʌlti'veiʃ(ə)n] *n.* culture *f*; **field under c.,** champ cultivé.

cultivator ['kʌltiveitər] *n. Agr:* **1.** (*pers.*) cultivateur, -trice. **2.** (*machine*) cultivateur *m*; motoculteur *m*.

cultural ['kʌltjər(ə)l] *a.* **1.** *Agr:* cultural, -aux. **2.** (institut, développement) culturel.

culture¹ ['kʌltjər] *n.* **1.** culture *f* (des champs, des abeilles, etc.). **2.** *Bac:* culture. **3. he lacks c.,** il n'a aucune culture.

culture² *v.tr. Bac:* faire une culture (d'un bacille). **cultured** *a.* (*a*) cultivé, lettré; **his c. mind,** son esprit cultivé; **highly c. man,** homme *m* de forte culture; (*b*) (perle) de culture.

culvert ['kʌlvət] *n.* **1.** *Civ.E:* canal *m*, -aux. **2.** *El:* conduit souterrain.

cum [kʌm] *Lt.prep.* avec; *St.Exch:* **c. dividend,** coupon attaché.

cumbersome ['kʌmbəsəm] *a.* encombrant, gênant.

cumin ['kʌmin, 'kju:-] *n. Bot:* cumin *m*.

cummerbund ['kʌməbʌnd] *n.* large ceinture *f*.

cumulative ['kju:mjulətiv] *a.* (*a*) cumulatif; *Jur:* **c. evidence,** accumulation *f* de témoignages; (*b*) *Com: etc:* (erreur) cumulée; **c. total,** cumul; *Fin:* **c. interest,** intérêts cumulatifs.

cumulonimbus ['kju:mjulou'nimbəs] *n. Meteor:* cumulo-nimbus *m inv.*

cumulus, *pl.* **-li** ['kju:mjuləs, -lai] *n. Meteor:* cumulus *m*.

cuneiform [kju'neiifɔ:m] *a. & n.* (écriture) cunéiforme (*m*).

cunning¹ ['kʌniŋ] *n.* (*a*) ruse *f*, finesse *f*; astuce *f*; (*b*) *Pej:* **(low) c.,** fourberie *f*, sournoiserie *f*.

cunning² *a.* **1.** rusé; fin; *F:* roublard; (*of look*) sournois. **2.** (dispositif) ingénieux. **-ly** *adv.* **1.** avec ruse; astucieusement. **2.** ingénieusement.

cunt (kʌnt] *n. V:* **1.** con *m*, chatte *f*. **2.** conard, -asse, salaud *m*, salope *f*.

cup¹ [kʌp] *n.* **1.** (*a*) tasse *f*; **coffee c.,** tasse à café; **c. of coffee, of tea,** tasse de café, de thé; *F:* **that's just my c. of tea,** c'est tout à fait dans mes cordes; **that's not everyone's c. of tea,** ce n'est pas au goût de tout le monde; (*b*) **(metal) c.,** gobelet *m*, timbale *f*. **2.** (*a*) *Lit:* coupe *f*; *Ecc:* calice *m* (du saint Sacrement); **c. bearer,** échanson *m*; **to drink a bitter c.,** vider un calice amer; *F:* **to be in one's cups,** être gris; (*b*) *Sp:* coupe; **to win a c.,** emporter une coupe; *Ten:* **the Davis C.,** la coupe Davis; *Fb:* **c. tie,** match *m* éliminatoire, de coupe; **c. final,** finale *f* du championnat, de coupe. **3. champagne c.,** marquise *f*; **cider c.,** boisson glacée au cidre (avec des fruits). **4.** (*a*) *Bot:* calice (d'une fleur); (*b*) *Anat:* emboîture *f* (d'un os); (*c*) *Mec.E:* **c.-and-ball joint,** joint *m* à rotule; (*d*) *Tchn:* godet *m*; **c. valve,** soupape *f* à cloche; (*e*) *Cost:* bonnet *m* (de soutien-gorge).

cup² *v.tr.* **(cupped) with one's chin cupped in one's hand,** le menton dans le creux de la main; **to c. one's hand behind one's ear,** mettre sa main en cornet; **to c. one's hands round one's mouth,** mettre les mains en porte-voix.

cupboard ['kʌbəd] *n.* armoire *f*; (*in wall*) placard *m*; **c. under the stairs,** soupente *f* d'escalier; **store c.,** armoire à provisions; **airing c.,** chauffe-linge *m inv*; *F:* **c. love,** amour intéressé.

cupful ['kʌpful] *n.* pleine tasse, pleine coupe (**of,** de); **add two cupfuls of milk,** ajouter deux tasses de lait.

Cupid ['kju:pid] **1.** *Pr.n.m.* Cupidon. **2.** *n. Art: etc:* Amour *m*.

cupidity [kju:'piditi] *n.* cupidité *f*; convoitise *f*.

cupola ['kju:pələ] *n. Arch:* coupole *f*, dôme *m*; *Navy:* coupole; *Metall:* **c. (furnace),** cubilot *m*.

cuppa ['kʌpə] *n. P:* tasse *f* de thé.

cupric ['kju:prik] *a. Ch:* (acide) cuprique.

cup-shaped ['kʌpʃeipt] *a. Bot:* cupulaire.

cur [kə:r] *n.* **1.** cabot *m*; chien *m* sans race. **2.** *F:* (*of pers.*) homme *m* méprisable, mufle *m*.

curable ['kjuərəbl] *a.* guérissable; (mal) curable.

curare [kjuə'rɑ:ri] *n.* curare *m*.

curate ['kjuərət] *n.* vicaire *m*; **c. in charge,** desservant *m*.

curative ['kjuərətiv] **1.** *a.* curatif. **2.** *n.* remède *m*.

curator [kjuə'reitər] *n.* **1.** conservateur *m* (de musée). **2.** *Jur: Scot:* tuteur, -trice; curateur (d'un dément).

curb¹ [kə:b] *n.* **1.** *Harn:* **c. (chain),** gourmette *f*; **c. bit,** mors *m* à gourmette; **c. reins,** rênes *fpl* de mors; **to put a c. on one's passions,** refréner, mettre un frein à, ses passions. **2.** *NAm:* bordure *f*, rebord *m* (de trottoir, etc.).

curb² *v.tr.* **1.** mettre la gourmette à (un cheval). **2.** réprimer, refréner (sa colère); maîtriser, brider (ses passions); modérer (son impatience); freiner (l'inflation, etc.).

curbstone ['kə:bstoun] *n. NAm:* pierre *f* de rebord (de trottoir).

curd [kə:d] *n.* (*a*) (lait) caillé (*m*); **curds and whey,** lait caillé sucré; (*b*) **lemon c.,** pâte composée d'œufs, de beurre et de jus de citron.

curdle ['kə:dl] **1.** *v.tr.* cailler (le lait); coaguler (un liquide); glacer, figer (le sang). **2.** *v.i.* (*of milk*) se cailler; (*of blood*) se figer; **my blood curdled,** mon sang s'est glacé.

cure¹ ['kjuər] *n.* **1.** guérison *f.* **2.** (*a*) cure *f*; **rest c.,** cure de repos; **to take a c.,** faire une cure; (*b*) remède *m*; **past c.,** (*of pers.*) incurable; (*of thg*) irrémédiable, irréparable; **the c. is worse than the disease,** le remède est pire que le mal. **3.** *Ecc:* **c. of souls,** cure, charge *f*, d'âmes.

cure² *v.tr.* **1.** guérir (qn) (**of an illness,** d'une maladie); corriger (qn) (d'une mauvaise habitude); remédier à (un mal); *Prov:* **what can't be cured must be endured,** où il n'y a pas de remède il faut se résigner. **2.** (*a*) saler, fumer (la viande, etc.); confire (des sardines); saurer (des harengs); (*b*) *Leath:* saler (les peaux). **curing** *n.* **1.** guérison *f.* **2.** salaison *f*; confiserie *f* (à l'huile).

cure-all ['kjuərɔ:l] *n.* panacée *f.*

curettage [kjuə'retidʒ] *n. Med:* curettage *m.*

curfew ['kə:fju:] *n.* couvre-feu *m*; **to ring the c. (bell),** sonner le couvre-feu.

curio ['kjuəriou] *n.* bibelot *m*; petit objet d'art.

curiosity [kjuəri'ɔsiti] *n.* **1.** curiosité *f*; **out of c., from c.,** par curiosité; **I was dying of c.,** je mourais de curiosité. **2.** (*a*) (*object*) curiosité, rareté *f.*

curious ['kjuəriəs] *a.* **1.** (*a*) curieux; **to be c. to see sth.,** être curieux de voir qch.; (*b*) *Pej:* indiscret, -ète. **2.** (*strange*) curieux, singulier; **c. sight,** chose curieuse à voir; **a c.-looking object,** un objet d'un aspect bizarre. **-ly** *adv.* **1.** curieusement, singulièrement; **c. enough . . .,** chose curieuse, singulière . . .. **2.** avec curiosité; indiscrètement.

curl¹ [kə:l] *n.* **1.** (*a*) boucle *f* (de cheveux); (*of hair*) **to fall in curls,** tomber en boucles; (*b*) spirale *f* (de fumée); crête recourbée (d'une vague); ronce *f* (dans le grain du bois); (*c*) *Metalw:* bordure *f* (d'une tôle, etc.). **2.** (*a*) action *f* de se recourber; **with a c. of the lips,** avec une moue dédaigneuse; (*b*) (*of hair*) **in curls,** bouclé, frisé. **3.** *Agr: etc:* **leaf c.,** enroulement *m* des feuilles.

curl² **1.** *v.tr.* (*a*) boucler, friser (les cheveux); (*b*) faire onduler (les vagues); **to c. one's lip,** faire une moue dédaigneuse; (*c*) *Metalw:* border (une tôle, etc.); (*d*) **to c. sth. round sth.,** enrouler qch. autour de qch. **2.** *v.i.* (*a*) (*of hair*) boucler, friser; (*of paper*) se recroqueviller; *F:* **stories that make your hair c.,** histoires *fpl* qui font dresser les cheveux; (*b*) (*of smoke*) s'élever en spirales; tourbillonner; (*of waves*) onduler ou déferler; (*of lip*) (i) se relever, (ii) s'abaisser, avec dédain; (*c*) (*of plant, etc.*) **to c. round sth.,** s'enrouler autour de qch. **3.** *v.i. Games:* jouer au *curling.* **curled** *a.* (*a*) (*of hair*) frisé; (*of leaf*) crépu; (moustache) en croc; (*b*) (tôle) bordée. **curling** *n.* **1.** (*a*) frisure *f* (des cheveux); ondulation *f* (des cheveux, des vagues); **c. irons, tongs,** fer *m* à friser; (*b*) *Metalw:* bordage *m* (des tôles, etc.); **2.** *Games:* curling *m.* **curl up** **1.** *v.tr.* (*a*) **c. up one's moustache,** porter la moustache en croc; (*b*) *v.pr. & i.* **to c. (oneself) up,** se rouler en boule; se pelotonner (**in an armchair,** dans un fauteuil); **curled up in bed,** couché en chien de fusil; **to c. (itself) up,** (*of cat, etc.*) se mettre en rond; se mettre en boule. **2.** *v.i.* (*a*) (*of leaves, paper, etc.*) s'enrouler; (*of thread, rope*) vriller; (*b*) *F:* (*of pers.*) se tortiller, se crisper (sous un sarcasme, etc.).

curler ['kə:lər] *n.* **1. (hair) c.,** bigoudi *m.* **2.** *Games:* joueur *m* de *curling.*

curlew ['kə:lju:] *n. Orn:* courlis *m.*

curlicue ['kə:likju:] *n.* trait *m* de plume en parafe.

curliness ['kə:linis] *n.* **1.** frisure *f.* **2.** sinuosité *f.*

curly ['kə:li] *a.* **1.** bouclé, frisé; en spirale; (laitue) frisée; **she had short c. hair,** elle était court bouclée. **2.** (bois) à grain ondulé.

curly-headed, -haired ['kə:lihedid, -hɛəd] *a.* à la tête bouclée, aux cheveux frisés; (*of negro*) crépu.

currant ['kʌrənt] *n.* **1.** *Hort:* groseille *f*; **c. bush,** groseiller *m.* **2.** raisin *m* de Corinthe, raisin sec; **c. bun,** petit pain aux raisins.

currency ['kʌrənsi] *n.* **1.** circulation *f*, cours *m* (de l'argent, des idées); **to give c. to a rumour,** mettre un bruit en circulation; répandre un bruit; (*of news, etc.*) **to gain c.,** s'accréditer. **2.** (terme *m* d') échéance (*f*) (d'une lettre de change). **3.** unité *f* monétaire (d'un pays); numéraire *m*; monnaie *f*; **foreign c.,** (i) monnaie étrangère; (ii) devise étrangère; **hard, soft, c.,** devise forte, faible.

current¹ ['kʌrənt] *a.* (*a*) courant, en cours; **c. month,** mois *m* en cours; **c. events,** actualités *fpl*; **c. number,** dernier numéro (d'une revue); **the c. treasurer,** l'actuel trésorier (de l'association); *Fin: etc:* **c. account,** compte courant; **c. assets,** actif *m* réalisable et disponible; **c. price,** prix courant; prix de marché; (*b*) courant, admis, reçu; **to be c.,** être accepté; avoir cours; **in c. use,** d'usage courant; **the word is in c. use,** le mot s'emploie couramment. **-ly** *adv.* (*a*) actuellement; (*b*) couramment, généralement.

current² *n.* **1.** courant *m* (d'un cours d'eau, de la marée, etc.); fil *m* de l'eau; *Meteor:* **air c.,** courant d'air; **to drift with the c.,** se laisser aller au fil de l'eau; *Fig:* suivre le courant. **2.** *El: etc:* **electric c.,** courant électrique; **direct, alternating, c.,** courant continu, alternatif.

curriculum, *pl.* **-a** [kə'rikjuləm, -ə] *n.* (*a*) *Sch:* programme *m* d'études; (*b*) **c. vitae** ['vi:tai], curriculum vitae *m.*

curry¹ ['kʌri] *n. Cu:* (*powder, dish*) cari *m*, curry *m.*

curry² *v.tr. Cu:* apprêter (des œufs, etc.) au cari, au curry; **curried eggs,** œufs *mpl* à l'indienne.

curry³ *v.tr.* **1.** étriller (un cheval). **2. to c. favour with s.o.,** s'insinuer dans les bonnes grâces de qn.

currycomb ['kʌrikoum] *n.* étrille *f.*

curse¹ [kə:s] *n.* **1.** malédiction *f*; **a c. on . . .!** maudit soit . . .! (*b*) chose maudite, abomination *f*; (*c*) imprécation *f*; juron *m*; **to let out a c.,** lâcher un juron. **2.** (*a*) fléau *m*; **here the rabbits are a c.,** ici les lapins sont un fléau; (*b*) *F:* (*of woman*) **to have the c.,** avoir ses règles.

curse² **1.** *v.tr.* maudire (qn, qch.); **he is cursed with a violent temper,** il est affligé d'un mauvais caractère; **c. (it)!** le diable l'emporte! **2.** *v.i.* blasphémer; sacrer, jurer; **to c. and swear,** jurer et sacrer. **cursed** ['kə:sid, kə:st] *a.* **1.** maudit; **the place is c.,** ce lieu est maudit. **2.** *F:* sacré, satané; **it's a c. nuisance,** c'est bigrement embêtant. **cursing** *n.* jurons *mpl*; gros mots *pl.*

cursive ['kə:siv] *a.* cursif; **c. handwriting,** *n.* **c.,** écriture courante, cursive.

cursory ['kə:səri] *a.* (coup d'œil) rapide, superficiel; (examen) fait à la hâte. **-ily** *adv.* à la hâte; superficiellement.

curt [kə:t] *a.* (*of manner*) brusque; (ton) cassant; (réponse) sèche. **-ly** *adv.* brusquement; d'un ton cassant.

curtail [kə:'teil] *v.tr.* **1.** raccourcir, abréger, écourter (une visite). **2.** diminuer, restreindre (la liberté de qn); amoindrir (l'autorité de qn); réduire (ses dépenses).

curtailment [kə:'teilmənt] *n.* restriction *f*, diminution *f* (d'autorité, etc.); réduction *f* (de dépenses).

curtain¹ ['kə:t(ə)n] *n.* **1.** rideau *m*; **to draw the c.,** tirer, (i) ouvrir, (ii) fermer, le rideau; *Pol:* **the Iron C.,** le rideau de fer; **c. ring, rod,** anneau *m*, tringle *f*, de rideau; **c. hook,** crochet *m* de rideau. **2.** *Th:* rideau; **safety c.,** rideau de fer; *P:* **it'll be curtains for you if . . .,** vous y laisserez votre peau si . . .; **c. call,**

rappel *m*; **to take three c. calls,** être rappelé trois fois; (*short play*) **c. raiser,** lever *m* de rideau. **3.** *Fort:* courtine *f*.

curtain² *v.tr.* **1.** garnir (une alcôve, etc.) de rideaux. **2. to c. off,** masquer (une partie d'une pièce) par un rideau.

curtness ['kəːtnis] *n.* brusquerie *f* (de paroles); ton cassant.

curts(e)y¹ ['kəːtsi] *n.* révérence *f* (que fait une femme en pliant le genou); **to make a c. to s.o.,** faire une révérence à qn.

curts(e)y² *v.i.* (*of woman, girl*) faire une révérence (**to s.o.,** à qn).

curvaceous [kəː'veiʃəs] *a.* *F:* (*of woman*) bien roulée, bien carrossée.

curvature ['kəːvətjər] *n.* courbure *f*; sphéricité *f* (de la terre, etc.); *Ph: Opt:* courbure (de l'espace); *Med:* **c. of the spine,** déviation *f* de la colonne vertébrale.

curve¹ [kəːv] *n.* (*a*) courbe *f*; (*in road*) tournant *m*, virage *m*; (*b*) (*of pers.*) **curves,** rondeurs *fpl*, formes *fpl*; (*c*) *Mth: etc:* **to plot a c.,** tracer une courbe.

curve² **1.** *v.tr.* courber, recourber; cintrer. **2.** *v.i.* se courber; décrire une courbe; **the road curves round the castle,** la route décrit une (ligne) courbe autour du château; **to c. down, up(wards),** monter, descendre, en courbe. **'curved** *a.* courbé; cintré; (nez) busqué.

curvilinear ['kəːvi'liniər] *a.* curviligne.

cushion¹ ['kuʃ(ə)n] *n.* **1.** coussin *m*; **scatter c.,** petit coussin décoratif. **2.** *Bill:* bande *f*; **off the c.,** par la bande; **stroke off the c.,** doublé *m*. **3.** (*a*) *Mch:* **steam c.,** matelas *m* de vapeur (dans le cylindre); vapeur *f*; (*b*) *Tchn:* coussin (d'air, etc.).

cushion² *v.tr.* **1.** (*a*) garnir (un siège, etc.) de coussins. **2.** amortir (un coup, un choc, une chute etc.); *Mch:* matelasser (le piston). **3.** *Bill:* acculer (une bille) à la bande. **cushioned** *a.* **1.** garni de coussins. **2.** (coup, choc) amorti.

cushy ['kuʃi] *a.* *F:* (vie, etc.) facile, pépère; **c. job,** fromage *m*, filon *m*.

cusp [kʌsp] *n.* **1.** *Astr:* corne *f* (de la lune). **2.** *Mth:* sommet *m* (d'une courbe). **3.** *Anat:* cuspide *f*.

cuspidor ['kʌspidɔːr] *n.* *esp. NAm:* crachoir *m*.

cuss [kʌs] *n.* *F:* **1.** juron *m*; **it isn't worth a (tinker's) c.,** ça ne vaut pas un clou. **2.** (*of pers.*) individu *m*, type *m*; **an awkward c.,** un mauvais coucheur.

cussed ['kʌsid] *a.* *F:* (*a*) sacré; **it's a c. nuisance,** c'est bigrement embêtant; (*b*) (*of pers.*) entêté.

cussedness ['kʌsidnis] *n.* *F:* perversité *f*, entêtement *m*; **out of sheer c.,** par esprit de contradiction.

custard ['kʌstəd] *n.* **1. (egg) c.** = crème anglaise; **baked c.,** crème cuite au four; flan *m*; **c. powder,** poudre *f* pour faire la crème anglaise; **c. tart,** flan. **2.** *Cin: etc:* **c. pie,** tarte à la crème (utilisée comme projectile). **3.** *Bot:* **c. apple,** anone réticulée.

custodian [kʌs'toudiən] *n.* gardien, -ienne; (*of museum, etc.*) conservateur *m*.

custody ['kʌstədi] *n.* **1.** garde *f* (d'enfants, etc.); **to have c. of s.o., of sth.,** avoir la garde de qn, de qch.; **in safe c.,** sous bonne garde. **2.** détention *f*; **to take s.o. into c.,** arrêter qn; mettre qn en état d'arrestation; **to be in c.,** être en détention préventive.

custom ['kʌstəm] *n.* **1.** coutume *f*, usage *m*; habitude *f*; **according to c.,** selon l'usage; **it is the c. of the country,** c'est la pratique du pays; **it was a c. with him to . . .,** il avait l'habitude de . . .; **the manners and customs,** les us *mpl* et coutumes (d'un pays). **2.** *Jur:* droit coutumier, coutume (d'un pays). **3.** *Adm:* **customs,** douane *f*; **custom(s) officer,** douanier *m*; **custom(s) duties,** droits *mpl* de douane; **customs declaration,** déclaration *f* de, en, douane; **customs union,** union douanière; **to go through the customs,** passer la douane, par la douane; **customs examination, formalities,** visite douanière; **customs clearance,** expédition en douane. **4.** *Com:* (*a*) (*of business*) clientèle *f*; (*b*) patronage *m* (du client); **to lose s.o.'s c.,** perdre un client; (*c*) *attrib.* **c. built, designed, made,** fait, fabriqué, sur commande; personnalisé; *Aut:* **c.-built body,** carrosserie spéciale; **c. car,** voiture *f* à carrosserie spéciale.

customary ['kʌstəm(ə)ri] *a.* (*a*) accoutumé, habituel, d'usage; **at the c. hour,** à l'heure accoutumée; **it is c. to . . .,** il est de coutume, d'usage de . . .; **as is c.,** comme il est d'usage; (*b*) *Jur:* **c. law,** droit coutumier; **c. right,** droit *m* d'usage. **-ily** *adv.* habituellement, d'habitude; ordinairement.

customer ['kʌstəmər] *n.* **1.** (*of shop, etc.*) client, -ente; (*of public house, etc.*) consommateur *m*; (*of restaurant, etc.*) **regular c.,** habitué, -ée. **2.** *F:* individu *m*, type *m*; **a queer c.,** un drôle de type; **an ugly c.,** un sale type; **an awkward c.,** un type pas commode.

customization [kʌstəmai'zeiʃ(ə)n] *n.* adaptation *f* aux besoins du client; personnalisation *f*.

customize ['kʌstəmaiz] *v.tr.* faire sur commande; personnaliser.

cut¹ [kʌt] *n.* **1.** (*a*) coupe *f*; **to make a clean c.,** trancher net; **the first c.,** l'entame *f*; (*b*) **power, electricity c.,** coupure *f* de courant; (*c*) coupure (dans un film, etc.); *Journ: etc:* coupe (dans un article); (*d*) *Cin:* **c. from one shot to another,** raccord *m* de deux plans; (*e*) *Com: etc:* réduction *f* (de prix, de dépenses); **wage cuts,** réductions de salaires; (*f*) *Cards:* coupe; **c. for partners,** tirage *m* pour les places; (*g*) *Cr: Ten:* coup tranchant. **2.** (*a*) coup *m* (de couteau, d'épée); (*b*) **c. with a whip,** coup de fouet; (*c*) coup, revers *m* (de fortune); sarcasme blessant; **the unkindest c. of all,** le coup de pied de l'âne. **3.** *Metalw: etc:* (*a*) taille *f*, entaille *f* (d'une lime); (*b*) passe *f* (de machine-outil); (*c*) **saw c.,** trait *m* de scie. **4.** (*wound*) coupure, estafilade *f*; balafre *f*; *Surg:* incision *f*; **c. across the cheek,** balafre à la joue. **5.** (*a*) gravure *f*, vignette *f*; (*b*) diagramme *m*, schéma *m*. **6.** *Th:* trappillon *m* (pour les fermes). **7.** coupe (d'un vêtement, des cheveux); taille (d'une pierre précieuse); *Hairdr:* **crew c.,** cheveux (coupés) en brosse. **8.** *F:* **to be a c. above s.o., sth.,** être supérieur à qn. **9.** (*a*) *Cu:* **c. off the joint,** tranche *f* de rôti; **prime c.,** morceau de (premier) choix; **cheap cuts,** bas morceaux; *NAm:* **cold cuts,** assiette anglaise; (*b*) *F:* commission *f*; gratte *f*; **he gets his c.,** il a part au gâteau. **10. short c.,** raccourci *m*; **to take a short c.,** couper au plus court; prendre (par) un raccourci.

cut² **I.** *v.tr. & i.* (*p.t. & p.p.* **cut;** *pr.p.* **cutting**) **1.** couper, tailler; (*in slices*) trancher; hacher (le tabac, etc.); faucher (les foins); tondre (le gazon); *Bookb:* rogner (les bords); (*of wind*) couper, cingler (le visage); **to c. one's finger,** se couper le, au, doigt; **to c. one's nails,** se couper les ongles; **to have one's hair c.,** se faire couper les cheveux; **this remark c. him to the quick,** cette parole l'a piqué au vif; (*with passive force*) **cloth that cuts easily,** tissu *m* qui se coupe facilement; **fog you could c. with a knife,** brouillard à couper au couteau; **atmosphere you could c. with a knife,** atmosphère très tendue; **that cuts both ways,** c'est un argument à deux tranchants; **to c. into a cake,** entamer un gâteau; **to c. into the bark,** inciser l'écorce; **this work cuts into my free time,** ce travail empiète sur mes heures de loisir; **the string is cutting (into) me,** le cordon me coupe la chair; *Com:* **to c. prices,** baisser les prix; *Aut: etc:* **to c. a corner,** prendre un virage à la corde; **to c. corners,** (i) faire des économies (de temps, etc.); (ii) contourner les règlements; *F:* **to c. and run,** filer (en vitesse); décamper, se sauver; *F:* **c. along (now)!** sauve-toi! file! *U.S:* **to c. loose,** (i) s'émanciper; (ii) s'évader. **2.** (*a*) **to c. sth.**

in two, couper qch. en deux; **to cut sth. to pieces,** couper qch. en morceaux; dépecer (un poulet, etc.); tailler en pièces (une armée); *F:* critiquer sévèrement (un livre, une pièce); **to c. an animal loose,** délier une bête; **to c. oneself loose from sth.,** se libérer de qch.; (*b*) faire des coupures dans (un film, etc.); abréger, raccourcir (un discours); couper, réduire (les nombres, ses dépenses); diminuer (la production); **to c. a speech, a visit, short,** écourter un discours, une visite; **to c. s.o. short,** couper la parole à qn; **to c. a long story short, bref;** pour dire la chose en deux mots; *F:* **c. it short!** soyez bref! *Cin: Rec: etc:* **c.!** coupez! (*c*) *Cin:* (*edit*) procéder au montage (d'un film). **3.** (*a*) couper, tailler (une pierre, du verre, etc.); percer, creuser (un canal); graver, ciseler (des caractères sur le métal ou la pierre); tailler (un habit); *Rec:* faire (un disque); (*b*) fileter (une vis). **4.** (*a*) **to c. one's way through the wood,** se frayer un chemin à travers le bois; **to c. across the fields,** couper à travers champs; **to c. through the waves,** fendre les eaux; (*b*) **to c. into the conversation,** intervenir dans, interrompre brusquement, la conversation. **5. to c. a tooth,** faire une dent. **6.** *Cards:* (*for deal*) tirer pour les places, pour la donne. **7.** *Cr: Ten:* trancher, couper (la balle). **8. to c. s.o. (dead),** faire semblant de ne pas voir qn; **he c. me dead,** il m'a passé raide (sans me saluer). **9.** *F:* manquer exprès à (un rendezvous); *Sch:* sécher (un cours, une classe). **II.** *a.* **1. c. glass,** cristal taillé; **c. diamond,** diamant taillé; **well-c. suit,** complet *m* de bonne coupe; **low-c. dress,** robe décolletée; **c. and dried,** (opinions) toutes faites. **2.** (prix) réduit; **c.-price goods,** marchandises vendues au rabais. **3. cut away** *v.tr.* (*a*) couper, ôter, retrancher; (*b*) évider, entailler. **cut back 1.** *v.tr.* (*a*) élaguer (un arbre, etc.); (*b*) baisser (les prix); diminuer (la production, etc.). **2.** *v.i.* (*a*) s'en retourner; rebrousser chemin; (*b*) *Cin:* (*of action*) revenir en arrière. **cut down 1.** *v.tr.* (*a*) (i) couper, abattre (un arbre); couper (le blé); (ii) abattre (un adversaire); faucher (les troupes ennemies); (*b*) abréger (un discours, etc.); tronquer (un ouvrage); couper, réduire (des dépenses); (*c*) **to c. down a man who is hanging,** couper la corde d'un pendu; (*d*) **to c. down trousers (to make shorts),** raccourcir un pantalon. **2.** *v.i.* **to c. down on sth.,** réduire (la consommation de) qch.; **to c. down on cigarettes,** fumer moins. **cut in 1.** *v.i.* (*a*) *Cards:* (r)entrer dans le jeu (à la place du joueur écarté au sort); (*b*) (i) intervenir dans la conversation; (ii) *Tp:* faire intrusion (dans une conversation); (*c*) *Danc:* enlever la danseuse de qn; (*d*) *Aut:* couper la route à qn (après avoir doublé). **2.** *v.tr.* (*a*) *El:* intercaler (une résistance); (*b*) *F:* **to c. s.o. in,** donner à qn sa part du gâteau. **cut off** *v.tr.* (*a*) couper, découper (un morceau); **to c. off s.o.'s head,** couper, trancher, la tête à qn; *Lit:* **to be c. off in one's prime,** être emporté, fauché, à la fleur de l'âge; (*b*) **to c. off s.o.'s retreat,** couper la retraite à qn; **to c. off the enemy,** couper la ligne de retraite de l'ennemi; **to be c. off,** se trouver isolé; **to c. oneself off from the world,** se retirer du monde; (*c*) *Tp:* couper (qn); **I've been c. off,** on m'a coupé; (*d*) couper, supprimer, (la vapeur, etc.); *El:* couper, interrompre, (le courant); *I.C.E:* couper (l'allumage); **to c. off s.o.'s water, supplies,** couper, supprimer, l'eau, les vivres à qn; **to c. s.o. off with a shilling,** déshériter qn. **cut out 1.** *v.tr.* (*a*) (i) couper, enlever (qch.); retrancher (un passage d'un livre); *Surg:* exciser (une tumeur, etc.); (ii) *F:* **he's trying to c. me out with my girlfriend,** il voudrait m'évincer auprès de mon amie; (*b*) (i) découper (des images); couper, tailler, découper (un vêtement); **to be c. out for sth.,** être fait, taillé, pour qch.; avoir des dispositions pour qch.; **he's not c. out to be a leader,** il n'est pas de taille à être chef; (ii) échancrer (une robe, etc.); (iii) **to c. a statue out of wood,** tailler une statue dans le bois; (*c*) supprimer (qch.); **to c. out luxuries,** se retrancher tout luxe; **to c. out smoking,** renoncer à fumer; *F:* **c. it out!** ça suffit maintenant! ça va comme ça! **2.** *v.i.* (*a*) *El:* (*of cutout*) s'ouvrir; (*b*) (*of engine*) caler; (*of sound, etc.*) s'arrêter. **cutting 1.** *a.* (*a*) **c. edge,** arête tranchante; coupant *m*, tranchant *m*; (*b*) (*of wind, rain*) cinglant, glacial; (*c*) (*of remark, etc.*) mordant, blessant; (*of criticism*) incisif. **2.** *n.* (*a*) (i) coupe *f*, coupage *m* (d'une branche, des foins, etc.); *Metalw:* cisaillage *m* (d'une barre de fer, etc.); *Bookb:* rognage *m* (des bords); *Surg:* **c. out,** excision *f*; **c. off, suppression** *f* (des vivres, etc.); *Mec.E:* **c. action,** cisaillement; **c. angle,** angle *m* de coupe; **c. back,** ravalement *m* (d'un arbre); réduction *f* (de la production, d'un budget); **c. away,** enlèvement *m*, retranchement *m*; (ii) **c. (down),** abattage *m* (des arbres); (iii) taille *f* (d'un diamant, d'une haie, etc.); (iv) découpage *m* (de la viande, etc.); *Cin:* montage *m*; *Tail:* **c. out,** découpage *m*; **c. up,** découpage *m*, dépècement *m*; **c. (up) of timber,** débit *m* du bois; (v) réduction *f* (des salaires, des prix); rabais *m* (des prix); (*b*) (*piece cut off*) (i) coupon *m*, bout *m* (d'étoffe, etc.); **c. from a newspaper,** coupure prise dans un journal; (ii) **cuttings,** copeaux *mpl*, rognures *fpl*, recoupe *f* (de bois, de métal, etc.); (iii) *Hort:* bouture *f*; (*of vine*) sarment *m*; (*c*) (*i*) *Civ.E: etc:* tranchée *f*, déblai *m*; **railway c.,** (voie *f* en) déblai; (ii) (*in forest*) percée *f*, tranchée. **cuttingly** *adv.* caustiquement, d'un ton piquant. **cut up 1.** *v.tr.* couper, débiter (le bois, la viande); détailler (une pièce, etc.); découper, dépecer (une volaille, etc.); hacher (des légumes, etc.); *F:* **to be very c. up (about sth.),** être profondément affecté, affligé (pas qch.). **2.** *v.i.* *F:* **to c. up rough,** se fâcher; se mettre en colère.

cutaneous [kju'teiniəs] *a.* cutané.

cutaway ['kʌtəwei] **1.** *a.* entaillé; évidé. **2.** *a. & n.* **c. (coat),** jaquette *f*.

cutback ['kʌtbæk] *n.* réduction *f* (de la production, d'un budget).

cute [kjuːt] *a.* *F:* **1.** (*a*) (*of pers.*) malin, -igne; (*b*) (idée) originale. **2.** *esp. U.S:* (*of pers.*) gentil, mignon; coquet.

cuteness ['kjuːtnis] *n.* *F:* **1.** finesse *f*. **2.** charme *m*.

cuticle ['kjuːtikl] *n.* *Anat:* peau *f* (à la base d'un ongle); cuticule *f*; *Toil:* **c. pen,** repousse-peaux *m inv*, repoussoir *m*.

cutlass ['kʌtləs] *n.* *Nau:* sabre *m* d'abordage.

cutler ['kʌtlər] *n.* coutelier *m*.

cutlery ['kʌtləri] *n.* coutellerie *f* (et argenterie *f* de table); **canteen of c.,** ménagère *f*.

cutlet ['kʌtlit] *n.* *Cu:* **1.** côtelette *f* (d'agneau, de veau). **2.** croquette *f* (de volaille, etc.).

cutoff ['kʌtɔf] *n.* **1.** *esp. U.S:* chemin *m* de traverse; raccourci *m*. **2.** *Mch:* (*a*) obturateur *m* (du cylindre); (*b*) fermeture *f* de l'admission.

cutout ['kʌtaut] *n.* **1.** *Bookb:* carton (détaché d'une feuille entière). **2.** *El:* (*a*) coupe-circuit *m inv*; disjoncteur *m*; (*b*) fusible *m* (de sûreté). **3.** *I.C.E: Aut:* (soupape *f* d')échappement *m* libre (du silencieux). **5.** (*a*) *Th: Cin:* décor découpé; (*b*) (*child's game*) **to make cutouts,** faire des découpages *mpl*.

cutter ['kʌtər] *n.* **1.** (*pers.*) (*a*) coupeur *m*; tailleur *m* (de pierre, de diamants); **coal c.,** haveur *m*; (*b*) *Tail:* coupeur; (*c*) *Cin:* monteur, -euse. **2.** *Tls:* coupoir *m*, lame *f*, couteau *m*; **rotary c.,** roue *f* à couteaux; **coal c.,** haveuse *f*; **milling c.,** fraise *f*; *Cu:* **pastry c.,** emporte-pièce *m inv*. **3.** *Nau:* (*a*) canot *m* (d'un bâtiment de guerre); (*b*) **revenue c.,** vedette *f* de la douane.

cutthroat ['kʌtθrout] *n.* **1.** (*a*) (*pers.*) assassin *m*;

(*b*) **c. (razor),** rasoir *m* à manche. **2.** *attrib.* (*a*) **c. competition,** concurrence acharnée; (*b*) *Cards:* **c. (bridge),** bridge *m* à trois.

cuttlebone ['kʌtlboun] *n.* os *m* de seiche.

cuttlefish ['kʌtlfiʃ] *n.* seiche *f.*

cutwork ['kʌtwəːk] *n. Needlew:* broderie ajourée.

cyanide ['saiənaid] *n. Ch:* cyanure *m*; **potassium c.,** cyanure de potassium.

cyanosis [saiə'nousis] *n. Med:* cyanose *f.*

cybernetics [saibə'netiks] *n.* (*with sg. const.*) cybernétique *f.*

cyclamen ['sikləmən] *n. Bot:* cyclamen *m.*

cycle¹ ['saikl] *n.* **1.** cycle *m* (de mouvements, etc.); **trade c.,** cycle économique; *Astr:* **lunar c.,** cycle lunaire; *I.C.E:* **four-stroke c.,** cycle à quatre temps; *Physiol:* **menstrual c.,** cycle menstruel. **2. (pedal) c.,** bicyclette *f*, vélo *m*; **c. track,** piste *f* cyclable; **c. racing,** courses *fpl* cyclistes; **c.-racing track,** vélodrome *m.*

cycle² *v.i.* faire de la bicyclette, du vélo; aller à bicyclette. **cycling** *n.* cyclisme *m.*

cyclic(al) ['s(a)iklik(l)] *a.* (*of movement etc.*) cyclique.

cyclist ['saiklist] *n.* cycliste *mf.*

cyclone ['saikloun] *n. Meteor:* cyclone *m*; **eye of a c.,** œil *m* de cyclone.

cyclonic [sai'klɔnik]. *a* cyclonique; cyclonal, -aux.

cyclostyle ['saikloustail] *v.tr. O:* polycopier (au moyen d'un stencil).

cyclotron ['saikloutrɔn] *a. Atom.Ph:* cyclotron *m.*

cygnet ['signit] *n. Orn:* jeune cygne *m.*

cylinder ['silindər] *n.* **1.** *Mth:* cylindre *m.* **2.** *Tchn:* cylindre; barillet *m* (de pompe, etc.); *El:* tambour *m* (de bobine électrique); *Typew:* rouleau *m* porte-papier; *Mch: I.C.E:* **piston c.,** cylindre de piston; **c. head,** culasse *f*, calotte *f*; **four-c. engine,** moteur *m* à quatre cylindres; *Typ:* **c. press,** presse *f* à cylindre(s).

cylindrical [si'lindrikl] *a.* cylindrique.

cymbal ['simb(ə)l] *n.* cymbale *f.*

cynic ['sinik] *a.* & *n. n.* cynique *m.*

cynical ['sinikl] *a.* cynique. **-ally** *adv.* cyniquement.

cynicism ['sinisizm] *n.* **1.** cynisme; *m.* **2.** (*a*) mot *m* caustique; (*b*) **cynicisms,** sarcasmes *mpl.*

cypher ['saifər] *n.* & *v.* = CIPHER¹,².

cypress ['saiprəs] *n. Bot:* cyprès *m.*

Cypriot(e) ['sipriət] **1.** *a. Geog:* chypriote, cypriote. **2.** *n.* Chypriote *mf*, Cypriote *mf.*

Cyprus ['saiprəs] *Pr.n. Geog:* Chypre *f.*

cyst [sist] *n.* **1.** *Biol: Anat:* sac *m.* **2.** *Med:* kyste *m.*

cystitis [sis'taitis] *n. Med:* cystite *f.*

cytology [sai'tɔlədʒi] *n. Biol:* cytologie *f.*

Czech [tʃek] **1.** *a. Geog:* tchèque. **2.** *n.* (*a*) Tchèque *mf*; (*b*) *Ling:* tchèque *m.*

Czechoslovak [tʃekou'slouvæk], **Czechoslovakian** [tʃekouslou'vækiən] **1.** *a. Geog:* tchécoslovaque. **2.** *n.* Tchécoslovaque *mf.*

Czechoslovakia [tʃekouslə'vækiə] *Pr.n. Geog:* Tchécoslovaquie *f.*

D

D, d [diː] *n.* **1.** (la lettre) D, d *m*;. *Mil: etc:* **D day,** le jour. **2.** *Mus:* ré *m.* **3.** *A. Num:* **d.,** (*abbr. for Lt.* **denarius**) penny *m*; pence *mpl*; **6d.,** six pence.
dab¹ [dæb] *n.* **1.** coup léger, tape *f.* **2.** (*a*) tache *f* (d'encre, de peinture); petit morceau (de beurre); touche *f* (de couleur); (*b*) *F:* **dabs,** empreintes digitales.
dab² *v.tr.* **(dabbed) 1.** donner un petit coup, une tape, à (qn). **2.** tapoter; (*with pad*) tamponner; **to d. one's eyes (with a handkerchief),** se tamponner les yeux; **to d. paint on sth.,** donner un coup de peinture à qch.
dab³ *n. Ich:* limande *f.*
dab⁴ *a. & n. F:* **to be a d. (hand) at sth., at doing sth.,** être passé maître en (l'art de faire) qch.; être calé en qch.
dabble ['dæbl] **1.** *v.tr.* (*a*) humecter, mouiller; (*b*) tremper (ses mains dans l'eau). **2.** *v.i.* (*a*) barboter, tripoter (dans l'eau); (*b*) *F:* **to d. on the Stock Exchange,** boursicoter; **to d. in politics,** se mêler de politique.
dabbler ['dæblər] *n.* **d. on the Stock Exchange,** boursicoteur *m*, boursicotier *m.*
dace [deis] *n. Ich:* vandoise *f*; dard *m.*
dachshund ['dækshund] *n.* (*F:* **dachs** [dæks]) (*dog*) teckel *m.*
dactyl ['dæktil] *n. Pros:* dactyle *m.*
dad [dæd] *n. F:* papa *m.*
Dada ['dɑːdɑː] *n. Art: Lit:* dada *m*, dadaïsme *m.*
Dadaism ['dɑːdɑːizm] *n. Art: Lit:* dadaïsme *m.*
daddy ['dædi] *n. F:* papa *m*; **sugar d.,** protecteur âgé; papa gâteau.
daddy-longlegs ['dædi'lɔŋlegz] *n. F: Ent:* cousin *m.*
dado ['deidou] *n.* **1.** *Arch:* (*a*) de *m* (de piédestal). **2.** lambris *m* (d'appui) (d'une salle).
daff [dæf] *n. F:* = DAFFODIL.
daffodil ['dæfədil] **1.** *n. Bot:* (narcisse *m*) jonquille (*f*). **2.** *a.* **d. (yellow),** jonquille *inv.*
daffy ['dæfi] *a. F:* timbré, toqué.
daft [dɑːft] *a. F:* timbré, toqué, cinglé, maboul(e); *adv.* **don't talk d.!** ne dis pas de bêtises!
daftness ['dɑːftnis] *n. F:* stupidité *f*, bêtise *f.*
dagger ['dægər] *n.* **1.** poignard *m*, dague *f*; *F:* **to be at daggers drawn,** être à couteaux tirés (**with,** avec); **to look daggers at s.o.,** foudroyer qn du regard. **2.** *Typ:* croix *f.*
dago ['deigou] *n. P: Pej:* métèque *m.*
dahlia ['deiliə] *n. Bot:* dahlia *m.*
daily ['deili] **1.** *a.* journalier, quotidien, de tous les jours; **d. paper,** (journal) quotidien (*m*); *Dom. Ec:* **d. help,** femme *f* de ménage; *Ecc:* **give us this day our d. bread,** donne-nous aujourd'hui notre pain de ce jour. **2.** *adv.* (*a*) quotidiennement, tous les jours; (*b*) (attendre qch.) d'un jour à l'autre. **3.** *n.* (*a*) *Journ:* quotidien *m*; (*b*) *F:* femme de ménage.
daintiness ['deintinis] *n.* délicatesse *f* (de goût, etc.).
dainty¹ ['deinti] *n. Lit:* friandise *f*; mets délicat.
dainty² *a.* **1.** (*of dish, food*) friand, délicat. **2.** (*of pers., thg*) délicat; gentil. **3.** délicat, difficile; **these animals are d. feeders,** ces animaux sont délicats sur la nourriture. **-ily** *adv.* délicatement; **to eat d.,** manger d'une manière délicate.
dairy ['dɛəri] *n.* **1.** laiterie *f*; **d. farm,** ferme laitière; **d. farming,** industrie laitière; **d. herd,** (troupeau *m* de) vaches laitières; **d. butter,** beurre laitier; **d. produce,** produits laitiers. **2.** (*shop*) laiterie; crémerie *f.*
dairymaid ['dɛərimeid] *n.f.* fille de laiterie.
dairyman, *pl.* **-men** ['dɛərimən] *n.m.* **1.** *Husb:* nourrisseur *m* (de vaches laitières). **2.** *Com:* laitier; crémier.
dais ['deiis] *n.* estrade *f* (d'honneur); dais *m.*
daisy ['deizi] *n. Bot:* pâquerette *f*; marguerite *f*; **Michaelmas d.,** aster *m* œil-du-Christ; **as fresh as a d.,** frais, fraîche, comme une rose; *P:* **he's pushing up the daisies,** il mange les pissenlits par les racines.
Dalai Lama ['dælai'lɑːmə] *n.* Dalaï-lama *m.*
dale [deil] *n.* vallée *f*; vallon *m.*
dalliance ['dæliəns] *n. Lit:* échange *m* de tendresses; badinage *m.*
dally ['dæli] *v.i. esp. Lit:* **1.** (*a*) folâtrer, folichonner (**with s.o.,** avec qn); **to d. with an idea,** caresser une idée; (*b*) badiner, flirter (**with,** avec). **2.** tarder, lambiner, traînasser; **to d. over sth.,** s'attarder à qch.
Dalmatian [dæl'meiʃən] *a. & n.* **D. (dog),** dalmatien *m.*
dam¹ [dæm] *n. Hyd.E:* barrage *m* (de retenue); digue *f* (de canal); **storage d.,** barrage-réservoir *m.*
dam² *v.tr.* **(dammed) to d. (up),** construire un barrage en aval (d'une vallée); endiguer (un cours d'eau, un lac); obstruer (un caniveau, etc.).
dam³ *n.* mère *f* (en parlant des animaux).
damage¹ ['dæmidʒ] *n.* **1.** dommage(s) *m*(*pl*), dégâts *mpl*; (*to engine, ship, etc.*) avarie(s) *f* (*pl*); **storm d.,** dégâts causés par un orage; **to pay for the d.,** payer les dégâts; **there's no great d. done,** il n'y a pas grand mal. **2.** préjudice *m*; **to cause s.o. d.,** porter préjudice à qn; **to do d. to a cause,** faire du tort à une cause. **3.** *Jur:* **damages,** dommages-intérêts *mpl*, indemnité *f*; **to be liable for damages,** être tenu des dommages-intérêts.
damage² *v.tr.* **1.** endommager; avarier (une marchandise, une machine); abîmer (qch.); accidenter (une voiture). **2.** faire tort à (qn); léser (des intérêts); porter atteinte à, tarer (la réputation de qn, etc.). **damaged** *a.* endommagé, abîmé; (marchandises) avariées; (voiture) accidentée. **damaging** *a.* préjudiciable; **d. admission,** aveu *m* préjudiciable.
Damascus [də'mɑːskəs] *Pr.n. Geog:* Damas *m.*
damask ['dæməsk] *n.* **1.** *Tex:* damas *m*; **d. silk,** soie damassée. **2.** *Metall:* **d. steel,** acier damassé. **3. d. rose,** rose *f* de Damas. **4. d. (colour),** rose foncé *m inv*; incarnat *m.*
dame [deim] *n.* **1.** (*a*) *A: & F:* femme *f*; **an old d.,** une vieille femme; (*b*) *Th:* (*in pantomime*) vieille femme comique (rôle joué par un homme). **2.** dame (titre accordé aux femmes titulaires de certaines décorations).
dammit ['dæmit] *F: int.* sacristi! sacrebleu! **it was as near as d.,** il était moins une.
damn¹ [dæm] *n. F:* juron *m*, gros mot; **I don't give, care, a d.,** je m'en fiche éperdument.
damn² *v.tr.* **1.** (*a*) condamner (un livre, etc.); éreinter (une pièce de théâtre); (*b*) perdre, ruiner (qn, un projet). **2.** (*a*) *Theol:* damner; (*b*) *F:* **well I'll be damned!** ça alors! **I'm, I'll be, damned if I'll do it,** si

tu crois que je vais le faire! **3.** *F:* (*a*) jurer après (qn); envoyer (qn) au diable; **d. you!** que le diable t'emporte! va te faire fiche! (*b*) **d. (it)!** zut! **d. and blast (it)!** sacré nom d'un chien! **damned** [dæmd] **1.** *a.* damné; *n.pl.* **the d.,** les damnés; **to suffer the tortures of the d.,** souffrir comme un damné. **2.** *F:* (*a*) *a.* sacré, satané; **you d. fool!** sacré imbécile! espèce d'idiot! **he's a d. nuisance!** ce qu'il est embêtant, casse-pieds! (*b*) *adv.* diablement, vachement; **it's d. hot,** il fait rudement chaud; **you can do what you d. well like!** fais ce que tu veux, je m'en fiche! (*c*) *n.* **to do one's damn(e)dest** ['dæmdist] faire tout son possible. **damning** ['dæmiŋ] *a.* (fait, etc.) accablant.

damn³ *a. F:* **1.** = DAMNED 2 (*a*), (*b*). **2.** *adv.* **he's doing d. all,** il ne fiche rien; **he knows d. all about it,** il n'y connaît (absolument) rien.

damnable ['dæmnəbl] *a.* **1.** damnable. **2.** *F:* maudit. **-ably** *adv.* **1.** damnablement. **2.** diablement, rudement (difficile, etc.).

damnation [dæm'neiʃ(ə)n] **1.** *n.* damnation *f*; *Theol:* **eternal d.,** la peine du dam. **2.** *int. F:* zut!

Damocles ['dæməkli:z] *Pr.n.m.* **the sword of D.,** l'épée *f* de Damoclès.

damp¹ [dæmp] *n.* **1.** humidité *f* (de l'air, etc.); moiteur *f* (de la peau); **the evening d.,** le serein; **d. mark,** tache *f* d'humidité; *Const:* **d. course,** couche *f* d'isolement; couche hydrofuge. **2.** *Min:* **(choke) d.,** mofette *f*; **fire d.,** grisou *m*.

damp² *v.tr.* **1.** mouiller; humecter (le linge, etc.). **2.** étouffer (le feu); étouffer (un son); **to d. down a furnace,** boucher un haut fourneau. **3.** (*a*) (*of unpleasant sight, etc.*) **to d. the appetite,** couper l'appétit (à qn); (*b*) abattre (le courage de qn); rabattre (la joie de qn); **to d. s.o.'s spirits,** décourager qn.

damp³ *a.* humide; (*of skin*) moite; **his hands are always d.,** il a toujours les mains moites; **d. heat,** chaleur *f* humide; *F:* **d. squib,** affaire ratée; coup raté.

dampen [dæmp(ə)n] **1.** *v.tr.* = DAMP² 1, 4 (*b*). **2.** *v.i.* (*a*) devenir humide, moite; (*b*) (*of ardour, etc.*) se refroidir.

damper ['dæmpər] *n.* **1.** *F:* événement décourageant; douche froide (sur l'enthousiasme, etc.); **to put a d. on the company,** jeter un froid sur la compagnie. **2.** *Mus:* (*of piano, sound*) étouffoir *m*; **d. pedal,** grande pédale (du piano). **3.** (*a*) registre *m* (de foyer, de cheminée); soupape *f* de réglage, à papillon (d'un tuyau de poêle); (*b*) *Ind:* registre (de fourneau). **4.** *Mec.E: El:* amortisseur *m*; *W.Tel:* sourdine *f*. **5.** mouilleur *m* (pour timbres, enveloppes).

dampish ['dæmpiʃ] *a.* un peu humide.

dampness ['dæmpnis] *n.* humidité *f*; moiteur *f*.

damp-proof ['dæmppru:f] *a.* hydrofuge.

damp-proofing ['dæmppru:fiŋ] *n.* isolation *f* contre l'humidité.

damsel ['dæmz(ə)l] *n.* **1.** *A: & Lit:* demoiselle *f*. **2.** *Ent:* **d. fly,** demoiselle.

damson ['dæmz(ə)n] *n.* (*a*) prune *f* de Damas; (*b*) **d. tree,** prunier *m* de Damas.

dance¹ [dɑ:ns] *n.* **1.** (*a*) danse *f*; **to lead, begin, the d.,** mener la danse; *F:* **to lead s.o. a d.,** donner du fil à retordre à qn; **folk d.,** danse folklorique; **d. music,** musique *f* de danse; **d. band,** orchestre *m* de musique de danse; **d. hall,** salle *f* de danse; dancing *m*; (*b*) *Mus:* (air *m* de) danse. **2.** bal *m*, *pl.* bals.

dance² **1.** *v.i.* (*a*) danser; **to d. with s.o.,** danser avec qn; (*b*) **to d. for joy,** danser de joie; **to d. about,** gambader. **2.** *v.tr.* (*a*) danser (une valse, etc.); (*b*) **to d. attendance on s.o.,** faire l'empressé auprès de qn. **dancing** **1.** *a.* dansant; **d. dervish,** derviche tourneur. **2.** *n.* danse *f*; **d. school,** école *f* de danse; **d. partner,** cavalier *m*, dame *f*; partenaire *mf*.

dancer ['dɑ:nsər] *n.* danseur, -euse; **ballet d.,** danseur, -euse, de ballet; ballerine *f*.

dandelion ['dændilaiən] *n. Bot:* pissenlit *m*.

dander ['dændər] *n. F:* **to get s.o.'s, one's, d. up,** mettre qn, se mettre, en colère.

dandle ['dændl] *v.tr.* (*a*) faire sauter (un enfant sur ses genoux); (*b*) bercer (un enfant).

dandruff ['dændrəf] *n.* pellicules *fpl* (du cuir chevelu).

dandy ['dændi] **1.** *n.* (*pers.*) dandy *m*, élégant *m*. **2.** *a. NAm: F:* épatant, chouette; **everything's just d.,** tout marche à merveille.

Dane [dein] *n.* **1.** *Ethn: Geog:* Danois, -oise. **2.** (*dog*) **(Great) D.,** (grand) danois.

danger ['dein(d)ʒər] *n.* danger *m*; péril *m*; **out of d.,** hors de danger; **to keep out of d.,** rester à l'abri du danger; **to be in d. of falling,** courir le risque, être en danger, de tomber; **in d. of (losing) his life,** en danger de mort; **there is some, no, d. that . . .,** il y a quelque danger que . . . (ne), il n'y a pas de danger que . . ., + *sub.*; *Rail: etc:* **d. signal,** signal *m* à l'arrêt; *Ind: etc:* **d. money,** prime *f* de risque.

dangerous ['dein(d)ʒ(ə)rəs] *a.* (*a*) dangereux, périlleux; (maladie) grave; **you are on d. ground,** vous êtes sur un terrain brûlant; (*b*) (*of example, maxim*) pernicieux. **-ly** *adv.* dangereusement; **d. ill,** gravement malade.

dangle ['dæŋgl] **1.** *v.i.* pendiller; **with one's legs dangling,** les jambes ballantes. **2.** *v.tr.* balancer (qch. au bout d'un cordon, etc.).

Danish ['deiniʃ] **1.** *a.* danois. **2.** *n. Ling:* danois *m*.

dank [dæŋk] *a.* (temps, cachot) humide (et froid).

Danube (the) [ðə'dænju:b] *Pr.n. Geog:* le Danube.

dapper ['dæpər] *a.* pimpant, coquet.

dapple¹ ['dæpl] *n.* **1.** (*a*) tache *f* de couleur (sur la robe d'un cheval, etc.); (*b*) tacheture *f*. **2.** cheval pommelé; **d. grey,** (cheval) gris pommelé.

dapple² **1.** *v.tr.* tacheter. **2.** *v.i.* se tacheter; (*of sky*) se pommeler.

Darby ['dɑ:bi] *Pr.n.* **D. and Joan** = Philémon et Baucis; **D. and Joan club,** club *m* des vieux, du troisième âge.

dare¹ [dɛər] *v.* **1.** *modal aux.* (*3rd sg.pr.* **dare;** *p.t.* **dared, dare;** *no p.p.*; **d. not** *often contracted to* **daren't**) oser; **I d. not, daren't, speak to him,** je n'ose pas lui parler; **don't you d. touch him!** ne touchez pas un cheveu de sa tête! **I d. say that . . .,** je suppose que . . .; **I d. say,** sans doute; c'est bien possible. **2.** *v.tr.* (*3rd sg.pr.* **dares;** *p.t., p.p.* **dared**) (*a*) oser; **to d. to do sth.,** oser faire qch.; **how d. you!** vous avez cette audace! **let him do it if he dare(s)!** qu'il le fasse s'il l'ose! (*b*) braver, affronter (le danger, la mort, etc.); (*c*) **to d. s.o. to do sth.,** défier qn de faire qch.; **I d. you!** chiche! **daring** **1.** *a.* (i) audacieux, hardi; (ii) téméraire; (robe) provocante; **greatly d.,** bien osé, fort osé. **2.** *n.* (i) audace *f*; (ii) témérité *f*; **to lose one's d.,** perdre de son audace. **daringly** *adv.* audacieusement; témérairement.

dare² *n.* (*a*) coup *m* d'audace; (*b*) défi *m*; **to do sth. for a d.,** faire qch. pour relever un défi.

daredevil ['dɛədevl] **1.** *n.* casse-cou *m inv*; risque-tout *m inv*. **2.** *a.* audacieux,-euse.

dark¹ [dɑ:k] *a.* **1.** sombre, obscur; noir; **d. glasses,** lunettes noires, de soleil; **it's d.,** (i) il fait nuit, il fait noir; (ii) il fait sombre (dans la pièce); **it is getting, growing, d.,** il commence à faire sombre, à faire nuit; **everything became d.,** tout s'assombrit. **2.** (*of colour*) foncé, sombre; **d. blue dresses,** robes *fpl* bleu foncé. **3.** (*of pers.*) brun; (*of complexion*) basané; **she has d. hair,** elle est brune. **4.** (*a*) (pensée, etc.) triste; sombre (avenir, etc.); **to look on the d. side of things,** voir tout en noir; (*b*) (pensées, etc.) sinistres; **to harbour d. designs,** nourrir de noirs desseins. **5.** mystérieux; secret, -ète; **keep sth. d.,** tenir qch. secret; *Fig:* **a d.**

horse, un concurrent (i) inconnu, (ii) que l'on ne croyait pas dangereux; **he's a d. horse,** (i) on ne sait rien de lui; (ii) il a bien caché son jeu. **6.** *Hist:* **the D. Ages,** le haut moyen âge; **the D. Continent,** le Continent noir, l'Afrique *f*. **-ly** *adv*. (*a*) obscurément; (*b*) (regarder qn) d'un air menaçant.

dark² *n*. **1.** ténèbres *fpl*, obscurité *f*; **in the d.,** dans le noir; **the child is afraid of the d.,** l'enfant a peur du noir; **after d.,** à, après, la tombée de la nuit. **2. to be (kept) in the d.,** être (laissé) dans l'ignorance.

darken [ˈdɑːk(ə)n] **1.** *v.tr.* obscurcir (une chambre, etc.); assombrir (le ciel, l'avenir); foncer (une couleur); attrister (la vie de qn); troubler (la raison); **never d. my doors again!** ne remettez plus les pieds chez moi! **2.** *v.i.* s'obscurcir; (*of sky, brow*) s'assombrir; (*of colour*) se foncer. **darkening** *n*. assombrissement *m* (du ciel, etc.); noircissement *m* (d'un tableau, etc.).

dark-eyed [ˈdɑːkˈaid] *a*. aux yeux noirs.

darkish [ˈdɑːkiʃ] *a*. un peu sombre.

darkness [ˈdɑːknis] *n*. **1.** obscurité *f*; **the room was in complete d.,** il faisait tout à fait noir dans la pièce. **2.** (*of colour*) teinte foncée. **3.** ignorance *f*.

darkroom [ˈdɑːkruːm] *n*. *Phot:* cabinet noir.

dark-skinned [ˈdɑːkˈskind] *a*. à peau brune; qui a la peau brune.

darling [ˈdɑːliŋ] *n*. & *v*. favori, -ite; chéri(e); **(my) d.!** mon chéri! ma chérie! mon chou! **she's a little d.,** c'est un petit amour; **a mother's d.,** *F:* le chouchou de sa maman; **the d. of the people,** l'idole *f* du peuple; **a d. little place,** un petit endroit charmant.

darn¹ [dɑːn], *n*. reprise *f* (dans un bas, etc.).

darn² *v.tr.* repriser. **darning** *n*. reprise *f*; **invisible d.,** reprise perdue; **d. egg, wool, needle,** œuf *m*, laine *f*, aiguille *f*, à repriser.

darn³ *v.tr.* & *i*. *F:* **d. (it)!** zut!

darn⁴, darned [dɑːrnd] *a*. *F*; sacré; **it's a d. nuisance,** c'est vachement embêtant.

dart¹ [dɑːt] *n*. **1.** (*a*) dard *m*, trait *m*; **paper d.,** avion *m* en papier; (*b*) *Games:* fléchette; **game of darts,** jeu *m* de fléchettes; (*c*) dard (d'abeille, etc.); (*d*) *Dressm:* pince *f*. **2.** mouvement soudain en avant; élan *m*; **to make a sudden d.,** foncer, se précipiter.

dart² **1.** *v.tr.* lancer, darder (un regard, etc.). **2.** *v.i.* se précipiter, s'élancer, foncer (**at s.o., sth.,** sur qn, qch.); **he darted across the road,** il traversa la rue comme une flèche; **to d. in, out,** entrer, sortir, comme une flèche. **3.** *v.tr.* *Dressm:* faire des pinces à (une robe, etc.).

dartboard [ˈdaːtbɔːd] *n*. cible *f* (de jeu de fléchettes).

dash¹ [dæʃ] *n*. **1.** goutte *f*, larme *f* (de cognac, etc.); filet *m* (de vinaigre); **add a d. of lemon,** ajoutez-y un filet de citron. **2. d. of colour,** touche *f* de couleur (dans un tableau). **3.** trait *m* (de plume, de l'alphabet Morse); *Typ:* (i) tiret *m*; (ii) moins *m*. **4.** (*a*) (i) attaque soudaine; (ii) course *f* à toute vitesse; élan *m*; **to make a d. forward,** s'élancer en avant; **to make a d. at sth.,** se précipiter sur qch.; foncer (sur l'ennemi); **to make a d. for it,** saisir l'occasion de s'enfuir; (*b*) *U.S: Sp:* sprint *m*. **5.** élan, entrain *m*; *Mus:* **to play with d.,** jouer avec brio. **6. to cut a d.,** faire de l'épate.

dash² **1.** *v.tr.* (*a*) heurter violemment (qch. contre qch.); jeter, *F:* flanquer (qch. par terre); **the ship was dashed against a rock,** le navire fut jeté sur un écueil; **to d. sth. to pieces,** fracasser qch.; briser qch. en morceaux; (*b*) déconcerter (qn); détruire (les espérances); refroidir (l'enthousiasme); **to d. s.o.'s spirits,** abattre le courage de qn; **he saw his hopes dashed (to the ground),** il a vu tomber à l'eau ses espérances; (*c*) *F:* **d. (it)!** zut! **2.** *v.i.* **I must d.,** il faut que je file; **to come dashing up, in,** arriver, entrer, comme un bolide; **to d. up, down, the stairs,** monter, descendre, l'escalier quatre à quatre; **to d. into the room,** entrer précipitamment, en coup de vent, dans la salle. **dash away** *v.i.* partir en coup de vent; filer à toute vitesse. **dashed** *F:* **1.** *a*. sacré; **what a d. nuisance!** quel empoisonnement! **2.** *adv*. vachement; **it's d. hot,** il fait, rudement chaud. **dashing** *a*. (*of pers.*) impétueux; **d. young man,** beau cavalier. **dashingly** *adv*. (se conduire) avec fougue, avec brio. **dash off** **1.** *v.i.* partir en coup de vent; filer à toute vitesse. **2.** *v.tr.* faire (qch.) en vitesse; dessiner, faire (un croquis) rapidement; écrire (une lettre) en vitesse. **dash out** *v.i.* sortir en coup de vent, en trombe.

dashboard [ˈdæʃbɔːd] *n*. *Aut: etc:* tableau *m* de bord.

dastardly [ˈdæstədli] *a*. *Lit:* **1.** lâche. **2.** (crime, etc.) infâme, ignoble.

data [ˈdeitə] *n*. données *fpl*; renseignements *mpl*; *Cmptr: etc:* **d. processing,** (i) informatique *f*; (ii) traitement *m* de l'information; **d. bank,** banque *f* de données; **weather d.,** données météorologiques.

date¹ [deit] *n*. *Bot:* datte *f*; **d. palm,** dattier *m*.

date² *n*. (*a*) date *f*; (*on coins, books, etc.*) millésime *m*; (*of month*) quantième *m*; **d. of birth,** date de naissance; **what's the d. (today)?** quelle est la date (aujourd'hui)? **to fix a d. for sth.,** prendre date pour qch.; **d. stamp,** dateur *m*, timbre *m* à date; *Geog:* **d. line,** ligne *f* de changement de date (le méridien 180°); (*b*) **up to d.,** à jour; **to be up to d.,** (i) être à jour (**with one's work,** dans son travail); être au courant (**with the latest developments,** des derniers développements); (ii) être à la page; **to bring a diary, etc., up to d.,** mettre à jour son journal, etc.; **to d.,** à ce jour; (*c*) **out of d.,** périmé; **this style is out of d.,** ce style est démodé; (*d*) *Com: Fin:* terme *m*, échéance *f* (d'un billet); **d. of maturity, due d.,** (date d')échéance; (*e*) *F:* (i) rendez-vous *m inv*; (ii) ami(e) (avec qui on fixe un rendez-vous); **blind d.,** rendez-vous avec quelqu'un qu'on ne connaît pas; *U.S.:* **double d.,** rendez-vous entre deux couples; **to make a d.,** fixer un rendez-vous.

date³ **1.** *v.tr.* (*a*) dater (une lettre, etc.); millésimer (une bouteille de vin, etc.); composter (un billet); **to d. back,** antidater; **to d. forward,** postdater; (*b*) **work of art that is difficult to d.,** œuvre d'art à laquelle il est difficile d'assigner une date; (*c*) **his clothes d. him,** ses vêtements démodés montrent qu'il n'est pas jeune; (*d*) sortir avec (une fille, etc.); fréquenter (qn). **2.** *v.i.* (*a*) dater (**from,** de); **church dating from, back to, the XIIIth century,** église *f* qui remonte au, qui date du, XIIIe siècle; **friendship dating back to the days of their youth,** amitié *f* qui remonte à leur jeunesse; (*b*) **his style is beginning to d.,** son style commence à dater; (*c*) *F:* (*of couple*) se fréquenter. **dated** *a*. (*a*) démodé; **his style is rather d.,** son style commence à dater; (*b*) *Fin:* **long-d., short-d.,** à longue, à courte, échéance. **dating** *n*. (*a*) datage *m* (d'un document, etc.); compostage *m* (de billets); (*b*) *Archeol: etc:* datation *f*.

dative [ˈdeitiv] *a*. & *n*. *Gram:* **d. (case),** (cas) datif (*m*); **in the d.,** au datif.

datum [ˈdeitəm] *n*. (*pl*. **data**) donnée *f*, élément *m* (d'information); *Surv: etc:* **d. point,** (i) élément de base; (ii) point *m* de référence; (iii) (point de) repère (*m*).

daub¹ [dɔːb] *n*. **1.** *Const:* torchis *m*. **2:** (*picture*) croûte *f*, barbouillage *m*.

daub² *v.tr.* **1.** barbouiller (**with,** de). **2.** *Art: F:* barbouiller (une toile).

daughter [ˈdɔːtər] *n.f.* fille.

daughter-in-law [ˈdɔːtərinlɔː] *n.f.* belle-fille, *pl*. belles-filles; bru.

daunt [dɔːnt] *v.tr.* intimider (qn); **nothing daunted,** intrépide(ment); nullement intimidé. **daunting** *a.* intimidant.

dauntless ['dɔːntlis] *a.* intrépide; sans peur. **-ly** *adv.* intrépidement.

davit ['dævit] *n. Nau:* bossoir *m* (d'embarcation).

Davy ['deivi] *Pr.n.m.* (*dim. of David*) David; *Nau: F:* **to go to D. Jones's locker,** boire à la grande tasse.

dawdle ['dɔːdl] *v.i.* flâner, traînasser, lambiner. **dawdling** *n.* flânerie *f.*

dawdler ['dɔːdlər] *n.* flâneur, -euse; traînard, -arde.

dawn¹ [dɔːn] *n.* **1.** aube *f*, aurore *f*; **at d.,** à l'aube; **at crack of d.,** à la pointe du jour; **the d. chorus,** le chant des oiseaux à l'aube. **2.** aurore, aube (de la vie); commencement *m* (de la civilisation).

dawn² *v.i.* (*of day, morning*) poindre; (commencer à) paraître; **day is dawning,** le jour se lève; **when the truth dawned on him,** quand il a compris la vérité; **it dawned on me that . . .,** j'ai commencé à me rendre compte que . . . . **dawning** *a.* (jour) naissant.

day [dei] *n.* **1.** (*a*) jour *m;* (*as a day's work, etc.*) journée *f*; **it's been a sunny d.,** il a fait une journée de soleil; **to work d. and night,** travailler nuit et jour; **all d. (long),** toute la journée; **to work, to be paid, by the d.,** travailler, être payé, à la journée; **it's all in a day's work,** ça fait partie de ma routine; **eight hour d.,** journée de huit heures; **in the course of the d.,** dans la journée; **twice a d.,** deux fois par jour; **I remember it to this (very) d.,** je m'en souviens encore aujourd'hui; **this d. last year,** il y a aujourd'hui un an; **the d. before, after, he came,** la veille, le lendemain, de son arrivée; **two days before, after, his wedding,** l'avant-veille *f*, le surlendemain, de son mariage; **two days later,** deux jours après, plus tard; le surlendemain; **every other d.,** tous les deux jours; un jour sur deux; **d. after d., d. in d. out,** jour après jour; **d. by d.,** jour par jour; **from d. to d.,** de jour en jour, d'un jour à l'autre; **to live from d. to d.,** vivre au jour le jour; **he's sixty if he's a d.,** il a soixante ans bien sonnés; *Mil: etc:* **officer of the d.,** officier *m* de jour; **pay d.,** jour de paie; *Mil:* jour de solde; *St.Exch:* jour de liquidation, de règlement; *F:* **let's call it a d.,** ça suffit pour aujourd'hui; (*b*) **to carry, win, the d.,** gagner la journée, la bataille; *F:* **that'll be the d.!** demain on rase gratis! (*c*) **d. labourer,** journalier *m*, ouvrier *m* à la journée; *Ind:* **d. shift,** équipe *f* du jour; (*of workman*) **to be on d. shift,** être de jour; *Med:* **d. nurse,** infirmier, -ière, qui est de service de jour; *Sch:* **d. school,** externat *m*; **d. pupil, d. boy, girl,** externe *mf*; **d. nursery,** crèche *f*; garderie *f* d'enfants; *Meteor:* **d. temperature,** température *f* diurne; *Rail: etc:* **d. return,** (billet *m* d')aller et retour *m* valable pour la journée; *Fin:* **d. bill,** effet *m* à date fixe. **2.** (*a*) (*dawn*) **before d.,** avant le jour; **at break of d.,** au point du jour; (*b*) (*daylight*) **in the full light of d.,** en plein jour; **to travel by d.,** voyager le jour, de jour, pendant le jour. **3.** (*24 hours*) jour (solaire, astronomique); *Jur: etc:* **ten clear days' notice,** préavis *m* de dix jours francs. **4.** (*a*) **d. of the month,** quantième *m* du mois; **what d. (of the week) is it (today)?** quel jour de la semaine sommes-nous? **to pass the time of d. with s.o.,** échanger quelques paroles de politesse avec qn; **one d., some d., one of these days,** un jour ou l'autre; un de ces jours; **the other d.,** l'autre jour; *Sch:* **parents' d., open d.,** journée portes ouvertes (dans un lycée, etc.); **to take, get, a d. off,** prendre, obtenir, un jour de congé; **wedding d.,** jour de mariage; *F:* **to name the d.,** fixer le jour du mariage; *Ecc:* **the d. of judgement,** le jour du jugement; (*b*) fête *f*; **All Saints' D.,** la Toussaint; **All Souls' D.,** le Jour des Morts; **Christmas D.,** le jour de Noël; *F:* **let's make a d. of it!** allons faire la fête! **5.** (*time*) **the good old days,** le bon vieux temps; **in the days of . . .,** au, du, temps de . . .; **in my young days,** au, du, temps de ma jeunesse; **in those days,** en ce temps-là; à cette époque; alors; **(in) these days,** de notre temps; **those were the days,** c'était la la belle vie (alors); **in his d.,** en son (i) temps, (ii) vivant; **he ended his days in poverty,** il a fini ses jours pauvre; **in days to come,** à l'avenir; (*of theory, fashion, etc.*) **to have had its d.,** avoir fait son temps; être démodé; *Prov:* **everything has its d.,** chaque chose a son temps.

daybed ['deibed] *n.* lit *m* de repos.

daybook ['deibuk] *n. Com:* (livre) journal (*m*), -aux; main courante, brouillard *m.*

daybreak ['deibreik] *n.* point *m* du jour; lever *m* du jour; **at d.,** au jour levant; au point du jour.

daydream¹ ['deidriːm] *n* rêverie *f*, songerie *f.*

daydream² *v.i.* rêver tout éveillé; rêvasser, songer. **daydreaming** *n.* rêverie *f*, songerie *f*, rêvasserie *f.*

daylight ['deilait] *n.* **1.** (*a*) jour *m*; lumière *f* du jour; **d.,** de jour, le jour; **in broad d.,** en plein jour; au grand jour; (*b*) l'aube *f*; le point du jour; **before d.,** avant le jour. **2.** *Fig:* **to (begin to) see d.,** (i) apercevoir la fin (du travail); (ii) (commencer à) voir clair (dans une affaire). **3.** *F:* **to beat the living daylights out of s.o.,** rosser, tabasser, qn; **to scare the living daylights out of s.o.,** flanquer la trouille, une peur bleue, à qn.

daytime ['deitaim] *n.* jour *m*, journée *f*; **in the d.,** pendant la journée; de jour.

daze¹ [deiz] *n.* étourdissement *m*, ahurissement *m*; **to be in a d.,** être hébété, ahuri.

daze² *v.tr.* (*a*) (*of drug, etc.*) stupéfier, hébéter; (*b*) (*of blow*) étourdir; (*c*) abasourdir, ahurir (qn). **dazed** *a.* (*a*) stupéfié (par un narcotique); hébété; (*b*) tout étourdi (par un coup); (*c*) abasourdi, sidéré.

dazzle¹ ['dæzl] *n.* éblouissement *m*; aveuglement *m.*

dazzle² *v.tr.* éblouir, aveugler; **dazzled with, by, the light,** aveuglé par la lumière. **dazzling** *a.* (*light, beauty*) éblouissant; (*light*) aveuglant; (*success*) éclatant. **dazzlingly** *adv.* **d. beautiful,** d'une beauté éblouissante.

deacon ['diːkən] *n. Ecc:* diacre *m.*

deaconess ['diːkənis] *n.f.* diaconesse.

dead [ded] **I.** *a.* **1.** mort; (*a*) **he is d.,** il est mort, décédé; **the d. man, woman,** le mort, la morte; **to drop, fall, (down) d.,** tomber (raide) mort; *P:* **drop d.!** allez au diable! **to shoot s.o. d.,** tuer qn net (d'un coup de revolver); *F:* **d. as a doornail, d. as mutton,** mort et bien mort; **d. and gone, d. and buried,** mort et enterré; **half d. with fright,** plus mort que vif; **d. to the world,** profondément endormi; (*b*) **d. water,** eau stagnante; *Nau:* remous *m* de sillage; *Geog:* **the D. Sea,** la Mer Morte; (*of regulation*) **to become a d. letter,** tomber en désuétude; rester lettre morte; *Post:* **d. letters,** lettres de rebut; **d.-letter office,** bureau *m* des rebuts; **d. language,** langue morte; (*c*) (*of tree, flower*) mort; **d. wood,** (i) bois mort; (ii) *N.Arch:* bois de remplissage; (iii) personnel *m* incapable; **to get rid of some of the d. wood in the office,** se débarrasser du personnel inutile; (*d*) (doigt) mort, engourdi par le froid; (*of limb*) **to go d.,** s'engourdir. **2.** (*hardened*) **d. to all sense of honour,** insensible à tout sentiment d'honneur. **3.** (feu) mort; (charbon) éteint; (couleur) terne; (son) mat; *El:* (fil) (i) hors courant, (ii) sans tension, sans courant; (pile) épuisée. **4.** (*a*) (ville) morte; **d. season,** morte-saison, *pl.* mortes-saisons; (*b*) **d. centre,** (i) *Mch:* point mort (du piston); (ii) (*of lathe*) centre *m* fixe; **d. end,** (i) cul-de sac *m*, *pl.* culs-de sac; impasse *m*; (ii) (*of pipe*) bout aveugle; **d. end job,** emploi *m* sans avenir; *Civ.E:* **d. load,** poids mort; *Fb:* **d. ball,** ballon mort; *Mil:* **d. angle,** angle mort. **5. d. stop,** arrêt *m* brusque, halte *f* subite; *Nau:* **d. calm,**

calme plat; **d. silence,** silence *m* de mort; **d. secret,** profond secret; **d. level,** niveau parfait; **d. loss,** (i) perte sèche; (ii) *F:* (*pers.*) propre *m* à rien. **II.** *n.* **1.** *pl.* **the d.,** les morts *mpl*; **to rise from the d.,** ressusciter des morts; **d. march,** marche *f* funèbre. **2.** **at d. of night,** au plus profond de la nuit; **in the d. of winter,** au plus fort de l'hiver. **III.** *adv.* (*a*) absolument; **d. drunk,** ivre mort; **d. tired,** mort de fatigue; **d. sure,** absolument certain; **d. on the hour,** à l'heure tapante; **he was d. right,** il avait absolument raison; **he was d. set on doing it,** il voulait le faire à tout prix; *F:* **d. broke,** fauché; **d. beat,** (i) mort de fatigue; (ii) éreinté; *Nau:* **wind d. ahead,** vent droit debout; **d. slow,** aussi lentement que possible; *P.N:* au pas; (*b*) **to stop d.,** s'arrêter net; (*c*) **with the tide running d. against us,** avec le courant en plein contre nous; (*of pers.*) **to be d. against sth.,** être absolument opposé à qch.; (*d*) **d. smooth surface,** surface parfaitement plane.

dead-and-alive ['ded(ə)ndə'laiv] *a.* mort, triste; **a d.-and-a. hole,** un trou perdu; un bled.

deaden ['ded(ə)n] *v.tr.* amortir (un coup); assourdir, étouffer, feutrer (un son); émousser (les sens); calmer (les nerfs). **deadening** *n.* amortissement *m*; assourdissement *m* (du bruit, d'un son).

deadhead ['dedhed] *n.* **1.** tête *f* de fleur morte. **2.** *F:* (*a*) *esp. U.S: Th: Rail:* personne *f* en possession d'un billet de faveur, d'un titre de transport gratuit; (*b*) (*pers.*) nullité *f*.

deadline ['dedlain] *n.* date *f* limite; heure *f* limite.

deadliness ['dedlinis] *n.* (*a*) nature mortelle (d'un poison, etc.); (*b*) ennui mortel.

deadlock ['dedlɔk] *n.* **1.** serrure *f* à pêne dormant. **2.** impasse *f*; situation *f* inextricable, insoluble.

deadly ['dedli] **1.** *a.* (*a*) (*of poison, blow, etc.*) mortel; (arme) meurtrière; (haine) implacable; (combat) à mort; **the seven d. sins,** les sept péchés capitaux; (*b*) (pâleur, silence, etc.) de mort; (*c*) **to be in d. earnest,** être tout à fait sérieux; (*d*) (*of play, book, etc.*) ennuyeux, rasant. **2.** *adv.* comme la mort; **d. pale,** d'une pâleur mortelle; *F:* **d. dull,** rasant.

deadman, *pl.* **-men** ['dedmæn, men] *n. Rail: etc:* **deadman's handle,** l'homme mort.

deadpan ['dedpæn] *a.* (visage) impassible, figé; (humour) de pince-sans-rire.

deadweight ['dedweit] *n.* **1.** poids mort, poids inerte. **2.** *Nau:* chargement *m*, port *m*, en lourd.

deaf [def] (*a*) *a.* sourd; **d. in one ear,** sourd d'une oreille; **d. and dumb,** sourd-muet, *f.* sourde-muette; **d. as a (door)post,** sourd comme un pot; **d. to entreaties,** sourd aux supplications; *Prov:* **there are none so d. as those that will not hear,** il n'y a pire sourd que celui qui ne veut (pas) entendre; **to turn a d. ear (to s.o., sth.),** refuser d'écouter (qn); rester sourd (aux prières); (*b*) *npl.* **the d.,** les sourds.

deaf-aid ['defeid] *n.* appareil *m* acoustique.

deafen ['defn] *v.tr.* assourdir (qn); **you're deafening me,** vous me percez les oreilles. **deafening** *a.* (bruit) assourdissant.

deaf-mute ['def'mju:t] *n.* sourd-muet, *f.* sourde-muette, *pl.* sourds-muets, sourdes-muettes.

deafness ['defnis] *n.* surdité *f*.

deal¹ [di:l] *n.* **a good d.,** beaucoup; **I have a great, good, d. to do,** j'ai beaucoup, bien des choses, à faire; **there's a great d. of truth in that,** il y a beaucoup de vrai là-dedans; **I think a great d. of him,** je l'estime beaucoup; **he is a good d. better,** il va beaucoup mieux.

deal² *n.* **1.** *Cards:* donne *f*; main *f*; **whose d. is it?** à qui de donner? **your d.!** à vous la donne! **2.** *Com: etc:* affaire *f*; marché *m*; **d. on the Stock Exchange,** coup *m* de Bourse; **cash d.,** transaction *f* au comptant; **package d.,** contrat global; **big d.,** (i) grosse affaire; (ii) *F: Iron:* la belle affaire! **it's a d.!** d'accord! entendu! *Pol:* **d. between parties,** tractation *f* entre partis; **to give s.o. a fair d.,** agir loyalement envers qn; **to give s.o. a raw d.,** en faire voir de dures à qn.

deal³ *v.* (*p.t. & p.p.* **dealt** [delt]) **I.** *v.tr.* **1. to d. out,** distribuer (des vivres, des dons) **(to, among,** entre); **to d. out justice,** rendre la justice. **2. to d. s.o. a blow,** porter un coup à qn. **3.** donner, distribuer (les cartes). **II.** *v.i.* **1.** (*a*) **to d. with s.o.,** avoir affaire à, avec, qn; **man easy, difficult, to d. with,** homme commode, pas commode; **I refuse to d. with him,** je refuse de traiter avec lui; (*b*) (*of book, etc.*) **to d. with a subject,** traiter, s'occuper, d'un sujet. **2.** (*a*) **to d. with (sth.),** conclure, terminer (une affaire); aviser à (une situation); *Com:* donner suite à (une commande); (*b*) **I know how to d. with him,** je sais comment il faut le traiter. **3.** *Com:* **to d. with (s.o.),** traiter, négocier, commercer, avec (qn); se fournir chez (un épicier, etc.); **to d. in leather,** *Fin:* **in options,** faire le commerce des cuirs, *Fin:* des primes. **4.** *Cards:* faire la donne; donner; *F:* faire. **dealing** *n.* **1. d. (out),** distribution *f* (de dons, etc.); distribution, donne *f* (de cartes). **2.** *Com:* **d. in wool, in wines,** commerce *m* des laines, des vins; *St.Exch:* **dealings for the account, for the settlement,** négociations *fpl* à terme. **3.** *pl.* (*a*) relations *fpl*, rapports mpl; **to have dealings with s.o.,** avoir des rapports avec qn; faire des affaires, traiter d'affaires, avec qn; (*b*) *Pej:* tractations *fpl* **(with,** avec); **underhand dealings,** menées sourdes. **4.** (*a*) conduite *f*, manière *f* d'agir; **fair d.,** loyauté *f*, honnêteté *f* (en affaires); (*b*) **d. with s.o.,** traitement *m* de qn, conduite *f* envers qn.

deal⁴ *n.* **1.** madrier *m*. **2.** (bois *m* de) pin *m*, sapin *m*.

dealer ['di:lər] *n.* **1.** *Cards:* donneur *m*. **2.** *Com:* (*a*) négociant *m* **(in,** en); distributeur *m* **(in,** de); *Aut: etc:* stockiste *m*; (*b*) marchand, -ande, fournisseur *m* **(in,** de); **secondhand d.,** brocanteur, -euse; (*c*) *St.Exch:* marchand de titres; (*d*) **double d.,** homme *m* à deux visages; trompeur, -euse.

dean [di:n] *n. Ecc: Sch:* doyen *m*.

deanery ['di:nəri] *n. Ecc:* **1.** doyenné *m*. **2.** résidence *f* du doyen.

dear [diər] **I.** *a.* **1.** (*a*) cher, chère **(to,** à); **he is d. to me,** il m'est cher; **all that I hold d.,** tout ce qui m'est cher; **what a d. little child!** quel amour d'enfant! **a d. little house,** une petite maison coquette; **to run for d. life,** courir aussi vite que possible; (*b*) *Corr:* **D. Sir,** Monsieur; **D. Madam,** Madame, Mademoiselle; **D. Mr Thomas,** Cher Monsieur; **My d. Alice,** Ma chère Alice. **2.** cher, coûteux; **these cigars are too d.,** ces cigares sont trop chers. **II.** *n.* cher, *f.* chère; chéri, chérie; **my d.,** (i) cher ami; chère amie; (ii) mon petit chou; **you're a d.!** tu es un amour! **be a d. and . . .,** sois gentil(le) et . . .. **III.** *adv.* **1.** (vendre, acheter, coûter, payer) cher. **2. he sold his life d.,** il vendit chèrement sa vie. **IV.** *int.* **d. d.! d. me!** mon Dieu, mon Dieu! **oh d.!** (i) oh là là! (ii) hélas! **oh d. no!** (oh) que non! **dearly** *adv.* **1.** cher, chèrement; **you shall pay d. for this,** cela vous coûtera cher. **2. I love him d.,** je l'aime tendrement; **he d. loves to play jokes on people,** il trouve tout son plaisir à jouer des tours aux gens.

dearie ['diəri] *F:* **1.** *n.* mon (petit) chéri; ma (petite) chérie. **2.** *int.* **d. me!** mon Dieu!

dearness ['diənis] *n.* cherté *f* (des vivres, etc.).

dearth [də:θ] *n.* disette *f*, pénurie *f* (de vivres, d'idées, de livres, etc.); pauvreté *f* (d'idées).

death [deθ] *n.* (*a*) mort *f*; *Hist:* **the Black D.,** la peste noire; **to be at death's door, on the verge, of d.,** être sur le point de mourir; **to die a violent d.,** mourir de mort violente; **at (the time of) his d.,** à sa mort; **until d.,** pour la vie; *F:* **to be sick to d. of sth.,** en avoir marre de qch.; *Psy:* **d. wish,** pulsion *f* de mort; **d.**

rattle, râle *m* de la mort; **d. mask,** masque *m* mortuaire; **death's head,** tête *f* de mort; *Ent:* **death's head moth,** (sphinx *m*) atropos (*m*); **d. knell,** glas *m*; **he fell to his d.,** il a fait une chute mortelle; **you'll catch your d. of cold if you go out in this weather,** vous allez crever de froid si vous sortez par ce temps; *F:* **he'll be the d. of me,** il me fera mourir; **it would be the d. of him,** ce serait sa mort; **to put s.o. to d.,** mettre qn à mort; exécuter qn; **condemned to d., under sentence of d.,** condamné à mort; **to drink oneself to d.,** se tuer à force de boire; **to die the d.,** se faire massacrer; **d. to traitors!** à mort les traîtres! **to be in at the d.,** assister au dénouement (d'une affaire); *F:* **to look like d. (warmed up),** avoir une figure de cadavre; (*b*) *Jur: Adm:* décès *m*; **d. certificate,** extrait *m* d'(acte) *m* de décès; **register of births, marriages and deaths,** registre *m* de l'état civil; *Journ:* **deaths,** nécrologie *f*; **d. duties,** *U.S:* **d. taxes,** droits *mpl* de succession; *Jur:* **d. warrant,** ordre *m* d'exécution; (*c*) *Jur:* **civil d.,** mort civile; (*d*) *Rept:* **d. adder,** acanthopis *m*; (*e*) *Fung:* **d. cap,** amanite *f* phalloïde.

deathbed ['deθbed] *n.* lit *m* de mort.

deathblow ['deθblou] *n.* coup mortel, fatal.

deathless ['deθlis] *a.* impérissable, immortel.

deathlike ['deθlaik] *a.* (pâleur, etc.) de mort.

deathly ['deθli] **1.** *a.* de mort; cadavérique; **d. silence,** silence *m* de mort. **2.** *adv.* comme la mort; **d. pale,** d'une pâleur mortelle.

deathtrap ['deθtræp] *n.* endroit, véhicule, dangereux.

deathwatch ['deθwɔtʃ] *n.* **1.** veillée de corps. **2.** *Ent:* **d. (beetle),** vrillette *f*, *F:* horloge *f* de la mort.

deb [deb] *n.f. F:* débutante.

debag [diː'bæg] *v.tr.* **(debagged)** *F:* déculotter.

debar [diː'bɑːr] *v.tr.* **(debarred) to d. s.o. from sth.,** exclure qn de qch.; interdire qch. à qn; **to d. s.o. from doing sth.,** interdire, à qn de faire qch.

debase [di'beis] *v.tr.* **1.** avilir, dégrader (qn); rabaisser (son style). **2.** (*a*) altérer (le métal); (*b*) **to d. the currency,** déprécier la monnaie.

debasement [di'beismənt] *n.* **1.** avilissement *m* (de qn). **2.** dépréciation *f* (des monnaies).

debatable [di'beitəbl] *a.* contestable, discutable.

debate¹ [di'beit] *n.* débat *m*, discussion *f*; délibération *f*.

debate² **1.** *v.tr.* débattre contradictoirement, discuter, agiter (une question, etc.); mettre (un sujet) en discussion; **a much debated question,** une question fort controversée; **I was debating with myself, in my mind, whether I would go or not,** je délibérais si j'irais ou non. **2.** *v.i.* discuter, disputer **(with s.o. on sth.,** avec qn sur qch.). **debating** *n.* **d. society,** société *f* de débats contradictoires.

debauch¹ [di'bɔːtʃ] *n.* débauche *f*.

debauch² *v.tr.* débaucher, corrompre (qn). **debauched** *a.* débauché, corrompu.

debauchery [di'bɔːtʃəri] *n.* débauche *f*; dérèglement *m* de(s) mœurs.

debenture [di'bentjər] *n. Fin:* obligation *f*; **d. bond,** titre *m* d'obligation; **d. stock,** obligations sans garantie; **d. holder,** obligataire *mf*.

debilitate [di'biliteit] *v.tr.* débiliter.

debility [di'biliti] *n. Med:* débilité *f*, asthénie *f*.

debit¹ ['debit] *n. Book-k:* débit *m*; **d. and credit,** doit *m* et avoir *m*; **d. entry,** article *m* au débit; **to enter sth. on the d. side of an account,** porter qch. au débit d'un compte; **d. note,** bordereau *m* de débit; **d. account,** compte débiteur.

debit² *v.tr. Book-k:* **1.** débiter (un article, un compte). **2. to d. s.o. with a sum,** porter une somme au débit de qn; débiter qn d'une somme.

debonair [debə'nɛər] *a. Lit:* jovial, -aux.

debrief [diː'briːf] *v.tr. Mil: Av: etc:* faire faire un compte-rendu (de fin de mission) à (un pilote, etc.); **to be debriefed,** faire rapport. **debriefing** *n.* rapport *m* (de fin de mission); debriefing *m*.

debris ['debriː] *n.* débris *mpl*; détritus *mpl*.

debt [det] *n.* dette *f*; **bad d.,** mauvaise créance; **d. of honour,** dette d'honneur; **to be in d.,** être endetté; avoir des dettes; *F:* **to be up to the ears in d.,** être criblé de dettes; **I shall always be in your d.,** je vous serai toujours redevable; **to get, run, into d.,** s'endetter, faire des dettes; **to be out of d.,** n'avoir plus de dettes; **d. collector,** agent *m* de recouvrements.

debtor ['detər] *n.* débiteur, -trice.

debug [diː'bʌg] *v.tr.* (*a*) éliminer les erreurs (d'un prototype, etc., *Cmptr:* d'un programme) dépanner (une machine); (*b*) éliminer les microphones clandestins (dans une pièce).

debunk [diː'bʌŋk] *v.tr. F:* **1.** déboulonner (qn). **2.** démentir (qch.).

début ['deibjuː] *n.* début *m*; (*in society*) entrée *f* dans le monde; **to make one's d.,** débuter.

débutante ['debjutɑ̃t, -tænt] *n.f.* débutante.

decade ['dekeid] *n.* **1.** (*a*) décennie *f*, décade *f*; (*b*) *Fr.Hist:* décade (du calendrier républicain). **2.** *Ecc:* dizaine *f* (d'un chapelet).

decadence ['dekədəns] *n.* **1.** décadence *f*. **2.** *Lit: Art:* décadentisme *m*.

decadent ['dekədənt] **1.** *a.* en décadence; décadent. **2.** *n. Lit: Art:* décadent *m*.

decaffeinate [diː'kæfiːneit] *v.tr.* décaféiner.

decagram(me) ['dekəgræm] *n. Meas:* décagramme *m*.

decalcification [diːkælsifi'keiʃ(ə)n] *n.* décalcification *f*.

decalcify [diː'kælsifai] *v.tr.* décalcifier (les os, etc.)

decamp [diː'kæmp] *v.i.* **1.** *Mil:* lever le camp. **2.** *F:* décamper, filer; ficher le camp.

decant [di'kænt] *v.tr.* transvaser (un liquide); décanter (une bouteille de vin) dans une carafe.

decanter [di'kæntər] *n.* carafe *f* (à liqueur, à vin).

decapitate [di'kæpiteit] *v.tr.* décapiter.

decapitation [dikæpi'teiʃ(ə)n] *n.* décapitation *f*.

decapod ['dekəpɔd] *n. Crust:* décapode *m*.

decarbonize [diː'kɑːbənaiz] *v.tr.* **1.** décarburer, décarboniser (l'acier, etc.). **2.** *I.C.E:* décalaminer (une culasse).

decathlon [di'kæθlɔn] *n. Sp:* décathlon *m*.

decay¹ [di'kei] *n.* **1.** décadence *f*, déchéance *f* (d'une famille, d'un pays, etc.); déclin *m* (de la beauté, etc.); délabrement *m* (d'un bâtiment); **moral d.,** déchéance morale; **senile d.,** affaiblissement sénile; **to fall into d.,** (*of house*) tomber en ruine, se délabrer; (*of state*) tomber en décadence. **2.** (*a*) pourriture *f*, corruption *f*, décomposition *f* (du bois, etc.); (*b*) carie *f* (des dents); (*c*) *Cmptr:* **d. time,** période *f* d'extinction.

decay² **1.** *v.i.* (*a*) (*of nation, family*) tomber en décadence; (*of building*) tomber en ruine; se délabrer; (*of race, tree*) dépérir; (*of empire*) décliner; (*of beauty, flowers*), (se) passer, se flétrir; (*b*) (*of meat, fruit*) se gâter, pourrir; (*of timber*) pourrir; (*of teeth*) se carier. **2.** *v.tr.* carier (les dents). **decayed** *a.* (*a*) en ruines; (*b*) (bois) pourri; (dent) cariée. **decaying** *a.* (*a*) en décadence; (*b*) en pourriture.

decease¹ [di'siːs] *n. Jur: Adm:* décès *m*.

decease² *v.i. Jur: Adm:* décéder. **deceased** *esp. Jur:* **1.** *a.* décédé; **son of Robert Martin, d.,** fils de feu M. Robert Martin. **2.** *n.* **the d.,** le défunt, la défunte.

deceit [di'siːt] *n.* **1.** supercherie *f*, tromperie *f*; *Jur:* fraude *f*. **2.** = DECEITFULNESS.

deceitful [di'siːtf(u)l] *a.* trompeur, -euse; fourbe. **-fully** *adv.* avec duplicité.

deceitfulness [di'siːtf(u)lnis] *n.* fausseté *f*, duplicité *f*.

deceive [di'si:v] *v.tr.* (*a*) tromper, abuser (qn); tromper, décevoir (les espérances de qn); **to d. oneself,** s'abuser; **I thought my eyes were deceiving me,** je ne pouvais pas en croire mes yeux; (*b*) tromper (son mari, sa femme).

deceiver [di'si:vər] *n.* trompeur, -euse.

decelerate [di:'seləreit] *v.i. & tr.* décélérer; ralentir.

deceleration [di:selə'reiʃ(ə)n] *n.* décélération *f*; ralentissement *m.*

December [di'sembər] *n.* décembre *m*; **in D.,** au mois de, en, décembre; **(on) the third of D.,** le trois décembre.

decency ['di:sənsi] *n.* **1.** décence *f* (de costume, etc.). **2.** bienséance, convenance(s) *f* (*pl*); **common d.,** les convenances (sociales).

decent ['di:s(ə)nt] *a.* **1.** (*a*) bienséant, convenable; **are you d.?** es-tu habillé (convenablement)? (*b*) décent, honnête. **2.** passable; **this wine is quite d.,** ce vin est très buvable, se laisse boire. **3.** *F:* **a d. (sort of) chap,** un bon type; **it's very d. of you,** c'est très gentil de votre part. **4.** *adv.* (*in compound adjs*) **d.-sized house,** maison *f* d'une grandeur raisonnable. **-ly** *adv.* **1.** décemment, convenablement; avec bienséance, avec décence. **2.** *F:* passablement; **he pays quite d.,** il ne paie pas mal.

decentralization [di:sentrəlai'zeiʃ(ə)n] *n.* décentralisation (administrative, etc.).

decentralize [di:'sentrəlaiz] *v.tr.* décentraliser (l'administration, etc.).

deception [di'sepʃ(ə)n] *n.* tromperie *f*, supercherie *f.* fraude *f.*

deceptive [di'septiv] *a.* (*a*) (*of thg, appearance*) trompeur, -euse; **appearances are d.,** les apparences sont trompeuses; (*b*) **he, his manner, is very d.,** on ne peut jamais deviner ce qu'il va faire, dire. **-ly** *adv.* **he has a d. quiet manner,** il a un air tranquille (bien) trompeur.

deceptiveness [di'septivnis] *n.* caractère trompeur (de qch.).

decibel ['desibel] *n. Ph:* décibel *m.*

decide [di'said] **1.** *v.tr.* (*a*) trancher (une question); juger (un différend); (*b*) décider de (qch.); **to d. s.o.'s fate,** décider du sort de qn; **event that decided his career,** événement *m* qui décida de sa carrière; **nothing has been, is, decided yet,** il n'y a encore rien de décidé; (*c*) **that decided me (to leave),** cela me décida (à partir); (*d*) **to d. to do sth.,** se décider, se résoudre, à faire qch.; décider, résoudre, de faire qch.; **it was decided to wait for his reply,** on a décidé d'attendre sa réponse. **2.** *v.i.* **to d. on (sth.),** se décider à (qch.); arrêter (un plan de conduite); déterminer (une méthode de travail; fixer (un jour); **to d. against sth.,** se prononcer contre qch.; **have you decided?** êtes-vous décidé? **decided** *a.* **1.** (ton) net, résolu; (refus) catégorique; **they are quite d. about it,** ils sont tout à fait décidés (à agir, etc.). **2.** (différence) marquée, prononcée; (changement) sensible; (succès) incontestable. **decidedly** *adv.* **1.** (agir) résolument. **2.** décidément; incontestablement; **he is d. better,** il va décidément mieux. **deciding** *a.* (facteur) décisif; *Sp:* **the d. game, set,** la belle.

decider [di'saidər] *n.* **1.** (*pers.*) arbitre *m.* **2.** facteur décisif; *Sp:* but, point, décisif; *Games:* la belle.

deciduous [di'sidjuəs] *a. Bot:* à feuilles caduques. *Z:* (*of antlers, etc.*) caduc.

decilitre, *NAm:* **deciliter** ['desili:tər] *n. Meas:* décilitre *m.*

decimal ['desim(ə)l] **1.** *a.* (*of fraction, system, coinage, etc.*) décimal, -aux; *Mth:* **d. point,** virgule (décimale); **d. place,** (i) décimale *f*; (ii) *Cmptr:* position décimale; *F:* **to go d.,** adopter le système décimal. **2.** *n.* (*a*) **correct to five decimal places,** exact jusqu'à la cinquième décimale.

decimalization [desiməlai'zeiʃ(ə)n] *n.* décimalisation *f.*

decimate ['desimeit] *v.tr.* (*of disease, etc.*) décimer (la population, etc.).

decimation [desi'meiʃ(ə)n] *n.* décimation *f.*

decimetre, *NAm:* **decimeter** ['desimi:tər] *n. Meas:* décimètre *m.*

decipher [di'saifər] *v.tr.* déchiffrer (des hiéroglyphes); déchiffrer, décoder (une dépêche chiffrée); déchiffrer (une écriture difficile).

decipherable [di'saif(ə)rəbl] *a.* déchiffrable.

decision [di'siʒ(ə)n] *n.* **1.** (*a*) décision *f* (d'une question, de faire qch.); vote *m* (sur une question); (*b*) décision, jugement *m*, arrêt *m*; **to give a d. on a case,** décider, statuer sur, un cas. **2.** (*a*) décision, résolution *f*; **to come to, arrive at, reach, a d. (about sth.),** arriver à une décision (quant à, touchant, qch.); se décider, se prononcer; (*b*) **d. maker,** personne *f* qui prend des décisions; **d. making,** prise *f* de décisions. **3.** résolution (de caractère); fermeté *f.*

decisive [di'saisiv] *a.* **1.** (*of question, battle, etc.*) décisif; (*of experiment, etc.*) concluant; (preuve) victorieuse. **2.** (*of manner, etc.*) décidé; (ton) tranchant, net. **-ly** *adv.* d'une façon décisive.

decisiveness [di'saisivnis] *n.* **1.** caractère décisif, concluant (d'une expérience, etc.). **2.** = DECISION 3.

deck[1] [dek] *n.* **1.** (*a*) *Nau:* pont *m*; **after d.,** pont arrière; **lower, upper, d.,** pont inférieur, supérieur; **promenade d.,** pont promenade; **boat d.,** pont des embarcations; **d. officer,** officier *m* de pont; **d. cargo, load,** pontée *f*; **mess d.,** poste *m* de l'équipage; **on d.,** sur le pont; **below deck(s),** dans l'entrepont; **to come, go, on d.,** monter sur le pont; **to clear the decks for action,** (i) faire le branle-bas de combat; (ii) se préparer à agir; *F:* **to hit the d.,** tomber à plat ventre; (*b*) *Veh:* plateforme *f*, *pl.* plates-formes; (*of bus*) **top d.,** impériale *f*; **single-d. bus,** autobus *m* sans impériale. **2.** *Civ.E:* tablier *m*; plancher *m* (d'un pont). 3. (*a*) *NAm:* **d. of cards,** jeu *m* de cartes; (*b*) *Cmptr:* paquet *m* (de cartes). **4.** *Rec:* platine *f*; **cassette d.,** platine à cassette; **tape d.,** platine de bande magnétique. **5.** *U.S:* *Aut:* (*a*) coffre *m*; (*b*) couvercle *m* du coffre.

deck[2] *v.tr.* **1.** parer, orner (**sth. with sth.,** qch. de qch.); **to d. oneself out,** s'endimancher. **2.** *N.Arch:* **to d. (over, in) a ship,** ponter un navire.

decker ['dekər] *n. comb. fm. Trans:* **single-d. (bus),** autobus *m* sans impériale; **double-d. (bus),** autobus à impériale; *Comest:* **double-d. sandwich,** sandwich *m* double.

deckhand ['dekhænd] *n.* matelot *m* de pont.

deckhouse ['dekhaus] *n. Nau:* rouf *m.*

deckle ['dekl] *n. Paperm:* cadre volant, rebord *m* (de la forme); **d. edge,** barbes *fpl* (du papier).

declaim [di'kleim] **1.** *v.i.* déclamer (**against,** contre). **2.** *v.tr.* déclamer (des vers, etc.).

declamation [deklə'meiʃ(ə)n] *n.* déclamation *f.*

declaration [deklə'reiʃ(ə)n] *n.* (*a*) déclaration *f* (de guerre, etc.); **d. of the poll,** proclamation *f* du résultat du scrutin; (*b*) **statutory d.,** attestation *f*; **d. of income,** déclaration de revenu: **customs d.,** déclaration de, en, douane; (*c*) *Cards:* annonce *f.*

declare [di'klɛər] *v.tr.* (*a*) déclarer (**sth. to s.o.,** qch. à qn); **to d. war,** déclarer la guerre (**on, against,** à); *Cust:* **have you anything to d.?** avez-vous quelque chose à déclarer? **to d. a strike,** proclamer la grève; *Fin:* **to d. a dividend of ten per cent,** déclarer un dividende de dix pour cent; (*b*) **to d. s.o. guilty,** déclarer qn coupable; (*c*) *v.i. Cr:* **to d.,** fermer son jeu (avant la chute des dix guichets); (*d*) *Cards:* appeler (l'atout, une couleur); *v.i.* **to d.,** annoncer son jeu; *Fig:* **to d. one's hand,** avouer ses intentions; (*e*) **to d. oneself,** (i) prendre parti; (ii) (*of lover*) faire sa déclaration; (*of disease*) **to d. itself,** se déclarer. **declared** *a.* avoué, déclaré.

declassify [diː'klæsifai] *v.tr.* remettre en circulation (un document secret, etc.).
declension [di'klenʃ(ə)n] *n. Gram:* déclinaison *f.*
declinable [di'klainəbl] *a. Gram:* déclinable.
declination [dekli'neiʃ(ə)n] *n.* **1.** *Astr:* déclinaison *f.* **2.** *NAm:* refus courtois, formel.
decline¹ [di'klain] *n.* déclin *m* (du jour, d'un empire); baisse *f* (de prix); ralentissement *m* (des affaires); **to be on the d.,** être sur le déclin; décliner; (*of prices*) être en baisse.
decline² **1.** *v.tr.* (*a*) refuser courtoisement (une invitation); décliner (un honneur); *v.i.* s'excuser; se faire excuser; (*b*) refuser; repousser (l'intervention de qn); **to d. to do sth.,** refuser de faire qch. **2.** *Gram:* décliner (un nom, etc.). **3.** *v.i.* (*a*) (*of day, sun, etc.*) décliner; (*of day*) tirer à sa fin; baisser; (*b*) (*of health, influence,* etc.) décliner, baisser; *Com:* (*of prices, business*) être en baisse. **declining** *a.* (*a*) (soleil) couchant, baissant; *Lit:* **in one's d. years,** au déclin de la vie; (*b*) *Pol.Ec:* (industrie) déclinante; (marché) en baisse.
declivity [di'kliviti] *n.* déclivité *f*, pente *f.*
declutch [diː'klʌtʃ] *v.i. Aut:* débrayer.
decoction [di'kɔkʃ(ə)n] *n.* décoction *f.*
decode [diː'koud] *v.tr.* déchiffrer, décoder, transcrire en clair (une dépêche); **decoded message,** message transcrit *m* en clair. **decoding** *n.* déchiffrement *m*, décodage *m*, transcription *f* en clair.
decoder [diː'koudər] *n.* décodeur *m*; déchiffreur *m.*
décolleté [dei'kɔltei] **1.** *a.* (*of dress, woman*) décolleté. **2.** *n.* décolletage *m.*
decompose [diːkəm'pouz] **1.** *v.tr.* (*a*) décomposer, (un composé, la lumière, etc.); *Ch:* dédoubler (un sel double); (*b*) décomposer (la matière). **2.** *v.i.* (*a*) se décomposer; (*b*) entrer en décomposition.
decomposition [diːkɔmpə'ziʃ(ə)n] *n.* décomposition *f.*
decompress [diːkəm'pres] *v.tr.* décomprimer (un gaz, etc.); faire séjourner (qn) dans la chambre de décompression.
decompression [diːkəm'preʃ(ə)n] *n. Mch: etc:* décompression *f*; séjournement *m* (de qn) dans la chambre de décompression; **d. chamber,** chambre *f* de décompression; *Med:* **d. sickness,** maladie *f* des caissons.
decongestion [diːkən'dʒestj(ə)n] *n. Med:* décongestion *f.*
decontaminate [diːkən'tæmineit] *v.tr.* **1.** désinfecter. **2.** décontaminer.
decontamination [diːkəntæmi'neiʃ(ə)n] *n.* **1.** désinfection *f.* **2.** décontamination *f.*
decontrol¹ [diːkən'troul] *v.tr.* (*a*) libérer (le commerce, etc.) des contraintes du gouvernement; (*b*) *Adm:* **decontrolled road,** route non soumise à la limite de vitesse minimum.
decontrol² *n. NAm:* libération *f* (des prix, etc.).
décor ['deikɔːr] *n. Th:* décor *m.*
decorate ['dekəreit] *v.tr.* **1.** (*a*) décorer, orner (**sth. with sth.,** qch. de qch.); pavoiser (une rue); (*b*) peindre et tapisser, décorer (un appartement). **2.** décorer, remettre une décoration à (qn.). **decorating** *n.* décoration *f* (de qch.).
decoration [dekə'reiʃ(ə)n] *n.* **1.** (*a*) décoration *f*; pavoisement *m* (des rues, etc.); peinture *f* et collage *m* de la tapisserie, décoration (d'une pièce); **interior d.,** décoration d'intérieur; (*b*) remise *f* d'une décoration (à qn). **2.** (*a*) *usu. pl.* (les) décorations (d'une ville en fête, etc.); (*b*) décoration, médaille *f.*
decorative ['dek(ə)rətiv] *a.* (art, ornement) décoratif; (dessin) d'ornement. **-ly** *adv.* décorativement.
decorator ['dekəreitər] *n.* décorateur *m*; **(painter and) d.,** peintre décorateur; **interior d.,** décorateur-ensemblier *m, pl.* décorateurs-ensembliers.
decorous ['dekərəs] *a.* bienséant, convenable. **-ly** *adv.* avec bienséance; convenablement.
decorticate [diː'kɔːtikeit] *v.tr.* décortiquer (le riz, etc.).
decorum [di'kɔːrəm] *n.* décorum *m*, bienséance *f*; **a breach of d.,** une inconvenance; **to have a sense of d.,** avoir de la tenue.
decoy¹ ['diːkɔi] *n.* **1.** appât *m*, leurre *m*; **d. (bird),** moquette *f*; (oiseau) appelant (*m*). **2.** compère *m*; **police d.,** policier *m* en civil (pour tromper un criminel).
decoy² [di'kɔi] *v.tr.* **1.** leurrer (des oiseaux). **2.** leurrer (qn); **to d. s.o. into a trap,** attirer, qn dans un piège.
decrease¹ ['diːkriːs] *n.* diminution *f*, décroissement *m*, décroissance *f*, amoindrissement *m*; **d. in price,** baisse *f* de prix; **d. in speed,** ralentissement *m*; **to be on the d.,** diminuer.
decrease² [di'kriːs] **1.** *v.tr.* (*a*) diminuer; (*b*) *Knit:* **d. three stitches,** diminuer de trois mailles. **2.** *v.i.* (*a*) diminuer; décroître; (*b*) *Knit:* diminuer, faire des diminutions. **decreasing** *a.* décroissant, diminuant. **decreasingly** *adv.* de moins en moins.
decree¹ [di'kriː] *n.* **1.** *Adm:* décret *m*, édit *m*, arrêté *m*; **to issue a d.,** promulguer un décret. **2.** *Theol: Ecc:* décret. **3.** *Jur:* décision *f*, arrêté, arrêt *m*, jugement *m*; **d. nisi** ['naisai], jugement provisoire (en matière de divorce); **d. absolute,** jugement *m* irrévocable.
decree² *v.tr.* **1.** décréter, ordonner; *Jur:* arrêter (**that,** que). **2.** décerner, accorder par décret (des honneurs, un prix) (**to,** à).
decrepit [di'krepit] *a.* **1.** (*of pers.*) décrépit. **2.** (*of thg*) vermoulu; qui tombe en ruine; délabré.
decrepitude [di'krepitjud] *n.* **1.** décrépitude *f.* **2.** état délabré (d'un mobilier, etc.).
decry [di'krai] *v.tr.* décrier, dénigrer (qn, qch.).
dedicate ['dedikeit] *v.tr.* **1.** (*a*) dédier, consacrer (une église); **to d. oneself, one's life, to s.o., to sth.,** se vouer à qn, à qch.; se consacrer à qch.; (*b*) *esp. NAm:* inaugurer (un édifice, etc.). **2.** dédicacer (un livre, etc.) (**to,** à). **dedicated** *a.* (*of pers.*) dédié (à sa profession, etc.); (médecin, professeur) par vocation; (vie) de dédication.
dedication [dedi'keiʃ(ə)n] *n.* **1.** consécration *f* (d'une église). **2.** dédicace *f* (d'un livre); **to write a d. in a book,** dédicacer un livre. **3.** attachement *m* (**to,** à).
deduce [di'djuːs] *v.tr.* déduire, conclure (**from,** de); **to d. sth. from a fact,** arguer qch. d'un fait.
deduct [di'dʌkt] *v.tr.* déduire (**from,** de); **to d. sth. from the price,** rabattre qch. sur le prix; **to be deducted,** à déduire.
deductible [di'dʌktibl] *a.* déductible.
deduction [di'dʌkʃ(ə)n] *n.* **1.** déduction *f* (**from a** quantity, sur une quantité); (*of pay*) retenue *f*; **d. from wages,** prélèvement *m* sur le salaire. **2.** déduction, conclusion *f* (**from,** tirée de); **by a process of d.,** par déduction.
deductive [di'dʌktiv] *a.* (raisonnement) déductif, par déduction.
deed [diːd] *n.* **1.** (*a*) action *f*, acte *m*; *Scout:* **to do one's good d. for the day,** faire sa bonne action, sa B.A., quotidienne; (*b*) *Lit:* **d. of valour,** haut fait; **foul d.,** forfait *m.* **2.** *Jur:* acte notarié; **mortgage d.,** acte hypothécaire; **d. poll,** acte unilatéral; contrat *m* à titre gratuit; **to change one's name by d. poll,** changer légalement son nom.
deem [diːm] *v.tr. A: & Lit:* **I do not d. it necessary, proper, to . . .,** je ne juge pas, crois pas, nécessaire, convenable, de . . . .
deep [diːp] **I.** *a.* **1.** (*a*) (*of water, well, etc.*) profond; **to be ten metres d.,** avoir dix mètres de profondeur, avoir une profondeur de dix mètres; **d. end,** bout le plus profond (d'une piscine); *F:* **to go off the d. end,** (i) s'emporter, (ii) s'affoler; **d. in debt,** criblé de dettes; **d. in thought,** plongé dans ses pensées; (*b*)

(blessure) profonde; (*of weapon*) **to inflict a d. wound,** pénétrer très avant; (*c*) **d. shelves,** rayons *mpl* larges; *Mil:* **two, four, d.,** sur deux, quatre, rangs; (*d*) (*of sigh, sleep, etc.*) profond; **d. thinker,** penseur profond; **his d. learning,** ses connaissances profondes. **2.** (*a*) (*of colour*) foncé, sombre; **d. blue,** bleu foncé; (*b*) (*of sound*) grave; **in a d. voice,** d'une voix profonde. **3.** (*of despair*) profond; **d. concern,** vive préoccupation; (*c*) (*of conduct*) difficile à pénétrer; (*of pers.*) malin, astucieux. **II.** *adv.* **1.** profondément; **d.-lying causes,** causes profondes; *Prov:* **still waters run d.,** il n'y a pire eau que l'eau qui dort. **2. the harpoon sank d. into the flesh,** le harpon pénétra très avant dans la chair; **to work d. into the night,** travailler tard dans la nuit. **III.** *n.* **the d.,** l'océan *m*; **to commit a body to the d.,** immerger un mort. **deeply** *adv.* profondément; **to go d. into sth.,** pénétrer, entrer, fort avant dans qch.; approfondir qch.; **to fall d. in love with s.o.,** tomber profondément amoureux de qn; **d. interesting,** fort intéressant; **d. offended,** grièvement offensé.

deepen ['di:p(ə)n] **1.** *v.tr.* (*a*) approfondir, creuser (un puits, etc.); (*b*) rendre (un sentiment) plus intense; **this only deepened his resentment,** cela n'a fait qu'augmenter son ressentiment; (*c*) foncer (une couleur); rendre (un son) plus grave. **2.** *v.i.* (*a*) (*of river, etc.*) devenir plus profond; (*b*) (*of colour*) devenir plus foncé; (*of sound*) devenir plus grave; (*c*) (*of shadows*) s'épaissir; (*of silence*) devenir plus profond.

deep-freeze¹ ['di:p'fri:z] *v.tr.* congeler, surgeler.

deep-freeze² *n.* congélateur *m.*

deep-fry ['di:p'frai] *v.tr.* faire cuire (du poisson, etc.) dans la friture.

deep-fryer ['di:p'fraiər] *n. Dom.Ec:* friteuse *f.*

deepness ['di:pnis] *n.* profondeur *f* (de la voix, etc.); *Mus:* gravité *f* (d'un son).

deep-rooted ['di:p'ru:tid] *a.* (arbre) à enracinement profond; (affection) profonde; (préjugé) vivace.

deep-sea ['di:p'si:] (plante, animal) pélagique; **d.-s. fishery, fishing,** (i) pêche hauturière; (ii) grande pêche.

deep-seated ['di:p'si:tid] *a.* profond, enraciné; (affection) profonde; (conviction) intime.

deep-set ['di:p'set] *a.* (yeux) enfoncés, creux.

deer ['diər] *n. inv.* **(red) d.,** cerf commun; **fallow d.,** daim *m*; **roe d.,** chevreuil *m*; **d. park, forest,** chasse gardée pour le cerf.

deerhound ['diəhaund] *n. Z:* lévrier *m* d'Écosse.

deerskin ['diəskin] *n.* peau *f* de daim; *Com:* daim *m*; **d. gloves,** gants *mpl* de daim.

deerstalker ['diəstɔ:kər] *n.* **1.** chasseur *m* (de cerf) à l'approche. **2.** *Cost:* chapeau *m* de chasse (à la Sherlock Holmes).

deerstalking ['diəstɔ:kiŋ] *n.* chasse *f* (au cerf) à l'approche.

deface [di'feis] *v.tr.* défigurer (qch.); mutiler (une statue); barbouiller (une affiche).

de facto [di:'fæktou] *Lt. phr: Jur:* de facto; *Jur:* **de f. and de jure,** de droit et de fait.

defamation [defə'meiʃ(ə)n] *n.* diffamation *f.*

defamatory [di'fæmət(ə)ri] *a.* diffamatoire, diffamant.

defame [di'feim] *v.tr.* diffamer (qn).

default¹ [di'fɔ:lt] *n.* **1.** *Jur:* défaut *m*; non comparution *f*; (*criminal law*) contumace *f*; **judgment by d.,** jugement *m* par contumace; *Sp:* **match won by d.,** match gagné par forfait. **2.** (*a*) *Com:* **d. in paying,** défaut de paiement; (*b*) **in d. of . . .,** à, au, défaut de . . ., faute de . . ..

default² *v.i.* (*a*) *Jur:* être en état de contumace; ne pas comparaître; (*b*) *St.Exch:* manquer à ses engagements.

defaulter [di'fɔ:ltər] *n.* **1.** *Jur:* défaillant, -ante; contumace *mf.* **2.** *Mil: Navy:* (*a*) retardataire *m*, réfractaire *m*; (*b*) (*undergoing punishment*) consigné *m.* **3.** *St.Exch:* défaillant *m*, failli *m.*

defeat¹ [di'fi:t] *n.* **1.** (*a*) défaite *f* (d'une armée); (*b*) **to suffer a d.,** essuyer une défaite. **2.** (*a*) renversement *m* (d'un projet); (*b*) *Parl: etc:* échec *m* (d'une mesure); défaite (du gouvernement).

defeat² *v.tr.* **1.** (*a*) battre, vaincre (une armée); (*b*) **this defeats me,** cela me dépasse. **2.** (*a*) déjouer, faire échouer (un projet); frustrer (une espérance); **to d. the ends of justice,** contrarier la justice; **to d. one's own object,** aller à l'encontre de ses propres intentions; (*b*) *Parl: etc:* mettre en minorité *f* (le gouvernement, etc.); faire échouer (une mesure).

defeatism [di'fi:tizm] *n.* défaitisme *m.*

defeatist [di'fi:tist] *a. & n.* défaitiste (*mf*).

defecate ['defəkeit] *v.i.* déféquer.

defecation [defə'keiʃ(ə)n] *n.* défécation *f.*

defect¹ ['di:fekt] *n.* défaut, imperfection *f* (de construction); tare *f*; **d. in pronunciation,** défaut de prononciation.

defect² [di'fekt] *v.i. Mil: etc:* passer à l'ennemi.

defection [di'fekʃ(ə)n] *n. Mil: etc:* défection *f.*

defective [di'fektiv] *a.* (*a*) défectueux, imparfait; (*of development*) vicieux; (enfant) anormal; (mémoire) infidèle; (freins) en mauvais état; *Ind:* (pièce) défectueuse; **to be d. in sth.,** manquer de qch.; (*b*) *Gram:* (verbe, etc.) défectif. **2.** *n.* **mental d.,** arriéré, -ée.

defector [di'fektər] *n. Mil: etc:* transfuge *mf.*

defence, *NAm:* **defense** [di'fens] *n.* **1.** (*a*) défense *f*, protection *f*; **to put up a stubborn d.,** se défendre avec acharnement; **self d.,** autodéfense *f*; *Mil: etc:* **civil d.** = défense passive, protection civile; **air d.,** défense aérienne. **2.** (*a*) dispositif défensif; (*of port*) **seaward defences,** ouvrages de défense face à la mer; (*b*) *Mil: Sp: etc:* **the d.,** les défenseurs *mpl.* **3.** (*a*) défense, justification *f*; **to speak in d. of s.o.,** défendre qn; (*b*) *Jur:* défense; **counsel for the d.,** défenseur *m*; (*in civil law*) avocat *m* de la défense; **witness for the d.,** témoin *m* à décharge; **to conduct one's own d.,** défendre soi-même sa cause.

defenceless, *NAm:* **defenseless** [di'fenslis] *a.* sans défense.

defend [di'fend] *v.tr.* **1.** défendre, protéger (**from, against,** contre). **2.** défendre, justifier (une opinion). **3.** *Jur:* défendre (un accusé); assumer, soutenir, la défense de (qn). **defending** *a.* **d. champion,** champion, -ionne, en titre.

defendant [di'fendənt] *a. & n. Jur:* (*a*) défendeur, -eresse; (*b*) (*on appeal*) intimé, -ée; (*c*) (*in criminal case*) accusé, -ée.

defender [di'fendər] *n.* défenseur *m.*

defense [di'fens] *n. NAm:* = DEFENCE.

defensible [di'fensəbl] *a.* **1.** (cause) défendable; (position) tenable. **2.** (opinion) justifiable, soutenable.

defensive [di'fensiv] **1.** *a.* défensif, de défense; *Mil: etc:* **d. action,** action défensive; **d. position,** position de défense. **2.** *n.* défensive *f*; **to be on the d.,** se tenir sur la défensive.

defer¹ [di'fə:r] *v.* **(deferred)** *v.tr.* (*a*) différer, ajourner, remettre (une affaire); reculer (un paiement); suspendre (un jugement); **to d. sth. to a later date,** remettre, reporter, qch. à plus tard; (*b*) *Mil: etc:* mettre (qn) en sursis (d'appel); **to d. s.o. on medical grounds,** réformer qn. **deferred** *a.* (*of share, etc.*) différé; **d. payment,** paiement (i) différé, (ii) par versements échelonnés.

defer² *v.i.* déférer (**to s.o.'s opinion,** à l'opinion de qn); se soumettre (**to s.o.'s wishes,** à la volonté de qn).

deference ['defərəns] *n.* déférence *f*; **to pay, show, d. to s.o.,** témoigner de la déférence à, envers, qn.; **in, out of, d. to . . .,** par déférence pour . . ..

deferential [defə'renʃ(ə)l] *a.* (air, ton) de déférence;

respectueux; **to be d. to s.o.,** se montrer plein de déférence envers qn. **-ally** *adv.* avec déférence.
deferment [di'fə:mənt] *n.* (*a*) ajournement *m*, remise *f* (d'une affaire); (*b*) *Mil: etc:* réformation *f* (pour raison de santé); **to apply for d. (of call up),** faire une demande de sursis (d'appel).
defiance [di'faiəns] *n.* défi *m*; **to bid d. to s.o.,** lancer un défi à qn; **in d. of,** au mépris de (la loi, un ordre).
defiant [di'faiənt] *a.* (*a*) provocant; (regard, parole) de défi; (*b*) intraitable; réfractaire. **-ly** *adv.* d'un air, d'un ton, provocant; d'un air de défi.
deficiency [di'fiʃənsi] *n.* **1.** manque *m*, insuffisance *f* (**of,** de). **2.** défaut *m*, imperfection *f*. **3.** (*a*) manquant *m*, déficit *m*; *Com:* découvert *m*; (*b*) déficit budgétaire; découvert. **4.** *Med:* carence *f* (**in, of,** de); déficience *f*.
deficient [di'fiʃənt] *a.* (*a*) défectueux, insuffisant, incomplet; **to be d. in sth.,** manquer de qch., être dépourvu de qch.; **mentally d.,** arriéré.
deficit ['defisit] *n.* *Fin: Com:* déficit *m*; découvert *m*; **budget that shows a d.,** budget déficitaire; **to make up the d.,** combler le déficit.
defile¹ ['di:fail] *n.* défilé *m*.
defile² [di'fail] *v.i.* *Mil: etc:* (*of troops, etc.*) défiler.
defile³ *v.tr.* souiller (qch., la mémoire de qn); salir (qch.); profaner (un lieu saint).
defilement [di'failmənt] *n.* **1.** souillure *f*; profanation *f* (d'un lieu saint). **2.** souillure, salissure *f*.
definable [di'fainəbl] *a.* définissable; déterminable.
define [di'fain] *v.tr.* **1.** définir (un mot, un objet). **2.** préciser (son attitude politique, etc.); formuler (sa position). **3.** déterminer (l'étendue, les limites, de qch.); délimiter (des pouvoirs); **well-defined limits,** limites bien déterminées. **4. well-defined outlines,** contours nettement dessinés, nettement dégagés.
definite ['definit] *a.* **1.** défini; bien déterminé; (réponse) précise, catégorique; *Com:* (commande) ferme; **at a d. time,** à une heure déterminée; **you are not d. enough,** vous ne précisez pas assez. **2.** *Gram:* (article) défini; **past d.,** passé défini. **-ly** *adv.* précisément; nettement; catégoriquement; **d. superieur,** nettement supérieur; **he is d. better,** il va décidément mieux; **he is d. mad,** il n'y a pas de doute qu'il est fou; **are you going? – d.!** est-ce que vous y allez?—bien sûr que oui!
definition [defi'niʃ(ə)n] *n.* **1.** définition *f*; **by d.,** par définition; **to give the d. of sth.,** donner la définition de, définir, qch. **2.** (*a*) *Opt:* netteté *f* (de l'image); (*b*) *TV:* définition.
definitive [di'finitiv] *a.* (*of verdict, result*) définitif; **d. edition,** édition définitive **-ly** *adv.* définitivement; en définitive.
deflate [di:'fleit] **1.** *v.tr.* (*a*) dégonfler (un ballon, un pneu); (*b*) *Pol.Ec:* **to d. the currency,** *v.i.* **to d.,** amener la déflation de la monnaie; (*c*) *F:* remettre (qn) à sa place. **2.** *v.i.* (*of tyre, etc.*) se dégonfler.
deflation [di:'fleiʃ(ə)n] *n.* **1.** dégonflement *m* (d'un ballon, d'un pneu). **2.** *Fin:* déflation *f*.
deflationary [di:'fleiʃən(ə)ri] *a.* *Pol.Ec:* (politique, etc.) de déflation; (mesure) déflationniste.
deflect [di'flekt] **1.** *v.tr.* (faire) dévier; détourner, défléchir; *Artil:* (*of projectile*) **to be deflected,** dériver. **2.** *v.i.* (se) dévier, se détourner, défléchir.
deflection [di'flekʃ(ə)n] *n.* **1.** déflexion *f* (de la lumière); déviation *f* (de l'aiguille du compas). **2.** *El: Elcs:* (*of voltmeter, etc.*) déviation, déflexion.
deflector [di'flektər] *n.* *Tchn:* déflecteur *m*; **sound d.,** abat-son *m inv.*
deflower [di:flauər] *v.tr.* **1.** déflorer (une vierge). **2.** défleurir (une plante, etc.).
defoliant [di:'fouliənt] *n.* défoliant *m*.
defoliate [di:'foulieit] *v.tr.* défeuiller (des arbres, etc.).
defoliation [di:fouli'eiʃ(ə)n] *n.* défoliation *f*.
deforest [di:'fɔrist] *v.tr.* déboiser.
deform [di'fɔ:m] *v.tr.* **1.** défigurer, enlaidir (qn, qch.). **2.** déformer; *Mec.E:* fausser (une poutre, etc.).
deformation [di:fɔ:'meiʃ(ə)n] *n.* **1.** défiguration *f*. **2.** déformation *f* (d'un os, etc.).
deformity [di'fɔ:miti] *n.* difformité *f*.
defraud [di'frɔ:d] *v.tr.* **1.** frauder (le fisc, etc.). **2.** (*a*) *Jur:* léser (qn); (*b*) **to d. s.o. of sth.,** frustrer qn de qch.; escroquer qch. à qn.
defrauder [di'frɔ:dər] *n.* fraudeur, -euse.
defray [di'frei] *v.tr.* **to d. s.o.'s expenses,** rembourser les frais de qn; **to d. the cost of sth.,** couvrir les frais de qch.
defreeze [di:'fri:z] *v.tr.* décongeler.
defrost [di:'frɔst] *v.tr.* **1.** dégivrer (un réfrigérateur, etc.). **2.** décongeler (la viande, etc.).
deft [deft] *a.* adroit; **with a d. hand,** d'une main exercée. **-ly** *adv.* adroitement; d'une main exercée.
deftness ['deftnis] *n.* adresse *f*, habileté *f*, dextérité *f*.
defunct [di'fʌŋkt] *a.* défunt, -e; décédé, -ée; *n.* **the d.,** le défunt, la défunte.
defuse [di:'fju:z] *v.tr.* désamorcer (une bombe, *Fig:* une crise).
defy [di'fai] *v.tr.* défier (qn); mettre (qn) au défi; braver (qn, un ordre, la loi); **to d. description,** échapper à toute description.
degenerate¹ [di'dʒen(ə)rət] *a.* & *n.* dégénéré, -ée.
degenerate² [di'dʒenəreit] *v.i.* dégénérer (**from,** de; **into,** en).
degeneration [didʒenə'reiʃ(ə)n] *n.* dégénérescence *f*, dégénération *f*; *Med:* **fatty d.,** dégénérescence graisseuse.
degradation [degrə'deiʃ(ə)n] *n.* **1.** *Mil:* dégradation *f*. **2.** avilissement *m*, dégradation *f*; **to live a life of d.,** vivre dans la dégradation. **3.** *Geol:* désagrégation *f*; *Ph:* dégradation.
degrade [di'greid] *v.tr.* (*a*) dégrader, casser (un officier, etc.); (*b*) avilir, dégrader (qn); (*c*) *Ph:* dégrader (l'énergie); *Geol:* désagréger (des roches). **degrading** *a.* avilissant, dégradant.
degree [di'gri:] *n.* **1.** (*a*) degré *m*; **to some, to a certain, d.,** à un certain degré; (jusqu')à un certain point; **to, in, a high d.,** éminemment; **in the highest d.,** au plus haut, au dernier, degré; **to such a d. that . . .,** à tel point que . . .; **by degrees,** par degrés; *Gram:* **d. of comparison,** degré de comparaison; *Ph:* **d. of humidity,** titre *m* d'eau, d'humidité; *Jur:* **marriage within the prohibited, forbidden, degrees,** mariage *m* entre parents ou alliés au degré prohibé; (*b*) *F:* **third d.,** passage *m* à tabac; **to put a prisoner through the third d.,** passer un accusé à tabac; *Med:* **third-d. burns,** brûlures du troisième degré; (*c*) *Ph: Geog: etc:* degré (d'un cercle, de latitude, de température); **angle of 30 degrees,** angle *m* de 30 degrés: **ten degrees of frost,** dix degrés au-dessous de zéro; (*d*) *Mth:* **equation of the second, third, d.,** équation *f* du second, troisième, degré. **2.** *Sch:* grade *m* (universitaire); **bachelor's d.** = licence *f* (ès lettres, etc.).
dehumanize [di:'hju:mənaiz] *v.tr.* déshumaniser.
dehydrate [di:'haidreit] *v.tr.* déshydrater; **to become dehydrated,** se déshydrater.
dehydration [di:hai'dreiʃ(ə)n] *n.* déshydratation *f*.
de-ice [di:'ais] *v.tr.* dégivrer.
de-icer [di:'aisər] *n.* dégivreur *m*.
deification [di:ifi'keiʃ(ə)n, dei-] *n.* déification *f*.
deify ['di:ifai, dei-] *v.tr.* déifier (qn).
deign [dein] *v.tr.* **to d. to do sth.,** daigner faire qch.; condescendre à faire qch.; **without deigning to look at me,** sans daigner me regarder.

deity ['di:iti, dei-] *n.* **1.** divinité *f* (de Jésus-Christ, etc.). **2.** (*a*) dieu *m*, déesse *f*; déité *f*, divinité; (*b*) *Theol:* **the D.,** la Divinité; Dieu *m*.
deject [di'dʒekt] *v.tr.* abattre, décourager (qn). **dejected** *a.* abattu, découragé; **to become d.,** se décourager. **dejectedly** *adv.* d'un air abattu, découragé.
dejection [di'dʒekʃ(ə)n] *n.* découragement *m*.
de jure ['di:'dʒuəri] *Lt. adv. phr.* de jure.
dekko ['dekou] *n. P:* coup *m* d'œil; **let's have a d.,** fais, faites, voir.
delay¹ [di'lei] *n.* **1.** sursis *m*; délai *m*, retard *m*; **without d.,** sans délai; **without (any) further d.,** sans plus tarder; **an hour's d.,** une heure de retard. **2.** retardement *m*, entrave *f* (du progrès); **the road works caused traffic delays,** les travaux *mpl* ont retardé, entravé, la circulation.
delay² **1.** *v.tr.* (*a*) retarder, remettre (son départ); différer, arriérer (un paiement); **delayed-action fuse,** fusée *f* à retardement; (*b*) retenir, retarder (qn); entraver, retarder (le progrès, la circulation). **2.** *v.i.* (*a*) tarder (**in doing sth.,** à faire qch.); *Mil:* **delaying action,** action retardatrice, combat retardateur; (*b*) s'attarder.
delectable [di'lektəbl] *a.* délectable, délicieux.
delectation [di:lek'teiʃ(ə)n] *n.* délectation *f*.
delegate¹ ['deligət] *n.* délégué, -ée.
delegate² ['deligeit] *v.tr.* **1.** déléguer (qn) (**to do sth.,** pour faire qch.). **2.** déléguer (des pouvoirs).
delegation [deli'geiʃ(ə)n] *n.* **1.** (*a*) délégation *f*; (*b*) délégation (de qn). **2.** délégation; **to send a d.,** envoyer une délégation.
delete [di'li:t] *v.tr.* effacer, rayer (un mot, etc.); (*on form*) **d. where inapplicable,** rayer les mentions inutiles.
deleterious [deli'tiəriəs] *a.* nuisible (à la santé).
deletion [di'li:ʃ(ə)n] *n.* **1.** suppression *f* (d'un mot, d'un passage). **2.** passage effacé, supprimé.
delft [delft] *n. Cer:* faïence *f* de Delft; **d. blue,** bleu *m* de faïence.
deliberate¹ [di'lib(ə)rət] *a.* **1.** délibéré, réfléchi; intentionnel, voulu; (insolence) calculée; (insulte) préméditée. **2.** (*of pers.*) (*a*) circonspect, avisé; (*b*) lent, sans hâte. **-ly** *adv.* **1.** de propos délibéré; à dessein; avec intention; exprès. **2.** (agir) posément, délibérément.
deliberate² [di'libəreit] *v.tr. & i.* délibérer (**on,** de, sur); réfléchir (**on,** sur); **to d. over, on, a question,** délibérer une, d'une, question.
deliberation [dilibə'reiʃ(ə)n] *n.* **1.** (*a*) délibération *f*; **after due d.,** après mûre délibération; (*b*) **the deliberations of an assembly,** les débats *mpl* d'une assemblée. **2.** (*a*) **to act with d.,** agir avec circonspection, après réflexion; (*b*) sage lenteur *f*; mesure *f*; **with d.,** posément, sans hâte.
deliberative [di'libərətiv] *a.* (*of function*) délibératif; (assemblée) délibérante.
delicacy ['delikəsi] *n.* **1.** (*a*) délicatesse *f*; finesse *f* (de l'ouïe); sensibilité *f* (d'un instrument de précision); (*b*) fragilité *f* (de santé); (*c*) légèreté *f* (de touche); (*d*) tact *m*; **negotiations of the utmost d.,** négociations très délicates. **2.** mets délicat.
delicate ['delikət] *a.* **1.** (*a*) délicat; (traits) fins, délicats; **to have a d. touch,** avoir de la légèreté de touche; **d. piece of machinery,** mécanisme délicat; (*b*) (sentiments) de délicatesse. **2.** (situation) délicate, difficile; (question) épineuse; **to tread on d. ground,** toucher à des questions délicates. **3.** (santé) fragile. **-ly** *adv.* délicatement; avec délicatesse.
delicatessen [delikə'tes(ə)n] *n.* (*a*) (*shop*) épicerie fine; (*b*) plats cuisinés; = charcuterie *f*.
delicious [di'liʃəs] *a.* exquis; (mets) délicieux.
delight¹ [di'lait] *n.* **1.** délices *fpl*, délice *m*; plaisir *m*; **it is such a d. to . . .,** c'est si bon de ...; **to be s.o.'s d.,** faire le bonheur de qn. **2.** joie *f*; **much to the d. of . . ., to the great d. of . . .,** au grand plaisir de . . ., à la grande joie de . . .. **3. to take d. in (doing) sth.,** prendre grand plaisir à faire qch.
delight² **1.** *v.tr.* enchanter, ravir (qn); (*of music*) charmer (les oreilles); **I'm delighted with it,** j'en suis ravi, enchanté. **2.** *v.i.* **to d. in sth., in doing sth.,** se délecter à, de (qch.); aimer beaucoup (faire) qch. **delighted** *a.* ravi, enchanté.
delightful [di'laitf(u)l] *a.* délicieux, ravissant; charmant. **-fully** *adv.* délicieusement; **she sings d.,** elle chante à ravir.
delimit [di:'limit] *v.tr.* délimiter.
delimitation [dilimi'teiʃ(ə)n] *n.* délimitation *f*.
delineate [di'linieit] *v.tr.* (*a*) tracer (un triangle, etc.); (*b*) dessiner (les traits de qn); délinéer (un profil).
delinquency [di'liŋkwənsi] *n.* délinquance *f*; **juvenile d.,** délinquance juvénile.
delinquent [di'liŋkwənt] *a. & n.* délinquant, -ante; **juvenile d.,** délinquant juvénile.
delirious [di'liriəs] *a.* (malade) en délire, dans le délire; délirant; **to be d.,** avoir, être dans, le délire; délirer; **-ly** *adv.* frénétiquement; **d. happy,** délirant de joie.
delirium [di'liriəm] *n.* délire *m*; **d. tremens,** delirium *m* tremens.
deliver [di'livər] *v.tr.* **1.** délivrer (**s.o. from his enemies,** qn de ses ennemis); **to d. s.o. from death,** sauver qn de la mort; *Ecc:* **d. us from evil,** délivrenous du mal. **2.** (*a*) *Obst:* **to d. a woman (of a child),** (faire) accoucher une femme; (*b*) **to be delivered of a child,** accoucher d'un enfant. **3.** (*a*) **to d. sth. to s.o.,** livrer, délivrer, qch. à qn; (*b*) **to d. up,** restituer, rendre (**to,** à); (*c*) **to d. over,** céder, transférer, transmettre (un bien, etc.) (**to** à). **4.** remettre, délivrer (un paquet, un télégramme, etc.); distribuer (des lettres); livrer (des marchandises); *Jur:* signifier (un acte); **to d. a message,** faire une commission; **to d. sth. at s.o.'s house,** livrer qch. à domicile; *Com:* **delivered free,** livraison franco; **to d. the goods,** (i) livrer les marchandises; (ii) *F:* remplir ses engagements. **5.** porter, donner (un coup); lancer (la balle, etc.); *Navy:* lâcher (une bordée). **6.** faire, prononcer (un discours); faire (une conférence); *Jur:* prononcer, rendre (un jugement). **7.** (*of machine, dynamo, etc.*) débiter, fournir (du courant).
deliverance [di'liv(ə)rəns] *n.* délivrance *f* (**from,** de).
deliverer [di'livərər] *n.* **1.** libérateur, -trice; sauveur *m*. **2.** livreur *m* (de marchandises).
delivery [di'liv(ə)ri] *n.* **1.** *Obst:* accouchement *m* (d'une femme). **2.** reddition *f* (d'un prisonnier). **3.** (*a*) exécution *f* (d'une commission); (*b*) livraison *f* (d'un paquet, etc.); remise *f* (d'une lettre); distribution *f* (des lettres); *Jur:* signification *f* (d'un acte); **charge for d.,** (frais *mpl* de) port (*m*); *U.S:* **general d.,** poste restante; **parcels awaiting d.,** colis *mpl* en souffrance; **d. note,** bulletin *m* de livraison; **free d.,** livraison franco; **d. man, boy, girl,** livreur, -euse; **to pay on d.,** payer à, sur, livraison; **d. date,** date *f* de livraison; (*c*) *Fin:* cession *f*, remise (de titres); (*of stocks*) **for d.,** au comptant; (*d*) *Jur:* tradition *f* (d'un bien); délivrance (d'un legs, etc.) (**to,** à). **4.** (*a*) *Games:* (i) lancement *m*, envoi *m* (de la balle); (ii) manière *f* de lancer (la balle); (*b*) *Mil:* lancement (d'une fusée, etc.). **5.** (*a*) prononciation *f* (d'un discours); (*b*) diction *f* (d'un orateur); **to have a good d.,** avoir un bon débit. **6.** débit (d'eau, de courant, etc.); refoulement *m* (d'une pompe).
dell [del] *n.* vallon *m*.
delouse [di:'laus] *v.tr.* ôter les poux de (qch., qn); épouiller (qn).
delphinium [del'finiəm] *n. Bot:* pied-d'alouette *m*, *pl.* pieds-d'alouette.
delta ['deltə] *n.* **1.** *Gr.Alph:* delta *m inv.* **2.** *Geog:*

delta *m*, *pl.* deltas. **3.** *Av:* **d. wing,** aile *f* (en) delta.
delude [di'l(j)uːd] *v.tr.* tromper (qn); induire (qn) en erreur; **to d. oneself,** se faire des illusions.
deluge¹ ['deljuːdʒ] *n.* déluge *m*; (*a*) **a d. of rain,** une pluie diluvienne; (*b*) déluge (de paroles); avalanche *f* (de lettres, etc.).
deluge² *v.tr.* inonder (**with,** de).
delusion [di'luːʒ(ə)n] *n.* illusion *f*; **to be under a d.,** se faire illusion; s'abuser; **to suffer from delusions,** être sujet à des hallucinations; **delusions of grandeur,** folie *f* des grandeurs.
de luxe [di'lʌks] *a.* de luxe; (appartement) (de) grand standing.
delve [delv] *v.i.* fouiller; **to d. into one's pocket,** fouiller dans sa poche; **to d. into the past,** remonter dans le passé.
demagnetize [diː'mægnitaiz] *v.tr.* démagnétiser.
demagogic [demə'gɔgik] *a.* démagogique.
demagogue ['deməgɔg] *n.* démagogue *m.*
demand¹ [di'mɑːnd] *n.* **1.** demande *f*, réclamation *f*; **payable on d.,** payable sur demande; **d. note,** avertissement *m*. **2.** *Pol.E:* demande; **supply and d.,** l'offre *f* et la demande; **to be in (great, little) d.,** être (très, peu) demandé, recherché. **3. demands,** nécessités *fpl*; exigences *fpl;* **to make great demands on s.o.'s patience,** exiger de qn beaucoup de patience; **I have many demands on my time,** je suis très pris.
demand² *v.tr.* **1. to d. sth. of, from, s.o.,** réclamer qch. à qn; **to d. to know whether . . .,** insister pour savoir si . . .; **to d. that . . .,** exiger que + *sub.* **2.** (*of thg*) demander, exiger; **the matter demands great care,** l'affaire *f* exige, réclame, beaucoup de soin. **demanding** *a.* (*a*) exigeant; (*b*) revendicatif.
demarcation [diːmɑː'keiʃ(ə)n] *n.* démarcation *f*; délimitation *f*; **line of d.,** ligne de démarcation; *Ind:* **d. dispute,** conflit *m* d'attributions.
demean [di'miːn] *v.pr.* **to d. oneself,** s'abaisser, s'avilir.
demeanour, *NAm:* **demeanor** [di'miːnər] *n.* comportement *m*; attitude *f*, conduite *f*; maintien *m*.
demented [di'mentid] *a.* fou, *f.* folle; dément; **to become d.,** tomber en démence; *F:* **like one d.,** (hurler, etc.) comme un fou.
dementia [di'menʃiə] *n. Med:* démence *f*; **senile d.,** démence sénile.
demerara [demə'rɛərə] *n.* **d. (sugar)** = cassonade *f.*
demerit [diː'merit] *n.* démérite *m*; tort *m.*
demesne [də'mein] *n.* **1.** *Jur:* possession *f.* **2.** domaine *m.*
demigod ['demigɔd] *n.* demi-dieu *m*, *pl.* demi-dieux.
demijohn ['demidʒɔn] *n. Ind: etc:* dame-jeanne *f*, *pl.* dames-jeannes; bonbonne *f.*
demilitarization [diːmilit(ə)rai'zeiʃ(ə)n] *n.* démilitarisation *f.*
demilitarize [diː'militəraiz] *v.tr.* démilitariser.
demise¹ [di'maiz] *n.* **1.** *Jur:* cession *f* (i) à bail, (ii) par testament; transfert *m* (d'un titre, etc.). **2.** *Adm:* décès *m*, mort *f* (de qn).
demise² *v.tr. Jur:* céder (i) à bail, (ii) par testament; transmettre (un titre, etc.).
demisemiquaver ['demisemikweivər] *n. Mus:* triple croche *f.*
demist [diː'mist] *v.tr.* désembuer.
demister [diː'mistər] *n. Aut:* (dispositif *m*) antibuée (*m*).
demo ['demo] *n. F:* manif *f.*
demob [di'mɔb] *F:* **1.** *v.tr.* **(demobbed)** démobiliser. **2.** *n.* démobilisation *f.*
demobilization [diːmoubilai'zeiʃ(ə)n] *n.* démobilisation *f.*
demobilize [diː'moubilaiz] *v.tr. & i.* démobiliser.
democracy [di'mɔkrəsi] *n.* démocratie *f*; **people's d.,** démocratie populaire; **social d.,** social-démocratie *f.*
democrat ['deməkræt] *n.* démocrate *mf*; **social d.,** social-démocrate *mf*, *m.pl.* sociaux-démocrates; *U.S:* **the Democrats,** le parti démocrate.
democratic [demə'krætik] *a.* démocratique; *U.S:* **D. Party,** parti *m* démocrate. **-ally** *adv.* démocratiquement.
democratize [di'mɔkrətaiz] **1.** *v.tr.* démocratiser. **2.** *v.i.* se démocratiser.
demographer [di'mɔgrəfər] *n.* démographe *mf.*
demographic [demou'græfik] *a.* démographique.
demography [di'mɔgrəfi] *n.* démographie *f.*
demolish [di'mɔliʃ] *v.tr.* démolir; démanteler (des fortifications, etc.); **he had soon demolished most of the cake,** il eut bientôt dévoré les trois quarts du gâteau.
demolition [demə'liʃ(ə)n, diː-] *n.* démolition *f*; **d. contractor,** démolisseur *m.*
demon ['diːmən] *n.* démon, diable *m*; **the D.,** le Démon; *F:* **that child's a little d.,** cet enfant est un petit démon; **he's a d. for work,** c'est un travailleur acharné.
demonetize [di'mʌnitaiz] *v.tr.* démonétiser (une monnaie).
demoniac [di'mouniæk] *a. & n.* démoniaque (*mf*).
demoniacal [diːmə'naiəkl] *a.* démoniaque.
demonology [diːmə'nɔlədʒi] *n.* démonologie *f.*
demonstrable [di'mɔnstrəbl, 'demən-] *a.* démontrable. **-ably** *adv.* **statement d. true, false,** affirmation *f* dont la vérité, la fausseté, peut être prouvée.
demonstrate ['demənstreit] **1.** *v.tr.* (*a*) démontrer (une vérité); (*b*) décrire, expliquer (un système); donner une démonstration pratique du fonctionnement (d'un appareil). **2.** *v.i. Pol: etc:* manifester; faire une manifestation.
demonstration [demən'streiʃ(ə)n] *n.* **1.** (*a*) démonstration *f* (d'une vérité); (*b*) démonstration pratique (d'un appareil); **d. car,** voiture *f* de démonstration; (*c*) *Sch:* **d. (class, lecture),** (séance *f* de) démonstration. **2.** manifestation *f* (politique, etc.); **to hold a d.,** manifester.
demonstrative [di'mɔnstrətiv] *a.* **1.** (argument, etc.) démonstratif. **2.** (*of pers.*) démonstratif, expansif. **3.** *Gram:* (adjectif, etc.) démonstratif.
demonstrator ['demənstreitər] *n.* **1.** démonstrateur, -trice. **2.** manifestant, -ante (politique, etc.).
demoralization [dimɔrəlai'zeiʃ(ə)n] *n.* démoralisation *f.*
demoralize [di'mɔrəlaiz] *v.tr.* démoraliser (les troupes, etc.). **demoralizing** *a.* (échec, etc.) démoralisant.
demote [di'mout] *v.tr.* réduire à un grade inférieur, à une classe inférieure; rétrograder.
demotic [di'mɔtik] *a.* populaire; du peuple.
demotion [di'mouʃ(ə)n] *n.* réduction *f* à un grade inférieur, une classe inférieure; rétrogradation *f.*
demur¹ [di'məːr] *n.* hésitation *f*; **without d.,** sans faire d'objection; sans hésitation.
demur² *v.i.* **(demurred) 1.** soulever des objections (**at, to,** contre). **2.** *Jur:* opposer une exception.
demure [di'mjuər] *a.* (*of young women*) **1.** posé(e); modeste, réservé(e). **2.** d'une modestie affectée. **-ly** *adv.* **1.** d'un air posé. **2.** avec une modestie affectée.
demureness [di'mjuənis] *n.* **1.** modestie *f* (d'une jeune fille). **2.** modestie *f* affectée.
den [den] *n.* **1.** tanière *f*, antre *m*, repaire *m* (de bêtes féroces); *F:* nid *m* (de brigands); **d. of thieves,** retraite *f* de voleurs; **d. of vice,** lieu *m* de débauche. **2.** cabinet *m* de travail; fumoir *m*. **3.** bouge *m*; **gambling d.,** maison *f* de jeu; **opium d.,** fumerie *f* d'opium.
denationalization [diːnæʃnəlai'zeiʃ(ə)n] *n.* dénationalisation *f.*
denationalize [diː'næʃnəlaiz] *v.tr.* dénationaliser.
denature [diː'neitjər] *v.tr.* dénaturer (un produit).

dengue ['deŋgi] *n. Med:* **d. (fever),** dengue *f.*
denial [di'naiəl] *n.* **1.** refus *m* (d'un droit, d'une demande); **d. of justice,** déni de justice. **2.** démenti *m* (de la vérité de qch.); **absolute, flat, d.,** dénégation absolue. **3.** *B:* **Peter's d.,** le reniement de Pierre. **4.** *Mil:* interdiction *f* (d'une zone, de survol, etc.).
denier ['deniər] *n. Tex:* (*hosiery*) denier *m*; **a 30 d. stocking,** un bas 30 deniers.
denigrate ['denigreit] *v.tr. Lit:* dénigrer (qn, un projet).
denim ['denim] *n.* **1.** *Tex:* (toile *f* de) jean *m*; **d. skirt,** jupe *f* en jean. **2.** *Cost:* **denims,** (i) bleus *mpl* (de travail); (ii) (blue-)jeans *mpl.*
denizen ['deniz(ə)n] *n. Poet:* habitant, -ante.
Denmark ['denmɑːk] *Pr.n. Geog:* Danemark *m.*
denominate [di'nɔmineit] *n. v.tr.* dénommer.
denomination [dinɔmi'neiʃ(ə)n] *n.* **1.** denomination *f.* **2.** *Rel:* culte *m*, confession *f.* **3.** valeur *f*; **coins of all denominations,** pièces *fpl* de toutes valeurs; **(notes of) small denominations,** petites coupures.
denominator [di'nɔmineitər] *n. Mth:* dénominateur *m*; **common d.,** dénominateur commun.
denote [di'nout] *v.tr.* **1.** dénoter, montrer; indiquer (**sth.,** qch.; **that,** que). **2.** signifier.
denounce [di'nauns] *v.tr.* **1.** (*a*) dénoncer (un criminel, un crime); **to d. s.o. to the authorities,** signaler qn à la justice; (*b*) **to d. s.o. as an impostor,** taxer qn d'imposture. **2.** s'élever contre (un abus); condamner (l'art moderne, etc.). **3.** dénoncer (un traité).
dense [dens] *a.* **1.** *Ph:* (*of body, metal, etc.*) dense. **2.** (*of smoke, fog, etc.*) épais, -aisse; (foule) compacte; (population) nombreuse. **3.** stupide, bête. **-ly** *adv.* **d. wooded country,** pays couvert de forêts épaisses; **d. populated region,** région très peuplée.
denseness ['densnis] *n.* **1.** épaisseur *f* (du brouillard). **2.** (*of pers.*) stupidité *f.*
density ['densiti] *n.* **1.** *Ph: Ch: El: etc:* densité *f*; *Atom.Ph:* **ion, neutron, d.,** densité ionique, neutronique. **2.** densité (de la population, de la circulation routière). **3.** (*of pers.*) stupidité *f.*
dent¹ [dent] *n.* (*a*) bossellement *m*, bosselure *f* (d'une théière, etc.); creux *m*, renfoncement *m*; (*b*) **to make a d. in one's fortune,** faire une brèche à sa fortune.
dent² *v.tr.* bosseler, bossuer, cabosser. **dented** *a.* bosselé, cabossé; *Aut:* **d. wing,** aile bosselée, faussée.
dental ['dent(ə)l] *a.* **1.** dentaire; **d. surgeon,** chirurgien *m* dentiste; **d. practice, surgery,** *NAm:* **office,** cabinet *m* de dentiste. **2.** *Ling:* dental, -aux; **d. consonant,** (consonne) dentale (*f*).
dentifrice ['dentifris] *n.* dentifrice *m.*
dentist ['dentist] *n.* dentiste *mf*; **to go to the dentist's,** aller chez le dentiste.
dentistry ['dentistri] *n.* dentisterie *f.*
dentition [den'tiʃ(ə)n] *n.* dentition *f.*
denture ['dentjər] *n.* dentier *m*; prothèse *f* dentaire.
denude [di'njuːd] *v.tr.* dénuder, dépouiller (qch.).
denunciation [dinʌnsi'eiʃ(ə)n] *n.* **1.** dénonciation *f* (d'un complice, etc.). **2.** (*a*) condamnation *f* (d'un abus, de l'art moderne, etc.); (*b*) accusation publique (de qn). **3.** dénonciation (d'un traité).
deny [di'nai] *v.tr.* **1.** nier (un fait, une vérité); démentir (une nouvelle); repousser (une accusation); opposer un démenti à (une déclaration); **the accused denies the charge,** l'accusé nie; **to d. having done sth.,** nier avoir fait qch.; **there is no denying the fact,** c'est un fait indéniable; **there's no denying that . . .,** on ne saurait nier que . . .. **2.** renier (qn, sa foi). **3.** refuser (une prière, etc.); **to d. s.o. sth., sth. to s.o.,** refuser qch. à qn; **to be denied one's request,** se voir refuser sa demande. **4.** (*a*) **to d. oneself sth.,** se priver de qch.; (*b*) **to d. oneself for one's children,** se priver pour ses enfants.
deodorant [diː'oudərənt] *a. & n. Hyg:* déodorant (*m*), désodorisant (*m*).
deodorize [diː'oudəraiz] *v.tr.* désodoriser.
deoxidize [diː'ɔksidaiz] *v.tr. Ch: Ind:* désoxyder.
depart [di'pɑːt] *v.i.* **1.** (*a*) partir; **to d. from a place,** quitter un lieu; (*b*) **to d. (from) this life,** quitter cette vie, ce monde. **2. to d. from (sth.),** se départir, s'écarter, de (son devoir); déroger à (un usage); sortir de, s'écarter de (son sujet); manquer à (la vérité). **departed** *a.* **1.** (*of glory, etc.*) passé, évanoui. **2.** mort, défunt, décédé; *n.* **the d.,** le mort, la morte.
department [di'pɑːtmənt] *n.* **1.** (*a*) *Adm: etc:* département *m*, service *m*; **personnel, accounts, d.,** service du personnel, de la comptabilité; (*in hospital*) **outpatients' d.,** service des consultations externes; **head of d.,** chef *m* de service; (*b*) *Com:* (*in shop*) rayon *m*; comptoir *m*; **glove d.,** rayon des gants; **d. store,** grand magasin; (*d*) **that's not (really) my d.,** ce n'est pas mon rayon. **2.** ministère *m*; **D. of Education and Science** = Ministère de l'Éducation; *U.S:* **War D.,** Ministère de la Guerre. **3.** *Geog:* (*in Fr.*) département.
departmental [diːpɑːt'ment(ə)l] *a.* départemental, -aux; **d. manager,** chef *m* de service.
departure [di'pɑːtjər] *n.* **1.** départ *m* (de qn, d'un train, etc.); **d. time,** heure *f* de départ; *Av:* **d. lounge,** salle *f* de départ; **to take one's d.,** partir; prendre congé. **2.** déviation *f* (**from a principle,** d'un principe); exception *f* (à la règle générale); manquement *m* (à la vérité); **a d. from his usual habits,** action *f* contraire à ses habitudes. **3. a new d.,** une nouvelle tendance, direction, orientation.
depend [di'pend] *v.i.* **1.** dépendre (**on,** de); **that depends entirely on you,** cela ne tient qu'à vous; **that depends, it all depends,** ça dépend; **depending on whether . . .,** suivant que . . .. **2.** (*a*) **to d. on s.o.,** être à la charge de qn; (*b*) **to d. on imports from abroad,** être tributaire de l'étranger. **3. to d. on s.o., sth.,** compter sur qn, qch.; **you can d. on him,** vous pouvez avoir confiance en lui; **you can never d. on what he says,** on ne peut pas se fier à ce qu'il dit.
dependability [dipendə'biliti] *n.* (*a*) confiance *f* que l'on inspire; (*b*) sécurité *f* (de fonctionnement).
dependable [di'pendəbl] *a.* (*of pers.*) digne de confiance; (*of information*) sûr; (machine) d'un fonctionnement sûr; **he is not d.,** on ne peut pas compter sur lui.
dependant [di'pendənt] *n.* (*a*) pensionnaire *mf* (de qn); (*b*) personne *f* à charge; **dependants,** charges *fpl* de famille.
dependence [di'pendəns] *n.* **1. d. on s.o., on sth.,** dépendance *f* de qn, de qch. **2.** confiance *f* (**on,** en). **3.** *Med:* (état *m* de) dépendance (d'une drogue).
dependency [di'pendənsi] *n.* dépendance, annexe *f* (d'une ville, d'un État).
dependent [di'pendənt] *a.* (*a*) dépendant (**on,** de); sujet (**on,** à); *Jur:* relevant (**on,** de); **to be d. on s.o., on sth.,** dépendre, relever, de qn, de; qch.; **institution d. on voluntary contributions,** institution soutenue par des contributions bénévoles; (*b*) *Gram:* (proposition) subordonnée; (*c*) **to be d. on s.o.,** être à la charge de qn; **two d. children,** deux enfants à charge; (*d*) *Med:* adonné (**on a drug,** à une drogue).
depict [di'pikt] *v.tr.* dépeindre, représenter.
depiction [di'pikʃ(ə)n] *n.* peinture *f*, description *f.*
depilate ['depileit] *v.tr. Toil:* épiler.
depilatory [di'pilətəri] *a. & n. Toil:* (crème, etc.) épilatoire (*m*).
deplane [diː'plein] *v.i.* descendre d'avion.
deplete [di'pliːt] *v.tr.* (*a*) épuiser (des provisions, etc.); **the stock is very depleted,** les stocks sont très bas; (*b*) démunir (une garnison de ses troupes).
depletion [di'pliːʃ(ə)n] *n.* épuisement *m*, diminution *f.*
deplorable [di'plɔːrəbl] *a.* déplorable, lamentable. **-ably** *adv.* déplorablement, lamentablement.

deplore [di'plɔːr] *v.tr.* déplorer; regretter vivement.
deploy [di'plɔi] *Mil: etc:* **1.** *v.tr.* déployer (une unité); articuler (des troupes sur le terrain). **2.** *v.i.* se déployer; (*of troops*) s'articuler (sur le terrain).
deployment [di'plɔimənt] *n. Mil: etc:* déploiement *m* (d'une unité); articulation *f* (de troupes sur le terrain).
depolarization [diːpouləraiˈzeiʃ(ə)n] *n. Opt: El:* dépolarisation *f.*
depolarize [diːˈpouləraiz] *v.tr. Opt: El:* dépolariser.
deponent [di'pounənt] *a. & n.* **1.** *Gram:* (verbe) déponent (*m*). **2.** *Jur:* (témoin) déposant (*m*).
depopulate [diːˈpɔpjuleit] *v.tr.* dépeupler.
depopulation [diːpɔpjuˈleiʃ(ə)n] *n.* dépopulation *f*, dépeuplement *m* (d'un pays).
deport [di'pɔːt] *v.tr.* (*a*) expulser (un étranger); (*b*) déporter (un condamné politique, etc.).
deportation [diːpɔˈteiʃ(ə)n] *n.* (*a*) expulsion *f* (d'un étranger); **d. order,** arrêté *m* d'expulsion; (*b*) déportation *f* (d'un condamné politique, etc.).
deportment [di'pɔːtmənt] *n.* tenue *f*, maintien *m.*
depose [di'pouz] *v.tr.* **1.** déposer (un roi, etc.). **2.** *Jur:* (*a*) déposer, attester (**that,** que + *ind.*); (*b*) *v.i.* faire une déposition.
deposit¹ [di'pɔzit] *n.* **1.** *Bank:* dépôt *m*; **bank d.,** dépôt bancaire, en banque; **on d.,** en dépôt: **d. account,** compte *m* à terme; **safe d.,** dépôt en coffre-fort. **2.** consignation *f* (d'une somme); cautionnement *m*; arrhes *fpl*; **to leave a d. on sth.,** verser une somme, un acompte, en garantie de qch.; **to pay a d.,** verser des arrhes; *Pol:* (*of candidate*) **to lose his d.** = perdre sa caution. **3.** (*a*) dépôt(s); précipité *m*; **alluvial deposits,** alluvions *fpl*; (*b*) *Geol:* gisement *m*; couche *f*; **coal d.,** gisement houiller; (*c*) *Tchn:* (*coating*) apport *m*; **d. of silver,** précipité d'argent.
deposit² *v.tr.* **1.** déposer, poser (**sth. on sth.,** qch. sur qch.). **2.** déposer (de l'argent à la banque); mettre (des documents) en dépôt (**with a bank,** dans une banque). **3.** *v.tr. & i.* (*of liquid*) déposer (un sédiment); **the flood waters deposited a layer of mud,** les inondations ont laissé un dépôt de boue.
deposition [diːpəˈziʃ(ə)n] *n.* **1.** déposition *f* (d'un roi, etc.). **2.** *Jur:* déposition, témoignage *m.*
depositor [di'pɔzitər] *n. Bank:* déposant, -ante.
depository [di'pɔzit(ə)ri] *n.* dépôt *m*, magasin *m*, entrepôt *m*; **furniture d.,** garde-meubles *m inv.*
depot ['depou] *n.* **1.** (*a*) *Mil:* dépôt *m*; **supply, ammunition, d.,** dépôt de ravitaillement, de munitions; (*b*) *Com: etc:* dépôt, entrepôt *m*; **goods d.,** dépôt des marchandises. **2.** *U.S:* (*a*) **(railroad) d.,** gare *f* (de chemin de fer); **freight d.,** gare des marchandises; (*b*) **bus d.,** gare routière.
depravation [deprəˈveiʃ(ə)n] *n.* dépravation *f.*
deprave [di'preiv] *v.tr.* dépraver. **depraved** *a.* (homme, goût) dépravé.
depravity [di'præviti] *n.* dépravation *f.*
deprecate ['deprikeit] *v.tr.* désapprouver (une action). **deprecating** *a.* désapprobateur, -trice.
depreciate [di'priːʃieit] **1.** *v.tr.* (*a*) déprécier, rabaisser (la valeur de qch.); dévaloriser (la monnaie); (*b*) *Com: Ind:* amortir (le mobilier, l'outillage, etc.). **2.** *v.i.* se déprécier; diminuer de valeur; (*of prices, shares, etc.*) baisser.
depreciation [dipriːʃiˈeiʃ(ə)n] *n.* (*a*) dépréciation *f* (de l'argent, *Ind:* du matériel, etc.); moins-value *f*; dévalorisation *f* (de la monnaie); (*b*) *Ind: Book-k:* **annual d.,** dépréciation annuelle, dénigrement *m* (d'une bonne action, de qn).
depredation [depriˈdeiʃ(ə)n] *n. usu. pl.* déprédation(s) *f*(*pl*); pillage *m.*
depress [di'pres] *v.tr.* **1.** (a)baisser (qch.); *Aut: etc:* appuyer sur (la pédale). **2.** (*a*) faire languir (le commerce); faire baisser (le prix de qch.); (*b*) déprimer, décourager (qn). **depressed** *a.* **1.** *Arch:* (arc) surbaissé. **2.** (*a*) *Com:* (marché) languissant, déprimé; **d. area,** région touchée par la crise; (*b*) (*of pers.*) déprimé; **to feel d.,** être déprimé, *F:* avoir le cafard. **depressing** *a.* déprimant; (paysage) triste. **depressingly** *adv.* d'une manière déprimante.
depression [di'preʃ(ə)n] *n.* **1.** (*a*) abaissement *m* (de qch.); *Aut:* enfoncement *m* (d'une pédale); (*b*) *Artil:* **angle of d.,** angle *m* de dépression; (*c*) *Astr:* dépression *f* (d'un astre). **2.** *Meteor:* dépression; zone *f* dépressionnaire. **3.** (*a*) dépression, enfoncement, creux *m* (de terrain). **4.** *Com:* crise *f*, affaissement *m* (des affaires); **economic d.,** dépression économique. **5.** dépression; *F:* le cafard; *Med:* **state of d.,** état dépressif.
depressive [di'presiv] *a.* dépressif.
depressurize [diːˈpreʃəraiz] *v.tr. & i. Av:* dépressuriser.
deprivation [depriˈveiʃ(ə)n] *n.* **1.** privation *f* (de droits, etc.). **2.** destitution *f* (de fonction).
deprive [di'praiv] *v.tr.* **1. to d. s.o. of sth.,** priver qn de qch., enlever qch. à qn; **to d. oneself,** s'infliger des privations. **2.** déposséder (qn) d'une charge. **deprived** *a.* (enfant) déshérité.
depth [depθ] *n.* **1.** profondeur *f* (d'une rivière, de la pensée, etc.); **in d.,** (i) en profondeur; (ii) (étudier qch.) à fond; **a study in d. of . . .,** une étude approfondie, très poussée, de . . .; **at a d. of 50 fathoms,** par 50 brasses de fond; *Oc:* **d. finder,** sondeur *m*; *Navy:* **d. charge,** grenade sous-marine. **2.** fond *m*, hauteur *f* (de l'eau); **to go, get, out of one's d.,** (i) perdre pied; (ii) *Fig:* sortir de sa compétence; **to be out of one's d.,** (i) avoir perdu pied; (ii) *Fig:* ne plus être sur son terrain. **3.** hauteur (d'un piston, etc.); épaisseur *f* (d'une couche). **4.** (*a*) gravité *f* (d'un son); (*b*) portée *f* (de l'intelligence); (*c*) vigueur *f*, intensité *f* (de coloris). **5.** fond (d'une forêt, etc.); milieu *m* (de la nuit); **in the depths of winter,** en plein hiver. **6.** *Tchn:* (*a*) *Mec.E:* **d. of cut,** profondeur de passe, de coupe (d'une machine-outil); (*b*) *Opt:* **d. of focus,** profondeur de foyer. **7. the depths,** (*a*) *Lit:* l'abîme *m*; (*b*) les profondeurs (de l'océan, etc.); les ténèbres *fpl* (de l'ignorance, etc.); **in the depths of despair,** dans le plus profond désespoir; **the lowest depths,** le dernier degré (de la honte, etc.).
deputation [depjuˈteiʃ(ə)n] *n.* **1.** députation *f*, délégation *f* (de qn). **2.** *coll.* députation.
depute [di'pjuːt] *v.tr.* **1.** déléguer (des pouvoirs) (**to s.o.,** à qn). **2.** députer, déléguer (qn) (**to do sth.,** pour faire qch.).
deputize ['depjutaiz] *v.i.* **to d. for s.o.,** faire l'intérim de qn, remplacer qn; remplir une suppléance.
deputy ['depjuti] *n.* fondé *m* de pouvoir; substitut *m*, suppléant *m* (d'un juge etc.); délégué *m* (d'un fonctionnaire); **to act as d. for s.o.,** suppléer qn; **d. governor,** sous-gouverneur *m*; **d. judge,** juge *m* suppléant; **d. manager,** sous-directeur; **d. director,** directeur adjoint.
derail [di'reil] *v.tr.* faire dérailler (un train); **to be derailed,** dérailler.
derailment [di'reilmənt] *n.* déraillement *m.*
derange [di'rein(d)ʒ] *v.tr.* **1.** dérégler, détraquer (une machine). **2.** aliéner (l'esprit); déranger le cerveau de (qn); **he, his mind, is deranged,** il a le cerveau détraqué; c'est un détraqué.
derangement [di'rein(d)ʒmənt] *n.* **1.** déréglage *m* (d'un appareil). **2. d. of mind,** dérangement *m* d'esprit; aliénation mentale.
Derby ['dɑːbi] *n.* **1.** *Sp:* (*a*) *Turf:* **the D.,** le derby d'Epsom; (*b*) **donkey D.,** course *f* d'ânes; (*c*) *Fb:* **local d.,** derby. **2.** *Cost: U.S:* ['dəːbi] chapeau *m* melon.

derelict [ˈderəlikt] **1.** *a.* abandonné; (tombé) en ruines. **2.** *n.* (*a*) *Jur:* épave *f*; *esp. Nau:* navire abandonné (en mer); épave; (*b*) délaissé, -ée; épave humaine. **3.** *a. U.S:* (*of pers.*) **to be d. (in one's duty),** être négligent de son devoir.
dereliction [deriˈlikʃ(ə)n] *n.* **1.** abandon *m*, délaissement *m*. **2. d. of duty,** négligence dans le service.
derestricted [diːriˈstriktid] *a.* (route) sans limitation de vitesse minimum.
deride [diˈraid] *v.tr.* tourner (qn, qch.) en dérision; railler, ridiculiser (qn).
derision [diˈriʒ(ə)n] *n.* dérision *f*; **object of d.,** objet *m* de risée.
derisive [diˈraisiv], **derisory** [diˈraisəri] *a.* **1.** (*of laughter*) moqueur. **2.** (offre) dérisoire. **derisively** *adv.* d'un air moqueur; d'un air, d'un ton, de dérision.
derivation [deriˈveiʃ(ə)n] *n.* **1.** dérivation *f*; **d. of a word from Latin,** dérivation d'un mot du latin **2.** *Mth:* dérivation (d'une fonction).
derivative [diˈrivətiv] **1.** *a.* & *n. Gram:* (mot) dérivé (*m*). **2.** *n.* (*a*) *Ch: Ind:* dérivé *m*; **petroleum d.,** dérivé du pétrole; (*b*) *Mth:* dérivée *f*.
derive [diˈraiv] *v.tr.* & *i.* **1.** (*a*) **to d. sth. from sth.,** tirer (son origine, etc.) de qch.; tirer (des revenus, etc.) de qch.; prendre (du plaisir) à qch.; **income derived from an investment,** revenu *m* provenant d'un placement; (*b*) *Ch:* **to d. one compound from another,** dériver un composé d'un autre; (*c*) *Ling:* (faire) dériver (un mot du latin, etc.); **word derived from Latin,** mot qui vient du latin. **2. to be derived,** *v.i.* **to d.,** dériver, (pro)venir (**from,** de).
dermatitis [dəːməˈtaitis] *n. Med:* dermite *f*, dermatite *f*.
dermatologist [dəːməˈtɔlədʒist] *n.* dermatologue *mf*, dermatologiste *mf*.
dermatology [dəːməˈtɔlədʒi] *n.* dermatologie *f*.
derogate [ˈderougeit] *v.i.* déroger (**from one's position, one's dignity, etc.,** à son rang, à sa dignité, etc.).
derogation [derouˈgeiʃ(ə)n] *n.* **1.** dérogation *f* (**of a law,** à une loi). **2. d. from a right,** atteinte portée à un droit.
derogatory [diˈrɔgət(ə)ri] *a.* **1.** dérogeant, qui déroge (**to,** à) **2.** qui abaisse (**to s.o.,** qn); (sens) péjoratif (d'un mot); **d. remark,** remarque désobligeante.
derrick [ˈderik] *n.* (*a*) derrick *m*; tour *f* de forage; (*b*) *Nau:* mât *m* de charge.
derring-do [ˈderiŋˈduː] *n. A:* bravoure *f*; **deeds of d.,** hauts faits.
derv [dəːv] *n. Aut:* gas-oil *m*.
dervish [ˈdəːviʃ] *n.* derviche *m*; **whirling, dancing, d.,** derviche tourneur.
desalinate [diːˈsælineit] *v.tr.* dessaler.
desalination [diːsæliˈneiʃ(ə)n] *n. Ind:* dessalaison *f*; dessalement *m* (de l'eau de mer).
descale [diːˈskeil] *v.tr.* détartrer.
descant [ˈdeskænt] *n. Mus:* déchant *m*; dessus *m*.
descend [diˈsend] **1.** *v.i.* (*a*) descendre; (*of rain*) tomber; **a feeling of sadness descended upon him,** un sentiment de tristesse s'empara de lui; (*b*) **to d. on s.o.,** (i) s'abattre sur qn; (ii) *F:* faire irruption chez qn; (*c*) **to d. to s.o's level, to doing sth.,** s'abaisser au niveau de qn, (jusqu')à faire qch.; (*d*) **to d., be descended, from s.o.,** descendre de qn; (*e*) (*of property, privilege*) **to d. from s.o. to s.o.,** passer de qn à qn. **2.** *v.tr.* descendre (une colline, un escalier). **descending** *a.* **1.** (*of scale, etc.*) descendant; *Mth:* (progression) décroissante; **in d. order,** en ordre décroissant. **2.** (mouvement) de descente.
descendant, -ent [diˈsendənt] *n.* descendant, -ante.
descent [diˈsent] *n.* **1.** descente *f* (d'un alpiniste, d'un aéronaute, etc.). **2.** descente, pente *f*. **3.** (*attack*) irruption *f* (**on,** dans, à, sur). **4.** (*a*) descendance *f*; **to trace one's d. back to . . .,** faire remonter sa famille à . . .. **5.** *Jur:* transmission *f* (d'un bien) par droit de succession, par héritage.
describe [disˈkraib] *v.tr.* **1.** (*a*) décrire, dépeindre (qn, qch.); (*b*) **to d. s.o., sth., as . . .,** qualifier qn, qch., de . . .; **to d. oneself as an actor,** se représenter comme acteur; (*c*) *Com:* désigner (des marchandises, etc.); (*d*) donner le signalement (d'un homme recherché par la police). **2.** décrire (une courbe, un cercle); tracer (un triangle).
description [disˈkripʃ(ə)n] *n.* **1.** (*a*) description *f* (de qn, de qch.); **beyond d.,** indescriptible; (*b*) (i) (*for police purposes*) signalement *m*; (*in a card index*) fiche *f* signalétique; (ii) (*on passport, etc.*) profession *f*; **to answer to the d.,** répondre au signalement; (iii) *Com:* désignation *f* (de marchandises). **2.** sorte *f*, espèce *f*; **people of this d.,** les gens *mpl* de cette espèce.
descriptive [disˈkriptiv] *a.* descriptif; (catalogue) raisonné.
descry [disˈkrai] *v.tr. Lit:* discerner.
desecrate [ˈdesikreit] *v.tr.* profaner, souiller.
desecration [desiˈkreiʃ(ə)n] *n.* profanation *f*.
desegregate [diːˈsegrigeit] *v.tr.* mettre fin à la ségrégation *esp.* raciale (dans un pays, une école, etc.).
desegregation [diːsegriˈgeiʃ(ə)n] *n.* déségrégation *f*.
desensitize [diːˈsensitaiz] *v.tr. Phot: Med:* désensibiliser.
desert¹ [diˈzəːt] *n. usu. pl.* mérites; *mpl*; dû *m*; **he has got his (just) deserts,** il n'a que ce qu'il mérite.
desert² [ˈdezət] **1.** *a.* (région, flore) désertique. **2.** *n.* désert *m*; **the Sahara D.,** le désert du Sahara. **3. d. rat,** (i) *Z:* gerboise *f*; (ii) *Mil: F:* (*World War II*) militaire *m* qui a fait la campagne de l'Afrique du Nord.
desert³ [diˈzəːt] *v.tr.* (*a*) déserter, quitter (un lieu); déserter, abandonner (son poste); *v.i. Mil:* déserter; **to d. from the army,** déserter l'armée; (*b*) abandonner (qn); **to d. one's party,** tourner casaque; **his courage deserted him,** son courage l'a abandonné. **deserted** *a.* (*of pers.*) abandonné; (*of place*) désert.
deserter [diˈzəːtər] *n.* déserteur *m*.
desertion [diˈzəːʃ(ə)n] *n.* **1.** abandon *m*, délaissement (de qn); *Jur:* abandon criminel de l'épouse. **2.** *Mil:* désertion *f*; abandon *m* de poste.
deserve [diˈzəːv] *v.tr.* mériter (qch.); être digne d'(éloges, etc.); **he deserves to be punished,** il mérite qu'on le punisse; **he thoroughly deserves it!** il ne l'a pas volé! **deserved** *a.* (bien) mérité. **deservedly** [diˈzəːvidli] *adv.* justement; à juste titre. **deserving** *a.* (*of pers.*) méritant, de mérite; (*of action*) méritoire.
desiccate [ˈdesikeit] *v.tr.* dessécher; **desiccated coconut,** noix de coco déshydratée.
design¹ [diˈzain] *n.* **1.** dessein *m*, intention *f*; **by d.,** à dessein; **to have designs on s.o., sth.,** avoir des desseins sur qn, qch. **2.** dessin *m* (d'ornement); (*in embroidery*) modèle *m*. **3.** (*a*) plan *m* (d'un roman, etc.); grandes lignes, ébauche *f* (d'un tableau, etc.); (*b*) *Ind: etc:* étude *f*, avant-projet *m* (d'une machine, etc.); **industrial d.,** esthétique industrielle; **d. office,** service *m* d'études. **4.** (*a*) dessin (d'une machine, etc.); **machine of faulty d.,** machine de construction fautive; (*b*) type *m*; modèle *m*; *Com:* **our latest d.,** notre dernier modèle; **d. centre,** centre *m* d'exposition (de modèles).
design² *v.tr.* **1.** destiner (**for,** à); **boats designed for river traffic,** bateaux destinés à la navigation fluviale; **machine designed for a special purpose,** machine construite dans un but spécial. **2.** (*a*) préparer (un projet); (*b*) étudier, concevoir; établir le plan (d'un bâtiment, d'un avion, etc.); créer (une robe); établir (un mécanisme, etc.); **well designed furniture,** meubles *mpl* aux lignes étudiées. **designedly** [diˈzainidli] *adv.* à dessein; exprès.
designate¹ [ˈdezigneit] *a.* (évêque, etc.) désigné.
designate² *v.tr.* (*a*) désigner, nommer (**s.o. to an office,** qn à une fonction); (*b*) **to d. s.o. as, for, one's successor,** désigner qn pour, comme, son successeur.

designation [dezig'neiʃ(ə)n] *n.* **1.** *Adm:* désignation *f* (d'une personne). **2.** désignation, nomination *f* (d'un successeur); **d. to a post,** nomination à un emploi. **3.** désignation, nom *m.*
designer [di'zainər] *n.* (*a*) *Art: Ind:* dessinateur, -trice; *Th:* **stage d.,** décorateur *m* de théâtre; (*b*) auteur *m,* inventeur, -trice (d'un projet).
desirability [dizaiərə'biliti] *n.* caractère *m* désirable; avantage *m* (d'une ligne de conduite); attrait *m* (d'une femme).
desirable [di'zaiərəbl] *a.* (*a*) désirable; souhaitable; *Com:* **d. property,** belle maison; (*b*) (*of pers., esp. of woman*) attrayant.
desire¹ [di'zaiər] *n.* (*a*) désir *m,* souhait *m;* **to have a d. to do sth.,** avoir le désir, avoir envie, de faire qch.; **I feel no d. to . . .,** je n'éprouve aucune envie de . . .; (*b*) appétit (charnel); désir.
desire² *v.tr.* **1.** (*a*) désirer (qch.); avoir envie de (qch); **to d. to do sth.,** désirer faire qch.; **it is to be desired that . . .,** il est souhaitable que + *sub.*; **it leaves much, nothing, to be desired,** cela laisse beaucoup, ne laisse rien, à désirer; (*b*) désirer (une femme). **2.** *Lit:* (*a*) **to d. sth. of s.o.,** demander qch. à qn; désirer qch. de qn; (*b*) **to d. s.o. to do sth.,** prier qn de faire qch.
desirous [di'zaiərəs] *a.* désireux (**of,** de).
desist [di'zist] *v.i. Lit:* cesser.
desk [desk] *n.* **1. (office) d.,** bureau *m;* **(writing) d.,** secrétaire *m;* **(school) d.,** pupitre *m* (d'écolier); **reading d.,** pupitre; *Ecc:* lutrin *m.* **2.** *Com:* caisse *f;* **pay at the d.,** payez à la caisse. **3.** *Cmptr: etc:* **control d.,** pupitre de commande.
desolate¹ ['desələt] *a.* désolé. **1.** abandonné. **2.** (lieu) désert, vide. **3.** (*a*) affligé(e); (*b*) (cri) de désolation. **-ly** *adv.* **1.** dans la solitude. **2.** d'un air désolé.
desolate² ['desəleit] *v.tr.* désoler. **1.** (*a*) ravager (un pays, etc.); (*b*) (*of epidemic, etc.*) dépeupler (une ville). **2.** affliger (qn).
desolation [desə'leiʃ(ə)n] *n.* **1.** désolation *f,* dévastation *f* (d'un pays vaincu, etc.). **2.** (*a*) désolation (d'un paysage, etc.); (*b*) désolation, chagrin *m.*
despair¹ [dis'pɛər] *n.* **1.** désespoir *m;* **to be in d.,** être au désespoir; **to drive s.o. to d.,** réduire qn au désespoir. **2.** *F:* **child who is the d. of his parents,** enfant qui fait le désespoir de ses parents.
despair² *v.i.* (*a*) désespérer (**of,** de); **to d. of doing sth.,** désesperer de faire qch.; **his life is despaired of,** on désespère de sa vie; (*b*) perdre espoir; (se) désespérer. **despairing** *a.* désespéré. **despairingly** *adv.* désespérément; avec désespoir.
despatch [dis'pætʃ] *n. & v.* = DISPATCH[1,2].
desperado [despə'rɑːdou] *n.m.* desperado *m,* hors-la-loi *m.*
desperate ['desp(ə)rət] *a.* **1.** (*a*) (*of condition, illness, etc.*) désespéré; sans espoir; (*b*) (remède) désespéré. **2.** (*a*) **a d. man,** un désespéré; (*b*) (lutte) désespérée; (résistance, lutte) acharnée; **to do something d.,** faire un malheur. **3.** (*intensive*) terrible, affreux. **-ly** *adv.* **1.** (lutter, etc.) désespérément. **2. d. ill,** gravement malade. **3.** éperdument; **to be d. in love with s.o.,** aimer qn à la folie; **to be d. sorry,** être navré.
desperation [despə'reiʃ(ə)n] *n.* désespoir *m;* **to drive s.o. to d.,** pousser qn à bout, réduire qn au désespoir; **in d.,** en désespoir de cause.
despicable [des'pikəbl] *a.* (conduite, action) méprisable. **-ably** *adv.* bassement.
despise [di'spaiz] *v.tr.* (*a*) mépriser (qn, qch.); (*b*) dédaigner (qch.); **these things are not to be despised,** cela n'est pas à dédaigner.
despite [dis'pait] *prep.* en dépit de, malgré (qch.); **d. what she says,** quoi qu'elle en dise.
despoil [dis'pɔil] *v.tr.* dépouiller, piller, spolier.
despondency [dis'pɔndənsi] *n.* découragement *m,* abattement *m.*
despondent [dis'pɔndənt] *a.* découragé, abattu; **to become d.,** se laisser abattre; **to feel d.,** se sentir déprimé. **-ly** *adv.* d'un air découragé, abattu.
despot ['despɔt] *n.* despote *m;* tyran *m.*
despotic [dis'pɔtik] *a.* **1.** (gouvernement, pouvoir) despotique. **2.** (*of pers.*) arbitraire, despote. **-ally** *adv.* despotiquement; arbitrairement.
despotism ['despətizm] *n.* despotisme *m.*
dessert [di'zəːt] *n.* dessert *m;* entremets sucré; **d. knife, spoon, plate,** couteau *m,* cuillère *f,* assiette *f,* à dessert; **d. wine,** vin *m* de liqueur.
destination [desti'neiʃ(ə)n] *n.* destination *f;* **to reach one's d.,** arriver à sa destination.
destine ['destin] *v.tr.* **1.** destiner (qn, qch.) (**for,** à; **to a calling,** à une carrière); **he was destined for the Church,** il fut destiné à l'église. **2.** (*usu. in pass.*) **he he was destined never to see her again,** il ne devait plus la revoir.
destiny ['destini] *n.* destin *m;* sort *m;* **such was his d.,** telle fut sa destinée.
destitute ['destitjuːt] *a.* **1.** dépourvu, dénué (**of,** de). **2.** indigent; sans ressources; *n.pl.* **the d.,** les pauvres; **to be utterly d.,** être dans la misère.
destitution [desti'tjuːʃ(ə)n] *n.* dénuement *m,* indigence *f,* misère *f.*
destroy [dis'trɔi] *v.tr.* **1.** détruire, annihiler (qch.); anéantir (des espérances, etc.). **2.** tuer, abattre (un animal); **to d. oneself,** se suicider.
destroyer [dis'trɔiər] *n.* **1.** destructeur, -trice. **2.** *Navy:* contre-torpilleur *m;* destroyer *m.*
destruct [dis'trʌkt] *v.tr.* détruire.
destructible [dis'trʌktibl] *a.* destructible.
destruction [dis'trʌkʃ(ə)n] *n.* **1.** destruction *f,* anéantissement *m* (de qch.); consomption *f* (par le feu). **2. the d. caused by the fire, by the storm,** les ravages *mpl* du feu, de la tempête.
destructive [dis'trʌktiv] *a.* destructeur, -trice; (effet) destructeur; **d. child,** enfant qui détruit tout. **-ly** *adv.* d'une manière destructice.
destructiveness [dis'trʌktivnis] *n.* **1.** effet, pouvoir, destructeur (d'un explosif, etc.). **2.** (*of child, etc.*) penchant *m* à détruire.
destructor [dis'trʌktər] *n.* (**refuse**) **d.,** incinérateur *m* (à ordures).
desuetude [di'sjuitjuːd] *n.* désuétude *f.*
desultory ['desəlt(ə)ri] *a.* qui saute d'un sujet à un autre; décousu, sans suite. **-ily** *adv.* d'une manière décousue.
detach [di'tætʃ] *v.tr.* **1.** détacher, séparer (**from,** de); dételer (des wagons); décoller (un timbre, etc.). **2.** *Mil: Navy:* détacher (des troupes, un navire, etc.). **detached** *a.* **1.** détaché, séparé (**from,** de); *Med:* **d. retina,** rétine décollée; **d. house,** maison séparée; (*b*) *Mil:* (officier), en affectation spéciale. **2.** (*a*) (*of pers.*) désintéressé; (*b*) (manière) désinvolte; (air) détaché, indifférent.
detachable [di'tætʃəbl] *a.* détachable; (*of machine part*) amovible.
detachment [di'tætʃmənt] *n.* **1.** (*a*) action *f* de détacher; séparation *f* (**from,** de); dételage *m* (de wagons); (*b*) décollement *m* (d'un timbre, *Med:* de la rétine). **2.** (*a*) détachement *m* (de l'esprit) (**from,** de); désintéressement *m;* (*b*) indifférence *f* (**from,** envers); insouciance *f.* **3.** *Mil:* détachement; **gun d.,** peloton *m* (des servants); **on d.,** détaché.
detail¹ ['diːteil] *n.* **1.** détail *m;* particularité *f;* **to go, enter, into all the details,** donner, entrer dans, tous les détails; **in d.,** en détail; **in every d.,** dans le moindre détail; **in the fullest d.,** dans le plus grand détail; **points, questions, of d.,** questions de détail; **minor details,** (i) menus détails; (ii) l'accessoire *m;* **I can't give you any details,** je ne peux vous donner aucune

précision. **2.** *Mil:* extrait *m* de l'ordre du jour; **details,** l'ordre *m* du jour. **3.** détachement *m* (*Mil:* de corvée, etc., *esp. U.S:* de policiers).

detail² *v.tr.* **1.** détailler; raconter en détail; énumérer (les faits). **2.** *Mil: etc:* **to d. s.o. for a duty,** désigner qn pour un service; affecter qn à un service. **detailed** *a.* détaillé; (récit) circonstancié, détaillé; (travail) minutieux; **to give a d. account of sth.,** raconter qch. en détail.

detain [di'tein] *v.tr.* **1.** détenir (qn en prison); garder (qn à l'hôpital). **2.** (*a*) retenir, arrêter (qn); empêcher (qn) de partir; **this question need not d. us,** cette question ne nous retiendra pas; (*b*) *Sch:* consigner (un élève).

detainee [di:tei'ni:] *n.* détenu, -ue; prisonnier, -ière.

detect [di'tekt] *v.tr.* (*a*) découvrir (le coupable, une erreur, etc.); déceler (un crime, etc.); dépister (une maladie); (*b*) percevoir (un son); apercevoir (un mouvement, etc.).

detectable [di'tektəbl] *a.* discernable; perceptible.

detection [di'tekʃ(ə)n] *n.* **1.** découverte *f*; **to escape d.,** (i) se dérober aux recherches; (ii) (*of mistake, etc.*) passer inaperçu. **2.** (*a*) **radar d.,** détection radar; **sound d.,** détection par le son; (*b*) *Mil: etc:* détection (des mines, des avions, etc.).

detective [di'tektiv] *n.* agent *m* de la police judiciaire; détective *m*; **private d.,** détective (privé); **d. story,** roman policier.

detector [di'tektər] *n. Tchn:* détecteur *m*; (*a*) **smoke d.,** détecteur de fumée; **metal d.,** détecteur de métaux; *Mil:* **mine d.,** détecteur de mines; **sound d.,** détecteur (d'armes, d'engins) par le son; *Jur:* **lie d.,** détecteur de mensonges; (*b*) détecteur *m* (d'ondes, etc.).

detention [di'tenʃ(ə)n] *n.* **1.** (*a*) détention *f* (en prison); *n. Mil:* **six weeks' d.,** six semaines de prison; (*b*) *Sch:* retenue *f*; **to give a boy d.,** consigner un élève. **2.** *Nau:* arrêt *m* (d'un navire). **3.** *Jur:* détention (d'une somme due, etc.).

deter [di'tər] *v.tr.* **(deterred)** détourner, décourager, empêcher (**s.o. from doing sth.,** qn de faire qch.).

detergent [di'tə:dʒənt] **1.** *a.* détersif. **2.** *n.* détergent *m*, lessive *f*.

deteriorate [di'tiəriəreit] **1.** *v.tr.* (*a*) détériorer, altérer; (*b*) déprécier; enlever de la valeur à (une terre, etc.). **2.** *v.i.* (*a*) (se) détériorer, s'altérer; dépérir; (*b*) diminuer de valeur; perdre de sa valeur.

deterioration [ditiəriə'reiʃ(ə)n] *n.* (*a*) détérioration *f*, altération *f*; dépérissement *m*; **d. in quality,** baisse *f* de qualité; (*b*) diminution *f* de valeur.

determination [ditə:mi'neiʃ(ə)n] *n.* **1.** détermination *f* (d'une date, de la position d'un astre); **2.** (*of pers.*) détermination, résolution *f*; **air of d.,** air résolu, décidé, déterminé. **3.** *Jur:* (*a*) décision *f* (d'une affaire); (*b*) arrêt *m*. **4.** *Jur:* résolution, résiliation *f* (d'un contrat, etc.).

determine [di'tə:min] *v.tr. & i.* **1.** (*a*) déterminer, fixer (une date, des règles, etc.); (*b*) délimiter (une frontière); (*c*) déterminer, constater (la nature, les dimensions, de qch.). **2.** décider, résoudre (une question, etc.); régler (un point en litige); **to d. s.o.'s fate,** décider du sort de qn. **3.** (*a*) **to d. to do sth., to d. on doing sth.,** se décider, se déterminer, se résoudre, à faire qch.; (*b*) **to be determined to do sth.,** être résolu à faire qch. **4.** *Jur: v.tr.* résoudre, résilier (un contrat, un bail). **determined** *a.* **1.** (*of price, limit*) déterminé. **2.** (*of pers.*) résolu. **determining** *a.* (facteur) déterminant.

deterrent [di'terənt] **1.** *a.* (effet) préventif (d'une peine). **2.** *n.* (*a*) (*of penalty, etc.*) **to act as a d. (of crime),** exercer un effet préventif contre le crime; (*b*) *Mil: Pol:* arme *f* de dissuasion.

detest [di'test] *v.tr.* détester; abhorrer; **I d. being interrupted,** je déteste être dérangé.

detestable [di'testəbl] *a.* détestable. **-ably** *adv.* détestablement.

detestation [di:tes'teiʃ(ə)n] *n.* **1.** haine *f*. **2.** chose *f* détestable; abomination *f*.

dethrone [di'θroun] *v.tr.* détrôner.

dethronement [di'θrounmənt] *n.* détrônement *m*.

detonate ['detəneit] **1.** *v.tr.* faire détoner (un explosif); faire sauter (une mine). **2.** *v.i.* (*a*) détoner.

detonation [detə'neiʃ(ə)n] *n.* détonation *f*, explosion *f*.

detonator ['detəneitər] *n.* (*a*) *Exp:* détonateur *m*; amorce *f*; **percussion d.,** détonateur à percussion; (*b*) *Rail:* (*fog signal*) détonateur.

detour¹ ['di:tuər] *n.* (*a*) détour *m*; (*b*) *NAm:* déviation *f* (d'itinéraire, etc.).

detour² *v.i. NAm:* faire un détour.

detract [di'trækt] **1.** *v.i.* **to d. from (sth.),** rabaisser, amoindrir (le mérite de qn); diminuer (le plaisir de qn). **2.** *v.tr.* (*a*) **to d. a great deal from s.o.'s pleasure,** diminuer de beaucoup le plaisir de qn.

detrain [di:'trein] **1.** *v.tr.* débarquer (des troupes) d'un train. **2.** *v.i.* (*of troops*) débarquer (du train).

detriment ['detrimənt] *n.* détriment *m*, préjudice *m*; **to the d. of . . .,** au détriment de . . .; **without d. to . . .,** sans nuire à . . ..

detrimental [detri'ment(ə)l] *a.* nuisible, préjudiciable (**to,** à); **it would be d. to my interests,** cela desservirait mes intérêts.

detritus [di'traitəs] *n. Geol:* détritus *m*(*pl*).

deuce¹ [dju:s] *n.* **1.** (*of dice, dominoes, cards*) deux *m*. **2.** *Ten:* quarante à, quarante partout.

deuce² *n. F: O:* diable *m*; **what the d. does he mean?** que diable veut-il dire?

deuced ['dju:sid] *a. F: O:* sacré.

devaluation [di:vælju'eiʃ(ə)n] *n. Pol.Ec:* dévaluation *f*.

devalue [di:'vælju] *v.tr. Pol.Ec:* dévaluer.

devastate ['devəsteit] *v.tr.* dévaster, ravager; *Fig:* terrasser, foudroyer (qn). **devastating** *a.* **1.** (*of storm, etc.*) dévastateur, -trice; ravageur, -euse. **2.** (argument) accablant; (charme) irrésistible; (choc, etc.) foudroyant. **devastatingly** *adv.* **d. beautiful,** d'une beauté incomparable.

devastation [devəs'teiʃ(ə)n] *n.* dévastation *f*.

develop [di'veləp] *v.* **(developed** [di'veləpt]**) I.** *v.tr.* **1.** *Mth:* développer (une surface, une fonction). **2.** (*a*) développer (les facultés, etc.); (*b*) développer, élargir (une pensée, etc.); (*c*) *Chess:* déployer (son jeu). **3.** (*a*) exploiter, mettre en valeur (une région); développer les ressources (d'une région); **to d. a building site,** (re)construire; (*b*) *Tchn:* réaliser (un nouveau dessin, etc.). **4.** *Ph: etc:* engendrer (de la chaleur). **5.** (*a*) contracter (une maladie); faire (de la fièvre); (*b*) contracter (une mauvaise habitude); manifester (un tendance à . . .). **6.** (*a*) *Phot:* développer (une épreuve). **II.** *v.i.* **1.** (*of the body, the faculties, etc.*) se développer. **2.** (*a*) se manifester, se révéler; (*of crisis*) se produire; (*b*) (*of fever*) se déclarer. **developing 1.** *a.* qui se développe, qui fait des progrès; (pays) en voie de développement. **2.** *n.* (*a*) exploitation *f*, mise en valeur (d'une région); (*b*) *Phot:* développement; **d. bath,** (bain) révélateur (*m*); **d. tray,** cuvette *f*.

developer [di'veləpər] *n.* **1.** (*a*) personne *f* qui met en valeur (une région, etc.); promoteur *m*; (*b*) *Phot:* (*pers.*) développeur *m*; (*c*) **late d.,** enfant *m* qui se développe tard. **2.** *Phot:* (agent) révélateur (*m*).

development [di'veləpmənt] *n.* **1.** *Mth:* (*a*) développement *m* (d'une surface, d'une fonction); (*b*) développée *f* (d'une spirale). **2.** (*a*) développement (du corps, des facultés); (*b*) développement, amplification *f* (d'un sujet); élargissement *m* (d'une idée);

(*c*) *Chess:* déploiement *m* (de ses pièces); (*d*) *Mus:* développement. **3.** (*a*) exploitation *f*, mise *f* en valeur (d'une région, etc.); *Town P:* aménagement *m*; (re)construction *f*; **d. area,** zone *f* à urbaniser en priorité; (*b*) *Tchn:* réalisation *f*, mise au point (d'un nouveau dessin, etc.). **4.** *Phot:* développement. **5.** (*a*) développement, progrès *m*; déroulement *m* (des événements, etc.); (*b*) évolution *f* (des événements, de la pensée). **6.** fait nouveau; **to await further developments,** attendre les événements.

deviant ['di:viənt] *a.* & *n. Psy:* déviant, -ante.

deviate ['di:vieit] *v.i.* dévier, s'écarter (**from,** de); dériver.

deviation [di:vi'eiʃ(ə)n] *n.* déviation *f* (d'une aiguille aimantée, etc.); écart *m* (de la norme, etc.).

deviationism [di:vi'eiʃənizm] *n. Pol:* déviationnisme *m.*

deviationist [di:vi'eiʃənist] *a.* & *n. Pol:* déviationniste (*mf*).

device [di'vais] *n.* **1.** (*a*) expédient *m*; (*b*) **devices,** inclination *f*; **to leave s.o. to his own devices,** laisser qn s'occuper comme bon lui semble; (*c*) stratagème *m.* **2.** dispositif *m*, appareil *m*, mécanisme *m*; **locking d.,** système *m* de verrouillage; **safety d.,** dispositif de sécurité. **3.** emblème *m*, devise *f.*

devil[1] ['dev(ə)l] *n.* **1.** (*a*) diable *m*; **devil's advocate,** avocat *m* du diable; **to be between the d. and the deep (blue) sea,** être pris entre deux feux; **talk of the d. (and he's sure to appear),** quand on parle du loup, on en voit la queue; *O:* **d. take it!** que le diable l'emporte! *F:* **go to the d.!** allez au diable! **to play the d. with sth.,** mettre la confusion dans qch.; (*b*) *F:* **what the d. are you doing?** que diable faites-vous là? **how the d. . . .?** comment diable . . .? **like the d.,** (travailler) avec acharnement; **to have the d. of a job (to do sth.),** avoir un mal de chien, un mal de tous les diables (à faire qch.); **he's got the d. of a temper,** il a un fichu caractère. **2.** démon *m*; **she-d.,** (i) diablesse *f*; (ii) *F:* mégère *f.* **3.** *F:* (*a*) **that child's a little d.,** cet enfant est un petit démon; **he's a bit of a d.,** il est quelque peu rageur; (*b*) **poor d.!** pauvre diable! **the silly d.!** quel espèce d'idiot! **4.** *F: Typ:* **printer's d.,** apprenti imprimeur. **5.** *Meteor:* **dust d.,** tourbillon *m* de poussière.

devil[2] *v.* (**devilled,** *NAm:* **deviled**) **1.** *v.i. F:* **to d. for s.o.,** servir de nègre à (un avocat, etc.). **2.** *v.tr. Cu:* faire griller et poivrer fortement (de la viande); **devilled eggs,** œufs durs au curry.

devilfish ['dev(ə)lfiʃ] *n.* **1.** *Ich:* raie *f* manta. **2.** *Moll:* pieuvre *f.*

devilish ['devliʃ] **1.** *a.* (*a*) diabolique; (*b*) *F:* sacré; de diable, du diable. **2.** *adv. F: O:* **it's d. hot!** il fait rudement chaud!

devil-may-care ['dev(ə)lmei'kɛər] *a.* insouciant, je-m'en-foutiste; **d.-m.-c. spirit,** esprit (i) téméraire, (ii) insouciant.

devilment ['dev(ə)lmənt], **devilry** ['dev(ə)lri] *n.* **1.** méchanceté *f.* **2.** diablerie *f*, espièglerie *f.*

devious ['di:viəs] *a.* **1.** (*of course, way*) détourné, tortueux; **to achieve one's ends by d. means,** prendre des voies détournées pour arriver à son but. **2.** (*of pers.*) retors. **-ly** *adv.* d'une façon détournée.

deviousness ['di:viəsnis] *n.* **1.** détours *mpl.* **2.** caractère retors (d'une personne).

devise[1] [di'vaiz] *n. Jur:* legs (immobilier).

devise[2] *v.tr.* **1.** combiner (un projet); inventer, imaginer (un appareil); tramer (un complot). **2.** *Jur:* léguer (des biens immobiliers).

devoid [di'vɔid] *a.* dénué, dépourvu (**of,** de).

devolution [di:və'l(j)u:ʃ(ə)n] *n.* **1.** *Biol:* dégénérescence *f.* **2.** *Jur:* dévolution *f*; transmission *f* par succession. **3.** *Pol:* décentralisation administrative.

devolve [di'vɔlv] **1.** *v.tr.* déléguer, transmettre (des fonctions, des pouvoirs) (**to s.o.,** à qn). **2.** *v.i.* (*a*) (*of responsibility, duty, etc.*) revenir, incomber (**on, upon,** à); (*b*) *Jur:* (*of property*) **to d. to, upon, s.o.,** être dévolu à qn.

devote [di'vout] *v.tr.* consacrer, dévouer (son temps, son argent, etc., à qn, à qch.); accorder (du temps à qch.); **review specially devoted to history,** revue spéciale à l'histoire; **to d. oneself to sth.,** se vouer, se consacrer (à une occupation); s'adonner, se livrer (à l'étude, etc.). **devoted** *a.* dévoué, attaché (**to,** à); **they are d. to each other,** ils sont dévoués l'un à l'autre. **devotedly** *adv.* avec dévouement; **to serve s.o. d.,** servir qn avec dévouement.

devotee [devou'ti:] *n.* fervent, -ente; **a d. of classical music,** un passionné de la musique classique.

devotion [di'vouʃ(ə)n] *n.* **1.** dévotion *f* (à Dieu, à un saint). **2.** *pl.* dévotions, prières *f.* **3.** dévouement *m* (**to s.o.,** à, pour, qn); **d. to duty,** dévouement; **d. to work,** assiduité *f* au travail.

devotional [di'vouʃən(ə)l] *a.* (livre, etc.) de dévotion; **d. articles,** articles *mpl* de piété.

devour [di'vauər] *v.tr.* dévorer; *F:* **to d. s.o. with one's eyes,** dévorer qn des yeux; **to d. a book,** dévorer un livre. **devouring** *a.* **a d. passion,** une passion dévorante, dévoratrice.

devout [di'vaut] *a.* **1.** dévot. **2.** (*of wish, etc.*) fervent, sincère. **-ly** *adv.* **1.** dévotement, avec dévotion. **2.** sincèrement.

devoutness [di'vautnis] *n.* dévotion *f*, piété *f.*

dew [dju:] *n.* **(morning) d.,** rosée *f*; **evening d.,** serein *m*; **d. is falling,** il tombe de la rosée; **d. point,** point *m* de rosée, de condensation.

dewclaw ['dju:klɔ:] *n. Z:* ergot *m* (des chiens, etc.).

dewdrop ['dju:drɔp] *n.* goutte *f* de rosée.

dewlap ['dju:læp] *n.* **1.** fanon *m* (de la vache). **2.** *F:* peau flasque et pendante (sous le menton de qn).

dewy ['dju:i] *a.* couvert de rosée; humecté de rosée; **d. -eyed,** les yeux brillants de larmes.

dexterity [deks'teriti] *n.* dextérité *f*, doigté *m*; habileté *f*; **manual d.,** habileté manuelle.

dext(e)rous ['dekst(ə)rəs] *a.* adroit, habile (**in doing sth.,** à faire qch.). **-ly** *adv.* adroitement; avec dextérité.

dextrin ['dekstrin] *n. Ch: Ind:* dextrine *f.*

dextrose ['dekstrous] *n. Ch:* dextrose *m.*

diabetes [daiə'bi:ti:z] *n. Med:* diabète *m.*

diabetic [daiə'betik] *a.* & *n. Med:* diabétique (*mf*).

diabolic(al) [daiə'bɔlik(l)] *a.* (cruauté, grimace, etc.) diabolique, atroce; (complot) infernal; (ricanement) satanique. **-ally** *adv.* diaboliquement.

diacritic [daiə'kritik] *a.* & *n. Gram:* (signe) diacritique (*m*).

diacritical [daiə'kritik(ə)l] *a. Gram:* (signe) diacritique.

diadem ['daiədem] *n.* diadème *m.*

diaeresis, *NAm: also* **dieresis,** *pl.* **-eses** [dai'erəsis, -əsi:z] *n. Gram:* tréma *m.*

diagnose ['daiəgnouz] *v.tr.* diagnostiquer (une maladie, une panne du moteur, etc.) faire le diagnostic (d'une maladie).

diagnosis, *pl.* **-ses** [daiəg'nousis, -si:z] *n. Med:* (*a*) diagnostic *m* (d'une maladie); (*b*) (*art*) diagnose *f.*

diagnostic [daiəg'nɔstik] *a.* diagnostique.

diagonal [dai'ægən(ə)l] **1.** *a. Mth:* diagonal, -aux; *Const:* (*of beam, etc.*) en écharpe. **2.** *n. Mth:* diagonale *f.* **-ally** *adv.* diagonalement, en diagonale.

diagram ['daiəgræm] *n.* **1.** diagramme *m*, schéma *m*; **geometrical d.,** figure géométrique; **block d.,** bloc-diagramme *m*, *pl.* blocs-diagrammes. **2.** (*a*) *Ph: etc:* graphique *m*, courbe *f* (de température, etc.); (*b*) *Mec.E: Mch:* diagramme, caractéristique *f* du moteur, etc.).

diagrammatic [daiəgrə'mætik] *a.* schématique.

dial¹ ['daiəl] *n.* (*a*) cadran *m* (d'horloge, de baromètre, etc.); (*b*) *Nau:* **compass d.,** rose *f* des vents; (*c*) *Tp:* cadran (d'appel); (*d*) cadran (d'un instrument scientifique, etc.).

dial² *v.tr.* **(dialled,** *NAm:* **dialed)** (*a*) *Tp:* composer, faire (un numéro); **to d. 999** = appeler Police Secours; (*b*) *Cmptr:* composer (un cadran). **dialling,** *NAm:* **dialing** *n. Tp:* composition *f* du numéro; **d. tone,** tonalité *f*; **d. code,** indicatif (départemental).

dialect ['daiəlekt] *n.* dialecte *m*; **provincial d.,** patois *m.*

dialectic(al) [daiə'lektik(l)] *a. Phil:* dialectique; **d. materialism,** matérialisme *m* dialectique.

dialectic(s) [daiə'lektik(s)] *n. Phil:* dialectique *f.*

dialogue ['daiəlɔg] *n.* dialogue *m.*

dialyse ['daiəlaiz] *v.tr. Ch:* dialyser.

dialysis, *pl.* **-es** [dai'ælisis, -i:z] *n. Ch: Surg:* dialyse *f.*

diamanté [daiə'mæntei] *n.* broderie diamantée.

diameter [dai'æmitər] *n.* diamètre *m*; **the wheel is 60 cm in d.,** la roue a 60 cm de diamètre; **internal d.,** calibre *m* (d'un tube); *I.C.E: etc:* alésage *m* (d'un cylindre, etc.).

diametric(al) [daiə'metrik(l)] *a.* (*of opinions, etc.*) **in d. opposition,** diamétralement opposés **(to,** à). **-ally** *adv.* (*of opinions, etc.*) **d. opposed,** diamétralement opposés.

diamond ['daiəmənd] *n.* **1.** (*a*) diamant *m*; **d. of the first water,** diamant de première eau; **rough, cut, d.,** diamant brut, taillé; **he's a rough d.,** ses manières frustes cachent beaucoup de qualités; **d. necklace, ring,** collier *m*, bague *f*, de diamants; **d. cutting,** taille *f* du diamant; (*pers.*) **d. cutter,** tailleur *m* de diamants; **d. wedding,** noces *fpl* de diamant; (*b*) *Tls:* **(cutting) d.,** diamant de vitrier; (*c*) *Rec:* diamant. **2.** (*a*) losange *m*; **d. pattern,** dessin *m* en losanges; (*b*) *Cards:* carreau *m*; (*c*) *Sp:* terrain *m* de baseball.

diamond-shaped ['daiəməndʃeipt] *a.* en losange.

diapason [daiə'peisən] *n. Mus:* **1.** diapason *m.* **2.** principaux jeux de fond (d'un orgue).

diaper ['daiəpər] *n. NAm:* couche *f*, lange *m* (de bébé).

diaphanous [dai'æfənəs] *a.* diaphane.

diaphragm ['daiəfræm] *n.* **1.** *Anat:* diaphragme *m.* **2.** (*a*) diaphragme, membrane *f*; (*b*) *Phot:* **Iris d.,** diaphragme iris; (*c*) *Med:* diaphragme (contraceptif).

diarist ['daiərist] *n.* auteur *m* d'un journal (intime).

diarrhoea [daiə'riə] *n. Med:* diarrhée *f.*

diary ['daiəri] *n.* **1.** journal *m* (intime). **2.** agenda *m*; **desk d.,** bloc *m* calendrier.

Diaspora (the) [ðədai'æspərə] *n. Jew.Rel:* la Diaspora.

diatribe ['daiətraib] *n.* diatribe *f* **(against,** contre).

dibber ['dibər], **dibble¹** ['dibl] *n. Tls:* plantoir *m.*

dibble² **1.** *v.tr.* semer (des graines), repiquer (des plantes), au plantoir. **2.** *v.i.* semer, repiquer, au plantoir.

dibs [dibz] *n.pl.* (*a*) (*game*) osselets *m*; *Cards:* jetons *m*; (*b*) *F:* argent *m*, fric *m.*

dice¹ [dais] *n.pl.* (*pl. of* **die¹** I.) *Games:* dés *mpl.*

dice² **1.** *v.i.* (*a*) jouer aux dés; (*b*) **to d. with death,** risquer sa vie. **2.** *v.tr. Cu:* couper (des légumes) en cubes. **dicing** *n.* (*a*) le jeu des dés; (*b*) les dés *mpl*, le jeu.

dicey ['daisi] *a. F:* hasardeux; risqué.

dichotomy [dai'kɔtəmi] *n.* dichotomie *f.*

Dick¹ [dik] *Pr.n.m. F:* Richard; **any Tom, D. or Harry,** le premier venu; **clever D.,** petit malin.

dick² *n. F:* détective *m*, flic *m.*

dickens ['dikinz] *n. F:* **what the d. are you doing?** que diable fais-tu? **the d. of a row,** un bruit de tous les diables.

dicky¹ ['diki] *n. F:* **1.** (*child's language*) **d. (bird),** (petit) oiseau, zoziau. **2.** *Cost:* faux plastron (de chemise). **3.** (*a*) *A.Veh:* **d. (seat),** siège *m* du cocher; (*b*) *A.Aut:* spider *m.*

dicky² *a. F:* (*a*) défectueux; (*b*) (*of heart*) malade, qui flanche; **to feel d.,** se sentir tout chose.

Dictaphone ['diktəfoun] *n. R.t.m:* Dictaphone *m.*

dictate¹ ['dikteit] *n.* ordre *m*; **to follow the dictates of one's conscience,** écouter sa conscience; **the dictates of fashion,** les exigences *fpl* de la mode.

dictate² [dik'teit] **1.** *v.tr.* (*a*) dicter (une lettre, un passage); (*b*) dicter (des conditions de paix, etc.); (*c*) **his words are dictated by wisdom,** c'est la sagesse qui inspire, ses paroles. **2.** *v.i.* faire la loi; **I won't be dictated to,** on ne me donne pas d'ordres. **dictating** *n.* **d. machine,** machine *f* à dicter.

dictation [dik'teiʃ(ə)n] *n.* dictée *f*; (*a*) **to write at, from, to, s.o.'s d.,** écrire sous la dictée de qn; (*b*) *Sch:* **to do d.,** faire la dictée.

dictator [dik'teitər] *n. Pol: etc:* dictateur *m.*

dictatorial [diktə'tɔ:riəl] *a.* **1.** (pouvoir) dictatorial, -aux. **2.** (ton) impérieux; (personne, ton) autoritaire. **-ally** *adv.* dictatorialement; impérieusement; autoritairement.

dictatorship [dik'teitəʃip] *n.* dictature *f.*

diction ['dikʃ(ə)n] *n.* **1.** style *m* (d'un orateur). **2.** diction *f.*

dictionary ['dikʃən(ə)ri] *n.* dictionnaire *m*; **English-French d.,** dictionnaire anglais-français.

dictum, *pl.* **-ums, -a** ['diktəm, -əmz, -ə] *n.* **1.** affirmation *f*, dire *m.* **2.** maxime *f*, dicton *m.*

didactic [d(a)i'dæktik] *a.* didactique. **-ally** *adv.* didactiquement.

diddle ['didl] *v.tr. F:* duper, refaire, rouler (qn); **he diddled me out of £1000,** il m'a refait, roulé, de £1000.

diddler ['didlər] *n. F:* carotteur, -euse.

die¹ [dai] *n.* **I.** (*pl.* **dice,** *q.v.*) dé *m* (à jouer); **the d. is cast,** le sort est jeté, les dés sont jetés. **II.** (*pl.* **dies** [daiz]) **1.** *Num:* (*in minting*) coin *m.* **2.** (*a*) *Metalw:* matrice *f*; coquille *f* (de moulage); **stamping, embossing, d.,** matrice, machine *f* à estamper; **screw-cutting d.,** mère *f* (de filet de vis); **d. casting,** moulage *m* en coquille; **d. stamping,** matriçage *m*; **d. sinker,** graveur *m* d'étampes, de matrices; (*b*) poinçonneuse *f* (à main).

die² *v.i.* (*p.t. & p.p.* **died** [daid]; *pr.p.* **dying** ['daiiŋ]) **1.** mourir; **to be dying,** mourir; **he died yesterday,** il est mort hier; **to d. a natural death,** (i) mourir de mort naturelle; (*of old age*) mourir de sa belle mort; (ii) (*of fashion, etc.*) passer de mode; *Aut: F:* **the engine died on me,** le moteur a calé; **to d. rich, a millionaire,** mourir riche, millionnaire; **they died like heroes,** ils sont morts en héros; **to d. of grief, of starvation,** mourir de chagrin, de faim; **to d. from, of, a wound,** mourir des suites d'une blessure; **old superstitions d. hard,** les vieilles superstitions ont la vie dure; **never say d.!** (i) il ne faut jamais désespérer; (ii) courage! tenez bon! **2.** (*a*) **I nearly died laughing,** je mourais de rire; **we were dying of cold,** nous mourions de froid; (*b*) **to be dying to do sth.,** brûler, mourir, d'envie de faire qch.; **I'm dying for a drink, for a cigarette,** je meurs de soif, je meurs d'envie de fumer une cigarette. **3. day is dying,** le jour s'en va; **his secret died with him,** il a emporté son secret dans le tombeau. **die away** *v.i.* se mourir; (*of sound*) s'affaiblir; (*of voice*) s'éteindre; (*of wind*) tomber; *Mus:* **to let the sound d. away,** éteindre le son. **die down** *v.i.* (*of fire, etc.*) baisser; (*of wind*) tomber; (*of sound*) s'éteindre; (*of excitement, storm*) se calmer. **die off** *v.i.* (*a*) (*of leaves*) se faner; (*b*) *F:* **they're dying off like flies,** ils meurent les uns après les autres, comme des mouches. **die out** *v.i.* se mourir; (*of family, etc.*) s'éteindre; (*of species*) disparaître. **dying 1.** *a.* mourant, agonisant; **in a d. voice,** d'une voix éteinte. **2.** *n.pl.* **the dead and the d.,** les morts *mpl* et les moribonds *mpl*; **prayers for the d.,** prières *fpl* des agonisants. **3.** *n.* (*a*) agonie *f*; mort *f*; **d. words,** dernières paroles; **with his d. breath,** de sa voix agonisante; **I shall remember it to my d. day,** je m'en souviendrai jusqu'à la mort; (*b*) **d. away,** affaiblissement *m* (d'un son); (*c*) **d. down,** extinction graduelle (du feu); (*d*) **d. out,** extinction graduelle (d'une race, d'une famille).

diehard ['daiha:d] *n.* *Pol:* conservateur *m* à outrance; immobiliste *m*; intransigeant *m*; **d. policy,** (politique *f* d')immobilisme (*m*); politique outrancière.

dieresis [dai'erəsis] *n.* *NAm:* = DIAERESIS.

diesel ['di:z(ə)l] **1.** *a.* (moteur, locomotive) diesel; **d. oil, fuel,** gas-oil *m.* **2.** *n.* diesel *m.*

diesel-electric [di:zəli'lektrik] *a.* diesel-électrique, *pl.* diesel-électriques.

diet¹ ['daiət] *n.* **1.** alimentation *f*; **their d. consists mainly of fish,** leur nourriture se compose essentiellement de poisson. **2.** *Med:* (*a*) régime *m* (alimentaire); **to be on a d.,** être au régime; **milk d.,** régime lacté; (*b*) **starvation d.,** diète absolue; régime affamant.

diet² *v.i.* se mettre, être, au régime.

diet³ *n.* *Pol:* diète *f.*

dietary ['daiət(ə)ri] **1.** *n.* régime *m* (alimentaire) (d'un malade, d'une prison, etc.). **2.** *a.* diététique.

dietetic [daiə'tetik] *a.* diététique.

dietetics [daiə'tetiks] *n.pl.* (*usu. with sg. const.*) diététique *f.*

dietician [daiə'tiʃ(ə)n] *n.* diététicien, -ienne.

differ ['difər] *v.i.* **1.** différer (**from,** de); être différent (de). **2.** (*disagree*) **to d. in opinion,** différer d'opinion, d'avis; **I beg to d.,** permettez-moi d'être d'un autre avis; **to agree to d.,** garder chacun son opinion.

difference [dif(ə)rəns] *n.* **1.** (*a*) différence *f*, écart *m* (**between,** entre); **d. in age, in altitude,** différence d'âge, d'altitude; **d. in temperature,** écart de température; **I don't quite see the d.,** je ne saisis pas la nuance; (*of schoolmistress, etc.*) **she doesn't make any d. between the children,** elle ne fait pas de distinction entre les enfants; **it doesn't make any d.,** cela ne fait aucune différence; **it makes no d. (to me),** cela ne (me) fait rien, m'est parfaitement égal; **that makes all the d.,** voilà qui change complètement les choses; **he's a businessman, but with a d.,** c'est bien un homme d'affaires, mais pas comme les autres; (*b*) différence (entre deux nombres, etc.); **differences in price,** écarts de prix; **to split the d.,** (i) *Com:* partager le différend; (ii) faire un compromis. **2.** désaccord *m*, différend *m* (**about sth., au sujet de qch.**); **to settle a d.,** régler un différend; se mettre d'accord; **we have our differences,** nous ne sommes pas toujours d'accord.

different ['dif(ə)rənt] *a.* différent (**from,** *NAm: also* **than,** de); (*a*) **entirely d. ideas,** des idées tout à fait différentes; (*b*) **I feel a d. man,** je ne me sens plus le même; **that dress makes you look d.,** cette robe vous change; (*c*) **I do it in a d. way,** je m'y prends tout autrement; **that's quite a d. matter,** ça c'est une autre affaire; (*d*) **d. colours,** couleurs diverses, variées; **d. kinds of . . .,** diverses, différentes, espèces de . . .; **at d. times,** à différentes, diverses, reprises; (*e*) au-dessus de l'ordinaire; *F:* **he just wants to be d.,** il cherche à se faire remarquer. **-ly** *adv.* différemment.

differential [difə'renʃ(ə)l] **1.** *a.* (*of tariff charges, diagnosis, etc.*) différentiel; *Mth:* **d. calculus,** calcul différentiel; *Aut: etc.* **d. gear,** engrenage différentiel; *Cmptr:* **d. analyser,** analyseur différentiel. **2.** *n.* (*a*) *Mth:* différentielle *f*; (*b*) *Aut:* différentiel *m*; (*c*) **weight d.,** différence *f* de poids; (*d*) écart *m* (des prix, des salaires); **wage differentials,** hiérarchie salariale.

differentiate [difə'renʃieit] **1.** *v.tr.* (*a*) différencier (**sth. from sth.,** qch. de qch.); (*b*) *Mth:* différentier (une fonction). **2.** *v.i.* faire la différence (**between two things,** entre deux choses).

differentiation [difərenʃi'eiʃ(ə)n] *n.* différenciation *f.*

difficult ['difikəlt] *a.* (*a*) (tâche, problème) difficile; **this question is d. to answer,** il est difficile de répondre à cette question; **I find it d., it is d. for me, to . . .,** j'ai de la peine à . . ., j'ai du mal à . . .; **it is d. to believe that . . .,** on a peine à croire que . . . + *sub.*; (*b*) (*of pers.*) difficile, peu commode; **he's d. to get on with,** il est peu commode; **don't be so d.!** ne fais pas le, la, difficile!

difficulty ['difikəlti] *n.* **1.** difficulté *f*; **to have d. in doing sth.,** éprouver de la difficulté à faire qch.; avoir du mal à faire qch.; **to have d. in breathing,** avoir de la gêne dans la respiration; **there will be no d. about that,** cela ne fera pas de difficultés; **the d. is to . . .,** le difficile, c'est de . . .; **with d.,** avec difficulté, difficilement. **2.** obstacle *m*, difficulté; **I see no d. about it,** je n'y vois pas d'inconvénient; **to raise, make, difficulties,** soulever des objections *fpl*; **there's the d.!** voilà la difficulté! **3.** embarras *m*, ennui *m*; **to be in d.,** être dans l'embarras, dans une situation difficile; **ship in difficulties,** navire *m* en détresse; **financial difficulties,** embarras pécuniaire; **to get into difficulties,** (i) s'attirer des ennuis; (ii) se mettre dans un mauvais pas; **to get out of one's difficulties,** se tirer d'affaire.

diffidence ['difidəns] *n.* manque *m* de confiance en soi-même; manque d'assurance.

diffident ['difidənt] *a.* qui manque d'assurance, de confiance en soi-même; (sourire) timide. **-ly** *adv.* timidement.

diffract [di'frækt] *v.tr.* *Opt:* diffracter.

diffraction [di'frækʃ(ə)n] *n.* *Opt:* diffraction *f.*

diffuse¹ [di'fju:s] *a.* (*of light, style, etc.*) diffus.

diffuse² [di'fju:z] **1.** *v.tr.* répandre (la lumière, une nouvelle, etc.); diffuser (la lumière). **2.** *v.i.* se répandre; (*of light, gas, etc.*) se diffuser. **diffused** *a.* **d. lighting,** éclairage diffusé.

diffuseness [di'fju:snis] *n.* prolixité *f*, caractère diffus (du style).

diffusion [di'fju:ʒ(ə)n] *n.* diffusion *f* (d'un fluide, du style, etc.); rayonnement *m* (des idées); *Ph:* dispersion *f* (des rayons); *W.Tel: etc:* diffusion (de nouvelles).

diffusive [di'fju:siv] *a.* **1.** diffusif. **2.** (style) diffus, prolixe.

dig¹ [dig] *n.* **1.** (*a*) coup *m* de bêche (au jardin, etc.); (*b*) *Archeol:* fouille *f*; **to go on a d.,** faire des fouilles. **2.** *F:* (*a*) **a d. in the ribs,** un coup de coude dans les côtes; (*b*) allusion (critique) (**at s.o.,** a qn); **to get in a d. at s.o.,** lancer un coup de patte à qn; **that's a d. at you,** cette remarque est à votre intention.

dig² *v.* (*p.t. & p.p.* **dug** [dʌg]; *pr.p.* **digging** ['digiŋ]) **1** *v.tr.* (*a*) bêcher (la terre); labourer (la terre) à la bêche; (*b*) arracher (des pommes de terre); creuser (la tourbe); (*c*) creuser (un trou, etc.); (*d*) *v.i.* travailler la terre; *Archeol:* faire des fouilles; **to d. for gold,** faire des fouilles pour trouver de l'or. **2.** *v.tr.* enfoncer (**sth. into sth.,** qch. dans qch.); *F:* **to d. s.o. in the ribs,** donner un coup de coude à qn. **3.** *v.tr.* *P:* (*a*) comprendre, piger (qch.); (*b*) aimer (qn, qch.); **I d. that,** ça me plaît, me botte. **digging** *n.* **1.** (*a*) bêchage *m* (de la terre); labour *m* à la bêche; creusement *m* (de fossés, etc.); excavation *f* (d'un puits, etc.); (*b*) *Archeol:* fouilles *fpl.* **dig in 1.** *v.tr.* enterrer (le fumier, etc.); **to d. one's toes, heels, in,** s'entêter; *F:*

to d. oneself in, s'incruster. **2.** *v.i.* (*a*) *Mil:* s'établir (en creusant des tranchées); (*b*) *F:* manger, bouffer; piocher (dans le plat). **dig out** *v.tr.* (*a*) extraire, déterrer (qch.); (*b*) déterrer (de vieux manuscrits, etc.). **dig up** *v.tr.* déraciner (une plante, etc.); mettre à jour (un trésor); piocher (la rue, etc.); déterrer, exhumer (un corps); *F:* **where did you d. that up?** où as-tu déniché ça?

digest[1] ['daidʒest] *n.* **1.** abrégé *m*, résumé *m* (d'une science). **2.** digeste *m*; recueil *m* de lois. **3.** *Journ:* condensé *m*, *F:* digest *m*.

digest[2] [d(a)i'dʒest] *v.tr.* (*a*) *Physiol:* digérer (les aliments); (*b*) *F:* digérer, avaler (une insulte, un affront); (*c*) digérer, assimiler (ce qu'on lit).

digestible [di'dʒestəbl] *a.* digestible; **easily d.,** d'une digestion facile; digeste.

digestion [d(a)i'dʒestʃ(ə)n] *n.* (*a*) *Physiol:* digestion *f*; **sluggish d.,** digestion laborieuse; (*b*) digestion, assimilation *f* (de ce qu'on a lu).

digestive [d(a)i'dʒestiv] **1.** *a.* (appareil, suc, etc.) digestif; **d. troubles,** troubles digestifs, de digestion. **2.** *n.* (*a*) *Pharm: etc:* digestif *m*; (*b*) *a. & n.* **d. (biscuit),** (sorte de) sablé *m*.

digger ['digər] *n.* **1.** (*with spade*) bêcheur *m*; **(gold, etc.) d.,** chercheur *m* (d'or, etc.). **2.** (*a*) *Tls:* truelle *f*; (*b*) *Civ.E:* **(mechanical) d.,** excavateur *m*. **3.** *Ent:* **d. (wasp),** guêpe fouisseuse.

digit ['didʒit] *n.* **1.** (*a*) doigt *m*; (*b*) orteil *m*. **2.** (*a*) *Mth:* chiffre *m* (arabe); **the ten digits,** les neuf chiffres et le zéro; (*b*) *Cmptr:* **binary d.,** chiffre binaire, bit *m*; **d. selector,** sélecteur *m* d'indice.

digital ['didʒit] *a.* (*a*) *Anat: etc:* digital, -aux; (*b*) *Cmptr: etc:* (calculateur, etc.) numérique; **d. watch, clock,** montre *f*, horloge *f*, à affichage digital.

digitalis [didʒi'teilis] *n.* **1.** *Bot:* digitale *f*. **2.** *Pharm:* digitaline *f*.

dignify ['dignifai] *v.tr.* (*a*) donner de la dignité à (qch.); (*b*) **to d. s.o. with the name of . . . ,** honorer qn du nom de . . . . **dignified** *a.* plein de dignité; (air) digne; **to have a d. manner,** avoir de la dignité.

dignitary ['dignit(ə)ri] *n.* dignitaire *m*.

dignity ['digniti] *n.* **1.** dignité *f*; (*a*) **to preserve one's d.,** soutenir sa dignité; **to be, stand, on one's d.,** se retrancher derrière sa dignité; (*b*) **the d. of labour,** la dignité du travail. **2. d. of chancellor,** dignité de chancelier.

digress [dai'gres] *v.i.* faire une digression, des digressions (**from,** de); s'écarter (du sujet).

digression [dai'greʃ(ə)n] *n.* digression *f*, écart *m* (du sujet).

digs [digz] *n.pl.* *F:* logement *m*; **to live in d.,** loger en garni, en meublé.

dihedral [dai'hi:drəl] *a. & n.* dièdre (*m*).

dike [daik] *n. & v.tr.* = DYKE[1,2].

dilapidated [di'læpideitid] *a.* (*of building, etc.*) délabré; dans un état de délabrement; (chapeau) dépenaillé.

dilapidation [dilæpi'deiʃ(ə)n] *n.* délabrement *m*, dégradation *f* (d'un bâtiment, etc.).

dilate [dai'leit] **1.** *v.tr.* dilater. **2.** *v.i.* (*a*) (*of eyes, etc.*) se dilater; (*b*) **to d. on a topic,** s'étendre sur un sujet.

dilation [dai'leiʃ(ə)n] *n.* dilatation *f; Med:* **d. and curettage,** dilatation et curetage.

dilatoriness ['dilət(ə)rinis] *n.* lenteur *f* (à agir).

dilatory ['dilət(ə)ri] *a.* **1.** (*of pers.*) lent (à agir); (*of action*) tardif. **2.** *Jur: etc:* **d. means,** moyens dilatoires.

dilemma [dai'lemə] *n.* **1.** *Log:* dilemme *m*; **to be on the horns of a d.,** être pris dans un dilemme. **2.** embarras *m*; **to be in a d.,** être fort embarrassé.

dilettante, *pl.* **-ti** [dili'tænti, -ti] **1.** *n.* dilettante *m*; amateur *m*. **2.** *a.* **in a d. manner,** (faire qch.) en dilettante, en amateur.

dilettantism [dili'tæntizm] *n.* dilettantisme *m*.

diligence ['dilidʒ(ə)ns] *n.* assiduité *f*, application *f*, zèle *m*.

diligent ['dilidʒ(ə)nt] *a.* (*of pers., work*) assidu, appliqué. **-ly** *adv.* avec assiduité; assidûment.

dill [dil] *n.* *Bot:* aneth *m*; fenouil *m*.

dillydally ['dili'dæli] *v.i.* **(dillydallied) 1.** traîner, traînasser, lambiner. **2.** hésiter; tergiverser.

dilute[1] [dai'lju:t, di-] *a.* **1.** (*of acid, etc.*) dilué, étendu. **2.** (*of colour*) délayé. **3.** atténué.

dilute[2] *v.tr.* **1.** diluer (un acide); allonger (une sauce) (**with,** de); **to d. wine with water,** couper du vin avec de l'eau; **to become diluted,** se diluer. **2.** délayer, adoucir (une couleur). **3.** atténuer (une doctrine, etc); **diluted radicalism,** radicalisme *m* à l'eau de rose.

dilution [dai'lju:ʃ(ə)n, di-] *n.* dilution *f*; réduction *f* (d'un acide); délayage *m* (d'une couleur).

dim[1] [dim] *a.* **(dimmer, dimmest)** (*of light*) faible, pâle; (*of colour*) effacé; (*of sight*) faible, trouble; (*of forest, room, lighting*) sombre; (*of sound*) sourd, mat; (*of outline, memory*) vague, faible, estompé; (*of intelligence*) vague, confus; *F:* (*of pers.*) bête; **to grow d.,** (*of light, faculties*) baisser, s'éteindre; (*of recollection*) s'effacer; (*of understanding*) s'affaiblir; (*of sight*) se troubler; (*of colour*) s'effacer; (*of outline*) s'effacer, s'estomper; *F:* **to take a d. view of sth.,** avoir une piètre opinion de qch.; **don't be so d.!** sois pas si bête! **-ly** *adv.* (brûler) faiblement; (voir) indistinctement; (sentir, se souvenir) vaguement; **d. lit room,** pièce mal éclairée.

dim[2] *v.* **(dimmed) 1.** *v.tr.* (*a*) obscurcir (la vue); troubler (la mémoire, l'intelligence); ternir (la beauté de qn, la surface d'un miroir); (*b*) atténuer, réduire (la lumière); **to d. the lights,** baisser les lumières; *NAm: Aut:* **to d. one's headlights,** se mettre en code; **dimmed headlights,** phares *mpl* code; (*c*) éclipser (la gloire de qn). **2.** *v.i.* (*of light*) baisser; s'éteindre; (*of eyes*) s'obscurcir; (*of outlines*) s'effacer, s'estomper.

dime [daim] *n.* *U.S:* dime *f* (= un dixième de dollar); **d. store,** magasin *m* bon marché.

dimension [dai'menʃ(ə)n, di-] *n.* **1.** dimension *f*; **of large dimensions,** de grandes dimensions. **2.** *Mth:* dimension; **the fourth d.,** la quatrième dimension.

dimensional [dai'menʃən(ə)l, di-] *a.* dimensionnel; **two-, three-d.,** (figure) à deux, à trois, dimensions *fpl*; *Cin:* **three-d.** (*also* **3D** ['θri:'di:]) **film,** film *m* en relief.

diminish [di'miniʃ] **1.** *v.tr.* diminuer, réduire. **2.** *v.i.* diminuer, s'atténuer. **diminished** *a.* diminué; *Mus:* (intervalle) diminué; *Jur:* **d. responsability,** responsabilité diminuée. **diminishing** *a.* décroissant; qui diminue; (*of value, etc.*) baissant; *Pol.Ec:* **law of d. returns,** loi *f* des rendements nonproportionnels, décroissants.

diminution [dimi'nju:ʃ(ə)n] *n.* diminution *f*; réduction *f*.

diminutive [di'minjutiv] **1.** *a. & n.* *Gram:* diminutif (*m*). **2.** *a.* tout petit; minuscule.

dimmer ['dimər] *n.* *El:* interrupteur *m* à gradation de lumière; *Cin:* obscurateur *m* de salle; **d. bulb,** ampoule *f* veilleuse.

dimness ['dimnis] *n.* **1.** faiblesse *f* (d'éclairage, de la vue); obscurité *f* (d'une pièce). **2.** imprécision *f*, vague *m* (d'un souvenir). **3.** *F:* stupidité *f*, bêtise *f*.

dimple[1] ['dimpl] *n.* **1.** (*on cheek, chin*) fossette *f*. **2.** (*on water, ground*) ride *f*.

dimple[2] **1.** *v.tr.* (*a*) (*of smile*) former des fossettes *fpl* dans (les joues de qn); (*b*) (*of wind*) rider (la surface de l'eau). **2.** *v.i.* (*of cheeks*) se former en fossettes; (*of water*) onduler. **dimpled** *a.* (joues) à fossettes.

dimwit ['dimwit] *n.* *F:* idiot, -ote; **you d.!** imbécile!

dimwitted [dim'witid] *a.* *F:* idiot, bête.

din[1] [din] *n.* tapage *m*, vacarme *m*, chahut *m*; **what a d.!** quel boucan!

din[2] *v.* **(dinned)** *v.tr.* **to d. sth. into s.o.,** seriner qch. à qn; **you have to d. it into him,** il faut le lui enfoncer à coups répétés dans la tête.

dine [dain] **1.** *v.i.* dîner; **to d. out,** dîner (i) en ville, à un restaurant, (ii) chez des amis. **2.** *v.tr.* **to wine and d. s.o.,** fêter qn. **dining** *attrib.* **d. room,** salle *f* à manger; **d. table,** table *f* de salle à manger; *Sch: etc:* **d. hall,** réfectoire *m*; *Rail:* **d. car,** wagon-restaurant *m, pl.* wagons-restaurants.

diner ['dainər] *n.* **1.** (*pers.*) dîneur, -euse. **2.** (*a*) *Rail:* wagon-restaurant *m, pl.* wagons-restaurants; (*b*) *NAm:* petit restaurant (au bord d'une route).

dinette [dai'net] *n.* coin-repas *m*.

ding-dong ['diŋ'dɔŋ] **1.** *n.* tintement *m* (des cloches); digue-din-don *m inv.* **2.** *a.* **d.-d. match,** partie où l'avantage passe constamment d'un côté à l'autre.

dinghy ['diŋ(g)i] *n. Nau:* (*a*) **(ship's) d.,** youyou *m*; (*b*) dinghy *m, pl.* dinghies; **sailing d.,** dinghy à voile; (*c*) **rubber, inflatable, d.,** canot *m* pneumatique.

dinginess ['dindʒinis] *n.* aspect miteux; aspect sombre.

dingo ['diŋgou] *n. Z:* dingo *m* (de l'Australie).

dingy ['dindʒi] *a.* (*of room, furniture, etc.*) défraîchi; (*of colour*) terne; (*of sky*) fuligineux; (hôtel) peu confortable.

dinkum ['diŋkəm] *Austr: F: a.* (*of pers.*) sincère; (*of thg*) authentique; **fair d.,** régulier, vrai de vrai.

dinky ['diŋki] *a. F: O:* mignon, gentil.

dinner ['dinər] *n.* (*a*) (*evening meal*) dîner *m*, *Fr.C:* souper *m*; **to go out to d.,** dîner (i) en ville, dans un restaurant, (ii) chez des amis; **public d.,** banquet *m*; *Mil:* **regimental d.,** repas *m* de corps; **to give a d. party,** donner un dîner; **d. dance,** dîner-dansant *m, pl.* dîners-dansant; **d. service,** service *m* de table; **d. table,** table *f* de salle à manger; **after-d. speech,** discours *m* d'après-dîner; (*b*) (*midday*) **d.,** déjeuner *m*; *Sch:* **d. hour,** l'heure du déjeuner; (*c*) **to give the dog his d.,** donner à manger au chien; *P:* **to be got up like a dog's d.,** être tout fringué.

dinosaur ['dainousɔːr] *n. Paleont:* dinosaure *m*.

dint [dint] *n.* (*used in the prep. phr.*) **by d. of (doing) sth.,** à force de (faire) qch.

diocese ['daiəsis] *n. Ecc:* diocèse *m*.

diode ['daioud] *n. Elcs:* (lampe *f*) diode (*f*).

diopter [dai'ɔptər] *n. Opt.Meas:* dioptrie *f*.

dioxide [dai'ɔksaid] *n. Ch:* dioxyde *m*, bioxyde *m*.

dip[1] [dip] *n.* **1.** plongement *m*, immersion *f* (de qch. dans un liquide, etc). **2.** (*a*) inclinaison *f* (d'une aiguille aimantée); (*b*) inclinaison, dépression *f* (du terrain); (*in road*) caniveau *m*; (*c*) dépression (de l'horizon); (*d*) *esp. NAm:* baisse *f* (dans les prix, etc.). **3.** *Nau:* salut *m* (avec le pavillon). **4.** baignade *f*; **I'm going for a d.,** je vais me baigner. **5.** (*a*) *Ind:* solution *f*, bain *m* de dorure, etc.); (*b*) **(sheep) d.,** bain parasiticide (pour moutons); (*c*) *Cu:* **cheese d.,** hors d'œuvre *m* au fromage.

dip[2] *v.* **(dipped) I.** *v.tr.* **1.** plonger, tremper (les mains, etc., dans l'eau). **2.** (*a*) *Ind:* immerger, décaper (un métal); teindre (la laine, un tissu); *Tan:* confire (les peaux); (*b*) **to d. sheep,** baigner les moutons (dans un bain parasiticide); (*c*) plonger (des chandelles). **3.** baisser (qch.) subitement; *Aut:* **to d. one's headlights,** se mettre en code; *Nau:* **to d. a flag,** (faire) marquer un pavillon. **II.** *v.i.* **1.** (*a*) plonger (dans l'eau, etc.); (*b*) **to d. into (sth.),** feuilleter (un livre); effleurer (un sujet); prendre dans (son capital); **I'm always dipping into my pocket,** je suis toujours à débourser. **2.** (*a*) (*of compass needle*) incliner; (*of scale*) pencher; (*of ground*) s'abaisser, descendre; **the road dips sharply,** la route descend brusquement; (*b*) **the sun dipped below the horizon,** le soleil est descendu derrière l'horizon; (*c*) *esp. NAm:* (*of prices, etc.*) baisser; (*d*) (*of bird in flight*) piquer. **dipped** *a.* (*a*) incliné; (*b*) *Aut:* **d. headlights,** phares *mpl* code. **dipping 1.** *a.* incliné; **steeply d.,** plongeant. **2.** *n.* (*a*) plongée *f*, immersion *f*; *Metalw:* décapage *m*; (*b*) **sheep d.,** baignage *m* des moutons; (*c*) *Fish:* **d. net,** épuisette; (*d*) *Aut:* mise *f* en code (des phares).

diphtheria [dif'θiəriə] *n. Med:* diphtérie *f*.

diphthong ['difθɔŋ] *Ling:* diphtongue *f*.

diploid ['diplɔid] *a. Biol:* diploïde.

diploma [di'ploumə] *n.* diplôme *m*; *Sch:* **teacher's d.** = C.A.P. (Certificat d'aptitude pédagogique); **D. of Education** (*usu.* **Dip Ed.,** ['dip'ed]) = C.A.P.E.S. (Certificat d'aptitude au professorat de l'enseignement secondaire).

diplomacy [di'ploumәsi] *n.* (*a*) diplomatie *f*; (*b*) diplomatie, tact *m*; **to attain one's ends by d.,** user d'adresse pour atteindre son but.

diplomat ['dipləmæt] *n.* diplomate *m*.

diplomatic [diplə'mætik] *a.* **1.** (corps, etc.) diplomatique; **d. bag,** valise *f* diplomatique; **to enter the d. service,** entrer dans la diplomatie, *F:* dans la carrière. **2.** politique, diplomatique; **d. answer,** réponse *f* politique; **he knows how to be d.,** il a beaucoup de souplesse. **-ally** *adv.* **1.** diplomatiquement. **2.** avec tact.

diplomatist [di'ploumətist] *n.* diplomate *mf*.

dipole ['daipoul] *n. El:* dipôle *m*.

dipper ['dipər] *n.* **1.** *Orn: F:* (*a*) cincle plongeur (*b*) *esp. NAm:* martin-pêcheur *m, pl.* martins-pêcheurs. **2.** (*a*) cuillère *f* à pot; louche *f*; (*b*) *Astr: NAm:* **the Great, Big, D.,** la Grande Ourse; (*c*) (*on fairground*) **big d.,** le grand huit. **4.** *Aut:* **d. (switch),** basculeur *m* de phares.

dippy ['dipi] *a. F: O:* toqué.

dipsomania [dipsə'meiniə] *n.* dipsomanie *f*.

dipsomaniac [dipsə'meiniæk] *n.* dipsomane *mf*.

dipstick ['dipstik] *n. Aut:* jauge *f* (de niveau) d'huile.

dipswitch ['dipswitʃ] *n. Aut:* basculeur *m* de phares.

dire ['daiər] *a.* néfaste, affreux; (pressentiment) lugubre; **d. necessity,** dure nécessité; **to be in d. straits,** se trouver dans la plus grande détresse; **this decision will have d. consequences,** cette décision aura des conséquences néfastes.

direct[1] [d(a)i'rekt] *v.tr.* **1.** adresser (une lettre, des observations, etc.) **(to s.o.,** à qn). **2.** conduire (une armée, ses affaires); diriger, mener, gérer (une entreprise); *NAm: Th:* mettre (une pièce) en scène. **3.** (*a*) **to d. s.o.'s attention to sth.,** appeler, attirer, l'attention de qn sur qch.; (*b*) **accusation directed against s.o.,** accusation *f* visant, qui vise, qn; (*c*) **to d. one's steps towards . . .,** diriger ses pas, se diriger, vers . . .. **4. can you d. me to the station?** pouvez-vous m'indiquer le chemin de la gare? **5.** (*a*) **to d. s.o. to do sth.,** ordonner, dire, à qn de faire qch.; **as directed,** (i) conformément aux ordres; (ii) selon les instructions; (*b*) *Jur:* (*of judge*) **to d. the jury,** instruire le jury (sur un point de droit).

direct[2] **1.** *a.* (*a*) direct; (cause) immédiate; **to be a d. descendant of s.o.,** descendre de qn en ligne directe; **in d. contradiction,** en contradiction directe; *Gram:* **d. object, speech,** complément, discours, direct; *Artil: etc:* **d. hit,** coup *m* au but; *Pol.Ec:* **d. tax,** impôt direct; (*b*) (*of pers.*) franc, *f.* franche; ouvert; (*c*) absolu, formel; (réponse) catégorique; (*d*) *El:* **d. current,** courant continu. **2.** *adv.* (aller) directement, tout droit; **to dispatch goods d. to s.o.,** expédier des marchandises directement à qn; *W.Tel: T.V:* **the concert will be broadcast d. from Paris,** ce concert sera transmis en direct de Paris. **-ly 1.** *adv.* (*a*) (aller) directement, tout droit; (descendre de qn) en ligne directe; **to come d. to the point,** aller droit au fait; **I am not d. concerned,** cela ne m'intéresse pas personnellement; (*b*) absolument nettement; **d. opposite the church,** juste en face de l'église; (*c*) tout à l'heure; **I'm coming d.,** je viens tout de suite. **2.** *conj.* aussitôt que, dès que; **I'll come d. I've finished,** je viendrai dès que j'aurai fini.

direction [d(a)i'rekʃ(ə)n] *n.* **1.** (*a*) direction *f*, administration *f* (d'une société, etc.); **under the d. of . . .,** sous la direction, la conduite, de . . .; (*b*) réglementation *f* (de la circulation). **2.** (*a*) direction, sens *m*; *Aut:* **d. sign,** panneau *m* de signalisation; **in the d. of . . .,** dans la direction de . . .; **we were going in the d. of Paris,** nous nous dirigions vers Paris; **in every d.,** dans tous les sens; **in the opposite d.,** en sens inverse; **in which d.?** de quel côté? **you are not looking in the right d.,** vous ne regardez pas du bon côté; **to lose one's sense of d.,** perdre le sens de l'orientation; **change of d.,** changement *m* de direction; *Aer: Nau:* changement de cap; *Elcs:* **d. finder,** radiogoniomètre *m*; (*b*) **improvements in many directions,** améliorations *fpl* sous bien des rapports. **3.** (*a*) **directions,** instructions *fpl*; **you have been given the wrong directions,** on vous a mal renseigné; **stage directions,** indications *fpl* scéniques; **directions (for use),** notice (explicative); (*b*) *Jur:* **d. to the jury,** exposé *m* de la loi fait par le juge au jury.

directional [d(a)i'rekʃən(ə)l] *a. Elcs:* directionnel.

directive [d(a)i'rektiv] *n. Mil: etc:* directive *f*.

directness [d(a)i'rektnis] *n.* (*a*) franchise *f* (d'une réponse, etc.); (*b*) franchise bourrue; **his d. of speech,** son parler carré.

director [d(a)i'rektər] *n.* (*a*) administrateur *m*, directeur *m* (d'une société, etc.); gérant *m* (d'une entreprise); **managing d.,** administrateur délégué, gérant; **d. of music,** (i) *Ecc:* maître *m* de chapelle; (ii) *Mil: etc:* chef de musique; (*b*) *R.C.Ch:* directeur de conscience; (*c*) *Jur:* **d. of public prosecutions,** *approx.* = chef de parquet; (*d*) *Th: Cin:* metteur *m* en scène.

directorate [d(a)i'rektər(e)it] *n.* conseil *m* d'administration.

directorship [d(a)i'rektəʃip] *n.* **1.** poste *m*, fonctions *fpl*, de directeur, d'administrateur. **2. during my d.,** au cours de mon administration.

directory [d(a)i'rektəri] *n.* répertoire *m* d'adresses; (*in France*) = le Bottin; annuaire *m* (des téléphones, etc.); guide *m* des rues; **commercial d.,** annuaire du commerce; **he, his number, is ex d.,** son numéro ne figure pas dans l'annuaire.

dirge [də:dʒ] *n.* hymne *m*, chant *m*, funèbre.

dirigible ['diridʒibl] *a. & n.* **d. (balloon),** (ballon *m*) dirigeable (*m*).

dirk [də:k] *n.* poignard *m* (des Écossais).

dirt [də:t] *n.* **1.** saleté *f*; boue *f*, crotte *f*; (*unwashed*) crasse *f*; (*from drains*) curure *f*; (*excrement*) ordure *f*; **hands ingrained with d.,** mains encrassées; (*of material*) **to show the d.,** être salissant; **to treat s.o. like d.,** traiter qn comme le dernier des derniers; *Ind: etc:* **d. money,** indemnité *f*, prime *f*, de salissure; **d. cheap,** à vil prix; (*b*) corps étranger(s), saletés (dans une machine, une solution, etc.); (*c*) **d. road,** chemin *m* en terre, de terre battue; *NAm:* **d. farmer, farming,** exploitant *m*, exploitation *f*, agricole; *Sp:* **d. track,** piste *f* en cendrée; **d.-track racing,** courses *fpl* (motocyclistes) sur cendrée. **2.** (*a*) saleté, malpropreté; **to live in a state of d.,** vivre dans la saleté; (*b*) *F:* obscénités *fpl*; **to talk d.,** raconter des cochonneries; *P:* **to do d. on s.o.,** faire un sale coup à qn.

dirtiness ['də:tinis] *n.* saleté *f*, malpropreté *f*.

dirty¹ ['də:ti] *a.* **1.** (*a*) sale, malpropre, souillé, crasseux; (*with mud*) crotté; (*of valves, pistons, etc.*) encrassé; **d. clothes,** linge *m* sale; (*b*) **d. weather,** sale temps; *Nau:* gros temps; (*c*) *Typ:* **d. copy,** manuscrit brouillé, peu clair; (*d*) **d. money,** (i) *Ind: etc:* indemnité *f* de salissure; (ii) argent mal acquis; gratte *f*. **2.** (*a*) (esprit) cochon; (histoire, etc.) sale; (livre, film) pornographique; **d. word,** mot grossier; **work is a dirty w. nowadays,** personne ne veut plus travailler de nos jours; **d. old man,** vieux cochon; **to tell d. stories,** raconter des saletés; (*b*) *F:* **d. trick,** sale tour *m*; **to play a d. trick on s.o.,** *n.* **to do the d. on s.o.,** jouer un sale tour, un sale coup, à qn; **it's a d. business,** c'est une sale affaire, une affaire louche; **d. look,** sale coup *m* d'œil. **3.** *adv. F:* (*intensive*) **a d. great lorry,** un camion monstre. **-ily** *adv.* **1.** salement. **2.** grossièrement.

dirty² **1.** *v.tr.* salir (ses habits, etc.); **to d. one's hands,** se salir les mains. **2.** *v.i.* se souiller, se salir; (*of material*) **to d. easily,** se salir facilement.

disability [disə'biliti] *n.* **1.** (*a*) incapacité *f*, impuissance *f* (**to do, for doing, sth.,** de faire qch.); **under a d.,** incapable; (*b*) **(physical) d.,** infirmité *f*; (*c*) *Adm:* invalidité *f*; **d. pension,** pension *f* d'invalidité. **2.** *Jur:* incapacité légale; inhabilité *f* (à faire qch.).

disable [dis'eibl] *v.tr.* mettre (qn) hors de combat; estropier (qn); désemparer (un navire); mettre (une machine) hors de service; (*of ship*) **to be disabled,** être avarié, désemparé. **disabled** *a.* infirme; (*as result of accident, etc.*) estropié; mutilé; **d. ex-serviceman,** mutilé *m* de guerre; *n.pl.* **the badly d.,** les grands infirmes; les grands mutilés.

disablement [dis'eiblmənt] *n.* **1.** mise *f* hors de combat. **2.** invalidité *f*; *Adm:* **degree of d.,** coefficient *m* d'invalidité.

disabuse [disə'bju:z] *v.tr.* désabuser (**of,** de).

disadvantage¹ [disəd'vɑ:ntidʒ] *n.* désavantage *m*; inconvénient *m*; **to take s.o. at a d.,** prendre qn au dépourvu; **to be at a d. owing to sth.,** être désavantagé par qch.; **to be seen at a d.,** être vu sous un jour désavantageux.

disadvantage² *v.tr.* désavantager (qn).

disadvantageous [disædvæn'teidʒəs] *a.* désavantageux, défavorable (**to,** à).

disaffected [disə'fektid] *a.* mécontent; mal disposé (**to,** envers).

disaffection [disə'fekʃ(ə)n] *n.* désaffection *f* (**to,** envers); mécontentement *m*.

disagree [disə'gri:] *v.i.* **1.** (*a*) être en désaccord, ne pas être d'accord (**with,** avec); (*of accounts*) différer, ne pas concorder; (*b*) **to d. with s.o.,** ne pas être du même avis que qn; **I d.,** je ne suis pas de cet avis. **2.** (*a*) (*quarrel*) se brouiller (**with,** avec); (*b*) être en mésintelligence (**with s.o.,** avec qn). **3.** ne pas convenir (**with,** à); **the climate disagrees with him,** le climat ne lui convient pas, ne lui va pas; **wine disagrees with him,** le vin lui est contraire.

disagreeable [disə'gri:əbl] *a.* (*a*) désagréable, déplaisant (**to,** à); (*b*) fâcheux, incommode; (*c*) désagréable, maussade; (personne) désobligeante. **-ably** *adv.* désagréablement; fâcheusement.

disagreeableness [disə'gri:əblnis] *n.* **1.** désagrément *m*. **2.** (*a*) mauvaise humeur; maussaderie *f*; (*b*) désobligeance *f* (**to,** envers).

disagreement [disə'gri:mənt] *n.* **1.** différence *f* (**between,** entre). **2.** désaccord *m* (**with s.o. about sth.,** avec qn sur qch.); conflit *m* d'opinions; **to be in d. with s.o.,** ne pas partager l'avis de qn. **3.** (*a*) brouille *f*, différend *m*; (*b*) mésentente *f* (**between,** entre).

disallow [disə'lau] *v.tr.* **1.** ne pas admettre, reconnaître (une hypothèse, etc.); *Jur:* rejeter (un témoignage). **2.** *Fb: etc:* annuler (un but).

disappear [disə'piər] *v.i.* disparaître (**from a place,** d'un endroit); **to d. in, into, the crowd,** se perdre dans la foule; **since he disappeared,** depuis sa disparition.

disappearing *n.* disparition *f*; **to do a d. act,** (i) (*of conjurer*) faire disparaître qn, qch.; (ii) *F:* partir, s'esquiver.
disappearance [disə'piərəns] *n.* disparition *f.*
disappoint [disə'pɔint] *v.tr.* (*a*) désappointer (qn); (*after promising*) manquer de parole à (qn); (*b*) décevoir (qn); **he was bitterly disappointed,** il a eu une grave déception; **to be disappointed in love,** avoir des chagrins d'amour; (*c*) tromper (les espérances, de qn); **I am disappointed in, with, you,** vous avez trompé, démenti, mes espérances; **I was very much disappointed in it, with it,** cela m'a beaucoup déçu. **disappointed** *a.* déçu; (candidat) refusé; **d. customers,** clients mal satisfaits. **disappointing** *a.* décevant; **how d.!** (i) quelle déception! (ii) quel contretemps!
disappointment [disə'pɔintmənt] *n.* déception *f*; déboire *m*; contretemps *m*; **bitter d.,** vive contrariété; **to suffer many disappointments,** essuyer bien des déboires.
disapprobation [disæprou'beiʃ(ə)n] *n.* désapprobation *f* (**of,** de).
disapproval [disə'pruːv(ə)l] *n.* désapprobation *f* (**of,** de); **look of d.,** regard désapprobateur.
disapprove [disə'pruːv] **1.** *v.tr.* désapprouver, réprouver (qn); trouver mauvais (un usage, etc.). **2.** *v.i.* (*a*) **to d. of sth.,** désapprouver qch; **to d. of sth. being done,** désapprouver que l'on fasse qch.; (*b*) **she disapproves of her son-in-law,** son gendre n'est pas à son goût. **disapproving** *a.* désapprobateur, -trice. **disapprovingly** *adv.* avec désapprobation; d'un air, d'un ton, désapprobateur.
disarm [dis'ɑːm] **1.** *v.tr.* désarmer (un prisonnier, etc.); désamorcer (une bombe, etc.). **2.** *v.i.* désarmer. **disarming** *a.* (sourire, etc.) désarmant. **disarmingly** *adv.* **he was d. frank**, il montrait une franchise désarmante.
disarmament [dis'ɑːməmənt] *n.* désarmement *m.*
disarrange [disə'reindʒ] *v.tr.* déranger (qch.); mettre (qch.) en désordre; **to d. s.o.'s plans,** déranger, bouleverser, les projets de qn.
disarrangement [disə'reindʒmənt] *n.* dérangement *m*, désajustement *m*; désordre *m.*
disarray [disə'rei] *n.* désarroi *m*; désordre *m*; **in complete d.,** en plein désarroi; (*of troops*) en déroute.
disassociate [disə'souʃieit] *v.tr.* dissocier.
disaster [di'zɑːstər] *n.* désastre *m*; (*by shipwreck, fire*) sinistre *m*; **d. area,** région sinistrée; **railway d.,** catastrophe *f* de chemin de fer; **our journey was a series of disasters**, notre voyage n'a été qu'une suite de malheurs *mpl*; **he is heading for d.,** il court à sa perte; **it would be a d.!** ce serait le désastre!
disastrous [di'zɑːstrəs] *a.* désastreux. **-ly** *adv.* désastreusement.
disavow [disə'vau] *v.tr.* désavouer, renier.
disband [dis'bænd] **1.** *v.tr.* licencier (des troupes, etc.); dissoudre (un comité, etc.). **2.** *v.i.* (*of troops*) (i) se débander; (ii) être licencié; (*of committee*) être dissout.
disbar [dis'bɑːr] *v.tr.* **(disbarred)** rayer (un avocat) du barreau, du tableau de l'ordre.
disbarment [dis'bɑːmənt] *n.* radiation *f* (d'un avocat) du tableau de l'ordre, de la liste du barreau.
disbelief [disbi'liːf] *n.* incrédulité *f* (**in sth.,** à l'égard de qch.).
disbelieve [disbi'liːv] **1.** *v.tr.* ne pas croire, refuser de croire (qn, qch.). **2.** *v.i.* **to d. in s.o., in sth.,** ne pas croire à qn, à qch. **disbelieving** *a.* incrédule.
disbeliever [disbi'liːvər] *n.* incrédule *mf.*
disbud [dis'bʌd] *v.tr. Hort:* ébourgeonner.
disburse [dis'bəːs] *v.tr.* débourser (de l'argent).
disbursement [dis'bəːsmənt] *n.* **1.** déboursement *m.* **2.** *pl.* débours *m.*
disc [disk] *n.* (*a*) disque *m* (de la lune, etc.); (*b*) *Mil: etc:* **identity, identification, d.,** plaque *f* d'identité; *Aut:* **parking d.,** disque de stationnement; (*c*) *Tchn:* disque, plateau *m*; rondelle *f* (en carton, etc.); *Aut:* **d. brakes,** freins *mpl* à disque; **d. wheel,** roue pleine, à voile plein; (*d*) *Agr:* **d. harrow,** pulvériseur *m*; **d. plough,** charrue *f* à disques; (*e*) *Rec:* disque; *W.Tel:* **d. jockey,** disc-jockey *m*; (*f*) *Anat:* **intervertebral d.,** disque intervertébral; *Med:* **slipped d.,** hernie discale; **to slip a d.,** se faire une hernie discale.
discard¹ ['diskɑːd] *n.* **1.** *Cards:* (*a*) (*at cribbage*) écart *m* (action ou carte); (*b*) (*at bridge*) défausse *f.* **2.** pièce *f* de rebut.
discard² [dis'kɑːd] *v.tr.* **1.** *Cards:* (*a*) (*at cribbage*) écarter (une carte); (*b*) (*at bridge, etc.*) défausser (d'une couleur); *v.i.* **to d.,** se défausser. **2.** mettre (qch.) de côté; abandonner (un projet); mettre au rebut (un vêtement).
discern [di'səːn] *v.tr.* (*a*) distinguer, discerner, percevoir; **to d. a distant object,** discerner, reconnaître, un objet dans le lointain; (*b*) **to d. good from bad,** discerner le bien d'avec le mal. **discerning** *a.* (*of pers.*) éclairé; plein de discernement; (*of intelligence*) pénétrant; (*of taste*) délicat.
discernible [di'səːnibl] *a.* perceptible. **-ibly** *adv.* perceptiblement.
discernment [di'səːnmənt] *n.* **1.** discernement *m* (**between . . . and . . .,** de . . . et de . . .). **2.** discernement; jugement *m.*
discharge¹ ['distʃɑːdʒ] *n.* **1.** déchargement *m* (d'un navire, d'une cargaison). **2.** décharge *f* (d'artillerie); départ *m* (d'une arme à feu). **3.** (*a*) décharge, évacuation *f* (d'eau, etc.); décharge, dégagement *m* (de gaz); échappement *m* (de vapeur); débit *m* (d'une pompe); **d. pipe,** tuyau *m* de décharge, de débit; **d. pump,** pompe *f* d'extraction, d'épuisement; (*b*) *El:* décharge (d'électricité); (*c*) *El:* décharge (d'une pile); (*d*) *Med:* (i) perte *f*; (ii) suppuration *f*; (*e*) (*from factory, etc.*) eaux usées. **4.** (*a*) renvoi *m*, congé *m* (d'un employé); (*b*) libération (temporaire ou définitive); congé; (*after active service*) démobilisation *f*; *Mil: Navy:* **to take one's d.,** prendre son congé; (*c*) *Mil: Navy:* (*for unfitness*) réforme *f*; (*d*) (*from hospital*) renvoi (d'un malade guéri). **5.** *Jur:* (*a*) mise *f* en liberté, libération (d'un prisonnier); (*b*) acquittement *m* (d'un accusé); (*c*) **d. in bankruptcy,** réhabilitation *f* (d'un failli); **to apply for one's d.,** demander, obtenir, sa réhabilitation. **6.** accomplissement *m* (d'un devoir); **in the d. of his duties,** dans l'exercice *m* de ses fonctions. **7.** (*a*) paiement *m* (d'une dette); (*b*) quittance *f*, décharge, acquit.
discharge² [dis'tʃɑːdʒ] **I.** *v.tr.* **1.** décharger (un navire, un réservoir, etc.). **2.** (*a*) décharger, tirer, faire partir (une arme à feu); (*b*) *El:* décharger (une pile, etc.); **discharged battery,** accu *m* à vide. **3.** (*a*) décharger, débarquer (une cargaison); (*b*) (*of vehicle*) déposer (des voyageurs). **4.** (*a*) congédier, renvoyer (un employé); débaucher (un ouvrier); destituer (un fonctionnaire); (*b*) licencier (des troupes); congédier, mettre en congé, donner son congé à, désenrôler (un militaire); **to be discharged from the force,** être congédié; (*c*) *Mil: Navy:* (*for unfitness*) réformer (un homme); (*d*) (*from hospital*), renvoyer (un malade guéri); **he was discharged from hospital yesterday,** il est sorti de l'hôpital hier; (*e*) *Jur:* **to d. the jury,** congédier les jurés. **5.** *Jur:* (*a*) libérer, mettre en liberté (un prisonnier); (*b*) acquitter (un accusé). **6.** (*a*) décharger, libérer, acquitter (qn) **(of an obligation,** d'une obligation); (*b*) *Jur:* réhabiliter, décharger (un failli); **discharged bankrupt,** failli réhabilité. **7.** (*a*) lancer (un projectile); (*b*) (*of abscess*) **to d. pus,** suppurer; (*c*) (*of chemical reaction*)

dégager (un gaz); dégager (de la vapeur); (*of gland*) sécréter (des hormones); (*d*) (*of reservoir, etc.*) déverser (de l'eau); (*of pump*) débiter (de l'eau); **river that discharges its water into a lake,** rivière qui déverse ses eaux dans un lac. **8.** (*a*) accomplir (un devoir); s'acquitter de (son devoir); (*b*) liquider, solder (une dette); payer (une amende); apurer (un compte, une obligation). **II.** *v.i.* **1.** (*of ship, etc.*) se décharger; être en déchargement. **2.** (*of gun*) partir, se décharger. **3.** (*of abscess, wound*) suppurer. **4.** (*of river*) se jeter, déboucher (**into a lake,** dans un lac).

disciple [di'saipl] *n.* disciple *m.*

disciplinarian [disipli'nɛəriən] *n.* **1.** disciplinaire *m*; **he is a strict d.,** il est strict en matière de discipline. **2.** partisan, -ane, d'une forte discipline.

disciplinary ['disiplinəri] *a.* disciplinaire.

discipline[1] ['disiplin] *n.* (*a*) discipline *f*; **iron d.,** discipline de fer; **to keep children under d.,** soumettre les enfants à la discipline; (*b*) (*branch of learning*) discipline.

discipline[2] *v.tr.* (*a*) discipliner (des élèves, des troupes); (*b*) former (le caractère).

disclaim [dis'kleim] *v.tr.* **1.** *Jur:* se désister de, renoncer à (un droit, etc.). **2.** désavouer, dénier (qch.); **to d. all knowledge of sth.,** nier toute connaissance de qch. **3.** rejeter, renier (l'autorité de qn).

disclaimer [dis'kleimər] *n.* (*a*) *Jur:* désistement *m*; renonciation *f* (**of a right,** à un droit); (*b*) dénégation *f* (de responsabilité); **d. of authorship (of a work),** désaveu *m* (d'une œuvre).

disclose [dis'klouz] *v.tr.* **1.** révéler (qch.). **2.** divulguer, déceler, dévoiler (un secret, etc.).

disclosure [dis'klouʒər] *n.* **1.** mise *f* à découvert (d'un trésor, etc.); révélation *f* (de sa pensée, etc.); divulgation *f* (d'un secret). **2.** (*fact disclosed*) révélation *f*.

disco ['diskou] *n. F:* discothèque *f*.

discolour, *NAm:* **discolor** [dis'kʌlər] **1.** *v.tr.* (*a*) décolorer; (*b*) ternir, délaver (un tissu, etc.); **to become discoloured,** (i) se décolorer; (ii) se ternir. **2.** *v.i.* (*a*) se décolorer; (*b*) se ternir.

discolo(u)ration [diskʌlə'reiʃ(ə)n] *n.* **1.** décoloration *f*. **2.** ternissure *f*.

discombobulate [diskəm'bɔbjuleit] *v.tr. U.S: F:* déranger, confondre (qn).

discomfiture [dis'kʌmfitjər] *n.* déconvenue *f* (de qn); embarras *m*, trouble *m*.

discomfort [dis'kʌmfət] *n.* (*a*) manque *m* de confort, inconfort *m*; (*b*) malaise *m*, gêne *f*.

discomposure [diskəm'pouʒər] *n.* trouble *m*, agitation *f*; perturbation *f* (d'esprit).

disconcert [diskən'səːt] *v.tr.* déconcerter, troubler (qn). **disconcerting** *a.* déconcertant, troublant. **disconcertingly** *adv.* d'une manière déconcertante.

disconnect [diskə'nekt] *v.tr.* **1.** disjoindre, séparer, détacher (**sth. from sth.,** qch. de qch.); décrocher (des wagons); débrayer, désembrayer (une machine, etc.). **2.** *El:* mettre (un accumulateur, etc.) hors circuit; débrancher (un accu, etc.); *Tp:* couper (la ligne); **I've been disconnected,** on a coupé la communication. **disconnected** *a.* **1.** (*a*) détaché, isolé; (*b*) *Mec.E:* débrayé; *El:* débranché. **2.** (*of speech, style, etc.*) décousu, sans suite; (histoire) sans queue ni tête. **disconnecting** *n.* **1.** désunion *f* (des parties d'une machine); décrochage *m* (d'un wagon, etc.); débrayage *m*, désembrayage *m* (d'une machine, etc.). **2.** *El:* mise *f* (d'un accu, etc.) hors circuit.

disconnection, disconnexion [diskə'nekʃ(ə)n] *n.* **1.** = DISCONNECTING; *see* DISCONNECT. **2.** séparation *f* (**between,** entre).

disconsolate [dis'kɔnsələt] *a.* tout triste; inconsolable; désolé. **-ly** *adv.* tristement; d'un air désolé.

discontent [diskən'tent] *n.* mécontentement *m*; **general d.,** mécontentement général.

discontented [diskən'tentid] *a.* mécontent (**with,** de); peu satisfait (de son sort, etc.); aigri.

discontinue [diskən'tinju] *v.tr.* (*a*) **to d. (doing) sth.,** discontinuer (de faire) qch.; (*b*) *Jur:* abandonner (un procès).

discontinuity [diskɔnti'nju(ː)iti] *n.* discontinuité *f*; manque *m* de suite (dans les idées).

discontinuous [diskən'tinjuəs] *a.* (i) discontinu; (ii) intermittent.

discord ['diskɔːd] *n.* **1.** discorde *f*, désaccord *m*. **2.** bruit discordant; discordance *f*, désaccord *m* (des voix, etc.). **3.** *Mus:* (i) dissonance *f* (de deux notes); (ii) accord dissonant.

discordance [dis'kɔːdəns] *n.* **1.** discordance *f* (des sons). **2.** désaccord *m* (d'opinions, etc.).

discordant [dis'kɔːd(ə)nt] *a.* **1.** (*a*) (*of sound*) discordant; (voix) criarde; (*b*) *Mus:* dissonant. **2. d. opinions,** opinions opposées.

discotheque ['diskətek] *n.* discothèque *f*.

discount[1] ['diskaunt] *n.* **1.** *Com:* remise *f*; **to sell sth. at a d.,** vendre qch. au rabais; **cash d.,** escompte *m* de caisse; **trade d.,** remise d'usage; **to allow a d. of 10%,** consentir un rabais de 10%; **d. price,** prix *m* faible; **d. store,** magasin *m* de demi-gros. **2.** (*a*) *Fin:* escompte; **d. bank,** banque *f* d'escompte; **to be at a d.,** (i) (*of shares*) être en perte; se trouver en moins-value; (ii) *Fig:* (*of politeness, etc.*) être en défaveur.

discount[2] [dis'kaunt, 'diskaunt] *v.tr.* **1.** *Fin:* escompter; prendre (un effet) à l'escompte. **2.** (*a*) ne pas tenir compte de (qn, qch.); (*b*) faire peu de cas de (l'avis de qn, un avertissement); **you must d. half of what he says,** il faut rabattre la moitié de ce qu'il dit.

discourage [dis'kʌridʒ] *v.tr.* **1.** décourager, abattre (qn); **to become discouraged,** se décourager. **2.** (*a*) décourager (un projet, etc.); rebuter (un soupirant, la critique, etc.); (*b*) **to d. s.o. from (doing) sth.,** décourager qn de (faire) qch. **discouraging** *a.* décourageant.

discouragement [dis'kʌridʒmənt] *n.* **1.** découragement *m*. **2.** désapprobation *f* (d'un projet).

discourse[1] ['diskɔːs] *n. Lit:* (*a*) discours *m*; (*b*) dissertation *f* (**on,** sur).

discourse[2] [dis'kɔːs] *v.i. Lit:* (*a*) discourir (**on, of,** sur); (*b*) parler, s'entretenir (de).

discourteous [dis'kəːtiəs] *a.* discourtois, impoli. **-ly** *adv.* impoliment; d'une façon impolie.

discourtesy [dis'kəːtəsi] *n.* incivilité *f*, impolitesse *f*.

discover [dis'kʌvər] *v.tr.* (*a*) découvrir (une planète, la cause d'une maladie, etc.); **we have discovered a good gardener,** nous avons déniché un bon jardinier; (*b*) **I discovered too late that . . .,** je me suis rendu compte trop tard que . . ..

discoverer [dis'kʌvərər] *n.* découvreur *m* (de l'Amérique, etc.).

discovery [dis'kʌvəri] *n.* (*a*) découverte *f* (d'une planète, etc.); **voyage of d.,** voyage *m* d'exploration *f*; (*b*) **to make a d.,** faire une découverte; **great d.,** (i) grande découverte; (ii) (*of a find*) trouvaille *f*.

discredit[1] [dis'kredit] *n.* **1.** doute *m*; **to throw d. on a statement,** mettre en doute une affirmation. **2.** (*a*) discrédit *m* (de qn, de qch.); **to bring d. on s.o., sth.,** jeter le discrédit sur qn, qch.; discréditer qn, qch.; **to bring sth. into d.,** discréditer qch.; **to bring d. on oneself,** se discréditer.

discredit[2] *v.tr.* **1.** ne pas croire (un bruit); mettre en doute (un bruit). **2.** discréditer (qn, une opinion); déconsidérer (qn); **his conduct has discredited him with the public,** sa conduite lui a fait perdre la considération du public.

discreditable [dis'kreditəbl] *a.* **1.** peu digne, peu honorable; **conduct d. to a barrister,** conduite *f* indigne d'un avocat. **2.** (composition, ouvrage) qui ne fait pas honneur (à son auteur); **her performance was far from d.,** elle ne s'est pas mal acquittée.

discreet [dis'kri:t] *a.* **1.** avisé, prudent; **a d. smile,** un petit sourire contenu. **2.** discret, -ète; **to maintain a d. silence,** observer un silence discret. **-ly** *adv.* **1.** prudemment. **2.** discrètement, avec discrétion.

discrepancy [dis'krepənsi] *n.* désaccord *m*; écart *m*; **there is a d. between the two stories,** les deux récits ne cadrent pas; **there is a d. in the accounts,** les comptes *mpl* ne sont pas justes.

discrete [dis'kri:t] *a. Mth: etc:* discret, ète.

discretion [dis'kreʃ(ə)n] *n.* **1.** (*liberty of action*) discrétion *f*; **I shall use my own d.,** je ferai comme je jugerai à propos; **to leave sth. to s.o.'s d.,** laisser qch. à la discrétion de qn; **at your d.,** comme vous voudrez; *Jur:* **fine at, left to, the d. of the judge,** amende *f* arbitraire. **2.** (*judgment*) jugement *m*, prudence *f*; **the age of d.,** l'âge *m* de raison; **d. is the better part of valour,** l'essentiel du courage c'est la prudence. **3.** discrétion, réserve *f*; **he is the soul of d.,** il est la discrétion même.

discretionary [dis'kreʃən(ə)ri] *a. Jur:* (pouvoir) discrétionnaire.

discriminate [dis'krimineit] **1.** *v.tr.* distinguer (**from,** de, d'avec). **2.** *v.i.* (*a*) distinguer, établir une distinction (**between,** entre); faire la différence (entre deux choses); (*b*) **to d. in favour of s.o., against s.o.,** faire des distinctions en faveur de qn, contre qn. **discriminating** *a.* **1.** (*of pers.*) plein de discernement; capable de juger; (acheteur) avisé, averti; (oreille) fine. **2.** (loi) qui fait la distinction des personnes; *Adm:* (droit, tarif) différentiel.

discrimination [diskrimini'neiʃ(ə)n] *n.* **1.** discrimination *f*, discernement *m* (**between . . . and,** entre . . . et). **2.** jugement *m*, discernement. **3.** discrimination, distinction *f*; mesures *fpl* discriminatoires; **without d.,** sans discrimination; **race, racial, d.,** discrimination raciale.

discursive [dis'kə:siv] *n.* (style, etc.) décousu.

discus ['diskəs] *n. Sp:* disque *m*; **d. thrower,** lanceur, -euse, de disque.

discuss [dis'kʌs] *v.tr.* discuter, débattre (un problème, etc.); délibérer (d'une question); **I know they were discussing me,** je sais qu'on parlait de moi.

discussion [dis'kʌʃ(ə)n] *n.* discussion *f*; **a subject for d.,** un sujet de discussion; **question under d.,** question *f* en discussion; **after much d. of sth.,** après avoir longtemps discuté qch.

disdain¹ [dis'dein] *n.* dédain *m* (**of,** de).

disdain² *v.tr.* dédaigner (qn, qch.); **to d. to do sth.,** dédaigner de faire qch.

disdainful [dis'deinful] *a.* dédaigneux (**of,** de). **-ly** *adv.* dédaigneusement.

disease [di'zi:z] *n.* **1.** (*a*) maladie *f*; **to die of a d.,** mourir d'une maladie; **skin d.,** maladie de la peau; **Parkinson's d.,** maladie de Parkinson; *Vet:* **foot and mouth d.,** fièvre aphteuse; (*b*) maladie (des pommes de terre, des vins, etc.).

diseased [di'zi:zd] *a.* malade.

disembark [disem'bɑ:k] *v.tr. & i.* débarquer (**from,** de).

disembarkation [disembɑ:'keiʃ(ə)n] *n.* débarquement *m*.

disembodied [dizim'bɔdid] *a.* (esprit) désincarné.

disembowel [disim'bauəl] *v.tr.* éventrer; éviscérer.

disenchant [disin'tʃɑ:nt] *v.tr.* désillusionner (qn). **disenchanted** *a.* désillusionné.

disenchantment [disin'tʃɑ:ntmənt] *n.* désillusion *f*.

disengage [disin'geidʒ] **1.** *v.tr.* (*a*) dégager, débarrasser (**s.o., sth., from sth.,** qn, qch., de qch.); (*b*) *Mec.E:* désengrener (une roue dentée); débrayer, désembrayer (un organe). **2.** *v.i.* (*a*) se dégager; (*b*) *Mec.E:* (*of catch, etc:*) se déclencher, se défaire. **disengaged** *a. Mec.E: etc:* debrayé.

disengagement [disin'geidʒmənt] *n.* **1.** détachement *m*, dégagement *m* (**from,** de). **2.** *Mec.E:* débrayage *m* (d'un organe). **3.** *Pol: Mil:* désengagement *m*.

disentangle [disin'tæŋgl] **1.** *v.tr.* démêler; (*a*) débarrasser (**s.o., sth., from sth.,** qn, qch., de qch.); (*b*) débrouiller (une ficelle); dénouer (une intrigue). **2.** *v.i.* se démêler, se débrouiller.

disestablish [disis'tæbliʃ] *v.tr.* séparer (l'Église) de l'État.

disestablishment [disis'tæbliʃmənt] *n.* **d. of the Church,** séparation *f* de l'Église et de l'État.

disfavour, *NAm:* **disfavor** [dis'feivər] *n.* défaveur *f*; **to fall into d.,** tomber en disgrâce; **at the risk of incurring s.o.'s d.,** au risque de déplaire à qn.

disfigure [dis'figər] *v.tr.* défigurer (qn, une statue, etc.); (*of buildings, etc.*) gâter, abîmer (le paysage). **disfigured** *a.* défiguré.

disfigurement [dis'figəmənt] *n.* défiguration *f* (de qn, d'une statue); enlaidissement *m*.

disfranchise [dis'fræn(t)ʃaiz] *v.tr.* priver (qn) du droit électoral, de ses droits civiques; priver (un bourg) de ses droits de représentation.

disgorge [dis'gɔ:dʒ] *v.tr.* (*a*) dégorger, rendre (la nourriture); (*b*) *v.i.* **river that disgorges into . . .,** rivière *f* qui se décharge, dans . . .

disgrace¹ [dis'greis] *n.* **1.** disgrâce *f*, défaveur *f*; **to be in d.,** être en disgrâce; (*of child*) être en pénitence *f*. **2.** (*a*) honte *f*, déshonneur *m*; **there is no d. in doing that,** il n'y a pas honte à faire cela; **to bring d. on one's family,** déshonorer sa famille; (*b*) **to be a d. to one's family,** être la honte de sa famille; faire honte à sa famille; *F:* **it's a d.!** c'est une honte, un scandale!

disgrace² *v.tr.* **1.** (*esp. in passive*) **to be disgraced,** être disgrâcié (**for,** pour). **2.** déshonorer; faire déshonneur à (qn); **to d. oneself,** (i) se conduire indignement; (ii) se couvrir de honte.

disgraceful [dis'greisful] *a.* honteux, infâme; **it's d.,** c'est scandaleux. **-fully** *adv.* honteusement; d'une manière scandaleuse.

disgruntled [dis'grʌntld] *a.* contrarié, mécontent (**at,** de); maussade.

disguise¹ [dis'gaiz] *n.* **1.** déguisement *m*; **in d.,** déguisé. **2.** feinte *f*; **to throw off all d.,** laisser tomber le masque, lever le masque.

disguise² *v.tr.* **1.** déguiser, travestir (qn); **to d. oneself as a clown,** se déguiser en clown. **2.** (*a*) déguiser (sa pensée, ses sentiments); déguiser, contrefaire (sa voix, son écriture); masquer (une odeur); (*b*) déguiser (la vérité); **there is no disguising the fact that . . .,** il faut avouer que . . .; (*c*) dissimuler (ses sentiments).

disgust¹ [dis'gʌst] *n.* **1.** dégoût profond; répugnance *f* (**at, for, towards,** pour). **2.** profond mécontentement.

disgust² *v.tr.* **1.** dégoûter; donner la nausée à (qn). **2.** indigner; **to be disgusted at, with, by, sth.,** être écœuré de qch.; **he is disgusted that . . .,** il est indigné, révolté, scandalisé, que + *sub.*, de ce que + *ind.* **disgusting** *a.* dégoûtant; écœurant; **it's d.!** c'est dégoûtant! **disgustingly** *adv.* dégoûtamment; **d. dirty,** d'une saleté répugnante.

dish¹ [diʃ] *n.* **1.** (*a*) plat *m*; (*earthenware*) terrine *f*; **vegetable d.,** légumier *m*; **butter d.,** beurrier *m*; (*b*) **to wash, do, the dishes,** faire la vaisselle; (*c*) (*contents*) **a. d. of strawberries,** un plat de fraises. **2.** *Cu:* plat (de viande, de légumes, etc.); mets *m*; **it's not a d. I often make,** ce n'est pas une recette, un plat, que je prépare souvent. **3.** (*a*) récipient *m*; *Phot:* cuvette *f*; (*b*) creux *m*, dénivellement *m* (de terrain, etc.); (*c*) *Rad: etc:* **d. antenna,** antenne *f* paraboloïde. **4.** *P:*

belle fille, jolie pépée; **she's a real d.,** ce qu'elle est belle.

dish² *v.tr. F:* achever, désarçonner, enfoncer (qn). **dish out** *v.tr.* (*a*) servir (la viande, etc.); (*b*) distribuer; **to d. out punishment,** (i) (*of boxer*) assener des coups (à son adversaire); (ii) (*of schoolmaster, etc.*) punir (ses élèves). **dish up** *v.tr.* (*a*) (i) mettre (la viande, etc.) sur un plat; (ii) servir (un plat, un repas); **shall I d. up?** je peux servir? je sers? (*b*) *F:* sortir tout un tas d'excuses, etc.

disharmony [dis'hɑːməni] *n.* **1.** désaccord *m*; manque *m* d'harmonie. **2.** (*of sound*) dissonance *f*.

dishcloth ['diʃklɔθ] *n.* torchon *m* (i) à laver, (ii) à essuyer, la vaisselle.

dishearten [dishɑːt(ə)n] *v.tr.* décourager, abattre, rebuter; **to become disheartened,** perdre courage. **disheartening** *a.* décourageant.

dishevelled [di'ʃevəld] *a.* (*a*) (*of pers.*) échevelé, dépeigné; les cheveux ébouriffés; (*b*) (cheveux) ébouriffés.

dishmop ['diʃmɔp] *n.* lavette *f* (à vaisselle).

dishonest [dis'ɔnist] *a.* malhonnête, peu honnête. **-ly** *adv.* malhonnêtement.

dishonesty [dis'ɔnisti] *n.* improbité *f*; malhonnêteté *f*.

dishonour¹, *NAm:* **dishonor¹** [dis'ɔnər] *n.* **1.** déshonneur *m*; **to bring d. on one's family,** déshonorer sa famille. **2.** chose déshonorante. **3.** non-paiement *m* (d'un chèque); non-acceptation *f* (d'un effet de commerce).

dishonour², *NAm:* **dishonor²** *v.tr.* **1.** déshonorer. **2.** (*a*) manquer à (sa parole); (*b*) *Com:* ne pas accepter (un effet); refuser de payer (un effet); **dishonoured cheque,** chèque impayé.

dishonourable, *NAm:* **dishonorable** [dis'ɔnərəbl] *a.* **1.** (*of pers.*) sans honneur; dépourvu d'honneur. **2.** (*of action*) honteux, indigne. **-ably** *adv.* avec déshonneur, de façon déshonorante.

dishrag ['diʃræg] *n.* torchon *m* à laver la vaisselle.

dishwasher ['diʃwɔʃər] *n.* **1.** (*in restaurant*) plongeur, -euse. **2.** lave-vaisselle *m inv*; *Fr.C:* laveuse *f* à vaisselle.

dishwater ['diʃwɔːtər] *n.* **1.** eau *f* de vaisselle. **2.** *F:* (*tasteless soup, coffee, etc.*) lavasse *f*.

dishy ['diʃi] *a. F:* séduisant; sexy; **he's, she's, very d.,** ce qu'il, qu'elle, est beau, belle.

disillusion [disi'ljuːʒən] *v.tr.* désillusionner, désabuser, désenchanter. **disillusioned** *a.* désillusionné, désenchanté.

disillusionment [disi'ljuːʒənmənt] *n.* désillusionnement *m*, désenchantement *m*.

disincentive [disin'sentiv] *n. Pol.Ec: etc:* facteur décourageant; **heavy taxation is a d. to expansion,** les taxes élevées découragent toute expansion.

disinclination [disiŋkli'neiʃ(ə)n] *n.* répugnance *f*, aversion *f* (**for, to,** pour); **to have, show, a d. to do sth.,** montrer peu d'empressement à faire qch.

disinclined [disin'klaind] *a.* peu disposé, peu enclin (à faire qch.).

disinfect [disin'fekt] *v.tr.* désinfecter.

disinfectant [disin'fektənt] *a. & n.* désinfectant (*m*).

disinfection [disin'fekʃ(ə)n] *n.* désinfection *f*.

disingenuous [disin'dʒenjuəs] *a.* (*of pers.*) sans franchise; insincère, finaud.

disingenuousness [disin'dʒenjuəsnis] *n.* manque *m* de franchise; sournoiserie *f*.

disinherit [disin'herit] *v.tr.* déshériter.

disintegrate [dis'intigreit] **1.** *v.tr.* désagréger. **2.** *v.i.* (*a*) (*of stone, etc.*) se désagréger, se désintégrer, s'effriter; (*b*) *Atom.Ph:* se désintégrer.

disintegration [disinti'greiʃ(ə)n] *n.* (*a*) désagrégation *f*, désintégration *f*; effritement *m* (de la pierre); (*b*) *Atom.Ph:* désintégration *f*.

disinter [disin'təːr] *v.tr.* (**disinterred**) déterrer, exhumer (un mort, des antiquités).

disinterested [dis'intərestid] *a.* **1.** (*of action, etc.*) désintéressé. **2.** (*of pers.*) indifférent (**in,** à).

disinterestedness [dis'intərestidnis] *n.* **1.** désintéressement *m*. **2.** indifférence *f*.

disinterment [disin'təːmənt] *n.* déterrement *m*; exhumation *f*.

disjointed [dis'dʒɔintid] *a.* (discours) sans suite, incohérent; (style) haché, décousu.

disk [disk] *n.* = DISC.

dislike¹ [dis'laik] *n.* aversion *f*, dégoût *m*, répugnance *f* (**to, of, for,** pour); **to take, conceive, a d. to s.o.,** prendre qn en grippe; **to conceive a d. for sth.,** prendre qch. en dégoût.

dislike² *v.tr.* ne pas aimer; **I don't d. him,** il ne me déplaît pas; **to d. doing sth.,** détester faire qch.

dislocate ['disləkeit] *v.tr.* (*a*) désorganiser (les affaires); bouleverser (un projet); (*b*) *Med:* luxer, démettre, disloquer (un membre); **to d. one's jaw,** se décrocher la mâchoire.

dislocation [dislə'keiʃ(ə)n] *n.* (*a*) bouleversement *m* (d'un projet, etc.); désorganisation *f* (des affaires); (*b*) *Med:* luxation *f*, déboîtement *m*, dislocation (d'un membre).

dislodge [dis'lɔdʒ] *v.tr.* **1.** déloger, débusquer (l'ennemi) (**from,** de). **2.** détacher; **several bricks had become dislodged,** plusieurs briques s'étaient détachées.

disloyal [dis'lɔiəl] *a.* infidèle (à son roi, à l'amitié); déloyal, -aux.

disloyalty [dis'lɔiəlti] *n.* infidélité *f*, déloyauté *f*.

dismal ['dizm(ə)l] *a.* lugubre, sombre, triste; (paysage, avenir) morne; (échec) lamentable. **-ally** *adv.* tristement; **to fail d.,** échouer lamentablement.

dismantle [dis'mæntl] *v.tr.* (*a*) démanteler (une forteresse); (*b*) démonter (une machine, un fusil, etc.).

dismast [dis'mɑːst] *v.tr. Nau:* démâter.

dismay¹ [dis'mei] *n.* consternation *f*, effarement *m*; **in d.,** consterné, atterré.

dismay² *v.tr.* consterner; **we were dismayed at the news,** cette nouvelle nous jeta dans la consternation.

dismember [dis'membər] *v.tr.* démembrer.

dismemberment [dis'membəmənt] *n.* démembrement *m*.

dismiss [dis'mis] *v.tr.* **1.** congédier, renvoyer (qn); chasser (un domestique); révoquer (un fonctionnaire); **to be dismissed,** recevoir son congé; *Mil:* **to d. s.o. from the service,** (i) rayer qn des cadres *mpl* de l'armée; (ii) réformer qn. **2.** (*a*) congédier (aimablement) (qn); donner à (qn) la permission de se retirer; (*b*) congédier, éconduire (un importun, etc.); (*c*) dissoudre (une assemblée). **3. to d. sth. from one's mind,** chasser, éloigner, qch. de ses pensées; **to d. a threat,** ne tenir aucun compte d'une menace. **4.** quitter, abandonner (un sujet de conversation, etc.). **5.** écarter (une proposition); *Jur:* rejeter (une demande, un appel); **to d. a case,** (i) classer une affaire; (ii) rendre une fin de non-recevoir; **to d. a charge,** rendre une ordonnance de non-lieu. **6.** *Mil:* **to d. a parade,** faire rompre les rangs *mpl* (aux troupes); **dismiss!** rompez (les rangs)! **7.** *Cr:* (*of batsman*) **dismissed for ten,** mis hors jeu quand il n'a marqué que dix points.

dismissal [dis'mis(ə)l] *n.* **1.** congédiement *m*, renvoi *m* (d'un employé); révocation *f* (d'un fonctionnaire). **2.** *Jur:* fin *f* de non-recevoir; rejet *m* (d'une demande, d'un appel).

dismount [dis'maunt] **1.** *v.i.* **to d. (from a horse, bicycle),** descendre (de cheval, de bicyclette). **2.** *v.tr.* (*a*) démonter, désarçonner (un cavalier); (*b*) démonter (un canon, une machine).

disobedience [disə'bi:diens] *n.* désobéissance *f* (**to s.o.,** à qn); **civil d.,** résistance passive.
disobedient [disə'bi:diənt] *a.* désobéissant; **to be d. to s.o.,** désobéir à qn.
disobey [disə'bei] *v.tr.* désobéir (à qn, à un ordre); enfreindre (un ordre, la loi).
disobliging [disə'blaidʒiŋ] *a.* désobligeant (**to,** envers).
disorder[1] [dis'ɔ:dər] *n.* **1.** désordre *m*, confusion *f*; **in d.,** en désordre; **they fled in d.,** ils s'enfuirent à la débandade. **2.** désordre, trouble *m*; **serious disorders have broken out,** de graves désordres ont éclaté. **3.** *Med:* **nervous d.,** troubles nerveux, affection nerveuse; **personality d.,** trouble caractériel.
disorder[2] *v.tr.* **1.** déranger; mettre (qch.) en désordre. **2.** déranger (l'estomac). **disordered** *a.* (estomac) dérangé; (foie, esprit) malade.
disorderliness [dis'ɔ:dəlinis] *n.* **1.** désordre *m*. **2.** conduite *f* contraire aux bonnes mœurs. **3.** turbulence *f*.
disorderly [dis'ɔ:dəli] *a.* **1.** qui manque d'ordre; désordonné; en désordre. **2.** (*of mob, etc.*) turbulent, tumultueux. **3.** (*of pers., behaviour*) désordonné, déréglé; **to lead a d. life,** vivre dans le dérèglement. **4.** *Jur:* **d. house,** (i) maison *f* de débauche; (ii) maison de jeu.
disorganization [disɔ:gənai'zeiʃ(ə)n] *n.* désorganisation *f*.
disorganize [dis'ɔ:gənaiz] *v.tr.* désorganiser; **to become disorganized,** se désorganiser.
disorientate [dis'ɔ:riənteit] *v.tr.* désorienter.
disown [dis'oun] *v.tr.* désavouer (une œuvre); **to d. a child,** refuser de reconnaître la paternité.
disparage [dis'pæridʒ] *v.tr.* **1.** déprécier, décrier, dénigrer (qn, qch). **2.** déshonorer, discréditer (qn, qch.). **disparaging** *a.* **1.** (terme) de dénigrement; **d. remark,** remarque désobligeante. **2.** désavantageux; peu flatteur, -euse. **disparagingly** *adv.* d'un ton, d'un air, dépréciateur; **to speak d. of s.o.,** parler de qn en termes de mépris.
disparagement [dis'pæridʒmənt] *n.* dénigrement *m*, dépréciation *f*.
disparate ['dispəreit] *a.* disparate.
disparity [dis'pæriti] *n.* **1.** inégalité *f*, disconvenance *f* (**of,** de); **d. of age,** différence *f* d'âge. **2.** disparité *f*, écart *m* (**between,** entre).
dispassionate [dis'pæʃənət] *a.* **1.** sans passion; calme. **2.** impartial, -aux: **to take a d. view of things,** juger impartialement les choses. **-ly** *adv.* **1.** sans passion. **2.** sans parti pris; impartialement.
dispatch[1] [dis'pætʃ] *n.* **1.** expédition *f*, envoi *m* (de qch.); **d. note,** bulletin *m*, bordereau *m*, d'expédition. **2.** exécution *f* (d'un condamné). **3.** (*a*) expédition (d'une affaire); (*b*) promptitude *f*; **with d.,** promptement. **4.** dépêche *f* (diplomatique, etc.); *Dipl: Adm: etc:* **d. box,** boîte *f* à documents; **d. case,** serviette *f* (en cuir); *Mil:* **d. rider,** estafette *f*; *Mil: etc:* **to be mentioned in dispatches,** être cité à l'ordre (du jour).
dispatch[2] *v.tr.* **1.** dépêcher (un courrier); expédier (une lettre); envoyer (qn). **2.** (*a*) achever (un animal); (*b*) expédier (qn) dans l'autre monde. **3.** *F:* expédier (un repas).
dispatcher [dis'pætʃər] *n.* (*a*) *Com: etc:* expéditeur, -trice; (*b*) régulateur *m*, contrôleur *m* (du mouvement des trains, des avions, etc.).
dispel [dis'pel] *v.tr.* **(dispelled)** chasser, dissiper.
dispensable [dis'pensəbl] *a.* **1.** dont on peut se passer. **2.** *Ecc:* (vœu, etc.) dispensable.
dispensary [dis'pensəri] *n.* (*a*) officine *f* (d'une pharmacie); (*b*) pharmacie *f*.
dispensation [dispen'seiʃ(ə)n] *n.* **1.** dispensation *f*, distribution *f* (des récompenses, des aumônes). **2.** décret *m* arrêt *m* (de la Providence). **3.** *Jur: Ecc:* **d. from sth.,** dispense *f* de qch.; **d. from fasting,** dispense du jeûne.
dispense [dis'pens] **1.** *v.tr.* (*a*) dispenser, distribuer (des aumônes); (*b*) administrer, rendre (la justice); (*c*) *Pharm:* préparer (des médicaments); exécuter (une ordonnance); **dispensing chemist,** pharmacien diplômé. **2.** (*a*) *v.tr.* dispenser, exempter (qn de faire qch.); *Ecc:* **to d. s.o. from fasting,** dispenser qn du jeûne. **3.** *v.i.* **to d. with s.o., sth.,** se passer de qn, de qch. **dispensing** *n.* **1.** dispensation *f*, distribution *f* (des aumônes, etc.). **2.** *Pharm:* préparation *f* (des médicaments).
dispenser [dis'pensər] *n.* **1.** (*a*) dispensateur, -trice, distributeur, -trice (d'aumônes, etc.); (*b*) pharmacien, -ienne. **2.** (*machine*) distributeur *m* (de cigarettes, de bonbons, etc.).
dispersal [dis'pə:s(ə)l] *n.* *Mil:* dispersion *f* (de troupes, etc.)
disperse[1] [dis'pə:s] **1.** *v.tr.* (*a*) disperser, éparpiller (l'ennemi); dissiper, chasser (les nuages); (*b*) disperser (ses troupes, etc.); (*c*) *Med:* résoudre, dissoudre (une tumeur); (*e*) (*of prism, etc.*) disperser (la lumière). **2.** *v.i.* (*of crowd*) se disperser, s'éparpiller; (*of light*) se disperser; (*of darkness*) se dissiper.
dispersion [dis'pə:ʃ(ə)n] *n.* dispersion *f*; *Rel.H:* **the D.,** la dispersion des Juifs.
dispirit [dis'pirit] *v.tr.* décourager, abattre (qn). **dispirited** *a.* découragé, abattu.
displace [dis'pleis] *v.tr.* **1.** déplacer (qch.); **weight of water displaced by a body,** poids *m* de l'eau déplacée par un corps. **2.** (*a*) destituer (un fonctionnaire, etc.); (*b*) remplacer (**by,** par); (*c*) évincer (qn); **to d. s.o. (in s.o.'s affections),** supplanter qn; (*d*) *Pol:* **displaced persons,** personnes déplacées.
displacement [dis'pleismənt] *n.* **1.** (*a*) déplacement *m* (de qch.); (*b*) **volumetric d.,** déplacement volumétrique; *N.Arch:* déplacement (d'un navire); tonnage *m* (d'un navire de guerre); **ship of five thousand tons d.,** navire *m* d'un déplacement de 5000 tonnes. **2. d. of A by B,** remplacement *m* de A par B; substitution *f* de B à A.
display[1] [dis'plei] *n.* (*a*) étalage *m*, exposition *f* (de marchandises); **d. case,** vitrine *f*; *Com:* **d. unit,** présentoir *m;* (*b*) affichage *m*, étalage (de sentiments, d'opinions, etc.); démonstration *f* (de force); (*c*) étalage (de luxe); **to be fond of d.,** aimer l'ostentation; (*d*) manifestation (artistique, etc.); **air d.,** fête *f* aéronautique; (*e*) *Typ:* lignes *fpl* en vedette; (*f*) *Rad:* indicateur *m*; **d. screen,** écran *m* de visualisation; (*g*) *Elcs: etc:* affichage *m*; représentation visuelle (des données); (*h*) *Orn:* parade *f*.
display[2] **1.** *v.tr.* (*a*) étaler, exposer (des marchandises); afficher (un avis); (*b*) afficher, déployer, étaler, manifester (un sentiment, une opinion etc.); **to d. courage,** faire preuve de courage; (*c*) *Typ:* mettre (une ligne, etc.) en vedette; (*c*) *Elcs: etc:* afficher, visualiser. **2.** *v.i.* *Orn:* parader.
displease [dis'pli:z] *v.tr.* fâcher, contrarier (qn); **to be displeased at, with, s.o., sth.,** être mécontent de qn, de qch.; être fâché contre qn, de qch. **displeasing** *a.* déplaisant, désagréable (**to,** à).
displeasure [dis'pleʒər] *n.* déplaisir *m*; **to incur s.o.'s d.,** s'attirer le mécontentement de qn.
disport [dis'pɔ:t] *v.pr. & i.* **to d. (oneself),** s'amuser, s'ébattre; folâtrer.
disposable [dis'pouzəbl] *a.* (*a*) (fonds, revenu, etc.) disponible; (*b*) (serviettes, etc.) à jeter, jetable; **d. wrapping,** emballage perdu.
disposal [dis'pouz(ə)l] *n.* **1.** (*a*) mise *f* au rebut; évacuation *f* (des ordures, etc.); **(refuse) d. plant,** dépotoir *m*; **bomb d.,** désamorçage *m* et enlèvement des bombes non éclatées; **bomb d. expert,** démineur

m; (*b*) **to be at s.o.'s d.,** être à la disposition de qn; **I am entirely at your d.,** vous pouvez disposer de moi; **to put sth. at s.o.'s d.,** mettre qch. à la disposition de qn; **to have a boat at one's d.,** disposer d'un bateau. **2.** (*a*) vente *f* (de biens); **for d.,** à vendre; à céder; (*b*) *Jur:* **d. of property,** dispositions testamentaires. **3.** arrangement *m* (des objets).

dispose [dis'pouz] *v.tr. & i.* **1.** (*a*) disposer, arranger (des objets); *Prov:* **man proposes, God disposes,** l'homme propose et Dieu dispose; (*b*) **to d. of one's time,** employer son temps. **2. to d. of (sth., s.o.),** se débarrasser de (qch., qn); mettre (qch.) au rebut; *F:* tuer, expédier (qn); régler (une affaire). **3.** *Com:* (*sell*) **to d. of (sth.),** écouler (des marchandises); vendre (un article); céder (son fonds, un bail). **4.** disposer, porter (**s.o. to sth., to do sth.,** qn à faire qch.); **I am not disposed to help him,** je ne suis pas disposé, prêt, à l'aider. **disposed** *a.* **1.** intentionné disposé; **well, ill, d. to s.o., towards s.o.,** bien, mal, intentionné envers, pour, qn. **2. d. to sth.,** enclin, porté, à qch.

disposition [dispə'ziʃ(ə)n] *n.* **1.** (*a*) disposition *f*, arrangement *m*; (*b*) *Jur:* disposition (testamentaire). **2.** nature *f*, humeur *f*; **child of a pleasant d.,** enfant *mf* d'un bon naturel; **he is of a kindly d.,** c'est une bonne nature. **3.** (*a*) désir *m*, intention *f* (de faire qch); inclination *f* (à faire qch.); (*b*) penchant *m*, tendance *f* (**to sth., to do sth.,** à qch., à faire qch.).

dispossess [dispə'zes] *v.tr.* (*a*) déposséder (qn); **to d. s.o. of sth.,** déposséder, *Jur:* dessaisir, qn de qch.; (*b*) exproprier (qn).

dispossession [dispə'zeʃ(ə)n] *n.* (*a*) dépossession *f*; *Jur:* dessaisissement *m*; (*b*) expropriation *f*.

disproportion [disprə'pɔːʃ(ə)n] *n.* disproportion *f*.

disproportionate [disprə'pɔːʃənət] *a.* disproportionné (**to,** à). **-ly** *adv.* d'une façon disproportionnée.

disprove [dis'pruːv] *v.tr.* (*p.p.* **disproved,** *Jur:* **disproven** [dis'prouvn]) réfuter (un dire); démontrer la fausseté (d'un dire).

disputable [dis'pjuːtəbl] *a.* contestable, disputable.

disputation [dispju'teiʃ(ə)n] *n.* (*a*) discussion *f* (d'un sujet); (*b*) controverse *f*, débat *m*.

dispute¹ ['dispjut, dis'pjuːt] *n.* **1.** contestation *f*, controverse *f*; **the matter in d.,** l'affaire contestée, en contestation; **the fact is beyond d.,** le fait est incontestable. **2.** querelle *f*, dispute *f* (**as to,** relatif, -ive, à); **to settle a d.,** régler une querelle; **industrial d.,** conflit *m* du travail.

dispute² [dis'pjuːt] **1.** *v.i.* se disputer, se quereller. **2.** *v.tr.* (*a*) discuter (une question); contester (une affirmation, etc.); (*b*) **to d. (the possession of) sth. with s.o.,** disputer qch. à qn.

disqualification [diskwɔlifi'keiʃ(ə)n] *n.* **1.** incapacité *f*; *Jur:* inhabilité *f* (**to act,** à agir). **2.** cause *f* d'incapacité (**for,** à). **3.** (*a*) mise *f* en état d'incapacité; (*b*) *Sp:* disqualification *f* (d'un concours).

disqualify [dis'kwɔlifai] *v.tr.* **1.** rendre incapable (**for sth.,** de faire qch.). **2.** (*a*) *Jur:* frapper (qn) d'incapacité; **disqualified from making a will,** inhabile à tester; (*b*) **to be disqualified from a competition,** être exclus d'un concours; (*c*) **to d. s.o. from driving,** retirer le permis de conduire à qn. **3.** *Sp:* disqualifier (un joueur).

disquiet¹ [dis'kwaiət] *n. Lit:* inquiétude *f*.

disquiet² *v.tr.* inquiéter; troubler. **disquieting** *a.* inquiétant; troublant.

disregard¹ [disri'gɑːd] *n.* indifférence *f* (**of, for,** à l'égard de); inobservation *f* (de la loi).

disregard² *v.tr.* ne tenir aucun compte de, ne pas faire attention à (qn, qch.); négliger (qn, qch.); enfreindre (un ordre); *Mil:* manquer à (la consigne).

disrepair [disri'pɛər] *n.* (*no pl.*) délabrement *m*; **to fall into d.,** tomber en ruine; se délabrer.

disreputable [dis'repjutəbl] *a.* **1.** (*of action*) déshonorant; peu honorable. **2.** (*a*) (*of pers.*) de mauvaise réputation; (*b*) **d. neighbourhood,** quartier (i) sordide, (ii) mal famé. **-ably** *adv.* **1.** honteusement; d'une façon peu honorable.

disrepute [disri'pjuːt] *n.* déshonneur *m*; mauvaise réputation; **to bring s.o. into d.,** ruiner la réputation de qn; **to bring the law into d.,** discréditer la loi.

disrespect [disri'spekt] *n.* irrévérence *f*, irrespect *m*; manque *m* de respect (**for,** envers); **to treat s.o., sth., with d.,** manquer de respect à qn, pour qch.

disrespectful [disri'spektful], *a.* irrespectueux, irrévérencieux; **to be d. to s.o.,** manquer de respect à qn. **-fully** *adv.* (parler de qn) sans respect.

disrobe [dis'roub] **1.** *v.tr.* aider (un magistrat, un prêtre) à se dévêtir de sa robe. **2.** *v.i.* (*of judge, clergyman, etc.*) se dévêtir de sa robe.

disrupt [dis'rʌpt] *v.tr.* désorganiser (une administration, un plan, etc.); rompre (une coalition); interrompre (une séance, etc.).

disruption [dis'rʌpʃ(ə)n] *n.* rupture *f*; interruption *f* (d'une séance, de la circulation, etc.).

disruptive [dis'rʌptiv] *a.* (élément) perturbateur; (élève) turbulent; **d. strike,** grève paralysante.

dissatisfaction [disætis'fækʃ(ə)n] *n.* insatisfaction *f*, mécontentement *m* (**with,** de).

dissatisfy [di'sætisfai] *v.tr.* mécontenter. **dissatisfied** *a.* mécontent, peu satisfait (**with,** de).

dissect [di'sekt] *v.tr.* disséquer; éplucher (un livre).

dissection [di'sekʃ(ə)n] *n.* dissection *f*.

dissemble [di'sembl] **1.** *v.tr.* dissimuler, cacher, (ses sentiments, etc.). **2.** *v.i.* agir avec dissimulation; déguiser sa pensée.

disseminate [di'semineit] *v.tr.* disséminer, propager, répandre (des opinions, etc.).

dissemination [disemi'neiʃ(ə)n] *n.* dissémination *f*, propagation *f*.

dissension [di'senʃ(ə)n] *n.* dissension *f*; **to sow d.,** semer la dissension, le désaccord.

dissent¹ [di'sent] *n.* **1.** dissentiment *m*; avis *m* contraire. **2.** *Ecc:* dissidence *f*.

dissent² *v.i.* **1.** différer (**from s.o. about sth.,** de qn sur qch.). **2.** *Ecc:* être dissident. **dissenting** *a.* dissident.

dissenter [di'sentər] *n.* dissident, -ente; *esp. Ecc:* personne qui n'appartient pas à l'Église anglicane.

dissertation [disə'teiʃ(ə)n] *n.* dissertation *f*.

disservice [di'səːvis] *n.* mauvais service rendu; **to do s.o. a d.,** rendre un mauvais service à qn.

dissidence ['disidəns] *n.* dissidence *f*; désaccord *m*.

dissident ['disidənt] *a. & n.* dissident, -ente.

dissimilar [di'similər] *a.* dissemblable (**to,** à, de).

dissimilarity [disimi'læriti] *n.* dissemblance *f*, dissimilarité *f* (**to,** de; **between,** entre).

dissimulate [di'simjuleit] **1.** *v.tr.* dissimuler. **2.** *v.i.* dissimuler, feindre; cacher ses pensées.

dissimulation [disimju'leiʃ(ə)n] *n.* dissimulation *f*.

dissipate ['disipeit] **1.** *v.tr.* dissiper (les nuages, etc.); gaspiller (une fortune). **2.** *v.i.* (*of cloud, heat, etc.*) se dissiper; *Ph:* (*of energy*) se dégrader. **dissipated** *a.* (vie) dissipée; **to be d.,** vivre dans la dissipation.

dissipation [disi'peiʃ(ə)n] *n.* **1.** dissipation *f* (du brouillard, de ses biens); gaspillage *m* (d'une fortune). **2.** dissipation; vie désordonnée.

dissociate [di'sousieit] **1.** *v.tr.* (*a*) dissocier (**from,** de); **to d. oneself from (s.o., sth.),** se désolidariser de (qn, d'une politique, etc.); (*b*) *Ch:* dissocier (un composé, etc.). **2.** *v.i. Ch:* se dissocier.

dissociation [disousi'eiʃ(ə)n] *n.* dissociation *f*.

dissoluble [di'sɔljubl] *a.* **1.** *Ph: etc:* dissoluble (**in,** dans). **2.** (mariage, etc.) dissoluble.

dissolute ['disəljut] *a.* dissolu, débauché; (conduite) licencieuse; (vie) déréglée; **to lead a d. life,** vivre dans la débauche.

dissoluteness ['disəljutnis] *n.* débauche *f.*

dissolution [disə'lju:ʃ(ə)n] *n.* **1.** dissolution *f.* **2.** dissolution (d'un mariage, etc.).

dissolve [di'zolv] **1.** *v.tr.* (*a*) (faire) dissoudre, faire fondre (qch.); **dissolved in tears,** tout en larmes; (*b*) dissiper (un nuage); dissiper (une illusion); (*c*) dissoudre (un mariage, etc.). **2.** *v.i.* (*a*) se dissoudre; fondre; **to d. into tears,** fondre en larmes; (*b*) se dissiper; (*of crowd*) se disperser; **to d. into thin air,** partir, s'en aller, en fumée; (*c*) (*of Parliament*) se dissoudre.

dissonance ['disənəns] *n. Mus:* dissonance *f.*

dissonant ['disənənt] *a. Mus:* dissonant.

dissuade [di'sweid] *v.tr.* **to d. s.o. from (doing) sth.,** dissuader qn de (faire) qch.

dissuasion [di'sweiʒ(ə)n] *n.* dissuasion *f* (**from,** de).

distaff ['distɑ:f] *n.* quenouille *f*; **the d. side,** le côté maternel (d'une famille).

distance¹ ['distəns] *n.* **1.** (*a*) distance *f*; **at a d. of . . .,** à une distance de . . .; **within five minutes walking d.,** à cinq minutes de marche; **a short d. away,** tout près; à deux pas; **to see sth. from a d.,** voir qch. de loin; *Mil:* **within striking d.,** à portée des coups de fusil, de canon, etc.; à portée de l'ennemi; (*b*) lointain *m*; **in the middle d.,** au second plan; (*c*) **at this d. of time,** à cet intervalle de temps. **2.** (*a*) distance (entre deux endroits); **to go part of the d. on foot,** faire une partie du trajet à pied; (*b*) distance, intervalle (qui sépare deux choses); **to keep s.o. at a d.,** tenir qn à distance; (*c*) *Sp:* (i) parcours; (ii) durée *f* (d'un match de boxe); **long-d., medium-d., race,** course *f* de fond, de demi-fond; **to go, last, stay, the d.,** (i) *Sp:* tenir la distance; (ii) *Fig:* tenir jusqu'au bout. **3.** réserve *f*; air distant; **to keep one's d., to keep at a d.,** se tenir sur la réserve; garder ses distances.

distance² *v.tr.* distancer (un concurrent).

distant ['distənt] *a.* **1.** *O:* **three miles d.,** à trois milles de distance; **not far d. from . . .,** à peu de distance de . . .. **2.** (*a*) (endroit, objet, parent) éloigné; (pays) lointain; *Rail:* **d. signal,** signal à distance; (*b*) faible, vague (ressemblance, etc.); **d. look,** regard perdu dans le vague; (*c*) (*in time*) éloigné; (souvenir) lointain; **in the d. future,** dans un avenir lointain. **3.** (*of pers., manner*) réservé, distant; **to be d. with s.o.,** tenir qn à distance; se montrer réservé avec qn. **-ly** *adv.* **1.** de loin; **d. related,** d'une parenté éloignée. **2.** avec réserve.

distaste [dis'teist] *n.* dégoût *m* (**for,** de); répugnance *f* (**for,** pour).

distasteful [dis'teistful] *a.* **1.** (*of food, etc.*) désagréable au goût. **2.** désagréable, déplaisant.

distastefulness [dis'teistfulnis] *n.* caractère désagréable, répugnant (d'une tâche, etc.).

distemper¹ [dis'tempər] *n. Vet:* maladie des jeunes chiens.

distemper² *n. Art: etc:* détrempe *f.*

distemper³ *v.tr.* peindre (un tableau, un mur) en détrempe; badigeonner (un mur) en couleur.

distend [dis'tend] **1.** *v.tr.* (*a*) gonfler (un ballon, les joues); dilater (les narines); (*b*) distendre, ballonner (l'estomac). **2.** *v.i.* (*a*) se dilater, enfler, se gonfler; (*b*) (*of stomach*) se ballonner, se distendre.

distension [dis'tenʃ(ə)n] *n.* (*a*) dilatation *f*, distension *f.*

distich ['distik] *n. Pros:* distique *m.*

distil, *NAm:* **distill** [dis'til] *v.* **(distilled) 1.** *v.tr. Ch: Ind:* distiller (de l'eau, etc.); raffiner (le pétrole); **to d. sth. off, out,** chasser qch. par la distillation. **2.** *v.i.* (*a*) *Ch: Ind:* se distiller, passer; (*b*) (*of liquid, secretion, etc.*) distiller (**from,** de).

distillation [disti'leiʃ(ə)n] *n.* **1.** distillation *f*; **fractional d.,** distillation fractionnée. **2.** produit *m* de la distillation.

distiller [dis'tilər] *n.* (*pers.*) *Ind:* distillateur *m.*

distillery [dis'tiləri] *n. Ind:* distillerie *f.*

distinct [dis'tiŋ(k)t] *a.* **1.** distinct, différent (**from,** de); **to keep two things d.,** distinguer entre deux choses. **2.** distinct, net, *f.* nette, clair; (souvenir) clair, net, précis; (ordres) formel, précis; (promesse) formelle; **the coast becomes more d.,** la côte se précise. **3.** (*of preference*) marqué. **-ly** *adv.* **1.** (*a*) (parler, entendre, voir) distinctement, clairement; (*b*) **I told him d.,** je le lui ai dit expressément. **2.** décidément; **he is d. better,** il va sensiblement mieux.

distinction [dis'tiŋ(k)ʃ(ə)n] *n.* **1.** (*difference*) distinction *f* (**between,** entre); **to make a d. between two things,** faire une distinction entre deux choses; **without d. of age,** sans distinction d'âge; **class d.,** distinction des classes. **2.** (*honour*) **academic distinctions,** distinctions académiques. **3.** (*excellence*) distinction; **to gain d.,** se distinguer; **man of d.,** homme distingué; *Sch:* **with d.,** avec mention.

distinctive [dis'tiŋ(k)tiv] *a.* distinctif. **-ly** *adv.* distinctivement.

distinctness [dis'tiŋ(k)tnis] *n.* clarté *f*, netteté *f.*

distinguish [dis'tiŋgwiʃ] **1.** *v.tr.* (*a*) discerner (un objet, un son); **I could not d. him among the crowd,** je n'ai pu le distinguer dans la foule; (*b*) distinguer, différencier (**from,** de); **reason distinguishes man from the other animals,** la raison sépare l'homme des autres animaux; **distinguishing mark,** signe distinctif; (*c*) **to d. oneself by . . .,** se distinguer, se signaler, se faire remarquer, par . . .. **2.** *v.i.* **to d. between two things,** faire une distinction entre deux choses. **distinguished** *a.* distingué; (écrivain, etc.) de distinction; **to look d.,** avoir l'air distingué.

distinguishable [dis'tiŋgwiʃəbl] *a.* **1.** que l'on peut distinguer, qui se distingue (**from,** de). **2.** reconnaissable; **hardly d. sound,** son *m* à peine perceptible; **the coast was hardly d.,** c'est à peine si l'on distinguait la côte.

distort [dis'tɔ:t] **1.** *v.tr.* (*a*) tordre (qch.); décomposer, déformer (les traits, le visage); distordre (les membres); déformer (la réception radiophonique, etc.); fausser, déjeter (une surface); (*b*) déformer (la vérité); fausser, dénaturer (les faits, des paroles); **to d. the meaning of a text,** dénaturer un texte. **2.** *v.i.* se déformer, se fausser. **distorted** *a.* tordu; déformé; *El:* (champ) tors, déformé; **face d. by rage,** visage convulsé de fureur. **distorting** *a.* déformant.

distortion [dis'tɔ:ʃ(ə)n] *n.* **1.** (*a*) distorsion *f*; altération *f* (des traits); (*b*) contorsion *f* (du corps); (*c*) altération (d'un texte); déformation *f* (des faits, de la vérité). **2.** (*a*) *Opt:* déformation, distorsion; (*b*) *Mec.E:* distorsion (d'un organe); torsion *f*, déformation; (*c*) *Elcs: W.Tel: etc:* distorsion, déformation (de la transmission); (*of sound*) distorsion sonore; (*d*) déviation *f* (du champ magnétique).

distract [dis'trækt] , *v.tr.* **1.** (*a*) distraire, détourner (l'esprit, l'attention) (**from,** de); (*b*) diviser (l'attention); **go away! you're distracting me!** va-t'en! tu me déranges! **2.** troubler, affoler (qn). **distracted** *a.* affolé, bouleversé; éperdu. **distractedly** *adv.* **1.** comme un affolé, comme un fou. **2.** (aimer qn) follement, éperdument. **distracting** *a.* **1.** qui distrait l'attention; **I find noise d. when I'm working,** le bruit me dérange quand je travaille. **2.** affolant.

distraction [dis'trækʃ(ə)n] *n.* **1.** distraction *f*; (*a*) divertissement *m*; **he's seeking d.,** il cherche à se distraire; (*b*) interruption *f* (au milieu du travail, etc.). **2.** confusion *f*, désordre *m.* **3. to drive s.o. to d.,** rendre qn fou; faire perdre la tête à qn; **to love s.o.**

to d., aimer qn éperdument, à la folie.

distrain [dis'trein] *v.i. Jur:* **to d. upon s.o.,** contraindre qn par saisie de biens; **to d. upon a debtor,** exécuter un débiteur.

distraint [dis'treint] *n. Jur:* saisie *f*, (saisie-)exécution *f, pl.* (saisies-)exécutions.

distraught [dis'trɔːt] *a.* (*a*) angoissé; **to look d.,** avoir l'air affolé; (*b*) fou, folle (**with grief,** de douleur).

distress¹ [dis'tres] *n.* **1.** (*a*) angoisse *f*; (*b*) misère (profonde) **2.** détresse *f*, embarras *m*; **companions in d.,** compagnons *mpl* d'infortune; *Nau:* **ship in d.,** navire *m* en détresse; **d. signal,** signal *m* de détresse. **3.** *Jur:* (*a*) saisie *f*; **d. warrant,** mandat *m* de saisie; (*b*) biens saisis.

distress² *v.tr.* affliger, angoisser; faire de la peine à (qn). **distressed** *a.* **1.** affligé, désolé; **to be d. about sth.,** être désolé d'apprendre qch. **2.** dans la détresse, dans la misère; **d. area,** (i) région frappée par une crise économique; (ii) zone sinistrée. **3.** *Jur:* saisi. **distressing** *a.* affligeant; pénible.

distribute [dis'tribju(ː)t] *v.tr.* **1.** distribuer, répartir; faire la distribution de (qch.); *Com:* être concessionnaire (d'un produit); *Fin:* répartir (un dividende). **2.** disperser, répartir (qch.) (sur une surface, etc.); **load evenly distributed,** charge uniformément répartie.

distribution [distri'bjuːʃ(ə)n] *n.* **1.** (*a*) (mise *f* en) distribution (*f*); répartition *f*; *Com:* **d. channel,** circuit *m* de distribution; (*b*) *El: etc:* **d. (switch)board,** tableau *m* de distribution; **d. box,** boîte *f* de dérivation, de jonction. **2.** répartition (de la population, de la main-d'œuvre, etc.); **d. of wealth,** distribution des richesses.

distributive [dis'tribjutiv] *a. & n.* distributif (*m*).

distributor [dis'tribjutər] *n.* **1.** (*a*) distributeur, -trice; (*b*) concessionnaire *m* (d'une marque d'automobiles, etc.). **2.** *El: etc:* distributeur *m*; **d. box,** boîte *f* de dérivation, de jonction.

district ['distrikt] *n.* (*a*) région *f*, territoire *m*; **mining d.,** région minière; *Bank: etc:* **d. manager,** directeur régional; (*b*) région (militaire, etc.); (*c*) *Adm:* district, secteur *m;* **urban d.,** district urbain; **postal d.,** secteur postal; **electoral d.,** *U.S:* **congressional d.,** circonscription électorale; *U.S: Jur:* **d. court** = tribunal *m* d'instance; **d. attorney** = procureur *m* de la République; **d. nurse,** infirmière visiteuse; (*d*) quartier *m* (d'une ville); *Adm:* = arrondissement *m* (d'une grande ville).

distrust¹ [dis'trʌst] *n.* méfiance *f*, défiance *f* (**of,** de).

distrust² *v.tr.* se méfier, se défier, de (qn, qch.); **to d. one's own eyes,** n'en pas croire ses propres yeux.

distrustful [dis'trʌstful] *a.* **1.** défiant, méfiant (**of,** de). **2. he was d. of his own capabilities,** il manquait de foi en ses propres capacités.

disturb [dis'təːb] *v.tr.* **1.** déranger (qn, des papiers); troubler (le repos, etc.); agiter, remuer (une surface, la terre); **don't d. him,** ne le dérangez pas. **2.** *Ph:* perturber (le champ magnétique); affoler (l'aiguille aimantée). **3.** (*a*) inquiéter, troubler (qn); (*b*) *Jur:* inquiéter, troubler (qn) dans la jouissance d'un droit. **disturbing** *a.* (*a*) perturbateur, -trice; (*b*) inquiétant, troublant.

disturbance [dis'təːbəns] *n.* **1.** trouble *m*; dérangement *m*; **atmospheric d.,** perturbation atmosphérique. **2.** (*a*) bruit *m*, tumulte *m*; (*b*) bagarre *f*; émeute *f*; **political disturbances,** troubles politiques; **to make, create, a d.,** troubler l'ordre public. **3. emotional disturbances,** troubles émotifs. **4.** *Jur:* trouble de jouissance.

disunite [disju'nait] **1.** *v.tr.* désunir; jeter la désunion dans (une famille). **2.** *v.i.* se désunir.

disunity [dis'juːniti] *n.* désunion *f*.

disuse [dis'juːs] *n.* désuétude *f* (d'un terme, etc.). abandon *m*, mise *f* au rancart (d'une machine, etc.); **to fall into d.,** (i) (*of word, custom*) tomber en désuétude; (*of law*) s'abroger; (ii) (*of object*) être mis au rancart.

disused [dis'juːzd] *a.* hors d'usage; mis au rancart; (*of public building*) désaffecté; (*of mine, well, railway line*) abandonné.

disyllabic [disi'læbik] *a.* dissyllabe, dissyllabique.

ditch¹ [ditʃ] *n.* fossé *m*; (*along roadside*) caniveau *m*; (*between fields*) douve *f*; **drainage d.,** rigole d'écoulement; *Rac:* **open d.,** douve.

ditch² **1.** *v.tr.* (*a*) entourer (un champ) de fossés; creuser des fossés dans (un champ); (*b*) *F:* jeter (qch.); mettre (qch.) au rancart; se débarrasser de (qch.); abandonner (un projet, etc.); plaquer (qn). **2.** *v.i. Av:* faire un amerrissage forcé. **ditching** *n.* **1. hedging and d.,** entretien *m* des haies et fossés. **2.** *Av:* amerrissage forcé.

ditchwater ['ditʃwɔːter] *n.* eaux stagnantes (d'un fossé); *F:* **it's as clear as d.,** c'est la bouteille à l'encre; **as dull as d.,** ennuyeux comme la pluie, comme un jour de pluie.

dither¹ ['diðər] *n. F:* **to be all of a d.,** ne plus savoir où donner de la tête; paniquer.

dither² *v.i. F:* hésiter; tergiverser; **stop dithering!** décide-toi!

dithery ['diðəri] *a. F:* **to feel d.,** se sentir nerveux.

ditto ['ditou] *F:* **1.** *a. & n.* idem; de même; *Com:* dito (*m inv*).

ditty ['diti] *n.* chanson *f*, chansonnette *f*.

diuretic [daiju'retik] *a. & n. Med:* diurétique (*m*).

diurnal [dai'əːn(ə)l] **1.** *a.* (*a*) *Astr:* mouvement) diurne; (*b*) *Nat.Hist:* (oiseau, papillon, etc.) diurne. **2.** *n. Ecc:* diurnal *m*, -aux.

divan [di'væn] *n. Furn:* divan *m*; **d. bed,** lit *m* à sommier tapissier.

dive¹ [daiv] *n.* **1.** (*a*) *Swim:* plongeon *m*; **high d.,** plongeon de haut vol; (*b*) *Nau:* plongée *f* (d'un sous-marin, d'un scaphandrier); (*c*) *Av:* **vertical d., nose d.,** piqué *m*; **to pull out of a d.,** effectuer un rétablissement; **d. bombing, bomber,** bombardement *m*, bombardier *m*, en piqué; (*d*) **he made a d. for the shelter,** il s'est précipité vers l'abri. **2.** *F:* **(low) d.,** bouge *m*.

dive² *v.i.* (*p.t.* **dived,** *U.S: F:* **dove** [douv]; *p.p.* **dived**) (*a*) plonger (**into,** dans); (*head first*) piquer une tête; **to d. for pearls,** pêcher des perles; (*b*) *Av:* **to d. down on an enemy,** piquer de haut sur un ennemi; (*c*) (*of submarine*) plonger, effectuer une plongée; (*d*) **to d. into one's pocket,** plonger (la main) dans sa poche; **to d. into a doorway for shelter,** se précipiter dans une entrée pour s'abriter. **diving** *n.* (*a*) *Swim:* **d. board,** plongeoir *m*; (*b*) plongée (sous-marine); **skin d., scuba d.,** plongée sous-marine autonome; **d. suit,** scaphandre *m*; **d. bell,** cloche *f* à plongeurs; (*c*) *Nau:* **d. rudder,** gouvernail *m* de profondeur (de sous-marin).

dive-bomb ['daivbɔm] *v.tr. Av:* attaquer en piqué.

diver ['daivər] *n.* **1.** (*a*) plongeur, -euse; **pearl d.,** pêcheur *m* de perles; (*b*) scaphandrier *m*; **skin d.,** plongeur sous-marin autonome. **2.** *Orn:* plongeon *m*, plongeur.

diverge [dai'vəːdʒ] **1.** *v.i.* (*of roads, lines, etc.*) diverger, s'écarter. **2.** *v.tr.* faire diverger (des rayons, etc.). **diverging** *a.* divergent.

divergence [dai'vəːdʒəns] *n.* divergence *f*.

divergent [dai'vəːdʒənt] *a.* divergent; **we take d. views on certain points,** nos opinions *fpl* divergent, diffèrent, sur certains points.

divers ['daivəz] *a. pl. A:* divers, plusieurs.

diverse [d(a)i'vəːs] *a.* **1.** divers, différent. **2.** divers, varié, changeant. **-ly** *adv.* diversement.

diversification [d(a)ivəːsifi'keiʃ(ə)n] *n.* **1.** diversité *f* (de goûts, etc.). **2.** *Fin: etc:* diversification *f*.

diversify [d(a)i'vəːsifai] *v.tr.* diversifier, varier.

diversion [d(a)i'vəːʃ(ə)n] *n.* **1.** (*a*) déviation *f*, détournement *m* (de la circulation, etc.); (*b*) *Hyd.E: El:* dérivation *f*. **2.** *Mil:* diversion *f*. **3.** (*a*) **to create, make, a d.,** faire diversion; **to seek d. from sth.,** chercher à se distraire de qch.; (*b*) divertissement *m*, distraction *f*.

diversionary [d(a)i'vəːʃən(ə)ri] *a.* (activité) destinée à faire diversion; *Mil:* (manœuvre) de diversion.

diversity [d(a)i'vəːsiti] *n.* diversité *f*; variété *f*.

divert [dai'vəːt, di-] *v.tr.* **1.** détourner, dériver (un cours d'eau, la circulation); parer, écarter (un coup); *Nau:* dérouter; détourner (l'attention) (**from,** de); *El:* dévier (le courant); détourner (la conversation); distraire (l'attention, de qn). **2.** divertir, amuser (qn); **to d. oneself by doing sth.,** faire qch. pour se distraire. **diverting** *a.* divertissant, amusant.

divest [d(a)i'vest] *v.tr.* (*a*) priver, dénuer (qn de qch.); **to d. oneself of (sth.),** se dévêtir de (son autorité); se désinvestir (d'une fonction); renoncer à (un droit); (*b*) *Jur:* déposséder (qn) (**of,** de).

divide[1] [di'vaid] *n.* *Geog:* ligne *f* de partage des eaux.

divide[2] **1.** *v.tr.* (*a*) diviser (un héritage, etc.); **to d. (up),** démembrer (un royaume); détailler (de la viande, etc.); morceler (un terrain); **to d. in two,** couper, diviser, en deux; **to d. into parts,** diviser en parties; *Pol:* **to d. the House,** faire voter la Chambre; (*b*) partager, répartir (**among,** entre); **we d. the work among us,** nous nous partageons le travail; (*c*) *Mth:* diviser; (*with passive force*) **twelve divides by three,** douze est divisible par trois; (*d*) séparer (**from,** de); **the mountains that d. France from Spain,** les montagnes *fpl* qui séparent la France d'avec l'Espagne; (*e*) mettre le désaccord dans (une famille); (*a*) **house divided against itself,** maison désunie; (*f*) **opinions are divided,** les avis sont partagés. **2.** *v.i.* (*a*) se diviser, se partager (**into,** en); se séparer; (*of political party*) se scinder; (*of road*) fourcher; (*b*) *Pol:* aller aux voix. **divided** *a.* (*a*) divisé; partagé; (attention) distraite; *Cost:* **d. skirt,** jupe-culotte *f*, *pl.* jupes-culottes; (*b*) *El:* **d. circuit,** circuit partagé; réseau *m* multiple; (*c*) (*of scale, thermometer, etc.*) gradué. **dividing** *a.* (ligne, etc.) de démarcation; **d. wall,** mur mitoyen; mur de séparation, de cloison; *El:* **d. box,** boîte *f* de dérivation.

dividend ['dividend] *n.* **1.** *Mth:* dividende *m*. **2.** *Fin:* (*a*) **d. on shares,** dividende d'actions; (*in insolvency*) (*a*) **d. paid to each creditor,** dividende payé à chaque créancier; *Fig:* (*of action, etc.*) **to pay dividends,** porter des fruits.

dividers [di'vaidəz] *n.pl.* compas *m* à pointes sèches.

divination [divi'neiʃ(ə)n] *n.* divination *f*.

divine[1] [di'vain] **1.** *a.* (*a*) divin; (*b*) *F:* **you look d. in that dress,** vous êtes divine, adorable, dans cette robe. **2.** *n.* théologien *m*. **-ly** *adv.* divinement.

divine[2] **1.** *v.tr.* deviner (l'avenir); pressentir (un malheur). **2.** *v.i.* prédire. **divining** *n.* (*a*) divination *f*; (*b*) **water d.,** radiesthésie *f*; **d. rod,** baguette *f* divinatoire, de sourcier.

diviner [di'vainər] *n.* (*a*) devin *m*, devineresse *f*; (*b*) **water d.,** radiesthésiste *m*; sourcier *m*.

divinity [di'viniti] *n.* **1.** (*a*) (*divine nature*) divinité *f* (**of,** de); (*b*) **the D.,** la Divinité. **2.** (*a*) **Doctor of D.,** docteur *m* en théologie; (*b*) *Sch:* enseignement religieux.

divisible [di'vizibl] *a.* divisible (**by,** par).

division [di'viʒ(ə)n] *n.* **1.** (*a*) division *f*, partage *m* (**into,** en); scission *f* (d'un parti); morcellement *m* (des terres); (*b*) graduation *f* (d'une échelle, etc.). **2.** répartition *f*, partage (des bénéfices, etc.); **d. of labour,** division du travail. **3.** (*discord*) division, désunion *f*; **to bring d. into a family,** amener la désunion dans une famille. **4.** *Mth:* division. **5.** *Parl:* vote *m*; **to come to a d.,** voter; **without a d.,** sans aller aux voix; sans scrutin. **6.** (*section*) (*a*) division (d'un livre, d'un pays); subdivision *f* (d'un casier, etc.); (*b*) *Biol:* groupe *m*, classe *f*; (*c*) *Jur:* section *f* (de la cour); (*d*) *Mil: etc:* division; **airborne, armoured, d.,** division aéroportée, blindée; (*e*) *Pol:* **parliamentary d.,** circonscription électorale; (*f*) *esp. U.S: Rail:* section de ligne; (*g*) (*of scale*) degré *m* (d'une échelle, d'un thermomètre, etc.). **7.** *Const: etc:* cloison *f*, séparation *f*.

divisive [di'vaisiv] *a.* qui sème la discorde.

divisor [di'vaizər] *n.* *Mth:* diviseur *m*.

divorce[1] [di'vɔːs] *n.* **1.** *Jur:* divorce *m*; **to sue for (a) d., to file a petition for d.,** demander le divorce; **to take, start, d. proceedings,** intenter une action en divorce. **2.** divorce, séparation *f* (**between sth. and sth.,** de qch. et de qch.).

divorce[2] *v.tr.* (*a*) *Jur:* (*of judge*) prononcer le divorce (des époux); (*b*) (*of husband or wife*) **to be divorced from s.o., to d. s.o.,** divorcer d'avec qn; **they are divorced,** ils sont divorcés; (*c*) **passage divorced from the context,** passage isolé du contexte.

divorcee [divɔː'siː] *n.* divorcé, -ée.

divot ['divət] *n.* motte *f* (de terre).

divulge [d(a)i'vʌldʒ] *v.tr.* divulguer.

dixie, dixy ['diksi] *n. esp. Mil: F:* gamelle.

dizziness ['dizinis] *n.* étourdissement *m*, vertige(s) *m(pl)*; **fit of d.,** éblouissement *m*.

dizzy ['dizi] *a.* **1.** pris de vertige; **d. spell,** éblouissement *m*; **to feel d.,** avoir le vertige; **to make s.o. d.,** donner le vertige à qn. **2.** (*of height, speed, etc.*) vertigineux. **3.** (*of wheel, etc.*] tournoyant, tourbillonnant. **4.** *F:* **a d. blonde,** une blonde évaporée. **-ily** *adv.* **1.** avec une sensation de vertige. **2.** vertigineusement.

do[1] [duː] *v.* **I** *v.tr.* (**he does** [dʌz]; *p.t.* **did** [did]; *pr.sub.sg. & pl.* **do**; *p.p.* **done** [dʌn]; *in the aux. use* **don't** [dount], **didn't** [didnt] *are common for* **do not, did not; doesn't,** *for* **does not) 1.** (*a*) faire (un travail, une bonne action, son devoir; **what do you do (for a living)?** qu'est-ce que vous faites (dans la vie)? **what are you doing?** qu'est-ce que vous faites? **to do right, wrong,** bien, mal, faire; bien, mal, agir; **he did brilliantly well (in his exam),** il a réussi brillamment (son examen); **you would do well to . . .,** vous feriez bien de . . .; **do as you're told,** faites ce qu'on vous dit; **he's doing medicine,** il fait la médecine; **the car was doing sixty,** la voiture faisait du soixante; **to do ten years (in prison),** faire dix ans de prison; **it isn't done,** cela ne se fait pas; **it is quite commonly done,** c'est de pratique courante; **it's as good as done,** c'est une affaire faite ou autant vaut; *F:* **that's done it!** ça y est! **it gives me something to do,** cela me donne de l'occupation; **don't do it again!** ne recommencez pas! **what is to be done?** que faire? **it can't be done,** cela n'est pas possible; c'est (chose) impossible; **there's nothing to be done,** il n'y a rien à faire; **she did nothing but cry,** elle n'a fait que pleurer; **I don't know what to do,** je ne sais que faire; je ne sais pas quoi faire; *F:* **this music doesn't do anything for me,** cette musique ne me dit rien; **what can I do for you?** que puis-je faire pour vous? **what are you going to do about it?** que proposez-vous de faire? **what would he do without you?** que deviendrait-il sans vous? **it was all I could do to lift it,** c'est à peine si j'ai pu le soulever; **do-or-die attitude,** attitude *f* de détermination inébranlable; **when in Rome do as the Romans do,** il faut hurler avec les loups; **well done!** très bien! bravo! (*b*) (*with passive force*) **there's nothing doing,** les affaires *fpl* ne vont pas; c'est le marasme; c'est la morte-saison; *F:* **nothing doing!** rien à faire! ça ne prend pas! **2.** (*a*) faire (une chambre, le ménage); **to do s.o.'s, one's, hair,** coiffer qn, se coiffer; **he does**

repairs, il fait des réparations; (*b*) cuire, faire cuire (de la viande, etc.); **meat well done,** viande bien cuite; **done to a turn,** cuit à point; (*c*) *Mth: etc:* faire (un calcul; résoudre (un problème); (*d*) faire (une traduction); (*e*) *F:* faire (Hamlet, etc.); **to do the interpreter,** faire l'interprète; (*f*) *F:* visiter, faire (une ville, un musée); (*g*) *F:* (*cheat*) **to do s.o. (down),** refaire, faire, qn; **I've been done!** j'ai été roulé! on m'a eu! **to do s.o. out of sth.,** soutirer, carotter, qch. à qn; frustrer, refaire, qn de qch.; **to do s.o. out of a job,** supplanter qn; (*h*) *F:* **they do you very well at this hotel,** on est très bien servi à cet hôtel; (*i*) *Com: F:* **we can do you this article at . . .,** nous pouvons vous faire cet article à . . .. **3.** (*in perfect tenses and past participle*) (*finish*) (*a*) **to have done,** avoir fini; *Lit:* **the day is done,** la journée tire à sa fin; *F:* **have you done?** avez-vous fini? (*b*) (*after a bargain made*) **done!** entendu! d'accord! **4. how do you do?** (i) comment allez-vous? (ii) (*on first introduction*) enchanté (de faire votre connaissance); **to be doing well,** (*of pers.*) être en bonne voie, faire de bonnes affaires; prospérer; (*of patient*) être en voie de guérison; (*of business*) bien aller, réussir; (*of plant*) bien pousser; **that young man will do well,** c'est un garçon qui réussira. **5.** (*serve, suffice*) **that will do,** (i) c'est bien (comme cela); c'est bon; (ii) ça suffit; c'est assez; en voilà assez! **this room will do for the office,** cette pièce ira bien pour le bureau; **that will never do,** cela n'ira jamais, ça n'ira pas du tout; **to make do with what one has,** s'arranger avec ce qu'on a; **that will do me,** cela fera mon affaire; **it would never do for them to see me,** il ne faudrait pas qu'ils me voient. **II.** *verb substitute.* **1.** (*replacing v.tr. or i.*) **they work in the fields as their fathers did,** ils travaillent aux champs comme le faisaient leurs pères; **he writes better than I do,** il écrit mieux que moi. **2.** (*replacing v.tr. and taking its construction*) **he envies me as much as I do him,** il me porte autant d'envie que je lui en porte. **3.** (*replacing v.tr. and obj.*) **if you understood the question as well as I do,** si vous compreniez la question aussi bien que moi. **4.** (*elliptical auxiliary*) **may I open these letters?—(please) do,** puis-je ouvrir ces lettres?— je vous en prie! **did you see him?—I did,** l'avez-vous vu?—oui (, je l'ai vu); **do you like her?—no I don't,** l'aimez-vous?—non (, je ne l'aime pas); **don't you like it?—yes, I do,** vous ne l'aimez pas?—mais si; **you like him, don't you?** vous l'aimez, n'est-ce pas? **he lives here, doesn't he?** il habite ici, n'est-ce pas? **that does you good, doesn't it?** ça fait du bien, hein? **don't!** ne faites pas ça! **5. you like Paris? so do I,** vous aimez Paris? moi aussi; **they have always existed and still do,** ils ont toujours existé et existent encore; **if you want to speak to him, do it now,** si vous désirez lui parler, faites-le maintenant. **III.** *v.aux.* (*used with inf. for simple pr. and past*) **1.** (*for emphasis*) **he** *did* **go,** il y est bien allé; **I** *do* **believe he is a thief,** je crois vraiment que c'est un voleur; **it doesn't matter—it** *does* **(matter)!** ça ne fait rien.— si, ça fait quelque chose! **why don't you work?—I** *do* **(work)!** pourquoi ne travaillez-vous pas?—mais si, je travaille! **do you remember him?—do I** *remember* **him!** vous souvenez-vous de lui?—si je m'en souviens! *do* **sit down,** asseyez-vous donc! **yes, people** *did* **live there,** oui, des gens ont vécu là; **I don't like coffee, but I** *do* **like tea,** je n'aime pas le café, mais j'aime bien le thé. **2. rarely does it happen that . . .,** il arrive rarement que . . .. **3.** *Jur:* **charged that he did on the 15th of August utter threats,** accusé d'avoir, le 15 août, proféré des menaces. **4.** (*usual form in questions and negative statements except with 'have', but cf.* HAVE, BE, *and modal verbs; also in negative commands*) **did you see him?** l'avez-vous vu? **we do not know,** nous ne le savons pas; **do not speak!** ne parlez pas! **don't do it!** n'en faites rien! **don't be afraid,** n'ayez pas peur; **do you, d'you, mind?** (i) ça ne vous fait rien? (ii) *Iron:* vous permettez? **do away,** *v.i.* **to do away with (sth., s.o.),** abolir, proscrire, abandonner (un usage); supprimer, éliminer (des frais, etc.); tuer, *F:* supprimer (qn); se défaire de (qn). **do by** *v.tr.* **to do well, badly, by s.o.,** bien, mal, agir, se bien, mal, conduire, envers qn; **he has been hard done by,** il a été traité durement. **do for** *v.tr. F:* (*a*) **to do for s.o.,** faire, tenir, le ménage de qn; (*b*) (i) tuer (qn); faire son affaire à (qn); (ii) ruiner (qn); **he's done for,** (i) c'est un homme mort; (ii) il est fichu. **do in** *v.tr. P:* (*a*) tuer, assassiner (qn); *F:* faire son affaire à (qn); (*b*) **I'm absolutely done in,** je suis fourbu, vanné. **doing** ['du:iŋ] *n.* **1.** (*a*) **d. of sth.,** action *f* de faire qch.; **talking is one thing, d. is another,** autre chose est de parler, autre chose d'agir; **that takes some d.,** ça ne se fait pas en un tour de main; (*b*) **this is his d.,** c'est son ouvrage; **all this is your d.,** c'est vous qui êtes la cause de tout cela; **it was none of my d.,** ce n'est pas à moi qu'il faut s'en prendre. **2. doings,** ce qu'on fait; (*a*) *Pej:* agissements *mpl* (de qn); **to be informed of s.o.'s doings,** être au courant des faits et gestes de qn; (*b*) événements *mpl*; *F:* **there have been great doings at their house,** il y a eu bien du mouvement chez eux. **3.** *F:* **the doings,** les machins *mpl,* les trucs *mpl.* **4.** (*a*) **d. away with sth.,** suppression *f,* abandon *m,* de qch.; (*b*) **d. out,** nettoyage *m* (d'une chambre); (*c*) **d. up,** remise *f* à neuf. **do up** *v.tr.* (*a*) réparer (qch.); remettre (qch.) à neuf; décorer (une maison, etc.); *F:* **to do oneself up,** faire toilette; (*b*) faire, envelopper, ficeler (un paquet); emballer, empaqueter (des marchandises); fermer, boutonner, agrafer (un vêtement); **the dress does up at the back,** la robe s'agrafe par derrière. **do with** *v.tr.* (*a*) **what did you do with my umbrella?** qu'avez-vous fait de mon parapluie? **she didn't know what to do with herself,** elle ne savait que faire, à quoi s'occuper; (*for joy*) elle ne se tenait pas de joie; (*for awkwardness*) elle était gênée; (*b*) **I want nothing to do with him,** je ne veux pas avoir affaire à lui; **he's something to do with insurance,** il est dans les assurances; **to have nothing to do with sth.,** (i) (*of pers.*) n'être pour rien dans, n'avoir rien à voir avec, qch. (ii) (*of thg*) n'avoir rien à faire avec, n'avoir pas de rapport à, avec, qch.; **it's nothing to do with you,** vous n'avez rien à voir là-dedans; **I had nothing to do with it,** je n'y suis pour rien; (*c*) **to have done with sth.,** en avoir fini avec qch.; **let's have done with it!** finissons-en! **to have done with s.o.,** avoir rompu avec qn; en avoir fini avec qn; **I haven't done with him yet!** je n'en ai pas encore fini avec lui! **that's all over and done with!** c'est fini, tout ça! (*d*) **I can do with little,** je sais me contenter de peu; (*e*) **I could do with a cup of tea,** je prendrais bien une tasse de thé; **we can do with your help,** vous n'êtes pas de trop. **do without** *v.tr.* se passer de (qn, qch.); **to do without food,** se passer de nourriture; *F:* **I could do without him,** je me passerais bien de lui.

do² [du:] *n.* **1.** (*a*) **the do's and don'ts of society,** ce qui se fait et ce qui ne se fait pas dans le monde; (*b*) *F:* manière *f* de traiter qn; **come on, fair do's!** dis donc, (i) donne-moi ma part! (ii) sois juste! **2.** *F:* réception *f*; soirée *f.*

do³ [dou] *n. Mus:* (*fixed*) do *m,* ut *m.*

doc [dɔk] *n. F:* (= DOCTOR) toubib *m.*

docile ['dousail] *a.* docile; (animal) sage.

docility [dou'siliti] *n.* docilité *f.*

dock¹ [dɔk] *n. Bot:* patience *f.*

dock² *n.* **1.** tronçon *m,* partie charnue (de la queue d'un cheval ou d'un chien). **2.** *Harn:* **d. (piece),** culeron *m,* trousse-queue *m inv.*

dock³ *v.tr.* **1. to d. a horse('s tail), a dog('s tail),**

couper la queue à un cheval, un chien. **2.** (*a*) diminuer, supprimer (le traitement de qn).

dock[4] *n.* **1.** *Nau:* (*a*) bassin *m* (d'un port); **to go into d.,** entrer au bassin; **the docks,** les docks *mpl*; *F:* (*of car, plane*) **in d.,** en réparation; (*b*) **dry d., graving d.,** cale sèche; **ship in dry d.,** navire *m* en radoub; (*c*) **floating d.,** dock flottant; chantier *m* à flot; (*d*) **naval docks** = DOCKYARD. **2.** *Th:* **scene d.,** remise *f* à décors.

dock[5] **1.** *v.tr.* (*a*) *Nau:* faire entrer (un navire) au bassin; (*b*) faire entrer (un navire) en cale sèche; (*c*) (*on canal, river*) garer (une péniche, etc.); (*d*) arrimer (deux engins spatiaux). **2.** *v.i.* (*a*) (*of ship*) entrer (i) au bassin, aux docks, (ii) en cale sèche; (*b*) (*of two spacecraft*) s'arrimer. **docking** *n.* (*a*) mise *f* au bassin; (*for repairs*) radoubage *m*; (*b*) arrimage *m* (de deux engins spatiaux); **d. manœuvre,** manœuvre *f* d'abordage.

dock[6]*n.* *Jur:* banc *m* des accusés, des prévenus; **prisonner in the d. Martin,** accusé Martin.

docker ['dɔkər] *n.* docker *m.*

docket[1] ['dɔkit] *n.* **1.** *Jur:* (*a*) registre *m* des jugements rendus; (*b*) *U.S:* rôle *m* des causes; (*c*) bordereau *m* (des pièces d'un dossier). **2.** étiquette *f*, fiche *f* (d'un document, d'une lettre); **wages d.,** bordereau de paye. **3.** *Adm:* récépissé *m* de douane.

docket[2] *v.tr.* **1.** *Jur:* (*a*) enregistrer (un jugement rendu); (*b*) *U.S:* porter (une cause) sur le rôle des causes. **2.** étiqueter, classer (des papiers).

dockland ['dɔklænd] *n.* les quartiers *mpl* des docks.

dockyard ['dɔkjɑ:d] *n.* chantier naval, de constructions navales; *esp.* **naval d.,** arsenal *m* maritime.

doctor[1] ['dɔktər] *n.* **1.** *Sch:* **D. of Divinity, of Laws,** docteur *m* en théologie, en droit; **D. of Medicine,** docteur en médecine; **D. of Literature, of Science,** docteur ès lettres, ès sciences; **doctor's degree,** doctorat *m.* **2.** médecin *m*, docteur; **woman d.,** femme médecin; **family d.,** médecin de famille; **ship's d.,** médecin du bord; **army d.,** médecin militaire; **National Health (Service) d.,** médecin conventionné; *F:* **just what the d. ordered,** la bonne formule.

doctor[2] *v.tr.* **1.** (*a*) soigner (un malade); (*b*) *Turf: Pej:* doper (un cheval); (*c*) châtrer (un chat, etc.). **2.** *F:* falsifier, fausser (des comptes, un texte); piper (un dé, des cartes); frelater, (du vin, etc.). **doctoring** *n.* **1.** (*a*) soins *mpl* (**of s.o.,** donnés à qn); (*b*) *F:* doping *m* (d'un cheval); (*c*) castration *f* (d'un chat). **2.** *F:* profession *f* de médecine. **3.** *F:* falsification *f*.

doctorate ['dɔkt(ə)rət] *n.* *Sch:* doctorat *m.*

doctrinaire [dɔktri'nɛər] *a. & n.* doctrinaire (*mf*).

doctrinal [dɔk'train(ə)l] *a.* doctrinal, -aux.

doctrine ['dɔktrin] *n.* doctrine *f*.

docudrama ['dɔkjudrɑ:mə] *n.* *T.V:* docudrame *m.*

document[1] ['dɔkjumənt] *n.* document *m*, pièce *f*; **legal d.,** acte *m* authentique; *Jur:* **documents relating to a case,** dossier *m* d'une affaire; **to draw up a d.,** rédiger un acte; **d. case,** porte-documents *m inv.*

document[2] ['dɔkjument] *v.tr.* documenter; **well documented book,** livre bien documenté.

documentary [dɔkju'ment(ə)ri] **1.** *a.* documentaire. **2.** *a. & n.* *Cin: TV:* **d. (film),** documentaire *m.*

documentation [dɔkjumen'teiʃ(ə)n] *n.* documentation *f*.

dodder ['dɔdər] *v.i.* (*of aged pers.*) trembloter; marcher d'un pas branlant. **doddering** *a.* **1.** (démarche) branlante. **2.** (*of pers.*) gaga *inv*, gâteux.

dodderer ['dɔdərər] *n.* gâteux, -euse; croulant, -ante.

doddery ['dɔdəri] *a.* *F:* branlant, tremblotant.

doddle [dɔdl] *n.* *F:* **it's a d.,** (i) c'est couru d'avance; (ii) c'est simple comme bonjour.

dodge[1] [dɔdʒ] *n.* **1.** mouvement *m*, saut *m*, de côté. **2.** (*a*) ruse *f*, artifice *m*; (*b*) truc *m*, combine *f*.

dodge[2] **1.** *v.i.* (*a*) se jeter de côté; **to d. behind a tree,** sauter, se glisser, derrière un arbre; (*b*) *Box: Fb:* esquiver, éviter; (*c*) biaiser, ruser, user d'artifices. **2.** *v.tr.* esquiver (un coup); éviter (qn); esquiver, tourner, éluder (une difficulté); escamoter (une question); **to d. military service,** se soustraire, *F:* couper, au service militaire.

dodgem ['dɔdʒəm] *a. & n.* **d. cars, dodgems,** autos tamponneuses.

dodger ['dɔdʒər] *n.* *F:* (*a*) *O:* **an artful d.,** un fin matois; (*b*) tire- au-flanc *m*; *US:* **draft d.,** réfractaire *m.*

dodgy ['dɔdʒi] *a.* *F:* **1.** roublard. **2.** (*situation*) délicat, épineux.

dodo, *pl.* **-oes, -os** ['doudou, -z] *n.* **1.** *Orn:* dronte *m*, dodo *m.* **2.** *F:* **(as) dead as a d.,** mort et enterré.

doe [dou] *n.* *Z:* **1.** daine *f*; biche *f*; **d.-eyed,** aux yeux de biche. **2.** (*of rabbit*) lapine *f*; (*of wild rabbit and hare*) hase *f*.

doer ['du:ər] *n.* (*a*) personne dynamique; **she's a d.,** c'est une femme très active; (*b*) auteur *m* (d'une action).

doeskin ['douskin] **1.** *n.* (*a*) peau *f* de daim; (*b*) *Tex:* simili-daim *m.* **2.** *attrib.* en peau de daim.

doesn't = **does not;** *see* DO[1].

doff [dɔf] *v.tr.* *Lit:* enlever, ôter (son chapeau).

dog[1] [dɔg] *n.* **1.** (*a*) chien *m*; **sporting d.,** chien de chasse; **sheep d.,** chien de berger; **police d.,** chien policier; **guide d.,** chien d'aveugle; *P. N:* **beware of the d.,** (attention) chien méchant; **d. racing,** *F:* **the dogs,** courses *fpl* de lévriers; *F:* **to go to the dogs,** aller aux courses de lévriers; (ii) gâcher sa vie; (*of business*) aller à la ruine; **d. show,** exposition canine; **d. collar,** (i) collier *m* de chien; (ii) *F:* faux col (d'ecclésiastique); *U.S:* **d. tag,** plaque *f* d'identité (de chien, *F:* de militaire); *Comest:* **hot d.,** (petit pain fourré d'une) saucisse de Francfort chaude; *F:* **d. Latin,** latin *m* de cuisine; **to lead a dog's life,** mener une vie de chien; **to die like a d.,** mourir comme un chien; **to follow s.o. about like a d.,** faire le chien après qn; **you can't teach an old d. new tricks,** on ne peut pas apprendre aux vieux singes à faire des grimaces; *F:* **he doesn't stand a dog's chance,** il n'a pas l'ombre d'une chance; *F:* **to see a man about a d.,** (i) aller aux toilettes; (ii) aller boire un pot; **give a d. a bad name,** qui veut noyer son chien l'accuse de la rage; **let sleeping dogs lie,** ne réveillez pas le chat qui dort; **its a case of d. eat d.,** c'est un cas où les loups se mangent entre eux; (*b*) *Z:* **(Cape) hunting d.,** lycaon *m*; **prairie d.,** cynomys *m.* **2.** mâle *m* (de certains animaux); **d. fox,** renard *m* mâle. **3.** *F:* *O:* **sly d.,** rusé coquin, fin renard; **gay d.,** coureur *m* (de femmes); **dirty d.,** salaud *m*, sale type *m.* **4.** *Astr:* **the D. Star,** Sirius *m.* **5.** *Tchn:* (*a*) (*pawl*) cliquet *m*; (*b*) (*of lathe*) toc *m* (d'entraînement); (*c*) *Mec.E:* crabot *m*; (*d*) *Metall:* agrafe *f* (de châssis de moulage); (*e*) sergent *m* (de tonnelier). **6. (fire) d.,** chenet *m.*

dog[2] *v.tr.* (**dogged** [dɔgd]) suivre (qn) à la piste; **to d. s.o.'s footsteps,** marcher sur les talons de qn; **he is dogged by misfortune,** il est poursuivi par la malchance.

dogcart ['dɔgkɑ:t] *n.* *Veh:* dog-cart *m*, *pl.* dog-carts.

doge [doudʒ] *n.* *Hist:* doge *m.*

dog-eared ['dɔgiəd] *a.* (livre) aux pages cornées; (page) cornée.

dogfight ['dɔgfait] *n.* **1.** combat *m* de chiens. **2.** *Mil.Av:* combat aérien. **3.** bagarre *f*.

dogfish ['dɔgfiʃ] *n.* *Ich:* chien *m* de mer, roussette *f*.

dogfood ['dɔgfu:d] *n.* pâtée *f* (pour chiens).

dogged ['dɔgid] *a.* obstiné, résolu; tenace; (attache-

ment) inébranlable. **-ly** *adv.* obstinément; avec ténacité; **to work d.,** travailler sans relâche.
doggedness ['dɔgidnis] *n.* obstination *f*; entêtement *m.*
doggerel ['dɔgərəl] *a. & n.* **d. (verse),** (i) (poésie *f*) burlesque; (ii) (vers *mpl*) de mirliton.
doggie ['dɔgi] *n. F:* toutou *m*, chienchien *m*; *U.S.* **d. bag,** petit sac fourni par certains restaurants pour emporter les restes.
doggone ['dɔgɔn] *a. U.S: F:* sacré.
doggy ['dɔgi] **1.** *a.* (*a*) de chien; (*b*) *F:* qui se connaît en chiens; qui adore les chiens. **2.** *n. F:* = DOGGIE.
doghouse ['dɔghaus] *n.* (*a*) *esp. U.S:* chenil *m*; (*b*) *F:* **to be in the d.,** être en défaveur, en disgrâce.
dogleg ['dɔgleg] *n.* coude *m* (dans un tuyau, un chemin, etc.).
doglike ['dɔglaik] *a.* (fidélité) de chien.
dogma, *pl.* **-as** ['dɔgmə, -əz] *n* dogme *m.*
dogmatic [dɔg'mætik] *a.* **1.** dogmatique. **2.** autoritaire, tranchant; **to be very d.,** trancher sur tout. **-ally** *adv.* d'un ton autoritaire, tranchant.
dogmatism ['dɔgmətizm] *n.* **1.** dogmatisme *m.* **2.** tour d'esprit autoritaire, positif.
dogmeat ['dɔgmiːt] *n.* viande *f* pour chiens.
do-gooder ['duː'gudər] *n. F: Pej:* âme *f* charitable; faiseur, -euse, de bonnes œuvres.
dogpaddle¹ ['dɔgpædl] *n. Swim:* nage *f* à la chien.
dogpaddle² *v.i.* nager à la chien.
dogrose ['dɔgrouz] *n. Bot:* **1.** églantine *f*, rose *f* sauvage. **2.** (*bush*) églantier *m*, rosier *m* sauvage.
dogsbody ['dɔgzbɔdi] *n. F:* factotum *m*; **she's the general d.,** elle est la bonne à tout faire.
dog-tired ['dɔg'taiəd] *a. F:* claqué; mort, brisé, de fatigue.
dogtooth ['dɔgtuːθ] *n.* (*a*) *Arch:* dent-de-chien *f*, *pl.* dents-de-chien; (*b*) *Bot:* **d. violet,** érythrone *m*, dent-de-chien.
dog-watch ['dɔgwɔtʃ] *n. Nau:* petit quart.
dogwood ['dɔgwud] *n. Bot: Com:* cornouiller *m.*
doh [dou] *n.* = DO³.
doily ['dɔili] *n.* **1.** petit napperon. **2.** dessus *m* d'assiette.
do-it-yourself [duitjə'self] *n.* bricolage *m*; **a do-it-y. enthusiast,** un bricoleur passionné; **do-it-y. kit,** panoplie *f* de construction (d'une table, etc.).
doldrums (the) [ðə'dɔldrəmz] *n. pl.* le cafard; idées noires; **to be in the d.,** (i) (*of pers.*) broyer du noir; avoir le cafard; (ii) (*of business*) être dans le marasme.
dole¹ [doul] *n. F:* indemnité *f* de chômage; **to go on the d.,** s'inscrire au chômage.
dole² *v.tr.* **to d. out sth.,** distribuer qch au compte-gouttes.
doleful ['doulful] *a.* (mine) lugubre; (cri) plaintif; (*of pers.*) triste. affligé. **-fully** *adv* plaintivement; tristement.
doll¹ [dɔl] *n.* **1.** (*a*) poupée *f*; **baby d.,** baigneur *m*; **to play with a d.,** jouer à la poupée; **doll's house,** (i) maison *f* de poupée; (ii) jolie petite maisonnette; (*b*) marionnette *f* (de ventriloque). **2.** *F:* (*a*) jolie femme; (*b*) femme, jeune fille; (*c*) *U.S:* amoureuse *f.*
doll² *v.tr.* **to d. up,** bichonner (qn); **to d. oneself up,** (*of woman*) se pomponner; **to be all dolled up,** être sur son trente et un, en grand tralala.
dollar ['dɔlər] *n. Num:* (*a*) dollar (canadien, australien, malais, etc.); (*b*) dollar (des États-Unis); *F:* **I bet my bottom d. that . . .,** je parie jusqu'à mon dernier sou que . . .; *Pol.Ec:* **d. area,** zone *f* dollar.
dollop ['dɔləp] *n. F:* **a d. of butter,** un gros morceau de beurre; **a good d. of cream,** une bonne cuillerée de crème.
dolly ['dɔli] *n.* **1.** *F:* (*a*) poupée *f*; (*b*) **d. (-bird),** jolie femme, *F:* poupée *f.* **2.** *Laund:* agitateur *m* (pour le linge); **d. tub,** (i) baquet *m* à lessive; (ii) *Min:* cuve *f* à rincer (l'or). **3.** *Metalw:* tas *m* à river (de riveur). **4.** *Civ.E:* avant-pieu *m*, *pl.* avant-pieux. **5.** *Rail:* (*shunting engine*) diabolo *m.* **6.** *Cin:* travelling *m*; chariot *m.*
dolmen ['dɔlmen] *n. Prehist:* dolmen *m.*
dolomite ['dɔləmait] **1.** *n.* (*a*) *Miner:* dolomite *f*; (*b*) *Geol:* (*rock*) dolomie *f.* **2.** *Pr.n.pl. Geog:* **the Dolomites,** les Dolomites.
dolphin ['dɔlfin] *n. Z: Her:* dauphin *m*; **bottlenose(d) d.,** tursiops *m*; souffleur *m.*
dolphinarium [dɔlfi'nɛəriəm] *n.* aquarium *m* pour dauphins.
dolt [doult] *n.* sot *m*, lourdaud *m*, nigaud *m*, gourde *f.*
doltish ['doultiʃ] *a.* sot, lourdaud, bête.
domain [də'mein] *n.* (*a*) domaine *m*; terres *fpl*; (*b*) *Mth: Ph:* domaine (d'une fonction).
dome [doum] *n.* **1.** *Arch:* dôme, *m.* coupole *f.* **2.** *Metall:* dôme, voûte *f* (de fourneau) **3.** (*a*) *Fig:* dôme, calotte *f* (des cieux); sommet arrondi (d'une colline); calotte (du crâne); (*b*) *NAm: P:* tête *f.*
domed [doumd] *a.* (*a*) (édifice) à dôme, à coupole; (*b*) en forme de dôme.
Domesday ['duːmzdei] *attrib. Hist:* **D. Book,** (livre *m* du) cadastre de l'Angleterre (établi en 1086 par Guillaume le Conquérant).
domestic [də'mestik] **I.** *a.* **1.** (vertu, malheur) domestique; (drame, charbon) de ménage; **d. duties,** les affaires *fpl*, les soins *mpl*, de ménage; **d. life,** la vie de famille; **d. servant,** domestique *mf*; bonne *f*; **d. science,** (i) les arts ménagers; (ii) *Sch:* enseignement ménager; **water for d. use,** eau ménagère. **2.** (*a*) (commerce, etc.) intérieur; (production) nationale; **d. products,** denrées *fpl* du pays; *Post: U.S:* **d. mail,** correspondance *f* à destination de l'intérieur; (*b*) *Pol:* (*of dissension*) intérieur; (guerre) intestine; (*c*) (animal) domestique. **3.** (*of pers.*) casanier; (femme) d'intérieur. **II.** *n.* (*in formal speech*) domestique *mf*; bonne *f.*
domesticate [də'mestikeit] *v.tr.* **1.** domestiquer, apprivoiser (un animal). **2.** acclimater (un animal, une plante). **3.** (*of pers.*) **to be domesticated,** aimer la vie d'intérieur; **to become domesticated,** prendre goût à la vie d'intérieur.
domesticity [doumes'tisiti] *n.* (*a*) attachement *m* au foyer; goûts *mpl* domestiques; (*b*) vie de famille; (*c*) simplicité *f* (d'un intérieur).
domicile¹ ['dɔmisail] *n. Com: Jur:* domicile *m.*
domicile² *v.tr.* (*a*) *Com:* domicilier (un effet); **bills domiciled in France,** traites *fpl* payables en France; (*b*) établir (qn) (dans un pays); **domiciled at Leeds,** domicilié, demeurant, à Leeds.
domiciliary [dɔmi'siljəri] *a.* (visite, etc.) domiciliaire; (assistance) à domicile.
dominance ['dɔminəns] *n.* **1.** dominance *f* (d'une maladie, etc.); prédominance *f* (d'une race). **2.** *Biol:* dominance (d'un gène).
dominant ['dɔminənt] **1.** *a.* dominant; dominateur, -trice; (hauteur) qui domine le paysage; *Biol:* (gène) dominant; *a. & n.* **d. (character),** caractère dominant. **2.** *n. Mus:* dominante *f*; **d. chord,** accord *m* de dominante; **d. seventh,** septième *f* de dominante. **-ly** *adv.* d'une manière dominante.
dominate ['dɔmineit] *v.tr. & i.* **1. to d. (over)/s.o., a people,** dominer (sur) qn, un peuple; **to be dominated by s.o.,** subir la loi de qn; **man dominated by ambition,** homme en proie à l'ambition. **2.** (*of mountain, etc.*) **to d. (over) the landscape,** dominer le paysage; **the fortress dominates the town,** la forteresse commande la ville. **dominating** *a.* (*of feature, colour, etc.*) dominant; (*of personality*) dominateur, -trice.
domination [dɔmi'neiʃ(ə)n] *n.* domination *f* **(over,** sur); **to be under s.o.'s d.,** être dominé par qn.

domineer [dɔmiˈniər] *v.i.* se montrer autoritaire; **to d. over s.o.,** tyranniser qn. **domineering** *a.* (*of pers., character, etc.*) dominateur, -trice, autoritaire.

dominical [dəˈminik(ə)l] *a. Ecc:* dominical, -aux.

Dominican [dəˈminikən] **1.** *a. & n. Ecc:* dominicain, -aine. **2.** *Geog:* (*a*) *a.* dominicain; **the D. Republic,** la République Dominicaine; (*b*) *n.* Dominicain, -aine.

dominion [dəˈminjən] *n.* **1.** autorité *f*, empire *m*; **to have, hold, d. over . . .,** exercer son empire, dominer, sur . . . **2.** dominion *m*; **the D. of Canada,** le Dominion (du Canada).

domino, *pl.* **-oes** [ˈdɔminou, -ouz] *n.* **1.** *Cost:* domino *m* (de bal masqué). **2.** *Games:* (*a*) domino; (*b*) (*game*) **dominoes,** (*usu. with sing. const.*) (jeu *m* de) dominos; **to play dominoes,** jouer aux dominos; **game of dominoes,** partie *f* de dominos. **3. the d. theory,** la théorie des dominos.

don¹ [dɔn] *n.m.* **1.** (*Spanish title*) Don. **2.** *Sch: F:* professeur (d'université).

don² *v.tr.* **(donned)** revêtir, endosser (un uniforme); mettre, coiffer (un chapeau).

donate [dəˈneit] *v.tr.* faire un don de (qch.); *Med:* **to d. blood,** donner du sang, son sang.

donation [dəˈneiʃ(ə)n] *n.* donation *f*, don *m*.

donator [dəˈneitər] *n.* donateur, -trice.

done. *see* DO¹.

donkey [ˈdɔŋki] *n.* **1.** âne *m*, *f.* ânesse; baudet *m*; **d. race,** course *f* d'ânes; **d. work,** (i) le gros travail; (ii) le plus gros d'un travail; **d. jacket,** grosse veste; *F:* **she would talk the hind leg off a d.,** elle est bavarde comme une pie; **I haven't seen him for donkey's years,** je ne l'ai pas vu depuis une éternité. **2.** *F:* imbécile *mf.* **3. d. engine,** petit-cheval, *pl.* petits-chevaux; *Nau:* **d. boiler,** chaudière *f* auxiliaire.

donnish [ˈdɔniʃ] *a.* (*a*) pédant; **he's a bit d.,** il a un petit air professoral; (*b*) (air, ton) d'érudit.

donor [ˈdounər] *n.* **1.** *Jur:* donateur, -trice. **2.** *Med:* donneur, -euse (de sang, etc.).

don't. *see* DO¹.

don't know [ˈdountˈnou] *n. F:* votant indécis.

doodah [ˈduːdɑː] *n. P:* truc *m*, machin *m*.

doodle¹ [ˈduːdl] *v.tr. F:* crayonner, griffoner (distraitement).

doodle² *n. F:* crayonnage *m*, griffonage *m*.

doodlebug [ˈduːdlbʌg] *n. Hist: F:* bombe volante.

doom¹ [duːm] *n.* **1.** destin *m* (funeste); sort (malheureux); **he met his d.,** il trouva la mort. **2.** perte *f*, ruine *f*.

doom² *v.tr.* **1.** condamner **(to,** à); *esp. in p.p.* **doomed,** (*of town*) condamné; (*of pers.*) perdu; **attempt doomed to failure,** tentative condamnée à l'insuccès, vouée à l'échec.

doomsday [ˈduːmzdei] *n.* le (jour du) jugement dernier; *F:* **till d.,** indéfiniment; **to put off sth. till d.,** renvoyer qch. aux calendes grecques.

door [dɔːr] *n.* **1.** (a) porte *f* (de maison, etc.); **doors of a wardrobe,** portes, battants *mpl*, d'une armoire; **front d.,** porte d'entrée; **back d.,** porte de service; **to get into a profession by the back d.,** entrer dans une profession par la petite porte; **folding d.,** porte brisée; **sliding d.,** porte coulissante; **revolving d.,** porte tournante, tambour *m*; **behind closed doors,** (à) portes closes; *Jur:* à huis clos; **two doors away,** deux portes plus loin; **the house next d.,** la maison à côté; **to show s.o. the d.,** éconduire qn; **to show s.o. to the d.,** conduire qn à la porte; reconduire qn; **out of doors,** dehors, en plein air; **to shut the d. in s.o.'s face,** fermer la porte au nez de qn; **to leave the d. open to, for, negotiations**, laisser la porte ouverte à des négociations; **to close the d. on any discussion,** rendre impossible aucune discussion; **to lay a charge at s.o.'s d.,** imputer qch. à qn; **from d. to d.,** de domicile à domicile; **d.-to-d. canvassing, selling,** porte-à-porte *m*; **to be a d.-to-d. salesman,** être placier *m*; faire du porte-à-porte; (*b*) **d. frame,** chambranle *m*, châssis *m*, de porte; **d. chain,** chaîne *f* de sûreté; **d. curtain,** portière *f*; **d. handle,** poignée *f*, bouton *m*, de porte; **d. knocker,** marteau *m* de porte, heurtoir *m*. **2.** (*a*) portière *f* (de wagon, de voiture, etc.); porte (de voiture); (*b*) porte (de réfrigérateur, etc.).

doorbell [ˈdɔːbel] *n.* sonnette *f*.

doorkeeper [ˈdɔːkiːpər] *n.* portier *m*, concierge *mf*.

doorknob [ˈdɔːnɔb] *n.* poignée (ronde) de porte.

doorman, *pl.* **-men** [ˈdɔːmən] *n.m.* portier.

doormat [ˈdɔːmæt] *n.* **1.** paillasson *m* (d'entrée). **2.** *F:* (*pers.*) lavette *f*; chiffe molle.

doornail [ˈdɔːneil] *n. F:* **(as) dead as a d.,** mort et bien mort.

doorpost [ˈdɔːpoust] *n.* montant *m* de porte.

doorstep [ˈdɔːstep] *n.* **1.** seuil *m*, pas *m* (de la porte). **2.** *F:* grosse tranche de pain.

doorstop [ˈdɔːstɔp] *n.* **1.** butoir *m*. **2.** cale-porte *m*, *pl.* cale-portes.

doorway [ˈdɔːwei] *n.* (baie *f* de) porte (*f*); encadrement *m* de la porte; **in the d.,** sous la porte.

dope¹ [doup] *n.* **1.** *Av: Aut:* enduit *m*. **2.** *Exp:* absorbant *m*. **3.** (*a*) drogue *f*; **d. addict,** drogué(e); toxico *mf*; **d. peddler,** trafiquant, -ante, de, en, stupéfiants; (*b*) *Rac:* doping *m*, stimulant *m*. **4.** *Petr:* additif *m*, dopant *m*. **5.** *P: Rac: etc:* renseignement *m; P:* rencard *m*, tuyau *m*. **6.** *P:* crétin *m*; **what a d.!** quelle nouille! quel andouille!

dope² *v.tr.* **1.** enduire. **2.** (*a*) doper (qn, un cheval); verser une drogue dans (une boisson). **3.** *Petr:* **doped fuel,** carburant dopé, additionné d'anti-détonant. **doping** *n.* **1.** enduisage *m*. **2.** *Petr:* dopage *m* (d'un combustible). **3.** (*a*) administration *f* d'un narcotique **(of s.o.,** à qn); (*b*) doping *m* (d'un cheval, etc.).

dopey [ˈdoupi] *a. F:* **1.** (*a*) drogué, dopé; (*b*) (à moitié) endormi. **2.** abruti, stupide.

Doric [ˈdɔrik] *a. & n. Arch:* dorique.

dorm [dɔːm] *n. Sch: F:* dortoir *m*.

dormant [ˈdɔːmənt] *a.* **1.** (*a*) (*of passion, etc.*) assoupi, endormi; **to lie d.,** être en sommeil; (*b*) (*of plant, bud*) dormant; (*c*) (volcan) en repos. **2.** (titre) tombé en désuétude; (loi) inappliquée.

dormer [ˈdɔːmər] *n.* **d. (window),** lucarne *f*; (fenêtre *f* en) mansarde (*f*).

dormitory [ˈdɔːmit(ə)ri] *n.* **1.** dortoir *m*; **d. town,** cité-dortoir *f*, *pl.* cités-dortoirs. **2.** *NAm:* maison *f*, foyer *m*, d'étudiants.

dormouse, *pl.* **-mice** [ˈdɔːmaus, -mais] *n.* Z: loir *m*.

dorsal [ˈdɔːs(ə)l] *a. Nat.Hist:* dorsal, -aux; **d. fin,** nageoire dorsale (d'un poisson).

dory [ˈdɔːri] *n.* **1.** *Ich:* **(John) D.,** dorée *f*, saint-pierre *m inv.* **2.** doris *m*.

dosage [ˈdousidʒ] *n.* **1.** administration *f* d'un médicament **(of s.o.,** à qn). **2.** dosage *m*, posologie *f* (d'un médicament).

dose¹ [dous] *n.* (*a*) *Med:* dose *f* (d'un médicament); (*b*) *Atom.Ph:* dose; (*c*) *F:* attaque *f* (de grippe, etc.). (*d*) *P:* vérole *f*.

dose² *v.tr.* **1.** doser (un médicament). **2.** administrer un médicament (à qn); **to d. oneself with quinine,** se bourrer de quinine. **3.** *Winem:* doser (le champagne).

doss¹ [dɔs] *n. P:* (*a*) lit *m*, pieu *m*; **d. house,** asile *m* de nuit; (*b*) somme *m*, roupillon *m*.

doss² *v.i. P:* **1.** (*a*) coucher à l'asile de nuit. **2. to d. down,** se coucher; se pieuter.

dosser [ˈdɔsər] *n.m. P:* clochard.

dossier [ˈdɔsiei, -iər] *n.* dossier *m* (d'une affaire).

dot¹ [dɔt] *n.* **1.** (*a*) point *m* (d'un trait pointillé); *Tg:* **dots and dashes,** points et traits *mpl*; **on the d.,** (arriver) à l'heure tapante; (payer) argent comptant; **three o'clock on the d.,** trois heures pile; **since the year d.,** il y a des siècles; (*b*) point (d'un i, d'un j); (*c*) point (de ponctuation, etc.); **three dots,** trois points; points de suspension. **2.** *Mus:* point d'augmentation.

dot² *v.tr.* **(dotted) 1.** mettre un point sur (un i); *F:* **to d. one's i's (and cross one's t's),** mettre les points sur les i. **2.** marquer (une surface) avec des points; pointiller (une ligne, un dessin); (*of surface, etc.*) **dotted with,** parsemé de (fleurs, etc.); **the islands are dotted all round the coast,** les îles sont éparpillées tout autour de la côte. **3.** *Mus:* pointer (une note). **4.** *F:* **to d. and carry one,** boiter (en marchant). **5.** *P:* **to d. s.o. one,** flanquer un gnon à qn. **dotted** *a.* **1.** (contour) pointillé; **d. line,** (ligne *f* en) pointillé (*m*); ligne pointillée; **to sign on the d. line,** (i) signer à la place indiquée (sur une formule); (ii) donner son consentement. **2.** *Mus:* (note) pointée.

dotage ['doutidʒ] *n.* gâtisme *m*; **to be in one's d.,** être gâteux.

dote [dout] *v.i.* **1.** être gâteux. **2. to d. on s.o.,** aimer qn à la folie; être fou, folle, de qn. **doting** *a.* **1.** gâteux, -euse. **2.** qui montre une tendresse ou une indulgence ridicule; qui aime follement.

dottle ['dɔtl] *n. F:* culot *m* (de pipe).

dotty ['dɔti] *a. F:* toqué, piqué; **he's d. about her,** il est toqué, fou, d'elle.

double¹ ['dʌbl] **I.** *a.* **1.** (*a*) double; **d. chin,** double menton *m*; **d. daffodil,** narcisse *m* double; **d. boiler, d. saucepan,** bain-marie *m, pl.* bains-marie; **with a d. meaning,** (i) à deux, double, sens; (ii) ambigu, -uë; **d. bed,** grand lit; lit pour deux personnes; **d. bedroom,** chambre *f* pour deux personnes; **"all" is spelt "a, d. l",** "all" s'écrit "a, deux l"; **to reach d. figures,** atteindre les deux chiffres; (*dicing, dominoes*) **d. ace,** double-as *m, pl.* doubles-as; *Ten:* **d. fault,** double faute *f*; **to d. fault,** faire une double faute; **to play a d. game,** jouer double jeu; **d. agent,** agent *m* double; **to lead a d. life,** mener une vie double; (*b*) de grandeur double; **d. whisky, d. Scotch,** double (consommation *f* de) whisky *m*; *Mus:* **d. bassoon,** contrebasson *m.* **2.** (*of material, etc.*) (plié) en deux; **to fold a sheet (of paper) d.,** plier une feuille en deux; (*of pers.*) **bent d.,** courbé en deux. **3. d. the number,** le double, deux fois autant; **to pay d. the value,** payer le double de la valeur; **I am d. your age,** je suis deux fois plus âgé que vous. **4.** *Mil: etc:* **d. time,** pas redoublé; pas de course; **in d. time,** au pas gymnastique. **II.** *adv.* **to see d.,** voir double. **III.** *n.* **1.** double *m*; **to toss d. or quits,** jouer (à) quitte ou double. **2.** (*a*) (*of pers.*) double; *F:* sosie *m* (de qn); (*b*) *Th: Cin:* doublure *f.* **3.** *F:* chambre *f* à deux personnes. **4.** (*a*) crochet *m* (d'un animal poursuivi); (*b*) *Bill:* doublé *m.* **5.** *Mil: etc:* **to break into the d.,** prendre le pas de course; **at the d.,** au pas gymnastique. **6.** *Ten:* **men's, women's, mixed, doubles,** double messieurs, dames, mixte. **7.** *Turf:* (i) coup *m* (de deux); (ii) pari couplé; **to bring off a d.,** réussir un double. **8.** *Cards:* (*at bridge*) contre *m.* **9.** (*dominoes*) double. **doubly** *adv.* doublement; **to be d. careful,** redoubler de prudence.

double² **I.** *v.tr.* **1.** (*a*) doubler (un nombre, etc.); porter (un chiffre) au double; *Gaming:* **to d. the stakes,** doubler la mise; (*b*) *Tex:* doubler (le fil). **2.** *Nau:* doubler (un cap). **3.** plier en deux, replier (du papier, etc.). **4.** *Cards:* (*at bridge*) contrer. **5.** *Bill:* **to d. the red,** doubler la rouge. **II.** *v.i.* **1.** (*of population, etc.*) (se) doubler. **2.** *Mil: etc:* prendre le pas gymnastique. **3.** (*a*) (*of pers., hunted animal, etc.*) faire un brusque crochet; (*b*) (*of road, etc.*) faire un détour, un crochet. **4. to d. for s.o.,** remplacer qn; *Th:* doubler qn. **double back 1.** *v.tr.* replier, rabattre (une couverture, etc.). **2.** *v.i.* (*of pers., hunted animal, etc.*) revenir sur ses pas. **double over 1.** *v.i.* se plier. **2.** *v.tr.* replier, rabattre. **double up 1.** *v.i.* se plier (en deux); se courber (en deux); **to d. up with laughter,** se tordre de rire. **2.** *v.tr.* (*a*) replier (du papier, de l'étoffe, etc.); (*b*) (*of blow, etc.*) faire plier (qn) en deux; asseoir (qn) par terre. **3.** *v.i.* **to d. up with s.o.,** partager une chambre avec qn. **doubling** *n.* **1.** doublement *m* (d'un nombre, etc.). **2.** doublage *m* (du fil). **3.** crochet *m.*

double-acting ['dʌbl'æktiŋ] *a. Mec.E:* (cylindre, machine à vapeur) à double effet.

double-barrelled ['dʌbl'bærəld] *a.* (fusil) à deux coups; **d.-b. name,** patronymique *m* double (*p.ex.* Mr J. Wynn-Jones).

double-bass ['dʌbl'beis] *n. Mus:* contrebasse *f* à cordes.

double-bottomed ['dʌbl'bɔtəmd] *a.* (casserole, etc.) à double fond; (canot, etc.) à double coque.

double-breasted ['dʌbl'brestid] *a.* (veston) croisé.

double-check ['dʌbl'tʃek] *v.tr.* revérifier.

double-cross¹ ['dʌbl'krɔs] *v.tr. F:* duper (qn).

double-cross² *n. F:* duperie *f* (d'un associé).

double-dealing ['dʌbl'diːliŋ] *n.* duplicité *f.*

double-decker ['dʌbl'dekər] *n.* **1.** autobus *m* à impériale. **2.** *F:* sandwich *m* double.

double-edged ['dʌbl'edʒd] *a.* (épée, compliment, argument) à deux tranchants.

double entendre ['duːblɑ̃n'tɑ̃ndr̥] *n. usu. Pej:* ambiguïté *f*, double entente *f.*

double-faced ['dʌbl'feist] *a.* **1.** *Tex:* réversible. **2.** (*of pers.*) à double face, à deux visages; hypocrite.

double-glazed ['dʌbl'gleizd] *a.* à double vitrage.

double-glazing ['dʌbl'gleiziŋ] *n.* double vitrage *m*; **to put in d.-g.,** faire mettre des doubles fenêtres.

double-headed ['dʌbl'hedid] *a.* **1.** à deux têtes; bicéphale. **2.** *Her:* **d.-h. eagle,** aigle *f* à deux têtes. **3. d.-h. coin,** pièce *f* de monnaie à deux faces.

double-jointed ['dʌbl'dʒɔintid] *a.* (*of pers., limb*) désarticulé.

double-lock ['dʌbl'lɔk] *v.tr.* fermer (une porte, etc.) à double tour.

double-park ['dʌbl'pɑːk] *v.tr. & i. Aut:* stationner en double file. **double parking** *n.* stationnement *m* en double file.

double-quick ['dʌbl'kwik] *a. & adv.* **in d.-q. time, d.-q.,** (i) au pas gymnastique; (ii) *F:* en moins de rien.

double-stop ['dʌbl'stɔp] *v.i.* **(-stopped)** *Mus:* (*on violin*) faire des doubles-cordes. **double stopping** *n.* double-corde *f.*

doublet ['dʌblit] *n.* **1.** *Cost: A:* pourpoint *m*, justeaucorps *m.* **2.** *Ling:* doublet *m.*

double-talk ['dʌbltɔːk] *n.* propos *mpl* nègre-blanc.

doubt¹ [daut] *n.* doute *m*; **to be in d.,** être en doute, dans le doute; **when in d.,** dans le doute; **to cast doubts on sth.,** mettre qch. en doute; **to have one's doubts about sth.,** avoir des doutes sur, au sujet de, qch.; **I have my doubts whether this is true,** je doute que cela soit vrai; **beyond d.,** hors de doute; **facts beyond d.,** faits avérés; **no d. he will come,** il viendra sans doute; **there is, seems to be, no d. that . . .,** il ne semble faire aucun doute, que + *ind.*; **without (a, any) d.,** sans aucun doute.

doubt² **1.** *v.tr.* douter de (qn, la parole de qn); mettre en doute (la parole de qn); **I d. it,** j'en doute. **2.** *v.i.* **I d. whether, if, he will come,** je doute qu'il vienne. **doubting** *a.* incrédule, sceptique; **d. Thomas,** Thomas l'incrédule.

doubtful ['dautful] *a.* **1.** (*of thg*) (*a*) douteux; **it is d. whether . . .,** il est douteux, à douter, que . . .; (*b*) *Com:* **d. debt,** créance douteuse. **2.** (*of pers.*) (*a*) indécis, incertain; **I was still d. about speaking to him,** j'hésitais encore à lui parler; (*b*) **to be d. of, about, sth.,** avoir des doutes sur qch. **3.** (caractère) équivoque, suspect; (question) discutable; **in d. taste,** d'un goût douteux. **-fully** *adv.* **1.** d'un air de doute. **2.** en hésitant; d'une façon indécise.

doubtless ['dautlis] *adv.* **1.** sans aucun doute. **2.** sans doute; très probablement.

douche¹ [du:ʃ] *n.* **1.** (*a*) *Toil:* douche *f*; (*b*) *Med:* lavage *m* interne; (*as contraceptive*) injection vaginale. **2.** *Med:* poire *f* à injection.

dough [dou] *n.* **1.** pâte *f* (à pain). **2.** *P:* fric *m*, pognon *m*.

doughnut ['dounʌt] *n. Cu:* sorte *f* de beignet fait avec de la pâte; *Fr.C:* beigne *f*.

doughty ['dauti] *a. A: & Lit:* vaillant.

doughy ['doui] *a.* **1.** (pain) pâteux. **2.** *F:* (visage) terreux.

dour [duər] *a.* austère, sévère.

douse [daus] *v.tr.* **1.** plonger, tremper (qch.) dans l'eau. **2.** arroser, asperger (qn) d'eau. **3.** *F:* éteindre (la lumière).

dove [dʌv] **1.** *n.* (*a*) *Orn:* colombe *f*; **ring d.,** (pigeon) ramier (*m*); palombe *f*; (*b*) *F:* **my d.!** ma chérie! (*c*) *NAm:* femme douce; (*d*) *Pol: F:* **the doves and the hawks,** les colombes et les faucons. **2.** *a.* **d.(-coloured, -grey),** colombin; gorge-de-pigeon *inv.*

dovecote ['dʌvkɔt] *n.* colombier *m*, pigeonnier *m*.

Dover ['douvər] *Pr.n. Geog:* Douvres; **the Straits of D.,** le Pas de Calais.

dovetail¹ ['dʌvteil] *n. Carp:* (*a*) queue-d'aronde *f*, *pl.* queues-d'aronde; (*b*) **d. (joint),** assemblage *m* à queue-d'aronde.

dovetail² **1.** *v.tr.* (*a*) assembler à queue-d'aronde; **dovetailed joint,** assemblage *m* à queue-d'aronde; (*b*) **to d. two schemes (together, into each other),** opérer le raccord entre deux entreprises. **2.** *v.i.* (*of schemes, etc.*) se rejoindre, se raccorder.

dowager ['dauədʒər] *n.f.* douairière; **d. duchess,** duchesse douairière.

dowdiness ['daudinis] *n.* manque *m* d'élégance, de chic.

dowdy ['daudi]. *a.* peu élégant; (*of dress*) démodé; (*of woman*) mal habillé.

dowel¹ ['dauəl] *n. Carp:* **1. d. (pin),** goujon *m* (d'assemblage); cheville *f* (en bois); **2. d. (wood),** fenton *m*.

dowel² *v.tr.* **(dowelled,** *NAm:* **doweled)** *Carp:* goujonner (des planches); enlacer (un joint); **dowelled joint,** enlaçure *f*.

dower ['dauər] *n.* douaire *m* (de veuve); **d. house,** maison assignée en douaire.

down¹ [daun] *n. Geog: usu.pl.* **downs,** chaîne *f* de collines crétacées; **the (North, South) Downs,** les Downs *mpl*.

down² *n.* **1.** duvet *m*. **2.** (*on pers.*) duvet. **3.** (*on plants*) poil *m*, coton *m*, duvet; (*on fruit*) duvet.

down³ **I.** *adv.* **1.** (*motion*) vers le bas; (de haut) en bas; (*a*) **to go d.,** aller en bas; descendre; **to lay d. one's arms,** mettre bas les armes; **to shoot, bring, d. an aircraft,** abattre, *F:* descendre, un avion; **to fall d.,** tomber (i) à terre, (ii) par terre; **money d., cash d.,** argent *m* (au) comptant, sur table; **d. to the ground,** jusqu'à terre; **it suits me d. to the ground,** ça me va parfaitement; (*b*) (*imperative*) **d. with the traitors!** à bas les traîtres! (*of medicine, etc.*) **d. with it!** avalez! (*to dog*) **d.!** couché! (*c*) (*crosswords*) verticalement. **2.** (*position*) **d. below,** en bas, en contre-bas; **d. there,** là-bas; **further d.,** plus bas; **d. under,** aux antipodes; *U.S:* **d. South,** aux États du sud; **the blinds were d.,** les stores étaient baissés; **to lay sth. face d.,** placer qch. face en dessous, à l'envers; **head d.,** la tête en bas; **to hit a man when he's d.,** frapper un homme à terre; **to put sth. d.,** coucher qch. par écrit; écrire qch.; **he's d. for £20,** il est inscrit pour (une cotisation de) £20; **he's £20 d.,** il a un déficit de £20; **he's d. with flu,** il est grippé; *F:* **that gets me d.,** ça me déprime; **the wind is d.,** le vent est tombé, s'est apaisé; **the river is d.,** la rivière est basse; **the price of gold is d.,** le prix de l'or a baissé; (*of ship*) **to go d. by the bows,** piquer de l'avant; **d. by the stern,** enfoncé par l'arrière. **3.** (*order, time*) **from prince d. to beggar,** du prince jusqu'au mendiant; **d. to recent times,** jusqu'au temps présent; **d. to here,** (en descendant) jusqu'ici. **4.** *phrases:* **to be d. on s.o.,** en vouloir à qn; *F:* **to come d. on s.o. like a ton of bricks,** rembarrer vertement qn; **to be d. in the mouth,** être découragé, déprimé; *F:* **to be d. and out,** être sans le sou; être sur la paille. **II.** *prep.* **to slide d. the wall,** se laisser couler le long du mur; **the tears ran d. his face,** les larmes lui coulaient le long des joues; **to go d. the street, d. a hill,** descendre la rue, une colline; **to go d. the river,** descendre le fleuve; **to fall d. the stairs,** tomber en bas de l'escalier; *Rail:* **d. the line,** en aval. **III.** *a.* **1. d. leap,** saut *m* en bas, à terre. **2.** *Rail:* **d. train,** train descendant. **3.** *W.Tel:* **d. lead** [li:d] descente *f* d'antenne; **4.** *Mus:* (*violin*) **d. bow,** tirez; **with the d. bow,** en tirant. **5. d. payment,** acompte *m*; versement *m* à la commande. **6.** découragé; déprimé. **IV.** *n.* **1. ups and downs,** ondulations *fpl* (du terrain); **the ups and downs of life,** les vicissitudes *fpl*, les hauts et les bas, de la vie; **the ups and downs of politics,** les avatars *mpl* de la politique. **2.** *F:* **to have a d. on s.o.,** en vouloir à qn.

down⁴ *v.tr.* **1.** terrasser, abattre (qn); descendre (un avion); *Box: etc:* abattre (un adversaire). **2.** *Ind:* **to d. tools,** débrayer; cesser le travail. **3.** *F:* **to d. a drink,** s'envoyer un verre.

down-and-out ['daunən(d)'aut] **1.** *a.* **to be d.-a.-o.,** être sans le sou. **2.** *n.* clochard *m*; sans-le-sou *m inv.*

down-at-heel ['daunət'hi:l] *a.* (*a*) (*of shoe*) éculé; (*b*) (*of pers.*) râpé; *F:* miteux.

downbeat¹ ['daunbi:t] *n. Mus:* (temps) frappé (*m*).

downbeat² *a. F:* triste, déprimé.

downcast ['daunkɑ:st] *a.* **1.** (*of pers.*) abattu, déprimé; **to look d.,** avoir l'air découragé. **2.** (*of look, eyes, etc.*) baissé.

downfall ['daunfɔ:l] *n.* **1.** chute *f* (de neige, etc.). **2.** ruine *f* (d'une personne); écroulement *m*, effondrement *m* (d'un ministère etc.); **drink was his d.,** la boisson l'a perdu.

downgrade¹ ['daungreid] *n.* (*a*) *Rail: etc:* pente descendante; descente *f*, déclivité *f*; (*b*) décadence *f*; **to be on the d.,** baisser, être sur le déclin, *F:* sur le retour; (*of business*) péricliter.

downgrade² *v.tr.* **1.** minimiser l'importance de (qch.). **2.** (*a*) classer (des marchandises) dans une catégorie inférieure; (*b*) déclasser (un employé) à une échelle de salaire inférieure. **downgrading** *n.* **1.** baisse *f* de l'importance (de qch.). **2.** (*a*) classement *m* (des marchandises) dans une catégorie inférieure; (*b*) déclassement *m* (d'un employé) à une échelle de salaire inférieure.

downhearted [daun'hɑ:tid] *a.* découragé; déprimé; **to become d.,** se décourager.

downhill ['daunhil] **1.** *n.* (*a*) descente *f*, pente *f*; (*b*) *Ski:* descente *f*. **2.** *a.* en pente, incliné. **3.** [daun'hil] *adv.* **to go d.,** (*of road*) aller en descendant; (*of car, etc.*) descendre (la côte); *F:* (*of pers.*) être sur le déclin; (*of business, etc.*) péricliter.

downpipe ['daunpaip] *n.* tuyau *m* de descente.

downpour ['daunpɔ:r] *n.* forte pluie, averse.

downright ['daunrait] **1.** *adv.* (*a*) tout à fait, complètement; (*b*) nettement, carrément; (nier, refuser) catégoriquement. **2.** *a.* (*a*) (*of pers., language*) direct; franc, *f.* franche; (*b*) complet, absolu; (mensonge) éclatant; **d. fool,** franc imbécile; **a d. no,** un non catégorique.

downstage [ˈdaunsteidʒ] *Th:* **1.** *adv. & a.* sur le devant (de la scène); à l'avant-scène. **2.** *n.* avant-scène *f.*

downstairs 1. *adv.* [daunˈstɛəz] (*a*) en bas (de l'escalier); **to come, go, d.,** descendre (l'escalier); (*b*) en bas, au rez-de-chaussée; **our neighbours d.,** nos voisins (i) de l'étage au-dessous, (ii) du rez-de-chaussée; nos voisins d'en bas. **2.** [ˈdaunstɛəz] (*a*) *a.* **the d. rooms,** les pièces *fpl* d'en bas, du bas, du rez-de-chaussée; (*b*) *n.* rez-de-chaussée *m inv.*

downstream 1. *adv.* [daunˈstriːm] en aval, à l'aval (**from,** de). **2.** *a.* [ˈdaunstriːm] d'aval.

downstroke [ˈdaunstrouk] *n.* **1.** (*in writing*) plein *m.* **2.** *Mch:* course descendante; mouvement *m* de descente (du piston). **3.** *Orn:* abaissée *f* (d'ailes).

downswept [ˈdaunswept] *a.* (châssis) surbaissé.

downtime [ˈdauntaim] *n. NAm:* heures *fpl* de loisirs.

down-to-earth [ˈdauntuˈəːθ] *a.* terre(-)à(-)terre *inv,* réaliste.

downtown [ˈdaunˈtaun] *NAm:* **1.** *adv.* vers (le centre de) la ville; **he gave me a lift d.,** il m'a descendu en ville. **2.** *a.* **d. New York,** le centre de New York. **3.** *n.* centre (d'une ville); quartier *m* des affaires.

downtrodden [ˈdauntrɔd(ə)n] *a.* **1.** (*of grass, etc.*) piétiné. **2.** (*of people*) opprimé, tyrannisé.

downward [ˈdaunwəd] **1.** *a.* (mouvement, sentier) descendant; (regard) dirigé en bas; **d. curve,** courbe descendante; **d. tendency (of prices),** tendance *f* à la baisse. **2.** *adv.* = DOWNWARDS.

downwards [ˈdaunwədz] *adv.* (*a*) de haut en bas; vers le bas, en descendant; (*on river*) en aval; (regarder) en bas; **to lay sth. face d.,** placer qch. face en dessous; (*b*) **from the twelfth century d.,** à partir du, depuis le, douzième siècle; (*c*) **children of five and d.,** enfants *mpl* de cinq ans et au-dessous.

downwind 1. *adv.* [ˈdaunˈwind] *Av:* (atterrir, etc.) vent arrière. **2.** *a.* [ˈdaunwind] (atterrissage) vent arrière.

downy [ˈdauni] *a.* (*a*) duveteux, duveté; couvert de duvet; (*b*) (of fruit) velouté.

dowry [ˈdauri] *n.* dot *f.*

dowse¹ [dauz] *v.i.* employer la baguette de sourcier; faire de la radiesthésie. **dowsing** *n.* radiesthésie *f;* **d. rod,** baguette *f* divinatoire de sourcier.

dowse² [daus] *v.tr.* = DOUSE¹·².

dowser [ˈdauzər] *n.* sourcier *m;* radiesthésiste *mf.*

doyen [ˈdɔijən] *n.m.* doyen (d'âge).

doze¹ [douz] *n.* petit somme; **to have a d.,** faire un petit somme.

doze² *v.i.* sommeiller, somnoler; **to d. off,** s'assoupir. **dozing** *n.* assoupissement *m.*

dozen [ˈdʌz(ə)n] *n.* douzaine *f.* **1.** (*inv. in pl.*) **a d. eggs,** une douzaine d'œufs; **half a d.,** une demi-douzaine; **six d. bottles of wine,** six douzaines de bouteilles de vin; **by the d.,** à la douzaine; *F:* **the daily d.,** la gymnastique matinale, quotidienne. **2.** (*pl.* **dozens) they arrived in their dozens,** ils arrivèrent par douzaines; **dozens of people think as I do,** des douzaines de gens pensent comme moi; **dozens and dozens of times,** maintes et maintes fois; **a baker's d., thirteen to the d.,** treize à la douzaine; *F:* **to talk nineteen to the d.,** bavarder comme une pie.

dozenth [ˈdʌz(ə)nθ] *a.* douzième.

doziness [ˈdouzinis] *n.* somnolence *f.*

dozy [ˈdouzi] *a.* somnolent, assoupi.

drab [dræb] **1.** *a. & n.* (i) gris (*m*); (ii) beige (*m*). **2.** *a.* (*a*) (couleur) terne; (vêtement) de couleur terne; (*b*) morne, monotone; (existence) terne, décolorée.

drachm [dræm] *n. Meas:* drachme *f.*

drachma, *pl.* **-mas, -mae** [ˈdrækmə, -məz, -miː] *n. Num:* drachme *f.*

draconian [drəˈkouniən] *a.* draconien.

draft¹ [drɑːft] *n.* **1.** *Mil:* (*a*) détachement *m* (de troupes); contingent *m* (de recrues); (*b*) *U.S:* conscription *f;* **to be d. age,** être en âge de faire son service; *F:* **d. dodger,** réfractaire *m.* **2.** *Com:* (*a*) tirage *m* (d'un effet); (*b*) traite *f;* lettre *f* de change; **banker's d.,** chèque *m* bancaire. **3.** *Arch: Mec.E: etc:* dessin *m* schématique; plan *m;* tracé *m;* (*of map, etc.*) **rough d.,** canevas *m;* ébauche *f.* **4.** (*a*) projet *m* (de loi); avant-projet *m, pl.* avant-projets (de traité); brouillon *m* (de lettre); **first d. of a novel,** premier jet d'un roman; (*b*) *attrib.* provisoire; **d. contract,** projet de contrat.

draft² *v.tr.* **1.** *Mil:* (*a*) détacher, envoyer en détachement (des troupes); affecter (un militaire à un service); **to d. troops into . . .,** faire passer des troupes dans . . .; (*b*) *U.S:* appeler (des soldats) sous les drapeaux. **2. to d. s.o. to a post,** désigner qn pour, à, un poste. **3.** rédiger (un acte, un projet); faire le brouillon (d'une lettre); **to d. a bill,** établir un projet de loi.

draft³ *n. NAm:* = DRAUGHT¹.

draftsman *pl.* **-men** [ˈdrɑːftsmən] *n.m.* **1.** *NAm:* = DRAUGHTSMAN 1. **2.** rédacteur (d'un acte).

drafty [ˈdrɑːfti] *a. NAm:* = DRAUGHTY.

drag¹ [dræg] *n.* **1.** (*a*) *Agr:* herse *f;* (*b*) traîneau (grossier). **2.** (*a*) (*for dredging*) drague *f;* (*b*) (*for retrieving lost object*) araignée *f; Nau:* grappin *m* à main; (*for drowning persons*) gaffe *f* de sauvetage. **3.** (*a*) enrayure *f;* **d. (shoe),** sabot *m;* **to put a d. on a wheel,** enrayer une roue; (*b*) *F:* ennui *m;* scie *f;* **it was a frightful d.,** c'était la barbe; (*c*) *F:* (*pers.*) raseur, -euse; casse-pieds *m inv;* **the party was a d.,** la soirée était rasante. **4.** (*a*) tirage *m,* résistance *f* (à l'avancement); frottement excessif; (*b*) **uphill d.,** montée fatigante; **there is still a long d. ahead,** il y a encore toute une tirée; (*c*) *Av:* traînée *f;* résistance à l'avancement; (*d*) *Bill:* effet *m* rétrograde; (*e*) ralentissement *m* (d'un moteur à ressort, etc.). **5.** *P:* **to have a d.,** tirer une bouffée (d'une cigarette). **6.** *Ven:* (i) voie artificielle; (ii) **d. (hunt),** chasse *f* à courre où la meute suit une voie artificielle; drag *m.* **7.** (*a*) *P:* costume féminin (porté par un homme); **he was in d.,** il portait des vêtements de femme; (*b*) **d. show,** spectacle *m* de travesti. **8.** *NAm: F:* **to have d.,** avoir du piston. **9.** *NAm: Aut:* **d. (race),** concours *m* d'accélération.

drag² *v.* (**dragged** [drægd]) **1.** *v.tr.* (*a*) traîner, tirer (qn, qch.); entraîner (qn) (contre sa volonté); **to d. one's feet,** (i) traîner les pieds; (ii) *F:* (*also* **to d. one's heels**) montrer peu d'empressement (à faire qch.); **he dragged himself to the door,** il se traîna jusqu'à la porte; (*b*) draguer (un étang, un fleuve); (*c*) *Agr:* herser (le terrain); (*d*) (*of ship*) **to d. its anchor,** déraper. **2.** *v.i.* (*a*) (*of thg*) traîner (à terre); (*of lawsuit, Th: of scene, etc.*) traîner en longueur; (*of conversation, action*) traîner, languir; **time is dragging,** les heures *fpl* traînent; (*b*) offrir de la résistance; (*of brakes*) frotter (sur les roues); (*c*) draguer (**for sth.,** à la recherche de qch.); *Nau:* draguer (un câble); (*d*) *Fish:* pêcher à la drague; **to d. for oysters,** pêcher les huîtres à la drague; (*e*) *F:* **to d. on, at, a cigarette,** tirer des bouffées d'une cigarette. **drag along** *v.tr.* traîner, entraîner (qn, qch.). **drag away** *v.tr.* (*a*) entraîner, emmener (qn) de force; (*b*) arracher (qn, qch.) (**from,** de). **drag down** *v.tr.* entraîner (qn, qch.) en bas; faire descendre (qn) de force; **he dragged me down with him,** il m'a entraîné dans sa chute. **dragging 1.** *a.* **d. step,** pas traînant. **2.** *n.* (*a*) traînage *m,* traînement *m* (d'un fardeau derrière soi, etc.); *Nau:* **d. of the anchor,** dérapage *m;* (*b*) dragage *m* (d'un étang, etc.); (*c*) *Fish:* pêche *f* à la drague, au traîneau. **drag in** *v.tr.* (*a*) faire entrer de force (qn, qch.); (*b*) traîner (un colis, etc.) (dans une pièce, etc.) **drag off** *v.tr.* = DRAG AWAY. **drag on** *v.i.* (*of affair, etc.*) s'éterniser; **to let a matter d. on,** laisser traîner une affaire. **drag out** *v.tr.* (*a*) faire sortir (qn, qch.) de force; **to d. s.o. out of bed,** tirer qn de son lit; **to d. the truth out of s.o.,** arracher la vérité à qn; (*b*) faire traîner (une affaire); (*c*) **to d. out a wretched existence,** traîner une existence misérable. **drag up** *v.tr.* (*a*) entraîner, tirer, (qn, qch.) jusqu'en haut; (*b*) repêcher (un cadavre, etc.) à la drague; *F:* **why do you d. up that old story?** pourquoi déterrer cette vieille histoire?

dragnet ['drægnet] *n.* **1.** *Fish:* drague *f*; seine *f*, drège *f*. **2.** cordon *m* de police; **twenty suspects were picked up in the d.,** vingt personnes suspectes furent arrêtées dans la rafle.

dragon ['drægən] *n.* **1.** (*a*) *Myth: & F:* dragon *m*; (*b*) *Rept:* dragon; draco *m*. **2.** *Mil:* (*a*) tracteur *m*; (*b*) **dragon's teeth,** rangées *fpl* de tétraèdres de béton (comme défense antichar).

dragonfly ['drægənflai] *n. Ent:* libellule *f*.

dragoon[1] [drə'gu:n] *Mil:* dragon *m*.

dragoon[2] *v.tr. F:* tyranniser (qn); **to d. s.o. into doing sth.,** forcer qn à faire qch.

dragrope ['drægroup] *n.* **1.** *Artil:* bricole *f*, combleau *m*. **2.** *Aer:* guide-rope *m*, *pl.* guide-ropes (d'un ballon).

drain[1] [drein] *n.* **1.** (*a*) canal *m*, -aux (de décharge); caniveau *m*, rigole *f*; *Agr:* fossé d'assainissement; (*b*) *Civ.E:* cunette *f* (d'égout). **2.** (*a*) égout *m*; **smell of drains,** odeur *f* d'égout; *F:* **to throw money down the d.,** jeter son argent par la fenêtre; **that's five years' work down the d.,** voilà cinq années de travail perdues; **to laugh like a d.,** rire à gorge déployée; (*b*) canalisation *f* sanitaire (d'une maison). **3.** (*a*) *Mec.E: etc:* tuyau *m* d'écoulement; **overflow d.,** (tube *m* de) trop-plein (*m*), *pl.* trop-pleins; (*b*) *Med:* drain *m*. **4.** perte *f*, fuite *f* (d'énergie, etc.); drainage *m* (de capitaux, etc.); **constant d. on the resources,** hémorragie *f* continuelle; **the brain d.,** l'exode *m*, le drainage, des cerveaux.

drain[2] **1.** *v.tr.* (*a*) **to d. water (away, off),** (i) évacuer, faire écouler, des eaux; (ii) faire égoutter l'eau; **to d. the wealth of a country,** épuiser les richesses d'un pays; (*b*) boire (un liquide) jusqu'à la dernière goutte; vider (une coupe); (*c*) assécher (un terrain); drainer (un terrain); mettre à sec, vider (un étang); assainir (un champ); saigner (un fossé); désamorcer (une pompe); (faire) égoutter (des bouteilles, des légumes); *I.C.E:* vidanger (le carter); *Med:* vider, drainer (un abcès); (*d*) épuiser (qn, la bourse); **to d. s.o. of his strength,** épuiser les forces de qn. **2.** *v.i.* (*a*) (*of water, etc.*) **to d. away,** s'écouler; (*b*) (*of sponge, bottle, etc.*) (s')égoutter. **3.** *v.tr.* creuser des rigoles d'assèchement dans (une prairie, etc.). **draining** *n.* (*a*) écoulement *m* (des eaux); assèchement *m* (d'un marais); drainage *m*, assainissement *m* (d'un terrain); égouttement *m* (des bouteilles, etc.); vidange *f* (d'un carter etc.); *Med:* drainage (d'ue plaie); *Dom.Ec:* **d. board,** égouttoir *m* (d'évier); (*b*) creusage *m* des rigoles d'assèchement (dans une prairie, etc.).

drainage ['dreinidʒ] *n.* **1.** = DRAINING, *see* DRAIN[2]; (*a*) **d. ditch,** rigole *f* d'écoulement; (*b*) *Geog:* **d. area, basin,** bassin *m* hydrographique; (*c*) *Med:* drainage *m*; **d. tube,** drain *m*. **2.** *Civ.E:* (i) système *m* d'écoulement des eaux; (ii) système d'égouts; **main d.,** tout-à-l'égout *m inv*. **3.** (i) eaux *fpl* de surface; (ii) eaux d'égout.

drainer ['dreinər] *n.* égouttoir *m*.

drainpipe ['dreinpaip] *n.* tuyau *m* d'écoulement, de drainage; *F:* **d. trousers,** pantalon étroit, en tuyau de poêle.

drake [dreik] *n. Orn:* canard *m* mâle; **wild d.,** malard *m*.

dram [dræm] *n.* **1.** *Pharm.Meas:* drachme *f* (= un seizième d'once = 1.77 grammes). **2.** *F:* goutte *f* (à boire); **to take a d.,** prendre un petit verre.

drama ['drɑ:mə] *n. Th:* **1.** drame *m*; **to make a d. out of a trivial incident,** faire un drame d'un incident sans importance. **2. (the) d.,** l'art *m* dramatique, le théâtre; **the masterpieces of French d.,** les chefs-d'œuvre de la scène française.

dramatic [drə'mætik] *a.* (*a*) (ouvrage, situation) dramatique; **the d. works of Corneille,** le théâtre de Corneille; **d. effect(s),** dramaturgie *f*; (*b*) (geste, effet) théâtral. **-ally** *adv.* (*a*) dramatiquement; (*b*) théâtralement.

dramatics [drə'mætiks] *n.pl.* (*usu. with sg. const.*) le théâtre; **this is no time for d.,** ce n'est pas le moment de faire un drame, de dramatiser.

dramatist ['dræmətist] *n.* auteur *m* dramatique.

dramatization [dræmətai'zeiʃ(ə)n] *n.* dramatisation *f*; adaptation *f* (d'un roman, etc.) à la scène.

dramatize ['dræmətaiz] **1.** *v.tr.* (*a*) dramatiser; adapter (un roman) à la scène; (*b*) (*with passive force*) **novel that would d. well,** roman qui s'adapterait bien à la scène. **2.** *v.tr. & i.* **there's no need to d. (it),** il ne faut pas en faire un drame.

drape[1] [dreip] *v.tr.* (*a*) draper, tendre (**with, in,** de); **the hall was draped in black,** la salle était tendue de noir; (*b*) *Art:* draper (une étoffe); (*c*) **she was d. over the sofa,** elle s'était étalée sur le canapé.

drape[2] *n.* **1.** *Cost:* drapé *m* (d'une robe, etc.). **2. drapes,** (*a*) tentures *fpl*; (*b*) *NAm:* rideaux *mpl*.

draper ['dreipər] *n.* marchand, -ande, de tissus.

drapery ['dreipəri] *n.* **1.** (*a*) **d. (trade),** commerce *m* des tissus; (*b*) **d. (shop),** magasin *m* de tissus; (*c*) **linen d.,** (articles *mpl* de) blanc *m*. **2.** (*a*) tentures *fpl*; (*b*) *NAm:* **draperies,** rideaux *mpl*.

drastic ['dræstik] *a.* **1.** violent; énergique; (mesure) énergique, rigoureuse, draconienne; **to make d. cuts,** faire des coupes sombres. **2.** *Med:* (remède) (i) drastique, (ii) énergique, de cheval. **-ally** *adv.* énergiquement; rigoureusement.

drat [dræt] *v.tr. F:* (*used only in third pers. sing. sub.*) **d. (it)!** sacristi! nom de nom! **d. the child!** au diable cet enfant! **dratted** *a. F:* maudit (garçon, etc.).

draught[1], *NAm:* **draft** [drɑ:ft] *n.* **1.** traction *f*, tirage *m*; **d. animal,** bête *f* de trait. **2.** *Fish:* coup *m* de filet. **3.** (*drinking*) trait *m*, gorgée *f*. **4.** *A: Med:* potion *f*; **poisoned d.,** potion empoisonnée. **5.** *Nau:* tirant *m* d'eau (d'un navire). **6. draughts,** (jeu *m* de) dames (*fpl*); **d. board,** damier *m*. **7.** (*a*) courant *m* d'air; **I'm in a d., I feel a d.,** je suis dans un courant d'air; **d. excluder,** bourrelet *m* de porte; brise-bise *m inv*; **d. screen,** paravent *m*; **d.-proof,** à l'épreuve des courants d'air; *F:* (*of firm, etc.*) **we're feeling the d.,** les affaires vont mal; (*b*) tirage (d'une cheminée); *Ind: etc:* entrée *f* d'air; venue *f* du vent. **8. beer on d.,** bière *f* à la pression; **d. beer,** bière au tonneau.

draught[2] *n. & v.tr. see* DRAFT[1,2].

draughtsman, *NAm:* **draftsman,** *pl.* **-men** ['drɑ:ftsmən] *n.* **1.** (*a*) *Ind:* dessinateur *m*, traceur *m* (de plans, d'épures, etc.); (*b*) *Art:* **he is a good d.,** il est bon dessinateur. **2.** rédacteur *m* (d'un acte).

draughtsmanship, *NAm:* **draftsmanship** ['drɑ:ftsmənʃip] *n.* **1.** l'art *m* du dessin industriel; *Ind:* le dessin. **2.** talent *m* de dessinateur.

draughty, *NAm:* **drafty** ['drɑ:fti] *a.* **1.** plein de courants d'air. **2.** (coin de rue, etc.) exposé à tous les vents.

draw[1] [drɔ:] *n.* **1.** tirage *m*; **it's your d.,** c'est à vous de tirer; **to take a d. at one's pipe,** tirer une bouffée de sa pipe; *F:* **to be quick on the d.,** (i) avoir la gâchette facile; (ii) avoir la répartie facile. **2.** (*a*) tirage au sort; *F:* **that's just the luck of the d.,** ça c'est la vie! (*b*) loterie *f*; tombola *f*; (*c*) *Sp:* tableau *m* des concurrents à chaque tour d'une série d'épreuves de championnat, etc. **3.** attraction *f*; clou *m* (de la fête, etc.); *Th:* pièce *f* qui fait recette. **4.** *Sp:* partie nulle; match *m* nul; **the game ended in a d.,** ils ont fait partie nulle.

draw² *v.* (**drew** [dru:] , **drawn** [drɔ:n]) **I.** *v.tr.* **1.** (*pull*) (*a*) tirer (un verrou); hâler (un filet) à bord; lever (un pont-levis); tendre (un arc); baisser (un store); **to d. the curtains,** tirer les rideaux; (i) fermer, (ii) ouvrir, les rideaux; (*b*) tirer (une remorque, etc.); **drawn by a locomotive,** remorqué par une locomotive. **2.** (*a*) tirer, aspirer (l'air dans ses poumons); (*b*) (*attract*) attirer (une foule, etc.); **a pretty girl drew his eye,** une jolie fille attira ses regards; *v.i.* (*of play, etc.*) **to d.,** attirer le public; **to d. s.o. into conversation,** entamer une conversation avec qn; **to d. s.o. into the conversation,** faire entrer qn dans la conversation; **to feel drawn to s.o.,** se sentir attiré vers qn. **3.** (*a*) retirer, ôter (**sth. from, out of, sth.,** qch. de qch.); ôter (une vis); retirer, tirer, faire sauter (un bouchon); **to d. one's sword,** tirer l'épée; dégainer; **to d. one's revolver,** sortir son revolver de l'étui, de sa poche; dégainer; **to d. a card (from the pack),** tirer une carte; (*dominoes*) **to d. (from the pool),** piocher; **to d. lots for sth.,** tirer qch. au sort; **number five was drawn,** le numéro cinq sortit au tirage; **to d. a prize at a lottery,** gagner un lot à une loterie; *Fin:* (*of bonds*) **to be drawn,** sortir au tirage; **to d. a blank,** (i) tirer un mauvais numéro; (ii) éprouver une déception; (iii) *U.S:* avoir un trou de mémoire; **to d. straws,** tirer à la courte paille; (*b*) arracher (un clou, une dent, etc.); **to d. a confession from s.o.,** arracher un aveu à qn; (*c*) **to d. water from the river,** puiser, tirer, de l'eau à la rivière; **to d. wine (from a barrel),** tirer du vin (d'un tonneau); **to d. consolation from sth.,** tirer consolation de qch.; **to d. a conclusion from sth.,** tirer, déduire, une conclusion de qch.; (*d*) toucher (un salaire, *Mil:* des rations); **to d. (one's) supplies from s.o.,** tirer des approvisionnements de qn; *v.i.* **to d. on one's savings, the reserves,** prendre sur ses économies; mettre à contribution les réserves; **to d. on s.o.'s experiences for a novel,** s'inspirer des expériences de qn pour un roman; (*e*) *Tchn:* éteindre (les feux); *Cer:* défourner (une fournée de poterie); *Metall:* démouler (un modèle); (*f*) *Cards:* **to d. trumps,** faire tomber les atouts; **to d. the enemy's fire,** (i) *Mil:* attirer sur soi le feu de l'ennemi; (ii) *Fig:* provoquer une attaque sur soi-même; **his accusation drew an instant denial,** son accusation provoqua un démenti immédiat; **the government refused to be drawn,** le gouvernement refusa de se commettre. **4.** (*a*) vider (une volaille, etc.); (*b*) pêcher (un étang) au filet. **5.** *Med:* faire aboutir (un abcès). **6.** *Metall:* étirer, tirer (du fil, des tubes, etc.). **7.** (*a*) tracer (un cercle, un plan); tirer, mener (une ligne); construire (des figures géométriques); *F:* **I d. the line at that,** je n'accepte pas ça; (*b*) **to d. a map,** (i) (*of surveyor*) dresser une carte; (ii) (*of schoolboy*) dessiner une carte; (*c*) dessiner (un paysage, une figure); faire (le portrait de qn); **the author has drawn the characters skilfully,** l'auteur a tracé les personnages avec adresse; (*d*) faire, établir (une comparaison) (**between two things,** entre deux choses). **8.** libeller, rédiger (un chèque); **to d. a cheque on a bank,** tirer un chèque sur une banque. **9.** *Nau:* (*of ship*) **to d. twenty feet of water,** tirer, jauger, vingt pieds d'eau; avoir vingt pieds de tirant d'eau. **10. to d. (a game) with s.o.,** faire partie nulle, match nul, avec qn. **II.** *v.i.* **1.** (*move*) (*a*) **to d. near, close, to s.o.,** se rapprocher de qn; s'approcher de qn; **when they drew near . . .,** à leur approche . . .; **the train drew into the station,** le train entra en gare; **to d. level with a competitor,** arriver à (la) hauteur d'un concurrent; (*b*) **to d. to an end,** tirer, toucher, à sa fin. **2.** (*a*) (*of chimney, pipe, etc.*) tirer; (*of pump*) aspirer; (*b*) *Med:* (*of plaster*) tirer. **3.** *Nau:* **the sails were drawing well,** les voiles *fpl* portaient plein. **4.** dessiner; **he draws extremely well,** c'est un dessinateur de premier ordre. **draw apart 1.** *v.tr.* séparer, écarter. **2.** *v.i.* se séparer, s'écarter. **draw aside 1.** *v.tr.* (*a*) détourner, écarter (qch.); tirer, écarter (les rideaux); (*b*) tirer, prendre, (qn) à l'écart. **2.** *v.i.* s'écarter; se ranger. **draw away 1.** *v.tr.* (*a*) entraîner (qn); (*b*) détourner (**s.o. from sth.,** qn de qch.). **2.** *v.i.* s'éloigner; *Sp:* **to d. away from a competitor,** prendre de l'avance sur un concurrent. **draw back 1.** *v.tr.* (*a*) tirer (qch., qn) en arrière; (*b*) tirer, ouvrir (les rideaux). **2.** *v.i.* (*a*) reculer; se retirer en arrière; (*b*) se dédire; **it is too late to d. back now,** le vin est tiré, il faut le boire. **draw forward** *v.i.* (*of pers.*) s'avancer, s'approcher. **draw in 1.** *v.tr.* (*a*) (*of cat, etc.*) rentrer, rétracter (ses griffes); (*of horseman*) serrer (les reines, la bride); (*b*) aspirer (l'air); (*c*) *F:* **to d. in one's horns,** faire des économies. **2.** *v.i.* (*a*) **the days are drawing in,** les jours diminuent, raccourcissent; (*b*) **a car drew in to the kerb,** une voiture s'est rangée le long du trottoir. **drawing** *n.* **1.** (*a*) tirage *m*; (*of water*) puisage *m*; (*of teeth*) extraction *f*; (*of lots*) tirage; vidage *m* (d'une volaille); (*b*) attraction *f* (**towards,** vers); **d. power,** pouvoir attractif, attirant; *U.S:* **d. card,** attraction, clou *m* (d'une fête, etc.); (*c*) *Metall:* démoulage *m* (des modèles); (*d*) *Metalw:* étirage *m* (des métaux); (*e*) *Fin:* traite *f* (de chèques, d'effets). **2.** *Com: Fin:* **drawings,** prélèvements *mpl*, levées *fpl*. **3.** dessin *m*; (*a*) **line d.,** dessin au trait; **rough d.,** ébauche *f*, croquis *m*; **pencil d.,** dessin au crayon; **d. board,** planche *f* à dessin; **still on the d. board,** (avion, projet) encore à l'étude; **d. book,** cahier *m* de dessin; **d. paper,** papier *m* à dessin; **d. pin,** punaise *f*; (*b*) *Ind: Mec.E:* dessin; **engineering d.,** dessin industriel; **sectional d.,** (vue *f* en) coupe *f*; **to make a d. of sth.,** tracer qch.; **d. office,** atelier *m*, bureau *m*, d'études. **4. d. off,** soutirage *m* (du vin). **5. d. up,** (*a*) rédaction *f*, dressement *m* (d'un acte); relèvement *m* (d'un compte); (*b*) élaboration *f* (d'une constitution); indication *f* (d'une procédure). **drawn** *a.* **1. with d. sword(s),** sabre *m* au clair. **2.** (*a*) (visage) hagard, abattu; (traits) tirés; (*b*) *Needlew:* **d.(-thread) work,** ouvrage *m*, travail *m*, à jour(s). **3.** (bataille) indécise; **d. match,** partie nulle, remise. **draw off** *v.tr.* (*a*) retirer (des troupes); ramener (des troupes) en arrière; (*b*) détourner (l'attention); (*c*) soutirer (un liquide). **draw on 1.** *v.tr.* **to d. s.o. on to do sth.,** entraîner, amener, qn à faire qch. **2.** *v.i.* (*a*) s'avancer; (*b*) **evening was drawing on,** la nuit approchait; **as time drew on his health improved,** avec le temps sa santé s'améliora. **draw out 1.** *v.tr.* (*a*) sortir, retirer (qch. de qch.); arracher (un clou); **to d. out money from the bank,** retirer de l'argent de la banque; (*b*) encourager (qn) à sortir de sa réserve; faire parler (qn); (*c*) allonger (un cordage); étirer (le fer); étendre (l'or); (*d*) prolonger (un repas, un discours); tirer (une affaire) en longueur; (faire) traîner (une affaire); **long drawn out tale,** récit prolongé, à n'en plus finir; (*e*) tracer (un plan). **2.** *v.i.* **the days are drawing out,** les journées se prolongent. **draw to** *v.tr.* **to d. the curtains to,** tirer, fermer, les rideaux. **draw together 1.** *v.tr.* (*a*) rassembler, réunir (des personnes, des choses); **the child's illness had drawn them together,** la maladie de l'enfant les avait rapprochés; (*b*) tirer, fermer (les rideaux). **2.** *v.i.* se rassembler; se mettre en groupe. **draw up 1.** *v.tr.* (*a*) tirer (qch.) vers le haut; relever (ses manches); tirer, aspirer (de l'eau); **he drew the blankets up to his chin,** il ramena les couvertures jusqu'à son menton; **to d. oneself up,** se (re)dresser; *Nau:* **to d. up a boat (on the beach),** tirer un bateau à sec; (*b*) **to d. up a chair,** approcher une chaise (de la table); (*c*) ranger, aligner (des troupes); (*d*) dresser, rédiger (un document); établir (un compte, un budget); **document drawn up before a lawyer,** acte passé devant (un) notaire; (*e*) dresser, rédiger, arrêter (un programme); indiquer (une procédure); élaborer (un projet); établir (un itinéraire). **2.** *v.i.* (*a*) **to d. up to the table,** s'approcher de la table; **to d. up with s.o.,** arriver à la hauteur de qn; (*b*) (*of car, etc.*) s'arrêter, stopper; **to d. up at the kerb,** ranger la voiture le long du trottoir; (*c*) (*of troops*) se ranger, s'aligner; **to d. up in line,** se mettre en ligne.

drawback ['drɔːbæk] *n.* **1.** inconvénient *m*, désavantage *m*. **2.** *Cust:* remboursement (à la sortie) des droits d'importation.

drawbridge ['drɔːbridʒ] *n.* **1.** pont-levis *m*, *pl.* ponts-levis. **2.** *Civ.E:* pont basculant, à bascule.

drawcard ['drɔːkɑːd] *n. U.S:* attraction *f*, *F:* clou *m* (d'une fête, etc.).

drawcord ['drɔːkɔːd] *n.* cordon *m* (de rideaux, etc.).

drawee [drɔː'iː] *n. Com:* tiré *m*, accepteur *m*, payeur *m* (d'une lettre de change).

drawer ['drɔːər] *n.* **1.** (*pers.*) (*a*) tireur, -euse; (*of water*) puiseur, -euse; (*b*) *Com:* tireur (d'une lettre de change); (*c*) dessinateur *m*, traceur *m*; (*d*) **d. (up),** rédacteur *m* (d'un document). **2.** [drɔːr] (*a*) tiroir *m*; **chest of drawers,** commode *f*; **bottom d.,** trousseau *m* (de mariage); *F:* **they're not really (out of the) top d.,** ils n'appartiennent pas vraiment à l'élite; (*b*) *Com:* **cash d.,** tiroir-caisse *m*, *pl.* tiroirs-caisses. **4.** *Cost: A:* **(pair of) drawers,** (*for men*) caleçon *m*; (*for women*) culotte *f*.

drawing-room ['drɔːiŋruːm] *n.* (*a*) salon *m*; salle *f* de réception; (*b*) *NAm: Rail:* voiture *f* salon, compartiment *m* salon.

drawl¹ [drɔːl] *n.* voix traînante; ton traînant; **to speak with an affected d.,** traîner la voix avec affectation.

drawl² **1.** *v.i.* traîner la voix en parlant; parler d'une voix traînante; traîner ses paroles. **2.** *v.tr.* **to d. out sth.,** dire, prononcer, qch. avec une voix traînante, avec une nonchalance affectée. **drawling 1.** *a.* (*of voice, tone*) traînant. **2.** *n.* affectation *f* de langueur dans le débit.

drawsheet ['drɔːʃiːt] *n. Med:* alaise *f*, alèse *f*.

drawstring ['drɔːstriŋ] *n.* cordon *m*.

dray [drei] *n. Veh:* camion *m*, haquet *m* (de brasseur); **d. horse,** cheval *m* de roulage.

dread¹ [dred] *n.* crainte *f*; terreur *f*, épouvante *f*; **to be, stand, in d. of s.o., of sth.,** craindre, redouter, qn, qch.

dread² *v.tr.* redouter, appréhender, craindre (qn, qch.); **to d. that . . .,** redouter que (ne) + *sub.*; **I d. to think of it,** j'ai horreur d'y penser.

dreadful ['dredful] **1.** *a.* terrible, redoutable. **2.** *a.* (*a*) (douleur, bruit, etc.) atroce, épouvantable; **it is d. that nothing can be done,** c'est affreux qu'on ne puisse rien faire; (*b*) *F:* (*intensive*) **it's a d. bore!** c'est assommant! **3.** *n. A:* **penny d.,** roman *m* à deux sous. **-fully** *adv.* **1.** terriblement, horriblement; **I was d. frightened,** j'avais horriblement peur. **2.** *F:* (*intensive*) **d. ugly,** affreusement laid; **I am d. sorry,** je regrette infiniment.

dream¹ [driːm] *n.* rêve *m*; (*a*) songe *m*; **to have a d.,** faire un rêve; **to have beautiful, bad, dreams,** faire de beaux, mauvais, rêves; **sweet dreams!** faites de beaux rêves! **to see sth. in a d.,** voir qch. en songe; (*b*) **day-d.,** rêve éveillé; **to cherish a d.,** caresser un rêve; **to be in a d.,** être dans un rêve; **my d. house, the house of my dreams,** la maison de mes rêves; *F:* **a d. of a car,** la voiture rêvée; **it's a d.,** c'est le rêve; **it worked like a d.,** cela a réussi à merveille.

dream² *v.tr. & i.* (*p.t. & p.p.* **dreamt** [dremt], **dreamed** [driːmd, dremt]) **1. to d. of, about, s.o., sth.,** rêver de qn, de qch.; **you must have been dreaming! you must have dreamt it!** vous l'avez rêvé! **I dreamt (that) you were ill,** j'ai rêvé que vous étiez malade. **2.** laisser vaguer ses pensées; rêver creux; rêvasser; **to d. of one's youth,** rêver à sa jeunesse. **3. I shouldn't d. of doing it,** jamais je ne m'aviserais de faire cela; **no one would have dreamt of suspecting him,** personne n'aurait songé à le soupçonner; **little did I d. that . . .,** je ne songeais guère que . . .. **dream away** *v.tr.* passer (son temps) à rêver. **dreaming** *n.* rêves *mpl*. **dream up** *v.tr. F:* inventer, imaginer (une idée, etc.); **what have you dreamed up now?** qu'est-ce que tu as combiné?

dreamer ['driːmər] *n.* **1.** rêveur, -euse. **2.** (esprit) songeur (*m*). **3.** *Pej:* visionnaire *mf*; songe-creux *m inv*.

dreamland ['driːmlænd] *n.* le pays, le monde, des rêves; le pays des songes.

dreamless ['driːmlis] *a.* (sommeil) sans rêves.

dreamworld ['driːmwəːld] *n.* monde *m* imaginaire.

dreamy ['driːmi] *a.* (*of pers., mood*) rêveur, -euse; songeur, -euse; **d. look,** (i) air rêveur; (ii) *Pej:* air distrait. **2.** *P:* magnifique, superbe. **-ily** *adv.* **1.** d'un air, d'un ton, rêveur; **to think d. of the future,** rêvasser à l'avenir. **2.** (vaguer) comme dans un rêve.

dreariness ['driərinis] *n.* tristesse *f* (de l'existence, etc.); aspect *m* morne (d'un paysage, etc.); manque *m* d'éclat (d'un livre, d'un discours, etc.).

dreary ['driəri] *a.* (temps, paysage) triste, morne; (discours, etc.) morne, ennuyeux; (régime) monotone. **-ily** *adv.* tristement; d'un air, d'un ton, morne.

dredge¹ [dredʒ] *n.* **1.** *Fish: Nau:* **d. (net),** (filet *m* de) drague (*f*). **2.** (*a*) (bateau *m*) dragueur (*m*); (*b*) = DREDGER¹ 2(*b*); **d. bucket,** godet *m* de drague.

dredge² *v.tr. & i.* **1. to d. (out),** draguer, dévaser (un canal); **to d. away mud,** enlever la vase avec une drague. **2. to d. for sth.,** draguer à la recherche de qch.; **3. to d. (up),** enlever (la vase) avec une drague; pêcher, recueillir, (un objet submergé) avec une drague. **dredging** *n.* dragagé *m*.

dredge³ *v.tr. Cu:* saupoudrer; **to d. flour over meat,** saupoudrer la viande de farine.

dredger¹ ['dredʒər] *n.* **1.** (*pers.*) (ouvrier) dragueur (*m*); **oyster d.,** dragueur d'huîtres. **2.** (*a*) (bateau *m*) dragueur; (*b*) (*machine*) drague *f*; **bucket d.,** drague à godets; **grab d.,** drague à benne piocheuse.

dredger² *n. Cu:* saupoudroir *m* (à sucre, etc.).

dregs [dregz] *n.pl.* lie *f*, fond *m* (de la coupe); *F:* **the d. of society,** les bas-fonds *mpl* de la société.

drench¹ [dren(t)ʃ] *n. Vet:* breuvage *m*, purge *f*.

drench² *v.tr.* **1.** tremper, mouiller (**with,** de); **to get drenched (with rain),** se faire tremper, *F:* se faire saucer; **drenched to the skin,** trempé jusqu'aux os. **2.** arroser abondamment (le sol). **3.** *Vet:* administrer un breuvage à (une bête). **drenching 1.** *a* (pluie) battante, diluvienne. **2.** *n.* (*a*) *Vet:* administration *f* d'un breuvage *m* (à une bête); (*b*) **we got a d.,** nous avons été trempés, saucés.

Dresden ['drezdən] *Pr.n.* **D. (china),** porcelaine *f* de Saxe.

dress¹ [dres] *n.* **1.** (*attire*) costume *m*; toilette *f*, mise *f*; (*a*) **in full d.,** en grande tenue; (*of women*) en grande toilette; **evening d.,** tenue de soirée; **it's a d. affair,** il faudra se mettre en tenue de soirée; **d. shirt,** chemise *f* de soirée; **d. suit,** habit *m* (de soirée); (*b*) *Mil:* **fatigue d.,** tenue de corvée; (jeu *m* de) treillis (*m*); **mess d., formal d.,** uniforme de cérémonie, de soirée; **full d.,** grande tenue; uniforme de parade; **(full) d. parade,** parade *f* en grande tenue; **walking-out d.,** tenue de ville; (*c*) **bird in its winter d.,**

oiseau *m* dans son plumage d'hiver. **2.** (*single garment*) robe *f*; **ball d.,** robe de bal; *Com:* **ladies' dresses,** modes *fpl*; **d. designer,** dessinateur, -trice, de robes; modéliste *mf*; **d. materials,** tissus *mpl* pour robes; **d. preserver, shield,** dessous-de-bras *m inv*.

dress² *v.* (**dressed** [drest]) **1.** (*a*) *v.tr.* habiller, vêtir (qn); *Th:* costumer (une pièce); **to be dressed in black, in silk,** être vêtu de noir, de soie; **well, badly, dressed,** bien, mal, habillé; **to be plainly dressed,** avoir une mise simple; (*b*) *v.pr.* & *i.* **to d. (oneself),** s'habiller; **she's dressing,** elle est à sa toilette; **to d. in black,** s'habiller de noir; **to d. (for dinner),** (i) (*of man*) se mettre en habit, (ii) se mettre en toilette du soir (pour dîner). **2.** *v.tr.* orner, parer (**sth. with sth.,** qch. de qch.); *Nau:* pavoiser (un navire); *Com:* **to d. the window,** faire la vitrine; (*of ship*) **dressed over all,** sous le grand pavois. **3.** *v.tr. Mil:* aligner (des troupes, des tentes, etc.); *v.i.* (*of troops*) **to d. on the right, left,** s'aligner sur la droite, la gauche. **4.** *v.tr. Med:* panser (une blessure, un blessé); faire un pansement à (un blessé). **5.** *v.tr.* (*a*) *Tchn:* apprêter (une surface); corroyer (le cuir); apprêter (les peaux); dresser, tailler, (des pierres); dresser, corroyer (le bois); trier (le minerai); préparer (une matière première, le coton, etc.); *Metall:* nettoyer (une pièce coulée); **to d. timber roughly,** dégrossir le bois; **to d. cloth,** (i) apprêter, (ii) garnir, l'étoffe; (*b*) **to d. s.o.'s hair,** coiffer qn; (*c*) *Cu:* (i) habiller (une volaille, la viande); (ii) apprêter, accommoder (des plats); assaisonner, garnir (une salade); **dressed poultry,** volaille prête à cuire, parée; (*d*) *Fish:* monter (une mouche). **dress down** *v.tr.* (*a*) panser (un cheval); (*b*) *F:* (i) flanquer une raclée à (qn); (ii) passer un savon à (qn); (*c*) *Metalw: etc:* dégrossir (une pièce). **dressing** *n.* **1.** (*a*) habillement *m*, toilette *f*; **d. case,** nécessaire *m*, trousse *f*, de toilette; **d. gown,** robe *f* de chambre; (*for women*) peignoir *m*; **d. room,** (i) cabinet *m* de toilette; (ii) *Th: Cin:* loge *f* (d'acteur, d'actrice); (iii) *Sp:* vestiaire *m*; **d. table,** (table *f* de) toilette; coiffeuse *f*; **d.-table set,** garniture *f* de toilette; (*b*) arrangement *m* (des cheveux); (*c*) *Agr: Hort:* façon *f*; (*d*) *Cu:* habillage *m* (d'une volaille); accommodage, assaisonnement *m* (des plats); présentation *f*; (*e*) *Med:* pansement *m* (d'une blessure); (*f*) *Mil:* alignement *m* (des troupes); (*g*) *Nau:* pavoisement *m* (d'un navire); (*h*) *Fish:* montage *m* (d'une mouche); (*i*) *Tchn:* apprêt *m*, habillage *m* (des peaux); apprêtage *m* (des étoffes); dressage *m*, taille *f* (des pierres); dressage, corroyage (du bois); préparation *f* mécanique (du minerai); rhabillage *m* (d'une meule); *Metall:* nettoyage *m* (d'une pièce coulée); *Civ.E:* **surface d.,** enduisage *m* de surface. **2.** (*a*) *Cu:* **(salad) d.,** assaisonnement *m* (pour la salade); **French d.,** vinaigrette *f*; (*b*) produit *m* d'entretien; enduit *m* (pour cuirs, etc.); *Agr: Hort:* engrais *m*; fumure *f*; **a heavy d. of manure,** un gros apport de fumier; **surface d., top d.,** engrais en couverture, couche *f* d'engrais; (*c*) *Med:* pansement *m*; **to apply a d.,** mettre, faire, un pansement; **surgical d. case,** trousse de pansement; *Mil:* **d. station,** poste *m* de secours; (*d*) *Tex:* apprêt, empois *m*; (*e*) *Arch:* **dressings,** moulures *fpl*. **3. d. down,** (*a*) *F:* (i) raclée *f*, volée *f*; (ii) verte semonce; savon *m*; **to give s.o. a d. down,** (i) flanquer une raclée à qn; (ii) semoncer qn; (*b*) *Metalw: etc:* dégrossissage *m*. **4. d. up,** (*a*) action *f* de faire toilette; **an occasion for d. up,** une occasion pour sortir en grande toilette; (*b*) déguisement *m*; **d.-up clothes,** vêtements *mpl* de mascarade. **dress up** *v.tr.* & *i.* (i) habiller (un enfant); (ii) costumer, déguiser (qn) **(as sth.,** en qch.); **to d. (oneself) up,** (i) se mettre en travesti; (ii) se faire beau, belle; **children love to d. up,** les enfants aiment se déguiser; *F:* **to be dressed up to the nines,** être sur son trente et un.

dressage ['dresɑːʒ] *n. Equit:* dressage (supérieur).

dresser¹ ['dresər] *n.* **1.** buffet *m*; vaisselier *m*. **2.** *NAm:* (table *f* de) toilette (*f*); coiffeuse *f*.

dresser² *n.* **1.** *Ind:* apprêteur, -euse. **2.** *Th:* habilleur, -euse. **3.** *Med: Surg:* panseur, -euse. **4. window d.,** étalagiste *m*. **5. a smart d.,** personne *f* qui s'habille avec chic. **6.** (*tool*) (*for wood*) raboteuse *f*; (for stone) rabotin *m*.

dressmaker ['dresmeikər] *n.* (i) couturière *f*; (ii) couturier *m*.

dressmaking ['dresmeikiŋ] *n.* couture *f*; confection *f* de robes.

dressy ['dresi] *a.* **1.** (*of pers.*) trop habillé. **2.** (*of clothes, etc.*) chic, élégant; (robe) habillée.

drib [drib] *n. only used in:* **in dribs and drabs,** petit à petit; peu à peu.

dribble¹ ['dribl] *n.* **1.** (*a*) petite(s) goutte(s) (d'eau, etc.); (*b*) (*of pers.*) bave *f*. **2.** *Fb: etc:* dribble *m*.

dribble² **1.** *v.i.* (*a*) (*of water, etc.*) dégoutter, tomber goutte à goutte; (*b*) (*of pers.*) baver; (*c*) *Bill:* (*of ball*) **to d. into the pocket,** rouler doucement dans la blouse. **2.** *v.tr.* (*a*) **to d. (out),** laisser couler (un liquide) goutte à goutte; (*b*) *Fb: etc:* dribbler (le ballon); (*c*) *Bill:* **to d. the ball into the pocket,** faire rouler tout doucement la bille dans la blouse. **dribbling** *n.* **1.** écoulement *m* de bave. **2.** *Fb: etc:* dribbling *m*.

dribbler ['driblər] *n. Fb: etc:* dribbleur *m*.

driblet ['driblit] *n.* **1.** petite somme d'argent. **2.** gouttelette *f*, petite goutte (d'eau, etc.); **in driblets,** goutte à goutte, au compte-gouttes.

drier ['draiər] *n.* **1.** (*pers.*) *Dom.Ec:* **d.(-up),** essuyeur, -euse (de vaisselle). **2.** (*thg*) *Ind:* sécheur *m*, séchoir *m*; **hair d.,** (i) (*held in hand*) séchoir (à cheveux), sèche-cheveux *m inv*; (ii) casque *m* sèche-cheveux; **clothes d.,** séchoir (de plafond, pliant, etc.); **spin d.,** essoreuse (centrifuge); **tumble(r) d.,** séchoir rotatif (à air chaud); *Phot:* **plate d.,** sèche-cliché *m*, *pl.* sèche-clichés. **3.** *Paint: etc:* siccatif *m*.

drift¹ [drift] *n.* **1.** (*a*) mouvement *m*; **continental d.,** dérive *f* des continents; **the d. from the land,** la lente désertion des campagnes; (*b*) (i) direction *f*, sens *m* (d'un courant); (ii) vitesse *f* (d'un courant); (*c*) cours *m* (des affaires, des événements). **2.** (*a*) dérive *f* (d'un avion, d'un navire); **d. current,** courant *m* de surface; **d. ice,** glaces flottantes; **policy of d.,** politique *f* de laisser-faire; (*b*) dérivation *f* (d'un projectile, etc.); *Civ.E:* déviation *f* (d'un trou de sonde); (*c*) *Elcs:* glissement *m*; **d. transistor,** drift *m*. **3.** sens général, portée *f* (des paroles de qn); **I see his d.,** je vois où il veut en venir; *F:* **I get the d.,** je pige. **4.** (*a*) objet flottant (à la dérive); (*b*) rafale *f* (de pluie, de neige); traînée *f* (de nuages). **5.** amoncellement *m* (de sable, etc.); *Geog:* apport(s) *m*(*pl*) (de sable); congère *f* (de neige). **6.** *Fish:* **d. (net),** filet traînant. **7.** *Min:* (i) direction (d'une galerie); (ii) (galerie de) chassage (*m*); (iii) galerie d'exploration. **8.** *Tls:* (*a*) **d. (punch),** chasse-clef *m*, *pl.* chasse-clefs; (*b*) (*for rivet holes*) **d. (pin),** broche *f* (d'assemblage).

drift² **1.** *v.i.* (*a*) flotter; être entraîné; dériver, aller en dérive; *Av:* déporter, marcher en crabe; **to d. with the current,** se laisser aller au fil de l'eau; **wisps of smoke are drifting across the sky,** des fumées se traînent dans le ciel; **conversation drifted from one subject to another,** la conversation passait d'un sujet à un autre; **to d. apart,** (*of friends*) se perdre de vue; (*of married couple*) se séparer peu à peu; **the audience started to d. towards the exit,** les spectateurs filaient lentement vers la sortie; (*b*) **to d. into crime,** être entraîné vers le crime; **to let things d.,** laisser aller les choses; (*c*) (*of sand, etc.*) s'amonceler, s'amasser; (*of snow*) se former en congères, s'amasser; (*d*) *Min:* chasser; percer en direction; (*e*) (*of questions, events*) tendre (**towards sth.,** vers un but). **2.** *v.tr.* (*a*) flotter (du bois); (*of current*) entraîner (qch.); (*b*) (*of wind*) amonceler, entasser (la neige, le sable); (*c*) *Mec.E:* brocher, mandriner (un trou de rivet). **drifting 1.** *a.* (navire, etc.) en dérive; (nuage) traînant. **2.** *n.* (*a*) entraînement *m* par le courant, par le vent; (*b*) amoncellement *m* (des neiges); (*c*) *Mec.E:* brochage *m*, mandrinage *m*.

drifter ['driftər] *n.* **1.** *Fish:* bâteau *m* de pêche à filets traînants. **2.** personne *f* qui se laisse aller.

driftwood ['driftwud] *n.* bois flottant, flotté.

drill¹ [dril] *n.* **1.** *Metalw: Carp:* (*a*) foret *m*, mèche *f*; **spoon d.,** cuiller *f*, cuillère *f*; (*b*) foreuse *f*, foret, drille *f*; (*power-driven*) perceuse *f*; **electric d.,** perceuse électrique; **percussion d.,** perceuse percuteuse; **d. chuck,** mandrin *m* (de tour) porte-mèche. **2.** *Dent:* fraise *f*. **3.** *Min: Civ.E:* (*a*) (i) perforateur *m*, perforatrice *f*; (ii) (*taking borings*) sondeuse *f*, sonde *f*; **pneumatic d.,** marteau-piqueur *m* (à air comprimé); (*b*) **d. (bit),** burin *m*. **4.** (*a*) exercice(s) *m*(*pl*); **fire d.,** exercices de sauvetage (en cas d'incendie); *Mil:* **recruit d.,** école du soldat; **firing d.,** instruction *f* du tir; **rifle d.,** maniement *m* du fusil; **to do punishment d.,** faire la pelote; *F:* **to know the d.,** savoir ce qu'il faut faire, comment s'y prendre; **d. ground,** terrain *m* d'exercice, de manœuvres; **d. sergeant,** sergent instructeur; (*b*) *Sch:* **verb d.,** exercices oraux sur les verbes.

drill² **1.** *v.tr.* (*a*) forer (un puits, etc.); perforer (une plaque); percer (un trou); *Min:* (per)forer (la roche, etc.); (*b*) *Dent:* fraiser (une dent); (*c*) *v.ind. tr.* **to d. for oil,** forer pour rechercher du pétrole. **2.** *v.tr. Gym: etc:* faire faire l'exercice à (des hommes); *Mil:* instruire, exercer (des soldats); *Nau:* **well-drilled crew,** équipage bien exercé; *F:* **to d. s.o. (in what he has to do, say),** faire la leçon à qn (sur ce qu'il doit faire, dire); **I can't d. (it) into him that ...,** je ne peux pas le faire comprendre que ...; *Sch:* **to d. the boys in French verbs,** faire faire aux élèves des exercices oraux sur les verbes français. **3.** *v.i.* (*of troops, etc.*) faire l'exercice. **drilling** *n.* **1.** (*a*) *Metalw:* forage *m*, perçage *m*; *Min:* perforation *f* (des roches, etc.); **d. machine,** machine *f* à percer; perceuse *f*, foreuse *f*; (*b*) *Min:* forage, sondage *m* (d'un puits); **d. machine,** sondeuse *f*, sonde *f*; *Petr:* **oil d.,** forage pétrolier; **d. rig,** installation *f* de forage; **offshore d. rig,** île *f* de forage; (*c*) *Dent:* fraisage *m*. **2.** *Mil:* exercices *mpl*, manœuvres *fpl*.

drill³ *n. Agr: Hort:* **1.** rayon *m*, sillon *m*; **to sow the grain in drills,** semer la graine en rayons. **2.** semoir *m* (à cuillers); **d. harrow,** herse *f* à semer; **d. hoe,** rigoleur *m*.

drill⁴ *v.tr. Agr:* semer en rayons.

drill⁵ *n. Tex:* coutil *m*; (*for denims, etc.*) treillis *m*.

drily ['draili] *adv.* = DRYLY, *see* DRY¹.

drink¹ [driŋk] *n.* **1.** (*a*) boire *m*; **to give s.o. food and d.,** donner à boire et à manger à qn; (*b*) **to give s.o. a d.,** donner à boire à qn; **to have a d.,** boire quelque chose; (*c*) consommation *f*; **to have a d.,** prendre quelque chose; *F:* prendre un pot; **to pay for the drinks,** payer les consommations; *F:* **long d.,** (grand) verre de bière, etc.; gin *m*, whisky *m*, à l'eau; **short d.,** apéritif *m*; verre d'alcool, etc.; (*d*) *F:* **the d.,** (i) *Nau:* la mer, la grande tasse; (ii) l'eau (d'un lac, d'une rivière); **to fall into the d.,** tomber (i) à la mer, (ii) dans l'eau. **2.** (*beverage*) boisson *f*; **strong d.,** spiritueux *mpl*; **soft drinks,** boissons sans alcool; **come round for a d.,** venez prendre l'apéritif. **3.** boisson; **to take to d.,** s'adonner à la boisson, se mettre à boire; **to be under the influence of d.,** avoir trop bu; *Jur:* **to drive a car while under the influence of d.,** conduire en état d'ébriété; **to drive s.o. to d.,** pousser qn à l'ivrognerie.

drink² *v.tr. & i* (*p.t.* **drank** [dræŋk]; *p.p.* **drunk** [drʌŋk], *Poet:* **drunken** ['drʌŋkən]) boire. **1.** (*a*) **will you have something to d.?** voulez-vous boire, prendre, quelque chose? **fit to d.,** bon à boire; potable; **to d. (to) s.o.'s health,** boire à la santé de qn; (*b*) boire (sa paie); **to d. s.o. under the table,** mettre qn sous la table. **2.** *v.i.* être adonné à la boisson; **to d. heavily,** s'alcooliser; **to d. like a fish,** boire comme un trou. **drink down** *v.tr.* boire, avaler (une boisson). **drink in** *v.tr.* (*a*) absorber, boire (l'eau); s'imbiber (d'eau); (*b*) boire (les paroles de qn). **drinking 1.** *a.* **hard-d.,** adonné à la boisson; **I'm not a d. man,** je n'ai pas l'habitude de boire. **2.** *n.* (*a*) boire *m*; **d. fountain,** (i) fontaine publique; (ii) *Ind: etc:* poste *m* d'eau potable; **d. glass,** verre *m* à boire; **d. trough,** abreuvoir *m*; **d. water,** eau *f* potable; (*b*) (*of alcoholic drinks*) (i) **d. saloon,** débit *m* de boissons; **d. song,** chanson *f* à boire; (ii) (*to excess*) ivrognerie *f*; alcoolisme *m*; **d. bout,** beuverie *f*. **drink off** *v.tr.* boire (un verre) d'un coup; avaler (une coupe de champagne). **drink up** *v.tr.* achever de boire; vider (un verre); *v.i.* **d. up!** videz vos verres! **drunk 1.** *a.* (*a*) ivre, gris; soûl (**with,** de); **to get d.,** se soûler; **to make s.o. d.,** soûler qn; **dead d.,** ivre mort; **blind d.,** soûl perdu; **d. as a lord,** soûl comme un Polonais; *Jur:* **d. and disorderly** = en état d'ivresse manifeste dans un lieu public; (*b*) enivré (**with success,** par le succès); **d. with joy,** ivre de joie. **2.** *n.* ivrogne *m*. **drunken** *a.* **1. d. man,** (i) homme ivre; (ii) ivrogne *m*; **d. brawl,** querelle *f* d'ivrognes. **2. d. state,** état *m* d'ivresse; *Jur:* **d. driving,** conduite *f* en état d'ébriété. **drunkenly** *adv.* en ivrogne; comme un ivrogne.

drinkable ['driŋkəbl] *a.* (*a*) buvable; **the wine's very d.,** ce vin se laisse boire; (*b*) (eau) potable.

drinker ['driŋkər] *n.* buveur, -euse; (*a*) **wine, beer, tea, drinkers,** buveurs de vin, de bière, de thé; (*b*) **he's a heavy, hard, d.,** il boit beaucoup.

drip¹ [drip] *n.* **1.** bruit *m* de l'eau qui tombe, qui s'écoule; bruit d'un robinet qui goutte. **2.** goutte *f*; **the drips from the trees,** l'égoutture *f* des arbres. **3. d. cup,** cuvette *f* d'égouttage; **d. feed,** distributeur *m* compte-gouttes (d'huile); **d.-feed lubricator,** (graisseur *m*) compte-gouttes *m inv*; **d. mat,** dessous *m* de bouteille, de verre. **4.** *Med:* goutte-à-goutte *m inv*. **5.** *P:* **he's, she's, a d.,** c'est une nouille.

drip² *v.* (**dripped**) **1.** *v.i.* dégoutter, s'égoutter; tomber goutte à goutte; **the perspiration was dripping from his forehead,** la sueur lui dégouttait du front; son front était ruisselant de sueur. **2.** *v.tr.* faire dégoutter (du liquide); laisser tomber (du liquide) goutte à goutte. **dripping 1.** *a.* ruisselant; (robinet) qui goutte; **to be d. wet,** être trempé; **d. with perspiration, with blood,** ruisselant de sueur, de sang. **2.** *n.* (*a*) égouttement *m*; (*b*) **drippings,** l'égoutture *f* (des arbres); (*c*) *Cu:* graisse *f* de rôti; **bread and d.,** tartine *f* à la graisse.

drip-dry ['dripdrai] *a.* ne nécessitant aucun repassage; lavé-repassé *inv*.

drip-feed ['dripfi:d] *v.tr.* (**drip-fed**) *Med:* nourrir, alimenter (un malade) par perfusion. **drip-feeding** *n.* alimentation *f* par perfusion; drip-feeding *m*.

drive¹ [draiv] *n.* **1.** promenade *f* en voiture; course *f*; **a 50 km d.,** un parcours, un trajet, de 50 km; **it's an hour's d. away,** c'est à une heure en voiture; **to go for a d.,** aller faire une promenade, *F:* un (petit) tour, en voiture; *Aut:* **test d.,** conduite *f* d'essai. **2.** (*a*) conduite (du bétail); (*b*) *Ven:* battue *f* (du gibier); (*c*) *NAm:* (i) (transport *m* du bois par le) flottage; *Fr.C:* drave *f*; (ii) train *m* (de bois flotté). **3.** (*a*) *Mec.E:* (mouvement *m* de) propulsion (*f*); commande *f* (par un organe); transmission *f*, actionnement *m*; **belt, chain, d.,** entraînement, transmission, par courroie, par chaîne; **gear d.,** commande par engrenages; (*b*) *Aut:* **direct d.,** prise directe; **front wheel d.,** traction *f* avant; **vehicle with four wheel d.,** véhicule *m* à quatre roues motrices. **4.** *Aut:* conduite; **left-hand d.,** conduite à gauche. **5.** *Sp:* (*a*) *Golf:* drive *m*; (*b*) *Ten:* drive; **(forearm) d.,** (drive de) coup droit; (*c*) *Cr:* coup droit long et appuyé. **6.** énergie *f*; dynamisme *m*; **to have plenty of d.,** être énergique, entreprenant. **7.** (*a*) offensive *f* (contre une place forte, un abus); (*b*) campagne *f*; **sales d.,** campagne de vente. **8.** *Psy:* pulsion (sexuelle, etc.). **9.** (*a*) allée *f* (dans un parc, etc.) pour les voitures; (*b*) avenue *f* (d'un château, etc.); route *f* de plaisance. **10.** *Min:* galerie *f* en direction. **11.** *Cards:* tournoi *m* (de bridge, de whist).

drive² *v.* (*p.t* **drove** [drouv]; *p.p.* **driven** ['drivn]) **I.** *v.tr.* **1.** (*a*) chasser, faire aller (devant soi); conduire, mener (le bétail); **to d. the enemy from his positions,** déloger l'ennemi; **the wind is driving the rain against the window panes,** le vent chasse la pluie contre les vitres; **the waves drove the ship onto the rocks,** les vagues ont poussé le navire contre les rochers; (*b*) *Ven:* rabattre (le gibier); **to d. the country (for game),** battre la campagne. **2.** (*a*) faire marcher (une machine); conduire une voiture, une locomotive); *Rac:* driver (un trotteur); piloter (une voiture de course); *v.i. & tr.* **can you d. (a car)?** savez-vous conduire? **who was driving?** qui était au volant? **to test d. a car,** faire l'essai d'une voiture; (*b*) **to d. s.o. to a place,** conduire qn en voiture quelque part; **to d. s.o. home,** reconduire qn chez lui (en voiture); (*c*) diriger (un flottage de bois). **3.** (*a*) pousser (qn à une action); **I was driven to resign,** j'ai été forcé de démissionner; **he won't be driven,** on ne le mène pas comme on veut; (*b*) réduire (qn au désespoir, etc.); **to d. s.o. out of his mind,** rendre qn fou; **to d. s.o. wild,** pousser qn à bout. **4.** surcharger (qn) de travail; exploiter (qn); surmener (ses employés); **to d. oneself too hard,** se surmener. **5.** enfoncer (un clou, un pieu); serrer (une vis). **6.** (*a*) percer, forer (un tunnel); pratiquer (une galerie); (*b*) **to d. a railway through the desert,** tracer, construire, une ligne de chemin de fer à travers le désert. **7. to d. a bargain,** conclure un marché; **to d. a hard bargain,** chercher à gagner le dernier centime. **8.** *Sp:* **to d. the ball,** *abs.* **to d.,** *Cr:* chasser la balle; *Ten:* jouer un drive; driver; *Golf:* driver. **9.** *Mec.E: Mch:* actionner, faire marcher (une machine); (*of part*) actionner (un organe); **driven by compressed air,** commandé par l'air comprimé. **II.** *v.i.* **1.** (*of clouds, etc.*) **to d. before the wind,** chasser devant le vent; **the rain driving against the window panes,** la pluie qui fouette les vitres. **2. to d. along the road,** rouler sur la route; **to d. to a place,** se rendre en voiture à un endroit; **to d. slowly,** rouler à petite allure, lentement; **to d. on the right (of the road),** circuler à droite; tenir la droite. **3.** (*with passive force*) **car that drives well,** voiture *f* facile à conduire. **drive along 1.** *v.tr.* chasser (qn, qch.). **2.** *v.i.* rouler (en voiture); **I was driving along slowly,** je roulais lentement. **drive at** *v.i.* **what are you driving at?** où voulez-vous en venir? **drive away 1.** *v.tr.* chasser, éloigner, écarter (qn, qch.). **2.** *v.i.* partir s'en aller, en voiture; démarrer. **drive back 1.** *v.tr.* (*a*) repousser, faire reculer (qn, qch.); (*b*) reconduire, ramener (qn) en voiture. **2.** *v.i.* rentrer, revenir, en voiture. **drive down 1.** *v.tr.* **to d. s.o. down to, into, the country,** conduire qn (en voiture) à la campagne. **2.** *v.i.* se rendre en voiture (de la ville à la campagne, de Londres en province). **drive in 1.** *v.tr.* enfoncer, renfoncer (un clou); visser (une vis). **2.** *v.i.* entrer (en voiture). **driven** *a.* **1. d. snow,** neige *f* vierge. **2. electrically d.,** actionné par l'électricité; à commande électrique. **drive off 1.** *v.tr.* chasser, éloigner, écarter, repousser (qn, qch.). **2.** *v.i.* partir, s'en aller, en voiture; démarrer. **drive on** *v.i.* continuer sa route; s'avancer; **d. on!** continuez! **drive out** *v.tr.* chasser (qn, qch.); faire sortir (qn). **drive through 1.** *v.tr.* **to d. one's sword through s.o.'s body,** passer son sabre à travers le corps à qn. **2.** *v.i.* passer (par une ville) en voiture. **drive up** *v.i.* s'approcher; **a car drove up to the door,** une voiture vint s'arrêter devant la porte. **driving 1.** *a.* (*a*) *Mec.E:* (*of wheel, etc.*) moteur, - trice; menant; **d. force,** force motrice; **the d. force behind the scheme,** le moteur d'un projet; *Mec.E:* **d. belt,** courroie *f* de commande; **d. gear,** (i) (engrenage *m* de) transmission (*f*); **d. shaft,** arbre *m* de transmission; **d. wheel,** (i) roue motrice (de locomotive, etc.); (ii) roue de transmission; (*b*) (pluie) battante; **d. snow,** neige fouettée par le vent. **2.** *n.* (*a*) conduite *f* (d'une voiture, etc.); *Aut:* **d. lessons,** leçons *fpl* de conduite; **d. school,** auto-école *f*, *pl.* auto-écoles; **d. test,** (examen *m* pour) permis *m* de conduire; **to pass one's d. test,** avoir son permis (de conduire); **d. licence,** permis de conduire; **d. seat,** du conducteur; *F:* **he's in the d. seat,** c'est lui qui mène l'affaire; (*b*) **log d.,** flottage *m* du bois; *Fr.C:* drave *f*; (*c*) *Mch: Mec.E:* commande *f*, transmission *f*; (*d*) enfoncement *m* (d'un clou, d'un pieu); serrage *m* (d'une vis); (*e*) *Min:* percement *m* (d'une galerie); (*f*) *Golf:* **d. iron,** grand fer, driver *m*.

drive-in ['draivin] *n. NAm:* **d.-in (cinema),** cinéma en plein air auquel on assiste en voiture; drive-in *m inv*; **d.-in (restaurant),** restaurant *m* où les clients sont servis dans leurs voitures; **d.-in bank,** banque *f* dont les guichets sont accessibles aux clients dans leurs voitures.

drivel¹ ['driv(ə)l] *n. F:* radotage *m*; bêtises *fpl*, balivernes *fpl*; **to talk d.,** radoter.

drivel² *v.i.* **(drivelled,** *NAm:* **driveled)** *F:* radoter; **what are you drivelling about?** qu'est-ce que tu radotes? **drivelling,** *NAm:* **driveling** *a. F:* radoteur, -euse; **you d. imbecile!** espèce d'idiot!

driver ['draivər] *n.* **1.** (*a*) mécanicien *m* (de locomotive); mécanicien, wattman *m* (de tramway); conducteur *m* (d'autobus); chauffeur, -euse (de taxi); conducteur, -trice (d'automobile); **racing d.,** coureur *m* (automobile); (*b*) (*of horse-drawn vehicle*) conducteur, - trice; cocher *m* (de fiacre, etc.); *Rac:* driver *m* (de sulky); *F:* **to be in the driver's seat,** tenir les rênes; (*c*) conducteur (de bestiaux); (*d*) **log d.,** flotteur *m*, driver; *Fr.C:* draveur *m*; (*e*) **slave d.,** (i) surveillant *m* d'esclaves; (ii) homme, femme, qui fait marcher, trimer, son personnel. **2.** *Tls:* (*a*) poinçon *m*; (*b*) chassoir *m*. **3.** *Mec.E:* (*a*) roue *f* de transmission; (*b*) poulie *f* de commande; (*c*) tige *f* d'entraînement; (*d*) *I.C.E:* heurtoir *m* (d'une soupape). **4.** *Golf:* driver *m*.

driveway ['draivwei] *n.* (*a*) allée *f* pour les voitures; (*b*) entrée *f* (d'une demeure, etc.).

drizzle¹ ['drizl] *n.* bruine *f*, crachin *m*; **the rain came down in a steady d.,** il pleuvait dru et menu.

drizzle² *v.i.* bruiner; **it was drizzling,** il bruinait; il faisait de la bruine.

drizzly ['drizli] *a.* (jour) bruineux.

drogue [droug] *n.* **1.** *Nau:* cône-ancre *m*, *pl.* cônes-ancres. **2.** *Av:* parachute *m* de queue (pour freinage rapide).

droll [droul] *a.* drôle, comique; bizarre, curieux.

dromedary ['drɔməd(ə)ri] *n.* dromadaire *m*.

drone¹ [droun] *n.* **1.** (*a*) *Ent:* abeille *f* mâle; faux-bourdon *m*, *pl.* faux-bourdons; (*b*) fainéant *m*, parasite *m*. **2.** (*a*) bourdonnement *m* (des abeilles); débit *m* monotone (d'un pasteur, etc.); ronronnement *m*, vrombissement *m* (d'un avion); (*b*) *Mus:* bourdon *m* (de cornemuse). **3.** *Mil.Av:* avion téléguidé; drone *m*.

drone² **1.** *v.i.* (*a*) (*of bee, etc.*) bourdonner; (*b*) (*of pers.*) parler d'un ton monotone; **he droned on for hours,** il n'a pas cessé de sa voix monotone. **2.** *v.tr.* **to d. (out),** dire (qch.) d'un ton monotone.

drool [dru:l] *v.i.* **1.** baver. **2.** radoter; **to d. over sth.,** s'extasier sur qch.

droop¹ [dru:p] *n.* **1.** attitude penchée (de la tête). **2.** langueur *f*, abattement *m*.

droop² **1.** *v.i.* (*a*) (*of head, etc.*) (se) pencher; (*of shoulders*) tomber; (*of eyelids*) s'abaisser; (*of feathers*) pendre; (*b*) (*of flower*) pencher; (*c*) (*of pers.*) languir; s'affaisser. **2.** *v.tr.* baisser, pencher (la tête). **drooping** *a.* (*a*) (*of shoulders*) tombant; (*of moustache*) tombant; (*of head*) baissé, penché; (*of eyelids*) abaissé; (*b*) (*of flower*) qui commence à faner; (*of pers.*) languissant; **to revive s.o.'s d. spirits,** remonter le moral à qn.

drop¹ [drɔp] *n.* **1.** (*a*) goutte *f* (d'eau, de sang); **d. by d.,** goutte à goutte; *F:* **it's only a d. in the ocean,** ce n'est qu'une goutte d'eau dans la mer; (*b*) *Pharm:* **drops,** gouttes; **nasal drops,** gouttes pour le nez; (*c*) doigt *m*, larme *f* (de vin); *Cu:* filet *m* (de vinaigre); (*d*) *F:* **to take a d.,** boire la goutte; **he likes a wee d.,** il aime bien prendre la goutte; (*e*) (*of necklace, chandelier, etc.*) pendant *m*, pendeloque *f*; (*f*) **acid d.,** bonbon acidulé; **chocolate d.,** pastille *f* de chocolat. **2.** (*a*) chute *f*; **a d. of a hundred metres,** un à-pic de cent mètres; *F:* **at the d. of a hat,** sans hésiter, sans hésitation; *Surv:* **d. in the ground,** dénivellation *f* du terrain; (*b*) *Av:* parachutage, *m*, droppage *m*; **delayed d.,** ouverture retardée (d'un parachute); (*c*) chute, baisse *f* (de prix, etc.); **sales show a d. of 10%,** les ventes accusent une régression de 10%; **d. in value, in takings,** moins-value *f*; **d. in voltage, in pressure,** perte *f* de charge, de pression. **3.** (*a*) (*of lock*) cache-entrée *m inv*; (*b*) *Th:* **d. (curtain),** rideau *m* d'entr'acte; (*c*) (*of gallows*) bascule *f*, trappe *f*; *F:* **the d.,** la potence. **4.** (*a*) *Fb:* **d. kick,** coup tombé; coup de pied à ras de terre; **d. goal,** drop-goal *m*, *pl.* drop-goals; drop *m*; (*b*) *Ten:* **d. shot, stroke,** volée amortie; amorti *m*. **5.** *Arch:* **d. arch,** arc-ogive surbaissé, *pl.* arcs-ogives; *Furn:* **d.-leaf table,** table *f* à battants; *Metall:* **d. hammer,** marteau-pilon *m*, *pl.* marteaux-pilons; mouton *m*; **d. stamp,** martinet *m*; *Nau:* **d. keel,** dériveur *m*; aile *f* de dérive; *Th:* **d. scene,** (i) toile *f* de fond; (ii) rideau d'entr'acte.

drop² *v.* (**dropped** [drɔpt]) **I.** *v.i.* **1.** tomber goutte à goutte, dégoutter (**from,** de). **2.** tomber; (*of pers.*) se laisser tomber; (*of ground*) s'abaisser; *Med:* (*of womb, etc.*) descendre; **the book dropped from, out of, his hands,** le livre lui tomba des mains; **his jaw dropped,** son visage s'allongea; **to d. into a chair,** s'affaler dans un fauteuil; **I am ready to d.,** (i) je tombe de fatigue; je ne tiens plus sur mes jambes; (ii) je tombe de sommeil; **to d. (down) dead,** tomber (raide) mort; *P:* **d. dead!** allez au diable! **3.** (*of prices, temperature, etc.*) baisser; (*of wind*) tomber. **4. there the matter dropped,** l'affaire en resta là; *F:* **let it d.!** n'en parlons plus! **5.** (*a*) **to d. to the rear,** rester en arrière; (*of boat*) **to d. downstream,** naviguer en aval; (*b*) **to d. into the habit, the way, of . . .,** prendre l'habitude de . . .. **II.** *v.tr.* **1.** verser (une larme, etc.). **2.** (*a*) laisser tomber; lâcher (qch.); baisser (un voile, un rideau); lancer (une bombe); lâcher (un parachutiste); *Nau:* débarquer (le pilote); jeter, mouiller (l'ancre); (*in knitting*) sauter (une maille); (*to dog*) **d. it!** lâche ça! (*b*) (*of sheep, etc.*) mettre bas (des petits); (*c*) **to d. a word in s.o.'s ear,** couler, glisser, un mot à l'oreille de qn; (*d*) **to d. a letter into the pillar box,** jeter une lettre à la poste; **to d. s.o. a line, a card,** envoyer, écrire, un mot, une carte, à qn. **3.** (*a*) perdre (de l'argent) (**over sth.,** sur qch.); (*b*) *Sp:* perdre (un point). **4.** (*lower*) **to d. the folding seat (of a taxi),** rabattre le strapontin; **to d. the hem of a dress,** allonger une robe; *Av:* **to d. a wing,** piquer de l'aile. **5.** (*set down*) déposer, descendre, (qn) (de voiture). **6.** (*a*) omettre, supprimer (une lettre, une syllabe); **cases in which the article is dropped,** cas où l'on supprime l'article; (*b*) ne pas prononcer (les r, etc.). **7.** baisser, laisser tomber (les yeux, le bras, la voix, etc.). **8.** (*of woman*) **to d. a curtsey,** faire une révérence. **9.** (*a*) abandonner, délaisser (un travail); cesser, lâcher (une poursuite); quitter (une habitude); **to d. the idea of doing sth.,** renoncer à (l'idée de) faire qch.; **let's d. the subject,** ne parlons plus de cela! brisons là! *F:* **d. it!** cessez donc! en voilà assez! (*b*) **to d. s.o.,** cesser de voir qn; laisser tomber qn; *F:* **to d. s.o. like a hot brick, a hot potato,** cesser du jour au lendemain toutes relations avec qn; *Sp:* **to d. a player,** laisser tomber un équipier. **drop back** *v.i.* (*a*) retomber; (*b*) retourner en arrière; (*c*) = DROP BEHIND. **drop behind** *v.i.* rester en arrière; se laisser distancer, dépasser. **drop by** *v.i.* passer chez qn. **drop down** *v.i.* (*a*) tomber par terre; **to d. down dead,** tomber (raide) mort; (*b*) (*of flap, etc.*) s'abaisser. **drop in** **1.** *v.tr.* ajouter (qch.) goutte à goutte; laisser tomber (qch.) dedans. **2.** *v.i.* entrer en passant; **to d. in on s.o.,** (i) faire une petite visite à qn; (ii) venir en visite chez qn (sans être attendu). **drop off** **1.** *v.i.* (*a*) (*of leaves, etc.*) tomber, se détacher; (*b*) *F:* **to d. off (to sleep),** s'assoupir, s'endormir; (*c*) (*of membership, attendance, etc.*) diminuer. **2.** *v.tr.* **d. me off at the corner,** déposez-moi au coin de la rue. **drop out** **1.** *v.tr.* (*a*) laisser tomber (qch.) dehors; (*b*) omettre (une syllable, un nom dans une liste, etc.). **2.** *v.i.* (*a*) tomber dehors; (*b*) **to d. out (of a contest),** se retirer; **to d. out (of a class),** abandonner un cours; (*c*) refuser la société; vivre en marge de la société; (*d*) *Mil:* sortir des rangs; rester en arrière; (*e*) *Typ: etc:* **the letter s has dropped out,** la lettre s a disparu. **dropped** *a.* **1.** *Med:* **d. eyelid,** chute *f* de la paupière. **2.** *Aut: etc:* (essieu, etc.) surbaissé; *Cy:* (guidon) renversé. **3.** *Fb:* (*Rugby*) **d. goal,** drop-goal *m*, *pl.* drop-goals. **dropping** *n.* **1.** (*a*) égouttement *m* (d'un liquide); **d. tube,** pipette *f*, compte-gouttes *m inv*; (*b*) descente *f*, chute *f* (d'un objet); baisse *f*, chute (des prix); suppression *f* (d'un mot); abandon *m* (d'un projet); (*c*) *Husb:* **d. (of young),** mise *f* bas; agnelage *m*, vêlage *m*, etc.; (*d*) *Aut: etc:* surbaissement *m* (du châssis); (*e*) *Av:* lâchage *m* (d'un parachutiste, de colis); **d. zone,** zone *f* de largage, de droppage; (*f*) **d. off,** (i) chute *f* (des feuilles); (ii) diminution *f* (de l'assistance, etc.); (iii) assoupissement *m*; (*j*) **d. out,** (i) abandon *m* (d'un cours, etc.); (ii) désinsertion sociale. **2. droppings,** (*a*) (*of animals, birds*) fiente *f*; (*of stags*) fumées *fpl*; (*of sheep*) crottes *fpl*.

drop-forge ['drɔpfɔ:dʒ] *v.tr.* *Metalw:* étamper, estamper. **drop-forging** *n.* **1.** estampage *m*. **2.** pièce *f* emboutie, étampée.

drophead ['drɔphed] *n.* *Aut:* capote *f* rabattable; **d. coupé,** coupé décapotable.

droplet ['drɔplit] *n.* gouttelette *f*.

dropout ['drɔpaut] *n.* *F:* (*a*) étudiant, -ante qui abandonne ses études; (*b*) marginal, -ale.

dropper ['drɔpər] *n.* compte-gouttes *m inv*.

dropsical ['drɔpsik(ə)l] *a.* *Med:* hydropique.

dropsy ['drɔpsi] *n.* *Med:* hydropisie *f*.

dross [drɔs] *n.* **1.** *Metall:* scories *fpl*, crasse *f* (du métal en fusion). **2.** (*a*) impuretés *fpl*; déchets *mpl*; (*b*) *F:* rebut *m*.

drought [draut] *n.* sécheresse *f*.

drove [drouv] *n.* (*a*) troupeau *m* (de bœufs, etc.) en marche; (*b*) foule *f* (de personnes en marche); **they walk about in droves,** ils se promènent en grandes bandes.

drover ['drouvər] *n.* conducteur *m*, toucheur *m*, de bestiaux.

drown [draun] *v.tr.* **1.** noyer; **to d. oneself,** se noyer; **to be drowned,** *v.i.* **to d. (by accident),** se noyer, être noyé; **drowned at sea,** noyé en mer; **to d. one's sorrow (in drink),** noyer son chagrin dans la boisson. **2.** inonder, submerger (une prairie); *F:* **eyes drowned in tears,** yeux noyés de larmes. **3.** étouffer (un son); **the noise of the waterfall drowns the voice,** le bruit de la cascade couvre la voix. **drowned** *a.* **1.** noyé; **a d. man, woman,** un noyé, une noyée; *F:* **he came home like a d. rat,** il est rentré trempé comme une soupe. **2.** (terrain) inondé. **drowning 1.** *a.* **a d. man,** un homme qui se noie. **2.** *n.* (*a*) **(case of) d.,** noyade *f*; **to save s.o. from d.,** sauver qn qui se noye; (*b*) inondation *f* (des champs).

drowse [drauz] *v.i.* somnoler, s'assoupir.

drowsiness ['drauzinis] *n.* somnolence *f*, assoupissement *m*.

drowsy ['drauzi] *a.* assoupi, somnolent; **to be, feel, d.,** avoir envie de dormir; avoir sommeil. **-ily** *adv.* d'un air, d'un ton, somnolent; à demi endormi.

drub [drʌb] *v.tr.* **(drubbed)** (*a*) battre, rosser (qn, l'ennemi); (*b*) **to d. sth. into s.o.,** faire entrer qch. de force dans la tête de qn. **drubbing** *n.* (*a*) volée *f* de coups (de bâton, de poing); (*b*) défaite *f*; **to give an opponent a d.,** battre un adversaire à plates coutures.

drudge¹ [drʌdʒ] *n.* femme *f*, homme *m*, de peine; **the household d.,** la cendrillon.

drudge² *v.i.* trimer, peiner.

drudgery ['drʌdʒəri] *n.* travail pénible, ingrat; corvée(s) *f*(*pl*).

drug¹ [drʌg] *n.* **1.** produit *m* pharmaceutique; drogue *f*. **2.** (*a*) narcotique *m*, stupéfiant *m*; **to take drugs,** se droguer; **d. addict,** drogué, -ée; toxicomane *mf*; **d. addiction,** toxicomanie *f*; **d. traffic,** *F:* **pushing, peddling,** trafic *m* des stupéfiants; (*b*) *F:* **the truth d.,** le sérum de vérité. **3. a d. on the market,** article *m* invendable.

drug² *v.* **(drugged)** *v.tr.* (*a*) donner, administrer, un narcotique, des stupéfiants, à (qn); doper (un cheval); **to d. oneself,** (i) prendre un narcotique; (ii) (*habitually*) se droguer; (*b*) **they had drugged his wine,** on avait mis un narcotique à son vin.

druggist ['drʌgist] *n.* pharmacien *m*; **wholesale d.,** pharmacien en gros; droguiste *m*.

drugstore ['drʌgstɔːr] *n. NAm:* drugstore *m*.

druid ['dru(ː)id] *n.m.* druide.

drum¹ [drʌm] *n.* **1.** *Mus:* tambour *m*; **big d., bass d.,** grosse caisse; *Mil:* **the drums,** la batterie; **d. beat,** coup *m*, roulement *m*, batterie, de tambour; **to beat the d.,** battre du tambour; *F:* **to bang the big d.,** battre la (grosse) caisse. **2.** *Anat:* tympan *m* (de l'oreille). **3.** tonneau *m* en fer, fût *m*; bidon *m*, tambour (à huile); **air d.,** réservoir *m* d'air comprimé. **4.** *Arch:* tambour (d'une colonne). **5.** (*a*) *Mec.E: etc:* tambour, barillet *m*; (*b*) *Civ.E: etc:* tambour, cylindre (pour malaxage, etc.); **concrete mixing d.,** mélangeur *m* à béton; bétonnière *f*; (*c*) cylindre (de treuil); tambour (de moulinet); **cable d.,** tambour, dévidoir *m* (pour câble électrique).

drum² *v.* **(drummed) 1.** *v.i.* tambouriner; battre du tambour; *F:* (*of pers., rain*) **to d. on the window panes,** tambouriner sur les vitres; **her fingers were drumming on the table,** elle battait le rappel sur la table. **2.** *v.tr.* **to d. a tune on sth.,** tambouriner un air sur qch.; **to d. sth. into s.o.'s head,** enfoncer qch. dans la tête de qn. **drumming** *n.* **1.** (*a*) tambourinage *m*, bruit *m* de tambour; (*b*) *Orn:* tambourinage *m* (du pic). **2. d. out,** (*a*) *Mil:* expulsion *f* (d'un militaire) au son du tambour; (*b*) expulsion (de qn d'un club, etc.) avec ignominie. **3. d. up,** recrutement *m*. **drum out** *v.tr.* (*a*) *Mil:* expulser (un militaire) au son du tambour; dégrader (un militaire); (*b*) expulser (qn d'un club, etc.) avec ignominie. **drum up** *v.tr.* racoler (des partisans); *F:* faire le rappel de (ses amis); **to d. up customers,** rechercher de la clientèle.

drumhead ['drʌmhed] *n.* (i) peau *f*, (ii) dessus *m*, de tambour; *Mil:* **d. service,** office divin en plein air.

drum-major [drʌm'meidʒər] *n. Mil:* tambour-major *m*, *pl.* tambours-majors.

drum-majorette ['drʌmmeidʒə'ret] *n.f. U.S:* majorette.

drummer ['drʌmər] *n.* tambour *m* (qui joue du tambour; (*player of kettle-drum*) timbalier *m*; (*jazz*) batteur *m*.

drumstick ['drʌmstik] *n.* **1.** *Mus:* baguette *f* de tambour, de timbale. **2.** *Cu:* pilon *m*, (bas *m* de la) cuisse (d'une volaille).

drunk. *see* DRINK².

drunkard ['drʌŋkəd] *n.* ivrogne *m*.

drunken *a.*, **drunkenly** *adv. see* DRINK².

drunkenness ['drʌŋk(ə)nnis] *n.* **1.** ivresse *f*. **2.** (*habitual*) ivrognerie *f*.

drunkometer [drʌn'kɔmitər] *n. NAm:* alcoo(l)test *m*.

drupe [druːp] *n. Bot:* drupe *m*.

dry¹ [drai] *a.* **(drier, driest)** sec, *f.* sèche. **1.** (*a*) (*of well, etc.*) tari, à sec; (*of weather, cold*) sec; (*of country*) aride; **d. land,** terre *f* ferme; **to pump a well d.,** épuiser l'eau d'un puits; **to run d., go d.,** (*of channel*) se dessécher; (*of spring, well*) s'épuiser, (se) tarir; (*of pump*) se désamorcer; (*of speaker*) **at the end of five minutes he had run d.,** au bout de cinq minutes il était à sec; *n.* **to stay in the d.,** rester au sec, à couvert; *Com:* **d. wine,** vin sec; **medium d. wine,** vin demi-sec, *pl.* demi-secs; **extra d. champagne,** champagne brut; (*b*) *Ind. Ch: etc:* (procédé, analyse) par voie sèche; **d. walling,** (i) murs *mpl* en pierres sèches; (ii) construction *f* en pierres sèches; (*c*) **d. clothing,** vêtements secs; **d. bread,** pain sec; **d. rot,** pourriture sèche (du bois); (*on container*) **to be kept d.,** craint l'humidité; *F:* **d. as a bone, bone d.,** sec comme une allumette; *Fish:* **d. fly,** mouche sèche; (*d*) *F:* (*of pers.*) **to be, feel, d.,** avoir la gorge sèche; **d. work,** travail qui donne soif. **2.** *F:* **d. country,** pays sec (où les boissons alcooliques sont prohibées); **to go d.,** prohiber la consommation des boissons alcooliques. **3.** (*a*) (*of subject, etc.*) aride, sans intérêt; (*b*) **the d. facts,** les faits purs et simples. **4.** (*a*) (ton) sec; **he has a d. manner,** il est d'une approche froide; (*b*) (sourire) teinté d'ironie; **to answer with d. sarcasm,** répondre d'un air de pince-sans-rire; **d. humour,** esprit caustique; **a man of d. humour,** un pince-sans-rire. **5. d. run,** (i) *Mil:* exercices *mpl* d'entraînement avec munitions à blanc; (ii) *F:* coup *m* d'essai. **6.** *Com:* **d. goods,** (i) marchandises sèches; (ii) *NAm:* articles *mpl* de nouveauté; étoffes *fpl*, tissus *mpl*; **d. goods store,** magasin *m* de nouveautés. **dryly, drily** *adv.* **1.** d'un ton sec; sèchement. **2.** avec une pointe d'ironie; (répondre) d'un air de pince-sans-rire.

dry² *v.* **(dried** [draid]**) 1.** *v.tr.* sécher (qch.); faire sécher (le linge); (*with spin drier*) essorer (le linge); étancher (le terrain); (*of wind*) sécher (les chemins); dessécher (la peau); **to d. the dishes,** essuyer la vaisselle; *abs.* **it's my turn to d.,** c'est à moi d'essuyer le vaisselle; **to d. one's eyes,** s'essuyer les yeux; **to d. (away) one's tears,** sécher ses larmes. **2.** *v.i.* (*a*) se sécher, se dessécher; **to put sth. out to d.,** mettre qch. à sécher dehors; **ink that dries black,** encre qui vire au noir en séchant; (*b*) *Husb:* (*of cow*) tarir, se sécher. **dried** *a.* séché, desséché; (fruits) secs; (lait, œufs) en poudre. **drying 1.** *a.* (*a*) (vent, etc.) desséchant; (*b*) (*of oil, varnish*) **quick-d.,** siccatif. **2.** *n.* (*a*) séchage *m*; dessèchement *m*; (*with a cloth*) essuyage *m*; **d. rack,** châssis *m* de séchage; séchoir *m*; (*for tobacco*) **d. barn,** suerie *f*; (*b*) **d. out,** (i) assèchement *m*, dessèchement *m*; (ii) désintoxication *f* (d'un alcoolique); (*c*) **d. up,** (i) tarissement *m* (d'un cours d'eau, etc.); (ii) essuyage *m* (de la vaisselle). **dry out 1.** *v.tr.* (*a*) faire évaporer (l'eau, etc.); (*b*) désintoxiquer (un alcoolique). **2.** *v.i.* (*a*) (*of moisture*) s'évaporer, sécher; (*b*) (*of alcoholic, drug addict*) se faire désintoxiquer. **dry up 1.** *v.i.* (*a*) (*of well, pool, etc.*) se dessécher, tarir; **the well has dried up,** le puits est à sec; (*b*) (*of author, etc.*) épuiser son inspiration; *F:* (*of speaker, etc.*) cesser de parler; rester en carafe; *P:* **d. up!** la ferme! ta gueule! **2.** *v.tr.* essuyer (la vaisselle); étancher (le terrain); (*of wind*) sêcher (les chemins); dessécher (la peau).

dryad ['draiæd] *n.f. Myth:* dryade.

dry-clean ['drai'kli:n] *v.tr.* nettoyer à sec. **dry-cleaning** *n.* nettoyage *m* à sec.

dry-cleaner ['drai'kli:nər] *n.* nettoyeur *m* à sec; teinturier *m*; **take it to the d.-cleaner's,** portez-le à la teinturerie, au pressing.

dry-dock ['drai'dɔk] **1.** *v.tr.* mettre (un navire) en cale sèche. **2.** *v.i.* (*of ship*) entrer en cale sèche.

dryer ['draiər] *n.* = DRIER.

dry-eyed ['drai'aid] a. les yeux secs, à l'œil sec.

dryness ['drainis] *n.* **1.** sécheresse *f* (d'une région, du temps); aridité *f* (du sol). **2.** sévérité *f* (de ton); aridité (d'un discours); causticité *f* (de l'esprit).

dual ['dju(:)əl] *a.* **1.** double; **d.-purpose,** (voiture, etc.) à double emploi; *Aut:* **d. carriageway,** route à quatre voies; **d. wheels,** roues jumelées; *Av:* **d. wheel (assembly),** diabolo *m*; *Aut:* **d.-control car,** voiture *f* à double commande; *Psy:* **d. personality,** dédoublement *m* de la personnalité; *Cmptr:* **d. processor computer,** ordinateur *m* biprocesseur. **2.** *Mth:* (nombre) dual.

dualism ['dju(:)əlizm] *n.* **1.** dualité *f.* **2.** *Phil:* dualisme *m.*

duality [dju(:)'æliti] *n.* dualité *f*; dédoublement *m* (de la personnalité, etc.).

dub¹ [dʌb] *v.tr.* **(dubbed) 1.** (*a*) **to d. s.o. (a) knight,** armer, adouber, qn chevalier; donner l'accolade à qn; (*b*) **he was dubbed the king of tennis,** on l'a surnommé le roi du tennis. **2.** *Leath:* préparer (le cuir) avec le dégras.

dub² *v.tr. Cin:* doubler (un film). **dubbing** *n.* doublage *m.*

dubbin¹ ['dʌbin] *n. Leath:* dégras *m.*

dubbin² *v.tr.* enduire (des chaussures) de dégras.

dubious ['dju:biəs] *a.* **1.** douteux; (*a*) (résultat) incertain; (lumière) douteuse, vague; (avantage) contestable; (*b*) (honneur) équivoque; (compagnie) douteuse, louche; **financiers of d. character,** financiers véreux. **2.** qui doute; **d. expression,** air de doute; **d. as to what he should do,** ne sachant trop ce qu'il devait faire; **we were d. about the scheme,** nous avions des doutes sur le projet. **-ly** *adv.* d'un ton, d'un air, de doute.

dubiousness ['dju:biəsnis] *n.* **1.** incertitude *f* (du résultat, etc.). **2.** équivoque *f* (d'un compliment, etc.).

ducal ['dju:k(ə)l] *a.* ducal, -aux.

ducat ['dʌkət] *n. A.Num:* ducat *m.*

duchess ['dʌtʃis] *n.f.* duchesse.

duchesse [dʌ'tʃes] *n. Cu:* **d. potatoes,** pommes *fpl* (de terre) duchesse.

duchy ['dʌtʃi] *n.* duché *m.*

duck¹ [dʌk] *n.* **1.** (*a*) (*female*) cane *f*; (*b*) (*generic*) canard *m*; **wild d.,** canard sauvage; **d. pond,** canardière; mare *f* aux canards; *F:* **to look like a dying d. (in a thunderstorm),** faire la carpe pâmée; avoir l'air pitoyable; **to take to sth. like a d. to water,** mordre à qch.; **criticism runs off him like water off a duck's back,** il est impénétrable à la critique; **to play at ducks and drakes,** faire des ricochets (sur l'eau); (*c*) (*d*) *Cu:* **Peking d.,** canard à la Pékinoise; **Bombay d.,** poisson sec assaisonné de cari. **2.** *F:* (*a*) **a sitting d.,** une cible facile; **dead d.,** (i) pauvre type *m*; (ii) (*pers.*) raté, -ée; (*thg*) fiasco *m*; **lame d.,** (i) malheureux, -euse; (ii) *Com:* maison, industrie, qui marche mal; (iii) *St. Exch:* spéculateur insolvable; failli *m*; (*b*) *P:* **what do you want, ducks?** et pour vous, ma petite dame? (*c*) *Cr:* zéro *m*; **to make a d.,** faire chou blanc.

duck² *n. Tex:* coutil *m*; toile fine; *Cost:* **ducks,** (i) pantalon *m*, (ii) complet *m*, de coutil, de toile.

duck³ *n.* **1.** plongeon *m*, bain (inattendu, involontaire). **2.** mouvement instinctif de la tête (pour se dérober à un coup, etc.); *Box:* esquive *f.*

duck⁴ 1. *v.i.* (*a*) plonger dans l'eau; (*b*) baisser la tête, se baisser (pour se dérober à un coup, etc.); *Box:* esquiver de la tête. **2.** *v.tr.* (*a*) plonger (qn) dans l'eau, faire faire le plongeon à (qn); (*b*) baisser subitement (la tête); (*c*) *F:* se dérober à (ses obligations, etc.); **to d. the issue,** s'esquiver; user de faux-fuyants. **ducking** *n.* plongeon *m* (involontaire); **to give s.o. a d.,** faire boire une tasse à qn.

duckbill ['dʌkbil] *n. Z:* ornithorynque *m.*

duck-billed ['dʌkbild] *a. Z:* **d. platypus,** ornithorynque *m.*

duckboards ['dʌkbɔ:dz] *n.pl.* caillebotis *m.*

duckling ['dʌkliŋ] *n. Orn:* canardeau *m*; (*drake*) caneton *m*; (*duck*) canette *f*; **the Ugly D.,** le vilain petit Canard.

duckweed ['dʌkwi:d] *n. Bot:* lentille *f* d'eau.

ducky ['dʌki] *n. F:* mon petit chou; ma cocotte.

duct¹ [dʌkt] *n.* **1.** conduit *m*; *Civ.E: etc:* caniveau *m*, -aux (pour câbles, etc.); **air d.,** manche *f* à air; gaine *f* (d'installation de ventilation). **2.** *Anat:* canal *m*, -aux, vaisseau *m*, -aux; **bile d.,** canal, biliaire; **auditory d.,** conduit auditif. **3.** *Bot:* trachée *f.*

ductile ['dʌktail] *a.* (*a*) (métal) ductile; (*b*) (caractère) docile, malléable, souple.

ductility [dʌk'tiliti] *n.* (*a*) ductilité *f* (d'un métal); (*b*) docilité *f*, souplesse *f* (de caractère).

dud [dʌd] *n. & a. F:* (*a*) incapable (*mf*); **I'm a d. at history,** je suis nul en histoire; (*b*) *Artil:* **d. (shell),** obus non éclaté; **d. cheque,** chèque *m* sans provision; **the note was a d.,** le billet était faux.

dude [dju:d] *n. U.S: F:* **1.** gommeux *m.* **2.** hôte *m* d'un ranch-hôtel; **d. ranch,** ranch-hôtel. **3.** type *m.*

dudgeon ['dʌdʒən] *n. Lit:* **in high d.,** fort en colère; fort indigné.

due [dju:] **I.** *a.* **1.** (*owing*) *Com: Fin:* (*of debt*) exigible; (*of bill*) échéable, échu; **bill d. on 1st May,** effet *m* payable le premier mai; **balance d.,** solde dû; **debts d. to us,** dettes actives; créances *fpl*; **debts d. by us,** dettes passives; **bond d. for repayment,** obligation amortie; (*of bill, etc.*) **to fall, become, d.,** échoir, devenir payable; **falling d.,** échéance *f*; **redemption before d. date,** remboursement anticipé. **2.** (*merited, proper*) dû, juste, mérité; **the first place is d. to Milton,** la première place revient à Milton; **to give s.o. d. warning,** avertir qn dans les formes; **with d. care,** avec tout le soin requis; **he was received with d. ceremony,** il fut reçu avec tout le cérémonial qui lui était dû; **in d. form** en bonne et due forme: **after d. consideration,** après mûre réflexion. **3.** (*a*) **d. to . . .,** causé par . . ., attribuable à . . .; **it is d. to his negligence,** c'est sa négligence qui en est (la) cause; **what is it d. to?** à quoi cela tient-il? (*b*) **d. to . . .,** par suite de . . .; **d. to fog the boat arrived late,** par suite du brouillard, le bateau est arrivé en retard. **4. the train is d. (to arrive) at two o'clock,** le train arrive à deux heures; **he is d. to arrive this evening,** il doit arriver ce soir; *F:* **I'm d. for a rise,** j'attends une augmentation de salaire. **II.** *adv.* **d. north,** droit vers le nord, plein nord. **III.** *n.* **1.** dû *m*; **to give s.o. his d.,** donner à qn ce qui lui est dû, ce qui lui revient; **one must give the devil his d.,** il faut faire la part du diable; **to pay one's dues,** payer ce qu'on doit. **2. dues,** (*a*) droits *mpl*, frais *mpl*; **market dues,** hallage *m*; *Nau:* **harbour dues,** droits de port; (*b*) (*club subscription*) cotisation annuelle. **duly** ['dju:li] *adv.* **1.** dûment; justement; **d. appointed,** (membre) régulièrement désigné. **2.** en temps voulu; **rent d. paid,** loyer payé exactement.

duel¹ ['dju(:)əl] *n.* **1.** duel *m*; affaire *f* d'honneur; **to fight a d.,** se battre en duel. **2.** lutte *f*, contestation *f*.

duel² *v.i.* **(duelled,** *NAm:* **dueled)** se battre en duel. **duelling,** *NAm:* **dueling** *n.* le duel; **d. pistols,** pistolets *mpl* de combat.

duellist, *NAm:* **duelist** ['dju(:)əlist] *n.* duelliste *m*.

duet [dju(:)'et] *n.* duo *m*; (*for piano*) morceau *m* à quatre mains.

duettist [dju(:)'etist] *n. Mus:* duettiste *mf*.

duff¹ [dʌf] *n.* **(plum) d.,** pudding *m* aux raisins.

duff² *v.tr. F:* **1.** bousiller (une affaire, etc.). **2. to d. up,** rosser (qn).

duff³ *a. F:* de mauvaise qualité; qui marche mal.

duffel ['dʌf(ə)l] *n.* = DUFFLE.

duffer ['dʌfər] *n. F:* (*a*) bousilleur, -euse; *Sch:* cancre *m* **to be a d. at (sth.),** être nul en (histoire, etc.); (*b*) cruche *f*, gourde *f*.

duffle ['dʌfl] *n.* **1.** *Cost:* **d. coat,** duffle-coat *m*, *pl.* duffle-coats. **2. d. bag,** sac marin, de campeur.

dug [dʌg] *n.* mamelle *f*, tétine *f*; pis *m* (de vache).

dugout ['dʌgaut] *n.* **1.** canot creusé dans un tronc d'arbre; pirogue *f*. **2.** *Mil: etc:* tranchée-abri *f*, *pl.* tranchées-abris.

duke¹ [dju:k] *n.* duc *m*.

duke² *v.i. U.S.* **to d. it out,** se bagarrer (avec qn).

dukedom ['dju:kdəm] *n.* **1.** duché *m*. **2.** (i) titre *m*, (ii) dignité *f*, de duc.

dulcet ['dʌlsit] *a. Lit:* (son) doux, suave, agréable.

dulcimer ['dʌlsimər] *n. A.Mus:* tympanon *m*.

dull¹ [dʌl] *a.* **1.** (*of pers.*) lent, lourd; **to be d.-witted,** avoir l'esprit lourd, engourdi; *Prov:* **all work and no play makes Jack a d. boy,** à toujours travailler les enfants s'abrutissent. **2.** (*a*) (*of pain*) sourd; (*b*) (bruit) sourd, étouffé. **3.** *Com: Fin:* (marché) calme, inactif; **the d. season,** la morte-saison; **business is d.,** les affaires languissent. **4.** (*depressed*) triste, morne. **5.** (*tedious*) triste, ennuyeux; (vie) monotone; (soirée) assommante; **as d. as ditchwater,** ennuyeux comme la pluie; **deadly d.,** abrutissant, assommant; **it's deadly d. here,** on s'ennuie à mourir ici. **6.** (*blunt*) émoussé; (*of tool, etc.*) **to become d.,** s'émousser. **7.** (*of colour, surface*) terne, mat; (style) terne; (yeux) sans éclat; **paper with a d. finish,** papier mat, non satiné. **8.** (*of weather*) triste, sombre. **dully** *adv.* **1.** lourdement, lentement. **2.** d'une manière ennuyeuse; tristement. **3.** sourdement, faiblement; sans éclat.

dull² **I.** *v.tr.* **1.** engourdir, alourdir (l'esprit); émousser (les sens). **2.** émousser (un outil). **3.** (*a*) amortir, assourdir (le son); ternir (les couleurs); dépolir (une surface); mater (un métal); (*b*) amortir (une douleur); rendre moins vif (le plaisir); **sorrow is dulled by the passage of time,** le temps émousse la douleur. **II.** *v.i.* **1.** (*of senses, etc.*) s'hébéter, s'engourdir. **2.** (*of colour*) se ternir; (*of metal, etc.*) se dépolir.

dullard ['dʌləd] *n.* lourdaud *m*; *Sch:* cancre *m*.

dul(l)ness ['dʌlnis] *n.* **1.** lourdeur *f* d'esprit; émoussement *m* (des sens). **2.** ennui *m*, tristesse *f*; monotonie *f* (de la vie, d'un discours). **3.** *Com: Fin:* stagnation *f* (des affaires); inactivité *f* (du marché). **4.** manque *m* de tranchant (d'une lame, etc.); émoussement (d'une pointe). **5.** manque d'éclat (d'une couleur); faiblesse *f* (d'un son, d'une lumière); bruit sourd (d'un coup).

duly *adv. see* DUE.

dumb [dʌm] *a.* **1.** muet, *f.* muette; **deaf and d.,** sourd-muet, *f.* sourde-muette; **d. animals,** les bêtes *fpl*; **I was struck d. with astonishment,** la stupeur me rendit muet; **d. show,** pantomime *f*; jeu muet. **2.** *F:* bête, sot, *f.* sotte; **d. cluck,** imbécile *mf*; **d. blonde,** blonde évaporée; **to play, act, d.,** faire le niais.

dumbbell ['dʌmbel] *n.* **1.** haltère *m*. **2.** *P:* sot *m*.

dumbfound [dʌm'faund] *v.tr.* abasourdir, ahurir, ébahir (qn). **dumbfounded** *a.* abasourdi, ahuri, ébahi **(at,** de); **I am d.,** je n'en reviens pas; **we were d. at the news,** la nouvelle nous frappa de stupeur.

dumbness ['dʌmnis] *n.* **1.** mutisme *m*; **deaf and d.,** surdi-mutité *f*. **2.** *F:* sottise *f*; bêtise *f*.

dumbwaiter ['dʌmweitər] *n.* **1.** (*a*) *Furn:* servante *f*; (*b*) plateau tournant. **2.** *NAm:* monte-plats *m inv*.

dumdum ['dʌmdʌm] *n. Mil:* **d. (bullet),** (balle *f*) dum-dum (*f*), *pl.* dum-dums.

dummy ['dʌmi] *n.* **1.** (*a*) homme *m* de paille; prête-nom *m inv;* (*b*) sot *m*, lourdaud *m*. **2.** (*a*) *Dressm: Tail:* mannequin *m*; (*in shop window*) figure *f* de cire; *F:* **standing there like a stuffed d.,** planté comme un piquet; (*b*) marionnette *f* (de ventriloque); (*c*) chose *f* factice, faux paquet; *Mil:* simulacre *m* (de grenade, etc.); *Publ:* maquette *f* (d'un livre); (*d*) **(baby's) d.,** sucette *f*; tétine *f*. **3.** *Cards:* (*player or hand at bridge, whist*) mort *m*; **to be, play, d.,** faire le mort; **d. bridge,** bridge *m* à trois personnes; **d. whist,** whist *m* avec un mort. **4.** *attrib.* (*a*) factice; faux, *f.* fausse; **d. run,** (i) *Navy:* évolution *f* d'entraînement; (ii) *Mil.Av:* incursion aérienne sans bombardement; (iii) *F:* coup *m* d'essai. **5.** *Sp:* feinte *f*.

dump¹ [dʌmp] *n.* **1.** tas *m*, amas *m* (de déchets, etc.). **2.** (*a*) chantier *m* de dépôt; dépôt *m* des déblais; (lieu *m* de) décharge (*f*); **refuse, rubbish, d.,** décharge; (*b*) *F:* taudis *m*; **what a d.!** (i) (*of place*) quel trou! quel bled! (ii) (*of office, etc.*) quelle boîte! **3.** dépôt (de vivres, etc.); *Mil:* **ammunition d.,** dépôt de munitions; parc *m* à munitions. **4.** *Cmptr:* **memory, storage, d.,** vidage *m* (de) mémoire. **5.** (*a*) *Civ.E: etc:* basculeur *m*, culbuteur *m*; (*b*) **d. truck,** tombereau *m*, dumper *m*.

dump² *v.tr.* **1.** (*a*) décharger, déverser (une charretée de sable, etc.); jeter (les ordures) à la voirie; (*b*) **to d. (down),** laisser tomber lourdement (un ballot, etc.); déposer (qn) rudement (sur une chaise, etc.); (*c*) *Av:* se délester de (la cargaison); (*d*) *F:* **to d. s.o.,** (i) se débarrasser de qn; (ii) abandonner qn, *F:* planquer qn. **2.** faire un dépôt de (vivres, etc.). **3.** *Com:* **to d. goods on a foreign market,** écouler à perte des marchandises à l'étranger; faire du dumping. **4.** *Cmptr:* (i) vider, (ii) mettre en réserve (un stockage). **dumping** *n.* **1.** (*a*) **d. bucket,** benne basculante; (*b*) dépôt *m*, déversement *m*; **d. ground,** (lieu *m* de) décharge (*f*); déversement *m*. **2.** *Com:* dumping *m* (du trop-plein de la production). **3.** *Cmptr:* vidage *m* (d'une mémoire).

dumper ['dʌmpər] *n. Civ.E: etc:* **d. (truck),** tombereau *m*, dumper *m*.

dumpling ['dʌmpliŋ] *n. Cu:* (*a*) boulette de pâte (servie avec un ragoût, etc.); (*b*) **apple d.,** pomme enrobée (dans de la pâte et cuite au four); (*c*) *F:* (*pers*) boulot, -otte.

dumps [dʌmps] *n.pl. F:* cafard *m*; idées noires; **to be down in the d.,** broyer du noir; avoir le cafard.

dumpy ['dʌmpi] *a.* (*of pers., etc.*) trapu, boulot.

dun[1] [dʌn] **1.** *a.* brun grisâtre. **2.** *a.* & *n.* (cheval) gris louvet.

dun[2] *v.tr.* **(dunned)** importuner, harceler (un débiteur); **dunned by his creditors,** pressé par ses créanciers.

dunce [dʌns] *n. Sch:* cancre *m*; **dunce's cap,** bonnet *m* d'âne.

dunderhead ['dʌndəhed] *n. F:* imbécile *mf.*

dune [dju:n] *n.* **(sand) d.,** dune *f.*

dung [dʌŋ] *n.* **1.** fiente *f*, crotte *f*; (*of wild animal*) fumées *fpl*; bouse *f* (de vache); crottin *m* (de cheval); *Ent:* **d. beetle,** bousier *m.* **2.** *Agr:* fumier *m*, engrais *m.*

dungaree [dʌŋgə'ri:] *n.* **1.** *Tex:* treillis *m.* **2. dungarees,** combinaison *f*; *F:* salopette *f*; bleus *mpl* (de mécanicien).

dungeon ['dʌn(d)ʒ(ə)n] *n.* **1.** cachot *m* (d'un château du moyen âge). **2.** (*tower*) donjon *m.*

dunghill ['dʌŋhil] *n.* tas *m* de fumier; fumier *m.*

dunk [dʌŋk] *v.tr.* tremper (du pain, un croissant) (dans son café, etc.); *F:* faire trempette.

Dunkirk [dʌn'kə:k] *Pr.n. Geog:* Dunkerque *f.*

dunlin ['dʌnlin] *n. Orn:* bécasseau *m* variable.

dunno [dʌ'nou] *P:* (*corruption de* **don't know**) sais pas!

dunnock ['dʌnək] *n. Orn:* accenteur *m* mouchet.

duo ['dju(:)ou] *n. Mus:* duo *m.*

duodecimal [dju(:)ou'desim(ə)l] **1.** *a.* duodécimal, -aux. **2.** *n.pl. Mth:* **duodecimals,** multiplication duodécimale; calcul *m* par le système duodécimal.

duodenal [dju(:)ou'di:n(ə)l] *a. Anat: Med:* (ulcère, etc.) duodénal, -aux.

duodenum, *pl.* **-na, -nums** [dju(:)ou'di:nəm, -nə, -nəmz] *n. Anat:* duodénum *m.*

dupe[1] [dju:p] *n.* dupe *f.*

dupe[2] *v.tr.* duper, tromper; **to be duped,** se laisser duper.

duple ['dju:pl] *a. Mus:* **d. time,** mesure *f* à deux temps.

duplex ['dju:pleks] *a.* **1.** double; duplex *inv*; (*a*) *Mec.E:* **d. lathe,** tour *m* à double outil; **d. crank,** manivelle *f* double; (*b*) *El: Tp:* (ligne, voie) duplex; (exploitation, etc.) en duplex. **2.** *a.* & *n. NAm:* **d. (house),** maison *f* pour deux familles; **d. (apartment),** appartement *m* à deux étages; duplex *m.*

duplicate[1] ['dju:plikət] **1.** *a.* (en) double; *Jur:* (document) ampliatif; **d. set of tools,** outils *mpl* de rechange; **d. receipt,** duplicata *m* d'un. **2.** *n.* (*a*) double *m*, répétition *f* (d'une œuvre d'art, etc.); (*b*) duplicata (d'un chèque, etc.); double, contrepartie *f* (d'un écrit); ampliation *f* (d'un acte); **in d.,** (en) double; en duplicata; en double exemplaire.

duplicate[2] ['dju:plikeit] *v.tr.* (*a*) faire le double de (qch.); copier (un document); reproduire (un document) en double exemplaire; (*b*) tirer plusieurs exemplaires (d'une lettre circulaire) au duplicateur; polycopier (une lettre circulaire). **duplicating** *n.* **1.** duplication *f.* **2.** tirage *m* de plusieurs exemplaires (d'une lettre, etc.) au duplicateur; **d. machine,** duplicateur *m*; machine *f* à polycopier.

duplication [dju:pli'keiʃ(ə)n] *n.* duplication *f*; répétition *f*, reproduction *f.*

duplicator ['dju:plikeitər] *n.* duplicateur *m*; machine *f* à polycopier.

duplicity [dju'plisiti] *n.* duplicité *f*; mauvaise foi.

durability [dju:rə'biliti] *n.* durabilité *f*; *Ind:* résistance *f* (des matériaux, etc.).

durable ['dju:rəbl] *a.* (*a*) durable; résistant; (tissu) résistant; (*b*) *Com:* **d. goods,** *n.pl.* **(consumer) durables,** biens.

duration [dju'reiʃ(ə)n] *n.* durée *f*; étendue *f* (de la vie); **the peace was of short d.,** la paix fut de courte durée; **for the d.,** (i) *Mil:* (s'engager) pour la durée de la guerre; (ii) *F:* jusqu'à la Saint-Glinglin.

duress [dju'res] *n.* **1.** emprisonnement *m.* **2.** *Jur:* contrainte *f*, coercition *f*; **to act under d.,** agir sous la contrainte.

during ['dju:riŋ] *prep.* pendant, durant; **d. his life,** pendant sa vie; **d. the whole week,** toute la semaine; **d. the winter,** au cours de l'hiver; **d. the journey,** en cours de route; **d. the last year,** dans le courant de l'année dernière; **killed d. a brawl,** tué au cours d'une rixe; **d. that time,** pendant ce temps.

dusk [dʌsk] *n.* crépuscule *m*; **at d.,** à la nuit tombante à la tombée de la nuit.

duskiness ['dʌskinis] *n.* **1.** demi-jour *m.* **2.** (*of complexion*) teint (i) brun, bistré, (ii) noiraud.

dusky ['dʌski] *a.* **1.** sombre, obscur. **2.** (*a*) (*of complexion*) brun foncé *inv*; mat; (*b*) noirâtre.

dust[1] [dʌst] *n.* **1.** poussière *f*; (*a*) **to cover sth. with d.,** couvrir qch. de poussière; **to raise a cloud of d.,** soulever un nuage de poussière; **to reduce sth. to d.,** réduire, qch. en poussière; **to trample s.o. in the d.,** fouler qn aux pieds; **to bite the d.,** mordre la poussière; **to shake the d. off one's feet,** secouer la poussière de ses pieds; **to throw d. in s.o.'s eyes,** jeter de la poudre aux yeux de qn; **to kick up, raise, a d.,** faire une scène, *P:* faire du foin; (*b*) poussière (de brique); sciure *f* (de marbre); *Ph:* **cosmic d.,** poussière cosmique; (*c*) **d. bag,** sac *m* à poussière; (*of bird*) **to take a d. bath,** s'ébrouer dans la poussière; *Mec.E:* **d. collector,** capteur *m* de poussières; **d. jacket, wrapper** = DUSTCOVER 2; **d. sheet,** housse *f* (pour meubles); *Mec.E: etc:* **d. trap,** (i) *Ind:* attrape-poussières *m inv*; (ii) nid *m* à poussière; *Geog:* **d. bowl,** zone *f* semi-aride, semi-désertique. **2.** cendres *fpl* (d'un mort); **ashes to ashes, d. to d.,** cendres aux cendres, poudre à la poudre; **all their hopes had turned to d. and ashes,** tous leurs espoirs s'étaient anéantis.

dust[2] *v.tr.* **1.** saupoudrer (un gâteau, etc.) **(with,** de). **2.** épousseter (une pièce, un meuble). **dusting** *n.* **1.** (*a*) saupoudrage *m* (d'un gâteau, etc.); *Phot:* poudrage *m*; **d. powder,** (i) *Toil:* (poudre *f* de) talc (*m*); (ii) *Med:* poudre antiseptique. **2.** (*a*) époussetage *m* (d'une pièce, d'un meuble, etc.).

dustbin ['dʌs(t)bin] *n.* poubelle *f.*

dustcart ['dʌs(t)kɑ:t] *n.* camion *m* d'enlèvement des ordures ménagères; camion des boueux.

dustcloud ['dʌstklaud] *n.* nuage *m* de poussière.

dustcoat ['dʌs(t)kout] *n. Cost: O:* cache-poussière *m inv.*

dustcover ['dʌs(t)kʌvər] *n.* **1.** housse *f* (pour fauteuil, etc.). **2.** *Bookb:* chemise *f*, jaquette *f* (d'un livre); couverture *f* (en papier).

duster ['dʌstər] *n.* **1.** chiffon *m* (à épousseter); torchon *m*; **feather d.,** plumeau *m f*; *Sch:* **blackboard d.,** chiffon (à effacer). **2.** *Nau: P:* pavillon *m*; **red d.** = pavillon marchand. **3.** *NAm: Cost:* **d. (coat),** manteau léger; *O:* cache-poussière *m inv.*

dustiness ['dʌstinis] *n.* état poudreux, poussiéreux.

dustman, *pl.* **-men** ['dʌs(t)mən] *n.m.* boueur, boueux, éboueur.

dustpan ['dʌs(t)pæn] *n.* pelle *f* à poussière.

duststorm ['dʌst(st)ɔ:m] *n.* tempête *f* de poussière.

dustup ['dʌstʌp] *n. F:* querelle *f*; *F:* coup *m* de torchon; **to have a d. with s.o.,** se quereller avec qn.

dusty ['dʌsti] *a.* **1.** poussiéreux, poudreux; recouvert de poussière; **to get d.,** se couvrir de poussière. **2.** *P: O:* **it's not so d.,** ce n'est pas si mauvais; *F:* c'est pas mal du tout. **4.** *F:* **d. answer,** réponse décevante; **I gave him a d. answer,** je l'ai enyoyé promener.

Dutch[1] [dʌtʃ] **1.** *a.* (*a*) (costume, etc.) hollandais; (fromage, etc.) de Hollande; (Gouvernement) néerlandais; **D. barn,** hangar *m* à récoltes; **D. oven,** cocotte *f*; (*b*) *F:* **D. courage,** bravoure *f* après boire; **D. treat,** régal *m* où chacun paie son écot; *adv.* **to go D.,** payer son écot; **to talk to s.o. like a D. uncle,** faire la morale à qn; (*c*) *U.S:* allemand, de souche allemande. **2.** *n.* (*a*) **the D. (people),** les Hollandais *mpl*; (*b*) *Ling:* (i) le hollandais; (ii) *S. Africa:* **Cape D.,** afrikaans *m*; (iii) *F:* **to talk double D.,** baragouiner; **it's all double D. to me,** (i) je ne peux rien comprendre à ce baragouin; (ii) c'est de l'hébreu pour moi.

dutch² *n. P:* **my old d.,** ma femme; ma vieille.

Dutchman, *pl.* **-men** ['dʌtʃmən] *n.m.* **1.** Hollandais; *F:* **if that's a real diamond (then) I'm a D.,** si c'est un vrai diamant je mange mon chapeau. **2.** *U.S:* Allemand; Américain de souche allemande.

dutiable ['dju:tiəbl] *a.* soumis à des droits; imposable, taxable; *Cust:* soumis aux droits de douane.

dutiful ['dju:tif(u)l] *a.* (*of child, etc.*) respectueux; soumis; **a d. husband,** un mari plein d'égards pour sa femme. **-fully** *adv.* avec soumission; respectueusement.

duty ['dju:ti] *n.* **1.** obéissance *f*, respect *m*; **to pay one's d. to s.o.,** présenter ses hommages à qn. **2.** devoir *m* (**to,** envers); **to do one's d.,** faire son devoir; **to fail in one's d.,** manquer à son devoir; **to do one's d. by s.o.,** remplir son devoir envers qn; **I shall make it my d. to ...,** je considérerai de mon devoir de ...; **you are (in) d. bound to do it,** votre devoir vous y oblige; **from a sense of d.,** par devoir; **to pay a d. call,** faire une visite de politesse. **3.** (*a*) *usu.pl.* fonction(s) *f* (*pl*); attributions *fpl*; **public duties,** fonctions publiques; **to take up one's duties,** entrer en fonctions, en charge; **to hand over one's duties,** (i) résigner ses fonctions; (ii) remettre ses fonctions (**to,** à); (*b*) *Mil:* mission *f*; tâche *f*; **to be on detached d.,** *U.S:* **on temporary d.,** être en mission. **4.** service *m*; (*a*) **to be on d.,** être de service; (*in factory, playground, etc.*) être de surveillance; *Navy:* être de service, de corvée; **to be off d.,** ne pas être de service; **to do d. for s.o.,** remplacer qn (dans son service); **d. chart, roster,** tableau *m* de service; (*b*) *Mil: Navy: etc:* **while on d.,** dans l'exécution du service; **active d.,** (i) service actif; (ii) activité *f* de service; **on guard d.,** de service de garde; **fatigue d.,** corvée *f*; **d. officer, d. N.C.O.,** officier *m*, sous-officier *m*, de service; **tour of d.,** tour *m* de service. **5.** droit *m*; (*a*) **customs d.,** droit(s) de douane; **liable to d.,** passible de droits; **d. paid,** franc de douane; (*b*) **stamp d.,** droit de timbre. **6.** *Mec.E: etc:* **heavy-d.,** (machine) à grand rendement, à fort débit; (appareil) soumis à un travail très dur; (cric, etc.) pour poids lourds.

duty-free ['dju:ti'fri:] *a.* exempt de droit; franc de tout droit; *Cust:* **d.-f. shop,** magasin *m* hors taxes.

duvet ['dju:vei] *n.* couette *f*; *Sw.Fr:* duvet *m*; **d. cover,** housse *f* de couette.

dwarf¹ [dwɔ:f] (*a*) *n. Myth:* nain *m*; (*b*) *n. & a.* (*of pers.*) nain, *f.* naine; (*of plant*) (i) nain; (ii) rabougri; **d. tree,** arbre nain.

dwarf² *v.tr.* **1.** empêcher (qn, qch.) de croître; rabougrir (une plante). **2.** rapetisser (par contraste); **tower that dwarfs the main building,** tour *f* dont la hauteur écrase le corps de bâtiment.

dwarfish ['dwɔ:fiʃ] *a.* (de) nain; chétif.

dwell [dwel] *v.i.* (*p.t. & p.p.* **dwelt** [dwelt]) **1.** *Lit:* **to d. in a place,** habiter (dans) un lieu. **2.** rester; se fixer; **this hope dwells within our hearts,** cet espoir repose dans notre cœur; **to let one's eye d. on s.o.,** arrêter son regard, sur qn. **3. to d. on (sth.),** insister sur, s'étendre sur (un sujet); appuyer sur (une syllabe, etc.); faire ressortir (les difficultés). **dwelling** *n.* **d. (place),** (i) *Lit:* lieu *m* de séjour; (ii) domicile *m*, demeure *f*; **d. house,** maison *f* d'habitation.

dweller ['dwelər] *n.* habitant, -ante (**in, on,** de); **cave d.,** troglodyte *mf*.

dwindle ['dwindl] *v.i.* **to d. (away),** diminuer, dépérir; (*of political party*) s'amenuiser; **to d. to nothing,** se réduire à rien. **dwindling 1.** *a.* diminuant, faiblissant. **2.** *n.* diminution *f*, dépérissement *m*; amenuisement *m* (d'un parti politique); *Fin:* déperdition *f* (de capital).

dye¹ [dai] *n.* **1.** (*a*) *Dy:* teinture *f*, teint *m*; **fast d.,** bon teint; (*b*) teinte *f*; *Lit:* **villain of the deepest d.,** coquin fieffé. **2.** matière colorante; teinture, colorant *m*; *Phot:* **d. solution,** bain colorant.

dye² *v.* (*pr.p.* **dyeing**) **1.** *v.tr.* teindre; **to d. sth. black,** teindre qch. en noir; **to have a dress dyed,** faire teindre une robe. **2.** *v.i.* (se) teindre; **material that dyes well,** tissu qui prend bien la teinture. **dyeing** *n.* **1.** teinture *f* (d'étoffes, des cheveux). **2.** (*trade*) teinturerie *f*.

dyed-in-the-wool ['daidinðə'wul] *a.* (drap) teint en laine; *Fig:* invétéré; inébranlable; **a d.-in-t.-w. Englishman,** un Anglais pur sang.

dyer ['daiər] *n.* teinturier *m*; **d. and cleaner,** teinturier dégraisseur.

dyestuff ['daistʌf] *n.* matière colorante; colorant *m*.

dyeworks ['daiwə:ks] *n.pl.* (*usu. with sg. const.*) teinturerie *f*.

dying. *see* DIE².

dyke¹ [daik] *n.* **1.** (*a*) *Hyd.E:* digue *f*, levée *f*; (*b*) chaussée surélevée, en remblai. **2.** fossé *m*, chenal *m*, -aux.

dyke² *v.tr.* endiguer (un cours d'eau); protéger (un terrain) par des digues.

dynamic [dai'næmik] *a.* (*a*) *Ph:* (pouvoir, etc.) dynamique; (*of force, etc.*) **to become d.,** se dynamiser; (*b*) *Fig:* **d. personality, character,** caractère *m* dynamique; (*c*) *Mus:* **d. range,** dynamique *f* (d'un instrument). **-ally** *adv.* dynamiquement.

dynamics [dai'næmiks] *n.pl.* (*usu. with sg. const.*) dynamique *f*.

dynamism ['dainəmizm] *n.* dynamisme *m*.

dynamite¹ ['dainəmait] *n.* dynamite *f*; *F:* **subject that is political d.,** sujet explosif; *P:* **it's d.!** c'est du tonnerre!

dynamite² *v.tr.* faire sauter (des roches, etc.) à la dynamite; dynamiter (un édifice, etc.).

dynamo, *pl.* **-os** ['dainəmou, -ouz] *n.* dynamo *f*; génératrice *f*, générateur *m* (de courant); *F:* **he's a human d.,** il a une énergie extraordinaire.

dynastic [di'næstik] *a.* dynastique.

dynasty ['dinəsti] *n.* dynastie *f*.

dyne [dain] *n. Ph.Meas:* dyne *f*.

dysentery ['disəntri] *n. Med:* dysenterie *f*; **amoebic d.,** dysenterie amibienne.

dyslectic [dis'lektik], **dyslexic** [dis'leksik] *a. & n. Med:* dyslexique (*mf*).

dyslexia [dis'leksiə] *n. Med:* dyslexie *f*.

dysmenorrhoea, *NAm:* **dysmenorrhea** [dismenə'riə] *n. Med:* dysménorrhée *f*.

dyspepsia [dis'pepsiə] *n. Med:* dyspepsie *f*; **acid d.,** aigreurs *fpl*, *F:* brûlures *fpl*, d'estomac.

dyspeptic [dis'peptik] **1.** *a. & n. Med:* dyspepsique (*mf*), dyspeptique (*mf*). **2.** *a. F:* mélancolique.

dystrophy ['distrəfi] *n. Med:* dystrophie *f*; **muscular d.,** dystrophie musculaire progressive.

E

E, e [iː] *n.* **1.** (la lettre) E, e *m.* **2.** *Mus:* mi *m*; **key of E flat,** clef *f* de mi bémol.
each [iːtʃ] **1.** *a.* chaque; **e. day,** chaque jour; tous les jours; **e. elector has two votes,** chaque électeur a deux voix; **e. one of us,** chacun, chacune, de nous, d'entre nous. **2.** *pron.* (*a*) chacun, -une; **e. of us,** chacun, chacune, d'entre nous; (*b*) **we e. earn £10, we earn £10 e.,** nous gagnons £10 chacun; **peaches at 5p e.,** pêches à 5p chacune, 5p pièce; **a little of e.,** un peu de chaque; (*c*) **e. other,** l'un l'autre, l'une l'autre; les uns les autres, les unes les autres; **separated from e. other,** séparés l'un de l'autre; **to fight e. other,** se battre; **they flatter e. other,** ils se flattent réciproquement.
eager [ˈiːgər] *a.* passionné; vif (désir, espoir); (regard) avide; **to be e. to do sth.,** être impatient de faire qch.; *F:* **an e. beaver,** un(e) zélé(e). **-ly** *adv.* passionnément, avidement; **to desire sth. e.,** désirer qch. passionnément; **to listen e.,** écouter avidement, avec empressement.
eagerness [ˈiːgənis] *n.* impatience *f* (de voir qn); empressement *m* (à se rendre utile, etc.); vif désir (d'apprendre qch. etc.); **to show e. in doing sth.,** montrer un intérêt très vif à faire qch.; **e. to succeed,** ardent désir de réussir.
eagle [ˈiːgl] *n.* **1.** *Orn:* (*a*) aigle *m*; **golden e.,** aigle royal; (*b*) **sea e.,** pygargue *m.* **2.** (*a*) *Her:* aigle *f*; **double-headed e.,** aigle à deux têtes; (*b*) *Mil: U.S:* aigle (insigne de grade de colonel); (*c*) *Ecc:* **e. lectern,** aigle. **5.** *Golf:* deux coups *mpl* sous la normale; eagle *m*, Fr.C: aiglon *m.*
eagle-eyed [ˈiːglˈaid] *a.* aux yeux d'aigle.
eaglet [ˈiːglit] *n. Orn:* aiglon *m.*
ear¹ [ˈiər] *n.* **1.** oreille *f*; (*a*) *Anat:* **the external e.,** (i) l'oreille externe; (ii) le pavillon de l'oreille; **the middle e.,** l'oreille moyenne; **the internal e.,** l'oreille interne; *Med:* **e., nose and throat specialist,** oto-rhino-laryngologiste *mf*; (*b*) **e. trumpet,** cornet *m* acoustique; **e. muff,** protège-oreilles *m inv.*, cache-oreilles *m inv.*; **e. protector,** (i) protège-tympan *m inv*; (ii) *Rugby Fb:* protège-oreilles; **a smile from e. to e.,** un sourire épanoui jusqu'aux deux oreilles; (*of words*) **to go in at one e. and out at the other,** entrer par une oreille et sortir par l'autre; **your ears must have been burning,** les oreilles ont dû vous tinter; **to prick (up) one's ears,** (i) (*of animal*) dresser les oreilles; (ii) (*of pers.*) tendre, dresser, l'oreille; **up to one's ears in work,** accablé de travail; *F:* **to be thrown out on one's e.,** se faire sortir; **to send s.o. away with a flea in his e.,** (i) renvoyer qn avec un refus net et catégorique; (ii) éconduire qn avec une verte semonce; **to box s.o.'s ears,** gifler, *F:* talocher, qn; *P:* **to get a thick e.,** recevoir une gifle, une taloche; **walls have ears,** les murs ont des oreilles; **dog's e.,** corne faite à la page d'un livre; (*c*) **to have sharp ears,** avoir l'ouïe fine; **deaf in one e.,** sourd(e) d'une oreille; **to have an e. for music,** avoir l'oreille musicale; **to play by e.,** jouer d'oreille; *F:* **to play it by e.,** aller au pifomètre; **to keep one's ears open, one's e. to the ground,** se tenir aux écoutes; **I'm all ears,** j'écoute; **to lend an e., lend one's e., to s.o.,** prêter l'oreille à qn; **to close one's ears to the truth,** fermer l'oreille à la vérité; **you might drop this hint into his e.,** glissez-lui cet avis à l'oreille; (*of sound*) **to greet the e.,** frapper l'oreille. **2.** *Tchn:* (*a*) anse *f*, oreille (de vase); anse (de cloche); (*b*) *Conch:* oreillette *f* (d'un coquillage).
ear² *n.* épi *m* (de blé); **wheat in the e.,** blé en épi.
earache [ˈiːəreik] *n.* mal *m* d'oreille(s); *Med:* otalgie *f*; **to have e.,** avoir mal à l'oreille, aux oreilles.
eardrum [ˈiːədrʌm] *n. Anat:* tympan *m* (de l'oreille).
eared [ˈiːəd] *a.* (*in compounds*) **long-, short-e.,** aux oreilles longues, courtes.
earflap [ˈiːəflæp] *n.* oreillette *f* (de casquette).
earful [ˈiːəful] *n.* **I got an e. of water,** j'ai eu l'oreille pleine d'eau; *F:* **to give s.o. an e.,** (i) donner une verte semonce à qn; (ii) dire son fait à qn.
earhole [ˈiːəhoul] *n.* trou *m* de l'oreille.
earl [əːl] *n.m.* (*f.* **countess,** *q.v.*) comte.
earldom [ˈəːldəm] *n.* **1.** comté *m.* **2.** titre *m* de comte.
early [ˈəːli] **I.** *a.* **(earlier, earliest) 1.** (*a*) (heure, silence, etc.) matinal(e); **in the e. morning,** de bon matin; **e. morning walk,** promenade matinale; **in the e. afternoon,** au commencement de l'après-midi; **to have an e. dinner,** dîner de bonne heure; **e. rising,** l'habitude *f* de se lever de bonne heure; **to be an e. riser,** être matinal; se lever de bon matin; **I'm going to have an e. night,** je vais me coucher de bonne heure; *Prov:* **the e. bird catches the worm,** heure du matin, heure du gain; **in (the) e. summer, in the e. part of summer,** dans les, aux, premiers jours de l'été; au commencement de l'été; *Com: etc:* **e. closing day,** jour où les magasins sont fermés l'après-midi; **it's e. days yet,** il est encore trop tôt (to, pour); (*b*) **the earliest times,** les temps les plus reculés; **the e. Church,** l'Église primitive; **e. Christians,** les premiers chrétiens; **in the e. nineteenth century,** au début du XIXᵉ siècle; **in the early sixties,** au début des années soixante; **from the earliest times,** de toute ancienneté; **the earliest legends,** les premières légendes; *Art:* **the e. masters,** les primitifs; (*c*) **e. youth,** première jeunesse; **e. age,** âge tendre; **at an e. age,** tout jeune; **from the earliest age,** dès la plus tendre enfance; **my earliest recollections,** mes souvenirs les plus lointains; **he received his e. education at . . .,** il reçut sa première éducation à . . .. **2.** précoce, hâtif; (mort) prématurée; **e. beans,** (i) haricots précoces; (ii) haricots de primeur; **e. vegetables, fruit, produce,** primeurs *fpl*; **we're having an e. winter,** l'hiver *m* est précoce. **3.** prochain, rapproché; **at an e. date,** prochainement; à une date prochaine; **at an earlier date,** (i) à une date antérieure; (ii) à une date plus rapprochée; **to take an e. opportunity to do sth.,** faire qch. à la première occasion; **at the earliest possible moment,** dans le plus bref délai possible; **next week at the earliest,** la semaine prochaine au plus tôt; **at your earliest convenience,** au premier moment favorable; le plus tôt possible. **II.** *adv.* **1.** (*a*) de bonne heure; tôt; **earlier,** plus tôt; **as I mentioned earlier,** comme j'ai mentionné (i) plus tôt, (ii) ci-dessus, plus haut; **too e.,** trop tôt; **to arrive five minutes (too) e.,** arriver avec cinq minutes d'avance; **I am half an hour e.,** je suis en avance d'une demi-heure; **e. in the morning,** le matin de bonne heure; de grand matin; **e. in the evening,** très tôt dans la soirée; **to get up e.,** se lever de bonne heure; **e. in the winter,** à l'entrée de l'hiver; **e. in the year,** au début de l'année; **e. on it was apparent**

that . . ., dès l'abord il a apparu que . . .; **e. in (his) life,** dans ses jeunes années; dans sa jeunesse; **e. in his career,** au début de sa carrière; **as e. as the tenth century,** dès le dixième siècle; **as e. as possible,** le plus tôt possible; (*b*) **to die e.,** mourir (i) jeune, (ii) prématurément; **this flower blooms very e.,** cette fleur s'épanouit trés précocement. **2. e. in the list,** tout au commencement de la liste.

early-warning ['ɜːli'wɔːniŋ] *a. Mil: etc:* **e.-w. system,** réseau *m* de radars de guet, de pré-alerte.

earmark¹ ['iːəmɑːk] *n. Husb:* marque *f* à l'oreille (d'un mouton, etc.).

earmark² *v.tr.* **1.** *Husb:* marquer (les moutons, etc.) à l'oreille. **2.** (*a*) faire une marque au coin (d'un document, un chèque); (*b*) donner (à des fonds) une affectation spéciale; **to e. funds for a purpose,** assigner des fonds à un projet; *F:* **to e. sth. for oneself,** se réserver qch.

earn [ɜːn] *v.tr.* **1.** gagner (de l'argent); **to e. one's living by writing,** gagner sa vie à écrire; *Ind:* **earning capacity,** rapport *m* (d'une entreprise). **2.** mériter, gagner (l'affection de qn); **his conduct earned him universal praise,** sa conduite lui valut les éloges de tous. **earnings** ['ɜːniŋz] *n.pl.* **1.** salaire *m*; appointements *mpl*; **my e.,** ce que je gagne; *Jur:* **living on immoral e.,** vagabondage spécial. **2.** profits *mpl*, bénéfices *mpl* (d'une entreprise); **gross e.,** bénéfices bruts; **net(t) e.,** bénéfices nets.

earnest¹ ['ɜːnist] **1.** *a.* (*a*) (*of pers.*) sérieux; (air) pénétré, grave; (*b*) (demande) pressante; (prière) fervente; sérieux (effort); profond (désir). **2.** *n.* **in e.,** sérieusement; pour de bon; **to be in e.,** être sérieux; ne pas plaisanter; **are you in e.?** parlez-vous sérieusement? **to speak in e.,** parler sérieusement; **I thought you were in e.,** je vous ai pris au sérieux; **to set to work in e.,** se mettre sérieusement à l'ouvrage; **half in jest, half in e.,** moitié plaisantant, moitié sérieux. **-ly** *adv.* (parler) sérieusement; **we e. hope that . . .,** nous espérons bien sincèrement que . . ..

earnest² *n. Com: etc: O:* arrhes *fpl.*

earnestness ['ɜːnistnis] *n.* caractère sérieux (d'une discussion); gravité *f*, sérieux *m* (de ton); ferveur *f* (d'une prière).

earphone ['iːəfoun] *n. W.Tel: Tp:* écouteur *m.*

earpiece ['iːəpiːs] *n. Tp:* écouteur *m* (de récepteur).

earpiercing ['iːəpiːəsiŋ] *a.* (cri) qui vous perce les oreilles.

earplug ['iːəplʌg] *n.* (*a*) (*for sleeping*) boule *f* Quiès (*R.t.m.*); (*b*) protège-tympan *m inv.*

earring ['iːəriŋ] *n.* boucle *f* d'oreille; **stud e.,** dormeuse *f*; **drop e.,** pendant *m* d'oreille.

earshot ['iːəʃɔt] *n.* **within, out of, e.,** à portée de voix, hors de portée de la voix.

earsplitting ['iːəsplitiŋ] *a.* (cri) qui vous fend les oreilles; (bruit) à briser, crever, le tympan.

earth¹ [ɜːθ] *n.* **1.** terre *f*; (*a*) le monde; **the earth's crust,** l'écorce *f* terrestre; **the earth's atmosphere,** l'atmosphère *f* terrestre; **on e.,** sur terre; *B:* **in e. as it is in heaven,** sur la terre comme au ciel; *F:* **where, why, on e. . . .?** où, pourquoi, diable . . .? **there's no reason on e.,** il n'y a absolument aucune raison; **it wouldn't cost the e.,** ça ne coûterait pas les yeux de la tête; (*b*) le sol; *F:* **to come back to e.,** revenir sur terre; **down to e.,** (i) réaliste, qui a les pieds sur terre; (ii) terre à terre. **2.** (*a*) *Agr: etc:* terre; **loose, heavy, e.,** terre(s) meuble(s), lourde(s); (*b*) *Ch:* **fuller's e.,** terre à foulon. **3.** *El:* (*a*) terre, masse *f*; **e. cable, wire,** câble *m*, fil *m*, de terre; **e. connection,** prise *f* de terre; (*b*) mise *f* à la terre; **dead e.,** contact parfait avec le sol; (*of car, etc.*) **e. to frame,** contact à la masse. **4.** terrier *m*, tanière *f* (de renard); (*of fox*) **to go to e.,** se terrer; **to run to e.,** (i) chasser (un renard) jusqu'à son terrier; (ii) découvrir la source d'une erreur de calcul, etc.; dénicher (qn); découvrir la retraite de (qn).

earth² **1.** *v.tr.* (*a*) *Hort:* **to e. (up),** butter, chausser (une plante); (*b*) *El:* mettre (le courant) à la terre; (*c*) *Ven:* poursuivre (un renard) jusqu'à son terrier. **2.** *v.i.* (*of fox*) se terrer.

earthbound ['ɜːθbaund] *a.* (*a*) terre à terre *inv*; (*b*) **e. spirit,** fantôme *m* qui ne peut pas quitter le monde des vivants; (*c*) qui se dirige vers la terre.

earthen ['ɜːθ(ə)n] *a.* en, de, terre (cuite).

earthenware ['ɜːθ(ə)nwɛər] *n.* poterie *f* (de terre); argile cuite; **glazed e.,** (i) faïence *f*; (ii) grès flambé; **e. jug,** cruche *f* en, de, terre (cuite).

earthfall ['ɜːθfɔːl] *n.* éboulement *m* de terres.

earthlight ['ɜːθlait] *n. Astr:* lumière cendrée (de la lune).

earthling ['ɜːθliŋ] *n.* habitant, -ante, de la terre.

earthly ['ɜːθli] *a.* **1.** terrestre; **the E. Paradise,** le Paradis terrestre. **2.** *F:* **there's no e. reason for . . .,** il n'y a pas la moindre raison du monde pour . . .; **it's of no e. use to me,** ça ne me sert, ne me servirait, à rien; **he hasn't an e. chance,** *F:* **an e.,** il n'a pas la moindre chance (de réussir).

earthmover ['ɜːθmuːvər] *n.* bulldozer *m.*

earthquake ['ɜːθkweik] *n.* tremblement *m* de terre; séisme *m.*

earthwork ['ɜːθwɜːk] *n.* **1.** (travaux *mpl* de) terrassement (*m*); **e. embankment,** terrassement en remblai. **2. earthworks,** (i) *Prehist:* fortifications *fpl* en terre; (ii) *Civ.E: etc:* travaux en terre, de terrassement.

earthworm ['ɜːθwɜːm] *n.* lombric *m*; ver *m* de terre.

earthy ['ɜːθi] *a.* **1.** terreux; **to have an e. smell,** sentir la terre. **2.** (*of pers.*) terre à terre; (*of humour*) truculent.

earwig ['iːəwig] *n. Ent:* perce-oreille *m*, *pl.* perce-oreilles.

ease¹ [iːz] *n.* **1.** (*a*) tranquillité *f* (d'esprit); repos *m*, bien-être *m* (du corps); **to be at e.,** avoir l'esprit tranquille; **to be, feel, ill at e.,** (i) être mal à l'aise; (ii) être inquiet (**about,** au sujet de); **to be at one's e.,** (i) être à son aise; (ii) être tranquille; **to put s.o. at e.,** (i) mettre qn à son aise; (ii) tranquilliser qn; **set your mind at e.,** rassurez-vous; soyez tranquille; **to take one's e.,** se mettre à l'aise; *Mil: etc:* **to stand at e.,** se mettre, se tenir, au repos; **stand at e.!** repos! (*b*) **e. from pain,** soulagement *m*; **chapel of e.,** (chapelle *f* de) secours (*m*); annexe *f*. **2.** (*a*) loisir *m*; (*b*) oisiveté *f*. **3.** (*a*) aisance (de manières, etc.); moelleux *m* (des mouvements); (*b*) facilité *f* (d'élocution, etc.); simplicité *f* (de réglage); douceur *f*, facilité (de manœuvre); **with e.,** facilement; aisément; **with the utmost e., the greatest of e.,** avec la plus grande facilité.

ease² **1.** *v.tr.* (*a*) (i) adoucir, calmer, alléger (la souffrance); soulager, apporter du soulagement à (un malade); (ii) tranquilliser (l'esprit); **to e. s.o.'s anxiety,** calmer les inquiétudes de qn; (*b*) débarrasser, délivrer (**s.o. of, from, sth.,** qn de qch.); **to e. oneself of a burden,** se soulager d'un fardeau; (*c*) (i) détendre, relâcher (un cordage, un ressort); desserrer (une vis); *Mch: etc:* modérer, soulager (la pression); **to e. the congestion in a street,** décongestionner la circulation d'une rue; (ii) *Dressm:* donner plus d'ampleur à (une robe); *Mec.E:* donner du jeu à (un organe); *Const:* ajuster (une porte); (*d*) (i) déplacer doucement; **to e. a load off a cart,** faire glisser à terre la charge d'une charrette; (ii) **to e. one's way through a crowd,** se faufiler à travers la foule. **2.** *v.i.* (*a*) (*of pain, rain, etc.*) s'atténuer; (*b*) (*of tension, St.Exch: of market, etc.*) se détendre; **the situation has eased,** la situation s'est détendue. **ease off 1.**

v.tr. (*a*) *Nau:* filer, choquer (un cordage); (*b*) dégager (une surface d'appui, etc.). **2.** *v.i.* (*a*) (*of pers.*) se relâcher; moins travailler; (*of pain, rain*) s'atténuer; (*b*) *St.Exch:* (*of rates*) se détendre; (*c*) *Nau:* s'éloigner un peu du rivage. **ease up 1.** *v.tr. Nau:* soulager (un palan). **2.** *v.i.* (*a*) se relâcher; moins travailler; (*b*) diminuer la vitesse; ralentir. **easing** *n.* **1.** (*a*) soulagement *m* (de la souffrance); (*b*) allègement *m* (d'une poutre, etc.). **2.** *Civ.E:* adoucissement (d'une courbe). **3. e. of tension,** détente *f* (politique, etc.); **e. of the market,** détente du marché. **4. e. off,** (*a*) atténuation *f* (de la douleur, etc.); (*b*) relâchement *m* (**from work,** du travail); (*c*) *St.Exch:* détente.

easel ['i:zl] *n.* chevalet *m* (de peintre, etc.).

easiness ['i:zinis] *n.* **1.** bien-être *m*, commodité *f.* **2.** grâce *f* (du style, etc.). **3.** indifférence *f*, insouciance *f.* **4.** facilité *f* (d'un travail). **5.** (*a*) complaisance *f*, humeur *f* facile (de qn); (*b*) jeu *m* facile (d'une machine). **6.** *Pol.Ec:* aisance *f*, facilité; **monetary e.,** aisance monétaire (du marché).

east [i:st] **1.** *n.* (*a*) est *m*; **house facing (the) e.,** maison exposée à l'est; **on the e., to the e.,** à l'est (**of,** de); (*b*) **the E.,** l'Orient; **the Middle E.,** le Moyen-Orient; **the Far E.,** l'Extrême-Orient; (*c*) **the e. of England,** l'est de l'Angleterre. **2.** *adv.* à l'est; **to travel e.,** voyager vers l'est; **e. of the Rhine,** à l'est du Rhin; **the wind blows e.,** le vent vient de l'est. **3.** *a.* (côte, etc.) est; (vent) d'est; (pays) de l'est; (mur, fenêtre) qui fait face à l'est; **e. coast,** côte *f* est; **e. end,** chevet *m* (d'une église); **the E. End,** les quartiers pauvres et populeux de la partie est (de Londres).

eastbound ['i:stbaund] *a.* (*of train, etc.*) allant vers l'est; (*on underground*) en direction de la banlieue est.

Easter ['i:stər] *n.* **1.** Pâques *m*; **E. Day, E. Sunday,** le jour, le dimanche, de Pâques; **E. week,** (i) la semaine de Pâques; (ii) la semaine sainte; **E. egg,** œuf *m* de Pâques. **2.** *Geog:* **E. Island,** l'île *f* de Pâques.

easterly ['i:stəli] **1.** *a.* (vent) d'est, qui vient de l'est; (courant) qui se dirige vers l'est; (point) situé à, vers, l'est. **2.** *adv.* vers l'est. **3.** *n.* vent *m* d'est.

eastern ['i:stən] **1.** *a.* (*a*) est, de l'est; oriental, -aux; **the E. Church,** l'Église d'Orient. **2.** *n. U.S:* oriental, -ale.

Easterner ['i:stənər] *n.* (*a*) oriental, -ale; (*b*) *U.S:* habitant, -ante, des États de l'est.

Eastertide ['i:stətaid] *n.* Pâques *m.*

eastward ['i:stwəd] **1.** *a.* (*a*) à l'est; dans l'est; (*b*) du côté de l'est. **2.** *adv.* = EASTWARDS.

eastwards ['i:stwədz] *adv.* à l'est; vers l'est.

easy ['i:zi] **I.** *a.* **(easier, easiest) 1.** (*a*) à l'aise; *F:* **she's e. on the eye,** elle n'est pas mal du tout; (*b*) sans inquiétude; (vie) sans souci; **to be e. in one's mind,** avoir l'esprit tranquille; **with an e. conscience,** la conscience tranquille. **2.** (*a*) (*of manners, etc.*) libre, dégagé; (style) facile, naturel; (*b*) **my coat is an e. fit,** mon veston est ample; (*c*) (mouvement) moelleux; *Mec.E:* **e. fit,** ajustage *m* lâche. **3.** (*a*) (travail) facile, aisé; (méthode, solution) simple; **that is e. to see,** cela se voit; **it is e. for him to . . .,** il lui est facile de . . .; **it's e. to say . . .,** on a vite fait de dire . . .; **this will make your job easier,** ce procédé facilitera votre tâche; **within e. distance, within e. reach, of . . .,** à distance commode de . . .; *F:* **as e. as A B C, as e. as falling off a log,** simple comme bonjour; **it isn't e.,** ce n'est pas facile; *F:* **e. money,** argent gagné sans peine; (*b*) (*of pers.*) facile, accommodant; **e. to get on with,** d'un commerce facile; **e. to live with,** facile à vivre; *F:* **I'm e.!** ça m'est égal! **woman of e. virtue,** femme de mœurs faciles; (*c*) **by e. stages,** (voyager) à petites étapes; **at an e. pace,** à petite vitesse; *Com:* **by e. payments, on e. terms,** avec facilités *fpl* de paiement; *Sp: etc:* **to come in an e. first,** arriver bon premier; *F:* **to have an e. time,** se la couler douce. **4.** *Com:* (marché) tranquille; **prices are (getting) easier,** on accuse une détente dans les prix; **cotton was easier,** le coton a accusé une détente. **II.** *adv.* **1.** (*a*) **to take things e., to take it e.,** prendre les choses en douceur; **take it e.!** ne vous en faites pas! **you'll have to go e. for a bit,** il va falloir freiner un peu; **to take life e.,** se laisser vivre; **to go e. with sth., s.o.,** ménager qch., qn; **e. does it!** (allez-y) doucement! **go e. on the electricity,** allez-y doucement avec l'électricité; (*b*) *Nau: Row:* **e. (ahead)!** (en avant) doucement! (*c*) *Mil:* **stand e.!** repos! **2.** *F:* **I can do it e.,** cela me sera facile; **easier said than done,** c'est plus facile à dire qu'à faire; *Prov:* **e. come e. go,** ce qui vient par la flûte s'en va par le tambour. **easily** *adv.* **1.** à son aise; **to take things, life, e.,** prendre le temps comme il vient; se laisser vivre; se la couler douce. **2.** (*a*) doucement; sans effort; **the door shuts e.,** la porte se ferme sans effort; (*b*) avec confort; **the car holds six people e.,** on tient à l'aise six personnes dans cette voiture. **3.** facilement, sans difficulté; **you can e. imagine my disappointment,** vous concevez sans peine ma déception; **he is not e. satisfied,** il n'est pas facile, aisé, à satisfaire; **e. moved,** facile à émouvoir; **he came in e. first,** il est arrivé bon premier; **he is e. forty,** il a bien quarante ans.

easy-going ['i:zi'gouiŋ] *a.* **1.** (*of horse*) à l'allure douce. **2.** (*of pers.*) (*a*) qui prend les choses tranquillement; qui ne se fait pas de bile; (*b*) accommodant, coulant; peu exigeant; (*c*) d'humeur facile; **an e.-g. man,** un homme facile à vivre; (*d*) qui a la conscience élastique.

eat [i:t] *v.tr.* **(ate** [et, *esp. NAm:* eit]; **eaten** ['i:tn]**) 1.** (*a*) manger (du pain, de la soupe, etc.); **to e. one's breakfast, dinner, supper,** déjeuner, dîner, souper; **to e. a good dinner,** faire un bon dîner; *Prov:* **you can't have your cake and e. it,** on ne peut pas avoir le drap et l'argent; **fit to e.,** bon à manger; mangeable; **to e. like a horse,** manger comme un ogre; **to e. one's fill,** manger à sa faim; *Fig:* **to e. one's heart out,** se ronger le cœur; *F:* **he eats out of my hand,** il fait tout ce que je veux; **he won't e. you,** il ne vous mangera pas; **to e. one's words,** se rétracter; *F:* **to e. humble pie,** s'humilier (devant qn); **if it comes off, I'll e. my hat,** si ça réussit, je mange mon chapeau; **to e. s.o. out of house and home,** ruiner qn en nourriture; (*of insect, worm*) **to e. into wood,** ronger le bois; (*b*) prendre ses repas; dîner; **we e. at seven,** nous dînons à sept heures; *F:* **let's e.!** à table! **2.** *F:* **what's eating you?** quelle mouche vous pique? qu'est-ce qui vous prend? **eat away** *v.tr.* éroder, miner (des roches, une falaise); saper (des fondations); (*of acid*) dissoudre, attaquer (un métal). **eating** *n.* **1.** manger *m*; **e. chocolate,** chocolat *m* à croquer; **e. apple,** pomme *f* à couteau, de dessert. **2. e. away,** corrosion *f* (du métal, etc.); érosion *f* (du littoral). **eat off** *v.tr.* (*of horse, etc.*) **to e. its head off,** coûter plus à nourrir qu'il ne vaut; *F:* (*of pers.*) **to e. one's head off,** s'empiffrer. **eat up** *v.tr.* (*a*) manger jusqu'à la dernière miette (un gâteau, etc.); **e. up your bread!** finis ton pain! **to e. up the miles,** dévorer la route; (*b*) épuiser les provisions de (qn); (*c*) consumer (qch.) sans profit; **stove that eats up the coal,** poêle qui mange beaucoup de charbon; (*d*) **to be eaten up (with sth.),** être dévoré (d'orgueil); consumé (par l'ambition).

eatable ['i:təbl] **1.** *a.* mangeable, bon à manger; **fruit that is quite e.,** fruit *m* qui se laisse manger. **2.** *n.pl.* **eatables,** provisions *fpl* de bouche; comestibles *mpl.*

eater ['i:tər] *n.* **1.** mangeur, -euse; **small, big, e.,** petit, gros, mangeur. **2.** fruit *m* à couteau, de dessert.

eatery [ˈiːtəri] *n. F:* café-restaurant *m.*
eating-house [ˈiːtiŋhaus] *n.* restaurant *m*; **cheap e.-h.,** gargote *f.*
eats [iːts] *n.pl. F:* le manger; **plenty of e.,** amplement de quoi manger.
eau-de-Cologne [ˈoudəkəˈloun] *n. Toil:* eau *f* de Cologne.
eaves [iːvz] *n.pl. Const:* avant-toit *m.*
eavesdrop [ˈiːvzdrɔp] *v.i.* **(eavesdropped)** écouter aux portes; **to e. on a conversation,** écouter indiscrètement une conversation privée.
eavesdropper [ˈiːvzdrɔpər] *n.* oreille indiscrète.
ebb¹ [eb] *n.* **1.** reflux *m*; baisse *f* (de la marée); **the e. and flow,** le flux et le reflux; **e. tide,** marée descendante; marée de jusant; **the tide is on the e.,** la marée baisse. **2.** déclin *m* (de la fortune, de la vie); **the patient is at a low e.,** le malade est très bas; **to be at one's lowest e.,** (i) être dans un très grand abattement; (ii) être à bout de ressources.
ebb² *v.i.* **1.** (*of tide*) baisser; **to e. and flow,** monter et baisser. **2.** (*of life, etc.*) décliner; être sur le déclin; **to e. away,** s'écouler; **his life was ebbing away,** il baissait d'heure en heure. **ebbing** *a.* (*a*) (eaux) qui refluent; (*b*) (fortune, etc.) sur le déclin; **e. strength,** forces diminuantes.
ebonite [ˈəbənait] *n.* ébonite *f*; vulcanite *f.*
ebony [ˈebəni] *n.* (*a*) (bois *m* d')ébène (*f*); **e. box,** boîte en bois d'ébène; (*b*) **e. (tree),** ébénier *m.*
ebullience [iˈbʌliəns] *n.* bouillonnement *m*, effervescence *f* (de la colère, de la jeunesse, etc.).
ebullient [iˈbʌliənt] *a.* enthousiaste, exubérant.
eccentric [ekˈsentrik] **1.** *a.* (*a*) *Mth: Astr:* (cercle, etc.) excentrique; (*b*) *Mec.E:* (came) désaxée; (arbre) excentré; (*c*) (*of pers.*) excentrique; original, -aux. **2.** *n.* (*a*) *Mec.E:* excentrique *m*; (*b*) (*of pers.*) excentrique; original, -ale. **-ally** *adv.* excentriquement.
eccentricity [eksenˈtrisiti] *n.* **1.** (*a*) excentricité *f* (d'une ellipse); (*b*) *Mec.E:* excentricité, désaxage *m.* **2.** (*a*) excentricité (de caractère); originalité *f* **(in,** de); (*b*) **eccentricities,** excentricités (de qn).
ecclesiastic [ikliːziˈæstik] *a.* & *n.* ecclésiastique (*m*).
ecclesiastical [ikliːziˈæstikl] *a.* (habit, etc.) ecclésiastique.
echelon [ˈeʃəlɔn] *n.* **1.** *Mil:* échelon *m*; **in e.,** en échelon. **2. the higher echelons of industry,** les niveaux supérieurs de l'industrie.
echo¹, *pl.* **-oes** [ˈekou, -ouz] *n.* écho *m*; **e. sounding,** sondage *m* par ultra-sons; **e. sounder,** écho-sondeur *m, pl.* écho-sondeurs; **e. chamber,** chambre *f* sonore.
echo² **1.** *v.tr.* répéter (en écho); **to e. s.o.'s opinions,** se faire l'écho des opinions de qn. **2.** *v.i.* (*a*) faire écho; **the woods echoed with the songs of birds,** les bois retentissaient des chants des oiseaux; **room that does not e.,** pièce sourde; (*b*) retentir; **his voice echoes through the room,** sa voix résonne dans la salle.
éclair [eiˈklɛər] *n. Cu:* éclair *m*; **chocolate e.,** éclair au chocolat.
eclectic [eˈklektik] *a.* & *n.* éclectique (*m*).
eclecticism [eˈklektisizm] *n.* éclecticisme *m.*
eclipse¹ [iˈklips] *n.* (*a*) *Astr:* éclipse *f*; **solar, lunar, e.,** éclipse de soleil, de lune; **total, partial, e.,** éclipse totale, partielle; (*b*) *Nau:* éclipse (d'un phare); (*c*) **to suffer an e.,** être éclipsé.
eclipse² *v.tr.* (*a*) éclipser (la lune, la lumière d'un phare, etc.); (*b*) éclipser, surpasser (qn).
ecliptic [iˈkliptik] *a. Astr:* écliptique.
ecological [iːkəˈlɔdʒikl] *a.* écologique.
ecologist [iːˈkɔlədʒist] *n.* écologiste *m.*
ecology [iːˈkɔlədʒi] *n.* écologie *f.*
economic [iːkəˈnɔmik] *a.* **1.** économique; **European E. Community,** Communauté Économique Européenne. **2.** (loyer) rentable.
economical [iːkəˈnɔmikl] *a.* (*a*) (*of pers.*) économe; **to be e. with sth.,** économiser qch.; (*b*) (*of apparatus, etc.*) économique; **e. speed,** vitesse *f* économique (d'un navire, etc.). **-ally** *adv.* économiquement; **to use sth. e.,** ménager qch.
economics [iːkəˈnɔmiks] *n.pl.* (*usu. with sg. const.*) **1.** les sciences *fpl* économiques; l'économie *f* politique. **2.** rentabilité *f* (d'un projet); **the e. of town planning,** les aspects financiers de l'urbanisme.
economist [i(ː)ˈkɔnəmist] *n.* **1.** personne *f* économe **(of,** de). **2. (political) e.,** économiste *m.*
economize [i(ː)ˈkɔnəmaiz] **1.** *v.tr.* économiser, ménager (le temps, l'argent, etc.). **2.** *v.i.* économiser, faire des économies; **to e. on sth.,** économiser sur qch.
economy [i(ː)ˈkɔnəmi] *n.* **1.** économie *f* (d'argent, etc.); **e. in fuel consumption,** économie de combustible; **to practise e.,** économiser; *Nau: Av:* **e. class,** classe *f* économique. **2.** (*a*) **political e.,** économie politique; **planned e.,** économie planifiée; (*b*) économie, régime *m* économique (d'un pays). **3. domestic e.,** économie domestique.
ecstasy [ˈekstəsi] *n.* **1.** transport *m* (de joie), joie délirante; ravissement *m*; **to be in an e. of joy,** se pâmer de joie; **to go into ecstasies over sth.,** s'extasier devant qch. **2.** extase (religieuse, etc.).
ecstatic [ekˈstætik] *a.* extatique. **-ally** *adv.* avec extase; **e. happy,** heureux jusqu'au ravissement.
ectoplasm [ˈektouplæzm] *n.* ectoplasme *m.*
Ecuador [ˈekwədɔːr] *Pr.n. Geog:* (la République de) l'Équateur *m.*
Ecuadorian [ekwəˈdɔːriən] *Geog:* **1.** *a.* écuadorien, équatorien. **2.** *n.* Écuadorien, -ienne; Équatorien, -ienne.
ecumenical [iːkjuˈmenikl] *a. Ecc:* (conseil) œcuménique.
eczema [ˈeksimə] *n. Med:* eczéma *m.*
eddy¹ [edi] *n.* **1.** (*of water, wind*) remous *m*; tourbillon *m.* **2.** *El:* **e. currents,** courants *m* de Foucault; courants parasites.
eddy² *v.i.* (*of water*) faire des remous; (*of wind*) tourbillonner, tournoyer.
edelweiss [ˈeid(ə)lvais] *n. Bot:* édelweiss *m.*
edema [iːˈdiːmə] *n. esp. NAm:* œdème *m.*
Eden [ˈiːdn] *Pr.n. B:* **(the Garden of) E.,** l'Éden *m*; le Paradis terrestre.
edge¹ [edʒ] *n.* **1.** (*a*) fil *m*, tranchant *m* (d'une lame); angle *m* (d'un outil); **to give s.o. the rough e. of one's tongue,** dire son fait à qn; (*b*) **knife with a keen e. on it,** couteau à tranchant aigu; **to put an e. on a tool,** aiguiser, affiler, un outil; **e. tool,** outil tranchant; **to take the e. off (sth.),** émousser (l'appétit); gâter (le plaisir); couper tout l'effet (d'un argument). **2.** (*a*) arête *f*, angle (d'une pierre, etc.); **sharp, rounded, e.,** arête vive mousse; *Carp: etc:* **feather e.,** biseau *m*; (*b*) (*of skating*) carre *f* (de patin); **inside, outside, e.,** dedans *m*, dehors *m*; (*c*) lèvre *f* (d'une plaie); (*d*) *Tls: Carp:* **straight e.,** limande *f.* **3.** bord *m*, rebord *m* (de table, de vase); tranche *f* (d'une planche); tranche (d'une médaille); *Bookb:* tranche (de livre); **gilt edges,** tranches dorées; **with gilt edges,** doré sur tranches; *Num:* **milled e.,** crénelage *m*, grènetis *m*; *Av:* **leading, trailing, e.,** bord d'attaque, de fuite (de l'aile); **on e.,** (i) (*of brick*) de chant, de can; (ii) (*of pers.*) énervé, nerveux; **to set on e.,** (i) mettre de chant, de can; (ii) faire grincer (les dents à qn); agacer (les nerfs); crisper, énerver (qn); **it sets my teeth on e.,** cela me fait mal aux dents; **she is on e. today,** elle est nerveuse aujourd'hui; *F:* **to have an, the, e. on s.o.,** être avantagé par rapport à qn. **4.** lisière *f*, bordure *f*, orée *f* (d'un bois); bord, rive (d'une rivière); bordure *f* (d'un route); marge *f* (d'un chemin); limite *f* (d'une plaine); liséré *m*, bord (d'une

étoffe, etc.); *Phot: etc:* (*of print*) **white e.,** liséré blanc; *Hort:* **e. trimmer, cutter,** coupe-bordure *m*, *pl.* coupe-bordure(s); **at the water's e.,** au bord de l'eau; **at the e. of a precipice,** au bord d'un précipice.

edge² *v.tr. & i.* **1.** (*a*) affiler, aiguiser (un couteau); affûter (un outil); (*b*) repiquer (une meule); (*c*) *Metalw:* tomber (un bord de tôle). **2.** border (une étoffe, la route) (**with,** de); lisérer (une jupe). **3. to e. (one's way) into a room,** se faufiler, se glisser, dans une pièce; **to e. one's chair nearer,** rapprocher, avancer, sa chaise peu à peu; **to e. towards s.o., sth.,** s'approcher tout doucement de qn, qch. **edge away** *v.i.* s'éloigner, s'écarter, tout doucement (**from s.o.,** de qn). **edged** *a.* **1.** (*of tool, etc.*) tranchant, acéré. **2.** (*in compound adjs.*) (*a*) à tranchant; **chisel-e.,** taillé en lame; (*b*) **gilt-e.,** doré sur tranche; **deckle-e.,** (papier) à bords non ébarbés; (*c*) **double-e.,** (épée, compliment) à deux tranchants. **edging** *n.* **1.** pose *f* d'un liséré, d'une ganse (à une robe, etc.); entretien *m* de la bordure (d'une pelouse, etc.); **e. tool,** coupe-gazon *m inv*, tranche-gazon *m inv*, molette *f*; **e. shears,** cisaille *f* à bordures. **2.** *Dressm: Furn: etc:* liséré *m*, passement *m*, ganse *f*; *Mil:* contour *m* (d'épaulette); *Hort:* bordure *f* (de parterre, etc.).

edgeways, edgewise ['edʒweiz, -waiz] *adv.* **1.** (vu) latéralement, de côté. **2.** de chant; **to lay, set, a plank e.,** placer une planche de chant; *F:* **I can't get a word in e.,** impossible de placer un mot (dans la conversation). **3.** (*of two things*) côte à côte; (*of two boards*) affronté.

edginess ['edʒinis] *n. F:* nervosité *f*.

edgy ['edʒi] *a. F:* (*of pers.*) énervé; **to get e.,** s'énerver.

edible ['edibl] **1.** *a.* comestible; bon à manger; mangeable; **e. oil,** huile *f* comestible. **2.** *n.pl.* **edibles,** comestibles *mpl*.

edict ['i:dikt] *n. Hist:* édit *m*; *Hist:* **the E. of Nantes,** l'Édit de Nantes.

edification [edifi'keiʃ(ə)n] *n.* édification *f* (de la jeunesse, etc.); instruction *f*.

edifice ['edifis] *n.* édifice *m*.

edify ['edifai] *v.tr.* édifier (qn); **edifying,** (spectacle, livre, etc.) édifiant.

Edinburgh ['edinbrə] *Pr.n. Geog:* Édimbourg.

edit ['edit] *v.tr.* (*a*) préparer (un texte) pour la publication; annoter (le texte d'un auteur); donner une édition annotée (d'une œuvre); diriger (une série de textes, etc.); (*b*) rédiger, diriger (un journal, une revue); **edited by . . .,** (série, journal, etc.) sous la direction de . . .; (*c*) *Cin:* monter (un film). **editing** *n.* (*a*) préparation *f*, annotation *f* (d'un texte); (*b*) rédaction *f*, direction *f* (d'un journal); (*c*) *Cin:* montage *m* (d'un film).

edition [i'diʃ(ə)n] *n. Publ:* édition *f* (d'un ouvrage); **limited e.,** édition à tirage limité; **school e.,** édition scolaire **cheap e.,** édition populaire; **book in its fourth e.,** livre à sa quatrième édition; **first e.,** édition originale.

editor ['editər] *n.* **1.** éditeur *m* (d'un texte); auteur *m* (d'une édition critique). **2.** (*a*) surveillant *m* de la publication; directeur *m* (d'une série, d'un dictionnaire); (*b*) rédacteur *m* en chef, directeur (d'une revue, d'un journal); **news e.,** rédacteur au service des informations; (*c*) *Journ:* titulaire *m* d'une rubrique, chroniqueur *m*; **sports e.,** rédacteur sportif; (*d*) *W.Tel:* **programme e.,** éditorialiste *mf*; (*e*) *Cin:* monteur *m* (d'un film).

editorial [edi'tɔ:riəl] **1.** *a.* éditorial, -aux; **e. office,** (salle *f* de) rédaction (*f*); **the e. staff,** la rédaction. **2.** *n. Journ:* article *m* de fond; éditorial *m*.

educable ['edjukəbl] *a.* éducable.

educate ['edjukeit] *v.tr.* **1.** (*a*) donner de l'instruction à, instruire (qn); **he was educated in France,** il a fait ses études en France; (*b*) faire faire ses études à (son enfant). **2.** former (qn, le goût de qn). **educated** *a.* (homme) instruit, lettré; **self e.,** autodidacte.

education [edju'keiʃ(ə)n] *n.* **1.** éducation *f*; **a man without e.,** un homme sans éducation. **2.** enseignement *m*, instruction *f*; **compulsory e.,** enseignement obligatoire; **primary, secondary, e.,** enseignement primaire, secondaire; **higher, university, e.,** enseignement supérieur; études supérieures; **further e.,** enseignement post-scolaire; **adult e.,** enseignement des adultes; **Department of E. and Science,** Ministère *m* de l'Éducation nationale; **he has a good e.,** il a reçu une bonne instruction.

educational [edju'keiʃən(ə)l] *a.* (maison, ouvrage) d'éducation, d'enseignement; (ouvrage) éducateur; (programme) scolaire; (procédé) éducatif, pédagogique; **e. film,** film éducatif; **for e. purposes,** pour l'enseignement. **-ally** *adv.* (*of child*) **e. subnormal,** arriéré.

education(al)ist [edju'keiʃən(əl)ist] *n.* educateur, -trice; pédagogue *mf*.

educator ['edjukeitər] *n.* éducateur, -trice.

Edward ['edwəd] *Pr.n.m.* Édouard.

Edwardian [ed'wɔ:diən] *a.* qui a rapport à l'époque du roi Édouard VII; **the E. era,** la belle époque.

eel [i:l] *n. Ich:* **1.** (*a*) anguille *f*; **e. basket, pot,** nasse *f* à anguilles; *Cu:* **jellied eels,** anguilles en gelée; **he's as slippery as an e.,** il vous glisse entre les doigts; (*b*) **conger e.,** congre *m*, anguille de mer. **2. electric e.,** anguille électrique. **3.** *Ann:* **e. worm,** anguillule *f*.

eerie, eery ['iəri] *a.* surnaturel; qui donne le frisson. **-ily** *adv.* étrangement; à donner le frisson.

eeriness ['iərinis] *n.* étrangeté surnaturelle (d'un lieu, d'un son, etc.).

efface [i'feis] *v.tr.* (*a*) effacer; oblitérer (une inscription, la mémoire de qch., etc.); (*b*) **to e. oneself,** s'effacer; se tenir à l'écart.

effacement [i'feismənt] *n.* effacement *m*; **self-e.,** effacement (de soi-même).

effect¹ [i'fekt] *n.* **1.** (*a*) effet *m*; résultat *m*, conséquence *f* (d'un fait); **the e. of heat on metals,** l'action de la chaleur sur les métaux; **cause and e.,** la cause et l'effet; **the effects of the economic crisis,** les effets de la crise économique; **after effects,** suites *fpl*, répercussions *fpl* (d'un événement); séquelles *fpl* (d'une maladie); **side effects,** réactions secondaires; *Ch: etc:* réactions latérales; **to have an e. on s.o., sth.,** faire, produire, de l'effet sur qn, sur qch.; affecter qn, qch.; **to have no e.,** ne faire, ne produire, aucun effet; (*b*) réalisation *f*; **to take e.,** (i) faire (son) effet; (ii) (*of regulation, etc.*) entrer en vigueur; (iii) (*of drugs*) agir, opérer; (*of vaccination*) prendre; **law that takes, comes into, e. today,** loi qui entre en vigueur à partir d'aujourd'hui; **to no e.,** en vain, sans résultat; **to bring, carry (sth.) into e.,** mettre (qch.) à exécution; exécuter, effectuer, réaliser (qch.); donner suite à (une décision, etc.); (*c*) sens *m*, teneur *f* (d'un document); **to the e. that . . .,** (clause) portant que . . .; **we have made provisions to this e.,** nous avons pris des dispositions dans ce sens; **that is what he said, or words to that e.,** voilà ce qu'il a dit, ou quelque chose d'approchant; (*d*) *Elcs: etc:* **flicker e.,** effet de scintillation; *Ph:* **Joule e.,** effet Joule. **2.** (*a*) **moonlight e.,** effet de lune; *Th: etc:* **stage effects,** jeux *mpl* scéniques; **sound effects,** bruitage *m*; *Cin: T.V: etc:* **special effects,** trucage *m*; (*b*) **words meant for e.,** phrases à effet; **it has a good e.,** cela fait bon effet. **3. in e.,** en fait, en réalité; **that is in e. a refusal,** c'est de fait un refus. **4. personal effects,** effets, biens, personnels; **household effects,** *Jur:* **movable effects,** biens mobiliers.

effect² *v.tr.* effectuer, réaliser, exécuter (qch.); *Mil:* opérer (une retraite); **to e. a payment,** effectuer un paiement.

effective [i'fektiv] **1.** *a.* (*a*) (moyen, remède, etc.) efficace; **the medicine was e.,** le médicament a produit son effet; (*b*) *Pol.Ec: etc:* (rendement) effectif; *El:* (charge) efficace; (fréquence) utile; *Mec.E:* **e. power,** rendement; **e. range,** (i) *Elcs:* étendue *f* de mesure; (ii) portée *f* utile (d'une arme à feu); (iii) *Av:* rayon *m* d'action; (*c*) (contraste) frappant, saisissant; (réponse) pleine d'à-propos; (discours) qui fait de l'effet; (orateur) dont les paroles portent; (*d*) *Adm:* **e. date,** date *f* d'entrée en vigueur; (*of decree, etc.*) **to become e.,** entrer en vigueur; **e. as from October 10,** applicable à partir du 10 octobre. **2.** *npl. Mil:* **effectives,** effectifs *mpl.* **-ly** *adv.* **1.** efficacement, utilement. **2.** effectivement, en réalité. **3.** d'une façon frappante.

effectiveness [i'fektivnis] *n.* **1.** efficacité *f.* **2.** effet heureux.

effectual [i'fektjuəl] *a.* **1.** efficace. **2.** (contrat) valide; (réglement) en vigueur. **-ally** *adv.* efficacement.

effeminacy [i'feminəsi] *n.* caractère efféminé.

effeminate [i'feminət] *a.* & *n.* effeminé (*m*).

effervesce [efə'ves] *v.i.* (*a*) être, entrer, en effervescence; (*of drinks*) mousser; (*b*) (*of pers.*) pétiller de joie, d'animation.

effervescence [efə'vesəns] *n.* (*a*) effervescence *f* (d'un liquide); (*b*) pétillement *m* (de la jeunesse, etc.).

effervescent [efə'vesənt] *a.* **1.** effervescent; (boisson) gazeuse. **2.** (*of pers.*) effervescent.

effete [i'fi:t] *a.* (*of civilization, method, etc.*) caduc, -uque; (*of pers.*) mou, veule.

efficacious [efi'keiʃəs] *a.* efficace.

efficaciousness [efi'keiʃəsnis], **efficacy** ['efikəsi] *n.* efficacité *f.*

efficiency [i'fiʃənsi] *n.* **1.** (*a*) efficacité *f*; (*b*) rendement (d'une machine, etc.); *Mec.E:* effet *m* utile; **e. expert,** expert *m* en organisation; (*c*) bon fonctionnement (d'une administration, etc.). **2.** (*of pers.*) capacité *f*; compétence *f.*

efficient [i'fiʃənt] *a.* (*a*) (*of method, work*) effectif, efficace; (*b*) *Mec.E:* (machine) (i) à bon rendement, (ii) d'un fonctionnement sûr; (*c*) (*of pers.*) capable, compétent; **to be e. in one's work,** se montrer capable dans son travail. **-ly** *adv.* (*a*) efficacement; (*b*) avec compétence.

effigy ['efidʒi] *n.* effigie *f*; **to burn, hang, s.o. in e.,** brûler, pendre, qn en effigie.

efflorescence [eflə'resəns] *n.* **1.** *Bot:* floraison *f.* **2.** *Ch: Med: etc:* efflorescence *f.*

efflorescent [eflə'resənt] *a. Bot:* efflorescent.

effluence ['efluəns] *n.* émanation *f*, effluence *f.*

effluent ['efluənt] *n.* **1.** *a.* effluent; **e. drain,** canalisation *f* de sortie (d'un collecteur d'eaux d'égout, etc.). **2.** *n.* effluent *m* (de collecteur d'eaux d'égout).

effluvium, *pl.* **-ia** [e'flu:viəm, -iə] *n.* (*a*) effluve *m*, émanation *f*; (*b*) *Pej:* émanation désagréable, fétide.

effort ['efət] *n.* **1.** (*a*) effort *m*; **physical e.,** effort physique; **without e.,** sans effort; **to make an e. to do sth.,** faire (un) effort pour faire qch.; **wasted e.,** peine perdue; (*b*) essai *m*; **that's not a bad e.,** ce n'est pas mal réussi; (*c*) **literary, artistic, e.,** œuvre *f* littéraire, artistique; *F:* **what do you think of his latest e.?** qu'est-ce que vous pensez de ce qu'il vient de faire? **2.** *Mec:* effort (de traction, etc.); poussée *f*, travail *m.*

effortless ['efətlis] *a.* **1.** qui ne fait aucun effort. **2.** (*a*) sans effort; (*b*) facile. **-ly** *adv.* sans effort.

effrontery [i'frʌntəri] *n.* effronterie *f.*

effusion [i'fju:ʒ(ə)n] *n.* effusion *f.*

effusive [i'fju:siv] *a.* démonstratif, expansif; (style) exubérant; (compliments) sans fin; **to be e. in one's thanks,** se confondre en remerciements. **-ly** *adv.* avec effusion; **to thank s.o. e.,** se confondre en remerciements.

effusiveness [i'fju:sivnis] *n.* effusion *f*; volubilité *f.*

egalitarian [igæli'tɛəriən] *a.* & *n.* égalitaire (*mf*).

egalitarianism [igæli'tɛəriənizm] *n.* égalitarisme *m.*

egg¹ [eg] *n.* **1.** (*a*) *Biol:* œuf *m*; **e. tooth,** dent *f* d'éclosion; (*b*) œuf (de poule, etc.); *Comest:* **free-range eggs,** œufs de ferme; *Cu:* **boiled e.,** œuf à la coque; **hard-boiled, soft-boiled, e.,** œuf dur, mollet; **fried e.,** œuf sur le plat; **poached e.,** œuf poché; **scrambled eggs,** œufs brouillés; **Scotch e.,** œuf dur entouré de chair à saucisse; **eggs and bacon,** œufs au jambon, au bacon; **e. flip, e. nog** = lait *m* de poule; **e. beater, whisk,** batteur *m*, fouet *m*, à œufs; **e. timer,** sablier *m*; **e. spoon,** cuillère *f* à œufs; **e. and spoon race,** course dans laquelle les coureurs doivent porter un œuf dans une cuillère; **e. white,** blanc *m* d'œuf; **e. yolk,** jaune *m* d'œuf; *F:* **as sure as eggs is eggs,** aussi sûr que deux et deux font quatre; **to have e. on one's face,** être couvert de ridicule; **you can't teach your grandmother to suck eggs,** ce n'est pas aux vieux singes qu'on apprend à faire des grimaces; **a bad e.,** un vaurien; *F: O:* **a good e.,** un type épatant; *Prov:* **don't put all your eggs into one basket,** il ne faut pas mettre tous ses œufs dans le même panier; (*c*) œuf (d'insecte); lente *f* (de pou). **2.** (*a*) **darning e.,** œuf à repriser; (*b*) **tea e.,** boule *f* à thé.

egg² *v.tr.* **to e. s.o. on (to do sth.),** pousser, inciter, qn (à faire qch.).

eggcup ['egkʌp] *n.* coquetier *m.*

egghead ['eghed] *n. F:* intellectuel, -elle, cerveau *m.*

egg-laying ['egleiiŋ] **1.** *a.* ovipare. **2.** *n.* ponte *f.*

eggplant ['egplɑ:nt] *n. Bot:* aubergine *f.*

egg-shaped ['egʃeipt] *a.* ovoïde; ovoïdal, -aux.

eggshell ['egʃel] *n.* coquille *f* (d'œuf); *Cer:* **e. china,** coquille d'œuf; *Paint:* **e. finish,** fini *m* coquille d'œuf.

eggy ['egi] *a. F:* taché, souillé, de jaune d'œuf.

egis ['i:dʒis] *n. NAm:* = AEGIS.

eglantine ['egləntain] *n. Bot:* églantier *m.*

ego ['egou, 'i:gou] *n.* **the e.,** le moi, l'ego *m*; *F:* **e. trip,** glorification *f* de soi-même.

egocentric [egou'sentrik] *a. Psy:* égocentrique.

egocentricity [egousen'trisiti] *n.* égocentrisme *m.*

egoism ['egouizm] *n.* égoïsme *m.*

egoist ['egouist] *n.* egoïste *mf.*

egoistic(al) [egou'istik(l)] *a.* égoïste. **-ally** *adv.* égoïstement.

egomania [egou'meiniə] *n.* manie *f* égocentrique.

egotism ['egoutizm] *n.* égotisme *m.*

egotist ['egoutist] *n.* égotiste *mf.*

egotistic(al) [egou'tistik(l)] *a.* égotiste.

egregious [i'gri:dʒiəs] *a. Pej: O:* fameux (sot); **e. blunder,** maladresse *f* insigne.

egress ['i:gres] *n.* **1.** sortie *f*, issue *f.* **2.** *Astr:* émersion *f.*

egret ['i:gret] *n. Orn:* aigrette *f.*

Egypt ['i:dʒipt] *Pr.n. Geog:* Égypte *f.*

Egyptian [i'dʒipʃ(ə)n] **1.** *a. Geog:* égyptien, d'Égypte. **2.** *n. Geog:* Égyptien, -ienne.

eh [ei] *int.* eh! hé! hein?

eider ['aidər] *n. Orn:* **e. (duck),** eider *m* à duvet.

eiderdown ['aidədaun] *n.* **1.** duvet *m* d'eider. **2.** édredon (piqué, américain).

eight [eit] **1.** *num. a.* & *n.* huit (*m*); **twenty-e.,** vingt-huit; **at e.,** à huit heures; **at e.-thirty,** à huit heures et demie; **a boy of e.,** un garçon de huit ans; **a mother of e.,** la mère de huit enfants; *Cards:* **the e. of**

spades, le huit de pique; **to take eights in gloves,** avoir huit de pointure (pour les gants); **e.-day clock,** huitaine *f*; *F:* **to have had one over the e.,** avoir bu un coup de trop; *Sp:* (*skating*) **to cut figures of e.,** faire des huit. **2.** *n. Sp: Row:* (i) équipe *f* de huit rameurs; (ii) canot *m* à huit rameurs; **to be in the last e.,** être en huitième de finale.

eighteen [ei'ti:n] *num. a. & n.* dix-huit (*m*); **she is e. (years old),** elle a dix-huit ans; **at e.-thirty,** à dix-huit heures trente.

eighteenth [ei'ti:nθ] **1.** *num. a. & n.* (*a*) dix-huitième; (*b*) **(on) the e. (of May),** le dix-huit (mai); **Louis the Eighteenth,** Louis Dix-huit. **2.** *n.* (*fractional*) dix-huitième *m*.

eightfold ['eitfould] **1.** *a.* octuple. **2.** *adv.* huit fois autant; **to increase e.,** octupler.

eighth [eitθ] **1.** *num. a. & n.* (*a*) huitième; **in the e. place,** huitièmement; (*b*) **(on) the e. (of April),** le huit (avril); **Henry the E.,** Henri Huit. **2.** *n.* (*fractional*) huitième *m*; **three eighths,** trois huitièmes.

eightieth ['eitiəθ] *num. a. & n.* quatre-vingtième (*m*); *Sw.Fr:Belg:* huitantième (*m*); *Sw.Fr: Fr.C:* octantième (*m*).

eighty ['eiti] *num. a. & n.* quatre-vingts (*m*); *Sw.Fr: Belg:* huitante (*m*); *Sw.Fr: Fr.C:* octante (*m*); **e.-one,** quatre-vingt-un; **page e.,** page quatre-vingt; **in the eighties,** dans les années quatre-vingt; **she is in her eighties,** elle a quatre-vingts ans passés.

Eire ['ɛərə] *Pr.n. Geog:* Eire *f*.

either ['aiðər, *esp. NAm:* 'i:ðər] **1.** *a. & pron.* (*a*) (*each of the two*) l'un(e) et l'autre; **on e. side,** de chaque côté; des deux côtés; (*b*) (*one or other*) l'un(e) ou l'autre; **e. of them,** soit l'un(e), soit l'autre; **I don't believe e. of you,** je ne vous crois ni l'un ni l'autre; **e. candidate may win,** l'un ou l'autre candidat pourra l'emporter; **there is no evidence e. way,** les preuves manquent de part et d'autre; **I do not want e. of them,** je ne veux ni l'un(e) ni l'autre. **2.** *conj. & adv.* (*a*) **e. . . ., or . . .,** ou . . ., ou . . .; **e. you or your brother,** (ou) vous ou votre frère; soit vous, soit votre frère; **e. come in or go out,** entrez ou sortez; (*b*) **not . . . e.,** ne . . . non plus; **if you don't go, I won't go e.,** si vous n'y allez pas je n'irai pas non plus; **nor I e.!** ni moi non plus; (*c*) **she's caught cold, and she isn't very strong e.,** elle s'est enrhumée, elle qui n'est déjà pas si forte.

ejaculate [i'dʒækjuleit] *v.tr. & i.* **1.** *Physiol:* éjaculer. **2.** pousser (un cri); s'écrier.

ejaculation [idʒækju'leiʃ(ə)n] *n.* **1.** *Physiol:* éjaculation *f*. **2.** cri *m*, exclamation *f* (de joie, etc.).

eject [i'dʒekt] *v.tr.* **1.** (*a*) jeter, émettre (des flammes, etc.); (*of volcano*) projeter (des cendres, etc.); (*b*) expulser (un agitateur, etc.) (d'une salle, d'une réunion); *Jur:* évincer (un locataire). **2.** *v.i. Av:* (*of pilot*) s'éjecter.

ejection [i'dʒekʃ(ə)n] *n.* (*a*) jet *m* (de flammes); rejet *m* (de lave); (*b*) expulsion *f* (de qn); *Av:* éjection (du pilote); *Jur:* évincement *m*, éviction *f* (d'un locataire).

ejector [i'dʒektər] *n.* **1.** *Sm.a:* éjecteur *m* (d'étuis vides). **2.** *Av:* **e. seat,** siège *m* éjectable.

eke [i:k] *v.tr.* **to e. out,** suppléer à l'insuffisance de, (ses revenus, etc.); économiser, faire durer (les vivres); **to e. out a living,** subsister pauvrement.

elaborate¹ [i'læbərət] *a.* (*of tool, etc.*) compliqué; (*of work*) soigné; (*of style*) travaillé; (*of work of art*) fouillé; (*of inspection, research, etc.*) minutieux; (*of dress, etc.*) recherché; (*of hairstyle*) compliqué. **-ly** *adv.* minutieusement; d'une façon compliquée; d'une manière approfondie. **2.** *v.i.* donner plus de détails (**on sth.,** sur qch.).

elaboration [ilæbə'reiʃ(ə)n] *n.* élaboration *f*.

élan [ei'lɑ̃ŋ] *n.* élan *m*, impétuosité *f*.

eland ['i:lənd] *n. Z:* **common e.,** éland *m* du Cap.

elapse [i'læps] *v.i.* (*of time*) s'écouler; (se) passer; **years have elapsed since then,** des années ont passé depuis.

elastic [i'læstik] **1.** *a.* (*a*) *Ph: Mec:* (corps) élastique; (bois, etc.) flexible, **e. band,** élastique *m*, (bande *f* en) caoutchouc (*m*); **to be e.,** faire ressort; (*b*) (pas) élastique; *Pol.Ec:* **e. supply, demand,** offre *f*, demande *f*, élastique; (*c*) *Anat:* (tissu) élastique; (*d*) *Pej:* **e. conscience,** conscience *f* élastique. **2.** *n.* (*a*) élastique *m*; (bande *f* en) caoutchouc (*m*).

elasticity [i:læs'tisiti] *n.* **1.** élasticité *f* (d'un corps); flexibilité *f* (du bois, d'un métal); souplesse *f* (de corps); *Med:* tonicité *f* (des muscles); *Mec:* **coefficient of e.,** coefficient *m* d'élasticité. **2.** (*a*) (*of pers.*) élasticité; résilience *f*; (*b*) **e. of interpretation,** élasticité (d'une loi); (*c*) *Pol.Ec:* **the e. of supply and demand,** l'élasticité de l'offre et de la demande.

elate¹ [i'leit] *v.tr.* exalter; **to be elated with success,** être enivré de succès. **elated** *a.* transporté; exalté; **to feel e.,** se sentir plein de joie.

elation [i'leiʃ(ə)n] *n.* **1.** exaltation *f*; ivresse *f* (du succès). **2.** joie *f*, gaieté *f*.

Elba ['elbə] *Pr.n. Geog:* **the island of E.,** l'île *f* d'Elbe.

elbow¹ ['elbou] *n.* **1.** (*a*) coude *m* (du bras); **e. joint,** articulation *f* du coude; **to lean one's e. on sth.,** s'accouder sur qch.; **e. to e.,** (se tenir) coude à coude; **to be at s.o.'s e.,** être, se tenir, aux côtés de qn; **to rub elbows with all sorts of people,** fréquenter toutes sortes de gens; **to have (enough) e. room,** avoir ses coudées franches; *F:* **e. grease,** huile *f* de coude; **to lift the e.,** lever le coude; *Cost:* **e.-length gloves,** gants longs (montant jusqu'au coude); (*b*) *Dressm: etc:* coude (d'une manche). **2.** (*a*) coude, tournant *m* (d'une route, etc.); (*b*) coude, genou *m* (d'un conduit, d'un tuyau); *Mec.E:* **e. joint,** joint articulé; raccord coudé.

elbow² *v.tr.* (*a*) coudoyer (qn); pousser (qn) du coude; **to e. s.o. aside,** écarter qn d'un coup de coude; (*b*) **to e. one's way through the crowd,** se frayer un passage à travers la foule en jouant des coudes.

elder¹ ['eldər] **1.** *a.* aîné, plus âgé (de deux personnes); **my e. brother,** mon frère aîné; **Pliny the E.,** Pline l'Ancien; *Pol:* **E. Statesmen,** les doyens des hommes politiques. **2.** *n.* (*a*) aîné, -ée; plus âge, -ée (de deux personnes); **he is my e. by two years,** il est de deux ans mon aîné; **children should obey their elders,** les enfants devraient obéir à leurs aînés; (*b*) *Hist: Ecc:* ancien *m*.

elder² *n. Bot:* **e. (tree),** sureau *m*.

elderberry ['eldəberi] *n. Bot:* baie *f* de sureau; **e. wine,** vin *m* de sureau.

elderflower ['eldəflauər] *n.* fleur *f* de sureau.

elderly ['eldəli] *a.* d'un certain âge; assez âgé.

eldest ['eldist] *a.* aîné; **my e. (son, daughter),** mon (fils) aîné, ma fille aînée, mon aînée.

elect¹ [i'lekt] *a.* élu; **the president e.,** le président élu; *n.pl.Ecc:* **the e.,** les élus.

elect² *v.tr.* **1. to e. to do sth.,** choisir de faire qch. **2.** (*a*) élire (qn); **to e. s.o. to the presidency,** élire qn à la présidence; (*b*) *Jur:* **to e. domicile,** élire domicile.

election [i'lekʃ(ə)n] *n.* (*a*) élection *f* (d'un candidat, etc.); **to stand for e.,** poser sa candidature, se porter candidat; (*b*) *Pol:* **general e.,** élections législatives; **by-e.,** *U.S:* **special e.,** élection partielle; **e. committee,** comité électoral.

electioneering [ilekʃə'niəriŋ] *n.* propagande électorale.

elective [i'lektiv] *a.* **1.** (*a*) (*of office, etc.*) électif; (*b*) (*of body, etc.*) électoral, -aux. **2.** *NAm: Sch:* (*of subject*) facultatif.

elector [i'lektər] *n.* électeur, -trice; votant, -ante.

electoral [i'lektər(ə)l] *a.* électoral, -aux; **e. body,** corps électoral.

electorate [i'lektərət] *n. Pol:* le corps électoral; les électeurs *mpl.*

electric [i'lektrik] *a.* (*a*) (courant, etc.) électrique; **e. wave,** onde *f* électrique; onde hertzienne; **e. power station,** centrale *f* électrique; **e. generator,** générateur *m,* génératrice *f,* d'électricité; (*b*) (lumière, cuisinière) électrique; **e. motor,** moteur *m* électrique; *U.S: Jur:* **e. chair,** chaise *f* électrique; (*c*) **e. blue,** bleu *m* électrique; (*d*) *Fig:* **the atmosphere of the meeting was e.,** l'atmosphère de la réunion était orageuse.

electrical [i'lektrikl] *a.* électrique; **e. engineering,** (i) électromécanique *f;* (ii) industrie *f* de l'équipement électrique; **e. engineer,** (i) ingénieur électricien; (ii) électromécanicien *m.*

electrician [ilek'triʃ(ə)n] *n.* électricien *m;* (*a*) électrotechnicien, -ienne; (*b*) électromécanicien *m.*

electricity [ilek'trisiti] *n.* électricité *f;* **static e.,** électricité statique; **lit by e.,** éclairé à l'électricité.

electrification [ilektrifi'keiʃ(ə)n] *n.* **1.** électrisation *f* (d'un corps, etc.). **2.** électrification *f* (d'une voie de chemin de fer, etc.).

electrify [i'lektrifai] *v.tr.* **1.** électriser (un corps, *Fig:* un auditoire). **2.** électrifier (une ligne de chemin de fer, etc.). **electrifying** *a.* (effet, etc.) électrisant.

electrocardiogram [ilektrou'kɑːdiougræm] *n. Med:* électrocardiogramme *m.*

electrocardiography [ilektroukɑːdi'ɔgrəfi] *n. Med:* électrocardiographie *f.*

electrochemistry [ilektrou'kemistri] *n.* électrochimie *f.*

electroconvulsive [ilektroukən'vʌlsiv] *a. Med:* **e. therapy,** électrochoc *m.*

electrocute [i'lektrəkjuːt] *v.tr.* électrocuter.

electrocution [ilektrə'kjuːʃ(ə)n] *n.* électrocution *f.*

electrode [i'lektroud] *n.* électrode *f;* **e. holder,** porte-électrodes *m inv.*

electrodynamics [ilektroudai'næmiks] *n.* (*usu. with sg. const.*) électrodynamique *f.*

electroencephalogram [ilektrouen'sefəlougræm] *n. Med:* électroencéphalogramme *m.*

electrolysis [ilek'trɔlisis] *n.* électrolyse *f.*

electrolyte [i'lektroulait] *n. El:* électrolyte *m.*

electrolytic [ilektrou'litik] *a.* électrolytique.

electromagnet [ilektrou'mægnit] *n.* électro-aimant *m, pl.* électro-aimants.

electromagnetic [ilektroumæg'netik] *a.* (champ, onde, etc.) électromagnétique.

electromagnetism [ilektrou'mægnitizm] *n.* électromagnétisme *m.*

electromotive [ilektrou'moutiv] *a.* électromoteur, -trice; **e. force,** force électromotrice.

electron [i'lektrɔn] *n. Ph:* électron *m;* **positive e.,** électron positif; **negative e.,** électron négatif; **e. microscope,** microscope *m* électronique.

electronic [ilek'trɔnik] *a.* électronique; **e. computer,** calculateur *m* électronique; **e. brain,** cerveau *m* électronique. **-ally** *adv.* électroniquement.

electronics [ilek'trɔniks] *n.pl.* (*usu. with sg. const.*) électronique *f;* **e. specialist, engineer,** ingénieur électronicien; électronicien, -ienne; **e. industry,** industrie *f* électronique.

electroplate¹ [i'lektroupleit] *n.* (métal) plaqué (*m*); articles (i) plaqués, (ii) argentés.

electroplate² *v.tr.* (i) plaquer, (ii) argenter (un métal).

electroshock [ilektrou'ʃɔk] *n. Med: etc:* électrochoc *m.*

electrostatic [ilektrou'stætik] *a.* (générateur, etc.) électrostatique.

electrostatics [ilektrou'stætiks] *n.pl.* (*usu. with sg. const.*) électrostatique *f.*

electrotechnic(al) [ilektrou'teknik(l)] *a.* électrotechnique.

electrotherapy [ilektrou'θerəpi] *n. Med:* électrothérapie *f.*

electrotype¹ [i'lektroutaip] *n. Typ:* électrotype *m;* galvanotype *m.*

electrotype² *v.tr. Typ:* électrotyper; galvanotyper.

elegance ['eligəns] *n.* élégance *f.*

elegant ['eligənt] *a.* **1.** élégant; **e. furniture,** meubles *mpl* d'un goût raffiné. **2.** *NAm: F:* excellent; de premier ordre. **-ly** *adv.* élégamment, avec élégance; **e. dressed,** habillé(e) avec élégance.

elegiac [eli'dʒaiək] **1.** *a.* élégiaque. **2.** *n.pl.* **elegiacs,** vers *mpl* élégiaques.

elegy ['elidʒi] *n.* élégie *f.*

element ['elimənt] *n.* élément *m.* **1. the four elements,** les quatre éléments; **to brave the elements,** braver les éléments; **exposed to the elements,** exposé aux intempéries *fpl;* **to be in one's e.,** être dans son élément. **2.** (*a*) **e. of uncertainty,** élément d'incertitude; **disturbing e.,** élément d'instabilité; **the personal e.,** le facteur humain; (*b*) élément, partie *f* (d'un tout); *El:* élément; *Cmptr:* **data e.,** élément d'information; *Atom.Ph:* (*for charging reactor*) **fuel e.,** charge *f.* **3.** *Ch:* corps *m* simple. **4. elements,** rudiments *mpl* (d'une science).

elemental¹ [eli'ment(ə)l] *a.* **1.** qui appartient aux éléments, aux forces de la nature; (esprit) élémental. **2.** élémentaire, primitif. **3.** (*of substance*) élémentaire. **4.** fondamental, essentiel.

elemental² *n.* esprit *m.*

elementary [eli'ment(ə)ri] *a.* élémentaire; **e. body,** (i) *Ch:* corps *m* simple; (ii) *Med:* corps élémentaire; *Sch:* **e. algebra,** rudiments *mpl* d'algèbre.

elephant ['elifənt] *n.* (*a*) *Z:* éléphant *m;* **bull e.,** éléphant mâle; **cow e.,** éléphant femelle; **e. calf,** *F:* **baby e.,** éléphanteau *m;* **white e.,** objet *m,* cadeau *m,* d'une certaine valeur mais inutile et encombrant; *F:* **to see pink elephants,** voir double; (*b*) **e. seal,** éléphant de mer.

elephantiasis [elifæn'taiəsis] *n. Med:* éléphantiasis *f.*

elephantine [eli'fæntain] *a.* **1.** éléphantin; (mouvement, etc.) gauche; **e. wit,** esprit lourd. **2.** (*of proportions, etc.*) éléphantesque.

elevate ['eliveit] *v.tr.* **1.** élever (l'hostie, l'esprit); relever (son style); *Artil:* pointer (un canon) en hauteur; **to e. s.o. to a high rank,** élever qn à un haut rang. **2.** exalter (qn); élever (l'âme de qn). **elevated** *a.* **1.** élevé; **e. position,** position élevée; **e. thoughts,** hautes pensées. **2.** (*overhead*) surélevé; **e. railway,** *U.S:* **railroad,** (i) chemin de fer aérien; (ii) métro aérien; **e. highway,** route surélevée. **elevating 1.** *a.* (*a*) (*of discourse, etc.*) qui élève l'esprit; **e. principles,** principes moralisateurs; (*b*) *Aer:* (force) ascensionnelle. **2.** *n.* élévation *f;* levage *m.*

elevation [eli'veiʃ(ə)n] *n.* **1.** (*a*) élévation *f* (de qch. à une certaine hauteur, de qn à un rang supérieur); (*b*) *Ecc:* **the E. (of the Host),** l'Élévation. **2.** *Geog: Surv:* **e. above sea level,** altitude, hauteur, au-dessus du niveau de la mer. **3.** (*hill*) élévation, éminence *f.* **4.** (*a*) *Astr:* élévation (d'un astre, etc.); (*b*) *Artil:* hausse *f;* pointage *m* en hauteur; **angle of e.,** angle *m* de hausse; **e. mechanism,** dispositif *m* de pointage en hauteur. **5.** *Draw: Arch: etc:* élévation (d'un édifice, etc.); **front e.,** façade *f* (d'un édifice). **6.** élévation, dignité *f* (du style); noblesse *f,* grandeur *f* (du caractère).

elevator ['eliveitər] *n.* **1.** (*a*) élévateur *m U.S:* (*for goods*) monte-charge(s) *m;* **bucket e.,** élévateur à godets; (*b*) *NAm:* ascenseur *m;* (*c*) **grain e.,** (i) élévateur à grains; (ii) silo *m*. **2.** *Av:* gouvernail *m* de profondeur, d'altitude; **e. angle,** angle *m* de braquage.

eleven [i'lev(ə)n] **1.** *num. a & n.* onze (*m*); **the e. o'clock train,** le train d'onze heures. **2.** *n. Sp: Cr: Fb: etc:* équipe *f* de onze joueurs; le onze.

elevenses [i'lev(ə)nziz] *n.pl. F:* collation *f*, casse-croûte *m inv*, de onze heures (du matin).

eleventh [i'lev(ə)nθ] **1.** *num. a. & n.* onzième (*m*); **at the e. hour,** au dernier moment; à la dernière heure. **2.** *n.* (*fractional*) onzième.

elf, *pl.* **elves** [elf, elvz] *n. Myth:* elfe *m*, lutin *m*, lutine *f*.

elfin ['elfin] *a.* d'elfe, de lutin; (paysage) féerique.

elicit [i'lisit] *v.tr.* découvrir (la vérité); tirer (les faits) au clair; obtenir (une réponse de qn); provoquer (une réponse).

elide [i'laid] *v.tr.* élider (une voyelle, etc.).

eligibility [elidʒi'biliti] *n.* **1.** éligibilité *f* (en droit). **2.** acceptabilité *f* (d'un prétendant, etc.).

eligible ['elidʒibl] *a.* **1.** éligible (en droit) (**to,** à); **to be e.,** avoir droit (**for,** à). **2.** digne d'être élu, choisi; acceptable; **e. young man,** bon parti.

eliminate [i'limineit] *v.tr.* éliminer (des matières toxiques, des noms d'une liste, etc.); supprimer, écarter (des possibilités d'erreur, etc.); *Mth:* **to e. x, y,** éliminer x, y. **eliminating** *a.* éliminateur, trice; *Sp:* **e. heats,** épreuves *fpl* éliminatoires.

elimination [ilimini'neiʃ(ə)n] *n.* élimination *f*; **by process of e.,** en procédant par élimination.

eliminator [i'limineitər] *n.* éliminateur *m*.

elision [i'liʒ(ə)n] *n.* élision *f* (d'un voyelle, etc.).

élite [ei'li:t] *n.* élite *f*.

elitism [ei'li:tizm] *n.* élitisme *m*.

elitist [ei'li:tist] *a. & n.* élitiste (*m*).

elixir [i'liksər] *n.* élixir *m*; **the e. of life,** l'élixir de longue vie.

Elizabethan [ilizə'bi:θ(ə)n] *a.* élisabéthain.

elk [elk] *n. Z:* (*a*) **Scandinavian e.,** élan *m*; (*b*) **American e.,** wapiti *m*.

ell [el] *n. A.Meas:* aune *f*.

ellipse [i'lips] *n. Mth:* ellipse *f*.

ellipsis, *pl.* **-ipses** [i'lipsis, -si:z] *n. Gram:* ellipse *f*.

ellipsoid [i'lipsɔid] *n. Mth:* ellipsoïde *m*.

elliptic(al) [i'liptik(ə)l] *a. Gram: Mth:* elliptique. **-ally** *adv.* elliptiquement.

elm [elm] *n. Bot:* orme *m*; **e. grove,** ormaie *f*; **Dutch e. disease,** maladie *f* des ormes.

elocution [elə'kju:ʃ(ə)n] *n.* élocution *f*, diction *f*.

elocutionist [elə'kju:ʃənist] *n.* (*a*) déclamateur, -trice; récitateur, -trice; (*b*) professeur *m* de diction.

elongate ['i:lɔŋgeit] **1.** *v.tr.* allonger, étendre. **2.** *v.i.* s'allonger, s'étendre. **elongated** *a.* allongé, prolongé.

elongation [i:lɔŋ'geiʃ(ə)n] *n.* **1.** *Astr:* élongation *f*. **2.** (*a*) allongement *m*; (*b*) prolongement *m* (d'une ligne).

elope [i'loup] *v.i.* s'enfuir de la maison paternelle, du domicile conjugal, avec un amant; se laisser enlever (**with s.o.,** par qn); (*of lovers*) s'enfuir (ensemble).

elopement [i'loupmənt] *n.* fuite *f* de la maison paternelle, du domicile conjugal.

eloquence ['eləkwəns] *n.* éloquence *f*.

eloquent ['eləkwənt] *a.* éloquent; **to be an e. speaker,** être éloquent; avoir de l'éloquence. **-ly** *adv.* éloquemment.

else [els] **1.** *adv.* autrement; ou bien; **come tomorrow or e. it will be too late,** venez demain, autrement il sera trop tard; **he must be joking or e. he's mad,** il plaisante, ou bien alors il est fou; **do what I tell you or e. . . .!** fais ce que je te dis, sinon . . .! **2.** (*a*) *a. or adv.* (*with indef. or interr. pron. or adv.*) **anyone, anybody, e.,** (i) toute autre personne; n'importe qui d'autre; **he is no more stupid than anyone e.,** il n'est pas plus bête qu'un autre; (ii) (*interrog.*) **can I speak to anyone e.?** y a-t-il quelqu'un d'autre à qui je puisse parler? **anything e.,** (i) n'importe quoi d'autre; (ii) (*interrog.*) **have you anything e. to do?** avez-vous autre chose à faire? *Com:* **anything e., madam?** et avec cela, madame? **someone, somebody, e.,** quelqu'un d'autre, un autre; **you are taking me for someone e.,** vous me prenez pour quelqu'un d'autre; **something e.,** quelque chose *m* d'autre; autre chose *m*; **I was thinking of something e.,** je pensais à autre chose; **no one e., nobody e.,** personne *m* d'autre, aucun autre **no one e. could do it,** il n'y a que lui qui puisse le faire; **nothing e.,** rien *m* d'autre; **nothing e., thank you,** plus rien, merci; **who e.?** qui d'autre? qui encore? **what e.?** quoi encore? quoi de plus? **what e. can I say?** qu'est-ce que je puis dire de plus? **everything e.,** tout le reste; **everyone, everybody, e. knows it,** tous les autres le savent; **little e.,** pas grand-chose *m* d'autre; **he eats bread but little e.,** il ne mange guère que du pain; **there isn't much e. to be done,** il ne reste pas beaucoup à faire; (*b*) *adv.* **where e.?** (i) où encore? (ii) en quel autre lieu? **everywhere e.,** partout ailleurs; **somewhere e.,** autre part; ailleurs; **nowhere e.,** nulle part ailleurs; **anywhere e.,** (i) n'importe où (ailleurs); (ii) (*interrog.*) **can I find some anywhere e.?** puis-je en trouver ailleurs?

elsewhere ['els(h)wɛər] *adv.* ailleurs, autre part.

elucidate [i'l(j)u:sideit] *v.tr.* élucider, éclaircir, tirer au clair (un fait, une question); dégager le sens (d'un passage).

elucidation [il(j)u:si'deiʃ(ə)n] *n.* élucidation *f*, éclaircissement *m* (**of,** de).

elude [i'l(j)u:d] *v.tr.* éluder (une question); esquiver, éviter (un coup); échapper à (la mort); se soustraire à (la justice); **to e. s.o.'s grasp,** échapper aux mains de qn.

elusive [i'l(j)u:siv] *a.* insaisissable, intangible; (personnalité) fuyante, flottante.

elusiveness [i'l(j)u:sivnis] *n.* nature *f* insaisissable.

elver ['elvər] *n. Ich:* civelle *f*.

Elysian [i'liziən] *a. Myth:* élyséen.

emaciate [i'meisieit] *v.tr.* amaigrir; émacier, dessécher (le corps); **emaciated,** émacié, décharné.

emaciation [imeisi'eiʃ(ə)n] *n.* amaigrissement *m*, émaciation *f*, dessèchement *m* (du corps).

emanate ['eməneit] *v.i.* émaner, découler (**from,** de).

emanation [emə'neiʃ(ə)n] *n.* émanation *f*; effluve *m*.

emancipate [i'mænsipeit] *v.tr.* émanciper (un mineur, les femmes, etc.); affranchir (un esclave). **emancipated** *a.* emancipé; (esclave) affranchi.

emancipation [imænsi'peiʃ(ə)n] *n.* émancipation *f*; affranchissement *m* (d'un esclave, etc.).

emasculate [i'mæskjuleit] *v.tr.* émasculer; châtrer.

emasculation [imæskju'leiʃ(ə)n] *n.* émasculation *f*; castration *f*.

embalm [im'ba:m] *v.tr.* embaumer. **embalming** *n.* embaumement *m*.

embalmer [im'ba:mər] *n.* embaumeur *m*.

embankment [im'bæŋkmənt] *n.* **1.** endiguement *m* (d'un fleuve). **2.** (*a*) digue *f*; levée *f* de terre; (*b*) remblai *m*; talus *m*; berge *f*, quai *m* (d'un fleuve).

embargo¹, *pl.* **-oes** [im'ba:gou, -ouz] *n.* embargo *m*, séquestre *m*; **to be under an e.,** être séquestré; **to put an e. on (sth.),** mettre un embargo sur (des marchandises, etc.)

embargo² *v.tr.* mettre l'embargo sur, séquestrer.

embark [im'ba:k] **1.** *v.tr.* (*a*) embarquer (des troupes, etc.); (*b*) (*of ship*) prendre à bord (des troupes, etc.). **2.** *v.i.* s'embarquer (à bord d'un navire); **to e. (up)on (sth.),** s'embarquer dans (une aventure).

embarkation [embɑːˈkeiʃ(ə)n] *n. Nau:* embarquement *m*; **e. card,** carte d'accès à bord.

embarrass [imˈbærəs] *v.tr.* embarrasser, gêner (qn). **embarrassed** *a.* embarrassé; gêné; **to be, feel, e.,** être, se sentir, gêné. **embarrassing** *a.* embarrassant. **embarrassingly** *adv.* d'une manière embarrassante.

embarrassment [imˈbærəsmənt] *n.* embarras *m*; gêne *f*; **blushing with e.,** rouge de confusion; **to be in a state of financial e.,** avoir des embarras d'argent.

embassy [ˈembəsi] *n.* **1.** ambassade *f*; **the French E.,** l'ambassade de France. **2. special e.,** mission spéciale.

embattled [imˈbætld] *a.* attaqué, encerclé (par l'ennemi).

embed [imˈbed] *v.tr.* **(embedded)** enfoncer (un clou dans un mur); poser (un câble dans le sable); encastrer (un châssis dans un mur); **embedded in concrete,** noyé dans le béton.

embellish [imˈbeliʃ] *v.tr.* embellir, orner (qch.); enjoliver (un récit); colorier (son style).

embellishment [imˈbeliʃmənt] *n.* embellissement *m*, ornement *m*; enjolivure *f*.

ember[1] [ˈembər] *n.* (*usu. pl.*) braise *f*; charbons ardents; cendres ardentes.

Ember[2] *attrib. Ecc:* **E. days,** les Quatre-Temps *mpl*.

embezzle [imˈbezl] **1.** *v.tr.* détourner, distraire, s'approprier (des fonds). **2.** *v.i.* commettre des détournements.

embezzlement [imˈbezəlm(ə)nt] *n.* détournement *m* (de fonds); appropriation *f* de fonds.

embezzler [imˈbezlər] *n.* détourneur *m* de fonds; auteur *m* d'un détournement.

embitter [imˈbitər] *v.tr.* remplir d'amertume; aigrir (le caractère); empoisonner (les plaisirs); envenimer (une querelle, etc.). **embittered** *a.* aigri (**by,** par).

emblazon [imˈbleiz(ə)n] *v.tr.* blasonner; décorer d'armoiries; **emblazoned with the arms of the town,** peint aux armes de la ville. **emblazoned** *a.* blasonné.

emblem [ˈembləm] *n.* **1.** emblème *m.* **2.** (*a*) *Her:* emblème, devise *f*; (*b*) **sporting e.,** insigne sportif; (*c*) *Aut:* écusson *m* (de radiateur).

emblematic [embləˈmætik] *a.* emblématique.

embodiment [imˈbɔdimənt] *n.* incarnation *f*; personnification *f*; **he is the e. of kindness,** il est la bonté même.

embody [imˈbɔdi] *v.tr.* **(embodied; embodying) 1.** incarner. **2.** personnifier (une qualité). **3.** incorporer (un article dans une loi); renfermer, rédiger (ses principes dans un traité). **embodied** *a.* concrétisé; (art) mis en pratique.

embolden [imˈbouldən] *v.tr.* enhardir (**s.o. to do sth.,** qn à faire qch.).

embolism [ˈembəlizm] *n. Med:* embolie *f*.

embonpoint [ɑ̃bɔ̃ˈpwɛ̃] *n.* embonpoint *m*, rondeurs *fpl*.

emboss [imˈbɔs] *v.tr.* travailler en relief; bosseler (le métal); repousser, estamper (le métal, le cuir). **embossed** *a.* (métal) gravé en relief, travaillé en bosse; bosselé; (métal, cuir) estampé, repoussé; **e. work,** travail *m* en relief, en repoussé. **embossing** *n.* **1.** bosselage *m* (du métal); estampage *m*, repoussage *m* (du cuir) **e. punch,** repoussoir *m*; *Paper m:* **e. press,** presse *f* à imprimer en relief. **2.** relief *m*, repoussé *m*, bosselure *f*.

embrace[1] [imˈbreis] *n.* (*a*) étreinte *f*; **iron e.,** étreinte de fer; (*b*) étreinte amoureuse.

embrace[2] *v.tr.* **1.** embrasser, étreindre; donner une accolade à (qn); *v.i.* **they embraced,** ils s'embrassèrent. **2.** embrasser (une religion); adopter (une cause). **3.** (*include*) embrasser (**in,** dans); contenir (**in,** dans); comprendre (des sujets). **4. the view from the terrace embraces the whole valley,** de la terrasse, la vue s'étend sur toute la vallée, embrasse toute la vallée. **embracing** *a.* qui embrasse, qui renferme; (geste) ample, compréhensif; **all-e. knowledge,** vaste érudition *f*.

embrasure [imˈbreiʒər] *n.* **1.** *Arch:* embrasure *f*, ébrasement *m*. **2.** *Artil:* embrasure, sabord *m*.

embrocation [embrəˈkeiʃ(ə)n] *n. Med:* embrocation *f*.

embroider [imˈbrɔidər] *v.tr.* **1.** *Needlew:* (*a*) broder; (*b*) *v.i.* faire de la broderie. **2.** enjoliver (un récit). **embroidering** *n.* **1.** = EMBROIDERY [1]. **2.** enjolivement *m* (d'un récit).

embroidery [imˈbrɔidəri] *n.* **1.** *Needlew:* broderie *f*; **e. frame,** métier *m* à broder. **2.** enjolivure *f* (d'un récit).

embroil [imˈbrɔil] *v.tr.* **1.** (*a*) brouiller, embrouiller (une affaire); (*b*) **embroiled in a quarrel,** entraîné dans une querelle.

embroilment [imˈbrɔilmənt] *n.* (*a*) embrouillement *m* (d'une affaire); (*b*) brouille *f* (entre deux personnes).

embryo, *pl.* **-os** [ˈembriou, -ouz] *n. Biol:* embryon *m*; **in e.,** (i) à l'état embryonnaire; (ii) (artiste) en herbe; (projets) embryonnaire, encore en germe.

embryology [embriˈɔlədʒi] *n.* embryologie *f*.

embryonic [embriˈɔnik] *a.* **1.** *Biol:* embryonnaire. **2.** en germe.

embus [imˈbʌs] **1.** *v.tr.* embarquer (des troupes) en autobus. **2.** *v.i.* s'embarquer dans un autobus.

emcee [ˈemˈsiː] *n. NAm: F:* **1.** maître *m* de cérémonies. **2.** *W.Tel: TV:* animateur, -trice.

emend [iˈmend], **emendate** [ˈiːmendeit] *v.tr.* corriger, apporter des émendations à (un texte).

emendation [iːmenˈdeiʃ(ə)n] *n.* **1.** émendation *f*, correction *f* (d'un texte). **2.** variante proposée.

emerald [ˈem(ə)rəld] **1.** *n. Miner:* émeraude *f*. **2.** *a. & n.* **e. (green),** (vert *m* d')émeraude; *Lit:* **the E. Isle,** la verte Irlande.

emerge [iˈməːdʒ] *v.i.* **1.** émerger (**from,** de); surgir (de l'eau, etc.). **2.** déboucher (**from,** de); sortir (d'un trou, de l'obscurité); **the moon is emerging from behind the clouds,** la lune se dégage des nuages. **3.** (*a*) (*of difficulty, etc.*) se dresser; surgir; (*b*) **from these facts it emerges that . . .,** de ces faits il ressort que . . . .

emergence [iˈməːdʒəns] *n.* émergence *f* (d'une théorie, etc.); apparition *f* (d'un nouvel état, d'un nouveau leader).

emergency [iˈməːdʒənsi] *n.* circonstance *f* critique; cas urgent; **to provide for emergencies,** parer aux éventualités, à l'imprévu; **to meet an e.,** faire face à une situation critique; **in case of e.,** en cas d'urgence; **e. repairs,** réparations *fpl* d'urgence; **e. brake,** frein *m* de secours; **e. tank,** réservoir *m* auxiliaire; **e. exit,** sortie *f* de secours; *Cin: etc:* **e. light, lighting,** éclairage *m* de sécurité; **e. supply,** en-cas *m inv*; **e. ration,** vivres *m* de réserve; **state of e.,** état *m* d'urgence; **e. regulations,** mesures *fpl* d'exception; **national e.,** catastrophe nationale; *Med:* **an e.,** une urgence; **e. ward,** salle d'urgence; **e. operation,** opération *f* à chaud.

emergent [iˈməːdʒənt] *a.* émergent; **e. nations,** nations en voie de développement.

emery [ˈeməri] *n.* émeri *m*; **e. paper,** papier d'émeri; *Toil:* **e. board,** lime *f* émeri; **e. powder,** poudre *f* d'émeri; **e. wheel,** meule *f* (en) émeri.

emetic [iˈmetik] *a. & n. Med:* émétique (*m*).

emigrant [ˈemigrənt] *a. & n.* émigrant, -ante.

emigrate [ˈemigreit] *v.i.* émigrer. **emigrating** *a.* émigrant.

emigration [emiˈgreiʃ(ə)n] *n.* émigration *f*.

émigré ['emigrei] *n.* émigré, -ée.
eminence ['eminəns] *n.* **1.** (*a*) éminence *f*, élévation *f* (de terrain); (*b*) *Anat:* éminence, saillie *f*. **2.** grandeur *f*, distinction *f* (d'une charge); position éminente; **to rise to e.,** parvenir à une haute position, **3.** *Ecc:* (*title of cardinal*) Éminence; **your E.,** votre Éminence.
eminent ['eminənt] *a.* éminent; (docteur, etc.) distingué. **-ly** *adv.* éminemment; **an e. respectable family,** une famille des plus honorables.
emir [e'miər] *n.* émir *m.*
emirate ['emireit] *n.* émirat *m.*
emissary ['emisəri] *n.* émissaire *m*; messager, -ère.
emission [i'miʃ(ə)n] *n.* **1.** émission *f*, dégagement *m* (de gaz, de chaleur, etc.); **e. current,** courant d'émission; **e. efficiency,** efficacité *f* (d'une cathode thermoélectronique). **2.** *Bank: etc:* émission (de billets de banque, etc.).
emit [i'mit] *v.tr.* **1.** dégager (de la chaleur, etc.); exhaler, dégager (une odeur); lancer, jeter (des étincelles); rendre (un son). **2.** émettre (du papier-monnaie).
emitter [i'mitər] *n.* *Atom.Ph:* émetteur.
emollient [i'mɔliənt] *a.* & *n.* *Med:* émollient (*m*).
emolument [i'mɔljumənt] *n.* (*usu. pl.*) émoluments *mpl*, appointements *mpl*; honoraires *fpl*.
emotion [i'mouʃ(ə)n] *n.* émotion *f*; emoi *m*; **to appeal to the emotions,** faire appel aux sentiments; **without showing the least e.,** sans montrer le moindre signe d'émotion; **voice touched with e.,** voix émue.
emotional [i'mouʃən(ə)l] *a.* **1.** (trouble) émotif; **for e. reasons,** pour des raisons émotives. **2.** (*liable to emotion*) émotif; **to be e.,** s'attendrir facilement. **-ally** *adv.* **1.** avec beaucoup d'émotion. **2. I am e. involved,** cela me concerne de trop près; **to be e. involved with s.o.,** avoir des liens affectifs avec qn.
emotionless [i'mouʃənlis] *a.* indifférent; impassible.
emotive [i'moutiv] *a.* émotif.
empanel [im'pæn(ə)l] *v.tr.* (**empanelled,** *NAm:* **empaneled**) *Jur:* **to e. a jury,** constituer le jury; **to e. a juror,** inscrire un juré sur la liste du jury.
empathy ['empəθi] *n.* *Psy:* empathie *f*.
emperor ['empərər] *n.* **1.** empereur *m.* **2.** (*a*) *Ent:* **e. moth,** saturnie *f*; *F:* paon *m* de nuit; (*b*) *Orn:* **e. penguin,** manchot empereur.
emphasis ['emfəsis] *n.* **1.** force *f*; accentuation *f*; **oratorical e.,** accent *m* oratoire. **2.** insistance *f*; **to lay e. on (sth.),** appuyer, insister, sur (un fait); souligner (un mot). **3.** (*a*) *Gram:* mise *f* en relief; (*b*) *Ling:* accent *m* d'insistance (sur un mot ou une syllabe).
emphasize ['emfəsaiz] *v.tr.* accentuer, appuyer sur (un mot, un fait); attirer l'attention sur (un fait); faire ressortir, mettre en relief (une qualité, etc.).
emphatic [im'fætik] *a.* **1.** (*a*) (manière) énergique (de s'exprimer); (geste) énergique; (orateur) vigoureux; (refus) positif, net; (*b*) (syllabe) accentuée. **2.** (style, mot, etc.) emphatique. **-ally** *adv.* **1.** énergiquement; (refuser) carrément, catégoriquement. **2.** en termes pressants. **3.** (*intensive*) **he is most e. a leader,** c'est un chef s'il en fut jamais.
empire ['empaiər] *n.* (*a*) empire *m*; *Hist:* **the Holy Roman E.,** le Saint Empire Romain Germanique; **e. builder,** constructeur *m* d'empires; (*b*) *Arch: Furn:* **E. style,** style Empire; **E. furniture,** meubles *mpl* Empire.
empiric [em'pirik] **1.** *a.* empirique. **2.** *n.* empiriste *m.*
empirical [em'pirik(ə)l] *a.* empirique; **e. formula,** formule *f* empirique.
empiricism [em'pirisizm] *n.* empirisme *m.*
emplacement [im'pleismənt] *n.* *Mil:* emplacement *m* (d'un canon).
emplane [im'plein] **1.** *v.i.* monter en avion. **2.** *v.tr.* faire monter (qn, des troupes) en avion.
employ¹ [im'plɔi] *n.* emploi *m*; **to be in s.o.'s e.,** être au service de qn; être employé par qn.
employ² *v.tr.* **1.** employer (des moyens, etc.); se servir de (la force, etc.). **2.** employer (qn) à son service; **to e. s.o. as secretary,** employer qn comme secrétaire. **3. to e. oneself, to be employed (in doing sth.),** s'occuper, être occupé (à faire qch.). **employed** *a.* employé; **gainfully e.,** rémunéré; *n.pl.* **employers and e.,** le patronat et le salariat.
employee [implɔi'iː, im'plɔiː] *n.* employé, -ée; **relations between management and employees,** relations *fpl* entre la direction et le personnel.
employer [im'plɔiər] *n.* *Ind:* patron, patronne; employeur, -euse; **body of employers,** patronat *m*; **employers' association,** organisation patronale, syndicat patronal.
employment [im'plɔimənt] *n.* **1.** emploi *m* (de l'argent, etc.). **2.** emploi, travail *m*; place *f*, situation *f*; **to be without e.,** être sans emploi, sans travail; **e. agency,** bureau *m*, agence *f*, de placement; (*for workmen*) service *m* d'embauche.
emporium [im'pɔːriəm] *n.* **1.** centre *m* de commerce. **2.** grand magasin.
empower [im'pauər] *v.tr.* **1.** *Jur:* donner pouvoir, donner procuration, à (qn). **2. to e. s.o. to do sth.,** autoriser qn à faire qch.; donner, conférer, plein(s) pouvoir(s) à qn pour faire qch.
empress ['empres] *n.f.* impératrice.
emptiness ['em(p)tinis] *n.* vide *m* (d'une chambre, etc.); *F:* **to feel an e.,** se sentir l'estomac creux.
empty¹ ['em(p)ti] **1.** *a.* vide (**of,** de); (*a*) (rue) déserte; (bourse) vide; (immeuble) inoccupé; (estomac) creux; (wagon) sans chargement; (*of lorry, etc.*) **to come back e.,** revenir à vide; **to be taken on an e. stomach,** à prendre à jeun; **to feel e.,** se sentir l'estomac creux; **e. handed,** les mains vides; (*b*) (tête) vide; (esprit) nul; **e.-headed,** sans cervelle; (*c*) vaines (paroles, menaces); (*d*) **word e. of meaning,** mot vide de sens. **2.** *n.pl.* *Com:* **empties,** caisses *fpl* vides; bouteilles *fpl* vides; **returned empties,** retournés *mpl* vides.
empty² **1.** *v.tr.* vider (un verre, etc.) (**into,** dans); décharger, *Min:* verser (un wagon); dépeupler (les rues); vidanger (une fosse d'aisance, un carter). **2.** *v.i.* (*a*) (*of river, etc.*) se déverser (**into,** dans); (*b*) (*of theatre*) se vider. **emptying** *n.* vidage *m* (d'un verre, etc.); vidange *f* (d'un tonneau, etc.); déchargement *m* (d'un wagon); dépeuplement *m* (des rues).
emu ['iːmjuː] *n.* *Orn:* émeu *m.*
emulate ['emjuleit] *v.tr.* être l'émule de (qn); imiter (qn, qch.).
emulation [emju'leiʃ(ə)n] *n.* émulation *f*.
emulsify [i'mʌlsifai] *v.tr.* émulsionner.
emulsion [i'mʌlʃ(ə)n] *n.* émulsion *f*; **e. paint,** peinture mate; *Phot:* **plate e.,** émulsion pour plaques.
enable [in'eibl] *v.tr.* **to e. s.o. to do sth.,** (i) mettre qn à même, mettre qn en état, de faire qch.; (ii) *Jur:* habiliter qn à faire qch.; **this legacy enabled him to retire,** cet héritage lui permit de prendre sa retraite. **enabling** *a.* *Jur:* habilitant; **e. act,** loi *f* qui habilite une personne juridique.
enact [in'ækt] *v.tr.* **1.** *Jur:* décréter (une loi); ordonner, décréter (une mesure). **2.** *Lit:* jouer, représenter (une tragédie).
enactment [in'æktmənt] *n.* **1.** établissement *m*, promulgation *f* (d'une loi). **2.** ordonnance *f*; décret *m.*; acte législatif; **by legislative e.,** par un texte législatif.
enamel [i'næm(ə)l] *n.* **1.** émail *m*, *pl.* émaux; (*a*) *Art:* **e. work,** (i) émaillure *f*; (ii) peinture *f* sur émail; **e. ware,** ustensiles *mpl* en fer émaillé; (*b*) *Anat:* émail

(des dents). 2. (*a*) vernis *m*; émail, *pl*. émails; **e. paint,** peinture *f* au vernis; (*b*) **to finish a bicycle in baked e.,** émailler une bicyclette à chaud, au four.

enamel² *v.tr.* (**enamelled,** *NAm:* **enameled**) **1.** émailler (la porcelaine, etc.). **2.** ripoliner (une porte, etc.); vernir (le fer, le cuir). **enamelled** *a.* (brique, etc.) émaillé; (carreau) vernissé; **e. saucepan,** casserole en fer émaillé. **2.** peint en émail. **enamelling** *n.* (*a*) émaillage *m*; (*b*) (*art of enamelling*) émaillure *f*; (*c*) peinture *f* en émail.

enamoured [i'næməd] *a. Lit:* amoureux (**of s.o.,** de qn); passionné (**of sth.,** pour qch.); **to become e. of s.o.,** s'éprendre de qn.

encage [in'keidʒ] *v.tr.* encager; mettre (un animal) en cage.

encamp [in'kæmp] **1.** *v.tr.* (faire) camper (une armée). **2.** *v.i.* camper.

encampment [in'kæmpmənt] *n.* campement *m*; camp *m*.

encapsulate [in'kæpsjuleit] *v.tr.* capsuler.

encase [in'keis] *v.tr.* **1.** encaisser, enfermer (**in,** dans); mettre (un objet) dans un étui. **2.** (*a*) munir (qch.) d'une enveloppe; (*b*) revêtir (**s.o. in sth.,** qn de qch.).

encash [in'kæʃ] *v.tr.* **1.** encaisser (un chèque, de la monnaie). **2.** toucher (un chèque, une somme).

encaustic [en'kɔːstik] **1.** *a.* (*a*) *Art:* (tableau, etc.) à l'encaustique; (peinture) encaustique; (*b*) *Cer:* **e. tile,** carreau *m* céramique. **2.** *n. Art:* encaustique *f*.

encephalitis [ensefə'laitis] *n. Med:* encéphalite *f*.

enchant [in'tʃɑːnt] *v.tr.* **1.** ensorceler. **2.** enchanter, ravir. **enchanted** *a.* **1.** enchanté, ensorcelé. **2.** enchanté, (**with,** de). **enchanting** *a.* enchanteur, -eresse; ravissant, charmant. **enchantingly** *adv.* à ravir.

enchantment [in'tʃɑːntmənt] *n.* enchantement *m*. **1.** ensorcellement *m*. **2.** ravissement *m*; *Lit:* **distance lends e. (to the view),** tout paraît beau (vu) de loin.

enchantress [in'tʃɑːntris] *n.f.* enchanteresse.

encircle [in'səːkl] *v.tr.* ceindre, encercler; cerner, entourer (une armée). **encircling** *n.* encerclement *m*; *Mil:* **e. movement,** manœuvre *f* de débordement.

encirclement [in'səːkəlmənt] *n.* encerclement *m*.

enclave ['enkleiv] *n.* enclave *f*.

enclose [in'klouz] *v.tr.* **1.** (*a*) clôturer (un champ) (**with,** de); entourer, investir (l'ennemi, une ville); **garden enclosed with, in, by, high walls,** jardin entouré de hauts murs; (*b*) blinder (un moteur électrique, etc.); enfermer (un mécanisme) dans un carter. **2.** inclure, (r)enfermer (**in,** dans); **to e. sth. in a letter,** joindre qch. à une lettre; **letter enclosing a cheque,** lettre contenant un chèque; **enclosed herewith,** sous ce pli; **enclosed please find . . .,** veuillez trouver ci-inclus, ci-joint . . .. **enclosed** *a.* **1.** (*a*) (*of field, etc.*) clos, enclos; (*of army*) entouré, cerné; (*of city*) investi; **e. space,** espace clos; (*b*) (*of order, monk, etc.*) cloîtré. **2.** *Mec.E: etc:* recouvert, enfermé; en carter.

enclosure [in'klouʒər] *n.* **1.** enceinte *f*, clôture. **2.** (*a*) enclos *m*, clos *m*, enceinte; (*b*) *Turf:* le pesage; **the public enclosures,** la pelouse. **3.** *Com:* pièce annexée, incluse; annexe *f*; le document ci-joint; **enclosures,** pièces jointes.

encode [en'koud] *v.tr.* chiffrer (un texte, etc.).

encompass [in'kʌmpəs] *v.tr.* **1.** entourer (**with,** de). **2.** envelopper, renfermer (**with, within,** dans).

encore¹ [ɔŋ'kɔːr] *n. & int.* (*a*) bis *m*; **e.!** bis! (*b*) chanson *f*, morceau, etc., exécuté à la fin d'un spectacle, d'un concert, etc., par un artiste que l'on a bissé; **to call for an e.,** bisser.

encore² **1.** *v.tr.* bisser (un passage, un acteur). **2.** *v.i.* crier bis, bisser.

encounter¹ [in'kauntər] *n.* **1.** rencontre *f* (d'amis, etc.). **2.** (*a*) rencontre (hostile); combat *m*; (*b*) duel *m*; (*c*) *Sp: Journ:* confrontation *f*.

encounter² *v.tr.* rencontrer (qn, un obstacle); éprouver, (des difficultés); affronter (l'ennemi); trouver (de la résistance); essuyer (une tempête).

encourage [in'kʌridʒ] *v.tr.* **1.** encourager, (qn). **2.** encourager, inciter (**s.o. to do sth.,** qn à faire qch.). **3.** appuyer (une bonne œuvre); favoriser (les arts, le commerce)); encourager (une croyance). **encouraging** *a.* encourageant. **encouragingly** *adv.* d'une manière encourageante.

encouragement [in'kʌridʒmənt] *n.* encouragement *m*.

encroach [in'kroutʃ] *v.i.* **to e. (up)on (sth.),** empiéter sur (une terre, etc.); usurper, *Jur:* léser (les droits de qn); **the sea is encroaching on the land,** la mer gagne du terrain.

encroachment [in'kroutʃmənt] *n.* **1.** *Jur:* (*a*) **e. upon s.o.'s rights,** usurpation *f* des droits de qn, empiètement *m* sur les droits de qn. **2.** ingression *f* (de la mer).

encrust [in'krʌst] *v.tr.* (*a*) incruster; (*b*) couvrir d'une croûte, incruster (**with,** de).

encumber [in'kʌmbər] *v.tr.* **1.** encombrer (**with,** de); gêner (qn, le mouvement). **2. encumbered estate,** propriété grevée (i) de dettes, (ii) d'hypothèques.

encumbrance [in'kʌmbrəns] *n.* **1.** embarras *m*, charge *f*; **to be an e. to s.o.,** être à charge à qn; **man without family encumbrances,** homme sans charges de famille. **2.** *Jur:* (*a*) charges (d'une succession); **to free an estate from encumbrances,** dégrever une propriété; (*b*) servitude *f*.

encyclic(al) [in'siklik(l)] *a. & n. R.C.Ch:* encyclique (*f*).

encyclopaedia, *NAm:* **encyclopedia** [insaiklə'piːdiə] *n.* encyclopédie *f*; *F:* **walking e.,** encyclopédie vivante.

encyclopaedic, *NAm:* **encyclopedic** [insaiklə'piːdik] *a.* encyclopédique.

end¹ [end] *n.* **1.** (*a*) bout *m*, extrémité *f* (d'un bâton, d'une rue, etc.); fin *f* (d'un livre); queue *f* (d'une procession, etc.); about *m* (d'une poutre); **the e. of the table,** le bout de la table; *Rail:* **e. of line,** tête *f* de ligne; **to come to the e. of the road,** (i) arriver au bout de la route; (ii) arriver au bout de sa carrière, de sa vie; (ii) être dans une impasse; *Ecc. Arch:* **east e.,** chevet *m* (d'une église); *Rail:* **the e. carriage,** le wagon de queue; *Tchn:* **e. piece,** embout *m*; *F:* **to get hold of the wrong e. of the stick,** prendre quelque chose à contre-sens; *F:* **to be at the receiving e.** recevoir les coups, les reproches, etc.; **to be at a loose e.,** être désœuvré; avoir du temps à perdre; *Fb: etc:* **to change ends,** changer de camp; (*of swimming pool*) **the deep, the shallow, e.,** le grand, le petit, fond; *F:* **to be thrown in at the deep e.,** être mis en pleine eau; *F:* **to go off the deep e.,** se mettre en colère, sortir de ses gonds; **to keep one's e. up,** (i) ne pas se laisser démonter; (ii) y mettre du sien; **e. to e.,** bout à bout; **to make (both) ends meet,** joindre les deux bouts; **from e. to e.,** d'un bout à l'autre; (*of barrel, etc.*) **on e.,** debout, sur bout; **to stand a box (up) on e.,** dresser une boîte debout; **his hair was standing on e.,** ses cheveux se dressaient sur sa tête, se hérissaient; **five hours on e.,** cinq heures de suite, d'affilée; **e. on,** bout à bout; (*b*) *I.C.E:* **big e., small e.,** tête *f*, pied *m*, de bielle; (*c*) tronçon *m* (de mât, etc.); tronche *f* (de câble); bout (de chandelle); bout, *F:* mégot *m* (de cigarette). **2.** limite *f*, borne *f*; **to the ends of the earth,** jusqu'au bout du monde. **3.** (*a*) bout, fin (du mois); fin (de travail); issue *f* (d'une réunion); terme *m* (d'un procès, etc.); **the third from the e.,** le troisième avant la fin; **we shall never hear the e. of it,** on n'entendra jamais la fin; **and that's the e. of it!** et voilà tout! **there's no e. to it,** cela n'en finit pas; *P:* **no e. of . . .,** infiniment de . . .; **it'll do you no e. of good,** ça te fera énormément de bien; **to make an e. of, put an e. to, (sth.),** en finir avec (qch.); achever (qch.); mettre fin à (un abus, etc.); supprimer (la concurrence); **to draw to an e.,** tirer, toucher, à sa fin; **to come to an e.,** prendre fin; (*of meeting, etc.*) se clore; **the war was at an e.,** la guerre était terminée; **to be at the e. of one's resources,** être au bout de ses ressources; **at the e. (of sth.),** à la fin (du mois, de l'hiver); à l'expiration (de cette période); au bout (de six mois); **in the e.,** (i) à la longue (ii) à la fin; enfin; **e. product,** (i) produit manufacturé, fabriqué; (ii) suite *f,* résultat *m;* (*b*) **e. of the world,** fin du monde; **until the e. of time,** jusqu'à la consommation des temps; *Ecc:* **world without e.,** pour les siècles des siècles; **it's not the e. of the world,** ce n'est pas la fin du monde; (*c*) fin, terme (de la vie); **to come to a bad e.,** mal finir; **to meet one's e.,** trouver la mort. **4.** (*aim, purpose*) fin, but *m,* dessein *m;* **to attain, achieve, one's e., one's ends,** en arriver, parvenir, à ses fins; atteindre son but; **to this e., with this e. in view,** dans cette intention; avec cet objectif en vue; *Prov:* **the e. justifies the means,** la fin justifie les moyens.

end² **1.** (*a*) *v.tr.* finir, terminer, achever (un ouvrage, etc.); conclure (un discours); clore (une séance); **to e. one's days peacefully,** terminer ses jours en paix; **to e. a speech with a quotation,** terminer un discours avec une citation; (*b*) *v.i.* **I must e. by thanking Mr X,** pour conclure je dois remercier M. X; **let us e. with a song,** finissons par une chanson. **2.** *v.i.* finir, se terminer (**at, in,** dans, en); (*of word*) se terminer (**in,** en); (*of subscription*) expirer; **the path ends at the lakeside,** le chemin aboutit au bord du lac; (*of stick*) **to e. in a point,** se terminer en pointe; (*of story*) **to e. happily,** avoir une issue heureuse; **his extravagance will e. (up) by ruining him,** son extravagance aboutira à sa ruine; **all's well that ends well,** tout est bien qui finit bien. **3.** *v.tr.* embouter (une canne, etc.). **ended** *a.* **1.** fini, terminé. **2.** (*with adj. or num. prefixed*) **round-e.,** à bout rond; **double-e.,** à deux bouts. **ending** *n.* **1.** terminaison *f,* achèvement *m.* **2.** fin *f,* conclusion *f* (d'un livre); **happy e.,** dénouement heureux; **to come to an abrupt e.,** terminer court. **3.** *Gram:* désinence *f,* terminaison (d'un mot); **case e.,** flexion casuelle.

end-all ['endɔ:l] *n. used in the phr.* **the be-all and e.-a.,** le but suprême, la fin des fins.

endanger [in'deindʒər] *v.tr.* mettre (qn, qch.) en danger; exposer, risquer (sa vie, etc.); compromettre (des intérêts).

endear [in'diər] *v.tr.* rendre (qn, qch.) cher (**to,** à); **he has endeared himself to all,** il s'est fait universellement aimer. **endearing** *a.* **1.** qui inspire l'affection; (qualité) qui rend qn sympathique. **2.** affectueux; (mot) tendre.

endearment [in'diəmənt] *n.* (*a*) **term of e.,** expression *f* de tendresse; (*b*) **endearments,** mots *mpl* tendres.

endeavour¹ [in'devər] *n.* effort *m,* tentative *f;* **to use, make, every e. to . . .,** faire tout son possible, tous les efforts possibles, pour . . ..

endeavour² *v.i.* **to e. to do sth.,** s'efforcer, tenter, essayer, de faire qch.; chercher à faire qch.

endemic [en'demik] **1.** *a. Bot: Med:* endémique. **2.** *n. Med:* endémie *f.* **-ally** *adv.* endémiquement.

endive ['endiv] *n. Bot: Hort:* **1. (curled) e.,** chicorée frisée. **2.** *U.S:* endive *f.*

endless ['endlis] *a.* **1.** (*in space*) (*a*) (voyage, etc.) sans fin, interminable; (câble, vis) sans fin; (*b*) sans bornes, infini; **e. space,** l'infini *m;* **to take e. pains to do, over, sth.,** se donner une peine infinie à faire qch. **2.** (*in time*) (*a*) sans fin; (discussion) à n'en plus finir, interminable; **it's an e. task, it's e.,** cela n'en finit pas; (*b*) (*of pain*) continuel, incessant; (*of chatter*) intarissable. **-ly** *adv.* sans fin, sans cesse; éternellement.

endocarp ['endouka:p] *n.* endocarpe *m.*

endocrine ['endoukrain] *a. & n.* glande *f* endocrine.

endorse [in'dɔ:s] *v.tr.* **1.** *Adm: Fin: etc:* endosser (un document, un chèque); viser (un passeport); avaliser (un effet); **to e. a driving licence,** inscrire les détails d'un délit sur le permis de conduire. **2.** appuyer, sanctionner (une opinion, une action); souscrire à (une décision, une opinion); *Jur:* approuver (un appel); **I e. all you have done,** j'approuve tout ce que vous avez fait.

endorsement [in'dɔ:smənt] *n.* **1.** (*a*) *Fin: etc:* endossement *m,* endos *m* (d'un chèque); aval *m* (d'un effet); *Adm:* contravention *f* inscrite sur le permis de conduire; (*on passport*) mention spéciale; (*b*) *Ins:* avenant *m.* **2.** approbation *f* (d'une action); adhésion *f* (à une opinion).

endorser [in'dɔ:sər] *n. Fin:* endosseur *m.*

endosperm ['endouspə:m] *n. Bot:* endosperme *m.*

endow [in'dau] *v.tr.* **1.** doter (qn, une société) (**with,** de); assurer un revenu à (sa fille, etc.); fonder (un lit dans un hôpital). **2.** (*of pers.*) **endowed with great talents,** doué de grands talents; **woman endowed with great beauty,** femme dotée d'une grande beauté; *F:* (*of woman*) **well endowed,** aux formes plantureuses.

endowment [in'daumənt] *n.* **1.** (*a*) dotation *f* (l'action ou le fonds); (*b*) fondation (léguée à un hospice); (*c*) *Ins:* **(pure) e. assurance, policy,** assurance *f* en cas de vie; assurance à capital différé; **(ordinary) e. assurance,** assurance mixte. **2.** don (naturel); talent *m.*

endpaper ['endpeipər] *n.* (page *f* de) garde (*f*).

endue [in'dju:] *v.tr. Lit:* revêtir (**with,** de).

endurable [in'dju:rəbl] *a.* supportable.

endurance [in'dju:rəns] *n.* **1.** (*a*) résistance *f;* **physical e.,** endurance *f* (physique); **beyond e.,** insupportable, intolérable; (*b*) **e. test,** (i) *Mec.E:* essai *m* de durée; (ii) *Sp:* épreuve *f* d'endurance. **2.** patience *f;* longanimité *f.*

endure [in'dju:ər] **1.** *v.tr.* supporter, endurer, souffrir avec patience (des insultes, etc.); soutenir (des reproches, etc.); *Prov:* **what can't be cured must be endured,** où il n'y a pas de remède il faut se résigner. **2.** *v.i.* durer, rester; **work that will e.,** ouvrage qui vivra. **enduring** *a.* durable, qui dure, permanent; (paix) stable; (mal) persistant, qui persiste.

endways, endwise ['endweiz, -waiz] *adv.* **1.** (*a*) de chant, debout; (*b*) **e. on,** avec le bout en avant. **2.** (*end to end*) bout à bout. **3.** longitudinalement.

enema ['enəmə] *n. Med:* **1.** lavement *m.* **2.** appareil *m* à lavements.

enemy ['enəmi] **1.** *n.* (*a*) ennemi, -e; **man without an e.,** homme sans ennemis; **to be one's own (worst) e.,** se desservir soi-même; (*b*) *coll.* **the e.,** l'ennemi, l'adversaire *m;* *Mil:* **e.-occupied territories,** territoires occupés par l'ennemi. **2.** *a.* (pays, navire, etc.) ennemi; **e. alien,** ressortissant, -ante, d'un pays ennemi.

energetic [enə'dʒetik] **1.** *a.* (homme, mesure) énergique. **2.** *n.pl.* (*usu. with sg. const.*) **energetics,** l'énergétique *f.* **-ally** *adv.* énergiquement; avec énergie.

energize ['enədʒaiz] *v.tr.* (*a*) donner de l'énergie à (qn); stimuler (qn); (*b*) *El:* alimenter; amorcer (une dynamo); aimanter (l'âme d'une bobine).

energy ['enədʒi] *n.* **1.** énergie *f,* vigueur *f;* **to have no e.,** ne pas avoir d'énergie; manquer d'allant; **man of e.,** homme énergique; **to devote, apply, all one's**

energies to a task, consacrer, apporter, appliquer, tous ses efforts, toute son énergie, à une tâche; **e.-producing foods,** aliments *mpl* énergétiques. **2.** (*a*) *Mec:* énergie, travail *m*; travail mécanique; **e. consumed,** puissance absorbée; **kinetic e.,** énergie cinétique; **to store up e.,** emmagasiner du travail; *Elcs:* **e. band,** bande *f* d'énergie; (*b*) **atomic e.,** énergie *f* atomique; (*c*) *Pol:* **E. Minister,** *in Eng:* **E. Secretary,** ministre *m* de l'Énergie; **the e. crisis,** la crise de l'énergie.

enervate ['enəveit] *v.tr.* affaiblir (le corps, la volonté). **enervating** *a.* (climat) débilitant.

enervation [enə'veiʃ(ə)n] *n.* **1.** affaiblissement *m.* **2.** mollesse *f.*

enfeeble [in'fibl] *v.tr.* (*of pain, age*) affaiblir.

enfilade¹ ['enfileid] *n. Mil:* tir *m* d'enfilade.

enfilade² *v.tr. Mil:* enfiler, prendre en enfilade.

enfold [in'fould] *v.tr.* envelopper (**sth. in sth.,** qch. dans qch.); **to e. s.o. in one's arms,** étreindre, embrasser, qn.

enforce [in'fɔːs] *v.tr.* **1.** donner de la force à, faire valoir (un argument); appuyer (une demande). **2.** mettre en vigueur (une loi, etc.); faire valoir (ses droits); faire respecter, faire obéir (la loi); appliquer (la loi); imposer, faire observer (un réglement); **to e. obedience,** se faire obéir. **enforced** *a.* (silence, etc.) forcé.

enforceable [in'fɔːsəbl] *a.* (contrat) exécutoire.

enforcement [in'fɔːsmənt] *n. Jur:* exécution *f*, mise *f* en vigueur, application *f* (d'une loi); **law e. officers,** fonctionnaires chargés de l'application de la loi.

enfranchise [in'fræn(t)ʃaiz] *v.tr.* **1.** affranchir (un esclave). **2.** *Pol:* admettre au suffrage (un citoyen); accorder le droit de vote à (qn).

enfranchisement [in'fræn(t)ʃizmənt] *n.* **1.** affranchissement *m* (d'un esclave). **2.** *Pol:* admission *f* (d'un citoyen) au suffrage.

engage [in'geidʒ] *v.tr. & i.* **1.** (*a*) engager (sa parole, son honneur); **to e. (oneself) to do sth.,** s'engager à faire qch.; (*b*) **to be engaged (to be married),** être fiancé(e); **to become engaged,** se fiancer. **2.** (*a*) engager (un domestique, etc.); embaucher (des ouvriers); *Navy:* recruter (des hommes); (*b*) louer (un taxi); **this seat is engaged,** cette place est retenue, occupée, prise; (*b*) *Tp:* occuper (la ligne); **the number is engaged,** la ligne est occupée. **3.** occuper (qn); fixer (l'attention); attirer, gagner (l'affection de qn); **to e. in conversation with s.o., to e. s.o. in conversation,** entrer en conversation avec qn; engager la conversation avec qn; **I can't come tonight as I am (otherwise) engaged,** je ne puis pas venir ce soir parce que je suis pris; **to be engaged in writing a novel,** être occupé à écrire un roman. **4.** *Mil:* **to e. (in) combat, to e. in action, to e. the enemy,** engager le combat; **to** e. an enemy aircraft, ouvrir le feu sur un appareil ennemi. **5.** *Mec.E:* (*a*) mettre en prise (un engrenage, une vitesse); **to e. first (gear),** mettre en première (vitesse); (*b*) *v.i.* (*of cog wheel*) (s')engrener, (s')engager (**with,** avec); s'embrayer. **engaged** *a.* **1.** fiancé; **the e. couple,** les fiancés. **2.** (*a*) **heavily e.,** très occupé; (*b*) *Tp:* **to get the e. signal,** entendre le signal de ligne occupée. **3.** *Mec.E:* (*of gear wheels*) en prise. **engaging** *a.* (sourire, ton) engageant, attrayant, attirant; (ton) liant; **to have an e. manner,** avoir du liant. **engagingly** *adv.* d'une manière engageante; (sourire) gentiment.

engagement [in'geidʒmənt] *n.* **1.** engagement *m*; (*a*) promesse *f*, obligation *f*; *Com:* **to carry out, meet, one's engagements,** faire face à ses engagements; remplir ses engagements; (*b*) rendez-vous *m*; **owing to a previous e.,** à cause d'une promesse antérieure; **public e.,** engagement à paraître en public; **she has many social engagements,** elle sort beaucoup; **to have an e.,** être pris, être occupé; **e. book,** agenda *m.* **2.** engagement (de domestiques); recrutement *m.* **3.** fiançailles; *fpl.* **e. ring,** anneau *m*, bague *f*, de fiançailles. **4.** *Mil:* (*a*) combat *m*, engagement *m*; (*b*) intervention (d'une unité dans la bataille). **5.** *Mec.E:* (*a*) mise *f* en prise; embrayage *m*; (*b*) prise *f* (d'un pignon avec une roue, etc.).

engender [in'dʒendər] *v.tr.* faire naître, produire (un effet); engendrer (une maladie, un sentiment).

engine ['endʒin] *n.* **1.** machine *f*, appareil *m*; **fire e.,** pompe *f* à incendie. **2.** *Mec.E: etc:* (*a*) moteur *m*; machine; **petrol,** *U.S:* **gas, e.,** moteur à essence; **steam e.,** machine à vapeur; **internal combustion e.,** moteur à combustion interne, à explosion; **two-stroke, four-stroke, e.,** moteur à deux, à quatre, temps; **jet e.,** moteur à réaction; **traction e.,** locomobile *f*; tracteur *m*; **(railway) e.,** locomotive *f*; (*b*) **e. house,** bâtiment *m* des machines, des moteurs; dépôt *m* (de pompes à incendie, etc.); **e. room,** salle *f* des machines; *Nau:* chambre *f* des machines; **e.-room telegraph,** chadburn *m*; *Rail:* **e. shed,** garage *m*, dépôt *m*, remise *f*, des locomotives; **circular e. shed,** rotonde *f*; **e. driver,** conducteur *m*, mécanicien *m* (de locomotive).

engineer¹ [endʒi'niər] *n.* **1.** ingénieur *m*; (*a*) **civil e.,** (i) ingénieur des travaux publics; (ii) = ingénieur des ponts et chaussées; **marine e.,** ingénieur du génie maritime; **mechanical, electrical, e.,** ingénieur mécanicien, électricien; **mining e.,** ingénieur des mines; (*b*) **consulting e.,** ingénieur conseil; **production e.,** ingénieur (chargé) de la production. **2.** (*a*) *Nau:* ingénieur, mécanicien *m*; **chief e.,** chef mécanicien; *Navy:* **e. officer,** ingénieur mécanicien; **second e.,** officier mécanicien en second; (*b*) *Av:* **flight e.,** (i) *Mil:* mécanicien navigant; (ii) (civil) mécanicien de bord; **aircraft e.,** mécanicien de piste; (*c*) *Mil:* soldat *m* du génie, sapeur *m*; **the engineers,** le génie, l'arme *f* du génie; **the Royal Engineers,** *U.S:* **the Corps of Engineers** = le Génie; **electrical, mechanical, e.,** sapeur électricien, mécanicien; (*d*) *Rail: NAm:* conducteur *m*, mécanicien (de locomotive); (*e*) *Fig:* l'âme *f*, l'instigateur *m* (d'un projet, d'un complot).

engineer² *v.tr.* **1.** construire (en qualité d'ingénieur) (des ponts, des routes). **2.** arranger (un spectacle); *usu. Pej:* machiner (un coup); manigancer (une affaire). **engineering** *n.* (*a*) technique *f*, science *f*, de l'ingénieur; **civil e.,** génie civil; **marine e.,** génie maritime; **electrical e.,** électrotechnique *f*; **agricultural e.,** génie agricole, rural; (*b*) **(mechanical) e.,** mécanique *f*; **precision e.,** mécanique de précision; **light e.,** petite mécanique; **e. works,** atelier *m* de constructions mécaniques; **electrical e. industry,** industrie *f* de l'équipement électrique; (*c*) **industrial e.,** organisation industrielle; **production e.,** technique de la production; **e. department,** service *m* technique; **e. and design department,** bureau *m* d'études; **e. consultant,** ingénieur *m* conseil; **human e.,** psychanalyse (industrielle); (*d*) *Fig: usu. Pej:* machinations *fpl*, manœuvres *fpl.*

engineman, *pl.* **men** ['endʒinmæn, -men] *n.m. Rail: NAm:* mécanicien.

England ['iŋglənd] *Pr.n. Geog:* l'Angleterre *f*; **in E.,** en Angleterre; **to go to E.,** aller en Angleterre.

English ['iŋgliʃ] **1.** *a.* anglais; **E. born, by birth,** de naissance anglaise; **E. history,** histoire *f* d'Angleterre; **the E. Channel,** la Manche; *Arch:* **early E. (style),** premier style gothique. **2.** *n.* (*a*) *pl.* **the E.,** les Anglais *mpl*; (*b*) *Ling:* anglais *m*, la langue anglaise; **E. E., British E.,** l'anglais d'Angleterre; **American, Australian, E.,** l'anglais américain, australien; **the King's, Queen's, E.,** l'anglais correct; **E. speaking,** anglophone, de langue anglaise; **to study E.,** étudier l'anglais; **to speak E.,** parler anglais; **in E.,** en anglais; **E. teacher,** professeur *m* d'anglais; **in plain E.,** en bon anglais; **let me tell you in plain E. that . . .,** je vais vous dire en mots de deux syllabes que . . .; **pidgin E.** = petit nègre.

Englishman, *pl.* **-men** ['iŋgliʃmən] *n.* Anglais *m.*

Englishwoman, *pl.* **-women** ['iŋgliʃwumən, -wimin] *n.f.* Anglaise.

engrave [in'greiv] *v.tr.* graver; **to e. on wood,** graver sur bois; **engraved on the memory,** gravé dans la mémoire. **engraving** *n.* (*process or print*) gravure *f*; (*print*) estampe *f*; **copper-plate e.,** chalcographie *f*; **line e.,** gravure au burin; **half-tone e.,** similigravure; **wood e.,** gravure sur bois.

engraver [in'greivər] *n.* (*pers.*) graveur *m*; **wood e.,** graveur sur bois.

engross [in'grous] *v.tr.* **1.** *Jur:* (i) grossoyer, (ii) rédiger (un document). **2.** absorber, occuper (qn); **engrossed in her reading,** toute à sa lecture; **to become engrossed in sth.,** s'abstraire, s'absorber, dans qch. **engrossing** *a.* (*of study, etc.*) absorbant.

engrossment [in'grousmənt] *n.* **1.** *Jur:* rédaction *f* de la grosse. **2.** absorption *f* (de l'attention) **(in,** dans).

engulf [in'gʌlf] *v.tr.* engloutir, engouffrer; **to be engulfed by the waves,** sombrer dans les flots.

enhance [in'hɑːns, -'hæns] *v.tr.* rehausser (le mérite de qch.); accroître (le plaisir); mettre en valeur (la beauté de qn); agrandir (la réputation).

enhancement [in'hɑːnsmənt, -'hæns-] *n.* renchérissement *m*, rehaussement *m* (de prix); augmentation *f* (de plaisir, etc.).

enharmonic [enhɑː'mɔnik] *a.* enharmonique.

enigma [i'nigmə] *n.* (*a*) énigme *f*; (*b*) personne énigmatique, mystérieuse.

enigmatic [enig'mætik] *a.* énigmatique; mystérieux. **-ally** *adv.* énigmatiquement, mystérieusement.

enjoin [in'dʒɔin] *v.tr.* enjoindre **(sth. on s.o.,** qch. à qn); **to e. s.o. to do sth.,** enjoindre à qn de faire qch.

enjoy [in'dʒɔi] *v.tr.* **1.** aimer, prendre plaisir à (qch.); savourer (une pipe); goûter (la musique, etc.); **to e. the fine weather,** jouir du beau temps; **to e. oneself,** s'amuser, se divertir; **e. yourself!** amusez-vous bien! **to e. doing sth.,** aimer, trouver du plaisir, à faire qch.; **I e. cooking,** j'aime (bien) faire la cuisine. **2.** (*a*) jouir de, posséder (une fortune, la confiance de qn); (*b*) **to e. good health,** jouir d'une bonne santé; *F:* **to e. bad health,** avoir la santé faible.

enjoyable [in'dʒɔiəbl] *a.* (séjour, excursion) agréable; **we had a most e. evening,** nous avons passé une excellente soirée. **-ably** *adv.* agréablement.

enjoyment [in'dʒɔimənt] *n.* **1.** jouissance *f* (d'un droit, etc.). **2.** plaisir *m.*

enlarge [in'lɑːdʒ] **1.** *v.tr.* (*a*) agrandir; étendre (une propriété); accroître, augmenter (sa fortune); (i) élargir, (ii) aléser (un trou); *Med:* hypertrophier (le cœur, le foie); *Phot:* agrandir (un cliché, etc.); **enlarged edition,** édition augmentée; *Med:* **enlarged tonsils,** amygdales hypertrophiées; (*b*) développer (une idée). **2.** *v.i.* (*a*) s'agrandir, s'étendre, s'élargir; (*b*) **to e. on . . .,** s'étendre sur, discourir longuement sur (un sujet, l'importance de qch.).

enlargement [in'lɑːdʒmənt] *n.* **1.** agrandissement *m*; extension *f* (d'une propriété); accroissement *m* (d'une fortune); (i) élargissement *m*, (ii) alésage *m* (d'un trou); augmentation *f.* **2.** *Phot:* agrandissement. **3.** *Med:* hypertrophie *f* (du cœur, de la rate).

enlarger [in'lɑːdʒər] *n. Phot:* agrandisseur *m.*

enlighten [in'lait(ə)n] *v.tr.* **to e. s.o. on a subject, as to sth.,** éclairer qn sur un sujet. **enlightened** *a.* (*of pers.*) éclairé; **e. criticism,** critique éclairée.

enlightenment [in'laitənmənt] *n.* **1.** (*a*) éclaircissement *m* **(on,** sur); (*b*) **for your e.,** pour votre édification. **2. the age of E.,** le siècle des lumières.

enlist [in'list] **1.** *v.tr.* (*a*) *Mil:* enrôler, engager (un soldat); (*b*) recruter (des partisans); s'assurer (le concours de qn); **to e. s.o.'s support for a cause,** rallier qn à une cause. **2.** *v.i. Mil:* (*of soldier*) s'engager. **enlisted** *a.* enrôlé, engagé, appelé (sous les drapeaux); *U.S:* **e. man,** (i) homme de troupe; (ii) gradé *m*; **e. men,** les hommes de troupe et les gradés.

enlistment [in'listmənt] *n. Mil:* engagement *m.*

enliven [in'laiv(ə)n] *v.tr.* (*a*) animer (qn, qch.); **to e. business,** stimuler les affaires; (*b*) égayer (une fête).

en masse ['ɑ̃ː'mæs] *adv.phr.* en masse, tous ensemble.

enmesh [in'meʃ] *v.tr.* (*a*) prendre au filet; (*b*) prendre (qn) dans un piège.

enmity ['enmiti] *n.* inimitié *f*, haine *f*, hostilité *f.*

ennoble [i'noubl] *v.tr.* **1.** anoblir (un roturier). **2.** ennoblir (qn, le caractère).

ennoblement [i'noublmənt] *n.* **1.** anoblissement *m* (d'un roturier). **2.** ennoblissement *m* (du caractère).

enormity [i'nɔːmiti] *n.* (*a*) énormité *f* (d'un crime, etc.); (*b*) **enormities,** énormités, atrocités *fpl.*

enormous [i'nɔːməs] *a.* énorme; colossal, -aux; monumental, -aux; (succès) fou. **-ly** *adv.* énormément.

enormousness [i'nɔːməsnis] *n.* grandeur démesurée.

enough [i'nʌf] **1.** *a.* & *n.* assez; **(not) e. money,** (pas) assez d'argent; *F:* **I've had e. of it, of them,** j'en ai assez; **I've had e. to drink,** j'ai assez bu; **that's e. for me,** cela me suffit; **that's e.,** (i) c'est assez, ça suffit; (ii) en voilà assez! **more than e.,** plus qu'il n'en faut; plus que suffisant; **there was more than e.,** il y en avait de reste; **have you e. to pay the bill?** avez-vous de quoi payer? **wages that are not e. to live on,** salaire qui ne suffit pas pour vivre; **he has e. to live on,** il a de quoi vivre; **e. said!** assez parlé! **e. of this nonsense!** assez de ces bêtises! **one word was e. to prove that . . .,** il a suffi d'un mot pour prouver que . . .; **it was e. to drive one crazy,** c'était à vous rendre fou; *Prov:* **e. is as good as a feast,** assez vaut (un) festin. **2.** *adv.* (*a*) **good e.,** assez bon; **fair e.!** ça va! d'accord! **it's a good e. reason,** c'est une raison comme une autre; **she is not strong e.,** elle n'est pas assez forte; **to be near e. to see,** être assez près pour voir; (*b*) (*intensive*) **you know well e. what I mean,** vous savez très bien ce que je veux dire; **curiously, oddly, e., nobody knew anything about it,** chose curieuse, personne n'en savait rien; (*c*) (*disparaging*) **well e.,** assez bien, pas mal; **the house is comfortable e.,** la maison est assez confortable.

en passant [ɑ̃ː'pasɑ̃] *adv.* en passant.

enquire [iŋ'kwaiər] *v.tr.* & *i.* demander (qch.); s'informer **(about sth.,** de qch.); se renseigner **(about sth.,** sur qch.); faire des recherches **(into sth.,** sur qch.).

enquiry [in'kwai(ə)ri] *n.* **1.** enquête *f*, recherche *f*, investigation *f.* **2.** demande *f* de renseignements.

enrage [in'reidʒ] *v.tr.* rendre furieux; exaspérer (qn).

enrapture [in'ræptjər] *v.tr.* ravir, enchanter (un auditoire, etc.). **enraptured** *a.* ravi, enchanté (d'admiration).

enrich [in'ritʃ] *v.tr.* enrichir (qn, une langue, etc.); fertiliser, amender (la terre); *I.C.E:* **to e. the mixture,** enrichir le mélange. **enriched** *a.* **e. with gold,** rehaussé d'or; *Atom.Ph:* **e. uranium,** uranium enrichi.

enrichment [in'ritʃmənt] *n.* enrichissement *m.*

enrol, *NAm:* **enroll** [in'roul] *v.tr.* & *i.* **(enrolled)** *Mil:* enrôler, encadrer (des recrues); embaucher (des ouvriers); immatriculer (des étudiants); **to e. (oneself),** s'enrôler, s'engager **(in the army,** dans l'armée); s'inscrire **(in a society,** à une société); **to e. for a course of lectures,** se faire inscrire pour un cours.

enrolment, *NAm:* **enrollment** [in'roulmənt] *n.*

enrôlement *m* (de soldats, etc.); embauche *f* (d'ouvriers, etc.); immatriculation *f* (d'étudiants).

ensconce [in'skɔns] *v.tr.* **to e. oneself,** se blottir, se nicher **(in a corner,** dans un coin); se camper **(in an armchair,** dans un fauteuil).

ensemble [ɑ̃:'sɑ̃:bl] *n. Mus: Cost: etc:* ensemble *m.*

enshrine [in'ʃrain] *v.tr.* enchâsser **(in,** dans).

ensign ['ensain, 'ens(ə)n] *n.* **1.** drapeau *m*; *Nau:* pavillon national; **white e.,** pavillon de la Marine anglaise et du Royal Yacht Squadron; **red e.** = pavillon marchand. **2.** (*pers.*) *U.S. Navy:* enseigne *m* (de vaisseau de deuxième classe).

ensilage [en'silidʒ] *n. Agr:* ensilage *m*, silotage *m.*

enslave [in'sleiv] *v.tr.* réduire à l'esclavage; asservir; rendre (qn) esclave.

enslavement [in'sleivmənt] *n.* réduction *f* (d'une nation, etc.) à l'esclavage; asservissement *m.*

ensnare [in'snɛər] *v.tr.* prendre (qn) au piège; (*of woman*) séduire (un homme).

ensue [in'sju:] *v.i.* s'ensuivre; **a long silence ensued,** il se fit un long silence. **ensuing** *a.* (année) qui suit; (événement) subséquent; **in the e. years,** au cours des années qui suivirent.

ensure [in'ʃuər] *v.tr.* assurer (le succès); réaliser (la guérison); **I have taken steps to e. that . . .,** j'ai pris des mesures pour que . . . (+ *sub.*).

entail[1] ['enteil] *n.* **1.** *Jur:* substitution *f* (d'héritiers). **2.** (*a*) *Jur:* bien substitué; (*b*) héritage *m* inéluctable.

entail[2] [en'teil] *v.tr.* **1.** *Jur:* **to e. an estate (on s.o.),** substituer un bien (au profit de qn); **entailed estate,** bien substitué. **2.** (*of action*) entraîner, occasionner (des dépenses); imposer (beaucoup de travail) **(on,** à); comporter (des difficultés).

entangle [in'tæŋgl] *v.tr.* **1.** (*a*) empêtrer; **to get, become, entangled in the seaweed,** s'empêtrer dans les algues; (*b*) embarrasser, empêtrer (qn); **to get entangled with a woman,** avoir une affaire avec une femme. **2.** emmêler (les cheveux, du fil); enchevêtrer (du fil de fer); **to get entangled,** s'emmêler, s'embrouiller.

entanglement [in'tæŋglmənt] *n.* **1.** embrouillement *m*, enchevêtrement *m*; **barbed wire e.,** réseau(x) *m(pl)* de fil de fer barbelé. **2. emotional entanglements,** complications sentimentales; **an e. with a woman,** une affaire avec une femme.

entente [ɑ̃:'tɑ̃:t] *n.* entente *f*; **e. cordiale,** entente cordiale.

enter ['entər] *v.* **(entered) I.** *v.i.* **1.** entrer **(into, through, etc.,** dans, par, etc.); *Th:* **e. Hamlet,** entre Hamlet. **2. to e. for (sth.),** se faire inscrire pour (une course); se présenter à (un examen). **II.** *v.tr.* **1.** entrer dans (une maison, un pays); **the bullet had entered his heart,** la balle lui avait pénétré dans le cœur; **it never entered my head that . . .,** il ne m'est pas venu à l'esprit que . . . **2.** (*a*) **to e. the Army, the Navy,** se faire soldat, se faire marin; **to e. the Church,** entrer dans les ordres; **to e. a university, a convent,** entrer à une université, dans un couvent; **to e. s.o.'s service,** entrer au service de qn; (*b*) **to e. one's sixtieth year,** entrer dans sa soixantième année. **3.** (*a*) **to e. a name on a list,** inscrire, porter, un nom sur une liste; **to e. a student at a university,** admettre un étudiant à une université; **to e. a horse for a race,** engager un cheval dans une course; *Cust:* **to e. goods,** déclarer des marchandises en douane; (*b*) *Com:* **to e. (up) an item in the ledger,** inscrire, porter, un article au grand livre; **to e. (sth.) to, against, s.o.,** porter, inscrire, (qch.) au compte de qn; (*c*) *Jur: etc:* **to e. an action against s.o.,** intenter un procès à qn; **to e. a protest,** protester formellement. **entering** *n.* **1.** entrée *f* (dans un endroit). **2.** (*a*) admission *f* (d'un étudiant); inscription *f* (d'un nom, etc.); (*b*) *Com:* **e. (up),** inscription, enregistrement *m.* **enter into** *v.i.* (*a*) entrer en (service); entrer dans (les affaires); entrer en (relations) **(with,** avec); engager (des négociations) **(with,** avec); conclure (un engagement) **(with,** avec); passer (un contrat) **(with,** avec); **to e. into partnership with s.o.,** s'associer avec qn; **to e. into a conversation with s.o.,** engager une conversation avec qn; (*b*) prendre part à (un complot, etc.); **factors that do not e. into the question,** facteurs qui sont en dehors de l'affaire; **to e. into the spirit of the game,** entrer dans le jeu. **enter upon** *v.i. Jur:* entrer en possession, prendre possession d'(un bien).

enteric [en'terik] *a. Med:* entérique; **e. fever,** *n.* **e.,** fièvre *f* typhoïde.

enteritis [entə'raitis] *n. Med:* entérite *f.*

enterprise[1] ['entəpraiz] *n.* **1.** (*a*) entreprise difficile; (*b*) **free e.,** la libre entreprise; **private e.,** l'entreprise privée; le secteur privé. **2. to show e.,** faire preuve d'un esprit entreprenant; **man of great e.,** homme entreprenant.

enterprising ['entəpraiziŋ] *a.* entreprenant. **-ly** *adv.* (*a*) d'une façon entreprenante; (*b*) hardiment.

entertain [entə'tein] *v.tr.* **1.** (*a*) amuser, divertir (qn); (*b*) faire la conversation à (qn). **2.** (*a*) régaler, fêter (qn); **to e. s.o. to dinner,** donner à dîner, offrir un dîner, à qn; (*b*) *v.i.* offrir une réception; **they e. a great deal,** its reçoivent beaucoup (de monde). **3.** admettre, accueillir (une proposition, une opinion); faire un accueil favorable à (une demande). **4.** concevoir (une idée, des doutes); éprouver (des craintes, des soupçons); nourrir (un espoir, une idée); chérir (une illusion). **entertaining 1.** *a.* amusant, divertissant. **2.** *n.* (*a*) réception *f* (de convives); (*b*) admission *f* (d'une proposition, d'une idée). **entertainingly** *adv.* (parler) d'une manière amusante, divertissante.

entertainer [entə'teinər] *n.* artiste *mf* de cabaret; diseur, -euse (de monologues); fantaisiste *mf.*

entertainment [entə'teinmənt] *n.* **1.** (*a*) divertissement *m*, amusement *m*; **much to the e. of the crowd,** au grand amusement de la foule; (*b*) *Th:* spectacle *m*, divertissement; **e. tax,** taxe *f* sur les spectacles. **2.** (*a*) hospitalité *f*; *Adm: Com:* **e. expenses,** frais *mpl* de représentation *f*; (*b*) réception *f*, fête *f.*

enthral, *esp. NAm:* **enthrall** [in'θrɔ:l] *v.tr.* **(enthralled)** captiver, passionner. **enthralling** *a.* (spectacle, etc.) captivant, passionnant.

enthrone [in'θroun] *v.tr.* (*a*) introniser (un évêque); (*b*) mettre (un roi) sur le trône.

enthronement [in'θrounmənt] *n.* intronisation *f.*

enthuse [in'θju:z] *v.i.* s'enthousiasmer **(over, about, sth.,** pour qch.); se passionner (de, pour, qch.).

enthusiasm [in'θju:ziæzm] *n.* enthousiasme *m* **(for, about,** pour).

enthusiast [in'θju:ziæst] *n.* enthousiaste *mf* **(for,** de); fanatique *mf* (de golf); passionné(e) (de musique).

enthusiastic [inθjuzi'æstik] *a.* enthousiaste; (pêcheur) passionné; **to become e. about sth.,** s'enthousiasmer pour qch. **-ally** *adv.* avec enthousiasme; **to accept e.,** accepter d'enthousiasme.

entice [in'tais] *v.tr.* attirer, séduire (qn); **to e. s.o. away,** entraîner qn à sa suite; **to e. s.o. into a place,** attirer qn dans un endroit. **enticing 1.** *a.* (*of offer, etc.*) séduisant, tentant, attrayant; (*of dish*) alléchant. **2.** *n. Jur:* séduction *f.* **enticingly** *adv.* d'une manière séduisante, attrayante.

enticement [in'taismənt] *n.* **1.** séduction *f.* **2.** attrait *m*, charme *m.* **3.** appât *m.*

entire [in'taiə] *a.* (*a*) entier, tout; **the e. population,** la population (tout) entière; **the e. day,** toute la journée; (*b*) entier, complet; **to enjoy s.o.'s e. confidence,** jouir de l'entière confiance de qn. **-ly** *adv.* entièrement, tout à fait, complètement; **to agree e. with s.o.,** être entièrement, tout à fait, d'accord avec qn; **e.**

unnecessary, absolument inutile; **you are e. mistaken,** vous vous trompez du tout au tout.

entirety [in'taiərəti] *n.* (*a*) intégralité *f*, intégrité *f*; **in its e.,** en entier; intégralement; **to tell a story in its e.,** raconter une histoire d'un bout à l'autre; (*b*) totalité *f* (d'un domaine, etc.).

entitle [in'taitl] *v.tr.* **1.** intituler (un livre, un chapitre). **2.** donner à (qn) le titre de (duc, prince, etc.). **3.** donner à (qn) le droit (**to,** à); **to e. s.o. to do sth.,** donner (le) droit à qn de faire qch.; **to be entitled to sth.,** avoir droit à qch.; **to be entitled to do sth.,** avoir le droit de faire qch.; *Jur:* être apte, avoir habilité (à hériter).

entitlement [in'taitlmənt] *n.* ce qui revient de droit à qn; allocation à laquelle on a droit; **(annual) holiday e.,** congé annuel (auquel on a droit).

entity ['entiti] *n.* entité *f.*

entomb [in'tu:m] *v.tr.* **1.** mettre dans la tombe; mettre au tombeau. **2.** (*of ruins, etc.*) ensevelir (qn).

entombment [in'tu:mmənt] *n.* ensevelissement *m*; mise *f* au tombeau.

entomological [entəmə'lɔdʒik(ə)l] *a.* entomologique.

entomologist [entə'mɔlədʒist] *n.* entomologiste *mf.*

entomology [entə'mɔlədʒi] *n.* entomologie *f.*

entourage [ɔntu:'rɑ:ʒ] *n.* entourage *m.*

entracte ['ɑ̃(n)trækt] *n. Th:* entracte *m.*

entrails ['entreilz] *n.pl.* entrailles *fpl* (d'un animal).

entrain [in'trein] **1.** *v.tr.* embarquer, faire embarquer (des troupes, etc.) en chemin de fer. **2.** *v.i.* s'embarquer (en chemin de fer).

entrance[1] ['entrəns] *n.* **1.** entrée *f*; (*a*) **to make one's e.,** faire son entrée (dans une salle, etc.); **actor's e. on the stage,** entrée en scène d'un acteur; **to force an e. into a house,** forcer l'entrée d'une maison; **e. gate,** grille *f* d'entrée; **e. hall,** vestibule *m* (d'une maison); hall *m* (d'un grand hôtel); (*b*) admission *f*, accès *m*; **to give e. to sth.,** donner accès à qch.; (*to club*) **e. fee,** droit *m* d'inscription; **e. examination,** examen *m* d'entrée. **2.** (*way in*) **wide, narrow, e.,** entrée large, étroite; **main e.,** entrée principale; (*of bus, etc.*) **the e. is at the rear,** l'entrée s'effectue par l'arrière.

entrance[2] [in'trɑ:ns] *v.tr.* extasier, ravir, transporter (qn); **to be entranced by . . .,** s'extasier sur, être en extase devant . . .; **I was entranced with the music,** j'étais enchanté par la musique. **entrancing** *a.* (rêve) enchanteur; (conte) passionnant; (mélodie) ravissante. **entrancingly** *adv.* à ravir.

entrant ['entrənt] *n.* (*a*) débutant, -ante (dans une profession, etc.); (*b*) inscrit, -ite (pour une course, etc.); candidat, -ate (à un examen).

entrap [in'træp] *v.tr.* **(entrapped)** prendre (qn) au piège.

entreat [in'tri:t] *v.tr.* **to e. s.o. to do sth.,** prier, implorer, supplier, qn de faire qch.; **they entreated him to stay,** ils lui demandèrent avec instance de rester. **entreating** *a.* (ton, regard) suppliant.

entreaty [in'tri:ti] *n.* prière *f*, supplication *f*; **at s.o.'s urgent e.,** sur les vives instances de qn; **look of e.,** regard suppliant.

entrée ['ɑ̃(n)trei] *n.* **1.** entrée *f* (**to, into,** dans). **2.** *Cu:* (*a*) entrée; (*b*) *NAm:* plat *m* de résistance.

entrench [in'tren(t)ʃ] *v.tr. Mil:* retrancher (un camp, une ville); **to e. oneself behind, in (sth.),** se retrancher, se terrer, derrière (des remparts, un prétexte).

entrenchment [in'tren(t)ʃmənt] *n. Mil:* retranchement *m.*

entrepôt ['ɑ̃(n)trəpou] *n.* entrepôt *m.*

entrepreneur [ɑ̃(n)trəprə'nœ:r] *n.* entrepreneur *m.*

entrepreneurial [ɑ̃(n)trəprə'nœ:riəl] *a.* d'un entrepreneur.

entropy ['entrəpi] *n.* entropie *f.*

entruck [en'trʌk] *U.S:* **1.** *v.i.* embarquer en camion. **2.** *v.tr.* embarquer (des troupes, etc.) en camion.

entrust [in'trʌst] *v.tr.* **to e. s.o. with sth.,** charger qn (d'une tâche, etc.), investir qn (d'une mission); **to e. (sth.) to s.o.,** confier (un secret, un enfant) à qn; **to e. s.o. with the care of sth.,** commettre qch. à la garde de qn; **to be entrusted with the sale of sth.,** être chargé de la vente de qch.

entry ['entri] *n.* **1.** (*a*) entrée *f*; **right of free e.,** droit *m* de passer librement les frontières; *P.N:* **no e.,** (i) sens interdit; (ii) passage interdit (au public); (*b*) **to make one's e.,** faire son entrée; (*of actor*) entrer en scène; (*c*) *Mus:* (i) entrée (d'un instrument); (ii) prise *f* (d'un sujet dans une fugue); (*d*) début *m* (dans la politique, etc.). **2.** *Jur:* (*a*) prise de possession; (*b*) **illegal e. (of a dwelling),** violation *f* de domicile. **3.** (*way in*) entrée (**to a mine,** d'une mine). **4.** (*a*) enregistrement *m* (d'un acte, etc.); inscription *f* (d'un nom sur une liste); (*b*) *Book-k:* (i) inscription (dans un livre de commerce); **single, double, e.,** comptabilité *f* en partie simple, en partie double; (ii) (*item*) article *m*, poste *m*, écriture *f*; **to make an e.,** porter un article à compte; **to make an e. against s.o.,** débiter qn; (*c*) (*in cataloguing*) **author, subject, entries,** fiches *fpl* auteur, sujet; (*d*) *Nau:* **e. in the log,** élément *m* du journal de bord. **5.** *Sp:* (*a*) liste *f* des concurrents; (*b*) inscription (d'un concurrent); **e. form,** feuille *f* d'inscription; **there are twenty entries,** il y a vingt (i) coureurs, (ii) candidats.

entwine [in'twain] **1.** *v.tr.* (*a*) entrelacer (des rameaux, etc.); **with arms entwined,** les bras entrelacés; (*b*) enlacer (**with,** de). **2.** *v.i.* (*a*) s'entrelacer; (*b*) s'enlacer (**round,** autour de).

enumerate [i'nju:məreit] *v.tr.* énumérer, détailler, dénombrer (les raisons, ses services).

enumeration [inju:mə'reiʃ(ə)n] *n.* enumération *f*, dénombrement *m*, recensement *m.*

enunciate [i'nʌnsieit] **1.** *v.tr.* énoncer, déclarer (une opinion, etc.). **2.** (*a*) *v.tr.* prononcer, articuler (des sons); (*b*) *v.i.* **to e. clearly,** articuler distinctement.

enunciation [inʌnsi'eiʃ(ə)n] *n.* **1.** énonciation *f* (d'une opinion, etc.); *Mth:* énoncé *m* (d'un problème). **2.** prononciation *f* (d'un mot); articulation *f.*

enuresis [enjuə'ri:sis] *n. Med:* énurésie *f.*

envelop [in'veləp] *v.tr.* **(enveloped)** envelopper (**in,** dans, de); **enveloped in mist,** (paysage) enveloppé, voilé, de brume.

envelope ['envəloup, *occ.* 'ɔnvəloup] *n.* (*a*) (*covering*) enveloppe *f*; *Nat.Hist:* enveloppe, tunique *f* (d'un organe); (*b*) enveloppe (d'une lettre); **adhesive e.,** enveloppe gommée; **window e.,** enveloppe à fenêtre; **to put a letter in an e.,** mettre une lettre sous enveloppe; **in a sealed e.,** sous pli cacheté; **e. file,** chemise *f* (de carton).

envelopment [in'veləpmənt] *n.* enveloppement *m.*

envenom [in'venəm] *v.tr.* envenimer.

enviable ['enviəbl] *a.* enviable, digne d'envie. **-ably** *adv.* d'une manière enviable.

envious ['enviəs] *a.* envieux; **e. glances,** (regards) d'envie; **to be e. of s.o.,** envier qn; **to look at s.o. with e. eyes,** regarder qn d'un œil jaloux; (*of things*) **to make s.o. e.,** faire envie à qn. **-ly** *adv.* (parler) avec envie; (regarder qch.) d'un œil jaloux.

environment [in'vaiərənmənt] *n.* milieu *m*, entourage *m*; milieu ambiant; influences ambiantes; environnement *m*; *Pol:* **Department, Ministry, of the E.** = ministère *m* de (la Protection de la Nature et de) l'Environnement.

environmental [invaiərən'ment(ə)l] *a.* (conditions) qui ont rapport à l'environnement; (modifications) (i) de l'environnement, (ii) produites par l'environnement.

environmentalist [invaiərən'mentəlist] *n.* écologiste *mf.*
environs [in'vaiərənz] *n.pl.* environs *mpl*, alentours *mpl* (d'une ville); abords *mpl*; voisinage *m*.
envisage [in'vizidʒ] *v.tr.* envisager (une difficulté).
envision [en'viʒən] *v.tr. NAm:* envisager.
envoy ['envɔi] *n.* (*pers.*) envoyé, -ée (diplomatique); ambassadeur, -drice.
envy¹ ['envi] *n.* **1.** envie *f*, jalousie *f*; **to be green with e.,** être dévoré d'envie. **2.** objet *m* d'envie; **to be the e. of s.o.,** être un objet d'envie pour qn.
envy² *v.tr.* envier, porter envie à (qn); **to e. s.o. sth.,** envier qch. à qn.
enzyme ['enzaim] *n. Bio-Ch:* enzyme *f*, diastase *f*.
Eocene ['i(:)ousi:n] *a. & n. Geol:* éocène (*m*).
eon ['i:ɔn] *n. NAm:* éon *m*.
epaulette ['epɔlet] *n. Mil:* épaulette *f*.
ephedrine ['efidri(:)n] *n. Pharm:* éphédrine *f*.
ephemera, *pl.* **-ae, -as** [i'femərə, -i:, -əz] *n.* **1.** *Ent:* éphémère *m*. **2.** chose *f* éphémère.
ephemeral [i'femərəl] *a.* éphémère; (passion) fugitive; (beauté) passagère.
ephemerid [i'femərid] *n. Ent:* éphémère *m*.
epic ['epik] **1.** *a.* épique; légendaire. **2.** *n.* (*a*) poème *m* épique; épopée *f*; (*b*) film *m* à grand spectacle.
epicarp ['epikɑ:p] *n. Bot:* épicarpe *m*.
epicentre ['episentər] *n.* épicentre *m* (d'une séisme).
epicure ['epikjuər] *n.* **1.** épicurien, -ienne. **2.** gourmet *m*, gastronome *m*.
epicurean [epikju'riən] *a. & n.* épicurien, -ienne.
epidemic [epi'demik] **1.** *a.* (maladie) épidémique. **2.** *n.* épidémie *f*.
epidermis [epi'də:mis] *n. Anat:* épiderme *m*.
epidural [epi'dju:r(ə)l] *a. Anat:* épidural, -aux.
epiglottis [epi'glɔtis] *n.* épiglotte *f*.
epigram ['epigræm] *n.* épigramme *f*.
epigrammatic [epigrə'mætik] *a.* épigrammatique. **-ally** *adv.* épigrammatiquement.
epigraph ['epigræf] *n.* épigraphe *f*.
epilepsy ['epilepsi] *n.* épilepsie *f*.
epileptic [epi'leptik] *a. & n.* épileptique (*mf*); **e. fit,** crise *f* épileptique.
epilogue ['epilɔg] *n.* épilogue *m*.
Epiphany [i'pifəni] *n. Ecc:* l'Épiphanie *f*.
episcopacy [i'piskəpəsi] *n.* épiscopat *m*.
episcopal [i'piskəp(ə)l] *a.* épiscopal, -aux; **e. palace,** évêché *m*; **e. ring,** anneau pastoral; (*in NAm: & Scot:*) **the E. Church,** l'Église épiscopale.
episcopalian [ipiskə'peiliən] *a. & n.* (*in NAm: & Scot:*) épiscopalien, -ienne; (membre *m*) de l'Église épiscopale.
episcopate [i'piskəpeit] *n.* épiscopat *m*.
episode ['episoud] *n.* épisode *m*.
episodic(al) [epi'sɔdik(l)] *a.* épisodique.
epistle [i'pisl] *n.* (*a*) *Ecc:* épître *f*; **e. side (of altar),** côté *m* de l'épître; (*b*) épître, lettre *f*.
epistolary [i'pistələri] *a.* (style) épistolaire.
epitaph ['epitæf] *n.* épitaphe *f*.
epithelium [epi'θi:liəm] *n. Anat:* épithélium *m*.
epithet ['epiθet] *n.* épithète *f*.
epithetic(al) [epi'θetik(l)] *a.* épithétique.
epitome [i'pitəmi] *n.* **1.** épitomé *m*, abrégé *m*. **2. to be the e. of sth.,** incarner qch.; **he is the e. of elegance,** il est l'élégance même.
epitomize [i'pitəmaiz] *v.tr.* **1.** abréger, résumer (un discours, etc.). **2.** incarner (qch.).
epizootic [epizou'ɔtik] *Vet:* **1.** *a.* (maladie) épizootique. **2.** *n.* épizootie *f*.
epoch ['i:pɔk] *n.* époque *f*, âge *m*; **to mark an e.,** faire époque, faire date.
epoch-making ['i:pɔkmeikiŋ] *a.* (découverte, événement) qui fait époque.
eponym ['epənim] *n.* éponyme *m*.
eponymous [i'pɔniməs] *a.* éponyme.
Epsom ['epsəm] *Pr.n. Pharm:* **E. salts,** sel *m* d'Epsom.
equability [ekwə'biliti, i:k-] *n.* uniformité (de climat, de température, etc.); égalité *f* (d'humeur).
equable ['ekwəbl, i:k-] *a.* uniforme, régulier; **e. temperament,** humeur égale. **-ably** *adv.* d'humeur égale.
equal¹ ['i:kwəl] **1.** *a.* (*a*) égal, -aux (**to, with,** à); **on e. terms,** à conditions égales; **to be on e. terms, on an e. footing, with s.o.,** être sur un pied d'égalité avec qn; **e. distribution of taxes,** péréquation *f* de l'impôt; **cinema e. to any in London,** cinéma à l'instar de Londres; **all things being e.,** toutes choses égales (d'ailleurs); **e. pay for e. work,** à travail égal, salaire égal; *Mth:* **e. sign,** signe *m* d'égalité; (*b*) **to be e. to (doing) sth.,** être de force à, à même de, (faire) qch.; **I don't feel e. to (doing) it,** je ne m'en sens pas le courage, la force; **to be e. to the occasion,** être à la hauteur d'une situation; **not to be e. to a task,** être au-dessous de la tâche. **2.** *n.* égal, -ale; pair *m*; **your equals,** vos pareils, vos égaux; **you won't find his e.,** vous ne trouverez pas son semblable; **to treat s.o. as an e.,** traiter qn en égal à égal. **-ally** *adv.* également, pareillement; **e. exhausted,** tout aussi fatigué(s); **to contribute e. to the expenses,** contribuer pour une part égale à la dépense.
equal² *v.tr.* (**equalled,** *NAm:* **equaled**) (*a*) égaler, être égal à (qn, qch.) (**in,** en); **nothing can e. this splendour,** rien ne saurait égaler cette splendeur; **not to be equalled,** sans égal; qui n'a pas son égal; (*b*) **four fives, four times five, equals twenty,** quatre fois cinq font vingt; *Mth:* **equals sign,** signe *m* d'égalité.
equality [i(:)'kwɔliti] *n.* égalité *f*.
equalization [i:kwəlai'zeiʃ(ə)n] *n.* **1.** égalisation *f*; *Adm:* péréquation *f* (de contributions). **2.** (*a*) compensation *f*; (*b*) *Civ. E:* compensation (de terrassements); *Mec.E:* équilibrage *m*.
equalize ['i:kwəlaiz] **1.** *v.tr.* (*a*) égaliser (**sth. with sth.,** qch. avec qch.); faire la péréquation (des salaires); *Fb:* *v.i.* **to e.,** marquer égalité de points; égaliser; (*b*) compenser, équilibrer (des forces, etc.). **2.** *v.i.* (*a*) s'égaliser; (*b*) se compenser, s'équilibrer. **equalizing** *a.* (courant, etc.) compensateur; (pression) de compensation.
equalizer ['i:kwəlaizər] *n.* (*a*) *El:* égaliseur *m* de potentiel; (*b*) *Mec.E:* compensateur *m*; (*c*) *Fb:* but égalisateur.
equanimity [i:kwə'nimiti, ek-] *n.* égalité *f* d'âme; équanimité *f*; **to disturb s.o.'s e.,** troubler la sérénité de qn; **to recover one's e.,** se ressaisir; **with e.,** d'une âme égale.
equate [i'kweit] *v.tr.* **1.** (*a*) égaler (**to, with,** à); (*b*) *Mth:* mettre (deux expressions, etc.) en équation. **2. to e. Jupiter with Zeus,** donner Jupiter comme l'équivalent de Zeus. **equating** *n.* **1.** égalisation *f*. **2.** *Mth:* mise *f* en équation.
equation [i'kweiʃ(ə)n] *n.* **1.** égalisation *f* (des dépenses au revenu, etc.). **2.** *Mth:* équation *f*; **simple, quadratic, e.,** équation du premier, du deuxième, degré. **3.** *Ch:* équation. **4.** *Astr:* équation (du temps, du centre).
equator [i'kweitər] *n.* équateur *m* (de la terre); **at the e.,** sous l'équateur.
equatorial [ekwə'tɔ:riəl] *a.* équatorial, -aux.
equerry ['ekwəri] *n.m.* **1.** écuyer. **2.** officier de la maison du roi, de la reine.
equestrian [i'kwestriən] **1.** *a.* (statue, etc.) équestre; **e. performances,** exercices *mpl* d'équitation. **2.** *n.* (*a*) (*f. occ.* **equestrienne**) cavalier, -ière; (*b*) écuyer, -ère (de cirque).
equidistant [i:kwi'distənt] *a.* équidistant (**from,** de).
equilateral [i:kwi'læt(ə)rəl] *a.* équilatéral, -aux.

equilibrate [iːˈkwilibreit] **1.** *v.tr.* (*a*) équilibrer; (*b*); faire contrepoids à (une force, etc.). **2.** *v.i.* (*a*) s'équilibrer; (*b*) (*of two forces, etc.*) se faire contrepoids.

equilibration [iːkwiliˈbreiʃ(ə)n] *n.* équilibration *f.*

equilibrium [iːkwiˈlibriəm] *n.* équilibre *m*, aplomb *m*; **stable, unstable, e.,** équilibre stable, instable; **to lose one's e.,** perdre l'équilibre.

equine [ˈiːkwain, ˈekwain] *a.* équin; (race) chevaline; *n.pl.* **zebras are equines,** les zèbres sont des équidés.

equinoctial [iːkwiˈnɔkʃ(ə)l, ek-] *a.* (*a*) (ligne, année, etc.) équinoxiale; (*b*) (tempête, etc.) d'équinoxe; **e. tides,** marées d'equinoxe, les grandes marées.

equinox [ˈiːkwinɔks, ˈek-] *n.* équinoxe *m*; **spring, vernal, e.,** équinoxe du printemps; point vernal; **autumn(al) e.,** équinoxe d'automne.

equip [iˈkwip] *v.tr.* **(equipped)** (*a*) équiper (un soldat); meubler, monter (une maison); outiller, monter (une usine); **to e. s.o. with sth.,** munir, équiper, qn de qch.; (*b*) préparer (qn) (pour faire qch.). **equipped** *a.* (*a*) (*of pers.*) (i) capable, (ii) préparé (pour faire qch.); (*b*) **well-e.,** bien équipé; (laboratoire, etc.) bien installé; (ménage) bien monté; (magasin) bien approvisionné.

equipage [ˈekwipidʒ] *n. Veh:* équipage *m.*

equipment [iˈkwipmənt] *n.* **1.** équipement *m* (d'une expédition); aménagement *m* (d'une maison); outillage *m* (d'une usine, etc.); installation *f* (d'un laboratoire, etc.). **2.** (*a*) équipement; appareils *mpl*; installations, matériel *m*; **heavy e.,** matériel lourd; **standby, emergency, e.,** matériel, installations, de secours; **electrical e.,** équipement électrique; *Sp:* **sports e.,** équipement sportif; **camping e.,** matériel de camping; *Mil:* **regulation, standard, e.,** matériel réglementaire; **surplus e.,** matériel en excédent; (*b*) **intellectual e.,** capacité intellectuelle.

equitable [ˈekwitəbl] *a.* équitable, juste. **-ably** *adv.* équitablement; avec justice.

equitation [ekwiˈteiʃ(ə)n] *n.* équitation *f.*

equity [ˈekwiti] *n.* **1.** équité *f*, justice *f.* **2.** *Jur:* équité; recours *m* aux principes mêmes de la justice (lorsque celle-ci se trouve en conflit avec le droit commun ou écrit). **3.** *Fin:* **equities,** actions *fpl* ordinaires. **4.** *Pr.n.* **E.,** le syndicat des artistes de la scène.

equivalence [iˈkwivələns] *n.* équivalence *f.*

equivalent [iˈkwivələnt] **1.** *a.* équivalent; **to be e. to sth.,** être équivalent, équivaloir, à qch. **2.** *n.* équivalent *m*; **to drink the e. of one glass of wine,** boire la valeur d'un verre de vin.

equivocal [iˈkwivək(ə)l] *a.* équivoque; (*a*) ambigu, -uë; (mot) à double entente; (réponse) équivoque; (*b*) incertain, douteux; (*c*) suspect, douteux; (affaire) un peu louche. **-ally** *adv.* d'une manière équivoque.

equivocate [iˈkwivəkeit] *v.i.* user d'équivoque, tergiverser.

equivocation [ikwivəˈkeiʃ(ə)n] *n.* tergiversation *f*; **to resort to equivocations,** user d'equivoque, tergiverser.

era [ˈiərə] *n.* ère *f* (géologique, etc.); **to mark an e.,** faire époque.

eradicate [iˈrædikeit] *v.tr.* extirper, déraciner.

eradication [irædiˈkeiʃ(ə)n] *n.* éradication *f*, extirpation *f* (d'un préjugé, d'un abus, etc.).

erase [iˈreiz] *v.tr.* effacer (un mot, un enregistrement sur bande); raturer, gommer (un mot); oblitérer (un souvenir). **erasing** *n.* effacement *m*; *Rec: Cmptr:* **e. head,** tête *f* d'effacement.

eraser [iˈreizər] *n.* gomme *f* (à effacer); **ink e.,** gomme à encre.

erasure [iˈreiʒər] *n.* **1.** effaçure *f*; effacement *m.* **2.** mot, chiffre, effacé.

ere [ˈɛər] *A: & Lit:* **1.** *prep.* avant; **e. now,** auparavant; déjà; **e. long,** bientôt. **2.** *conj.* avant que + *sub.*

erect¹ [iˈrekt] *a.* (*of pers.*) droit, debout; **with head e.,** la tête haute, relevée; **to stand e.,** se tenir droit.

erect² *v.tr.* **1.** dresser (un mât); **2.** ériger, construire (un édifice); élever (une statue) (**to,** à); dresser (un échafaudage, un autel); installer (une machine).

erectile [iˈrektail] *a. Physiol:* (tissu) érectile.

erection [iˈrekʃ(ə)n] *n.* **1.** (*a*) redressement *m* (du corps); dressage *m* (d'un mât); (*b*) construction *f*, érection *f* (d'un édifice); érection (d'une statue); installation *f* (d'une machine); (*c*) *Physiol:* érection (d'un organe). **2.** bâtisse *f*, construction, édifice *m.*

erectness [iˈrektnis] *n.* attitude droite.

erector [iˈrektər] *n.* **1.** (*pers.*) constructeur *m* (de bâtiments). **2.** *Anat:* **e. (muscle),** (muscle *m*) érecteur (*m*).

erg [əːg] *n. Ph.Meas:* erg *m.*

ergo [ˈəːgou, ˈɛəgou] *Lt.adv. Log:* ergo, donc.

ergonomics [əːgouˈnɔmiks] *n.pl.* (*usu. with sg. const.*) ergonomie *f.*

ergot [ˈəːgɔt] *n. Agr: Pharm:* ergot *m* (de seigle).

ergotism [ˈəːgətizm] *n. Med:* ergotisme *m.*

Erie [ˈiəri] *Pr.n. Geog:* **Lake E.,** le lac Érié.

erigeron [iˈridʒərən] *n. Bot:* érigéron *m.*

Erin [ˈerin] *Pr.n. A: & Lit:* l'Irlande *f.*

ermine [ˈəːmin] *n.* hermine *f.*

erode [iˈroud] *v.tr.* éroder; ronger; corroder.

erogenous [eˈrɔdʒinəs] *a.* (zone, etc.) érogène.

Eros [ˈiərɔs] *Pr.n.* Éros *m.*

erosion [iˈrouʒ(ə)n] *n.* (*a*) érosion (marine, etc.); **wind e.,** érosion éolienne; (*b*) détérioration *f*; **the e. of real earnings by inflation,** la diminution du salaire réel causée par l'inflation.

erotic [iˈrɔtik] *a.* érotique. **-ally** *adv.* érotiquement.

erotica [iˈrɔtikə] *n.pl.* écrits, dessins, etc., érotiques.

eroticism [iˈrɔtisizm] *n.* érotisme *m.*

err [əːr] *v.i.* (*a*) s'égarer, s'écarter (**from,** de); **to e. from the straight and narrow path,** s'égarer du droit chemin; (*b*) pécher; **he does not e. on the side of modesty,** il ne pèche pas par la modestie; (*c*) errer; faire erreur; **to e. is human,** tout le monde peut se tromper. **erring** *a.* dévoyé, égaré; tombé dans l'erreur; (mari, femme) infidèle.

errand [ˈerənd] *n.* commission *f*, course *f*; **to go on, run, errands,** (aller) faire des commissions, des courses; *Com:* **e. boy,** (i) garçon *m* de courses; (ii) garçon livreur.

errant [ˈerənt] *a.* (*a*) errant; *A:* **knight e.,** chevalier errant; (*b*) dévoyé; (mari) infidèle.

erratic [iˈrætik] *a.* **1.** *Med:* (douleur) erratique. **2.** (*a*) irrégulier; **e. working,** irrégularité *f* de marche (d'une machine); (*b*) *Aut:* **e. driving,** conduite mal assurée. **3.** (*of pers.*) capricieux, bizarre, velléitaire; (vie) désordonnée. **-ally** *adv.* sans méthode, sans règle; **to work e.,** (i) (*of pers.*) travailler irrégulièrement, par boutade; (ii) (*of machine*) fonctionner irrégulièrement, par à-coups; *Aut:* **to drive e.,** conduire d'une façon mal assurée.

erratum, *pl.* **-ta** [iˈrɑːtəm, -tə] *n.* erratum *m*, *pl.* errata.

erroneous [iˈrouniəs] *a.* (calcul) erroné, faux; (supposition) fausse; **arguments resting on e. premises,** arguments *mpl* qui portent à faux. **-ly** *adv.* par erreur.

erroneousness [iˈrouniəsnis] *n.* erreur *f*, fausseté *f.*

error [ˈerər] *n.* **1.** (*a*) erreur *f*, faute *f*; **e. of judgement,** erreur de jugement; **human e.,** défaillance humaine; **printer's e.,** faute *f* d'impression; *Com:* **errors and omissions excepted,** sauf erreur ou omission; **by e.,** par erreur; (*b*) *Tchn:* erreur, écart *m*, aberration *f*, déviation *f*; **allowable e.,** erreur permise; tolérance *f*;

vertical e., écart en hauteur; **compass e.,** déviation du compas; *Cmptr:* **e. tape,** bande *f* recevant les erreurs; **e. routine,** sous-programme *m* de correction d'erreurs. **2.** (*a*) (*being wrong*) **to be in e.,** être dans l'erreur; avoir tort; **to fall into e.,** tomber dans l'erreur; **he has seen the e. of his ways,** il est revenu de ses égarements; (*b*) (*wrongdoing*) écart (de conduite); **errors of youth,** erreurs, écarts, de jeunesse.

ersatz [ɛə:'zæts, 'ə:zæts] *a. & n.* succédané; **the coffee is e.,** le café n'est qu'un ersatz, un succédané.

Erse [ə:s] *a. & n. Ling:* (*a*) erse (*m*), gaélique (*m*); (*b*) irlandais (*m*).

erstwhile ['ə:st(h)wail] *A: & Lit:* **1.** *adv.* autrefois, jadis. **2.** *a.* ancien (élève, etc.).

eructation [i:rʌk'teiʃ(ə)n] *n.* éructation *f*, renvoi *m*.

erudite ['eru(:)dait] *a.* érudit, savant.

erudition [eru(:)'diʃ(ə)n] *n.* érudition *f*; **work of monumental e.,** vrai monument d'érudition.

erupt [i'rʌpt] *v.i.* **1.** (*of teeth*) percer. **2.** (*a*) (*of volcano*) entrer en éruption; faire éruption; (*b*) (*of violence, anger*) éclater; (*of pers.*) **to e. (in anger),** exploser.

eruption [i'rʌpʃ(ə)n] *n.* **1.** (*a*) éruption *f*; **volcano in e.,** volcan en activité; (*b*) éclat *m*, accès *m* (de colère, de gaieté, etc.). **2.** (*a*) *Med:* éruption, poussée *f* (de boutons); (*b*) éruption (des dents).

erysipelas [eri'sipiləs] *n. Med:* érysipèle *m*.

erythrocyte [e'riθrousait] *n. Physiol:* érythrocyte *m*.

escalate ['eskəleit] *v.i.* **1.** (*of prices, etc.*) monter (en flèche). **2.** (*of conflict, etc.*) s'aggraver; **small incidents can easily e. into a world war,** de simples incidents (militaires) peuvent facilement mener à une guerre mondiale.

escalation [eskə'leiʃ(ə)n] *n.* **1.** *Pol.Ec:* augmentation *f* (rapide) (des prix, etc.); escalade *f* (des taux d'intérêt). **2.** *Mil: Pol:* escalade.

escalator ['eskəleitər] *n.* (*a*) escalier mécanique; escalator *m*; (*b*) *Pol.Ec:* **e. clause,** échelle *f* mobile.

escalope ['eskələp] *n. Cu:* escalope *f* (de veau).

escapade ['eskəpeid] *n.* escapade *f*, frasque *f*, fredaine *f*.

escape¹ [is'keip] *n.* **1.** (*a*) fuite *f*, évasion *f*; **to make one's e.,** s'échapper, se sauver; **to make good one's e.,** réussir à s'échapper; (*b*) **to have a narrow e.,** l'échapper belle; **to have a miraculous e.,** échapper comme par miracle; **e. hatch,** trappe *f* de secours; *Com: etc:* **e. clause,** clause *f* échappatoire; (*c*) échappement *m*, fuite, dégagement *m* (de gaz, d'eau, etc.); (*d*) **e. velocity,** vitesse *f* de libération de l'attraction terrestre. **2. fire e.,** échelle *f* de sauvetage. **3.** *Hyd.E:* déversoir *m*; *Mec.E: etc:* **e. valve,** soupape *f* d'échappement, de trop-plein; *Clockm:* **e. wheel,** roue *f* d'échappement.

escape² **1.** *v.i.* (*a*) échapper, s'échapper, prendre la fuite; **to e. from prison,** s'échapper de prison; s'évader; **escaped prisoner,** évadé, -ée; (*b*) **to e. by the skin of one's teeth,** échapper tout juste; **to e. uninjured,** s'en tirer indemne; **he escaped with a fright,** il en a été quitte pour la peur; (*c*) (*of gases, fluids*) se dégager; s'échapper, fuir. **2.** *v.tr.* (*a*) (*of pers.*) échapper à (un danger); **he narrowly escaped death,** il a échappé tout juste à la mort; **he just escaped being killed,** il a bien failli être tué; il a manqué (de) se faire tuer; (*b*) (*of thgs*) **to e. notice,** échapper à l'attention; passer inaperçu; (*c*) **a cry escaped him,** il laissa échapper un cri; (*d*) (*of name, date, etc.*) échapper à (qn); **his name escapes me,** son nom m'échappe.

escapee [eskei'pi:] *n.* évadé, -ée.

escapement [is'keipmənt] *n.* échappement *m* (d'une pendule, d'un piano, etc.).

escaper [is'keipər] *n.* fugitif, -ive.

escapism [is'keipizm] *n.* évasion *f* (de la réalité).

escapist [is'keipist] *n.* personne *f* qui cherche à fuir la réalité; **e. literature,** littérature *f* d'évasion.

escapologist [iskei'pɔlədʒist] *n.* prestidigitateur *m* spécialiste de l'évasion.

escarpment [is'kɑ:pmənt] *n.* escarpement *m*.

eschatology [eskə'tɔlədʒi] *n. Theol:* eschatologie *f*.

escheat [is'tʃi:t] *v.i. Jur:* (*of estate*) tomber en déshérence; revenir à l'État, à la Couronne.

eschew [is'tʃu:] *v.tr. A: & Lit:* éviter (qch.); renoncer à (qch.); s'abstenir de (qch.).

escort¹ ['eskɔ:t] *n.* **1.** (*pers.*) (*a*) (*group of pers.*) escorte *f*; suite *f* (d'attendants); (*b*) (*single pers.*) escorte; guide *m*; (*to a woman*) cavalier *m*. **2.** (*escorting*) escorte; **under the e. of . . .,** sous l'escorte de . . .; **to conduct a prisoner under e.,** conduire un prisonnier sous escorte. **3.** *Nau:* (*ship*) escorteur *m*; bâtiment *m* d'escorte; *Mil.Av:* **e. fighter,** chasseur *m* d'escorte.

escort² [is'kɔ:t] *v.tr.* escorter, faire escorte à, servir d'escorte à (un convoi); servir de cavalier à (une dame); conduire (un prisonnier) sous escorte.

escutcheon [is'kʌtʃ(ə)n] *n.* écu *m*, écusson *m*.

Eskimo, *pl.* **-o(e)s**, *also* **-o** ['eskimou, -ouz] *Ethn:* **1.** *a.* esquimau, -aude, -aux (*occ. inv. inf.*); eskimo *inv*; **E. woman,** Esquimaude, femme esquimau; **E. dog,** chien *m* esquimau. **2.** *n.* Esquimau, -aude.

esophagus [i'sɔfəgəs] *n. NAm: Anat:* œsophage *m*.

esoteric [esou'terik] *a.* ésotérique; secret.

espadrille [espæ'dril] *n. Bootm:* espadrille *f*.

espalier [is'pæliər, -iei] *n. Hort:* espalier *m*.

esparto [es'pɑ:tou] *n.* **e. (grass),** sparte *m*; alfa *m*.

especial [is'peʃ(ə)l] *a.* spécial, -aux; particulier; **of e. importance,** d'une importance toute particulière. **-ally** *adv.* surtout; **we were e. lucky with the weather,** le temps nous était particulièrement favorable.

Esperanto [espə'ræntou] *n. Ling:* espéranto *m*.

espionage ['espiənɑ:ʒ] *n.* espionnage *m*.

esplanade [esplə'neid] *n.* (*a*) esplanade *f*; (*b*) (*in seaside town*) digue *f*.

espouse [is'pauz] *v.tr.* épouser, embrasser (une cause, un parti, etc.).

espresso [es'presou] *a. & n.* **e. (coffee),** (café *m*) express (*m*).

espy [is'pai] *v.tr. A: & Lit:* apercevoir, aviser.

esquire [is'kwaiər] *n. Corr:* (*titre honorifique, abr.* **Esq.**) **David Thomas, Esq.** = Monsieur David Thomas.

essay ['esei] *n.* **1.** essai *m*, tentative *f* (**at,** de). **2.** (*a*) *Lit:* essai; (*b*) *Sch:* dissertation *f*; composition *f*.

essayist ['eseiist] *n. Lit:* essayiste *mf*; auteur *m* d'essais.

essence ['esəns] *n.* **1.** *Phil: Theol: etc:* essence *f*; fond *m* (d'une affaire); **the very e. of authority,** l'autorité même; **in e.,** essentiellement. **2.** *Ch: Cu: etc:* essence, extrait *m*; **meat e.,** extrait de viande.

essential [i'senʃ(ə)l] **1.** *a.* (*a*) (*of difference, etc.*) essentiel; (*b*) essentiel, indispensable; capital, -aux; **e. foodstuffs,** denrées *fpl* de première nécessité; **e. part,** essence *f* (d'une doctrine, etc.); **e. feature,** fond *m* (d'une politique, etc.); **it is e. to do that,** il est essentiel, absolument nécessaire, de faire cela; **the e. thing,** l'essentiel *m*; **prudence is e.,** la prudence s'impose; (*c*) (huile) essentielle. **2.** *n.usu. pl.* **reduced to its essentials,** dépouillé; **to concentrate on essentials,** s'attacher à l'essentiel; **one of the essentials of a business man,** une des qualités indispensables à un homme d'affaires. **-ally** *adv.* essentiellement.

establish [is'tæbliʃ] *v.tr.* **1.** (*a*) affermir (sa foi); asseoir (son pouvoir); instaurer (le règne de la justice); (*b*) *Jur:* confirmer, ratifier (un testament); **to e. one's right,** faire apparoir son bon droit. **2.** établir (un gouvernement); édifier (un système); fonder (une maison de commerce); créer (une agence); constituer (une société); mettre sur pied (une paix); **to e. close relations with s.o.,** nouer des relations avec qn; **to e. s.o.'s reputation as an author,** faire la réputation de qn comme auteur; **to e. oneself in business,** s'établir dans les affaires; *Pej:* **to e. oneself in s.o.'s house,** s'installer, s'ancrer, chez qn. **3.** établir (un fait); démontrer (l'identité de qn); constater (la réalité d'un fait); établir (l'innocence de qn); **the facts established by the inquiry,** les faits qui résultent des informations. **4.** ériger (une Église) en Église d'État. **established** *a.* établi; (réputation) solide, bien établie; (maison, amitié) solide; (fait) avéré; **e. scientific fact,** fait acquis à la science; **the E. Church,** (i) l'Église établie; (ii) la religion d'État; **the e. order,** l'ordre établi.

establishment [is'tæbliʃmənt] *n.* **1.** (*a*) affermissement *m* (de sa foi); ratification *f* (d'un testament); constatation *f* (d'un fait, etc.); (*b*) établissement *m* (d'un gouvernement, d'une Église); création *f* (d'un système); fondation *f* (d'une maison de commerce); constitution *f* (d'une société); assiette *f* (d'un impôt). **2.** établissement, maison *f*; **business e.,** maison de commerce; **private e.,** maison particulière. **3.** (*a*) personnel *m* d'une maison; **to be on the e.,** faire partie du personnel; (*b*) *Mil: etc:* effectif *m* (d'une unité, etc.); **peacetime e.,** effectifs de paix. **4.** (*a*) **the (Church) E.,** l'Église établie; (*b*) **the E.,** (i) les institutions *fpl* (d'un pays); (ii) le monde traditionnel; **to be against the E., to be anti-E.,** être anticonformiste.

estate [is'teit] *n.* **1.** état *m*, condition *f*; **man's e.,** l'âge d'homme. **2.** *Lit:* **of high, low, e.,** de haut rang, d'humble condition. **3.** *Fr.Hist:* **the Estates (of the Realm),** les états, les ordres (de l'ancien régime); **the Third E.,** le Tiers (État). **4.** *Jur:* (*a*) bien *m*, domaine *m*, immeuble *m*; **real e.,** biens immobiliers; **landed e.,** propriété foncière; (*b*) succession *f*, biens (d'un défunt); **e. duty,** droits *mpl* de succession; (*c*) actif *m* (d'un failli). **5.** (*a*) terre *f*, propriété *f*; **country house and e. for sale,** à vendre château et domaine; (*b*) **housing e.,** (i) lotissement *m*; (ii) cité ouvrière; groupe *m* de H.L.M.; (*c*) **e. agent, agency,** agent immobilier, agence immobilière; (*d*) *Aut:* **e. car,** familiale *f*; commerciale *f*, break *m*.

esteem¹ [is'ti:m] *n.* estime *f*, considération *f*; **to hold s.o. in high e.,** avoir qn en haute estime; **to go up, down, in s.o.'s e.,** monter, baisser, dans l'estime de qn.

esteem² *v.tr.* **1.** estimer (qn); priser (qch.); **to e. sth. lightly,** faire peu de cas de qch.; **highly esteemed,** (homme) fort estimé. **2.** estimer, regarder (**sth. as sth.,** qch. comme qch.); **to e. it an honour that . . .,** se sentir honoré que . . .

ester ['estər] *n. Bio-Ch:* ester *m*.

esthete ['i:sθi:t] *n.*, **esthetic** [i:s'θetik] *a.*, *etc. NAm:* = AESTHETE, AESTHETIC, etc.

estimable ['estiməbl] *a.* estimable, digne d'estime.

estimate¹ ['estimət] *n.* **1.** appréciation *f*, évaluation *f*, calcul *m* (du contenu de qch., de la force de qch.); **rough e.,** approximation grossière; **at a rough e.,** à vue de nez; **at the lowest e.,** au bas mot. **2.** *Com:* devis (estimatif); **building e.,** devis de construction; **preliminary e.,** devis de prévision; **to put in an e.,** donner un devis, soumissionner; *Pol:* **the Estimates,** les prévisions *fpl* budgetaires.

estimate² ['estimeit] *v.tr.* estimer, évaluer (les frais, etc.); **to e. sth. at so much,** estimer, calculer, qch. à tant; **his fortune is estimated at . . .,** on évalue sa fortune à . . .; **I e. that it will take three years,** j'estime que cela prendra trois ans. **estimated** *a.* (coût) estimatif; (valeur) estimée; **it is only an e. figure,** ce n'est qu'une estimation; **e. time of arrival,** heure prévue d'arrivée.

estimation [esti'meiʃ(ə)n] *n.* **1.** estimation *f*, appréciation *f*, évaluation *f*; calcul *m* (des frais, etc.). **2.** (*a*) jugement *m*; **in my e.,** d'après moi; à mon avis; (*b*) estime *f*, considération *f*; **he is rising in the e. of the public,** il remonte dans l'estime du public.

Estonia [es'touniə] *Pr.n. Geog: Hist:* Estonie *f*.

Estonian [es'tounion] *Geog:* **1.** *a.* estonien. **2.** *n.* Estonien, -ienne.

estrange [is'trein(d)ʒ] *v.tr.* s'aliéner l'affection de (qn); **to become estranged from s.o.,** se détacher de qn; (*of married couple*) **to be estranged,** être séparés. **estranged** *a.* **an e. couple,** des époux séparés; **her e. husband,** son mari dont elle est séparée.

estrangement [is'trein(d)ʒmənt] *n.* aliénation *f* (de qn); éloignement *m* (de deux personnes); brouille *f* (**between,** entre); (*of married couple*) séparation *f*.

estrogen ['i:strədʒen] *n. Bio-Ch:* œstrogène *m*.

estrous ['i:strəs] *a. Biol:* (cycle) œstral, -aux.

estrus ['i:strəs] *n. Biol:* œstrus *m*.

estuary ['estju(ə)ri] *n.* estuaire *m*.

etcetera [et'setrə] **1.** *Lt.phr.* (*abbr.* **etc.**) et cætera. **2.** *n.pl.* **etceteras,** extras *mpl*; **roast turkey with all the etceteras,** dinde rôtie avec tout ce qui s'ensuit.

etch [etʃ] **1.** *v.tr.* graver (un dessin, etc.) à l'eau-forte; graver (une planche); **to e. away the metal,** enlever le métal à l'eau-forte. **2.** *v.i.* faire de la gravure à l'eau-forte. **etching** *n.* **1.** art *m* de graver à l'eau-forte. **2.** gravure à l'eau-forte; eau-forte *f*, *pl.* eaux-fortes.

etcher ['etʃər] *n.* graveur *m* à l'eau-forte.

eternal [i(:)'tə:n(ə)l] **1.** *a.* (*a*) éternel; **e. life,** la vie éternelle; (*b*) continuel, sans fin; (querelles) incessantes. **2.** *n.* **the E.,** l'Éternel *m*. **-ally** *adv.* éternellement; **I shall be e. grateful to you,** je vous en aurai une reconnaissance éternelle.

eternity [i(:)'tə:niti] *n.* éternité *f*; *F:* **I waited an e.,** j'ai attendu pendant une éternité.

ethane ['i:θein] *n. Ch:* éthane *m*.

ether ['i:θər] *n.* **1.** éther *m*. **methyl e.,** éther méthylique; **e. addict,** éthéromane *mf*. **2.** *Ph:* **waves in the e.,** ondes *fpl* de l'éther. **3.** *A. & Poet:* **the e.,** la voûte éthérée.

ethereal [i'θiəreəl] *a.* (*of regions, etc.*) éthéré; (*of form*) léger, impalpable. **-ally** *adv.* **e. beautiful,** d'une beauté éthérée.

etherize ['i:θəraiz] *v.tr. Med:* éthériser.

ethic(al) ['eθik(l)] *a.* **1.** moral, -aux; **ethical writer,** moraliste *m*. **2.** *Gram:* **ethic dative,** datif *m* éthique. **3.** *U.S: Pharm:* **ethical drug,** remède vendu uniquement sur l'ordonnance d'un médecin. **-ally** *adv.* d'après (les doctrines de) l'éthique.

ethics ['eθiks] *n.pl.* (*usu. with sg. const.*) éthique *f*, morale *f*.

Ethiopia [i:θi'oupiə] *Pr.n. Geog:* Éthiopie *f*.

Ethiopian [i:θi'oupiən] *Geog:* **1.** *a.* éthiopien. **2.** *n.* Éthiopien, (ienne.

ethnic(al) ['eθnik(l)] *a.* ethnique. **-ally** *adv.* du point de vue ethnique.

ethnographer [eθ'nɔgrəfər] *n.* ethnographe *mf*.

ethnography [eθ'nɔgrəfi] *n.* ethnographie *f*.

ethnological [eθnə'lɔdʒik(ə)l] *a.* ethnologique. **-ally** *adv.* ethnologiquement.

ethnologist [eθ'nɔlədʒist] *n.* ethnologue *mf*.

ethnology [eθ'nɔlədʒi] *n.* ethnologie *f*.

ethological [i:θə'lɔdʒik(ə)l] *a.* éthologique.

ethology [i(:)'θɔlədʒi] *n.* éthologie *f*.

ethos ['i:θɔs] *n.* génie *m* (d'un peuple, etc.).

ethyl ['eθil] *n. Ch:* éthyle *m*; **e. alcohol,** alcool *m* éthylique.

ethylene ['eθili:n] *n. Ch:* éthylène *m*.

etiolate ['i:tiouleit] *v.tr.* étioler (une plante).

etiology [i:ti'ɔlədʒi] *n. esp. NAm:* étiologie *f*.

etiquette ['etiket] *n.* (*a*) etiquette *f*; **court e.,** le cérémonial de cour; (*b*) **the e. of the Bar,** les règles *fpl* du Barreau.
Etonian [i:'tounian] *n.m.* élève (du collège) d'Eton; **Old E.,** ancien élève d'Eton.
Etruscan [i'trʌskən] *A.Hist:* **1.** *a.* étrusque. **2.** *n.* Étrusque *mf.*
etymological [etimə'lɔdʒik(ə)l] *a.* étymologique. **-ally** *adv.* étymologiquement.
etymologist [eti'mɔlədʒist] *n.* étymologiste *mf.*
etymology [eti'mɔlədʒi] *n.* étymologie *f.*
eucalyptus, *pl.* **-ti, -tuses** [jukə'liptəs; -tai, -ti:; -təsiz] *n.* **1.** *Bot:* eucalyptus *m.* **2.** *Pharm:* **e. oil,** essence *f* d'eucalyptus.
Eucharist (the) [ðə'ju:kərist] *n. Ecc:* l'eucharistie *f*; **to receive the E.,** recevoir l'eucharistie.
Euclidean [ju'klidiən] *a.* (géométrie) euclidienne.
eugenics [ju'dʒeniks] *n.pl.* (*usu. with sg. const.*) eugénique *f*, eugénisme *m.*
eulogize ['ju:lədʒaiz] *v.tr.* faire l'éloge, le panégyrique, de (qn, qch.).
eulogy ['ju:lədʒi] *n.* panégyrique *m*; **to pronounce a e. on s.o.,** faire l'éloge, le panégyrique, de qn.
eunuch ['ju:nək] *n.* eunuque *m.*
euphemism ['ju:fimizm] *n.* euphémisme *m.*
euphemistic [jufi'mistik] *a.* euphémique. **-ally** *adv.* euphémiquement; par euphémisme.
euphonious [ju'founiəs] *a.* euphonique.
euphonium [ju'founiəm] *n. Mus:* saxhorn *m* basse; basse *f* (des cuivres); **e. player,** bassiste *m.*
euphony ['ju:fəni] *n.* euphonie *f*; **for the sake of e.,** par euphonie.
euphorbia [ju'fɔ:biə] *n. Bot:* euphorbe *f.*
euphoria [ju'fɔ:riə] *n.* euphorie *f.*
euphoric [ju'fɔ:rik] *a.* euphorique.
Eurasia [ju'reiʃə, -ʒə] *Pr.n. Geog:* Eurasie *f.*
Eurasian [ju'reiʃən, -ʒən] **1.** *a. Ethn:* eurasien; (faune, etc.) eurasiatique. **2.** *n. Ethn:* Eurasien, -ienne.
eurhythmics [ju'riθmiks] *n.pl.* (*usu. with sg. const.*) gymnastique *f* rhythmique.
Eurocrat ['ju:roukræt] *n.* eurocrate *mf.*
Eurodollar ['ju:roudɔlər] *n. Fin:* Eurodollar *m.*
Europe ['ju:rəp] *Pr.n. Geog:* Europe *f*; **Council of E.,** Conseil *m* de l'Europe; **in E.,** en Europe.
European [jurə'pi:ən] **1.** *a.* européen; **E. Economic Community,** Communauté économique européenne. **2.** *n.* (*a*) Européen, -éenne; (*b*) *F:* blanc, blanche.
Eustachian [jus'teiʃən] *a. Anat:* **E. tube,** trompe *f* d'Eustache.
eutectic [ju'tektik] *a. & n. Ch:* eutectique (*m*).
euthanasia [juθə'neiziə] *n.* euthanasie *f.*
evacuate [i'vækjueit] *v.tr.* (*a*) évacuer (un lieu); (*b*) évacuer (la population); (*c*) *Physiol:* évacuer; (*d*) *Mch:* refouler (les gaz brûlés d'un moteur, etc.); *Ph:* faire le vide dans (un tube).
evacuation [ivækju'eiʃ(ə)n] *n.* (*a*) évacuation *f* (d'un lieu); (*b*) évacuation (des gens); (*c*) *Physiol:* évacuation (du ventre); (*d*) *Mch:* refoulement *m* (des gaz brûlés d'un moteur, etc.); *Ph:* production *f* du vide (dans un tube).
evacuee [ivækju:'i:] *n.* évacué, -ée.
evade [i'veid] *v.tr.* éviter (un coup, un danger); esquiver (un coup, ses créanciers); se soustraire à (la justice); éluder, tourner (un obstacle, la loi); déjouer (la vigilance de qn); **to e. customs duty,** passer qch. en fraude; **to e. tax,** frauder le fisc.
evader [i'veidər] *n.* éludeur *m* (**of,** de); **tax e.,** fraudeur, -euse, du fisc.
evaluate [i'væljueit] *v.tr.* évaluer (les dommages), estimer le montant (des dommages).
evaluation [ivælju'eiʃ(ə)n] *n.* évaluation *f* (du dommage); *Mil:* **e. of information,** critique *f* du renseignement.
evanescent [i:væ'nesənt] *a.* évanescent; éphémère.
evangelical [i:væn'dʒelik(ə)l] **1.** *a. Ecc:* évangélique, conforme à l'Évangile. **2.** (*a*) *a.* qui appartient à la religion réformée; **the E. Church,** l'Église évangelique; (*b*) *n.* protestant *m* évangélique.
evangelicalism [i:væn'dʒelikəlizm] *n. Ecc:* évangélisme *m*; doctrine *f* de l'Église évangélique.
evangelism [i'vændʒilizm] *n. Ecc:* évangélisme *m*, prédication *f* de l'Évangile.
evangelist [i'væn(d)ʒilist] *n.* évangéliste *m.*
evangelize [i'væn(d)ʒilaiz] **1.** *v.tr.* évangéliser; prêcher l'Évangile à (qn). **2.** *v.i.* prêcher l'Évangile.
evaporate [i'væpəreit] **1.** *v.tr.* (faire) évaporer (un liquide); **evaporated milk,** lait évaporé. **2.** *v.i.* (*a*) (*of liquid, etc.*) s'évaporer, se vaporiser; (*of acid*) se volatiliser; (*b*) (*of thg*) s'évaporer; (*of money*) disparaître comme par enchantement. **evaporating** *n.* évaporation *f.*
evaporation [ivæpə'reiʃ(ə)n] *n.* évaporation *f*, vaporisation *f* (d'un liquide, d'un parfum); volatilisation *f* (d'un acide, etc.).
evaporator [i'væpəreitər] *n. Ind:* évaporateur *m.*
evasion [i'veiʒ(ə)n] *n.* **1.** (*a*) évasion *f*, fuite *f*; (*b*) dérobade *f*; **tax e.,** fraude fiscale. **2.** subterfuge *m*, échappatoire *f*, faux-fuyant *m*, *pl.* faux-fuyants; **without e.,** sans détours.
evasive [i'veisiv] *a.* évasif; (personnalité) fuyante; **to give an e. answer,** faire une réponse évasive; répondre évasivement; **to take e. action,** faire une manœuvre d'évitement. **-ly** *adv.* évasivement.
evasiveness [i'veisivnis] *n.* caractère évasif.
Eve[1] [i:v] *Pr.n.f.* Ève; *F:* **a daughter of E.,** une fille d'Ève.
eve[2] *n.* **1.** *A: & Poet:* soir *m.* **2.** (*a*) *Ecc:* vigile *f* (de fête); (*b*) veille *f*; **Christmas E.,** la veille de Noël; **New Year's E.,** la Saint-Sylvestre; **on the e. of . . .,** à la veille de . . .; **to be on the e. of success,** être à la veille du succès.
even[1] ['i:v(ə)n] *a.* **1.** (*of surface, ground, etc.*) uni; égal, -aux; uniforme; **to be e. with sth.,** être au niveau de, à ras de, qch.; **to make e.,** araser (les assises d'une construction); aplanir (une surface); affleurer (les bords de deux planches, etc.); égaliser (des entre-deux, etc.). **2.** (pouls) égal, régulier; **e. temperature,** température égale; **e. temper,** caractère *m* calme; (*d*) **with an e. hand,** impartialement. **3.** (*a*) **e money,** pari *m* avec enjeu égal; *n.* **to lay evens,** parier à égalité; **horse quoted at evens, at e. money,** cheval coté à égalité; **to break e.,** ne faire ni pertes ni profits; **he has an e. chance of succeeding,** il a une chance sur deux de réussir; (*b*) *Games:* **to be e.,** être but à but, tant à tant, point à point, *F:* point à; **e. match,** partie égale; **to get e. with s.o.,** (i) arriver, se mettre, à la hauteur de qn; (ii) prendre sa revanche sur qn; **to be e. with s.o.,** être quitte avec qn; **I'll be e. with him yet,** je la lui rendrai; (*c*) **e. bargain,** marché *m* équitable, juste. **4.** (*a*) (nombre) pair; **odd or e.,** pair ou impair; (*b*) **e. money,** compte rond; **to make up the e. money,** faire l'appoint. **-ly** *adv.* **1.** (étendre, filer) uniment. **2.** (respirer, tourner) régulièrement; (diviser) également; **e. matched,** (i) de grandeur égale; (ii) de force égale.
even[2] *adv.* **1.** même; (*with comparative*) encore; (*with negative*) même; **or e. . . .,** ou même . . ., **e. the cleverest,** même les plus habiles; **e. the children knew,** même les enfants le savaient; **I never e. saw it,** je ne l'ai même pas vu; **e. supposing that . . .,** même en supposant que . . .; **that would be e. worse, better,** ce serait encore pis, mieux; **e. more, less,** encore plus, moins; **he seemed e. sadder than usual,** il paraissait encore plus triste que d'habitude; **without e. speaking,** sans dire un mot; **e. if he failed,** même s'il éc-

houait; **he always goes by bus, e. though he has a car,** il prend toujours l'autobus, bien qu'il ait une voiture; **e. so,** mais cependant, quand même; **e. then he wouldn't believe me,** même alors il ne voulait pas me croire. **2. e. now,** à l'instant même; **e. then,** déjà (à cette époque).

even³ *v.tr.* **1.** aplanir, niveler, égaliser (une surface, etc.); affleurer (deux planches, etc.); araser (les assises d'un mur). **2.** rendre égal; *Typ:* **to e. (out) the spacing,** égaliser l'espacement; **that will e. things up,** cela rétablira l'équilibre.

evening [ˈiːvniŋ] *n.* **1.** (*a*) soir *m*; (*duration*) soirée *f*; **tomorrow e.,** demain (au) soir; **in the e.,** le soir, au soir; **at nine o'clock in the e.,** à neuf heures du soir; **(on) that e.,** ce soir-là; **(on) the e. before, (on) the previous e.,** la veille au soir; **the next e.,** le lendemain soir; **one, on a, fine summer e.,** (par) un beau soir d'été; **every e.,** tous les soirs; **every Monday e.,** tous les lundis soir; **all (the) e.,** toute la soirée; **during the e.,** pendant la soirée; **e. paper,** journal *m* du soir; *Th:* **e. performance,** représentation de soirée; *Astr:* **e. star,** étoile *f* du soir; (*b*) *Lit:* **in the e. of life,** au déclin de la vie. **2.** (*a*) (*evening party*) soirée; **musical e.,** soirée musicale; (*b*) **e. dress,** (i) (*for men*) tenue *f* de soirée; (ii) (*for women*) robe *f* du soir; **in e. dress,** en tenue de soirée.

evenness [ˈiːvənnis] *n.* **1.** égalité *f*; régularité *f* (de mouvement). **2.** calme *m* (d'esprit); égalité (d'humeur).

even-numbered [ˈiːvənˈnʌmbəːd] *a.* (portant un nombre) pair.

evensong [ˈiːv(ə)nsɔŋ] *n. R.C.Ch:* vêpres *fpl* et salut *m*; *Ch. of Eng:* office *m* du soir.

event [iˈvent] *n.* **1.** cas *m*; **in the e. of his refusing,** au cas, dans le cas, où il refuserait; pour le cas où il refuserait; **in the e. of his death,** en cas de décès; **unforeseen e.,** occurrence imprévue. **2.** (*a*) événement *m*; **it's quite an e.,** c'est un véritable événement; *Com:* **great coat e.!** grandes soldes de manteaux! *F:* **a happy e.,** un heureux événement; **in the course of events,** par la suite; (*b*) issue *f*, résultat *m*; **in either e.,** dans l'un ou l'autre cas; **wise after the e.,** sage après coup; **at all events,** en tout cas; (*c*) *Ph:* phénomène *m*. **3.** *Sp:* (*a*) réunion sportive; **sporting e.,** manifestation sportive; (*b*) (*athletics*) **field events,** épreuves *fpl* sur terrain; **track events,** courses *fpl*, épreuves, sur piste; (*c*) rencontre *f* (de boxe, à l'épée, etc.).

even-tempered [ˈiːv(ə)nˈtempəd] *a.* d'humeur égale.

eventful [iˈventful] *a.* (*a*) (*of life*) plein d'incidents; mouvementé; (*b*) (*of day, year*) mémorable.

eventide [ˈiːv(ə)ntaid] *n. Lit:* soir *m*.

eventual [iˈventjuəl] *a.* **1.** éventuel; **the e. profits of this new deal,** les profits éventuels de cette nouvelle affaire. **2.** définitif; **his prodigality and his e. ruin,** sa prodigalité et sa ruine finale. **-ally** *adv.* en fin de compte; par la suite; **he e. became a judge,** il finit par être nommé juge.

eventuality [iventjuˈæliti] *n.* éventualité *f*.

ever [ˈevər] *adv.* **1.** (*a*) jamais; **the best mother that e. was,** la meilleure mère qui fût jamais; **I read seldom if e.,** je lis rarement, pour ne pas dire jamais; **if e. I catch him,** si jamais je l'attrape; **nothing e. happens,** il n'arrive jamais rien; **hardly e., scarcely e.,** presque jamais; **he's a liar if e. there was one,** c'est un menteur s'il en fut jamais; **it started to rain faster than e.,** il s'est mis à pleuvoir de plus belle; **without e. having thought of it,** sans jamais y avoir pensé; **worst e., best e.,** sans précédent; *P:* **did you e.!** par exemple! (*b*) **they lived happily e. after,** ils ont vécu heureux à tout jamais; (*c*) **e. since (then),** dès lors, depuis; **I have been here e. since lunch,** je suis là depuis le déjeuner. **2.** (*a*) toujours; **e.-increasing influence,** influence toujours plus étendue; *Corr:* **yours e., e. yours,** bien cordialement à vous; tout(e) à vous; (*b*) **for e.,** pour toujours; à jamais; **to go away for e.,** partir sans retour; **for e. and e.,** à tout jamais; **Scotland for e.!** vive l'Écosse! **to live for e.,** vivre éternellement; **he's for e. grumbling,** il ne cesse pas de se plaindre. **3.** (*intensive*) (*a*) **as quickly as e. you can,** aussi vite que possible; **as soon as e. he comes home,** aussitôt qu'il rentrera; **it was the funniest sight e.,** c'était à se tordre; (*b*) *F:* **e. so pretty,** joli comme tout; **it was e. so long ago,** ça fait tellement longtemps; **e. so many times,** je ne sais combien de fois; **thank you e. so much,** merci mille fois; **I'm e. so pleased,** j'en suis tellement content; (*c*) (*emphasized*) **how e. you manage I don't know,** je me demande comment vous faites; **what e. shall we do?** qu'est-ce que nous allons bien faire? **what ever's the matter with you?** mais qu'est-ce que vous avez donc? **what e. can it be?** qu'est-ce que ça peut bien être? **when e. will he come?** quand donc viendra-t-il? **where e. have you been?** mais d'où venez-vous? **who e. told you that?** qui est-ce qui a bien pu vous dire cela? **why e. not?** mais pourquoi pas?

evergreen [ˈevəgriːn] **1.** *a.* toujours vert; *Bot:* à feuilles persistantes; **e. oak,** chêne vert; *O:* **e. topic,** question *f* toujours d'actualité. **2.** *n.* (*a*) arbre à feuilles persistantes; (*b*) **evergreens,** plantes vertes.

everlasting [evəˈlɑːstiŋ] **1.** *a.* (*a*) éternel; *B:* **the mighty God, the e. Father,** le Dieu tout-puissant, le Père éternel; (*b*) *Bot:* **e. flower,** immortelle *f*; **e. pea,** pois *m* vivace; (*c*) (*of material*) inusable, solide; (*d*) perpétuel, continuel; **I am tired of her e. complaints,** je suis las de ses plaintes sans fin. **2.** *n.* **the E.,** l'Éternel. **-ly** *adv.* **1.** éternellement. **2.** perpétuellement; **he's e. complaining,** il est toujours à se plaindre.

evermore [evəˈmɔːr] *adv.* toujours; **for e.,** à jamais.

every [ˈevri] *a.* (*a*) chaque; tout; tous les . . .; **e. week,** toutes les semaines; chaque semaine; **e. word he says is a lie,** tout ce qu'il dit est mensonge; **I have copied e. word of it,** je l'ai copié mot pour mot; **his desire to meet your e. wish,** son désir d'aller au-devant de chacun de vos désirs; **e. action of his,** *Lit:* **his e. action,** chacune de ses actions; **e. day,** chaque jour, tous les jours; **confidence is increasing e. day,** la confiance s'accroît de jour en jour; **e. other, second, day,** tous les deux jours; un jour sur deux; **e. other Sunday,** un dimanche sur deux; **e. second or third day,** tous les deux ou trois jours; **e. third man was chosen,** on choisissait un homme sur trois; **at e. quarter past the hour,** toutes les heures, au quart; **e. few minutes,** toutes les cinq minutes; **e. time he comes,** chaque fois qu'il vient; **perseverance wins e. time,** la persévérance l'emporte toujours; (*b*) (*intensive*) **he was e. inch a republican,** il était républicain jusqu'au bout des doigts; **I have e. reason to believe that . . .,** j'ai tout lieu de croire que . . .; **e. bit as good, as intelligent, as . . .,** tout aussi bon, intelligent, que . . .; **I shall give you e. assistance,** je vous aiderai de tout mon pouvoir; **I look forward with e. confidence to the future,** j'envisage l'avenir avec une pleine confiance; (*c*) **e. one,** chacun, chacune; **e. one of us was there,** nous étions tous là; **they are my friends, e. one of them,** ils sont tous mes amis; **e. man for himself,** (i) chacun pour soi; (ii) (*in danger*) sauve qui peut! **e. person has this right,** chacun a ce droit; **e. man Jack of them,** tous sans exception.

everybody [ˈevribɔdi] *indef.pron.* tout le monde; **e. has his own way, a way of his own,** chacun a sa manière à lui; **e. else,** tous les autres; **e. knows that,** tout le monde, n'importe qui, sait cela; **not e. can do it,** ce n'est pas tout le monde qui pourrait le faire; **e. else knows it,** tous les autres le savent.

everyday [ˈevridei] *a.* **1.** journalier, quotidien; **e. occurrence,** (i) fait journalier; (ii) fait banal; **e. life,** la vie quotidienne. **2.** de tous les jours; (vêtements) de la semaine. **3.** usuel; banal, -aux; ordinaire, (expression) courante; **e. English,** l'anglais usuel; **words in e. use,** mots d'usage courant.
everyone [ˈevriwʌn] *indef.pron.* = EVERYBODY.
everything [ˈevriθiŋ] *indef.pron.* (*a*) tout; **he has eaten e.,** il a tout mangé; **(a place for e., and) e. in its place,** chaque chose à sa place; **e. good,** tout ce qu'il y a de bon; **they sell e.,** on y vend de tout; *Com:* **e. for cyclists,** tout ce qui concerne le cyclisme; *F:* **we're in a bad way with strikes and e.,** ça marche mal à cause des grèves et de tout ça; (*b*) de première importance; **money is not e.,** l'argent n'est pas tout; **she is very pretty—beauty isn't e.,** elle est très jolie—il n'y a pas que la beauté (qui compte); **she's e. to me,** je ne vis que pour elle.
everywhere [ˈevri(h)wɛər] *adv.* partout; en tout lieu; en tous lieux; **to look e. for s.o.,** chercher qn partout; **e. you go,** partout où vous allez.
evict [iˈvikt] *v.tr.* évincer, expulser (un locataire) **(from,** de); **evicted tenant,** locataire évincé.
eviction [iˈvikʃ(ə)n] *n. Jur:* éviction *f*, expulsion *f* (d'un locataire).
evidence[1] [ˈevidəns] *n.* **1.** (*a*) évidence *f*; **to fly in the face of the e.,** se refuser à l'évidence; (*b*) (*of pers., etc.*) **to be in e.,** être en évidence. **2.** signe *m*, marque *f*; **to bear, give, e. of sth.,** porter la marque de qch.; **there was no e. of his stay in the house,** rien ne marquait qu'il eût séjourné dans la maison. **3.** (*a*) preuve *f*; **internal e.,** preuves intrinsèques; **external e.,** preuves extrinsèques; (*b*) *Jur:* témoignage *m*; **oral e.,** preuve orale; **written, documentary, e.,** preuve littérale, documentaire; **to bear, give, e.,** témoigner, déposer (en justice); faire une déposition; porter témoignage; **to give e. in s.o.'s favour,** témoigner en faveur de qn; **to call s.o. in e.,** appeler qn en témoignage; **the e. was strongly against him,** les témoignages pesaient contre lui; **if you can't believe the e. of your eyes!** si vous n'êtes pas convaincu par ce que vous voyez devant vous! **4.** *Jur:* (*pers.*) témoin(s) *m(pl)*; **to turn King's, Queen's, e.,** *U.S:* **State's e.,** témoigner contre ses complices (sous promesse de pardon).
evidence[2] *v.tr.* prouver, manifester, démontrer (qch.).
evident [ˈevidənt] *a.* évident; (*of fact, truth*) patent; **it was e. that . . .,** il était evident, clair, que . . . **-ly** *adv.* évidemment, manifestement; **he was e. afraid,** il était évident, clair, qu'il avait peur.
evil [ˈiːv(ə)l] **1.** *a.* (*a*) mauvais; (jour malheureux; (moment) funeste; **house of e. repute,** lieu mal famé; **e. omen,** présage *m* de malheur; **to fall on e. days,** tomber dans l'infortune, dans le malheur; (*b*) méchant; (esprit) malfaisant, malin; **the E. One,** le Mauvais, le Malin; **e. influence,** influence néfaste; **e. eye,** mauvais œil; **e. tongue,** mauvaise langue; **to silence e. tongues,** faire taire la médisance. **2.** *n.* mal *m*, *pl.* maux; **a social e.,** une plaie sociale; **to speak e. of s.o.,** dire du mal de qn. **evilly** *adv.* avec malveillance; (regarder qn) d'un mauvais œil, d'un air méchant.
evil-doer [ˈiːv(ə)lduːər] *n.* malfaiteur *m*.
evil-looking [ˈiːv(ə)llukiŋ] *a.* de mauvaise mine; (homme) louche; **he drew an e.-l. knife,** il tira un vilain couteau.
evil-minded [ˈiːv(ə)lˈmaindid] *a.* porté au mal: malintentionné, malveillant; malin, -igne.
evil-smelling [ˈiːv(ə)lˈsmeliŋ] *a.* nauséabond.
evince [iˈvins] *v.tr.* montrer, témoigner (une qualité, etc.); manifester (de la curiosité, etc.).
eviscerate [iˈvisəreit] *v.tr.* **1.** éviscérer, éventrer. **2.** émasculer (un ouvrage littéraire, etc.).
evisceration [ivisəˈreiʃ(ə)n] *n.* éviscération *f*.
evocation [evouˈkeiʃ(ə)n] *n.* évocation *f*.
evocative [iˈvɔkətiv] *a.* évocateur, -trice.
evoke [iˈvouk] *v.tr.* (*a*) évoquer (un souvenir); (*b*) **this remark evoked a smile,** cette observation a provoqué, suscité, un sourire.
evolution [iːvəˈl(j)uːʃ(ə)n] *n.* **1.** (*a*) *Biol:* évolution *f*, développement *m* (d'une espèce, d'un projet, etc.); (*b*) **the e. of events,** le déroulement des événements. **2.** évolution (d'un acrobate, de troupes, etc.).
evolutionary [iːvəˈl(j)uːʃən(ə)ri] *a. Biol:* évolutionnaire, évolutif.
evolutionism [iːˈvəˈl(j)uːʃənizm] *n. Biol:* évolutionnisme *m*.
evolve [iˈvɔlv] **1.** *v.tr.* (*a*) dérouler, développer (un projet); (*b*) développer, déduire (une théorie, une vérité) **(from,** de); (*c*) développer (par évolution). **2.** *v.i.* (*a*) (*of events*) se dérouler; (*b*) (*of gas, etc.*) se dégager; (*c*) (*of race*) se développer, évoluer.
ewe [juː] *n.* brebis *f*.
ewer [ˈjuər] *n. O:* pot *m* à eau; broc *m* de toilette.
ex[1] [eks] *prep.* **1.** *Com:* (*out of*) **price ex works,** prix *m* départ usine, prix sortie d'usine. **2.** (*without*) *Fin:* **shares quoted ex dividend, ex coupon,** actions citées ex-dividende, coupon détaché, ex-coupon.
ex-[2] **1.** *pref.* (*former*) ancien; ex-; **ex-minister,** ex-ministre; **an ex-teacher,** un ancien professeur; **ex-wife,** ex-femme. **2.** *n. F:* **my ex,** mon ex.
exacerbate [egˈzæsəbeit] *v.tr.* exacerber, aggraver (une douleur, etc.); irriter, exaspérer (qn).
exact[1] [egˈzækt] *a.* exact. **1.** (*a*) précis; **to give e. details,** donner des détails précis, des précisions *fpl*; préciser; **the e. sciences,** les sciences exactes; (*b*) **the e. word,** le mot juste; (*on bus*) **to tender the e. amount,** faire l'appoint; (*c*) (*of discipline*) strict, rigoureux. **2.** (*of pers.*) **to be e. in sth., in doing sth.,** être exact (dans ses paiements); être strict (en affaires). **-ly** *adv.* exactement, précisément; (*of time*) juste; **I don't know e. what happened,** je ne sais pas au juste ce qui est arrivé; **e.!** précisément! parfaitement! **it is e. five,** il est cinq heures juste; **he is not e. a scholar,** ce n'est pas exactement un savant.
exact[2] *v.tr.* **1.** (*a*) exiger (un impôt) **(from,** de); (*b*) extorquer (une rançon à qn). **2.** exiger, réclamer, (l'obéissance) **(from,** de). **exacting** *a.* (*of pers.*) exigeant; (*of work*) astreignant; **to be too e.,** se montrer trop exigeant.
exaction [egˈzækʃ(ə)n] *n.* exaction *f*.
exactitude [egˈzæktitjuːd] *n.* exactitude *f*, précision *f*; justesse *f* (d'un raisonnement, d'un calcul).
exaggerate [egˈzædʒəreit] *v.tr.* exagérer; agrandir, amplifier (les fautes, etc.); grandir (un incident); charger (un récit); *v.i.* **let's not, don't, e.!** n'exagérons rien! **exaggerated** [egˈzædʒəreitid] *a.* exagéré (*of praise*) outré; **to have an e. opinion of oneself,** avoir une très haute opinion de soi-même; **to attach e. importance to sth.,** prêter une importance excessive à qch. **exaggeratedly** *adv.* exagérément.
exaggeration [egzædʒəˈreiʃ(ə)n] *n.* **1.** exagération *f*. **2. that's an e.!** vous exagérez!
exalt [egˈzɔːlt] *v.tr.* **1.** élever (qn en rang, etc.). **2.** exalter, vanter (les vertus de qn); **to e. s.o. to the skies,** porter qn jusqu'aux nues. **exalted** *a.* **1.** (rang) élevé; (personnage) haut placé. **2.** exalté; (ton) élevé.
exam [egˈzæm] *n. F:* = EXAMINATION 2.
examination [egzæmiˈneiʃ(ə)n] *n.* examen *m*. **1.** inspection *f*, visite *f* (des machines, etc.); vérification *f* (de comptes); dépouillement *m* (d'un rapport); *Jur:* compulsation *f* (de dossiers, etc.); **on e.,** après examen, examen fait; **on further e.,** après un examen plus approfondi; *Jur:* **the case is under e.,** l'affaire

est soumise à vérification; **to undergo a medical e.,** passer une visite médicale. **2.** *Sch: etc:* **entrance e.,** examen d'entrée; **competitive e.,** concours *m*; **written, oral, e.,** épreuves écrites, orales; **to take, sit, an e.,** passer, subir, un examen; **to pass, fail, an e.,** être reçu, refusé, à un examen. **3.** *Jur:* (*a*) interrogatoire *m* (d'un accusé, etc.); audition *f* (de témoins); (*b*) instruction *f* (d'une cause).

examine [eg'zæmin] *v.tr.* **1.** (*a*) examiner, inspecter (une machine); *Cust:* visiter (les bagages); vérifier (des comptes); contrôler, viser (un passeport); compulser (des dossiers, etc.); dépouiller (un inventaire, un compte); **to e. one's conscience,** faire son examen de conscience; **to e. a question thoroughly,** examiner une question à fond; **to get examined,** se faire examiner; *Nau:* **to stop and e. a ship,** arraisonner un navire; (*b*) *Med:* examiner (un malade). **2.** examiner, faire passer un examen à (qn); **to e. a candidate in Latin,** examiner un candidat en latin. **3.** *Jur: etc:* (*a*) interroger, faire subir un interrogatoire à (un prévenu, un témoin); (*b*) instruire (une cause). **examining** *a.* examinateur, -trice; **e. body,** jury *m* d'examen; **e. magistrate** = juge *m* d'instruction.

examinee [egzæmi'ni:] *n. Sch:* candidat, -ate.

examiner [eg'zæminər] *n.* **1.** inspecteur, -trice, visiteur, -euse (de bagages, etc.); compulseur *m* (de dossiers, etc.). **2.** *Sch:* examinateur, -trice; **the examiners,** le jury (d'examen).

example [eg'zɑ:mpl] *n.* exemple *m.* **1. to quote sth. as an e.,** citer qch. à titre d'exemple; **he showed me some examples of his work,** il m'a montré des spécimens *mpl* de son travail; **for e., by way of e.,** par exemple; **large towns, as for e. London,** les grandes villes, telles que Londres (par exemple). **2.** précédent *m*; **without e.,** sans exemple, sans précédent. **3. to give, set, an e.,** donner l'exemple; **to make an e. of s.o.,** faire un exemple de qn; punir qn pour l'exemple; **to take s.o. as an e.,** prendre exemple sur qn; **to follow s.o.'s e.,** suivre l'exemple de qn.

exasperate [eg'zɑ:spəreit, -zæ-] *v.tr.* exaspérer, irriter; **exasperated at, by, his insolence,** poussé à bout par son insolence. **exasperating** *a.* exaspérant, irritant. **exasperatingly** *adv.* d'une manière exaspérante, irritante.

exasperation [egzɑ:spə'reiʃ(ə)n, -zæ-] *n.* exaspération *f*; **to drive s.o. to e.,** pousser qn à bout.

excavate ['ekskəveit] *v.tr.* excaver, creuser (un tunnel); fouiller (la terre); approfondir (un canal); déterrer (des ruines, etc.); *Archeol:* **to e. (a site),** faire des fouilles (dans un endroit).

excavation [ekskə'veiʃ(ə)n] *n.* excavation *f.* **1.** fouillement *m* (de la terre, etc.); approfondissement *m.* **2.** terrain excavé; fouille *f*; **the excavations at Pompeii,** les fouilles de Pompéi.

excavator ['ekskəveitər] *n.* (*a*) *Civ.E:* excavateur, -trice, pelleteuse *f*; (*b*) (*pers.*) fouilleur, -euse.

exceed [ek'si:d] *v.tr.* (*a*) excéder, dépasser (des limites, etc.); **not exceeding ten pounds,** ne dépassant pas dix livres; *Post:* **not exceeding 250 gr.,** jusqu'à 250 gr.; **to e. one's instructions,** dépasser ses instructions; **to e. one's rights, one's powers,** sortir des limites de son droit, sortir de sa compétence; *Aut:* **to e. the speed limit,** dépasser la limite de vitesse; **he was fined for exceeding the speed limit,** il a eu une contravention pour excès de vitesse; (*b*) surpasser (qn, qch.) **(in,** en); **the outcome exceeded all our hopes,** le résultat a dépassé toutes nos espérances. **exceedingly** *adv.* extrêmement; excessivement.

excel [ek'sel] *v.* **(excelled) 1.** *v.i.* exceller **(in doing sth.,** à faire qch.); **to e. at a game,** exceller à un jeu. **2.** *v.tr.* surpasser (qn); **to e. oneself,** se surpasser.

excellence ['eksələns] *n.* excellence *f.* **1.** perfection *f.* **2.** mérite *m*, qualité *f*, supériorité *f* (de qn, de qch.).

excellency ['eksələnsi] *n.* (*title*) **Your E.,** votre Excellence *f*; **his E. the French Ambassador,** son Excellence l'ambassadeur de France.

excellent ['eksələnt] *a.* excellent, parfait. **-ly** *adv.* admirablement, d'une manière excellente.

except¹ [ek'sept] *v.tr.* excepter, exclure **(from,** de); **present company excepted,** les présents exceptés; **errors and omissions excepted,** sauf erreur ou omission. **excepting** *prep. & conj.* = EXCEPT²; **not e. my wife,** sans excepter ma femme.

except² **1.** *prep.* (*a*) excepté; à l'exception de; **nobody e. him,** personne excepté lui; **all e. the doctor,** tous, à l'exception du docteur; **nobody heard it e. me,** il n'y a que moi qui l'aie entendu; **e. by agreement between the parties,** sauf accord entre les parties; **e. when, if,** sauf quand, si; (*b*) **e. for,** à part, si ce n'est; **the dress is ready e. for the buttons,** la robe est prête, à l'exception des boutons. **2.** *conj.phr.* **e. that,** excepté que, si ce n'est que; **he came out of it unscathed, e. that he lost his hat,** il en est sorti indemne, sauf qu'il a perdu son chapeau.

exception [ek'sepʃ(ə)n] *n.* **1.** exception *f*; **to make an e. to a rule,** faire une exception à une règle; **the e. proves the rule,** l'exception confirme la règle; **without e.,** sans (aucune) exception; **with the e. of . . .,** à l'exception de . . ., exception faite de . . .; **with a few exceptions,** sauf de rares exceptions, à quelques exceptions près; **with certain exceptions,** sauf exceptions. **2.** objection *f*; **to take e. to sth.,** (i) trouver à redire à qch.; (ii) se formaliser, s'offenser, de qch.; **to take e. to s.o.'s doing sth.,** trouver mauvais que qn fasse qch.

exceptionable [ek'sepʃ(ə)nəbl] *a.* (*usu. with a negative*) (rien de) blâmable, critiquable; **to find nothing e. in sth.,** ne rien trouver à redire à qch.

exceptional [ek'sepʃən(ə)l] *a.* **1.** (*a*) (*of case, etc.*) exceptionnel; (*b*) **jurisdiction of an e. court,** juridiction *f* d'exception. **2.** (*outstanding*) (*of beauty, etc.*) exceptionnel; **an e. man,** un homme exceptionnel, remarquable. **-ally** *adv.* exceptionnellement. **1.** par exception. **2.** (*unusually*) extraordinairement; **e. cheap,** d'un bon marché exceptionnel; **e. gifted child,** enfant remarquablement doué.

excerpt ['eksə:pt] *n.* (*a*) extrait *m*, citation *f*; (*b*) *Mus:* **excerpts from** *Carmen,* extraits de *Carmen.*

excess [ek'ses] *n.* **1.** (*a*) excès *m* (de lumière, de zèle, etc.); **to eat, drink, to e.,** manger, boire, à l'excès; **indulgence carried to e.,** indulgence poussée trop loin; (*b*) excès; abus *m*; **to commit excesses,** commettre des excès, des cruautés. **2.** excédent *m* (de dépenses, etc.); **e. weight,** excédent de poids; surpoids *m*; **sum in e.,** somme *f* en surplus; **sum in e. of £50,** somme au-dessus de £50; *Rail:* **e. fare,** supplément *m*; **to pay the e. (on one's ticket),** prendre un supplément; **e. luggage,** excédent de bagages *mpl* en surpoids.

excessive [ek'sesiv] *a.* (*of heat, etc.*) excessif; (*of zeal*) immodéré; (*of virtue, etc.*) outré, exagéré; (*of ambition*) démesuré; **to be an e. drinker, smoker,** boire, fumer, à l'excès; **e. expenses,** dépenses exagérées. **-ly** *adv.* (souffrir, etc.) excessivement, extrêmement; (manger) à l'excès; **to be e. generous,** être par trop généreux.

exchange¹ [eks'tʃeindʒ] *n.* **1.** (*a*) échange *m* (de prisonniers, de coups, etc.); **in e. (for sth.),** en échange (de qch.); **car taken in part e.,** reprise *f*; *Adm:* **e. of posts,** permutation *f* (de deux fonctionnaires); (*b*) *Atom.Ph:* **e. reaction,** réaction *f* d'échange. **2.** *Fin:* (*a*) **foreign e.,** change *m*; **e. bank,** banque s'occupant d'opérations de change; **dollar e.,** change du dollar, en dollars; **e. rate, rate of e.,** cours *m*, taux *m*, du change; **e. control,** contrôle *m* des changes; **at the current rate of e.,** au change du jour; **(foreign) e.**

broker, cambiste *m*, agent *m* de change; **foreign e. office,** bureau *m* de change; (*b*) **bill of e.,** effet *m*, traite *f*; lettre *f* de change; (*c*) *coll.* (*U.S: usu.* **exchanges**) lettres de change, traites. **3.** (*a*) bourse *f* (des valeurs); **Commodities E.,** (*in London*) **the Royal E.,** Bourse de commerce; **Corn E.,** bourse des céréales; halle *f* aux blés; (*b*) *U.S: Mil:* **post e.,** économat *m* de l'armée. **4.** *Typ:* **(telephone) e.,** central *m* téléphonique; **e. office,** bureau central (téléphonique); **local e. area** = réseau urbain.

exchange² *v.tr.* échanger (des coups, des paroles, des prisonniers); troquer (des denrées, etc.); **to e. sth. for sth.,** échanger, troquer, qch. pour, contre, qch., faire un échange de qch. pour, contre, qch.; **to e. glances,** échanger un regard; *Adm:* **to e. posts with s.o.,** permuter avec qn.

exchangeable [eks'tʃeindʒəbl] *a.* échangeable (**for,** pour, contre).

exchequer [eks'tʃekər] *n.* (*a*) *Adm:* **the E.,** (i) la trésorerie, le fisc; (ii) le Trésor public; (iii) = le Ministère des Finances; **the Chancellor of the E.** = le Ministre des Finances; (*b*) *F:* budget *m* (d'un particulier).

excise¹ ['eksaiz] *n. Adm:* **1.** contributions indirectes; *Belg:* accise *f*. **2.** service *m* des contributions indirectes; la régie; **Customs and E.,** la Régie; **e. duties,** droits *mpl* de régie.

excise² ['eksaiz] *v.tr.* (*a*) *Surg:* exciser, couper (un organe); (*b*) retrancher (un passage d'un livre).

exciseman, *pl.* **-men** ['eksaizmən] *n.m.* employé de l'excise, de la régie.

excision [ek'siʒ(ə)n] *n.* excision *f*, coupure *f*; *Surg:* excision, abscission *f*, ablation *f*.

excitable [ek'saitəbl] *a.* **1.** (*of pers., temperament*) émotionnable, surexcitable; émotif; **to be terribly e.,** être vif comme la poudre. **2.** *El: Physiol:* excitable.

excite [ek'sait] *v.tr.* **1.** (*a*) provoquer, exciter, soulever; inspirer, allumer (un sentiment); susciter (de l'intérêt); piquer (la curiosité de qn); (*b*) *Physiol:* exciter, stimuler (un nerf); (*c*) *El:* exciter, amorcer (une dynamo, etc.). **2.** (*a*) exciter, animer (un sentiment, une passion); stimuler (l'appétit); (*b*) agiter, énerver, surexciter (qn); mettre (qn) en émoi; **easily excited,** surexcitable, emotionnable. **excited** *a.* **1.** *El: Physiol:* excité; **e. state,** (i) *Atom.Ph:* état excité, d'excitation; (ii) *El:* état d'amorçage. **2.** (*of pers.*) (i) troublé; (ii) impatient; (iii) énervé, surexcité; **e. children,** enfants excités; **e. crowd,** foule (i) surexcitée, en émoi, (ii) impatiente; **to get e.,** s'émotionner, s'énerver; **don't get e.!** ne vous énervez pas! du calme! **he gets e. over nothing,** il s'emballe pour un rien. **excitedly** *adv.* d'une manière agitée; avec agitation. **exciting** *a.* **1.** (*of story, etc.*) passionnant; (*of situation, scene*) sensationnel; (roman) plein de suspense; *Sp:* **e. finish,** arrivée palpitante; **an e. game,** une partie mouvementée. **2.** (*a*) *Med:* (cause) excitatrice; (*b*) *El:* **e. dynamo,** dynamo *f* d'excitation; **e. coil,** bobine inductrice. **excitingly** *adv.* d'une manière sensationnelle.

excitement [ek'saitmənt] *n.* **1.** *Physiol:* surexcitation *f* (d'un organe). **2.** agitation *f*, vive émotion; surexcitation; **the thirst for e.,** la soif des sensations fortes; **the e. of departure,** l'émoi *m* du départ; **to cause great e.,** faire (grande) sensation; **to be in a state of e.,** être dans tous ses états.

exclaim [eks'kleim] **1.** *v.i.* s'écrier, s'exclamer. **2.** *v.tr.* **"leave me alone," he exclaimed,** "laissez-moi," s'écria-t-il.

exclamation [eksklə'meiʃ(ə)n] *n.* exclamation *f*; **e. mark,** *U.S:* **e. point,** point *m* d'exclamation.

exclamatory [eks'klæmət(ə)ri] *a.* exclamatif.

exclude [eks'klu:d] *v.tr.* (*a*) exclure (**from,** de); empêcher (l'air) d'entrer; **to e. s.o. from a society,** (i) bannir qn d'une société; (ii) refuser à qn l'entrée d'une société; **excluding . . .,** à l'exclusion de . . .; (*b*) écarter (le doute, les soupçons); **this excludes all possibility of doubt,** le doute n'est plus permis.

exclusion [eks'klu:ʒ(ə)n] *n.* **1.** exclusion *f* (**from,** de); **to the e. of . . .,** à l'exclusion de . . .. **2.** refus *m* d'admission (**from,** à).

exclusive [eks'klu:siv] *a.* **1.** exclusif; **two qualities that are mutually e.,** deux qualités qui s'excluent. **2.** (*a*) (droit, etc.) exclusif; **to have e. rights in a production,** avoir l'exclusivité *f* d'une production; *Journ:* **e. interview,** interview accordée exclusivement à un journal; (*b*) seul, unique; **it has been his e. occupation for ten years,** ç'a été son occupation unique pendant dix ans; (*c*) (robe, etc.) exclusive; (*d*) (*of club, etc.*) très fermé. **3.** *adv.* (*a*) exclusivement; **chapters one to twenty e.,** chapitres un à vingt exclusivement; (*b*) sans compter les extras; **rent (of a flat), £1000 a year e.,** loyer (d'un appartement) £1000 par an, contributions et charges en plus; (*c*) **e. of wrappings,** sans compter, non compris, l'emballage; **price of dinner e. of wine,** prix *m* du dîner, vin non compris. **4.** *n. Journ:* article *m* en exclusivité. **-ly** *adv.* exclusivement.

excommunicate¹ [ekskə'mju:nikət] *a. & n.* excommunié, -ée.

excommunicate² [ekskə'mju:nikeit] *v.tr.* excommunier.

excommunication [ekskəmju:ni'keiʃ(ə)n] *n.* excommunication *f*.

excrement ['ekskrimənt] *n.* excrément *m*.

excrescence [eks'kresəns] *n.* excroissance *f*.

excrescent [eks'kresənt] *a.* **1.** qui forme une excroissance. **2.** superflu, redondant.

excreta [eks'kri:tə] *n.pl.* excréta *mpl*, excrétions *fpl*.

excrete [eks'kri:t] *v.tr.* excréter; (*of plant*) sécréter.

excretion [eks'kri:ʃ(ə)n] *n.* excrétion *f*; sécrétion *f* (d'une plante).

excruciating [eks'kru:ʃieitiŋ] *a.* (*of pain*) atroce, horrible; *F:* **e. music,** musique *f* atroce. **-ly** *adv.* atrocement; *F:* **e. funny,** (histoire) tordante; **e. boring,** à en mourir d'ennui.

exculpate ['ekskʌlpeit] *v.tr.* disculper, exonérer (**from,** de); justifier (qn).

exculpation [ekskʌl'peiʃ(ə)n] *n.* disculpation *f*, exonération *f* (**from,** de); justification *f* (de qn).

excursion [eks'kə:ʃ(ə)n] *n.* **1.** excursion *f*; voyage *m* d'agrément; *Aut: Cy: etc:* randonnée *f*; **to make an e.,** faire une excursion; *Rail:* **e. ticket,** billet *m* d'excursion. **2.** digression *f* (dans un discours).

excursionist [eks'kə:ʃənist] *n.* excursionniste *mf*.

excusable [eks'kju:zəbl] *a.* (erreur, etc.) excusable, pardonnable. **-ably** *adv.* excusablement.

excuse¹ [eks'kju:s] *n.* **1.** excuse *f*; **there is no e. for his behaviour,** sa conduite est inexcusable; **there was no e. for (doing) that,** il n'y avait aucun prétexte à (faire) cela; **ignorance of the law is no e.,** nul n'est censé ignorer la loi. **2.** (*a*) excuse, prétexte *m*; **poor, feeble, e.,** faible excuse; **to make excuses,** s'excuser; **to look for an e.,** (i) chercher des excuses; (ii) (*in order not to do sth.*) chercher des faux-fuyants, une échappatoire; **to find an e. for sth.,** trouver une excuse à qch.; (*b*) **a poor e. for a letter,** un semblant de lettre; **a poor e. for a car,** un vieux tacot délabré.

excuse² [eks'kju:z] *v.tr.* **1.** (*a*) excuser, pardonner; **to e. s.o.'s laziness, to e. s.o.'s being lazy,** excuser la paresse de qn; **e. my being late,** excusez-moi d'être en retard; *F:* **e. me yawning,** je vous demande pardon si je bâille; **to e. the absence of s.o.,** excuser l'absence de qn; **he may be excused for laughing,** il est excusable d'avoir ri; **if you will e. the expression,** si vous voulez me pardonner l'expression; **e. me!** (i) excusez-moi! (ii) pardon! je vous demande pardon!

pardonnez-moi! (*expressing contradiction*) **e. me, it was yesterday that . . .,** pardon, c'était hier que . . .; (*b*) **to e. s.o. from doing sth.,** excuser, exempter, dispenser, qn de faire qch.; **to e. s.o. from attendance,** excuser qn; **e.-me dance,** danse *f* où on change de partenaire; *Mil: Navy:* **to be excused a fatigue,** être exempté d'une corvée; *Sch:* **may I be excused?** est-ce que je peux sortir? **2. his youth excuses him,** sa jeunesse l'excuse, peut lui servir d'excuse.

execrable ['eksikrəbl] *a.* exécrable, abominable. **-ably** *adv.* exécrablement, abominablement.

execrate ['eksikreit] *v.tr.* **1.** exécrer, détester. **2.** maudire; anathématiser.

execration [eksi'kreiʃ(ə)n] *n.* exécration *f.* **1.** détestation *f* (**of,** de). **2.** malédiction *f.*

execute ['eksikju:t] *v.tr.* **1.** (*a*) exécuter (un travail); mettre à exécution (un projet); accomplir (une opération); donner suite à, exécuter (un ordre); *Fin:* effectuer (une transfert); *Jur:* exécuter (un testament); souscrire, signer (un acte); (*b*) *Mus:* exécuter, jouer (un morceau). **2.** exécuter (un criminel).

execution [eksi'kju:ʃ(ə)n] *n.* **1.** (*a*) exécution *f* (d'un projet, d'un ordre); accomplissement *m* (d'un dessein, etc.); **to put, carry, a plan into e.,** mettre un projet à exécution; **in the e. of one's duty,** dans l'exercise de ses fonctions; (*b*) *Jur:* souscription *f* (d'un acte); exécution (d'un testament); (*c*) (i) exécution (d'un morceau de musique); (ii) jeu *m* (d'un musicien). **2.** *Jur:* saisie-exécution *f*, pl. saisies-exécutions. **3.** exécution (d'un criminel).

executioner [eksi'kju:ʃənər] *n.* bourreau *m*; exécuteur *m* des hautes œuvres.

executive [eg'zekjutiv] **1.** *a.* (*a*) exécutif; **e. powers,** pouvoirs exécutifs; *Furn:* **e. suite,** mobilier du directeur; *Cin:* **e. producer,** producteur délégué; *Mil:* **e. duties,** service *m* de détail; (*b*) *Pol: U.S:* **e. session,** séance *f* à huis clos. **2.** *n.* (*a*) pouvoir exécutif, exécutif *m* (d'un gouvernement); (*b*) agents exécutifs; (*c*) agent exécutif; directeur, - trice; cadre *m*; chef *m* de service; **sales e.,** directeur commercial; *Adm:* **e. (officer)** = rédacteur, -trice (de ministère).

executor [eg'zekjutər] *n.* *Jur:* exécuteur, -trice, testamentaire; **literary e.,** exécuteur littéraire.

executrix, *pl.* **-trices** [eg'zekjutriks, -trisi:z] *n.f.* *Jur:* exécutrice testamentaire.

exegesis [eksi'dʒi:sis] *n.* exégèse *f.*

exemplary [eg'zempləri] *a.* **1.** (conduite) exemplaire; (époux) modèle. **2.** (*of punishment*) exemplaire; *Jur:* **e. damages,** dommages-intérêts *m* exemplaires. **3.** typique. **-ily** *adv.* exemplairement.

exemplify [eg'zemplifai] *v.tr.* **1.** démontrer par des exemples; exemplifier. **2.** servir d'exemple à (une règle).

exempt¹ [eg'zem(p)t] *a.* exempt, dispensé, exempté (**from,** de); franc, *f.* franche, (d'impôts); *Mil:* **to be e. from fatigues,** être dispensé des corvées.

exempt² *v.tr.* **to e. s.o. (from sth.),** exempter, dispenser, qn (d'un impôt, du service militaire); **to e. s.o. from doing sth.,** exempter qn de faire qch.; *Mil:* **exempted from military service,** dispensé du service militaire.

exemption [eg'zem(p)ʃ(ə)n] *n.* **e. (from sth.),** exemption *f*, dispense *f* (d'un impôt, du service militaire).

exercise¹ ['eksəsaiz] *n.* **1.** exercice *m* (d'une faculté, de ses fonctions); pratique *f* (d'un métier, d'une religion); **in the e. of one's duties,** dans l'exercice de ses fonctions; *St.Exch:* **e. of an option,** levée *f* d'une prime. **2.** (*a*) **mental e.,** exercice de l'esprit; **outdoor e.,** exercice au grand air; **to take e.,** prendre de l'exercice; **e. yard,** préau *m* (de prison); (*b*) *Mil: Navy:* exercice; **tactical exercises,** évolutions *fpl* tactiques; (*c*) **school e.,** exercice scolaire; **written e.,** exercice écrit; devoir *m*; **e. book,** cahier *m*; **piano exercises,** exercices pour piano; *Gym:* **physical exercises,** exercices physiques; **breathing exercises,** gymnastique *f* respiratoire; (*d*) **religious exercises,** pratiques religieuses.

exercise² *v.tr.* **1.** exercer (un droit, ses fonctions); exercer, pratiquer (un métier); user d'(un droit); **to e. one's will, one's authority,** faire acte de volonté, d'autorité; *Fin:* **to e. an option,** lever une prime. **2.** (*a*) exercer (le corps, l'esprit); faire faire l'exercice à (des troupes); (i) exercer, (ii) promener (un cheval); (*b*) *v.i.* (i) prendre de l'exercice; (ii) s'entraîner. **3.** tracasser; mettre à l'épreuve (la patience de qn).

exert [eg'zə:t] *v.tr.* **1.** employer, faire usage de (la force); déployer (son talent); exercer (une influence, une pression). **2. to e. oneself,** se remuer; se donner du mal; **to e. oneself to do sth.,** s'efforcer de, faire des efforts pour, faire qch.

exertion [eg'zə:ʃ(ə)n] *n.* **1.** usage *m*, emploi *m* (de la force, d'un talent). **2.** effort *m*; **without great e.,** sans grand effort.

exeunt ['eksiənt] *v.i.* *Th:* **e. Romeo and Juliet,** Roméo et Juliette sortent.

exfoliate [eks'foulieit] *v.i.* s'exfolier.

exfoliation [eksfouli'eiʃ(ə)n] *n.* exfoliation *f.*

ex gratia [eks'greiʃiə] *a. & adv.* à titre de faveur.

exhalation [eks(h)ə'leiʃ(ə)n] *n.* **1.** (*a*) exhalation *f* (d'odeurs); (*b*) expiration *f* (du souffle). **2.** effluve *m*, exhalaison *f.*

exhale [eks'heil] **1.** *v.tr.* (*a*) exhaler, émettre (un gaz, des odeurs); (*b*) expirer (l'air des poumons); exhaler (son dernier souffle, etc.). **2.** *v.i.* (*a*) (*of vapour, etc.*) s'exhaler; (*b*) expirer (l'air des poumons).

exhaust¹ [eg'zɔ:st] *n.* **1.** *I.C.E: Mch:* (*a*) échappement *m* (des gaz); **e. fumes,** gaz *mpl* d'échappement; **e. pipe,** *I.C.E:* (tuyau *m* d')échappement; **e. stroke,** course *f* d'échappement; (*b*) gaz d'échappement. **2.** production *f* du vide (dans un cylindre, etc.). **3.** *I.C.E:* (tuyau d')échappement.

exhaust² *v.tr.* (*a*) aspirer (l'air, un gaz); (*b*) épuiser (les réserves, un sujet de conversation); (*c*) épuiser, éreinter, exténuer (qn); **to e. oneself in useless efforts,** se consumer en efforts inutiles. **exhausted** *a.* (*a*) (*of resources, etc.*) épuisé; (terre) usée; (*b*) (*of pers.*) épuisé, exténué; *F:* éreinté; **I'm e.,** je n'en peux plus. **exhausting** *a.* (effort, climat) épuisant; *F:* (travail) éreintant.

exhaustion [eg'zɔ:stʃ(ə)n] *n.* **1.** *Ph:* aspiration *f* (d'un gaz). **2.** épuisement *m* (du sol, des ressources). **3. (state of) e.,** épuisement; **to be in a state of complete e.,** être complètement à bout de forces; **I was ready to drop with e.,** je tombais de fatigue.

exhaustive [eg'zɔ:stiv] *a.* exhaustif; complet, - ète; (enquête) approfondie; **to make an e. study of a subject,** traiter un sujet à fond. **-ly** *adv.* exhaustivement; à fond.

exhibit¹ [eg'zibit] *n.* **1.** *Jur:* pièce *f* à conviction (en procédure criminelle); pièce ou document *m* à l'appui. **2.** objet exposé (à une exposition, en vitrine).

exhibit² *v.tr.* **1.** exhiber, montrer, faire voir (un objet); faire preuve (de courage, de mauvaise volonté). **2.** offrir, présenter (qch. à la vue). **3.** (*a*) exposer (des tableaux, etc.); (*b*) *v.i.* (*of artist*) exposer. **4.** *Jur:* exhiber, produire (des pièces à l'appui).

exhibition [eksi'biʃ(ə)n] *n.* **1.** (*a*) exposition *f*, étalage *m* (de marchandises, etc.); manifestation *f* (d'un talent); *F:* **to make an e. of oneself,** se donner en spectacle; (*b*) démonstration *f* (d'un procédé, etc.); (*c*) *Jur:* production *f* (des pièces). **2.** (*a*) exposition; **great international e.,** grande exposition internationale; **Ideal Home E.** = Salon *m* des Arts ménagers; (*b*) *Com:* **e. room,** salon d'exposition (d'automobiles, etc.); (*c*) *Sch: U.S:* séance (musicale, etc.) donnée par les élèves, et à laquelle sont invités les parents. **3.** *Sch:* bourse *f*.

exhibitionism [eksi'biʃənizm] *n.* (*a*) *Psy:* exhibitionnisme *m*; (*b*) désir *m* de se faire remarquer.

exhibitionist [eksi'biʃənist] *n.* (*a*) *Psy:* exhibitionniste *mf*; (*b*) **he's an e.,** il aime se faire remarquer.

exhibitor [eg'zibitər] *n.* **1.** exhibiteur, -trice. **2.** (*at exhibition*) exposant, -ante.

exhilarate [eg'ziləreit] *v.tr.* vivifier, ragaillardir; émoustiller. **exhilarated** *a.* ragaillardi, émoustillé. **exhilarating** *a.* vivifiant; (nouvelles) qui vous remontent le cœur.

exhilaration [egzilə'reiʃ(ə)n] *n.* gaieté *f* de cœur, joie *f* de vivre.

exhort [eg'zɔːt] *v.tr.* exhorter, encourager (**s.o. to do sth.,** qn à faire qch.).

exhortation [egzɔː'teiʃ(ə)n] *n.* exhortation *f* (**to do sth.,** à faire qch.).

exhumation [eks(h)juː'meiʃ(ə)n] *n.* exhumation *f*.

exhume [eks'hjuːm] *v.tr.* exhumer, dé(sen)terrer.

exigence ['eksidʒəns], **exigency** ['eksidʒənsi] *n.* **1.** exigence *f*, nécessité *f*. **2.** situation *f* critique; cas pressant; **in this e.,** dans cette situation urgente.

exigent ['eksidʒənt] *a. Lit:* **1.** urgent, pressant. **2.** exigeant.

exiguity [eksi'gjuiti] *n.* exiguïté *f* (d'un logement, etc.); modicité *f* (d'un revenu, etc.).

exiguous [eg'zigjuəs] *a.* exigu, -uë; fort petit; (revenu) modique.

exile¹ ['eksail] *n.* exil *m*, bannissement *m*; **to send s.o. into e.,** envoyer qn en exil; bannir qn; **to go into e.,** partir en exil, pour l'exil; s'exiler.

exile² *n.* (*pers*) exilé, -ée; banni, -ie.

exile³ *v.tr.* exiler, bannir (**from,** de).

exist [eg'zist] *v.i.* exister. **1.** être; (*of conditions, etc.*) régner; **I think, therefore I e.,** je pense, donc je suis; **to cease to e.,** cesser d'exister; **to continue to e.,** subsister. **2.** se maintenir en vie; **I can't e. on that,** cela ne me suffit pas pour vivre. **existing** *a.* existant; actuel, présent; **in e. circumstances,** dans les circonstances actuelles.

existence [eg'zistəns] *n.* **1.** existence *f*; **to be in e.,** exister; **the oldest manuscript in e.,** le plus ancien manuscrit existant; **the firm has been in e. for fifty years,** la maison existe depuis cinquante ans; **to come into e.,** naître; **to spring into e.,** naître soudainement. **2.** existence, vie *f*; **to lead a pleasant e.,** mener une existence agréable.

existent [eg'zistənt] *a.* **1.** existant. **2.** d'aujourd'hui.

existential [egzis'tenʃəl] *a.* existentiel, -elle.

existentialism [egzis'tenʃəlizm] *n. Phil:* existentialisme *m*.

existentialist [egzis'tenʃəlist] *a. & n. Phil:* existentialiste (*mf*).

exit¹ ['eksit] *n.* sortie *f*. **1.** (*going out*) (*a*) **to make one's e.,** *Th: etc:* sortir; quitter la scène; (*b*) **the audience must have free e. at all times,** le public doit pouvoir sortir librement à tout moment; **e. staircase,** escalier *m* de sortie; (*c*) *Adm:* **e. visa, permit,** visa *m*, permis *m*, de sortie. **2.** (*way out*) sortie, issue *f* (d'un théâtre, etc.); **emergency e.,** sortie, issue, de secours; **e. only,** (passage, etc.) strictement réservé à la sortie.

exit² *v.i.* **(exited) 1.** *Th:* **e. Macbeth,** Macbeth sort. **2.** *F:* sortir; faire sa sortie.

exocrine ['eksoukrain] *a.* (glande) exocrine.

exodus ['eksədəs] *n.* (*a*) exode *m* (des Hébreux, etc.); *B:* **(the Book of) Exodus,** l'Exode; (*b*) départ *m*, sortie *f* (d'un groupe de gens, etc.); **there was a general e.,** il y eut une sortie générale; **e. of capital,** évasion *f* des capitaux.

ex officio ['eksə'fiʃiou] *adv.phr.* (membre) de droit, à titre d'office; **to act ex o.,** agir d'office.

exonerate [eg'zɔnəreit] *v.tr.* **1.** exonérer, décharger (**s.o. from an obligation,** qn d'une obligation). **2. to e. s.o. (from blame),** disculper, justifier, qn.

exoneration [egzɔnə'reiʃ(ə)n] *n.* **1.** exonération *f*, décharge *f* (**from,** de). **2. e. from blame,** disculpation *f*, justification *f*.

exorbitance [eg'zɔːbit(ə)ns] *n.* énormité *f* (des prix).

exorbitant [eg'zɔːbit(ə)nt] *a.* exorbitant, exagéré, excessif; (intérêt) usuraire; **e. price,** prix exorbitant; **-ly** *adv.* d'une manière exorbitante; excessivement.

exorcism ['eksɔːsizm] *n.* exorcisme *m*.

exorcist ['eksɔːsist] *n.* exorciste *m*.

exorcize ['eksɔːsaiz] *v.tr.* exorciser (un démon, un possédé, etc.); conjurer (un esprit).

exotic [eg'zɔtik] **1.** *a.* exotique; **a taste for the e.,** le goût de l'exotique. **2.** *n. Bot:* plante *f* exotique. **-ally** *adv.* exotiquement.

expand [eks'pænd] **1.** *v.tr.* (*a*) dilater (un gaz); étendre (les limites d'un empire); développer (une idée, une formule algébrique, la poitrine); élargir (l'esprit); (*b*) déployer (les ailes, etc.). **2.** *v.i.* (*a*) (*of solid, air, gas*) se dilater; (*of balloon*) se gonfler; (*of steam*) se détendre; (*of chest*) se développer; **as the Empire expanded,** à mesure que l'Empire grandissait, s'étendait; (*b*) (*of sail, etc.*) s'étendre, se déployer; (*c*) *Mec.E:* (*of belt*) s'allonger. **expanded** *a.* allongé; étendu; (polystyrène) expansé; *Metalw:* (métal) déployé. **expanding** *a.* **1.** en expansion; (gaz) qui se dilate; (ballon, etc.) qui se gonfle, qui enfle; (commerce) qui se développe, qui prend de l'extension; **the e. universe,** l'univers en expansion. **2.** (bracelet) extensible; (valise) à soufflets.

expander [eks'pændər] *n. Gym:* **(chest) e.,** extenseur *m*.

expanse [eks'pæns] *n.* étendue *f* (de pays, d'eau, etc.); **a vast e.,** vaste étendue (d'eau, de neige, etc.); une mer (de sable, etc.).

expansion [eks'pænʃ(ə)n] *n.* **1.** (*making larger*) dilatation *f* (d'un gaz); développement *m* (d'un sujet, de la poitrine, etc.). **2.** (*becoming larger*) (*a*) expansion *f* (d'un solide, d'un liquide, d'un commerce, etc.); dilatation *f* (d'un gaz, d'un métal, etc.); **colonial e.,** expansion coloniale; (*b*) épanouissement *m* (d'une fleur, du cœur); (*c*) *Pol.Ec:* relance *f*. **3.** (*a*) *Mec.E:* **e. joint,** (i) fourreau compensateur; (joint) compensateur (*m*); (ii) (*in concrete work*) joint de dilatation; *Tls:* **e. bit,** foret *m*, mèche *f*, extensible; (*b*) *Mch:* expansion (de la vapeur, des gaz, etc.).

expansionism [iks'pænʃənizm] *n. Pol.Ec:* expansionnisme *m*.

expansionist [eks'pænʃənist] *a. & n. Pol: etc:* expansionniste (*mf*).

expansive [eks'pænsiv] *a.* **1.** (*a*) (*of force*) expansif; (*b*) (*of gas*) expansible, dilatable. **2.** (*of pers.*) expansif; **in an e. mood,** en veine d'épanchement.

expansiveness [eks'pænsivnis] *n.* expansibilité *f*. **2.** expansivité *f*, nature expansive (de qn).

expatiate [eks'peiʃieit] *v.i.* discourir (longuement) (**on,** sur).

expatriate¹ [eks'pætrieit] *v.tr.* expatrier (qn); **to e. oneself,** (i) s'expatrier; (ii) renoncer à sa nationalité.

expatriate² [eks'pætriət] *a. & n.* expatrié, -iée.

expatriation [ekspætri'eiʃ(ə)n] *n.* **1.** expatriation *f*. **2.** renonciation *f* à sa nationalité.

expect [iks'pekt] *v.tr.* **1.** attendre (qn, qch.); s'attendre à (un événement); compter sur (l'arrivée de qn, etc.); **to e. s.o. to dinner,** attendre qn à dîner; **I expected as much,** je m'y attendais; **I knew what to e.,** je savais à quoi m'attendre; **to e. the worst,** s'attendre au pire; **as one might e., as might be expected,** comme on doit s'y attendre; comme de raison; **to e.**

that s.o. will do sth., that sth. will happen, s'attendre à ce que qn fasse qch., à ce que qch. arrive; **to e. to do sth.,** compter, espérer, faire qch.; **he is not expected to recover,** on ne compte pas le sauver; **she's expecting a baby,** *F:* **she's expecting,** elle attend un bébé. **2. to e. sth. from s.o.,** exiger qch. de qn; **I e. you to be punctual,** je vous demanderai d'arriver à l'heure; **how do you e. me to do it?** comment voulez-vous que je le fasse? **it's too much to e. of a child,** c'est trop attendre d'un enfant; **I know what is expected of me,** je sais ce qu'on attend de moi. **3.** penser, croire (que); **I e. he'll pay,** je pense qu'il payera; **I e. so,** je crois bien que oui. **expected** *a.* attendu; espéré.

expectancy [eks'pektənsi] *n.* **1.** attente *f*; **eager e.,** vive impatience. **2.** *Jur:* expectative *f* (d'un héritage, etc.); **life e.,** espérance de vie.

expectant [eks'pekt(ə)nt] *a.* (*a*) (qui est) dans l'attente (**of sth.,** de qch.); **e. mother,** femme enceinte, future mère; (*b*) *Jur:* (bien, héritier, etc.) en expectative. **-ly** *adv.* dans l'expectative, dans l'attente.

expectation [ekspek'teiʃ(ə)n] *n.* **1.** (*a*) attente *f*, espérance *f*; **to come up to, fall short of, s.o.'s expectations,** remplir, répondre à, tromper, l'attente de qn; **to succeed beyond one's expectations,** réussir au delà de ses espérances; **contrary to all expectations,** contrairement à, contre, toute attente; contre toute prévision; **in (the) e. of,** dans l'attente de; (*b*) (*expectancy*) **with eager e.,** avec une vive impatience; **to live in e.,** vivre dans l'expectative. **2.** (*a*) *Jur:* expectative *f* d'héritage; (*b*) **expectations,** espérances; **uncle from whom one has expectations,** oncle à héritage. **3.** probabilité *f* (d'un événement); *Ins:* **e. of life,** espérance de vie.

expectorant [eks'pektərənt] *a.* & *n.* *Med:* expectorant (*m*).

expectorate [eks'pektəreit] **1.** *v.tr.* expectorer (des mucosités, etc.). **2.** *v.i.* cracher.

expedience [eks'pi:diəns], **expediency** [eks'pi:diənsi] *n.* **1.** convenance *f*, opportunité *f* (d'une mesure, etc.); **on grounds of expediency,** pour des raisons de convenance. **2.** *Pej:* opportunisme *m*.

expedient [eks'pi:diənt] **1.** *a.* expédient, convenable; à propos; **do what you think e.,** faites ce que vous jugerez à propos. **2.** *n.* expédient *m*, moyen *m*.

expedite ['ekspidait] *v.tr.* **1.** activer, pousser, hâter (une mesure); accélérer (un procédé). **2.** expédier, dépêcher (une affaire).

expedition [ekspə'diʃ(ə)n] *n.* **1.** expédition *f*. **2.** *O:* promptitude *f*.

expeditionary [ekspə'diʃ(ə)nəri] *a.* *Mil:* (corps, etc.) expéditionnaire.

expeditious [ekspə'diʃəs] *a.* (procédé) expéditif; (résponse) prompte. **-ly** *adv.* promptement.

expel [eks'pel] *v.tr.* **(expelled; expelling)** (*a*) expulser (qn); chasser, expulser (un corps étranger, l'ennemi, etc.); chasser, refouler (un liquide, un gaz); **to e. a boy from school,** renvoyer, chasser, un élève (de l'école); (*b*) *Adm:* expulser, refouler (un étranger).

expendable [eks'pendəbl] **1.** *a.* consommable, dépensable; non récupérable; (matériel) de consommation courante. **2.** *n.pl.* **expendables,** (i) troupes sacrifiables, sacrifiées; (ii) (*thgs*) matériel non récupérable.

expenditure [iks'penditʃər] *n.* **1.** dépense *f* (d'argent, etc.); consommation *f* (de munitions). **2.** (*amount*) dépense(s); **heavy e.,** une forte dépense, de fortes dépenses.

expense [iks'pens] *n.* **1.** (*a*) dépense *f*, frais *mpl*; **regardless of e.,** sans regarder à la dépense; **at great, little, e.,** à grands, à peu de, frais; **at my own e.,** à mes propres frais; **book published at author's e.,** livre édité à compte d'auteur; **to go to great e.,** faire beaucoup de dépense; **to put s.o. to e.,** faire faire des dépenses à qn; **don't go to any e. over . . .,** ne faites pas de frais pour . . .; (*b*) **expenses,** dépenses, débours *mpl*, frais; *Com:* sorties *fpl*; **travelling, living, expenses,** frais de déplacement, de séjour; **general expenses,** frais généraux; **incidental expenses,** faux frais; **to incur expenses,** faire des dépenses; **to have all expenses paid,** être défrayé de tout. **2.** dépens *m*; **a laugh at my e.,** un éclat de rire à mes dépens. **3. to be a great e. to s.o.,** être une grande charge pour qn. **4.** (*allowance*) **expenses,** indemnité *f* (pour débours); **travelling expenses,** indemnité de voyage; **to offer s.o. £100 and expenses,** offrir à qn £100, tous frais payés; **e. account,** indemnité pour frais professionnels.

expensive [eks'pensiv] *a.* (objet) coûteux, cher; (procédé) dispendieux; *F:* (marchand, etc.) (qui prend) cher; (passe-temps) onéreux; **e. wife,** femme qui coûte cher à son mari; **to be, come, e.,** revenir cher *inv*; **travelling is e.,** les voyages coûtent cher. **-ly** *adv.* (s'habiller) coûteusement; **to live e.,** mener la vie large.

expensiveness [eks'pensivnis] *n.* cherté *f* (d'une denrée, etc.); prix élevé (de qch.).

experience¹ [eks'piəriəns] *n.* **1.** épreuve personnelle; aventure *f*; **to have a nasty e.,** (i) passer (par) un mauvais quart d'heure; (ii) faire une mauvaise rencontre; **it was a new e. for them,** ce fut une nouveauté pour eux; **it was his first e. of love,** c'était la première fois qu'il est tombé amoureux. **2.** expérience *f*; **to gain e. of life,** faire l'apprentissage de la vie; **practical e.,** la pratique; **to have much e.,** avoir beaucoup d'expérience; **driving e.,** expérience de la route; **he still lacks e.,** il manque encore de pratique; **a man of e.,** un homme d'expérience; **e. shows that . . .,** l'expérience démontre que . . .; **to know sth. from e.,** savoir qch. par experience; **I know from bitter e. that . . .,** je sais, pour l'avoir éprouvé cruellement, que . . .; **have you had any previous e.?** avez-vous déjà travaillé dans ce métier? *F:* **she is not without e.,** elle n'est pas innocente; **I have enough business e. to . . .,** j'ai assez de pratique des affaires pour . . ..

experience² *v.tr.* **1.** éprouver; faire l'expérience de (qch.); **to e. difficult times,** passer par des temps difficiles. **2.** apprendre (par expérience) (**that,** que). **experienced** *a.* qui a de l'expérience; (général) expérimenté; (observateur) averti; (œil) exercé (**in,** à); **to be e. in sth.,** avoir l'expérience de qch.; s'y connaître à qch.; **e. in business,** rompu aux affaires.

experiment¹ [eks'perimənt] *n.* expérience *f*; essai *m*; **to make, carry out, an e.,** faire, procéder à, une expérience; **as an e., by way of e.,** à titre d'essai, d'expérience.

experiment² [eks'periment] *v.i.* expérimenter, faire une expérience, des expériences (**on, with,** sur, avec); **to e. on dogs,** expérimenter sur les chiens.

experimental [eksperi'ment(ə)l] *a.* **1.** (savoir) expérimental, -aux; fondé sur l'expérience. **2.** (sujet) d'expérience; (physique) expérimentale; **e. research,** recherche (expérimentale); **e. rocket,** fusée expérimentale; **this new reactor is at the e. stage,** ce nouveau réacteur est à l'essai, en cours d'expérimentation. **-ally** *adv.* **1.** (découvrir qch.) expérimentalement. **2.** à titre d'essai.

experimentation [eksperimen'teiʃ(ə)n] *n.* expérimentation *f*.

expert ['ekspə:t] **1.** *a.* expert, habile; **to be e. in, at, sth.,** être expert en qch.; connaître à fond qch. **2.** *n.* expert *m*; spécialiste *mf*; *Jur:* **medical e.,** médecin légiste; **the experts,** les spécialistes; **he is an e. in this field,** il est expert dans la matière; **the eye of an e.,** un œil expert; **expert's report,** expertise *f*; **e. advice,** avis autorisé; **according to the experts,** à dire d'experts. **-ly** *adv.* habilement; en expert.

expertise [ekspə'ti:z] *n.* **1.** expertise *f*. **2.** adresse *f*, habileté *f* (**in,** à); connaissances *fpl* techniques.

expiate ['ekspieit] *v.tr.* expier (un péché, une faute).

expiation [ekspi'eiʃ(ə)n] *n.* expiation *f*; **in e. of his crime,** pour expier, en expiation de, son crime.

expiration [ekspi'reiʃ(ə)n, -pai-] *n.* **1.** expiration *f* (de l'air des poumons). **2.** cessation *f*, expiration (d'un bail); échéance *f* (d'un marché à prime); fin *f* (d'un terme); *Ins:* expiration, déchéance *f* (d'une police); **date of e.,** date d'expiration (d'une garantie, etc.).

expire [eks'paiər] **1.** *v.tr.* expirer, exhaler (l'air des poumons). **2.** *v.i.* (*a*) expirer, mourir; (*of hope*) s'évanouir; (*b*) (*of law, treaty, etc.*) expirer, cesser; venir à expiration; *Ins:* **expired policy,** police déchue; **(the validity of) this passport expires on . . .,** ce passeport expire le . . .; **expired passport,** passeport périmé. **expiring** *a.* **1.** expirant, qui se meurt; **with an e. voice,** d'une voix mourante. **2.** (*of lease, contract*) qui expire; qui est à son terme.

expiry [eks'paiəri] *n.* expiration *f*, fin *f* (d'un terme); terme *m* (d'une période).

explain [eks'plein] **1.** *v.tr.* (*a*) expliquer (une règle, etc.); **that explains everything,** voilà qui explique tout; **that is easily explained,** cela s'explique facilement; **to e. sth. away,** donner une explication satisfaisante de qch.; (*b*) justifier (sa conduite, etc.). **2. to e. (oneself),** (i) s'expliquer; (ii) se justifier; **you'd better e.,** allons, expliquez-vous. **3.** *v.i.* donner des explications.

explainable [eks'pleinəbl] *n.* (conduite, etc.) explicable; **it's easily e.,** cela s'explique facilement.

explanation [eksplə'neiʃ(ə)n] *n.* explication *f*, éclaircissement *m*; **to give explanations,** fournir des explications; **to give an e. of one's behaviour,** justifier sa conduite.

explanatory [eks'plænət(ə)ri] *a.* explicatif; explicateur, -trice; (note) interprétative.

expletive [eks'pli:tiv] **1.** *a. Gram: etc:* explétif. **2.** *n.* (*a*) *Gram: etc:* particule explétive; explétif *m*; (*b*) juron *m*.

explicable [eks'plikəbl] *a.* explicable.

explicit [eks'plisit] *a.* explicite; formel; **to be more e. (in one's statements),** préciser (ses affirmations). **-ly** *adv.* explicitement.

explode [eks'ploud] **1.** *v.tr.* (*a*) démontrer la fausseté de (qch.); discréditer (une théorie); (*b*) faire éclater (un obus); faire sauter (une mine); faire exploser (un gaz). **2.** *v.i.* faire explosion; (*a*) (*of boiler, shell, etc.*) éclater; (*of mine*) sauter; *F:* (*of pers.*) **to e. with laughter,** éclater de rire; **if he finds out he'll e.,** s'il découvre ça, il explosera, il va sortir de ses gonds; (*b*) (*of gas, dynamite, etc.*) exploser, détoner. **exploded** *a.* **1.** (théorie) abandonnée, reconnue pour fausse. **2.** (obus) éclaté; (mine) qui a sauté. **3.** *Draw: Tchn:* **e. view,** (vue) éclatée (*f*).

exploit¹ ['eksplɔit] *n.* exploit *m*; haut fait.

exploit² [eks'plɔit] *v.tr.* (*a*) exploiter (une mine, une forêt, etc.); (*b*) exploiter (qn, les talents de qn).

exploitation [eksplɔi'teiʃ(ə)n] *n.* exploitation *f*.

exploration [eksplə'reiʃ(ə)n] *n.* **1.** (*a*) exploration *f*; **voyage of e.,** voyage *m* de découverte; (*b*) exploration, reconnaissance *f* (du terrain); **e. work,** travaux *mpl* de recherches. **2.** *Med:* exploration (d'une plaie).

explorative [eks'plɔrətiv] *a.* explorateur, -trice.

exploratory [eks'plɔrət(ə)ri] *a.* **1.** (puits, sondage) d'exploration. **2.** (voyage) de découverte. **3.** (conversations) préliminaires; **e. surgery,** opération exploratoire.

explore [eks'plɔ:r] *v.tr.* (*a*) explorer (une région); aller à la découverte dans (un continent); faire l'exploration (d'un pays); tâter (le terrain); (*b*) *Med:* explorer, sonder (une plaie).

explorer [eks'plɔrər] *n.* **1.** (*pers.*) explorateur, -trice; voyageur, -euse. **2.** (*apparatus*) instrument explorateur; *esp. Med:* sonde *f*.

explosion [eks'plouʒ(ə)n] *n.* **1.** explosion *f* (d'un mélange gazeux, d'un obus, etc.); déflagration *f* (d'un gaz); *Min:* **firedamp e.,** coup de grisou; **to cause an e.,** provoquer une explosion. **2.** (*noise*) détonation. **3.** *F:* débordement *m* (de fureur); explosion (de rires).

explosive [ek'splousiv] **1.** *a.* (*a*) explosif, détonant; **e. mixture,** mélange détonant; *Atom.Ph:* **e. fission,** fission explosive; (*b*) *Ling:* (consonne) explosive; (*c*) (situation) explosive. **2.** *n.* (*a*) explosif *m*; poudre *f*; **high e.,** explosif détonant; explosif à grande puissance; (*b*) *Ling:* (consonne) explosive (*f*).

exponent [eks'pounənt] *n.* **1.** interprète *mf* (d'un système, etc.); *Mus:* interprète, exécutant, -ante (d'une œuvre); protagoniste *mf* (d'un sport). **2.** *Mth:* exposant *m* (d'une quantité).

exponential [ekspou'nenʃəl] *a.* exponentiel; *Mth:* **e. curve,** courbe exponentielle.

export¹ ['ekspɔ:t] *n.* **1.** marchandise exportée; **exports,** (i) articles *mpl* d'exportation; (ii) exportations *fpl* (d'un pays); **visible, invisible, exports,** exportations visibles, invisibles. **2.** exportation *f*, sortie *f*; **e. trade,** commerce *m* d'exportation; **a flourishing e. trade,** une exportation florissante; **e. duty,** droit(s) de sortie.

export² [eks'pɔ:t] *v.tr.* exporter (des marchandises).

exportation [ekspɔ:'teiʃ(ə)n] *n.* exportation *f*.

exporter [eks'pɔ:tər] *n.* exportateur, -trice.

expose [eks'pouz] *v.tr.* exposer. **1.** (*a*) laisser sans abri; exposer, abandonner (un nouveau-né); (*b*) **to e. s.o., oneself, to danger,** exposer qn, s'exposer, au danger; **to e. one's flank to the enemy,** prêter le flanc à l'ennemi; **to e. oneself to ridicule,** s'exposer à la risée publique; (*c*) *Phot:* exposer (un film). **2.** (*a*) mettre (qch.) à découvert, à nu, à jour; afficher (son ignorance); (*b*) étaler (des marchandises à vendre); (*c*) *Ecc:* exposer (le saint Sacrement); (*d*) **to e. oneself,** faire de l'exhibitionnisme. **3.** éventer (un secret); dévoiler (un crime); dénoncer (qn, un vice). **exposed** *a.* **1.** (*a*) exposé (à la vue, aux éléments); (engrenages) à découvert; *Mil:* **e. position,** endroit exposé; (*of troops*) **to be e.,** être en l'air; (*b*) (*laid bare*) à nu. **2.** *Phot:* (film, etc.) exposé, impressionné.

exposé [eks'pouzei] *n.* (*a*) exposé *m*; (*b*) révelation *f* (d'un scandale, etc.).

exposition [ekspɔ'ziʃ(ə)n] *n.* **1.** exposition *f* (d'un enfant, *Ecc:* du saint Sacrement). **2.** exposition, exposé *m*, interprétation *f*. **3.** *NAm:* exposition (de peinture, etc.).

expostulate [eks'pɔstjuleit] *v.i.* **to e. with s.o.,** faire des remontrances à qn (**about,** sur, au sujet de).

expostulation [ekspɔstju'leiʃ(ə)n] *n.* remontrance(s) *f* (*pl*).

exposure [eks'pouʒər] *n.* **1.** (*a*) exposition *f* (à l'air, au froid, à un danger); **to die of e.,** mourir de froid; (*b*) *Phot:* prise *f* de vue; **time e.,** pose *f*; **e. time,** temps *m* de pose; **e. meter,** posemètre *m*; **e. counter,** compteur *m* de prises de vue; (*c*) *Atom.Ph:* **e. (to radiation),** irradiation *f*. **2.** exposition, abandon *m* (d'un nouveau-né). **3.** (*a*) *Min: etc:* mise *f* à nu, à découvert (du minerai, etc.); (*b*) exposition, étalage *m* (de marchandises à vendre); (*c*) *Jur:* **indecent e.,** outrage public à la pudeur; (*d*) dévoilement *m* (d'un crime, etc.); dénonciation *f* (d'un escroc); **to threaten s.o. with e.,** menacer qn d'un scandale. **4.** exposition, orientation *f* (d'un lieu, d'un bâtiment).

expound [eks'paund] *v.tr.* **1.** exposer (une doctrine, ses principes). **2.** interpréter (les Écritures saintes).

express¹ [eks'pres] **1.** *a.* (*a*) (image) exacte, fidèle (**of,** de); (*b*) (*of law, stipulation, etc.*) exprès, *f.* expresse; (*of order*) formel, explicite; **for this e. purpose,**

dans ce but même; (*c*) **e. train,** (train) express (*m*), rapide (*m*); **e. delivery,** envoi *m* par exprès; **e. letter,** lettre *f*, messager *m*, exprès; *Post:* **by e. messenger,** par exprès; (*d*) *U.S:* **e. company,** *F:* **the e.,** compagnie *f* de messageries. **2.** *adv.* sans arrêt; **lift that goes e. to the twentieth floor,** ascenseur *m* qui monte sans arrêt au vingtième étage. **3.** *n. Rail:* express *m*, rapide *m*. **-ly** *adv.* **1.** expressément, formellement (défendu). **2.** (faire qch.) dans le seul but (**to,** de).

express² *v.tr.* **1.** exprimer (l'huile) (**out of, from,** de). **2.** énoncer (un principe); exprimer, rendre (ses sentiments); dire (son sentiment); manifester (sa volonté); émettre (une opinion); formuler (un souhait); témoigner (sa reconnaissance); **well, badly, expressed,** bien, mal, rendu. **3. to e. oneself,** s'exprimer; **he has difficulty in expressing himself,** il a du mal à s'exprimer.

express³ *v.tr.* **1.** *U.S:* envoyer, expédier (un colis) par les messageries. **2.** envoyer (une lettre) par exprès.

expression [eks'preʃ(ə)n] *n.* **1.** expression, manifestation *f* (d'une pensée, de la joie, etc.); **beyond e.,** au delà de toute expression; inexprimable; **freedom of e.,** liberté *f* d'expression. **2.** (*a*) expression, locution *f*; (*b*) **algebraical e.,** expression, formule *f*, algébrique. **3.** (*a*) expression (du visage, des yeux); (*b*) *Mus:* **with e.,** (chanter, jouer) avec expression.

expressionism [eks'preʃənizm] *n. Art: etc:* expressionnisme *m*.

expressionist [eks'preʃənist] *a.* & *n.* expressionniste (*mf*).

expressionless [eks'preʃ(ə)nlis] *a.* (figure, voix) sans expression; (visage) impassible.

expressive [eks'presiv] *n.* (*a*) expressif, plein d'expression; (geste, silence) éloquent; (*b*) **attitude e. of disdain,** attitude *f* qui exprime le dédain. **-ly** *adv.* avec expression.

expressiveness [eks'presivnis] *n.* caractère expressif, force *f* d'expression (d'un visage, etc.).

expropriate [eks'prouprieit] *v.tr.* exproprier (un propriétaire, une propriété).

expropriation [eksproupri'eiʃ(ə)n] *n.* expropriation *f* (d'un propriétaire, d'une propriété).

expulsion [eks'pʌlʃ(ə)n] *n.* expulsion *f* (d'un étranger, etc.); renvoi *m* (d'un élève).

expunge [eks'pʌndʒ] *v.tr.* effacer, rayer (un nom d'une liste, un passage dans un livre).

expurgate ['ekspə:geit] *v.tr.* (*a*) expurger (un livre); épurer (un texte); **expurgated edition,** édition expurgée; (*b*) supprimer (un passage, etc.).

expurgation [ekspə:'geiʃ(ə)n] *n.* (*a*) expurgation *f* (d'un livre); épuration *f* (d'un texte, d'une association); (*b*) suppression *f* (d'un passage).

exquisite ['ekskwizit] *a.* (*a*) (plat, vin) exquis; (*b*) (*of pleasure, etc.*) vif; (supplice) raffiné; (*c*) très sensible, délicat, subtil. **-ly** *adv.* **1.** d'une manière exquise; (*of needlework, etc.*) **e. done,** perlé. **2.** excessivement, extrêmement (petit, sensible, etc.).

exquisiteness ['ekskwizitnis] *n.* **1.** perfection délicate (d'une œuvre d'art). **2.** caractère vif (du plaisir, etc.); acuité *f* (de la douleur). **3.** finesse *f* (de l'oreille).

ex-serviceman, *pl.* **-men** [eks'sə:vismən] *n.m.* ancien combattant.

extant [ek'stænt] *a.* existant; qui existe encore.

extemporaneous [ekstempə'reinjəs] *a.* improvisé, impromptu. **-ly** *adv.* (parler, etc.) impromptu.

extempore [eks'tempəri] **1.** *adv.* (parler) impromptu, sans préparation; **to speak e.,** improviser (un discours). **2.** *a.* (*a*) (discours) improvisé, impromptu; (*b*) (orateur) qui parle sans préparation.

extemporization [ekstempərai'zeiʃ(ə)n] *n.* improvisation *f*.

extemporize [eks'tempəraiz] **1.** *v.tr.* improviser (un discours); faire (une prière) à l'impromptu. **2.** *v.i.* (*a*) improviser, parler à l'impromptu; (*b*) *Mus:* improviser (**on the organ, etc.,** à l'orgue, etc.).

extend [eks'tend] **1.** *v.tr.* (*a*) (i) étendre, allonger (le corps); prolonger (une ligne); (ii) *Sp:* faire rendre son maximum à, pousser (un cheval, un coureur, etc.); **to e. oneself,** donner son maximum; (*b*) prolonger (une période de temps, *Rail:* un billet); *Com:* proroger (l'échéance d'un billet); continuer (des recherches); (*c*) étendre, porter plus loin (les limites); étendre (la signification d'un mot); accroître (des connaissances); agrandir, augmenter (son pouvoir, ses terres); reculer (les frontières d'un État); **we are going to e. our premises,** nous allons nous agrandir; (*d*) (i) tendre (la main); (ii) **to e. a welcome to s.o.,** souhaiter la bienvenue à qn. **2.** *v.i.* (*a*) s'étendre, s'allonger (**to, over, across,** jusqu'à, au delà de); **to e. beyond the wall,** s'avancer en dehors du mur; (*b*) (*of period of time*) se prolonger, continuer; **enquiries extending over a number of years,** investigations prolongées pendant un grand nombre d'années. **extended** *a.* **1.** (*a*) (corps, bras) étendu, allongé; *Equit:* **e. trot,** trot allongé; (*b*) *Mil:* (troupes) déployées; **in e. order,** en ordre dispersé. **2.** (*a*) (bail, etc.) prolongé; (*b*) long, prolongé; (voyage) de quelque durée; *Rec:* **an e. play record,** un super 45 tours. **3.** augmenté, agrandi. **extending 1.** *a.* (table) à rallonges; (échelle) à coulisse. **2.** *n.* extension *f*, allongement *m*; prolongation *f*.

extension [eks'tenʃ(ə)n] *n.* **1.** (*a*) extension *f* (du bras); prolongement *m* (d'un canal, d'un chemin de fer, etc.); agrandissement *m*, extension (d'une usine, etc.); *Surg:* extension (d'une jambe cassée); *Mec:* **e. piece,** pièce *f* formant prolongement; (r)allonge *f* (de table, de cric, etc.); **e. ladder,** échelle *f* à coulisse; (*b*) *Av:* sortie *f* (du train d'atterrissage, etc.); (*c*) *Phot:* tirage *m* du soufflet, d'un appareil). **2.** (*growing*) extension, accroissement *m* (des affaires, etc.); **there has been a considerable e. of his business,** son commerce a pris une extension considérable. **3.** (*a*) (r)allonge (de table, etc.); allonge (de câble); *Tp:* poste *m* supplémentaire; **e. 35,** poste 35; *El:* **e. light,** baladeuse *f*; *Elcs:* **e. loudspeaker,** haut-parleur séparé; (*b*) annexe *f* (d'un bâtiment); (*c*) *Gram:* complément *m* (du sujet, de l'attribut). **4.** prolongation *f* (de congé, d'un billet de chemin de fer); **to get an e. of time,** obtenir un délai; **arrangement for an e. of time,** atermoiement *m*. **5.** *Sch:* **e. courses,** cours *mpl* du soir organisés par une université.

extensive [eks'tensiv] *a.* **1.** étendu, vaste, ample; **e. knowledge,** vastes connaissances; **e. researches,** travaux approfondis; **to make e. use of sth.,** faire un usage considérable de qch. **2.** (agriculture) extensive. **-ly** *adv.* **to use sth. e.,** se servir beaucoup de qch.; faire un usage considérable de qch.

extent [eks'tent] *n.* étendue *f* (d'un terrain, des connaissances, etc.); importance *f* (du dommage, etc.); **vast e. of ground,** grande superficie de terrain; **credit to the e. of £50,** crédit jusqu'à concurrence de £50; **to a certain e., to some e.,** jusqu'à un certain point; dans une certaine mesure; **to a great e., to a large e.,** en grande partie; dans une large mesure; **to such an e. that . . .,** à tel point que . . ..

extenuate [eks'tenjueit] *v.tr.* atténuer, amoindrir (la faute de qn). **extenuating** *a.* (circonstance) atténuante.

extenuation [ekstenju'eiʃ(ə)n] *n.* atténuation *f* (d'une faute); **circumstances in e. of his fault,** circonstances *fpl* qui atténuent sa faute.

exterior [eks'tiəriər] **1.** *a.* extérieur (**to,** à), en dehors (**to,** de); *Mth:* **e. angle,** angle (i) extérieur, (ii) externe. **2.** *n.* (*a*) extérieur *m*, dehors *mpl*; **on the e.,** à l'extérieur; **house with an imposing e.,** maison aux dehors imposants; **despite his stern e. he is very likeable,** (*b*) malgré un extérieur sévère il est très sympathique; *Th: Cin:* extérieur.

exteriorize [eks'tiəriəraiz] *v.tr.* extérioriser.

exterminate [eks'tə:mineit] *v.tr.* exterminer (des insectes, une population, etc.).

extermination [ekstə:mi'neiʃ(ə)n] *n.* extermination *f* (d'une population, etc.).

exterminator [eks'tə:mineitər] *n.* (*pers.*) exterminateur, -trice.

extern [eks'tə:n] *n. Sch: Med:* externe *mf.*

external [eks'tə:n(ə)l] **1.** *a.* (*a*) (médicament, angle) externe; *Med:* **for e. use only,** pour l'usage externe; (*b*) (mur) extérieur; (affaires) du dehors, de l'extérieur; (*c*) (*of trade*) extérieur; étranger, -ère; (*d*) (étudiant) libre. **2.** *n.* (*usu. in pl.*) (*a*) extérieur *m*, formes extérieures, dehors *mpl*; **to judge by externals,** juger les choses selon les apparences; (*b*) choses secondaires. **-ally** *adv.* extérieurement; à l'extérieur.

extinct [eks'tiŋ(k)t] *a.* (*a*) (*of volcano, passion*) éteint; (*b*) (*of animal, plant*) disparu, qui n'existe plus; (*of office, title*) aboli, tombé en désuétude; (*of race*) **to become e.,** s'éteindre, disparaître.

extinction [eks'tiŋ(k)ʃ(ə)n] *n.* extinction *f* (d'un incendie, d'une race); anéantissement *m* (d'une espérance); **race threatened with e.,** race *f* en passe de disparaître.

extinguish [eks'tiŋgwiʃ] *v.tr.* éteindre (le feu, un incendie, une race); souffler (la chandelle); anéantir (une espérance).

extinguisher [eks'tiŋgwiʃər] *n.* (*a*) appareil *m* d'extinction; (appareil) extincteur (*m*) (d'incendie); **foam e.,** extincteur à mousse; (*b*) (*for candle*) éteignoir *m.*

extirpate ['ekstə:peit] *v.tr.* extirper, déraciner (un arbre, un abus).

extirpation [ekstə:'peiʃ(ə)n] *n.* extirpation *f*, éradication *f* (d'un arbre, d'un vice).

extol, *NAm: also* **extoll** [eks'ətoul] *v.tr.* **(extolled)** exalter, vanter, prôner; célébrer, chanter (la beauté de qch.); **to e. s.o. to the skies,** porter qn aux nues.

extort [eks'tɔ:t] *v.tr.* extorquer (de l'argent, etc.) **(from s.o.,** à qn); arracher (une promesse, un aveu) **(from s.o.,** à qn).

extortion [eks'tɔ:ʃ(ə)n] *n.* extorsion *f* (d'argent, etc.); arrachement *m* (d'une promesse, d'un aveu).

extortionate [eks'tɔ:ʃənit] *a.* **1.** (*of pers.*) extorsionnaire, rapace. **2.** (prix) exorbitant.

extortioner [eks'tɔ:ʃənər], **extortionist** [eks'tɔ:ʃənist] *n.* extorqueur, -euse.

extra ['ekstrə] **1.** *a.* (*a*) en sus, de plus; supplémentaire; d'extra; **e. charge,** prix *m* en sus; supplément *m* de prix; **e. pay,** prime *f*, supplément *m* de salaire; *Mil: Navy:* supplément de solde; **e. work,** (i) heures *fpl* supplémentaires; (ii) surcroît *m* de travail; **e. time,** (i) *Ind: etc:* heures supplémentaires; (ii) *Sp:* prolongation *f*; **as an e. precaution,** pour plus de précaution; *Sch:* **e. subject,** matière facultative; **to make an e. effort,** faire un surcroît d'effort; (*b*) de réserve, de rechange; (*c*) de qualité supérieure; exceptionnel; **rope of e. strength,** corde *f* d'une solidité exceptionnelle; corde extra-solide. **2.** *adv.* (*a*) plus que d'ordinaire; extra-; **e. strong binding,** reliure extra-solide; **e. white,** extra-blanc; **e. smart,** ultra-chic; (*b*) en plus; **meals taken in the bedroom are charged (for) e.,** il y a un supplément pour les repas servis dans la chambre; **packing e.,** emballage compté à part, non compris. **3.** *n.* (*a*) supplément (de menu); édition spéciale (d'un journal); (*b*) (*pers.*) extra *m*; *Th: Cin:* figurant, -ante; **to be, work as, an e.,** faire de la figuration; (*c*) **extras,** frais *mpl*, dépenses *fpl*, supplémentaires; suppléments; *Typ:* surcharge *f*; (*d*) **little extras,** les petits à-côtés.

extract[1] ['ekstrækt] *n.* (*a*) extrait *m*; concentré *m*; **malt, beef, e.,** extrait de malt, de bœuf; **meat e.,** concentré de viande; (*b*) *Lit: Sch:* **extracts,** morceaux choisis.

extract[2] [eks'trækt] *v.tr.* (*a*) extraire (de l'huile, du métal, etc.); (*b*) extraire, arracher (une dent); **to e. a passage from a book,** extraire un passage d'un livre; **to e. a bullet from a wound,** retirer une balle d'une plaie; **to e. money, a confession, from s.o.,** arracher de l'argent, un aveu, à qn; tirer de l'argent, un aveu, de qn.

extraction [eks'trækʃ(ə)n] *n.* **1.** (*a*) expression *f*, extraction *f* (du jus d'un citron, etc.); (*b*) **e. of stone from a quarry,** extraction de la pierre d'une carrière; (*c*) arrachage *m* (d'un clou); extraction (d'une dent). **2.** extraction; origine *f*; **of humble e.,** de basse extraction.

extractor [eks'træktər] *n.* **1.** (*pers.*) extracteur *m* (de dents, etc.). **2.** (*a*) *Tls:* pince *f*; *Dent:* davier *m*; *Surg:* extracteur (de calculs, etc.); (*b*) **e. fan,** aérateur *m*; (*c*) **juice e.,** presse-fruit *m, pl.* presse-fruits.

extra-curricular ['ekstrəkə'rikjulər] *a. Sch:* hors-programme *inv*; **e.-c. activities,** activités *fpl* périscolaires.

extraditable [ekstrə'daitəbl] *a.* **1.** (*of pers.*) passible d'extradition. **2.** (crime) qui justifie l'extradition.

extradite ['ekstrədait] *v.tr. Jur:* **1.** extrader (un criminel). **2.** obtenir l'extradition (d'un criminel).

extradition [ekstrə'diʃ(ə)n] *n.* extradition *f.*

extra-dry ['ekstrə'drai] *a.* (vin) très sec.

extra-fine ['ekstrə'fain] *a.* extra-fin.

extrajudicial ['ekstrədʒu(:)'diʃ(ə)l] *a.* extrajudiciaire.

extra-marital ['ekstrə'mærit(ə)l] *a.* extra-conjugal, -aux.

extramural ['ekstrə'mju:r(ə)l] *a.* **1.** (quartier) extra-muros *inv.* **2.** *Sch:* **e. lecturer,** conférencier en dehors de la Faculté accrédité pour certains cours; **e. course,** cours *m* supplémentaire.

extraneous [eks'treiniəs] *a.* étranger (**to,** à); (considérations) en dehors de la question.

extraordinariness [eks'trɔ:dənrinis, ekstrə'ɔ:dənrinis] *n.* caractère *m*, nature *f*, extraordinaire.

extraordinary [eks'trɔ:dənri, ekstrə'ɔ:d(ə)nri] *a.* extraordinaire; (*a*) **ambassador e.,** ambassadeur *m* extraordinaire; **to call an e. meeting of the shareholders,** convoquer une assemblée générale extraordinaire; (*b*) (conduite) extraordinaire; **the e. thing is that . . .,** ce qu'il y a d'étrange, de singulier, c'est que . . .; (*c*) *F:* phénoménal, -aux; prodigieux. **-ily** *adv.* extraordinairement.

extrapolate [ek'stræpəleit] *v.tr.* extrapoler.

extrasensory ['ekstrə'sensəri] *a.* extra-sensoriel; **e. perception,** la perception extra-sensorielle.

extra-special ['ekstrə'speʃ(ə)l] **1.** *a.* & *n. Journ:* **e.-s. (edition),** deuxième édition spéciale. **2.** *a. F:* **e.-s. wine,** du vin extra; **suit for e.-s. occasions,** costume *m* pour les grandes occasions; **sth. e.-s.,** de l'extra.

extraterrestrial ['ekstrəte'restriəl] *a.* extra-terrestre.

extraterritorial ['ekstrəteri'tɔ:riəl] *a.* (privilège) d'exterritorialité.

extravagance [iks'trævəgəns] *n.* **1.** extravagance *f*, exagération *f.* **2.** folles dépenses, prodigalités *fpl*; **a piece of e., an e.,** une dépense inutile; une folie.

extravagant [iks'trævəgənt] *a.* **1.** extravagant; (prétentions) exagérées, déraisonnables; (éloges) outrés; (style) exagéré. **2.** (*of pers.*) dépensier, gaspilleur; (goûts) dispendieux; **don't be so e. with the butter,** ne gaspillez pas le beurre. **3.** (*of price*) exorbitant, prohibitif. **-ly** *adv.* **1.** d'une façon extravagante; **to talk, act, e.,** dire, faire, des folies, des extravagances. **2.** excessivement, à l'excès; **e. furnished house,** maison meublée avec un luxe exagéré.

extravaganza [ekstrævə'gænzə] *n.* **1.** œuvre (musicale, littéraire) d'une extravagance bouffonne; œuvre fantaisiste. **2.** (*conduct*) folie *f.*

extravert ['ekstrəvəːt] *a. & n. Psy:* extraverti, -ie.

extreme [eks'triːm] **1.** *a.* extrême; (*a*) **at the e. end of the quay,** tout au bout du quai; **the e. penalty,** le dernier supplice; *R.C.Ch:* **e. unction,** extrême-onction *f*; *Pol:* **the e. left,** l'extrême gauche *f*; (*b*) (chaleur, etc.) extrême; *Pol:* (nationalisme) outrancier; (opinions) extrémistes; **to be in e. peril,** être en (très) grand danger; **to behave with e. awkwardness,** se conduire avec la dernière gaucherie; **an e. case,** un cas exceptionnel; **the question is one of e. delicacy,** le problème est délicat entre tous. **2.** *n.* extrême *m*; **to go from one e. to the other,** passer d'un extrême à l'autre; **in the e.,** au dernier degré; **to go to extremes,** pousser les choses à l'extrême. **-ly** *adv.* extrêmement; au dernier degré, au dernier point; **to be e. witty,** avoir énormément d'esprit.

extremism [eks'triːmizm] *n. Pol:* extrémisme *m.*

extremist [eks'triːmist] *a. & n. Pol:* extrémiste (*mf*).

extremity [eks'tremiti] *n.* **1.** extrémité *f*; point *m* extrême; bout *m* (d'une corde, d'une rue); sommité *f* (d'une plante, d'une branche). **2. the extremities,** les extrémités (du corps). **3.** gêne *f*; **to be reduced to the last e.,** en être réduit à la dernière extrémité.

extricate ['ekstrikeit] *v.tr.* dégager, tirer (**s.o. from a critical position,** qn d'un mauvais pas); **to e. oneself from a danger,** se tirer d'un danger; **to e. oneself from difficulties,** se débrouiller; se tirer d'affaire.

extrinsic [eks'trinsik] *a.* extrinsèque.

extrovert ['ekstrəvəːt] *a. & n. Psy:* extroverti, -ie.

extrude [eks'truːd] **1.** *v.tr.* (*a*) expulser, faire jaillir (**from,** de); (*b*) *Metalw:* filer, profiler; **extruded section, shape,** profilé *m*; (*c*) *Ind:* (*plastics*) boudiner (à chaud). **2.** *v.i. Geol:* (*of rock, etc.*) s'épancher.

extrusion [eks'truːʒ(ə)n] *n.* (*a*) expulsion *f* (de qch.); émission *f* (d'une sécrétion); (*b*) *Geol: f,* épanchement *m* (volcanique); (*c*) *Metalw:* extrusion *f*; filage *m* (à chaud); (*d*) *Ind:* (*plastics*) boudinage *m*, extrusion.

exuberance [eg'zjuːb(ə)r(ə)ns] *n.* exubérance *f*; (*a*) richesse *f* (de végétation); (*b*) (*of pers.*) gaieté débordante.

exuberant [eg'zjuːb(ə)r(ə)nt] *a.* exubérant; (*a*) (*of vegetation*) riche; (*of health, vitality*) débordant; (*b*) (*of pers.*) débordant de vie. **-ly** *adv.* avec exubérance; **e. healthy,** débordant de santé.

exude [eg'zjuːd] **1.** *v.tr.* exsuder. **2.** *v.i.* exsuder, suinter; (*of sap*) couler, s'écouler.

exult [eg'zʌlt] *v.i.* **1.** exulter, se réjouir (**at, in,** de). **2. to e. over s.o.,** triompher de qn.

exultant [eg'zʌltənt] *a.* (sentiment) joyeux; (cri) de triomphe; **to be e.,** exulter. **-ly** *adv.* (parler, etc.) d'un air de triomphe.

exultation [egzʌl'teiʃ(ə)n] *n.* exultation *f.*

ex-voto [eks'voutou] *n. Ecc:* **ex-voto (offering),** ex-voto *m inv.*

eye¹ [ai] *n.* **1.** (*a*) œil *m*, *pl.* yeux; *Z:* **simple e.,** œil simple, ocelle *m*; **compound e.,** œil composé, à facettes; **e. hospital,** hôpital *m* ophtalmologique, pour les maladies des yeux; **e. bank,** banque *f* des yeux; **to have blue eyes,** avoir les yeux bleus; *F:* **black e.,** œil poché; **to give s.o. a black e.,** pocher l'œil à qn; **glass e.,** œil artificiel, œil de verre; *B:* **an e. for an e., a tooth for a tooth,** œil pour œil, dent pour dent; **to open, close, one's eyes,** ouvrir, fermer, les yeux; **to open one's eyes wide,** ouvrir les yeux tout grands; **to do sth. with one's eyes open,** faire qch. les yeux ouverts, en connaissance de cause; **to keep one's eyes and ears open,** avoir l'œil et l'oreille au guet; **to keep one's eyes open,** *F:* **peeled, skinned,** avoir l'œil ouvert, les yeux ouverts; **he could not keep his eyes open,** il dormait debout; **to open s.o.'s eyes (to sth.),** ouvrir les yeux à qn; dessiller les yeux à qn; **to shut, close, one's eyes to s.o.'s faults,** s'aveugler, fermer les yeux, sur les défauts de qn; **to have the sun, the light, in one's eyes,** avoir le soleil, la lumière, dans les yeux; **at e. level,** à la hauteur des yeux; (*on cooker*) **e.-level grill,** gril *m* à hauteur des yeux; **to be up to the eyes in work, in debt,** avoir du travail, des dettes, par-dessus la tête; **with tears in one's eyes,** les larmes aux yeux; **dry your eyes,** essuyez vos larmes: *F:* **that's one in the e. for him!** ça lui fait les pieds! *F:* **my e.!** mon œil! *F:* **that's all my e. (and Betty Martin),** tout ça c'est de la blague, des histoires; (*b*) (*of thg*) **to strike, catch, the e.,** frapper, attirer, l'œil, les regards; (*of pers., thg*) **to catch s.o.'s e.,** attirer l'attention de qn; (*in Parliament*) **to catch the Speaker's e.,** obtenir la parole; **it pleases, delights, the e.,** cela charme, réjouit, les yeux, les regards; **he has eyes at the back of his head,** il a des yeux d'Argus; **he has eyes for nobody but her,** il n'a d'yeux que pour elle; **to set eyes on sth.,** apercevoir, voir, qch.; **to see sth. with one's own eyes,** voir qch. de ses propres yeux; **it took place before my (very) eyes,** cela s'est passé sous mes yeux; **to see sth. in one's mind's e.,** voir qch. en imagination, en idée; **where are your eyes?** êtes-vous aveugle? (*c*) **with jealous eyes,** d'un œil jaloux; **to make eyes at s.o.,** *F:* **to give s.o. the (glad) e.,** lancer des œillades, faire de l'œil à qn; *F:* **to make sheep's eyes at s.o.,** lancer des œillades amoureuses à qn; **to see e. to e. with s.o.,** voir les choses du même œil que qn; **you can see that with half an e.,** cela saute aux yeux; **to run, cast, one's e. over sth.,** jeter un coup d'œil sur qch.; *Mil:* **eyes right, left!** tête (à) droite, (à) gauche! **eyes front!** fixe! (*d*) **to keep an e. on sth., on s.o.,** surveiller qch., qn; **to have one's e., to keep a sharp, a strict, e., on s.o.,** avoir l'œil sur qn; surveiller qn de près; **keep your e. on him!** ne le quittez pas des yeux! *Games:* **to keep one's e. on the ball,** suivre, *Golf:* fixer, la balle; **under the e. of . . .,** sous la surveillance de . . .; **with an e. to . . .,** en vue de . . .; **to be all eyes,** être tout yeux; (*e*) **to have an e. for a horse,** s'y connaître en chevaux; être bon juge des chevaux; **with the e. of a painter,** d'un œil de peintre; (*f*) **equal in the eye(s) of the law,** égaux devant la loi; **in the eyes of all he is guilty,** aux yeux de tous il est coupable; **to be very much in the public e.,** occuper une position très en vue; (*g*) **private e.,** détective, enquêteur, privé. **2.** (*a*) **eyes in a peacock's tail,** yeux, miroirs *mpl*, de la queue d'un paon; (*in mahogany, etc.*) **bird's eyes,** tourbillons *mpl*; (*b*) *Hort:* (i) œil, bourgeon *m*; germe *m* (de pomme de terre); (ii) (*in grafting*) œilleton *m*. **3.** (*a*) œil (*pl.* œils) (d'un outil); œil, trou *m*, (d'une aiguille); œil, boucle *f* (d'un cordage); collet *m*, œillet *m*, (d'un étai); anneau *m* (pour tringle, etc.); **to pass through the e. of a needle,** passer par le trou d'une aiguille; (*b*) piton *m*; **e. end,** œil, piton (de câble). **4.** (*a*) *Phot:* œilleton *m* (de viseur iconomètre); (*b*) *Elcs:* **electric e., magic e.,** cellule *f* photoélectrique, œil magique. **5.** *Meteor:* œil (d'un typhon).

eye² *v.tr.* **(eyed; eyeing)** regarder, observer (d'un œil jaloux, avec dégoût); mesurer (qn, un obstacle, etc.) des yeux; **to e. s.o. up and down, from head to foot,** toiser qn (de haut en bas).

eyeball ['aibɔːl] *n.* bulbe *m*, globe *m*, de l'œil.

eyebath ['aibɑːθ] *n. Med:* œillère *f*; bain *m* d'œil.

eyebrow ['aibrau] *n.* sourcil *m*; **to knit one's eyebrows,** froncer le(s) sourcil(s); *F:* **he never raised an e.,** il n'a pas sourcillé.

eye-catching ['aikætʃiŋ] *a. F:* accrocheur, -euse; (publicité) tapageuse; **an e.-c. title,** un titre accrocheur.
eyecup ['aikʌp] *n.* = EYEBATH.
eyeful ['aiful] *n. F:* **to get an e., se rincer l'œil; she's quite an e.,** elle vaut le coup d'œil.
eyeglass ['aiglɑ:s] *n.* monocle *m*; **watchmaker's e.,** loupe *f* d'horloger.
eyehole ['aihoul] *n.* (*a*) (*of mask*) **eyeholes,** ouvertures *fpl* pour les yeux; (*b*) petite ouverture; judas *m* (d'une porte, etc.); *Tchn:* trou *m* de regard, de visite.
eyelash ['ailæʃ] *n. Anat:* cil *m*.
eyelet ['ailit] *n.* **1.** œillet *m*; petit trou. **2.** œillet (métallique); *Bootm:* œillet; *Nau:* (*in rope*) cosse *f*.
eyelid ['ailid] *n. Anat:* paupière *f*; **he didn't bat an e.,** il n'a pas sourcillé.
eyeliner ['ailainər] *n. Toil:* eye-liner *m*.
eye-opener ['aioup(ə)nər] *n. F:* **that was an e.-o. for him,** cela lui a ouvert les yeux; ç'a été une révélation pour lui.
eyepiece ['aipi:s] *n.* **1.** *Opt:* (*a*) oculaire *m* (de microscope, etc.); (*b*) viseur *m* (de théodolite, etc.); (*c*) œilleton *m* (de viseur iconomètre, etc.). **2.** (*a*) *Metall:* lunette *f* de regard (d'un fourneau, d'un cubilot); (*b*) lunette (de masque à gaz).
eyeshade ['aisheid] *n.* visière *f*.
eyeshadow ['aiʃædou] *n.* ombre *f* à paupières.
eyesight ['aisait] *n.* vue *f*; **to have good e.,** avoir une bonne vue, de bons yeux; **my e. is failing,** ma vue baisse.
eyesore ['aisɔ:r] *n.* ce qui blesse la vue; **the building is an e.,** le bâtiment est une horreur.
eyespot ['aispɔt] *n.* ocelle *f* (de papillon, etc.).
eyestrain ['aistrein] *n.* **to suffer from e.,** avoir les yeux fatigués.
eyetooth, *pl.* **-teeth** ['aitu:θ, -ti:θ] *n.* dent canine; **to cut one's eyeteeth,** (i) faire ses canines; (ii) *F:* sortir de sa première enfance.
eyewash ['aiwɔʃ] *n.* **1.** *Pharm:* collyre *m* liquide. **2.** *F:* **that's all e.,** tout ça c'est du boniment.
eyewitness ['aiwitnis] *n.* témoin *m* oculaire.
eyrie ['aiəri] *n.* aire *f* (d'un aigle).

F

F, f [ef] *n.* **1.** (la lettre) F, f *f.* **2.** *Mus:* fa *m*; **F clef,** clef *f* de fa.

fa [fɑː] *n. Mus:* **1.** (*fixed*) fa *m.* **2.** (*movable*) la sous-dominante.

fab [fæb] *a. F:* sensass.

fable [ˈfeibl] *n.* fable *f*, conte *m.*

fabled [ˈfeib(ə)ld] *a.* célèbre dans la fable; légendaire.

fabric [ˈfæbrik] *n.* **1.** édifice *m*, bâtiment *m*; **the f. of society,** l'édifice social. **2.** *Tex: etc:* tissu *m*; étoffe *f*; **dress fabrics,** tissus pour robes; **silk, woollen and cotton fabrics,** soieries *fpl*, lainages *mpl* et cotonnades *fpl.* **3.** structure *f*, fabrique (d'un édifice, d'un système); gros œuvre (d'un bâtiment).

fabricate [ˈfæbrikeit] *v.tr.* inventer, fabriquer (une nouvelle); forger (un document).

fabrication [fæbriˈkeiʃ(ə)n] *n.* **1.** invention *f* (d'une nouvelle); contrefaçon *f* (d'un document); **it's pure f.,** c'est de la pure fabrication. **2. a pure f.,** une histoire inventée de toute pièce.

fabulous [ˈfæbjuləs] *a.* **1.** (conte) fabuleux; (personnage) légendaire. **2.** *F:* prodigieux; (prix) fou; **we had a f. evening,** on a passé une soirée merveilleuse. **-ly** *adv.* fabuleusement; prodigieusement (riche, etc.).

façade [fæˈsɑːd] *n. Arch:* façade *f.*

face[1] [feis] *n.* **1.** (*a*) figure *f*, visage *m*; *P:* **what a f.!** quelle gueule! **I shall never be able to look him in the f. again,** je ne pourrai jamais plus le regarder dans les yeux; **he won't show his f. here again!** il ne se risquera pas à remettre les pieds ici! **full-f. portrait,** portrait *m* de face; **f. to f.,** face à face; **to bring s.o. f. to f. with s.o.,** confronter qn avec qn; **to come f. to f. with s.o.,** se trouver vis-à-vis avec qn; **to set one's f. against sth.,** s'opposer résolument à qch.; **in the f. of danger,** devant le danger; **I told him so to his f.,** je le lui ai dit au nez, à sa barbe; (*b*) **f. cream,** crème *f* de beauté; **f. pack,** masque (hydratant, etc.); **f. flannel** = gant *m* de toilette; *Cards: NAm:* **f. card,** figure *f.* **2.** (*a*) mine *f*, physionomie *f*; **to make, pull, faces (at s.o.),** faire des grimaces (à qn); **to keep a straight f.,** garder son sérieux; **to put a good f. on it,** faire contre mauvaise fortune bon cœur; (*b*) *F:* front *m*, toupet *m*; **he had the f. to tell me so,** il a eu le culot de me le dire. **3.** apparence *f*, aspect *m* (de qch.); **on the f. of it,** au premier aspect, à première vue; **f. value,** valeur nominale; **I took him at his f. value,** je l'ai jugé sur les apparences; **to save f.,** sauver la face; **to lose f.,** perdre la face; **loss of f.,** humiliation *f.* **4.** surface *f* (de la terre); **they disappeared from the f. of the earth,** ils ont disparu de la surface du globe. **5.** (*a*) face (d'une pièce de monnaie); endroit *m* (d'un tissu); recto *m* (d'un document); **f. up, f. down,** face en dessus, en dessous; (*b*) devant *m*, façade *f* (d'un immeuble); face (d'une falaise); *Min:* **coal f., working f.,** front *m* de taille (du charbon); (*c*) face (d'un polyèdre, etc.); facette *f*, plan *m* (d'un cristal); (*d*) plat *m* (d'un marteau); table *f* (d'une enclume); tranche *f* (d'une meule); semelle *f* (d'un rabot); *Sp:* face (d'une crosse de golf); (*e*) *Mec.E:* plateau *m* (de tour); (*f*) *Civ.E: Mec.E:* surface; **bearing f.,** (sur)face portante; (*g*) cadran *m* (d'une horloge, d'une montre); (*h*) *Typ:* œil *m* (d'un caractère); **bold f.,** (caractère) gras (*m*); **light f.,** (caractère) maigre (*m*).

face[2] *v.tr.* **1.** affronter, braver, faire face à (un danger, un ennemi); **to f. facts,** regarder les choses en face; **let's f. it,** voyons les choses comme elles sont; **the problem that faces us,** le problème qui se pose; **to be faced with a difficulty,** se heurter à une difficulté; **he dared not f. me,** il n'a pas osé me rencontrer face à face; *F:* **to f. the music,** faire front. **2.** (*a*) faire face à, se tenir devant (qn, qch.); se présenter de face devant (qn); **sunflowers always f. the sun,** le tournesol regarde toujours le soleil; **hotel facing the square,** hôtel *m* en façade sur la place; **the picture facing page 10,** la gravure en regard de la page 10; **facing each other,** l'un en face de l'autre; *Rail:* **seat facing the engine,** place dans le sens de la marche; (*b*) *v.i.* **the house faces north,** la maison est exposée au nord, regarde le nord; **terrace facing south,** terrasse orientée au sud; **to f. both ways,** (i) faire face des deux côtés; (ii) ménager la chèvre et le chou; *Mil:* **right f.!** face à droite! **left f.!** face à gauche! **3.** *Cards:* retourner (une carte). **4.** *Tchn:* (*a*) *Metalw: etc:* dresser, planer, surfacer; (*b*) revêtir (un mur, etc.) (**with,** de). **face about** *v.i. Mil:* faire demi-tour. **face out** *v.tr.* (*a*) surmonter par soi-même (une situation difficile); (*b*) **to f. it out,** ne pas broncher. **face up** *v.i.* **to f. up to s.o., to a danger,** affronter qn, un danger. **facing** *n.* **1.** *Mil: etc:* mouvement *m* de front; **f. about,** volte-face *f.* **2.** *Join: Metalw: etc:* dressage *m* (d'une surface); **f. tool,** outil *m.* à surfacer. **3.** (*a*) revers *m* (d'un habit, etc.); *Mil:* **regimental facings,** parements (de la manche ou du col) servant à distinguer les différents corps; (*b*) *Const:* revêtement *m* (d'un mur, etc.); perré *m* (d'un talus, d'une tranchée); **f. brick,** brique *f* de parement; (*c*) *Civ.E: Mec.E:* surface *f* de portée; (*d*) garniture *f* (de frein, d'embrayage).

faceless [ˈfeislis] *a.* (*a*) sans visage; (*b*) anonyme; nonidentifiable; **f. men in government offices,** fonctionnaires *mpl* anonymes.

facelift [ˈfeislift] *n.* (*a*) lifting *m*, chirurgie *f* esthétique (du visage); (*b*) restauration *f* (de la façade d'un bâtiment); rénovation *f*, retapage *m.*

facer [ˈfeisər] *n. F:* **1.** gifle *f.* **2. that's a f.!** quelle tuile!

facet[1] [ˈfæsit] *n.* **1.** facette *f* (d'un diamant, *Ent:* de l'œil, etc.). **2.** aspect *m* (d'une situation, etc.).

facet[2] *v.tr.* **(facet(t)ed)** facetter (une pierre précieuse). **facet(t)ed** *a.* à facettes.

facetious [fəˈsiːʃəs] *a.* facétieux, plaisant, gouailleur; (style) bouffon. **-ly** *adv.* facétieusement.

facetiousness [fəˈsiːʃəsnis] *n.* caractère facétieux; bouffonnerie *f*; humeur facétieuse.

facial [ˈfeiʃ(ə)l] **1.** *a.* facial, -aux; (expression) du visage. **2.** *n.* (i) massage facial; (ii) traitement *m* esthétique (pour le visage).

facile [ˈfæsail, -il] *a. usu. Pej:* facile; **to be a f. liar,** être habile à controuver des mensonges.

facilitate [fəˈsiliteit] *v.tr.* faciliter (une action).

facility [fəˈsiliti] *n.* **1.** (*a*) facilité *f*; **f. in speaking, in writing,** facilité à parler, à écrire; **to do sth. with great f.,** faire qch. avec une grande facilité; (*b*) **facilities for payment,** facilités de paiement; **they are given every f. for improving their French,** on leur accorde toutes facilités de se perfectionner en français. **2.** *usu. pl.* aménagements *mpl*; **storage facilities,** installations de stockage; **cooking facilities,** installations de cuisine; **we have no facilities for it,** nous ne sommes pas équipés pour cela; *Av:* **ground facilities,** installations au sol. **3.** souplesse *f* de caractère.

facsimile [fæk'simili] *n.* fac-similé *m*, *pl.* fac-similés; *Jur:* copie figurée (d'un testament, etc.); **to reproduce sth. in f., to make a f. of sth.,** fac-similer qch.; **f. signature,** signature autographiée.

fact [fækt] *n.* **1.** fait *m*; **an accomplished f.,** un fait accompli. **2.** (*a*) fait; **f. and fiction,** le réel et l'imaginaire *m*; **scientific facts,** les vérités *fpl* scientifiques; **to stick to the facts,** s'en tenir aux faits; **the facts of a case,** les faits d'une cause; **owing to the f. that . . .,** du fait que . . .; **it's a f. that . . .,** il est de fait que . . .; **to know for a f. that . . .,** savoir pertinemment que . . .; **apart from the f. that . . .,** hormis que . . .; **in f.,** de fait; **in point of f.,** en fait; **as a matter of f.,** (i) en réalité; (ii) en effet; (*b*) *Jur:* **the jury only decides issues of f.,** les jurés *mpl* ne sont juges que du fait.

fact-finding ['fæktfaindiŋ] *a.* (mission, etc.) d'information, d'enquête.

faction¹ ['fækʃ(ə)n] *n.* faction *f*, cabale *f*.

faction² *n. Cin: TV:* docudrame *m*.

factitious [fæk'tiʃəs] *a.* factice, artificiel.

factor ['fæktər] *n.* **1.** (*pers.*) (*a*) *Com:* agent *m* (dépositaire); commissionnaire *m* en gros; (*b*) *Scot:* intendant *m* (d'un domaine). **2.** (*a*) *Mth:* diviseur *m*, facteur *m*; **the highest common f.,** le plus grand commun diviseur; (*b*) **amplification f.,** coefficient d'amplification; **demand f.,** facteur de consommation; (*c*) **safety f.,** marge *f* de sécurité; **load f.,** coefficient de charge. **3.** facteur (concourant à un résultat); **an important f. in the life of a nation,** un facteur important dans la vie d'une nation; **the human f.,** l'élément humain.

factory ['fækt(ə)ri] *n. Ind:* usine *f*, fabrique *f*; **munitions f.,** fabrique de munitions; **biscuit f.,** biscuiterie *f*; *Fish: etc:* **f. ship,** navire-usine *m*, *pl.* navires-usines; **f. farming,** élevage industriel.

factotum [fæk'toutəm] *n.* factotum *m*; homme *m* à tout faire.

factual ['fæktjuəl] *a.* (connaissance) des faits; (considération) pratique. **-ally** *adv.* en ce qui concerne les faits.

facultative ['fæk(ə)ltətiv] *a.* facultatif, -ive.

faculty ['fæk(ə)lti] *n.* **1.** (*a*) faculté *f*, pouvoir *m*; **the f. of speech,** le don de la parole; **to be in possession of all one's faculties,** jouir de toutes ses facultés; (*b*) facilité *f*, talent *m*; **to have the f. of observation,** savoir bien observer. **2.** *Sch: etc:* (*a*) faculté (des lettres, de droit, etc.); (*b*) (i) *NAm:* professorat *m*, corps enseignant (d'une université, d'un collège); (ii) **the medical f.,** les physiciens et les chirurgiens.

fad [fæd] *n.* manie *f*, lubie *f*, dada *m*; **it's only a passing f.,** c'est un caprice dont on reviendra.

faddiness ['fædinis] *n.* maniaquerie *f*.

faddist ['fædist] *n. F:* **food f.,** (i) maniaque *mf* en fait de nourriture; (ii) partisan, -ane, d'un (certain) régime alimentaire.

faddy ['fædi] *a.* capricieux, maniaque; **he's f. about his food,** il est difficile sur la nourriture.

fade [feid] **1.** *v.i.* (*a*) (*of flowers, colour, etc.*) se faner, se flétrir; (*of material*) se décolorer, déteindre; (*b*) (*of hope*) s'éteindre; (*of light*) **to f. (away),** s'affaiblir; **the light is fading,** le jour s'éteint; **colours that f. into each other,** couleurs qui se fondent; **summer fades into autumn,** peu à peu l'automne succède à l'été; **to f. from memory,** s'effacer de la mémoire; (*c*) (*of sound*) s'évanouir. **2.** *v.tr.* (*a*) faner; décolorer; **curtains faded by the sun,** rideaux décolorés par le soleil; (*b*) *Cin:* **to f. one scene into another,** enchaîner deux scènes. **faded** *a.* (*of flower, colour, etc.*) fané, flétri; (*of material*) décoloré; (*of beauty, etc.*) défraîchi, passé; (*of photograph*) jauni. **fade in** *Cin: etc:* **1.** *v.i.* arriver dans un fondu. **2.** *v.tr.* faire arriver (une scène) dans un fondu. **fade out** *Cin: etc:* **1.** *v.i.* (*of scene*) s'effacer dans un fondu. **2.** *v.tr.* faire partir (une scène) dans un fondu; *W.Tel: etc:* diminuer l'intensité de (la musique, etc.). **fading 1.** *a.* (fleur) qui se fane; (lumière) pâlissante. **2.** *n.* (*a*) flétrissure *f* (d'une plante); décoloration *f* (d'une étoffe); (*b*) *W.Tel: etc:* fading *m*; (*c*) *Cin: etc:* (fermeture *f* en) fondu (*m*).

faecal, *NAm:* **fecal** ['fi:k(ə)l] *a.* fécal, -aux; **f. matter,** matières fécales; déjections *fpl*.

faeces, *NAm:* **feces** ['fi:si:z] *n.pl. Physiol:* fèces *fpl*; matières fécales.

fag¹ [fæg] *n.* **1.** *F:* corvée *f*. **2.** *Sch:* jeune élève attaché au service d'un grand. **3.** *F:* cigarette *f*, sèche *f*. **4. f. end,** (i) bout *m* (d'un morceau d'étoffe, etc.); (ii) queue *f* (de l'hiver etc.); (iii) *F:* mégot *m* (d'une cigarette).

fag² *v.* **(fagged) 1.** *F:* (*a*) *v.i. O:* travailler dur, s'échiner; (*b*) *v.tr.* (*of work, etc.*) éreinter (qn); **fagged out,** épuisé, éreinté. **2.** *Sch: v.i.* (*of young pupil*) **to f. for a senior,** faire les corvées d'un grand.

faggot¹ ['fægət] *n.* **1.** fagot *m*; bourrée *f* (de bois); *Fort:* fascine *f*. **2.** *Metall:* faisceau *m* (de fer en barres). **3.** *Cu:* boulette *f* (de viande). **4.** *P:* (*a*) **old f.,** vieille chipie; (*b*) vieux homosexuel.

faggot² *v.tr.* **(faggoted)** mettre en fagots (du bois); *Metall:* mettre en faisceaux (le fer, l'acier).

fah [fɑ] *n.* = FA.

Fahrenheit ['færənhait] *a. Ph.Meas:* (échelle, thermomètre) fahrenheit.

faience [fa'jɑ̃:s] *n.* faïence *f*; poterie vernissée.

fail¹ [feil] *n. used in adv.phr.* **without f.,** à coup sûr.

fail² 1. *v.i.* (*a*) manquer, faillir, faire défaut; **when all else failed,** en désespoir de cause; **to f. in one's duty,** manquer à son devoir; **to f. to do sth.,** négliger de faire qch.; **he failed to mention that . . .,** il a omis de faire remarquer que . . .; (*b*) **the engine failed to start,** le moteur a refusé de démarrer; **the brakes failed,** les freins ont lâché; (*c*) (*of light*) baisser, s'éteindre; **the patient is failing visibly,** le malade décline à vue d'œil; **his sight is beginning to f.,** sa vue commence à faiblir; **his memory is failing,** sa mémoire baisse; (*d*) ne pas réussir; manquer son coup; (*of negotiations, etc.*) ne pas aboutir; (*of play*) faire fiasco; **enterprise which failed,** entreprise qui a échoué; **I f. to see why . . .,** je ne vois pas pourquoi . . .; *Sch:* **to f. in an examination,** être refusé, recalé, à un examen; (*e*) *Com:* faire faillite; tomber en faillite. **2.** *v.tr.* (*a*) *Sch:* refuser, recaler (un candidat); être refusé à (un examen); (*b*) **words f. me to express my thanks,** je ne sais comment vous exprimer mes remerciements; (*c*) **I won't f. you,** vous pouvez compter sur moi. **failed** *a. Com:* (maison) en faillite; (candidat) refusé, recalé; (artiste) raté. **failing 1.** *a.* (*of sight, etc.*) défaillant, baissant. **2.** *n.* (*a*) (i) manquement *m*; **his f. to report the accident,** son silence sur l'accident; (ii) défaillance *f* (de forces, etc.); baisse *f* (de la vue, etc); (iii) non-réussite *f*; échec *m*; (iv) *Com:* faillite *f*; (*b*) faiblesse *f*, défaut *m*; **with all his failings,** avec tous ses défauts. **3.** *prep.* à, au, défaut de; **f. a satisfactory reply,** faute de réponse satisfaisante; **f. which,** faute de quoi; **f. all else,** en désespoir de cause.

fail-safe ['feilseif] *a.* **f.-s. device, system,** dispositif *m* de sécurité positive.

failure ['feiljər] *n.* **1.** (*a*) manque *m*; **f. to keep a promise,** manquement à une promesse; **f. to pay a bill,** défaut de paiement d'un effet; (*b*) non-fonctionnement *m*; panne *f*; **mechanical f.,** défaillance *f* mécanique; *El:* **power f.,** panne de courant; *Med:* **heart f.,** syncope (mortelle). **2.** (*a*) insuccès *m*, non-réussite *f*; échec *m* (à un examen, d'une pièce); **it's a f.,** c'est raté; (*b*) *Com:* faillite *f*. **3.** (*a*) (*of pers.*) raté, -ée; *Sch:* **there are too many failures,** trop de candidats ont été recalés; (*b*) *Th: etc:* four *m*, fiasco *m*; **the play was a f.,** la pièce a été un four; **the experiment was, proved, turned out, a f.,** l'expérience *f* n'a pas réussi, a raté.

fain [fein] *adv. A: & Lit:* volontiers.

faint¹ [feint] *a.* **1.** *A: & Lit:* timide; **f. heart never won fair lady,** jamais honteux n'eut belle amie. **2.** (*a*) (*of hope, etc.*) faible; (*of praise*) tiède; **to give a f. smile,** sourire du bout des lèvres; (*b*) (*of colour*) pâle, délavé; (*of sound, touch, etc.*) léger; (*of idea*) vague, peu précis; (*of mark, etc.*) à peine visible; (*of inscription*) indistinct; **a f. tinge of blue,** une légère nuance bleuâtre; **I haven't the faintest idea,** je n'en ai pas la moindre idée; **the sound of the footsteps grew fainter,** le bruit des pas s'affaiblit. **3. to feel f.,** se sentir mal; être pris d'une défaillance **-ly** *adv.* **1.** faiblement; mollement. **2.** légèrement; **f. visible,** à peine visible; **to smile f.,** esquisser un sourire.

faint² *n.* évanouissement *m*, défaillance *f*; **to fall down in a f.,** tomber évanoui.

faint³ *v.i.* **to f. (away),** s'évanouir, défaillir. **fainting** *n.* évanouissement *m*; **f. fit,** syncope *f*.

faint(-)hearted ['feint'hɑ:tid] *a.* pusillanime.

faintness ['feintnis] *n.* (*of voice, etc.*) faiblesse *f*; (*of breeze, etc.*) légèreté *f*.

fair¹ [fɛər] *n.* **1.** foire *f*; **world f.,** exposition universelle; **fun f.** = fête foraine. **2. village f.,** kermesse *f*.

fair² **I.** *a.* **1.** beau, *f.* belle; **the f. sex,** le beau sexe. **2.** spécieux; **f. promises,** de belles promesses. **3.** (*of pers., hair*) blond; (*of skin*) blanc, *f.* blanche. **4.** (*a*) net, sans tache; (*b*) (*intensive*) *P:* **it's a f. old do,** c'est une pure escroquerie; (*c*) juste, équitable; (prix) raisonnable; (salaire) équitable; **f. play,** jeu loyal, franc jeu, fair-play *m inv*; **fair's f.,** il faut être juste; **that's only f.,** ce n'est que juste; **it's not f.,** ce n'est pas juste; **f. enough!** ça va! d'accord! **it's all f. and above board, all f. and square,** c'est de la bonne guerre; **he is strict but f.,** il est sévère mais sans parti pris; **it is only f. to say that . . .,** il faut dire que . . .; **by f. means or foul,** d'une manière ou d'une autre; *Prov:* **all's f. in love and war,** en amour la ruse est de bonne guerre. **5.** assez bon; **in f. condition,** acceptable; **a f. number of . . .,** un nombre respectable de . . .; **he has a f. chance of success,** il a des chances de réussir; **how are you?—f. to middling,** comment ça va?—comme ci comme ça. **6.** (*a*) (*of wind, etc.*) propice, favorable; (*b*) **f. weather,** beau temps; **the barometer is at set f.,** le baromètre est au beau fixe. **II.** *adv.* **1.** (agir) loyalement; **to play f.,** jouer beau jeu; **to fight f.,** faire la bonne guerre. **2.** *F:* (*a*) complètement; (*b*) **struck f. (and square) on the chin,** frappé en plein menton. **fairly** *adv.* **1.** (juger, etc.) équitablement, avec justice; **to treat s.o. f.,** traiter qn avec impartialité. **2.** (agir, jouer, etc.) honnêtement; **to come by sth. f.,** obtenir qch. par des moyens honnêtes. **3.** (*a*) bien; **once the ship was f. under way,** une fois le navire en bonne route; (*b*) *F:* complètement, absolument. **4.** assez (riche, habile, etc.); **f. good wine,** vin passablement bon; **it is f. certain that . . .,** il est à peu près certain que . . .; **to do sth. f. well,** faire qch. d'une façon passable. **fairing** *n. Av: Aut:* profilage *m*; carénage *m*.

fairground ['fɛəgraund] *n.* champ *m* de foire.

fair-haired ['fɛə'hɛəd] *a.* blond; aux cheveux blonds.

fairish ['fɛəriʃ] *a.* **1.** (*of hair*) plutôt blond. **2.** assez bon.

fair-minded ['fɛə'maindid] *a.* équitable, juste.

fairness ['fɛənis] *n.* **1.** *A: & Poet:* beauté *f*. **2.** couleur blonde (des cheveux); blancheur *f* (de la peau). **3.** équité *f*, honnêteté *f*; **in all f.,** en toute justice.

fair-sized ['fɛə'saizd] *a.* assez grand.

fairway ['fɛəwei] *n.* **1.** *Nau:* chenal *m*, passe *f*, passage *m*. **2.** *Golf:* fairway *m*.

fair-weather ['fɛə'weðər] *a.* (bateau) qui convient seulement pour le beau temps; (*b*) **f.-w. friends,** amis *mpl* des beaux jours.

fairy ['fɛəri] **1.** *n.* (*a*) fée *f*; **the wicked f.,** la fée Carabosse; (*b*) P: pédé *m*, tapette *f*, tante *f*. **2.** *a.* féerique; **f. footsteps,** pas légers; **f. queen,** reine *f* des fées; **f. godmother,** (i) marraine *f* fée; (ii) *F:* marraine gâteau; **f. story, tale,** conte *m* de fées; **f. light,** lampion *m*.

fairyland ['fɛərilænd] *n.* (*a*) le pays, le royaume, des fées; (*b*) féerie *f*; **at night the garden became a f.,** le soir, le jardin se transforma en pays enchanté.

faith [feiθ] *n.* **1.** (*a*) foi *f*; **to have f. in s.o., in sth.,** avoir confiance en qn, en qch.; **to have f. in God,** avoir foi en Dieu; **to put one's f. in s.o.,** accorder toute sa confiance à qn; **f. healer, healing,** guérisseur *m*, guérison *f*, par la prière; (*b*) religion *f*; **the Christian f.,** la foi chrétienne. **2.** (*a*) **to keep f. with s.o.,** tenir ses engagements envers qn; **to break f. with s.o.,** manquer de foi, de parole, à qn; (*b*) **good faith,** bonne foi; **to say sth. in good f.,** dire qch. en toute bonne foi; **to do sth. in all good f.,** faire qch. en tout honneur; **bad f.,** perfidie *f*.

faithful ['feiθf(u)l] **1.** *a.* fidèle; (*a*) (*of friend, etc.*) loyal, -aux; **to remain f. to s.o.,** rester fidèle à qn; **f. promise,** promesse formelle; (*b*) (*of copy*) exact, juste; (traduction) fidèle; **f. in every detail,** exact jusqu'au moindre détail. **2.** *n.pl. Ecc:* **the f.,** les fidèles *mpl*; (*Islam*) les croyants *mpl*. **-fully** *adv.* **1.** fidèlement, loyalement; *Corr:* **we remain yours f.,** recevez l'expression de nos sentiments distingués; **he promised f. to come tomorrow,** il a promis formellement de venir demain. **2.** (traduire, copier, etc.) exactement.

faithfulness ['feiθf(u)lnis] *n.* **1.** fidélité *f*, loyauté *f* (**to,** envers). **2.** fidélité, exactitude *f* (d'un récit, etc.).

faithless ['feiθlis] *a.* **1.** infidèle, sans foi. **2.** infidèle (**to,** à). **3.** déloyal, -aux; perfide.

faithlessness ['feiθlisnis] *n.* **1.** infidélité (**to,** à). **2.** déloyauté *f*; manque *m* de foi.

fake¹ [feik] *n.* article faux, truqué; **it's a f.,** c'est du trucage.

fake² *v.tr.* truquer (des calculs, etc.); **faked balance sheet,** bilan truqué; **to f. a story,** inventer une histoire. **faking** *n.* trucage *m*.

faker ['feikər] *n.* truqueur *m*.

fakir ['fæ'kiər, 'feikiər] *n.* fakir *m*.

falcon ['fɔ:(l)kən] *n. Orn:* faucon *m*; **peregrine f.,** faucon pèlerin.

falconer ['fɔ:(l)kənər] *n.* fauconnier *m*.

falconry ['fɔ:(l)kənri] *n.* fauconnerie *f*.

Falkland ['fɔ:klənd] *Pr.n. Geog:* **the F. Islands,** les (îles) Malouines (*fpl*), les îles Falkland.

fall¹ [fɔ:l] *n.* **1.** (*a*) chute *f* (d'un corps, etc.); *Th:* baisser *m* (du rideau); **free f.,** chute libre; **to have a f.,** faire une chute; (*b*) *Wr:* tomber *m*; (*c*) quantité tombée (de neige, de pluie); **there has been a heavy f. of snow,** il est tombé beaucoup de neige. **2.** *NAm:* **the f.,** l'automne *m or f*. **3.** (*a*) *usu. pl.* chute (d'eau); **the Victoria Falls,** les Chutes Victoria; **the Niagara Falls,** les Chutes du Niagara; (*b*) *Hyd.E:* hauteur *f* de chute (d'un barrage). **4.** (*a*) décrue *f*, baisse *f* (des eaux); reflux *m*, jusant *m* (de la marée); pente *f* (d'une route, etc.); diminution *f* (de poids, etc.); chute (du baromètre, etc.); baisse (de la température); cadence *f* (de la voix); (*b*) dénivellation *f*; (*c*) *Com: Fin:* baisse (des prix, des actions); dépréciation *f* (de la monnaie); **heavy f.,** forte baisse; **f. in prices,** chute de prix. **5.** perte *f*, ruine *f* (de qn). **6.** chute (d'une ville); déchéance (d'un empire, etc.); renversement *m* (d'un gouvernement, etc.). **7.** éboulement *m* (de terre).

fall² *v.i.* (*p.t.* **fell** [fel]; *p.p.* **fallen** ['fɔːl(ə)n]) **1.** (*a*) tomber; **to f. to the ground,** tomber à terre; **to f. off a ladder,** tomber à bas d'une échelle; **to f. out of the window,** tomber par la fenêtre; **to f. on one's feet,** retomber sur ses pieds; avoir de la chance; **to f. into a trap,** donner dans un piège; **to f. into s.o.'s hands,** tomber entre les mains de qn; **night is falling,** la nuit tombe; (*b*) *Astr:* (*of star*) filer; (*c*) (*hang down*) **his fair fell to his shoulders,** ses cheveux *mpl* lui descendaient jusqu'aux épaules; (*d*) **Christmas falls on a Thursday,** Noël tombe un jeudi. **2.** (*from standing or perpendicular position*) (*a*) **to f. to the ground,** tomber par terre; **to f. on one's knees,** tomber à genoux; **to f. (to temptation),** succomber à la tentation; (*b*) (*of building*) s'écrouler, s'effondrer; **to f. to pieces,** tomber en morceaux; (*c*) **when Liège fell,** lorsque Liège capitula; **the government has fallen,** le gouvernement a été renversé. **3.** (*a*) (*of tide, etc.*) baisser; (*of wind*) tomber; (*of price, etc.*) diminuer; (*of price, exchange, etc.*) baisser, se déprécier; *Fig:* **his stock is falling,** son crédit est en baisse; **the thermometer has fallen ten degrees,** le thermomètre a baissé de dix degrés; (*b*) (*of ground*) aller en pente; s'incliner; *Mth:* (*of curve*) décroître; **her eyes fell,** elle a baissé les yeux; **his face fell,** sa figure s'allongea; **my spirits fell,** j'ai perdu tout courage; (*c*) *Nau:* (*of ship*) **to f. to leeward,** tomber sous le vent; (*d*) **to f. from one's position,** déchoir de sa position; **to f. in s.o.'s estimation,** perdre dans l'estime de qn. **4.** (*a*) **a shadow fell on the wall,** une ombre se projeta sur le mur; **the accent falls on the last syllable,** l'accent tombe sur la dernière syllabe; (*b*) **to f. (up)on the enemy,** attaquer l'ennemi; (*c*) **suspicion fell on him,** les soupçons retombèrent sur lui. **5.** (*a*) **to f. to s.o.'s share,** échoir (en partage) à qn; **the blame, responsibility, falls on . . .,** le blâme, la responsabilité, retombe sur . . .; **these facts f. under another category,** ces faits entrent dans une autre catégorie; (*b*) (*of pers.*) **to f. under suspicion,** devenir l'objet des soupçons; devenir suspect; **to f. in with (s.o., sth.),** (i) rencontrer (qn) par hasard; (ii) accéder à (une requête); accepter (une proposition); **to f. on evil days,** connaître de mauvais jours; (*c*) **I soon fell into their ways,** (i) je me suis vite accoutumé à leur manière de faire; (ii) j'ai bientôt appris la routine; **to f. into a habit,** contracter une habitude; **to f. into error,** être induit en erreur. **6.** (*a*) (*with adj. complement*) **to f. ill, sick,** tomber malade; **to f. asleep,** s'endormir; (*of post*) **to f. vacant,** se trouver vacant; (*b*) **to f. a victim to . . .,** être victime de . . . . **7.** (*to begin*) **they fell to work (again),** ils se (re)mirent au travail. **fall about** *v.i.* tomber de côté et d'autre; **to f. about laughing,** se tordre de rire. **fall apart** *v.i.* se désintégrer; tomber en morceaux. **fall away** *v.i.* (*a*) (*of ground, etc.*) s'affaisser brusquement; (*b*) (*of followers, etc.*) déserter; (*of prejudices, etc.*) disparaître. **fall back** *v.i.* (*a*) tomber à la renverse, en arrière; **to f. back on the cushions,** retomber sur les coussins; (*b*) (*of troops*) se replier, reculer; **to f. back a pace,** reculer d'un pas; (*c*) *St.Exch: Fin:* se replier; (*d*) **to have some money to f. back on,** avoir de l'argent en réserve comme en-cas; **you can always f. back on me,** en dernière ressource vous pouvez compter sur moi. **fall behind** *v.i.* s'arriérer; rester en arrière; **to f. behind with the rent,** être en retard pour payer son loyer. **fall down** *v.i.* (*a*) tomber à terre, par terre; (*b*) (*of building, etc.*) s'écrouler, s'effondrer; (*c*) *F:* **to f. down on the job,** louper le travail. **fallen 1.** *a.* (*a*) (feuilles) tombées; (*b*) **f. woman,** femme déchue; fille perdue. **2.** *n.pl.* **the f.,** les morts *mpl* (sur le champ de bataille). **fall for** *v.i. F:* (*a*) tomber amoureux de (qn); (*b*) **to f. for a trick,** s'y laisser prendre. **fall in** *v.i.* (*a*) (i) (*of building, roof, etc.*) s'écrouler, s'effondrer; (*of trench, etc.*) s'ébouler; (ii) (*of cheeks*) se creuser; (*b*) *Mil:* former les rangs; **f. in!** rassemblement! (*c*) (*of lease, etc.*) expirer; (*of debt*) arriver à échéance. **falling 1.** *a.* (*of darkness, etc.*) tombant; *Astr:* (étoile) filante; (température) en baisse; *Com:* (prix) qui baisse; (marché) avec tendance à la baisse. **2.** *n.* (*a*) (i) chute *f*; (ii) baisse *f* (de prix, du baromètre, etc.); (*b*) **f. away,** (i) affaissement *m* brusque (du terrain); (ii) défection *f* (de partisans); (*c*) *Mil: etc:* **f. back,** repli *m*, repliement *m*; (*d*) **f. in,** (i) éboulement *m*, effondrement *m* (d'un bâtiment, d'une tranchée); (ii) *Mil:* rassemblement *m*; (iii) expiration *f* (d'un bail, etc.); échéance *f* (d'une dette, etc.); (iv) acquiescement *m* (**with sth.,** à qch.); acceptation *f* (**with sth.,** de qch.); (*e*) **f. off,** (i) défection *f* (de partisans); (ii) diminution *f* (de chiffres, de taux, etc.); déclin *m* (de pouvoir, de popularité); relâchement *m* (de zèle); ralentissement (de commandes, des affaires). **fall off** *v.i.* (*a*) (*of thg*) tomber; (*b*) *Nau:* abattre sous le vent; (*c*) (*of followers, etc.*) faire défection; (*d*) (*of profits*) diminuer; (*of speed*) ralentir; (*of zeal*) se relâcher; (*e*) (*deteriorate*) décliner; (*of skill*) baisser; **his popularity is falling off,** sa popularité baisse. **fall out** *v.i.* (*a*) tomber dehors; (*b*) (*of hair*) tomber; (*c*) *Mil:* (i) quitter les rangs; (ii) rompre les rangs; **f. out!** rompez! (*d*) se brouiller, se fâcher (**with,** avec); **they have fallen out,** ils sont fâchés. **fall over 1.** *v.i.* (*a*) (*of pers.*) tomber (par terre); (*of thg*) se renverser, être renversé. **2.** *v.tr. & pron.* trébucher sur (un obstacle); *F:* **publishers were falling over each other for his new book,** les éditeurs se disputaient avec acharnement son prochain livre; **he was falling over himself in his anxiety to please her,** il se mettait en quatre pour lui plaire. **fall through** *v.i.* (*of scheme, etc.*) ne pas aboutir; échouer; *F:* tomber à l'eau. **fall to** *v.i. F: O:* s'attaquer au repas.

fallacious [fə'leiʃəs] *a.* trompeur, -euse; (espoir, paix) illusoire.

fallacy ['fæləsi] *n.* **1.** (*a*) *Log:* sophisme *m*; (*b*) erreur *f*. **2.** fausseté *f* (d'un argument, etc.).

fall-guy ['fɔːlgai] *n. esp. NAm: F:* bouc *m* émissaire; souffre-douleur *m inv.*

fallibility [fæli'biliti] *n.* faillibilité *f*.

fallible ['fælibl] *a.* faillible.

Fallopian [fə'loupiən] *a.* (trompe, etc.) de Fallope.

fallout ['fɔːlaut] *n.* retombées (radioactives).

fallow¹ ['fælou] *Agr:* **1.** *n.* jachère *f*, friche *f*. **2.** *a.* (*of land*) en friche; en jachère; **to lie f.,** être en jachère, en friche.

fallow² *a.* **f. deer,** daim *m*.

false [fɔːls] *a.* **1.** (*incorrect*) faux, *f.* fausse; (idée) erronée; **f. report,** fausse nouvelle, *F:* canard *m*; **f. modesty,** (i) fausse pudeur; (ii) fausse modestie; **f. alarm,** fausse alerte; **to take a f. step,** faire un faux pas; **f. start,** faux départ; *Mus:* **f. note,** fausse note. **2.** perfide; infidèle; (*of promise, etc.*) mensonger; **f. witness,** faux témoin; **to bear f. witness,** rendre faux témoignage; *adv.* **his memory played him f.,** sa mémoire l'a mal servi. **3.** (*of hair, etc.*) artificiel, postiche; (*of action, etc.*) feint, prétendu; (*of document, etc.*) forgé; (*of coin, seal, etc.*) faux, contrefait; **f. bottom,** double fond (d'une boîte, etc.). **-ly** *adv.* faussement; à faux.

falsehood ['fɔːlshud] *n.* **1. to distinguish truth from f.,** distinguer le vrai du faux. **2. to tell a f.,** faire un mensonge.

falseness ['fɔːlsnis] *n.* **1.** fausseté *f* (d'un rapport, etc.). **2.** *O:* infidélité *f* (d'un amant, etc.).

falsetto [fɔːl'setou] **1.** *n. & a. Mus:* **f. (voice),** voix *f* de fausset. **2.** *n.* (*singer*) fausset *m*.

falsies ['fɔːlsiz] *n.pl. F:* faux seins, faux nichons.

falsification [fɔːlsifi'keiʃ(ə)n] *n.* falsification *f*.

falsify ['fɔːlsifai] *v.tr.* **(falsified; falsifying) 1.** falsifier (un document); fausser (un bilan); dénaturer (des faits, etc.). **2.** prouver la fausseté de (qch.).

falsity ['fɔːlsiti] *n.* fausseté *f* (d'une doctrine, etc.).

falter ['fɔːltər] *v.i.* **1.** (*a*) (*of voice*) hésiter, trembler; **he faltered in his speech,** il eut un moment d'hésitation; (*b*) (*of pers.*) chanceler; (*c*) (*of pers. or courage*) défaillir. **2.** *v.tr.* dire (qch.) d'une voix hésitante; **to falter out,** balbutier (une excuse, etc.). **faltering** *a.* (*a*) (*of voice, etc.*) hésitant; **to speak in a f. voice,** parler d'une voix mal assurée; (*b*) (*of legs*) chancelant; **with f. steps,** d'un pas mal assuré; (*c*) (*of courage, memory, etc.*) défaillant.

fame [feim] *n.* renom *m,* renommée *f,* réputation *f;* **to win f.,** se faire un grand nom; **house of ill f.,** maison mal famée.

famed [feimd] *a.* célèbre; bien connu **(for,** pour).

familiar [fə'miliər] **1.** *a.* (*a*) familier, intime; **to be on f. terms with s.o.,** avoir des rapports d'intimité avec qn; **you are rather too f.,** vous prenez trop de privautés; (*b*) **f. spirit,** démon familier; (*c*) (*of thg*) familier, bien connu; **a f. face,** une figure de connaissance; **it strikes one as f.,** cela fait l'effet du déjà vu, du déjà entendu; **to be on f. ground,** être sur son terrain; **his voice sounded f. to me,** il me sembla reconnaître sa voix; (*d*) (*of pers.*) **to be f. with sth.,** bien connaître qch.; **to be f. with the customs,** être au courant des usages. **2.** *n.* démon familier. **-ly** *adv.* familièrement.

familiarity [fəmili'æriti] *n.* **1.** familiarité *f;* intimité *f; Prov:* **f. breeds contempt,** la familiarité engendre, fait naître, le mépris. **2.** connaissance *f* **(with,** de); **his f. with French,** sa connaissance du français.

familiarization [fəmiliərai'zeiʃ(ə)n] *n.* accoutumance *f* **(with,** à); habitude *f* **(with,** de).

familiarize [fə'miliəraiz] *v.tr.* **1.** rendre (qch.) familier. **2. to f. s.o. with sth.,** faire connaître qch. à qn; **to f. oneself with a language,** se familiariser avec une langue.

family ['fæm(i)li] *n.* **1.** (*a*) famille *f;* **large f.,** famille nombreuse; **a friend of the f.,** un ami de la maison; **to be one of the f.,** être de la maison; **it runs in the f.,** cela tient de famille; **disease that runs in the f.,** maladie *f* héréditaire; (*b*) **a f. dinner,** un dîner en famille; **f. tree,** arbre *m* généalogique; **f. portraits,** portraits *mpl* d'ancêtres; **f. hotel,** hôtel *m* de famille; **in a f.-size(d) jar,** en pot familial; **f. likeness,** air *m* de famille; **f. butcher,** boucher *m* du coin; **f. life,** vie familiale; **f. man,** (i) père *m* de famille; (ii) homme d'intérieur; *Adm:* **f. allowance,** allocation familiale; **f. planning,** limitation *f* des naissances, planning familial; *P:* **she's in the f. way,** elle est enceinte. **2.** famille (de plantes, de mots, etc.).

famine ['fæmin] *n.* (*a*) famine *f;* **to die of f.,** mourir de faim; (*b*) disette *f* (d'eau, etc.).

famished ['fæmiʃd] *a.* affamé; *F:* **to be, feel, f.,** mourir de faim. **famishing** *a. F:* **to be f.,** mourir de faim.

famous ['feiməs] *a.* **1.** célèbre, renommé **(for,** pour, par); **f. in history,** célèbre dans l'histoire; **town f. for its monuments,** ville *f* célèbre par ses monuments. **2.** parfait, fameux. **-ly** *adv. F:* fameusement, à merveille; **I get on f. with him,** on s'entend à merveille.

fan¹ [fæn] *n.* **1.** *Agr:* tarare *m.* **2.** (*a*) éventail *m; Geog:* **alluvial f.,** cône *m* d'alluvions; *Arch:* **f. vaulting,** voûte(s) *f* (*pl*) en éventail; *Av:* **f. marker,** radiobalise *f* à faisceau en éventail; (*b*) *Bot:* **f. palm,** palmier-éventail *m.* **3.** ventilateur (rotatif, à ailes, soufflant); *Ind:* soufflet *m;* **extractor f.,** aérateur *m; Aut:* **radiator f.,** ventilateur; *Dom.Ec:* **f. heater,** radiateur soufflant; **f.-cooled,** refroidi par ventilateur. **4.** aile *f,* pale *f,* d'hélice; gouvernail *m* (d'un moulin à vent).

fan² *v.tr.* **(fanned) 1.** *Agr:* vanner (le grain). **2.** (*a*) éventer (qn); **terraces fanned by cool sea breezes,** terrasses rafraîchies par les brises de mer; (*b*) souffler (le feu); attiser, exciter (les passions); attiser, envenimer (une querelle). **fan out** *v.i.* se déployer, s'étaler en éventail.

fan³ *n. F:* fanatique *mf,* fana *m* (de la télévision, du sport, etc.); **football f.,** fana de football; **f. club,** club *m* des fanas.

fanatic [fə'nætik] *a. & n.* fanatique (*mf*).

fanatical [fə'nætikl] *a.* fanatique. **-ally** *adv.* fanatiquement.

fanaticism [fə'nætisizm] *n.* fanatisme *m.*

fancier ['fænsiər] *n.* connaisseur, -euse (en chiens, etc.).

fanciful ['fænsif(u)l] *a.* **1.** (*a*) (*of pers.*) capricieux, fantasque; (*b*) (travail, etc.) fantaisiste; (portrait) de fantaisie. **2.** (projet) chimérique. **-fully** *adv.* d'une manière fantasque.

fancy¹ ['fænsi] **I.** *n.* **1.** (*a*) imagination *f,* fantaisie *f;* **the realm of f.,** le domaine de l'imagination; (*b*) chose *f* imaginaire; **it's only f.!** c'est pure imagination! (*c*) idée *f;* **idle fancies,** vaines imaginations. **2.** (*a*) fantaisie, caprice *m;* **just as the f. takes me,** comme l'idée me prend, *F:* comme ça me chante; (*b*) fantaisie, goût *m;* **to take a f. to sth.,** prendre goût à qch.; **to take a f. to s.o.,** (i) prendre qn en affection; (ii) s'éprendre, s'enticher, de qn; **it took, caught, my f. at once,** cela m'a séduit du premier coup; **to be f. free,** avoir le cœur libre. **II.** *a.* (*a*) de fantaisie; **f. biscuits,** biscuits assortis; **f. goods,** nouveautés *fpl;* **f. dress,** travesti *m,* déguisement *m;* **f. dress ball,** bal travesti; *F:* **to cut out the f. stuff,** élaguer; (*b*) **f. price,** prix trop élevé; (*c*) *P:* **f. man,** (i) gigolo *m;* (ii) souteneur *m;* **f. woman, f. piece,** maîtresse *f.*

fancy² *v.tr.* **1.** (*a*) s'imaginer, se figurer (qch.); *F:* **f. now! just f.! f. (that)!** qui l'aurait dit? figurez-vous ça! **f. meeting you!** je ne m'attendais guère à vous rencontrer! (*b*) croire, penser; **I f. I have seen him before,** j'ai l'impression de l'avoir déjà vu; **he fancied he heard footsteps,** il a cru entendre des pas. **2.** (*a*) **to f. sth.,** se sentir attiré vers qch.; **I don't f. his offer,** son offre *f* ne me dit rien; **I f. a bit of chicken,** je mangerais volontiers un morceau de poulet; *Turf:* **strongly fancied horse,** cheval très coté; (*b*) **to f. s.o.,** se sentir attiré vers qn; (*c*) **to f. oneself,** être infatué de sa petite personne; se gober; **he fancies himself as a speaker,** il se croit orateur. **fancied** *a.* imaginaire, imaginé.

fancywork ['fænsiwəːk] *n. Needlew:* ouvrage(s) *m*(*pl*) d'agrément; broderie *f.*

fanfare ['fænfɛər] *n.* fanfare *f* (exécutée par des cors de chasse); sonnerie *f* (de trompettes).

fang [fæŋ] *n.* (*a*) croc *m* (de chien, etc.); (*b*) crochet *m* (de vipère); dent *f* à venin.

fanlight ['fænlait] *n.* imposte *f.*

fanmail ['fænmeil] *n. F:* courrier *m* des admirateurs et admiratrices (d'une vedette, etc.).

Fanny ['fæni] **1.** *Pr.n.f. P:* **sweet F. Adams,** rien du tout, nib de nib. **2.** *n.* (*a*) *NAm: P:* **f.,** derrière *m,* fesses *fpl;* (*b*) *V:* vagin *m,* minou *m.*

fan-shaped ['fænʃeipt] *a.* en éventail.

fantail ['fænteil] *n. Orn:* pigeon *m* paon.

fantailed ['fænteild] *a. Orn:* **f. pigeon,** pigeon *m* paon.

fantasia [fæn'teiziə] *n. Mus:* fantaisie *f.*

fantasize ['fæntəsaiz] *v.i.* fantasmer.

fantastic [fæn'tæstik] *a.* (*a*) (*of pers., thg*) fantasque, bizarre; (*of pers.*) original, -aux; (*of thg*) fantastique, grotesque; (*b*) *F:* formidable; incroyable; *Com:* **f. reductions,** baisses phénoménales. **ally** *adv.* (*a*) d'une manière fantasque; (*b*) *F:* **f. beautiful,** incroyablement beau.

fantasy ['fæntəzi] *n.* **1.** fantaisie *f;* (*a*) imagination capricieuse; (*b*) caprice *m.* **2.** (*a*) vision *f,* idée *f,* bizarre; (*b*) idée fantasque. **3.** (*a*) œuvre *f*, édifice *m*, fantastique; (*b*) *Mus:* fantaisie *f*.

far¹ [fɑːr] *adv.* (**farther, -est** [ˈfɑːðər, -ist]; **further, -est** [ˈfəːðər, -ist]) **1.** (*place*) loin; (*a*) **to go f.,** aller loin; faire du chemin; **this young man will go f.,** ce jeune homme ira loin; **to go too f.,** aller trop loin; **is it f. from here?** est-ce loin d'ici? **as f. as the eye can see,** à perte de vue; **to live f. away,** demeurer au loin; **his thoughts were f. away,** sa pensée était ailleurs; **f. and wide,** de tous côtés; **f. and near,** partout; **f. from . . .,** loin de . . .; **not f. from . . .,** à peu de distance de . . .; *Journ:* **the story so f.** = résumé *m* des chapitres précédents; (*b*) **a pound does not go very f. nowadays,** on ne va pas loin avec une livre de nos jours; **to go so f. as to do sth.,** aller jusqu'à faire qch.; **I'll go so f. as to say that . . .,** je vais jusqu'à dire que . . .; **things went so f. that . . .,** les choses sont allées si loin que . . .; **that is going too f.,** cela passe la mesure; **how f. have you got?** où en êtes-vous (de votre lecture, etc.)? **as f. as I can judge . . .,** autant que je puis en juger . . .; **as f. as I know,** autant que je sache; **I will help you as f. as I can, as f. as possible,** je vous aiderai dans la mesure de mes moyens; **so f. so good,** c'est fort bien jusque-là; jusqu'ici ça va bien; **in so f. as . . .,** dans la mesure où . . .; **f. from admiring him I loathe him,** bien loin de l'admirer je le déteste; **f. from it,** loin de là; **not f. from it,** peu s'en faut; **f. be it from me to put pressure on you!** loin de moi l'idée de vous influencer! **he is not f. off sixty,** il approche de la soixantaine; **by f.,** de loin; **by f. the best,** de beaucoup le meilleur. **2.** (*time*) **so f.,** jusqu'ici; **have you seen him?—not so f.,** l'avez-vous vu?—pas jusqu'ici; **as f. back as I can remember,** aussi loin que je puisse me rappeler; **as f. back as 1900,** déjà en 1900; **as f. as I can see,** autant que je puisse prévoir; **to work f. into the night,** travailler bien avant dans la nuit. **3.** (*with qualifying adjectives, adverbs, etc.*) beaucoup; **it is f. better,** c'est beaucoup mieux; **f. and away the best,** de beaucoup le meilleur; **the night was f. advanced,** la nuit était fort avancée.

far² *a.* (**farther, -est** [ˈfɑːðər, -ist]; **further, -est** [ˈfəːðər, -ist] **1.** lointain, éloigné; **a f. country,** un pays lointain; **in the f. distance,** tout au loin; *Geog:* **the F. East,** l'Extrême-Orient *m*. **2. the f. end,** le bout le plus éloigné (d'une planche, etc.); **the f. bank of the river,** la rive opposée de la rivière.

farad [ˈfæræd] *n. El.Meas:* farad *m*.

faraway [ˈfɑːrəwei] *a.* lointain, éloigné; **his eyes had a f. look,** il avait le regard perdu dans le vague.

farce [fɑːs] *n. Th:* farce *f*; **knockabout f.,** grosse farce; **the trial was a f.,** le procès a été grotesque.

farcical [ˈfɑːsik(ə)l] *a.* (*a*) *Th:* bouffon, burlesque; (*b*) (*of incident*) absurde, grotesque; **this accusation is f.,** cette accusation est grotesque. **-ally** *adv.* d'une manière absurde, grotesque.

fare¹ [ˈfɛər] *n.* **1.** (*a*) *Rail: etc:* prix *m* du voyage; (*in taxi*) prix de la course; **half f.,** demi-place *f*, *pl.* demi-places; **single f.,** billet simple, (prix d')aller *m*; **return f.,** aller et retour *m*; **excess f.,** supplément *m*; **to pay one's f.,** payer son billet, sa course; (*in bus*) **fares, please!** les places, s'il vous plaît! (*b*) (*in taxi*) client, -ente; voyageur, -euse. **2.** chère *f*, manger *m*; **good f.,** bonne chère; **prison f.,** régime *m* de prison; **bill of f.,** carte *f* du jour.

fare² *v.i.* **to f. well,** aller bien; **he went out in the snow to see how the lambs were faring,** il est sorti sous la neige pour voir ce que devenaient les agneaux.

farewell [fɛəˈwel] *int. & n.* adieu (*m*); **to bid s.o. f.,** dire adieu à qn; **a f. dinner,** un dîner d'adieu.

far-fetched [ˈfɑːˈfetʃt] *a.* (*of example, etc.*) forcé, outré; tiré par les cheveux.

far-flung [ˈfɑːflʌŋ] *a.* (*of empire, etc.*) très étendu.

farinaceous [færiˈneiʃəs] *a.* farineux, farinacé.

farm¹ [fɑːm] *n.* **1.** (*a*) ferme *f*, exploitation *f* agricole; **sheep, trout, f.,** élevage *m* de moutons, de truites; **dairy f.,** ferme laitière; **poultry f.,** exploitation avicole; **stud f.,** haras *m*; (*b*) **f. machinery,** machines *fpl* agricoles; **f. labourer, worker,** ouvrier *m* agricole; **f. horse,** cheval *m* de ferme; **f. buildings,** dépendances *fpl* (d'une ferme). **2. sewage f.,** champs *mpl* d'épandage.

farm² **1.** *v.tr.* cultiver, exploiter (une propriété); **to f. 400 acres** = exploiter 160 hectares. **2.** *v.i.* être cultivateur. **farming 1.** *a.* **f. communities,** agglomérations rurales. **2.** *n.* exploitation *f* agricole; agriculture *f*; **mixed f.,** polyculture *f*; **sheep f.,** élevage *m* de moutons; **poultry f.,** aviculture *f*. **farm out** *v.tr.* (*a*) mettre (des enfants) en nourrice; (*b*) *F:* **to f. o. work,** sous-traiter; faire appel à des collaborateurs extérieurs.

farmer [ˈfɑːmər] *n.* agriculteur *m*; cultivateur, -trice; **(tenant) f.,** fermier, -ière; **sheep f.,** éleveur, -euse, de moutons; **poultry f.,** aviculteur, -trice.

farmhand [ˈfɑːmhænd] *n.* ouvrier *m* agricole.

farmhouse [ˈfɑːmhaus] *n.* (maison *f* de) ferme (*f*).

farmstead [ˈfɑːmsted] *n.* ferme *f*.

farmyard [ˈfɑːmjɑːd] *n.* cour *f* de ferme.

Faroe [ˈfɛərou] *Pr.n. Geog:* **the F. Islands, the Faroes,** les îles *fpl* Féroé.

far-off [ˈfɑːrɔf] *a.* lointain, éloigné, reculé.

far-out [ˈfɑːraut] *a.* avant-garde; outré.

far-reaching [ˈfɑːˈriːtʃiŋ] *a.* de grande envergure, d'une grande portée; **to have a f.-r. influence,** avoir une grande portée.

farrier [ˈfæriər] *n.* maréchal-ferrant *m*, *pl.* maréchaux-ferrants.

farrow¹ [ˈfærou] *n.* portée *f* de cochons.

farrow² **1.** *v.tr.* mettre bas (des cochons). **2.** *v.i.* (*of sow*) **to f. (down),** faire des petits; cochonner.

far-seeing [ˈfɑːˈsiːiŋ], **far-sighted** [ˈfɑːˈsaitid] *a.* prévoyant, clairvoyant, perspicace; **to be f.-s.,** voir loin; *F:* avoir bon nez.

far-sightedness [ˈfɑːˈsaitidnis] *n.* prévoyance *f*; perspicacité *f*.

fart¹ [fɑːt] *n. P:* pet *m*.

fart² *v.i. P:* péter; lâcher un pet.

farther [ˈfɑːðər] (*comp. of* **far**) **1.** *adv.* (*a*) plus loin (**than,** que); **f. off,** plus éloigné; plus loin; **f. on,** (i) plus en avant; (ii) plus en avance; **I can go no f.,** (i) je ne saurais aller plus loin; (ii) je n'en peux plus! (*b*) **f. (back),** plus en arrière; **f. back than 1500,** antérieurement à 1500. **2.** *a.* plus lointain; **at the f. end of the room,** à l'autre bout de la salle; au fond de la salle.

farthest [ˈfɑːðist] (*sup. of* **far**) **1.** *a.* (*a*) **f. (off),** le plus éloigné, le plus reculé; (*b*) (*of way, etc.*) le plus long. **2.** *adv.* le plus loin.

farthing [ˈfɑːðiŋ] *n. A.Num:* quart *m* d'un penny; *F:* **not to have a f.,** n'avoir pas le sou; *F:* **I don't care a brass f.,** je m'en moque éperdument.

fascia, *pl.* **-s** [ˈfeiʃə, -z] *n.* (*a*) *Arch:* bandelette *f*, bande *f*; (*b*) *Com:* enseigne *f* en forme d'entablement; (*c*) *Aut:* tableau *m* de bord.

fascicle [ˈfæsikl], **fascicule** [ˈfæsikjuːl] *n. Nat.Hist: Bookb: etc:* fascicule *m*.

fascinate [ˈfæsineit] *v.tr.* fasciner, charmer, séduire (qn); **to be fascinated by sth.,** être fasciné par qch. **fascinating** *a.* fascinateur, -trice; séduisant.

fascination [fæsiˈneiʃ(ə)n] *n.* fascination *f*, attrait *m*.

fascism [ˈfæʃizm] *n. Pol:* fascisme *m*.

fascist [ˈfæʃist] *a. & n. Pol:* fasciste (*mf*).

fash [fæʃ] *v.tr. Scot:* agacer, ennuyer (qn); **dinna f. yourself,** ne te fais pas de la bile.

fashion¹ [ˈfæʃ(ə)n] *n.* **1.** manière *f* (de faire qch.); **crabs walk in a peculiar f.,** les crabes marchent d'une façon étrange; **after a f.,** tant bien que mal. **2.** (*of clothes, etc.*) mode *f*, vogue *f*; **in f.,** à la mode, en vogue; **out of f.,** passé de mode; démodé; **in the latest f.,** à la dernière mode; **to set the f.,** (i) faire école; (ii) fixer, mener, la mode; **to become the f., come into f.,** devenir la mode; **it's all the f.,** c'est la grande vogue; *Com:* **f. house,** maison *f* de haute couture; **f. show,** présentation *f* de collections; **f. magazine,** journal *m* de modes.

fashion² *v.tr.* (*a*) façonner, former; confectionner (une robe, etc.); (*b*) **fully fashioned,** (entièrement) diminué, proportionné.

fashionable ['fæʃ(ə)nəbl] *a.* à la mode, en vogue; **blue is very f. this year,** le bleu se porte beaucoup cette année. **-ably** *adv.* (habillé) à la mode.

fast¹ [fɑːst] *n.* jeûne *m*; *Ecc:* **f. day,** jour *m* de jeûne; **to break one's f.,** rompre le jeûne.

fast² *v.i.* (*a*) jeûner; (*b*) *Med:* être à la diète. **fasting** *n.* (*a*) jeûne *m*; (*b*) *Med:* diète (absolue).

fast³ I. *a.* **1.** (*a*) (*of stake, etc.*) ferme, fixe, solide; (*of grip, etc.*) tenace; *Nau: etc:* **to make a rope f.,** amarrer un cordage; (*b*) *Nau:* **to make f. (to a buoy),** prendre le corps-mort; **to make f. (alongside),** s'amarrer; (*c*) (*of door, lid, etc.*) bien fermé; (*d*) (*of colour*) solide, résistant; **these colours are not f.,** ces couleurs ne résistent pas. **2.** (*a*) rapide; **you're a f. walker,** vous marchez vite; *Rail:* **f. train,** rapide *m*; express *m*; (*b*) *Games:* (billard, court) qui rend bien; (*c*) *Phot:* (pellicule) rapide; (*d*) *F:* **he pulled a f. one on me,** il m'a joué un mauvais tour. **3.** (*of clock, watch*) en avance; **my watch is five minutes f.,** ma montre avance de cinq minutes. **4.** *F: O:* (*of pers.*) (trop) émancipé; **to lead a f. life,** mener une vie dissolue. **II.** *adv.* **1.** ferme, solidement; **to hold f.,** tenir ferme; tenir bon; **to stand f.,** tenir bon; ne pas bouger; **to stick f.,** (i) bien tenir; (ii) rester pris, rester collé; *Tex:* **f. dyed,** grand teint *inv*; **to be f. asleep,** dormir d'un profond sommeil; *F:* **to play f. and loose,** jouer double jeu (**with s.o.,** avec qn). **2.** vite, rapidement; **to run f.,** courir vite; **not so f.!** pas si vite! doucement! **bad news travels f.,** les mauvaises nouvelles courent vite.

fastback ['fɑːstbæk] *a.* & *n. Aut:* (à) arrière profilé.

fasten ['fɑːs(ə)n] **1.** *v.tr.* (*a*) (*attach*) attacher (**to, on,** à); **to f. papers together with a clip,** attacher des papiers (ensemble) avec une agrafe; **to f. one's eyes on s.o.,** fixer le regard sur qn; (*b*) (*hold securely*) fixer, assurer; **to f. a door with a bolt,** fermer une porte au verrou. **2.** *v.i.* s'attacher, se fixer; (*a*) (*with passive force*) (*of garment*) s'agrafer, se boutonner (*at the back,* par derrière); (*of door, etc.*) se fermer; **door that fastens with a bolt,** porte qui se ferme au verrou; (*b*) **the crab fastened on to his leg,** le crabe s'accrocha à sa jambe. **fasten down** *v.tr.* fixer (qch.) à terre ou en place. **fastening** *n.* **1.** action *f* d'attacher; fixage *m*, fixation *f* (de qch. sur qch.); (*with bolts*) boulonnage *m*; agrafage *m* (d'un vêtement). **2.** (*a*) = FASTENER; (*b*) **fastenings,** attaches *fpl.* **fasten up** *v.tr.* agrafer, boutonner (sa robe, etc.).

fastener ['fɑːsnər] *n.* **1.** attache *f*; (*of garment*) agrafe *f*; (*of purse*) fermoir *m*; (*of window, etc.*) fermeture *f*; (*of French window*) espagnolette *f*; **zip f.,** fermeture à glissière, *R.t.m:* fermeture éclair; **snap f.,** bouton (fermoir) à pression.

fastidious [fæ'stidiəs] *a.* difficile, délicat (**about sth.,** sur qch.); **to be f.,** être difficile à contenter; faire le difficile. **-ly** *adv.* avec une délicatesse exagérée.

fastidiousness [fæs'tidiəsnis] *n.* goût *m* difficile.

fast-moving ['fɑːst'muːviŋ] *a.* rapide.

fastness ['fɑːstnis] *n.* (*a*) solidité *f* (d'une couleur, etc.); (*b*) rapidité *f*, vitesse *f*; (*c*) **mountain f.,** repaire *m* (de brigands).

fat¹ [fæt] *a.* **(fatter; fattest) 1.** (*a*) (*of pers.*) gros, *f.* grosse; gras, *f.* grasse; corpulent; (*of meat*) gras; (*of tissue*) adipeux; **to get f.,** engraisser; **to grow f. at the expense of others,** s'engraisser aux dépens d'autrui; **f. volume,** gros tome; **f. wallet,** portefeuille bien garni; *U.S: Pol: F:* **f. cat,** richard *m* (qui donne beaucoup d'argent au parti); (*b*) (*of clay, lime, etc.*) gras; **f. coal,** houille grasse, bitumineuse. **2.** (*of land*) riche, fertile, gras; **f. living,** prébende *f* qui rapporte gros; *F:* **a f. lot of good that'll do you!** cela vous fera une belle jambe! **a f. lot you know about it!** comme si vous en saviez quelque chose!

fat² *n.* **1.** (*a*) graisse *f*; *Com:* **fats,** matières grasses; **animal, vegetable, f.,** graisse animale, végétale; *F:* **the fat's in the fire!** le feu est aux poudres! (*b*) (*of pers.*) **to put on f.,** engraisser. **2.** gras *m* (de viande); **to live off the f. of the land,** vivre comme un coq en pâte.

fatal ['feit(ə)l] *a.* **1.** fatal, -als; **the f. hour,** l'heure fatale. **2.** (*a*) (*of blow, accident*) mortel; (*b*) **f. decision,** décision *f* funeste; **f. error, mistake,** erreur fatale, faute capitale. **-ally** *adv.* **1.** fatalement. **2.** mortellement (blessé).

fatalism ['feitəlizm] *n.* fatalisme *m.*

fatalist ['feitəlist] *a.* & *n.* fataliste (*mf*).

fatalistic [feitə'listik] *a.* fataliste.

fatality [fə'tæliti] *n.* **1.** caractère *m* funeste (**of,** de). **2.** accident mortel; sinistre *m*; **there were no fatalities,** il n'y a pas eu de mort.

fate [feit] *n.* destin *m*, sort *m*; *f*; (*a*) **stroke of f.,** coup *m* du destin, du sort; *Myth:* **the Fates,** les Parques *fpl*; (*b*) **to leave s.o. to his f.,** abandonner qn à son sort; (*c*) **to meet one's f.,** trouver la mort.

fated ['feitid] *a.* **1.** (*of day, etc.*) fatal, -als. **2.** destiné, condamné (**to do sth.,** à faire qch.). **3.** voué à la destruction.

fateful ['feitf(u)l] *a.* **1.** (voix, etc.) prophétique; (parole) fatidique. **2.** (jour, etc.) décisif, fatal, -als. **3.** (événement, etc.) fatal, inévitable.

fathead ['fæthed] *n. F:* imbécile *mf.*

father¹ ['fɑːðər] *n.* **1.** père *m*; **from f. to son,** de père en fils; **he's his father's son,** c'est bien le fils de son père; **on the father's side,** du côté paternel; **like a f.,** paternellement; **yes, F.,** oui, (mon) père; **like f. like son,** tel père tel fils; **F. Christmas,** le père Noël; *F:* **we had the f. and mother of a row,** nous avons eu une de ces empoignades! **2. our fathers,** nos ancêtres *mpl*, nos aïeux *mpl.* **3.** (*a*) père, fondateur *m* (d'une science, d'un art, etc.); (*b*) **the Fathers of the Church,** les Pères de l'Église. **4.** *Theol:* **God the F.,** Dieu le Père; **Our F. which, who, art in Heaven,** notre Père qui es aux cieux. **5.** *Ecc:* (*a*) **the Holy F.,** le Saint-Père; **F. confessor,** père spirituel; directeur *m* (de conscience); (*b*) **Father Martin,** (i) (*in monastic order*) le Père Martin; (ii) (*priest*) l'abbé Martin; (*in address*) **yes, F.,** (i) oui, mon Père; (ii) oui, monsieur l'Abbé. **6.** doyen *m* (de la Chambre, etc.); *Typ: etc:* **f. of the chapel,** chef *m* de l'atelier.

father² *v.tr.* engendrer (un enfant); inventer, produire (qch.); concevoir (un projet).

fatherhood ['fɑːðəhud] *n.* paternité *f.*

father-in-law, *pl.* **fathers-in-law** ['fɑːðərinlɔː, 'fɑːðəzinlɔː] *n.m.* beau-père, *pl.* beaux-pères.

fatherland ['fɑːðəlænd] *n.* patrie *f.*

fatherless ['fɑːðəlis] *a.* sans père; orphelin, -ine, de père.

fatherly ['fɑːðəli] *a.* (*of pers., tone, manner, etc.*) paternel; **to behave in a f. way towards s.o.,** se montrer paternel pour qn; être un père pour qn.

fathom¹ ['fæðəm] *n. Nau: Meas:* brasse *f* (= 6 feet = 1 m. 829).

fathom² *v.tr.* sonder; pénétrer, sonder (un mystère); **I can't f. him (out),** je ne le comprends pas.

fatigue¹ [fə'tiːg] *n.* **1.** (*a*) fatigue *f*; **mental f.,** fatigue cérébrale; **to be dropping with f.,** tomber de fatigue; (*b*) *Tchn:* **metal f.,** fatigue des métaux. **2.** *Mil:* **f. (duty),** corvée *f*; **cookhouse f.,** corvée de cuisine(s); **f.**

party, (détachement *m* de) corvée; **f. dress,** tenue *f* de corvée; treillis *m*.

fatigue² *v.tr.* **1.** fatiguer (qn); **to f. oneself doing sth.,** se fatiguer à faire qch. **2.** *Tchn:* fatiguer (un métal, etc.). **fatiguing** *a.* fatigant.

fatness ['fætnis] *n.* adiposité *f* (de la chair, etc.); embonpoint *m*, corpulence *f* (de qn).

fatted ['fætid] *a.* **to kill the f. calf,** tuer le veau gras.

fatten ['fæt(ə)n] **1.** *v.tr.* **to f. (up),** engraisser (des moutons, des veaux, etc.). **2.** *v.i.* engraisser; devenir gras. **fattening 1.** *a.* (*of food*) qui fait grossir. **2.** *n. Husb:* engraissement *m*, engraissage *m*.

fatty ['fæti] **1.** *a.* (*a*) graisseux; **f. foods,** aliments gras; (*b*) *Ch:* **f. acid,** acide gras; (*c*) (*of tissue, etc.*) adipeux. **2.** *n. F:* (i) gros enfant; (ii) gros bonhomme, patapouf *m*; **hi, f.!** ohé, mon gros!

fatuity [fæ'tju:iti] *n.* sottise *f*; imbécillité *f*.

fatuous ['fætjuəs] *a.* imbécile, idiot; (sourire) béat. **-ly** *adv.* sottement; d'un air imbécile.

fatuousness ['fætjuəsnis] *n.* = FATUITY.

faucet ['fɔ:sit] *n. NAm:* robinet *m*.

fault¹ [fɔ:lt] *n.* **1.** (*a*) défaut *m*; imperfection *f*; **to shut one's eyes to s.o.'s faults,** fermer les yeux sur les défauts de qn; **in spite of all his faults,** malgré tous ses travers; **scrupulous to a f.,** scrupuleux à l'excès; **to find f. with s.o., sth.,** trouver à redire contre qn, à qch.; (*b*) *Tchn:* défaut, vice *f* (de construction). **2.** (*a*) faute *f*; **to be at f.,** être en défaut; être coupable; **whose f. is it?** à qui la faute? **I am afraid it was my f.,** je crains bien que ce ne soit de ma faute; **through no f. of mine,** sans que je sois en cause; (*b*) **spelling f.,** faute d'orthographe. **3.** *Ten:* faute; **double f.,** double faute; **foot f.,** faute de pied. **4.** *Geol:* faille *f*; **f. line, plane,** ligne *f*, plan *m*, de faille.

fault² *v.tr.* prendre (qn) en défaut; trouver un défaut dans (qch.).

faultfinder ['fɔ:ltfaindər] *n.* (*pers.*) critiqueur, -euse; (*device*) détecteur *m* de fuites.

faultfinding ['fɔ:ltfaindiŋ] **1.** *a.* censeur, -euse. **2.** *n.* (*a*) disposition *f* à critiquer; (*b*) localisation *f* des défauts.

faultiness ['fɔ:ltinis] *n.* défectuosité *f*, imperfection *f*.

faultless ['fɔ:ltlis] *a.* (*of work, etc.*) sans défaut, sans faute; parfait; (*of dress*) impeccable, irréprochable. **-ly** *adv.* parfaitement; d'une manière impeccable.

faultlessness ['fɔ:ltlisnis] *n.* perfection *f*.

faulty ['fɔ:lti] *a.* (*of work, etc.*) défectueux, imparfait; (*of style, etc.*) incorrect; (*of reasoning, etc.*) erroné; *Gram:* (*of construction, etc.*) vicieux; **f. workmanship,** mauvaise construction.

faun [fɔ:n] *n. Myth:* faune *m*.

fauna ['fɔ:nə] *n.* faune *f* (d'une région, d'un pays).

faux pas ['fou'pɑ:] *n.* faux pas, gaffe *f*.

favour¹, *NAm:* **favor¹** ['feivər] *n.* **1.** faveur *f*, approbation *f*; **to find f. with s.o.,** trouver grâce aux yeux de qn; **to gain s.o.'s f.,** gagner la faveur de qn; **to be restored, to return, to f.,** rentrer en grâce; **to fall out of f. with s.o.,** perdre les bonnes grâces de qn. **2.** grâce *f*, bonté *f*; **to ask s.o. a f., a f. of s.o.,** solliciter une grâce, une faveur, de qn; **to do s.o. a f.,** faire une faveur à qn; obliger qn; **will you do me a great f.?** voulez-vous me rendre un grand service? **as a f.,** à titre gracieux. **3.** partialité *f*, préférence *f*; **to show f. towards s.o.,** favoriser qn; **without fear or f.,** sans distinction de personnes. **4.** *prep.phr.* **in f. of . . .,** en faveur de . . .; **to speak in s.o.'s f.,** parler en faveur de qn, pour qn; **to have everything in one's f.,** avoir tout pour soi; **to be in f. of sth.,** être partisan de qch.; préconiser qch. **5.** faveur *f*, cocarde *f*.

favour², *NAm:* **favor²** *v.tr.* **1.** approuver, préférer (qch.); accorder une préférence à (qn); être pour (un projet). **2.** favoriser (qn); accorder une grâce à (qn); to f. s.o. with a smile, gratifier qn d'un sourire. **3.** (*a*) avantager (qn); montrer de la partialité pour (qn); (*b*) faciliter (qch.); **to be favoured by circumstances,** avoir les circonstances en sa faveur. **4.** (*of fact, etc.*) soutenir (une théorie, etc.). **favoured,** *NAm:* **favored** *a.* (*of pers.*) **1.** favorisé, avantagé; **the most-f. nation,** la nation la plus favorisée; **the f. few,** les élus (du patron, etc.). **2.** *O:* **ill-f.,** laid, de mauvaise mine.

favourable, *NAm:* **favorable** ['feiv(ə)rəbl] *a.* favorable: (*of weather, wind, etc.*) propice; (*of reception, etc.*) bienveillant; (*of terms, etc.*) bon, avantageux; (*of a report, etc.*) bon, rassurant; **in a f. light,** sous un jour favorable; *Com:* **on f. terms,** à bon compte. **-ably** *adv.* favorablement.

favourite, *NAm:* **favorite** ['feiv(ə)rit] **1.** *n.* favori, *f.* favorite; (*a*) **the youngest daughter is his f.,** c'est la plus jeune qui est sa préférée; *Rac:* **to back the f.,** jouer le favori; (*b*) **old favourites,** vieilles chansons populaires. **2.** *a.* (fils, auteur, etc.) favori, préféré; **my f. opera,** mon opéra de prédilection.

favouritism, *NAm:* **favoritism** ['feiv(ə)ritizm] *n.* favoritisme *m*.

fawn¹ [fɔ:n] *n.* **1.** *Z:* faon *m*. **2. f. (colour),** couleur *f* fauve; *a.* **f.(-coloured),** fauve.

fawn² *v.ind.tr.* **to f. on s.o.,** (i) (*of dog*) caresser qn., faire des caresses à qn; (ii) (*of pers.*) aduler qn; faire le chien couchant auprès de qn. **fawning 1.** *a.* (*of pers.*) adulateur, -trice; servile. **2.** *n.* adulation *f*.

fealty ['fiəlti] *n. Hist:* féauté *f*; fidélité *f*.

fear¹ ['fiər] *n.* **1.** crainte *f*, peur *f*; **a sudden f.,** une alarme; **deadly f.,** effroi *m*; **to be overcome by, with, f.,** être en proie à la frayeur, à la terreur; **to be, stand, go, in f. of s.o., of sth.,** avoir peur de, redouter, craindre, qn, qch.; **to go in f. of one's life,** craindre pour sa vie; **for f. of making a mistake,** de crainte d'erreur; **there is no f. that he will come back,** il n'y a pas de danger qu'il revienne; *F:* **no f.!** pas de danger! jamais de la vie! **2.** respect *m*, crainte (de Dieu, des lois, etc.); *F:* **to put the f. of God into s.o.,** faire à qn une semonce dont il se souviendra longtemps.

fear² *v.tr.* **1.** craindre, avoir peur de (qn, qch.). **2.** (*a*) appréhender, craindre (un événement); **to f. for s.o., sth.,** s'inquiéter au sujet de qn, de qch.; **I f. it is too late,** j'ai peur, je crains, qu'il ne soit trop tard; **I f. he will not come,** je crains qu'il ne vienne pas; (*b*) **I f. he's out,** je crois qu'il n'y est pas; **I f. I'm late,** je crois bien être en retard. **3.** craindre (Dieu, etc.). **feared** *a.* (*of pers., etc.*) redouté.

fearful ['fiəful] *a.* **1.** (*of noise, etc.*) affreux, effrayant; *F:* **a f. mess,** un désordre effrayant, formidable. **2.** (*of pers.*) (*a*) peureux, craintif; (*b*) **f. of . . .,** qui craint de . . . . **-fully** *adv.* **1.** affreusement, terriblement. **2.** peureusement.

fearfulness ['fiəfulnis] *n.* **1.** caractère terrifiant (de qch.). **2.** crainte *f*; appréhension *f*.

fearless ['fiəlis] *a* intrépide, courageux; sans peur (of, de); **he was f. of danger,** il ne reculait devant aucun danger. **-ly** *adv.* intrépidement; sans peur.

fearlessness ['fiəlisnis] *n.* intrépidité *f*, courage *m*.

fearsome ['fiəsəm] *a.* effrayant, redoutable.

feasibility [fi:zə'biliti] *n.* **1.** praticabilité *f*; faisabilité *f* (d'un plan, etc.). **2.** plausibilité *f*, vraisemblance *f* (d'une histoire, etc.).

feasible ['fi:zəbl] *a.* **1.** (*of plan, etc.*) faisable, réalisable, praticable. **2.** (*of story, etc.*) vraisemblable.

feast¹ [fi:st] *n.* **1.** *Ecc: etc:* **f. (day),** (jour *m* de) fête (*f*); **movable f.,** fête mobile. **2.** festin *m*, banquet *m*.

feast² **1.** *v.i.* faire festin; festoyer; **to f. (up)on sth.,** se régaler de qch. **2.** *v.tr.* régaler, fêter (qn); **to f. one's eyes on sth.,** repaître ses yeux de qch. **feasting** *n.* festoiement *m*.

feat [fi:t] *n.* **1.** exploit *m*; **f. of arms,** fait d'armes. **2.**

(*a*) tour *m* de force; **feats of engineering,** triomphes *mpl* de l'ingénieur; (*b*) **f. of skill,** tour d'adresse.

feather¹ ['feðər] *n.* **1.** (*a*) plume *f*; (*of tail, wing*) penne *f*; **feathers of an arrow,** (em)pennes *fpl* d'une flèche; **to show the white f.,** manquer de courage; **you could have knocked me down with a f.,** j'ai pensé tomber de mon haut; *F:* **that's a f. in his cap,** il peut en être fier; (*b*) **f. bed,** (i) lit *m* de plume; (ii) *F:* sinécure *f*; **f. duster,** plumeau *m.* **2.** plumage *m*; *Prov:* **birds of a f. flock together,** qui se ressemble s'assemble. **3.** (*in gem*) paillette *f*, crapaud *m.* **4.** *Mec.E:* languette *f*; clavette plate. **5.** *Row:* nage plate.

feather² **1.** *v.tr.* (*a*) empenner (une flèche); **to tar and f. s.o.,** emplumer qn; *Fig:* **to f. one's nest,** faire sa pelote, son beurre; (*b*) *Row:* ramener (l'aviron) à plat; nager plat; **f. (your oars)!** avirons à plat! (*c*) *Av:* mettre (une hélice) en drapeau. **2.** *v.i.* (*of young bird*) **to f. (out),** s'emplumer. **feathering** *n.* **1.** (*of birds*) plumage *m.* **2.** empennage *m* (d'une flèche). **3.** *Row:* nage plate. **4.** *Av:* mise *f* en drapeau (de l'hélice).

featherbed ['feðəbed] *v.tr.* *F:* subventionner (excessivement). **featherbedding** *n.* réduction *f* de la productivité des ouvriers pour éviter le chômage.

featherbrained ['feðəbreind] *a.* *F:* étourdi.

featheredge ['feðəredʒ] *n.* *Carp: etc:* biseau *m.*

featheredged ['feðəredʒd] *a.* taillé en biseau.

featherstitch ['feðəstitʃ] *n.* *Needlew:* point *m* d'épines.

featherweight ['feðəweit] *n.* *Box:* poids *m* plume.

feathery ['feðəri] *a.* (*of snow, wheat, etc.*) plumeux.

feature¹ ['fiːtʃər] *n.* **1.** (*a*) trait *m* (du visage); **prominent features,** traits accusés; (*b*) trait (de caractère, etc.). **2.** (*a*) trait, caractéristique *f* (d'un paysage, etc.); **main features,** grands traits; **physical features of a country,** topographie *f* d'un pays; **special f.,** particularité; **prominent f.,** trait saillant; **the redeeming f.,** le beau côté (de qch.); (*b*) **paper that makes a f. of sports,** journal qui fait une large place aux sports; (*c*) *Cin:* **f. (film),** long métrage, *F:* grand film; **double-f. programme,** programme à deux longs métrages; (*d*) *Journ:* article *m* vedette, grand reportage; *W.Tel: etc:* numéro *m* vedette; *Com:* article *m* réclame.

feature² *v.tr.* **1.** caractériser, marquer, distinguer (qch.). **2.** *Cin:* (i) représenter (qn); (ii) **film featuring X,** film avec X en vedette. **3.** *Journ:* mettre (une nouvelle) en manchette.

featureless ['fiːtʃəlis] *a.* sans traits bien marqués.

febrifuge ['febrifjuːdʒ] *a.* & *n.* *Med:* fébrifuge (*m*).

febrile ['fiːbrail] *a.* (pouls, etc.) fébrile, fiévreux.

February ['februəri] *n.* février *m*; **in F.,** au mois de février, en février; **(on) the first, the seventh, of F.,** le premier, le sept, février.

fecal ['fiːk(ə)l], **feces** ['fiːsiːz] *n.pl.* *NAm:* = FAECAL, FAECES.

feckless ['feklis] *a.* (*a*) propre à rien; incapable; (*b*) étourdi, irréfléchi.

fecklessness ['feklisnis] *n.* (*a*) incapacité *f*; (*b*) étourderie *f.*

fecundity [fi'kʌnditi] *n.* fécondité *f*, productivité *f.*

fed. *see* FEED².

federal ['fedərəl] **1.** *a.* (*of government, etc.*) fédéral, -aux. **2.** *n.* *U.S.Hist:* fédéral *m*, nordiste *m.*

federalism ['fedərəlizm] *n.* fédéralisme *m.*

federalist ['fedərəlist] *n.* fédéraliste *mf.*

federalize ['fedərəlaiz] *v.tr.* **1.** fédéraliser. **2.** *U.S:* charger le gouvernement fédéral du contrôle de (qch.).

federate¹ ['fedərət] *a.* (*of states, etc.*) fédéré(s).

federate² ['fedəreit] **1.** *v.tr.* fédérer. **2.** *v.i.* se fédérer.

federation [fedə'reiʃ(ə)n] *n.* fédération *f*; **Federations of Employers,** syndicats patronaux.

fee [fiː] *n.* **1.** (*a*) *Hist:* fief *m*; (*b*) *Jur:* propriété *f* héréditaire. **2.** (*a*) honoraires *mpl* (d'un médecin consultant, d'un avocat, etc.); cachet *m* (d'un acteur); jeton *m* de présence (d'un administrateur); (*b*) *Jur:* **property held in f. simple,** propriété *f* sans conditions, libre; (*c*) **school fees,** frais de scolarité; **boarding-school fees,** pension *f*; **entrance f.,** droit d'entrée; *f* **registration f.,** (i) *Post:* taxe de recommandation; (ii) droit d'inscription; **for a small f.,** moyennant une légère redevance.

feeble ['fiːbl] *a.* (*a*) (*of pers.*) faible, infirme, débile; (*of action, etc.*) faible; (*of light*) douteux; *F:* **that's pretty f.,** ça, c'est bien médiocre; (*b*) *F:* (*of pers.*) mou, peu capable. **-bly** *adv.* faiblement.

feeble-minded ['fiːbl'maindid] **1.** *a.* d'esprit faible; arriéré. **2.** *n.pl.* **the f.-m.,** les débiles mentaux.

feeble-mindedness ['fiːbl'maindidnis] *n.* faiblesse *f* d'esprit; arriération *f.*

feebleness ['fiːblnis] (*of pers.*) faiblesse *f*, débilité *f.*

feed¹ [fiːd] *n.* **1.** (*a*) alimentation *f* (d'un animal, etc.); pâturage *m* (des moutons, etc.); (*b*) nourriture *f*, pâture *f* (pour les animaux); fourrage *m* (pour les chevaux, etc.); **horse off his f.,** cheval *m* qui boude sur son avoine; *F:* (*of pers.*) **to be off one's f.,** bouder sur la nourriture; **it's time for baby's f.,** il faut donner à manger au bébé; (*c*) mesure *f*, ration *f* (de nourriture pour les animaux); **f. of oats,** picotin *m* d'avoine; (*d*) *F:* repas *m*; **to have a good f.,** bien manger; (*e*) *Th: etc:* acteur, -trice, qui donne la réplique; (*of comedian*) faire-valoir *m*; **f. line,** réplique *f.* **2.** *Tchn:* (*a*) alimentation *f* (d'une machine, etc.); **gravity f.,** alimentation par gravité; **f. pump,** pompe *f* d'alimentation; **f. pipe,** tuyau *m* d'alimentation; *Cmptr:* **card f.,** mécanisme *m* d'alimentation de cartes; (*b*) appareil *m*, système *m*, d'alimentation; conduit *m* d'alimentation.

feed² *v.* (*p.t.* & *p.p* **fed** [fed]) **I.** *v.tr.* **1.** (*a*) nourrir; donner à manger à (qn); alimenter (une famille, etc.); approvisionner (un pays, etc.); ravitailler (une armée); faire manger (un chien, etc.); affourrager (des bestiaux); allaiter (un bébé); (*of mother bird*) donner la becquée à (ses petits); (*b*) **field that feeds three cows,** champ *m* qui nourrit trois vaches; (*c*) **manure feeds the ground,** le fumier nourrit la terre; **to f. the mind,** nourrir l'esprit; (*d*) alimenter (une machine, le feu, etc.); charger (un fourneau, etc.); *Cmptr:* faire avancer, alimenter (une carte perforée); (*e*) *Fb: etc:* **to f. the forwards,** alimenter les avants; (*f*) *Th:* donner la réplique à (un acteur). **2.** *v.i.* manger; (*of cattle, sheep*) paître, brouter; **to f. on sth.,** se nourrir, vivre, de qch. **feed back** *v.tr.* *Cmptr:* réintroduire, réinjecter (des cartes). **feeding** *n.* **1.** (*a*) alimentation *f* (de qn, d'une machine, etc.); affourragement *m* (des bestiaux); **force(d) f.,** gavage *m*; *Med:* **f. cup,** biberon, canard *m*; (*b*) *Ind:* **f. mechanism,** mécanisme alimentateur. **2.** *Mec.E:* avance *f*, avancement *m* (du travail à l'outil, de l'outil au travail, etc.). **feed up** *v.tr.* (*a*) engraisser (les animaux); (*b*) *F:* **to be fed up,** en avoir assez; en avoir plein le dos; **I'm fed up with it,** j'en ai marre.

feedback ['fiːdbæk] *n.* *Elcs: etc:* réaction *f*, rétroaction *f*, *F:* feed-back *m inv*; *Cmptr:* réaction, rétroaction.

feeder ['fiːdər] *n.* **1.** (*pers.*) (*a*) nourrisseur *m* (de bestiaux); (*b*) *Ind:* alimenteur, -euse (d'une machine, etc.); chargeur, -euse (d'un fourneau, etc.); (*c*) mangeur, -euse; **heavy f.,** gros mangeur. **2.** bavette *f*, bavoir *m* (d'enfant). **3.** (*a*) *Geog:* affluent *m* (d'un cours d'eau); *Hyd.E:* canal *m* d'alimentation, d'amenée; *Trans:* route *f* de raccordement; *Rail:* embranchement *m*; (*b*) canalisation *f* (de gaz, etc.); (*c*) *El:* câble *m*, ligne *f*, d'alimentation.

feel¹ [fiːl] *n.* **1.** toucher *m*, tact *m*; **rough to the f.,**

rude au toucher. **2.** (*a*) toucher, manier *m* (du papier, etc.); **to recognize sth. by the f. of it,** reconnaître qch. au toucher; (*b*) sensation *f*; **the f. of a collar round my neck,** la sensation d'un faux-col autour de mon cou; (*c*) **he has the f. of his car,** il a sa voiture bien en main; **you'll soon get the f. of the work,** vous allez bientôt vous habituer au travail.

feel[2] *v.* (*p.t. & p.p.* **felt** [felt]) **1.** (*a*) *v.tr.* toucher (qch. avec la main); promener les doigts sur (qch.); tâter (le pouls, etc.); palper un membre cassé); manier (une étoffe, etc.); (*b*) *v.tr. & i.* **to f. (about) for sth.,** chercher qch. à tâtons; **to f. one's way,** (i) avancer, marcher, à tâtons; (ii) explorer le terrain; y aller doucement; **to f. one's way towards sth.,** avancer vers qch. à tâtons; **to f. in one's pockets for sth.,** chercher qch. dans ses poches. **2.** (*a*) *v.tr.* sentir (qch.); **I felt the floor trembling,** je sentais trembler le plancher; **she felt his arms around her,** elle se sentait pressée dans ses bras; (*b*) *v.tr. & i.* éprouver (de la douleur, etc.); ressentir (une injure); **to f. the heat,** être incommodé par la chaleur; **to f. the cold,** être sensible au froid; être frileux; **to make one's authority felt,** affirmer son autorité; **to f. for s.o. in his sorrow,** partager la douleur de qn; **I f. for him,** il a toute ma sympathie; (*c*) *v.tr.* avoir conscience de (qch.); **I f. it in my bones that I shall succeed,** quelque chose me dit que je réussirai; **I felt it necessary to intervene,** j'ai jugé nécessaire d'intervenir; **what I f. about it is that . . .,** mon sentiment là-dessus c'est que . . .. **3.** *v.i.* (*of pers.*) (*a*) **to f. hot, cold,** avoir chaud, froid; **to f. ill, tired,** se sentir malade, fatigué; **my foot feels better,** mon pied va mieux; **to f. all the better for it,** s'en trouver mieux; **I f. ten years younger,** je me sens dix ans de moins; **I f. quite myself again,** je me sens tout à fait rétabli; **to f. up to doing sth.,** se sentir (i) assez bien pour faire qch., (ii) de taille à faire qch.; **to f. certain that . . .,** être certain que . . .; (*b*) **I f. as if . . .,** j'ai l'impression que . . .; **to f. like doing sth.,** se sentir d'humeur à faire qch.; **I felt like crying,** j'avais envie de pleurer; **if you f. like it,** si le cœur vous en dit; **I don't f. like it,** ça ne me dit rien; **I f. like a cup of tea,** je prendrais bien une tasse de thé. **4.** *v.i.* (*of thgs, with passive force*) **to f. hard, soft,** être dur, doux, au toucher; **the wall felt hot,** le mur était chaud au toucher; **the room feels damp,** la pièce (me) paraît humide; **it feels like . . .,** cela donne la sensation de . . .. **feeling 1.** *a.* (*of pers.*) sensible. **2.** *n.* (*a*) tâtage *m* (de qch. avec les mains); maniement *m* (du drap); (*b*) **(sense of) f.,** toucher *m*, tact *m*; **to have no f. in one's arm,** avoir le bras mort; (*c*) sensation (douloureuse, de froid, etc.); *F:* **I've got that sinking f.,** (i) j'ai le coup de pompe (de onze heures); (ii) j'ai le trac; (*d*) sentiment *m*; (i) **his feelings towards me,** ses sentiments envers moi; **public f. ran high against the proposal,** le sentiment populaire s'élevait contre cette proposition; **feelings are running very high,** les esprits sont très montés; **no hard feelings!** sans rancune! (ii) **I had a f. of danger,** j'avais le sentiment d'être en danger; **there is a general f. that . . .,** l'impression règne (dans le public) que . . .; (*e*) sensibilité *f*; **a f. for nature,** le sentiment de la nature; **to have a f. for music,** être sensible à la musique; **to have no feelings,** (i) être dépourvu de toute sensibilité; (ii) n'avoir point de cœur; **to suppress one's feelings,** se contenir; **with f.,** (parler, etc.) (i) avec émotion, (ii) avec chaleur; (chanter, etc.) avec âme. **feelingly** *adv.* avec émotion; d'un air ému.

feeler ['fiːlər] *n.* **1.** *Biol:* antenne *f* (d'un insecte, etc.); corne *f* (d'escargot); tentacule *m* (d'un mollusque etc.). **2.** ballon *m* d'essai; **to throw out a f.,** (i) lancer un ballon d'essai; (ii) tâter le terrain; **peace feelers,** sondages de paix. **3.** *Mec.E:* calibre *m* d'épaisseur (à lames).

feet. *see* FOOT[1].

feign [fein] *v.tr.* feindre, simuler (une maladie, etc.); affecter (la surprise).

feint[1] [feint] *n.* (*a*) *Mil:* fausse attaque; (*b*) *Box: Fenc: etc:* feinte *f*; (*c*) **his anger is only a f.,** sa colère n'est qu'une simulation.

feint[2] *v.i.* (*a*) *Mil:* faire une fausse attaque; (*b*) *Box: etc:* feinter; **to f. with the right,** feinter du droit.

feldspar ['feldspɑːr] *n. Miner:* feldspath *m.*

felicitous [fi'lisitəs] *a.* heureux; (*a*) (*of word, etc.*) bien trouvé, à propos; (*b*) (*of pers.*) **f. in his choice of words,** heureux dans le choix de ses mots.

felicity [fi'lisiti] *n.* **1.** félicité *f*, bonheur *m.* **2.** à-propos *m*, bien-trouvé *m* (d'une observation, etc.).

feline ['fiːlain] **1.** *a.* (*a*) *Z:* félin; (*b*) **f. grace,** grâce féline; grâce de chat. **2.** *n. Z:* félin *m.*

fell[1] [fel] *n.* **1.** fourrure *f*; peau *f* (de bête). **2.** toison *f.*

fell[2] *n.* (*N. of Eng.*) colline, montagne, rocheuse.

fell[3] *v.tr.* (*a*) abattre, terrasser (un adversaire, etc.); (*b*) abattre, couper (un arbre); **felled wood, timber,** abattis *m*, bois gisant, vente *f*. **felling** *n.* abattage *m* (d'un bœuf); abattage *m*, coupe *f* (de bois).

fell[4] *a. A: & Lit:* **1.** (*of pers., etc.*) féroce. **2.** (*of thg*) sinistre; **at one f. swoop,** d'un seul coup.

fell[5]. *see* FALL[2].

fellow ['felou] *n.* **1.** camarade *m*, compagnon *m*; **f. passenger, sufferer,** compagnon de voyage, de misère; **f. being, creature,** semblable *mf*; **f. citizen,** concitoyen, -enne; **f. countryman, -woman,** compatriote *mf*; **f. soldier,** compagnon *m* d'armes; camarade *m* de régiment; **f. student,** camarade *mf* d'études; *Pol:* **f. traveller,** communisant, -ante; **f. feeling,** sympathie *f.* **2.** (*of pers., etc.*) semblable *m*, pareil *m*; (*of thg*) pendant *m*; **a vase and its f.,** un vase et son pendant. **3.** (*a*) (*at university*) chargé de cours; (*b*) membre, associé, -ée (d'une société savante); **F. of the Royal Society,** membre de la Société royale (de Londres). **4.** *F: O:* homme *m*; **a good f.,** un brave garçon; **a decent f.,** un bon gars; **he's a queer f.,** c'est un drôle de type; **the poor little f.,** le pauvre petit.

fellowship ['felouʃip] *n.* **1.** communion *f*, communauté *f.* **2. (good) f.,** amitié *f*, camaraderie *f.* **3.** association *f*, corporation *f.* **4.** (*a*) *Sch:* bourse *f* universitaire (avec obligation de faire un cours, des recherches); (*b*) titre *m* de membre, d'associé (d'une société savante).

felon ['felən] *n. Jur:* criminel, -elle.

felonious [fe'louniəs] *a. Jur:* criminel; **f. act,** action *f* qui constitue un crime.

felony ['feləni] *n. Jur:* crime *m*; **to compound a f.,** pactiser avec un crime.

felspar ['felspɑːr] *n.* = FELDSPAR.

felt[1] [felt] *n. Tex: etc:* feutre *m*; **roofing f., tarred f.,** feutre bitumé; **f. (-tipped) pen,** crayon *m* feutre.

felt[2] *v.tr.* (*a*) *Tex:* feutrer (de la laine, des poils); (*b*) couvrir (un toit, etc.) de feutre bitumé.

felt[3]. *see* FEEL[2].

female ['fiːmeil] **1.** *a.* (*a*) (*of pers.*) féminin; (voix, etc.) de femme; **male and f. patients,** malades hommes et femmes; *Jur:* **male and f. heirs,** héritiers *mpl* mâles et femelles; (*b*) (*of animals, plants, etc.*) femelle; (*c*) *Tchn:* femelle; **f. screw,** écrou *m.* **2.** *n.f.* (*a*) *Jur:* (*of pers.*) femme; **a young f.,** une jeune femme; (*b*) (*of animals, plants*) femelle.

feminine ['feminin] *a.* féminin; *Gram:* **in the f. gender,** *n.* **in the f.,** au féminin; **this word is f.,** ce mot est du féminin.

femininity [femi'niniti] *n.* féminéité *f*, féminité *f.*

feminism ['feminizm] *n.* féminisme *m.*

feminist ['feminist] *a. & n.* féministe (*mf*).

femoral ['femərəl] *a. Anat:* fémoral, -aux.

femur, *pl.* **femurs, femora** ['fiːmər, -əz, 'femərə] *n. Anat: etc:* fémur *m.*

fen [fen] *n.* marais *m*, marécage *m*; *Geog:* **the Fens,** les plaines marécageuses de l'Angleterre de l'est.

fence[1] [fens] *n.* **1.** (*a*) clôture *f*; **wire f.,** clôture en fil métallique; **electric f.,** clôture électrique; **sunk f.,** saut *m* de loup; **to sit on the f.,** ménager la chèvre et le chou; se réserver; **to be on the other side of the f.,** être (i) de l'autre côté de la barricade, (ii) *Pol:* du parti opposé; (*b*) *Equit:* obstacle *m*, (i) haie *f*, (ii) barrière *f*; **to put a horse over the fences,** mettre un cheval sur les obstacles. **2.** *Tchn:* (*a*) guide *m* (d'une scie circulaire, etc.); (*b*) garde *f* (d'une machine-outil, etc.). **3.** *F:* receleur, -euse (d'objets volés).

fence[2] **1.** *v.i.* faire de l'escrime; **to f. with a counsel,** répondre en éludant les questions d'un avocat. **2.** *v.tr.* (*a*) protéger; **building fenced from the wind,** bâtiment abrité du vent; (*b*) **to f. off,** parer (une attaque, etc.). **3.** *v.tr.* **to f. in,** clôturer (un terrain, etc.); **to f. off one corner of a field,** séparer un coin d'un champ par une clôture. **4.** *v.i.* faire le recel. **fencing** *n.* **1.** escrime *f*; **f. bout,** assaut *m* d'armes; **f. school,** école *f* d'escrime. **2. f. (in),** action *f* de clôturer (un terrain, etc.). **3.** (*a*) clôture, barrière *f*; **wire f.,** treillage *m* en fil de fer; (*b*) matériaux *mpl* pour clôture. **4.** *F:* recel *m*, recèlement *m*.

fencer ['fensər] *n.* escrimeur *m*.

fend [fend] **1.** *v.tr.* **to f. off,** parer, détourner (un coup, etc.). **2.** *v.i.* **to f. for oneself,** se débrouiller.

fender ['fendər] *n.* (*a*) (i) *NAm:* pare-choc(s) *m inv* (de locomotive, de tramway); (ii) chasse-pierres *m inv*; (*b*) *Nau:* bourrelet *m* de défense; (*c*) *NAm: Aut:* garde-boue *m inv*; (*d*) (*protecting wall, door post, etc.*) bouteroue *f*; (*e*) *Furn:* garde-cendre *m inv*.

fenland ['fenlænd] *n.* pays marécageux.

fennel ['fen(ə)l] *n.* fenouil *m*; **sweet f.,** fenouil officinal.

ferment[1] ['fə:ment] *n.* **1.** ferment *m*. **2.** (*a*) fermentation *f* (des liquides); (*b*) agitation populaire, ouvrière; **the whole town was in a (state of) f.,** toute la ville était en effervescence, dans un état d'agitation.

ferment[2] [fə'ment] **1.** *v.i.* (*a*) (*of liquids, etc.*) fermenter; (*of wine*) travailler; (*b*) (*of sedition, etc.*) fermenter. **2.** *v.tr.* fermenter (un liquide, etc.).

fermentation [fə:men'teiʃ(ə)n] *n.* (*a*) fermentation *f* (d'un liquide, etc.); travail *m* (du vin); (*b*) *Fig:* agitation *f*.

fern [fə:n] *n. Bot:* fougère *f*; *coll.* **hillside covered with f.,** coteau couvert de fougères.

ferocious [fə'rouʃəs] *a.* (*of animal, pers., look, etc.*) féroce. **-ly** *adv.* férocement, avec férocité.

ferocity [fə'rɔsiti] *n.* férocité *f*.

ferret[1] ['ferit] *n. Z:* furet *m*.

ferret[2] *v.* **(ferreted; ferreting) 1.** *v.i.* fureter; chasser au furet; **to f. (about) in one's pockets,** fureter, fouiller, dans ses poches (**for sth.,** pour trouver qch.). **2.** *v.tr.* chasser (les lapins, etc.) au furet; **to f. out,** dénicher (qn, qch.); déterrer (un secret). **ferreting** *n.* chasse *f* au furet.

ferrety ['feriti] *a.* de furet; *Pej:* **f. eyes,** yeux de fouine.

ferric ['ferik] *a. Ch:* ferrique; **f. ammonium salt,** sel *m* ferrico-ammonique.

Ferris wheel ['feris(h)wi:l] *n.* la grande roue (dans les parcs d'attractions).

ferrite ['ferait] *n.* ferrite *m*.

ferro-concrete ['ferou'kɔŋjri:t] *n.* béton armé.

ferromagnetic ['feroumæg'netik] *a.* ferromagnétique.

ferrous ['ferəs] *a. Ch:* (oxyde, etc.) ferreux; **f. sulphide,** pyrite *f* de fer.

ferrule ['fer(ə)l, 'ferju:l] *n.* frette *f* (d'un manche d'outil, etc.); bout ferré, embout *m* (de canne).

ferry[1] ['feri] *n.* (*a*) (endroit *m* de) passage *m* (d'un cours d'eau en bac); *F:* le bac; **to cross the f.,** passer le bac; (*b*) bac *m*; **passenger, car, f.,** bac à piétons, à voitures; **train f.,** bac transbordeur; ferry-boat *m*, *pl.* ferry-boats; **air f.,** avion transbordeur; **to take the f.,** prendre le bac; (*c*) *Jur:* **f. (right),** droit *m* de bac.

ferry[2] *v.tr.* **to f. s.o., a car, across a river,** passer qn, une voiture, en bac; transborder qn, une voiture; **he spent the day ferrying voters to the poll,** il a passé la journée à transporter des électeurs aux urnes. **ferrying** *n.* **1.** transport *m* en, par, bac. **2. f. across,** passage *m* en bac.

ferryboat ['feribout] *n.* bac *m*.

ferryman, *pl.* **-men** ['ferimən] *n.m.* passeur.

fertile ['fə:tail] *a.* (*a*) (sol, etc.) fertile, fécond (**in,** en); productif (**of,** de); **f. imagination,** imagination *f* fertile; (*b*) (œuf) fécondé.

fertility [fə:'tiliti] *n.* fertilité *f*, fécondité *f* (du sol, de l'imagination de qn, etc.); productivité *f* (du sol).

fertilization [fə:tilai'zeiʃ(ə)n] *n.* fertilisation *f*, fécondation *f* (d'un œuf, etc.); **cross f.,** fécondation croisée; *Biol:* **self f.,** autofécondation *f*.

fertilize ['fə:tilaiz] *v.tr.* **1.** fertiliser, féconder (un œuf, une plante, etc.); *Bot:* **to cross f.,** hybrider (deux espèces). **2.** fertiliser, engraisser (le sol).

fertilizer ['fə:tilaizər] *n. Agr:* engrais *m*; **artificial fertilizers,** engrais chimiques.

fervent ['fə:vənt] *a.* ardent, fervent; **f. prayer,** prière ardente, fervente. **-ly** *adv.* (prier, etc.) avec ferveur; (désirer, etc.) avec ardeur.

fervour, *NAm:* **fervor** ['fə:vər] *n.* ferveur *f*, ardeur *f*.

fescue ['feskju:] *n. Bot:* **f. (grass),** fétuque *f*.

fess(e) [fes] *n. Her:* fasce *f*.

fester ['festər] *v.i.* (*a*) (*of wound, etc.*) suppurer, s'envenimer; (*b*) (*of resentment, etc.*) couver. **festering 1.** *a.* (*of wound, etc.*) ulcéreux, suppurant. **2.** *n.* suppuration *f*, ulcération *f* (d'une blessure, etc.).

festival ['festiv(ə)l] *n.* (*a*) fête *f*; *Ecc:* **harvest f.,** office d'action de grâces (célébré après la rentrée des récoltes); (*b*) *Mus:* festival *m*, -als; **film f.,** festival du film.

festive ['festiv] *a.* **1.** (jour, etc.) de fête; (table, etc.) du festin; **the f. season,** l'époque *f* des fêtes. **2.** (*of pers.*) **to be in f. mood,** avoir le cœur en fête.

festivity [fes'tiviti] *n.* fête *f*, réjouissance *f*, festivité *f*.

festoon[1] [fes'tu:n] *n.* feston *m*, guirlande *f*.

festoon[2] *v.tr.* (*a*) festonner (qch.) (**with,** de) (*b*) disposer (des fleurs, etc.) en festons.

fetal ['fi:tl] *a. NAm:* = FOETAL.

fetch [fetʃ] *v.tr.* **1.** aller chercher (qn, qch.); **to f. water from the river,** aller puiser de l'eau dans la rivière; (*b*) apporter (qch.); amener (qn); (*to dog*) **f. (it)!** va chercher! (*of pers.*) **to f. and carry for s.o.,** être aux ordres de qn. **2.** *Com: etc:* (i) rapporter, (ii) atteindre (un certain prix); **it fetched a high price,** cela s'est vendu cher. **3.** pousser (un soupir, un gémissement). **4.** *P:* **to f. s.o. a blow,** flanquer un coup à qn. **fetch back** *v.tr.* ramener (qn); rapporter (qch.). **fetching** *a.* (sourire, air) séduisant, attrayant; (chapeau) ravissant. **fetch up 1.** *v.tr.* faire monter (qn, qch.). **2.** *v.i. Nau:* **to f. up at a port,** parvenir, arriver, à un port; *F:* **they finally fetched up at our house,** ils ont finalement abouti chez nous; **the car fetched up against a wall,** la voiture s'est (finalement) arrêtée en heurtant un mur.

fête[1] [feit] *n.* fête *f*; **village f.,** fête communale.

fête[2] *v.tr.* fêter (qn, un événement); faire fête à (qn).

fetid ['fetid, 'fi:tid] *a.* fétide, puant.

fetish ['fetiʃ] *n.* fétiche *m*.

fetishism ['fetiʃizm] *n.* fétichisme *m*.

fetishist ['fetiʃist] *n.* fétichiste *mf*.

fetlock ['fetlɔk] *n.* fanon *m* (du cheval); **f. joint,** boulet *m*.

fetter[1] ['fetər] *n. usu. in pl.* chaînes *fpl*, fers *mpl*. (d'un prisonnier, etc.); **in fetters,** enchaîné; dans les fers; **to burst one's fetters,** rompre ses liens, ses fers.

fetter² *v.tr.* enchaîner (qn); entraver (un cheval).
fettle¹ ['fetl] *n.* **to be in fine, good, f.,** être en condition, en forme, en bon état.
fettle² *v.tr. Metall:* ébarber; abavurer.
fetus ['fi:təs] *n. NAm:* = FOETUS.
feud¹ [fju:d] *n.* inimitié *f* (entre familles, clans, etc.); **family blood f.,** vendetta *f.*
feud² *v.i.* se quereller (**over,** au sujet de).
feudal ['fju:d(ə)l] *a. Hist:* (régime, service, etc.) féodal, -aux. **-ally** *adv.* féodalement.
feudalism ['fju:dəlizm] *n.* le système féodal.
fever ['fi:vər] *n.* (*a*) *Med:* (*high temperature*) fièvre *f;* **high f.,** forte fièvre; (*b*) *Med:* (*disease*) fièvre; **yellow f.,** fièvre jaune; **hay f.,** rhume *m* des foins; **scarlet f.,** scarlatine *f; Vet:* **swine f.,** rouget *m* du porc; (*c*) **f. of joy, of excitement,** joie, excitation, fébrile, fiévreuse; **expectation was f. high, had reached f. pitch,** l'attente *f* était fiévreuse; *Hist:* **gold f.,** fièvre de l'or.
fevered ['fi:vəd] *a.* enfiévré, fiévreux.
feverish ['fi:v(ə)riʃ] *a. Med:* fiévreux, fébrile; **to feel f.,** se sentir fiévreux; *Fig:* **f. activity,** activité fébrile, fiévreuse. **-ly** *adv.* fiévreusement, fébrilement.
feverishness ['fi:v(ə)riʃnis] *n.* état *m* fébrile.
few [fju:] *a.* **1.** (*a*) peu de (personnes, choses); **he has f. friends,** il a peu d'amis; **with f. exceptions,** à de rares exceptions près; **trains every f. minutes,** trains *mpl* à quelques minutes d'intervalle; **every f. days,** tous les deux ou trois jours; (*b*) **a f.,** quelques; **I have only a f. pounds,** je n'ai que quelques livres; **he had a good f. enemies,** il avait pas mal d'ennemis; **in a f. minutes,** dans quelques minutes; (*c*) peu nombreux, rares; **his visits are f. and far between,** ses visites sont rarissimes. **2.** (*with noun function*) (*a*) peu (de gens, etc.); **there are very f. of us,** nous sommes peu nombreux; **the fortunate f.,** une minorité de gens heureux; (*b*) quelques-uns, -unes; **a f. of these cakes, of these oranges,** quelques-uns de ces gâteaux, quelques-unes de ces oranges; **a f. of the survivors,** quelques-uns des survivants; **I know a f. of them,** j'en connais quelques-uns; **a f. of us,** quelques-uns d'entre nous.
fewer ['fju:ər] *a.* (*comp. of* FEW) **1.** moins (de); **there are f. (of them) than I thought,** il y en a moins que je n'avais pensé. **2.** plus rares, moins nombreux; **the houses became f.,** les maisons devenaient plus rares.
fewest ['fju:ist] *a.* (*sup. of* FEW) **1.** le moins (de); **the f. people possible,** le moins de gens possible. **2.** les plus rares; **the area where there are the f. houses,** la région où les maisons sont les moins nombreuses.
fey [fei] *a. Scot:* **1.** (*a*) qui a des pressentiments de mort, des visions de l'au-delà; (*b*) qui est doué de seconde vue. **2.** un peu idiot.
fez [fez] *n. Cost:* fez *m.*
fiancé, *f.* **-ée** [fi'ɑ̃:nsei] *n.* fiancé, -ée.
fiasco [fi'æskou] *n.* fiasco *m* (*of play*); **to be a f.,** faire four.
fib¹ [fib] *n. F:* petit mensonge; conte *m,* blague *f.*
fib² *v.i.* **(fibbed)** *F:* mentir; blaguer; en conter (à qn).
fibber ['fibər] *n. F:* menteur, -euse; blagueur *m.*
fibre, *NAm:* **fiber** ['faibər] *n.* **1.** (*a*) fibre *f;* **muscle f.,** fibre musculaire; **every f. of his being revolted at the idea,** chaque fibre de son être se révoltait à cette idée; (*b*) **our moral f.,** notre nature *f;* (*c*) *Metall:* fibre, nerf *m* (de l'acier). **2.** *Com:* **vegetable f.,** crin végétal; **wood f.,** fibre de bois; **glass f.,** fibre de verre.
fibreboard ['faibəbɔ:d] *n.* panneau *m* de fibres agglomérées.
fibreglass ['faibəglɑ:s] *n.* fibre *f* de verre.
fibrillation [faibri'leiʃ(ə)n] *n.* fibrillation *f.*
fibroid ['faibrɔid] **1.** *a.* (tumeur, etc.) fibroïde. **2.** *n. Med:* fibrome *m.*
fibroma, *pl.* **-mata** [fai'broumə(tə)] *n. Med:* fibrome *m.*
fibrositis [faibrou'saitis] *n. Med:* fibrosite *f.*
fibrous ['faibrəs] *a.* (tissu, etc.) fibreux.
fickle ['fikl] *a.* inconstant, volage, capricieux; (caractère) changeant, versatile.
fickleness ['fik(ə)lnis] *n.* inconstance *f;* humeur *f* volage.
fiction ['fikʃ(ə)n] *n.* **1.** fiction *f,* création *f* de l'imagination; *Jur:* **legal f.,** fiction légale; **these tales are pure f.,** tous ces contes sont de pure invention. **2.** **(works of) f.,** romans *mpl;* **light f.,** romans de lecture facile; **science f.,** science-fiction *f;* (*in library, bookshop*) **fiction,** romans.
fictional ['fikʃən(ə)l] *a.* fictif.
fictionalize ['fikʃənəlaiz] *v.tr.* romancer.
fictitious [fik'tiʃəs] *a.* **1.** fictif; *Com:* **f. assets,** actif fictif. **2.** (récit) inventé. **-ly** *adv.* fictivement.
fiddle¹ ['fidl] *n.* **1.** *F:* (*a*) violon *m;* **bass f.,** contrebasse *f;* (*b*) (joueur, -euse, de) violon; **to play second f. (to s.o.),** jouer un rôle secondaire (auprès de qn). **2.** *Nau:* violon de mer; fiche *f* de roulis. **3.** *F:* combine *f;* **to be on the f.,** faire du fricotage.
fiddle² *v. F:* **1.** *v.i.* (i) jouer du violon; (ii) *Pej:* racler du violon; *Fig:* **to f. while Rome burns,** s'occuper de choses futiles au lieu de lutter contre une calamité. **2.** (*a*) *v.i.* bricoler; fignoler; **to f. with one's watch,** jouer avec sa montre; **don't f. with the mechanism,** laissez le mécanisme tranquille; ne trifouillez pas le mécanisme; (*b*) (i) *v.i.* combiner, fricoter; (ii) *v.tr.* bricoler (un compteur, etc.); **to f. the accounts,** truquer les comptes; **he fiddled a week's leave,** il a carotté huit jours de permission. **fiddling** *F:* **1.** *a.* (*a*) (*of thg*) futile, insignifiant; (*b*) (besogne) agaçante. **2.** *n.* (*a*) raclage *m* (de violon); (*b*) **f. about,** tripotage *m;* (*c*) combines *fpl;* fricotage *m.*
fiddlededee [fidldi'di:] *int. F: O:* bah! turlututu!
fiddlefaddle ['fidlfædl] *F:* **1.** *n.* bagatelles *fpl,* balivernes *fpl,* fadaises *fpl.* **2.** *int.* = FIDDLEDEDEE.
fiddler ['fidlər] *n.* **1.** *F:* (*a*) violoneur *m;* joueur *m* de violon; (*b*) **strolling f.,** violoneux *m.* **2.** *F:* (*a*) bricoleur, -euse; (*b*) combinard, -arde.
fiddlestick ['fid(ə)lstik] *F: O:* **1.** *n.* archet *m* (de violon). **2.** *int.* **fiddlesticks!** balivernes! quelle blague!
fiddly ['fidli] *a.* (travail) délicat, minutieux.
fidelity [fi'deliti] *n.* **1.** fidélité *f* (d'un ami, etc.); loyauté *f* (de qn). **2.** fidélité, exactitude *f* (d'une traduction); *Rec:* **high f.,** haute fidélité.
fidget¹ ['fidʒit] *n. F:* **1.** *usu. pl.* **the fidgets,** agitation nerveuse; **to have the fidgets,** ne pas tenir en place. **2.** (*of pers.*) **he's a f.,** il ne tient pas en place; **what a f. you are!** mais tiens-toi donc tranquille!
fidget² *v.* **(fidgeted)** *v.i.* (*a*) **to f. (about),** remuer continuellement; ne pas tenir en place; (*to child*) **don't f.!** tiens-toi tranquille! (*b*) s'énerver.
fidgetiness ['fidʒitinis] *n.* agitation nerveuse.
fidgety ['fidʒiti] *a. F:* **1.** qui ne tient pas en place; qui remue continuellement. **2.** nerveux; impatient.
fiduciary [fi'dju:ʃəri] **1.** *a. Jur: Fin:* fiduciaire. **2.** *n.* (*a*) héritier *m* fiduciare; (*b*) dépositaire *m.*
fief [fi:f] *n. Hist:* fief *m.*
field [fi:ld] *n.* **1.** (*a*) *Agr: etc:* champ *m;* (*under pasture*) pré *m;* **f. of wheat,** champ de blé; **strawberry f.,** plantation *f* de fraisiers; **in the open f.,** en plein champ; (*b*) district *m,* région *f;* (*in comb. fm.*) champ (pétrolifère, etc.); gisement (houiller, pétrolifère); (*c*) *Mil:* **f. (of battle),** champ de bataille; **in the f.,** en campagne; **to hold the f.,** (i) *Mil:* (*of army*) se maintenir sur ses positions; (ii) (*of theory, etc.*) faire autorité; **f. of honour,** champ d'honneur; **f. service,** service *m* en campagne; **f. hospital,** ambulance *f* divisionnaire; **f. artillery,** artillerie *f* de campagne; **f. gun,** canon *m* de campagne; **f. telegraph,** télégraphe *m* militaire; **f. exercise,** exercice *m* en campagne; manœuvre *f;* **f. rations,** ration *f* de guerre; **f. day,** (i) jour *m* de grandes manœuvres, de revue; (ii) *esp. NAm:*

réunion *f* athlétique; (iii) journée *f* de grands événements, grande occasion; (*e*) *Av:* **landing f.,** terrain *m* d'atterrissage. **2.** (*a*) *Fb: Cr: etc:* terrain; (*baseball*) champ; (*b*) *Cr:* l'équipe du bôleur; (*c*) **f. events,** épreuves *fpl* d'athlétisme. **3.** *Turf:* (i) **the f.,** le champ; les partants; **big f.,** champ fourni; *Fig:* **there are three candidates in the f.,** il y a trois candidatures de déposées; (ii) **the f. (of runners),** le peloton; **to lead the f.,** mener le peloton. **4.** (*a*) étendue *f*, espace *m* (de mer, de ciel, etc.); (*b*) *Her:* champ, sol *m*; (*c*) *Art:* champ, fond *m* (d'un tableau, etc.); *Num:* champ (d'une médaille). **5.** (*a*) théâtre *m*, champ (d'opération, etc.); domaine *m* (d'une science); **in the political f.,** sur le plan politique; (*b*) *Com:* marché *m* (pour un produit); (*c*) **f. work,** (i) travaux *mpl*, recherches *fpl*, sur le terrain, sur les lieux; (ii) *Min: etc:* exploration *f*; (iii) *Com:* démarchage *m* auprès de la clientèle; **f. study,** étude *f* sur le terrain, sur les lieux; **f. engineer,** ingénieur *m* de chantier, sur le terrain. **6.** (*a*) *Opt: Phot:* champ; **f. of view, of vision,** champ visuel; **f. glasses,** jumelles *fpl*; (*b*) *Ph:* **f. of force,** champ de force; **magnetic f.,** champ magnétique; **f. coil,** bobine *f* d'excitation, d'inducteur; bobine inductrice.

field[2] **1.** *v.i. Cr:* tenir le champ (pour relancer la balle). **2.** *v.tr.* (*a*) *Cr:* **to f. a ball,** arrêter (et relancer) une balle (dans le champ); (*b*) *Sp:* réunir (une équipe); (*c*) *Mil: etc:* **to be able to f. 50,000 men,** pouvoir mettre 50.000 hommes en ligne; *Pol:* **to f. 500 candidates,** présenter 500 candidats.

fielder ['fi:ldər] *n. Sp: Cr: etc:* chasseur *m*.

fieldmouse, *pl.* **-mice** ['fi:ldmaus, -mais] *n.* mulot *m*.

fiend [fi:nd] *n.* **1.** (*a*) démon *m*, diable *m*; (*b*) monstre *m* (de cruauté); *F:* **he's a perfect f.,** c'est un vrai suppôt de Satan. **2.** *F:* **fresh-air f.,** maniaque *mf*, fanatique *mf*, du plein air; **dope f.,** toxicomane *mf*.

fiendish ['fi:ndiʃ] *a.* diabolique; satanique; **to take a f. pleasure in sth.,** prendre un plaisir diabolique à qch. **-ly** *adv.* **1.** infernalement. **2.** *F:* **it was f. cold,** il faisait un froid de tous les diables.

fierce ['fiəs] *a.* (*a*) (*of pers.*) violent; brutal, -aux; (*of animal*) féroce; (*of fire, etc.*) ardent; (*of battle, etc.*) acharné; (*of wind, etc.*) furieux, violent; **f. encounter,** rencontre violente; (*b*) *Aut: etc:* **f. brake,** frein brutal; (*c*) *NAm: F:* désagréable; **the weather has been f.,** il a fait un temps de chien. **-ly** *adv.* violemment; avec acharnement.

fierceness ['fiəsnis] *n.* violence *f*, véhémence *f* (de qn); férocité *f* (d'un animal); ardeur *f* (du feu, etc.); acharnement *m* (de la bataille); fureur *f* (du vent, etc.); *Aut: etc:* brutalité *f* (des freins).

fieriness ['faiərinis] *n.* **1.** (*a*) ardeur *f* (du soleil); (*b*) saveur cuisante (d'une boisson spiritueuse). **2.** ardeur, fougue *f*, impétuosité *f*, emportement *m*.

fiery ['faiəri] *a.* **1.** ardent, brûlant, enflammé; **f. furnace,** fournaise ardente; **f. red,** rouge ardent, rouge feu; **f. sky,** ciel embrasé; **f. taste,** saveur cuisante. **2.** (*of pers.*) (i) fougueux, emporté, impétueux; (ii) colérique, bouillant; **to make f. speeches against s.o.,** vomir feu et flamme contre qn.

fife [faif] *n. Mus:* fifre *m*.

fifteen [fif'ti:n, 'fifti:n] *num.a.* & *n.* quinze (*m*); **she is f. (years old),** elle a quinze ans; **the plane will land at f. thirty (15.30),** l'avion va atterrir à quinze heures trente (15h.30); *Rugby Fb:* **the French f.,** le quinze français.

fifteenth [fif'ti:nθ, 'fifti:nθ] **1.** *num.a.* & *n.* quinzième; **Louis the F.,** Louis Quinze; **(on) the f. (of the month),** le quinze du mois. **2.** *n.* quinzième *m*.

fifth [fifθ] **1.** *num.a.* & *n.* cinquième; **Henry the F.,** Henri Cinq; *Sch:* **f. form,** *approx.* = classe *f* de seconde; *Pol:* **f. column,** cinquième colonne. **2.** *n.* (*a*) cinquième *m*; **two fifths,** deux cinquièmes; (*b*) *Mus:* quinte *f*; **diminished f.,** quinte diminuée.

fifthly ['fifθli] *adv.* cinquièmement.

fifth-rate ['fifθreit] *a.* médiocre.

fiftieth ['fiftiəθ] *num.a.* & *n.* cinquantième (*m*).

fifty ['fifti] *num.a.* & *n.* cinquante (*m*); **f.-one, -two,** cinquante et un, cinquante-deux; **f.-f.** moitié-moitié; **to go f.-f. with s.o.,** se mettre de moitié avec qn; **about f. books,** une cinquantaine de livres; **the fifties,** les années cinquante (1950–1959); **she is in her fifties,** elle a passé la cinquantaine.

fig [fig] *n.* **1.** figue *f*; **green figs,** figues fraîches; **dried figs,** figues sèches; *F:* **a f. for him,** zut pour lui! **2. f. (tree),** figuier *m*.

fight[1] [fait] *n.* **1.** (*a*) *Mil: etc:* combat *m*; engagement *m*, action *f*; (*b*) combat (entre deux personnes, deux animaux, etc.); *Box:* assaut *m* (de boxe); **hand to hand f.,** (lutte *f*) corps à corps (*m*); **f. to the death,** lutte à mort; **free f.,** (i) rixe *f*, bagarre *f*; (ii) mêlée générale; **they had a f.,** ils se sont battus. **2.** (*a*) **the f. for life,** la lutte pour la vie; **to carry on a stubborn f. against s.o.,** soutenir une lutte opiniâtre contre qn; (*b*) **to show f.,** résister; offrir de la résistance; *Sp: etc:* **to put up a good f.,** bien se défendre; **there was no f. left in him,** il n'avait plus de cœur à se battre.

fight[2] *v.* (*p.t.* & *p.p.* **fought** [fɔ:t]) **1.** *v.i.* (*a*) se battre; lutter; **to f. against the enemy,** combattre l'ennemi; **to f. against adversity,** lutter contre l'adversité; **to f. against sleep,** lutter contre le sommeil; **to f. for s.o.,** se battre pour qn; **to f. for sth.,** (i) se battre pour une cause, etc.; (ii) se battre pour avoir qch.; **two dogs fighting over a bone,** deux chiens *mpl* qui se disputent un os; **to f. fair,** faire la bonne guerre; (*b*) (*with cogn. acc.*) **to f. a battle,** livrer (une) bataille; **to f. the good fight,** combattre pour la bonne cause; **the match was fought yesterday,** le match (de boxe, etc.) s'est disputé hier; **to f. s.o.'s battles,** prendre le parti de qn; **to f. one's way (out),** se frayer un passage (pour sortir); **to f. an action (at law),** se défendre dans un procès. **2.** *v.tr.* se battre avec, contre (qn); combattre (qn, un incendie, une maladie). **fight back 1.** *v.tr.* lutter contre (une émotion, etc.); refouler (ses larmes); **to f. one's way back again,** remonter le courant. **2.** *v.i.* résister; se battre; **to f. back against an illness,** combattre une maladie. **fight down** *v.tr.* vaincre (une passion, la résistance, etc.). **fighting 1.** *a.* militant, de combat; *Mil:* **f. men,** combattants *mpl*; **f. forces,** effectifs *mpl* sous les armes. **2.** *n.* combat *m*; *Box:* pugilat *m*, boxe *f*; **close f.,** (lutte *f*) corps à corps (*m*); **f. cock,** coq *m* de combat; *Mil:* **f. unit,** unité combattante; **f. strength,** effectif *m* de combat; *F:* **I still have a f. chance,** j'ai encore une chance si je résiste jusqu'au bout; **f. drunk,** dans un état d'ivresse agressive. **fight off** *v.tr.* (*a*) résister (avec effort) à (une maladie, etc.); **to f. off a cold with aspirin,** juguler un rhume à force d'aspirine; (*b*) repousser (l'ennemi). **fight out** *v.tr.* **to f. it out,** (i) se battre jusqu'à une décision; (ii) vider une querelle.

fighter ['faitər] *n.* **1.** combattant *m*; **he is not a f.,** il n'a rien de combatif. **2.** *Mil.Av:* chasseur *m*, avion *m* de chasse; **f. bomber,** chasseur-bombardier *m*, *pl.* chasseurs-bombardiers.

figleaf ['figli:f] *n.* **1.** feuille *f* de figuier. **2.** *Art:* feuille de vigne.

figment ['figmənt] *n.* fiction *f*, invention *f*; **figments of the imagination,** imaginations *fpl*.

figuration [figju'reiʃ(ə)n] *n.* **1.** figuration *f* (d'une idée, etc.). **2.** représentation figurative. **3.** *Mus:* contrepoint fleuri.

figurative ['figjurətiv] *a.* **1.** (*of language, etc.*) figuré, métaphorique; **in the f. sense,** au figuré. **2.** (art) figuratif; **f. writing,** écriture *f* en images. **-ly** *adv.* **1.** figurativement. **2.** au figuré; métaphoriquement.

figure¹ ['figər, *NAm: also* 'figjər] *n.* **1.** (*a*) figure *f*; (*b*) (*of pers.*) taille *f*, silhouette *f*; **to have a good f.,** être bien fait de sa personne; (*of woman*) avoir une jolie taille; **to look after, keep, one's f.,** soigner, garder, sa ligne. **2.** (*a*) forme humaine; **a fine f. of a man, of a woman,** un bel homme, une belle femme; **a f. of fun,** un grotesque; (*b*) personnage *m*; **a distinguished f.,** une personnalité; (*c*) figure, apparence *f*, air *m*; **to cut a sorry f.,** faire piètre figure. **3.** *Art: etc:* image *f*, représentation *f* (de la forme humaine); **the central f. of a painting,** le personnage principal d'un tableau. **4.** (*a*) illustration *f* (dans un livre); **geometrical f.,** figure géométrique; (*b*) dessin *m* (sur un tissu); (*c*) **the figures of a dance,** les figures d'une danse; **f. skating, skater,** patinage *m*, patineur, -euse, artistique. **5.** (*a*) *Mth: etc:* chiffre *m*; **in round figures,** en chiffres ronds; **to carry a f.,** retenir un chiffre; **to be good at figures,** être bon en calcul; **f. of eight,** *Mth:* huit-de-chiffre(s) *m*, *pl.* huits-de-chiffres; figure en forme de huit; *Com:* **sales figures,** chiffres de vente; **to fetch a high f.,** se vendre cher; **our takings have reached four figures,** nous avons décroché les quatre chiffres; (*b*) **figures,** détails chiffrés (d'un projet, etc.); statistiques *fpl*; **the figures for 1975,** les statistiques de 1975. **6. f. of speech,** (i) figure de rhétorique; (ii) façon *f* de parler.

figure² **1.** *v.tr.* (*a*) figurer, représenter (qn, un paysage, etc.); **f. to yourself a happy family,** imaginez une famille heureuse; (*b*) *NAm:* estimer, évaluer; **I f. that it will take three years,** j'estime que cela prendra trois ans; (*c*) brocher, gaufrer (la soie, etc.); imprimer (le coton, etc.); (*d*) *Mus:* chiffrer (la basse). **2.** *v.i.* (*a*) chiffrer, calculer; faire des chiffres; (*b*) (*appear*) figurer; **his name figures on the list,** son nom se trouve sur la liste; (*c*) *NAm: F:* sembler logique, normal; **that figures,** ça colle. **figured** *n.* **1.** (*of material, etc.*) façonné; (*of silk, etc.*) broché. **2.** (bois) ronceux. **3.** *Mus:* (*a*) (contrepoint) figuré; (*b*) (basse) chiffrée. **figure on** *v.tr. NAm: F:* (*a*) compter sur, s'attendre à (qch.); (*b*) compter sur (qn); (*c*) **to f. on doing sth.,** avoir l'intention de, compter, faire qch. **figure out** *F:* **1.** *v.i.* **it will f. out at about £100,** cela coûtera une centaine de livres. **2.** *v.tr.* calculer (une somme); résoudre (un problème); **he couldn't f. out what she meant,** il ne pouvait pas comprendre ce qu'elle voulait dire. **figure up** *v.tr. esp. U.S:* additionner, calculer (des comptes, etc.).

figurehead ['figəhed, *NAm:* 'figjəhed] *n.* **1.** *N.Arch:* figure *f* de proue. **2.** (*a*) homme *m* de paille; prête-nom *m*, *pl.* prête-noms; (*b*) personnage purement décoratif.

figurine ['figəri:n, *NAm:* 'figjəri:n] *n.* figurine *f*.

Fiji ['fi:dʒi:] *Pr.n.* **the F. Islands,** les îles *fpl* Fidji.

Fijian [fi:'dʒi:ən] **1.** *a.* fidjien. **2.** *n.* Fidjien, -ienne.

filament ['filəmənt] *n.* **1.** *Nat.Hist:* filament *m*, filet *m*. **2.** *El:* filament; **f. lamp,** lampe à incandescence.

filbert ['filbət] *n.* aveline *f*; grosse noisette.

filch [fil(t)ʃ] *v.tr.* chiper **(sth. from s.o.,** qch. à qn).

file¹ [fail] *n. Tls:* lime *f*; *Toil:* **nail f.,** lime à ongles.

file² *v.tr.* limer (le métal, etc.); **to f. down,** enlever (une saillie, etc.) à la lime; adoucir (une surface) à la lime; *Farr:* raboter (le sabot d'un cheval); *Toil:* **to f. one's nails,** se donner un coup de lime aux ongles. **filing** *n.* **1.** limage *m*; **f. down,** adoucissement *m* à la lime; rabotage *m* (des sabots de cheval). **2. filings,** limaille *f*.

file³ *n.* **1.** classeur *m*; casier *m*; **cardboard f.,** chemise *f*; **card-index f.,** fichier *m*; **f. card,** fiche *f* (de classeur); **card f.,** fichier sur cartes; **master f.,** fichier permanent; *esp. NAm:* **f. clerk,** documentaliste *mf*. **2.** collection *f*, liasse *f* (de papiers); **files,** archives *fpl*; *Jur: etc:* dossier *m*; **we have placed your report on our files,** nous avons ajouté votre rapport au dossier; **f. copy,** exemplaire *m* d'archives; **f. number,** cote *f* (d'un document dans un dossier).

file⁴ *v.tr.* **1.** classer (des fiches, des lettres, etc.). **2.** (*a*) *Jur:* **to f. a petition,** (i) enregistrer une requête; (ii) déposer une requête; **to f. one's petition (in bankruptcy),** déposer son bilan; (*b*) *esp. U.S: Adm:* déposer (un document, une plainte). **filing** *n.* **1.** classement *m* (de documents, de fiches, etc.); **f. system,** méthode *f* de classement; **f. cabinet,** fichier *m*; **f. tray,** corbeille *f* pour correspondance à classer; **f. clerk,** documentaliste *mf*. **2.** *Jur:* (*a*) enregistrement *m* (d'une requête); (*b*) dépôt *m* (d'une demande).

file⁵ *n.* file *f*; **in single, Indian, f.,** en file indienne; **to walk in single f.,** marcher à la file, en file indienne; *Mil:* **in f.,** (en colonne) par deux.

file⁶ *v.i.* marcher à la file, en ligne de file; **to f. off,** défiler; **to f. past a catafalque,** défiler devant un catafalque; **to f. in, out,** entrer, sortir, un à un.

filial ['filiəl] *a.* filial, -aux. **-ally** *adv.* filialement.

filibuster¹ ['filibʌstər] *n.* **1.** *Hist:* flibustier *m*. **2.** *Parl:* obstruction *f*.

filibuster² *v.i.* **1.** *Hist:* faire le flibustier. **2.** *Parl:* faire de l'obstruction; **filibustering tactics,** manœuvres obstructionnistes. **filibustering** *n.* obstruction *f*.

filigree ['filigri:] *n.* filigrane *m*; **f. work,** (travail *m* en) filigrane.

fill¹ [fil] *n.* **1. to have one's f. of sth.,** avoir assez de qch.; **to eat one's f.,** manger à sa faim. **2.** (*a*) charge *f*, plein *m*; **a f. of tobacco,** une pipe de tabac; (*b*) *Tchn:* matériau *m* de remplissage; *Civ.E:* remblai *m*.

fill² **I.** *v.tr.* **1.** (*a*) remplir, emplir (une cruche, etc.) **(with,** de); bourrer (sa pipe); entonner (des saucisses); charger (un wagon, etc.); **to f. s.o.'s glass,** (i) servir à boire à qn; (ii) (*to the brim*) verser une rasade à qn; (*b*) **to f. the air with one's cries,** remplir l'air de ses cris; **an odour of cooking filled the house,** une odeur de cuisine envahissait la maison; **to f. one's head with useless things,** se farcir la tête de choses inutiles; **to be filled with admiration,** être rempli d'admiration. **2.** (*a*) combler (une brèche, une lacune, etc.); plomber (une dent); **to f. woodwork** mastiquer les boiseries (avant de les peindre); (*b*) pourvoir à (une vacance); **two places remain to be filled,** deux postes restent à pourvoir. **3.** occuper; (*a*) **a post he has filled for some time,** un poste qu'il occupe depuis quelque temps; **to f. s.o.'s shoes,** (i) succéder à qn; (ii) prendre les fonctions de qn; (*b*) **the thoughts that filled his mind,** les pensées qui occupaient son esprit; **reading fills my evenings,** la lecture remplit toutes mes soirées. **4.** (*a*) (*fulfil*) **to f. every requirement,** répondre à tous les besoins; (*b*) *Pharm:* exécuter (une ordonnance). **5.** verser; **to f. concrete into a coffering,** remplir un coffrage de béton. **II.** *v.i.* **1.** se remplir, se combler; **her eyes filled with tears,** ses yeux se remplissaient de larmes; **the hall is beginning to f.,** la salle commence à se garnir. **2.** *Nau:* (*of sails*) se gonfler. **fill in** *v.tr.* (*a*) combler, boucher (un trou); condamner (une porte); remblayer (un fossé); (*b*) combler (des lacunes); remplir (un formulaire); insérer (la date); *F:* **to f. s.o. in on the details,** éclaircir qn sur les détails (d'une affaire). **filling** **1.** *a.* (*of food*) rassasiant. **2.** *n.* (*a*) (i) (r)emplissage *m* (d'une mesure); chargement *m* (d'un wagon, etc.); bourrage *m* (d'une pipe à tabac); mise *f* en eau (d'un réservoir); *Aut:* **f. station,** poste *m* d'essence; station-service *f*, *pl.* stations-service; (ii) peuplement *m* (d'un étang); (*b*) (i) comblement *m* (d'un vide); remblayage *m* (d'un fossé, etc.); *Civ.E: Const:* remplissage; *Dent:* plombage *m* (d'une dent); (ii) **f. of a vacancy,** nomination *f* de quelqu'un à un poste; (*c*) occupation *f* (d'un poste, etc.); (*d*) (i) **f. in,** comblement *m* (d'un trou); remblayage *m* (d'un fossé, etc.); rédaction *f* (d'un formulaire); (ii) **f. out,** gonflement *m* (d'un ballon, etc.); (iii) **f. up,** remplissage *m* (d'un tonneau, etc.); comblement (d'une lacune); bouchage *m* (d'un trou, etc.); remblayage (d'un fossé, etc.); (*e*) (matière *f* de) remplissage; tripe *f* (d'un cigare); *Dent: Carp:* mastic *m*; *Civ.E: Const:* remplissage; (*rubble*) blocage *m*; (*liquid*) coulis *m*; *Cu:* garniture *f* (d'un sandwich); **cake with a chocolate f.,** gâteau fourré au chocolat. **fill out 1.** *v.tr.* (*a*) gonfler (un ballon, etc.); (*b*) étoffer (un discours, etc.); *NAm:* remplir (un formulaire). **2.** *v.i.* se gonfler; (*of pers.*) engraisser, grossir; **her cheeks are filling out,** ses joues se remplissent. **fill up 1.** *v.tr.* (*a*) remplir (un verre) jusqu'au bord; combler (une mesure, etc.); *v.i.* **to f. up with petrol, with water,** faire le plein d'essence, d'eau; (*b*) boucher (un trou avec du mastic, etc.); remblayer (un fossé, etc.); (*c*) remplir (un formulaire). **2.** *v.i.* se remplir, se combler.

filler ['filər] *n.* **1.** (*a*) (*pers.*) remplisseur, -euse; (*in supermarket, etc.*) **shelf f.,** réassortisseur, -euse; (*b*) (*thg*) remplisseuse *f*; **oil f.,** entonnoir *m*. **2.** (*a*) (matière *f* de) remplissage (*m*); tripe *f* (d'un cigare); (*b*) *Tchn:* bouche-pores *m inv* (de bois); *Paint:* mastic *m*.

fillet[1] ['filit] *n.* **1.** *Cost:* filet *m*, bandelette *f* (pour maintenir les cheveux). **2.** *Cu:* (*a*) filet (de bœuf, de sole); (*b*) rouelle *f* (de veau). **4.** (*a*) *Arch: etc:* filet; bande *f*; (*b*) *Join:* baguette *f*, listel *m* (de panneau); (*c*) *Mec.E:* collet *m*, boudin *m* (sur un tuyau, etc.). **5.** (*a*) *Her:* filet; (*b*) *Bookb: Typ:* filet.

fillet[2] *v.tr.* **(filleted) 1.** orner (qch.) d'un filet, d'une baguette. **2.** *Cu:* détacher les filets (d'un poisson); désosser (un poisson); **filleted sole,** filets *mpl* de sole.

fillip ['filip] *n.* **1.** chiquenaude *f*. **2.** stimulant *m*, encouragement *m*; coup de fouet (donné au sang, etc.); **to give a f. to business,** stimuler les affaires.

filly ['fili] *n.* **1.** pouliche *f*. **2.** *F:* jeune fille *f*.

film[1] [film] *n.* **1.** (*a*) pellicule *f*, couche *f* (de glace, d'huile); *Med:* taie *f* (sur l'œil); (*b*) voile (de brume, de fumée, etc.). **2.** *Phot:* (*a*) pellicule, film; **roll f.,** pellicule, film, en bobine; **colour f.,** film (en) couleur(s); **f. cassette,** cartouche *f* de pellicule, de film; (*b*) couche *f* sensible (de la pellicule); (*c*) *Cmptr:* **f. card,** microfiche *f*. **3.** *Cin:* (*a*) film; bande *f*; **silent f.,** film muet; **full-length, short(-length) f.,** long métrage, court métrage; **supporting f.,** film supplémentaire; **news f.,** actualités *fpl*; **f. script,** scénario *m*, script *m*; **to act, play in, a f.,** jouer dans un film; **to shoot a f.,** tourner un film; **to have a f. test,** tourner une bande d'essai; (*b*) **the films,** le cinéma; **the f. industry,** l'industrie cinématographique, du cinéma; **f. actor, actress,** acteur, -trice, de cinéma; **f. library,** cinémathèque *f*; **f. club,** ciné-club *m*; **f. critic,** critique *m* du cinéma.

film[2] **1.** *v.tr.* (*a*) recouvrir (qch.) (i) d'une pellicule, (ii) d'un voile; (*b*) *Cin:* filmer, tourner (une scène, etc.); porter (un roman) à l'écran. **2.** *v.i.* **to f. (over),** (i) (*of lake, etc.*) se couvrir d'une pellicule; (ii) (*of the eyes*) se couvrir d'une taie. **filming** *n. Cin:* filmage *m*; tournage *m*.

filmstar ['filmstɑːr] *n.* vedette *f* de cinéma.

filmstrip ['filmstrip] *n.* film *m* fixe (d'enseignement).

filmy ['filmi] *a.* **1.** (*a*) (*of substance*) qui forme une pellicule; (*b*) (*of thg*) couvert d'une pellicule; (*of eye*) couvert d'une taie. **2.** (*of lace, cloud, etc.*) léger.

filter[1] ['filtər] *n.* **1.** filtre *m*; épurateur *m* (d'essence, etc.); **air f.,** filtre à air; épurateur d'air; **coffee f.,** filtre à café; **f. paper,** papier filtre; **f. tip (of cigarette),** bout filtre (d'une cigarette); *Hyd.E:* **f. bed,** bassin de filtration. **2.** *Opt: Phot:* **colour f.,** filtre de couleur; écran *m* filtre. **3.** *El: Elcs: etc:* **frequency f.,** filtre de fréquences; **f. circuit,** circuit *m* de filtrage.

filter[2] **1.** *v.tr.* filtrer (l'eau); épurer (l'air, etc.); **to f. out,** séparer (des impuretés) par filtrage. **2.** *v.i.* (*a*) (*of water, etc.*) filtrer **(through,** à travers); (*seep*) suinter; **the light filtered through the branches,** la lumière filtrait à travers les branches; **the news soon filtered through,** les nouvelles se divulguèrent bientôt; (*b*) *Aut: etc:* changer de file; **to f. to the right, to the left,** glisser à droite, à gauche. **filtering** *n.* filtrage *m*, filtration *f*.

filterable ['filtərəbl] *a. Med:* (virus) filtrant.

filth [filθ] *n.* **1.** (*a*) ordure *f*; immondices *mpl*; (*b*) **to live in f.,** vivre dans la saleté. **2.** (*a*) corruption morale; (*b*) propos orduriers; **to talk f.,** dire des obscénités.

filthy ['filθi] **1.** *a.* (*a*) sale, immonde; **f. weather,** temps de chien; (*b*) **in a f. temper,** d'une humeur massacrante; (*c*) (*of book, talk, etc.*) ordurier, obscène; (*of pers.*) crapuleux. **2.** *adv. F:* **f. dirty,** crasseux; **f. rich,** pourri de fric.

filtration [fil'treiʃ(ə)n] *n.* filtration *f*, filtrage *m*.

fin [fin] *n.* **1.** (*a*) *Nat.Hist:* nageoire *f* (d'un poisson, d'une baleine); aileron *m* (d'un requin); (*b*) *Swim:* **fins,** palmes *fpl*; (*c*) *P:* main *f*, pince *f*. **2.** (*a*) *N.Arch:* dérive *f*; **stabilizer f.,** aileron stabilisateur; (*b*) *Av:* empennage *m*; (*c*) (*of bomb, etc.*) ailette *f*; (*d*) *Aut:* ailette (de radiateur, etc.); **cooling fins,** ailettes de refroidissement.

final ['fain(ə)l] **1.** *a.* final, -als; (*a*) dernier; **f. preparations,** derniers préparatifs; **to make a f. effort,** faire un dernier effort; **to put the f. touches to sth.,** mettre la dernière main à qch.; *Com: Fin:* **f. date (for payment),** terme fatal; **f. instalment,** dernier versement; versement de libération; (*b*) définitif; **f. text,** texte définitif; *Jur:* **f. judgment,** jugement définitif, sans appel; **the umpire's decision is f.,** la décision de l'arbitre est sans appel; **take this as f.,** tenez-le-vous pour dit; (*c*) *Gram:* (proposition) finale. **2.** *n.* (*a*) (lettre) finale (*f*) (d'un mot); (*b*) *Sp:* **the f.,** les (épreuves) finales; la finale; *Fb:* **cup f.,** finale de coupe; (*c*) *Sch:* **to sit, take, one's finals** = passer son dernier examen de licence. **-ally** *adv.* finalement. **1.** enfin. **2.** définitivement. **3.** en somme.

finale [fi'nɑːli] *n.* **1.** *Mus:* finale *m*. **2.** conclusion *f*; *Th:* **grand f.,** apothéose *f*.

finalist ['fainəlist] *m. Sp:* finaliste *mf*.

finality [fai'næliti] *n.* **1.** *Phil:* finalité *f*. **2.** caractère définitif, irrévocabilité *f*.

finalize ['fainəlaiz] *v.tr.* mener (qch.) à bonne fin; mettre la dernière main à (qch.).

finance[1] [fai'næns, fi-] *n.* **1.** finance *f*; **high f.,** (i) la haute finance; (ii) *coll.* la haute banque; **f. company,** société *f* de crédits. **2. his finances are low,** ses fonds sont bas.

finance[2] *v.tr.* financer, commanditer (qn, une entreprise, etc.); supporter tous les frais (d'une entreprise). **financing** *n.* financement *m*.

financial [fai'nænʃ(ə)l, fi-] *a.* financier; **f. year,** exercice (financier); année *f* budgétaire; **f. resources,** ressources fiscales. **-ally** *adv.* financièrement.

financier [fai'nænsiər, fi-] *n.* financier *m*.

finch [fin(t)ʃ] *n. Orn:* fringille *f*.

find[1] [faind] *n.* **1.** découverte *f*. **2.** trouvaille *f*.

find[2] *v.tr.* (*p.t. & p.p.* **found** [faund]) **1.** (*a*) trouver, découvrir; **to f. happiness with s.o.,** rencontrer le bonheur auprès de qn; **to f. some difficulty in doing sth.,** éprouver quelque difficulté à faire qch.; **the bullet found its mark,** la balle a atteint son but; (*b*) **to f. s.o. at home, in,** trouver qn chez lui; **they found him dead,** on l'a trouvé mort; **we must leave everything as we find it,** il faut tout laisser tel quel; **I found him waiting in the hall,** je l'ai trouvé qui m'attendait dans le vestibule; **I often f. myself smiling,** je me surprends souvent à sourire. **2.** (*discover by searching*) (*a*) **the (lost) key has been found,** la clef s'est retrouvée; **to try to f. sth.,** chercher qch.; **I ran to f. a doctor,** j'ai couru à la recherche d'un médecin;

to f. a job for s.o., trouver un emploi à qn; **to f. a leak in a main,** localiser une fuite dans une conduite; **I can f. no reason for . . .,** je ne vois pas de raison pour . . .; **to f. a way to do sth.,** trouver le moyen de faire qch.; **to f. it in one's heart to do sth.,** avoir le cœur de faire qch.; (*b*) obtenir (une sûreté); **to f. favour with s.o.,** gagner la faveur de qn. **3.** (*a*) (*perceive*) constater; **you will f. that I am right,** vous verrez que j'ai raison; **I was surprised to f. that . . .,** j'ai été surpris de constater que . . .; **I found that she had left the house,** j'ai appris qu'elle avait quitté la maison; (*b*) **they will f. it easy, difficult,** cela leur sera facile, difficile; **to f. it impossible, necessary, to do sth.,** se trouver dans l'impossibilité, dans la nécessité, de faire qch.; **how do you f. this wine?** comment trouvez-vous ce vin? (*c*) **they found an unexpected supporter in Mr X,** ils ont trouvé en M. X un partisan inattendu. **4.** *Jur:* (*a*) **to f. s.o. guilty,** déclarer qn coupable; (*b*) **to f. for s.o.,** prononcer, rendre, un verdict en faveur de qn. **5.** (*provide*) (*a*) **to f. the money for an undertaking,** procurer les capitaux, fournir l'argent, pour une entreprise; (*b*) **wages £20, all found,** gages *mpl* £20, tout fourni. **finding** *n.* (*a*) **he published his findings in a scientific journal,** il a fait publier les résultats de ses recherches dans un journal scientifique; (*b*) *Jur:* conclusion *f* (du tribunal, du jury) sur un point de fait; **his f. is that . . .,** il est arrivé à la conclusion que . . . . **find out** *v.tr. & i.* (*a*) se rendre compte (des faits); découvrir (la vérité); (*b*) **to f. out about sth.,** se renseigner sur qch.; **I have found out all about it,** j'ai pu établir tous les faits; **I'll f. out,** je le saurai; (*c*) **to f. s.o. out,** (i) découvrir le vrai caractère de qn; (ii) prendre qn en défaut.

finder ['faindər] *n.* **1.** (*pers.*) trouveur, -euse; *Jur:* inventeur, -trice (d'un objet perdu); *Prov:* **finders keepers,** ce qui tombe dans le fossé est pour le soldat. **2.** (*of telescope*) chercheur *m.*

fine¹ [fain] *n. Jur:* (*a*) pas *m* de porte; (*b*) amende *f*; **to impose a f. on s.o.,** infliger une amende à qn.

fine² *v.tr.* condamner (qn) à une amende; **to f. s.o. £20,** frapper qn d'une amende de £20.

fine³ *a.* **1.** (*a*) (*of metals, oil, etc.*) fin; **gold twenty-two carats f.,** or à vingt-deux carats de fin; (*b*) fin; **f. distinction,** distinction subtile. **2.** beau, bel, belle, beaux; (*a*) **a f. statue,** une belle statue; **a f. piece of writing,** une belle page; **the f. arts,** les beaux-arts *mpl*; (*b*) **to appeal to s.o.'s finer feelings,** faire appel aux sentiments élevés de qn; **it is a f. thing to see . . .,** il fait beau voir . . .; (*c*) (*of manners*) affecté; **a f. lady,** (i) une dame élégante; (ii) une grande dame. **3.** (*a*) bel (exemple de qch.); **meat of the finest quality,** viande de premier choix; (*b*) excellent, magnifique; **f. display,** étalage *m* superbe; **we had a f. time,** nous nous sommes bien amusés; **that's f.!** voilà qui est parfait; (*c*) *Iron:* **you're a f. one, you are!** vous êtes joli, vous! **you're a f. one to talk!** c'est bien à vous de parler! (*d*) *F:* (*intensive*) **he was in a f. (old) temper!** ce qu'il rageait! **4.** (*of weather*) beau; **when the weather is f.,** quand il fait beau; **a f. day,** une belle journée; **one of these f. days,** un de ces beaux jours. **5.** (*a*) (*of texture*) fin; (*of gravel, dust, etc.*) menu; **f. rain,** pluie fine; **to chop meat f.,** hacher menu la viande; (*b*) effilé; (*of writing*) délié, mince; (aiguille) fine; (tranchant) affilé, aigu; (plume) pointue; **f. print,** petits caractères; **not to put too f. a point on it,** pour parler carrément. **6. to cut it f.,** arriver de justesse; *Bill:* **to cut the ball too f.,** prendre la bille trop fin, trop fine. **-ly** *adv.* **1.** finement; (*a*) habilement; (*b*) délicatement; (*c*) **f. powdered,** finement pulvérisé; **f. chopped,** haché fin. **2.** magnifiquement.

fine⁴ *int.* bon! entendu! d'accord!

fine⁵ **1.** *v.tr.* (*a*) **to f. (down),** clarifier (la bière); (*b*) affiner (l'or, etc.); (*c*) **to f. (down, off),** amincir (qch.); alléger (une planche, etc.). **2.** *v.i.* (*of liquid*) se clarifier, devenir clair.

fine-cut ['fain'kʌt] *a.* **1.** finement ciselé; délicatement ciselé. **2.** (tabac) haché fin.

fine-draw ['fain'drɔː] *v.tr.* **(fine-drew; fine-drawn)** *Needlew:* rentraire; faire une reprise perdue à (une déchirure). **fine-drawn** *a.* **1.** (*a*) *Needlew:* **f.-d. seam, mend,** reprise perdue; rentraiture *f*; (*b*) (*of wire*) finement étiré; (*of thread*) délié; (*c*) (*of features, etc.*) fin. **2.** (*of distinction*) subtil.

fine-grained ['fain'greind] *a.* à grain fin.

fine-looking ['fain'lukiŋ] *a.* beau, bel, belle.

fineness ['fainnis] *n.* **1.** titre *m*, aloi *m* (de l'or); pureté *f* (du vin, etc.). **2.** qualité supérieure, excellence *f*. **3.** splendeur *f*, magnificence *f* (d'un costume, etc.). **4.** finesse *f* (des cheveux, d'un tissu, etc.); délicatesse *f*, subtilité *f* (des sentiments, etc.).

finery ['fainəri] *n.* parure *f*; fanfreluches *fpl*; **decked out in all her f.,** parée de ses plus beaux atours.

fine-spun ['fain'spʌn] *a.* **1.** *Tex:* au fil ténu, délié. **2.** (raisonnement, etc.) subtil.

finesse [fi'nes] *n.* **1.** finesse *f*, délicatesse *f*, subtilité *f* (du style, etc.). **2.** finesse, ruse *f*. **3.** *Cards:* impasse *f*.

fine-tooth ['fain'tuːθ] *a.* (peigne) fin; **to go through sth. with a f.-t. comb,** passer qch. au peigne fin.

fine-tune ['faintjuːn] *v.tr. U.S:* peaufiner.

finger¹ ['fiŋgər] *n.* **1.** (*a*) doigt *m* (de la main); **first f.,** index *m*; **middle f.,** médius *m*, doigt du milieu; **ring f.,** annulaire *m*; **little f.,** petit doigt; auriculaire *m*; **to eat sth. with one's fingers,** manger qch. avec ses doigts; **to lay, put, one's f. on the source of the trouble,** mettre le doigt sur la source du mal; *F:* **don't you dare lay a f. on him,** je vous défends de le toucher; **he wouldn't lift a f. to help you,** il ne remuerait pas le petit doigt pour vous aider; **they could be counted on the fingers of one hand,** on pourrait les compter sur les doigts de la main; **to keep one's fingers crossed** = toucher du bois; *P:* **get, pull, take, your f. out!** grouille-toi! **he has a f. in every pie,** il est mêlé à tout; **f. board,** (i) touche *f* (de violon, etc.); **f. exercises,** (exercices *mpl* de) doigté (*m*); (*b*) (*measure, etc.*) **f. of brandy,** doigt de cognac; **f. of bread,** mouillette *f*; (*c*) doigt (d'un gant); (*d*) *Coel: F:* **dead man's fingers,** alcyon *m*; (*e*) **f. alphabet,** alphabet *m* des sourds-muets; **f. plate,** plaque *f* de propreté; *Mus:* **f. hole,** trou *m* (de flûte, etc.); *Dom.Ec:* **f. bowl,** rince-doigts *m inv*; *Cu:* **f. biscuit,** biscuit *m* à la cuiller. **2.** *Tchn: Mec.E:* doigt (de guidage).

finger² *v.tr.* **1.** toucher, tâter, *F:* tripoter (qch.). **2.** (*a*) **to f. the piano,** tapoter sur le piano; (*b*) *Mus:* doigter (un morceau). **fingering** *n.* **1.** maniement *m.* **2.** *Mus:* doigté *m.*

fingermark ['fiŋgəmɑːk] *n.* empreinte *f* de doigt sale.

fingernail ['fiŋgəneil] *n.* ongle *m* (de la main).

fingerprint¹ ['fiŋgəprint] *n. Adm:* empreinte digitale; **f. identification,** dactyloscopie *f*.

fingerprint² *v.tr.* prendre les empreintes digitales de (qn).

fingerstall ['fiŋgəstɔːl] *n. Med:* doigtier *m.*

fingertip ['fiŋgətip] *n.* bout *m* du doigt; **f. control,** commande *f* au doigté; **he is a Frenchman to his fingertips,** il est Français jusqu'au bout des ongles; **to have sth. at one's fingertips,** savoir qch. sur le bout du doigt.

finicky ['finiki] *a.* (*of pers., style, etc.*) méticuleux, vétilleux.

finish¹ ['finiʃ] *n.* **1.** (*a*) fin *f* (de la vie, etc.); *Sp:* arrivée *f* (d'une course); *Sp:* **he has a fast f.,** il a un bon finish; *F:* **that was the f. (of him),** ce fut le coup de grâce; (*b*) *Sp:* la ligne d'arrivée; l'arrivée. **2.** (*a*) fini *m*, finesse *f* de l'exécution (d'un travail, etc.); (*b*) apprêt *m*; **paint with a gloss, matt, f.,** peinture *f* vernis, mate; (*c*) *Tchn:* finition *f*.

finish² **1.** *v.tr.* finir; (*a*) terminer, achever; mettre fin à (une affaire, etc.); compléter (un ouvrage, etc.); **to f. doing sth.,** achever de faire qch.; **to f. off a wounded animal,** donner le coup de grâce à une bête; *F:* **to f. s.o. off,** donner son reste à qn; **he's finished!** il est fini, achevé! **f. (up) your soup!** finis ta soupe! (*b*) perfectionner, donner du fini à (un ouvrage, etc.); *Tex:* apprêter (un tissu); *Metalw:* usiner (une pièce); *Needlew:* **to f. (off) a buttonhole,** brider une boutonnière. **2.** *v.i.* (*a*) finir, cesser, se terminer, s'achever; **the meeting finished in a brawl,** le meeting se termina par des coups; *Tp:* **have you finished?** terminé? (*b*) **to f. in a point,** se terminer en pointe; (*c*) **he finished by calling me a liar,** il a fini par me traiter de menteur; (*d*) **I've finished with it,** je n'en ai plus besoin; *F:* **I'm finished with it,** j'en ai marre; *F:* **I've finished with you,** tout est fini entre nous; (*e*) **wait until I've finished with him,** attendez que je lui aie réglé son compte! (*f*) **to f. fourth,** finir, arriver, quatrième. **finished** *a.* **1.** (article, etc.) fini, apprêté; (produit) ouvré; **machine f.,** apprêté à la machine; **badly f. goods,** marchandises mal finies. **2.** (*of pers., appearance, etc.*) soigné, parfait. **finishing 1.** *a.* dernier; **the f. stroke,** le coup *m* de grâce; **f. touches,** finitions *fpl.* **2.** *n.* (*a*) achèvement *m* (d'une tâche, etc.); **f. school,** école *f* d'arts d'agrément pour les jeunes filles; (*b*) *Tchn:* finition *f*; apprêtage *m* (du cuir, du papier); **f. coat,** dernière couche (de peinture, etc.); dernier enduit (de chaux, etc.); *Ind:* **f. shop,** atelier *m* de finitions; *Metalw:* **f. pass,** passe *f* de finissage; (*c*) *Const:* **finishings,** menuiserie *f* (d'une maison, etc.); (*d*) *Sp:* **f. line,** ligne *f* d'arrivée.

finisher ['finiʃər] *n.* (*pers.*) (*a*) *Ind:* finisseur, -euse; (*b*) *Sp:* finisseur, -euse; **he's a fast f.,** c'est un bon finisseur.

finite ['fainait] **1.** *a.* (*a*) (*of nature, etc.*) fini, limité; (*b*) *Gram:* (verbe) à un mode fini. **2.** *n.* **the f. and the infinite,** le fini et l'infini.

Finland ['finlənd] *Pr.n. Geog:* Finlande *f*.

Finn [fin] *n. Geog:* Finlandais, -aise; Finnois, -oise.

Finnish ['finiʃ] **1.** *a.* finlandais. **2.** *n. Ling:* finnois *m*.

fiord [fjɔːd] *n. Geog:* fjord *m*, fiord *m*.

fir [fəːr] *n.* **1. f. (tree),** sapin *m*; **Douglas f.,** sapin de Douglas; **Scots f.,** pin d'Écosse; **f. cone,** pomme *f* de pin. **2.** (bois *m* de) sapin; (bois de) pin.

fire¹ ['faiər] *n.* **1.** feu *m*; (*a*) **to make a f.,** faire du feu; **f. worship,** culte *m* du feu; (*b*) **open f.,** feu dans la cheminée; **camp f.,** feu de camp; **wood f.,** feu de bois; **gas, electric, f.,** radiateur *m* à gaz, électrique; **to light a f.,** faire du feu; **to throw sth. into the f.,** jeter qch. au feu; **a roaring f.,** une belle flambée; **f. screen,** (i) devant *m* de cheminée; (ii) écran ignifuge; **f. irons,** garniture *f* de foyer; (*c*) **blacksmith's f.,** feu de forge; **f. box,** foyer, boîte *f* à feu (d'une locomotive); (*d*) incendie *m*; **bush f.,** feu de brousse; **to cause, start, a f.,** provoquer un incendie; **to catch f.,** prendre feu; **the house, her dress, caught f.,** le feu a pris à la maison, à sa robe; **fire!** au feu! **on f.,** en feu; **the house, the ship, is on f.,** la maison, le navire, brûle; *F:* **to get on like a house on f.,** (i) (*of work, etc.*) marcher rondement; (ii) (*with pers.*) s'entendre à merveille; **f. raiser,** incendiaire *mf*; **f. fighting,** lutte *f* contre l'incendie; **f.-fighting equipment,** matériel *m* d'incendie; **f. insurance,** assurance *f* contre l'incendie; **f. brigade,** *NAm:* **f. department,** (corps *m* de) sapeurs-pompiers (*mpl*), *F:* les pompiers; **f. station,** poste *m* d'incendie; caserne *f* de (sapeurs-)pompiers; **f. engine,** pompe *f* à incendie; **f. extinguisher,** extincteur *m* d'incendie; **f. hose,** tuyau *m* de pompe, manche *f*, à incendie; **f. escape,** (i) échelle *f* à incendie; (ii) escalier *m* de secours; **f. drill,** exercice *m* de sauvetage en cas d'incendie; **f. door,** porte *f* coupe-feu; *Nau: Av:* **f. bulkhead,** cloison *f* pare-feu; (*e*) *Pyr:* **blue f.,** feu de Bengale; (*f*) lumière *f*, éclat *m*. **2.** enthousiasme *m*; fougue *f*; **the f. of youth,** l'enthousiasme de la jeunesse. **3.** *Mil: etc:* feu, tir *m*; coups *mpl* de feu; **individual f., f. at will,** tir à volonté; **to open f.,** ouvrir, commencer, le feu; **to cease f.,** cesser le feu; **under enemy f.,** sous le feu de l'ennemi; **we are under f.,** on tire sur nous; **to come under f.,** (i) être exposé au feu (de l'ennemi); (ii) s'attirer des attaques (**from s.o.,** de qn).

fire² *v.tr. & i.* **1.** (*a*) mettre le feu à (une maison, etc.); (*b*) animer, enthousiasmer (qn); exciter (l'imagination); **to be fired with enthusiasm for sth.,** brûler d'enthousiasme pour qch. **2.** cuire (de la poterie, etc.). **3.** *Mch: etc:* chauffer (une locomotive, etc.); allumer (une chaudière); **oil fired central heating,** chauffage au mazout. **4.** (*a*) *I.C.E:* enflammer (le mélange); (*b*) lancer (une fusée, une torpille); (*c*) **to f. at, on, s.o., sth.,** tirer sur qn, qch.; **to f. at s.o. with a revolver,** tirer un coup de revolver sur qn; **fire!** feu! **to f. a gun at s.o.,** lâcher un coup de fusil à qn; **to f. a gun,** tirer un coup de canon; **without firing a shot,** sans tirer un coup; **we were fired on,** nous avons reçu des coups de feu; **to f. a question at s.o.,** poser une question à qn à brûle-pourpoint. **5.** *F:* renvoyer, congédier (un employé, etc.). **6.** *v.i.* (*a*) (*of shot*) partir; **the revolver failed to f.,** le revolver a fait long feu; (*b*) *I.C.E:* **the engine is firing evenly, badly,** le moteur tourne régulièrement, mal. **fire away** *v.i.* (*a*) **to f. away at the enemy,** tirer à l'ennemi à feu continu; (*b*) *F:* **f. away!** allez-y! commencez! **fire off** *v.tr.* (*a*) tirer (un coup de fusil, etc.); (*b*) poser (des questions) à brûle-pourpoint. **firing** *n.* **1.** cuisson *f* (des briques, de la poterie, etc.). **2.** chauffage *m*, chauffe *f* (d'un four, d'une locomotive, etc.); **coal, oil, f.,** chauffe au charbon, au mazout. **3.** (*a*) *Min: Exp:* allumage *m* (d'un coup de mine); **f. mechanism, wire,** mécanisme *m*, fil *m*, de mise à feu; (*b*) *I.C.E:* allumage; **f. order, sequence,** ordre *m* d'allumage (des cylindres); (*c*) *Mil: etc:* tir (d'une fusée). **4.** *Artil: Sm.a:* tir, feu *m*; **f. position,** (i) (*of weapon*) position *f* de tir; (ii) position du tireur; **f. practice,** exercice *m* de tir; **f. pin,** percuteur *m*; **f. range,** (i) distance *f* de tir; (ii) stand *m*, travée *f*, de tir; **f. party, squad,** (i) peloton *m* d'exécution; (ii) peloton chargé de tirer la salve d'honneur; **heavy f. could be heard,** on entendait une vive fusillade.

firearm ['faiərɑːm] *n.* arme *f* à feu.

fireball ['faiəbɔːl] *n. Meteor:* (*a*) bolide *m*; (*b*) éclair *m* en boule.

fireboat ['faiəbout] *n.* bateau-pompe *m*, *pl.* bateaux-pompes.

firebrand ['faiəbrænd] *n.* **1.** tison *m*, brandon *m*. **2.** (*pers.*) brandon de discorde.

firebreak ['faiəbreik] *n. For:* coupe-feu *m inv*.

firebrick ['faiəbrik] *n.* brique *f* réfractaire.

firebug ['faiəbʌg] *n. F:* incendiaire *mf*, pyromane *mf*.

fireclay ['faiəklei] *n.* argile *f* réfractaire.

firedamp ['faiədæmp] *n. Min:* grisou *m*.

firedog ['faiədɔg] *n. Furn:* chenet *m*.

fire-eater ['faiəriːtər] *n.* **1.** (saltimbanque) avaleur *m* de feu. **2.** *F:* batailleur *m*, exalté *m*.

firefly ['faiəflai] *n. Ent:* luciole *f*.

fireguard ['faiəgɑːd] *n.* **1.** pare-étincelles *m inv*; garde-feu *m inv*. **2.** (*pers.*) *U.S.* guetteur *m* d'incendies.

firelight ['faiəlait] *n.* lumière *f* du feu; **by, in, the f.,** à la lumière du feu.

firelighter ['faiəlaitər] *n.* allume-feu *m inv*.

fireman, *pl.* **-men** ['faiəmən] *n.m.* **1.** chauffeur (d'une machine à vapeur, etc.) **2.** (sapeur-)pompier.

fireplace ['faiəpleis] *n.* cheminée *f*, âtre *m*, foyer *m*.

fireproof¹ ['faiəpruːf] *a.* (*a*) incombustible, ignifuge; **f. material,** matière ignifugée; **f. vault,** salle blindée; **f. door,** porte *f* coupe-feu; (*b*) **f. dish,** plat *m* allant au feu.

fireproof² *v.tr.* ignifuger (un tissu, etc.); rendre (qch.) ininflammable.

fireranger [ˈfaiəreindʒər] *n. NAm:* guetteur *m* d'incendies (dans une forêt).

fireside [ˈfaiəsaid] *n.* cheminée *f,* foyer *m;* coin *m* du feu; **f. chair,** chaise *f* de coin du feu.

firetrap [ˈfaiətræp] *n.* **this building's a real f.,** ce bâtiment est une véritable souricière (en cas d'incendie).

firewall [ˈfaiəwɔːl] *n.* cloison *f* pare-feu.

firewarden [ˈfaiəwɔːdən] *n.* guetteur *m* d'incendies.

firewatcher [ˈfaiəwɔtʃər] *n.* guetteur *m* d'incendies.

firewatching [ˈfaiəwɔtʃiŋ] *n.* surveillance *f* contre les incendies.

firewater [ˈfaiəwɔːtər] *n. F:* gnole *f,* gnôle *f.*

firewood [ˈfaiəwud] *n.* bois *m* de chauffage; bois à brûler; **bundle of f.,** margotin *m.*

firework [ˈfaiəwəːk] *n.* **1.** pièce *f* d'artifice. **2. fireworks,** feu *m* d'artifice; **grand display of fireworks,** grand feu d'artifice; *F:* **whenever they get together there's fireworks,** quand ils se rencontrent il y a du grabuge.

firm¹ [fəːm] *n. Com:* **1.** raison sociale, nom social. **2.** maison (de commerce); entreprise *f;* firme *f;* **a large f.,** une grosse entreprise; **f. of solicitors** = étude *f* de notaire.

firm² *a.* **1.** (*of flesh, etc.*) ferme; (*of post, nail, etc.*) solide, fixe; (*of tread, etc.*) assuré; **as f. as a rock,** inébranlable; **to rule with a f. hand,** gouverner d'une main ferme; **to walk with a f. step,** marcher d'un pas assuré. **2.** (*of friendship, etc.*) constant, inaltérable; (*of intention, etc.*) résolu, déterminé; (*of person, tone, etc.*) décidé, résolu; **to be f. about sth.,** tenir bon sur qch.; **to have a f. belief that . . .,** avoir la ferme conviction que . . . . **3.** *Com: Fin:* (*of offer, sale*) ferme; **these shares remain f. at . . .,** ces actions se maintiennent à . . . . **4.** *adv.* **to stand f.,** tenir bon; tenir ferme; **to stand f. about sth.,** tenir bon sur qch. **-ly** *adv.* **1.** fermement; (marcher) d'un pas assuré; **I f. believe that . . .,** j'ai la ferme conviction que . . . . **2.** d'un ton ferme.

firm³ **1.** *v.tr.* (*a*) **to f. the soil,** affermir, tasser, le sol; (*b*) **to f. up a post,** raffermir un poteau. **2.** *v.i.* (*of prices, etc.*) **to f. (up),** se raffermir.

firmness [ˈfəːmnis] *n.* fermeté *f;* force *f* (de caractère, etc.); constance *f* (d'une amitié); *Com: Fin:* raffermissement *m* (des valeurs, etc.).

first [fəːst] **I.** *a.* **1.** premier; (*a*) (*in time, order*) **the f. (day) of the month,** le premier (jour) du mois; *Post:* **f.-day cover,** (enveloppe *f* de) premier jour (d'émission); **the f. of April,** le premier avril; **the f. three years,** les trois premières années; **on the f. floor,** (i) au premier étage; (ii) *NAm:* au rez-de-chaussée; **Charles the F.,** Charles Premier; **at f. sight,** à première vue; **at the f. attempt,** au premier, de prime, abord; **to use, wear, sth. for the f. time,** étrenner qch.; **it was my f. flight,** c'était mon baptême de l'air; **to fall head f.,** tomber la tête la première; **to be the f. person to do sth.,** être le premier, la première, à faire qch.; **to come out f. in an examination,** être reçu premier à un examen; **f. name,** prénom *m;* **to be on f.-name terms with s.o.,** appeler qn par son prénom; **f. cousin,** cousin(e) germain(e); *Th: etc:* **f. night, f. performance,** première *f;* *Med:* **f. aid,** secourisme *m;* premiers secours; **f.-aid outfit, kit,** trousse *f* de secours; **f.-aid station, post,** poste *m* de (premiers) secours; **f.-aid dressing,** paquet individuel de pansement; *Gram:* **in the f. person,** à la première personne; *Sch:* **f. form** = (classe *f* de) sixième *f;* *Aut:* **f. gear,** première vitesse; *Publ:* **f. edition,** édition princeps, originale; **the F. World War,** la première guerre mondiale; (*b*) **to put f. things f.,** mettre en avant les choses essentielles; **to travel f. class,** voyager en première (classe); **f. lieutenant,** lieutenant *m* en premier; (*c*) **to have news at f. hand,** tenir une nouvelle de première main, d'original. **2.** unième; **twenty-f.,** vingt et unième; **seventy-f.,** soixante et onzième; **eighty-f.,** quatre-vingt-unième; **ninety-f.,** quatre-vingt-onzième; **one hundred and f.,** cent unième. **II.** *n.* **1.** (le) premier, (la) première; **we were the very f. to arrive,** nous sommes arrivés les tout premiers; *Sp: etc:* **to come in an easy f.,** arriver bon premier; **to be the f. to do sth.,** être le premier à faire qch.; *Sch:* (*of degree*) **to get a f.** = avoir une mention (très) bien. **2.** commencement *m;* **from f. to last,** depuis le début jusqu'à la fin; **from the f.,** dès le commencement; **at f.,** d'abord. **3. to travel f.,** voyager en première (classe); *Aut:* **to climb a hill in f.,** monter une côte en première (vitesse). **III.** *adv.* premièrement, d'abord; **f. and foremost,** surtout et avant tout; **f. of all,** pour commencer; en premier lieu; **f. forget that . . .,** commencez par oublier que . . . . **2.** pour la première fois; **when did you f. see him?** quand l'avez-vous vu pour la première fois? **3.** plutôt; *F:* **I'll see him damned f.,** qu'il aille au diable. **4.** le premier, la première; **he arrived f.,** il arriva le premier; **to claim the right to speak f.,** réclamer la priorité; **you go f.!** passez devant! **f. come f. served,** les premiers vont devant; **ladies f.!** place aux dames! **women and children f.!** les femmes et les enfants d'abord! **-ly** *adv.* premièrement; en premier lieu.

firstborn [ˈfəːstbɔːn] *a. & n.* (enfant) premier-né, *pl.* premiers-nés.

first(-)class [ˈfəːst(ˈ)klɑːs] **1.** *a.* (*a*) (wagon) de première classe; (article) de première qualité; (hôtel, etc.) de premier ordre; (*b*) *Post:* à tarif normal; **f.-c. mail,** (i) lettres, etc. envoyées à tarif normal; (ii) *NAm:* lettre close. **2.** *adv.* **to travel f.-c.,** voyager en première; *Post:* **to send a letter f.-c.,** envoyer une lettre à tarif normal.

first-degree [ˈfəːstdiˈgriː] *a.* (brûlure) au premier degré; *U.S.:* **f.-d. murder,** assassinat *m.*

firsthand [ˈfəːst(ˈ)hænd] *a.* (nouvelle) de première main.

first(-)rate [ˈfəːst(ˈ)reit] *a.* excellent; de première classe; **of f.-r. quality,** de toute première qualité; **f.-r. idea,** fameuse idée.

firth [fəːθ] *n. Geog: Scot:* estuaire *m;* **the F. of Forth,** le golfe du Forth.

fiscal [ˈfisk(ə)l] **1.** *a. Fin:* fiscal, -aux; **f. year,** année *f* budgétaire; année d'exercice. **2.** *n. Scot:* **(procurator) f.,** procureur général.

fish¹, *pl.* **fishes,** *coll.* **fish** [fiʃ, ˈfiʃiz] *n.* **1.** poisson *m;* **f. farming,** pisciculture *f;* **f. farm,** établissement *m* piscicole; **f. tank,** vivier *m;* **f. market,** marché *m* au poisson; **f. shop,** poissonnerie *f;* *Cu:* **fried f.,** poisson frit; **f. and chips,** poisson frit avec des frites; **f.-and-chip shop,** friterie *f;* **f. fingers,** *NAm:* **sticks,** filets de poisson panés; **f. meal,** farine *f* de poisson; *Dom.Ec:* **f. kettle,** poissonnière *f;* **f. knife and fork,** couvert *m* à poisson; **I've other f. to fry,** j'ai d'autres chats à fouetter; **neither f., flesh nor good red herring,** ni chair ni poisson. **2.** *Astr:* **the Fish(es),** les Poissons.

fish² **1.** *v.i.* pêcher; **to f. for trout, for pearls,** pêcher la truite, des perles; *F:* **to f. for compliments,** chercher des compliments. **2.** *v.tr.* (*a*) pêcher (un saumon, etc.); (*b*) **to f. up, out, a dead body,** (re)pêcher un cadavre; **to f. up a mine,** relever une mine; **he fished a pencil out of his pocket,** il a fouillé dans sa poche et en a tiré un crayon; (*c*) pêcher (une rivière). **fishing** *n.* la pêche; **trout f.,** pêche à la truite; **pearl f.,** pêche des perles; **fly f.,** pêche à la mouche; **f. ground,** pêcherie *f;* **f. tackle,** articles *mpl* de pêche; **f. line,** ligne *f* (de pêche); **f. rod,** canne *f* à pêche; **f. net,** filet *m* de pêche; **f. boat, smack,** bateau *m,* de pêche; **f. port,** port *m* de pêche.

fish³, *pl.* **fishes** *n. Rail: Const:* éclisse *f.*
fishbone ['fiʃboun] *n.* arête *f* (de poisson).
fishcake ['fiʃkeik] *n. Cu:* croquette *f* de poisson.
fisherman, *pl.* **-men** ['fiʃəmən] *n.m.* pêcheur.
fishery ['fiʃəri] *n.* **1.** pêche *f*; **f.-protection vessel,** garde-pêche *m inv.* **2.** pêcherie *f.*
fish-hook ['fiʃhuk] *n. Fish:* hameçon *m.*
fishmonger ['fiʃmʌŋgər] *n.* poissonnier *m*; **fishmonger's (shop),** poissonnerie *f.*
fishplate ['fiʃpleit] *n. Rail:* éclisse *f.*
fishpond ['fiʃpɔnd] *n.* (*a*) vivier *m*; (*b*) étang.
fishtail ['fiʃteil] *n.* queue *f* de poisson.
fishwife, *pl.* **-wives** ['fiʃwaif, -waivz] *n.f.* marchande de poisson; **she swears like a f.,** elle jure comme un charretier.
fishy ['fiʃi] *a.* **1.** (odeur, goût) de poisson. **2.** *F:* (*of business, etc.*) douteux, louche; **f. story,** histoire *f* qui ne tient pas debout.
fissile ['fisail] *a.* fissile.
fission ['fiʃ(ə)n] *n.* **1.** *Biol:* scissiparité *f.* **2.** *Ph:* fission *f*; **nuclear, thermal, f.,** fission nucléaire, thermique.
fissure¹ ['fiʃər] *n.* fissure *f*, fente *f* (dans un mur, etc.).
fissure² **1.** *v.tr.* fissurer, fendre (un rocher, etc.). **2.** *v.i.* (*of rock, etc.*) se fissurer, se fendre.
fist [fist] *n.* **1.** poing *m*; **he went for them with his fists,** il tomba sur eux à coups de poing; **to clench one's f.,** serrer le poing; **to shake one's f. at s.o.,** menacer qn du poing. **2.** *P:* main *f.*
fistful ['fistful] *n. F:* poignée *f* (d'argent, etc.).
fisticuffs ['fistikʌfs] *n.pl.* coups *m.pl* de poing.
fistula ['fistjulə] *n. Med:* fistule *f.*
fit¹ [fit] *n.* **1.** (*a*) accès *m* (de folie, etc.); quinte *f* (de toux); (*b*) (i) crise *f* épileptique; (ii) attaque d'apoplexie; **fainting f.,** évanouissement *m*; **to have,** *F:* **throw, a f.,** piquer une crise; *F:* **he'll have a f. when he knows,** il en aura une congestion quand il le saura. **2.** accès, mouvement *m* (de mauvaise humeur, etc.); **in a f. of temper,** dans un mouvement de colère; **f. of crying,** crise de larmes; **f. of laughter,** accès de rire; **to be in fits of laughter,** avoir le fou rire; **in a f. of idleness,** dans un moment de paresse; **to have sudden fits of energy,** avoir des élans d'énergie; **to work by fits and starts,** travailler par à-coups.
fit² *a.* **(fitter, fittest) 1.** bon, propre **(for sth.,** à qch.); **f. to eat,** bon à manger, mangeable; **f. to drink,** buvable, potable; **I've nothing fit to wear,** je n'ai rien à me mettre; **story that is not f. to be repeated,** histoire qu'il ne serait pas convenable de répéter; **I'm not f. to be seen,** je ne suis pas présentable; **to think f., see f., to do sth.,** juger convenable, trouver bon, de faire qch.; **do as you see, think, f.,** faites comme bon vous semble; **she cried f. to break her heart,** elle pleurait à gros sanglots. **2.** (*a*) capable; **f. for sth.,** en état de faire qch.; **f. for duty,** bon pour le service; *Mil:* valide; **f. to do sth.,** capable de faire qch.; **that's all he's f. for,** il n'est bon qu'à cela; (*b*) disposé (à faire qch.); **I felt f. to drop,** je me sentais prêt à tomber (de fatigue). **3.** (*of pers.*) **to be (fighting) fit,** avoir une bonne constitution; être en forme; **to keep f.,** rester en forme; **he is not yet f. to go back to work,** il n'est pas encore en état de reprendre son travail; *F:* **to be as f. as a fiddle,** être en parfaite santé.
fit³ *n.* (*a*) ajustement *m*; **your coat is a perfect f.,** votre manteau vous va parfaitement; **it was a tight f.,** on tenait tout juste; (*b*) *Mec.E:* ajustage *m* (d'un assemblage, etc.).
fit⁴ *v.* **(fitted) 1.** *v.tr.* (*a*) s'accorder avec (qch.); (*b*) (*of clothes, etc.*) être à la taille de (qn); **key that fits the lock,** clef qui va à la serrure; (*c*) (i) adapter, ajuster **(sth. to sth.,** qch. à qch.); **to f. a nozzle on the end of a pipe,** adapter un ajutage à l'extrémité d'un tuyau; **to f. a handle to a broom,** emmancher un balai; **to f. one part into another,** emboîter une pièce dans une autre; **I'm going to be fitted for my new dress,** je vais faire l'essayage de ma nouvelle robe; **to make the punishment f. the crime,** proportionner les peines aux délits; (ii) **to f. parts together,** monter, assembler, des pièces; **to f. a machine together,** assembler une machine; (*d*) **to f. sth. with sth.,** munir, pourvoir, qch. de qch.; **fitted with two propellers,** pourvu de deux hélices. **2.** *v.i.* (*a*) **to f. (together),** s'ajuster, s'adapter; **pieces that f. together,** pièces *fpl* rapportables; **to f. on sth.,** s'adapter sur qch.; **to f. into sth.,** s'emboîter dans qch.; **piece that fits into another,** pièce qui entre dans une autre; (*b*) **your dress fits well, badly,** votre robe vous va, ne vous va pas, bien. **fit in 1.** *v.tr.* (*a*) emboîter (des tubes, etc.); (*b*) faire cadrer (des projets, etc.). **2.** *v.i.* (*a*) **to f. in between two things,** s'emboîter entre deux choses; (*b*) **to f. in with sth.,** être en harmonie avec qch.; **your plans don't f. in with mine,** vos projets ne cadrent pas avec les miens; **he doesn't f. in,** il ne sait pas s'adapter. **fit out** *v.tr.* équiper **(sth. with sth.,** qch. de qch.); armer (un navire); équiper (un navire neuf); **to f. s.o. out,** équiper qn (de vêtements, etc.). **fitted** *a.* **1.** (*a*) ajusté; (*b*) *Dressm:* ajusté; (*c*) (tapis) cloué; **f. sheet,** drap *m* housse. **2.** (*of pers., thg*) **to be f. for sth., to do sth.,** être fait pour qch. **fitting 1.** *a.* convenable; approprié **(to,** à); (remarque) à propos. **2.** *n.* (*a*) (i) ajustement *m* (d'une pièce, etc.); emboîtement *m* (d'un pignon, etc.); installation *f* (d'appareils); **f. of sth. on sth.,** adaptation de qch. à qch.; *Ind:* **f. shop,** atelier *m* d'ajustage; (ii) *Tail: etc:* essayage *m*, ajustage (de vêtements); **f. room,** cabine *f* d'essayage; (iii) *Com:* **made in three fittings,** fabriqué en trois tailles, (*of shoes*) en trois largeurs; (iv) **f. out,** équipement *m* (d'une expédition, etc.); armement *m* (d'un navire); (*b*) *usu. pl.* agencements *mpl*, installations (d'un bureau, etc.); accessoires *mpl* (sanitaires, etc.); **door fittings,** ferrures *fpl* de porte; **brass fittings,** garnitures en cuivre; *El:* **light f.,** appareil *m* d'éclairage; **ceiling f.,** plafonnier *m*; **wall f.,** applique *f.* **fittingly** *adv.* convenablement, à propos. **fit up** *v.tr.* aménager **(sth. for sth.,** qch. pour qch.).
fitter ['fitər] *n.* **1.** *Mec.E: Aut: etc:* ajusteur *m*; assembleur, -euse; **electrical f.,** installateur *m* d'appareils électriques. **2.** *Dressm: Tail:* essayeur, -euse.
five [faiv] **1.** *num.a & n.* cinq (*m*); **a f.-pound note,** un billet de cinq livres; **he leaves his office at f.,** il quitte son bureau à cinq heures; *Pol.Ec:* **the F. Year Plan,** le Plan quinquennal. **2.** *n. Games:* **fives** = balle *f* au mur.
five-figure ['faiv'figər] *a. Mth:* (nombre) de cinq chiffres.
five-finger ['faiv'fiŋgər] *a. Mus:* **f.-f. exercises,** exercices *mpl* de doigté.
fivefold ['faivfould] **1.** *a.* quintuple. **2.** *adv.* cinq fois autant; au quintuple; **to increase f.,** quintupler.
fivepence ['faifpəns] *n.* (somme *f* de) cinq pence.
fiver ['faivər] *n. F:* billet *m*, somme *f*, de cinq livres, *U.S:* de cinq dollars.
fix¹ [fiks] *n.* **1.** *F:* embarras *m*, difficulté *f*; **to be in a f.,** être dans une situation embarrassante; **to get into a f.,** se mettre dans l'embarras. **2.** *P:* piqûre *f* de drogue; **to give oneself a f.,** se piquer.
fix² *v.tr.* **1.** fixer; caler, monter (une roue sur l'essieu, une poulie, etc.); assurer (une planche avec des clous, etc.); attacher (un hameçon à une ligne, etc.); **to f. sth. in one's memory,** se graver qch. dans la mémoire; **to f. one's attention on sth.,** fixer son attention sur qch.; **to f. one's eye(s) on s.o.,** fixer qn (du regard). **2.** (*a*) *Ch: Phot: etc:* fixer (le mercure, une teinture, etc.); (*b*) *v.tr. Med:* stériliser (à la formaline, etc.). **3.** (*a*) établir (un camp); **to f. one's residence in a place,** établir son domicile dans un endroit; (*b*) **to f. oneself somewhere,** s'installer, se

caser, quelque part. **4.** (*a*) fixer, établir (une limite, le taux de l'intérêt, etc.); désigner (l'endroit pour un rendez-vous); régler (l'itinéraire d'un voyage, etc.); **the date is not yet fixed,** la date n'est pas encore certaine; **there's nothing fixed yet, nothing is fixed yet,** il n'y a encore rien de décidé; *F:* **how are you fixed for money, for time?** tu as assez d'argent, de temps? (*b*) *v.ind.tr.* **to f. on sth.,** se décider pour qch.; (*c*) *U.S:* **to be fixing to do sth.,** être décidé, déterminé, de faire qch. **5.** (*a*) **to f. sth. with s.o.,** arranger qch. avec qn; **I've fixed it with him,** je me suis arrangé avec lui; (*b*) *F:* réparer, retaper (qch.); **just wait while I f. my hair,** attends que je me coiffe; (*c*) *F:* préparer (un repas, etc.). **6.** *F:* (*a*) **I'll f. him!** je lui ferai son affaire! (*b*) graisser la patte à (qn); (*c*) truquer (un match, etc.). **fixed** *a.* **1.** fixe, immobile, stationnaire; **f. pulley,** poulie *f* fixe. **2.** (*a*) fixe, constant, invariable; (règle) établie, absolue; **of f. length,** de longueur constante; **f. price,** prix *m* fixe, forfaitaire; **f. income,** revenu fixe; (*b*) (idée) fixe; **to have f. ideas,** avoir des idées (bien) arrêtées; **to have no f. plans,** ne pas avoir des projets bien déterminés; (*c*) (regard) fixe; (sourire) figé; (*d*) **f. point,** point *m* fixe, point de repère; **f. assets,** immobilisations *fpl.* **3.** *Ch:* (huile, sel) fixe. **4.** *F:* (match, etc.) truqué. **fixedly** ['fiksidli] *adv.* fixement. **fixing** *n.* **1.** (*a*) fixation *f*, mise *f* en place (d'un appareil, etc.); fixage *m* (d'une épreuve photographique); ancrage *m* (de crampons, etc.); pose *f* (d'une serrure); *Phot:* **f. solution, bath,** solution *f*, bain *m*, de fixage; (*b*) *Av: Nau:* relevé *m*, relèvement *m* (d'une position); (*c*) *Com:* établissement *m* (des prix, etc.). **2.** *esp. NAm:* **fixings,** accessoires *mpl*; *Cu:* **roast turkey with all the fixings,** dinde rôtie avec tout ce qui s'ensuit. **fix up** *v.tr.* (*a*) **to f. up a room as a study,** transformer une pièce en bureau; (*b*) arranger (une affaire); **it's all fixed up,** c'est une affaire réglée; (*c*) *F:* réparer, retaper (qch.); (*d*) **to f. s.o. up with (sth.),** trouver (un travail, une chambre) pour qn.

fixation [fik'seiʃ(ə)n] *n.* **1.** fixation *f* (de l'impôt, du mercure, etc.). **2.** *Psy:* fixation.

fixative ['fiksətiv] *a.* & *n.* *Art: Toil:* fixatif (*m*).

fixer ['fiksər] *n.* **1.** (*pers.*) (*a*) *Pej:* combinard *m*; (*b*) pourvoyeur *m* de drogues. **2.** (*a*) *Art:* fixatif *m*; (*b*) *Phot:* fixateur *m.*

fixity ['fiksiti] *n.* fixité *f*; **f. of purpose,** détermination *f.*

fixture ['fikstjər] *n.* **1.** (*a*) appareil fixe; **to make sth. a f.,** fixer qch. (à demeure); ancrer qch. en place; *F:* (*of pers.*) **he's become a f. here,** il s'est bien ancré chez nous; il fait partie des meubles; (*b*) **fixtures,** aménagements *mpl* (d'une maison, etc.); appareils (électriques, etc.); **£1000 for fixtures and fittings,** £1000 de reprise; **bathroom fixtures and fittings,** installations *fpl* et accessoires *mpl* de salles de bain. **2.** *Sp:* rencontre (prévue); match (prévu); **list of fixtures,** calendrier *m* (de la saison).

fizz¹ [fiz] *n.* **1.** pétillement *m* (du champagne, etc.); *Mch:* sifflement *m* (de la vapeur). **2.** *F:* (i) champagne *m*; (ii) boisson gazeuse.

fizz² *v.i.* (*of champagne*) pétiller; (*of steam*) siffler.

fizzle ['fizl] *v.i.* (*of wine*) pétiller; (*of gas burner, etc.*) siffler. **fizzle out** *v.i.* *F:* ne pas aboutir.

fizzy ['fizi] *a.* (*of mineral water*) gazeux; (*of wine*) mousseux.

fjord [fjɔːd] *n.* *Geog:* fjord *m*, fiord *m.*

flabbergast ['flæbəgɑːst] *v.tr.* *F:* abasourdir, ahurir (qn); **I was flabbergasted,** j'en étais sidéré.

flabbiness ['flæbinis] *n.* flaccidité *f*, manque *m* de fermeté (de la chair, etc.); mollesse *f* (de qn).

flabby ['flæbi] *a.* (*of muscles, etc.*) flasque; mou, *f.* molle; (*of cheeks*) pendant; (*of pers.*) mollasse.

flaccid ['flæksid] *a.* mou, *f.* molle; (chair) flasque.

flag¹ [flæg] *n.* *Bot:* iris *m.*

flag² *n.* *Const:* carreau *m*, dalle *f.*

flag³ *v.tr.* daller (un trottoir, etc.); paver de carreaux. **flagged** *a.* (*of floor*) carrelé, dallé. **flagging** *n.* carrelage *m*, dallage *m.*

flag⁴ *n.* (*a*) drapeau *m*; **f. day,** (i) jour de quête pour une œuvre de bienfaisance; (ii) *U.S:* le 14 juin; (*b*) *Mil:* drapeau; **white f.,** drapeau blanc; **f. signals,** signalisation *f* par fanions; *Fig:* **to keep the f. flying,** ne pas se laisser abattre; (*c*) *Nau:* pavillon *m*; **yellow f.,** pavillon de quarantaine; **pilot f.,** pavillon (de) pilote; **black f.,** pavillon noir; **f. of convenience,** pavillon de complaisance; *Navy:* **f. officer,** officier général; **f. captain,** commandant *m* du navire amiral; (*d*) *Ski:* **pair of flags,** porte *f*; (*e*) drapeau (de taximètre); **taxi with the f. up,** taxi *m* libre.

flag⁵ *v.tr.* **1.** pavoiser (un édifice). **2.** transmettre des signaux à (qn) au moyen de fanions; arrêter (un taxi); **to f. down a motorist, a car,** arrêter, stopper, un automobiliste, une voiture. **3.** *Sp:* **to f. out,** jalonner (un champ de course).

flag⁶ *v.i.* **1.** (*of thg*) pendre mollement; (*of sail*) battre. **2.** (*of plant*) languir; (*of pers.*) s'alanguir; (*of conversation*) traîner, languir; (*of attention*) faiblir, fléchir; (*of courage*) s'amollir; **his strength was flagging,** il était à bout de forces. **flagging 1.** *a.* (*of conversation, etc.*) languissant. **2.** *n.* amolissement *m* (du courage); ralentissement *m* (du zèle).

flagellate¹ ['flædʒəleit] *a.* & *n.* *Prot:* flagellé (*m*).

flagellate² *v.tr.* flageller; fouetter.

flagellation [flædʒə'leiʃ(ə)n] *n.* flagellation *f.*

flageolet ['flædʒəlet, flædʒə'let] *n.* flageolet *m.*

flagon ['flægən] *n.* **1.** flacon *m*; *Ecc:* burette *f.* **2.** grosse bouteille ventrue. **3.** pot *m* (à anse).

flagpole ['flægpoul] *n.* mât *m* de drapeau.

flagrant ['fleigrənt] *a.* (*of offence*) flagrant, scandaleux; (*of offender*) notoire; **a f. injustice,** une injustice criante. **-ly** *adv.* d'une manière flagrante.

flagrante delicto (in) [inflə'græntidi'liktou] *Lt.adv.phr.* *Jur:* en flagrant délit.

flagship ['flægʃip] *n.* *Navy:* (navire *m*) amiral (*m*).

flagstaff ['flægstɑːf] *n.* **1.** mât *m* de drapeau. **2.** *Nau:* mât de pavillon.

flagstone ['flægstoun] *n.* dalle *f*; **f. pavement,** dallage *m* en pierre.

flail¹ [fleil] *n.* *Agr:* fléau *m.*

flail² **1.** *v.tr.* *Agr:* battre au fléau. **2.** *v.i.* **to f. around,** s'agiter; se débattre des mains et des pieds.

flair ['flɛər] *n.* (*a*) flair *m*; (*b*) aptitude *f* (**for,** à); **to have a f. for languages,** avoir le don des langues.

flak [flæk] *n.* (*a*) artillerie anti-aérienne; (*b*) tir *m* contre-avions; (*c*) **f. jacket,** gilet *m* de protection; (*d*) *F:* critique *f.*

flake¹ [fleik] *n.* (*a*) flocon *m* (de neige); (*b*) écaille *f*, éclat *m*, paillette *f* (de métal, etc.); **soap flakes,** savon *m* en paillettes.

flake² *v.i.* (*a*) (*of snow, etc.*) tomber en flocons; (*b*) (*of metal, mineral, etc.*) **to f. (away, off),** s'écailler; **the paint is flaking off,** la peinture s'écaille. **flaking 1.** *a.* (peinture) qui s'écaille. **2.** *n.* écaillement *m* (de la peinture).

flake³ *v.i.* *F:* **to f. out,** (i) s'évanouir; tomber dans les pommes; (ii) s'endormir (après avoir trop bu, etc.); **to be flaked (out),** être vidé, crevé.

flaky ['fleiki] *a.* **1.** (*of snow, etc.*) floconneux. **2.** (*of mineral, etc.*) écailleux; **f. pastry,** pâte feuilletée. **3.** *U.S:* *F:* (*of pers.*) (un peu) toqué, timbré.

flamboyance [flæm'bɔiəns] *n.* qualité flamboyante.

flamboyant [flæm'bɔiənt] *a.* (*a*) *Arch:* (style) flamboyant; (*b*) (*of pers., speech, etc.*) flamboyant.

flame¹ [fleim] *n.* **1.** (*a*) flamme *f*; **in flames,** en flammes, en feu; **to burst into flame(s), to go up in flames,** s'enflammer brusquement, se mettre à flamber; (*b*) *Metalw:* **f. cutter,** chalumeau *m* à découper;

(*c*) *a.* **f.(-coloured),** ponceau *inv*; couleur de feu *inv*. **2.** éclat *m* (d'une pierre précieuse). **3.** (*a*) *Lit:* passion *f*, ardeur *f*; (*b*) *F: O:* (*pers.*) béguin *m*; **he, she, is an old f. of mine,** c'est une de mes anciennes amours.

flame² **1.** *v.i.* (*a*) (*of fire, etc.*) flamber, flamboyer; *Lit:* (*of passions, etc.*) flamber; (*b*) (*of diamond, etc.*) briller. **2.** *v.tr. Med: etc:* flamber (un instrument). **flame up** *v.i.* (*a*) s'enflammer; (*b*) *F:* (*of pers.*) se mettre en colère. **flaming** *a.* **1.** (feu) flambant, flamboyant. **2.** (soleil) ardent; **f. red,** rouge feu *inv*; *F:* **in a f. temper,** d'une humeur massacrante. **3.** *P:* sacré; **you f. idiot!** sacré imbécile!

flamenco [flə'meŋkou] *n. Danc:* flamenco *m*.

flameproof ['fleimpru:f] *a.* (*a*) ignifuge; ininflammable; (*b*) antidéflagrant.

flamethrower ['fleimθrouər] *n. Mil: Hort:* lance-flammes *m inv*.

flamingo, *pl.* **-o(e)s** [flə'miŋgou, -ouz] *n. Orn:* flamant *m* (rose).

flammable ['flæməbl] *a. NAm:* inflammable.

flan [flæn] *n. Cu:* tarte *f* aux fruits.

Flanders ['flɑ:ndəz] *Pr.n. Geog:* la Flandre.

flange¹ [flændʒ] *n.* **1.** (*a*) bourrelet *m*, collerette *f* (d'un tube, d'un tuyau); collet *m*, rebord *m* (d'une tôle); **f. coupling,** raccordement *m* à bride; (*b*) boudin *m*, rebord (d'une roue); (*c*) aile *f* (d'une poutre); *Rail:* patin *m* (de rail). **2.** *I.C.E:* **cooling f.,** ailette *f* de refroidissement.

flange² *v.tr. Tchn:* brider (qch.); border (une tôle); bourreler (une roue). **flanged** *a.* **1.** (tube) à bride(s); (roue) à boudin; (rail) à patin; (poutre) à aile; (tôle) à bord tombé. **2.** *Aut:* (radiateur) à ailettes.

flank¹ [flæŋk] *n.* **1.** (*a*) flanc *m* (d'une personne, d'un animal); (*b*) *Cu:* flanchet *m* (de bœuf). **2.** (*a*) côté *m*, flanc (d'une montagne, etc.); (*b*) *Mil:* flanc (d'une armée, etc.); **to protect one's flanks,** se couvrir sur les flancs.

flank² *v.tr.* **1.** flanquer; soutenir (qch.) sur le flanc; **to f. sth. with, by, sth.,** flanquer qch. de qch.; **flanked by two policemen,** encadré de deux gendarmes. **2.** *Mil:* prendre (l'ennemi, etc.) de flanc; *Artil:* enfiler (une tranchée, etc.).

flannel ['flæn(ə)l] *n.* (*a*) *Tex:* flanelle *f*; *Cost:* **f. trousers,** *npl.* **flannels,** un pantalon de flanelle; (*b*) *Toil:* **(face) f.** = gant *m* de toilette.

flannelette [flæn(ə)'let] *n. Tex:* pilou *m*, veloutine *f*.

flap¹ [flæp] *n.* **1.** battement *m*, coup *m* (d'aile); clapotement *m*, claquement *m* (d'une voile); *F:* affolement *m*; **to get into a f.,** s'agiter, s'affoler; **to be in a f.,** ne plus savoir où donner de la tête. **2.** (*a*) rabat *m* (d'une enveloppe); patte (d'une poche); pan *m* (d'un vêtement); rabat *m* (de la jaquette d'un livre, etc.); (*b*) *Mec.E:* clapet *m* (à charnière); (*c*) abattant *m* (de table); trappe *f* (de cave); **desk with a writing f.,** secrétaire *m*; (*d*) *Av:* volet; **landing f.,** volet d'atterrissage; (*e*) *Surg:* lambeau *m*.

flap² *v.* **(flapped) 1.** *v.tr.* battre; **the bird flaps its wings,** l'oiseau bat des ailes; **to f. one's arms about,** agiter les bras. **2.** *v.i.* (*a*) (*of sail*) battre, claquer; (*of wings*) battre; (*b*) *F:* s'agiter sans but; s'affoler. **flapping** *n.* (*a*) battement *m* (des ailes); clapotement *m*, claquement *m* (d'une voile); (*b*) *F:* affolement *m*; agitation *f*.

flapper ['flæpər] *n. A:* jeune femme (des années 20).

flare¹ [flɛər] *n.* **1.** (*a*) flamboiement irrégulier, flamme vacillante (de gaz, etc.); (*of jet engine, etc.*) flammes *fpl*; (*b*) *Mil: Av:* feu *m* de signal; fusée éclairante; **f. pistol,** pistolet *m* de signalisation; **f. path,** piste éclairée; (*c*) *Phot:* **f. (spot),** spectre *m* secondaire. **2.** évasement *m*; godet *m* (d'une jupe).

flare² **1.** *v.i.* (*a*) (*of lamp, etc.*) flamboyer; (*b*) (*of skirt, etc.*) s'évaser. **2.** *v.tr.* évaser (un tube, une jupe, etc.). **flared** *a.* (*a*) (jupe) evasée; (*b*) (tube, etc.) évasé. **flare up** *v.i.* (*a*) (*of candle, etc.*) s'enflammer brusquement; (*b*) (*of anger, fighting, etc.*) éclater; **to f. up again,** éclater de nouveau; reprendre; (*c*) (*of pers.*) s'emporter; **he flares up at the slightest thing,** il monte comme une soupe au lait.

flare-up ['flɛərʌp] *n.* (*a*) flambée soudaine; (*b*) (i) déclenchement *m* (d'une guerre); éruption *f* (de la colère); (ii) recrudescence *f* (de la colère, d'une guerre); (*c*) *F:* altercation *f*; (ii) éclat *m* de colère.

flash¹ ['flæʃ] *n.* **1.** (*a*) éclair *m*; lueur soudaine; éclat *m*; **a f. of lightning,** un éclair; **f. of wit,** saillie *f*; **f. of inspiration,** éclair de génie; **f. of hope,** rayon *m* d'espoir; **in a f.,** en un rien de temps, en un clin d'œil; **f. flood,** crue subite; (*b*) lueur, éclair (d'une arme à feu); *Fig:* **a f. in the pan,** un feu de paille; (*c*) *Petr:* détente *f*; (*d*) *Metalw:* **f. welding,** soudure *f* par étincelage; (*e*) *Atom.Ph:* **f. burn,** brûlure *f* par irradiation; (*f*) *Phot:* flash *m* (*pl.* flashes) (électronique); **f. cube,** flash cube; **f. bulb,** ampoule *f* (de) flash; (*g*) *Journ:* flash; **news f.,** flash d'information; (*h*) *Cin:* scène de raccord (très courte). **2.** *Metalw:* bavure *f* (d'une pièce brute de fonderie). **3.** *Mil:* écusson *m*.

flash² **1.** *v.i.* (*a*) (*of fire, eyes, etc.*) jeter des éclairs; lancer des étincelles; (*of diamonds, etc.*) briller; (*of lake, etc.*) miroiter; **his eyes flashed with anger,** ses yeux lançaient des éclairs de colère; (*b*) **to f. past,** passer comme un éclair; **it flashed across my mind that . . .,** l'idée m'est venue tout d'un coup que . . .. **2.** *v.tr.* (*a*) (i) faire étinceler (ses bijoux); étaler (son argent); (ii) projeter (une image sur l'écran, etc.); lancer (un sourire, un regard) **(at s.o.,** à qn); **to f. a light in s.o.'s eyes,** diriger une lumière dans les yeux de qn; (iii) **to f. a piece of news all over Europe,** répandre une nouvelle en éclair à travers l'Europe; (*b*) montrer (qch.) rapidement. **flash back** *v.i.* (*of gas stove, etc.*) avoir un retour de flamme. **flashing** **1.** *a.* (*of torch, etc.*) éclatant, flamboyant; (yeux) étincelants; (feu, signal) clignotant; (phare) à éclats. **2.** *n.* (*a*) flamboiement *m* (du feu); éclat *m* (d'un diamant); miroitement *m* (d'un miroir); clignotement *m* (d'un signal); (*b*) projection *f* (d'un rayon de lumière). **flash over** *v.i.* (*of conductor, etc.*) cracher des étincelles.

flashback ['flæʃbæk] *n.* **1.** retour *m* de flamme. **2.** *Cin:* retour en arrière; flash-back *m*; **a f. to prewar days,** un coup d'œil rétrospectif sur les années d'avant-guerre.

flasher ['flæʃər] *n.* **1.** clignotant *m*. **2.** *F:* exhibitionniste *m*.

flashgun ['flæʃgʌn] *n.* (*a*) projecteur *m* de signalisation à main; (*b*) *Phot:* flash *m*, *pl.* flashes.

flashlamp ['flæʃlæmp] *n.* torche *f* (électrique).

flashlight ['flæʃlait] *n.* **1.** (*of lighthouse, etc.*) feu *m* à éclats. **2.** *Phot:* ampoule *f* de flash; **f. photography,** prise de vues au flash. **3.** torche *f* (électrique).

flashover ['flæʃouvər] *n.* étincelle *f* de rupture.

flashpoint ['flæʃpɔint] *n.* **1.** (*of oil, etc.*) point *m* d'inflammabilité. **2.** *Fig:* situation explosive, critique.

flashy ['flæʃi] *a.* voyant, tapageur, -euse; **f. young man,** jeune homme à toilette tapageuse. **flashily** *adv.* **f. dressed,** à toilette tapageuse.

flask [flɑ:sk] *n.* (*a*) flacon *m*; **brandy f.,** flacon à cognac; **vacuum f.,** bouteille isolante; (*b*) *Ch:* (i) fiole *f*; (ii) ballon *m*.

flat¹ [flæt] **I.** *a.* **1.** (*a*) plat; horizontal, -aux; (toit) plat, en terrasse; *Med:* (pied) plat; (*b*) (*of curve, etc.*) aplati; *Arch:* (voûte) plate; (arc) déprimé; (*c*) (*of surface*) plat, uni; (nez) camus; **f. country,** pays plat; pays de plaine; **f. chest,** poitrine plate; **f. tyre,** pneu dégonflé, à plat; **to beat sth. f.,** aplatir qch.; *Turf:* **f. racing,** le plat; **f. race,** course plate, de plat; *Bookb:*

f. sheets, feuilles *fpl* à plat; **as f. as a pancake,** plat comme une galette; (*d*) (*of picture*) sans relief; (*e*) *Paint:* (couleur) mate. **2.** net, *f.* nette; positif; (démenti) formel, absolu; (refus) net, catégorique; **to give a f. refusal,** refuser net; *F:* **that's f.!** voilà qui est net! **3.** (*a*) (*of existence, etc.*) monotone, ennuyeux; (*of style, etc.*) terne; (*of pers.*) ennuyeux; (voix) terne, blanche; *Nau:* **f. calm,** calme plat; (*b*) (*of drink*) éventé, plat; (vin) mou; (*c*) (*of battery*) à plat. **4.** invariable, uniforme; **f. rate,** taux *m*, tarif *m* uniforme; (*on bus, etc.*) **f. fare, f.-rate fare,** tarif unique; **f.-rate subscription,** abonnement *m* à forfait. **5.** (*a*) (son, etc.) sourd; (*b*) *Mus:* (i) bémol *inv*; **symphony in D f.,** symphonie *f* en ré bémol; (ii) **you're f.,** vous chantez, jouez, en dessous du ton. **II.** *adv.* **1.** à plat; dans une position horizontale; **to fall f. on one's face,** (i) tomber à plat ventre; (ii) *F:* essuyer une humiliation; **stretched out f. on the ground,** étendu à plat sur le sol. **2.** (*a*) nettement, positivement; *F:* **he told me f. that . . .,** il m'a dit carrément que . . .; **to be f. broke,** être à sec; (*b*) **to work f. out,** travailler d'arrache-pied; **to go f. out,** filer à toute allure. **3. to fall f.,** (i) (*of joke, etc.*) manquer son effet; tomber à plat; (ii) (*of play, etc.*) faire four. **4.** *Mus:* (chanter, etc.) en dessous du ton. **III.** *n.* **1.** plat *m* (d'un sabre, etc.); **blow with the f. of the hand,** coup donné avec la main plate. **2.** (*a*) plaine *f*; marécage *m*; (*b*) (*left exposed at low tide*) sèche *f*. **3.** (*a*) **on the f.,** horizontalement; *Rail:* (voie) en palier; *Rac:* sur le plat; (*b*) *Turf:* **the f.,** la saison du plat. **4.** appartement *m*; **furnished, unfurnished, f.,** appartement meublé, non meublé; **service f.,** appartement avec service; **block of flats,** immeuble divisé en appartements. **5.** *Th:* ferme *f*. **6.** *Mus:* bémol *m*. **7.** *F:* pneu dégonflé, à plat; pneu crevé. **flatly** *adv.* nettement, carrément; (refuser) net; (nier) absolument. **2.** d'une façon monotone.

flat-bottomed ['flæt'bɔtəmd] *a.* à fond plat.

flatcar ['flætkɑːr] *n. NAm:* wagon *m* en plateforme.

flatfish ['flætfiʃ] *n. Ich:* poisson plat.

flatfoot ['flætfut] *n.* **1.** *Med:* pied plat. **2.** *F:* agent *m* de police.

flat-footed ['flæt'futid] *a.* **1.** à pied plat, aux pieds plats. **2.** *F:* (*of answer, etc.*) franc, *f.* franche; carré; (refus) absolu. **3.** *F:* bête, stupide.

flatiron ['flætaiən] *n.* fer *m* à repasser.

flatlet ['flætlit] *n.* petit appartment; studio *m*.

flatmate ['flætmeit] *n.* colocataire *mf* (d'un appartement).

flatness ['flætnis] *n.* **1.** égalité *f*, nature plate (d'une surface, etc.); manque *m* de relief. **2.** aplatissement *m* (d'une courbe, etc.). **3.** netteté *f* (d'un refus). **4.** (*a*) monotonie *f* (de l'existence, etc.); insipidité *f* (du style, etc.); (*b*) (*of beer, etc.*) évent *m*.

flatten ['flæt(ə)n] *v.* **(flattened) 1.** *v.tr.* (*a*) aplatir, aplanir (qch.); (*of wind, rain*) coucher (le blé, etc.); **to f. oneself against a wall,** se plaquer, se coller, contre un mur; *F:* **to f. s.o.,** écraser qn; remettre qn à sa place; (*b*) rendre (qch.) fade, insipide; (*c*) *Mus:* bémoliser (une note). **2.** *v.i.* (*a*) s'aplatir, s'aplanir; (*b*) devenir fade, insipide; (*of wine, etc.*) s'éventer; (*c*) *Av:* **to f. out,** se redresser (après un vol piqué); reprendre le vol horizontal. **flattened** *a.* **1.** (*a*) aplati, aplani; (nez) épaté. **2.** (voûte) surbaissée. **3.** *Mus:* (note) bémolisée.

flatter ['flætər] *v.tr.* flatter; **he flatters himself that he will succeed,** il se flatte de réussir. **flattering** *a.* (*of words, etc.*) flatteur, -euse; (*exaggerated*) adulatoire; **to speak in f. terms of s.o., to make f. remarks about s.o.,** parler de qn en termes flatteurs. **flatteringly** *adv.* en termes flatteurs.

flatterer ['flætərər] *n.* flatteur, -euse; flagorneur, -euse.

flattery ['flætəri] *n.* flatterie *f*; (*exaggerated*) flagornerie *f*.

flatulence ['flætjuləns,] *n.* **1.** *Med:* flatulence *f*; flatuosité *f*; **to suffer from f.,** avoir des vents. **2.** emphase *f* (de style, etc.).

flatulent ['flætjulənt] *a.* **1.** *Med:* (*of pers., etc.*) flatulent. **2.** (style) boursouflé.

flatware ['flætwɛər] *n. NAm:* vaisselle plate.

flaunt [flɔːnt] **1.** *v.i.* (*of pers.*) **to f. oneself,** parader, s'afficher. **2.** *v.tr.* étaler, afficher, faire parade de (sa richesse). **3.** *v.tr. U.S:* faire fi de (l'autorité de qn); se moquer (d'un ordre).

flautist ['flɔːtist] *n. Mus:* flûtiste *mf*.

flavour¹, *NAm:* **flavor¹** ['fleivər] *n.* saveur *f*; goût *m*; (*of tea, etc.*) arôme *m*; (*of ice cream, etc.*) parfum *m*.

flavour², *NAm:* **flavor²** *v.tr.* assaisonner, parfumer (un mets, etc.); **to f. a sauce with garlic,** relever une sauce avec de l'ail; **vanilla flavoured,** (parfumé) à la vanille. **flavouring**, *NAm:* **flavoring** *n.* **1.** assaisonnement *m*. **2.** parfum *m*.

flavourless, *NAm:* **flavorless** ['fleivəlis] *a.* (*of food, etc.*) sans saveur; fade, insipide; (*of wine*) plat.

flaw¹ [flɔː] *n.* **1.** (*a*) défaut *m*, défectuosité *f*, imperfection *f*; point *m* faible (d'un projet); (*b*) (*in glass, etc.*) fêlure *f*; (*in wood, etc.*) fente *f*; (*in metal*) brisure *f*. **2.** *Jur:* (*in document, etc.*) vice *m* de forme (entraînant la nullité).

flaw² *v.tr.* endommager, défigurer. **flawed** *a.* défectueux; (bois) gercé; (diamant) qui a un crapaud.

flawless ['flɔːlis] *a.* sans défaut; parfait; (technique) impeccable. **-ly** *adv.* parfaitement.

flawlessness ['flɔːlisnis] *n.* perfection *f*.

flax [flæks] *n. Bot: Tex:* lin *m*; **f. field,** linière *f*.

flax-coloured ['flækskʌləd] *a.* couleur de lin *inv*.

flaxen ['flæks(ə)n] *a.* **1.** (toile, etc.) de lin. **2.** (*of hair*) blond de lin *inv*; blond filasse *inv*.

flay [flei] *v.tr.* (*a*) écorcher (un animal); **to be flayed alive,** être écorché vif; (*b*) *F:* fouetter, étriller (qn); **the critics flayed him,** les critiques l'ont éreinté.

flea [fliː] *n.* **1.** *Ent:* puce *f*; *Crust:* **sand f.,** crevettine *f*; **he sent him away with a f. in his ear,** il l'a envoyé promener. **2.** *F:* **f. market,** marché *m* aux puces.

fleabag ['fliːbæg] *n. P:* (*a*) (*animal*) sac *m* à puces; (*b*) *U.S:* hôtel pouilleux.

fleabite ['fliːbait] *n.* **1.** morsure *f* de puce. **2.** *F:* (*trifle*) vétille *f*, bagatelle *f*.

fleabitten ['fliːbit(ə)n] *a.* (*of pers.*) mordu par les puces.

fleapit ['fliːpit] *n. P:* cinéma, etc., pouilleux.

fleck¹ [flek] *n.* **1.** petite tache (de lumière, etc.); moucheture *f* (de couleur). **2.** particule *f* (de poussière).

fleck² *v.tr.* tacheter; **hair flecked with grey,** cheveux qui commencent à grisonner; **flecked material,** tissu moucheté.

fled. *see* FLEE.

fledged [fledʒd] *a.* (oiseau) qui a toutes ses plumes; *F:* **he's a fully-f. doctor now,** il a tous ses diplômes.

fledgling ['fledʒliŋ] *n.* **1.** oisillon *m*. **2.** novice *mf*.

flee [fliː] *v.* (*p.t. & p.p.* **fled** [fled]) **1.** *v.i.* (*a*) (*of pers.*) s'enfuir, prendre la fuite; **to f. from a place,** s'enfuir d'un endroit; **to f. to America,** se réfugier en Amérique; (*b*) (*of time, etc.*) fuir. **2.** *v.tr.* s'enfuir de (qn, un pays, etc.); fuir (la tentation, etc.). **fleeing 1.** *a.* (*of army, etc.*) en fuite. **2.** *n.* fuite *f*.

fleece¹ [fliːs] *n.* **1.** toison *f*; *Lit:* **the Golden F.,** la Toison d'or. **2.** moutonnement *m* de nuages. **3.** *Tex:* molleton *m*; **f. lining,** doublure *f* de molleton.

fleece² *v.tr. F:* écorcher (qn); **I've been fleeced,** je me suis fait estamper. **fleecing** *n.* écorcherie *f*.

fleecy ['fliːsi] *a.* (*of wool*) floconneux; (*of material, etc.*) laineux; (*of cloud*) moutonné; **f.-lined,** doublé de molleton.

fleet[1] [fliːt] *n.* **1.** (*a*) *Navy:* flotte *f*; (*naval unit*) escadre *f*; **the F.** = la Marine nationale; **the Atlantic F.,** l'escadre de l'Atlantique; **battle f.,** flotte de ligne; **the F. Air Arm** = l'Aéronavale *f*; (*b*) **merchant f.,** flotte de commerce; **a fishing f.,** une flottille de pêche. **2.** (*a*) **air f.,** flotte aérienne; (*b*) parc *m* (de voitures, de taxis); **a f. of coaches took the tourists to their hotel,** une caravane de cars a amené les touristes à leur hôtel.

fleet[2] *a. Lit:* vite, leste; **f. of foot,** au pied léger.

Fleet *n. Journ:* **F. Street,** la presse.

fleet-footed ['fliːt'futid] *a. Lit:* au pied léger.

fleeting ['fliːtiŋ] *a.* (*of time*) fugitif, fugace; (*of beauty*) passager; (*of happiness*) éphémère; **to pay s.o. a f. visit,** faire une courte visite à qn.

Fleming ['flemiŋ] *n. Geog:* Flamand, -ande.

Flemish ['flemiʃ] **1.** *a.* flamand. **2.** *n.* le flamand.

flense [flenz] *v.tr.* dépecer (une baleine).

flesh[1] [fleʃ] *n.* chair *f.* **1.** (*a*) **to make s.o.'s f. creep,** donner la chair de poule à qn; **to put on f.,** (*of animal*) prendre chair; (*of pers.*) grossir, prendre de l'embonpoint; **f. wound,** blessure légère, en séton; **he exacts his pound of f. from his debtors,** il traite ses débiteurs en usurier; (*b*) *occ.* viande *f*; *Ecc:* **to eat f.,** faire gras; (*c*) chair (d'une pêche, etc.). **2. to mortify the f.,** châtier son corps; **it was he in the f.,** c'était lui en chair et en os; **his own f. and blood,** la chair de sa chair; **it is more than f. and blood can stand, bear,** c'est plus que la nature humaine ne saurait endurer; **the spirit is willing but the f. is weak,** l'esprit est prompt, mais la chair est faible; **to go the way of all f.,** payer sa dette à la nature; **the sins of the f.,** le péché de la chair. **3. f. colour,** couleur *f* (de) chair; **f.-coloured,** (couleur) chair; *Th: etc:* **f. tights,** maillot *m* chair; *Art:* **f. tints,** carnations *fpl.*

flesh[2] *v.i.* **to f. (out),** engraisser, prendre de l'embonpoint.

fleshpots ['fleʃpɔts] *n.pl.* **the f. (of Egypt),** la bonne chère.

fleshy ['fleʃi] *a.* (*of limb, fruit, etc.*) charnu; (*of leaf*) succulent.

fleur-de-lis, *pl.* **fleurs-de-lis** ['flәːdә'liː] *n. Her:* fleur *f* de lis.

flew. *see* FLY[3].

flex[1] [fleks] **1.** *v.tr.* fléchir (le bras, etc.); faire jouer (ses muscles). **2.** *v.i.* (*of spring*) fléchir.

flex[2] *n. El:* cordon *m*, câble *m*; fil *m* souple.

flexibility [fleksi'biliti] *n.* flexibilité *f*; élasticité *f*; souplesse *f*; **f. of character,** souplesse de caractère.

flexible ['fleksibl] *a.* flexible, souple; **f. character,** caractère souple; **f. working hours,** horaire *m* souple.

flexion ['flekʃ(ә)n] *n.* **1.** flexion *f*, courbure *f* (d'un ressort, etc.). **2.** courbe *f.*

flextime ['flekstaim] *n. Ind: etc:* horaire *m* souple.

flibbertigibbet [flibәti'dʒibit] *n. F:* écervelé, -ée; évaporé, -ée; hurluberlu *m.*

flick[1] [flik] *n.* petit coup (de fouet, de queue, etc.); (*with finger*) chiquenaude *f*; **a f. of the wrist,** un tour de main; **at the f. of a switch,** juste en appuyant sur un bouton.

flick[2] *v.tr.* (*with whip, etc.*) effleurer (un cheval, etc.); (*with finger*) donner une chiquenaude à (qch.); **to f. sth. away, off, with a duster,** faire envoler qch. d'un coup de torchon; **to f. a duster over sth.,** donner un coup de torchon à qch.; *Aut:* **to f. on the lights,** allumer les phares; **to f. through a book,** feuilleter un livre.

flicker[1] ['flikәr] *n.* (*a*) petit mouvement vacillant; battement *m* (des paupières); (*b*) **a f. of light,** une petite lueur tremblotante; (*c*) *Cin:* scintillement *m* (de la reproduction); *T.V:* papillotement *m.*

flicker[2] *v.i.* (*of flame, etc.*) trembloter, vaciller; (*of eyelids*) cligner; (*of light*) clignoter; (*of snake's tongue*) onduler; (*of needle, etc.*) osciller; *Cin:* (*of reproduction*) scintiller; **the candle flickered out,** la bougie vacilla et s'éteignit; **a smile flickered on his lips,** un sourire voltigeait sur ses lèvres. **flickering 1.** *a.* (*of light*) tremblotant. **2.** *n.* tremblotement *m*, clignotement *m*; *Cin:* scintillement *m*; *T.V:* papillotement *m.*

flick-knife ['fliknaif] *n.* (*with folding blade*) couteau *m* à cran (d'arrêt); (*with retractable blade*) couteau à lame rentrable.

flier ['flaiәr] *n.* = FLYER.

flight[1] [flait] *n.* **1.** vol *m* (d'un oiseau, d'un avion, etc.); course *f* (d'un projectile, d'un astre, etc.); (*a*) *Orn:* **f. feather,** penne *f*; (*b*) *Av:* **blind, instruments, f.,** vol sans visibilité, aux instruments; **level f.,** vol horizontal, en palier; **f. path,** trajectoire *f* de vol; **f. trainer,** appareil *m* d'entraînement au vol; **f. personnel,** personnel navigant; **f. engineer,** mécanicien de bord; **f. deck,** (i) poste *m* de pilotage (d'un avion); (ii) pont *m* d'envol (d'un porte-avions); (*c*) **f. of fancy,** essor *m* de l'imagination. **2.** (*distance*) (*a*) volée *f*, distance parcourue (par un oiseau, etc.); migration *f* (d'oiseaux, etc.); (*b*) trajectoire *f* (d'un projectile); **time of f.,** durée *f* du trajet (d'un projectile, etc.); (*c*) *Av:* **it's an hour's f. from London,** c'est à une heure de vol de Londres. **3.** (*specific trip*) (*a*) *Av:* **maiden f.,** vol inaugural, premier vol (d'un avion); (*of pers.*) **first f.,** baptême *m* de l'air; **solo f.,** vol en solo; **f. A to Brussels,** vol A pour Bruxelles; **connecting f.,** (vol de) correspondance (*f*); **f. plan,** plan *m* de vol; **f. clearance,** autorisation *f* de vol; **f. recorder,** enregistreur *m* de vol; **f. log,** journal *m* de vol; **f. control,** (i) conduite *f* (d'un avion); (ii) contrôle *m* de la navigation aérienne; (iii) *Mil:* contrôle des missions aériennes; (*b*) *Mil.Av:* **reconnaissance f.,** vol de reconnaissance; **f. formation,** *U.S:* **f. pattern,** formation *f* de vol; (*c*) *Mil.Av:* **f. lieutenant,** capitaine aviateur. **4.** (*group*) (*a*) vol, volée (d'oiseaux, etc.); *Fig:* **in the top f.,** parmi les tout premiers; (*b*) escadrille *f* (d'avions); **the Queen's, King's, F.,** avions au service de la famille royale. **5.** (*a*) *Const:* **f. of stairs,** escalier *m*; (*b*) *Rac:* **f. of hurdles,** série de haies (dans une course d'obstacles); *Hyd.E:* **f. of locks,** suite *f* de biefs.

flight[2] *n.* fuite *f*; **headlong f.,** sauve-qui-peut *m inv*; **to take to f.,** prendre la fuite; **to put the enemy to f.,** mettre l'ennemi en fuite; **in full f.,** en pleine déroute; *Fin:* **the f. of capital,** l'exode *m* des capitaux.

flightiness ['flaitinis] *n.* inconstance *f.*

flighty ['flaiti] *a.* (*a*) frivole, étourdi; (*b*) (conduite) instable.

flimsiness ['flimzinis] *n.* (*a*) manque de consistance (d'un tissu, etc.); (*b*) faiblesse *f* (d'une excuse, etc.).

flimsy ['flimzi] **1.** *a.* sans solidité; fragile; (*a*) (*of paper, etc.*) léger; peu solide; (*b*) (*of excuse*) pauvre; (*of style*) superficiel; (*of evidence*) peu convaincant; **to condemn s.o. on the flimsiest evidence,** condamner qn sur les indices les plus faibles. **2.** *n.* (*a*) papier *m* pelure; (*b*) *Journ:* copie *f* (de reporter). **-ily** *adv.* d'une manière peu solide.

flinch [flin(t)ʃ] *v.i.* (*a*) fléchir; **I flinched at the thought of it,** j'ai reculé en y pensant; (*b*) tressaillir, sursauter (de douleur); **to bear pain without flinching,** supporter la douleur sans broncher.

fling[1] [fliŋ] *n.* **1.** (*a*) jet *m*, coup *m*; (*b*) *F:* **I'll have a f. at it,** je vais essayer. **2.** *Danc:* **(highland) f.,** pas seul écossais. **3.** *F:* **to have one's f.,** faire la fête; **youth will have its f.,** il faut que jeunesse se passe.

fling[2] *v.* (*p.t. & p.p.* **flung** [flʌŋ]) **1.** *v.tr.* jeter (qch.); lancer (une balle, etc.); **to f. s.o. into prison,** jeter qn en prison; **to f. oneself into s.o.'s arms, into an arm-**

chair, se jeter dans les bras de qn, dans un fauteuil. **2.** *v.i.* se précipiter; **he flung out of the house,** il est sorti brusquement de la maison. **fling about** *v.tr.* jeter (des objets) de côté et d'autre; **to f. one's arms about,** gesticuler violemment; **to f. one's money about,** gaspiller son argent. **fling away** *v.tr.* jeter (qch.) de côté; se défaire de (qch.); **to f. away one's money,** gaspiller son argent. **fling down** *v.tr.* jeter (qch.) à terre; **he flung the books down on the table,** il a jeté les livres sur la table. **fling off** *v.tr.* (*a*) secouer (le joug); (*b*) retirer brusquement (son manteau, etc.). **fling open** *v.tr.* ouvrir toute grande (la fenêtre, etc.); **to f. open the door,** ouvrir la porte d'un mouvement brusque. **fling out 1.** *v.tr.* (*a*) jeter (qch.) dehors; *F:* **to f. s.o. out,** flanquer qn à la porte; (*b*) **to f. out one's arm,** étendre le bras d'un grand geste. **2.** *v.i.* (*of horse*) ruer; *F:* (*of pers.*) **to f. out at s.o.,** invectiver, injurier, qn. **fling up** *v.tr.* (*a*) jeter (qch.) en l'air; (*b*) *F:* abandonner, renoncer à (un projet); démissionner.

flint [flint] *n.* (*a*) *Miner:* silex *m*; (*b*) pierre *f* à feu; (*for cigarette lighter*) pierre à briquet; *Prehist:* **f. implements,** outils *mpl* en silex taillés; (*c*) **f. glass,** flint(-glass) *m.*

flinty ['flinti] *a.* **1.** de silex. **2.** (cœur) dur.

flip^1 [flip] *n.* (*drink*) flip *m.*

flip^2 *n.* **1.** chiquenaude *f*, pichenette *f.* **2.** (*a*) petite secousse vive; **f. of the tail,** coup *m* de queue; (*b*) *F:* **f. side,** revers *m* (d'un disque).

flip^3 *v.tr.* **(flipped) 1.** (*a*) donner une chiquenaude, une pichenette, à (une boulette de papier, etc.); **to f. a coin,** jouer à pile ou face; (*b*) *El:* basculer (un interrupteur). **2.** donner une secousse vive à (sa ligne en pêchant, etc.). **3.** *U.S:* retourner (un disque). **4.** *v.i.* **to f. through a book,** feuilleter un livre. **5.** *v.tr.* & *v.i.* *P:* **to f. (one's lid),** sortir de ses gonds. **flipping** *a. F:* fichu; **a f. nuisance,** un fichu embêtement.

flip-flop ['flipflɔp] *n.* **1. flip-flops,** claquettes *fpl* (en plastique pour la plage). **2.** saut périlleux. **3.** *Elcs:* **f.-f. (circuit),** (circuit) basculeur *m* monostable.

flippancy ['flipənsi] *n.* légèreté *f*, désinvolture *f.*

flippant ['flipənt] *a.* léger, désinvolte. **-ly** *adv.* d'une manière désinvolte.

flipper ['flipər] *n.* **1.** (*a*) nageoire *f* (de cétacé, de phoque); aileron *m* (de requin); (*b*) palme *f* (de nageur sous-marin, etc.). **2.** *P:* main *f*, patte *f.*

flirt^1 [flə:t] *n.* (*pers.*) flirteur *m*; (*woman*) coquette *f.*

flirt^2 *v.i.* (*a*) flirter; **to f. with s.o.,** (*of woman*) faire la coquette avec qn; (*of man*) faire le galant auprès (d'une femme); (*b*) flirter (**with an idea,** avec une idée).

flirtation [flə:'teiʃ(ə)n] *n.* flirt *m.*

flirtatious [flə:'teiʃəs] *a. F:* (*of man*) flirteur; (*of woman*) coquette.

flit^1 [flit] *n. F:* **to do a moonlight f.,** déménager à la cloche de bois; mettre la clef sous la porte.

flit^2 *v.i.* **(flitted) 1.** (*a*) **to f. (away),** partir; (*b*) *Scot:* déménager. **2.** *F:* mettre la clef sous la porte; déménager à la cloche de bois. **3.** (*of bird, etc.*) **to f. by,** passer légèrement; **to f. about,** aller et venir d'un pas léger.

flitch [flitʃ] *n.* flèche *f* (de lard).

float^1 [flout] *n.* **1.** (*a*) train *m* (de bois); (*b*) radeau *m.* **2.** (*a*) *Mec.E: etc:* flotteur *m* (de chaudière, de carburateur, etc.); *I.C.E:* **f. chamber,** *U.S:* **f. bowl,** chambre *f* du flotteur; (*b*) flotteur, bouchon *m* (d'une ligne, d'un filet de pêche); galet *m* (de filet); (*c*) *Nat.Hist:* flotteur (de plante aquatique); vessie *f* natatoire (de poisson). **3.** (*a*) *Th: Cin:* portant *m* mobile; (*b*) *Th:* (*lighting*) **the floats,** la rampe. **4.** (*a*) wagon *m* en plate-forme; (*b*) char *m* de carnaval; **milk f.,** voiture *f* de livraison du lait. **5.** *Com:* (*a*) petite caisse; (*b*) fonds *mpl* de roulement.

float^2 **I.** *v.i.* **1.** (*a*) flotter, surnager; (*of boat*) être à flot; **cork floats on the surface of water,** le liège surnage à la surface de l'eau; **to f. down the stream,** descendre le courant; (*b*) *Swim:* faire la planche. **2.** (*a*) **to f. to the surface,** revenir à la surface; (*b*) **to f. in the air,** planer dans l'air; **there were rumours floating about that . . .,** le bruit courait que . . .. **3.** *Mec.E:* (*of part of machine*) avoir du jeu. **4.** (*a*) *Pol:* (*of voter*) être indécis; (*b*) **she floated out of the room,** elle est sortie de la pièce d'un pas léger. **II.** *v.tr.* **1.** (*a*) flotter (des bois, etc.); (*b*) (i) mettre (un navire) à flot, à l'eau; (ii) renflouer (un navire). **2.** (*a*) *Com:* lancer (une compagnie, etc.); *Fin:* émettre, lancer (un emprunt); (*b*) **to f. a rumour,** lancer une rumeur. **floating 1.** *a.* (*a*) (i) flottant, à flot; **f. light,** veilleuse *f* (à flotteur, à huile); **f. bridge,** pont de bateaux, de radeaux; **f. crane,** ponton-grue *m*, *pl.* pontons-grues; (ii) *Com:* **f. cargo,** cargaison *f* sur mer; (*b*) (i) (population) flottante; *Fin:* (*of exchange rate*) flottant; (capital) circulant, mobile; (ii) *Anat:* **f. ribs,** côtes flottantes; *Med:* **f. kidney,** rein mobile, flottant; (*c*) *Mec.E: etc:* (*of bearing*) flottant; (*d*) *Pol:* (voteur) indécis. **2.** *n.* (*a*) flottement *m* (d'un bâtiment); *Swim:* la planche; (*b*) mise *f* à flot (d'un navire); **f. (off),** renflouage *m* (d'une épave, etc.); (*c*) flottage *m* (du bois); (*d*) *Com:* lancement *m* (d'une société commerciale, etc.); *Fin:* émission *f* (d'un emprunt). **float off 1.** *v.i.* (*of ship*) se déséchouer. **2.** *v.tr.* renflouer (une épave).

floater ['floutər] *n.* **1.** (*pers.*) (*a*) baigneur qui fait la planche; (*b*) *Fin:* lanceur *m* (d'une compagnie, etc.). **2.** *Tchn:* flotteur *m.*

flocculent ['flɔkjulənt] *a.* floconneux.

flock^1 [flɔk] *n.* **1.** bourre *f* (de laine); **f. mattress,** matelas *m* en bourre de laine. **2. f. wallpaper,** papier tontisse.

flock^2 *n.* bande *f* (d'animaux); troupeau *m* (de moutons, d'oies); volée *f* (d'oiseaux); **a pastor and his f.,** un pasteur et ses ouailles *fpl*; **a f. of visitors,** une foule de visiteurs.

flock^3 *v.i.* **to f. (together),** s'attrouper, s'assembler; **everybody is flocking to see the exhibition,** tout le monde se précipite pour voir l'exposition; **in summer people f. to the sea,** en été les gens vont en foule au bord de la mer.

floe [flou] *n.* masse *f* de glaces flottantes; banquise *f.*

flog [flɔg] *v.tr.* **(flogged) 1.** flageller (qn); battre (qn) à coups de fouet; **to f. a horse,** cravacher un cheval; *F:* **to f. a dead horse,** se dépenser en pure perte; **to f. a subject to death,** ne pas savoir se taire sur une question. **2.** *F:* vendre, bazarder (qch.). **flogging** *n.* flagellation *f*; *Jur: Sch:* le châtiment du fouet.

flood^1 [flʌd] *n.* **1. f. (tide),** flux *m* (de la marée); marée montante. **2.** (*a*) inondation *f*; déluge *m*; **the river was in f.,** la rivière débordait; **crops ruined by the floods,** récoltes perdues à cause des inondations; **the victims of the f.,** les inondés; *B:* **the F.,** le Déluge; (*b*) **the floods of the Nile,** les crues du Nil; (*c*) **a f. of light,** des flots de lumière; **floods of tears, of abuse,** un torrent de larmes, d'injures.

flood^2 **1.** *v.tr.* (*a*) inonder (un terrain, etc.); *Nau:* noyer (les soutes); (*of house, ship, etc.*) **to be flooded,** être envahi par l'eau; (*b*) *Agr:* irriguer (un champ, etc.); (*c*) *I.C.E:* noyer (le carburateur); étouffer (le moteur); **to f. a (cigarette) lighter,** noyer la mèche d'un briquet; (*d*) **to f. the market with . . .,** inonder le marché de . . .; **to be flooded with letters,** être inondé, submergé, de lettres. **2.** *v.i.* (*a*) (*of rivers, etc.*) (i) déborder; (ii) être en crue; (*b*) **the sun's rays came flooding through the window,** les rayons du soleil entraient à flots par la fenêtre. **flooded** *a.* (*a*) (terrain) inondé; (*b*) (carburateur) noyé. **flooding** *n.* (*a*) inondation *f* (d'un terrain, etc.); débordement *m* (d'une rivière, etc.); *P.N:* **road liable to f.,** route inondable; (*b*) *Agr:* irrigation *f* (d'un champ, etc.); *Nau: etc:* noyage *m* (des soutes, etc.).

floodgate ['flʌdgeit] *n.* vanne (de décharge); porte *f* d'écluse; **to open, close, the floodgates,** lever, mettre, les vannes; **to open the floodgates of one's passions,** lâcher les écluses à ses passions.

floodlight¹ ['flʌdlait] *n.* (*a*) projecteur *m* (pour l'illumination des monuments); (*b*) lumière *f* de grande intensité; (*c*) *Phot:* (lampe *f*) flood (*f*).

floodlight² *v.tr.* (*p.t. & p.p.* **floodlighted** *or* **floodlit**) illuminer par projecteurs. **floodlit** *a.* illuminé (par des projecteurs). **floodlighting** *n.* illumination *f* par des projecteurs.

floor¹ [flɔːr] *n.* **1.** (*a*) parquet *m*; plancher *m*; **parquet f.** = parquet à l'anglaise; **tiled f.,** carrelage *m*; **f. polish,** cire *f* à parquet; *F:* **to wipe the f. with s.o.,** battre qn à plate couture; (*b*) parquet (d'un tribunal, d'une assemblée législative); **to take the f.,** prendre la parole; (*c*) **dance f.,** piste *f* de danse; **to take the f.,** se joindre aux danseurs; **f. show,** spectacle *m* de cabaret; (*d*) **the factory f., shop f.,** l'atelier *m*. **2.** étage *m*; palier *m*; **house on two floors,** maison *f* avec étage; **the ground f.,** le rez-de-chaussée; **first f.,** (i) premier étage; (ii) *NAm:* rez-de-chaussée; **to live on the fifth f.,** habiter (i) au cinquième, (ii) *NAm:* au sixième; **we live on the same f.,** nous habitons sur le même palier, nous sommes voisins de palier; *F:* **to get in on the ground f.,** (i) acheter des actions dès leur émission, au plus bas prix; (ii) s'assurer une situation privilégiée; **f. waiter,** garçon *m* d'étage (dans un hôtel). **3.** (*a*) fond *m* (de l'océan); (*b*) *Min:* sole *f* (d'une galerie de mine); (*c*) **threshing f.,** aire *f* (d'une grange).

floor² *v.tr.* **1.** *Const:* (i) planchéier, (ii) parqueter, (iii) carreler (une pièce). **2.** (*a*) terrasser (un adversaire); envoyer (un adversaire) au tapis; (*b*) *F:* réduire (qn) à quia; clouer le bec à (qn). **flooring** *n.* **1.** planchéiage *m*; parquetage *m*; carrelage *m*, dallage *m*. **2.** (*a*) plancher *m*; **parquet f.** = parquet *m* à l'anglaise; (*b*) *Veh:* plancher (d'une voiture, d'un avion, etc.).

floorboard ['flɔːbɔːd] *n.* planche *f* (du plancher, à planchéier).

floorcloth ['flɔːklɔθ] *n. Dom.Ec:* serpillière *f*.

floorspace ['flɔːspeis] *n.* surface (couverte), superficie *f* (d'une pièce, etc.); *Veh:* surface du plancher.

floorwalker ['flɔːwɔːkər] *n.* chef *m* de rayon.

floozie, floozy ['fluːzi] *n. P:* pouffiasse *f*.

flop¹ [flɔp] *n.* **1.** coup mat; bruit sourd. **2.** *F:* four *m*, fiasco *m*. **3.** *F:* (*pers.*) raté, -ée.

flop² *int. & adv.* **1.** plouf! patapouf! floc! **to fall f.,** faire patapouf. **2. to go f.,** faire échec.

flop³ *v.i.* **(flopped) 1.** (*a*) (*of stone, etc.*) faire plouf; faire floc; (*b*) (*of pers.*) **to f. (down),** se laisser tomber; s'affaler; **to f. down on(to) a seat,** tomber lourdement sur un siège; se laisser tomber comme un sac sur un siège; (*c*) **to f. about,** faire des sauts de carpe. **2.** *F:* échouer; (*of play, etc.*) faire four.

floppy ['flɔpi] *a.* (*of hat, etc.*) pendant, souple; (*of garment*) lâche, trop large; **with f. ears,** à oreilles pendantes.

flora ['flɔːrə] *n.* **the f. and fauna of a region,** la flore et la faune d'une région.

floral ['flɔːrəl] *a.* floral, -aux; **dress with a bold f. design,** robe *f* à grands ramages.

floret ['flɔːrit] *n. Bot:* fleuron *m*.

floribunda [flɔri'bʌndə] *a. & n. Hort:* (rose *f*, rosier *m*) floribunda *inv*.

florid ['flɔrid] *a.* (*of style, etc.*) fleuri; orné à l'excès; (*of dress, etc.*) flamboyant; (*of complexion*) coloré.

Florida ['flɔridə] *Pr.n. Geog:* Floride *f*.

florin ['flɔrin] *n. Num: A:* (pièce *f* de) deux shillings.

florist ['flɔrist] *n.* fleuriste *mf*.

floss [flɔs] *n. Tex:* **f. silk,** bourre *f* de soie; *Dent:* **dental f.,** fil *m* (de soie) dentaire.

flotation [flou'teiʃ(ə)n] *n.* **1.** *Nau:* flottaison *f*. **2.** flottage *m* (du bois, etc.). **3.** *Com:* lancement *m* (d'une compagnie); *Fin:* émission *f* (d'un emprunt).

flotilla [flə'tilə] *n. Navy: Nau:* flottille *f*; escadrille *f*.

flotsam ['flɔtsəm] *n. Jur:* épave(s) flottante(s); **f. and jetsam,** choses *fpl* de flot et de mer.

flounce¹ [flauns] *n.* mouvement vif (d'indignation).

flounce² *v.i.* s'élancer, se jeter (avec un mouvement d'indignation, d'impatience); **to f. in, out, off,** entrer, sortir, partir, brusquement.

flounce³ *n. Dressm:* volant *m*.

flounce⁴ *v.tr.* garnir de volants; **flounced skirt,** jupe à volants.

flounder¹ ['flaundər] *n. Ich:* flet *m*, carrelet *m*.

flounder² *v.i.* patauger, barboter (dans la boue, etc.); **to f. about in the water,** se débattre dans l'eau; **to f. along,** avancer en trébuchant; **to f. in a speech,** patauger dans un discours. **floundering 1.** *a.* qui patauge, barbote (dans la boue, etc.). **2.** *n.* barbotement *m*, pataugeage *m*.

flour¹ ['flauər] *n.* **1.** farine *f*; **f. mill,** minoterie *f*; **f. dredger,** saupoudroir *m* à farine; **to dust sth. with f.,** (en)fariner qch. **2.** (*a*) farine (de riz, etc.); **potato f.,** fécule *f* de pommes de terre; (*b*) fleur (de soufre).

flour² *v.tr.* (en)fariner (qn, qch.); saupoudrer (une pâte, etc.) de farine.

flourbin ['flauəbin] *n.* farinière *f*, huche *f*, maie *f*.

flourish¹ ['flʌriʃ] *n.* **1.** (*a*) trait *m* de plume; (*after signature*) parafe *m*; (*b*) fioriture *f* (de style). **2.** grand geste; brandissement *m* (d'épée); **to take off one's hat with a f.,** saluer d'un grand geste; **to carry things off with a f.,** y mettre du panache. **3.** *Mus:* (*a*) fanfare *f* (de trompettes); (*b*) fioriture(s), ornement *m*.

flourish² 1. *v.i.* (*a*) (*of plant*) croître, se développer, bien venir; **to f. in a sandy soil,** se plaire dans un terrain sablonneux; (*b*) (*of pers., business, etc.*) être florissant, prospérer; (*of arts*) fleurir; **trade is flourishing,** le commerce est prospère; (*c*) être dans tout son éclat; battre son plein; (*d*) *Mus:* faire des fioritures; (*e*) (*of trumpets*) sonner une fanfare. **2.** *v.tr.* brandir (une épée, un bâton). **flourishing** *a.* (*of plant, industry, etc.*) florissant; (commerce) prospère.

floury ['flauəri] *a.* **1.** enfariné; couvert de farine. **2.** (*of potatoes, etc.*) farineux.

flout [flaut] *v.tr.* (*a*) railler (qn); narguer (ses ennemis); (*b*) faire fi de (l'autorité de qn).

flow¹ [flou] *n.* **1.** (*flowing*) (*a*) coulée *f* (d'un liquide); (*b*) *Mch:* courant *m*, flux *m* (de vapeur); (*c*) *Metall: etc:* fluage *m*; **f. point,** point *m* de fluage; limite *f* d'écoulement; (*d*) *Geog: Geol:* écoulement (d'un cours d'eau, d'une couche); (*e*) *El:* passage *m* (d'un courant); (*f*) passage, arrivée *f* (d'air, d'essence, etc.); (*g*) flot *m*, flux (de la marée); **ebb and f.,** flux et reflux; (*h*) *Med:* écoulement (du sang); (*i*) *Fin:* mouvement *m* (de capital); **f. of money,** flux monétaire; **cash f.,** cash-flow *m*; (*j*) *Cmptr:* circulation *f* (de l'information); **f. path,** branche *f* de traitement; **f. diagram,** organigramme *m*; (*k*) **a steady f. of immigrants,** un courant ininterrompu d'immigration. **2.** (*quantity*) (*a*) volume *m* (de liquide débité); débit *m* (d'une rivière, d'une pompe, d'un courant électrique); **the f. of traffic,** le débit de la circulation; **there was a heavy f. of traffic,** il y avait une grande circulation. **3.** (*sth. that flows*) (*a*) courant, cours *m* (d'eau); (*b*) coulée *f* (de lave); (*c*) flot (de sang, etc.); (*d*) *Physiol:* **menstrual f.,** règles *fpl*; (*e*) lignes tombantes (d'une robe); drapé *m* (d'un vêtement).

flow² *v.i.* **1.** (*stream along*) (*a*) couler; s'écouler; (*of river*) **to f. into the sea,** se verser dans la mer; **lava**

that flows down the mountains, lave qui dévale de la montagne; (b) (*of tide*) monter, remonter; (c) (*of blood, etc.*) circuler; **blood flowing to the head,** sang *m* qui afflue à la tête; (d) (*of people*) aller, venir, en masse; (*of conversation, etc.*) aller son train; (*of literary style*) couler facilement; (e) (*of hair, etc.*) flotter. **2.** (*stream out*) (*of blood, tears, etc.*) se répandre, jaillir. **3.** (*result*) dériver, découler (**from,** de); **God, from Whom all blessings f.,** Dieu, de qui découlent toutes les grâces. **4.** *Lit:* **land flowing with milk and honey,** pays où coulent le lait et le miel. **flow away** *v.i.* (*of liquid*) s'écouler. **flow back** *v.i.* refluer; (*of water*) regorger (dans un tuyau, etc.). **flow in** *v.i.* (a) (*of liquid*) entrer; (b) (*of people, money*) affluer. **flowing 1.** *a.* (a) (*of stream, etc.*) coulant; (b) (*of style, etc.*) coulant, fluide; (*of movement*) gracieux; (c) (*of hair*) tombant (dans le cou); (barbe) longue. **2.** *n.* (a) coulement *m* (d'une rivière, etc.); (b) écoulement *m* (de l'eau). **flow out** *v.i.* sortir, s'écouler.

flowchart ['floutʃɑːt] *n.* (a) *Cmptr:* organigramme *m*; (b) diagramme *m* des opérations successives.

flower¹ ['flauər] *n.* **1.** *Bot:* fleur *f*; **wild flowers,** fleurs sauvages, des champs; **bunch of flowers,** bouquet *m* (de fleurs); **cut flowers,** fleurs coupées; **to put flowers on a grave,** fleurir une tombe; **no flowers by request,** ni fleurs ni couronnes; **f. garden,** jardin d'agrément; **f. bed,** plate-bande *f*, *pl.* plates-bandes; (*round*) corbeille *f*; **f. market,** marché *m* aux fleurs; **f. seller, f. girl,** marchande *f* de fleurs (dans la rue); **f. vase,** vase *m* à fleurs; **f. show,** exposition *f* horticole; floralies *fpl.* **2.** *Ch: etc:* **flowers of sulphur,** fleur de soufre. **3.** (*ornament*) *Typ:* fleuron *m.* **4.** fine fleur, crème *f* (de l'armée, etc.). **5.** (*of plant*) **in f.,** en fleur; **in full f.,** en plein épanouissement; **to burst into f.,** fleurir; **in the f. of youth,** dans la première fleur de la jeunesse.

flower² *v.i.* (*of plant*) fleurir, être en fleur. **flowered** *a.* (a) (jardin, talus, etc.) fleuri; (b) **white-f.,** à fleurs blanches; **many-f.,** multiflore; (c) *Tex:* (tissu) à fleurs. **flowering 1.** *a.* (a) (*of garden, plant*) fleuri, en fleur; (b) (arbrisseau) à fleurs. **2.** *n.* fleuraison *f* (d'une plante).

flowerhead ['flauəhed] *n. Bot:* capitule *m.*

flowerpot ['flauəpɔt] *n.* pot *m* à fleurs; (*ornamental*) cache-pot *m inv.*

flowery ['flauəri] *a.* **1.** (pré, etc.) couvert de fleurs; (tapis, etc.) orné de fleurs, de ramages. **2.** *Pej:* (*of style, etc.*) fleuri; **f. phrases,** fleurs *fpl* de rhétorique.

flowline ['floulain] *n.* (a) *Cmptr:* ligne de jonction de symboles (sur un organigramme); (b) *Ind:* **f. production,** travail *m* à la chaîne.

flowmeter ['floumiːtər] *n.* débitmètre *m*; indicateur *m* d'écoulement, de débit (des liquides, etc.).

flown. *see* FLY³.

flu [fluː] *n. Med: F:* grippe *f*; **Asian f.,** grippe asiatique.

flub¹ [flʌb] *v.tr. & i.* (**flubbed**) *NAm: F:* faire une gaffe.

flub² *n. NAm:* gaffe *f*, bourde *f.*

fluctuate ['flʌktjueit] *v.i.* **1.** fluctuer; (*of conditions, etc.*) varier; **prices f. between . . . and . . .,** les prix flottent entre . . . et . . . . **2.** (*of pers.*) vaciller (dans ses opinions, etc.). **fluctuating** *a.* (*of temperature, etc.*) variable; (*of prices, etc.*) oscillant.

fluctuation [flʌktju'eiʃ(ə)n] *n.* variations *fpl* (de température); **exchange f.,** fluctuation(s) *f* du change.

flue [fluː] *n.* **1.** (a) *Const:* tuyau *m* de cheminée; conduit *m* de fumée; (b) *Mch:* **f. boiler,** chaudière *f* à tubes-foyers; (c) **f. brush,** torche-tubes *m inv*; hérisson *m.* **2.** *Mus:* bouche *f* (de tuyau d'orgue); **f. pipe,** tuyau à bouche; **f. stop,** jeu *m* de flûte.

fluency ['fluːənsi] *n.* facilité *f* (de parole, de style).

fluent ['fluːənt] *a.* (*of speech, etc.*) coulant, facile; **to be a f. speaker,** avoir la parole facile; **he is a f. speaker of French,** il parle le français couramment. **-ly** *adv.* (parler, lire) couramment; (s'exprimer) avec facilité.

fluff¹ [flʌf] *n.* **1.** (a) duvet *m* (d'étoffe); coton *m* (de laine); **a bit of f.,** (i) une peluche; (ii) *F:* (*girl*) une poule; (b) (*under bed, etc.*) **(pieces of) f.,** moutons *mpl.* **2.** fourrure douce (d'un lapin, etc.). **3.** *Th: F:* loup *m.*

fluff² *v.tr.* **1.** lainer (un drap, etc.); **to f. (out) one's hair,** faire bouffer ses cheveux; **bird that fluffs (up) its feathers,** oiseau *m* qui hérisse ses plumes. **2.** *Th: F:* rater, louper (son entrée); *Sp:* **to f. a shot,** rater un coup.

fluffy ['flʌfi] *a.* (drap) pelucheux; (poussin, etc.) duveteux; **f. hair,** cheveux flous.

fluid ['fluːid] **1.** *a.* (a) fluide, liquide; (b) *Mec.E:* (embrayage) hydraulique; (transmission) fluide; (c) (*of style, etc.*) coulant, facile; (*of opinions, etc.*) changeant, inconstant; **industry in a f. state,** industrie *f* en voie de transformation rapide; **f. situation,** situation *f* fluide. **2.** *n.* (a) fluide *m*, liquide *m*, solution *f*; *Aut:* **brake f.,** liquide pour freins; *Med:* **sterilizing f.,** solution stérilisante; (b) **body fluids,** sécrétions *fpl.*

fluidify [fluː'idifai] *v.tr.* liquéfier (un solide).

fluidity [fluː'iditi] *n.* (a) fluidité, facilité *f* (de style, etc.); (b) caractère changeant (des opinions, etc.).

fluidize ['fluːidaiz] *v.tr.* rendre fluide.

fluke¹ [fluːk] *n.* **1.** *Ich:* flet *m.* **2. f. (worm),** douve *f* (du foie).

fluke² *n.* **1.** *Nau:* patte *f*, aile *f* (d'ancre). **2.** *Z:* **flukes,** nageoires *fpl* (de la queue d'une baleine).

fluke³ *n.* (a) *Bill:* point volé; **by a f.,** par raccroc; (b) coup de veine; chance *f*; **his success was due to a f.,** c'est un hasard qu'il ait réussi.

fluke⁴ *v.tr. Bill:* raccrocher (la balle).

flume¹ [fluːm] *n.* **1.** buse *f* (d'un moulin à eau). **2.** (*for logs, etc.*) canal *m* d'amenée. **3.** *U.S: Geog:* ravin *m.*

flummox ['flʌməks] *v.tr. F:* réduire (qn) à quia.

flung. *see* FLING².

flunk [flʌŋk] *esp. NAm: F:* **1.** *v.i.* se faire recaler, se faire coller (à un examen). **2.** *v.tr.* (a) recaler, coller (qn à un examen); (b) rater, se faire coller à (un examen).

flunkey ['flʌŋki] *n. A: or Pej:* laquais *m.*

fluoresce [fluːə'res] *v.i.* entrer en fluorescence.

fluorescence [fluə'resəns] *n.* fluorescence *f.*

fluorescent [fluə'resənt] *a.* fluorescent; **f. lighting,** éclairage fluorescent, par fluorescence.

fluoridation [fluəri'deiʃ(ə)n] *n. Ch:* fluoration *f.*

fluoride ['fluəraid] *n. Ch:* fluorure *f.*

fluorine ['fluːəriːn] *n. Ch:* fluor *m.*

fluoroscope ['fluərəskoup] *n.* fluoroscope *m.*

flurry¹ ['flʌri] *n.* **1.** rafale *f* (de neige); *NAm: occ.* averse *f.* **2.** agitation *f*, bouleversement *m*, émoi *m.*

flurry² *v.tr.* **to get flurried,** perdre la tête.

flush¹ [flʌʃ] *n. Ven:* envolée *f* (d'oiseaux).

flush² *v.tr. Ven:* (faire) lever, faire partir (des perdrix, etc.).

flush³ *n.* **1.** (a) *Hyd.E:* chasse *f* (d'eau); (b) curage *m* (d'un égout). **2.** accès *m*, élan *m* (d'émotion, etc.); **in the first f. of victory,** dans l'ivresse de la victoire. **3.** (a) éclat *m* (de lumière, de la beauté, etc.); **in the first f. of youth,** dans le premier éclat de la jeunesse; (b) rougeur *f*, flot *m* de sang (au visage); *Med:* suffusion *f*; **hot f.,** bouffée *f* de chaleur; **the words brought a f. to her cheeks,** ces mots l'ont fait rougir.

flush⁴ *v.* **1.** *v.tr.* faire jaillir (l'eau); **to f. (out) a drain,** donner une chasse à un égout; **to f. the lavatory,**

tirer la chasse d'eau; **to f. sth. away,** jeter qch. à l'égout. **2.** *v.i.* (*a*) (*of light, etc.*) éclater; (*b*) (*of pers.*) rougir; (*of blood*) monter (au visage); **he, his face, flushed,** il a rougi. **3.** *v.tr.* **the exercise had flushed their cheeks,** l'exercice leur avait fait monter le sang au visage. **flushed** *a.* (visage) empourpré, congestionné; **f. with anger,** rouge de colère; **f. with success,** exalté par le succès.

flush[5] *n. Cards:* (*poker*) flush *m*; longue couleur; **straight f.,** séquence *f* flush.

flush[6] *a.* **1.** *F:* (*of pers.*) **to be f. (with money),** être en fonds. **2.** (*of surface, etc.*) ras; de niveau; (*of door lock, etc.*) encastré; (*of screw, nail*) noyé; (*of rivet*) à tête noyée, perdue; **f. mounted,** monté à fleur; **to be f. with sth.,** être à fleur de qch.; être de niveau avec qch.; **f. with the ground,** à ras de sol.

flush[7] *v.tr.* affleurer (deux surfaces, etc.).

fluster[1] ['flʌstər] *n.* agitation *f*, trouble *m*; **in a f.,** tout en émoi, déconcerté.

fluster[2] **1.** *v.tr.* faire perdre la tête à (qn); rendre (qn) nerveux; **to be, get, flustered,** se troubler. **2.** *v.i.* s'agiter; s'énerver.

flute[1] [flu:t] *n.* **1.** *Mus:* (*a*) flûte *f*; **transverse f.,** flûte traversière; *Th:* **the Magic F.,** la Flûte enchantée; (*b*) **f. stop,** jeu *m* de flûte (de l'orgue). **2.** *Mus:* **f. (player),** (joueur, -euse, de) flûte. **3.** (*a*) (*in wood, etc.*) cannelure *f* (de colonne); (*b*) **f. (glass),** flûte.

flute[2] *v.* **1.** (*a*) *v.i.* (i) jouer de la flûte; (ii) (*of birds*) flûter; (*b*) *v.tr.* jouer (un air) sur la flûte. **2.** *v.tr.* canneler (une colonne). **fluted** *a.* (*of wood, etc.*) à cannelures; (*of column*) cannelé. **fluting** *n.* **1.** (*a*) façonnage *m* des cannelures. **2.** *coll.* (*a*) cannelures *fpl.*

flutist ['flu:tist] *n. esp. NAm:* flûtiste *mf.*

flutter[1] ['flʌtər] *n.* **1.** (*a*) volètement *m*, trémoussement *m* (d'un oiseau); battement *m* (des ailes, des paupières); palpitation *f* (du cœur); flottement *m* (d'un drapeau, etc.); (*b*) pulsation *f* (du son); (*c*) *T.V:* scintillation *f*. **2.** agitation *f*, trouble *m*; **to be in a f. of excitement,** *F:* **all in a f.,** être tout en émoi. **3.** *Fin: F:* petite spéculation; **to have a little f.,** risquer de petites sommes au jeu; faire un ou deux petits paris.

flutter[2] **1.** *v.i.* (*of birds, insects*) voleter; battre des ailes; (*of flag, etc.*) flotter, s'agiter (au vent); (*of heart*) palpiter; (*of pulse*) battre irrégulièrement; **to make s.o.'s heart f.,** faire tressaillir le cœur de qn; **the letter fluttered to the ground,** la lettre a volé par terre. **2.** *v.tr.* (*of bird*) **to f. its wings,** battre des ailes.

fluvial ['flu:viəl] *a.* fluvial, -aux.

flux[1] [flʌks] *n.* **1.** (*a*) *Med:* flux *m* (de sang, etc.); (*b*) *Oc:* flux, montant *m* (de la marée); **f. and reflux,** flot et jusant; (*c*) courant *m* (d'eau, etc.). **2.** (*a*) changement continuel; **to be in a state of f.,** être sujet à des changements fréquents, à des vicissitudes; (*b*) flux (magnétique, etc.). **3.** (*a*) *Metall:* fondant *m*, flux; (*b*) *Glassm:* **gold f.,** aventurine *f*.

flux[2] **1.** *v.i.* (*of metal*) fondre; devenir liquide. **2.** *v.tr. Metall:* fondre, mettre en fusion (un métal).

fluxion ['flʌkʃ(ə)n] *n. Med:* fluxion *f* (de sang, etc.).

fluxmeter ['flʌksmi:tər] *n. Ph:* fluxmètre *m.*

fly[1], *pl.* **flies** [flai(z)] *n.* **1.** (*a*) *Ent:* mouche *f*; **Spanish f.,** mouche d'Espagne, cantharide *f*; **horse f.,** taon *m*; **tsetse f.,** (mouche) tsé-tsé (*f*); **f. whisk,** chasse-mouches *m inv*; **f. swatter,** tapette *f* à mouches; **they were dying like flies,** on mourait comme des mouches; **he wouldn't hurt a f.,** il ne ferait pas de mal à une mouche; *F:* **a f. in the ointment,** un cheveu (sur la soupe); **to catch flies,** bayer aux corneilles; **there are, there's, no flies on him,** il n'est pas bête; (*b*) *Fish:* mouche (artificielle ou naturelle); **wet f.,** mouche mouillée, noyée; **wet-f., dry-f., fishing,** pêche à la mouche noyée, sèche; (*c*) *Bot:* **f. orchis,** ophrys *f* mouche; *Fung:* **f. agaric,** fausse oronge. **2.** *Typ:* receveur mécanique.

fly[2] *n.* **1.** vol *m.* **2.** (*a*) (*also pl.* **flies**) braguette *f* (de pantalon); (*b*) (i) auvent *m*, (ii) toit *m* (de tente). **3.** *Th:* **the flies,** les cintres *mpl.* **4.** (*a*) *Tchn:* régulateur *m*, contrepoids *m* (de sonnerie d'horloge, etc.); (*b*) *Tex:* **f. shuttle,** navette volante.

fly[3] *v.* (*p.t.* **flew** [flu:]; *p.p.* **flown** [floun]) **I.** *v.i.* **1.** (*a*) (*of bird, etc.*) voler; *F:* **the bird has flown,** l'oiseau s'est envolé; **to f. high,** (i) voler haut; (ii) (*of pers.*) avoir de l'ambition; **as the crow flies,** à vol d'oiseau; (*b*) *Av:* voler; effectuer un vol; **to f. blind,** voler sans visibilité; **to f. over London,** survoler Londres. **2.** (*of hair, etc.*) flotter. **3.** (*a*) (*of pers., etc.*) courir, aller à toute vitesse; (*of time*) fuir, filer; **to f. to s.o.'s help,** courir à l'aide de qn; **it's late, I must f.,** il se fait tard, il faut que je me sauve; **time is flying,** le temps s'envole; **to f. into a temper,** se mettre en colère; **the door flew open,** la porte s'ouvrit en coup de vent; (*b*) (*of cork, etc.*) voler, sauter en l'air; (*of sparks*) jaillir; **to make the fur f.,** (i) se battre avec acharnement; (ii) faire une scène; **to f. off the handle,** (i) (*of axe head, etc.*) se démancher; (ii) *F:* s'emporter; sortir de ses gonds; *F:* **to send s.o. flying,** envoyer rouler qn; (*c*) **to f. to pieces, to bits,** éclater; voler en éclats. **4.** **to let f.,** lancer (une flèche); décocher (un trait); lâcher (une volée d'injures); **to let f. at s.o.,** (i) décharger son fusil sur qn; (ii) *F:* flanquer un coup à qn; (iii) s'en prendre à qn. **5.** (= FLEE, *in pres. tenses only*) (*a*) fuir, s'enfuir; (*b*) *v.tr.* **to f. the country,** s'enfuir du pays. **II.** *v.tr.* **1.** *Nau:* battre (un pavillon). **2.** (*a*) **to f. pigeons,** faire un lancer des pigeons voyageurs; (*b*) **to f. a kite,** (i) faire voler un cerf-volant; (ii) *Fig:* lancer un ballon d'essai. **3.** *Av:* piloter (un avion); emmener qn, qch., en avion; transporter qn, qch., par avion. **fly about** *v.i.* (*of bird*) voler çà et là; (*of butterfly, etc.*) voltiger. **fly away** *v.i.* (*a*) (*of bird, etc.*) s'envoler; (*b*) (*of pers.*) se sauver. **fly by** *v.i.* (*a*) passer à toute vitesse; **as the days flew by,** à mesure que les jours s'enfuyaient; (*b*) *Av:* (*of aircraft*) passer. **fly in 1.** *v.i.* arriver en avion. **2.** *v.tr.* amener (qn, qch.) en avion. **flying 1.** *a.* (*a*) (i) (oiseau, poisson, etc.) volant; **f. fox,** roussette *f*; (ii) *U.S: Av:* **f. corps,** corps d'armée aérien; **unidentified f. object,** objet volant non identifié; (*b*) (ruban, etc.) volant, léger; (*c*) (i) (course, etc.) rapide; (camp) temporaire; **f. column,** *Mil:* colonne *f* mobile, groupement *m* mobile; (ii) **to pay a f. visit to London,** faire une visite éclair à Londres; (iii) **f. start,** départ en flèche; **we got off to a f. start,** nous nous sommes lancés (dans ce projet, etc.) sans anicroche; **to take a f. leap over sth.,** franchir qch. d'un saut; (*d*) *Civ.E: etc:* (échafaudage) à bascule; **f. bridge,** pont volant; (*e*) (*fleeing*) en fuite; *Lit: Mus:* **the F. Dutchman,** le Vaisseau fantôme. **2.** *n.* (*a*) (i) vol *m* (d'un oiseau, d'une flèche, etc.); (ii) *Av:* aviation *f*; pilotage *m* (d'un avion); **blind f.,** vol sans visibilité; **instrument f.,** navigation aux instruments; **f. club,** aéro-club *m*, *pl.* aéro-clubs; **f. boat,** hydravion monocoque; **he is interested in anything connected with f.,** il s'intéresse à tous les aspects de l'aviation; (*b*) jaillissement *m* (d'étincelles); (*c*) fuite *f* (de qn); (*d*) (i) lancement *m* (des pigeons, d'un cerf-volant); (ii) déploiement *m* (d'un drapeau). **fly off** *v.i.* (*a*) (*of bird, etc.*) s'envoler; (*b*) (*of pers.*) partir en avion; (*c*) (*of button, etc.*) sauter. **fly out 1.** *v.i.* (*a*) sortir en volant; (*b*) partir en avion. **2.** *v.tr.* emmener (qn, qch.) en avion. **fly past** *v.i. Mil.Av:* exécuter un défilé aérien. **fly up** *v.i.* s'élever; se projeter en l'air.

fly[4] *a. F: O:* malin, -igne; **he's very f.,** c'est un malin.

flyaway ['flaiəwei] *a.* (*a*) (*of bow, etc.*) flottant, négligé; (*b*) (*of pers.*) léger, étourdi.

flybill ['flaibil] *n.* **1.** feuille volante; prospectus *m.* **2.** (*poster*) papillon *m.*

flyblow ['flaiblou] *n.* (*a*) œufs *mpl* de mouche (dans la viande); (*b*) *F:* chiures *fpl* de mouche.
flyblown ['flaibloun] *a.* (*a*) plein, couvert, d'œufs de mouches; (*b*) *F:* couvert de chiures de mouche.
fly-by-night ['flaibainait] *n. F:* (*a*) oiseau *m* de nuit; (*b*) *a. & n.* **f.-by-n. (firm),** entreprise véreuse.
flycatcher ['flaikætʃər] *n.* **1.** attrape-mouche(s) *m inv.* **2.** *Orn:* (*a*) gobe-mouches *m inv;* **spotted f.,** gobe-mouches gris; (*b*) *NAm:* moucherolle *f.*
flyer ['flaiər] *n.* **1.** aviateur, -trice. **2. to take a f. over the handlebars,** se trouver projeté par-dessus le guidon. **3.** feuille volante, prospectus *m.*
flyleaf ['flaili:f] *n. Bookb:* (feuille *f* de) garde (*f*).
flyover ['flaiouvər] *n.* **1.** *Civ.E:* saut-de-mouton *m, pl.* sauts-de-mouton; **f. crossing,** croisement *m* à niveaux différents. **2.** *Av.* (*a*) survol *m;* (*b*) défilé aérien.
flypaper ['flaipeipər] *n.* papier *m* tue-mouches.
flypast ['flaipɑ:st] *n. Mil.Av:* défilé aérien.
flypost ['flaipoust] *v.tr.* coller illicitement des papillons, des affichettes.
flysheet ['flaishi:t] *n.* **1.** feuille volante; prospectus *m.* **2.** double toit *m* (d'une tente).
flyweight ['flaiweit] *n. Box:* poids *m* mouche.
flywheel ['flai(h)wi:l] *n. Mec.E: etc:* volant *m* (d'entraînement, de commande).
foal¹ [foul] *n.* poulain *m,* pouliche *f;* (*of donkey*) ânon *m,* bourriquet *m;* **mare in, with, f.,** jument pleine.
foal² *v.tr.* mettre bas (un poulain); *abs.* pouliner.
foam¹ [foum] *n.* **1.** écume *f;* (*on beer*) mousse *f;* **waves white with f.,** vagues moutonneuses; (*of wave*) **to break into f.,** déferler; **f.-flecked,** moucheté d'écume; *Toil:* **f. bath,** bain *m* de mousse. **2.** bave *f;* écume (à la bouche). **3.** mousse; (*a*) **f. fire extinguisher,** extincteur *m* à mousse carbonique; (*b*) **f. rubber,** caoutchouc *m* mousse.
foam² *v.i.* (*of sea, etc.*) écumer; (*of beer, etc.*) mousser; **to f. at the mouth,** (i) avoir l'écume aux lèvres; (*of dog, etc.*) baver; (ii) *F:* écumer (de rage). **foaming** *a.* (*of sea, horse, etc.*) écumant; (*of sea*) moutonnant; (*of beer, etc.*) moussant; (*of blood, saliva*) spumeux.
foamy ['foumi] *a.* (*of sea*) écumant; (*of drink*) mousseux.
fob¹ [fɔb] *n.* **f. (pocket),** gousset *m* (de pantalon).
fob² *v.tr.* **(fobbed) to f. s.o. off with sth., to f. sth. off on s.o.,** refiler qch. à qn.
focal ['fouk(ə)l] *a.* (*a*) *Ph: Opt: Mth:* focal, -aux; **f. point,** foyer *m* (d'un miroir, etc.); **f. length,** distance, longueur, focale; (*b*) *Med:* (infection) focale.
focalization [foukəlai'zeiʃ(ə)n] *n.* **1.** focalisation *f.* **2.** *Med:* localisation *f* (d'une maladie) à son foyer.
focalize ['foukəlaiz] *v.tr.* **1.** = FOCUS² 1. **2.** mettre au point (l'œil). **3.** (*a*) localiser (une maladie) à son foyer; (*b*) *v.i.* (*of illness*) se localiser à son foyer.
fo'c'sle ['fouksl] *n. Nau:* **1.** gaillard *m;* **f. deck,** pont de gaillard. **2.** (*in merchant vessel*) poste *m* de l'équipage.
focus¹, *pl.* **foci, focuses** ['foukəs, 'fousai, 'foukəsiz] *n.* **1.** *Mth: Opt: etc:* foyer *m* (de lentille, etc.); *Opt:* **depth of f.,** (i) profondeur *f* de foyer; (ii) profondeur de champ; **in f.,** (i) (*of image*) au point; (ii) (*of instrument*) réglé; **out of f.,** (i) (*of image*) pas au point; (ii) (*of instrument*) non réglé, déréglé; (iii) (*of headlamp bulb, etc.*) mal réglé; **to bring sth. into f.,** mettre qch. au point; *Phot:* **fixed-f. camera,** appareil *m* à mise au point fixe. **2.** centre *m* (d'un tremblement de terre, etc.); *Med:* siège *m* (d'une maladie); **f. of infection,** foyer d'infection.
focus² *v.tr.* **(focused) 1.** concentrer (les rayons de lumière, etc.) **(in, on,** dans, sur); faire converger (des rayons); *v.i.* (*of light, sound, etc.*) converger (**on,** sur); **all eyes were focused on him,** il était le point de mire de tous les yeux. **2.** (*a*) mettre au point (un microscope, etc.); *v.i. Phot:* **to f. on an object,** mettre au point sur un objet; (*b*) mettre au point (un objet). **focusing** *n.* **1.** convergence *f* (de rayons, etc.). **2.** (*a*) mise *f* au point (d'une jumelle, etc.); (*b*) focalisation *f.*
fodder¹ ['fɔdər] *n.* fourrage *m;* **green, dry, f.,** fourrage (en) vert, (en) sec; *F:* **cannon f.,** chair *f* à canon.
fodder² *v.tr.* donner le fourrage à (une bête).
foe [fou] *n. Lit:* ennemi *m,* adversaire *m.*
foetal, *NAm:* **fetal** ['fi:t(ə)l] *n. Biol:* fœtal, -aux.
foetid ['fi:tid] *a.* = FETID.
foetus, *NAm:* **fetus,** *pl.* **-uses** ['fi:təs, -əsiz] *n. Biol:* fœtus *m.*
fog¹ [fɔg] *n.* **1.** (*a*) brouillard *m;* brume *f;* **in the f.,** par le brouillard; *Fig:* **I'm in a f.,** je ne sais plus où j'en suis; *Av: etc:* **f. dispersal,** dénébulation *f;* **f. light,** (i) projecteur *m* pour le brouillard; (ii) *Aut:* (phare) antibrouillard (*m*); **f. signal,** (i) *Nau:* signal *m,* -aux, de brume; (ii) *Rail:* pétard *m;* (*b*) *Phot:* (*on negative*) voile *m.* **2.** buée *f* (sur les vitres, etc.).
fog² *v.* **(fogged) 1.** *v.tr.* (*a*) embrumer (un endroit); *F:* brouiller (les idées); embrouiller (qn); **I am a bit fogged,** je ne sais plus où j'en suis; (*b*) embuer (une glace, etc.); (*c*) *Phot:* voiler (un cliché). **2.** *v.i.* (*a*) (*of spectacles*) **to f. (up),** se couvrir de buée; (*b*) *Phot:* (*of negative*) se voiler. **fogging** *n.* **1.** ternissement *m* (d'une glace). **2.** *Phot:* voile *m.*
fogbound ['fɔgbaund] *a.* pris dans le brouillard.
fogey ['fougi] *n. F:* **old f.,** vieille baderne.
fogginess ['fɔginis] *n.* **1.** état brumeux (du temps). **2.** confusion *f* (des idées de qn); *Phot:* voile *m.*
foggy ['fɔgi] *a.* **1.** brumeux; **f. weather,** temps *m* de brume; temps brumeux; **on a f. day,** par un jour de brouillard; **it's f.,** il y a, il fait, du brouillard. **2.** (*of photograph, etc.*) voilé; **to have only a f. idea of sth.,** n'avoir qu'une vague idée de qch.; *F:* **I haven't the foggiest (idea)!** je n'en ai pas la moindre idée.
foghorn ['fɔghɔ:n] *n. Nau:* corne *f* de brume; sirène *f; F:* **voice like a f.,** voix *f* de taureau.
foglamp ['fɔglæmp] *n.* (phare *m*) antibrouillard (*m*).
foible ['fɔibl] *n.* côté *m* faible, point *m* faible.
foil¹ [fɔil] *n.* **1.** *Arch:* lobe *m* (d'un arc, etc.). **2.** *Metalw:* (*a*) feuille *f* (d'or, etc.); **silver f.,** feuille d'argent; *Cu:* **household f., cooking f.,** feuille d'aluminium; (*b*) tain *m* (d'une glace). **3.** patin *m,* aile *f* (d'un hydrofoil). **4.** (*of pers., thg*) repoussoir *m;* **to serve as a f. to s.o.'s beauty,** servir de repoussoir à la beauté de qn.
foil² *n. Fenc:* **1.** fleuret *m.* **2. foils,** escrime *f* au fleuret.
foil³ *v.tr.* faire échouer, faire manquer (une tentative, etc.); contrecarrer (un plan, un complot); (*of pers.*) **to be foiled at all points,** échouer sur toute la ligne.
foist [fɔist] *v.tr.* refiler (**sth. on s.o.,** qch. à qn); **to f. oneself on s.o.,** s'imposer à qn, chez qn.
fold¹ [fould] *n.* **1.** *Husb:* **sheep f.,** parc *m* à moutons. **2.** sein *m* (i) de l'Église, (ii) de la famille; **to bring back a lost sheep to the f.,** ramener au bercail une brebis égarée; **to return to the f.,** (*of member of family*) rentrer au bercail; (*of politician, etc.*) revenir à son parti.
fold² *v.tr.* (em)parquer (les moutons).
fold³ *n.* (*a*) pli *m,* repli *m* (du papier, etc.); *Dressm:* **box folds,** plis rentrés; **folds of fat,** bourrelets *mpl* de graisse; (*b*) *Geol:* pli, plissement *m.*
fold⁴ 1. *v.tr.* (*a*) plier (une feuille de papier, etc.); **to f. sth. in two,** plier qch. en deux; (*b*) **to f. sth. (up) in paper,** envelopper qch. dans du papier; **to f. s.o. in one's arms,** enlacer, serrer, qn dans ses bras; (*c*) **to f. one's arms,** (se) croiser les bras; **with folded arms,** les bras croisés; **to f. one's hands,** joindre les mains **2.** *v.i.* (*a*) (*of screen*) se (re)plier, se briser; (*b*) = FOLD UP 2. (*b*). **fold back 1.** *v.tr.* rabattre (un col, etc.);

retourner (les couvertures d'un lit). **2.** *v.i.* (*of door, etc.*) se rabattre. **fold down 1.** *v.tr.* retourner (les couvertures d'un lit). **2.** *v.i.* (*of seat, etc.*) se rabattre. **fold in** *v.tr.* (*a*) replier (les bords) en dedans; (*b*) **literary supplement folded in with each number,** supplément littéraire encarté dans chaque numéro; (*c*) *Cu:* **to f. in the whites of the eggs,** incorporer le blanc des œufs. **folding 1.** *a.* pliant; rabattable; (joint, volet) brisé; **f. bed,** (i) lit pliant, à rabattement; (ii) lit de sangle; **f. camera,** appareil *m* à soufflet; **f. chair,** chaise pliante; **f. door,** porte brisée; **f. screen,** paravent *m*; **f. stool,** pliant *m*; **f. table,** (i) table pliante; (ii) table à battants; **car with a f. top,** voiture *f* décapotable. **2.** *n.* (*a*) pliage *m* (de l'étoffe, etc.); *Bookb:* pliure *f* (de feuilles); (*b*) enveloppement *m* (**of sth. in sth.,** de qch. dans qch.); (*c*) croisement *m* (des bras). **3.** *Geol:* plissement *m* (du terrain). **fold under** *v.tr.* replier (les bords) en dessous. **fold up 1.** *v.tr.* (re)plier (un siège, une table); replier, fermer (un paravent). **2.** *v.i.* (*a*) se replier; **seat that folds up,** siège pliant; (*b*) *F:* (*of business, etc.*) cesser les affaires; *Th:* **the play folded up after a week,** la pièce a été retirée au bout d'une semaine.

-fold[5] *comb. fm.* -uple; **tenfold,** décuple; **a hundredfold,** centuple, cent fois.

foldaway ['fouldəwei] *a.* repliable, escamotable; (siège) pliant, rabattable; **f. bed,** lit *m* escamotable.

folder ['fouldər] *n.* **1.** (*pers.*) plieur, -euse (de journaux, etc.). **2.** *Tls:* plioir *m.* **3.** *Com:* prospectus (plié). **4.** (*for papers, etc.*) chemise *f*, dossier *m.*

fold-out ['fouldaut] *n.* dépliant *m.*

foliage ['fouliidʒ] *n.* feuillage *m*, frondaison *f*; **f. plant,** plante *f* à feuillage.

foliate ['foulieit] *a. Bot:* feuillu.

foliation [fouli'eiʃ(ə)n] *n.* **1.** (*a*) foliation *f*, feuillaison *f* (d'une plante); (*b*) *Arch:* (ornementation *f* en) rinceaux (*mpl*). **2.** *Geol:* foliation (d'une roche, etc.). **3.** foliotage *m* (d'un livre).

folio, *pl.* **-os** ['fouliou, -ouz] *n.* **1.** (*a*) *Bookb:* folio *m*, feuille *f* (de manuscrit); (*b*) *Typ: etc:* numéro *m* (d'une page). **2.** *n.* & *a.* **(book in) f., f. book,** (livre *m*) in-folio (*m*).

folk [fouk] *n.* **1.** (*pl.* **folk,** *occ., esp. NAm:* **folks**) gens *mfpl*; **country f.,** campagnards *mpl*; **my f., your f.,** les miens, les vôtres; ma famille, votre famille; *esp. NAm: F:* **hi, folks!** salut, tout le monde! **2.** *attrib.* folklorique, traditionnel; **f. singer,** (i) chanteur, -euse, de chansons folkloriques; (ii) (*modern*) folk-singer *m*, *pl.* folk-singers; **f. song,** (i) chanson traditionnelle, folklorique; (ii) (*modern*) folk-song *m*, *pl.* folk-songs.

folklore ['fouklɔːr] *n.* folklore *m*; tradition *f.*

folkloric ['fouklɔːrik] *a.* folklorique.

folksy ['fouksi] *a. F:* **1.** sociable. **2.** folklorique.

follicle ['fɔlikl] *n. Anat: Bot: etc:* follicule *m.*

follow ['fɔlou] **I.** *v.tr.* **1.** (*a*) suivre, marcher derrière qn, etc.); **to f. s.o. about,** suivre qn partout; **a man followed by his dog,** un homme suivi de son chien; *F:* **to f. one's nose,** aller tout droit devant soi; (*b*) (*go along*) suivre (un chemin); **boat that follows the coast,** bateau qui longe la côte; (*c*) succéder à (qn, qch.); **the years f. one another,** les années se succèdent, se suivent; **George IV was followed by William IV,** Guillaume IV succéda à Georges IV; **dinner followed by a dance,** dîner suivi d'un bal; **following our correspondence,** comme suite à notre échange de lettres. **2.** être le disciple de (qn); imiter (les anciens maîtres). **3.** poursuivre (l'ennemi, etc.). **4.** suivre (la mode, etc.); s'assujettir à (un régime); suivre (l'exemple de qn). **5.** exercer, suivre (une profession); poursuivre (une carrière). **6.** (*a*) aller aussi vite que (qn); **he went too fast for me to f.,** il allait trop vite pour que je puisse le suivre; (*b*) suivre, comprendre (une explication, etc.); **I don't quite f. you,** je ne vous comprends pas très bien; (*c*) prêter attention à (un discours, un sermon). **7. to f. a tragedy with a light comedy,** faire suivre une tragédie d'une comédie légère. **II.** *v.i.* **1. to f. (after),** suivre; venir à la suite; **a long silence followed,** il s'ensuivit un long silence; **as follows,** ainsi qu'il suit; **our method is as follows,** notre méthode est la suivante. **2. to f. in s.o.'s footsteps,** marcher sur les traces de qn; **to f. close behind s.o.,** emboîter le pas à qn. **3.** s'ensuivre, résulter (**from,** de); **it follows that . . .,** il s'ensuit que . . .; **it does not f. that . . .,** ce n'est pas à dire que + *sub.* **following 1.** *a.* (*a*) qui suit; (*b*) (i) suivant; **on the f. day,** le jour suivant; le jour d'après; le lendemain; (ii) **the f. resolution,** la résolution que voici; **the f. persons,** les personnes dont les noms suivent; **the f. is the full list,** voici la liste complète; (iii) **two days f.,** deux jours de suite. **2.** *n.* (i) suite *f* (d'un prince); (ii) *Pol: etc:* parti *m* (d'un chef); **to have a big f.,** avoir un grand nombre de partisans, de disciples; **television programme that commands a wide f.,** programme de télévision très suivi. **follow on** *v.i.* (*a*) continuer (dans la même direction); (*b*) *Cr:* reprendre la garde du guichet au commencement de la seconde partie du match (au lieu d'alterner avec l'autre équipe). **follow out** *v.tr.* exécuter (des ordres). **follow through 1.** *v.tr.* **to f. a project through (to the end),** poursuivre un projet jusqu'à sa conclusion. **2.** *v.i. Sp:* suivre le coup. **follow up** *v.tr.* (*a*) poursuivre (avec énergie); *Com:* faire suivre (une lettre) d'une seconde lettre; poursuivre (un avantage); exploiter (un succès); **to f. up a clue,** suivre une piste; (*b*) donner suite immédiate à (une victoire, etc.).

follower ['fɔlouər] *n.* (*a*) serviteur *m* (d'un prince, etc.); **the King and his followers,** le roi et sa suite; (*b*) partisan, -ane, disciple *mf.*

follow-my-leader ['fɔloumi'liːdər] *n.* jeu *m* de la queue leu leu.

follow-on ['fɔlou'ɔn] *n.* continuation *f*, suite *f*; *Cr:* **to try to save the f.-o.,** s'efforcer de marquer le nombre de points requis pour ne pas avoir à reprendre la garde du guichet.

follow-through ['fɔlou'θruː] *n. Sp:* fin *f* du coup.

follow-up ['fɔlou'ʌp] *n.* (*a*) poursuite *f*; suite *f*; *Com: etc:* relance *f* (de la publicité, etc.); **f.-up letter,** lettre *f* de rappel; (*b*) *Med:* examens *mpl* de contrôle à long terme; **f.-up care,** soins post-hospitaliers; (*c*) *Mil:* soutien *m*; poursuite; **f.-up action,** action *f* de soutien.

folly ['fɔli] *n.* **1.** folie *f*, sottise *f*; **an act of f., a f.,** une folie; **it would be the height of f. to . . .,** ce serait la plus grande folie de . . .. **2.** *Arch:* folie.

foment [fou'ment] *v.tr.* **1.** *Med:* fomenter (une plaie). **2.** fomenter (la discorde, des troubles).

fomentation [foumen'teiʃ(ə)n] *n.* **1.** *Med:* fomentation *f.* **2.** fomentation (de la discorde, etc.).

fond [fɔnd] *a.* **1.** (*a*) (parent, etc.) indulgent; (*b*) affectueux, tendre; (sourire) attendri; (*c*) (souvenir, etc.) doux; (espoir) dont on se flatte. **2.** (*a*) **to be f. of s.o., sth.,** aimer qn, qch.; **they are f. of each other,** ils s'aiment; **he was very f. of me,** il me portait beaucoup d'affection; **to become f. of s.o.,** s'attacher à qn; (*b*) **to be f. of music,** être amateur de musique; **f. of sweets,** friand de sucreries; **he is passionately f. of reading,** il adore la lecture. **-ly** *adv.* **1.** crédulement, naïvement. **2.** tendrement, affectueusement.

fondant ['fɔndənt] *n.* fondant *m.*

fondle ['fɔndl] *v.tr.* caresser, câliner (qn); faire des mamours à (qn).

fondness ['fɔndnis] *n.* **1.** indulgence excessive (d'une mère, etc.). **2.** affection *f*, tendresse *f* (**for,** pour, envers). **3.** penchant *m*, prédilection *f*, goût *m* (**for**

sth., pour qch.); amour *m* (**for sth.**, de qch).
fondue ['fɔndju] *n. Cu:* fondue *f*.
font [fɔnt] *n.* fonts baptismaux.
fontanel(le) [fɔntə'nel] *n. Anat:* fontanelle *f*.
food [fu:d] *n.* **1.** (*a*) nourriture *f*; aliments *mpl*; vivres *mpl*; **f. and clothing,** le vivre et le vêtement; **hotel where the f. is good,** hôtel où la cuisine, la table, est bonne; **to be off one's f.,** ne pas avoir d'appétit: **f. counter,** (*in large store*) **f. hall, f. department,** rayon *m* d'alimentation; **f. poisoning,** intoxication *f* alimentaire; **the f. industry,** l'industrie *f* alimentaire; **f. value,** valeur nutritive; (*b*) aliment; **canned, tinned, foods,** aliments de conserve (en boîte); **health foods,** (i) produits *mpl* diététiques; (ii) produits alimentaires naturels; *Toil:* **skin f.,** aliment pour la peau; (*c*) *Husb:* pâture *f* (d'animaux); mangeaille *f* (de volaille); (*of animal*) **to hunt, search, for f.,** chercher sa nourriture; (*d*) **plant f.,** (i) *Bot:* aliments des plantes; (ii) *Hort:* engrais *m*; (*e*) **f. for the mind,** nourriture de l'esprit; **to give s.o. f. for thought,** donner à penser à qn. **2.** (*as opp. to drink*) manger *m*; **f. and drink,** le boire et le manger.
foodstore ['fu:dstɔ:r] *n.* alimentation *f*.
foodstuff(s) ['fu:dstʌf(s)] *n.* (*pl.*) produits *mpl* alimentaires, d'alimentation.
fool¹ [fu:l] *n.* **1.** imbécile *mf*; idiot, -ote; **to play, act, the f.,** faire l'idiot; **to make a f. of oneself,** se couvrir de ridicule; **I felt such a f.,** je me sentais vraiment idiot; *F:* **silly f.!** espèce d'idiot! **what a f.!** quel idiot! **he's no f.,** il n'est pas bête; **any f. knows that,** le premier imbécile venu sait cela; **some f. (of a) politician,** quelque imbécile d'homme politique . . .; *Prov:* **there's no f. like an old f.,** un vieux fou est le pire des fous. **2.** fou *m*, bouffon *m*; **fool's cap,** bonnet *m* de fou. **3.** dupe *f*; **to make a f. of s.o.,** se moquer de qn; *F:* mettre qn en boîte; **he's nobody's f.,** c'est un malin, un rusé; **to go on a fool's errand,** y aller pour des prunes, pour le roi de Prusse; **to send s.o. on a fool's errand,** envoyer qn décrocher la lune; **All Fool's Day,** le premier avril. **4. fool's gold,** pyrite *f* de fer; *Bot:* **fool's parsley,** petite ciguë.
fool² **1.** *v.i.* (*a*) faire l'idiot; **stop fooling (about)!** assez de bêtises! (*b*) dire des blagues; **I was only fooling,** je plaisantais. **2.** *v.tr.* duper (qn); faire marcher (qn); **you can't f. me,** on ne m'a pas comme ça; **to (allow oneself to) be fooled,** se laisser duper; **to be fooled into doing sth.,** être amené par duperie à faire qch. **fool about, fool around** *v.i.* (*a*) courir la ville (**with,** avec); (*b*) **to f. a. with (sth.),** tripoter (un appareil, etc.); jouer avec (un fusil, etc.).
fool³ *n. Cu:* marmelade *f* à la crème; **gooseberry f.,** marmelade de groseilles (à maquereau) à la crème.
foolery ['fu:ləri] *n.* **1. (piece of) f.,** sottise *f*, folie *f*. **2.** bouffonnerie *f*; pitrerie *f*.
foolhardiness ['fu:lhɑ:dinis] *n.* témérité *f*, imprudence *f*.
foolhardy ['fu:lhɑ:di] *a.* téméraire, imprudent.
foolish ['fu:liʃ] *a.* **1.** (*a*) insensé; fou, *f.* folle; **it is f. of him to . . .,** c'est fou de sa part, de . . .; **a f. hope,** un fol espoir; (*b*) bête; **to do sth. f.,** faire une bêtise. **2.** absurde, ridicule; **to look f.,** avoir l'air penaud: **to feel f.,** se sentir idiot. **-ly** *adv.* **1.** follement. **2.** bêtement.
foolishness ['fu:liʃnis] *n.* **1.** folie *f*. **2.** bêtise *f*.
foolproof ['fu:lpru:f] *a.* (mécanisme) indéréglable, indétraquable, de sûreté, à toute épreuve.
foolscap ['fu:lskæp] *n.* papier *m* ministre.
foot¹, *pl.* **feet** [fut, fi:t] *n.* **1.** pied (humain); (*a*) **to put one's best f. forward,** (i) avancer vite, à toute allure; (ii) pousser la besogne; **to sit at s.o.'s feet,** être le disciple de qn; **to set f. on an island,** mettre pied sur une île; **I shall never set f. in his house again,** jamais je ne remettrai les pieds chez lui; **to put one's feet up,** (i) surélever les pieds; (ii) se reposer; *F:* **to sweep s.o. off his feet,** enthousiasmer qn; **to be swept off one's feet by s.o.,** s'emballer pour qn; (*in debate*) **to rise to one's feet,** prendre la parole; **he jumped to his feet,** d'un bond il fut debout; **to be on one's feet,** se tenir debout; **she is on her feet all day,** elle est sur ses jambes du matin au soir; **he's on his feet again,** il est de nouveau sur pied; **to set s.o. on his feet,** (re)-mettre qn sur pied, (r)établir qn; **he's beginning to find his feet,** il commence à s'acclimater; **to put one's f. down,** (i) faire acte d'autorité; (ii) *Aut: F:* accélérer; **to get one's f. in (the door),** s'implanter (chez qn); *F:* **to put one's f. in it,** mettre les pieds dans le plat; faire une gaffe; **idol with feet of clay,** statue *f* aux pieds d'argile; *F:* **to have, get, cold feet,** avoir la frousse; **to have one's feet firmly on the ground,** avoir les pieds sur terre; **not to put a f. wrong,** ne faire aucune erreur; **to catch s.o. on the wrong f.,** (i) *Ten: etc:* prendre qn à contre-pied; (ii) prendre qn au dépourvu; **to start off on the wrong f.,** partir du pied gauche; *F:* **my f.!** mon œil! (*b*) marche *f*; (*c*) *adv.phr.* **on f.,** à pied; **to go on f.,** aller à pied; **to set negotiations on f.,** ouvrir, mettre en train, des négociations; **under f.,** sous les pieds; **to trample, tread, sth. under f.,** fouler qch. aux pieds. **2.** pied (d'animaux à sabot); patte *f* (de chien, etc.); **the fore, hind, feet,** le bipède antérieur, postérieur (du cheval); *Vet:* **f. and mouth disease,** fièvre aphteuse. **3.** *coll. Mil:* fantassins *mpl*; soldats *mpl* d'infanterie. **4.** (*a*) pied, semelle *f* (d'un bas); (*b*) bas bout (d'une table); pied (d'un lit, d'une tombe); extrémité inférieure (d'un lac); (*c*) base *f* (de colonne, etc.); pied (de verre à boire); (*d*) pied, bas (de montagne, d'échelle); *Typ:* pied (d'une lettre); **at the f. of the stairs,** au bas, en bas, de l'escalier; **at the f. of the page,** au bas de la page; **at the f. of the list, of the class,** à la queue de la liste, de la classe. **5.** (*a*) *Pros:* pied; (*b*) *Meas:* pied anglais (de 30 cm 48); **square, cubic, f.,** pied carré, pied cube; **to be five f., five feet, high,** avoir cinq pieds de haut(eur). **6.** *attrib.* (*a*) (*on foot*) **f. passenger,** voyageur *m* à pied; **f. soldier,** soldat *m* d'infanterie; fantassin *m*; (*b*) (*for, of, the feet*) **f. scraper,** gratte-pieds *m inv*; *Ecc:* **f. washing,** lavement *m* des pieds; (*c*) (*worked by the foot*) **f. brake,** frein *m* à pédale, à pied; **f. control,** commande *f* au pied; **f. pump,** pompe *f* à pied.
foot² *v.tr.* **1.** *F:* **to f. it,** marcher (à pied). **2.** mettre un pied, faire un pied, à (un bas). **3.** *F:* **to f. the bill,** payer la note, les dépenses. **4.** *N.Am: F:* **to f. (up),** additionner (un compte). **footing** *n.* **1.** (*a*) *Fenc: Danc: etc:* pose *f* des pieds; (*b*) = FOOTHOLD; (*in bathing, etc.*) **to lose one's f.,** perdre pied, perdre terre; **to miss one's f.,** poser le pied à faux (en descendant, etc.) **2.** (*a*) situation sûre; pied *m*; **to gain a f.,** s'implanter, prendre pied (quelque part); (*b*) position *f*, condition *f* (d'une personne); condition, état *m* (d'une institution, etc.); **on a war f.,** sur le pied de guerre; en état de guerre; **to place (two people) on the same f.,** mettre (deux personnes) sur le même rang; **to be on an equal f.,** être de pair, sur un pied d'égalité (**with,** avec); (*c*) entrée *f* (dans une société, etc.); admission *f* (à une société, etc.). **3.** *Const:* empattement *m*, socle *m* (d'un mur).
footage ['futidʒ] *n.* longueur *f* (en pieds); métrage *m* (d'un film, etc.).
football ['futbɔ:l] *n.* **1.** ballon *m* (de football). **2.** (i) (*soccer*) football *m*; *F:* foot *m*; (ii) **Rugby f.,** rugby *m*; **f. ground,** terrain *m* de football.
footballer ['futbɔ:lər] *n.* footballe(u)r *m*.
footbath ['futbɑ:θ] *n.* bain *m* de pieds.
footbridge ['futbridʒ] *n.* passerelle *f*; pont *m* pour piétons.

footfall ['futfɔːl] *n.* (bruit *m* de) pas (*m*); **I heard a light f.,** j'ai entendu un pas léger.
foot-fault¹ ['futfɔːlt] *n. Ten:* faute *f* de pied.
foot-fault² *Ten:* **1.** *v.i.* faire une faute de pied. **2.** *v.tr.* (*of umpire*) **to f. a player,** décider qu'un joueur a fait une faute de pied.
footgear ['futgiər] *n.* chaussures *fpl.*
foothills ['futhilz] *n.pl.* collines basses, avancées (d'une chaîne); avant-monts *mpl.*
foothold ['futhould] *n.* prise *f*, assiette *f*, pour le pied; **to get a f.,** prendre pied; **to keep one's f.,** préserver l'équilibre; **to lose one's f.,** perdre pied.
footle ['fuːtl] *v.i. F:* **to f. about,** perdre son temps à des futilités. **footling** *a. F:* insignifiant.
footlights ['futlaits] *n.pl. Th:* rampe *f.*
footloose ['futluːs] *a.* (personne) libre.
footman, *pl.* **-men** ['futmən] *n.m.* valet de pied.
footmuff ['futmʌf] *n.* chancelière *f*; chaufferette *f.*
footnote ['futnout] *n.* note *f*, renvoi *m*, en bas de page.
footpath ['futpɑːθ] *n.* (*a*) sentier *m* pour piétons; (*b*) (*by canal, railway*) banquette *f*, accotement *m*; (*c*) (*in street*) trottoir *m.*
footplate ['futpleit] *n. Mch:* plate-forme *f*, *pl.* plates-formes, tablier *m* (de locomotive).
footplateman, *pl.* **-men** ['futpleitmən] *n.m. Rail:* mécanicien de locomotive.
foot-pound ['futpaund] *n.* (*pl.* **foot-pounds**) *Mec.Meas:* pied-livre *m*, *pl.* pieds-livres.
footprint ['futprint] *n.* empreinte *f* de pas; **footprints on the sands,** pas sur le sable.
footrest ['futrest] *n.* (*a*) *Cy:* repose-pied(s) *m inv*; cale-pied(s) *m inv*; *Furn:* bout *m* de pied; *Med:* porte-pieds *m inv*; (*b*) sellette *f* (de décrotteur).
footrot ['futrɔt] *n. Vet:* fourchet *m*, piétin *m.*
footrule ['futruːl] *n.* règle *f* (d'un pied).
foot-second ['fut'sekənd] *n.* (*pl.* **foot-seconds**) *Mec.Meas:* pied *m* par seconde.
footsie ['futsi] *n. P:* **to play f. with s.o.,** faire du pied avec qn.
footslog ['futslɔg] *v.i.* **(footslogged)** *P:* marcher; faire la route à pied.
footsore ['futsɔːr] *n.* qui a mal aux pieds.
footstall ['futstɔːl] *n. Arch:* socle *m.*
footstep ['futstep] *n.* **1.** pas *m*; **I hear footsteps,** j'entends un bruit de pas. **2.** (empreinte *f* de) pied; **to follow, tread, walk, in s.o.'s footsteps,** marcher sur les traces, pas, de qn; **to follow in one's father's footsteps,** suivre les traces de son père.
footstool ['futstuːl] *n.* tabouret *m* (pour les pieds).
footwarmer ['futwɔːmər] *n.* chancelière *f.*
footway ['futwei] *n.* chemin *m* pour piétons.
footwear ['futwɛər] *n.* chaussures *fpl.*
footwork ['futwəːk] *n.* **1.** *Sp:* jeu *m* des pieds, des jambes. **2. job that requires a lot of f.,** emploi qui exige qu'on se déplace beaucoup.
fop [fɔp] *n. A:* bellâtre *m*, fat *m*; dandy *m.*
foppish ['fɔpiʃ] *a.* (*a*) (homme) qui apporte trop de recherche à sa toilette; (*b*) (*of clothes*) d'une élégance affectée.
for [fɔːr, *unstressed* fər] **I.** *prep.* pour. **1.** (*a*) (i) (*representing*) *Tp:* **A f. Andrew,** A comme André; (ii) (*instead of*) **to act f. s.o.,** agir pour qn, au nom de qn; **he took me f. my brother,** il m'a pris pour mon frère; (*b*) (*introducing predicative complement*) **to have s.o. f. a teacher,** avoir qn comme professeur; **they left him f. dead,** on le laissa pour mort; (*c*) **to be paid f. one's services,** recevoir des gages pour ses services; **claim f. loss of . . .,** réclamation *f* résultant de la perte de . . .; (*d*) (*in exchange for*) **you can hire a car f. five pounds a day,** on peut louer une voiture moyennant cinq livres par jour; **to exchange one thing f. another,** échanger une chose contre une autre; **to sell sth. f. ten francs,** vendre qch. dix francs; (*e*) *F:* **to get sth. f. free,** obtenir qch. gratis; **this time it's f. real,** cette fois c'est pour de vrai. **2. he is f. free trade,** il est partisan du libre-échange; il est pour le libre-échange; **judgment f. the plaintiff,** arrêt *m* en faveur du demandeur. **3.** (*a*) (*purpose*) **what f.?** pourquoi (faire)? **what's that gadget f.?** à quoi sert ce truc-là? **garments f. men,** vêtements pour hommes; **f. sale,** à vendre; **f. example,** par exemple; **a cure f. indigestion,** un remède contre l'indigestion; **it is f. your own good,** c'est pour votre bien; *F:* **he's f. it** ['fɔːrit], **he's in f. it** ['infərit], qu'est-ce qu'il va prendre! (*b*) (*because of*) (i) **to marry s.o. f. his money,** épouser qn pour son argent; **to choose s.o. f. his ability,** choisir qn en raison de sa compétence; **to die f. one's country,** mourir pour la patrie; **art f. art's sake,** l'art pour l'art; **to jump f. joy,** sauter de joie; **to criticize s.o. f. doing sth.,** critiquer qn d'avoir fait qch.; (ii) (*with comparative*) **if you owned millions, would you be any (the) happier f. it?** si vous aviez des millions en seriez-vous plus heureux? (*c*) (*considering*) **f. all the use he is he might as well go and play,** pour ce qu'il fait d'utile il peut aussi bien aller jouer. **4.** (*direction*) (*a*) **ship (bound) f. America,** navire à destination de l'Amérique; **the train f. London,** le train allant à Londres, le train de Londres; **I'm leaving f. France,** je pars pour la France; (*b*) **his feelings f. you,** ses sentiments envers vous, à votre égard. **5.** (*extent in space*) **the road is lined with trees f. two miles,** la route est bordée d'arbres pendant deux milles; *P.N:* **bends f. one mile,** virages sur un mille. **6.** (*extent of time*) (*a*) (*future*) **I'm going away f. a fortnight,** je pars pour quinze jours; **he will be away f. a year,** il sera absent pendant un an; **we have food f. three days,** nous avons des vivres pour trois jours; (*b*) (*past*) **I lived there f. five years,** j'y ai vécu (pendant) cinq ans; **I have not seen him f. three years,** il y a trois ans que je ne l'ai vu; (*c*) (*past extending to pres.*) **I have been here f. three days,** il y a trois jours que je suis ici; je suis ici depuis trois jours; **I had known him f. years,** je le connaissais depuis des années; il y avait des années que je le connaissais. **7.** (*intention, destination*) (*a*) **this box is f. you,** cette boîte est pour vous; **I'll come f. you tomorrow,** je viendrai vous prendre demain; **to make a name f. oneself,** se faire un nom; **to act f. the best,** agir pour le mieux; (*b*) **your job f. tomorrow,** votre travail pour demain; **can you give him an appointment f. three o'clock?** pouvez-vous lui donner un rendez-vous pour trois heures? **8. to care f. s.o., sth.,** aimer qn, qch.; **you are the man f. me,** vous êtes mon homme; **that is just the thing f. you,** c'est juste ce qu'il vous faut; **eager f. praise,** avide d'éloges; **it's time f. school,** c'est l'heure de la classe; **too stupid f. words,** d'une bêtise indicible; **oh, f. some peace and quiet!** que ne donnerais-je pour la paix! **now f. it!** (i) allons-y! (ii) ça y est! **9.** (*to the amount of*) **a cheque f. £50,** un chèque de £50; **put me down f. £1,** inscrivez-moi pour £1. **10.** (*a*) (*with regard to*) **he is big f. his age,** il est grand pour son âge; **not bad f. a beginner!** pour un débutant ce n'est pas si mal! **as f. him,** quant à lui; **as f. that,** pour ce qui est de cela; **f. myself, f. my part, I shall do nothing of the sort,** pour moi, quant à moi, pour ma part, je n'en ferai rien; **see f. yourself!** voyez par vous-même! (*b*) (*in spite of*) **f. all that,** malgré tout, malgré cela, tout de même; **she loved him, f. all his faults,** elle l'aimait malgré ses défauts; (*c*) (*owing to*) **were it not f. her, I should have died,** sans elle, je serais mort; (*d*) (*corresponding to, in opposition to*) **word f. word,** mot pour mot; (traduire) mot à mot; **they sell twenty red bikes for every black one,** pour chaque vélo noir vendu, il y en a vingt rouges. **II.** *prep.* (*introducing an infinitive*

clause) **1. it is easy, difficult, impossible, f. him to come,** il lui est facile, difficile, impossible, de venir; **it is too late f. us to start,** il est trop tard pour que nous partions. **2. they made way f. him to pass,** on se rangea pour le laisser passer; **I have brought it f. you to see,** je l'ai apporté pour que vous le voyiez; **it is not f. me to decide, to criticize him,** ce n'est pas à moi de décider, de le critiquer. **3. it is usual f. the mother to accompany her daughter,** il est d'usage que la mère accompagne sa fille; **it's no good f. Mr X to talk,** M. X a beau dire. **4. I am delighted f. Miss X to know,** je suis enchanté que Mlle X le sache. **5. he gave orders f. the trunks to be packed,** il donna l'ordre de faire les malles; **to arrange f. sth. to be done,** prendre des dispositions pour que qch. se fasse; **to wait f. sth. to be done,** attendre que qch. se fasse. **6. it took an hour f. the taxi to get to the station,** le taxi a mis une heure pour aller jusqu'à la gare; **the best plan will be f. you to go away for a time,** le mieux sera que vous vous absentiez pour quelque temps; **it would be a disgrace f. you to back out now,** vous retirer maintenant serait honteux. **III.** *conj.* car.

forage[1] ['fɔridʒ] *n.* **1.** fourrage(s) *m(pl)*, affouragement *m.* **2.** fourragement *m*; **to go on the f.,** aller au fourrage; *Mil:* **f. cap,** bonnet *m* de police; calot *m.*

forage[2] *v.i.* (*a*) fourrager, aller au fourrage; *F:* **to f. for sth.,** fouiller pour trouver qch.; **to f. about, around, in a drawer,** fouiller dans un tiroir; **never mind me, I'll f. for myself,** ne t'occupe pas de moi, je me débrouillerai.

foray[1] ['fɔrei] *n.* razzia *f*, incursion *f*, raid *m*; **to make a brief f. into the business world,** faire une courte incursion dans le monde des affaires.

foray[2] *v.i.* faire des incursions, des raids.

forbear[1] ['fɔ:bεər] *n.* aïeul *m*, -eux; ancêtre *m.*

forbear[2] [fɔ:'bεər] *v.* (*p.t.* **forbore** [fɔ:'bɔ:r]; *p.p.* **forborne** [fɔ:'bɔ:n]) *Lit:* **1.** *v.tr.* s'abstenir de (qch.). **2.** *v.i.* **to f. from doing sth.,** s'abstenir de, se garder de, faire qch.; **to f. from mentioning sth.,** se taire sur, de, qch. **forbearing** *a.* patient, indulgent.

forbearance [fɔ:'bεərəns] *n.* **1. f. from doing sth.,** abstention *f* de faire qch. **2.** patience *f*, longanimité *f*; **to show f. towards s.o.,** montrer de l'indulgence envers qn.

forbid [fə'bid] *v.tr.* (*p.t.* **forbade** [fə'bæd, -'beid]; *p.p.* **forbidden** [fə'bidn]) **1.** défendre, interdire; proscrire (un usage, etc.); *Jur:* prohiber (qch.); **to f. s.o. sth.,** défendre qch. à qn; **I am forbidden (to drink) tea,** le thé m'est défendu. **2.** empêcher (qch.); **Heaven f. that I should do such a thing!** Dieu me préserve de faire une telle chose! **God f.!** à Dieu ne plaise (**that,** que + *sub.*)! **forbidden** *a.* défendu, interdit; **tread on f. ground,** (i) empiéter sur un terrain défendu; (ii) toucher à un sujet tabou. **forbidding** *a.* (visage, aspect) sinistre; (caractère) mal avenant; (ciel, temps) sombre; (rocher) menaçant.

force[1] [fɔ:s] *n.* force *f.* **1.** (*a*) violence *f*, contrainte *f*; **by sheer, brute, f.,** de vive force; **by sheer f. of will,** à force de volonté; **owing to the f. of circumstances,** par la force des choses; **to resort to f.,** (i) faire appel à la force; (ii) se porter à des voies de fait; (*b*) influence *f*, autorité *f*; **f. of example,** influence de l'exemple; **moral f.,** force morale. **2.** énergie *f*; effort *m* (d'un choc, etc.); intensité *f* (du vent); vigueur *f* (de l'imagination, etc.); **a blow with plenty of f. behind it,** un coup bien appuyé, bien asséné. **3.** *Mec:* force, effort; (*a*) **f. exerted by an engine,** effort d'un moteur; **f. of gravity,** (force de la) pesanteur; (*b*) *Atom.Ph:* **nuclear f.,** force nucléaire; (*c*) *Meteor:* **f. ten on the Beaufort scale,** la force dix de l'échelle Beaufort. **4.** (*a*) *Mil:* force, troupe *f*, élément(s) *m(pl)*; **an armed f.,** une force (armée); **the armoured forces,** les blindés; **the land forces,** l'armée de terre; **strike f.,** *Av:* force de frappe; *Navy:* force d'intervention; **task f.,** *Mil:* groupement opérationnel, tactique; *Navy:* force (navale) opérationnelle, tactique; (*b*) **the (armed) forces,** les forces armées; **the naval forces,** l'armée de mer; la marine de guerre; (*c*) **the police f.,** *F:* **the F.,** la Police; (*d*) **a strong f. of police,** un fort détachement de police; **to join forces with s.o. in doing sth.,** se joindre à qn pour faire qch.; **we turned out in (full) f.,** nous étions là en masse. **5.** (*a*) vertu *f*, valeur *f*, efficacité *f* (d'un remède, d'un argument, etc.); (*b*) signification *f* (d'un mot, d'un document); valeur *f* (d'un mot, d'une expression); **verb used with passive f.,** verbe employé avec la valeur d'un passif. **6.** (*of law, rule, etc.*) **to be in f.,** être en vigueur; **to put the law into f.,** appliquer la loi; **to come into f.,** entrer en vigueur.

force[2] *v.tr.* **1.** (*a*) **to f. s.o.'s hand,** forcer la main à qn; **to f. the pace,** forcer l'allure, le pas; **she forced a smile,** elle s'est forcée à sourire; **to f. (the meaning of) a word,** tordre le sens d'un mot; (*b*) prendre (qn, qch.) par force, de force; forcer, enfoncer (une porte, une fenêtre); forcer (une serrure); **to f. one's way into a house,** pénétrer de force dans une maison; (*c*) pousser, faire avancer (qch.); **to f. sth. into sth.,** faire entrer qch. de force dans qch.; *I.C.E:* **to f. air into the carburettor,** refouler l'air dans le carburateur; (*d*) **to f. a plant,** forcer une plante; *Aut:* **to f. the engine,** trop pousser le moteur. **2.** (*a*) **to f. s.o. to do sth., into doing sth.,** forcer, contraindre, qn à faire qch.; **I am forced to conclude that . . .,** je suis forcé de conclure que . . .; **to be forced to give way,** céder à la force; (*b*) **to f. s.o. into, out of, the room,** faire entrer, faire sortir, qn de force; (*c*) **to f. sth. on s.o.,** imposer qch. à qn; **to f. drink on s.o.,** contraindre qn à boire; (*d*) **to f. sth. from s.o.,** arracher (une promesse, etc.) à qn. **force back** *v.tr.* (*a*) repousser, faire reculer (l'ennemi, etc.); (*b*) refouler (l'air, l'eau, etc.). **forced** *a.* **1.** forcé; **f. sale,** vente forcée; **f. labour,** travail forcé; *Av:* **f. landing,** atterrissage forcé. **2.** (*a*) forcé, contraint; (rire) forcé, faux; **to give a f. laugh,** rire du bout des lèvres; (*b*) *Mil:* **f. march,** marche forcée; (*c*) *Mec.E: Mch:* **f. circulation,** circulation forcée (d'une chaudière); **f. draught,** tirage forcé; **f. feed (of oil),** graissage sous pression; (*d*) *Husb:* **f. feeding,** gavage *m.* **3. f. vegetables, f. fruit,** légumes *mpl*, fruits *mpl* forcés; primeurs *fpl.* **force down** *v.tr.* faire descendre (qch.) de force; **to f. air down into a mine shaft,** refouler de l'air dans un puits de mine; **to f. prices down,** faire baisser les prix; *Av:* **the plane was forced down,** on a forcé l'avion à atterrir. **force out** *v.tr.* pousser (qn, qch.) dehors; faire sortir (qn, qch.) de force; *I.C.E:* refouler au dehors (les gaz brûlés); **to f. out a few words of congratulation,** féliciter qn du bout des lèvres. **force up** *v.tr.* faire monter (qch.) de force; **to f. prices up,** faire monter (les prix). **forcing** *n.* **1.** (*a*) **f. (open),** forcement *m* (d'une serrure); enfoncement *m* (d'une porte); (*b*) *Cu:* **f. bag,** poche *f* à douille. **2.** *Hort:* forçage *m*; culture forcée; **f. frame,** châssis *m.*

force-feed[1] ['fɔ:s'fi:d] *a. Mec.E: etc:* **f.-f. oiler,** burette *f* à pompe, à piston; **f.-f. lubrication,** graissage *m* sous pression.

force-feed[2] *v.tr.* (*p.t. & p.p.* **-fed** [-fed]) gaver (une oie); nourrir (qn) de force.

forceful ['fɔ:sful] *a.* plein de force; énergique. **-fully** *adv.* avec force; vigoureusement.

force-land ['fɔ:s'lænd] *v.i. Av:* faire un atterrissage forcé.

forcemeat ['fɔ:smi:t] *n. Cu:* farce *f*, hachis *m.*

forceps ['fɔ:seps] *n. inv.* **a (pair of) f.,** une pince; *Surg:* forceps *m*; *Dent:* davier *m.*

forcible ['fɔ:sibl] *a.* **1.** (entrée, etc.) de force; *Jur:* **f.**

entry, prise de possession illégale et par la violence. 2. vigoureux, plein de force. **-ibly** *adv.* 1. de force; **to detain s.o. f.,** retenir qn de force. 2. vigoureusement.

ford[1] [fɔːd] *n.* gué *m* (d'une rivière).

ford[2] *v.tr.* guéer, traverser à gué (une rivière).

fordable ['fɔːdəbl] *a.* guéable.

fore [fɔːr] **I.** *a.* (*a*) antérieur; de devant; **the f. side of sth.,** la partie antérieure, le devant, de qch.; (*b*) *Nau:* (de l')avant; **f. hatch,** panneau *m* avant. **II.** *n.* (*a*) *Nau:* avant *m*; **at the f.,** au mât de misaine; (*b*) (*of pers., etc.*) **to the f.,** (i) en vue, en évidence, en vedette; (ii) présent; **to come to the f.,** commencer à être connu. **III.** *int. Golf:* gare devant!

fore(-)and(-)aft ['fɔːrənd'ɑːft] *a. & adv.* 1. de bout en bout; *Nau:* de l'avant à l'arrière; **f.-and-a. sail,** voile *f* aurique; **f.-and-a. bulkhead,** cloison médiane. 2. (dans le sens) longitudinal; *Mil:* **f.-and-a. cap,** calot *m.*

forearm[1] ['fɔːrɑm] *n.* avant-bras *m inv.*

forearm[2] [fɔːr'ɑːm] *v.tr.* prémunir (qn).

forebear ['fɔːbɛər] *n.* = FORBEAR[1].

forebode [fɔː'boud] *v.tr.* 1. (*of thg*) présager (le malheur); **policy that forebodes disaster,** politique qui laisse prévoir le désastre. 2. (*of pers.*) pressentir (un malheur). **foreboding** *n.* 1. mauvais augure. 2. (mauvais) pressentiment.

forecast[1] ['fɔːkɑːst] *n.* prévision *f*; **racing f.,** pronostic *m* des courses; **weather f.,** prévision météorologique; **long-range, short-range, f.,** prévision à longue échéance, sur période courte.

forecast[2] *v.tr.* (*p.t. & p.p.* **forecast(ed)**) prévoir (les événements, etc.); *Meteor:* pronostiquer (le temps); prévoir (un orage, etc.); *Sp:* pronostiquer (le résultat). **forecasting** *n.* pronostication *f* (d'un résultat, etc.); prévision *f* (du temps).

forecaster ['fɔːkɑːstər] *n.* pronostiqueur, -euse; **weather f.,** prévisionniste *mf.*

forecastle ['fouksl] *n.* *Nau:* 1. gaillard *m.* 2. (*in merchant vessel*) poste *m* de l'équipage.

foreclose [fɔː'klouz] *v.tr.* *Jur:* **to f. (the mortgage),** saisir l'immeuble hypothéqué.

foreclosure [fɔː'klouʒər] *n.* *Jur:* saisie *f* (d'une hypothèque).

forecourt ['fɔːkɔːt] *n.* avant-cour *f, pl.* avant-cours; devant *m* de garage.

foredoomed [fɔː'duːmd] *a.* condamné d'avance (**to,** à).

forefather ['fɔːfɑːðər] *n.m.* aïeul, -eux.

forefinger ['fɔːfiŋgər] *n.* index *m.*

forefoot, *pl.* **-feet** ['fɔːfut, -fiːt] *n.* (*of animal*) pied antérieur; patte *f* de devant.

forefront ['fɔːfrʌnt] *n.* premier rang; **this question is still in the f.,** cette question occupe toujours le premier plan.

foregather [fɔː'gæðər] *v.i.* = FORGATHER.

foregoing ['fɔːgouiŋ] *a.* précédent, antérieur; déjà cité; **the f.,** ce qui précède.

foregone ['fɔːgɔn] *n.* décidé d'avance; **it was a f. conclusion,** c'était prévu.

foreground ['fɔːgraund] *n.* *Art: Phot: etc:* premier plan; **in the f.,** au premier plan.

forehand ['fɔːhænd] *Ten:* (*a*) *a.* **f. stroke,** coup *m* d'avant-main; coup droit; **f. drive,** drive *m* de coup droit; (*b*) *n.* **to serve on to one's opponent's f.,** servir sur le coup droit adverse; **to take a ball on the f.,** jouer le coup droit.

forehead ['fɔrid, 'fɔːhed] *n.* *Anat:* front *m*; **wide, receding, f.,** front large, fuyant.

foreign ['fɔrin] *a.* étranger. 1. **f. to (sth.),** qui n'appartient pas à (qch.); **such feelings are f. to his nature,** de tels sentiments lui sont étrangers; *Med: etc:* **f. body,** corps étranger. 2. qui n'est pas du pays; (*a*) (*situated abroad*) **f. countries, f. parts,** pays étrangers, l'étranger *m*; **our relations with f. countries,** nos rapports avec l'extérieur; **f. travel,** voyages à l'étranger; **the F. Service,** le corps diplomatique; (*b*) (*dealing with foreign countries*) **f. trade,** commerce extérieur; **f. correspondent,** correspondant à l'étranger; *Pol:* **F. Affairs,** les Affaires étrangères; **the F. Office** = le Ministère des Affaires étrangères; **the F. Secretary** = le Ministre des Affaires étrangères.

foreign-built ['fɔrin'bilt] *a.* (voiture) de marque étrangère; (navire) construit à l'étranger.

foreigner ['fɔrinər] *n.* étranger, -ère.

foreignness ['fɔrinnis] *n.* air étranger; exotisme *m.*

foreknowledge [fɔː'nɔlidʒ] *n.* préconnaissance *f*; prescience *f.*

foreland ['fɔlənd] *n.* cap *m*, promontoire *m.*

foreleg ['fɔːleg] *n.* jambe *f*, patte *f*, de devant.

forelock ['fɔːlɔk] *n.* (*of pers.*) mèche *f* (de cheveux) sur le front; **to take time by the f.,** saisir l'occasion par les cheveux; **to touch one's f.,** porter la main à son front (pour saluer qn).

foreman, *pl.* **-men** ['fɔːmən] *n.m.* 1. *Jur:* chef (du jury). 2. (*a*) *Ind: etc:* contremaître; **f. of a gang of workmen,** chef d'équipe, de brigade; **works f.,** conducteur de travaux; (*b*) *Typ:* **printer's f.,** prote *m.*

foremast ['fɔːmɑːst] *n.* *Nau:* mât *m* de misaine; (arbre *m* de) trinquet (*m*).

forementioned ['fɔː'menʃənd] *a.* dont il a déjà été fait mention; *Jur: Adm:* précité.

foremost ['fɔːmoust] 1. *a.* premier; le plus avancé; le plus en avant; **in the f. rank,** au tout premier rang; **I know I shall only leave this room feet f.,** je sais que je ne quitterai cette chambre que les pieds devant. 2. *adv.* **first and f.,** tout d'abord; en premier lieu.

forename ['fɔːneim] *n.* prénom *m.*

forenoon ['fɔːnuːn] *n.* (*esp. Scot. & Irish*) matinée *f*; **in the f.,** dans, pendant, la matinée.

forensic [fə'rensik, fɔ-] *a.* (éloquence) du barreau; (médecine, chimie) légale; **f. scientist,** expert *m* légiste.

foreordain ['fɔːrɔː'dein] *v.tr.* prédestiner (**s.o. to sth., to do sth.,** qn à qch., à faire qch.).

forepart ['fɔːpɑːt] *n.* avant *m*, devant *m.*

forequarter ['fɔːkwɔːtər] *n.* quartier *m* de devant (de bœuf, etc.); **forequarters of a horse,** avant-main *m*, avant-train *m*, d'un cheval.

forerunner ['fɔːrʌnər] *n.* avant-coureur *m, pl.* avant-coureurs; précurseur *m.*

foresail ['fɔːseil, 'fɔːsl] *n.* (voile *f* de) misaine (*f*).

foresee [fɔː'siː] *v.tr.* (*p.t.* **foresaw** [fɔː'sɔ], *p.p.* **foreseen** [fɔː'siːn]) prévoir, entrevoir (un malheur); **it was an accident which should have been foreseen,** c'était un accident à prévoir.

foreseeable [fɔː'siːəbl] *a.* (conséquence, etc.) que l'on peut prévoir; (l'avenir, etc.) prévisible.

foreshadow [fɔː'ʃædou] *v.tr.* présager, annoncer, faire pressentir (un événement, etc.).

foreshore ['fɔːʃɔːr] *n.* 1. plage *f.* 2. laisse *f* de mer.

foreshorten [fɔː'ʃɔːt(ə)n] *v.tr.* dessiner (un objet) en raccourci, en perspective; **foreshortened figure,** figure vue en raccourci. **foreshortening** *n.* raccourci *m.*

foresight ['fɔːsait] *n.* 1. prévoyance *f*; **lack of f.,** imprévoyance *f*, imprévision *f.* 2. *Sm.a:* guidon *m*; bouton *m* de mire.

foreskin ['fɔːskin] *n.* *Anat:* prépuce *m.*

forest[1] ['fɔrist] *n.* 1. (*a*) forêt *f*; **deciduous, coniferous, f.,** forêt à feuilles caduques, de conifères; **tropical rain f.,** forêt tropicale humide; **f.-covered hills,** collines boisées; *Geog:* **the Black F.,** la Forêt Noire; *Fig:* **a f. of masts, of telegraph poles,** une forêt de mâts, de poteaux télégraphiques; (*b*) **f. ranger, guard,** garde forestier. 2. chasse royale; chasse seigneuriale.

forest² *v.tr.* boiser (une région).
forestall [fɔː'stɔːl] *v.tr.* anticiper, devancer, prévenir.
forestay ['fɔːstei] *n. Nau:* étai *m* de misaine.
forester ['fɔristər] *n.* garde forestier; forestier *m.*
forestry ['fɔristri] *n.* sylviculture *f*; *Adm:* **F. Commission,** service *m* des Eaux et Forêts.
foretaste ['fɔːteist] *n.* avant-goût *m*, *pl.* avant-goûts.
foretell [fɔː'tel] *v.tr.* (*p.t. & p.p.* **foretold** [fɔː'tould]) **1.** (*of pers.*) prédire. **2.** présager; **the sky foretells fine weather,** le ciel annonce le beau temps.
forethought ['fɔːθɔːt] *n.* prévoyance *f*, prudence *f.*
foretoken [fɔː'toukən] *v.tr.* présager, annoncer (une tempête, etc.).
foretop ['fɔːtɔp] *n. Nau:* hune *f* de misaine.
foretopsail ['fɔːtɔpseil, -sl] *n. Nau:* petit hunier.
forever [fɔr'evər] **1.** *adv.* (*a*) pour toujours, à jamais; (*b*) éternellement, sans cesse. **2.** *n. F:* **to take f. to do sth.,** prendre une éternité à faire qch.
forewarn [fɔː'wɔːn] *v.tr.* prévenir; **to f. s.o. of sth.,** avertir qn de qch.; *Prov:* **forewarned is forearmed,** un homme averti en vaut deux.
forewoman, *pl.* **-women** ['fɔːwumən, -wimin] *n.f.* **1.** *Jur:* porte-parole *m inv* (d'un jury). **2.** *Ind: etc:* contremaîtresse; *F:* première.
foreword ['fɔːwəːd] *n.* (*to book*) avant-propos *m inv,* préface f.
forfeit¹ ['fɔːfit] *a. Hist: Jur:* confisqué; **his lands were f.,** on confisqua ses terres.
forfeit² *n.* (*a*) amende *f*; (*for non-performance of contract*) dédit *m*; *Sp: esp. Turf:* forfait *m*; **f. clause (of a contract),** clause *f* de dédit; **to have to pay a f.,** être mis à l'amende; (*b*) *Games:* gage *m*; **to play forfeits,** jouer aux gages.
forfeit³ *v.tr.* **1.** perdre (qch.) par confiscation; être déchu d'(un droit). **2.** perdre (qch.); **to f. one's life,** payer de sa vie; **to f. one's honour,** forfaire à l'honneur.
forfeiture ['fɔːfitʃər] *n.* perte *f* (de biens) par confiscation; perte (de la vie, de l'honneur, etc.); *Jur: Fin:* déchéance *f*, forfaiture *f* (de titres, d'un droit).
forgather [fɔː'gæðər] *v.i.* **1.** s'assembler; se réunir. **2. to f. with s.o.,** rencontrer qn.
forge¹ [fɔːdʒ] *n.* (*a*) atelier *m* de forgeron, forge *f*; (*b*) *Metall:* **f. (shop),** atelier de forge; forge; **f. hammer,** marteau-pilon *m*, *pl.* marteaux-pilons.
forge² *v.tr.* **1.** (*a*) forger (un fer à cheval, etc.); (*b*) *Metall:* forger, cingler (le fer). **2.** contrefaire (une signature, des billets de banque); fabriquer, inventer (une calomnie, etc.); *v.i.* commettre, faire, un faux. **forged** *a.* **1.** *Metall:* (fer) forgé. **2.** (document, billet de banque, etc.) faux, contrefait; **f. document,** forgerie *f.* **forging** *n.* **1.** *Metalw:* travail *m* de forge; **f. mill,** forge *f*; **f. press,** marteau-pilon *m*, *pl.* marteaux-pilons. **2.** pièce forgée. **3.** contrefaçon *f* (de documents, etc.).
forge³ *v.i.* **to f. ahead,** (i) *Nau:* courir de l'avant; avancer à toute vitesse; (ii) (*of pers.*) dépasser tous ses concurrents; (*in business*) pousser de l'avant; *Rac:* foncer.
forger ['fɔːdʒər] *n.* contrefacteur *m* (de billets de banque); (*of signature, etc.*) faussaire *mf.*
forgery ['fɔːdʒəri] *n.* **1.** contrefaçon *f*; falsification *f* (de documents); *Jur:* **to be guilty of f.,** être coupable de faux. **2.** document fabriqué; faux *m*; **the signature was a f.,** la signature était contrefaite.
forget [fə'get] *v.tr.* (*p.t.* **forgot** [fə'gɔt]; *p.p.* **forgotten** [fə'gɔt(ə)n]; *pr.p.* **forgetting**) oublier. **1.** oublier (un fait); désapprendre (son latin); **f. (about) it!** (i) n'y pensez plus! (ii) (*in reply to apology*) il n'y a pas de quoi! **he warned me of the danger but I forgot (all) about it,** il m'a averti du danger mais je n'y ai plus pensé; **I had forgotten it,** j'en avais perdu le souvenir; **don't f. that he is only ten years old,** faites attention qu'il n'a que dix ans; **to f. how to do sth.,** oublier comment faire qch.; ne plus savoir faire qch.; **to be forgotten,** tomber dans l'oubli; **it's best forgotten,** il vaut mieux ne plus en parler; **things best forgotten,** choses qu'il vaut autant ne pas rappeler; **never to be forgotten,** inoubliable; **a never-to-be-forgotten day,** un jour mémorable. **2.** (*a*) omettre, oublier (un nom sur une liste, etc.); **to f. to do sth.,** oublier, omettre, de faire qch.; **don't f. to . . .,** ne manquez pas de . . .; (*b*) oublier (son mouchoir, ses gants, (etc.); (*c*) négliger (son devoir, etc.). **3.** *F:* **to f. oneself,** s'oublier; **to f. oneself so far as to do sth.,** s'oublier au point de faire qch.
forgetful [fə'getf(u)l] *a.* **1.** oublieux (**of,** de); **he is very f.,** il a très mauvaise mémoire. **2.** négligent.
forgetfulness [fə'getf(u)lnis] *n.* **1.** (*a*) manque (habituel) de mémoire; (*b*) **a moment of f.,** un moment d'oubli *m*. **2.** négligence *f.*
forget-me-not [fə'getminɔt] *n. Bot:* myosotis *m*; ne m'oubliez pas *m inv.*
forgivable [fə'givəbl] *a.* excusable, pardonnable.
forgive [fə'giv] *v.tr.* (*p.t.* **forgave** [fə'geiv]; *p.p.* **forgiven** [fə'giv(ə)n]) **1.** (*a*) pardonner, *A: & Ecc:* remettre (une faute, une injure); **to f. s.o. sth.,** pardonner qch. à qn; (*b*) **to f. s.o. a debt,** faire grâce d'une dette à qn. **2. to f. s.o.,** pardonner à qn; **he asked me to f. him,** il m'a demandé pardon; **one might perhaps be forgiven for thinking that . . .,** il n'est pas interdit de penser que . . .; **f. and forget,** il faut oublier et pardonner. **forgiving** *a.* indulgent, peu rancunier.
forgiveness [fə'givnis] *n.* **1.** (*a*) pardon *m*, rémission *f* (d'une faute, etc.); **to ask s.o.'s f.,** demander pardon à qn; (*b*) remise *f* (d'une dette). **2.** indulgence *f*; absence *f* de rancune.
forgo [fɔː'gou] *v.tr.* (*p.t.* **forwent** [fɔː'went]; *p.p.* **forgone** [fɔː'gɔn]) renoncer à (qch.); s'abstenir de (qch.).
fork¹ [fɔːk] *n.* **1.** *Agr:* fourche *f*; **garden f.,** fourche à bêcher. **2.** fourchette *f* (de table); **carving f.,** fourchette à découper; *F:* **f. lunch, f. buffet,** repas *m* à la fourchette. **3.** (*a*) (*to support branch, etc.*) poteau fourchu; (*b*) (*of water diviner*) baguette *f* divinatoire; (*c*) branche fourchue, bifurquée (d'un arbre). **4.** (*a*) *Cy:* **front fork(s),** fourche avant, de direction; (*b*) *Mus:* **tuning f.,** diapason *m*. **5.** (*a*) (i) bifurcation *f*, jonction *f*; (ii) **take the left f.,** prenez la route, le sentier, à gauche; (*b*) fourche (de branches, des jambes, de pantalon); (*c*) **f. of lightning,** zigzag *m* (d'éclair).
fork² **1.** *v.i.* (*of tree, etc.*) fourcher; (*of road*) fourcher, faire la fourche, (se) bifurquer; *P.N:* **f. right for York,** prenez à droite pour York. **2.** *v.tr.* fourcher (le sol); remuer (le sol, le foin) à la fourche; **to f. in,** enfouir (du fumier) en fourchant; **to f. over,** retourner légèrement (un parterre) à la fourche. **3.** (*a*) *v.tr. F:* **to f. out money,** allonger, abouler, de l'argent; (*b*) *v.i.* **he had to f. out,** il a dû s'exécuter. **forked** *a.* (*of branch, pipe*) fourchu, bifurqué, en fourche; (*of road*) bifurqué, à bifurcation; (langue) fourchue; (éclair) ramifié. **forking** *n.* bifurcation *f*, fourchement *m* (d'un arbre, d'une route, etc.)
forkful ['fɔːkful] *n.* **1.** fourchée *f* (de foin, etc.). **2.** fourchetée *f.*
forklift ['fəɔːklift] *n.* **f. (truck),** chariot (élévateur) à fourche.
forlorn [fə'lɔːn] *a. Lit:* **1.** désespéré, perdu; **f. hope,** aventure désespérée. **2.** (*a*) (endroit) abandonné, délaissé; (*b*) (mine) triste; (*c*) *NAm:* **f. of hope,** privé de tout espoir.
form¹ [fɔːm] *n.* **1.** (*a*) forme *f*, conformation *f*, configuration *f* (d'un objet); **to take f.,** prendre forme; (*b*) figure *f*, silhouette *f* (d'un homme, d'un animal).

2. (*a*) forme, nature *f*; **tonic taken in the f. of pills,** remontant pris sous la forme de pilules; **poverty in every f.,** la misère sous toutes ses formes; (*b*) (i) *Biol:* forme (spéciale) (d'une variété); (ii) sorte *f*, espèce *f*; **it's a f. of disease,** c'est une forme spéciale de maladie; **the different forms of worship,** les différentes façons d'adorer Dieu; (*c*) *Gram: Lit: Mus:* forme; **work that lacks f.,** œuvre qui manque de forme. **3.** forme, formalité *f*; (*a*) *Jur: etc:* **in due, proper, f.,** en bonne (et due) forme; dans les formes; **receipt in due f.,** quittance régulière; **to go through the f. of refusing,** faire la simagrée de refuser; **for form's sake, as a matter of f.,** pour la forme; par manière d'acquit; **it is a mere matter of f.,** c'est une pure formalité; *F:* **to know the f.,** savoir ce qu'il faut faire; (*b*) les convenances *fpl*; l'étiquette *f*; **it is good f.,** c'est de bon ton; **good f. demands that . . .,** la politesse exige que . . .; **it is not good f., it's bad f.,** c'est de mauvais ton, de mauvais genre. **4.** (*a*) formule *f*, forme (d'un acte, etc.); **correct f. of words,** tournure correcte de phrase; **forms of address,** titres *mpl* de politesse; (*b*) formule, formulaire *m*; **printed f.,** imprimé *m*; **f. 20,** modèle *m* numéro 20; **application f.,** (i) bulletin de demande; (ii) (*for shares*) bulletin de souscription; **order f.,** bulletin de commande; **to fill in, up, a f.,** remplir une formule, un formulaire. **5.** (*a*) *Sp:* forme; état *m*, condition *f* (d'entraînement); **to be in f., out of f.,** être, ne pas être, en forme; **to be in good f., in excellent f.,** être en train, dans une forme excellente; **he felt in good f.,** il se sentait gaillard; (*b*) *Turf:* (i) performances *fpl* (d'un cheval); (ii) tableau *m* des performances (des chevaux); (*d*) *F:* (*of pers.*) **he's got f.,** son casier judiciaire n'est pas vierge. **6.** *Sch:* classe *f*; **first f.** = *approx.* (classe de) sixième *f*; **sixth f.** = *approx.* (classe de) première; **f. master,** professeur principal; **f. room,** salle *f* de classe; la classe. **7.** banc *m*, banquette *f*; (*in amphitheatre*) gradin *m*. **8.** (*a*) *Metall:* forme, moule *m*; (*b*) *Civ.E: etc:* coffrage *m*, coffre *m* (pour béton armé); (*c*) *Typ:* forme; **to lock up a f.,** serrer une forme. **9.** gîte *m*, forme (du lièvre).

form² **1.** *v.tr.* (*a*) (i) former, faire, façonner (qch.); développer (l'esprit); (ii) *Metalw:* former, emboutir (une pièce); (*b*) (i) former, organiser (une société, etc.); instituer, établir (une république, etc.); **they formed themselves into a committee,** ils se constituèrent en comité; (ii) former, faire (un nouveau mot, etc.); **the past tense is formed by the addition of** *-ed*, le passé se forme par l'addition de *-ed*; (iii) se former, se faire (une idée, etc.); concevoir (des doutes); (iv) contracter (une liaison, etc.); (v) arrêter (un plan); **he had formed a plan to . . .,** il avait projeté de . . .; (*c*) (i) former, faire; **the walls f. a square,** les murs forment un carré; (ii) **to f. part of sth.,** faire partie de qch.; **the ministers who f. the cabinet,** les ministres qui composent, constituent, le gouvernement. **2.** *v.i.* **1.** prendre forme, se former, se produire; **his style is forming,** son style se fait. **2.** *Mil:* **to f. (up),** se former en rangs; **to f. into line,** se mettre en ligne. **forming** *n.* **1.** (*a*) formation *f* (d'une lettre); formation, développement *m* (du caractère); (*b*) *Metalw:* formage *m*, façonnage *m* (d'une pièce). **2.** constitution *f* (d'une société, etc.). **3.** *Mil:* **f. up,** rassemblement *m*.

formal ['fɔːm(ə)l] *a.* **1.** *Log: Theol:* formel. **2.** (*of procedure*) formel, en règle; (*of order*) positif, explicite; (contrat) en due forme; **to give s.o. a f. warning,** avertir qn dans les formes. **3.** (*a*) (*of occasion, etc.*) cérémonieux, solennel; **f. dress,** tenue *f* de (i) cérémonie, (ii) soirée; **f. dinner,** dîner officiel; grand dîner; **f. style,** style empesé; (*b*) *n. NAm:* (i) robe *f* de soirée; (ii) soirée formelle; bal formel. **4.** (*a*) (*of pers.*) pointilleux, formaliste; guindé; **he's always very f.,** il est toujours très compassé; (*b*) conventionnel; **he had no f. schooling,** il n'a pas fait des études conventionnelles; (*c*) (jardin) à la française. **-ally** *adv.* **1.** formellement. **2.** avec formalité. **3. f. correct,** correct quant à la forme.

formaldehyde [fɔː'mældihaid] *n. Ch:* formaldéhyde *m*; aldéhyde *m* formique.

formalin ['fɔːməlin] *n. Ch:* formol *m*.

formalism ['fɔːməlizm] *n.* formalisme *m*.

formality [fɔː'mæliti] *n.* **1.** formalité *f*; **legal formalities,** formes *fpl* juridiques; **a mere f.,** une pure formalité. **2.** (*a*) raideur *f* (de maintien); compassement *m* (d'un discours); (*b*) cérémonie *f*, formalité(s).

formalize ['fɔːməlaiz] *v.tr.* **1.** donner une forme exacte à (un contrat, etc.). **2.** donner une forme conventionnelle à (son art, etc.).

format ['fɔːmæt] *n.* format *m* (d'un livre, etc.).

formation [fɔː'meiʃ(ə)n] *n.* **1.** (*a*) formation *f* (du pluriel, de la houille, etc.); développement *m* (de l'esprit d'un enfant); (*b*) constitution *f* (d'une société, etc.); établissement *m* (d'une république, etc.). **2.** *Mil: etc:* (*a*) formation, dispositif *m* (des troupes); **battle f.,** *U.S:* **combat f.,** formation de combat; **close f.,** dispositif serré; *Av:* **f. flying,** vol *m* de groupe; **to break f.,** décrocher; (*b*) unité *f*; **armoured f.,** formation blindée. **3.** *Geol:* **granite f.,** formation granitique.

formative ['fɔːmətiv] **1.** *a.* formateur, -trice; **the f. years,** les années *fpl* de formation. **2.** *n. Ling:* élément formateur.

forme [fɔːm] *n. Typ:* = FORM¹ 8 (*c*).

former¹ ['fɔːmər] *a.* **1.** antérieur, -eure, précédent; ancien; **my f. pupils,** mes anciens élèves; **a f. convict,** un repris de justice; **in f. times,** autrefois; **he is a mere shadow of his f. self,** il n'est plus que l'ombre de ce qu'il était autrefois. **2.** (*as opposed to the latter*) **I prefer the f. alternative to the latter,** je préfère la première alternative à la dernière; (*b*) *pron.* celui-là, celle-là, ceux-là, celles-là; **of the two methods I prefer the f.,** des deux méthodes je préfère celle-là. **-ly** *adv.* autrefois, jadis; **Mr Martin, f. a liberal,** M. Martin, ci-devant libéral; **Mrs X, f. Miss Y,** Madame X, auparavant Mademoiselle Y.

former² *n.* **1.** (*pers.*) fondateur, -trice (d'une alliance, etc.). **2.** *Mec.E:* gabarit *m*, calibre *m* (de forme).

formic ['fɔːmik] *a. Ch:* (acide) formique.

formidable ['fɔːmidəbl] *a.* formidable, redoutable; **a f. adversary,** un rude adversaire.

formless ['fɔːmlis] *a.* informe, sans forme.

Formosa [fɔː'mousə] *Pr.n. Geog:* Formose *f*.

formula, *pl.* **-as, -ae** ['fɔːmjulə, -əz, -iː] *n.* formule *f*. **1. hackneyed formulas,** formules stéréotypées; **to find a f. acceptable to all parties,** découvrir une formule qui soit acceptable à tous les partis. **2.** (*pl. usu.* **formulae**) *Ch: etc:* formule. **3.** *NAm:* lait *m* en boîte (pour bébés).

formulate ['fɔːmjuleit] *v.tr.* **1.** formuler (une loi, une doctrine, etc.); élaborer (un projet). **2.** formuler, exprimer (son opinion, des objections).

formulation [fɔːmju'leiʃ(ə)n] *n.* **1.** formulation *f*, élaboration *f* (d'un projet). **2.** expression *f* (d'une opinion).

formwork ['fɔːmwəːk] *n.* coffrage *m* (pour béton armé).

fornicate ['fɔːnikeit] *v.i.* forniquer.

fornication [fɔːni'keiʃ(ə)n] *n.* fornication *f*.

forsake [fə'seik], *v.tr.* (*p.t.* **forsook** [fə'suk]; *p.p.* **forsaken** [fə'seik(ə)n]) **1.** abandonner, délaisser (qn). **2.** renoncer à, abandonner (une croyance, etc.). **forsaking** *n.* **1.** abandon(nement) *m*. **2.** renoncement *m* (**of,** à).

forsooth [fə'suːθ] *adv. A: & Lit:* **1.** en vérité. **2.** *Iron:* par exemple! ma foi!

forswear [fɔːˈswɛər] *v.tr.* (*p.t.* **forswore** [fɔːˈswɔːr]; *p.p.* **forsworn** [fɔːˈswɔːn]). **1.** abjurer, renier (qch.); renoncer à (qch.). **2. to f. oneself,** se parjurer.
forsythia [fɔːˈsaiθiə] *n. Bot:* forsythia *m.*
fort [fɔːt] *n. Mil:* **1.** fort *m.* **2.** place fortifiée; forteresse *f*; *F:* **to hold the f.,** gérer la maison, assurer la permanence (en l'absence des chefs).
forte¹ [fɔːt, ˈfɔːti] *n.* fort *m*; **singing is not his f.,** le chant n'est pas son fort.
forte² [ˈfɔːti] *a., adv. & n. Mus:* forte (*m*) *inv.*
forth [fɔːθ] *adv.* **1.** en avant; **to walk back and f.,** marcher de long en large. **2.** *A:* (*time*) **from this time f.,** désormais, dorénavant. **3. and so f.,** et ainsi de suite; et cætera.
forthcoming [fɔːθˈkʌmiŋ] *a.* **1.** (*a*) qui arrive; **help is f.,** des secours sont en route; (*b*) prochain, à venir; **the f. session,** la prochaine session. **2.** *Publ:* (livre) en préparation. **3. to be f.,** ne pas se faire attendre; **the money will be f.,** on trouvera l'argent nécessaire; **the promised help was not f.,** les secours promis ont fait défaut. **4.** (*of pers.*) (*a*) sociable, expansif; (*b*) ouvert, franc, *f.* franche; **not (very) f.,** réservé, renfermé (**about,** au sujet de).
forthright [ˈfɔːθrait] *a.* (*of pers.*) franc, *f.* franche.
forthrightness [ˈfɔːθraitnis] *n.* franchise *f.*
forthwith [fɔːθˈwiθ] *adv.* tout de suite, immédiatement, aussitôt; **the Council must be summoned f.,** il faut convoquer le Conseil d'urgence.
fortieth [ˈfɔːtiiθ] *num.a. & n.* quarantième (*m*).
fortification [fɔːtifiˈkeiʃ(ə)n] *n.* **1.** (*a*) fortification *f* (d'une ville, etc.); (*b*) affermissement *m* (du courage, etc.). **2. fortifications,** fortifications (d'une ville).
fortify [ˈfɔːtifai] *v.tr.* **1.** (*a*) renforcer, fortifier (un navire, etc.); (*b*) fortifier (qn); affermir, fortifier (qn, la résolution de qn); **fortified with the rites of the Church,** muni des sacrements de l'Église; **to f. oneself against the cold,** (i) se garantir contre le froid; (ii) boire une goutte. **2.** (*a*) alcooliser (un vin); (*b*) augmenter la valeur nutritive d'(un aliment). **3.** *Mil:* fortifier (une place); **fortified town,** ville fortifiée; place forte. **fortifying 1.** *a.* fortifiant; (*of drink, etc.*) remontant. **2.** *n.* (*a*) (i) renforcement *m* (d'un navire, etc.); (ii) affermissement *m* (du courage, etc.); (*b*) (i) *Winem:* alcoolisage *m*; (ii) augmentation *f* de la valeur nutritive (d'un aliment); (*c*) fortification *f* (d'une ville).
fortissimo [fɔːˈtisimou] *adv. & n. Mus:* fortissimo (*m inv*).
fortitude [ˈfɔːtitjuːd] *n.* force morale; force d'âme.
fortnight [ˈfɔːtnait] *n.* quinzaine *f*; quinze jours *mpl*; **today f.,** (d')aujourd'hui en quinze; **a f. ago,** il y a quinze jours; **to adjourn a case for a f.,** remettre une cause à quinzaine; **to take a fortnight's holiday,** prendre quinze jours de vacances.
fortnightly [ˈfɔːtnaitli] **1.** *a.* bimensuel, semi-mensuel. **2.** *adv.* bimensuellement; tous les quinze jours.
fortress [ˈfɔːtris] *n.* forteresse *f*; place forte.
fortuitous [fɔːˈtju(ː)itəs] *a.* fortuit, imprévu. **-ly** *adv.* fortuitement; par hasard.
fortunate [ˈfɔːtjənət, -tʃ-] *a.* **1.** (*of pers., etc.*) heureux; **to be f.,** avoir de la chance; **to be f. enough to . . .,** avoir la chance de . . . . **2.** (*of occasion, etc.*) propice, favorable, heureux; **how f.!** quel bonheur! quelle chance! **-ly** *adv.* **1.** heureusement. **2.** par bonheur.
fortune [ˈfɔːtʃən, -tʃuːn] *n.* fortune *f.* **1.** (*a*) hasard *m*, chance *f*; **piece of good f.,** coup *m* de bonheur; **by good f.,** par bonheur; **f. favours him,** la fortune lui sourit; (*b*) *Myth:* le Sort, le Destin; (*c*) destinée *f*, sort; **the fortunes of war,** le sort des armes; **to tell fortunes,** dire la bonne aventure; **to tell s.o.'s f. by cards,** tirer les cartes à qn. **2.** (*a*) bonne chance; (*b*) prospérité *f*, richesse *f*; **a man of f.,** un homme riche; (*c*) richesses *fpl*, biens *mpl*; **to make a f.,** faire fortune; **to come into a f.,** hériter une fortune; **her jewels are worth a f.,** ses bijoux valent une fortune; *F:* **it cost me a (small) f.,** cela m'a coûté un argent fou; (*d*) **her face is her f.,** jolie fille porte sur son front sa dot.
fortune-hunter [ˈfɔːtʃənhʌntər] *n.* chercheur *m* de richesses, de fortune; *esp.* coureur *m* de dot.
fortune-teller [ˈfɔːtʃəntelər] *n.* diseur, -euse, de bonne aventure; (*with cards*) tireur, -euse, de cartes.
fortune-telling [ˈfɔːtʃənteliŋ] *n.* la bonne aventure; (*with cards*) cartomancie *f.*
forty [ˈfɔːti] *num.a. & n.* quarante (*m*); **f.-one, f.-two,** quarante et un, quarante-deux; **about f. guests,** une quarantaine d'invités; **to be f. (years old),** avoir quarante ans; **the forties,** les années quarante (1940–50); **she's in her forties,** elle a passé la quarantaine; **the roaring forties,** les parages océaniques situés entre les 40 et 50 degrés de latitude nord; *F:* **to have f. winks,** piquer, faire, un petit somme.
forty-five [ˈfɔːtiˈfaiv] *n.* disque *m* quarante-cinq tours.
fortyish [ˈfɔːtiiʃ] *a.* d'une quarantaine d'années.
forum [ˈfɔːrəm] *n.* tribune *f* libre, forum *m.*
forward¹ [ˈfɔːwəd, *Nau:* ˈfɔrəd] **I.** *a.* **1.** (*a*) de devant, situé en avant; *Nau:* (de l')avant, sur l'avant; *Navy:* **f. turret,** tourelle *f* avant; (*b*) (mouvement, etc.) progressif, en avant; **f. motion,** marche *f* (en) avant; **f. and backward movement,** mouvement *m* d'avance et de recul; *Rail: etc:* **the f. journey,** l'aller *m.* **2.** (*of plants, child, etc.*) avancé; précoce. **3.** (*of opinions, etc.*) avancé. **4.** effronté, hardi. **5.** *Com:* (*of price, etc.*) à terme; *St.Exch:* **f. deals,** opérations *fpl* à terme. **II.** *adv.* (*occ.* **forwards** [ˈfɔːwədz]) **1.** (*a*) (*of extent of time*) **from that day f.,** à partir de ce jour-là; **to look f. to sth., to doing sth.,** attendre qch. avec plaisir, avec impatience; (*b*) *Com:* **to date f. a cheque,** postdater un chèque; **carriage f.,** (en) port dû; **charges f.,** frais *mpl* à percevoir à la livraison; (*c*) *Com: Fin:* **to sell f.,** vendre à terme. **2.** (*a*) (*direction*) en avant; **to go, move, f.,** (s')avancer; **to rush f.,** se précipiter (en avant); **to come, step, f.,** se détacher (des autres); faire un pas en avant; **f.!** en avant! (*b*) (*position*) à l'avant; **the seat is too far f.,** la banquette est trop avancée; *Nau:* **f. of the beam,** sur l'avant du travers; **the crew's quarters are f.,** le logement de l'équipage est à l'avant; (*c*) *Com: Book-k:* **to carry the balance f.,** reporter le solde à nouveau; **(carried) f.,** à reporter; report *m.* **3. new doctrines were put f., brought f.,** on mit en avant de nouvelles doctrines; **to come f.,** se proposer, s'offrir (pour un emploi, etc.); se présenter (**as a candidate,** comme candidat). **III.** *n. Fb: etc:* (*player*) avant *m.*
forward² *v.tr.* **1.** avancer, favoriser (les intérêts de qn, etc.). **2.** (*a*) expédier, envoyer, *Com:* transiter (des marchandises, etc.); **to f. sth. to s.o.,** faire parvenir qch. à qn; **to f. goods to Paris,** diriger des marchandises sur Paris; (*b*) faire suivre (une lettre); **please f.,** prière de faire suivre; à faire suivre. **forwarding** *n.* **1.** avancement *m* (d'une affaire, etc.). **2.** expédition *f*, envoi *m*; **f. address,** nouvelle adresse (pour faire suivre une lettre); **f. instructions,** indications *fpl* concernant l'expédition; **f. agent,** entrepreneur *m* de transports; transitaire *m*; **f. house,** maison d'expédition; maison de transit.
forward-looking [ˈfɔːwədlukiŋ] *a.* progressiste.
forwardness [ˈfɔːwədnis] *n.* **1.** avancement *m*, progrès *m* (d'un travail, etc.). **2.** état avancé, précocité *f* (de la saison, d'un élève, etc.). **3.** empressement *m*, ardeur *f.* **4.** hardiesse *f*, présomption *f.*
forwards [ˈfɔːwədz] *adv. see* FORWARD¹ II.

forwent. *see* FORGO.

fossil ['fɔs(i)l] **1.** *n.* fossile *m*; *F:* **an old f.,** une vieille croûte, un vieux fossile. **2.** *a.* (flore, etc.) fossile.

fossilization [fɔsilai'zeiʃ(ə)n] *n.* fossilisation *f.*

fossilize ['fɔsilaiz] **1.** *v.tr.* fossiliser. **2.** *v.i.* se fossiliser; *F:* (*of pers.*) s'encroûter; se fossiliser. **fossilized** *a.* (*a*) fossilisé; (*b*) (*of ideas, etc.*) fossile.

foster ['fɔstər] *v.tr.* **1.** (*a*) prendre (un enfant) en nourrice; (*b*) *Adm:* parrainer (un enfant). **2.** entretenir, nourrir (une idée, etc.); encourager, favoriser (les plans, de qn); protéger (les arts, etc.); **to f. friendship between peoples,** stimuler l'amitié entre les peuples. **fostering** *n.* **1.** (*a*) prise *f* (d'un enfant) en nourrice; (*b*) *Adm:* parrainage *m* (d'un enfant). **2.** entretien *m* (d'une idée, etc.); patronage *m*, encouragement *m* (des arts, etc.).

fosterchild ['fɔstətʃaild] *n.* (*a*) enfant en nourrice; (*b*) *Adm:* enfant placé dans une famille qui n'est pas la sienne.

fosterhome ['fɔstəhoum] *n.* foyer *m* (i) des parents nourriciers, (ii) des parrains; **placing of children in fosterhomes,** placement familial des enfants.

fostermother ['fɔstəmʌðər] *n.f.* (*a*) (mère) nourricière; nourrice; (*b*) *Adm:* femme qui accueille dans sa famille un enfant qui n'est pas le sien.

fosterparents ['fɔstəpɛərənts] *n.pl.* (*a*) parents nourriciers; (*b*) *Adm:* parrains *mpl.*

fought. *see* FIGHT².

foul¹ [faul] **I.** *a.* **1.** (*a*) infect, fétide; répugnant; **f. breath,** mauvaise haleine; **f. air,** air vicié; (*b*) (*of thoughts*) immonde, impur, corrompu; (*of language*) grossier, ordurier; (*c*) (*of deed, etc.*) noir, infâme, odieux; **f. deed,** infamie *f*; (*d*) *F:* horrible; **what f. weather!** quel sale temps! quel temps infect! **2.** (*a*) (linge, etc.) sale, souillé; (eau) croupie; (*b*) (*clogged*) (*of gun, sparking-plug, etc.*) encrassé; (*of pump*) engorgé; (*of tongue*) chargé; *Nau:* (*of ship*) **f. bottom,** carène *f* sale; (*c*) *Typ:* (copie) peu claire, illisible; **f. proof,** (i) mauvaise épreuve; (ii) épreuve en première. **3.** *Nau:* (*a*) engagé; **to run f. of another ship,** aborder, heurter, entrer en collision avec, un autre navire; *F:* **to fall f. of the law,** se brouiller avec la justice; (*b*) **f. weather,** gros temps; (*c*) **f. bottom,** mauvais fond (pour mouiller). **4.** *Sp: etc:* déloyal, -aux, illicite; **f. play,** (i) *Sp:* jeu déloyal; tricherie *f*; (ii) intrigue déloyale; malveillance *f*; (iii) action criminelle; **f. play is not suspected,** on ne croit pas à un crime. **II.** *n.* **1.** *Nau:* collision *f*, entrechoquement *m.* **2.** *Sp:* coup illicite, déloyal; *Fb:* poussée irrégulière; *Box:* coup bas. **III.** *adv.* irrégulièrement; déloyalement; **to fight f.,** se battre déloyalement; **to play s.o. f.,** faire une crasse à qn. **-lly** *adv.* **1.** salement. **2.** (parler, etc.) grossièrement. **3.** bassement; **he was f. murdered,** il fut ignoblement assassiné.

foul² **I.** *v.tr.* **1.** (*a*) salir, souiller (un endroit, sa réputation, etc.); (*b*) encrasser (un canon de fusil, *I.C.E:* les bougies). **2.** (*a*) embarrasser, obstruer (une ligne de chemin de fer, etc.); *Nau* surjaler (une ancre); engager (un cordage, etc.); (*b*) *F:* **to f. up,** déranger, dérégler (une machine); mettre (une machine) en panne; embrouiller, gâcher (un projet); (*c*) (*of ship, etc.*) entrer en collision avec, (se) heurter contre (un autre navire, etc.). **3.** (*a*) *Sp:* commettre une faute contre (qn); *Fb:* gêner ou plaquer (l'adversaire) en dehors des règles; *Turf:* couper (un cheval); (*b*) *v.i. Mec.E:* (*of moving part*) toucher. **II.** *v.i.* **1. to f. (up),** (*of gun barrel, etc.*) s'encrasser; (*of pump*) s'engorger. **2.** *Nau:* (*of anchor, rope, etc.*) s'engager; (*of anchor*) surjaler. **fouling** *n.* **1.** encrassement *m* (d'un fusil, *I.C.E:* des bougies); engorgement *m* (d'une pompe). **2.** (*a*) engagement *m* (d'une ancre, d'une hélice, etc.); (*b*) abordage *m* (de deux navires, etc.). **3.** *Artil: Sm.a:* crasse *f.*

foulbrood ['faulbru:d] *n. Ap:* loque *f.*

foul-mouthed ['faul'mauðd] *a.* (*of pers.*) au langage ordurier.

foulness ['faulnis] *n.* **1.** (*a*) impureté *f*, fétidité *f* (de l'air, etc.); (*b*) saleté *f.* **2.** grossièreté *f*, obscénité *f* (de langage, etc.). **3.** infamie *f* (d'un acte).

foul-up ['faulʌp] *n. F:* (*a*) déréglement *m*, dérangement *m* (d'un instrument, etc.); (*b*) embrouillement *m*; *P:* cafouillage *m*; **there's been a f.-up somewhere,** il y a eu un contretemps quelque part.

found¹ [faund] *v.tr.* (*a*) fonder (un édifice, une ville); (*b*) fonder, créer (un collège, etc.); établir (une maison de commerce, etc.); fonder (une famille); **to f. a fortune,** (i) établir les bases d'une fortune; (ii) élever une fortune (**on,** sur); (*c*) baser, fonder (ses soupçons, etc.) (**on,** sur); (*of novel, etc.*) **founded on fact,** reposant sur des faits véridiques; **well founded,** (bruit) bien fondé; (peur) légitime; **ill-founded,** (bruit) mal fondé. **founding** **1.** *a.* (*of member*) fondateur, -trice; *U.S: Hist:* **F. Father,** membre de la Convention constituante de 1787. **2.** *n.* = FOUNDATION 1.

found² **1.** *see* FIND². **2.** *a.* (*with adv. prefixed*) (*of ship, etc.*) **well-f.,** bien équipé (**in,** de).

found³ *v.tr. Metall:* fondre (les métaux); mouler (la fonte). **founding** *n.* fonderie *f*, moulage *m.*

foundation [faun'deiʃ(ə)n] *n.* **1.** (*a*) fondation *f* (d'un édifice, d'une ville, etc.); établissement *m*, institution *f* (d'un empire, d'une maison de commerce); (*b*) fondation et dotation *f* (d'un hôpital). **2.** (*a*) massif *m* de base, soubassement *m*; fondement *m*, fondation (d'un édifice); assiette *f* (d'une chaussée); assise *f* (d'une machine, etc.); **the foundations of a building,** le gros œuvre d'un édifice; **to lay the f. of an alliance,** jeter les bases d'une alliance; *Const:* **to lay the f. stone,** poser la première pierre; (*b*) *Fig:* **the foundations of modern society,** les assises de la société moderne. **3.** (*a*) fond (d'une robe, etc.); **embroidery on a silk f.,** broderie *f* sur fond de soie; (*b*) *Paint:* fond de teint (d'une toile); *Th: Toil:* **make-up f., f. cream,** base de maquillage, fond de teint; (*c*) *Cost:* **f. garment,** gaine *f*; combiné *m.* **4.** fondement, base (d'une théorie, etc.); motif *m*, cause *f* (d'un doute); **rumour without f.,** bruit dénué de fondement. **5.** (*a*) institution dotée; fondation; **f. school,** école dotée; *Sch:* **f. scholar,** élève boursier; (*b*) capital légué pour œuvres de bienfaisance; fondation.

founder¹ ['faundər] *n.* fondateur *m* (d'un hôpital, etc.); **f. member,** membre fondateur.

founder² *n. Metall:* fondeur *m.*

founder³ **1.** *v.i.* (*a*) (*of hopes, horse*) s'effondrer; (*b*) *Nau:* (*of ship*) sombrer; couler. **2.** *v.tr.* courbaturer (un cheval). **foundering** *n.* effondrement *m.*

foundling ['faundliŋ] *n.* enfant trouvé, -ée; *Hist:* **f. hospital,** hospice *m* des enfants trouvés.

foundry ['faundri] *n. Metall:* fonderie *f* (de fer, etc.); **f. iron,** fonte *f* de moulage.

fount¹ [faunt] *n. Poet: Lit:* source *f* (d'eau); source, cause *f*, principe *m* (du bonheur, etc.); **the f. of all knowledge,** la source de toute science.

fount² [faunt, *among printers* fɔnt], *n. Typ:* fonte *f*; **wrong f.,** lettre *f* d'un autre œil.

fountain ['fauntin] *n.* fontaine *f*; (*a*) *A: & Lit:* source *f* (d'eau); **f. of wisdom,** source de sagesse; (*b*) **drinking f.,** (i) fontaine publique; (ii) poste *m* d'eau potable; **soda f.,** bar *m* pour glaces et rafraîchissements non alcooliques; (*c*) jet *m* d'eau (de jardin public, etc.).

fountainhead ['fauntinhed] *n.* **the f. of all knowledge,** la source de toute science.
fountain-pen ['fauntinpen] *n.* stylo *m* à encre.
four [fɔːr] *num.a. & n.* **1.** quatre (*m*); **twenty-f.,** vingt-quatre; **f. fives, five fours, are twenty, f. times five is twenty,** quatre fois cinq, cinq fois quatre, font vingt; **we have tea at f. thirty,** nous prenons le thé à quatre heures et demie; **to be f. (years old),** avoir quatre ans; **scattered to the f. corners of the earth,** éparpillés aux quatre coins du monde; **to run on all fours,** courir à quatre pattes. **2.** *Sp:* (*a*) *Row:* **a f.,** un quatre; (*b*) *Cr:* **to hit a f.,** marquer quatre points; (*c*) *Golf:* **a f.-ball (match),** une partie à quatre joueurs et quatre balles.
four-colour ['fɔː'kʌlər] *a. Engr: etc:* à quatre couleurs; **f.-c. work,** quadrichromie *f.*
four-cornered ['fɔː'kɔːnəd] *a.* à quatre coins; carré, quadrangulaire.
four-engined ['fɔːr'endʒind] *a. Av:* (avion) quadrimoteur.
four-figure ['fɔː'figər] *a. Mth:* (nombre) à quatre chiffres; (logarithme) à quatre décimales.
fourfold ['fɔːfould] **1.** *a.* quadruple. **2.** *adv.* quatre fois autant; au quadruple; **to increase f.,** quadrupler.
four-footed ['fɔː'futid] *a.* (animal) quadrupède; à quatre pattes.
four-handed ['fɔː'hændid] *a.* **1.** (singe) à quatre mains, quadrumane. **2.** (*a*) (jeu) à quatre (personnes); (*b*) *occ.Mus:* (morceau) à quatre mains.
four-in-hand ['fɔːin'hænd] **1.** *n.* (*a*) véhicule *m* à quatre chevaux; (*b*) *NAm: Cost:* **f.-in-h. (tie),** cravate-plastron *f, pl.* cravates-plastrons. **2.** *adv.* **to drive f.-in-h.,** conduire à quatre (chevaux).
four-leaved ['fɔː'liːvd] *a. Bot:* quadrifolié; (trèfle) à quatre feuilles.
four-legged ['fɔː'legid] *a.* (*a*) (table) à quatre pieds; (*b*) (animal) quadrupède.
four-letter ['fɔː'letər] *a. F:* **f.-l. word,** obscénité *f.*
four-master ['fɔː'mɑːstər] *n.* quatre-mâts *m inv.*
four-part ['fɔː'pɑːt] *a. Mus:* à quatre parties; à quatre voix.
fourpence ['fɔːpəns, -pens] *n.* (somme *f* de) quatre pence.
fourpenny ['fɔːp(ə)ni] *a.* qui vaut quatre pence; **10 f. stamps,** 10 timbres à quatre pence; *P:* **to give s.o. a f. one,** flanquer un gnon, une beigne, à qn.
four-phase ['fɔː'feiz] *a. El:* (système) tétraphasé.
four-poster ['fɔː'poustər] *a. & n.* (lit *m*) à colonnes.
four-seater [fɔː'siːtər] *n. Aut:* voiture *f* à quatre places.
foursome ['fɔːsəm] *n.* groupe *m* de quatre personnes; *Golf:* partie (de) double, à deux contre deux.
four-speed ['fɔː'spiːd] *a. Aut:* à quatre vitesses.
foursquare ['fɔː'skwɛər] *a. & adv.* (i) carré(ment); (ii) solide(ment).
four-stroke ['fɔːstrouk] *a. & n. I.C.E:* (moteur *m*) à quatre temps.
fourteen ['fɔːtiːn] *num.a. & n.* quatorze (*m*); **she is f.,** elle a quatorze ans; **the plane will arrive at fourteen thirty,** l'avion arrivera à quatorze heures trente.
fourteenth [fɔː'tiːnθ] **1.** *num.a. & n.* quatorzième (*mf*); **Louis the F.,** Louis Quatorze; **(on) the f. (of May),** le quatorze (mai). **2.** *n.* (*fractional*) quatorzième *m.*
fourth [fɔːθ] **1.** *num.a. & n.* quatrième (*mf*); **Henry the F.,** Henri Quatre; **he's f. in his class,** il est le quatrième de sa classe; *Aut:* **in f. (gear),** en quatrième (vitesse); **the f. of January, January the f.,** le quatre janvier; *Sch:* **the f. form,** *approx.* = la classe de troisième; *Cards: etc:* **to make a f.,** faire le quatrième. **2.** *n.* (*a*) (*fractional*) quart *m*; **three-fourths of the globe,** les trois quarts du globe; (*b*) *Mus:* quarte *f.*
fourthly ['fɔːθli] *adv.* quatrièmement, en quatrième lieu.
four-wheel ['fɔː(h)wiːl] *a.* **1.** (*also* **four-wheeled** ['fɔː'(h)wiːld]) (véhicule) à quatre roues. **2.** *Aut:* **tractor with a f.-w. drive,** tracteur *m* à quatre roues motrices.
four-wheeler ['fɔː'(h)wiːlər] *n.* voiture *f* à quatre roues.
fowl¹ [faul] *n.* **1.** (*a*) *Lit:* oiseau *m*; (*b*) *coll.* oiseaux; **water f.,** gibier d'eau. **2.** (*a*) poule *f*, coq *m*, volaille *f*; **to keep fowls,** élever des poules; *Vet:* **f. pest,** peste aviaire, des poules; **f. pox,** diphtérie *f* aviaire; (*b*) *Cu:* volaille; **boiling f.,** poule (au pot).
fowl² *v.i.* faire la chasse au gibier ailé. **fowling** *n.* chasse *f* aux oiseaux; **f. piece,** fusil *m* de chasse (à petit plomb).
fox¹ [fɔks] *n.* (*a*) renard *m*; **f. cub,** renardeau *m*; **red f.,** renard commun; **Arctic f.,** renard bleu; **silver f.,** renard argenté; **f. brush,** queue *f* de renard; **fox's earth,** renardière *f*; terrier *m* de renard; *Cost:* **f. fur,** (fourrure en) renard; (*b*) *F:* **an old f.,** un vieux madré; **a sly f.,** un fin renard; un roublard.
fox² **1.** *v.tr.* (*a*) tacher de roux (les feuilles d'un livre); maculer (une gravure); (*b*) mystifier, tromper (qn). **2.** *v.i.* feindre; ruser; renarder. **foxing** *n.* **1.** feinte *f*; finasserie *f.* **2.** (*on paper*) macules *fpl* (d'une estampe).
foxglove ['fɔksglʌv] *n. Bot:* digitale (pourprée).
foxhole ['fɔkshoul] *n.* **1.** renardière *f*; terrier *m* de renard. **2.** *Mil:* trou *m* de tirailleur; abri individuel.
foxhound ['fɔkshaund] *n.* chien courant (pour la chasse au renard); fox-hound *m, pl.* fox-hounds.
foxhunt ['fɔkshʌnt] *n.* chasse *f* au renard.
foxhunting ['fɔkshʌntiŋ] *n.* chasse *f* au renard.
foxiness ['fɔksinis] *n.* **1.** astuce *f*; roublardise *f.* **2.** état maculé (des pages). **3.** goût foxé (du vin).
foxmark ['fɔksmɑːk] *n.* tache *f* de roux (sur une feuille d'un livre).
foxtail ['fɔksteil] *n.* **1.** queue *f* de renard. **2.** *Bot:* **f. (grass),** vulpin *m.*
fox-terrier ['fɔks'teriər] *n.* fox-terrier *m, pl.* fox-terriers; *F:* fox *m.*
foxtrot¹ ['fɔkstrɔt] *n. Danc:* fox-trot *m inv.*
foxtrot² *v.i.* **(fox-trotted)** danser le fox-trot.
foxy ['fɔksi] *a.* **1.** (*a*) (visage, etc.) qui ressemble à un renard; au nez pointu; (*b*) rusé, astuce. **2.** (*of hair, complexion*) roux, *f.* rousse. **3.** (*of wine, beer*) foxé.
foyer ['fɔiei, 'fwajei] *n. Th:* foyer *m* du public; *Cin:* (hall *m* d')entrée (*f*).
fraction ['frækʃ(ə)n] *n.* **1.** petite portion, petite partie (de qch.); fragment *m.* **2.** (*a*) *Mth:* fraction; **vulgar, common, f.,** fraction ordinaire; **decimal f.,** fraction décimale; **compound f.,** fraction de fraction; **he escaped death by a f. of a second,** il a été à deux doigts de la mort; (*b*) *Fin:* fraction, rompu *m* (d'action, d'obligation). **3.** *Ch:* fraction (de distillation). **4.** *Pol:* fraction; groupe *m* fractionnaire (d'un parti).
fractional ['frækʃən(ə)l] *a.* **1.** *Mth:* fractionnaire; *F:* **the difference is only f.,** la différence est minime. **2.** *Ch:* fractionné; **f. distillation,** distillation fractionnée; fractionnement *m.* **-ally** *adv.* **f. larger, heavier,** plus grand, plus lourd, d'un tout petit peu.
fractionate ['frækʃəneit] *v.tr. Ch: Ind:* fractionner (le pétrole, etc.).
fractionize ['frækʃənaiz] *v.tr. Mth:* fractionner.
fractious ['frækʃəs] *a.* (*a*) revêche; (*b*) de mauvaise humeur; (bébé) pleurnicheur.
fractiousness ['frækʃəsnis] *n.* mauvaise humeur; (*of baby*) pleurnicherie *f*, pleurnichage *m.*
fracture¹ ['fræktʃər] *n.* **1.** (*a*) fracture *f*, rupture *f* (d'un essieu, etc.); (*b*) fracture (d'un os, etc.); **simple f.,** fracture simple; **compound f.,** fracture compliquée; **to set a f.,** réduire une fracture. **2.** *Geol:* cassure *f*,

fracture. **3.** *Ling:* fracture (d'une voyelle).

fracture² **1.** *v.tr.* (*a*) casser, briser (qch.); (*b*) fracturer (un os); **fractured skull,** crâne fracturé; **fractured ribs,** côtes enfoncées; (*c*) *U.S:* enfreindre (la loi, etc.). **2.** *v.i.* (*a*) se casser, se briser; (*b*) (*of limb*) se fracturer.

fragile ['frædʒail] *a.* **1.** (*of thg*) fragile. **2.** (*of pers.*) faible; délicat; *F:* **I'm feeling a bit f. this morning,** j'ai mal aux cheveux ce matin. **-ly** *adv.* fragilement.

fragility [frə'dʒiliti] *n.* **1.** (*of thg*) fragilité *f*; *Metall:* frangibilité *f*. **2.** (*of pers.*) faiblesse *f*; délicatesse *f*.

fragment¹ ['frægmənt] *n.* **1.** fragment *m*, morceau *m* (de porcelaine, etc.); éclat *m* (d'obus); brin *m* (de papier). **2.** *Lit:* fragment; (*a*) œuvre inachevée (d'un auteur); (*b*) extrait *m* (d'un livre).

fragment² [fræg'ment] *v.tr.* réduire en fragments; briser en morceaux.

fragmentary ['frægmənt(ə)ri] *a.* fragmentaire.

fragmentation [frægmən'teiʃ(ə)n] *n.* fragmentation *f*.

fragrance ['freigrəns] *n.* parfum *m*.

fragrant ['freigrənt] *a.* parfumé, odorant, fragrant; (odeur) embaumée; **to be f.,** sentir bon; **woods f. with wild strawberries,** bois parfumés de fraises sauvages.

frail [freil] *a.* **1.** (*a*) peu solide; fragile; frêle; (*b*) (bonheur) transitoire; éphémère. **2.** (*of pers.*) faible, frêle.

frailness ['freilnis] *n.* **1.** (*a*) fragilité *f* (du verre, etc.); (*b*) caractère éphémère, transitoire (de la beauté, etc.). **2.** (*a*) faiblesse *f*, débilité *f*, *esp.* faiblesse de l'âge; (*b*) faiblesse morale.

frailty ['freilti] *n.* **1.** = FRAILNESS 2 (*b*). **2.** faible *m*; défaut *m*.

frame¹ [freim] *n.* **1.** (*a*) construction *f*, structure *f*, disposition *f*; **f. of mind,** état *m*, disposition, d'esprit; **he is in a bad f. of mind,** il est mal disposé; (*b*) système *m*, forme *f* (de gouvernement); ordre *m* (de la société); plan *m* (de l'univers). **2.** (*a*) ossature *f* (d'une personne, d'un animal); **man of gigantic f.,** homme d'une taille colossale; (*b*) charpente *f* (d'un bâtiment, d'un pont, etc.); *NAm:* **f. house,** maison *f* en bois; (*c*) ossature *f* (de l'aile d'un avion); cadre *m* (d'une bicyclette, etc.); châssis *m* (d'une locomotive, d'une automobile); bâti *m* (d'une machine); monture (d'un parapluie); armature *f* (d'une raquette); monture (d'une paire de lunettes); **f. of a bed,** châlit *m*; bois *m* de lit; **f. saw,** scie montée, à châssis; (*d*) *N.Arch:* membrure *f*, carcasse *f* (d'un navire); (*e*) *Mth:* **f. of reference, reference f.,** système *m* de coordonnées; référentiel *m*. **3.** (*a*) cadre, encadrement *m* (d'un tableau, miroir, etc.); **gilded f.,** cadre doré; (*b*) chambranle *m*, châssis dormant (d'une fenêtre, d'une porte); (*c*) *Cin:* image *f* (de film); *T.V:* (i) trame *f* (double), (ii) image; *T.V:* **f. frequency,** fréquence *f* des trames; *U.S:* fréquence des images. **4.** (*a*) *Needlew:* métier *m* (à broder); tambour *m* (à broder); (*b*) *Tex:* métier (à filer). **5.** *Hort:* châssis (de couches); **hot f., cold f.,** châssis chaud, froid. **6.** *Sp:* (*bowling, etc.*) reprise *f*, coup *m* (de jeu de quilles). **7.** *F:* coup monté (contre qn).

frame² *v.tr.* **1.** former, régler (ses pensées, etc.); *v.i.* **he is framing well,** il montre des dispositions; il donne de grandes espérances. **2.** (*a*) faire la charpente d'(un toit); construire la carcasse d'(un navire); (*b*) charpenter (un roman, etc.); composer (un poème, une réponse, etc.); *Jur:* rédiger (une loi). **3.** (*a*) se faire (une opinion); (*b*) fabriquer (une histoire, etc.); *F:* **to f. s.o.,** monter une accusation, un coup, contre qn; **I've been framed,** c'est un coup monté (contre moi). **4.** (*a*) encadrer (un tableau, etc.); **black hair framed her pale face,** des cheveux noirs encadraient son pâle visage; (*b*) *T.V:* cadrer, centrer (l'image). **framing** *n.* **1.** (*a*) construction *f* (de qch.); (*b*) composition *f* (d'un poème, etc.); *Jur:* rédaction *f* (d'une loi); (*c*) invention *f*, fabrication *f* (d'une accusation); (*d*) *F:* accusation à tort; (*e*) encadrement *m* (d'un tableau, etc.); (*f*) *T.V:* cadrage *m*, centrage *m* (de l'image). **2.** = FRAME¹ 2; **metal f. (for window),** vitrière *f*.

framemaker ['freimmeikər] *n.* carcassier *m* (de parapluies, etc.).

frame-up ['freimʌp], *n. F:* coup monté.

framework ['freimwə:k] *n.* **1.** (*a*) charpente *f*, bâti *m*, ossature *f*, carcasse *f*, squelette *m*; charpente (d'un roman); **it comes within the f. of the U.N.,** cela rentre dans le cadre de l'O.N.U.; (*b*) construction *f* en cloisonnage; coffrage *m* (de travaux en béton); **open f.,** treillis *m*. **2.** fabrication *f* de cadres.

franc [fræŋk] *n. Num:* franc *m*.

France [frɑ:ns] *Pr.n. Geog:* France *f*; **in F.,** en France.

Frances ['frɑ:nsis] *Pr.n.f.* Françoise.

franchise ['fræn(t)ʃaiz] *n.* **1.** (*a*) concession (octroyée à une compagnie d'utilité publique); (*b*) *Com:* contrat *m* de franchisage; **to have the f., a f., for sth. in a given territory,** avoir le droit (exclusif) de vendre qch. dans un territoire déterminé. **3.** *Pol:* droit de vote; électorat *m*. **franchising** *n.* franchisage *m*.

Francis ['frɑ:nsis] *Pr.n.m.* François.

Franciscan [fræn'siskən] *n. & a.* franciscain (*m*).

francophile ['fræŋkoufail] *a. & n.* francophile (*mf*).

francophobe ['fræŋkoufoub] *a. & n.* francophobe (*mf*).

frangible ['frændʒibl] *a.* frangible, cassant, fragile.

frank¹ [fræŋk] *a.* (*of pers., feelings*) franc, *f.* franche; sincère; (*of speech*) direct, ouvert; **to be quite f.,** parler franchement, à cœur ouvert. **-ly** *adv.* franchement, avec franchise; ouvertement; (parler) à cœur ouvert; **f. incredible,** tout bonnement incroyable; **I tell you f. that . . .,** je vous dis carrément que . . .; **(quite) f., no!** franchement, non!

frank² *v.tr.* affranchir (une lettre) (*esp.* à la machine). **franking** *n.* affranchissement *m* (*esp.* à la machine); **f. machine,** machine *f* à affranchir.

Frank³ *Pr.n.m.* (*dim. of Francis*) François.

Frankfurter ['fræŋkfə:tər] *n.* saucisse *f* de Francfort.

frankincense ['fræŋkinsens] *n.* encens *m* (mâle).

Frankish ['fræŋkiʃ] *a. Hist:* franc, *f.* franque.

frankness ['fræŋknis] *n.* franchise *f*, sincérité *f*.

frantic ['fræntik] *a.* **1.** frénétique, forcené; fou, *f.* folle; **f. efforts,** efforts effrénés; **f. with pain,** fou de douleur; **it drives him f.,** cela le met hors de lui. **2.** *F:* affreux, terrible. **-ally,** *NAm:* **franticly** *adv.* **1.** frénétiquement, follement, avec frénésie; **to rush f. around,** courir çà et là comme un affolé. **2.** *F:* affreusement, terriblement; **I'm f. busy,** j'ai tellement à faire que je ne sais où donner de la tête.

fraternal [frə'tə:n(ə)l] *a.* fraternel; **-ally** *adv.* fraternellement.

fraternity [frə'tə:niti] *n.* **1.** fraternité *f*. **2.** confrérie *f*. **3.** *NAm:* association *f* de camarades de classe.

fraternization [frætənai'zeiʃ(ə)n] *n.* fraternisation *f* (**with,** avec).

fraternize ['frætənaiz] *v.i.* fraterniser (**with,** avec).

fraud [frɔ:d] *n.* **1.** (*a*) *Jur:* fraude *f*, dol *m*; **to obtain sth. by f.,** obtenir qch. par fraude, frauduleusement; **guilty of f.,** coupable de manœuvres frauduleuses; **the f. squad,** la brigade de la police chargée de la répression des fraudes; (*b*) supercherie *f*, tromperie *f*. **2.** *F:* (*a*) (*pers.*) truqueur, -euse; imposteur *m*; **he's a f.,** c'est un imposteur; (*b*) attrape *f*; **this place is a f.,** cet endroit ne répond pas à la réputation qu'on lui a faite.

fraudulence ['frɔ:djuləns] *n.* (*a*) caractère frauduleux (d'une transaction); (*b*) infidélité *f* (d'un dépositaire, etc.).

fraudulent ['frɔːdjulənt] *a. Jur:* frauduleux; (transaction) entachée de fraude; **f. bankrupt,** banqueroutier frauduleux. **-ly** *adv.* frauduleusement, par fraude.

fraught [frɔːt] *a.* **1.** *Lit:* fertile (**with,** en); gros (**with,** de); **f. with danger,** qui entraîne des conséquences funestes. **2.** (*of thg*) désolant, pénible; (*of pers.*) désolé.

fray¹ [frei] *n.* (*a*) bagarre *f,* échauffourée *f,* mêlée *f;* **in the thick of the f.,** au plus épais de la mêlée; (*b*) rixe *f;* **to enter the f.,** descendre dans l'arène; **to return to the f.,** rentrer en lice.

fray² **1.** *v.tr.* érailler, effiler (un tissu, etc.); **my nerves are frayed,** je suis à bout de nerfs. **2.** *v.i.* (*of material*) s'érailler, s'effiler; (*of rope*) s'étriper; **my collar is fraying,** mon col s'effrange au bord. **frayed** *a.* **1.** (*of cloth, garment, etc.*) éraillé, frangé; (*of rope*) étripé, usé; **shirt f. at the cuffs,** chemise élimée aux manchettes. **2.** (*of nerves*) à vif; **tempers were getting a little f.,** on commençait à se fâcher.

frazzle ['fræzl] *n.* **to be worn to a f.,** être complètement éreinté; **to beat s.o. to a f.,** battre qn à plate(s) couture(s); **a joint cooked to a f.,** un rôti calciné.

freak¹ [friːk] *n.* **1.** caprice *m,* fantaisie *f,* lubie *f;* **f. of fortune,** jeu *m* de la fortune. **2.** (*a*) **f. (of nature),** monstre *m,* phénomène *m;* **f. show,** exhibition *f* de monstres; **he's a f.,** c'est un grotesque; (*b*) *P:* **drugs f.,** toxicomane *mf;* **jazz f.,** fana *mf* du jazz. **3.** *attrib.* (*of storm, etc.*) complètement inattendu; **f. weather,** temps anormal; **f. accident,** accident *m* incroyable.

freak² *v.i. P:* **to f. out,** (i) (*of drug taker*) se défoncer; être du voyage; (ii) se défouler; (iii) devenir hippie.

freakish ['friːkiʃ] *a.* capricieux, fantasque, bizarre; (imagination) libertine; **f. notion,** fantaisie *f.*

freckle¹ ['frekl] *n.* tache *f* de rousseur.

freckle² **1.** *v.tr.* marquer (qn, la peau) de taches de rousseur. **2.** *v.i.* (*of the skin*) se couvrir de taches de rousseur. **freckled** *a.* **1.** couvert de taches de rousseur. **2.** (*of animal's coat*) tacheté.

Fred [fred], **Freddy** ['fredi] *Pr.n.m. F:* (*dim. of Frederick*) Frédéric.

Frederic(k) ['fred(ə)rik] *Pr.n.m.* Frédéric.

free¹ [friː] *a. & adv.* **1.** (*a*) libre; *Nau:* (port) franc; **f. house,** débit *m* de boissons qui est libre de vendre les produits de n'importe quelle brasserie; **of one's own f. will,** de (son) propre gré; **man is a f. agent,** l'homme est libre; *F:* **it's a f. country,** vous avez (le droit d'agir selon) votre libre arbitre; (*b*) en liberté; **to set f.,** mettre (qn) en liberté; affranchir (un esclave); laisser s'envoler (un oiseau); délivrer, libérer (un prisonnier); **to break f.,** (i) se dégager de ses liens; (ii) s'échapper; **to be allowed to go f.,** être mis en liberté; être relâché. **2.** (*unoccupied*) libre; *Tp:* (ligne) dégagée; **is this table f.?** est-ce que cette table est libre? **f. time,** temps libre; moment de loisir; **to have some time f.,** avoir du temps de libre; **I am f. tomorrow,** je suis libre demain. **3.** (*unrestricted*) (*a*) libre, sans entraves; (amour) libre; **f. speech,** libre parole; **right of f. entry,** droit de passer librement les frontières; **f. trade,** libre-échange *m;* **f. trader,** libre-échangiste *mf, pl.* libre-échangistes; **to have a f. hand,** avoir pleine liberté d'action, avoir ses coudées franches (**to,** pour); **to give, allow, s.o. a f. hand,** donner carte blanche à qn; **as f. as the air,** libre comme l'air; **to be (entirely) f. to do sth.,** être (entièrement) libre de faire qch.; **I am f. to do what I please,** je suis libre de mes mouvements; (*b*) (*of style, etc.*) franc, *f.* franche; aisé; (*of bearing*) souple, désinvolte; **she's f. and graceful in all her actions,** elle fait tout avec aisance et grâce; (*c*) **with his f. hand,** avec sa main libre; **f. end,** brin *m* libre (d'un cordage); **f. diving,** plongée sous-marine autonome; *Cy:* **f. wheel,** roue *f* libre; **f. fall,** chute *f* libre (d'un poids, d'un parachutiste); (*d*) **f. from, of, sth.,** débarrassé de qch.; **to be f. from care, worry, anxiety,** être sans souci; **wood f. from knots,** bois exempt de nœuds; **style f. from affectation,** style dénué de toute recherche; **at last I am f. of him,** enfin je suis débarrassé de lui; (*e*) franc (**of,** de); **interest f. of tax,** intérêts nets, exempts d'impôt; *Cust:* **f. of duty,** exempt de droits d'entrée; **to import sth. f. of duty,** faire entrer qch. en franchise; **you are allowed to bring in half a litre f.,** il y a une tolérance d'un demi-litre; **f. zone,** zone franche. **4.** (*a*) *Ch:* (*of gas, etc.*) (à l'état) libre, non-combiné; **f. gold,** or *m* à l'état natif; (*b*) (*of power, energy*) libre, disponible. **5.** (*a*) (*of action, etc.*) libre, spontané, volontaire; (choix) arbitraire; **as a f. gift,** en pur don; **f. translation,** traduction libre; *Pros:* **f. verse,** vers libres; *Sch:* **f. composition,** composition libre (en langue étrangère); (*b*) (*of pers.*) libéral, généreux; **to be f. with one's money,** être prodigue de son argent; **he was very f. with his advice,** il a été très libéral de conseils; (*c*) (*of supply*) abondant, copieux; (*d*) (*of pers., speech*) franc, ouvert, sans réserve; **f. and easy,** désinvolte; sans gêne; sans façon; **to be f. and easy,** prendre ses aises; (*e*) libre de contrainte; **to make f. with sth.,** se servir de qch. sans se gêner; **he made very f. with my whisky,** il ne se gênait pas pour boire mon whisky; (*f*) (*of language*) libre, licencieux; **to be rather f. in one's conversation,** tenir des propos peu convenables. **6.** *F:* **feel f.,** faites comme chez vous. **7.** (*without charge*) (concert, échantillon) gratuit; *Th:* (billet) de faveur; **admission f.,** entrée gratuite, gratis; **f. demonstration in the home,** démonstration gracieuse à domicile; *Publ:* **f. copy,** spécimen *m;* **f. luggage allowance,** bagage(s) *m(pl)* en franchise; *Com:* **delivery f.,** livré franco *inv;* **post f.,** franco de port; **f. on board,** franco à bord. **8.** *adv.* (*a*) franco, gratuitement; **catalogue sent f. on request,** catalogue franco sur demande; **the gallery is open f. on Saturdays,** l'entrée du musée est gratuite le samedi; (*b*) *Nau:* **vessel running f.,** navire *m* courant largue; (*c*) *adv.phrs. F:* **for f., f. gratis and for nothing,** gratis; **to get sth. for f.,** obtenir qch. pour rien; (*d*) (*followed by a present participle*) = FREELY; **f. flowing,** qui coule abondamment; **f. flowering,** qui fleurit abondamment. **-ly** *adv.* **1.** (donner, faire, qch.) librement; **to give f. to s.o.,** faire des libéralités à qn. **2.** (parler, agir, etc.) franchement, en toute liberté; **to speak f. to s.o.,** parler à qn à cœur ouvert. **3.** (*a*) (couler, etc.) abondamment, copieusement; (*b*) **to see that a mechanism works f.,** s'assurer du bon fonctionnement d'un mécanisme.

-free² *a.* (*with noun prefixed*) **knot-f. timber,** bois sans nœuds; **accident-f. driving record,** passé *m* de chauffeur vierge d'accidents.

free³ *v.tr.* (**freed; freeing**) (*a*) affranchir (un esclave, etc.); libérer, élargir (un prisonnier, etc.); **to f. oneself from s.o.'s grasp,** se dégager des mains de qn; **I couldn't f. my foot,** je ne pouvais pas dégager mon pied; **to f. s.o. from an obligation,** libérer qn d'une obligation; **to f. oneself from one's commitments,** se délier de tous ses engagements; (*b*) débarrasser (**from, of,** de); dégager (un sentier, etc.); déblayer (le terrain); (*c*) *Mec.E: etc:* dégager (une pièce); (*d*) désobstruer (un filtre engorgé); dégorger (une pompe); (*e*) **to f. a property (from mortgage),** déshypothéquer une propriété; (*f*) *Adm:* (i) mettre (des denrées réglementées) en vente libre; (ii) détaxer (des denrées taxées). **freeing** *n.* **1.** libération *f,* délivrance *f* (d'un prisonnier); affranchissement *m* (d'un esclave); exemption *f* (de qn d'un impôt). **2.** dégagement *m* (d'un cordage); débarrassement *m* (d'un passage, etc.); dégorgement *m* (d'un tuyau, etc.).

freebie, freebee ['friːbiː] *n.* prime (accordée à un journaliste, etc.).

freeboard ['fri:bɔ:d] *n. Nau:* (franc-)bord *m.*
freeborn ['fri:bɔ:n] *a.* libre de naissance; né libre.
freedom ['fri:dəm] *n.* **1.** (*a*) liberté *f*, indépendance *f*; **in f.,** en liberté; (*b*) liberté d'action; liberté de penser; **f. of speech,** la liberté d'expression; **f. to do sth.,** liberté de faire qch. **2.** (*a*) franchise *f*, familiarité *f* (d'une conversation, etc.); (*b*) hardiesse *f*; sans-gêne *m.* **3.** (*of action, etc.*) facilité *f*, liberté. **4.** (*a*) exemption *f*, franchise; **f. from tax,** exemption d'impôts; (*b*) **f. of a city,** (i) droit *m* de cité; (ii) citoyenneté *f* d'honneur d'une ville; **to receive the f. of a town,** être nommé citoyen, -enne, d'honneur d'une ville. **5.** libre usage *m* (de qch.); **the f. of the seas,** la liberté de la haute mer; **to give s.o. the f. of one's library,** mettre sa bibliothèque à la disposition de qn.
freefone ['frifoun] *n. Tp:* libre appel *m.*
free-for-all ['fri:fərɔ:l] *a. & n. F:* **f.-f.-a. (race, competition),** concours auquel tout le monde peut participer; **f.-f.-a. (fight),** rixe *f*, bagarre *f*, mêlée *f*.
freehand ['fri:hænd] **1.** *a.* (dessin) à main levée. **2.** *adv.* (dessiner) à main levée.
freehanded [fri:'hændid] *a.* généreux.
freehold ['fri:hould] **1.** *a.* tenu en propriété perpétuelle et libre. **2.** *n.* propriété foncière perpétuelle et libre.
freeholder ['fri:houldər] *n.* propriétaire foncier (à perpétuité).
freelance¹ ['fri:lɑ:ns] **1.** *n.* (journaliste, etc.) indépendant(e). **2.** *a.* (journaliste, etc.) indépendant; *Journ:* **f. work,** travail indépendant. **3.** *adv.* **to work f.,** faire du travail indépendant.
freelance² *v.i.* être un journaliste, acteur, etc., indépendant.
freeloader [fri:'loudər] *n. NAm: F:* pique-assiette *mf inv*; écornifleur, -euse.
freeman, *pl.* **-men** ['fri:mən] *n.m.* **1.** homme libre. **2.** citoyen d'honneur.
freemason ['fri:meis(ə)n] *n.m.* franc-maçon, *pl.* francs-maçons.
freemasonry ['fri:meis(ə)nri] *n.* franc-maçonnerie *f*.
freepost ['fri:poust] *n.* libre-réponse *f*.
free-range ['fri:'reindʒ] *a.* (œufs, poulet) de ferme.
freesia ['fri:ʒə] *n. Bot:* freesia *m.*
free-spoken ['fri:'spouk(ə)n] *a.* (*of pers.*) franc, *f.* franche; qui parle ouvertement.
freestanding ['fri:'stændiŋ] *a.* (mur, etc.) autosupportant; *Arch:* (colonne) isolée.
freestyle ['fri:stail] *n. Swim:* nage *f* libre.
freethinker ['fri:θiŋkər] *n.* libre penseur, -euse.
freeway ['fri:wei] *n.* (*a*) route *f* à grande circulation avec interdiction de stationner; (*b*) *NAm:* autoroute *f* sans péage.
free(-)wheel ['fri:'(h)wi:l] *v.i.* **1.** (*a*) *Cy:* faire roue libre; **to f. down a hill,** descendre une côte en roue libre; (*b*) *Aut:* marcher, rouler, en roue libre. **2.** aller son petit bonhomme de chemin.
freeze¹ [fri:z] *n.* **1.** gel *m*, gelée *f*; **the big freeze,** la grande gelée. **2. price and wage f.,** blocage *m* des prix et des salaires.
freeze² *v.* (*p.t.* **froze** [frouz]; *p.p.* **frozen** [frouz(ə)n]) **1.** *v.i.* (*a*) *impers.* **it's freezing,** il gèle; **it's freezing hard,** il gèle ferme; (*b*) (*of liquid*) (se) geler; se congeler; **the river is, has, frozen,** la rivière est prise; *F:* **I'm freezing,** j'ai très froid, je gèle; **the smile froze on his lips,** le sourire se figea sur ses lèvres; (*c*) **to f. to death,** mourir de froid; (*d*) (*of pers.*) (i) rester cloué sur place; se figer; (ii) se raidir; se guinder; **f.!** ne bougez pas! **2.** *v.tr.* (*a*) geler, congeler (qch.); congeler (la viande); **to f. the blood (in one's veins),** glacer le sang, le cœur; **to be frozen to death,** mourir de froid; (*b*) geler (des crédits, des devises); bloquer (les salaires); (*c*) *Med:* insensibiliser avec une anesthésie locale. **freeze out** *v.tr.* (*a*) évincer (qn); supplanter (un rival); (*b*) boycotter (qn). **freeze over** *v.i* **the pond has, is, frozen over,** l'étang a, est, gelé d'un bout à l'autre. **freeze up** *v.i.* **the river has frozen up,** la rivière est prise; **the radiator froze up,** le radiateur a gelé. **freezing 1.** *a.* réfrigérant, congelant; (temps, etc.) glacial, -als. **2.** *n.* (*a*) (*becoming frozen*) congélation *f*, gel *m*; *Ph:* **f. point,** point *m* de congélation; **the thermometer is at f. point,** le thermomètre est à zéro; (*b*) (*making frozen*) réfrigération *f* (d'un liquide, etc.); congélation (de la viande, etc.); **f. compartment,** congélateur *m*, freezer *m* (d'un réfrigérateur); **f. mixture,** mélange réfrigérant; (*c*) blocage *m* (des salaires, etc.). **frozen** *a.* **1.** gelé, glacé; (viande) congelée; **f. foods,** (produits) surgelés (*mpl*), congelés (*mpl*); *F:* **my hands are f.,** j'ai les mains gelées, glacées; **I've got f. waiting for you,** je me suis gelé à vous attendre. **2.** (*of assets, etc.*) non liquide, gelé.
freeze-dry ['fri:z'drai] *v.tr.* lyophiliser (un sérum, etc.). **freeze-drying** *n.* lyophilisation *f*.
freezer ['fri:zər] *n.* **1.** congélateur *m*; **upright f.,** congélateur vertical; **chest f.,** congélateur bahut. **2. f. compartment,** congélateur, freezer *m* (d'un réfrigérateur).
freeze-up ['fri:zʌp] *n.* gelée *f*; gel *m.*
freight¹ [freit] *n.* **1.** (*a*) fret *m*; (*b*) transport *m* (de marchandises); **air f.,** transport par air. **2.** (*a*) fret, cargaison *f*, chargement *m* (d'un navire); **to take in f.,** prendre du fret; (*b*) marchandises (transportées); **f. train,** train *m* de marchandises; *Av:* **f. plane,** avion-cargo *m*, *pl.* avions-cargos; *NAm:* **f. car,** wagon *m* à, de, marchandises. **3.** fret; prix *m* du transport de marchandises; **to pay the f.,** payer le fret.
freight² *v.tr.* **1.** (af)fréter (un navire). **2. to f. (out) a ship,** donner un navire à fret. **3.** charger (un vaisseau).
freightage ['freitidʒ] *n.* **1.** (af)frètement *m* (d'un vaisseau). **2.** fret *m*, cargaison *f*. **3.** transport *m* des marchandises.
freighter ['freitər] *n.* **1.** affréteur *m* (d'un vaisseau). **2.** *NAm:* consignateur, -trice (de marchandises pour transport par voie de terre). **3.** entrepreneur *m* de transports; exportateur *m.* **4.** (*a*) cargo *m*; navire *m* de charge; (*b*) *Rail: NAm:* wagon *m* de marchandises; (*c*) *Av:* avion-cargo *m*, *pl.* avions-cargos.
freightliner ['freitlainər] *n.* train *m* de marchandises en conteneurs.
French [fren(t)ʃ] **I** *a.* **1.** (*a*) français; **the F. Ambassador,** l'ambassadeur de France; **of F. make,** de fabrication française: (*b*) (*of dish, fashion, etc.*) à la française; *Cu:* **F. dressing,** vinaigrette *f*; *Const:* **F. window,** porte-fenêtre *f*, *pl.* portes-fenêtres; **F. polish,** vernis *m* au tampon; *P:* **F. letter,** capote anglaise; (*c*) *Sch:* **F. master, mistress,** professeur *m* de français; **F. lesson,** leçon *f* de français. **2. F. Canadian,** canadien français; **F. Canada,** le Canada français. **II.** *n.* **1.** *Ling.* (*a*) le français; la langue française; **to speak F.,** parler français; **to learn, know, F.,** apprendre, connaître, le français; **say it in F.,** dites-le en français; (*b*) **F. Canadian, Canadian F.,** le français canadien, du Canada. **2.** (*a*) *pl.* **the F.,** les Français; (*b*) **F. Canadian,** Canadien, -ienne, français(e).
Frenchify ['fren(t)ʃifai] **1.** *v.tr.* franciser (son style, etc.). **2.** *v.i.* se franciser.
Frenchman, *pl.* **-men** ['fren(t)ʃmən] *n.* Français *m.*
French-polish ['fren(t)ʃ'pɔliʃ] *v.tr.* vernir (un meuble, etc.) au tampon.
French-speaking ['fren(t)ʃ'spi:kiŋ] *a.* francophone.
Frenchwoman, *pl.* **-women** ['fren(t)ʃwumən, -wimin] *n.f.* Française.

frenetic [frə'netik] *a.* (*of pers., action, etc.*) frénétique; fou, *f.* folle. **-ally** *adv.* frénétiquement.
frenzied ['frenzid] *a.* (*a*) (*of pers.*) affolé, forcené; (*b*) (*of rage*) fou, *f.* folle; (*of applause*) frénétique, délirant.
frenzy ['frenzi] *n.* frénésie *f*, folie *f* (du désespoir).
frequency ['fri:kwənsi] *n.* **1.** (*of letters, etc.*) fréquence *f*; *Mth:* **f. of errors,** répartition *f* des erreurs. **2.** (*a*) *Ph:* fréquence; *F:* **I'm not on your f.,** je ne suis pas sur la même longueur d'onde que vous; (*b*) *El:* **high, low, f.,** haute, basse, fréquence; **very high f.,** très haute fréquence; (*c*) *T.V: Rad:* **radio f.,** fréquence radio(électrique); (*d*) **f. band,** bande *f* de fréquences; **f. modulation,** modulation *f* de fréquence; **f. range,** gamme *f* de fréquences.
frequent¹ ['fri:kwənt] *a.* **1.** (*a*) très répandu; **it's quite a f. practice,** c'est une coutume assez répandue; (*b*) *Med:* (pouls) rapide. **2.** (*of visits, etc.*) fréquent; qui arrive souvent; **f. visits to the theatre,** fréquentation *f* du théâtre. **3.** (*of visitor*) familier; (*of customer*) habituel. **-ly** *adv.* fréquemment; souvent.
frequent² [fri'kwent] *v.tr.* fréquenter, hanter (les théâtres, les cafés, etc.); **to f. s.o.,** fréquenter qn.
frequentation [fri:kwen'teiʃ(ə)n] *n.* fréquentation *f.*
frequenter [fri'kwentər] *n.* habitué *m*, familier *m* (d'une maison, etc.).
fresco, *pl.* **-o(e)s** ['freskou(z)] *n. Art:* **1.** fresque *f*; **to paint in f.,** peindre à fresque; **f. painter,** fresquiste *mf.* **2.** (peinture *f* à) fresque; **the frescoes of Raphael,** les fresques de Raphaël.
fresh [freʃ] **I.** *a.* **1.** (*a*) nouveau, -el, -elle; **f. paragraph,** nouveau paragraphe; **to put f. courage into s.o.,** ranimer le courage de qn; **to let f. air into a room,** renouveler l'air d'une pièce; **f. outbreak of fire,** recrudescence *f* de feu; (*b*) (*of news, etc.*) frais, *f.* fraîche; récent; **it is still f. in my mind,** je l'ai encore frais à la mémoire; **f. from London,** nouvellement arrivé de Londres; **the bread was f. from the oven,** le pain sortait du four. **2.** (*of pers.*) inexpérimenté; **to be a f. hand at sth.,** être novice dans qch. **3.** (*a*) **f. or tinned peas,** pois frais ou en boîte; **f. vegetables,** légumes verts; (*b*) (air) frais, pur; **in the f. air,** au grand air, en plein air; *F:* **f.-air fiend,** fanatique *mf* de l'air frais; **f. water,** eau douce; (*c*) (*colours, etc.*) frais. **4.** (*a*) (teint) frais, fleuri; (*b*) (*of pers.*) vigoureux, alerte; dispos; (*of horse, etc.*) fougueux, animé; **f. troops,** troupes fraîches; **as f. as a daisy,** frais et dispos; (*c*) *F:* effronté; **to get f. with a girl,** prendre des libertés avec une jeune fille; **don't (you) get f. with me!** ne te fiche pas de moi! **5.** *Nau:* **f. breeze,** bonne brise. **6.** *F:* (*of pers.*) éméché; un peu gris. **II.** *adv.* fraîchement, nouvellement, récemment (arrivé, peint, etc.); **f.-cut flowers,** fleurs nouvellement cueillies; **f.-killed poultry,** volaille fraîchement tuée du jour. **III.** *n.* fraîcheur *f* (du matin, etc.); fraîche *f* (du soir). **freshly** *adv.* **1.** (*with p.p. only*) fraîchement, de frais; **f. picked peaches,** des pêches fraîches cueillies. **2.** vigoureusement, vivement.
freshen ['freʃ(ə)n] **1.** *v.i.* (*a*) (*of temperature*) (se) rafraîchir; (*b*) (*of wind, weather*) fraîchir; (*c*) (*of pers.*) **to f. (up),** faire un bout de toilette. **2.** *v.tr.* (*a*) rafraîchir (l'air, la mémoire, etc.); **to f. up paint,** (r)aviver la couleur; (*b*) *Nau:* rafraîchir (une amarre, les remorques).
fresher ['freʃər] *n. F:* étudiant(e) de première année.
freshman, *pl.* **-men** ['freʃmən] *n.m. & f.* (*at university*) étudiant, -ante, de première année.
freshness ['freʃnis] *n.* **1.** caractère récent (d'un événement). **2.** (*a*) fraîcheur *f* (d'un visage, d'une impression, etc.); (*b*) fraîcheur, froideur *f* (du vent, etc.). **3.** (*of pers.*) (*a*) vigueur *f*, vivacité *f*; (*b*) naïveté *f*, inexpérience *f*; (*c*) *F:* effronterie *f.*
freshwater ['freʃwɔ:tər] *a.* (poisson, etc.) d'eau douce; *F:* **f. sailor,** marin d'eau douce.
fret¹ [fret] *n. Arch:* **(Greek) f.,** grecque *f*; frette *f.*
fret² *v.tr.* **(fretted) 1.** découper (le bois). **2.** *Arch:* sculpter, orner (un plafond, etc.).
fret³ *n. Mus:* touchette *f*, touche *f* (de guitare, etc.).
fret⁴ *n.* (*a*) agitation *f*; (*b*) irritation *f*; état *m* d'agacement; **to be in a f.,** se faire du mauvais sang, de la bile.
fret⁵ *v.* **(fretted) 1.** *v.tr.* (*a*) ronger (qch.); **to f. a rope,** érailler un cordage; (*b*) inquiéter, tracasser (qn). **2.** *v.pr. & i.* se tourmenter, s'inquiéter; se faire du mauvais sang; **don't f.!** (i) ne vous faites pas de bile! ne vous faites pas de mauvais sang! (ii) ne vous inquiétez pas! **child fretting for his mother,** enfant qui réclame sa mère (en pleurnichant); **to f. over, about, trifles,** s'irriter pour des sujets futiles; **to f. and fume,** se ronger d'impatience; rager. **fretting** *n.* **1.** usure *f.* **2.** rongement *m* d'esprit; inquiétude *f.*
fretful ['fretf(u)l] *a.* (*of pers.*) qui se fait du mauvais sang; **f. baby,** bébé agité. **-fully** *adv.* d'un air chagrin; d'un ton maussade.
fretfulness ['fretf(u)lnis] *n.* irritabilité *f.*
fretsaw ['fretsɔ:] *n.* scie *f* à découper.
fretwork ['fretwə:k] *n.* **1.** (*of ceilings, etc.*) ornementation *f*, sculpture *f.* **2.** *Woodw:* découpage *m*; travail ajouré; bois découpé.
Freudian ['frɔidiən] *a. Psy:* freudien; **F. slip,** lapsus *m.*
friable ['fraiəbl] *a.* (terre, etc.) friable.
friar ['fraiər] *n.* **1.** *R.C.Ch:* moine *m*, frère *m*, religieux *m*; **Grey Friars,** Franciscains *mpl*; **Black Friars,** Dominicains *mpl*; **White Friars,** Carmes *mpl.* **2.** *Pharm:* **friar's balsam,** baume *m* de benjoin.
friary ['fraiəri] *n.* monastère *m.*
fricassee¹ [frikə'si:] *n. Cu:* fricassée *f*; (*of rabbit or hare*) gibelotte *f.*
fricassee² *v.tr. Cu:* fricasser.
fricative ['frikətiv] *Ling:* **1.** *a.* (*of consonant*) fricatif, sifflant, soufflant. **2.** *n.* fricative *f*, sifflante *f.*
friction ['frikʃ(ə)n] *n.* **1.** *Med: Hairdr:* friction *f*; **f. gloves,** gants *mpl* de crin. **2.** frottement *m* (de deux corps); **f. surface,** frottoir *m* (d'une boîte d'allumettes); *NAm:* **f. tape,** chatterton *m.* **3.** *Mec: Ph:* frottement, friction. **f. brake,** frein à friction; **f. drive,** entraînement *m* par friction. **4.** friction, désaccord *m*; **there's f. between them,** il y a du tirage entre eux.
frictional ['frikʃən(ə)l] *a. Ph:* à, de, friction.
Friday ['fraidi] *n.* vendredi *m*; **he's coming (on) F.,** il viendra vendredi; **he comes every F.,** il vient tous les vendredis; **Good F.,** (le) Vendredi saint; **Man F.,** (i) *Lit:* Vendredi (le domestique de Robinson Crusoé); (ii) *F:* factotum *m*; homme à tout faire; *F:* **girl F.,** aide *f* de bureau.
fridge [fridʒ] *n. F:* réfrigérateur *m*, *F:* frigo *m.*
fried. *see* FRY².
friend [frend] *n.* **1.** (*a*) ami, *f.* amie; **I am speaking to you as a f.,** je vous parle en ami(e); **boy f.,** petit ami; **girl f.,** petite amie; **bosom f.,** ami(e) intime; **to be friends with s.o.,** être ami avec qn; **to make friends,** se faire des amis; **to make friends with s.o.,** se lier d'amitié avec qn; *Prov:* **a f. in need is a f. indeed,** au besoin on connaît l'ami; (*b*) (*not an enemy*) *F:* **you'd better be, keep, friends with them,** vous ferez bien de ne pas vous brouiller avec eux; **let us part friends,** séparons-nous (en) bons amis; **he's no f. of mine,** (i) il n'est nullement mon ami; (ii) il ne me veut pas de bien. **2.** connaissance *f*; *F:* **a f. at court,** un ami en haut lieu, bien placé; **to have friends at court,** avoir des protections; **to dine with a few friends,** dîner en petit comité; *Parl:* **my honourable f.,** *Jur:* **my learned f.,** mon (cher) confrère. **3.** (*a*) **f. of the poor,** bienfaiteur, -trice, des pauvres; (*b*) ami, partisan *m* (de l'ordre, etc.); (*c*) patron, -onne (des arts, etc.); **the**

Friends of Canterbury Cathedral, la Société des Amis, les Amis, de la Cathédrale de Cantorbéry. **4.** *Rel:* Quaker, -eresse; Ami, -ie; **the Society of Friends,** la Société des Amis; les Quakers.

friendless ['frendlis] *a.* sans amis, sans appui.

friendliness ['frendlinis] *n.* bienveillance *f,* bonté *f,* dispositions amicales (**to, towards,** envers).

friendly ['frendli] **I.** *a.* **1.** (*a*) amical, -aux; sympathique; **piece of f. advice,** avis amical; **f. gathering,** réunion d'amis; **to be f. with s.o.,** être ami avec qn; **they became very f.,** il se sont pris d'amitié l'un pour l'autre; **in a f. manner,** amicalement; (*b*) (*not hostile*) **to be on f. terms with s.o.,** être en bons termes, en relations d'amitié, avec qn; **f. nation,** pays ami; *Sp:* **f. match,** match amical. **2.** (*of pers.*) bienveillant, favorablement disposé. **3. f. society,** association *f* de bienfaisance; société *f* de mutualité. **II.** *n. Sp:* match amical.

Friendly Islands (the) [ðə'frendliailəndz] *Pr.n.pl. Geog:* Tonga *m;* les îles *fpl* des Amis.

friendship ['frendʃip] *n.* amitié *f;* **to form a f. with s.o.,** se lier (d'amitié) avec qn.

fries [fraiz] *n.pl. F:* **French f.,** frites *fpl.*

frieze¹ [fri:z] *n. Tex:* frise *f;* ratine *f.*

frieze² *n.* **1.** *Arch:* frise *f.* **2.** bordure *f* (de papier peint).

frigate ['frigət] *n.* **1.** *Navy:* frégate *f,* escorteur *m.* **2.** *Orn:* **f. (bird),** frégate.

fright [frait] *n.* **1.** peur *f,* effroi *m;* **he was seized with f.,** l'effroi l'a saisi; **to take f.,** s'effrayer (**at,** de); **to give s.o. a f.,** faire peur à qn; *F:* **I got an awful f.,** j'ai eu une peur bleue. **2.** *F:* (*esp. of woman*) personne *f* laide, grotesque; **what a f. you look!** comme vous voilà fagotée!

frighten ['frait(ə)n] *v.tr.* effrayer (qn); faire peur à (qn); **it frightens him, her,** cela lui fait peur; **these animals are easily frightened,** ces animaux s'effarouchent d'un rien; **you f. me to death,** vous me faites mourir de peur. **frighten away** *v.tr.* effaroucher (qn, un animal); **don't f. away the birds,** n'effarouchez pas les oiseaux. **frightened** *a.* (*of pers., etc.*) apeuré; **easily f.,** peureux; **I wasn't as f. as you were,** je n'avais pas aussi peur que vous; **to feel f.,** avoir peur; **f. out of one's wits,** terrifié; **f. to death,** en proie à une frayeur mortelle. **frightening** *a.* effrayant. **frighteningly** *adv.* à faire peur. **frighten off** *v.tr.* effaroucher (qn, un animal); (*of dog, etc.*) chasser (des voleurs, etc.).

frightful ['fraitf(u)l] *a.* effroyable, épouvantable; *F:* **to have a f. headache,** avoir un mal de tête affreux. **-fully** *adv.* affreusement; **he is f. ugly,** il est laid à faire peur; *F:* **I am f. sorry,** je regrette énormément; **f. rich,** colossalement riche.

frightfulness ['fraitfulnis] *n.* horreur *f;* atrocité *f.*

frigid ['fridʒid] *a.* **1.** (*a*) glacial, -als; (très) froid; (*b*) (style) glacial; (réponse) glacée. **2.** *Med:* (femme) frigide. **-ly** *adv.* glacialement; **f. polite,** d'une politesse glaciale.

frigidity [fri'dʒiditi] *n.* **1.** frigidité *f;* froideur (de style). **2.** froideur (sexuelle); frigidité.

frill¹ [fril] *n. Cost: etc:* (*a*) volant *m,* ruche *f;* **shirt f.,** jabot *m;* *Cu:* (*on ham, etc.*) papillote *f;* (*b*) *F:* **a plain meal without frills,** un repas simple sans présentation compliquée.

frill² *v.tr.* plisser, froncer, rucher (le linge, etc.). **frilled** *a.* (*a*) (*of ribbon, etc.*) froncé, ruché; (*of shirt*) à jabots; (*b*) *Rept:* **f. lizard,** iguane australien.

frilly ['frili] *a.* froncé, ruché.

fringe¹ [frindʒ] *n.* **1.** *Tex:* frange *f.* **2.** (*a*) bordure *f,* bord *m;* **the outer fringe(s) of London,** la banlieue excentrique de Londres; **to live on the f. of society,** vivre en marge de la sociéte; **f. benefits,** avantages *mpl* accessoires; (*for employees*) compléments *mpl* de salaire en nature; **f. theatre,** petit théâtre expérimental; *T.V:* **f. area,** zone *f* limitrophe; (*b*) *Hairdr:* frange; cheveux *mpl* à la chien; **to wear a f.,** être coiffée à la chien.

fringe² **1.** *v.tr.* franger (un tapis, etc.); **eyes fringed with black lashes,** yeux bordés de cils noirs. **2.** *v.i.* **to f. upon sth.,** border qch.; **boldness that fringes on insolence,** hardiesse *f* qui frise l'insolence. **fringing** *a.* marginal, -aux; (récif) frangeant.

frippery ['fripəri] *n.* parure *f* sans valeur.

Frisco ['friskou] *Pr.n. Geog: F:* San Francisco.

frisk¹ [frisk] *n.* **with a f. of its tail,** en donnant un coup de queue.

frisk² **1.** *v.i.* **to f. (about),** (*of lambs, etc.*) s'ébattre; gambader, folâtrer; (*of horse*) cabrioler. **2.** *v.tr.* (*of dog, etc.*) **to f. its tail,** frétiller de la queue. **3.** *v.tr. F:* (i) palper, (ii) fouiller (un suspect, etc.). **frisking** *n.* palpation *f* (d'un suspect, d'un voyageur).

friskiness ['friskinis] *n.* folâtrerie *f;* vivacité *f.*

frisky ['friski] *a.* vif, folâtre; (cheval) qui fait des cabrioles; (*of pers.*) **to feel f.,** se sentir plein d'entrain.

fritillary [fri'tiləri] *n.* **1.** *Bot:* fritillaire *f.* **2.** *Ent:* damier *m.*

fritter¹ ['fritər] *n. Cu:* beignet *m;* **apple f.,** beignet aux pommes.

fritter² *v.tr.* **to f. (sth.) away,** dissiper (sa fortune); gaspiller (son argent, son temps).

frivolity [fri'vɔliti] *n.* **1.** frivolité *f;* légèreté *f* d'esprit. **2.** frivolité, chose frivole.

frivolous ['frivələs] *a.* **1.** (*of pers., etc.*) frivole. **2.** (*of complaint, etc.*) vain, futile. **-ly** *adv.* **1.** frivolement. **2.** futilement.

frivolousness ['frivələsnis] *n.* **1.** frivolité *f;* légèreté *f* d'esprit. **2.** futilité *f* (d'une objection, etc.).

frizz¹ [friz] *n.* (*a*) crêpelure *f* (des cheveux); (*b*) cheveux crêpelés.

frizz² *v.tr.* (*a*) crêper, frisotter (les cheveux); (*b*) *v.i.* (*of hair*) frisotter.

frizziness ['frizinis] *n.* crêpelure *f* (des cheveux).

frizzle ['frizl] **1.** *v.i.* (*a*) grésiller (dans la poêle); (*b*) crépiter. **2.** *v.tr. Cu:* (*a*) faire frire (le lard); (*b*) griller (le lard).

frizzy ['frizi] *a.* (*of hair*) crêpelé, crêpelu, frisotté.

fro [frou] *adv.* en s'éloignant; **to go to and f.,** aller et venir.

froing ['frouiŋ] *n. F:* **toing and froing,** va-et-vient *m.*

frock [frɔk] *n. Cost:* **1.** robe *f* (d'enfant, de femme). **2.** froc *m,* bure *f* (de moine).

frock-coat ['frɔk'kout] *n. Cost:* redingote *f.*

frog¹ [frɔg] *n.* **1.** *Amph:* (*a*) grenouille *f;* **tree f.,** rainette (verte); **frog('s) spawn,** (i) œufs de grenouille; (ii) *P:* tapioca *m* au lait; (*b*) *F:* **Frog,** Français, -aise. **2.** *F:* **to have a f. in one's throat,** avoir un chat dans la gorge.

frog² *n. Mil: etc:* **1.** porte-epée *m inv;* porte-baïonnette *m inv.* **2.** *Cost:* **frogs,** brandebourgs *mpl.*

frogged [frɔgd] *a. Cost:* orné de brandebourgs.

frogman, *pl.* **-men** ['frɔgmən] *n.* homme-grenouille *m, pl.* hommes-grenouilles.

frogmarch² ['frɔgmɑ:tʃ] *v.tr.* porter (qn) à quatre, le derrière en l'air.

frolic¹ ['frɔlik] *n.* (*a*) ébats *mpl,* gambades *fpl;* (*b*) fredaine *f,* divertissement *m.*

frolic² *v.i.* (**frolicked**) s'ébattre, folâtrer, gambader.

from [frɔm, *unstressed* frəm] *prep.* de. **1.** (*a*) (*place*) de; **he returned f. London,** il est revenu de Londres; **f. Paris to London,** de Paris à Londres; **f. town to town,** de ville en ville; **f. side to side,** d'un côté à l'autre; (*b*) **the bird lays f. four to six eggs,** l'oiseau pond de quatre à six œufs; **wines, f. four francs a bottle,** vins à partir de quatre francs la bouteille. **2.** (*time*) depuis, dès, à partir de; **f. that day,** depuis ce jour; à partir de ce jour; **f. tomorrow on,** à partir de demain; **house let f. June 1st,** maison louée à compter du premier juin; **f. his childhood,** depuis, dès, son enfance; **f. morning till night,** du matin au soir; **f. time to time,** de temps en temps. **3.** (*distance*) **he is away f. home,** il est en voyage; **not far f. . . .,** pas loin de . . .; **ten kilometres f. Paris,** à dix kilomètres de Paris. **4.** (*a*) de, à; **separation f. s.o.,** séparation d'avec qn; **he stole a pound f. her,** il lui a volé une livre; **to dissuade s.o. f. doing sth.,** dissuader qn de faire qch.; (*b*) (*protection*) contre; **to shelter f. the rain,** s'abriter contre la pluie. **5.** (*a*) (*change*) **f. bad to worse,** de mal en pis; **the price has been increased f. five pence to ten pence,** on a augmenté le prix de cinq pence à dix pence; (*b*) (*difference*) d'avec, de; **he can't distinguish the good f. the bad,** il ne sait pas distinguer le bon d'avec le mauvais; (*c*) **he grabbed a revolver f. the table,** il saisit un revolver sur la table; **to drink f. the stream,** boire au ruisseau; **to drink f. the bottle,** boire à même la bouteille; **to take sth. f. one's pocket,** prendre qch. dans sa poche. **6.** (*a*) (*origin*) **a train f. the North,** un train en provenance du nord; **wheat f. Russia,** blé venant de Russie; **a quotation f. Shakespeare,** une citation tirée de Shakespeare; **to draw a conclusion f. sth.,** tirer une conclusion de qch.; **f. your point of view,** à votre point de vue; (*b*) (*sender*) **a letter f. my father,** une lettre de mon père; **I have brought it to you f. a friend,** je vous l'apporte de la part d'un ami; **tell him that f. me,** dites-lui cela de ma part; (*on parcel*) **f. . . .,** expéditeur, -trice . . .; (*c*) d'après; **painted f. nature,** peint d'après nature. **7. to act f. conviction,** agir par conviction; **I know him f. seeing him at the club,** je le reconnais pour l'avoir vu au cercle; **f. his looks you might suppose that . . .,** à le voir on dirait que . . .; **f. what I heard . . .,** d'après ce que j'ai entendu dire . . .; **f. what I can see . . .,** à ce que je vois . . .. **8.** (*a*) (*with adv., prep.*) **f. above,** d'en haut; **I saw him f. a long way off,** je l'ai vu de loin; **f. among . . ., f. amidst . . .,** de parmi . . .; (*b*) (*after adv.*) **to come down f. one's room,** descendre de sa chambre; **to move away f. s.o.,** s'éloigner de qn.

frond [frɔnd] *n.* fronde *f* (de fougère); feuille *f* (de palmier).

front¹ [frʌnt] **I.** *n.* **1.** (*a*) contenance *f*, face *f*; **to put a bold f. on it,** faire bonne contenance; (*b*) **to have the f. to do sth.,** avoir l'effronterie, le front, de faire qch.; (*c*) prétexte *m*; **it's only a f. on his part,** ce n'est qu'une façade de sa part; (*d*) *NAm:* prête-nom *m, pl.* prête-noms. **2.** (*a*) *Mil:* front; **to be sent to the f.,** être envoyé au front; (*b*) *Pol:* **common f.,** front commun; **popular f.,** front populaire; (*c*) *Fig:* **to make progress on all fronts,** faire des progrès de tous côtés: (*d*) *Meteor:* **warm, cold, f.,** front chaud, froid. **3.** (*a*) devant *m*; façade *f* (d'un bâtiment); *Arch.Draw:* élévation *f*; devanture *f* (d'un magasin); étalage *m* (de boutique); avant *m* (d'une voiture); devant (de chemise); **carriage in the f. of the train,** voiture *f* en tête du train; (*b*) (*at seaside*) **the f.,** la promenade; **house on the f.,** maison faisant face à la mer. **4.** premier rang; **to push one's way to the f.,** se frayer un chemin jusqu'au premier rang; se pousser (en avant). **5.** *adv.phr.* **in f.,** devant, en avant; **to send s.o. on in f.,** envoyer qn devant; *Th:* **out f.,** dans la salle; *prep.phr.* **in f. of,** *U.S:* **f. of,** (i) en face de; (ii) devant; **he stood right in f. of me,** (i) il se trouvait juste en face de moi; (ii) il s'est mis juste devant moi. **II.** *a.* (*a*) antérieur, de devant, d'avant; **f. seat,** siège d'avant; **to have a f. seat,** être aux premières loges; **f. door,** porte d'entrée (principale); **f. room,** chambre sur la rue; **f. carriage,** voiture *f* de tête; **artists in the f. rank,** artistes *mfpl* de premier plan; **f. view,** vue *f* de face; *Arch:* élévation; **f. wheel,** roue *f* (d')avant; **f.-wheel drive,** traction *f* avant; *Journ:* **f. page,** première page; *F:* la une; **f.-page news,** nouvelles sensationnelles; **f.-loading washing machine,** machine *f* à laver avec chargement en façade; *Mil:* **f. line,** ligne *f* de contact, de feu; **f.-line troops,** troupes *fpl* du front; (*b*) *NAm:* **f. man,** (i) prête-nom *m, pl.* prête-noms; (ii) représentant *m* (d'une société), porte-parole *m inv* (d'une délégation); (*in election, etc.*) **f. runner,** favori *m*.

front² **1.** *v.tr. & i.* **to f. (on, onto) sth.,** faire face à qch.; être tourné vers qch.; **the house fronts north,** la maison est exposée, orientée, au nord; **the river and the houses fronting on it,** le fleuve et les maisons donnant dessus. **2.** *v.tr.* donner une (nouvelle) façade à (un édifice). **3.** *v.i. Mil:* faire front; **left f.!** à gauche front! à gauche, gauche!

frontage [ˈfrʌntidʒ] *n.* **1.** terrain *m* en bordure (d'un fleuve, etc.). **2.** longueur *f* de façade (d'un édifice); devanture *f* (d'un magasin). **3.** façade *f*; **premises with frontages on two streets,** local avec façades sur deux rues.

frontal¹ [ˈfrʌnt(ə)l] *n.* **1.** *Ecc:* devant *m* d'autel; fronteau *m*. **2.** façade *f* (d'un bâtiment).

frontal² *a.* (*a*) *Anat:* frontal, -aux; (*b*) *Arch:* (vue, etc.) de face; *Mil:* (attaque, etc.) de front; **full f. nudity,** état de nudité vue de face.

front-bencher [ˈfrʌntˈben(t)ʃər] *n. Parl:* membre *m* de la Chambre siégeant aux premières banquettes (réservées aux ministres).

frontier [ˈfrʌntiər] *n.* frontière *f*; **natural frontiers,** frontières naturelles; **the frontiers of human knowledge,** les bornes *fpl* des connaissances humaines; **f. guard,** garde-frontière *m, pl.* gardes-frontière; **f. town,** ville *f* frontière.

frontispiece [ˈfrʌntispiːs] *n. Typ:* frontispice *m*.

frosh [frɔʃ] *n. U.S: Sch: F:* étudiant, -ante, de première année.

frost¹ [frɔst] *n.* (*a*) *Meteor:* gelée *f*, gel *m*; **ground f.,** gelée blanche; **ten degrees of f.,** dix degrés de froid; (*b*) **hoar f.,** givre *m*; *Lit:* frimas *m*.

frost² *v.tr.* **1.** geler (un arbre fruitier). **2.** (*a*) givrer (les vitres, etc.); (*b*) *v.i.* (*of windscreen, etc.*) **to f. over, up,** se givrer, se couvrir de givre. **3.** saupoudrer (qch.) de sucre, etc.; glacer, givrer (un gâteau, etc.). **4.** dépolir (le verre). **frosted** *a.* **1.** (*of window panes*) givré. **2.** saupoudré (**with,** de); (gâteau) glacé. **3.** (*of glass*) dépoli. **frosting** *n.* **1.** (*a*) givrage *m*; (*b*) dépolissage *m* (du verre). **2.** sucre pilé (pour glaçage).

frostbite [ˈfrɔstbait] *n. Med:* (*of feet, etc.*) gelure *f*, froidure *f*.

frostbitten [ˈfrɔstbit(ə)n] *a.* **1.** (*of nose, etc.*) gelé. **2.** (*of plants*) brûlé par le froid; grillé (par la gelée).

frostbound [ˈfrɔstbaund] *a.* (sol) gelé.

frostiness [ˈfrɔstinis] *n.* **1.** froid glacial (du temps). **2.** manière glaciale (de qn).

frostproof [ˈfrɔstpruːf] *a.* résistant à la gelée.

frosty [ˈfrɔsti] *a.* **1.** glacial, -als; (temps) de gelée. **2.** (accueil) glacial; (réponse) glacée. **3.** (*of window*) couvert de givre. **-ily** *adv.* d'une manière glaciale.

froth¹ [frɔθ] *n.* **1.** écume *f*; mousse *f* (de la bière, etc.). **2.** *F:* paroles creuses.

froth² *v.i.* écumer, mousser; (*of waves*) moutonner; **to f. up,** mousser fortement; **he was frothing at the mouth,** il avait l'écume aux lèvres.

frothy [ˈfrɔθi] *a.* **1.** (*a*) écumeux; mousseux; (*of waves*) moutonneux; (*b*) (tissu) léger, bouffant. **2.** *F:* (*of speech*) vide, creux.

frown¹ [fraun] *n.* **1.** froncement *m* de sourcils; regard sévère. **2.** air désapprobateur.

frown² *v.i. & tr.* (*of pers.*) froncer les sourcils; se renfrogner; **to f. at, on, s.o.,** regarder qn en fronçant les sourcils; **to f. upon a suggestion,** désapprouver une suggestion. **frowning** *a.* (*of looks, face, etc.*) renfrogné, rechigné; (*of brow*) sourcilleux.

frowsty [ˈfrausti] *a. F:* qui sent le renfermé.

frowzy ['frauzi] *a.* **1.** (salle) qui sent le renfermé. **2.** (*of pers., clothes, etc.*) mal tenu, peu soigné.
froze, frozen. *see* FREEZE².
fructify ['frʌktifai] **1.** *v.i.* fructifier; (i) produire du fruit; (ii) produire des bénéfices. **2.** *v.tr.* faire fructifier.
fructose ['frʌktous] *n. Ch:* fructose *m.*
frugal ['fru:g(ə)l] *a.* **1.** (*of pers., life*) frugal, -aux; (femme) économe; **to be f. of sth.,** ménager qch. **2.** (*of meal, etc.*) frugal, sobre; **f. eater,** homme sobre. **-ally** *adv.* frugalement.
frugality [fru'gæliti] *n.* frugalité *f*; (i) économie *f*; (ii) sobriété *f.*
fruit¹ [fru:t] *n.* fruit *m.* **1.** (*a*) **apples and other fruit(s),** les pommes et autres fruits; **a stone f.,** un fruit à noyau; (*b*) *coll.* **eat more f.,** mangez plus de fruits; **soft f.,** *NAm:* **small f.,** petits fruits; **dried f.,** fruits secs; **stewed f.,** compote *f* de fruits; **to bear f.,** (i) (*of tree*) donner des fruits; porter fruit; (ii) *Fig:* (*of labour*) porter fruit; **my enquiries bore f.,** mes recherches furent couronnées de succès; (*c*) **f. bud,** bourgeon *m* à fruit; **f. cup,** boisson glacée avec fruits; **f. dish,** (i) compotier *m*; (ii) corbeille *f* à fruits; **f. drop,** pastille parfumée de fruits; **f. farmer, grower,** pomiculteur *m*; **f. farming,** pomoculture *f*; *Ent:* **f. fly,** drosophile *f*; mouche *f* à fruits; **f. juice,** jus *m* de fruits; **f. knife,** couteau *m* à fruit(s); **f. machine,** machine *f* à sous; *P:* tire-pognon *m, pl.* tire-pognons; **f. salad,** macédoine *f*, salade *f*, de fruits; **f. tree,** arbre fruitier, à fruit. **2.** (*a*) **the fruits of the earth,** les fruits, les biens *mpl*, de la terre; **the f. of her womb,** le fruit de ses entrailles; (*b*) **the fruits of industry,** les fruits, les produits *mpl*, de l'industrie; (*c*) **his knowledge is the f. of much study,** son savoir est le fruit de longues études.
fruit² *v.i.* fruiter; porter des fruits. **fruiting** *a.* (*of tree, etc.*) frugifère, fructifère.
fruit-bearing ['fru:tbɛəriŋ] *a.* frugifère, fructifère.
fruit-eating ['fru:ti:tiŋ] *a. Nat.Hist:* frugivore.
fruiterer ['fru:tərər] *n.* fruitier, -ière; **fruiterer's (shop),** fruiterie *f.*
fruitful ['fru:tf(u)l] *a.* **1.** (*of tree, etc.*) fructueux, productif; (*of soil, etc.*) fertile, fécond. **2.** *A:* fécond; prolifique. **3.** (*of work*) fructueux, profitable. **-fully** *adv.* fructueusement, à profit.
fruitfulness ['fru:tf(u)lnis] *n.* productivité *f* (d'un arbre, etc.); fertilité *f* (du sol, etc.); caractère fructueux, utilité *f* (d'un travail, etc.).
fruition [fru(:)'iʃ(ə)n] *n.* réalisation *f* (d'un projet, d'un espoir); **to come to f.,** porter fruit; **to bring sth. to f.,** réaliser qch.
fruitless ['fru:tlis] *a.* sans fruit, stérile, infructueux; **f. efforts,** efforts sans résultat.
fruity ['fru:ti] *a.* **1.** (*a*) (goût, etc.) de fruit; (*b*) (vin) fruité, fruiteux. **2.** *F:* (*a*) **f. voice,** voix (trop) étoffée; (*b*) (roman, scandale, etc.) corsé; (*c*) *U.S:* (*of pers.*) toqué, cinglé.
frump [frʌmp] *n. F:* femme mal attifée.
frumpish ['frʌmpiʃ], **frumpy** ['frʌmpi] *a.* (femme) mal attifée, *F:* mal fagotée.
frustrate [frʌs'treit] *v.tr.* (*a*) faire échouer (un projet); **to f. s.o.'s hopes,** frustrer qn dans son espoir; frustrer l'espoir de qn; (*b*) contrecarrer (qn). **frustrated** *a.* frustré. **frustrating** *a.* frustrant.
frustration [frʌs'treiʃ(ə)n] *n.* **1.** anéantissement *m* (des projets de qn); frustration *f* (d'un espoir). **2.** *Psy:* frustration.
fry¹ [frai] *n. coll.* **1.** *Ich:* (*a*) frai *m*, fretin *m*, alevin *m*; **small f.,** menu fretin; (*b*) **salmon f.,** saumoneaux *mpl* dans la deuxième année. **2.** *F:* **the small f.,** (i) le menu fretin, les gens insignificants; (ii) les gosses *mpl.*
fry² *v.* **(fried) 1.** *v.tr.* (*a*) **to f.,** (faire) frire, (faire) cuire en friteuse (du poisson, etc.); **French fried potatoes,** pommes frites; frites *fpl*; (*b*) **fried potatoes,** pommes (de terre) sautées; **fried eggs,** œufs sur le plat; **to f. an egg,** faire cuire un œuf sur le plat. **2.** *v.i.* (*of food*) frire. **frying** *n.* friture *f*; **f. pan,** poêle *f* à frire; *F:* **to jump out of the f. pan into the fire,** tomber d'un mal dans un pire; tomber de Charybde en Scylla.
fry³ *n.* **1.** *Cu:* plat *m* de viande frite; friture *f.* **2.** issues *fpl*; fressure *f* (d'agneau, de porc).
fryer ['fraiər] *n.* **1.** (*pers.*) friturier, -ière. **2.** *Dom.Ec:* bassine *f* à friture; poêle *f* à frire; **deep f.,** friteuse *f.*
frypan ['fraipæn] *n. NAm:* poêle *f* à frire.
fry-up ['fraiʌp] *n.* (plat *m* de) friture *f.*
fuchsia ['fju:ʃə] *n. Bot:* fuchsia *m.*
fuck [fʌk] *v.* (*not in decent use*) **1.** *v.tr.* foutre, baiser (une femme); **f. it!** merde! **2.** *v.i.* **to f. about,** déconner; **f. off!** va te faire foutre! **fucking 1.** *a.* foutu; **this f. car,** cette putain de voiture. **2.** *adv.* bougrement (froid, etc.).
fuddled ['fʌdld] *a. F:* **1.** soûl; **to get f.,** s'enivrer; **slightly f.,** un peu gris. **2.** brouillé (dans ses idées).
fuddy-duddy ['fʌdidʌdi] *F:* **1.** *a.* vieux jeu *inv.* **2.** *n.* vieil encroûté.
fudge¹ [fʌdʒ] *n.* (*a*) bêtise(s) *f*; (*b*) *Journ:* dernières nouvelles; (*c*) *Cu:* fondant américain.
fudge² *v.tr.* (*a*) bousiller (un travail, etc.); (*b*) cuisiner (des comptes, etc.); (*c*) **to f. an issue,** éluder une question.
fuel¹ ['fjuəl] *n.* combustible *m*; (*a*) **domestic, household, f.,** combustible de ménage; **solid f.,** combustible solide; *Fig:* **to add f. to the flames,** jeter de l'huile sur le feu; **to add fresh f. to a quarrel,** alimenter une querelle; (*b*) carburant *m*; **jet f.,** carburéacteur *m*; **f. tank,** réservoir *m* à carburant, d'essence; (*c*) **nuclear f.,** combustible nucléaire.
fuel² *v.* **(fuelled,** *NAm:* **fueled) 1.** *v.tr.* (*a*) alimenter, charger (un fourneau, etc.); (*b*) ravitailler, alimenter (un véhicule, une machine, etc.) en combustible, en carburant, en essence. **2.** *v.i.* **to f. (up),** se ravitailler en combustible, en carburant, en essence. **fuelling,** *NAm:* **fueling** *n.* ravitaillement *m* en combustible, en carburant, en essence.
fuel-oil ['fjuəlɔil] *n.* fuel(-oil) *m*; mazout *m.*
fug [fʌg] *n. F:* forte odeur de renfermé; air empesté de tabac.
fuggy ['fʌgi] *a. F:* (salle, etc.) qui sent le renfermé.
fugitive ['fju:dʒitiv] **1.** *a.* (*a*) (*of prisoner*) fugitif, fuyard; (*b*) (*of happiness*) fugitif, fugace, éphémère. **2.** *n.* (*a*) fugitif, -ive; fuyard *m*; **a f. from justice,** un fugitif recherché par la justice; (*b*) réfugié, -ée.
fugue [fju:g] *n. Mus: Psy:* fugue *f.*
fulcrum, *pl.* **-cra, -crums** ['fʌlkrəm, -krə, -krəmz] *n.* pivot *m* (d'un levier); couteau *m* (de balance).
fulfil, *NAm:* **fulfill** [ful'fil] *v.tr.* **(fulfilled) 1.** (*a*) accomplir (une prophétie); répondre à, remplir (l'attente de qn); **to f. oneself,** trouver sa vocation; remplir sa destinée; (*b*) satisfaire (un désir); exaucer (une prière); (*c*) accomplir (une tâche); remplir, s'acquitter d'(une obligation); (*d*) remplir (les conditions requises); **to f. the purpose in view,** répondre au but envisagé; (*e*) obéir à (un commandement); remplir (les instructions de qn). **2.** achever, compléter (une période de temps). **fulfilling** *a.* (travail, etc.) satisfaisant.
fulfilment, *NAm:* **fulfillment** [ful'filmənt] *n.* (*a*) accomplissement *m* (d'une prophétie, d'un devoir, etc.); (*b*) exaucement *m* (d'une prière); accomplissement (d'un désir); **to have a feeling of f.,** sentir qu'on a réussi; (*c*) exécution *f* (d'un projet, contrat); *Jur:* accomplissement (d'une condition).
full¹ [ful] **I.** *a.* **1.** (*a*) (*of receptacle*) plein, rempli, comble; (jour) chargé; **f. to the brim,** rempli jusqu'au bord; **f. to overflowing,** plein à déborder; **don't speak**

with your mouth f., ne parle pas la bouche pleine; (*b*) **to be f. of sth.,** être plein de qch.; **to have one's pockets f. of money,** avoir ses poches pleines d'argent; **her eyes were f. of tears,** elle avait les yeux pleins de larmes; **exercise f. of mistakes,** devoir plein de fautes; **f. of holes,** plein de trous; **look f. of hatred,** regard chargé, animé, de haine; **to be f. of hope,** être rempli d'espoir; **to be f. of praise of s.o.,** se répandre en éloges sur qn; **to be f. of ideas,** remuer beaucoup d'idées. **2.** (*of bus, etc.*) plein, complet; **f. house,** (i) salle *f* comble; (ii) *Cards:* (*poker*) main pleine; **f. session (of a committee, etc.),** réunion plénière; **the bus is f. up,** l'autobus *m* est au complet; **f. up!** complet! *Cards:* (*poker*) **f. hand,** main pleine. **3.** (*of pers.*) (*a*) **to be f. of sth.,** être pénétré de qch.; **to be f. of one's own importance,** être pénétré de sa propre importance; **f. of oneself,** plein de soi-même; (*b*) (*of pers.*) **to be f. (up),** être repu, rassasié. **4.** (*of notes, etc.*) ample, copieux; **she received her f. share of the money,** elle a eu sa bonne part de l'argent; **in the fullest detail,** dans le plus grand détail; **to ask for fuller information,** demander des précisions sur qch. **5.** complet, entier; (*a*) **f. meal,** repas complet; **in f. retreat,** en pleine retraite; **f. pay,** paie entière; **leave on f. pay,** congé *m* à solde entière; **f. price,** prix fort; *Th:* **to pay f. price,** *Rail:* **to pay f. fare,** payer place entière; **f. weight, measure,** poids *m* juste; mesure comble; **we were under f. sail,** nous avions toutes voiles dehors; **f. cargo,** plein chargement; **f. text,** texte intégral; (*b*) **in f. flower,** en pleine fleur; **roses in f. bloom,** roses larges épanouies; **in f. uniform,** en grande tenue; **to give f. scope to s.o.,** donner libre carrière à qn; **in f. flight,** en pleine déroute; (*c*) **I waited two f. hours,** j'ai attendu deux bonnes heures; (*d*) **f. brother, f. sister,** frère germain, sœur germaine; *Sch:* **f. professor,** professeur *m* titulaire; **f. member,** membre *m* titulaire; (*e*) (*in punctuation*) **f. stop,** point *m* (final); *F:* **to come to a f. stop,** s'arrêter net. **6.** (*a*) (*of face*) plein; rond; (lèvres) grosses, fortes; (*b*) (*of sleeve, etc.*) large, bouffant; **too f.,** trop large; (*c*) **f. voice,** voix pleine, ronde. **7.** (*of sail*) plein, gonflé; **the sails are f.,** les voiles portent bien. **II.** *n.* **1.** cœur *m*, fort *m* (de la saison, etc.); apogée *f* (de la gloire, etc.); **the moon is at the f.,** la lune est dans son plein. **2.** *adv.phr.* (*a*) **to publish a letter in f.,** publier une lettre intégralement; **money refunded in f.,** on rembourse intégralement l'argent, l'argent en totalité; **name in f.,** nom *m* et prénoms; **to write out a word in f.,** écrire un mot en toutes lettres; (*b*) **to the f.,** tout à fait; **to indulge one's tastes to the f.,** donner libre carrière à ses goûts. **III.** *adv.* **1. I know it f. well,** je le sais bien, parfaitement. **2.** (*a*) **lying f. in the sun,** couché en plein (au) soleil; **f. in the centre,** en plein dans le centre; **hit f. in the face,** atteint en pleine figure; (*b*) **to turn a tap f. on,** ouvrir un robinet en grand; **to turn the wireless f. on,** mettre la radio au plus fort de sa puissance; **to drive a car f. out,** conduire à toute vitesse; **to make a f.-out effort to do sth.,** faire l'effort maximum pour faire qch. **fully** *adv.* **1.** (*a*) pleinement, entièrement; **to be f. satisfied,** être pleinement satisfait; **f. armed,** armé de toutes pièces; **f. paid,** payé intégralement; **capital f. paid (up),** capital entièrement versé; (*b*) **to treat a subject f.,** traiter un sujet à fond; **I will write you more f.,** je vous écrirai plus longuement. **2. it takes f. two hours,** cela prend bien, au moins, deux heures.

full² *v.tr.* fouler (l'étoffe). **fulling** *n.* foulage *m.*

fullback ['fulbæk] *n. Fb:* arrière *m.*

full-blooded ['ful'blʌdid] *a.* **1.** de race pure; (cheval) de sang, pur-sang *inv*; **f.-b. Indians,** Indiens *mpl* pur sang. **2.** vigoureux; robuste. **3.** (tempérament) sanguin.

fullblown [ful'bloun] *a.* **1.** (*of rose, etc.*) épanoui; en pleine fleur. **2.** *F:* (*of doctor, etc.*) qualifié; **he is a f. lawyer,** il a (obtenu) tous ses diplômes.

fullbodied [ful'bɔdid] *a.* **1.** (*of pers.*) replet, corpulent. **2.** (vin) corsé, qui a du corps.

fullbred ['ful'bred] *a.* de race pure.

full-dress ['ful'dres] *a.* (tenue) de cérémonie, de parade; *Mil: Navy:* **f.-d. uniform,** tenue numéro un; *F:* **f.-d. debate,** débat solennel.

fuller ['fulər] *n. Tex:* fouleur, -euse; **fuller's earth,** terre à foulon; *Bot:* **fuller's teasel,** cardère *f* à foulon.

full-faced ['ful'feist] *a.* **1.** (*of pers.*) à la figure ronde; au visage plein. **2.** (*of portrait*) de face.

full-fledged ['ful'fledʒd] *a.* (*a*) (*of bird*) qui a toutes ses plumes; (*b*) *F:* (*of doctor, etc.*) qualifié.

full-grown ['ful'groun] *a.* (*a*) (arbre) qui a atteint son développement complet; (*b*) (*of pers.*) adulte.

full-length ['ful'leŋθ] *a.* (*a*) (portrait) en pied; (miroir) qui permet de se voir en pied; (fenêtre) qui descend du plafond au parquet; (robe de soirée) longue; (*b*) **f.-l. film,** grand film; long métrage.

ful(l)ness ['fulnis] *n.* **1.** état plein (d'un récipient); **out of the f. of his heart,** comme son cœur débordait. **2.** plénitude, perfection *f*, totalité *f* (de la force, etc.); **in the f. of time,** quand les temps seront révolus. **3.** (*a*) ampleur *f* (d'un vêtement); (*b*) ampleur (d'un compte rendu, etc.); abondance *f* (de détail); (*c*) rondeur *f* (de la forme); (*d*) richesse *f* (du style, etc.).

full-page ['ful'peidʒ] *a.* (illustration) hors texte; (réclame) d'une page entière.

full-scale ['ful'skeil] *a.* **1.** = FULL-SIZE(D). **2.** (*of reform*) complet, intégral; (*of attack*) de grande envergure.

full-size(d) ['ful'saiz(d)] *a.* (dessin, etc.) (i) grandeur nature, (ii) *Ind:* à la dimension exacte.

full-time ['ful'taim] **1.** *adv.* **to work f.-t.,** travailler à plein temps. **2.** *a.* (emploi) à temps complet, à plein temps; *F:* **looking after the baby is a f.-t. job,** soigner le bébé occupe toute la journée.

fully-fashioned ['fuli'fæʃ(ə)nd] *a.* (*of stockings*) entièrement diminué; proportionné.

fully-fledged ['fuli'fledʒd] *a.* = FULL-FLEDGED.

fulmar ['fulmər] *n. Orn:* pétrel glacial.

fulminate ['fʌlmineit] *v.i.* fulminer (**against,** contre).

fulmination [fʌlmi'neiʃ(ə)n] *n.* fulmination *f.*

fulsome ['fulsəm] *a.* (*of praise, etc.*) excessif; **f. flattery,** flagornerie *f*, adulation *f*. **-ly** *adv.* à l'excès.

fumarole ['fju:məroul] *n. Geol:* fumerolle *f.*

fumble ['fʌmbl] **1.** *v.i.* fouiller (au hasard); tâtonner; **to f. in a dark room for sth.,** chercher qch. à tâtons dans une chambre obscure; **to f. for words,** chercher ses mots; **to f. with sth.,** manier qch. maladroitement. **2.** *v.tr.* manier (qch.) maladroitement; *Sp:* **to f. the ball,** arrêter, attraper, la balle maladroitement. **fumbling 1.** *a.* maladroit, gauche. **2.** *n.* (*a*) maniement maladroit; (*b*) tâtonnement *m.*

fume¹ [fju:m] *n.* vapeur *f*; gaz *m*; **petrol fumes,** vapeurs d'essence; *I.C.E:* **exhaust fumes,** gaz d'échappement.

fume² **1.** *v.tr.* exposer (qch.) à la fumée; **fumed oak,** chêne patiné. **2.** *v.i.* (*a*) fumer; émettre de la fumée, des vapeurs; (*b*) *F:* (*of pers.*) rager; fumer (**with rage,** de colère); **I was fuming,** j'étais exaspéré (**at,** de).

fumigate ['fju:migeit] *v.tr.* fumiger (qch.); désinfecter (un appartement, etc.) par fumigation.

fumigation [fjumi'geiʃ(ə)n] *n.* fumigation *f*; désinfection *f* (d'une chambre).

fumigator ['fju:migeitər] *n.* **1.** (*pers.*) fumigateur. **2.** appareil *m* fumigatoire.

fumitory ['fju:mitəri] *n. Bot:* fumeterre *f.*

fun [fʌn] *n.* amusement *m*, gaieté *f*; plaisanterie *f*; **to make f. of, poke f. at, s.o., sth.,** se moquer de qn, de qch.; rire de qn; **for f., in f.,** (i) pour rire; par plaisanterie; (ii) pour se distraire; **I did it for the f. of the thing, of it,** je l'ai fait (i) histoire de rire, (ii) pour le plaisir; **he is great f., full of f.,** il est très drôle; **it was great f.,** c'était très amusant; **to have f.,** s'amuser, se divertir; *F:* **a f. party,** une fête amusante; **we had lots of f. and games,** (i) on s'est bien amusé; (ii) *Iron:* on a eu bien des ennuis; **that's when the f. began,** c'est là que ça a commencé à barder; **all the f. of the fair,** toutes les attractions de la foire; **what f.!** (i) chouette alors! (ii) *Iron:* je vous en félicite!

function¹ ['fʌŋ(k)ʃ(ə)n] *n.* **1.** fonction *f*; (*a*) **vital functions,** fonctions vitales; (*b*) **the spring performs the f. of a shock absorber,** le ressort joue le rôle d'(un) amortisseur. **2.** (*a*) fonction, charge *f*; **in his f. as a magistrate,** en sa qualité de magistrat; **he combines the functions of servant and gardener,** il tient le double emploi de domestique et de jardinier; (*b*) **to discharge one's functions,** s'acquitter de ses fonctions. **3.** (*a*) cérémonie (religieuse); (*b*) réception *f*, réunion *f*; **society f.,** réception mondaine; (*c*) cérémonie *f* publique; solennité *f*. **4.** *Mth: etc:* fonction; **the resistance is a f. of the pressure,** la résistance est fonction de la pression.

function² *v.i.* **1.** fonctionner; *F:* **this gadget won't f.,** ce truc ne marche pas. **2. adjective that functions as an adverb,** adjectif qui fait fonction d'adverbe.

functional ['fʌŋ(k)ʃən(ə)l] *a.* (*a*) *Mth:* fonctionnel; (*b*) (mobilier) fonctionnel, utilitaire.

functionary ['fʌŋ(k)ʃənəri] *n. Pej:* fonctionnaire *m.*

fund¹ [fʌnd] *n.* **1.** fonds *m*, capacité *f* (d'esprit); **unfailing f. of humour,** fonds d'humour intarissable. **2.** *Fin: etc:* (*a*) fonds, caisse *f*; **International Monetary F.,** Fonds Monétaire International; **old-age pension f., retirement f.,** caisse des retraites pour la vieillesse; **fighting f.,** caisse de défense (d'un syndicat, etc.); **slush f.,** caisse noire; **to start a f.,** lancer une souscription; **f.-raising scheme,** projet *m* (d'un hôpital, etc.) pour se procurer des fonds; (*b*) **funds,** fonds; ressources *fpl* pécuniaires; **to be in funds,** être en fonds; **funds are low,** les fonds sont bas; *Bank:* **"no funds",** "défaut *m* de provision," "manque *m* de fonds"; (*c*) **funds,** la dette publique; les fonds publics; **to buy funds,** acheter de la rente; **f.-holder,** rentier, -ière.

fund² *v.tr. Fin:* **1.** consolider (une dette publique). **2. to f. money,** placer de l'argent dans les fonds publics. **3.** pourvoir (une société, etc.) de fonds. **funded** *a.* (biens) en rentes; (capitaux) investis; **f. debt,** dette consolidée. **funding** *n.* consolidation *f* (d'une dette); assiette *f* (d'une rente).

fundamental [fʌndə'ment(ə)l] **I.** *a.* **1.** (*a*) fondamental, -aux; essentiel; (question) principale, de fond; **of f. importance,** d'une importance capitale; (*b*) (*of colours, etc.*) primitif. **2.** *Mus:* **f. note,** note fondamentale. **II.** *n.* **1. fundamentals,** principe(s) *mpl*; notions fondamentales, fondements *mpl* (d'une science, etc.); partie essentielle (d'un système, etc.); **fundamentals of arithmetic,** notions fondamentales d'arithmétique; **to reach agreement on fundamentals,** réaliser un accord sur les points essentiels. **2.** *Mus:* son fondamental. **-ally** *adv.* fondamentalement.

fundamentalist [fʌndə'mentəlist] *n. Theol:* fondamentaliste *m.*

funeral ['fju:nərəl] *n.* **1.** (*a*) funérailles *fpl*; obsèques *fpl*; enterrement *m*; **to attend s.o.'s f.,** assister à l'enterrement de qn; *F:* **that's your f.!** ça c'est votre affaire! (*b*) convoi *m* funèbre. **2. f. ceremony,** cérémonie *f* funèbre; **the f. procession,** le convoi (funèbre); **f. service,** office *m* des morts; **f. director,** entrepreneur de pompes funèbres; *NAm:* **f. home, parlor,** établissement *m* de pompes funèbres; *F:* **to proceed at a f. pace,** avancer à un pas d'enterrement.

funereal [fju'niəriəl] *a. F:* lugubre, funèbre, triste; (*of voice*) lugubre, sépulcral, -aux; (*of pace*) lent.

fun-fair ['fʌn'fɛər] *n.* (*a*) fête foraine; foire *f*; (*b*) parc *m* d'attractions.

fungicide ['fʌndʒisaid] *n.* fongicide *m.*

fungoid ['fʌŋgɔid] *a.* **1.** *Bot:* fongoïde. **2.** *Med:* fongueux.

fungous ['fʌŋgəs] *a.* fongueux.

fungus, *pl.* **-uses, -i** ['fʌŋgəs, -əsiz, -gai; 'fʌndʒai] *n.* **1.** *Bot:* champignon *m*; **edible, poisonous, f.,** champignon comestible, vénéneux. **2.** *Med:* fongus *m.*

funicular [fju'nikjulər] *a. & n.* **f. (railway),** funiculaire *m.*

funk¹ [fʌŋk] *n. P:* **1.** frousse *f*; **to be in a (blue) f.,** avoir une peur bleue; avoir une frousse de tous les diables; **to get into a f.,** caner. **2.** (*pers.*) froussard, - arde.

funk² *v.tr. & i. P:* **to f. (it),** caner; se dégonfler; **to f. sth., doing sth.,** avoir peur de qch., de faire qch.

funk-hole ['fʌŋkhoul] *n. Mil: F:* abri *m*, planque *f*.

funky ['fʌŋki] *a.* (*a*) *F:* froussard; (*b*) *P:* amusant.

funnel¹ ['fʌn(ə)l] *n.* **1.** (*a*) entonnoir *m*; (*b*) *Ind:* **(loading) f.,** trémie *f*, hotte *f*. **2.** (*a*) tuyau *m*, cheminée *f*, d'aération; (*b*) cheminée (d'une locomotive, d'un bateau à vapeur).

funnel² *v.* **(funnelled) 1.** *v.i.* **the crowd funnelled into a narrow passage,** la foule s'engouffra dans un passage étroit. **2.** *v.tr.* canaliser; **complaints are funnelled to the head office,** les réclamations sont dirigées vers le bureau central.

funniness ['fʌninis] *n.* **1.** drôlerie *f*; caractère amusant, comique (de qch.). **2.** bizarrerie *f*.

funny ['fʌni] **I.** *a.* drôle. **1.** comique, amusant; **it was really too f.! it was too f. for words!** c'était vraiment trop drôle! c'était tordant! **none of your f. tricks! don't try to be f.,** pas de farces! **the f. thing about it is . . .,** le comique de la chose c'est que . . .; *Cin:* **f. film,** film *m* comique. **2.** curieux, bizarre; **he is a f. person,** c'est un drôle d'homme; **he was f. that way,** il était comme ça; **a f. idea,** une drôle d'idée; **well, that's f.!** voilà qui est curieux, étrange; **there's something f. about it,** il y a quelque chose de louche dans cette affaire; *F:* **no f. business!** (i) pas de blagues! (ii) pas d'histoires! (iii) à bas les pattes! **this butter tastes f.,** ce beurre a un drôle de goût. **3.** *P:* **I came over all f.,** je me suis senti(e) tout(e) chose; **he went a bit f. in his old age,** il devint un peu bizarre dans sa vieillesse. **II.** *n.pl.* **funnies,** bandes dessinées, pages comiques (d'un périodique). **-ily** *adv.* drôlement; (i) comiquement; (ii) curieusement; **f. enough . . .,** chose curieuse . . . .

funnybone ['fʌniboun] *n. F:* le petit Juif (à l'articulation du coude).

fur¹ [fə:r] *n.* **1.** (*a*) fourrure *f*; **to line a garment with f.,** doubler un vêtement de fourrure; **f. coat,** manteau *m* de fourrure; **f. fabric,** fourrure synthétique; **f. farm,** élevage *m* d'animaux à fourrure; **f.-lined coat,** manteau doublé de fourrure; **f. skins,** pelleterie *f*; **f. trade,** commerce *m* de fourrures; pelleterie; (*b*) poil *m* (de lapin, etc.); *F:* **to make the f. fly,** (i) se battre avec acharnement; (ii) faire une scène violente; (*c*) *Ven:* **f. and feather,** gibier à poil et à plume; (*d*) **furs,** peaux *fpl* (d'animaux). **2.** *Her:* fourrure. **3.** (*a*) (*in bottles*) dépôts *mpl*; (*in kettle*) tartre *m*; (*b*) *Med:* (*on tongue*) enduit *m.*

fur² *v.* **(furred) 1.** *v.tr.* entartrer, incruster (une chaudière, etc.); *Med:* charger (la langue). **2.** *v.i.* **to f. (up),** (*of boiler, etc.*) s'incruster, s'entartrer; (*of tongue*) se charger, s'empâter. **furred** *a.* (*a*) (animal) à poil; (*b*) (*of boiler, etc.*) entartré, encrusté; (langue) chargée. **furring** *n.* (*a*) incrustation *f* (d'une chaudière, etc.); chargement *m* (de la langue); (*b*) (*in boiler, etc.*) tartre *m.*

furbish ['fə:bɪʃ] *v.tr.* **1. to f. (up),** fourbir, polir, astiquer (une pièce de métal). **2. to f. up,** remettre à neuf (des meubles); revoir (son français). **furbishing** *n.* **1. f. (up),** fourbissage *m*, astiquage *m*. **2. f. up,** remise *f* à neuf; révision *f*.

furious ['fjuəriəs] *a.* furieux; (*of look*) furibond; (*of battle, etc.*) acharné, forcené; **to drive at a f. speed,** conduire à une allure folle; **to get f.,** entrer en fureur; **to be f. with s.o.,** être furieux contre qn; *adv.* **he was going at it fast and f.,** il y allait frénétiquement. **-ly** *adv.* furieusement; (combattre) avec acharnement, avec furie; (conduire) à une allure folle; **the fire was blazing f.,** l'incendie faisait rage.

furl [fə:l] **1.** *v.tr.* (*a*) *Nau:* serrer, ferler (une voile); (*b*) rouler (un parapluie, etc.); fermer (un éventail); replier (les ailes, etc.). **2.** *v.i.* se rouler.

furlong ['fə:lɔŋ] *n.* *A. Meas:* furlong *m* (= 201 mètres).

furlough ['fə:lou] *n.* *Mil: etc:* congé *m*, permission *f*; **to be, go, on f.,** être, aller, en permission.

furnace ['fə:nis] *n.* **1.** (*a*) fourneau *m*, four *m*; (*b*) *Fig:* fournaise *f*; **this room is like a f.,** cette chambre est une (vraie) fournaise. **2. (central-heating) f.,** calorifère *m*.

furnish ['fə:niʃ] *v.tr.* **1.** (*a*) fournir, donner (des renseignements); pourvoir (les fonds nécessaires); produire, alléguer (des raisons); offrir, présenter, fournir (une occasion); (*b*) **to f. s.o. with sth.,** fournir, pourvoir, munir, qn de qch. **2.** meubler (une maison, etc.); **to f. one's room, one's home,** se meubler. **furnished** *a.* **1.** pourvu, fourni, équipé (**with,** de); **well f. shop,** magasin bien achalandé. **2. f. flat, room,** appartement meublé; chambre meublée; **to live in f. rooms,** loger en meublé. **furnishing** *n.* **1.** (*a*) fourniture *f*, provision *f* (des choses nécessaires, etc.); prestation *f* (de capitaux); allégation *f* (d'une raison, etc.); (*b*) action de meubler (une maison, etc.); **f. fabrics,** tissus *mpl* d'ameublement. **2** (*thg furnished*) (*a*) garniture *f*; (*b*) **furnishings,** ameublement *m* (d'une maison); **soft furnishings,** (i) tissus d'ameublement; (ii) tapis *mpl* et rideaux *mpl*.

furnisher ['fə:niʃər] *n.* fournisseur *m* (**of,** de); *esp.* marchand *m* d'ameublement.

furniture ['fə:nitʃər] *n.* **1.** meubles *mpl*, mobilier *m* (d'une maison, etc.); **piece of f.,** meuble; **set of dining-room f.,** mobilier, meubles, de salle à manger; **f. polish,** encaustique *f* pour les meubles; **f. remover,** déménageur *m*; **f. shop,** maison *f* d'ameublement; **f. van,** camion *m* de déménagement. **2.** ferrures *fpl* (d'une porte, d'un cercueil, etc.).

furore [fju(ə)'rɔ:ri], *NAm:* **furor** ['fjuərɔ:r] *n.* *F:* enthousiasme démesuré; **to create a f.,** (i) (*in popularity*) faire fureur; (ii) provoquer un tumulte.

furrier ['fʌriər] *n.* pelletier, -ière; fourreur *m*.

furriery ['fʌriəri] *n.* pelleterie *f*.

furrow¹ ['fʌrou] *n.* **1.** *Agr:* **(open) f.,** sillon *m*; tranche (de terre) retournée par la charrue; *Fig:* **to plough a lonely f.,** poursuivre seul une idée; faire bande à part. **2.** (*on face*) ride profonde; sillon.

furrow² *v.tr* **1.** creuser des sillons dans (la terre). **2.** rider profondément (le front, etc.); **his brow is furrowed with wrinkles,** des rides profondes lui sillonnent le front. **furrowed** *a.* (front, visage) coupé de rides profondes.

furry ['fə:ri] *a.* **1.** (animal) à poil; (insecte, etc.) velu; (mousse, etc.) qui ressemble à (de) la fourrure. **2.** (langue) chargée.

further¹ ['fə:ðər] **1.** *adv.* (*a*) plus loin (**than,** que); **to penetrate f. into the country,** pénétrer plus avant dans le pays; **I can go no f.,** (i) je ne saurais aller plus loin; (ii) je n'en peux plus; **to move f. away,** s'éloigner; (*b*) davantage, plus; **I didn't question him any f.,** je ne l'ai pas interrogé davantage; **until you hear f.,** jusqu'à nouvel avis; (*c*) **to go no f. into the matter,** en rester là; **to add water to the wine to make it go f.,** allonger le vin d'eau; **that doesn't get us much f.,** cela ne nous avance pas beaucoup; (*d*) (*in time*) **f. back,** à une période plus reculée; **f. back than the last century,** antérieurement au siècle dernier; (*e*) d'ailleurs, de plus; **we would f. add that . . .,** nous nous permettons d'ajouter en outre que . . .. **2.** *a.* (*a*) **at the f. end of the room,** à l'autre bout, au fond, de la salle; **the f. bank of the river,** la rive opposée de la rivière; (*b*) additionnel, supplémentaire; **without f. loss of time,** sans autre perte de temps; sans perdre plus de temps; **without f. ado,** sans plus de cérémonie; **upon f. consideration,** après plus ample(s) réflexion(s); **one or two f. details,** encore un ou deux détails; **f. information,** renseignements *m* complémentaires (**about,** au sujet de); **to await f. news,** attendre de plus amples nouvelles; *Com:* **f. orders,** commandes ultérieures; nouvelles commandes; **f. education,** enseignement *m* postscolaire.

further² *v.tr.* avancer (les intérêts de qn); seconder (un dessein).

furtherance ['fə:ðərəns] *n.* avancement *m* (d'un travail, etc.); **for the f., in f., of sth.,** pour avancer qch.

furthermore [fə:ðə'mɔ:r] *adv.* en outre, au surplus, de plus, du reste, par ailleurs.

furthermost ['fə:ðəmoust] *a.* (endroit, etc.) le plus lointain, le plus reculé, le plus éloigné; **to the f. ends of the earth,** jusqu'aux extrémités *fpl* de la terre.

furthest ['fə:ðist] *adv.* & *a.* **he went f.,** il est allé le plus loin; **the f. part of the cave,** la partie la plus reculée de la caverne.

furtive ['fə:tiv] *a.* (*a*) (*of manner, pers.*) sournois, cachottier; (*b*) (*of smile, etc.*) furtif, dérobé. **-ly** *adv.* (*a*) sournoisement; (*b*) furtivement.

fury ['fjuəri] *n.* **1.** furie *f*, fureur *f*; déchaînement *m*, violence *f* (du vent, etc.); **to get into a f.,** entrer en fureur, s'emporter; *F:* **to work like f.,** travailler avec acharnement. **2.** (*a*) *Myth:* **the Furies,** les Furies *fpl*; (*b*) *F:* mégère *f*.

furze [fə:z] *n.* *Bot:* ajonc *m*.

fuse¹, *NAm:* **fuze¹** [fju:z] *n.* **1.** *Artil: Pyr: etc:* fusée *f* (d'obus, etc.); amorce *f*; **time f.,** fusée à retard(ement); **to set a f.,** régler une fusée. **2.** *Min: etc:* étoupille *f*, mèche *f*; **safety f.,** cordeau *m* (bickford).

fuse², *NAm:* **fuze²** *v.tr.* amorcer (une bombe); *Min: etc:* étoupiller (un trou de mine).

fuse³ *n.* *El:* **(safety) f.,** fusible *m* (de sécurité); plomb *m*; **f. box,** boîte *f* à fusibles; **f. wire,** fil *m* à fusible; **to blow a f.,** faire sauter un plomb; **the f. has blown,** *F:* **gone,** le plomb a sauté.

fuse⁴ **1.** *v.tr.* (*a*) fondre, mettre en fusion (un métal, etc.); **to f. two pieces together,** réunir deux pièces par fusion; (*b*) fusionner, amalgamer (deux partis, etc.); (*c*) *El:* faire sauter les plombs (d'un circuit). **2.** *v.i.* (*a*) (*of metals, etc.*) fondre; (*b*) (*of parties, etc.*) fusionner; s'amalgamer; (*c*) *El:* **the lights have fused,** les plombs ont sauté. **fused** *a.* pourvu d'un fusible.

fusee, *NAm:* **fuzee** [fju:'zi:] *n.* *Clockm:* fusée *f* (d'une montre, etc.).

fuselage ['fju:zəlɑ:ʒ] *n.* *Av:* fuselage *m*.

fusilier [fju:zi'liər] *n.* *Mil:* fusilier *m*.

fusillade [fju:zi'leid] *n.* *Mil:* fusillade *f*.

fusion ['fju:ʒ(ə)n] *n.* fusion *f*. **1.** (*a*) fonte *f* (d'un métal); (*b*) *Atom.Ph:* **controlled f.,** fusion contrôlée; *Mil:* **f. bomb,** bombe *f* thermonucléaire. **2.** fusionnement *m* (de plusieurs banques, etc.); *Pol:* fusion (de deux partis, etc.).

fuss¹ [fʌs] *n.* **1.** bruit exagéré; **what's all this f. about?** (i) qu'est-ce que c'est que toutes ces histoires? (ii) qu'est-ce qui cloche? **without any f.,** sans bruit; **a lot**

of f. about nothing, beaucoup de bruit pour rien; **to make,** *F:* **kick up, a f.,** faire un tas d'histoires. **2.** façons *fpl*; **a great f.,** bien des cérémonies; **without (any) f.,** sans cérémonies; **don't make such a f. about it,** ne faites pas tant d'embarras; **to make a f. of s.o.,** (i) être aux petits soins pour qn; (ii) mettre qn en avant; **he likes to be made a f. of,** (*of pers.*) il aime qu'on fasse grand cas de lui; (*of dog*) il aime qu'on le caresse.

fuss² **1.** *v.i.* faire des embarras; faire des histoires; **to f. about, around,** s'affairer; **to f. over, around, s.o.,** être aux petits soins pour qn; **she never stops fussing with her hair,** elle ne cesse pas d'arranger nerveusement ses cheveux. **2.** *v.tr.* tracasser, agiter (qn); *F:* **I'm not fussed,** ça ne me fait rien.

fussiness [ˈfʌsinis] *n.* **1.** (*of pers.*) (i) embarras *mpl*; (ii) esprit tracassier. **2.** manque *m* de simplicité.

fusspot [ˈfʌspɔt] *n. P:* (i) tatillon, -onne; (ii) faiseur, -euse, d'embarras; chichiteux, -euse.

fussy [ˈfʌsi] *a.* **1.** (*of pers.*) tatillon, -onne; tracassier, méticuleux; **to be f.,** (i) faire des difficultés à propos de rien; (ii) *F:* faire des embarras; **to be f. about one's food,** être difficile sur la nourriture. **2.** (*of dress*) trop pomponné; (style) qui manque de simplicité. **-ily** *adv.* **1.** (*a*) d'une manière tatillonne; (*b*) d'un air important; en faisant des embarras. **2. f. dressed,** vêtu avec trop de recherche.

fustian [ˈfʌstiən] *n.* (*a*) *Tex:* futaine *f*; (*b*) grandiloquence *f*, emphase *f*.

fustiness [ˈfʌstinis] *n.* **1.** odeur *f* de renfermé, de moisi. **2.** caractère démodé (d'une théorie).

fusty [ˈfʌsti] *a.* **1.** (pain) qui sent le moisi; (maison, vêtement) qui sent le renfermé; (odeur) de renfermé. **2.** (*of ideas, etc.*) suranné, démodé.

futile [ˈfjuːtail] *a.* **1.** vain; **f. attempt,** vaine tentative. **2.** (prétexte, etc.) puéril, futile; **f. ideas,** idées creuses.

futility [fjuːˈtiliti] *n.* **1.** futilité *f*; impuissance *f* (des efforts de qn). **2. to utter futilities,** dire des futilités.

future [ˈfjuːtʃər] **1.** *a.* (*a*) futur; (*of events*) à venir; **my f. wife,** ma future; **at some f. date,** dans l'avenir; *Com:* **goods for f. delivery,** marchandises *fpl* livrables ultérieurement; *Fin:* **to sell for f. delivery,** vendre livrable à terme; (*b*) *Gram:* **f. tense,** temps futur. **2.** *n.* (*a*) avenir *m*; **in (the) f., for the f.,** à l'avenir; **in the near f.,** dans un proche avenir, sous peu; **in the distant f.,** dans un avenir lointain; **to think of the f.,** songer au lendemain; (*b*) *Gram:* (temps) futur; **f. perfect,** futur antérieur; **verb in the f.,** verbe au futur; (*c*) avenir (de qn); **job with a (good) f.,** situation d'avenir; **to ruin one's f.,** briser son avenir; **he has a brilliant f. before him,** il a devant lui un bel avenir; (*d*) *Fin:* **futures,** opérations *fpl* à terme.

futurism [ˈfjuːtʃərizm] *n. Art:* futurisme *m*.

futuristic [ˈfjuːtʃəˈristik] *a. Art:* futuriste.

futurologist [fjuːtʃəˈrɔlədʒist] *n.* futurologue *m*.

futurology [fjuːtʃəˈrɔlədʒi] *n.* futurologie *f*.

fuze [fjuːz] *n. & v.tr. NAm:* = FUSE$^{1, 2}$.

fuzee [fjuːˈziː] *n. NAm:* = FUSEE.

fuzz¹ [fʌz] *n.* **1.** (*on blankets, etc.*) peluches *fpl*, bourre *f*. **2.** duvet *m*.

fuzz² *n. P:* (i) flic *m*; (ii) *coll.* **the f.,** les flics.

fuzziness [ˈfʌzinis] *n.* **1.** crêpelure *f* (des cheveux). **2.** manque *m* de netteté (d'un contour); *Art: Phot:* flou *m* (d'un cliché, etc.).

fuzzy [ˈfʌzi] *a.* **1.** (*of hair*) crêpelu; (*of cloth, etc.*) floconneux. **2.** (*of outline, etc.*) sans netteté; *W.Tel: Rec:* (enregistrement) qui manque de netteté; *Art: Phot:* flou; **everything looks f. to me,** j'ai une vue confuse de tout.

G

G, g [dʒiː] *n.* **1.** (la lettre) G, g *m.* **2.** *Mus:* sol *m;* **G clef,** clef *f* de sol; **in G minor,** en sol mineur; **G string,** (i) *Mus:* corde *f* de sol; (ii) *Cost:* cache-sexe *m inv.* **3.** *U.S:* **G.-man,** agent *m* de la police fédérale. **4. G.-suit,** combinaison spatiale.

gab¹ [gæb] *n. F:* faconde *f;* **to have the gift of the g.,** (i) avoir la langue bien pendue; (ii) avoir du bagou(t).

gab² *v.i.* **(gabbed)** *F:* jaser; caqueter; bavarder.

gabardine [gæbə'diːn, 'gæbədiːn] *n.* = GABERDINE.

gabble¹ ['gæbl] *n.* bredouillement *m* (de paroles prononcées trop vite).

gabble² **1.** *v.i.* bredouiller, manger ses mots. **2.** *v.tr.* **to g. (out),** débiter (un discours) à toute vitesse.

gaberdine [gæbə'diːn, 'gæbədiːn] *n.* garbardine *f.*

gable ['geibl] *n. Arch: Const:* **g. (end),** pignon *m;* **g. roof,** comble *m* sur pignon(s); **g. window,** faîtière *f;* **ornamental g.,** gable, gâble *m.*

gabled ['geib(ə)ld] *a.* (*of house*) à pignon(s); (*of wall*) en pignon; (*of roof*) sur pignon(s).

Gabon ['gæbən] *Pr.n. Geog:* le Gabon.

Gabonese [gæbə'niːz] *Geog:* **1.** *a.* gabonais. **2.** *n.* Gabonais, -aise.

gad [gæd] *v.i.* **(gadded) to g. about,** courir le monde, la ville; se baguenauder.

gadfly ['gædflai] *n. Ent:* (*a*) taon *m;* (*b*) œstre *m.*

gadget ['gædʒit] *n.* (*a*) accessoire *m* (de machine); dispositif *m;* gadget *m;* (*b*) *F:* chose *m,* machin *m.*

gadgetry ['gædʒitri] *n.* (*a*) gadgets *mpl;* dispositifs *mpl;* (*b*) *F:* trucs *mpl.*

Gaelic ['geilik] **1.** *a.* gaélique. **2.** *n. Ling:* gaélique *m.*

gaff¹ [gæf] *n.* **1.** *Fish:* (*a*) gaffe *f;* (*b*) harpon *m.* **2.** *Nau:* corne *f;* **g. topsail,** voile *f* de flèche.

gaff² *v.tr.* gaffer (un saumon, etc.).

gaff³ *n. F:* **to blow the g.,** vendre la mèche; **to blow the g. on s.o.,** dénoncer qn; vendre qn.

gaffe [gæf] *n.* gaffe *f,* bourde *f.*

gaffer ['gæfər] *n. F:* (*a*) contremaître *m,* chef *m* d'équipe; (*b*) le patron, le singe; (*c*) le vieux.

gag¹ [gæg] *n.* **1.** bâillon *m; Med:* ouvre-bouche *m inv.* **2.** *F:* (*in Parliament*) clôture *f* (des débats). **3.** *Th: Cin: F:* (i) interpolation (faite par l'acteur); (ii) idée *f* drôle; *F:* gag *m.*

gag² *v.* **(gagged) 1.** *v.tr.* (*a*) bâillonner (qn, la presse); (*b*) *Pol: F:* clôturer (un débat). **2.** *v.i. Th: F:* faire des gags. **3.** *v.i. F:* avoir des haut-le-cœur. **gagging** *n.* **1.** (*a*) bâillonnement *m;* (*b*) *Pol: F:* clôture *f* (d'un débat). **2.** *Th: etc:* (i) interpolations *fpl* comiques (dans un rôle); (ii) gags *mpl.* **3.** *F:* haut-le-cœur *m.*

gaga ['gɑːgɑː] *a. F:* gaga, gâteux.

gage¹ [geidʒ] *n.* gage *m,* garantie *f.*

gage² *n. & v.tr.* = GAUGE[1, 2].

gage³ *n. Hort: F:* reine-claude *f, pl.* reine(s)-claudes.

gaggle¹ ['gægl] *n.* **1.** (*a*) troupeau *m* (d'oies); (*b*) *F:* troupe *f* (de femmes bavardes).

gaggle² *v.i.* (*of goose*) cacarder.

gagman ['gægmən] *n.m. NAm:* créateur de gags.

gaiety ['geiəti] *n.* **1.** gaieté *f;* allégresse *f.* **2.** *usu.pl.* amusement *m,* fête *f;* réjouissances *fpl.*

gain¹ [gein] *n.* **1.** gain *m,* profit *m,* avantage *m;* **eager for g.,** âpre au gain; **ill-gotten gains,** bien mal acquis; **my g. is your loss,** le profit de l'un est le dommage de l'autre. **2.** augmentation *f;* **g. in weight,** accroissement de poids; hausse *f* (de valeur).

gain² *v.tr. & i.* gagner. **1.** acquérir (une réputation); gagner (du temps); (re)prendre (des forces); obtenir (des renseignements); **you will g. nothing by it,** vous n'y gagnerez rien. **2.** gagner (des adhérents à une cause); s'acquérir (la sympathie); gagner (le cœur de qn); **to g. s.o.'s affection,** s'affectionner qn. **3. to g. weight,** prendre du poids; **to g. (in) popularity,** gagner de la popularité; **he has gained prestige through this action,** cette action a rehaussé son prestige. **4.** (*a*) gagner (une bataille); **to g. the upper hand,** prendre le dessus; (*b*) **to g. (ground) on s.o.,** gagner du terrain sur qn; *Sp:* **to g. on a competitor,** prendre de l'avance sur un concurrent. **5.** (*of clock*) prendre de l'avance; **to g. five minutes a day,** avancer de cinq minutes par jour.

gainful ['geinf(u)l] *a.* profitable; rémunérateur, -trice; (emploi) rémunéré. **-fully** *adv.* (*of population*) **g. employed, actif.**

gainsay [gein'sei] *v.tr.* (*p.p. & p.t.* **gainsaid** [gein'sed]) *usu. Lit:* contredire, démentir (qn, qch.).

gait [geit] *n.* (*a*) allure *f,* démarche *f;* **unsteady g.,** pas, mal assuré; (*b*) train *m* (d'un cheval).

gaiter ['geitər] *n. Cost:* guêtre *f.*

gala ['gɑːlə] *n.* fête *f;* gala *m;* **swimming g.,** grand concours de natation; **in g. dress,** en habit de gala; **g. evening,** soirée de gala; **g. performance,** représentation de gala.

galactic [gə'læktik] *a. Astr:* (pôle, etc.) galactique.

galaxy ['gæləksi] *n.* **1.** galaxie *f;* **the G.,** la Voie lactée. **2.** assemblée brillante (de femmes); constellation *f* (d'hommes illustres, etc.).

gale [geil] *n.* grand (coup de) vent, vent fort; **g. force winds,** vents forts; **g. warning,** avis *m,* signal *m,* de tempête; **it's blowing a g.,** le vent souffle en tempête.

galena [gə'liːnə] *n. Miner:* galène *f.*

Galilean [gæli'liːən] *B.Hist:* **1.** *a.* galiléen. **2.** *n.* Galiléen, -éenne.

Galilee ['gælili:] *Pr.n. Geog:* Galilée *f;* **the Sea of G.,** la mer, le lac, de Galilée.

Galileo [gæli'leiou] *Pr.n.m.* Galilée.

gall¹ [gɔːl] *n.* (*a*) fiel *m,* bile *f* (d'animal); (*b*) **g. bladder,** vésicule *f* biliaire; (*c*) *F:* effronterie *f,* culot *m.*

gall² *n.* (*a*) *Bot:* galle *f,* cécidie *f;* **g. nut,** noix *f* de galle; (*b*) *Ent:* **g. wasp,** cynips *m.*

gall³ *n.* (*a*) écorchure, excoriation (causée par le frottement); (*b*) humiliation *f;* blessure (faite à l'amour-propre).

gall⁴ *v.tr.* (*a*) écorcher (par le frottement); excorier; (*b*) irriter, vexer (qn); froisser, blesser (qn). **galling** *a.* irritant, exaspérant; (*of remark*) blessant, humiliant.

gallant ['gælənt] *a.* **1.** (*a*) brave, vaillant; **g. deed,** acte *m* de bravoure; (*b*) (*of ship, horse, etc.*) beau, *f.* belle; noble, fier; superbe. **2.** (*usu.* [gə'lænt]) galant. **-ly** *adv.* **1.** ['gæləntli] bravement, vaillamment. **2.** [gə'læntli, 'gæləntli] en homme galant.

gallantry ['gæləntri] *n.* **1.** vaillance *f,* valeur *f,* bravoure *f.* **2.** galanterie *f* (auprès des femmes).

galleon ['gæliən] *n. A.Nau:* galion *m.*

gallery ['gæləri] *n.* **1.** (*a*) galerie *f* (d'une salle, etc.); (*in Houses of Parliament*) **strangers', public, g.,** tribune réservée au public; **press g.,** tribune de la presse; (*b*) **the g.**, (i) *Th:* la (troisième) galerie; *F:* le paradis; (ii) l'ensemble *m* des spectateurs; la galerie; **to play to the g.**, jouer pour la galerie; (*c*) *NAm:* (i) balcon *m*; (ii) véranda *f*. **2. (art) g.**, (i) galerie; (ii) musée *m* (d'art); **portrait g.**, galerie, musée, de portraits. **3.** (*a*) *Min:* galerie; (*b*) **shooting g.**, stand *m* de tir.

galley ['gæli] *n.* **1.** *Nau:* (*a*) *A:* galère *f*; **g. slave,** galérien *m*; *F:* **I'm nothing but a g. slave,** c'est à moi de faire toutes les sales besognes; (*b*) yole *f* (d'amiral). **2.** *Nau: Av:* cuisine *f*. **3.** *Typ:* (*a*) galée *f*; (*b*) **g. (proof),** (épreuve *f* en) placard (*m*).

Gallic ['gælik] *a.* (*a*) *Hist:* gaulois; (*b*) français.

gallicism ['gælisizm] *n. Ling:* gallicisme *m*.

gallicize ['gælisaiz] **1.** *v.tr.* franciser. **2.** *v.i.* se franciser.

gallivant ['gælivænt] *v.i.* (*a*) courir la prétentaine; (*b*) **to be always gallivanting about,** être toujours en voyage, en visite.

gallon ['gælən] *n.* gallon *m* (= 4 lit. 54; *U.S:* = 3 lit. 78); *Aut:* **miles per g.** = consommation *f* d'essence aux cent kilomètres; *F:* **they drink gallons of beer,** ils boivent de la bière à tire-larigot.

gallop[1] ['gæləp] *n.* **1.** galop *m*; **at a g.,** au galop (allongé); **(at) full g.,** au grand galop. **2.** galopade *f*; **to have, go for, a g.,** faire une galopade.

gallop[2] *v.* **(galloped) 1.** *v.i.* (*a*) (*of horse*) galoper; (*of horse or rider*) aller au galop; **to g. away, off,** s'éloigner au galop; *F:* **to g. through prayers,** réciter les prières au grand galop. **2.** *v.tr.* faire galoper (un cheval). **galloping** *a.* **1.** au galop. **2. g. inflation,** inflation galopante.

gallophile ['gæloufail] *a. & n.* gallophile (*mf*).

gallophobe ['gæloufoub] *a. & n.* gallophobe (*mf*).

Gallo-Roman ['gælou'roumən] *a.* gallo-romain, *pl.* gallo-romains.

gallows ['gælouz] *n.* (*often with sg. const.*) potence *f*, gibet *m*; *F:* **g. bird,** réchappé *m* de potence.

gallstone ['gɔːlstoun] *n. Med:* calcul *m* biliaire.

Gallup ['gæləp] *Pr.n.* **G. poll,** sondage *m* Gallup.

galore [gə'lɔːr] *adv. F:* en abondance, à profusion; à gogo; **children g.,** une flopée d'enfants; **books g.,** des livres en masse; **money g.,** de l'argent à gogo.

galosh [gə'lɔʃ] *n.* caoutchouc *m*.

galumph [gə'lʌmf] *v.i. F:* galoper lourdement (et avec bruit).

galvanic [gæl'vænik] *a. El:* galvanique.

galvanism ['gælvənizm] *n. El:* galvanisme *m*.

galvanization [gælvənai'zeiʃ(ə)n] *n.* **1.** galvanisation *f* (d'un nerf). **2.** *Metalw:* galvanisation.

galvanize ['gælvənaiz] *v.tr.* **1. to g. s.o., sth., into life,** galvaniser qn, qch. **2.** *Metalw:* galvaniser; **galvanized iron,** fer galvanisé. **galvanizing** *n. Metalw:* galvanisation *f*.

galvanometer [gælvə'nɔmitər] *n.* galvanomètre *m*.

Gambia (the) [ðə'gæmbiə] *Pr.n. Geog:* la Gambie.

gambit ['gæmbit] *n.* (*a*) *Chess:* gambit *m*; (*b*) *Fig:* tour *m*; **opening g.,** manœuvre d'approche.

gamble[1] ['gæmbl] *n.* (*a*) jeu *m* de hasard; (*b*) affaire *f* où l'on risque fort de perdre; **pure g.,** pure spéculation, affaire de chance.

gamble[2] **1.** *v.i.* jouer de l'argent; **to g. on a throw of the dice,** miser sur un coup de dé(s); **to g. on the Stock Exchange,** agioter; **to g. on a rise in prices,** jouer à la hausse; **she's gambling on getting home by 8 o'clock,** elle compte rentrer avant 8 heures. **2.** *v.ind.tr.* (*a*) **to g. away,** perdre (sa fortune, etc.) au jeu; (*b*) *v.tr.* **to g. one's money on horses,** jouer aux courses. **gambling** *n.* le jeu; jeux d'argent; **g. on the Stock Exchange,** agiotage *m*; **g. debts,** dettes *fpl* de jeu; **g. den, house,** *U.S:* **g. joint,** maison *f* de jeu; tripot *m*.

gambler ['gæmblər] *n.* joueur, -euse (pour de l'argent); **g. on the Stock Exchange,** spéculateur, -trice.

gambol[1] ['gæmb(ə)l] *n.* gambade *f*, cabriole *f*.

gambol[2] *v.i.* **(gambolled,** *NAm:* **gamboled)** gambader, cabrioler; faire des gambades.

gambrel ['gæmbrəl] *n. Arch:* toit *m* en croupe.

game[1] [geim] *n.* **1.** (*a*) amusement *m*, divertissement *m*, jeu *m*; *F:* **what a g.!** quelle farce! (*b*) jeu; **g. of skill, of chance,** jeu d'adresse, de hasard; **card games,** jeux de cartes; **ball g.,** (i) jeu à la balle, au ballon; (ii) *NAm:* le baseball; **outdoor games,** jeux de plein air; (*c*) **Olympic games,** jeux olympiques; *Sch:* **games,** sports *mpl*; **games master, mistress,** maître, maîtresse, d'éducation sportive; **he's good at games,** c'est un sportif; (*d*) **he plays a good g. of cards, of billiards,** il joue bien aux cartes, au billard; **to play the g.,** jouer franc jeu; jouer selon les règles; **that's not playing the g.,** ce n'est pas loyal; **to play a dangerous g.,** jouer un jeu dangereux; **to beat s.o. at his own g.,** battre qn avec ses propres armes; **two can play at that g.,** à bon chat bon rat; (*e*) *F:* **what's his g.?** où veut-il en venir? **I know your (little) g.!** je sais bien où vous voulez en venir! **so that's your g.!** voilà donc ce que vous manigancez! **he's at his old games again,** voilà qu'il refait des siennes; **that's a dirty g. you're playing!** vous faites là un vilain métier; (*of prostitute, etc.*) **to be on the g.,** travailler, turbiner; **to spoil s.o.'s g.,** déjouer les plans de qn; **the game's up,** l'affaire est dans l'eau; (*f*) partie *f* (de cartes, d'échecs, etc.); manche *f* (d'une partie de cartes); **how's the g. going?** (i) comment marche, (ii) où en est, la partie? *Ten:* **g., set, and match,** jeu, set, et partie; *Chess: etc:* **opening, end, g.,** début *m*, fin *f*, de partie. **2.** (*a*) gibier *m*; **big g.,** (i) gros gibier; (ii) les grands fauves; **big-g. hunting,** la chasse aux grands fauves; **small g.,** menu gibier; **g. birds,** gibier à plumes; **g. preserve,** parc *m* à gibier; **g. licence,** permis *m* de chasse; *Fig:* **he's fair g.,** c'est une bonne proie; (*b*) *Cu:* gibier; **g. pie,** pâté de gibier en croûte.

game[2] *v.i.* jouer (de l'argent). **gaming** *n.* le jeu; **g. table,** table *f* de jeu; **g. house,** maison *f* de jeu.

game[3] *a.* courageux, résolu; **to be g.,** (i) avoir du cran; (ii) être d'attaque; **I'm g.!** d'accord! j'en suis! **he's g. for anything,** il est prêt à tout, capable de tout. **-ly** *adv.* courageusement.

game[4] *a.* (jambe) boiteuse, percluse.

gamecock ['geimkɔk] *n.* coq *m* de combat.

gamekeeper ['geimkiːpər] *n.* garde-chasse *m*, *pl.* gardes-chasse(s); garde forestier.

gameness ['geimnis] *n.* courage *m*, *F:* crânerie *f*.

gamesmanship ['geimzmənʃip] *n.* l'art *m* de gagner (sans enfreindre les règles du jeu).

gamete ['gæmiːt, gæ'miːt] *n. Biol:* gamète *m*.

gamma ['gæmə] *n.* (*a*) *Gr.Alph:* gamma *m*; (*b*) **g. rays,** rayons *mpl* gamma; **g.-ray therapy,** gammathérapie *f*; (*c*) **g. globulin,** gammaglobuline *f*.

gammon ['gæmən] *n.* (*a*) quartier *m* (du porc); (*b*) quartier de lard fumé; (*c*) jambon fumé.

gammy ['gæmi] *a. F:* = GAME[4].

gamp [gæmp] *n. F:* parapluie *m*, pépin *m*.

gamut ['gæmət] *n.* **1.** *Mus:* (*a*) gamme *f*; (*b*) étendue *f* (de la voix). **2.** gamme (de couleurs, etc.).

gander ['gændər] *n.* **1.** jars *m*. **2.** *P:* coup *m* d'œil; **just take a g.!** mate-moi ça!

gang[1] [gæŋ] *n.* (*a*) groupe *m*, troupe *f* (de personnes); *Ind:* équipe *f*; convoi *m* (de prisonniers); (*b*) bande *f*, *F:* gang *m* (de voleurs, etc.); **the whole g.,** toute la bande; **g. war(fare),** lutte *f* entre bandes rivales.

gang[2] *v.i.* **to g. up with s.o.,** s'allier avec qn; **to g. up on s.o.,** se liguer contre qn.

ganger ['gæŋər] *n. Rail:* chef *m* d'équipe.

Ganges (the) [ðə'gæn(d)ʒiːz] *Pr.n.* le Gange.

gangland ['gæŋlænd] *n.* (*a*) la zone des gangsters (dans une grande ville); (*b*) le monde criminel, le milieu; **g. warfare,** lutte *f* entre gangsters.

gangling [ˈgæŋgliŋ] *a.* dégingandé.
ganglion, -ia [ˈgæŋgliən, -iə] *n. Anat:* ganglion *m.*
gangplank [ˈgæŋplæŋk] *n. Nau:* passerelle *f;* (*between two ships*) traversine *f.*
gangrene¹ [ˈgæŋgriːn] *n.* (*a*) *Med:* gangrène *f*, nécrose *f;* (*b*) *Fig:* pourriture *f.*
gangrene² **1.** *v.tr.* gangrener, nécroser. **2.** *v.i.* se gangrener.
gangrenous [ˈgæŋgrinəs] *a.* gangreneux, gangrené.
gangster [ˈgæŋstər] *n.* gangster *m;* **g. film,** film *m* de gangsters.
gangsterism [ˈgæŋstərizm] *n.* gangstérisme *m.*
gangway [ˈgæŋwei] *n.* **1.** passage *m;* couloir central (d'autobus, etc.); **central g.,** allée centrale; **g. please!** dégagez, s'il vous plaît! **2.** *Nau:* (*a*) passerelle *f* de service (pour débarquement, etc.); (*b*) (*opening or port*) coupée *f* (dans la muraille).
gannet [ˈgænit] *n. Orn:* fou *m* (de Bassan).
gantry [ˈgæntri] *n.* **1.** chantier *m* (pour fûts). **2.** *Ind:* (*a*) pont roulant (pour grue mobile); *Rail:* **signal g.,** pont à signaux; **g. crane,** grue *f* à portique; **travelling g.,** portique roulant; (*b*) portique de lancement (des fusées).
gaol¹ [dʒeil] *n.* prison *f;* **six months' g.,** six mois de prison; **to be in g.,** être en prison.
gaol² *v.tr.* mettre (qn) en prison; écrouer (qn).
gaolbird [ˈdʒeilbəːd] *n.* (i) prisonnier *m;* (ii) criminel *m;* récidiviste *m.*
gaolbreak [ˈdʒeilbreik] *n.* évasion *f* de prison.
gaolbreaker [ˈdʒeilbreikər] *n.* évadé *m* de prison.
gaoler [ˈdʒeilər] *n.* gardien *m* de prison.
gap [gæp] *n.* **1.** (*a*) trou *m;* trouée *f*, ouverture *f*, vide *m* (dans une haie, etc.); brèche *f* (dans un mur, etc.); discontinuité *f* (d'une surface); **to fill (in, up), to stop, a g.,** boucher, colmater, un trou; combler un vide; (*b*) *Geog:* trouée *f; esp. U.S:* col *m;* (*c*) interstice *m;* intervalle *m;* écart *m;* distance *f* (entre deux convois); **gaps between the planks,** des jours *mpl* entre les planches; **there's a g. in the curtains,** les rideaux bâillent; *I.C.E:* **starter g.,** intervalle d'allumage; (*d*) trou, lacune *f*, vide (dans des souvenirs, etc.); **his death leaves a g. in the family circle,** sa mort laisse un vide dans la famille; **to fill the gaps in one's education,** combler les lacunes de son éducation; **to bridge the g.,** combler le fossé, le déficit; *Com:* **g. in the market,** créneau *m; Pol.Ec:* **trade g.,** déficit commercial; **credibility g.,** manque de crédit (accordé à un gouvernement, etc.); crise *f* de confiance; (*f*) *Rec:* blanc *m* sonore; (*in recorded tape*) plage *f* de silence; (*g*) (*in time*) **age g.,** écart d'âge; **a g. of over twenty years,** un intervalle de plus de vingt ans. **2.** *Mec.E:* coupure *f*, rompu *m* (d'un banc de tour).
gape¹ [geip] *n.* bâillement *m; F:* **to give s.o. the gapes,** faire bâiller qn.
gape² *v.i.* **1.** (*a*) (*of pers.*) (i) ouvrir la bouche toute grande; (ii) bâiller (d'ennui); (*b*) (*of thg*) **to g. (open),** s'ouvrir (tout grand); (*of hole*) être béant; (*of seam, etc.*) bâiller; **these boards g.,** ces planches ne joignent pas. **2.** (*of pers.*) être, rester, bouche bée; **to g. at s.o., sth.,** regarder qn, qch., bouche bée. **gaping 1.** *a.* (*of hole, etc.*) béant. **2.** *n.* (*a*) contemplation *f* bouche bée; (*b*) bâillement *m.*
gap-toothed [ˈgæptuːθt] *a.* aux dents écartées.
garage¹ [ˈgærɑːʒ] *n. Aut:* garage *m;* **lock-up g.,** box *m, pl.* boxes; **g. proprietor, owner,** garagiste *m;* **g. mechanic,** mécanicien *m* de garage, *F:* garagiste.
garage² *v.tr.* (i) garer, (ii) remiser (une voiture).
garageman, *pl.* **-men** [ˈgærɑːʒmæn, -men] *n.m.* mécanicien de garage, *F:* garagiste.
garb¹ [gɑːb] *n. Lit:* costume *m*, habit *m;* **in clerical g.,** en habit ecclésiastique.
garb² *v.tr. Lit:* habiller, vêtir (**in,** de); **garbed all in black,** vêtu tout de noir.
garbage [ˈgɑːbidʒ] *n.* (*a*) immondices *fpl*, détritus *mpl;* déchets *mpl;* (*b*) *esp. NAm:* ordures ménagères; **g. heap,** tas *m* d'ordures; **g. can,** poubelle *f;* **g. disposal unit,** broyeur *m* à ordures; **g. man, g. collector,** (é)boueur *m.*
garble [ˈgɑːbl] *v.tr.* fausser (des nouvelles, une citation); dénaturer (les faits); altérer (un texte); **garbled account,** compte rendu trompeur, mensonger; **garbled message,** message embrouillé.
garden¹ [ˈgɑːd(ə)n] *n.* jardin *m;* **flower g.,** jardin d'agrément; jardin de fleurs; **kitchen g., vegetable g.,** (jardin) potager (*m*); **market g.,** *NAm:* **truck g.,** jardin maraîcher; **(market-)g. produce,** produits maraîchers; **g. centre,** pépinière *f;* **rock g.,** jardin alpin; **g. of remembrance** = cimetière *m* d'un crématorium; **botanical g.,** jardin botanique; **zoological gardens,** jardin zoologique; **public garden(s),** jardin public; parc *m;* **beer g.** = café *m* en plein air; *F:* **to lead s.o. up the g. path,** duper, faire marcher, qn; **g. plants,** plantes *fpl* de jardin; **g. tools,** outils *mpl* de jardinage; **g. furniture, chair,** meubles *mpl*, chaise *f*, de jardin; **g. party,** réception *f* en plein air; garden-party *f, pl.* garden-parties; **g. suburb, g. city,** cité-jardin *f, pl.* cités-jardins; *a. phr. F:* **common or g.,** (i) ordinaire; (ii) banal.
garden² *v.i.* jardiner; faire du jardinage. **gardening** *n.* jardinage *m;* horticulture *f;* **landscape g.,** l'art *m* de dessiner les jardins; **market g.,** *NAm:* **truck g.,** maraîchage *m;* **g. tools,** outils *mpl* de jardinage.
gardener [ˈgɑːdnər] *n.* jardinier *m;* **landscape g.,** jardinier paysagiste; **market g.,** *NAm:* **truck g.,** maraîcher, -ère; **nursery g.,** pépiniériste *mf.*
gardenia [gɑːˈdiːniə] *n. Bot:* gardénia *m.*
gargantuan [gɑːˈgæntjuən] *a.* gargantuesque.
gargle¹ [ˈgɑːgl] *n. Med:* gargarisme *m.*
gargle² **1.** *v.i.* se gargariser. **2.** *v.tr.* **to g. one's throat,** se gargariser la gorge.
gargoyle [ˈgɑːgɔil] *n. Arch: etc:* gargouille *f.*
garish [ˈgɛəriʃ] *a.* **1.** (*of dress, etc.*) voyant; d'un faste de mauvais goût. **2.** (lumière) crue.
garishness [ˈgɛəriʃnis] *n.* **1.** luxe criard. **2.** crudité *f* (d'une couleur, de l'éclairage).
garland¹ [ˈgɑːlənd] *n.* guirlande *f;* couronne *f* (de fleurs).
garland² *v.tr.* (en)guirlander; **garlanded with flowers,** paré de guirlandes de fleurs.
garlic [ˈgɑːlik] *n. Bot:* ail *m, pl.* ails *or* aulx; **clove of g.,** gousse *f* d'ail; **g. sausage,** saucisson *m* à l'ail.
garlicky [ˈgɑːliki] *a. F:* qui sent l'ail.
garment [ˈgɑːmənt] *n.* vêtement *m.*
garner [ˈgɑːnər] *v.tr. NAm: & Lit:* mettre (le grain) en grenier, en grange.
garnet [ˈgɑːnit] *n. Miner:* grenat *m.*
garnish¹ [ˈgɑːniʃ] *n. Cu: etc:* garniture *f.*
garnish² *v.tr.* garnir, orner, embellir (**with,** de); *Cu:* garnir (un plat). **garnishing** *n.* **1.** garnissage *m.* **2.** garniture *f* (d'un plat).
garnishee [gɑːniˈʃiː] *n. Jur:* tiers-saisi *m, pl.* tiers-saisis; **g. order,** ordonnance *f* de saisie-arrêt.
garret [ˈgærət] *n.* mansarde *f*, soupente *f;* **to live in a g.,** habiter sous les combles.
garrison¹ [ˈgæris(ə)n] *n.* garnison *f;* **g. duty,** service *m* de place, de garnison; **g. town,** ville *f* de garnison.
garrison² *v.tr.* **1. to g. a town,** (i) mettre une garnison dans une ville; (ii) être en garnison dans une ville. **2.** mettre (des troupes) en garnison; **troops garrisoned at Lille,** troupes *fpl* en garnison à Lille.
garrotte¹, *NAm:* **garrote** [gəˈrɔt] *n.* **1.** supplice *m* du garrot. **2.** strangulation *f.*
garrotte² *v.tr.* **(ga(r)rotted) 1.** faire subir le supplice du garrot à (qn). **2.** étrangler (qn). **garrotting,** *NAm:* **garroting** *n.* **1.** supplice *m* du garrot. **2.** strangulation *f.*

garrulity [gæ'ru:liti], **garrulousness** ['gæruləsnis] *n.* **1.** loquacité *f.*
garrulous ['gæruləs] *a.* loquace, bavard. **-ly** *adv.* avec volubilité.
garter ['gɑ:tər] *n.* (*a*) jarretière *f*; **the Order of the G.,** l'Ordre *m* de la Jarretière; **Knight of the G.,** chevalier *m* de l'Ordre de la Jarretière; (*b*) *NAm:* jarretelle *f*; (*for socks*) fixe-chaussettes *mpl*; **g. belt,** porte-jarretelles *m inv*; (*c*) *Knit:* **g. stitch,** point *m* mousse.
gas¹, *pl.* **gases** [gæs, 'gæsiz] *n.* **1.** gaz *m*; (*a*) **natural g.,** gaz naturel; **marsh g.,** méthane *m*; (*b*) **the g. industry,** l'industrie du gaz; **g. furnace,** fourneau *m* à gaz; **g. holder, tank,** gazomètre *m*; réservoir *m* à gaz; **g. cylinder,** bouteille *f* à gaz; (*c*) **town g.,** gaz de ville; **g. main, pipe,** tuyau *m* à gaz; conduite *f* de, du, gaz; **g. burner,** bec *m* de gaz; (*in street*) **g. lamp,** réverbère *m*; **to cook by g.,** faire la cuisine au gaz; **g. cooker, stove,** cuisinière *f* à gaz; **g. oven,** four *m* à gaz; **g. ring,** (i) réchaud *m* à gaz (à un feu); (ii) brûleur *m* à couronne; **g. fire,** radiateur *m* à gaz; **g. lighter,** (i) allume-gaz *m inv*; (ii) briquet *m* (à gaz); **g. fitter,** gazier *m*; poseur *m*, ajusteur *m*, d'appareils à gaz; (*d*) **laughing g.,** gaz hilarant; *Dent:* **to have g.,** se faire anesthésier (pour l'extraction d'une dent); (*e*) *Mil: etc:* gaz de combat; **g. warfare,** guerre chimique; **tear g.,** gaz lacrymogène; **mustard g.,** ypérite *f*; **blister g.,** gaz vésicant; **g. chamber,** chambre *f* à gaz; **g. attack,** attaque *f* par gaz; (*g*) *Min:* grisou *m*. **2.** *NAm:* essence *f*; **to fill up with g.,** faire le plein d'essence; **to step on the g.,** (i) *Aut:* appuyer sur le champignon; (ii) se presser; se grouiller. **3.** *F:* (*a*) bavardage *m*; verbiage *m*; (*b*) *NAm:* **what a g.!** (i) c'est bien rigolo! (ii) quel emmerdement!
gas² *v.* **(gassed) 1.** *v.tr.* asphyxier, intoxiquer (par un gaz); *Mil:* gazer; **to g. oneself,** s'asphyxier; **gassed,** atteint par les gaz asphyxiants; *Mil:* gazé. **2.** *v.i. F:* jaser, bavarder. **gassing** *n.* **1.** asphyxie *f*, intoxication *f*, (i) par les gaz de combat, (ii) par le gaz d'éclairage. **2.** *F:* bavardage *m*; jaserie *f*.
gasbag ['gæsbæg] *n.* (*a*) ballon *m* à gaz (pour oxygène, etc.); (*b*) *F:* bavard, -arde; vantard *m*.
Gascony ['gæskəni] *Pr.n. Geog:* la Gascogne.
gaseous ['gæsiəs, 'geisiəs] *a.* gazeux.
gash¹ [gæʃ] *n.* coupure *f*, entaille *f* (faite dans la chair); estafilade *f*, taillade *f*; (*on face*) balafre *f*.
gash² *v.tr.* entailler, couper; balafrer (le visage); **to g. one's chin,** se faire une entaille au menton.
gasholder ['gæshouldər] *n.* réservoir *m* à gaz.
gasification [gæsifi'keiʃ(ə)n] *n.* gazéification *f*.
gasify ['gæsifai] **1.** *v.tr.* gazéifier. **2.** *v.i.* se gazéifier.
gasket ['gæskit] *n.* **1.** *Nau:* raban *m* (de ferlage). **2.** *Mec.E:* joint *m* d'étanchéité; garniture *f* (de joint); *I.C.E:* **cylinder-head g.,** joint de culasse.
gaslight ['gæslait] *n.* lumière *f* du gaz; **by g.,** à la lumière du gaz.
gasman, *pl.* **-men** ['gæsmæn, -men] *n.m. F:* (*a*) gazier; (*b*) contrôleur, employé, du gaz.
gasmask ['gæsmɑ:sk] *n.* masque *m* à gaz.
gasmeter ['gæsmi:tər] *n.* compteur *m* à gaz.
gasoline ['gæsəli:n] *n. NAm:* essence *f*.
gasometer [gæ'sɔmitər] *n.* gazomètre *m*; réservoir *m* à gaz.
gasp¹ [gɑ:sp] *n.* hoquet *m*, sursaut *m* (de surprise); **to be at one's last g.,** agoniser; être à l'agonie; **to give one's last g.,** rendre le dernier soupir; **to defend sth. to the last g.,** défendre qch. jusqu'à son dernier souffle.
gasp² *v.i. & tr.* (*a*) avoir un hoquet (de surprise); sursauter (de terreur); **to make s.o. g.,** couper le souffle à qn; **to g. out sth.,** dire qch. d'une voix entrecoupée; (*b*) **to g. for breath, for air,** haleter, suffoquer; *F:* **I'm gasping for a drink,** je meurs de soif.
gassy ['gæsi] *a.* (*a*) gazeux; (*of wine*) mousseux, crémant; (*b*) *Min:* grisouteux.
gastric ['gæstrik] *a.* gastrique; **g. ulcer,** ulcère *m* simple de l'estomac; gastrite ulcéreuse; **g. flu,** grippe gastro-intestinale.
gastritis [gæs'traitis] *n. Med:* gastrite *f*.
gastro-enteritis [gæstrouentə'raitis] *n. Med:* gastro-entérite *f*.
gastronome ['gæstrənoum] *n.* gastronome *m*.
gastronomic(al) [gæstrə'nɔmik(l)] *a.* gastronomique.
gastronomy [gæs'trɔnəmi] *n.* gastronomie *f*.
gastropod ['gæstroupod] *a. & n. Moll:* gastéropode (*m*).
gasworks ['gæswə:ks] *n.pl.* (*usu. with sg. const.*) usine *f* à gaz.
gate¹ [geit] *n.* **1.** (*a*) porte *f* (d'une ville, d'un château fort, etc.); **the gate(s) of hell,** les portes de l'enfer; (*b*) (*at exhibition, etc.*) entrée *f*; **to pay at the g.,** payer à l'entrée; **the g.,** (i) le public (à un match); (ii) (*also* **g. money**) la recette; les entrées; (*c*) (*in airport*) **g. no. 15,** porte 15. **2.** (*a*) barrière *f*, porte à claire-voie; (*metal*) grille *f* (d'entrée); **level-crossing,** *NAm:* **grade-crossing, g.,** barrière du passage à niveau; **toll g.,** barrière *f* (de péage); (*b*) *Rac:* **starting g.,** starting-gate *m*; (*c*) *Ski:* porte. **3.** *Hyd.E:* **(lock) g.,** vanne *f* (d'écluse). **4.** *Aut:* **g. (quadrant),** grille (de changement de vitesse).
gate² *v.tr.* **1.** *Sch:* **to be gated,** se faire consigner. **2.** *Hyd.E:* vanner (une écluse).
gâteau ['gætou] *n.* gros gâteau à la crème.
gatecrash ['geitkræʃ] *v.tr. & i. F:* resquiller; faire l'intrus. **gatecrashing** *n. F:* resquillage *m*.
gatecrasher ['geitkræʃər] *n. F:* resquilleur, -euse.
gatehouse ['geithaus] *n.* **1.** loge *f* (à l'entrée d'un parc). **2.** corps-de-garde *m inv* (d'un château).
gatekeeper ['geitki:pər] *n.* **1.** portier, -ière. **2.** *Rail:* garde-barrière *mf*, *pl.* gardes-barrière(s).
gatelegged ['geitlegd] *a.* (table) à abattants.
gatepost ['geitpoust] *n.* montant *m* (de barrière); *F:* **between you and me and the g.,** soit dit entre nous.
gateway ['geitwei] *n.* **1.** porte *f*, entrée *f*, passage *m*; **the g. to the Continent,** la porte du Continent. **2.** porte monumentale; voûte *f* d'entrée; portail *m*.
gather ['gæðər] **I.** *v.tr.* **1.** (*a*) assembler, rassembler (des personnes); rassembler, recueillir (des choses); **to g. one's thoughts,** se recueillir; **to g. all one's strength (in order) to ...,** rassembler, ramasser, toutes ses forces pour ...; (*b*) **to g. (up),** ramasser (des papiers, etc.); recueillir (les miettes); retrousser (ses jupes); *Bookb:* rassembler (les feuilles d'un livre); **to g. (up) one's hair into a knot,** tordre ses cheveux en chignon; (*c*) cueillir (des fleurs); récolter (du blé); recueillir (des informations); ramasser (du bois); faire la cueillette de (fraises, etc.); **to g. (in) the harvest,** rentrer la moisson; (*of bees*) **to g. honey from the flowers,** butiner les fleurs; (*d*) **tiger gathered for a spring,** tigre accroupi avant de sauter; (*e*) *Equit:* rassembler (un cheval). **2. to g. speed,** acquérir, prendre, de la vitesse; (*of pers.*) **to g. strength,** reprendre des forces; **to g. dirt,** s'encrasser. **3.** (*a*) serrer; **to g. the blankets round one,** se serrer dans les couvertures; **he gathered her (up) in his arms,** il l'a serrée dans ses bras; (*b*) *Needlew:* froncer (une jupe, etc.). **4.** conclure; **so far as I can g.,** à ce que je comprends; **I g. from the papers that ...,** à en croire les journaux ...; **I g. he has been ill,** on me dit qu'il a été malade; **I g. from the evidence that ...,** j'infère, je déduis, de ces témoignages que .... **II.** *v.i.* **1.** (*of pers.*) (*a*) se réunir, s'assembler, se rassembler; **to g. round s.o.,** se rassembler autour de qn; **g. round!** approchez-vous! (*b*) s'attrouper (en foule); **a crowd**

gathered, une foule se forma. **2.** (*of thgs*) s'accumuler, s'amonceler, s'amasser; (*a*) **the clouds are gathering,** les nuages s'amoncellent, s'amassent; **a storm is gathering,** un orage se prépare; (*b*) **in the gathering darkness,** dans la nuit grandissante; **with gathering force,** avec une force croissante. **3.** *Med:* (*of wound*) abcéder; (*of abscess*) aboutir, mûrir; **the pus gathers,** le pus s'accumule. **gathered** *a.* (*a*) *Needlew:* (volant, etc.) froncé, à fronces; (*b*) *Bookb:* (feuilles) assemblées. **gathering** *n.* **1.** (*a*) rassemblement *m*, attroupement *m* (d'une foule); (*b*) accumulation *f* (de choses); *Bookb:* assemblage *m* (des feuilles); (*c*) cueillette *f* (des fruits, etc.); **g. (in) of the crops,** (rentrage *m* de la) récolte (*f*); (*d*) gain *m*, augmentation *f* (de vitesse); reprise *f* (de forces); (*e*) *Needlew:* fronçure *f* (d'une robe, etc.); (*f*) accumulation *f*, amoncellement *m* (de nuages); (*g*) *Med:* collection *f* (du pus). **2.** (*a*) assemblée *f*, réunion *f* (dans une salle); assemblage, rassemblement, attroupement (dans les rues); **family g.,** réunion de famille; (*b*) *Needlew:* fronces *fpl*; (*c*) *Med:* abcès *m*; (*d*) *Bookb:* cahier *m*.

gathers ['gæðəz] *n.pl. Needlew:* fronces *fpl*.

gauche [gouʃ] *a.* gauche, maladroit.

gaucheness ['gouʃnis] *n.* gaucherie *f*, maladresse *f*.

gaudiness ['gɔːdinis] *n.* éclat criard (d'une couleur); ostentation *f*; clinquant *m*.

gaudy ['gɔːdi] *a.* (*of colours*) voyant, criard, éclatant; (*of display*) de mauvais goût. **-ily** *adv.* d'une manière voyante; (peint) en couleurs criardes.

gauge¹ [geidʒ] *n.* **1.** (*a*) calibre *m* (d'un écrou, etc.); *a. phr.* **fine g., heavy g.,** (bas) de jauge fine, de grosse jauge; (*b*) *Veh:* espacement *m* (des roues); *Rail:* écartement *m*, largeur *f* (de la voie); **narrow-g. track,** voie étroite; (*c*) *Cin:* pas *m* (de l'image, de la perforation). **2.** (appareil *m*) vérificateur (*m*); calibre, jauge *f* (pour mesurer qch.); **standard g.,** calibre étalon; **cal(l)iper g.,** jauge à coulisse; calibre, de précision; **wire g.,** calibre pour fils métalliques. **3.** indicateur *m*, contrôleur *m*; (*a*) *Ph:* **vacuum g.,** indicateur, jauge, du vide; (*b*) *Mch:* **water, oil, g.,** (indicateur de) niveau (*m*) d'eau, d'huile; **pressure g.,** manomètre *m*; *Aut:* **petrol, fuel, g.,** jauge d'essence; **tyre(-pressure) g.,** manomètre (pour pneus). **4.** *Nau:* (*a*) tirant *m* d'eau (d'un navire); (*b*) **weather g.,** avantage *m* du vent.

gauge² *v.tr.* calibrer (un écrou, etc.); jauger, mesurer (l'huile); *Fig:* prévoir (l'avenir, etc.); **to g. sth. by the eye,** mesurer qch. à l'œil. **gauging** *n.* calibrage *m*; jaugeage *m*; **g. rod, stick,** jauge *f*.

Gaul [gɔːl] *A. Geog:* **1.** *Pr.n.* Gaule *f*. **2.** *n.* Gaulois, -oise.

Gaullist ['goulist] *a. & n. Pol:* gaulliste (*mf*).

gaunt [gɔːnt] *a.* **1.** maigre, décharné. **2.** lugubre, désolé.

gauntlet¹ ['gɔːntlit] *n.* **1.** *Arm:* gantelet *m*, gant *m*; **to throw, fling, down the g.,** jeter le gant; **to take up the g.,** relever le gant. **2. g. (glove),** gant à crispins, à manchette.

gauntlet² *n.* **to run the g.,** (i) *Mil:* passer par les baguettes; *Nau:* courir la bouline; (ii) soutenir un feu roulant (de critiques adverses).

gauntness ['gɔːntnis] *n.* maigreur *f*; aspect *m* hâve (de qn, du visage de qn).

gauze [gɔːz] *n.* (*a*) gaze *f*; *Med:* **antiseptic g.,** gaze aseptique; (*b*) **wire g.,** toile *f* métallique.

gave. *see* GIVE².

gavel ['gæv(ə)l] *n.* marteau *m* (de commissaire-priseur, *NAm:* de juge).

gavotte [gə'vɔt] *n. Danc: Mus:* gavotte *f*.

gawk¹ [gɔːk] *n. F:* godiche *mf*; **big g.,** grand dadais.

gawk² *v.i. F:* = GAWP.

gawker ['gɔːkər] *n. NAm:* badaud *m*, curieux, -euse.

gawkiness ['gɔːkinis] *n.* gaucherie *f*; air empoté.

gawky ['gɔːki] *a.* dégingandé, gauche; *F:* empoté.

gawp [gɔːp] *v.i. F:* rester bouche bée; *F:* gober des mouches.

gay [gei] **(gayer, gayest) 1.** *a.* (*a*) gai, allègre; (rire) enjoué; (*b*) **to lead a g. life,** mener une vie de plaisir(s); (*c*) *P:* homosexuel; (*d*) gai, splendide; (couleurs) vives, gaies. **2.** *n. P:* homosexuel *m*. **gaily** *adv.* **1.** gaiement, allègrement. **2.** de couleurs gaies; **g. coloured,** aux couleurs vives.

gaze¹ [geiz] *n.* regard *m* fixe; **exposed to the public g.,** exposé aux regards inquisiteurs de tous.

gaze² *v.i.* regarder fixement; **to g. at, on, s.o.,** fixer, contempler, considérer, qn.

gazebo [gə'ziːbou] *n.* belvédère *m*.

gazelle [gə'zel] *n. Z:* gazelle *f*.

gazette¹ [gə'zet] *n.* journal officiel, *esp.* la *London Gazette*; **the Police G.,** la Gazette des tribunaux.

gazette² *v.tr.* annoncer, publier (une faillite, une nomination, etc.) dans un journal officiel.

gazetteer [gæzi'tiər] *n.* répertoire *m* géographique.

gazump [gə'zʌmp] *v.tr. F:* revenir sur une promesse de vente faite à (qn) pour accepter une suroffre. **gazumping** *n.* le fait de revenir sur une promesse de vente (pour accepter une suroffre).

gear¹ [giər] *n.* **1.** (*a*) harnais *m*, harnachement *m* (de cheval de trait); (*b*) attirail *m*, équipement *m*, appareil *m*; *Nau:* apparaux *mpl*; attirail (de pêche); matériel *m* (de camping); **photographic g.,** équipement photographique; **fishing g.,** attirail de pêche; **lifting g.,** matériel de levage; (*c*) *F:* (i) fringues *fpl*; (ii) effets *mpl*; **he arrived with all his g.,** il est arrivé avec tout son attirail, tous ses bagages. **2.** *Mec.E:* (*a*) appareil, mécanisme *m*; **control g.,** appareils, organes *mpl*, de commande; *Av:* dispositif *m*, organe(s), de manœuvre; *Av:* **landing g.,** train *m* d'atterrissage; (*b*) **(driving, transmission) g.,** transmission *f*, commande *f*; **g. drive,** transmission par engrenages; **in g.,** (i) embrayé, engagé, en prise; (ii) (*of machine*) en action, en marche; **out of g.,** (i) débrayé, désengrené, hors de prise; (ii) (*of machine*) au repos; (iii) dérangé, détraqué; (iv) *Fig:* (*of organization*) désorganisé, perturbé; **to throw, put, (sth.) out of g.,** (i) débrayer, désengrener; (ii) mettre (une machine) au repos; (iii) déranger, détraquer; (iv) *Fig:* désorganiser, perturber (une organisation, etc.); (*c*) **g. ratio,** rapport *m* d'engrenages, des dentures; (*d*) *Aut:* vitesse *f*; **neutral g.,** point mort; **first, bottom, g.,** première vitesse; **top g.,** prise (directe); **g. changes,** changements *mpl* de vitesse; **to change g.,** changer (i) *Aut:* de vitesse, (ii) *Cy:* de braquet; *Aut:* **g. lever,** levier *m* de (changement de) vitesse.

gear² **1.** *v.i.* s'embrayer, s'engrener. **2.** *v.tr.* (*a*) *Mec.E:* **to g. up, down,** multiplier, démultiplier (la vitesse de révolution); *F:* **to be geared up for sth.,** être préparé pour, prêt à, qch.; (*b*) **wages geared to the cost of living,** salaires indexés au coût de la vie; **this book is geared to the needs of students,** ce livre est spécialement adapté aux besoins des étudiants. **gearing** *n.* **1.** (*a*) engrenage *m*, embrayage *m*; (*b*) **g. up,** multiplication *f*; *Cy:* développement *m*; **g. down,** démultiplication *f*. **2.** transmission *f*, commande *f*; système *m*, jeu *m*, d'engrenages. **3.** *Fin:* ratio *m* d'endettement.

gearbox ['giəbɔks] *n.* (i) *Aut:* boîte *f* de changement de vitesse, boîte de vitesses; (ii) *Mec.E:* boîte, carter *m*, d'engrenage, de transmission.

gearshift ['giəʃift] *n. Aut: NAm:* (*a*) changement *m* de vitesse; **automatic g.,** changement de vitesse automatique; (*b*) levier *m* de vitesse.

gearwheel ['giə(h)wiːl] *n.* (*a*) *Mec.E:* (roue *f* d')engrenage (*m*); (*b*) *Cy:* pignon *m*.

gecko, *pl.* **-os, -oes** ['gekou, -ouz] *n.* gecko *m*.

gee¹ [dʒiː] *int.* (*to horse*) **g.-up!** hue! huhau!

gee² *int. NAm:* **g. (whiz(z))!** ça alors! mince alors!

gee-gee ['dʒiːdʒi] *n. F:* (*child's language*) cheval *m.*

geese. *see* GOOSE.

geezer ['giːzər] *n. F:* **old g.,** vieux type; **funny old g.,** drôle *m* de bonhomme.

Geiger ['gaigər] *Pr.n. Atom.Ph:* **G. counter,** compteur *m* (de) Geiger.

geisha ['geiʃə] *n.* geisha *f*, ghesha *f.*

gel¹ [dʒel] *n. Ch:* colloïde (coagulé); gel *m.*

gel² *v.i.* **(gelled)** (*of colloid*) se coaguler.

gelatine [dʒelə'tiːn] *n.* (*a*) gélatine *f*; *Phot:* **g. paper,** papier gélatiné; (*b*) *Exp:* **explosive g.,** plastic *m.*

gelatinize [dʒi'lætinaiz] **1.** *v.tr.* gélatiniser. **2.** *v.i.* se gélatiniser.

gelatinous [dʒi'lætinəs] *a.* gélatineux.

geld [geld] *v.tr.* châtrer (un animal); hongrer (un cheval).

gelding ['geldiŋ] *n.* (*a*) animal châtré; (*b*) cheval *m* hongre; hongre *m.*

gelignite ['dʒelignait] *n. Exp:* gélignite *f.*

gem [dʒem] *n.* **1.** (*a*) pierre précieuse; joyau *m*; **g. stone,** pierre gemme; (*b*) **the g. of the collection,** le joyau de la collection; *F:* **he's a g. of a husband,** c'est la perle des maris; (*c*) *Sch: F:* (= *mistake*) perle *f*; (*d*) *Type:* diamant *m.* **2.** pierre gravée.

Gemini ['dʒeminai] *Pr.n.pl. Astr:* les Gémeaux *mpl.*

gen¹ [dʒen] *n. F:* renseignements *mpl*, tuyaux *mpl.*

gen² *F:* **1.** *v.tr.* **to g. s.o. up on sth.,** rencarder qn sur qch. **2.** *v.i.* **to g. up on sth.,** se rencarder sur qch.

gender ['dʒendər] *n.* **1.** *Gram:* genre *m.* **2.** *F:* sexe *m.*

gene [dʒiːn] *n. Biol:* gène *m*; facteur *m* (d'hérédité); **dominant, recessive, g.,** gène, dominant, récessif.

genealogical [dʒiːniə'lɔdʒik(ə)l] *a.* (tableau, arbre) généalogique.

genealogist [dʒiːni'ælədʒist] *n.* généalogiste *mf.*

genealogy [dʒiːni'ælədʒi] *n.* généalogie *f.*

genera. *see* GENUS.

general ['dʒen(ə)r(ə)l] **I.** *a.* général, -aux. **1.** (paralysie, grève) générale; **the rain has been pretty g.,** il a plu un peu partout; **g. effect,** effet *m* d'ensemble. **2.** (*a*) **g. meeting,** assemblée générale; (*in agenda*) **g. business,** questions diverses; *Pol:* **g. election,** élections générales; *Ecc:* **g. confession,** confession *f* en commun; (*b*) **word in g. use,** mot généralement employé, couramment employé; **to come into g. use,** se généraliser; **as a g. rule,** en règle générale; **speaking in a g. way,** (parlant) d'une manière générale; **the g. public,** le grand public; (*c*) **g. knowledge,** connaissances générales; *Publ:* **g. books,** livres *mpl* pour le grand public; (*d*) (ressemblance) générale, vague; **in g. terms,** en termes généraux. **3.** (*a*) **inspector g.,** inspecteur général, en chef; (*Fr.Hist: & Channel Is.*) **States G.,** États généraux; (*b*) *Mil:* (officier) général. **4.** *adv.phr.* **in g.,** en général, généralement. **II.** *n.* **1.** **to argue from the g. to the particular,** arguer du général au particulier. **2.** (*a*) *Mil:* (i) général *m*; (ii) (*rank*) général d'armée; **major g.,** général de division; (*b*) *Ecc:* général (d'un ordre religieux). **-ally** *adv.* **1.** généralement, universellement. **2.** généralement; **to make oneself g. useful,** se rendre généralement utile; **g. speaking,** (parlant) d'une façon générale. **3.** en règle générale; généralement, en général.

generality [dʒenə'ræliti] *n.* généralité *f*; (*a*) caractère général; (*b*) **to confine oneself to generalities,** s'en tenir aux généralités; (*c*) **the g. of mankind,** la plupart des hommes.

generalization [dʒen(ə)rəlai'zeiʃ(ə)n] *n.* généralisation *f*; **to make generalizations,** généraliser.

generalize ['dʒen(ə)rəlaiz] **1.** *v.tr.* (*a*) généraliser (des faits, etc.); (*b*) répandre (un usage, etc.). **2.** *v.i.* généraliser, faire des généralisations.

general-purpose ['dʒen(ə)r(ə)l'pəːpəs] *a.* (à) toutes fins, (pour) tous usages; (d'usage) universel.

generate ['dʒenəreit] *v.tr.* **1.** produire un courant électrique, de la chaleur, etc.). **2.** *Mth:* engendrer (une surface, etc.). **3.** amener, produire (un résultat); provoquer (un sentiment); **environment that generates crime,** ambiance génératrice de crime. **4.** *Cmptr:* créer, générer. **generating 1.** *a.* générateur, -trice; *El:* **g. station,** centrale *f* électrique. **2.** *n.* génération *f.*

generation [dʒenə'reiʃ(ə)n] *n.* **1.** (*a*) *Biol:* **spontaneous g.,** génération spontanée; (*b*) génération, production *f* (de la chaleur, etc.); (*c*) *Mth:* génération (d'une surface, etc.); (*d*) génération, formation *f* (des idées, etc.); (*e*) *Cmptr:* création *f*, génération; **data g.,** élaboration *f* des données. **2.** (*a*) génération; **from g. to g.,** de génération en génération; de père en fils; **for generations there had always been a doctor in the family,** ils étaient médecins de père en fils; (*b*) **the rising g.,** la jeune, la nouvelle, génération; **the present g.,** la génération actuelle; **the g. gap,** l'écart *m*, le fossé, entre les générations.

generator ['dʒenəreitər] *n.* (*a*) *Tchn:* générateur, appareil producteur (de chaleur, etc.); (*b*) *El:* génératrice *f*, dynamo; **electric g.,** générateur électrique; (*c*) *Cmptr:* (programme) générateur.

generatrix, *pl.* **-ices** ['dʒenəreitriks, -isiːz] *n. Mth:* génératrice *f* (d'une surface, etc.).

generic [dʒi'nerik] *a.* (nom, etc.) générique. **-ally** *adv.* génériquement.

generosity [dʒenə'rɔsiti] *n.* générosité *f*; (*a*) magnanimité *f*; **in a spirit of g.,** (agir) par générosité; (*b*) libéralité *f*; **the library was founded thanks to the g. of Mr X,** la fondation de la bibliothèque a été due au don généreux de M. X.

generous ['dʒen(ə)rəs] *a.* généreux; (*a*) magnanime; **he has a g. nature,** c'est une âme généreuse; (*b*) libéral, -aux; **g. gift,** don généreux; **he's g. with his money,** il n'est pas avare de son argent; (*c*) (vin) généreux; (*d*) **he took a g. helping of the stew,** il s'est servi amplement de ragoût; *F:* **she's built on g. lines,** elle a des formes généreuses. **-ly** *adv.* généreusement; (*a*) magnanimement; (*b*) libéralement; (*c*) **he helped himself g. to the stew,** il s'est servi libéralement de ragoût.

genesis ['dʒenisis] *n.* **1.** genèse *f*, origine *f.* **2.** *B:* **(the Book of) G.,** la Genèse.

genetic [dʒi'netik] *a. Biol:* génétique. **-ally** *adv.* génétiquement.

geneticist [dʒi'netisist] *n.* généticien, -ienne.

genetics [dʒi'netiks] *n.pl.* (*usu. with sg. const.*) génétique *f.*

Geneva [dʒi'niːvə] *Pr.n.* Genève *f*; **the Lake of G.,** le lac Léman; *Hist:* **the G. Convention,** la Convention de Genève.

genial ['dʒiːniəl] *a.* **1.** (*a*) (*of climate*) doux, *f.* douce; clément; (*of fire*) réconfortant; (*b*) plein de bienveillance; plein de bonne humeur; **2.** (*of talent*) génial, -aux; de génie. **-ally** *adv.* affablement.

geniality [dʒiːni'æliti] *n.* (*a*) douceur *f*, clémence *f* (d'un climat); (*b*) bienveillance *f*; bonne humeur.

genie, *pl.* **genii** [dʒiːni, 'dʒiːniai] *n. Myth:* djinn *m.*

genital ['dʒenit(ə)l] **1.** *a.* génital, -aux. **2.** *n.pl.* **genitals,** organes génitaux externes.

genitive ['dʒenitiv] *a. & n. Gram:* génitif (*m*); **in the g.,** au génitif.

genius ['dʒiːniəs] **1.** (*a*) (*only in sg.*) génie *m*, esprit *m* tutélaire (d'un lieu, etc.); **she is his good g., evil g.,** c'est son bon, mauvais, génie; (*b*) (*with pl.* **genii** ['dʒiːniai]) démon *m*, djinn *m.* **2.** (*no pl.*) génie particulier, esprit (d'une époque, d'une nation, etc.). **3.** (*no pl.*) (*ability*) (*a*) aptitudes naturelles; **to have a g. for business,** avoir le génie des affaires; **to have a g. for doing sth.,** avoir le don de faire qch.; (*b*) **man of g.,** homme *m* de génie; **work of g.,** œuvre géniale; **to**

show g., faire preuve de génie. **4.** (*pers.*) (*pl.* **geniuses** [ˈdʒiːniəsiz]) **to be a g.,** être un génie.

Genoa [ˈdʒenouə] *Pr.n. Geog:* Gênes *f.*

genocidal [dʒenəˈsaid(ə)l] *a.* (guerre, etc.) génocide.

genocide [ˈdʒenəsaid] *n.* génocide *m.*

Genoese [dʒenouˈiːz] **1.** *a.* génois. **2.** *n.* Génois, -oise.

genotype [ˈdʒiːnoutaip] *n. Biol:* génotype *m.*

genre [ˈʒɔnrə] *n.* genre *m*; **g. painting,** peinture *f* de genre.

gent [dʒent] *n.* (*a*) *P:* monsieur *m*; (*b*) *Com:* **gents' footwear,** chaussures *fpl* pour hommes; (*c*) *P.N:* **gents,** hommes; **where's the gents?** où sont les toilettes?

genteel [dʒenˈtiːl] *a.* (*a*) *A:* comme il faut; (*b*) **g. poverty,** pauvreté qui s'efforce de sauver les apparences; (*c*) *Pej:* maniéré.

gentian [ˈdʒenʃiən] *n. Bot:* gentiane *f*; **g. bitter,** (amer *m* de) gentiane.

Gentile [ˈdʒentail] *a.* & *n.* gentil, -ile; **the Gentiles,** les Gentils.

gentility [dʒenˈtiliti] *n.* (*a*) *A:* distinction *f*; manières distinguées; (*b*) **shabby g.,** la misère en habit noir; (*c*) *Pej:* prétention *f* au bon ton; manières affectées.

gentle [ˈdʒentl] *a.* **(gentler, gentlest) 1.** (*a*) *A:* **of g. birth,** bien né; (*b*) *Lit:* **the g. art,** la pêche à la ligne; *Iron:* **the g. art of smuggling,** le noble art de la contrebande. **2.** doux, *f.* douce; (réprimande) peu sévère; (tape) légère; (exercice physique) modéré; (pente) douce, faible; **g. as a lamb,** doux comme un agneau; **to be g. with one's hands,** avoir la main légère; **the gentle(r) sex,** le sexe faible; **g. breeze,** brise molle. **-tly** *adv.* doucement; **to speak g.,** parler d'un ton doux, avec douceur; **to deal g. with s.o.,** traiter qn avec indulgence; **g. (does it)!** allez-y doucement!

gentlefolk [ˈdʒent(ə)lˈfouk] *n.pl.* personnes *fpl* de bonne famille, de la meilleure bourgeoisie.

gentleman, *pl.* **-men** [ˈdʒent(ə)lmən] *n.m.* **1.** *A:* gentilhomme, *pl.* gentilshommes; *still so used in* **G. in waiting,** gentilhomme de service (près du roi). **2.** homme bien élevé; gentleman; **gentleman's agreement,** convention verbale, où n'est engagée que la parole d'honneur entre les deux parties; **to act, behave, like a g.,** se conduire en gentleman; **he's no g.,** il est mal élevé. **3.** (*a*) *Jur:* **g. (of independent means),** rentier; **g. farmer,** gentleman-farmer, *pl.* gentlemen-farmers; (*b*) *Sp:* amateur. **4.** monsieur, homme; (*to audience*) **Ladies and Gentlemen!** mesdames et messieurs! **there's a g. to see you,** il y a un monsieur qui voudrait vous parler; *Com:* **gentlemen's hairdresser,** coiffeur *m* pour hommes; *P.N:* (*on public convenience*) **gentlemen,** messieurs; **gentleman's g.,** valet de chambre.

gentlemanly [ˈdʒent(ə)lmənli] *a.* bien élevé; **it would have been more g. to say nothing,** un homme bien élevé, un gentleman, n'aurait rien dit.

gentleness [ˈdʒent(ə)lnis] *n.* douceur *f.*

gentry [ˈdʒentri] *n. coll.* **1.** petite noblesse; **landed g.,** aristocratie terrienne. **2.** *Pej:* gens *mpl.*

genuflect [ˈdʒenjuflekt] *v.i.* faire une génuflexion.

genuflection, genuflexion [dʒenjuˈflekʃ(ə)n] *n.* génuflexion *f.*

genuine [ˈdʒenjuin] *a.* (*a*) (manuscrit, etc.) authentique, véritable; *Com:* (article) garanti d'origine; (bourgogne) authentique; (diamant) véritable; (*b*) sincère; franc, *f.* franche; (croyance) sincère; (ami) loyal; (personne) sans affectation; (acheteur) sérieux; **g. surprise,** véritable surprise *f.* **-ly** *adv.* **1.** authentiquement. **2.** sincèrement.

genuineness [ˈdʒenjuinnis] *n.* **1.** authenticité *f* (d'un manuscrit, etc.). **2.** sincérité *f*, loyauté *f.*

genus, *pl.* **genera** [ˈdʒiːnəs, ˈdʒenərə] *n. Nat.Hist:* genre *m.*

geode [ˈdʒiːoud] *n. Geol:* géode *f.*

geodesic [dʒiouˈdiːsik] *a.* géodésique.

geodesy [dʒiːˈɔdisi] *n.* géodésie *f.*

geographer [dʒiˈɔgrəfər] *n.* géographe *mf.*

geographic(al) [dʒiəˈgræfik(l)] *a.* géographique. **-ally** *adv.* géographiquement.

geography [dʒiˈɔgrəfi] *n.* (*a*) géographie *f*; **physical g.,** géographie physique; *F:* **I'll show you the g. of the house,** je vais vous montrer la toilette; (*b*) **g. (book),** (livre *m* de) géographie.

geologic(al) [dʒiəˈlɔdʒik(l)] *a.* géologique. **-ally** *adv.* géologiquement.

geologist [dʒiˈɔlədʒist] *n.* géologue *mf.*

geology [dʒiˈɔlədʒi] *n.* (*a*) géologie *f*; (*b*) **g. (book),** (livre *m* de) géologie.

geometer [dʒiːˈɔmitər] *n.* **1.** géomètre *m.* **2.** *Ent:* (*a*) (chenille) arpenteuse *f*; (*b*) (*moth*) géomètre *f.*

geometric(al) [dʒiəˈmetrik(l)] *a.* géométrique. **-ally** *adv.* géométriquement.

geometry [dʒiˈɔmitri] *n.* (*a*) géométrie *f*; **plane g.,** géométrie plane; (*b*) **g. (book),** (livre *m* de) géométrie.

geomorphologic(al) [dʒioumɔːfəˈlɔdʒik(l)] *a.* géomorphologique.

geomorphology [dʒioumɔːˈfɔlədʒi] *n.* géomorphologie *f.*

geophysical [dʒiouˈfizik(ə)l] *a.* géophysique.

geophysics [dʒiouˈfiziks] *n. pl.* (*usu. with sg. const.*) géophysique *f*; physique *f* du globe.

geopolitics [dʒiouˈpɔlitiks] *n.pl.* (*usu. with sg. const.*) géopolitique *f.*

Geordie [ˈdʒɔːdi] *n. F:* habitant, -ante, originaire *mf*, du Tyneside.

George [dʒɔːdʒ] **1.** *Pr.n.m.* Georges; *F: O:* **by G.!** sapristi! **2.** *n. Av:* pilote *m* automatique, *F:* George *m.*

georgette [dʒɔːˈdʒet] *n. Tex:* crêpe *m* georgette.

Georgia [ˈdʒɔːdʒiə] *Pr.n. Geog:* Géorgie *f.*

Georgian¹ [ˈdʒɔːdʒiən] *a. Eng.Hist:* (i) du règne des quatre rois Georges; (ii) du règne de Georges V.

Georgian² *Geog:* **1.** *a.* géorgien. **2.** *n.* Géorgien, -ienne.

geotropism [dʒiˈɔtrəpizm] *n.* géotropisme *m.*

geranium [dʒəˈreiniəm] *n.* **1.** *Bot:* géranium *m.* **2.** *Hort:* pélargonium *m*; géranium. **3.** *a.* **g. (red),** vermeil.

gerbil [ˈdʒəːbil] *n. Z:* gerbille *f.*

geriatric [dʒeriˈætrik] *a.* (hospice, salle, etc.) des vieillards; **g. medicine,** gériatrie *f.*

geriatrics [dʒeriˈætriks] *n.pl. Med:* (*usu. with sg. const.*) gériatrie *f.*

germ¹ [dʒəːm] *n.* **1.** *Biol:* germe *m* (d'un organisme); **g. cell,** cellule *f*; (i) spermatozoïde *m*; (ii) ovule *m*; *Fig:* **the g. of an idea,** le germe d'une idée. **2.** *Med:* germe, microbe *m* (d'une maladie), bacille *m*; **g. warfare,** guerre *f* bactériologique.

germ² *v.i.* germer.

german¹ [ˈdʒəːmən] *a.* **cousin g.,** cousin(e) germain(e).

German² **1.** *a. Geog:* allemand; **West-G., East-G.,** ouest-allemand, est-allemand. **2.** *n.* Allemand, -ande. **3.** *n. Ling:* allemand *m*; **High G., Low G.,** haut, bas, allemand.

germander [dʒəːˈmændər] *n. Bot:* germandrée *f.*

germane [dʒəːˈmein] *a.* se rapportant (**to,** à).

Germanic [dʒəːˈmænik] **1.** *a.* allemand. **2.** *a. Hist:* germanique, germain. **3.** *n. Ling:* germanique *m.*

Germanist [ˈdʒəːmənist] *n. Ling:* germaniste *mf.*

Germanize [ˈdʒəːmənaiz] *v.tr.* germaniser.

Germany [ˈdʒəːməni] *Pr.n. Geog:* Allemagne *f*; **West, East, G.,** l'Allemagne de l'ouest, de l'est.

germ-free [ˈdʒəːmfriː] *a.* (milieu, etc.) stérile.

germicidal [dʒəːmiˈsaid(ə)l] *a.* germicide.

germicide [ˈdʒəːmisaid] *n.* germicide *m.*

germinate [ˈdʒəːmineit] **1.** *v.i.* (*of seed, Fig: of idea*) germer. **2.** *v.tr.* faire germer (des graines, etc.).

germination [dʒəːmiˈneiʃ(ə)n] *n.* germination *f.*

gerontologist [dʒərɔnˈtɔlədʒist] *n.* gérontologue *mf.*

gerontology [dʒerɔnˈtɔlədʒi] *n.* gérontologie *f.*

gerrymander [ˈdʒerimændər] *v.tr.* **to g. constituencies,** découper ou remanier arbitrairement les circonscriptions électorales (dans un but politique). **gerrymandering** *n.* truquage électoral.

gerund [ˈdʒerənd] *n. Gram:* gérondif *m*; substantif verbal; **in the g.,** au gérondif.

gerundive [dʒiˈrʌndiv] *Gram:* **1.** *a.* du gérondif. **2.** *n. Lt.Gram:* adjectif verbal.

gesso [ˈdʒesou] *n.* **1.** plâtre *m* de Paris; gypse *m.* **2.** *Art:* enduit de plâtre (pour les fresques).

gestate [dʒesˈteit] *v.i.* être en gestation.

gestation [dʒesˈteiʃ(ə)n] *n. Physiol:* gestation *f.*

gesticulate [dʒesˈtikjuleit] *v.i.* gesticuler.

gesticulation [dʒestikjuˈleiʃ(ə)n] *n.* gesticulation *f.*

gesture¹ [ˈdʒestjər] *n.* geste *m*, signe *m*; **to make a g.,** faire un geste; **with a sweeping g.,** d'un geste large; **g. of defiance,** geste de défi; **as a g. of friendship,** en témoignage d'amitié.

gesture² **1.** *v.i.* faire des gestes. **2.** *v.tr.* exprimer (qch.) par gestes.

get [get] *v.* (*p.t.* **got** [gɔt]; *p.p.* **got,** *A: & NAm: also* **gotten** [ˈgɔtn]; *pr.p.* **getting** [ˈgetiŋ]) **I.** *v.tr.* **1.** (*a*) procurer, obtenir; **to g. sth. for s.o.,** procurer qch. à qn; acheter qch. pour qn; **where did you g. that?** où avez-vous trouvé, acheté, cela? **to g. sth. to eat,** (i) trouver de quoi manger; (ii) manger qch. (au restaurant, etc.); **I got this car cheap,** j'ai eu, j'ai acheté, cette voiture (à) bon marché; (*b*) acquérir (une fortune); gagner, remporter (un prix); **to g. £5,000 a year,** gagner £5,000 par an; **to g. 10% interest,** recevoir 10% d'intérêt; **to g. nothing by it, out of it,** n'y rien gagner; **I don't think I've got the right answer,** je n'ai pas trouvé la solution; (*c*) **to g. s.o.'s permission to do sth.,** obtenir la permission de qn de faire qch.; **to g. one's own way,** faire valoir sa volonté; **I'll do it if I g. the time,** je le ferai si j'ai le temps, si je trouve un moment; **you g. a fine view from the top of the mountain,** il y a une vue magnifique du sommet de la montagne; (*d*) *W.Tel:* **we can't g. Moscow,** nous ne pouvons pas avoir Moscou; *Tp:* **I had a job to g. you,** j'ai eu du mal à vous joindre. **2.** (*a*) recevoir (un cadeau, etc.); **room that gets no sun,** pièce où le soleil ne donne pas; **he gets his shyness from his mother,** il tient sa timidité de sa mère; (*b*) attraper (un rhume, une maladie); **he got a bullet in his shoulder,** il a reçu une balle dans l'épaule; **to g. ten years,** attraper dix ans de prison; **to g. the sack,** être congédié, mis à la porte. **3.** (*a*) prendre, attraper; *F:* **we'll g. them yet!** on les aura! **you've got me this time,** (i) cette fois-ci vous m'avez eu; (ii) je donne ma langue au chat; (*b*) *F:* émouvoir (qn); **the play didn't really g. me,** la pièce ne m'a pas dit grand-chose; **that gets me, gets my goat,** ça me met en boule; (*c*) *F:* **I don't g. you, your meaning,** je ne vous comprends pas; **g. me?** tu y es? tu piges? **4. he went and got a book from the library,** il est allé chercher un livre dans la bibliothèque; **go and g. a doctor,** allez chercher un médecin. **5.** (*a*) faire parvenir; faire transporter; **how can I g. it to you?** comment vous le faire parvenir? **how am I to g. this parcel home?** comment vais-je faire transporter ce paquet chez moi? **to g. the children to bed,** faire coucher les enfants; **to g. s.o. on (to) a subject,** amener qn à parler de qch.; (*b*) **to g. the answer right,** trouver la bonne réponse; **to g. lunch (ready),** préparer le déjeuner; **to g. s.o. into trouble,** attirer des histoires à qn; *F:* **to g. a woman into trouble,** mettre une femme à mal; *F:* **it gets me down,** ça me décourage. **6.** (*a*) **to g. sth. done by s.o., to get s.o. to do sth. (for one),** faire faire qch. à, par, qn; **to g. sth. mended,** faire raccommoder qch.; **to g. oneself noticed,** se faire remarquer; (*b*) **g. him to read it,** faites-le-lui lire; **to g. s.o. to agree,** décider qn à consentir; **we must g. him to come and see us,** il faut le persuader de venir nous voir; **I can't g. the door to shut,** je n'arrive pas à fermer la porte; (*c*) **to g. one's work finished,** venir à bout de son travail; **to g. one's dress torn,** déchirer sa robe; (*d*) *Aut:* **to g. the engine running,** mettre le moteur en marche; *F:* **that got him guessing,** ça l'a intrigué. **7. have got** (*a*) avoir; (i) **what have you got there?** qu'avez-vous là? **what's that got to do with it!** qu'est-ce que cela y fait? **he's got measles,** il a la rougeole; *F:* **you've got it!** vous y êtes! (ii) (**got** *is redundant, and would be omitted in formal style*) **have you got any children?** avez-vous des enfants? **I haven't got any,** je n'en ai pas; **have you got a light?** avez-vous du feu? (*b*) être obligé (de faire qch.); **it has got to be done,** il faut que cela se fasse; **have you really got to work on Sundays?** est-ce que vous êtes vraiment obligé de travailler le dimanche? **II.** *v.i.* **1.** (*a*) (*with adj. complement*) devenir (riche, etc.); **to g. old,** devenir vieux; vieillir; **I'm getting used to it,** je commence à m'y habituer; **to g. angry,** se mettre en colère; **to g. better,** (i) s'améliorer; (ii) (*after illness*) se remettre; **it's getting late,** il se fait tard; **it's getting dark,** il commence à faire nuit; (*b*) (*usu. classified v.i.*) **to g. dressed,** s'habiller; **to g. married,** se marier; **to g. shaved,** (i) se raser; (ii) se faire raser; **to g. killed,** se faire tuer; **to g. drowned,** se noyer; **to g. caught,** se laisser prendre (par la police, etc.); être surpris (par une averse, etc.); **he got dismissed,** il a reçu son congé; (*c*) **to g. going,** (i) partir, se mettre en route; (ii) se mettre au travail; (iii) se dépêcher; **let's g. going,** *F:* **g. cracking,** allons-y! en route! **to g. talking with s.o.,** entrer en conversation avec qn. **2.** (*a*) arriver, se rendre (à un endroit, etc.); **how does one g. there?** comment fait-on pour y aller? (*asking one's way*) **how do I g. to the station?** le chemin de la gare, s'il vous plaît? *F:* **to g. there,** (i) comprendre; (ii) arriver, réussir; **we're not getting anywhere, we're getting nowhere,** nous n'aboutissons à rien; **to g. to the top of a tree, of a ladder,** monter jusqu'au haut d'un arbre, d'une échelle; **where have you got to?** où en êtes-vous (dans votre travail, etc.)? **where has he got to?** qu'est-ce qu'il est devenu? *P:* **g. the hell out of here!** fiche(-moi) le camp! **he got as far as saying . . .,** il a été jusqu'à dire . . .; **we got on to (the subject of) divorce,** nous en sommes venus à parler du divorce; **he gets on my nerves,** il m'agace; *F:* **it's getting beyond a joke,** ça dépasse la plaisanterie; (*b*) **to g. behind a tree,** se mettre derrière un arbre; **to g. to work,** (i) se mettre au travail; (ii) arriver à son (lieu de) travail; (*c*) **to g. to do sth.,** finir par faire qch.; **you'll g. to like him,** vous finirez par l'aimer; **to g. to know sth.,** apprendre qch.; **when you g. to know him,** quand on le connaît mieux; **they got to be friends,** ils sont devenus amis. **get about** *v.i.* (*a*) (*of pers.*) circuler; **he gets about a great deal,** il se déplace beaucoup; (*of invalid*) **he can't g. about yet,** il ne peut pas encore sortir; (*b*) (*of news*) se répandre, circuler. **get across** **1.** *v.i.* traverser (une rue), passer (une rivière); *Th: F:* **the play failed to g. across,** la pièce n'a pas passé la rampe; *F:* **to g. across to s.o.,** se faire comprendre par qn. **2.** *v.tr.* faire passer, faire traverser; *F:* **I couldn't g. it across to him,** je n'ai pas réussi à le lui faire comprendre. **get along** *v.i.* (*a*) s'avancer (dans son chemin); **it's time for me to be getting along,** il est temps que je parte; *F:* **g. along with you!** (i) allez-vous-en! (ii) allons donc! vous plaisantez! (*b*) faire des progrès (dans son travail, etc.); (*c*) s'entendre (avec qn). **get around** *v.i.* (*a*) circuler, voyager; rouler sa bosse; **she gets around a great deal,** elle est toujours par ci, par là; (*b*) **to g. around to doing sth.,** trouver le temps de faire qch.; (*c*) surmonter (des difficultés, etc.). **get at** *v.tr. & i.* (*a*) atteindre (un endroit, qn); **the study is locked and I can't g. at my books,** le bureau est fermé à clef et je ne puis pas prendre mes livres; **to g. at the truth,** découvrir la vérité; **that's what I'm trying to g. at,** c'est là que je veux en venir; *F:* **just let me g. at him!** si jamais il me tombe sous la patte! (*b*) *F:* acheter (qn); suborner (un témoin); (*c*) *F:* attaquer (qn); **she's always getting at her husband,** elle est toujours à dénigrer son mari. **get away 1.** *v.i.* (*a*) partir; (*of prisoner, etc.*) s'échapper, se sauver; **to g. away early from the office,** quitter le bureau de bonne heure; **to g. away for a few days,** (parvenir à) s'absenter pendant quelques jours; **how wonderful to g. away from it all!** quel plaisir de tout quitter! **g. away!** allez-vous-en! *P:* **g. away (with you)!** tu plaisantes! ça ne prend pas! **there's no getting away from it,** il faut bien l'admettre; (*b*) *Aut:* démarrer; **car that gets away quickly,** voiture qui a une bonne reprise; (*c*) **the burglars got away with £10,000,** les cambrioleurs ont raflé £10.000; *F:* **to g. away with it,** (i) faire accepter quelque chose; (ii) s'en tirer à bon compte. **2.** *v.tr.* éloigner (qn); **I managed to g. her away at eleven,** j'ai réussi à l'emmener à onze heures. **get back 1.** *v.i.* (*a*) reculer; (*b*) revenir, retourner; **to g. back home,** rentrer chez soi; **to g. back into bed,** se recoucher; **to g. back to nature,** retourner à la nature. **2.** *v.tr.* (*a*) se faire rendre (qch.); recouvrer (ses biens); reprendre (ses forces); **to g. one's money back,** (i) rentrer dans ses fonds; (ii) se faire rembourser; *F:* **to g. one's own back,** *v.i. NAm:* **to g. back at s.o.,** prendre sa revanche (sur qn); (*b*) faire revenir (qch); (*c*) remettre (qch.); **to g. sth. back into its box,** faire rentrer qch. dans sa boîte. **get by** *v.i.* (*a*) passer; **there wasn't enough room to g. by,** il n'y avait pas assez de place pour passer; (*b*) *F:* se débrouiller; **we just g. by,** on s'en tire, voilà tout. **get down 1.** *v.i.* (*a*) descendre (**from, off,** de); **to g. down on one's knees,** se mettre à genoux; (*to dog*) **g. down!** couché! (*b*) **to g. down to work,** se mettre au travail; **we'd better g. down to the facts,** il faut en venir aux faits. **2.** *v.tr.* (*a*) descendre (un livre d'un rayon, etc.); (*b*) **to g. sth. down (in writing, on paper),** noter qch. (par écrit); (*c*) avaler (une bouchée, etc.). **get in 1.** *v.i.* (*a*) entrer; **we got in at about eleven,** nous sommes rentrés (chez nous) vers onze heures; **he got in through the window,** il est entré par la fenêtre; **to g. in a train,** monter dans un train; **water had got in everywhere,** l'eau avait pénétré partout; **if the train gets in on time,** si le train arrive à l'heure; (*b*) *F:* **to g. in with s.o.,** s'insinuer dans les bonnes grâces de qn; (*c*) *Pol:* être élu député (pour une circonscription); **he's sure to g. in,** il sera certainement élu. **2.** *v.tr.* (*a*) rentrer (la moisson, etc.); *Nau:* rentrer (une embarcation); **to g. coal in for the winter,** faire une provision de charbon pour l'hiver; **to g. a man in to mend a window,** faire venir un homme pour réparer une fenêtre; (*b*) **I can't g. a word in (edgeways),** je n'arrive pas à placer un mot; (*c*) **to g. one's hand in,** se faire la main; (*d*) semer (des graines, etc.). **get into** *v.tr. & i.* (*a*) (*mainly prepositional*) entrer dans (une maison, etc.); pénétrer dans (un bois, etc.); monter dans (une voiture, un train, etc.); **to g. into parliament,** être élu député; **to g. into a university,** entrer en faculté; (*b*) mettre (ses vêtements); endosser (un pardessus, etc.); **I can't g. into this dress any more,** je n'entre plus dans cette robe; **to g. into a rage,** se mettre en rage; **to g. into a bad habit,** acquérir, prendre, une mauvaise habitude; **to g. into the way of doing sth.,** (i) apprendre à faire qch.; (ii) prendre l'habitude de faire qch.; (*c*) **to g. sth. into sth.,** (faire) (r)entrer qch. dans qch.; **to g. the key into the lock,** mettre, introduire, la clef dans la serrure; **to g. an article into a paper,** faire accepter un article par un journal. **get off 1.** *v.i.* (*a*) descendre (d'un autobus, etc.); *P:* **I told him where to g. off,** je lui ai dit ses quatre vérités; (*b*) se faire exempter (d'une corvée, etc.); (*c*) se tirer d'affaire; être acquitté; **to g. off lightly,** s'en tirer à bon compte; **to g. off with a fine,** en être quitte pour une amende; (*d*) partir; *Av:* décoller; **to g. off to sleep,** s'endormir. **2.** *v.tr.* (*a*) enlever (des vêtements, etc.); ôter, enlever (des taches); (*b*) expédier (une lettre); **we managed to g. him off on time,** nous avons réussi à le faire partir à l'heure; (*c*) **to g. sth. off one's hands,** se débarrasser de qch.; *F:* **he's got his daughter off his hands,** il a marié sa fille; (*d*) faire acquitter (un prévenu); tirer (qn) d'affaire; (*e*) *Nau:* renflouer, déséchouer (un navire). **get on 1.** *v.tr.* mettre (ses chaussures, etc.); enfiler (ses bas, etc.); **I can't g. these trousers on any more,** je n'entre plus dans ce pantalon. **2.** *v.i.* (*a*) **to g. on (to) a ladder, a train,** monter sur une échelle, dans un train; (*b*) se mettre en route; **to be getting on (in years),** prendre de l'âge; **to be getting on for forty,** approcher de, friser, la quarantaine; **time's getting on,** l'heure s'avance; **it's getting on for midnight,** il est presque minuit; (*c*) faire des progrès; réussir (dans la vie); **to g. on with one's work,** continuer son travail; **how are you getting on?** comment allez-vous? comment va votre travail? **how did you g. on in your exam(ination)?** comment votre examen a-t-il marché? **I'll let you know how he's getting on,** je vous donnerai de ses nouvelles; **I can't g. on without him,** je ne peux pas me passer de lui; (*d*) **to g. on (well) with s.o.,** s'entendre avec qn; **we don't g. on very well (together),** nous ne nous entendons pas très bien; (*e*) *F:* **g. on with you!** (i) pour qui me prends-tu? (ii) va te promener! (*f*) *F:* **to g. on to s.o.,** (i) contacter qn; (ii) découvrir le vrai caractère de qn. **get out 1.** *v.tr.* (*a*) arracher (un clou, etc.); retirer (un bouchon); faire disparaître (une tache); **to g. sth. out of sth.,** faire sortir qch. de qch.; **I can't g. the idea out of my mind,** je ne peux pas me débarrasser de l'idée; **to g. a secret out of s.o.,** arracher un secret à qn; **I can't g. anything out of him,** je ne peux rien tirer de lui; **to g. money out of s.o.,** tirer de l'argent de qn; **to g. s.o. out of a difficulty,** tirer qn d'une difficulté; (*b*) sortir (ses outils, etc.); **to g. out one's car,** sortir sa voiture; **I got out a pencil to write the address,** j'ai sorti un crayon pour écrire l'adresse; **to g. out a book from the library,** emprunter un livre à la bibliothèque; **he could hardly g. a word out,** c'est à peine s'il a pu sortir un mot. **2.** *v.i.* (*a*) **to g. out of sth.,** sortir de qch.; descendre (d'un train, etc.); (*of lion*) s'échapper (de sa cage, etc.); **the secret got out,** le secret s'est fait jour; **to g. out of s.o.'s way,** faire place à qn; **to g. out of bed,** se lever; *F:* **g. out!** fiche(-moi) le camp! (*b*) **to g. out of a difficulty,** se tirer d'une position difficile; **to g. out of doing sth.,** se faire exempter de faire qch.; **there's no getting out of it,** il faut passer par là; **to g. out of the habit of doing sth.,** perdre l'habitude de faire qch. **get over** *v.tr. & i.* (*a*) escalader, passer par-dessus (un mur, etc.); (*b*) **to g. sth. over (and done with),** en finir avec qch.; **it's best to g. it over,** il vaut mieux en finir; (*c*) **to g. over (sth.),** se remettre (d'une maladie); venir à bout de (ses difficultés); revenir de (sa surprise); **she can't g. over it,** (*of illness*) elle ne se remet pas; (*of surprise, shock, etc.*) elle n'en revient pas; (*of loss*) elle est inconsolable; **it will take her a long time to g. over it,** elle s'en ressentira longtemps. **get round** *v.i. & tr.*

(*a*) tourner (un coin); contourner (une difficulté); tromper (la loi); persuader (qn); (*b*) **to g. round to doing sth.,** trouver le temps de faire qch. **get through** *v.tr. & i.* (*a*) (*prepositional*) (i) passer par (un trou, une fenêtre); se frayer un chemin à travers (la foule, etc.); (ii) achever, arriver au bout de (son travail, etc.); **to g. through a lot of work,** abattre du travail; **to g. through the day,** faire passer la journée; **we shall never g. through all this food,** nous ne viendrons jamais à bout de toute cette nourriture; **to g. through (an examination),** être reçu (à un examen); (*b*) (*adverbial*) parvenir à franchir un obstacle; **the news got through to them,** la nouvelle leur est parvenue; **to g. through (to s.o.),** (i) *Tp:* obtenir la communication (avec qn); (ii) *F:* faire comprendre (qn); (*c*) **to g. a bill through (parliament),** faire adopter un projet de loi; **to g. sth. through the customs,** (faire) passer qch. à la douane. **get together 1.** *v.i.* (*of people*) se réunir, se rassembler. **2.** *v.tr.* rassembler, ramasser (des objets); réunir (des amis, etc.); **let me g. my thoughts together,** laissez-moi rassembler mes idées. **get up 1.** *v.tr. & i.* (*a*) **to g. up a ladder,** monter à une échelle; **to g. s.o. up the stairs,** aider qn à monter l'escalier; **to g. a trunk up to the attic,** monter une malle au grenier; (*b*) **to g. up to Chapter 5,** arriver au chapitre 5; **where have you got up to?** où en êtes-vous? (*c*) **to g. up speed,** donner de la vitesse. **2.** *v.i.* (*a*) se lever, se mettre debout; **g. up!** levez-vous! **to g. up from a chair, from the table,** se lever de sa chaise, de table; (*b*) se lever (du lit); **I g. up at seven,** je me lève à sept heures; (*c*) (*of wind*) se lever; (*of sea*) grossir. **3.** *v.tr.* (*a*) réveiller (qn); (*b*) organiser (une fête, etc.); (*c*) *Com:* apprêter, présenter (un article pour la vente); (*d*) *F:* **to g. oneself up as a sailor,** se déguiser en marin.

getatable, get-at-able [get'ætəbl] *a. F:* accessible, d'accès facile.

getaway ['getəwei] *n.* **1.** fuite *f*; évasion *f*; **g. car,** voiture *f* de fuite; **to make one's g.,** s'enfuir. **2.** (*a*) *Rac:* démarrage *m* (d'un coureur); (*b*) *Aut:* démarrage; **smart g.,** bonne accélération.

Gethsemane [geθ'seməni] *Pr.n.* Gethsémani *m.*

get-rich-quick ['get'ritʃ'kwik] *a. F:* (projet) qui promet une fortune.

get-together ['get(t)əgeðər] *n. F:* réunion *f*; **you and I must have a little g.-t.,** il faut qu'on se voie, qu'on se réunisse, un jour.

getup, get-up ['getʌp] *n.* (*a*) habillement *m*, tenue *f*, toilette *f*; **what a g.!** quel costume! (*b*) (*fancy dress*) déguisement *m*; (*c*) *Com:* présentation *f* (des marchandises).

gewgaw ['gju:gɔ:] *n.* babiole *f.*

geyser ['gi:zər] *n.* **1.** *Geol:* geyser *m.* **2.** chauffe-eau *m inv* à gaz.

Ghana ['gɑ:nə] *Pr.n. Geog:* Ghana *m.*

Ghanaian, Ghanian [gɑ:'neiən, 'gɑ:niən] *Geog:* **1.** *a.* ghanéen. **2.** *n.* Ghanéen, -enne.

ghastliness ['gɑ:stlinis] *n.* horreur *f* (d'un crime); aspect *m* sinistre (de qch.).

ghastly ['gɑ:stli] **1.** *a.* (*a*) horrible, affreux, épouvantable; (*b*) *F:* **what g. weather!** quel temps abominable! **a g. mistake,** une erreur monstrueuse; (*c*) blême; (pâleur) mortelle; (lumière) blafarde; **he looked g.,** il avait l'air d'un déterré. **2.** *adv.* (*a*) horriblement, affreusement; (*b*) **g. pale,** pâle comme un mort.

Ghent [gent] *Pr.n. Geog:* Gand *m.*

gherkin ['gə:kin] *n.* cornichon *m*; *Comest:* **pickled gherkins,** cornichons confits (au vinaigre).

ghetto ['getou] *n.* ghetto *m.*

ghost¹ [goust] *n.* **1.** *A:* âme *f*; (*still used in*) **to give up the g.,** rendre l'âme; expirer. **2. the Holy G.,** l'Esprit Saint, le Saint-Esprit. **3.** (*a*) fantôme *m*, spectre *m*; **to believe in ghosts,** croire aux revenants; **you look as if you'd seen a g.,** vous avez l'air d'un déterré; **g. ship,** vaisseau *m* fantôme; **g. story,** histoire *f* de revenants; (*b*) **to be the mere g. of one's former self,** n'être plus que l'ombre de soi-même; **not the g. of a chance,** pas la moindre chance; **g. of a smile,** sourire *m* vague. **4.** *F:* **g. (writer),** collaborateur, -trice, anonyme; nègre *m* (d'un auteur, etc.). **5.** (*a*) *Opt:* spectre *m* secondaire; image blanche; (*b*) *T.V:* écho *m*; *Rad: T.V:* **g. image,** image fantôme.

ghost² **1.** *v.i.* servir de nègre (**for an author,** à un écrivain); prêter à qn une collaboration anonyme. **2.** *v.tr.* écrire (les discours de qn); **to g. a book,** servir de nègre à l'auteur d'un livre; **ghosted work,** ouvrage *m* hétéronyme.

ghostly ['goustli] *a.* spectral, -aux; de fantôme.

ghoul [gu:l] *n.* **1.** *Myth:* goule *f.* **2.** *F:* (*a*) déterreur *m* de cadavres; (*b*) amateur du macabre.

ghoulish ['gu:liʃ] *a.* de goule; (humour) macabre.

giant ['dʒaiənt] **1.** *n.* géant *m.* **2.** *a.* (chêne, carton) géant; **with g. strides,** à pas de géant.

giantess ['dʒaiəntes] *n.f.* géante.

gibber ['dʒibər] *v.i.* (*a*) produire des sons inarticulés (comme un singe, un idiot); **he was gibbering with rage,** il bégayait de rage; (*b*) baragouiner.

gibberish ['dʒibəriʃ] *n.* baragouin *m*, charabia *m.*

gibbet ['dʒibit] *n.* gibet *m*, potence *f.*

gibbon ['gibən] *n. Z:* gibbon *m.*

gibbous ['gibəs] *a.* gibbeux; *Astr:* **g. moon,** lune *f* au troisième, dernier, quartier.

gibe¹ [dʒaib] *n.* raillerie *f*; moquerie *f*; quolibet *m.*

gibe² *v.tr. & i.* **to g. (at) s.o.,** railler qn; se moquer de qn.

giblets ['dʒiblits] *n.pl.* abattis *mpl* (de volaille).

Gibraltar [dʒi'brɔ:ltər] *Pr.n. Geog:* Gibraltar; **the Straits of G.,** le détroit de Gibraltar.

giddiness ['gidinis] *n.* **1.** étourdissement *m*, vertige *m*; **fits of g.,** des étourdissements, des vertiges. **2.** (*a*) étourderie *f*; (*b*) frivolité *f* (de caractère); légèreté *f.*

giddy¹ ['gidi] *a.* **1.** (*a*) étourdi; **to be, feel, g.,** être pris de vertige; **I feel g.,** la tête me tourne; **it makes me (feel) g.,** cela me donne le vertige; (*b*) (*of height*) vertigineux, qui donne le vertige; **g. round of pleasures,** tourbillon *m* de plaisirs. **2.** frivole, étourdi. **-ily** *adv.* **1.** d'une manière vertigineuse. **2.** étourdiment.

gift [gift] *n.* (*a*) don *m*; **to make a g. of sth. to s.o.,** faire don de qch. à qn; *Jur:* **as a g.,** à titre d'avantage; *F:* **he thinks he's God's g. to mankind,** il se prend pour le nombril du monde; (*b*) cadeau *m*; **Christmas g.,** cadeau de Noël; **it was a g.,** (i) c'était un cadeau; (ii) (*of bargain*) c'était donné; **g. shop,** magasin *m* de nouveautés; **g.-wrapped,** (article) emballé en paquet cadeau; **I wouldn't have it as a g.,** je n'en voudrais pas quand bien même on me le donnerait; *Prov:* **never look a g. horse in the mouth,** à cheval donné on ne regarde pas à la bride; (*c*) *Com:* (*on presentation of coupons*) prime *f*; (*d*) talent *m*; **to have a g. for mathematics,** avoir le don, *F:* la bosse, des mathématiques.

giftbook ['giftbuk] *n.* livre d'étrennes.

gifted ['giftid] *a.* bien doué; (artiste) de talent.

gig¹ [gig] *n.* **1.** *Veh:* cabriolet *m.* **2.** *Nau:* yole *f.*

gig² *n. Mus:* engagement *m* d'un soir; gig *f.*

gigantic [dʒai'gæntik] *a.* géant, gigantesque; (bâtiment, etc.) colossal, -aux. **-ally** *adv.* gigantesquement.

giggle¹ ['gigl] *n.* petit rire bête; **to have (a fit of) the giggles,** avoir le fou rire; *F:* **to do sth. for a g.,** faire qch. pour rire, pour rigoler.

giggle² *v.i.* rire bêtement. **giggling 1.** *a.* qui rit bêtement. **2.** *n.* rires *mpl* bébêtes; fou rire.

giggly ['gigli] *a.* qui pousse des petits rires bêtes.
gigolo ['dʒigəlou] *n.m. Pej:* gigolo.
gild [gild] *v.tr.* (*p.t.* **gilded;** *p.p.* **gilded,** *occ.* **gilt** [gilt]) dorer; **to g. the lily,** faire œuvre de superfétation; orner la beauté même; **to g. the pill,** dorer la pilule. **gilding** *n.* dorure *f.* **gilt** *a.* (cadre, etc.) doré.
gill[1] [gil] *n.* **1.** *usu.pl.* ouïe(s) *f(pl)*, branchie(s) *f(pl)* (de poisson). **2. gills,** (*a*) lames *fpl*, lamelles *fpl* (d'un champignon); (*b*) *F:* bajoues *fpl* (de qn); **to be, look, green about the gills,** avoir le teint vert; avoir l'air malade.
gill[2] [dʒil] *n. Meas:* (0.142l.) = canon *m* (de vin).
gillie ['gili] *n. Scot:* serviteur *m* (d'un chasseur, d'un pêcheur).
gillyflower ['dʒiliflauər] *n. Bot:* **1. (clove) g.,** œillet *m* giroflée. **2.** *F:* giroflée *f* jaune, des murailles.
gilt[1] [gilt]. *see* GILD.
gilt[2] *n.* dorure *f*; doré *m*; *Bookb:* **g.-edged,** doré sur tranche; *St.Exch:* **g.-edge(d) stock(s),** *n.pl.* **gilts,** fonds *mpl* d'État; valeurs *fpl* de tout repos, de premier ordre, *F:* de père de famille; *F:* **that takes the g. off the gingerbread,** voilà qui enlève le charme, l'attrait.
gilt[3] *n. Z:* cochette *f*, jeune truie *f.*
gimbals ['dʒimb(ə)lz] *n.pl. Av: Nau: etc:* (suspension *f* à la) cardan (*m*).
gimcrack ['dʒimkræk] **1.** *a.* (meubles) de pacotille, de camelote; (maison) de carton; (bijoux) en toc.
gimlet ['gimlit] *n. Tls: Carp:* vrille *f*; foret *m* à bois; *Fig:* **g. eyes,** yeux perçants, en trou de vrille.
gimmick ['gimik] *n. F:* truc *m*, astuce *f*; **advertising g.,** artifice *m*, astuce, truc, publicitaire.
gimmickry ['gimikri] *n. F:* astuces *fpl*; combinaisons *fpl* (pour attirer l'attention du public).
gimmicky ['gimiki] *a. F:* plein de trucs, d'astuces.
gin[1] [dʒin] *n.* **1.** *Ven:* piège *m.* **2.** *Tex:* **(cotton) g.,** égreneuse *f* de coton.
gin[2] *n.* gin *m*; (*made in Holland*) genièvre *m.*
ginger[1] ['dʒindʒər] **1.** *n.* (*a*) gingembre *m*; **preserved g.,** gingembre confit; **g. wine,** vin *m* de gingembre; **g. ale, beer,** boisson gazeuse au gingembre; (*b*) *F:* entrain *m*, énergie *f*; *Pol:* **g. group,** groupe *m* de pression; les militants *mpl* (d'un parti). **2.** *a. F:* (*of hair*) roux, *f.* rousse; rouquin; *n.* **hi, g.,** ohé, poil de carotte!
ginger[2] *v.tr.* **to g. up,** *F:* mettre du cœur au ventre de (qn); émoustiller (qn); activer (la production, etc.).
gingerbread ['dʒindʒəbred] *n.* **1.** *n.* pain *m* d'épice; **g. man,** bonhomme *m* de, en, pain d'épice. **2.** *attrib. F:* (architecture) prétentieuse et sans solidité.
gingerly ['dʒindʒəli] *adv. & a.* **g., in a g. fashion,** doucement, avec précaution; **to proceed, to go about it, g.,** y aller doucement.
gingernut, -snap ['dʒindʒənʌt, -snæp] *n.* biscuit *m* au gingembre.
gingery ['dʒindʒəri] *a.* **1.** (*of temperament*) irascible, coléreux. **2.** *F:* (*of hair*) roux, *f.* rousse.
gingham ['giŋəm] *n. Tex:* guingan *m.*
gingivitis [dʒindʒi'vaitis] *n. Med:* gingivite *f.*
ginseng ['dʒinseŋ] *n.* ginseng *m.*
gipsy ['dʒipsi] *n.* **1.** bohémien, -ienne; romanichel, -elle; (*Spanish*) gitan, -ane; **g. music,** musique tzigane. **2.** (*a*) *Ent:* **g. moth,** zigzag *m.*
gipsyish ['dʒipsiiʃ] *a.* (*a*) comme un bohémien, un romanichel; (*b*) noiraud.
giraffe [dʒi'ræf, -'rɑːf] *n. Z:* girafe *f.*
gird [gəːd] *v.tr.* (*p.t. & p.p.* **girded, girt** [gəːt]) *A: & Lit:* **1.** ceindre; **to g. up one's loins,** se ceindre les reins; **to g. (on) one's sword,** ceindre son épée. **2.** ceindre (**with,** de); **sea-girt Britain,** la Grande-Bretagne encerclée par les mers.
girder ['gəːdər] *n. Const:* poutre *f* (métallique).
girdle[1] ['gəːdl] *n.* (*a*) ceinture *f*; (*b*) *Cost:* gaine *f*; (*c*) *Anat:* **pelvic g., pectoral g.,** ceinture pelvienne, scapulaire.
girdle[2] *v.tr.* ceindre, entourer.
girdle[3] *n. Cu:* tôle (sur laquelle ou cuit des galettes); **g. cake,** galette *f.*
girl [gəːl] *n.f.* (*a*) fille; **little g.,** petite fille, fillette; **when I was a g.,** quand j'étais petite; **girl's name,** prénom féminin; **girls' school,** école *f* de filles; **old g.,** ancienne élève; (*b*) **a French g., an Indian g.,** une jeune Française, une jeune Indienne; **a blind g.,** une jeune aveugle; (*c*) jeune fille, jeune femme; *F:* **his g. friend,** son amie, sa petite amie; **my dear g.!** ma chère! *P:* **the old g.,** (i) ma femme, la bourgeoise; (ii) ma mère; (iii) la patronne; (iv) *F:* ma vieille voiture, bagnole; (*d*) **my eldest, youngest, g.,** ma fille aînée, cadette; (*e*) **chorus g.,** girl.
girlhood ['gəːlhud] *n.* jeunesse *f* (d'une femme).
girlie ['gəːli] *n.f. F:* **g. magazines,** revues *fpl* qui contiennent de nombreuses photos de femmes nues.
girlish ['gəːliʃ] *a.* **1.** (*of behaviour, figure, etc.*) de petite fille, de jeune fille. **2.** (*of boy*) mou, efféminé.
giro ['dʒairou] *n. Post: Bank:* (*a*) **National G.** = service *m* de chèques postaux; **g. account,** compte *m* chèque postal; (*b*) **bank g.,** virement *m* bancaire.
girt. *see* GIRD.
girth [gəːθ] *n.* **1.** *Harn:* sangle *f*; **saddle g.,** sangle de selle. **2.** circonférence *f* (d'un arbre, etc.); tour *m* (de poitrine, de taille); (*of pers.*) **of considerable g.,** d'une belle corpulence.
gist [dʒist] *n.* fond *m*, substance *f*, essence *f* (d'une conversation); point essentiel (d'une question); **to get the g. of the matter,** saisir l'essentiel.
give[1] [giv] *n.* **1.** élasticité *f*; jeu *m* (dans un mécanisme, etc.); **shoes with no g. in them,** chaussures qui ne prêtent pas. **2. g. and take,** accommodement *m*; concessions mutuelles.
give[2] *v.* (*p.t.* **gave** [geiv]; *p.p.* **given** ['givn]) **I.** *v.tr.* donner. **1.** (*a*) **to g. sth. to s.o., to g. s.o. sth.,** donner qch. à qn; **to g. s.o. a present,** faire, donner, un cadeau à qn; **to g. alms,** faire l'aumône; **to g. a dinner,** donner un dîner; **g. me the good old days!** parlez-moi du bon vieux temps! (*b*) *Tp:* **g. me Mr X,** passez-moi, donnez-moi, M. X; (*c*) **to g. and take,** faire des concessions mutuelles; **we'll get there in two hours, g. or take a few minutes,** on fera le trajet en deux heures, ou à quelques minutes près. **2.** (*a*) **to g. s.o. sth. to eat, to drink,** donner à manger, à boire, à qn; **to g. s.o. six months' imprisonment,** condamner qn à six mois de prison; **to g. a child a name,** donner un nom à un enfant; **to g. s.o. a job to do,** assigner une tâche, un rôle, à qn; (*b*) **to g. s.o. a note from s.o.,** remettre à qn un petit mot de qn; (*c*) **g. her my love,** embrasse-la pour moi; **to g. s.o. one's support,** prêter son appui à qn; (*d*) engager (son honneur, etc.); **to g. one's word,** donner sa parole. **3. to g. sth. in exchange for sth.,** donner qch. contre qch.; **to g. a good price for sth.,** donner, payer, un bon prix pour qch.; **I'll g. you £10 for it,** je vous en donnerai £10; **I would g. a lot, a great deal, to know . . .,** je donnerais beaucoup pour savoir . . .. **4.** (*a*) **to g. one's mind, oneself, to one's studies,** s'adonner, s'appliquer, à ses études; (*b*) (*of woman*) **to g. herself,** se donner. **5.** (*a*) **to g. a jump,** (i) sauter, faire un saut; (ii) tressauter; **to g. a laugh,** rire; laisser échapper un rire; **to g. a sigh,** soupirer, pousser un soupir; **to g. s.o.'s hand a squeeze,** serrer la main à qn; **to g. s.o. a smile,** adresser un sourire à qn; **he gave me an odd look,** il m'a lancé un regard singulier; (*b*) faire (une réponse); donner (des ordres); **he gave his age as twenty,** il a déclaré avoir vingt ans; (*at shop*) **to g. an order,** faire une commande; **to g. s.o. the lie,** accuser qn de mentir. **6.** (*a*) **to g. s.o. one's hand,** donner, tendre, la main à qn; **she gave him her hand**

(in marriage), elle lui a accordé sa main; (*b*) **to g. one's attention to s.o.,** faire attention à qn; **he gave it considerable thought,** il l'a considéré avec beaucoup de soin. **7.** (*a*) donner (son avis); donner, fournir (des détails); **to g. a description of sth.,** faire une description de qch.; décrire qch.; **to g. a decision,** (i) faire connaître sa décision; (ii) *Jur:* rendre un arrêt; (*b*) **to g. no sign of life,** ne donner aucun signe de vie; **to g. an average of . . .,** rendre une moyenne de . . .; (*c*) donner (un exemple); **given these facts, explain why . . .,** à partir de ces données, expliquez pourquoi . . .; **given a triangle ABC,** soit un triangle ABC; (*d*) donner (un concert, etc.); **to g. a recitation,** réciter, dire des vers; *Th:* **they're giving** *Macbeth* **this week,** on joue *Macbeth* cette semaine; (*e*) **to g. a toast,** proposer un toast; **I g. you our host,** je bois à la santé de notre hôte. **8.** (*a*) **he gave me his cold,** il m'a donné, passé, son rhume; **that gave me the idea of travelling,** cela m'a donné l'idée de voyager; (*b*) faire, causer (de la peine, du plaisir); **to g. oneself trouble,** se donner du mal; (*c*) **to g. s.o. to believe, understand, that . . .,** faire croire, donner à entendre, à qn que . . .; (*d*) rendre; **investment that gives 10%,** placement *m* qui rend, rapporte, 10%; **this lamp gives a poor light,** cette lampe éclaire mal. **9.** (*a*) *F:* **to g. it (to) s.o.,** (i) laver la tête à qn; (ii) rosser qn; **g. it them!** allez-y! *P:* **I gave him what for!** je l'ai arrangé de la belle façon! (*b*) *F:* **to g. as good as one gets,** rendre coup pour coup. **10.** (*a*) **to g. way,** céder, succomber; (*of ladder*) se casser, se rompre; (*of cable*) partir; **the ground gave way under our feet,** le sol s'est affaissé, s'est dérobé, sous nos pieds; **my legs are giving way (under me),** mes jambes fléchissent, mollissent, se dérobent, sous moi; **his health is giving way,** sa santé s'affaiblit; (*b*) **to g. way to s.o.,** céder à qn; **to g. way to despair, to grief,** s'abandonner au désespoir, à la douleur; **to g. way to temptation,** céder à la tentation; (*c*) **to g. way to s.o., to a car,** céder la place à qn, le passage à une voiture; *P.N: Aut:* **g. way,** cédez le pas. **II** *v.i.* **1.** (*a*) (*of cloth, elastic*) prêter, donner; **the springs don't g. enough,** les ressorts manquent de souplesse; (*b*) céder, fléchir; **the door will g. if you push hard enough,** la porte cédera si vous la poussez assez fort. **2. the window gives on (to) the garden,** la fenêtre donne sur le jardin; **this door gives into the yard,** cette porte donne accès à la cour. **3.** *F:* **what gives?** (i) salut! (ii) qu'est-ce qui se passe, se fricote? (iii) quoi de neuf? **4.** *P:* **g.!** vide ton sac! **give away** *v.tr.* (*a*) donner (qch. à qn); **to g. away the prizes,** distribuer les prix; (*b*) **to g. away the bride,** conduire la mariée à l'autel; (*c*) trahir, vendre (qn); **to g. oneself away,** se révéler; se trahir; **to g. the game away,** lâcher le secret; vendre la mèche. **give back** *v.tr.* (*a*) rendre, restituer; **to g. s.o. back his liberty,** rendre la liberté à qn; (*b*) renvoyer (un écho); refléter (une image). **give in 1.** *v.tr.* **to g. in one's name,** donner son nom; **to g. in one's examination paper,** remettre sa copie d'examen. **2.** *v.i.* céder; se soumettre; **to g. in to s.o.,** céder à qn. **given** *a.* (*a*) donné; **in a g. time,** dans un délai donné, prescrit; **at a g. point,** à un point donné; (*b*) *esp.* **g. name,** prénom *m*; nom *m* de baptême. **give off** *v.tr.* dégager, émettre (une odeur); répandre (la chaleur); *Ch:* dégager (un gaz). **give out 1.** *v.tr.* (*a*) distribuer (du ravitaillement, des livres, etc.); (*b*) dégager (une odeur); répandre (la chaleur); (*c*) **to g. out a notice,** lire une communication; **it was given out that . . .,** on a annoncé, dit, que . . .. **2.** *v.i.* manquer, faire défaut; (*of supplies*) s'épuiser; **my strength was giving out,** j'étais à bout de forces. **give over** *v.tr.* (*a*) **to g. sth. over to s.o.,** remettre qch. entre les mains de qn; (*b*) **given over to despair,** abandonné, en proie, au désespoir; (*c*) *P:* **g. over, will you?** c'est vraiment assez! est-ce fini, par exemple! **give up** *v.tr.* (*a*) rendre (sa proie); abandonner (ses biens, ses prétentions); **to g. up one's seat to s.o.,** céder sa place à qn; (*b*) renoncer à (un projet, etc.); **to g. up the idea of doing sth.,** renoncer à (l'idée de) faire qch.; **to g. up smoking,** cesser de fumer; **to g. up one's job,** résigner son emploi, ses fonctions; **to g. up the game, the struggle,** abandonner la partie; renoncer à la lutte; **don't g. up!** tenez bon! (*of riddle*) **I g. (it) up,** je donne ma langue au chat; (*c*) **to g. s.o. up (for lost),** considérer qn comme perdu; **the doctors have given him up,** les médecins l'ont condamné; **I'd given you up!** je ne vous attendais plus! (*d*) livrer (qn à la justice, etc.); **to g. oneself up,** se constituer prisonnier; **to g. oneself up to (sth.),** se livrer à (qch.); s'absorber dans (la lecture, etc.); s'adonner à (l'étude, etc.); **his mornings were given up to business,** ses matinées étaient consacrées aux affaires. **giving 1.** *a.* (*of pers.*) donnant; **of a g. nature,** généreux. **2.** *n.* don *m*, donation *f*; *Sch:* **prize g.,** distribution *f* des prix.

giveaway ['givəwei] *n. F:* (*a*) révélation *f* involontaire; **it was a dead g.,** c'était un geste, un mot, qui en disait long; (*b*) *Com:* **g. price,** prix défiant toute concurrence.

giver ['givər] *n.* donneur, -euse; donateur, -trice.

gizmo ['gizmou] *n. U.S: F:* machin *m*, truc *m*.

gizzard ['gizəd] *n.* gésier *m*; *F:* **that sticks in my g.,** je ne peux pas avaler, digérer, ça.

glacé ['glæs(e)i] *a.* (*a*) (cuir) glacé; (*b*) *Cu:* **g. fruits,** fruits glacés.

glacial ['gleisiəl, -ʃəl] *a.* **1.** *Geol:* (érosion, vallée, etc.) glaciaire. **2.** (vent, etc.) glacial, -als.

glaciation [gleisi'eiʃ(ə)n, -ʃi'ei-] *n.* glaciation *f*.

glacier ['glæsiər] *n. Geol:* glacier *m*.

glad [glæd] *a.* **(gladder, gladdest) 1.** (*of pers.*) heureux; joyeux; content; **to be g. to hear sth.,** apprendre qch. avec plaisir; être heureux, bien content, d'apprendre qch.; **I'm g. you like him,** je suis content que vous l'aimiez; **he is only too g. to help you,** il ne demande pas mieux que de vous aider; **they would be g. of your help,** ils seraient bien heureux d'avoir votre aide; **it makes my heart g. to hear him,** cela me réjouit le cœur de l'entendre. **2.** (*a*) (cri) de plaisir; (sourire) de contentement; (*b*) **g. news,** *Lit:* **g. tidings,** bonne nouvelle; (*c*) *U.S:* **to give s.o. the g. hand,** faire un accueil chaleureux à qn (souvent dans un but intéressé); (*d*) *F:* **to put on one's g. rags,** (i) mettre ses plus beaux habits; (ii) (*of woman*) mettre une robe de soirée. **-ly** *adv.* avec plaisir, volontiers, avec joie; **I accept g.,** j'accepte avec grand plaisir.

gladden ['glæd(ə)n] *v.tr.* réjouir; rendre (qn) bien heureux; **it gladdens my heart to see them,** cela me réjouit le cœur de les voir.

glade [gleid] *n.* clairière *f*, éclaircie *f* (dans une forêt).

glad-hand ['glædhænd] *v.tr. & i. U.S:* (i) faire un accueil chaleureux (à qn), (ii) serrer la main à tout le monde (souvent dans un but intéressé).

gladiator ['glædieitər] *n.* gladiateur *m*.

gladiatorial [glædiə'tɔːriəl] *a.* gladiatorial, -aux; (combats) de gladiateurs.

gladiolus, *pl.* **-luses, -li** [glædi'ouləs, -ləsiz, -lai] *n. Bot:* glaïeul *m*.

gladness ['glædnis] *n.* joie *f*, allégresse *f*.

Gladstone ['glædstən] *Pr.n.* **G. bag,** sac américain.

glamorize ['glæməraiz] *v.tr.* donner une beauté factice à (qn); donner un faux éclat à (qch.); *Com:* donner du cachet à (des marchandises); **to g. war,** peindre la guerre sous de belles couleurs.

glamorous ['glæmərəs] *a.* enchanteur, -eresse, fascinateur, -trice; prestigieux, -euse.

glamour, *NAm: also* **glamor** ['glæmər] *n.* (*a*) fascination *f*; prestige *m* (d'un nom); éclat *m*; **the false g. of war,** le faux éclat de la guerre; (*b*) *F:* **g. boy,** beau mâle; **g. girl,** belle fille séduisante, pin up *f*.

glance¹ [glɑːns] *n.* **1.** coup *m* qui ricoche; coup en biais; ricochet *m*. **2.** regard *m*, coup d'œil; **at a g.,** d'un coup d'œil; **at first g.,** à première vue; au premier coup d'œil. **3.** trait *m* de lumière; éclat *m*.

glance² *v.i.* **1.** (*of bullet, etc.*) **to g. off,** dévier, ricocher. **2. to g. at s.o., at sth.,** jeter un regard sur qn, sur qch.; lancer un coup d'œil à qn; **to g. around,** jeter un regard autour de soi; **to g. through, over, sth.,** examiner rapidement qch.; parcourir, feuilleter (un livre). **3.** (*of steel, weapons*) étinceler; jeter des lueurs. **glancing** *a.* (*of blow*) oblique.

gland¹ [glænd] *n.* glande *f*; **lymphatic glands,** ganglions *mpl* lymphatiques; *Rept:* **poison g.,** glande à venin.

gland² *n. Mec.E:* **packing g.,** bague *f* de presse-étoupe.

glanders ['glændəz] *n.pl.* (*with sg. const.*) *Vet:* morve *f*.

glandular ['glændjulər] *a. Physiol: Med:* glandulaire; *Med:* **g. fever,** mononucléose infectieuse.

glare¹ ['glɛər] *n.* **1.** (*a*) éclat *m*, éblouissement *m*, lumière éblouissante (du soleil, etc.); **in the full g. of publicity,** sous les feux de la rampe; (*b*) éblouissement *m*, aveuglement *m* (d'un phare, etc.). **2.** fausse splendeur (de cirque forain). **3.** regard fixe et irrité.

glare² *v.i.* **1.** (*of sun, etc.*) briller d'un éclat éblouissant. **2. to g. at s.o.,** lancer un regard furieux, furibond, à qn. **glaring** *a.* **1.** (*a*) (*of light*) éblouissant, éclatant; (soleil) aveuglant; (*b*) (*of colour, etc.*) voyant; cru. **2.** (*of fact*) manifeste, patent, qui saute aux yeux; (*of injustice*) flagrant; (abus) scandaleux, choquant; (faute) grossière. **3. with g. eyes,** (i) d'un œil furieux; (ii) aux yeux menaçants.

glass¹ [glɑːs] *n.* **1.** verre *m*; (*a*) **the g. industry,** l'industrie *f* du verre; **cut g.,** verre taillé; **plate g.,** glace *f* de vitrage; **g. wool, paper,** laine *f*, papier *m*, de verre; **broken g.,** éclats *mpl* de verre; (*b*) **Bohemian g.,** verre de Bohême; **clear, frosted, g.,** verre clair, dépoli; **stained-g. window,** vitrail *m*, *pl.* vitraux; verrière *f*; **the stained g. of a church,** les vitraux, les verrières, d'une église; (*c*) vitre *f* (de fenêtre); glace (de voiture); verre (de montre, de lampe); **pane of g.,** vitre, glace; carreau *m*; (*d*) **g. cutting,** (i) taillage *m* de glaces; (ii) taille *f* du verre; **g. cutter,** (i) (*pers.*) coupeur *m* de verre, vitrier *m*; (ii) *Tls:* diamant *m* (de vitrier); coupe-verre *m inv*; **g. blowing,** soufflage *m* du verre; **g. blower,** souffleur *m* de verre; **g. manufacture,** verrerie *f*. **2.** (*a*) **(drinking) g.,** verre (à boire); **wine g.,** verre à vin; **g. of wine,** verre de vin; **liqueur g.,** verre à liqueur; **stem g.,** verre à pied; (*b*) *coll.* **table, oven, g.,** verrerie de table, allant au four; *Post: etc:* **g. with care,** fragile. **3.** (*a*) lentille *f* (d'un instrument d'optique); (*b*) **magnifying g.,** loupe *f*; verre grossissant; (*c*) **(field) g.,** lunette *f* d'approche; longue-vue *f*, *pl.* longues-vues; **field glasses,** jumelles *fpl*; **opera glasses,** jumelles de théâtre; (*d*) **glasses,** lunettes, verres; **dark glasses, sun glasses,** lunettes de soleil; **to wear glasses,** porter des lunettes. **4. (looking) g.,** glace, miroir *m*. **5.** baromètre *m* (à cadran); **the g. is falling,** le baromètre baisse. **6.** *Hort:* (i) châssis *m*; (ii) serre(s) *f*(*pl*); **grown under g.,** cultivé sous verre, en serre, sous châssis. **7. musical glasses,** harmonica *m*. **8.** *attrib.* de, en, verre; **g. bottle,** bouteille *f* de, en, verre; **g. door,** porte vitrée; porte de, en, verre; **g. partition,** cloison *m* de, en, verre; **g. roof,** verrière *f* (de gare, etc.); **g. case,** vitrine *f*; **to keep, display, sth. in a g. case, under g.,** garder, exposer, qch. sous verre; *Prov:* **people who live in g. houses shouldn't throw stones,** il faut être sans défauts pour critiquer autrui.

glass² *v.tr.* **to g. in,** vitrer (un balcon, etc.).

glasscloth ['glɑːsklɔθ] *n.* torchon *m* essuie-verres.

glassful ['glɑːsful] *n.* (plein) verre (d'eau, etc.)

glasshouse ['glɑːshaus] *n.* **1.** *Hort:* serre *f*. **2.** *Tchn:* verrerie *f*. **3.** *F:* prison *f* militaire, ours *m*.

glassware ['glɑːswɛər] *n.* articles *mpl* de verre; cristaux *mpl*; verrerie *f*.

glassworks ['glɑːswəːks] *n.pl.* (*usu. with sg. const.*) verrerie *f*, glacerie *f*; (*for crystal*) cristallerie *f*.

glassy ['glɑːsi] *a.* vitreux; **g. look, eye,** regard, œil, vitreux.

Glaswegian [glæs'wiːdʒiən] *a. & s.* (originaire, habitant, -ante) de Glasgow.

Glauber ['glɔːbər] *Pr.n. Pharm:* **Glauber's salt(s),** sel *m* (admirable) de Glauber; sulfate *m* de soude.

glaucoma [glɔː'koumə] *n. Med:* glaucome *m*.

glaucous ['glɔːkəs] *a.* glauque.

glaze¹ [gleiz] *n.* **1.** (*a*) lustre *m*, glacé *m* (du drap, du cuir); (*b*) aspect vitreux (de l'œil). **2.** *Cer:* glaçure *f*, vernis (luisant). **3.** *Cu:* glace *f* ((i) de jus de viande, (ii) de blanc d'œuf); dorure *f*. **4.** *Paint:* glacis *m*. **5.** *U.S:* verglas *m*.

glaze² **1.** *v.tr.* (*a*) vitrer (une fenêtre, une maison); (*b*) (i) glacer, lustrer (un tissu); vernir, vernisser, glacer (le cuir); lisser (le papier); (ii) *Cer:* glacer, vernisser, émailler (la poterie); vitrifier (les tuiles, etc.); (iii) *Cu:* glacer, dorer; (iv) *Paint:* glacer (un tableau); (v) *Phot:* émailler (une épreuve). **2.** *v.i.* **to g. (over),** (*of eye*) devenir vitreux. **glazed** *a.* (*a*) (*of roof, door*) vitré; **g.-in light,** verrine *f*; (*b*) (i) (tissu) glacé, lustré; (cuir) glacé, verni, vernissé; (papier) brillant, satiné; (ii) *Cer:* glacé, émaillé; (*of brick*) vitrifié; (iii) *Cu:* glacé, doré; (*c*) (œil, regard) vitreux. **glazing** *n.* **1.** (*a*) pose *f* des vitres; (*b*) glaçage *m*, lustrage *m*, vernissage *m*, satinage *m*; *Cer: Phot:* émaillage *m*. **2.** vitrerie *f*; **double g.,** double vitrage *m*.

glazier ['gleiziər] *n.* vitrier *m*.

gleam¹ [gliːm] *n.* (*a*) rayon *m*, lueur *f*, trait *m* (de lumière); **g. of hope,** lueur d'espoir; (*b*) reflet *m* (d'un couteau, etc.); miroitement *m* (d'un lac, etc.).

gleam² *v.i.* luire, reluire, rayonner; (*of water*) miroiter, brasiller. **gleaming** **1.** *a.* rayonnant, luisant, miroitant; **g. eyes,** yeux luisants. **2.** *n.* rayonnement *m*, miroitement *m*.

glean [gliːn] *v.tr.* glaner (du blé, des renseignements, etc.); *v.i.* faire la glane. **gleaning** *n.* **1.** glanage *m*, glane *f*. **2. gleanings,** (*a*) glanes *fpl*; (*b*) **gleanings from the newspapers,** glanures prises dans les journaux.

gleaner ['gliːnər] *n.* glaneur, -euse.

glebe [gliːb] *n. Ecc:* terre assignée à un bénéfice.

glee [gliː] *n.* **1.** joie *f*, allégresse *f*; **in high g.,** tout joyeux. **2.** *Mus:* petit chant à trois ou quatre parties (pour voix d'hommes); **g. club,** chorale *f*.

gleeful ['gliːful] *a.* joyeux, allègre. **-fully** *adv.* allègrement; plein de joie.

glen [glen] *n.* vallée étroite; gorge *f* (de montagne).

glib [glib] *a. Pej:* (*a*) (*of answer*) spécieux; (*b*) (*of speaker*) qui a de la faconde; **to have a g. tongue,** avoir la langue bien pendue. **-ly** *adv.* (*a*) spécieusement; (*b*) (parler) avec aisance; (répondre) sans hésiter.

glibness ['glibnis] *n.* **1.** spéciosité *f* (d'une excuse, etc.). **2.** faconde *f*; facilité *f* (de parole); bagou *m*.

glide¹ [glaid] *n.* **1.** (*a*) glissement *m*; (*b*) *Danc:* glissade *f*, glissé *m*. **2.** *Av:* (i) vol plané; (ii) descente *f* en (vol) plané; **g. path,** (i) trajectoire *f* de (vol) plané; (ii) trajectoire de descente, d'atterrissage. **3.** *Mus:* port *m* de voix; glissade. **4.** *Ling:* son *m* transitoire.

glide² *v.i.* (*a*) (se) glisser, couler; **to g. (along) over the water,** glisser sur l'eau; (*b*) (*of birds*) planer (dans l'air); (*c*) *Av:* (i) planer; faire un vol plané; (ii) faire du vol à voile. **gliding** *n.* (*a*) glissement *m*; (*b*) *Av:* (i) (vol *m*) plané (*m*); (ii) vol à voile; **g. club,** club *m* de vol à voile.

glider ['glaidər] *n. Av:* (*a*) (*pers.*) spécialiste *mf* du vol à voile; (*b*) (*machine*) planeur *m*.

glimmer¹ ['glimər] *n.* faible lueur *f* (d'une chandelle, etc.); reflet *m* (de l'eau, etc.); **g. of hope,** rayon *m*, lueur, d'espoir; **not the slightest g. of intelligence,** pas la moindre trace d'intelligence.

glimmer² *v.i.* jeter une faible lueur; (*of water*) miroiter; (*of sea*) brasiller. **glimmering 1.** *a.* (*of light*) faible; (*of water*) miroitant. **2.** *n.* émission *f* d'une faible lueur; miroitement *m*.

glimpse¹ [glim(p)s] *n.* vision momentanée (de qch.); **to catch a g. of s.o., sth.,** entrevoir qn, qch.

glimpse² *v.tr.* avoir une vision fugitive de (qch.); entrevoir (qn, qch.).

glint¹ [glint] *n.* trait *m*, lueur *f*, éclair *m* (de lumière); reflet *m* (d'un couteau, etc.); **hair with glints of gold,** chevelure *f* à, aux, reflets d'or.

glint² *v.i.* étinceler; (*of lights*) miroiter (dans l'eau); **his eyes were glinting with fury,** ses yeux étincelaient de fureur.

glisten ['glis(ə)n] *v.i.* étinceler, reluire, scintiller; (*of sea*) miroiter; **his forehead was glistening with perspiration,** la sueur perlait sur son front. **glistening** *a.* étincelant, luisant, scintillant; miroitant.

glitter¹ ['glitər] *n.* scintillement *m*, éclat *m*, brillant *m*.

glitter² *v.i.* briller, scintiller, (re)luire; *Prov:* **all that glitters is not gold,** tout ce qui brille n'est pas or. **glittering** *a.* brillant, éclatant, reluisant, resplendissant; (bijoux) qui lancent des éclairs.

gloaming ['gloumiŋ] *n.* crépuscule *m* (du soir); **in the g.,** à la brune.

gloat [glout] *v.i.* **to g. over, on, sth.,** (i) couver, dévorer, qch. des yeux; (ii) contempler qch. avec un plaisir mauvais, méchant; **to g. over s.o.'s misfortune,** triompher du malheur de qn. **gloating** *a.* (i) (œil) avide; (ii) (sourire, regard) d'exultation méchante.

global ['gloub(ə)l] *a.* **1.** (poids) global, -aux. **2.** mondial, -aux; planétaire; **g. war(fare),** guerre mondiale.

globe [gloub] *n.* globe *m*; (*a*) sphère *f*; (*b*) globe terrestre; **to go round the g.,** faire le tour du globe; (*c*) *Sch:* **terrestrial g., celestial g.,** globe terrestre, céleste; (*d*) globe (de lampe); (*e*) bocal *m*, -aux (pour poissons rouges); (*f*) *Anat:* globe (de l'œil); (*g*) *Hort:* **g. artichoke,** artichaut *m*; (*h*) *Meteor:* **g. lightning,** éclair *m* en boule.

globeflower ['gloubflauər] *n. Bot:* trolle *m*.

globetrotter ['gloubtrɔtər] *n. F:* touriste *mf* qui court le monde; globe-trotter *m*.

globetrotting ['gloubtrɔtiŋ] *n. F:* parcours *m* du monde (en globe-trotter); tourisme *m* à l'échelle mondiale.

globular ['glɔbjulər] *a.* globulaire, globuleux.

globule ['glɔbju:l] *n.* globule *m*, gouttelette *f* (d'eau, etc.).

globulin ['glɔbjulin] *n. Bio-Ch:* globuline *f*; **gamma g.,** gammaglobuline *f*.

glockenspiel ['glɔkənʃpi:l] *n. Mus:* glockenspiel *m*.

gloom [glu:m] *n.* **1.** obscurité *f*, ténèbres *fpl*; (*of landscape*) **shrouded in g.,** enténébré. **2.** assombrissement *m*, mélancolie *f*; tristesse *f* pessimiste; **to cast, throw, a g. over, on, the company,** jeter une ombre, un voile de tristesse, sur l'assemblée; **there is g. in the City,** la Bourse est pessimiste.

gloominess ['glu:minis] *n.* assombrissement *m*; (*a*) obscurité *f* (du temps, etc.); (*b*) tristesse *f*, air *m* sombre.

gloomy ['glu:mi] *a.* **1.** sombre, ténébreux. **2.** lugubre, morne, sombre; (pensées) noires; (front) ténébreux; **the weather is g.,** il fait sombre; **g. picture,** tableau poussé au noir; (*of pers.*) **to become g.,** se rembrunir. **-ily** *adv.* sombrement, mélancoliquement.

glorification [glɔ:rifi'keiʃ(ə)n] *n.* glorification *f*.

glorify ['glɔ:rifai] *v.tr.* (*a*) glorifier; rendre gloire à (Dieu, etc.); (*b*) exalter, célébrer; chanter les louanges de (qn). **glorified** *a.* **1.** *Theol:* glorifié; (corps) glorieux. **2.** (*of thg*) en plus grand, en mieux, embelli.

glorious ['glɔ:riəs] *a.* **1.** (règne, martyr) glorieux; (action) éclatante. **2.** (*a*) resplendissant, radieux; **g. in her youth and beauty,** resplendissante de jeunesse et de beauté; (*b*) magnifique, splendide; **what g. weather!** quel temps superbe! **-ly** *adv.* **1.** glorieusement. **2.** *F: O:* **g. drunk,** complètement ivre.

glory¹ ['glɔ:ri] *n.* gloire *f*. **1.** (*a*) honneur *m*, renommée *f*; **to cover oneself with g.,** se couvrir de gloire; (*b*) **to give g. to God,** rendre gloire à Dieu; **g. be to God!** gloire à Dieu! *F:* **g. be!** Dieu merci! (*c*) sujet *m* de gloire; **to be the g. of the age,** faire la gloire du siècle; (*d*) **eternal g.,** gloire éternelle; **the saints in g.,** les glorieux. **2.** splendeur *f*, éclat *m* (d'un spectacle, etc.); *F:* **in all her g.,** parée de ses plus beaux atours; **Spain, in the days of her g.,** l'Espagne, aux jours de sa splendeur. **3.** gloire (d'un saint, etc.).

glory² *v.i.* **to g. in sth.,** se glorifier de qch.; se faire gloire de qch.

glory(-)hole ['glɔ:rihoul] *n. F:* (*a*) capharnaüm *m*, (chambre *f* de) débarras (*m*); (*b*) *Nau:* poste *m* (i) des chauffeurs, (ii) des garçons de cabine.

gloss¹ [glɔs] *n.* (*a*) glose *f*; (*b*) commentaire *m*; (*c*) traduction *f* interlinéaire.

gloss² *v.tr.* gloser sur, annoter (un texte).

gloss³ *n.* **1.** lustre *m*, vernis *m*, poli *m*; brillant *m*; *Tex:* cati *m*; **to take the g. off sth.,** délustrer qch.; *Tex:* décatir (une étoffe); **g. paint,** peinture *f* vernis. **2.** vernis (de légalité, etc.).

gloss⁴ *v.tr.* **1.** lustrer, glacer; *Tex:* catir (l'étoffe); brillanter (le fil). **2.** farder, déguiser (la vérité); **to g. over,** farder (les faits); glisser sur, vernir (les défauts de qn); passer (un fait) sous silence.

glossary ['glɔsəri] *n.* glossaire *m*, lexique *m*.

glossiness ['glɔsinis] *n.* glacé *m*, lustre *m*, vernis *m*.

glossy ['glɔsi] *a.* lustré, glacé, brillant; (poil) lustré, (re)luisant; *Phot:* (papier) brillant; (épreuve) glacée; **g. magazine,** *n.* **glossy** (*pl.* **glossies**), revue illustrée.

glottal ['glɔt(ə)l] *a.* (*a*) *Anat: Ling:* glottal, -aux, glottique; *Ling:* **g. stop,** coup *m* de glotte.

glottis ['glɔtis] *n. Anat:* glotte *f*.

glove¹ [glʌv] *n.* (*a*) gant *m*; **you have to handle him with kid gloves (on),** il faut prendre des gants pour l'approcher; **rubber gloves,** gants en caoutchouc; **to put on one's gloves,** mettre ses gants, se ganter; **to take off one's gloves,** se déganter; (*b*) *Sp:* **boxing gloves,** gants de boxe; *Fig:* **the gloves were off,** on y allait carrément, sans ménagement; (*c*) *Aut:* **g. compartment,** boîte *f* à gants; **g. maker, manufacturer,** gantier, -ière; (*in large store*) **g. counter, department,** ganterie *f*.

glove² *v.tr.* ganter; **she is always well gloved,** elle est toujours bien gantée.

glover ['glʌvər] *n.* gantier, -ière.

glow¹ [glou] *n.* **1.** (*a*) lueur *f* (rouge); incandescence *f*; **the g. of the setting sun,** l'embrasement *m* du soleil couchant; (*b*) *El:* lueur, luminescence *f*, incandescence. **2.** (*a*) *Physiol:* sensation *f* de douce chaleur; réaction *f* (après un bain, etc.); (*b*) ardeur *f*, chaleur *f* (d'une passion). **3.** teint *m* rouge (de qn); vermeil *m* (des joues, etc.); **g. of health,** éclat *m* du teint dû à la santé.

glow² *v.i.* **1.** luire rouge, rougeoyer. **2.** (*a*) rayonner; **her face was glowing with pleasure,** son visage rayonnait de plaisir; (*of painting*) **to g. with colour,** rayonner de couleur; (*b*) **to be glowing with health,** éclater de santé; (*c*) **his cheeks were glowing,** il avait les joues en feu. **3.** sentir une douce chaleur (dans le corps); **to g. with enthusiasm,** brûler d'enthousiasme. **glowing** *a.* **1.** (chauffé au) rouge; incandescent, rougeoyant. **2.** (*of coal*) embrasé; (yeux) de braise. **3.** rayonnant; (joues) rouges. **4.** (*of colours, words*) chaleureux; (*of pers.*) ardent, enthousiaste; (description) en termes chaleureux; **to paint sth. in g. colours,** présenter qch. sous un jour des plus favorables; **to speak in g. terms of s.o.,** dire merveille de qn.

glower [ˈglauər] *v.i.,* braquer, fixer, les yeux (**at s.o.,** sur qn) (d'un air maussade, menaçant). **glowering** *a.* (air) maussade; (regard) farouche.

glow-worm [ˈglouwəːm] *n. Ent:* (*a*) ver luisant; (*b*) luciole *f.*

gloxinia [glɔkˈsiniə] *n. Bot:* gloxinia *m.*

glucose [ˈgluːkous] *n.* glucose *m.*

glue¹ [gluː] *n.* colle (forte); **fish g.,** colle de poisson *F:* **he sticks to me like g.,** il me suit partout.

glue² *v.* **(glued; gluing) 1.** (*a*) coller (à la colle forte); (*b*) **she watched the crowds passing, her face glued to the window,** son visage collé à la fenêtre, elle regardait passer la foule. **2.** *v.i.* **wood that glues well,** bois qui prend bien la colle.

gluepot [ˈgluːpɔt] *n.* pot *m* à colle.

gluey [ˈgluːi] *a.* gluant, poisseux.

glug¹ [glʌg] *n.* **g. (g.),** glouglou *m.*

glug² *v.i.* **(glugged)** faire glouglou.

glum [glʌm] *a.* (visage) renfrogné, maussade; (air) morne; **to look g.,** se renfrogner, *F:* faire une tête. **-ly** *adv.* d'un air maussade.

glumness [ˈglʌmnis] *n.* air *m* maussade.

glut¹ [glʌt] *n. Com:* (*a*) encombrement *m* (du marché); **it's a g. on the market,** c'est un article dont tout le monde est pourvu, dont personne ne veut plus; (*b*) surabondance *f* (d'une denrée, etc.); **there is a g. of pears,** le marché regorge de poires.

glut² *v.tr.* **(glutted)** (*a*) rassasier, assouvir (qn, sa faim, etc.); **to g. oneself,** se rassasier, se gorger (**on,** de); (*b*) *Com:* encombrer, inonder (le marché); **the market is glutted with this article,** le marché regorge de cet article.

glutamine [ˈgluːtəmain] *n. Ch:* glutamine *f.*

gluten [ˈgluːtən] *n.* gluten *m.*

glutinous [ˈgluːtinəs] *a.* glutineux.

glutton [ˈglʌt(ə)n] *n.* **1.** (*a*) glouton, -onne; goulu, -e, *F:* goinfre *m,* bâfreur, -euse; (*b*) **he's a g. for work,** c'est un bourreau de travail; **g. for punishment,** encaisseur *m.* **2.** *Z:* glouton, goulu.

gluttonous [ˈglʌtənəs] *a.* glouton, goulu. **-ly** *adv.* gloutonnement.

gluttony [ˈglʌtəni] *n.* gloutonnerie *f, F:* goinfrerie *f.*

glycerin(e) [ˈglisərin, -iːn], **glycerol** [ˈglisərɔl] *n. Ch: etc:* glycérine *f,* glycérol *m.*

glycol [ˈglaikɔl] *n. Ch:* glycol *m.*

gnarled [nɑːld] *a.* **1.** (*of tree*) (*a*) noueux, rugueux; (*b*) tordu. **2.** (*of hands, fingers*) noueux, déformé.

gnash [næʃ] *v.tr.* **to g. one's teeth,** grincer des dents. **gnashing** *n.* grincement *m* (des dents).

gnat [næt] *n. Ent:* moucheron *m*; moustique *m.*

gnaw [nɔː] *v.tr. & i.* (*p.t.* **gnawed;** *p.p.* **gnawed, gnawn**) (*a*) (*of rodent*) **to g. (at, into) sth.,** ronger qch.; (*of dog*) **to g. a bone,** ronger un os; (*b*) **gnawed by hunger, by remorse,** tenaillé par la faim, rongé par le remords. **gnawing** *a.* (*a*) (*of animal*) rongeur, -euse; (*b*) (*of hunger*) dévorant; tenaillant; (*of anxiety*) rongeant; **the g. pains of hunger,** les tiraillements de la faim.

gneiss [nais] *n. Geol:* gneiss *m.*

gnome [noum] *n. Myth:* gnome *m*; *F:* **the gnomes of Zürich,** les banquiers internationaux de Zürich.

gnosis [ˈnousis] *n. Theol:* gnose *f.*

gnostic [ˈnɔstik] *a. & n. Rel.H:* gnostique (*mf*).

gnosticism [ˈnɔstisizm] *n. Rel.H:* gnosticisme *m.*

gnu [nuː] *n. Z:* gnou *m.*

go¹ [gou] *n.* (*pl.* **goes**) *F:* **1.** (*a*) aller *m*; **to be always on the go,** être toujours à trotter, à courir; **to keep s.o. on the go,** faire trimer qn; (*b*) **it's all go,** on n'a pas une minute à soi; ça n'arrête pas. **2. to be full of, have plenty of, go,** être plein d'entrain; avoir de l'allant; **music full of go,** musique pleine de vie, de brio. **3.** (*a*) coup *m,* essai *m*; **to make a go of it,** y réussir; *Games:* **(it's) your go!** à vous de jouer! **to have a go at sth.,** (i) essayer (de faire qch.); (ii) s'attaquer à (un rôti, un pâté, etc.); **let's have a go!** essayons le coup! allons-y! **(it's) no go!** rien à faire! **at one go,** d'un (seul) coup; *Typew:* **she can do six copies at one go,** elle peut faire six exemplaires en une seule frappe; (*b*) (*at fair, etc.*) tour *m* (de manège, etc.); (*c*) *F:* accès *m* (de fièvre, etc.); attaque *f* (de grippe). **4.** *O:* **it's all the go,** ça fait fureur, rage. **5.** *a. Space: F:* **all systems are go,** tout est paré et en ordre de marche (pour le départ).

go² *v.* **(he goes;** *p.t.* **went** [went]; *p.p.* **gone** [gɔn]) (*the aux. is usu.* **have,** *occ.* **be) I.** *v.i.* **1.** aller; (*a*) **to go to a place,** aller, se rendre, à un endroit; **to go to Paris, to the country,** aller à Paris, à la campagne; **to go to France, to Japan,** aller en France, au Japon; **to go to church, to mass,** aller à l'église, à la messe; **to go to the doctor's,** aller consulter, aller chez, le médecin; **to go to prison,** être mis en prison; **to go to the lavatory,** aller aux toilettes; **to come and go,** aller et venir; **to go to s.o.'s house,** aller chez qn; **to go on a journey,** faire un voyage; aller en voyage; **to go for a walk,** aller se promener; faire une promenade; **to go on foot, by train, by car,** aller à pied, par le train, en voiture; **there he goes!** le voilà (qui passe)! **who goes there?** qui va là? **to go at 100 km an hour,** faire 100 km, du cent, à l'heure; **to go at full speed,** se lancer à toute vitesse; **you go first!** (i) partez le premier; (ii) à vous d'abord; (*b*) (*s.a. the compound verbs*) **to go up, down, across, along, a street,** monter, descendre, traverser, passer par, une rue; **to go into a room,** entrer dans une pièce; **to go behind s.o.'s back,** faire qch. derrière le dos de qn; **to go over, across, a bridge,** traverser un pont; **the ball went over the wall,** la balle a passé par-dessus le mur; **to go forward,** avancer; **to go ahead of s.o.,** devancer qn; (*c*) **which road goes to London?** quel est le chemin qui va à Londres? (*d*) **to go to school,** (i) aller à, (ii) fréquenter, l'école; **to go to sea,** se faire marin; **to go into the army,** (i) s'engager (dans l'armée); (ii) (*conscription*) partir au régiment; (*e*) **to go hungry, thirsty,** souffrir de la faim, de la soif; **wine that goes to the head,** vin qui monte à la tête; (*f*) *F:* (*of woman*) **to be six months gone,** être enceinte de six mois; (*g*) **to go one's own way,** faire à sa guise; *F:* **anything goes,** on fait ce qu'on veut; **to go one better (than s.o.),** surenchérir (sur qn); (*h*) **promotion goes by seniority,** l'avancement se fait à l'ancienneté. **2.** marcher; (*a*) **to set, get, a piece of machinery going,** mettre une machine en marche, en mouvement; *F:* **get going!** file! vas-y! **my watch won't go,** ma montre ne marche pas; **enough timber to keep three sawmills going,** assez de bois pour alimenter trois scieries; **to keep the conversation going,** entretenir la conversation; (*b*) **everything's going well,** tout marche bien; **things are going badly,** cela ne marche pas; **how are things going?** comment ça va? **if all goes well,** si tout va bien; **the rehearsal went well, badly,** la répétition a bien, mal, marché; **the way things are going,** au train où vont les choses; *F:* **when he gets going he never stops,** quand il est lancé, une fois lancé, il ne sait pas s'arrêter; **what he says goes,** c'est lui qui commande; (*c*) **the bell is going,** la cloche sonne; **it has just gone eight,** huit heures viennent de sonner; **it has gone four,** il est passé quatre heures; (*d*) **to go crack, bang,** faire crac, pan; **go like this with your left foot,** faites comme ça du pied gauche; (*e*) **I forget how the tune goes,** l'air m'échappe; **how does the chorus go?** quelles sont les paroles du refrain? (*f*) **which way will the decision go?** comment décidera-t-on? **I don't know how things will go,** je ne sais pas comment cela tournera; **judgment went for, against, the plaintiff,** l'arrêt fut prononcé en faveur du, contre le, demandeur; (*g*) **these colours don't go (together),** ces couleurs jurent; **the carpet doesn't go with the furniture,** le tapis n'est pas assorti aux meubles. **3.** (*a*) (*of time*) passer; **there were only five minutes to go before . . .,** il ne restait que cinq minutes avant . . .; **how's the time going?** combien de temps nous reste-t-il? (*b*) **the story goes that . . .,** à ce que l'on raconte; **as the saying goes,** selon le dicton; **as things go today,** par le temps qui court; **that's not dear as things go,** ce n'est pas cher au prix où sont les choses; (*c*) **to go by, under, a false name,** être connu sous un faux nom; (*d*) **it goes without saying that . . .,** il va de soi que . . .; **that goes without saying,** cela va sans (le) dire. **4.** (*a*) partir; s'en aller; **after, when, I had gone,** après mon départ; **we must go, must be going,** il est temps de partir; **let me go,** laissez-moi partir; **go!** (i) allez-vous-en! (ii) *Sp:* partez! **from the word go,** dès le commencement; (*b*) **a hundred employees will have to go,** il va falloir mettre cent employés à la porte; (*c*) disparaître; **my hat has gone,** mon chapeau a disparu; **it's all gone,** il n'y en a plus; **that's the way the money goes,** voilà comme l'argent file; **her sight is going,** elle est en train de perdre la vue; (*d*) se casser; (*of cable*) partir; **the spring went,** le ressort s'est cassé; *El:* **a fuse went,** un plomb a sauté; **my dress is going at the seams,** ma robe se déchire aux coutures; (*e*) **to going cheap,** se vendre (à) bon marché; **they are going at ten francs each,** ils sont en vente, en solde, à dix francs pièce; **the lot went for £20,** le lot fut adjugé à £20; **going! going! gone!** une fois! deux fois! adjugé! (*f*) **let's see if there's any lunch going,** allons voir si le déjeuner est prêt; **there are drinks going in the drawing room,** on sert l'apéritif dans le salon; (*g*) mourir; **his wife went first,** sa femme est morte avant lui; **when I am gone, after I have gone,** après ma mort. **5.** (*a*) **to go and do sth.,** aller faire qch.; **to go to dinner with s.o.,** aller dîner avec qn, chez qn; **to go to see, go and see, s.o.,** aller voir qn; **to go and look for sth.,** aller chercher qch.; *F:* **and then he went and got married!** et puis il a eu l'idée de se marier! *P:* **now you've (been and) gone and done it!** vous en avez fait une belle! ça y est cette fois-ci! (*b*) **he went (forward) to help her, but . . .,** il est allé pour l'aider, il a fait un mouvement pour l'aider, mais . . .; (*c*) **I'm going to have my own way,** je veux faire à ma tête; **I'm not going to be cheated,** je ne me laisserai pas abuser; (*d*) (*intention*) **I was going to walk,** j'avais l'intention d'y aller à pied; **I'm going to France for my holiday,** je compte passer mes vacances en France; (*e*) (*aux. forming an immediate future*) **I'm going to tell you a story,** je vais vous raconter une histoire; **the shortage is not going to last,** la disette ne durera pas; (*f*) **to go riding,** (aller) se promener à cheval; **to go hunting, fishing,** aller à la chasse, à la pêche; **to go looking for sth.,** partir à la recherche de qch.; **there you go again!** vous voilà reparti! **6.** (*a*) **to go to law,** avoir recours à la justice; **to go to war,** entrer en guerre; **to go to press,** mettre sous presse; **I will go up to £100,** je veux bien payer jusqu'à £100; (*b*) *Gaming:* **to go £10,** risquer £10; (*c*) *Cards:* **to go two, three, no trumps,** annoncer deux, trois, sans atout; **to go one better,** renchérir. **7.** (*a*) **too big to go into the basket,** trop grand pour entrer dans le panier; **the key won't go in(to) the lock,** la clef n'entre pas dans la serrure; (*b*) **where does this book go?** où faut-il mettre, où est la place de, ce livre? (*c*) *Mth: F:* **six into twelve goes twice,** douze divisé par six fait deux; **four into three won't go,** trois n'est pas divisible par quatre. **8. the proceeds will go to charity,** les bénéfices seront distribués, iront, à des œuvres charitables; **his estate will go to his eldest son,** son fils aîné va hériter de la propriété. **9.** contribuer (à qch.); **the qualities that go to make a great man,** les qualités qui constituent un grand homme; **ingredients that go to make a good dish,** ingrédients qui contribuent à faire un bon plat; **to go to prove sth.,** servir à prouver qch.; **it only goes to show that you can't be too careful,** cela montre qu'on ne peut jamais prendre trop de précautions. **10.** s'étendre; **the garden goes down to the river,** le jardin s'étend jusqu'à la rivière; **the difference goes deep,** il y a une profonde différence; **as far as the style goes,** quant au style; pour ce qui est du style. **11.** (*a*) devenir; **to go mad,** devenir fou; **to go Communist,** devenir communiste; **he went cold all over,** son sang s'est glacé; **to go white, red,** rougir, blanchir; **my hair is going grey,** mes cheveux grisonnent, deviennent gris; (*b*) (*of pers.*) **to go to the bad,** mal tourner; (*c*) *F:* **let the rest of them go hang!** tant pis pour les autres! **12.** (*a*) **to let go,** lâcher prise; **let me go!** lâchez-moi! *Nau:* **to let a rope go,** laisser aller, lâcher, un cordage; (*b*) **to let oneself go,** (i) s'abandonner; se laisser aller; (ii) donner carrière à ses sentiments, etc.; (*c*) **we'll let it go at that,** tenons-nous-en là; cela ira comme ça; **well, let it go at that!** passons! **13.** *F:* (*a*) **to go it,** aller grand train; se lancer; (*b*) **to go it alone,** agir tout seul. **go about** *v.i.* (*a*) (i) circuler; aller çà et là; (*of rumour*) courir; (ii) *Nau:* virer de bord; (iii) *Mil: etc:* faire demi-tour; (*b*) (*with cogn. acc.*) (i) **to go about the country,** parcourir le pays; **to go about the streets,** circuler dans les rues; (ii) **to go about one's work,** vaquer à son travail; **how to go about it,** comment s'y prendre. **go along** *v.i.* (*a*) suivre son chemin; **I check the figures as I go along,** je vérifie les chiffres à mesure; (*b*) **to go along with s.o.,** coopérer avec qn; **to go along with sth.,** approuver, accepter, qch. **go around** *v.i.* circuler; voyager; (*of rumour*) courir. **go at** *v.* s'attaquer à (qn, qch.); **to go at it hard,** ne pas y aller de main morte. **go away** *v.i.* (*a*) s'en aller, partir; **to go away on business, for the weekend,** s'absenter pour affaires, pour le week-end; (*b*) **to go away with sth.,** emporter qch; (*c*) *F:* **go away!** va t'en! **go back** *v.i.* (*a*) (i) s'en retourner; **to go back home,** rentrer chez soi; (ii) retourner en arrière; rebrousser chemin; **to go back the same way,** revenir, retourner, par le même chemin; (iii) reculer; **to go back two paces,** faire deux pas en arrière; **to go back to the beginning,** recommencer; **he went back to his reading,** il s'est replongé dans sa lecture; **to go back to sleep,** se rendormir; **to go back to one's old ways,** retomber dans ses anciennes habitudes; (*b*) remonter (à l'origine de qch.); **his family goes back to the Crusades,** sa famille descend des Croisés; (*c*) **to go back on one's word,** revenir sur sa parole; manquer à sa parole. **go by** *v.i.* (*a*) passer; (*of time*) s'écouler; **as the years go by,** à mesure que les années passent; **to watch people going by,** regarder passer les gens; **to let an opportunity go by,** laisser passer une occasion; (*b*) **to go by s.o., sth.,** se régler sur qn, sur qch.; **to go by appearances,** juger d'après les apparences. **go down** *v.i.* (*a*) descendre; (*in lift*) **going down!** on descend! pour descendre! *Sch:* **to go down (from the university),** (i) quitter l'université (à la fin de ses études); (ii) partir en vacances (à la fin du trimestre); (*b*) (*of sun*) se coucher; (*c*) (*of ship*) sombrer; (*d*) **to go down well,** (i) (*of drink*) se laisser boire; (*of food*) se laisser manger; (ii) (*of entertainment, speech*) plaire; être bien reçu; (*e*) **he went down with a thud,** il est tombé lourdement; **to go down on one's knees,** se mettre, se jeter, à genoux; *F:* **to go d. with flu,** attraper la grippe; (*f*) *Cards:* (*bridge*) perdre le coup; ne pas faire autant de levées qu'on en a annoncé; (*g*) (*of floods, temperature*) baisser, s'abaisser; (*of wind*) baisser, tomber; (*of prices, value*) baisser; **to go d. in s.o.'s estimation,** baisser dans l'estime de qn; (*h*) (*of swelling*) se désenfler, se dégonfler; (*of tyre, balloon*) se dégonfler; (*i*) continuer (jusqu'à la fin de la page, etc.); (*j*) *U.S: F:* **what's going down?** qu'est-ce qui se passe? **go for** *v.tr. F:* (*a*) (i) attaquer, tomber sur (qn); (*to dog*) **go for him!** pille! pille! (ii) attaquer (qn), chercher noise à (qn); **they went for each other in court,** ils se sont empoignés, engueulés, devant le tribunal; (*b*) **I don't go for him much,** il ne me dit pas grand-chose. **go in** *v.i.* (*a*) entrer; rentrer; **let's go in!** entrons! (*b*) (*of sun*) se cacher; (*c*) *Cr:* prendre son tour au guichet; (*d*) **to go in for sth.,** faire qch.; s'occuper de qch.; **to go in for painting,** faire de la peinture; **to go in for teaching,** entrer dans l'enseignement; **to go in for an examination,** se présenter à un examen; **to go in for a competition,** prendre part à un concours; (*e*) **to go in with s.o.,** se joindre à qn (dans une entreprise, etc.); (*f*) *Mil: etc: F:* attaquer. **going 1.** *a.* (*a*) qui marche; **to start, set, sth. g.,** mettre qch. en marche; **the business is a g. concern,** la maison est en plein activité; **to be sold as a g. concern,** à vendre avec fonds; (*b*) **the g. price, rate,** le prix courant, actuel; (*c*) (*in compounds*) **slow-g., fast-g.,** qui marche lentement, vite; **theatre-g.,** qui fréquente les théâtres. **2.** *n.* (*a*) (i) aller *m*; **comings and goings,** allées *fpl* et venues *fpl*; (ii) marche *f* (de qn, d'une machine); **that's very good g.!** c'est une bonne allure! voilà qui n'est pas mal du tout! *Typ:* **g. to press,** mise *f* sous presse; **g. to law, to war,** recours *m* à la justice, à la guerre; **theatre g.,** visites *fpl* au théâtre; (*b*) départ *m*; (*c*) état *m* du sol; **the g. is rough,** le chemin est rude; *Rac:* **good, heavy, g.,** terrain bon, lourd; **to get out while the going's good,** partir pendant que la voie est libre; **it's heavy g. getting him to talk,** on a du mal à le faire parler; (*d*) *attrib.* **g.-away dress,** robe *f* de voyage de noces; (*e*) **g. back,** (i) retour *m*; (ii) recul *m*; **g. back on one's word,** manque *m* de parole; (*f*) **g. out,** sortie(s) *f* (*pl*); (*g*) *F:* **to give s.o. a g. over,** (i) fouiller qn; (ii) battre qn; (*h*) *F:* **goings on,** (i) événements *mpl*; (ii) activités *fpl*; **strange goings on,** des choses étranges qui se passent; **what extraordinary goings on!** (i) quelles histoires extraordinaires! (ii) voilà une conduite extraordinaire! **go into** *v.tr.* (*a*) **to go into details,** entrer dans des détails; (*b*) **to go into mourning,** prendre le deuil; **to go into hysterics,** avoir une crise de nerfs; **to go into fits of laughter,** éclater de rire; (*c*) examiner, étudier (une question); mettre (une question) à l'étude; **I shall go into the matter,** je vais m'occuper de l'affaire. **gone** *a.* (*a*) *F:* **to be g.,** être (i) fichu, (ii) endormi, (iii) mort; **to be pretty far g.,** être dans un état avancé (d'ivresse, etc.); (*b*) *P:* **g. on s.o.,** amoureux, toqué, de qn. **go off** *v.i.* (*a*) partir, s'en aller, s'éloigner; *Th:* quitter la scène; *F:* **she's gone off and left him,** elle l'a quitté; **to go off with sth.,** emporter, enlever, qch.; (*b*) (*of gun*) partir, se décharger; **the pistol didn't go off,** le pistolet a raté; (*c*) *F:* s'endormir; (*d*) *F:* (*of feeling*) passer; (*of tennis player*) perdre de sa forme; (*of woman*) perdre de sa beauté; (*e*) *F:* (*of food*) se détériorer; (*of wine*) perdre de son arôme; (*of milk*) tourner; (*of butter*) rancir; (*of fish, meat*) se gâter; (*f*) **everything went off well,** tout a bien marché, tout s'est bien passé; (*g*) perdre le goût de (qch.); **I've gone off cheese,** je n'aime plus le fromage; **I've completely gone off him,** j'ai commencé à le prendre en grippe. **go on** *v.i.* (*a*) continuer; **time goes on,** le temps passe; **I must go on with my work,** il me faut continuer mon travail; **go on looking!** cherchez toujours! **I have enough to be going on with,** j'en ai assez pour le moment; **how he goes on!** impossible de l'arrêter! **he's going on for forty,** il va sur la quarantaine; (*b*) **to go on to another question,** passer à une autre question; *P:* **go on (with you)!** allons donc! (*c*) marcher; **this has been going on for years,** cela dure depuis des années; **what's going on here?** qu'est-ce qui se passe ici? (*d*) *F:* se conduire; **you mustn't go on like that,** il ne faut pas vous laisser aller comme ça; (*e*) *P:* faire une scène; **he's always going on at me,** il est toujours à me gronder; (*f*) *Th:* monter en scène; entrer en scène. **go out** *v.i.* (*a*) (i) sortir; *W.Tel: TV:* (*of programme*) être diffusé; **she was dressed to go out,** elle était en tenue de ville; **to go out for a walk,** faire une promenade (à pied); **to go out to dinner with friends,** (aller) dîner chez des amis; **he doesn't go out much,** il sort peu; **to go out (on strike),** se mettre en grève; *F:* **he was going out with her for two years before they got married,** il l'a fréquentée pendant deux ans avant de l'épouser; *Fig:* **my heart went out to him,** (i) je l'ai trouvé tout de suite sympathique; (ii) j'ai ressenti de la pitié pour lui; (*b*) passer de mode; se démoder; (*c*) (*of fire*) s'éteindre; (*d*) (*of tide*) baisser, se retirer. **go over** *v.i.* (*a*) examiner, revoir (un compte, un rapport, etc.); passer (des papiers, etc.) en revue; relire (un document); repasser, revoir (une leçon); **to go over sth. in one's mind,** repasser qch. dans son esprit; (*b*) **to go over to the enemy,** passer à l'ennemi; **to go over to the other side,** changer de parti; (*c*) (*of play*) faire son petit effet, passer la rampe; *F:* **to go over big,** décrocher le grand succès. **go round** *v.i.* (*a*) faire un détour; **to go a long way round,** faire un grand détour; (*b*) (*of wheel*) tourner; **my head's going round,** la tête me tourne; (*c*) (*of rumour*) circuler, courir; (*of bottle*) circuler; (*d*) **to make the food go round,** ménager la nourriture; **there isn't enough to go round,** il n'y en a pas assez pour tout le monde. **go through** *v.i.* (*a*) remplir (des formalités); subir, essuyer (de rudes épreuves); (*b*) examiner (des documents); repasser (une leçon, des comptes); trier (sa garde-robe); *Cust:* visiter, fouiller (des valises); **to go through s.o.'s pockets,** fouiller dans les poches de qn; **to go through all one's money,** dépenser tout son argent; (*c*) **the bill has gone through,** la loi a passé; **the deal didn't go through,** le marché n'a pas été conclu; **I mean to go through with it,** j'irai jusqu'au bout. **go under** *v.i.* (*a*) (*of drowning man*) couler, enfoncer; (*b*) succomber, sombrer; faire faillite. **go up** *v.i.* (*a*) monter; **to go up to bed,** monter se coucher; **to go up in an aircraft,** monter en avion; (*in lift*) **going up!** on monte! pour monter! *Th:* **before the curtain goes up,** avant le lever du rideau; **a shout went up from the crowd,** un cri s'éleva de la foule; (*b*) *Sch:* **to go up (to Oxford),** entrer à l'université (d'Oxford); (*c*) (*of prices, temperature, etc.*) monter; hausser; **bread is going up,** le pain augmente; **to go up in s.o.'s estimation,** monter dans l'estime de qn; (*d*) (*of mine*) sauter; **to go up in flames,** se mettre à flamber. **go with** *v.i.* (*a*) marcher, aller, de pair avec (qch.); (*b*) s'accorder avec (qch.); (*of colours*) se marier avec (une teinte); s'assortir. **go without** *v.i.* (*a*) se passer de (qch.); (*b*) manquer de (qch.); être privé de (qch.).

goad[1] [goud] *n.* aiguillon *m*; pique-bœuf *m*, *pl.* pique-bœufs.

goad[2] *v.tr.* aiguillonner, piquer (les bœufs); piquer, stimuler (la curiosité de qn); **to g. s.o. on,** aiguillonner, inciter, qn; **to g. s.o. into doing sth.,** talonner qn jusqu'à ce qu'il fasse qch.

go-ahead ['gouəhed] *F:* **1.** *a.* (*a*) plein d'allant; actif; entreprenant; **g.-a. business man,** homme d'affaires entreprenant; (*b*) **go-a. signal,** feu vert. **2.** *n.* **to give s.o. the go-a.,** donner à qn le feu vert.

goal [goul] *n.* but *m*; (*a*) **my g. is in sight,** j'approche de mon but, du but; (*b*) *Fb:* **to score a g.,** marquer un but; **to keep g.,** garder le but; **g. line,** ligne *f* de but; **g. mouth,** entrée *f* du but.

goalkeeper ['goulki:pər], *F:* **goalie** ['gouli] *n. Sp:* gardien *m* de but, *F:* le goal.

goalless ['goullis] *a. Sp:* **g. draw,** match *m* sans but marqué; match nul.

goalpost ['goulpoust] *n.* montant *m*, poteau *m*, de but.

goat [gout] *n.* **1.** chèvre *f*; **she g.,** bique *f*; **he g.,** bouc *m*; **goat's milk,** lait *m* de chèvre; **g. cheese, goat's milk cheese,** fromage *m* de chèvre; *F:* **it gets my g.,** ça me met en boule, me tape sur les nerfs. **2.** *Astr:* **the G.,** le Capricorne.

goatee [gou'ti:] *n.* barbiche *f*; bouc *m*.

goatherd ['goutha:d] *n.* chevrier, -ière.

goatskin ['goutskin] *n.* **1.** peau *f* de chèvre; peau de bique. **2.** (*bottle*) outre *f* (en peau de bouc).

goatsucker ['goutsʌkər] *n. Orn:* engoulevent *m*.

gob [gɔb] *n.* **1.** *F:* gros morceau (de qch.). **2.** *P:* crachat *m*. **3.** *P:* bouche *f*, gueule *f*; **shut your g.!** fermé-la! ta gueule!

gobble¹ ['gɔbl] *v.tr. & i.* **to g. sth. (up),** avaler qch. gloutonnement; dévorer, bâfrer, *F:* bouffer, qch.; (*to child*) **don't g.!** mange plus lentement!

gobble² *n.* (*of turkey*) glouglou *m*.

gobble³ *v.i.* (*of turkey*) glouglouter.

gobbledegook, gobbledygook ['gɔb(ə)ldigu:k] *n. F:* charabia *m*; jargon administratif.

go-between ['goubitwi:n] *n.* intermédiaire *mf*; **to act, serve, as a go-b.,** servir d'intermédiaire (**to,** à).

goblet ['gɔblit] *n.* **1.** *Lit:* coupe *f*. **2.** *Com:* verre *m* à pied.

goblin ['gɔblin] *n.* gobelin *m*, lutin *m*.

gobstopper ['gɔbstɔpər] *n. F:* gros bonbon en boule.

go-by ['goubai] *n. F:* **to give s.o., sth., the go-by,** (i) éviter (qn) (ii) oublier (qn, qch).

gocart, go-cart ['gouka:t] *n.* **1.** (*a*) (*for babies*); poussette *f*; (*b*) charrette à bras. **2.** *Sp:* kart *m*.

god [gɔd] *n.* **1.** (*a*) dieu *m*; **the g. of war,** le dieu des combats; **feast (fit) for the gods,** festin *m* digne des dieux; *F:* **little tin g.,** petit dieu en toc; **to make a g. of money,** se faire un dieu de l'argent; (*b*) *Th: F:* **the gods,** le poulailler, le paradis. **2. God,** Dieu; **G. willing,** s'il plaît à Dieu; **I wish to G. . . .,** plût à Dieu . . .; **in God's name, in the name of G.,** au nom de Dieu; *F:* **what in God's name are you doing?** que faites-vous là, grand Dieu! **thank G.!** Dieu merci! *P:* **oh G.! my G.!** mon Dieu! grand Dieu!

god-awful ['gɔdɔ:ful] *a. P:* dégueulasse.

godchild, *pl.* **-children** ['gɔdtʃaild, -tʃildrən] *n.* filleul, *f.* filleule.

God-damn ['gɔd(d)æm] **1.** *int. A:* sapristi! nom de Dieu! **2.** *a.* (*more often* **god-damned**) *P:* sacré; **this g. idiot,** ce sacré imbécile.

god(-)daughter ['gɔddɔ:tər] *n.f.* filleule.

goddess ['gɔdis] *n.f.* déesse.

godfather ['gɔdfa:ðər] *n.m.* parrain.

God-fearing *a.* (homme) craignant Dieu.

godforsaken ['gɔdfəseik(ə)n] *a.* misérable; *F:* (endroit) perdu; **what a g. country!** quel bled!

godhead ['gɔdhed] *n.* divinité *f*.

godless ['gɔdlis] *a.* (*of pers., action, etc.*) impie.

godlike ['gɔdlaik] *a.* de Dieu; d'un dieu; divin.

godliness ['gɔdlinis] *n.* piété *f*.

godly ['gɔdli] *a.* dévot, pieux, saint; **to lead a g. life,** vivre pieusement, saintement.

godmother ['gɔdmʌðər] *n.f.* marraine.

godparent ['gɔdpɛərənt] *n.* parent spirituel; **my godparents,** mon parrain et ma marraine.

godsend ['gɔdsend] *n.* aubaine *f*; **this money is a g. to him,** cet argent lui tombe du ciel.

godson ['gɔdsʌn] *n.m.* filleul.

goer ['gouər] *n.* (*a*) (*of horse, vehicle, etc.*) **good, bad, g.,** bon, mauvais, marcheur; (*b*) **cinema, theatre, g.,** habitué, -ée, du cinéma, du théâtre; (*c*) personne active; **he's a g.,** il est plein d'allant.

goffer¹ ['gɔfər, 'goufər] *n.* **1.** *Cost:* godron *m*, tuyau *m*. **2.** fer *m* à tuyauter, à gaufrer; godron *m*.

goffer² *v.tr. Laund:* godronner, tuyauter. **goffering** *n.* **1.** (*a*) *Laund:* gaufrage *m*; tuyautage *m*; **g. tongs, g. iron(s),** fer *m* à tuyauter.

go-getter ['gougetər] *n. F:* arriviste *mf*.

goggle ['gɔgl] *v.i.* (*a*) rouler de gros yeux; **to g. at s.o.,** regarder qn en roulant de gros yeux; (*b*) (*of eyes*) être saillants.

gogglebox ['gɔg(ə)lbɔks] *n. F:* la télé.

goggle-eyed ['gɔg(ə)laid] *a. F:* (*a*) qui a des yeux à fleur de tête, en boules de loto; (*b*) (regarder) les yeux écarquillés.

goggles ['gɔg(ə)lz] *n.pl.* lunettes (protectrices); *Ind:* lunettes de travail; **snow g.,** lunettes d'alpiniste.

go-go ['gougou] *n.* **g.-g. dancer,** danseuse *f* (dans une boîte de nuit, etc.).

goitre, *NAm:* **goiter** ['gɔitər] *n. Med:* goitre *m*.

go-kart ['gouka:t] *n. Sp:* kart *m*; **go-k. racing,** karting *m*.

gold [gould] *n.* or *m*; (*a*) **g. digger,** (i) chercheur *m* d'or; (ii) *F:* (*woman*) croqueuse *f* de diamants; *F:* **fool's g.,** pyrite *f* de fer; *Hist:* **the g. rush,** la ruée vers l'or; (*b*) *Metall:* **fine g.,** or fin; **pure g.,** or pur; **g. content,** teneur *f* en or; (*c*) or massif; **g. plate,** or orfévré; **g.-plated,** plaqué (d')or; **g. leaf, g. foil,** feuille *f* d'or; or en feuille; **g. brooch, necklace,** broche *f*, collier *m*, d'or, en or; **g. medal,** (*at Olympic Games, etc.*) *n.* **gold,** médaille d'or; *Cost:* **g. lace,** galon *m* d'or; **g. lamé dress,** robe lamée d'or; **g.-rimmed spectacles,** lunettes *fpl* à monture d'or; (*d*) *Hist:* **the Field of the Cloth of G.,** le camp du Drap d'or; (*e*) *Dent:* **g. filling, stopping,** obturation *f* à l'or, en or; **g. crown,** couronne *f* en or; (*f*) *Fin:* **g. currency, money,** monnaie *f* d'or; pièces *fpl* d'or, en or; **g. coin,** pièce d'or; **g. bullion,** or en barres, en lingots; **to pay s.o. in g.,** payer qn en or; **g. reserve,** réserve *f* d'or; **the g. standard,** l'étalon *m* d'or, l'étalon-or *m*; (*g*) *a. & n.* (couleur *f* de l')or; **g. dress,** robe *f* couleur de l'or; **the reds and golds of autumn,** les rouges *mpl* et les ors de l'automne; **old g.,** vieil or *inv*.

goldbeater ['gouldbi:tər] *n.* batteur, -euse, d'or.

goldcrest ['gouldkrest] *n. Orn:* roitelet huppé.

golden ['gould(ə)n] *a.* (*a*) d'or; **the G. Fleece,** la Toison d'or; **to worship the g. calf,** adorer le veau d'or; (*b*) **g. hair,** cheveux *mpl* d'or; *Geog:* **the G. Horn,** la Corne d'Or; *Orn:* **g. eagle,** aigle royal; **g. pheasant,** faisan doré; *Bot:* **g. rod,** verge *f* d'or; (*c*) **the g. age,** l'âge d'or; **g. rule,** règle *f* d'or; **g. opportunity,** occasion *f* magnifique; **the g. mean,** le juste milieu; (*d*) **g. wedding,** noces *fpl* d'or; (*e*) (sourire) radieux, accueillant.

goldeneye ['gouldənai] *n. Orn:* garrot *m* à œil d'or, canard *m* garrot.

goldfield ['gouldfi:ld] *n.* champ *m*, région *f*, aurifère.

goldfinch ['gouldfin(t)ʃ] *n. Orn:* chardonneret *m*.

goldfish ['gouldfiʃ] *n. Ich:* poisson *m* rouge.

goldmine ['gouldmain] *n.* mine *f* d'or; *F:* **a regular g.,** une vraie mine d'or; une affaire d'or.

goldsmith ['gouldsmiθ] *n.* orfèvre *m*; **goldsmith's work,** orfèvrerie *f*.

gold-tipped ['gould'tipt] *a.* à bout doré.

golf¹ [gɔlf] *n.* golf *m*; **clock g.,** jeu *m* de l'horloge; **g. ball,** balle *f* de golf; **g. club,** (i) crosse *f* de golf, club *m*; (ii) club de golf; **g. course, links,** terrain *m*, parcours *m*, de golf; un golf.

golf² *v.i.* jouer au golf; **I went golfing yesterday,** hier j'ai fait du golf.

golfer [ˈgɔlfər] *n.* golfeur, -euse; joueur, -euse, de golf.

Goliath [gəˈlaiəθ] *Pr.n.m. B.Hist:* Goliath.

golliwog [ˈgɔliwɔg] *n.* poupée *f* en étoffe représentant un nègre.

golly [ˈgɔli] *int. F: O:* fichtre! mince (alors)!

golosh [gəˈlɔʃ] *n.* = GALOSH.

gonad [ˈgɔnæd, ˈgou-] *n. Biol:* gonade *f*.

gondola [ˈgɔndələ] *n.* **1.** *Nau:* gondole *f*. **2.** (*a*) gondole, nacelle *f* (d'un ballon); (*b*) *NAm:* nacelle, cabine *f*, téléphérique. **3.** *NAm: Rail:* **g. (car),** wagon plat.

gondolier [gɔndəˈliər] *n.* gondolier *m*.

gone. *see* GO².

goner [ˈgɔnər] *n. F:* (*a*) mort, morte; **I thought he was a g.,** je pensais qu'il allait mourir, crever; (*b*) type fini, fichu; **he's a g.,** il est fichu, foutu.

gong [gɔŋ] *n.* (*a*) gong *m*; **to sound the g.,** faire retentir le gong; (*b*) *F:* médaille *f*; **he was wearing all his gongs,** il exhibait toute sa batterie de cuisine.

gonorrhoea [gɔnəˈriə] *n. Med:* gonorrhée *f*.

goo [guː] *n. F:* **1.** substance collante. **2.** sentimentalité excessive, à l'eau de rose.

good [gud] **I.** *a.* **(better, best)** bon. **1.** (*a*) **g. wine,** bon vin; **g. handwriting,** belle écriture; **g. weather,** beau temps; **g. to eat,** bon à manger; **this looks g.,** cela a l'air bon; **that smells g.,** cela sent bon; **this is g. enough for me,** cela fera mon affaire; (*of story, joke*) **that's a g. one,** en voilà une bonne; **to have a g. time,** s'amuser (bien); **he's too g. for that job,** il mérite une meilleure situation; **g. doctor,** un médecin de premier ordre; **to have g. sight,** avoir une bonne vue, de bons yeux; **g. nature,** bon naturel; **g. living,** bonne chère; (*b*) (*of food*) bon (à manger), en bon état; **is the meat still g.?** est-ce que la viande est encore bonne? (*c*) **g. reason,** bonne raison, raison valable; **he, his credit, is g. for £25,000,** il peut payer jusqu'à £25.000, il est bon pour £25.000; **this car ought to be g. for another five years,** cette voiture devrait me faire encore cinq ans; *F:* **he's g. for another ten years,** il en a encore bien pour dix ans à vivre; (*d*) avantageux; **g. opportunity,** bonne occasion; **to be in a g. position to do sth.,** être bien placé pour faire qch.; **it is not always g. to . . .,** il n'est pas toujours bon de . . .; **to earn g. money,** gagner largement sa vie; (*e*) heureux; **g. news,** bonnes, heureuses, nouvelles; **too g. to be true,** trop beau pour y croire, pour être vrai; **g. for you! g. show!** *Austr:* **g. on you!** tant mieux pour toi, pour vous! **very g.!** (i) très bien! parfait! (ii) très bien, je m'en charge; **it's g. to be alive!** il fait bon vivre! (*f*) **g. morning! g. day! g. afternoon!** bonjour (monsieur, etc.); **to wish s.o. a g. night,** souhaiter une bonne nuit à qn; (*g*) **this medicine is very g. for coughs,** ce remède est très bon pour la toux; **beer is not g. for me,** la bière ne me vaut rien; **to drink more than is g. for one,** boire plus que de raison; (*h*) **to be g. with one's hands,** être adroit, habile, de ses mains; **g. for nothing,** bon à rien; **to be g. at maths,** être bon, fort, en math; (*i*) *F:* **to feel g.,** se sentir en bonne forme, bien en train; **I don't feel too g.,** je ne suis pas dans mon assiette. **2.** (*a*) **g. Christian,** bon chrétien, bonne chrétienne; **to lead a g. life,** vivre en homme de bien; **g. conduct, behaviour,** bonne conduite; **he proved to be a g. friend,** il s'est montré un véritable ami; *n.pl.* **the g. and the bad,** les bons et les méchants; (*b*) (*of child*) sage; **be g.!** sois sage! **as g. as gold,** sage comme une image; (*c*) *O:* **his g. lady,** sa femme; (*d*) aimable; **that's very g. of you,** c'est bien aimable, gentil, de votre part; **would you be g. enough to . . .?** auriez-vous l'amabilité, la gentillesse, de . . .? **he has always been g. to me,** il s'est toujours montré bon pour moi; **he's a g. sort,** c'est un bon type; *F:* **g. Lord! g. heavens! g. gracious!** grand Dieu! par exemple! **g. grief!** fichtre alors! **3.** (*a*) **a g. half,** une bonne moitié; **a g. two hours,** deux bonnes heures; **a g. while, a g. time,** pas mal de temps; **a g. round sum,** une somme rondelette; **a g. twenty years ago,** il y a bien vingt ans, vingt ans bien comptés; **a g. deal, a g. many,** beaucoup; **a g. few,** pas mal; **to come in a g. third,** arriver bon troisième; (*b*) *adv. F:* **they beat us g. and proper,** ils nous ont battus à plates coutures; **he was g. and mad,** il était absolument furieux; **he was g. and sorry,** il le regrettait amèrement. **4. it's as g. a way as any other,** c'est une façon qui en vaut une autre; **to give s.o. as g. as one gets,** rendre la pareille à qn; rendre coup pour coup; **it's as g. as new,** c'est pour ainsi dire neuf; c'est quasi neuf; **to make sth. as g. as new,** remettre qch. à neuf; **it's as g. as settled,** c'est une affaire faite ou autant vaut; **it is as g. as saying that . . .,** autant vaut dire que . . .. **5. to make g.,** (i) se rattraper de (ses pertes, etc.); réparer (une injustice, des dégâts); combler (un déficit, une perte); (ii) remplir (sa promesse); (iii) effectuer (sa retraite, etc.); (iv) assurer (sa position); faire prévaloir (ses droits); (v) (*of pers.*) prospérer, faire son chemin; (vi) se refaire une vie. **II.** *n.* **1.** bien *m*; (*a*) **to return g. for evil,** rendre le bien pour le mal; **to do g.,** faire du, le, bien; **that will do more harm than g.,** cela fera plus de mal que de bien; **he's up to no g.,** il prépare quelque mauvais coup; (*b*) **I did it for your g.,** je l'ai fait pour votre bien; **for the g. of one's health,** en vue de sa santé; **to act for the common g.,** agir dans l'intérêt commun; **it will do you g. to spend a week in the country,** cela vous fera du bien de passer une semaine à la campagne; **what g. will that do you? what g. will it be to you?** à quoi cela vous avancera-t-il? **that won't be much g.,** ça ne servira pas à grand-chose; **what's the g. of that?** à quoi bon (faire) cela? **(it's) no g. talking about it,** inutile d'en parler; **that's no g.,** (i) cela ne sert à rien; (ii) cela ne vaut rien; **he's no g.,** il est nul; (*c*) **to be five pounds to the g.,** avoir cinq livres de gagné, de profit; **it is all to the g.,** c'est autant de gagné; (*d*) *adv.phr.* **he is gone for g.,** il est parti pour (tout) de bon; **to settle down for g.,** se fixer définitivement. **2. goods** (*a*) *Jur:* biens, effets *mpl*; (*b*) *Com: Pol.Ec:* marchandises *fpl*; articles *mpl*; **manufactured goods,** produits fabriqués; **leather goods,** articles en cuir; maroquinerie *f*; **knit(ted) goods,** bonneterie *f*; **consumer goods,** biens de consommation; **stolen goods,** objets volés; **to deliver the goods,** (i) livrer la marchandise, les marchandises; (ii) *F:* remplir ses engagements; tenir parole; (*c*) *Rail:* **goods train, station, depot,** train *m*, gare *f*, dépôt *m*, de marchandises; (*d*) *P:* **a nice bit of goods,** un beau brin de fille; une jolie poupée.

goodbye [gudˈbai] *int. & n.* au revoir; **g. for now!** à bientôt! **to say g. to s.o.,** dire au revoir à qn.

good-for-nothing [ˈgudfənʌθiŋ] **1.** *a.* (*of pers.*) qui n'est bon à rien. **2.** *n.* (*a*) propre *mf* à rien; bon *m* à rien; (*b*) vaurien, -ienne.

good-hearted [gudˈhɑːtid] *a.* (personne) qui a bon cœur; compatissant.

good-humoured, *NAm:* **-humored** [gudˈhjuːməd] *a.* (personne) d'un caractère facile; (sourire, etc.) de bonne humeur; (plaisanterie, etc.) sans malice; **he is always g.-h.,** il a bon caractère. **-ly** *adv.* avec bonhomie; (rire) avec bonne humeur.

goodish [ˈgudiʃ] *a.* **1.** assez bon, passable. **2.** assez grand (nombre, etc.); **it's a g. step from here,** c'est à un bon bout de chemin d'ici.

good-looking [gud'lukiŋ] *a.* beau, *f.* belle; **he's very g.-l.,** il est beau garçon; **she's quite g.-l.,** elle n'est pas mal.

goodly ['gudli] *a.* large, ample (portion, etc.); (nombre) considérable.

good-natured [gud'neitjəd] *a.* (*of pers.*) au bon naturel, accommodant, de bon caractère; (rire) jovial. **-ly** *adv.* avec bonhomie.

goodness ['gudnis] *n.* **1.** (*a*) bonté *f* (de cœur, etc.); (*b*) bonne qualité (d'un article, etc.). **2. to extract all the g. out of sth.,** extraire de qch. tout ce qu'il y a de bon. **3. g. gracious!** bonté divine! **my g.!** mon Dieu! **thank g.!** Dieu merci! **for goodness' sake, be quiet!** taisez-vous, pour l'amour de Dieu! **g. (only) knows what I must do,** Dieu seul sait ce que je dois faire.

goodnight [gud'nait] **1.** *int.* (i) bonsoir! (ii) bonne nuit! **2.** *n.* **after they had said their goodnights,** après s'être dit (i) bonsoir, (ii) bonne nuit.

good-tempered [gud'tempəd] *a.* de caractère facile, égal; placide; qui a bon caractère.

goodwill ['gud'wil] *n.* **1.** bonne volonté; bienveillance *f*; bon vouloir (**towards,** pour, envers); **to retain s.o.'s g.,** conserver les bonnes grâces de qn. **2.** bon cœur; **to set to work with g.,** se mettre à l'œuvre de bon cœur. **3.** *Com:* clientèle *f*; actif incorporel.

goody ['gudi] *F:* **1.** *n.* (*a*) (*pers.*) bon type; **the goodies and the baddies,** les bons et les vauriens *mpl*; (*b*) **goodies,** friandises *fpl.* **2.** *int.* chouette!

goody-goody ['gudigudi] *a.* & *n. F: Pej:* (personne *f*) d'une piété affectée; **she's awfully g.-g.,** elle fait la prude, la sainte nitouche.

gooey ['gu:i] *a. F:* **1.** gluant, collant. **2.** (sentimentalité) à l'eau de rose.

goof [gu:f] *v.i. F:* gaffer, faire une gaffe.

goofy ['gu:fi] *a. F:* loufoque.

goon [gu:n] *n. F:* **1.** imbécile *mf.* **2.** *NAm:* gorille *m.*

goosander [gu:'sændər] *n. Orn:* harle *m* bièvre.

goose, *pl.* **geese** [gu:s, gi:s] *n. Orn:* (*a*) (*female*) oie *f*; (*b*) (*generic*) oie; **wild g.,** oie sauvage; **flock of geese,** troupeau *m* d'oies; **goose's egg,** œuf *m* d'oie; **g. fat,** graisse *f* d'oie; *F:* **g. pimples,** *NAm:* **g. bumps,** chair *f* de poule; *Fig:* **all his geese are swans,** d'après lui, tout ce qu'il fait tient du prodige; (*c*) *Bot:* **g. grass,** (i) grateron *m*, (ii) potentille *f* ansérine; (*d*) *F:* (*pers.*) niais, *f.* niaise; bébête *f*; *O:* **I'm not such a g.,** je ne suis pas si bête que ça.

gooseberry ['guzb(ə)ri] *n.* **1.** groseille *f* à maquereau, groseille verte; **g. bush,** groseillier *m* (à maquereau); *Cu:* **g. fool,** crème *f* de groseilles (à maquereau); *F:* **to play g.,** (i) faire le chaperon; (ii) se trouver en tiers (avec deux amoureux). **2.** *Bot:* **Cape g.,** souris végétale. **Chinese g.,** coqueret *m* du Pérou;

gooseflesh ['gu:sfleʃ] *n.* **1.** chair *f* d'oie. **2.** *F:* chair de poule.

goosefoot ['gu:sfut] *n.* (*pl.* **goosefoots**) *Bot:* chénopode *m.*

goosestep¹ ['gu:sstep] *n. Mil:* pas *m* de l'oie.

goosestep² *v.i.* (**goosestepped**) faire le pas de l'oie.

goos(e)y ['gu:si] *a. F:* **to go g.,** avoir la chair de poule.

gopher ['goufər] *n. Z:* (*a*) géomys *m*; (*b*) spermophile *m.*

Gordian ['gɔ:diən] *a. Fig:* **to cut the G. knot,** trancher le nœud gordien.

gore¹ [gɔ:r] *n.* (*a*) *Dressm:* (i) soufflet *m*; (ii) godet *m*; (*b*) *Nau:* pointe *f* (de voile); (*c*) *Arch:* pan *m* (d'un dôme); (*d*) *Aer:* fuseau *m* (d'un ballon, d'un parachute).

gore² *v.tr. Dressm:* faire, mettre, des soufflets à (une robe, etc.); **gored skirt,** jupe à godets.

gore³ *n. Lit:* sang versé; **he lay in his g.,** il baignait dans son sang.

gore⁴ *v.tr.* blesser (qn) avec les cornes, encorner (qn); **gored to death,** tué d'un coup de corne.

gorge¹ [gɔ:dʒ] *n.* **1.** *A:* & *Lit:* gosier *m*; **it makes my g. rise,** cela me soulève le cœur. **2.** *Geog:* gorge, défilé *m.* **3.** *Mec.E:* gorge (de poulie).

gorge² **1.** *v.i.* **to g. (oneself),** se gorger, se repaître (**on,** de); se rassasier; s'empiffrer (**on,** de). **2.** *v.tr.* (*a*) rassasier (qn); (*b*) avaler, engloutir (sa nourriture); (*c*) gaver (une oie).

gorgeous ['gɔ:dʒəs] *a.* (*a*) magnifique, fastueux; **a g. sunset,** un coucher de soleil splendide; (*b*) *F:* épatant, superbe; (repas) somptueux; (*to girl*) **hello g.!** bonjour ma belle! **-ly** *adv.* magnifiquement, splendidement; somptueusement.

gorgon ['gɔ:gən] *n. Gr.Myth:* gorgone *f.*

gorilla [gə'rilə] *n. Z:* gorille *m.*

gormandize ['gɔ:məndaiz] **1.** *v.tr.* bâfrer, manger goulûment. **2.** *v.i.* goinfrer; *P:* s'empiffrer. **gormandizing** *n.* goinfrerie *f.*

gormandizer ['gɔ:məndaizər] *n.* glouton, -onne.

gormless ['gɔ:mlis] *a. F:* idiot, bête; **he's g.,** c'est une nouille.

gorse [gɔ:s] *n. Bot:* ajonc *m.*

gory ['gɔ:ri] *a.* sanglant, ensanglanté.

gosh [gɔʃ] *int. F:* sapristi! mince (alors)!

goshawk ['gɔshɔ:k] *n. Orn:* autour *m.*

gosling ['gɔzliŋ] *n.* oison *m.*

go-slow ['gou'slou] *n.* **go-s. (strike),** grève perlée.

gospel ['gɔsp(ə)l] *n.* évangile *m*; (*a*) **St Mark's G., the G. according to St Mark,** l'Évangile selon saint Marc; **g. oath,** serment prêté sur l'évangile; *F:* **to take sth. for g.,** accepter qch. comme parole d'évangile; **it's the g. truth,** c'est (vrai comme) parole d'évangile; (*b*) *Ecc:* **the g. for the day,** l'évangile du jour; (*c*) **to preach the g.,** prêcher l'évangile; **to preach the g. of economy,** prêcher l'économie.

gospeller ['gɔspələr] *n.* **(hot) g.,** évangélisateur *m.*

gossamer ['gɔsəmər] **1.** *n.* (*a*) fils *mpl* de la Vierge; filandres *fpl*; **g. thread,** freluche *f*, filandre *f*; (*b*) *Tex:* gaze légère; (*c*) *NAm:* imperméable léger. **2.** *a.* (tissu) très léger, arachnéen.

gossip¹ ['gɔsip] *n.* **1.** (*pers.*) (*a*) bavard, -arde; (*b*) (*ill-natured*) commère; cancanier, -ière. **2.** (*a*) bavardage *m*; commérage(s) *m*(*pl*); *Journ:* **g. column,** chronique mondaine; échos *mpl*; **g. writer,** échotier *m*; (*b*) (*ill-natured*) cancans *mpl*; potins *mpl.*

gossip² *v.i.* (*a*) bavarder, caqueter; (*b*) (*ill-naturedly*) cancaner, potiner, commérer; **to g. about s.o.,** faire des commérages sur qn. **gossiping** *n.* (*a*) bavardage *m*; (*b*) commérage *m.* **gossipy** *a.* (style) anecdotique; **g. letter,** lettre pleine de racontars.

got. *see* GET.

Gothic ['gɔθik] **1.** *a.* gothique. **2.** *n.* (*a*) *Art:* gothique *m*; (*b*) *Ling:* gotique *m*, gothique.

gotten. *see* GET.

gouache [gu'ɑ:ʃ] *n. Art:* gouache *f.*

gouge¹ [gaudʒ] *n. Tls: Carp: Surg:* gouge *f.*

gouge² *v.tr.* **1.** gouger (le bois). **2. to g. out,** creuser (une cannelure, etc.) à la gouge; **to g. s.o.'s eye out,** faire sauter un œil à qn.

goulash ['gu:læʃ] *n. Cu:* goulache *f.*

gourd ['guəd] *n.* **1.** *Bot:* courge *f*, gourde *f.* **2.** (*bottle*) gourde, calebasse *f.*

gourmand ['guəmənd] **1.** *a.* (*a*) glouton; (*b*) gourmand. **2.** *n.* (*a*) glouton *m*; (*b*) gourmet *m.*

gourmandism ['guəməndizm] *n.* gourmandise *f.*

gourmet ['guəmei] *n.* gourmet *m*; gastronome *m.*

gout [gaut] *n. Med:* goutte *f.*

gouty ['gauti] *a.* (*of pers., joint, etc.*) goutteux.

govern ['gʌvən] *v.tr.* **1.** (*a*) gouverner, régir (un État, etc.); administrer (une province, etc.); *v.i.* **to g.,** gouverner; (*b*) **laws that g. chemical reactions,** lois *fpl* qui régissent les réactions chimiques; (*c*) *Gram:* se construire avec (l'accusatif). **2.** maîtriser, gouverner, contenir (ses passions, etc.). **governing 1.** *a.* gouvernant; **g. body,** conseil *m* d'administration. **2.** *n.* gouvernement *m.*

governance ['gʌvənəns] *n.* **1.** gouvernement *m* (d'une province, etc.). **2.** maîtrise *f,* empire *m.*

governess ['gʌvənis] *n.f.* gouvernante; institutrice (privée).

government ['gʌv(ə)nmənt] *n.* **1.** gouvernement *m;* (*a*) **form of g.,** régime *m;* **local g.,** gouvernement local; **self g.,** autonomie *f* (d'un État); (*b*) **the British G.,** le Gouvernement anglais; **g. offices,** bureaux *mpl* du Gouvernement; **g. loan,** emprunt public; (*c*) ministère *m;* **to form a g.,** former un ministère, un gouvernement; **the G. party,** le parti gouvernemental. **2. G. house,** résidence (officielle) (du gouverneur).

governmental [gʌvən'ment(ə)l] *a.* gouvernemental, -aux.

governor ['gʌv(ə)nər] *n.* **1.** (*a*) gouverneur *m* (d'une colonie, d'une banque, d'une prison); **g. general,** gouverneur général; (*b*) directeur *m* (d'une école de réforme, etc.); (*c*) membre *m* du conseil d'administration (d'une école, etc.); (*d*) *F:* **the g.,** (i) le patron, le singe. **2.** (*device*) *Mec.E:* régulateur *m;* modérateur *m* (de vitesse).

governorship ['gʌvənəʃip] *n.* poste *m,* fonctions *fpl,* de gouverneur.

gown¹ [gaun] *n.* **1.** *Com:* robe *f* (de femme); **dinner g.,** robe de soirée. **2.** robe, toge *f* (de magistrat, universitaire, etc.); blouse *f* (de chirurgien).

gown² *v.tr.* revêtir (qn) d'une robe, d'une toge.

grab¹ [græb] *n.* **1.** mouvement vif de la main pour saisir qch.; **to make a g. at sth.,** faire un mouvement pour saisir qch. **2.** *Civ.E:* **g. (bucket),** benne preneuse, piocheuse.

grab² *v.tr. & i.* **(grabbed) to g. (hold of) sth., s.o.,** saisir qch. (d'un geste brusque); empoigner qch., qn; **he grabbed a revolver from the table,** il a saisi un revolver sur la table; **to save oneself by grabbing a rope,** se raccrocher à un cordage; **to g. at s.o.,** s'agripper à qn.

grace¹ [greis] *n.* **1.** grâce *f;* (*a*) élégance *f* (d'un mouvement, etc.); (*b*) **to do sth. with good, bad, g.,** faire qch. de bonne, mauvaise, grâce; **to have the g. to apologize,** avoir la bonne grâce de faire des excuses; (*c*) *Gr.Myth:* **the Graces,** les Grâces. **2.** (*a*) faveur *f,* gracieuseté *f;* **to be in, get into, s.o.'s good graces,** être dans, entrer dans, les bonnes grâces de qn; (*b*) *Theol:* **the g. of God,** la grâce de Dieu; **in a state of g.,** en état de grâce; **to fall from g.,** perdre la grâce; **it has the saving g. that . . .,** cela a au moins ce mérite que . . .; **in the year of g. 1066,** en l'an de grâce 1066. **3.** (*a*) *A:* grâce, pardon *m;* (*still used in*) **act of g.,** (i) lettres *fpl* de grâce; (ii) loi *f* d'amnistie; (*b*) *Com: Ins:* **days of g.,** délai (accordé pour le paiement d'un effet, d'une prime); **to give a creditor seven days' g.,** accorder à un créancier sept jours de grâce, de faveur; **last day of g.,** terme fatal. **4. grace,** (i) (*before meal*) bénédicité *m;* (ii) (*after meal*) grâces. **5.** (*address*) **His G.,** Monsieur (le duc de . . .); Monseigneur (l'archevêque de . . .). **6.** *Mus:* **g. note,** note *f* d'agrément.

grace² *v.tr.* (*a*) honorer (**with,** de); **to g. a meeting with one's presence,** honorer une réunion de sa présence; (*b*) embellir, orner.

graceful ['greisf(u)l] *a.* **1.** gracieux, élégant; **g. figure,** taille élégante; **she is a g. dancer,** elle danse avec grâce. **2.** (discours) gracieux, poli, bien tourné. **-fully** *adv.* avec grâce; avec élégance.

gracefulness ['greisf(u)lnis] *n.* grâce *f,* élégance *f.*

graceless ['greislis] *a.* (*a*) gauche, inélégant; (*b*) impie, dépravé; (*c*) *F:* effronté.

gracious ['greiʃəs] *a.* **1.** (*a*) gracieux, indulgent, bienveillant; **to be g. to s.o.,** être affable avec, envers, qn; (*b*) **our g. King, Queen,** notre gracieux souverain. **2.** (*of God*) plein de grâce, de compassion (**to,** envers). **3.** (*of living, etc.*) élégant. **4. g. (me)! good(ness) g.!** miséricorde! mon Dieu! **good g. no!** jamais de la vie! **-ly** *adv.* gracieusement; **to be g. pleased to do sth.,** daigner faire qch.

graciousness ['greiʃəsnis] *n.* **1.** grâce *f;* aménité *f* (de style). **2.** gracieuseté *f,* bienveillance *f* (**to, towards,** envers). **3.** bonté *f,* miséricorde *f* (de Dieu). **4.** élégance *f* (de vie, maison, etc.).

gradate [grə'deit] **1.** *v.i.* (*of colours*) se dégrader. **2.** *v.tr.* (*a*) dégrader (des teintes); (*b*) graduer (qch.).

gradation [grə'deiʃ(ə)n] *n.* **1.** (*a*) gradation *f,* progression *f;* (*b*) classification *f* par degrés; (*c*) *Art:* (dé)gradation *f* (des teintes). **2.** degré *m.* **3.** *Ling:* **(vowel) g.,** mutation *f* vocalique.

grade¹ [greid] *n.* **1.** (*a*) grade *m,* rang *m,* degré *m* (d'une hiérarchie, etc.); échelon *m* (d'une administration); (*b*) qualité *f;* classe *f;* (*of oil*) grade; *Com: etc:* **high-g., low-g.,** de qualité supérieure, inférieure; *Aut:* **high-g. petrol** = supercarburant *m, F:* super *m;* (*c*) *Sch: NAm:* **to get high grades** = avoir de bonnes notes. **3.** *Breed:* **g. cattle, grades,** bétail amélioré par le croisement. **4.** (*a*) *NAm:* (*gradient*) pente *f,* rampe *f;* montée *f* ou descente *f* (d'une voie ferrée, etc.); **to make the g.,** atteindre le niveau requis; se montrer à la hauteur; (*b*) *NAm:* niveau *m;* **g. level,** palier *m;* *Rail:* **g. crossing,** passage *m* à niveau; (*c*) *Sch:* (i) *NAm:* classe *f* (*esp.* dans une école primaire); (ii) *U.S:* **g. school, the grades** = école primaire.

grade² *v.tr.* **1.** (*a*) classer, trier (des marchandises, etc., selon leurs qualités); **to g. up, down,** classer (qch.) dans une catégorie supérieure, inférieure; (*b*) *Sch: NAm:* **to g. essays** = corriger des dissertations (et leur donner une note). **2.** *Breed:* (*a*) **to g. (up),** améliorer (une race, etc.). **3.** (*a*) graduer (des exercices, etc.); **graded tax,** impôt (i) progressif, (ii) dégressif; (*b*) *Art:* fondre (des teintes). **4.** *NAm:* (*a*) *Civ.E: Rail:* ménager, régulariser, la pente de (la voie, etc.); (*b*) *Civ.E:* niveler (un terrain). **grading** *n.* **1.** (*a*) classement *m,* gradation *f;* triage *m* (du minerai, etc.); (*b*) *NAm: Sch:* correction *f* (des dissertations, etc., avec notes). **2.** *Breed:* amélioration *f* par le métissage. **3.** (dé)gradation *f* (des teintes). **4.** *NAm:* (a)ménagement *m* (d'une pente).

gradient ['greidiənt] *n.* **1.** *Civ.E: etc:* inclinaison *f;* dénivellation *f;* **downward g.,** pente *f,* déclivité *f;* **upward g.,** rampe *f,* montée *f;* **angle of g.,** angle *m* de gradient; **steep, low, g.,** forte, faible, pente. **2.** *Mth: Ph:* gradient *m* (de température, etc.).

gradual ['grædju(ə)l] **1.** *a.* graduel; progressif; (pente) douce; (transition) ménagée (**from . . . to . . .,** de . . . à . . .); **g. process,** gradation *f.* **2.** *n.* *Ecc:* graduel *m.* **-ally** *adv.* graduellement; par degrés; petit à petit.

graduate¹ ['grædjuət] *n.* *Sch:* diplômé, -ée; = licencié, -ée.

graduate² ['grædjueit] **1.** *v.i.* (*a*) *Sch:* (i) recevoir ses diplômes; = être reçu licencié(e); **he graduated from Oxford,** il a fait ses études à Oxford; (ii) *NAm:* **to g. from high school,** terminer ses études au lycée; (*b*) **to g. into sth.,** se changer graduellement en . . . . **2.** *v.tr.* (*a*) graduer (une échelle, un thermomètre, etc.); **graduated in centimetres,** gradué en centimètres; (*b*) graduer (des exercices, etc.); **graduated income tax,** impôt progressif.

graduation [grædju'eiʃ(ə)n] *n.* **1.** *Sch:* (*a*) remise *f* des diplômes; **g. ceremony,** cérémonie *f* de la remise des diplômes; (*b*) (*by student*) réception *f* d'un diplôme. **2.** (*a*) graduation *f* (d'un thermomètre, etc.); (*b*) **graduations,** degrés *mpl,* grades *mpl.*

graffiti [græ'fi:ti:] *n. pl.* graffiti *mpl*; **obscene graffiti on the wall,** graffiti obscènes sur le mur.

graft[1] [grɑ:ft] *n.* (*a*) *Arb: Hort:* (i) greffon *m*, ente *f*; (ii) greffe *f*, greffage *m*; (*b*) *Surg:* **bone, skin, g.,** greffe osseuse, épidermique.

graft[2] *v.tr.* (*a*) *Arb:* greffer, enter (un greffon, une souche); (*b*) *Surg:* greffer, implanter. **grafting** *n.* (*a*) *Arb:* greffe *f*, greffage *m*; (*b*) *Surg:* greffe (humaine); **skin g.,** greffe épidermique.

graft[3] *n. F:* **1.** gratte *f*, graissage *m* de patte, pots-de-vin *mpl*. **2. hard g.,** travail *m*, boulot *m*.

graft[4] *v.i. F:* **1.** gratter; faire de la gratte; donner ou recevoir des pots-de-vin. **2.** travailler dur.

Grail [greil] *n. Lit:* **the Holy G.,** le Saint-Graal.

grain[1] [grein] *n.* **1.** (*a*) grain *m* (de blé); (*b*) *coll.* **g. crop,** récolte *f* de grains, de céréales; **g. market,** marché *m* aux grains. **2.** (*a*) grain (de poivre, etc.); (*b*) grain (de sel, de sable, etc.); **not a g. of common sense,** pas un grain, un brin, pas une once, de bon sens; (*c*) *Meas:* grain (= 0 gramme 0648). **3.** (*a*) grain (du bois, etc.); **close g.,** grain fin; *Phot:* **coarse g.,** gros grain; **fine g.,** grain fin; (*b*) fil *m* (du bois, de la viande); **against, across, the g.,** contre le fil; à contre-fil; **it goes against the g. for me to do it,** c'est à contrecœur que je le fais; (*c*) *Leath:* grain, grenure *f* (du cuir).

grain[2] *v.tr.* **1.** grener (le sel, etc.); granuler (la poudre). **2.** greneler, grainer (le cuir, le papier, etc.). **3.** *Paint:* (*a*) veiner (une surface) façon bois; (*b*) marbrer (une surface). **graining** *n.* **1.** *Leath:* grenure *f*. **2.** veinage *m* (de la peinture); décor *m* imitant le bois, le marbre; décor en bois, en marbre.

gram [græm] *n. Meas:* gramme *m*.

grammar ['græmər] *n.* (*a*) grammaire *f*; **to speak, write, bad g.,** parler, écrire, peu grammaticalement; **that's not (good) g.,** ce que vous dites là n'est pas grammatical; (*b*) (livre *m*, traité *m*, de) grammaire; **a French g.,** une grammaire française; (*c*) **g. school** = lycée *m*.

grammarian [grə'mɛəriən] *n.* grammairien, -ienne.

grammatical [grə'mætikl] *a.* grammatical, -aux. **-ally** *adv.* grammaticalement.

gramme [græm] *n. Meas:* gramme *m*.

gramophone ['græməfoun] *n.* gramophone *m*.

grampus ['græmpəs] *n. Z:* épaulard *m*, orque *f*.

gran [græ'n] *n.f. F:* grand-maman, mamie.

granary ['grænəri] *n.* grenier *m*; *Com:* entrepôt *m* de grain; **Egypt was the g. of the ancient world,** l'Égypte était le grenier de l'ancien monde.

grand [grænd] *a.* **1.** grand; **g. duke,** grand-duc *m*, *pl.* grands-ducs; **g. duchess,** grande-duchesse *f*, *pl.* grandes-duchesses. **2.** (*a*) grand; **G. Hotel,** le Grand Hôtel; **G. Cross,** grand-croix *f inv*; **g. master,** (i) grand maître (d'un ordre de chevalerie); (ii) vénérable *m* (d'une loge de francs-maçons); (iii) champion *m* (aux échecs); (*b*) (total) global, général. **3.** (*a*) **g. concert,** grand concert; **g. display of fireworks,** grand feu d'artifice; (*b*) **g. piano,** *n.* **grand,** piano *m* à queue; **concert g.,** piano à queue de concert; **baby g.,** (piano) quart de queue. **4.** (*a*) grandiose, imposant, magnifique; **the g. manner,** la grande manière; **g. old man of trade unionism,** vétéran *m* du syndicalisme; (*b*) **a g. lady,** une grande dame. **5.** *F:* (*a*) excellent, splendide; (dîner) magnifique; **he's g.,** c'est un type épatant; (*b*) **I'm not feeling too g.,** je ne suis pas dans mon assiette. **6.** *n. F:* (i) *NAm:* mille dollars *mpl*; (ii) *U.K:* mille livres (sterling). **-ly** *adv.* (*a*) grandement, magnifiquement, splendidement; (*b*) grandiosement.

grandchild, *pl.* **-children** ['græn(d)tʃaild, -tʃildrən] *n.* petit-fils *m* ou petite-fille *f*, *pl.* petits-enfants *m*.

grand-dad ['græn(d)dæd] *n.m. F:* grand-papa, *pl.* grands-papas; pépé *m*.

grand-daughter ['græn(d)dɔ:tər] *n.f.* petite-fille, *pl.* petites-filles.

grandee [græn'di:] *n.* (*a*) grand *m* (d'Espagne); (*b*) *F:* grand personnage.

grandeur ['grændjər] *n.* grandeur *f*; (*a*) noblesse *f*, éminence *f*; **delusions of g.,** folie *f* des grandeurs; (*b*) splendeur *f*, magnificence *f*; **the g. of the landscape,** la majesté du paysage; (*c*) pompe *f*, éclat *m* (d'une cérémonie, d'un train de vie).

grandfather ['græn(d)fɑ:ðər] *n.m.* grand-père, *pl.* grands-pères; aïeul.

grandiloquence [græn'diləkwəns] *n.* grandiloquence *f*; emphase *f*.

grandiloquent [græn'diləkwənt] *a.* grandiloquent; (ton) magnifique, pompeux; (style) emphatique.

grandiose ['grændious, -ouz] *a.* (*a*) grandiose, magnifique; (*b*) pompeux.

grandma ['græn(d)mɑ:] *n.f. F:* grand-maman, *pl.* grands-mamans; mémé, mamie.

grandmother ['græn(d)mʌðər] *n.f.* grand-mère, *pl.* grands-mères; aïeule.

grand-nephew ['græn(d)'nefju] *n.m.* petit-neveu, *pl.* petits-neveux.

grandness ['grændnis] *n.* **1.** grandeur *f*. **2.** *Pej:* affectation *f* de grandeur; air important.

grand-niece ['græn(d)'ni:s] *n.f.* petite-nièce, *pl.* petites-nièces.

grandpa ['grænpɑ:] *n.m. F:* grand-papa, *pl.* grands-papas; pépé.

grandparent ['græn(d)pɛərənt] *n.* grand-père *m*, aïeul *m*; grand-mère *f*, aïeule; *pl.* grands-parents *m*.

grandson ['græn(d)sʌn] *n.m.* petit-fils, *pl.* petits-fils.

grandstand ['græn(d)stænd] *n. Sp:* tribune *f* (d'honneur), grande tribune; *Rac:* **g. finish,** arrivée palpitante.

grange [greindʒ] *n.* **1.** grange *f*. **2.** manoir *m* (avec ferme); château *m*.

granite ['grænit] *n.* granit(e) *m*.

granitic [græ'nitik] *a.* granitique, graniteux.

grannie, granny ['græni] *n. F:* (*a*) grand-maman *f*, *pl.* grands-mamans; mémé *f*; (*b*) **an old g.,** une vieille commère; (*c*) **g. knot,** nœud de ménagère, de soldat.

grant[1] [grɑ:nt] *n.* **1.** (*a*) concession *f*, octroi *m* (d'une permission, etc.); délivrance *f* (d'un brevet); (*b*) *Jur:* don *m*, cession *f* (d'un bien, etc.); (*c*) *Jur:* acte *m* de donation. **2.** aide *f* pécuniaire; subvention *f*; *Sch:* allocation *f* d'études; **g. in aid,** subvention; **to make a g. to s.o.,** accorder une subvention à qn; **to receive a State g.,** être subventionné par l'État.

grant[2] *v.tr.* **1.** (*a*) accorder, concéder, octroyer (une permission, etc.); délivrer (une autorisation, un brevet); **he was granted permission to . . .,** il reçut la permission de . . .; **the countries that have been granted autonomy,** les pays qui se sont vu accorder l'autonomie; **God g. that . . .,** Dieu veuille que . . .; (*b*) **to take sth. for granted,** considérer qch. comme admis, comme convenu; **you take too much for granted,** vous présumez trop; **he takes it for granted that he can borrow my books,** il se croit permis d'emprunter mes livres; **we take all this for granted,** tout cela nous semble normal; (*c*) exaucer (une prière); accéder à (une requête); (*d*) *Jur:* faire cession de (qch.). **2.** accorder, allouer (une subvention à qn); consentir (un prêt). **3.** admettre (un argument); **it must be granted that . . .,** il faut reconnaître que . . .; **I g. you that he is lazy,** il est paresseux, je le veux bien.

granular ['grænjulər] *a.* (*of surface, texture*) granulaire, granuleux.

granulate ['grænjuleit] **1.** *v.tr.* granuler; grener, grainer (la poudre, etc.); cristalliser (le sucre); grenailler (un métal, etc.); **granulated sugar,** sucre cristallisé. **2.** *v.i.* (*a*) se former en grains; se grenailler; (*of sugar, etc.*) se cristalliser; (*b*) *Med:* (*of wound*) bourgeonner.

granulation [grænju'leiʃ(ə)n] *n.* granulation *f*; granulage *m* (de la poudre, etc.); grenaillement *m* (d'un métal).

granule ['grænjul] *n.* granule *m.*

grape [greip] *n.* (*a*) (grain *m* de) raisin (*m*); (*b*) *Hort:* **a (variety of) g.,** un raisin; (*c*) **bunch of grapes,** grappe *f* de raisin; **I'll have grapes,** je prendrai du raisin; **to gather the grapes,** faire la vendange; *F:* **sour grapes!** ils sont trop verts! (*d*) **g. picker,** vendangeur, -euse; **g. harvest,** vendange *f*; *Bot:* **g. hyacinth,** muscari *m.*

grapefruit ['greipfru:t] *n.* pamplemousse *m*; **g. tree,** pamplemoussier *m.*

grapejuice ['greipdʒu:s] *n.* jus *m* de raisin.

grapeshot ['greipʃɔt] *n.* mitraille *f.*

grapevine ['greipvain] *n.* **1.** *NAm:* vigne *f*, treille *f.* **2.** *F:* téléphone *m* arabe; **I heard on the g. that . . .,** la rumeur publique voudrait que . . ..

graph¹ [grɑ:f] *n.* graphique *m*, graphe *m*, diagramme *m*, courbe *f*, tracé *m* (d'une équation, etc.); **g. paper,** papier *m* pour graphique, papier millimétré.

graph² *v.tr.* graphiquer (une courbe); tracer (une courbe) graphiquement.

graphic ['græfik] *a* **1.** *Mth: etc:* (*also* **graphical**) (représentation, etc.) graphique. **2.** (*of description*) pittoresque, vivant; **g. artist,** graphiste *mf*; **g. art,** art *m* graphique. **-ally** *adv.* **1.** (résoudre un problème) graphiquement. **2.** (décrire) d'une manière pittoresque.

graphics ['græfiks] *n.pl.* (*usu. with sg. const.*) la graphique.

graphite ['græfait] *n.* graphite *m*; mine *f* de plomb.

graphologist [græ'fɔlədʒist] *n.* graphologue *mf.*

graphology [græ'fɔlədʒi] *n.* graphologie *f.*

grapnel ['græpnəl] *n.* *Nau:* grappin *m*, crochet *m*; *Hyd.E:* araignée *f*; *Aer:* ancre *f* (de ballon).

grapple¹ ['græpl] *n.* = GRAPNEL.

grapple² **1.** *v.tr.* accrocher, agripper (qn, qch.). **2.** *v.i.* **to g. with s.o., a difficulty,** en venir aux prises avec qn, une difficulté. **grappling** *n.* **1.** accrochage *m.* **2.** *Nau:* **g. iron, hook,** grappin *m*, crochet *m.* **3.** (lutte *f*) corps à corps (*m*) (**with,** avec).

grasp¹ [grɑ:sp] *n.* (*a*) poigne *f*; **to have a strong g.,** avoir de la poigne; (*b*) prise *f*; **to wrest sth. from s.o.'s g.,** arracher qch. des mains de qn; **to have sth. within one's g.,** avoir qch. à sa portée; tenir (le succès) entre ses mains; (*c*) compréhension *f*; **to have a good g. of modern history,** avoir une bonne connaissance de l'histoire moderne.

grasp² **1.** *v.tr.* (*a*) saisir; empoigner (un outil, etc.); serrer (qch.) dans sa main; **to g. s.o.'s hand,** serrer la main à qn; **I grasped his arm,** je lui ai saisi le bras; (*b*) s'emparer de (qch.); saisir (la couronne); se saisir de (qch.); **to g. the opportunity,** saisir l'occasion (de faire qch.). **2.** *v.tr.* comprendre (une difficulté, etc.); se rendre compte (de l'importance de qch.); **I did not quite g. what he said,** je n'ai pas tout à fait saisi ce qu'il disait. **3.** *v.i.* **to g. at sth.,** (i) tâcher de saisir, d'atteindre, qch.; (ii) saisir avidement (une occasion, une offre). **grasping** *a.* avide, cupide.

grass¹ [grɑ:s] *n.* **1.** (*a*) herbe *f*; **blade of g.,** brin *m* d'herbe; **he doesn't let the g. grow under his feet,** il ne perd pas son temps; **g. seed,** (i) graine fourragère; (ii) graine pour gazon; *F:* **g. widow,** (i) femme dont le mari est absent, en voyage; (ii) *NAm:* femme divorcée ou séparée (de son mari); (*b*) *Bot:* **quaking g.,** brize *f*; (*c*) *Rept:* **g. snake,** couleuvre *f* à collier, serpent *m* d'eau. **2.** (*a*) herbage *m*, pâture *f*, fourrage *m* en vert; **to put, turn, a horse out to g.,** mettre un cheval à l'herbe; **to be (out) at g.,** (i) (*of animal*) être au vert; (ii) *F:* (*of pers.*) être à la retraite; **to put land under g.,** enherber une terre; (*b*) gazon *m*; **keep off the g.,** (i) *P.N:* défense de marcher sur le gazon, sur les pelouses; (ii) *F:* n'empiétez pas sur mes plates-bandes. **3.** *Rad: F:* parasites *mpl.* **4.** *F:* marijuana *f*, thé (vert). **5.** *P:* dénonciateur, -trice; cafardeur, - euse.

grass² *v.tr.* **1.** mettre en herbe, enherber (un champ); gazonner (un terrain). **2.** *v.i.* *P:* chanter; cafarder; **to g. on s.o.,** dénoncer qn.

grassbox ['grɑ:sbɔks] *n.* panier *m* à herbes (d'une tondeuse de gazon).

grasscloth ['grɑ:sklɔθ] *Tex:* (toile *f* de) ramie (*f*).

grass(-)green ['grɑ:s'gri:n] *a.* vert pré *inv.*

grasshopper ['grɑ:shɔpər] *n.* *Ent:* sauterelle *f.*

grassland ['grɑ:slænd] *n.* prairies *fpl*, prés *mpl.*

grassroots ['grɑ:sru:ts] *n.pl.* (*with sg. or pl. const.*) **1. the g.,** la population rurale; **g. democracy,** le populisme. **2.** fondation *f*, source *f*; **to attack a problem at the g.,** remonter à la source d'un problème.

grassy ['grɑ:si] *a.* herbu, herbeux; (*of pasture land*) herbageux; (chemin) vert; (plaines) verdoyantes.

grate¹ [greit] *n.* (*a*) grille *f* (de foyer); (*b*) foyer *m*, âtre *m*; **let's have a fire in the g.!** faisons un feu dans la cheminée!

grate² **1.** *v.tr.* râper; **grated cheese,** fromage râpé. **2.** (*a*) *v.tr.* **to g. one's teeth,** grincer des dents; (*b*) **to g. sth. on sth.,** frotter qch. contre qch. (avec un grincement). **3.** *v.i.* (*a*) (*of machinery*) grincer; (*of chalk on blackboard*) crisser; **the door grated on its hinges,** la porte grinçait, criait, sur ses gonds; (*b*) **to g. on the ear,** écorcher, affliger, l'oreille; **to g. on the nerves,** taper sur les nerfs. **grating 1.** *a.* (bruit) discordant, grinçant; (voix) rude; **g. sound,** grincement *m*; crissement *m*; **g. laugh,** ricanement *m.* **2.** *n.* (*a*) (i) râpage *m*; (ii) **gratings,** râpure(s) *f*(*pl*); (*b*) grincement *m*, crissement *m* (d'un gond).

grateful ['greitf(u)l] *a.* **1.** (*of pers.*) reconnaissant (**to, towards, s.o. for sth.,** à, envers, qn de qch.); **to be g. to s.o. for sth.,** savoir (bon) gré à qn de qch. **-fully** *adv.* avec reconnaissance.

grater ['greitər] *n.* râpe *f*; **cheese g.,** râpe à fromage.

gratification [grætifi'keiʃ(ə)n] *n.* **1.** satisfaction *f*, plaisir *m*; **to do sth. for one's own g.,** faire qch. pour son propre contentement. **2.** satisfaction, assouvissement *m* (des passions).

gratify ['grætifai] *v.tr.* **1.** faire plaisir à (qn). **2.** satisfaire, contenter (une passion, etc.); **to g. s.o.'s whims,** satisfaire aux caprices de qn. **gratified** *a.* satisfait, content (**with,** de); (sourire) de satisfaction. **gratifying** *a.* agréable; (perspective, etc.) qui donne de la satisfaction.

grating ['greitiŋ] *n.* (*a*) grille *f*, grillage *m* (de fenêtre); (*b*) *Nau:* caillebot(t)is *m.*

gratis ['grɑ:tis] **1.** *a.* gratis, gratuit. **2.** *adv.* gratis, gratuitement, à titre gratuit.

gratitude ['grætitju:d] *n.* gratitude *f*, reconnaissance *f* (**to,** envers).

gratuitous [grə'tju(:)itəs] *a.* **1.** gratuit; (service, etc.) bénévole. **2.** (*of insult, lie*) gratuit, sans motif. **-ly** *adv.* **1.** gratuitement; à titre gratuit. **2.** sans motif.

gratuity [grə'tju(:)iti] *n.* **1.** gratification *f*, pourboire *m*; **no gratuities,** défense de donner des pourboires. **2.** *Mil:* prime *f* de démobilisation.

grave¹ [greiv] *n.* tombe *f*, tombeau *m*; **mass g.,** tombe collective; **to be in one's g.,** être enterré; *F:* **he must have turned in his g.,** il a dû frémir dans sa tombe; **someone's walking over my g.,** j'ai le frisson; **to have one foot in the g.,** avoir un pied dans la tombe; **from beyond the g.,** d'outre-tombe.

grave² *v.tr.* (*p.t.* **graved;** *p.p.* **graven, graved**) *A:* graver (une inscription); **graven on his memory,** gravé dans sa mémoire; *B:* **graven image,** image taillée.

grave³ *a* (*a*) grave, sérieux; (ton) solennel; (*b*) (situation) grave; lourde (erreur); **to make a g. mistake,** se tromper lourdement; **g. news,** de graves nouvelles. **-ly** *adv.* gravement; (*a*) solennellement; (*b*) **g. ill,** gravement malade; **g. wounded,** grièvement blessé.

grave⁴ [grɑːv] *a. Ling:* **g. accent,** accent *m* grave.

grave⁵ [greiv] *v.tr. Nau:* radouber (un navire). **graving** *n.* radoub *m*; **g. dock,** bassin *m* de radoub.

gravedigger ['greivdigər] *n.* fossoyeur *m.*

gravel¹ ['grævəl] *n.* **1.** gravier *m*; **g. pit,** carrière *f* de gravier; **g. path,** allée sablée. **2.** *Med:* gravelle *f, F:* graviers, sable *m.*

gravel² *v.tr.* **(gravelled) 1.** couvrir de gravier; **gravelled path,** allée sablée. **2.** *esp. NAm: F:* embarrasser (qn).

gravelly ['grævəli] *a.* **1.** graveleux; (lit de rivière) pierreux; (chemin) sablonneux; *F:* **g. voice,** voix râpeuse. **2.** *Med:* (*of urine, etc.*) graveleux.

graven. *see* GRAVE².

graveness ['greivnis] *n.* gravité *f* (du maintien, etc.).

gravestone ['greivstoun] *n.* pierre tombale.

graveyard ['greivjɑːd] *n.* (*a*) cimetière *m*; (*b*) cimetière (de vieilles voitures, etc.); **this firm is the g. of personal initiative,** cette maison est le tombeau, la fin, de toute initiative individuelle.

gravitate ['græviteit] *v.i.* graviter (**towards,** vers; **round,** autour de); **most of the guests had gravitated to the bar,** la plupart des invités s'étaient dirigés vers le bar.

gravitation [grævi'teiʃ(ə)n] *n.* gravitation *f*; attraction universelle; **law of g.,** la loi de la pesanteur.

gravitational [grævi'teiʃən(ə)l] *a.* gravitationnel; (champ) de gravitation; **g. pull,** gravitation *f.*

gravity ['græviti] *n.* **1.** (*a*) gravité *f*, sérieux *m*; **to lose one's g.,** perdre son sérieux; (*b*) gravité (d'une situation, d'une blessure). **2.** (*a*) *Ph:* gravité, pesanteur *f*; (force *f* de) gravitation (*f*); **law of g.,** la loi de la pesanteur; **centre of g.,** centre *m* de gravité; **force of g.,** force gravifique; **specific g.,** poids *m*, gravité, spécifique; (*b*) *Tchn:* **g. feed,** alimentation *f* en charge, par gravité.

gravy ['greivi] *n.* **1.** *Cu:* (*a*) jus *m* (qui sort de la viande); (*b*) sauce *f* (au jus); **g. boat,** saucière *f.* **2.** *P:* profit *m* illicite; gratte *f*; **the g. train,** l'assiette *f* au beurre; un bon filon.

gray [grei] *a. & n.* = GREY.

grayling ['greiliŋ] *n.* **1.** *Ich:* ombre *m* (de rivière). **2.** *Ent:* (papillon *m*) agreste (*m*).

graze¹ [greiz] **1.** *v.i.* paître, brouter, pâturer; **to g. on a field,** pâturer un champ. **2.** *v.tr.* (*a*) (faire) paître (un troupeau); (*b*) pacager, mettre en pacage (un champ); (*c*) (*of cattle, etc.*) pâturer (un champ); paître (l'herbe). **grazing** *n.* **1.** pâturage *m* (de troupeaux, etc.); **g. rights,** droit *m* de pâturage, de pacage. **2. g. (land, ground),** pâture *f*, pacage *m.*

graze² *n.* écorchure *f*, éraflure *f.*

graze³ *v.tr.* **1.** écorcher, érafler (ses genoux, etc.). **2.** effleurer; **the bullet grazed his shoulder,** la balle lui rasa l'épaule.

grease¹ [griːs] *n.* **1.** *Mec.E:* graisse; (*dirty*) cambouis *m*; **axle g.,** graisse pour essieux; *Mch:* **g. box,** boîte *f* à graisse, de graissage; **g. gun,** pistolet *m* graisseur. **2.** *Arb:* glu *f* horticole; **g. band,** bande enduite de glu horticole.

grease² [griːs] *v.tr.* **1.** graisser, encrasser (ses habits). **2.** (*a*) graisser, lubrifier (une machine), suiffer (un mât); **to keep a mechanism well greased,** entretenir un mécanisme au gras; *F:* **to g. s.o.'s palm,** graisser la patte à qn; (*b*) *Cu:* beurrer (un moule à gâteau).

greasepaint ['griːspeint] *n.* fard *m*; *Th:* **stick of g.,** crayon gras (de maquillage); **white g.,** blanc gras.

greaseproof ['griːspruːf] *a.* (papier) parcheminé; *F:* (papier) jambon, (papier) beurre.

greaser ['griːsər] *n.* **1.** (*pers.*) (*a*) graisseur *m*; (*b*) *Nau: F:* chef *m* de chauffe; mécanicien *m*, graisseur. **2.** (*instrument*) *Mec.E:* graisseur; godet à graisse.

greasiness ['griːsinis] *n.* **1.** état graisseux, gras. **2.** *F:* (*of manner*) onctuosité *f.*

greasy ['griːsi] *a.* **1.** (*a*) graisseux, huileux; **to taste g.,** sentir le graillon; (*b*) taché de graisse; **to make one's clothes g.,** graisser ses habits. **2.** (*a*) gras, *f.* grasse; glissant; **g. road,** chemin gras, glissant; **g. pole,** mât *m* de cocagne (de fête villageoise, etc.); (*b*) (*of manner*) onctueux, patelin.

great [greit] *a* grand; (*a*) **a g. crowd,** une grande foule, une foule énorme; *Geog:* **the G. Lakes,** les Grands Lacs; **Greater London,** le grand Londres, l'agglomération londonienne; (*b*) **a g. deal,** beaucoup (**of,** de); une grande quantité; **a g. many,** beaucoup (de + *pl.*); **a g. many people,** beaucoup de gens; beaucoup de monde; **the g. majority, the greater part,** la plupart, la majeure partie (**of,** de); **to a g. extent,** en grande partie; **to reach a g. age,** parvenir à un âge avancé; (*c*) **his greatest fault,** son plus grand défaut; son défaut capital; **to take g. care,** prendre grand soin (**of,** de); **g. difference,** grande, forte, différence; **with g., with the greatest of, pleasure,** avec grand, avec le plus grand, plaisir; **the G. War,** la Grande Guerre; (*d*) **g. artist,** grand artiste; *F:* **G. Scott!** grands dieux! **Alexander the G.,** Alexandre le Grand; (*e*) **g. scoundrel,** grand fripon; **they are g. friends,** ils sont grands amis; *F:* **to be g. at tennis,** être fort au tennis; (*f*) **it is no g. matter,** ce n'est pas une grosse affaire; **to have no g. opinion of s.o.,** tenir qn en médiocre estime; **the g. thing is that . . .,** le grand avantage, le principal, c'est que . . .; **to have a g. time,** s'amuser follement; **(that's) g!** fameux! magnifique! **isn't he g.!** quel homme! **-ly** *adv.* grandement; **g. irritated,** trés irrité; fortement irrité; **I would g. prefer . . .,** je préférerais (de) beaucoup . . .; **to contribute g. to a result,** contribuer puissamment à un résultat.

great-aunt ['greit'ɑːnt] *n.f.* grand-tante, *pl.* grand(s)-tantes.

greatcoat ['greitkout] *n.* **1.** pardessus *m.* **2.** *Mil:* (*a*) manteau *m* (de cavalerie); (*b*) capote *f* (d'infanterie); (*c*) **hooded g.,** capot *m.*

great-grandchild, *pl.* **-children** ['greit'græn(d)tʃaild, -tʃildrən] *n.* arrière-petits-fils *m*, arrière-petite-fille *f*, *pl.* arrière-petits-enfants *m.*

great-granddaughter ['greit'græn(d)dɔːtər] *n.f.* arrière-petite-fille, *pl.* arrière-petites-filles.

great-grandfather ['greit'græn(d)fɑːðər] *n.m.* arrière-grand-père, *pl.* arrière-grands-pères; bisaïeul, *pl.* bisaïeuls.

great-grandmother ['greit'græn(d)mʌðər] *n.f.* arrière-grand-mère, *pl.* arrière-grand-mères; bisaïeule.

great-grandparents ['greit'græn(d)pɛərənts] *n.pl.* arrière-grands-parents *mpl.*

great-grandson ['greit'græn(d)sʌn] *n.m.* arrière-petit-fils, *pl.* arrière-petits-fils.

great-great-grandfather ['greit'greit'græn(d)-fɑːðər] *n.m.* trisaïeul, *pl.* trisaïeuls.

great-great-grandmother ['greit'greit'græn(d)-mʌðər] *n.f.* trisaïeule.

great-nephew ['greit'nefjuː] *n.m.* petit-neveu, *pl.* petits-neveux.

greatness ['greitnis] *n.* grandeur *f*; (*a*) élévation *f*, noblesse *f* (de pensée); **g. of soul,** grandeur d'âme; (*b*) importance *f*, étendue *f*, intensité *f.*

great-niece ['greit'niːs] *n.f.* petite-nièce, *pl.* petites-nièces.

great-uncle ['greit'ʌŋkl] *n.m.* grand-oncle, *pl.* grands-oncles.

grebe [gri:b] *n. Orn:* grèbe *m*; **great crested g.,** grèbe huppé.

Grecian ['gri:ʃ(ə)n] *a.* grec, *f.* grecque; **in the G. style,** à la grecque.

Greece [gri:s] *Pr.n. Geog:* Grèce *f.*

greed [gri:d] *n.* **1.** avidité *f*, cupidité *f*; âpreté *f* au gain. **2.** gourmandise *f*, gloutonnerie *f.*

greediness ['gri:dinis] *n.* **1.** avidité *f*, cupidité *f*; âpreté *f* au gain. **2.** gourmandise *f*, gloutonnerie *f.*

greedy ['gri:di] *a.* **1.** avide; âpre (au gain); cupide. **2.** gourmand; glouton, -onne; goulu. **-ily** *adv.* **1.** avidement, cupidement. **2.** (manger) goulûment, gloutonnement.

greedyguts ['gri:digʌts] *n. P:* goinfre *m*, bâfreur *m.*

Greek [gri:k] **1.** *a.* (*a*) grec, *f.* grecque; (*b*) **the G. Church,** l'Église grecque; l'Église orthodoxe. **2.** *n. Geog:* Grec, Grecque. **3.** *n. Ling:* grec *m*; **modern G.,** le grec moderne; *F:* **it's all G. to me,** c'est de l'hébreu pour moi.

green¹ [gri:n] *a. & n.* **1.** *a.* vert; (*a*) **as g. as grass,** vert comme pré; **to grow g.,** verdir; (*of grass*) verdoyer; (*b*) *Husb:* **g. crop,** récolte *f* de fourrages verts; (*c*) **g. old age,** verte vieillesse; **to keep s.o.'s memory g.,** entretenir la mémoire de qn; (*d*) (fruits) verts; *Tan:* (peau) verte; **g. bacon,** lard (salé et) non fumé; (*e*) (*of complexion*) blême; **to go, turn, g.,** blêmir; verdir; **to make s.o. g. with envy,** faire pâlir qn d'envie; (*f*) (i) jeune, inexpérimenté; (ii) naïf, serin; **he's not as g. as he looks,** il n'est pas si niais qu'il en a l'air; (*g*) **she has g. fingers,** *NAm:* **a g. thumb,** en jardinage, tout lui sourit, elle a la main heureuse. **2.** *n.* vert *m*; (*a*) **the greens of a picture,** les verts d'un tableau; (*b*) verdure *f*, feuillage *m*; (*c*) **greens,** légumes verts; (*d*) pelouse *f*, gazon *m*; **village g.,** pelouse communale, pré communal; = place *f* du village; *Turf:* **the g.,** la pelouse; *Golf:* **putting g.,** pelouse d'arrivée; le vert; **bowling g.,** (terrain *m* pour) jeu *m* de boules. **3.** *n. & a.* (*in Fr. a.inv.*) **grass(-)g.,** vert pré; **sea(-)g.,** vert de mer, d'eau; *a.* glauque; **bottle(-)g.,** vert bouteille; **olive(-)g.,** (couleur *f* d')olive (*m*).

green² **1.** *v.i.* verdir, verdoyer. **2.** *v.tr.* verdir; faire verdoyer (les champs).

greenery ['gri:nəri] *n.* verdure *f*, feuillage *m.*

green-eyed ['gri:naid] *a.* aux yeux verts; *Lit:* **the g.-e. monster,** la sombre jalousie.

greenfinch ['gri:nfinʃ] *n. Orn:* verdier *m.*

greenfly ['gri:nflai] *n. Ent:* **1.** puceron *m* (du rosier); aphis *m.* **2.** *coll.* aphidés *mpl*, aphidiens *mpl.*

greengage ['gri:ngeidʒ, gri:n'geidʒ] *n.* reine-claude *f*, *pl.* reines-claudes.

greengrocer ['gri:ngrousər] *n.* marchand, -ande, de légumes; fruitier, -ière; **greengrocer's (shop),** magasin *m* de marchand de légumes; fruiterie *f.*

greenhorn ['gri:nhɔ:n] *n. F:* blanc-bec *m*, *pl.* blancs-becs; bleu *m*, cornichon *m.*

greenhouse ['gri:nhaus] *n. Hort:* serre *f.*

greenish ['gri:niʃ] *a.* verdâtre; tirant sur le vert.

Greenland ['gri:nlənd] *Pr.n. Geog:* Groenland *m*; in G., au Groenland.

Greenlander ['gri:landər] *n.* Groenlandais, -aise.

greenness ['gri:nnis] *n.* **1.** verdeur *f*; (*a*) couleur verte; (*b*) immaturité *f* (d'un fruit, etc.); (*c*) (i) inexpérience *f*; (ii) naïveté *f*, simplicité *f.* **2.** verdure *f* (du paysage, etc.).

greenroom ['gri:nru:m] *n. Th:* foyer *m* des artistes.

greenstuff ['gri:nstʌf] *n.* (*a*) verdure *f*; herbages *mpl*; (*b*) fourrage *m*; (*c*) légumes verts.

greensward ['gri:nswɔ:d] *n. Lit:* pelouse *f*; (tapis *m* de) gazon (*m*).

Greenwich ['grinidʒ] *Pr.n.* Greenwich; *Hor:* **G. mean time,** temps moyen de Greenwich.

greenwood ['gri:nwud] *n.* bois *m*, forêt *f* (en été).

greet [gri:t] *v.tr.* (*a*) saluer, aborder, accueillir (qn) avec quelques paroles aimables; **to g. a speech with cheers,** acclamer un discours; (*b*) **to g. the ear,** frapper l'oreille; **to g. the eyes,** s'offrir à l'œil. **greeting** *n.* salutation *f*, salut *m*; **greetings card,** carte *f* de vœux; **to send greetings to s.o.,** envoyer ses salutations à qn; **new-year greetings,** compliments *mpl* du jour de l'an; **greetings to all!** salut à tous!

gregarious [gri'gɛəriəs] *a.* (*a*) *Z: Bot:* grégaire; **the g. instinct,** l'instinct *m* grégaire; (*b*) (*of pers.*) sociable. **-ly** *adv. Z:* (vivre) en troupes, par bandes.

gregariousness [gri'gɛəriəsnis] *n.* grégarisme *m.*

Gregorian [gri'gɔ:riən] *a. Ecc:* (chant, etc.) grégorien.

gremlin ['gremlin] *n. F:* lutin *m.*

grenade [grə'neid] *n. Mil:* grenade *f*; **hand g.,** grenade à main.

grenadier [grenə'diər] *n. Mil:* grenadier *m.*

grenadine ['grenadi:n] *n.* **1.** *Tex:* grenadine *f.* **2.** (*syrup*) grenadine.

grew. *see* GROW.

grey¹ [grei] *a. & n.* **1.** *a.* (*a*) gris; *Anat:* **g. matter,** substance grise (du cerveau); (*b*) (*of hair*) gris; **to turn, go, g.,** grisonner; (*c*) (*of complexion*) blême; **to turn g.,** blêmir; (*d*) (*of outlook, etc.*) sombre, morne. **2.** *n.* (*a*) gris *m*; **hair touched with g.,** cheveux grisonnants; (*b*) cheval gris. **3.** *n. & a.* (*Fr. a.inv.*) **charcoal g.,** gris anthracite; **dapple(-)g.,** (cheval) gris pommelé; **iron(-)g.,** gris (de) fer; **slate(-)g.,** gris ardoise.

grey² *v.i.* (*of hair*) grisonner. **greying** *a.* grisonnant.

greybeard ['greibiəd] *n.* grison *m*; vieux barbon.

grey-eyed ['grei'aid] *a.* aux yeux gris.

grey-haired, -headed ['grei'hɛəd, 'hedid] *a.* aux cheveux gris; grisonnant.

greyhound ['greihaund] *n.* lévrier *m*; **g. racing,** courses *fpl* de lévriers; **g.(-racing) track,** cynodrome *m.*

greyish ['greiiʃ] *a.* grisâtre.

greylag ['greilæg] *n. Orn:* **g. (goose),** oie cendrée.

greyness ['greinis] *n.* **1.** teinte grise; **the g. of London,** la grisaille de Londres. **2.** caractère *m* morne, sombre; tristesse *f.*

grid¹ [grid] *n.* **1.** (*a*) grille *f*, grillage *m*; *El:* grille, grillage (d'accumulateur); **cattle g.,** grille sur la route permettant aux voitures mais non au bétail de passer; (*b*) grille (d'un tube électronique, etc.); **g. valve,** tube à grille. **2.** = GRIDIRON. **3.** (*a*) *Mapm:* quadrillage *m* (d'une carte); **g. system,** réseau *m* de quadrillage; **g. lines,** droites *fpl* du quadrillage; (*b*) **the g.,** le réseau électrique national; (*c*) *Town P:* **g. layout,** quadrillage, damier *m.* **4. (starting) g.** ligne *f* de départ (d'une piste automobile).

griddle ['gridl] *n. Cu:* tôle (sur laquelle on cuit des galettes); **g. cake,** galette *f.*

gridiron ['gridaiən] *n.* **1.** (*a*) *Cu:* gril *m*; (*b*) *Cy:* **g. carrier,** porte-bagages *m inv* en tubes d'acier; (*c*) *Nau:* gril de carénage; (*d*) *Th:* gril (pour la manœuvre des décors). **2.** *NAm:* terrain *m* de football.

grief [gri:f] *n.* chagrin *m*, douleur *f*, peine *f*; **to die of g.,** mourir de chagrin; **to come to g.,** (i) se voir accablé de malheurs; faire de mauvaises affaires; (ii) (*of plan, etc.*) échouer, mal tourner; (iii) avoir un accident; (*of rider*) faire une chute; *F:* **good g.!** mon Dieu!

grief-stricken ['gri:fstrik(ə)n] *a.* pénétré, accablé, de douleur; en proie à la douleur.

grievance [ˈgriːvəns] *n.* **1.** grief *m*; **to have a g. against s.o.,** avoir un grief contre qn; **to air, state, one's grievances,** conter, exprimer, ses doléances. **2.** injustice *f*; **to redress a g.,** réparer un tort.

grieve [griːv] **1.** *v.tr.* chagriner, affliger, peiner (qn); **we are grieved to learn . . .,** nous apprenons avec peine . . .. **2.** *v.i.* se chagriner, s'affliger (**over, about, sth.,** de qch.); **the whole nation grieved at his death,** la nation entière pleura sa mort. **grieved** *a.* chagriné, affligé, désolé (**at,** de); **deeply g.,** navré (**at,** de).

grievous [ˈgriːvəs] *a.* **1.** douloureux, pénible; (perte) cruelle. **2.** (blessure, etc.) grave; *Jur:* **to cause g. bodily harm,** causer de graves blessures. **3.** (*of news*) affligeant, douloureux. **-ly** *adv.* **1.** douloureusement, péniblement, cruellement. **2.** gravement; grièvement (blessé).

griffin [ˈgrifin] *n. Myth:* griffon *m.*

griffon [ˈgrifən] *n.* **1.** (chien) griffon *m.* **2.** *Myth:* griffon *m.* **3.** *Orn:* **g. (vulture),** vautour griffon.

grift [grift] *v.i. NAm: P:* escroquer.

grifter [ˈgriftər] *n. NAm: P:* escroc *m.*

grill¹ [gril] *n.* **1.** *Cu:* grillade *f.* **2. g. (room),** grill-room *m* (de restaurant); rôtisserie *f.*

grill² *n. Cu:* gril *m*; grilloir *m.*

grill³ **1.** *v.tr.* griller (la viande); faire cuire (qch.) sur le gril; *F:* cuisiner (un détenu, etc.). **2.** *v.i.* griller, être grillé; cuire sur le gril. **grilled** *a.* grillé; **g. meat,** viande grillée; grillade *f*; **charcoal-g. meat,** carbonnade *f.* **grilling** *n.* cuisson *f* sur le gril; *F:* cuisinage *m* (d'un détenu, etc.); **to give s.o. a g.,** cuisiner qn.

grill⁴ *n.* = GRILLE ¹.

grille¹ [gril] *n.* grille *f* (de porte); **(counter) g.,** grille de comptoir (d'un bureau de banque, etc.); *Aut:* **radiator g.,** calandre *f.*

grille² *v.tr.* grillager. **grilled** *a.* grillagé, à grille.

grim [grim] *a.* menaçant, sinistre; (paysage) lugubre; (sourire) sardonique; (humour) macabre; **to hold on like g. death,** se cramponner en désespéré; **g. determination,** volonté *f* inflexible; (*of pers.*) **to look g.,** avoir une mine sévère; *F:* **how do you feel?—pretty g.!** comment ça va?—plutôt mal; **things are looking g.,** ça marque mal, s'annonce mal. **-ly** *adv.* sinistrement; sévèrement; (se battre, se cramponner) avec acharnement.

grimace¹ [griˈmeis] *n.* grimace *f*; **to make a g.,** faire la grimace.

grimace² *v.i.* grimacer; faire la grimace.

grime [graim] *n.* saleté *f*; poussière *f* de charbon, de suie (qui vous entre dans la peau).

griminess [ˈgraiminis] *n.* saleté *f*, noirceur *f.*

grimness [ˈgrimnis] *n.* caractère *m* sinistre, aspect *m* redoutable (de qch.); sévérité *f* (de visage); acharnement *m* (d'un combat).

grimy [ˈgraimi] *a.* sale, encrassé, noirci; noir (de suie).

grin¹ [grin] *n.* **1.** grimace *f* qui découvre les dents. **2.** large sourire; sourire épanoui; **to give a broad g.,** se fendre la bouche en un large sourire.

grin² *v.i.* **(grinned) 1.** grimacer en montrant les dents. **2.** rire, sourire, d'une oreille à l'autre; **he grinned broadly,** son visage s'est épanoui en un large sourire; **to g. and bear it,** (tâcher de) garder le sourire; *F:* encaisser (sans broncher); **to g. like a Cheshire cat,** sourire jusqu'aux oreilles.

grind¹ [graind] *n.* **1.** grincement *m*, crissement *m.* **2.** *F:* (*a*) labeur *m* monotone et continu; **the daily g.,** le boulot journalier; **what a g.!** quelle corvée!

grind² (*p.t. & p.p.* **ground** [graund]) **1.** *v.tr.* (*a*) moudre (du blé, du café); concasser (du poivre); broyer (des couleurs); piler (qch. dans un mortier); **to g. sth. (down) to dust,** pulvériser qch.; **to g. sth. under one's heel,** écraser qch. sous ses pieds; **to g. the faces of the poor,** opprimer les pauvres; (*b*) meuler (une pièce coulée); dépolir (le verre, un bouchon); (*c*) aiguiser, émoudre, affûter (un outil); passer (un couteau, etc.) à la meule; mettre le tranchant à (une lame); (*d*) **to g. one's teeth,** grincer des dents; (*e*) jouer (d'un orgue de Barbarie); **to g. (out) a tune,** tourner un air. **2.** *v.i.* (*a*) (*of wheels*) grincer, crisser; (*b*) *F:* bûcher, turbiner; *Sch:* bachoter. **grinding 1.** *a.* (*a*) **g. sound,** grincement *m*, crissement *m*; (*b*) (*of pain*) déchirant; (*of worry*) rongeur, rongeant; **g. poverty,** misère écrasante. **2.** *n.* (*a*) mouture *f* (du blé); broyage *m*, broiement *m* (des couleurs); pilage *m* (dans un mortier); *Ind:* **g. mill,** broyeur *m*; (*b*) (i) meulage *m*; rodage *m*; polissage *m* à la meule; (ii) aiguisage *m*, affûtage *m*; (*c*) grincement *m*, crissement *m.* **ground** *a.* **1.** (café, blé) moulu; **g. rice,** semoule *f* de riz; *NAm:* **g. beef,** bœuf hâché. **2.** (acier) meulé; (verre) dépoli.

grinder [ˈgraindər] *n.* **1.** (*a*) broyeur, -euse; **organ g.,** joueur, -euse, d'orgue de Barbarie; (*b*) rémouleur *m* (de couteaux, de ciseaux). **2.** (dent) molaire (*f*). **3.** (*a*) appareil broyeur; broyeuse *f*; **coffee g.,** moulin *m* à café; (*b*) meule courante (d'un moulin); (*c*) *Mec.E:* rectifieuse *f*; machine *f* à rectifier; (*d*) machine *f* à aiguiser, à affûter; affûteuse *f*; (*e*) *F:* **to put s.o. through the g.,** faire passer un mauvais quart d'heure à qn. **4.** *U.S: F:* gros sandwich.

grindstone [ˈgraindstoun] *n.* meule *f* (en grès) à aiguiser; *F:* **he keeps our noses to the g.,** il ne nous laisse aucun répit.

gringo [ˈgriŋgou] *n. usu. Pej:* (*in Latin America*) Anglo-américain, -aine.

grip¹ [grip] *n.* **1.** prise *f*, serrage *m*; serrement *m* (d'un outil); étreinte *f* (des mains); adhérence *f* (des roues sur la route); **to have a strong g.,** avoir une bonne poigne; **to come to grips,** en venir aux prises (**with,** avec); **to get a g. on sth.,** prendre prise à qch.; **to lose one's g.,** (i) lâcher prise; (ii) *F:* baisser (du point de vue mental); **in the g. of a disease,** en proie à une maladie; **to have a firm g. on sth.,** tenir qch. bien en main; **to get, take, keep, a g. on oneself,** se maîtriser; se contrôler. **2.** (*a*) poignée *f* (d'aviron, etc.); poignée, crosse *f* (de pistolet); (*b*) *Ten:* manchon *m* (pour raquette); *Cy:* poignée (de guidon). **3.** (*a*) *Mec.E: etc:* douille *f* de serrage; pince *f*; griffe *f*; (*b*) *Hairdr:* **(hair) g.,** pince (à cheveux). **4.** *NAm:* valise *f*; mallette *f.*

grip² *v.tr.* **(gripped)** (*a*) saisir, prendre (qch.); empoigner, agripper (qch.); **to g. sth. in a vice,** serrer, pincer, qch. dans un étau; (*b*) *v.i.* **the wheels are not gripping,** les roues *fpl* n'adhèrent pas (sur la route); (*c*) **fear gripped him,** la peur le saisit; **play that grips the audience,** pièce *f* qui passionne les spectateurs. **gripping** *a.* (*of book, story*) passionnant.

gripe¹ [graip] *n.* **1.** *F:* **gripes,** colique *f.* **2.** *F:* ronchonnerie *f*, rouspétance *f.*

gripe² **1.** *v.tr. F:* (*a*) affliger (qn); (*b*) donner la colique à (qn). **2.** *v.i. F:* ronchonner, rouspéter. **griping** *F:* **1.** *a.* **g. pains,** coliques *fpl.* **2.** *n.* ronchonnerie *f*, rouspétance *f.*

grisly [ˈgrizli] *a. Lit:* (*a*) affreux, horrible; (*b*) effrayant, sinistre.

grist [grist] *n.* blé *m* à moudre; **all is g. to the mill,** ça fait venir l'eau au moulin; **all is g. that comes to his mill,** il fait profit de tout.

gristle [ˈgrisl] *n.* cartilage *m*; croquant *m.*

gristly [ˈgrisli] *a.* cartilagineux; plein de croquant.

grit¹ [grit] *n.* **1.** (*a*) grès *m*, sable *m*; (*b*) *Mec.E: etc:* corps étrangers; impuretés *fpl.* **2.** grès (dur); **millstone g.,** grès à meule(s). **3.** grain *m* (d'une pierre). **4.** *F:* cran *m*, courage *m*; **man of g., who has plenty of g.,** homme qui a du cran.

grit² *v.* **(gritted) 1.** *v.i.* grincer, crisser. **2.** *v.tr.* **to g. one's teeth,** grincer des dents. **3.** *v.tr.* sabler (un pavé glissant, etc.).
grits [grits] *n.pl. NAm:* gruau *m* d'avoine; grosse farine d'avoine.
gritstone ['gritstoun] *n.* grès (dur); pierre *f* de grès.
gritty ['griti] *a.* **1.** (*a*) (sol) gréseux, sablonneux, cendreux; (crayon) graveleux; (poire) graveleuse; (*b*) abrasif. **2.** *NAm: F:* qui a du cran; résolu.
grizzle ['grizl] *v.i.* **1.** se faire de la bile; grognonner. **2.** pleurnicher, geindre. **grizzling** *n.* **1.** grognonnerie *f.* **2.** pleurnicherie *f*, pleurnichement *m.*
grizzled ['griz(ə)ld] *a.* (*of hair, pers.*) grisonnant.
grizzly ['grizli] **1.** *a.* (*of hair, pers.*) grisonnant. **2.** *n. Z:* **g. (bear),** grizzli *m*, grizzly *m.*
groan¹ [groun] *n.* **1.** gémissement *m*; **to give, utter, a deep g.,** pousser un profond gémissement. **2.** (*at meeting*) **groans,** murmures *mpl* de désapprobation.
groan² **1.** *v.i.* gémir; pousser un gémissement; **to g. inwardly,** étouffer une plainte, un gémissement; **the cart is groaning under the load,** la charrette gémit sous le fardeau. **2.** *v.tr.* **he groaned out the whole story,** il a raconté entre ses gémissements ce qui était arrivé.
groats [grouts] *n.pl.* gruau *m* d'avoine, de froment.
grocer ['grousər] *n.* épicier, -ière; **the grocer's will be closed,** l'épicerie sera fermée.
grocery ['grousəri] *n.* **1.** épicerie *f*; **to be in the g. business,** être dans l'épicerie. **2. groceries,** (articles *mpl* d')épicerie.
grog [grɔg] *n.* grog *m.*
groggy ['grɔgi] *a. F:* (*a*) chancelant, titubant; (boxeur) groggy; **to feel g.,** avoir des jambes en coton; (*b*) **I'm feeling a bit g.,** je ne suis pas dans mon assiette.
groin [grɔin] *n.* **1.** *Anat:* aine *f.* **2.** *Arch:* arête *f* (de voûte).
grommet ['grɔmit] *n.* **1.** *Nau:* erse *f*, erseau *m.* **2.** *Mec.E:* bague *f* d'étoupe.
groom¹ [gru:m] *n.m.* **1.** gentilhomme, valet (de la Chambre du Roi, etc.). **2.** palefrenier; garçon d'écurie. **3.** (*at wedding*) le marié.
groom² *v.tr.* **1.** panser (un cheval). **2.** dresser (un candidat) (en vue d'un poste, d'une fonction dans la politique). **groomed** *a.* **well-g.,** (i) (cheval) bien entretenu; (ii) (homme, etc.) bien soigné, soigné de sa personne.
groove¹ [gru:v] *n.* **1.** (*a*) rainure *f*; rayure *f* (d'un canon, etc.); cannelure *f* (d'une colonne, etc.); (*of penknife, etc.*) **thumbnail g.,** onglet *m*; (*b*) *Carp: Mec.E:* rainure; **g. and tongue joint,** assemblage *m* à rainure et languette; (*c*) *Mec.E:* creux *m* (d'une vis); (*for sliding shutter, etc.*) coulisse *f*, glissière *f*; cannelure (d'une poulie); (*d*) *Rec:* **(sound) g.,** sillon sonore. **2.** *F:* routine *f*; **to get into a g.,** s'encroûter; devenir routinier.
groove² *v.tr.* rainer; rayer (un canon, etc.); canneler (une colonne); **to g. and tongue,** assembler à rainure et languette.
groovy ['gru:vi] *a. F:* formidable, épatant.
grope [group] *v.i.* tâtonner; marcher à tâtons; **to g. for sth.,** chercher qch. à tâtons, à l'aveuglette; **to g. one's way,** avancer à tâtons, se diriger en tâtonnant (**towards sth.,** vers qch.). **groping 1.** *a.* tâtonnant. **2.** *n.* tâtonnement *m.*
grosbeak ['grousbi:k] *n. Orn:* gros-bec *m.*
grosgrain ['grougrein] *n. Tex:* gros-grain *m.*
gross¹ [grous] *n. inv.* douze douzaines *fpl*; grosse *f.*
gross² *a.* **1.** gras, *f.* grasse; gros, *f.* grosse; bouffi. **2.** (*a*) grossier; (ignorance) crasse; (injustice) flagrante; (abus) choquant; (*b*) **g. pleasures,** plaisirs grossiers; **g. feeder,** goulu, -ue; (*c*) (*of joke, etc.*) grossier. **3.** (*a*) *Com: Fin:* (bénéfice, revenu) brut; **g. national product,** produit national brut; (*b*) *Com:* **g. weight,** poids brut; brut *m*; (*c*) *Nau:* (déplacement) global, total; **g. (register) tonnage,** (tonnage *m* de) jauge brute, tonnage brut. **-ly** *adv.* grossièrement; énormément (exagéré); **to be g. mistaken,** se tromper grossièrement.
gross³ *v.tr. Com: etc:* produire (tant de francs) brut; **they grossed £10 million,** cela leur a rapporté brut 10 millions de livres.
grossness ['grousnis] *n.* grossièreté *f*; **1.** énormité *f* (d'un abus). **2.** crudité *f* (d'une histoire).
grotesque [grou'tesk] **1.** *a. & n.* grotesque (*m*). **2.** *a.* absurde; bizarre. **-ly** *adv.* grotesquement.
grotto, *pl.* **-oes, -os** ['grɔtou, -ouz] *n.* grotte *f.*
grotty ['grɔti] *n. P:* moche; dégueulasse.
grouch¹ [grautʃ] *n.* **1.** maussaderie *f*; **to have a g. against s.o.,** en vouloir à qn. **2.** (*pers.*) grogneur, -euse.
grouch² *v.i.* grogner, grommeler, ronchonner.
grouchy ['grautʃi] *a.* maussade, grognon.
ground¹ [graund]. *see* GRIND².
ground² *n.* **1.** (*a*) fond *m* (de la mer); *Nau:* (*of ship*) **to touch g.,** talonner; (*b*) *Nau:* **g. swell,** houle *f*, lame *f*, de fond; *Fish:* **g. line,** ligne *f* de fond; **g. bait,** amorce *f* de fond. **2. grounds,** marc *m* (du café, etc.); lie *f* (du vin). **3.** (*a*) fond, champ *m* (d'un tableau); **light colour on a dark g.,** couleur claire sur un fond sombre; (*b*) *Art:* **the middle g.,** le second plan (d'un tableau). **4.** (*a*) raison *f*, cause *f*, motif *m*; base *f* (de soupçons, etc.); **g. for complaint,** grief *m*; **what grounds have you for saying that?** sur quoi vous fondez-vous pour affirmer cela? **on what grounds?** à quel titre? **on personal grounds,** pour des raisons personnelles; (*b*) *Jur:* **grounds for divorce,** motifs de divorce; **grounds for appeal,** voies *fpl* de recours. **5.** (*a*) sol *m*, terre *f*; **sitting on the g.,** assis par terre; **to fall to the g.,** (i) tomber à, par, terre; (ii) (*of scheme*) tomber à l'eau; *Veh:* **g. clearance,** hauteur *f* du châssis au-dessus du sol; **above g.,** sur terre; *Min:* au jour, à la surface; **under g.,** sous terre; **at g. level,** au niveau du sol; **curtains down to the g.,** rideaux qui pendent jusqu'à terre; **burnt (down) to the g.,** brûlé de fond en comble; *F:* **that suits me down to the g.,** *U.S:* **from the g. up,** (i) cela me va à merveille; (ii) ça m'arrange le mieux du monde; *Const:* **g. plan,** plan horizontal; projection horizontale; **to be on sure, firm, g., to be sure of one's g.,** connaître le terrain; être sûr de son fait; **to cut the g. from under s.o.'s feet,** couper l'herbe sous le pied à qn; (*b*) *Av:* **g. crew, personnel, staff,** personnel *m* au sol, personnel non navigant; **g. speed,** vitesse *f* par rapport au sol; (*c*) *Ven:* (*of fox*) **to run, go, to g.,** se terrer; **to run a fox to g.,** poursuivre un renard jusqu'à son terrier; (*d*) terrain *m*; (i) **rocky, rough, g.,** terrain rocheux, raboteux; **open g.,** terrain découvert; (ii) **country house with extensive grounds,** château *m* avec domaine; **g. rent,** loyer *m* de la terre; redevance *f* emphytéotique; (*as source of income*) rente foncière; (iii) **football g.,** terrain de football; *Mil:* **parade g.,** terrain d'exercice, de manœuvre; *Fig:* **to find a common g. for negotiations,** trouver un terrain d'entente en vue de négocier; **to change, shift, one's g.,** changer d'arguments; **to cover a lot of g.,** (i) faire beaucoup de chemin; (ii) parcourir un champ très vaste; **to gain g.,** gagner du terrain, progresser; (*of idea*) faire son chemin; (*of news*) se répandre; **to give, lose, g.,** céder, perdre, du terrain; (*of troops*) se replier; **to hold, stand, one's g.,** tenir bon, tenir ferme. **6.** *El: NAm:* (i) terre; (ii) masse *f*; **to connect to g.,** mettre (un pôle) à la masse; **g. connection,** prise *f* de terre. **7.**

attrib. fondamental, -aux; *Mus:* **g. note,** son fondamental; **g. bass,** basse contrainte.

ground³ **1.** *v.tr.* (*a*) fonder, baser, appuyer (**on, in, sth.,** sur qch.); asseoir (sa conviction) (**on,** sur); (*b*) **to g. a pupil in Latin,** enseigner à fond les rudiments du latin à un élève; (*c*) préparer le fond (d'un tableau); (*d*) mettre (qch.) à terre; *Mil:* **g. arms!** l'arme au pied! reposez armes! (*e*) *NAm: El:* mettre (le courant) à la terre, à la masse; (*f*) *Nau:* jeter (un navire) à la côte; (*g*) *Av:* interdire de vol (un avion). **2.** *v.i.* (*a*) *Nau:* (*of ship*) échouer, s'échouer (**on,** sur); (*b*) (*of balloon*) atterrir. **grounded** *a.* **1. well g., ill g.,** (croyance) bien, mal, fondée; **well g. rumour,** bruit consistant. **2.** *NAm: El:* (mis) à la terre, à la masse. **grounding** *n.* **1.** (*a*) assise *f* (d'un argument sur qch.); (*b*) *NAm: El:* mise *f* (du courant) à la terre, à la masse; (*c*) *Nau:* échouage *m*; (*d*) atterrissage *m* (d'un ballon); (*d*) *Av:* interdiction *f* de vol. **2.** (*a*) **to have a good g. in Latin,** avoir une connaissance solide des rudiments du latin; (*b*) *Paint:* première couche.

groundhog ['graundhɔg] *n. Z:* marmotte *f* d'Amérique.

groundless ['graundlis] *a.* (soupçon, etc.) mal fondé, sans fondement; **my suspicions were g.,** mes soupçons étaient sans motif.

groundnut ['graundnʌt] *n. Bot:* arachide *f.*

groundsel ['graun(d)səl] *n. Bot:* séneçon *m.*

groundsheet ['graundʃi:t] *n.* tapis *m* de sol.

groundsman, *pl.* **-men** ['graundzmən] *n.m.* préposé à l'entretien d'un terrain de jeux.

groundwork ['graundwə:k] *n.* **1.** couleur *f* de fond (d'un tableau, etc.). **2.** (*a*) fondement *m*, fond; base *f*; (*b*) plan *m*, canevas *m* (d'un roman, etc.); (*c*) *Fig:* **to do the g.,** préparer le terrain.

group¹ [gru:p] *n.* (*a*) groupe *m* (de personnes); **to form a g.,** se grouper; **g. action, decision,** action, décision, collective; *Pol:* **political g.,** groupe(ment) politique; **pressure g.,** groupe de pression; **blood g.,** groupe sanguin; *Psy:* **g. therapy,** sociatrie *f*; *Mus:* **pop g.,** groupe pop; (*b*) *Mil.Av:* (i) commandement aérien tactique; (ii) zone *f* de défense aérienne; (iii) *U.S:* escadre aérienne; **g. captain,** colonel *m*; (*c*) groupe, ensemble *m* (de choses); *Mec.E:* ensemble; **(arranged) in groups of three,** (objets, etc.) disposés en groupes de trois.

group² **1.** *v.tr.* grouper, disposer en groupes; combiner (des idées). **2.** *v.i.* se grouper (**round,** autour de). **grouping** *n.* groupage *m* (de colis, etc.); groupement *m* (de figures, etc.); **blood g.,** groupage sanguin.

grouper ['gru:pər] *n. Ich:* mérou *m.*

groupie ['gru:pi] *n.f. F:* minette (qui suit les groupes de rock); groupie.

grouse¹ [graus] *n. inv. in pl. Orn:* tétras *m*, grouse *m or f*; **red g.,** lagopède *m* (rouge) d'Écosse; **black g.,** tétras lyre.

grouse² *n.* **1.** grogne *f*; **he enjoys a good g.,** il aime à grogner. **2. to have a g. against s.o.,** avoir un grief contre qn.

grouse³ *v.i.* ronchonner, grogner (**at, about,** contre). **grousing** *n.* grognonnerie *f.*

grouser ['grausər] *n.* grognon *mf.*

grout¹ [graut] *n. Const: etc:* coulis *m*; mortier clair, liquide; **cement g.,** lait *m*, laitance *f*, de ciment.

grout² *v.tr. Const:* jointoyer (des pierres).

grove [grouv] *n.* futaie *f*, bosquet *m*; **beech g.,** hêtraie *f*; **orange g.,** orangeraie *f*; **olive g.,** oliveraie *f.*

grovel ['grɔv(ə)l] *v.i.* **(grovelled,** *NAm:* **groveled)** ramper; **to g. in the dirt,** se vautrer, se traîner, dans la boue; **to g. to, before, s.o.,** ramper, se prosterner, devant qn. **grovelling** **1.** *a.* rampant; bas, vil. **2.** *n.* (*a*) rampement *m*; prosternation *f* (devant qn).

grow [grou] *v.* (*p.t.* **grew** [gru:]; *p.p.* **grown** [groun]) **I.** *v.i.* **1.** (*a*) (*of plants*) croître, pousser; **to g. again,** recroître, repousser; (*of plants, hair*) revenir; (*of nail*) **to g. in,** s'incarner; (*b*) (*of seeds*) germer; **the custom has grown up,** la coutume s'est établie; (*c*) **olives do not g. in England,** l'olivier ne pousse pas en Angleterre; *F:* (*esp. of money*) **it doesn't g. on trees,** ça ne pousse pas sur les arbres. **2.** (*of pers.*) grandir; **to g. tall,** devenir grand; grandir; **he had grown into a man,** il était devenu homme; **to g. up,** grandir; **to g. out of one's clothes,** devenir trop grand pour ses vêtements; **he's mischievous, but he will g. out of it,** s'il est espiègle, cela passera avec l'âge. **3.** (*a*) s'accroître, grandir; **the crowd grew,** la foule augmentait, grossissait; **his influence grew,** son influence a grandi; **the rumour was growing,** la rumeur grandissait; **to g. in wisdom, in beauty,** croître en sagesse, en beauté; (*b*) **habit that grows on one,** habitude *f* qui vous gagne; (*c*) *F:* **that picture grows on me,** plus je regarde ce tableau plus il me plaît. **4.** (*a*) devenir; **to g. old,** devenir vieux; vieillir; **to g. younger,** rajeunir; **to g. big, bigger,** (i) grandir; (ii) grossir; (iii) augmenter; **to g. smaller,** (i) rapetisser; (ii) diminuer; **to g. alarmed, excited,** s'alarmer, s'exciter; **to g. angry,** se fâcher; **to g. less,** diminuer; **it is growing dark,** il commence à faire sombre; (*b*) **I have grown to think that . . .,** j'en suis venu à penser que . . .. **II.** *v.tr.* **1.** cultiver (des roses); planter (des choux); **soil that will not g. asparagus,** sol *m* qui se refuse aux asperges. **2.** laisser pousser (sa barbe, etc.); **the stag grows fresh antlers every year,** le cerf renouvelle ses andouillers chaque année. **growing** **1.** *a.* (*a*) croissant; qui pousse; (*b*) grandissant; (i) (enfant) en cours de croissance; (ii) (dette) qui augmente; (opinion) de plus en plus répandue; **there was a g. fear that . . .,** on craignait de plus en plus que . . .; (*c*) **wheat-g., potato-g., district,** région *f* à blé, à pommes de terre. **2.** *n.* (*a*) croissance *f*; **g. pains,** douleurs *fpl* de croissance; (*b*) culture *f* (de légumes, etc.). **grown** *a.* **(full-) g.,** grand; **to be g. up,** être adulte; *n.pl.* **the g.-ups,** les grands; les grandes personnes.

grower ['grouər] *n.* **1.** (*of plant*) **fast g., slow g.,** plante *f* qui croît vite, lentement. **2.** (*pers.*) cultivateur, -trice; **rose g.,** rosiériste *mf.*

growl¹ [graul] *n.* grondement *m*, grognement *m.*

growl² *v.i. & tr.* **1.** (*of animal*) grogner; (*of cat*) feuler; gronder (**at,** contre). **2.** (*of pers.*) gronder, grogner, grommeler. **growling** *n.* grognement *m*, grondement *m*; (*of cat*) feulement *m.*

grown. *see* GROW.

growth [grouθ] *n.* **1.** croissance *f*, venue *f*; **plant of quick g.,** plante *f* qui pousse vite. **2.** accroissement *m*; développement *m* (des affaires); extension *f* (des affaires, d'une maison de commerce); expansion *f* (de la population); **economic g.,** développement, croissance, économique; **rate of g.,** taux *m* d'expansion, de croissance. **3.** (*a*) **yearly g.,** pousse annuelle; (*b*) poussée *f* (de cheveux, etc.); **a week's g. on his chin,** le menton couvert d'une barbe de huit jours. **4.** *Med:* tumeur *f*, excroissance *f*; **benign, malignant, g.,** tumeur bénigne, maligne.

groyne [grɔin] *n.* brise-lames *m inv.*

grub¹ [grʌb] *n.* **1.** *Ent:* (*a*) larve *f*; (*b*) *F:* ver (blanc); asticot *m.* **2.** *P:* boustifaille *f*; **grub's up!** à la soupe!

grub² **1.** *v.tr.* (*a*) fouir, travailler superficiellement (la terre); (*b*) défricher (un terrain). **2.** *v.i.* fouiller (dans la terre). **grub about** *v.i.* fouiller, farfouiller. **grubbing** *n.* (*a*) fouillage *m*; (*b*) **g. up,** extirpation *f* (des racines); défrichage *m*, défrichement *m* (d'un terrain). **grub out** *v.tr.* extirper (des racines, etc.). **grub up** *v.tr.* (*a*) extirper (une racine); déraciner (une plante); (*b*) défricher (un terrain).

grubber ['grʌbər] *n. Agr:* (*a*) extirpateur *m*; (*b*) hoyau *m*; (*c*) arrachoir *m*.
grubbiness ['grʌbinis] *n.* saleté *f*; malpropreté *f*.
grubby ['grʌbi] *a.* sale, crasseux, malpropre.
grubstake ['grʌbsteik] *n. NAm:* provisions *fpl* données à un prospecteur (contre un pourcentage de ses profits).
grudge¹ [grʌdʒ] *n.* rancune *f*; **to bear s.o. a g., to have a g. against s.o.,** en vouloir à qn.
grudge² *v.tr.* **1.** donner (qch. à qn) à contrecœur, à regret; **to g. s.o. the food he eats,** lésiner sur la nourriture de qn. **2. to g. s.o. his pleasures,** voir d'un mauvais œil les plaisirs de qn. **grudging** *a.* (*of praise, gift*) fait, donné, à contrecœur. **grudgingly** *adv.* (faire qch.) à contrecœur, de mauvaise grâce.
gruel ['gru(:)əl] *n.* gruau *m* (d'avoine); (*thin*) brouet *m*.
gruelling ['gru(:)əliŋ] *a.* éreintant, épuisant; (match) âprement disputé; **we had a g. time,** ç'a été tout ce qu'il y a de plus dur.
gruesome ['gru:səm] *a.* horrible, macabre, affreux. **-ly** *adv.* horriblement, affreusement.
gruff [grʌf] *a.* (ton) bourru, rébarbatif, brusque; **g. voice,** grosse voix. **-ly** *adv.* d'un ton bourru.
gruffness ['grʌfnis] *n.* ton bourru; brusquerie *f*.
grumble¹ ['grʌmbl] *n.* (*a*) grommellement *m*, grognement *m*, grondement *m*; (*b*) murmure *m* (de mécontentement); **to obey without a g.,** obéir sans murmurer; (*c*) *F:* **to have a good old g.,** rouspéter.
grumble² *v.i.* grommeler, grogner; *F:* rouspéter; **to g. about the food,** se plaindre de la nourriture; trouver à redire à la nourriture; **to g. at s.o.,** grommeler, rouspéter, contre qn. **grumbling 1.** *a.* (*a*) grognon; grondeur, -euse; (*b*) **g. appendix,** appendicite *f* chronique. **2.** *n.* (*a*) rouspétance *f*; (*b*) mécontentement *m*.
grumbler ['grʌmblər] *n.* **1.** grognon *m*, grommeleur, -euse, rouspéteur, -euse. **2.** mécontent, -ente.
grummet ['grʌmit] *n.* = GROMMET.
grumpiness ['grʌmpinis] *n.* mauvaise humeur; maussaderie *f*; caractère *m* désagréable.
grumpy ['grʌmpi] *a.* maussade, renfrogné; **a g. old man,** un vieux grincheux. **-ily** *adv.* maussadement; d'un ton, d'un air, maussade.
grunt¹ [grʌnt] *n.* grognement *m* (de porc, de qn); **to give a g.,** pousser, faire entendre, un grognement.
grunt² **1.** *v.i.* (*of pig, of pers.*) grogner; pousser un grognement. **2.** *v.tr.* **to g. (out) an answer,** grogner une réponse. **grunting** *n.* grognement(s) *m*(*pl*).
Guadeloupe [gwɑ:dəlu:p] *Pr.n.* Guadeloupe *f*.
guano ['gwɑ:nou] *n.* guano *m*.
guarantee¹ [gærən'ti:] *n.* **1.** (*pers.*) (*a*) (*guarantor*) garant, -ante; caution *f*; (*b*) créancier *m* à qui est donné caution; garanti, -ie. **2.** garantie *f* (**against,** contre); **clock with g. for two years,** pendule *f* avec une garantie de deux ans. **3.** (*security*) garantie, caution, gage *m*; **to leave sth. as a g.,** laisser qch. en gage.
guarantee² *v.tr.* **1.** garantir, cautionner (qn, qch.); se porter garant, caution, pour (qn, qch.); garantir (une dette); **watch guaranteed for two years,** montre garantie pour deux ans; **I won't g. that he'll come,** je ne garantis pas qu'il viendra. **2. to g. s.o. against loss,** garantir les pertes à qn.
guarantor [gærən'tɔ:r] *n.* garant, -ante; caution *f*; **to stand as g. for s.o.,** appuyer qn de sa garantie.
guaranty ['gærənti] *n.* = GUARANTEE¹ 2, 3.
guard¹ [gɑ:d] *n.* **1.** garde *f*; (*a*) *Fenc: Box:* **on g.!** en garde! (*b*) **to be on one's g.,** être, se tenir, sur ses gardes; **to be on one's g. against sth.,** être sur ses gardes contre qch.; **to put s.o. on his g.,** mettre qn en garde; **to be caught off one's g.,** être pris au dépourvu; (*c*) (*of sentry, etc.*) **to be on g. (duty),** être en, de, faction; être de garde; **to go on g., to mount g.,** monter la garde; **to come off g.,** descendre de garde; **to keep g.,** faire la garde, être de garde; **to keep a prisoner under g.,** garder un prisonnier à vue; **he was marched off under g.,** il fut emmené sous escorte. **2.** *coll.* (*a*) *Mill:* garde *f*; **main g.,** gros *m* d'avant-garde; **mounting of the g.,** parade *f*; **one of the old g.,** un vieux de la vieille; **g. of honour,** garde d'honneur; **to form a g. of honour,** faire la haie; (*b*) **to set a g. on a bridge,** faire surveiller un pont. **3.** (*pers.*) (*a*) chef *m* de train; **frontier g.,** garde-frontière *m*, *pl.* gardes-frontière; (*b*) *Mil:* **the Guards,** les Gardes *mpl* du corps; **Home G.** = milice *f*; (*c*) *U.S:* **prison g.,** gardien *m* de prison. **4.** (*a*) dispositif protecteur; protecteur *m* (d'une machine); carter *m* (d'engrenages, etc.); garde-fou *m*, *pl.* garde-fous (de passerelle, etc.); **fire g.,** garde-feu *m inv*; **g. rail,** (i) garde-corps, garde-fou; (ii) *Rail:* contre-rail *m*, *pl.* contre-rails; (iii) balustrade *f*; (*b*) garde *f* (d'un fleuret).
guard² **1.** *v.tr.* (*a*) garder; **to g. s.o. from, against, a danger,** garder, protéger, qn d'un danger; (*b*) surveiller (sa langue); mesurer (ses paroles); (*c*) *Ind:* protéger (un engrenage, etc.); mettre un carter à (un mécanisme). **2.** *v.i.* **to g. against sth.,** se garder de qch.; parer à qch.; **to g. against an error,** se méfier d'une erreur. **guarded** *a.* **1.** (*of speech*) prudent, mesuré, circonspect; (réponse) qui n'engage à rien. **2.** (mécanisme etc.) protégé. **3.** (prisonnier) gardé à vue. **guardedly** *adv.* avec circonspection, avec précaution. **guarding** *n.* garde *f* (de qn, qch.).
guardhouse ['gɑ:dhaus] *n.* corps-de-garde *m inv*.
guardian ['gɑ:diən] *n.* **1.** (*a*) gardien, -ienne; (*b*) conservateur, -trice (d'un musée, etc.). **2.** tuteur, -trice (de mineur); conseil *m* judiciaire (d'un prodigue). **3. g. angel,** ange gardien.
guardianship ['gɑ:diənʃip] *n.* **1.** garde *f*. **2.** *Jur:* gestion *f* tutélaire; tutelle *f*.
guardroom ['gɑ:dru:m] *n. Mil:* **1.** corps-de-garde *m inv*. **2.** salle *f*, poste *m*, de police.
guardsman, *pl.* **-men** ['gɑ:dzmən] *n.m.* (i) officier, (ii) soldat, de la Garde.
Guatemala [gwæti'mɑ:lə) *Pr.n.* Guatemala *m*.
Guatemalan [gwæti'mɑ:lən] *Geog:* **1.** *a.* guatémaltèque. **2.** *n.* Guatémaltèque *mf*.
guava ['gwɑ:və] *n. Bot:* **1.** goyave *f*. **2. g. (tree),** goyavier *m*.
gudgeon¹ ['gʌdʒən] *n. Ich:* goujon *m*.
gudgeon² *n. Mec.E:* goujon *m*, tourillon *m*, axe *m*; **g. pin,** (i) *I.C.E:* axe de pied de bielle; (ii) *Mch:* tourillon de la crosse.
guelder-rose ['geldə'rouz] *n. Bot:* boule-de-neige *f*.
Guernsey ['gə:nzi] **1.** *Pr.n. Geog:* Guernesey. **2.** *n.* (*a*) **g.,** tricot *m*; jersey *m*; (*b*) vache *f* de Guernesey.
guer(r)illa [gə'rilə] *n. Mil:* guérillero *m*; **troop, band, of guer(r)illas,** guérilla *f*; **g. warfare,** guérilla.
guess¹ [ges] *n.* conjecture *f*, estimation *f*; **to have, make, a g.,** (i) hasarder une conjecture; (ii) tâcher de deviner; **you've made a lucky g.,** vous êtes bien tombé; **your g. is as good as mine,** j'en sais autant que toi; **it's anybody's g.,** qui sait? Dieu seul le sait; **I give you three guesses,** tu devines? **at a g.,** au jugé.
guess² *v.tr. & i.* **1. to g. at sth.,** (tâcher de) deviner qch.; **to g. the length of sth.,** estimer la longueur de qch.; **g. who did it!** devinez qui l'a fait! **I guessed him to be twenty-five,** je lui ai donné vingt-cinq ans. **2. to g. right, wrong,** bien, mal, deviner; **you've guessed**

it! you've guessed right! vous l'avez deviné! to g. sth. from s.o.'s manner, juger qch. d'après l'attitude de qn. 3. *esp. NAm:* croire, penser; I g., à ce que je pense; I g. you're right, m'est avis que vous avez raison. **guessing** *n.* estimation *f*; g. games, devinettes *fpl.*

guesswork ['geswɔːk] *n.* estime *f*, conjecture *f*; **it's pure g.**, c'est pure conjecture; **by g.**, à l'estime; au jugé; **by sheer g.**, à vue de nez.

guest [gest] *n.* **1.** convive *mf*; invité, -ée; **g. artist**, artiste invité(e); *Iron:* **be my g.!** faites comme chez vous! **2.** client, -ente (d'un hôtel); **the landlord and his guests**, l'hôtelier *m* et ses hôtes; **paying g.**, pensionnaire *mf.*

guesthouse ['gesthaus] *n.* **1.** hôtellerie *f* (d'un monastère, etc.). **2.** pension *f* de famille.

guestroom ['gestruːm] *n.* chambre *f* d'ami(s).

guffaw¹ [gʌ'fɔː] *n.* gros rire (bruyant); pouffement *m.*

guffaw² *v.i.* pouffer de rire; s'esclaffer.

Guiana [gi'ɑːnə] *Pr.n. Geog: Hist:* Guyane *f.*

guidance ['gaidəns] *n.* **1.** direction *f*, gouverne *f*, conduite *f*; **under the g. of . . .**, sous la direction de . . .; **sent for your g.**, envoyé à titre d'indication; *Sch:* **vocational g.**, orientation professionnelle. **2.** *Ball:* guidage *m*; **radio g.**, radioguidage *m.*

guide¹ [gaid] *n.* **1.** (*pers.*) (*a*) guide *m*; **museum g.**, guide de musée; **to take sth. as a g.**, prendre qch. pour règle; (*b*) *Scout:* **(girl) g.**, éclaireuse *f*; *R.C.Ch:* guide de France. **2.** (*book*) guide; livret *m* (de musée); indicateur *m* (des chemins de fer); **g. to Switzerland**, guide de la Suisse. **3.** (*a*) indication *f*, exemple *m*; **as a g.**, à titre indicatif; (*b*) *Mec.E: etc:* guide (d'ascenseur, etc.); **g. rope**, (i) câble *m* de guidage; (ii) *Aer:* guiderope *m*; *Rail:* **g. rail**, contre-rail *m*, *pl.* contre-rails; (*c*) **g. line**, ligne *f* pour guider la main (en écrivant); **g. lines**, (i) transparent (rayé); (ii) directives *fpl*; (*of card index*); **g. (card)**, intercalaire *m.*

guide² *v.tr.* guider, conduire, diriger; **to g. a child's first steps**, guider les premiers pas d'un enfant; **I will be guided by your advice**, je suivrai vos conseils. **guided** *a.* (*a*) (*of tour, etc.*) guidé; sous la conduite d'un guide; (*b*) *Ball:* (missile, etc.) guidé; **radio-g.**, radioguidé. **guiding 1.** *a.* qui sert de guide; (principe) directeur; **the g. principles of his life**, les principes sur lesquels se guide sa vie; **g. star**, guide *m*. **2.** *n.* guidage *m*, conduite *f*, direction *f.*

guideline ['gaidlain] *n. Pol: etc:* directive *f*; indication *f* d'une politique à suivre.

guild [gild] *n.* **1.** *Hist:* corporation *f*; **merchant g.**, guilde *f* de commerçants. **2.** association *f*, confrérie *f*; **church g.**, cercle *m.*

guilder ['gildər] *n. Num:* florin *m.*

guildhall ['gildhɔːl] *n.* **1.** salle *f* de réunion d'une guilde. **2.** hôtel *m* de ville.

guile [gail] *n.* artifice *m*, ruse *f*, astuce *f.*

guileless ['gaillis] *a.* **1.** franc, *f.* franche; sincère. **2.** candide, naïf.

guillemot ['gilimɔt] *n. Orn:* guillemot *m.*

guillotine¹ ['gilətiːn] *n.* **1.** guillotine *f.* **2.** *Bookb:* guillotine, massicot *m*; presse *f* à rogner. **3.** *Parl:* clôture *f* par tranches.

guillotine² *v.tr.* **1.** guillotiner (qn). **2.** *Bookb:* guillotiner, massicoter (du papier, etc.). **3.** *Parl:* appliquer la clôture par tranches à (un projet de loi).

guilt [gilt] *n.* culpabilité *f*; **the g. does not lie with him alone**, il n'y a pas que lui de coupable.

guiltless ['giltlis] *a.* innocent **(of sth.**, de qch.).

guilty ['gilti] *a.* (*a*) coupable **(of theft**, de vol); **g. person**, coupable *mf*; **he is not the only g. party**, il n'y a pas que lui de coupable; *Jur:* **to plead g., not g.**, plaider coupable, non coupable; **to find s.o. g., not g.**, prononcer, déclarer, qn coupable, innocent; **verdict of g., not g.**, verdict *m* de culpabilité, d'acquittement; (*b*) qui se sent coupable; **g. conscience**, mauvaise conscience; conscience chargée; **g. look**, regard confus; (*c*) (acte) coupable. **-ily** *adv.* coupablement; d'un air coupable.

Guinea ['gini] **1.** *Pr.n. Geog:* Guinée *f*; *Orn:* **g. cock**, pintade *f* mâle; **g. hen**, pintade. **2.** *n. A:* **g.**, (pièce *f* d'or d'une) guinée (= 21 shillings).

guineafowl ['ginifaul] *n.* (*a*) *Orn:* pintade *f*; (*b*) *Cu:* pintadon *m.*

guineapig ['ginipig] *n.* cobaye *m*; cochon *m* d'Inde; **to be a g.**, servir de cobaye.

guise [gaiz] *n.* dehors *m*, apparence *f*; **under, in, the g. of friendship**, sous l'apparence, sous le masque, de l'amitié; **under the g. of religion**, sous le manteau, le couvert, de la religion.

guitar [gi'tɑːr, *NAm: also* 'gitɑːr] *Mus:* guitare *f*; **electric g.**, guitare électrique.

guitarist [gi'tɑːrist] *n. Mus:* guitariste *mf.*

gulch [gʌltʃ] *n. NAm:* ravin *m.*

gulf [gʌlf] *n.* **1.** *Geog:* golfe *m*; **the G. Stream**, le Gulfstream. **2.** gouffre *m*, abîme *m*; **there is a g. between the two ideologies**, un abîme sépare les deux idéologies.

gull¹ [gʌl] *n. Orn:* mouette *f*, goéland *m*; **black-headed g.**, mouette rieuse; **herring g.**, goéland argenté.

gull² *n. O: F:* gogo *m*, jobard *m.*

gull³ *v.tr. O: F:* duper, rouler (qn).

gullet ['gʌlit] *n. Anat:* œsophage *m*, *F:* gosier *m.*

gullibility [gʌli'biliti] *n.* crédulité *f*, jobarderie *f.*

gullible ['gʌlibl] *a.* facile à duper; crédule.

gully¹ ['gʌli] *n.* **1.** *Geol:* (petit) ravin. **2.** *Civ.E:* caniveau *m*; rigole *f*; **g. hole**, bouche *f* d'égout.

gully² *v.tr.* raviner; creuser.

gulp¹ [gʌlp] *n.* **1.** coup *m* de gosier; **to swallow sth. at one g.**, avaler qch. d'un coup. **2.** grosse bouchée.

gulp² *v.* **1.** *v.tr.* (*a*) **to g. sth. down**, avaler qch. à grosses bouchées; ingurgiter (une huître); **he gulped it down**, il n'en fit qu'une bouchée; (*of drink*) il n'en fit qu'une gorgée; (*b*) **to g. down, back, one's tears**, avaler, refouler, ses larmes. **2.** *v.i.* essayer d'avaler; **he gulped**, sa gorge se serra.

gum¹ [gʌm] *n.* **1.** (*a*) gomme *f*; (*b*) (*adhesive*) gomme, colle. **2.** (*a*) **g. arabic**, gomme arabique. **3.** *Comest:* (*a*) chewing-gum *m*; **bubble g.**, chewing-gum qui fait des bulles; (*b*) boule *f* de gomme. **4.** (*of eye*) chassie *f.* **5.** (*disease of fruit trees*) gomme. **6.** *Bot:* **g. tree**, gommier *m*; *F:* **to be up a g. tree**, être dans le pétrin.

gum² *v.* **(gummed) 1.** *v.tr.* (*a*) gommer, encoller (le papier, la toile); (*b*) coller (une page dans un livre, etc.); **to g. two pages together**, réunir deux feuilles avec de la colle; (*c*) **to g. (up)**, (i) *I.C.E:* gommer (un piston); (ii) encrasser (une lime); *F:* **to g. up the works**, mettre des bâtons dans les roues. **2.** *v.i.* (*of piston*) **to g. (up)**, (se) gommer. **gummed** *a.* **1.** (*of label*) gommé. **2. g. up**, (piston) gommé; *F:* (projet) qui ne marche plus.

gum³ *n.* gencive *f*; *Box:* **g. shield**, protège-dents *m inv.*

gum⁴ *int. F: O:* **by g.!** fichtre! mazette!

gumboil ['gʌmbɔil] *n.* abcès *m* à la gencive; *Med:* parulie *f.*

gumboot ['gʌmbuːt] *n.* botte *f* de caoutchouc.

gumdrop ['gʌmdrɔp] *n. Comest:* boule *f* de gomme.

gummy ['gʌmi] *a.* gommeux; gluant.

gumption ['gʌm(p)ʃ(ə)n] *n. F:* jugeotte *f*, sens *m* pratique; **he's got plenty of g.**, c'est un débrouillard.

gumshoe ['gʌmʃuː] *n. U.S:* **1.** (*rubber overshoe*) caoutchouc *m*. **2.** *F:* détective *m*, flic *m.*

gun¹ [gʌn] *n.* **1.** (*a*) *Artil:* canon *m*, bouche *f* à feu, pièce *f* (d'artillerie); **the guns**, l'artillerie *f*, le canon; **the big guns**, la grosse artillerie, les grosses pièces; *F:*

g. fodder, chair *f* à canon; **do you hear the guns?** entendez-vous le canon? **g. carriage,** affût *m* de canon; (*at military funeral*) prolonge *f* d'artillerie; (*b*) **machine g.,** mitrailleuse *f*; (*c*) coup *m* de canon; **salute of six guns,** salve *f* (d'honneur) de six coups de canon; (*d*) *Elcs:* **electron g.,** canon à électrons; (*e*) *F:* (*pers.*) **big g.,** gros manitou, grosse légume; **it was blowing great guns,** il faisait un vent à décorner les bœufs; **to be going great guns,** (i) marcher tambour battant; (ii) être en pleine forme; (iii) être en plein succès; *O:* **son of a g.,** coquin *m*. **2.** (*a*) fusil *m*, *esp.* fusil de chasse non rayé; **single-barrelled, double-barrelled, g.,** fusil à un coup, à deux coups; **air g.,** fusil, carabine *f*, à air comprimé; **harpoon g.,** fusil harpon; **automatic g.,** fusil mitrailleur automatique; *F:* **to jump the g.,** brûler le feu; **to stick to one's guns,** tenir bon; ne pas en démordre; **g. barrel,** canon de fusil; **g. runner,** contrebandier *m* d'armes; **g. running,** contrebande *f* d'armes; (*b*) (*pers.*) chasseur *m*; **a party of six guns,** une bande de six chasseurs. **3.** revolver *m*; pistolet *m*. **4.** (*a*) *Mec.E:* seringue *f*, injecteur *m* (à graisse); (*b*) *Paint:* **spray g.,** pistolet (à peinture); *Hort:* **flame g.,** agriflamme *m*.

gun² *v.* **(gunned) 1.** *v.i.* (*a*) **to g. for game,** chasser le gibier au tir; (*b*) *F:* **to g. for sth., s.o.,** pourchasser qch., qn; **he's gunning for us,** c'est à nous qu'il en veut. **2.** *v.tr. F:* **to g. s.o. down,** tuer (qn) d'un coup de revolver. **3.** *v.tr. Aut:* (faire) emballer (son moteur).

gunboat ['gʌnbout] *n.* aviso-torpilleur *m*, *pl.* avisos-torpilleurs.

guncotton ['gʌnkɔt(ə)n] *n. Exp:* fulmicoton *m*.

gundeck ['gʌndek] *n. Navy:* batterie *f*.

gundog ['gʌndɔg] *n.* chien *m* d'arrêt.

gunfight ['gʌnfait] *n.* bagarre *f* entre bandits armés.

gunfire ['gʌnfaiər] *n. Artil:* (*a*) canonnade *f*; feu *m* (des pièces); (*b*) tir *m* rapide.

gunmaker ['gʌnmeikər] *n.* armurier *m*.

gunman, *pl.* **-men** ['gʌnmən] *n.m.* (*a*) partisan armé; (*b*) voleur armé; bandit *m*; terroriste *m*.

gunmetal ['gʌnmet(ə)l] *n.* **1.** bronze *m* à canon. **2.** *Com: F:* métal oxydé. **3. g. (grey),** gris acier (foncé).

gunner ['gʌnər] *n.* (*a*) artilleur *m*; (*b*) **machine g.,** mitrailleur *m*; (*c*) *Navy:* (*warrant officer*) canonnier.

gunnery ['gʌnəri] *n.* artillerie *f*; tir *m* au canon.

gunny ['gʌni] *n.* **1.** toile *f* de jute. **2.** sac *m* en jute.

gunplay ['gʌnplei] *n.* coups *mpl* de revolver.

gunpoint ['gʌnpɔint] *n.* **at g.,** sous la menace d'un pistolet, d'un fusil; **to hold s.o. at g.,** menacer qn d'un pistolet, d'un fusil.

gunport ['gʌnpɔ:t] *n. Navy:* sabord *m* de batterie.

gunpowder ['gʌnpaudər] *n.* poudre *f* (à canon); *Hist:* **the G. Plot,** la Conspiration des Poudres.

gunroom ['gʌnru:m] *n.* **1.** *Navy:* poste *m* des aspirants. **2.** salle *f* aux fusils (d'un chasseur).

gunship ['gʌnʃip] *n.* **(helicopter) g.,** hélicoptère *m* de protection.

gunshot ['gʌnʃɔt] *n.* **1.** coup *m* de fusil, de canon; coup de feu; **g. wound,** blessure *f* de balle; **to receive a g. wound,** recevoir un coup de feu. **2. within, out of, g.,** à, hors de, portée de fusil.

gunslinger ['gʌnsliŋər] *n. F:* vaurien armé.

gunsmith ['gʌnsmiθ] *n.* armurier *m*; **gunsmith's shop,** armurerie *f*.

gunstock ['gʌnstɔk] *n.* fût *m* (de fusil).

gunwale ['gʌn(ə)l] *n. Nau:* (*a*) plat-bord *m*, *pl.* plats-bords; (*b*) **gunwales,** fargues *fpl* (de canot).

guppy ['gʌpi] *n. Ich:* guppy *m*.

gurgle¹ ['gə:gl] *n.* (*a*) (*of liquid*) glouglou *m*; gargouillis *m* (de l'eau qui tombe); murmure *m* (d'un ruisseau); (*b*) (*of pers.*) gloussement *m*, roucoulement *m*; **gurgles of laughter,** des roucoulements de rire.

gurgle² **1.** *v.i.* (*of liquid*) (*a*) glouglouter; faire glouglou (en sortant de la bouteille); (*b*) gargouiller (en tombant); (*c*) (*of stream*) murmurer. **2.** *v.i. & tr.* (*of pers.*) glousser, roucouler; **he gurgled with laughter,** il a gloussé de rire. **gurgling 1.** *a.* (*a*) (*of liquid in bottle*) glougloutant; qui fait glouglou; (*b*) (ruisseau) murmurant; (*c*) **a g. laugh,** un gloussement de rire. **2.** *n.* (*a*) glouglou *m*; (*b*) gargouillement *m*; (*c*) roucoulement *m*.

Gurkha ['gə:kə] *n. Ethn:* Go(u)rkha *m*.

gurnard ['gə:nəd], **gurnet** ['gə:nit] *n.* grondin *m*.

guru ['guru:] *n.m. Hindu Rel:* gourou.

gush¹ [gʌʃ] *n.* **1.** effusion *f* (d'une source, de larmes); bouillonnement *m* (d'un torrent). **2.** jet *m*, flot *m* (de sang). **3.** épanchement *m* de sentiments; débordement sentimental.

gush² **1.** *v.i.* (*a*) **to g. (forth, out),** jaillir, couler à flots; (*of torrent*) bouillonner; **tears gushed from her eyes,** des pleurs jaillirent de ses yeux; (*b*) faire de longs discours sentimentaux; *F:* la faire au sentiment; **she gushed over their baby,** elle s'attendrissait sur leur bébé. **2.** *v.tr.* **to g. water, oil,** lancer des jets d'eau, un jet de pétrole. **gushing** *a.* **1.** (*of water*) jaillissant, vif; (*of torrent*) bouillonnant. **2.** (*of pers.*) exubérant, expansif; (compliments) chaleureux; **she's rather g.,** elle se jette à votre tête.

gusher ['gʌʃər] *n.* **1.** personne exubérante. **2.** *Petr:* source (de pétrole) jaillissante; puits jaillissant.

gusset ['gʌsit] *n.* pièce *f* triangulaire (d'étoffe, etc.); *Dressm:* soufflet *m*; gousset (de manche, etc.).

gust¹ [gʌst] *n.* **1.** bouffée *f* (de fumée, de colère, etc.). **2.** (*a*) **g. of rain,** ondée *f*, giboulée *f*; (*b*) **g. of wind,** coup *m* de vent; rafale *f*, bourrasque *f*, *Nau:* grain *m*.

gust² *v.i.* (*of wind*) souffler par rafales.

gusto ['gʌstou] *n.* délectation *f*, goût *m*; **to eat sth. with g.,** manger qch. en savourant; *F:* **to do sth. with g.,** faire qch. (i) avec plaisir, (ii) avec élan.

gusty ['gʌsti] *a.* (temps, lieu) venteux; (vent) à rafales; (journée) de grand vent.

gut¹ [gʌt] *n.* **1.** *Anat:* boyau *m*, intestin *m*; **small g.,** intestin grêle. **2. guts,** (*a*) boyaux, intestins, entrailles *fpl*; *P:* **to sweat, work, one's guts out,** se casser les reins; *Fig:* **g. reaction,** réaction *f* dans son for intérieur; (*b*) *P:* (*of pers.*) **to have guts,** avoir du cran, du cœur au ventre; **he hasn't any guts,** il manque de cran. **3.** corde *f* de boyau (pour violons, etc.). **4.** (*a*) goulet *m* (dans un port, etc.); (*b*) passage étroit, défilé *m*.

gut² *v.tr.* **(gutted) 1.** (*a*) étriper (un animal); vider (un poisson, une volaille); (*b*) (*of fire*) ne laisser que les quatre murs (d'une maison). **2.** résumer (un livre); extraire l'essentiel (d'un livre).

gutless ['gʌtlis] *a. P:* mou, *f.* molle; mollasse; qui manque de cran.

gutsy ['gʌtsi] *a. P:* **1.** goinfre. **2.** qui a du cran.

gutter¹ ['gʌtər] *n.* **1.** gouttière *f*, chéneau *m* (de toit); **g. pipe,** tuyau *m* de descente; **g. tile,** tuile creuse. **2.** ruisseau *m* (de rue); caniveau *m*; **open g.,** cassis *m*; **to end up in the g.,** tomber, rouler, dans le ruisseau; **g. language,** langage *m* des rues; *Journ: F:* **g. press,** bas-fonds *mpl* du journalisme. **3.** (*a*) rigole *f*; sillon (creusé par la pluie); (*b*) cannelure *f* (dans une tôle); (*c*) *Bookb:* les petits fonds (de deux pages en vis-à-vis).

gutter² *v.i.* (*of candle*) couler. **guttering** *n.* **1.** coulage *m* (d'une bougie). **2.** *coll. Const:* gouttières *fpl* (d'une maison).

guttersnipe ['gʌtəsnaip] *n.* gamin, -ine, des rues.

guttural ['gʌtərəl] **1.** *a.* guttural, -aux. **2.** *n. Ling:* gutturale *f*.

guv [gʌv], **guv'nor** ['gʌvnər] *n. P:* **the g.,** (i) le patron, le singe; (ii) le vieux, le paternel.

guy¹ [gai] **1.** *n.* (*a*) effigie *f* burlesque de Guy Fawkes, le chef de la Conspiration des Poudres (1605); (*b*) *F:* (*pers.*) épouvantail *m*; **dressed like a g.,** fichu(e) comme l'as de pique. **2.** *F:* type *m*, individu *m*; **who's that g.?** qu'est-ce que c'est que ce type-là? **a great g.,** un chic type; **a tough g.,** un dur; **a wise g.,** un donneur de conseils; un je-sais-tout; *esp. U.S:* **fall g.,** (i) bouc *m* émissaire; (ii) dupe *f*, pigeon *m*.

guy² *v.* **(guyed; guying) 1.** *v.tr.* (*a*) se moquer de (qn); *F:* charrier (qn); mettre (qn) en boîte; (*b*) *Th:* charger, travestir, cascader (un rôle).

guy³ *n.* corde *f* de tente.

Guyana [gai'ænə] *Pr.n. Geog:* Guyane *f*.

Guyanese [gaiə'ni:z] Geog: **1.** *a.* guyanais. **2.** *n.* Guyanais, -aise.

guyrope ['gairoup] *n.* cordon *m* (de tente).

guzzle ['gʌzl] *v.tr. & i. F:* (*a*) (*eating*) bâfrer, bouffer (la nourriture); s'empiffrer, goinfrer; (*b*) (*drinking*) boire avidement, lamper (la boisson).

guzzler ['gʌzlər] *n. F:* (*a*) bâfreur, -euse; goinfre *m*; (*b*) buveur, -euse; pochard, -arde.

gym [dʒim] *n. F:* **1.** = GYMNASIUM 1. **2.** = GYMNASTICS.

gymkhana [dʒim'kɑ:nə] *n.* (*a*) gymkhana *m* équestre; (*b*) *esp. NAm:* gymkhana automobile.

gymnasium, *pl.* **-iums, -ia** [dʒim'neiziəm, -iəmz, -iə] *n. Sp:* gymnase *m*.

gymnast ['dʒimnæst] *n.* gymnaste *mf*.

gymnastic [dʒim'næstik] **1.** *a.* gymnastique. **2.** *n.pl.* (*usu. with sg. const.*) **gymnastics,** gymnastique *f*; **to do gymnastics,** faire de la gymnastique; **mental gymnastics,** gymnastique intellectuelle.

gynaecologic(al), *NAm:* **gynecologic(al)** [gainikə'lɔdʒik(l)] *a.* gynécologique.

gynaecologist, *NAm:* **gynecologist** [gaini'kɔlədʒist] *n.* gynécologue *mf*.

gynaecology, *NAm:* **gynecology** [gaini'kɔlədʒi] *n.* gynécologie *f*.

gyp [dʒip] *n. F:* **to give s.o. g.,** (i) flanquer une raclée à qn; (ii) (*of aching tooth, etc.*) faire souffrir qn.

gypsum ['dʒipsəm] *n. Miner:* gypse *m*.

gypsy ['dʒipsi] *n.* = GIPSY.

gyrate [dʒai'reit] *v.i.* tourner; tournoyer.

gyration [dʒai'reiʃ(ə)n] *n.* giration *f*, gyration *f*.

gyratory ['dʒaiərət(ə)ri, dʒai'reitəri] *a.* giratoire, gyratoire; *Adm:* **g. (traffic) system,** (système *m* de) circulation en sens giratoire.

gyrfalcon ['dʒə:fɔ:(l)kən] *n. Orn:* gerfaut *m*.

gyro ['dʒairou] **1.** *attrib.* gyroscopique; **g. control,** commande *f* gyroscopique. **2.** *n.* (*a*) = GYROSCOPE; (*b*) = GYROCOMPASS.

gyrocompass [dʒairou'kʌmpəs] *n. Nau:* gyrocompas *m*; compas *m* gyroscopique.

gyromagnetic [dʒairoumæg'netik] *a.* gyromagnétique.

gyropilot ['dʒairoupailət] *n.* (*a*) *Av:* pilote *m* automatique, gyropilote *m*; (*b*) *Nau:* (*compass*) gyropilote.

gyroplane ['dʒairəplein] *n. Av:* giravion *m*; autogyre *m*.

gyroscope ['dʒairəskoup] *n.* gyroscope *m*, gyro *m*.

gyroscopic [dʒairə'skɔpik] *a.* gyroscopique.

gyrostat ['dʒairəstæt] *n.* gyrostat *m*.

H

H, h [eitʃ] *n.* (la lettre) H, h *mf*; **to drop one's h's** ['eitʃiz] ne pas aspirer les h. **2.** *Mil:* **H bomb,** bombe *f* H.
ha (ha:] *int.* ha!
habeas corpus ['heibiəs'kɔ:pəs] *n. Jur:* **(writ of) h.c.,** habeas corpus *m.*
haberdasher ['hæbədæʃər] *n. Com:* **1.** mercier *m.* **2.** *NAm:* chemisier *f.*
haberdashery ['hæbədæʃəri] *n. Com:* **1.** mercerie *f.* **2.** *NAm:* chemiserie *f.*
habit ['hæbit] *n.* **1.** *(a)* habitude *f*, coutume *f*; **to be in the h., to make a h., of doing sth.,** avoir l'habitude de faire qch.: **it's a h. with him,** c'est une habitude chez lui; **to get into the h. of doing sth.,** prendre l'habitude de faire qch.; **to get into bad habits,** prendre de mauvaises habitudes; **to get out of a h.,** perdre une habitude; **from force of h.,** poussé par l'habitude; **to do sth. by sheer force of h.,** faire qch. par pure habitude; *(b) F:* (i) **the h.,** l'usage *m* des drogues; (ii) dose habituelle de drogues. **2.** constitution *f* physique. **3.** *Cost:* *(a)* habit *m* (de religieuse); *(b)* **riding h.,** amazone *f*; habit de cheval.
habitable ['hæbitəbl] *a.* habitable.
habitat ['hæbitæt] *n.* habitat *m.*
habitation [hæbi'teiʃ(ə)n] *n.* **1.** habitation *f* (d'une maison); **fit for h.,** habitable. **2.** habitation, demeure *f.*
habit-forming ['hæbitfɔ:miŋ] *a.* *(of drug)* qui cause, crée, une accoutumance.
habitual [hə'bitjuəl] *a.* **1.** *(customary)* habituel, d'usage. **2.** (menteur, ivrogne) invétéré; **h. criminal, offender,** récidiviste *mf.* **-ally** *adv.* habituellement, d'habitude; par habitude.
habituate [hə'bitjueit] *v.tr.* **to h. s.o. to sth., to doing sth.,** habituer, accoutumer, qn à qch., à faire qch.
hack¹ [hæk] *n.* **1.** pic *m*, pioche *f* (de mineur, etc.). **2.** *(a)* taillade *f*, entaille *f*; *(b) Fb:* coup *m* de pied (sur le tibia).
hack² **1.** *v.tr. & i.* *(a)* hacher; **to h. sth. to pieces,** couper, tailler, qch. en pièces; **to h. (away) at a tree,** entailler un arbre à coups de hache; **to h. one's way through the jungle,** se frayer un chemin à coups de hache dans la jungle; *(b) Fb: etc:* **to h. s.o.'s shins,** donner déloyalement à un adversaire un coup de pied sur le tibia. **2.** *v.i.* émettre une toux sèche. **hacking** **1.** *a.* (toux) sèche et pénible. **2.** *n.* *(a)* hachage *m*, hachement *m*; *(b) Fb: etc:* coups *mpl* de pied (sur le tibia).
hack³ *n.* **1.** *(a)* cheval *m*, -aux, de louage; *(b) F:* rosse *f*; *(c)* cheval de selle (à toutes fins). **2.** *NAm: F:* (i) taxi *m*; (ii) chauffeur *m* de taxi. **3.** *(a)* homme *m* de peine; **h. writer, literary h.,** écrivain *m* à la tâche; nègre *m.*
hack⁴ **1.** *v.tr.* banaliser (qch.); **to h. an argument to death,** ressasser, rabâcher, un argument. **2.** *v.tr. & i.* **to h. (a horse) along the road,** cheminer à cheval; se promener à cheval. **hacking,** *s.* promenade(s) *f(pl)* à cheval.
hackle ['hækl] *n. Orn:* plume *f* de cou (des gallinacés); **hackles,** camail *m*: *F:* *(of pers.)* **when his hackles are up,** quand il monte sur ses ergots.
hackney ['hækni] *n.* **1.** *(a)* cheval *m*, -aux, de louage; *(b)* cheval de route; bidet *m*; *(c)* (cheval) trotteur *m* (de course). **2.** *Adm:* **h. carriage,** taxi *m.*
hackneyed ['hæknid] *a.* (discours) rebattu, usé, banal; **h. phrase,** formule stéréotypée; cliché *m.*
hacksaw ['hæksɔ:] *n.* scie *f* à métaux.
hackwork ['hækwə:k] *n.* **1.** travail *m* d'écrivain à gages. **2.** travail (de plume) bâclé au jour le jour; besogne *f* alimentaire.
haddock ['hædək] *n. Ich:* aiglefin *m*, eglefin, *m*; *Cu:* **smoked h.,** haddock (fumé).
Hades ['heidi:z] *n. Gr.Myth:* Hadès *m*, les Enfers *mpl.*
hadn't = **had not;** *see* HAVE².
Hadrian ['heidriən] *Pr.n.m. Rom.Hist:* Adrien, Hadrien; **Hadrian's Wall,** le Mur d'Adrien.
haematology, *NAm:* **hematology** [hi:mə'tələdzi) *n. Physiol:* hématologie *f.*
haematoma, *NAm:* **hematoma** [hi:mə'toumə] *n. Med:* hématome *m.*
haemoglobin, *NAm:* **hemoglobin** [hi:mou'gloubin] *n. Physiol:* hémoglobine *f.*
haemophilia, *NAm:* **hemophilia** [hi:mou'filiə] *n. Med:* hémophilie *f.*
haemophiliac, *NAm:* **hemophiliac** [hi:mou'filiæk] *Med:* *a. & n.* hémophile *(mf).*
haemorrhage, *NAm:* **hemorrhage** ['hemərid3] *n. Med:* hémorragie *f.*
haemorrhoids, *NAm:* **hemorrhoids** ['hemərɔidz] *n.pl. Med:* hémorroïdes *fpl.*
haft [ha:ft] *n.* manche *m*, poignée *f* (d'un outil, etc.).
hag¹ [hæg] *n.* (vieille) sorcière; *F:* **she's an old h.,** c'est une vieille taupe.
haggard ['hægəd] *a.* *(a)* hâve; (visage) décharné; *(b)* (visage) égaré, hagard.
haggis ['hægis] *n. Scot.Cu:* estomac *m* de mouton farci d'un hachis d'abats et de farine d'avoine très épicé.
haggle ['hægl] *v.i.* marchander, *F:* chipoter; **to h. about, over, the price of sth.,** chicaner sur le prix de qch. **haggling** *n.* marchandage *m.*
hagiographer [hægi'ɔgrəfər] *n.* hagiographe *mf.*
hagiography [hægi'ɔgrəfi] *n.* hagiographic *f.*
hagridden ['hægridn] *a.* *(a)* tourmenté de cauchemars; *(b)* obsédé, tourmenté (par une idée, etc.).
Hague (the) [ðə'heig] *Pr.n. Geog:* la Haye.
hah [hɑ:] *int.* ah! ha!
ha-ha¹ [hɑ:'hɑ:] *int.* ha, ha!
ha-ha² ['hɑ:hɑ:] *n.* saut *m* de loup; haha *m.*
hail¹ [heil] *n.* *(a)* grêle *f*; *(b)* grêle, volée *f* (de coups, de pierres).
hail² *v.i. & tr.* grêler; *(a) impers.* **it's hailing,** il grêle; *(b)* **to h. down blows on s.o.,** faire pleuvoir des coups sur qn.
hail³ **1.** *int.* salut! *R.C.Ch:* **hail, Mary, full of grace!** je te salue, Marie, pleine de grâce! *n.* **the H. Mary,** l'Ave Maria *m inv.* **2.** *n.* appel *m*; **within h.,** à portée de (la) voix.
hail⁴ **1.** *v.tr.* *(a)* saluer (qn); **to h. s.o. (as) king,** acclamer qn roi; *(b)* héler (qn, un navire); *Nau:* arraisonner (un navire); **to h. a taxi,** appeler, héler, un taxi (qui passe); **within hailing distance,** à portée de (la) voix. **2.** *v.i. Nau* *(of ship)* **to h. from a port,** (i) dépendre d'un port; (ii) venir d'un port; **where does he h. from?** d'où vient-il?
hail-fellow-well-met ['heilfelouwel'met] *a.* **to be h.-f.-w.-m. with everyone,** être à tu et à toi avec tout le monde.
hailstone ['heilstoun] *n.* grêlon *m.*

hailstorm ['heilstɔːm] *n.* averse *f* de grêle.

hair ['hɛər] *n.* **1.** (*of human head*) (*a*) cheveu *m*; (*in metal*) **h. crack,** gerçure *f*; **h. stroke,** (i) empattement *m* (de lettre); (ii) (*in handwriting*) délié *m*; **to split hairs,** ergoter; couper les cheveux en quatre; (*b*) *coll.* **the h.,** les cheveux, la chevelure; **long fair h.,** de longs cheveux blonds; **h. tonic, lotion,** lotion *f* capillaire; **h. cream,** crème coiffante; **h. oil,** brillantine *f*; **h. spray,** laque *f*; **h. grip,** pince *f* (à cheveux); **to comb one's h.,** se peigner; **to have, get, one's h. cut,** se faire couper les cheveux; **to do one's h.,** se coiffer; **to wash one's h.,** se laver la tête; **to have one's h. set,** *F:* **done,** se faire faire une mise en plis; **to let down one's h.,** défaire, laisser tomber, ses cheveux; *F:* **to let one's h. down,** (i) se mettre à son aise; (ii) s'amuser follement; **to tear one's h.,** s'arracher les cheveux; **it was enough to make your h. stand on end,** c'était à faire dresser les cheveux (sur la tête); *F:* **keep your h. on!** calmez-vous! *F:* **to get in s.o.'s h.,** (i) taper sur les nerfs à qn; (ii) enquiquiner qn. **2.** (*a*) (*of human face & body, animals, plants*) poil *m*; **removal of superfluous h.,** épilation *f*, dépilation *f*; (*b*) *coll.* (*of animal*) poil, pelage *m*; (*c*) crin *m* (de cheval); soie *f* (de porc); **h. mattress,** matelas *m* de crin. **3.** *Opt:* cheveu, fil *m* (de réticule d'appareil de visée); **cross hairs,** réticule *m*.

hairbreadth ['hɛəbredθ] **1.** *n.* = HAIR'S BREADTH. **2.** *attrib.* **to have a h. escape,** l'échapper belle.

hairbrush ['hɛəbrʌʃ] *n.* brosse *f* à cheveux.

haircut ['hɛəkʌt] *n.* (*a*) coupe *f* de cheveux; **to have a h.,** se faire couper les cheveux; (*b*) coiffure *f*.

hairdo ['hɛəduː] *n. F:* coiffure *f*.

hairdresser ['hɛədresər] *n* coiffeur, -euse.

hairdressing ['hɛədresiŋ] *n.* coiffure *f*; **h. salon,** salon *m* de coiffure.

hairdrier, hairdryer ['hɛədraiər] *n.* séchoir *m* à cheveux, sèche-cheveux *m inv*.

hairless ['hɛəlis] *a.* (*of pers.*) sans cheveux; chauve; (*of animal*) sans poils; (visage) glabre, nu.

hairline ['hɛəlain] *n.* **1.** délié *m*; **h. distinction,** distinction subtile. **2.** *Typ:* **h. type,** capillaires *fpl*. **3.** *Tchn:* (*in metal*) gerçure *f*. **4.** *Opt:* cheveu *m*, fil *m* (de réticule d'appareil de visée); **hairlines,** réticule *m*. **5.** naissance *f* des cheveux; **his h. is receding,** il commence à se déplumer.

hairnet ['hɛənet] *n.* filet *m* pour cheveux.

hairpiece ['hɛəpiːs] *n.* mèche *f* postiche.

hairpin ['hɛəpin] *n.* épingle *f* à cheveux; (*on road*) **h. bend,** lacet *m*; virage *m* en épingle à cheveux.

hair-raising ['hɛəreiziŋ] *a.* effrayant; (aventure) effroyable; (récit), à vous faire dresser les cheveux sur la tête.

hair's breadth ['hɛəzbredθ] *n.* épaisseur *f* d'un cheveu; **he escaped death by a h. b.,** il a été à deux doigts de la mort, il a frisé la mort; **to be within a h. b. of disaster,** être à un cheveu de la ruine.

hair-splitting ['hɛəsplitiŋ] **1.** *n.* ergotage *m*, ergoterie *f*; chicane(rie) *f*. **2.** *a.* (*of argument, etc.*) (trop) subtil.

hairstyle ['hɛəstail] n. coiffure *f*.

hairy ['hɛəri] *a.* (*a*) (*of hands, chest, etc.*) velu, poilu; (*of scalp*) chevelu; (*of pers.*) hirsute; (*b*) *F:* (*of situation, etc.*) périlleux, épineux.

Haiti ['heiti, 'hai-] *Pr.n. geog:* Haïti *m or f*.

Haitian ['heiʃ(ə)n, 'heitiən] *Geog:* **1.** *a.* haïtien. **2.** *n.* Haïtien, -ienne.

hake [heik] *n. Ich:* merluche *f*, colin *m*.

halcyon ['hælsiən] **1.** *n.* (*a*) *Myth:* alcyon *m*; (*b*) *Orn:* halcyon *m*; martin-chasseur *m*, *pl.* martins-chasseurs. **2.** *attrib.* **h. days,** jours alcyoniens; jours de calme, de bonheur paisible.

hale [heil] *a.* (vieillard) vigoureux, robuste, encore gaillard; **to be h. and hearty,** être frais et gaillard.

half, *pl.* **halves** [hɑːf, hɑːvz] **1.** *n.* (*a*) moitié *f*; **what is h. of twelve?** quelle est la moitié de douze? **h. the time he isn't there,** la moitié du temps, il n'est pas là; **the first h. of the year,** la première moitié de l'année; **to fold, cut, sth. in h., in halves,** plier, couper, qch. en deux; **to go halves with s.o.,** partager avec qn; se mettre de moitié avec qn; **bigger by h.,** plus grand de moitié; *F:* **he is too clever by h.,** il est beaucoup trop malin; (*b*) demi *m*, demie *f*; **two halves,** (i) deux demis; (ii) *Rail: etc:* deux demi-places; (iii) deux bières, = deux demis; **three and a h.,** trois et demi; **I waited for two and a h. hours,** j'ai attendu pendant deux heures et demie; (*c*) (*pers.*) *F:* **my better h.,** ma (chère) moitié; (*d*) *Rail:* (*of ticket*) **outward h., return h.,** coupon *m* d'aller, de retour; (*e*) *Fb:* (i) **the first h. (of the game),** la première mi-temps; **the second h.,** la seconde mi-temps; la reprise; (ii) **in our h. (of the ground),** dans notre camp; (iii) (*pers.*) demi; **wing halves,** demi aile; **scrum h.,** demi de mêlée; **centre h.,** demi centre; (*f*) *Sch:* trimestre *m*. **2.** *a.* demi; (*a*) **h. an hour,** une demi-heure; **I'll be with you in h. a second,** *F:* **h. a tick,** je reviens en moins de rien; **h. a dozen,** une demi-douzaine; **at h. price,** à moitié prix; *Mil:* **h. right, left,** demi à-droite *m*, à-gauche *m*; **h. day,** demi-journée *f*; **h. time,** (i) *Adm: Ind: etc:* travail *m* à mi-temps, à la demi-journée; (ii) *Fb: etc:* (la) mi-temps. **3.** *adv.* à moitié, à demi; mi; (*a*) **he only h. understands,** il ne comprend qu'à moitié; **he h. opened the door,** il entrouvrit la porte; **the bottle was h. full, h. empty,** la bouteille était à moitié pleine, vide; **h. dressed,** à demi vêtu; **h. naked,** à moitié nu; **h. asleep,** à moitié endormi; **h. dead,** à moitié mort; **h. done,** (i) (ouvrage, etc.) à moitié fait; (ii) (rôti, etc.) à moitié cuit; **h. laughing, h. crying,** moitié riant, moitié pleurant; **I was h. afraid that you wouldn't come,** j'avais quelque crainte que vous ne veniez pas; *F:* **it isn't h. bad,** ce n'est pas mauvais du tout; ce n'est pas si mal; *P:* (*intensive*) **it isn't h. cold!** il fait rudement froid! **not h.!** tu parles! et comment! (*b*) **it is h. past two,** *F:* **h. two,** il est deux heures et demie; **h. past twelve,** midi, minuit, et demi; (*c*) **h. as big,** moitié aussi grand; **he gets h. as much money as you,** il reçoit moitié moins d'argent que vous; **h. as big again,** plus grand de moitié.

half-and-half ['hɑːfənd'hɑːf] **1.** (*a*) *adv.* moitié l'un moitié l'autre, *F:* moitié-moitié: (*b*) *a. & adv.* **how shall I mix them?—h.-and-h.,** comment faut-il les mélanger?—à doses égales; **how do you like your coffee?—h.-and-h.,** comment prenez-vous le café?—moitié café, moitié lait. **2.** *n.* mélange *m*.

halfback ['hɑːfbæk] *n. Fb:* demi-arrière *m*, *pl.* demi-arrières; demi*m*.

half-baked [hɑːf'beikt] *a. F:* (*a*) (*of pers.*) (i) inexpérimenté; (ii) niais; (*b*) insuffisamment étudié; incomplet; (projet) qui ne tient pas debout.

half-blood ['hɑːfblʌd] *n.* **1.** parenté *f* d'un seul côté. **2.** (*a*) parent, -ente, d'un seul côté; (*b*) = HALFBREED.

halfbreed ['hɑːfbriːd] *n.* **1.** métis, -isse. **2.** cheval *m* demi-sang, *pl.* chevaux demi-sang.

half-brother ['hɑːfbrʌðər] *n.m.* demi-frère, *pl.* demi-frères; (*through mother*) frère utérin, de mère; (*through father*) frère consanguin, de père.

halfcaste ['hɑːfkɑːst] *a. & n.* métis, -isse.

half-circle ['hɑːf'səːkl] *n.* demi-cercle *m*, *pl.* demi-cercles; *Nau:* **to turn a h.-c.,** faire demi-tour.

half(-)cock ['hɑːf'kɔk] *n. Sm.a.* **(gun) at h. c.,** (fusil etc.) au demi-armé; **h.-c. notch,** cran *m* de repos; *F:* **to go off at h. c.,** mal partir, mal démarrer.

halfcrown [hɑːf'kraun] *n. Num:* demi-couronne *f*.

halfhearted [hɑːf'hɑːtid] *a.* sans enthousiasme; (effort) timide, hésitant. **-ly** *adv.* sans enthousiasme.

halfheartedness [hɑːf'hɑːtidnis] *n.* tiédeur *f*, manque *m* d'enthousiasme.

half-hourly [hɑːf'auəli] **1.** *adv.* toutes les demi-heures. **2.** *a.* de toutes les demi-heures.
half-length ['hɑf'leŋθ] *n.* demi-longueur *f*, *pl.* demi-longueurs; **h.-l. portrait,** portrait *m* en buste.
half-life ['hɑːflaif] *n. Atom. Ph: etc:* demi-vie *f* (d'un isotope, etc.), *pl.* demi-vies.
half-light ['hɑːf'lait] *n.* demi-jour *m*, *pl.* demi-jours; pénombre *f*.
half-mast ['hɑf'mɑːst] *n. in the adv. phr.* **at h.,** à mi-mât; **flag at h. m.,** pavillon *m* en berne.
half-moon ['hɑːf'muːn] *n.* **1.** demi-lune *f*, *pl.* demi-lunes. **2.** lunule *f* (des ongles).
half(-)Nelson ['hɑːf'nels(ə)n] *n Wr:* simple prise *f* de tête à terre.
half(-)pay ['hɑːf'pei] *n.* demi-solde *f*; solde *f* de non-activité; **on h. p.,** en demi-solde, en disponibilité.
halfpenny ['heipni, 'hɑːfpeni] *n.* demi-penny *m*; *F:* = sou *m*.
half-seas-over ['hɑːfsiːz'ouvər] *a. F:* gris, ivre, soûl.
half-sister ['hɑːfsistər] *n.f.* demi-sœur, *pl.* demi-sœurs; (*through the father*) sœur consanguine, de père; (*through the mother*) sœur utérine, de mère.
half-term [hɑːf'təːm] *n. Sch:* congé *m* de mi-trimestre.
half-timbered [hɑːf'timbəd] *a.* (maison) à colombage.
half-title ['hɑːf'taitl] *n. Typ:* avant-titre *m* (d'un livre), *pl.* avant-titres.
half-tone [hɑːf'toun] *n.* **1.** *Art:* demi-teinte *f*, *pl.* demi-teintes; *Phot. Engr:* similigravure (tramée); *F:* simili *m*. **2.** *Mus:* demi-ton *m*, *pl.* demi-tons.
halftrack ['hɑːftræk] *n. Veh:* (auto)chenille *f*, half-track *m*.
half-truth ['hɑːftruːθ] *n.* demi-vérité *f*, *pl.* demi-vérités.
half-volley ['hɑːf'vɔli] *n. Ten:* demi-volée *f*, *pl.* demi-volées.
halfway [hɑːf'wei] **1.** *adv.* à moitié chemin; à mi-chemin; (*of piston*) à mi-course; **h. between the two towns,** à mi-chemin entre les deux villes; **h. to Paris,** à mi-chemin de Paris; **h. up, h. down, the hill,** à mi-côte, à mi-pente; **I was h. up, down, the stairs,** j'étais à mi-hauteur de l'escalier; **h. through (a period of time),** à mi-terme; **to meet s.o. h.,** (i) rencontrer qn a mi-distance; (ii) *F:* faire la moitié des avances. **2. h. house,** (i) maison *f*, auberge *f*, à mi-chemin; (ii) centre *m* de réadaptation (pour drogués, etc.); *Fb:* **h. line,** ligne des cinquante mètres. **3.** *n.* **there's no h. with him,** avec lui il n'y a pas de demi-mesures.
halfwit ['hɑːfwit] *n.* faible *mf* d'esprit; simple *mf*.
halfwitted [hɑːf'witid] *a.* faible d'esprit, simple.
half-yearly [hɑːf'jiəli] **1.** *a.* semestriel. **2.** *adv.* par semestre; tous les six mois.
halibut ['hælibət] *n. Ich:* flétan *m*; halibut *m*.
halitosis [hæli'tousis] *n. Med:* mauvaise haleine.
hall [hɔːl] *n.* (grande) salle; (*a*) **(dining) h.,** (i) salle à manger (d'un château, etc.); (ii) *Sch:* (*of college, etc.*) réfectoire *m*; (*b*) **the servants' h.,** l'office *f*; (*c*) **lecture h.,** salle de conférences; **assembly h.,** salle d'assemblée; **concert h.,** salle de concert; **dance h.,** salle de danse, de bal; dancing *m*; **music h.,** (i) music-hall *m*; (ii) *NAm:* salle de concert; (*d*) **parish h.,** salle d'œuvres de la paroisse. **2.** (*a*) (*usu. as Pr.n.*) = manoir *m*; (*b*) maison *f* (d'un corps de métier, etc.); **town h.,** hôtel *m* de ville; (*c*) *Sch:* (i) fondation *f* universitaire (à Oxford et Cambridge): (ii) = maison d'étudiants. **3.** (*a*) **(entrance) h.,** entrée *f* (d'une maison); hall *m* (d'un grand hôtel): **h. porter,** concierge *m*; (*b*) *NAm:* couloir *m*, corridor *m*.
hallelujah [hæli'luːjə] *int. & s.* alléluia (*m*).
hallmark¹ ['hɔːlmɑːk] *n.* (cachet *m* de) contrôle (*m*) (sur les objets d'orfèvrerie); **the h. of genius,** l'empreinte *f*, du génie.
hallmark² *v.tr.* contrôler, poinçonner (l'orfèvrerie).
hallo [hə'lou] *int.* (*a*) bonjour! (*b*) (*calling attention*) holà! ohé! (*c*) (*indicating surprise*) tiens! (*d*) *Tp:* allô!
hallow¹ ['hælou] *n. Ecc:* **All Hallows' (Day),** (le jour de) la Toussaint.
hallow² *v.tr.* sanctifier, consacrer; **hallowed** [haloud, *occ.* 'halouid] **be Thy name,** que Ton nom soit sanctifié; **hallowed ground,** terre sainte.
Hallowe'en [hælou'iːn] *n.* veille *f* de la Toussaint.
hallstand ['hɔːlstænd] *n.* porte-habits(s) *m*.
hallucinate [hə'l(j)uːsineit] **1.** *v.tr.* halluciner. **2.** *v.i.* avoir des hallucinations.
hallucination [həl(j)uːsi'neiʃ(ə)n] *n.* hallucination *f*.
hallucinatory [hə'l(j)uːsinət(ə)ri] *a.* hallucinatoire.
hallucinogenic [hali(j)usinou'dʒenik] *a.* hallucinogène.
hallway ['hɔːlwei] *n.* **1.** vestibule *m*, entrée *f*. **2.** *NAm:* corridor *m* d'étage.
halo, *pl.* **-os, -oes** ['heilou, -ouz] *n.* **1.** *Astr: Opt: Phot:* halo *m*; auréole *f* (de la lune). **2.** auréole, nimbe *m* (d'un saint).
halogen ['hælədʒən] *n. Ch:* halogène *m*.
halt¹ [hɔlt] *n.* **1.** arrêt *m*, temps *m* d'arrêt; interruption (momentanée); halte *f*, pause *f*; (*a*) (*of machine, vehicle*) **to bring to a h.,** faire marquer un temps d'arrêt, une pause (à un processus, etc.); provoquer l'interruption momentanée (d'un mouvement, d'une action); arrêter, faire stopper (un véhicule, une foule, etc.); **to come to a h.,** (i) marquer un temps d'arrêt, s'interrompre momentanément; s'arrêter, stopper; (ii) (*on journey*) faire halte; (iii) (*in a speech*) rester sans pouvoir rien dire; *Aut:* **h. sign,** stop *m*; (*b*) *Mil:* **at the h.,** de pied ferme, sur place. **2.** stationnement *m* (d'un véhicule, d'une troupe, etc.). **3.** *Rail:* (*small station*) halte.
halt² **1.** *v.i.* faire halte; s'arrêter; **to h. at . . .,** faire un arrêt, s'arrêter, à . . .; *Mil:* **company h.!** compagnie halte! **2.** *v.tr.* faire faire halte à (qn). **halting** **1.** *a.* (*of words, speech, etc.*) hésitant; (style) heurté. **2.** *n.* hésitation *f*. **haltingly** *adv.* en hésitant.
halt³ *a. A: & B:* boiteux; *n.pl.* **the h.,** les estropiés.
halter¹ ['hɔːltər] *n.* **1.** (*a*) licou *m* (pour chevaux). **2.** corde *f* (de pendaison). **3.** *Cost:* (*a*) **h. (neck),** encolure *f* bain-de-soleil; (*b*) *NAm:* corsage *m*, haut *m*, bain-de soleil.
halter² *v.tr.* **to h. (up) a horse,** mettre un licou à un cheval.
halve [hɑːv] *v.tr.* (*a*) diviser en deux; couper en deux moitiés; (*b*) partager (qch. en deux); (*c*) réduire (les dépenses, etc.) de moitié. **halving** *n.* partage *m* en deux, division *f* en deux, mipartition *f*.
halves. *see* HALF.
halyard ['hæljəd] *n. Nau:* drisse *f*.
ham¹ [hæm] *n.* **1.** *F:* **the hams,** les fesses *fpl*, le derrière. **2.** *Cu:* jambon *m*; **h. and eggs,** œufs *mpl* au jambon. **3.** *F:* (*a*) *Th:* **h. actor,** cabotin *m*; (*b*) **radio h.,** amateur *m* de radio.
ham² *Th: F:* **1.** *v.i.* jouer comme un pied. **2.** *v.tr.* **he hams all his parts,** il joue tous ses rôles en charge.
Hamburg ['hæmbəːg] *n. Pr.n. Geog:* Hambourg.
Hamburger ['hæmbəːgər] *n.* **1.** *Geog:* Hambourgeois, -oise. **2.** *n.m. Cu:* hamburger *m*.
hamfisted [hæm'fistid] *a.* maladroit.
Hamitic [hə'mitik] *a.* chamitique.
hamlet ['hæmlit] *n.* hameau *m*.
hammer¹ ['hæmər] *n.* **1.** *Tls:* marteau *m*; (*heavy*) masse *f*; (*a*) **wooden h.,** maillet *m*; *Civ.E:* **bush h.,** boucharde *f*; (*b*) *F:* **to go at it h. and tongs,** (i) y aller de bon cœur, ne pas y aller de main morte; (ii) se quereller; se bagarrer. **2.** marteau (de commissaire-

priseur); **to come under the h.,** être mis aux enchères. **3.** (*a*) *Mus:* marteau (de piano, etc); (*b*) *Mus:* **tuning h.,** accordoir *m*; clef *f* d'accordeur; (*c*) *Clockm: El:* marteau (de sonnerie *f* d'horloge, de sonnette électrique); (*d*) *Anat:* marteau (de l'oreille interne). **4.** *Sm.a:* chien *m* (d'une arme à feu). **5.** *Sp:* **throwing the h.,** lancement *m* du marteau. **6.** *Med:* **h. toe,** orteil *m* en marteau.

hammer² **1.** *v.tr.* (*a*) marteler; battre au marteau; **to h. sth. into shape,** (i) façonner (un pot, etc.) à coups de marteau; (ii) *F:* perfectionner (un projet, etc.); *F:* **to h. sth. into s.o.,** faire entrer qch. dans la tête à qn; *F:* **to h. (s.o., sth.),** (i) bourrer (qn) de coups; (*of boxer, etc.*) cogner dur sur (son adversaire); (ii) battre (son adversaire) à plate(s) couture(s); (iii) critiquer (qn, un livre, etc.); (*b*) **to h. prices,** faire baisser les prix. **2.** *v.i.* travailler avec le marteau; **to h. at, on, the door,** frapper à la porte à coups redoublés. **hammer in** *v.tr.* enfoncer (un clou) à coups de marteau. **hammering** *n.* **1.** (*a*) martelage *m*, martèlement *m*; battage *m* (du fer); (*b*) *F:* dégelée *f* de coups); **to give (s.o., sth.) a h.,** (i) cogner dur sur (qn); bourrer (qn) de coups; (ii) battre (qn) à plate(s) couture(s); (iii) critiquer (qn, un livre, etc.). **2.** *Mec. E: Mch:* tambourinage *m*, martèlement *m* (d'un coussinet, etc.). **hammer out** *v.tr.* (*a*) étendre (l'or, etc.) sous le marteau; panner (le cuivre); (*b*) *F:* perfectionner (un projet, etc.).

hammerhead ['hæməhed] *n.* **1.** (*a*) tête *f* de marteau; (*b*) **h. crane,** grue *f* marteau. **2.** *Ich:* **h. (shark),** requin *m* marteau. **3.** *Orn:* ombrette *f* (du Sénégal).

hammock ['hæmək] *n.* hamac *m*.

hamper¹ ['hæmpər] *n.* manne *f*, mannequin *m*; calais *m* (à provisions, etc.); bourriche *f* (d'huîtres, etc.); **Christmas h.,** panier *m* de Noël.

hamper² *v.tr.* embarrasser, gêner, empêtrer (qn); **to h. the progress of business,** entraver la marche des affaires; **she was hampered by her long cloak,** elle était empêtrée dans son grand manteau.

hamster ['hæmstər] *n.* *Z:* hamster *m*.

hamstring¹ ['hæmstriŋ] *n.* *Anat:* tendon *m* du jarret.

hamstring² *v.tr.* (*p.t. & p.p.* **hamstringed** *or* **-strung**) **1.** couper le(s) jarret(s) à (qn, un cheval). **2.** couper les moyens à (qn); donner un coup de Jarnac à (qn).

hand¹ [hænd] *n.* **1.** main *f*; (*a*) **he writes with his left h.,** il écrit de la main gauche; **the h. of God,** le doigt de Dieu; **on one's hands and knees,** à quatre pattes; **to vote by show of hands,** voter à main levée; **to have one's hands tied,** (i) avoir les mains liées; (ii) se trouver dans l'impossibilité d'agir; **to hold (sth.) in one's h.,** tenir (une épée, son chapeau) à la main, (des graines) dans la main, (le succès) entre les mains; **to take s.o. by the h.,** prendre qn par la main; **give me your h.,** donnez-moi la main; *F:* **to put, dip, one's h. in the till,** puiser dans la caisse; **I can't put my h. on it,** je ne peux pas le retrouver; **to lay hands on sth.,** mettre la main sur qch.; s'emparer de qch.; **to lay hands on s.o.,** faire violence à qn; **hands off!** (i) n'y touchez pas! (ii) bas les mains! **hands up!** haut les mains! **to rule with a firm h.,** gouverner d'une main ferme; *Fb:* **hands,** (faute *f* de) main; *F:* **I'll soon have him eating out of my h.,** je l'amènerai bientôt à faire exactement ce que je veux; (*b*) **to try one's h. at sth.,** essayer (de faire) qch., y mettre la main; **to get one's h. in,** se faire la main; **he can turn his h. to anything,** c'est un homme qui peut tout faire; **to have a h. in sth.,** y être pour quelque chose; se mêler de qch.; **to give, lend, s.o. a (helping) h.,** aider qn; **to lend a h.,** mettre la main à la pâte; (*c*) **to have one's hands full,** avoir fort à faire; **to have s.o., sth., on one's hands,** avoir qn, qch., à sa charge, sur les bras; **to have an hour on one's hands,** avoir une heure à tuer; **to change hands,** (i) (*of goods, etc.*) passer en d'autres mains; (ii) (*of business, etc.*) changer de propriétaire; **to fall into enemy hands,** tomber entre les mains de l'ennemi; **to be in good hands,** être en bonnes mains; **to put oneself in s.o.'s hands,** se confier à qn; *Jur:* **to put a matter in the hands of a lawyer,** confier une affaire à un avocat; (*d*) applaudissement(s) *m(pl)*; *F:* **to give s.o. a big h.,** applaudir vivement qn. **2.** *phrs.* (*a*) **to be (near) at h.,** (i) (*of object, etc.*) être sous la main, à portée de la main; (ii) (*of event, etc.*) approcher, être prochain; **the hour is at h.,** l'heure est proche; **there is always a doctor at h.,** il y a toujours un médecin de service; (*b*) **made, done, by h.,** fait à la main; **h. operated,** à commande manuelle; **to send a letter by h.,** envoyer une lettre par porteur; (*c*) **sword in h.,** sabre au poing; **to have so much money in h.,** avoir tant d'argent disponible; *Com:* **cash in h.,** espèces *fpl* en caisse; **stock in h.,** marchandises *fpl* en magasin; **I've five minutes in h.,** j'ai encore cinq minutes; **the matter in h.,** la chose en question; **work in h.,** travail *m* en cours, en chantier; **to have one's car well in h.,** être maître de sa voiture; **the situation is well in h.,** la situation est bien en main; (*d*) (i) **work on h.,** travail en cours, à faire; (ii) **I'm on h. if you need me,** je suis à votre disposition si vous avez besoin de moi; (iii) **on (the) one h.,** d'une part; **on the other h.,** d'autre part; par contre; (*e*) (i) **to do sth. out of h.,** faire qch. sur-le-champ; **to shoot s.o. out of h.,** abattre qn sans autre forme de procès; (ii) (*of troops, children, etc.*) **to get out of h.,** perdre toute discipline; (*f*) (i) (*of letter, etc.*) **to come to h.,** arriver à destination; **your parcel came to h. this morning,** votre paquet m'est parvenu ce matin; (ii) **the first excuse to h.,** le premier prétexte venu; (*g*) **to be h. in glove with s.o.,** être d'intelligence, *Pej:* de mèche, avec qn; (*h*) **to wait on s.o. h. and foot,** être aux petits soins avec qn; (*i*) **to go h. in h. with s.o.,** (i) marcher avec qn la main dans la main; (ii) agir de concert avec qn; (*j*) **h. over h., h. over fist,** main sur main (en grimpant, etc.); *F:* **to make money h. over fist,** s'enrichir rapidement; (*k*) (i) **to fight h. to h.,** combattre corps à corps; **h.-to-h. fight,** corps-à-corps *m inv.*; (ii) **to pass sth. from h. to h.,** passer qch. de main en main; (*l*) **to be living from h. to mouth,** vivre au jour le jour; (*m*) *Rac: etc.* **to win hands down,** gagner haut la main; **to beat s.o. hands down,** battre qn à plate(s) couture(s). **3.** (*a*) (*pers.*) ouvrier, -ière; manœuvre *m*; *Nau:* matelot *m*; *pl.* **(the ship's) hands,** l'équipage *m*; *Ind: etc:* **to take on hands,** embaucher de la main-d'œuvre; *Nau:* **all hands on deck!** tout le monde sur le pont! (*of ship*) **to be lost with all hands,** périr corps et biens; (*b*) **to be a good,** *F:* **dab, h. at sth., at doing sth.,** être adroit, avoir de l'habileté, à qch., à faire qch.; **an old h.,** un expert, un spécialiste. **4.** (*a*) écriture *f*; **round h., running h.,** écriture ronde, cursive; **he writes a very good h.,** il a une belle écriture; **in one's own h.,** (écrire une lettre) de sa propre main; (*b*) signature *f*; *Jur:* **to set one's h. to a deed,** apposer sa signature à un acte; **note of h.,** billet *m* à ordre. **5.** *Cards:* (*a*) jeu *m*; **to have a good h.,** avoir beau jeu; avoir du jeu; (*b*) la main, le coup; **to win the h.,** gagner la main; (*c*) joueur, -euse; **first h., fourth h.,** premier, dernier, en cartes; (*d*) partie *f*; **to finish the h.,** finir le coup. **6.** *Meas: Farr:* paume *f*; **horse fifteen hands high,** cheval de quinze paumes. **7.** (*a*) *Typ:* index *m*; (*b*) (*of signpost*) indicateur *m*; (*c*) indicateur (de baromètre, etc.); aiguille *f* (de montre). **8.** (*a*) *Cu:* **h. of pork,** jambonneau *m*; (*b*) régime *m* (de bananes). **9.** **h. luggage,** bagages *mpl* à main; **(wash) h. basin,** lavabo *m*; **h. sewn, stitched,** cousu (à la) main; *Aut: etc:* **h. brake,** frein *m* à main.

hand² *v.tr.* **1.** (*a*) passer, remettre, donner (qch. à qn); **he handed her the letter to read,** il lui a donné la lettre à lire; (*b*) *F:* **to h. it to s.o.,** reconnaître la supériorité de qn; **you've got to h. it to him,** devant lui, chapeau! **2.** *Nau:* serrer (une voile). **hand down** *v.tr.* (*a*) donner la main à (qn) pour l'aider à descendre; (*b*) descendre (qch.) (et le remettre à qn); (*c*) transmettre (une tradition). **hand in** *v.tr.* (*a*) remettre, déposer (un paquet, un télégramme); **to h. in one's resignation,** démissionner; (*b*) *Nau:* **to h. in the sail,** crocher dans la toile. **handing** *n.* (*a*) remise *f* (de qch.) (**to s.o.,** à qn); (*b*) **h. down, on,** transmission *f* (d'une tradition); (*c*) **h. over,** (i) remise (de qch.) entre les mains de qn; (ii) cession *f* (de biens); transmission (de pouvoirs). **hand on** *v.tr.* transmettre (une coutume); passer (une nouvelle) (to, à). **hand out** *v.tr.* (*a*) tendre, remettre (qch. à qn); (*b*) **to h. out the wages,** distribuer la paie. **hand over** *v.tr.* remettre (qch. à qn); céder (son bien à qn); transmettre (des pouvoirs à qn); **to h. over the money,** remettre l'argent; **to h. s.o. over to justice,** livrer, remettre, qn aux mains de la justice; **to h. over the command to . . .,** remettre le commandement à . . . **hand round** *v.tr.* faire passer, faire circuler (la bouteille, etc.)

handbag [ˈhændbæg] *n.* sac *m* à main.

handball [ˈhændbɔːl] *n. Games:* hand-ball *m.*

handbell [ˈhændbel] *n.* sonnette *f*, clochette *f.*

handbill [ˈhændbil] *n.* prospectus *m.*

handbook [ˈhændbuk] *n.* **1.** *Sch: etc:* manuel *m* (de sciences, etc.). **2.** guide *m* (du voyageur, du touriste); livret *m* (d'un musée, etc.).

handcart [ˈhændkɑːt] *n.* charrette *f* à bras; baladeuse *f.*

handcuff [ˈhændkʌf] *v.tr.* mettre les menottes à, menotter (qn).

handcuffs [ˈhændkʌfs] *n.pl.* menottes *fpl.*

handful [ˈhændful] *n.* **1.** poignée *f* (de sable, etc.); **there was only a h. there,** il n'y avait là que quelques personnes. **2.** *F:* **that child is a h.,** cet enfant-là me donne du fil à retordre.

handglass [ˈhændglɑːs] *n.* **1.** loupe *f* à main (pour la lecture). **2.** miroir *m* à main. **3.** *Hort:* cloche *f.*

handgrip [ˈhændgrip] *n.* **1.** prise *f.* **2.** poignée *f* de main. **3.** *Cy:* poignée.

handhold [ˈhændhould] *n.* prise *f.*

handicap¹ [ˈhændikæp] *n.* **1.** (*a*) *Sp:* handicap *m*; (*of racehorse*) **(weight) h.,** surcharge *f*; **time, distance, h.,** rendement *m* de temps, de distance; (*b*) *Turf:* (*race*) handicap; (*c*) désavantage *m*; **to have a severe h.,** être fort handicapé. **2.** rendement (accordé à un concurrent); *Golf:* handicap; marge *f* d'erreur.

handicap² *v.tr.* **(handicapped) 1.** *Sp:* handicaper. **2.** **to be handicapped,** être handicapé, désavantagé; *n.pl.* **the physically, mentally, handicapped,** les handicapés physiques, mentaux.

handicraft [ˈhændikrɑːft] *n.* **1.** travail manuel. **2.** (*a*) (*trade*) métier manuel; **productions of the local handicrafts,** produits *mpl* d'artisanat régional; (*b*) artisanat *m* d'expression.

handiness [ˈhændinis] *n.* **1.** adresse *f*, dextérité *f*; habileté (manuelle). **2.** (*a*) commodité *f* (d'un outil, etc.); (*b*) maniabilité *f* (d'un navire, etc.).

handiwork [ˈhændiwəːk] *n.* (*a*) travail manuel; (*b*) ouvrage *m*, travail *m*, œuvre *f.*

handkerchief [ˈhæŋkətʃif] *n.* **(pocket) h.,** mouchoir *m* (de poche); **garden the size of a pocket h.,** jardin grand comme un mouchoir de poche.

handle¹ [ˈhænd(ə)l] *n.* (*a*) manche *m* (de balai, etc.); bras *m*, balancier *m* (de pompe); brancard *m* (de civière); bras (de brouette); (*b*) (*grip*) manche (de couteau, d'outil); queue *f* (de poêle); poignée *f* (d'épée, de levier, etc.); clef *f* (de robinet); *F:* **to fly off the h.,** s'emporter, s'emballer; *F:* **to have a h. to one's name,** (i) avoir un titre (de noblesse); (ii) avoir un nom à particule; **you're giving him a h. against you,** vous lui donnez des armes, un avantage, contre vous; (*c*) anse *f* (de corbeille, de seau, etc.); portant *m* (de boîte, de valise); (*d*) (*crank handle*) manivelle *f*; *Aut:* **starting h.,** manivelle (de mise en marche).

handle² *v.tr.* **1.** tâter des mains; **to h. a material,** tâter un tissu. **2.** (*a*) manier, manipuler (qch.); manœuvrer (un navire, les voiles, etc.); gouverner (un navire); conduire (une voiture); **how to h. a gun,** comment se servir d'un fusil; *Post:* **h. with care** = fragile; (*b*) manier, manipuler (une affaire); **to h. s.o. roughly,** malmener, rudoyer, qn; **to h. a situation,** prendre en main une situation; (*c*) **to h. a lot of business,** brasser beaucoup d'affaires; **to h. large orders,** s'occuper de grandes commandes; **to h. a lot of money,** avoir un maniement considérable. **handling** *n.* (*a*) maniement *m* (d'un outil, etc.); manipulation *f* (des explosifs, etc.); manutention *f* (de marchandises, etc.); manœuvre *f* (d'un navire); conduite *f* (d'une voiture); **industrial h.,** manutention industrielle; (*b*) traitement *m* (de qn, d'un sujet, etc.); **rough h.,** traitement brutal; (*c*) maniement (de fonds); (*d*) *Com:* distribution *f*; (*e*) *Fb:* (faute *f* de) main (*f*).

handlebar [ˈhænd(ə)lbɑːr] *n.* guidon *m* (de bicyclette); *F:* **h. moustache,** moustaches *fpl* en guidon (de bicyclette).

handler [ˈhændlər] *n.* (*a*) manipulateur, -trice; *Com:* manutentionnaire *mf*; (*b*) **(dog) h.,** dresseur *m* de chiens; (*c*) *Box:* second *m*; soigneur *m.*

handmade [ˈhændˈmeid] *a.* fait, fabriqué, à la main.

hand-me-downs [ˈhændmidaunz] *n.pl. F:* vêtements usagés, d'occasion; frusques *fpl.*

handout [ˈhændaut] *n. F:* **1.** (i) aumône *f*; (ii) nourriture distribuée aux mendiants; **state h.,** allocation faite par l'assistance publique. **2.** (*a*) *Journ:* compte rendu communiqué à la presse; (*b*) *Sch: etc:* notes (polycopiées) (données aux élèves). **3.** *Com:* (*a*) prospectus *m*, circulaire *m* publicitaire; (*b*) cadeau *m* publicitaire.

hand-pick [ˈhændpik] *v.tr.* trier (le charbon, etc.) à la main; éplucher (la laine, etc.) à la main; *F:* **hand-picked,** (réunion) triée sur le volet, très sélecte.

handrail [ˈhændreil] *n.* garde-fou *m*, *pl.* garde-fous; garde-corps *m inv*; rampe *f*, main courante (d'escalier, etc.); (*on wall side of staircase*) écuyer *m*; *Nau: Rail:* rambarde *f.*

handsaw [ˈhændsɔː] *n.* scie *f* à main.

handset [ˈhændset] *n. Tp:* combiné *m.*

handshake [ˈhændʃeik] *n.* poignée *f*, serrement *m*, de main; *F:* **golden h.,** indemnité *f* de départ, pont *m* d'or.

handsome [ˈhænsəm] *a.* (*a*) beau, *f.* belle; **a h. man,** un bel homme; **she was still a h. woman,** elle était toujours belle; (*b*) (*of conduct, etc.*) gracieux, généreux; **he received very h. treatment,** on l'a traité d'une façon généreuse; (*c*) (*considerable*) belle (fortune); bon (prix); (cadeau) généreux; **to make a h. profit,** faire, réaliser, de beaux bénéfices. **-ly** *adv.* (*a*) bien (habillé, meublé, etc.); (*b*) (agir) généreusement; (payer) libéralement.

handsomeness [ˈhænsəmnis] *n.* (*a*) beauté *f*, grâce *f* (d'une personne, d'un monument, etc.); (*b*) générosité *f* (d'une action); libéralité *f* (d'une récompense).

handspring [ˈhændspriŋ] *n. Gym:* saut *m* de mains.

handstand [ˈhændstænd] *n. Gym:* **to do a h.,** faire l'arbre droit.

hand-tooling [ˈhændtuːliŋ] *n.* **1.** *Ind:* travail *m* à la main (sur le tour, etc.). **2.** *Bookb:* dorure à froid faite à la main.

handwork [ˈhændwəːk] *n.* travail *m* à la main, travail manuel.

handwriting [ˈhændraitiŋ] *n.* écriture *f*; **h. expert,** expert *m* en écritures; **this letter is in the h. of . . .,** cette lettre a été écrite par . . ., est de la main de. . ..

handwritten [ˈhændrit(ə)n] *a.* (*of letter, etc.*) manuscrit.

handy [ˈhændi] *a.* **1.** (*of pers.*) adroit (de ses mains); habile: **he's very h. about the house,** (i) il aide bien au ménage; (ii) c'est un bon bricoleur; **h. at sth., at doing sth.,** adroit à qch., à faire qch.; **to be h. with one's fists,** savoir se servir de ses poings. **2.** (*of tool, etc.*) maniable, bien en main(s); (navire) maniable. **3.** commode; **that would come in very h.,** cela serait très utile, ferait bien l'affaire. **4.** à portée (de la main); **I always keep my tools h.,** j'ai toujours mes outils sous la main.

handyman, *pl.* **-men** [ˈhændimæn, -men] *n.m.* homme à tout faire, à toute main; bricoleur.

hang[1] [hæŋ] *n.* **1.** (*a*) pente *f*, inclinaison *f* (d'une falaise, etc.); (*b*) ajustement *m* (d'un vêtement); drapé *m* (d'un tissu); (*c*) *F:* **to get the h. of sth.,** (i) attraper le coup, saisir le truc, de, pour faire, qch.; (ii) comprendre, piger, qch.; **when you've got the h. of things,** quand vous serez au courant. **2.** *F:* **I don't give, care, a h.,** je m'en moque, m'en fiche.

hang[2] *v.* (*p.t. & p.p.* **hung** [hʌŋ]) **I.** *v.tr.* **1.** pendre, accrocher, suspendre (**on, from,** à); monter (un porte); **to h. sth. on the wall,** pendre qch. au mur; **to h. a picture,** (i) suspendre un tableau; (ii) exposer un tableau (au Salon, etc.); *Aut: etc:* **low-hung,** (essieu, etc.) surbaissé. **2.** (*droop*) **to h. one's head,** baisser la tête. **3.** *Cu:* faire faisander (la viande, le gibier). **4.** (*a*) **to h. a room with tapestries,** tendre une salle de tapisseries; **hall hung with flags,** salle ornée de drapeaux; (*b*) coller (du papier à tapisser). **5. to h. fire,** (i) (*of firearms*) faire long feu; (ii) (*of undertaking, etc.*) traîner (en longueur). **6.** (*p.t. & p.p.* **hanged**) pendre (un criminel); **he hanged himself,** il s'est pendu; *F:* **I'm hanged if I know!** je n'en sais fichtre rien! **h. it!** zut! mince alors! *Prov:* **as well be hanged for a sheep as for a lamb,** autant vaut être pendu pour un mouton que pour un agneau. **II.** *v.i.* **1.** pendre, être suspendu; *Cu:* (*of game*) se faisander; **picture hanging on the wall,** tableau pendu, accroché, au mur; **to h. out of the window,** (*of pers.*) se pencher par la fenêtre, (*of thg*) pendre à la fenêtre. **2. a thick fog hangs over the town,** un épais brouillard plane sur la ville; **a heavy silence hung over the meeting,** un silence pesait sur l'assemblée. **3.** (*a*) **to h. on s.o.'s arm,** (*of thg*) pendre au bras de qn; (*of pers.*) se pendre au bras de qn; **to h. on s.o.'s lips, words,** être suspendu aux lèvres de qn; **the children hung on his every word,** les enfants l'écoutaient avidement; (*b*) (*depend*) **everything hangs on his answer,** tout dépend de sa réponse. **4. horse that hangs on the bit,** cheval *m* qui appuie sur le mors; **time hangs heavy (on my hands),** le temps me pèse, me semble long. **5.** fainéanter, flâner; **to h. about, around, the house doing nothing,** traîner à la maison sans rien faire; **to keep s.o. hanging about, around,** faire poireauter qn. **6.** (*a*) (*of drapery, clothes, etc.*) tomber, se draper; **to h. loose, limply,** pendiller; **his clothes h. loosely on him,** il flotte dans ses vêtements; (*b*) **this door hangs badly,** cette porte est mal suspendue (sur ses gonds). **7.** (*of criminal*) être pendu; *F:* **if he doesn't like it he can go h.,** si ça ne lui plait pas, qu'il aille se faire pendre. **hang back** *v.i.* (*a*) rester en arrière; (*b*) hésiter; renâcler. **hang down** *v.i.* (*a*) pendre; (*b*) pencher (sous le poids de qch.). **hanging 1.** *a.* (*a*) (crochet, lustre, etc.) pendant; (pont) suspendu; (échafaudage) volant; *Geog:* (vallée) suspendue; **h. cupboard,** armoire murale; **the h. gardens of Babylon,** les jardins suspendus de Babylone; (*b*) *F:* **h. judge,** juge *m* féroce, qui condamne les accusés à la potence. **2.** *n.* (*a*) (i) suspension *f* (d'une lampe, d'un tableau, etc.). montage *m*, accrochage *m* (d'une porte); *Cu:* faisandage *m*, (du gibier); (ii) tenture *f*, pose *f* (d'une tapisserie); (iii) pendaison *f* (d'un criminel); *F:* **hanging's too good for him,** il ne vaut par la corde pour le pendre; (iv) **h. committee,** comité *m* de réception, jury *m* d'admission, des tableaux au Salon (à Paris), à la *Royal Academy* (à Londres); (*b*) **hangings,** tenture(s) *f* (*pl*), tapisserie(s) *f* (*pl*). **hang on** *v.i.* se cramponner, s'accrocher; **to h. on to sth.,** (i) s'accrocher, se crampouner, à qch.; (ii) ne pas lâcher, abandonner, qch.; *Tp:* **h. on!** ne quittez pas! **h. on for a moment,** attendez un moment; **to h. on like grim death,** se cramponner; tenir tout juste. **hang out 1.** *v.tr.* pendre, mettre, (qch.) au dehors; étendre (le linge); arborer (un pavillon). **2.** *v.i.* (*a*) pendre (au dehors); **his shirt was hanging out,** sa chemise passait; *F:* **where do you h. out?** où nichez-vous? (*b*) **the rocks h. out over the gully,** les rochers surplombent le ravin. **hang together** *v.i.* (*a*) (*of persons*) rester unis; (*b*) (*of statements, etc.*) s'accorder, *F:* tenir debout. **hang up** *v.tr.* (*a*) (i) accrocher, pendre (son chapeau, un tableau, etc.); (ii) *Tp:* raccrocher (l'appareil); *F:* **to h. up on s.o.,** couper la communication avec qn; (*b*) **to work is hung up,** le travail est suspendu.

hangar [ˈhæŋər] *n. esp. Av:* hangar *m.*

hangdog [ˈhæŋdɔg] *a.* **h. look,** air *m* de chien battu.

hanger [ˈhæŋər] *n.* **1.** (*device*) (*a*) crochet *m* (de suspension); **(coat) h.,** cintre *m*; (*b*) *Cost:* attache *f* (de manteau, etc.); (*c*) *Mec.E:* suspenseur *m*; **bearing h.,** chaise suspendue. **2.** (*pers.*) **h.-on,** *pl.* **hangers-on,** parasite *m*; écornifleur *m.*

hang-glide [ˈhæŋglaid] *v.i.* faire du deltaplane. **hang-gliding** *n.* (sport *m* du) deltaplane.

hang-glider [ˈhæŋglaidər] *n.* (*a*) deltaplane *m*; (*b*) (*pers.*) deltaplaneur *m.*

hangman, *pl.* **-men** [ˈhæŋmən] *n.m.* bourreau.

hangnail [ˈhæŋneil] *n.* envie *f* (de l'ongle).

hangout [ˈhæŋaut] *n. F:* (*a*) logement *m*; (*b*) repaire *m*, nid *m* (de criminels, etc.).

hangover [ˈhæŋouvər] *n. F:* **1.** reliquat *m* (de superstition, d'une habitude, etc.). **2. to have a h.,** avoir la gueule de bois, avoir mal aux cheveux.

hang-up [ˈhæŋʌp] *n.* (*a*) *Cmptr:* arrêt imprévu (de la machine); (*b*) *F:* trouble *m* psychique.

hank [hæŋk] *n.* écheveau *m* (de laine, etc.); torchette *f*, peignée *f* (de fil).

hanker [ˈhæŋkər] *v.i.* **to h. after sth.,** avoir bien envie de, soupirer après, convoiter, qch. **hankering** *n.* vif désir, grande envie (**after, for,** de).

hankie, hanky [ˈhæŋki] *n. F:* mouchoir *m.*

hanky-panky [ˈhæŋkiˈpæŋki] *n.* **1.** tour *m* de passe-passe. **2.** *F:* supercherie *f*; finasseries *fpl.*

Hanoverian [hænəˈviəriən] *Geog:* **1.** *a.* hanovrien. **2.** *n.* Hanovrien, -ienne.

Hansard [ˈhænsɑːd] *n.* compte rendu officiel des débats parlementaires.

Hanseatic [hænsiˈætik] *a. Hist:* **the H. League,** la Ligue hanséatique.

ha'penny, *pl.* **ha'pence** [ˈheipəni, -pəns] *n. F:* = HALFPENNY.

haphazard [hæpˈhæzəd] **1.** *adv.* par, au, hasard; au petit bonheur. **2.** *a.* (tentative) au petit bonheur; (disposition) fortuite; **to choose in a h. way,** choisir à l'aveuglette. **-ly** *adv.* au petit bonheur; à l'aveuglette.

hapless [ˈhæplis] *a. A: & Lit:* infortuné, malheureux.

happen [ˈhæp(ə)n] *v.i.* **1.** (*take place*) (*a*) arriver, se passer; advenir, survenir, se produire; **it happened ten years ago,** cela s'est passé il y a dix ans; **accidents will h.,** les accidents arrivent; *F:* **worse things h. at sea,** il y a pire; **it happens over and over again,** c'est toujours la même chose; **don't let it h. again!** que cela n'arrive plus! **just as if nothing had happened,** comme si de rien n'était; **whatever happens,** quoi qu'il arrive; **as it happens,** justement, précisément; **as often happens,** comme il est fréquent; (*b*) **what has happened to him?** (i) qu'est-ce qui lui est arrivé? (ii) qu'est-ce qu'il est devenu? **what's happened to my pen?** qu'est-ce qu'on a fait de mon stylo? **2.** (*chance*) **he happened to pass that way,** il s'est trouvé passer par là; **a taxi happened to be passing,** par hasard, par bonheur, un taxi passait; **I h. to know that . . .,** il se trouve que je sais que . . .; **do you h. to know whether . . .?** sauriez-vous par hasard si . . .? **if you h. to find it,** s'il arrive que vous le trouviez. **3. to h. on sth., on s.o.,** tomber sur qch., qn. **happening** *n.* (*a*) événement *m*; (*b*) *Th:* happening *m*.

happenstance [ˈhæp(ə)nstæns] *n. U.S: F:* événement fortuit.

happiness [ˈhæpinis] *n.* bonheur *m*, félicité *f*.

happy [ˈhæpi] *a.* heureux. **1.** (*a*) (circonstance) heureuse; **in happier circumstances,** dans des circonstances plus favorables; (*b*) **h. life,** vie heureuse; **to be as h. as the day is long,** être heureux comme un poisson dans l'eau; **h. Christmas!** joyeux Noël! *F:* (*as toast*) **h. days!** à votre santé! *Games:* **h. families,** jeu *m* des métiers; **I'm very h. with his work,** je suis très satisfait, content, de son travail; **I'm not at all h. about it,** cela ne me plait pas du tout; **to make s.o. h.,** (i) rendre qn heureux; (ii) faire le joie de qn; **to be h. to do sth.,** être heureux, content, de faire qch.; (*c*) *F: O:* **to be h.,** être un peu gris. **2.** (expression) bien choisie, à propos. **-ily** *adv.* heureusement; (i) dans le bonheur; (ii) par bonheur; **to live h.,** vivre heureux; **a h. married couple,** un ménage heureux.

happy-go-lucky [ˈhæpigouˈlʌki] *a.* sans souci, insouciant; **to do sth. in a h.-go-l. fashion,** faire qch. au petit bonheur.

Hapsburg [ˈhæpsbəːg] *Pr.n. Hist:* Habsbourg.

harangue¹ [həˈræŋ] *n.* harangue *f*.

harangue² **1.** *v.tr.* haranguer (la foule, etc.). **2.** *v.i.* prononcer, faire, une harangue.

harass [ˈhærəs] *v.tr.* **1.** *Mil:* harceler, tenir en alerte (l'ennemi). **2.** tracasser, tourmenter (qn).

harassment [ˈhærəsmənt] *n.* **1.** harcèlement *m*. **2.** tracasserie *f*, tourment *m*.

harbinger [ˈhɑːbindʒər] *n. Lit:* avant-coureur *m*, *pl.* avant-coureurs; messager, -ère; précurseur *m*.

harbour¹, *U.S:* **harbor¹** [ˈhɑːbər] *n. Nau:* port *m*; **tidal h.,** port à, de, marée; **h. master,** capitaine *m*, officier *m*, de port; (*of small port*) lieutenant *m* de port; **h. dues,** droits *mpl* de mouillage.

harbour², *NAm:* **harbor²** **1.** *v.tr.* héberger; donner asile à (qn): receler (un criminel); retenir (la saleté); entretenir, nourrir (des soupçons); **to h. a grudge against s.o.,** garder rancune à qn. **2.** *v.i.* chercher asile, se réfugier (**in,** dans).

hard [hɑːd] **I.** *a.* **1.** (*firm*) dur; (*a*) **h. substance,** substance dure; (*of cement, etc.*) **to become, get, h.,** durcir; **to become harder,** se rendurcir; **h. snow,** neige durcie; *Metall:* **h. lead,** plomb *m* aigre; **to be as h. as nails,** (i) être musclé; (ii) être dur; (*b*) *Fin:* (*of stock, rates, etc.*) tendu, tenu, soutenu; (*c*) (*of ship*) **h. and fast,** à sec; bien pris; **h. and fast rule,** règle absolue, rigoureuse. **2.** (*difficult*) difficile; (tâche, chemin) pénible; **to be h. to please,** être exigeant, difficile à contenter; **to be h. of hearing,** être dur d'oreille; **the h. of hearing,** les malentendants; **article that is h. to sell,** article peu vendable; *esp. NAm:* **the h. sell,** publicité poussée à fond; battage *m* publicitaire; **I find it h. to believe that . . .,** j'ai peine à croire que + *sub.*; **it is h. to understand,** c'est difficile à comprendre; **the hardest part of the job is done,** le plus dur est fait. **3.** (*severe; harsh*) (*a*) (*of pers., manner, etc.*) dur, sévère (**to, towards,** envers); (maître) sévère, exigeant; (cœur) dur; **to be h. on s.o.,** être sévère envers qn; (*b*) **to say h. things to s.o.,** dire des duretés à qn; **h. fact,** fait brutal; **times are h.,** les temps sont durs, difficiles; **to have a h. time of it,** en voir de dures; **h. luck! h. lines!** pas de chance! quelle guigne! (*c*) rude (**to the touch,** au toucher); (voix, *Ling:* consonne) dure; (lumière) crue; *Phot:* (épreuve) heurtée, contrastée; **h. water,** eau calcaire; **h. liquor,** spiritueux *mpl*; *F:* **a drop of the h. stuff,** une goutte d'alcool, d'eau-de-vie; **h. drugs,** drogues dures. **4.** (*strenuous*) **h. work,** (i) travail assidu; (ii) travail ingrat; **it was h. work to convince him,** j'ai eu fort à faire pour le convaincre; **it is h. work for me to . . ., I find it h. work to . . .,** j'ai beaucoup de peine, bien du mal à . . .; **h. gallop,** galop soutenu; **h. drinker,** grand buveur; **h. fight,** rude combat *m*; **it's a h. blow for him,** c'est un rude coup pour lui; **to try one's hardest,** faire tout son possible; **h. labour,** travaux forcés; *n. F:* **fifteen years' h.,** quinze longes *fpl* des durs. **5.** (*extreme*) (hiver) rigoureux; **h. frost,** forte gelée. **II.** *adv.* **1.** (*a*) (*vigorously*) fort; **as h. as one can,** de toutes ses forces; **to hit, strike, h.,** cogner dur; **he goes at it h.,** il n'y va pas de main morte; **to jam on the brakes h.,** serrer les freins à bloc; **to look, gaze, stare, h. at s.o.,** regarder fixement qn; **to think h.,** réfléchir profondément; **to work h. (at sth.),** travailler dur, ferme (à qch.); **he works too h.,** il se surmène; **to be h. at work,** être en plein travail; **it's raining h.,** il pleut à verse; (*b*) **it will go h. with him if . . .,** cela sera sérieux (pour lui) si . . .; (*c*) *Nau:* **h. over!** la barre toute! (*d*) **to be h. up (for money), to be h. pushed,** être dans la gêne; être à court (d'argent). **2.** (*with difficulty*) difficilement, avec peine; **h.-earned wages,** salaire péniblement gagné. **3.** (*near*) **h. by,** tout près, tout contre; **to follow h. (up)on, after, behind, s.o.,** suivre qn de près. **III.** *n.* **1.** tabac *m* en carotte. **2.** *Nau:* cale *f* (de débarquement). **3. hards,** déchets *mpl* de chanvre, de lin. **hardly** *adv.* **1. sévèrement; to deal h. with s.o.,** user de rigueur envers qn. **2.** (*a*) à peine; ne . . . guère; **she can h. read,** c'est à peine si elle sait lire; **I need h. say . . .,** il va sans dire . . .; **h. anyone, anything,** presque personne, presque rien; **h. ever,** presque jamais; (*b*) sûrement pas; **he could h. have said that,** il n'aurait sûrement pas dit cela.

hardback [ˈhɑːdbæk] *n.* livre cartonné.

hard-bitten [ˈhɑːdbit(ə)n] *a. F:* (*of pers.*) tenace, boucané, dur à cuire.

hardboard [ˈhɑːdbɔːd] *n. Const:* carton dur, Isorel *m* (*R.t.m.*).

hardboiled [hɑːdˈbɔild] *a.* (*a*) (œuf) dur; (*b*) *F:* = HARD-BITTEN.

hardcore [ˈhɑːdkɔːr] *n.* **1.** *Const:* blocaille *f*. **2.** *Fig:* noyeau *m* (de résistance, etc.); **h. pornography,** pornographie dure.

hard-earned [hɑːdˈəːnd] *a.* (*of money, etc.*) péniblement gagné; (*of prize, holiday, etc.*) bien mérité.

harden [ˈhɑːd(ə)n] **1.** *v.tr.* (*a*) durcir, (r)endurcir (qch.); tremper (l'acier, etc.); *Med:* scléroser (les muscles, etc.); **to h. oneself, to become hardened, to the cold,** s'endurcir, s'aguerrir, au froid; **to h. s.o.'s heart,** endurcir le cœur de qn; (*b*) *Hort:* **to h. (off) seedlings,** fortifier de jeunes plants; (*c*) *Metall:* **to (case-)h.,** cémenter (l'acier). **2.** *v.i.* (*a*) (*of substance*) (se) durcir, s'endurcir; (*b*) *Fin:* (*of shares, etc.*) **to h. (up),** se raffermir; **prices are hardening,** les prix sont en hausse; (*c*) (*of the constitution*) s'endurcir; s'aguerrir; (*d*) **scientific opinion has hardened to the**

view that . . ., le monde savant est de plus en plus d'avis que . . .. **hardened** *a.* (*of substance*) durci, endurci; (*of steel, glass*) trempé; (criminel) endurci. **hardening** *n.* (*a*) durcissement *m*, (r)endurcissement *m*, affermissement *m*; *Metall:* trempe *f*; (*b*) *Metall:* **(case) h.,** cémentation *f* (de l'acier); (*c*) durcissement (des artères).

hard-faced, -featured [hɑːd'feist, -'fiːtjəd] *a.* (personne) aux traits durs, sévères.

hardfisted [hɑːd'fistid] *a. F:* avare.

hard-fought ['hɑːd'fɔːt] *a.* vivement, chaudement, contesté; âprement disputé.

hard-headed [hɑːd'hedid] *a.* (*of pers.*) (*a*) positif, pratique; **h.-h. business man,** homme d'affaires réaliste; (*b*) obstiné, têtu.

hardhearted [hɑːd'hɑːtid] *a.* (*of pers.*) impitoyable, au cœur dur; (père) dénaturé.

hard-hitting [hɑːd'hitiŋ] *a.* qui frappe dur; *Box: etc:* **h.-h. opponent,** adversaire cogneur.

hardiness ['hɑːdinis] *n.* robustesse *f*, vigueur *f*.

hard-liner [hɑːd'lainər] *n. Pol: etc:* faucon *m*, épervier *m*.

hardness ['hɑːdnis] *n.* **1.** (*a*) dureté *f* (d'une substance); (*b*) trempe *f* (de l'acier); (*c*) tons heurtés (d'un cliché, d'un tableau); dureté (de style); (*d*) crudité *f* (de l'eau). **2.** *Fin:* tension *f* (du marché, des actions). **3.** (*a*) difficulté *f* (d'un travail, d'un problème, etc.): (*b*) **h. of hearing,** dureté d'oreille. **4.** (*a*) sévérité *f*, rigueur *f* (d'une règle, etc.); (*b*) caractère *m* insensible (de qn); dureté, brutalité *f*.

hard-pressed, -pushed [hɑːd'prest, -'puʃt] *a.* (*of debtor, etc.*) aux abois, fort embarrassé.

hardship ['hɑːdʃip] *n.* privation *f*; fatigue *f*; (dure) épreuve; tribulation *f*; **he has suffered great hardships,** il en a vu de dures.

hardtack ['hɑːdtæk] *n. Nau:* biscuit *m* de mer.

hardtop ['hɑːdtɔp] *n. Aut:* hard-top *m*.

hard-up [hɑːd'ʌp] *a. F:* **to be h.-up,** être à sec, être fauché; **to be h.-up for sth.,** manquer de qch.

hardware ['hɑːdwɛər] *n.* **1.** (*a*) quincaillerie *f*; **h. dealer,** quincaillier *m*; **h. shop, store,** quincaillerie *f*; (*b*) *F:* armes *fpl*. **2.** (*a*) éléments *mpl*, parties *fpl* métalliques (d'un appareil, d'une installation); ferrures *fpl*; (*b*) *Cmptr:* matériel *m*, hardware *m*.

hard-wearing [hɑːd'wɛəriŋ] *a.* (vêtements, etc.) de bon usage, de bon service; (tissu) durable.

hard-won [hɑːd'wʌn] *a.* (*of trophy, victory*) chaudement disputé, remporté de haute lutte.

hardwood ['hɑːdwud] *n.* bois dur.

hard-working [hɑːd'wəːkiŋ] *a.* laborieux, travailleur, -euse, assidu.

hardy ['hɑːdi] *a.* **1.** hardi, courageux, audacieux. **2.** (*a*) robuste; endurci (à la fatigue, etc.); (*b*) *Bot:* résistant; (arbuste) vivace; (plante) de pleine terre; **h. annual,** (i) *Bot:* plante annuelle de pleine terre; (ii) *F:* question *f* qui revient régulièrement sur le tapis.

hare¹ ['hɛər] *n.* lièvre *m*; **doe h.,** hase *f*; *Cu:* **jugged h.,** civet *m* de lièvre; **to run with the h. and hunt with the hounds,** ménager la chèvre et le chou; jouer double jeu; **to start a h.,** (i) *Ven:* lever un lièvre; (ii) donner un nouveau tour à la conversation; *Sp:* **h. and hounds,** rallye-paper *m* (à pied), *pl.* rallye-papers.

hare² *v.i. F:* (*of pers.*) courir comme un lièvre, à toutes jambes; **to h. off after s.o.,** s'élancer à la poursuite de qn.

harebell ['hɛəbel] *n. Bot:* campanule *f*.

harebrained ['hɛəbreind] *a.* écervelé, étourdi; **h. scheme,** projet insensé.

harelip ['hɛəlip] *n. Med:* bec-de-lièvre *m*, *pl.* becs-de-lièvre.

harem [hɑː'riːm] *n.* harem *m*.

haricot ['hærikou] *n.* **1.** *Cu:* **h. mutton,** haricot *m* de mouton. **2. h. (bean),** *Bot:* haricot blanc.

hark [hɑːk] *v.i.* **1.** prêter l'oreille **(at, to,** à un son, etc.); **h.!** écoutez! **h. at him!** ta, ta, ta, comme il y va! **2.** (*of pers.*) **to h. back to sth.,** ramener la conversation sur un sujet; **to h. back to the past,** ressasser le passé.

harlequin ['hɑːlikwin] *n. Th:* arlequin *m*; **h. coat,** habit bigarré ou mi-parti.

harlot ['hɑːlət] *n. A:* prostituée *f*.

harm¹ [hɑːm] *n.* mal *m*, tort *m:* **to do h. to s.o.,** faire du tort à qn; **what h. has she done you?** quel mal vous a-t-elle fait? **to see no h. in sth.,** ne pas voir de mal à qch.; **you will come to no h.,** il ne vous arrivera pas de mal; **out of harm's way,** (i) à l'abri du danger, en sûreté; (ii) mis dans l'impossibilité de nuire à personne; **it will do more h. than good,** cela fera plus de mal que de bien; **that won't do any h.,** cela ne gâtera rien; **it won't do him any h.,** cela ne lui fera pas de mal; **there's no h. in saying so,** il n'y a pas de mal à le dire; **there's no h. in trying,** on peut toujours essayer.

harm² *v.tr.* faire du mal, du tort, à (qn); causer du tort à (qn); nuire à (qn); léser (les intérêts de qn).

harmful ['hɑːmf(u)l] *a.* malfaisant, pernicieux; nocif, nuisible **(to,** à).

harmfulness ['hɑːmf(u)lnis] *n.* nocivité *f*; nature *f* nuisible **(of,** de).

harmless ['hɑːmlis] *a.* (animal) inoffensif; (homme) sans malice; (passe-temps) innocent; (médicament) anodin; **h. talk,** conversation anodine. **-ly** *adv.* sans (faire de) mal; (s'amuser) innocemment.

harmonic [hɑː'mɔnik] **1.** *a.* harmonique; **h. series,** (i) *Mus:* échelle *f* harmonique; (ii) *Mth:* série *f* harmonique; *Mth: Ph:* **h. motion,** mouvement sinusoïdal. **2.** *n.* (*a*) *Mus:* harmonique *m* (d'un son fondamental); (*on stringed instrument*) harmonique, son flûté; **harmonics,** sons harmoniques; (*b*) *Mth: Ph:* harmonique (d'un mouvement ondulatoire).

harmonica [hɑː'mɔnikə] *n.* harmonica *m*.

harmonious [hɑː'mouniəs] *a.* harmonieux. **1.** accordant, en bon accord. **2.** mélodieux. **-ly** *adv.* harmonieusement; (travailler, vivre) en harmonie.

harmonium [hɑː'mouniəm] *n.* harmonium *m*.

harmonization [hɑːmənai'zeiʃ(ə)n] *n. Mus:* harmonisation *f*.

harmonize ['hɑːmənaiz] **1.** *v.tr.* (*a*) harmoniser (des idées, etc.); faire accorder (des textes, etc.); allier (des couleurs, etc.) **(with,** avec); (*b*) *Mus:* harmoniser (une mélodie). **2.** *v.i.* (*of sounds, colours, etc.*) s'harmoniser; (*of facts, thgs*) s'accorder; (*of pers., ideas, etc.*) se mettre en harmonie, s'accorder; **colours that h. well,** couleurs qui vont bien ensemble; **to h. with sth.,** s'adapter harmonieusement à qch.

harmony ['hɑːməni] *n.* **1.** *Mus:* harmonie *f*; (*a*) **to study h.,** étudier l'harmonie; (*b*) **songs full of h.,** chants mélodieux. **2.** (*a*) (*of pers., ideas, etc.*) harmonie *f*, accord *m*; (*of voices, instruments*) concert *m*; **to live in perfect h.,** vivre en parfaite intelligence; **in h. with . . .,** qui s'harmonise, qui s'accorde, avec . . .; (*b*) concordance *f* (de textes).

harness¹ ['hɑːnis] *n.* **1.** (*a*) harnais *m*, harnachement *m* (d'un cheval); **h. horse,** cheval d'attelage; **draught h.,** harnais d'attelage; **h. room,** sellerie *f*; **to go in single h.,** (i) (*of horse*) être attelé par un; (ii) (*of pers.*) être célibataire; (*of pers.*) **to get back into h. (again),** reprendre le collier; **to die in h.,** mourir à la peine; (*b*) *U.S: Turf:* **h. race,** course *f* au trot; (*c*) **parachute h.,** ceinture *f*, harnais, de parachutiste; *Ind: Aut: etc:* **safety h.,** harnais de sécurité. **2.** *Tex:* harnais (de métier à tisser).

harness² *v.tr.* **1.** harnacher (un cheval); **to h. a horse to a cart,** atteler un cheval à une charrette. **2.** aménager (une chute d'eau, etc.); **to h. atomic energy for industrial purposes,** mettre l'énergie atomique au service de l'industrie. **harnessing** *n.* **1.** harnachement *m*; attelage *m*. **2.** aménagement *m* (d'une chute d'eau, etc.).

harp¹ [hɑːp] *n. Mus:* (*a*) harpe *f*; **to play the h.,** jouer de la harpe; (*b*) **Jew's h.,** guimbarde *f*.

harp² *v.i.* jouer de la harpe: *F:* **to be always harping on the same string,** rabâcher toujours la même chose; chanter toujours le même refrain.

harpist ['hɑːpist] *n. Mus:* harpiste *mf*.

harpoon¹ [hɑː'puːn] *n.* harpon *m*, lance *f*; **pronged h.,** foëne *f*; **h. gun,** (i) canon *m* lance-harpon; (ii) fusil *m* à harpon.

harpoon² *v.tr.* harponner.

harpsichord ['hɑːpsikɔːd] *n. Mus:* clavecin *m*.

harpsichordist ['hɑːpsikɔːdist] *n.* claveciniste *mf*.

harpy ['hɑːpi] *n.* **1.** *Myth:* harpie *f*; *F:* **old h.,** vieille mégère. **2.** *Orn:* **h. eagle,** harpie.

harridan ['hærid(ə)n] *n. F:* vieille sorcière.

harrier¹ ['hæriər] *n.* **1.** pilleur *m*, pillard *m*. **2.** *Orn:* busard *m*.

harrier² *n.* **1.** (*a*) *Ven:* (*dog*) harrier *m*; (*b*) *Sp:* (*pers.*) harrier, coureur *m*. **2. harriers,** (*a*) *Ven:* meute *f* (de chiens pour la chasse au lièvre); (*b*) *Sp:* club *m* de coureurs, de cross.

harrow¹ ['hærou] *n. Agr:* herse *f*.

harrow² *v.tr. Agr:* herser (un terrain); *Fig:* **to h. s.o.'s feelings, to h. s.o.,** déchirer le cœur à qn. **harrowing** *a.* (conte, etc.) poignant, navrant; (cri) déchirant.

Harry¹ ['hæri] *Pr.n.m.* **1.** (*dim.*) = Henri; *F:* **any, every, Tom, Dick and H.,** tout le monde. **2.** *F:* **to play old H. with s.o.,** en faire voir des vertes et des pas mûres à qn.

harry² *v.tr.* **1.** attaquer, harceler (l'ennemi). **2.** pourchasser, harceler (un débiteur).

harsh [hɑːʃ] *a.* **1.** dur, rêche, rude (au toucher); âpre (au goût); strident (à l'oreille); (bruit) désagréable; (voix) rude, rauque; (vin) âpre. **2.** (caractère) bourru; (traitement) dur; (maître, réponse) rude; **to say h. things to s.o.,** en dire de dures à qn. **-ly** *adv.* (répondre, etc.) durement, rudement; (traiter qn) sévèrement.

harshness ['hɑːʃnis] *n.* **1.** dureté *f*, rudesse *f* (au toucher); stridence *f* (d'un son); aspérité *f* (du style, de la voix). **2.** sévérité *f* (d'une punition, d'une loi).

hart [hɑːt] *n.* cerf *m*; *Ven:* cerf âgé de plus de cinq ans.

harum-scarum ['hɛərəm'skɛərəm] *F:* **1.** *a.* étourdi, écervelé. **2.** *n.* écervelé(e); **she's a h.-s.,** c'est une évaporée.

harvest¹ ['hɑːvist] *n.* **1.** moisson *f* (du blé); récolte *f* (des fruits); fenaison *f* (du foin); vendange *f* (du vin); **to get in the h.,** faire la moisson. **2.** (temps *m*, époque *f*, de) la moisson. **3. h. thanksgiving, festival,** action *f* de grâces (après la rentrée des récoltes); **h. home,** fête *f* de la moisson; **h. moon,** lune *f* de la moisson; *Z:* **h. mouse,** souris *f* des moissons.

harvest² **1.** *v.tr.* moissonner (les blés); récolter (les fruits). **2.** *v.i.* rentrer, faire, la moisson. **harvesting** *n.* (rentrée *f* de la) moisson.

harvester ['hɑːvistər] *n.* **1.** (*pers.*) moissonneur, -euse. **2.** (*machine*) moissonneuse *f*; **combine h.,** moissonneuse-batteuse *f*, *pl.* moissonneuses-batteuses.

has-been ['hæzbiːn] *n. F:* (*a*) (*pers.*) vieux ramolli; **he's a h.-b.,** c'est une (vieille) croûte; (*b*) homme fini.

hash¹ [hæʃ] *n.* **1.** *Cu:* (*a*) hachis *m*; (*b*) *F:* nourriture *f*, boustifaille *f*. **2.** *F:* **to make a h. of sth.,** gâcher, gâter, un travail; faire un beau gâchis de qch.; **he make a h. of it,** il a tout bousillé, saboté; **to settle s.o.'s h.,** régler son compte à qn. **3.** *F:* **h.(-up),** réchauffé *m* (de vielles idées, etc.); compilation *f* (de l'œuvre d'autrui).

hash² *v.tr.* (*a*) **to h. (up) meat,** hacher de la viande (en petits morceaux); (*b*) *F:* **we've hashed over this question long enough,** on a déjà mis assez de temps à considérer cette question; (*c*) **to h. up,** bousiller (qch.).

hashish ['hæʃiːʃ] *n.* hachisch *m*.

hasn't = **has not;** *see* HAVE².

hasp [hɑːsp] *n.* **1.** (*for padlocking*) **(staple) h.,** moraillon *m*. **2.** (*a*) loquet *m* (de porte); (*b*) espagnolette *f* (de porte-fenêtre); (*c*) fermoir *m f* (d'album, etc.).

hassle¹ ['hæsl] *n. F:* **1.** dispute *f*; chamaillerie *f*. **2.** pagaïe *f*. **3.** tracas *m*; embêtement *m*.

hassle² *F:* **1.** *v.i.* se quereller; se disputer; se chamailler. **2.** *v.tr.* ennuyer, embêter (qn.).

hassock ['hæsək] *n. Ecc:* agenouilloir *m*.

haste¹ [heist] *n.* hâte *f*, célérité *f*; **to do sth. in h.,** faire qch. à la hâte en hâte; **a note written in h.,** un billet écrit à la hâte; **to make h.,** se hâter, se presser, se dépêcher (**to do sth.,** de faire qch.); *Prov:* **more h. less speed,** plus on se hâte moins on avance.

hasten ['heis(ə)n] *esp. Lit:* **1.** *v.tr.* (*a*) accélérer, hâter, presser (le pas, etc.); avancer (le départ de qn); (*b*) activer (la combustion). **2.** *v.i.* se hâter, se depêcher, se presser (**to do sth.,** de faire qch.).

hastiness ['heistinis] *n.* **1.** précipitation *f*, hâte *f*. **2.** (*of temper*) emportement *m*, *f*, brusquerie *f*.

hasty ['heisti] *a.* **1.** (départ, adieu) précipité; (croquis) fait à la hâte; (repas) sommaire; **I sent him a h. note,** je lui ai envoyé un billet écrit à la hâte; **to be too h. in doing sth.,** mettre trop de hâte à faire qch. **2.** (aveu) irréfléchi; **to jump to a h. conclusion,** conclure à la légère. **3.** emporté, vif. **-ily** *adv.* **1.** à la hâte, précipitamment. **2.** (parler) sans réfléchir; (juger qch.) à la légère. **3.** brusquement.

hat [hæt] *n.* chapeau *m*; **top h.,** chapeau haut de forme; **straw h.,** chapeau de paille; **paper h.,** chapeau de papier, coiffure *f* de cotillon; **h. trick,** (i) (*conjuring*) tour *m*, coup *m*, du chapeau; (ii) *Cr:* mise *f* hors jeu de trois batteurs avec trois balles de suite; *Fb: etc:* trois buts marqués de suite par le même joueur; **to put on, take off, one's h.,** mettre, enlever, son chapeau; **I take my h. off to him, you!** chapeau! **hats off!** chapeaux bas! *F:* **to pass the h. round (for s.o., sth.),** faire passer le chapeau, faire la quête, (pour qn, qch.); *F:* **my h.!** mon Dieu! **to talk through one's h.,** parler à tort et à travers; **to keep sth. under one's h.,** garder qch. pour soi; **if that comes off I'll eat my h.,** si ça réussit, je mange mon chapeau; **that's old h.,** ça c'est vieux jeu.

hatband ['hætbænd] *n.* ruban *m* de chapeau.

hatbox ['hætbɔks] *n.* boîte *f*, carton *m*, à chapeau.

hatch¹ [hætʃ] *n.* **1.** partie basse d'une porte coupée; demi-porte *f*, *pl.* demi-portes. **2.** *Nau:* (*a*) descente *f*, écoutille *f*; **cargo h.,** panneau *m* de chargement, de déchargement; (*b*) **h. (cover),** panneau de descente, panneau (d'écoutille); opercule *m*; **to batten down the hatches,** condamner les descentes; (*c*) *F:* **down the h.!** cul sec! **3.** (*a*) trappe *f*; panneau d'accès; **service h.,** passe-plats *m inv*; (*b*) *Av: etc:* **escape h.,** panneau d'évacuation. **4.** *Hyd: E:* vanne *f* d'écluse.

hatch² *n. Husb:* **1.** éclosion *f* (d'un œuf, d'une couvée). **2.** couvée *f*.

hatch³ **1.** *v.tr.* (*a*) faire éclore (des poussins); incuber, (faire) couver (des œufs); ourdir, tramer (un complot); (*b*) *Pisc:* incuber (les œufs). **2.** *v.i.* (*of young birds or eggs*) **to h. (out),** éclore; **newly hatched chickens,** poussins *mpl* qui sortent de la coquille.

hatch⁴ *n. Engr:* hachure *f*.

hatch⁵ *v.tr. Engr: Her:* hacher, hachurer (un dessin). **hatching** *n.* hachure(s) *f*(*pl*).

hatchback ['hætʃbæk] *n. Aut:* (voiture *f* à) hayon *m* arrière.

hatchery ['hætʃəri] *n. Husb:* couvoir *m*, couveuse *f*; *Pisc:* appareil *m* à éclosion.

hatchet [ˈhætʃit] *n.* (*a*) hachette *f*, cognée *f*; hache *f* à main; **to bury the h.,** enterrer la hache de guerre; faire la paix; (*b*) **h. man,** (i) tueur *m* (à gages); (ii) *Pol: etc:* homme *m* à main; (*c*) **h. face,** visage *m* en lame de couteau.
hatchway [ˈhætʃwei] *n. Nau:* descente *f*, écoutille *f*.
hate¹ [heit] *n.* **1.** haine *f*. **2.** objet *m* d'aversion; **his pet h.,** sa bête noire.
hate² *v.tr.* **1.** haïr, détester, exécrer (qn, qch.); **I h. him,** il m'est odieux; **I h. myself for agreeing to it,** je m'en veux d'y avoir consenti. **2. to h. to do sth.,** détester (de) faire qch.; **she hates to be contradicted,** elle ne peut pas souffrir qu'on la contredise; **she hates being kissed,** elle a horreur qu'on l'embrasse.
hateful [ˈheitf(u)l] *a.* (*of pers., thg*) odieux, détestable **-fully** *adv.* odieusement, détestablement.
hater [ˈheitər] *n.* haïsseur, -euse; ennemi *m* (**of,** de).
hatless [ˈhætlis] *a.* (homme, etc.) sans chapeau, tête nue.
hatpeg [ˈhætpeg] *n.* patère *f*.
hatpin [ˈhætpin] *n.* épingle *f* à chapeau.
hatrack [ˈhætræk] *n.* porte-chapeaux *m inv*.
hatred [ˈheitrid] *n.* haine *f* (**of s.o.,** de contre, qn); **to incur s.o.'s h.,** s'attirer la haine de qn.
hatshop [ˈhætʃɔp] *n.* (*for men*) chapellerie *f*; (*for women*) boutique *f* de modiste.
hatstand [ˈhætstænd] *n.* porte-chapeaux *m inv*.
hatter [ˈhætər] *n.* chapelier, -ière.
haughtiness [ˈhɔːtinis] *n.* arrogance *f*, hauteur *f*.
haughty [ˈhɔːti] *a.* hautain, arrogant, altier. **-ily** *adv.* hautainement; d'une manière hautaine, arrogante.
haul¹ [hɔːl] *n* **1.** amenée *f*; effort *m* (pour tirer, haler, amener, qch.). **2.** *Fish:* (*a*) **at one h.,** d'un seul coup de filet; (*b*) prise *f*, pêche *f*; **to make, get, a good h.,** (i) faire (une) bonne pêche; (ii) *F:* (*of financier, etc.*) faire son butin. **3.** (i) chemin parcouru par un objet traîné; (ii) parcours *m*, trajet *m*; (iii) transport *m*; *Av: etc:* **short, long, h.,** étape, distance, courte, longue; **long-h. transport aircraft,** (avion *m*) long-courrier (*m*); **there's still a long h. ahead,** il y a encore toute une tirée.
haul² **1.** *v.tr.* (*a*) tirer; traîner (une charge); remorquer (un bateau, un train); *F:* **to h. s.o. over the coals,** réprimander qn; laver la tête à qn; (*b*) transporter (des marchandises) par camions. **2.** *v.i. Nau:* (*a*) **to h. on a rope,** haler sur une manœuvre; (*b*) **to h. alongside,** accoster. **haul down** *v.tr.* descendre (qch.); *Nau:* haler bas, affaler (les voiles, etc.); rentrer (un pavillon). **haul in** *v.tr.* tirer (qch.) en dedans; *Nau:* haler en dedans. **hauling** *n.* (*a*) traction *f*; remorquage *m*; (*b*) *Nau:* halage *m*; **h. rope,** câble *m* de halage. **haul up** *v.tr.* (*a*) monter (qch.); *Nau:* hisser (un pavillon); **to h. up a boat,** rentrer une embarcation; (*on the beach*) haler une embarcation à sec; (*b*) *F:* **to h. s.o. up (for sth., for doing sth.),** demander compte à qn (de qch.); **to be hauled up before the court,** être sommé de comparaître.
haulage [ˈhɔːlidʒ] *n.* **1.** (*a*) (transport *m* par) roulage *m*, charriage *m*, camionnage *m*; **road h.,** transports routiers; **h. contractor,** entrepreneur *m* de transports; (*b*) traction *f*, remorquage *m*. **2.** (*costs*) frais *mpl* de roulage, de transport.
haulier [ˈhɔːliər] *n.m.* camionneur; routier; entrepreneur de transports.
haunch [hɔːn(t)ʃ] *n.* (*a*) *Anat:* hanche *f*; (*b*) *Cu:* cuissot *m* (de chevreuil); (*c*) **haunches,** arrière-train *m*; **sitting on his haunches,** (*of pers.*) accroupi; (*of dog*) assis (sur son derrière).
haunt¹ [hɔːnt] *n.* lieu fréquenté (par une personne, un animal); retraite *f*; repaire *m* (de bêtes féroces, de voleurs, etc.); rendez-vous *m* (de bons compagnons).
haunt² *v.tr.* (*a*) (*of pers., animal*) fréquenter, hanter (un endroit, qn); (*b*) (*of ghost*) hanter (une maison, etc.); **the red room is haunted,** il y des revenants dans la chambre rouge; (*c*) (*of thoughts, etc.*) obséder, poursuivre (qn); troubler, hanter (l'esprit, le sommeil); **to be haunted by memories,** être obsédé par des souvenirs. **haunted** *a* (*a*) (château, etc.) hanté; (*b*) **he has a h. look,** il a l'air égaré. **haunting 1.** *a.* (mélodie, souvenir, etc.) qui vous hante; (souvenir, etc.) obsédant; **h. memory,** hantise *f*. **2.** *n.* hantement *m* (d'un lieu, etc.).
Havana [həˈvænə, -ˈvɑː-] **1.** *Pr.n. Geog:* la Havane. **2. a H. (cigar),** un havane.
have¹ [hæv] *n. F:* **the haves and the h.-nots,** les riches *mpl* et les pauvres *mpl*.
have² *v.tr.* (*pr. ind.* **have;** *3rd pers.* **has** [hæz]; *pl.* **have;** *pr. sub. sg. & pl.* **have;** *past ind. & sub.* **had** [hæd]; *pl.* **had;** *pr.p.* **having;** *p.p.* **had;** *have not, has not, had not, are frequently shortened into* **haven't, hasn't, hadn't;** *I have, he has, we have, etc., into* **I've, he's, we've,** *etc.; I had, etc., into* **I'd,** *etc.*). **1.** (*a*) avoir; **a week has seven days,** une semaine a sept jours; **he had no friends,** il n'avait pas d'amis; **all I h.,** tout ce que je possède; **he has a shop,** il tient une boutique; **my bag has no name on it,** ma valise ne porte pas de nom; **I h. nothing to do,** je n'ai rien à faire; **I h. work to do,** j'ai à travailler; **to h. a right,** jouir d'un droit; **I h. it!** j'y suis! *F:* **to h. it in for s.o.,** garder à qn un chien de sa chienne; (*b*) **we're having visitors tomorrow,** nous attendons des invités demain; **to h. friends (in) to dinner,** avoir des amis à dîner; **we shall h. the painters in next week,** la semaine prochaine nous aurons les peintres; **we had to h. the doctor in,** nous avons dû appeler le médecin. **2.** (*a*) (*give birth to*) **how many children has she had?** combien d'enfants a-t-elle eus? **our cat has had kittens,** notre chatte a fait des petits; (*b*) (*beget*) **he had two children by her,** il a eu d'elle deux enfants. **3.** (*obtain*) (*a*) **there was no work to be had,** on ne pouvait pas obtenir de travail; **to h. one's wish,** obtenir ce que l'on désire; (*b*) **to h. news from s.o.,** recevoir des nouvelles de qn; **I h. it on good authority,** je l'ai appris de bonne source; (*c*) **I will let you h. it for £5,** je vous le cèderai pour cinq livres; **let me h. your keys,** donnez-moi vos clefs; **you shall h. it back tomorrow,** je vous le rendrai demain; *F:* **to h. it out with s.o.,** s'expliquer avec qn; *F:* **I let him h. it,** (i) je lui ai dit son fait; (ii) je lui ai flanqué une raclée; *P:* **you've had it!** (i) tu es fait! (ii) tu es foutu! *P:* (= *dead, dying*) **he's had it,** il a sa dose. **4.** prendre (un repas); **to h. tea with s.o.,** prendre le thé avec qn; **what will you h., sir?—I'll h. a chop,** que prendra monsieur?—donnez-moi une côtelette; **to h. a cigarette,** fumer une cigarette; *F:* **I'm not having any!** on ne me la fait pas! **5.** (*in numerous verbal phrases; e.g.*) (*a*) **to h. measles,** avoir la rougeole; **to h. a cold,** être enrhumé; **to h. dealings with s.o.,** avoir affaire à qn; **to h. the choice,** avoir le choix; **to h. an idea,** avoir une idée; **to h. a taste for sth.,** avoir le goût de qch.; **to h. a right to sth.,** avoir droit à qch.; (*b*) **to h. a dream,** faire un rêve; **to h. a game,** faire une partie; **to h. a fall,** faire une chute; (*c*) **to h. a lesson,** prendre une leçon; **to h. a bath,** prendre un bain; **to h. a wash,** se laver; **to h. a shave,** se raser; (*d*) **I had a pleasant evening,** j'ai passé une soirée agréable; **I didn't h. any trouble in finding it,** je n'ai eu aucune peine à le trouver; **we had a rather strange adventure,** il nous est arrivé une aventure assez étrange; (*e*) **to h. fine, wet, weather,** avoir du beau temps, de la pluie. **6.** (*a*) prétendre, soutenir, affirmer; **rumour has it that . . .,** le bruit court que . . .; (*b*) **as Plato has it,** comme dit Platon. **7.** (*a*) **to h. s.o. in one's power,** avoir qn en son pouvoir; *F:* **to h. s.o.,** monter un coup à qn; faire marcher qn; **he had me by the throat,** il me tenait à la gorge; (*b*) **you h.**

me there! voilà où vous me prenez en défaut! (*c*) *F:* (*outwit*) avoir, attraper (qn); **to be had,** donner dans le panneau; *F:* donner dedans; **you've been had!** on vous a eu! (*for a purchase*) on vous a passé un rossignol. **8.** (*a*) (*causative*) **to h. sth. done,** faire faire qch.; **to h. s.o. do sth.,** faire faire qch. à qn; **to h. one's hair cut,** se faire couper les cheveux; (*b*) **three houses had their windows shattered,** trois maisons ont eu leurs fenêtres brisées; **I had my watch stolen,** je me suis fait voler ma montre; **to h. a tooth out,** se faire arracher une dent; (*c*) **I shall h. everything ready,** je veillerai à ce que tout soit prêt; (*d*) **to h. one's hands full,** avoir les mains pleines. **9.** (*a*) **which one will you h.?** lequel voulez-vous? **she won't h. him,** elle ne veut pas de lui; **as luck would h. it he arrived too late,** la malchance voulut qu'il arrivât trop tard; (*b*) **what would you h. me do?** que voulez-vous que je fasse? **I would h. you know that . . .,** sachez que . . .; (*c*) (*allow*) **I will not h. such conduct,** je ne supporterai pas une pareille conduite; **I won't h. you coming in here,** je ne veux pas que vous entriez ici. **10.** (*a*) (*of pers.*) (*be compelled*) **to h. to do sth.,** être obligé, forcé, de faire qch.; **I had to go away,** j'ai dû m'en aller; **I don't h. to work,** moi je n'ai pas besoin de travailler; *Iron:* **of course you *had* to go and tell him about that!** il te fallait bien sûr lui parler de ça! (*b*) **the clock will h. to be mended,** la pendule a besoin d'être réparée. **11. to h. sth. on a horse,** miser sur un cheval. **12.** (*as auxiliary*) (*a*) **to h. been, to h. given, to h. done,** avoir été, avoir donné, avoir fait; **to h. hurt oneself,** s'être blessé; **I h. lived in London for three years,** j'habite Londres depuis trois ans; (*emphatic*) **well, you *have* grown!** ce que tu as grandi! (*b*) **you h. forgotten your gloves—so I h.!** vous avez oublié vos gants—en effet! tiens, c'est vrai! **you h. been in prison before—I haven't!** vous avez déjà fait de la prison—c'est faux! **13.** (*past sub.* **had** = *would have*) **I had better say nothing,** je ferais mieux de ne rien dire; **I'd much rather start at once,** j'aimerais bien mieux partir tout de suite. **have up** *v.tr. F:* (*a*) faire assigner (qn) (en justice); citer (qn) en justice; (*b*) (*of magistrate*) assigner, citer (qn) en justice; **to be had up for an offence,** être cité devant les tribunaux pour un délit.

haven ['heiv(ə)n] *n.* (*a*) *Lit:* havre *m*, port *m*; (*b*) abri *m*, asile *m*, refuge *m*.

haven't = **have not;** *see* HAVE².

haversack ['hævəsæk] *n.* **1.** *Mil:* musette *f*. **2.** havresac *m* (de camping).

havoc ['hævək] *n.* ravage *m*, dégâts *mpl*, dévastation *f*; **to cause, wreak, make, h.,** faire de grands dégâts, de grands ravages (dans un pays, etc.); **to play h. with (sth.),** ravager (les récoltes, etc.); déranger, detraquer (la santé, etc.); désorganiser complètement (les plans de qn, etc.).

haw¹ [hɔː] *n. Bot:* cenelle *f*.

haw² *v.i.* bégayer; **to hum and h.,** (i) bafouiller; (ii) se montrer indécis; tourner autour du pot.

Hawaii [hə'waiiː] *Pr.n. Geog:* Hawaï.

Hawaiian [hə'waiən] *Geog:* **1.** *a.* hawaïen; *Mus:* **H. guitar,** guitare hawaïenne. **2.** *n.* Hawaïen, -ïenne.

haw-haw ['hɔː'hɔː] *n.* rire bruyant; gros rire.

hawk¹ [hɔːk] *n.* **1.** *Orn:* faucon *m*; **to have eyes like a h.,** avoir des yeux d'aigle. **2.** *F:* (*pers.*) (*a*) vautour *m*, homme *m* rapace; (*b*) *Pol: etc:* belliciste *m*, faucon.

hawk² *v.i. Ven:* chasser au faucon. **hawking** *n.* chasse *f* au faucon; fauconnerie *f*.

hawk³ *v.i. & tr. F:* graillonner; **to h. up,** expectorer.

hawk⁴ *v.tr.* colporter (qch.); crier (des marchandises) dans les rues. **hawking** *n.* colportage *m*.

hawker¹ ['hɔːkər] *n.* fauconnier *m*.

hawker² *n.* colporteur *m*, démarcheur, -euse.

hawk-eyed ['hɔːkaid] *a.* (personne) aux yeux d'aigle.

hawkmoth ['hɔːkmɔθ] *n. Ent:* sphinx *m*; crépusculaire *m*, smérinthe *m*.

hawknosed ['hɔːknouzd] *a.* (personne) au nez aquilin.

hawser ['hɔːzər, 'hɔːs-] *n. Nau:* (*a*) aussière *f*, grelin *m*; (*b*) amarre *f*; **steel h.,** amarre, aussière, en fil d'acier; (*c*) câble *m* de remorque.

hawthorn ['hɔːθɔːn] *n. Bot:* aubépine *f*.

hay¹ [hei] *n.* foin *m*: **h. rake,** râteau *m*, fauchet *m*; **to make h.,** faire le(s) foin(s); faner; *Prov:* **to make h. while the sun shines,** battre le fer pendant qu'il est chaud; *F:* **to hit the h.,** se coucher.

hay² *v.i.* faire les foins. **haying** *n.* fenaison *f*.

haycart ['heikɑːt] *n.* fourragère *f* de foin.

haycock ['heikɔk] *n.* tas *m*, meulette *f*, de foin.

hayfever ['heifiːvər] *n. Med:* rhume *m* des foins.

hayfork ['heifɔːk] *n.* fourche *f* à foin.

hayloft ['heilɔft] *n.* fenil *m*; grange *f* à foin.

haymaker ['heimeikər] *n.* **1.** (*pers.*) faneur, -euse. **2.** (*machine*) faneuse *f*, tourne-foin *m inv*.

haymaking ['heimeikiŋ] *n.* fenaison *f*.

hayrack ['heiræk] *n.* râtelier *m* d'écurie.

hayrick ['heirik], **haystack** ['heistæk] *n.* meule *f* de foin; (*small*) meulette *f*; (*square*) barge *f*.

haywire ['heiwaiər] *a. F:* (*a*) confus, embrouillé; **to go h.,** (*of plan*) être loupé, finir en queue de poisson; (*of mechanism, etc.*) se détraquer; (*b*) (*of pers.*) emballé, excité; **he's gone h.,** il déménage.

hazard¹ ['hæzəd] *n.* **1.** (*a*) hasard *m*; (*b*) risque *m*, danger *m*, péril *m*; *Aut: etc:* point dangereux. **2.** *Golf:* accident *m* de terrain.

hazard² *v.tr.* hasarder, risquer, aventurer (sa vie, sa fortune); hasarder (une opinion).

hazardous ['hæzədəs] *a.* (coup, commerce) hasardeux, chanceux, hasardé; (profit, etc.) aléatoire; (projet) aventureux.

haze¹ [heiz] *n.* (*a*) brume légère; brumasse *f*; (*b*) obscurité *f*, incertitude *f* (de l'esprit).

haze² *v.tr.* (*a*) tourmenter (qn); (*b*) *NAm:* brimer (un nouvel étudiant, etc.)

hazel ['heiz(ə)l] *n*, **1. h. (tree),** noisetier *m*, coudrier *m*, avelinier *m*. **2.** *attrib.* **h. eyes,** yeux *mpl* (couleur de) noisette.

hazelnut ['heiz(ə)lnʌt] *n. Bot:* noisette *f*, aveline *f*.

haziness ['heizinis] *n.* état brumeux, nébuleux (du temps, de l'esprit); imprécision *f* (d'un souvenir).

hazy ['heizi] *a.* **1.** (*of weather*) brumeux, embrumé. **2.** (*a*) (contour, etc.) flou, estompé; (*b*) (*of ideas, etc.*) vaporeux, nébuleux; (souvenir, connaissance) vague; **to be h. about sth.,** n'avoir qu'une connaissance imprécise de qch.; n'avoir qu'un souvenir vague d'un événement. **-ily** *adv.* vaguement.

he [hiː] *pers. pron. nom. m.* **1.** (*unstressed*) il; (*a*) (*of pers., male animal, Lit: of certain things personified*) **he loves her,** il l'aime; **what is he saying?** que dit-il? (*b*) **here he comes,** le voici qui vient; **he's a strange man,** c'est un homme étrange. **2.** (*stressed*) (*a*) lui; **he and I,** lui et moi; **I am as tall as he (is),** je suis aussi grand que lui; (*b*) *esp. Lit:* (*antecedent to a rel.pron.*) celui; **he who believes,** celui qui croit. **3.** (*as substantive*) (*a*) *F:* mâle; **it's a he,** (i) (*of newborn child*) c'est un garçon; (ii) (*of animal*) c'est un mâle; (*b*) **he bear,** ours mâle; **he goat,** bouc; (*c*) *Games:* (jeu *m* de) chat *m*; **you're he!** c'est toi le chat!

head¹ [hed] *n.* **1.** tête *f* (*a*) **bald h.,** tête chauve; **from h. to foot,** de la tête aux pieds, des pieds à la tête; **he gave orders over my h.,** il a donné des ordres sans me consulter; **h. down,** la tête baissée; **h. first,** la tête la première; **to stand on one's h.,** faire le poirier; **I could do it standing on my h.,** c'est simple comme bonjour; **to turn h. over heels,** (i) faire la culbute; (ii) tomber à la renverse; **to fall h. over heels in love with s.o.,** tomber follement amoureux de qn; *Turf:* (*of horse*) **to win by a h.,** gagner d'une tête; **to win by a short h.,** gagner de justesse; **to let s.o. have his h.,** lâcher les rênes à qn; donner (libre) carrière à qn; **his blood will be upon your h.,** son sang retombera sur votre tête; **to cut off s.o.'s h.,** décapiter qn; *F:* **to talk s.o.'s h. off,** bavarder comme une pie; **to bite, snap, s.o.'s h. off,** rembarrer qn; **a fine h. of hair,** une belle chevelure; *Mus:* **h. voice, h. register,** voix *f* de tête; (voix de) fausset *m*; (*b*) *Anthr:* **h. hunter,** chasseur *m* de têtes; **h. shrinker,** (i) (Indien) réducteur *m* de têtes; (ii) *F:* psychiatre *mf*; (*c*) (*pers.*) **crowned h.,** tête couronnée; (*d*) *Art: etc:* **coinage bearing the h. of George III.** monnaie (frappée) à l'effigie de Georges III; (*e*) *Cu:* **sheep's h., calf's h.,** tête de mouton, de veau; **potted h.,** *NAm:* **h. cheese,** fromage *m* de tête; (*f*) *Ven:* (*antlers*) bois *mpl*, tête (de cerf); **deer of the first, second, h.,** cerf *m* à la première, deuxième, tête. **2.** (*a*) (*intellect, mind*) **to have a good h. for business,** avoir l'entente des affaires; s'entendre aux affaires; **to get sth. into one's h.,** se mettre qch. dans la tête; **I can't get that into his h.,** je ne peux pas lui enfoncer ça dans la tête; **he has taken it into his h. that . . .,** il s'est mis dans la tête, en tête, que . . .; **it never entered my h. that . . .,** je n'aurais jamais pensé que . . .: **put ideas into s.o.'s h.,** donner des idées à qn; **his name has gone right, clean, out of my h.,** j'ai complètement oublié son nom; **we put our heads together,** nous avons conféré ensemble; *Prov:* **two heads are better than one,** deux conseils valent mieux qu'un; **I think he made it up out of his own h.,** je crois que c'est lui qui a inventé ça; **to have a good, strong, h. for drink,** avoir la tête solide, bien porter le vin; **wine that goes to one's h.,** vin qui coiffe; vin qui monte à la tête; (*of speech, lecture, etc.*) **to be over the heads of the audience,** dépasser l'entendement de l'auditoire; **to lose one's h.,** perdre la tête, *F:* la boule, la boussole; **he's off his h.,** il est fou, *F:* timbré, toqué; **to go off one's h.,** devenir fou; **he's not quite right in the h., a bit weak in the h.,** il est faible d'esprit, un peu timbré; (*b*) *F:* **I've got a bad h., an awful h.,** j'ai mal à la tête, un de ces maux de tête; (*after drinking*) j'ai mal aux cheveux. **3.** (*a*) tête (d'arbre, de fleur, etc.); pomme *f* (de chou); pointe *f* (d'asperge); pied *m* (de céleri); épi *m* (de blé); (*b*) tête (de violon, d'épingle, etc.); pomme (de canne); **rivet h.,** rivure *f*; (*c*) (*detachable end*) tête *f* (de marteau); fer *m* (de lance, etc.); *Rec:* **pick-up h.,** tête de lecture; (*d*) (*top section*) tête (de volcan, etc.); haut *m* (de page); chapiteau *m* (de colonne, etc.); (*e*) haut (de l'escalier, etc.); *Min:* (i) carreau *m* (de carrière); (ii) bouche *f* (de puits de mine); (*f*) (*rounded end, cover*) tête, culasse *f* (de cylindre); chapiteau (d'alambic, de fusée, etc.); cône *m* (de torpille); (*g*) (*flat end*) tête (de piston); fond (de barrique, etc.); peau *f* (de tambour); (*h*) chevet *m*, tête (de lit); haut bout (de la table); source *f* (d'une rivière); **at the h. of the lake,** à l'amont du lac; *Hyd. E:* **h. gate,** porte *f* d'amont (d'une écluse); *Min:* **h. frame,** chevalement *m*; (*i*) *Med:* tête (d'un furoncle); (*of abscess, etc.*) **to come to a h.,** mûrir, aboutir; **to bring matters to a h.,** forcer une décision; **things are coming to a h.,** une crise est proche; (*j*) *Ch: Brew:* (*on fermenting liquid*) chapeau *m*; **h. on beer,** mousse *f*, *F:* faux-col *m*, *pl.* faux-cols; **beer with no h.,** bière éventée; (*k*) tête, intitulé *m* (d'un chapitre, etc.); en-tête *m*, *pl.* en-têtes (d'une page, etc.); *Book-k: etc:* rubrique *f*; *Ten:* tête (d'une raquette). **4.** (*projecting part*) (*a*) nez *m*, avant *m* (de navire); (*of ship*) **to collide with a ship h. on,** aborder un navire par l'avant; *Nau: F:* (*latrines*) **the heads,** (*for officers*) les bouteilles *fpl*: (*for crew*) les poulaines, les corneaux *mpl*; (*b*) *Cy:* colonne *f* de direction (du cadre); (*c*) = HEADLAND. **5.** (*a*) (*front or chief place*) **at the h. of a procession,** à la tête d'un cortège; **to be at the h. of the list,** venir en tête de liste; (*b*) (*pers.*) chef *m* (de famille, de l'Église, d'une entreprise); directeur, -trice (d'une école); **h. of state,** chef d'État; **h. of department,** chef de service; (*in store*) chef de rayon; *Sch:* **h. boy, girl,** élève choisi(e) parmi les grand(e)s pour maintenir la discipline, etc.; (*c*) (*in genealogy*) souche *f* (d'une famille); (*d*) **h. clerk,** premier commis; chef de bureau; **h. gardener,** jardinier *m* en chef; **h. foreman,** chef d'atelier; **h. post office,** bureau central (des postes). **6.** (*a*) (*unit*) *inv.* **six h. of cattle,** six têtes de bétail; **thirty h. of oxen,** trente bœufs *mpl*; (*b*) **to pay so much per h., a h.,** payer tant par tête, par personne. **7. h. of a coin,** face *f*; **to toss heads or tails,** jouer à pile ou face; **heads I win, tails you lose,** je gagne de toutes les façons; *F:* **I can't make h. or tail of this,** je n'y comprends rien; ça n'a ni queue ni tête. **8.** *Ph: Hyd. E: Mec. E:* charge *f*, pression *f* (d'un fluide, gaz, etc.); **h. of water,** (i) charge, pression, d'eau; (ii) chute *f* (d'eau); *Mch:* **h. of steam,** charge, pression, de vapeur; *Ph:* **loss of h.,** perte *f* de pression.

head² *v.tr. & i.* **1.** *Arb:* **to h. (down),** étêter, écimer (un arbre, une branche). **2.** (*put a head on*) (*a*) entêter, mettre une tête à (une épingle, un clou, etc.); (*b*) **to h. (up) a barrel,** mettre un fond à un tonneau; (*c*) **the article is headed . . .,** l'article est intitulé . . .. **3.** (*a*) conduire, mener (un cortège); être à la tête (d'un parti); venir en tête (d'un cortège); venir en tête (du scrutin); **to h. the list,** (i) s'inscrire en tête de la liste (de souscriptions, etc.); (ii) être, venir, en tête de (la) liste; (*b*) (*of thg*) surmonter, couronner, coiffer. **4.** (*oppose*) s'opposer à, affronter (un danger). **5.** *Nau:* **to h. the ship for Southampton,** mettre le cap sur Southampton. **6.** contourner (un lac) par l'amont, (une rivière) par sa source. **7.** *Fb:* jouer (le ballon) de la tête. **8.** *v.i.* (*a*) (*move forward*) **to h. for a place,** (i) *Nau:* piquer, avoir le cap, sur un endroit; (ii) s'avancer, se diriger, vers un endroit; **we were heading for . . .,** nous étions en route pour . . .: (*of ship*) **to h. (to the) East,** faire de l'Est; (*b*) *Min:* avancer. **9.** *v.i.* (*form a head*) (*of cabbage, etc.*) pommer; (*of grain*) épier; (*of abscess*) aboutir, mûrir. **head back.** *v.i.* rentrer; retourner. **headed** *a.* **1.** muni (i) d'une tête , (ii) d'un en-tête: (chou) pommé, cabus; **h. (note) paper,** papier *m* à en-tête. **2.** (*with noun or adj. prefixed*) (*of pers., animal, etc.*) **double-h. monster,** monstre *m* à deux têtes; **black-h.,** (i) (personne) aux cheveux noirs; (ii) (oiseau, etc.) à tête noire. **heading** *n.* **1.** (*a*) écimage *m* (d'un arbre); fonçage *m* (d'un baril); (*b*) façonnement *m* des têtes (de clous, etc.). **2.** *Fb:* (jeu *m* de) tête (*f*). **3.** tête (d'un chapitre, d'un article); rubrique *f* (d'un article); chapeau *m* (de passage cité, d'un rapport); en-tête *m*, *pl.* en-têtes (d'une page, etc.); *Book-k:* poste *m*, rubrique; **this subject comes under the h. of rhetoric,** ce sujet ressortit à la rhétorique. **4.** *Min:* (i) avancée *f*, avancement *m*; (ii) galerie *f* d'avancement. **5.** *Coop:* fond *m*, fonçailles *fpl* (de tonneau). **6.** *Const:* **h. (course),** assise *f* de boutisses. **7.** *Av: Ball:* cap *m*; **collision h.,** cap de collision. **head off** *v.tr.* (*a*) barrer la route à (qn); détourner, intercepter (des fugitifs); rabattre (le gibier); faire rebrousser chemin à (qn); couper la retraite à (l'ennemi); (*b*) détourner (qn) (**from doing sth.,** de faire qch.); parer à (une question).

headache ['hedeik] *n.* (*a*) mal *m* de tête, *pl.* maux de tête; **to have a h.,** avoir mal à la tête; *F:* **you give me a h.,** vous me cassez la tête; (*b*) *F:* embêtement *m*, casse-tête *m*; **this job's an awful h.,** ça c'est un travail à vous rendre fou.

headband ['hedbænd] *n.* bandeau *m*.

headboard ['hedbɔːd] *n. Furn:* dosseret *m* (d'un lit).
head-dress ['heddres] *n. Cost:* coiffure *f*, coiffe *f*.
header ['hedər] *n.* **1.** (*a*) **to take a h.,** piquer une tête; (i) plonger (dans l'eau) la tête la première; (ii) *F:* tomber (par terre) la tête la première; (*b*) *Fb:* coup *m* de tête. **2.** *Const:* boutisse *f*.
headgear ['hedgiːər] *n.* couvre-chef *m*.
headiness ['hedinis] *n.* **1.** emportement *m*, impétuosité *f*. **2.** qualité capiteuse (d'un vin).
headlamp ['hedlæmp] *n.* = HEADLIGHT.
headland ['hedlənd] *n. Geog:* cap *m*, promontoire *m*.
headless ['hedlis] *a.* (*a*) sans tête; (corps) décapité; (*b*) *Nat.Hist:* (animal, etc.) acéphale.
headlight ['hedlait] *n.* phare *m* (d'automobile); feu *m* d'avant (de locomotive); **to dip the headlights,** se mettre en code; **dipped headlights,** phares *mpl* code; feux de croisement.
headline¹ ['hedlain] *n. Typ:* en-tête *m,pl.* en-têtes; ligne *f* de tête; *Journ:* titre *m*, soustitre *m* (de rubrique, etc.); titre en vedette; **banner headlines,** gros titres; **to get into,** *F:* **hit, the headlines,** tenir la manchette (des journaux).
headline², *v.tr.* mettre en vedette, en première page.
headlong ['hedlɔŋ] **1.** *adv.* **to fall h.,** tomber la tête la première; **to rush h. to one's ruin,** courir à corps perdu à sa ruine. **2.** *a.* (*a*) (chute) la tête la première; **to take a h. dive,** piquer une tête; (*b*) (*of pers., action*) précipité, irréfléchi, impétueux; **h. flight,** sauve-qui-peut *m inv*; panique *f*.
headman, *pl.* **-men** ['hedmən] *n.m.* chef (d'une tribu, etc.).
headmaster [hed'mɑːstər] *n.m.* directeur (d'une école); principal (d'un collège); proviseur (d'un lycée).
headmistress [hed'mistris] *n.f.* directrice (d'une école).
head-on ['hed'ɔn] *a. & adv.* de front; (collision) frontale, de plein fouet; (réunion) en face à face; **they met h.-on,** ils se sont abordés de front.
headphones ['hedfounz] *n.pl. Tp: W.Tel:* casque *m* (téléphonique, d'écoute).
headquarters [hed'kwɔːtəz] *n.pl.* (*often with sg. const.*) **1.** *Mil:* (*a*) (*lower units*) poste *m* de commandement; (*b*) (*higher units*) quartier général; (*c*) état-major *m*, *pl.* états-major; **company, platoon, h.,** groupe *m* de commandement de la compagnie, de la section. **2.** *Adm: Com: etc:* siège social, résidence (administrative), bureau principal; administration centrale (de l'O.N.U., etc.); **to have its h. at . . .,** siéger, avoir son siège, à . . ..
headrest ['hedrest] *n.* appui-tête *m*, *pl.* appuis-tête; support *m* de tête; *Aut:* repose-tête *m inv*.
headroom ['hedruːm] *n.* encombrement vertical; tirant *m* d'air; échappée *f* (d'un arc).
headscarf ['hedskɑːf] *n.* foulard *m*.
headset ['hedset] *n.* casque *m* (radio, téléphonique).
headship ['hedʃip] *n.* direction *f* (d'un collège, etc.).
headstall ['hedstɔːl] *n. Harn:* têtière *f*, licou *m*.
headstand ['hedstænd] *n. Gym:* poirier *m*, arbre fourchu; **to do a h.,** faire le poirier.
headstone ['hedstoun] *n.* **1.** pierre tombale. **2.** *Arch: Const:* (*a*) clef *f* de voûte; (*b*) pierre angulaire.
headstrong ['hedstrɔŋ] a. volontaire, têtu, entêté.
headway ['hedwei] *n.* progrès *m*; **to make h.,** avancer; faire des progrès; (*of ship*) faire de la route; siller; **to make no h.,** ne pas avancer.
headwind ['hedwind] *n. Nau:* vent *m* contraire; vent debout.
headword ['hedwəːd] *n.* (mot *m*) en-tête *m*, *pl.* en-têtes; entrée *f* (dans un dictionnaire).
heady ['hedi] *a.* **1.** (*of pers., action*) impétueux, emporté, violent. **2.** (*a*) (parfum, vin, etc.) capiteux; (parfum) troublant; (*b*) (*of height, etc.*) vertigineux.
heal [hiːl] **1.** *v.tr.* guérir (**s.o. of a disease,** qn d'une maladie); guérir, cicatriser (une blessure); **to h. the breach (between two people),** amener une réconciliation (entre deux personnes). **2.** *v.i.* (*of wound*) **to h. (up, over),** se cicatriser, se refermer. **healing 1.** *a.* (*a*) (remède, etc.) curatif; (onguent) cicatrisant; (plante, remède) vulnéraire; (*b*) (plaie) qui se cicatrise. **2.** *n.* (*a*) guérison *f*; (*b*) cicatrisation *f* (d'une plaie).
healer ['hiːlər] *n.* guérisseur, -euse.
health [helθ] *n.* santé *f*; (*a*) **to restore s.o. to h.,** rendre la santé à qn; **to regain one's h.,** recouvrer la santé; **h. foods,** (i) produits *mpl* diététiques, de régime; (ii) produits alimentaires naturels; **h. food shop,** magasin *m* diététique; (*b*) **good h.,** bonne santé; **ill h., poor h.,** mauvaise santé; **chronic ill h.,** invalidité *f*; **to be in good h.,** être en bonne santé, bien portant; **to be in bad, poor, h.,** se porter mal, être mal portant; **public h.,** santé, hygiène, publique; **the Department of H. and Social Security** = le Ministère de la Santé publique; **(public) h. officer, inspector,** inspecteur *m* de la santé publique; (*c*) **to drink to s.o.'s h.,** boire à la santé de qn; **(your very) good h.!** (à votre) santé!
health-giving ['helθgiviŋ] *a.* (effet, etc.) bien faisant, salutaire; (air, etc.) tonifiant, vivifiant.
healthiness ['helθinis] *n.* salubrité *f* (d'un endroit, d'un climat).
healthy ['helθi] *a.* **1.** (*a*) (*of pers.*) sain; en bonne santé; bien portant; (peau) saine; (*b*) (*of climate, food, etc.*) salubre, sain. **2.** (appétit) robuste; **he showed a h. interest in sports,** il manifestait pour les sports un intérêt tout viril; **it is a h. sign that . . .,** il est encourageant que + *sub.* **-ily** *adv.* **1.** sainement. **2.** salubrement.
heap¹ [hiːp] *n.* (*a*) tas *m*, monceau *m*, amas *m*, amoncellement *m* (de bois, de pierres); **h. of junk,** tas de ferraille; *U.S: P:* **h.,** (i) vieille auto de rebut; (ii) bagnole *f*, tacot *m*; (*of pers.*) **to fall in a h.,** s'affaisser (sur soi même); *F:* **to be struck all of a h.,** en rester abasourdi, stupéfait; (*b*) *F:* (*large number*) **she had heaps of children,** elle avait une ribambelle d'enfants; **I've got heaps of things to do,** j'ai un tas de choses à faire: **you've got heaps of time,** vous avez largement le temps.
heap², *v.tr.* **1.** (*a*) **to h. (up),** entasser, amonceler, mettre en tas (des pierres, du bois); amasser (des richesses); (*b*) **to h. insults on s.o.,** accabler qn d'injures. **2. to h. sth., s.o., with sth.,** combler qch., qn. de qch.; **she heaped my plate with cherries,** elle a rempli mon assiette de cerises. **heaped** *a.* **1.** entassé, amoncelé. **2.** (mesure) comble; (cuillère) bien pleine.
hear [hiər] *v.tr.* (*p.t. & p.p.* **heard** [həːd]) **1.** entendre; **I heard a ring,** j'ai entendu sonner; **let's h. it,** dites (donc); racontez-nous ça; **I heard my name (mentioned),** j'ai entendu dire mon nom; **to h. s.o. speak,** entendre parler qn; **I could hardly make myself heard,** je pouvais à peine me faire entendre; *F:* **I've heard that one before!** connu! *F:* **you heard!** ne faites pas le sourd! **2.** (*listen to*) (*a*) écouter; **they refused to h. me,** on n'a pas voulu m'écouter; **h. me out,** écoutez-moi jusqu'au bout; (*at meeting*) **h.! h.!** très bien! très bien! *Ecc:* **to h. mass,** assister à la messe; *Jur:* **to h. a case,** (i) connaître d'un différend; (ii) entendre une cause; (*b*) exaucer, écouter (une prière). **3.** (*learn*) apprendre (une nouvelle); apprendre, savoir (la vérité); **I have heard that . . .,** j'ai appris, on m'a appris, que . . .. **4.** (*a*) **to h. from s.o.,** recevoir des nouvelles, une lettre, de qn; **let me h. how you get on,** donnez-moi de vos nouvelles; (*as threat*) **you'll**

h. from me! vous aurez de mes nouvelles! (*b*) **to h. of about, s.o. sth.,** avoir des nouvelles de qn, entendre parler de qn, de qch.; **he has not been heard of since,** depuis on n'en a plus entendu parler; **this is the first I have heard of it,** c'est la première fois que j'en entends parler; **I only heard of it yesterday,** je n'en ai eu connaissance qu'hier; **I have heard a great deal about him,** on m'a beaucoup parlé lui; **I never heard of such a thing!** a-t-on jamais entendu une chose pareille! je n'ai jamais vu une chose pareille! **hearing** *n.* **1.** (*a*) audition *f* (d'un son); (*b*) audition, audience *f*; **he was refused a h.,** on a refusé de l'entendre; **to condemn s.o. without a h.,** condamner qn sans connaissance de cause; (*c*) *Jur:* **h. of witnesses,** audition des témoins; témoignages *mpl*; **h. of the case,** (i) l'audience; (ii) l'audition de la cause par le juge (sans jury); **the case comes up for hearing tomorrow,** la cause sera entendue demain. **2.** ouïe *f*; *Med:* **h. aid,** audiophone *m*; **within h.,** à portée d'oreille; **out of h.,** hors de portée de la voix; **it was said in my h.,** on l'a dit devant moi, en ma présence.

hearer [ˈhiərər] *n.* auditeur, -trice; **hearers,** auditoire *m.*

hearken [ˈhɑːk(ə)n] *v.i. A: & Lit:* écouter.

hearsay [ˈhiəsei] *n.* ouï-dire *m inv*; **I know it, have it, only from h.,** je ne le sais que par ouï-dire; *Jur:* **h. evidence,** déposition *f* sur la foi d'autrui.

hearse [həːs] *n.* corbillard *m*, fourgon *m* mortuaire.

heart [hɑːt] *n.* **1.** (*a*) cœur *m*; *Med:* **h. disease,** maladie *f* de cœur; **to have h. trouble, a weak h.,** être cardiaque; **h. attack,** crise *f* cardiaque; **h. failure,** systolie *f*, insuffisance *f* mécanique du cœur; **h.-lung machine,** cœur-poumon artificiel; *F:* **to have one's h. in one's mouth,** avoir un serrement de cœur; **to press, clasp, s.o. to one's h.,** serrer, presser, qn sur son cœur; **to cry one's h. out,** pleurer à chaudes larmes; **to break s.o.'s h.,** briser le cœur à qn; **it was enough to break your h.,** c'était à fendre le cœur, l'âme; (*b*) *R.C.Ch:* **the Sacred H.,** le Sacré-Cœur. **2.** (*a*) **h. of gold,** cœur d'or; **h. of stone,** cœur de pierre; **have a h.!** ayez un peu de cœur! **his h. was full, heavy,** il avait le cœur gros; **with a heavy h.,** le cœur serré; (*b*) (*innermost being, core*); **in my h. of hearts,** au plus profond de mon cœur; **from the bottom of one's h.,** (remercier qn, féliciter qn) de tout son cœur; **to be sick at h.,** avoir le cœur gros, serré; **to learn, know, sth. by h.,** apprendre, savoir, qch. par cœur; (*c*) **to love s.o. with all one's h.,** aimer qn de tout son cœur; **to win s.o.'s h.,** gagner le cœur de qn; **to have s.o.'s welfare at h.,** avoir à cœur le bonheur de qn; **to take sth. to h.,** prendre qch. à cœur; (*d*) (*desire*) **to have set one's h. on sth., on doing sth.,** avoir qch. à cœur; avoir, prendre, à cœur de faire qch.; **I have set my h. on it,** j'y tiens; **he's a man after my own h.,** c'est un homme selon mon cœur; **to one's heart's content,** à cœur joie, à souhait; **to eat, drink, to one's heart's content,** manger, boire, tout son soûl; (*e*) (*enthusiasm, interest*) **to put (all) one's h. into sth.,** y aller de tout son cœur; **his, my, h. isn't in it,** le cœur n'y est pas; **to put one's h. and soul, to throw oneself h. and soul, into sth.,** se donner corps et âme à une affaire; (*f*) (*courage*) **to put new h. into s.o.,** donner du courage, du cœur, à qn; **to take h.,** (re)prendre courage; **to lose h.,** perdre courage; se décourager; **my h. sank at the news,** à cette nouvelle mon courage s'évanouit; **not to have the h. to do sth.,** ne pas avoir le cœur, le courage, de faire qch. **3.** cœur (d'un chou); cœur, vif *m* (d'un arbre); âme *f*, mèche *f* (d'un câble); **h. of oak,** homme courageux; **the h. of the matter,** le fond du problème; **in the h. of . . .,** au cœur (d'une ville, d'un pays), au (beau) milieu (d'une forêt), au (fin) fond (d'un désert). **4.** *Cards:* **heart(s),** cœur; **to play a h., hearts,** jouer (du) cœur; **king, queen, of hearts,** roi, dame, de cœur. **5.** *Her:* **h. (point),** cœur, abîme *m* (de l'écu).

heartache [ˈhɑːteik] *n.* chagrin *m*, peine *f* de cœur.

heartbeat [ˈhɑːtbiːt] *n.* battement *m*, pulsation *f*, du cœur.

heartbreak [ˈhɑːtbreik] *n.* déchirement *m* de cœur.

heartbreaking [ˈhɑːtbreikiŋ] *a.* navrant, accablant, déchirant; **it was h.,** c'était à fendre l'âme.

heartbroken [ˈhɑːtbrouk(ə)n] *a.* **to be h.,** avoir le cœur brisé.

heartburn [ˈhɑːtbəːn] *n. Med:* brûlures *fpl* d'estomac.

heartburning [ˈhɑːtbəːniŋ] *n.* rancœur *f*; jalousie *f*; animosité *f*.

hearten [ˈhɑːt(ə)n] **1.** *v.tr.* encourager (qn); donner du courage à (qn). **2.** *v.i.* **to h. (up),** reprendre courage. **heartening** *a.* (conseil, mot) encourageant.

heartfelt [ˈhɑːtfelt] *a.* (émotion, vœu) sincère; qui vient, part, du cœur; **to express one's h. thanks to s.o.,** exprimer ses remerciements sincères à qn.

hearth, *pl.* **hearths** [hɑːθ, hɑːs] *n.* **1.** foyer *m*, âtre *m*; **without h. or home,** sans feu ni lieu. **2.** (*a*) *Metall:* aire *f*, foyer, sole *f* (de four à réverbère); creuset *m* (de haut fourneau); **open-h. furnace,** four *m* à sole; four Martin; (*b*) **smith's h.,** forge *f*.

hearthrug [ˈhɑːθrʌg] *n.* devant *m* de foyer.

hearthstone [ˈhɑːθstoun] *n.* pierre *f* de la cheminée; (marbre *m* du) foyer.

heartiness [ˈhɑːtinis] *n.* cordialité *f*, chaleur *f* (d'un accueil); sincérité *f* (d'un consentement); vigueur *f* (de l'appétit); ardeur *f*, empressement *m*.

heartland [ˈhɑːtlænd] *n. Pol: Pol. Ec:* centre (i) important, (ii) stratégique.

heartless [ˈhɑːtlis] *a.* (personne) sans cœur, insensible; (traitement, mot) dur, cruel. **-ly** *adv.* sans cœur, sans pitié; cruellement.

heartlessness [ˈhɑːtlisnis] *n.* manque *m* de cœur; cruauté *f*; insensibilité *f*.

heartrending [ˈhɑːtrendiŋ] *a.* (soupir, nouvelle) à fendre le cœur; (spectacle) navrant; **h. cries,** cris déchirants.

heartsearching [ˈhɑːtsəːtʃiŋ] *a.* (question, regard) qui sonde le(s) cœur(s).

heartsick [ˈhɑːtsik] *a.* écœuré; **to be, feel, h.,** avoir la mort dans l'âme; avoir le cœur navré.

heartstrings [ˈhɑːtstriŋz] *n.pl. Fig:* **to tug at s.o.'s h.,** serrer le cœur de qn.

heartthrob [ˈhɑːtθrɔb] *n. F:* idole *f*, coqueluche *f*.

heart-to-heart [ˈhɑːtəˈhɑːt] *a.* (conversation) intime, à cœur ouvert; **to have a h.-to-h. talk,** *F: n.* **a h.-to-h., with s.o.,** parler avec qn à cœur ouvert.

hearty [ˈhɑːti] *a.* **1.** cordial, *pl.* -aux; (sentiment) sincère, qui part du cœur; (rire) jovial; **my heartiest congratulations,** mes félicitations les plus chaleureuses; **h. cheers,** acclamations nourries. **2.** (*a*) vigoureux, robuste, bien portant; **he is still (hale and) h.,** il est encore gaillard; (*b*) (repas) copieux, abondant; **h. appetite,** gros, rude, appétit; **he's a h. eater,** c'est un gros mangeur; (*c*) (*of land*) productif, d'un bon rapport. **-ily,** *adv.* **1.** (saluer) cordialement; (accueillir qn, applaudir) chaleureusement; (travailler, rire) de bon cœur; (se réjouir) sincèrement; *F:* **to be h. sick of sth.,** être profondément dégoûté de qch. **2.** (dîner) copieusement; (manger) de bon appétit, avec appétit.

heat[1] [hiːt] *n.* **1.** (*a*) chaleur *f*; ardeur *f* (du soleil, d'un foyer); **in the h. of the day,** au plus chaud de la journée; **h. haze,** brume due à la chaleur; (*b*) *Ph: Ch: etc:* chaleur; **h. of combustion,** chaleur de combustion; **latent h.,** chaleur latente; **radiant h.,** chaleur radiante; **h. constant,** constante *f* calorifique; (*c*) *Tchn:* **h. engine,** machine *f*, moteur *m*, thermique; **h. shield,** bouclier *m* thermique (d'un véhicule spatial, etc.); *Ind:* **h. treatment,** traitement *m* thermique; (*d*) **blood h.,** température *f* du sang; *Med:* **h. treatment,** thermothérapie *f*; (*e*) *Metall:* (i) (*temperature*) chaleur, chaude *f*; **red h.,** chaude, chaleur, rouge; **white h.,** chaleur d'incandescence; chaleur blanche; (ii) (*heating*) chaude; (*f*) *Cu:* intensité *f* de chauffe; température. **2.** (*a*) (*passion*) **to get into a h.,** s'échauffer, s'emporter; **to reply with some h.,** répondre avec une certaine vivacité; **h. of a discussion,** feu *m* d'une discussion; **the h. of passion,** la fougue des passions; **in the h. of the moment,** dans la chaleur du moment; *F:* **to turn on the h.,** (i) s'enflammer, s'échauffer; (ii) faire pression sur qn. **3.** (*of animal*) rut *m*, œstrus *m*, chaleur; **to be in, on, h.,** être en chaleur. **4.** *Med:* rougeur *f* (sur la peau); **prickly h.,** miliaire *f*, sudamina *mpl*; **h. rash,** échauffaison *f*, échauffure *f*. **5.** *Sp:* *Rac:* (*a*) épreuve *f*, manche *f*; **qualifying, eliminating, h.,** (épreuve *f*, série *f*) éliminatoire (*f*); (*b*) **dead h.,** course *f* à égalité.

heat² **1.** *v.tr.* (*a*) chauffer (l'eau, une maison, etc.); **to h. sth. to (a temperature of) 80°,** porter qch. à 80°; **to h. a house with gas,** chauffer une maison au gaz; (*b*) échauffer (le sang, etc.); échauffer, enflammer (l'imagination, les passions); (*c*) (*ferment*) échauffer (le foin, etc.). **2.** *v.i.* (*a*) (*of water, etc.*) chauffer; (*b*) (*of bearing, etc.*) chauffer, s'échauffer; (*c*) (*of hay, etc.*) s'échauffer, fermenter. **heated** *a.* **1.** chaud, chauffé. 2. (*a*) *Mec.E:* (palier) échauffé, qui chauffe; (*b*) (discussion) chaude, animée. **heatedly** *adv.* avec chaleur, avec emportement. **heating** **1.** *a.* (*a*) de chauffage, de réchauffage; chauffant, réchauffant; **h. power,** puissance *f*, pouvoir *m*, calorifique; rendement *m* calorique; *El:* puissance de chauffage; *Tchn:* **h. apparatus,** appareil *m* de chauffage, calorifère *m*; *Mec.E: etc:* **h. coil,** serpentin *m* de chauffage, réchauffeur *m*; *El: etc:* **h. element, unit,** élément chauffant; (*b*) échauffant. **2.** *n.* (*a*) (*making hot*) (i) chauffage *m*; **electric h.,** chauffage électrique; **oil h.,** chauffage au mazout; **central h.,** chauffage central; *Metall:* **white, red, h.,** chauffage au blanc, au rouge; (ii) réchauffage *m* (d'un plat, etc.); (*b*) (*becoming hot*) (i) échauffement *m* (d'un outil, etc.); (ii) échauffement, fermentation *f* (du fourrage, du grain, etc.). **heat up** **1.** *v.tr.* (faire) réchauffer (un plat, etc.). **2.** *v.i.* chauffer.

heat-conducting [ˈhiːtkəndʌktiŋ] *a.* thermoconductible.

heater [ˈhiːtər] *n.* (*a*) radiateur *m*; **electric h.,** radiateur électrique; **fan h.,** radiateur soufflant; (*b*) **water h.,** chauffe-eau *m inv*; **immersion h.,** thermoplongeur *m*; (*c*) *I.C.E: etc:* réchauffeur *m*; (*d*) réchaud *m*; (*e*) *U.S:* *P:* revolver *m*.

heath [hiːθ] *n.* **1.** (*tract of land*) bruyère *f*, lande *f*. **2.** *Bot:* bruyère.

heathen [ˈhiːð(ə)n] *a. & n.* (*a*) païen, -ïenne; *coll.* **the h.,** les païens; (*b*) sauvage; barbare.

heathenish [ˈhiːðəniʃ] *a.* (*a*) païen; (*b*) barbare.

heathenism [ˈhiːðənizm] *n.* paganisme *m*.

heather [ˈheðər] *n.* *Bot:* bruyère *f*, brande *f*; **Scotch h., bell h.,** bruyère cendrée.

heatproof [ˈhiːtpruːf] *a.* calorifuge; (vernis, etc.) allant au feu.

heat-resistant, -resisting [ˈhiːtrizistɑnt, -rizistiŋ] *a.* résistant à la chaleur; thermorésistant.

heatstroke [ˈhiːtstrouk] *n.* *Med:* *Vet:* coup *m* de chaleur.

heatwave [ˈhiːtweiv] *n.* *Meteor:* vague *f* de chaleur; canicule *f*.

heave¹ [hiːv] *n.* soulèvement *m*. **1.** effort *m* (pour soulever); **with a mighty h.,** d'un effort puissant. **2.** haut-le-cœur *m inv*. **3.** *Nau:* **h. of the sea,** poussée *f*, entraînement *m*, des lames; houle *f*.

heave² *v.* (*p.t. & p.p.* **heaved** *or esp. Nau:* **hove** [houv]) **I.** *v.tr.* **1.** (*lift*) lever, soulever (un fardeau); *Nau:* **to h. (up) the anchor,** lever l'ancre. **2.** (*utter*) pousser (un soupir, etc.). **3.** (*a*) (*haul*) (i) porter, (ii) décharger (le charbon); (*b*) *Nau:* **to h. the ship ahead, astern,** virer le navire de l'avant, de l'arrière. **4.** (*throw*) lancer, jeter (**sth. at s.o., sth.,** qch. contre qn, qch.); balancer (des pierres, etc.); *Nau:* jeter (la sonde, le plomb). **5.** *Sp:* **to h. oneself up,** faire un rétablissement. **II.** *v.i.* **1.** (*a*) (*swell*) (se) gonfler, se soulever; (*of sea*) s'agiter, se soulever; (*of ship*) se soulever sur la lame; (*of bosom*) palpiter; (*b*) (*retch*) (*of pers.*) avoir des haut-le-cœur; (*of the stomach*) se soulever. **2.** *Nau:* (*of land, ship*) **to h. in sight,** paraître (à l'horizon); **h. to,** *v.tr. & i.* *Nau:* (se) mettre en panne, à la cape; (*in gale*) caranguer.

heave-ho [ˈhiːvˈhou] **1.** *int.* *Nau:* ohé! ô hisse! **2.** *n.* *P:* **to give s.o. the h.-ho,** sacquer, virer, qn.

heaven [ˈhev(ə)n] *n.* ciel *m*, *pl.* cieux; **in h.,** au ciel; dans le ciel; **to go to h.,** aller au ciel, en paradis; **it's h. on earth,** c'est le paradis sur terre; **to move h. and earth to do sth.,** remuer ciel et terre pour faire qch.; **the heavens opened,** il a commencé à pleuvoir à torrents; *F:* **it stinks to high h.,** ça pue; **(good) heavens! heavens above!** juste ciel! bonté divine! **thank h. (for that)!** Dieu merci! **for heaven's sake!** pour l'amour de Dieu! **where in the name of h. is he?** où diable est-il?

heavenly [ˈhev(ə)nli] *a.* (musique, etc.) céleste; (don) du ciel; **h. body,** astre *m*; **our h. Father,** notre Père céleste; *F:* **what h. peaches!** quelles pêches délicieuses!

heaven-sent [ˈhev(ə)nsent] *a.* providentiel.

heaviness [ˈhevinis] *n.* (*a*) lourdeur *f*, pesanteur *f* (d'un corps, de l'allure); poids *m* (d'un fardeau); lourdeur (d'un aliment); (*b*) poids (des impôts); (*c*) engourdissement *m*, lassitude *f*, abattement *m* (des membres, de l'esprit); **h. of heart,** serrement *m* de cœur.

heavy [ˈhevi] *a.* **1.** lourd; (*a*) (paquet) lourd, pesant; **to weigh h.,** peser lourd; **h. blow,** (i) coup violent; (ii) rude coup (du sort, etc.); **food that lies h. on the stomach,** nourriture lourde, indigeste; (*b*) (pas) pesant, lourd, alourdi; (style) lourd, monotone; (*c*) (*of animal*) **h. with young,** gravide; (*d*) *Ph:* (corps) grave; *Atom. Ph:* (atome, noyau) lourd; **h. water,** eau lourde. **2.** (*a*) gros, *f*, grosse; **h. luggage,** gros bagages; **h. wire,** fil *m* (de) grosse épaisseur; *Navy:* **h. armament,** artillerie de gros calibre; (*b*) **h. features,** gros traits; (*c*) fort; **h. beard,** forte barbe; **h. meal,** repas lourd à digérer; *Mil:* **h. fire,** feu nourri; feu intense; **h. rain,** pluie battante; **h. shower,** grosse averse; **h. losses,** lourdes, fortes, pertes; **h. pressure,** haute pression; **h. cold,** gros rhume; (*d*) (silence) profond; **h. sleep,** profond sommeil; sommeil de plomb. **3.** (*oppressive*) (odeur) lourde; (ciel) sombre, morne; **air h. with scent,** air chargé de parfums; **h. responsibility,** lourde responsabilité; **h. fine,** lourde amende; **to rule with a h. hand,** gouverner d'une main rude, sévère. **4. h. eyes,** yeux battus; **h. with sleep,** accablé de sommeil. **5.** (*a*) (travail) pénible, difficile, dur, laborieux; (respiration) pénible; lourde (tâche); (journée) chargée; **he did the h. work,** c'est lui qui a fait le gros travail; **this book is h. reading,** ce livre est indigeste; **to find it h. going,** avancer avec difficulté; **h. soil,** sol gras; (*b*) **h. weather,** gros temps; **he made h. weather of it,** il s'est compliqué la tâche; **h. sea,** forte mer, grosse mer. **6.** *Th:* **h. parts,** rôles sombres, sérieux; **h. father,** père noble; *F:* **to come the h. father,** prendre un ton de père autoritaire. **7.** gros (mangeur); franc (buveur); **to be a h. sleeper,** avoir le sommeil dur. **8.** *n.* (*a*) *Th:* (i) rôle *m* sérieux, sombre; (ii) rôle de scélérat, de traître; (*b*) *Journ:* **heavies,** journaux sérieux. **-ily** *adv.* **1.** (marcher, tomber) lourdement; **time hangs h. on his hands,** le temps lui pèse; **he walked h.,** il avançait d'un pas pesant. **2.** fortement, fort; **h. underlined,** fortement souligné; **to drink h.,** boire beaucoup; **to lose h.,** perdre gros; **to be h. hit,** être gravement atteint (par ses pertes, etc.); **to be h. taxed,** être fortement imposé. **3.** (soupirer) profondément; **to sleep h.,** dormir profondément; dormir d'un sommeil de plomb. **4.** (respirer) péniblement.

heavy-duty [hevi'djuti] *a.* (machine) à grand, à fort, rendement, de grande puissance; (pneus) tous-terrains; (cric) pour poids lourds; (huile) à haute tenue.

heavy-eyed [hevi'aid] *a.* aux yeux battus.

heavy-handed [hevi'hændid] *a.* **1.** (*a*) à la main lourde; (*b*) oppressif, cruel. **2.** maladroit, gauche.

heavy-headed [hevi'hedid] *a.* **to feel h.-h.,** (i) se sentir la tête lourde; (ii) avoir envie de dormir.

heavy-hearted [hevi'hɑːtid] *a.* qui a le cœur lourd, gros.

heavy-laden [hevi'leid(ə)n] *a.* **1.** lourdement chargé. **2.** chargé de soucis.

heavyweight ['heviweit] **1.** *n. Box:* poids lourd. **2.** *a. Box:* (catégorie (des)) poids lourd; *Tex:* lourd.

Hebrew ['hiːbruː] **1.** *a. B.Hist:* hébreu, *f*, hébraïque. **2.** *n.* (*a*) *B.Hist:* Hébreu *m*; (*b*) *Ling:* hébreu *m*.

Hebrides (the) [ðə'hebridiːz] *Pr.n.pl. Geog:* les Hébrides *fpl*.

heck *F:* (*a*) *int.* sapristi! zut! (*b*) *n.* **what the h. are you doing there?** que diable fais-tu là? **a h. of a lot,** tout un tas (de).

heckle ['hek(ə)l] *v.tr.* (*at public meetings*) interpeller; poser des questions embarrassantes à (qn). **heckling** *n.* interpellation(s) *f(pl)*.

heckler ['heklər] *n. Pol: etc:* interpellateur, -trice; adversaire *m* qui cherche à embarrasser le candidat.

hectare ['hektɑːr] *n. Meas:* hectare *m*.

hectic ['hektik] *a.* **1.** *Med:* (fièvre) hectique. **2.** agité, fiévreux; (existence) bousculée; (matinée) mouvementée; **we had a h. time,** nous ne savions où donner de la tête **-ally** *adv.* fiévreusement.

hectolitre ['hektəliːtər] *n.* hectolitre *m*; *F:* hecto *m*.

hector ['hektə] *v.tr. & i.* faire de l'esbroufe; prendre un ton autoritaire avec (qn); intimider, rudoyer (qn). **hectoring** *a.* (ton, etc.) autoritaire, impérieux.

he'd = (i) **he had;** *see* HAVE[2]; (ii) **he would;** *see* WILL[3].

hedge¹ [hedʒ] *n.* **1.** haie *f*; **h. clippers, shears,** taille-buissons *m inv*. **2.** haie (d'agents de police, etc.). **3.** *St.Exch:* arbitrage *m*; couverture *f*.

hedge² **1.** *v.tr.* **to h. in,** mettre une haie autour (d'un terrain); enfermer, enclore (un terrain); **hedged in with difficulties,** entouré de difficultés; **to h. off a piece of ground,** séparer un terrain par une haie **(from,** de); (*c*) **to h. one's bets,** (i) parier pour et contre; (ii) se couvrir; éviter de se compromettre. **2.** *v.i.* (*a*) *Turf:* parier pour et contre; (*b*) *St.Exch:* arbitrer, se couvrir; (*c*) (*in discussion*) se réserver; éviter de se compromettre. **hedging** *n.* **1.** entretien *m* des haies. **2.** bordure *f*. **3.** (*a*) *Turf:* pari *m* pour et contre; (*b*) *St.Exch:* arbitrage *m*; *U.S:* contrepartie *f*; (*c*) hésitation *f* à prendre des décisions.

hedgehog ['hedʒhɔg] *n.* **1.** hérisson *m*; **to curl up like a h.,** se hérisser; se mettre en boule. **2.** *NAm:* porc-épic *m*, porcs-épics.

hedgehop ['hedʒhɔp] *v.i.* **(hedgehopped)** *Av: F:* voler en rase-mottes, *F:* faire du rase-mottes.

hedgerow ['hedʒrou] *n.* bordure *f* d'arbres, d'arbustes, formant une haie.

hedonism ['hiːdənizm] *n. Phil:* hédonisme *m*.

hedonist ['hiːdənist] *n. Phil:* hédoniste *mf*.

heeby-jeebies ['hiːbi'jiːbiz] *n.pl. P:* **to have the h.-j.,** (i) avoir le cafard; (ii) avoir la frousse.

heed¹ [hiːd] *n. esp. Lit:* attention *f*, garde *f*, soin *m*; **to give, pay, h. to sth., to s.o.,** faire attention à qch.; **to take h.,** prendre garde.

heed² *v.tr. esp. Lit:* faire attention à, prendre garde à, tenir compte de (qch.); **his advice was not heeded,** on n'a tenu aucun compte de ses conseils.

heedful ['hiːdf(u)l] *a. Lit:* vigilant, prudent, circonspect; **h. of advice,** attentif aux conseils.

heedless ['hiːdlis] *a.* **1.** étourdi, insouciant, imprudent. **2. to be h. of (sth.),** être inattentif à (ce qui se passe); être peu soucieux de (l'avenir, etc.). **-ly** *adv.* étourdiment; avec insouciance.

hee-haw¹ ['hiːhɔː] *n.* hi-han *m*.

hee-haw² *v.i.* braire; faire hi-han.

heel¹ [hiːl] *n.* **1.** (*a*) talon *m* (du pied); **to have the police at one's heels,** avoir la police à ses trousses; **to tread on s.o.'s heels,** marcher sur les talons de qn; **to follow close on s.o.'s heels,** suivre qn de près; emboîter le pas à qn; **to take to one's heels,** prendre ses jambes à son cou; *F:* **to kick one's heels,** croquer le marmot; poireauter; **to kick up one's heels,** sauter de joie; **to come to h.** (*of dog*) venir derrière à l'ordre; *F:* (*of pers.*) se soumettre; (*to dog*) **h.!** au pied! **to bring s.o. to h.,** rappeler qn à l'ordre; (*b*) talon d'une chaussure); **high, low, heels,** talons hauts, bas; **stiletto heels,** *U.S:* **spike heels,** talons aiguille; **down at h.,** (soulier) éculé; *F:* (*of pers.*) **to be down at h.,** être dans la dèche; (*c*) croûton *m* (de pain); (*d*) *P:* (*pers.*) chameau *m*, salaud *m*. **2.** *Tchn:* talon (d'outil, etc.). queue *f* (du dos d'un livre); pied *m*, caisse *f* (de mât); diamant *m* (de pince); *Nau:* talon (du gouvernail). **3.** derrière *m* du sabot (d'un cheval, etc.).

heel² **1.** *v.i.* taper du talon. **2.** *v.tr.* (*a*) (i) mettre un talon à (une chaussure); (ii) réparer le talon (d'une chaussure); refaire le talon (d'un bas); (*b*) *Rugby Fb:* talonner (le ballon) pour le sortir de la mêlée. **heeled** *a.* **1.** (chaussures) à talons; (*with adj. prefixed*) **high-h., low-h., shoes,** chaussures à hauts talons, à talons bas. **2.** *F:* **well h.,** riche. **heeling** *n.* **1.** (*a*) pose *f* du talon (à une chaussure, etc.); (*b*) réparation *f* du talon; **soling and h.,** ressemelage complet. **2.** *Rugby Fb:* talonnage *m*.

heel³ *n. Nau:* bande *f*, gîte *f*, inclinaison *f* (d'un navire).

heel⁴ *v.i. Nau:* **to h. (over),** avoir, donner, de la bande; pencher sur le côté; prendre de la gîte.

heelcap ['hiːlkæp] *n.* contrefort *m* du talon (d'une chaussure).

heeltap ['hiːltæp] *n. Bootm:* rondelle *f* en cuir (pour talon).

heft [heft] *v.tr. NAm: F:* (*a*) soupeser (qch.); (*b*) soulever (qch.).

hefty ['hefti] *a. F:* **1.** (homme) fort, solide, costaud. **2.** lourd, pesant. **3.** gros, important; **a h. bill,** une note de taille.

hegemony [hi'geməni] *n.* hégémonie *f*.

hegira [hi'dʒairə] *n.* hégire *f*.

heifer ['hefər] *n. Husb:* génisse *f*, taure *f*.

heigh-ho ['hei'hou] *int.* eh bien!

height [hait] *n.* **1.** (*a*) hauteur *f*, élévation *f*; **wall two metres in h.,** mur *m* qui a deux mètres de haut; (*of vehicle*) **overall h.,** hauteur totale; (*b*) flèche *f*, montée *f* (d'un arc); **maximum h. (of bridge),** hauteur libre (d'un pont); (*c*) taille *f*, grandeur *f*, stature *f* (de qn); **of average h.,** de taille moyenne. **2.** altitude *f*; **h. above sea level,** altitude au-dessus du niveau de la mer; *Av:* **cruising h.,** altitude de croisière; **h. indicator,** altimètre *m*; **to have a good head for heights,** ne pas avoir le vertige. **3.** (*hill, mountain*) hauteur; éminence *f* (de terrain). **4.** (*highest point*) apogée *m* (de la gloire, etc.); faîte *m* (des grandeurs); comble *m* (de la folie, etc.); sommet *m* (de l'éloquence); **this is the h. of insolence!** c'est de la plus haute insolence!

at the h. of the storm, au (plus) fort de l'orage; **in the h. of summer,** en plein été; **the season is at its h.,** la saison bat son plein; **it's the h. of fashion,** c'est la dernière mode, le dernier cri.

heighten ['hait(ə)n] **1.** *v.tr.* (*a*) surélever, surhausser (un mur, etc.); augmenter (un prix); (*b*) accroître, augmenter (un plaisir); aggraver (un mal); accentuer (un contraste); relever, faire ressortir (une couleur, etc.); renchérir sur (une histoire); **to h. the interest in sth.,** augmenter l'intérêt pour qch. **2.** *v.i.* s'élever; se rehausser; augmenter. **heightening** *n.* **1.** surélévation *f*, surhaussement *m* (d'un mur, des prix). **2.** accroissement *m* (d'un plaisir); aggravation *f* (d'un mal); rehaussement *m* (d'une couleur).

heinous ['heinəs] *a.* (crime) odieux, atroce, abominable.

heir ['ɛər] *n.* héritier *m*; **to be h. to an estate,** être le légataire d'une propriété; **h. apparent,** héritier présomptif; **h. presumptive,** héritier présomptif (sauf naissance d'un héritier en ligne directe); **h.-at-law,** *pl.* **heirs-at-law, rightful h.,** héritier légitime.

heiress ['ɛəris] *n.f.* héritière.

heirloom ['ɛəlu:m] *n.* héritage *m*; meuble *m*, bijou *m*, de famille.

Helen ['helin] *Pr.n.f.* Hélène.

helianthus [hi:li'ænθəs] *n. Bot:* hélianthe *m*, tournesol *m*.

helical ['helik(ə)l] *a.* **1.** *Conch:* **h. shell,** hélice *f*, coquille contournée. **2.** *Mec.E:* (*of gear, etc.*) hélicoïdal, -aux; (*of spring*) hélicoïde, en hélice.

helicopter ['helikɔptər] *n. Av:* hélicoptère *m*.

heliograph ['hi:liəgræf] *n.* **1.** héliographe *m* (de signalisation); héliostat *m*. **2.** *Phot.Engr:* héliogravure *f*.

heliotrope ['hi:liətroup] **1.** *n. Bot:* héliotrope *m*. **2.** *a.* héliotrope *inv*.

heliport ['helipɔ:t] *n.* héliport *m*.

helium ['hi:liəm] *n. Ch:* hélium *m*.

helix, *pl.* **helices** ['hi:liks, 'hi:lisi:z] *n.* **1.** (*a*) *Mth:* hélice *f*; (*b*) *Arch: etc:* spirale *f*; volute *f*. **2.** *Anat:* hélix *m* (de l'oreille). **3.** *Moll:* (*snail*) hélice, colimaçon *m*.

hell [hel] *n.* **1.** *Myth:* les enfers *mpl*. **2.** (*a*) enfer *m*; *F:* **it was all h. let loose,** c'était infernal; **to make s.o.'s life h., a h. on earth,** faire un enfer de la vie de qn; *F:* **it's as cold as h.,** il fait un froid de canard; (*b*) *F:* **(oh) h.!** zut alors! *F:* **hell's bells!** (sacré) nom de nom! *P:* **go to h.!** va(-t-en) au diable! **to h. with him!** qu'il aille au diable! **get the h. out of here!** fiche-moi le camp d'ici! *P:* **like h. I will!** jamais de la vie! *F:* **I feel like h.,** je me sens au cent mille dessous; *F:* **come h. or high water,** advienne que pourra; **to work like h.,** travailler comme un dératé; **to go h. for leather,** galoper ventre à terre; **like a bat out of h.,** à une vitesse vertigineuse; (*b*) *F:* **a. h. of a price,** un prix salé; *P:* **you've got a h. of a (helluva) nerve!** tu as un culot du diable! **a h. of a row,** (i) un vacarme infernal; (ii) une dispute violente; **he's a h. of a guy,** c'est un type formidable; (*c*) *P:* **what the h. do you think you're doing?** que diable es-tu en train de fabriquer? **what the h. (does it matter, do I care)?** diable si ça me regarde!

he'll = **he will**; *see* WILL[3].

hellbender ['helbendər] *n. U.S: F:* (séance *f* de) beuverie *f*.

hellbent ['hellbent] *a. F:* d'une détermination féroce, têtue; **to be h. on doing sth.,** vouloir à tout prix faire qch.

hellcat ['helkæt] *n. F:* sorcière *f*, mégère *f*.

hellebore ['helibɔ:r] *n. Bot:* ellébore *m*, varaire *m or f*.

Hellene ['heli:n] *n.* Hellène *mf*.

Hellenic [he'li:nik] *a.* (race) hellène; (langue, histoire) hellénique.

hellfire [hel'faiər] *n.* feu *m* de l'enfer.

hellhole ['helhoul] *n.* (*a*) *Fig:* enfer *m*; (*b*) *F:* bouge *m*.

hellish ['heliʃ] *a.* (*a*) infernal, -aux; d'enfer; diabolique; (*b*) *F:* **it was (simply) h.,** c'était infernal. **-ly** *adv.* infernalement; diaboliquement.

hello [he'lou] *int.* (*a*) bonjour! (*b*) (*calling attention*) **h. there, wake up!** holà! debout! hé, là-bas, debout! (*c*) (*indicating surprise*) **h., is that you?** tiens! c'est vous! (*d*) *Tp:* allô!

hell-raiser ['helreizər] *n. F:* chahuteur *m*.

helm [helm] *n. Nau:* barre *f* (du gouvernail); gouvernail *m*, timon *m*; **the man at the h.,** (i) l'homme de barre; (ii) l'homme qui tient le gouvernail, qui dirige l'entreprise; **to be at the h.,** être à la barre; **to take the h.,** prendre la direction des affaires.

helmet ['helmit] *n.* casque *m* (de soldat, de pompier, etc.); **crash h.,** casque protecteur.

helmsman, *pl.* **-men** ['helmzmən] *n.m. Nau:* homme de barre; timonier.

help[1] [help] *n.* **1.** aide *f*, assistance *f*, secours *m*; **with God's h.,** Dieu aidant; grâce à Dieu; **to shout for h.,** crier au secours; appeler à l'aide; **he's past h.,** il est perdu; **can I be of (any) h.?** puis-je vous aider? **2. to come to s.o.'s h.,** venir au secours de qn. **3.** (*a*) **to be a h. to s.o.,** être d'un grand secours à qn; rendre service à qn; (*b*) (*pers.*) (i) aide *mf*; **daily h.,** femme *f* de ménage; **home h.,** aide ménagère; **mother's h.,** aide familiale; (ii) *esp. NAm:* (*pl.* **help**) ouvrier, -ière; employé, -ée.

help[2] *v.tr.* **1.** (*a*) aider, secourir, assister (qn); **can I, may I, h. you?** puis-je vous aider? **so h. me God!** que Dieu me juge si je ne dis pas la vérité! **come and h. me,** venez m'aider, me donner un coup de main; **to h. s.o. to do sth.,** aider qn à faire qch.; **he helped the old lady up the stairs,** il a aidé la vieille dame a monter l'escalier; **to h. one another,** s'entraider; *Prov:* **God helps him who helps himself,** aide-toi et le ciel t'aidera; **h.!** au secours! **h.! I'm late!** mon Dieu! je suis en retard! (*b*) faciliter (la digestion, le progrès); **that doesn't h. the situation, doesn't h. much,** cela ne nous avance pas; *Iron:* **to h. matters, we had a puncture,** ce qui n'était pas pour arranger les choses, nous avons eu une crevaison. **2.** (*at table*) servir (qn); **to h. s.o. to soup, to wine,** servir du potage, verser du vin, à qn; **h. yourself,** servez-vous; *F:* **to h. oneself to sth.,** voler, prendre, chiper, qch. **3.** (*with negation expressed or implied*) (*a*) empêcher; **I can't h. it,** je n'y peux rien; **it can't be helped!** tant pis! il n'y rien à faire; (*b*) s'empêcher, se défendre (de faire qch.); **I can't h. laughing,** je ne peux pas m'empêcher de rire; **I can't h. it,** c'est plus fort que moi; (*c*) **don't be away longer than you can h.,** tâchez d'être absent le moins de temps possible. **helping 1.** *a.* **to lend a h. hand,** prêter son aide; **to give s.o. a h. hand,** prêter la main à qn. **2.** *n.* portion *f* (de nourriture); **two helpings of soup,** deux assiettées *fpl* de soupe; **I had two helpings, a second h.,** j'en ai repris. **help out** *v.tr.* aider (qn) à sortir d'une difficulté; tirer (qn) d'embarras; dépanner (qn); parer à l'insuffisance de (qch.).

helper ['helpər] *n.* aide *mf*; assistant, -ante; auxiliaire *mf*.

helpful ['helpf(u)l] *a.* **1.** (personne) secourable, serviable; **he always tries to be h.,** il essaie toujours de rendre service. **2.** (livre, etc.) utile; (avis) utile, salutaire; **the dictionary is not a bit h.,** le dictionnaire ne sert pas à grand-chose. **-fully** *adv.* utilement.

helpfulness ['helpf(u)lnis] *n.* **1.** serviabilité *f*. **2.** utilité *f*, aide *f*.

helpless ['helplis] *a.* **1.** (orphelin, etc.) sans appui, délaissé. **2.** (*a*) faible, impuissant; **I am h. in the**

matter, je n'y puis rien; *F:* **he's one of the h. sort,** il n'a aucune initiative; (*b*) (navire) désemparé. **-ly** *adv.* faiblement; sans faire preuve d'aucune iniative; **to watch h.,** regarder en spectateur impuissant.

helplessness ['helplisnis] *n.* **1.** abandon *m*, délaissement *m.* **2.** faiblesse *f*, impuissance *f.*

helter(-)skelter ['heltər'skeltər] **1.** *adv.* (courir, fuir) pêle-mêle, à la débandade. **2.** *a.* **h.-s. flight,** fuite désordonnée; débandade *f.* **3.** *n.* (*a*) tohu-bohu *m*; (*b*) toboggan *m* (dans une foire).

hem¹ [hem] *n.* **1.** bord *m* (d'un vêtement). **2.** ourlet *m* (d'un mouchoir, etc.).

hem² *v.tr.* **1.** (*a*) border, mettre un bord à (un vêtement); (*b*) *Nau:* gainer (une voile). **2.** ourler (un mouchoir, etc.). **3. to h. in,** entourer, cerner (l'ennemi); investir (une place); **hemmed in by high mountains,** enserré entre de hautes montagnes.

hem³ *int.* hem!

hem⁴ *v.i.* **1.** faire hem, hum; toussoter. **2. to h. and haw,** (i) bredouiller, bafouiller; (ii) hésiter (à prendre une décision, etc.).

he-man, *pl.* **-men** ['hi:mæn, -men] *n.m.* *F:* homme viril.

hemicycle ['hemisaikl] *n.* *Arch:* hémicycle *m.*

hemiplegia [hemi'pli:dʒiə] *n.* *Med:* hémiplégie *f.*

hemisphere ['hemisfiər] *n.* hémisphère *m*; *Geog:* **the northern, southern, h.,** l'hémisphère nord, boréal; l'hémisphère sud, austral.

hemispheric(al) [hemi'sferik(l)] *a.* hémisphérique.

hemline ['hemlain] *n.* *Dressm:* hauteur *f* de l'ourlet.

hemlock ['hemlɔk] *n.* *Bot:* ciguë *f.*

hemp [hemp] *n.* **1.** (*a*) *Bot:* chanvre *m*; (*b*) *Tex:* chanvre, filasse *f.* **2.** *Pharm: etc:* **Indian h.,** chanvre indien, hachisch *m.*

hemstitch¹ ['hemstitʃ] *n.* *Needlew:* ourlet *m* à jour.

hemstitch² *v.tr.* ourler (un mouchoir) à jour.

hen [hen] *n.* **1.** poule *f*; *Cu:* **boiling h.,** poule au pot; *F:* **h. party,** réunion de femmes seules. **2.** femelle *f* (d'oiseau, etc.); **h. bird,** oiseau *m* femelle.

henbane ['henbein] *n.* *Bot:* jusquiame *f*; herbe *f* aux poules.

hence [hens] *adv.* **1.** *A: & Lit:* (*of place*) **(from) h.,** d'ici; **five miles h.,** à deux lieues d'ici. **2.** (*of time*) dorénavant, désormais; à partir d'aujourd'hui; **five years h.,** dans cinq ans (d'ici). **3.** (*of issue, consequence*) de là, en conséquence; **h. his anger,** de là sa fureur.

henceforth [hens'fɔ:θ], **henceforward** [hens'fɔ:wəd] *adv.* désormais, dorénavant, à l'avenir.

henchman, *pl.* **-men** ['henʃmən] *n.m.* (*a*) *Hist:* écuyer; (*b*) *Pol: etc:* partisan, acolyte.

hencoop ['henku:p] *n.* cage *f* à poules.

henhouse ['henhaus] *n.* poulailler *m.*

henna ['henə] *n.* *Bot: etc:* henné *m.*

henpeck ['henpek] *v.tr.* *F:* (*of wife*) gouverner (son mari); mener (son mari) par le bout du nez; **henpecked husband,** mari mené par sa femme.

henroost ['henru:st] *n.* (*a*) juchoir *m*, perchoir *m*; (*b*) *F:* poulailler *m.*

Henry ['henri] *Pr.n.m.* Henri.

hep [hep] *a.* *F:* à la page, dans le vent.

hepatic [he'pætik] *a.* *Anat: etc:* hépatique.

hepatitis [hepə'taitis] *n.* *Med:* hépatite *f.*

her¹ [*unstressed* hər; *stressed* hə:r] *pers. pron. f*; *objective case* **1.** (*unstressed*) (*a*) (*direct*) la, (*before a vowel sound*) l'; (*indirect*) lui; **I hate h.,** je la déteste; **have you seen h.?** l'avez-vous vue? **I shall tell h. so.,** je le lui dirai; **look at h.,** regardez-la; **tell h.,** dites-lui; (*b*) **I am thinking of h.,** je pense à elle; **I remember h.,** je me souviens d'elle; (*c*) (*reflexive*) elle; **she closed the door behind h.,** elle referma la porte derrière elle. **2.** (*stressed*) (*a*) elle; **I can forgive her parents but not** *her*, je puis pardonner à ses parents, mais pas à elle; (*b*) (*with dem. force*) *Lit:* celle; **to h. who should take offence at this I would say . . .,** à celle qui s'en offenserait je dirais . . .. **3.** (*complement of verb* **to be**) **it's h.!** c'est elle! **that's h.!** la voilà!

her² *poss.a.* (*denoting a f. possessor*) (*a*) son, *f*; sa, *pl.* ses; **h. hat,** son chapeau; **h. dress, h. dresses,** sa robe, ses robes; **h. father and mother,** son père et sa mère; **h. eyes are blue,** elle a les yeux bleus; **she has hurt h. hand,** elle s'est fait mal à la main; (*b*) **H. Majesty,** sa Majesté.

herald¹ ['herəld] *n.* (*a*) héraut *m*; **the Heralds' College,** le Collège héraldique (à Londres); (*b*) avant-coureur, *pl.* avant-coureurs; précurseur *m.*

herald² *v.tr.* annoncer, proclamer (l'arrivée, etc., de qn, de qch.); **to h. (in) the dawn,** annoncer l'aube du jour.

heraldic [hi'rældik] *a.* héraldique; **h. bearing,** armoirie *f*, blason *m.*

heraldry ['herəldri] *n.* l'art *m*, la science, héraldique; l'héraldique *f*; le blason; **book of h.,** armorial *m*, *pl.* -aux.

herb [hə:b] *n.* *Bot:* (*a*) herbe *f*; (*b*) (*for seasoning*) **(sweet) herbs,** (fines) herbes; **medicinal herbs,** plantes médicinales; simples *mpl*; **h. tea,** infusion *f*, tisane *f* (d'herbes).

herbaceous [hə'beiʃəs] *a.* *Bot:* herbacé; **h. border,** bordure de plantes hercacées.

herbage ['hə:bidʒ] *n.* **1.** herbes fpl; herbage(s) *m(pl).* **2.** *Jur:* droit(s) *m(pl)* de pacage.

herbal ['hə:b(ə)l] **1.** *n.* herbier *m.* **2.** *a.* (breuvage) fait avec des herbes; (infusion) d'herbes.

herbalist ['hə:bəlist] *n.* herboriste *mf.*

herbarium [hə:'bɛəriəm] *n.* herbier *m.*

herbivorous [hə:'bivərəs] *a.* *Z:* herbivore.

Herculean [hə:kju'liən] *a.* (travail, effort) herculéen; (taille, force) d'Hercule.

Hercules ['hə:kjuli:z] **1.** *Pr.n.m.* *Myth:* *Astr:* Hercule. **2.** *n.* homme *m* d'une grande force; hercule *m.*

herd¹ [hə:d] *n.* (*a*) troupeau *m* (de gros bétail, de porcs); harde *f* (de cerfs); troupe *f*, bande *f* (de chevaux, etc.); bande (de buffles); **the h. instinct,** (i) l'instinct *m* grégaire; (ii) l'instinct qui gouverne le troupeau; (*b*) troupeau, foule *f* (de gens); *O:* **the common h.,** le populaire, le peuple.

herd² **1.** *v.i.* **to h. together,** (*of animals*) (i) vivre en troupeaux; (ii) s'assembler en troupeau; *F:* (*of people*) s'associer, se déplacer, en grands groupes. **2.** *v.tr.* garder, surveiller (le bétail, etc.); *F:* diriger (un groupe de touristes, etc.); **to h. together,** (r)assembler (le bétail, etc.) en troupeau; **the candidates were all herded into the waiting room,** on avait entassé les candidats dans l'antichambre.

herdsman, *pl.* **-men** ['hə:dzmən] *n.m.* gardien *m* de troupeau.

here [hiər] *adv.* **1.** (*a*) ici; là; **come h.!** (venez) ici! **in h., please,** par ici, s'il vous plaît; **near h.,** près d'ici; **over h.,** ici; **from h. to there,** d'ici à là; (*of fashion, etc.*) **it's h. to stay,** cela restera; **h. and now,** immédiatement, tout de suite; **h. goes!** allons-y! (*b*) (*on tombstone*) **h. lies . . .,** ci-gît . . .; (*c*) (*at roll call*) présent! (*d*) *esp. Lit:* (*on this earth*) **h. below,** ici-bas. **2. here's your hat!** voici, voilà, votre chapeau! **h. you are!** (i) vous voici! vous voilà! (ii) tenez! **h. she comes!** la voici (qui vient)! **h. I am!** me voici! me voilà! **3.** (*esp. over aperitif, etc.*) **here's to you!** à votre santé! **4. my friend h. will tell you,** mon ami que voici vous le dira. **5. h. and there,** par-ci, par-là; çà et là; **h., there and everywhere,** (un peu) partout; **neither h. nor there,** ni ici ni ailleurs; **that's neither h. nor there,** cela n'a aucun rappport.

hereabout(s) ['hiərəbaut(s)] *adv.* *F:* près d'ici, par ici.

hereafter [hiər'ɑ:ftər] **1.** *adv.* (*a*) (*of position*) (*in *book, writings, etc.*) ci-après, ci-dessous; (*b*) *esp. Jur:* (*of time*) dorénavant, désormais; ultérieurement; (*c*) *Lit: O:* dans la vie à venir; dans l'autre monde. **2.** *n. Lit:* l'au-delà *m*; **in the h.,** dans l'autre monde.

hereby [hiə'bai, 'hiəbai] *adv.* (*a*) par ceci, par ce moyen, par là; (*b*) *Jur:* par ces présentes; **the council h. declares that . . .,** le conseil déclare par le présent acte que . . ..

hereditary [hi'redit(ə)ri] *a.* héréditaire.

heredity [hi'rediti] *n.* hérédité *f.*

herein [hiər'in] *adv. Lit: & Jur:* **1.** (*of place, position*) ici, dans ce livre, dans ce lieu; **the letter enclosed h.,** la lettre ci-incluse. **2.** (*in this matter*) sur ce point.

heresy ['herəsi] *n.* hérésie *f*; (*of opinion*) **to smack of h.,** sentir l'hérésie, le brûlé, le fagot.

heretic ['herətik] *n.* hérétique *mf.*

heretical [hi'retik(ə)l] *a.* hérétique.

hereto [hiə'tu:, 'hiətu:] *adv. Jur:* **annexed h., h. annexed,** ci-joint.

heretofore ['hiətu'fɔ:r] *adv. A: & Lit:* jusqu'ici; **as h.,** comme par le passé.

hereunder [hiər'ʌndər] *adv. Jur: etc:* ci-dessous.

hereupon ['hiərəpɔn] *adv. Jur: etc:* là dessus; sur ce.

herewith [hiə'wiθ] *adv. Com:* **price list h. enclosed,** prix-courant ci-inclus, sous ce pli.

heritable ['heritəbl] *a.* **1.** *Biol:* (maladie, vice) héréditaire. **2.** *Jur:* (*a*) (droit) héréditaire; (propriété) héritable; (*b*) (*of pers.*) capable d'hériter.

heritage ['heritidʒ] *n.* héritage *m*, patrimoine *m.*

hermaphrodite [hə:'mæfrədait] *a. & n. Z: Bot:* hermaphrodite (*m*).

hermetic [hə:'metik] *a.* **h. sealing,** scellement *m* hermétique; bouchage *m* hermétique. **-ally** *adv.* (scellé) hermétiquement.

hermit ['hə:mit] *n.* **1.** ermite *m*; **to live like a h.,** vivre en solitaire, en ermite. **2.** *Crust:* **h. crab,** bernard-l'ermite *m.*

hermitage ['hə:mitidʒ] *n.* ermitage *m.*

hernia ['hə:niə] *n. Med:* hernie *f*; **strangulated h.,** hernie étranglée.

hero, *pl* **-oes** ['hiərou, -ouz] *n.m.* héros.

Herod ['herəd] *Pr.n.m. Hist:* Hérode.

heroic [hi'rouik] **1.** *a.* héroïque; **h. deed,** action *f* d'éclat; **h. poem,** poème *m* épique; **h. verse, couplet,** vers *m* décasyllabe; distique héroïque. **2.** *n.pl.* **heroics,** (*a*) vers héroïques; (*b*) grandiloquence *f*; emphase *f*. **-ally** *adv.* heroïquement.

heroin ['herouin] *n. Ch: Pharm:* héroïne *f.*

heroine ['herouin] *n.f.* héroïne.

heroism ['herouizm] *n.* héroisme *m.*

heron ['herən] *n. Orn:* héron *m.*

hero-worship ['hiərouwə:ʃip] **1.** *n.* culte *m* des héros. **2.** *v.tr.* idolâtrer (qn).

herpes ['hə:pi:z] *n. Med:* herpès *m.*

herring ['heriŋ] *n. Ich:* hareng *m*; *Com:* **salted h.,** hareng salé, braillé; **red h.,** (i) hareng saur; (ii) diversion *f*; **h. boat,** harenguier *m.*

herringbone ['heriŋboun] *n.* (*a*) arête *f* de hareng; **h. pattern,** dessin *m* à chevrons; *Needlew:* **h. (stitch),** point croisé; point d'épine; (*b*) *Ski:* montée *f* en ciseaux, en pas de canard.

hers [hə:z] *poss. pron. f.* le sien, la sienne, les siens, les siennes; **this book is h.,** ce livre est à elle, lui appartient; **a friend of h.,** un(e) de ses ami(e)s; un(e) ami(e) à elle; **it's no business of h.,** ce n'est pas son affaire.

herself [hə(:)'self] *pers. pron.* (*a*) (*emphatic*) elle-même; en personne; (*after illness*) **she's looking (quite) h. again,** elle paraît complètement remise; (*b*) (*reflexive*) se; **she hurt h.,** elle s'est fait mal; **she was living by h.,** elle vivait seule.

hertz [hə:ts] *n. El. Meas:* hertz.

he's = (i) **he is;** *see* BE; (ii) **he has;** *see* HAVE[2].

hesitancy ['hezitənsi] *n.* hésitation *f.*

hesitant ['hezitənt] *a.* hésitant, irrésolu; **he's a very h. speaker,** il hésite beaucoup en parlant. **-ly** *adv.* avec hésitation.

hesitate ['heziteit] *v.i.* (*a*) hésiter (en parlant, en agissant); **to h. before taking a decision,** hésiter avant de prendre une décision; **he didn't h. for a moment,** il n'a pas hésité un instant; **without hesitating,** sans hésiter; (*b*) (*to be reluctant*) **to h. to do sth.,** hésiter à faire qch.

hesitation [hezi'teiʃ(ə)n] *n.* hésitation *f*; **without (the slightest) h.,** sans (la moindre) hésitation; **he has no h. about it,** il n'hésite pas du tout.

hessian ['hesiən] *n. Tex:* toile *f* de jute.

het [het] *a. F:* **h. up,** (i) chauffé; (ii) fâché; **don't get h. up about it,** ne t'en fais pas pour cela.

heterodox ['hetəroudɔks] *a.* hétérodoxe.

heterogeneous [hetərə'dʒi:niəs] *n.* hétérogène.

heteronym ['hetərənim] *n. Ling:* homographe *m*; homogramme *m.*

heterosexual [hetərou'seksjuəl] *a. & n.* hétérosexuel, -elle.

hew [hju:] *v.tr.* (*p.t.* **hewed** [hju:d]; *p.p.* **hewed, hewn** [hju:n]) (*a*) couper, tailler (avec une hache, un ciseau, etc.); tailler, dresser, équarrir (une pierre); (*b*) **to h. down,** abattre (un arbre); **to h. off, away,** abattre, élaguer (une branche).

hewer ['hju:ər] *n.* tailleur *m*, coupeur *m* (de pierres, etc.).

hex[1] [heks] *n. NAm: F:* sortilège *m*; sort *m.*

hex[2] **1.** *v.i.* pratiquer la sorcellerie. **2.** *v.tr.* jeter un sort sur (qn, qch.).

hexagon ['heksəgən] *n. Mth:* hexagone *m.*

hexagonal [hek'sægən(ə)l] *a.* hexagonal, -aux.

hexameter [hek'sæmitər] *n. Pros:* hexamètre *m.*

hey [hei] *int.* **1.** hé! holà! **2.** hein? **3. h. presto!** passez muscade!

heyday ['heidei] *n.* apogée *m* (de ses forces, de la gloire, etc.); **to be in the h. of youth,** être dans, à, la fleur de l'âge.

hi [hai] *int.* (*a*) hé! là-bas! ohé! (*b*) *esp. NAm:* salut!

hiatus, *pl.* **-uses** [hai'eitəs, -əsiz] *n.* **1.** lacune *f* (dans une série, un récit, etc.). **2.** *Gram:* hiatus.

hibernate ['haibəneit] *v.i.* hiberner.

hibernation [haibə'neiʃ(ə)n] *n. Z:* hibernation *f.*

hibiscus [hi'biskəs] *n. Bot:* ketmie *f*, hibiscus *m.*

hiccough[1], hiccup[1] ['hikʌp] *n.* hoquet *m*; **to have the hiccoughs,** avoir le hoquet.

hiccough[2], hiccup[2]. **1.** *v.i.* avoir le hoquet; hoqueter. **2.** *v.tr.* dire (qch.) en hoquetant.

hick [hik] *NAm: F:* **1.** *n.* paysan *m*, rustaud *m.* **2.** *a.* **a h. town,** un bled.

hickey ['hiki] *n. NAm: F:* **1.** *Med:* bouton *m.* **2.** machin *m*, truc *m.*

hickory ['hikəri] *n.* (*tree or wood*) noyer (blanc) d'Amérique; hickory *m.*

hide[1] [haid] *n.* affût *m* (de chasseur); cachette *f.*

hide[2] *v.* (*p.t.* **hid** [hid]; *p.p.* **hidden** ['hid(ə)n]) **1.** *v.tr.* (*a*) cacher (**from,** a); enfouir (qch. dans la terre); **where has he hidden himself?** où est-il allé se fourrer? **to h. one's face,** se cacher la figure, se voiler la face; **to h. one's light under a bushel,** cacher son talent; **to h. sth. from s.o.,** (i) cacher qch. à qn; (ii) taire qch. à qn; (*b*) **to h. sth. from sight,** soustraire qch. aux regards; **clouds hid the sun,** des nuages voilaient le soleil. **2.** *v.i.* se cacher; (i) se tenir caché; se blottir (dans un coin, etc.); (ii) aller se cacher; **I didn't know where to h.,** je ne savais où me fourrer; **to h. (away) from s.o.,** se cacher de qn. **hidden** *a.* (trésor, etc.) caché; *Fin:* **h. reserves,** réserve latente; *Fig:* **h. hand,** influence *f* occulte. **hiding** *n.* (*a*) dissimulation *f* (de la joie, etc.); *Jur:* recel *m* (d'un criminel);

to go into h., se cacher; to be in h., se tenir caché; to come out of h., sortir de sa cachette; (*b*) h. place, cachette *f*.

hide³ *n*. **1.** peau *f*, dépouille *f* (d'un animal); *Com:* cuir *m* **2.** *F:* peau (de qn); **to save one's h.,** sauver sa peau.

hide-and-seek, *U.S:* **hide and go seek** [haidən(gou)'si:k] *n. Games:* cache-cache *m*.

hideaway ['haidəwei] *n*. cachette *f*; *F:* planque *f*.

hidebound ['haidbaund] *a*. (*of pers.*) aux vues étroites; plein de préjugés; (idées) étroites.

hideous ['hidiəs] *a*. hideux, affreux, effroyable; (crime) horrible, odieux; **what a h. picture!** quelle peinture abominable! **-ly** *adv*. hideusement, affreusement.

hideousness ['hidiəsnis] *n*. hideur *f*, laideur *f*.

hideout ['haidaut] *n*. cachette *f*; *F:* planque *f*.

hiding ['haidiŋ] *n*. *F:* raclée *f*, rossée *f*, volée *f*; **to give s.o. a good h.,** donner une raclée à qn.

hidyhole ['haidihoul] *n*. *F:* cachette *f*.

hierarchic(al) [haiə'rɑ:kik(l)] *a*. hiérarchique; **in h. order,** par ordre hiérarchique.

hierarchy ['haiərɑ:ki] *n*. hiérarchie *f*.

hieroglyph ['haiərəglif] *n*. hiéroglyphe *m*.

hieroglyphic [haiərə'glifik] *a*. hiéroglyphique.

hieroglyphics [haiərə'glifiks] *n.pl.* hiéroglyphes *mpl*, signes *mpl* hiéroglyphiques.

hi-fi ['hai'fai] *a*. & *n*. *Rec: etc: F:* (de) haute fidélité; *F:* hi-fi (*f inv*).

higgledy-piggledy ['hig(ə)ldi'pig(ə)ldi] *adv*. *F:* sans ordre, en pagaïe, pêle-mêle.

high [hai] **I.** *a*. **1.** (*a*) haut; **house built on h. ground,** maison construite sur un terrain élevé; **wall two metres h.,** mur haut de deux mètres, qui a une hauteur de deux mètres; **at h. water, h. tide,** à la marée haute; (*b*) *Cost:* (corsage, col) montant; (col) haut; **h.-necked dress,** robe montante; (*c*) (pommettes) saillantes; (épaules) montantes. **2.** haut, élevé; (*a*) **sun h. above the horizon,** soleil haut sur l'horizon; **h.-flying,** haut vol; *Av:* vol à grande hauteur; **with one's head h.,** la tête haute; (*b*) **of h. rank,** de haut rang; **to be in a h. position,** être haut placé; **higher posts,** postes, emplois, supérieurs; *Sch:* **higher education,** études supérieures; **higher mathematics,** mathématiques supérieures; **the h. table,** la table d'honneur; *Sch:* la table des professeurs (au réfectoire); **h. and mighty,** haut et puissant; (*c*) (pensées) élevées, nobles; **h. ideals,** haut idéalisme; (*d*) (prix) élevé; gros (pourcentage); grande (vitesse); **to fetch a h. price,** se vendre cher; **to make a higher bid,** faire une offre supérieure; **to play for h. stakes,** jouer gros (jeu); *Cards:* **h. cards,** cartes hautes; **ore with a h. mineral content,** minerai à haute teneur; **h. latitudes,** les hautes latitudes; **highest speed,** vitesse maximum; vitesse de pointe; (*e*) **to have a h. opinion of s.o.,** tenir qn en haute estime; **to a h. degree,** à un haut degré; **to, in, the highest degree,** au dernier degré; **of the highest importance,** de première importance; *Rec: etc:* **h. fidelity,** haute fidélité; (*f*) forte, grosse, (fièvre); (vent) fort, violent; **h. treason,** haute trahison; (*g*) **h. colour,** (i) couleur vive; (ii) vivacité *f* du teint; **to be in h. spirits,** être plein d'entrain *m*; **the h. spot of the match,** le point culminant du match; (*h*) **h. voice,** (i) voix élevée, haute; (ii) voix grêle; *Mus:* **to set a song half a tone higher,** hausser un chant d'un demi-ton. **3.** (*principal*) **the H. Street,** la Grand-rue, la Grande rue; *Ecc:* **h. mass,** la grand-messe, la grande messe; **h. altar,** maître autel. **4.** (*far advanced*) (*a*) **h. noon,** plein midi; **its h. time he went to school,** il est grand temps qu'il aille à l'école; (*b*) (*of meat, etc.*) avancé, gâté; (*of game*) faisandé; (*of game*) **to get h.,** se faisander; **to smell h.,** avoir une forte odeur; (*c*) *F:* (*of pers.*) **to be h.,** (i) être ivre; (ii) être dans un état d'euphorie. **5.** (*of ship*) **h. and dry,** échoué au plein; à sec (sur la plage, etc.); *F:* (*of pers.*) **to be left h. and dry,** être laissé en plan. **II.** *adv*. **1.** (*a*) haut; en haut; **higher (up),** plus haut; **higher and higher,** de plus en plus haut; **to aim h.,** (i) viser haut; (ii) *Fig:* avoir de hautes visées; **to rise h. in the public esteem,** monter très haut dans l'estime publique; **to hunt h. and low for sth.,** chercher qch. partout; (*b*) **higher up the river,** en amont. **2. to go as h. as £2000,** aller jusqu'à £2000; *Cards: etc:* **to play, stake, h.,** jouer gros jeu. **3.** fort, fortement; **to run h.,** (i) (*of sea*) être grosse, houleuse; (ii) (*of feeling*) s'échauffer; (iii) (*of prices*) être élevés; **tempers were running h.,** la querelle s'échauffait. **III.** *n*. **1.** (*a*) **the Most H.,** le Très-Haut, le Tout-Puissant; (*b*) **on h.,** en haut; dans le ciel; **from on h.,** d'en haut; de là-haut. **2.** *Meteor:* aire anticyclonique. **3.** *St.Exch:* **highs and lows,** hausses *fpl* et baisses *fpl*; **prices have reached a new h.,** les prix ont atteint un nouveau maximum. **highly** *adv*. **1. h. placed official,** haut fonctionnaire. **2. his services are h. paid,** on paie très cher ses services; **to think h. of s.o.,** avoir une haute opinion de qn. **3.** fort, très, bien, fortement; **h. amusing,** très amusant; **h. displeased,** fort mécontent; **h. seasoned,** fortement assaisonné; **h. coloured,** (tableau, style) haut en couleur; (récit) coloré; (*of pers.*) **h. strung,** nerveux, impressionnable.

high-born ['haibɔ:n] *a*. de haute naissance.

highbrow ['haibrau] *n*. *F:* **1.** intellectuel, -elle; grosse tête. **2.** *a*. (littérature) pour les intellectuels.

highchair ['haitʃεər] *n*. chaise haute (de bébé).

high-class ['hai'klɑ:s] *a*. (marchandises, etc.) de premier ordre, de première qualité; (hôtel) de première classe; **h.-c. cooking,** la haute cuisine.

highfalutin(g) [haifə'lu:tin, -iŋ] *a*. *F:* (style, discours) ampoulé, prétentieux, pompeux.

high-fidelity [haifi'deliti] *a*. *Rec: etc:* de haute fidélité.

highflown ['haifloun] *a*. (style, discours) ampoulé, pompeux, déclamatoire.

high-frequency [hai'fri:kwənsi] *a*. *El:* (courant, lampe) à haute fréquence; (amplificateur) de haute fréquence.

high-grade ['hai'greid] *a*. (minerai, etc.) à haute teneur; (marchandises) de première qualité, de (premier) choix; **h.-g. petrol,** supercarburant *m*.

high-handed [hai'hændid] *a*. autoritaire; (autorité) tyrannique.

high-hat ['haihæt] *a*. & *n*. arrogant (*m*); snob (*m*).

highjack, highjacker ['haidʒæk, -jækər] *v.tr.*, *n*. = HIJACK, HIJACKER.

highland ['hailənd] **1.** *n*. pays montagneux; *Geog:* **the Highlands,** (la) Haute Écosse; les Highlands *mpl*. **2.** *a*. (*a*) des montagnes; (*b*) des Highlands; **h. cattle,** race bovine des Highlands.

highlander ['hailəndər] *n*. **1.** montagnard, -arde. **2. Highlander,** (i) Highlander *m*; habitant, -ante, de la Haute Écosse; (ii) soldat *m* d'un régiment écossais.

highlight¹ ['hailait] *n*. (*a*) **highlights,** rehauts *mpl*, clairs *mpl* (d'une peinture); (*b*) grand moment; clou *m* (de la fête, etc.); point culminant (d'un match, etc.).

highlight² *v.tr.* mettre en vedette; mettre (un problème) au premier plan.

high-minded ['hai'maindid] *a*. aux sentiments nobles, généreux; (action, nature) magnanime.

high-mindedness ['hai'maindidnis] *n*. noblesse *f* de sentiments; magnanimité *f*; grandeur *f* d'âme.

highness ['hainis] *n*. **1.** (*a*) élévation *f* (des prix, etc.); (*b*) grandeur *f* (d'âme); (*c*) force *f*, violence *f* (du vent). **2.** (*title*) Altesse *f*; **His, Her, Royal H.,** son Altesse Royale.

high-octane ['hai'ɔktein] *a*. **h.-o. petrol,** essence *f* à indice d'octane élevé; supercarburant *m*.

high-pitched [ˈhaipitʃt] *a.* **1.** (*of sound*) aigu, -uë; (*of voice*) aigu, criard. **2.** *Const:* **h.-p. roof,** comble *m* à forte inclinaison, à forte pente.
high-powered [ˈhaiˈpauəd] *a.* (*a*) gros (moteur); (voiture) de haute puissance; *W.Tel: etc:* (poste) de haute puissance, de grande portée; (*b*) *Opt:* (jumelles) à fort grossissement; (*c*) (*of pers.*) très important.
high-pressure [ˈhaiˈpreʃər] *a.* (*a*) (cylindre, machine) à haute pression, à haute tension; *Meteor:* (aire) anticyclonique; (*b*) (vendeur) importun, agressif.
high-principled [ˈhaiˈprinsip(ə)ld] *a.* aux principes élevés.
high-rise [ˈhaiˈraiz] *a.* **h.-r. building,** immeuble-tour *m.*
highroad [ˈhairoud] *n.* grande route, route nationale.
high-sounding [ˈhaisaundiŋ] *a.* (titre, éloge) pompeux, prétentieux; ronflant.
high-speed [ˈhaiˈspiːd] *a.* (*a*) ultra-rapide; (machine) à marche rapide; (moteur) grande vitesse; (*b*) *Phot:* (objectif) à très grande ouverture.
high-spirited [haiˈspiritid] *a.* plein d'ardeur, de feu; (cheval) fougueux.
high-strung [ˈhaistrʌŋ] *a.* (tempérament) nerveux, impressionnable; (personne) au tempérament nerveux.
high-up [ˈhaiʌp] *n. F:* personnage important; gros bonnet, grosse légume.
highway [ˈhaiwei] *n.* (*a*) grande voie de communication; grande route; artère *f*; **h. patrolman,** motard *m*; **highways and byways,** chemins et sentiers; (*b*) *Adm:* voie publique; **h. engineer** = ingénieur *m* des Ponts et Chaussées; **the H. Code,** le Code de la Route.
highwayman *pl.* **-men** [ˈhaiweimən] *n.m.* voleur de grand(s) chemin(s); détrousseur.
hijack [ˈhaidʒæk] *v.tr. F:* s'emparer de force (d'un véhicule); détourner (un avion en vol) (en menaçant l'équipage). **hijacking** *n.* (*a*) vol armé d'un véhicule et de son contenu; (*b*) détournement *m* (d'avion); piraterie *f* de l'air.
hijacker [ˈhaidʒækər] *n. F:* (*a*) pirate *m* de la route (qui s'empare d'un véhicule et de son contenu); (*b*) pirate de l'air.
hike¹ [haik] *n. F:* **1.** (longue) promenade *f* à pied; randonnée *f.* **2.** *NAm:* augmentation *f* (de prix, de salaire); hausse *f* (de prix).
hike² *F:* **1.** *v.i.* faire une (longue) promenade à pied; faire du footing. **2.** *v.tr.* (*a*) **to h. oneself up on to sth.,** grimper (avec difficulté) jusqu'à qch.; (*b*) *NAm:* augmenter (les prix, les salaires). **hiking** *n.* tourisme *m* à pied; footing *m.*
hiker [ˈhaikər] *n. F:* randonneur, -euse (à pied).
hilarious [hiˈlɛəriəs], *a.* gai, hilare; *F:* rigoleur, -euse; **it was h.!** c'était à se tordre (de rire)! **-ly** *adv.* avec hilarité; (rire) aux éclats; **it was h. funny,** c'était à se tordre (de rire).
hilariousness [hiˈlɛəriəsnis], **hilarity** [hiˈlæriti] *n.* hilarité *f*, gaieté *f.*
hill [hil] *n.* **1.** (*a*) colline *f*, coteau *m*; **up h. and down dale,** par monts et par vaux; **h. country,** pays *m* de montagne(s); (*in India*) **h. station,** station *f* de montagne; (*b*) éminence *f*; monticule *m*; (*c*) *Mil: Surv:* **h. 304,** la cote 304. **2.** (*on road*) côte *f*; (i) montée *f*; (ii) descente *f*; **steep h.,** (i) montée, (ii) descente, abrupte; **h. start,** départ *m* en côte; **to go down the h.,** (i) descendre la colline; descendre la côte; (ii) *Fig:* baisser, décliner.
hillbilly [ˈhilbili] *n. U.S: F:* montagnard *m*, rustaud *m*; **h. songs,** chants *mpl* imitant le folklore.
hilliness [ˈhilinis] *n.* montuosité *f*; vallonnement *m.*
hillock [ˈhilək] *n.* petite colline; butte *f*, tertre *m.*
hillside [ˈhilsaid] *n.* flanc *m* de coteau; coteau *m.*
hilltop [ˈhiltɔp] *n.* **1.** sommet *m* de (la) colline; hauteur *f*, éminence *f.* **2.** le haut de la côte.
hilly [ˈhili] *a.* **1.** (pays) montagneux, (terrain) accidenté. **2.** (chemin) montueux, à fortes pentes.
hilt [hilt] *n.* **1.** poignée *f*, garde *f* (d'épée); *F:* **right up to the h.,** jusqu'à la gauche; **mortgaged up to the h.,** fortement hypothéqué. **2.** manche *m* (de dague, de couteau, etc.); crosse *f* (de pistolet).
him [him] *pers.pron.m., objective case.* **1.** (*unstressed*) (*a*) (*direct*) le, (*before a vowel sound*) l'; (*indirect*) lui; **I hate h.,** je le déteste; **do you love h.?** l'aimez-vous? **I shall tell h. so,** je le lui dirai; **tell h. I have come,** dites-lui que je suis là; (*b*) (*reflexive*) lui; **he took his luggage with h.,** il a pris ses bagages avec lui. **2.** (*stressed*) (*a*) lui; **she is thinking of h.,** elle pense à lui; (*b*) (*with dem. force*) celui; **the prize goes to h. who comes in first,** le prix est pour celui qui arrivera le premier. **3.** (*as complement of v.* **to be**) **it's h.!** c'est lui!
Himalayas [himəˈleiəz] *Pr.n. pl. Geog:* (les montagnes de) l'Himalaya *m.*
himself [himˈself] *pers.pron. m.* (*a*) (*emphatic*) lui-même; **he doesn't want to do it h.,** il ne veut pas le faire lui-même; (*after illness*) **he's not (quite) h. again yet,** il n'est pas encore complètement remis; (*b*) (*reflexive*) se; **he hurt h.,** il s'est fait mal; **he lives by h.,** il vit seul; (*c*) (*used impersonally*) soi(-même); **everyone for h.,** chacun pour soi.
hind¹ [haind] *n. Z:* biche *f*; **h. calf,** faon *m* femelle.
hind² *a.* de derrière; postérieur; **hind legs, feet,** jambes *fpl*, pattes *fpl*, de derrière; *F:* **to get on one's h. legs,** se lever (pour prononcer un discours).
hinder¹ [ˈhaindər] *a.* de derrière; postérieur.
hinder² [ˈhindər] *v.tr.* **1.** (*impede*) gêner, embarrasser (qn); retarder, entraver (qch.); faire obstacle à (un mouvement). **2.** (*prevent*) empêcher, retenir, arrêter (**s.o. from doing sth.,** qn de faire qch.).
Hindi [ˈhindiː] *n. Ling:* hindi *m.*
hindmost [ˈhaindmoust] *a.* dernier.
hindquarters [ˈhaindkwɔːtəz] *n.pl.* arrière-train *m.*
hindrance [ˈhindrəns] *n.* empêchement *m*, obstacle *m*, entrave *f*; **he is a h.,** il gêne.
hindsight [ˈhaindsait] *n.* sagesse *f* d'après coup.
Hindu [hinˈduː] (*a*) *a.* hindou; (*b*) *n.* Hindou, -oue.
Hinduism [ˈhinduːizm] *n.* (h)indouisme *m.*
Hindustan [hinduˈstɑːn] *Pr.n. Geog:* Hindoustan *m.*
Hindustani [hinduˈstɑːni] *a. & n. Ling:* hindoustani (*m*).
hinge¹ [hindʒ] *n.* gond *m* (de porte); paumelle *f*; **butt h.,** charnière *f*; **the door came off its hinges,** la porte est sortie hors de ses gonds; **h. pin,** broche *f* de charnière.
hinge² **1.** *v.tr.* (i) monter (une porte, etc.) sur ses gonds; (ii) mettre les charnières à (une boîte, etc.). **2.** *v.i.* (*a*) tourner, pivoter (**on,** autour de); (*of seat, etc.*) **to h. forward,** basculer vers l'avant; (*b*) (*in novel, etc.*) **everything hinges on his answer,** tout dépend de sa réponse. **hinged** *a.* (porte, couvercle, etc.) à charnière(s); **h. flap,** (i) (*of counter, etc.*) battant *m* rabattable; (ii) (*of aircraft*) volet articulé.
hint¹ [hint] *n.* **1.** (*a*) insinuation *f*, allusion indirecte; **broad h.,** (i) allusion évidente, claire; (ii) avis peu voilé; **gentle h.,** allusion discrète; **to give, drop, s.o. a h.,** toucher un mot à qn; **to know how to take a h.,** entendre (qn) à demi-mot; (*b*) (*sign*) signe *m*, indication *f*, suggestion *f*; **not a h. of surprise,** pas une **ombre de surprise; not the slightest h. of . . .,** pas le moindre soupçon de . . .. **2. can you give me some hints?** (i) pouvez-vous me donner quelques conseils? (ii) pouvez-vous me mettre sur la voie?
hint² *v.tr. & i.* insinuer (qch.); suggérer, dire (qch.) à mots couverts; **to h. to s.o. that . . .,** faire entendre à

qn que . . .; **to h. at sth.,** laisser entendre qch. à mots couverts; faire une allusion voilée à qch.
hinterland ['hintəlænd] *n.* arrière-pays *m.*
hip¹ [hip] *n.* **1.** *Anat:* hanche *f*; **h. bone,** os iliaque; **h. size, measurement,** tour *m* de hanches; **h. pocket,** poche *f* revolver, *F:* poche fessière. **2.** *Const:* **h. (piece, rafter),** arêtier *m*, arête *f* (d'un comble).
hip² *n. Bot:* cynor(r)hodon *m*, fruit *m* du rosier; *Pharm:* **rose h. syrup,** sirop *m* de cynor(r)hodon.
hip³ *a. F:* à la page, dans le vent.
hip⁴ *int.* **h.! h.! hurray!** hip! hip! hourra!
hipped [hipt] *a.* (*with adj. prefixed*) **broad-h.,** à fortes hanches.
hippie ['hipi] *n. F:* hippie *mf.*
hippo ['hipou] *n. F:* hippopotame *m.*
Hippocrates [hi'pɔkrəti:z] *Pr.n.m. Med.Hist:* Hippocrate.
Hippocratic [hipə'krætik] *a. Med:* hippocratique; **H. oath,** serment *m* d'Hippocrate.
hippodrome ['hipədroum] *n.* **1.** hippodrome *m.* **2.** *NAm:* arène *f* (où on donne des spectacles équestres).
hippopotamus, *pl.* **-muses, -mi** [hipə'pɔtəməs, -məsiz, mai] *n. Z:* hippopotame *m.*
hippy ['hipi] *n. F:* hippy *mf.*
hipster ['hipstər] *n. Cost:* pantalon *m* taille basse.
hire¹ [haiər] *n.* **1.** (*a*) *NAm:* louage *m* (d'un domestique); embauchage *m* (de main-d'œuvre); location *f* (d'une maison); **on h.,** à louer; (*b*) location (d'une voiture, d'une salle); (*taxi sign*) **for h.,** libre; (*c*) **h. purchase,** (i) location-vente *f*; (ii) achat *m* à crédit, à tempérament. **2.** *esp. NAm:* (i) salaire *m*, gages *mpl*; (ii) loyer *m.*
hire² *v.tr.* **1.** (*a*) *esp. NAm:* engager (un ouvrier, etc.); prendre à son service (un domestique); (*b*) soudoyer (un assassin); (*c*) louer (une voiture, etc.). **2. to h. (sth.) out,** louer (qch.), donner (qch.) en location (**to s.o.,** à qn). **hired** *a.* **1.** (*pers.*) (*a*) *NAm:* **h. man,** (i) domestique *m*; (ii) (*also* **h. hand**) ouvrier agricole; (*b*) (assassin) à gages. **2.** (*thg*) (voiture) de location. **hiring** *n.* (*a*) *NAm:* embauchage *m* (d'un ouvrier, etc.); (*b*) louage (d'une voiture, etc.).
hireling ['haiəliŋ] *n. Pej:* stipendié *m*; laquais *m.*
hirsute ['hə:sju:t] *a.* hirsute, velu, poilu.
his¹ [hiz] *poss.a.* (*denoting a m. possessor*) (*a*) son, *f.* sa, *pl.* ses; **one of h. friends,** un de ses amis, un ami à lui; **h. father and mother,** son père et sa mère; *Adm:* ses père et mère; **h. own son,** son propre fils; **he has hurt h. hand,** il s'est fait mal à la main; **h. eyes are brown,** il a les yeux bruns; (*b*) **H. Majesty,** sa Majesté.
his² *poss. pron.* (*denoting a m. possessor*) le sien, la sienne, les siens, les siennes; **he took my pen as well as h.,** il a pris mon stylo avec le sien; **this book is h.,** ce livre est appartient à lui; c'est son livre à lui; **a friend of h.,** un de ses amis; un ami à lui; **it is no business of h.,** ce n'est pas son affaire.
Hispanic [his'pænik] **1.** *a.* hispanique. **2.** *n. U.S:* Américain, -aine, de langue espagnole; Hispano-Américain.
Hispano-American [hi'spænouə'merik(ə)n] **1.** *a.* hispano-américain. **2.** *n.* Hispano-américain, -aine.
hiss¹ [his] *n.* **1.** sifflement *m*; *Th: etc:* sifflets *m.* **2.** *Ling:* fricative sourde; sifflante *f.*
hiss² *v.tr. & i.* (*of pers., steam, etc.*) siffler; (*of steam, gas*) chuinter; dire (qch.) d'une voix sifflante; **to h. (at) an actor,** siffler un acteur; **to be hissed,** être sifflé. **hissing 1.** *a.* (voix) sifflante; (gaz) qui chuinte; **h. noise,** sifflement *m*; chuintement *m*; bruissement *m.* **2.** *n.* sifflement *m*; chuintement *m.*
histamin(e) ['histəmin, -mi:n] *n. Physiol:* histamine *f.*
historian [his'tɔ:riən] *n.* historien, -ienne.
historic [his'tɔrik] *a.* **1.** historique; **h. building,** monument *m* historique; **an h. occasion,** une occasion mémorable. **2.** *Gram:* **h. tense,** temps *m* historique; *Lt. & Fr.Gram:* **past h.,** passé simple.
historical [his'tɔrik(ə)l] *a.* **1.** historique, de l'histoire; **h. character,** personnage *m* historique; **h. record, account,** historique *m.* **2.** (tableau) d'histoire; (pièce roman) historique. **3.** (linguistique) historique. **-ally** *adv.* historiquement.
historiographer [histɔ:ri'ɔgrəfər] *n.* historiographe *m.*
historiography [histɔ:ri'ɔgrəfi] *n.* historiographie *f.*
history ['hist(ə)ri] *n.* **1.** (*a*) l'histoire *f*; **French h.,** l'histoire de France; **ancient, modern, h.,** l'histoire ancienne, moderne; **that's ancient h.,** ça c'est une vieille histoire; **we're making h.,** nous faisons l'histoire; (*b*) passé *m*; **this ship has an interesting h.,** l'histoire de ce navire est intéressante; (*c*) *Sch:* **h. (book),** livre *m* d'histoire; (*d*) historique *m*; **regimental h.,** historique du régiment. **2. natural h.,** histoire naturelle **3.** *Med:* **case h.,** dossier médical (d'un malade).
histrionic [histri'ɔnik] *a.* **1.** théâtral, -aux. **2.** histrionique; peu sincère.
histrionics [histri'ɔniks] *n.pl.* **1.** l'art *m* du théâtre. **2.** *Pej:* parade *f* d'émotion, d'affection, de colère, etc.; **it is mere h. on her part,** c'est une comédie qu'elle nous joue.
hit¹ [hit] *n.* **1.** (*a*) coup *m*; *F:* **that's a h. at you,** c'est à vous que s'adresse l'allusion; (*b*) *Artil: etc:* (i) impact *m*; (ii) coup au but; (*c*) *Fenc:* touche *f*, coup; **to score a h.,** toucher; (*d*) *Bill:* touche; (*e*) (*hockey*) coup de crosse; **free h.,** coup franc; (*f*) (*baseball*) coup de batte; frappe *f.* **2.** (*a*) coup réussi; succès *m*; **to make a lucky h.,** (i) avoir de la chance; (ii) (*in guessing, etc.*) tomber juste; **to make, be, a h.,** (*of thg*) réussir en plein; (*of pers.*) faire sensation; (*b*) *Th: T.V: etc:* spectacle *m*, etc., à succès; **h. song,** chanson *f* à succès; tube *m*; *T.V: etc:* **h. parade,** palmarès *m.*
hit² *v.* (*p.t. & p.p.* **hit; hit;** *pr.p.* **hitting**) **1.** *v.tr.* (*a*) frapper; **to h. s.o. in the face,** frapper qn au visage; *v.i.* **to h. hard,** frapper, cogner, fort; (*b*) **to h. one's foot against a stone,** se cogner le pied contre une pierre; buter contre une pierre; *Nau:* **to h. a rock,** heurter un récif; (*c*) atteindre; *Fenc: Bill:* toucher; *Mus:* **to h. the wrong note,** (i) frapper à faux (sur le piano, etc.); (ii) attaquer faux; **to be h. by a bullet,** être atteint d'une balle; (*of allusion, etc.*) **to h. home,** porter (coup); piquer (qn) au vif; **to be hard h.,** être sérieusement touché (par ses pertes, etc.); **the strike has h. several factories,** la grève a atteint plusieurs usines; (*d*) **to strike out, to answer, h. or miss,** frapper, répondre, au hasard, au petit bonheur; **it's h. or miss!** c'est tout ou rien! (*e*) *U.S: F:* **he h. his friend for 100 dollars,** il a tapé son ami de 100 dollars. **2.** (*a*) *v.tr. & i.* **to h. on sth.,** découvrir, trouver (un moyen); rencontrer (un indice, etc.); **to h. on the idea of doing sth.,** avoir l'idée de faire qch.; **to h. (on) the right word,** trouver le mot juste; **you've h. it!** vous y êtes! vous avez mis le doigt dessus! *Journ: F:* **to h. the headlines,** défrayer la chronique; **to h. the nail on the head,** tomber juste; *F:* **to h. the roof,** être furieux; *P:* **to h. the bottle,** picoler; *P:* **to h. the hay,** *U.S:* **the sack,** se coucher, se pieuter; (*b*) *v.tr. U.S:* arriver à (un endroit); **to h. the trail, the road,** se mettre en route; (*c*) *v.tr.* **we h. a terrible snowstorm,** nous nous sommes trouvés dans une tempête de neige terrible; (*d*) *v.tr. F:* **how did it h. you?** quelle impression cela vous a-t-il fait? **he didn't know what had h. him,** il se demandait ce qui lui était arrivé. **hit back** *v.i.* se défendre; rendre coup pour coup (**at s.o.,** à qn). **hit off** *v.tr.* (*a*) imiter (qn); faire un portrait (satirique)

de (qn, qch.); (*b*) **to h. it off with s.o.,** s'accorder, s'entendre, avec qn. **hit out** *v.i.* **to h. out at s.o.,** (i) décocher un coup à qn; (ii) *Fig:* lancer une attaque contre qn.

hit-and-run ['hit(ə)n(d)'rʌn] *a.* (*a*) *Mil:* **h.-a.-r. raid,** raid *m* éclair; (*b*) **h.-a.-r. accident,** accident *m* dont l'auteur est coupable du délit de fuite; **killed by a h.-a.-r. driver,** tué par un chauffard qui a pris la fuite.

hitch¹ [hitʃ] *n.* **1.** (*a*) saccade *f*, secousse *f*; (*b*) (*of horse*) léger boitement. **2.** (*a*) *Nau:* nœud *m*; **half h.,** demi-clef *f*; (*b*) *NAm:* (dispositif *m* d')attelage (*m*); accrochage *m*; attache *f*. **3.** empêchement *m*, anicroche *f*, contretemps *m*; **there's a h. somewhere,** il y a quelque chose qui cloche; **without a h.,** sans à-coup, sans accroc; *W.Tel: T.V: etc:* **technical h.,** incident *m* technique. **4.** *NAm: F:* (*a*) service *m* militaire; (*b*) **to do a three-year h. in prison,** faire trois ans de prison.

hitch² **1.** *v.tr.* remuer (qch.) par saccades; **to h. up one's trousers,** remonter son pantalon. **2.** (*a*) *v.tr.* accrocher, attacher, *Nau:* amarrer (**sth. to sth.,** qch. à qch.); (*b*) *v.i.* faire de l'auto-stop, du stop; *v.tr.* **we hitched a ride to Paris,** on nous a pris en stop jusqu'à Paris. **3.** *v.i.* **to h. on to sth.,** s'accrocher à qch. **4.** *v.i. P:* **to get hitched,** se marier.

hitch-hike ['hitʃhaik] *v.i.* faire de l'auto-stop, du stop; **to h.-h. to Paris,** aller à Paris en stop. **hitch-hiking** *n.* auto-stop *m.*

hitch-hiker ['hitʃhaikər] *n.* auto-stoppeur, -euse.

hither ['hiðər] *adv.* ici (exprimant la venue); **h. and thither,** çà et là.

hitherto ['hiðə'tuː] *adv.* jusqu'ici, jusqu'à présent.

hive¹ [haiv] *n.* **1.** ruche *f*; **a h. of industry,** une véritable ruche, fourmilière. **2.** (*swarm*) essaim *m.*

hive² **1.** *v.tr.* (*a*) (re)cueillir (un essaim) dans une ruche; **to h. sth. off,** détacher, séparer, qch. d'un tout; **to h. off work,** sous-traiter. **2.** *v.i.* (*a*) (*of swarm*) entrer dans la ruche; (*b*) **to h. off,** essaimer.

hives [haivz] *n.pl. Med:* urticaire *f.*

h'm [hm] *int.* (*expressing doubt*) heu! hum!

ho¹ [hou] *int.* **1.** (*expressing surprise, amusement, etc.*) ho! **2.** (*to attract attention*) hé! ohé! *Nau:* **land ho!** la terre en vue!

hoard¹ [hɔːd] *n.* amas *m*, approvisionnement secret (de vivres, etc.); **h. of money,** trésor *m*, *F:* magot *m.*

hoard² *v.tr.* amasser, accaparer (le blé, etc.); mettre, tenir, en réserve (des vivres, etc.); **to h. up treasure,** *v.i.* **to h.,** thésauriser (de l'argent). **hoarding** *n.* mise *f* en réserve (de provisions); thésautisation *f* (d'argent).

hoarder ['hɔːdər] *n.* amasseur, -euse, accumulateur, -trice; **h. of money,** thésauriseur, -euse.

hoarding ['hɔːdiŋ] *n.* (*a*) clôture *f* en planches; palissade *f* (de chantier, etc.); (*b*) panneau *m* d'affichage.

hoarfrost ['hɔːfrɔst] *n.* gelée blanche.

hoarse [hɔːs] *a.* (*of voice, etc.*) enroué, rauque; **to be h.,** être enroué; **to shout oneself h.,** s'enrouer à force de crier. **-ly** *adv.* d'une voix rauque, enrouée.

hoarseness ['hɔːsnis] *n.* enrouement *m.*

hoary ['hɔːri] *a.* **1.** (*a*) (*of hair*) blanchi, chenu; (*b*) *Bot: Ent:* (feuillage, insecte) couvert d'un duvet blanc. **2.** vénérable, séculaire.

hoax¹ [houks] *n.* canular *m*, farce *f*, tour *m*; *Journ: F:* canard *m*; **to play a h. on s.o.,** jouer un tour à qn.

hoax² *v.tr.* monter un canular à (qn).

hoaxer ['houksər] *n.* faceur, -euse.

hob [hɔb] *n.* (*a*) plaque *f* de côte (d'une grille de cheminée); (*b*) table de cuisson (de cuisinière électrique).

hobble¹ ['hɔbl] *n.* **1.** boitillement *m.* **2.** (*a*) entrave *f*, (pour chevaux, etc.); (*b*) *A. Cost:* **h. skirt,** jupe entravée.

hobble² **1.** *v.i.* boitiller, clopiner; **to h. along,** marcher en boitillant. **2.** *v.tr.* entraver (un cheval, etc.).

hobby ['hɔbi] *n.* passe-temps (favori); violon *m* d'Ingres; **my main h. is photography,** ma principale distraction c'est la photographie.

hobbyhorse ['hɔbihɔːs] *n.* dada *m*; cheval *m* de bois; *Th: etc:* cheval-jupon *m*, *pl.* chevaux-jupons.

hobgoblin ['hɔbgɔblin] *n.* lutin *m*, gobelin *m.*

hobnail¹ ['hɔbneil] *n.* caboche *f*; clou *m* à ferrer (les souliers).

hobnail² *v.tr.* ferrer (un soulier); **hobnailed boot,** soulier ferré; gochillot *m.*

hobnob ['hɔbnɔb] *v.i.* (**hobnobbed**) **to h. with s.o.,** être de pair à compagnon avec qn; **to h. with the great,** frayer avec les grands; fréquenter les grands.

hobo ['houbou] *n. NAm:* (*a*) ouvrier ambulant; (*b*) chemineau *m*, trimardeur *m.*

Hobson ['hɔbsən] *Pr.n.m.* **Hobson's choice,** choix *m* qui ne laisse pas d'alternative.

hock¹ [hɔk] *n.* jarret *m* (de quadrupède).

hock² *n.* vin *m* du Rhin.

hock³ *n F:* **in h.,** (i) (*of watch, etc.*), au clou; (ii) (*of pers.*) en prison.

hock⁴ *v.tr* engager (sa montre, etc.); mettre (sa montre) au clou.

hockey ['hɔki] *n.* **hockey,** *U.S:* **field h.,** *Can:* **grass h.,** (jeu *m* de) hockey *m*; **ice h.,** *NAm:* **hockey,** hockey sur glace, *Fr.C:* hockey; **h. stick,** crosse *f* de hockey.

hockshop ['hɔkʃɔp] *n. NAm: F:* crédit municipal; mont-de-piété *m.*

hocus-pocus ['houkəs'poukəs] *n.* **1.** (*a*) passe-passe *m* (formule du prestidigitateur); (*b*) tour *m* de passe-passe. **2.** tromperie *f*, supercherie *f.*

hod [hɔd] *n.* **1.** oiseau *m*, hotte *f* (de maçon). **2.** seau *m*, caisse *f* (à charbon).

hoe¹ [hou] *n.* (*a*) *Hort: Agr:* houe *f*, binette *f*; **weeding h.,** sarcloir *m*; **Dutch h.,** griffe-bineuse *f*, *pl.* griffes-bineuses; (*b*) **miner's h.,** sape *f.*

hoe² *v.tr.* (**hoed; hoeing**) houer, biner (le sol); sarcler (les mauvaises herbes). **hoeing** *n.* houement *m*, binage *m* (du sol); sarclage *m* (de mauvaises herbes).

hog¹ [hɔg] *n.* **1.** (*a*) porc châtré; (*b*) porc, cochon *m*, pourceau *m*; *F:* **to go the whole h.,** aller jusqu'au bout; tout risquer. **2.** (*pers.*) *F:* (*a*) goinfre *m*, glouton *m*; (*b*) sale cochon.

hog² *v.* (**hogged**) **1.** *v.i.* (*of ship, keel*) s'arquer; (*of pipes, etc.*) cintrer. **2.** *v.tr.* (*a*) *Nau:* donner de l'arc à (un navire); (*b*) anglaiser (la crinière d'un cheval); (*c*) *F:* prendre plus que sa part de (qch.); **to h. the limelight,** accaparer la vedette; *Aut:* **to h. the road,** tenir toute la route.

Hogmanay ['hɔgmənei] *n. Scot:* la Saint-Sylvestre.

hogshead ['hɔgzhed] *n.* tonneau *m*, barrique *f.*

hogtie ['hɔgtai] *v.tr. U.S:* (*a*) lier les quatre pattes (d'un animal); (*b*) *Fig:* entraver (l'économie, etc.).

hogwash ['hɔgwɔʃ] *n.* (*a*) eaux grasses (que l'on donne aux porcs); (*b*) *F:* foutaise *f.*

hogweed ['hɔgwiːd] *n. Bot:* berce commune.

hoi polloi ['hɔipə'lɔi] *n.pl.* **the h. p.,** la foule, les masses.

hoist¹ [hɔist] *n.* **1.** (*a*) levage *m*; coup *m* de treuil; (*b*) **to give s.o. a h. (up),** aider qn à monter; faire la courte échelle à qn. **2.** (*a*) appareil *m*, engin *m*, de levage; treuil *m*, grue *f*, palan *m*; *Min:* bourriquet *m*; (*b*) (*for goods*) monte-charge *m inv*; (*for cars*) monte-voiture *m*, *pl.* monte-voitures. **3.** *Nau:* guindant *m* (de pavillon, de voile).

hoist² *v.tr.* (*a*) *Civ.E: etc:* lever, hisser (un fardeau, etc.); *Nau:* hisser (une embarcation, un pavillon); **to h. boats in, out,** embarquer, débarquer, les canots; **h. away!** hissez! (*b*) *F:* **to h. oneself up a wall,** se hisser le long d'un mur. **hoisting** *n.* (*a*) *Civ.E: etc:* levage *m*, hissage *m*; (*by windlass*) guindage *m*; **h. gear, tackle,** appareil *m*, engin *m*, de levage, de hissage; (*b*) *Mil:* **h. the colours,** lever *m* des couleurs.

hoity-toity ['hɔiti'tɔiti] **1.** *int.* ta, ta, ta! taratata! **2.** *a.* (*a*) qui se donne des airs; qui fait l'important; (*b*) qui se froisse facilement; susceptible.

hokum ['houkəm] *n. NAm:F:* **1.** niaiseries *fpl*, paroles sentimentales. **2.** bêtises *fpl*.

hold¹ [hould] *n.* **1.** (*a*) prise *f*; **to have h. of s.o., sth.,** tenir qn, qch.; **to catch, get, take, h. of s.o., sth.,** saisir, empoigner, qn, qch.; **where did you get h. of that?** où vous êtes-vous procuré cela? **it's difficult to get h. of this book,** ce livre est difficile à trouver; **to relax one's h.,** relâcher son étreinte *f*; **to lose, let go, one's h.,** lâcher prise; **to lose one's h. on reality,** perdre le sens des réalités; (*b*) **to have a h. on, over, s.o.,** avoir prise sur qn; **to gain a firm h. over s.o.,** acquérir un grand pouvoir sur qn; (*c*) *Box:* tenu *m*; *Wr:* prise; **no holds barred,** toutes prises autorisées. **2.** soutien *m*; point *m* d'appui.

hold² *v.* (*p.t. & p.p.* **held** [*held*]). **I.** *v.tr.* **1.** tenir; (*a*) **to h. sth. in one's hand,** tenir qch. à, dans, la main; **to h. sth., s.o., tight(ly),** serrer qch., qn; tenir qch., qn, serré; **they held (each other's) hands,** ils se tenaient (par) la main; **to h. one's sides with laughter,** se tenir les côtes de rire; **to h. one's nose,** se boucher le nez; (*b*) **to h. sth. in position,** tenir qch. en place; (*c*) **to h. s.o. at bay, in check,** tenir qn aux abois, en respect; **to h. s.o. prisoner,** tenir qn prisonnier; **to h. s.o. (as) hostage,** retenir qn en otage; **to h. stocks as security,** détenir des titres en garantie; **to h. s.o. to his promise,** obliger, contraindre, qn à tenir sa promesse. **3.** (*a*) **to h. one's ground,** tenir bon, ne pas lâcher pied; **to h. one's own,** se maintenir, se défendre; *Mil:* **to h. a fort, a position,** défendre une forteresse, tenir une position; *F:* **I'll h. the fort while you're away,** je m'occuperai de tout pendant votre absence; **to be able to h. one's drink,** avoir la tête solide; bien porter le vin; **to h. the stage,** (i) (*of actor*) retenir l'attention de l'auditoire; (ii) (*of play*) tenir l'affiche (pendant longtemps); (*b*) *Nau: etc:* **to h. course,** tenir la route; *Tp:* **h. the line!** ne quittez pas! **car that holds the road well,** voiture *f* qui tient bien la route. **4.** porter; **to h. one's head high,** porter la tête haute; **to h. oneself straight,** se tenir droit; **to h. oneself well,** avoir de la tenue. **5.** (*a*) (*contain*) contenir, renfermer (une quantité de qch.); **barrel that holds twenty litres,** tonneau *m* d'une contenance de vingt litres; **car that holds six people,** voiture *f* à six places; (*b*) **what the future holds,** ce que l'avenir nous réserve. **6.** tenir (une séance, etc.); avoir (une consultation); célébrer (une fête, etc.); **the meeting will be held at 8 p.m.,** la réunion aura lieu à 8 heures du soir; **to h. a conversation with s.o.,** s'entretenir avec qn. **7.** retenir; arrêter; empêcher; (*a*) **to h. one's breath,** retenir sa respiration; **there's no holding him,** (une fois lancé) il n'y a pas moyen de l'arrêter; **h. your tongue!** taisez-vous! **h. it! h. your horses!** arrêtez! attendez! stop! (*at photographer's*) **h. it!** ne bougez plus! (*b*) **to h. water,** (i) (*of cask, etc.*) tenir l'eau, être étanche; (ii) (*of theory, story, etc.*) tenir debout; (*c*) retenir (l'attention); **to h. one's audience,** retenir l'attention de l'auditoire; (*d*) *Mil:* **to h. the enemy,** contenir l'ennemi. **8.** avoir, posséder (un titre, un emploi); détenir (une charge); occuper (une position); être titulaire (d'une médaille); *Fin:* détenir (des actions). **9.** (*consider*) (*a*) **to h. sth. lightly,** faire peu de cas de qch.; attacher peu d'importance à qch.; **to h. sth. sacred,** tenir qch. pour sacré; **to h. s.o. responsible,** tenir qn responsable; *F:* **he was left holding the baby,** on l'a laissé payer les pots cassés; **to be held in respect,** être respecté de tous; (*b*) avoir, professer (une opinion). **10.** *Mus:* **to h. a note,** tenir, prolonger (une note). **II.** *v.i.* **1.** (*of rope, nail, etc.*) tenir (bon); être solide; (*on bus, etc.*) **h. tight!** = attention au départ! **2.** durer, persister; (*of weather*) se maintenir; **if your luck holds,** si votre chance dure. **3. to h. (good, true),** être vrai, valable; **the same holds true in respect of . . .,** il en est de même pour . . .. **4. to h. to a belief,** rester attaché à une croyance; **to h. by, to, one's decision,** s'en tenir à, maintenir, sa décision. **hold back 1.** *v.tr.* retenir (qn, ses larmes); cacher, dissimuler (la vérité). **2.** *v.i.* (*a*) rester en arrière; (*b*) hésiter; se retenir (**from doing sth.,** de faire qch.); **buyers are holding back,** les acheteurs s'abstiennent. **hold down** *v.tr.* (*a*) baisser (la tête); (*b*) maintenir (un homme) à terre; **to h. down a job,** (i) se montrer à la hauteur d'un emploi; (ii) occuper un emploi; (*c*) maintenir le niveau (des prix). **hold forth** *v.i. F:* disserter, pérorer; **hold in** *v.tr.* serrer la bride à (un cheval); contenir (un cheval); réprimer (ses désirs); maîtriser (une passion); **to h. oneself in,** se contenir, se retenir. **holding** *n.* **1.** (*a*) tenue *f* (d'un objet, etc., à la main); (*b*) tenue (d'un congrès, etc.). **2.** (*a*) *Mec.E:* fixation *f*; maintien *m* (en position); (*b*) *Mil:* **h. operation,** opération *f* de fixation (de l'adversaire). **3.** conservation *f*; prolongation *f* (d'un mouvement, d'une action); (*a*) *Mil:* conservation (du terrain conquis); (*b*) *Mus:* prolongation (d'une note); (*c*) *Av:* attente (imposée à un avion avant d'atterrir). **4.** (*a*) *Hist:* possession *f* (de terres), tenure *f*; (*b*) *Agr:* terre affermée; ferme *f*. **5.** *Fin:* avoir *m* (en actions); effets *mpl* en portefeuille; holding *m*; **he has holdings in several companies,** il est actionnaire de plusieurs sociétés; **h. company,** (société) holding *m*. **hold off 1.** *v.tr.* tenir (qn, qch.) à distance. **2.** *v.i.* (*a*) se tenir à distance (**from,** de); *Nau:* tenir le large; (*b*) **the rain is holding off,** jusqu'ici il ne pleut pas; (*c*) s'abstenir; se réserver. **hold on** *v.i.* **to h. on to sth.,** (i) s'accrocher, se tenir, à qch.; (ii) ne pas lâcher, ne pas abandonner, qch.; **h. on (a minute)!** (i) tenez bon! (ii) *Tp:* ne quittez pas! (iii) attendez (un instant)! pas si vite! **how long can you h. on?** combien de temps pouvez-vous tenir? **hold out 1.** *v.tr.* tendre, offrir (la main, etc.); offrir, laisser voir (des espérances). **2.** *v.i.* durer; **to h. out against an attack,** soutenir une attaque; **to h. out for a higher price,** exiger un prix plus élevé. **hold over** *v.tr.* remettre (à plus tard); ajourner (une décision, etc.); arriérer (un paiement); **bills held over,** effets *mpl* en souffrance, en suspens. **hold together 1.** *v.tr.* maintenir (deux choses) ensemble. **2.** *v.i.* tenir (ensemble); garder de la cohésion; **the story doesn't h. together,** l'histoire ne tient pas debout. **hold up 1.** *v.tr.* (*a*) soutenir (qn, qch.); (*b*) lever (qch.) (en l'air); (*c*) **to h. s.o. up as an example,** citer qn comme exemple; **to h. s.o. up to ridicule,** tourner qn en ridicule; (*d*) arrêter (qn, un train, etc.); bloquer (la circulation, etc.); immobiliser (qn, qch.); **the car was held up at the traffic lights,** la voiture a dû s'arrêter au feu rouge; **goods held up at the customs,** marchandises *fpl* en consigne à la douane; (*e*) attaquer (qn, une banque); arrêter (un train) à main armée. **2.** *v.i.* (i) se soutenir; (ii) (*of weather*) se maintenir. **hold with** *v.i.* (*usu. neg.*) **I don't h. with his opinions,** je ne partage pas ses opinions; **I don't h. with such behaviour,** je n'approuve pas une telle conduite.

hold³ *n. Nau:* cale *f*.

holdall ['houldɔ:l] *n.* sac *m* de voyage; fourre-tout *m inv.*

holder ['houldər] *n.* **1.** (*pers.* (*a*) teneur, -euse (de qch.); (*b*) détenteur, -trice (*Fin:* de titres, d'une lettre de change, *Sp:* du record); tenant *m* (d'un championnat); porteur, -euse (*Fin:* de titres, d'un effet); titulaire *mf* (d'un droit, d'un poste, etc.); propriétaire *mf* (d'une terre); détenteur *m* (d'un terrain, etc., hypothéqué). **2.** (*device*) support *m*, monture *f*, patte *f*; (*a*) **drill h.,** porte-foret *m*, *pl.* porte-forets; **tool h.,** porte-outil(s) *m*; (*b*) **toothbrush h.,** porte-brosses *m inv* à dents; **cigarette h.,** porte-cigarette *m inv*. **3.** (*vessel*) récipient *m*.

holdup ['houldʌp] *n.* **1.** (*a*) arrêt *m*, embouteillage *m* (de voitures); (*b*) panne *f* (du métro, etc.). **2.** attaque *f*, hold-up *m*, à main armée; braquage *m*.

hole¹ [houl] *n.* **1.** (*a*) trou, creux *m*, cavité *f*; **to dig a h.,** creuser un trou; (*b*) *Golf:* trou; (*c*) terrier *m* (de lapin); tanière *f* (de renard); trou (de souris, etc.); (*d*) *F:* **what a h.!** (i) (*of room, etc.*) quel (sale) trou! (ii) (*of house*) quel taudis! (iii) (*of town*) quel bled! **2.** trou; orifice *m*, ouverture *f*; perforation *f* (dans une plaque de métal, etc.); point *m* (d'une courroie); perce *f* (d'une flûte); (*a*) *Tchn:* **punched h.,** trou poinçonné; **inspection h.,** orifice trou, de visite; *Min:* **blast h.,** trou de mine; (*b*) *Cmptr:* **(punch) h.,** perforation; (*c*) *Med:* *F:* **h. in the heart,** trou dans le cœur; (*e*) **to bore a h.,** percer un trou; **to stop (up) a h.,** boucher un trou; **to make a h. (in sth.),** faire un trou (à qch.); trouer (un vêtement); **this jersey is full of holes,** ce tricot est tout troué; **to pick holes in a theory,** relever les points faibles d'une théorie.

hole² *v.* **1.** *v.tr.* (*a*) trouer, percer (qch.); pratiquer, faire, un trou dans (qch.); (*b*) faire entrer, mettre, (qch.) dans un trou; *Bill:* bloquer, blouser (la bille); *Golf:* **to h. the ball,** *v.i.* **to hole (out),** envoyer, mettre, la balle dans le trou; *F:* **holed in one!** vous avez deviné juste! **2.** *v.i.* (*of stockings, etc.*) se trouer, se percer.

hole-and-corner ['houl(ə)n(d)'kɔːnər] *a.* *F:* clandestin, secret; (affaire) conclue en sous-main.

holey ['houli] *a.* (tout) troué; plein de trous.

holiday¹ ['hɔlidi, -dei] *n.* (*a*) (jour *m* de) fête (*f*); jour férié; **public, bank, h.,** fête légale; (*b*) (jour de) congé (*m*); *Sch:* **half h.,** après-midi *m* de congé; **I'm going to take a h. today,** je vais prendre un congé aujourd'hui; (*c*) **a month's h.,** un mois de vacances; **the summer holidays,** les grandes vacances; **when are you going on h.?** quand est-ce que vous allez prendre vos vacances? **camping h.,** vacances passées à faire du camping; **h. camp,** (i) camp *m* de vacances; (ii) (*for children*) colonie *f* de vacances; **the h. season,** la période des vacances.

holiday² ['hɔlidei] *v.i.* passer les vacances.

holidaymaker ['hɔlideimeikər] *n.* vacancier, -ière; estivant, -ante.

holier-than-thou ['houliəðən'ðau] *a.* (*of attitude, etc.*) hypocritement pieux.

holiness ['houlinis] *n.* (*a*) sainteté *f*; (*b*) (*of the Pope*) **His, Your, H.,** Sa, Votre, Sainteté.

holism ['houlizm] *n.* *Phil:* holisme *m*.

holistic [hou'listik] *a.* *Phil:* holistique.

Holland ['hɔlənd] **1.** *Pr.n.* *Geog:* Hollande *f*. **2.** *n.* *Tex:* **h.,** toile *f* de Hollande; toile bise.

holler ['hɔlər] *v.i.* *P:* crier à tue-tête; brailler.

hollow¹ ['hɔlou] **I.** *a.* **1.** creux, caverneux; (dent) creuse; (joues) creuses, rentrées; (yeux) caves; **h.-cheeked, h.-eyed,** aux joues creuses, aux yeux caves; *Mil:* **h. square,** carré *m*; *F:* **to feel h.,** avoir le ventre, l'estomac, creux; avoir faim; *F:* **he's got h. legs,** il boit comme un trou. **2.** (son) sourd; **in a h. voice,** d'une voix caverneuse. **3.** (*of promise, friendship, etc.*) faux, *f.* fausse; trompeur, -euse. **II.** *adv.* **1. to sound h.,** sonner creux. **2. to beat s.o. h.,** battre qn à plate(s) couture(s). **III.** *n.* (*a*) creux *m* (de la main, d'un arbre, etc.); cavité *f* (d'une dent); excavation *f*; (*b*) enfoncement *m*, dépression *f* (du sol); bas-fond *m*, *pl.* bas-fonds; cuvette *f*.

hollow² *v.tr.* **to h. (out),** creuser, évider; canneler (une rainure); (*undermine*) caver (un rocher, etc.); (*of water*) **to h. out the ground,** raviner le terrain.

hollowness ['hɔlounis] *n.* **1.** creux *m*, concavité *f* (d'un arbre, etc.). **2.** timbre caverneux (de la voix). **3.** manque *m* de sincérité (d'une promesse, etc.).

holly ['hɔli] *n.* *Bot:* (*a*) **h. (tree),** houx *m*; **h. berry,** cenelle *f*.

hollyhock ['hɔlihɔk] *n.* *Bot:* rose trémière.

holm¹ [houm] *n.* petite île, îlot *m* (de rivière).

holm² *n.* *Bot:* **h. (oak),** yeuse *f*.

holocaust ['hɔləkɔːst] *n.* holocauste *m*.

hologram ['hɔləgræm] *n.* *Phot:* hologramme *m*.

holograph ['hɔləgræf] **1.** *a.* (document, testament) (h)olographe. **2.** *n.* (h)olographie *f*; document, testament, (h)olographe.

hols [hɔlz] *n.pl.* *Sch:* *F:* vacances *fpl*.

holster ['houlstər] *n.* fonte *f* (de selle); étui *m* de revolver (de selle, de ceinturon).

holy ['houli] **1.** *a.* **(holier, holiest)** (*a*) saint, sacré; **the H. Trinity,** la Sainte Trinité; **the H. Ghost,** le Saint-Esprit; **the H. Father,** le Saint-Père; le Pape; **the H. Land,** la Terre Sainte; **h. war,** guerre sainte; **h. bread, water,** pain bénit, eau bénite; **h. place,** lieu saint; **h. ground,** terre sacrée; **to swear by all that is h.,** jurer ses grands dieux; *F:* **to have a h. fear of sth.,** avoir une crainte salutaire de qch; *P:* **h. cow! h. smoke! h. mackerel!** sapristi! (*b*) (*of pers.*) saint, pieux. **2.** *n.* **the H. of Holies,** le saint des saints.

holystone¹ ['houlistoun] *n.* *Nau:* brique *f* à pont, à briquer.

holystone² *v.tr.* *Nau:* briquer (le pont).

homage ['hɔmidʒ] *n.* hommage *m*; **to pay, do, h. to s.o.,** rendre, faire, hommage à qn.

homburg ['hɔmbəːg] *n.* **h. (hat),** chapeau mou; feutre *m* souple.

home¹ [houm] **I.** *n.* **1.** (*a*) chez-soi *m inv*; logis *m*; foyer (familial); intérieur *m*; **I've come straight from h.,** je viens (directement) de chez moi; **the Ideal H. Exhibition,** *U.S:* **the H. Show** = le Salon des Arts Ménagers; **to have a h. of one's own,** avoir un chez-soi; **television brings the world into your own h.,** la télévision vous apporte le monde à domicile; **to make one's h. in France,** s'établir en France; **it's a h. from h.,** on y est comme chez soi; (*b*) **there's no place like h.,** on n'est nulle part si bien que chez soi; **to leave h.,** (i) quitter la maison; (ii) partir (définitivement); quitter la famille; **to be away from h.,** être parti, absent, en voyage; **at h.,** (i) à la maison, chez soi; (ii) *Sp:* (jouer) sur le terrain du club; **to stay at h.,** rester à la maison; **how are things at h.?** comment ça va chez vous? **to find no one at h.,** trouver porte close; **to feel at h. with s.o.,** se sentir à l'aise avec qn; **I don't feel at h. here,** je me sens dépaysé ici; **he is at h. on, with, any topic,** tous les sujets lui sont familiers; **to make oneself at h.,** (i) s'installer (dans un fauteuil, etc.); (ii) faire comme chez soi. **2.** (*a*) patrie *f*; pays (natal); terre natale; **at h. and abroad,** dans notre pays et à l'étranger; **our policy at h. and abroad,** notre politique intérieure et extérieure; (*b*) **to take an example nearer h.,** sans aller chercher si loin; (*c*) **Greece, the h. of the arts,** la Grèce, patrie des beaux-arts. **3.** *Nat. Hist:* habitat *m* (d'un animal, d'une plante). **4.** asile *m*, hospice *m*; **old people's h.,** maison de retraite (pour les vieillards); **rest h.,** maison de repos; **nursing h.,** clinique *f*; **children's h.,** home *m* d'enfants. **5.** (*in games*) le but. **6.** (*a*) **h. life,** vie *f* de famille; **h. address,** adresse personnelle; **h. cooking,** (i) cuisine bourgeoise; (ii) cuisine familiale; **h.-brewed,** (bière) brassée à la maison; (cidre) de ménage; (*b*) **the H. Counties,** les comtés *mpl* avoisinant Londres; *Sp:* **h. side,** équipe *f* qui reçoit; **h. ground,** terrain *m* du club; **h. match,** match *m* à domicile; *Rac:* **the h. straight, stretch,** la dernière ligne droite; (*c*) **h. journey,** voyage *m* de retour; (*d*) (coup, etc.) qui porte; (question) qui touche au vif; **to tell s.o. a few h. truths,** dire son fait, ses quatre vérités, à qn; (*e*) **h. town,** ville natale; (*f*) **h. trade,** (i) commerce intérieur; (ii) cabotage national; **h. market,** marché intérieur; **h. products,** produits du pays; **h. news,** nouvelles *fpl* de l'intérieur; **the H. Guard** = la milice; **the H. Office** = le Ministère de l'Intérieur; **the H. Secretary** = le Ministre de l'Intérieur; (*g*) *Hist: Pol:* **h. rule,** autonomie *f*; indépendance législative. **II.** *adv.* **1.** (*a*) à la maison, chez soi, au logis; **to go, come, h.,** (i) rentrer (à la maison); (ii) (*after period of absence*) rentrer dans sa famille; **on his way h.,** en rentrant, en revenant, chez lui; **to bring work h.,** emporter du travail à faire à la maison; (*b*) au pays; **to go, come, h.,** retourner au pays; **to send s.o. h. (from abroad),** rapatrier qn; (*c*) **to be h.,** être de retour; **he's h. again!** il est de retour! **2.** (*a*) (*of bullet, etc.*) **the blow went h.,** le coup a porté; *F:* **his speech went h.,** son discours fit impression; **it will come h. to him some day,** il s'en rendra compte un jour; **to drive sth. h. to s.o.,** faire entrer qch. dans la tête à qn; (*b*) à fond; **to screw a piece h.,** visser, serrer, une pièce à bloc.

home² *v.* **1.** *v.i.* (*a*) retourner à son gîte; (*of pigeon*) revenir au colombier; (*b*) (*of aircraft*) revenir à, rallier, sa base; (*c*) (*of aircraft, missile, etc.*) **to h. on, towards . . .,** mettre le cap sur . . ., se diriger vers, sur . . . **2.** *v.tr.* diriger (un avion, un missile, etc., sur un point ou un objectif (déterminé) par radioguidage ou autoguidage. **homing 1.** *a.* (*a*) *Orn:* **h. pigeon,** pigeon voyageur; (*b*) *Tchn:* directionnel, de radioguidage; **h. device,** appareil, dispositif, autodirecteur; autodirecteur *m.* **2.** *n.* (*a*) *Nat.Hist:* retour *m* au gîte; (*of pigeon*) retour *m* au colombier; (*b*) (*of aircraft*) (radio-)ralliement *m*; **h. to base,** retour à la base.

home-baked ['houm'beikt] *a.* (pain, gâteau) fait, cuit, à la maison; (pain) de ménage.

homebird ['houmbə:d] *n. F:* (*pers.*) casanier, -ière.

homebody ['houmbɔdi] *n. esp. U.S: F:* casanier, -ière.

homecoming ['houmkʌmiŋ] **2.** *n.* retour *m* au foyer, à la maison, au pays.

homecraft ['houmkrɑ:ft] *n.* les arts ménagers.

homegrown ['houm'groun] *a.* (denrée) du pays; (produit) indigène; (vin) du cru; (fruits, légumes) du jardin.

homeland ['houmlænd] *n.* patrie *f.*

homeless ['houmlis] *a.* sans foyer; sans abri; **to be h.,** être sur le pavé; *n.pl.* **the h.,** les sans-logis *mpl.*

homeloving ['houmlʌviŋ] *a.* casanier, -ière.

homely ['houmli] *a.* **1.** (nourriture) simple, ordinaire; (goûts) bourgeois, modestes; (atmosphère) accueillante. **2.** *NAm:* (*of pers.*) plutôt laid; (visage) ingrat.

homemade [hou(m)'meid] *a.* (gâteau, vin) fait à la maison; (pain) de ménage.

Homer ['houmər] *Pr.n.m.* Homère.

Homeric [hou'merik] *a.* (poème, rire, etc.) homérique.

homesick ['houmsik] *a.* nostalgique; qui a le mal du pays.

homesickness ['houmsiknis] *n.* mal *m* du pays; nostalgie *f.*

homespun ['houmspʌn] **1.** *a.* (*a*) (tissu de laine) de fabrication domestique; (drap) fait, filé, à la maison; (toile) de ménage; (*b*) *O:* simple, sans apprêt. **2.** *n.* tissu fait à la maison; brouelle *f.*

homestead ['houmsted] *n.* **1.** ferme *f* (avec dépendances). **2.** *NAm:* bien *m* de famille; la concession statutaire de 160 acres.

homeward ['houmwəd] **1.** *a.* qui se dirige (i) vers sa maison, (ii) (*from abroad*) vers son pays, (*of ship*) vers son port d'attache; **h. voyage,** voyage *m* de retour. **2.** *adv.* = HOMEWARDS.

homeward-bound ['houmwəd'baund] *a. Nau:* (*navire*) à destination de son port d'attache, retournant au port, sur le retour; (cargaison) de retour; (*of pers., etc.*) **to be h.-b.,** rentrer chez soi.

homewards ['houmwədz] *adv.* vers sa maison, vers sa demeure; (*from abroad*) vers son pays; *Nau:* **cargo h.,** cargaison *f* de retour.

homework ['houmwərk] *n. Sch:* devoirs *mpl; F:* **it was plain that the chairman had not done his h.,** il était évident que le président n'avait pas préparé son discours.

homey ['houmi] *a.* accueillant.

homicidal [hɔmi'said(ə)l] *a.* homicide, meurtrier.

homicide¹ ['hɔmisaid] *n.* (*pers.*) homicide *mf.*

homicide² *n.* (*crime*) homicide *m*; *Jur:* **wilful, culpable, h.,** homicide volontaire; meurtre *m*; **justifiable h., h. in self defence,** homicide par légitime défense.

homily ['hɔmili] *n.* homélie *f.*

hominy ['hɔmini] *n. NAm: Cu:* maïs concassé et bouilli.

homo ['houmou] *n. F:* homosexuel *m*, pédé *m.*

homoeopath, *NAm:* **homeopath** ['houmioupæθ] *n.* homéopathe *mf.*

homoeopathic, *NAm:* **homeopathic** [houmiou'pæθik] *a.* homéopathique.

homoeopathy, *NAm:* **homeopathy** [houmi'ɔpəθi] *n.* homéopathie *f.*

homogeneity [homoudʒi'ni:iti] *n.* homogénéité *f.*

homogeneous [hɔmou'dʒi:niəs] *a.* homogène.

homogenize [hɔ'mɔdʒənaiz] *v.tr.* homogénéiser.

homograph ['hɔməgræf] *n.* homographe *m.*

homologous [hə'mɔləgəs] *a. Biol: Mth: etc:* homologue.

homonym ['hɔmənim] *n. Ling:* homonyme *m.*

homosexual [hɔmou'seksjuəl] *a.* & *n.* homosexuel, -uelle.

homosexuality [hɔmouseksju'æliti] *n.* homosexualité *f.*

hone¹ [houn] *n.* pierre *f* à aiguiser.

hone² *v.tr.* aiguiser, affiler.

honest ['ɔnist] *a.* **1.** (*a*) (*of pers.*) honnête, probe, droit; loyal, -aux (en affaires); **he has an h. face,** il a une figure d'honnête homme; (*b*) vrai, sincère, de bonne foi; **the h. truth,** la pure vérité, la vérité vraie; **an h. piece of work,** un travail consciencieux; *P:* **I couldn't help it, h.,** c'était plus fort que moi, vraiment; (*c*) juste, légitime; (moyens) légitimes; **to earn an h. living,** gagner honnêtement sa vie. **2.** (*a*) *in the phr.* **to make an h. woman of s.o.,** rendre l'honneur à une femme (en l'épousant); (*b*) *O:* (*usu. used condescendingly*) brave, honnête; **they are h. folk,** ce sont de braves gens. **-ly** *adv.* (*a*) honnêtement, loyalement; avec probité; de bonne foi; (*b*) sincèrement; **quite h.,** en toute sincérité; **I can h. say that . . .,** je peux dire franchement que . . ..

honesty ['ɔnisti] *n.* **1.** (*a*) honnêteté *f*, probité *f*; loyauté *f* (en affaires); *Prov:* **h. is the best policy,** l'honnêteté est la meilleure des tactiques; (*b*) véracité *f*, sincérité *f*, bonne foi; franchise *f* (d'un discours); **in all h.,** en toute sincérité. **2.** *Bot:* lunaire *f*; *F:* monnaie *f* du pape.

honey ['hʌni] *n.* **1.** (*a*) miel *m*; **clear, thick, h.,** miel liquide, grenu; **comb h.,** miel en rayon; **h. coloured,** miellé; (*b*) douceur *f* (de mots, de caresses); **he was all h.,** il a été tout sucre et tout miel. **2.** (*term of endearment*) chéri, *f.* chérie. **3.** *Z:* **h. bear,** kinkajou *m.*

honeybee ['hʌnibi:] *n. Ent:* abeille *f.*

honeybun(ch) ['hʌnibʌ(tʃ)] *n. U.S: F:* mon, ma, chéri(e), mon amour.

honeycomb¹ ['hʌnikoum] *n.* **1.** (*a*) rayon *m* de miel;

(*b*) gâteau *m* de miel; (*c*) *Tex:* nid d'abeilles *m*; *Geol:* **h. structure, formation,** structure, formation, alvéolée, alvéolaire. **2.** (*in metal*) chambre *f*, soufflure *f*.

honeycomb² **1.** *v.tr.* (*a*) cribler (de petits trous); (*b*) marquer en nid d'abeilles. **2.** *v.i.* (*of metal*) se chambrer, s'affouiller.

honeydew ['hʌnidju] *n.* **1.** miellée *f*, miellure *f* (exsudée par les plantes). **2. h. melon,** melon d'hiver.

honeymoon¹ ['hʌnimu:n] *n.* (*a*) lune *f* de miel; (*b*) **h. (trip),** voyage *m* de noces; **h. couple,** couple *m* en voyage de noces.

honeymoon² *v.i.* aller, être, en voyage de noces.

honeymooners ['hʌnimu:nəz] *n.pl. F:* couple *m* en voyage de noces.

honeypot ['hʌnipɔt] *n.* pot *m* à miel.

honeysuckle ['hʌnisʌkl] *n. Bot:* chèvrefeuille *m*.

honk¹ [hɔŋk] *n.* **1.** cri *m* de l'oie sauvage. **2.** *Aut:* coup *m* de klaxon.

honk² *v.* **1.** *v.i.* (*a*) (*of goose, seal, etc.*) pousser un cri; (*b*) (*of foghorn, etc.*) retentir. **2.** *v.tr.* **to h. the horn,** klaxonner.

honky-tonk ['hɔŋki'tɔŋk] *a. & n. NAm: F:* **h.-t. (joint),** bouge *m*, bastringue *m*, boui-boui *m*.

honor ['ɔnər] *n. & v.tr. NAm:* = HONOUR¹,².

honorable ['ɔnərəbl] *a. NAm:* = HONOURABLE.

honorarium, *pl.* **-ia, -iums** [ɔnə'rɛəriəm, -iə, -iəmz] *n.* honoraires *mpl* (d'un docteur, d'un avocat).

honorary ['ɔnərəri] *a.* **1.** (*a*) (emploi, service) honoraire, bénévole; (*b*) (président) d'honneur; **h. member,** membre *m* honoraire; associé, -ée (d'un cercle, etc.); **h. membership,** honorariat *m*; (*c*) *Mil:* **h. rank,** grade *m* honorifique; *Sch:* **h. degree,** grade honorifique, honoris causa. **2.** (*depending on honour*) (engagement, contrat) d'honneur.

honorific [ɔnə'rifik] *a.* (épithète) honorifique.

honour¹, *NAm:* **honor¹** ['ɔnər] *n.* honneur *m*. **1. in the seat of h.,** assis à la place d'honneur; **to put up a statue in h. of s.o.,** ériger une statue à la gloire de qn; **dinner in your h.,** dîner *m* en votre honneur; *Prov:* **h. to whom h. is due, h. where h. is due,** à tout seigneur tout honneur. **2.** (*privilege*) (*a*) **to consider it an h. to do sth.,** tenir à honneur de faire qch.; **to whom have I the h. of speaking?** à qui ai-je l'honneur de parler? (*b*) *Games:* **to have the h.,** (*at bowls*) avoir la boule; (*at golf*) avoir l'honneur. **3.** (*good name*) (*a*) **to come out of an affair with h.,** se tirer galamment d'une affaire; **to lose one's h.,** perdre son honneur; se déshonorer; **to make (it) a point of h. to do sth.,** mettre son (point d')honneur à faire qch.; **to be in h. bound to . . .,** être obligé par l'honneur à . . .; **man of h.,** homme d'honneur; **debt of h.,** dette *f* d'honneur; **to swear on one's h.,** jurer sur, par, sa foi; **to give one's word of h.,** engager sa parole (d'honneur); **on my (word of) h.!** je vous donne ma parole! sur l'honneur! **h. is satisfied,** l'honneur est satisfait; (*b*) l'honneur, la réputation (d'une femme). **4.** distinction *f* honorifique; *Sch:* **Honours list,** palmarès *m*; tableau *m* d'honneur. **5.** *Sch:* **honours course,** programme *n* d'études spécialisées au niveau de la licence; **honours degree** = licence. **6. honours,** (*a*) (*civilities*) **to receive s.o. with full honours,** recevoir qn avec tous les honneurs qui lui sont dus; **to do the honours (of one's house),** faire les honneurs (de sa maison); (*b*) *Cards:* (*bridge, etc.*) honneurs (as, roi, dame, et valet d'atout). **7.** (*of pers.*) (*a*) **to be an h. to one's country,** faire honneur à sa patrie; (*b*) **Your H., His H.,** Monsieur le juge, Monsieur le président. **8.** *Com:* **acceptance for h.,** acceptation *f* par intervention.

honour², *NAm:* **honor²** *v.tr.* **1.** (*a*) honorer (qn, la mémoire de qn); (*b*) **to h. s.o. with a title,** honorer qn d'un titre. **2.** faire honneur à (sa signature, *Com:* un effet); payer, accepter (un effet); **honoured bill,** traite payée, acquittée. **honoured,** *NAm:* **honored** *a.* honoré.

honourable, *NAm:* **honorable** ['ɔnərəbl] *a.* **1.** honorable; **he is an h. man,** c'est un homme d'honneur. **2. the H.,** *abbrev.* **the Hon.,** l'honorable . . .; **the H. member for Caithness,** l'honorable membre représentant Caithness. **-ably** *adv.* honorablement.

hooch [hu:tʃ] *n. P:* gnôle *f*, gniole *f*.

hood¹ [hud] *n.* **1.** *Cost:* (*a*) capuchon *m* (de moine, etc.); cagoule *f* (de pénitent); capuche *f* capeline *f* (de femme, d'enfant); (*b*) *Sch:* chaperon *m* (de toge universitaire) (= épitoge *f*); (*c*) *Ven:* chaperon (de faucon); *Harn:* camail *m* (de cheval); (*e*) *Nat.Hist:* casque *m* (de fleur, d'insecte); coiffe *f* (de cobra). **2.** (*a*) *Veh: etc:* **(folding) h.,** capote *f* (de voiture, de landau; (*b*) *Nau:* capot *m* (d'écoutille, etc.); (*c*) *Phot:* parasoleil *m* (d'objectif); (*d*) hotte *f* (de forge, etc.); chapeau *m* (de lampe); parapluie *m* (de cheminée); *El:* cloche *f* (d'isolateur); *NAm: Aut:* capot (du moteur).

hood² *v.tr. Ven:* chaperonner (un faucon). **hooded** *a.* (*a*) (*of pers.*) encapuchonné; **hooded men,** cagoulards *mpl*; (*b*) (vêtement) à capuchon; (oiseau, etc.) mantelé; (fleur) capuchonnée.

hood³ *n. NAm: P:* = HOODLUM.

hoodlum ['hu:dləm] *n. F:* (*a*) voyou *m*; (*b*) gangster *m*.

hoodoo ['hu:du:] *n.* (*a*) vaudou *m*; envoûtement *m*; (*b*) *F:* porteur, -euse, de malheur, de guigne; (*c*) *F:* malheur *m*, guigne *f*.

hoodwink ['hudwiŋk] *v.tr. F:* tromper (qn); donner le change à (qn); en mettre plein les yeux à (qn).

hooey ['hu:i] *F:* **1.** *n.* bêtises *fpl*. **2.** *int.* (tout ça c'est des) bêtises!

hoof¹, *pl.* **-s, hooves** [hu:f, -s, hu:vz] *n.* (*a*) sabot *m* (de cheval, etc.); (*b*) *F:* pied *m*.

hoof² *F:* **1.** (*a*) *v.tr. & i.* **to h. (it),** aller à pied, pedibus; (*b*) *v.i. NAm:* danser. **2.** *v.tr.* **to h. s.o. out,** chasser qn à coups de pied.

hoo-ha ['hu:ha:] *n. F:* **what's (all) the hoo-ha about?** qu'est-ce qu'il y a de cassé? qu'est-ce qui se passe?

hook¹ [huk] *n.* **1.** crochet *m*; croc *m*; griffe *f*; (*a*) **butcher's h.,** croc de boucherie; **chimney, pot, h.,** crémaillère *f*; **coat h.,** patère *f*; *Jp:* **to take, leave, the phone off the h.,** décrocher le téléphone, laisser le récepteur décroché; **h. nail,** (i) clou *m* à croc, à crochet; (ii) clou barbelé; (*b*) croc (pour happer qch.); *Av: Nau:* **arrester h.,** crosse *f* d'appontage; **by h. or (by) crook,** d'une manière ou d'une autre; coûte que coûte; (*c*) *Cost:* agrafe *f*; crochet de couturière; **h. and eye,** agrafe et œillet. **2.** *Fish:* hameçon *m*; **baited h.,** (i) hameçon garni; (ii) *F:* piège; attrape-nigaud *m inv*; *F:* **to let s.o. off the h.,** faire grâce à qn. **3.** (*a*) **(reaping) h.,** faucille *f*; **pruning h.,** émondoir *m*, ébranchoir *m*; (*b*) **(painter's) shave h.,** grattoir *m*, ébardoir *m*. **4.** *Mus:* crochet (d'une croche, etc.). **5.** (*a*) *Box:* **right, left, h.,** crochet du droit, du gauche; (*b*) *Golf: Cr:* coup tourné à gauche; *Golf:* coup tiré. **6.** cap *m*; pointe *f* de terre; coude *m* (d'une rivière); crochet (d'un chemin). **7.** *F:* **to sling one's h.,** décamper, plier bagage; *NAm:* **to get the h.,** être congédié, mis à la porte.

hook² *v.tr.* **1.** courber (le doigt). **2. to h. sth. (on, up) to sth.,** accrocher, suspendre, qch. à qch. **3. to h. (up) a dress,** agrafer une robe. **4.** (*a*) crocher, gaffer (un bateau, etc.); (*b*) *F:* voler (qch.), mettre le grappin sur (qch.). **5.** (*a*) *Fish:* prendre (un poisson) à l'hameçon; accrocher (un poisson); (*b*) *F:* attraper (un mari, etc.); (*c*) *F:* **to be hooked on sth.,** être entiché de qch.; **he got hooked on morphine,** il est devenu morphinomane. **6.** (*a*) **to h. the ball,** *Cr: etc:*

renvoyer (la balle) d'un coup tourné à gauche; *Golf:* faire un coup tiré; (*b*) *Box:* donner un coup en crochet à (son adversaire). **7.** *F:* **to h. it,** filer, décamper. **hooked** *a.* **1.** (bec, nez) crochu. **2.** muni de crochets, d'hameçons. **hook up** *v.tr & i.* (*a*) assembler (les pièces d'un appareil); installer (un appareil, etc.); (*b*) *P:* **to get hooked up,** se marier.

hookah ['hukə] *n.* narghileh *m,* narguilé *m.*

hooker [hukər] *n.* **1.** *Rugby Fb:* talonneur *m.* **2.** *P:* putain *f.*

hookey ['huki] *n.* = HOOKY.

hooknose ['huknouz] *n.* nez crochu.

hook-nosed ['huknouzd] *a.* au nez crochu.

hookup ['hukʌp] *n. Tchn:* liaison *f; W.Tel:* conjugaison de postes; postes conjugués.

hookworm ['hukwəːm] *n. Ann:* ankylostome *m.*

hooky ['huki] *n. esp. NAm: F:* **to play h.,** faire l'école buissonnière.

hooligan ['huːligən] *n.* vandale *m.*

hooliganism ['huːligənizm] *n.* vandalisme *m.*

hoop [huːp] *n.* **1.** (*a*) *Coop:* cercle *m,* cerceau *m* (de tonneau); (*b*) cercle, cerceau (de mât, etc.); anneau *m* (de moyeu, etc.); cerce *f* (de tamis, etc.); *Av:* cerce (de fuselage); (*c*) jante *f* (de roue); (*d*) cercle, vergette *f* (de tambour); (*e*) forme *f* (à fromage). **2.** cerceau (d'enfant, de cirque); (*in circus*) **paper h.,** ballon *m;* **to go through the h.,** (i) (*of dog, etc.*) passer à travers le cerceau; (ii) *F:* sauter le bâton; **to put s.o. through the h.,** rendre la vie dure à qn. **3.** (*a*) (*croquet*) arceau *m.*

hoop-la ['huːplɑː] *n.* **1.** (*at fairs*) jeu *m* des anneaux. **2.** *NAm: F:* brouhaha (joyeux); tapage *m.*

hoopoe ['huːpou] *n. Orn:* huppe *f* (d'Europe).

hoot¹ [huːt] *n.* **1.** (*a*) ululation *f,* (h)ululement *m* (de hibou); (*b*) huée *f* (de dérision, etc.); (*c*) *F:O:* **what a h.!** c'est à se tordre (de rire)! (*d*) *Aut:* coup *m* de klaxon; coup *m* de sifflet (d'une locomotive); coup de sirène (de bateau, d'une usine); mugissement *m* (d'une sirène). **2.** *F:* **not to care a h., not to give two hoots (about s.o., sth.),** se ficher éperdument (de qn, de qch.).

hoot² **1.** *v.i.* (*a*) (*of owl*) (h)ululer, huer; (*b*) (*of pers.*) huer; *F:* **to h. with laughter,** rire aux éclats; (*c*) *Aut:* klaxonner; (*d*) (*of locomotive, etc.*) siffler; lancer un coup de sifflet; (*of siren*) mugir; (*of ship*) faire marcher la sirène. **2.** *v.tr.* huer, conspuer (qn); siffler (une pièce de théâtre). **hooting** *n.* (*a*) (h)ululement *m* (de hibou); (*b*) (*of pers.*) huées *fpl;* (*c*) *Aut:* coups *mpl* de klaxon.

hootenanny ['huːtnæni] *n. NAm:* réunion *f* de chanteurs folkloriques.

hooter ['huːtər] *n.* (*a*) *Nau: Ind:* sirène *f;* sifflet *m;* (*b*) *Aut: etc:* klaxon *m;* (*c*) *P:* nez *m,* trompette *f.*

Hoover¹ ['huːvər] *n. R.t.m:* aspirateur *m.*

hoover² *v.tr. F:* passer l'aspirateur sur (un plancher, etc.).

hooves. *see* HOOF¹.

hop¹ [hɔp] *n. Bot:* houblon *m; Brew:* **hops,** le houblon; **h. grower,** houblonnier *m;* **h. field,** houblonnière *f;* **h. picker,** cueilleur, -euse, de houblon.

hop² *v.* (**hopped** [hɔpt]) **1.** *v.tr.* houblonner (la bière). **2.** *v.i.* cueillir le houblon. **hopping** *n.* **1.** cueillette *f* de houblon. **2.** houblonnage *m* (de la bière).

hop³ *n.* **1.** (*a*) petit saut; sautillement *m;* (*b*) saut à clochepied; *Sp:* **h., skip and jump,** triple saut; *F:* **to catch s.o. on the h.,** prendre qn au pied levé; **to keep s.o. on the h.,** ne pas laisser chômer qn; (*c*) *Av:* étape *f.* **2.** *F:* (*dance*) sauterie *f.*

hop⁴ **1.** *v.i.* (*a*) sauter, sautiller; **to h. on one leg,** sauter à cloche-pied; *F:* **to h. off,** filer; ficher le camp; (*b*) *F:* danser; (*c*) **to h. out of bed,** sauter à bas de son lit; **to h. on a bus,** sauter dans un autobus. **2.** *v.tr. F:* sauter (un obstacle); *F:* **to h. it,** filer, ficher le camp; **h. it!** allez, ouste! va-t'-en! **3.** *v.tr. esp. U.S: F:* **to h. a ride (on a train),** voyager (en chemin de fer) sans payer. **hopping** **1.** *n.* sautillement *m,* sauts *mpl.* **2.** *adv. F:* **to be h. mad,** être fou de colère.

hope¹ [houp] *n.* **1.** (*a*) espérance *f,* espoir *m;* **to be full of h.,** avoir bon espoir; **to lose h.,** perdre (l')espoir; **to h. against h.,** espérer contre toute espérance; **to put one's h. in the future,** compter sur l'avenir; **to set one's hopes on s.o., on sth.,** mettre tout son espoir en qn, en qch.; *NAm:* **h. chest,** trousseau *m* (de mariage); *Geog:* **the Cape of Good H.,** le cap de Bonne Espérance; (*b*) **in the h. of . . .,** dans l'attente de . . ., dans l'espoir de . . . **2. my last h.,** mon dernier espoir; ma dernière planche de salut; **to have hopes of sth., of doing sth.,** avoir qch. en vue; avoir l'espoir de faire qch.; **to live, be, in hopes that . . .,** caresser l'espoir que . . .; *Iron:* **what a h.! some h.!** si vous comptez là-dessus!

hope² **1.** *v.i.* espérer; **we must h. against h.,** il faut espérer contre toute espérance; **to h. for sth.,** espérer qch.; **hoped-for victory,** victoire espérée, désirée. **2.** *v.tr.* (*a*) **I h. and pray, that . . .,** j'espère avec confiance que . . .; **I h. to see you again,** j'espère vous revoir; *Corr* **hoping to hear from you,** dans l'attente de vos nouvelles; (*b*) **I h. your brother is better,** j'espère que votre frère va mieux; **I h. you may be right,** je souhaite que vous ayez raison.

hopeful ['houpf(u)l] *a.* **1.** plein d'espoir; **we must remain h.,** il faut continuer d'espérer; **to be h. that . . .,** avoir bon espoir que . . .. **2.** (*a*) (avenir, carrière) qui promet; *n. F:* (*usu. Iron:*) **young h.,** l'espoir de la famille; (*b*) **the situation looks more h.,** la situation est plus encourageante. **-fully** *adv.* **1.** (parler, attendre, etc.) avec bon espoir, avec optimisme. **2.** *F:* **h. the sun will shine tomorrow,** espérons qu'il fera du soleil demain.

hopefulness ['houpf(u)lnis] *n.* **1.** bon espoir; confiance *f.* **2.** bons présages (de la situation, etc.).

hopeless ['houplis] *a.* **1.** sans espoir; désespéré; **h. grief,** douleur *f* inconsolable. **2.** (*a*) qui ne permet aucun espoir; (passion, etc.) incurable; (situation) désespérée; (projet) qui n'a aucune chance de réussir; (*of patient, etc.*) **to be in a h. condition,** être dans un état désespéré; **to give sth. up as h.,** renoncer à faire qch.; **it is h. to try to . . .,** on aurait beau essayer de . . .; (*b*) *F:* (ivrogne) incorrigible; **you're h.!** vous êtes impossible! **-ly** *adv.* **1.** (vivre) sans espoir. **2.** (vaincu) irrémédiablement; (amoureux) sans retour; **h. drunk,** soûl perdu.

hopelessness ['houplisnis] *n.* **1.** désespoir *m.* **2.** état désespéré (d'une situation).

hophead ['hɔphed] *n. U.S: P:* toxicomane *mf;* drogué, -ée.

hopper ['hɔpər] *n.* **1.** (*a*) (*pers., animal*) sauteur, -euse; (*b*) *F:* sauterelle *f.* **2.** (*a*) trémie *f,* huche *f,* hotte *f* (de moulin); (*b*) *Agr:* semoir *m;* (*c*) *Husb:* mangeoire *f;* trémie (pour poulets, etc.). **3.** *Nau:* **h. barge,** marie-salope *f.pl.* maries-salopes; *Rail:* **h. car,** wagon-trémie *m.*

hopscotch ['hɔpskɔtʃ] *n. Games:* marelle *f.*

Horace ['hɔris] *Pr.n.m.* Horace.

horde [hɔːd] *n.* horde *f* (de barbares, etc.).

horizon [hə'raiz(ə)n] *n.* horizon *m;* (*a*) **on the h.,** à l'horizon; **this discovery opens up new horizons,** cette découverte ouvre de nouveaux horizons; (*b*) *Astr: Av: Nau:* **celestial h.,** horizon astronomique; *Av:* **artificial h.,** horizon artificiel; **h. bar,** barre *f* d'horizon (du directeur de vol).

horizontal [hɔri'zɔnt(ə)l] **1.** *a.* horizontal, -aux; *Gym:* **h. bar,** barre *f* fixe; *U.S:* **h. increase in salaries**

of 10%, augmentation *f* uniforme de 10% sur toutes les rétributions. **2.** *n.* horizontale *f.* **-ally** *adv.* horizontalement.

hormonal [hɔː'moun(ə)l] *a. Physiol:* hormonal, -aux.

hormone ['hɔːmoun] *n. Physiol:* hormone *f.*

horn¹ [hɔːn] *n.* **1.** (*a*) corne *f* (de bétail, de bélier, etc.); bois *mpl* (d'un cerf); (*b*) *Nat. Hist:* antenne *f* (de cerf-volant); corne (de limaçon); aigrette *f* (de hibou); *F:* **to draw in one's horns,** (i) rentrer les cornes; (ii) restreindre son ardeur, rabattre (de) ses prétentions; (*c*) corne (de la lune, etc.); branche *f* (d'un estuaire); *Nau:* oreille *f* (de taquet); (*d*) *Log:* corne (d'un dilemme); (*e*) *Geog:* **Cape H., the H.,** le cap Horn; **the h. of Africa,** la péninsule des Somalis. **2.** (*horny matter*) corne; (*a*) **h. comb,** peigne *m* en corne; (*b*) *Farr: etc:* corne (de sabot de cheval, etc.). **3.** *Mus:* (*a*) cor *m*, cornet *m*; **French h.,** cor d'harmonie; **hunting h.,** trompe *f* de chasse; **h. player,** cor, corniste *m*; **to sound, blow, the h.,** sonner du cor; (*b*) **English h.,** cor anglais. **4.** *Aut:* klaxon *m*; **to sound one's h.,** klaxonner. **5.** pavillon *m* (de haut-parleur, etc.). **6.** *Lit:* **h. of plenty,** corne d'abondance.

horn² **1.** *v.tr.* écorner (un bœuf). **2.** *v.tr.* (*of animals*) encorner (qn); donner un coup de corne à (qn). **3.** *v.i. F:* **to h. in,** intervenir sans façon (**on a conversation,** dans une conversation). **horned** [hɔːnd; *Lit:* 'hɔːnid] *a.* (animal) à cornes; (serpent, etc.) cornu.

hornbeam ['hɔːnbiːm] *n.* charme *m*; hêtre blanc.

hornbill ['hɔːnbil] *n. Orn:* calao *m.*

hornet ['hɔːnit] *n. Ent:* frelon *m*; **to stir up a hornets nest,** tomber dans un guêpier.

hornpipe ['hɔːnpaip] *n. Danc: Mus:* matelote *f.*

horn-rimmed ['hɔːnrimd] *a.* (lunettes) à monture en corne.

horny ['hɔːni] *a* (*a*) corné; (bec, etc.) de corne, en corne; (*b*) (*of hand, etc.*) calleux; **to grow h.,** se racornir; (*c*) *P:* (i) lascif; (ii) (sexuellement) excité.

horology [hɔ'rɔlədʒi] *n.* **1.** horlogerie *f.* **2.** horométrie *f.*

horoscope ['hɔrəskoup] *n.* horoscope *m*; **to cast s.o.'s h.,** faire, dresser, l'horoscope de qn.

horrendous [hɔ'rendəs] *a. F:* terrible, affreux, horrible.

horrible ['hɔrəbl] *a.* horrible, affreux, atroce; (bruit) épouvantable; (temps) abominable; **how h.!** quelle horreur! **-ily** *adv.* horriblement, affreusement.

horrid ['hɔrid] *a.* **1.** horrible, affreux; **h. sight,** chose *f* horrible à voir. **2.** *F:* méchant; **to be h. to s.o.,** être méchant envers qn; **to say h. things about s.o.,** dire des méchancetés de qn; **don't be h.!** (i) ne dites pas des horreurs pareilles! (ii) ne faites pas le vilain! **-ly** *adv.* **1.** affreusement. **2.** *F:* (se conduire) méchamment.

horrific [hɔ'rifik] *a.* horrifique; horrible.

horrify ['hɔrifai] *v.tr.* (*a*) horrifier (qn); faire horreur à (qn); **to be horrified,** être horrifié; être saisi d'horreur; (*b*) scandaliser (qn). **horrifying** *a.* horrifiant.

horror ['hɔrər] *n.* **1.** horreur *f*; **paralysed with h.,** glacé d'horreur; **to my h.,** à ma grande horreur; **to have a h. of s.o., of sth., of doing sth.,** avoir horreur de qn, de qch., de faire qch.; **h. film,** film *m* d'épouvante. **2.** (*a*) chose horrible, affreuse; horreur; **Chamber of Horrors,** Chambre *f* des Horreurs (d'un musée); (*b*) **that child's a little h.,** cet enfant est un petit monstre; (*c*) *F:* **to have the horrors,** (i) grelotter de peur; (ii) être en proie au délire alcoolique; **it gives me the horrors,** cela me donne le frisson.

horrorstricken, horrorstruck ['hɔrəstrik(ə)n, -strʌk] *a.* saisi d'horreur; glacé, frappé, d'horreur.

horse¹ [hɔːs] *n.* **1.** (*a*) cheval, -aux *m*; **draught h.,** cheval de trait; **saddle h.,** cheval de selle; monture *f*; **one-h., two-h., carriage,** voiture *f* à un cheval, à deux chevaux; *F:* **one-h. town,** petite ville de rien du tout; bled *m*; **to mount a h.,** monter à cheval; monter un cheval; **to fall of one's h.,** tomber de cheval; **to get on one's high h.,** monter sur ses grands chevaux; *F:* **to eat like a h.,** manger comme un ogre; **I could eat a h.!** j'ai une faim de loup! **h. blanket, rug,** couverture *f* de cheval; **h. collar,** collier *m* de cheval; *F:* **h. doctor,** vétérinaire *m*; **h. laugh,** gros rire bruyant; **h. sense,** gros bon sens; **h. dealer, trader,** maquignon *m*; **h. trading,** maquignonnage *m*; **h. fair,** foire *f* aux chevaux; **h. show,** concours *m* hippique; **h. box,** (i) *Rail:* wagon *m* à chevaux; wagon-écurie *m, pl.* wagons-écuries; (ii) *Veh:* van *m*; (*b*) *Breed:* cheval mâle, cheval entier; **stud h.,** étalon *m*; **to take a mare to h.,** faire couvrir une jument; (*c*) *Ich:* **sea h.,** hippocampe *m*; (*d*) *Bot:* **h. chestnut,** marron *m* d'Inde; (*e*) **white horses,** vagues *fpl* à crêtes d'écume; moutons *mpl.* **2.** *coll. Mil:* cavalerie *f*; troupes montées; **a regiment of five hundred h.,** un régiment de cinq cents chevaux; **h. artillery,** artillerie montée; **the (Royal) H. Guards,** la Garde du corps (à cheval). **3.** (*a*) **wooden h.,** cheval de bois; **rocking h.,** cheval à bascule; (*b*) *Gym:* **(vaulting) h.,** cheval(-sautoir) *m*; **pommel h.,** cheval d'arçons. **4.** (*a*) **clothes h.,** (i) chevalet pour linge; séchoir *m*; (ii) *F: Pej:* élégant, -ante; (*b*) *Tchn:* chevalet, tréteau *m*, chèvre *f.* **5.** *Nau:* marchepied *m.* **6.** *NAm: Cin: T.V:* **h. opera,** western *m.*

horse² *v.i. NAm: F:* **to h. around,** faire des bêtises.

horseback ['hɔːsbæk] *n.* **on h.,** à (dos de) cheval; **to ride on h.,** aller à cheval.

horsebreaker ['hɔːsbreikər] *n.* dresseur, -euse, de chevaux.

horse-drawn ['hɔːsdrɔːn] *a.* tiré par des chevaux; **h.-d. vehicle,** véhicule attelé.

horseflesh ['hɔːsfleʃ] *n.* **1.** chair *f*, viande *f*, de cheval. **2.** *coll.* chevaux *mpl.*

horsefly ['hɔːsflai] *n. Ent:* taon *m.*

horsehair ['hɔːshɛər] *n.* crin *m* (de cheval); *Tex:* tissu *m* de crin; **h. mattress,** matelas *m* de crin.

horseman, *pl.* **-men** ['hɔːsmən] *n.m.* cavalier, écuyer; **to be a good h.,** bien monter à cheval; être bon cavalier.

horsemanship ['hɔːsmənʃip] *n.* équitation *f*; l'art *m* de monter à cheval.

horsemeat ['hɔːsmiːt] *n.* viande *f* de cheval.

horseplay ['hɔːsplei] *n.* jeu brutal, jeu de main(s); **no h.!** doucement! pas de brutalité!

horsepower ['hɔːspauər] *n. Mec:* (i) puissance *f* en chevaux; (ii) *Meas:* cheval-vapeur *m, pl.* chevaux-vapeur; **brake h., actual h.,** puissance effective en chevaux; puissance au frein.

horseradish ['hɔːsrædiʃ] *n. Bot:* raifort *m*, cran *m*; *Cu:* **h. sauce,** raifort à la crème.

horseshoe ['hɔː(s)ʃuː] *n.* (*a*) fer *m* à cheval; (*b*) *attrib.* (table, broche, etc.) en (forme de) fer à cheval.

horsetail ['hɔːsteil] *n.* queue *f* de cheval.

horsewhip¹ ['hɔːs(h)wip] *n.* cravache *f.*

horsewhip² *v.tr.* (**horsewhipped**) cravacher, sangler (qn); administrer une cravachée à (qn).

horsewoman, *pl.* **-women** ['hɔːswumən, -wimin] *n.f.* amazone, cavalière, écuyère.

horsy ['hɔːsi] *a.* (*also* **horsey**) **1.** chevalin. **2.** (*of pers.*) (*a*) hippomane; **she's terribly h.,** elle ne parle que chevaux; (*b*) **h. face,** figure chevaline.

horticultural [hɔːti'kʌltʃər(ə)l] *n.* (outil) horticole, d'horticulture; **h. show,** exposition *f* d'horticulture.

horticulture ['hɔːtikʌltjər] *n.* horticulture *f.*

horticulturist [hɔːti'kʌltjərist] *n.* horticulteur *m.*

hose¹ [houz] *n.* **1.** *coll. Cost: Com:* bas *mpl*; **half h.,**

chaussettes *fpl* (d'hommes). **2.** (*pl.* **hoses**) (*a*) *Tchn:* tuyau *m* souple; boyau *m*; manche *f* (d'arrosage, etc.); **fire h.,** tuyau de pompe à incendie; **garden h.,** tuyau d'arrosage; **h. reel,** chariot *m* à tuyaux; (*b*) *Mec.E:* **(flexible) h.,** tuyau flexible, durite *f*; **air h.,** tuyau d'air flexible.

hose² *v.tr.* (*a*) laver (qch.) à grande eau; **to h. (down) the car,** laver la voiture au jet d'eau; (*b*) arroser (un gazon, etc.) (au jet d'eau).

hosepipe ['houzpaip] *n.* tuyau *m*, flexible *m* (de lavage, d'incendie, etc.).

hosier ['houziər] *n.* bonnetier, -ière.

hosiery ['houziəri] *n.* **h. (trade),** bonneterie *f*; **h. counter, department,** rayon *m* des bas et chaussettes.

hospice ['hɔspis] *n.* hospice *m.*

hospitable [hɔs'pitəbl] *a.* hospitalier; accueillant. **-ably** *adv.* avec hospitalité.

hospital ['hɔspit(ə)l] *n.* **1.** hôpital, -aux *m*; **to send s.o. to h.,** hospitaliser qn; **teaching h.** = centre hospitalier universitaire; (*in wartime*) **Red Cross h.,** hôpital auxiliaire; **h. train,** train *m* sanitaire; **h. ship,** navire-hôpital *m*, *pl.* navires-hôpitaux. **2.** (*as Pr.n.*) **Greenwich H.,** l'Hospice de Greenwich (pour les invalides de la marine).

hospitality [hɔspi'tæliti] *n.* hospitalité *f*; *F:* **to enjoy His, Her, Majesty's h.,** faire de la prison.

hospitalization [hɔspitəlai'zeiʃ(ə)n] *n.* hospitalisation *f* (des malades).

hospitalize ['hɔspitəlaiz] *v.tr.* hospitaliser (un malade).

host¹ [houst] *n.* (*a*) *A: & Poet:* armée *f*, multitude *f*, foule *f*; (*b*) **a (whole) h.,** (toute) une armée (de domestiques, etc.).

host² *n.* (*a*) hôte *m*; (*b*) hôtelier *m*, aubergiste *m*; **to reckon without one's h.,** compter sans son hôte; (*c*) *Biol:* hôte.

host³ *v.tr.* (*a*) *esp. U.S:* recevoir (qn), donner l'hospitalité à (qn); (*b*) *T.V: etc:* animer (un programme, etc.).

host⁴ *n. Ecc:* hostie *f.*

hostage ['hɔstidʒ] *n.* otage *m*; **as (a) h.,** en otage, pour otage.

hostel ['hɔstəl] *n.* (*a*) foyer *m* (sous la direction d'une œuvre sociale, etc.); (*b*) **youth h.,** auberge *f* de jeunesse.

hosteller ['hɔstələr] *n.* **(youth) h.,** ajiste *mf.*

hostelling ['hɔstəliŋ] *n.* **(youth) h.,** ajisme *m.*

hostess ['houstis] *n.f.* (*a*) hôtesse; (*b*) hôtelière, aubergiste *f*; (*c*) *Av:* **air h.,** hôtesse de l'air.

hostile ['hɔstail] **1.** *a.* (*a*) hostile (acte) d'hostilité; (*b*) hostile, opposé (**to,** à); ennemi (**to,** de); **to be h. to s.o.,** être hostile à, envers, qn. **2.** *n. U.S:* ennemi *m.*

hostility [hɔs'tiliti] *n.* **1.** hostilité *f* (**to,** contre); **to feel no h. towards s.o.,** n'avoir aucune animosité contre qn. **2. hostilities,** hostilités.

hot¹ [hɔt] *a.* **(hotter, hottest) 1.** (*a*) chaud; (soleil) ardent; (feu) vif; **boiling h.,** bouillant; **burning h.,** brûlant; **to be very h.,** (*of thg*) être très chaud; être brûlant; (*of pers.*) avoir très chaud; (*of weather*) faire très chaud; **it was a h. day,** il faisait chaud; **to get, grow, h.,** (i) (*of thg*) devenir chaud, chauffer; (ii) (*pers.*) commencer à avoir chaud; (iii) (*of weather*) commencer à faire chaud; (iv) (*of discussion, contest*) s'échauffer; **to keep a dish h.,** tenir un plat au chaud; *Comest:* **h. dog,** petit pain fourré d'une saucisse chaude; hot-dog *m*; **h. water bottle,** bouillotte *f*; *F:* **to be in h. water,** être dans le pétrin; **to get into h. water,** s'attirer, se créer, des ennuis; **h.-air engine,** moteur *m*, machine *f*, à air chaud; *F:* **he was letting off a lot of h. air,** il débitait des platitudes; *F:* **h. spot,** (i) boîte *f* de nuit; (ii) coin *m*, endroit *m*, névralgique; *adv.* **to blow h. and cold,** (i) souffler le chaud et le froid; (ii) parler, agir, de façons contradictoires; *F:* **to get all h. and bothered,** s'échauffer; se faire du mauvais sang; *F:* **to get h. under the collar,** (i) être embarrassé; (ii) se mettre en colère; **how are you?—not so h.!** comment ça va?—ce n'est pas terrible, fameux! (*b*) brûlant, cuisant; **h. flush,** rougeur brûlante, vive rougeur; **h. tears,** larmes cuisantes; (*c*) (poivre) cuisant; (moutarde) piquante; (assaisonnement) épicé; *F:* **he's h. stuff at tennis,** au tennis c'est un as; (*d*) (*of colour*) trop vif. **2.** (*a*) **cakes h. from the oven,** gâteaux *mpl* sortant du four; **news h. from the press,** nouvelles *fpl* sortant tout droit de la presse; nouvelles de la dernière heure; (*b*) **to be h. on the scent, on the trail,** être sur la bonne piste (d'un animal, d'un criminel); *Games:* **you're getting h.,** tu brûles. **3.** (*a*) violent, chaleureux; **to have a h. temper,** s'emporter facilement; **h. words,** paroles violentes; (*b*) **to be in h. pursuit of s.o.,** poursuivre qn de près; (*c*) *Turf:* **h. favourite,** grand favori; **h. tip,** tuyau *m* increvable; (*d*) *F:* **h. rod,** voiture gonflée; bolide *m.* **4.** *F:* (*a*) **the place was getting too h. for me,** je me trouvais dans un véritable guêpier; **to make things, it, too h. for s.o.,** rendre la vie intolérable à qn; *U.S:* **h. seat,** (i) *F:* chaise électrique; (ii) situation *f* difficile; (*b*) (travail) urgent, prioritaire; *Tp:* **h. line,** ligne directe; (*U.S.A. to Kremlin*) ligne rouge; (*Élysée to Kremlin*) ligne verte; (*c*) (*of stolen property, etc.*) recherché par la police; (*d*) *Fin:* **h. money,** capitaux flottants, errants. **5.** *Atom.Ph:* radio-actif. **-ly** *adv.* **1.** (répondre, protester) vivement, avec chaleur. **2.** (poursuivre) avec acharnement, de près; **h. contested,** chaudement disputé.

hot² *F:* **1.** *v.tr.* (*a*) **to h. sth. up,** chauffer qch.; (*b*) *Aut:* gonfler (un moteur); (*c*) **to h. up the pace,** forcer l'allure. **2.** *v.i.* (*of campaign, etc.*) s'échauffer; (*of affair, etc.*) chauffer; **things are beginning to h. up,** l'affaire se corse.

hotbed ['hɔtbed] *n.* **1.** *Hort:* couche *f* (de fumier, de terreau). **2.** foyer (ardent) (de corruption, d'intrigue).

hot-blooded ['hɔt'blʌdid] *a.* emporté, ardent, passionné; (race) au sang fougueux.

hotchpotch ['hɔtʃpɔtʃ] *n.* **2.** mélange confus; méli-mélo *m*, *pl.* mélis-mélos.

hotel [(h)ou'tel] *n.* hôtel *m*; **private, residential, h.** = pension *f* de famille; **h. keeper,** hôtelier, -ière; **the h. trade,** l'industrie hôtelière; l'hôtellerie *f.*

hôtelier [(h)ou'teliei] *n.* hôtelier *m.*

hotfoot ['hɔt'fut] *adv.* (s'en aller, arriver) à toute vitesse, en (toute) hâte.

hothead ['hɔthed] *n.* exalté, -ée; tête ardente; tête chaude, emballée.

hotheaded ['hɔt'hedid] *a.* **1.** exalté, impétueux, à la tête chaude. **2.** emporté, violent; **he's h.,** il est vif, prompt, à s'irriter.

hothouse ['hɔthaus] *n.* **1.** serre chaude; **h. plant,** (i) plante *f* de serre chaude; (ii) *F:* (*pers.*) plante de serre. **2.** = HOTBED 2.

hotplate ['hɔtpleit] *n. Dom.Ec:* (*a*) plaque chauffante; (*b*) chauffe-plats *m inv.*

hotpot ['hɔtpɔt] *n. Cu:* ragoût de viande aux pommes de terre, cuit à l'étuvée.

hotshot ['hɔtʃɔt] *U.S: F:* **1.** *a.* magnifique, terrible. **2.** *n.* (*pers.*) as *m*, crack *m.*

hotspur ['hɔtspə:r] *n. F:* tête chaude; cerveau brûlé.

hot-tempered ['hɔt'tempəd] *a.* colérique, coléreux; vif.

Hottentot ['hɔt(ə)ntɔt] *Ethn:* **1.** *a.* hottentot. **2.** *n.* Hottentot, -ote.

hound¹ [haund] *n.* (*a*) chien *m*; (*b*) *Ven:* chien de meute; chien courant; braque *m*; **the pack of hounds, the hounds,** la meute, l'équipage *m*; **master of hounds,** maître *m* d'équipage; grand veneur; **to ride to**

hounds, chasser (le renard); chasser à courre; (*c*) *Sp:* coureur *m*, poursuivant *m* (dans un rallye-paper); (*d*) *F: Pej:* (*pers.*) canaille *f*.

hound² *v.tr.* **1.** (*a*) *Ven:* chasser (le gibier) au chien courant; (*b*) **to h. s.o. down,** poursuivre qn avec acharnement, traquer qn; **hounded from place to place,** pourchassé d'un endroit à l'autre; **he was hounded out of France,** il fut chassé de France. **2. to h. the dogs on,** exciter les chiens à la poursuite.

hour ['auər] *n.* heure *f*. **1. an h. and a half,** une heure et demie; **half an h.,** une demi-heure; **a quarter of an h.,** un quart d'heure; **h. by h.,** d'heure en heure; **to pay s.o. by the h.,** payer qn à l'heure; **to be paid £2 an h.,** être payé £2 de l'heure; *Ind: etc:* **output per h.,** puissance *f* horaire; **to take hours over sth.,** mettre des heures à faire qch.; **eight-h. day,** journée *f* (de travail) de huit heures; **office hours,** heures de bureau; **to work long hours,** faire de longues journées (de travail); (*b*) **h. hand,** petite aiguille (de montre, de pendule). **2.** (*a*) l'heure, le moment; **in the h. of need, of death,** à l'heure du besoin, de la mort; **his h. has come,** son heure est venue; (*b*) **the small hours,** les premières heures (après minuit); **well on into the small hours,** bien avant, très avant, dans la nuit; **to keep late hours,** (i) rentrer à des heures indues; (ii) se coucher très tard; (*c*) *Ecc:* **Book of Hours,** livre *m* d'Heures.

hourglass ['auəglɑːs] *n.* sablier *m*.

hourly ['auəli] **1.** *a.* (*a*) de toutes les heures; (service de trains, etc.) à chaque heure; **three-h. doses,** une dose toutes les trois heures; (*b*) (débit, rendement) par heure, horaire; (salaire) à l'heure; (*c*) continuel. **2.** *adv.* (*a*) toutes les heures; d'heure en heure; (*b*) constamment, continuellement.

house¹, *pl.* **houses** [haus, 'hauziz] *n.* **1.** maison *f*; **detached h.,** maison séparée; **semi-detached houses,** maisons jumelles, jumelées; **country h.,** château *m*; *NAm:* **apartment h.,** immeuble divisé en appartements; **private h.,** maison particulière; **the White H.,** la Maison Blanche; **we invited him to our h.,** nous l'avons invité à venir chez nous; **from h. to h.,** de porte en porte; **to keep h. for s.o.,** tenir, diriger, la maison de qn; **to keep open h.,** tenir table ouverte; **dolls' h.,** maison de poupée; **the son, daughter, of the h.,** le fils, la fille, de la maison; **to move h.,** déménager; **h. of cards,** château de cartes; **h. property,** immeubles *mpl*; **h. agent,** agent immobilier; **h. painter,** peintre *m* en bâtiments; peintre décorateur. **2.** (*a*) **the h. of God,** la maison de Dieu; **h. of prayer, of worship,** église *f*, temple *m*; **the H. of Commons,** la Chambre des Communes; *Parl:* **bill before the H.,** loi *f* en cours de vote; (*b*) *Com: etc:* maison; **publishing h.,** maison d'édition; (*in restaurant*) **h. speciality,** *F:* **h. special,** spécialité *f* de la maison; **to have a drink on the h.,** prendre une consommation aux frais du patron; *Nau:* **h. flag,** pavillon *m* d'armateur, de compagnie (de navigation); (*c*) *Sch:* (i) (*in boarding school*) maison d'élèves; (ii) (*in day school*) groupe *m* d'élèves (qui rivalise avec un autre); (*d*) *Med:* **h. surgeon, physician,** interne *m* en chirurgie, en médecine (d'un hôpital); (*e*) *Astrol:* maison. **3.** (*a*) **hen h.,** poulailler *m*; (*b*) *Tchn:* cabine *f* (d'une grue); *Nau:* rouf *m* (sur le pont); kiosque *m* (de la barre, etc.). **4.** (*a*) (*members of household*) maison; **the whole h. was down with influenza,** toute la maison avait la grippe; *Parl: etc:* (*of assembly*) **to make a h.,** être en nombre; (*b*) famille *f*, maison, dynastie *f*; **the H. of Stuart, of Bourbon,** les Stuarts *mpl*, les Bourbons *mpl*. **5.** *Th:* salle *f*, auditoire *m*, assistance *f*; **a full h.,** une salle pleine; **'h. full'**, 'complet'; **to play to an empty h.,** jouer devant les banquettes (vides); *Cin:* **the first h.,** la première séance.

house² [hauz] *v.tr.* (*a*) loger, héberger (qn); pourvoir au logement de (la population); (*b*) faire rentrer (les troupeaux); rentrer, engranger (le blé); (*c*) mettre à l'abri, à couvert (une locomotive, etc.); emmagasiner (un avion, etc.); *Nau:* rentrer (une voile). **housing** *n.* **1.** (*a*) logement *m* (de personnes); **the h. problem, shortage,** la crise du logement; (*b*) rentrée *f* (des troupeaux, du blé, etc.); emmagasinage *m* (du blé); (*c*) mise à l'abri, à couvert (d'une locomotive, etc.); *Nau:* rentrée (d'une voile). **2.** *Nau:* partie *f* (du mât) au-dessous du pont; partie (du beaupré) en dedans de l'étrave. **3.** (*a*) *Carp:* logement, ruinure *f* (d'une poutre, etc.); (*b*) *Mec.E: etc:* bâti *m*, cage *f* (d'un laminoir); coquille *f* (de moteur); carter *m* (de l'engrenage); *Aut:* carter (du différentiel).

houseboat ['hausbout] *n.* péniche (aménagée).

housebound ['hausbaund] *a.* (*of invalid*) obligé de garder la maison; immobilisé à la maison.

housebreaker ['hausbreikər] *n.* **1.** voleur *m* avec effraction; cambrioleur *m*. **2.** *Const:* démolisseur *m*.

housebreaking ['hausbreikiŋ] *n.* **1.** cambriolage *m*. **2.** démolition *f*.

housecoat ['hauskout] *n.* robe *f* d'intérieur.

housefly ['hausflai] *n.* mouche domestique, commune.

houseful ['hausful] *n.* maisonnée *f*; pleine maison (d'invités, etc.).

household ['haushould] *n.* **1.** (membres *mpl* de la) maison; famille *f*; ménage *m*; **h. articles,** articles ménagers; **h. expenses,** frais *mpl* de, du, ménage; **h. duties,** (affaires *fpl* du) ménage; **h. goods,** meubles *mpl*, mobilier *m*; **his name is a h. word,** son nom est connu de tous. **2.** (*a*) les domestiques; **to have a large h.,** avoir une nombreuse domesticité; (*b*) **the H.,** la Maison du souverain; **the H. troops,** la Garde.

householder ['haushouldər] *n.* (i) propriétaire *mf*, (ii) locataire *mf*, de maison; chef *m* de famille.

housekeeper ['hauskiːpər] *n.* **1.** concierge *mf*. **2.** femme *f* de charge; gouvernante *f* (d'un prêtre, etc.); économe *f*, intendante *f* (d'un château, etc.). **3.** ménagère *f*.

housekeeping ['hauskiːpiŋ] *n.* **1.** le ménage; **to set up h.,** se mettre, entrer, en ménage. **2.** économie *f* domestique; les soins *mpl* du ménage; **she knows nothing of h.,** ce n'est pas une femme d'intérieur; **h. book,** carnet *m* de dépenses; **h. allowance, money,** *F:* **h.,** l'argent *m* pour le ménage.

housemaid ['hausmeid] *n.f.* bonne; femme de chambre; *F:* **housemaid's knee,** hygroma *m* du genou.

houseman *pl.* **-men** ['hausmən] *n.m.* (*a*) domestique; (*b*) *Med:* interne *m* (d'un hôpital).

housemaster, housemistress ['hausmɑːstər, -mistris] *n.* professeur chargé de la surveillance (i) d'un internat, (ii) (*in day school*) d'un groupe d'élèves (nommé *house*).

houseparty ['hauspɑːti] *n.* (*a*) partie *f* de campagne; (*b*) les invités *mpl* à une partie de campagne.

housephone ['hausfoun] *n.* téléphone intérieur.

houseproud ['hauspraud] *a.* **she is very h.,** c'est une femme d'intérieur méticuleuse.

houseroom ['hausruːm] *n.* place *f* (pour loger qn, qch.); logement *m*; *F:* **I wouldn't give it h.,** je n'en voudrais pas quand même on me le donnerait.

house-to-house ['haustə'haus] *a.* (quête, vente, etc.) à domicile; **h.-to-h- canvassing,** le porte à porte; **the police made a h.-to-h. search,** la police a fait une fouille maison par maison.

housetop ['haustɔp] *n.* toit *m*; *F:* **to proclaim sth. from the housetops,** crier qch. sur les toits.

housetrain ['haustrein] *v.tr.* dresser (un chien, etc.) à la propreté; **housetrained,** (chien, etc.) propre.

housewarming ['hauswɔːmiŋ] *n.* pendaison *f* de la

crémaillère; **to give, have, a h.,** pendre la crémaillère.
housewife, *pl.* **-wives 1.** *n.f.* ['hauswaif, -waivz] maîtresse de maison; femme au foyer. **2.** *n.* ['hʌzif, -vz] *O:* trousse *f* de couture.
housewifery ['hauswif(ə)ri] *n.* économie *f* domestique; soins *mpl* du ménage.
housework ['hauswə:k] *n.* travaux *mpl* domestiques, de ménage; **to do the h.,** faire le ménage.
housey-housey ['hausi'hausi] *n.* (jeu de) loto *m.*
hove. *see* HEAVE².
hovel ['hɔv(ə)l] *n.* taudis *m,* bouge *m,* masure *f.*
hover ['hɔvər] *v.i.* **1.** (*a*) (*of bird, insect*) planer, se balancer; **danger is hovering over him,** le danger le menace; (*b*) (*of aircraft*) planer, effectuer un vol stationnaire; (*c*) *F:* (*of pers.*) faire un vol, une traversée, en aéroglisseur. **2.** (*of pers.*) (*a*) **to h. round s.o.,** errer, rôder, autour de qn; (*b*) **to h. between two courses,** hésiter entre deux partis. **hovering** *n. Av:* vol *m* stationnaire; (*of bird, etc.*) vol en suspension.
hovercraft ['hɔvəkrɑ:ft] *n. inv.* aéroglisseur *m*; *F:* hovercraft *m.*
hoverport ['hɔvəpɔrt] *n.* hoverport *m*; gare *f* aéroglisseur.
hovertrain ['hɔvətrein] *n.* aérotrain *m.*
how [hau] *adv.* **1.** (*a*) comment; **h. does one spell this word?** comment écrit-on ce mot? *F:* **h. the devil . . ., h. on earth . . ., h. in the world . . .?** comment diable . . .? **tell me h. he did it,** dites-moi comment il l'a fait; **h. are you?** comment allez-vous? *F:* comment ça va? **h. do you, d'you, do?** (i) comment allez-vous? (ii) enchanté (de faire votre connaissance); **h. is it that . . .?** comment se fait-il que . . .? **h. so?** comment ça? **how's that?** (i) comment ça? (ii) *Cr:* appel à l'arbitre, pour savoir si le guichet est sauf, ou si la balle a été bien attrapée; *F:* **and h.!** et comment! **h. could you!** vous n'avez pas honte? **to learn h. to do sth.,** apprendre comment faire qch.; apprendre à faire qch.; (*b*) **h. do you like this wine?** comment trouvez-vous ce vin? **2.** (*to what extent* (*a*) **h. much, h. many,** combien (de); **h. many times? h. often?** combien de fois? **h. many are there of you?** vous êtes combien de personnes? **you know h. useful he is to me,** vous savez à quel point il m'est utile; **you don't know h. right you are,** vous ne savez pas combien vous dites vrai; **h. wide is this room?** quelle est la largeur de cette pièce? **h. old are you?** quel âge avez-vous? (*b*) (*in exclamations*) comme, que; **h. pretty she is!** comme elle est jolie! qu'elle est jolie! **h. kind!** comme, que, c'est aimable! **h. she has changed!** ce qu'elle a changé! **h. I wish I could!** si seulement je pouvais! **h. surprised he was when . . .!** quelle ne fut pas sa surprise lorsque . . .! **3.** (*introducing indirect statement*) que; **I told him h. there had been a great storm,** je lui ai dit qu'il y avait eu un grand orage. **4.** *n.* **the hows, whys and the wherefores,** les comment et les pourquoi; tous les détails.
howdy ['haudi] *int. NAm: F:* salut!
however [hau'evər] *adv.* **1.** (*a*) de quelque manière que . . .; **h. that may be,** quoi qu'il en soit; (*b*) quelque . . . que . . ., si . . . que . . .; **h. good his work is,** quelque excellent que soit son travail; **h. little,** si peu qu'il soit; si peu que ce soit. **2.** toutefois, cependant, pourtant; **if h. you don't agree,** si toutefois cela ne vous convient pas.
howitzer ['hauitsər] *n. Artil:* obusier *m.*
howl¹ [haul] *n.* hurlement *m* (de loup, etc.); braillement *m* (de bébé); huée *f* (de la foule); mugissement *m* (du vent); **to give a h. of rage,** hurler de rage; **there were howls of laughter,** on riait à gorge déployée.
howl² *v.i. & tr.* **1.** (*of animals, people*) hurler; pousser des hurlements; (*of wind*) mugir, rugir; *F:* **to h. with laughter,** rire à gorge déployée; **to h. down a speaker,** faire taire un orateur en poussant des huées. **2.** *F:* beugler (une chanson, etc.). **howling 1.** *a.* (*a*) (enfant) qui hurle; (foule) hurlante; (vent) furieux; (*b*) *F:* (*intensive*) énorme; (succès) fou. **2.** *n.* hurlement *m*; braillement *m* (de bébé); mugissement *m* (du vent, de la tempête).
howler ['haulər] *n.* **1.** hurleur, -euse. **2.** *F:* grosse gaffe, bourde *f* énorme; **schoolboy h.,** perle *f.*
hoyden ['hɔi(ə)dn] *n.f.* garçon manqué.
hoydenish ['hɔid(e)niʃ] *a.* (*of manner, etc.*) garçonnier, -ière.
hub [hʌb] *n.* **1.** moyeu *m* (de roue, d'hélice). **2.** centre *m* d'activité; **the h. of the universe,** le pivot, le centre, de l'univers.
hubbub ['hʌbʌb] *n.* remue-ménage *m,* vacarme *m,* tohu-bohu *m*; **h. of voices,** brouhaha *m* de voix.
hubby ['hʌbi] *n. F:* (petit) mari *m.*
hubcap ['hʌbkæp] *n. Veh:* couvre-moyeu *m, pl.* couvre-moyeux; *Aut:* enjoliveur *m.*
huckleberry ['hʌk(ə)lberi] *n. Bot: NAm:* airelle *f* myrtille.
huckster ['hʌkstər] *n.* (*a*) colporteur *m*; (*b*) mercanti *m,* profiteur *m*; **political h.,** trafiquant *m* politique.
huddle¹ ['hʌdl] *n.* (*b*) tas confus, méli-mélo *m* (de choses); (petit) groupe (de personnes); (*b*) *F:* **to go into a h.,** se réunir en petit comité.
huddle² *v.tr. & i.* **1. to h. things (up, together),** entasser des choses pêle-mêle; (*of people, animals*) **to h. together,** s'entasser, se tasser; se serrer les uns contre les autres. **2.** (*of pers.*) **to h. (oneself) up,** se replier sur soi-même; se pelotonner; **huddled (up) in bed,** couché en chien de fusil; **huddled (up) in a corner,** blotti dans un coin.
hue¹ [hju:] *n.* teinte *f,* couleur *f,* nuance *f.*
hue² *n.* **h. and cry,** clameur *f* de haro; *Jur:* clameur publique; **a h. and cry was raised against this reform,** cette réforme provoqua un tollé général.
huff¹ [hʌf] *n.* **to be in a h.,** être froissé, fâché; **to get into a h.,** s'offusquer; **he went off in a h.,** il prit la mouche et s'en alla.
huff² 1. *v.i.* (*a*) (*still used in*) **he huffed and puffed,** il soufflait et haletait; (*b*) s'offenser; prendre la mouche. **2.** *v.tr.* froisser (qn); **to be, feel, huffed,** être offensé, fâché.
huffy ['hʌfi] *a.* faché, vexé.
hug¹ [hʌg] *n.* **1.** étreinte *f*; **to give s.o. a h.,** serrer qn dans ses bras; étreindre qn. **2.** (*a*) étreinte (de l'ours); (*b*) *Wr:* prise *f.*
hug² *v.tr.* **(hugged) 1.** (*a*) étreindre, embrasser, serrer (qn); serrer (qn) sur son cœur; (*b*) (*of bear*) étouffer, enserrer (sa victime); *F:* **to h. s.o. to death,** embrasser qn à l'étouffer; (*c*) chérir (ses défauts); **to h. a belief,** ne pas démordre d'une conviction; (*d*) **to h. oneself for doing sth.,** se féliciter d'avoir fait qch. **2.** (*a*) *Nau:* raser, longer (la côte); (*b*) longer, serrer (le mur); *Aut:* **to h. the kerb,** serrer le trottoir; (*c*) *F:* **to h. the fire,** se blottir au coin du feu.
huge [hju:dʒ] *a.* immense, énorme; (bâtiment) énorme, vaste; (succès) immense, formidable; (homme) colossal; (différence) énorme, capitale; **h. undertaking,** vaste entreprise *f.* **-ly** *adv.* énormément; extrêmement.
hugeness ['hju:dʒnis] *n.* énormité *f,* immensité *f.*
hugger-mugger ['hʌgəmʌgər] **1.** *n.* désordre *m,* confusion *f.* **2.** *a.* (collection) sans ordre; (arrangement) confus. **3.** *adv.* en désordre; confusément, pêle-mêle.
Hugh [hju:], **Hugo** ['hju:gou] *Pr.n.m.* Hugues.
Huguenot [hju:gənɔt, -nou] *n. Rel:H:* Huguenot, -ote.
hulk [hʌlk] *n.* **1.** *Nau:* carcasse *f* de navire; ponton *m.* **2.** *F:* (*of pers.*) gros pataud; lourdaud *m,* mastoc *m.*

hulking [ˈhʌlkiŋ] *a.* gros, lourd; **h. great creature,** gros pataud; lourdaud *m*, mastoc *m*.

hull¹ [hʌl] *n.* **1.** cosse *f*, gousse *f* (de pois, de fève). **2.** (*a*) *N.Arch: Av: Mil:* coque (de navire, de char); (*b*) *M.Ins:* corps *m*; **h. insurance,** assurance *f* sur corps.

hull² *v.tr.* **1.** écosser (des pois); monder (de l'orge); baller (de l'avoine); décortiquer (le riz, l'orge). **2.** *Nau:* percer la coque (d'un navire).

hullabaloo [hʌləbəˈluː] *n.* tintamarre *m*, vacarme *m*; boucan *m*.

hullo [hʌˈlou] *int.* (*a*) (*calling attention*) ohé! holà! **h. you!** hé, là-bas! (*b*) (*expressing surprise*) **h.! that's curious!** tiens! tiens! c'est curieux; (*c*) (*greeting*) bonjour! **h. everybody!** salut à tous! (*d*) *Tp:* allô!

hum¹ [hʌm] *n.* bourdonnement *m* (d'abeille); ronflement *m* (de machine); vrombissement *m* (d'un avion, d'une toupie); murmure *m* (d'approbation); bruit sourd (de voix); *W.Tel: etc:* bourdonnement, ronflement; brouhaha *m* (de conversation).

hum² *v.* **(hummed) 1.** *v.i.* (*a*) (*of insect, etc.*) bourdonner; (*of top*) ronfler, vrombir; (*of aircraft*) vrombir; *W.Tel:* (*of set*) ronronner, ronfler; **town humming with activity,** ville bourdonnante d'activité; *F:* **to make things h.,** faire marcher rondement les choses; (*b*) (*of pers.*) (i) dire hum; (ii) hésiter, ânonner (en parlant); **to h. and haw,** (i) bredouiller, bafouiller; (ii) hésiter (à prendre un parti). **2.** *v.tr.* fredonner, chantonner (un air); *v.i.* fredonner, chantonner. **humming 1.** *a.* bourdonnant; **h. top,** toupie *f* d'Allemagne. **2.** *n.* (*a*) = HUM¹; fredonnement *m* (d'un air); **h. noise,** bourdonnement *m*; (*b*) **h. and hawing,** hésitation *f*.

hum³ *int.* hmm! hum!

human [ˈhjuːm(ə)n] **1.** *a.* humain; **h. being,** être humain; **h. nature,** la nature humaine; **h. error,** erreur humaine. **2.** *n.* être humain; **humans,** les humains *mpl.* **-ly** *adv.* humainement; **to do everything h. possible,** faire tout ce qui est humainement possible.

humane [hjuˈmein] *a.* (*a*) humain, compatissant; (œuvre) humanitaire; (mesures) bienfaisantes; **the Royal H. Society,** la Société de sauvetage, de secours aux noyés; (*b*) clément; qui évite de faire souffrir. **-ly** *adv.* humainement, avec humanité.

humanism [ˈhjuːmənizm] *n. Lit: Phil:* humanisme *m*.

humanist [ˈhjuːmənist] *n.* humaniste *m*.

humanistic [hjuməˈnistik] *a.* humaniste.

humanitarian [hjumæniˈtɛəriən] *a. & n.* humanitaire *mf*).

humanity [hjuˈmæniti] *n.* humanité *f*. **1.** (*a*) nature humaine; (*b*) le genre humain; les hommes *mpl.* **2. to treat s.o. with h.,** traiter qn avec humanité. **3.** *Lit: Phil:* **the humanities,** les humanités, les lettres *fpl.*

humanize [ˈhjuːmənaiz] *v.tr.* humaniser.

humanoid [ˈhjuːmənɔid] *a. & n.* humanoïde (*m*).

humble¹ [ˈhʌmbl] *a.* humble. **1.** (*meek*) **h. prayer,** humble prière *f*; **in my h. opinion,** à mon humble avis. **2.** (*unpretentious*) modeste; **to be of h. origin,** être d'origine modeste. **-bly** *adv.* **1.** (parler) humblement, avec humilité. **2.** (vivre) modestement.

humble² *v.tr.* humilier, mortifier (qn); (r)abattre (l'orgueil de qn); **to h. oneself,** s'humilier. **humbling 1.** *a.* humiliant **2.** *n.* humiliation *f* (de qn); abaissement *m* (des grands, etc.).

humble³ *n.* **to eat h. pie,** s'humilier (devant qn); faire amende honorable.

humble-bee [ˈhʌmb(ə)lbiː] *n. Ent:* bourdon *m*.

humbleness [ˈhʌmb(ə)lnis] *n.* humilité *f*.

humbug [ˈhʌmbʌg] *n.* **1.** (i) charlatanisme *m*; (ii) blagues *fpl*; **(that's all) h.!** tout cela c'est de la blague. **2.** (*pers.*) (*a*) enjôleur, -euse; (*b*) charlatan *m*. **3.** *Comest:* berlingot *m*; = bêtise *f* de Cambrai.

humdinger [ˈhʌmdiŋər] *n. esp. U.S: F:* quelque chose d'extraordinaire, de fantastique; **a h. of a speech,** un discours formidable, sensationnel.

humdrum [ˈhʌmdrʌm] **1.** *a.* monotone; banal, -als; (existence) monotone; **h. daily life,** le train-train quotidien. **2.** *n.* monotonie *f* (de l'existence, etc.).

humerus *pl.* **-i** [ˈhjuːmərəs, -ai, -iː] *n. Anat:* humérus *m*.

humid [ˈhjuːmid] *a.* humide; (*of heat, skin*) moite.

humidifier [hjuˈmidifaiər] *n.* humidificateur *m*.

humidify [hjuˈmidifai] *v.tr.* humidifier (l'air, etc.).

humidity [hjuˈmiditi] *n.* humidité *f*.

humidor [ˈhjuːmidɔːr] *n.* boîte à cigares (pourvue d'un humidificateur).

humiliate [hju(ː)ˈmilieit] *v.tr.* humilier, mortifier (qn). **humiliating** *a.* humiliant, mortifiant.

humiliation [hjumiliˈeiʃ(ə)n] *n.* humiliation *f*.

humility [hjuˈmiliti] *n.* humilité *f*.

hummingbird [ˈhʌmiŋbəːd] *n. Orn:* colibri *m*, oiseau-mouche *m*, *pl.* oiseaux-mouches.

hummock [ˈhʌmək] *n.* **1.** tertre *m*, mamelon *m* (de terre); monticule *m*. **2.** (*in ice field*) hummock *m*.

humor [ˈhjuːmər] *n. & v.tr. NAm:* = HUMOUR¹, ².

humorist [ˈhjuːmərist] *n.* **1.** (*a*) farceur *m*; (*b*) comique *m*. **2.** écrivain *m* humoristique; humoriste *m*.

humorous [ˈhjuːm(ə)rəs] *a.* (*of pers.*) plein d'humour; comique, drôle; (*of writer, etc.*) humoriste, humoristique; (*of drawing, etc.*) humoristique. **-ly** *adv.* drôlement, comiquement; humoristiquement.

humour¹, *NAm:* **humor¹** [ˈhjuːmər] *n.* **1.** *Anat:* humeur *f*. **2.** (*mood, temper*) humeur, disposition *f*; **to be in the h. for doing sth.,** être disposé à faire qch.; **good h.,** bonne humeur. **3.** (*a*) humour *m*; **broad h.,** grosse gaieté; (*b*) **the h. of the situation,** le côté comique de la situation; (*c*) sens *m* de l'humour; **to have no sense of h.,** ne pas avoir le sens de l'humour.

humour², *NAm:* **humor²** *v.tr.* **to h. s.o.,** complaire à qn; se prêter, se plier, à tous les caprices de qn; ménager qn.

humourless, *NAm:* **humorless** [ˈhjuːməlis] *a.* dépourvu d'humour, du sens de l'humour.

hump¹ [hʌmp] *n.* **1.** (*a*) bosse *f* (de bossu, de chameau); **to have a h.,** être bossu; (*b*) **h. in the road,** dos *m* d'âne; (*c*) *Rail:* butte *f* de triage; (*d*) *Fig:* obstacle *m*; **we're over the h. now,** le plus difficile est passé maintenant. **2.** *F:* **to have the h.,** avoir le cafard.

hump² **1.** *v.tr.* (*a*) courber, arquer, cambrer; (*of pers., animal*) arrondir, arquer (le dos); voûter (les épaules); (*b*) *F:* porter (un fardeau) sur son dos.

humpback [ˈhʌmpbæk] *n.* (*a*) bossu, -ue; (*b*) **to have a h.,** être bossu.

humpbacked [ˈhʌmpbækt] *a.* bossu; **h. bridge,** pont en dos d'âne.

humph [hʌmf, hm] *int.* hum! hmm!

humus [ˈhjuːməs] *n. Agr: Hort:* humus *m*; terreau *m*.

Hun [hʌn] *n.* **1.** *Hist:* **the Huns,** les huns *mpl.* **2.** *F:* (*in 1914–18 War*) boche *m*.

hunch¹ [hʌn(t)ʃ] *n.* **1.** bosse *f*. **2.** gros morceau (de pain, de fromage). **3. to have a h.,** avoir une idée, un pressentiment.

hunch² *v.tr.* arrondir (le dos); voûter (les épaules); **to sit hunched up,** se tenir accroupi le menton sur les genoux.

hunchback [ˈhʌn(t)ʃbæk] *n.* bossu, -ue.

hunchbacked [ˈhʌn(t)ʃbækt] *a.* bossu.

hundred [ˈhʌndrəd] *num. a. & n.* (*a*) cent (*m*); **a h. and one,** cent un; **about a h. houses,** une centaine de maisons; **two h. apples,** deux cents pommes; **to live to be a h.,** atteindre la centaine; **they were dying in hundreds,** ils mouraient par centaines; *Cu:* **hundreds and thousands** = vermicelles *fpl*, perlages *mpl*; **to**

drive at a h. kilometres an hour, faire du cent à l'heure; **a h. per cent,** cent pour cent; **to sell by the h.,** vendre au cent; *Sp:* **the h. metre race, the h. metres,** le cent mètres; (*b*) **not a h. miles away,** pas si loin d'ici; **a h. and one details,** mille et un détails; **I've told you hundreds of times,** je vous l'ai dit je ne sais combien de fois; **a h. to one it will be a failure,** ça fera four à coup sûr.

hundredfold ['hʌndrədfould] **1.** *a.* centuple. **2.** *adv.phr.* **a h.,** cent fois autant; **to increase a h.,** centupler.

hundredth ['hʌndrədθ] **1.** *num.a. & n.* centième (*mf*); *Th:* **h. performance,** centième *f.* **2.** *n.* (*fractional*) centième *m*; **three hundredths,** trois centièmes.

hundredweight ['hʌndrədweit] *n. Meas:* (*a*) poids *m* de 112 livres. = 50 kg 802; (*approx.* =) quintal *m*; (*b*) *U.S:* poids de 100 livres, = 45 kg 359.

Hungarian [hʌŋ'gɛəriən] **1.** *a. Geog:* hongrois. **2.** *n.* (*a*) Hongrois, -oise; (*b*) *Ling:* hongrois *m*.

Hungary ['hʌŋgəri] *Pr.n. Geog:* Hongrie *f.*

hunger[1] ['hʌŋgər] *n.* (*a*) faim *f*; **h. pains,** tiraillements *mpl* d'estomac; **h. strike, striker,** grève *f*, gréviste *mf*, de la faim; **to go on h. strike,** faire la grève de la faim; (*b*) **h. for sth.,** ardent désir de qch.; soif *f* de qch.

hunger[2] *v.i. esp. Lit:* (*a*) avoir faim; (*b*) **to h. after, for, sth.,** être affamé de, avoir soif de, qch.

hungry ['hʌŋgri] *a.* **1.** affamé, qui a faim; **to be, feel, h.,** avoir faim; **to be ravenously h., as h. as a wolf,** *U.S:* **a bear,** avoir une faim de loup; **I was getting h.,** je commençais à avoir faim; **to look h.,** avoir l'air famélique. **2.** (regard, œil) avide; **to be h. for knowledge,** être avide d'apprendre. **-ily** *adv.* avidement, voracement.

hunk [hʌŋk] *n.* gros morceau (de gâteau, de fromage, etc.); quignon *m* (de pain).

hunky-dory ['hʌŋki'dɔːri] *a. F:* excellent, au poil.

hunt[1] [hʌnt] *n.* **1.** (*a*) chasse *f* (*esp.* à courre); **fox h., tiger h.,** chasse au renard, au tigre; (*b*) équipage *m* de chasse; (*c*) terrain *m* de chasse. **2.** recherche *f*; **he continued his h. for work,** il continuait à chercher un emploi.

hunt[2] **1.** *v.i.* (*a*) *Ven:* chasser au chien courant; chasser à courre; (*b*) **to h. (about) for sth., s.o.,** chercher (à découvrir) qch., qn; **to h. for treasure,** aller à la recherche d'un trésor. **2.** *v.tr.* (*a*) chasser (le cerf, etc.); pêcher (la baleine); (*b*) **to h. a thief,** (i) poursuivre un voleur; (ii) être à la recherche d'un voleur; **he had a hunted look,** il avait l'air persécuté; (*c*) parcourir, battre (un terrain); (*d*) monter (un cheval) à la chasse; diriger, conduire (la meute). **hunt down** *v.tr.* (*a*) traquer, forcer (une bête); *F:* mettre (qn) aux abois; (*b*) *F:* persécuter (qn). **hunting 1.** *a.* **h. man,** fervent *m* de la chasse à courre; grand chasseur. **2.** *n.* (*a*) (i) chasse *f* (à courre); poursuite *f* (du gibier); **fox h.,** chasse au renard; **h. lodge,** pavillon *m* de chasse; **h. horn,** cor *m*, trompe *f*, de chasse; **h. ground,** terrain *m* de chasse; **the Happy H. Grounds,** le Paradis des Peaux-Rouges; (ii) **house h.,** recherche *f* d'une maison, d'un logement; **bargain h.,** la chasse aux soldes; **a happy h. ground for collectors,** un paradis pour les collectionneurs; (*b*) (*science*) vénerie *f.* **hunt out** *v.tr.* (*a*) chasser, expulser (qn); débusquer (qn); (*b*) déterrer, dénicher (qch.) (à force de recherches); découvrir (la vérité); arriver à retrouver (qn, qch.). **hunt up** *v.tr.* rechercher (qn, qch.).

hunter ['hʌntər] *n.* **1.** (*a*) chasseur *m*; tueur *m* (de lions, etc.); (*b*) *F:* pourchasseur *m* **(of,** de); **curio h.,** dénicheur *m* d'antiquités; **dowry h.,** coureur *m* de dots. **2.** cheval *m* de chasse; hunter *m*. **3.** (montre *f* à) savonnette (*f*); **half h.,** montre à guichet.

huntress ['hʌntris] *n.f.* chasseuse; *Poet:* chasseresse.

huntsman *pl.* **-men** ['hʌntsmən] *n.m.* **1.** chasseur (à courre). **2.** veneur, piqueur.

hunt-the-slipper ['hʌntðə'slipər] *n. Games:* jeu *m* du furet.

hurdle[1] ['həːdl] *n.* (*a*) *Agr:* claie *f*, clôture *f*; (*b*) *Sp:* *Turf:* haie *f*; **h. race,** course *f* de haies; **400 metre hurdles,** 400 mètres haies; (*c*) *Fig:* obstacle *m*.

hurdle[2] **1.** *v.tr.* (*a*) entourer (qch.) de claies; (*b*) sauter (un obstacle); *Sp:* franchir (une haie). **2.** *v.i. Sp:* courir une course de haies. **hurdling** *n. Sp: Turf:* (i) saut *m* de haies; (ii) courses *fpl* de haies.

hurdler ['həːdlər] *n. Sp:* coureur *m* de courses de haies; *Turf:* cheval *m* de courses de haies.

hurdy-gurdy ['həːdigəːdi] *n. F:* orgue *m* de Barbarie.

hurl[1] [həːl] *n.* **1.** lancée *f*, lancement *m*; *esp. U.S:* **a h. of angry water,** un torrent impétueux d'eau. **2.** *Sp:* crosse *f* de *hurling*.

hurl[2] **1.** *v.tr.* lancer (qch.) avec force, avec violence **(at,** contre); lancer (des reproches) **(at s.o.,** à qn); **to h. oneself at s.o.,** se ruer sur qn; **to h. oneself into the fray,** se jeter à corps perdu dans la mêlée; **to h. abuse,** vociférer des injures. **2.** *v.i. Sp:* jouer au *hurling*. **hurl back** *v.tr.* refouler, repousser (l'ennemi, etc.). **hurl down** *v.tr.* précipiter; jeter bas. **hurling** *n.* **1.** lancement *m* (d'un projectile, etc.). **2.** *Sp:* (*Ireland*) variété de jeu de hockey.

hurly-burly ['həːlibəːli] *n.* charivari *m*, tohu-bohu *m*.

hurrah [hu'rɑː], **hurray** [hu'rei] *int. & n.* hourra (*m*); **h. for the holidays!** vive(nt) les vacances!

hurricane ['hʌrikən, -kein] *n. Meteor:* ouragan *m*; (*in W. Indies*) hurricane *m*; **it was blowing a h.,** le vent soufflait en ouragan; **h. lamp,** lampe-tempête *f*, *pl.* lampes-tempête.

hurry[1] ['hʌri] *n.* hâte *f*, précipitation *f*; **to go out in a h.,** sortir à la hâte, en courant; **to be always in a h.,** être toujours pressé; **to be in no h.,** ne pas être pressé; avoir le temps; **you won't see him again in a h.,** vous ne le reverrez pas de sitôt. **he was in no h. to leave,** il n'était pas pressé de partir.

hurry[2] **1.** *v.tr.* (*a*) hâter, presser (qn); (*b*) hâter, activer, presser (le travail); **work that cannot be hurried,** travail qui demande du temps. **2.** *v.i.* (*a*) se hâter, se presser; se dépêcher; **don't h.,** ne vous pressez pas; **there's no need to h.,** on a tout son temps; (*b*) presser le pas; **she hurried home,** elle s'est dépêchée de rentrer; **to h. into, out of, a room,** entrer dans une pièce, sortir d'une pièce, en toute hâte; **to h. after s.o.,** courir après qn; (*c*) **to h. into one's clothes,** s'habiller en toute hâte. **hurried** *a.* **1.** (pas) pressé, précipité; (ouvrage) fait à la hâte; **a few h. words,** quelques mots dits, écrits, à la hâte. **2. to be h.,** être pressé; être bousculé. **hurriedly** *adv.* à la hâte, en toute hâte; précipitamment. **hurry along 1.** *v.tr.* entraîner (qn) précipitamment. **2.** *v.i.* marcher d'un pas pressé. **hurry away 1.** *v.tr.* emmener (qn) précipitamment. **2.** *v.i.* partir précipitamment. **hurry back 1.** *v.tr.* faire revenir, faire rentrer (qn) en toute hâte. **2.** *v.i.* revenir, retourner, à la hâte. **hurry off 1.** *v.tr.* emmener, entraîner (qn) en toute hâte. **2.** *v.i.* partir précipitamment. **hurry on 1.** *v.tr.* faire hâter le pas à (qn); pousser (qn) en avant; avancer (un travail); précipiter (une affaire). **2.** *v.i.* presser le pas. **hurry up 1.** *v.tr.* hâter, presser (qn); faire hâter le pas à (qn). **2.** *v.i.* se dépêcher, se hâter; **h. up!** dépêchez-vous! dépêche-toi!

hurt[1] [həːt] *n.* mal *m*. **1.** blessure *f.* **2.** tort *m*, détriment *m*; **what h. can it do you?** quel tort cela peut-il vous faire?

hurt² *v.tr.* (*p.t. & p.p.* **hurt**) **1.** faire (du) mal à, blesser (qn); **to h. oneself,** se faire (du) mal; **to h. one's foot,** se blesser au pied; **to get h.,** (i) être blessé; recevoir une blessure; (ii) se faire du mal; **my wound hurts (me),** ma blessure me fait mal; **that hurts,** ça fait mal. **2.** faire de la peine à (qn); **to h. s.o.'s feelings,** blesser, peiner, qn; offenser qn; **the thing that hurts him most,** la chose qui lui tient au cœur. **3.** (*to injure*) (*of things*) gâter, abîmer, endommager (qch.).

hurtful [ˈhəːtf(u)l] *a.* **1.** (*a*) nuisible, nocif; pernicieux; (*b*) préjudiciable (**to,** à); blessant, offensant; **there is nothing so h. as ingratitude,** il n'y a rien qui blesse comme l'ingratitude.

hurtle [ˈhəːt(ə)l] **1.** *v.tr.* lancer, faire dévaler (des pierres, etc.). **2.** *v.i.* (*a*) se précipiter, s'élancer (avec bruit, comme un bolide); (*of car, etc.*) **to h. along,** dévorer la route; (*b*) (*of rocks, etc.*) **to h. down,** dévaler avec fracas.

husband¹ [ˈhʌzbənd] *n.* mari *m*, époux *m*; **h. and wife,** les (deux) époux, les conjoints *mpl*; **to live as h. and wife,** vivre maritalement.

husband² *v.tr.* ménager, économiser (ses ressources, ses forces); bien gérer (ses ressources).

husbandry [ˈhʌzbəndri] *n.* **1.** agronomie *f*, économie rurale, agriculture *f*; **animal h.,** élevage *m*. **2. good h.,** bonne gestion; sage administration *f* (de son bien).

hush¹ [hʌʃ] *n.* **1.** silence *m*, calme *m*. **2. h. money,** argent donné à qn pour acheter son silence; prime *f* du silence; pot-de-vin *m*.

hush² **1.** *v.tr.* (*a*) calmer, faire taire (un enfant); imposer silence à (qn); (*b*) étouffer (un bruit); **hushed conversation,** conversation étouffée, discrète; **to talk in a hushed voice,** chuchoter. **2.** *v.i.* se taire, faire silence. **hush up** *v.tr.* étouffer (un scandale, etc.).

hush³ *int.* chut! silence!

hush-hush [ˈhʌʃhʌʃ] *a. F:* archi-secret, -ète.

husk¹ [hʌsk] *n.* cosse *f*, gousse *f* (de pois, etc.); brou *m* (de noix); hérisson *m* (de châtaigne); coque *f* (de grain de café); tégument *m*, pellicule *f* (de grain); enveloppe *f* (de l'épi du maïs); *Husb:* **husks,** vannure *f*.

husk² *v.tr.* décortiquer; écosser (des pois); ébrouer (des noix); perler, monder (le riz, l'orge); éplucher (le maïs); vanner (le grain).

huskiness [ˈhʌskinis] *n.* enrouement *m* (de la voix, d'un son); empâtement *m* (de la voix).

husky¹ [ˈhʌski] *a.* **1.** (pois, etc.) cossu. **2. h. voice,** voix enrouée, voilée. **3.** *a. & n. F:* (homme) fort, costaud. **-ily** *adv.* (parler) d'une voix enrouée.

husky² *n.* chien *m* esquimau.

hussar [huˈzɑːr] *n. Mil:* hussard *m*.

hussy [ˈhʌzi] *n.f. F: A:* coquine, friponne; **you little h.!** petite coquine!

hustings [ˈhʌstiŋz] *n.pl.* plate-forme électorale; **to mount the h.,** se présenter aux élections (pour la Chambre des Communes).

hustle¹ [ˈhʌsl] *n.* **1.** bousculade *f*. **2.** hâte *f*, activité *f* énergique; **h. and bustle,** tourbillon *m* d'activité.

hustle² **1.** *v.tr.* (*a*) bousculer, pousser, presser (qn); **to be hustled away,** être emmené précipitamment; (*b*) **to h. things on,** pousser le travail; *F:* faire activer les choses; (*c*) **to h. s.o. into a decision,** forcer qn à se décider sans lui donner le temps de respirer; **I won't be hustled,** je ne veux pas qu'on me bouscule. **2.** *v.i.* (*a*) se dépêcher, se presser; (*b*) **to h. through the crowd,** se frayer un passage à travers la foule.

hustler [ˈhʌslər] *n.* **1.** bousculeur, -euse. **2.** débrouillard *m*; brasseur *m*, remueur *m*, d'affaires.

hut [hʌt] *n.* hutte *f*, cabane *f*; **mud h.,** hutte de terre; **Alpine h.,** chalet-refuge *m*, *pl.* chalets-refuges.

hutch [hʌtʃ] *n.* **1.** coffre *m*. **2. rabbit h.,** clapier *m*, lapinière *f*. **3.** *NAm: Furn:* vaisselier *m*.

hutments [ˈhʌtmənts] *n.pl.* baraquements *mpl*.

hyacinth [ˈhaiəsinθ] *n.* **1.** *Miner:* hyacinthe *f*. **2.** *Bot:* jacinthe *f*; **wood, wild, h.,** jacinthe des bois. **3.** *a. & n.* (*colour*) bleu jacinthe *inv*, bleu violet *inv*.

hyaena [haiˈiːnə] *n.* = HYENA.

hybrid [ˈhaibrid] *Biol: Hort: Ling: etc:* **1.** *n.* (*a*) hybride *m*; (*b*) (*of pers.*) mêtis, -isse. **2.** *a.* (*a*) hybride; (*b*) hétérogène.

hybridism [ˈhaibridizm] *n.* hybridisme *m*.

hybridization [haibridaiˈzeiʃ(ə)n] *n. Biol:* hybridation *f*.

hybridize [ˈhaibridaiz] **1.** *v.tr.* hybrider. **2.** *v.i.* s'hybrider.

Hydra [ˈhaidrə] *n.* **1.** *Gr. Myth:* Hydre *f* (de Lerne). **2.** *Coel:* **h.,** (*pl.* **hydrae** [ˈhaidri]) hydre.

hydrangea [haiˈdreindʒə] *n. Bot:* hortensia *m*.

hydrant [ˈhaidrənt] *n.* prise *f* d'eau; **fire h.,** bouche *f* d'incendie.

hydrate¹ [ˈhaidreit] *n. Ch:* hydrate *m*.

hydrate² *v.tr. Ch:* hydrater.

hydraulic [haiˈdrɔːlik] *a.* **1.** (force, frein, etc.) hydraulique; **h. engineering,** technique *f* hydraulique. **2.** *Const:* (ciment, etc.) hydraulique.

hydraulics [haiˈdrɔːliks] *n.pl.* (*usu. with sg. const.*) hydraulique *f*, hydromécanique *f*.

hydro [ˈhaidrou] *n.* **1.** établissement *m* hydrothérapique. **2.** *Can:* (*a*) énergie hydraulique; (*b*) centrale *f* d'énergie hydraulique.

hydrocarbon [haidrouˈkɑːbən] *n. Ch:* hydrocarbure *m*.

hydrochloric [haidrouˈklɔ(ː)rik] *a. Ch:* (acide) chlorhydrique.

hydrochloride [haidrouˈklɔ(ː)raid] *n. Ch:* chlorhydrate *m*.

hydrodynamics [haidroudaiˈnæmiks] *n.pl.* (*usu. with sg. const.*) hydrodynamique *f*.

hydroelectric [haidrouiˈlektrik] *a.* hydro(-)électrique; **h. power,** énergie hydraulique.

hydrofoil [ˈhaidroufɔil] *n.* hydrofoil *m*.

hydrogen [ˈhaidrədʒən] *n. Ch:* hydrogène *m*; **h. bomb,** bombe *f* à hydrogène; **h. peroxide,** eau oxygénée.

hydrography [haiˈdrɔgrəfi] *n.* hydrographie *f*.

hydrolysis [haiˈdrɔlisis] *n. Ch:* hydrolyse *f*.

hydrometer [haiˈdrɔmitər] *n.* hydromètre *m*.

hydrometry [haiˈdrɔmitri] *n. Ph:* hydrométrie *f*.

hydropathy [haiˈdrɔpəθi] *n.* hydropathie *f*.

hydrophobia [haidrəˈfoubiə] *n.* **1.** *Med:* hydrophobie *f*. **2.** phobie *f* de l'eau.

hydrophobic [haidrəˈfoubik] *a.* hydrophobe.

hydroplane [ˈhaidrəplein] *n.* **1.** *Av:* hydravion *m*. **2.** *Nau:* (*a*) hydroplane *m*; (*b*) hydroglisseur *m*.

hydroponics [haidrouˈpɔniks] *n.pl.* (*usu. with s.g. const.*) culture *f* hydroponique.

hydrostat [ˈhaidroustæt] *n.* hydrostat *m*.

hydrostatics [haidrouˈstætiks] *n.pl.* (*usu. with sg. const.*) hydrostatique *f*.

hydrotherapy [haidrouˈθerəpi] *n. Med:* hydrothérapie *f*.

hydroxide [haiˈdrɔksaid] *n. Ch:* hydroxyde *m*, hydrate *m*.

hyena [haiˈiːnə] *n. Z:* hyène *f*; **laughing h.,** hyène moqueuse.

hygiene [ˈhaidʒiːn] *n.* hygiène *f*.

hygienic [haiˈdʒiːnik] *a.* hygiénique. **-ally** *adv.* hygiéniquement.

Hymen [ˈhaimen] **1.** *Pr.n.m. Myth:* Hymen, Hyménée. **2.** *n. Anat:* **h.,** hymen *m*.

hymn [him] *n.* **1.** *Ecc:* hymne *f*, cantique *m*; **h. book,** livre *m* de cantiques. **2.** hymne *m* (national, etc.).

hymnal [ˈhimn(ə)l] *n.* livre *m* d'hymnes, de cantiques.

hype¹ [haip] *n. P:* **1.** seringue *f* hypodermique. **2.** drogué, -ée. **3.** grand battage publicitaire.
hype² *v.tr. F:* **1. hyped up,** drogué, défoncé. **2.** pousser la vente de (qch.) par un grand battage publicitaire.
hyperacidity [haipərə'siditi] *n.* hyperacidité *f.*
hyperactive [haipə'ræktiv] *a.* hyperactif.
hyperbola [hai'pəːbələ] *n. Mth:* hyperbole *f.*
hyperbole [hai'pəːbəli] *n. Rh:* hyperbole *f.*
hyperbolic(al) [haipə'bɔlik(əl)] *a. Mth: Rh:* hyperbolique.
hypercritical ['haipə'kritik(ə)l] *a.* hypercritique.
hypermarket ['haipəmɑːkit] *n.* hypermarché *m.*
hypersensitive [haipə'sensitiv] *a.* hypersensible.
hypertension [haipə'tenʃ(ə)n] *n. Med:* hypertension (artérielle, etc.).
hyphen¹ ['haif(ə)n] *n.* trait *m* d'union.
hyphen², hyphenate ['haifəneit] *v.tr.* mettre un trait d'union à (un mot); **hyphenated word,** mot *m* à trait d'union; *U.S:* **hyphenated American,** étranger naturalisé (Germano-Américain, Hispano-Américain, etc.).
hypnosis [hip'nousis] *n.* hypnose *f.*
hypnotic [hip'nɔtik] **1.** *a. Psy: Pharm:* hypnotique; **h. state,** état *m* d'hypnose. **2.** *n.* (*a*) *Psy:* (*pers.*) hypnotique *mf*; (*b*) *Pharm:* hypnotique *m.*
hypnotism ['hipnətizm] *n.* hypnotisme *m.*
hypnotist ['hipnətist] *n.* hypnotiseur, -euse.
hypnotize ['hipnətaːiz] *v.tr.* hypnotiser.
hypochondria [haipou'kɔndriə] *n. Med:* hypocondrie *f.*
hypochondriac [haipou'kɔndriæk] *a. & n.* hypocondriaque (*mf*).
hypocrisy [hi'pɔkrisi] *n.* hypocrisie *f.*
hypocrite ['hipəkrit] *n.* hypocrite *mf*, *F:* tartufe *m.*
hypocritical [hipə'kritik(ə)l] *a.* hypocrite. **-ally** *adv.* hypocritement.
hypodermic [haipə'dəːmik] *a.* **1.** (injection, etc.) hypodermique; **h. syringe,** *n.* **h.,** seringue *f* hypodermique. **2.** *Anat:* sous-cutané.
hypotenuse [hai'pɔtənjuːz] *n. Mth:* hypoténuse *f.*
hypothermia [haipou'θəːmiə] *n. Med:* hypothermie *f.*
hypothesis [hai'pɔθəsis] *n.* hypothèse *f.*
hypothesize [hai'pɔθəsaiz] *v.i. & tr.* supposer (une notion); faire des hypothèses, des suppositions; admettre comme hypothèse (**that,** que).
hypothetic(al) [haipə'θetik(l)] *a.* hypothétique, supposé. **-ally** *adv.* hypothétiquement, par hypothèse.
hysterectomy [histə'rektəmi] *n. Surg:* hystérectomie *f.*
hysteria [his'tiriə] *n. Med:* hystérie *f*; crise *f* de nerfs; **mass h.,** hystérie collective.
hysteric [his'terik] *a. & n.* hystérique (*mf*).
hysterical [his'terik(ə)l] *a.* **1.** *Med:* hystérique; atteint(e) d'hystérie. **2.** (*a*) sujet à des crises de nerfs; (sanglots) convulsifs; (rire) nerveux, énervé; (*b*) en proie à une crise de nerfs; **she was h.,** elle était dans tous ses états. **-ally** *adv.* sans pouvoir maîtriser ses émotions; **to weep h.,** avoir une crise de larmes; **to laugh h.,** (i) être pris d'un rire nerveux; (ii) avoir le fou rire.
hysterics [his'teriks] *n.pl.* **1.** attaque *f* de nerfs; crise *f* de nerfs; **to go into h.,** avoir une crise de nerfs. **2.** (i) fou rire; (ii) sanglots convulsifs; **to go into h.,** avoir le fou rire.

I

I[1] [ai] *n.* (la lettre, I, i *m*; *F:* **to dot one's i's (and cross one's t's),** mettre les points sur les i.

I[2] **1.** *pers.pron.* (*a*) (*unstressed*) je *mf*, (*joined to vowel*) j'; **I sing,** je chante; **I accuse,** j'accuse; **here I am,** me voici; **what have I said?** qu'ai-je dit? (*b*) (*stressed*) moi *mf*; **he and I,** lui et moi; **I too,** moi aussi. **2.** *n.* **another I,** un autre moi(-même).

iambic [ai'æmbik] *Pros:* **1.** *a.* & *n.* **i. (foot),** ïambe *m*; vers *m* ïambique. **2.** *n.* (*poem*) ïambe.

Iberia [ai'biːriə] *Pr.n. Geog:* Ibérie *f.*

Iberian [ai'biːriən] **1.** *a.* (peuple) ibérien, ibérique; **the I. peninsula,** la Péninsule ibérique. **2.** *n.* Ibère *mf.*

ibex, *pl.* **-exes** ['aibeks, -eksiz] *n. Z:* ibex *m*; bouquetin *m* (des Alpes).

ibis, *pl.* **-ises** ['aibis, -isiz] *n. Orn:* ibis *m.*

ice[1] [ais] *n.* glace *f.* **1.** (*a*) **my feet are as cold as i.,** j'ai les pieds glacés; *Fig:* **to break the i.,** briser la glace; **to be on, skate on, thin i.,** être sur, toucher à, un sujet délicat; *F:* **to cut no i. with s.o.,** ne faire aucune impression sur qn; (*b*) *Dom.Ec:* glace (à rafraîchir); *F:* **to put a project on i.,** mettre un projet en veilleuse; (*c*) *Geog:* **the i. regions, seas,** les régions, mers, glaciales; **drift i.,** glace(s) flottante(s); **pack i.,** glace de banquise; pack *m*; (*d*) *Meteor:* givre *m*; **black i.,** verglas *m* (sur les routes); (*e*) *Geol:* **i. age,** période *f* glaciaire; *Geog:* **i. floe,** banquise *f*, banc *m* de glace; **i. cap,** calotte *f* glaciaire; **i. bucket,** seau *m* à glace, à rafraîchir; **i.-cold,** froid comme la glace; (eau) glacée; (vent) glacial; **i. cube,** glaçon *m*; *Sp:* **i. hockey,** hockey *m* sur glace, *Fr.C:* hockey; **i. skating,** patinage *m* sur glace; **i. rink,** patinoire *f*; **show on i.,** spectacle sur glace; **i. pick,** (i) *Mount:* pioche *f* à glace; (ii) *Dom.Ec:* poinçon *m* à glace. **2.** *Cu:* **strawberry i.,** glace à la fraise; **water i.,** sorbet *m*. **3.** *Ch:* **dry i.,** neige *f* carbonique. **4.** *P:* diamants *mpl.*

ice[2] **1.** *v.tr.* (*a*) congeler, geler; (*b*) rafraîchir (l'eau, un melon, etc.) avec de la glace; frapper (du champagne); (*c*) glacer (un gâteau). **2.** *v.i.* (*of pond, etc.*) **to i. (up, over),** geler; (*of windscreen, propeller, etc.*) **to i. (up),** se givrer. **iced** *a.* **1.** (*of cream*) glacé, à la glace; (melon) rafraîchi; (champagne) frappé; (café) glacé. **2.** (gâteau) glacé. **icing** *n.* **1.** (*a*) congélation *f*; (*b*) givrage *m*; (*c*) glaçage *m* (d'un gâteau); **i. sugar,** sucre glace. **2.** glace *f* (de sucre).

iceberg ['aisbəːg] *n.* **1.** iceberg *m*. **2.** *F:* (*pers.*) glaçon *m.*

icebound ['aisbaund] *a.* (i) (navire) retenu, bloqué, par les glaces; (ii) (port, etc.) fermé par les glaces.

icebox ['aisbɔks] *n.* **1.** glacière *f* (domestique); compartiment *m* à glace. **2.** *NAm:* réfrigérateur *m.*

icecream ['aiskriːm] *n.* glace *f* (à la crème); **i.-c. man,** glacier *m*; **i.-c. parlour,** salon *m* de dégustation de glaces.

icehouse ['aishaus] *n.* glacière *f.*

Iceland ['aislənd] *Pr.n. Geog:* Islande *f.*

Icelander ['aisləndər] *n. Geog:* Islandais, -aise.

Icelandic [ais'lændik] **1.** *a.* islandais, d'Islande. **2.** *n. Ling:* islandais *m.*

iceman, *pl.* **-men** ['aismæn, -men] *n.m.* **1.** fabricant de glace. **2.** glacier, marchand de glaces.

ichthyology [ikθi'ɔlədʒi] *n.* icht(h)yologie *f.*

ichthyosaur(us) [ikθiou'sɔːr(əs)] *n. Paleont:* icht(h)yosaure *m.*

icicle ['aisikl] *n.* petit glaçon; chandelle *f* de glace.

icky ['iki] *a. U.S: F:* (*childish language*) collant.

icon ['aikɔn] *n. Ecc:* icône *f.*

iconoclast [ai'kɔnouklæst] *n.* iconoclaste *mf.*

iconoclastic [aikɔnou'klæstik] *a.* iconoclaste.

icy ['aisi] *a.* **1.** couvert de glace; glacial, -als; (route) verglacée. **2.** (froid, *Fig:* accueil) glacial; (mains) glacées. **-ily** *adv.* **1.** d'un air glacial. **2. it's i. cold,** il fait un froid glacial.

I'd = (i) **I had,** *see* HAVE[2]; (ii) **I would,** *see* WILL[3].

idea [ai'diːə] *n.* idée *f*; (*a*) **general i.,** idée générale; aperçu *m* (d'un livre); **I can't bear the i. (of it),** je ne peux pas en souffrir l'idée; **I have an i. that I've seen him before,** j'ai l'impression de l'avoir déjà vu; **it's not my i. of pleasure,** ce n'est pas là ma conception du plaisir; **I had no i. that . . .,** je ne soupçonnais pas que . . .; je n'avais aucune idée que . . .; **you have no i. how anxious I was,** vous ne vous rendez pas compte combien j'étais inquiet; **he has some i. of chemistry,** il a des notions de chimie; (*b*) **a bright i.,** une idée lumineuse; **what a funny i.!** quelle drôle d'idée! **what a good i.!** quelle bonne idée! **to be full of ideas,** avoir de l'idée; **man of ideas,** homme d'idées; **to get an i. that . . .,** s'imaginer que . . .; **to get ideas into one's head,** se faire des idées; **what put that i. into your head?** qu'est-ce qui vous a donné cette idée? *F:* **what an i.!** en voilà une idée! **the (very) i.!** quelle idée! **get the idea?** vous comprenez? (*c*) **I had some i. of going as far as Paris,** j'avais quelque idée de pousser jusqu'à Paris.

ideal [ai'diːəl] **1.** *a.* idéal, *pl.* idéaux; **it's i.!** c'est le rêve! c'est l'idéal! **2.** *n.* idéal *m*, *pl.* -als, -aux; (*a*) **the i. of beauty,** le beau idéal; l'idéal de la beauté; (*b*) **a man with no ideals,** un homme sans idéal; **his high ideals,** sa hauteur de vues; (*c*) *Mth:* idéal. **-ally** *adv.* idéalement; **i., everyone should share alike,** l'idéal serait le partage égal pour tout le monde.

idealism [ai'diəlizm] *n.* idéalisme *m.*

idealist [ai'diəlist] *n.* idéaliste *mf.*

idealistic [aidiə'listik] *a.* idéaliste.

idealize [ai'diəlaiz] *v.tr.* idéaliser.

identical [ai'dentik(ə)l] *a.* identique (**with,** à); même; **i. copy (of a text),** copie textuelle; **i. twins,** vrais jumeaux, vraies jumelles. **-ally** *adv.* identiquement.

identification [aidentifi'keiʃ(ə)n] *n.* identification *f*; (*a*) **i. of sth. with sth.,** identification de qch. avec qch; (*b*) identification (d'un cadavre, d'un malfaiteur); **i. parade,** séance *f* d'identification d'un suspect; **i. papers,** pièces *fpl* d'identité; *Av: Nau:* **i. marks,** (lettres *fpl* et numéros *mpl* d')immatriculation *f.*

identify [ai'dentifai] *v.tr.* **1.** identifier; (*a*) **to i. oneself with a cause,** s'identifier à, avec, s'assimiler à, une cause; (*b*) identifier (qn, qch.); reconnaître (qn, qch, un navire.). **2.** *Nat.Hist:* déterminer (un spécimen). **3.** *v.i.* s'identifier (**with,** avec, à); **I can't i. (with it),** ça n'a rien à voir avec moi.

identikit [ai'dentikit] *n.* **i. (picture),** portrait-robot *m*, photo-robot *m*, *pl.* portraits-, photos-robots.

identity [ai'dentiti] *n.* identité *f*; (*a*) **i. between two things,** identité entre deux choses, de deux choses; (*b*) **to establish the i. of s.o.,** identifier qn; **to prove one's i.,** établir son identité; **mistaken i.,** erreur *f* sur la personne; *Adm:* **i. card,** carte *f* d'identité; *Mil:* **i. disk, bracelet,** plaque *f*, bracelet *m*, d'identité.

ideogram ['idiəgræm], **ideograph** ['idiəgræf] *n.* idéogramme *m.*

ideological [aidiə'lɔdʒik(ə)l] *a. Phil: etc:* idéologique.

ideologist [aidi'ɔlədʒist] *n.* idéologue *mf.*

ideology [aidi'ɔlədʒi] *n.* idéologie *f.*

ides [aidz] *n.pl. Rom.Ant:* ides *fpl.*

idiocy ['idiəsi] *n.* **1.** **(congenital) i.,** idiotie (congénitale); idiotisme *m.* **2.** bêtise *f,* stupidité *f.*

idiom ['idiəm] *n.* **1.** (*a*) dialecte *m*; idiome *m* (d'une région); (*b*) langue *f,* idiome (d'un pays). **2.** idiotisme *m,* locution *f* (d'une langue); **a French i.,** un gallicisme; **an English i.,** un anglicisme.

idiomatic [idiə'mætik] *a.* **1.** idiomatique; **i. phrase,** idiotisme *m*; expression *f* idiomatique. **2.** qui appartient à la langue courante, à la langue familière; **his French is not very i.,** son français n'est pas le français tel qu'on le parle. **-ally** *adv.* (s'exprimer, etc.) de façon idiomatique.

idiosyncrasy [idiou'siŋkrəsi] *n.* **1.** *Med: etc:* idiosyncrasie *f.* **2.** particularité *f*; petite manie; tic *m.*

idiosyncratic [idiousiŋ'krætik] *a.* **1.** idiosyncrasique. **2.** particulier, caractéristique.

idiot ['idiət] *n.* **1.** *Med:* idiot, -ote; imbécile *mf*; **congenital i.,** idiot congénital. **2.** imbécile; **what an i. I've been!** comme j'ai été bête! **you i.!** espèce d'imbécile, d'idiot!

idiotic [idi'ɔtik] *a.* bête, idiot; **that's i.,** c'est stupide, c'est idiot; **don't be i.!** ne fais pas l'idiot! **-ally** *adv.* idiotement.

idiotism ['idiətizm] *n. NAm:* idiotisme *m,* locution *f* (d'une langue).

idle[1] ['aid(ə)l] *a.* **1.** (*a*) (*of pers.*) inoccupé, oisif, désœuvré; **to be, stand, i.,** rester à ne rien faire; **in my i. moments,** à mes heures perdues; (*b*) (*of machinery, employees*) qui chôme, en chômage; (*of machine*) au repos; **to run i.,** (i) (*of machine*) marcher à vide; (ii) *I.C.E:* (*of engine*) tourner au ralenti; (*of money*) **to lie i.,** dormir; (*c*) *Mec.E:* (roue) folle, décalée; (pignon) fou, intermédiaire; **i. period,** période *f* d'inactivité; (*in mechanical cycle*) temps mort; (*d*) *El:* (courant) déwatté. **2.** (*of pers.*) paresseux, fainéant, indolent; **the i. rich,** les riches désœuvrés. **3.** (*of actions, feelings, etc.*) inutile, vain, futile; (larmes) inutiles; (idée, menace) en l'air; (rumeur) sans fondement; **out of i. curiosity,** par simple curiosité. **idly** *adv.* **1.** sans rien faire, sans travailler; **to stand i. by,** rester là à ne rien faire. **2.** inutilement; d'une façon futile; (parler) en l'air. **3.** (*a*) paresseusement; (*b*) nonchalamment; **to do sth. i.,** faire qch. pour passer le temps.

idle[2] *v.i.* **1.** fainéanter, musarder; *v.tr.* **to i. one's time away,** perdre son temps à ne rien faire. **2.** *Aut:* (*of engine*) tourner au ralenti. **idling** **1.** *a. I.C.E:* (moteur) au ralenti. **2.** *n.* (*a*) fainéantise *f*; (*b*) *I.C.E:* (marche *f* au) ralenti (*m*).

idleness ['aid(ə)lnis] *n.* **1.** (*a*) inaction *f,* oisiveté *f,* désœuvrement *m*; *Prov:* **i. is the root of all evil,** l'oisiveté est (la) mère de tous les vices; (*b*) chômage *m* (involontaire) (d'une fabrique, etc.). **2.** futilité *f* (d'une menace, d'un projet, etc.). **3.** (*of pers.*) paresse *f,* fainéantise *f.*

idler ['aidlər] *n.* **1.** (*a*) oisif, -ive; flâneur, -euse; (*b*) fainéant, -ante. **2.** *Mec.E:* (i) roue folle, décalée; (ii) pignon fou, intermédiaire.

idol ['aid(ə)l] *n.* idole *f*; (*a*) **i. worship,** idolâtrie *f*; (*b*) **to make an i. of wealth,** faire son idole de l'argent.

idolater [ai'dɔlətər], *f.* **idolatress** [ai'dɔlətris] *n.* **1.** idolâtre *mf.* **2.** *F:* adorateur, -trice (**of,** de).

idolatrous [ai'dɔlətrəs] *a.* (vénération) idolâtre; (culte) idolâtrique.

idolatry [ai'dɔlətri] *n.* idolâtrie *f*; culte *m* des idoles.

idolize ['aidəlaiz] *v.tr.* idolâtrer, adorer (qn, qch.); faire une idole de (qn, l'argent). **idolizing** **1.** *a.* (regard, etc.) plein d'adoration. **2.** *n.* idolâtrie *f.*

idyll ['(a)idil] *n.* idylle *f.*

idyllic [(a)i'dilik] *a.* idyllique.

if [if] *conj.* si. **1.** (*conditional*) (*a*) **if I am late, I apologize,** si je suis en retard, je fais mes excuses; (*b*) **if he does it, he will be punished,** s'il le fait, il sera puni; **let him do it if he dare(s)!** qu'il le fasse s'il ose! **if you hesitate (at all),** pour peu que vous hésitiez; **if (it is) necessary,** s'il est nécessaire; s'il le faut; au besoin; **if (it is) possible,** si c'est possible; si possible; **if (it be) so,** s'il en est ainsi; **modifications, if any, will have to be made later,** les modifications éventuelles devront être apportées plus tard; **if not,** sinon; **go and see him, if only to please me,** allez le voir ne serait-ce que pour me faire plaisir; (*c*) **if I were** you, si j'étais vous; à votre place; **if it were so,** même s'il en était ainsi; **even if he did say so,** quand même il l'aurait dit; (*d*) (*exclamatory*) **if I had only known!** si seulement je l'avais su! **if only he comes in time!** pourvu qu'il vienne à temps! (*e*) **as if,** comme si; **he looks as if he were drunk,** il a l'air d'être ivre; **as if to show it,** comme pour le montrer; **as if by chance,** comme par hasard; **as if I would allow it!** comme si je le permettrais! **2.** (*concessive*) **pleasant weather, if rather cold,** temps agréable, bien qu'un peu froid; **well-paid, if uninteresting, work,** travail bien rémunéré à défaut d'être intéressant. **3.** (*introducing a noun clause,* = WHETHER) **I asked if it was true,** j'ai demandé si c'était vrai. **4.** *n.* si *m inv*; **your ifs and buts make me tired,** je suis fatigué de vos si et de vos mais; **it's a very big if,** c'est une condition qui n'est pas aisément remplie.

igloo ['iglu:] *n.* igloo *m*

igneous ['igniəs] *a.* (roche) éruptive, ignée.

ignite [ig'nait] **1.** *v.tr.* mettre feu à (qch.); allumer (une charge de mine); enflammer (un mélange explosif). **2.** *v.i.* prendre feu, s'enflammer, s'allumer.

ignition [ig'niʃ(ə)n] *n.* **1.** ignition *f* (d'une charge de mine, etc.). **2.** *I.C.E:* allumage *m*; **to cut, switch, off the i.,** couper l'allumage; **delayed retarded, i.,** retard *m* à l'allumage; allumage retardé; **i. cable, lead, wire,** fil *m* d'allumage, de bougie; **i. spark,** étincelle *f* d'allumage; **i. switch,** contact *m.*

ignoble [ig'noubl] *a.* (*of act, etc.*) ignoble, bas, *f.* basse; infâme, vil.

ignominious [ignə'miniəs] *a.* **1.** ignominieux, honteux. **-ly** *adv.* ignominieusement; honteusement.

ignominy ['ignəmini] *n.* ignominie *f,* honte *f.*

ignoramus [ignə'reiməs] *n.* ignorant, -ante; ignare *mf.*

ignorance ['ignərəns] *n.* ignorance *f.* **1.** **through i.,** par ignorance; **to keep s.o. in i. of sth.,** laisser qn dans l'ignorance de qch.; **I am in complete i. of his intentions,** j'ignore tout de ses intentions; *Jur:* **i. of the law is no excuse,** nul n'est censé ignorer la loi. **2.** **crass i.,** ignorance crasse.

ignorant ['ignərənt] *a.* ignorant. **1.** (*unaware*) **to be i. of a fact,** ignorer un fait; *Jur:* être ignorant du fait. **2.** (*a*) (*unlearned*) **he is i. of the world,** il ne connaît pas le monde; (*b*) (question) qui trahit l'ignorance; **an i. person,** un ignorant. **-ly** *adv.* **1.** par ignorance. **2.** (discourir) avec ignorance.

ignore [ig'nɔ:r] *v.tr.* **1.** feindre d'ignorer (qch.); ne tenir aucun compte de (qch.); passer (qch.) sous silence; ignorer (qn); feindre de ne pas voir (qn); méconnaître (les faits); ne pas répondre à (une invitation); ne pas relever (une injure); sortir (d'une règle); ne tenir aucun compte (d'un ordre); *Rail:* brûler (un signal). **2.** *Jur:* rejeter (une plainte).

iguana [i'gwɑ:nə] *n. Rept:* iguane *m.*

ikon ['aikɔn] *n. Ecc:* icône *f.*

ilex, *pl.* **-exes** [ˈaileks, -eksiz] *n. Bot:* ilex *m.*
ilk [ilk] *n.* (*a*) *Scot:* (*of landowner bearing the name of his property*) **Moray of that i.,** Moray du domaine de Moray; (*b*) *Pej:* **and others of that i.,** et d'autres du même genre.
ill [il] *a., adv., & n.* (*comp.* **worse,** *sup.* **worst**) **I.** *a.* **1.** (*a*) (*of reputation, health, etc.*) mauvais; (effet) pernicieux; **i. breeding,** manque *m* de savoir-vivre; **i. luck, fortune,** mauvaise chance; **house of i. fame,** maison mal famée; *Prov:* **it is an i. wind that blows nobody any good,** à quelque chose malheur est bon; (*b*) (*of deed, nature, etc.*) méchant, mauvais; **i. will,** malveillance *f*; **i. feeling,** rancune *f.* **2.** (*a*) malade, souffrant; **to be, feel, i.,** être malade; se sentir souffrant; **to fall, get, be taken, i.,** tomber malade; **he was seriously i. last year,** il a fait une grave maladie l'année dernière; **to look i.,** avoir mauvaise mine; (*b*) *F:* **to be i.,** vomir; avoir mal au cœur. **II.** *adv.* mal. **1.** *Lit:* **to take sth. i.,** prendre qch. en mauvaise part. **2. to be i. provided with sth.,** être mal pourvu de qch.; **I can i. afford the expense,** je peux difficilement supporter cette dépense; **it i. becomes you to . . .,** il vous sied mal de . . . **3. to be, feel, i. at ease,** (i) être mal à l'aise; (ii) être, se sentir, inquiet (**about,** au sujet de). **III.** *n.* **1.** mal *m*; **to speak i. of s.o.,** dire du mal de qn. **2.** (*a*) dommage *m,* tort *m*; **I have suffered no i. at his hands,** il ne m'a fait aucun tort; (*b*) **ills,** maux *mpl,* malheurs *mpl.*
I'll = (i) **I will;** (ii) **I shall.**
ill-advised [ˈiləd'vaizd] *a.* **1.** (*of pers.*) malavisé. **2.** (*of action*) impolitique, peu judicieux.
ill-assorted [ˈiləˈsɔːtid] *a.* mal assorti; disparate.
ill-behaved [ˈilbiˈheivd] *a.* qui se conduit, se tient, mal.
ill-bred [ˈilˈbred] *a.* mal élevé, malappris.
ill-concealed [ilkənˈsiːld] *a.* mal dissimulé.
ill-considered [ilkənˈsidəd] *a.* (*of action, view, etc.*) peu réfléchi; (*of measure, etc.*) hâtif.
ill-disposed [ildisˈpouzd] *a.* **1.** malintentionné, malveillant; **i.-d. towards s.o.,** mal disposé envers qn. **2. to be i.-d. to do sth.,** être peu disposé à faire qch.
illegal [iˈliːg(ə)l] *a.* illégal, -aux. **-ally** *adv.* illégalement.
illegible [iˈledʒibl] *a.* illisible. **-ibly** *adv.* illisiblement.
illegitimacy [iliˈdʒitiməsi] *n.* illégitimité *f.*
illegitimate [iliˈdʒitimət] *a.* **1.** (conclusion) illégitime; (déclaration) non autorisée. **2.** illégal, -aux. **3.** *Jur:* (enfant) illégitime, bâtard. **-ly** *adv.* illégitimement.
ill-fated [ilˈfeitid] *a.* (enfant) infortuné; (jour) fatal.
ill-founded [ilˈfaundid] *a.* (*of rumour*) mal fondé, sans fondement.
ill-gotten [ilˈgɔtn] *a.* mal acquis.
ill-humoured, *NAm:* **-humored** [ilˈhjuːməd] *a.* de mauvaise humeur.
illiberal [iˈlibər(ə)l] *a.* peu libéral, -aux; (*a*) mal élevé; sans distinction; (*b*) borné, petit (d'esprit); (*c*) peu généreux, mesquin.
illiberality [ilibəˈræliti] *n.* illibéralité *f*; (*a*) petitesse *f* (d'esprit); (*b*) manque *m* de générosité.
illicit [iˈlisit] *a.* illicite. **-ly** *adv* illicitement.
illimitable [iˈlimitəbl] *a.* illimité.
ill-informed [ilinˈfɔːmd] *a.* **1.** mal renseigné. **2.** peu instruit; (*of criticism, etc.*) ignorant.
ill-intentioned [ilinˈtenʃ(ə)nd] *a.* malintentionné (**towards,** envers).
illiteracy [iˈlit(ə)rəsi] *n.* analphabétisme *m.*
illiterate [iˈlit(ə)rət] *a. & n.* illettré, -ée; analphabète (*mf*).
ill-judged [ilˈdʒʌdʒd] *a.* (*of action*) malavisé; peu sage.
ill-kempt [ilˈkempt] *a.* (*of hair, etc.*) mal peigné; (*of pers., garden, etc.*) peu soigné; négligé.
ill-mannered [ilˈmænəd] *a.* grossier, malappris; **to be i.-m.,** être mal élevé.
ill-natured [ilˈneitʃəd] *a.* d'un mauvais caractère; méchant; désagréable.
illness [ˈilnis] *n.* maladie *f.*
illogical [iˈlɔdʒik(ə)l] *a.* illogique; peu logique. **-ally** *adv.* illogiquement.
illogicality [ilɔdʒiˈkæliti] *n.* illogisme *m.*
ill-starred [ˈilˈstɑːd] *a.* né sous une mauvaise étoile; (jour) malheureux, néfaste.
ill-suited [ilˈs(j)uːtid] *a.* mal assorti.
ill-tempered [ilˈtempəd] *a.* (*of pers.*) de mauvais caractère; hargneux, maussade, grincheux.
ill-timed [ilˈtaimd] *a.* mal à propos, hors de propos; (arrivée) inopportune; (plaisanterie) hors de saison.
ill-treat [ilˈtriːt] *v.tr.* maltraiter, brutaliser (qn, un chien); rudoyer (un cheval).
ill-treatment [ilˈtriːtmənt] *n.* mauvais traitements.
illuminate [iˈl(j)uːmineit] *v.tr.* **1.** éclairer (une salle, etc.). **2.** illuminer (un édifice). **3.** enluminer (un manuscrit). **4.** (*a*) éclairer, élucider (un sujet, une question); (*b*) *Rel: Phil:* illuminer (l'esprit). **illuminated** *a.* **1.** éclairé; (enseigne) lumineuse. **2.** (manuscrit) enluminé. **illuminating 1.** *a.* (*a*) éclairant; (effet) lumineux; (*b*) (discours, entretien) qui éclaire la situation. **2.** *n.* (*a*) éclairage *m*; (*b*) illumination *f* (d'un édifice); (*c*) enluminure *f* (d'un manuscrit); (*d*) élucidation *f* (d'un sujet, etc.).
illumination [il(j)umiˈneiʃ(ə)n] *n.* **1.** (*a*) éclairage *m* (d'une salle, etc.); (*b*) illumination *f* (d'un édifice); (*c*) enluminure *f* (d'un manuscrit). **2.** (*a*) **we went out to see the illuminations,** nous sommes sortis voir les illuminations; (*b*) enluminure (d'un manuscrit). **3.** *Ph:* (*a*) **(degree of) i.,** éclairement *m*; (*b*) *Opt:* éclat *m* (d'une lentille, etc.). **4.** *Theol:* illumination.
illuminator [iˈl(j)uːmineitər] *n.* (*pers.*) (*a*) illuminateur, -trice; (*b*) *Art:* enlumineur, -euse.
ill-use [ilˈjuːz] *v.tr.* (*a*) maltraiter (un enfant, une femme); malmener (un adversaire); (*b*) mal agir envers (qn).
illusion [iˈluːʒ(ə)n] *n.* illusion *f*; **optical i.,** (i) illusion, (ii) truc *m,* d'optique; **to be under an i.,** être (la) victime d'une illusion; **to cherish an i.,** se bercer d'une illusion; **I have no illusions on this point,** je ne me fais aucune illusion sur ce point.
illusionist [iˈluːʒənist] *n.* prestidigitateur *m,* illusionniste *mf.*
illusory [iˈluːs(ə)ri] *a.* illusoire; trompeur.
illustrate [ˈiləstreit] *v.tr.* **1.** éclairer, expliquer, démontrer (qch.) par des exemples; **lectures illustrated by slides,** conférences illustrées par des projections. **2.** illustrer (le texte d'un livre, d'un journal); **illustrated magazine,** (journal, magazine) illustré (*m*).
illustration [iləsˈtreiʃ(ə)n] *n.* **1.** explication *f,* exemple *m,* preuve *f* (d'un principe, etc.); **by way of i.,** à titre d'exemple. **2.** illustration *f*; (*a*) art *m* d'illustrer (les livres, etc.); (*b*) gravure *f,* image *f* (dans le texte d'un livre, etc.); **text i.,** vignette *f.*
illustrative [ˈiləstr(ə)tiv] *a.* qui sert à expliquer; **i. of sth.,** qui explique, illustre, qch.
illustrator [ˈiləstreitər] *n.* illustrateur *m.*
illustrious [iˈlʌstriəs] *a.* illustre, fameux, célèbre. **-ly** *adv.* illustrement.
I'm = **I am,** *see* BE.
image [ˈimidʒ] *n.* **1.** (*a*) image (sculptée); représentation *f,* statue *f* (d'un dieu, etc.); (*for worship*) idole *f*; (*b*) *Num:* image. **2.** *Opt:* image; (*a*) **ghost i.,** image blanche; *Phot:* **latent i.,** image latente; (*b*) *Elcs: T.V:* **i. distortion,** distorsion *f* d'image. **3.** image; portrait *m*; **God created man in his own i.,** Dieu créa l'homme à son image; **he's the very, living,** *F:* **spitting, i. of his**

father, c'est le portrait vivant de son père; *F:* c'est son père tout craché. **4.** (*a*) image; idée *f*, conception *f*; **he dismissed her i. from his mind,** il chassa son image de sa pensée; (*b*) *Com:* **brand i.,** image de marque; (*of politician, etc.*) **(public) i.,** image (de marque). **5.** image, métaphore.

imagery [ˈimidʒ(ə)ri] *n.* **1.** *coll.* images sculptées; idoles *fpl.* **2.** figures *fpl* de rhétorique; images.

imaginable [iˈmædʒinəbl] *a.* imaginable; **the finest thing i.,** la plus belle chose qu'on puisse imaginer.

imaginary [iˈmædʒin(ə)ri] *a.* imaginaire; de pure fantaisie.

imagination [imædʒiˈneiʃ(ə)n] *n.* imagination *f*; **to have no i.,** manquer d'imagination; **that's your i.!** vous l'avez rêvé!

imaginative [iˈmædʒinətiv] *a.* **1.** (*of pers., faculty, etc.*) imaginatif. **2.** (poème, etc.) d'imagination.

imaginativeness [iˈmædʒinətivnis] *n.* **1.** nature imaginative (d'un poème, etc.). **2.** imagination *f*; esprit inventif.

imagine [iˈmædʒin] *v.tr.* **1.** (*a*) imaginer, concevoir (qch.); se figurer, se représenter (qch.); se faire une idée de (qch.); **as may (well) be imagined,** comme on peut (se) l'imaginer; **i. meeting you here!** qui aurait jamais pensé vous rencontrer ici! **just i. my despair,** représentez-vous, imaginez(-vous) un peu, mon désespoir; **you can't i. it!** vous n'avez pas idée! (*b*) (*suppose*) **I i. them to be fairly rich,** je les crois assez riches; **don't i. that I'm satisfied,** n'allez pas croire que je sois satisfait. **2.** s'imaginer, se figurer; **to i. all sorts of things, to be always imagining things,** se faire des idées.

imbalance [imˈbæləns] *n.* déséquilibre *m.*

imbecile [ˈimbisiːl] **1.** *a.* imbécile. **2.** *n.* imbécile *mf.*

imbecility [imbiˈsiliti] *n.* **1.** imbécillité *f.* **2.** stupidité *f*; imbécillité.

imbibe [imˈbaib] **1.** *v.tr.* (*a*) (*of pers.*) absorber, s'assimiler (des connaissances, des idées); (*b*) (*of pers.*) boire, avaler (une boisson); aspirer (l'air frais); (*c*) (*of thg*) imbiber (qch.); s'imprégner de (qch.). **2.** *v.i.* *F:* boire trop; picoler.

imbue [imˈbjuː] *v.tr.* *Lit:* **to i. s.o. with an idea,** pénétrer qn d'une idée; **imbued with false principles,** pénétré, imprégné, de faux principes.

imitable [ˈimitəbl] *a.* imitable.

imitate [ˈimiteit] *v.tr.* imiter; (*a*) copier; suivre l'exemple de (qn); **to i. s.o.'s style,** attraper la manière de qn; *Art: Lit: Mus:* pasticher le style de qn; (*b*) singer, mimer (qn); contrefaire (le cri d'un oiseau, etc.); (*c*) (*of insect, etc.*) **to i. its surroundings,** prendre l'aspect de son milieu.

imitation [imiˈteiʃ(ə)n] *n.* **1.** imitation *f*; **in i. of s.o., sth.,** à l'imitation de, imitant, qn, qch. **2.** (*a*) copie *f*, imitation; *Com:* contrefaçon *f*; (*b*) **i. leather,** cuir artificiel; similicuir *m*; **i. silver, gold,** similargent *m*, similor *m*; **i. jewellery,** bijoux *mpl* en faux, en toc; **to wear i. jewellery,** porter du faux.

imitative [ˈimitətiv] *a.* (*a*) (son, etc.) imitatif; (*b*) **manner, style, i. of s.o.,** manière *f*, style *m*, qui imite qn.

imitator [ˈimiteitər] *n.* **1.** (*a*) imitateur, -trice; (*b*) *Com:* contrefacteur *m*; (*c*) *Lit: etc:* pasticheur, -euse. **2.** *F:* singeur, *f.* singeuse.

immaculate [iˈmækjulət] *a.* **1.** immaculé; sans tache; *Theol:* **the I. Conception,** l'Immaculée Conception. **2.** (*of dress*) impeccable. **-ly** *adv.* **1.** sans tache. **2.** (vêtu) impeccablement.

immanent [ˈimənənt] *a. Phil:* immanent.

immaterial [iməˈtiəriəl] *a.* **1.** (esprit, etc.) immatériel, incorporel. **2.** (*a*) peu important; sans conséquence; **that fact is (quite) i.,** cela n'a aucune importance; (*b*) qui n'a aucun rapport.

immature [iməˈtjuər] *a.* (*a*) (qui n'est) pas mûr; (adulte) qui manque de maturité; (*b*) **the project is i.,** le projet n'est pas suffisamment mûri; **i. work,** œuvre *f* de jeunesse, d'apprenti; (*c*) *Biol:* immature.

immaturity [iməˈtjuəriti] *n.* immaturité *f*; manque *m* de maturité (d'un projet).

immeasurable [iˈmeʒ(ə)rəbl] *a.* (espace, abîme) incommensurable; (temps) immesurable, infini. **-ably** *adv.* infiniment.

immediacy [iˈmiːdiəsi] *n.* **1.** relation directe, intime **(of sth. with sth.,** entre qch. et qch.). **2.** caractère immédiat **(of,** de); imminence *f* (d'un danger); urgence *f* (d'un besoin).

immediate [iˈmiːdiət] *a.* immédiat. **1.** (*a*) direct; **my i. object,** mon premier but; **what are your i. plans?** que proposez-vous faire d'abord? **in the i. future,** dans un avenir immédiat; dans l'immédiat; (*b*) **my i. neighbour,** mon voisin immédiat; **the i. family, relations,** les proches parents. **2.** instantané; sans retard; **i. answer, delivery,** réponse, livraison, immédiate; **house for sale with i. possession,** maison *f* à vendre avec jouissance immédiate. **3.** (besoin, danger) pressant, urgent; **work of i. urgency,** travail *m* de première urgence. **-ly 1.** *adv.* immédiatement; (*a*) directement; **it does not affect me i.,** cela ne me touche pas directement; (*b*) tout de suite; sans délai; **please send i. . . .,** veuillez (bien) envoyer d'urgence . . .; **i. after,** aussitôt après. **2.** *conj.* **i. he received the money, he paid me,** dès qu'il eut reçu l'argent il me paya.

immemorial [imiˈmɔːriəl] *a.* immémorial, -aux; **from time i.,** de toute antiquité; de temps immémorial.

immense [iˈmens] *a.* **1.** (étendue) immense, vaste; (quantité) énorme. **2.** magnifique; **it was an i. success,** c'était un succès fou. **-ly** *adv.* **1.** immensément (vaste); énormément (riche). **2. to enjoy oneself i.,** s'amuser énormément.

immensity [iˈmensiti] *n.* **1.** immensité *f* (de l'univers, d'une fortune, etc.). **2.** énormité *f* (d'un crime).

immerse [iˈməːs] *v.tr.* **1.** (*a*) immerger, plonger (qn, qch.) (dans un liquide); (*b*) baptiser (qn) par immersion. **2. to be immersed in one's work, in one's thoughts,** être plongé, absorbé, dans son travail, dans ses pensées.

immersion [iˈməːʃ(ə)n] *n.* **1.** (*a*) immersion *f*; **i. (water) heater,** chauffe-eau *m inv* à immersion; (*b*) baptême *m* par immersion. **2.** absorption *f* (d'esprit) **(in,** dans).

immigrant [ˈimigrənt] *a. & n.* immigrant, -ante; immigré, -ée.

immigrate [ˈimigreit] *v.i.* immigrer.

immigration [imiˈgreiʃ(ə)n] *n.* immigration *f*; **i. officer,** agent *m* du service de l'immigration.

imminence [ˈiminəns] *n.* imminence *f* **(of,** de).

imminent [ˈiminənt] *a.* (danger, etc.) imminent.

immobile [iˈmoubail] *a.* immobile.

immobility [iməˈbiliti] *n.* immobilité *f.*

immobilize [iˈmoubilaiz] *v.tr.* **1.** (*a*) immobiliser (un membre blessé, etc.); (*b*) immobiliser, arrêter (une armée, la circulation, etc.). **2.** *Fin:* rendre (des capitaux) indisponibles; immobiliser (des espèces monnayées).

immoderate [iˈmɔd(ə)rət] *a.* immodéré, intempéré, outré; (soif) démesurée; (gaieté) exubérante. **-ly** *adv.* immodérément.

immodest [iˈmɔdist] *a.* (femme, tenue) impudique, sans pudeur. **-ly** *adv.* impudiquement.

immolate [ˈimouleit] *v.tr.* immoler (qn, qch.).

immoral [iˈmɔr(ə)l] *a.* immoral, -aux; (*a*) (*of pers., life*) dissolu; **i. conduct,** débauche *f*; (*b*) (ouvrage) contraire à la morale; (*c*) *Jur:* **for i. purposes,** aux fins de débauche; **(the crime of) living on i. earnings,** (le délit de) vagabondage spécial. **-ally** *adv.* immoralement.

immorality [imɔ'ræliti] *n.* immoralité *f*; (i) débauche *f*; (ii) acte immoral; **to incite to i.**, inciter à la débauche.

immortal [i'mɔːt(ə)l] *a. & n.* immortel (*m*); **the i. memory of . . .**, le souvenir impérissable de . . ..

immortality [imɔː'tæliti] *n.* immortalité *f*.

immortalize [i'mɔːtəlaiz] *v.tr.* immortaliser (le nom d'un auteur, etc.); éterniser, perpétuer (la mémoire de qn).

immovable [i'muːvəbl] **1.** *a.* (*a*) fixe; *Ecc:* **i. feast**, fête *f* fixe; (*b*) (opinion, volonté) immuable, inébranlable; (*c*) (visage) impassible; (*d*) *Jur:* **i. property**, biens immobiliers, immeubles. **2.** *n.pl. Jur:* **immovables**, biens immobiliers, immeubles.

immune [i'mjuːn] *a.* (*a*) *Med:* **i. against, from, to, a poison**, immunisé contre un poison; (*b*) **i. from criticism**, à l'abri de la critique; **i. from taxation**, exempt d'impôts.

immunity [i'mjuːniti] *n.* **1.** exemption *f* (**from**, de); **diplomatic i.**, immunité *f* diplomatique. **2.** *Med:* immunité (**from a disease**, contre une maladie).

immunization [imjunai'zeiʃ(ə)n] *n. Med:* immunisation *f* (**against**, contre).

immunize ['imjunaiz] *v.tr. Med:* immuniser (**s.o. against sth.**, qn contre qch.).

immunology [imju'nɔlədʒi] *n. Med:* immunologie *f*.

immure [i'mjuər] *v.tr.* **1.** enfermer, cloîtrer (qn). **2.** emmurer (une victime).

immutability [imjuːtə'biliti] *n.* immu(t)abilité *f*.

immutable [i'mjuːtəbl] *a.* immuable; inaltérable. **-ably** *adv.* immuablement.

imp [imp] *n.* (*a*) diablotin *m*, lutin *m*, gobelin *m*; (*b*) *F:* (*of child*) petit espiègle, petite espiègle.

impact¹ ['impækt] *n.* **1.** choc *m*, impact *m*, collision *f*; (*a*) *Ph: Mec:* **i. of one body on, against, another**, choc d'un corps contre un autre; (*b*) *Artil: Ball:* impact; point *m* de chute (d'un projectile); **on i.**, à l'impact, à l'arrivée; **point of i.**, point d'impact. **2.** *Fig:* répercussion(s) *f*(*pl*), impact; **the i. of a publicity campaign**, la force d'impact d'une campagne publicitaire; **his speech made a great i. on the audience**, son discours eut un effet retentissant sur l'auditoire.

impact² [im'pækt] *v.tr.* encastrer (**into**, dans); loger, fixer (solidement) (**into**, dans). **impacted** *a.* encastré; *Surg:* (fracture) avec impaction; *Dent:* (dent) barrée.

impair [im'pɛər] *v.tr.* affaiblir (la vue, l'esprit); altérer, abîmer (la santé); faire perdre, diminuer (les forces); ébrécher (sa fortune); compromettre (l'autorité de qn); **seriously impaired health**, santé gravement atteinte.

impairment [im'pɛəmənt] *n.* affaiblissement *m* (de la vue, de la mémoire); altération *f*, ébranlement *m* (de la santé); diminution *f* (des forces).

impala [im'pɑːlə] *n. Z:* impala *m*.

impale [im'peil] *v.tr.* **to be impaled**, être empalé, s'empaler (sur une grille, etc.).

impalpable [im'pælpəbl] *a.* **1.** impalpable, intangible. **2.** insaisissable (à l'esprit).

impanel [im'pænəl] *v.tr.* (**impanelled**, *NAm:* **impaneled**) constituer (d'office) (un comité, etc.); *Jur:* **to i. a jury**, former, dresser, la liste du jury.

impart [im'pɑːt] *v.tr.* **1.** (*a*) donner (du courage, etc.), imprimer, communiquer (un mouvement) (**to**, à); (*b*) transmettre (de la chaleur). **2.** communiquer (des connaissances); faire connaître, annoncer, confier (une nouvelle); transmettre (la vérité) (**to**, à).

impartial [im'pɑːʃ(ə)l] *a.* (*of pers., conduct*) impartial, -aux; sans prévention (**towards**, envers); **to be i.**, être impartial, équitable. **-ally** *adv.* impartialement; avec impartialité; (juger) équitablement.

impartiality [impɑːʃi'æliti] *n.* impartialité *f* (**to**, envers).

impassable [im'pɑːsəbl] *a.* (rivière) infranchissable; (barrière) impassable; (route) impraticable.

impasse ['æmpɑːs] *n.* impasse *f*.

impassioned [im'pæʃ(ə)nd] *a.* (orateur, discours, etc.) passionné; (style) chaleureux.

impassive [im'pæsiv] *a.* impassible; (visage) composé. **-ly** *adv.* impassiblement.

impatience [im'peiʃəns] *n.* (*a*) impatience *f*; (*b*) **i. of sth.**, intolérance *f* de qch.; (*c*) **i. to do sth.**, désir impatient de faire qch.; hâte *f* (de partir, etc.).

impatient [im'peiʃənt] *a.* (*a*) impatient; (réponse) vive, emportée; (ton) d'impatience; **to get, grow, i.**, s'impatienter; **to get i. with sth., s.o.**, s'impatienter de qch., contre qn; (*b*) **to be i. of advice**, ne pas supporter les conseils; (*c*) **to be i. for sth.**, être désireux, avide, de qch.; **to be i. to do sth.**, être impatient, *F:* brûler, de faire qch. **-ly** *adv.* (attendre) avec impatience; (répondre) sur un ton, d'un ton, d'impatience.

impeach [im'piːtʃ] *v.tr.* **1.** (*a*) attaquer, mettre en doute (la véracité, la probité, de qn); (*b*) *Jur:* récuser, reprocher (un témoin); révoquer (un témoignage) en doute. **2.** (*a*) **to i. s.o. of, with, a crime**, accuser qn d'un crime; (*b*) *Jur:* **to i. s.o. for high treason**, mettre qn en accusation pour haute trahison. **3.** blâmer, censurer (les motifs, la conduite, de qn).

impeachment [im'piːtʃmənt] *n.* **1.** (*a*) dénigrement *m* (de l'honneur de qn); (*b*) reproche *m*, récusation *f* (d'un témoin). **2.** *Jur:* mise *f* en accusation (d'un ministre, etc.).

impeccable [im'pekəbl] *a.* impeccable, irréprochable. **-ably** *adv.* irréprochablement, impeccablement.

impecunious [impi'kjuːniəs] *a.* impécunieux.

impedance [im'piːdəns] *n. El:* impédance *f*.

impede [im'piːd] *v.tr.* mettre obstacle à, empêcher, entraver (le progrès, l'activité, etc.); entraver (la circulation); contrarier (les mouvements de l'ennemi).

impediment [im'pedimənt] *n.* (*a*) entrave *f*, empêchement *m* (**to**, à); obstacle *m* (**to**, à); (*b*) **speech i.**, trouble *m* de la parole; **to have an i. in one's speech**, avoir la parole, la prononciation, embarrassée.

impedimenta [impedi'mentə] *n.pl.* impedimenta *mpl*; **all the i. of war**, tout l'attirail de la guerre.

impel [im'pel] *v.tr.* (**impelled**) **1.** pousser, forcer (**s.o. to do sth.**, qn à faire qch.). **2.** pousser (en avant); faire marcher. **impelling** *a.* (*a*) (*of force, etc.*) impulsif; (*b*) (besoin, etc.) urgent.

impending [im'pendiŋ] *a.* (danger, etc.) imminent, menaçant; **her impending arrival**, son arrivée prochaine.

impenetrability [impenitrə'biliti] *n.* impénétrabilité *f*.

impenetrable [im'penitrəbl] *a.* impénétrable (**to, by**, à); (mystère) insondable.

impenitence [im'penitəns] *n.* impénitence *f*.

impenitent [im'penitənt] *a. & n.* impénitent, -ente. **-ly** *adv.* sans repentir.

imperative [im'perətiv] **1.** *a. & n. Gram:* **i. (mood)**, (mode) impératif (*m*); **in the i. (mood)**, à l'impératif. **2.** *a.* (*a*) (ton) impératif, impérieux, péremptoire; (*b*) (besoin, etc.) urgent; **it is i. that he should come**, il faut absolument qu'il vienne. **-ly** *adv.* (parler) impérativement; (exiger) impérieusement.

imperceptible [impə'septibl] *a.* imperceptible; (bruit, différence) insaisissable; (différence) insensible. **-ibly** *adv.* imperceptiblement, insensiblement.

imperfect [im'pəːfikt] **1.** *a.* imparfait; *Mus:* (cadence) imparfaite. **2.** *a. & n. Gram:* **i. (tense)**, (temps) imparfait (*m*); **verb in the i.**, verbe *m* à l'imparfait. **-ly** *adv.* imparfaitement.

imperfection [impə'fekʃ(ə)n] *n.* **1.** imperfection *f*, défectuosité *f.* **2.** état incomplet; caractère imparfait.
imperial [im'piəriəl] **1.** *a.* (*a*) (gouvernement, etc.) impérial; **the i. crown,** la couronne impériale; **His (Her) I. Majesty,** sa Majesté Impériale; (*b*) (poids et mesures) qui ont cours légal dans le Royaume-Uni; **i. pint,** pinte légale; (*c*) majestueux, altier. **2.** *n.* (*a*) (*beard*) impériale *f*; (*b*) (papier) grand jésus. **-ally** *adv.* **1.** impérialement. **2.** majestueusement.
imperialism [im'piəriəlizm] *n.* impérialisme *m.*
imperialist [im'piəriəlist] *a.* & *n.* impérialiste (*mf*).
imperialistic [impiəriə'listik] *a.* impérialiste.
imperil [im'peril] *v.tr.* (**imperilled,** *NAm:* **imperiled**) mettre en péril, en danger; exposer (sa vie, etc.) au danger; compromettre (sa réputation).
imperious [im'piəriəs] *a.* **1.** (homme, ton, caractère) impérieux, dictatorial, -aux; (ton) impératif. **2.** urgent; (besoin) pressant. **-ly** *adv.* (parler, agir) impérieusement.
imperishable [im'periʃəbl] *a.* impérissable.
impermanent [im'pə:mənənt] *a.* impermanent.
impermeable [im'pə:miəbl] *a.* imperméable.
impersonal [im'pə:s(ə)n(ə)l] *a.* **1.** (style, etc.) impersonnel. **2.** *Gram:* (verbe) impersonnel. **-ally** *adv.* impersonnellement.
impersonate [im'pə:səneit] *v.tr.* **1.** personnifier (la vertu, etc.). **2.** (*a*) *Th:* représenter, jouer le rôle de (qn); (*b*) se faire passer pour (qn).
impersonation [impə:sə'neiʃ(ə)n] *n.* **1.** personnification *f.* **2.** *Th:* (*a*) création *f*, interprétation *f* (d'un rôle); (*b*) **to do impersonations,** faire des imitations *fpl* (de personnages).
impersonator [im'pə:səneitər] *n.* **1.** celui, celle, qui se fait passer pour un(e) autre. **2.** *Th:* (*a*) créateur, -trice, interprète *mf* (d'un rôle); (*b*) imitateur, -trice (de personnages, etc.); **male, female, i.,** actrice, acteur, qui joue un rôle travesti.
impertinence [im'pə:tinəns] *n.* **1.** (*a*) impertinence *f*, insolence *f*; (*b*) **an i., a piece of i.,** une impertinence. **2.** *Jur:* impertinence.
impertinent [im'pə:tinənt] *a.* **1.** impertinent, insolent; (remarque) déplacée; **to be i. to s.o.,** être insolent envers qn. **2.** *Jur:* (sujet, récit) impertinent, hors de propos. **-ly** *adv.* **1.** impertinemment, insolemment; d'un ton insolent. **2.** *Jur:* (répondre) en dehors de la question.
imperturbable [impə(:)'tə:bəbl] *a.* imperturbable.
impervious [im'pə:viəs] *a.* **1.** (*of material, etc.*) **i. (to water),** imperméable, étanche; *Geol:* **i. stratum,** couche *f* étanche. **2. i. to reason,** inaccessible, rebelle, à la raison; **he's i. to criticism,** il est indifférent à la critique.
impetigo [impi'taigou] *n. Med:* impétigo *m*; *F:* gourme *f.*
impetuosity [impetju'ɔsiti] impétuosité, fougue *f* (d'une personne).
impetuous [im'petjuəs] *a.* (caractère) fougueux, emporté, impétueux. **-ly** *adv.* impétueusement, avec impétuosité.
impetus ['impitəs] *n.* vitesse acquise; élan *m*; **to give an i. to sth.,** donner l'impulsion à qch.; **carried away by my own i.,** emporté par mon propre élan.
impiety [im'paiəti] *n.* impiété *f.*
impinge [im'pin(d)ʒ] *v.i.* **to i. on sth.,** (i) *O:* se heurter à, contre, qch.; (ii) empiéter sur (les droits d'autrui, etc.).
impingement [im'pindʒmənt] *n.* (*a*) *O:* heurt *m*; (*b*) empiètement *m* (sur les droits de qn, etc.).
impious ['impiəs] *a.* impie. **-ly** *adv.* avec impiété.
impish ['impiʃ] *a.* de petit diable; d'espiègle; (rire) espiègle, malicieux. **-ly** *adv.* en espiègle.
impishness ['impiʃnis] *n.* espièglerie *f.*
implacable [im'plækəbl] *a.* implacable (**towards,** à, pour, à l'égard de). **-ably** *adv.* implacablement.
implant¹ [im'plɑ:nt] *v.tr.* **1.** (*of bones, minerals*) **to be implanted,** être implanté (**in,** dans). **2.** inculquer (**an opinion in s.o.,** une opinion à qn); implanter (**an idea in s.o.,** une idée dans la tête de qn); insinuer (**a principle in s.o.,** un principe à qn); **from his youth this ideal had been implanted in his mind,** dès sa jeunesse il avait été pénétré de cet idéal. **3.** *Med:* implanter.
implant² ['implɑ:nt] *n. Surg:* implant *m.*
implausible [im'plɔ:zibl] *a.* peu plausible; invraisemblable. **-ibly** *adv.* invraisemblablement.
implement¹ ['implimənt] *n.* outil *m*, instrument *m*, ustensile *m*; **gardening implements,** outils de jardinage.
implement² ['impliment] *v.tr.* **1.** rendre effectif (un traité, etc.); exécuter, remplir (un engagement); mettre en œuvre (un accord); mettre à exécution (un projet); donner suite à (une décision). **2.** augmenter (qch.); suppléer à (qch.).
implementation [implimen'teiʃ(ə)n] *n.* exécution *f* (d'un engagement); mise *f* en œuvre (d'un accord).
implicate ['implikeit] *v.tr.* impliquer; (*a*) renfermer; **words implicating contradiction,** mots *m* qui renferment une contradiction; (*b*) **to i. s.o. in a crime,** impliquer, mêler, qn dans un crime; **without implicating anyone,** sans compromettre personne.
implication [impli'keiʃ(ə)n] *n.* **1.** implication *f*; **by i.,** implicitement; par induction; **the full i. of these words,** la portée de ces paroles. **2.** insinuation *f*, sous-entendu *m*, *pl.* sous-entendus.
implicit [im'plisit] *a.* **1.** (condition, etc.) implicite; (reconnaissance) tacite. **2.** (obéissance) absolue; **i. faith,** (i) *Theol:* foi *f* implicite; (ii) confiance *f* aveugle (**in,** dans). **-ly** *adv.* **1.** implicitement; tacitement. **2.** (obéir) aveuglément; **to trust s.o. i.,** avoir une foi implicite en qn.
implode [im'ploud] *v.i.* (*of vacuum tube, etc.*) imploser, faire implosion.
implore [im'plɔ:r] *v.tr.* implorer (le pardon, etc.); conjurer, supplier (qn) (**to do sth.,** de faire qch.). **imploring** *a.* (regard, ton, etc.) implorant, suppliant. **imploringly** *adv.* d'un ton, air, suppliant.
implosion [im'plouʒ(ə)n] *n.* implosion *f* (d'un tube à vide, etc.).
imply [im'plai] *v.tr.* **1.** impliquer; **conclusion implied from the evidence,** conclusion *f* qui découle (implicitement) des dépositions. **2.** donner à entendre; **you seem to i. that . . .,** ce que vous dites fait supposer que . . .. **implied** *a.* (consentement) implicite, tacite; **i. meaning,** signification impliquée; sous-entendu *m*, *pl.* sous-entendus.
impolite [impə'lait] *a.* impoli (**to, towards,** envers). **-ly** *adv.* impoliment.
impoliteness [impə'laitnis] *n.* impolitesse *f.*
impolitic [im'pɔlitik] *a.* impolitique, imprudent.
imponderability [impɔnd(ə)rə'biliti] *n.* impondérabilité *f.*
imponderable [im'pɔnd(ə)rəbl] *a.* & *n.* impondérable *m.*
import¹ ['impɔ:t] *n.* **1.** sens *m*, signification *f* (d'un mot); teneur *f* (d'un document). **2.** importance *f* (d'un événement); portée *f* (d'une observation); valeur *f* (d'une découverte, etc.); **matter of great i.,** affaire *f* de toute importance. **3.** *Com:* (*a*) **imports,** (i) (*collective imports*) importations *fpl*; (ii) (*individual imports*) articles *mpl* d'importation; (*b*) **i. ban,** interdiction *f* d'importation; **i. duty,** droit *m* d'entrée; **i.-export (trade),** import-export *f.*
import² [im'pɔ:t] *v.tr.* **1.** *Com:* importer (des marchandises); **imported goods,** importations *fpl*; **imported from England,** de provenance anglaise. **2.**

Lit: indiquer; (*a*) signifier, vouloir dire; (*b*) déclarer, faire savoir (**that,** que); (*c*) présager, augurer (des changements, etc). **importing 1.** *a.* (pays) importateur. **2.** *n.* importation *f* (de marchandises).

importance [im'pɔːtəns] *n.* (*a*) importance *f*; **to give i. to a word,** mettre un mot en valeur; **to be of i.,** avoir de l'importance; **of vital i.,** d'une importance capitale; **it is of the highest i. to remember that . . .,** il importe fort de se souvenir que . . .; **it is of no great i.,** cela importe peu; **detail of no i.,** détail *m* négligeable, sans importance; **to attach i. to sth.,** mettre, attacher, de l'importance à qch.; (*b*) (*of pers.*) importance; **to be full of one's own i.,** être pénétré de son importance.

important [im'pɔːtənt] *a.* (*a*) important; (*of nation, etc.*) **to become more i.,** s'agrandir; **it is i. for you to know that . . ., that you should know that . . .,** il est important, il importe, que vous sachiez que . . .; il importe de savoir que . . .; (*b*) (*of pers.*) important; **to look i.,** prendre, se donner, des airs (d'importance). **-ly** *adv.* d'un air, ton, d'importance.

importation [impɔːteiʃ(ə)n] *n.* **1.** importation *f* (de marchandises). **2.** importation; article *m* d'importation.

importer [im'pɔːtər] *n.* importateur, -trice.

importunate [im'pɔːtjunit] *a.* (créancier) importun; (visiteur) excédant, ennuyeux.

importune [im'pɔːtjuːn] *v.tr.* importuner (qn); harceler, presser, qn.

importunity [impɔː'tjuːniti] *n.* importunité *f*.

impose [im'pouz] **1.** *v.tr.* (*a*) *Ecc:* (*of priest*) **to i. hands on s.o.,** imposer les mains à qn, sur qn; (*b*) *Typ:* imposer (une feuille); mettre (la matière) en pages. **2.** *v.tr.* (*a*) imposer (le silence, etc.) (**on s.o.,** à qn); **his bearing imposes respect,** *abs.* **imposes,** son maintien impose le respect, en impose; (*b*) **to i. a tax on sugar,** imposer, taxer, le sucre; **to i. the maximum penalty provided,** appliquer le maximum de la peine. **3.** *v.i.* **to i. on, upon, s.o.,** (i) en imposer à qn; en faire accroire à qn; (ii) abuser de l'amabilité de qn; **to i. upon s.o.'s kindness,** abuser de la bonté de qn. **imposing** *a.* (air, ton) imposant; (spectacle) impressionnant.

imposition [impə'ziʃ(ə)n] *n.* **1.** (*a*) *Ecc:* imposition *f* (des mains); (*b*) *Typ:* imposition (d'une feuille); mise *f* en pages; (*c*) imposition (d'une tâche, etc.). **2.** imposition, impôt *m*, taxe *f*. **3.** abus *m* de la bonne volonté de qn; **this is an i. on your kindness,** c'est abuser de votre bonté. **4.** *Sch:* punition *f*.

impossibility [imposi'biliti] *n.* **1.** impossibilité *f* (de qch.). **2. physical i.,** chose *f* matériellement impossible.

impossible [im'pɔsibl] **1.** *a.* (*a*) impossible; **it is i. for me to do it,** il m'est impossible de le faire; **to make it i. for s.o. to do sth.,** mettre qn dans l'impossibilité de faire qch.; (*b*) (histoire, récit) invraisemblable; (*c*) *F:* **i. hat,** chapeau *m* impossible, grotesque; **you're i.!** vous êtes impossible! **2.** *n.* **to attempt the i.,** tenter l'impossible. **-ibly** *adv.* **1. not i.,** peut-être bien. **2.** *F:* (habillé) d'une façon impossible, grotesque; **i. long,** insupportablement long.

impostor [im'pɔstər] *n.* imposteur *m*.

imposture [im'pɔstjər] *n.* imposture *f*, tromperie *f*.

impotence ['impətəns] *n.* **1.** (*a*) impuissance *f*; (*b*) faiblesse *f*, impotence *f*. **2.** *Jur:* *Med:* impuissance (sexuelle).

impotent ['impətənt] *a.* **1.** (*a*) impuissant; (*b*) impotent, faible. **2.** *Med:* *Jur:* impuissant.

impound [im'paund] *v.tr.* **1.** mettre (une bête, une voiture, etc.) en fourrière. **2.** *Jur:* confisquer, saisir. **impounding** [im'paundiŋ] *n.* **1.** mise *f* en fourrière (de bêtes, etc.). **2.** *Jur:* (*a*) arrêt *m*, saisie *f* (de marchandises); (*b*) prise *f* de possession (de documents).

impoverish [im'pɔv(ə)riʃ] *v.tr.* appauvrir (qn, un pays). **impoverished** *a.* appauvri, pauvre.

impracticability [impræktikə'biliti] *n.* impraticabilité *f*.

impracticable [im'præktikəbl] *a.* infaisable, impraticable; (théorie) inapplicable, irréalisable.

impractical [im'præktik(ə)l] *a.* (*of pers.*) peu pratique; (projet, etc.) peu réaliste.

imprecation [impri'keiʃ(ə)n] *n.* imprécation *f*, malédiction *f*.

imprecise [impri'sais] *a.* imprécis, vague.

imprecision [impri'siʒ(ə)n] *n.* imprécision *f*, manque *m* de précision.

impregnable [im'pregnəbl] *a.* (*a*) (forteresse) imprenable, inexpugnable; (*b*) (vérité, etc.) invincible.

impregnate ['impregneit] *v.tr.* **1.** *Biol:* féconder (une femelle). **2.** (*a*) imprégner, imbiber, saturer (**sth. with sth.,** qch. de qch.); **to i. wood,** injecter le bois; (*b*) **to become impregnated with false principles,** s'imprégner, se pénétrer, de faux principes.

impregnation [impreg'neiʃ(ə)n] *n.* **1.** *Biol:* fécondation *f*. **2.** imprégnation *f* (d'un tissu, etc.); injection *f*, pénétration *f* (du bois, etc.).

impresario [impre'sɑːriou] *n.* impresario *m*.

impress[1] ['impres] *n.* (*a*) impression *f*, empreinte *f*; (*b*) marque distinctive; cachet *m*.

impress[2] [im'pres] *v.tr.* **1. to i. sth. on, upon, sth.,** imprimer, empreindre, qch. sur qch.; **to i. sth. on the mind,** graver qch. dans la mémoire. **2. to i. sth. upon s.o.,** faire bien comprendre qch. à qn; inculquer (une idée) à qn; **you must i. on him that . . .,** il faut bien lui faire sentir que . . .. **3. to i. sth. with a seal,** faire une impression sur qch. avec un cachet; *Fig:* **to i. s.o. with the idea that . . .,** pénétrer qn de l'idée que . . .. **4.** (*a*) faire une impression à (qn); **he impressed me favourably,** il m'a fait une impression favorable; (*b*) **to i. s.o.,** frapper, impressionner, qn; **I was deeply impressed by it,** cela m'a fait une grande impression; j'en ai été profondément impressionné; *F:* **I'm not impressed,** cela me laisse froid; *v.i.* **he doesn't i.,** il ne fait pas impression.

impression [im'preʃ(ə)n] *n.* **1.** (*action*) impression *f* (d'un cachet sur la cire, *Typ:* d'un livre, etc.). **2.** empreinte *f*, impression (d'un cachet); **to take an i. of sth.,** prendre l'empreinte, l'impression, de qch. **3.** *Typ:* empreinte (des caractères sur le papier); **i. cylinder,** cylindre *m* de rotative. **4.** *Publ:* tirage *m* (d'un livre, etc.). **5.** *Engr:* impression; **proof i.,** épreuve *f* avant la lettre. **6.** (*a*) impression (sur qn, sur les sens); **to make a good, bad, i. (on s.o.),** faire (une) bonne, mauvaise, impression (sur qn); **to make an i.,** faire impression; **tell us your impressions,** dites-nous vos impressions; (*b*) idée *f*; **I'm under the i. that I've seen him before,** j'ai l'impression de l'avoir déjà vu; **to create the i. that . . .,** donner, produire, l'impression que . . ..

impressionable [im'preʃ(ə)nəbl] *a.* impressionnable, susceptible; **to be at an i. age,** être à un âge impressionnable.

impressionism [im'preʃənizm) *n.* *Art:* impressionnisme *m*.

impressionist [im'preʃənist] *a.* & *n.* *Art:* impressionniste (*mf*).

impressive [im'presiv] *a.* (spectacle, langage) impressionnant; **his speech was very i.,** son discours a fait impression. **-ly** *adv.* d'une manière impressionnante.

imprint[1] ['imprint] *n.* **1.** empreinte *f* (d'un cachet, des pattes d'un animal, etc.); **to take an i. of sth.,** prendre l'empreinte de qch. **2. publisher's i.,** firme *f*, rubrique *f*, de l'éditeur; **printer's i.,** nom *m* de l'imprimeur.

imprint² [im'print] *v.tr.* imprimer; (*a*) **to i. sth. on the memory,** graver, fixer, qch. dans la mémoire; (*b*) **to i. sth. with sth.,** marquer, empreindre, qch. de qch.

imprison [im'priz(ə)n] *v.tr.* emprisonner (qn); mettre (qn) en prison; **to keep s.o. imprisoned,** tenir qn en prison.

imprisonment [im'prizənmənt] *n.* emprisonnement *m*; **ten days' i.,** dix jours de prison.

improbability [imprɔbə'biliti] *n.* (*a*) improbabilité *f*; (*b*) invraisemblance *f*.

improbable [im'prɔbəbl] *a.* improbable; **it's highly i. that he'll come,** il est très improbable, très peu probable, qu'il vienne. **-ably** *adv.* improbablement, invraisemblablement.

impromptu [im'prɔm(p)tju:] **1.** *adv.* (faire qch.) sans préparation, (à l')impromptu. **2.** *a.* (poème, discours) impromptu; (bal, etc.) improvisé; **to make an i. speech,** improviser un discours. **3.** *n. Th: Mus:* impromptu *m*.

improper [im'prɔpər] *a.* **1.** (partage) incorrect; (expression, dérivation) impropre; (terme) inexact; **to use a word in an i. sense,** donner à un mot un sens abusif. **2.** malséant, indécent, inconvenant. **3.** déplacé; **it would be i. to refuse,** il serait de mauvaise grâce de refuser. **-ly 1.** (se servir d'une expression) improprement, incorrectement; **word i. used,** mot employé abusivement. **2.** (se conduire) d'une manière inconvenante, malséante. **3.** (parler, se conduire) d'une façon déplacée.

impropriety [imprə'praiəti] *n.* (*a*) impropriété *f*, inexactitude *f* (de langage, etc.); (*b*) inconvenance *f*, indécence *f* (de conduite, d'un geste, etc.).

improve [im'pru:v]. **1.** *v.tr.* (*a*) améliorer, rendre meilleur (qch.); apporter des perfectionnements à (une invention); (r)abonnir, bonifier (le vin, etc.); nourrir, cultiver (l'esprit); étendre, élargir (ses connaissances); affiner (son goût); *Agr:* bonifier, amender (le sol); **to i. the appearance of s.o., sth.,** embellir qn, qch.; (*b*) **to i. the occasion,** *F:* **the shining hour,** profiter de l'occasion; mettre l'occasion à profit; (*c*) *v.ind.tr.* **to i. on s.o.,** faire mieux que qn, surpasser qn; **to i. on sth.,** améliorer qch.; *Com:* **to i. on s.o.'s offer,** enchérir sur l'offre de qn. **2.** *v.i.* (*a*) s'améliorer, devenir meilleur; (*of wine, etc.*) se bonifier, (s')abonnir; **wine improves with age,** le vin acquiert en vieillissant; **the situation has improved,** la situation s'est améliorée; **business is improving,** les affaires reprennent; **his health is improving,** sa santé s'améliore; (*b*) *Com:* (*of prices, markets*) monter; être en hausse. **improved** *a.* (*a*) (*of situation, etc.*) amélioré; (*of invention*) perfectionné; (*b*) *Com:* (offre) supérieure.

improvement [im'pru:vmənt] *n.* **1.** (*a*) amélioration *f* (de la situation, etc.); perfectionnement *m* (d'une invention); embellissement *m* (d'une ville); culture *f*, affinage *m* (de l'esprit); **i. in health,** amélioration de la santé; (*b*) **moral i.,** édification *f* (du peuple). **2.** (*a*) (*usu. pl.*) **improvements,** améliorations, embellissements (dans une propriété, etc.); **i. grant,** aide financière, subvention *f*, pour la modernisation (d'une maison); (*b*) **to be an i. on s.o., sth.,** surpasser qn, qch.; **my new car is a great i. on the old one,** ma nouvelle voiture est bien supérieure à l'ancienne.

improvidence [im'prɔvidəns] *n.* imprévoyance *f*.

improvident [im'prɔvidənt] *a.* (*a*) imprévoyant; (*b*) prodigue. **-ly** *adv.* sans prévoyance.

improvisation [imprəvai'zeiʃ(ə)n] *n. Lit: Mus: etc:* improvisation *f*.

improvise ['imprəvaiz] *Lit: Mus: etc:* **1.** *v.tr.* (*a*) improviser; **improvised speech,** discours improvisé, impromptu *inv*; (*b*) improviser (un bal, etc.); **hastily improvised,** sommairement organisé; **i. raft,** radeau *m* de fortune. **2.** *v.i.* improviser; parler, jouer, sans préparation; **to i. on the piano,** improviser au piano.

improviser ['imprəvaizər] *n.* improvisateur, -trice.

imprudence [im'pru:d(ə)ns] *n.* imprudence *f*.

imprudent [im'pru:d(ə)nt] *a.* imprudent, malavisé; **i. action,** imprudence *f*. **-ly** *adv.* imprudemment.

impudence ['impjud(ə)ns] *n.* impudence *f*, effronterie *f*, insolence *f*, audace *f*.

impudent ['impjudənt] *a.* effronté, audacieux, insolent; **he's an i. fellow,** c'est un insolent. **-ly** *adv.* effrontément, insolemment.

impugn [im'pju:n] *v.tr.* attaquer, contester (une proposition, etc.); mettre en doute, en question (la véracité de qch., l'honneur de qn); *Jur:* récuser (un témoignage).

impulse ['impʌls] *n.* **1.** (*a*) impulsion *f*; poussée motrice; *Ph:* quantité *f* de mouvement; (*b*) *El:* **electrical impulses,** impulsions électriques; (*c*) *Fig:* **to give an i. to sth.,** donner une impulsion, de l'impulsion, à qch. (au commerce, etc.). **2.** (*a*) impulsion, mouvement spontané, élan *m*; **to feel an i. to do sth.,** se sentir poussé à faire qch.; **on the, a, first i.,** tout d'abord; à première vue; **rash, sudden, i.,** coup *m* de tête; **to act on i.,** agir spontanément; **i. buying,** achat spontané; (*b*) *Psy:* pulsion (sexuelle, etc.). **3.** *Physiol:* **nerve i.,** signal nerveux.

impulsion [im'pʌlʃ(ə)n] *n.* impulsion *f*.

impulsive [im'pʌlsiv] *a.* **1.** *Mec:* impulsif, propulsif; **i. force,** force impulsive, projective. **2.** (*a*) (geste, etc.) involontaire, spontané; **i. action,** coup *m* de tête; (*b*) (*of pers.*) impulsif, velléitaire, primesautier. **-ly** *adv.* (agir) par impulsion; spontanément.

impulsiveness [im'pʌlsivnis] *n.* impulsivité *f*, caractère impulsif.

impunity [im'pju:niti] *n.* impunité *f*; **to do sth. with i.,** faire qch. impunément, en toute impunité.

impure [im'pjuər] *a.* **1.** (sang, air, lait) impur. **2.** *Rel: Poet:* (*of hands, etc.*) impur, souillé. **3.** (*of pers., desire, etc.*) impur, impudique.

impurity [im'pju:riti] *n.* **1.** (*a*) impureté *f* (de l'eau, etc.); (*b*) **moral i.,** souillure morale. **2.** impureté, saleté *f*.

imputation [impju(:)'teiʃ(ə)n] *n.* imputation *f*.

impute [im'pju:t] *v.tr.* imputer, attribuer (une action, etc.) (**to s.o.,** à qn).

in¹ [in] **I.** *prep.* **1.** (*of place*) (*a*) en, à, dans; **in France,** en France; **in Japan,** au Japon; **in the United States,** aux États-Unis; **in Paris,** à Paris; **in the provinces,** en province; **to be in town, in the country,** être en ville, à la campagne; **in his country,** dans son pays; **in prison,** en prison; **in church,** à l'église; **in bed,** au lit; **in the house,** dans la maison; **in the water,** dans l'eau; **the key is in the door,** la clef est sur la porte; **in this book,** dans ce livre; **in my hand,** dans ma main; **with a cigar in his mouth,** le cigare à la bouche; **in the distance,** au loin; **in your place,** à votre place; **wounded in the shoulder,** blessé à l'épaule; (*b*) (*among*) **in the crowd,** dans la foule; **in the thirties,** (i) entre trente et quarante; (ii) dans les années trente; **he is in his sixties,** il a passé la soixantaine. **2.** (*in respect of*) **blind in one eye,** aveugle d'un œil; **expert in economics,** expert en économie politique; **two metres in length,** long de deux mètres. **3.** (*of ratio*) **one in ten,** un sur dix; **once in ten years,** une fois tous les dix ans. **4.** (*in time*) (*a*) **in 1927,** en 1927; **in the night,** pendant la nuit; de nuit; **in the afternoon,** dans l'après-midi; **at four o'clock in the afternoon,** à quatre heures de l'après-midi; **in the evening,** le soir; **in summer, autumn, winter,** en été, en automne, en hiver; **in spring,** au printemps; **in (the month of) April,** au mois d'avril, en avril; **in the future,** à l'avenir; **never in my life,** jamais de ma vie; **in my time,** de mon temps; (*b*) **to do sth. in three hours,** faire qch. en trois heures; **he'll be here in three hours,** il sera là dans trois heures; **in a little while,** sous peu; *F:* **I haven't seen you in years,** ça fait des années que je ne t'ai vu; (*c*) (*introducing a gerund*) **in crossing the river,** en traversant la rivière. **5.** (*of condition, state*) **in good health,** en bonne santé; **in tears,** en larmes; **in despair,** au désespoir; **cow in calf,** vache pleine; **the person in question,** la personne en question. **6.** (*clothed in*) **in his shirt,** en chemise; **in slippers,** en pantoufles; **dressed in white,** habillé de blanc. **7. to go out in the rain, the snow,** sortir par la pluie, la neige; **in this warm weather,** par ce temps chaud; **to work in the rain,** travailler sous la pluie; **in the sun,** au soleil; **in the dark,** dans l'obscurité. **8.** (*engaged in*) **to be in politics,** être dans la politique; **killed in action,** tué à l'ennemi. **9.** (*according to*) **in my opinion,** à mon avis. **10.** (*a*) (*of manner*) **in a gentle voice,** d'une voix douce; **in a businesslike manner,** en bon homme d'affaires; **in the French style,** à la française; **to be in fashion,** être à la mode; (*b*) (*of medium*) **to write in French,** écrire en français; **in writing,** par écrit; **to talk in whispers,** parler en chuchotant; (*c*) (*of arrangement*) **to walk in groups,** se promener par groupes; **to stand in a circle,** se tenir en cercle; **in alphabetical order,** par ordre alphabétique; (*d*) **I've nothing in your size,** je n'ai rien à votre taille; (*e*) **in the form of a pill,** sous forme de pilule; **money in gold,** espèces *fpl* en or; (*f*) (*of degree, extent*) **in large quantities,** en grandes quantités; **in part,** en partie; **in places,** par endroits. **11.** (*of purpose*) **in reply to . . .,** en réponse à . . .; **in honour of . . .,** en l'honneur de . . .; **in search of . . .,** à la recherche de . . .; **in the cause of humanity,** pour la cause de l'humanité. **12.** (*a*) (*with reflexive pronoun*) **this product is not a poison in itself,** ce produit n'est pas un poison en lui-même; (*b*) **I was sure he had something in him,** je savais bien qu'il avait quelque chose dans le ventre. **13. in that,** par ce que, puisque, vu que. **II.** *adv.* **1.** (*a*) (*at home*) à la maison, chez soi; **is your mother in?** est-ce que votre mère est à la maison? (*b*) *F:* en prison; **what is he in for?** pour quel crime est-il en prison? (*c*) *Agr:* **the harvest is in,** la moisson est rentrée; (*d*) (*of train, etc.*) **to be in,** être arrivé; **the train is in,** le train est en gare; **the mail is in,** le courrier est arrivé; (*e*) *Nau:* **the sails are in,** les voiles sont serrées, ferlées; (*f*) **in with you!** (i) allons, rentrez! (ii) allez-y! (*g*) *Ten:* **the ball is in,** la balle est bonne. **2.** (*a*) (*in power, in office*) élu; **the Liberals were in,** le parti libéral était au pouvoir; (*b*) (*in season*) **strawberries are in,** c'est la saison des fraises; (*c*) (*in fashion*) **stripes are in this year,** les rayures *f* sont à la mode, la rage, cette année; (*d*) (*in practice*) **I've got my hand in,** je suis bien en train; je suis en main (pour dessiner, etc.); (*e*) (*in favour*) **to be (well) in with s.o.,** être en bons termes avec qn; être bien avec qn; **those who are in,** ceux qui sont acceptés par la société; (*f*) *Turf:* **horse that is well in,** cheval *m* qui a un handicap avantageux; **my luck is in,** je suis en veine; (*g*) *Cr:* **to be in,** battre la balle; *F:* être à la batte. **3.** (*a*) **to be in for a thousand pounds,** en avoir, y être, pour mille livres; **we're in for a storm,** nous aurons sûrement de l'orage; **he's in for a surprise,** il va être surpris; *F:* **he's in for it,** qu'est-ce qu'il va prendre! **(now) we're in for it!** ça va commencer! **to have it in for s.o.,** avoir une dent contre qn; (*b*) **to be in on a secret,** être dans le secret; **I wasn't in on it,** je n'étais pas dans le coup. **4.** (*phrases*) (*a*) **day in, day out, year in, year out,** tous les jours, chaque année (sans exception); (*b*) **all in,** (i) tout compris; **it will cost you £100, all in,** cela vous coûtera cent livres tout compris; (ii) *F:* **I'm absolutely all in,** je suis absolument éreinté, fourbu; (*c*) *Ten:* **advantage in,** avantage dedans, au servant; (*d*) (i) **(to go) in and out,** entrer et sortir; **he is always in and out of the house,** il entre et sort comme chez lui; (ii) **to know s.o. in and out,** connaître qn à fond. **III.** *a.* **1.** (*a*) *Com:* **in tray,** entrées *fpl*; *Fin:* **in book,** livre *m* du dedans; (*b*) **in patient,** (malade) hospitalisé, -ée; (*c*) *Cr:* **the in side,** l'équipe *f* qui est à la batte. **2. an in joke,** une plaisanterie de coterie; **it's the in thing these days,** c'est la rage aujourd'hui. **IV.** *n.* **1.** *F:* **to know the ins and outs of a matter,** connaître tous les coins et recoins d'une affaire; connaître une affaire dans tous ses détails; **the ins and outs of a house,** les aîtres *mpl* d'une maison. **2.** *Pol:* **the ins,** le parti au pouvoir. **3.** *U.S:* *F:* **to have an in,** avoir de l'influence; **he has an in with the senator,** il a ses entrées chez le sénateur.

in² *Lt. prep.* (*occurs in many phrases, e.g. the following*) **in extremis,** in extremis; à l'article de la mort; **in flagrante delicto,** en flagrant délit; **in memoriam,** en mémoire (de); **in situ,** in situ; en place.

inability [inə'biliti] *n.* incapacité *f* (**to do sth.,** de faire qch.); impuissance *f* (**to do sth.,** à faire qch.).

inaccessibility [inæksesi'biliti] *n.* inaccessibilité *f.*

inaccessible [inæk'sesibl] *a.* (*a*) (point, port) inaccessible (**to,** à); (*b*) (personne) inabordable.

inaccuracy [in'ækjurəsi] *n.* inexactitude *f,* imprécision *f*; infidélité *f* (d'une traduction); **full of inaccuracies,** (ouvrage) plein d'inexactitudes.

inaccurate [in'ækjurət] *a.* (calcul, esprit) inexact; (esprit) imprécis; (avis, sens) incorrect; (récit) infidèle. **-ly** *adv.* (calculer) inexactement; (juger, citer) incorrectement; (traduire) infidèlement.

inaction [in'ækʃ(ə)n] *n.* inaction *f*; inertie *f*; **policy of i.,** politique *f* de laisser-faire.

inactive [in'æktiv] *a.* **1.** inactif; (esprit) inerte. **2.** *Mil:* en non-activité.

inactivity [inæk'tiviti] *n.* inactivité *f*; passivité *f.*

inadequacy [in'ædikwəsi] *n.* insuffisance *f* (d'un revenu); imperfection *f* (d'un système, etc.); **to be fully conscious of one's own i.,** connaître bien son insuffisance.

inadequate [in'ædikwət] *a.* **1.** inadéquat, insuffisant; (*of thg*) **to be i.,** être insuffisant (pour (faire) qch.) **2.** (style) inapproprié au sujet. **-ly** *adv.* insuffisamment.

inadmissible [inəd'misibl] *a.* (théorie, prétention) inadmissible; (offre) inacceptable; *Jur:* (témoignage) irrecevable.

inadvertence [inəd'vəːtəns] *n.* **1.** inattention *f*; **through i.,** par inadvertance. **2.** étourderie *f.*

inadvertent [inəd'vəːtənt] *a.* **1.** (*of pers.*) inattentif (**to,** à); négligent (**to,** de). **2.** (*of mistake, etc.*) commis par inadvertance. **-ly** *adv.* par inadvertance; par étourderie.

inadvisability [inədvaizə'biliti] *n.* imprudence *f,* inopportunité *f* (d'une action).

inadvisable [inəd'vaizəbl] *a.* (*of action*) peu sage; imprudent.

inalienable [in'eiliənəbl] *a.* (bien, droit) inaliénable.

inane [i'nein] *a.* (*of pers., action*) inepte, stupide, bête; (sourire) bête, niais; (réponse) inepte, saugrenue; **i. remark,** ineptie *f.* **-ly** *adv.* bêtement, stupidement.

inanimate [in'ænimət] *a.* (corps, style, etc.) inanimé, sans vie; **i. nature,** le monde inanimé.

inanition [inæ'niʃ(ə)n] *n.* *Med:* inanition *f.*

inanity [i'næniti] *n.* inanité *f,* niaiserie *f.*

inapplicable [in'æplikəbl] *a.* inapplicable (**to,** à).

inappropriate [inə'proupriət] *a.* peu approprié, qui ne convient pas (**to,** à); (*of word*) impropre; (*of speech*) déplacé. **-ly** *adv.* d'une façon mal à propos; improprement.

inapt [in'æpt] *a.* inapte. **1.** (*a*) incapable; (*b*) inhabile, inexpert. **2.** peu approprié (**to,** à).

inaptitude [in'æptitju:d] *n.* **1.** inaptitude *f* (**for,** à). **2.** incapacité *f.*

inarticulate [inɑ:'tikjulət] *a.* **1.** *Nat.Hist:* inarticulé. **2.** (*a*) (son) inarticulé; (désir) inexprimé; (*b*) (animal, etc.) qui n'a pas le don de la parole; muet, -ette; (*pers.*) qui manque la facilité de s'exprimer; (*c*) (malade) incapable de parler; **i. with rage,** bégayant de colère.

inartistic [inɑ:'tistik] *a.* (*a*) (*of production, etc.*) peu artistique; sans valeur artistique; (*b*) (*of pers.*) dépourvu de sens artistique.

inasmuch [inəz'mʌtʃ] *conj.phr.* **i. as,** attendu que, vu que, en ce sens que.

inattention [inə'tenʃ(ə)n] *n.* inattention *f*; manque *m* d'attention.

inattentive [inə'tentiv] *a.* **1.** inattentif, distrait; (élève) inappliqué. **2.** négligent (**to,** de). **3.** peu attentionné (**to, towards, s.o.,** pour qn); peu prévenant. **-ly** *adv.* sans attention; distraitement.

inaudible [in'ɔ:dibl] *a.* inaudible; (son) imperceptible; (réponse) insaisissable; **it, he, is almost i.,** on l'entend à peine. **-ibly** *adv.* de manière inaudible.

inaugural [i'nɔ:gjur(ə)l] **1.** *a.* inaugural, -aux; (discours) d'inauguration. **2.** *n. U.S:* discours d'inauguration.

inaugurate [i'nɔ:gjureit] *v.tr.* (*a*) inaugurer (un monument; faire l'inauguration (d'une fête); (*b*) inaugurer, commencer (une ère nouvelle); mettre en vigueur (un nouveau système); (*c*) installer (un chef d'état, etc.).

inauguration [inɔ:gju'reiʃ(ə)n] *n.* (*a*) inauguration *f* (d'un édifice, etc.); (*b*) commencement *m*, mise en vigueur (d'un nouveau système, etc.).

inauspicious [inɔ:s'piʃəs] *a.* peu propice; malheureux; (moment) malencontreux. **-ly** *adv.* sous de mauvais auspices; peu favorablement.

in-between [inbi'twi:n] **1.** *a.* intermédiaire, au milieu. **2.** *n.* entre-deux *m.*

inborn ['inbɔ:n] *a.* (*a*) (instinct, mérite) inné, infus, naturel; (*b*) *Med:* congénital, -aux.

inbreed ['inbri:d] *v.* (**inbred**) **1.** *v.tr.* accoupler (des chevaux, etc.) consanguins. **2.** *v.i.* (*of animals*) s'accoupler avec des consanguins; (*of people*) s'accoupler avec des membres de la même famille. **inbred** *a.* **1.** inné. **2.** *Breed:* (*of horses, etc.*) consanguin. **inbreeding** *n.* accouplement *m* d'animaux consanguins; consanguinité *f.*

incalculable [in'kælkjuləbl] *a.* **1.** incalculable; (perte) inestimable. **2.** (*of temper*) inégal, changeant. **-ably** *adv.* incalculablement.

incandescence [inkæn'desəns] *n.* incandescence *f*; *Metall:* chaleur blanche.

incandescent [inkæn'desənt] *a.* incandescent; (lumière, lampe, etc.) à incandescence.

incantation [inkæn'teiʃ(ə)n] *n.* incantation *f.*

incapability [inkeipə'biliti] *n.* incapacité *f.*

incapable [in'keipəbl] **1.** *a.* **i. of,** incapable de; (*a*) (*of pers.*) **i. of movement,** incapable de bouger; **he's i. of doing such a spiteful thing,** il n'est pas capable de faire une méchanceté pareille; *Jur:* **declared i. of managing his own affairs,** en état d'incapacité légale; (*b*) (*of thg*) **i. of improvement,** peu susceptible d'amélioration; (*c*) *Jur:* (*of pers.*) **i. of succeeding (to an estate, etc.),** incapable de succéder. **2.** *a.* & *n.* incapable (*mf*), incompétent, -ente.

incapacitate [inkə'pæsiteit] *v.tr.* **1.** rendre (qn) incapable (**for work,** de travailler). **2.** *Jur:* priver (qn) de capacité légale; frapper (qn) d'incapacité.

incapacity [inkə'pæsiti] *n.* **1.** incapacité *f*, incompétence *f.* **2.** *Jur:* incapacité légale.

incarcerate [in'kɑ:səreit] *v.tr.* incarcérer, mettre en prison, emprisonner.

incarceration [inkɑ:sə'reiʃ(ə)n] *n.* incarcération *f*, emprisonnement *m.*

incarnate¹ [in'kɑ:neit] *a. Theol:* **the Word I.,** le Verbe incarné; **the devil i.,** le diable incarné.

incarnate² ['inkɑ:neit] *v.tr.* incarner.

incarnation [inkɑ:'neiʃ(ə)n] *n.* **1.** *Theol: etc:* incarnation *f* (du Christ, d'une idée). **2.** (*of pers.*) **to be the i. of wisdom,** incarner la sagesse du monde.

incautious [in'kɔ:ʃəs] *a.* imprudent; inconsidéré; **in an i. moment,** dans un moment d'irréflexion. **-ly** *adv.* imprudemment.

incendiary [in'sendjəri] **1.** *a.* (*a*) (matériel, etc.) incendiaire; (*b*) (discours) séditieux. **2.** *n.* (*a*) incendiaire *mf*; auteur *m* volontaire (d'un incendie); (*b*) incendiaire; séditieux *m*; (*c*) *F:* bombe *f* incendiaire.

incense¹ ['insens] *n.* encens *m*; *Ecc:* **i. bearer,** thuriféraire *m*; **i. burner,** cassolette *f*; brûle-parfums *m inv*; *Ecc:* encensoir *m.*

incense² ['insens] *v.tr.* encenser (qn, qch.).

incense³ [in'sens] *v.tr.* exaspérer, courroucer, irriter (qn); **to i. s.o. against s.o.,** mettre qn en colère contre qn. **incensed** *a.* enflammé de colère; courroucé; **to become, get, i. (against, at, with, s.o.),** s'irriter, se courroucer (contre qn).

incentive [in'sentiv] **1.** *a.* (*a*) provocant, excitant; (*b*) stimulant; *Com: Ind:* **i. pay,** primes *fpl* de rendement. **2.** *n.* stimulant *m*, aiguillon *m*; *Com: Ind:* **production incentives,** primes de rendement.

inception [in'sepʃ(ə)n] *n.* commencement *m*, début *m* (d'une entreprise, etc.).

incessant [in'sesənt] *a.* (bruit) incessant, continuel; (soucis) éternels. **-ly** *adv.* sans cesse, sans relâche; continuellement.

incest ['insest] *n.* inceste *m.*

incestuous [in'sestjuəs] *a.* incestueux.

inch¹ [in(t)ʃ] *n. Meas:* pouce *m* (= 2 centimètres 54); **square, cubic, i.,** pouce carré, cube; **he couldn't see an i. in front of him, of his nose,** il n'y voyait pas à deux pas devant lui; **he's every i. a soldier,** il est soldat jusqu'au bout des ongles; **he won't give way an i.,** il ne reculera pas d'une semelle; **by inches, i. by i.,** peu à peu, petit à petit; **I know every i. of the neighbourhood,** je connais la région comme ma poche; **give him an i. and he'll take an ell,** donnez-lui-en grand comme le doigt, et il en prendra long comme le bras.

inch² **1.** *v.i.* **to i. forward, along,** (s')avancer peu à peu, petit à petit. **2.** *v.tr.* **to i. sth. forward,** faire avancer qch. petit à petit.

incidence ['insidəns] *n.* **1.** incidence *f* (d'un événement, d'un impôt) (**on,** sur). **2.** fréquence *f* (des vols, etc.); **the i. of cancer has increased,** les cas de cancer se sont multipliés. **3.** *Opt: Elcs: Av: etc:* **(angle of) i.,** angle *m* d'incidence.

incident¹ ['insidənt] *n.* **1.** incident *m*; **diplomatic i.,** incident diplomatique; **journey full of incidents,** voyage mouvementé. **2.** *Jur:* (i) servitude attachée, (ii) privilège attaché, à une tenure.

incident² *a.* **1.** qui arrive; qui appartient, qui tient (**to,** à). **2.** (*a*) *Opt: Elcs:* (rayon, etc.) incident.

incidental [insi'dent(ə)l] **1.** *a.* (*a*) (événement) fortuit, accidentel; (*of circumstance, etc.*) incidentel; (*of observation, etc.*) incident; **i. expenses,** faux frais; dépenses imprévues; **i. music for a play,** la musique pour une pièce; (*b*) auquel on peut s'attendre; **i. to sth.,** qui résulte de qch. **2.** *n.* (*a*) chose fortuite; éventualité *f*; (*b*) **incidentals,** faux frais; dépenses imprévues. **-ally** *adv.* **1.** incidemment. **2.** soit dit en passant, entre parenthèses.

incinerate [in'sinəreit] *v.tr.* incinérer.

incineration [insinə'reiʃ(ə)n] *n.* incinération *f.*

incinerator [in'sinəreitər] *n. Ind: Hort:* incinérateur *m*; four *m* crématoire.

incipient [in'sipiənt] *a.* naissant; qui commence; **i. madness,** folie naissante.

incise [in'saiz] *v.tr.* **1.** inciser, faire une incision dans (qch.); *Surg:* inciser, débrider (une plaie, un tissu). **2.** *Art: etc:* graver (une inscription, etc.).

incision [in'siʒ(ə)n] *n.* incision *f*, entaille *f*; **to make an i. in sth.,** inciser qch.; *Hort:* **i. for a graft,** enture *f*; *Surg:* **buttonhole i.,** boutonnière *f.*

incisive [in'saisiv] *a.* (instrument, ton) incisif, tranchant; (ton) mordant; (esprit) pénétrant. **-ly** *adv.* incisivement; d'un ton tranchant, mordant.

incisor [in'saizər] *n. Anat:* (dent) incisive (*f*).

incite [in'sait] *v.tr.* inciter, instiguer, animer **(to sth., to do sth.,** à qch., à faire qch.); **to i. s.o. to crime,** pousser qn au crime; **to i. workmen against their employers,** monter les ouvriers contre le patronat.

incitement [in'saitmənt] *n.* **1.** incitation *f*, instigation *f*, encouragement *m* **(to,** à). **2.** stimulant *m*, aiguillon *m*; mobile *m*, motif *m* **(of,** de).

incivility [insi'viliti] *n.* incivilité *f.*

inclemency [in'klemənsi] *n.* inclémence *f*, rigueur *f.*

inclement [in'klemənt] *a.* (juge, sort, etc.) inclément; (climat, etc.) inclément, rigoureux, rude.

inclination [inkli'neiʃ(ə)n] *n.* **1.** inclination *f* (de la tête, du corps). **2.** inclinaison *f* (d'un talus, d'un plan, etc.); pente *f* (d'un coteau); déversement *m*, dévers *m* (d'un mur); dévoiement *m* (d'un tuyau). **3.** (*a*) inclination, penchant *m* **(to, for,** à, pour); **to follow only one's own i.,** ne faire que ce qui fait envie; **to have an i. for sth.,** avoir un penchant pour qch.; **to have lost all i. for sth.,** être revenu de qch.; **to do sth. from i.,** faire qch. par goût; (*b*) tendance *f* (à qch.).

incline[1] ['inklain] *n.* pente *f*; plan incliné.

incline[2] [in'klain] **1.** *v.tr.* (*a*) incliner, pencher, faire pencher (la tête, un vase); (*b*) **to feel, be, inclined to do sth.,** pencher, avoir de l'inclination, à faire qch.; se sentir disposé à faire qch.; **I am inclined to think that he's right,** je suis porté à croire qu'il a raison; **to be favourably inclined towards sth.,** être favorable à qch.; **if ever you should feel so inclined,** si jamais l'envie vous en prenait; **prices are inclined to fall,** les prix *m* tendent à baisser; **he's inclined to put on weight,** il a une tendance à grossir. **2.** *v.i.* (*a*) (*of thg*) incliner, pencher **(to, towards,** à, vers); se déverser; **inclined at an angle of 45°,** incliné à un angle de 45°; (*b*) avoir un penchant **(to,** pour qch., à faire qch.); être enclin, porté, disposé **(to,** à); **to i. to the belief that . . .,** incliner à croire que . . .; (*c*) **to i. to the left,** tirer sur la gauche. **inclined** *a.* **1.** *Mth: etc:* (plan, etc.) incliné; (mur, etc.) penchant. **2.** (*a*) (*momentarily*) disposé, porté **(to,** à); (*b*) (*permanently*) enclin, incliné; **i. to laziness, to be lazy,** enclin à la paresse. **3.** (*with adv. prefixed*) **to be well-i. towards s.o.,** être bien disposé envers qn.

inclose, inclosure [in'klouz, in'klouʒər] = ENCLOSE, ENCLOSURE.

include [in'klu:d] *v.tr.* comprendre, renfermer; comporter; **men above seventy are not included,** les hommes de plus de soixante-dix ans ne sont pas compris; **there are five of us, not including the children,** nous sommes cinq, sans compter les enfants; **up to and including December 31st,** jusqu'à et y compris le 31 décembre; **up to and including page 5,** jusqu'à la page 5 incluse; **to i. s.o. among one's friends,** compter qn parmi ses amis. **included** *a.* (y) compris; **all his property was sold, his house i.,** tous ses biens furent vendus, y compris sa maison; (*at hotel, etc.*) **service i.,** service compris.

inclusion [in'klu:ʒ(ə)n] *n.* inclusion *f.*

inclusive [in'klu:siv] *a.* qui comprend; **five i. of the driver,** cinq y compris le chauffeur; (*at hotel, etc.*) **i. terms,** (prix) tout compris; **from the 4th to the 12th February i.,** du 4 au 12 février inclusivement. **-ly** *adv.* inclusivement.

incognito [inkɔg'ni:tou] **1.** *a. & adv.* **to be, travel, i.,** être, voyager, incognito. **2.** *n.* (*a*) (*pers.*) inconnu, -ue; (*b*) incognito *m.*

incoherence [inkou'hiərəns] *n.* incohérence *f.*

incoherent [inkou'hiərənt] *a.* incohérent; (raisonnement) qui ne tient pas debout; (style) décousu. **-ly** *adv.* d'une manière incohérente; sans cohérence.

incombustible [inkəm'bʌstibl] *a.* (gaz, etc.) incombustible.

income ['inkəm] *n.* **1.** revenu *m*, revenus *mpl*; **source of i.,** source(s) *f*(*pl*) de revenu; **earned i.,** revenus salariaux; traitements *mpl*; **unearned i., private i.,** rente(s) *f*(*pl*); **to have a private i. of £3000 a year,** avoir trois mille livres de rente; **i. group,** tranche *f* de salaire, de revenus; *Pol:* **incomes policy,** politique *f* des revenus; *Pol.Ec:* **gross, net, national i.,** revenu national brut, net; **i. tax,** impôt *m* (cédulaire) sur le revenu; **i.-tax return,** déclaration de revenu, fiscale. **2.** *Com:* recettes *fpl*, revenus; rentrées *fpl.*

incoming ['inkʌmiŋ] **1.** *a.* (*a*) qui entre, qui arrive; (locataire, navire) entrant; (marée) montante; **i. mail,** courrier *m* à l'arrivée; *Tp:* **i. call,** enregistrement *m* d'appel; communication *f* d'arrivée; (*b*) **i. profit,** profits accrus, réalisés. **2.** *n.* (*a*) entrée *f*, arrivée *f*; **the i. and outgoing of the tide,** le flux et le reflux; (*b*) **incomings,** recettes *fpl*, revenus *mpl*; rentrées *fpl.*

incommensurable [inkə'menʃ(ə)rəbl] *a. Mth:* (*a*) incommensurable **(with,** avec); (*b*) (nombre) irrationnel.

incommensurate [inkə'menʃ(ə)rət] *a.* pas en rapport, pas en proportion **(with,** avec); disproportionné **(with,** à).

incommode [inkə'moud] *v.tr.* incommoder, déranger (qn); gêner, empêcher (la marche, etc.).

incommodious [inkə'moudiəs] *a.* (*a*) incommode; peu confortable; (*b*) (appartement, etc.) où l'on est à l'étroit.

incommunicado [inkəmju:ni'kɑ:dou] *adv.* **to be held i.,** être tenu, gardé, au secret.

incomparable [in'kɔmp(ə)rəbl] *a.* incomparable **(to, with,** à); (artiste) incomparable, sans pareil. **-ably** *adv.* incomparablement.

incompatibility [inkəmpæti'biliti] *n.* incompatibilité *f* **(with,** avec; **between,** entre); inconciliabilité *f* (de deux théories).

incompatible [inkəm'pætibl] *a.* (*a*) incompatible, inconciliable **(with,** avec); (*of ideas, etc.*) inalliable. (*b*) (*of metals, fluids, etc.*) non, peu, alliable **(with,** avec); (*c*) *Pharm:* (médicaments) incompatibles.

incompetence [in'kɔmpitəns] *n.* **1.** *Jur:* incompétence *f* (d'un tribunal); incompétence, incapacité *f*, inhabilité *f* (d'une personne). **2.** incompétence (de qn); insuffisance *f* (du personnel, etc.).

incompetent [in'kɔmpitənt] *a.* **1.** *Jur:* (juge, tribunal) incompétent (à connaître d'une cause); (personne) inhabile (à accomplir un acte); **I am i. to act,** je n'ai pas qualité pour agir. **2.** incompétent, incapable; *n.* **the incompetents,** les incapables.

incomplete [inkəm'pli:t] *a.* incomplet, inachevé; imparfait. **-ly** *adv.* incomplètement; imparfaitement.

incompleteness [inkəm'pli:tnis] *n.* imperfection *f*, inachèvement *m.*

incomprehensible [inkɔmpri'hensibl] *a.* incompréhensible; indéchiffrable. **-ibly** *adv.* incompréhensiblement.

incomprehension [inkɔmpri'henʃ(ə)n] *n.* défaut *m*, manque *m*, de compréhension; incompréhension *f.*

inconceivable [inkən'siːvəbl] *a.* inconcevable. **-ably** *adv.* inconcevablement.
inconclusive [inkən'kluːsiv] *a.* (raisonnement, témoignage) peu concluant, inconcluant. **-ly** *adv.* d'une manière peu concluante.
incongruity [inkɔŋ'gru(ː)iti] *n.* **1.** désaccord *m*; manque *m* d'harmonie (**with,** avec); inconséquence *f.* **2.** absurdité *f*, incongruité *f.* **3.** inconvenance *f*; incongruité.
incongruous [in'kɔŋgruəs] *a.* **1.** qui ne s'accorde pas (**with,** avec); qui détonne (**with,** avec); sans rapport (**to, with,** avec); (mélange) hétéroclite. **2.** (*of remark*) incongru, déplacé, absurde. **-ly** *adv.* **1.** mal à propos. **2.** incongrûment; (se conduire) absurdement.
inconsequence [in'kɔnsikwəns] *n.* inconséquence *f.*
inconsequent [in'kɔnsikwənt] *a.* **1.** inconséquent, (idées) sans suite; (raisonnement) illogique. **2.** = INCONSEQUENTIAL 2.
inconsequential [inkɔnsi'kwenʃ(ə)l] *a.* **1.** = INCONSEQUENT 1. **2.** (circonstance, affaire) sans importance.
inconsiderate [inkən'sid(ə)rət] *a.* **1.** inconsidéré; irréfléchi; (opinion) peu réfléchie. **2.** (personne) sans égards pour les autres; **it was most i. of you to do that,** vous avez manqué d'égards en agissant ainsi. **-ly** *adv.* **1.** inconsidérément; sans réfléchir. **2. to behave i. to s.o.,** manquer d'égards envers qn.
inconsistency [inkən'sistənsi] *n.* **1.** inconsistance *f*, contradiction *f* (**between two things,** entre deux choses). **2.** inconséquence *f*, inconsistance, illogisme *m* (d'une personne); incohérence *f* (d'un argument).
inconsistent [inkən'sistənt] *a.* **1.** incompatible, en contradiction, en désaccord (**with,** avec); contradictoire (**with,** à); **his words are i. with his conduct,** sa conduite ne cadre pas avec ses paroles. **2.** (*of pers.*) inconsistant; inconséquent, illogique. **-ly** *adv.* inconséquemment, illogiquement.
inconsolable [inkən'souləbl] *a.* inconsolable.
inconspicuous [inkən'spikjuəs] *a.* peu en évidence; peu frappant; discret, -ète; peu voyant; **to be, remain, i.,** rester dans l'obscurité. **-ly** *adv.* d'une manière discrète, peu frappante.
inconstancy [in'kɔnstənsi] *n.* inconstance *f*; instabilité *f*, caractère changeant (du temps, etc.).
inconstant [in'kɔnstənt] *a.* **1.** (homme, caractère) inconstant, volage. **2.** (vent) mobile, variable.
incontestable [inkən'testəbl] *a.* incontestable, indéniable. **-ably** *adv.* incontestablement.
incontinence [in'kɔntinəns] *n.* (*a*) incontinence *f*; (*b*) *Med:* incontinence.
incontinent [in'kɔntinənt] *a.* (*a*) (*unchaste*) incontinent; (*b*) *Med:* incontinent.
incontrovertible [inkɔntrə'vəːtibl] *a.* (vérité) incontroversable, incontestable; (preuve) irrécusable.
inconvenience¹ [inkən'viːnjəns] *n.* (*a*) inconvénient *m*, incommodité *f*, dérangement *m*; désagrément *m*; **to cause i., to be an i., to s.o.,** incommoder, déranger, qn; **I am putting you to a great deal of i.,** je vous donne beaucoup d'embarras; **without the slightest i.,** sans le moindre inconvénient, dérangement; (*b*) **the i. of living so far from town,** les inconvénients qu'il y a à vivre si loin de la ville.
inconvenience² *v.tr.* déranger, incommoder, gêner (qn).
inconvenient [inkən'viːnjənt] *a.* (*of house, etc.*) incommode, malcommode; (*of pers.*) gênant; (*of time*) inopportun; **if it is not i. to you,** si cela ne vous gêne pas. **-ly** *adv.* incommodément; (arriver) à un moment inopportun.
inconvertible [inkən'vəːtibl] *a. Fin:* inconvertible.
incorporate [in'kɔːpəreit] **1.** *v.tr.* (*a*) incorporer, mêler, unir (**with,** à, avec); **to i. a paragraph in a chapter,** incorporer un paragraphe dans un chapitre; (*b*) **work that incorporates all the latest discoveries,** ouvrage *m* où se trouvent incorporées toutes les découvertes les plus récentes; (*c*) *Com:* constituer (une association) en société commerciale; réunir (des banques) en société. **2.** *v.i.* (*a*) s'incorporer (**in one body,** en un seul corps; **with others,** avec, à, d'autres); (*b*) *U.S:* se constituer en société commerciale. **incorporated** *a.* **1.** incorporé (**in one body,** en un seul corps); faisant corps (**with others,** avec d'autres). **2.** *U.S: Com:* **i. company,** association constituée en société commerciale; société autorisée.
incorporation [inkɔːpə'reiʃ(ə)n] *n.* **1.** incorporation *f* (**in, with, into,** à, avec, dans). **2.** *Com: Jur:* constitution *f* (d'une association) en société commerciale.
incorrect [inkə'rekt] *a.* **1.** (*a*) (*of statement, account, etc.*) inexact; (*b*) **i. expression,** locution vicieuse, incorrecte; *Com:* **i. endorsement,** endos défectueux. **2.** (*of style, behaviour, etc.*) incorrect; **it is i. to . . .,** c'est contraire (i) à la politesse, (ii) au protocole, de . . .. **-ly** *adv.* **1.** inexactement; (parler) incorrectement; **i. addressed,** (lettre) mal adressée. **2.** (se conduire, etc.) incorrectement.
incorrigible [in'kɔridʒibl] *a.* (enfant, paresse, etc.) incorrigible; **he's i.,** il est incorrigible.
incorruptible [inkə'rʌptibl] *a.* (matière, juge) incorruptible.
increase¹ ['inkriːs] *n.* (*a*) augmentation *f* (de prix, de recettes, etc.); accroissement *m* (de vitesse, de la douleur, etc.); gain *m* (de vitesse); renouvellement *m* (de zèle, d'attention); redoublement *m* (d'efforts, de gaieté); multiplication *f* (des êtres, de l'espèce); **i. in the cost of living,** renchérissement (du coût) de la vie; **i. in value,** plus-value *f* (d'une propriété, etc.); **I've had an i. in salary,** j'ai été augmenté; (*b*) *adv.phr.* **to be on the i.,** être en augmentation; **crime is on the i.,** le nombre des crimes augmente beaucoup; **unemployment is on the i.,** le chômage s'accentue.
increase² [in'kriːs] **1.** *v.i.* (*a*) augmenter, s'augmenter; grandir, s'agrandir; croître, s'accroître; (*in bulk*) grossir; **his efforts increased,** ses efforts *m* redoublaient; **to i. in size, value,** augmenter de grandeur, de valeur; **to i. in price,** renchérir; (*of earth, lime*) **to i. in volume,** foisonner; (*b*) se multiplier; **the population is increasing,** la population grossit, augmente; (*c*) *Knit:* **i. two in the next row,** augmenter de deux points au rang suivant. **2.** *v.tr.* augmenter (la vitesse, la production); grossir (le nombre, la dépense); accroître (sa fortune); relever (les salaires); agrandir (l'importance); majorer (les prix); allonger (la distance); accentuer (le mécontentement); **to i. s.o.'s salary,** augmenter (le salaire de) qn; **to i. the dose,** forcer la dose (d'un médicament); **to i. one's efforts,** redoubler d'efforts; **increased cost of living,** renchérissement *m* (du coût) de la vie. **increasing** *a.* croissant; **ever-i. influence,** influence toujours plus étendue. **increasingly** *adv.* de plus en plus (difficile, grand, etc.).
incredible [in'kredibl] *a.* incroyable; *F:* **it's i.!** c'est incroyable, *F:* renversant. **-ibly** *adv.* incroyablement; **he's i. stupid,** il est d'une sottise incroyable.
incredulity [inkri'djuːliti] *n.* incrédulité *f.*
incredulous [in'kredjuləs] *a.* incrédule (**of,** à l'égard de); (sourire) d'incrédulité. **-ly** *adv.* d'un air, ton, incrédule.
increment ['inkrimənt] *n.* **1.** augmentation *f*; *Mth:* différentielle *f.* **2.** profit *m*; (*of land, shares*) **unearned i.,** plus-value *f.*
incriminate [in'krimineit] *v.tr.* **1.** accuser (qn) d'un crime. **2.** impliquer (un complice, etc.) (dans une

accusation); mêler (qn) à une affaire. **incriminating** *a.* (circonstance, etc.) qui tend à prouver la culpabilité (de qn); **i. documents,** pièces *fpl* à conviction.

incrimination [inkrimi'neiʃ(ə)n] *n.* incrimination *f*; accusation *f* (de qn).

incrustation [inkrʌs'teiʃ(ə)n] *n. Mch:* (*a*) entartrage *m* (d'une chaudière); (*b*) tartre *m*, dépôt *m* calcaire.

incubate ['inkjubeit] **1.** *v.tr.* couver, incuber (des œufs). **2.** *v.i.* (*a*) (*of eggs*) être soumis à l'incubation; (*b*) (*of disease*) couver.

incubation [inkju'beiʃ(ə)n] *n.* incubation *f*; *Med:* **i. period,** période *f* d'incubation (d'une maladie).

incubator ['inkjubeitər] *n.* incubateur *m*; (i) *Husb:* couveuse artificielle; couvoir *m* (pour volaille), poussinière *f* (pour poussins); (ii) *Bac:* incubateur (iii) (*for premature babies*) couveuse.

incubus ['inkjubəs] **1.** *Myth:* incube *m*. **2.** *Fig:* cauchemar *m*.

inculcate ['inkʌlkeit] *v.tr.* inculquer (une leçon, etc.); **to i. sth. on s.o.,** inculquer qch. à qn.

inculcation [inkʌl'keiʃ(ə)n] *n.* inculcation *f*.

incumbent¹ [in'kʌmbənt] *n.* **1.** *Ecc:* bénéficier *m*, bénéficiaire *m*, titulaire *m* (d'une charge). **2.** *esp. NAm:* titulaire (d'une fonction administrative).

incumbent² *a.* **to be i. on s.o. to do sth.,** incomber, appartenir, à qn de faire qch.

incunabulum, *pl.* **-a** [inkju(:)'næbjuləm, -ə] *n.* incunable *m*.

incur [in'kər] *v.tr.* **(incurred)** courir (un risque); encourir (un blâme); subir (une perte); s'attirer (le courroux de qn); contracter (des dettes); s'attirer (la haine); **to i. expenses,** encourir des frais.

incurable [in'kju:rəbl] **1.** *a.* (maladie) incurable, inguérissable; (ivrogne) invétéré. **2.** *n.* (*usu. in pl.*) **home for incurables,** hospice *m* des incurables. **-ably** *adv.* incurablement; **i. lazy,** d'une paresse incurable.

incurious [in'kju:riəs] *a.* incurieux, sans curiosité.

incursion [in'kə:ʃ(ə)n] *n.* incursion *f*.

indebted [in'detid] *a.* **1.** endetté; **to be heavily i. to s.o.,** devoir une forte somme à qn. **2.** redevable (**to s.o. for sth.,** à qn de qch.); **I am indebted to Mr Martin for this information,** c'est à M. Martin que je dois ce renseignement.

indebtedness [in'detidnis] *n.* dette(s) *f*(*pl*).

indecency [in'di:sənsi] *n.* indécence *f*; *Jur:* **(public act of) i.,** attentat *m* aux mœurs; outrage (public) aux mœurs.

indecent [in'di:sənt] *a.* peu décent, indécent; **i. behaviour,** attentat *m* aux mœurs; **i. assault,** attentat *m* à la pudeur. **-ly** *adv.* indécemment.

indecipherable [indi'saif(ə)rəbl] *a.* indéchiffrable.

indecision [indi'siʒ(ə)n] *n.* indécision *f*, irrésolution *f*.

indecisive [indi'saisiv] *a.* **1.** (*of argument*) indécisif; (*of battle*) indécis. **2.** (*of pers.*) indécis, irrésolu.

indeclinable [indi'klainəbl] *a. Gram:* indéclinable.

indecorous [in'dekərəs] *a.* inconvenant, peu convenable. **-ly** *adv.* d'une manière peu convenable.

indecorum [indi'kɔ:rəm] *n.* (*a*) inconvenance *f*; (*b*) manque *m* de décorum, de maintien.

indeed [in'di:d] *adv.* **1.** (*a*) en effet; en vérité; vraiment; de fait; **he was i. a man of genius,** c'était vraiment un homme de génie; (*b*) (*intensive*) **I am very glad i.,** je suis très très content; **thank you very much i.,** merci infiniment; merci mille fois; (*c*) (*concessive*) **I may i. be wrong,** il se peut toutefois que j'aie tort. **2.** même, à vrai dire; **I think so, i. I am sure of it,** je le pense et même j'en suis sûr. **3.** (*a*) (*with affirmation or negation*) **yes i.!** (i) mais certainement! pour sûr! (ii) (*contradicting*) si fait! **does that surprise you?—it does i.!** cela vous étonne?—bien sûr que oui! (*b*) (*interrogatively*) **I have lived in Paris—i.?** j'ai vécu à Paris—vraiment?

indefatigable [indi'fætigəbl] *a.* infatigable, inlassable. **-ably** *adv.* infatigablement.

indefensible [indi'fensibl] *a.* (place, théorie) indéfendable, indéfensible; (conduite) inexcusable; (argument) insoutenable.

indefinable [indi'fainəbl] *a.* **1.** indéfinissable. **2.** (sentiment) vague.

indefinite [in'definit] *a.* **1.** (*of ideas, promises, etc.*) indéfini, vague. **2.** (*a*) (*of distance, time, number*) indéfini, indéterminé; (congé) illimité, indéfini; (*b*) *Gram:* (article, pronom) indéfini. **-ly** *adv.* **1.** (promettre) indéfiniment, vaguement. **2. to postpone sth. i.,** remettre qch. indéfiniment; **I could go on i.,** je pourrais continuer à l'infini.

indelible [in'delibl] *a.* indélébile, ineffaçable; (crayon) violet, à encre indélébile. **-ibly** *adv.* de façon indélébile; ineffaçablement.

indelicacy [in'delikəsi] *n.* (*a*) indélicatesse *f*, manque *m* de délicatesse; (*b*) inconvenance *f*.

indelicate [in'delikət] *a.* (*a*) indélicat; qui manque de délicatesse; peu délicat; (*b*) inconvenant.

indemnification [indemnifi'keiʃ(ə)n] *n.* **1.** indemnisation *f*, dédommagement *m* (**of s.o. for sth.,** de qn de qch.). **2.** indemnité *f*, dédommagement.

indemnify [in'demnifai] *v.tr.* **1.** garantir (qn) (**from, against,** contre); *Pol:* accorder à (un ministre) un bill d'indemnité. **2.** indemniser, dédommager (qn) (**for a loss,** d'une perte).

indemnity [in'demniti] *n.* **1.** garantie *f*, assurance *f* (contre une perte, etc.); *Pol:* **bill, act, of i.,** bill *m* d'indemnité. **2.** indemnité *f*, dédommagement *m*, compensation *f*.

indent¹ ['indent, in'dent] *n.* **1.** (*a*) dentelure *f*, entaille *f*; (*b*) *Carp:* adent *m*. **2.** commande *f* de marchandises (*esp.* reçue de l'étranger).

indent² [in'dent] **1.** *v.tr.* (*a*) denteler, entailler (le bord de qch.); (*b*) *Carp:* endenter (une poutre); (*c*) *Typ:* renfoncer, (faire) rentrer (une ligne); **indented line,** ligne *f* en alinéa, en retrait; (*d*) *Jur:* passer (un document) en partie double.

indent³ ['indent] *n.* (*a*) empreinte creuse; creux *m*, bosselure *f*; (*b*) *Metalw: etc:* brouture (laissée par l'outil).

indent⁴ [in'dent] *v.tr.* empreindre (en creux); bosseler, bossuer (une surface).

indentation [inden'teiʃ(ə)n] *n.* **1.** (*a*) découpage *m* (des bords de qch.); (*b*) *Carp:* endentement *m* (de deux poutres); (*c*) impression *f* (du sable par les roues, etc.). **2.** dentelure *f*; entaille *f*, découpure. **3.** = INDENT³.

indenture¹ [in'dentjər] *n. Jur:* contrat *m* synallagmatique; contrat bilatéral; (*b*) **indentures,** contrat, brevet *m*, d'apprentissage.

indenture² *v.tr.* **1.** lier (qn) par contrat. **2.** mettre (qn) en apprentissage (**to s.o.,** chez qn); engager (qn) par un brevet d'apprentissage.

independence [indi'pendəns] *n.* indépendance *f* (**of,** de, à l'égard de); autonomie *f* (d'un état); **the American War of I.,** la Guerre de l'Indépendance (des États-Unis).

independent [indi'pendənt] **1.** *a.* (*a*) indépendant; (état, pays) autonome; **to be i. of s.o., sth.,** ne pas dépendre de qn, qch.; **to be i.,** être indépendant; *Adm:* **i. school** = école *f* libre; *Aut:* **i. suspension,** suspension indépendante; (*b*) (i) **a man of i. means,** un rentier, un homme renté; (ii) **his children are i. now,** ses enfants peuvent maintenant pourvoir eux-mêmes à leurs besoins; (*c*) (caractère, air) indépendant. **2.** *n. Pol: etc:* indépendant, -ante. **-ly** *adv.* **1.** indépendemment. **2.** avec indépendance.

indescribable [indis'kraibəbl] *a.* (fureur, misère) indescriptible; (joie) indicible. **-ably** *adv.* indescriptiblement, indiciblement.
indestructible [indis'trʌktəbl] *a.* indestructible.
indeterminate [indi'tə:minət] *a.* (*of space, etc.*) indéterminé; (*of thought*) vague, imprécis; *Mth:* (quantité) indéterminée. **-ly** *adv.* de façon indéterminée; vaguement.
index¹, *pl.* **indexes, indices** ['indeks, 'indeksiz, 'indisi:z] *n.* **1.** (*pl.* **(indexes) i. (finger),** index *m.* **2.** *Tchn:* (*pl.* **indexes**) (*a*) aiguille *f* (de cadran, etc.); style *m* (de cadran solaire); (*b*) *Typ:* main *f.* **3.** (*pl.* **indices**) indice *m*, signe (indicateur). **4.** (*pl.* **indexes**) repère *m*; (dispositif) indicateur (*m*); **i. mark,** (marque *f*) repère, point *m* de repère. **5.** (*pl.* **indexes**) index; table *f* alphabétique, répertoire *m* (d'un livre). **6.** (*pl.* **indices**) (*a*) *Mth:* exposant *m*; (*b*) coefficient *m*, indice; *Opt:* **i. of refraction,** indice de réfraction; (*c*) *Com: Pol.Ec:* **i. number,** chiffre indicateur; indice; **cost of living i.,** indice du coût de la vie; **retail, wholesale, price i.,** indice des prix de détail, de gros. **7.** *Cmptr:* **modulation i.,** indice de modulation.
index² *v.tr.* (*a*) faire, dresser, l'index (d'un livre); indexer (un livre); (*b*) répertorier, classer (un article).
indexation [indek'seiʃ(ə)n] *n.* indexation *f.*
index-linked ['indeks'liŋkt] *a.* (*of wages, etc.*) indexé.
India ['indiə] *Pr.n. Geog:* l'Inde *f*; **I. ink,** encre *m* de Chine.
Indian ['indiən] **1.** (*a*) *a.* de l'Inde; des Indes; indien; **the I. Ocean,** l'océan Indien; (*b*) *n.* Indien, -ienne. **2.** (*a*) *a.* indien; des Indiens (d'Amérique); amérindien; (*b*) *n.* Indien, -ienne (d'Amérique); Amérindien, -ienne; **Red Indians,** Peaux-Rouges *mpl.*
indiarubber [indiə'rʌbər] *n.* (*a*) **i. (eraser),** gomme *f* à effacer; (*b*) caoutchouc *m*; gomme élastique.
indicate ['indikeit] *v.tr.* **1.** (*a*) indiquer, montrer; **to i. sth. with the hand,** indiquer qch. de la main; (*b*) **at the time indicated,** à l'heure dite, indiquée; (*c*) *Med:* **a certain treatment is indicated,** un certain traitement est indiqué; **strong measures were clearly indicated,** il était évident que la situation demandait des mesures rigoureuses. **2.** (*a*) indiquer, dénoter, témoigner (qch.); **face that indicates energy,** visage *m* qui révèle qui dénote, l'énergie; (*b*) faire savoir (qch.) en termes brefs.
indication [indi'keiʃ(ə)n] *n.* **1.** indication *f* (**of sth. to s.o.,** de qch. à qn). **2.** (*a*) indice *m*, signe *m*; **there is every i. of his speaking the truth,** tout porte à croire qu'il dit vrai; **he gave early indications of his talent,** il laissa de bonne heure entrevoir son talent; (*b*) **to give clear i. of one's intentions,** faire connaître clairement ses intentions.
indicative [in'dikətiv] **1.** *a. & n. Gram:* **i. (mood),** (mode) indicatif (*m*); **in the i.,** à l'indicatif. **2.** *a.* (*also* ['indikeitiv]) indicatif (**of,** de).
indicator ['indikeitər] *n.* **1.** (*pers.*) indicateur, -trice (**of,** de). **2.** (*a*) table *f* d'orientation (au sommet d'une montagne, etc.); (*b*) **i. (panel),** tableau indicateur; *Rail:* **train i.,** tableau, indicateur, des arrivées, des départs. **3.** (*a*) index *m*, aiguille *f* (de baromètre, etc.); *Aut:* **direction i.,** flèche *f* de direction; (*flashing*) clignotant *m*; (*b*) *Mec.E: etc:* indicateur; (*c*) *Nau: Av:* indicateur, compteur *m* (de vitesse, etc.); (*d*) *Tp: etc:* **i. board,** tableau indicateur; (*e*) *Atom.Ph:* **radiation i.,** indicateur, signaleur *m*, de rayonnement. **4.** *Com:* **retail-price i.,** indice *m* des prix de détail.
indict [in'dait] *v.tr. Jur:* accuser, inculper (qn) (**for,** de); traduire, poursuivre (qn) en justice (**for,** pour).
indictable [in'daitəbl] *a. Jur:* **1.** (personne) traduisible en justice. **2. i. offence,** délit *m.*
indictment [in'daitmənt] *n. Jur:* **1.** accusation *f*, incrimination *f*, inculpation *f*; (*by public prosecutor*) réquisitoire *m.* **2.** acte *m* d'accusation (au criminel); **to draw up an i.,** rédiger un acte d'accusation.
Indies (the) [ðiˈindiz] *Pr.n.pl. Geog:* les Indes *fpl*; **the East I.,** l'Insulinde *f*; **the West I.,** les Antilles *fpl*, les Indes occidentales.
indifference [in'dif(ə)rəns] *n.* **1.** indifférence *f*, manque *m* d'intérêt, apathie *f* (**to, towards, sth., s.o.,** pour qch., à l'égard de qn); **it's a matter of complete i. to me,** cela m'est parfaitement indifférent. **2.** médiocrité *f* (de talent, etc.). **3.** *Pol.Ec:* **i. curve,** courbe *f* d'indifférence.
indifferent [in'dif(ə)rənt] *a.* **1.** indifférent (**to,** à); **I am, feel, i. about him,** il m'est indifférent. **2.** médiocre, passable; **to be an i. painter,** peindre pauvrement. **-ly** *adv.* **1.** indifféremment. **2.** médiocrement; ni bien ni mal; (peindre) pauvrement.
indigence ['indidʒəns] *n.* indigence *f*, pauvreté *f.*
indigenous [in'didʒinəs] *a.* (*of plant, product, etc.*) indigène (**to,** à); du pays.
indigent ['indidʒənt] *a.* indigent, pauvre.
indigestible [indi'dʒestibl] *a.* indigeste.
indigestion [indi'dʒestʃ(ə)n] *n.* dyspepsie *f*; **to have an attack of i.,** avoir une indigestion.
indignant [in'dignənt] *a.* (air) indigné; (cri) d'indignation; **to be, feel, i. at sth.,** être indigné, s'indigner, de qch.; **to make s.o. i.,** indigner qn. **-ly** *adv.* avec indignation; d'un ton, air, indigné.
indignation [indig'neiʃ(ə)n] *n.* indignation *f*; **righteous i.,** une juste indignation.
indignity [in'digniti] *n.* indignité *f*; **to suffer indignities,** souffrir des affronts.
indigo, *pl.* **-o(e)s** ['indigou, -ouz] *n.* **1.** *Dy: Com:* indigo *m*; inde *m*; **i. blue,** (i) (*colour*) (bleu) indigo *m inv*; (ii) *Dy:* indigo bleu. **2.** *Bot:* **i. (plant),** indigotier; anil *m.*
indirect [indi'rekt] *a.* **1.** (*of influence, result, etc.*) indirect; *Gram:* **i. speech,** discours indirect; **i. object,** complément indirect. **2.** (moyen, etc.) détourné, oblique. **-ly** *adv.* indirectement.
indiscernible [indi'sə:nibl] *a.* (*a*) indiscernable; (*b*) imperceptible.
indiscipline [in'disiplin] *n.* indiscipline *f.*
indiscreet [indis'kri:t] *a.* **1.** indiscret, -ète; **would it be i. to ask you what you are going to do?** peut-on vous demander sans indiscrétion ce que vous comptez faire? **2.** peu judicieux; imprudent; (démarche) inconsidérée. **-ly** *adv.* **1.** indiscrètement. **2.** imprudemment.
indiscretion [indis'kreʃ(ə)n] *n.* **1.** (*a*) manque *m* de discrétion; (*b*) indiscrétion *f.* **2.** (*a*) action inconsidérée; imprudence *f*; (*b*) écart *m* de conduite; faux pas; **to be guilty of an i.,** (i) commettre une inconséquence; (ii) se compromettre (avec qn).
indiscriminate [indis'kriminət] *a.* (vengeance, admirateur) aveugle, qui ne fait pas de distinction; **i. slaughter,** tuerie générale. **-ly** *adv.* (censurer, frapper) sans faire de distinction; (admirer) aveuglément.
indispensable [indis'pensəbl] *a.* **1.** (loi, devoir) obligatoire, qu'on ne peut négliger. **2.** indispensable; de première nécessité (**to s.o.,** à qn; **for sth.,** pour, à qch.); **no one is i.,** personne n'est indispensable.
indisposed [indis'pouzd] *a.* **1.** peu enclin, peu disposé (**to do sth.,** à faire qch.). **2. to be, feel, i.,** être indisposé, souffrant; se sentir mal en train.
indisposition [indispə'ziʃ(ə)n] *n.* **1.** peu d'inclination (**to do sth.,** à faire qch.). **2.** indisposition *f*, malaise *m.*
indisputable [indis'pju:təbl] *a.* incontestable, indiscutable, indisputable. **-ably** *adv.* indiscutablement, incontestablement.
indissoluble [indi'sɔljubl] *a.* (union, amitié) indissoluble.

indistinct [indis'tiŋ(k)t] *a.* (objet, bruit, etc.) indistinct, peu distinct; (bruit) confus; (souvenir) vague. **-ly** *adv.* (voir, parler) indistinctement; (sentir) vaguement; **to speak i.,** manger ses mots.
indistinguishable [indis'tiŋgwiʃəbl] *a.* indiscernable, que l'on ne peut distinguer (**from,** de).
individual [indi'vidjuəl] **1.** *a.* (*a*) individuel, particulier; **his pupils get i. attention,** il s'occupe de ses élèves individuellement; (*b*) qui se distingue des autres; **he's so i. in his views,** il a des idées si originales. **2.** *n.* individu *m*; **a private i.,** un simple particulier. **-ally** *adv.* individuellement.
individualism [indi'vidjuəlizm] *n.* individualisme *m.*
individualist [indi'vidjuəlist] *n.* individualiste *mf.*
individualistic [individjuə'listik] *a.* individualiste.
individuality [individju'æliti] *n.* individualité *f.*
individualize [indi'vidjuəlaiz] *v.tr.* individualiser.
indivisible [indi'vizibl] *a.* indivisible, insécable.
Indochina ['indou'tʃainə] *Pr.n. Geog:* Indochine *f.*
indoctrinate [in'dɔktrineit] *v.tr.* endoctriner; **to i. s.o. with an idea,** inculquer une idée à qn.
indoctrination [indɔktri'neiʃ(ə)n] *n.* endoctrinement *m.*
Indo-European ['indoujuərə'pi:ən] **1.** *a. Ling: Ethn:* indo-européen. **2.** *n.* (*a*) Indo-Européen, -enne; (*b*) *Ling:* indo-européen *m.*
indolence ['indələns] *n.* indolence *f*, paresse *f.*
indolent ['indələnt] *a.* indolent, paresseux. **-ly** *adv.* indolemment.
indomitable [in'dɔmitəbl] *a.* indomptable; (courage, etc.) invincible.
Indonesia [indou'ni:ziə, -ʒə] *Pr.n. Geog:* Indonésie *f.*
Indonesian [indou'ni:ziən, -ʒ(ə)n] **1.** *a. Geog:* indonésien. **2.** *n.* (*a*) Indonésien, -ienne; (*b*) *Ling:* indonésien *m.*
indoor ['indɔ:*r*] *a.* (robe, etc.) d'intérieur; (décoration, plante) d'appartement; (photographie) en appartement; **i. games,** (i) jeux *mpl* de salle; (ii) jeux de société; **i. swimming pool,** piscine couverte.
indoors [in'dɔ:z] *adv.* à la maison; **to go i.,** (r)entrer (dans la maison); **to stay i.,** rester à la maison.
indorse [in'dɔ:s] *v.tr.* = ENDORSE.
indrawn ['indrɔ:n] *a.* (air) aspiré; **i. breath,** aspiration *f.*
indubitable [in'dju:bitəbl] *a.* indubitable; hors de doute, incontestable. **-ably** *adv.* indubitablement; sans aucun doute.
induce [in'dju:s] *v.tr.* **1. to i. s.o. to do sth.,** induire, amener, déterminer, qn à faire qch.; **nothing will i. him to change his mind,** rien ne le fera changer d'idée. **2.** (*a*) amener, produire, occasionner, causer; provoquer (le sommeil); (*b*) *El: etc:* amorcer, induire (un courant, etc.). **3.** induire (une loi, etc.). **induced** *a.* (*a*) (hypnose) provoquée; (*b*) **i. draught,** tirage par induction; (*c*) *El:* **i. current,** courant induit, d'induction.
inducement [in'dju:smənt] *n.* **1.** (*a*) motif *m*, mobile *m*, qui décide, pousse, qn à faire qch.; (*b*) *Jur:* incitation *f* (**to,** à). **2.** *Jur:* motif (d'un acte judiciaire); cause *f* (d'un contrat).
induct [in'dʌkt] *v.tr.* (*a*) *Ecc:* mettre (un ecclésiastique) en possession d'un bénéfice; (*b*) installer (un fonctionnaire) dans sa charge.
induction [in'dʌkʃ(ə)n] *n.* **1.** installation *f* (d'un ecclésiastique, d'un fonctionnaire). **2. i. of facts,** énumération *f* des faits (pour prouver qch.); apport *m* de preuves. **3.** *Log: Mth:* induction *f.* **4.** *El:* induction; **i. coil,** bobine *f* d'induction, bobine de self. **5.** *Mch: I.C.E:* admission *f*, entrée *f* (de la vapeur, des gaz); aspiration *f* (de gaz); **i. stroke,** course *f*, temps *m*, d'admission.
inductive [in'dʌktiv] *a.* **1.** *Log: Mth:* (raisonnement) inductif, par induction. **2.** *El:* (courant, etc.) inducteur.
indulge [in'dʌldʒ] **1.** *v.tr.* (*a*) avoir, montrer, trop d'indulgence pour (qn); gâter (qn); **to i. oneself,** ne rien se refuser; **to i. s.o.'s fancies,** flatter les caprices de qn; (*b*) s'abandonner à (une fantaisie); nourrir (un espoir); se livrer, donner libre cours, à (une passion); (*c*) *R.C.Ch:* accorder une indulgence à (qn); (*d*) *Com:* accorder un délai (au payeur d'une lettre de change). **2.** *v.i.* **to i. in a practice,** s'adonner à une habitude; **to i. in a cigar,** se permettre un cigare; **to i. in a glass of port,** s'offrir un verre de porto.
indulgence [in'dʌldʒ(ə)ns] *n.* **1.** indulgence *f*, complaisance *f* (**to,** envers); **a mother's i. for her children,** faiblesse *f* d'une mère pour ses enfants. **2. sexual i.,** plaisirs sensuels. **3.** *R.C.Ch:* indulgence.
indulgent [in'dʌldʒənt] *a.* indulgent; (*a*) **i. to s.o.,** indulgent envers, pour, qn; (*b*) faible; **over-i. father,** père trop indulgent. **-ly** *adv.* avec indulgence.
industrial [in'dʌstriəl] *a.* industriel; (*a*) (centre) industriel; **i. exhibition,** salon *m* de l'industrie; (*b*) (conflit) ouvrier, du travail; (agitation) ouvrière; (maladie) professionnelle; **to take i. action,** se mettre en grève; **i. relations,** relations humaines dans l'entreprise.
industrialism [in'dʌstriəlizm] *n.* industrialisme *m.*
industrialist [in'dʌstriəlist] *n.* industriel *m.*
industrialization [indʌstriəlai'zeiʃ(ə)n] *n.* industrialisation *f.*
industrialize [in'dʌstriəlaiz] **1.** *v.tr.* industrialiser. **2.** *v.i.* s'industrialiser.
industrious [in'dʌstriəs] *a.* industrieux, travailleur. **-ly** *adv.* industrieusement.
industriousness [in'dʌstriəsnis] *n.* assiduité *f* (au travail); application *f.*
industry ['indʌstri] *n.* **1.** application *f*, assiduité *f* au travail; diligence *f.* **2.** industrie *f*; **growth i.,** industrie en plein essor; **cottage i.,** industrie artisanale; artisanat *m*; **light i.,** l'industrie légère; **aircraft, mining, i.,** industrie aéronautique, minière; **the shipping i.,** l'armement *m.*
inebriate[1] [in'i:briət] **1.** *a.* ivre, gris, enivré. **2.** *n.* ivrogne, -esse; alcoolique *mf.*
inebriate[2] [in'i:brieit] *v.tr.* enivrer, griser; **to be inebriated,** être gris, ivre.
inebriation [ini:bri'eiʃən] *n.* **1.** enivrement *m.* **2.** ivresse *f*, ébriété *f.*
inedible [in'edibl] *a.* **1.** immangeable. **2.** non comestible.
ineducable [in'edjukəbl] *a.* inéducable.
ineffable [in'efəbl] *a.* **1.** (*of joy, etc.*) ineffable, indicible. **2.** (*of sacred name, etc.*) qu'on n'ose pas prononcer.
ineffective [ini'fektiv] *a.* **1.** (moyen, remède) inefficace, ineffectif. **2.** (travail, architecture) qui manque d'effet artistique; (discours) sans effet; (orateur) terne; (style) plat, terne. **3.** (*of pers.*) incapable. **-ly** *adv.* ineffectivement, vainement.
ineffectual [ini'fektjuəl] *a.* **1.** (*a*) (effort, raisonnement) inefficace, sans effet, vain; (traitement) sans résultat; (*b*) qui donne une impression de faiblesse; terne. **2. i. person,** personne incapable; velléitaire *mf.*
inefficacious [inefi'keiʃəs] *a.* inefficace.
inefficaciousness [inefi'keiʃəsnis], **inefficacy** [in'efikəsi] *n.* inefficacité *f.*
inefficiency [ini'fiʃənsi] *n.* **1.** inefficacité *f.* **2.** incapacité (professionnelle); incompétence *f*, insuffisance *f* (de qn).
inefficient [ini'fiʃənt] *a.* (*of measure, etc.*) inefficace, ineffectif. **2.** (*of pers.*) incapable, incompétent, insuffisant. **-ly** *adv.* **1.** inefficacement **2.** sans compétence.

inelastic [ini'læstik] *a.* (*a*) sans élasticité; raide; qui ne prête pas; (*b*) *Fig:* rigide, raide.
inelegant [in'eligənt] *a.* (style) inélégant; (personne) sans élégance. **-ly** *adv.* sans élégance, inélégamment.
ineligible [in'elidʒibl] *a.* (*a*) (candidat) inéligible; (*b*) inacceptable; **i. for military service,** inapte au service militaire.
ineluctable [ini'lʌktəbl] *a.* inéluctable, inévitable.
inept [in'ept] *a.* (*of remark, etc.*) (i) déplacé; mal à propos; (ii) inepte, absurde; **he's hopelessly i.,** c'est un parfait incapable. **-ly** *adv.* ineptement.
ineptitude [in'eptitju:d] *n.* **1.** manque *m* de justesse, d'à-propos (d'une observation). **2.** ineptie *f*, sottise *f*.
inequality [ini(:)'kwɔliti] *n.* inégalité *f*; variabilité *f*, inégalité (du climat); **social inequalities,** inégalités sociales.
inequitable [in'ekwitəbl] *a.* inéquitable.
ineradicable [ini'rædikəbl] *a.* indéracinable, inextirpable.
inert [i'nə:t] *a.* **1.** (*a*) (masse, substance) inerte; (*b*) (esprit) inerte, apathique. **2.** *Ch:* inactif, inerte.
inertia [i'nə:ʃiə] *n.* inertie *f*; (*a*) *Ph: Mec:* **mass i.,** inertie de masse; *I.C.E:* **i. starter,** démarreur *m* à inertie; (*b*) *Aut:* **i. reel seat belt,** ceinture *f* (de sécurité) à enrouleur; (*c*) (*of pers.*) paresse *f*; veulerie *f*; (*d*) *Phot: Com:* **i. selling,** vente *f* par obtention abusive, frauduleuse, de commande.
inescapable [ini'skeipəbl] *a.* inéluctable, inévitable.
inessential [ini'senʃ(ə)l] *a.* qui n'est pas essentiel; superflu; négligeable.
inestimable [in'estiməbl] *a.* **1.** (*of damage, etc.*) inestimable, incalculable. **2.** (*of help, etc.*) inappréciable.
inevitability [inevitə'biliti] *n.* inévitabilité *f*.
inevitable [in'evitəbl] *a.* (*a*) inévitable, inéluctable; (*b*) fatal, -als; obligé; **his promotion is i.,** il va de soi qu'il sera promu; **the i. latecomer,** le retardataire fatal; *Lit:* (*of a play, novel*) **the i. conclusion,** le dénouement fatal. **-ably** *adv.* inévitablement; inéluctablement.
inexact [inig'zækt] *a.* (récit, etc.) inexact. **-ly** *adv.* inexactement.
inexactitude [inig'zæktitju:d] *n.* **1.** inexactitude *f* (d'un récit, etc.). **2.** erreur *f*.
inexcusable [iniks'kju:zəbl] *a.* inexcusable; sans excuse; impardonnable. **-ly** *adv.* inexcusablement, impardonnablement.
inexhaustible [ineg'zɔ:stibl] *a.* **1.** inépuisable, inexhaustible; (source) intarissable. **2.** infatigable.
inexorable [in'eks(ə)rəbl] *a.* (personne, destin) inexorable; (personne) inflexible, implacable. **-ably** *adv.* inexorablement; implacablement.
inexpedient [iniks'pi:diənt] *a.* inopportun, malavisé.
inexpensive [iniks'pensiv] *a.* peu coûteux; bon marché; (qui ne coûte) pas cher; **house i. to run,** maison *f* économique. **-ly** *adv.* (à) bon marché, à bas prix; (vivre) économiquement, à peu de frais.
inexperience [iniks'piəriəns] *n.* inexpérience *f*.
inexperienced [iniks'piəriənst] *a.* **1.** inexpérimenté, sans expérience; **he is still i.,** il est encore novice; **he's i. in handling staff,** il n'a pas l'habitude de diriger le personnel. **2.** inaverti; (œil) inexercé.
inexpert [in'ekspə:t] *a.* inexpert, maladroit; peu habile (**in,** à). **-ly** *adv.* d'une manière inexperte; maladroitement.
inexplicable [iniks'plikəbl] *a.* (mystère) inexplicable; (ingratitude) inconcevable. **-ably** *adv.* inexplicablement.
inexpressible [iniks'presibl] *a.* (plaisir) inexprimable; (charme) indicible.
inexpressive [iniks'presiv] *a.* inexpressif, sans expression.
inextinguishable [iniks'tiŋgwiʃəbl] *a.* (feu, rire) inextinguible.
inextricable [iniks'trikəbl, in'eks-] *a.* inextricable. **-ably** *adv.* inextricablement.
infallibility [infæli'biliti] *n.* *Theol: etc:* infaillibilité *f*.
infallible [in'fælibl] *a.* (jugement, remède, etc.) infaillible. **-ibly** *adv.* infailliblement.
infamous ['infəməs] *a.* **1.** (personne, conduite) infâme; (conduite) abominable; (endroit) mal famé. **2.** *Jur:* (crime) infamant.
infamy ['infəmi] *n.* infamie *f* (d'un crime, etc.).
infancy ['infənsi] *n.* **1.** (*a*) première enfance, petite enfance; **from i.,** dès la plus tendre enfance; (*b*) débuts *mpl*, première période, enfance (d'un art, d'une industrie). **2.** *Jur:* minorité *f*.
infant ['infənt] *n.* **1.** enfant *mf* du premier âge; nourrisson *m*; nouveau-né *m*, nouveau-née *f*; **i. mortality,** mortalité *f* infantile; *Sch:* **i. class,** la classe enfantine; **i. school,** école *f* pour les enfants de cinq à huit ans. **2.** *Jur:* mineur, -eure.
infanticide [in'fæntisaid] *n.* **1.** (*pers.*) infanticide *mf*. **2.** (crime *m* d')infanticide (*m*).
infantile ['infəntail] *a.* **1.** (*a*) (esprit, imagination) d'enfant; (*b*) (raisonnement, etc.) enfantin; (remarque) puérile. **2.** *Med:* (maladie) infantile.
infantry ['infəntri] *n.* *Mil:* (*a*) infanterie *f*; (*b*) fantassins *mpl*.
infantryman, *pl.* **-men** ['infəntrimən] *n.m.* soldat d'infanterie; fantassin.
infatuated [in'fætjueitid] *a.* infatué, entiché; **to become i. with s.o., sth.,** s'engouer, s'enticher, de qn, de qch.
infatuation [infætju'eiʃ(ə)n] *n.* engouement *m*; **to have an i. for s.o.,** avoir le béguin pour qn.
infect [in'fekt] *v.tr.* **1.** infecter, corrompre, vicier (l'air, les mœurs, etc.). **2.** (*a*) *Med:* contaminer (qn); infecter (une plaie, une ville); **to i. s.o. with a disease,** communiquer une maladie à qn; **infected clothing,** vêtements porteurs de germes; (*b*) **to i. s.o. with one's high spirits,** communiquer sa gaieté à qn.
infection [in'fekʃ(ə)n] *n.* **1.** (*a*) *Med:* infection *f*, contamination *f*, contagion *f*; **viral i.,** infection virale; **source of i.,** foyer *m* d'infection; **to spread i.,** répandre l'infection; (*b*) *Fig:* contagion.
infectious [in'fekʃəs] *a.* (*a*) *Med:* (*of disease*) (i) infectieux; (ii) contagieux; **is it an i. disease?** est-ce que c'est une maladie contagieuse? (*b*) (rire) contagieux, communicatif.
infectiousness [in'fekʃəsnis] *n.* (*a*) nature infectieuse (d'une maladie); (*b*) contagion *f* (du rire).
infelicitous [infi'lisitəs] *n.* malheureux.
infelicity [infi'lisiti] *n.* **1.** malheur *m*; infélicité *f*. **2.** expression malheureuse; gaffe *f*.
infer [in'fə:r] *v.tr.* **(inferred)** inférer, déduire, conclure (**sth. from sth.,** qch. de qch.; **that,** que).
inference ['inf(ə)rəns] *n.* *Log: etc:* **1.** inférence *f*; **by i.,** par induction. **2.** inférence, déduction *f*, conclusion *f*; **to draw an i. from sth.,** tirer une conclusion, une conséquence, de qch.
inferior [in'fiəriər] **1.** *a.* (*a*) inférieur; (ouvrage) de second ordre; **i. quality,** qualité inférieure; **to be in an i. position,** être dans une position inférieure, subordonnée; (*b*) *Astr:* **the i. planets,** les planètes inférieures; (*c*) *Bot:* (calice, ovaire) infère; (*d*) *Typ:* **i. letter,** *n.* **i.,** petite lettre inférieure. **2.** *n.* (*a*) (*in school position*) inférieur, -eure; (*b*) (*in rank, grade*) inférieur, subordonné, -ée, subalterne *m*.
inferiority [infiəri'ɔriti] *n.* infériorité *f* (**to,** par rapport à); *Psy:* **i. complex,** complexe *m* d'infériorité.
infernal [in'fə:n(ə)l] *a.* **1.** infernal, -aux; **the i. re-**

gions, l'enfer *m.* **2.** *F:* (*a*) infernal, abominable, diabolique; (*b*) (*intensive*) (chaleur, etc.) d'enfer; (bruit) infernal; **it's an i. nuisance,** c'est diablement embêtant. **-ally** *adv. F:* diablement; **it's i. hot,** il fait une chaleur d'enfer, à crever.

inferno, *pl.* **-os** [in'fəːnou, -ouz] *n.* enfer *m*; *Lit:* **Dante's I.,** l'Enfer de Dante; **the building was a raging i.,** la maison était un véritable brasier.

infertile [in'fəːtail] *a.* (*a*) (terrain) stérile, infertile, infécond; (esprit) stérile; (*b*) (œuf) clair, non fécondé.

infertility [infəː'tiliti] *n.* infertilité *f*, stérilité *f*.

infest [in'fest] *v.tr.* (*of vermin, etc.*) infester.

infestation [infes'teiʃ(ə)n] *n.* invasion *f* (des plantes par les parasites, etc.); *Med:* infestation *f*.

infidel ['infidəl] *a. & n.* **1.** *Hist:* infidèle (*mf*); mécréant, -ante. **2.** *Pej:* incroyant, -ante.

infidelity [infi'deliti] *n.* **1.** incroyance *f*. **2.** (*a*) infidélité, déloyauté *f* (d'un serviteur, etc.); (*b*) **his frequent infidelities,** ses fréquentes infidélités.

infiltrate ['infiltreit] **1.** *v.tr.* (*a*) faire pénétrer (un liquide, etc.) dans (qch.); (*b*) (*of liquid*) s'infiltrer, pénétrer, dans (une substance); imprégner (une substance); (*c*) (*of troops*) s'infiltrer dans (l'ennemi, etc.); *Pol: etc:* (*of subversionists, etc.*) noyauter (un syndicat, etc.). **2.** *v.i.* (*of fluid*) s'infiltrer (**into,** dans; **through,** à travers).

infiltration [infil'treiʃ(ə)n] *n.* (*a*) infiltration *f* (d'un liquide, etc.) (**through,** à travers); (*b*) (*of troops, etc.*) **to advance by i.,** s'infiltrer; *Pol:* **the i. of communists into the trade unions,** le noyautage des syndicats par les communistes.

infiltrator ['infiltreitər] *n.* agent *m* qui s'infiltre (dans un parti politique, etc.).

infinite ['infinit] **1.** *a.* infini; (*a*) illimité; *Mth:* (série) infinie; (*b*) **truth of i. importance,** vérité *f* d'une très grande importance; **to have i. trouble in doing sth.,** avoir une peine infinie à faire qch.; (*c*) (*with n. in pl.*) **i. ways of doing sth.,** une infinité de façons de faire qch.; **i. varieties,** variétés *fpl* sans nombre; (*d*) [in'fainait] *Gram:* **i. verb, verb i.,** formes substantives du verbe. **2.** *n.* (*a*) *Theol:* **the I.,** l'infini *m*; (*b*) *Mth:* **the i.,** l'infini. **-ly** *adv.* infiniment.

infinitesimal [infini'tesim(ə)l] *a.* infinitésimal, -aux; (*a*) *Mth:* **i. calculus,** calcul infinitésimal; (*b*) (quantité) infinitésimale; (majorité) infime.

infinitive [in'finitiv] *a. & n. Gram:* infinitif (*m*); **in the i.,** à l'infinitif.

infinity [in'finiti] *n.* **1.** infinité *f*, infinitude *f* (de l'espace, etc.). **2.** *Mth: etc:* infini *m*; **to i.,** à l'infini; *Phot:* **to focus on, for, i.,** mettre au point sur l'infini.

infirm [in'fəːm] *a.* **1.** (*of pers.*) infirme, débile. **2.** (esprit, jugement) irrésolu, flottant.

infirmary [in'fəːməri] *n.* **1.** infirmerie *f* (d'une école, prison, etc.). **2.** hôpital *m*, -aux.

infirmity [in'fəːmiti] *n.* **1.** (*a*) infirmité *f*, débilité *f*, (du corps, de l'esprit); (*b*) infirmité; **the infirmities of old age,** les infirmités de la vieillesse. **2. i. of purpose,** irrésolution *f*.

inflame [in'fleim] **1.** *v.tr.* (*a*) mettre le feu à, enflammer (une substance); (*b*) enflammer (le courage); allumer (les désirs); attiser (la discorde); envenimer (une querelle); (*c*) *Med:* enflammer (une plaie). **2.** *v.i.* (*a*) s'enflammer, prendre feu; (*b*) *Med:* (*of wound, tissue*) s'enflammer. **inflamed** *a.* **1.** enflammé (**with,** de); **i. with passion,** brûlant d'amour. **2.** *Med:* (*of wound, eye, etc.*) enflammé; **to become i.,** s'enflammer.

inflammable [in'flæməbl] **1.** *a.* (*a*) (substance, etc.) inflammable; (*b*) (*of pers., crowd*) prompt à s'échauffer; inflammable. **2.** *n.pl.* **inflammables,** substances *fpl* inflammables.

inflammation [inflə'meiʃ(ə)n] *n.* **1.** (*a*) inflammation *f* (d'un combustible); (*b*) inflammation, excitation *f* (des esprits). **2.** *Med:* inflammation.

inflammatory [in'flæmət(ə)ri] *a.* **1.** (discours, brochure) incendiaire, provocateur, -trice. **2.** *Med:* (fièvre) inflammatoire. **3.** (*of projectile, etc.*) inflammateur, -trice; incendiaire.

inflatable [in'fleitəbl] *a.* (*of balloon, etc.*) gonflable; (radeau) pneumatique.

inflate [in'fleit] *v.tr.* **1.** (*a*) gonfler (un ballon, un pneu); gonfler (une voile); **to i. the lungs with air,** remplir les poumons d'air; souffler dans les poumons; (*b*) **to i. s.o. with pride,** bouffir, qn d'orgueil. **2.** (*a*) *Com:* grossir, charger (un compte); (*b*) hausser, faire monter (les prix); (*c*) *Pol.Ec:* **to i. the currency,** accroître artificiellement la circulation fiduciaire. **inflated** *a.* **1.** (*a*) (ballon, etc.) gonflé, enflé; **to become i.,** se gonfler (d'air); (*b*) (*of pers.*) **i. with pride,** bouffi d'orgueil. **2.** (*a*) *Com:* (prix) exagéré; (*b*) *Pol.Ec:* **i. currency,** circulation fiduciaire artificiellement accrue. **3.** *Lit:* (style) enflé.

inflation [in'fleiʃ(ə)n] *n.* **1.** (*a*) gonflement *m*, gonflage *m* (d'un ballon, pneu, etc.); (*b*) *Med:* inflation *f* (de l'estomac); (*c*) *Pol.Ec:* (i) hausse *f* (des prix, des salaires); (ii) inflation; **rate of i.,** taux *m* d'inflation. **2.** *Lit:* enflure *f*, emphase *f* (du style).

inflationary [in'fleiʃ(ə)nəri] *a.* (politique, etc.) inflationniste, d'inflation.

inflect [in'flekt] *v.tr.* **1.** fléchir, courber (en dedans); *Opt:* infléchir (un rayon). **2.** *Gram:* donner (i) des inflexions, (ii) des flexions, à (un mot). **3.** (*a*) moduler (la voix); (*b*) *Mus:* altérer (une note). **inflected** *a.* **1.** (position) courbée; *Arch:* (arc) renversé; *Opt:* (rayon) infléchi. **2.** *Ling:* (langue) à flexions, flexionnelle; (voyelle) infléchie. **3.** *Mus:* (note) altérée.

inflection [in'flekʃ(ə)n] *n.* = INFLEXION.

inflexibility [infleksi'biliti] *n.* inflexibilité *f*, rigidité *f*.

inflexible [in'fleksibl] *a.* inflexible; (courage) inébranlable; **i. code of morals,** morale *f* rigide.

inflexion [in'flekʃ(ə)n] *n.* **1.** (*a*) inflexion *f*, fléchissement *m* (du corps, etc.); (*b*) *Opt: Mth:* inflexion. **2.** *Ling:* (i) inflexion, (ii) flexion *f* (d'un mot). **3.** (*a*) inflexion (de la voix); (*b*) *Mus:* altération *f* (d'une note).

inflict [in'flikt] *v.tr.* infliger (**sth. on s.o.,** qch. à qn); faire (une blessure à qn); faire subir, occasionner (du chagrin à qn); *Jur:* infliger (une punition à qn); *F:* **to i. oneself on s.o.,** s'imposer.

infliction [in'flikʃ(ə)n] *n.* **1.** *Jur:* infliction *f* (d'une peine). **2.** (*a*) peine infligée; châtiment *m*; (*b*) affliction *f*.

inflorescence [inflə'resəns] *n. Bot:* **1.** inflorescence *f*. **2.** (*a*) floraison *f*; (*b*) fleurs *fpl* (d'un arbre, etc.).

inflow ['inflou] *n.* **1.** (*a*) entrée *f*, affluence *f* (d'un cours d'eau); **i. pipe,** arrivée *f* d'eau; (*b*) affluence *f*, afflux *m* (de gens, de marchandises); flot *m* (d'idées nouvelles). **2.** vitesse *f* d'appel (d'air).

influence[1] ['influəns] *n.* **1.** (*a*) influence *f*, action *f* (**upon, on,** sur); **to exert, exercise, an i. on s.o.,** exercer une influence sur qn; influencer qn; **to use one's i. with s.o.,** user de son influence auprès de qn; **to have great i. over s.o.,** avoir beaucoup d'influence sur qn; **under the i. of drink,** *F:* **under the i.,** sous l'empire de la boisson; *Jur:* **undue i.,** intimidation *f*; (*b*) (*of pers.*) **to have i.,** (i) avoir de l'influence, de l'autorité; (ii) avoir de la protection, du crédit (**with s.o.,** auprès de qn); **man of i.,** homme influent; **outside i.,** influence étrangère; *F:* piston *m*; **he owes his position to i.,** il doit sa situation au piston, au pistonnage. **2.** *El:* induction *f*.

influence[2] *v.tr.* (*of pers.*) influencer (qn); (*of thg*) influer sur (qch., qn); **to i. one's friends,** influencer, exercer une influence sur, ses amis.

influential [influ'enʃ(ə)l] *a.* influent; **to be i.,** avoir de l'influence; avoir le bras long.

influenza [influ:'enzə] *n. Med:* grippe *f.*

influx ['inflʌks] *n.* (*a*) entrée *f*, affluence *f* (d'un cours d'eau, etc.); (*b*) affluence *f*, afflux *m* (de gens, de marchandises); afflux (de gaz); flot *m* (d'idées nouvelles); *Pol.Ec:* **i. of gold,** entrée, afflux, d'or.

info ['infou] *n. F:* renseignements *mpl*, tuyaux *mpl.*

inform [in'fɔ:m] **1.** *v.tr.* (*a*) **to i. s.o. of sth.,** informer, avertir, aviser, qn de qch.; apprendre, faire savoir, qch. à qn; renseigner qn sur qch.; **to keep s.o. informed of what is happening,** tenir qn au courant de ce qui se passe; **to i. the police,** avertir la police; **we are writing to i. you of the dispatch of . . .,** nous vous avisons de l'envoi de . . .; **I regret to have to i. you that . . .,** j'ai le regret de vous annoncer que . . .; **we are informed that . . .,** on nous fait savoir, que . . .; (*b*) **to i. s.o. on, about, sth.,** renseigner qn sur qch. **2.** *v.i. Jur:* **to i. against s.o.,** dénoncer qn. **informed** *a.* bien renseigné; **i. public opinion,** l'opinion publique bien renseignée, bien au courant; **i. estimate,** une évaluation bien renseignée.

informal [in'fɔ:m(ə)l] *a.* **1.** (*a*) *Jur:* irrégulier; (*b*) (réunion, séance) en dehors des statuts; (renseignement) officieux. **2.** (dîner, etc.) sans cérémonie, simple, en famille; **i. clothes,** tenue *f* de sport, de loisirs. **-ally** *adv.* **1.** (*a*) en dehors des règles; irrégulièrement; (*b*) officieusement; à titre non officiel. **2.** sans cérémonie; sans formalités; en famille.

informality [infɔ:'mæliti] *n.* absence *f* de formalité, de cérémonie; caractère intime (d'un dîner, etc.).

informant [in'fɔ:mənt] *n.* informateur, -trice; **I have it from a reliable i.,** je le tiens de bonne source.

information [infə'meiʃ(ə)n] *n.* **1.** renseignement(s) *m(pl)*, information(s) *f(pl)*; (*a*) **I am sending you this brochure for your i., . . .,** je vous envoie cette brochure à titre d'information; *Adm:* **(strictly) confidential i.,** renseignements (strictement) confidentiels; **to ask for i. on, about, s.o., sth.,** demander des renseignements sur qn, qch.; se renseigner sur qn, qch., *Adm:* **i. bureau,** bureau *m* de renseignements; centre *m* d'information; **Central Office of I.** = Commissariat *m* à l'Information; (*b*) *Cmptr:* **i. processing industry,** l'informatique *f*; **i. theory,** théorie *f* de l'information. **2.** instruction *f*, savoir *m*, connaissances *fpl*; **for my own i.,** pour mon instruction. **3.** *Jur:* dénonciation *f* (**against s.o.,** contre qn); délation *f* (**against s.o.,** de qn); **to lay (an) i. against s.o. with the police,** dénoncer qn à la police; informer contre qn.

informative [in'fɔ:mətiv] *a.* instructif; (livre) éducatif; (influence) informante.

informer [in'fɔ:mər] *n.* dénonciateur, -trice; informateur, -trice; *Jur:* **common i.,** délateur, -trice; **to turn i.,** dénoncer ses complices.

infraction [in'frækʃ(ə)n] *n.* infraction *f* (d'un droit); transgression *f*; violation *f* (de la loi); **minor i. of the law, i. of regulations,** contravention *f.*

infra dig ['infrə'dig] *adj.phr.* (*from Lt. Phr.* **infra dignitatem**) *F:* **it would be i. d. for us to reply,** ce serait au-dessous de notre dignité, au-dessous de nous, de répondre.

infrared [infrə'red] *a. Ph:* infra(-)rouge; **i. radiation, rays,** radiation *f* infra(-)rouge; infra(-)rouge *m*; *Med:* **i. lamp,** lampe *f* à rayons infra(-)rouges.

infrequency [in'fri:kwənsi] *n.* rareté *f.*

infrequent [in'fri:kwənt] *a.* rare, peu fréquent. **-ly** *adv.* rarement; **not i.,** assez souvent.

infringe [in'frindʒ] **1.** *v.tr.* enfreindre, violer (une loi, un serment); transgresser (la loi); **to i. an author's copyright,** violer, empiéter sur, les droits d'un auteur. **2.** *v.ind.tr.* **to i. on s.o.'s rights,** empiéter sur les droits de qn.

infringement [in'frindʒmənt] *n.* **1.** infraction *f* (d'un règlement); violation *f* (d'une loi, d'un droit); **i. of s.o.'s rights,** infraction, atteinte *f*, aux droits de qn. **2. i. of copyright,** contrefaçon.

infuriate [in'fjuərieit] *v.tr.* rendre (qn, un taureau, etc.) furieux. **infuriated** *a.* furieux, en fureur; **to become i.,** entrer en fureur. **infuriating** *a.* qui rend furieux; exaspérant; **at times I find him i.,** quelquefois il me met hors de moi. **-ly** *adv.* d'une façon exaspérante; à rendre furieux.

infuse [in'fju:z] *v.tr.* **1.** (*a*) **to i. courage, new life, into s.o.,** infuser du courage, une nouvelle vie, à qn; (*b*) **to i. s.o. with ardour,** inspirer de l'ardeur à qn. **2.** infuser, faire infuser (du thé, des herbes).

infuser [in'fju:zər] *n.* infusoir *m.*

infusion [in'fju:ʒ(ə)n] *n.* **1.** *Theol:* infusion *f* (de la vérité, etc.). **2.** (*a*) infusion (d'une tisane); (*b*) tisane, infusion (de camomille, etc.); *Pharm:* infusé *m.*

ingenious [in'dʒi:njəs] *a.* (homme, mécanisme) ingénieux. **-ly** *adv.* ingénieusement.

ingenuity [indʒi'nju(:)iti] *n.* ingéniosité *f* (de qn, d'une invention).

ingenuous [in'dʒenjuəs] *a.* **1.** franc, *f.* franche; sincère. **2.** ingénu, simple, candide; naïf, *f.* naïve. **-ly** *adv.* **1.** franchement, sincèrement. **2.** ingénument, naïvement; avec candeur.

ingenuousness [in'dʒenjuəsnis] *n.* ingénuité *f*, naïveté *f*, candeur *f.*

ingest [in'dʒest] *v.tr. Physiol:* ingérer (un aliment).

ingestion [in'dʒestjən] *n. Physiol:* ingestion *f.*

inglenook ['iŋglnuk] *n.* coin *m* du feu.

inglorious [in'glɔ:riəs] *a.* **1.** (*of pers.*) humble, obscur. **2.** (combat, etc.) déshonorant, honteux. **-ly** *adv.* **1.** humblement. **2.** sans gloire; ignominieusement.

ingot ['iŋgət] *n.* lingot *m* (d'or, d'argent).

ingrain [in'grein] *v.tr.* fixer; **certain habits are ingrained in one's nature,** certaines habitudes constituent une partie essentielle de sa nature; **prejudices that become ingrained,** préjugés *mpl* qui s'incrustent. **ingrained** *a.* (*a*) **i. with dirt,** encrassé; **i. dirt,** crasse *f*; (*b*) (préjugé) enraciné; (habitude) invétérée.

ingratiate [in'greiʃieit] *v.tr.* **to i. oneself with s.o.,** s'insinuer dans les bonnes grâces de qn. **ingratiating** *a.* insinuant, prévenant; (sourire) engageant; **to act, speak, in an i. manner,** agir, parler, d'une manière insinuante. **ingratiatingly** *adv.* d'une manière insinuante.

ingratitude [in'grætitju:d] *n.* ingratitude *f.*

ingredient [in'gri:diənt] *n.* ingrédient *m*; élément *m.*

ingress ['ingres] *n. Jur:* entrée *f*; **free i.,** droit *m* de libre accès.

ingrowing ['ingrouiŋ] *a. Med:* **i. (toe)nail,** ongle incarné.

inhabit [in'hæbit] *v.tr.* habiter, habiter dans (une maison, une ville).

inhabitable [in'hæbitəbl] *a.* habitable.

inhabitant [in'hæbitənt] *n.* habitant, -ante.

inhalant [in'heilənt] *n. Med:* inhalation *f.*

inhalation [in(h)ə'leiʃ(ə)n] *n.* (*a*) inhalation *f* (de chloroforme, etc.); (*b*) aspiration *f* (d'un parfum).

inhale [in'heil] **1.** *v.tr.* (*a*) *Med:* inhaler (de l'éther, etc.); (*b*) aspirer, humer (un parfum); (*c*) respirer, avaler (la fumée d'une cigarette). **2.** *v.i.* avaler la fumée. **inhaling** *n.* inhalation *f.*

inhaler [in'heilər] *n.* **1.** (*pers.*) fumeur *m* qui avale la fumée de sa cigarette. **2.** (*device*) (*a*) *Med:* inhalateur *m*; (*b*) *Ind:* respirateur *m.*

inherent [in'hiərənt] *a.* **1.** inhérent, naturel, propre (**in,** à); **i. stability,** stabilité *f* propre (d'un avion, d'un navire, etc.). **2. power i. in an office,** pouvoir assigné, qui appartient, à une fonction. **-ly** *adv.* par héritance; **i. lazy,** né paresseux.

inherit [in'herit] **1.** *v.tr.* (*a*) hériter de (qch.); succéder à (une fortune); (*b*) **to i. sth. from s.o.,** hériter qch. de qn. **2.** *v.i.* **to i. equally,** hériter de parts égales; **to i. jointly,** cohériter. **inherited** *a.* (bien, trait, goût) hérité.

inheritance [in'heritəns] *n.* **1.** succession *f*; **right of i.,** droit *m* de succession; **law of i.,** droit successif. **2.** patrimoine *m*, héritage *m*; **to come into an i.,** faire un héritage; *NAm:* **i. tax,** droits *mpl* de succession.

inhibit [in'hibit] *v.tr.* **1.** *Jur: etc:* **to i. s.o. from doing sth.,** interdire, défendre, à qn de faire qch. **2.** (*a*) *Med:* paralyser (une sécrétion, etc.); (*b*) *Psy:* inhiber (un sentiment); **inhibited person,** inhibé(e). **inhibiting** *a.* (*of influence, etc.*) inhibiteur, -trice.

inhibition [in(h)i'biʃ(ə)n] *n.* **1.** *Jur: etc:* défense expresse; prohibition *f.* **2.** *Med: Psy:* inhibition *f*; **person with inhibitions,** inhibé(e).

inhibitive [in'hibitiv] *a.* (mandat) prohibitif; (jugement) inhibitoire.

inhibitory [in'hibit(ə)ri] *a.* **1.** (mandat) prohibitif. **2.** (nerf, reflexe) inhibiteur.

inhospitable [inhɔ'spitəbl, in'hɔs-] *a.* inhospitalier. **-ably** *adv.* d'une manière inhospitalière.

inhuman [in'hjuːmən] *a.* inhumain; brutal, -aux; (coutume) barbare.

inhumane [inhju(:)'mein] *a.* inhumain, cruel.

inhumanity [inhju(:)'mæniti] *n.* inhumanité *f*, cruauté *f*, barbarie *f* (d'une personne, d'une action).

inhumation [inhju(:)'meiʃ(ə)n] *n.* inhumation *f*, enterrement *m* (d'un cadavre).

inimical [i'nimik(ə)l] *a.* (*a*) (peuple) ennemi, hostile; (*b*) défavorable, contraire, adverse (**to,** à).

inimitable [i'nimitəbl] *a.* inimitable. **-ably** *adv.* d'une manière inimitable.

iniquitous [i'nikwitəs] *a.* inique. **-ly** *adv.* iniquement.

iniquity [i'nikwiti] *n.* iniquité *f.*

initial¹ [i'niʃ(ə)l] **1.** *a.* (*a*) initial, -aux; premier; **the disease is only in the i. stages,** la maladie ne fait que commencer; **the i. difficulties,** les difficultés du début; les premières difficultés; *Com:* **i. cost,** coût initial; (*of manufactured product*) prix *m* de revient; *El:* **i. charge,** charge principale (d'un accumulateur); (*b*) *Typ:* **i. letter,** *n.* **initial,** lettre initiale; lettrine *f.* **2.** *n. usu. pl.* **initials,** initiales *f*; (*to alteration of cheque, etc.*) paraphe *m*; (*of supervisor, etc.*) visa *m*; (*for sewing on garment, etc.*) monogramme *m.* **-ally** *adv.* au commencement, au début.

initial² *v.tr.* **(initialled)** parapher (un traité, une correction); viser (un acte, etc.); mettre son paraphe au bas (d'un acte).

initiate [i'niʃieit] *v.tr.* **1.** (*a*) commencer, ouvrir (des négociations, etc.); lancer, amorcer (une entreprise, etc.); instaurer (des mesures,etc.); instituer (une expérience, etc.); inaugurer (une politique nouvelle); être l'initiateur (d'une réforme); *Jur:* **to i. proceedings against s.o.,** instituer des poursuites contre qn; (*b*) *Cmptr:* lancer, faire démarrer (un programme). **2.** initier (qn); (*a*) **to i. s.o. into a secret,** initier qn à un secret; (*b*) **to i. s.o. into a secret society,** initier qn à, admettre qn dans, une société secrète. **initiated** *a.* initié; *n.pl.* **the i.,** les initiés.

initiation [iniʃi'eiʃ(ə)n] *n.* **1.** (*a*) commencement(s) *m(pl)*, début(s) *m(pl)* (d'une entreprise); instauration *f*, inauguration *f* (d'un usage); (*b*) *Cmptr:* lancement *m*, déclenchement *m* (d'un programme, etc.). **2.** initiation *f* (de qn) (**into,** à).

initiative [i'niʃiətiv] *n.* initiative *f*; (*a*) **to take the i. in doing sth.,** prendre l'initiative pour faire qch.; (*b*) **to do sth. on one's own i.,** faire qch. de sa propre initiative; **to show, lack, i.,** faire preuve, manquer, d'initiative; **person with plenty of i.,** personne entreprenante.

initiator [i'niʃieitər] *n.* initiateur, -trice; lanceur *m* (d'une mode, etc.).

inject [in'dʒekt] *v.tr.* (*a*) **to i. a fluid into a cavity,** injecter un liquide dans une cavité; **to i. capital into a business,** injecter du capital dans une entreprise; (*b*) **to i. a cavity with a fluid,** injecter une cavité d'un, avec, un liquide; **to i. s.o. with morphia,** faire une piqûre de morphine à qn.

injection [in'dʒekʃ(ə)n] *n.* injection *f.* **1.** *Const:* **i. of cement,** injection de ciment; *Mch:* **i. pump,** pompe *f* à injection; **(fuel) i. pump,** pompe d'injection (de carburant). **2. i. of capital into a business,** injection, apport *m*, du capital dans une entreprise. **3.** *Med:* **antitetanus i.,** piqûre *f* antitétanique; **intravenous i.,** injection intraveineuse; **course of injections,** série *f* de piqûres; **to give s.o. an i.,** faire une injection, une piqûre, à qn; piquer qn.

injudicious [indʒu(:)'diʃəs] *a.* peu judicieux, malavisé. **-ly** *adv.* d'une façon peu judicieuse.

Injun ['indʒən] *n. F:* (*a*) *NAm:* Indien, -ienne (d'Amérique); (*b*) **honest I.!** vrai de vrai! sans blague!

injunction [in'dʒʌŋkʃ(ə)n] *n.* **1.** injonction *f*, ordre *m*, recommandation *f*; **to give s.o. strict injunctions to do sth.,** enjoindre formellement à qn de faire qch. **2.** *Jur:* arrêt *m* de suspension; arrêt de sursis; **I shall ask for an i.,** je vais mettre opposition.

injure ['indʒər] *v.tr.* **1.** nuire à, faire tort à (qn, la réputation de qn); léser (qn); *Jur:* porter préjudice à (qn); compromettre (les intérêts de qn). **2.** (*a*) blesser (qn); faire mal à (qn); **to i. oneself,** se blesser; se faire du mal; **fatally injured,** blessé mortellement; **to i. s.o.'s pride,** blesser qn dans son amour-propre; (*b*) endommager, abîmer, gâter (qch.); *Com:* avarier (des marchandises); **to i. one's health,** s'abîmer la santé. **injured** *a.* **1.** (*of pers.*) offensé, outragé; (femme) trompée, trahie; **the i. party,** l'offensé, -ée; *Jur:* la partie lésée; **in an i. (tone of) voice,** d'une voix offensée. **2.** (bras, etc.) blessé; *n.pl.* **the i.,** les blessés *mpl*; (*from accident*) les accidentés *mpl.*

injurious [in'dʒuəriəs] *a.* **1.** (*a*) nuisible, pernicieux, préjudiciable (**to,** à); (*b*) **i. to (the) health,** nocif; nuisible à la santé. **2.** (langage) injurieux, offensant.

injury ['indʒ(ə)ri] *n.* **1.** tort *m*, mal *m*, préjudice *m*; *Jur:* lésion *f*; **to do s.o. an i.,** faire du tort à qn; **to suffer i.,** subir un préjudice. **2.** (*a*) blessure *f* (au corps); *Med:* lésion; **to do oneself an i.,** se blesser; se faire du mal; **he escaped without i.,** il n'a eu aucun mal; **internal injuries,** lésions internes; (*b*) (*damage*) dommage *m*, dégât *m*; *Nau: Mch:* avarie *f.*

injustice [in'dʒʌstis] *n.* **1.** injustice *f* (d'une loi, etc.). **2. you do him an i.,** vous êtes injuste envers lui.

ink¹ [iŋk] *n.* **1.** encre *f*; (*a*) **written in i.,** écrit à l'encre; **indelible, waterproof, i.,** encre indélébile; **Indian i.,** encre de Chine; **marking i.,** encre à marquer le linge; (*b*) **i. blot, i. stain,** tache *f* d'encre; pâté *m*; *Psy:* **i.-blot test,** test *m* de la tache d'encre; **i. bottle,** bouteille d'encre; **i. pad,** tampon (encreur). **2.** *Moll:* noir *m*, encre (de seiche); sépia *f*; **i. bag, sac,** glande *f*, poche *f*, du noir.

ink² *v.tr.* **1.** noircir d'encre, barbouiller d'encre, tacher d'encre. **2.** *Typ:* encrer (les lettres); toucher (la forme). **ink in** *v.tr.* tracer à l'encre (des lignes faites au crayon); mettre (un dessin) à l'encre. **inking** *n.* (*a*) *Typ:* encrage *m* (des rouleaux); (*b*) **i. in,** mise *f* à l'encre. **ink out,** *v.tr.* oblitérer, rayer, biffer, (un mot, etc.) à l'encre. **ink over** *v.tr.* = INK OUT.

inkling ['iŋkliŋ] *n.* soupçon *m*; **to give s.o. an i. of sth.,** faire pressentir qch. à qn; **he had an i. of the truth,** il entrevoyait la vérité; **he has no i. of the matter,** il ne se doute de rien.

inkpot ['iŋkpɔt] *n.* encrier *m.*

inkstand ['iŋkstænd] *n.* (grand) encrier.

inkwell ['iŋkwel] *n.* encrier *m* (de pupitre).

inky ['iŋki] *a.* **1.** taché d'encre; barbouillé d'encre. **2.** **i. (black),** noir comme (de) l'encre; **the night was i. black,** il faisait noir comme dans un four.

inlaid. *see* INLAY².

inland ['inlænd] **1.** *n.* (l')intérieur *m* (d'un pays). **2.** *a.* (*a*) intérieur; **i. waterways,** voies navigables; **i. navigation,** navigation intérieure, fluviale; (*b*) du pays; (commerce) intérieur; (produits) indigènes, du pays; (courrier) intérieur; **i. postage rates,** (tarif *m* d')affranchissement (*m*) en régime intérieur; **i. revenue,** contributions (directes et indirectes); **the I. Revenue,** le fisc. **3.** *adv.* **to go, march, i.,** pénétrer vers l'intérieur, dans les terres.

in-laws [in'lɔːz] *n.pl.* parents *mpl* par alliance; belle-famille *f*; beaux-parents.

inlay¹ ['inlei] *n.* (*a*) incrustation *f* (de nacre, etc.); marqueterie *f*; (*b*) *Dent:* inlay *m*, incrustation (de métal, en céramique, etc.).

inlay² ['inlei, in'lei] *v.tr.* **(inlaid)** incruster (**with,** de); marqueter (une table, etc.); **to i. with enamel,** nieller; **table inlaid with mother-of-pearl,** table incrustée de nacre. **inlaid** *a.* incrusté, marqueté; (plancher) parqueté; **i. work,** marqueterie *f*; **i. enamel work,** nielle *f*, niellage *m*.

inlet ['inlet] *n.* **1.** entrée *f*, arrivée *f*, admission *f* (d'air, etc.); **i. pipe,** tuyau *m* d'arrivée (de vapeur, etc.). **2.** (*a*) *Tchn:* (orifice *m* d')entrée, (orifice d')admission (d'air, etc.); ouïe *f* (de ventilateur, etc.); (*b*) *Geog:* goulet *m* (d'entrée dans un port, etc.). **3.** *Geog:* petit bras de mer; crique *f*, anse *f*.

inmate ['inmeit] *n.* (*a*) habitant, -ante (d'une maison); (*b*) pensionnaire *mf* (d'une maison de santé); hôte *m* (d'un hospice); (*c*) détenu, -ue (dans une prison).

inmost ['inmoust] *a.* le plus profond; **our i. thoughts, feelings,** nos pensées les plus secrètes, nos sentiments *m* les plus intimes; **our i. being,** le tréfonds, l'arrière-fond *m*, de notre être.

inn [in] *n.* **1.** (*a*) auberge *f*; (*fashionable*) hôtellerie *f*, hostellerie *f*; (*b*) (*restaurant*) hôtellerie, hostellerie. **2.** *Jur:* **Inns of Court,** les quatre Écoles de droit de Londres qui seules confèrent le droit d'être avocat.

innards ['inədz] *n.pl.* *P:* entrailles *fpl*, intestins *mpl*.

innate [i'neit] *a.* inné, infus; **i. common sense,** bon sens foncier, naturel; *Phil:* **i. ideas,** idées innées.

inner ['inər] **1.** *a.* intérieur; (écorce, etc.) interne, de dedans; **on the i. side,** à l'intérieur, en dedans; *Anat:* **the i. ear,** l'oreille *f* interne; **i. harbour,** arrière-port *m*, *pl.* arrière-ports; *Cy: Aut:* **i. tube,** chambre *f* à air; **the i. circle,** le cercle intime (d'amis); le groupe dirigeant (d'un parti politique). **2.** *n.* premier cercle autour de la mouche (d'une cible).

innermost ['inəmoust] *a.* = INMOST.

innings ['iniŋz] *n.* (*pl. inv.*) *Sp:* (*Cr: baseball*) tournée *f*, tour *m* de batte ((i) de chaque équipe, (ii) de chaque membre de l'équipe); **to have had a good i.,** (i) avoir vécu longtemps; (ii) avoir eu de la chance.

innkeeper ['inkiːpər] *n.* aubergiste *mf*; hôtelier, -ière.

innocence ['inəsəns] *n.* (*a*) innocence *f* (d'un accusé); (*b*) naïveté *f*, simplicité *f*, innocence; **to take advantage of s.o.'s i.,** abuser de l'innocence de qn; **in all i.,** en toute innocence.

innocent ['inəsənt] *a.* **1.** (*a*) innocent; pas coupable; **i. of a crime,** innocent d'un crime; **an i. person,** un(e) innocent(e); (*b*) dépourvu, vierge (**of,** de); **to be quite i. of Latin,** ne pas savoir un mot de latin. **2.** (*a*) pur; sans péché; innocent; **as i. as a newborn babe,** innocent comme un enfant qui vient de naître; **Holy Innocents' Day,** la fête des saints Innocents; (*b*) naïf, *f.* naïve; sans malice; innocent; **to put on an i. air,** faire l'innocent(e). **3.** (*a*) (jeu, remède) innocent, inoffensif; (*b*) (commerce) légitime, permis; *Jur:* **i. purchase,** acquisition *f* de bonne foi. **-ly** *adv.* innocemment; en toute innocence.

innocuous [i'nɔkjuəs] *a.* inoffensif, anodin, banal. **-ly** *adv.* inoffensivement.

innovate ['inəveit] *v.i.* innover (**in,** à, en, dans).

innovation [inə'veiʃ(ə)n] *n.* innovation *f*, changement *m* (dans une méthode, etc.).

innovative ['inəveitiv] *a.* innovateur, -trice.

innovator ['inəveitər] *n.* innovateur, -trice; novateur, -trice.

innuendo, *pl.* **-o(e)s** [inju(ː)'endou, -ouz] *n.* **1.** *Jur:* insinuation *f*, mot couvert (destiné à atteindre qn dans son honneur). **2.** allusion (malveillante); **to discredit s.o. by i.,** discréditer qn par sous-entendus.

innumerable [i'njuːm(ə)rəbl] *a.* innombrable; (*usu. with pl. n.*) **i. books,** des livres *m* innombrables, sans nombre; **the successes have been i.,** les réussites *f* ne se comptent plus.

inoculate [i'nɔkjuleit] *v.tr.* *Med:* (*a*) **to i. s.o. with a virus,** inoculer un virus à qn; (*b*) **to i. s.o.,** inoculer, vacciner, qn (contre une maladie).

inoculation [inɔkju'leiʃ(ə)n] *n.* *Med:* inoculation *f*.

inoffensive [inə'fensiv] *a.* **1.** (médicament, animal) inoffensif. **2.** (odeur, etc.) sans rien de désagréable; (observation, etc.) qui n'a rien d'offensant.

inoperable [in'ɔp(ə)rəbl] *a.* *Med:* inopérable.

inoperative [in'ɔp(ə)rətiv] *a.* *Jur:* inopérant.

inopportune [in'ɔpətjuːn] *a.* inopportun; intempestif; **i. remarks,** (propos) hors de saison. **-ly** *adv.* inopportunément; mal à propos.

inordinate [i'nɔːdinət] *a.* démesuré, excessif, immodéré, désordonné. **-ly** *adv.* démesurément; excessivement.

inorganic [inɔː'gænik] *a.* inorganique.

input ['input] *n.* **1.** (*a*) consommation *f* (d'une usine, d'une machine); énergie, puissance, absorbée; (*b*) *El: Elcs:* (i) puissance *f* à l'entrée, d'alimentation; (ii) entrée *f*; **i. transformer,** courant *m*, transformateur *m*, d'entrée. **2.** *Cmptr:* (i) entrée, introduction *f* (des données); (ii) **i. (data),** données introduites; **i. programme,** programme *m* d'introduction.

inquest ['inkwest] *n.* enquête (criminelle); *esp.* **coroner's i.,** enquête judiciaire par-devant jury (en cas de mort violente ou suspecte).

inquire [in'kwaiər] **1.** *v.tr.* **to i. the price of sth.,** s'informer du prix de qch.; **to i. of s.o. what is happening,** s'informer auprès de qn de ce qui se passe. **2.** *v.i.* s'enquérir, se renseigner, se faire renseigner (**about,** sur); prendre des renseignements (**about,** sur); **i. within,** s'adresser ici; **to i. after s.o.,** demander des nouvelles de qn; **to i. after s.o.'s health,** s'informer de la santé de qn; **to i. into sth.,** faire des recherches sur qch.; *Jur:* enquêter, faire une enquête, sur (une affaire). **inquiring** *a.* investigateur, -trice; curieux; (coup d'œil) interrogateur. **inquiringly** *adv.* d'un air, d'un ton, interrogateur; **to look i. at s.o.,** interroger qn du regard.

inquiry [in'kwaiəri] *n.* **1.** enquête *f*; recherche *f*; investigation *f*; **to conduct, hold, an i. into sth.,** procéder, se livrer, à une enquête sur qch. **2.** demande *f* de renseignements; **to make inquiries,** aller aux renseignements; **to make inquiries about s.o.,** prendre des renseignements sur qn; s'informer, se renseigner, sur qn; **private i. agent,** détective (privé); **to make inquiries after s.o.,** s'enquérir de qn; **to make inquiries into sth.,** faire des recherches sur qch.; **i. desk, office, inquiries,** bureau *m* de renseignements.

inquisition [inkwi'ziʃ(ə)n] *n.* (*a*) recherche *f*, investigation *f*; (*b*) *Jur:* enquête *f* (judiciaire); (*c*) *Rel.H:* **the I.,** l'Inquisition *f*.

inquisitive [in'kwizitiv] *a.* (*a*) investigateur, -trice;

curieux; (regard) inquisiteur; (*b*) *Pej:* curieux, questionneur. **-ly** *adv.* avec curiosité; d'un œil inquisiteur.

inquisitiveness [in'kwizitivnis] *n.* curiosité *f.*

inquisitor [in'kwizitər] *n.* **1.** *Jur:* enquêteur, -euse. **2.** *Rel. H:* inquisiteur *m.*

inroad ['inroud] *n.* (*a*) *Mil:* incursion *f*; (*b*) empiétement *m* (sur la liberté, les droits, de qn); **to make inroads on one's capital,** entamer, ébrécher, son capital.

inrush ['inrʌʃ] *n.* irruption *f* (d'eau, de voyageurs, etc.); entrée soudaine (d'air, de gaz).

insalubrious [insə'lu:briəs] *a.* insalubre, malsain.

insane [in'sein] *a.* **1.** (*of pers.*) fou, *f.* folle; (esprit) dérangé, aliéné; **to become i.,** perdre la raison; *NAm:* **i. asylum,** hospice *m*, asile *m*, d'aliénés; *n.pl.* **the i.,** les aliénés *mpl.* **2.** (désir, etc.) insensé, fou. **-ly** *adv.* follement.

insanitary [in'sænit(ə)ri] *a.* insalubre; malsain.

insanity [in'sæniti] *n.* **1.** *Med:* folie *f*, démence *f*, insanité *f*; aliénation mentale. **2.** folie (d'une démarche, etc.).

insatiable [in'seiʃiəbl] *a.* (faim, désir, etc.) insatiable, inassouvissable. **-ably** *adv.* insatiablement.

inscribe [in'skraib] *v.tr.* **1.** (*a*) inscrire, graver (**sth. on stone,** qch. sur la pierre); (*b*) **to i. a tomb with a name,** graver un nom sur un tombeau. **2.** dédier (une œuvre littéraire) (**to,** à).

inscription [in'skripʃ(ə)n] *n.* **1.** (*a*) **i. of a name,** inscription *f* d'un nom (sur une pierre, dans un registre); (*b*) inscription (sur un monument, etc.); inscription, légende *f* (d'une pièce de monnaie). **2.** dédicace *f* (d'un livre, etc.).

inscrutability [inskru:tə'biliti] *n.* inscrutabilité *f.*

inscrutable [in'skru:təbl] *a.* (dessein) impénétrable, inscrutable; (visage) fermé.

insect ['insekt] *n.* insecte *m*; **i. eater,** insectivore *m*; **i. powder,** poudre *f* insecticide.

insecticide [in'sektisaid] *a.* & *n.* insecticide (*m*).

insectivorous [insek'tivərəs] *a. Bot: Z:* insectivore.

insecure [insi'kjuər] *a.* **1.** (verrou, etc.) peu sûr; (glace, etc.) peu solide; (terrain) dangereux; (pont) mal affermi; (espoir) incertain, peu ferme. **2.** exposé au danger; **to feel i.,** éprouver un manque de sécurité, d'assurance.

insecurity [insi'kjuəriti] *n.* insécurité *f*; danger *m* (d'une position); **to have a feeling of i.,** éprouver un manque de sécurité, d'assurance.

inseminate [in'semineit] *v.tr. Biol:* inséminer.

insemination [insemi'neiʃ(ə)n] *n. Biol:* insémination *f*; *Breed:* **artificial i.,** insémination (artificielle).

insensate [in'senseit] *a.* **1.** (corps) insensible. **2.** (projet, etc.) insensé.

insensibility [insensi'biliti] *n.* **1.** défaillance *f.* **2.** insensibilité *f* (**to,** à); indifférence *f* (**to,** pour).

insensible [in'sensibl] *a.* **1.** insensible, imperceptible; (transition) à peine sensible. **2.** sans connaissance; évanoui; **to become i.,** perdre connaissance. **3.** insensible, indifférent (**to pain,** à la douleur); **he was quite i. of the danger he was in,** il ne se doutait pas du danger qui le menaçait.

insensitive [in'sensitiv] *a.* **1.** insensible (**to,** à). **2.** (*of pers.*) **he remains i. and cold,** il reste insensible et froid.

insensitiveness [in'sensitivnis], **insensitivity** [insensi'tiviti] *n.* insensitivité *f.*

inseparable [in'sep(ə)rəbl] *a.* inséparable (**from,** de); (*of pers.*) **they are i.,** *n.* **inseparables,** ils sont inséparables; ce sont deux inséparables. **-ably** *adv.* inséparablement.

insert¹ ['insə:t] *n.* **1.** *Typ: etc:* insertion *f* (dans une épreuve). **2.** (*a*) pièce rapportée; *Cin:* scène-raccord *f, pl.* scènes-raccords; (*b*) garniture intérieure (en caoutchouc, etc.); (*c*) *Publ:* encartage *m.* **3.** *Dressm:* incrustation *f.*

insert² [in'sə:t] *v.tr.* **1.** insérer (une page dans un livre, etc.); insérer, introduire, apposer (une clause dans un acte); *Typ:* intercaler (une ligne). **2.** introduire, enfoncer (une clef dans un serrure, etc.).

insertion [in'sə:ʃ(ə)n] *n.* **1.** insertion *f*, introduction *f* (de qch. dans qch.); insertion (d'une annonce, etc. dans un journal). **2.** (*a*) *Typ:* insertion; **i. mark,** renvoi *m*; (*b*) *Needlew:* entre-deux *m inv* (de dentelle, etc.); (*c*) *Dressm:* incrustation *f*; (*d*) *Ind:* pièce *f* d'insertion; *Mec.E:* garniture *f* (de joint).

inset¹ ['inset] *n.* **1.** *Bookb:* (*a*) encart *m*, carton *m* (de 4 ou 8 pages); (*b*) (*leaf, advertisement*) encartage *m.* **2.** *Typ:* gravure *f* hors texte; hors-texte *m inv*; médaillon *m* (en coin de page). **3.** *Dressm:* incrustation *f.*

inset² ['in'set] *v.tr.* (*p.t.* & *p.p.* **inset, insetted**) **1.** *Bookb:* encarter (des feuillets, des annonces). **2.** *Typ:* insérer en cartouche, en médaillon. **3.** *Dressm:* insérer (une pièce d'étoffe, etc.); faire des incrustations de (dentelle, etc.). **4.** *Typ:* renfoncer (les lignes, un alinéa).

inshore *Nau:* **1.** *adv.* [in'ʃɔ:r] près de terre; (dirigé) vers la côte; **to keep close i.,** naviguer près de terre; serrer la terre. **2.** *a.* ['inʃɔ:r] (navigation, pêche) côtière; **i. wind,** vent *m* du large.

inside I. *n.* [in'said] (*a*) dedans *m*, (côté) intérieur (*m*) (d'un habit, etc.); **the door opens from (the) i.,** la porte s'ouvre de dedans; **on the i.,** en, au, dedans; à l'intérieur; **to walk on the i. (of the pavement),** prendre le côté du mur; *F:* **to know the i. of an affair,** connaître les dessous *mpl* d'une affaire; *adv.phr.* **i. out** ['insaid'aut], à l'envers; **to turn sth. i. out,** mettre qch. à l'envers; *Fig:* **to turn everything i. out,** mettre tout sens dessus dessous; **to know sth. i. out,** savoir qch. à fond; **to know Paris i. out,** connaître Paris comme le fond de sa poche; (*b*) intérieur (d'une maison, etc.); (*c*) *F:* ventre *m*; **to have pains in one's inside(s),** avoir mal au ventre; (*d*) *Fb:* **the insides,** les inters *mpl.* **II.** *a.* ['insaid] (*a*) intérieur; d'intérieur; (mesure, etc.) dans œuvre; (diamètre) interne; (escalier) dans œuvre; **to have an i. accomplice,** avoir un complice intérieur; **it's a i. job,** c'est un coup monté par qn de la maison; *Rac:* **to be on the i. track,** tenir la corde; *Fb:* **i. left,** intérieur, *F:* inter, gauche; (*b*) **i. information,** renseignements privés; **I speak with i. knowledge,** ce que je dis je le sais de bonne source; **to know the i. story,** connaître le dessous des cartes. **III.** *adv.* [in'said] (*a*) intérieurement; (fermé) en dedans; (propre) à l'intérieur; **with the fur i.,** le côté poil en dedans; **there's nothing i.,** il n'y a rien dedans; **i. and out** ['insaidənd'aut] au dedans et au dehors; à l'intérieur et à l'extérieur; (*b*) dans la maison, la chambre, la salle, etc.; **to push s.o. i.,** pousser qn à l'intérieur, dedans; **come i.!** entrez! *P:* **to put s.o. i.,** mettre qn en taule; (*c*) *NAm: F:* **to be i. on a matter,** connaître les dessous d'une affaire; *F:* & *NAm:* **i. of three hours,** (faire qch.) en moins de trois heures. **IV.** *prep.* [in'said] **1.** à l'intérieur de, dans l'intérieur de, dans (la maison, etc.); *Th: F:* **to get right i. a part,** entrer dans la peau d'un personnage. **2. i. a week, an hour,** en moins d'une semaine, d'une heure.

insidious [in'sidiəs] *a.* (*of disease, etc.*) insidieux; (raisonnement) captieux, astucieux. **-ly** *adv.* insidieusement.

insight ['insait] *n.* **1.** perspicacité *f*, pénétration *f*; **i. into character,** finesse *f* psychologique. **2.** aperçu *m*; **to get an i. into sth.,** prendre un aperçu de qch.

insignia [in'signiə] *n.pl.* insignes *mpl* (de la royauté, etc.); *Mil:* **i. of rank,** signes distinctifs de grade.

insignificance [insig'nifikəns] *n.* insignifiance *f.*
insignificant [insig'nifikənt] *a.* **1.** (mot, geste) insignifiant, qui ne signifie rien. **2.** (perte, etc.) de peu d'importance; (personne) sans importance.
insincere [insin'siər] *a.* (*a*) peu sincère; *Lit:* insincère; (*b*) (*of smile, etc.*) faux, *f.* fausse.
insincerity [insin'seriti] *n.* manque *m* de sincérité; fausseté *f.*
insinuate [in'sinjueit] *v.tr. & i.* insinuer. **1. to i. sth., into a place,** insinuer, glisser, qch. dans un endroit; **to i. oneself into s.o.'s favour,** s'insinuer dans les bonnes grâces de qn. **2.** donner adroitement à comprendre (qch.); laisser entendre, sous-entendre (qch.).
insinuation [insinju'eiʃ(ə)n] *n.* **1.** insinuation *f,* introduction *f* (**of sth. into sth.,** de qch. dans qch.). **2.** insinuation; sous-entendu *m, pl.* sous-entendus.
insipid [in'sipid] *a.* (mets, conversation) insipide, fade, sans saveur; (style) décoloré.
insipidity [insi'piditi] *n.* insipidité *f*; fadeur *f.*
insist [in'sist] *v.tr. & i.* insister. **1.** *v.i.* (*a*) **to i. on a point,** insister, appuyer, sur un point; **to i. upon one's innocence,** affirmer son innocence avec insistance; **I won't i.,** je n'insiste pas; (*b*) **to i. on doing sth.,** mettre une grande insistance à faire qch.; **he insists on your coming,** il insiste pour que vous veniez; **I i. on it,** je l'exige; **to i. on one's rights,** revendiquer ses droits. **2.** *v.tr.* **people insisted that they had seen him,** on affirmait avec insistance l'avoir vu; **he insisted that it was so,** il maintenait qu'il en était ainsi.
insistence [in'sistəns] *n.* insistance *f*; **he did it at her i.,** il l'a fait parce qu'elle a insisté.
insistent [in'sistənt] *a.* qui insiste, insistant; (*of creditor*) importun; (réclamations) instantes; **to be very i.,** insister très fort; **don't be too i.,** n'appuyez, n'insistez, pas trop. **-ly** *adv.* instamment; avec insistance.
insofar [insou'fa:r] *adv.* **i. as,** dans la mesure où.
insole ['insoul] *n. Bootm:* (*a*) première semelle; (*b*) semelle intérieure (de liège, feutre, etc.).
insolence ['insələns] *n.* insolence *f* (**to,** envers).
insolent ['insələnt] *a.* insolent (**to,** envers); **an i. boy,** un (jeune) insolent. **-ly** *adv.* insolemment.
insolubility [insəlju'biliti] *n.* insolubilité *f.*
insoluble [in'səljubl] *a.* **1.** (sel, etc.) insoluble. **2.** (problème) insoluble, irrésoluble.
insolvency [in'səlvənsi] *n.* (*a*) insolvabilité *f*; *Jur:* carence *f*; (*b*) faillite *f.*
insolvent [in'səlvənt] **1.** *a.* (débiteur) insolvable; *Com:* (débiteur, société) en (état de) faillite; **to declare oneself i.,** se déclarer insolvable; *Com:* déposer son bilan. **2.** *n.* débiteur *m* insolvable; *Com:* failli *m.*
insomnia [in'səmniə] *n.* insomnie *f.*
insomniac [in'səmniæk] *n.* insomniaque *mf.*
insomuch [insou'mʌtʃ] *Lit: conj. phr.* **1. i. as** = INASMUCH. **2. i. that ...,** à un tel point que ....
inspect [in'spekt] *v.tr.* **1.** (*a*) examiner (qch.), regarder (qch.) de près; (*b*) inspecter (une école, etc.). contrôler, vérifier (les livres d'un négociant); vérifier, inspecter (une machine, etc.); *Sp:* **to i. the pitch,** visiter le terrain (avant le match). **2.** faire la revue, faire l'inspection (d'un régiment); passer (un régiment) en revue; (*of troops*) **to be inspected,** passer en revue. **inspecting** *a.* **i. officer,** inspecteur *m.*
inspection [in'spekʃ(ə)n] *n.* **1.** (*a*) examen *m*; vérification *f* (de documents, etc.); **on close, closer, i.,** en y regardant de plus près; *Publ:* **i. copy,** spécimen *m*; (*b*) inspection *f,* visite *f* (d'un établissement, etc.); contrôle *m* (des billets, du matériel, etc.); **tour of i.,** inspection; **general i.,** inspection générale; **the I. of Mines,** le Service du Contrôle des Mines; **sanitary i.,** contrôle sanitaire; **medical i.,** visite médicale; *Tchn:* **i. hole, port,** orifice *m,* trou *m,* regard *m,* de visite; fenêtrelle *f.* **2.** *Mil:* revue *f*; **kit i.,** revue d'habillement; **to make, hold, an i.,** passer une revue.
inspector [in'spektər] *n.* inspecteur *m* (des écoles, de police, des mines, etc.); *Rail:* surveillant *m*; **detective i.,** inspecteur de la Sûreté; **i. of taxes,** inspecteur, contrôleur *m,* des contributions directes; *Mil: etc:* **i. general,** inspecteur général.
inspectorate [in'spekt(ə)rət] *n.* **1.** inspectorat *m.* **2.** corps *m* d'inspecteurs; *F:* l'inspection *f.*
inspiration [inspi'reiʃ(ə)n] *n.* **1.** aspiration *f,* inspiration *f* (d'air, etc.). **2.** inspiration; (*a*) **divine i.,** inspiration divine; **he is the i. of the movement,** c'est l'âme *f* du mouvement; (*of poet*) **to lack i.,** manquer d'inspiration; (*b*) **to have a sudden i.,** avoir une inspiration subite.
inspire [in'spaiər] *v.tr.* **1.** aspirer, inspirer (l'air, etc.). **2.** inspirer; (*a*) **to be inspired to do sth.,** être inspiré de faire qch.; **to i. a thought, a feeling, in, into, s.o.,** inspirer une pensée, un sentiment, à qn; **to i. s.o. with confidence,** inspirer (de la) confiance à qn; **to i. s.o. with hope,** donner de l'espoir à qn; **inspired with hope,** animé d'espoir; (*b*) **I don't know what inspired me to turn back,** je ne sais pas ce que c'est qui m'a donné l'inspiration de revenir sur mes pas. **inspired** *a.* **1.** (air etc.) aspiré, inspiré. **2.** (*a*) (*of poet, verse, etc.*) inspiré, plein d'inspiration; **to make an i. guess,** bien tomber; tomber juste; (*b*) (*of rumour, etc.*) officieux. **inspiring** *a.* (discours, exemple, etc.) inspirant; (influence) vivifiante.
instability [instə'biliti] *n.* instabilité *f.* **1.** (*a*) *Ph: Mec:* **thermal i.,** instabilité thermique; (*b*) *Mec.E:* déséquilibrage *m*; (*c*) *Meteor:* instabilité (atmosphérique). **2.** mobilité *f,* instabilité (de caractère); **mental i.,** instabilité mentale. **3.** manque *m* de solidité (d'un pont, etc.).
install, *NAm: also* **instal** [in'stɔ:l] *v.tr.* **1.** (*a*) installer (un évêque, qn dans une fonction); (*b*) **she installed herself in an armchair,** elle s'installa dans un fauteuil. **2.** installer, monter (une machine, etc.); installer (l'électricité, etc.).
installation [instə'leiʃ(ə)n] *n.* **1.** installation *f* (d'un évêque, etc.). **2.** (*a*) installation (du chauffage central dans la maison, etc.); (*b*) installation, montage *m* (d'une machine, etc.); mise *f* en place (d'un téléviseur, etc.). **3.** installation; **electrical installations,** installations électriques.
instalment, *NAm:* **installment** [in'stɔ:lmənt] *n.* **1.** *Com: etc:* fraction *f* (de paiement); acompte *m*; versement partiel; traite *f*; **final i.,** paiement *m* pour solde; **to pay in, by, instalments,** échelonner, fractionner, les paiements; **payable in monthly instalments,** payable par mensualités *fpl*; **i. plan,** vente *f* à tempérament. **2.** *Publ:* fascicule *m,* livraison *f* (d'un ouvrage à paraître en fascicules); (*b*) *W.Tel: T.V:* épisode *m* (d'un feuilleton).
instance¹ ['instəns] *n.* **1.** exemple *m,* cas *m*; **an isolated i.,** un cas isolé; **in many instances,** dans bien des cas; **for i.,** par exemple. **2.** (*a*) *Jur:* procès *m,* poursuite *f,* instance *f*; (*b*) **in the first i.,** en (tout) premier lieu; **in the present i., in this i.,** dans le cas actuel; dans cette circonstance; *Jur:* dans l'espèce.
instance² *v.tr.* **1.** citer (qch., qn) en exemple. **2.** (*usu. in passive*) **his cruelty is well instanced by ...,** sa cruauté est bien illustrée par ....
instant¹ ['instənt] *a.* **1.** instant, pressant, urgent. **2.** (*abbr.* **inst.**) courant; de ce mois; **on the 5th inst.,** le 5 courant. **3.** (*a*) immédiat; **this calls for i. remedy,** il faut y remédier tout de suite, sur-le-champ; (*b*) (café) soluble; **i. potatoes,** pommes de terre déshydratées; (*c*) (risque, etc.) imminent. **-ly** *adv.* tout de suite; immédiatement; sur-le-champ; à l'instant.
instant² *n.* instant *m,* moment *m*; **come this i.!** venez immédiatement! **not an i. too soon,** juste à temps.

instantaneous [inst(ə)n'teinjəs] *a.* instantané; *Phot:* **i. exposure,** pose instantanée; instantané *m.* **-ly** *adv.* instantanément.

instead [in'sted] **1.** *prep.phr.* **i. of sth.,** au lieu de qch.; **to stand i. of sth.,** tenir lieu de qch.; **i. of s.o.,** à la place de qn; **i. of doing sth.,** au lieu de faire qch.; **i. of diminishing, crime has increased,** loin d'avoir diminué, les crimes ont augmenté. **2.** *adv.* au lieu de cela; **if John can't come, take me i.,** si Jean ne peut pas venir, emmenez-moi à sa place; **he did not go to Rome but went to Venice i.,** au lieu d'aller à Rome il est allé à Venise.

instep ['instep] *n.* (*a*) cou-de-pied *m*, *pl.* cous-de-pied; **foot with a high i.,** pied, cou-de-pied, très cambré; (*b*) *Bootm:* cambrure (d'une chaussure).

instigate ['instigeit] *v.tr.* **1.** inciter, pousser, provoquer (**s.o. to do sth.,** qn à faire qch.). **2. to i. revolt,** inspirer, susciter, la révolte.

instigation [insti'geiʃ(ə)n] *n.* instigation *f*, incitation *f* (**to a crime,** à un crime); **at s.o.'s i.,** à l'instigation de qn.

instigator ['instigeitər] *n.* **1.** instigateur, -trice (d'un crime, etc.). **2.** auteur *m* (d'une révolte, etc.); fauteur, -trice (d'une émeute).

instil, *NAm:* **instill** [in'stil] *v.tr.* **(instilled)** faire pénétrer (goutte à goutte); instiller (le courage) (**into s.o.,** à qn.); inspirer (un sentiment) (**into s.o.,** à qn); faire pénétrer (une idée) (**into s.o.,** dans l'esprit de qn).

instillation [insti'leiʃ(ə)n] *n.* inspiration *f* (d'une idée, d'un sentiment).

instinct ['instiŋ(k)t] *n.* instinct *m*; **by i., from i.,** d'instinct, par instinct; **to have an i. for business,** avoir l'instinct des affaires.

instinctive [in'stiŋ(k)tiv] *a.* instinctif. **-ly** *adv.* instinctivement; d'instinct.

institute¹ ['institju:t] *n.* (*a*) institut *m*; **i. for the blind,** établissement *m* pour aveugles; (*b*) cercle *m*, foyer *m*.

institute² *v.tr.* **1.** instituer, établir (un ordre, une loi); fonder, constituer (une société). **2.** *Jur:* ordonner, instituer, (une enquête); **to i. (legal) proceedings against s.o.,** entamer, engager, des poursuites contre qn. **3.** (*a*) *Ecc:* **to i. s.o. to a benefice,** investir qn d'un bénéfice; (*b*) *Jur:* **to i. s.o. as heir,** instituer qn héritier.

institution [insti'tju:ʃ(ə)n] *n.* **1.** (*a*) institution *f*, établissement *m* (d'une loi, etc.); constitution *f* (d'un comité); création *f* (d'un État); (*b*) commencement *m*, établissement (d'une enquête, etc.); (*c*) *Ecc:* investiture *f* (d'un ecclésiastique); (*d*) *Jur:* institution (d'un héritier). **2.** institution; pratique passée dans les mœurs. **3.** (*a*) institution (d'éducation, etc.); **charitable i.,** établissement, œuvre *f*, de bienfaisance; *Adm:* établissement d'intérêt public (qui ne paie pas d'impôts); (*b*) établissement (public, financier, etc.); (*c*) association *f* (d'ingénieurs, etc.).

institutional [insti'tju:ʃən(ə)l] *a.* qui se rapporte à une institution; institutionnel; **i. life,** la vie dans un établissement (de charité, etc.); **he needs i. care,** il a besoin de soins hospitaliers.

institutionalize [insti'tju:ʃ(ə)nəlaiz] *v.tr.* (*a*) institutionnaliser (qch.); (*b*) placer (qn) dans un établissement; faire interner qn; **she's become institutionalized,** elle est marquée par sa vie dans un établissement.

instruct [in'strʌkt] *v.tr.* **1.** instruire (qn); **to i. s.o. in sth.,** instruire qn en, dans, qch. **2.** (*a*) informer (qn) (**that,** que); (*b*) *Jur:* **to i. a solicitor,** donner ses instructions à un avoué; **to i. counsel,** constituer avocat. **3. to i. s.o. to do sth.,** charger qn de faire qch.; **I am instructed by the Board to inform you that . . .,** la Direction me charge de vous faire savoir que . . . .

instruction [in'strʌkʃ(ə)n] *n.* **1.** instruction *f*, enseignement *m*; *Aut:* **driving i.,** leçons *fpl* de conduite. **2.** *usu. pl.* instructions, indications *fpl*, directives *fpl*; (*a*) ordres *mpl*; (*to sentry, etc.*) consigne *f*; (*to representative, etc.*) mandat *m*; **oral, written, instructions,** instructions verbales, écrites; **(book of) standing instructions,** règlement *m*; **strict instructions,** des instructions formelles, des ordres formels; **to carry out instructions,** exécuter des ordres; **to act in accordance with, contrary to, one's, s.o.'s instructions,** se conformer, ne pas se conformer, aux instructions reçues; **to follow s.o.'s instructions,** suivre les instructions de qn; **to obey s.o.'s instructions,** obéir aux ordres de qn; *Com: etc:* **we await your instructions,** nous attendons vos instructions; (*b*) **instructions for use,** mode *m*, notice *f*, d'emploi; **i. manual, i. book(let),** livret *m* d'instruction(s); manuel *m* d'entretien (d'une machine, etc.); (*c*) *Cmptr:* instruction (du programme); (*d*) *Jur:* **to give instructions to a solicitor, a counsel,** donner ses instructions à un avoué; constituer un avocat.

instructive [in'strʌktiv] *a.* instructif.

instructor [in'strʌktər] *n.* maître enseignant; précepteur *m*; *Mil:* instructeur *m*; *Ski:* moniteur, - trice; *Aut:* **driving i.,** moniteur, trice, de conduite; **swimming i.,** professeur *m* de natation.

instructress [in'strʌktris] *n.f.* maîtresse; professeur *m*; monitrice (de ski, de conduite).

instrument¹ ['instrumənt] *n.* instrument *m.* **1.** (*means, agent*) **to serve as the i. of s.o.'s vengeance,** servir d'instrument à la vengeance de qn. **2.** (*a*) **scientific, precision, i.,** instrument scientifique, de précision; **optical, surgical, i.,** instrument d'optique, de chirurgie, chirurgical; (*b*) **aircraft instruments,** instruments de bord; **flying, landing, on instruments, i. flying, landing,** vol *m*, atterrissage *m*, aux instruments, sans visibilité; **i. board, panel,** (i) *Av: Aut:* tableau *m* de bord; (ii) tableau de commande, de contrôle; (*c*) **musical i.,** instrument de musique; **wind, stringed, i.,** instrument à vent, à cordes. **3.** (*a*) *Jur:* acte *m* juridique (de cession, etc.); instrument, document officiel; (*b*) *Com:* **negotiable i.,** effet *m* de commerce; titre *m* au porteur.

instrument² ['instrumənt, instru'ment] **1.** *v.i. Jur:* instrumenter. **2.** *v.tr.* (*a*) *Mus:* orchestrer, instrumenter (un opéra, etc.); (*b*) équiper, munir, (un atelier, etc.) d'instruments.

instrumental [instru'ment(ə)l] *a.* **1.** contributif (**to,** à); **to be i. in doing sth.,** contribuer à faire qch.; jouer un rôle décisif dans qch. **2.** *Tchn:* de l'instrument, d'instruments; (équipement) en instruments; **i. error,** erreur (de lecture) due à l'instrument. **3.** *Mus:* (musique) instrumentale; **i. performer,** instrumentiste *mf*.

instrumentalist [instru'mentəlist] *n. Mus:* instrumentiste *mf*.

instrumentation [instrumen'teiʃ(ə)n] *n. Mus:* instrumentation *f*.

insubordinate [insə'bɔ:dinət] *a.* insubordonné, insoumis; (soldat, etc.) mutin.

insubordination ['insəbɔ:di'neiʃ(ə)n] *n.* insubordination *f*, insoumission *f*.

insubstantial [insəb'stænʃ(ə)l] *a.* insubstantiel; (*a*) imaginaire; (*b*) (i) (corps) immatériel; (ii) qui manque de substance; (argument) vide, sans substance.

insufferable [in'sʌf(ə)rəbl] *a.* insupportable, intolérable. **-ably** *adv.* insupportablement, intolérablement.

insufficiency [insə'fiʃənsi] *n.* insuffisance *f*.

insufficient [insə'fiʃənt] *a.* insuffisant; **i. food supplies,** manque *m* de vivres. **-ly** *adv.* insuffisamment.

insular ['insjulər] *a.* (*a*) (climat, etc.) insulaire; (*b*) (vie, etc.) d'insulaire; (esprit) étroit, borné; **to be very i. in one's views,** avoir les idées très bornées.

insularity [insju'læriti] *n.* insularité *f.*

insulate ['insjuleit] *v.tr.* (*a*) *El:* isoler (un fil, etc.); (*b*) calorifuger (une conduite); (*c*) *W.Tel: etc:* insonoriser (un studio); **to i. against vibration,** protéger contre les vibrations. **insulated** *a.* isolé; (*a*) *El:* (i) (fil) isolé, étanche; (ii) isolant; (*b*) **(heat-)i.,** calorifugé; (*c*) **(sound-)i.,** insonore, insonorisé. **insulating** *a.* isolant; isolateur, -trice; (*a*) *El:* **i. material,** matériau isolant; matière isolante; isolant *m* électrique; **i. tape,** ruban isolant; chatterton *m*; (*b*) **(heat-)i.,** calorifuge; (*c*) **(sound-)i.,** insonore.

insulation [insju'leiʃ(ə)n] *n.* **1.** (*action, state*) isolation *f*, isolement *m* (électrique, thermique, acoustique); **poor i.,** mauvais isolement; **heat, thermal, i.,** isolation thermique; calorifugeage *m*; **sound i.,** isolation acoustique; insonorisation *f* (d'un salle, etc.). **2.** (*substance*) isolant *m* (électrique, thermique, acoustique).

insulator ['insjuleitər] *n.* **1.** *El:* (*a*) (*substance*) isolant *m*; (*b*) (*device*) isolateur *m*. **2.** (*a*) **heat i.,** isolant thermique; matériau *m*, matière *f*, calorifuge; (*b*) **sound i.,** isolant acoustique; matériau, matière, insonore.

insulin ['insjulin] *n.* *Med:* insuline *f*; **i. treatment,** insulinothérapie *f.*

insult¹ ['insʌlt] *n.* **1.** insulte *f*, affront *m*; **to add i. to injury,** doubler ses torts d'un affront; **it's an i. to the intelligence,** c'est un outrage à l'intelligence. **2.** *NAm: Med:* blessure *f*, lésion *f* (du corps).

insult² [in'sʌlt] *v.tr.* **1.** insulter (qn); faire affront, faire injure, à (qn); **to i. s.o.'s intelligence,** faire outrage à l'intelligence de qn. **2.** *NAm: Med:* **foods that i. the body,** nourriture *f* qui nuit à la santé. **insulting** *a.* (geste, mot) insultant, offensant, injurieux; **to use i. language,** dire des injures; **to be guilty of i. behaviour towards s.o.,** (i) s'être conduit insolemment à l'égard de qn; (ii) *Jur:* être coupable d'outrages (à un agent, un magistrat). **insultingly** *adv.* d'une façon insultante, offensante.

insuperable [in'sju:p(ə)rəbl] *a.* (difficulté, etc.) insurmontable; (obstacle) infranchissable.

insupportable [insə'pɔ:təbl] *a.* insupportable.

insurance [in'ʃuərəns] *n.* assurance *f.* **1.** *Com:* (*a*) **to take out an i. on sth., against a risk,** prendre une assurance; s'assurer sur qch., contre un risque; **accident i.,** assurance contre les accidents; assurance-accidents *f, pl.* assurances-accidents; **fire i.,** assurance contre l'incendie; assurance-incendie *f, pl.* assurances-incendie; **personal liability i.,** assurance responsabilité civile; **third-party i.,** assurance aux tiers; **all risks i., comprehensive i.,** assurance tous risques; (*b*) **marine i.,** assurance maritime; **cargo i.,** assurance de la cargaison; (*c*) **i. agent,** agent *m* d'assurance(s); **i. broker,** courtier *m* d'assurance(s); **i. policy,** police *f* d'assurance; (*d*) *F:* prime *f* d'assurance; **to pay the i. on a car,** payer l'assurance d'une voiture; (*e*) **he's in i.,** il est dans les assurances. **2.** *Adm:* **national i.,** assurance sociale; **unemployment i.,** assurance chômage.

insure [in'ʃuər] *v.tr.* **1.** *Com: etc:* (i) assurer, (ii) faire assurer (des marchandises, etc.); **to i. one's life,** s'assurer, se faire assurer, sur la vie; *v.i.* **to i. against a risk,** s'assurer, se faire assurer, contre un risque. **2.** *v.i.* **to i. against a danger,** se garantir d'un danger. **insured** [in'ʃuə:d] *a. & n.* assuré, -ée; *Ins:* **i. value,** valeur assurée; *Post:* **parcel i. for £5,** colis chargé avec valeur déclarée £5.

insurer [in'ʃuərər] *n.* *Com:* assureur *m.*

insurgent [in'sə:dʒənt] **1.** *a.* insurgé, révolté. **2.** *n.* insurgé, -ée; révolté, -ée.

insurmountable [insə(:)'mauntəbl] *a.* (difficulté, obstacle) insurmontable; (obstacle) infranchissable.

insurrection [insə'rekʃ(ə)n] *n.* insurrection *f*; soulèvement *m*, rébellion *f.*

insurrectional [insə'rekʃən()l], **insurrectionary** [insə'rekʃənəri] *a.* insurrectionnel.

insurrectionist [insə'rekʃənist] *n.* insurgé, -ée; rebelle *mf.*

intact [in'tækt] *a.* intact, indemne; **to keep one's reputation i.,** conserver sa réputation entière.

intaglio [in'tɑ:liou] *n.* *Lap: etc:* intaille *f*; **i. engraving,** gravure *f* en creux.

intake ['inteik] *n.* **1.** prise *f* (d'air, d'eau, *El:* de courant); arrivée *f*, adduction *f*, admission *f* (de vapeur); *I.C.E:* entrée *f* (d'air); *Min:* galerie *f* d'appel d'air; (*b*) *Hyd.E:* aire *f* d'alimentation. **2.** consommation *f*; **food i.,** ration *f* alimentaire. **3.** (*a*) *Mil:* contingent *m*; (*b*) *Sch:* admission(s) *f(pl).*

intangible [in'tæn(d)ʒibl] *a.* intangible, impalpable; *Com:* **i. assets,** *n.pl.* **intangibles,** valeurs immatérielles; actif incorporel; *Jur:* **i. property,** biens incorporels.

integer ['intidʒər] *n.* *Mth:* (nombre) entier (*m*).

integral ['intigr(ə)l] **1.** *a.* (*a*) intégrant; **to be, form, an i. part of sth.,** faire partie intégrante de qch.; **to become an i. part of sth.,** s'intégrer dans qch.; (*b*) *Mth:* **i. number,** nombre entier; **i. calculus,** calcul intégral; (*c*) *Tchn:* (i) d'une seule pièce; en un seul bloc; (ii) incorporé (**with,** à); structural, -aux; qui fait partie intégrante (**with,** de). **2.** *n.* *Mth:* intégrale *f.*

integrate ['intigreit] *v.tr.* **1.** compléter, rendre entier (qch. d'incomplet). **2.** (*a*) intégrer (une minorité dans un groupe); **to become integrated,** *v.i.* **to i.,** s'intégrer (dans un milieu social, ethnique, etc.); (*b*) *U.S:* **to i. a school,** imposer la déségrégation raciale dans une école; *v.i.* **to i.,** pratiquer la déségrégation raciale. **3.** *Mth:* intégrer (une fonction, etc.); déterminer l'intégrale (d'une fonction).

integration [inti'greiʃ(ə)n] *n.* intégration *f*; (*a*) **the i. of ethnic minorities,** l'intégration des minorités ethniques; **raciale i.,** déségrégation raciale; (*b*) *Mth:* **i. by parts,** intégration par parties.

integrity [in'tegriti] *n.* **1.** intégrité *f*, totalité *f* (d'un texte, etc.). **2.** intégrité, honnêteté *f*, probité *f* (de qn, d'un motif, etc.); **man of i.,** homme intègre.

integument [in'tegjumənt] *n.* *Nat.Hist:* tégument *m.*

intellect ['intilekt] *n.* **1.** intelligence *f*, esprit *m*, entendement *m*, intellect *m*; **man of i.,** homme intelligent; **he was one of the best intellects of his time,** c'était une des meilleures intelligences de son époque. **2.** *coll.* **the i. of the country,** tous les meilleurs esprits du pays.

intellectual [inti'lektjuəl] **1.** *a.* intellectuel. **2.** *n.* intellectuel, -elle. **-ally** *adv.* intellectuellement.

intelligence [in'telidʒəns] *n.* **1.** intelligence *f*; (*a*) esprit *m*; (*b*) entendement *m*, sagacité *f*; **person of good i.,** personne intelligente; *Psy:* **i. test,** test *m* d'intelligence; **i. quotient,** quotient intellectuel. **2.** renseignement(s) *m(pl)*; (*a*) **to give, receive, i. of sth.,** donner, avoir, avis de qch.; (*b*) *Mil: etc:* **i. (service),** service *m* de renseignements; le deuxième Bureau; **i. officer,** officier *m* de renseignements.

intelligent [in'telidʒənt] *a.* (*of child, animal, etc.*) intelligent; (*of answer, etc.*) avisé, intelligent. **-ly** *adv.* intelligemment, avec intelligence.

intelligentsia [inteli'dʒentsiə] *n.* intelligentsia *f.*

intelligibility [intelidʒi'biliti] *n.* intelligibilité *f.*

intelligible [in'telidʒibl] *a.* intelligible; **he was hardly i.,** on le comprenait à peine. **-ibly** *adv.* intelligiblement.

intemperance [in'temp(ə)rəns] *n.* intempérance *f*; *esp.* alcoolisme *m*.
intemperate [in'temp(ə)rət] *a.* (*of pers.*) intempérant; (*a*) immodéré; (*b*) **person of i. habits,** personne intempérante, *esp.* adonnée à la boisson.
intend [in'tend] *v.tr.* **1.** (*a*) **to i. doing sth., to i. to do sth.,** avoir l'intention de faire qch.; se proposer, de faire qch.; compter faire qch.; **was that intended?** était-ce fait avec intention, à dessein? (*b*) **I i. to be obeyed,** je veux être obéi. **2. book intended for students,** livre destiné à l'usage des étudiants; **this remark is intended for you,** c'est à vous que cette observation s'adresse. **3. I intended it as a compliment,** mon intention était de vous faire un compliment. **intended** *a.* **1.** (*a*) (voyage, etc.) projeté; **my i. husband, bride,** *n. F:* **my i.,** mon fiancé, ma fiancée; mon futur, ma future; (*b*) **the i. effect,** l'effet voulu. **2.** intentionnel; fait avec intention.
intense [in'tens] *a.* (*a*) (*of feeling, anxiety*) vif, *f.* vive; (*of heat, colour, etc.*) intense; (douleur) vive, aiguë; (haine) profonde; (*b*) **i. expression,** expression concentrée; **she's too i.,** elle est trop sérieuse. **-ly** *adv.* (*a*) excessivement; **it was i. hot,** il faisait une chaleur intense; **i. blue eyes,** yeux *mpl* d'un bleu très vif; (*b*) (regarder) avec intensité; intensément.
intensification [intensifi'keiʃ(ə)n] *n.* intensification *f* (d'un son, etc.); *Phot:* renforcement *m* (d'un cliché).
intensify [in'tensifai] **1.** *v.tr.* (*a*) intensifier, augmenter, accroître (un son, un sentiment); amplifier (un son); renforcer (une couleur); (*b*) *Phot:* renforcer (un cliché faible). **2.** *v.i.* s'augmenter, s'accroître; devenir plus fort, plus vif, plus intense.
intensity [in'tensiti] *n.* **1.** intensité *f* (du froid, etc.); force *f* (d'une passion); violence *f* (d'une douleur); **with i.,** intensément. **2.** (*a*) *Ph:* intensité (d'un son, *El:* du courant, etc.); **luminous i.,** intensité lumineuse; (*b*) *Ch:* énergie *f* (d'une réaction); (*c*) *Phot:* densité *f* (d'un cliché).
intensive [in'tensiv] *a.* (*of work, cultivation, etc.*) intensif; (étude) serrée; *Med:* **i. care unit,** service *m* de soins intensifs; *Gram:* **i. verb, pronoun,** (verbe, pronom) intensif (*m*). **-ly** *adv.* intensivement, intensément.
intent¹ [in'tent] *n.* **1.** intention *f*, dessein *m*, but *m*; **with good i.,** dans une bonne intention; **with i. to defraud,** dans l'intention de frauder; **declaration of i.,** déclaration *f* d'intention. **2. to all intents and purposes,** virtuellement; de fait; à tous égards.
intent² *a.* **1.** (*a*) **to be i. on sth.,** être tout entier à qch., être absorbé par qch.; **to be i. on doing sth.,** être résolu, déterminé, à faire qch.; (*b*) attentif. **2.** (*of faculties, etc.*) ardent, acharné; (regard) profond; (application) soutenue. **-ly** *adv.* (écouter) attentivement; (regarder) fixement; (réfléchir) profondément.
intention [in'tenʃ(ə)n] *n.* intention *f.* **1.** (*a*) **I had no i., not the slightest i., of accepting,** je n'avais nullement l'intention d'accepter; **he acted with the best and most honourable intentions,** il a agi en tout bien (et) tout honneur; *Prov:* **the road to hell is paved with good intentions,** l'enfer est pavé de bonnes intentions; (*b*) *pl. O:* **his intentions are honourable,** il a l'intention de l'épouser. **2.** *Ecc:* **to celebrate mass for a special i.,** dire une messe à l'intention spéciale (de qn, qch.).
intentional [in'tenʃən(ə)l] *a.* intentionnel, voulu; fait à dessein, fait exprès. **-ally** *adv.* avec intention; à dessein; exprès; de propos délibéré.
inter [in'tə:r] *v.tr.* **(interred)** enterrer, ensevelir, inhumer (un mort).
interact [intər'ækt] *v.i.* réagir réciproquement.
interaction [intər'ækʃ(ə)n] *n.* action mutuelle, réciproque; *Ph: etc:* interaction *f.*
interbreed [intə(:)'bri:d] *v.* **(interbred) 1.** *v.tr.* (*a*) (entre)croiser (des races); (*b*) *Husb:* accoupler (des animaux consanguins). **2.** *v.i.* (*a*) se reproduire par croisement; se croiser; (*b*) se reproduire par (i) mariages, (ii) accouplements, consanguins.
intercalate [in'tə:kəleit] *v.tr.* intercaler.
intercalation [intə(:)kə'leiʃ(ə)n] *n.* intercalation *f.*
intercede [intə(:)'si:d] *v.i.* intercéder; **to i. (with s.o.) for s.o.,** intercéder, plaider (auprès de qn) en faveur de qn, pour qn.
intercept [intə(:)'sept] *v.tr.* intercepter (la lumière, une lettre, etc.); arrêter (qn) au passage; *W.Tel: etc:* capter (un message); *Fb:* **to i. a pass,** *v.i.* **to i.,** intercepter une passe.
interception [intə(:)'sepʃ(ə)n] *n.* interception *f* (de lettres, etc.); *W.Tel: etc:* captation *f* (de messages, de conversations, etc.); *Fb:* interception (d'une passe).
interceptor [intə(:)'septər] *n.* **1.** personne *f* qui intercepte (un message, etc.). **2.** *Av: Mil:* **i. (aircraft),** avion *m* d'interception; intercepteur *m.*
intercession [intə(:)'seʃ(ə)n] *n.* intercession *f.*
interchange¹ ['intətʃein(d)ʒ] *n.* **1.** échange *f* (de compliments, d'objets, d'idées); communication *f* (d'idées). **2.** *Civ.E: Adm:* échangeur *m* (d'autoroute).
interchange² [intə(:)'tʃein(d)ʒ] **1.** *v.tr.* (*a*) échanger (des compliments, etc.) (**with,** avec); (*b*) échanger (des parties d'une machine, etc.); **all parts of these machines can be interchanged,** toutes les pièces de ces machines sont interchangeables; (*c*) **to i. the position of two things,** changer deux choses de place. **2.** *v.i.* s'interchanger.
interchangeable [intə(:)'tʃein(d)ʒebl] *a.* interchangeable.
intercity [intə(:)'siti] *a. Trans:* (service, etc.) interurbain, intervilles *inv.*
intercom ['intə(:)kɔm] *n. Tp: F:* interphone *m.*
intercommunicate [intə(:)kə'mju:nikeit] *v.i.* **1.** (*of rooms, etc.*) communiquer. **2.** (*of prisoners, etc.*) communiquer entre eux.
intercommunion [intəkɔ'mju:njən] *n.* **1.** intercommunication *f.* **2.** *Ecc:* intercommunion *f.*
interconnect [intə(:)kə'nekt] *El: Cmptr:* **1.** *v.tr.* interconnecter (des circuits, des calculateurs). **2.** *v.i.* être interconnectés.
interconnection [intə(:)kə'nekʃ(ə)n] *n.* interconnexion *f.*
intercontinental [intə(:)kɔnti'nent(ə)l] *a.* intercontinental, -aux.
intercourse ['intəkɔ:s] *n.* **1.** commerce *m*, relations *fpl*, rapports *mpl*; **social i.,** la fréquentation du monde. **2. (sexual) i.,** rapports sexuels; **to have i. with a woman,** avoir des relations avec une femme. **3. i. with God,** communion *f* avec Dieu.
interdenominational ['intədinɔmi'neiʃən(ə)l] *a.* *Ecc:* interconfessionnel.
interdepartmental ['intə(:)di:pɑ:t'ment(ə)l] *a.* interdépartemental, -aux; entre services; entre départements.
interdependence [intə(:)di'pendəns] *n.* interdépendance *f.*
interdependent [intə(:)di'pendənt] *a.* interdépendant.
interdict¹ ['intədikt] *n.* **1.** *Jur:* défense *f*, interdiction *f.* **2.** *Ecc:* interdit *m.*
interdict² [intə(:)'dikt] *v.tr.* **1.** *Jur:* interdire, prohiber. **2.** *Ecc:* frapper d'interdit (un prêtre, une ville); interdire (un prêtre).
interdiction [intə(:)'dikʃ(ə)n] *n.* **1.** interdiction *f.* **2.** = INTERDICT¹ 2.
interest¹ ['int(ə)rest] *n.* intérêt *m.* **1.** (*a*) participa-

tion *f*; **to have a direct i. in sth.,** avoir un intérêt personnel dans qch.; **I have no financial i. in the business,** je ne suis pas intéressé dans cette entreprise; (*b*) **the shipping i.,** les armateurs *mpl*; le commerce maritime; **we look after British interests,** nous défendons les intérêts britanniques. **2.** avantage *m*, profit *m*; **the public i.,** l'intérêt public; **to act in, against, one's (own) interest(s),** agir dans, contre, son propre intérêt; **to act in s.o.'s best interest(s),** agir dans l'intérêt de qn; **it's in my i. to do this,** j'ai intérêt à faire ceci. **3.** (*a*) **this may be of i. to you,** ceci peut vous intéresser; **to take an i. in s.o., sth.,** s'intéresser, porter intérêt, à qn; **to take no (further) i. in sth.,** se désintéresser de qch.; (*b*) **I have many interests,** beaucoup de choses m'intéressent; **to have an i. in politics,** s'intéresser à la politique. **4.** *Fin:* intérêt(s) (de l'argent); **simple i.,** intérêts simples; **fixed i.,** intérêt fixe; **back i.,** arrérages *mpl* (d'une rente, etc.); **i. on capital,** intérêt du capital; **i. on a loan,** intérêt sur prêt; **to bear, yield, i.,** porter intérêt, des intérêts; **to yield 5% i.,** rapporter du 5%, un intérêt de 5%; *Fig:* **to repay an injury with i.,** rendre le mal avec usure.

interest² *v.tr.* **1.** intéresser (**s.o. in a business,** qn à, dans, une affaire). **2.** éveiller l'intérêt de (qn); **to be interested in painting, music,** s'intéresser à la peinture, à la musique; **I am not interested,** cela ne m'intéresse pas; **I should be interested to hear the end of the story,** je serais curieux d'apprendre la fin de l'histoire. **interested** *a.* intéressé. **1.** *Com:* **the i. parties,** les parties intéressées; *Jur:* **i. party,** ayant droit *m*, *pl.* ayants droit. **2.** (motif) intéressé; **to act from i. motives,** agir par calcul. **interesting** *a.* (livre, travail, etc.) intéressant. **interestingly** *adv.* de façon intéressante; **i. enough. . . .,** ce qui est intéressant c'est que . . . .

interfacing [ˈintə(:)feisiŋ] *n.* *Dressm:* entoilage *m.*

interfere [intəˈfiər] *v.i.* **1.** (*a*) (*of pers.*) s'ingérer, s'immiscer, intervenir (**in a matter,** dans une affaire); s'interposer (dans une querelle); **to i. with s.o.'s affairs,** se mêler des affaires de qn; **don't i. with what doesn't concern you,** ne vous mêlez pas de ce qui ne vous regarde pas; **he's always interfering,** il fourre son nez partout; (*b*) **someone has interfered with the clock,** on a touché à la pendule; (*c*) (*of thg*) **to i. with (sth.),** gêner, contrarier (les projets de qn); gêner (la circulation, etc.); entraver (la marche des affaires); **pleasure should not be allowed to i. with business,** il ne faut pas que les plaisirs empiètent sur les affaires; **it interferes with my plans,** cela dérange mes projets. **2.** (*a*) *Ph:* *etc:* (*of light waves, etc.*) interférer; *Ch:* perturber; (*b*) *Elcs:* *W.Tel:* **to i. with a signal,** brouiller, parasiter, un signal. **interfering** *a.* **1.** (*of pers.*) importun; qui se mêle à ce qui ne le regarde pas; **he's so i.,** il fourre son nez partout. **2.** (*a*) *Ph:* *etc:* (*of waves*) interférent; (*of chemical reagent, etc.*) perturbateur, -trice; (*b*) *Elcs:* *W.Tel:* qui brouille; parasite.

interference [intəˈfiərəns] *n.* **1.** (*a*) intervention *f*; intrusion *f*, ingérence *f* (**in,** dans); (*b*) *Sp:* obstruction *f* (d'un adversaire). **2.** (*a*) *Ph:* interférence *f* (des ondes lumineuses, etc.); *Ch:* perturbation *f*; *Opt:* **i. figure, pattern,** figure *f* d'interférence; (*b*) *Elcs:* *W.Tel:* interférence(s), parasite(s) *m*(*pl*), brouillage *m*.

interim [ˈintərim] **1.** *n.* intérim *m*; *Pol:* intérimat; *m* **in the i.,** dans l'intérim. **2.** *a.* (rapport, etc.) intérimaire; **the i. period,** l'intérim; *Jur:* **i. order,** avant faire droit *m inv.*

interior [inˈtiəriər] **1.** *a.* (*a*) (côté, commerce) intérieur; (terres, etc.) de l'intérieur; *Mth:* (angle) interne; (*b*) **i. decoration,** décoration d'intérieur. **2.** *n.* (*a*) intérieur *m* (du pays, des terres); **the i. of a building,** l'intérieur d'un édifice; (*b*) *Art:* (tableau *m* d')intérieur.

interject [intə(:)ˈdʒekt] *v.tr.* **to i. a remark, a protest,** lancer une remarque; émettre une protestation.

interjection [intə(:)ˈdʒekʃ(ə)n] *n.* **1.** action *f* de lancer (une remarque, etc.), d'émettre (une protestation). **2.** *Gram:* interjection *f*.

interlace [intə(:)ˈleis] **1.** *v.tr.* (*a*) entrelacer (des branches, etc.); entrecroiser (des fils); (*b*) intremêler (**with,** de). **2.** *v.i.* s'entrelacer, s'entrecroiser; s'entremêler.

interlard [intə(:)ˈlɑ:d] *v.tr.* (entre)larder, entremêler (un discours, ses récits) (**with,** de).

interleave [intə(:)ˈli:v] *v.tr.* interfolier (un livre); *Typ:* intercaler (des feuilles).

interline¹ [intə(:)ˈlain] *v.tr.* (*a*) interligner (un document, un manuscrit).

interline² *v.tr.* *Tail:* *etc:* mettre une doublure intermédiaire à (un vêtement, etc.). **interlining** *n.* doublure *f* intermédiaire.

interlock [intə(:)ˈlɔk] **1.** *v.tr.* enclencher (un mécanisme); engrener (des roues dentées); emboîter (les parties d'un mécanisme). **2.** *v.i.* (*a*) (*of questions, etc.*) s'entrecroiser, s'entremêler; (*b*) (*of mechanism*) s'enclencher; (*of pinions*) s'engrener; (*of parts*) s'emboîter. **interlocking** *a.* (*a*) entrecroisé, entrelacé, entremêlé; (*b*) *Mec.E:* (roues) qui s'engrènent, s'enclenchent.

interlocutor [in ə(:)ˈlɔkju:tər] *n.* interlocuteur, -trice.

interloper [ˈintəloupər] *n.* intrus, -use.

interlude [ˈintə(:)lu:d] *n.* *Th:* *etc:* intermède *m*; **musical i.,** interlude *m*; intermède musical.

intermarriage [intə(:)ˈmæridʒ] *n.* mariage *m* entre les membres de différentes familles, castes; intermariage *m* entre les membres d'une même famille.

intermarry [intə(:)ˈmæri] *v.i.* (*of different tribes, etc.*) se marier les uns avec les autres, entre eux.

intermediary [intə(:)ˈmi:diəri] *a.* & *n.* intermédiaire (*m*); **to act as i.,** servir d'intermédiaire.

intermediate¹ [intə(:)ˈmi:diət] *a.* intermédiaire; (*a*) **i. stops,** arrêts *mpl* intermédiaires (au cours d'un voyage); (*b*) (taille, etc.) intermédiaire; *El:* **i. frequency,** fréquence moyenne; (*c*) *Sch:* (cours, etc.) (de niveau) moyen.

intermediate² [intə(:)ˈmi:dieit] *v.i.* s'entremettre; servir de médiateur (**between,** entre).

interment [inˈtə:mənt] *n.* enterrement *m*, inhumation *f*.

interminable [inˈtə:minəbl] *a.* (discussion, voyage) interminable, sans fin; (histoires) à n'en plus finir. **-ably** *adv.* interminablement.

intermingle [intə(:)ˈmiŋgl] **1.** *v.tr.* entremêler; mélanger (des couleurs). **2.** *v.i.* s'entremêler, se mêler, se confondre (**with,** avec).

intermission [intə(:)ˈmiʃ(ə)n] *n.* **1.** interruption *f*, pause *f*; *Med:* intermission *f*, rémission *f* (de la fièvre); **without i.,** sans arrêt. **2.** *Th:* entracte *m.*

intermittent [intə(:)ˈmitənt] *a.* intermittent. **-ly** *adv.* par intervalles, par intermittance.

intern¹ [inˈtə:n] *v.tr.* interner (des étrangers, etc.).

intern² [ˈintə:n] *n.* *NAm:* interne *m* (des hôpitaux).

internal [inˈtə:n(ə)l] *a.* **1.** (*a*) intérieur, interne; (*b*) *Med:* hémorragie, etc.) interne; (maladie) organique; (*c*) *Tp:* **i. cable,** câble *m* d'immeuble; **i. telephone,** téléphone intérieur. **2.** (*a*) (valeur, preuve) intrinsèque; (*b*) secret, intime; **the i. workings of the mind,** les opérations secrètes de l'esprit. **3.** (*a*) (commerce) intérieur; (droit) interne; (législation) nationale, interne; **i. revenue,** recettes fiscales; **i. security,** sécurité intérieure; (*b*) *Sch:* **i. student,** étudiant, -ante, d'une université. **-ally** *adv.* intérieurement; (*a*) **i. fired boiler,** chaudière *f* à chauffage intérieur; (*b*) *Med:* **not to be taken i.,** pour usage externe.

international [intə(:)ˈnæʃən(ə)l] **1.** *a.* international,

-aux; **i. law,** droit international. **2.** *Sp:* (*a*) (joueur) international (*m*); (*b*) concours international. **-ally** *adv.* internationalement.

Internationale (the) [ðiːintənæʃiəˈnɑːl] *n.* l'Internationale *f.*

internationalism [intə(ː)ˈnæʃ(ə)nəlizm] *n.* internationalisme *m.*

internationalize [intə(ː)ˈnæʃ(ə)nəlaiz] *v.tr.* internationaliser.

internecine [intə(ː)ˈniːsain] *a.* (guerre, etc.) de destruction réciproque.

internee [intəːˈniː] *n.* interné, -ée.

internist [inˈtəːnist] *n. esp. U.S: Med:* specialiste *mf* des maladies organiques.

internment [inˈtəːnmənt] *n.* **1.** internement *m*; **i. camp,** camp *m* d'internement. **2. penal i.,** réclusion *f.*

interphone [ˈintəfoun] *n.* interphone *m.*

interplanetary [intə(ː)ˈplænit(ə)ri] *a.* (espace, etc.) interplanétaire.

interplay [ˈintəplei] *n.* interaction *f*; effet *m* réciproque; effets, jeux, combinés.

interpolate [inˈtəːpəleit] *v.tr.* (*a*) interpoler, intercaler (un mot, un passage); *Bookb:* **interpolated sheet,** feuille *f* intercalaire; (*b*) altérer (un texte) par interpolation.

interpolation [intəːpəˈleiʃ(ə)n] *n.* interpolation *f.*

interpose [intə(ː)ˈpouz] **1.** *v.tr.* (*a*) interposer (un objet entre deux autres); (*b*) opposer (son veto); (*c*) **to i. a remark,** *abs.* **to i.,** faire une observation (dans une conversation) **2.** *v.i.* s'interposer, intervenir.

interpret [inˈtəːprit] *v.tr.* **1.** interpréter (une loi, un songe, etc.); expliquer (un texte); interpréter (un signal, etc.) **to i. s.o.'s words as a threat,** interpréter les paroles de qn comme, pour, une menace. **2.** (*a*) traduire (un discours, etc.); (*b*) *v.i.* faire l'interprète. **3.** *Th: Mus:* interpréter. **interpreting** *n.* interprétation *f.*

interpretation [intəːpriˈteiʃ(ə)n] *n.* **1.** interprétation *f* (d'un texte, d'un songe, etc.); **to put a wrong i. on sth.,** donner une fausse interprétation à qch. **2.** traduction orale; interprétation.

interpretative [inˈtəːpritətiv] *a.* interprétatif.

interpreter [inˈtəːpritər] *n.* interprète *mf*; **to act as i.,** servir d'interprète.

interracial [intə(ː)ˈreiʃəl] *a.* (mariage, etc.) entre des races différentes.

interregnum, *pl.* **-ums, -a** [intə(ː)ˈregnəm, -əmz, -ə] *n.* interrègne *m.*

interrelated [intə(ː)riˈleitid] *a.* (faits) étroitement reliés entre eux, en relation mutuelle, en corrélation.

interrelation [intə(ː)riˈleiʃ(ə)n] *n.* relation mutuelle; corrélation *f.*

interrogate [inˈterəgeit] *v.tr.* interroger, questionner (qn); faire subir un interrogatoire à (un prévenu); consulter (un ordinateur, etc.).

interrogation [interəˈgeiʃ(ə)n] *n.* **1.** interrogation *f* (d'un candidat, etc.); interrogatoire *m* (d'un prévenu); *Mil:* **i. centre,** centre *m* d'interrogation (des prisonniers de guerre). **2.** *Gram:* **i. mark,** *NAm:* **i. point,** point *m* d'interrogation.

interrogative [intəˈrɔgətiv] **1.** *a.* (*of tone, look, etc.*) interrogateur, -trice. **2.** *a. & n. Gram:* **i. (pronoun, etc.),** (pronom, etc.) interrogatif (*m*). **-ly** *adv.* interrogativement; d'un air interrogateur.

interrogator [inˈterəgeitər] *n.* (*pers.*) interrogateur, -trice.

interrogatory [intəˈrɔgət(ə)ri] *a.* (*of look, etc.*) interrogateur, -trice.

interrupt [intəˈrʌpt] *v.tr.* **1.** interrompre (une action, une conversation, etc.); **to i. s.o.,** interrompre qn; couper la parole à qn. **2.** (*a*) suspendre (la circulation); couper (les communications); interrompre (un circuit électrique); rompre (la cadence); (*b*) interrompre, former obstacle à (la vue, etc.).

interruption [intəˈrʌpʃ(ə)n] *n.* interruption *f*; dérangement *m* (de qn); **without i.,** sans interruption; sans arrêt.

intersect [intə(ː)ˈsekt] **1.** *v.tr.* entrecouper, intersecter, entrecroiser (**with, by,** de); croiser; **line that intersects another,** ligne qui en coupe une autre; (*of lines, surfaces*) **to i. one another,** se couper, s'intersecter. **2.** *v.i. Mth: etc:* se couper, s'intersecter, se croiser; s'entrecouper, s'entrecroiser; **streets that i.,** rues qui s'entrecroisent.

intersection [intə(ː)ˈsekʃ(ə)n] *n.* **1.** *Mth:* intersection *f* (de deux plans, etc.); *Surv:* recoupement *m*, intersection. **2.** (*a*) **(point of) i.,** point *m* d'intersection, de recoupement; (*b*) carrefour *m*; croisement *m* de chemins.

interspace [ˈintə(ː)ˈspeis] *v.tr.* espacer (des caractères, etc.).

intersperse [intə(ː)ˈspəːs] *v.tr.* entremêler (**between, among,** entre; **with,** de); **to i. a speech with quotations,** émallier un discours de citations.

interstate [ˈintə(ː)ˈsteit] *a.* (commerce, etc.) entre États (des États-Unis, de l'Australie, etc.).

interstellar [intə(ː)ˈstelər] *a. Astr:* (espace, etc.) interstellaire; (espace) intersidéral, -aux, interastral, -aux.

interstice [inˈtəːstis] *n.* interstice *m.*

intertwine [intə(ː)ˈtwain] **1.** *v.tr.* entrelacer. **2.** *v.i.* s'entrelacer, s'accoler.

interurban [intərˈəːbən] *a.* interurbain.

interval [ˈintəv(ə)l] *n.* intervalle *m.* **1.** (*time*) (*a*) **at intervals,** par intervalles; **after an i. of time,** après un laps de temps; **an hour's i. between two lectures,** une heure de battement entre deux conférences; **rainy weather with bright intervals,** temps pluvieux avec éclaircies; (*b*) *Sch:* (période *f* de) récréation (*f*); *Ind: etc:* **meal i.,** pause *f*; (*c*) (i) *Th:* entracte *m*; (ii) *Fb: etc:* mi-temps *f inv*, pause. **2.** (*a*) (*space*) **i. between two beams,** écartement *m* de deux poutres; **trees growing at regular intervals along the road,** arbres *mpl* qui jalonnent la route; (*b*) *Mus:* intervalle; (*c*) *Mapm:* **contour i.,** équidistance *f* des courbes; **vertical i.,** distance verticale.

intervene [intə(ː)ˈviːn] *v.i.* **1.** (*of pers., thg*) intervenir, s'interposer; **to i. in a quarrel,** intervenir dans une querelle. **2.** (*of event*) survenir, arriver. **3.** (*in time and space*) **ten years intervened,** dix ans s'écoulèrent. **intervening** *a.* **1.** (*of pers.*) intervenant. **2.** (événement) survenu. **3.** (époque, distance) intermédiaire; **during the i. week,** pendant la semaine qui s'écoula.

intervention [intə(ː)ˈvenʃ(ə)n], *m.* intervention *f*; interposition *f* (d'un corps); *Med:* **surgical intervention**, intervention chirurgicale.

interview¹ [ˈintə(ː)vjuː] *n.* **1.** entrevue *f*; *Adm:* **to invite s.o. to an i.,** convoquer qn. **2.** *Journ: etc:* interview *f.*

interview² *v.tr.* **1.** avoir une entrevue avec (qn); **to i. candidates for a post,** examiner les candidats à un poste; **he's being interviewed tomorrow,** on le convoque demain. **2.** *Journ: etc:* interviewer (qn).

interviewee [intə(ː)vjuːˈiː] *n.* interviewé, -ée.

interviewer [ˈintəvjuːər] *n. Journ: etc:* interviewer *m*, intervieweur *m*; (*for research*) enquêteur, -euse.

inter-war [ˈintə(ː)ˈwɔːr] *a.* **the i.-w. years, period,** l'entre-deux-guerres *m or f*; l'interguerre *f.*

interweave [intə(ː)ˈwiːv] *v.* (*p.t.* **interwove** [intə(ː)-ˈwouv]; *p.p.* **interwoven** [intə(ː)ˈwouvn]) **1.** *v.tr.* (*a*) tisser ensemble (des fils d'or et de laine, etc.); entrelacer (des branches); **material interwoven with gold threads,** tissue broché d'or; (*b*) entremêler (des sentiments, etc.); **closely interwoven systems,** systèmes étroitement liés l'un à l'autre. **2.** *v.i.* s'entrelacer, s'entremêler.

intestate [in'testeit] **1.** *a.* (*a*) intestat *inv*; **she died i.,** elle est morte intestat; (*b*) **i. estate, succession,** succession *f* ab intestat. **2.** *n.* intestat *mf.*
intestinal [in'testin(ə)l] *a. Anat:* intestinal, -aux.
intestine [in'testin] *n. Anat:* intestin *m*; **the large i.,** le gros intestin; **the small i.,** l'intestin grêle.
intimacy ['intiməsi] *n.* **1.** intimité *f*; **in the i. of the family,** dans l'intimité de la famille. **2.** *Jur:* rapports *mpl* sexuels; **evidence that i. took place,** preuve *f* de relations intimes.
intimate¹ ['intimət] **1.** *a.* (*a*) (amitié, ami) intime; **to be very i. with s.o.,** être très intime avec qn; **a few i. friends,** quelques intimes; **the i. nature of their conversation,** l'intimité de leur conversation; (*b*) (restaurant) intime; (*c*) **to be i. with a woman,** avoir des relations intimes avec une femme; (*d*) (journal) intime; (*e*) **to have an i. knowledge of sth.,** avoir une connaissance approfondie de qch. **2.** *n.* (*usu. pl.*) intime *mf.* **-ly** *adv.* intimement; **i. connected,** étroitement lié.
intimate² ['intimeit] *v.tr.* **1.** intimer (un ordre); signifier (ses intentions); **to i. sth. to s.o.,** notifier qch. à qn. **2.** donner à entendre, indiquer, suggérer (**sth. to s.o.,** qch. à qn).
intimation [inti'meiʃ(ə)n] *n.* **1.** avis *m* (de décès, etc.); **at the first i.,** au premier avis. **2.** avis à mots couverts; suggestion *f.*
intimidate [in'timideit] *v.tr.* intimider. **intimidating** *a.* intimidateur, -trice; intimidant.
intimidation [intimi'deiʃ(ə)n] *n.* intimidation *f*; *Jur:* menaces *fpl*; **guilty of i.,** coupable de menaces.
into ['intu, 'intə] *prep.* dans, en. **1.** (*motion, direction*) (*a*) **to go i. a house,** entrer dans une maison; **to fall i. the hands of the enemy,** tomber entre les mains de l'ennemi; **the door opens i. the garden,** la porte donne sur le jardin; **to come i. a property,** hériter d'un bien; **to get i. difficulties,** s'attirer des ennuis; **to work far i. the night,** travailler bien tard dans la nuit; (*b*) *F:* **to be i. sth.,** donner à fond dans qch.; **I'm not really i. that sort of thing,** ces choses-là ne me disent rien. **2.** (*change, result*) **to change sth. i. sth.,** changer, transformer, qch. en qch.; **to grow i. a man,** devenir un homme; **to divide i. four,** diviser en quatre; **to break sth. i. pieces,** briser qch. en morceaux; **to burst i. tears,** fondre en larmes. **3.** *Mth:* **three i. six goes two,** six divisé par trois fait deux.
intolerable [in'tɔl(ə)rəbl] *a.* intolérable, insupportable. **-ably** *adv.* insupportablement.
intolerance [in'tɔlərəns] *n.* intolérance *f* (**of,** de); *Med:* **i. of a drug,** intolérance d'un remède.
intolerant [in'tɔlərənt] *a.* (*a*) intolérant; **to be very i.,** être d'une extrême intolérance; (*b*) *Med:* **to be i. of a drug,** ne pas supporter un médicament. **-ly** *adv.* avec intolérance.
intonation [intə'neiʃ(ə)n] *n.* intonation *f.*
intone [in'toun] *v.tr. Ecc:* **1.** psalmodier (des litanies, etc.). **2.** entonner (le chant).
intoxicate [in'tɔksikeit] *v.tr.* enivrer, griser, rendre ivre. **intoxicated** *a.* ivre, gris; **to become i.,** s'enivrer (**with,** de); **i. with praise,** grisé d'éloges. **intoxicating** *a.* (vin, parfum) enivrant, grisant; **i. liquors,** boissons *fpl* alcooliques; spiritueux *mpl.*
intoxication [intɔksi'keiʃ(ə)n] *n.* **1.** *Med:* intoxication *f.* **2.** (*a*) ivresse *f*; (*b*) *Fig:* griserie *f.*
intractability [intræktə'biliti] *n.* indocilité *f* (d'un enfant, d'un animal); opiniâtreté *f.*
intractable [in'træktəbl] *a.* (enfant, animal) intraitable, insoumis, indocile; (cheval) rebours; (maladie) opiniâtre, intraitable; (problème) très difficile.
intramural [intrə'mjuːr(ə)l] *a.* intra-muros *inv.*
intransigence [in'trænsidʒəns] *n.* intransigeance *f.*
intransigent [in'trænsidʒənt] *a.* intransigeant.
intransitive [in'trænsitiv] *a. & n. Gram:* **i. (verb),** (verbe) intransitif (*m*). **-ly** *adv.* intransitivement.
intra-uterine ['intrə'juːtərain] *a. Anat:* intra-utérin, *pl.* intra-utérins.
intravenous [intrə'viːnəs] *a. Physiol:* intraveineux.
intrepid [in'trepid] *a.* intrépide, brave, courageux. **-ly** *adv.* intrépidement.
intrepidity [intre'piditi] *n.* intrépidité *f.*
intricacy ['intrikəsi] *n.* (*a*) complexité *f*, nature compliquée (d'un mécanisme, etc.); caractère embrouillé (d'une affaire); (*b*) **the intricacies of the law,** les dédales *mpl* de la loi.
intricate ['intrikət] *a.* (*a*) (mécanisme) compliqué; (question, affaire) difficile à démêler; (dessin) intriqué; (*b*) (*of thoughts, statements*) enchevêtré, embrouillé, confus; **i. details,** détails compliqués. **-ly** *adv.* d'une manière compliquée, embrouillée.
intrigue¹ [in'triːg] *n.* **1.** intrigue *f*, cabale, *f*, machination *f.* **2.** *Th:* intrigue (d'un drame, etc.); **comedy of i.,** comédie *f* d'intrigue.
intrigue² **1.** *v.i.* intriguer; mener des intrigues; **to i. against s.o.,** intriguer contre qn. **2.** *v.tr.* intriguer (qn); éveiller, piquer, la curiosité de (qn); **I'm greatly intrigued by the idea,** l'idée m'intrigue énormément. **intriguing** *a.* (paroles) mystérieuses, intrigantes; **all this is very i.,** tout cela nous intrigue beaucoup.
intrinsic [in'trinsik] *a.* (vice, valeur) intrinsèque. **-ally** *adv.* intrinsèquement.
introduce [intrə'djuːs] *v.tr.* **1.** introduire; (*a*) faire entrer (une clef dans une serrure); **to i. a subject,** mettre une question sur le tapis; (*b*) **to i. s.o. into s.o.'s presence,** introduire qn auprès de qn; (*c*) établir, faire adopter (une loi, un usage); **this fashion was introduced in the fifteenth century,** cette mode fut introduite au quinzième siècle; (*d*) *Parl:* **to i. a bill,** déposer un projet de loi; (*e*) (*of conjunction, adverb*) commencer (une phrase); (*f*) *Com:* lancer (une marchandise); *St.Exch:* introduire (des actions). **2.** (*a*) présenter; **to i. s.o. to s.o.,** présenter qn à qn; **to i. oneself (by name),** se faire connaître; **who is going to i. us?** qui est-ce qui va faire les présentations? (*b*) (*of débutante*) **to be introduced to society,** faire son entrée dans le monde. **3. to i. s.o. to sth.,** faire connaître qch. à qn; **he introduced me to Greek,** il m'a initié au grec.
introduction [intrə'dʌkʃ(ə)n] *n.* **1.** introduction *f* (**of sth. into sth.,** de qch. dans qch.). **2.** présentation *f* (**of s.o. to s.o.,** de qn à qn); **to do the introductions,** faire les présentations; **letter of i.,** (lettre *f* d')introduction, de recommandation. **3.** avant-propos *m inv*, introduction (d'un livre). **4.** manuel *m* élémentaire (**to,** de); introduction (**to,** à). **5.** introduction (dans le monde); premier contact (avec qch.).
introductory [intrə'dʌktəri] *a.* (qui sert) d'introduction; (page, épître) liminaire; **after a few i. words,** après quelques mots d'introduction; *Com:* **i. price,** prix *m* de lancement.
introit ['intrɔit] *n. Ecc:* introït *m.*
introspection [introu'spekʃ(ə)n] *n.* introspection *f.*
introspective [introu'spektiv] *a.* introspectif.
introversion [introu'vəːʃ(ə)n] *n.* recueillement *m* (d'esprit); retour *m* sur soi-même; *Psy:* introversion *f.*
introvert ['intrəvəːt] *n.* introverti, -ie.
introverted [intrə'vəːtid] *a.* (esprit) recueilli, *Psy:* introverti.
intrude [in'truːd] **1.** *v.tr.* (*a*) **to i. sth. into sth.,** introduire qch. de force dans qch.; (*b*) **to i. sth. on s.o.,** imposer qch. à qn; **he tries to i. himself on us,** il voudrait s'imposer. **2.** *v.i.* faire intrusion (**on s.o.,** auprès de qn); être importun; **I hope I am not intruding,** j'espère que je ne vous dérange pas; **to i. on**

s.o.'s privacy, s'ingérer dans la vie privée de qn.

intruder [in'tru:dər] *n.* **1.** intrus, -use; importun, -une; **she felt like an i.,** elle se sentait de trop. **2.** *Mil.Av:* chasseur *m* de pénétration.

intrusion [in'tru:ʒ(ə)n] *n.* (*a*) intrusion *f*; **to make an i. upon s.o.,** faire (une) intrusion auprès de qn; (*b*) intrusion; **I hope I am not guilty of an i.,** j'espère que je ne suis pas indiscret, que je ne dérange pas.

intrusive [in'tru:siv] *a.* **1.** (*of pers.*) importun, indiscret. **2.** *Ling: etc:* intrusif.

intuition [intju(:)'iʃ(ə)n] *n.* intuition *f*.

intuitive [in'tju:itiv] *a.* intuitif. **-ly** *adv.* intuitivement, par intuition.

inundate ['inʌndeit] *v.tr.* inonder (**with,** de); **to be inundated with letters,** être débordé de lettres.

inundation [inʌn'deiʃ(ə)n] *n.* inondation *f*.

inure [i'njuər] *v.tr.* habituer, endurcir, aguerrir (**to,** à); **inured to hardships,** habitué aux privations.

invade [in'veid] *v.tr.* **1.** (*a*) envahir; faire une invasion dans (un pays, etc.); (*b*) **to i. s.o.'s privacy,** violer la retraite de qn. **2.** empiéter sur (les droits de qn); porter atteinte à (un privilège). **invading** *a.* envahissant; (armée) d'invasion.

invader [in'veidər] *n.* envahisseur *m*.

invalid¹ [in'vælid] *a.* (*a*) *Jur:* (mariage) invalide, non valide; (clause) non-valable; (décision) nulle et non avenue; (*b*) (*of argument, etc.*) peu valable.

invalid² ['invəli(:)d] **1.** *a.* & *n.* (*suffering from illness*) malade (*mf*); (*from disability*) invalide (*mf*), infirme (*mf*); **she has an i. sister,** elle a une sœur (i) infirme, (ii) *O:* d'une santé délicate; **i. car,** voiture *f* d'infirme; **i. chair,** fauteuil roulant. **2.** *n.* *Mil: etc:* (*disabled man*) invalide.

invalid³ ['invəli:d] *v.tr.* *Mil:* **to i. a man out of the army,** réformer un homme.

invalidate [in'vælideit] *v.tr.* *Jur:* **1.** invalider, rendre nul (un testament); vicier (un acte, un contrat). **2.** casser, infirmer (un jugement).

invalidation [invæli'deiʃ(ə)n] *n.* *Jur:* **1.** invalidation *f* (d'un document, d'un contrat). **2.** infirmation *f*, cassation *f* (d'un jugement).

invalidity [invə'liditi] *n.* **1.** invalidité *f* (d'un passeport, d'un contrat, etc.). **2.** invalidité *f*; **i. pension,** pension *f* d'invalidité.

invaluable [in'væljuəbl] *a.* inestimable; (trésor) d'un prix incalculable; **it's i.,** cela ne se paie pas; c'est inestimable, inappréciable.

invariable [in'vɛəriəbl] *a.* invariable; *Gram:* **i. particle,** particule *f* invariable. **-ably** *adv.* invariablement, immanquablement; toujours.

invasion [in'veiʒ(ə)n] *n.* **1.** (*a*) invasion *f*, envahissement *m*; (*b*) invasion; **these invasions of my privacy,** ces intrusions *fpl* dans mon intimité. **2. i. of s.o.'s rights,** violation des droits, empiétement *m* sur les droits, de qn.

invective [in'vektiv] *n.* invective *f*; **a torrent of invective(s),** un flot d'invectives, d'injures.

inveigh [in'vei] *v.i.* invectiver (**against,** contre).

inveigle [in'veigl, -'vi:-] *v.tr.* attirer, séduire, leurrer, enjôler (qn); **to i. s.o. into doing sth.,** entraîner, amener, qn à faire qch.

invent [in'vent] *v.tr.* inventer (une machine, une histoire, etc.); **recently invented,** d'invention récente.

invention [in'venʃ(ə)n] *n.* **1.** invention *f* (d'une machine, etc.); **a story of his own i.,** une histoire de son cru. **2.** (*a*) chose inventée; invention; (*b*) invention, mensonge *m*; **this is pure i.,** c'est une pure invention; (*c*) *Mus:* invention.

inventive [in'ventiv] *a.* (esprit) inventif.

inventiveness [in'ventivnis] *n.* esprit inventif, d'invention; don *m* d'invention.

inventor [in'ventər] *n.* inventeur, -trice.

inventory¹ ['invənt(ə)ri] *n.* **1.** *Com:* inventaire *m*; **to take, draw up, an i.,** faire, dresser, un inventaire. **2.** *NAm:* (*a*) stock(s) *m*(*pl*); (*b*) (établissement *m*, levée *f*, d')inventaire.

inventory² *v.tr.* inventorier (les biens de qn); dresser l'inventaire (des biens de qn).

inverse [in'və:s] **1.** *a.* inverse; (corrélation) négative; **in i. order,** en sens inverse; *Mth:* **i. function,** fonction *f* inverse; **in i. ratio, proportion,** en raison, proportion, inverse (**to,** de). **2.** *n.* inverse *m*, contraire *m* (**of,** de). **-ly** *adv.* inversement.

inversion [in'və:ʃ(ə)n] *n.* **1.** renversement *m* (d'une image, de l'utérus, etc.); *Mus:* **i. of a chord,** (i) renversement d'un accord; (ii) accord dérivé. **2.** inversion (des mots d'une phrase, *Mth:* d'une intégrale, etc.). **3.** *Ch:* inversion (du sucre, etc.). **4.** *Psy:* **sexual i.,** inversion sexuelle; homosexualité *f*.

invert¹ ['invə:t] **1.** *a.* & *n.* **i. (sugar),** sucre inverti. **2.** *n.* *Psy:* inverti, -ie.

invert² [in'və:t] *v.tr.* **1.** renverser, retourner (un objet) (le haut en bas); *Mus:* renverser (un accord). **2.** (*a*) invertir, intervertir, renverser (l'ordre, les positions); *Gram:* inverser (le sujet, etc.); (*b*) *Ch:* invertir (le sucre). **3.** retourner; mettre à l'envers. **inverted** *a.* **1.** (*a*) inversé, renversé; **i. commas** = guillemets *mpl*; (*b*) *Dressm:* **i. pleat,** pli inverti, creux; (*c*) *Mus:* (accord) renversé; (*d*) *Opt:* (image) renversée. **2.** (ordre, siphon) inverse. **3.** *Psy:* (instinct) inverti.

invertebrate [in'və:tibrət] *a.* & *n.* *Z:* invertébré (*m*).

invest [in'vest] *v.tr.* **1.** revêtir (**with,** de); **to i. a subject with interest,** rendre un sujet intéressant. **2.** investir (qn de l'autorité, etc.); **to i. s.o. with an office,** investir qn d'une fonction. **3.** *Mil:* investir, cerner (une place forte). **4.** (*a*) *Fin:* placer, investir (son argent, des fonds); **to i. one's money in real estate,** faire des placements immobiliers; **capital invested,** mise *f* de fonds; capital engagé, investi; *v.i.* **to i. in house property,** faire des placements en immeubles; (*b*) *F:* *v.i.* **to i. in a new refrigerator,** acheter, se payer, un nouveau réfrigérateur.

investigate [in'vestigeit] *v.tr.* examiner, étudier, sonder, remuer (une question); faire une enquête sur, enquêter sur (un crime); *v.i.* *F:* **I'll go and i.,** j'irai voir ce qui se passe. **investigating** *n.* investigation *f*; recherches *fpl*; **i. committee,** commission *f* d'enquête.

investigation [investi'geiʃ(ə)n] *n.* investigation *f*; approfondissement *m* (**of,** de); enquête *f* (**of,** sur); *Jur:* instruction *f* (d'un crime, etc.); **question under i.,** question *f* à l'étude; **scientific i.,** enquête scientifique; **on further i.,** en poursuivant les recherches; **the police made investigations,** la police a procédé aux constatations, à une enquête.

investigator [in'vestigeitər] *n.* investigateur, -trice; rechercheur, -euse; enquêteur, -euse.

investiture [in'vestitjər] *n.* (*a*) investiture *f* (d'un évêque, etc.); (*b*) remise *f* de décorations.

investment [in'vestmənt] *n.* **1.** *Mil:* investissement *m*, cernement *m* (d'une place forte). **2.** *Fin:* placement *m* (de fonds); mise *f* de fonds; investissement *m* (des capitaux); **good, safe, i.,** placement sûr; **long-term, short-t., i.,** placement à long, court, terme; **i. company,** société *f* de portefeuille, d'investissement.

investor [in'vestər] *n.* actionnaire *mf*, investisseur *m*.

inveterate [in'vetərət] *a.* (*a*) (mal, défaut) invétéré, enraciné; (*of disease, bad habit*) **to become i.,** s'invétérer, s'enraciner; (*b*) (ivrogne, joueur) invétéré; (fumeur) acharné, enragé; (ennemi) implacable.

invidious [in'vidiəs] *a.* **1.** haïssable, odieux; (tâche) ingrate, peu agréable. **2.** (i) qui incite l'envie; (ii) qui suscite la jalousie; (comparaison) désobligeante.

invigilate [in'vidʒileit] *v.i.* *Sch:* surveiller les can-

didats (à un examen).
invigilator [in'vidʒileitər] *n. Sch:* surveillant, -ante (des candidats à un examen).
invigorate [in'vigəreit] *v.tr.* (*a*) fortifier (qn), donner de la vigueur à (qn); (*b*) (*of the air, etc.*) vivifier, tonifier. **invigorating** *a.* (aliment, etc.) fortifiant; (air, etc.) vivifiant, tonifiant.
invincibility [invinsi'biliti] *n.* invincibilité *f.*
invincible [in'vinsibl] *a.* invincible.
inviolability [invaiələ'biliti] *n.* inviolabilité *f.*
inviolable [in'vaiələbl] *a.* inviolable. **-ably** *adv.* inviolablement.
inviolate [in'vaiələt] *a.* inviolé.
invisibility [invizi'biliti] *n.* invisibilité *f.*
invisible [in'vizibl] *a.* invisible; (encre) sympathique; **i. to the naked eye,** invisible, indiscernable, à l'œil nu; **i. mending,** stoppage *m.* **-ibly** *adv.* invisiblement; **to mend i.,** stopper (un trou, un vêtement).
invitation [invi'teiʃ(ə)n] *n.* (*a*) invitation *f* (**to do sth.,** à faire qch.); **at s.o.'s i.,** sur l'invitation de qn; **i. to lunch,** invitation à déjeuner; (*b*) **speech that is an i. to criticism,** discours *m* qui provoque la critique.
invite¹ [in'vait] *v.tr.* **1.** inviter; convier (des amis à dîner); **to i. s.o. in,** inviter qn à entrer; prier qn d'entrer; **to i. oneself,** s'inviter soi-même; **the invited guests,** les invités *mpl*; (*at table*) les convives *mpl.* **2.** engager, convier, inviter, appeler (**s.o. to do sth.,** qn à faire qch.). **3.** provoquer (le danger, la critique); **to i. trouble,** se préparer des ennuis. **inviting** *a.* invitant, attrayant; (mets) appétissant, ragoûtant; **not very i.,** peu invitant, peu attrayant. **invitingly** *adv.* d'une manière attrayante, tentante.
invite² ['invait] *n. F:* invitation *f.*
invocation [invə'keiʃ(ə)n] *n.* invocation *f.*
invoice¹ ['invɔis] *n. Com:* facture *f* (de débit); note *f* (de frais); **to make out an i.,** établir une facture; **as per i.,** suivant la facture; **i. clerk,** facturier, -ière.
invoice² *v.tr.* facturer (des marchandises). **invoicing** *n.* facturation *f* (de marchandises, etc.).
invoke [in'vouk] *v.tr.* **1.** (*a*) invoquer (Dieu, la mémoire de qn, etc.); (*b*) **to i. s.o.'s aid,** appeler qn à son secours; **to i. a blessing on an undertaking,** demander à Dieu de bénir une entreprise. **2.** évoquer (un esprit).
involuntary [in'vɔlənt(ə)ri] *a.* involontaire. **-ily** *adv.* involontairement.
involve [in'vɔlv] *v.tr.* **1.** (*a*) *Lit:* envelopper, entortiller (**in,** dans); (*b*) compliquer (un récit). **2.** (*a*) **to i. s.o. in a quarrel,** mêler qn à, dans, une querelle; **to i. s.o. in a crime,** impliquer qn dans un crime; **to i. oneself in debt,** s'endetter; (*b*) **to be involved in sth.,** être entraîné dans qch.; **he is involved in the plot,** il est compromis dans le complot; **the vehicle involved,** le véhicule impliqué, en cause (dans l'accident); (*c*) **to become involved in charitable work,** s'adonner aux œuvres de bienfaisance; **I am emotionally involved,** cela me concerne de trop près, me touche trop; (*d*) **he got involved with his friend's wife,** il a eu une liaison avec la femme de son ami. **3.** (*include, entail*) comporter, impliquer, comprendre, entraîner; **to i. much expense,** nécessiter de gros frais; **the difficulties which this would i.,** les difficultés *f* que cela comporterait. **involved** *a.* (style, discours) embrouillé, entortillé, compliqué.
involvement [in'vɔlvmənt] *n.* **1.** mise *f* en jeu (de forces, etc.). **2.** participation *f* (**in,** à); implication *f*, *Pej:* empêtrement *m* (de qn dans une affaire). **3.** confusion *f*, imbroglio *m.*
invulnerability [invʌlnərə'biliti] *n.* invulnérabilité *f.*
invulnerable [in'vʌlnərəbl] *a.* (*of pers.*) invulnérable; (*of position, etc.*) inattaquable, invincible.
inward ['inwəd] **1.** *a.* (*a*) intérieur; interne; (*b*) (orienté, se dirigeant) vers l'intérieur; **i. traffic of a port,** trafic *m* d'entrée (d'un port); *Book-k:* **i. payment,** paiement reçu; encaissement *m.* **2.** *adv.* = INWARDS; **i. opening door,** porte qui s'ouvre vers l'intérieur. **-ly** *adv.* en dedans, intérieurement; **I was i. pleased,** dans mon for intérieur j'étais content.
inwards ['inwədz] *adv.* **1.** (*a*) vers l'intérieur; en dedans; (*b*) *Com: Nau:* pour l'importation; **clearance i.,** (i) déclaration *f*, (ii) permis *m*, d'entrée. **2.** dans l'âme; intérieurement.
iodine ['aiədi:n] *n. Ch:* iode *m*; *Pharm:* **(tincture of) i.,** teinture *f* d'iode.
iodize ['aiədaiz] *v.tr. Med: Phot:* ioder.
iodoform [ai'ɔdoufɔ:m] *n. Ch:Pharm:* iodoforme *m.*
ion ['aiən] *n. Ph: Ch: El:* ion *m*; (*a*) **hydrogen i.,** ion d'hydrogène; (*b*) **i. beam,** faisceau *m* ionique.
Ionic¹ [ai'ɔnik] *a.* (*a*) *Arch: Pros:* (ordre, vers) ionique; (*b*) *Ling: Mus:* (dialecte, mode) ionien.
ionic² *a. Ph: Ch: El:* ionique.
ionization [aiənai'zeiʃ(ə)n] *n.* **1.** *Ph: El:* ionisation *f.* **2.** *Med:* (traitement *m* par) ionisation.
ionize ['aiənaiz] *Ph: El:* **1.** *v.tr.* ioniser (l'air, un gaz). **2.** *v.i.* (*of acid, etc.*) s'ioniser.
ionosphere [ai'ɔnəsfiər] *n.* ionosphère *f.*
iota [ai'outə] *n.* **1.** *Gr.Alph:* iota *m.* **2.** iota, rien *m*; **not one i.,** pas un iota; **not an i. of truth,** pas un brin de vérité.
IOU, *pl.* **IOUs** ['aiou'ju:, -ju:z] *n.* (= **I owe you**) reconnaissance *f* (de dette); **I'll give you an IOU,** je vais vous faire un billet.
Iran [i'rɑ:n] *Pr.n. Geog:* Iran *m.*
Iranian [i'reinjən] **1.** *a. Geog:* iranien. **2.** *n.* (*a*) Iranien, -ienne; (*b*) *Ling:* iranien.
Iraq [i'rɑ:k] *Pr.n. Geog:* Irak *m.*
Iraqi [i'rɑ:ki] **1.** *a. Geog:* irakien. **2.** *n.* (*a*) Irakien, -ienne; (*b*) *Ling:* irakien.
irascibility [iræsi'biliti] *n.* irascibilité *f.*
irascible [i'ræsibl] *a.* (homme) irascible, coléreux; (tempérament) colérique **-bly** *adv.* irasciblement.
irate [ai'reit] *a.* courroucé, en colère, furieux, irrité.
ire ['aiər] *n. A: & Lit:* courroux *m*, colère *f.*
Ireland ['aiələnd] *Pr.n. Geog:* Irlande *f*; **Northern I.,** l'Irlande du Nord; **the Republic of I.,** la République d'Irlande.
iridescence [iri'desəns] *n.* irisation *f*, chatoiement *m* (d'un plumage, etc.).
iridescent [iri'desənt] *a.* irisé, iridescent; chatoyant.
iris ['aiəris] **1.** *Pr.n.f. Myth:* **Iris,** Iris. **2.** *n.* (*pl.* **irides** ['aiəridi:z]) *Anat:* iris *m* (de l'œil). **3.** *n.* (*pl.* **irises** ['aiərisiz]) *Bot:* iris *m*; **yellow i.,** iris jaune, des marais.
Irish ['aiəriʃ] **1.** *a.* (peuple, etc.) irlandais; (beurre, etc.) d'Irlande; **I. American,** Américain, -aine, d'origine irlandaise; **I. coffee,** café noir au whiskey irlandais couronné de crème fraîche; **I. setter,** setter irlandais. **2.** *n.* (*a*) *Ling:* irlandais *m*; (*b*) *pl.* **the I.,** les Irlandais.
Irishman, *pl.* **-men** ['aiəriʃmən] *n.m.* Irlandais.
Irishwoman, *pl.* **-women** ['aiəriʃwumən, -wimin] *n.f.* Irlandaise.
irk [ə:k] *v.tr.* ennuyer, contrarier (qn).
irksome ['ə:ksəm] *a.* (travail) ennuyeux, ingrat.
iron¹ ['aiən] *n.* fer *m.* **1. old i.,** ferraille *f*; **(made) of i.,** de, en, fer; **he has an i. constitution,** il a une santé de fer; **man of i.,** homme dur, sans pitié; **will of i.,** volonté *f* de fer; *Metall:* **cast i.,** (fer de) fonte *f*; **crude i.,** fer cru, brut; **wrought i.,** fer forgé; **(sheet) i.,** tôle *f*; **corrugated i.,** tôle ondulée. **2.** (*a*) **i. bar,** barre *f* de fer; **i. bridge,** pont *m* en fer; **i. filings,** limaille *f* de fer; (*b*) *Miner: Ch:* **i. ore,** minerai *m* de fer; (*c*)

Metall: **i. foundry,** fonderie *f* de fonte; **the i. and steel industry,** l'industrie *f* sidérurgique, la sidérurgie; (*d*) *Fig:* **i. discipline,** discipline *f* de fer; **i. will,** volonté de fer; (*e*) *Med:* **i. lung,** poumon *m* d'acier. **3.** *Med:* **i. deficiency,** manque *m* de fer. **4.** (*a*) *Hairdr: A:* **curling i.,** fer à friser; **to have several irons in the fire,** s'occuper de plusieurs choses à la fois; (*b*) *F:* revolver *m*; pistolet *m*; (*c*) *Dom.Ec:* **(flat) i., laundry i.,** fer à repasser; **electric i.,** fer électrique; (*d*) *Carp:* **plane i.,** fer, couteau *m*, de rabot; (*e*) *Equit:* **(stirrup) i.,** étrier *m*; (*f*) *Golf:* (crosse *f* en) fer; **i. shot,** coup *m* de fer. **5.** *Const:* poutre *f* de fer. **6.** (*a*) **irons,** fers, chaînes *fpl*; (*b*) *Med:* **irons,** attelles *fpl*.

iron[2] *v.tr.* **1.** garnir (une porte, etc.) de fer; ferrer (une porte, etc.). **2.** repasser (le linge); donner un coup de fer à (un col); **to i. out a crease,** faire disparaître un faux pli au fer (chaud); *Fig:* **to i. out the difficulties,** aplanir les difficultés. **ironing** *n.* repassage *m*; **i. board,** planche *f* à repasser.

ironclad [ˈaiənklæd] *a.* (*a*) à enveloppe de fer; (vaisseau) cuirassé; (puits) blindé; (*b*) *NAm:* (serment, contrat, etc.) strict; (règlement) rigoureux.

iron-grey [ˈaiənˈgrei] *a. & n.* gris (de) fer (*m inv*).

ironic(al) [aiˈrɔnik(l)] *a.* ironique. **-ally** *adv.* ironiquement; (parler) avec ironie.

ironmonger [ˈaiənmʌŋgər] *n.* quincaillier *m*; **ironmonger's shop, ironmongers's,** quincaillerie *f*.

ironmongery [ˈaiənmʌŋg(ə)ri] *n.* (*a*) (*goods*) quincaillerie *f*; (i) ferronnerie *f*; (ii) ferblanterie *f*; (*b*) (*shop*) quincaillerie.

ironstone [ˈaiənstoun] *n.* **(clay) i.,** minerai *m* de fer (argileux).

ironware [ˈaiənwɛər] *n.* ferronerie *f*.

ironwork [ˈaiənwəːk] *n.* **1.** construction *f* en fer; (*a*) (*work in wrought iron*) serrurerie *f*; (travail *m* de) ferronnerie (*f*); (*b*) **heavy i.,** charpente *f* en fer, grosse serrurerie; (*c*) (*parts made of iron*) ferrure(s) *f*(*pl*); ferrerie *f*; ferrements *mpl* (d'un navire, d'un wagon); dentelle *f* (d'une balustrade, etc.). **2.** (*often with sg. const.*) **ironworks** (*a*) fonderie *f* de fonte; (*b*) usine sidérurgique; forges *fpl*.

irony [ˈairəni] *n.* ironie *f*; **i. of fate,** ironie du sort.

irradiate [iˈreidieit] *v.tr.* **1.** (*a*) (*of light, heat*) irradier (la terre, etc.); (*of light rays*) illuminer (une surface); (*b*) *Rad.-A:* irradier (une substance, etc.); *Med:* traiter (un malade) par irradiation. **2.** émettre comme des rayons; **presence that irradiates strength and courage,** présence *f* d'où irradient la force et le courage. **3.** (*of good humour, etc.*) faire rayonner (le visage, etc.). **4.** *v.i.* irradier.

irradiation [ireidiˈeiʃ(ə)n] *n.* **1.** (*a*) *Ph: Opt: Physiol:* irradiation *f*; illumination *f*; (*b*) *Atom.Ph:* irradiation; *Med:* (traitement *m* par) irradiation; radiothérapie *f*. **2.** rayonnement *m*, éclat *m* (d'une source de lumière).

irrational [iˈræʃən(ə)l] *a.* (*a*) (animal, etc.) dépourvu de raison, irraisonnable; (*b*) (*of fear, conduct, etc.*) déraisonnable, absurde, irrationnel; (*c*) *Mth:* (nombre) irrationnel. **-ally** *adv.* déraisonnablement; irrationnellement.

irreconcilable [irekənˈsailəbl] *a.* **1.** (ennemi) irréconciliable; (haine) implacable. **2.** (croyance, idée) incompatible, inconciliable (**with,** avec).

irrecoverable [iriˈkʌv(ə)rəbl] *a.* (créance) irrécouvrable; (perte) irréparable, irrémédiable.

irredeemable [iriˈdiːməbl] *a.* **1.** (*a*) (faute) irrachetable; (*b*) *Fin:* (fonds) irrachetable, irréalisable, irremboursable; (papier) non convertible. **2.** (*a*) (désastre, etc.) irrémédiable; (*b*) (escroc) incorrigible.

irreducible [iriˈdjuːsibl] *a.* irréductible.

irrefutable [iriˈfjuːtəbl] *a.* (témoignage, déclaration) irréfutable; (témoignage) irrécusable.

irregular [iˈregjulər] *a.* irrégulier. **1.** (*a*) contraire aux règles; (conduite) irrégulière; (vie) déréglée; *Jur:* (document) informe; (*b*) *Gram:* (pluriel, verbe) irrégulier. **2.** asymétrique; (*of outline, etc.*) anfractueux; (*of surface*) inégal, -aux; (forme) irrégulière; **i. features,** traits irréguliers. **3.** (pouls) irrégulier, déréglé, inégal; (respiration) saccadée. **4.** *Mil:* **i. troops,** *n.pl.* **irregulars,** troupes irrégulières; irréguliers *mpl*. **-ly** *adv.* irrégulièrement.

irregularity [iregjuˈlæriti] *n.* **1.** (*a*) irrégularité *f* (de conduite, etc.); (*b*) *Adm: etc:* **to commit irregularities,** commettre des irrégularités (dans les comptes, etc.). **2.** (*a*) irrégularité (des traits); (*b*) **irregularities,** accidents *mpl* (du terrain).

irrelevance [iˈrelivəns], **irrelevancy** [iˈrelivənsi] *n.* **1.** inapplicabilité *f* (**to,** à). **2.** inconséquence *f*; manque *m* d'à-propos. **3.** **irrelevancies,** à-côtés *mpl* qui n'ont rien à voir avec la question.

irrelevant [iˈrelivənt] *a.* non pertinent; (*of remark, etc.*) hors de propos; **that is i.,** cela n'a aucun rapport, n'a rien à voir, avec la question.

irreligious [iriˈlidʒəs] *a.* irréligieux.

irremediable [iriˈmiːdiəbl] *a.* (mal, faute, etc.) irrémédiable; sans remède; (perte, etc.) irrécupérable. **-ably** *adv.* irrémédiablement, sans remède.

irremovable [iriˈmuːvəbl] *a.* (*a*) immuable, fixe; (*b*) (fonctionnaire) inamovible.

irreparable [iˈrepərəbl] *a.* (mal, perte) irréparable; (perte) irrémédiable, irrécupérable. **-ably** *adv.* irréparablement, irrémédiablement.

irreplaceable [iriˈpleisəbl] *a.* irremplaçable.

irrepressible [iriˈpresibl] *a.* (bâillement) irrésistible, irréprimable; (force) irrépressible; (rire) inextinguible. **-ibly** *adv.* irrésistiblement.

irreproachable [iriˈproutʃəbl] *a.* irréprochable; (vêtement) impeccable. **-ably** *adv.* irréprochablement.

irresistible [iriˈzistibl] *a.* irrésistible. **-ibly** *adv.* irrésistiblement.

irresolute [iˈrezəl(j)uːt] *a.* **1.** indécis; **to be i.,** hésiter. **2.** (caractère) irrésolu; (homme) qui manque de résolution; (esprit) vacillant, hésitant. **-ly** *adv.* irrésolument.

irresoluteness [iˈrezəl(j)utnis], **irresolution** [iˈrezəl(j)uʃ(ə)n] *n.* indécision *f*; irrésolution *f*.

irrespective [iriˈspektiv] *a.* **1.** *a.* indépendant (**of,** de). **2.** *adv.* **i. of sth.,** indépendamment, sans tenir compte, de qch.

irresponsibility [ˈirispɔnsiˈbiliti] *n.* **1.** *Jur:* irresponsabilité *f* (d'un aliéné, etc.). **2.** irréflexion *f*.

irresponsible [iriˈspɔnsibl] *a.* **1.** *Jur:* (*of mental defective, etc.*) irresponsable. **2.** (*a*) (*of pers.*) étourdi, irréfléchi; (*b*) (*of action*) irréfléchi. **-ibly** *adv.* **1.** irresponsablement. **2.** étourdiment.

irretrievable [iriˈtriːvəbl] *a.* irréparable, irrémédiable. **-ably** *adv.* irréparablement; (perdu) à tout jamais.

irreverence [iˈrev(ə)rəns] *n.* irrévérence *f* (**towards,** envers, pour).

irreverent [iˈrev(ə)rənt] *a.* (*in religious matters*) irrévérent; (*in social intercourse*) irrévérencieux. **-ly** *adv.* irrévérencieusement.

irreversible [iriˈvəːsibl] *a.* **1.** (*of decision, etc.*) irrévocable. **2.** (*of process, gear, etc.*) irréversible.

irrevocable [iˈrevəkəbl] *a.* irrévocable; *Jur:* (décision) irréformable. **-ably** *adv.* irrévocablement.

irrigable [ˈirigəbl] *a.* (terre) irrigable.

irrigate [ˈirigeit] *v.tr.* **1.** (*a*) *Agr:* irriguer (des champs); (*b*) (*of river*) arroser (un bassin, une région). **2.** *Med:* irriguer (une plaie, etc.).

irrigation [iriˈgeiʃ(ə)n] *n.* **1.** irrigation *f* (des champs); arrosage *m* (des prés, etc.); **i. canal, ditch,** canal *m* d'irrigation. **2.** *Med:* irrigation (d'une plaie).

irritability [iritəˈbiliti] *n.* irritabilité *f*; irascibilité *f*.

irritable ['iritəbl] *a.* (caractère, esprit) irritable, irascible. **-ably** *adv.* d'un ton irrité; avec humeur.
irritant ['iritənt] *a. & n. Med:* irritant (*m*).
irritate ['iriteit] *v.tr.* **1.** irriter, agacer (qn, un animal); exciter (un animal). **2.** *Med:* irriter (un organe). **irritating** *a.* **1.** irritant, agaçant. **2.** *Med:* irritant.
irritation [iri'teiʃ(ə)n] *n.* **1.** irritation *f*; **state of nervous i.,** état *m* d'énervement. **2.** *Med:* irritation (de la gorge, etc.).
is. *see* BE.
isinglass ['aisiŋglɑːs] *n.* (*a*) ichtyocolle *f*, isinglass *m*; (*b*) *Cu:* gélatine *f*.
Islam ['izlɑːm] *n.* (i) (*religion*) islam *m*; (ii) (*people*) l'Islam; **to go over to I.,** embrasser l'islamisme.
Islamic [iz'læmik] *a.* islamique.
Islamism ['izləmizm] *n.* islamisme *m*.
island ['ailənd] *n.* **1.** île *f*; **small i.,** îlot *m*; **the Pacific Islands,** les îles du Pacifique. **2.** (*a*) îlot (de maisons, etc.); *Rail:* **i. platform,** quai *m* d'entre-voie; quai entre voies; (*b*) **traffic i.,** refuge *m* (pour piétons); (*c*) (*in supermarket*) gondole *f*; (*d*) *Navy:* îlot, superstructure *f* (d'un porte-avions); (*e*) *Fig:* **i. of resistance,** îlot de résistance.
islander ['ailəndər] *n.* insulaire *mf*; **Channel Islanders,** habitants *mpl* des îles de la Manche.
isle [ail] *n.* (*a*) (*poet, except in certain proper names*) île *f*; **the British Isles,** les Iles britanniques; **the I. of Man,** l'île de Man.
islet ['ailit] *n.* îlot *m*.
isn't = is not, *see* BE.
isobar ['aisoubɑːr] *n. Meteor: Ph:* isobare *f*.
isolate¹ ['aisəleit] *v.tr.* **1.** (*a*) isoler (un malade, un fil électrique, etc.) (**from,** de, d'avec); (*b*) faire le vide autour de (qn). **2.** *Ch:* isoler, dégager (un corps simple); *Biol:* isoler (une culture). **isolated** *a.* (*of house, etc.*) isolé, écarté; **i. instance,** cas isolé.
isolation [aisə'leiʃ(ə)n] *n.* **1.** isolement *m* (d'un malade); **i. hospital,** hôpital *m* d'isolement de contagieux; **i. ward,** salle *f* des contagieux. **2.** isolement, solitude *f*; **splendid i.,** *f* splendide isolement.
isolationism [aisə'leiʃənizm] *n.* isolationnisme *m*.
isolationist [aisə'leiʃənist] *a. & n.* isolationniste (*mf*).
Isolde [i'zɔldə] *Pr.n.f.* Yseu(l)t, Iseu(l)t.
isosceles [ai'sɔsiliːz] *a. Mth:* (triangle) isocèle.
isotherm ['aisouθəːm] *n. Meteor:* isotherme *f*.
isotope ['aisoutoup] *n. Ch: Ph:* isotope *m*.
Israel ['izreiəl] *Pr.n. Geog: B. Hist:* Israël *m*.
Israeli [iz'reili] *Geog:* **1.** *a.* israélien. **2.** *n.* (*pl.* **Israeli(s)**) Israélien, -ienne.
Israelite ['izriəlait] **1.** *a.* israélite. **2.** *n.* Israélite *mf*.
issue¹ ['isjuː] *n.* **1.** sortie *f*, décharge *f* (de fumée, etc.). **2.** *Med:* décharge (de sang, de pus). **3.** (*way out*) (*a*) issue *f*, sortie, débouché *m* (**out of,** de); (*b*) embouchure *f* (d'un fleuve). **4.** résultat *m*, dénouement *m*; **to await the i. (of events),** attendre la fin, le résultat; **in the i., nothing was decided,** à la fin, en fin de compte, il n'y avait rien de décidé. **5.** progéniture *f*, descendance *f*; **to die without i.,** mourir sans (laisser de) postérité *f*. **6.** (*a*) *Jur:* **i. (of fact, of law),** (i) question *f*, point *m* (de fait, de droit); (ii) conclusion *f*; *Fig:* **I don't want to make an i. of it,** je n'en fais pas une affaire; (*b*) **to join i. with s.o. about sth.,** discuter l'opinion de qn au sujet de qch.; **the point at i.,** la question pendante; **matters at i.,** matières *fpl* en contestation; **to be at i., take i., with s.o.,** être (i) en désaccord, (ii) en contestation, avec qn; **to evade, avoid, the i.,** prendre la tangente; **to confuse the issue,** brouiller les cartes. **7.** (*a*) *Adm: Fin:* émission *f* (de mandats, de billets de banque, de timbres-poste, etc.); **i. price,** taux *m* d'émission; (*b*) *Adm: Mil: etc:* distribution *f*, *Mil:* versement *m* (de matériel, etc.); *Mil: etc:* **i. boots, shirts,** bottes *fpl* chemises *fpl*, réglementaires; *U.S:* **government i. equipment,** matériel *m* réglementaire de l'armée; (*c*) (i) parution *f*, publication *f* (d'un livre); lancement *m* (d'un prospectus, etc.); (ii) *Mil:* **i. of orders,** publication des ordres; (*d*) *Rail: etc:* délivrance (de billets, etc.); *Th:* contrôle *m* (des billets); (*in library*) communication *f* (de livres). **8.** édition *f* (d'un livre); numéro *m* (d'un journal).
issue² **1.** *v.i.* (*a*) **to i. (out, forth),** (*of blood, water*) jaillir, s'écouler (**from,** de); (*of smoke*) sortir (de); (*of smell*) se dégager (de); (*b*) provenir, dériver (**from,** de); **the children issuing from this marriage,** les enfants provenant de ce mariage; (*c*) **to i. in sth.,** se terminer par, aboutir à (qch.). **2.** *v.tr.* (*a*) émettre (des billets de banque, etc.); créer (un effet de commerce); (*b*) publier, donner (une nouvelle édition, etc.); lancer (un prospectus, etc.); *Fin:* fournir (une lettre de crédit); *Mil:* publier, donner (un ordre); *Jur:* rendre (un arrêt); **to i. a summons,** décerner, lancer, une citation; (*c*) verser, distribuer (des provisions, etc.); délivrer (des billets de chemin de fer, etc.); (*of library*) communiquer (des livres); **each man will be issued with two uniforms,** chaque homme recevra deux tenues; **to i. s.o. with sth.,** délivrer qch. à qn. **issuing** **1.** *a.* émetteur, -trice; distributeur, -trice; *Post:* **i. office,** bureau *m* d'émission; *Fin:* **i. house,** banque *f* de placement. **2.** *n.* (*a*) émission *f* (d'un emprunt, etc.); publication *f* (d'un livre, d'un journal); (*b*) délivrance *f* (de billets); distribution *f* (de vivres); (*in library*) communication *f* (des livres).
Istanbul [istæn'buːl] *Pr.n. Geog:* Istanb(o)ul *m*.
isthmus, *pl.* **-muses** ['is(θ)məs, -məsiz] *n. Geog: Anat:* isthme *m*.
it [it] *pers.pron.* **1.** (*referring to inanimate objects, animals, and children, but in French taking the gender of the noun for which* it *stands*) (*a*) (*nom.*) il, *f.* elle; **the house is small but it is my own,** la maison est petite mais elle est à moi; **where is your hat?—it's in the cupboard,** où est votre chapeau?—il est dans l'armoire; (*b*) (*acc.*) le, *f.* la; **I don't believe it,** je ne le crois pas; (*c*) (*dat.*) lui *mf*; **fetch the dog and give it something to eat,** allez chercher le chien et donnez lui à manger; (*d*) (*reflexive*) **the Committee has devoted much care to the task before it,** le comité a donné beaucoup d'attention à la tâche qui lui incombait; (*e*) (*stressed*) *F:* **he thinks he's it,** il se croit sorti de la cuisse de Jupiter; **this book is absolutely** *it!* c'est un livre épatant! **this is** *it!* nous y voilà! ça y est! on est fait! **2.** (*a*) (*as vague object of a verb*) **to face it,** faire front; **blast it!** zut! sapristi! (*b*) (*as vague object of a preposition*) **now for it!** et maintenant allons-y! **there is nothing for it but to run,** il n'y a qu'une chose à faire, c'est de filer; *F:* **he's (in) for it!** qu'est-ce qu'il va prendre! **to have a bad time of it,** en voir de dures. **3.** ce, cela, il; **who is it?** qui est-ce? **that's it,** (i) c'est ça; (ii) ça y est! **it frightens me,** cela me fait peur; **it doesn't matter,** cela ne fait rien; **it's raining,** il pleut; **it's ten o'clock,** il est dix heures; **it's Monday,** c'est lundi. **4.** (*anticipatory*) (*a*) (*provisional subject*) **it's nonsense talking like that,** il est absurde de parler comme ça; **it is impossible to work in this heat,** il est impossible de travailler par cette chaleur; **it says in . . .,** on lit dans . . .; (*b*) (*provisional object*) **the fog made it difficult to see,** le brouillard rendait la vision difficile; **you may rely upon it that he will do his best,** vous pouvez compter qu'il fera de son mieux. **5.** (*with prepositions*) **to consent to it,** y consentir; **above it, over it,** au-dessus; dessus; **below it, under(neath) it,** au-dessous; dessous; **for it,** en, y; pour lui, pour elle, pour cela; **from it,** en; **he's not bad, far from it,** il n'est pas méchant, loin de là; **of it,** en, y; **give me half of it,** donnez-m'en la moitié; **think of it,** pensez-y; **on it,** y, dessus; **don't tread on**

it, ne marchez pas dessus; **with it,** avec cela, avec lui, avec elle; **I cracked his head with it,** je lui ai fendu la tête avec.

Italian [i'tæljən] *a.* (*a*) *Geog:* italien; (ciel) d'Italie; (*b*) **I. cooking,** cuisine *f* italienne; **I. hand,** écriture anglaise. **2.** *n.* (*a*) Italien, -ienne; (*b*) *Ling:* italien *m*; (*c*) *F:* vermouth italien.

italic [i'tælik] *Typ:* (*a*) *a.* (caractère) italique; (*b*) *n. usu. pl.* **to print in italic(s),** imprimer en italique(s); **the italics are mine,** c'est moi qui souligne.

italicize [i'tælisaiz] *v.tr. Typ:* imprimer, mettre, en italiques; (*in manuscript*) souligner; **italicized words,** mots en italiques.

Italy ['itəli] *Pr.n. Geog:* Italie *f.*

itch¹ [itʃ] *n.* **1.** démangeaison *f*; *F:* **to have an i. for sth., to do sth.,** avoir une envie de qch., de faire qch.; **the seven year i.,** l'écueil *m* des sept ans de mariage. **2.** *Med: F:* gale *f.*

itch² *v.i.* **1.** (*a*) démanger; (*of pers.*) éprouver des démangeaisons; **my hand itches,** la main me démange; *impers.* **where does it i.?** où est-ce que cela vous démange? (*b*) **bites that i.,** morsures *fpl* qui font éprouver des démangeaisons. **2.** *F:* **to i. to do sth.,** brûler d'envie de faire qch.; **I was itching to speak,** la langue me démangeait (de parler); **she is itching to be off,** les pieds lui brûlent. **itching 1.** *a.* (plaie, etc.) qui démange. **2.** *n.* démangeaison *f.*

itchy ['itʃi] *a.* **I've got an i., hand,** la main me démange; *F:* **to have i. feet,** brûler de partir; avoir la bougeotte.

it'd = **it would,** *see* WILL³.

item ['aitəm] **1.** *adv. Com: Book-k:* de même; de plus; item. **2.** *n.* (*a*) *Com:* article *m*; **please send us the following items,** prière de nous envoyer les articles suivants; (*b*) *Book-k:* écriture *f*, article, poste *m*, détail *m*; **i. of expenditure, expense i.,** article, chef *m*, de dépense; (*c*) **the second i. of the contract,** l'article deux du contrat; **the items on the agenda,** les questions *fpl* à l'ordre du jour; *Th: etc:* **the last i. on the programme,** le dernier numéro du programme; (*d*) *Journ:* entrefilet *m*; **news items,** faits divers, échos *mpl.*

itemize ['aitəmaiz] *v.tr.* détailler (une facture, etc.); **itemized account,** compte spécifié.

iterate ['itəreit] *v.tr.* réitérer; répéter (constamment).

itinerant [i'tinərənt, ai-] *a.* (marchand, comédien, musicien) ambulant; (pasteur) itinérant.

itinerary [ai'tinərəri] *n.* itinéraire *m.*

it'll = **it will.**

its [its] **1.** *poss.a.* son, *f.* sa, *pl.* ses; (*in the fem. before a vowel sound*) son; (*of animal*) **its nose, mouth, and eyes,** son nez, sa bouche, et ses yeux; (*of forest, etc.*) **its extent,** son étendue *f*; **a charm of its own,** un charme qui est à lui seul, à elle seule. **2.** *occ. poss.pron.* (*stressed*) le sien, *f.* la sienne, *pl.* les sien(ne)s.

it's = (i) **it is,** *see* BE; (ii) **it has,** *see* HAVE².

itself [it'self] *pers.pron.* lui-même, elle-même, soi-même; (*a*) (*emphatic*) **it is simplicity i.,** c'est tout ce qu'il y a de plus simple; **she is kindness i.,** elle est la bonté même; (*b*) (*reflexive*) **the dog hurt i.,** le chien s'est fait mal; **door that opens i.,** porte qui s'ouvre (d')elle-même, toute seule; (*c*) (*after prepositions*) **the child was left by i.,** l'enfant était laissé(e) tout(e) seul(e); **the thing in i.,** la chose en elle-même.

I've = **I have.**

ivory ['aivəri] *n.* **1.** (*a*) ivoire *m*; (*b*) (objet *m* d')ivoire; **a collection of ivories,** une collection d'ivoires; (*c*) *F:* **ivories,** (i) *Bill:* billes *fpl*; (ii) dés *mpl*; (iii) dents *fpl*; (iv) touches *fpl* (du piano). **2.** *attrib.* (*a*) d'ivoire, en ivoire; **i. trade,** ivoirerie *f*; *Lit:* **i. tower,** tour *f* d'ivoire; (*b*) **i.-white teeth,** dents *fpl* d'une blancheur d'ivoire; (*c*) *Geog:* **the I. Coast,** la Côte d'Ivoire.

ivy ['aivi] *n. Bot:* **1.** lierre *m.* **2. poison i.,** sumac vénéneux; *Fr.C:* herbe *f* à la puce; **ground i.,** lierre terrestre, rampant. **3.** *attrib. U.S:* **I. League,** qui fait partie, est caractéristique, du cercle des vieilles universités prestigieuses des états de l'est.

J

J, j [dʒei] *n.* (la lettre) J, j *m.*
jab¹ [dʒæb] *n.* **1.** (*a*) coup de pointe; (*b*) *Med: F:* piqûre *f.* **2.** *Box:* coup sec; un jab.
jab² *v.tr. & i.* **(jabbed; jabbing) 1. to j. s.o., sth., with sth.,** piquer qn, qch., du bout de qch.; **to j. at s.o., at sth.,** lancer un coup sec à qn, qch. **2.** *Box:* donner un coup sec, un jab, à (qn).
jabber¹ ['dʒæbər] *n.* **1.** baragouin *m.* **2.** jacasserie *f.*
jabber² **1.** *v.i.* (*a*) baragouiner; (*b*) jacasser; **she never stops jabbering,** elle jacasse comme une pie borgne. **2.** *v.tr.* **to j. French,** baragouiner le français. **jabbering** *n.* (*a*) baragouinage *m*; (*b*) jacasserie *f.*
jabot ['ʒæbou] *n.* *Cost:* jabot *m.*
jacaranda [dʒækə'rændə] *n.* *Bot:* jacaranda *m.*
jacinth ['dʒæsinθ] **1.** *n.* *Miner: Lap:* jacinthe *f*, hyacinthe *f.* **2.** *a. & n.* (*colour*) rouge orangé *inv.*
Jack, jack¹ [dʒæk] **I.** *Pr.n.m.* (*dim. of* **John**) **1.** Jean, Jeannot; **he was off before you could say J. Robinson,** il est parti sans qu'on ait le temps de dire ouf; *F:* **I'm all right, J.,** je m'en tire bien (et tant pis pour les autres). **2. J. (tar),** marin *m*; **an old j. tar,** un loup de mer. **II.** *n.* **1.** (*pers.*) **j. of all trades,** homme à tout faire; bricoleur *m*; **every man j.,** tout le monde; *Toys:* **j. in the box,** diable *m* (à ressort). **2.** *Cards:* valet *m.* **3.** *Clockm:* jaquemart *m.* **4.** *Ich:* (*a*) brocheton *m*; (*b*) **j. salmon,** saumoneau *m*, jeune saumon *m.* **5.** (*male of species*) âne *m*; **j. hare,** bouquin *m*; **j. rabbit,** (i) lapin (mâle); (ii) gros lièvre américain. **III.** *n.* **1.** (*a*) **roasting j.,** tournebroche *m*; (*b*) **chimney j.,** mitre *f* (de cheminée) à tête mobile; girouette *f* à fumée. **2.** support *m*; (*a*) *Ind:* **assembling j.,** support d'assemblage; (*b*) *Mec.E:* cric *m*; **car j.,** cric pour voiture; **wheel j.,** lève-roue *m inv*; **lifting j.,** vérin *m* de levage. **3.** *El: Tp:* jack *m*; fiche *f* femelle. **4.** *Games:* (*bowls*) cochonnet *m.*
jack² *v.tr.* **1. to j. up,** (*a*) (i) mettre à niveau, soulever, au moyen de vérins; (ii) soulever (une voiture, etc.) avec un cric; (*b*) *F:* augmenter (des prix, etc.). **2.** *F:* **to j. in, up,** abandonner (une entreprise, etc.).
jack³ *n.* *Nau:* pavillon *m* beaupré; **the Union J.,** le pavillon britannique, du Royaume-Uni; **black j.,** le pavillon noir (des pirates).
jackal ['dʒækɔːl] *n.* *Z:* chacal *m*, *pl.* chacals.
jackass ['dʒækæs] *n.* **1.** (*a*) âne (mâle) *m*; baudet *m*; (*b*) *F:* idiot, -ote, imbécile *mf.* **2.** *Orn:* **laughing j.,** dacélo *m.*
jackboots ['dʒækbuːts] *n.pl.* bottes *fpl* de cavalier, à genouillères.
jackdaw ['dʒækdɔː] *n.* *Orn:* choucas *m* des tours.
jacket¹ ['dʒækit] *n.* **1.** (*a*) *Cost:* veste *f*; veston *m* (d'homme); **single-breasted, double-breasted, j.,** veston droit, croisé; **dinner j.,** smoking *m*; **sheepskin j.,** canadienne *f*; **bed j.,** liseuse *f*; (*b*) robe *f* (d'un animal); pelure *f* (de fruit, etc.); *Cu:* **j. potatoes,** pommes *fpl* de terre en robe de chambre, en robe des champs. **2.** (*a*) **(filing) j.,** chemise *f*; (*b*) jaquette *f* (de livre); couverture *f*, pochette *f* (de disque); (*c*) *Mec.E: etc:* **cooling j.,** chemise, enveloppe *f* de refroidissement (d'un cylindre, d'un tuyau, etc.); **water j.,** chemise d'eau (d'un four à cuve); (*d*) *Artil:* **barrel j., gun j.,** jaquette *f* de canon; *Ball:* **bullet j.,** chemise, enveloppe, de la balle.
jacket² *v.tr.* **(jacketed)** garnir, envelopper (un cylindre, une chaudière, etc.) d'une chemise; chemiser.
jack(-)knife¹ ['dʒæknaif] *n.* **1.** couteau *m* de poche; couteau pliant, fermant; surin *m.* **2.** *Swim:* **j.-k. dive,** saut *m* de carpe.
jack(-)knife² *v.i.* (*a*) se plier en deux (pour entrer, sortir de, quelque part); (*b*) *Swim:* faire un saut de carpe; (*c*) *Aut:* (*esp. of trailer*) se mettre en travers de la route.
jackpot ['dʒækpɔt] *n.* (*a*) *Cards:* (*poker*) (jack-)pot *m*; (*b*) **to hit the j.,** gagner le gros lot.
jackrabbit ['dʒækræbit] *n.* gros lièvre américain.
jackstraw ['dʒækstrɔː] *n.* *Games:* fiche *f* de jonchets; **jackstraws,** (jeu *m* de) jonchets (*mpl*).
Jacob ['dʒeikəb] *Pr.n.m.* Jacob; **Jacob's ladder,** (i) *B:* l'échelle *f* de Jacob; (ii) *Bot:* polémonie bleue; valériane grecque; (iii) *Nau:* échelle de revers.
Jacobean [dʒækə'biən] *a.* *Arch: Furn: etc:* de l'époque de Jacques Ier.
Jacobite ['dʒækəbait] *a. & n.* *Eng.Hist:* jacobite (*mf*).
jade¹ [dʒeid] *n.* (*horse*) rosse *f*, haridelle *f.*
jade² *n.* **1.** *Miner:* jade *m*, néphrite *f.* **2. j. (green),** vert *m* de jade; vert olivâtre.
jaded ['dʒeidid] *a.* (*a*) (*of horse*) surmené, éreinté; (*b*) (*of pers.*) fatigué, excédé; **j. palate,** palais blasé.
jag¹ [dʒæg] *n.* pointe *f*, dent *f* (de rocher, etc.).
jag² *v.tr.* (**jagged** [dʒægd]) déchiqueter (une robe, etc.); ébrécher (un couteau, etc.). **jagged** ['dʒægid] *a.* (*of line, edge, etc.*) déchiqueté, entaillé, ébréché; (contour) haché; (pierre) aux arêtes vives; (rocher) pointu, dentelé; **j. outline of a coast,** dentelures *fpl* d'une côte.
jag³ *n.* *O:* soûlerie *f*; **to go on the j.,** se soûler; prendre une cuite.
jaguar ['dʒægjuər, -ɑːr] *n.* *Z:* jaguar *m.*
jail¹ [dʒeil] *n.* prison *f*; **to be in j.,** être en prison.
jail² *v.tr.* mettre (qn) en prison.
jailbird ['dʒeilbəːd] *n.* *F:* récidiviste *mf*; cheval *m* de retour.
jailbreak ['dʒeilbreik] *n.* évasion *f* de prison.
jailbreaker ['dʒeilbreikər] *n.* évadé *m* de prison.
jailer ['dʒeilər] *n.* gardien *m* de prison.
jalop(p)y [dʒə'lɔpi] *n.* *F:* vieux tacot; vieille guimbarde.
jam¹ [dʒæm] *n.* **1.** (*a*) blocage *m*; coincement *m*; enrayement *m* (d'une mitrailleuse, etc.); (*b*) *Mus: F:* **j. session,** jam-session *f*, séance *f* de jazz improvisé. **2.** (*a*) foule *f*, presse *f* (de gens); (*b*) **(traffic) j.,** encombrement *m*, embouteillage *m*, bouchon *m* (de circulation); *F:* **to be in a j.,** être dans le pétrin; (*c*) embâcle *m* (de bûches dans une rivière).
jam² *v.* **(jammed) 1.** *v.tr.* (*a*) serrer, presser; **to j. sth. into a box,** fourrer, enfoncer de force, qch. dans une boîte; (*b*) **to j. on the brakes,** bloquer les freins; serrer les freins à bloc; (*c*) coincer, caler, engager (une machine, etc.); enrayer (une mitrailleuse, une roue, etc.); *Nau:* coincer, engager (la barre); **to get jammed,** (se) coincer; (*d*) **people were jamming the corridor,** des gens obstruaient, bloquaient, le couloir; (*e*) *W.Tg:* brouiller (un message). **2.** *v.i.* (*of drawer, etc.*) se coincer, se caler; (*of machine part*) (se) coincer, gommer; (*of machine*) prendre; (*of rifle*) s'enrayer; (*of machine gun, wheel*) se caler, s'enrayer; (*of brake*) se bloquer; *Cin:* (*of film in its channel*) bourrer; *Nau:* (*of rope*) étriver; genoper; **the lift has**

jammed, l'ascenseur est coincé, en panne; **the cable is jammed,** le câble est mordu. **jamming** *n.* **1.** (*a*) serrement *m*, pressage *m*; coincement *m*, écrasement *m* (du doigt); **j. (on) (of a brake),** blocage *m* (d'un frein); (*b*) arrêt *m* de fonctionnement (d'une machine, etc.); coincement (d'une soupape, etc.); enrayage *m* (d'une mitrailleuse, etc.); (*c*) *W.Tel: etc:* brouillage *m* (d'un message). **2.** tassement *m* (de glaçons, etc.).

jam³ *n.* confiture *f*; **strawberry j.,** confiture de fraises; **j. jar,** pot *m* à confiture; *F:* **it's money for j.,** c'est donné; **what d'you want, j. on it?** ça ne te suffit pas? et avec ça?

jam⁴ *v.tr.* **(jammed)** mettre de la confiture sur (une tartine).

Jamaica [dʒə'meikə] *Pr.n. Geog:* la Jamaïque.

Jamaican [dʒə'meikən] *Geog:* **1.** *a.* jamaïquain. **2.** *n.* Jamaïquain, -aine.

jamb [dʒæm] *n.* jambage *m*, montant *m*, chambranle *m* (de porte, de cheminée); battée *f*, dosseret *m* (de porte).

jamboree [dʒæmbə'riː] *n.* **1.** réjouissances tapageuses. **2.** (*a*) *Scout:* jamboree *m*; (*b*) *F:* réunion générale (d'une association).

James [dʒeimz] *Pr.n.m.* Jacques.

jammy ['dʒæmi] *a.* *F:* veinard, bidard; **he's a j. bugger,** il a du pot.

jam-packed ['dʒæmpækd] *a.* (*of hall, bus, etc.*) bondé; noir de monde.

Jane [dʒein] **1.** *Pr.n.f.* Jeanne. **2.** *n.f.* *F:* femme, nana; **she's rather a plain J.,** elle n'est pas très jolie.

jangle¹ ['dʒæŋgl] *n.* sons discordants; cliquetis *m*.

jangle² **1.** *v.i.* rendre des sons discordants; cliqueter; s'entrechoquer. **2.** *v.tr.* faire cliqueter; faire entrechoquer (des clefs, etc.); **jangled nerves,** nerfs ébranlés.

janitor ['dʒænitər] *n.* portier *m*, concierge *m*.

January ['dʒænjuəri] *n.* janvier *m*; **in J.,** en janvier; **(on) the first, the seventh, of J.,** le premier, le sept, janvier.

Jap [dʒæp] *F:* **1.** *n.* Japonais, -aise. **2.** *a.* japonais.

Japan¹ [dʒə'pæn] **1.** *Pr.n. Geog:* Japon *m*; **in J.,** au Japon. **2.** *n.* **j.,** laque *m* (de Chine); vernis japonais; vernis du Japon.

japan² *v.tr.* **(japanned)** laquer (un métal, etc.); vernir avec du laque.

Japanese [dʒæpə'niːz] **1.** *a.* *Geog:* japonais; **the J. ambassador,** l'ambassadeur *m* du Japon. **2.** *n.* (*a*) Japonais, -aise; (*b*) *Ling:* japonais *m*.

japonica [dʒə'pɔnikə] *n.* *Bot:* cognassier *m* du Japon.

jar¹ [dʒɑːr] *n.* **1.** dissonance *f*; son discordant, dur. **2.** (*a*) ébranlement *m*; trépidation *f*; choc *m*; secousse *f*; **his fall gave him a nasty j.,** sa chute l'a fortement ébranlé; (*b*) manque *m* d'accord; choc (d'intérêts, etc.). **3.** *Min:* coulisse *f* (de perforateur).

jar² *v.* **(jarred) 1.** *v.i.* (*a*) rendre un son discordant, dur; **noise that jars (on the ear),** bruit *m* qui choque l'oreille; (*b*) heurter, cogner; (*of machine part, etc.*) **to j. on sth.,** se cogner à qch.; cogner sur qch.; **to j. on s.o.'s feelings,** froisser, choquer, les sentiments de qn; **the noise jarred on my nerves,** le bruit me crispait les nerfs; (*c*) (*of door, window, etc.*) vibrer, trembler; (*of machine*) marcher par à-coups; (*d*) être en désaccord **(with sth.,** avec qch.); **colours that j.,** couleurs *fpl* qui jurent **(with,** avec); couleurs qui détonnent; (*e*) *Mus:* (*of note*) détonner. **2.** *v.tr.* (*a*) choquer, heurter, cogner; **the fall jarred his spine,** la chute lui a ébranlé la colonne vertébrale; (*b*) choquer (l'oreille, etc.); agacer (les nerfs, etc.); froisser (les sentiments). **jarring** *a.* **1.** (*of sound*) discordant, dur; *Mus:* (note) qui détonne; **his remark struck a j. note,** sa remarque a troublé l'harmonie (de la réunion, etc.). **2.** (*of blow, etc.*) qui ébranle tout le corps; (*of incident, behaviour, etc.*) qui produit une impression désagréable. **3.** (*of door, window, etc.*) vibrant, tremblant. **4.** en désaccord, opposé; (couleurs) disparates, qui jurent.

jar³ *n.* (*a*) récipient *m*; pot *m* (à confitures, etc.); **(glass) j.,** bocal *m*; (*b*) *El:* verre *m*, vase *m* (de pile électrique); **Leyden j.,** bouteille *f* de Leyde; (*c*) *F:* **to have a j.,** prendre un pot.

jargon ['dʒɑːgən] *n.* **1.** jargon *m*, langage *m* (d'une profession, etc.). **2.** baragouin *m*, charabia *m*.

jasmin(e) ['dʒæzmin, 'dʒæs-] *n.* *Bot:* **(common, white) j.,** jasmin *m*; **winter j.,** jasmin d'hiver.

jasper ['dʒæspər] *n.* *Miner:* jaspe *m*.

jaundice ['dʒɔːndis] *n.* *Med:* jaunisse *f*, ictère *m*.

jaundiced ['dʒɔːndist] *a.* **1.** *Med:* ictérique, bilieux. **2. to look on the world with a j. eye,** (i) voir tout en noir; (ii) tout regarder d'un œil jaloux.

jaunt [dʒɔːnt] *n.* (petite) excursion, sortie *f*; **on a j.,** en excursion.

jauntiness ['dʒɔːntinis] *n.* **1.** désinvolture *f*. **2.** air effronté.

jaunty ['dʒɔːnti] *a.* **1.** (*of manner, etc.*) (*a*) insouciant, dégagé, désinvolte; **with a j. air,** d'un air dégagé; (*b*) effronté. **2.** enjoué, vif; **j. step,** démarche vive. **-ily** *adv.* **1.** d'une manière désinvolte. **2.** d'un air effronté.

Java ['dʒɑːvə] *Pr.n. Geog:* Java.

Javanese [dʒɑːvə'niːz] *Geog:* **1.** *a.* javanais. **2.** *n.* Javanais, -aise.

javelin ['dʒævlin] *n.* javelot *m*; **j. thrower, throwing,** lanceur *m*, lancer *m*, du javelot.

jaw¹ [dʒɔː] *n.* **1.** (*a*) mâchoire *f*; **upper, lower, j.,** mâchoire supérieure, inférieure; **to snatch s.o. from the jaws of death,** arracher qn des griffes de la mort; *F:* **his j. dropped,** il en resta bouche bée; (*b*) *Tchn:* mâchoire, mors *m*, mords *m*, mordache *f* (de tenailles, d'un étau, etc.); bec *m* (d'une clef anglaise); **gripping jaws, vice jaws,** mordaches; (*c*) *Nau:* mâchoire (de gui, de corne). **2.** (*a*) *F:* bavardage *m*; **to have a good j.,** bien papoter; (*b*) *esp. Sch:* *F:* sermon *m*, laïus *m*.

jaw² *F:* **1.** *v.i.* (*a*) bavarder; (*b*) *Sch:* piquer un laïus. **2.** *v.tr.* *esp. Sch:* sermonner (qn); faire la morale à (qn).

jawbone¹ ['dʒɔːboun] *n.* os *m* maxillaire; mâchoire *f*.

jawbone² *v.tr.* *U.S:* **to j. s.o. into doing sth.,** user de toute son influence pour forcer qn à faire qch.

jawbreaker ['dʒɔːbreikər] *n.* *NAm:* *Comest:* bonbon (dur).

jay [dʒei] *n.* **1.** *Orn:* geai *m* (des chênes); **blue j.,** geai bleu. **2.** *NAm:* *F:* (*a*) bavard, -arde; (*b*) idiot, -ote.

jaywalker ['dʒeiwɔːkər] *n.* *F:* piéton distrait, imprudent.

jaywalking ['dʒeiwɔːkiŋ] *n.* inattention *f* de la part des piétons.

jazz¹ [dʒæz] *n.* (*a*) *Mus:* jazz *m*; **j. band,** jazz-band *m*; (*b*) *F:* baratin *m*; **and all that j.,** et tout ce fatras; et tout le bataclan.

jazz² **1.** *v.i.* danser le jazz. **2.** *v.tr.* **to j. (up) a tune,** tourner une mélodie en jazz; *F:* **to j. s.o. up,** animer, émoustiller, qn; **jazzed up,** (i) *Pej:* modernisé; (ii) (*of pers.*) endimanché; sur son trente-et-un.

jazzman, *pl.* **-men** ['dʒæzmæn, -men] *n.* *Mus:* jazzman *m*, *pl.* jazzmen.

jazzy ['dʒæzi] *a.* *F:* **1.** (air) de jazz. **2.** (*of colour, etc.*) tapageur; voyant.

jealous ['dʒeləs] *a.* **1.** jaloux **(of,** de); **to be j. of s.o.,** être jaloux de qn; jalouser qn; **to be j. of one's good name,** être jaloux de sa réputation. **2.** (*zealous*) (soin) jaloux. **-ly** *adv.* jalousement.

jealousy ['dʒeləsi] *n.* jalousie *f*.

jean [dʒiːn] *n.* *Tex:* **1.** coutil *m*, treillis *m*. **2.** *Cost:* **(pair of) jeans,** jean *m*; **blue jeans,** blue-jean *m*, *pl.* blue-jeans.

jeep [dʒiːp] *n.* *Aut:* jeep *f*.

jeez(e) [ˈdʒiːz] *int. esp. U.S: F:* mon Dieu!

jeer¹ [ˈdʒiər] *n.* **1.** raillerie *f*, moquerie *f*. **2.** huée *f*.

jeer² **1.** *v.i.* **to j. at sth.,** se moquer de qch. **2.** *v.tr.* (i) se moquer de (qn); railler (qn); (ii) huer, conspuer (qn). **jeering** **1.** *a.* railleur, -euse; moqueur, -euse. **2.** *n.* raillerie *f*; moquerie *f*.

Jehovah [dʒiˈhouvə] *Pr.n.m.* **1.** *B:* Jéhovah. **2.** *Rel:* **Jehovah's Witness,** témoin *m* de Jéhovah.

jejune [dʒiˈdʒuːn] *a.* (*of author, etc.*) aride; (*of style, etc.*) fade.

jell [dʒel] *v.i.* **1.** prendre; se congeler. **2.** *F:* se cristalliser; réussir; **my idea didn't j.,** mon idée n'a pas pris.

jelly¹ [ˈdʒeli] *n.* **1.** *Cu:* (*a*) **table j.,** gelée *f*; **red-currant j.,** gelée de groseille(s); *F:* **to beat, pound, s.o. into a j.,** réduire qn en bouillie, en marmelade; (*b*) **meat j.,** glace *f*; gelée de viande. **2.** *Exp:* plastic *m*; **petroleum j.,** graisse minérale; vaseline *f*. **3.** *Ap:* **royal j.,** gelée royale.

jelly² **1.** *v.tr. Cu:* mettre en gelée; **jellied eels,** anguilles *fpl* en gelée; aspic *m* d'anguilles. **2.** *v.i.* prendre; se congeler.

jellybean [ˈdʒelibiːn] *n. NAm: Comest:* (genre de) bonbon mou au parfums variés.

jellyfish [ˈdʒelifiʃ] *n. Coel:* méduse *f*.

jemmy [ˈdʒemi] *n. Tls:* broche-levier *f*, *pl.* broches-leviers; **(burglar's) j.,** pince-monseigneur *f*, *pl.* pinces-monseigneur.

Jenny [ˈdʒeni] **1.** *Pr.n.f.* (*dim. of Jane*) Jeannette. **2.** *n.* (*a*) **j. wren,** roitelet *m*; (*b*) (*female*) **j. robin,** rouge-gorge *m* femelle, *pl.* rouges-gorges femelles. **3.** *n. Bot:* **creeping j.,** lysimaque *f*. **4.** *n. Mec.E:* chariot *m* de roulement (d'un pont roulant). **5.** *n. Tex:* **spinning j.,** métier *m* à filer.

jeopardize [ˈdʒepədaiz] *v.tr.* exposer (qn, qch.) au danger; compromettre, hasarder (sa vie); (i) faire péricliter, (ii) laisser péricliter (ses affaires).

jeopardy [ˈdʒepədi] *n.* danger *m*, péril *m*; **to be in j.,** (*of one's life*) être en danger, en péril; (*of one's happiness, etc.*) être compromis; (*of business, etc.*) péricliter.

jerboa [dʒəːˈbouə] *n. Z:* gerboise *f*; souris sauteuse.

jeremiad [dʒeriˈmaiæd] *n.* jérémiade *f*, plainte *f*.

jerk¹ [dʒəːk] *n.* **1.** saccade *f*, secousse *f*, à-coup *m* (d'une corde, etc.); *Nau:* coup *m* de fouet; **with one j.,** tout d'une tire. **2.** *Physiol:* secousse, trémoussement *m* (d'un membre); tic *m*; *Med:* réflexe tendineux; *Med:* **knee j.,** réflexe patellaire, rotulien. **3.** *Gym:* jeté *m* (de l'haltère); *F:* **physical jerks,** la gymnastique. **4.** *NAm: F:* idiot *m*; andouille *f*.

jerk² **1.** *v.tr.* (*a*) donner une secousse à (qch.); donner une saccade, des saccades, à (qch.); tirer (qch.) d'un coup sec; **to j. sth. out of s.o.'s hand,** arracher qch. de la main de qn (d'un coup sec); (*b*) lancer brusquement (une pierre, etc.). **2.** *v.i.* se mouvoir soudainement; **to j. along,** avancer par saccades, par à-coups.

jerkin [ˈdʒəːkin] *n.* (*a*) gilet *m*; (*b*) *A.Cost:* justaucorps *m*.

jerky [ˈdʒəːki] *a.* (*of movement, voice, etc.*) saccadé; (*of style*) décousu. **-ily** *adv.* d'une manière saccadée; par à-coups.

Jerry¹ [ˈdʒeri] **1.** *Pr.n.m.* (*dim. of Jeremy, Jeremiah*) Jérémie. **2.** *n. F:* pot *m* de chambre, Jules *m*.

Jerry² *n.* (*dim. of German*) *F: Pej: O:* boche *m*, Fritz *m*.

jerry-building [ˈdʒeribildiŋ] *n. Pej:* construction *f* de carton, de camelote.

jerry-built [ˈdʒeribilt] *a. Pej:* (maison) de camelote, de carton.

jerrycan [ˈdʒerikæn] *n.* jerrycan *m*, bidon *m*.

Jersey [ˈdʒəːzi] **1.** *Geog:* (*a*) (Ile de) Jersey *m*; (*b*) **J. (cow),** vache *f* de Jersey. **2.** *n.* **j.,** (*a*) *Cost:* jersey *m*; chandail *m*; tricot *m* (de laine); **(football, etc.) j.,** maillot *m*; (*b*) *Tex:* jersey; tricot de laine, de soie, etc.

Jerusalem [dʒəˈruːsələm] *Pr.n. Geog:* Jérusalem; *Hort:* **J. artichoke,** topinambour *m*.

jest¹ [dʒest] *n.* **1.** plaisanterie *f*, badinage *m*, badinerie *f*, farce *f*; **in j.,** (dire qch.) en plaisantant, pour rire, par plaisanterie. **2.** bon mot, facétie *f*.

jest² *v.i.* plaisanter (**about sth.,** sur qch.); badiner, railler. **jesting** **1.** *a.* (fait) pour plaisanter, pour rire. **2.** *n.* raillerie *f*, plaisanterie *f*.

jester [ˈdʒestər] *n.* **1.** plaisant *m*; farceur, -euse. **2.** *Hist:* **court j.,** bouffon *m* du roi.

Jesu [ˈdʒiːzjuː] *Pr.n.m. Poet:* Jésus.

Jesuit [ˈdʒeʒjuit, -zjuit] *n. R.C.Ch:* jésuite *m*; **J. college,** collège *m* de jésuites.

jesuitic(al) [dʒezjuˈitik(l)] *a.* jésuitique.

Jesus [ˈdʒiːzəs] *Pr.n.m.* **1.** Jésus; **J. Christ,** Jésus-Christ; *Ecc:* **the Society of J.,** la Compagnie de Jésus. **2.** *int. P:* **j.!** nom de Dieu!

jet¹ [dʒet] **1.** *n. Miner:* jais *m*. **2.** (*a*) **j. (black),** (i) *a.* noir comme (du) jais; (ii) *n.* noir *m* de jais.

jet² *n.* **1.** jet *m* (d'eau, de vapeur, etc.); *Ph:* veine *f* fluide (d'eau, de gaz); **j. of flame,** jet, dard *m*, de flamme. **2.** (*a*) ajutage *m*, jet (de tuyau d'arrosage, etc.); **spreader j.,** jet en éventail; (*b*) *I.C.E:* **(carburettor) j.,** gicleur *m*; (*c*) brûleur *m* (de foyer à mazout). **3.** *Metall:* (*a*) trou *m* de coulée; (*b*) jet de coulée (attenant à une pièce); coulée *f*. **4.** *I.C.E: etc:* (*a*) buse *f*, tuyère *f* (d'éjection des gaz); (*b*) jet (de gaz d'échappement); gaz *mpl* d'échappement; **j. propulsion,** propulsion *f* par réaction; (*c*) *Av: etc:* **j. engine,** moteur *m* à réaction; réacteur *m*; **j.-propelled aircraft, j. (plane),** avion *m* à réaction, *F:* jet; **j. liner,** avion commercial, de ligne, à réaction; **j. fighter,** chasseur *m* à réaction. **5.** *Meteor:* **j. stream,** jet-stream *m*, courant-jet *m*. **6. the j. set,** le monde des play-boys internationaux.

jet³ *v.* **(jetted; jetting)** **1.** *v.i.* (*of fluid*) s'élancer en jet. **2.** *v.tr.* (*a*) faire gicler (un fluide); (*b*) émettre un jet de (fluide). **3.** *v.i. F:* faire un voyage en avion à réaction, en jet.

jetsam [ˈdʒetsəm] *n. Jur:* **1.** marchandise jetée à la mer (pour alléger le navire). **2.** épaves jetées à la côte.

jettison [ˈdʒetis(ə)n] *v.tr.* **(jettisoned)** (*a*) *Jur: Nau:* jeter à la mer, se délester de (la cargaison); (*b*) *Av:* larguer par-dessus bord (des bombes, du carburant, etc.); (*c*) abandonner, renoncer à (un espoir, etc.).

jetty [ˈdʒeti] *n.* (*a*) jetée *f*, môle *m*; (*b*) **landing j.,** embarcadère *m*, débarcadère *m*.

Jew [dʒuː] *n.* **1.** juif *m*; **the Wandering J.,** le Juif errant. **2.** *Mus:* **Jew's harp,** guimbarde *f*.

jewel¹ [ˈdʒuːəl] *n.* **1.** (*a*) bijou *m*, joyau *m*; **j. case,** coffret *m*, écrin *m*, à bijoux; *F:* **she's a j.,** c'est une perle, un trésor; (*b*) **jewels,** pierres précieuses; gemmes *fpl*. **2.** *Clockm:* rubis *m*.

jewel² *v.tr.* **(jewelled,** *NAm:* **jeweled)** **1.** orner, parer, (qn) de bijoux. **2.** *Clockm:* monter (un rouage) sur rubis. **jewelled,** *NAm:* **jeweled** *a.* **1.** orné, paré, de bijoux. **2.** *Clockm:* monté sur rubis; à rubis.

jeweller, *NAm:* **jeweler** [ˈdʒuːələr] *n.* bijoutier *m*, joaillier *m*; **jeweller's (shop),** bijouterie *f*.

jewel(le)ry [ˈdʒuːəlri] *n.* bijoux *mpl;* bijouterie *f*, joaillerie *f*.

Jewess [ˈdʒuːes, -is] *n.f.* Juive.

Jewish [ˈdʒuːiʃ] *a.* juif, *f.* juive.

Jewry [ˈdʒuəri] *n.* la communauté juive; les Juifs.

jib¹ [dʒib] *n.* **1.** *Nau:* foc *m*; **storm j.,** trinquette *f*, tourmentin *m*; **j. boom,** bout-dehors *m*, *pl.* bouts-dehors, de foc. **2.** *Mec.E:* **(crane) j., derrick j.,** flèche *f*, bras *m* (de grue).

jib² *v.i.* **(jibbed)** (*a*) (*of horse*) regimber (**at sth.,** devant qch.); refuser; se dérober; (*b*) (*of pers.*) se regimber;

to j. at sth., regimber contre qch.; **to j. at doing sth.,** rechigner, répugner, à faire qch.

jibe¹ [dʒaib] *n.* & *v.* = GIBE¹,².

jibe² *v.i. NAm:* s'accorder (**with,** avec).

jiffy ['dʒifi] *n. F:* **in (half) a j.,** en un instant; en moins de rien; en un clin d'œil.

jig¹ [dʒig] *n.* **1.** *Danc: Mus:* gigue *f.* **2.** (*a*) *Mec.E:* calibre *m*, gabarit *m* (de forme, de réglage, etc.) montage *m*; (*b*) *Mch.Tls:* **j. drill,** machine *f* à pointer et à percer.

jig² *v.* **(jigged) 1.** *v.i.* (*a*) danser la gigue; (*b*) *F:* sautiller; **to j. up and down,** se trémousser (en dansant). **2.** *v.tr.* (*a*) secouer légèrement; (*b*) *Min:* cribler, sasser (le minerai); (*c*) *Mec.E:* travailler sur montage, sur gabarit.

jigger¹ ['dʒigər] *n.* **1.** danseur, -euse, de gigue. **2.** (*a*) *F:* machin *m*, truc *m*, chose *f*; (*b*) *El: W.Tel:* jigger *m*; transformateur *m* d'oscillations. **3.** *Min:* (*a*) (*pers.*) cribleur, -euse; (*b*) crible *m* (pour minerai); (*dry*) sasseur *m*; (*c*) tenaille *f* d'accrochage; pince *f* d'accrochage (de wagon). **4.** *Nau:* (*tackle*) palan *m* à fouet; cartahu *m.*

jigger² *n. Ent:* puce pénétrante, *F:* chique *f.*

jigger³ *v.tr. F: O:* (*used only in passive*) **well, I'm jiggered!** (i) pas possible! (ii) zut alors!

jiggery-pokery ['dʒigəri'poukəri] *n. F:* manigances *fpl*, micmacs *mpl.*

jiggle ['dʒigl] *v.tr.* & *i.* secouer, balancer, légèrement.

jigsaw ['dʒigsɔː] *n. Carp:* scie *f* à chantourner; scie anglaise; sauteuse *f*; *Games:* **j. (puzzle),** puzzle *m.*

jilt [dʒilt] *v.tr.* laisser tomber, *F:* plaquer (un amoureux).

Jim [dʒim] *Pr.n.m.* **1.** (*dim. of James*) Jacquot, Jim. **2.** *U.S: F:* **J. Crow,** (i) *Pej:* nègre *m*; (ii) *Hist:* politique *f* raciste.

jim-jams ['dʒimdʒæmz] *n.pl. F:* **to have the j.-j.,** avoir le frisson; avoir les nerfs en pelote.

Jimmy ['dʒimi] **1.** *Pr.n.m.* (*dim. of James*) Jacquot, Jimmy. **2.** *NAm:Tls:* pince-monseigneur *f*, pl. pinces-monseigneur.

jingle¹ ['dʒiŋgl] *n.* (*a*) tintement *m* (d'un grelot, etc.); bruit *m* d'anneaux; cliquetis *m* (de fourchettes, de verres, etc.); (*b*) petit couplet; *Com:* **(advertising) j.,** ritournelle *f* publicitaire.

jingle² **1.** *v.i.* (*of bells*) tinter, tintinnabuler; (*of keys, etc.*) cliqueter. **2.** *v.tr.* faire tinter (des grelots, etc.); faire sonner (son argent); agiter (ses clefs).

jingo ['dʒiŋgou] *int. O:* **by j.!** nom de nom! **by j., you're right!** tiens! mais vous avez raison!

jingoism ['dʒiŋgouizm] *n.* chauvinisme *m.*

jingoistic [dʒiŋgou'istik] *a.* chauvin(iste).

jinks [dʒiŋks] *n.pl. F:* **high j.,** rigolade *f.*

jinx¹ [dʒiŋks] *n. F:* **1.** porte-malheur *m inv.* **2.** maléfice *m*; **to break the j.,** échapper à la guigne.

jinx² *v.tr. F:* porter malheur, porter la guigne, à (qn); **to be jinxed,** avoir la guigne.

jitney ['dʒitni] *n. U.S:* **1.** pièce *f* de cinq cents. **2. j. (bus),** autobus *m* à itinéraire fixe et à prix modique.

jitter ['dʒitər] *n. F:* **the jitters,** la frousse; **to give s.o. the jitters,** flanquer la trouille à qn.

jittery ['dʒitəri] *a. F:* **to be j.,** avoir la frousse.

jiu-jitsu [dʒuː'dʒitsuː] *n.* jiu-jitsu *m.*

jive¹ [dʒaiv] *n. Danc:* jive *m.*

jive² *v.i. Danc:* faire du jive.

Joan [dʒoun] *Pr.n.f.* Jeanne; **J. of Arc,** Jeanne d'Arc.

job¹ [dʒɔb] *n.* **1.** tâche *f*, besogne *f*, ouvrage *m*; travail *m* (particulier); (*a*) **to do a j.,** exécuter un travail, faire une besogne; **my special j. is to . . .,** je m'occupe surtout de . . ., mon rôle consiste surtout à . . .; *F:* (*child's language*) **to do a big j.,** faire caca; **materials fit, unfit, for the j.,** matériaux *m* propres, impropres, à cet usage; **odd jobs,** petits travaux; bricoles *fpl*; **odd-j. man,** homme à tout faire; **j. worker,** ouvrier, -ière, aux pièces, à la tâche; (*b*) *Ind:* opération *f*; travail (particulier); **precision j.,** travail de précision; **j. specification,** données *fpl* d'exécution; **to be on the j.,** (i) être sur le tas; (ii) travailler avec acharnement, d'arrache-pied; **on-the-j. training,** apprentissage *m*, formation *f*, sur le tas; (*c*) **to make a good, a bad, j. of sth.,** bien faire, réussir, qch.; mal faire, *F:* bousiller, qch.; **it's a good j. that . . .,** il est fort heureux que . . .; **that's a good j.! and a good j. too!** tant mieux! à la bonne heure! **to give sth. up as a bad j.,** renoncer à faire qch.; y renoncer; (*d*) *Cmptr:* travail, job *m*; **j. scheduler,** programmateur *m* de travaux; (*e*) *F:* **my new car's a lovely j.,** ma nouvelle voiture, c'est du beau travail; **that's just the j.,** ça fait juste l'affaire; (*f*) tâche difficile; corvée *f*; **I had a j. to do it,** j'ai eu du mal à le faire; (*g*) **this pin isn't good enough for the j.,** cette goupille ne tiendra pas le coup; **the pill did its j.,** la pilule a fait son travail. **2.** emploi *m*, poste *m*; situation *f*; *F:* boulot *m*, job; **to look for a j.,** chercher un emploi, du travail; **to be out of a j.,** chômer; être en chômage; *Adm:* **j. description,** description *f* de la fonction; **he knows his j.,** il connaît son métier; il s'y entend; **every man to his j.,** (à) chacun son métier. **3.** *Com:* **j. lot,** soldes *mpl*; articles *mpl*, marchandises *fpl*, d'occasion; articles dépareillés; **to buy a j. lot of books,** acheter des livres en vrac. **4.** (i) intrigue *f*; (ii) affaire illégale, *esp.* cambriolage *m*; **put-up j.,** coup monté; **inside j.,** cambriolage perpétré avec des complices intérieurs. **5.** *Typ:* **j. (printing, work),** travail, -aux, de ville; **j. printer,** imprimeur *m* de travaux de ville.

job² *v.* **(jobbed) 1.** *v.i.* (*a*) faire des petits travaux; bricoler; (*b*) travailler à la tâche, à la pièce; (*c*) *St.Exch:* agioter, spéculer; (*d*) intriguer, tripoter. **2.** *v.tr.* (*a*) *F:* exécuter (une tâche); (*b*) *St.Exch:* **to j. shares,** faire le négoce (en bourse) d'actions (en gros et en détail). **jobbing 1.** *a.* qui travaille à la tâche, à la pièce; **j. tailor,** tailleur *m* à façon; **j. gardener,** jardinier *m* à la journée. **2.** *n.* (*a*) ouvrage *m* à la tâche; *Tail:* travail *m* à façon; (*b*) *St.Exch:* (i) courtage *m* (de titres en gros et en détail); *Pej:* **stock j.,** agiotage *m*; (ii) **j. in contangoes,** arbitrage *m* de reports.

Job³ [dʒoub] *Pr.n.m.* Job; **Job's comforter,** consolateur *m* pessimiste; ami *m* de Job.

jobber ['dʒɔbər] *n.* **1.** ouvrier, -ière, à la tâche. **2.** *St.Exch:* **(stock) j.,** marchand *m* de titres (en gros et en détail qui exécute les ordres que lui donnent les agents de change).

jobless ['dʒɔblis] *a.* sans travail; en chômage; *n.pl.* **the j.,** les chômeurs *mpl*; les sans-travail *mpl.*

Jock [dʒɔk] **1.** *Pr.n.m.* (*dim. of John*) *Scot:* Jean. **2.** *n.* Écossais *m.*

jockey¹ ['dʒɔki] *n.* (*a*) *Turf:* jockey *m*; **amateur j.,** gentleman-rider *m*, *pl.* gentlemen-riders; **j. cap,** casquette *f* de jockey; (*b*) *T.V: etc:* **disc j.,** présentateur *m* de disques.

jockey² **1.** *v.tr.* (*a*) tromper, duper (qn); **to j. s.o. out of sth.,** soutirer, escamoter, qch. à qn; **to j. s.o. into doing sth.,** amener sournoisement qn à faire qch.; (*b*) maquignonner (une affaire). **2.** *v.i.* (*a*) manœuvrer; (*b*) *Pej:* (*of pers.*) **to j. for a position,** intriguer pour se placer avantageusement.

jockstrap ['dʒɔkstræp] *n. Cost:* slip *m* de soutien (pour sportifs); support *m* athlétique.

jocose [dʒɔ'kous] *a.* facétieux; jovial, -aux. **-ly** *adv.* facétieusement; en plaisantant.

jocular ['dʒɔkjulər] *a.* facétieux, jovial, -aux; enjoué; **in a j. vein,** d'un ton rieur. **-ly** *adv.* facétieusement; jovialement.

jocund ['dʒɔkənd] *a. Lit:* jovial, -aux; enjoué.

jodhpurs ['dʒɔdpəːz] *n.pl. Cost:* pantalon *m*, culotte *f*, de cheval; jodhpurs *mpl*.

Joe [dʒou] **1.** *Pr.n.m.* (*dim. of Joseph*) Joseph. **2.** *n. F: esp. NAm:* homme *m*, type *m*.

jog¹ [dʒɔg] *n.* **1.** (*a*) coup *m* (de coude, etc.); (*b*) secousse *f*, cahot *m* (d'une voiture, etc.). **2.** petit trot; **to go along at an easy j.,** aller son petit bonhomme de chemin.

jog² *v.* **(jogged) 1.** *v.tr.* (*a*) pousser (d'un coup sec); **to j. s.o.'s elbow,** pousser le coude à qn; **to j. s.o.'s memory,** rafraîchir la mémoire de qn; (*b*) (*of vehicle*) secouer, cahoter (les voyageurs). **2.** *v.i.* (*a*) **to j. along,** (i) trottiner (à cheval); aller au petit trot; (ii) aller, faire, son petit bonhomme de chemin; (*b*) faire du jogging. **jogging** *n.* **1.** cahotage *m*, cahotement *m* (d'une voiture, etc.). **2.** (*a*) petit trot; (*b*) jogging *m*.

jogger ['dʒɔgər] *n.* joggeur *m*.

joggle¹ ['dʒɔgl] **1.** *v.tr. F:* secouer légèrement; **to j. sth. in, out,** faire entrer, sortir, qch. par petites secousses. **2.** *v.i.* (*a*) branler; (*b*) **to j. along,** (i) avancer par saccades; (ii) avancer cahin-caha.

joggle² *n.* légère secousse.

jogtrot ['dʒɔgtrɔt] *n.* (*a*) petit trot; **at a j.,** au petit trot; (*b*) vie routinière.

Johanna [dʒou'(h)ænə] *Pr.n.f.* Jeanne.

John [dʒɔn] **1.** *Pr.n.m.* Jean; **St J. the Baptist,** saint Jean-Baptiste. **2.** *Pr.n.m.* **J. Bull,** John Bull, l'Anglais typique; *F:* **J. Blunt,** l'homme qui dit carrément son fait. **3.** *n.* **j.,** *esp. U.S:* (*a*) *F:* homme *m*, type *m*; (*b*) *P:* client *m* d'une prostituée. **4.** *n.* (*a*) *Ich:* **J. Dory,** dorade *f*; (*b*) *F:* **J. Barleycorn,** le whisky; (*c*) *Cost: F:* **long johns,** caleçon long. **5.** *n. esp. NAm: F:* **the j.,** les cabinets *mpl*, les toilettes *fpl*.

Johnnie, Johnny ['dʒɔni] **1.** *Pr.n.m.* (*dim. of* **John**) Jeannot; *F:* **Johnny come lately,** nouveau venu. **2.** *n. F:* type *m*, individu *m*.

join¹ [dʒɔin] *n.* joint *m*, jointure *f*; soudure *f* (d'os, de chambre à air, etc.); ligne *f* de jonction (de deux feuilles d'une carte, etc.).

join² 1. *v.tr.* (*a*) joindre, unir, réunir (deux morceaux de drap, etc.); relier, assembler (deux madriers, etc.); rapprocher (les lèvres d'une plaie); souder (un os fracturé); **to j. (two things) end to end,** joindre (deux choses) bout à bout; ajoindre, rabouter, raboutir (des planches); raccorder (des tuyaux); **to j. sth. (on) to sth.,** rapporter, ajouter, attacher, qch. à qch.; **to j. hands with s.o.,** (i) prendre qn par la main; (ii) s'unir à qn, se joindre à qn (pour faire qch.); **joined in, by, marriage,** unis par le mariage; **to j. forces with s.o. in doing sth.,** se joindre à qn pour faire qch.; **to j. company with s.o.,** rejoindre qn; (*b*) ajouter; **the documents joined to the report,** les documents annexés au procès-verbal; (*c*) **straight line that joins two points,** droite *f* qui joint deux points. **2.** *v.tr.* (*a*) se joindre à, s'unir à (qn); rejoindre (qn); **will you j. us?** voulez-vous vous joindre à nous? **I will j. you at . . .,** je vous (re)joindrai à . . .; **to j. s.o. in sth.,** se joindre à qn dans (une entreprise, etc.); **to j. s.o. in a drink,** prendre un verre avec qn; (*b*) *Mil:* rallier, rejoindre (son unité); *Nau: Navy:* rejoindre (son navire); (*c*) entrer dans (un club, un régiment, etc.); adhérer à, s'affilier à (un parti); devenir membre (d'une société); s'inscrire pour (un cours du soir); s'engager dans (l'armée). **3.** *v.tr.* (*a*) se joindre, s'unir, à (qch.); **the place where the footpath joins the road,** l'endroit *m* où le sentier rejoint la route; (*b*) **to be joined to, to j., sth.,** être contigu à qch.; **in the past England was joined to France,** dans le passé l'Angleterre tenait à la France. **4.** *v.i.* se joindre, se rejoindre, s'unir (**with s.o., sth.,** à qn, qch.); **to j. together,** (*of thgs*) se souder; (*of pers.*) se réunir (pour faire qch.); **to j. with s.o. in doing sth.,** se joindre à qn pour faire qch. **join in** *v.i.* se mettre de la partie; s'associer, s'affilier à (un projet, etc.); prendre part à (une querelle, etc.); **to j. in (the singing),** participer (au chant); **to j. in the protest,** joindre sa voix aux protestations. **joining** *n.* **1.** (*a*) jonction *f*, (ré)union *f*, assemblement *m*, assemblage *m* (des morceaux de qch., etc.); suture *f* (d'os, etc.); liaison *f* (de sons, etc.); (*b*) *El:* **j. up,** connexion *f*. **2.** entrée (dans un club, etc.); **j. up,** engagement *m* (dans l'armée).

joinder ['dʒɔindər] *n.* réunion *f*, union *f*; *esp. Jur:* **j. of actions,** jonction *f* d'instances.

joiner ['dʒɔinər] *n.* menuisier *m*.

joinery ['dʒɔinəri] *n.* menuiserie *f*.

joint¹ [dʒɔint] *n.* **1.** (*a*) joint *m*, jointure *f*; *Mec.E: etc:* **soldered, welded, j.,** soudure *f*; (*b*) *El:* épissure *f*; **j. box,** boîte *f* de jonction (de câbles); (*c*) *Mec.E: etc:* **hinged j.,** articulation *f*, assemblage, à charnière; **universal j.,** joint universel; **toggle j.,** genouillère *f*; (*d*) *Bookb:* mors *m*; (*e*) *Carp:* assemblage, empatture *f*; **dovetail j.,** assemblage à queue d'aronde. **2.** *Anat:* (point *m* d')articulation; joint, jointure (du genou, etc.); **hip j.,** articulation de la hanche; **rheumatism in, of, the joints,** rhumatisme *m* articulaire; **out of j.,** (i) (bras, etc.) disloqué, démis; (ii) *F:* (système, mécanisme, etc.) désorganisé, dérangé, détraqué; **to put one's arm out of j.,** se démettre le bras; *F:* **to put s.o.'s nose out of j.,** jouer un mauvais tour à qn; dépiter qn. **3.** (*a*) partie *f* (du corps, d'une chose articulée) entre deux articulations; virole *f*, phalange *f* (du doigt); (*b*) *Cu:* morceau *m*, quartier *m*, de viande; **(roast) j.,** rôti *m*; **cut off the j.,** tranche *f* de rôti. **4.** *Bot:* nœud *m*, articulation (de tige). **5.** *P:* (*a*) endroit *m*; boîte *f*; **gambling j.,** tripot *m*; (*b*) (*drug*) joint.

joint² *v.tr.* **1.** (*a*) joindre, assembler (des pièces de bois, etc.); emmancher (des tuyaux, etc.); (*b*) articuler; **bone that is jointed with another,** os *m* qui s'articule avec un autre. **2.** découper, dépecer (un poulet, etc.). **3.** *Const:* jointoyer (un mur, etc.). **4.** *Carp:* varloper (deux planches, etc.). **jointed** *a.* (*a*) articulé; jointif; (canne) jointée; *Bot:* (tige) articulé; (*b*) (poulet, etc.) dépecé.

joint³ *a.* **1.** (*of work, etc.*) commun, combiné, coordonné; (efforts) réunis, en commun; (action) combinée, collective; (rapport) collectif; (commission) mixte; (entreprise) en participation; *Bank:* (compte) conjoint; *Fin:* **j. stock,** capital social; **j. stock bank,** société *f* de dépot. **2.** co-, associé; **j. author,** coauteur *m*; **j. director,** codirecteur; **j. heir,** cohéritier *m*; **j. holder,** codétenteur, -trice; **j. owner,** copropriétaire *mf*; **j. ownership,** copropriété *f*; **j.tenancy,** location indivise. **-ly** *adv.* ensemble, conjointement; **to inherit j.,** copartager une succession; *Jur:* **j. liable, responsible,** solidaire; **acting j.,** agissant solidairement; **j. and severally liable,** responsables conjointement et solidairement.

joist [dʒɔist] *n. Const:* solive *f*, soliveau *m*, poutre *f*, poutrelle *f*; **floor j.,** lambourde *f*, gîte *m*, de plancher.

joke¹ [dʒouk] *n.* (*a*) plaisanterie *f*, farce *f*, *F:* blague *f*; **to say, do, sth. for a j.,** dire, faire, qch. par plaisanterie, pour rire; **to make a j. of everything,** tourner tout en badinage, en blague; **the j. is that . . .,** le comique de l'histoire, c'est que . . .; **it's no j. waiting for hours,** ce n'est pas amusant d'attendre des heures; **practical j.,** tour *m*; **to play a practical j. on s.o.,** faire une farce à qn; jouer un tour à qn; **the joke's on me,** c'est à vous, à eux, de rire; (*b*) bon mot; facétie *f*, plaisanterie; **he is always ready with a j.,** il a toujours le mot pour rire; (*c*) sujet *m* de plaisanterie; risée *f*; **he's the j. of the town,** il est en butte aux railleries de toute la ville.

joke² 1. *v.i.* plaisanter, railler, badiner; **to j. at, about, sth.,** plaisanter de qch.; **I was only joking,** ce n'était qu'une plaisanterie; **you're joking! you must be,** *F:*

you've got to be, joking! vous voulez rire! **I'm not joking,** je ne plaisante pas; **to j. with s.o.,** plaisanter avec qn. **2.** *v.tr.* plaisanter, railler (qn); se moquer de (qn). **joking 1.** *a.* (ton, air) moqueur, de plaisanterie. **2.** *n.* plaisanterie *f*, badinage *m*. **jokingly** *adv.* en plaisantant; pour rire.

joker [ˈdʒoukər] *n.* **1.** farceur, -euse; plaisant *m*; *F:* blagueur, -euse. **2.** *F: Pej:* type *m*, individu *m*. **3.** *Cards:* joker *m*. **4.** *NAm: F:* (i) échappatoire *f*; (ii) subtilité *f*.

jollification [dʒɔlifiˈkeiʃ(ə)n] *n. F:* réunion joyeuse, gaie; partie *f* de plaisir.

jollity [ˈdʒɔliti] *n.* gaieté *f*.

jolly¹ [ˈdʒɔli] **1.** *a.* (*pers.*) joyeux, gai. **2.** *adv. F:* rudement; **I'll take j. good care,** je ferai rudement attention; **and a j. good job too!** tant mieux (pour ça)! **he did it j. quickly,** il l'a fait drôlement vite.

jolly² *v.tr.* plaisanter, railler (qn); **to j. s.o. along,** encourager qn par des plaisanteries, des flatteries.

jolly³ *n. Nau:* **j. (boat),** (petit) canot (à bord d'un navire).

jolt¹ [dʒoult] *n.* **1.** (*a*) cahot *m*, choc *m*, secousse *f*; (*b*) *Mec.E:* à-coup *m*, *pl.* à-coups; *Aut:* coup *m* de raquette. **2.** surprise *f*, choc; **it gave me a bit of a j.,** ça m'a donné un coup; ça m'a fait quelque chose.

jolt² **1.** *v.tr.* cahoter, ballotter, secouer; **to be jolted,** être cahoté; subir des chocs. **2.** *v.i.* (*a*) (*of vehicle*) cahoter, ballotter; **to j. along,** avancer avec des cahots, en cahotant; (*b*) *Mec.E:* avoir, donner, des à-coups; *Aut:* donner des coups de raquette. **jolting 1.** *a.* cahotant. **2.** *n.* (*a*) cahotement *m*, ballottement *m*; (*b*) *Mec.E:* à-coups *mpl*; *Aut:* coups *mpl* de raquette.

Jonah [ˈdʒounə] **1.** *Pr.n.m. B.Hist:* Jonas. **2.** *n.* guignard *m*, malchanceux *m*; porte-malheur *m inv*.

jonquil [ˈdʒɔŋkwil] **1.** *n. Bot:* jonquille *f*. **2.** *a. & n.* (couleur *f*) jonquille (*m*) *inv*.

Jordan [ˈdʒɔːd(ə)n] *Pr.n. Geog:* **1.** (*river*) le Jourdain. **2.** (*country*) Jordanie *f*.

Joseph [ˈdʒouzif] *Pr.n.m.* Joseph.

Josephine [ˈdʒouzifiːn] *Pr.n.f.* Joséphine.

josh [dʒɔʃ] *v.tr. NAm: F:* railler (qn); taquiner (qn).

joss [dʒɔs] *n.* (*in China*) idole *f*; **j. house,** temple (chinois); **j. stick,** bâton *m* d'encens.

jostle¹ [ˈdʒɔsl] *n.* bousculade *f*, presse *f* (d'une foule).

jostle² **1.** *v.i.* jouer des coudes; **to j. against s.o.,** bousculer qn; **to j. (one's way) to the front,** jouer des coudes pour arriver au premier rang. **2.** *v.tr.* (*a*) bousculer, coudoyer (qn); **to be jostled by the crowd,** être bousculé par la foule; **to j. s.o. out of the way,** écarter qn en jouant des coudes; (*b*) *Rac:* serrer (un concurrent). **jostling** *n.* **1.** = JOSTLE¹. **2.** *Rac:* action *f* de serrer un concurrent.

jot¹ [dʒɔt] *n.* (*a*) *A:* iota *m*; (*b*) **not a j.,** pas un iota.

jot² *v.tr.* **(jotted) to j. sth. down,** noter qch.; prendre note de qch.; prendre qch. en note. **jotting** *n.* **1. j. down,** prise *f* (d'une note). **2. jottings,** notes *fpl*; mémorandum *m*.

jotter [ˈdʒɔtər] *n.* bloc-notes *m*, *pl.* bloc-notes.

journal [ˈdʒəːn(ə)l] *n.* **1.** journal, -aux *m*; *Nau:* journal de bord; *Book-k:* (livre) journal. **2.** journal; feuille (quotidienne); revue (savante). **3.** *Mec.E:* tourillon *m* (d'arbre); fusée *f* (d'essieu); **j. bearing,** palier *m*.

journalese [dʒəːnəˈliːz] *n. F:* style *m* de journaliste, de journal.

journalism [ˈdʒəːnəlizm] *n.* journalisme *m*.

journalist [ˈdʒəːnəlist] *n.* journaliste *mf*.

journalistic [dʒəːnəˈlistik] *a.* journalistique.

journey¹, *pl.* **-eys** [ˈdʒəːni, -iz] *n.* voyage *m*; trajet *m*; parcours *m* (entre deux endroits); **return j.,** *Nau: Av:* **inward j.,** (voyage de) retour *m*; *Nau: Av:* **outward j.,** (voyage d')aller *m*; **to go on, make, undertake, a j.,** faire un voyage; voyager; **bus j.,** trajet d'autobus.

journey² *v.i.* **(journeyed; journeying)** voyager.

journeyman, *pl.* **-men** [ˈdʒəːnimən] *n. Ind:* compagnon *m*; **j. carpenter,** compagnon charpentier.

joust¹ [dʒaust] *n.* joute *f*.

joust² *v.i.* jouter.

Jove [dʒouv] *Pr.n.m.* Jupiter; *F: O:* **by J.!** (i) parbleu! (ii) mâtin! nom d'un tonnerre!

jovial [ˈdʒouvjəl] *a.* jovial, -aux; enjoué; **he's in a j. mood today,** il est de bonne humeur aujourd'hui. **-ally** *adv.* jovialement.

joviality [dʒouviˈæliti] *n.* jovialité *f*, enjouement *m*.

jowl [dʒaul] *n.* (*a*) mâchoire *f*; (*b*) joue *f*, bajoue *f* (d'homme, de porc, etc.); (*c*) fanon *m* (de bœuf, de dindon); jabot *m* (d'oiseau); (*d*) hure *f*, tête *f* (de saumon, d'esturgeon, etc.).

joy [dʒɔi] *n.* joie *f*, allégresse *f*; **to be full of j.,** être plein de joie; **to leap for j.,** sauter de joie; *F:* **any j.?** ça a marché? *F:* **no j.!** pas de chance! **a thing that is a j. to see,** une chose qui fait plaisir à voir; (*also Iron:*) **I wish you j. of it!** je vous en félicite!

joyful [ˈdʒɔif(u)l] *a.* joyeux, heureux; (*a*) **to be j.,** être allègre, être en joie, être plein de joie; (*b*) **j. news,** bonnes nouvelles. **-fully** *adv.* joyeusement, allégrement.

joyous [ˈdʒɔiəs] *a.* joyeux, heureux; (*of pers.*) allègre. **-ly** *adv.* joyeusement.

joyride [ˈdʒɔiraid] *n. F:* balade *f* en voiture (parfois volée).

joystick [ˈdʒɔistik] *n. Av:* levier *m* de commande; *F:* manche *m* à balai.

jubilant [ˈdʒuːbilənt] *a.* (*a*) (*of pers.*) réjoui (**at sth.,** de qch.); exultant; (*b*) (cri, etc.) joyeux, de joie; (visage) épanoui. **-ly** *adv.* avec joie.

jubilation [dʒuːbiˈleiʃ(ə)n] *n.* (*a*) joie *f*, allégresse *f*; exultation *f*; jubilation *f*; (*b*) réjouissance *f*, fête *f*.

jubilee [ˈdʒuːbiliː] *n.* **1.** *Jew.Rel: R.C.Ch:* jubilé *m*. **2.** jubilé; (fête *f* du) cinquantième anniversaire *m* (d'un événement); **silver, golden, diamond, j.,** fête du vingt-cinquième, cinquantième, soixantième, anniversaire (du couronnement d'un souverain, etc.).

Judaea [dʒuːˈdiə] *Pr.n. B.Geog:* Judée *f*.

Judah [ˈdʒuːdə] *Pr.n. B. Hist:* Juda *m*.

Judaic [dʒuːˈdeiik] *a.* judaïque.

Judaism [ˈdʒuːdeiizm] *n.* judaïsme *m*.

Judas [ˈdʒuːdəs] **1.** *Pr.n.m. B.Hist:* **J. (Iscariot),** Judas (Iscariot(e)); **J. kiss,** baiser *m* de Judas. **2.** *n.* (*a*) judas *m*, traître *m*; (*b*) **j. (hole, trap),** judas (dans une porte); *Bot:* **J. tree,** arbre *m* de Judée; arbre d'amour.

judder¹ [ˈdʒʌdər] *n. Aut:* trépidation *f* (du frein, etc.).

judder² *v.i.* (*of brakes, etc.*) trépider; (*of tool*) brouter.

judge¹ [dʒʌdʒ] *n.* **1.** (*a*) juge *m*; **presiding j.,** président *m* du tribunal; **the judges,** la magistrature assise; (*b*) *U.S:* magistrat *m*. **2.** *Sp: etc:* arbitre *m*, juge; *Rac:* commissaire *m* à l'arrivée; membre *m* du jury (d'une exposition canine, etc.). **3.** connaisseur, -euse; **to be a good j. of wine,** s'y connaître, s'y entendre, en vin.

judge² *v.tr.* **1.** (*a*) juger (un prisonnier, une affaire); **a man is judged by his actions,** un homme se juge par ses actions; (*b*) **to j. others by oneself,** mesurer les autres à son aune; **to j. sth. by sth. else,** juger qch. sur qch.; **judging by . . .,** à en juger par . . .; (*c*) *v.i.* arbitrer (à un comice agricole, etc.); faire fonction de juge. **2.** apprécier, estimer (une distance, etc.); **to j. distance by the eye,** mesurer la distance à la vue. **3. to j. it necessary to do sth.,** juger nécessaire de faire qch.; **it is for you to j.,** c'est à vous d'en juger; **j. for yourself,** jugez(-en) par vous-même.

judg(e)ment ['dʒʌdʒmənt] *n.* jugement *m.* **1.** (*a*) **the Last J., J. day,** le jugement dernier; **to sit in j. on s.o.,** juger qn; se poser en juge de qn; (*b*) décision *f* judiciaire; arrêt *m* (d'une cour de cassation, etc.); sentence *f* (d'une cour inférieure); **to pass, give, deliver, j.,** prononcer, rendre, un jugement; statuer sur une affaire; **it is not for me to pass j. on him,** ce n'est pas à moi de le juger; **it is a j. on you, on him,** (i) c'est le doigt de Dieu! (ii) *F:* ça vous, lui, apprendra! **2.** opinion *f*, avis *m*; **to give one's j. on sth.,** exprimer son avis, son sentiment, sur qch.; **against our better j.,** contrairement à notre opinion délibérée. **3.** bons sens; discernement *m*; **to have a sound, clear, good, j.,** avoir le jugement sain, le sens droit; **to show (sound) j.,** montrer du jugement.

judicature ['dʒu:dikətjər] *n.* **1.** judicature *f*; **court of j.,** cour *f* de justice. **2.** période *f* d'exercice (d'un juge). **3.** *coll.* la magistrature.

judicial [dʒu'diʃ(ə)l] *a.* **1.** (*a*) judiciaire; juridique; **j. inquiry,** enquête *f* judiciaire; **j. murder,** assassinat légal, juridique; (*b*) **to be invested with j. powers,** être investi de pouvoirs judiciaires. **2.** (*a*) impartial; **j. fairness,** impartialité *f*; (*b*) **j. faculty,** faculté *f* judiciaire; sens *m* critique.

judiciary [dʒu'diʃiəri] **1.** *a.* judiciaire. **2.** *n.* la magistrature; **officials of the j.,** fonctionnaires *mpl* de l'ordre judiciaire.

judicious [dʒu'diʃəs] *a.* (*of pers., thought, etc.*) judicieux; d'un jugement sain, sensé; (politique) sage. **-ly** *adv.* judicieusement.

judiciousness [dʒu'diʃəsnis] *n.* discernement *m*; bon sens.

judo ['dʒu:dou] *n.* judo *m.*

Judy ['dʒu:di] *Pr.n.f.* **1.** *F:* Judith. **2.** (*a*) la femme de Guignol, de Polichinelle; (*b*) *n.f. F:* femme, fille.

jug¹ [dʒʌg] *n.* **1.** (*a*) cruche *f*, broc *m*; (*for milk, etc.*) pot *m*; pichet *m*; (*b*) (*jug and contents*) **j. of milk,** pot de lait; **j. of wine,** pichet de vin. **2.** *F:* prison *f*, taule *f*; **to put s.o. in j.,** mettre qn dedans.

jug² *v.tr.* **(jugged) 1.** *Cu:* étuver, braiser; **jugged hare** = civet *m* de lièvre. **2.** *F:* emprisonner (qn).

Juggernaut ['dʒʌgənɔ:t] *n.* **1.** *Rel.H:* Jaggernath *m.* **2. j.,** (*a*) poids écrasant; force meurtrière; (*b*) *Veh:* mastodonte *m* (de la route).

juggins ['dʒʌginz] *n. F:* idiot, -ote; cruche *f*.

juggle¹ ['dʒʌgl] *n.* **1.** (*a*) jonglerie *f*; (*b*) tour *m* de passe-passe. **2.** *F:* supercherie *f*, fourberie *f*.

juggle² *v.i.* jongler (avec des boules, etc.); **to j. with figures, with words,** jongler avec les chiffres, avec les mots. **juggling** *n.* jonglerie *f*.

juggler ['dʒʌglər] *n.* **1.** (*a*) jongleur, -euse; (*b*) prestidigitateur *m.* **2.** *F:* homme *m* de mauvaise foi.

jugular ['dʒʌgjulər] *a.* & *n. Anat:* jugulaire (*f*).

juice¹ [dʒu:s] *n.* **1.** jus *m*, suc *m*, pressis *m* (de la viande, d'un fruit); eau *f* (d'un fruit); **fruit j.,** jus de fruit(s); *Physiol:* **gastric j.,** suc gastrique. **2.** suc, sève *f* (d'une science, d'un récit). **3.** *F:* jus, (i) *Aut:* essence *f*, (ii) *El:* courant *m.*

juice² *v.tr.* extraire le jus (des fruits).

juicer ['dʒu:sər] *n. U.S:* presse-fruits *m inv.*

juiciness ['dʒu:sinis] *n.* nature juteuse, succulence *f* (d'un fruit, etc.).

juicy ['dʒu:si] *a.* **1.** (*a*) succulent, juteux; fondant; (rôti) qui jute; (*b*) *F:* (*of pipe*) **to get j.,** super. **2.** (*a*) *U.S:* (temps) pluvieux; (*b*) (récit, style) savoureux; (*c*) *F:* **a nice j. scandal,** un scandale tout juteux.

jukebox ['dʒu:kbɔks] *n.* juke-box *m.*

julep ['dʒu:lep] *n.* **1.** *Pharm:* julep *m.* **2. (mint) j.,** whisky frappé à la menthe.

Julian¹ ['dʒu:ljən] *Pr.n.m. Ecc.Hist:* Julien.

Julian² *a.* Julien, de Jules César.

Juliet ['dʒu:liet] *Pr.n.f.* Juliette.

Julius ['dʒu:liəs] *Pr.n.m.* Jules; **J. Caesar,** Jules César.

July, *pl.* **-ys** [dʒu'lai, -aiz] *n.* juillet *m*; **in (the month of) J.,** en juillet; au mois de juillet; **(on) the first, seventh, of J.,** le premier, le sept, juillet.

jumble¹ ['dʒʌmbl] *n.* **1.** brouillamini *m*, pêle-mêle *m*, méli-mélo *m*, fouillis *m* (d'objets hétéroclites); entremêlement *m*, embrouillement *m* (d'idées); enchevêtrement *m* (de mots). **2.** objets usagés, de rebut; **j. sale,** vente *f* de charité (d'objets usagés).

jumble² **1.** *v.tr.* brouiller, mêler confusément, mettre pêle-mêle; **to j. everything up, together,** tout mettre en salade. **2.** *v.i.* se mêler confusément, se brouiller.

jumbo ['dʒʌmbou] *n. F:* **1.** (*a*) éléphant; (*b*) (*nickname for fat pers.*) gros lourdaud; = Patapouf. **2.** *a.* énorme; colossal, -aux; *a.* & *n. R.t.m.* **J. (jet),** (avion) gros porteur.

jump¹ [dʒʌmp] *n.* **1.** (*a*) saut *m*, bond *m*; **to take a j.,** faire un saut; sauter; *Sp:* **high j.,** saut en hauteur; **long j.,** saut en longueur; **j. suit,** combinaison *f* (de saut, etc.); cotte *f*; **to be a j. ahead of s.o.,** devancer qn; prendre l'avantage sur qn; *F:* **he's for the high j.!** qu'est-ce qu'il va prendre! *P:* **go (and) take a running j. (at yourself)!** va te faire voir! va te faire foutre! **j. in prices,** brusque hausse *f* des prix; (*b*) lacune *f*, vide *m* (dans une série, etc.). **2.** sursaut *m*, haut-le-corps *m inv*; **that gave me a j.,** cela m'a fait sursauter. **3.** *Tchn:* anomalie *f* (dans un processus, etc.). **4.** *Turf: Equit:* obstacle *m*; **to put a horse over a j.,** faire sauter un obstacle à son cheval.

jump² **I.** *v.i.* **1.** (*a*) sauter; bondir; *Av:* sauter (en parachute); (*to dog*) **j.!** allons, hop! houp là! **to j. for joy,** sauter de joie; **to j. at an offer, at the chance,** sauter sur une offre, l'occasion; *F:* **j. to it!** allez-y! grouillez-vous! **to j. from one subject to another,** sauter d'un sujet à un autre; **to j. to a conclusion,** arriver prématurément à une conclusion; **prices have jumped 10%,** les prix ont monté de 10% d'un coup; (*b*) **to j. over a hedge,** franchir, sauter par-dessus, une haie; **to j. off, down from, a wall,** sauter à bas d'un mur; **to j. down (on to the ground),** sauter à terre; *F:* **to j. down s.o.'s throat,** rembarrer, rabrouer, qn; *Aut: Rail:* **j. in!** montez (vite)! **to j. out of bed,** sauter à bas du lit; *F:* **I nearly jumped out of my skin,** cela m'a fait sursauter; (*c*) *El:* (*of spark*) jaillir. **2.** (*a*) sursauter, tressauter; **my heart jumped when I heard the news,** (i) mon cœur a bondi, (ii) j'ai eu un serrement de cœur, lorsque j'ai appris la nouvelle; (*b*) *Mec.E: etc:* (*of tool*) brouter. **II.** *v.tr.* **1.** (*a*) franchir, sauter (une haie, etc.); sauter (un passage d'un livre); (*of train*) **to j. the rails,** dérailler; **to j. the queue,** passer avant son tour, *F:* resquiller; *Aut: F:* **to j. the lights,** brûler, griller, le feu (rouge); *F:* **to j. the gun,** (i) *Sp:* voler le départ; (ii) commencer à faire quelque chose prématurément, avant son tour; (*b*) (*at draughts*) sauter (un pion). **2.** (*to cause to jump*) (*a*) faire sauter (un cheval); (*b*) **to j. a child (up and down) on one's knees,** faire sauter un enfant sur ses genoux. **3.** (*a*) saisir (qch.) à l'improviste; voler (qch.); *Min:* **to j. a claim,** s'emparer d'une concession (en l'absence de celui qui l'a délimitée); *F:* **to j. s.o.,** voler, rouler, qn; (*b*) *NAm:* **to j. a train,** (i) monter dans un, (ii) descendre d'un, train en marche. **jump back** *v.i.* sauter en arrière; reculer brusquement. **jumping 1.** *a.* sauteur, -euse; *Toys:* **j. jack,** pantin *m.* **2.** *n.* (*a*) (i) saut(s) *m(pl)*; bond(s) *m(pl)*; **j.-off place,** point *m* de départ (d'une expédition, etc.); (ii) *El:* jaillissement *m* (d'une étincelle); (iii) *Mec.E:* broutage *m* (d'un outil); (*b*) (i) franchissement *m* (d'une haie); *Equit:* monte *f* à l'obstacle; jumping *m*; *Turf:* **j. race,** course *f* d'obstacles; (ii) cahotage *m* (d'un appareil, etc.); (*c*) appropriation *f* (d'une concession, etc.). **jump off**

v.i. Equit: faire un barrage. **jump up** *v.i.* se (re)lever d'un saut; **j. up!** allons! debout!

jumped-up [ˈdʒʌmptˈʌp] *a. F:* parvenu.

jumper¹ [ˈdʒʌmpər] *n.* **1.** (*a*) (*pers.*) sauteur, -euse; *Sp:* **high, long, j.,** sauteur, -euse, en hauteur, en longueur; (*b*) *Equit:* jumper *m*; cheval *m* à obstacles. **2.** *Ent: F:* sauteur. **3.** *El: Tp: Tg:* cavalier *m*, bretelle *f*, liaison volante. **4.** *Min:* **j. (bar),** barre *f* de mine; fleuret *m*.

jumper² *n. Cost:* **1.** vareuse *f*, chemise *f* (de marin, etc.). **2.** tricot *m* (de femme), pull-over *m*, *F:* pull *m*. **3.** *NAm:* (*a*) robe *f* à bretelles, *Fr.C:* jumper *m*; (*b*) barboteuse *f* (pour enfants).

jumpiness [ˈdʒʌmpinis] *n. F:* **1.** nervosité *f*, agitation *f*. **2.** instabilité *f* (du marché, etc.).

jump-off [ˈdʒʌmpɔf] *n. Equit:* barrage *m*.

jumpy [ˈdʒʌmpi] *a. F:* **1.** (*of pers.*) agité, nerveux; **to be j.,** avoir les nerfs agacés, à vif. **2.** (*a*) (*of market, etc.*) instable; (*b*) (*of style*) sautillant, saccadé.

junction [ˈdʒʌŋ(k)ʃ(ə)n] *n.* **1.** jonction *f*; confluence *f* (de deux rivières, etc.); raccordement *m* (de tuyaux); *El:* connexion *f*, prise *f*, raccordement. **2.** (*a*) (point *m* de) jonction; carrefour *m*; embranchement *m*, bifurcation *f* (de route, de voie de chemin de fer); (*b*) *Rail:* gare *f* de jonction; (*c*) *Metalw: etc:* joint *m*, soudure *f*, raccord *m*; (*d*) *El:* **j. box,** boîte *f* de dérivation, de jonction.

juncture [ˈdʒʌŋ(k)tjər] *n.* **1.** jointure *f* (de deux plaques, etc.). **2.** conjoncture *f* (de circonstances); **at this j.,** (i) à ce moment (critique); en l'occurrence; (ii) dans les circonstances actuelles.

June [dʒuːn] *n.* juin *m*; **in (the month of) J.,** en juin, au mois de juin; **(on) the first, the seventh, of J.,** le premier, le sept, juin.

jungle [ˈdʒʌŋgl] *n.* jungle *f*, fourré *m*, brousse *f*; embrouillamini confus (de faits); **the law of the j.,** la loi de la jungle.

junior [ˈdʒuːnjər] *a. & n.* **1.** (*in age*) cadet, -ette; plus jeune; *Sp:* junior *m*; **he is three years my j., my j. by three years,** il est mon cadet de trois ans; il est plus jeune que moi de trois ans; **Martin J.,** Martin (i) le jeune, (ii) fils; *U.S:* **come on J.!** viens, mon fils! *Sch:* **j. school,** école *f* primaire; *Sp:* **j. event,** épreuve *f* des cadets. **2.** (*in rank*) moins ancien; subalterne (*m*); **j. partner,** associé en second, second associé, dernier associé; **j. officer,** officier *m* subalterne; *Jur:* **j. counsel,** avocat *m* en second.

juniper [ˈdʒuːnipər] *n. Bot:* **j. (tree),** genévrier *m*, genièvre *m*; *Pharm:* **j. oil,** essence *f* de genièvre.

junk¹ [dʒʌŋk] *n.* **1.** *a* (choses *fpl* de) rebut (*m*); déchet *m*; bric-à-brac *m inv*; camelote *f*; pacotille *f*; **j. heap,** dépotoir *m*; tas *m* de ferraille; **j. dealer,** brocanteur *m*; *U.S:* **j. jewellery,** bijoux *mpl* de fantaisie; (*b*) *F:* **that's all j.,** tout ça c'est des bêtises; (*c*) *U.S: P:* narcotiques *mpl*, came *f*. **2.** (*a*) *Nau:* bœuf salé; (*b*) *F:* **j. food,** aliments *mpl* minute.

junk² *n. Nau:* jonque *f*.

junket¹ [ˈdʒʌŋkit] *n.* **1.** *Cu:* lait caillé (souvent parfumé). **2.** *F:* (*a*) festin *m*, banquet *m*; (*b*) *esp. U.S:* partie *f* de plaisir; (*c*) *esp. U.S:* voyage officiel aux frais de la princesse.

junket² *v.i. F:* **1.** banqueter, festoyer. **2.** *esp. U.S:* (*a*) faire une partie de plaisir; (*b*) voyager aux frais de la princesse.

junkie [ˈdʒʌŋki] *n. P:* drogué, -ée, camé, -ée.

junkman [ˈdʒʌŋkmən] *n. NAm:* brocanteur *m*.

junkroom [ˈdʒʌŋkruːm] *n.* (pièce *f* de) débarras (*m*).

junkshop [ˈdʒʌŋkʃɔp] *n.* boutique *f* de brocanteur.

junkyard [ˈdʒʌŋkjɑːd] *n.* entrepôt *m* de marchand de ferraille.

Juno [ˈdʒuːnou] **1.** *Pr.n.f. Rom.Myth: Astr:* Junon. **2.** *n.* (*of a woman*) une Junon.

junta [ˈdʒʌntə] *n. Hist: Pol:* (*in Spain, Italy, etc.*) junte *f*.

Jupiter [ˈdʒuːpitər] *Pr.n.m. Rom Myth: Astr:* Jupiter.

juridical [dʒuːˈridik(ə)l] *a.* juridique.

jurisdiction [dʒuːrisˈdikʃ(ə)n] *n.* juridiction *f*; (*a*) **to have j. over s.o.,** avoir la juridiction sur qn; **area within, under, the j. of . . .,** territoire soumis à l'autorité judiciaire, à la juridiction, de . . .; (*b*) compétence *f* (d'une cour, etc.); (*of question*) **to come within the j. of a court,** rentrer dans la juridiction d'une cour; **this matter does not come within our j.,** cette matière n'est pas de notre compétence.

jurisprudence [dʒuːrisˈpruːdəns] *n.* jurisprudence *f*; **medical j.,** médecine légale.

jurist [ˈdʒuːrist] *n.* **1.** (*a*) juriste *m*, jurisconsulte *m*, légiste *m*; (*b*) *U.S:* homme *m* de loi. **2.** étudiant, -ante, en droit.

juror [ˈdʒuːrər] *n.* (*a*) *Jur:* juré *m*; membre *m* du jury; (*b*) membre du jury (d'une exposition, etc.).

jury¹ [ˈdʒuːri] *n.* **1.** *Jur:* jury *m*; jurés *mpl*; **to be, serve, on the j.,** être du jury; **foreman of the j.,** chef *m* du jury. **2.** jury (d'un concours, d'une exposition, etc.).

jury² *a. Nau:* (mât, gouvernail) de fortune.

juryman, *pl.* **-men, -woman,** *pl.* **-women** [ˈdʒuːrimən, -wumən, -wimin] *n.* = JUROR.

just [dʒʌst] **I.** *a. & n.* **1.** *a.* (*a*) (homme, jugement, etc.) juste, équitable; impartial, -aux; **j. reward,** juste récompense *f*, récompense bien méritée; **it is only j.,** ce n'est que justice; **as was only j.,** comme de juste; **to show j. cause for . . .,** donner une raison valable de . . .; (*b*) (observation) juste, judicieuse, à propos. **2.** *n.pl.* **the j.,** les justes *mpl*; **to sleep the sleep of the j.,** dormir du sommeil du juste. **II.** *adv.* **1.** (*a*) juste, justement, précisément; **j. at that spot, at that time,** juste à cet endroit, à ce moment; **j. here,** juste ici; **it is j. twelve o'clock,** il est midi juste; **not ready j. yet,** pas encore tout à fait prêt; **j. how many are there?** combien y en a-t-il au juste? **he's j. the man you want,** c'est précisément l'homme qu'il vous faut; **that's j. what happened,** voilà justement ce qui est arrivé; **that's j. it,** (i) c'est bien cela; (ii) justement! *F:* (*of pers.*) **very j. so,** très correct; **j. when the door was opening,** au moment même où la porte s'ouvrait; **j. over, under, fifty pounds,** un peu plus, moins, de cinquante livres; (*b*) **he's j. as clever as you,** il est tout aussi intelligent que vous; **that's j. as good,** c'est tout comme; **I would j. as soon have this one,** j'aimerais tout autant celui-ci; **I will take it j. as it is,** je le prends tel qu'il est, tel quel; **j. as he was starting out,** au moment (même) de partir; au moment où il partait; (*c*) **j. now,** (i) actuellement, à l'heure actuelle; (ii) en ce moment, pour le moment; (iii) tout à l'heure, à l'instant; (*d*) (*intensive*) **it was j. splendid,** c'était ni plus ni moins que merveilleux; *F:* **you remember?—don't I j.!** vous vous en souvenez?—si je m'en souviens! **j. you wait!** tu n'as qu'à attendre! tu verras bien! **2.** (*a*) **j. before I came,** immédiatement avant mon arrivée; **j. after,** immédiatement après; (*b*) **he has j. written to you,** il vient de vous écrire; **he has (only) j. come,** il arrive à l'instant; **he has j. left school,** il sort du collège; **j. cooked,** fraîchement cuit; (*of book*) **j. out,** vient de paraître. **3. hair j. turning grey,** cheveux *mpl* qui commencent à grisonner; **I'm j. coming!** j'arrive! **he is j. going out,** il est sur le point de sortir. **4. he j. managed to do it,** c'est tout juste s'il est arrivé à le faire; c'est à peine s'il a pu le faire; **they j. missed the train,** ils ont manqué de peu le train; **I've only j. enough to live on,** j'ai tout juste de quoi vivre; **you're j. in time to . . .,** vous arrivez juste à temps pour . . . . **5.** (*a*) seulement; **j. once,** seulement une fois; rien qu'une fois; **j. one,** un seul, rien qu'un; *F:* **I'll j. pop in,** je ne ferai qu'entrer et sortir; **I have come j. to see you,** je viens uniquement pour vous voir; **they will travel fifty miles j. to go to a dance,** ils font cinquante milles rien que pour aller à un bal; (*b*) **j. sit down, please,** veuillez donc vous asseoir; **j. look!** regardez-moi ça! **j. read that!** lisez donc ça! *F:* **j. (you) shut up!** vous, taisez-vous! **justly** *adv.* **1.** justement, avec justice; (traiter qn) équitablement; **j. famous,** célèbre à bon titre, à bon droit. **2.** avec justesse, avec juste raison.

justice [ˈdʒʌstis] *n.* **1.** justice *f*; (*a*) **the j. of a claim, a sentence,** le bien-fondé, la justice, d'une réclamation, d'un jugement; (*b*) **in j. to him it must be admitted that . . .,** pour lui rendre justice il faut avouer que . . .; **in all j. we must allow him to . . .,** en toute justice il faut lui permettre de . . .; **poetic j.,** justice idéale; **to dispense j.,** rendre la justice; **to do j. to s.o., to do s.o. j.,** rendre, faire, justice à qn; **to do oneself j.,** se faire valoir; **to do j. to a meal,** faire honneur à un repas; (*c*) **to bring s.o. to j.,** traduire qn en justice. **2.** magistrat *m*; (*a*) juge *m* (d'un tribunal d'ordre supérieur); **the Lords Justices,** les juges de la cour de cassation; (*b*) *U.S:* **Chief J.,** président *m* d'une cour suprême; (*c*) **the Justices,** les juges (du tribunal d'instance).

justifiable [ˈdʒʌstifaiəbl] *a.* (crime, etc.) justifiable, justifié, défendable; (acte, colère) légitime; (refus) motivé. **-ably** *adv.* justifiablement; légitimement.

justification [dʒʌstifiˈkeiʃ(ə)n] *n.* **1.** (*a*) justification *f*; raison *f* d'être; **there is no j. for such an action,** une pareille action est injustifiable; (*b*) *Jur:* (*in libel suit*) **to plead j.,** établir la défense sur la vérité des faits allégués par le défendeur. **2.** *Typ:* justification (des lignes).

justify [ˈdʒʌstifai] *v.tr.* **1.** justifier (qn, sa conduite, etc.); légitimer, motiver (une action); justifier, prouver le bien-fondé de (son dire); **he was justified in the event,** l'événement lui a donné raison. **2.** *Typ:* justifier (une ligne). **justified** *a.* justifié; **fully j. decision,** décision bien fondée. **justifying** *a.* justificatif; justificateur, -trice; *Theol:* (grâce, foi) justifiante.

justness [ˈdʒʌstnis] *n.* **1.** justice *f* (d'une cause, etc.). **2.** justesse *f* (d'une idée, d'une observation, etc.).

jut¹ [dʒʌt] *n.* saillie *f*, projection *f* (d'un toit, etc.).

jut² *v.i.* **(jutted) to j. (out),** être en saillie, faire saillie; dépasser; **to j. out over sth.,** surplomber qch.; **jutting (out)** *a.* saillant, en saillie.

jute [dʒuːt] *n. Bot: Tex:* jute *m.*

juvenile [ˈdʒuːvənail] **1.** *a.* juvénile; (œuvre) de jeunesse; **j. books,** *n.pl.* **juveniles,** livres *mpl* pour enfants, pour la jeunesse; **j. court,** tribunal *m* pour enfants; **j. offender,** accusé mineur. **2.** *n.* jeune *mf.*

juxtapose [ˈdʒʌkstəpouz] *v.tr.* juxtaposer. **juxtaposed** *a.* juxtaposé; en juxtaposition.

juxtaposition [dʒʌkstəpəˈziʃ(ə)n] *n.* juxtaposition *f*; **to be in j.,** se juxtaposer.

K

K, k [kei] *n.* (la lettre) K, k, *m.*
kaffeeklatsch ['kæfiklætʃ] *n. U.S:* réunion *f* où on sert du café.
Kaffir ['kæfər] *Ethn:* **1.** *a.* caf(f)re. **2.** *n.* Caf(f)re *mf.*
kaftan ['kæftæn] *n. Cost:* kaftan *m.*
kail [keil] *n.* = KALE.
kale [keil] *n.* **1.** *Hort:* **curly k.,** chou frisé. **2.** *Scot:* soupe *f* aux choux.
kaleidoscope [kə'laidəskoup] *n.* kaléidoscope *m.*
kaleidoscopic [kəlaidə'skɔpik] *a.* kaléidoscopique.
kamikaze [kæmi'kɑ:zi] *n. Japanese Hist:* kamikaze *m.*
kangaroo [kæŋgə'ru:] *n.* **1.** *Z:* kangourou *m.* **2.** **k. court,** tribunal irrégulier.
kaolin ['keiəlin] *n.* kaolin *m.*
kapok ['keipɔk] *n.* kapok *m;* **k. tree,** kapokier *m.*
kaput [kə'put] *a. F:* fichu, foutu.
karakul ['kærək(u)l] *n.* karakul *m,* caracul *m.*
karate [kæ'rɑ:ti] *n. Sp:* karaté *m.*
kart [kɑ:t] *n.* kart *m;* **k. racing,** *n.* **karting,** karting *m.*
Kashmir [kæʃ'miər] *Pr.n. Geog:* Cachemire *m.*
Katharine, Katherine ['kæθ(ə)rin], **Kathleen** ['kæθli:n] *Pr.n.f.* Catherine.
kayak ['kaiæk] *n. Nau:* kayac *m,* kayak *m.*
kebab [ki'bæb] *n. Cu:* kebab *m.*
kedge¹ [kedʒ] *n. Nau:* **k. (anchor),** ancre *f* à jet.
kedge² *Nau:* **1.** *v.tr.* haler, touer (un navire) sur une ancre à jet. **2.** *v.i.* se touer sur une ancre à jet.
kedgeree [kedʒə'ri:] *n. Cu:* mets *m* de riz accommodé avec du beurre, des œufs et du poisson.
keel¹ [ki:l] *n.* **1.** (*a*) *N.Arch:* quille *f;* **bilge k.,** quille latérale, de roulis; **drop k.,** dériveur *m,* aile *f,* quille, de dérive; **on an even k.,** (i) *Nau:* sans différence de tirant d'eau, de calaison; (ii) *Av:* dans une position horizontale; en ligne de vol; *Fig:* **to be back on an even k.,** (*of situation, etc.*) être de nouveau stable; (*of pers.*) avoir retrouvé son égalité d'âme; (*b*) *Aer:* quille (d'hydravion, etc.); (*c*) *Lit:* navire *m.* **2.** *Nat. Hist:* carène *f* (de feuille, de pétale, etc.).
keel² **1.** *v.tr.* (*a*) mettre (un navire) en carène; (*b*) **to k. over,** faire chavirer (un navire). **2.** *v.i.* **to k. over,** (i) (*of ship*) faire le tour; chavirer; (ii) *F:* (*of pers.*) s'évanouir, tomber dans les pommes.
keelhaul ['ki:lhɔ:l] *v.tr.* **1.** *Nau: A:* faire passer (un matelot) sous la quille. **2.** réprimander sévèrement, passer un savon à (qn).
keen¹ [ki:n] *n. Dial:* (*Irish*) mélopée funèbre (chantée en veillant le corps).
keen² *v.tr. & i. Dial:* (*Irish*) **to k. (a corpse),** chanter une mélopée en veillant un corps.
keen³ *a.* **1.** (couteau, etc.) affilé, aiguisé; **k. edge,** fil tranchant; **k. edged,** bien affilé; aiguisé, tranchant; **as k. as a razor,** affilé comme un rasoir. **2.** (froid, vent, air) vif, piquant, aigre; (son) aigu; (froid) perçant; (œil) pénétrant, perçant. **3.** (chagrin) aigu; (regret) poignant; (remords) cuisant; **k. pleasure,** vif plaisir; **k. appetite,** rude appétit. **4.** (*a*) (*of pers.*) ardent, assidu, zélé; **he is a k. businessman,** il est âpre aux affaires; **k. sportsman,** ardent sportif; **k. golfer,** enragé *m* de golf; **he's as k. as mustard,** il brûle de zèle; *F:* **to be k. on sth.,** être enthousiaste de qch.; avoir la passion de qch.; *F:* **to be k. on s.o.,** être emballé, béguin, pour qn; **he's k. on sport,** le sport le passionne; **he's not k. on it,** il n'y tient pas beaucoup; (*b*) **k. interest,** vif intérêt; **k. competition,** concurrence acharnée, âpre; **there is a k. demand for these stocks,** ces fonds sont activement recherchés; *Com:* **k. prices,** prix *mpl* au plus bas, prix étudiés. **5.** (œil, regard) perçant, pénétrant, vif; **to have a k. eye for a bargain,** être prompt à reconnaître une bonne affaire; **to have a k. ear,** avoir l'oreille, l'ouïe, fine. **6.** (esprit) fin, pénétrant, vif, perçant. **-ly** *adv.* **1. the wind was blowing k.,** il faisait un vent âpre. **2. it touched me k.,** cela me toucha profondément, douloureusement. **3.** âprement, vivement; **to be k. interested in . . .,** s'intéresser vivement à . . .
keenness ['ki:nnis] *n.* **1.** finesse *f,* acuité *f* (du tranchant d'un outil). **2.** âpreté *f,* rigueur *f* (du froid). **3.** ardeur *f,* vivacité *f,* empressement *m,* zèle *m* (de qn); mordant *m* (des troupes, etc.); **k. on doing sth.,** grand désir de faire qch. **4** acuité (de la vision); finesse (de l'ouïe). **5.** pénétration *f,* finesse (d'esprit).
keep¹ [ki:p] *n.* **1.** donjon *m* (d'un château fort). **2.** nourriture *f,* subsistance *f;* frais *mpl* de subsistance; **to earn one's k.,** subvenir à ses besoins. **3.** *F:* **for keeps,** pour de bon; pour toujours.
keep² *v.* (*p.t. & p.p.* **kept** [kept]) **I.** *v.tr.* **1.** (*observe*) observer, suivre (la loi, une règle); tenir, remplir (une promesse); rester fidèle à (un vœu); tenir, respecter, observer (un traité); ne pas manquer à (un rendez-vous); **to k. late hours,** se coucher tard; **to k. one's word,** tenir (sa) parole; *Ecc:* **to k. the commandments,** observer les commandements. **2.** célébrer (une fête); fêter, célébrer (son anniversaire); observer (le jeûne). **3.** (*protect*) (*a*) **God k. (you)!** Dieu vous garde! **God k. his soul!** (que) Dieu ait son âme! (*b*) préserver (**s.o. from evil,** qn du mal); (*c*) *Mil:* défendre (une forteresse, etc.); (*d*) *Sp:* **to k. goal,** garder le but; *Cr:* **to k. wicket,** garder le guichet. **4.** (*a*) garder (des moutons, des troupeaux); (*b*) entretenir (un jardin, etc.); **well, badly, kept road,** route bien, mal, entretenue; (*c*) tenir (un journal, des comptes, *Com:* les livres); **to k. note of sth.,** tenir note de qch.; (*d*) subvenir aux besoins de (qn); **he doesn't earn enough to k. himself,** il ne gagne pas de quoi vivre; **he has his parents to k.,** il a ses parents à sa charge; **to k. s.o. in clothes, in food,** fournir de l'habillement, de la nourriture, à qn; (*e*) avoir (une voiture, etc.); élever (des abeilles, de la volaille, etc.); entretenir (une maîtresse); *O:* **kept woman,** femme entretenue; (*f*) tenir (une école, un magasin, etc.); (*g*) *Com:* tenir, avoir en magasin (des marchandises); **do you k. nails?** est-ce que vous vendez des clous? **5.** (*a*) maintenir (l'ordre); garder (le silence, un secret); **to k. one's composure,** garder son sang-froid; *F:* **they k. themselves to themselves,** ils font bande à part; (*b*) **it's too warm to k. the central heating on,** il fait trop chaud pour maintenir le chauffage central; (*c*) **to k. a good table,** faire bonne chère; **to k. open house,** tenir maison ouverte. **6.** (*detain*) **to k. s.o. in prison,** tenir, retenir, qn en prison; **I kept him at home,** je l'ai gardé à la maison; **the doctor kept him in bed,** le médecin l'a obligé de garder le lit; **there was nothing to k. me in England,** il n'y avait rien pour me retenir en Angleterre; **what's keeping you?** qu'est-ce qui vous retient? **7.** (*restrain; prevent*) **to k. back an army,** retenir

une armée; **the police were trying to k. the crowd back,** la police essayait de contenir, de retenir, la foule; **to k. back one's tears,** refouler, retenir, ses larmes; **to k. prices down,** empêcher les prix d'augmenter; **to k. s.o. from falling,** empêcher qn de tomber; **the wind will k. the rain off, away,** le vent empêchera la pluie; **k. your hands off (that)!** n'y touchez pas! **k. your hands off (me), k. your hands to yourself,** (à) bas les mains, les pattes! **8.** (*reserve*) garder (**sth. for s.o., for oneself,** qch. pour qn, pour soi); **to k. sth. for later,** garder, conserver, réserver, qch. pour plus tard; **to k. sth. back from s.o.'s wages,** retenir une somme sur le salaire de qn. **9.** (*a*) garder (des provisions, etc.); **the cupboard where I k. the crockery,** l'armoire *f* où je mets la vaisselle; **she keeps her letters under lock and key,** elle garde ses lettres sous clef; **to k. matches away from the children,** tenir les allumettes hors de la portée des enfants; (*b*) **to k. fruit until it is ripe,** garder des fruits jusqu'à ce qu'ils mûrissent. **10.** (*retain*) (*a*) garder (qch.); conserver (son emprise sur qch.); retenir (l'attention de qn); garder (la page dans un livre); **you can k. the book I lent you,** vous pouvez garder le livre que je vous ai prêté; **I'll k. my coat on,** je vais garder mon manteau; **I can't k. my food (down),** chaque fois que je mange je vomis. **11. to k. sth. to oneself,** taire qch.; garder (ses impressions) pour soi; *F:* **you can k. your remarks to yourself!** j'en ai assez de vos observations! **to k. sth. from s.o.,** cacher qch. à qn. **12. to k. (on) one's course,** continuer, poursuivre, son chemin; **to k. (in) the middle of the road,** garder le milieu de la route. **13. to k. (to) one's bed, one's room,** garder le lit, la chambre. **14.** (*a*) **to k. the field against the enemy,** se maintenir contre les attaques de l'ennemi; **to k. the stage,** tenir la scène; (*b*) **to k. one's seat,** rester assis; (*c*) **to k. one's figure,** garder la ligne; (*of thg*) **to k. its shape, its colour,** conserver sa forme, sa couleur. **15.** (*a*) **to k. sth. clean, secret,** tenir qch. propre, secret; *F:* **k. it clean!** pas de grossièretés! **to k. oneself warm,** (i) se tenir au chaud; (ii) s'habiller chaudement; **to k. the door open, shut,** garder, laisser, la porte ouverte, fermée; **the noise kept me awake,** le bruit m'a empêché de dormir; **to k. s.o. waiting,** faire attendre qn; (*b*) **to k. one's hands in one's pockets,** garder les mains dans ses poches; **to k. one's eyes fixed on sth.,** fixer qch. du regard; **to k. sth. in reserve, in store,** tenir qch. en réserve. **II.** *v.i.* **1.** rester, se tenir; **she told the children to k. away from the river,** elle a dit aux en-fants de ne pas s'approcher de la rivière; **k. away (from me), k. back!** n'approchez pas! **k. off the grass!** défense de marcher sur le gazon! **k. out of this!** mêlez-vous de ce qui vous regarde! **to k. out of danger,** rester à l'abri du danger; **to k. to the left, to the right,** tenir la gauche, la droite; **to k. well,** rester en bonne santé; **how are you keeping?** comment allez-vous? **to k. quiet**, se tenir, rester, tranquille; **to k. awake, calm,** rester éveillé, calme; **to k. smiling,** garder le sourire; **the weather is keeping cool, fine,** le temps reste frais, se maintient au beau. **2.** continuer; (*a*) **to k. working,** continuer de travailler; **to k. hard at it,** travailler sans relâche; **to k. straight on,** continuer tout droit; (*b*) **to k. (on) doing sth.,** ne pas cesser de faire qch.; **don't k. (on) asking questions,** ne posez pas tout le temps des questions; *F:* **to k. on at s.o.,** être toujours sur le dos de qn; harceler, tracasser, qn. **3.** (*with passive force*) (*of food, etc.*) se garder, se conserver; **butter that will k.,** beurre *m* qu'on peut conserver; **I'll tell you the story later; it will k.,** je vous raconterai l'histoire plus tard; elle n'y perdra rien. **keep in 1.** *v.tr.* (*a*) empêcher (qn) de sortir; *Sch:* mettre (un élève) en retenue; (*b*) entretenir (un feu); (*c*) **to k. one's hand in,** s'entretenir la main; se tenir en haleine. **2.** *v.i.* (*a*) (*of fire*) rester allumé; (*b*) *F:* **to k. in with s.o.,** cultiver qn; rester en bons termes avec qn. **keeping** *n.* (*a*) (i) observation *f* (d'une règle, d'une promesse); (ii) célébration *f* (d'une fête); (*b*) conservation (de fruits, etc.); (*c*) garde *f*; **to have s.o., sth., in one's k.,** avoir qn, qch., en garde, sous sa garde; **in God's k.,** à la garde de Dieu; (*d*) **in k. with . . .,** en harmonie, en accord, avec . . .; **in k. with his principles,** conforme à ses principes; **out of k. with . . .,** en désaccord avec . . .. **keep up 1.** *v.tr.* (*a*) entretenir (un bâtiment, une route, un feu, etc.); (*b*) conserver (un usage); entretenir (une correspondance, son français, etc.); **we must k. it up,** il nous faut continuer nos efforts; **k. it up!** allez toujours! continuez! (*c*) soutenir (l'intérêt, etc.); soutenir, maintenir (son courage); **to k. up appearances,** garder, sauver, les apparences; (*d*) **I mustn't k. you up,** je ne veux pas vous empêcher de vous coucher. **2.** *v.i.* **to k. up with s.o.,** marcher de front avec qn; aller de pair avec qn; **I can't k. up with you,** vous marchez, parlez, etc., trop vite pour moi; *F:* **to k. up with the Joneses,** rivaliser de standing avec ses voisins; **to k. up with the times,** être à la page.

keeper ['ki:pər] *n.* **1.** (*pers.*) (*a*) garde *m*, gardien *m*; surveillant *m*, gardien (de prison); conservateur *m* (de musée, etc.); gardeur, -euse (de troupeaux); **park k., lighthouse k.,** gardien de parc, de phare; (*b*) garde-chasse *m*, *pl.* gardes-chasse(s); (*c*) tenancier, -ière (d'un établissement). **2.** *Tchn:* (*device*) (*a*) (*pawl, click*) détente *f*, cliquet *m*; (*b*) *Locksm:* gâche *f* (de serrure).

keepsake ['ki:pseik] *n.* souvenir *m.*

keg [keg] *n.* caque *f* (de harengs); barillet *m*, baricaut *m* (d'eau-de-vie, etc.); tonnelet *m* (d'eau); **powder k.,** baril *m* de poudre.

kelp [kelp] *n.* varech *m.*

ken [ken] *n.* **within s.o.'s k.,** (i) à portée de la vue de qn; (ii) dans les connaissances, dans la compétence, de qn; **out of, beyond, s.o.'s k.,** hors de (i) la vue, (ii) la compétence, de qn.

kennel ['ken(ə)l] *n.* **1.** (*a*) chenil *m* (de chiens de chasse); (*b*) **kennels,** établissement *m* d'élevage de chiens; **to put a dog into kennels,** mettre un chien en pension. **2.** (*a*) loge *f*, niche *f* (de chien de garde, etc.); (*b*) *Ven:* terrier *m* (de renard). **3.** *Ven:* **the k.,** la meute.

kennelmaid ['ken(ə)lmeid] *n.f.* employée d'éleveur de chiens, de chenil.

Kenya ['ki:njə, 'ken-] *Pr.n. Geog:* Kenya *m.*

Kenyan ['kenjən] *Geog:* **1.** *a.* kenyan. **2.** *n.* Kenyan, -ane.

kerb, *NAm:* **curb** [kə:b] *n.* (*a*) bordure *f*, bord *m*, de trottoir; **to draw up at the k.,** se mettre en stationnement (le long du trottoir); (*b*) *St.Exch: F:* **business done on the k.,** opérations *fpl* en coulisse, après clôture de Bourse; **k. broker,** coulissier *m*, courtier *m* en valeurs mobilières.

kerbstone ['kə:bstoun] *n.* (*a*) pierre *f* de parement (d'un trottoir); (*b*) *St.Exch: F:* **k. market,** la coulisse.

kerchief ['kə:tʃif] *n. Cost: O:* (*a*) mouchoir *m* de tête; (*b*) fichu *m*; (*c*) *A:* mouchoir.

kerfuffle [kə'fʌfl] *n. F:* remue-ménage *m*, tohu-bohu *m.*

kernel ['kə:n(ə)l] *n.* **1.** (*a*) amande *f* (de noisette, de noyau); pignon *m* (de pomme de pin); (*b*) grain *m* (de céréale); graine *f* (de légumineuse); (*c*) *Cu:* noix *f* (de veau). **2.** noyau (d'une organisation, etc.); fond *m*, essentiel *m* (d'un problème, etc.).

kerosene ['kerəsi:n] *n.* **1.** *Ch:* kérosène *m.* **2.** *NAm:* pétrole lampant.

kestrel ['kestrəl] *n. Orn:* (faucon *m*) crécerelle (*f*).

ketch [ketʃ] *n. Nau:* ketch *m*, dundee *m*, dindet *m.*

ketchup ['ketʃəp] *n.* **(tomato) k.,** ketchup *m.*

kettle [ketl] *n.* **1.** (*a*) (*for boiling water*) bouilloire *f*; (*b*) (*for cooking*) chaudron *m*; chaudière *f*; **fish k.,** poissonnière *f*; *Mil:* **mess k.,** gamelle *f*; *F:* **here's pretty, a fine, k. of fish!** nous voilà dans de beaux draps! **that's quite a different k. of fish,** c'est tout à fait autre chose; ça c'est une autre affaire. **2.** *Geol:* **giant's k.,** marmite *f*, chaudière, de géant(s).

kettledrum ['ket(ə)ldrʌm] *n. Mus:* timbale *f*.

key¹ [ki:] *n.* **1.** (*a*) clef *f*, clé *f* (de serrure, de porte, etc.); **master k.,** passe-partout *m inv*; **k. ring,** porte-clefs *m inv*; **k. case,** étui *m* porte-clefs; (*in hotel, etc.*) **k. rack,** tableau *m* (pour clefs); **k. money,** arrhes *fpl*, *F:* pas *m* de porte; *U.S:* **k. club,** club privé dont les membres possèdent chacun une clef; **to turn the k. (in the lock),** donner un tour de clef (à la porte); *F:* **to have the k. to the door,** atteindre sa majorité; **it was the k. to his success,** cela lui a ouvert les portes du succès; (*b*) *attrib.* d'une importance capitale, vitale; **k. factor, post, industry,** facteur *m*, poste *m*, industrie *f*, clef; **k. man,** cheville ouvrière, pilier *m*, pivot *m* (d'un établissement, d'une organisation); **k. point, k. position,** position *f* clef; verrou *m*; *Mil: etc:* point vital, point qui commande une position, une zone; (*c*) **the (House of) Keys,** le Parlement de l'Ile de Man. **2.** (*a*) clef (d'une énigme, d'un chiffre, etc.); (*b*) légende *f* (d'une carte, etc.); (*on squared map*) **k. numbers,** numéros *mpl* de repérage; (*c*) *Sch:* corrigé *m*; livre *m* du maître; solutions *fpl* (des problèmes); (*d*) *Cmptr:* indicatif *m*, critère *m* (de tri, d'identification, etc.). **3.** (*a*) *Mus:* **major, minor, k.,** ton majeur, mineur; **the k. of C,** le ton d'ut; **k. signature,** armature *f* (de la clef); (*b*) *Art: etc:* caractéristique de luminosité (d'un tableau, d'une image); **picture painted in a low k.,** tableau peint dans des tons sombres. **4.** (*a*) touche *f* (de piano, d'orgue); (*b*) touche (de machine à écrire, etc.); *Tp: Tg:* clef, touche (d'appel, etc.); *El:* manette *f*; *Tp: Tg:* **listening, speaking, k.,** clef d'écoute, de conversation; **Morse k.,** clef, manipulateur *m*, Morse; (*c*) clef (d'un instrument à vent). **5.** *Tchn:* (*a*) clef, carotte *f* (de robinet); (*b*) (*spanner*) **box k.,** clef à douille; (*c*) remontoir *m* (de pendule, de jouet mécanique, etc.). **6.** (*a*) *Carp:* clef; (*b*) *Mec.E: etc:* clavette *f*; cale *f*, coin *m* (d'arbre); *Rail:* coin (de coussinet de rail); **set k.,** coin prisonnier; (*c*) *El:* fiche *f*. **7.** (*a*) *Const:* rappointis *m*; (*b*) *Carp:* adent *m* (pour empêcher une poutre, etc., de glisser).

key² *v.tr.* **1.** (*a*) *Mec.E:* clavet(t)er, coincer, caler (une poulie sur un arbre); **to k. sth. with sth.,** lier qch. à qch.; *Rail:* **to k. the rails,** coincer les rails; (*b*) *Carp:* adenter (une planche). **2.** (*a*) *Mus:* **to k. (up) the strings of an instrument,** accorder un instrument; (*b*) **crowd keyed up for the match,** foule tendue dans l'attente du match; **he was all keyed up,** il était crispé, tendu; (*c*) *Tg:* manipuler. **3.** *Cmptr:* **to k. (in)** coder (l'information). **keying** *n.* **1.** *Mec.E:* claret(t)age *m*, calage *m*, coinçage *m*. **2.** accordage *m* (d'un piano). **3.** *Tg:* manipulation *f*. **4.** *Cmptr:* **k. (in),** introduction *f*, imposition *f*, au clavier.

keyboard ['ki:bɔ:d] *n.* clavier *m* (de piano, de machine à écrire, etc.).

keyhole ['ki:houl] *n.* trou *m* de serrure; **to look through the k.,** regarder par le trou de la serrure.

keynote ['ki:nout] *n.* (*a*) *Mus:* tonique *f*; (*b*) note dominante, idée dominante (d'un discours); mot *m* d'ordre (d'une politique); **k. speech,** discours d'ouverture.

keynoter ['ki:noutər] *n. U.S:* orateur *m* qui prononce le discours d'ouverture.

keypunch ['ki:pʌn(t)ʃ] *n. Cmptr:* perforatrice *f* à clavier; poinçonneuse *f*.

keystone ['ki:stoun] *n.* (*a*) *Arch:* clef *f* de voûte; (*b*) clef de voûte, pivot *m* (d'une politique).

keyword ['ki:wə:d] *n.* mot-clé *m*, *pl.* mots-clés; mot-clef *m*, *pl.* mots-clefs.

khaki ['kɑ:ki] **1.** *n. Tex:* kaki *m.* **2.** kaki *inv.*

kibbutz, *pl.* **-zim** [ki'buts, kibut'si:m] *n. Agr:* kibboutz, *pl.* kibboutzim.

kibitzer ['kibitsər] *n.* (*a*) celui, celle, qui donne des conseils non sollicités; mouche *f* du coche; (*b*) spectateur, -trice, d'une partie de cartes.

kibosh ['kaibɔʃ] *n. F:* **1.** bêtises *fpl.* **2. to put the k. on sth.,** mettre fin à qch.

kick¹ [kik] *n.* **1.** (*a*) coup *m* de pied; *Fb: etc:* **free k.,** coup de pied franc; **goal k.,** coup de pied de but; (*of motor cycle*) **k. starter,** kick(-starter) *m*; (*b*) ruade *f* (d'un cheval, etc.). **2.** (*a*) vigueur *f*, énergie *f*; (*b*) *F:* **a drink with a k. in it,** une boisson qui vous remonte; **to get a k. out of (doing) sth.,** prendre plaisir à qch.; **to do sth. for kicks,** faire qch. pour s'amuser. **3.** (*a*) recul *m*, réaction *f*, repoussement *m*, bourrade *f* (d'un fusil); cahot *m*, secousse *f* (d'un mécanisme, etc.); (*b*) *I.C.E:* = KICKBACK.

kick² **1.** *v.i.* (*a*) donner un coup de pied, des coups de pied; (*of animal*) ruer, lancer des ruades; (*b*) *Sp:* (*of athlete*) démarrer; (*c*) (*of pers.*) *F:* **to k. at, against, sth.,** regimber contre qch.; répugner à qch.; (*d*) (*of gun*) reculer, repousser. **2.** *v.tr.* donner un coup de pied, des coups de pied, à (qn, qch.); pousser (qn, qch.) du pied; (*of horse, etc.*) détacher un coup de pied à (qn); *Fb:* botter (le ballon); marquer (un but); **to get kicked,** recevoir des coups de pied; **to k. sth. away, aside,** repousser qch. du pied; écarter qch. à coups de pied, d'un coup de pied; *F:* **to k. s.o.'s behind,** flanquer à qn un coup de pied au cul; *P:* **to k. the bucket,** mourir, casser sa pipe, crever; **to k. a man when he's down,** donner le coup de pied de l'âne à qn; **I could k. myself,** je me serais donné des gifles. **kick around** *F:* **1.** *v.i.* traîner; rouler sa bosse; **there are plenty of people like that kicking around,** des gens comme ça, ce n'est pas ça qui manque. **2.** *v.tr.* traiter (qn) sans ménagements. **kick back 1.** *v.i.* (*a*) *I.C.E:* (*of engine*) donner des retours en arrière; (*b*) rendre un coup de pied (à qn); *F:* (*of pers.*) réagir; regimber. **2.** *v.tr.* relancer (un ballon). **kick in 1.** *v.tr.* enfoncer (la porte, etc.) à coups de pied. **2.** *v.i. F:* payer sa part, son écot. **kick off 1.** *v.tr.* enlever (qch.) d'un coup de pied; **to k. off one's shoes,** enlever ses chaussures d'un mouvement brusque du pied. **2.** *v.i.* (*a*) *Fb:* donner le coup d'envoi; mettre le ballon en jeu; (*b*) *F:* démarrer, partir. **kick out 1.** *v.tr.* chasser (qn) à coups de pied; *Fb:* renvoyer (le ballon); *F:* **to be kicked out,** être mis à la porte. **2.** *v.i.* (*of horse, etc.*) lancer des ruades. **kick over** *v.tr.* renverser (qch.) d'un coup de pied. **kick up** *v.tr. F:* **to k. up a fuss,** faire des histoires; **to k. up a row, a racket,** faire du tapage, du boucan.

kickback ['kikbæk] *n.* (*a*) *I.C.E:* retour *m* en arrière; (*b*) *F:* réaction violente, coup *m* en boomerang; (*c*) *F:* ristourne *f*, dessous-de-table *m inv.*

kicker ['kikər] *n.* **1.** (*a*) donneur *m* de coups de pied; (*b*) *Fb:* joueur *m*; (*c*) *F:* **high k.,** (i) *Th:* danseuse *f* de can-can, de chahut; (ii) chahuteur, -euse. **2.** cheval *m*, etc., qui rue; rueur, -euse.

kick-off ['kikɔf] *n. Fb:* coup *m* d'envoi; coup de pied de départ; *Fig: F:* démarrage *m*; **k.-o. at two o'clock,** la partie commence à deux heures.

kickstand ['kikstænd] *n.* béquille *f* (de bicyclette).

kickstart(er) ['kiksta:t(ər)] *n.* (*motorbike*) démarreur *m* au pied, kick *m*.

kid¹ [kid] *n.* **1.** (*a*) *Z:* chevreau *m*, *f.* chevrette; (*b*) (peau *f* de) chevreau, cabron *m*; **k. gloves,** gants *mpl* (en peau) de chevreau; **to handle s.o. with k. gloves,** ménager qn. **2.** *F:* (*a*) mioche *mf*, gosse *mf*; **my k.**

brother, mon petit frère; (*b*) *U.S.:* **say, k.!** dis-moi, mon petit, ma petite; (*c*) **it's kid's stuff,** (i) c'est facile à faire; (ii) c'est (bon) pour les gosses.

kid² *v.tr. F:* en conter à (qn); faire marcher (qn); **you're kidding us,** tout ça c'est des blagues; **no kidding!** sans blague! **to k. s.o. that . . .,** faire croire à qn que . . .; **to k. oneself,** se faire des illusions.

kiddie, kiddy ['kidi] *n. F:* petit(e) gosse; mioche *mf.*

kidnap ['kidnæp] *v.tr.* **(kidnapped)** enlever (qn) de vive force; voler (un enfant); kidnapper (qn). **kidnapping** *n.* kidnapping *m*; enlèvement *m*; *Jur:* rapt *m* (d'enfant).

kidnapper ['kidnæpər] *n.* ravisseur, -euse (d'enfant); kidnappeur, -euse.

kidney ['kidni] *n.* **1.** (*a*) *Anat:* rein *m*; *Med:* **k. stone,** calcul rénal; **k. machine,** rein artificiel; **k. -shaped,** en forme de haricot; réniforme; (*b*) **a man of his k.,** un homme de sa trempe; (*c*) *Med:* **k. tray,** cuvette *f* à pansements réniforme, *F:* haricot *m.* **2.** (*a*) *Cu:* rognon *m*; **devilled kidneys,** rognons à la diable; (*b*) *Geol:* rognon (de silex, etc.); **k. stone,** néphrite *f*; (*c*) *Hort:* **k. bean,** (i) haricot nain; (ii) haricot d'Espagne, à grappes; *Bot:* **k. vetch,** (anthyllide *f*) vulnéraire *f*; trèfle *m* jaune.

kill¹ *n.* **1.** *Ven:* (*a*) mise *f* à mort (du renard, du cerf, etc.); (*b*) gibier tué; le tableau. **2.** (*a*) *Mil: etc:* destruction *f*, élimination *f* (de l'ennemi); (*b*) *F:* assassinat *m*; descente *f* (d'avion ennemi); coulée *f* (d'un navire ennemi).

kill² *v.tr.* **1.** (*a*) tuer, faire mourir (qn, une plante); faire périr (qn); *Mil:* détruire (l'ennemi); tuer, abattre (un animal); descendre (une perdrix, un homme); **to k. oneself,** se suicider; **k. or cure remedy,** remède *m* héroïque; **this superstition will be hard to k.,** cette superstition aura la vie dure; **to k. two birds with one stone,** faire d'une pierre deux coups; faire coup double; **to k. s.o. with kindness,** faire du mal à qn par excès de bonté; **to k. oneself with work,** se tuer à (force de) travailler; *F:* **to be dressed to k.,** porter une toilette irrésistible; être en grand tralala; (*b*) (*of butcher*) abattre, tuer (un bœuf, etc.); (*with passive force*) (*of beast*) **to k. well,** donner un bon rendement (de viande); (*c*) tuer (le nerf d'une dent); (*d*) *Ven:* servir (la bête). **2.** tuer (le temps); éteindre (l'ambition); détruire, étouffer (tout sentiment d'humanité); *Pol:* couler (un projet de loi); *Publ: Journ:* supprimer (un passage). **3.** (*a*) amortir (le son); (*b*) *Ch:* neutraliser (un acide, etc.); *Plumb: etc:* décomposer (l'esprit de sel); éteindre, amortir (la chaux); neutraliser (les odeurs). **4.** *Sp:* (*a*) *Fb:* bloquer (le ballon); (*b*) *Ten:* tuer, massacrer (la balle). **killed** *a.* tué, abattu; *F:* descendu. **killing 1.** *a.* (*a*) (i) meurtrier, assassin; (ii) (*in compounds*) **germ-k.,** microbicide; (*b*) (métier) tuant, assommant, écrasant; (*c*) *F:* (histoire) crevante; **it's too k. for words,** c'est à mourir de rire; c'est à se tordre les côtes. **2.** *n.* (*a*) (i) tuerie *f*, abattage *m* (d'animaux); (ii) meurtre *m*; (iii) *Mil:* destruction *f* (de l'ennemi); (iv) *F:* **to make a k.,** faire un bénéfice énorme, une affaire à tout casser; (*b*) *Tchn:* amortissement *m* (des sons); *Ch:* neutralisation *f* (d'un acide, etc.). **kill off** *v.tr.* (*a*) exterminer (toute une population, etc.); (*b*) **the author kills off his hero in the last chapter,** l'auteur fait mourir son héros au dernier chapitre.

killer ['kilər] *n.* **1.** (*a*) tueur, -euse; meurtrier *m*; **k. disease,** maladie meutrière; (*b*) *Z:* **k. whale,** épaulard *m.* **2.** (*in slaughtering*) **humane k.,** revolver *m* d'abattage. **3. insect, fly, k.,** insecticide *m.*

killjoy ['kildʒɔi] *n.* rabat-joie *m inv.*

kiln [kiln] *n.* **1.** (*a*) four *m* (céramique); **brick k.,** four à briques; **lime k.,** four à chaux, chaufour *m*; (*b*) séchoir *m*, sécherie *f*, étuve *f*; **hop k.,** four, séchoir, à houblon; *Brew:* **malt k.,** touraille *f*; **k. drying, seasoning,** séchage *m* au four; étuvage *m*; *Brew:* touraillage *m* (du malt). **2. charcoal k.,** meule *f* (de charbon de bois).

kilo ['ki:lou] *n. Meas: F:* kilo *m.*

kilocalorie [kilou'kæləri] *n. Ph.Meas:* kilocalorie *f.*

kilocycle ['kiləsaikl] *n. Ph: El:* kilocycle *m*; kilohertz *m.*

kilogram(me) ['kiləgræm] *n. Meas:* kilogramme *m.*

kilohertz ['kilouhə:ts] *n. Meas:* kilohertz *m.*

kilometre, *NAm:* **kilometer** ['kiləmi:tər, *esp. NAm:* ki'lɔmitər] *n. Meas:* kilomètre *m*; **distance in kilometres,** distance *f* kilométrique.

kilometric [kilə'metrik], *a.* kilométrique.

kilovolt ['kiləvoult] *n. El.Meas:* kilovolt *m.*

kilowatt ['kiləwɔt] *n. El.Meas:* kilowatt *m*; **k.-hour,** kilowatt-heure *m*, *pl.* kilowatt-heures.

kilt [kilt] *n. Cost:* kilt (écossais).

kilter ['kiltər] *n. NAm: F:* bonne condition; **out of k.,** en panne; détraqué.

kimono [ki'mounou] *n. Cost:* kimono *m.*

kin [kin] *n.* **1.** souche *f* (d'une famille). **2.** (*a*) parents *mpl*; **his k.,** ses parents, sa parenté; (*b*) **to be k. to s.o.,** être parent de qn, apparenté avec qn; **next of k.,** la famille, le parent le plus proche; **to inform the next of k.,** prévenir la famille.

kind¹ [kaind] *n.* **1.** (*race*) espèce *f*, genre *m.* **2.** (*a*) (*class, sort*) genre, espèce, sorte *f*; **(of) what k. is it?** de quelle sorte (est-ce)? **what k. of tree is this?** quelle sorte d'arbre est-ce? **what k. of man is he?** quel genre d'homme est-ce? **people of all kinds,** des gens de toutes sortes; **something of the k.,** quelque chose de ce genre; **nothing of the k.,** rien de la sorte; **in a k. of a way,** en quelque façon; *Theol:* **communion in both kinds,** communion *f* sous les deux espèces; (*b*) **this k. of man,** ce genre d'hommes; les hommes de cette sorte; *P:* **k. of** (*occ. pronounced* **kinda** ['kaində]), **I k. of expected it,** je m'en doutais presque; **he looks k. of stupid,** il a l'air plutôt bête. **3.** (*a*) **difference in k.,** différence *f* spécifique; (*b*) **payment in k.,** paiement *m*, livraison *f*, en nature; **to repay s.o. in k.,** (i) rembourser qn en nature; (ii) payer qn de la même monnaie; rendre à qn la monnaie de sa pièce.

kind² *a.* **1.** bon, aimable, bienveillant; **k. hearted,** qui a bon cœur; un **they are k. people,** ce sont des gens aimables; **k. words,** paroles bienveillantes; **give him my k. regards,** faites-lui mes amitiés; **to be k. to s.o.,** se montrer bon pour, envers, qn; être plein de bontés pour qn; **it's very k. of you to . . .,** c'est bien aimable de votre part, à vous, de . . .; **(would you) be k. enough to, so k. as to . . .,** soyez assez bon pour . . .; ayez la bonté de . . .; veuillez (bien) . . .; **you are really too k.,** vous êtes vraiment trop aimable. **2.** (*of detergents, etc.*) **k. to the skin,** qui n'irrite pas la peau. **kindly 1.** *adv.* avec bonté; **he spoke very k. of you,** il a dit des choses très aimables à votre égard; **to be k. disposed towards s.o., sth.,** être bien disposé envers qn; *Com:* **k. remit by cheque,** prière de nous couvrir par chèque; **not to take k. to s.o., sth.,** ne pas aimer qn, qch. **2.** *a* (*a*) bon, bienveillant; (ton, conseil) paternel; (*b*) (climat) doux.

kindergarten ['kindəga:t(ə)n] *n. Sch:* jardin *m* d'enfants; école maternelle.

kindle ['kindl] **1.** *v.tr.* (*a*) allumer (une flamme, un feu); enflammer, embraser (du charbon, une forêt); (*b*) allumer (la haine); faire naître, susciter (les passions); enflammer (le courage, les désirs); embraser (le cœur); aviver (les soupçons, le chagrin); exciter (le zèle). **2.** *v.i.* (*of fire, wood, passions, etc.*) s'allumer, s'enflammer. **kindling** *n.* **1.** embrasement *m*, enflammement *m.* **2. k. (wood),** bois *m* d'allumage, petit bois; allume-feu *m inv.*

kindliness ['kaindlinis] *n.* bonté *f*, bienveillance *f.*

kindness ['kaindnis] *n.* **1.** bonté *f* (**towards s.o.,** pour qn); bienveillance *f*, amabilité *f* (**towards,** envers); **thanks for your k.,** merci de votre complaisance; **to show k. to s.o.,** témoigner de la bonté à qn; **will you have the k. to . . .?** voulez-vous avoir la bonté de . . .? **the milk of human k.,** le lait de la tendresse humaine. **2. a k.,** un service (rendu); un bienfait; **to do s.o. a k.,** rendre service à qn.

kindred ['kindrid] **1.** *n.* (*a*) (i) parenté *f* (de qn avec qn); (ii) affinité *f* (**with,** avec); (*b*) *coll.* parents *mpl*; famille *f*. **2.** *a.* de la même nature; du même genre; **k. souls,** âmes *fpl* sœurs; **he has found a k. spirit,** il a trouvé une âme qui a des affinités avec la sienne.

kinematic [kinə'mætik, kain-] *a. Ph:* cinématique.

kinetic [ki'netik, kai-] *a. Ph: etc:* (énergie, etc.) cinétique.

king [kiŋ] *n.* **1.** roi *m*; (*a*) **the kings and queens of England,** les souverains *mpl* d'Angleterre; *B:* **K. of Kings,** Roi des rois; **the three Kings,** les Rois Mages; **the Book of Kings,** le livre des Rois; **to crown s.o. k.,** couronner qn roi; **dish fit for a k.,** morceau *m* de roi; (*b*) *Her:* **K. of Arms,** roi d'armes; (*c*) *Ind: etc:* magnat *m*; **one of the oil kings,** un des rois du pétrole; (*d*) *Crust:* **k. crab,** limule *m*, crabe *m* des Moluques; *Rept:* **k. cobra,** cobra royal. **2.** (*a*) *Chess: Cards:* roi; (*b*) (*at draughts*) dame *f*.

kingbolt ['kiŋboult] *n. Const: Mec.E:* cheville maîtresse, ouvrière; pivot central.

kingcup ['kiŋkʌp] *n. Bot:* **1.** bouton *m* d'or. **2.** populage *m*, souci *m* d'eau.

kingdom ['kiŋdəm] *n.* **1.** royaume *m*; **the United K.,** le Royaume-Uni; **the k. of heaven,** le royaume des cieux. **2.** règne (animal, végétal, minéral); **in the animal k.,** chez les animaux. **3.** (*a*) *Theol:* règne; **Thy k. come,** que Ton règne vienne; (*b*) *F:* **k. come,** le paradis; **to send s.o. to k. come,** expédier qn dans l'autre monde; **until k. come,** jusqu'à l'éternité.

kingfisher ['kiŋfiʃər] *n. Orn:* martin-pêcheur *m*, *pl.* martins-pêcheurs.

kingly ['kiŋli] *a.* de roi; royal, -aux.

kingpin ['kiŋpin] *n.* **1.** (*a*) axe *m* de rotule; (*b*) = KINGBOLT[1]; (*c*) cheville ouvrière (d'une organisation, d'une entreprise). **2.** *Games:* quille *f* du milieu.

kingpost ['kiŋpoust] *n. Const:* poinçon *m*, aiguille *f* (d'une ferme de comble).

kingship ['kiŋʃip] *n.* royauté *f*.

king-size(d) ['kiŋ'saizd] *a. Com:* géant; (*cigarettes*) long.

kink[1] [kiŋk] *n.* **1.** (*a*) vrillage *m*; tortillement *m* (dans un fil, dans une corde); grigne *f* (dans le feutre); crêpelure *f* (des cheveux); *Nau:* coque *f* (dans un cordage); *Tex:* vrille *f*, boucle *f*; *Mec.E: etc:* pliure *f* (d'une pièce mécanique). **2.** déséquilibre *m*, abérration *f*; **he's got a k.,** il a des goûts sexuels excentriques.

kink[2] *v.i.* (*of rope*) se nouer, se tortiller, vrillonner; *Nau:* faire des coques; (*of thread*) vriller.

kinky ['kiŋki] *a.* (*a*) (*of rope, etc.*) noué; (*of hair*) crêpelé, crépu; (*b*) *F:* (*of pers.*) (i) fantasque, extravagant; timbré; (ii) qui a des goûts sexuels excentriques; (*c*) *F:* (*of clothes, etc.*) bizarre, extravagant.

kinsfolk ['kinzfouk] *n.pl.* parents *mpl* et alliés *mpl*.

kinship ['kinʃip] *n.* parenté *f*.

kinsman, *pl.* **-men** ['kinzmən] *n.m.* parent.

kinswoman, *pl.* **-women** ['kinzwumən, -wimin] *n.f.* parente.

kiosk ['kiɔːsk] *n.* kiosque *m*; **newspaper k.,** kiosque à journaux; **telephone k.,** cabine *f* téléphonique.

kip[1] [kip] *n. Leath:* peau *f* de veau, d'agneau.

kip[2] *n. P:* (*a*) lit *m*, pieu *m*, plumard *m*; (*b*) **to have a k.,** piquer un roupillon.

kip[3] *v.i.* **(kipped)** *P:* (*a*) coucher; **to k. down,** se pieuter; (*b*) dormir, roupiller.

kipper[1] ['kipər] *n. Com:* hareng légèrement salé et fumé; kipper *m*.

kipper[2] *v.tr.* saler et fumer (des harengs); **kippered herring** = KIPPER[1].

kirk [kəːk] *n. Scot:* (*a*) église *f*; (*b*) **the K.,** l'Église (presbytérienne) d'Écosse.

kiss[1] [kis] *n.* baiser *m*; **to give s.o. a k.,** donner un baiser à qn; (*to child*) **give mother a k.!** fais une bise à maman! *Med: F:* **k. of life,** bouche-à-bouche *m*; **k. curl,** accroche-cœur *m*, *pl.* accroche-cœurs.

kiss[2] *v.tr.* **1.** donner un baiser à, embrasser (qn); baiser (le front, la main, de qn, un objet sacré); (*ceremonially*) donner l'accolade à (qn); **they kissed (each other),** ils se sont embrassés; *F:* **to k. and make up,** se réconcilier; **to k. the book,** baiser la Bible (pour prêter serment); *Lit:* **to k. the dust,** mordre la poussière; **to k. s.o. goodbye,** dire au revoir à qn en l'embrassant. **2.** *Bill:* (*a*) (*of ball*) frapper (une autre) par contrecoup; (*b*) *v.i.* (*of balls*) se frapper par contrecoup. **kissing** *n.* baisers *mpl*, embrassade *f*; **k. of hands,** baisemain *m*.

kisser ['kisər] *n.* **1.** embrasseur, -euse. **2.** *P:* bouche *f*, museau *m*.

kit[1] [kit] *n.* (*a*) effets *mpl*, bagages *mpl*; *Mil: etc:* petit équipement; effets (personnels); **to pack up one's k.,** plier bagage, faire ses paquets; *Mil: etc:* **k. inspection,** revue *f* de détail, d'inspection; *F:* **the whole k. and caboodle,** tout le bataclan; (*b*) matériel *m*, équipement *m*; trousseau *m*, trousse *f* (d'outils, etc.); **repair k.,** nécessaire *m*, trousse, de réparations; **first-aid k.,** trousse de première urgence; (*c*) **riding k.,** tenue *f* de cheval; **troops in full battle k.,** troupes *fpl* en tenue de campagne.

kit[2] *v.tr.* **(kitted)** équiper, fournir son équipement à (un soldat, etc.); **(all) kitted up,** complètement équipé; *Mil:* **to be kitted out, up,** toucher son paquetage.

kitbag ['kitbæg] *n.* sac *m* de voyage; sac (de) marin; *Mil:* sac à paquetage, sac de grande monture.

kitchen ['kitʃin] *n.* **1.** cuisine *f*; **in the k.,** à la cuisine; **mobile k.,** cuisine roulante (de l'armée); *F:* **thieves' k.,** (i) repaire *m* de voleurs; (ii) officine *f* (d'intrigues). **2. k. table,** table *f* de cuisine; **k. unit,** bloc-cuisine *m*, *pl.* blocs-cuisines; **k. utensils,** batterie *f* de cuisine; **k. stove,** cuisinière *f*; **k. sink,** évier *m*; *F:* **k.-sink literature,** littérature *f* boîte à ordures; *F:* **everything but the k. sink,** tout, y compris la cage aux serins; **k. garden,** (jardin) potager *m*.

kitchenette [kitʃin'et] *n.* petite cuisine.

kitchenware ['kitʃinwɛər] *n.* faïence *f*, vaisselle *f*, de cuisine.

kite [kait] *n.* **1.** *Orn:* milan *m*. **2.** (*a*) (i) cerf-volant *m*, *pl.* cerfs-volants; (ii) *Fin: F:* cerf-volant; traite *f* en l'air; billet *m* de complaisance; **k. balloon,** ballon observateur; ballon cerf-volant; *F:* saucisse *f*; **to fly a k.,** lancer, enlever, faire voler, un cerf-volant; (*b*) *F:* **as high as a k.,** (i) ivre, soûl; (ii) drogué, camé. **3.** *Av: F:* avion *m*, taxi *m*.

kith [kiθ] *n. A: still used in* **our k. and kin,** nos parents et amis; **to have neither k. nor kin,** être seul sur la terre.

kitsch [kitʃ] *n.* kitsch *m*; art pompier.

kitten[1] ['kit(ə)n] *n.* (*a*) chaton *m*; petit(e) chat(te); **a cat and her kittens,** une chatte et ses petits; *F:* (*of pers.*) **to have kittens,** être dans tous ses états; (*b*) *esp. NAm:* jeune lapin *m*; jeune hamster *m*; (*c*) (*as term of endearment*) ma petite, ma mignonne.

kitten[2] *v.tr. & i.* (*of cat*) mettre bas (des petits); avoir des petits; chatonner.

kittenish ['kitəniʃ] *a.* **1.** (*of girl, disposition*) (*a*) coquette, chatte; (*b*) enjouée. **2.** (grâce) féline.

kittiwake ['kitiweik] *n. Orn:* mouette *f* tridactyle.

kitty[1] ['kiti] *n.* chaton *m*.

kitty² *n.* **1.** (*a*) *Cards: etc:* cagnotte *f*; (*b*) cagnotte, caisse commune (d'un groupe). **2.** (*at bowls*) cochonnet *m*.

kiwi ['ki:wi:] *n.* **1.** *Orn:* aptéryx *m*; kiwi *m*. **2.** *F:* **K.**, Néo-Zélandais(e).

kleptomania [kleptə'meiniə] *n.* kleptomanie *f*.

kleptomaniac [kleptə'meiniæk] *a.* & *n.* kleptomane (*mf*).

knack [næk] *n.* tour *m* de main; talent *m*, *F:* truc *m*; chic *m*; **to have the k. of, a k. for, doing sth.,** avoir le talent de faire qch.; avoir le coup, le tour de main, pour faire qch.; **to have lost the k. of sth.,** n'avoir plus l'habitude de qch.

knacker¹ ['nækər] *n.* **1.** abatteur *m* de chevaux; équarrisseur *m*; **knacker's yard,** chantier *m* d'équarrissage; équarrissoir *m*. **2.** (*a*) entrepreneur *m* de démolitions; (*b*) démolisseur *m* de vieux navires.

knacker² *v.tr.* *F:* éreinter; **I'm knackered,** je suis crevé, fourbu.

knapsack ['næpsæk] *n.* (*a*) havresac *m*, sac *m* (porté sur le dos); sac alpin, tyrolien; (*b*) *Mil:* sac d'ordonnance.

knave [neiv] *n.* **1.** *O:* fripon *m*, coquin *m*. **2.** *Cards:* valet *m*; **k. of clubs,** valet de trèfle; (*at loo, etc.*) mistigri *m*.

knavery ['neivəri] *n.* *O:* friponnerie *f*, coquinerie *f*.

knead [ni:d] *v.tr.* **1.** pétrir, malaxer, travailler (la pâte, l'argile). **2.** *Med:* masser, pétrir (les muscles). **kneading** *n.* **1.** pétrissage *m* (de la pâte); malaxage *m* (de l'argile, etc.); **k. trough,** pétrin *m*. **2.** *Med:* massage *m*, foulage *m* (des muscles).

knee¹ [ni:] *n.* **1.** (*a*) genou, -oux *m*; *Anat:* **k. reflex, k. jerk,** réflexe patellaire, rotulien; **to be k. deep in mud,** être enfoncé dans la boue jusqu'aux genoux; **to bend, bow, the k. to, before, s.o.,** fléchir le genou devant qn; **on one's (bended) knees, on bended k.,** (demander qch.) à genoux; **to go down, fall, drop, on one's knees,** s'agenouiller; tomber à genoux; **on your knees!** à genoux! **to bring s.o. to his knees,** (i) forcer qn à s'agenouiller; (ii) obliger qn à capituler; (*b*) *F:* **tennis k.,** foulure du genou (due au tennis); (*c*) *Vet:* (*of horse*) **broken knees,** couronnement *m*. **2.** (*a*) *Mec.E:* *Const:* genou, équerre *f*, sabot *m*; genouillère *f*; **k. bracket,** console-équerre *f*, *pl.* consoles-équerres; (*b*) *Carp: etc:* **k. timber,** bois courbant, coudé; (*c*) *N.Arch:* courbe *f* (de consolidation); **k. (plate),** gousset *m* (de charpente).

knee² *v.tr.* pousser (qch., qn) du genou.

kneecap ['ni:kæp] *n.* *Anat:* rotule *f*.

knee-high [ni:'hai] *a.* & *adv.* à hauteur du genou; *F:* **when I was k.-h. to a grasshopper,** quand j'étais petit, haut comme trois pommes.

kneel [ni:l] *v.i.* (*p.t.* & *p.p.* **knelt** [nelt], *occ.* **kneeled**) **to k. (down),** s'agenouiller; se mettre à genoux; **to k. to s.o.,** se mettre à genoux devant qn. **kneeling 1.** *a.* agenouillé, à genoux. **2.** *n.* agenouillement *m*.

knee-length ['ni:leŋθ] *a.* (robe, etc.) qui descend jusqu'au genou.

kneeler ['ni:lər] *n.* **1.** personne agenouillée. **2.** agenouilloir *m*; coussin *m* pour s'agenouiller.

kneepad ['ni:pæd] *n.* genouillère *f*.

knell [nel] *n.* glas *m*; **to toll the k.,** sonner le glas; **this rang the death k. of his hopes,** cette nouvelle, ce refus, etc., sonnait le glas de ses espérances.

knelt. *see* KNEEL.

knickerbockers ['nikəbɔkəz] *n.pl.* culotte (bouffante); knickerbockers *mpl*.

knickers ['nikəz] *n.pl.* culotte *f* (de femme).

knick-knack ['niknæk] *n.* colifichet *m*, babiole *f*, bibelot *m*.

knife¹, *pl.* **knives** [naif, naivz] *n.* **1.** (*a*) couteau *m*; **kitchen, table, k.,** couteau de cuisine, de table; **carving k.,** couteau à découper; **fish, dessert, k.,** couteau à poisson, à dessert; **k. and fork,** couvert *m*; **k. rest,** porte-couteau *m*, *pl.* porte-couteaux; **k. sharpener,** affiloir *m* (pour couteaux); **k. grinder,** (i) (*pers.*) rémouleur *m*; repasseur *m* de couteaux; (ii) (*instrument*) meule *f* à aiguiser; **before you could say k.,** en un rien de temps; en moins de rien; (*b*) **pocket k.,** couteau de poche, canif *m*; (*c*) couteau; poignard *m*; **to get, have, one's k. into s.o.,** s'acharner après, contre, sur, qn; en vouloir à qn; (*d*) *Surg:* bistouri *m*; scalpel *m*; inciseur *m*; **he was under the k. for two hours,** l'opération *f* a duré deux heures; (*e*) *Tchn:* **coopers' hollowing k.,** plane creuse de tonnelier; **putty k.,** spatule *f* de vitrier; couteau à palette, à mastiquer. **2.** couteau, lame *f* (d'un hache-paille, etc.); couperet *m* (de la guillotine); *Tex:* rasoir *m* (de tondeuse). **3.** *El:* **k. switch,** interrupteur *m*, commutateur *m*, à couteau, à lame(s).

knife² *v.tr.* **1.** donner un coup de couteau à (qn); poignarder (qn). **2.** *U.S:* dégringoler (un homme politique) (par des moyens déloyaux, occultes).

knife-edge ['naifedʒ] *n.* **1.** (*a*) arête *f* (de montagne) en lame de couteau; (*b*) *Tchn:* bord tranchant; pièce *f* (mécanique, etc.) en lame de couteau; couteau *m* (de balance, etc.). **2. trousers with a k.-e. crease,** pantalon *m* au pli cassant.

knight¹ [nait] *n.* **1.** chevalier *m*; (*a*) *Lit:* **the Knights of the Round Table,** les Chevaliers de la Table Ronde; (*b*) *Hist:* **k. service,** service *m* de haubert; **k. errant** [erənt] (*pl.* **knights errant**), chevalier errant; paladin *m*; (*c*) **K. of the Garter,** chevalier de l'Ordre de la Jarretière. **2.** *Chess:* cavalier *m*.

knight² *v.tr.* **1.** *Hist:* armer chevalier (un écuyer, etc.). **2.** faire, créer (qn) chevalier.

knighthood ['naithud] *n.* **1.** chevalerie *f*. **2. he has just been given a k.,** il vient d'être créé chevalier.

knightly ['naitli] *a.* (conduite, etc.) chevaleresque, de chevalier.

knit [nit] *v.* (*p.t.* & *p.p.* **knitted** *or* **knit**) **1.** *v.tr.* (*a*) tricoter (un vêtement); (*b*) faire les mailles à l'endroit; **k. two, purl two,** deux à l'endroit, deux à l'envers; (*c*) **to k. one's brows,** froncer le(s) sourcil(s); (*d*) faire souder (les os); lier (un liquide, un ciment); (*e*) joindre, unir, lier (des personnes); **knit (together) by close friendship,** liés d'une étroite amitié; (*f*) **to k. up,** assembler (un vêtement) (en le tricotant); rassembler les fils (d'un argument). **2.** *v.i.* (*a*) tricoter, faire du tricot; (*b*) (*of bones*) se souder, se rejoindre; (*of liquid, cement*) se lier, prendre. **knit, knitted** *a.* **1.** (écharpe) tricotée, de, en, tricot; (dentelle) au tricot; **knitted fabric,** tricot *m*; **knit(ted) goods,** tricots *pl*, articles *mpl* en tricot. **2. knit(ted) eyebrows,** sourcils froncés. **3. close-knit,** étroitement lié; **closely knit sentences,** phrases *fpl* d'une structure serrée. **knitting** *n.* **1.** (*a*) tricotage *m*; **k. needle,** aiguille *f* à tricoter; **k. machine,** machine *f* à tricoter; tricoteuse *f*; (*b*) soudure *f* (des os). **2.** tricot; **I've brought my k.,** j'ai apporté mon tricot.

knitter ['nitər] *n.* tricoteur, -euse.

knob¹ [nɔb] *n.* **1.** (*a*) (*on surface, forehead, etc.*) bosse *f*, protubérance *f*; (*b*) pomme *f* (de canne, de balustrade); bouton *m*, poignée *f* (de porte, de tiroir, etc.); (*c*) *Mec.E:* **(knurled) k.,** bouton (moleté) (d'appareil, etc.); **control k.,** bouton, molette *f*, de réglage; *Elcs:* *T.V:* *W.Tel:* **tuning k.,** bouton de réglage du son, de la tonalité; bouton d'accord; (*d*) *P:* **with knobs on,** et le pouce, et mèche, et le rab; **the same to you with knobs on!** que le diable t'emporte! **2.** *NAm:* = KNOLL. **3.** petit morceau (de fromage, etc.); noix *f*, noisette *f* (de beurre).

knobbed [nɔbd] *a.* **1.** (*of surface*) plein de bosses. **2.** (*of stick*) à pommeau.

knobbly ['nɔbli] *a.* couvert de bosses; noueux.

knock¹ [nɔk] *n.* **1.** coup *m*, heurt *m*, choc *m*; **to give s.o. a k. on the head,** (i) porter à qn un coup à la tête; (ii) assommer qn; **to get a nasty k.,** attraper un vilain coup; *F:* **to take the k.,** essuyer de grosses pertes. **2. k. at the door,** coup à la porte; **he heard a k.,** il a entendu frapper; **he gave a loud k.,** il a frappé très fort; **k., k.!** toc, toc! pan, pan! **3.** (*a*) *Mec.E: etc:* cognement *m*, cliquetis *m*; (*b*) *I.C.E:* détonation *f* (du carburant dans le moteur).

knock² **1.** *v.tr.* (*a*) frapper, heurter, cogner; **to k. s.o. on the head,** (i) frapper qn sur la tête; (ii) assommer qn; **our plans have been knocked on the head,** nos projets sont tombés à l'eau; **to k. one's head against sth.,** (i) se cogner la tête contre qch.; (ii) *Fig:* se heurter à, buter contre, un obstacle; **it's like knocking your head against a brick wall,** c'est peine perdue; (*b*) **to k. a hole in, through, sth.,** faire un trou dans qch.; **to k. holes in an argument,** démolir un argument; **to k. a nail into a wall,** enfoncer un clou dans un mur; *F:* **that'll k. a bit of sense into him!** ça le lui apprendra! **to k. a book off the table,** faire tomber un livre de la table; **I managed to get something knocked off the price,** j'ai réussi à faire rabattre quelque chose du prix; *F:* **to k. s.o.'s head, block, off,** flanquer une taloche à qn; **to k. sth., s.o., over,** faire tomber, renverser, qch., qn; (*c*) *F:* épater (qn); **to k. s.o. sideways,** renverser, abasourdir, stupéfier, qn; (*d*) *F:* critiquer (qn, qch.). **2.** *v.i.* (*a*) frapper, heurter (**at,** à); taper (**at,** sur); **to k. at the door,** frapper à la porte; (*b*) **to k. against sth.,** se donner un coup, se heurter, se cogner, contre qch.; (*c*) *I.C.E:* (*of engine*) cogner, cliqueter; (*of bearings*) tambouriner. **knock about** (*esp. U.S: also* **knock around**) **1.** *v.tr.* bousculer, maltraiter, malmener (qn); **the furniture has been badly knocked about,** les meubles ont été fort maltraités; **they were knocking each other about,** ils se cognaient, se battaient. **2.** *v.i.* **to k. about (the world),** rouler sa bosse; parcourir le monde; **I spent an hour knocking about waiting for him,** j'ai flâné pendant une heure en l'attendant. **knock back** *v.tr. F:* (*a*) **to k. back a drink,** s'enfiler un pot; s'envoyer, lamper, un verre; (*b*) coûter; **it knocked me back £200,** ça m'a coûté £200. **knock down** *v.tr.* (*a*) renverser (qch., qn); jeter (qch., qn) par terre; étendre (qn) par terre (d'un coup de poing); abattre (un mur, etc.); **he was knocked down by a car,** il a été renversé par une voiture; (*b*) adjuger, vendre (un article aux enchères); **to k. sth. down to s.o.,** adjuger qch. à qn. **knocking** *n.* **1.** coups *mpl* (à la porte, etc.). **2.** (*of engine*) tapage *m*, pilonnage *m*; cognement *m*. **knock off** **1.** *v.tr.* (*a*) achever (un travail); *F:* **k. it off!** arrêtez! (ça) suffit! (*b*) *P:* voler, faucher (qch.); (*c*) *P:* assassiner, zigouiller (qn). **2.** *v.i. Ind: etc:* s'arrêter de travailler; (*at end of day*) cesser le travail, débrayer; **we k. off at six,** nous finissons à six heures. **knock out** *v.tr.* (*a*) chasser, repousser (un rivet); **to k. s.o.'s brains out,** faire sauter la cervelle à qn; (*b*) assommer (qn) raide; *Box:* mettre (son adversaire) knock-out; knockouter (son adversaire); (*c*) *Sp:* (*in tournament, etc.*) **to be knocked out,** être éliminé. **knock together** *v.tr.* assembler à la hâte (un abri, un radeau, etc.). **knock up** **1.** *v.tr.* (*a*) construire (un hangar, etc.) à la hâte; improviser (un repas); (*b*) *v.tr. & i. Ten:* **to k. up (a few balls),** faire des balles (avant la partie); (*c*) *Cr:* **to k. up a century,** faire cent points; (*d*) réveiller, faire lever (qn); (*e*) éreinter, épuiser (qn). **2.** *v.tr. P:* mettre (une femme) enceinte.

knockabout [ˈnɔkəbaut] **1.** (*a*) *a.* (jeu, etc.) violent, bruyant; (*b*) *a. & n.* **k. (comedian),** bateleur *m*; clown *m*; **k. comedy,** (grosse) farce; (*c*) *a.* **k. clothes,** (i) tenue *f* de loisir, de sport; (ii) vêtements usagés (qu'on met pour faire du bricolage, etc.). **2.** *n.* petit voilier.

knockdown [ˈnɔkdaun] *a.* **1.** (*a*) **k. blow,** coup *m* d'assommoir; (*b*) (machine, etc.) démontable. **2. k. price,** prix *m* minimum; prix de réclame.

knocker [ˈnɔkər] *n.* **1. (door) k.,** marteau *m* (de porte); heurtoir *m*. **2.** *P:* **knockers,** seins *mpl*, nichons *mpl*.

knock-kneed [ˈnɔkˈniːd] *a.* cagneux; **k.-k. horse,** cheval serré du devant; cheval panard.

knock-on [ˈnɔkɔn] *a.* **k.-on effect,** répercussions *fpl*.

knockout [ˈnɔkaut] **1.** *a.* (*a*) (coup) d'assommoir; **k. drops,** soporifique (*esp.* ajouté à une boisson); (*b*) (concours) avec (épreuves) éliminatoires; (*c*) *F:* magnifique, mirobolant. **2.** *n.* (*a*) coup de grâce; *Box:* knock-out *m*, *pl.* knock-outs; (*b*) *F:* (*pers. or thg*) merveille *f*; phénomène *m*; **she's a k.!** ce qu'elle est belle! (*c*) (*at auction*) entente *f* (entre concurrents pour baisser les prix); revidage *m*; (*d*) *Sp:* élimination progressive (des concurrents, des équipes).

knockup [ˈnɔkʌp] *n. Ten:* **to have a k.,** faire quelques balles (avant la partie, pour se faire la main).

knoll [noul] *n.* mamelon *m*, tertre *m*, monticule *m*, butte *f*.

knot¹ [nɔt] *n.* **1.** (*a*) nœud *m*; **to tie, untie, a k.,** faire, défaire, un nœud; **to tie a k. in one's handkerchief,** faire un nœud à son mouchoir; faire un pense-bête; **reef k.,** nœud plat; **slip k.,** nœud coulant; (*b*) nœud (de rubans); **sailor's k.,** nœud régate (marine); (*c*) **k. of hair,** chignon *m*. **2.** *Nau:* (*a*) nœud, division *f*, de la ligne de loch; (*b*) (*of ship*) **to make 10 knots,** filer 10 nœuds. **3.** nœud (d'une question, d'un problème). **4. the marriage k.,** le lien conjugal, du mariage; *F:* (*of priest*) **to tie the k.,** prononcer le conjungo. **5.** (*a*) nœud (d'une tige, d'un ligament, etc.); nodus *m* (d'un ligament, etc.); nodosité *f* (arthritique, etc.); (*b*) nœud (du bois). **6.** groupe *m*, noyau *m* (de personnes); groupe (d'objets); bouquet *m* (d'arbres).

knot² *v.* (**knotted**) **1.** *v.tr.* (*a*) nouer; faire un nœud, des nœuds, à (une ficelle); **to k. together two ropes,** attacher deux cordages ensemble; (*b*) (*of gout, etc.*) nouer (les membres). **2.** *v.i.* (*of string*) se nouer, faire des nœuds; (*of joints*) se nouer. **knotting** *n.* nouement *m* (de cordes).

knotty [ˈnɔti] *a.* **1.** (*of rope, etc.*) plein de nœuds. **2.** (*of problem, etc.*) épineux, embrouillé; (*of question*) difficile, épineux. **3.** (*a*) (*of wood, etc.*) noueux, raboteux; (*b*) (mains) noueuses.

know¹ [nou] *n. F:* **to be in the k.,** avoir le mot de l'affaire; être au courant (de l'affaire); *Rac: etc:* avoir des tuyaux; **those who are in the k.,** les initiés.

know² *v. tr. & i.* (*p.t.* **knew** [njuː]; *p.p.* **known** [noun]) **1.** (*a*) (*recognize*) reconnaître; **don't you k. me?** est-ce que vous ne me reconnaissez pas? **I'd k. him anywhere,** je le reconnaîtrais n'importe où; **I knew him by his walk,** je l'ai reconnu à son allure, à sa démarche; **I knew him for a German,** je l'ai reconnu comme Allemand; (*b*) distinguer (**from,** de, d'avec); **to k. good from evil,** connaître le bien d'avec le mal; **I didn't k. the one from the other,** je ne pouvais pas les distinguer l'un de l'autre. **2.** (*a*) (*be acquainted with*) connaître (qn, un lieu); **to get, come, to k. s.o.,** faire le connaissance de qn; **when I first knew him,** quand j'ai fait sa connaissance; (*b*) **he doesn't k. what fear is,** il ne sait pas ce que c'est que d'avoir peur; (*c*) **to k. about sth.,** être informé de qch.; être au courant; **nobody knows anything about it,** personne n'en sait rien; **he knows all about cars,** il est très calé sur les voitures; **I don't k. about that,** je n'en suis pas sûr; (*d*) **to k. of s.o.,** connaître qn de réputation; avoir entendu parler de qn; **to get to k. of sth.,** apprendre qch.; **we knew nothing of it,** nous l'ignorions; *F:* **not that I k. of,** pas que je sache. **3.** (*to be intimate *with*) connaître, fréquenter (qn); **he is not a man to k.,** ce n'est pas un homme à fréquenter. **4.** savoir, connaître, posséder (un sujet, une langue); **to k. sth. by heart,** savoir qch. par cœur; **to k. how to read, swim, do sth.,** savoir lire, nager, faire qch.; **to k. how to behave,** savoir se conduire. **5.** (*a*) (*to have cognizance of*) savoir (qch.); **to k. more than one says,** en savoir plus long qu'on n'en dit; **had I known,** si j'avais su; **as far as I k., for all I k.,** autant que je sache; *F:* **I wouldn't k.,** je ne saurais dire; **well, what do you k.!** sans blague! **he knows all the answers,** il a réponse à tout; *F:* **to k. a thing or two, to k. one's way about, around,** être malin, roublard; **as everyone knows,** comme tout le monde le sait; **he knows his own mind,** il sait ce qu'il veut; **I would have you k. that . . .,** sachez que . . .; **everyone knows that . . .,** personne n'ignore que . . .; **I knew (that) he had talent,** je lui connaissais du talent; **how do you k. (that) he will come?** qui vous dit qu'il viendra? **do you k. when . . ., why . . .?** savez-vous quand . . ., pourquoi . . .? **heaven (only) knows when I shall get back,** Dieu sait quand je serai de retour; **he didn't quite k. what to say,** il ne savait trop que dire; (*b*) **I k. him to be a liar,** je sais que c'est un menteur; **he is known to be a good father,** on le sait bon père; **it has been known to happen,** c'est une chose que qu'on a vue se produire; **I have never known him tell a lie,** je ne sache pas qu'il ait jamais menti. **6. to get to k. sth.,** apprendre qch.; **how did you get to k. that?** comment avez-vous appris cela? **please let us k. whether . . .,** veuillez nous faire savoir si . . .; **I don't want it known,** je ne veux pas que cela se sache. **7.** *F:* **don't I k. it!** à qui le dites-vous! **not if I k. it!** pour rien au monde! **she is pretty and doesn't she k. it!** elle est jolie et elle le sait bien! **8. to k. better than to . . .,** se bien garder de . . .; **I k. better (than that),** (i) je m'y connais mieux que ça; (ii) on ne m'y prendra pas; *F:* pas si bête! **he is old enough to k. better,** à son âge il devrait être plus raisonnable; **you k. best,** vous en êtes le meilleur juge; **you k. best what should be done,** vous savez mieux que personne ce qu'il faut faire. **knowing** *a.* (*a*) intelligent, instruit; (*b*) fin, malin, rusé; (sourire) entendu. **knowingly** *adv.* (*a*) sciemment; en connaissance de cause; (*b*) finement; d'un air rusé; (sourire) d'un air entendu. **known** *a.* (*a*) connu, reconnu; su; **a k. fact,** un fait bien connu; un fait reconnu; (*b*) (voleur, ennemi) avéré; (*c*) *Mth:* (quantité) connue.

know-all ['nouwɔːl] *n. F:* (*U.S: also* **know-it-all**) je-sais-tout *mf.*

know-how ['nouhau] *n. F:* savoir-faire *m* (technique); connaissances *fpl* techniques; technique opérationnelle; habilité *f.*

knowledge ['nɔlidʒ] *n.* **1.** (*a*) connaissance *f* (d'un fait, d'une personne); **it has come to my k. that . . .,** il est venu, parvenu, à ma connaissance que . . .; j'ai appris que . . .; **I had no k. of it,** je ne le savais pas; je l'ignorais; **lack of k.,** ignorance *f* (**of,** de); **it is a matter of common k. that . . .,** c'est un fait notoire que . . .; **to (the best of) my k.,** à ma connaissance; (autant) que je sache; **not to my k.,** pas que je sache; **without my k.,** à mon insu; **to speak with full k. (of the facts),** parler en connaissance de cause, en pleine connaissance des faits; (*b*) **he had grown out of all k.,** il avait grandi au point d'être méconnaissable. **2.** savoir *m,* science *f,* connaissance(s); **to have a k. of several languages,** connaître plusieurs langues; **he has a little k., a working k., of Latin,** il a quelques connaissances en latin; **his k. is immense,** ses connaissances sont très étendues; **k. of the world,** la science du monde; **k. is power,** savoir c'est pouvoir; *B:* **the tree of k. of good and evil,** l'arbre *m* de la science du bien et du mal. **3. carnal k.,** connaissance charnelle.

knowledgeable ['nɔlidʒəbl] *a.* bien informé.

knuckle[1] ['nʌkl] *n.* **1.** articulation *f,* jointure *f,* du doigt; **to rap s.o. over the knuckles,** donner sur les doigts à qn. **2.** *Cu:* **k. of a leg of lamb,** (i) (*bone*) manche *m,* (ii) (*meat*) souris *f* (d'un gigot); **k. of veal, of pork,** jarret *m* de veau, de porc; **k. of ham,** jambonneau *m*; *Games:* **to play at k. bones,** jouer aux osselets. **3.** *Mec.E: etc:* **k. (joint),** articulation à genouillère, joint *m* en charnière; charnière universelle.

knuckle[2] *v.tr.* **1.** frapper ou frotter (qch.) avec le poing. **2.** (*at marbles*) caler (la bille). **knuckle down** *v.i.* (*a*) (*at marbles*) appuyer la main à terre (en lançant la bille); (*b*) s'y mettre sérieusement. **knuckle under** *v.i.* se soumettre; céder; mettre les pouces.

knuckleduster ['nʌkldʌstər] *n.* coup-de-poing (américain), *pl.* coups-de-poing.

knurl[1] [nəːl] *n.* **1.** nœud *m* (du bois). **2.** *Metalw:* (*a*) *Tls:* molette *f,* godronnoir *m*; (*b*) molet(t)age *m.*

knurl[2] *v.tr. Metalw:* molet(t)er, godronner.

koala [kou'ɑːlə] *n. Z:* **k. (bear),** koala *m.*

kohlrabi [koul'ræbai, -'rɑːbi] *n. Bot:* chou-rave *m, pl.* choux-raves; turnep(s) *m.*

kola ['koulə] *n. Bot:* cola *m,* kola *m,* **k. (tree),** kolatier *m*; **k. nut,** noix *f* de cola, de kola.

kolkhoz ['kɔlkɔz] *n.* kolkhoze *m,* ferme collective.

kook [kuk] *n. NAm: F:* personne *f* bizarre; drôle d'individu *m.*

Koran (the) [ðəkɔː'rɑːn] *n. Rel:* le Koran, le Coran.

Korea [kə'riə] *Pr.n. Geog:* Corée *f*; **North K., South K.,** Corée du Nord, du Sud.

Korean [kə'riən] *Geog:* **1.** *a.* coréen. **2.** *n.* Coréen, -enne.

kosher ['kɔʃər, ·kouʃər] *a.* (*a*) *Jew.Rel:* cacher, -ère; kascher, -ère; (*b*) *F:* légitime, comme il faut, impec.

kowtow[1] [kau'tau] *n.* prosternation *f,* prosternement *m* (à la chinoise).

kowtow[2] *v.i.* **1.** se prosterner, se courber (à la chinoise) (**to,** devant); saluer à la chinoise. **2. to k. to s.o.,** faire des courbettes devant qn.

kraft [krɑːft] *n. Paperm:* papier *m* d'emballage fort, papier Kraft.

Krakow ['krɑːkɔf] *Pr.n. Geog:* Cracovie *f.*

Kremlin (the) [ðə'kremlin] *n.* le Kremlin.

kudos ['kjuːdɔs] *n.* (*a*) prestige *m*; (*b*) célébrité *f.*

Kurd [kəːd] *Ethn:* **1.** *a.* k(o)urde. **2.** *n.* K(o)urde *mf.*

Kurdish ['kəːdiʃ] **1.** *a. Ethn:* k(o)urde. **2.** *n. Ling:* k(o)urde *m.*

Kurdistan [kəːdi'stɑːn] *Pr.n. Geog:* K(o)urdistan *m.*

Kuweit [kuː'weit] *Pr.n. Geog:* Koweït *m.*

Kuweiti [kuː'weiti] *Geog:* **1.** *a.* koweïtien. **2.** *n.* Koweïtien, -ienne.

kyrie ['kiriei] *n. Ecc:* **k. (eleison** [ei'lei(i)sɔn]), kyrie *m inv* (eleïson).

L

L, l [el] *n.* **1.** (la lettre) L, l *m or f*; *Ling:* **liquid l, palatal(ized) l,** l mouillée. **2. L iron,** fer *m* cornière, fer en équerre.
la [lɑː] *n. Mus:* **1.** (*fixed*) la *m.* **2.** (*movable*) la sus-dominante.
lab [læb] *n. F:* (= *laboratory*) labo *m.*
label¹ ['leibl] *n.* (*a*) étiquette *f*; **gummed l.,** étiquette gommée; **luggage l.,** étiquette à bagages; (*b*) *Com:* label *m*, étiquette; (*c*) *Cmptr:* label (de bande, de fichier); (*d*) désignation *f*, qualification *f* (de qn).
label² *v.tr.* (**labelled,** *NAm:* **labeled**) (*a*) étiqueter; coller une étiquette sur (un paquet, une bouteille, etc.); **a bottle labelled poison,** une bouteille marquée poison; (*b*) *Com:* attribuer un label (de garantie, de qualité, etc.) à (un produit); (*c*) **to l. s.o. a liar,** qualifier qn de menteur.
labellum, *pl.* **-bella** [lə'beləm, -ə] *n. Bot:* labelle *m.*
labial ['leibiəl] **1.** *a.* labial, -aux; *Mus:* **l. pipe,** tuyau *m* à bouche (d'un orgue); *Ling:* **l. consonant,** consonne labiale. **2.** *n. Ling:* labiale *f.*
labiate ['leibieit] *Bot:* **1.** *a.* labié. **2.** *n.* labiée *f.*
labium, *pl.* **-a** ['leibiəm, -ə] *n.* **1.** *Bot:* lèvre *f* (de corolle labiée). **2.** *Ent:* labium *m.* **3.** *Anat:* **labia,** labia, lèvres (de la vulve).
labor ['leibər] *n. & v. NAm:* = LABOUR[1,2].
laboratory [lə'bɔrətri, *esp. NAm:* 'læbrətɔːri] *n.* laboratoire *m*; **research l.,** laboratoire de recherches; **l. tested,** essayé, éprouvé, en laboratoire; **dental l.,** laboratoire de prothèse dentaire; *Sch:* **language l.,** laboratoire de langues; **l. assistant,** laborantin, -ine.
laborious [lə'bɔːriəs] *a.* laborieux. **1.** travailleur, -euse. **2.** pénible, fatigant. **-ly** *adv.* péniblement.
laboriousness [lə'bɔːriəsnis] *n.* peine *f* (d'un travail, d'une ascension, etc.); pénibilité *f.*
labour¹, *NAm:* **labor¹** ['leibər] *n.* **1.** (*a*) travail *m*, labeur *m*, peine *f*; **manual l.,** travail manuel; **division of l.,** division *f* du travail; (*b*) *Jur: A:* **hard l.,** réclusion criminelle, *A:* travaux forcés. **2.** (*a*) main-d'œuvre *f*; travailleurs *mpl*; **male, female, l.,** main-d'œuvre masculine, féminine; **skilled, semi-skilled, unskilled, l.,** main-d'œuvre qualifiée, spécialisée, non spécialisée; **cost of l.,** prix *m* de la main-d'œuvre; **shortage of l.,** pénurie *f*, crise *f*, de main-d'œuvre; *NAm:* **labor union,** syndicat (ouvrier); (*b*) **capital and l.,** le capital et la main-d'œuvre; **l. unrest,** agitation ouvrière; *Adm: A:* **l. exchange,** bureau *m* de placement; **minister of l.,** ministre *m* du travail; (*c*) *coll. Pol:* les travaillistes *m*; **the L. party,** le parti travailliste; **L. member (of Parliament),** député *m* travailliste. **3. the twelve labours of Hercules,** les douze travaux d'Hercule; **l. of love,** (i) travail à titre gracieux; (ii) travail fait avec plaisir. **4.** *Med:* travail; couches *fpl*; **premature l.,** accouchement *m* avant terme; **woman in l.,** femme *f* en couches, en travail (d'enfant); **l. pains,** douleurs *fpl* de l'enfantement.
labour², *NAm:* **labor²** **1.** *v.i.* (*a*) travailler, peiner; **to l. for sth.,** se donner de la peine pour obtenir qch.; **to l. at, over, sth.,** travailler à qch.; peiner sur qch.; (*b*) **to l. up a hill,** gravir péniblement une côte; (*c*) **to l. under great difficulties,** être aux prises avec de grandes difficultés; **to l. under a sense of injustice,** nourrir un sentiment d'injustice; **to l. under a misapprehension,** être dans l'erreur; être (la) victime d'une erreur; (*d*) *Mch: I.C.E: etc.* (*of engine*) fatiguer, peiner; (*of ship*) bourlinguer, fatiguer; (*of car*) **to l. uphill,** peiner en côte. **2.** *v.tr.* élaborer (un ouvrage); travailler (son style); **I won't l. the point,** je ne m'étendrai pas là-dessus. **laboured,** *NAm:* **labored** *a.* **1.** (style, etc.) travaillé, trop élaboré; (poème, etc.) martelé, qui sent l'huile; (plaisanterie) laborieuse. **2.** (respiration) pénible. **labouring,** *NAm:* **laboring** **1.** *a.* (*a*) *O:* **l. man,** ouvrier *m*; **the l. class,** la classe ouvrière; (*b*) (cœur) qui peine. **2.** *n.* (*a*) travail manuel; peine *f*; (*b*) battement(s) *m*(*pl*) (du cœur).
labourer, *NAm:* **laborer** ['leibərər] *n.* (*a*) travailleur *m*; *Prov:* **the l. is worthy of his hire,** toute peine, tout travail, mérite salaire; (*b*) *Ind:* manœuvre *m*; homme *m* de peine; **unskilled l.,** ouvrier non spécialisé; (*c*) **agricultural l.,** ouvrier agricole.
labour-saving, *NAm:* **labor-** ['leibəseiviŋ] *a.* (appareil) allégeant le travail.
Labrador ['læbrədɔːr] *Pr.n. Geog:* le Labrador. **2.** *n.* (*dog*) labrador *m.*
laburnum [lə'bɔːnəm] *n. Bot:* cytise *m* (à grappes).
labyrinth ['læbərinθ] *n.* **1.** *Arch: etc:* labyrinthe *m*, dédale *m.* **2.** *Anat:* labyrinthe (de l'oreille).
lac [læk] *n.* gomme *f* laque; laque *f.*
lace¹ [leis] *n.* **1.** lacet *m* (de corset, de soulier); cordon *m* (de soulier). **2. gold, silver, l.,** galon *m* d'or, d'argent. **3.** dentelle *f*, point *m*; **bobbin l., pillow l.,** dentelle aux fuseaux, au coussin; **l. manufacture,** dentellerie *f*; **l. collar,** col *m* de dentelle.
lace² *v.tr.* **1. to l. (up),** lacer (des chaussures); (*with passive force*) (*of boots, etc.*) **to l. (up),** se lacer; **l.-up shoes,** *n.* **lace-ups,** chaussures *fpl* à lacets. **2. to l. sth. with sth.,** entrelacer qch. de, avec, qch. **3.** garnir (un ouvrage) de dentelles; galonner. **4.** *F:* additionner d'alcool (une boisson); **milk laced with rum,** lait *m* au rhum.
lacemaker ['leismeikər] *n.* **1.** fabricant, -ante, de dentelles. **2.** ouvrier, -ière, en dentelles.
lacemaking ['leismeikiŋ] *n.* dentellerie *f.*
lacerate ['læsəreit] *v.tr.* lacérer; déchirer. **lacerated** *a.* **l. feelings,** sentiments profondément blessés.
laceration [læsə'reiʃ(ə)n] *n.* **1.** lacération *f*, déchirement *m.* **2.** *Med: etc:* déchirure *f.*
lacewing ['leiswiŋ] *n. Ent:* **l. (fly)** hémérobe *m.*
lacework ['leiswəːk] *n.* dentelles *fpl*; dentellerie *f.*
lachrymal ['lækrim(ə)l] *a. & n. Anat:* (canal, sac) lacrymal, -aux; **l. gland,** glande lacrymale.
lachrymose ['lækrimous] *a.* larmoyant.
lack¹ [læk] *n.* manque *m*, pénurie *f* (**of,** de); **l. of judgment,** manque de jugement; **l. of money,** pénurie d'argent; **she was tired from l. of sleep,** ayant peu dormi elle était fatiguée; **for l. of . . .,** faute de . . . .
lack² *v.tr. & i.* manquer de (qch.); être dénué de (qch.); **we l. nothing,** nous ne manquons de rien; il ne nous manque rien; **he lacks experience,** il manque d'expérience; *F:* **to be lacking,** être (un peu) simplet.
lackadaisical [lækə'deizik(ə)l] *a.* (*of pers., manner, etc.*) apathique; d'une nonchalance affectée.
lackey ['læki] *n.* laquais *m.*
lacklustre ['læklʌstər] *a.* terne, sans brillant.
laconic [lə'kɔnik] *a.* laconique; (*of answer, etc.*) bref, *f.* brève. **-ally** *adv.* laconiquement.
lacquer¹ ['lækər] *n.* **1.** vernis-laque *m inv*; laque *m.* **2.** émail *m*; peinture laquée. **3.** *Hairdr:* laque *f.*

lacquer² *v.tr.* **1.** vernir, laquer. **2.** émailler (des meubles, etc.).
lacquerwork ['lækəwə:k] *n.* laque(s) *m(pl)*.
lacrosse [lə'kros] *n. Sp:* crosse *f*.
lactation [læk'teiʃ(ə)n] *n.* **1.** *Physiol:* lactation *f*. **2.** allaitement *m*.
lacteal ['læktjəl] *a.* lactaire.
lactic ['læktik] *a. Ch:* lactique; caséique.
lactose ['læktous] *n. Ch:* lactose *f*; sucre *m* de lait.
lacuna, *pl.* **-ae, -as** [læ'kju:nə, -i:, -əz] *n.* lacune *f*; hiatus *m* (dans un ouvrage).
lacustrine [lə'kʌstrin] *a.* (plante, etc.) lacustre.
lacy ['leisi] *a.* de dentelle; fin comme de la dentelle.
lad [læd] *n.* (*a*) jeune homme; garçon; **come on, lads!** allons, les gars! (*b*) **he's a real l., quite a l.,** (i) c'est un gaillard; (ii) c'est un vrai garçon; **one of the lads,** un des gars; (*c*) *Turf:* **(stable) l.,** lad *m*.
ladder¹ ['lædər] *n.* **1.** échelle *f*; (*a*) **extending, telescopic, l.,** échelle à coulisse; **folding l.,** échelle pliante; *Nau:* **accommodation l.,** échelle de commandement de coupée; **gangway l.,** échelle de coupée, de côté; **the social l.,** l'échelle sociale; **to climb a rung of the social l.,** gravir un échelon social; **to reach the top of the l.,** atteindre le sommet de l'échelle; (*b*) *Pisc:* **fish l., salmon l.,** échelle à poissons. **2.** (*in stocking*) maille filée; **I've got a l.,** j'ai une maille qui file; **to mend a l.,** rem(m)ailler un bas.
ladder² **1.** *v.tr.* **I've laddered my stocking,** j'ai filé mon bas. **2.** *v.i.* (*of stocking, etc.*) se démailler; filer.
laddie ['lædi] *n.m. Scot: F:* (*a*) garçon; (*b*) (*term of endearment*) mon petit gars.
laden ['leid(ə)n] *a.* chargé. **1. fully l. ship,** navire *m* en pleine charge. **2. heavily l. tree,** arbre chargé de fruits.
la-di-da(h) ['la:di'da:] *a. F:* (air) affecté.
lading ['leidiŋ] *n.* (*a*) chargement *m* (d'un navire); (*b*) mise *f* à bord (de marchandises).
ladle¹ ['leidl] *n.* **1. soup l.,** louche *f*. **2.** (*a*) *Ind:* puisoir *m*, casse *f*; (*b*) *Metall:* **foundry l.,** poche *f* de fonderie.
ladle² *v.tr.* **1. to l. (out) the soup,** servir le potage (avec la louche); **to l. out information,** débiter des renseignements. **2.** *Metall:* couler (la fonte).
ladleful ['leid(ə)lful] *n.* pleine louche (of, de).
lady ['leidi] *n.f.* dame. **1.** (*a*) (*at court*) **l. in waiting,** dame d'honneur; **l. of the bedchamber,** dame des atours; (*b*) *O:* dame, femme bien élevée; **she's a real l.,** c'est une femme très comme il faut; (*c*) **a l. and a gentleman,** un monsieur et une dame; **a young l.,** une jeune fille; (*married*) une jeune dame; **an old l.,** une vieille dame; (*to child*) **how are you, young l.?** comment allez-vous, ma petite demoiselle? (*at meeting, etc.*) **ladies and gentlemen!** mesdames, mesdemoiselles, messieurs! **come in, ladies!** entrez donc, mesdames! (*on public convenience*) **ladies,** dames; (*d*) **the l. of the house,** la maîtresse de maison; (*e*) **lady's watch,** montre *f* de dame; **ladies' tailor,** tailleur pour dames; **lady's maid,** femme de chambre; **a ladies' man,** un homme galant. **2.** *Ecc:* **Our L.,** Notre-Dame, la sainte Vierge; **L. chapel,** chapelle *f* de la Vierge; **L. Day,** la fête de l'Annonciation (le 25 mars). **3.** (*a*) (*title*) (i) (*no Fr. equivalent*) **Lady X,** lady X (femme de Sir David X); (ii) (*informal address*) **Lady Y,** Madame (la Comtesse, la Marquise, etc.) de Y; (*b*) **the l. of the manor,** la châtelaine. **4.** (*a*) *A:* femme, épouse; (*b*) *P:* **how's your good l.?** comment va votre femme? **my young l.,** (i) ma bonne amie; (ii) ma fiancée, ma future. **5.** (*a*) *Ent:* **painted l.,** belle-dame *f*, *pl.* belles-dames; (*b*) *Bot:* **lady's slipper,** sabot *m* de Vénus.
ladybird, *NAm:* **ladybug** ['leidibə:d, -bʌg] *n. Ent:* coccinelle *f*; *F:* bête *f* à bon Dieu.
ladykiller ['leidikilər] *n. F:* bourreau des cœurs; casse-cœur *inv*; don Juan.
ladylike ['leidilaik] *a.* (air, etc.) distingué, de dame; (*of woman*) comme il faut; bien élevée.
ladyship ['leidiʃip] *n.* **her l., your l.,** madame (la comtesse, etc.)
lag¹ [læg] *n. Ph:* retard *m*; *Ind: etc:* **time l.,** décalage *m* (entre deux opérations); *I.C.E: etc:* **ignition l.,** retard à l'allumage; *El:* **time l.,** retard.
lag² *v.i.* **(lagged) 1. to l. (behind),** rester en arrière; se laisser distancer (par les autres); **wages are lagging behind the cost of living,** les salaires restent inférieurs au coût de la vie. **2.** *Tchn:* (*of tides, etc.*) retarder; *El:* (*of current*) être déphasé en arrière.
lag³ *n. F:* **an old l.,** un repris de justice, un récidiviste.
lag⁴ *n.* latte *f* (d'enveloppe de chaudière).
lag⁵ *v.tr.* envelopper, revêtir (une chaudière) d'un calorifuge; calorifuger, isoler (une chaudière). **lagging** *n.* **1.** garnissage *m*, calorifugeage *m* (d'une chaudière, etc.). **2.** revêtement *m* calorifuge (d'une chaudière, etc.).
lager ['la:gər] *n.* bière blonde allemande.
laggard ['lægəd] **1.** *a.* lent; en retard. **2.** *n.* traînard, -arde; retardataire *mf*.
lagoon [lə'gu:n] *n. Geog:* **1.** (*sand, shingle, etc.*) lagune *f*. **2.** lagon *m* (d'atoll).
lah [la:] *n.* = LA.
laid. *see* LAY⁴.
lain [lein]. *see* LIE⁴.
lair ['lɛər] *n.* tanière *f*, repaire *m*, antre *m* (de bête fauve); **brigands' l.,** repaire de brigands.
laird ['lɛəd] *n. Scot:* propriétaire (foncier).
laisser-faire, laissez-faire [lesei'fɛər] *n.* laisser-faire *m*; **l.-f. policy,** politique *f* de laisser-faire.
laity ['leiiti] *n. coll.* **the l.,** les laïques *mpl*; le laïcat.
lake¹ [leik] *n.* (*a*) lac *m*; **salt l.,** lac salé; **ornamental l.,** bassin *m*; pièce d'eau décorative; **(the) L. (of) Geneva,** le lac Léman; **the Great Lakes,** les Grands Lacs (d'Amérique du Nord); **the L. District,** la région des lacs (au nord-ouest de l'Angleterre); *P:* **go jump in the l.,** va te faire foutre; (*b*) *Prehist: etc:* **l. dwelling,** habitation *f* lacustre.
lake² *n. Paint:* laque *f*; **crimson l.,** laque carminée.
Lakeland ['leiklənd] *attrib.* de la région des lacs (du nord-ouest de l'Angleterre).
lam [læm] *v.tr. & i.* **(lammed)** *F:* **to l. (into) s.o.,** rosser, étriller, qn.
lama ['la:mə] *n. Rel:* lama *m*; **the Dalai, Grand, L.,** le dalaï, grand, Lama.
lamb¹ [læm] *n.* **1.** (*a*) agneau *m*; **ewe l.,** agnelle *f*; **ewe with l.,** brebis pleine; *Ecc:* **L. (of God),** Agneau (de Dieu); *F:* **he went like a l.,** il s'est laissé faire; (*b*) *F:* **my l.,** mon petit; (*c*) *Hort:* **lamb's lettuce,** mâche *f*; (*d*) *F:* **lambs' tails,** chatons *mpl* (du noisetier). **2.** *Cu:* agneau; **l. cutlet, chop,** côtelette *f* d'agneau. **3.** (*fur*) **Persian l.,** astrakan *m*, caracul *m*.
lamb² *v.i.* (*of ewe*) agneler, mettre bas. **lambing** *n.* agnelage *m*, agnèlement *m*.
lambast [læm'bæst], **lambaste** [læm'beist] *v.tr.* fustiger (qn).
lambskin ['læmskin] *n.* (*a*) *Leath:* peau *f* d'agneau; (*b*) (*fur*) agnelin *m*.
lambswool ['læmzwul] *n.* laine *f* d'agneau.
lame¹ [leim] *a.* **1.** (*a*) boiteux; (*through accident, etc.*) estropié; **l. leg,** jambe boiteuse; **l. horse,** cheval boiteux; **to be l. in one leg,** boiter d'une jambe; **to be l.,** boiter; **to go l.,** se mettre à boiter; (*b*) *Pros:* **l. verses,** vers *mpl* boiteux; vers qui boitent. **2. l. excuse,** mauvaise, faible, excuse. **-ly** *adv.* (s'excuser, etc.) faiblement.
lame² *v.tr.* (*a*) rendre (qn) boiteux; écloper (qn, un cheval); (*b*) estropier (qn).
lamé ['la:mei] *n. Tex:* **gold, silver, l.,** lamé *m* d'or, d'argent.

lamella, *pl.* **-ae** [lə'melə, -iː] *n.* lamelle *f.*

lameness ['leimnis] *n.* **1.** (*a*) claudication *f*; (*b*) boiterie *f* (d'un cheval). **2.** faiblesse *f* (d'une excuse, etc.).

lament[1] [lə'ment] *n.* **1.** lamentation *f.* **2.** *Mus: A:* complainte *f.*

lament[2] *v.tr. & i.* **to l. (for, over) sth., s.o.,** se lamenter sur qch.; pleurer qch., qn; **the late lamented X,** le regretté X.

lamentable ['læməntəbl] *a.* (perte, insuccès, etc.) lamentable, déplorable; **it's l.!** c'est lamentable! **-ably** *adv.* lamentablement.

lamentation [læmən'teiʃ(ə)n] *n.* lamentation *f*; *B:* **the Lamentations of Jeremiah,** les Lamentations de Jérémie.

laminate ['læmineit] **1.** *v.tr.* (*a*) *Ind:* laminer, lamifier; (*b*) diviser en lamelles; (*c*) feuilleter (du verre); stratifier (de la matière plastique); contreplaquer (du bois); (*d*) *Bookb: etc:* plastifier (du papier, etc.). **2.** *v.i.* (*a*) se laminer; (*b*) se diviser en lamelles. **laminated** *a.* **1.** (*a*) *Mec.E:* **l. spring,** ressort *m* à lames (superposées); (*b*) (*of glass*) feuilleté; (*of wood*) contreplaqué; **l. plate glass,** verre *m* (de sécurité) feuilleté; *Ind:* **l. plastics,** matières *fpl* plastiques stratifiées. **2.** (*of paper, etc.*) plastifié; *Bookb:* **l. jacket,** jaquette plastifiée.

Lammas ['læməs] *n.* **L. (Day),** le premier août.

lammergeier ['læməgaiər] *n. Orn:* gypaète barbu.

lamp [læmp] *n.* **1.** (*a*) lampe *f*; **oil, paraffin, l.,** lampe à huile, à pétrole; **miner's l.,** lampe de mineur; **safety l.,** lampe de sûreté; (*in garage, etc.*) **portable l., inspection l.,** baladeuse *f*; (*b*) **projector, projection, l.,** lampe de projection; (*c*) lampe (de bicyclette); *Aut: O:* phare *m*; *Rail:* **signal l.,** lanterne de signalisation; (*d*) **table l.,** lampe de table; **standard l.,** lampadaire *m*; lampe sur pied; **l. standard,** torchère *f*; **hanging l.,** suspension *f*; **wall l.,** (lampe d')applique *f*; *Med:* **head l.,** lampe frontale. **2.** *El:* (*bulb*) lampe, ampoule *f*; **filament l.,** lampe à filament; **neon l.,** lampe au néon; **incandescent l.,** lampe à incandescence; **ultra-violet l.,** lampe à rayons ultra-violets; **infra-red l.,** lampe infra-rouge.

lampblack ['læmpblæk] *n.* noir *m* de fumée.

lamplight ['læmplait] *n.* lumière *f* de la lampe; **to work by l.,** travailler à la lampe.

lampoon[1] [læm'puːn] *n.* libelle *m*, brocard *m.*

lampoon[2] *v.tr.* lancer des satires, des brocards, contre (qn); chansonner (qn); brocarder (qn).

lamp-post ['læmppoust] *n.* **1.** (*in street*) (montant *m*, poteau *m*, de) réverbère (*m*). **2.** *Ind: Civ.E:* (*high*) mât *m* d'éclairage; (*low*) poteau d'éclairage.

lamprey, *pl.* **-eys** ['læmpri, -iz] *n. Ich:* lamproie *f.*

lampshade ['læmpʃeid] *n.* abat-jour *m inv.*

lampstand ['læmpstænd] *n.* pied *m* de lampe.

lance[1] [lɑːns] *n.* **1.** lance *f*; haste *f*; *A: & Lit:* **to break a l. with s.o.,** rompre une lance avec qn. **2.** *Mil:* **l. corporal,** (i) soldat *m* de première classe; (ii) sous-brigadier *m* de police.

lance[2] *v.tr.* **1.** percer (qn) d'un coup de lance. **2.** *Med:* percer, inciser (un abcès).

lanceolate(d) ['lɑːnsiəleit(id)] *a. Bot:* lancéolé.

lancer ['lɑːnsər] *n.* **1.** *Mil:* lancier *m.* **2. lancers,** (quadrille *m* des) lanciers.

lancet ['lɑːnsit] *n.* **1.** *Med:* lancette *f*, bistouri *m.* **2.** *Arch:* **l. (arch),** lancette.

land[1] [lænd] *n.* **1.** (*a*) (*opposed to sea*) terre *f*; **dry l.,** terre ferme; *Geog:* **Land's End,** la pointe de Cornouaille; **to travel by l.,** voyager par voie de terre; **l. route,** voie *f* de terre; **l. breeze,** brise *f* de terre; *Nau:* **l. ho!** terre (en vue)! **to make l.,** reconnaître la terre; atterrir; *Fig:* **to see how the l. lies,** sonder, tâter, le terrain; *Mil:* **to attack by l., sea and air,** attaquer par terre, par mer et par air; **l. warfare,** guerre *f* sur terre; **l. army,** armée *f* de terre; (*b*) terre, terrain, sol *m*; **arable l.,** terre arable, labourable; **ploughed l.,** terre labourée; **waste l.,** terre inculte; terrain vague; **man lives off the l.,** c'est la terre qui nourrit les hommes; *Jur:* **l. act,** loi *f* agraire; **l. bank,** crédit foncier, crédit agricole. **2.** (*country*) terre, pays *m*; **distant, unknown, lands,** pays lointains, inconnus; **the Holy L.,** la Terre Sainte; **the l. of dreams,** le pays des rêves. **3.** *Jur:* terre(s); fonds *m* de terre; bien-fonds *m*, *pl.* biens-fonds; propriété foncière; **to buy l.,** acheter des terres; **l. tax,** contributions foncières (sur les propriétés non bâties); **l. register,** registre *m* du cadastre. **4.** (*a*) plat *m*, intervalle *m* (entre cannelures ou gorges); cloison *f* (entre les rayures d'un fusil); (*b*) *Rec:* partie vierge, non enregistrée (d'un disque).

land[2] **1.** *v.tr.* (*a*) mettre, faire descendre, (qn) à terre; mettre (qch.) à terre; débarquer (qn, qch.); (*of vehicle*) déposer (qn à l'hôtel, etc.); décharger (des marchandises); faire atterrir (un avion); (*b*) amener (un poisson) à terre; **to l. a prize,** remporter un prix; (*c*) amener, planter (**s.o. somewhere,** qn quelque part); **that will l. you in prison,** cela vous vaudra de la prison; **you've landed us in a nice mess!** vous nous avez mis dans de beaux draps! **to be landed with sth.,** rester avec qch. sur les bras; (*d*) *F:* **to l. s.o. a blow in the face,** allonger, flanquer, à qn un coup au visage. **2.** *v.i.* (*a*) (*of pers.*) descendre à terre; débarquer; (*of ship*) aborder, accoster la terre, atterrir; (*of aircraft, pilot*) atterrir; (*of aircraft on deck of aircraft carrier*) apponter; **to l. on the moon,** alunir; **to l. on the sea,** amerrir; (*b*) tomber (à terre); **he slipped and landed in a puddle,** il a glissé et est tombé dans une flaque d'eau; (*c*) (*from a vehicle*) mettre pied à terre; (*after jumping*) tomber, retomber; **to l. on one's feet,** retomber sur ses pieds; *F:* **he always lands on his feet,** il retombe toujours sur ses pattes; (*d*) *Equit:* (*of horse, after jumping*) se recevoir; (*e*) *Rac:* (*of horse*) **to l. first,** arriver (le) premier. **landed** *a.* **1.** (voyageur) débarqué. **2. l. property,** propriété foncière, territoriale, *Jur:* prédiale; **l. proprietor,** propriétaire terrien. **landing** *n.* **1.** (*a*) *Fish:* prise *f* (d'un poisson); **l. net,** épuisette *f*; (*b*) *Nau:* débarquement *m*, mise *f* à terre (de qn, de qch.); *Com:* déchargement *m*; **(passenger's) l. card, ticket,** ticket *m*, carte *f*, carton *m*, de débarquement; **l. stage,** débarcadère *m*, embarcadère *m*; (*c*) *Mil: Navy:* débarquement; **l. force, party,** troupes *fpl*, compagnie *f*, de débarquement; **l. operation,** opération *f* de débarquement; **l. craft,** chaland *m*, engin *m*, de débarquement; (*d*) *Av:* (*of aircraft*) (*on land*) atterrissage; (*on sea*) amerrissage *m*; (*on deck of ship*) appontage *m*; **blind l., instrument l.,** atterrissage sans visibilité, aux instruments; **visual l.,** atterrissage à vue; **forced, emergency, l.,** atterrissage forcé; **to make a crash l.,** faire un atterrissage, atterrir, en catastrophe; **l. gear,** train *m* (d'atterrissage); atterrisseur *m*; **to retract the l. gear,** relever, rentrer, le train; **l. strip,** bande *f*, piste *f*, d'atterrissage; *Mil.Av:* **l. zone,** zone *f* d'atterrissage (des troupes aéroportées); **l. flap,** volet *m* d'atterrissage; **l. lights,** feux *mpl*, rampe *f*, d'atterrissage. **2.** *Const:* palier *m* (d'un escalier).

landau ['lændɔː] *n. A.Veh:* landau *m*, *pl.* landaus.

landfall ['lændfɔːl] *n. Nau:* (i) atterrissage *m*; (ii) arrivée *f* en vue de terre; **to make a l.,** (i) atterrir; (ii) arriver en vue de terre.

landlady ['lændleidi] *n.f.* **1.** propriétaire *f* (d'un immeuble). **2.** (*keeping furnished apartments*) logeuse (en garni). **3.** aubergiste, hôtelière.

landlegs ['lændlegz] *n.pl. F:* (*of sailor*) **to get one's l.,** se familiariser de nouveau avec la terre.

landlocked ['lændlɔkt] *a.* enfermé entre les terres; (port, etc.) entouré de terre; **l. sea,** mer intérieure.

landlord ['lændlɔːd] *n. m.* **1.** propriétaire (foncier). **2.**

propriétaire (d'un immeuble). **3.** (*keeping furnished apartments*) logeur *m* (en garni). **4.** aubergiste *m*, hôtelier *m*.

landlubber ['lændlʌbər] *n. Nau: F:* marin *m* d'eau douce; terrien *m*.

landmark ['lændmɑːk] *n.* **1.** borne *f* limite. **2.** (*a*) (point *m* de) repère (*m*); (*b*) *Av:* repère, point de repérage (au sol); (*c*) *Nau:* amer *m*, indice *m* (à terre); point à terre. **3.** point décisif, événement marquant; (*of event*) **to be a l.,** faire époque.

landmine ['lændmain] *n.* mine *f* terrestre.

landowner ['lændounər] *n.* propriétaire foncier.

landscape¹ ['læn(d)skeip] *n.* (*a*) paysage *m*; **these factories are a blot on the l.,** ces usines déparent le paysage; (*b*) **l. design,** *U.S:* **architecture,** architecture *f* de paysage; **l. gardener,** jardinier *m* paysagiste; *Art:* **l. painter,** paysagiste *m*, peintre *m* de paysages.

landscape² *v.tr.* aménager (un terrain) en parc; **they had their garden landscaped,** ils ont employé un jardinier paysagiste pour aménager leur propriété.

landslide ['lændslaid] *n.* **1.** éboulement *m*, affaissement *m*, glissement *m* (de terrain). **2.** *Pol:* (*a*) débâcle *f*, défaite accablante (d'un parti politique aux élections); (*b*) **l. (victory),** victoire écrasante.

landslip ['lændslip] *n.* = LANDSLIDE 1.

landward ['lændwəd] **1.** *adv.* **(to) l.,** du côté de la terre; vers la terre. **2.** *a.* **on the l. side,** vers l'intérieur; du côté de la terre.

lane [lein] *n.* **1.** (*in country*) chemin vicinal, rural; (*in town*) ruelle *f*, passage *m*. **2.** (*a*) (*in icefield*) passage; (*b*) *Nau:* route *f* de navigation; *Av:* **air l.,** couloir aérien; (*c*) *Aut: etc:* **(traffic) l.,** voie *f*; **four l. road,** route à quatre voies (de circulation); **fast l., slow l.** = voie de gauche, de droite; **get into l.** = serrez à gauche, à droite; (*d*) *Sp:* couloir.

language ['læŋgwidʒ] *n.* **1.** (*a*) langue *f* (d'un peuple); **the English l.,** la langue anglaise; **foreign languages,** langues étrangères; **modern languages,** langues vivantes; (*b*) langage *m*; **the l. of flowers,** le langage des fleurs; (*c*) **code l.,** langage convenu; code *m*; **business l.,** langage, langue, des affaires; *Cmptr:* **computer l., machine l.,** langage machine. **2.** langage; **bad l.,** langage grossier; grossièretés *fpl*; **to use bad l.,** parler vertement; lâcher de gros mots; **mind your l.!** surveillez votre langage!

languid ['læŋgwid] *a.* languissant, langoureux, faible; (voix) traînante; (mouvements) lents, traînants. **-ly** *adv.* languissamment, langoureusement.

languidness [læŋgwidnis] *n.* langueur *f*.

languish ['læŋgwiʃ] *v.i.* languir. **1.** dépérir; (*of plant*) s'étioler. **2. to l. after, for, s.o., sth.,** languir après, pour, qn, qch.; **to l. in prison,** languir en prison. **languishing** *a.* languissant, langoureux.

languor ['læŋgər] *n.* langueur *f*.

languorous ['læŋgərəs] *a.* langoureux. **-ly** *adv.* langoureusement.

lank [læŋk] *a.* **1.** (*of pers.*) maigre; sec, *f.* sèche; efflanqué; (corps) décharné. **2. l. hair,** cheveux plats.

lankiness ['læŋkinis] *n.* taille grande et maigre (de qn); aspect efflanqué.

lanky ['læŋki] *a.* grand et maigre.

lanolin(e) ['lænəli(ː)n] *n. Ch: Pharm:* lanoline *f*, graisse *f* de laine.

lantern ['læntən] *n.* **1.** (*a*) lanterne *f*, falot *m*; *Nau:* fanal, -aux, *m*; **Chinese l.,** lanterne vénitienne; (*b*) *A:* **magic l.,** lanterne magique. **2.** *Arch:* lanterne, lanternau *m* (de dôme). **3. l. jaws,** (i) joues creuses; (ii) menton *m* en galoche.

lanyard ['lænjɑːd, -jəd] *n. Nau:* aiguillette *f*; ride *f* (de hauban); (*of knife, etc.*) amarrage *m*.

Laos ['leiɔs, laus] *Pr.n. Geog:* Laos *m*.

Laotian [lei'ouʃ(ə)n] **1.** *a.* laotian. **2.** *n.* Laotien, -ienne.

lap¹ [læp] *n.* genoux *mpl*; *Lit:* giron *m*; **to sit on s.o.'s l.,** s'asseoir sur les genoux de qn; **it's in the l. of the gods,** Dieu seul le sait; **he expects everything to fall into his l.,** il pense qu'il n'y a qu'à se baisser et à prendre.

lap² *n.* **1.** (*a*) *Mch:* recouvrement *m;* (*b*) *Const:* chevauchement *m*, recouvrement (des tuiles, des ardoises); *Metalw:* **l. joint,** ourlet *m*; **l. weld(ing),** soudure *f* à recouvrement. **2.** (*a*) tour *m* (d'une corde autour d'un cylindre, etc.); (*b*) *Sp:* tour (de piste, de circuit); **to do three laps,** faire trois tours de circuit; **to be on the last l.,** en être à la dernière étape; **l. of honour,** tour d'honneur.

lap³ *v.* **(lapped** [læpt]**) 1.** *v.tr.* (*a*) **to l. sth. round sth.,** enrouler qch. autour de qch.; (*b*) *Const:* enchevaucher (des planches); poser (des planches) à recouvrement; donner du recouvrement à (des tuiles, etc.); **to l. a joint with sheet metal,** chaperonner un assemblage; (*c*) *Sp:* (i) **to l. an opponent,** prendre un tour d'avance sur un concurrent; (ii) **to l. the course,** boucler le circuit. **2.** *v.i.* **to l. over sth.,** dépasser, recouvrir, qch.; (*of tiles, etc.*) chevaucher qch.

lap⁴ *n.* **1.** gorgée *f* (de lait, etc.). **2.** clapotement *m*, clapotis *m* (des vagues).

lap⁵ 1. *v.tr.* (*of animal*) **to l. (up) milk,** laper du lait; *F:* **it was sheer flattery but he lapped it all up,** c'était de la flatterie pure et simple mais il a tout gobé, avalé. **2.** *v.i.* (*of waves*) clapoter. **lapping** *n.* clapotement *m*, clapotis *m* (des vagues).

laparotomy [læpə'rɔtəmi] *n. Surg:* laparotomie *f*.

lapdog ['læpdɔg] *n.* chien *m* d'appartement.

lapel [lə'pel] *n. Tail:* revers *m* (d'un habit).

lapidary ['læpid(ə)ri] *a. & n.* lapidaire (*m*).

lapis lazuli ['læpis'læzul(a)i] *n. Miner:* lazulite *m*; lapis(-lazuli) *m inv*; ultramarine *f*, outremer *m*.

Lapland ['læplænd] *Pr.n. Geog:* Laponie *f*.

Laplander ['læplændər] *n. Geog:* Lapon, -one.

Lapp [læp] **1.** *a. Geog:* lapon. **2.** *n.* (*a*) Lapon, -one; *Ling:* lapon *m*.

lapse¹ [læps] *n.* **1.** (*a*) (*mistake*) erreur *f*, faute *f*; **l. of memory,** défaillance *f*, absence *f*, de mémoire; oubli *m*; (*b*) (*moral fault*) chute *f*, faute, défaillance; faux pas; écart *m* de conduite; **l. from one's duty,** manquement *m* à son devoir. **2.** (*a*) *Jur:* déchéance *f* (d'un droit); (*b*) *Ecc:* dévolu *m*, dévolution *f* (d'un bénéfice). **3.** cours *m*, marche *f* (du temps); laps *m* de temps; **after a l. of three months,** après un délai de trois mois. **4.** *Meteor:* décroissement *m* (de la température, etc., avec l'élévation de l'altitude).

lapse² *v.i.* **1.** (*a*) déchoir; faillir; **to l. from duty,** manquer au devoir; s'écarter de son devoir; **to l. into silence,** rentrer dans le silence; (*b*) manquer à ses devoirs; être coupable d'un écart de conduite; faire un faux pas. **2.** *Jur:* (*of right, passport, etc.*) périmer, se périmer; (*of estate*) devenir disponible; (*of legacy*) devenir caduc; (*of law*) s'abroger; *Ins:* (*of policy, etc.*) cesser d'être en vigueur; **to allow a right to l.,** laisser périmer, laisser tomber, un droit. **lapsed** *a.* **1.** déchu; **a l. Christian,** un chrétien déchu. **2.** (billet, mandat-poste) périmé; *Jur:* (droit) périmé; (legs) tombé en dévolu; (contrat, legs) caduc (*f.* caduque).

lapsus ['læpsəs] *n.* lapsus *m*.

lapweld ['læpweld] *v.tr. Metalw:* souder en écharpe.

lapwing ['læpwiŋ] *n. Orn:* vanneau (huppé).

larceny ['lɑːsəni] *n.* (*a*) vol *m*; (*b*) *Jur:* **petty l.,** vol simple; vol minime.

larch [lɑːtʃ] *n.* (*a*) *Bot:* mélèze *m*; (*b*) **l. (wood),** bois *m* de mélèze.

lard¹ [lɑːd] *n.* saindoux *m*; panne *f*; graisse *f* de porc.

lard² *v.tr. Cu:* larder, barder, piquer (la viande); **larded joint,** larde *f*; *F:* **to l. one's writings with quotations,** larder ses écrits de citations.

larder ['lɑːdər] *n.* garde-manger *m inv*.

large [lɑːdʒ] **I.** *a.* **1.** (*a*) grand; gros, vaste; **l.(-sized),** de grand format; **a l. woman,** une grosse femme; **l. town,** grande ville; **l. parcel,** gros paquet, paquet volumineux; **to grow larger,** grossir; **there she is as l. as life,** la voilà, c'est bien elle! (*b*) **a l. sum,** une grosse, forte, somme; **l. family,** famille nombreuse; **l. whisky,** double whisky *m*; **to a l. extent,** en grande partie; **to trade on a l. scale,** faire les affaires en grand. **2.** (*a*) (*liberal*) **l. views,** idées *fpl* larges; (*b*) (*wide, extensive*) **l. powers,** pouvoirs larges, étendus. **II.** *adv.* **by and l.,** à tout prendre; généralement. **III.** *n.* **1.** (*a*) **to set a prisoner at l.,** élargir, relaxer, un prisonnier; **to be at l.,** être libre, en liberté; **the murderer is still at l.,** l'assassin n'est pas encore arrêté; (*b*) **the people at l.,** le grand public; la grande masse du public; (*c*) **at l.,** tout au long; en détail; (*d*) **to talk at l.,** parler au hasard. **2. details shown in l.,** détails *mpl* en grand. **-ly** *adv.* **1.** en grande partie; pour une grande part. **2. that is l. sufficient,** cela suffit grandement, largement.

largeness ['lɑːdʒnis] *n.* **1.** (*a*) grosseur *f* (du corps); (*b*) grandeur *f*, importance *f* (des profits, d'une majorité, etc.). **2.** (*a*) étendue *f* (d'un pouvoir); (*b*) largeur *f* (d'idées); grandeur (d'âme).

large-scale ['lɑːdʒ'skeil] *a.* grosse (entreprise); (carte) à grande échelle; **l.-s. farmer,** gros agriculteur.

largesse(e) [lɑː'ʒes] *n.* largesse *f*.

largish ['lɑːdʒiʃ] *a.* assez grand; assez gros.

largo ['lɑːgou] *adv.* & *n.* *Mus:* largo (*m inv*).

lariat ['læriət] *n.* **1.** corde *f* à piquet. **2.** lasso *m*.

lark¹ [lɑːk] *n.* *Orn:* alouette *f*; **to rise with the l.,** se lever au chant du coq; **she sings like a l.,** elle chante comme un rossignol.

lark² *n.* *F:* (*a*) farce *f*, rigolade *f*, blague *f*; **to do sth. for a l.,** faire qch. histoire de rire, de rigoler; **what a l.!** quelle farce! (*b*) **I'd like to know what his little l. is,** je me demande ce qu'il tripote.

lark³ *v.i.* **to l. (about),** faire des farces; rigoler.

larkspur ['lɑːkspəːr] *n.* *Bot:* pied-d'alouette *m*, *pl.* pieds-d'alouette.

larva, *pl.* **-vae** ['lɑːvə, -viː] *n.* *Ent:* larve *f*.

larval ['lɑːv(ə)l] *a.* **1.** *Ent:* larvaire; de larve; en forme de larve. **2.** *Med:* (*of disease*) latent, larvé.

laryngitis [lærin'dʒaitis] *n.* *Med:* laryngite *f*.

laryngoscope [lə'riŋgəskoup] *n.* laryngoscope *m*.

larynx ['læriŋks] *n.* *Anat:* larynx *m*.

lascivious [lə'siviəs] *a.* lascif; (sourire) provocant. **-ly** *adv.* lascivement.

lasciviousness [lə'siviəsnis] *n.* lasciveté *f*.

laser ['leizər] *n.* laser *m*; **l. beam,** faisceau *m* laser.

lash¹ [læʃ] *n.* **1.** (*a*) coup *m* de fouet; (*b*) lanière *f* (de fouet); **the l.,** le supplice du fouet. **2.** *Anat:* cil *m*.

lash² *v.tr.* & *i.* (*a*) fouetter, cingler (un cheval, etc.); (*of rain*) **to l. (against) the windows,** fouetter les vitres; (*of waves*) **to l. (against) the shore,** battre, fouetter, le rivage; (*b*) (*verbally*) cingler; **to l. s.o. with one's tongue,** adresser à qn des paroles cinglantes. **lashing 1.** *a.* (*of rain*) cinglant. **2.** *n.* (*a*) (i) coups *mpl* de fouet; le fouet; (ii) fouettée *f*; (iii) **tongue l.,** verte réprimande; (*b*) *F:* **lashings of sth.,** des tas *mpl* de qch.

lash³ *v.tr.* lier, attacher; *Nau:* amarrer; **to l. down a load on a trailer,** lier, brider, une charge sur une remorque; **to l. two wires together,** ligaturer, ligoter, deux fils. **lashing** *n.* **1.** *Nau:* amarrage *m*; ligature *f* (de câbles, de fils). **2.** *Nau:* amarre *f*; point *m* d'amarrage; commande *f* (de pontons).

lass [læs] *n.f.* *esp. Scot:* & *N.Eng:* jeune fille; **country l.,** jeune campagnarde.

lassie ['læsi] *n.f.* *esp. Scot:* fillette; **a wee l.,** une petite fille.

lassitude ['læsitjuːd] *n.* lassitude *f*.

lasso¹ [læ'suː] *n.* lasso *m*.

lasso² *v.tr.* prendre au lasso.

last¹ [lɑːst] *n.* *Bootm:* forme *f* (à chaussure); *Prov:* **let the shoemaker stick to his l.,** cordonnier, mêlez-vous de votre pantoufle!

last² I. *a.* dernier. **1.** (*a*) **the l. guest to arrive,** le dernier des invités à arriver; **the l. but one,** l'avant-dernier, *pl.* avant-derniers; **the l. syllable but one,** la (syllabe) pénultième; **the l. but three,** le troisième avant le dernier; **l. but not least,** le dernier (nommé), mais non le moindre; **you are the l. one who should criticize,** vous devriez être le dernier à critiquer; **that's the l. thing that's worrying me,** ça c'est le cadet de mes soucis; **in the l. resort, as a l. resort,** en dernière ressource; en dernier recours; **in the l. place,** en dernier lieu; pour finir; **in the l. analysis,** en dernière analyse; **to have the l. word,** (i) parler le dernier; (ii) avoir le dernier mot; **hotel that is the l. word in comfort,** hôtel qui est le dernier mot du confort; **to pay one's l. respects to s.o.,** rendre les derniers devoirs à qn; **I'm down to my l. pound,** il ne me reste plus qu'une livre; *esp. NAm:* (*intensive*) **every l. scrap of bread had been eaten,** on avait mangé jusqu'à la dernière miette; **at the l. moment, minute,** au dernier moment; **l.-minute decision,** décision *f* de dernière heure, de dernière minute; **the l. day of the month,** le dernier jour du mois; (*b*) (*lowest*) **that isn't his l. price,** ce n'est pas son dernier prix. **2.** (*of past time*) **l. Tuesday, Tuesday l.,** mardi dernier; **l. January,** au mois de janvier dernier; **the l. time I saw him,** la dernière fois que je l'ai vu; **l. week,** la semaine dernière; la semaine passée; **l. night,** (i) la nuit dernière; (ii) hier soir; **I slept badly l. night,** j'ai mal dormi cette nuit; **in the l. fifty years,** dans les cinquante ans qui viennent de s'écouler; pendant les cinquante dernières années; **this day l. week,** il y a aujourd'hui huit jours; **this day l. year,** l'an dernier à pareil jour. **II.** *n.* **1. this l.,** ce dernier, cette dernière; *B:* **the l. shall be first,** les derniers seront les premiers. **2.** (*a*) **we shall never hear the l. of it,** on ne nous le laissera pas oublier; **we haven't heard the l. of it,** tout n'est pas dit; **that's the l. I saw of him,** je ne l'ai pas revu depuis; (*b*) **to, till, the l.,** jusqu'au bout, jusqu'à la fin; **faithful to the l.,** fidèle jusqu'au bout; (*c*) *adv.phr.* **at l., at long l.,** enfin; à la fin (des fins); **now at l. I understand,** finalement je comprends; (*d*) **to look one's l. on sth.,** voir qch. pour la dernière fois; (*e*) (*death*) fin *f*; **to be near one's l.,** toucher à sa fin; **towards the l.,** vers la fin. **III.** *adv.* (*a*) **when I l. saw him, when I saw him l.,** la dernière fois que je l'ai vu; **when did you l. eat?** de quand date, à quand remonte, votre dernier repas? (*b*) **he spoke l.,** il a parlé le dernier; (*c*) **l. but not least,** enfin et surtout. **lastly** *adv.* pour finir; en dernier lieu.

last³ 1. *v.i.* durer, se maintenir; **it's too good to l.,** c'est trop beau pour durer; **if the good weather lasts,** si le beau temps tient; **the supplies will not l. (out) two months,** les vivres *mpl* ne feront pas deux mois; **their friendship won't l. long,** leur amitié *f* ne fera pas long feu; **it will l. me a lifetime,** j'en ai pour la vie; **he won't l. long in that job,** il ne fera pas long feu dans cette situation. **2.** *v.tr.* **to l. s.o. out,** (i) (*of pers.*) survivre à qn; (ii) (*of thg*) durer autant que qn; **to l. the year out,** durer, aller, jusqu'au bout de l'année; **my overcoat will l. the winter out,** mon pardessus fera encore l'hiver. **lasting** *a.* (*a*) durable, permanent; (*of material, etc.*) résistant, de bon usage; **l. peace,** paix *f* durable; (*b*) persistant.

latch¹ [lætʃ] *n.* **1.** (*a*) loquet *m*; (*for shutters, etc.*) **small l.,** loqueteau; (*b*) pêne *m*, gâche *f* (de portière de véhicule, etc.); (*c*) serrure *f* de sûreté (avec clef de maison); **to leave the door on the l.,** (i) fermer la porte au loquet; (ii) fermer la porte (sans la verrouiller). 2. *Mec.E:* verrou *m* (de levier, d'une pièce mécanique mobile); chien *m* (d'arrêt).

latch² *v.tr.* 1. (*a*) fermer (la porte) au loquet; (*b*) fermer (la porte) sans mettre le verrou. 2. *Mec.E:* verrouiller, bloquer (un levier, une pièce mécanique mobile). 3. *F:* **to l. on to (s.o., sth.),** (i) s'attacher à (qn); saisir (qch.); s'emparer de (qch.); (ii) saisir, piger (qch.).

latchkey ['lætʃki:] *n.* clef *f* de maison; clef de porte d'entrée; **l. child,** enfant dont les parents travaillent, et qui doit rentrer seul après l'école.

late [leit] I. *a.* (**later; latest;** *n.a.* LATTER *and* LAST²) 1. (*a*) (*after the appointed time*) en retard; **to be l. (for sth.),** être en retard (pour qch.); se faire attendre; **the train is l., is ten minutes l.,** le train a du retard, a dix minutes de retard; (*b*) (*delayed*) retardé. 2. (*a*) (*far on in the day, etc.*) tard; **it is l.,** il est tard; **it is getting l.,** il se fait tard; **it is too l.,** il est trop tard; **the latest I can come,** le plus tard que je puisse venir; **I was l. going to bed,** je me suis couché tard; **in the l. afternoon,** tard dans l'après-midi; **in l. summer,** vers la fin de l'été; *Prov:* **it's never too l. to mend,** il n'est jamais trop tard pour s'amender; **later events proved that . . .,** la suite des événements a démontré que . . .; **at a later meeting,** dans une séance ultérieure; **later will,** testament subséquent; **in later life,** plus tard dans la vie; **on Wednesday at the latest,** mercredi au plus tard; **latest date,** (i) date *f* limite; (ii) *Jur:* terme fatal; (iii) *Com:* terme de rigueur, délai *m* de rigueur; (*b*) (*far on in period*) **l. stained glass,** vitraux *mpl* de la dernière époque (du moyen âge, etc.); **in the l. (eighteen) eighties,** dans les années approchant 1890. 3. (*fruit, etc.*) tardif; **l. frosts,** gelées tardives, printanières. 4. (*a*) ancien, ex-; **the l. minister,** l'ancien ministre, l'ex-ministre; *Com:* **Martin, l. Thomas,** Martin, ancienne maison Thomas; (*b*) feu, défunt, décédé; **my l. father,** feu mon père; **the l. queen,** feu la reine, la feue reine. 5. (*of recent date*) récent, dernier; **the l. war,** la guerre récente; **of l. years,** (dans) ces dernières années; **of l.,** dernièrement, récemment, depuis peu; **this author's latest work,** le dernier ouvrage de cet auteur; **his latest views on the subject,** ses vues les plus récentes sur ce sujet; *Com:* **latest novelties,** dernières nouveautés; **the very latest improvements,** les tout derniers perfectionnements; **the very latest news,** les informations de toute dernière heure; **have you heard the latest?** savez-vous la dernière nouvelle? II. *adv.* (**later; latest;** *see also* LAST⁴) 1. (*after the appointed time*) en retard; **to arrive too l.,** arriver trop tard; arriver après coup; *Prov:* **better l. than never,** mieux vaut tard que jamais. 2. (*far on in the day, etc.*) tard; **he came home very l.,** il est rentré fort tard; **sooner or later,** tôt ou tard; **to keep s.o. l.,** attarder qn; **to go to bed l.,** (se) coucher tard; **to sleep, stay in bed, l.,** faire la grasse matinée; **l. into the night,** jusqu'à une heure avancée de la nuit; **l. in the year,** vers la fin de l'année; **l. in life,** à un âge avancé; **he married l. in life,** il se maria tard, sur le tard; **no later than yesterday,** pas plus tard qu'hier; **a moment later,** l'instant d'après; **this happened later (on),** cela est arrivé après, plus tard, ultérieurement; **a few days later,** à quelques jours de là; **as we shall see later,** comme nous le verrons plus tard, dans la suite; *F:* **see you later!** à bientôt! 3. *Poet:* = LATELY. 4. (*formerly*) **l. of London,** dernièrement domicilié à Londres; autrefois établi à Londres. **lately** *adv.* dernièrement, récemment; dans ces derniers temps; **what have you been doing l.?** qu'avez-vous fait ces derniers temps? **it is only l. that the matter has become known,** la chose n'a été sue que ces jours-ci.

lateen [lə'ti:n] *a. Nau:* **l. sail,** voile latine.

latency ['leitənsi] *n.* latence *f*, état latent; **l. period,** temps *m* de latence.

lateness ['leitnis] *n.* 1. arrivée tardive (de qn); tardiveté *f* (d'un fruit, etc.). 2. **the l. of the hour,** l'heure avancée.

latent ['leitənt] *a.* latent; **l. period,** temps *m* de latence; *Ph:* **l. heat,** chaleur latente; *Med:* **l. disease,** maladie latente; (*b*) caché, invisible; *Jur:* **l. defect,** vice caché; *Bot:* **l. bud,** œil dormant.

lateral ['læt(ə)rəl] *a.* latéral, -aux; *Mec:* **l. motion,** mouvement latéral; **l. play,** jeu latéral; *Bot:* **l. bud,** *n.* **lateral,** bourgeon latéral. **-ally** *adv.* latéralement.

latex ['leiteks] *n. Bot:* latex *m.*

lath [læθ, lɑ:θ] *n.* 1. *Const:* latte *f*; **l.-and-plaster partition,** cloison lattée et plâtrée. 2. (*of Venetian blind*) lame *f.* 3. batte *f*, latte, sabre *m* de bois (d'Arlequin).

lathe [leið] *n. Mch.Tls:* (*a*) tour *m*; **precision l.,** tour de précision; **l. bed,** banc *m*, bâti *m*, de tour; **capstan, turret, l.,** tour (à) révolver; (*b*) touret *m*; **polishing l.,** touret à polir, de polisseur.

lather¹ ['læðər] *n.* 1. mousse *f* de savon; **to make a l.,** faire lever la mousse. 2. (*on horse*) écume *f*; **horse all in a l.,** cheval couvert d'écume; *F:* **to work oneself into a l.,** s'énerver.

lather² 1. *v.tr.* (*a*) savonner (**s.o.'s chin,** le menton à qn); **to l. one's face,** se savonner; (*b*) *F: O:* (*thrash*) rosser (qn). 2. *v.i.* (*a*) (*of soap*) mousser; (*b*) (*of horse*) jeter de l'écume.

lathe-turned ['leiðtə:nd] *a.* fait au tour; tourné.

Latin ['lætin] 1. (*a*) *a.* latin; **the L. races,** les races latines; *Geog:* **L. America,** Amérique latine; (*b*) (*in Paris*) **the L. Quarter,** le Quartier latin. 2. *n.* (*a*) Latin, -ine; (*b*) *Ling:* latin *m*; **written in L.,** écrit en Latin; *F:* **dog L.,** latin de cuisine.

Latin-American ['lætinə'merikən] 1. *a.* latino-américain, *pl.* latino-américains. 2. *n.* Latino-américain, -aine.

latinize ['lætinaiz] *v.tr.* latiniser.

latish ['leitiʃ] 1. *a.* (*a*) un peu en retard; (*b*) un peu tard; **at a l. hour,** à une heure assez avancée. 2. *adv.* (*a*) (arriver) un peu en retard; (*b*) (se réveiller, etc.) un peu tard.

latitude ['lætitju:d] *n.* 1. **to allow s.o. the greatest l.,** laisser à qn la plus grande latitude, la plus grande liberté d'action. 2. *Geog:* latitude; **in northern, southern, latitudes,** dans les latitudes boréales, australes; **at a l. of 30° north,** par 30° (de) latitude nord; **in these latitudes,** sous ces latitudes. 3. *Astr:* **celestial l.,** latitude céleste.

latrines [lə'tri:nz] *n.pl.* latrines *fpl.*

latter ['lætər] *a.* 1. (*second-mentioned*) dernier (des deux); **the l.,** ce, le, dernier; cette, la, dernière; ces, les, derniers, -ières; celui-ci, celle-ci; ceux-ci, celles-ci. 2. (*belonging to the end*) **the l. half, part, of June,** la deuxième moitié de juin. **-ly** *adv.* 1. dans les derniers temps; vers la fin (d'une époque). 2. récemment.

latter-day ['lætə'dei] *a.* (*a*) *O:* moderne, d'aujourd'hui; (*b*) *Rel.H:* **the L.-d. Saints,** les Mormons *mpl.*

lattice ['lætis] *n.* (*a*) treillis *m*, treillage *m*; **l. window,** (i) fenêtre treillagée, treillissée; (ii) fenêtre à losanges, à vitraux sertis de plomb; *Civ.E: etc:* **l. beam, girder,** poutre *f* en treillis, à croisillons; **l. bridge,** pont *m* en treillis; **l. mast,** (i) *N.Arch:* mât *m* en treillis; (ii) *Civ.E:* (*supporting electric wires, etc.*) pylône métallique; (*b*) lacis *m*, entrecroisement *m*; **l. of boughs,** lacis de branchages.

latticed ['lætist] *a.* treillissé, treillagé; (rameaux) entrecroisés.

latticework ['lætiswə:k] *n.* treillage *m*, treillis *m.*

Latvia ['lætviə] *Pr.n.* Lettonie *f.*

Latvian [ˈlætviən] **1.** *a.* lettonien, letton. **2.** *n.* Lettonien, -ienne; (*a*) Letton, -one; (*b*) *Ling:* letton *m.*
laud [lɔːd] *v.tr. Lit:* louer, panégyriser (qn).
laudable [ˈlɔːdəbl] *a.* louable; digne de louanges. **-ably** *adv.* louablement.
laudanum [ˈlɔːd(ə)nəm] *n. Pharm:* laudanum *m.*
laudatory [ˈlɔːdət(ə)ri] *a.* élogieux, louangeur, -euse.
laugh¹ [lɑːf] *n.* rire *m*; **to burst into a (loud) l.,** éclater de rire; partir d'un éclat de rire; **with a l.,** en riant; **he loves a l.,** il aime à rire; **to raise a l.,** faire rire; *F:* **to do sth. for a l.,** faire qch. histoire de rire; **that's a l.!** quelle blague! c'est marrant! **the laugh's on us,** on nous a bien refaits.
laugh² **1.** *v.i.* rire; (*a*) **to l. heartily,** rire de bon cœur; **to l. and cry at the same time,** pleurer d'un œil et rire de l'autre; **to l. till one cries, till the tears come,** rire (jusqu')aux larmes; **to l. to oneself,** rire tout seul; rire tout bas; *F:* **to l. all the way to the bank,** rire à la caisse; **to l. in, up, one's sleeve,** rire dans sa barbe; **to l. in s.o.'s face,** rire au nez, à la barbe, de qn; *F:* **I soon made him l. on the other side of his face,** je lui ai bientôt fait passer son envie de rire; *F:* **don't make me l.,** laissez-moi rire! *Prov:* **he laughs best who laughs last,** rira bien qui rira le dernier; (*b*) **to l. at, over, sth.,** rire de qch.; **there's nothing to l. at,** il n'y a pas de quoi rire; **to l. at s.o.,** se moquer, (se) rire, de qn; railler qn; **I'm afraid of being laughed at,** j'ai peur de prêter à rire. **2.** *v.tr.* (*a*) *with cogn. acc.* **he laughed a bitter l.,** il eut un rire amer; (*b*) **to l. down a proposal,** tuer une proposition par le ridicule; **to l. s.o. out of court,** se moquer des prétentions de qn; **he laughed the matter off,** il tourna la chose en plaisanterie. **laughing** **1.** *a.* riant; rieur. **2.** *n.* (*a*) rires *mpl*; **in a l. mood,** en humeur de rire; **I'm in no l. mood,** je n'ai pas le cœur à rire; **it's no l. matter,** il n'y a pas de quoi rire; (*b*) **l. gas,** gaz hilarant. **laughingly** *adv.* en riant.
laughable [ˈlɑːfəbl] *a.* risible, comique, ridicule; (offre) dérisoire. **-ably** *adv.* risiblement.
laughingstock [ˈlɑːfiŋstɔk] *n.* (objet *m* de) risée *f*; objet de raillerie; **to make a l. of oneself,** se faire moquer de soi.
laughter [ˈlɑːftər] *n.* rire(s) *m(pl)*; **peals of l.,** éclats *mpl* de rire; **to cause l.,** provoquer, exciter, les rires, l'hilarité *f*; **he made us cry with l.,** il nous a fait rire aux larmes; *F:* **to split one's sides with l.,** crever, mourir de rire; **uncontrollable fit of l.,** fou rire.
launch¹ [lɔːn(t)ʃ] *n. Nau:* chaloupe *f*; **motor l.,** vedette *f.*
launch² *n. Nau: Ball: etc:* lancement *m.*
launch³ **1.** *v.tr.* (*a*) lancer (un projectile, un coup, etc.) (**at s.o.,** à qn); (*b*) *Nau:* lancer (un navire, une torpille); mettre (un navire) à l'eau, à la mer; (*c*) lancer (qn, une affaire, une enquête); *Mil:* déclencher (une offensive). **2.** *v.i.* (*a*) **to l. out at, against, s.o.,** (i) lancer un coup à qn; (ii) faire une sortie à, contre, qn; (*b*) **to l. out,** mettre à la mer; (*c*) **to l. out on an enterprise,** se lancer dans une affaire; **to l. into abuse of s.o.,** se répandre en invectives contre qn; **once he is launched on this subject,** une fois lancé sur ce sujet; **to l. out (into expense),** se lancer dans la dépense. **launching** *n.* **1.** *Nau:* (*a*) lancement, mise *f* à l'eau (d'un navire); **l. cradle,** berceau *m* de lancement; (*b*) mise à l'eau (d'une embarcation); (*c*) *Navy:* lancement (d'une torpille). **2.** (*a*) *Ball:* lancement (d'un projectile, d'une fusée); **l. pad, platform,** plateforme *f* de lancement (de fusées, de missiles); **l. ramp,** rampe *f* de lancement; **l. site,** (i) aire *f* de lancement; (ii) *esp. U.S:* base *f*, complexe *m*, station *f*, de lancement (de fusées, de missiles); (*b*) *Av:* **l. catapult,** catapulte *f* de lancement. **3.** (*a*) *Com: Fin:* lancement (d'une affaire, d'un emprunt, etc.); (*b*) *Mil:* déclenchement *m*, lancement (d'une attaque, d'une offensive).
launcher [ˈlɔːn(t)ʃər] *n.* (*a*) appareil *m*, dispositif *m*, de lancement; lanceur *m* (de projectiles, de fusées); *Mil:* **grenade l.,** lance-grenades *m inv* (à fusil); **rocket l.,** lance-fusées *m inv*; (*b*) *Ball:* rampe *f*, plateforme *f*, de lancement (de fusées, de missiles); (*c*) *Av:* catapulte *f* de lancement (d'avions).
launder [ˈlɔːndər] *v.tr.* blanchir (le linge). **laundering** *n.* blanchissage *m.*
launderette [lɔːndəˈret] *n.* laverie *f* automatique.
laundress [ˈlɔːndres] *n.f.* blanchisseuse.
laundromat [ˈlɔːndroumæt] *n. NAm:* laverie *f* automatique.
laundry [ˈlɔːndri] *n.* **1.** blanchisserie *f*; *Fr.C:* buanderie *f.* **2.** lessive *f*; linge (i) blanchi, (ii) à blanchir; **l. list,** liste *f* de blanchissage.
laureate [ˈlɔːriət] **1.** *a.* lauréat; **Poet L.** (*pl.* **Poets Laureate**), poète lauréat (dignité conférée par la Couronne). **2.** *n.* lauréat, -ate.
laurel [ˈlɔrəl] *n.* **1.** *Bot:* laurier *m.* **2.** **l. wreath,** couronne *f* de lauriers; **crowned with laurel(s),** couronné, ceint, de lauriers; **to reap, win, laurels,** cueillir, moissonner, des lauriers; **to rest on one's laurels,** se reposer sur ses lauriers; **he must look to his laurels,** il est en passe d'être éclipsé.
lav [læv] *n. F:* petit coin, cabinets *mpl.*
lava [ˈlɑːvə] *n.* lave *f*; **l. stream, flow,** coulée *f* de lave.
lavabo, *pl.* **-os** *n.* (*a*) [ləˈveibou, -ouz] *Ecc:* lavabo *m*; (*b*) [ˈlævəbou, -ouz] *NAm: Dom.Ec:* lavabo.
lavatory [ˈlævətri] *n.* **1.** *A:* & *NAm:* (*a*) cabinet *m* de toilette; (*b*) lavabo *m.* **2.** (*a*) cabinets *mpl*; **public l.,** W.-C. *mpl*, toilette(s) *f(pl)*; **l. paper,** papier *m* hygiénique; (*b*) ensemble W.-C.; **l. pan,** cuvette *f* de W.-C.
lavender [ˈlævindər] **1.** *n. Bot:* lavande *f*; **oil of l.,** essence *f* de lavande; **l. water,** eau *f* de lavande. **2.** *a.* (*colour*) lavande *inv.*
lavish¹ [ˈlæviʃ] *a.* **1.** (*of pers.*) prodigue (**in, of,** de); **to be l. in praises,** prodiguer des louanges; se prodiguer en éloges; **l. in spending,** prodigue de son argent. **2.** (*of thg*) somptueux; abondant; (repas) plantureux; (dépenses) folles; (installation) princière; **to live in a l. style,** mener la vie à grandes guides. **-ly** *adv.* **1.** avec prodigalité; à pleines mains; **to spend l.,** dépenser de l'argent à profusion; être prodigue de son argent. **2.** somptueusement.
lavish² *v.tr.* prodiguer (son argent); répandre (son argent, etc.); **to l. sth. on s.o.,** prodiguer qch. à qn.
lavishness [ˈlæviʃnis] *n.* **1.** prodigalité *f.* **2.** somptuosité *f.*
law [lɔː] *n.* **1.** (*a*) loi *f*; **to pass, repeal, a l.,** voter, abroger, une loi; **labour laws,** législation *f* du travail; (*b*) loi (de la nature, etc.); *Ph:* **the laws of gravity,** les lois de la pesanteur; *Pol.Ec:* **l. of diminishing returns,** loi des rendements décroissants; (*c*) *Phil: etc:* principe *m*; (*d*) **laws of a game,** règles *fpl* d'un jeu. **2.** (*a*) **the l.,** la loi; **to carry out the l.,** appliquer la loi; **to keep, break, the l.,** observer, enfreindre, la loi; **custom that has become l.,** usage *m* qui a passé en loi; **to have the force of l.,** faire loi, avoir force de loi; **his word is l.,** sa parole fait loi, a force de loi; **to lay down the l.,** (i) expliquer la loi; (ii) faire la loi (à qn); **he thinks he's above the l.,** il se croit tout permis; **to be a l. unto oneself,** n'en faire qu'à sa tête; **to have one l. for the rich and another for the poor,** avoir deux poids et deux mesures; (*b*) **Divine l.,** la loi divine; (*c*) *Rel.H:* **the L., the l. of Moses,** la loi mosaïque. **3.** droit *m*; **civil l.** = droit civil; **common l.,** (i) droit coutumier; (ii) droit civil; **criminal l.,** droit pénal, criminel; législation criminelle; **commercial l.,** droit commercial; code *m* de commerce; **l. of contract** = droit des obligations; **Roman l.,** droit romain; **case l.,** droit jurisprudentiel; **judgment**

quashed on a point of l., arrêt cassé pour vice de forme; **to read, study, l.,** étudier le droit, faire son droit; **l. student,** étudiant, -ante, en droit; **Bachelor, Doctor, of Laws** = licencié(e), docteur, en droit; **to practise l.,** exercer une profession juridique; **l. officer,** conseiller *m* juridique; **l. lord,** membre *m* juriste de la Chambre des Lords. **4.** (*a*) (*justice*) **court of l.,** cour *f* de justice; tribunal *m*, -aux; **to go to l.,** avoir recours à la justice; recourir à la justice; *P:* **I'll have the l. on you!** je vais vous poursuivre en justice! **to hand s.o. over to the l.,** remettre qn à la justice; **action at l.,** action *f* en justice; **to be at l.,** être en procès; **to take the l. into one's own hands,** (i) se faire justice soi-même; (ii) agir de soi-même sans avoir recours à la justice; *Adm: Com:* **l. department,** bureau *m*, service *m*, du contentieux; le contentieux; **l. costs,** frais *mpl* de procédure; (*b*) *F:* **the l.,** (i) la police; (ii) un policier, un flic; **arm of the l.,** représentant *m* de la loi.

law-abiding ['lɔːəbaidiŋ] *a.* respectueux des lois; qui observe la loi; **l.-a. people,** amis *mpl* de l'ordre.

lawbook ['lɔːbuk] *n.* livre *m* de droit.

lawbreaker ['lɔːbreikər] *n.* transgresseur *m* de la loi.

lawbreaking ['lɔːbreikiŋ] *n.* infraction *f* à la loi.

lawcourt ['lɔːkɔːt] *n.* cour *f* de justice; tribunal *m*.

lawful ['lɔːf(u)l] *a.* légal, -aux. **1.** permis, licite; **l. trade,** trafic *m* licite. **2.** (droit, union, enfant, etc.) légitime; (contrat) valide; (*of inheritance*) **l. share,** portion virile. **3.** (revendication, etc.) juste. **-fully** *adv.* légalement, légitimement.

lawgiver ['lɔːgivər] *n.* législateur *m*.

lawless ['lɔːlis] *a.* **1.** sans loi; (temps) d'anarchie. **2.** sans frein; déréglé, désordonné.

lawlessness ['lɔːlisnis] *n.* dérèglement *m*, désordre *m*, licence *f*; anarchie *f*.

lawmaker ['lɔːmeikər] *n.* législateur *m*.

lawn[1] [lɔːn] *n. Tex:* batiste *f*; (*fine*) linon *m*.

lawn[2] *n.* pelouse *f*; (parterre *m* de) gazon (*m*); **l. sprinkler,** arrosoir *m* de pelouse; tourniquet arroseur; **to mow, cut, the lawn,** tondre le gazon.

lawnmower ['lɔːnmouər] *n.* tondeuse *f* (à gazon).

Lawrence ['lɔrəns] *n. Pr.n.m.* Laurent.

lawsuit ['lɔːsjuːt] *n.* procès *m*; action *f* judiciaire; **to bring a l. against s.o.,** intenter un procès à qn.

lawyer ['lɔːjər] *n.* homme *m* de loi; juriste *m*; jurisconsulte *m*; = (i) avocat *m*, (ii) avoué *m*, (iii) notaire *m*.

lax [læks] *a.* **1.** (*a*) (*of conduct, principles*) relâché; (*of pers.*) négligent, inexact; (discipline) lâche; **l. morals,** morale *f* facile, peu sévère; **to be l. in (carrying out) one's duties,** ne pas toujours observer ses devoirs; (*b*) (*of ideas, interpretation, etc.*) vague; peu exact; **l. use of a word,** emploi peu précis d'un mot; emploi abusif d'un mot. **2.** (*limp*) mou, *f.* molle; flasque. **3.** *Med:* (ventre) lâche, relâché.

laxative ['læksətiv] *a.* & *n. Med:* laxatif (*m*).

laxity, laxness ['læksiti, 'læksnis] *n.* (*a*) relâchement *m* (des mœurs, de la discipline); **l. in one's duties,** inexactitude *f* à remplir ses devoirs; (*b*) vague *m*, imprécision *f*, peu *m* d'exactitude (de langage, etc.).

lay[1] [lei] *n.* **1.** lai *m*, chanson *f*. **2.** poème *m* (lyrique). **3.** poème, chant, récité par un ménestrel.

lay[2] *a.* **1.** laïque, lai; (*a*) *Ecc:* **l. brother,** frère lai, frère convers. **l. sister,** sœur laie, sœur converse; **l. clerk,** chantre *m*; **l. preacher,** prédicateur laïque; (*b*) **to the l. mind it seems complicated,** aux yeux du profane cela est compliqué. **2.** *Art:* **l. figure,** mannequin *m* (en bois, etc.).

lay[3] *n.* **1.** *P:* genre *m* d'affaires, spécialité *f*; **that's not my l.,** ce n'est pas de ma partie. **2. l. of the land,** configuration *f*, disposition *f*, du pays, du terrain. **3. hens in full l.,** poules *fpl* en pleine ponte. **4.** *P:* **she's an easy l.,** c'est une môme facile, une Marie couche-toi-là.

lay[4] *v.* (*p.t.* & *p.p.* **laid** [leid]) **I.** *v.tr.* **1.** coucher; (*a*) **to l. s.o., sth., low, flat,** (i) coucher, étendre, qn, qch. (par terre); (ii) terrasser, abattre, qn; **laid low by sickness,** terrassé par la maladie; (*b*) (*of wind, rain*) coucher, abattre (le blé); (*c*) *Needlew:* remplier (un ourlet, etc.); (*d*) *P:* **to l. a girl,** s'envoyer une fille. **2.** (*cause to subside*) (*a*) abattre (la poussière, etc.); (*b*) exorciser, conjurer (un fantôme); **to l. a fear,** écarter à tout jamais un sujet d'inquiétude. **3.** (*deposit*) mettre, placer, poser (**sth. on sth.,** qch. sur qch.); **to l. one's hand on s.o.'s shoulder,** mettre la main sur l'épaule de qn; **to l. a book on the table,** poser un livre sur la table; **to have nowhere to l. one's head,** ne pas avoir où reposer la tête; **to l. s.o. to rest,** mettre, coucher, qn au tombeau. **4.** (*of hen, etc.*) pondre (un œuf); *v.i.* **hen beginning to l. again,** poule qui recommence à pondre. **5.** faire (un pari); parier (une somme); **to l. ten pounds,** y aller de dix livres. **6.** (*place*) (*a*) **to l. a ship alongside (the quay),** accoster un navire le long du quai; (*b*) pointer (une arme à feu, un missile, etc.) (**on,** sur). **7.** soumettre (une question, une demande) (**before s.o.,** devant qn); exposer (les faits); **he laid before me all the facts of the case,** il me présenta tous les faits; *Jur:* **to l. a complaint,** déposer une plainte; porter plainte; **to l. a matter before the court,** saisir le tribunal d'une affaire; **to l. an information,** présenter une information. **8.** (*a*) imposer (une peine, une obligation) (**upon s.o.,** à qn); infliger (une amende, etc.); (*b*) **to l. a tax on sth.,** frapper qch. d'un impôt; (*c*) *P:* **to l. into s.o.,** rosser qn; rouer qn de coups; **to l. about one,** frapper de tous côtés. **9.** (*dispose, arrange*) (*a*) poser, jeter, asseoir (des fondements); ranger (des briques); poser (une voie ferrée); poser, immerger (un câble); verser (le béton) en place; poser, tendre (un tapis); préparer (le feu); *Navy:* poser, mouiller (une mine); **to l. the table,** mettre la table; **to l. for three,** mettre la table pour trois personnes; mettre trois couverts; (*b*) dresser, tendre (un piège); disposer, dresser, placer, tendre (une embuscade); (*c*) former, faire (un projet); former, ourdir, tramer, concerter (un complot). **II.** *v.i. P:* (*incorrectly used for* **lie**) **to l. in bed,** rester couché. **laid** *a. Paperm:* (papier) vergé. **lay aside** *v.tr.* se dépouiller de (ses préjugés, sa réserve); abandonner, mettre de côté (un travail); mettre (un papier) de côté; remiser (qch.); mettre (de l'argent) de côté. **lay back** *v.tr.* retourner, rabattre (qch.); (*of horse*) rabattre, coucher (les oreilles). **lay by** *v.tr.* mettre (qch.) de côté; réserver (qch.); **to l. money by,** mettre de l'argent en réserve (pour l'avenir); mettre de l'argent de côté. **lay down 1.** *v.tr.* (*a*) déposer, poser (qch.); mettre bas, rendre (les armes); *Cards:* étaler, abattre (son jeu); (*b*) coucher, étendre (qn); **to l. oneself down,** se coucher; (*c*) quitter, se démettre de, résigner (ses fonctions); abdiquer, résigner (le pouvoir); (*d*) **to l. down one's life,** sacrifier sa vie, faire le sacrifice de sa vie (**for,** pour); (*e*) mettre (un navire) en chantier, sur cale; (*f*) poser, imposer, établir (un principe, une règle); fixer (des conditions); spécifier (des fonctions); indiquer, prescrire (une ligne de conduite); **to l. down that . . .,** stipuler que . . .; (*g*) tracer, marquer (qch. sur une carte, un plan); (*h*) mettre (du vin) en cave, sur chantier. **2.** *v.i. P:* = LIE DOWN. **lay in** *v.tr.* (*a*) faire provision, s'approvisionner, de (qch.); **to l. in provisions,** faire des provisions; *Com:* **to l. in goods, stock,** emmagasiner des marchandises; (*b*) rentrer (les avirons). **laying 1.** *a.* **l. hen,** poule pondeuse. **2.** *n.* (*a*) pose *f* (de rails, de tuyaux, de câbles, etc.); assise *f* (de fondements); immersion *f* (d'un câble sous-marin); mouillage *m* (d'une mine); (*b*) ponte *f* (des œufs); (*c*) pointage *m* (d'une arme à feu, d'un missile, etc.); (*d*) **l. down,** (i) établissement *m* (d'un principe, etc.); (ii) pose *f* (d'une canalisation, d'un câble); assiette *f* (d'une ligne); mise en chantier, sur cale (d'un navire); (iii) dépôt *m* (des armes); (*e*) **l. in,** emmagasinage *m* (de marchandises); approvisionnement *m*; (*f*) **l. off,** (i) licenciement *m* (de la main-d'œuvre); mise en repos (d'une machine); (ii) *Ins:* réassurance *f*; (*g*) **l. on,** (i) application *f* (d'un enduit, etc.); (ii) installation *f* (de l'eau, etc.); *Ecc:* **l.-on of hands,** imposition *f* des mains; (*h*) **l. out,** (i) disposition *f*; étalage *m*; (ii) toilette *f* (d'un mort); (*i*) **l. up,** désarmement *m* (d'un navire); mise sur cales (d'une voiture). **lay off 1.** *v.tr.* (*a*) licencier, renvoyer temporairement (des ouvriers); (*b*) *Nau:* **to l. off a bearing,** porter un relèvement (sur la carte); (*c*) *Ins:* **to l. off a risk,** effectuer une réassurance; *Turf: etc:* **to l. off a bet,** faire la contre-partie d'un pari. **2.** *v.i.* (*a*) *F:* se reposer; prendre, s'offrir, un congé; *P:* **l. off!** fiche-moi la paix! (*b*) *Nau:* rester au large. **lay on** *v.tr.* (*a*) étendre, coucher, appliquer (un enduit, etc.); *Art:* **to l. on the paint,** peindre dans la pâte, en pleine pâte; *F:* **to l. it on thick, with a trowel,** (i) flatter qn grossièrement; ne pas épargner les compliments; (ii) faire (qch.) à l'excès; exagérer; (*b*) (i) installer (le gaz, l'électricité); amener (l'eau, le gaz) (dans la maison); (ii) *F:* arranger, préparer, organiser (qch.); **I'll l. on a car for you at the station,** je vais vous faire chercher en voiture à la gare. **lay out** *v.tr.* (*a*) arranger, disposer (des objets); étaler, déployer (des marchandises); servir (un repas); (*b*) (i) faire la toilette (d'un mort); (ii) *F:* étendre (qn) d'un coup; coucher (qn) par terre, sur le carreau; *Box:* envoyer (l'adversaire) au tapis; (*c*) **to l. out money,** dépenser, débourser, de l'argent; (*d*) dresser, tracer, aligner (un camp); dessiner, disposer (un jardin); tracer (une avenue, une courbe); faire le tracé (d'une route); construire (une route). **lay up** *v.tr.* (*a*) mettre (qch.) en réserve; accumuler, amasser (des provisions, etc.); (*b*) désarmer, déséquiper (un navire); mettre (un navire) en rade; mettre (une voiture) sur cales; (*c*) **to be laid up,** être alité, obligé de garder le lit.

layabout ['leiəbaut] *n. F:* paresseux *m*; vaurien *m*.

layby ['leibai] *n.* (*a*) *Rail:* voie *f* de garage; (*b*) (*on road*) terre-plein *m*, bande *f*, de stationnement; (*on motorway*) = aire *f* (de stationnement).

layer¹ ['leiər] *n.* **1.** (*pers.*) (*a*) poseur *m* (de tuyaux, de rails, etc.); **l. out,** (i) dessinateur *m* (de jardins); (ii) ensevelisseuse *f* (d'un mort); (*b*) *Rac:* **layers and backers,** parieurs *mpl* contre et pour. **2.** (*hen, etc.*) **good l.,** bonne pondeuse. **3.** (*a*) couche *f* (de peinture, etc.); lit *m* (de fumier); *Cu:* **l. cake,** gâteau fourré (à la crème); (*b*) **the upper layers of the atmosphere,** les couches supérieures de l'atmosphère; **Heaviside l.,** couche de Heaviside; (*c*) *El:* **conducting l.,** couche conductrice; **magnetic l.,** feuillet *m* magnétique; (*d*) *Phot: etc:* **sensitive l.,** couche sensible; (*e*) *Const:* assise *f*, lit (de béton, de briques, etc.); *Geol:* couche, strate *f* (de roches, etc.). **4.** *Hort:* marcotte *f*.

layer² *v.tr.* (*a*) poser, disposer, en couches; (*b*) *Hort:* marcotter (un rosier, etc.).

layette [lei'et] *n.* layette *f*.

layman, *pl.* **-men** ['leimən] *n.m.* **1.** *Ecc:* laïque *m*, séculier *m*. **2.** personne *f* qui n'est pas du métier; profane *m*, civil *m*.

layoff ['leiɔf] *n. Ind:* licenciement *m* (temporaire).

layout ['leiaut] *n.* **1.** (*a*) tracé *m* (d'une construction, etc.); dessin *m* (d'un jardin); (*b*) agencement *m*, disposition *f*, des pièces (dans un ensemble mécanique); schéma *m* de montage; (*c*) *Typ:* disposition *f* typographique, (mode *m* de) présentation *f* (d'un texte, etc.). **2.** étude *f* (pour la construction d'une machine, etc.); *Aut:* **chassis l.,** étude de châssis.

laywoman, *pl.* **-women** ['leiwumən, -wimin] *n.f.* **1.** laïque. **2.** femme qui n'est pas du métier.

Lazarus ['læzərəs] *Pr.n.m. B:* Lazare.

laze [leiz] *v.tr. & i.* **to l. (about),** paresser, fainéanter; lézarder; **to l. in bed,** traînasser au lit; faire la grasse matinée.

laziness ['leizinis] *n.* paresse *f*, fainéantise *f*.

lazy ['leizi] *a.* **1.** (*a*) paresseux, fainéant; **a l. person,** un paresseux, une paresseuse; **I feel too l. to do it,** je n'ai pas l'énergie de le faire; (*b*) *NAm:* **l. Susan,** plateau tournant (placé au milieu de la table). **2.** (moments) de paresse. **-ily** *adv.* paresseusement; (vivre) en paresseux.

lazybones ['leizibounz] *n. F:* paresseux, -euse; fainéant, -ante.

lea [li:] *n. Lit:* prairie *f*, pâturage *m*.

leach [li:tʃ] **1.** *v.tr.* (*a*) filtrer (un liquide); (*b*) lessiver (du minerai, de l'écorce); (*c*) **to l. away, l. out, salts,** extraire des sels par lessivage. **2.** *v.i.* (*of liquid*) filtrer (**through,** à travers).

lead¹ [led] *n.* **1.** plomb *m*; (*a*) **l. ore,** minerai *m* de plomb; **white l.,** (i) (*ore*) plomb blanc, (ii) *Ch:* blanc *m* de plomb; **l. content,** indice *m* de plomb (dans un carburant); (*b*) *Metall:* **pig l.,** plomb en saumon; **l. wire,** fil *m* de plomb; **l. glass,** verre *m* de, au, plomb; **l. pipe,** tuyau *m* de plomb; (*c*) *Const:* **roof leads,** plombs de couverture; **window leads,** plombs de vitrail, de vitraux; (*d*) *Sm.a:* **l. shot,** grenaille *f* de plomb, petit plomb; (*e*) *Med:* **l. poisoning,** intoxication saturnine, par le plomb. **2.** mine *f* (de crayon); **l. pencil,** crayon *m* à la mine de plomb. **3.** *Nau:* (plomb de) sonde *f*; **l. line,** ligne *f* de sonde; *F:* **to swing the l.,** tirer au flanc. **4.** *Typ:* interligne *f*.

lead² [led] *v.tr.* (**leaded** ['ledid]; **leading** ['lediŋ]) (*a*) plomber (un toit); (*b*) *Fish:* plomber (une ligne, un filet); (*c*) enchâsser (des vitraux) dans les plombs; **leaded windows,** vitres plombées; (*d*) *Typ:* interligner (des lignes de composition).

lead³ [li:d] *n.* **1.** conduite *f*; **to follow s.o.'s l.,** suivre l'exemple de qn; prendre exemple sur qn; **to give s.o. a l.,** (i) amener qn sur un sujet; (ii) mettre qn sur la voie; (*b*) **to take the l.,** (i) prendre la tête; (ii) prendre la direction; (iii) *Sp: etc:* devancer ses concurrents; **to take the l. over s.o.,** prendre le pas, gagner les devants, sur qn; **to have a l. of ten metres,** avoir une avance de dix mètres. **2.** *Cards:* primauté *f*; **to have the l.,** jouer le premier; avoir la main; **your l.!** à vous de jouer (le premier)! **to follow the l. in clubs,** fournir du trèfle. **3.** *Th:* premier rôle; (rôle de) vedette *f*; **juvenile l.,** jeune premier, jeune première. **4.** (*a*) (*for dog, etc.*) laisse *f*; **dogs must be kept on a l.,** les chiens doivent être tenus en laisse; (*b*) *Harn:* **l. reins,** grandes guides. **5. mill l.,** bief *m* de moulin. **6.** *El:* câble *m*, branchement *m*, de canalisation; amenée *f* de courant; fil *m* électrique.

lead⁴ [li:d] *v.* (*p.t. & p.p.* **led** [led]) **I.** *v.tr.* **1.** (*a*) mener, conduire, guider (**s.o. to a place,** qn à un endroit); *Ecc:* **l. us not into temptation,** ne nous soumets pas à la tentation; **to be led astray,** se laisser entraîner; *Jur:* **to l. a witness,** poser des questions tendancieuses à un témoin; (*b*) **to l. the way,** montrer le chemin; marcher le premier, en tête; **to l. the conversation back to a subject,** ramener la conversation sur un sujet. **2.** conduire, guider (un aveugle, etc.) par la main; mener (un cheval) par la bride; tenir (un chien) en laisse; **he is easily led,** il va comme on le mène. **3.** induire, porter, pousser (**s.o. to do sth.,** qn à faire qch.); **that leads me to believe that . . .,** cela me mène à croire que . . .; **I was led to the conclusion that . . .,** je fus amené à conclure que . . .. **4.** amener (de l'eau à un endroit); faire passer (un cordage à travers une poulie). **5.** (*a*) mener (une vie heureuse, malheureuse); (*b*) **to l. s.o. a dog's life,** faire une vie de chien à qn. **6.** (*a*) commander (une armée); **leading his troops,** à la tête de ses troupes; (*b*) mener (la danse, le chant); **to l. a party,** être chef de parti; (*c*) *v.i.* (*of barrister*) être l'avocat principal (dans un procès). **7.** (*in race, etc.*) **to l. the field,** mener le champ; **to l. (s.o.) by eight points,** mener (qn) par huit points. **8.** *Cards:* (*a*) **to l. a card,** entamer, attaquer, d'une carte; **to l. clubs,** jouer, attaquer, trèfle; (*b*) *v.i.* ouvrir le jeu; jouer le premier, entamer. **II.** *v.i.* **1.** (*of road*) mener, conduire (**to,** à); **road that leads to the town,** chemin *m* qui mène, va, à la ville; **door that leads into the garden,** porte *f* qui communique avec le jardin, qui donne accès au jardin. **2. to l. to a good result,** aboutir à un bon résultat; produire un heureux effet; **to l. to a discovery,** conduire, aboutir, à une découverte; **one thing leads to another,** une chose mène à une autre; **to l. to nothing,** n'aboutir, ne mener, à rien; **action which led to criticism,** action qui a motivé des critiques. **leading 1.** *a.* (*a*) **l. question,** *Jur:* question posée au témoin de manière à suggérer la réponse; question tendancieuse; (*b*) (*chief*) premier; principal, -aux; important; **a l. man,** (i) un homme important; (ii) *Navy:* matelot *m* de première classe; **the l. statesmen of Europe,** les hommes d'État dirigeants de l'Europe; **a l. shareholder,** un des principaux actionnaires; **one of the l. firms of the country,** une des plus puissantes maisons du pays; **l. article,** (i) *Journ:* = LEADER 4 (*e*); (ii) *Com:* article *m* (de) réclame; spécialité *f* de réclame; *Th:* **l. role, part,** premier rôle; **l. man, lady,** premier rôle; vedette *f*; **to play a l. role in a matter,** jouer un rôle prépondérant dans une affaire; (*c*) (*in front*) (i) (voiture) de, en, tête; *Navy:* **the l. ship,** le chef de file; *Mil:* **l. patrol,** patrouille *f* de tête; (ii) *Veh:* **l. axle, wheels,** essieu porteur d'avant; *Av:* **l. edge,** bord *m* d'attaque (de l'aile); (iii) *El:* **l. current,** courant déphasé en avant; (iv) *Cards:* **l. card,** première carte; (v) *Hort:* **l. shoot,** pousse principale, terminale. **2.** *n.* conduite *f*, menage *m* (de chevaux, etc.); *Harn:* **l. rein,** longe *f*, plate-longe *f*, *pl.* plates-longes; (*b*) *Mil: etc:* conduite, commandement *m* (de la troupe, d'une unité); (*c*) direction *f* (d'une entreprise, etc.). **lead off** *v.i. & tr.* (*a*) commencer, débuter (**with,** par); (*b*) entamer les débats; jouer le premier; *Bill:* donner l'acquit; *Danc:* ouvrir le bal; **to l. off an attack,** lancer une attaque. **lead on 1.** *v.tr.* **to l. s.o. on to talk,** encourager qn à parler; *F:* **to l. s.o. on,** (i) entraîner qn; (ii) tromper, duper, qn. **2.** *v.i.* **l. on!** en avant! **lead up** *v.i.* **to l. up to a subject,** amener un sujet; **to l. up to the climax,** amener le dénouement.

lead-bearing ['ledbɛəriŋ] *a.* plombifère.

leaden ['led(ə)n] *a.* de plomb; (teint) plombé; **l. sky,** ciel *m* de plomb; **l.-eyed,** aux yeux ternes; **l.-footed,** à la démarche pesante; **l. limbs,** membres inertes.

leader ['li:dər] *n.* **1.** (*pers.*) (*a*) conducteur, -trice; guide *m*; (*b*) *Mil:* chef *m*; commandant *m* (de compagnie); (*c*) chef, directeur *m* (d'un parti); meneur *m* (d'une émeute); **L. of the House of Commons,** chef de la majorité ministérielle à la Chambre des Communes; *Sp:* **team l.,** chef d'équipe; (*d*) *Mus:* premier violon; (*of a group*) chef; (*e*) *Jur:* avocat principal (dans une cause); (*f*) chef, premier, -ière (d'un file); (*g*) **major group, l. in its field,** groupe important, leader *m* dans sa branche. **2.** cheval *m* de volée, de tête, d'avant; **the leaders,** l'attelage *m* de devant. **3.** question, observation, faite pour orienter la conversation. **4.** (*a*) *Agr:* conduit *m*; (*b*) *Rec: Cin:* amorce *f* (de bande magnétique, de film); (*c*) *Const:* tuyau *m* de descente; descente *f* d'eau; conduit d'eau; (*d*) *Hort:* pousse terminale; bourgeon terminal; (*e*) *Journ:* article principal, de fond, de tête; éditorial, -aux; *F:* leader; **l. writer,** éditorialiste *m*; (*f*) *Com:* **loss l.,** produit *m* d'appel (vendu à perte).

leadership ['li:dəʃip] *n.* **1.** (*a*) conduite *f*; **to be under s.o.'s l.,** être sous la conduite de qn; (*b*) qualités *fpl* de chef; (*c*) sens *m* de commandement. **2.** (*a*) *Mil:* commandement *m*; (*b*) fonctions *fpl* de chef; direction *f* (d'un parti, etc.).

lead-in ['li:din] *n.* **1.** (*a*) *El: Tp: etc:* entrée *f* (de câble, *W.Tel:* de poste); (*b*) *W.Tel: etc:* descente *f* d'antenne; *Rec:* **l.-in groove,** sillon initial (de disque). **2.** *Av:* guidage *m* (d'un avion vers une piste d'atterrissage, etc.).

lead-out ['li:daut] *n. El: Tp:* sortie *f* (de fils, etc.); *Rec:* **l.-o. groove,** sillon *m* de sortie (d'un disque).

leadsman, *pl.* **-men** ['ledzmən] *n.m. Nau:* sondeur.

leadwork ['ledwə:k] *n.* (*a*) plomberie *f*; (*b*) *Arch:* plombs *mpl* (d'un vitrail).

leaf¹, *pl.* **leaves** [li:f, li:vz] *n.* **1.** (*a*) feuille *f* (de plante, d'arbre); *Bot:* **l. bud,** bourgeon *m* à feuille; *Hort:* **l. mould,** terreau *m* de feuilles; (*of plant, tree*) **to put out leaves, to come into l.,** (se) feuiller; **to shed its leaves,** s'effeuiller; **in l.,** couvert de feuilles, en feuilles; (*b*) *F:* pétale *m* (de fleur); (*c*) **l. tobacco,** tabac *m* en feuilles; **outer l. of a cigar,** robe *f* d'un cigare; (*d*) *Ent:* **l. insect,** phyllie *f*; **l.-cutting bee,** (abeille) (dé)coupeuse *f* de feuilles; (*e*) *a. & n.* **l. green,** vert pré (*m*) *inv.* **2.** (*a*) feuillet *m* (de livre); *Bookb:* **single l.,** carton *m* de deux pages; **to turn over the leaves of a book,** feuilleter un livre; (*of pers.*) **to turn over a new l.,** (i) changer de conduite; faire peau neuve; (ii) faire plan neuf; **to take a l. out of s.o.'s book,** prendre exemple, modèle, sur qn; (*b*) **counterfoil and l.,** talon *m* et volant *m* (d'un carnet de chèques, etc.). **3.** feuille (d'argent, d'or, etc.). **4.** battant *m*, vantail, -aux *m* (de porte); battant (de contrevent); panneau, -eaux *m* (de paravent); *Mec.E: etc:* obturateur *m* (de vanne); aile *f* (de pignon); lame *f*, feuille, feuillet (de ressort); **l. of a table,** (i) (*inserted*) rallonge *f*, (ii) (*hinged, also* **drop l.,** *U.S:* **fall l.**) battant, de table).

leaf² *v.i.* **1.** (se) feuiller; pousser des feuilles. **2. to l. through a book,** feuilleter un livre.

leaflet ['li:flit] *n.* (*a*) feuillet *m* (de papier); imprimé *m*; (*b*) *Com: etc:* imprimé, papillon *m*, publicitaire; prospectus *m*; *Pol:* tract *m*.

leafstalk ['li:fstɔ:k] *n. Bot:* pétiole *m*.

leafy ['li:fi] *a.* feuillu; couvert de feuilles; *Lit:* **l. canopy,** dais *m* de feuillage, de verdure.

league¹ [li:g] *n. A.Meas:* lieue *f*.

league² *n.* (*a*) ligue *f*; **everyone is in l. against them,** tout le monde est ligué, s'est conjuré, contre eux; **he was in l. with them,** il était ligué, d'intelligence, avec eux; *Hist:* **the L. of Nations,** la Société des Nations; *Fb:* **l. matches,** matchs *mpl* de championnat (professionnels); (*b*) catégorie *f*; *F:* **I'm not in your l.,** je ne suis pas de votre classe.

league³ 1. *v.tr.* **to be leagued with s.o.,** être ligué avec qn; **to be leagued together,** être ligués, être d'intelligence. **2.** *v.i.* **to l. (together),** se liguer, se conjurer (**with, against,** avec, contre; **in order to,** pour).

leak¹ [li:k] *n.* (*a*) fuite *f*, écoulement *m* (d'un liquide); perte *f* d'eau; (*b*) infiltration *f*, rentrée *f* (d'eau, etc.); *Nau:* voie *f* d'eau; (*of ship*) **to spring a l.,** (se) faire une voie d'eau; (*c*) fuite (de secrets officiels, etc.).

leak² 1. *v.i.* (*a*) (*of tank, etc.*) avoir une fuite; fuir; perdre (son eau); (*of liquid*) fuir, couler; (*of truth, news, etc.*) **to l. (out),** s'ébruiter, transpirer; (*b*) (*of ship, etc.*) faire eau; avoir une voie d'eau; **roof that leaks,** toit qui laisse entrer la pluie; **my shoes l.,** mes chaussures prennent l'eau. **2.** *v.tr. F:* divulguer, laisser filtrer (des informations, etc.).

leakage [ˈliːkidʒ] *n.* **1.** (*a*) fuite *f* (d'eau, de gaz, d'un tonneau); perte *f*, coulage *m* (d'eau); perte, fuite, (d'électricité) (par dispersion); (*b*) fuites, pertes, coulage. **2.** (*a*) coulage (dans une maison de commerce); (*b*) fuite (de secrets officiels).

leaky [ˈliːki] *a.* (*a*) (tonneau) qui coule, qui perd, qui fuit; (*b*) (bateau) qui fait eau; (chaussures) qui prennent l'eau; (toit) qui laisse entrer la pluie.

lean¹ [liːn] **1.** *a.* maigre; (*a*) amaigri, décharné; (*of animal*) efflanqué, étique; (*b*) (viande) maigre; (*c*) (années) maigres, déficitaires; (années) de disette; (argile) pauvre; (houille) maigre; **l. diet,** maigre régime; régime frugal. **2.** *n.* maigre *m* (de la viande).

lean² *n.* inclinaison *f.*

lean³ *v.* (*p.t. & p.p.* **leaned** [liːnd] *or* **leant** [lent]) **1.** *v.i.* (*a*) s'appuyer (**against, on, sth.,** contre, sur, à, qch.); **to l. on one's elbow(s),** s'accouder; **leaning against a wall,** appuyé à, contre, un mur; **to l. back in one's chair,** se renverser dans son fauteuil; **to l. on s.o.,** (i) s'appuyer sur qn; (ii) *F:* serrer la vis à qn; (*b*) **to l. forward, out of the window,** se pencher en avant, par la fenêtre; **to l. over, towards, sth.,** se pencher sur, vers, qch.; **that wall is leaning towards the right,** ce mur incline, penche, déverse, vers la droite; (*c*) **to l. towards an opinion,** incliner pour une opinion; **to l. towards socialism,** pencher au socialisme; (*d*) *F:* **to l. over backwards to do sth.,** (i) se mettre en quatre pour faire qch.; (ii) aller aux concessions extrêmes pour faire qch. **2.** *v.tr.* appuyer (une échelle) (**against a wall,** contre, à, un mur); **to l. sth. against sth.,** (i) (*with its back*) adosser, (ii) (*with its side*) accoter qch. à, contre, qch. **leaning 1.** *a.* penché; penchant; (mur) qui penche; **the l. tower of Pisa,** la tour penchée de Pise. **2.** *n.* (*a*) inclination *f* (d'une tour, etc.); (*b*) inclination (**towards,** pour); penchant *m* (**towards,** pour, vers); tendance *f* (**towards,** à); **he has leanings towards communism,** il penche vers le communisme.

leanness [ˈliːnnis] *n.* maigreur *f.*

leant. *see* LEAN³.

lean-to [ˈliːntuː] **1.** *a.* **l.-to roof,** comble *m* en appentis. **2.** *n.* appentis *m*; abat-vent *m inv.*

leap¹ [liːp] *n.* **1.** saut *m*, bond *m*; **to take a l. in the dark,** faire un saut dans l'inconnu; **his heart gave a l.,** son cœur bondit; il eut un bondissement de cœur; **to advance by leaps and bounds,** avancer à pas de géant. **2.** obstacle *m* (à sauter); saut; **salmon l.,** chute *f* d'eau (que les saumons doivent sauter pour remonter). **3. l. day,** jour *m* intercalaire; le 29 février; **l. year,** année bissextile.

leap² *v.* (*p.t. & p.p.* **leaped** [liːpt] *or* **leapt** [lept]) **1.** *v.i.* (*a*) sauter, bondir; **to l. to one's feet,** se lever brusquement; **to l. over a ditch,** sauter un fossé; **to l. at the opportunity,** saisir l'occasion au vol; **to l. for joy,** sauter de joie; (*of the heart*) bondir, tressaillir, de joie; **he nearly leapt out of his skin,** il a sauté au plafond; (*b*) (*of flame, etc.*) **to l. (up),** jaillir. **2.** *v.tr.* (*a*) sauter (un fossé); franchir (un fossé) d'un saut; (*b*) (*cause to leap*) **to l. a horse over a ditch,** faire sauter, faire franchir, un fossé à un cheval.

leapfrog¹ [ˈliːpfrɔg] *n.* **to play l.,** jouer à saute-mouton *m.*

leapfrog² *v.tr. & i.* (**leapfrogged**) (*a*) sauter (qch.) comme à saute-mouton; (*b*) *Mil:* opérer une manœuvre de dépassement, un dépassement. **leapfrogging** *n.* (*a*) jeu *m* de saute-mouton; (*b*) *Mil:* (manœuvre de) dépassement (*m*).

leapt. *see* LEAP².

learn [ləːn] *v.tr. & i.* (*p.t. & p.p.* **learnt** [ləːnt], *occ.* **learned** [ləːnd]) **1.** apprendre (le français, les mathématiques, etc.); **to l. to read,** apprendre à lire; **to l. a new technique,** s'initier à une nouvelle technique; **he has learnt his lesson,** (i) il a appris sa leçon; (ii) *F:* il a eu une leçon; **to l. from one's mistakes,** mettre à profit les fautes commises; *Prov:* **it is never too late to l.,** on apprend à tout âge. **2.** apprendre (une nouvelle, etc.); **we are sorry to l. that . . .,** nous sommes désolés d'apprendre que . . .. **3.** *A. & P:* (= *teach*) **to l. s.o. sth.,** apprendre qch. à qn; *P:* **that'll l.** [lɑːn] **him!** ça lui apprendra! **learned** [ˈləːnid] *a.* savant, instruit, érudit, docte; **l. treatise,** traité savant; **l. profession,** profession libérale. **learning** *n.* **1.** action *f* d'apprendre, étude *f*; apprentissage *m.* **2.** science *f*, instruction *f*, érudition *f*, savoir *m*, connaissances *fpl*; **seat of l.,** centre intellectuel; **man of great l.,** homme de grand savoir.

learner [ˈləːnər] *n.* **1.** celui qui apprend; **to be a quick l.,** apprendre facilement. **2.** élève *mf*; débutant, -ante; apprenti *m*; *Aut:* **l. (driver),** apprenti conducteur.

learnt. *see* LEARN.

lease¹ [liːs] *n. Jur:* (*a*) bail *m*, *pl.* baux; **l. of a house,** bail à loyer; **l. of a farm, of land,** bail à ferme; **long l.,** bail à long terme, à longue échéance; **to take a new l., to renew the l., of a house,** renouveler le bail d'une maison; *Fig:* **to take on a new l. of life,** renaître à la vie, faire corps neuf; *F:* repartir pour un nouveau bail; (*b*) concession *f* (d'une source d'énergie, etc.).

lease² *v.tr.* **1. to l. (out),** louer; donner (une maison) à bail; affermer (une terre). **2.** prendre (une maison) à bail; louer (une maison); affermer (une terre). **leasing** *n.* location *f* à bail; affermage *m.*

leasehold [ˈliːshould] **1.** *n.* (*a*) tenure *f* à bail, *esp.* tenure en vertu d'un bail emphytéotique; (*b*) propriété *f*, immeuble *m*, loué(e) à bail. **2.** *a.* tenu à bail.

leaseholder [ˈliːshouldər] *n.* locataire *mf*, affermataire *mf*, à bail.

lease-lend [ˈliːsˈlend] *n. Pol.Ec:* prêt-bail *m* (*no pl.*).

leash¹ [liːʃ] *n.* laisse *f*, attache *f*; **to put a dog on the l.,** mettre un chien en laisse, à l'attache; **to strain at the l.,** (i) (*of dog*) tirer sur la laisse; (ii) (*of pers.*) ruer dans les brancards.

leash² *v.tr.* mettre (un chien) à l'attache.

least [liːst] **1.** *a.* (*a*) **(the) l.,** (le, la) moindre, (le, la) plus petit(e); **he flares up at the l. thing,** il se fâche pour un rien; **I'm not the l. bit musical,** je ne suis pas musicien pour un sou; *Mth:* **the l. common multiple,** le plus petit commun multiple; (*b*) le moins important; **that's the l. of my worries,** ça c'est le moindre de mes soucis. **2.** (*a*) *n.* **(the) l.,** (le) moins; **to say the l. (of it),** pour ne pas dire plus, mieux; pour ne rien dire de plus; **it's the l. I can do,** c'est la moindre des choses; *Prov:* **(the) l. said (the) soonest mended,** moins on en parle mieux cela vaut; (*b*) *adv. phrs.* **at l.,** (tout) au moins; **I can at l. try,** je peux toujours essayer; **it cost him at l. £1000,** cela lui a coûté £1,000 au bas mot; **not in the l.,** pas le moins du monde; aucunement, nullement; **it doesn't matter in the l.,** cela n'a pas la moindre importance. **3.** *adv.* **(the) l.,** (le) moins; **the l. unhappy,** le moins malheureux; **he deserves it l. of all,** il le mérite moins que personne.

leastways, *NAm:* **leastwise** [ˈliːstweiz, -waiz] *adv. Dial:* ou du moins . . ..

leather¹ [ˈleðər] *n.* **1.** cuir *m*; **l. shoes,** chaussures *fpl* en cuir; **fancy l. goods,** maroquinerie *f.* **2.** (*a*) cuir (de pompe, de soupape, etc.); (*of shoe*) **upper l.,** empeigne *f*; (*b*) **(stirrup) l.,** étrivière *f.*

leather² *v.tr.* **1.** garnir (qch.) de cuir. **leathering** *n. F:* **to give s.o. a l.,** tanner le cuir à qn.

leather-bound [ˈleðəbaund] *a.* (livre) relié (en) cuir.

leathercloth [ˈleðəklɔθ] *n.* toile *f* cuir.

leatherette [leðə'ret] *n. O:* similicuir *m.*

leatherjacket ['leðədʒækit] *n. Ent:* larve *f* de la tipule.

leatherneck ['leðənek] *n.m. F:* soldat *m* de l'infanterie de marine.

leatherwork ['leðəwəːk] *n.* **1.** travail *m* en cuir. **2.** (*a*) cuirs *mpl* (d'une carrosserie, etc.); (*b*) **fancy l.,** maroquinerie *f.*

leathery ['leðəri] *a.* qui ressemble au cuir; (*of food*) coriace.

leave¹ [liːv] *n.* **1.** permission *f*, autorisation *f*, permis *m*; **l. to go out,** permission (de sortir); exeat *m*; **to beg l. to do sth.,** (i) demander la permission de faire qch.; (ii) prendre la liberté de faire qch.; **to grant s.o. l. to do sth.,** donner, accorder, à qn la permission de faire qch.; **by, with, your l.,** avec votre permission; si vous le voulez bien; **without so much as a by your l.,** sans même en demander la permission. **2.** *Adm: Mil: etc:* congé *m*; **sick l.,** congé de maladie; **compassionate l.,** congé, permission *f*, pour affaires de famille; *Nau:* **shore l.,** sortie *f* à terre; *Mil: etc:* **absence without l.,** absence illégale. **3.** adieux *mpl*, congé; **to take one's l.,** prendre congé; **to take l. of s.o.,** faire ses adieux à qn; *F:* **to take French l.,** filer à l'anglaise.

leave² *v.tr.* (*p.t. & p.p.* **left** [left]) **1.** laisser; (*a*) **he left his pen behind,** il a oublié son stylo; **to l. things (lying) about,** laisser traîner des choses; *F:* **take it or l. it,** c'est à prendre ou à laisser; (*b*) **to l. a wife and three children,** laisser une femme et trois enfants; (*c*) **to l. one's money to s.o.,** laisser, léguer, sa fortune à qn; (*d*) (*with complement*) **to l. the door open,** laisser la porte ouverte; **to l. sth. unfinished,** laisser qch. inachevé; **to l. a page blank,** laisser une page en blanc; **l. me alone!** laissez-moi en paix, tranquille! **she had been left a widow at thirty,** elle était restée veuve à trente ans; **left to oneself,** livré à soi-même; **let's l. it at that, we'll l. it at that,** (i) demeurons-en là; (ii) n'en parlons plus; (*e*) **to l. hold, l. go, of sth.,** lâcher qch.; (*f*) **left luggage,** bagages déposés à la consigne; **left-luggage office,** consigne; **left-luggage lockers,** consigne automatique; **to l. sth. with s.o.,** confier qch. à qn; **to l. s.o. in charge of sth.,** laisser à qn la garde de qch.; **to l. a message for s.o.,** laisser un mot, un message, un billet, pour qn; (*g*) **to l. s.o. to do sth.,** laisser qn faire qch.; laisser à qn le soin de faire qch.; **I l. it to you,** je m'en remets à vous, je m'en rapporte à vous; **l. it to me,** remettez-vous-en à moi; je m'en charge; **nothing was left to accident,** on avait paré à toutes les éventualités; **I l. it to you to decide,** je vous laisse le soin de décider; (*h*) *Bill:* **to l. the balls in a good, bad, position,** donner un bon, mauvais, acquit; (*i*) **there are no strawberries left,** il ne reste plus de fraises; (*j*) *Mth:* **three from seven leaves four,** sept moins trois égale quatre. **2.** (*a*) quitter (un endroit, qn); **he has left London,** il est parti de Londres; il a quitté Londres; **she never leaves the house,** elle ne sort jamais de la maison; **to l. the room,** sortir (de la pièce); *Sch:* **may I l. the room?** puis-je sortir? **his eyes never left her,** il ne la quittait pas des yeux; **to l. the table,** se lever de table; **to l. one's job,** quitter son emploi; *Mil: etc:* **to l. the service,** quitter le service; *Nau:* **to l. harbour,** sortir du port; *v.i.* **we l. tomorrow,** nous partons demain; **we are leaving for Paris,** nous partons pour Paris; **I was just leaving when . . .,** j'étais sur mon départ lorsque . . .; (*b*) abandonner; **to l. one's wife,** quitter sa femme; (*c*) **they left me behind,** ils sont partis sans moi; **to be left behind, left standing,** être dépassé, distancé (par ses concurrents); (*d*) (*of train*) **to l. the rails,** dérailler; **the car left the road,** la voiture a quitté la route. **leave in** *v.tr.* inclure, retenir (un passage dans un article, etc.). **leave off 1.** *v.tr.* quitter, renoncer à (qch.); **to l. off work,** cesser le travail. **2.** *v.i.* cesser, s'arrêter; **where did we l. off?** où en sommes-nous restés (dans notre lecture, etc.)? *P:* **l. off!** ça suffit comme ça! arrête! **leave out** *v.tr.* (*a*) exclure (qn); (*b*) omettre (qch.); (*c*) oublier (qch.); sauter (une ligne). **leave over** *v.tr.* (*a*) remettre (qch.) à plus tard; (*b*) **what's left over?** qu'est-ce qui reste? **you can keep what is left over,** vous pouvez garder le surplus. **leaving** *n.* **1.** départ *m.* **2.** *pl.* **leavings,** restes *mpl* (d'un repas).

leaved [liːvd] *a.* (*a*) feuillé, feuillu; (*b*) (*with adj. or num. prefixed*) **three-l.,** (volet, paravent, etc.) à trois feuilles; **broad-l. tree,** arbre feuillu, à larges feuilles; **ivy-l.,** à feuilles de lierre.

leaven¹ ['lev(ə)n] *n.* levain *m.*

leaven² *v.tr.* **1.** faire lever (le pain, la pâte). **2.** modifier, transformer (le caractère d'un peuple, etc.) (**with,** par); imprégner (**with,** de).

leaver ['liːvər] *n.* **(school) leavers,** élèves sortants.

leavetaking ['liːvteikiŋ] *n.* adieux *mpl.*

Lebanese [lebə'niːz] *Geog:* **1.** *a.* libanais. **2.** *n.* Libanais, -aise.

Lebanon ['lebənən] *Pr.n. Geog:* le Liban; *Bot:* **cedar of L.,** cèdre *m* du Liban.

lecher ['letʃər] *n.* débauché *m.*

lecherous ['letʃərəs] *a.* lascif, libertin, lubrique, débauché; (*of old man*) paillard. **-ly** *adv.* lascivement.

lectern ['lektən] *n. Ecc:* lutrin *m*, aigle *m.*

lector ['lektɔːr] *n. Sch:* chargé *m* de cours.

lecture¹ ['lektjər] *n.* **1.** (*a*) conférence *f* (**on,** sur); **to give, attend, a l.,** faire, assister à, une conférence; **l. hall,** salle *f* de conférences; (*b*) *Sch:* cours *m*; **history l.,** cours d'histoire; **l. on Napoleon,** cours sur Napoléon. **2.** *F:* sermon *m*, semonce *f*, mercuriale *f*; **to read s.o. a l.,** faire une semonce, faire la morale, à qn; semoncer qn; sermonner qn.

lecture² **1.** *v.i.* faire une conférence, des conférences; *Sch:* faire un cours (**on,** sur); **he lectured on Eastern affairs,** il a traité des affaires d'Orient. **2.** *v.tr. F:* sermonner, semoncer (qn); faire la morale à (qn).

lecturer ['lektjərər] *n.* **1.** conférencier, -ière. **2.** *Sch:* **(junior, assistant) l.** = maître assistant; **(senior) l.** = maître de conférences.

lectureship ['lektjəʃip] *n. Sch:* maîtrise de conférences.

led. *see* LEAD⁴.

ledge [ledʒ] *n.* **1.** rebord *m*; saillie *f*; (*on wall, building*) corniche *f.* **2.** (*a*) **l. of rock,** plateforme rocheuse; (*b*) (*awash or under water*) banc *m* de rochers; (*c*) *Geol:* filon *m*, veine *f* (de minerai, etc.).

ledger ['ledʒər] *n.* **1.** *Book-k:* grand livre (de frais, de ventes, d'achats, etc.); **payroll l.,** grand livre de paie; *Navy:* cahier *m* de solde. **2.** *Mus:* **l. line,** ligne supplémentaire (à la portée).

lee [liː] *n.* (*a*) *Nau:* côté *m* sous le vent; **l. shore,** terre *f* sous le vent; (*b*) abri *m* (contre le vent); **in the l. of a rock,** abrité par un rocher.

leeboard ['liːbɔːd] *n. Nau:* aile *f*, semelle *f*, de dérive.

leech [liːtʃ] *n.* **1.** *Ann:* sangsue *f.* **2.** *Med:* **artificial l.,** sangsue artificielle; ventouse scarifiée. **3.** *F:* (*pers.*) importun, -e; sangsue, crampon *m.*

leek [liːk] *n. Bot:* poireau *m.*

leer¹ ['liər] *n.* (*a*) œillade *f* en dessous; (*b*) regard paillard, polisson.

leer² *v.i.* **to l. at s.o.,** (i) lorgner, guigner, (qn) d'un air méchant; (ii) lancer des œillades à qn; fixer sur qn un regard paillard, polisson.

lees [liːz] *n.pl.* lie *f* (de vin, etc.).

leeward ['luːəd, 'liːwəd] *Nau:* **1.** *a. & adv.* sous le vent; *Geog:* **the L. Islands,** les Iles *fpl* sous le Vent (i) de l'Océanie française, (ii) des Antilles. **2.** *n.* côté *m* sous le vent; **to pass to l. of a ship,** passer sous le vent d'un navire.

leeway ['li:wei] *n.* (*a*) *Nau:* dérive *f*; **to make l.,** dériver (à la voile); (*b*) **he has considerable l. to make up,** il a un fort retard à rattraper.

left [left] **1.** *a.* gauche; **on my l. hand,** à ma gauche. **2.** *adv. Mil:* **l. turn!** à gauche, gauche! **eyes l.!** tête (à) gauche! **3.** *n.* (*a*) (i) (*left hand*) gauche *f*; **on the l., to the l.,** à gauche; *Aut: etc:* **to keep (to the) l.,** tenir la gauche; (ii) (*left fist, arm*) *Box:* gauche *m*; (*b*) (*left wing*) *Mil:* gauche *f*; l'aile *f* gauche; (*c*) *Pol:* **the L.,** la gauche.

lefthand ['lefthænd] *a.* **1.** (poche, etc.) de gauche; **l. blow,** coup *m* de la main gauche; **on the l. side,** à gauche; **l. turn,** virage *m* à gauche. **2.** *Tchn:* (serrure, vis, foret) à gauche; (filin) commis à gauche; **l. thread (of a screw),** filet *m* à gauche, renversé (d'une vis).

lefthanded [left'hændid] **1.** *a.* (*a*) (*of pers.*) gaucher, -ère; (*b*) *F:* (*of pers.*) gauche, maladroit; (*c*) *F:* suspect, équivoque; (compliment) peu flatteur; (*d*) **l. marriage,** mariage *m* de la main gauche; (*e*) (club de golf, etc.) pour gaucher; (*f*) *Tchn:* = LEFTHAND 2. **2.** *adv.* (*a*) (virer, etc.) à gauche; (*b*) **to play tennis l.,** jouer au tennis de la main gauche.

lefthander [left'hændər] *n.* **1.** (*pers.*) gaucher, -ère. **2.** (*a*) *Box:* coup *m* du gauche; fausse garde, gaucher; (*b*) *F:* coup déloyal.

leftist ['leftist] *a. & n. Pol:* gauchiste (*mf*); (homme) de gauche.

leftover ['leftouvər] **1.** *a.* (provisions, etc.) de surplus, en surplus; *Com:* **l. stock,** restes *mpl.* **2.** *n.* (*a*) survivance *f* (des temps passés); (*b*) *Com: Cu:* **leftovers,** restes.

left-wing ['leftwiŋ] *a.* (politique) de gauche.

left-winger ['left'wiŋər] *n. Pol:* gauchiste *mf*; député *m* de la gauche; **the left-wingers,** les gauches *mpl,* les gauchistes; la gauche.

leg¹ [leg] *n.* **1.** jambe *f* (d'homme, de cheval); patte *f* (de chien, d'oiseau, d'insecte, de reptile); **wooden l.,** jambe de bois; **to take to one's legs,** prendre ses jambes à son cou; **to put one's best l. forward,** (i) avancer vite, à toute allure; (ii) pousser la besogne; faire de son mieux; (iii) se mettre à l'ouvrage; **to be on one's legs,** être debout; (*of public speaker*) être en train de parler; **to get on one's legs again,** (i) se relever; (ii) se rétablir; **to be on one's last legs,** tirer vers sa fin; **to feel, find, one's legs,** (i) se trouver en état de se tenir debout; (ii) prendre conscience de ses forces; **to give s.o. a l. up,** (i) faire la courte échelle à qn; (ii) aider qn à monter en selle; (iii) *F:* donner à qn un coup d'épaule; **to pull s.o.'s l.,** se payer la tête de qn; faire marcher qn; *F:* **l. show,** spectacle *m* de music-hall (où les girls montrent leurs jambes); *Cr:* **l. before wicket,** (mis hors jeu) à pied obstructif; *Wr:* **l. lock,** passement *m* de pied; **l. rest,** appui-jambes *m inv*; bout *m* de pied (d'une chaise longue); *Med:* étrier *m.* **2.** *Cu:* cuisse *f* (de poulet); cuisseau *m* (de veau); **roast l. of pork,** cuissot *m* de porc rôti; **frogs' legs,** cuisses de grenouille; **l. of lamb,** gigot *m.* **3.** jambe (de pantalon); tige *f* (de bas, etc.). **4.** (*a*) pied *m* (de table, de chaise); jambe (de trépied, etc.); montant *m* (de chevalet); (*b*) *Nau:* béquille *f* (pour étayer un bateau échoué); (*c*) branche *f* (de compas). **5.** *Cr:* le terrain à gauche et en arrière du joueur qui est au guichet; **l. drive,** coup *m* arrière à gauche. **6.** *Sp: etc:* manche *f*; **the first l.,** la première manche.

leg² *v.tr.* (**legged; legging**) **1.** *F:* **to l. it,** (i) faire la route à pied; *F:* aller pedibus; (ii) marcher, courir, rapidement; *F:* jouer des jambes. **2.** *Cr:* chasser (la balle) à gauche. **-legged** [-'legid, legd] *a.* (*with adj. or num. prefixed*) **short-l.,** aux jambes courtes; **two-l.,** à deux jambes; à deux pattes.

legacy ['legəsi] *n.* legs *m*; **to come into a l.,** faire un héritage; **this desk is a l. from my predecessor,** j'ai hérité ce bureau de mon prédécesseur.

legal ['li:g(ə)l] *a.* **1.** légal, -aux; (commerce) licite. **2.** (*a*) légal; judiciaire, juridique; selon les lois; **by l. process,** par voies légales; par voies de droit; **l. redress,** recours *m* à la justice; **l. security,** caution *f* judiciaire; **l. claim to sth.,** titre *m* juridique à qch.; **l. document,** acte *m* authentique; (*b*) **l. year,** année civile; **l. charges,** frais *mpl* judiciaires; (*of bank, etc.*) **l. department,** service *m,* bureau *m,* du contentieux; **to go into the l. profession,** faire une carrière juridique; **l. expert,** jurisconsulte *m*; avocat *m* conseil; **l. adviser,** conseiller, -ière, juridique; **to take l. advice** = consulter un avocat; **l. aid,** assistance *f* judiciaire; (*c*) **l. owner,** propriétaire *m* légitime. **-ally** *adv.* légalement; **l. responsible,** responsable en droit.

legalization [li:gəlai'zeiʃ(ə)n] *n.* légalisation *f.*

legalize ['li:gəlaiz] *v.tr.* rendre (un acte) légal; autoriser (un acte); légaliser, certifier, authentiquer (un document); dépénaliser (une drogue).

legate¹ ['legət] *n. Ecc: Rom.Ant:* légat *m.*

legate² [li'geit] *v.tr.* léguer.

legatee [legə'ti:] *n.* légataire *mf.*

legation [li'geiʃ(ə)n] *n. Dipl: Ecc:* légation *f.*

legato [li'gɑ:tou] *adv. Mus:* legato; coulé.

legend ['ledʒənd] *n.* **1.** légende *f.* **2.** (*a*) légende (sur une médaille, etc.); (*b*) légende (d'une carte, etc.).

legendary ['ledʒənd(ə)ri] *a.* légendaire.

legerdemain ['ledʒədəmein] *n.* (tours *mpl* de) passe-passe (*m*); tour d'adresse; prestidigitation *f.*

leggings ['legiŋz] *n.pl. Cost:* jambières *fpl*; leggin(g)s *mpl or fpl.*

leggy ['legi] *a.* aux longues jambes; **a l. girl,** une fille toute en jambes.

legibility [ledʒi'biliti] *n.* lisibilité *f* (d'une écriture).

legible ['ledʒibl] *a.* (écriture) lisible, nette. **-ibly** *adv.* (écrire) lisiblement.

legion ['li:dʒ(ə)n] *n.* légion *f*; **the Foreign L.,** la Légion étrangère; **the L. of honour,** la Légion d'honneur; *Lit:* **their name is L.,** ils sont innombrables.

legionary ['li:dʒənəri] **1.** *a.* qui se rapporte à une légion; légionnaire. **2.** *n.* légionnaire *m.*

legislate ['ledʒisleit] *v.i. & tr.* faire des, les, lois; légiférer.

legislation [ledʒis'leiʃ(ə)n] *n.* **1.** législation *f.* **2.** *Parl:* programme législatif.

legislative ['ledʒislətiv] *a.* (*a*) législatif; **the L. Assembly,** l'Assemblée législative; (*b*) **l. power,** la puissance législatrice.

legislator ['ledʒisleitər] *n.* législateur, -trice.

legislature ['ledʒislətjər] *n.* législature *f*; pouvoir législatif; corps législatif.

legist ['li:dʒist] *n.* légiste *m.*

legit [li'dʒit] *a. F:* légitime.

legitimacy [li'dʒitiməsi] *n.* légitimité *f* (d'un enfant, d'une opinion, etc.).

legitimate¹ [li'dʒitimət] *a.* **1.** (*a*) (enfant, autorité, etc.) légitime; (*b*) **l. stage,** le vrai théâtre; le théâtre régulier. **2.** (raisonnement, etc.) légitime. **-ly** *adv.* légitimement.

legitimate² [li'dʒitimeit] *v.tr.* légitimer (un enfant).

legitimatize [li'dʒitimətaiz] *v.tr.* légitimer (un enfant).

legitimize [li'dʒitimaiz] *v.tr.* = LEGITIMATIZE.

legless ['leglis] *a.* sans jambes; **l. cripple,** cul-de-jatte *m, pl.* culs-de-jatte; *P:* **to be l.,** être soûl.

legman, *pl.* **-men** ['legmæn, -mən] *n. NAm:* reporter qui fait la chronique des chiens écrasés.

leg-pull ['legpul] *n. F:* blague *f,* mystification *f.*

leg-puller ['legpulər] *n. F:* blagueur, -euse; mystificateur, -euse.

legume ['legjum] *n.* **1.** fruit *m* d'une légumineuse. **2. legumes,** légumineuses *fpl.*

leguminous [le'gju:minəs] *a. Bot:* légumineux; **l. plant,** légumineuse *f.*

legwork ['legwə:k] *n. F:* (*a*) travail actif; **he does all the l.,** c'est lui qui fait le plus dur; (*b*) *U.S:* voyages d'affaires fréquents et monotones.

leisure ['leʒər, *U.S:* 'li:ʒər] *n.* loisir(s) *m(pl)*; **to have enough l. for reading,** avoir le loisir, le temps, de lire; **to do sth. at one's l.,** faire qch. à loisir, dans ses moments de loisir; **l. hours,** heures *fpl* de loisir; *F:* **I'm a lady of l. at the moment,** je ne travaille pas à présent.

leisured ['leʒəd] *a.* **1.** (*of life, etc.*) de loisir; désœuvré. **2.** (*of pers.*) qui a des loisirs; **the l. classes,** les rentiers *mpl.*

leisurely ['leʒəli] **1.** *a.* (*of pers.*) qui n'est jamais pressé; (allure) mesurée, posée; (voyage) par petites étapes; **to do sth. in a l. fashion,** faire qch. sans se presser. **2.** *adv.* (*a*) à tête reposée; (*b*) sans se presser.

lemming ['lemiŋ] *n. Z:* lemming *m.*

lemon¹ ['lemən] **1.** *n.* (*a*) *Bot:* citron *m*; (*drink*) **fresh l.,** citron pressé; *Cu:* **l. cheese, curd,** (sorte de) confiture *f* au citron; **l. squeezer,** presse-citrons *m inv*; (*b*) **l. (tree),** citronnier *m*; (*c*) **the answer's a l.!** rien à faire! **I felt a real l.,** je me sentais bien bête; (*d*) personne *f*, chose *f*, qui ne vaut rien. **2.** *n. Bot:* **l. balm,** mélisse officinale; citronnelle *f*; **l. verbena,** verveine *f* citronnelle. **3.** *a.* **l. (coloured),** (jaune) citron *inv.*

lemon² *n. Ich:* **l. sole,** plie *f* sole; limande-sole *f.*

lemonade [lemə'neid] *n.* limonade *f.*

lemur ['li:mər] *n. Z:* maki *m.*

lend [lend] *v.tr.* (*p.t. & p.p.* **lent** [lent]) **1.** (*a*) prêter (**sth. to s.o., s.o. sth.,** qch. à qn); **to l. money at interest,** prêter de l'argent à intérêt; (*b*) **to l. (out) books,** tenir une bibliothèque de prêt. **2.** (*a*) **to l. s.o. a (helping) hand,** donner un coup de main à qn; (*b*) **to l. an ear to . . .,** prêter l'oreille à . . .; (*c*) **to l. dignity to sth.,** donner, prêter, de la dignité à qch.; **distance lends enchantment to the view,** tout paraît beau (vu) de loin. **3.** *v.pr.* **to l. oneself, itself, to sth.,** se prêter à qch. **lending** *n.* prêt *m* (d'un objet, de l'argent); *Fin:* prestation *f* (de capitaux); **l. (out) of books,** location *f* de livres; **l. library,** bibliothèque *f* de prêt; **l. bank,** banque *f* de crédit.

lender ['lendər] *n.* prêteur, -euse.

lend-lease ['lend'li:s] *n. Pol.Ec:* prêt-bail *m* (*no pl.*).

length [leŋθ] *n.* **1.** longueur *f*; *Row: Turf:* **to win by a l., by half a l.,** gagner d'une longueur, d'une demi-longueur; **throughout the l. and breadth of the country,** dans toute l'étendue du pays; **I fell full l. on the ground,** je suis tombé de tout mon long. **2.** longueur (d'un livre, d'un voyage, etc.); durée *f* (d'un bail); **l. of service,** ancienneté *f*; **the l. of time required to do sth.,** le temps qu'il faut pour faire qch.; *adv.phr.* **at l.,** (i) (parler) longuement; (expliquer qch.) en détail; (ii) enfin, à la fin. **3. to go to the l. of doing sth.,** aller jusqu'à faire qch.; **he would go to any lengths,** il ne reculerait devant rien. **4.** *Pros:* longueur (d'une voyelle, d'une syllabe). **5.** *Ten: Cr:* longueur de balle. **6.** morceau *m*, bout *m* (de ficelle, etc.); pièce *f*, coupon *m* (d'étoffe); morceau (de bois); tronçon *m* (de tuyau); *Dressm: Tail:* **dress, trouser, l.,** coupon de robe, de pantalon; **what l. do I need for . . .?** quel métrage faut-il pour . . .?

lengthen ['leŋθən] **1.** *v.tr.* allonger, rallonger (une jupe, une chaîne, etc.); prolonger (un intervalle, la vie, une voyelle, etc.); étendre (un récit). **2.** *v.i.* s'allonger, se rallonger; (*of days*) augmenter, croître, grandir; (*of time*) se prolonger. **lengthening** *n.* allongement *m*, rallongement *m*; agrandissement *m* (en long); prolongation *f* (d'un séjour, etc.)

lengthways, *NAm:* **lengthwise** ['leŋθweiz, -waiz] *adv.* longitudinalement; dans le sens de la longueur; en longueur; en long.

lengthy ['leŋθi] *a.* (discours, récit) long, plein de longueurs, prolixe. **-ily** *adv.* longuement; (raconter) tout au long.

leniency ['li:niənsi] *n.* clémence *f*; douceur *f*, indulgence *f* (**to, towards,** pour).

lenient ['li:niənt] *a.* clément; doux, *f.* douce; indulgent (**to, towards,** envers, pour). **-ly** *adv.* avec clémence; avec indulgence.

Leningrad ['leningræd] *Pr.n. Geog:* Léningrad *m.*

Leninism ['leninizm] *n. Pol:* léninisme *m.*

Leninist ['leninist] *n. Pol:* léniniste *mf.*

lenitive ['lenitiv] *a. & n. Med:* lénitif (*m*).

lens [lenz] *n.* **1.** *Opt:* (*a*) lentille *f*; **converging, diverging, l.,** lentille convergente, divergente; **concave, convex, l.,** lentille concave, convexe; (*b*) (*magnifying glass*) loupe *f*, verre grossissant; (*c*) verre (de lunettes); **contact l.,** verre de contact; (*d*) *Phot:* objectif *m* (photographique); **l. aperture,** ouverture *f* de l'objectif; (*e*) **mirror l.,** objectif à lentille spéculaire; (*f*) *Elcs:* **electron l.,** lentille électronique. **2.** *Anat:* **crystalline l.,** cristallin *m* (de l'œil); *F:* lentille.

Lent [lent] *n. Ecc:* le Carême; **to keep L.,** faire carême.

lentil ['lentil] *n. Bot: Comest:* lentille *f.*

Leo ['li:ou] *Pr.n.* **1.** Léon *m.* **2.** *Astr:* le Lion.

leonine ['li(:)ənain] *a.* de lion(s); léonin.

leopard ['lepəd] *n.* **1.** *Z:* léopard *m*; *F:* **can a l. change his spots?** il mourra dans sa peau. **2.** *Z:* **American l.,** jaguar *m*; **hunting l.,** guépard *m.*

leopardess ['lepədis] *n. Z:* léopard *m* femelle.

leotard ['li:ətɑ:d] *n. Cost:* maillot *m* (de danseur); justaucorps *m.*

leper ['lepər] *n.* lépreux, -euse; **l. hospital, colony,** léproserie *f.*

lepidopteran [lepi'dɔptərən] *a. & n. Ent:* lépidoptère (*m*).

leprechaun ['leprəkɔ:n, -hɔ:n] *n. Myth:* farfadet *m*, lutin *m.*

leprosy ['leprəsi] *n. Med:* lèpre *f.*

leprous ['leprəs] *a. Med:* lépreux.

Lesbian ['lezbiən] **1.** *Geog:* (*a*) *a.* lesbien; (*b*) *n.* Lesbien, -ienne. **2. l.,** (*a*) *a.* lesbien; (*b*) *n.* lesbienne *f.*

lesbianism ['lezbiənizm] *n.* lesb(ian)isme *m.*

lesion ['li:ʒ(ə)n] *n. Jur: Med:* lésion *f.*

less [les] **1.** *a.* (*comp.* **lesser**) (*a*) (*smaller*) moindre; **the distance is l. than I thought,** la distance est moindre que je ne le pensais; **to a lesser degree,** à un degré inférieur; (*b*) (*not so much, not so many*) **one mouth l. to feed,** une bouche de moins à nourrir; **in l. time than it takes to tell,** en moins de temps qu'il ne faut, n'en faut, pour le dire; **l. trouble, difficulty,** moins de peine, de difficulté; (*c*) (*younger*) **he is l. than thirty,** il a moins de trente ans. **2.** *prep.* moins; **eight l. five equals three,** huit moins cinq égale trois; **a year l. two days,** une année moins deux jours. **3.** *n.* moins *m*; **in l. than an hour,** en moins d'une heure; **in l. than no time,** en moins de rien; **I can't sell it at l. than cost price,** je ne peux pas le vendre à moins du prix de revient. **4.** *adv.* **l. (well) known,** moins (bien) connu; **I want nothing l.,** (i) je ne veux rien de moins; (ii) cela ne m'arrange pas du tout; **one man l.,** un homme de moins; **not a penny l.,** pas un sou de moins; **l. than six,** moins de six; **l. and l.,** de moins en moins; **no more, no l.,** ni plus ni moins; **the l. said about it the better,** moins on en parle mieux cela vaut; **still l., even l.,** encore moins; **he continued none the l.,** il n'en continua pas moins. **5.** (*a*) **nothing l. than,** (i) (*at the very least*) rien (de) moins que; pour le moins; **it's nothing l. than monstrous!** c'est absolument monstrueux! (ii) (*anything rather than*) rien moins que; (*b*) **this wall is no l. than a metre thick,** ce mur n'a pas moins d'un mètre d'épaisseur; **they have no l. than six cars,** ils ont six voitures, pas moins; **the letter was signed by X, no l.,** la lettre était signée de X, rien de moins! **he dislikes it no l. than I (do),** il ne le déteste pas moins que moi; **I expected no l. from you,** je n'en attendais pas moins de vous.

lessee [le'si:] *n.* **1.** locataire *mf* (à bail) (d'un immeuble, etc.); tenancier, -ière (d'un casino, etc.); fermier *m* (d'une ferme). **2.** concessionnaire *mf.*

lessen ['les(ə)n] **1.** *v.i.* s'amoindrir, diminuer; (*of symptoms, etc.*) s'atténuer. **2.** *v.tr.* amoindrir, diminuer; rapetisser; atténuer (le bruit, un crime); ralentir (son activité, son ardeur). **lessening** *n.* amoindrissement *m*, diminution *f*; atténuation *f.*

lesser ['lesər] *a.* **1.** petit. **2.** moindre; **to choose the l. of two evils,** de deux maux choisir le moindre.

lesson ['les(ə)n] *n.* **1.** leçon *f*; (*a*) *Sch:* cours *m*; (*in primary school*) leçon; **French l.,** cours de français; **swimming l.,** leçon de natation; **private lessons,** leçons particulières; **to be an object l. to s.o.,** servir d'exemple à qn; (*b*) **to learn a l. from sth.,** tirer une leçon de qch.; **let that be a l. to you!** que cela vous serve d'exemple, de leçon! **2.** *Ecc:* lecture *f* de l'Écriture sainte.

lessor [le'sɔ:r] *n.* bailleur, -eresse.

lest [lest] *conj.* **1.** *esp. Lit:* de peur, de crainte, que . . . (ne) + *sub.*; **l. we forget,** de peur que nous n'oubliions. **2.** *A:* (*after verbs of fearing*) **I feared l. he should fall,** je craignais qu'il (ne) tombât.

let¹ [let] *n. Ten:* **l. (ball),** balle *f* à remettre; balle de filet.

let² *n.* location *f*; *F:* **when I get a l. for the season I spend the time abroad,** quand je loue ma maison, etc., pour la saison je vais à l'étranger.

let³ *v.* (*p.t. & p.p.* **let**; *pr.p.* **letting**) **I.** *v.tr.* **1.** (*a*) (*allow*) permettre; laisser; **to l. s.o. do sth.,** laisser qn faire qch.; permettre à qn de faire qch.; **to l. oneself be guided,** se laisser guider; **l. me tell you that . . .,** permettez-moi de vous dire que . . .; **to l. fall,** laisser échapper (qch.); **he l. go (of) the rope,** il a lâché la corde; (*b*) (*cause*) **to l. s.o. know sth.,** faire savoir qch. à qn; faire part de qch. à qn; **l. me know when . . .,** faites-moi savoir quand . . .; **I will l. him know you are here,** je vais le prévenir que vous êtes ici; **l. me hear the story,** racontez-moi l'histoire; (*c*) **the police would not l. anyone pass,** la police ne laissait passer personne, ne permettait à personne de passer; (*d*) *A.Med:* **to l. blood,** pratiquer une saignée; saigner qn. **2.** louer (une maison, etc.); **house to l.,** maison à louer. **II.** *v.aux.* (*supplying 1st & 3rd pers. of imperative*) **let's hurry!** dépêchons-nous! **l. us pray,** prions; **don't let's start yet,** ne partons pas encore; **now, don't let's have any nonsense!** allons, pas de bêtises! **l. him do it at once!** qu'il le fasse tout de suite! *Mth:* **l. AB be equal to CD,** supposons que AB soit égal à CD; **l. me see!** voyons! attendez un peu! **l. them all come!** qu'ils viennent tous! **don't l. me see you here again!** que je ne vous retrouve plus ici! **let down** *v.tr.* (*a*) baisser (la glace, un store, etc.); **to l. down one's hair,** (i) laisser tomber ses cheveux; (ii) *F:* abandonner toute réserve; se laisser aller; (*b*) rallonger (une robe, etc.); (*c*) *F:* **to l. s.o. down gently,** ne pas être trop sévère avec qn; (*d*) *F:* laisser (qn) en panne; faire faux bond à (qn); **I won't l. you down,** vous pouvez compter sur moi; **he has been badly l. down,** il a été gravement déçu; (*e*) détendre, débander (un ressort); dégonfler (un pneu). **let in** *v.tr.* (*a*) laisser entrer, faire entrer, admettre (qn); laisser entrer (l'air, la pluie); **he's got a key, so he can l. himself in,** puisqu'il a une clef, il peut entrer dans la maison, etc.; **my shoes l. in water,** mes chaussures prennent l'eau; (*b*) **to l. s.o. in on a secret,** initier qn à un secret; (*c*) *Dressm: etc:* ajouter, introduire (une pièce); (*d*) *F:* **I didn't know what I was letting myself in for,** je ne savais pas à quoi je m'engageais. **let into** *v.tr.* (*a*) laisser entrer, faire entrer, (qn) dans la maison, etc.; **to l. s.o. into a secret,** dévoiler un secret à qn; mettre qn dans le secret; (*b*) *Dressm: etc:* **to l. a piece into a skirt,** mettre, ajouter, une pièce à une jupe. **let off** *v.tr.* (*a*) faire partir (un fusil, un pétard); tirer, faire partir (un feu d'artifice); décocher (une flèche, etc.); (*b*) lâcher, laisser échapper (de la vapeur); (*c*) **to l. s.o. off from (doing) sth.,** décharger qn d'une corvée, etc.; dispenser qn de faire qch.; **you l. him off too easily,** vous lui faites la part trop belle; (*d*) **to l. s.o. off,** faire grâce à qn; **I'll l. you off this time,** je vous pardonne (pour) cette fois-ci; **to be l. off with a fine,** en être quitte pour une amende. **let on** *v.tr. & i. F:* (*a*) **don't l. on that I was there,** n'allez pas dire que j'y étais; **he didn't l. on that he saw her,** (i) il n'a pas dit qu'il l'avait vue; (ii) il a fait semblant de ne pas la voir; **don't l. on!** pas un mot! (*b*) feindre; faire semblant; **he wasn't as ill as he l. on,** il faisait semblant d'être plus malade qu'il ne l'était. **let out** *v.tr.* (*a*) laisser sortir (qn); laisser échapper (un oiseau); élargir (un prisonnier); **to l. out the air from sth.,** laisser échapper l'air de qch.; dégonfler (un ballon, etc.); **to l. out the bath water,** vider la baignoire; *F:* **to l. out a yell,** laisser échapper un cri; (*b*) élargir, agrandir (un vêtement); *Nau:* lâcher (un cordage); larguer (une voile); (*c*) **to l. chairs out (on hire),** louer des chaises; (*d*) **to l. out a secret,** laisser échapper (un secret); révéler, divulguer (un secret). **let through** *v.tr.* laisser passer (qn, l'eau, la lumière). **letting** *n.* louage *m*; location *f* (d'une maison). **let up** *v.i.* (*of rain, pressure of business, etc.*) diminuer; (*of frost, etc.*) s'adoucir; (*of pers.*) **once he's started he never lets up,** une fois lancé il ne s'arrête plus.

let-down ['letdaun] *n. F:* déception *f*, déboire *m.*

lethal ['li:θ(ə)l] *a.* mortel; **l. dose,** dose mortelle; *Mil: etc:* **l. weapon,** arme meurtrière.

lethargic [li'θɑ:dʒik] *a.* léthargique. **-ally** *adv.* d'une manière léthargique.

lethargy ['leθədʒi] *n.* léthargie *f.*

let-out ['letaut] *n. F:* (i) excuse *f*; (ii) échappatoire *f.*

letter¹ [letər] *n.* **1.** (*a*) lettre *f* (de l'alphabet); *Typ:* lettre, caractère *m*; (*b*) **according to the l. of the law,** selon la lettre de la loi; **to obey to the l.,** obéir à la lettre, au pied de la lettre; (*c*) *Engr:* **proof before the l.,** épreuve *f* avant la lettre; (*d*) **code l.,** (i) lettre d'un code de chiffrement; lettre-code *f*, *pl.* lettres-code(s); (ii) *W.Tel:* indicatif littéral; *W.Tel: etc:* **call letters,** indicatif *m* d'appel (d'une station radio, etc.). **2.** (*a*) lettre, missive *f*; **business l.,** lettre d'affaires; **I've had a l. from him,** j'ai reçu une lettre de lui; *Post:* **registered l.,** lettre recommandée; **express l.,** lettre exprès; **airmail l.,** lettre par avion; **air l.,** aérogramme *m*; **l. bomb,** lettre piégée; **l. rate,** tarif *m* (d'affranchissement des) lettres; **l. opener,** coupe-papier *m inv*; **l. tray,** corbeille *f*, panier *m* (à lettres, à courrier); **l. file,** classeur *m* de lettres; classe-lettres *m inv*; *Hyg: P:* **French l.,** capote anglaise; (*b*) **letters patent,** lettres de patentes; **letters patent of nobility,** lettres de noblesse; (*c*) *Bank: Com:* **l. of credit, of exchange,** lettre de crédit, de change; **l. of advice,** lettre d'avis; **l. of acknowledgement,** accusé *m* de réception. **3. letters,** (belles-)lettres; littérature *f*; **man of letters,** homme de lettres, littérateur *m.*

letter² *v.tr.* **1.** marquer (un objet) avec des lettres; graver des lettres sur (un objet); estampiller. **2.** mettre le titre à (un livre). **lettered** *a.* **1.** marqué avec des lettres. **2.** (homme) lettré. **lettering** *n.* **1.** lettrage *m*; estampillage *m.* **2.** lettres *fpl*; inscription *f*; titre *m* (d'un livre).

letterbox ['letəbɔks] *n.* boîte *f* à, aux, lettres.

lettercard ['letəkɑːd] *n.* carte-lettre *f*, *pl.* cartes-lettres.

letterhead ['letəhed] *n.* en-tête *m inv* de lettre (imprimé).

letterpress ['letəpres] *n.* **1.** *Typ:* impression *f* typographique; **l. printing,** typographie *f.* **2.** texte *m* (accompagnant une illustration). **3.** presse *f* à copier.

lettuce ['letis] *n.* laitue *f*; **cabbage l.,** laitue pommée; **cos l.,** (laitue) romaine *f*; **lamb's l.,** mâche *f.*

let-up ['letʌp] *n. F:* diminution *f* (**in,** de); changement *m* (du temps); relâchement *m* (des efforts); **to work fifteen hours without a l.-up,** travailler quinze heures d'affilée.

leucocyte ['ljuːkousait] *n. Physiol:* leucocyte *m.*

leukaemia, *NAm:* **leukemia** [lju'kiːmiə] *n. Med:* leucémie *f.*

leukaemic, *NAm:* **leukemic** [lju'kiːmik] *a. Med:* leucémique.

Levant [li'vænt] *Geog:* **1.** *Pr.n.* **the L.,** le Levant. **2.** *attrib.* du Levant; levantin.

Levantine [lə'væntain] *Geog:* **1.** *a.* levantin. **2.** *n.* Levantin, -ine.

levee ['levi] *n. NAm: Civ.E:* levée *f*, digue *f* (d'une rivière).

level¹ ['lev(ə)l] **I.** *n.* **1.** *Tls: etc:* (*a*) niveau *m* (de charpentier, etc.); **spirit l.,** niveau à bulle d'air, à alcool; (*b*) **l. (rule),** latte *f*, règle *f*, de niveau; (*c*) *Mch:* **water l.,** niveau d'eau. **2.** (*a*) niveau (de la mer, d'un liquide dans un récipient, etc.); *Geog: Surv:* altitude *f*, niveau; **mean sea l.,** niveau moyen de la mer; *Surv:* **datum, reference, l.,** niveau de référence; **at a higher, lower, l.,** en contre-haut, en contre-bas **(than,** de); **at eye l.,** à (la) hauteur des yeux; **on a l. with sth.,** au niveau, à la hauteur, de qch.; de niveau avec qch.; **split l. house,** maison à ressaut, à paliers; *Adm: Can:* maison à mi-étages; (*b*) niveau (des prix, des salaires, etc.); **to maintain prices at a high l.,** maintenir les prix à un niveau élevé; (*c*) *Ph: etc:* **energy l.,** niveau énergétique; **noise l.,** niveau de bruit (d'un moteur, etc.); **radiation l.,** niveau de radiation; (*d*) *Mec.E:* **oil l.,** niveau d'huile; (*e*) niveau, étage *m* (de la société, etc.); **to be on a l. with s.o.,** être au niveau de qn; être sur un pied d'égalité avec qn; **to come down to s.o.'s l.,** se mettre au niveau, à la portée, de qn; **at ministerial l.,** à l'échelon ministériel. **3.** (*a*) surface *f*, trajectoire *f*, de niveau; terrain *m* de niveau; *Aut: Rail: Av:* palier *m*; **dead l.,** niveau parfait, palier absolu; **on the l.,** (i) sur un terrain plat; (ii) (*of pers.*) loyal, -aux; de bonne foi; (iii) *F:* en toute honnêteté; (*b*) *Min:* (i) niveau, étage; (ii) galerie *f*, voie *f* (de niveau); (*c*) *Geol:* étage. **II.** *a.* **1.** (*a*) (*not sloping*) horizontal, -aux; (terrain) de niveau, à niveau; (route, etc.) en palier; *Av:* **l. flight,** vol horizontal; (*b*) (*flat*) égal, -aux, uni; (*c*) **l. with . . .,** de niveau avec . . .; au niveau, à (la) hauteur, de . . .; *Rail:* **l. crossing,** passage *m* à niveau; **l. with the ground,** au ras du sol; à ras de terre; **l. spoonful,** cuillerée rase; *Sp:* **to draw l. with . . .,** arriver à (la) hauteur de . . .; (*in rowing*) venir bord à bord avec . . .. **2. l. tone,** ton soutenu, uniforme; **to keep a l. head,** garder sa tête, son sang-froid; **to do one's l. best,** faire tout son possible, de son mieux. **III.** *adv. Av:* **to fly l.,** (i) voler en palier; (ii) attaquer le palier.

level² *v.* **(levelled,** *NAm:* **leveled) 1.** *v.tr.* (*a*) niveler; mettre (un billard, etc.) de niveau; (*b*) niveler, égaliser (une surface); araser (un terrain, etc.); (*c*) **to l. a town (to the ground),** raser une ville. **2.** *v.tr.* pointer (un fusil), braquer (un canon), diriger (une longue-vue) (**at,** sur); **to l. one's gun at, against, s.o.,** ajuster, viser, qn avec son fusil; mettre, qn en joue; **to l. accusations at s.o.,** lancer des accusations contre qn; **to l. a blow at s.o.,** porter un coup à qn. **3.** *v.tr. Surv:* effectuer des opérations de nivellement dans (une région); niveler (une région). **4.** *v.i. esp. NAm: F:* **to l. with s.o.,** parler franchement. **level down** *v.tr.* (*a*) araser (un mur, etc.); (*b*) abaisser (qn, qch.) à son niveau; niveler par le bas. **levelling,** *NAm:* **leveling** *n.* **1.** (*a*) nivellement *m*; (i) mise *f* à niveau, de niveau; (ii) aplanissement *m* (d'une surface); égalisation *f* (de la chaussée); *Surv:* **l. pole,** mire *f* (de nivellement); (*b*) arasement *m* (d'un mur). **2.** pointage *m*, braquage *m* (d'une arme à feu). **level off 1.** *v.tr.* aplanir (qch.). **2.** *v.i.* (*a*) s'arrêter à un certain niveau; (*b*) *Av:* voler en palier. **level out 1.** *v.tr.* égaliser (une surface, etc.). **2.** *v.i.* (*a*) (*of prices*) s'équilibrer; (*b*) (*of aircraft*) attaquer le palier.

level-headed ['lev(ə)l'hedid] *n.* qui a la tête bien équilibrée; pondéré; **he's l.-h.,** il a l'esprit rassis.

leveller, *NAm:* **leveler** ['lev(ə)lər] *n.* (*a*) niveleur, -euse; (*b*) *Pol:* égalitaire *mf*; (*c*) *Lit:* **death is a great l.,** tous les hommes sont égaux devant la mort.

lever¹ ['liːvər, *NAm:* 'levər] *n.* **1.** (*a*) *Mec: Tls:* levier *m*; (*b*) *Mec.E:* levier; manette *f*; **control l., operating l.,** levier de commande, de manœuvre; *Aut:* **gear l.,** levier de changement de vitesse, levier des vitesses; (*c*) *Rail:* **point l., switch l.,** levier d'aiguille; (*d*) *Sm.a:* **arming l., cocking l.,** levier d'armement.

lever² 1. *v.i.* manœuvrer un levier. **2.** *v.tr.* **to l. sth. up,** soulever qch. au moyen, à l'aide, d'un levier.

leverage ['liːvəridʒ] *n.* **1.** (*a*) force *f*, puissance *f*, de levier; (*b*) **to bring l. to bear on (a door, etc.),** exercer des pesées *fpl* sur (une porte, etc.); (*c*) **we have no l. we could bring to bear on him,** nous n'avons pas de prise sur lui. **2.** système *m* de leviers.

leveret ['levərit] *n. Z:* levraut *m.*

leviathan [li'vaiəθ(ə)n] *n.* **1.** *B:* léviathan *m.* **2.** *F:* (navire *m*) monstre (*m*).

levitate ['leviteit] *Psychics:* **1.** *v.i.* se soulever (par lévitation). **2.** *v.tr.* soulever (qn, qch.) (par lévitation).

levitation [levi'teiʃ(ə)n] *n. Psychics:* lévitation *f.*

levity ['leviti] *n.* **1.** légèreté *f*; manque *m* de sérieux. **2.** *Ph: etc:* légèreté.

levy¹ ['levi] *n.* **1.** (*a*) levée *f* (d'un impôt); (*b*) *Mil:* levée (des troupes); réquisition *f* (des chevaux, etc.). **2.** impôt *m*, contribution *f*; cotisation *f*; **capital l.,** prélèvement *m* sur le capital.

levy² *v.tr.* **1.** lever, percevoir (un impôt); imposer (une amende); **to l. a duty on goods,** imposer des marchandises; **to l. a fine on s.o.,** frapper qn d'une amende. **2.** *Mil:* lever (des troupes).

lewd [ljuːd] *a.* impudique, lascif, lubrique, crapuleux; (sourire) lascif, égrillard. **-ly** *adv.* impudiquement, lascivement, crapuleusement.

lewdness ['ljuːdnis] *n.* **1.** impudicité *f*, lasciveté *f*, lubricité *f.* **2.** luxure *f*, débauche *f.*

lexicographer [leksi'kɔgrəfər] *n.* lexicographe *mf.*

lexicography [leksi'kɔgrəfi] *n.* lexicographie *f.*

lexicology [leksi'kɔlədʒi] *n.* lexicologie *f.*

lexicon ['leksikən] *n.* lexique *m.*

liability [laiə'biliti] *n.* **1.** *Jur:* responsabilité *f*; **employer's l.,** responsabilité patronale, de l'employeur (pour les accidents du travail); **civil l.,** responsabilité civile. **2.** (*a*) *Com: Fin:* **liabilities,** ensemble *m* des dettes; obligations *fpl*, valeurs passives, dettes passives; le passif; (*in bankruptcy*) masse passive (d'une liquidation après faillite); **assets and liabilities,** actif *m* et passif; **to meet one's liabilities,** faire face à ses engagements; (*b*) (*on bills of exchange*) encours *m*; (*c*) *Fig:* désavantage *m*; handicap *m.* **3.** (*a*) **l. to a fine,** risque *m* d'amende; **l. for military**

service, obligation *f* du service militaire; (*b*) disposition *f*, tendance *f* (**to sth., to do sth.,** à qch., à faire qch.); (*c*) (*of product, etc.*) **l. to explode,** danger *m* d'explosion.

liable ['laiəbl] *a.* **1.** *Jur:* responsable (**for,** de); **you are l. for the damage,** vous êtes responsable du dommage. **2.** sujet, assujetti, tenu, astreint (**to,** à); redevable, passible (**to,** de); **l. to a tax,** assujetti à un impôt; redevable d'un impôt; **l. to a fine,** passible d'une amende; **l. to military service,** astreint au service militaire. **3.** sujet, apte, exposé (**to,** à); **l. to make mistakes,** enclin à faire des fautes. **4. when he gets angry he is l. to do anything,** quand il se met en colère il est capable de tout.

liaise [li:'eiz] *v.i. F:* faire, effectuer, la liaison.

liaison [li'eizɔn] *n.* **1.** *Mil: etc:* **l. agent, officer,** agent *m*, officier *m*, de liaison. **2.** liaison (amoureuse). **3.** *Ling:* **to make a l.,** faire la liaison (entre deux mots).

liana [li'ɑ:nə] *n. Bot:* liane *f*.

liar ['laiər] *n.* menteur, -euse; **you l.!** menteur que tu es! quel menteur (tu fais)!

libation [lai'beiʃ(ə)n] *n.* libation *f*.

libel¹ ['laibl] *n.* (*a*) diffamation *f*; (*b*) *Jur:* diffamation (par écrit); écrit *m* diffamatoire; **to utter a l. against s.o.,** publier un article, un écrit, diffamant qn; **action for l., l. action,** procès *m* en diffamation.

libel² *v.tr.* (**libelled,** *NAm:* **libeled**) *Jur:* diffamer (qn) (par écrit); publier une calomnie contre (qn); calomnier (qn).

libellous, *NAm:* **libelous** ['laibələs] *a.* (écrit) diffamatoire, diffamant.

liberal ['lib(ə)rəl] *a.* **1.** (*a*) libéral, -aux; **l. education,** éducation libérale; (*b*) (*of pers.*) d'esprit large; sans préjugés. **2.** (*a*) libéral, généreux; **l. with one's money,** prodigue de son argent; (*b*) ample; **l. supply of food,** nourriture abondante. **3.** *a. & n. Pol:* libéral, -ale. **-ally** *adv.* libéralement.

liberalism ['lib(ə)rəlizm] *n.* libéralisme *m*.

liberality [libə'ræliti] *n.* libéralité *f*. **1.** largeur *f* (de vues). **2.** générosité *f*.

liberalize ['lib(ə)rəlaiz] *v.tr.* libéraliser (les idées, un peuple, etc.).

liberate ['libəreit] *v.tr.* **1.** libérer; mettre en liberté; élargir (un prisonnier); lâcher (des pigeons). **2.** *Ch:* libérer, dégager (un gaz). **3.** *Fin:* **to l. capital,** mobiliser des capitaux.

liberation [libə'reiʃ(ə)n] *n.* **1.** libération *f*; mise *f* en liberté; élargissement *m* (d'un prisonnier); *Hist:* **after the l.,** après la libération (de la France). **2.** *Ch: Ph:* dégagement *m* (d'un gaz, de chaleur). **3.** *Fin:* **l. of capital,** mobilisation *f* de capitaux.

liberator ['libəreitər] *n.* libérateur, -trice.

Liberia [lai'biəriə] *Pr.n. Geog:* Libéria *m*.

Liberian [lai'biəriən] *Geog:* **1.** *a.* libérien. **2.** *n.* Libérien, -ienne.

libertine ['libətain, -ti:n] *a. & n.* libertin, -ine.

liberty ['libəti] *n.* liberté *f*; (*a*) **l. of conscience,** liberté de conscience; **to be at l. to do sth.,** être libre de faire qch.; **Statue of L.,** statue *f* de la Liberté; *Navy:* **l. ticket,** permission *f* de terre, d'aller à terre; (*b*) **to take the l. of doing, to do, sth.,** prendre la liberté, se permettre, de faire qch.; (*c*) **to take liberties with s.o.,** prendre, se permettre, des libertés avec qn.

libidinous [li'bidinəs] *a.* libidineux.

libido [li'bi:dou, -'bai-] *n. Psy:* libido *f*.

Libra ['laibrə, 'li:-] *Pr.n. Astr:* la Balance.

librarian [lai'brɛəriən] *n.* bibliothécaire *mf*.

library ['laibrəri] *n.* bibliothèque *f*; (*a*) **lending l.,** bibliothèque de prêt; **reference l.,** bibliothèque d'ouvrages de référence; salle *f* de lecture; **mobile l.,** bibliobus *m*; **photographic l.,** photothèque *f*; **film l.,** cinémathèque *f*; **music l.,** musicothèque *f*; **record l.,** discothèque *f*; collection de disques; **tape l.,** magnétothèque *f*; (*b*) *F:* **he's a walking l.,** c'est une encyclopédie vivante.

librettist [li'bretist] *n. Th:* librettiste *mf*.

libretto, *pl.* **-i, -os** [li'bretou, -i:, -ouz] *n.* libretto *m*, *pl.* libretti, librettos; livret *m* (d'opéra, etc.).

Libya ['libiə] *Pr.n. Geog:* Libye *f*.

Libyan ['libiən] **1.** *a. Geog:* libyen, libyque; **the L. desert,** le désert de Libye. **2.** *n.* (*a*) Libyen, -yenne.

lice. *see* LOUSE.

licence, *NAm:* **license** ['laisəns] *n.* **1.** (*a*) permission *f*, autorisation *f*; **under l. from the inventor,** avec l'autorisation de l'inventeur; (*b*) **release on l.,** libération conditionnelle (d'un prisonnier); (*c*) *Adm:* permis *m*, autorisation, patente *f*, licence *f*, privilège *m*; **l. to sell beer, wine and spirits,** *esp. NAm:* **liquor l.,** permis, licence, de débit de boissons; **off l.,** (i) licence permettant exclusivement la vente des boissons à emporter; (ii) débit *m* où on vend les boissons à emporter; **trading l.,** carte *f* de commerce; **manufacturing l.,** brevet *m*, licence, de fabrication; **made, manufactured, under l.,** construit, fabriqué, sous licence; **television l.,** impôt (annuel) sur un téléviseur; **import, export, l.,** licence d'importation, d'exportation; **marriage l., special l.** = dispense *f* de bans; **shooting l.,** permis de chasse; **gun l.,** permis de port d'arme(s); **dog l.,** taxe *f* pour chien; **car l.,** permis de circulation, *F:* = carte grise; **l. number,** numéro *m* d'immatriculation; **driving l.,** *NAm:* **driver's l.,** permis de conduire; **heavy goods (vehicle) l.,** permis poids lourds; *Av:* **pilot's l.,** brevet de pilote. **2.** (*a*) (*abuse of freedom*) licence; **poetic l.,** licence poétique; (*b*) = LICENTIOUSNESS.

license¹ ['laisəns] *v.tr.* accorder un permis, une patente, un brevet, un privilège, à (qn); **to l. s.o. to sell drink,** autoriser qn à tenir un débit de boissons; **licensed to sell beer, wines and spirits,** autorisé, *Fr.C:* licencié, à vendre des boissons alcooliques. **licensed** *a. Adm:* autorisé, patenté; *Av:* (pilote) breveté; **l. house, premises,** débit *m* de boissons; **l. victualler,** débitant *m* de boissons, de spiritueux. **licensing** *n.* autorisation *f* (de qn à faire qch.); octroiement *m* d'un permis, d'une autorisation (à qn); **l. laws,** lois relatives aux débits de boissons alcooliques.

license² *n. NAm:* = LICENCE.

licensee [lais(ə)n'si:] *n.* détenteur, -trice, d'une patente, d'un permis; gérant, -ante, propriétaire *mf* (d'un pub, etc.).

licentiate [lai'senʃiət] *n.* **1.** *Sch:* diplômé, -ée. **2.** *Ecc:* aspirant *m* à un pastorat (de l'Église réformée).

licentious [lai'senʃəs] *a.* licencieux, dévergondé.

licentiousness [lai'senʃəsnis] *n.* licence *f*, dévergondage *m*.

lichen ['laikən, 'litʃən] *n.* lichen *m*.

lichgate ['litʃgeit] *n.* porche *m* d'entrée de cimetière surmonté d'un petit toit.

licit ['lisit] *a.* licite. **-ly** *adv.* licitement.

lick¹ [lik] *n.* **1.** (*a*) coup *m* de langue; **to give sth., s.o., a l.,** lécher qch., qn; *F:* **a l. and a promise,** un bout, un brin, de toilette; (*b*) *F:* petite quantité; **a l. of paint,** une petite couche de peinture; *F:* **at (a) great l., at full l.,** à toute allure; à toute vitesse. **2.** *Husb:* **salt l.,** (i) pain salé; salègre *m*; (ii) terrain *m* salifère (où les bêtes viennent lécher le sol).

lick² *v.tr.* **1.** lécher; **to l. one's lips,** *F:* **one's chops,** s'en lécher les babines; se (pour)lécher les babines; *F:* **to l. s.o.'s boots,** lécher les bottes à qn; **to l. s.o. into shape,** former, dégrossir, dégourdir, qn; **to l. sth. up,** (*of animal*) laper qch.; *F:* **to l. the platter, plate, clean,** faire les plats nets; torcher le plat. **2.** *F:* (*a*) battre, rosser (qn); (*b*) battre, vaincre, écraser (un adversaire); **this licks me,** ça me dépasse. **licking** *n.* **1.** léchage *m.* **2.** *F:* (*a*) raclée *f*, rossée *f*; (*b*) défaite *f*.

lickety-split ['likəti'split] *adv. U.S: F:* très vite; à toute vitesse.

lid [lid] *n.* **1.** (*a*) couvercle *m* (de boîte, etc.); *F:* **that puts the l. on it!** ça c'est le comble! (*b*) *F:* chapeau *m.* **2.** *Anat:* paupière *f.* **3.** *Nat.Hist:* opercule *m.*

lidded ['lidid] *a.* (*a*) (boîte, etc.) à couvercle; (*b*) *Nat.Hist:* (capsule, etc.) à opercule.

lie[1] [lai] *n.* (*a*) mensonge *m*; **white l.,** pieux mensonge; **it's all lies, a pack of lies!** c'est un tissu de mensonges! **to tell a l.,** dire un mensonge; **l. detector,** détecteur *m* de mensonges; (*b*) **to give s.o. the l. (direct),** donner un démenti (formel) à qn.

lie[2] *v.i.* & *tr.* (*p.t.* & *p.p.* **lied** [laid]; *pr.p.* **lying** ['laiiŋ]) mentir (**to s.o.,** à qn); **to l. about one's age,** tricher sur sa date de naissance. **lying 1.** *a.* (*of pers.*) menteur, -euse; (récit) mensonger. **2.** *n.* mensonge *m.*

lie[3] *n.* **1.** disposition *f* (du terrain, etc.); *Geol:* gisement *m*; *Civ.E:* tracé *m* (d'une route); **l. of the land,** configuration *f*, disposition, du terrain; topographie *f*; *Fig:* **to find out the l. of the land,** tâter le terrain. **2.** *Golf:* position *f*, assiette *f* (de la balle).

lie[4] *v.i.* (*p.t.* **lay** [lei]; *p.p.* **lain** [lein]; *pr.p.* **lying** ['laiiŋ]) **1.** (*of pers., animal*) (*a*) être couché (à plat); **to be lying ill in bed,** être (malade et) alité; **we found him lying dead,** nous l'avons trouvé mort; (*of gravestones*) **here lies . . .,** ci-gît . . .; (*b*) être, rester, se tenir; **to l. in bed,** rester au lit; **to l. awake,** rester éveillé; **to l. hidden,** rester, se tenir, caché; **to l. low,** (i) se tapir; rester tapi; (ii) *F:* rester, se tenir, coi; **to l. in wait for s.o.,** se tenir à l'affût de qn; attendre qn à l'affût. **2.** (*of thg*) (*a*) être, se trouver; **the papers lay on the table,** les papiers étaient (étendus) sur la table; (*of building*) **to l. in ruins,** être en ruines; **the obstacles that l. in our way,** les obstacles qui bloquent notre chemin; *Nau:* **ship lying at her berth,** navire mouillé, amarré, à son poste; (*b*) rester, séjourner; (*of money*) **to l. in the bank,** être déposé à la banque; **the snow did not l.,** la neige n'a pas tenu; (*c*) (*of food*) **to l. (heavy) on one's stomach,** peser sur l'estomac; **sins that l. heavy on the conscience,** péchés qui pèsent sur la conscience; (*d*) **the onus of proof lies with them,** c'est à eux qu'incombe le soin de faire la preuve; **the responsibility lies with the author,** la responsabilité incombe à l'auteur; (*e*) **town lying in a valley,** ville située dans une vallée; **he knows where his interests l.,** il sait où se trouve ses intérêts; **the difference lies in this, that . . .,** la différence consiste en ceci que . . .; **the fault lies with you,** la faute retombe sur vous; (*f*) **a vast plain lay before us,** une vaste plaine s'étendait devant nous; **a brilliant future lies before him,** un brillant avenir s'ouvre devant lui; (*g*) **our way lies through the woods,** notre chemin passe par les bois; **my talents do not l. in that direction,** je n'ai pas de dispositions, de talent, pour cela. **3.** *Jur:* (*of action, appeal*) être recevable; se soutenir. **lie about** *v.i.* (*of thg*) traîner (çà et là); **to leave one's papers lying about,** laisser traîner ses papiers. **lie back** *v.i.* (*a*) se laisser retomber; se renverser (dans son fauteuil); (*b*) **when you have finished you can l. back and take things easy,** quand vous aurez fini vous pourrez vous reposer. **lie down** *v.i.* (*a*) se coucher, s'étendre; **to l. down on one's bed,** s'étendre sur son lit; **to l. down on the ground,** se coucher, s'allonger, par terre; (*to dog*) **l. down!** couché! (*b*) **to take an insult lying down,** ne pas relever une insulte; **he won't take it lying down,** il ne se laissera pas faire. **lie in** *v.i.* (*a*) *O:* **lying-in hospital,** maternité *f*; (*b*) faire la grasse matinée. **lie off** *v.i.* (*of ship*) rester au large. **lie over** *v.i.* (*of thg*) être remis à plus tard; **to let a bill l. over,** différer l'échéance d'un effet. **lie to** *v.i.* (*of ship*) être à la cape; tenir la cape. **lie up** *v.i.* **1.** *F:* (*of pers.*) (*a*) garder le lit; garder la chambre; (*b*) se cacher. **2.** (*of ship*) désarmer. **lying 1.** *a.* couché; étendu. **2.** *n.* **l. (down) position,** position couchée.

lie-down ['lai'daun] *n.* **to have a l.-d.,** faire une sieste, un petit somme.

lief [li:f] *a.* & *adv.* **I would as l. . . .,** j'aimerais autant . . . .

lie-in ['lai'in] *n.* **to have a l.-in,** faire la grasse matinée.

lien [li:(ə)n] *n. Jur:* privilège *m* (sur un meuble, etc.); droit *m* de rétention; **to have a l. (up)on a cargo,** avoir un recours sur un chargement.

lieu [lju:, lu:] *n.* **in l. of . . .,** au lieu de . . .; en remplacement de . . .; **to stand in l. of . . .,** tenir lieu de . . .; **I'll take something else in l.,** je prendrai quelque chose d'autre à la place.

lieutenant [lef'tenənt, *esp. U.S:* lu:-] *n.* (*a*) *Mil:* lieutenant; **l.-colonel** (*pl.* **lieutenant-colonels),** lieutenant-colonel *m*, *pl.* lieutenants-colonels; **l. general** (*pl.* **lieutenant generals),** général *m* de corps d'armée; (*b*) *Navy:* lieutenant de vaisseau; **l. commander** (*pl.* **lieutenant commanders**) capitaine *m* de corvette; (*c*) *Mil.Av:* **flight l.,** capitaine (d'aviation).

life, *pl.* **lives** [laif, laivz] *n.* **1.** (*a*) (*existence*) vie *f*; **l. force,** force vitale; élan vital; **to give l. to s.o.,** donner la vie à qn; **to come to l.,** s'animer; **to come to l. again,** revenir à la vie; **it is a matter of l. and death,** c'est une question de vie ou de mort; **he is hovering between l. and death,** il est entre la vie et la mort; **l.-and-death struggle,** lutte désespérée; guerre *f* à mort; **to take s.o.'s l.,** tuer qn; **to take one's own l.,** se suicider; *Space:* **l. support system,** équipement *m* de survie; *Med:* respirateur artificiel; **to risk one's l., to risk l. and limb,** risquer sa peau; **to escape with one's l.,** s'en tirer la vie sauve; **to beat s.o. within an inch of his l.,** battre qn à le laisser pour mort; **to lose one's l.,** perdre la vie; périr; **there were no lives lost,** personne n'a été tué; **the catastrophe resulted in great loss of l.,** la catastrophe a fait beaucoup de victimes; **run for your lives!** sauve qui peut! **he was rowing for dear l.,** il ramait de toutes ses forces; *F:* **not on your l.!** jamais de la vie! (*b*) (*vivacity*) **full of l.,** plein de vie, d'entrain; (*of street, etc.*) plein de mouvement, d'animation; **to put new l. into (s.o., sth.),** ranimer (qn, une entreprise, etc.); **he's the l. and soul of the party,** c'est le boute-en-train de la compagnie; *F:* **there's no l. in this place,** ça manque d'entrain ici; (*c*) *Art: Lit:* **to draw from l.,** dessiner sur le vif, d'après nature; **l. class,** classe *f* où on dessine des académies; **characters taken from l.,** caractères pris sur le vif; **true to l.,** (roman, etc.) vécu, senti; (*d*) *coll.* **animal, vegetable, l.,** la vie animale, végétale; **bird l.,** les oiseaux *mpl*; *Art:* **still l.,** nature morte. **2.** (*period of existence*) (*a*) vie, vivant *m* (de qn); **he worked all his l.,** il a travaillé durant toute sa vie; **never in (all) my l.,** jamais de la vie; **in his early l.,** quand il était jeune; **married l.,** vie conjugale; **working l.,** période *f*, années *fpl*, d'activité, de travail; **appointed for l.,** nommé à vie; **l. annuity, pension,** pension, rente, viagère; **l. interest,** usufruit *m* (d'un bien); viager *m*; **l. imprisonment,** emprisonnement perpétuel; (*of animal, bird*) **to mate for l.,** s'unir pour la vie; (*b*) *Ins:* **l. assurance,** assurance *f* sur la vie, assurance-vie *f*; **expectation of l.,** vie moyenne, probable; (*c*) *Lit:* **l. (story),** biographie *f*; **to write s.o.'s l. (story),** écrire la vie de qn; (*d*) vie, durée *f* (d'un phénomène, d'une lampe, etc.); **useful l.,** vie, durée, utile (d'une machine, etc.); *Atom.Ph:* **average, mean, l.,** vie moyenne (d'un atome, d'un isotope). **3.** (*a*) **to**

depart this l., mourir, quitter ce monde; (*b*) **way of l.,** manière *f* de vivre; (train *m* de) vie; **the American way of l.,** la vie américaine; **high l.,** la vie mondaine; **night l.,** la vie nocturne; *F:* **how's l.?** comment ça va? **what a l.!** quelle vie! **such is l.!** c'est la vie! **to see l.,** (i) se frotter au monde; (ii) s'amuser; faire la noce; **he makes her l. a misery,** il lui rend la vie dure.

lifebelt ['laifbelt] *n.* ceinture *f* de sauvetage.

lifeblood ['laifblʌd] *n.* (*a*) *Lit:* sang *m* (de qn); (*b*) âme *f* (d'une entreprise, etc.); (*c*) (*of oil, etc.*) **the l. of the economy,** le pivot de l'économie.

lifeboat ['laifbout] *n.* (*a*) **(coastal) l.,** canot *m* de sauvetage; **l. station,** station *f*, poste *m*, de sauvetage; (*b*) **(ship's) l.,** embarcation *f* de sauvetage.

lifeboatman, *pl.* **-men** ['laifboutmən] *n.* sauveteur *m.*

lifebuoy ['laifbɔi] *n.* bouée *f* de sauvetage.

life-giving ['laifgiviŋ] *a.* vivifiant; (soleil) fécondant; (chaleur) féconde.

lifeguard, life guard ['laifgɑːd] *n.* **1.** *Mil:* (*in British Army*) **the L. Guards,** le corps de cavaliers appartenant à la maison du roi; les Gardes du corps. **2.** (*at the seaside*) gardien *m* de plage.

Life Guardsman, *pl.* **-men** ['laifgɑːdzmən] *n.m.* *Mil:* cavalier faisant partie des *Life Guards*; cavalier de la Garde.

lifejacket ['laifdʒækit] *n.* brassière *f*, gilet *m*, de sauvetage.

lifeless ['laiflis] *a.* sans vie; (style, etc.) mou, inanimé, froid. **-ly** *adv.* sans vie.

lifelessness ['laiflisnis] *n.* (*a*) absence *f*, de vie; (*b*) manque *m* d'animation.

lifelike ['laiflaik] *a.* (portrait, etc.) vivant, qui a de la vie; *Art:* **l. flesh,** chairs vraies.

lifeline ['laiflain] *n.* **1.** *Nau:* (*a*) ligne *f* de sauvetage; (*b*) (*aboard ship*) garde-corps *m inv*, attrape *f*; sauvegarde *f*; (*c*) corde *f* de communication (de scaphandrier); (*d*) ligne de pompier. **2.** (*in palmistry*) la ligne de vie.

lifelong ['laiflɔŋ] *a.* (amitié, etc.) de toute la vie; **a l. friend,** un ami de toujours.

lifepreserver ['laifprizəːvər] *n.* **1.** *Nau:* appareil *m* de sauvetage. **2.** casse-tête *m inv*; canne plombée.

lifer ['laifər] *n.* *F:* condamné(e) à perpétuité.

lifesaver ['laifseivər] *n.* **1.** (*pers.*) sauveteur *m.* **2.** *Fig:* planche *f* de salut.

lifesaving ['laifseiviŋ] *n.* sauvetage *m*; **l. apparatus,** appareils *mpl*, engins *mpl*, de sauvetage.

life-size(d) ['laifsaiz(d)] *a.* (portrait, etc.) de grandeur naturelle, grandeur nature; (statue) en grand.

lifetime ['laiftaim] *n.* (*a*) vie *f*; **in, during, his l.,** en, de, son vivant; **a l. of happiness,** toute une vie de bonheur; **it's the chance of a l.,** cette chance n'arrive qu'une fois dans la vie; (*b*) *Ph:* durée *f*, vie (d'un phénomène); *Atom.Ph:* durée de vie, longévité *f* (d'un atome, d'un isotope).

lifework ['laifwəːk] *n.* travail *m* de toute une vie.

lift¹ [lift] *n.* **1.** (*a*) (*act of raising*) haussement *m*; élévation *f* (du bras, etc.); levée *f* (d'un fardeau, etc.); **to give s.o. a l.,** (i) prendre, emmener, qn en voiture; (ii) *F:* remonter le moral à qn; **can I give you a l.?** est-ce que je peux vous conduire, déposer, quelque part? **to thumb a l.,** faire de l'auto-stop, du stop; (*b*) (*sth. raised*) palanquée (de marchandises, etc.); **fork l. truck,** chariot (élévateur) à fourche. **2.** (*a*) (*extent of rise*) hauteur *f* de levage (d'une grue, etc.); hauteur d'élévation (d'une pompe); *Mec.E:* levée *f* (d'un clapet, d'une came); (hauteur de) chute *f* (d'un bief); (*b*) différence *f* de niveau (entre paliers, etc.); *Min:* hauteur verticale (entre deux galeries). **3.** (*raising power*) (*a*) force ascensionnelle (d'un ballon, d'un gaz); (*b*) *Av: etc:* portance *f*, poussée *f* (aérodynamique); sustentation *f*. **4.** (*raising device*) (*a*) ascenseur *m*; **(goods) l.,** monte-charge *m inv*, élévateur *m*; **service l.,** monte-plats *m inv*; **l. shaft,** cage *f* d'ascenseur; (*b*) (*of aircraft carrier*) monte-charge; ascenseur; (*c*) **ski l.,** (re)monte-pente *m*, *pl.* remonte-pentes; **chair l.,** télésiège *m*; (*d*) *Mil: Av:* **bomb l.,** treuil *m* de chargement de bombes; (*e*) *Nau:* balancine *f* (de vergue, etc.).

lift² **I.** *v.tr.* **1.** (*a*) lever, soulever (un poids); lever, élever, hausser (le bras); lever, dresser (la tête); lever (les yeux); **to l. sth. up again,** soulever, relever, qch.; **to l. s.o. up,** (i) aider qn à se relever; (ii) prendre (un enfant) dans ses bras; **to l. up one's head,** (i) relever, redresser, la tête; (ii) reprendre courage; **to l. up one's voice,** élever la voix; **to l. sth. down,** descendre qch. (d'un rayon, etc.); **the wind lifted him off his feet,** il a été soulevé par le vent; (*b*) **to l. (up),** élever (l'âme, le cœur); (*c*) *Nau:* soulager (une voile). **2.** (*a*) *Agr:* arracher (les pommes de terre); dépiquer (les plants pour les repiquer); (*b*) *Min:* remonter (le minerai); (*c*) *Cer:* démouler (la porcelaine); (*d*) *Com:* enlever (des marchandises). **3.** *Cr: Golf:* donner de l'essor à (la balle); *Ten:* lifter (un coup). **4.** *F:* (*a*) voler, lever (qch.); **to l. a passage from an author,** plagier un auteur; (*b*) *Sp:* remporter (une coupe). **5.** lever (un embargo). **II.** *v.i.* **1.** (*a*) (*of valve, etc.*) se lever, se soulever; (*b*) (*of floor*) se soulever (sous l'action de l'humidité, etc.). **2.** (*a*) (*of fog*) s'élever; se dissiper; (*b*) *U.S:* (*of rain*) cesser. **3.** *Nau:* (*of vessel*) s'élever à la lame. **4.** (*of aircraft, rocket*) **to l. (off),** décoller. **lifting** *n.* **1.** levage *m*, relevage *m*, soulèvement *m* (d'un poids, etc.); *Aut:* **l. ramp, platform,** pont élévateur; **l. capacity,** force *f*, puissance *f*, de levage; *Av:* **l. force, power,** force de sustentation, puissance ascensionnelle. **2.** (*a*) *Agr:* arrachage *m* (des pommes de terre); (*b*) *Min:* remontée *f* (du minerai); (*c*) *Cer:* démoulage *m* (de la porcelaine). **3.** (*a*) levée *f* (d'un embargo); (*b*) *F:* vol *m*; (*c*) (*of literary work*) démarquage *m.*

liftgate ['liftgeit] *n.* *U.S:* *Aut:* hayon *m* arrière.

liftman, *pl.* **-men** ['liftmæn, -men] *n.m.* liftier.

lift-off ['liftɔf] *n.* *Space:* décollage *m.*

ligament ['ligəmənt] *n.* *Anat:* ligament *m.*

ligature¹ ['ligətjər] *n.* **1.** *Surg:* ligature *f*. **2.** *Typ:* ligature. **3.** *Mus:* liaison *f*.

ligature² *v.tr.* (*a*) *Surg:* ligaturer, barrer (une veine); (*b*) lier; (*c*) entrelacer (a et e).

light¹ [lait] *n.* **1.** lumière *f*; (*a*) **artificial, electric, l.,** lumière artificielle, électrique; **by the l. of the moon,** au clair, à la clarté, de la lune; **the l. of day,** la lumière du jour; le jour; **at first l.,** à l'aube; **to bring (sth.) to l.,** (i) mettre (qch.) à jour, au jour; déterrer, exhumer (qch.); (ii) mettre (qch.) en évidence; révéler (qch.); (*of crime, etc.*) **to come to l.,** se dévoiler, se découvrir; **to see the l.,** (i) voir le jour, la lumière; (ii) être convaincu, converti; (*b*) *Ph: etc:* **bright l.,** lumière vive; **infrared, ultraviolet, l.,** lumière infrarouge, ultraviolette; **source of l., l. source,** source lumineuse; **l. beam, ray,** faisceau, rayon, lumineux; **l. wave,** onde lumineuse; (*c*) *Astr:* **l. year,** année-lumière *f*, *pl.* années-lumière; (*d*) **good, bad, l.,** bon, mauvais, éclairage; **to put, turn, on the l.,** donner de la lumière; allumer; **picture hung in a good l.,** tableau accroché dans un bon jour; **against the l., with one's back to the l.,** à contre-jour; **to see sth. in a new l., in its true l.,** voir qch. sous un jour nouveau, sous son vrai jour; **the question should be considered in the l. of these facts,** on devrait considérer la question dans ce contexte; (*e*) **to throw, shed, l. on (sth.),** jeter du jour sur (qch.); éclairer, éclaircir (qch.); (*f*) *Rel:* **the inner l.,** la parole intérieure du Saint-Esprit. **2.** (*a*) lumière; bougie *f*; lampe *f*; *Mil:* **lights out,** (sonnerie *f* de) l'extinction *f* des feux; *F:* **to go out like a l.,** (i) s'évanouir; (ii) s'endormir aussitôt couché; *F:* **one**

of the leading lights of the town, une des personnalités de la ville; (*b*) **traffic lights,** feux *mpl* de circulation, de signalisation routière; feux de croisement, *F:* feu rouge; **turn right at the (traffic) lights,** tournez à droite au feu rouge; *Fig:* **to see the red l.,** se rendre compte du danger, sentir le danger; **to give s.o. the green l.,** donner le feu vert à qn; *Av:* **airport lights,** feux d'aéroport; **approach l.,** feu d'approche; **landing, runway, light(s),** feu(x) d'atterrissage, de piste; *Nau:* **harbour lights,** feux (d'entrée) de port; **flashing l.,** feu à éclats; (*c*) *Aut:* **rear lights,** feux rouges; **parking lights,** feux de position, de stationnement; **reversing l.,** phare *m* de recul; *Rail: etc:* **red l.,** lanterne *f* rouge; **signal l.,** fanal *m*; **warning l.,** fanal avertisseur; *Aut:* **dip your lights,** roulez en code; *Nau: Av:* **navigation, position, lights,** feux de navigation, de position; (*of ship*) **she was showing no lights,** il navigait, faisait route, tous feux éteints; (*d*) *Tchn:* **control, warning, l.,** voyant lumineux; *Aut:* **dashboard, panel, l.,** lampe du tableau de bord; (*in car*) **courtesy l.,** éclairage intérieur automatique; (*e*) **l. flare,** fusée éclairante; (*f*) (*in Pr.n.*) phare. **3.** (*a*) (*fire*) **to set l. to sth.,** mettre le feu à qch.; (*of smoker*) **could I have a l., please?** pouvez-vous me donner du feu, s'il vous plaît? (*b*) feu, éclat *m* (du regard). **4.** (*a*) fenêtre *f*; lucarne *f*; jour *m* (de fenêtre à meneaux); carreau *m* (de serre); vitre *f*; (*b*) *Jur:* **ancient lights,** servitude *f* de vue. **5.** *Art: Phot:* lumière, clair *m*; **l. effects,** effets *mpl* de lumière; **l. and shade,** les clairs et les ombres; le clair-obscur.

light² *v.tr. & i.* (*p.t. & p.p.* **lit** [lit], *occ.* **lighted**) **1.** (*a*) allumer (une lampe, etc.); **to l. a fire,** allumer un feu; faire du feu; (*b*) éclairer, illuminer (une pièce, une rue); (*c*) **to l. the way for s.o.,** éclairer qn. **2. to l. up,** (i) allumer; mettre la lumière; (ii) *Mch:* mettre les feux; (iii) *F:* allumer sa cigarette, sa pipe; **a smile lit up her face,** un sourire a illuminé son visage; **his eyes lit up,** ses yeux se sont animés. **lighting** *n.* **1.** allumage *m* (d'une lampe, etc.). **2.** éclairage *m*; illumination *f*; **fluorescent l.,** éclairage par fluorescence; **direct, indirect, l.,** éclairage direct, indirect; **emergency l.,** éclairage de secours; **street l.,** éclairage urbain, des rues; *Adm:* **l.-up time,** heure *f* d'éclairage; **l. engineer,** (ingénieur *m*) éclairagiste (*m*); *Th:* **stage l.,** éclairage scénique; éclairages; **l. effects,** jeux *mpl* de lumière. **3.** éclairage, exposition *f* (d'un tableau).

light³ *a.* **1.** (*a*) **it is l., will soon be l.,** il fait, fera bientôt, jour; (*b*) (*of room, etc.*) clair; (bien) éclairé. **2.** (*a*) **painted in l. tones,** peint en tons clairs, lumineux; (*b*) (*of hair, complexion*) blond; (*of colour*) clair; **l. blue,** bleu clair *inv.*

light⁴ I. *a.* **1.** (*a*) (fardeau, coup) léger; (terre) meuble; (chaise) volante; (*b*) **with a l. step,** d'un pas léger; **to be l. on one's feet,** avoir le pas léger; (*c*) **l. wine,** vin léger; **l. beer,** bière légère; **l. breeze,** brise faible, légère; (*d*) (*deficient*) (poids) faible. **2.** (*a*) *Mil:* **l. artillery,** artillerie légère, de petit calibre; **l. infantry,** infanterie légère; = les chasseurs *m* (à pied); **l. duty,** service réduit; *Metall:* **l. castings,** petites pièces (de fonderie); (*b*) non chargé; *Nau:* (bateau) lège; (*of engine*) **to run l.,** (i) *Mch:* marcher à vide, à blanc; (ii) *Rail:* aller haut-le-pied; (*c*) **l. crop,** faible récolte *f*; **to have a l. meal,** prendre un repas léger; (*d*) **to be a l. sleeper,** avoir le sommeil léger. **3.** (*a*) **l. punishment,** peine légère; **l. taxation,** faible imposition *f*; (*b*) (tâche) facile; **l. work,** petits travaux; travail peu fatigant. **4.** (*a*) (*of comedy, style, music, etc.*) léger; **l. reading,** lecture(s) récréative(s), délassante(s); (*b*) *O:* (femme) légère; **l. talk,** propos frivoles, légers; (*c*) **to make l. of sth.,** traiter qch. à la légère; attacher peu d'importance à (une accusation). **II.** *adv.* légèrement; **to sleep l.,** (i) avoir le sommeil léger; (ii) dormir d'un sommeil léger; **to travel l.,** voyager avec peu de bagages. **lightly** *adv.* **1.** légèrement, à la légère; (marcher) d'un pas léger; **to stroke sth. l.,** effleurer qch.; **to skip l. from rock to rock,** sauter agilement de rocher en rocher; **his responsibilities sit l. on him,** ses responsabilités ne lui pèsent pas; **to sleep l.,** dormir légèrement. **2. to get off l.,** s'en tirer à bon compte, à bon marché. **3. to speak l. of sth.,** parler de qch. à la légère.

light⁵ *v.i.* (*p.t. & p.p.* **lighted**) (*a*) **to l. on s.o., sth.,** rencontrer qn, qch.; trouver qn, qch., par hasard; **his eyes lighted on the picture,** ses yeux rencontrèrent le tableau; (*b*) *NAm: F:* **to l. out,** décamper.

light-coloured ['laitkʌləd] *a.* clair.

lighten¹ ['lait(ə)n] **1.** *v.tr.* (*a*) éclairer (les ténèbres, le visage); rendre plus claire (une habitation, etc.); (*b*) éclaircir (une couleur, le ciel). **2.** *v.i.* (*a*) s'éclairer, s'illuminer; (*b*) **it's thundering and lightening,** il fait du tonnerre et des éclairs.

lighten² **1.** *v.tr.* alléger; délester (un navire); réduire le poids de (qch.); soulager (une douleur); **to l. one's conscience,** décharger sa conscience. **2.** *v.i.* **my heart lightened,** mon cœur fut soulagé.

lighter¹ ['laitər] *n.* **1.** (*pers.*) allumeur, -euse. **2.** (*device*) allumeur, allumoir *m*; **(cigarette) l.,** briquet *m*; **gas l.,** (i) briquet à gaz; (ii) allume-gaz *m.*

lighter² *n. Nau:* allège *f*, gabare *f*.

lighter³ *v.tr.* décharger (des marchandises) par allèges.

lighterage ['laitəridʒ] *n. Nau:* **1.** déchargement *m* par allèges, par gabares; gabarage *m*. **2.** droits *mpl*, frais *mpl*, d'allège, de gabarage.

light-fingered [lait'fiŋgəd] *a.* **1.** à la main légère; aux doigts agiles. **2. he's l.-f.,** c'est un voleur.

lightfooted ['lait'futid] *a.* agile, leste; au pied léger.

lightheaded [lait'hedid] *a.* **1. to feel l.,** avoir, se sentir, le cerveau vide (par défaut de nourriture, etc.). **2.** à la tête légère; étourdi, écervelé.

lighthearted [lait'hɑːtid] *a.* au cœur léger; allègre.

lighthouse ['laithaus] *n. Nau:* phare *m*; **l. keeper,** gardien *m* de phare.

lightness ['laitnis] *n.* **1.** légèreté *f*; **l. of foot,** agilité *f*; **l. of heart,** gaieté *f* de cœur; **l. of touch,** légèreté de main (d'un médecin, etc.); légèreté de plume, de pinceau, de style. **2.** (i) facilité *f*, (ii) caractère peu fatigant (d'une tâche).

lightning ['laitniŋ] *n.* (*a*) éclairs *mpl*, foudre *f*; **a flash of l.,** un éclair; **struck by l.,** frappé par la foudre; **l. conductor,** paratonnerre *m*; **as quick as l., with l. speed,** *F:* **like greased l.,** aussi vite que l'éclair, (rapide) comme l'éclair; **l. attack,** attaque *f* éclair; **l. visit,** visite *f* éclair; (*b*) *NAm: Ent:* **l. bug,** luciole *f*.

lightproof ['laitpruːf] *a.* opaque.

lights [laits] *n.pl. Cu:* mou *m* (de bœuf, etc.).

light-sensitive ['lait'sensitiv] *a. Ph:* photosensible.

lightship ['laitʃip] *n. Nau:* bateau-feu *m*, *pl.* bateaux-feux; bateau-phare *m*, *pl.* bateaux-phares.

lightweight ['laitweit] **1.** *n. Box:* poids léger; **2.** *attrib.* (*of garment, etc.*) léger.

lignite ['lignait] *n. Miner:* lignite *m.*

likable ['laikəbl] = LIKEABLE.

like¹ [laik] **I.** *a.* **1.** semblable, pareil, tel; (*a*) **walking sticks and l. objects,** cannes et objets similaires; **l. father, l. son,** tel père tel fils; *Mth:* **l. terms, quantities,** termes *mpl*, quantités *fpl*, semblables; *El:* **l. poles,** pôles *mpl* semblables, de même nom; (*b*) ressemblant; **they are as l. as two peas,** ils se ressemblent comme deux gouttes d'eau. **2.** (*a*) **I want to find one l. it,** je veux trouver le pareil, la pareille; **people l. you,** des gens comme vous; **to be l. s.o., sth.,** être semblable à qn, à qch.; ressembler à qn, à qch.; **what's the weather l.?** quel temps fait-il? **you know what he is l.,** vous savez comme il est; **he was l.**

father to me, il fut pour moi un père; **when I hear things l. that,** quand j'entends des choses semblables; **I know plenty of people l. that,** je connais pas mal de gens comme ça; **something very much l. it,** quelque chose qui y ressemble beaucoup; **it costs something l. £10,** cela coûte quelque £10; **it's just l. (at) home,** c'est tout comme chez nous; *F:* **that's something l.!** voilà qui est réussi! **there's nothing l. it,** il n'y a rien de semblable, de pareil; **she is nothing l. as pretty as you,** elle est bien loin d'être aussi jolie que vous; (*b*) **that's just l. a woman!** voilà bien les femmes! **that's just l. him!** c'est bien de lui! voilà comme il est! **II.** *prep.* comme; **I think l. you,** je pense comme vous; **just l. anybody else,** tout comme un autre; *F:* **he ran l. blazes, l. hell, l. mad,** il courait comme un dératé; **don't talk l. that,** ne parlez pas comme ça. **III.** *adv.* **1.** (*a*) *F:* **l. enough, very l., (as) l. as not,** probablement, vraisemblablement; (*b*) *P:* **he looked angry l.,** il était comme en colère; il avait l'air furieux. **2.** *F:* (*a*) (= AS) comme; **do l. I do,** faites comme moi; **l. I said,** comme je l'ai dit; (*b*) (= AS IF) **he behaved l. he was scared,** il s'est conduit comme s'il avait peur. **IV.** *n.* semblable *mf*, pareil, -eille; **he and his l.,** *P:* **he and the likes of him,** lui et ses semblables; *P:* **it's too good for the likes of me,** c'est trop bon pour des personnes comme moi; **music, painting, and the l.,** la musique, la peinture, et autres choses du même genre; *F:* **I've never seen the l. of it,** je n'ai jamais vu chose pareille.

like² *n.* (*usu. pl.*) goût *m*, préférence *f*, inclination *f*; **likes and dislikes,** sympathies *fpl* et antipathies *fpl*.

like³ *v.tr.* **1.** aimer (qch.); aimer, avoir de la sympathie pour (qn); **I l. him,** je l'aime bien; il me plaît; **how do you l. him?** comment le trouvez-vous? **he likes school,** il se plaît à l'école; **I should l. time to consider it,** j'aimerais avoir le temps d'y réfléchir; **I should l. some tea,** je prendrais bien une tasse de thé; **I should l. nothing better,** je ne demande pas mieux; **do you l. tea?** aimez-vous le thé? **I don't l. it at all,** cela ne me plaît pas du tout; **if he doesn't l. it he can go elsewhere,** si ça ne lui va pas qu'il aille ailleurs; **whether he likes it or not,** qu'il le veuille ou non; **these plants don't l. the damp,** ces plantes craignent l'humidité; *F:* **(well) I l. that!** en voilà une bonne! elle est bien bonne, celle-là! **2.** (*a*) **I l. to see them now and again,** j'aime (à) les voir de temps à autre; **he doesn't l. people to talk about it,** il n'aime pas qu'on en parle; **would you l. a cigarette?** voulez-vous une cigarette? **I should very much l. to go,** j'aimerais beaucoup y aller; **would you l. me to go with you?** voulez-vous que je vous accompagne? **I should l. to know whether . . .,** je voudrais bien savoir si . . .; (*b*) **as you l.,** comme vous voudrez; **I can do as I l. with him,** je fais de lui ce que je veux; **he is free to do as he likes,** il est libre d'agir à sa guise, de faire comme il lui plaira; **to do just as one likes,** en faire à sa tête; **if you l.,** si vous voulez; **when you l.,** quand il vous plaira; **he thinks he can do anything he likes,** il se croit tout permis; **as much as you l.,** tant que vous voudrez. **liking** *n.* goût *m*, penchant *m*; **to one's l.,** à souhait; **is it to your l.?** cela est-il à votre goût? est-ce que cela vous plaît? **to have a l. for sth.,** avoir du goût pour qch.; aimer qch.; **I have taken a l. to him,** il m'est devenu sympathique.

likeable ['laikəbl] *a.* (*of pers.*) agréable, sympathique.

likelihood ['laiklihud] *n.* vraisemblance *f*, probabilité *f*, apparence *f*; **there is little l. of his succeeding,** il y a peu de chances qu'il réussisse; **in all l.,** selon toute probabilité; selon toute vraisemblance.

likely ['laikli] **I.** *a.* **1.** vraisemblable, probable; *F:* **that's a l. story!** la belle histoire! en voilà une bonne! **it's more than l.,** c'est plus que probable; **it's l. to rain,** il y a des chances pour qu'il pleuve; **he is quite l. to do it,** il est probable qu'il le fasse. **2. books l. to interest young people,** ouvrages *mpl* susceptibles d'intéresser les jeunes; **this plan is most l. to succeed,** ce projet offre le plus de chances de succès; **the likeliest place to find him in,** l'endroit où on a le plus de chances de le trouver. **3. a l. lad,** (i) un joyeux gaillard; (ii) un gars qui promet. **II.** *adv.* **most l., very l.,** *esp. NAm:* **l.,** vraisemblablement; très probablement; **as l. as not,** vraisemblablement; *F:* **not l.!** jamais de la vie!

like-minded [laik'maindid] *a.* dans les mêmes dispositions, du même avis; qui ont les mêmes goûts.

liken ['laik(ə)n] *v.tr.* assimiler, faire ressembler (**sth. to sth.,** qch. à qch.); rendre semblable (**to,** à).

likeness ['laiknis] *n.* **1.** ressemblance *f* (**between,** entre; **to,** à); similitude *f* (de deux personnes, de deux objets); **a close l.,** une ressemblance étroite; **family l.,** air *m* de famille. **2.** portrait *m*, image *f*; **the picture is a good l.,** le portrait est très ressemblant.

likewise ['laikwaiz] *adv.* **1.** (*moreover*) de plus, de même, aussi. **2.** (*similarly*) *only in the phr.* **to do l.,** faire de même; en faire autant.

lilac ['lailək] **1.** *n. Bot:* lilas *m*. **2.** *a.* **l.(-coloured),** lilas *inv*.

Lilliputian [lili'pjuːʃ(ə)n] *a. Lit:* lilliputien.

lilt¹ [lilt] *n.* **1.** *A. & Scot:* chant *m*; air *m*. **2.** rythme *m*, cadence *f* (des vers).

lilting ['liltiŋ] *a.* (rythme) musical; (air) cadencé, scandé.

lily ['lili] *n.* **1.** *Bot:* lis *m*; **tiger l.,** lis tigré. **2.** *Bot:* **l. of the valley,** muguet *m*.

lilywhite ['lili(h)wait] *a.* blanc, *f.* blanche, comme le lis; d'une blancheur de lis.

limb [lim] *n.* **1.** membre *m*; **the lower limbs,** les membres inférieurs; **to tear an animal l. from l.,** mettre un animal en pièces. **2. l. of the devil, of Satan,** tison *m* d'enfer, suppôt *m* de Satan. **3.** (*a*) (grosse) branche (d'un arbre); bras *m* (d'une croix); (*b*) *F:* **to be out on a l.,** être en plan; être sur la corde raide.

limber¹ ['limbər] *n. Artil:* avant-train *m*, *pl.* avant-trains (d'affût de canon).

limber² *v.tr. & i. Artil:* **to l. a gun,** attacher une pièce de canon à l'avant-train; **to l. up,** amener, accrocher, mettre, l'avant-train.

limber³ *a.* souple.

limber⁴ **1.** *v.tr.* assouplir. **2.** *v.i. Sp: etc:* **to l. up,** se chauffer les muscles; **limbering-up exercises,** exercices *mpl* d'assouplissement.

limbless ['limblis] *a.* (personne) (i) sans membres, (ii) à qui il manque un ou plusieurs membres; **l. ex-servicemen,** grands mutilés *mpl* de guerre.

limbo ['limbou] *n. Theol:* les limbes *mpl*.

lime¹ [laim] *n.* **1.** (= BIRDLIME) glu *f*; **l. twig,** gluau *m*. **2.** chaux *f*; **slaked l.,** chaux éteinte; **l. pit,** carrière *f* de pierre à chaux.

lime² *v.tr.* **1.** gluer (des ramilles); enduire (des ramilles) de glu; **to l. birds,** prendre des oiseaux à la glu, au gluau. **2.** *Agr:* chauler (un terrain).

lime³ *n. Bot:* **1.** lime *f*; **l. juice,** jus *m* de lime douce, de citron doux. **2. l.(-tree),** limettier *m*.

lime⁴ *n. Bot:* **l. (-tree),** tilleul *m*.

limeade ['laimeid] *n. NAm:* jus de citron vert additionné de sucre et d'eau.

limekiln ['laimkiln] *n.* four *m* à chaux, chaufour *m*.

limelight ['laimlait] *n.* (*a*) lumière *f* oxhydrique; (*b*) **in the l.,** sous les feux de la rampe; très en vue; en vedette.

limerick ['limərik] *n.* poème *m* en cinq vers, toujours comique et absurde, aux rimes a a b b a.

limestone ['laimstoun] *n.* (*a*) *Geol:* calcaire *m*; (*b*) *Ind: etc:* pierre *f* à chaux.

limewater ['laimwɔːtər] *n. Pharm:* eau *f* de chaux.

limey ['laimi] *n. esp. U.S: Austr: P:* (*a*) Anglais *m*; (*b*) matelot anglais.

limit¹ ['limit] *n.* **1.** limite *f*; borne *f*; (*a*) **within a ten kilometre l.,** dans un rayon de dix kilomètres; **the limits of decency,** les frontières de la bienséance; **to fix, set, a l., limits (to sth.),** fixer, mettre, une limite, des limites (à qch.); **age l.,** limite d'âge; **time l.,** (i) limite de temps (imposée à un orateur, etc.); (ii) délai *m* (de paiement, etc.); (iii) durée *f* (d'un privilège, etc.); **speed l.,** vitesse *f* limite, maximum, maximale; *Fin:* **credit l.,** limite, plafond *m*, du crédit; (*b*) *Mec:* limite (d'élasticité, etc.); (*c*) *Ins:* plein *m*; **to fix a l.,** fixer les pleins; (*d*) **there's a l. to everything!** il y a limite à tout! *F:* **the sky's the l.,** il n'y a pas de limite; **that's the l.!** ça c'est le comble! **he's the l.!** il est impossible! **2.** *Mec.E:* tolérance *f*; *Tls:* **l. gauge,** calibre *m* de tolérance; (*external*) bague *f* à tolérance; (*internal*) bouchon *m* à tolérance.

limit² *v.tr.* limiter, borner, restreindre (qn, qch.); **to l. oneself to . . .,** se borner à . . .; **to l. oneself to strict necessities,** se restreindre au strict nécessaire. **limited** *a.* (nombre, etc.) limité, restreint; (intelligence) bornée; *Com:* (marché) étroit, restreint; *Publ:* **l. edition,** (édition *f* à) tirage limité.

limitless ['limitlis] *a.* sans bornes, illimité.

limousine [limu'ziːn] *n. Aut:* limousine *f*.

limp¹ [limp] *n.* boitement *m*, clochement *m*, claudication *f*; **to walk with a l., to have a l.,** boiter.

limp² *v.i.* boiter, claudiquer; traîner la jambe; **to l. along,** aller en boitant, *F:* clopin-clopant; (*of ship, etc.*) avancer péniblement. **limping** *a.* boiteux.

limp³ *a.* mou, *f.* molle; flasque; *Bookb:* **l. binding,** cartonnage *m* souple, à l'anglaise; (*of linen*) **to become l.,** devenir mou; (*of starched linen*) se désempeser; (*of pers.*) **to feel l.,** se sentir mou, sans énergie; **l. with the heat,** abattu par la chaleur. **-ly** *adv.* **1.** mollement, flasquement. **2.** sans énergie.

limpet ['limpit] *n.* **1.** *Moll:* patelle *f*, arapède *m*. **2.** *F:* (*pers.*) crampon *m*.

limpid ['limpid] *a.* limpide, pellucide, clair.

limpness ['limpnis] *n.* mollesse *f*; manque *m* d'énergie.

linchpin ['lin(t)ʃpin] *n.* (*a*) *Veh:* esse *f*; cheville *f* d'essieu; (*b*) *Fig:* cheville ouvrière (d'une organisation, etc.).

linctus ['liŋktəs] *n. Pharm:* sirop *m*.

linden ['lindən] *n. Bot: Lit:* **l. (tree),** tilleul *m*.

line¹ [lain] *n.* **1.** (*cord, wire, etc.*) (*a*) *Nau:* ligne *f*, corde *f*, cordage *m*; amarre *f*; **lead, sounding, l.,** ligne de sonde; *Dom.Ec:* **clothes l.,** corde à linge; (*b*) *Fish:* ligne (de pêche); **ground l.,** ligne de fond; **l. fishing,** pêche *f* à la ligne; (*c*) *Tp:* **extension l.,** ligne supplémentaire; **shared, party, l.,** ligne partagée; *Pol:* **the hot l.,** (i) (*Élysée to Kremlin*) la ligne verte; (ii) (*U.S.A. to Kremlin*) la ligne rouge; **the line's very bad,** la communication est mauvaise; **I have X on the l.,** j'ai X au bout du fil; (*d*) *El:* **high-tension l.,** ligne à haute tension; *El: Tp:* **overhead, underground, l.,** ligne aérienne, souterraine; (*e*) *Surv: Const:* cordeau *m*; **laid out by the l., by rule and l.,** tiré au cordeau; (*f*) *F:* **it's hard lines on you!** c'est bien malheureux pour vous! **hard lines!** pas de chance! **2.** *Nau:* collecteur *m*. **3.** (*a*) ligne; trait *m*; raie *f*; **straight l.,** (ligne) droite (*f*); **perpendicular l.,** (ligne, droite) perpendiculaire (*f*); **l. drawing,** dessin *m* au trait; **broken l.,** (i) ligne brisée; (ii) trait discontinu; **wavy l.,** trait ondulé; **l. engraving,** gravure *f* au trait; *Nau:* **water l.,** ligne de flottaison; **load l.,** ligne de charge; **datum l.,** ligne de référence; (*supplied with writing pad*) **guide lines,** transparent *m*; *Ten:* **service l.,** ligne de service; **on the l.,** sur la raie; *T.V:* **definition of 625 lines,** définition *f* de 625 lignes (d'exploration); *Aut:* **white l.,** *U.S:* **yellow l.,** = ligne blanche, bande médiane; **double yellow lines** = ligne rouge (d'interdiction de stationnement); **(single) yellow l.** = stationnement limité; (*b*) *Geol: Geog:* **snow l.,** ligne, limite *f*, des neiges; **fault l.,** ligne de faille; (*of glacier*) **flow l.,** ligne de flux; (*c*) filet *m* (de lumière); *Ph:* raie (du spectre); **the lines of the hand,** les lignes de la main; **the lines on his forehead,** les rides *fpl* de son front; (*d*) *Geog:* **the l.,** la Ligne (équatoriale); l'équateur *m*; (*e*) *Opt:* **l. of sight,** ligne de visée; *Artil: Sm.a:* ligne de mire; **l. of vision,** ligne de visée; *Ball:* **l. of fire,** ligne de tir; (*f*) *F:* **to get a l. on sth.,** (i) obtenir des tuyaux sur qch.; (ii) se rendre compte de qch.; **to give s.o. a l. on sth.,** tuyauter qn sur qch.; **to get a l. on s.o.,** se renseigner sur qn; (*h*) (*contour*) ligne (de l'horizon); contours *mpl* (d'un rivage, d'un visage); lignes (d'une voiture, etc.); **the hard lines of his face,** ses traits durs; **to work on the same lines as s.o.,** travailler d'après le modèle tracé par qn; **to be working on the right lines,** être en bonne voie; (*i*) (*limit*) **demarcation l.,** ligne de démarcation; **one must draw the l. somewhere,** il y a une limite à tout; **to overstep the l.,** dépasser la mesure. **4.** (*row of pers. or thgs*) (*a*) (*side by side*) ligne, rangée *f* (de personnes, d'objets); alignement *m*; **to put (out) things in a l.,** aligner des objets; (*of pers.*) **to fall, get, into l., to form a l.,** se mettre en ligne; former les rangs; **out of l.,** désaligné; **to get out of l.,** se désaligner; (*of individual*) quitter les rangs, sortir des rangs; **to fall into l. with s.o.'s ideas,** se conformer aux idées de qn; **his decision is not in l., is out of l., with government policy,** sa décision ne se conforme pas, n'est pas d'accord, avec la politique du gouvernement; (*b*) (*one behind the other*) file *f*; *NAm:* queue *f*; **twenty cars in a l.,** vingt voitures à la file; **l. of traffic,** colonne *f* de véhicules; (*of vehicle*) **to get into the l. of traffic,** prendre la file; *Ind:* **assembly l.,** chaîne *f* de montage; **production l.,** chaîne de production; **to work on the assembly, the production, l.,** travailler à la chaîne; (*of pers.*) **to stand in a l.,** (i) se tenir à la file; (ii) faire la queue; (*c*) *Mil: etc:* **fighting l., l. of battle,** ligne de combat, de bataille; **l. of attack,** ligne d'attaque; **the front, rear, lines,** le front, l'arrière *m*; **to win all along the l.,** gagner sur toute la ligne; (*d*) *Mil:* **lines,** lignes (de fortification, etc.); (*e*) ligne (de mots écrits, imprimés); vers *m* (de poésie); **first l. of a paragraph,** alinéa *m*; (*in dictating*) **new l.,** à la ligne; *F:* **I'll drop you a l.,** je vous enverrai un petit mot; **just a l. to tell you . . .,** deux mots pour vous dire . . .; *Typ: Typew:* **l. space,** entre-ligne *m*, interligne *m*; **l. spacing,** interlignage *m*; *Typ: etc:* **l. printing,** impression *f* ligne par ligne; *Th:* (*of actor*) **he doesn't know his lines,** il ne sait pas son rôle; *F:* **marriage lines,** acte *m* de mariage. **5.** ligne, compagnie *f* (de paquebots, etc.); **shipping l.,** compagnie de navigation; messageries *fpl* maritimes. **6.** ligne de descendants, d'ascendants; ligne (généalogique); **male, female, l.,** ligne masculine, féminine; **long l. of ancestors,** longue suite d'ancêtres; **in direct l.,** en ligne directe. **7.** (*a*) ligne (de marche, d'intercommunication); voie *f* (de communication); *Mil: etc:* **l. of advance,** direction *f* de marche; (*b*) *Rail:* voie; ligne; **main l.,** voie principale; grande ligne; **single-track, double-track, l.,** ligne à voie unique, à double voie; (*c*) **l. of conduct,** ligne de conduite; **l. of thought,** suite *f* d'idées; **l. of argument,** raisonnement *m*; **what l. are you going to take?** quel parti allez-vous prendre? (*d*) *F:* genre *m* d'affaires; métier *m*; **what's his l.?** quel est son métier? qu'est-ce qu'il fait? **that's not my l.,** ce n'est pas mon rayon; **that's more (in) my l.,** cela est plus dans mon genre; (*e*) *Com:* série *f* (d'articles); article *m*; *F:* **a rice pudding or something in that l.,** un gâteau de riz ou quelque chose dans ce genre (-là).

line² *v.tr.* **1.** ligner, régler, rayer (un morceau de papier); (*of forehead, face*) **to become lined,** se rider. **2.** border; **to l. the roads with troops,** aligner des troupes sur les routes; **the crowd lined the street,** la foule s'alignait le long du trottoir. **3.** érafler, rayer; strier de lignes. **lined** *a.* ligné; (papier) réglé, rayé; **deeply l. forehead,** front creusé de rides. **line up 1.** *v.tr.* (*a*) aligner, mettre en ligne (des personnes, des objets); (*b*) *F:* prévoir (qch., qn); avoir (qch., qn) en vue; **what have you got lined up for us?** qu'est-ce que vous nous préparez? **2.** *v.i.* (*of pers.*) s'aligner; se mettre en ligne; se ranger; faire la queue.

line³ *v.tr.* (*a*) *Tail: Dressm: etc:* doubler (un vêtement) (**with,** de); **fur-lined gloves,** gants fourrés; (*b*) **to l. a box with paper,** tapisser une boîte de papier; *Cu:* **to l. a tin with pastry,** foncer un moule de pâte; **nest lined with moss,** nid garni de mousse; (*c*) *Tchn:* garnir, recouvrir (un palier); revêtir, incruster (un mur, un fourneau) (**with,** de); cuveler (un puits); **to l. a shaft with metal,** blinder un puits. **lined** *a.* (manteau) doublé; (gant) fourré; (frein) garni; *Min:* (galerie) coffrée; **steel-l.,** (cylindre) chemisé d'acier; **well l. purse,** bourse bien garnie. **lining** *n.* **1.** doublage *m*, garnissage *m*; revêtement intérieur. **2.** (*a*) doublure *f* (de robe); coiffe *f* (de chapeau); (*b*) *Tchn:* garniture *f*, fourrure *f* (de frein, de coussinet); chemise *f* (de fourneau, de pompe); cuvelage *m* (de puits); paroi *f* (d'un tunnel).

lineage ['liniidʒ] *n.* lignée *f*, lignage *m*; famille *f*; **to boast an ancient l.,** se vanter d'une longue généalogie.

lineal ['liniəl] *a.* linéal, -aux; (descendant, succession) en ligne directe.

lineaments ['liniəmənts] *n.pl.* traits *mpl*, linéaments *mpl.*

linear ['liniər] *a.* linéaire; **l. measure,** mesure *f* linéaire, mesure de longueur; *Ph:* **l. expansion,** dilatation *f* linéaire.

linen ['linin] *n.* **1.** (*a*) *Tex:* toile *f* (de lin); **l. sheets,** draps *mpl* fil; **l. industry,** industrie linière, toilière; (*b*) **l. paper,** papier toilé. **2.** linge *m*; lingerie *f*; **table l.,** linge de table; **dirty l.,** linge sale; *F:* **don't wash your dirty l. in public,** il faut laver son linge sale en famille; **l. cupboard,** armoire *f* à linge; **l. room,** lingerie.

liner¹ ['lainər] *n.* (paquebot *m*) transatlantique (*m*).

liner² *n.* (*a*) cale *f* d'épaisseur (en fer, en bois); (*b*) *Mch:* fourreau *m* (de cylindre); (*c*) **bin l.,** sac *m* à poubelle.

linesman, *pl.* **-men** ['lainzmən] *n.m.* *Fb: Ten:* arbitre de lignes; *Fb:* arbitre, juge de touche.

line-up ['lainʌp] *n.* (*a*) mise *f* en rang, en ligne; alignement *m*; (*b*) (i) *NAm:* queue *f* (de personnes); (ii) rangée *f* de personnes (assemblées par la police pour l'identification d'un suspect); (*c*) *Sp:* formation *f* (d'une équipe sur le terrain).

linework ['lainwəːk] *n.* *Art:* dessin *m* au trait.

ling¹ [liŋ] *n.* *Ich:* lingue *f*; morue longue; julienne *f*.

ling² *n.* *Bot:* bruyère commune; callune *f* vulgaire.

linger ['liŋgər] *v.i.* (*a*) tarder, s'attarder, traîner; **to l. over a meal,** s'attarder sur un repas; **a doubt still lingered in his mind,** un doute subsistait encore dans son esprit; (*b*) (*of invalid*) **to l. (on),** languir, traîner. **lingering** *a.* (regard) prolongé; (doute) qui subsiste encore; **there was a l. hope that . . .,** on conservait un vague espoir que . . .. **2.** (maladie) qui traîne, maladie chronique; (mort) lente.

lingerie ['læːʒəri(ː)] *n.* lingerie *f* (pour femmes).

lingo ['liŋgou], *pl.* **lingoes** ['liŋgouz] *n.* *F:* **1. the l. of the country,** (i) la langue du pays; (ii) le jargon, le patois, du pays. **2.** argot *m* (du théâtre, etc.).

linguist ['liŋgwist] *n.* linguiste *mf*; **to be a good l., no l.,** être, ne pas être, doué pour les langues.

linguistic [liŋ'gwistik] *a.* linguistique. **-ally** *adv.* linguistiquement.

linguistics [liŋ'gwistiks] *n.pl.* (*usu. with sg. const.*) linguistique *f*; **structural l.,** linguistique structurale.

liniment ['linimənt] *n.* liniment *m.*

link¹ [liŋk] *n.* **1.** (*a*) chaînon *m*, maillon *m*, maille *f*, anneau *m* (d'une chaîne); *Nau:* paillon *m* (de câble-chaîne); (*b*) maille (de tricot); (*c*) **cuff links,** boutons de manchette. **2.** *Mec.E: etc:* (*a*) pièce *f* de liaison, tige *f* d'assemblage; *Aut:* bielle d'accouplement (des roues avant); (*b*) **(fork) l.,** étrier *m*; (*c*) menotte *f* (de ressort); (*d*) *Mch:* coulisse *f* (de machine à vapeur). **3.** lien *m*, liaison *f* (**between,** entre); **air, radio, l.,** liaison aérienne, radiophonique; **he is a l. between the old world and the new,** il sert de trait d'union entre le vieux monde et le nouveau; **missing l.,** (i) vide *m*, lacune *f* (dans une théorie); (ii) *Biol:* forme intermédiaire disparue; *F:* (l')anneau manquant.

link² **1.** *v.tr.* enchaîner, (re)lier, (re)joindre, (r)attacher (**with, to,** à); **wages linked to the cost of living,** salaires indexés sur le coût de la vie; **facts closely linked together,** faits étroitement unis; **to l. hands, arms,** se donner la main, le bras. **2.** *v.i.* **to l. on to sth., to l. in, up, with sth.,** s'attacher, se joindre, s'unir, à qch. **linked** *a.* lié, joint; *Mec.E:* articulé; **l. traffic lights,** feux synchronisés. **linking** *n.* enchaînement *m*, liaison *f*; *Space:* **l. up,** jonction *f* (de deux engins spatiaux).

linkage ['liŋkidʒ] *n.* **1.** liaison *f*; raccord *m*. **2.** (*a*) *Ch:* liaison; (*b*) enchaînement *m* (de phénomènes).

linkman, *pl* **-men** ['liŋkmən] *n.m.* *U.S: Th: Cin:* commissionaire.

links [liŋks] *n.pl.* (*usu. with sg. const.*) **(golf) l.,** terrain *m*, parcours, *m* de golf.

link(-)up ['liŋkʌp] *n.* lien *m*, liaison *f* (**between,** entre).

linnet ['linit] *n.* *Orn:* linotte (mélodieuse).

lino ['lainou] *n.* *F:* linoléum *m.*

linoleum [li'nouliəm] *n.* linoléum *m.*

linseed ['linsiːd] *n.* graine *f* de lin; **l. oil,** huile *f* de lin.

lint [lint] *n.* **1.** *Med:* pansement ouatiné. **2.** peluche *f* (de coton, de chiffon, etc.).

lintel ['lint(ə)l] *n.* **1.** linteau *m*, sommier *m* (de porte, de fenêtre); *Arch:* **l. course,** plate-bande *f*, *pl.* plates-bandes. **2.** travers *m* (de manteau de cheminée).

lion ['laiən] *n.* **1.** *Z:* (*a*) lion *m*; **lion('s) cub,** lionceau *m*; **l. house,** fauverie *f*; **lion's den,** antre *m* du lion; **the lion's share,** la part du lion; **to put one's head into the lion's mouth,** se fourrer dans la gueule du loup; (*b*) **mountain l.,** lion d'Amérique; couguar *m*. **2.** *O:* personnage marquant; lion; **the l. of the day,** la célébrité du jour. **3.** *Astr:* **the L.,** le Lion.

lioness ['laiənes] *n.f.* *Z:* lionne.

lionheart ['laiənhɑːt] *n.* homme courageux; *Hist:* **(Richard) the L.,** Richard Cœur de lion.

lionhearted ['laiənhɑːtid] *a.* au cœur de lion.

lionize ['laiənaiz] *v.tr.* faire une célébrité de (qn).

lip [lip] *n.* **1.** (*a*) lèvre *f* (de qn); babine *f* (d'un animal); **to keep a stiff upper l.,** ne pas broncher; serrer les dents; **to do, pay, l. service to s.o., to sth.,** rendre à qn, à qch., des hommages peu sincères; **a cigar between his lips,** un cigare aux lèvres; **to bite one's lip(s),** se mordre les lèvres; **to smack, lick, one's lips over sth.,** se lécher les babines; **no complaint ever passes his lips,** jamais il ne se plaint; (*b*) *P:* effronterie *f*, insolence *f*; **none of your l.! don't give me any of your l.!** ne te fiche pas de moi! (*c*) lèvre (d'une plaie); *Bot:* lèvre (de corolle labiée); labelle *m* (d'orchidée). **2.** (*a*) (*rim*) bord *m*, rebord *m* (d'une tasse, d'une cavité); margelle *f* (de puits); bord (de cratère); (*b*) **pouring l.,** bec *m* (de cruche); (*c*) (*projection*) rebord, saillie *f*; couronne *f* (de came); (*d*) *Tls:* lèvre, tranchant *m* (de mèche anglaise).

lipped [lipt] *a.* **1.** (*with adj. prefixed*) **thin-l.,** aux lèvres minces; **thick-l.,** lippu; **red-l.,** aux lèvres rouges. **2.** *Bot:* labié. **3.** (tuyau, etc.) à rebord; (cruche) à bec.

lipread ['lipri:d] *v.i.* (*of the deaf*) lire sur les lèvres. **lipreading** *n.* lecture *f* sur les lèvres.

lipsalve ['lipsælv, -sɑ:v] *n.* pommade *f* pour les lèvres.

lipstick ['lipstik] *n.* rouge *m*, crayon *m*, à lèvres.

liquefaction [likwi'fækʃ(ə)n] *n.* liquéfaction *f.*

liquefy ['likwifai] **1.** *v.tr.* liquéfier (un gaz, etc.). **2.** *v.i.* (*of gas, etc.*) se liquéfier.

liqueur [li:'kɔ:r, li'kjuər] *n.* (*a*) liqueur *f* (de dessert); **l. glass,** verre *m* à liqueur; **l. brandy** = fine champagne; *F:* fine *f*; **l. chocolates,** bonbons *mpl* à la liqueur; (*b*) *Wine-m:* liqueur d'expédition.

liquid ['likwid] **1.** *a.* (*a*) (combustible, air, etc.) liquide; **to reduce sth. to a l. state,** liquéfier qch.; (*b*) (son) doux, harmonieux, clair; (*c*) *Fin:* (argent) liquide, disponible; **l. assets,** valeurs *fpl* disponibles; actif *m* liquide; disponible *m*; (*d*) *Ling:* (consonne) liquide. **2.** *n.* (*a*) liquide *m*; **l. measure,** mesure *f* de capacité pour les liquides; (*b*) **refrigerating l.,** liquide réfrigérant; *Dom.Ec:* **washing-up l.,** lave-vaisselle *m*; (*c*) *Ling:* (consonne) liquide (*f*).

liquidate ['likwideit] *v.* **1.** *v.tr.* (*a*) liquider (une société, une dette); amortir (une dette); mobiliser (des capitaux); (*b*) *F:* liquider (qn). **2.** *v.i.* entrer en liquidation; liquider.

liquidation [likwi'deiʃ(ə)n] *n.* liquidation *f* (d'une société, d'une dette); amortissement *m* (d'une dette); mobilisation *f* (de capitaux); (*of company*) **to go into l.,** entrer en liquidation.

liquidator ['likwideitər] *n.* liquidateur, -trice (d'une société en liquidation).

liquidity [li'kwiditi] *n.* **1.** liquidité *f* (d'une substance). **2.** *Fin:* liquidité (d'une dette).

liquidize ['likwidaiz] *v.tr.* liquéfier.

liquidizer ['likwidaizər] *n. Dom.Ec:* mixe(u)r *m.*

liquor ['likər] *n.* **1.** boisson *f* alcoolique; spiritueux *m*, alcool *m*; *NAm:* **l. store** = marchand *m* de vins; **to be the worse for l.,** être ivre. **2.** *Cu:* (i) *O:* jus *m* (d'un rôti); (ii) eau (des huîtres).

liquorice ['likəris] *n. Bot: Comest:* réglisse *f.*

Lisbon ['lizbən] *Pr.n. Geog:* Lisbonne *f.*

lisle [lail] *a. & n. Tex:* **l. (thread),** fil *m* d'Écosse; **l. stockings,** bas *mpl* de fil.

lisp¹ [lisp] *n.* zézaiement *m*, chuintement *m*; **to have a l., to speak with a l.,** zézayer, chuinter.

lisp² *v.i. & tr.* zézayer; chuinter.

lissom ['lisəm] *a.* souple, agile, leste.

list¹ [list] *n. A:* **lists,** lice *f*; **to enter the lists,** entrer en lice (**against s.o.,** contre qn).

list² *n.* (*a*) liste *f*; *Adm: etc:* bordereau *m*; **alphabetical l.,** liste par ordre alphabétique; **l. of names,** liste nominative; **shopping l.,** liste des achats; **check l.,** liste de contrôle, de vérification; (*in restaurant*) **wine l.,** carte *f* des vins; *St.Exch:* **l. of quotations,** bulletin *m* de cours; *Mil: etc:* **casualty l.,** état *m* des pertes; *Adm:* **civil l.,** liste civile; (*in hospital*) **to be on the danger l.,** être gravement malade; *Bank: etc:* **l. of investments,** (bordereau *m* de) portefeuille (*m*); **to make out, draw up, a l.,** établir, dresser, une liste; **to enter (sth.) on a l.,** porter (qch.) sur une liste; (*b*) *Com:* catalogue *m*; **mailing l.,** liste d'envoi, des abonnés; **price l.,** prix-courant *m*, *pl.* prix-courants; tarif *m*; **market price l.,** mercuriale *f.*

list³ *v.tr.* inscrire, porter, (des noms, etc.) sur une liste; enregistrer (qch.); inventorier (des marchandises, etc.); *Fin:* **listed securities, stock,** valeurs admises, inscrites, à la cote (officielle).

list⁴ *n. Nau:* faux bord; bande *f*, gîte *f*; **to have, take, a l.,** donner de la bande; prendre de la gîte; **l. to starboard,** gîte à tribord.

list⁵ *v.i. Nau:* donner de la bande (**to starboard,** à tribord); prendre de la gîte; **the ship is listing,** le navire penche sur le côté.

listel ['list(ə)l] *n. Arch:* listel *m*, *pl.* -eaux.

listen ['lis(ə)n] *v.ind.tr.* **1.** écouter; **to l. to s.o., to sth.,** écouter qn, qch.; **to l. with half an ear,** n'écouter que d'une oreille; **to l. to s.o. singing,** écouter chanter qn; **l.! I've got an idea,** écoutez donc, j'ai une idée. **2.** faire attention; écouter; **he wouldn't l.,** il n'a rien voulu savoir; **you've been listening to tales,** vous vous êtes laissé raconter des histoires. **3.** *W.Tel:* **to l. in,** écouter la radio; **to l. to the news,** écouter les informations; *Tp:* **to l. in to other people's conversations,** écouter les conversations d'autrui. **listening** *n.* écoute *f*; **l. apparatus,** appareil *m* d'écoute; écouteur *m*; **l. post, station,** poste *m*, station *f*, d'écoute.

listener ['lisnər] *n.* (*a*) (i) auditeur, -trice; (ii) écouteur, -euse; **he's a good l.,** il sait écouter; (*b*) *Mil: Tp:* écouteur; (*c*) *W.Tel:* **listener(-in),** auditeur.

listless ['listlis] *a.* indifférent; apathique, sans énergie. **-ly** *adv.* apathiquement.

listlessness ['listlisnis] *n.* apathie *f*; indifférence *f.*

litany ['litəni] *n. Ecc:* litanies *fpl.*

litchi ['li:tʃi:, 'lai-] *n. Bot:* litchi *m.*

liter ['li:tər] *n. NAm:* = LITRE.

literacy ['litərəsi] *n.* fait *m* de savoir lire et écrire; degré *m* d'instruction, d'alphabétisation.

literal ['litərəl] *a.* **1.** (*a*) littéral, -aux; (traduction) mot à mot; (*b*) **in the l. sense of the word,** au sens propre du mot; **to take sth. in a l. sense,** prendre qch. au pied de la lettre; (*c*) (*of pers.*) terre à terre; prosaïque. **2.** (*a*) *Mth:* (coefficient) littéral; (*b*) *Typ:* **l. error,** *n.* **literal,** coquille *f.* **-ally** *adv.* littéralement; (traduire) mot à mot; **l. speaking,** à proprement parler; **to take sth. l.,** prendre qch. au pied de la lettre.

literary ['litərəri] *a.* (œuvre, agent, propriété, etc.) littéraire; **l. man,** homme *m* de lettres.

literate ['litərət] **1.** *a.* (*a*) qui sait lire et écrire; (*b*) lettré.

literature ['litərətjər] *n.* **1.** littérature *f*; (*a*) la carrière des lettres; (*b*) œuvres *fpl* littéraires; (*c*) **French l.,** la littérature française. **2.** (*a*) **the l. of a subject,** la bibliographie d'un sujet; (*b*) *Com: etc:* prospectus *mpl*, brochures *fpl*; documentation *f.*

lithe [laið] *a.* souple, agile.

lithium ['liθiəm] *n. Ch:* lithium *m.*

lithograph ['liθəgræf] *n. Engr:* lithographie *f.*

lithographic [liθə'græfik] *a.* lithographique.

lithography [li'θɔgrəfi] *n.* lithographie *f*; procédés *mpl* lithographiques.

Lithuania [liθju'einiə] *Pr.n. Geog:* Lit(h)uanie *f.*

Lithuanian [liθju'einiən] *Geog: Hist:* **1.** *a.* lit(h)uanien. **2.** *n.* Lit(h)uanien, -ienne.

litigant ['litigənt] *Jur:* **1.** *a.* **l. parties,** parties plaidantes, en litige. **2.** *n.* plaideur, -euse.

litigate ['litigeit] **1.** *v.i.* plaider; être en procès. **2.** *v.tr.* contester (une question); mettre (une question, une propriété) en litige.

litigation [liti'geiʃ(ə)n] *n. Jur:* litige *m*; procès *mpl*; **in l.,** en litige.

litigious [li'tidʒəs] *a.* litigieux.

litmus ['litməs] *n. Dy: Ch:* tournesol *m*; **l. paper,** papier *m* (de) tournesol.

litre, *NAm:* **liter** ['li:tər] *n. Meas:* litre *m.*

litter¹ ['litər] *n.* **1.** (*a*) *Veh:* litière *f*; **to be carried in a l.,** être porté en litière; (*b*) civière *f* (pour le transport des blessés). **2.** *Agr:* (*a*) litière (de paille, etc.); (*b*) fumier *m* (d'écurie, etc.). **3.** (*a*) détritus *m*; papiers gras; (*in street*) **l. bin,** boîte *f* à ordures; (*b*) fouillis *m*, désordre *m*; fatras *m*. **4.** portée *f* (d'un animal); (*of pups*) chiennée *f*; (*of kittens*) chattée *f*; **five young at a l., in one l.,** cinq petits d'une portée.

litter² *v.* **1.** *v.tr.* (*a*) **to l. (down) a horse,** faire la litière à un cheval; (*b*) **to l. (down) a stable,** étendre de la paille dans une écurie. **2.** *v.tr.* mettre en désordre (une chambre, etc.); **table littered with papers,** table encombrée de papiers. **3.** *v.i.* (*of animal*) mettre bas, avoir une portée.

litterbug, litterlout [ˈlitəbʌg, -laut] *n. F:* personne *f* qui jette des ordures n'importe où.

little [ˈlitl] **I.** *a.* (*for comp. and sup.* **less, least, smaller, smallest,** *q.v., are used; F:* **littler, littlest**) **1.** petit; **l. girl,** petite fille; fillette *f*; **l. ones,** (i) enfants *mpl*, *F:* mioches *mpl*; (ii) petits *mpl* (d'un animal); **poor l. girl!** pauvre petite! *F:* **a tiny l. house,** une toute petite maison; **wait a l. while!** attendez un petit moment! **the l. finger,** le petit doigt. **2.** peu (de); **l. money,** peu d'argent; **a l. money,** un peu d'argent; **to gain l. advantage from sth.,** ne tirer que peu d'avantage de qch.; *F:* **be it ever so l.,** si peu que ce soit. **3.** mesquin; **a l. mind,** un petit esprit. **II.** *n.* (*comp. and sup.* **less, least**) **1.** peu *m*; **to eat l. or nothing,** manger peu ou point; **he knows very l.,** il ne sait pas grand-chose; **he has done l. for us,** il a peu fait pour nous; **I see very l. of him,** je ne le vois guère; **the l. I know,** le peu que je sais; **to think l. of s.o.,** tenir qn en médiocre estime; **to make, think, l. of sth.,** faire peu de cas de qch.; *adv. phr.* **l. by l.,** petit à petit; peu à peu; *Prov:* **every l. helps,** (i) les petits ruisseaux font les grandes rivières; (ii) il n'y a pas de petites économies; (iii) on fait feu de tout bois. **2.** (*a*) **a l. more,** encore un peu; **a l. more and he would have died,** peu s'en fallut qu'il ne meure; **for, after, a l.,** pendant, après, un certain temps; (*b*) (*used adverbially*) **he helped him a l.,** il l'a aidé un peu; **I was not a l. afraid,** j'avais très peur; **wait a l.!** attendez un peu! **III.** *adv.* (*comp. and sup.* **less, least**) peu; **l. known,** peu connu; **l. more than an hour ago,** il n'y a guère qu'une heure; **do you see him?—very l.,** le voyez-vous?—très peu; **he l. knows, thinks, suspects . . .,** il ne se doute guère . . . .

littoral [ˈlitərəl] **1.** *a.* littoral, -aux. **2.** *n.* littoral *m.*

liturgic(al) [liˈtəːdʒik(l)] *a.* liturgique.

liturgy [ˈlitədʒi] *n.* liturgie *f.*

livable [ˈlivəbl] *a.* = LIVEABLE.

live¹ [laiv] *a.* **1.** (*a*) vivant; en vie; **l. weight,** poids vif, vivant (d'un animal de boucherie); *F:* **a real l. burglar,** un cambrioleur en chair et en os; *Fish:* **l. bait,** amorce vive; (*b*) *T.V: W.Tel:* (émission) en direct; (*as distinct from film, etc.*) **l. show,** spectacle *m* sur une scène de théâtre; (*c*) (récit) vivant; (homme) plein de vie; (*d*) (question) d'actualité; (*e*) (charbons) ardents. **2.** (*a*) *Mil:* (munitions) (i) actives, (ii) de guerre; (bombe) active, amorcée, armée; (cartouche) à balle, réelle; (*b*) *El:* **l. wire,** câble *m*, fil *m*, sous tension, en charge, chargé; *F:* **he's a l. wire,** il est énergique; il a de l'allant. **3.** (*a*) *Tchn:* (charge) roulante, mobile; **l. weight,** charge utile; (*b*) *Mec.E:* (essieu) moteur.

live² [liv] **1.** *v.i.* vivre; (*a*) (*be alive*) **while my father lived,** du vivant de mon père; **long l. the king!** vive le roi! **as long, so long, as I l.,** tant que je vivrai; *Prov:* **you l. and learn,** (i) on apprend à tout âge; (ii) qui vivra verra; **l. and let l.,** il faut que tout le monde vive; (*b*) durer; **his name will l.,** son nom vivra, sera immortalisé; (*c*) (*subsist*) **to l. on vegetables,** vivre, se nourrir, de légumes; **he earns enough to l. on,** il gagne de quoi vivre; **to l. on one's capital,** vivre sur son capital; **to l. on s.o.,** vivre aux crochets de qn; **he lives by his pen,** il vit de sa plume; (*d*) (*pass life*) **to l. in style,** mener grand train; **to l. well,** faire bonne chère; ne rien se refuser; **to l. up to one's principles,** vivre selon ses principes; **to l. up to one's reputation,** faire honneur à sa réputation; **to l. up to one's promise,** remplir sa promesse; (*e*) (*reside*) **to l. in Paris, in the country,** habiter Paris; demeurer, habiter, à la campagne; **where do you l.?** où est-ce que vous habitez? **this house isn't fit to l. in,** cette maison est inhabitable; **the house doesn't seem to be lived in,** la maison ne paraît pas habitée; (*f*) **to l. with s.o.,** vivre, habiter, avec qn; **to l. happily with s.o.,** faire bon ménage avec qn; (*g*) (*cohabit*) **they l. together,** ils vivent ensemble, ils font ménage à deux. **2.** *v.tr.* (*a*) (*with cogn. acc.*) **to l. a happy life,** mener une vie heureuse; **once more life seemed worth living,** de nouveau la vie lui semblait bonne; (*b*) **to l. a lie,** vivre dans un perpétuel mensonge; *Th:* **to l. a part,** entrer dans la peau d'un personnage; (*c*) *F:* **to l. it up,** faire la noce. **live down** *v.tr.* **to l. down one's past,** faire oublier son passé. **live in** *v.i.* (*of servant*) coucher à la maison; **the employees l. in,** les employés sont logés et nourris. **live out** *v.i.* (*of servant*) coucher à son domicile; venir en journée. **living 1.** *a.* (*a*) vivant, vif; en vie; **while he was l.,** de son vivant; **l. or dead,** mort ou vif; **there is not a l. soul to be seen,** on ne rencontre pas âme qui vive, *F:* pas un chat; **he has done more for them than any man l.,** il a fait plus pour eux que n'importe qui; *n.pl.* **the l.,** les vivants; **he's still in the land of the l.,** il est encore vivant, de ce monde; **l. language,** langue vivante; **l. pictures,** tableaux vivants; **a l. death,** une vie pire que la mort; (*b*) **l. rock,** roc vif; **l. water,** eau vive; **l. force,** force vive; (*c*) (*with adj. prefixed*) **clean-l.,** de vie réglée; de bonnes mœurs. **2.** *n.* (*a*) vie *f*; **l. in the country,** la vie à la campagne; **style of l.,** train *m* de vie; *Pol.Ec:* **standard of l.,** niveau *m* de vie; **to be fond of good l.,** aimer la bonne chère; **l. space,** espace vital; (*b*) **l. in, l. out,** logement *m* (d'une bonne, etc.) chez l'employeur, hors de chez l'employeur; (*c*) (*livelihood*) **to earn one's l.,** gagner sa vie; **to work for one's l., for a l.,** travailler pour gagner sa vie; **to write for a l.,** vivre de sa plume; **what does he do for a l.?** qu'est-ce qu'il fait? quel est son métier? **to make a l.,** gagner de quoi vivre; **he makes a l. out of it,** il en vit; **l. wage,** minimum vital; (*d*) *Ecc:* bénéfice *m*, cure *f*.

liveable [ˈlivəbl] *a.* **1.** (*of house, room*) habitable. **2.** (*of life*) tenable, supportable. **3.** (*of pers.*) **l. (with),** accommodant; avec qui on peut vivre.

livelihood [ˈlaivlihud] *n.* vie *f*; moyens *mpl* d'existence; gagne-pain *m inv*; **to earn, gain, get, make, a l.,** gagner sa vie, son pain; gagner de quoi vivre.

liveliness [ˈlaivlinis] *n.* vivacité *f*, animation *f*, entrain *m*, vie *f*; *Fin:* animation (du marché).

livelong [ˈlivlɔŋ] *a. Lit:* **the l. day, night,** toute la journée; tout le long du jour; toute la nuit.

lively [ˈlaivli] *a.* **1.** (*a*) vif, animé; plein d'entrain; **l. imagination,** imagination vive; **l. conversation,** conversation animée; **l. music,** musique égayante, pleine d'entrain; (*b*) *F:* **to make it, things, l. for s.o.,** rendre la vie dure à qn; **things are getting l.,** ça chauffe; (*c*) (*of pleasure, satisfaction*) vif; **to take a l. interest in sth.,** s'intéresser vivement à qch. **2.** (*of colour*) vif. **3.** (*of pers.*) gai, enjoué; guilleret, -ette; **as l. as a cricket,** gai comme un pinson. **4.** *Nau:* (canot) léger sur l'eau; vif.

liven [ˈlaiv(ə)n] **1.** *v.tr.* **to l. (up),** animer, égayer (qn, une réunion, etc.); activer, *F:* chauffer (une affaire); *Th:* mouvementer (l'action); **to l. up the conversation,** ranimer la conversation. **2.** *v.i.* **to l. up,** s'animer, s'activer; *F:* s'échauffer.

liver¹ [ˈlivər] *n. Anat:* foie *m*; *Cu:* **calf's l.,** foie de veau; **l. pâté,** pâté *m* de foie.

liver² *n.* (*of pers.*) **fast l.,** viveur, -euse, noceur, -euse; **loose l.,** libertin *m*, débauché *m*.

liveried [ˈlivərid] *a.* en livrée.

liverish [ˈlivəriʃ] *a. F:* **to feel l.,** avoir une crise de foie.

Liverpudlian [livə'pʌdliən] *Geog:* **1.** *a.* de Liverpool. **2.** *n.* Liverpoolien, -ienne.
liverwurst ['livəwəːst] *n. NAm:* saucisse *f* de foie.
livery ['livəri] *n.* **1.** (*a*) livrée *f*; **full l.,** grande livrée; **in l.,** en livrée; (*b*) **l. company,** corporation *f* d'un corps de métier (de la cité de Londres). **2. l. horse,** cheval *m* de louage; **l. stables,** écuries *fpl* de chevaux de louage. **3.** *Jur:* mise *f* en possession.
livestock ['laivstɔk] *n. Husb:* bétail *m*, bestiaux *mpl*; *Jur:* cheptel *m*.
livid ['livid] *a.* (teint) livide, blême; (ciel) plombé; **to be l. with anger,** *F:* **absolutely l.,** être blême de colère, furieux; **it makes me l.!** ça me met en rage!
livingroom ['liviŋruːm] *n.* salle *f* de séjour.
Livy ['livi] *Pr.n.m. Lt.Lit:* Tite-Live.
lizard ['lizəd] *n. Rept:* lézard *m*.
Lizzie, Lizzy ['lizi] *n. Bot: F:* **busy L.,** balsamine *f*, impatiente *f*.
llama ['lɑːmə] *n. Z:* lama *m*.
lo [lou] *int. A. & Lit:* voici, voilà; *Hum:* **lo and behold there he was,** et voilà qu'il était là.
loach [loutʃ] *n. Ich:* loche *f*.
load¹ [loud] *n.* **1.** (*a*) fardeau *m*; **to carry a l. on one's back,** porter un fardeau sur son dos; **that's a l. off my mind!** quel soulagement! (*b*) charge *f*, chargement *m* (d'un camion, d'un navire, etc.); **useful l.,** charge utile; *Nau:* **l. line,** ligne *f* de charge; (*c*) (*contents of vehicle*) camion *m*, tombereau *m* (de gravier, etc.); charge (de bois); *F:* **it's a l. of rubbish, of nonsense,** c'est du bidon; *P:* **get a l. of that!** (i) écoute un peu ça! (ii) regarde ça! (*d*) *F:* **he's got loads of them,** il en a des quantités, des tas; **we've done it loads of times,** nous l'avons fait je ne sais combien de fois; **we've got loads of time,** nous avons largement le temps. **2.** *Mch: El:* charge; **safe l.,** charge de sécurité; **machine working at full l.,** machine *f* qui fonctionne, qui travaille, à pleine charge; **under l.,** en charge; *El:* **to shed the l.,** délester; **l. shedding,** délestage *m*.
load² **1.** *v.tr.* (*a*) charger (un camion, un navire, etc.); (*of bus*) **to l. passengers,** prendre des voyageurs; **to l. oneself up with luggage,** se charger de bagages; (*b*) **to l. s.o. with favours,** combler qn de faveurs; **loaded with cares,** accablé de soucis; (*c*) **to l. a gun,** charger un fusil (à balle); **my gun wasn't loaded,** mon fusil, mon revolver, n'était pas chargé; (*d*) *Mec.E:* serrer, bander (un ressort); (*e*) piper (des dés); (*f*) *Ins:* majorer (une prime). **2.** *v.i.* (*of ship, etc.*) **to l. (up),** prendre charge; faire la cargaison; **ship loading,** navire en chargement, en charge; *Aut:* (*in street*) **one can stop for a few minutes to l. and unload,** des arrêts brefs sont autorisés pour charger et décharger. **loaded** *a.* (*a*) (camion, navire, etc.) chargé; (*b*) *Mec.E:* (ressort) bandé. **2.** (*a*) (dés) pipés; *I.C.E:* **spring-l. valve,** soupape à ressort; (*b*) (*of pers.*) *P:* (i) soûl; (ii) richissime; (iii) drogué, camé. **3. a l. question,** une question insidieuse. **loading** *n.* (*a*) chargement *m* (d'un camion, d'un wagon, d'un navire, d'un avion); **bulk l.,** chargement en vrac; **l. ramp, bay,** rampe *f*, quai *m*, de chargement; (*b*) *Artil: Sm.a:* chargement (d'un canon, d'un fusil, etc.); **breech, muzzle, l.,** chargement par la culasse, par la bouche; (*c*) *Phot:* chargement (de l'appareil, des châssis); (*d*) *Atom.Ph:* chargement (du réacteur en combustible); (*e*) *Cmptr:* chargement (de programme); mise *f* en place (d'une bande magnétique).
loader ['loudər] *n.* **1.** (*pers.*) (*a*) chargeur *m*, manœuvre *m*; (*b*) (*with shooting party*) chargeur des fusils. **2.** (*device*) chargeuse *f*; *Civ.E:* chargeur; **bucket l.,** chargeuse à godets. **3. breech l., muzzle l.,** pièce *f* se chargeant par la culasse, par la bouche.
loaf¹, *pl.* **loaves** [louf, louvz] *n.* **1.** pain *m*; **tin l.,** pain moulé; **French l.,** baguette *f*; **sandwich l.,** pain de mie; **cottage l.** = double miche *f*; = calotte bretonne; *Prov:* **half a l. is better than no bread,** faute de grives on mange des merles. **2.** (*a*) **sugar l.,** pain de sucre; (*b*) *Cu:* **meat l.,** hachis *m* de viande moulé en forme de pain. **3.** *F:* tête, caboche *f*; **use your l.,** fais un peu travailler tes méninges.
loaf² **1.** *v.i.* **to l. (about, around),** flâner; fainéanter; traîner. **2.** *v.tr.* **to l. away the time,** passer son temps à flâner, à fainéanter.
loafer ['loufər] *n.* (*a*) (*pers.*) flâneur, -euse; fainéant, -ante; (*b*) (*shoe*) mocassin *m*.
loam [loum] *n. Agr: Geol:* terreau *m*; terre grasse, forte.
loamy ['loumi] *a.* (*of soil*) (i) gras; (ii) argileux.
loan¹ [loun] *n.* **1.** (*a*) prêt *m*; avance *f* (de fonds); **l. of money,** prêt, avance, d'argent; **on l. from the Louvre,** prêt du Louvre; (*b*) (*money advanced*) prêt, emprunt *m*; **long-term, short-term, l.,** prêt, emprunt, à long, court, terme; **secured l.,** prêt, emprunt, gagé, garanti; **unsecured l., l. without security,** prêt, emprunt, à découvert; **l. society,** société *f*, établissement, de crédit; *F:* **l. shark,** usurier *m*; **to raise a l. on an estate,** emprunter de l'argent sur une terre; (*c*) **it's a l., you can have it as a l.,** je vous le prête; c'est à titre de prêt. **2.** *Fin: etc:* emprunt; **government l.,** emprunt d'État; **issue of a l.,** émission *f* d'un emprunt.
loan² **1.** *v.tr. & i.* prêter (**sth. to s.o.,** qch. à qn); **loaned by the Louvre,** prêt *m* du Louvre. **2.** *v.tr. F:* emprunter (qch.).
loanword ['lounwəːd] *n. Ling:* mot *m* d'emprunt.
loath [louθ] *a.* **to be l. to do sth.,** répugner à faire qch.; faire qch. à contrecœur.
loathe [louð] *v.tr.* détester, exécrer (qn, qch.); avoir, éprouver, de l'aversion, du dégoût, pour (qn, qch.); **I l. milk,** j'ai horreur du lait; **to l. doing sth.,** détester faire qch. **loathing** *n.* dégoût *m*, répugnance *f* (**for,** pour); **to take, conceive, a l. for s.o.,** prendre qn en dégoût; **to have a l. for milk,** avoir horreur du lait.
loathsome ['louðsəm] *a.* repoussant, dégoûtant, répugnant; (*of smell*) nauséabond.
loathesomeness ['louðsəmnis] *n.* nature repoussante, dégoûtante (de qch.).
lob¹ [lɔb] *n. Sp:* lob *m*; chandelle *f*.
lob² *v.tr. Sp:* envoyer (la balle, etc.) en chandelle; lober (la balle, etc.).
lobby¹ ['lɔbi] *n.* **1.** (*a*) couloir *m*, antichambre *f*, vestibule *m*; promenoir *m* (d'un tribunal, etc.); entrée *f* (d'un théâtre); (*b*) (*in Parliament*) **the l. of the House,** la salle des pas perdus; les couloirs de la Chambre; **division lobbies,** vestibules où passent les députés lorsqu'ils se divisent pour voter. **2.** *Pol: etc:* lobby *m*, groupe *m* de pression.
lobby² *v.tr. & i.* **to l. (members),** fréquenter la salle des pas perdus de la Chambre (en quête de nouvelles, etc.); faire les couloirs.
lobe [loub] *n.* (*a*) *Arch: Bot:* lobe *m* (d'une rosace, d'un feuille); (*b*) *Anat:* lobe (de l'oreille, etc.).
lobelia [lə'biːliə] *n. Bot:* lobélie *f*.
lobster ['lɔbstər] *n. Crust:* homard *m*; **spiny l.,** langouste *f*; **Norway l.,** langoustine *f*; **l. boat,** (i) homardier *m*; (ii) langoustier *m*; **l. pot,** casier *m* (i) à homards, (ii) à langoustes.
local ['louk(ə)l] **1.** *a.* (*a*) local, -aux; régional, -aux; du pays, de la région; **l. authorities,** autorités locales, régionales; **l. government** = l'administration (i) départementale, (ii) communale; **l. news,** informations de la région; **l. wine,** vin *m* du pays; **l. colour,** couleur locale; **l. time,** heure légale; **the l. doctor,** le médecin du quartier; **a matter of l. politics,** une question de politique de clocher; **l. train,** (train *m*) omnibus (*m*); **l. showers,** averses éparses; (*b*) *Post:* **local,** en ville; *Bank: Com:* **l. bill,** effet *m* sur place; (*c*) (douleur) localisée; **l. anaesthetic,** anesthésique local. **2.** *n.* (*a*) **the locals,** (i) les gens *mpl*, les habitants *mpl*, du pays;

(ii) *Sp:* l'équipe locale, du pays; (*b*) *F:* anesthésique local; (*c*) *F:* **the l.,** le bistro du village, du coin. **-ally** *adv.* localement; **l. produced wine,** vin *m* du pays.

locale [lou'kɑːl] *n.* localité *f*; scène *f*, théâtre *m* (des événements).

locality [lou'kæliti] *n.* **1. to have a good sense of l., the bump of l.,** avoir le sens de l'orientation. **2.** (*a*) localité *f*; habitat *m* (d'une faune, d'une flore, etc.); emplacement *m* (d'un gisement, etc.); (*b*) localité; endroit *m*; voisinage *m*; **in our l.,** dans notre pays, notre région; (*c*) *Mil:* point *m* (sur le terrain).

localize ['loukəlaiz] *v.tr.* (*a*) localiser (une épidémie, etc); (*of disease*) **to become localized,** se localiser (dans un organe); (*b*) localiser (une légende).

locate [lou'keit] *v.tr.* localiser (qch.); situer (qch.); *El:* repérer, localiser (un dérangement, etc); *Nau:* **to l. a ship,** déterminer la position d'un navire (en mer).

location [lou'keiʃ(ə)n] *n.* **1.** localisation *f*; *El:* repérage *m* (d'un dérangement, etc.). **2.** situation *f*, emplacement *m.* **3.** (*in S. Africa*) réserve *f* indigène. **4.** *Cin:* **to be on l.,** tourner en extérieur; **l. shot,** extérieur *m.*

locative ['lɔkətiv] *a. & n. Gram:* locatif (*m*).

loch [lɔχ] *n. Scot:* **1.** lac *m.* **2. sea l.,** bras *m* de mer; fjord *m.*

lock¹ [lɔk] *n.* (*a*) mèche *f*, boucle *f* (de cheveux); (*b*) *A: & Lit:* **locks,** cheveux *mpl*; chevelure *f.*

lock² *n.* **1.** serrure *f*; fermeture *f*; **mortise l.,** serrure encastrée; **safety, combination, l.,** serrure de sûreté, à combinaisons; **under l. and key,** sous clef; (*of pers.*) sous les verrous; **to pick a l.,** crocheter une serrure. **2.** *Mec.E:* verrou *m*, *pl.* verrous; verrouillage *m*, blocage *m*; *Veh:* enrayage *m*, blocage (des roues); *Artil:* **breech l.,** verrou de culasse. **3.** (*a*) platine *f* (de fusil); (*b*) **l., stock and barrel,** tout sans exception; tout le fourbi. **4.** *Wr:* étreinte *f*, clef *f*; **arm l.,** clef de bras. **5.** *Aut: etc:* angle *m* de braquage; **on full l.,** braqué au maximum. **6.** (*a*) *Hyd.E:* écluse *f*; **l. chamber,** sas *m*, chambre *f* (d'écluse); **l. gate,** porte *f* d'écluse; (*b*) **air l.,** (i) sas à air, sas pneumatique; (ii) poche *f* d'air (dans un tuyau, etc.).

lock³ **I.** *v.tr.* **1.** (*a*) fermer à clef; donner un tour de clef à (une porte); (*with passive force*) **the door locks on the inside,** la serrure (de la porte) joue à l'intérieur; (*b*) **to l. s.o. in a room,** enfermer qn dans une chambre; **to l. sth. (away) in a drawer,** enfermer qch. dans un tiroir. **2.** (*a*) enrayer, bloquer, caler (les roues); enclencher (les pièces d'un mécanisme); *Sm.a:* verrouiller (la culasse); **ship locked in ice,** navire pris dans les glaces; (*b*) (*of pers.*) **to be locked (together) in a struggle,** être engagés corps à corps dans une lutte; **to be locked in each other's arms,** se tenir étroitement embrassés; (*c*) serrer (les dents); **his jaws were tightly locked,** il avait les dents serrées. **3.** *v.ind.tr. Elcs:* (*of radar, etc.*) **to l. on to (sth.),** accrocher (un objectif). **II.** *v.i.* **1.** (*a*) (*of wheels, etc.*) s'enrayer, se bloquer; (*b*) **the parts l. into each other,** les parties (i) s'enclavent, (ii) s'enclenchent. **2.** *Hyd.E:* (*of boat*) passer par une écluse. **3.** *Aut:* **to l. left, right,** braquer à gauche, à droite. **lock in** *v.tr.* enfermer (qn) à clef; mettre (qn) sous clef. **locking** *n.* **1.** fermeture *f* à clef; **l. up,** mise *f* sous clef; fermeture (d'une maison, etc.); *Fin:* immobilisation *f* (de capitaux). **2.** *Mec.E: etc:* blocage *m*, enclenchement *m*; **l. device, mechanism,** dispositif *m*, mécanisme *m*, de blocage. **3.** *Elcs:* (*of radar, etc.*) **l. on,** accrochage *m* (d'un objectif). **lock out** *v.tr.* (*a*) **to l. s.o. out,** fermer la porte à clef (quand il y a qn qui n'est pas rentré); **I found myself locked out,** en rentrant j'ai trouvé la porte fermée (à clef); (*b*) *Ind:* lock(-)outer (le personnel). **lock up** *v.tr.* (*a*) mettre, serrer, (qch.) sous clef; enfermer (qn, qch.); fermer (une maison) à clef; mettre (qn) sous les verrous, en lieu sûr; **it's time to l. up,** c'est l'heure de fermer la maison; (*b*) *Fin:* immobiliser, bloquer, engager (des capitaux).

locker ['lɔkər] *n.* **1.** armoire *f*, coffre *m* (fermant à clef); **l. room,** vestiaire *m* (d'une usine, d'un pavillon de sports, etc.). **2.** *Nau:* (*a*) caisson *m*, coffre; **signal l.,** coffre, caisson, à signaux; (*b*) soute *f.*

locket ['lɔkit] *n.* médaillon *m* (porté en parure).

lockjaw ['lɔkdʒɔː] *n. Med:* (i) trismus *m*, trisme *m*; (ii) *F:* tétanos *m.*

lock-keeper ['lɔkkiːpər] *n.* gardien *m* d'écluse; éclusier *m.*

locknut ['lɔknʌt] *n.* contre-écrou *m*, *pl.* contre-écrous.

lockout ['lɔkaut] *n.* lock-out *m inv*; grève patronale.

locksmith ['lɔksmiθ] *n.* serrurier *m.*

lockup ['lɔkʌp] *n.* **1.** hangar *m*, etc., fermant à clef; **l. shop,** (petit) magasin (construit sans habitation attenante); **l. garage,** box *m.* **2.** *F:* (*police cell*) le violon, le bloc.

loco¹ ['loukou] *n. F:* locomotive *f.*

loco² *a. F:* (*pers.*) fou, *f.* folle; maboul.

locomotion [loukə'mouʃ(ə)n] *n.* locomotion *f.*

locomotive [loukə'moutiv] **1.** *a.* locomotif, -ive; locomobile. **2.** *n. Rail:* locomotive *f*; **diesel l.,** locomotive (à moteur) diesel.

locomotor ['loukəmoutər] *a.* locomoteur, -trice.

locum ['loukəm] *n.* **l. (tenens** ['tenenz]), remplaçant, -ante (d'un médecin, d'un ecclésiastique).

locus, *pl.* **loci** ['loukəs, 'lousai, 'lousiː] *n.* **1.** *Mth:* lieu *m* géométrique. **2.** *Biol:* locus *m* (d'un chromosome).

locust ['loukəst] *n.* **1.** *Ent:* acridien *m*, criquet *m*; grande sauterelle d'Orient. **2.** *Bot:* (*a*) **l. (bean),** caroube *f*; (*b*) **l. (tree),** (i) caroubier *m*; (ii) robinier *m.*

locution [lou'kjuːʃ(ə)n] *n.* locution *f.*

lode [loud] *n. Geol: Min:* filon *m*, veine *f.*

lodestar ['loudstɑːr] *n.* **1.** étoile directrice; *esp.* **the l.,** l'étoile polaire. **2.** point *m* d'attraction, point de mire (de l'attention, etc.).

lodestone ['loudstoun] *n. Miner:* aimant naturel.

lodge¹ [lɔdʒ] *n.* **1.** (*a*) loge *f* (de concierge, etc.); (*b*) **keeper's l.,** maison *f* de garde-chasse; **(gate) l.,** pavillon *m* d'entrée (d'une propriété); pavillon du garde; **l. keeper,** portier *m.* **2. shooting l.,** pavillon de chasse. **3.** (*a*) loge, atelier *m* (des francs-maçons); **the Grand L. of France,** le Grand Orient (de France); (*b*) **l. (meeting),** tenue *f.* **4.** (*in University*) **master's l.,** résidence *f* du principal. **5.** terrier *m* (de loutre); hutte *f* (de castor). **6.** hutte (des Indiens de l'Amérique), wigwam *m.*

lodge² **I.** *v.tr.* **1.** (*a*) loger (qn); héberger (qn); (*b*) **to l. oneself,** s'établir; prendre position. **2.** (*a*) déposer, remettre; **to l. money with s.o.,** consigner, déposer (de l'argent) (**with s.o.,** chez qn); déposer (des titres) (**with a bank,** dans une banque); **securities lodged as collateral,** titres déposés, remis, en nantissement; (*b*) *Jur:* **to l. an appeal,** interjeter appel, faire appel; **to l. a complaint against s.o.,** porter plainte contre qn. **3.** (*of wind, rain*) verser, coucher, abattre (le blé). **II.** *v.i.* **1.** (*of pers.*) (se) loger (quelque part); **to l. with s.o.,** (i) louer une chambre, des chambres, chez qn; (ii) être en pension chez qn. **2.** (*of thg*) rester, se loger; **a fishbone lodged in his throat,** il a eu une arête coincée dans son gosier. **lodging** *n.* **1.** (*a*) hébergement *m* (de qn); **l. house,** hôtel garni; maison meublée; (*b*) dépôt *m*, consignation *f*, remise *f* (d'argent, de valeurs, etc.); (*c*) *Jur:* déposition *f* (d'une plainte), interjection *f* (d'appel). **2.** logement *m*; **to find a night's l.,** trouver où se coucher pour la nuit; **board and l.,** chambre *f* avec pension. **3.** (*usu. in pl.*) logement, logis *m*, appartement meublé; **to live, be, in lodgings,** loger, habiter, en garni, en (hôtel) meublé.

lodger ['lɔdʒər] *n.* locataire *mf* (en meublé); pensionnaire *mf*; **to take (in) lodgers,** louer des chambres; prendre des pensionnaires.

loft¹ [lɔft] *n.* **1.** grenier *m*, soupente *f*. **2. pigeon l.,** pigeonnier *m*. **3.** galerie *f*, tribune *f* (dans une église, une salle, etc.); **organ l.,** tribune de l'orgue.

loft² *v.tr. Golf:* donner de la hauteur à (la balle).

lofty ['lɔfti] *a.* **1.** (*of mountain, tree, building, etc.*) haut, élevé. **2.** (*of pers., manner*) hautain, orgueilleux, altier; (*b*) (air) condescendant, protecteur. **3.** (*a*) (*of aim, desire, etc.*) élevé; (*b*) (*of style, etc.*) élevé, relevé, sublime, soutenu. **-ily** *adv.* **1.** (situé) en hauteur. **2.** (répondre) avec (i) hauteur, (ii) condescendance.

log¹ [lɔg] *n.* **1.** grosse bûche; tronçon *m* de bois; rondin *m*; **l. cabin, hut,** hutte *f* de troncs d'arbre, cabane *f* de bois; **l. running,** flottage *m* du bois; *Veh:* **l. transporter,** fardier *m*; **to sleep like a l.,** dormir comme une souche. **2.** *Nau:* (*a*) loch *m*; **l. line,** ligne *f* de loch; (*b*) (*in engine room*) indicateur *m* de vitesse. **3.** carnet *m* de route, de bord; *Nau:* journal *m*, -aux; *Av:* carnet de vol; **ship's l.,** journal (i) de navigation, (ii) de bord; **to write up the l.,** noter les détails du voyage.

log² *v.tr.* **1.** tronçonner (le bois); débiter (le bois) en bûches. **2.** (*of ship*) filer (tant de nœuds). **3.** (*a*) *Nau: etc:* porter (un fait) au journal; (*b*) *Ind:* noter (des résultats, etc.) sur le registre. **4.** *W.Tel:* repérer, étalonner (une station). **logging** *n.* **1.** exploitation *f* des bois et forêts. **2.** inscription *f* (d'un fait) dans le journal, le carnet de route. **3.** *W.Tel:* étalonnage *m* (d'une station).

log³ *n. Mth: F:* log *m*.

loganberry ['lougənberi] *n. Hort:* ronce-framboise *f*, *pl.* ronces-framboises.

logarithm ['lɔgəriθm] *n.* logarithme *m*.

logarithmic [lɔgə'riθmik] *a.* **1.** (courbe, papier) logarithmique; (papier) à divisions logarithmiques. **2. l. table,** table *f* des logarithmes.

logbook ['lɔgbuk] *n.* **1.** *Nau:* livre *m* de loch. **2.** (*a*) *Nau:* **ship's l.,** journal *m* (i) de navigation, (ii) de bord; (*b*) *Aut:* carnet *m* de route; (*c*) *Av:* carnet de vol; (*d*) journal de travail (d'une machine); registre *m*; *W.Tel:* carnet d'écoute. **3.** *O: Aut: F:* = carte grise.

logger ['lɔgər] *n.* bûcheron *m*; forestier *m*.

loggerheads ['lɔgəheds] *n. F:* **to be at l. with s.o.,** être en conflit, en désaccord, avec qn; *F:* être à couteaux tirés avec qn.

loggia, *pl.* **-ias, -ie** ['lɔdʒiə, -iəz, -iei] *n. Arch:* loge *f*, loggia *f*.

logic ['lɔdʒik] *n.* logique *f*; *F:* **feminine l.,** logique féminine.

logical ['lɔdʒik(ə)l] *a.* (*of thg, pers.*) logique; **do be l.!** sois quand même logique! **-ally** *adv.* logiquement.

logistic [lə'dʒistik] *a. Phil: Mil:* logistique.

logistics [lə'dʒistiks] *n.pl.* (*usu. with sg. const.*) *Mil:* logistique *f*.

logjam ['lɔgdʒæm] *n.* (*a*) embâche *m* de bûches; (*b*) *Fig:* impasse *f*.

logo ['lougou] *n.* logo *m*.

logrolling ['lɔgrouliŋ] *n.* **1.** transport *m* des billes à la rivière. **2.** (*a*) alliance *f* politique dans un but intéressé; (*b*) camaraderie *f* littéraire.

logwood ['lɔgwud] *n. Bot:* (*a*) (*wood*) (bois *m* de) campêche (*m*); (*b*) (*tree*) campêcher *m*.

loin [lɔin] *n.* **1. loins,** reins *mpl*; *Anat:* lombes *mpl*; *Lit:* **to gird up one's loins,** se ceindre les reins; **sprung from the loins of . . .,** sorti des reins de . . . **2.** (*a*) esquine *f* (d'un cheval); (*b*) *Cu:* filet *m* (de mouton, de veau); longe *f* (de veau); carré *m* (de mouton); aloyau *m* et faux-filet (de bœuf); échine *f*, filet *m* (de porc); **l. chop,** côtelette *f* de filet.

loincloth ['lɔinklɔθ] *n.* pagne *m*.

loiter ['lɔitər] *v.i.* (*a*) flâner, traîner; s'attarder (en route); (*b*) *Jur:* **to l. (with intent),** rôder (d'une manière suspecte dans un endroit fréquenté). **loitering** *n. Jur:* **l. with intent,** délit *m* d'intention.

loll [lɔl] **1.** *v.i.* (*a*) (*of tongue*) **to l. (out),** pendre; (*b*) (*of pers.*) être étendu (paresseusement); **lolling back in an armchair,** étendu paresseusement dans un fauteuil; (*c*) **to l. about,** flâner, fainéanter. **2.** *v.tr.* (*of dog, etc.*) **to l. out its tongue,** laisser pendre la langue.

lollipop ['lɔlipɔp] *n.* (*a*) sucette *f*; (*b*) *F:* **l. man, woman,** gardien, -ienne, de passage clouté (pour les écoliers).

lollop ['lɔləp] *v.i. F:* **to l. along,** marcher lourdement.

lolly ['lɔli] *n. F:* **1.** (*a*) sucette *f*; **ice(d) l.,** sucette glacée; (*b*) *Austr:* bonbon *m*. **2.** (*money*) fric *m*.

London ['lʌndən] *Pr.n.* **1.** (*a*) *Geog:* Londres; **Greater L.,** le grand Londres; (*b*) *attrib.* londonien, de Londres; **a L. street,** une rue de Londres. **2.** *Bot:* **L. pride,** saxifrage ombreuse.

Londoner ['lʌndənər] *n.* Londonien, -ienne; habitant, -ante, de Londres; **a L. born and bred,** un vrai Londonien de Londres.

lone [loun] *a.* **1.** *esp.Lit:* (*of pers., thg*) solitaire, seul; (*of place*) isolé, désert. **2. to play a l. hand,** (i) (*at cards*) faire la chouette; (ii) agir tout seul; être seul contre tous.

loneliness ['lounlinis] *n.* **1.** solitude *f*, isolement *m*. **2.** sentiment *m* d'abandon.

lonely ['lounli] *a.* solitaire, isolé; (endroit) désert; **to feel very l.,** se sentir bien seul.

loner ['lounər] *n.* solitaire *mf*.

lonesome ['lounsəm] **1.** *a.* solitaire, seul; **to feel l.,** se sentir seul. **2.** *n. F:* **to be on one's l.,** être seul avec soi-même.

long¹ [lɔŋ] **I.** *a.* (**longer** ['lɔŋgər], **longest** ['lɔŋgist]) long, *f.* longue. **1.** (*a*) **how l. is the table?** quelle est la longueur de la table? **to make sth. longer,** allonger, rallonger, qch.; **to be six metres l.,** avoir six mètres de long; **the best by a l. way,** de loin le meilleur; (*b*) (robe) longue; (*c*) **a l. face,** (i) une figure allongée; (ii) une triste figure; **to pull a l. face,** faire une tête; **l. in the leg,** haut jambé. **2.** (*in time*) **the l. vacation,** les grandes vacances; **the days are getting longer,** les jours rallongent; **it will take a l. time,** cela prendra longtemps; ce sera long; **a l. time ago,** il y a (bien) longtemps; **to wait for a l. time,** attendre longtemps; **three days at the longest,** trois jours (tout) au plus; **a l. memory,** une mémoire tenace; **to have a l. talk with s.o.,** parler longuement avec qn; *Pros:* **l. syllable,** syllabe longue; *Mil:* **l. servicemen,** engagés *mpl* à long terme. **3.** *Com:* **l. hundred,** grand cent, cent vingt; **l. dozen,** treize. **II.** *n.* **1.** (*a*) **the l. and short of the matter is that . . .,** le fin mot de l'affaire c'est que . . .; **that's the l. and short of it,** voilà ni plus ni moins l'affaire; et voilà tout! (*b*) *Pros:* **longs and shorts,** longues *fpl* et brèves *fpl*. **2. before l.,** avant peu; sous peu; **for l.,** pendant longtemps; **it won't take l.,** cela ne prendra pas longtemps; cela ne sera pas long. **III.** *adv.* **1.** (*a*) longtemps; **I didn't wait l.,** je n'ai pas attendu longtemps; **l. live the King, the Queen!** vive le roi, la reine! **so l. as, as l. as,** (i) aussi longtemps que; (ii) tant que; (iii) pourvu que; **as l. as I live,** tant que je vivrai; **he was not l. in coming,** il n'a pas tardé à venir; **he won't be l.,** (i) il ne tardera pas; (ii) il l'aura vite fait; *F:* **so l.!** au revoir! à bientôt! (*b*) depuis longtemps; **I have l. been convinced of it,** j'en suis convaincu depuis longtemps; (*c*) **how l.?** combien de temps? **how much longer shall we be?** pour combien de temps avons-nous encore? **2. l. before, l.**

after, longtemps avant, après; **not l. before, after,** peu de temps avant, après; **l. ago,** il y a longtemps; **not (very) l. ago,** il n'y a pas longtemps; **in the days of l. ago,** autrefois; *Lit:* jadis. **3. all day, all night, l.,** tout le long du jour, de la nuit; pendant toute la journée, la nuit. **4. I could no longer see him,** je ne pouvais plus le voir; **I couldn't wait any longer,** je ne pouvais pas attendre plus longtemps; **five minutes longer,** cinq minutes de plus; encore cinq minutes.

long² *v.i.* **to l. for sth.,** désirer qch. fortement, ardemment; **to l. for home,** avoir la nostalgie du foyer; **to l. for s.o.'s return,** attendre impatiemment le retour de qn; **to l. to do sth.,** avoir bien envie de faire qch.; être impatient de faire qch.; rêver de faire qch. **longing 1.** *a.* qui désire, qui attend, ardemment. **2.** *n.* désir ardent, grande envie (**for,** de). **longingly** *adv.* avec envie; **to look l. at sth.,** couver qch. des yeux.

longboat ['lɔŋbout] *n. Nau:* grand canot; chaloupe *f.*

longbow ['lɔŋbou] *n. Mil.Hist:* arc *m* d'homme d'armes; *F:* **to draw the l.,** exagérer, hâbler.

long-dated ['lɔŋ'deitid] *a. Fin:* à longue échéance.

long-distance ['lɔŋ'distəns] *a. Tp:* à longue distance; (train) de grand parcours; (avion) long-courrier; *Sp:* **l.-d. runner,** coureur, -euse, de fond.

long-drawn-out ['lɔŋ'drɔːn'aut] *a.* (*of sigh, etc.*) prolongé; (*of story, explanation, etc.*) interminable.

long-established ['lɔŋis'tæbliʃt] *a.* établi depuis longtemps.

longevity [lɔn'dʒeviti] *n.* longévité *f.*

long-forgotten [lɔŋfə'gɔt(ə)n] *a.* oublié depuis longtemps.

longhair ['lɔŋhɛər] *a. U.S: F:* qui plaît aux intellectuels; **l. music,** musique *f* classique.

longhaired ['lɔŋhɛəd] *a.* (*a*) (homme) à cheveux longs; (chien, chat, etc.) à poil(s) long(s); (*b*) *NAm: F:* intellectuel.

longhand ['lɔŋhænd] *n.* écriture ordinaire, courante, non-abrégée; **in l.,** (écrire qch.) en clair.

longish ['lɔŋiʃ] *a.* assez long, plutôt long.

longitude ['lɔndʒitjuːd] *n. Astr: Geog:* longitude *f.*

longitudinal [lɔndʒi'tjuːdin(ə)l] *a.* longitudinal, -aux; en long; **l. beam,** longeron *m.* **-ally** *adv.* longitudinalement; en long.

long-legged ['lɔŋ'legid] *a.* à longues jambes; (*of horse*) haut-perché, *pl.* haut-perchés; (*of bird*) à longues pattes.

long-lived ['lɔŋ'livd] *a.* (*a*) qui vit longtemps; *Nat. Hist:* longévital, -aux; (*b*) (erreur) persistante, vivace; (célébrité) de longue durée.

long-lost ['lɔŋ'lɔst] *a.* perdu depuis longtemps; (*pers.*) disparu depuis longtemps.

long-playing ['lɔŋ'pleiiŋ] *a. Rec:* **l.-p. record,** disque *m* de longue durée, (disque) microsillon (*m*).

long-range ['lɔŋ'reindʒ] *a.* (avion) long-courrier; (canon, radar) à longue portée; *Meteor:* **l.-r. forecast,** prévision *f* à longue échéance.

longshoreman, *pl.* **-men** ['lɔŋʃɔːmən] *n.m. Nau:* homme qui travaille dans le port; débardeur.

longsighted [lɔŋ'saitid] *a.* **1.** (*a*) presbyte; (*b*) hypermétrope. **2.** prévoyant.

longsightedness [lɔŋ'saitidnis] *n.* **1.** (*a*) presbytie *f*; (*b*) hypermétropie *f.* **2.** prévoyance *f.*

longstanding [lɔŋ'stændiŋ] *a.* ancien; de longue date; de vieille date; **l. accounts,** vieux comptes.

longsuffering [lɔŋ'sʌf(ə)riŋ] *a.* (*a*) patient, endurant; (*b*) longanime, indulgent.

long-term ['lɔŋtəːm] *a.* **1.** (détenu) qui subit un emprisonnement de longue durée. **2.** *Fin:* (crédit, politique, etc.) à long terme.

longwinded [lɔŋ'windid] *a.* **1.** (histoire) de longue haleine, interminable. **2.** (*of speaker*) verbeux, prolixe. **3.** *Sp:* (*of pers., horse*) qui ne s'essouffle pas.

loo [luː] *n. F:* **the l.,** les cabinets, les toilettes; **to go to the l.,** aller aux cabinets; **l. paper,** papier *m* hygiénique.

loofah ['luːfə] *n. Bot: Toil:* loofa(h) *m,* luffa *m.*

look¹ [luk] *n.* **1.** regard *m;* **to have a l. at sth.,** regarder qch.; jeter un coup d'œil sur qch.; **to take a good l. at s.o.,** (i) scruter qn du regard; (ii) dévisager qn; **to have a l. round the town,** faire un tour dans la ville. **2.** (*a*) aspect *m,* air *m,* apparence *f* (de qn, de qch.); mine *f* (de qn); **the business has a suspicious l. about it,** l'affaire paraît suspecte, louche; **I like the l. of him,** il me plaît, je le trouve sympathique; **by, from, the l. of him I think it probable,** à le voir cela me paraît très probable; *Com:* **new l.,** nouvelle apparence, nouvelle mode; (*b*) **good looks,** belle mine; beauté *f.*

look² 1. *v.i.* regarder; (*a*) **to l. through, out of, the window,** regarder par la fenêtre; **to l. down a list,** parcourir une liste; **to l. the other way,** (i) regarder de l'autre côté; (ii) détourner les yeux; **to l. into s.o.'s eyes,** regarder dans les yeux de qn; regarder qn dans les yeux; *Prov:* **l. before you leap,** il faut réfléchir avant d'agir; (*b*) **l. where you're going!** regardez où vous allez, où vous marchez; (*c*) **I l. to you to help me,** je compte sur votre aide; (*d*) **the house looks south,** la maison est exposée au sud, orientée vers le sud; **the living room looks on to the garden,** le salon donne sur le jardin; (*e*) **to l. to, towards, the future,** envisager l'avenir. **2.** *v.tr.* **to l. s.o. (full, straight) in the face,** regarder qn (bien) en face, dans les yeux; **I can never l. him in the face again,** je me sentirai toujours honteux devant lui; **to l. s.o. up and down,** regarder qn de haut en bas. **3.** *v.i.* avoir l'air, paraître, sembler; **she looks tired,** elle a l'air bien fatigué(e); **to l. old,** paraître, faire, vieux; **he's not as stupid as he looks,** il est moins bête qu'il n'en a l'air; **she doesn't l. her age,** on ne lui donnerait pas son âge; **to l. ill,** avoir l'air malade; avoir mauvaise mine; **to l. well,** (i) (*of pers.*) avoir bonne mine; (ii) (*of thg*) faire bien; faire bon effet; **that dress looks well on you,** cette robe vous va bien; **the crops l. promising,** la récolte s'annonce bien; **things are looking bad, black,** les choses prennent une mauvaise tournure; **you l. as if you'd slept badly,** vous avez l'air d'avoir mal dormi; **it looks as if he didn't want to go,** il semble qu'il ne veuille pas y aller; **what does he l. like?** comment est-il? **it looks like an elephant,** on dirait un éléphant; **he looks the part,** il est fait pour ce rôle; **he looks like winning,** *esp. U.S:* **it looks like he'll win,** on dirait qu'il va gagner. **4. l. here!** écoutez donc! dites donc! voyons! *F:* **l. alive! l. sharp!** dépêchez-vous! grouillez-vous! **look after** *v.ind.tr.* soigner (qn, qch.); s'occuper de, avoir soin de (qn, qch.); veiller sur (qn, qch.); veiller à, ménager (ses intérêts); **you're well looked after,** vous êtes bien soigné; **he can l. after himself,** il sait se débrouiller; **the car has been well looked after,** la voiture a été bien entretenue. **look at** *v.ind.tr.* (*a*) regarder (qn, qch.); **what are you looking at?** qu'est-ce que vous regardez? **just l. at that!** regardez-moi ça! *F:* **she won't l. at a man,** elle dédaigne les hommes; **what's he like to l. at?** quel air a-t-il? (*b*) **if you l. at the result,** si vous considérez le résultat; **I don't like his way of looking at things,** je n'aime pas la manière dont il voit les choses. **look back** *v.i.* (*a*) regarder en arrière; **to l. back on the past,** faire un retour sur le passé; (*b*) *F:* **he has never looked back since that day,** depuis ce jour il a fait des progrès ininterrompus. **look down** *v.i.* **to l. down on s.o.,** mépriser, dédaigner, qn. **look for** *v.ind.tr.* (*a*) chercher (qn, qch.); **go and l. for him,** allez le chercher; (*b*) s'attendre à (qch). **look forward** *v.i.* **to l. forward to sth.,** (i) s'attendre à qch.; (ii) attendre qch. avec plaisir; **I'm looking forward to seeing her again,** ce sera un grand plaisir, il me tarde, de la revoir. **look in** *v.i.* entrer en passant; **I'll look in again tomorrow,** je repasserai demain. **look into** *v.ind.tr.* examiner, étudier (une question); prendre (une question) en considération. **look on 1.** *v.i.* être spectateur. **2.** *v.ind.tr.* considérer, envisager (qn, qch.); **I l. on him as a friend,** je le considère comme un ami. **look out 1.** *v.i.* (*a*) **to l. out for s.o.,** guetter (l'arrivée de) qn; (*b*) prendre garde; être sur ses gardes; **l. out!** attention! prenez garde! **2.** *v.tr.* chercher (qch.); **I'll l. you out some interesting books,** je vais vous choisir des livres intéressants. **look over** *v.tr.* jeter un coup d'œil sur (qch); examiner (qch.); parcourir (des papiers, etc.); visiter (une maison à vendre, etc.). **look round** *v.i.* (*a*) regarder autour de soi; faire un tour d'horizon; (*b*) tourner la tête; se retourner (pour voir); **don't l. round!** ne regardez pas en arrière! **look through** *v.tr.* (*a*) parcourir, examiner rapidement (des papiers, etc.); (*b*) **to l. s.o. through and through,** transpercer qn du regard. **look up 1.** *v.i.* (*a*) lever les yeux; relever la tête; (*b*) **to l. up to s.o.,** respecter, estimer, qn; (*c*) **to be looking up,** (*of business*) reprendre; (*of shares*) remonter. **2.** *v.tr.* (*a*) chercher (un mot dans un dictionnaire, un train dans l'indicateur, etc.); (*b*) **to l. s.o. up,** aller voir qn; passer chez qn; **(come and) l. me up,** venez me voir.

looker ['lukər] *n.* **1. l.-on,** *pl.* **lookers-on,** spectateur, -trice **(at,** de); assistant, -ante **(at,** à). **2.** *F:* **good l.,** bel homme, belle femme.

look-in ['lukin] *n.* **1.** courte visite; visite éclair. **2. he won't have, get, a l.-in,** il n'a pas la moindre chance.

looking-glass ['lukiŋglɑ:s] *n.* miroir *m*, glace *f*.

lookout ['lukaut] *n.* **1.** guet *m*, surveillance *f*, observation *f*; *Nau:* veille *f*; **to keep a l.,** être aux aguets; *Nau:* veiller; être en, de, vigie; **to be on the l. for s.o., sth.,** guetter qn; être à la recherche de qch. **2.** (*a*) *Mil: Nau:* poste *m* d'observation, de guet, de vigie; guérite *f*; (*b*) (*pers.*) (i) *Mil:* guetteur *m*; (ii) *Nau:* homme *m* de veille, de vigie. **3.** vue *f*, perspective *f*; *F:* **that's a poor l. for him,** c'est de mauvais augure pour lui; **that's his l.!** ça c'est son affaire! qu'il s'arrange!

look-see ['luksi:] *n.* *F:* visite *f*, coup *m* d'œil, d'inspection; **I'll go and a have a l.-s.,** je vais aller voir.

loom¹ [lu:m] *n.* *Tex:* métier *m* à tisser.

loom² *v.i.* apparaître indistinctement; **a ship loomed up out of the fog,** un navire surgit du brouillard; **dangers looming ahead,** dangers qui menacent; (*of event, etc.*) **to l. large,** paraître imminent; être tout proche.

loon [lu:n] *n.* **1.** *Orn:* (*a*) plongeon *m*, *Fr.C:* huart *m*; (*b*) grèbe *m*. **2.** *F:* fou, *f.* folle.

loony ['lu:ni] *a.* & *n.* *F:* fou, *f.* folle; loufoque, timbré, -ée; **l. bin,** maison *f* de fous.

loop¹ [lu:p] *n.* **1.** (*a*) boucle *f* (de ruban, etc.); **running l.,** boucle à nœud coulant; *Furn:* **curtain-l.,** embrasse *f* de rideau; *Needlew:* **l. stitch,** picot *m*; (*b*) *Anat:* anse *f*; (*c*) méandre *m*, boucle (de rivière); (*d*) *Rail:* **l. (line),** voie *f* d'évitement; voie de raccordement; (*at terminus*) boucle d'évitement; (*e*) *Sp:* (*skating*) croisé *m*; (*f*) *Av:* **(inside) l.,** boucle, looping *m*; (*g*) tour *m*, spire *f* (de spirale, de bobine); (*h*) *Cin:* boucle (de film). **2.** (*a*) *El:* boucle, bouclage *m*; **l. circuit,** circuit bouclé; **l. current,** courant *m* circulant dans un circuit bouclé; (*b*) *Atom.Ph:* boucle, circuit (de réacteur); (*c*) *Cmptr:* boucle (i) d'itération, (ii) de bande pilote; (*d*) *Tp:* circuit (branché); ligne dérivée; (*e*) *Elcs:* **l. antenna, aerial,** cadre d'antenne.

loop² 1. *v.tr.* (*a*) faire une boucle, des boucles, à (une ficelle, etc.); (*b*) enrouler **(sth. with sth.,** qch. de qch.); (*c*) **to l. back,** retenir (un rideau) avec une embrasse; (*d*) *Av: etc:* **to l. the loop,** faire un looping; boucler la boucle; *n.* **looping the loop,** looping *m*; (*e*) *El:* boucler. **2.** *v.i.* (*a*) faire une boucle; former des boucles; (*b*) *Cmptr:* tourner sur une boucle. **looped** *a.* *U.S: F:* (*of pers.*) ivre, soûl.

loophole ['lu:phoul] *n.* **1.** (*a*) *Fort:* meurtrière *f*, créneau *m*; (*b*) trou *m*, ouverture *f*. **2.** échappatoire *f*; **to find a l.,** trouver une échappatoire.

loopy ['lu:pi] *a.* *F:* toqué, timbré.

loose¹ [lu:s] *a.* **1.** (*a*) (*of fixed part*) dégagé, mal assujetti; branlant; (*of page*) détaché; (*of knot*) défait, délié; (planche) désajustée; (dent) qui branle, qui remue; *El:* (raccord) déconnecté, desserré; **to come l., to get l.,** se dégager, se détacher; (*of knot*) se défaire, se délier; (*of screw*) se desserrer; (*of iron bar from stonework, etc.*) se desceller; **to work l.,** (*of machine parts*) se desserrer; prendre du jeu; (*b*) (*of animal*) déchaîné, lâché; **to let a dog l.,** lâcher, détacher, un chien; **to let l. a torrent of abuse,** lâcher, déchaîner, un torrent d'injures; *Rac:* **l. horse,** cheval *m* sauvage; (*c*) non assujetti; mobile; (câble) volant; *Mec.E:* **l. pulley,** roue folle, décalée; **l. end,** bout pendant (d'une corde); **to be at a l. end,** se trouver désœuvré, sans rien à faire; avoir une heure à perdre; (*of rope, etc.*) **to hang l.,** pendre, flotter; (*d*) **l. cash, change,** menue monnaie; (*e*) *Ch:* (à l'état) libre, noncombiné; (*f*) **to buy sth. l.,** acheter qch. en vrac. **2.** (*slack*) (*a*) détendu; (câble) mou; (nœud) lâche; (peau) flasque; (vêtement) ample; (manteau) flottant; (*b*) *Med:* (toux) grasse; **l. bowels,** ventre *m* lâche. **3.** (terre) meuble; (terrain) sans consistance; (tissu) lâche, à claire-voie; *Mil:* (ordre) dispersé. **4.** vague, peu exact; (style) lâche, décousu; (traduction) approximative; *Sp:* **l. ball,** (i) *Cr:* balle mal lancée; (ii) *Ten:* coup *m* faible. **5.** dissolu, relâché, débauché; (femme) de mauvaise vie; **l. living,** mauvaise vie; inconduite *f*; **l. morals,** mœurs relâchées; *n.* **to be on the l.,** être en bordée, en vadrouille, en rupture de ban. **-ly** *adv.* **1.** (tenir qch.) sans serrer; **to be l. fixed,** être mal serré, mal ajusté; avoir du jeu; **her dress hung l. on her body,** elle flottait dans sa robe. **2.** (parler) inexactement, sans précision. **3.** (vivre) d'une manière dissolue.

loose² *v.tr.* **1.** délier, détacher; **to l. one's hold,** lâcher prise. **2.** délier, dénouer, défaire (un nœud, etc.); dénouer, détacher (ses cheveux); *Nau:* larguer (une amarre); déferler (une voile). **3.** (*a*) décocher (une flèche); (*b*) *v.i.* *Mil: F:* **to l. off,** tirer (avec une mitrailleuse); lâcher, envoyer, une giclée.

loose-fitting ['lu:sfitiŋ] *a.* non ajusté; (vêtement) ample, large; (col) dégagé.

loose-limbed ['lu:s'limd] *a.* (*of pers.*) démanché; dégingandé; (cheval) décousu.

loose-leaf ['lu:sli:f] *a.* (album, etc.) à feuilles mobiles; **l.-l. ledger,** grand livre biblorhapte; **l.-l. binder,** grebiche *f*.

loosen ['lu:s(ə)n] **1.** *v.tr.* (*a*) (i) défaire, délier (un nœud); (ii) relâcher (un nœud); desserrer, dégager, décoller (un écrou, etc.); relâcher, détendre (une corde); **to l. s.o.'s bonds,** dénouer les liens de qn; **to l. one's grip,** relâcher son étreinte; **to l. s.o.'s tongue,** délier, dénouer, la langue à qn; *Med:* **to l. the bowels,** relâcher le ventre; (*b*) détacher **(sth. from sth.,** qch. de qch.); (*c*) relâcher (la discipline). **2.** *v.i.* (*a*) (*of knot, etc.*) se délier, se défaire; (*of screw, etc.*) se desserrer; (*of rope*) se relâcher; (*of machinery*) prendre du jeu; (*b*) (*of pers.*) **to l. up,** (i) se dégourdir; (ii) se mettre à l'aise; ne plus se gêner.

looseness ['lu:snis] *n.* **1.** (*a*) état branlant (d'une dent, d'une pierre); desserrage *m* (d'un écrou); jeu *m* (d'une cheville, etc.); (*b*) flaccidité *f* (de la peau). **2.** relâchement *m* (d'une corde); ampleur *f* (d'un vêtement). **3.** (*a*) imprécision *f* (de terminologie); (*b*) relâchement (de la discipline, etc.); (*c*) licence *f*; vie dissolue.

loosestrife ['lu:sstraif] *n. Bot:* **(purple) l.,** salicaire commune.

loot¹ [lu:t] *n.* **1.** pillage *m*; **soldiers on the l.,** soldats *mpl* en maraude *f*. **2.** butin *m*.

loot² *v.tr.* **1.** piller, saccager, mettre à sac (une ville, etc.); *v.i.* se livrer au pillage. **2.** (*of soldiers, etc.*) voler (du bétail, etc.). **looting** *n.* pillage *m*.

looter ['lu:tər] *n.* pilleur, -euse; pillard, -arde.

lop [lɔp] *v.tr.* (**lopped** [lɔpt]) élaguer, ébrancher (un arbre); **to l. off a branch,** couper, élaguer, une branche.

lope [loup] *v.i.* **to l. along,** courir à petits bonds.

lop-eared ['lɔpi:əd] *a.* (lapin, etc.) aux oreilles pendantes.

lopsided [lɔp'saidid] *a.* qui manque de symétrie; déjeté, déversé; de guingois; (chaise) bancale.

loquacious [lɔ'kweiʃəs] *a.* loquace.

loquaciousness [lɔ'kweiʃəsnis], **loquacity** [lɔ'kwæsiti] *n.* loquacité *f*.

lord¹ [lɔ:d] *n.m.* **1.** seigneur; **our sovereign l. the king,** notre seigneur souverain, le roi; *F:* **her l. and master,** son seigneur et maître; son mari. **2.** *Ecc:* **L. God Almighty,** Seigneur Dieu Tout-puissant; **the L.,** le Seigneur; **in the year of our L. . . .,** en l'an de grâce . . .; **the Lord's Prayer,** l'oraison dominicale; *F:* **(good) L.! O L.!** mon Dieu! **L. knows if . . .,** Dieu sait si . . .. **3.** (*a*) (*title*) lord *m*; *Pol:* **the House of Lords,** *F:* **the Lords,** la Chambre des Lords; **to live like a l.,** mener une vie de grand seigneur; (*b*) **the L. Mayor,** le lord maire. **4.** *Bot:* **lords and ladies,** arum maculé; pied-de-veau *m*, *pl.* pieds-de-veau.

lord² *v.i. F:* **to l. it,** trancher du grand seigneur; **to l. it over s.o.,** vouloir en imposer à qn.

lordly ['lɔ:dli] *a.* **1.** de grand seigneur; noble. **2.** hautain, altier; (air) de grand seigneur; **in a l. manner,** avec hauteur.

lordship ['lɔ:dʃip] *n.* **1.** suzeraineté *f*; seigneurie *f* (**over,** de). **2.** domaine *m*, seigneurie. **3. your l.,** votre Seigneurie; (*to nobleman*) monsieur le comte, etc.; (*to bishop*) monseigneur.

lore [lɔ:r] *n.* science *f*, savoir *m*; **country l.,** connaissance *f* intime de la campagne.

lorgnette [lɔ:'njet] *n.* **1.** face-à-main *m*, *pl.* faces-à-main. **2.** jumelles *fpl* (de théâtre) à manche.

lorry ['lɔri] *n.* camion *m*; **articulated l.,** véhicule articulé; semi-remorque *f or m*, *pl.* semi-remorques; **l. driver,** conducteur *m*, (i) de camion, (ii) de poids lourd, *F:* routier *m*.

lose [lu:z] *v.tr.* (*p.t. & p.p.* **lost** [lɔst]; *pr.p.* **losing** [lu:ziŋ]) **1.** (*a*) perdre, égarer (son parapluie, etc.); (*b*) perdre (un droit, son argent, etc.); **I lost a £100, francs,** j'ai perdu £100; (*at cards, etc.*) **to l. heavily,** perdre une forte somme; **you will l. nothing by waiting,** vous ne perdrez rien pour attendre; **to l. in value,** perdre de sa valeur; (*c*) **he has lost an arm,** il a perdu un bras; **to l. one's voice,** perdre la voix; **to l. one's reason,** perdre la raison; **to l. one's reputation,** se perdre de réputation; **he had lost interest in his work,** son travail ne l'intéressait plus; **the patient is losing strength,** le malade baisse; **to l. weight,** perdre du poids; **I've lost 10 kilos,** j'ai maigri de 10 kilos; (*d*) perdre (son père, *Com:* un client, etc.); **to be lost at sea,** périr en mer; *v.i.* **both armies lost heavily,** les deux armées ont subi de fortes pertes. **2. to l. one's way, to get lost,** perdre son chemin; se perdre, s'égarer; **to l. oneself, to be lost, in the crowd,** se perdre, se dissimuler, dans la foule; se mêler à, dans, la foule; *F:* **I'm lost! you've lost me!** je n'y suis plus! *P:* **get lost!** fiche-moi le camp! **to l. oneself in a book,** s'absorber dans la lecture d'un livre; **to l. sight of s.o.,** perdre qn de vue. **3.** gaspiller, perdre (son temps); **lost labour,** peine perdue; **the joke was lost on him,** il n'a pas saisi la plaisanterie. **4. clock that loses five minutes a day,** pendule *f* qui retarde de cinq minutes par jour; *v.i.* **my watch is losing,** ma montre retarde. **5.** manquer (le train, etc.). **6.** perdre (une partie, une bataille, un procès); être battu dans (une course); (*in debate*) **the motion was lost,** la motion a été rejetée. **7.** faire perdre (qch. à qn); **that mistake lost him the match,** cette faute lui coûta la partie. **8.** *v.i.* **to l. out,** ne pas réussir; échouer. **losing 1.** *a.* perdant; **l. bargain,** mauvais marché; **l. battle,** bataille *f* de vaincu; **to play a l. game,** (i) jouer un jeu à perdre; (ii) défendre une cause perdue; **the l. side,** les vaincus; *Sp:* l'équipe perdante. **2.** *n.* (*a*) perte *f*; (*b*) *Sp:* défaite *f*. **lost** *a.* perdu; (*a*) **l. property office,** *U.S:* **l. and found department,** (service *m* des) objets trouvés; *U.S:* **l. river,** rivière souterraine; **to give s.o., sth., up for l.,** abandonner tout espoir de retrouver qn, qch.; (*b*) **l. soul,** âme perdue, âme damnée; **to wander (about) like a l. soul,** errer comme une âme en peine; (*c*) **he seems, looks, l.,** il a l'air dépaysé; (*d*) **when he's listening to music he's l. to the world,** quand il écoute la musique le monde n'existe plus pour lui.

loser ['lu:zər] *n.* **1. he'll be the l.,** c'est lui qui perdra; **he's a born l.,** il ne réussit jamais. **2.** (*a*) **to be the l. of a battle,** perdre une bataille; (*b*) *Sp: etc:* perdant, -ante; **the winners and the losers,** les gagnants et les perdants, les vainqueurs et les vaincus; **to be a good, bad, l.,** être bon, mauvais, joueur. **3.** *Sp:* coup perdant.

loss [lɔs] *n.* **1.** (*a*) perte *f* (d'un parapluie, etc.); égarement *m* (d'un document, etc.); (*b*) **l. of sight,** perte, privation *f*, de la vue; **l. of voice,** extinction *f* de voix; *Jur:* **l. of civil rights,** perte des droits civiques, dégradation *f* civique; *Theol:* **l. of grace,** amission *f* de la grâce. **2.** (*a*) **to sustain, suffer, heavy losses,** subir de grosses pertes; **dead l.,** perte sèche; *Com:* **to sell at a l.,** vendre à perte; **to cut one's losses,** faire la part du feu; (*b*) *Ins:* sinistre *m*; *M.Ins:* **(actual) total l.,** perte totale; (*c*) perte (de son père, etc.); *Mil: etc:* **to suffer heavy losses,** éprouver, subir, de grosses pertes. **3.** (*a*) déperdition *f*; perte (de poids, de chaleur, etc.); (*b*) *Ind: Trans:* freinte *f*, déperdition (d'un produit en cours de fabrication ou de transport); **l. in transit,** freinte, déchet *m*, de route; (*c*) *Med:* écoulement *m*, perte. **4. to be at a l.,** être désorienté; **he seemed at a l.,** il avait l'air dépaysé; **to be at a l. to . . .,** avoir de la peine à . . .; être en peine de . . .; **to be at a l. (to know) what to do, what to say,** ne savoir que faire, que dire; **he's never at a l. for an answer,** il a, il trouve, réponse à tout; **he's never at a l. for sth. to say,** il n'est jamais à court (de mots).

lot [lɔt] *n.* **1.** (*a*) **to draw, cast, lots for sth.,** tirer au sort pour qch.; tirer qch. au sort; **to throw, cast, in one's l. with s.o.,** partager le sort, la fortune, de qn; (*b*) sort *m*; tirage *m* au sort; **drawn by l.,** tiré au sort. **2.** (*a*) sort, part *f*, partage *m*; **it fell to my l. to decide,** c'était à moi de décider; (*b*) destin *m*, destinée *f*; **the poor man's l.,** la condition du pauvre. **3.** (*a*) (lot *m* de) terrain *m*; *Cin:* **(studio) l.,** terrain (de studio); **parking l.,** parcage *m*, *F:* parking *m*; (*b*) (*at auction*) lot; (*c*) *Com: etc:* lot (de marchandises); *Fin:* paquet *m* (de titres, d'actions); **in lots,** par parties; **to buy, sell, in one l.,** acheter, vendre, en bloc; (*d*) **a bad l.,** un mauvais sujet; un vaurien; (*woman*) une dévoyée; *Iron:* **you're a nice l.!** vous êtes admirables, vous! (*e*) **that's the l.,** c'est tout; **the whole l. of you,** vous tous (sans exception); **the whole l. of them,** toute la bande; *F:* **and the whole damn l.,** et tout le bazar. **4.** (*a*) **a l. of . . .,** beaucoup de . . .; **what a l. of people!** que de monde! **such a l. of people,** tant de monde; **quite a l.,** une quantité considérable; **I saw quite a l. of him in Paris,** je l'ai vu assez souvent pendant mon séjour à Paris; **not a l.,** pas beaucoup; **he would have given a l. to . . .,** il aurait donné gros pour . . .; *adv.* **times**

have changed a l., les temps ont bien changé; (*b*) *F:* **we've (got) lots of time,** nous avons tout le temps; **lots of people,** beaucoup de gens; **I've lots of things to do,** j'ai un tas de choses à faire; *adv.* **I feel lots better,** je me sens infiniment mieux.

loth [louθ] *a.* = LOATH.

lotion ['louʃ(ə)n] *n. Pharm: Toil:* lotion *f*; *Hairdr:* **setting l.,** lotion pour mise en plis.

lottery ['lɔtəri] *n.* loterie *f*.

lotto ['lɔtou] *n. Games:* loto *m*.

lotus, *pl.* **-uses** ['loutəs, -əsiz] *n.* (*a*) lotus *m*; **l. eater,** mangeur *m* de lotus; lotophage *m*; (*b*) (*yoga*) **l. position,** posture *f* de méditation.

loud [laud] **1.** *a.* (*a*) bruyant, retentissant; grand (bruit, cri); (détonation) violente; gros (rire); (voix) forte, haute; **in a l. voice,** à haute voix; **l. applause,** vifs applaudissements; (*b*) (*of pers., behaviour*) bruyant, tapageur; (*c*) (*of colour, etc.*) criard, voyant; (*of costume*) tapageur, affichant. **2.** *adv.* (crier, parler) haut, à haute voix; **to talk out l.,** parler tout haut; **louder!** parlez plus haut! **-ly** *adv.* (crier) haut, fort, à voix haute; (rire) bruyamment; (frapper) rudement.

loudhailer [laud'heilər] *n.* porte-voix *m inv.*

loudmouth ['laudmauθ] *n. F:* gueulard, -arde.

loudmouthed ['laudmauðd] *a. F:* gueulard.

loudness ['laudnis] *n.* **1.** force *f*, sonorité *f* (d'un bruit, etc.); grand bruit. **2.** conduite tapageuse.

loudspeaker [laud'spi:kər] *n.* haut-parleur *m*, *pl.* haut-parleurs.

Louisiana [lu(:)i:zi'ænə] *Pr.n. Geog:* Louisiane *f*.

lounge¹ [laundʒ] *n.* **1.** (*a*) promenoir *m*; (*in hotel*) hall *m*; **cocktail l., l. bar,** bar *m* (où l'on sert des cocktails, etc.); **l. suit,** complet veston *m*; (*b*) (*in house*) salon *m*; **sun l.,** véranda *m*; (*c*) *Th: Av: etc:* foyer *m* (du public). **2.** *NAm:* (*a*) *Furn:* canapé *m*; **l. chair,** fauteuil *m*; (*b*) *Rail:* **l. car,** voiture-salon *f*, *pl.* voitures-salons.

lounge² *v.i.* **1. to l. (about),** flâner; *v.tr.* **to l. away the time,** passer le temps en flânant, à flâner. **2.** s'étendre paresseusement (sur un canapé, etc.).

lounger ['laundʒər] *n.* **1.** flâneur, -euse; flemmard -arde. **2.** *Furn:* (*a*) *NAm:* canapé *m*; (*b*) **(sun) l.,** fauteuil *m* de relaxation.

louse¹ *pl.* **lice** [laus, lais] *n.* (*a*) *Ent:* pou *m*, *pl.* poux; **infested with lice,** pouilleux; (*b*) *P:* fripouille *f*; salaud *m*.

louse² *v.tr. F:* **to l. sth. up,** bousiller, gâcher, qch.

lousewort ['lauswə:t] *n. Bot:* herbe *f* aux poux.

lousy ['lauzi] *a.* **1.** pouilleux; plein de poux. **2.** *F:* (*a*) sale, ignoble; moche; **a l. trick,** un sale tour; **l. weather,** sale temps *m*, temps de chien; **a l. meal,** un repas dégoûtant; (*b*) **this place is l. with . . .,** ça grouille de . . .; **he's l. with money,** c'est un gros richard.

lout [laut] *n.* (*a*) lourdaud *m*; rustre *m*; **you clumsy l.!** espèce de lourdaud! (*b*) voyou *m*.

loutish ['lautiʃ] *a.* rustre, lourdaud.

louver, louvre ['lu:vər] *n.* (*a*) *Arch:* **l. (board),** abat-vent *m inv*, abat-son *m*, *pl.* abat-sons (de clocher); (*b*) *Nau:* louvre *m*; *Aut: Av:* persienne *f*, volet *m* (d'aérage, de capot); *Mec.E:* ouïe *f* (de prise d'air).

louvered ['lu:vəd] *a.* **1.** *Arch:* (clocher) à abat-sons. **2.** (*a*) *Nau:* muni d'un louvre, de louvres; (*b*) *Aut: Av:* (capot) à persiennes, à volet.

lovable ['lʌvəbl] *a.* (caractère) sympathique.

lovage ['lʌvidʒ] *n. Bot:* ache *f* de(s) montagne(s).

love¹ [lʌv] *n.* **1.** (*a*) amour *m*; affection *f*, tendresse *f*; **l. of, for, s.o., sth.,** amour de, pour, envers, qn, de qch.; **there's no l. lost between them,** ils ne peuvent pas se sentir; **for the l. of God,** pour l'amour de Dieu; **give my l. to your parents,** faites mes amitiés à vos parents; **I wouldn't do it for l. or money,** je ne le ferais pour rien au monde; (*b*) (*between lovers*) amour (*the pl. is fem. in Lit. use*); **first l.,** les premières amours; **it's l. at first sight,** c'est le coup de foudre; **l. life,** vie amoureuse; **l. match,** mariage *m* d'amour; **to marry for l.,** faire un mariage d'inclination; **l. letter,** billet doux; **l. story,** histoire *f*, roman *m*, d'amour; **l. child,** enfant naturel, illégitime; **to be, fall, in l. with s.o.,** être, tomber, amoureux de qn; **head over heels in l.,** amoureux fou, éperdument amoureux; **to make l. to s.o.,** (i) *O:* faire la cour à qn; (ii) faire l'amour avec qn. **2.** (*pers.*) (*a*) **(my) l.,** mon amour; (*b*) *F:* **more coffee, l.?** tu prends encore du café, mon petit, ma petite? *P:* **there you are, l.!** voilà, ma petite dame! **3. Love,** l'Amour, Cupidon *m*. **4.** *Ten: etc:* zéro *m*, rien *m*; **l. fifteen, fifteen l.,** rien à quinze, quinze à rien; **l. game,** jeu blanc.

love² *v.tr.* **1.** (*a*) aimer, affectionner (qn); **to l. one another,** s'aimer, s'entr'aimer; (*b*) aimer (d'amour); **I l. you!** je t'aime! **2.** aimer (passionnément) (qch.); adorer (la musique, etc.); **to l. to do sth., to l. doing sth.,** aimer (à) faire qch.; **will you come with me?—I should l. to,** voulez-vous m'accompagner?—avec le plus grand plaisir; **she'd l. to see you again,** elle serait enchantée, ravie, de vous revoir. **loving** *a.* **1.** affectueux, affectionné; *Corr:* **your l. mother,** ta mère affectueuse. **2.** (*with noun prefixed*) **home l.,** qui aime son chez-soi. **3. l. cup,** coupe *f* de l'amitié. **lovingly** *adv.* affectueusement, tendrement.

lovebird ['lʌvbə:d] *n.* (*a*) *Orn:* perruche *f* inséparable; (*b*) *F:* (*of pers.*) **lovebirds,** tourtereaux *mpl.*

love-in-a-mist ['lʌvinə'mist] *n. Bot:* nigelle *f* (de Damas); cheveux *mpl* de Vénus.

loveless ['lʌvlis] *a.* sans amour.

love-lies-bleeding ['lʌvlaiz'bli:diŋ] *n. Bot:* amarante *f* à fleurs en queue.

loveliness ['lʌvlinis] *n.* beauté *f*, charme *mf* (d'une femme, d'un paysage, etc.).

lovely ['lʌvli] *a.* **1.** (*a*) beau, *f.* belle; charmant, ravissant; **what a l. woman!** quelle femme ravissante! (*b*) beau (jour, temps, etc.); **it's been l. seeing you again,** ça a été charmant de vous revoir. **2.** *F:* (personne) très aimable.

lovemaking ['lʌvmeikiŋ] *n.* (*a*) *O:* cour (amoureuse); (*b*) rapports sexuels.

lover ['lʌvər] *n.* **1.** (*a*) (i) amoureux *m*, prétendant *m*; (ii) fiancé *m*; (*b*) amant *m*; **they were lovers,** ils étaient amants. **2.** amateur *m*, ami(e) (de la nature, etc.); **music l.,** mélomane *mf*.

lovesick ['lʌvsik] *a.* qui languit d'amour.

lovesickness ['lʌvsiknis] *n.* mal *m* d'amour.

lovey(-)dovey ['lʌvidʌvi] *P:* *a.* (parler) sentimental, mignard.

low¹ [lou] **I.** *a.* **1.** bas, *f.* basse; **l. relief,** bas-relief *m*; **dress with a l. neckline,** robe décolletée; **the fire is burning l.,** le feu baisse; **light turned l.,** lumière *f* en veilleuse; **l. tide,** marée basse; **my stocks are rather l.,** mes stocks sont un peu dégarnis. **2.** (*a*) (plafond) bas, peu élevé; **to make s.o. a l. bow,** saluer qn profondément; *Geog:* **the L. Countries,** les Pays-Bas; (*b*) **to bring s.o. l.,** humilier, abaisser, qn; **to lie l.,** (i) se tapir; rester tapi; (ii) rester coi; se tenir coi; (*c*) **lower part,** bas *m* (d'une échelle, etc.); **the lower Alps,** les basses Alpes; **the lower jaw,** la mâchoire inférieure; (*d*) *Ling:* **l. German,** le bas allemand. **3.** (*a*) **l. birth,** basse naissance; **all the people, high and l.,** tous, du haut en bas de l'échelle sociale; **the lower classes,** le bas peuple; **lower ranks,** rangs inférieurs (de l'armée, etc.); *Sch:* **the lower school, the lower forms,** les petites classes; (*b*) bas, peu élevé; **the lower animals,** les animaux inférieurs; (*c*) bas, vil; **l. company,** mauvaise compagnie; **the lowest of the l.,** le dernier des derniers; **that's a l. trick!** ça c'est un sale coup! **4.** (*of* *invalid*) **to be very l., in a very l. state,** être bien bas; aller très mal; **to feel l., to be in l. spirits,** se sentir déprimé; *F:* avoir le cafard; *Med:* **l. physical condition,** atonie *f*. **5. l. price,** bas prix; prix faible; **the lowest price,** le dernier prix; **£100 at the very lowest,** £100 au bas mot; **l. wages,** salaires peu élevés; **l. temperature,** basse température; **to cook sth. over a l. heat, a l. fire,** faire cuire qch. à feu doux; *Cards:* **the l. cards,** les basses cartes. **6. l. note,** note basse; **l. murmur,** faible murmure *m*; **in a l. voice,** à voix basse, à mi-voix. **7.** *Ecc:* **l. mass,** messe basse; **L. Sunday,** Pâques closes, dimanche *m* de Quasimodo. **II.** *adv.* **1.** (*a*) (pendre, viser) bas; **to bow l.,** s'incliner profondément; saluer très bas; **dress cut l. in the back,** robe décolletée dans le dos; *Box:* **to hit l.,** toucher bas; (*b*) (*of bird, aircraft*) **to fly l.,** voler bas. **2. to play l.,** jouer petit jeu; **the lowest paid employees,** les employés les moins payés. **3.** (*a*) (parler) à voix basse; (*b*) *Mus:* **to set (a song, etc.) lower,** baisser (une chanson, etc.). **III.** *n.* **all-time l.,** record le plus bas; **to reach a new l.,** descendre encore plus bas.

low² *v.i.* (*of cattle*) meugler. **lowing** *n.* meuglement *m*.

lowborn ['loubɔːn] *a.* **1.** de basse naissance. **2.** d'humble naissance.

lowbred ['loubred] *a.* mal élevé; grossier.

lowbrow ['loubrau] *F:* **1.** *a.* peu intellectuel. **2.** *n.* personne *f* terre à terre, dépourvue de sens artistique; philistin, -ine.

low-budget [lou'bʌdʒit] *a.* économique.

low-calorie [lou'kæləri] *a.* (régime, etc.) de basses calories; (régime) hypocalorique.

low-capacity ['loukə'pæsiti] *a.* à faible capacité.

low-class ['loukl ɑːs] *a.* vulgaire; sans distinction.

low-cut ['loukʌt] *a.* (*of dress*) décolleté.

lowdown¹ ['loudaun] *a.* **1.** bas, *f.* basse. **2.** bas, ignoble; **that's a l. trick,** ça c'est un coup rosse.

lowdown² *n. F:* **to give s.o. the l.,** renseigner qn; tuyauter qn (**on,** sur).

lower¹ ['louər] **1.** *v.tr.* (*a*) baisser (la tête, les yeux); abaisser (les paupières); abaisser, rabattre (son voile, son chapeau); *Th:* **to l. the curtain,** faire baisser le rideau; (*b*) descendre (un tonneau, etc.); *Nau:* amener, caler (un mât); mettre (une embarcation) à la mer; **l. away!** laissez aller! **to l. s.o. on a rope,** (faire) descendre qn au bout d'une corde; (*c*) abaisser (qch.); diminuer la hauteur de (qch.); (*d*) baisser, rabaisser (un prix); réduire (la pression); baisser (la lumière); abaisser (la température); (*e*) baisser (la voix, le ton); déprimer (le moral de l'ennemi); (*f*) (r)abaisser, faire baisser, (r)abattre (l'orgueil de qn); abaisser, avilir (qn); **to l. oneself,** s'abaisser, se ravaler (**to,** à). **2.** *v.i.* (*a*) (*of ground, etc.*) s'abaisser, descendre; (*b*) (*of prices, rents, etc.*) diminuer, baisser. **lowering** *n.* **1.** (*a*) abaissement *m*; baissement *m* (de la tête, etc.); (*b*) descente *f* (d'une échelle); *Nau:* calage *m* (d'un mât); mise *f* à la mer (d'une embarcation); (*c*) abaissement, diminution *f* de la hauteur (de qch.). **2.** rabattage *m*, rabais *m*, diminution (des prix); réduction *f* (de la pression).

lower² ['lauər] *v.i.* **1.** (*of pers.*) se renfrogner; froncer les sourcils; **to l. at s.o.,** regarder qn d'un mauvais œil; menacer qn du regard. **2.** (*of sky*) s'amonceler; (*of storm*) menacer. **lowering** *a.* **1.** (air) renfrogné, menaçant. **2.** (ciel) menaçant.

low-flying [lou'flaiiŋ] *a. Av:* (avion) volant à basse altitude.

low-grade ['lou'greid] *a.* de qualité inférieure.

lowland ['loulənd] *n.* plaine (basse); terre *f* en contrebas; *Geog:* **the Lowlands,** la Basse-Écosse.

lowliness ['loulinis] *n.* humilité *f*.

lowly *a. A: & Lit:* humble, modeste; (rang) infime; *n.pl.* **the l.,** les humbles *mpl*.

low-lying ['lou'laiiŋ] *a.* situé en bas; (terrain) bas, enfoncé.

low-necked ['lou'nekt] *a.* (of dress) décolleté.

lowness ['lounis] *n.* **1.** manque *m* de hauteur (d'un mur, etc.); petitesse *f* (d'un arbre, etc.); faible altitude *f* (d'une île, des collines). **2.** humilité *f* (d'une situation). **3.** (*a*) gravité *f* (d'un son); (*b*) faiblesse *f* (d'un bruit). **4.** bassesse *f* (de conduite). **5. l. (of spirits),** abattement *m*, découragement *m*, dépression *f*.

low-pitched ['lou'pitʃt] *a.* **1.** *a.* (*a*) (son) grave; (*b*) (piano) accordé à un diapason bas. **2.** (comble) à faible pente.

low-pressure ['lou'preʃər] *a.* (*a*) *Meteor:* (zone) de basse pression; (*b*) (cylindre, machine) à basse pression, tension.

low-speed ['lou'spiːd] *a.* (machine) à petite vitesse.

low-spirited ['lou'spiritid] *a.* abattu, triste, déprimé, découragé.

loyal ['lɔiəl] *a.* (*a*) (ami, etc.) fidèle, dévoué (**to,** à); loyal, -aux (**to,** envers); (*b*) fidèle au souverain; **to drink the l. toast,** boire le toast au souverain. **-ally** *adv.* fidèlement.

loyalist ['lɔiəlist] *n.* loyaliste *mf*.

loyalty ['lɔiəlti] *n.* fidélité *f* à la Couronne; loyalisme *m*; **l. to one's friends,** loyauté *f* envers ses amis.

lozenge ['lɔzindʒ] *n.* **1.** *Mth: Her:* losange *m*. **2.** *Pharm:* pastille *f*, tablette *f*.

lubricant ['luːbrikənt] *a. & n.* lubrifiant (*m*); lubrificateur, -trice; graisse *f*, huile *f* (pour machines).

lubricate ['luːbrikeit] *v.tr.* **1.** lubrifier; graisser, huiler; **to l. the wheels,** graisser les roues. **lubricating** *n.* lubrification *f*; **l. oil,** huile *f* de graissage.

lubrication [luːbri'keiʃ(ə)n] *n.* lubrification *f*; graissage *m*.

lubricator ['luːbrikeitər] *n.* graisseur *m*; appareil *m* de graissage; **gravity-feed l.,** graisseur par gravité.

lubricity [lu'brisiti] *n.* **1.** onctuosité *f*. **2.** lubricité *f*.

lucern(e)¹ [luː'səːn] *n. Bot: Agr:* luzerne *f*.

Lucerne² *Pr.n. Geog:* Lucerne *f*; **the Lake of L.,** le lac des Quatre-Cantons.

lucid ['luːsid] *a.* (*a*) (esprit, style) lucide; (explication) claire; (*b*) *Med:* (intervalle) lucide, de lucidité. **-ly** *adv.* lucidement.

lucidity [luː'siditi] *n.* lucidité *f*.

Lucifer ['luːsifər] *Pr.n.m. Astr: B:* Lucifer.

luck [lʌk] *n.* **1.** hasard *m*, chance *f*, fortune *f*; **good l.,** bonne chance; bonheur *m*; **good l. (to you)!** bonne chance! *Iron:* **good l. to him! and the best of (British) l. to him!** qu'il le fasse si ça lui chante! **bad l.,** malchance *f*, mauvaise fortune; malheur *m*; déveine *f*; **to be down on one's l.,** avoir de la guigne; **to bring s.o. bad, good, l.,** porter malheur, bonheur, à qn; **to try one's l.,** tenter sa chance; **just my l.!** c'est bien ma chance! pas de veine! **hard l.!** pas de chance! **by good l.,** heureusement; par bonheur; **as l. would have it,** par bonheur; **as l. would have it I was there,** le hasard a voulu que je fusse là. **2.** bonheur *m*, bonne fortune, (bonne) chance; **to keep sth. for l.,** garder qch. comme porte-bonheur; **bit, piece, stroke, of l.,** coup *m* de fortune, coup de veine; aubaine *f*; **to be in l.,** avoir de la chance, de la veine; **to be out of l.,** être en guigne; ne pas avoir de chance; **he has all the l.,** c'est un veinard; **to have the l. of the devil,** avoir une chance de tous les diables.

luckless ['lʌklis] *a.* **1.** (*of pers.*) malheureux, malchanceux. **2.** (jour) malencontreux; (heure) fatale.

lucky ['lʌki] *a.* (*a*) heureux, fortuné; chanceux, veinard; *F:* **the l. man,** le marié; *F:* **(you) l. devil! l. beggar!** veinard! **to be l.,** avoir de la chance; *Iron:* **you'll be l.!** tu peux toujours courir! **he was born l.,** il est né coiffé; **l. in love, at cards,** heureux en amour, au jeu; (*b*) (jour) de veine; (heure, moment) propice; **l. shot,** coup heureux, de veine; **to make a l. guess,** tomber juste; **it's not my l. day,** je n'ai pas de chance aujourd'hui; (*c*) **l. charm,** porte-bonheur *m inv*; (*of thg*) **it's l.,** ça porte bonheur; (*d*) **l. dip,** baquet rempli de son où l'on plonge la main pour en retirer une surprise. **-ily,** *adv.* heureusement; par bonheur.

lucrative ['lu:krətiv] *a.* lucratif.

lucre ['lu:kər] *n.* lucre *m*; **to do sth. for (filthy) l.,** agir par amour de gain, de lucre.

ludicrous ['lu:dikrəs] *a.* risible, comique, ridicule; grotesque. **-ly** *adv.* ridiculement; grotesquement.

ludo ['lu:dou] *n. Games:* jeu *m* des petits chevaux.

luff¹ [lʌf] *n. Nau:* **1.** lof *m*, ralingue *f* du vent, chute *f* avant (d'une voile). **2.** *N.Arch:* épaule *f* (de l'avant).

luff² *Nau:* **1.** *v.i.* lof(f)er; faire une aulof(f)ée. **2.** *v.tr.* **to l. the boat (up),** faire loffer la barque.

lug¹ [lʌg] *n.* = LUGWORM.

lug² *n. Nau:* = LUGSAIL.

lug³ *n. Tchn:* (*a*) oreille *f*; (*b*) patte *f*, bride *f*; (*c*) *Metall:* tasseau *m* (d'une pièce venue de fonderie).

lug⁴ *v.tr.* **(lugged)** traîner, tirer (qch. de pesant); **to l. sth. along, away,** entraîner qch.; **to l. sth. about with one,** promener, trimbaler, qch. avec soi.

luge [lu:dʒ] *n. Sp:* luge *f*.

luggage ['lʌgidʒ] *n.* bagage(s) *m*(*pl*); **hand l.,** bagages à main; **excess l.,** excédent *m* de bagages; *Rail:* **l. van,** fourgon *m* (aux bagages); *Nau:* **l. room, hold,** soute *f* aux bagages; *Av:* **l. bay, compartment,** compartiment *m*, soute, à bagages; **l. rack,** (i) *Rail:* filet *m*, porte-bagages *m inv*; (ii) *Aut:* galerie *f*.

lugger ['lʌgər] *n. Nau:* lougre *m*.

lughole ['lʌghoul] *n. F:* oreille *f*.

lugsail ['lʌgseil, 'lʌgsl] *n. Nau:* voile *f* à bourcet.

lugubrious [lu:'gu:briəs] *a.* lugubre. **-ly** *adv.* lugubrement.

lugworm ['lʌgwə:m] *n.* arénicole *f*.

Luke [lu:k] *Pr.n.m.* Luc; **Saint L.,** saint Luc.

lukewarm ['lu:kwɔ:m] *a.* (*of water, friendship, etc.*) tiède; **to become l.,** tiédir.

lull¹ [lʌl] *n.* moment *m* de calme; (*before storm*) bonace *f*; *Nau:* accalmie *f*, embellie *f*; **there was a l. in the conversation,** la conversation tomba.

lull² **1.** *v.tr.* (*a*) bercer, endormir (qn); **to l. a child to sleep,** endormir un enfant; (*b*) endormir (les soupçons de qn); assoupir (une douleur); (*c*) calmer, apaiser (la tempête). **2.** *v.i.* (*of storm, sea*) se calmer, s'apaiser; *Nau:* calmir.

lullaby ['lʌləbai] *n. Mus:* berceuse *f*.

lumbago [lʌm'beigou] *n. Med:* lumbago *m*.

lumbar ['lʌmbər] *a.* & *n. Anat:* lombaire (*f*).

lumber¹ ['lʌmbər] *n.* **1.** vieux meubles; objets encombrants; fatras *m*; **l. room,** (pièce *f* de) débarras (*m*). **2.** *NAm:* (*a*) bois *m* de charpente, de construction; (*b*) *Cost:* **l. jacket,** blouson *m*; canadienne *f*.

lumber² *v.tr.* **1.** (*a*) encombrer, embarrasser (un lieu); remplir (un lieu) de fatras; **to l. (up) a room with furniture,** encombrer une pièce de meubles; (*b*) entasser (des objets) pêle-mêle; (*c*) *F:* **I don't want to be lumbered with him for the whole evening,** je ne veux pas l'avoir à mes trousses pendant toute la soirée. **2.** *NAm:* abattre (des arbres); débiter (du bois).

lumber³ *v.i.* (*a*) **to l. along,** avancer à pas pesants, d'un pas lourd; (*b*) **to l. about,** se trimbaler çà et là.
lumbering *a.* lourd, pesant.

lumberjack ['lʌmbədʒæk] *n. esp. NAm:* bûcheron *m*.

lumberman ['lʌmbəmæn] *n. esp. NAm:* = LUMBERJACK.

luminary ['lu:minəri] *n.* **1.** corps lumineux; luminaire *m*, astre *m*. **2.** (*of pers.*) lumière *f*; flambeau *m* (de la science, etc.).

luminescence [lu:mi'nesəns] *n.* luminescence *f*.

luminescent [lu:mi'nesənt] *a.* luminescent.

luminosity [lu:mi'nɔsiti] *n.* luminosité *f*.

luminous ['lu:minəs] *a.* **1.** lumineux; (*a*) *Ph:* **l. density,** densité lumineuse; luminance *f*; (*b*) (cadran) lumineux; **l. paint,** peinture lumineuse. **2.** (génie, etc.) illuminant; (explication) lumineuse.

lumme ['lʌmi] *int. F:* mon Dieu!

lummox ['lʌməks] *n. NAm: F:* lourdaud, -e.

lump¹ [lʌmp] *n.* **1.** (*a*) gros morceau, bloc *m* (de pierre); motte *f* (de terre, d'argile); morceau (de sucre); masse *f* (de plomb, etc.); (*in porridge, etc.*) boule *f*, grumeau *m*; *Paperm:* pâton *m* (dans le papier); **l. sum,** (i) somme grosse, globale; prix global; (ii) prix à forfait; paiement *m* forfaitaire; **to have a l. in one's throat,** avoir la gorge serrée; (*b*) (*caused by bruise*) bosse *f* (au front, etc.); (*c*) *Med: etc:* excroissance *f*; grosseur *f*. **2.** *F:* (*of pers.*) empoté *m*, pataud *m*; **great lump of a girl,** grosse dondon. **3.** *F:* **the l.,** ouvriers indépendants (qui évitent le fisc).

lump² *v.tr.* (*a*) mettre en bloc, en masse, en tas; (*b*) **to l. things together,** réunir des choses ensemble; **to l. persons together,** considérer des personnes en bloc.

lump³ *v.tr. F:* **if he doesn't like it, he can l. it, he can like it or l. it,** si cela ne lui plaît pas, qu'il s'arrange.

lumpfish ['lʌmpfiʃ] *n. Ich:* lompe *m*, lump *m*.

lumpish ['lʌmpiʃ] *a.* **1.** gros, balourd, pataud; **great l. man,** lourdaud *m*. **2.** *F:* à l'esprit lent.

lumpy ['lʌmpi] *a.* (*a*) (*of earth*) rempli de mottes; (*of sauce*) grumeleux; (*b*) (mer) courte, houleuse; (*c*) couvert de protubérances; (front) couvert de bosses.

lunacy ['lu:nəsi] *n.* **1.** aliénation mentale; folie *f*; *Jur:* démence *f*. **2.** *F:* action, idée, folle; **it's sheer l.,** c'est de la folie (pure et simple).

lunar ['lu:nər] *a.* **1.** (cycle, etc.) lunaire. **2.** en forme de croissant.

lunaria [lu:'nɛəriə] *n. Bot:* lunaire *f*.

lunatic ['lu:nətik] **1.** *a.* (*a*) fou, *f.* folle; **l. asylum,** maison *f* de fous; **the l. fringe,** les originaux *mpl*; les cinglés *mpl.* **2.** *n.* fou, *f.* folle; aliéné, -ée.

lunch¹ [lʌn(t)ʃ] *n.* (*a*) déjeuner *m*; *Fr.C: Belg:* dîner *m*; **they have l. at one o'clock,** ils déjeunent à une heure; **we had a picnic l.,** nous avons pique-niqué à midi; (*b*) *NAm:* petit repas, casse-croûte (pris à n'importe quelle heure).

lunch² **1.** *v.i.* (*a*) déjeuner. **2.** *v.tr.* donner à déjeuner à (qn); faire déjeuner (qn).

luncheon ['lʌn(t)ʃ(ə)n] *n.* (*usu. formal meal*) déjeuner *m*; *Rail: etc:* **first, second, l.,** premier, deuxième, service; **l. basket,** (i) panier *m* à provisions; (ii) panier-repas *m*, *pl.* paniers-repas; *Com: etc:* **l. voucher,** chèque-repas *m*, *pl.* chèques-repas; chèque-restaurant *m*, *pl.* chèques-restaurant.

luncheonette ['lʌnʃə'net] *n. NAm:* petit restaurant, café-restaurant *m*.

lung [lʌŋ] *n.* poumon *m*; **to shout at the top of one's lungs,** crier à tue-tête; **l. cancer,** cancer *m* du poumon; *Med:* **iron l.,** poumon d'acier.

lunge¹ [lʌndʒ] *n.* **1.** *Fenc:* botte *f*; développement *m*; coup de pointe. **2.** mouvement (précipité) en avant.

lunge² *v.i.* **1.** (*a*) *Fenc:* se fendre; **to l. at the adversary,** porter, pousser, une botte à l'adversaire; (*b*) **to l. out at s.o.,** allonger un coup de poing à qn. **2. to l. forward,** se précipiter en avant; se jeter en avant.

lupin ['lu:pin] *n. Bot:* lupin *m*.

lurch¹ [lə:tʃ] *n. used in the phr.* **to leave s.o. in the l.,** laisser qn en panne, dans le pétrin; planter là qn.

lurch² *n.* **1.** embardée *f*, coup *m* de roulis (d'un navire). **2.** embardée (d'une voiture). **3.** pas titubant (d'un ivrogne).

lurch³ *v.i.* **1.** (*of ship, car, etc.*) faire une embardée. **2.** (*of pers.*) **to l. along,** marcher en titubant.

lurcher ['lə:tʃər] *n. Z:* lévrier bâtard.
lure¹ ['(j)uər] *n.* **1.** (*a*) *Ven:* leurre *m* (de fauconnier); (*b*) *Fish:* leurre; appât *m* factice. **2.** (*a*) piège *m*; (*b*) attrait *m*; **the l. of the sea,** l'attrait de la mer.
lure² *v.tr.* **1.** (*a*) *Ven:* leurrer (un faucon); (*b*) leurrer (un poisson, etc.). **2.** attirer, séduire, allécher; **to be lured into the trap,** être entraîné dans le piège.
lurid ['l(j)uərid] *a.* **1.** (*a*) (ciel) blafard, fauve; (teint) livide; **l. light,** lueur blafarde, sinistre; (*b*) *Nat.Hist:* luride, **2.** (*a*) cuivré; (flammes) rougeoyantes; (*b*) (récit, langage) corsé; (film, etc.) à effets corsés. **-ly** *adv.* **1.** avec une lueur blafarde; sinistrement. **2.** (*a*) en rougeoyant; (*b*) en corsant les effets.
lurk [lə:k] *v.i.* se cacher; se tenir caché. **lurking** *a.* caché; secret, -ète; **a l. suspicion,** un vague soupçon.
luscious ['lʌʃəs] *a.* succulent, savoureux; (fruit) fondant.
lusciousness ['lʌʃəsnis] *n.* succulence *f* (d'un fruit).
lush [lʌʃ] *a.* (*of grass, plant*) plein de sève; luxuriant.
lushness ['lʌʃnis] *n.* luxuriance *f* (de l'herbe, etc.).
lust¹ [lʌst] *n.* **1.** (*a*) *Theol:* appétit *m* (coupable); convoitise *f*; **lusts of the flesh,** concupiscence *f*; (*b*) luxure *f*; désir (charnel). **2. l. for power,** soif *f* du pouvoir.
lust² *v.ind.tr. Lit:* **1.** (*a*) **to l. for, after, sth.,** convoiter qch.; (*b*) **to l. after a woman,** désirer une femme. **2. to l. for power,** avoir soif du pouvoir.
luster ['lʌstər] *n. NAm:* = LUSTRE.
lustful ['lʌstf(u)l] *a.* lascif, libidineux. **-fully** *adv.* lascivement.
lustre, *NAm:* **luster** ['lʌstər] *n.* **1.** éclat *m*, brilliant *m*, lustre *m*; *Tex:* cati *m*, lustre (du drap); *Lit:* **to add fresh l. to a name,** ajouter un nouveau lustre á un nom. **2.** (*a*) pendeloque *f* (de lustre); (*b*) lustre (de plafond). **3.** *Tex:* **(cotton) l.,** lustrine *f*.
lustreless, *NAm:* **lusterless** ['lʌstəlis] *a.* mat, terne; (yeux) sans éclat.
lustreware, *NAm:* **lusterware** ['lʌstəwεər] *n.* *Cer:* poterie *f* à reflets métalliques; poterie lustrée.
lustrous ['lʌstrəs] *a.* brillant, éclatant; (*of material*) lustré, satiné.
lusty ['lʌsti] *a.* vigoureux, fort, robuste; puissant (de corps). **-ily** *adv.* (travailler) vigoureusement, de toutes ses forces; (chanter, crier) à pleine gorge.
lute¹ [lu:t] *n. Mus:* luth *m*; **l. maker,** luthier *m*; **l. player,** joueur, -euse, de luth; luthiste *mf*.
lute² *n.* lut *m*, mastic *m*.
lute³ *v.tr.* luter, boucher, mastiquer.
Lutheran ['lu:θərən] *a. & n. Rel.H:* luthérien, -ienne.
luxation [lʌk'seiʃ(ə)n] *n.* luxation *f*.
Luxemb(o)urg ['lʌksəmbə:g] *Pr.n. Geog:* **the Grand Duchy of L.,** le grand-duché de Luxembourg.
luxuriance [lʌg'zju:riəns, lʌk's-] *n.* exubérance *f*, luxuriance *f* (de la végétation, de style, etc.).
luxuriant [lʌg'zju:riənt, lʌk's-] *a.* exubérant, luxuriant; **l. growth of hair,** chevelure abondante. **-ly** *adv.* avec exubérance; en abondance.
luxuriate [lʌg'zju:rieit, lʌk's-] *v.i.* **1.** (*of vegetation*) croître avec exubérance; pousser dru. **2.** (*of pers.*) (*a*) **to l. in an armchair,** prendre ses aises dans un fauteuil; (*b*) **to l. in dreams,** se griser de rêves.
luxurious [lʌg'zju:riəs, lʌk's-] *a.* **1.** (appartement) luxueux, somptueux; (vie) de luxe. **2.** (*of pers.*) (*a*) adonné au luxe; (*b*) sensuel; voluptueux. **-ly** *adv.* **1.** luxueusement; avec luxe. **2.** avec volupté.
luxuriousness [lʌg'zjuəriəsnis, lʌn's-] *n.* luxe *m*.
luxury ['lʌkʃəri] *n.* **1.** luxe *m*; **to live in (the lap of) l.,** vivre dans le luxe. **2.** objet *m* de luxe; **l. flat,** appartement *m* de luxe; **l. car,** voiture *f* de (grand) luxe; **to indulge in the l. of a cigar,** se payer le luxe d'un cigare; **l. tax,** taxe *f* de luxe. **3.** luxe (d'un appartement, etc.).
lychee [lai'tʃi:] *n. Bot:* litchi *m*.
lychgate ['litʃgeit] *n.* = LICHGATE.
lye [lai] *n.* lessive *f* (de soude, de potasse).
lymph [limf] *n. Physiol:* lymphe *f*; **l. gland,** ganglion *m* lymphatique.
lymphatic [lim'fætik] *Physiol:* **1.** *a.* lymphatique; **l. gland,** glande *f*, ganglion *m*, lymphatique. **2.** *n.* (vaisseau) lymphatique (*m*).
lynch [lin(t)ʃ] *v.tr.* lyncher. **lynching** *n.* lynchage *m*.
lynx [liŋks] *n. Z:* lynx *m*.
lynx-eyed ['liŋksaid] *a.* aux yeux de lynx.
lyre ['laiər] *n. Mus:* lyre *f*.
lyrebird ['laiəbə:d] *n. Orn:* oiseau-lyre *m*, *pl.* oiseaux-lyres; ménure *m*.
lyric ['lirik] **1.** *a.* (poète, drame) lyrique. **2.** *n.* (*a*) poème *m* lyrique; (*b*) **lyrics,** paroles *fpl* (d'une chanson); **l. writer,** parolier *m*.
lyrical ['lirik(ə)l] *a.* (*a*) lyrique; (*b*) dit, écrit, sur un ton lyrique; *F:* **she got positively l. about it,** elle y a montré un enthousiasme fou. **-ally** *adv.* lyriquement.
lyricism ['lirisizm] *n.* lyrisme *m*.
lyricist ['lirisist] *n.* poète *m* lyrique.
lysergic [lai'sə:dʒik] *a.* (acide) lysergique.

M

M, m [em] *n.* (la lettre) M, m *f.*

ma [mɑː] *n.f.* maman.

ma'am [mɑːm] *n.* **1.** madame. **2.** *F:* **school-m.,** maîtresse *f* d'école.

mac[1] [mæk] *n. F:* imper *m.*

mac[2] *n. U.S: F:* **hey, m.!** hé, mon vieux, mon pote!

macabre [mə'kɑːbr] *a.* macabre.

macadam [mə'kædəm] *n. Civ.E:* macadam *m*; **tar m.,** macadam au goudron.

macadamize [mə'kædəmaiz] *v.tr. Civ.E:* macadamiser (une route); **macadamized road,** macadam *m.*

macaroni [mækə'rouni] *n. Cu:* macaroni *m*; **m. cheese,** macaroni au gratin.

macaroon [mækə'ruːn] *n. Cu:* macaron *m.*

macaw [mə'kɔː] *n. Orn:* ara *m.*

mace[1] [meis] *n.* masse *f.*

mace[2] *n. Bot: Cu:* macis *m*; fleur *f* de muscade.

macebearer ['meisbɛərər] *n.* massier *m.*

macerate ['mæsəreit] *v.tr. & i.* macérer.

Mach [mæk] *n. Ph: Meas:* **M. (number),** (nombre *m* de) Mach.

machete [mə'tʃeiti, -'tʃeti] *n.* machette *f.*

Machiavellian [mækiə'veliən] *a.* Machiavélique.

machination [mæki'neiʃ(ə)n] *n.* machination *f*, complot *m.*

machine[1] [mə'ʃiːn] *n.* (*a*) machine *f*; **sewing, washing, m.,** machine à coudre, à laver; **m. made,** fait à la machine; **m. tool,** machine-outil *m*, *pl.* machines-outils; *Med:* **kidney, heart-lung, m.,** rein, cœur, artificiel; *Com: etc:* **slot m.,** distributeur *m* automatique, *F:* machine à sous; *F:* **fruit m.,** tire-pognon *m*; (*b*) (*pers.*) automate *m*, robot *m*, machine; (*c*) *Pol:* **the party m.,** les rouages *mpl* du parti; **to get caught up in the m.,** être pris dans l'engrenage; (*d*) **m. gun,** mitrailleuse *f*; **to m.-gun,** mitrailler; **m. gunner, gunning,** mitrailleur *m*; mitraillage *m.*

machine[2] *v.tr.* **1.** *Ind:* (*a*) façonner (une pièce); travailler (qch.) à la machine; (*b*) usiner, ajuster; **to m. down,** amincir (le métal). **2.** *Dressm:* coudre, piquer, à la machine. **machining** *n.* **1.** usinage *m*; ajustage *m* mécanique; **m. down,** amincissement *m.* **2.** *Dressm:* couture *f* à la machine.

machinery [mə'ʃiːn(ə)ri] *n.* **1.** mécanisme *m*; machines *fpl*, machinerie *f*; appareil(s) *m(pl)*, outillage *m.* **2. the m. of government,** les rouages *mpl* du gouvernement; **administrative m.,** l'appareil administratif.

machinist [mə'ʃiːnist] *n. Ind:* (*a*) machiniste *m*; mécanicien *m*; (*b*) (*for sewing*) mécanicienne *f.*

machismo [mæ'tʃizmou] *n. F:* machisme *m.*

macho ['mɑːtʃou] *a. F:* d'une masculinité aggressive.

mackerel ['mæk(ə)rəl] *n.* (*a*) *Ich:* maquereau *m*; (*b*) **m. sky,** ciel pommelé, moutonné.

mackintosh ['mækintɔʃ] *n.* (manteau *m* en) caoutchouc (*m*); mackintosh *m*; imperméable *m.*

macramé [mə'krɑːmi] *n.* macramé *m.*

macrobiotics [mækroubai'ɔtiks] *n.pl.* (*usu. with sg. const.*) macrobiotique *f.*

macrocosm ['mækroukɔzm] *n.* macrocosme *m.*

macroeconomics [mækrouekə'nɔmiks] *n.pl* (*usu. with sg. const.*) macroéconomie *f.*

macroscopic [mækrə'skɔpik] *a.* macroscopique.

mad [mæd] *a.* **(madder, maddest) 1.** fou, *f.* folle; aliéné; dément; *F:* **(stark) raving m., as m. as a hatter, as a March hare,** fou à lier; **it is enough to drive you m.,** il y a de quoi devenir fou; c'est à vous rendre fou; **to go m.,** devenir fou; **nationalism gone m.,** nationalisme forcené; **m. with fear,** affolé (de peur); **a m. plan,** un projet insensé; *F:* **to run like m.,** courir comme un dératé. **2. m. for revenge,** assoiffé de revanche; **to be m. about, on, sth.,** être fou de qch.; avoir la folie, la rage, de qch.; **to be m. on sport,** avoir la passion des sports; être un sportif passionné. **3.** *F:* furieux, furibond; **to be m. with,** *U.S:* **at, s.o.,** être furieux contre qn; **hopping m.,** fou furieux, hors de soi. **4.** (*a*) **m. bull,** taureau furieux, enragé; (*b*) *Vet:* **m. dog,** chien enragé. **5.** *adv. F:* **m. keen on sth.,** fou de, emballé de, qch. **-ly** *adv.* **1.** follement; en fou; comme un fou, une folle. **2.** (aimer) à la folie, éperdument. **3.** *F:* très; beaucoup; *F:* drôlement; **it's m. expensive,** c'est fou ce que c'est cher.

Madagascan [mædə'gæskən] **1.** *a.* malgache. **2.** *n.* Malgache *mf.*

madam ['mædəm] *n.f.* **1.** madame, mademoiselle; **M. Chairman,** Madame la Présidente; *Corr:* **Dear M.,** Madame, Mademoiselle. **2.** (*pl.* **madams**) tenancière de bordel; maquerelle. **3.** *F:* (*pl.* **madams) she's a bit of a m.,** c'est une pimbêche.

madcap ['mædkæp] *a. & n.* écervelé, -ée; étourdi, -ie; **m. scheme,** projet insensé.

madden ['mæd(ə)n] *v.tr.* rendre (qn) fou; exaspérer (qn). **maddening** *a.* à rendre fou; exaspérant. **maddeningly** *adv.* à rendre fou.

madder ['mædər] *n.* (*a*) *Bot:* garance *f*; **m. root,** alizari *m*; (*b*) *Dy:* teinture *f* de garance.

madding ['mædiŋ] *a. Poet:* fou, *f.* folle; furieux; **far from the m. crowd,** loin de la foule et du bruit.

Madeira [mə'diːərə] **1.** *Pr.n. Geog:* Madère *f.* **2.** (*a*) *n.* vin *m* de Madère; madère *m*; (*b*) **M. cake,** gâteau *m* de Savoie.

madhouse ['mædhaus] *n.* maison *f* de fous; *F:* **this place is a m.!** on se croirait à Charenton!

madman, *pl.* **-men** ['mædmən, -men] *n.m.* fou, aliéné; **like a m.,** (se battre) en désespéré, comme un forcené; (crier) comme un perdu.

madness ['mædnis] *n.* folie *f*, fureur *f*; démence *f*; **in a fit of m.,** dans un accès, dans un moment, de folie; *F:* **it's sheer m.,** c'est insensé, c'est de la folie; **midsummer m.,** (i) le comble de la folie; (ii) une aberration qui passera.

madonna [mə'dɔnə] *n.f.* madone.

madrigal ['mædrig(ə)l] *n.* madrigal, -aux *m.*

maelstrom ['meilstroum] *n.* tourbillon *m*; gouffre *m*; **the m. of modern life,** le tourbillon de la vie moderne.

maestro, *pl.* **-tros, -tri** ['maistrou, -trouz, -triː] *n.m. Mus:* maestro, *pl.* maestros.

Mae West ['mei'west] *n. O:* gilet *m* de sauvetage.

maf(f)ia ['mɑːfiə, 'mæfiə] *n.* maf(f)ia *f.*

mag [mæg] *n. F:* = MAGAZINE 3.

magazine [mægə'ziːn] *n.* **1.** *Mil:* magasin *m*; dépôt (d'armes, etc.); **powder m.,** (i) *Mil:* poudrière *f*, dépôt d'explosifs; (ii) *Navy:* soute *f* aux poudres, à poudre. **2.** (*a*) *Sm.a:* chargeur *m*, magasin; **m. rifle,** fusil *m* à répétition, à chargeur; (*b*) *Phot:* magasin. **3.** (revue *f*) périodique (*m*); **illustrated m.,** revue illustrée,

magazine *m*; *W.Tel: T.V:* **m. (programme),** magazine.
magenta [mə'dʒentə] *n.* & *a.* (*colour*) magenta (*m*) *inv.*
Maggie ['mægi] *Pr.n.f.* (*dim. of* **Margaret**) Margot.
maggot ['mægət] *n.* ver *m*, asticot *m*.
maggoty ['mægəti] *a.* véreux, plein de vers.
Magi ['meidʒai] *n.pl. B.Hist:* **the Three M.,** les trois (rois) mages *m*.
magic¹ ['mædʒik] *n.* magie *f*, enchantement *m*; **black, white, m.,** magie noire, blanche.
magic² *a.* (*a*) magique, enchanté; **m. wand,** baguette *f* magique; (*b*) *Mth:* **m. square,** carré *m* magique.
magical ['mædʒik(ə)l] *a.* magique. **-ally** *adv.* magiquement; (comme) par enchantement.
magician [mə'dʒiʃ(ə)n] *n.* magicien, -ienne.
magisterial [mædʒis'tiəriəl] *a.* **1.** (air, ton) magistral, -aux; (air) de maître. **2.** de magistrat.
magistrate ['mædʒistreit] *n.* magistrat *m*, juge *m*; **police-court m.,** juge d'instance; **magistrate's court** = tribunal *m* d'instance.
Magna Carta ['mægnə'kɑ:tə] *n. Engl.Hist:* la Grande Charte (de l'année 1215).
magnanimity [mægnə'nimiti] *n.* (*a*) grandeur *f* d'âme; (*b*) magnanimité *f*, générosité *f*.
magnanimous [mæg'næniməs] *a.* (*a*) **to be m.,** faire preuve de grandeur d'âme; (*b*) magnanime. **-ly** *adv.* (*a*) noblement; (*b*) magnanimement.
magnate ['mægneit] *n.* magnat *m* (de l'industrie, etc.).
magnesia [mæg'ni:ʃə] *n.* **1.** *Ch:* magnésie *f*. **2.** *Pharm:* magnésie blanche; **milk of m.,** magnésie hydratée.
magnesium [mæg'ni:ziəm] *n. Ch:* magnésium *m*.
magnet ['mægnit] *n.* **1.** aimant *m*; **horseshoe m.,** aimant en fer à cheval. **2.** électro-aimant *m*, *pl.* électro-aimants.
magnetic [mæg'netik] *a.* **1.** (*a*) aimanté; **m. needle,** aiguille aimantée; (*b*) (attraction, etc.) magnétique; **m. pole,** pôle *m* magnétique; **m. tape,** bande *f* magnétique; *Cmptr:* **m. card,** carte *f* magnétique. **2.** (*of pers., power*) magnétique, hypnotique. **-ally** *adv.* magnétiquement.
magnetism ['mægnitizm] *n.* magnétisme *m*.
magnetization [mægnitai'zeiʃ(ə)n] *n. Ph:* aimantation *f*, magnétisation *f*.
magnetize ['mægnitaiz] *v.tr.* **1.** (*a*) aimanter (une aiguille, etc.); (*b*) (*with passive force*) (*of iron, etc.*) s'aimanter. **2.** magnétiser, attirer (qn, par magnétisme personnel). **magnetizing** *a.* (courant, champ, etc.) magnétisant.
magneto [mæg'ni:tou] *n. El:* magnéto *f*.
magneto-electric [mægni:toui'lektrik] *a. Ph:* magnéto-électrique.
magnificat [mæg'nifikæt] *n. Ecc:* magnificat *m*.
magnification [mægnifi'keiʃ(ə)n] *n. Opt: etc:* grossissement *m*, grandissement *m*; **high m.,** fort grossissement.
magnificence [mæg'nifisəns] *n.* magnificence *f*.
magnificent [mæg'nifisənt] *a.* magnifique; (repas) somptueux. **-ly** *adv.* magnifiquement.
magnifier ['mægnifaiər] *n.* verre grossissant; loupe *f*.
magnify ['mægnifai] *v.tr.* **1.** (*a*) grossir, agrandir (une image); amplifier (un son); (*b*) grossir, exagérer (un incident). **2.** *Ecc:* magnifier (le Seigneur). **magnifying** *n. Opt: etc:* grossissement *m*, amplification *f*; **m. power,** pouvoir grossissant, grossissement (d'une lentille, d'un objectif); **m. glass,** loupe *f*.
magnitude ['mægnitjud] *n.* (*a*) grandeur *f*, importance *f*; (*b*) *Astr:* magnitude *f*; **star of the first m.,** étoile *f* de première magnitude; (*c*) *Mth:* grandeur, valeur *f*.
magnolia [mæg'nouliə] *n. Bot:* (*a*) magnolia *m*; (*b*) **m. (tree),** magnolia, magnolier *m*.
magnum, *pl.* **-ums** ['mægnəm(z)] *n.* magnum *m* (de champagne, etc.).
magpie ['mægpai] *n.* (*a*) *Orn:* pie *f*; (*b*) *F:* (*pers.*) (i) bavard(e), pie; (ii) voleur *m*; chipeur *m*.
Magyar ['mægjɑ:r] **1.** *a.* magyar. **2.** *n.* Magyar, -are.
maharajah [mɑ:hə'rɑ:dʒə] *n.m.* maharajah.
maharani [mɑ:hə'rɑ:ni:] *n.f.* maharani.
mahogany [mə'hɔgəni] *n.* (*a*) *Bot:* acajou *m*; (*b*) (bois *m* d')acajou; **m. table,** table *f* en acajou.
Mahometan [mə'hɔmətən] *a.* & *n.* musulman, -ane; Mahométan, -ane.
maid [meid] *n.f.* **1.** *Lit:* (*a*) jeune fille; (*b*) vierge; **the M. of Orleans,** la Pucelle (d'Orléans). **2. old m.,** vieille fille; **to remain an old m.,** rester fille. **3.** bonne, domestique; **lady's m.,** femme de chambre. **4. m. of honour,** (i) fille d'honneur (de la reine); (ii) *NAm:* (*at wedding*) première demoiselle d'honneur.
maiden ['meid(ə)n] *n.* **1.** (*a*) jeune fille *f*; (*b*) vierge *f*. **2.** (*a*) **m. aunt,** tante non mariée; (*b*) **m. name,** nom *m* de jeune fille; (*c*) **m. voyage, flight,** premier voyage, vol; **m. speech,** premier discours; discours de début (d'un député).
maidenhair ['meid(ə)nhɛər] *n. Bot:* **m. (fern),** adiante *m*, capillaire *m*; cheveu *m* de Vénus.
maidservant ['meidsə:vənt] *n.f. A:* domestique.
mail¹ [meil] *n. Arm:* mailles *fpl*; **coat of m.,** cotte *f* de mailles.
mail² *n.* **1** courrier *m*; lettres *fpl*; **incoming outgoing, m.,** courrier (à l')arrivée, (au) départ; *U.S:* **m. drop,** boîte *f* aux lettres. **2.** (*a*) *A.Veh:* malle *f*; malle-poste *f*, *pl.* malles-poste(s); **m. coach,** malle-poste; (*b*) la poste; **m. van,** *Rail:* wagon-poste *m*, *pl.* wagons-poste; *Aut:* voiture *f*, fourgon *m*, des postes; **m. train,** train-poste *m*; *Com:* **m. order,** commande *f* par correspondance; **m. order catalogue,** tarif-album *m*, *pl.* tarifs-albums.
mail³ *v.tr.* envoyer par la poste, expédier (des lettres, des paquets); mettre (une lettre) à la poste. **mailing** *n.* (*a*) mise *f* à la poste; **m. list,** liste *f* de diffusion; liste d'adresses; (*b*) *U.S:* grande quantité de courrier (à expédier).
mailbag ['meilbæg] *n.* sac postal, sac de dépêches.
mailbox ['meilbɔks] *n. NAm:* boîte *f* aux lettres.
mailman ['meilmən] *n. NAm:* facteur *m*.
maim [meim] *v.tr.* estropier, mutiler (qn).
main¹ [mein] *n.* **1.** *still used in the phr.* **with might and m.,** de toutes mes, ses, forces. **2. in the m.,** en général, en gros, en somme, généralement (parlant). **3.** (*a*) *Civ.E:* canalisation maîtresse, principale; *El:* conducteur principal; câble *m* de distribution; **electric mains,** canalisations électriques; **gas mains,** conduites *fpl* de gaz; **water mains,** canalisations, conduites, d'eau; **mains water,** eau *f* de ville; *W.Tel:* **mains set,** poste *m* secteur; (*b*) *Nau:* grand-mât.
main² *a.* principal, -aux, premier, essentiel; (*a*) **m. body,** gros *m* (de l'armée, de la flotte, etc.); *Agr:* **m. crop,** culture principale; (*b*) **m. point, thing,** l'essentiel, le principal; **m. idea,** idée *f* mère (d'une œuvre, etc.); *Com: Ind:* **m. office,** direction générale; siège social; *Gram:* **m. clause,** proposition principale; *Cu:* **m. course, dish,** plat *m* de résistance; (*c*) **m. road,** grande route; **m. street,** *NAm: F:* **m. drag,** rue principale; **m. sewer,** égout collecteur; *Rail: etc:* **m. line,** voie principale, grande ligne; (*d*) *Nau:* **m. masts,** les mâts majeurs; **m. deck,** pont principal; premier pont. **-ly** *adv.* **1.** principalement, surtout. **2.** en grande partie.
mainbrace ['meinbreis] *n. Nau:* grand bras de vergue; *F:* **to splice the m.,** boire un coup.
mainland ['meinlænd] *n.* continent *m*; terre *f* ferme.
mainline ['meinlain] *v.i. F:* se piquer, se piquouser.
mainliner ['meinlainər] *n. F:* drogué(e) qui se fait des piqûres intraveineuses, piquouseur *m*.

mainmast ['meinmɑːst, -məst] *n. Nau:* grand mât.

mainsail ['meinseil, 'meinsl] *n. Nau:* grand-voile *f, pl.* grand(s)-voiles.

mainsheet ['meinʃiːt] *n. Nau:* grand-écoute *f, pl.* grand-écoutes.

mainspring ['meinspriŋ] *n.* **1.** grand ressort; ressort moteur (d'une pendule, etc.). **2.** mobile essentiel, cause principale.

mainstay ['meinstei] *n.* **1.** *Nau:* étai *m* de grand mât. **2.** soutien principal; point *m* d'appui (d'une cause).

mainstream ['meinstriːm] *n.* (*a*) courant principal; **the m. of French tradition,** l'axe *m* de la tradition française; (*b*) *Mus:* **m. jazz,** style *m* de jazz entre le traditionnel et le moderne.

maintain [mein'tein] *v.tr.* **1.** maintenir (l'ordre, la discipline); soutenir (une lutte, la conversation, etc.); entretenir (des relations, etc.); conserver (la santé); garder, observer (une attitude, le silence); **to m. the speed,** conserver l'allure. **2.** entretenir, soutenir, nourrir (une famille, etc.). **3.** entretenir (une armée, une route). **4.** soutenir, défendre (une cause). **5.** garder (un avantage); *Mil: etc:* se maintenir dans, tenir (une position). **6.** soutenir (une opinion, un fait); **to m. (that) . . .,** maintenir, soutenir, prétendre, que . . .; **he maintains that he is innocent,** il affirme qu'il est innocent.

maintenance ['meintinəns] *n.* **1.** maintien *m* (de l'ordre, de qn dans un emploi); *Com:* **resale price m.,** prix imposés. **2.** (*a*) entretien *m* (d'une famille, des troupes, etc.); *Sch:* **m. grant,** bourse *f* d'entretien; (*b*) *Jur:* pension *f* alimentaire; **m. order,** obligation *f* alimentaire; (*c*) *Adm: Fin:* alimentation *f*, financement *m* (d'un fonds, d'une caisse). **3.** (*a*) *Tchn:* entretien, conservation *f* (du matériel, des routes, etc.); **m. handbook,** manuel *m* d'entretien; **m. kit,** trousse *f* d'entretien; **m. engineer,** ingénieur *m* d'entretien; **m. vehicle,** camion-atelier *m, pl.* camions-ateliers; (*b*) *Rail: Tp: etc:* surveillance *f* (des voies, des lignes); *Tp:* **m. department,** service *m* de surveillance des lignes. **4.** défense *f* (de ses droits).

main-top ['meintɔp] *n. Nau:* grand-hune *f, pl.* grand-hunes.

maison(n)ette [meizə'net] *n.* appartement *m* prélevé sur un immeuble, *esp.* (appartement) duplex (*m*).

maize [meiz] *n.* maïs *m.*

majestic [mə'dʒestik] *a.* majestueux, auguste; (maintien) plein de majesté. **-ally** *adv.* majestueusement.

majesty ['mædʒəsti] *n.* majesté *f*; (*a*) **God in all His m.,** Dieu dans toute sa majesté; (*b*) **His M., Her M.,** Sa Majesté le Roi, Sa Majesté la Reine; **Your M.,** Votre Majesté; **on His, Her, M.'s Service** (pour le) service de Sa Majesté (= service de l'État); *Post:* en franchise.

major¹ ['meidʒər] *n. Mil:* (*a*) commandant *m*, chef *m* de bataillon (d'infanterie); **m. general,** général *m* de division; (*b*) chef d'escadron (de cavalerie, etc.).

major² **1.** *a.* (*a*) **the m. portion,** la majeure partie, la plus grande partie; **the m. prophets,** les grands prophètes; **m. decision,** décision capitale; **m. illness,** maladie *f* grave; *Mil:* **m. offensive,** vaste offensive; *Mus:* **m. key,** ton, mode, majeur; *Aut:* **m. road,** route principale, à priorité; (*b*) *Sch:* **Martin m.,** Martin aîné, l'aîné des deux Martin. **2.** *n.* (*a*) *Jur:* (*pers.*) majeur, -eure; (*b*) *Log:* majeure *f*; (*c*) *Sch: U.S:* (i) matière principale (d'un étudiant); (ii) **philology m.,** étudiant, -ante, en philologie.

major³ *v.i. Sch: U.S:* **to m. in a subject,** se spécialiser dans un sujet; **to m. in English** = faire sa licence d'anglais.

Majorca [mə'dʒɔːkə] *Pr.n. Geog:* Majorque *f.*

Majorcan [mə'dʒɔːkən] **1.** *a. Geog:* majorquin. **2.** *n.* Majorquin, -ine.

major-domo, *pl.* **-os** [meidʒə'doumou, -ouz] *n.* majordome *m.*

majorette [meidʒə'ret] *n.f. NAm:* **(drum) m.,** majorette.

majority [mə'dʒɔriti] *n.* **1.** majorité *f* (des voix); (*a*) **absolute m.,** majorité absolue; **a two-thirds m.,** une majorité de deux tiers, de deux contre un; **to be in a, the, m.,** être en majorité, avoir la majorité; **elected by a m.,** élu à la pluralité des voix; **by an overwhelming m.,** en nombre écrasant; **m. party,** parti *m* majoritaire; *Jur:* **m. verdict,** verdict *m* de la majorité (du jury); (*b*) la plus grande partie, le plus grand nombre (des hommes, etc.); (*c*) *U.S:* majorité absolue. **2.** *Jur:* majorité; **to attain one's m.,** atteindre sa majorité; devenir majeur. **3.** *Mil:* grade *m* de commandant.

make¹ [meik] *n.* **1.** (*a*) façon *f*, fabrication *f*, construction *f*; coupe *f* (d'une robe, etc.); (*b*) *Com: Ind:* marque *f* (d'un produit); **of French m.,** de fabrication française; **cars of all makes,** voitures *fpl* de toutes marques. **2.** caractère *m*, aspect *m* (de qn). **3.** *F:* **to be on the m.,** chercher à faire fortune par tous les moyens. **4.** *El:* fermeture *f* (du circuit); **at m.,** en circuit.

make² *v.* (*p.t. & p.p.* **made** [meid]) **I.** *v.tr.* **1.** (*a*) faire, construire (une machine, une boîte, etc.); façonner (un vase, etc.); fabriquer (du papier, etc.); confectionner (des vêtements, etc.); ménager (une ouverture, etc.); **God made man,** Dieu a créé l'homme; **they seem made for each other,** ils semblent créés l'un pour l'autre; *Knit:* **to m. one, two,** faire un jeté simple, double; (*b*) **bread is made of flour,** le pain est fait de farine; **what is it made of?** en quoi est-ce? c'est en quoi? **to m. a friend of s.o.,** faire de qn son ami; **I don't know what to m. of it,** je n'y comprends rien; **what do** *you* **m. of it?** et vous, qu'en pensez-vous? **to show what one is made of,** donner sa mesure; (*c*) faire (son testament); (*d*) faire (le lit, le thé, du feu); (*e*) **to m. trouble,** causer des ennuis **(for s.o.,** à qn); provoquer le désordre; **to m. a noise,** faire du bruit; **to m. peace,** faire, conclure, la paix; (*f*) faire (une loi); établir (une règle); **to m. a distinction,** faire une distinction; (*g*) effectuer, faire (un versement, une transaction); opérer (un changement); (*h*) faire (un discours, des excuses, etc.); commettre (une erreur); **to m. an attempt to do sth.,** essayer de faire qch.; **to m. war,** faire la guerre; **to m. one's escape,** s'échapper, se sauver. **2.** (*a*) établir, assurer (**a connection between . . .,** le raccordement de . . .); *El:* (*of contact points*) fermer (le circuit); (*b*) **two and two m. four,** deux et deux font quatre; **they m. a handsome couple,** ils font un beau couple. **3.** faire (de l'argent); **to m. £100 a week,** gagner, se faire, £100 par semaine; **to m. one's fortune,** faire fortune; *F:* **to m. a bit on the side,** se faire de la gratte; **to m. a name for oneself,** se faire un nom; **to m. friends,** (i) se faire des amis; (ii) devenir amis; se lier d'amitié (**with s.o.,** avec qn); *Cards:* **to m. a trick,** faire une levée; *F:* **to m. it,** réussir, y arriver; **he's got it made,** son avenir est assuré; *F:* **I just made my train,** j'ai eu mon train tout juste. **4.** (*a*) faire la fortune de (qn); **this book made him, made his name,** ce livre l'a rendu célèbre; **this will m. him or break him,** cela sera ou son succès ou sa ruine; (*b*) **that made my day,** ça m'a rendu heureux pour toute la journée; **it makes all the difference,** ça change tout. **5. to m. s.o. happy, rich,** rendre qn heureux, riche; **to m. s.o. hungry, sleepy,** donner faim, sommeil, à qn; **to m. s.o. angry,** fâcher qn; **to m. s.o. one's heir,** constituer qn son héritier; **to m. sth. known,** faire connaître qch.; **to m. oneself heard,** se faire entendre; **to m. oneself ill,** se rendre malade; **to m. oneself tired,** se fatiguer. **6. what time do you m. it?** quelle heure avez-vous? **I m. it five kilometres,** j'évalue la distance à cinq kilomètres. **7.** (*cause, compel*) **to m. s.o. speak, sleep,** faire parler, dormir, qn; **I made him stop,** je l'ai forcé de s'arrêter; **what made you say that?** pourquoi avez-vous dit cela? **8.** *Nau:* (*a*) arriver à (un port, etc.); (*b*) (*of ship*) **to m. twenty knots,** faire vingt nœuds. **II.** *v.i.* **1. to m. for, towards, a place,** se diriger vers un endroit; **to m. for the door,** se diriger vers la porte; **the crowd made for the square,** la foule s'est portée vers la place; *Nau:* **to m. for . . .,** faire route sur . . ., mettre le cap sur . . .; **ship making for Hull,** navire *m* à destination de Hull. **2. this cannot m. for happiness,** cela ne peut pas contribuer au bonheur; **these agreements m. for peace,** ces accords *mpl* tendent à maintenir la paix. **3. to m. as if, as though, to do sth.,** faire mine, faire semblant, de faire qch.; **he made as if to speak,** il a eu l'air de vouloir parler. **4.** (*of tide*) se faire; (*of floodtide*) monter; (*of ebb*) baisser. **5.** *El:* (*of current*) **to m. and break,** s'interrompre et se rétablir. **make away** *v.i. F:* **to m. away with sth.,** faire disparaître, enlever, qch.; voler (de l'argent, etc.); **to m. away with s.o.,** tuer, supprimer, qn; **to m. away with oneself,** se suicider. **make do 1.** *v.i.* **I need a hundred pounds but I could m. do with fifty,** j'ai besoin de cent livres mais cinquante feraient mon affaire. **2.** *v.tr.* **we'll have to m. the milk do,** il faut nous contenter du peu de lait que nous avons. **make off** *v.i. F:* se sauver; décamper; s'éclipser, filer; **to m. off with the cash,** filer avec l'argent; **somebody's made off with my overcoat,** on m'a volé, chipé, mon pardessus. **make out 1.** *v.tr.* (*a*) faire, établir, dresser (une liste, etc.); dresser, rédiger (un mémoire); établir, dresser, relever (un compte); établir (un chèque) (au nom de qn); (*b*) (i) établir, prouver (qch.); **how do you m. that out?** comment arrivez-vous à ce résultat, à cette conclusion? (ii) **to m. s.o. out to be richer than he is,** faire qn plus riche qu'il ne l'est; **he's not such a fool as people m. out,** il n'est pas aussi bête qu'on le croit; (*c*) (i) comprendre (une énigme, un problème); démêler (les raisons de qn, la signification de qch.); déchiffrer (une écriture); débrouiller (une affaire); **I can't m. the boy out,** ce garçon est une énigme pour moi; **I can't m. it out,** je ne puis m'y retrouver; je n'y comprends rien; (ii) distinguer, discerner (qch.). **2.** *v.i. F:* réussir, faire son chemin; faire des progrès; **he's making out very well,** il fait de bonnes affaires. **make over** *v.tr.* céder, transférer, transmettre (**sth. to s.o.,** qch. à qn). **make up 1.** *v.tr.* (*a*) compléter, parfaire (une somme); parfournir (des commandes); combler, suppléer à (un déficit); **to m. up the difference,** parfaire la différence; (*b*) **to m. up lost ground,** regagner le terrain perdu; **to m. it up to s.o. for sth.,** dédommager qn de qch.; indemniser qn; (*c*) faire (un paquet); *Pharm:* préparer, exécuter (une ordonnance); (*d*) (i) faire, confectionner, façonner (des vêtements); **customers' own material made up,** on travaille à façon; (ii) dresser (une liste); (iii) régler, établir, arrêter (un compte); régler, balancer (les livres); **to m. up one's accounts,** vider ses comptes; (iv) inventer, forger (une histoire, des excuses); **the whole thing is made up!** pure invention (que) tout cela! (*e*) rassembler, réunir (une compagnie); compléter (une somme d'argent); **to m. up the fire,** arranger le feu; *v.i. Typ:* **to m. up,** mettre en pages; (*f*) former, composer (un ensemble); (*g*) **to m. (oneself) up,** se maquiller; *Th:* se farder; (*of man*) se grimer; **to m. s.o. up,** maquiller qn; (*h*) **to m. up one's mind,** se décider, prendre son parti; (*i*) arranger, accommoder (un différend); **to m. it up (again),** se réconcilier. **2.** *v.i.* (*a*) **to m. up for lost time,** rattraper, réparer, le temps perdu; **to m. up for one's losses,** compenser ses pertes; **that makes up for it,** c'est une compensation; **to m. up for the lack of sth.,** suppléer au manque de qch.; (*b*) **to m. up to s.o.,** faire des avances, faire la cour, à qn; flatter qn. **made** *a.* **1.** fait, fabriqué. **2.** *F:* **he's a m. man,** son avenir est assuré; sa fortune est faite. **3. m.-up** (*a*) factice; faux, *f.* fausse; (histoire) inventée; (*b*) (vêtement) tout fait; (*c*) maquillé, fardé. **making** *n.* **1.** (*a*) fabrication *f* (de la toile, du papier); confection *f*, façon *f* (de vêtements); construction *f* (d'un pont, d'une machine); création *f* (d'un poste); **this failure was the m. of him,** cet échec a réformé son caractère; **history in the m.,** l'histoire *f* en train de se faire; (*b*) **to have the makings of . . .,** avoir tout ce qu'il faut pour devenir . . .; **he has the makings of a statesman,** il y a en lui l'étoffe d'un homme d'État; (*c*) *El:* **m. and breaking,** fermeture *f* et ouverture *f* (du circuit). **2.** *Th: etc:* **m. up,** maquillage *m.*

make-and-break ['meikənd'breik] *n. El:* conjoncteur-disjoncteur *m*, *pl.* conjoncteurs-disjoncteurs; *I.C.E:* dispositif *m*, levier *m*, de rupture.

make-believe ['meikbiliːv] **1.** *n.* semblant *m*, feinte *f*, trompe-l'œil *m inv*; **that's all m.-b.,** tout cela est (de la) pure fantaisie; **the land of m.-b.,** le pays des chimères. **2.** *a.* **a m.-b. world,** un monde imaginaire.

makefast ['meikfɑːst] *n. Nau:* amarre *f.*

maker ['meikər] *n.* **1.** faiseur, -euse; *Com: Ind:* fabricant *m* (de drap, etc.); constructeur *m* (de machines). **2.** *Rel:* **our M.,** le Créateur.

makeready ['meikredi] *n. Typ:* mise *f* en train.

makeshift ['meikʃift] *n.* expédient *m*; moyen *m* de fortune; **m. equipment,** installation *f* de fortune.

makeup ['meikʌp] *n.* **1.** (*a*) composition *f*, arrangement *m* (de qch.); confection *f* (des vêtements); (*b*) (*of pers.*) caractère *m.* **2.** maquillage *m*; fard *m*; **m. bag,** *Th: etc:* **m. box,** trousse *f*, boîte *f*, à maquillage; **m. remover,** démaquillant *m*; *Th: etc:* **m. man, girl,** maquilleur, -euse. **3.** *Typ:* mise *f* en pages; imposition *f.* **4.** *U.S: Sch:* examen *m* de rattrapage.

malachite ['mæləkait] *n. Miner:* malachite *f.*

maladjusted [mælə'dʒʌstid] *a. & n.* inadapté, -ée.

maladjustment [mælə'dʒʌstmənt] *n.* (*a*) *Mec.E:* (i) défaut *m* d'ajustage; (ii) mauvais réglage; (*b*) *El: Elcs:* déréglage *m* (d'un appareil); (*c*) inadaptation *f*; **emotional m.,** déséquilibre émotif.

maladministration [mælədminis'treiʃ(ə)n] *n.* mauvaise administration; mauvaise gestion (des affaires publiques, etc.); **m. of justice,** prévarication *f.*

maladroit [mælæ'drɔit] *a.* maladroit. **-ly** *adv.* maladroitement.

malaria [mə'lɛəriə] *n. Med:* malaria *f*, paludisme *m.*

malarial [mə'lɛəriəl] *a.* paludéen; **m. fever,** fièvre paludéenne; paludisme *m.*

Malawi [mə'lɑːwi] **1.** *Pr.n. Geog:* Malawi *m.* **2.** *n.* (*pers.*) Malawi *mf inv.*

Malay [mə'lei] **1.** *a. Geog:* malais; **the M. Peninsula,** la presqu'île Malaise. **2.** *n.* (*a*) Malais, -aise; (*b*) *Ling:* malais *m.*

Malaya [mə'leiə] *Pr.n. Geog:* Malaisie *f.*

Malayan [mə'leiən] **1.** *a. Geog:* malais. **2.** *n.* Malais, -aise.

Malaysia [mə'leiziə] *Pr.n. Geog:* Malaysia *f.*

malcontent ['mælkəntent] *a. & n.* mécontent, -ente.

male [meil] **1.** *a.* (*a*) (enfant, etc.) mâle; (sexe) masculin; **a m. friend,** un ami; **m. line (of descent),** ligne masculine; (*b*) (hormone, fleur, etc.) mâle; (*c*) *Tchn:* (vis) mâle. **2.** *n.m.* mâle.

malediction [mæli'dikʃ(ə)n] *n.* malédiction *f.*

malefactor ['mælifæktər] *n.* malfaiteur, -trice.

malevolence [mə'levələns] *n.* malveillance *f* (**towards,** envers).

malevolent [mə'levələnt] *a.* malveillant. **-ly** *adv.* avec malveillance; (regarder) d'un œil malveillant.
malformation [mælfɔː'meiʃ(ə)n] *n. Med: etc:* malformation *f*, difformité *f*; défaut *m*, vice *m*, de conformation.
malformed [mæl'fɔːmd] *a.* mal conformé; difforme.
malfunction¹ [mæl'fʌŋkʃən] *n.* fonctionnement défectueux, irrégulier (d'un mécanisme, d'un organe); dérèglement *m.*
malfunction² *v.i.* mal fonctionner.
Mali ['mɑːliː] **1.** *Pr.n. Geog:* (*country*) le Mali. **2.** *a. Geog:* malien. **3.** *n.* Malien, -ienne.
malice ['mælis] *n.* **1.** malice *f*, méchanceté *f*; rancune *f*; **out of m.,** par malice, par méchanceté; **to bear m. to, towards, s.o., to bear s.o. m.,** vouloir du mal à qn, en vouloir à qn; **no m., I hope,** sans rancune, j'espère. **2.** *Jur:* intention criminelle, délictueuse; **with m. aforethought,** avec intention criminelle; avec préméditation.
malicious [mə'liʃəs] *a.* **1.** (*a*) méchant, malveillant; (*b*) rancunier. **2.** *Jur:* fait avec intention criminelle, délictueuse; criminel; **m. intent,** intention délictueuse. **-ly** *adv.* **1.** (*a*) avec méchanceté; avec malveillance; (*b*) par rancune. **2.** *Jur:* avec intention criminelle; avec préméditation.
malign¹ [mə'lain] *a.* (*of thg*) pernicieux, nuisible.
malign² *v.tr.* calomnier, diffamer (qn); dire du mal de (qn); **much maligned man,** homme dont on dit beaucoup de mal.
malignancy [mə'lignənsi] *n.* **1.** malignité *f*, méchanceté *f*. **2.** *Med:* malignité, virulence *f* (d'une maladie).
malignant [mə'lignənt] *a.* **1.** malin, *f.* maligne; méchant. **2.** *Med:* malin; **m. tumour,** tumeur maligne. **-ly** *adv.* avec malignité; méchamment.
malinger [mə'liŋgər] *v.i.* faire le malade; simuler une maladie, *F:* tirer au flanc. **malingering** *n.* simulation *f* (de maladie); *F:* tirage *m* au flanc.
malingerer [mə'liŋgərər] *n.* faux malade, simulateur *m*; *F:* tireur *m* au flanc.
mall [mɔːl] *n.* **1.** *Games: A:* le (jeu de) mail *m*. **2.** (*a*) mail; promenade publique; (*b*) *NAm:* centre commercial (fermé à la circulation automobile).
mallard ['mælɑːd] *n. Orn:* col-vert *m*, *pl.* cols-verts; colvert *m*; canard *m* sauvage.
malleable ['mæliəbl] *a.* malléable.
mallet ['mælit] *n.* **1.** maillet *m*, mailloche *f*. **2.** *Games:* maillet (de croquet, de polo).
mallow ['mælou] *n. Bot:* (*a*) mauve *f*; (*b*) guimauve *f*, althée *f*.
malnutrition [mælnju'triʃ(ə)n] *n.* malnutrition *f*; sous-alimentation *f*.
malodorous [mæ'loudərəs] *a.* malodorant.
malpractice [mæl'præktis] *n.* **1.** méfait *m*. **2.** *Jur:* (*a*) négligence *f*, incurie *f* (d'un médecin); (*b*) malversation *f*.
malt¹ [mɔːlt] *n. Brew: etc:* malt *m*; **m. liquor,** bière *f*.
malt² **1.** *v.tr.* (*a*) *Brew:* malter (l'orge); (*b*) **malted milk,** lait malté. **2.** *v.i.* (*of grain*) se convertir en malt. **malting** *n.* **1.** maltage *m*. **2.** malterie *f*.
Malta ['mɔːltə] *Pr.n. Geog:* Malte *f*.
Maltese [mɔːl'tiːz] **1.** *a.* (*a*) *Geog:* maltais; (*b*) *Her: Mec.E: etc:* **M. cross,** croix *f* de Malte. **2.** *n.* (*a*) *Geog:* Maltais, -aise; (*b*) *Ling:* maltais *m*.
maltreat [mæl'triːt] *v.tr.* maltraiter, malmener (qn); maltraiter, déshonorer (un tableau, un arbre, etc.).
maltreatment [mæl'triːtmənt] *n.* mauvais traitement.
mam(m)a [mə'mɑː] *n.f. F:* maman.
mammal ['mæm(ə)l] *n.* mammifère *m*.
mammalian [mæ'meiliən] *a.* & *n.* mammifère (*m*).
mammary ['mæməri] *a.* & *n. Anat:* **the m. glands,** *n.* **the mammaries,** (les glandes *f*) mammaires (*f*).
Mammon ['mæmən] *Pr.n. B:* Mammon *m*; le Veau d'or.
mammoth ['mæməθ] **1.** *n. Paleont:* mammouth *m*. **2.** *a.* géant, monstre; énorme, gigantesque, colossal.
mammy ['mæmi] *n.f.* **1.** *F:* maman. **2.** *U.S:* (*a*) bonne d'enfants noire; (*b*) *Pej:* noire.
man¹, *pl.* **men** [mæn, men] *n.m.* **1.** (*a*) (*human being*) homme; **the rights of m.,** les droits de l'homme; **any man,** n'importe qui; **few men,** peu de gens; **no man's land,** (i) terrains *mpl* vagues; (ii) *Mil:* zone *f* neutre; (*b*) (*mankind*) l'homme; **m. proposes, God disposes,** l'homme propose et Dieu dispose; **m. does not live by bread alone,** on ne se nourrit pas que de pain; (*c*) *Theol:* **the inner m.,** l'homme intérieur; (*d*) *Ind: etc:* **m. hour,** heure *f* de travail, de main-d'œuvre; heure-homme *f*, *pl.* heures-homme. **2.** (*adult male*) homme; (*a*) **men and women,** les hommes et les femmes; *P.N:* (*on public convenience*) **men,** hommes; *Com:* **men's department,** rayon *m* hommes; **m. for m.,** homme pour homme; **they replied as one m.,** ils répondirent d'une seule voix; **to make a m. of s.o.,** faire un homme de qn; **he took it like a m.,** il a pris ça courageusement; **he's just the m. for me,** c'est mon homme; **to be one's own m.,** (i) être maître de soi; (ii) ne dépendre que de soi; **a lady's m.,** un galant; *F:* **look at that, m.!** regarde un peu, mon vieux! **come here, young m.!** venez ici (i) jeune homme, (ii) mon petit! **good m.!** bravo mon vieux! (*b*) **an old m.,** un vieillard; **an ambitious m.,** un ambitieux; **a dead m.,** (i) un mort; (ii) *F:* (*empty bottle*) un cadavre; *Rail: etc:* **dead man's handle,** l'homme-mort; (*c*) **an Oxford m.,** (i) un originaire, un habitant, d'Oxford; (ii) un étudiant de l'Université d'Oxford; (*d*) **odd-job m.,** homme à tout faire; *F:* **the weather m.,** Monsieur Météo. **3. m. and wife,** mari et femme; **to live as m. and wife,** vivre maritalement; *F:* **my old m.,** (i) mon mari, mon homme; (ii) mon père, le vieux; **my young m.,** (i) mon amoureux; (ii) mon fiancé. **4.** (*a*) *Hist:* (*vassal*) homme; (*b*) (*manservant*) domestique, valet; (*c*) *Ind: etc:* **employers and men,** les patrons et les ouvriers; (*d*) *Mil:* **officers and men,** officiers et hommes de troupe; (*e*) *Sp:* joueur; *Cr:* **twelfth m.,** le joueur de réserve. **5.** *Games:* (*chess*) pièce *f*; (*draughts*) pion *m*.
man² *v.tr.* **(manned) 1.** (*a*) fournir du personnel à (une organisation, etc.); être affecté à (une organisation, etc.); assurer le service (d'une machine), la manœuvre (d'un appareil); être membre de l'équipe (d'un avion, etc.); (*b*) *Mil:* occuper, garnir (un fort etc.); **to m. a gun,** servir, manœuvrer, une pièce; (*c*) *Nau:* armer, équiper (un canot); **to m. the pumps,** armer les pompes; *Navy:* (*in salute, etc.*) **to m. ship,** faire passer l'équipage à la bande. **2. to m. oneself,** se fortifier; s'armer de courage. **manned** *a.* (*of spacecraft*) habité.
Man³ *Pr.n. Geog:* **the Isle of M.,** l'île *f* de Man.
manacle¹ ['mænəkl] *n.* *usu. pl.* **manacles,** (i) menottes *fpl*; (ii) chaînes *fpl*; entraves *fpl*.
manacle² *v.tr.* mettre les menottes à (qn).
manage ['mænidʒ] *v.tr.* **1.** conduire (une entreprise, etc.); administrer, diriger, gérer (une affaire, une société, etc.); gouverner (une banque); régir (une propriété); **to m. s.o.'s business,** gérer les affaires de qn. **2. to know how to m. s.o.,** savoir prendre qn. **3. to m. to do sth.,** s'arranger pour faire qch.; arriver, parvenir, à faire qch.; trouver moyen de faire qch.; **I think I can m. it,** je crois que je pourrai le faire; **I shall never m. to learn it,** jamais ne n'arriverai à l'apprendre; **how do you m. not to dirty your hands?** comment faites-vous pour ne pas vous salir les mains? **£100 is the most that I can m.,** £100 c'est tout ce que je peux offrir, payer; **can you m. a few more**

cherries? pouvez-vous manger encore quelques cerises? **4.** *v.i.* **she manages well,** elle sait s'y prendre; **we shall m. better next time,** nous ferons mieux la prochaine fois; **he'll m. all right,** il se débrouillera; **we could just m.,** on vivait bien juste. **managing** *a.* **1.** directeur, -trice; gérant; **m. director,** directeur général. **2.** *usu. Pej:* autoritaire.

manageable ['mænidʒəbl] *a.* **1.** (*of thg*) maniable; (canot) manœuvrable. **2.** (*of pers.*) maniable, traitable, docile. **3.** (*of undertaking*) praticable, faisable.

management ['mænidʒmənt] *n.* **1.** (*a*) maniement *m* (d'un outil, etc.); (*b*) direction *f*, conduite *f* (d'une affaire); gérance *f*, gestion *f* (d'une usine, etc.); exploitation *f* (d'une carrière, etc.); **business m.,** gestion des affaires; **m. consultant,** conseil *m* en gestion; **bad m.,** mauvaise organisation; **under new m.,** (i) changement *m* de propriétaire; (ii) nouvelle direction. **2.** adresse *f*; savoir-faire *m*. **3.** *coll.* l'administration *f*, la direction.

manager ['mænidʒər] *n.* **1.** (*a*) directeur *m*, gérant *m* (d'une société, etc.); administrateur *m* (de biens); régisseur *m* (d'une propriété); *Cin: Sp: F:* manager *m*; **general m.,** directeur général; **sales m.,** directeur commercial; **personnel m.,** chef, directeur, du personnel; (*b*) *U.S:* chef (d'un parti politique). **2.** ménager, -ère; **she's a good m.,** elle est bonne ménagère. **3.** *Jur:* **receiver and m.,** administrateur (d'une faillite, etc.); syndic *m* de faillite.

manageress ['mænidʒəres] *n.f.* directrice, gérante.

managerial [mænə'dʒiəriəl] *a.* directorial, -aux; (poste) de commande; **m. staff,** les cadres *mpl*.

manatee [mænə'tiː] *n. Z:* lamantin *m*.

Manchuria [mæn'tʃuːriə] *Pr.n. Geog:* Mandchourie *f*.

Manchurian [mæn'tʃuːriən] **1.** *a. Geog:* mandchou. **2.** *n.* Mandchou, -oue.

Mancunian [mæŋ'kjuːniən] *a. & n.* (habitant, etc.) de Manchester.

mandarin¹ ['mændərin] *n.* **1.** *Chinese Hist:* mandarin *m*; *Toys:* **nodding m.,** branle-tête *m inv*. **2.** *F:* haut fonctionnaire; mandarin.

mandarin², mandarine ['mændəriːn] *n.* **1.** *Bot:* mandarine *f*. **2.** *a. & n.* (*colour*) mandarine *inv*.

mandate ['mændeit] *n. Pol:* (*a*) *Hist:* mandat *m*; (*b*) **electoral m.,** mandat de député.

mandatory ['mændət(ə)ri] *a.* (*a*) mandataire; **m. writ,** mandement *m*; (*b*) obligatoire.

mandible ['mændibl] *n.* **1.** *Z:* mandibule *f*. **2.** *Anat:* mâchoire inférieure.

mandolin(e) ['mændəlin] *n. Mus:* mandoline *f*.

mandrake ['mændreik] *n. Bot:* mandragore *f*.

mandrel, mandril ['mændril] *Mec.E:* **1.** mandrin *m*, arbre *m* (de tour). **2.** (*a*) *Metalw:* mandrin (pour évaser les tubes); (*b*) (*for rings*) triboulet *m*.

mandrill ['mændril] *n. Z:* mandrill *m*.

mane [mein] *n.* crinière *f* (du cheval, du lion, etc.).

maneater ['mæniːtər] *n.* (*pl.* **maneaters**) **1.** (*of pers.*) anthropophage *m*, cannibale *m*. **2.** (*of animal*) mangeur *m* d'hommes.

maneating ['mæniːtiŋ] *a.* **1.** (tribu etc.) anthropophage, cannibale. **2.** (tigre, etc.) mangeur d'hommes; **m. shark,** requin blanc, mangeur *m* d'hommes.

maneuver [mə'nuːvər] *n. & v. NAm:* = MANOEUVRE[1, 2].

manful ['mænful] *a.* vaillant, courageux, hardi. **-fully** *adv.* vaillamment, courageusement, hardiment.

manganese [mæŋgə'niːz] *n. Miner: Ch:* manganèse *m*; **m. steel,** acier *m* au manganèse.

mange [mein(d)ʒ] *n. Vet:* gale *f* (du chien, etc.).

mangel-wurzel ['mæŋgl'wəːzl] *n.* betterave *f* champêtre; betterave fourragère.

manger ['meindʒər] *n.* mangeoire *f*, crèche *f*; auge *f* d'écurie; *F:* **he's a dog in the m.,** il fait l'empêcheur de tourner en rond.

mangle¹ ['mæŋgl] *n. Laund:* essoreuse *f* (à rouleaux).

mangle² *v.tr.* essorer (le linge) (dans une essoreuse à rouleaux).

mangle³ *v.tr.* **1.** déchirer, lacérer, mutiler (qn, les membres de qn); charcuter, massacrer (un morceau de viande). **2.** mutiler, déformer (un mot); estropier (une citation); mutiler, dénaturer (un texte).

mango, *pl.* **-oes** ['mæŋgou, -ouz] *n. Bot:* **1.** mangue *f*. **2. m. (tree),** manguier *m*.

mangrove ['mæŋgrouv] *n. Bot:* **m. (tree),** manglier *m*, palétuvier *m*; **m. swamp,** mangrove *f*.

mangy ['meindʒi] *a.* **1.** galeux. **2.** *F:* (*of furniture, etc.*) minable, miteux.

manhandle ['mænhændl] *v.tr.* **1.** manutentionner (des marchandises, etc.); transporter, déplacer (qch.) à force de bras. **2.** brutaliser, malmener (qn).

manhole ['mænhoul] *n.* trou *m* d'homme (de chaudière); trou de visite, regard *m* (d'égout); **m. cover, lid,** plaque *f* d'égout.

manhood ['mænhud] *n.* **1.** humanité *f*; nature humaine. **2.** âge *m* d'homme; âge viril; virilité *f*.

manhunt ['mænhʌnt] *n.* chasse *f* à l'homme.

mania ['meiniə] *n.* **1.** *Med:* (i) manie *f*; folie *f*; (ii) folie furieuse; **suicidal m.,** folie du suicide. **2.** passion *f* (de qch.).

maniac ['meiniæk] *a. & n. Med:* fou furieux, folle furieuse; *Psy:* maniaque (*mf*); **sex m.,** obsédé sexuel.

manic ['mænik] *a. Psy:* (désir, etc.) qui tient de la folie; *a. & n.* **m. depressive,** maniaco-dépressif, -ive; **m. depression,** psychose maniaque dépressive.

manicure¹ ['mænikjuər] *n.* soin *m* des mains; **m. set,** trousse *f* de manucure; **to have a m.,** se faire soigner les mains.

manicure² *v.tr.* **1.** soigner les mains de (qn); faire les mains, les ongles, à (qn). **2. to m. one's nails,** se faire les ongles.

manicurist ['mænikjuərist] *n.* manucure *mf*.

manifest¹ ['mænifest] *a.* manifeste, évident; **to make sth. m.,** manifester qch. **-ly** *adv* manifestement.

manifest² *n.* (*a*) *Nau:* manifeste *m* (d'entrée, de sortie); (*b*) *Av:* état *m* de chargement.

manifest³ **1.** *v.tr.* (*a*) manifester, témoigner; (*b*) (*of symptom, etc.*) **to m. itself,** se manifester, se révéler; (*c*) *Nau:* faire figurer (une marchandise) sur le manifeste. **2.** *v.i. Psychics:* (*of ghost, spirit*) se manifester.

manifestation [mænifes'teiʃ(ə)n] *n.* manifestation *f*.

manifesto [mæni'festou] *n. Pol: etc:* manifeste *m*, proclamation *f*; déclaration publique.

manifold ['mænifould] **1.** *a.* (*a*) divers, varié; de diverses sortes; (*b*) multiple, nombreux; (*c*) **m. increase,** (i) dépassement *m* du taux normal; (ii) *Pharm:* surdosage *m*. **2.** *n.* (*a*) *Phil:* diversité *f*; (*b*) *I.C.E: etc:* tubulure *f*, tuyauterie *f*; collecteur *m*, culotte *f*.

Manil(l)a [mə'nilə] *Pr.n. Geog:* Manille *f*; **m. rope,** (cordage *m* en) manille *f*; *Paperm:* **m. paper,** papier *m* bulle.

manioc ['mæniɔk] *n.* **1.** *Bot:* manioc *m*. **2.** *Cu:* cassave *f*.

manipulate [mə'nipjuleit] *v.tr.* **1.** manipuler (un objet); manœuvrer, actionner (un dispositif mécanique); agir sur (un levier, une pédale). **2.** *Pej:* tripoter, cuisiner, arranger (des comptes); *St.Exch:* **to m. the market,** agir sur le marché; travailler le marché.

manipulation [mənipju'leiʃ(ə)n] *n.* **1.** manipulation *f*. **2.** manœuvre *f*; **wrong m.,** fausse manœuvre. **3.** *Pej:* tripotage *m*; *St.Exch:* agiotage *m*.

manipulator [mə'nipjuleitər] *n.* **1.** manipulateur. **2.**

Pej: tripoteur *m*; *St.Exch:* agioteur *m*.

mankind *n. coll.* **1.** [mæn'kaind] le genre humain; l'humanité *f*; l'espèce humaine. **2.** ['mænkaind] (*opp. to womankind*) les hommes *mpl*.

manlike ['mænlaik] *a.* **1.** (*a*) d'homme; mâle; (*b*) (*of woman*) hommasse. **2.** semblable à un homme.

manliness ['mænlinis] *n.* caractère viril; virilité *f*.

manly ['mænli] *a.* d'homme; mâle, viril.

man-made ['mænmeid] *a.* artificiel, synthétique; **m.-m. laws,** les lois faites par l'homme; **m.-m. fibres,** fibres *fpl* synthétiques.

manna ['mænə] *n.* **1.** *B: etc:* manne *f*; *Fig:* **it was m. from heaven,** cela tombait des mains des dieux. **2.** *Bot: Pharm: etc:* manne du frêne.

mannequin ['mænikin] *n.* (*pers.*) mannequin *m*.

manner ['mænər] *n.* **1.** manière *f*, façon *f* (de faire qch.); **the m. in which . . .,** la manière dont . . .; **in a m. of speaking,** en quelque sorte; dans un certain sens; **it's a m. of speaking,** c'est une façon de parler; *Gram:* **adverb of m.,** adverbe *m* de manière. **2.** *A: & Lit:* manière, coutume *f*; **he does it as (if) to the m. born,** il le fait comme s'il était né pour cela. **3.** *pl.* mœurs *fpl*, usages *mpl* (d'un peuple). **4.** maintien *m*, tenue *f*, air *m*, abord *m*; **I do not like his m.,** je n'aime pas son attitude. **5.** *pl.* (*a*) manières; **bad manners,** mauvaises manières; manque *m* de savoir-vivre; **it is bad manners to stare,** il est mal élevé de dévisager les gens; (*b*) **(good) manners,** bonnes manières, savoir-vivre *m*, politesse *f*; **to teach s.o. manners,** donner à qn une leçon de politesse, de bienséance; (*to child*) **where are your manners?** c'est comme ça qu'on se tient? en voilà une tenue! **6.** espèce *f*, sorte *f*; **all m. of people, of things,** toutes sortes de gens, de choses.

mannered ['mænəd] *a. Art: Lit:* maniéré; affecté; (style) recherché, précieux.

mannerism ['mænərizm] *n.* **1.** maniérisme *m*, affectation *f*. **2.** particularité *f* (d'un écrivain, etc.).

man(n)ikin ['mænikin] *n.* **1.** petit homme; homoncule *m*, nabot *m*. **2.** *Art: Med: Surg:* mannequin *m*.

mannish ['mæniʃ] *a.* (*of woman*) hommasse; **to be m. in one's dress,** s'habiller d'une manière masculine.

manœuvre¹, *NAm:* **maneuver¹** [mə'nuːvər] *n.* manœuvre *f*. **1.** *Mil: etc:* (*a*) (*action*) *Mil:* **encircling m.,** manœuvre d'encerclement; **evasive m.,** manœuvre de dérobement; (*b*) (*exercise*) **manœuvres,** manœuvres; **troops on manœuvres,** troupes *fpl* en manœuvre. **2.** (*a*) **a clever m.,** une manœuvre habile; (*b*) *pl. Pej:* menées *fpl*, intrigues *fpl*.

manœuvre², *NAm:* **maneuver²** **1.** *v.tr.* manœuvrer, faire manœuvrer (une armée, une flotte); **to m. s.o. into a corner,** (i) acculer qn dans un coin; (ii) amener adroitement qn dans une impasse. **2.** *v.i.* (*of troops, etc.*) manœuvrer; *Nau:* (*of ship*) évoluer.

manœuvrable, *NAm:* **maneuvrable** [mə'nuːvrəbl] *a.* (avion, etc.) manœuvrable, maniable.

man-of-war, *pl.* **men-of-war** ['mænəv'wɔːr, 'men-] *n.* **1.** *Nau: A:* vaisseau *m*, bâtiment *m*, de guerre. **2.** *Coel:* **Portuguese m.-of-w.,** physalie *f*, galère *f*.

manor ['mænər] *n.* (*a*) *Hist:* seigneurie *f*; (*b*) **m. (house),** manoir *m*.

manorial [mə'nɔːriəl] *a.* seigneurial, -aux.

manpower ['mænpauər] *n.* **1.** *Mec.E:* la force des bras. **2.** *coll. Ind: etc:* main-d'œuvre *f*; *Mil:* effectifs *mpl*; **shortage of m.,** crise *f* de main-d'œuvre, d'effectifs.

mansard ['mænsɑːd] *n.* **m. (roof),** toit *m*, comble *m*, en mansarde.

manse [mæns] *n. Ecc:* maison *f* du pasteur.

manservant, *pl.* **menservants** ['mænsəːvənt, 'mensəːvənts] *n.m.* domestique; valet (de chambre).

mansion ['mænʃ(ə)n] *n.* (*in country*) château *m*; (*in town*) hôtel (particulier); **m. (house),** manoir *m*, château *m*.

mansize(d) ['mænsaiz(d)] *a.* (*a*) de la grandeur d'un homme; (*b*) (*of handkerchief, helping of food, etc.*) qui convient à un homme; (*c*) (travail) d'homme.

manslaughter ['mænslɔːtər] *n. Jur:* homicide *m* (i) involontaire, par imprudence, (ii) sans préméditation.

mantel ['mænt(ə)l] *n.* = MANTELPIECE.

mantelpiece ['mænt(ə)lpiːs] *n.* **1.** manteau *m*, linteau *m*, chambranle *m*, de cheminée. **2.** dessus *m*, tablette *f*, de cheminée.

mantilla [mæn'tilə] *n. Cost:* mantille *f*.

mantis ['mæntis] *n. Ent:* mante *f*; **praying m.,** mante religieuse; prie-Dieu *f inv*.

mantle ['mænt(ə)l] *n.* **1.** *A: Cost:* mante *f*, pèlerine *f* (de femme). **2.** manteau *m* (de lave, de neige). **3.** (*a*) manchon *m* (de bec de gaz); (*b*) *Const:* parement *m* (d'un mur).

mantrap ['mæntræp] *n.* piège *m* à hommes.

manual ['mænjuəl] **1.** *a.* (travail, ouvrier, etc.) manuel; (travail) de manœuvre; **the m. alphabet,** l'alphabet *m* des sourds-muets. **2.** *n.* (*a*) (*handbook*) manuel *m*; (*b*) *Mus:* clavier *m* (d'un orgue). **-ally** *adv.* manuellement, à la main.

manufacture¹ [mænju'fæktʃər] *n.* **1.** fabrication *f*, élaboration *f* (d'un produit industriel); confection *f* (de vêtements). **2.** produit fabriqué, manufacturé.

manufacture² *v.tr.* fabriquer (un produit industriel); confectionner (des vêtements, etc.). **manufacturing 1.** *a.* industriel. **2.** *n.* fabrication *f*; confection *f* (de vêtements).

manufacturer [manju'fæktʃərər] *n.* fabricant *m*.

manure¹ [mə'njuər] *n.* engrais *m*; **farmyard m.,** fumier *m* (d'étable); **chemical m.,** engrais chimique; **liquid m.,** purin *m*; **m. heap,** tas *m* de fumier.

manure² *v.tr.* fumer, engraisser (la terre).

manuscript ['mænjuskript] **1.** *n.* manuscrit *m*. **2.** *a.* manuscrit; écrit à la main.

manway ['mænwei] *n. U.S.: Min:* galerie *f* de circulation.

Manx [mæŋks] **1.** *a. Geog:* de l'île de Man; **M. cat,** chat *m* sans queue de l'île de Man. **2.** *n.* (*a*) *Ling:* mannois *m*; (*b*) *pl.* **the M.,** les habitants *m* de l'île de Man.

many ['meni] *a.* **(more, most,** *q.v.*) un grand nombre (de); beaucoup (de); bien des; **m. times,** beaucoup de fois, bien des fois; **in m. cases,** dans bien des cas; **for m. years,** pendant de longues années; *Prov:* **m. hands make light work,** à plusieurs mains l'ouvrage avance; **m. of us,** beaucoup d'entre nous; **like so m. others,** comme tant d'autres; **he told me in so m. words that . . .,** il m'a dit en propres termes que . . .; **too m. people,** trop de monde; **a card too m.,** une carte de trop; **how m.?** combien? **I have as m. books as you,** j'ai autant de livres que vous; **as m. as you like,** autant que vous voulez; **as m. again, as m. more, twice as m.,** deux fois autant; **four accidents in as m. days,** quatre accidents en autant de jours; **a good m. things,** pas mal de choses.

many-coloured ['meni'kʌləd] *a.* multicolore.

many-sided ['meni'saidid] *a.* **1.** (figure) à plusieurs côtés. **2.** (problème) complexe, compliqué. **3.** (personne) aux talents variés.

Maoist ['mauist] *a. & n. Pol:* maoïste (*mf*).

Maori ['mɑːəri] **1.** *a. Ethn:* maori. **2.** *n.* (*a*) Maori, -ie; (*b*) *Ling:* maori *m*.

map¹ [mæp] *n.* (*a*) carte *f* (géographique); **relief m.,** carte topographique; **m. reading,** lecture *f* des cartes; **m. reference,** référence *f* topographique; coordonnées *fpl*; **m. maker,** cartographe *m*; (*b*) **to put a town**

on the m., mettre une ville en vedette; **the village was wiped off the m.,** le village a été rasé; **it's off the m.,** c'est à l'autre bout du monde.

map² *v.tr.* **(mapped) 1.** dresser une carte, un plan, de (la région, etc.). **2. to m. out,** tracer (un itinéraire); dresser, tracer (un programme). **mapping** *n.* cartographie *f*; levé *m* de carte, de plan.

maple ['meipl] *n. Bot:* **1. m. (tree),** érable *m*; **m. sugar,** sucre *m* d'érable; **m. syrup,** sirop *m* de sucre d'érable. **2.** (bois *m* d')érable.

mar [mɑːr] *v.tr.* **(marred)** gâter, gâcher (le plaisir de qn); troubler (la joie de qn); déparer (la beauté de qn); **to make or m. s.o.,** faire la fortune ou la ruine de qn.

marabou ['mærəbuː] *n. Orn:* marabout *m*.

maraschino [mærəs'kiːnou] *n. Dist:* marasquin *m*; **m. cherries,** cerises *fpl* au marasquin.

Marathon ['mærəθ(ə)n] *Pr.n.* (*a*) *Geog:* Marathon; (*b*) *Sp: etc:* **m. (race),** marathon *m*; **m. runner,** marathonien *m*; **m. speech,** marathon oratoire.

maraud [mə'rɔːd] *v.i.* **to go marauding,** marauder; aller à la maraude. **marauding 1.** *a.* maraudeur, -euse. **2.** *n.* maraude *f*.

marauder [mə'rɔːdər] *n.* maraudeur, -euse.

marble¹ ['mɑːbl] *n.* **1.** (*a*) marbre *m*; **m. statue,** statue *f* de marbre; (*pers.*) **m. cutter,** marbrier *m*; **m. quarry,** marbrière *f*; (*b*) *Art:* **(collection of) marbles,** (collection *f* de) marbres. **2.** *Games:* bille *f*; **to play marbles,** jouer aux billes.

marble² *v.tr.* marbrer (une boiserie, etc.); *Bookb:* marbrer, raciner (les plats); jasper, marbrer (les tranches).

March¹ [mɑːtʃ] *n.* mars *m*; **in M.,** en mars, au mois de mars; **(on) the first, the seventh, of M.,** le premier, le sept, mars.

march² *n.* **1.** *Mil: etc:* (*a*) marche *f*; **m. in step,** marche au pas; **m. past,** défilé *m*; **on the m.,** en marche; (*b*) pas *m*, allure *f*; **quick m.,** pas cadencé; **parade m., slow m.,** pas de parade. **2.** marche, progrès *m* (du temps, etc.). **3.** *Mus:* marche; **dead m.,** marche funèbre; **wedding m.,** marche nuptiale.

march³ 1. *v.i.* (*a*) *Mil: etc:* marcher; avancer; **to m. off,** se mettre en marche; **to m. by, past (s.o.),** défiler (devant qn); **quick . . . m.!** en avant . . . marche! (*b*) **time marches on,** l'heure *f* avance; le temps s'écoule. **2.** *v.tr.* (*a*) faire marcher, mettre en marche (des troupes); (*b*) **he was marched off to prison,** il a été emmené en prison. **marching** *n. Mil: etc:* marche *f*; **in m. order,** (i) en tenue de campagne; (ii) en formation de marche; **m. orders,** ordre *m* de mise en route; *F:* **to give s.o. his m. orders,** donner son congé à qn; mettre qn à la porte.

marchioness ['mɑːʃənes] *n.f.* marquise.

mare ['mɛər] *n.* jument *f*; **a mare's nest,** une illusion.

margarine [mɑːdʒə'riːn] *n.* margarine *f*.

marge [mɑːdʒ] *n. F:* margarine *f*.

margin ['mɑːdʒin] *n.* **1.** (*a*) marge *f*; bord *m*; lisière *f* (d'un bois); bord, rive *f* (d'un lac, etc.); *Nat.Hist:* marge (d'une feuille, etc.); *Anat:* bord, rebord *m* (d'une cavité, d'un orifice); (*b*) marge, écart *m*; **profit m.,** marge bénéficiaire; **to give s.o. some m.,** accorder quelque liberté à qn; **m. of error,** marge d'erreur; (*c*) *Com: Fin:* marge, couverture *f*; provision *f*; *St.Exch:* acompte (versé à un courtier); (*d*) *Mec.E: etc:* **tolerance, safety, m.,** marge de tolérance, de sécurité. **2.** marge, blanc *m* (d'une page, etc.); *Phot:* liseré *m* (d'une épreuve); **to write sth. in the m.,** écrire qch. en marge; *Typewr: etc:* **m. stop,** margeur *m*; curseur *m* de marges; **m. release,** déclenche-marge *m inv*.

marginal ['mɑːdʒin(ə)l] *a.* **1.** (*a*) marginal, -aux; *Geog:* **m. moraine,** moraine marginale; (*b*) **m. case,** cas *m* limite; *Pol:* **m. seat,** point chaud, siège chaudement disputé; (*c*) *Com: etc:* **m. profit,** bénéfice marginal. **2.** marginal, en marge; **m. note,** note, glose, marginale. **-ally** *adv.* d'une manière marginale; en marge; **the shares were m. lower,** les actions *f* avaient légèrement baissé.

marguerite [mɑːgə'riːt] *n. Bot:* grande marguerite, marguerite des champs.

Maria [mə'raiə] *Pr.n.f.* Maria; *F:* **black M.,** voiture *f* cellulaire; panier *m* à salade.

marigold ['mærigould] *n. Bot:* **1.** souci *m*. **2. African m.,** rose *f* d'Inde; **French m.,** œillet *m* d'Inde.

marihuana, marijuana [mæri'(h)wɑːnə] *n.* marihuana *f*, marijuana *f*.

marina [mə'riːnə] *n.* port *m* de plaisance, marina *f*.

marinade¹ [mæri'neid] *n. Cu:* marinade *f*.

marinade², marinate ['mærineid, -eit] *v.tr. Cu:* (faire) mariner.

marine [mə'riːn] **1.** *a.* (*a*) marin; **m. life,** vie marine; (*b*) **m. architect,** ingénieur *m* des constructions navales; **m. engineering,** ingénierie *f* de marine; mécanique navale; (*c*) **m. forces,** troupes *fpl* de marine; (*d*) **m. insurance, risk,** assurance *f*, risque *m*, maritime. **2.** *n.* (*a*) marine *f*; **merchant, mercantile, m.,** marine marchande, de commerce; (*b*) soldat *m* de marine; = fusilier marin; **the Royal Marines, the U.S. Marine Corps,** *approx.* = les fusiliers marins; *F:* **tell that to the marines!** allez raconter ça ailleurs, à d'autres!

mariner ['mærinər] *n. Nau:* marin *m*.

marionette [mæriə'net] *n.* marionnette *f*.

marital ['mærit(ə)l] *a.* **1.** marital, -aux. **2.** matrimonial, -aux.

maritime ['mæritaim] *a.* maritime.

marjoram ['mɑːdʒərəm] *n. Bot:* marjolaine *f*.

mark¹ [mɑːk] *n.* **1.** (*a*) (*target*) but *m*, cible *f*; **to hit the m.,** (i) atteindre le but, frapper juste; (ii) (*of pers.*) réussir; tomber, deviner, juste; **to miss the m.,** manquer le but; **wide of the m.,** (i) loin du but; (ii) loin de la réalité, de la vérité; (*b*) *F:* **an easy m.,** un crédule, une dupe. **2.** (*sign, proof*) (*a*) marque *f*, preuve *f*, signe *m*, témoignage *m*; **as a m. of respect,** en signe de respect; (*b*) (*of horse*) **m. of mouth,** marque d'âge (aux dents). **3.** (*trace*) (*a*) marque, tache *f*, signe, empreinte (de la souffrance, etc.); (*b*) **to make one's m.,** se faire un nom, une réputation; arriver. **4.** (*a*) **distinguishing m.,** marque distinctive; **identification m.,** marque d'identification; (*on gold, silver*) **(assay) m.,** poinçon *m* de garantie; *F:* **he's not up to the m.,** (i) il n'est pas dans son assiette; (ii) il n'est pas à la hauteur; (*b*) *Ind: Mil:* **m. II, III,** série *f* II, III; (*c*) **punctuation marks,** signes de ponctuation; **question m.,** point *m* d'interrogation; **as he couldn't write he made his m.,** ne sachant pas écrire il a fait une croix; (*d*) *Sch:* point, note *f*; **good m.,** bon point; **bad m., black m.,** mauvais point. **5.** (*reference on instrument, etc.*) (*a*) marque, repère *m*; **reference, guide, m.,** point de repère; (*b*) *Nau:* amer *m*, point de reconnaissance; (*on a buoy*) voyant *m*; **high-water m.,** niveau *m*, laisse *f*, de la marée haute; (*c*) *Sp:* ligne *f* de départ; **on your marks! get set! go!** à vos marques! prêts! partez! **to be quick off the m.,** démarrer vite.

mark² *v.tr.* **1.** (*a*) marquer, chiffrer (du linge, de l'argenterie, etc.); estampiller (des marchandises); *Tchn:* signer (de la bijouterie, etc.); biseauter, piper (les cartes); (*b*) (*usu. passive*) **face marked by, with, smallpox,** visage marqué de, par, la petite vérole. **2.** (*a*) **to m. (the price of) an article,** mettre le prix à un article; *St.Exch:* **to m. stock,** coter des valeurs; (*b*) *Sch:* corriger, noter (un devoir); **marked out of 10,** noté sur 10. **3. to m. s.o., sth., as . . .,** désigner, choisir, qn, qch., pour . . . **4.** (*a*) marquer, repérer, indiquer; **to m. a place on the map,** indiquer un lieu sur la carte; (*b*) **stream that marks the boundary of the estate,** ruisseau *m* qui marque la limite de la propriété; (*c*) indiquer; **X marks the spot,** X indique l'endroit. **5.** (*a*) témoigner, montrer (son approbation, son mécontentement); accentuer (le rythme); **to m. time,** (i) *Mil:* marquer le pas; (ii) *F:* piétiner sur place; attendre; (iii) *F:* vivre sur son acquis; **we're marking time,** on n'avance pas; (*b*) **to m. an era,** faire époque. **6.** *Sp:* marquer (un adversaire). **mark down** *v.tr.* baisser le prix de (qch.); démarquer (des marchandises); *Sch:* baisser la note (d'une copie). **marked** [mɑːkt] *a.* **1.** (*a*) (*after accident*) **badly m. face,** visage balafré; (*b*) (carte) marquée, biseautée. **2. m. man,** homme marqué (par ses ennemis); homme repéré; **he's a m. man,** son sort est réglé. **3.** marqué, prononcé, accusé; (différence) marquée, prononcée; (amélioration) sensible; **strongly m. features,** traits fortement accusés; **a very m. German accent,** un accent allemand très prononcé; **the change is becoming more m.,** le changement s'accentue. **markedly** [ˈmɑːkidli] *adv.* d'une façon marquée; nettement; **m. polite,** d'une politesse marquée. **marking,** *n.* **1.** (*a*) marquage *m* (du linge, du bétail, etc.); **m. ink,** encre *f* à marquer; (*b*) estampillage *m*; poinçonnage (de l'or, de l'argent, etc.); (*c*) *Mec.E: etc:* repérage *m* (du point mort, etc.). **2.** (*a*) **markings,** marques *fpl; (on animal)* taches *fpl*, rayures *fpl*; *Av:* **fuselage m.,** cocarde *f*; (*b*) estampille *f*. **3.** *Sch:* (*a*) correction *f* (d'un devoir); (*b*) copies *f* à corriger. **mark off** *v.tr. Surv:* jalonner (une ligne, une route); **to m. off a distance on the map,** (i) mesurer, (ii) rapporter, une distance sur la carte. **mark up** *v.tr. Com:* élever le prix de (qch.); *Sch:* hausser la note (d'une copie).

mark³ *n. Num:* mark *m*; **gold marks,** marks or.

Mark⁴ *Pr.n.m.* Marc; **the Gospel according to Saint M.,** l'évangile *m* selon saint Marc.

marker [ˈmɑːkər] *n.* **1.** (*pers.*) (*a*) marqueur, -euse (de linge, de bétail, etc.); (*b*) (*at games*) marqueur, pointeur *m*; (*c*) *Mil: etc:* (i) jalonneur *m*; (ii) (*at butts*) marqueur. **2.** (*a*) *Ind: Mec.E:* marqueuse *f*; machine *f* à marquer, à estampiller; (*b*) *Tls:* marquoir *m*. **3.** (*a*) jalon *m*; repère *m*; fanion *m*, piquet *m*, d'alignement, de jalonnement; *Av: etc:* (radio)-phare *m*, (radio)balise *f*; **boundary m.,** borne *f*, feu *m*, de balisage; balise de délimitation (d'aérodrome); **m. beacon,** (radio)phare de balisage; *Nau:* **m. buoy,** bouée *f* de balisage; (*b*) **(book) m.,** signet *m*.

market¹ [ˈmɑːkit] *n.* (*a*) marché *m*; **open-air m.,** marché en plein air; **covered m.,** halle(s) *f*(*pl*), marché couvert; **cattle, fish, m.,** marché aux bestiaux, aux poissons; **m. day,** jour *m* de marché; **m. square, place,** place *f* du marché; **m. town,** ville *f* de marché; **m. gardening,** culture maraîchère; maraîchage *m*; **m. garden,** jardin maraîcher; **m. gardener,** maraîcher, -ère; (*b*) **commodity m.,** marché des matières premières; **cotton m.,** marché du coton; (*c*) marché; débouchés *mpl* (d'un produit); **the home m.,** le marché intérieur; **foreign market,** marché extérieur; **the Common M.,** le Marché Commun; **black m.,** marché noir; **m. research,** étude *f* de marché; **buyers', sellers', m.,** marché à la baisse, à la hausse; **he put his flat on the m.,** il a mis son appartement en vente; (*of pers.*) **to be in the m. for sth.,** être acheteur de qch.; **to find a m. for sth.,** trouver un débouché, des acheteurs, pour qch.; **there's no m. for these products,** ces produits ne se vendent pas; **m. price,** prix courant; (*d*) *Fin: St.Exch:* **foreign exchange m.,** marché des changes; **stock m.,** marché des valeurs; la Bourse (des valeurs).

market² *v.tr.* **(marketed)** vendre; trouver des débouchés pour (ses marchandises); lancer (un produit). **marketing** *n.* (*a*) achat *m*, vente *f* (de qch.) au marché; (*b*) commercialisation *f*; (*c*) étude *f* des marchés; marketing *m*.

marketable [ˈmɑːkitəbl] *a.* (*of goods*) vendable.

marketeer [mɑːkiˈtiər] *n.* **black m.,** trafiquant *m* du marché noir; **(pro-)M.,** partisan, -ane, du Marché Commun.

marksman, *pl.* **-men** [ˈmɑːksmən] *n.* bon tireur; tireur d'élite.

marksmanship [ˈmɑːksmənʃip] *n.* adresse *f*, habileté *f*, au tir.

marl [mɑːl] *n. Agr:* marne *f*; **m. pit,** marnière *f*.

marlin [ˈmaːlin] *n. Ich:* poisson *m* épieu.

marline [ˈmɑːlin] *n. Nau:* lusin *m*.

marlinespike [ˈmɑːlinspaik] *n. Nau:* épissoir *m*.

marly [ˈmɑːli] *a.* (sol) marneux.

marmalade [ˈmɑːməleid] *n. Cu:* confiture *f* d'oranges.

marmoset [mɑːməˈzet] *n. Z:* ouistiti *m*, marmouset *m*.

marmot [ˈmɑːmət] *n. Z:* marmotte *f*.

maroon¹ [məˈruːn] **1.** *a. & n.* (*colour*) marron pourpré *inv*; rouge foncé *inv*. **2.** *n. Pyr:* marron *m*; fusée *f* à pétard.

maroon² *v.tr.* (*a*) abandonner (qn) dans une île déserte; (*b*) **marooned,** isolé (par des inondations).

marquee [mɑːˈkiː] *n.* grande tente.

marquess, marquis [ˈmɑːkwis] *n.* marquis *m*.

marquetry [ˈmɑːkitri] *n.* marqueterie *f*.

marram [ˈmærəm] *n. Bot:* **m. grass,** oyat *m*.

marriage [ˈmæridz] *n.* **1.** mariage *m*; union (conjugale); **proposal of m.,** demande *f* en mariage; **uncle by m.,** oncle *m* par alliance; **civil m.,** mariage civil; **m. settlement,** contrat *m* de mariage; **m. certificate,** *F:* **m. lines,** acte *m* de mariage. **2.** mariage, union (entre les choses). **3.** *Cards:* (*bezique*) mariage.

marriageable [ˈmæridʒəbl] *a.* (*a*) (fille, âge) nubile; **of m. age,** d'âge à se marier; (*b*) (fille) mariable, à marier.

marrow [ˈmærou] *n.* **1.** (*a*) moelle *f*; **to be frozen to the m.,** être transi de froid; être glacé jusqu'à la moelle; (*b*) moelle, essence *f* (de qch.). **2.** *Hort:* **vegetable m.,** courge *f*.

marrowbone [ˈmærouboun] *n.* os *m* à moelle.

marrowfat [ˈmæroufæt] *n.* **1.** graisse *f* de moelle. **2.** *Hort:* **m. (pea),** pois carré.

marry [ˈmæri] *v.tr.* (*p.t. & p.p.* **married** [mærid]) **1.** (*of priest, parent*) marier; unir (en mariage). **2.** (*a*) se marier avec (qn); épouser (qn); (*b*) *v.tr. & i.* **to m., to get married,** se marier; **to m. (for) money,** faire un mariage d'argent; **to m. again, a second time,** se remarier; *F:* **he is not the marrying kind,** il n'est pas enclin au mariage. **3.** *Nau:* marier (deux cordages). **married** *a.* (*a*) marié; **a m. couple,** un ménage; **the young, newly, m. couple,** les jeunes, nouveaux, mariés; (*b*) **m. life,** la vie conjugale; le mariage; **m. name,** nom *m* de femme mariée, de mariage.

marsh [mɑːʃ] *n.* (*a*) marais *m*, marécage *m*; **salt m.,** marais salant; (*b*) *Bot:* **m. marigold,** souci *m* d'eau; populage *m*; (*c*) **m. gas,** gaz *m* des marais.

marshal¹ [ˈmɑːʃ(ə)l] *n.* **1.** (*a*) *Mil:* **field m.** = maréchal *m* (de France); (*b*) *Mil: Av:* **M. of the R.A.F.** = Commandant *m* en Chef des Forces aériennes; **Air Chief M.** = général *m* d'armée aérienne; (*c*) **M. of the Diplomatic Corps,** Chef *m* du Protocole. **2.** (*a*) maître *m* des cérémonies; (*b*) *U.S:* fonctionnaire *m* ayant les attributions d'un shérif; (*c*) **fire m.,** chef du service d'incendie (dans une région, une usine).

marshal² *v.tr.* **(marshalled,** *NAm:* **marshaled)** (*a*) placer (des personnes) en ordre, en rang; (*b*) *Mil:* ranger (des troupes); (*c*) **to m. facts,** rassembler des faits et les mettre en ordre; (*d*) *Rail:* classer, trier, manœuvrer (des wagons); (*e*) (*of usher, footman, etc.*) introduire **(s.o. into a room,** qn dans une salle). **marshalling,** *NAm:* **marshaling** *n.* **1.** disposition *f* en ordre (de personnes, de choses). **2.** *Rail:*

classement *m*, triage *m* (des wagons); **m. yard,** gare *f* de triage.
marshland ['mɑːʃlænd] *n.* terrain marécageux; marécages *mpl.*
marshmallow [mɑːʃ'mælou] *n.* (*a*) *Bot:* guimauve *f*, althée *f*; (*b*) *Comest:* (pâte *f* de) guimauve.
marshy ['mɑːʃi] *a.* (sol, air) marécageux.
marsupial [mɑː's(j)uːpiəl] *a. & n.* marsupial (*m*).
mart [mɑːt] *n.* **1.** centre *m* de commerce; marché *m*. **2. (auction) m.,** salle *f* de vente; **car m.,** auto-marché *m*, *pl.* auto-marchés.
marten ['mɑːtin] *n. Z:* mart(r)e *f*; **beech, stone, m.,** fouine *f*; **pine m.,** martre des pins; martre commune.
martial ['mɑːʃ(ə)l] *a.* martial, -aux, guerrier; **m. law,** loi martiale; (*in a town*) **to declare m. law,** proclamer l'état *m* de siège.
Martian ['mɑːʃ(ə)n] *n.* Martien, -ienne.
martin ['maːtin] *n. Orn:* **(house) m.,** martinet *m*.
martinet ['mɑːtinet] *n. Mil: etc:* officier *m* à cheval sur la discipline; **she's a m.,** c'est un vrai gendarme.
martingale ['mɑːtiŋgeil] *n.* **1.** *Harn:* martingale *f*. **2.** *Nau:* **m. (guy, stay),** martingale du beaupré.
Martinmas ['mɑːtinmæs] *n.* la Saint-Martin.
martyr¹ ['mɑːtər] *n.* martyr *m*, *f.* martyre; **to be a m. to rheumatism,** souffrir (beaucoup) des rhumatismes; **to die a m. in, to, a cause,** mourir martyr d'une cause.
martyr² *v.tr.* martyriser (qn); **a martyred people,** un peuple martyr.
martyrdom ['mɑːtədəm] *n.* martyre *m*; supplice *m*, calvaire *m*.
martyrize ['mɑːtəraiz] *v.tr.* faire subir le martyre à qn; martyriser qn.
marvel¹ ['mɑːv(ə)l] *n.* (*a*) merveille *f*; (*b*) **to work marvels,** faire des merveilles; (*of treatment, etc.*) faire merveille; (*c*) *P:* **you're a bloody m.!** (i) tu es un as! (ii) espèce d'andouille!
marvel² *v.i.* **(marvelled,** *NAm:* **marveled)** *O:* s'émerveiller, s'étonner **(at,** de).
marvellous, *NAm:* **marvelous** ['mɑːv(ə)ləs] *a.* merveilleux, **it would be m. if . . .,** ce serait merveilleux si . . .; *Iron:* **isn't it m.!** ça c'est le bouquet, le comble! **-ly** *adv.* à merveille; merveilleusement.
Marxism ['mɑːksizm] *n. Pol.Ec:* marxisme *m*.
Marxist ['mɑːksist] *a. & n. Pol.Ec:* marxiste (*mf*).
Mary ['mɛəri] *Pr.n.f.* Marie; **M. Stuart, M. Queen of Scots,** Marie Stuart; **Bloody M.,** (i) *Hist: F:* Marie Tudor; (ii) *F:* cocktail composé de vodka et de jus de tomate.
marzipan [mɑːzi'pæn] *n. Cu:* massepain *m*, pâte *f* d'amandes.
mascara [mæs'kɑːrə] *n. Toil:* mascara *m*.
mascot ['mæskɔt] *n.* mascotte *f*; porte-bonheur *m inv*; *Aut:* **radiator m.,** enjoliveur *m* de capot.
masculine ['mæskjulin] *a.* **1.** masculin, mâle; (femme) masculine, hommasse. **2.** *Gram:* masculin; *n.* **in the m.,** au masculin.
masculinity [mæskju'liniti] *n.* masculinité *f*.
maser ['meizər] *n. Atom.Ph:* maser *m*.
mash¹ [mæʃ] *n.* **1.** *Brew:* fardeau *m* (de malt et d'eau chaude). **2.** *Husb:* mash *m* (pour chevaux); pâtée *f* (pour cochons, volaille); **bran m.,** pâtée de son. **3.** *F:* purée *f* de pommes de terre. **4.** mélange *m*; pâte *f*; bouillie *f*; **to reduce sth. to m.,** réduire (du papier, etc.) en pâte, en bouillie.
mash² *v.tr.* **1.** *Brew:* brasser, mélanger, démêler (le moût). **2. to m. (sth.) (up),** broyer, écraser (qch.); *Cu:* (en) faire une purée; **mashed potatoes,** purée de pommes de terre.
masher ['mæʃər] *n. Tchn:* (*device*) broyeur *m*, écraseur *m*, mélangeur *m*; *Dom.Ec:* **potato m.,** presse-purée *m*.
mashie, mashy ['mæʃi] *n. Golf:* mashie *m*.
mask¹ [mɑːsk] *n.* **1.** (*a*) masque *m*; (*silk or velvet*) loup *m*; **to put on a m.,** se masquer; **to throw off, drop, the m.,** lever le masque; se démasquer; **with the m. off,** à visage découvert; (*b*) **protective m.,** masque de protection; **fencing m.,** masque d'escrime; *Ind:* **welder's m.,** capot protecteur. **2.** moulage *m*, masque (d'un visage); **death m.,** masque mortuaire.
mask² *v.tr.* **1.** (se) masquer. **2.** (*a*) masquer (une batterie, un faisceau lumineux). **3.** cacher déguiser (ses sentiments, ses pensées); voiler (ses défauts, etc.). **masked** *a.* **1.** (homme, bal) masqué. **2.** *Mil:* (batterie) masquée. **3.** (sourire) caché. **masking** *n.* pose *f* d'un masque, d'un cache; *Paint:* **m. tape,** bande *f* de papier-cache.
masochism ['mæsoukizm] *n. Psy:* masochisme *m*.
masochist ['mæsoukist] *n. & a.* masochiste (*mf*).
masochistic [mæsou'kistik] *a.* masochiste.
mason ['meis(ə)n] *n.* **1.** maçon *m*. **2.** franc-maçon *m*, *pl.* francs-maçons.
masonic [mə'sɔnik] *a.* (franc-)maçonnique; des francs-maçons, de la franc-maçonnerie.
masonry ['meisənri] *n.* **1.** (*a*) maçonnerie *f*; (*b*) ouvrage *m* en pierre. **2.** franc-maçonnerie *f*.
masquerade¹ [mæskə'reid] *n.* mascarade *f*.
masquerade² *v.i.* se masquer, aller en masque, faire une mascarade; **to m. as . . .,** se déguiser en . . . .
mass¹ [mæs, mɑːs] *n.* (*a*) *Ecc:* messe *f*; **high m.,** grand-messe *f*; **low m.,** messe basse; **requiem m., m. for the dead,** messe de requiem, messe des morts; **to celebrate, say, m.,** célébrer, dire, la messe; (*b*) **black m.,** messe noire.
mass² [mæs] *n.* **1.** (*a*) masse *f*, amas *m*; **air m.,** masse d'air; (*b*) *Ch:* **molecular m.,** masse moléculaire; **atomic m.,** masse atomique, de l'atome; **m. number,** nombre *m* de masse (d'un noyau nucléaire); (*c*) *Mec:* **unit of m.,** unité *f* de masse. **2.** (*a*) foule *f*, multitude *f* (de gens); collection *f*, grande quantité (de choses, de lettres); *F:* **I've masses (of things) to do,** j'ai un tas de choses à faire; **he was a m. of bruises,** il était tout couvert de meurtrissures; **m. meeting,** réunion *f*, assemblée *f*, en masse; grand rassemblement *m*; **m. grave,** tombe collective; *Ind:* **m. production,** fabrication *f*, production *f*, en série; (*b*) **the (great) m. of the people,** la plus grande partie, la majorité, de la population; **the masses,** les masses; le grand public; **m. media,** les (mass) média *mpl*; **m. protest,** protestation *f* en masse.
mass³ [mæs] **1.** *v.tr.* masser (des troupes, etc.). **2.** *v.i.* (*of troops*) se masser; (*of clouds*) s'amonceler.
massacre¹ ['mæsəkər] *n.* massacre *m*, tuerie *f*.
massacre² *v.tr.* massacrer (des hommes, une langue); faire un massacre de (gibier).
massage¹ ['mæsɑːʒ] *n.* (*a*) massage *m*; (*b*) *Hairdr:* **(scalp) m.,** friction *f*.
massage² *v.tr.* masser (le corps).
masseur, *f.* **masseuse** [mæ'səːr, mæ'səːz] *n.* masseur, -euse.
massif ['mæsif] *n. Geog:* massif *m*.
massive ['mæsiv] *a.* (*a*) (monument, etc.) massif; (*b*) (entreprise) à grande échelle; *Pharm: etc:* **m. dose,** dose massive. **-ly** *adv.* massivement.
mass-produce [mæsprə'djuːs] *v.tr. Ind:* fabriquer en série.
mast¹ [mɑːst] *n.* **1.** (*a*) *Nau:* mât *m*; **the masts,** les mâts, la mâture; **to sail before the m.,** servir comme simple matelot; (*b*) **Venetian m.,** mât de pavoisement. **2.** *W.Tel:* pylône *m*.
mast² *v.tr. Nau:* **1.** mâter (un bâtiment). **2.** hisser haut (une vergue).
mast³ *n.* **(ground) m.,** faînes *fpl* (de hêtre); faînée *f*.
mastectomy [mæs'tektəmi] *n. Surg:* mastectomie *f*.
masted ['mɑːstid] *a. Nau:* (*a*) mâté; (*b*) **three-, four-m. ship,** navire *m* à trois, quatre, mâts.

-master ['mɑːstər] *n. Nau:* **three-, four-m.,** trois-mâts *m inv*, quatre-mâts *m inv*; navire *m* à trois, quatre, mâts.

master¹ ['mɑːstər] *n.* **1.** (*a*) maître *m*; **the m. of the house,** le maître de la maison; **to be m. in one's own house,** être maître chez soi; **to be one's own m.,** ne dépendre que de soi; **to be m. of the situation,** être maître de la situation; **to meet one's m.,** trouver son maître; (*b*) (*employer*) maître, patron *m*, chef *m*; **like m. like man,** tel maître tel valet; (*c*) (*esp. at Oxford, Cambridge*) directeur *m*, principal, -aux *m* (de certains collèges universitaires); (*d*) *Nau:* patron (d'un bateau de pêche); capitaine *m*, commandant *m* (d'un navire marchand); (*e*) *Ven:* **M. of foxhounds,** maître d'équipage; grand veneur; **m. of ceremonies,** maître des cérémonies; *Th:* **chorus m.,** répétiteur *m*; (*f*) (*freemasonry*) vénérable *m*. **2.** *Sch:* (*a*) (*primary*) maître; instituteur *m*; (*secondary*) professeur *m*; **form m.,** professeur principal (d'une classe); **French m.,** professeur de français; (*b*) **fencing, dancing, m.,** maître d'escrime, de danse; (*c*) **M. of Arts, of Science** = maître ès lettres, ès sciences. **3. to be a m. of one's art,** posséder son art en maître; *Art:* **old m.,** (i) maître; (ii) tableau *m* de maître. **4.** (*as title*) (*a*) *O:* (*form of address to small boys*) (i) **M. David Thomas,** Monsieur David Thomas; (ii) (*said by servant*) **M. David,** Monsieur David; (*b*) *Scot:* titre *m* de l'héritier d'une pairie au-dessous du rang de *earl*. **5.** (*a*) **m. carpenter, m. mason,** maître charpentier, maître maçon; **m. mariner,** capitaine au long cours; capitaine marchand; (*b*) **it is the work of a m. hand,** c'est fait de main de maître; **m. stroke,** coup *m* de maître; (*c*) *Cards:* **m. card,** carte maîtresse; (*d*) principal, -aux; **m. plan,** plan d'ensemble détaillé; **m. key,** passe-partout *m inv*; **m. race,** race supérieure; **m. gauge,** (i) *Mec.E:* calibre *m* mère, d'ensemble; (ii) *Rail:* gabarit *m* passe-partout; *El:* **m. switch,** commutateur, disjoncteur, principal; *Cmptr:* **m. file,** fichier permanent, maître; *Rec:* **m. record,** (disque) original (*m*); **m. tape,** bande *f* mère.

master² *v.tr.* **1.** dompter, maîtriser (qn); se rendre maître, maîtresse, de (qn); vaincre (un cheval). **2.** maîtriser, dompter (ses passions); surmonter (une difficulté, sa colère); apprendre (un sujet) à fond; **to have mastered a subject,** posséder un sujet à fond.

masterful ['mɑːstəf(u)l] *a.* (*of pers., manner, etc.*) impérieux, dominateur, -trice, autoritaire. **-fully** *adv.* impérieusement, avec autorité.

masterly ['mɑːstəli] *a.* de maître; magistral, -aux; **m. stroke,** coup *m* de maître; **m. work,** œuvre magistrale; **in a m. manner,** de main de maître.

mastermind¹ ['mɑːstəmaind] *n.* (*a*) esprit supérieur, magistral; (*b*) cerveau *m* (d'une entreprise, etc.).

mastermind² *v.tr.* diriger (un projet, etc.); tramer (un complot, etc.).

masterpiece ['mɑːstəpiːs] *n.* chef-d'œuvre *m*, *pl.* chefs-d'œuvre.

masterstroke ['mɑːstəstrouk] *n.* coup *m* de maître.

mastery ['mɑːst(ə)ri] *n.* **1.** maîtrise *f* (**of,** de); autorité *f*, domination *f* (**over,** sur). **2.** connaissance approfondie (d'un sujet).

masthead ['mɑːsthed] *n. Nau:* tête *f*, ton *m*, de mât; haut *m* du mât; **m. light,** feu *m* de tête de mât.

mastic ['mæstik] *n.* **1.** (*resin*) mastic *m*. **2.** (*cement*) mastic.

masticate ['mæstikeit] *v.tr.* **1.** mâcher, mastiquer (un aliment). **2.** *Ind:* triturer (le caoutchouc, etc.); malaxer.

mastiff ['mæstif] *n.* mâtin *m*; mastiff *m*.

mastitis [mæs'taitis] *n. Med:* mastite *f*.

mastodon ['mæstoudɔn] *n. Paleont:* mastodonte *m*.

mastoid ['mæstɔid] *a.* & *n. Anat:* **m. (process),** (apophyse *f*) mastoïde (*f*); *Med: F:* **mastoids,** mastoïdite *f*.

masturbate ['mæstəbeit] *v.i.* & *tr.* (se) masturber.

masturbation [mæstə'beiʃ(ə)n] *n.* masturbation *f*.

mat¹ [mæt] *n.* **1.** (*a*) natte *f* (de paille, de jonc); (*b*) (petit) tapis, carpette *f* (de laine, etc.); **prayer m.,** tapis à prière; (*c*) (*at entrance door*) paillasson *m*; essuie-pieds *m inv*; *F:* **to be on the m.,** être sur la sellette; (*d*) **table m.,** (i) dessous *m* de plat; (ii) (*also* **place m.**), rond *m* de table; (*e*) *Wr:* tapis. **2.** *Nau:* paillet *m*, sangle *f*, baderne *f*; **chafing m.,** paillet de portage.

mat² *v.* **(matted) 1.** *v.tr.* emmêler (les cheveux, etc.). **2.** *v.i.* (*of hair, fibres, etc.*) s'emmêler, se coller ensemble. **matted** *a.* (*of cloth, etc.*) feutré; **m. hair,** cheveux emmêlés, entremêlés. **matting** *n.* **1.** (*a*) enchevêtrement *m*, emmêlement *m* (de fils, etc.); (*b*) tressage *m* (de la paille). **2.** natte(s) *f* (*pl*), paillassons *mpl*.

mat³ 1. *a.* (*of colour, surface*) mat; *Phot:* **m. paper,** papier mat; **m. varnish,** (vernis *m*) mattolin (*m*). **2.** *n.* (*for gilding*) mat *m*, dorure mate.

mat⁴ *v.tr.* **(matted)** *Tchn:* matir (la dorure); mater (le cuivre, etc.); dépolir (le verre).

matador ['mætədɔːr] *n.* matador *m*.

match¹ [mætʃ] *n.* **1.** (*a*) (*of pers.*) égal, -ale, -aux; pareil, -eille; **to meet more than one's m.,** trouver, s'attaquer à, plus fort que soi; **to be more than a m. for s.o.,** (i) être trop fort pour qn; (ii) circonvenir qn; (*b*) (*of thgs*) **to be a bad, good, m.,** aller mal, bien, ensemble; **perfect m. of colours,** assortiment parfait de couleurs. **2.** *Sp:* lutte *f*, partie *f*, match *m*; **tennis m.,** partie de tennis; **football m.,** match de football; **to win the m.,** gagner la partie; **m. point,** balle *f* de match; **m. play,** (i) *Ten:* jeu *m* de match; (ii) *Golf:* partie *f* par trous. **3.** (*a*) mariage *m*; alliance *f*; **good m.,** beau mariage; (*b*) **he's a good m.,** c'est un bon, un excellent, parti.

match² 1. *v.tr.* (*a*) égaler (qn); être l'égal de (qn); rivaliser avec (qn); **evenly matched,** de force égale; **there's nobody to m. him,** il n'a pas son pareil; (*b*) **to m. s.o. against s.o.,** opposer qn à qn; *Sp:* **to m. opponents,** matcher des adversaires; (*c*) apparier (des gants, des bas); rappareiller (un service à thé, etc.); assortir, allier (des couleurs); **a well matched couple,** un couple bien assorti; **I need a new hat to m. my suit,** j'ai besoin d'un nouveau chapeau qui aille avec mon tailleur; (*d*) *Carp:* bouveter, embrever (des planches). **2.** *v.i.* s'assortir; s'harmoniser; **paper and envelopes to m.,** papier et enveloppes assortis. **matching 1.** *a.* (couleurs) assorties; **these pictures are a m. pair,** ces tableaux font pendant. **2.** *n.* assortiment *m* (de couleurs); appariement *m* (d'objets).

match³ *n.* **1.** allumette *f*; **safety m.,** allumette de sûreté; **box of matches,** boîte *f* d'allumettes; **to strike a m.,** frotter une allumette. **2.** *Min:* canette *f*, raquette *f*; **slow m.,** corde *f* à feu.

matchbox ['mætʃbɔks] *n.* boîte *f* à allumettes.

matchless ['mætʃlis] *a.* incomparable; sans égal, sans pareil.

matchmaker ['mætʃmeikər] *n.* faiseur, -euse, de mariages; marieur, -euse.

matchstick ['mætʃstik] *n.* allumette *f*.

matchwood ['mætʃwud] *n.* bois *m* d'allumettes; **smashed, reduced, to m.,** réduit en miettes.

mate¹ [meit] *n. Chess:* mat *m*.

mate² *v.tr. Chess:* mettre (le roi) échec et mat; mater.

mate³ *n.* **1.** camarade *mf*, compagnon, *f.* compagne; *F:* copain, *f.* copine; **(workman's) m.,** aide *mf*; *F:* **hi, m.!** dis donc, mon vieux! **2.** (*a*) (*one of a pair*) (*of pers., animals*) compagnon, compagne; (*of animals*) mâle *m* ou femelle *f*; (*b*) *Sp:* **team m.,**

coéquipier *m*. **3.** *Nau:* (*a*) (*on merchant vessel*) officier *m*; **first m., chief m.,** second *m*; **second m.,** lieutenant *m*; (*b*) *Navy:* second maître. **4.** *esp. U.S: Mec.E:* pièce *f* qui s'accouple (avec une autre), qui s'emboîte (dans une autre).

mate⁴ 1. *v.tr.* (*a*) *O:* marier, unir (**s.o. with s.o.,** qn à qn); (*b*) accoupler (des oiseaux, des animaux); (*c*) *Tchn: Mec.E:* assembler, réunir (des éléments). **2.** *v.i.* (*a*) (*of birds*) s'accoupler; (*b*) *Mec.E: etc:* (*of parts*) correspondre (**to,** à); s'accoupler (**to,** à); s'emboîter (**to,** dans). **mating** *n.* **1.** accouplement *m* (d'oiseaux); **the m. season,** la saison des amours; (*of domestic animals*) la monte. **2.** *Tchn:* accouplement *m*, raccordement *m*; (*of gears*) conjugaison *f*.

mater [ˈmeitər] *n.* **1.** *Anat:* **dura m.,** dure-mère *f*. **2.** *F: O:* **the m.,** ma mère; maman.

material [məˈtiəriəl] **I.** *a.* **1.** (*a*) *Phil: Ph: Theol:* matériel; (*b*) (*of point of view, etc.*) matériel, matérialiste; (*c*) (*of comfort, interests*) matériel; **to have enough for one's m. comfort, needs,** avoir de quoi vivre matériellement. **2.** (*a*) important, essentiel (**to,** pour); **m. witnesses,** témoins essentiels; (*b*) (fait, témoignage) pertinent. **II.** *n.* **1.** (*a*) matière *f*; matériau, -aux *m*; **raw material(s),** matière(s) première(s); *El:* **insulating m.,** matière isolante; isolant *m*; **building materials,** matériaux de construction; (*b*) **the m. for a play,** le matériau d'une pièce; **he was collecting m. for a book on China,** il se documentait pour écrire un livre sur la Chine. **2.** (*a*) **war m.,** matériel de guerre; (*b*) **photographic materials,** fournitures *fpl*, accessoires *mpl*, pour la photographie; **writing materials,** tout ce qu'il faut pour écrire; **artists' materials,** matériel de l'artiste. **3.** (*a*) *Tex:* tissu *m*; étoffe *f*; **dress m.,** tissu pour robes; **customers' own m. made up,** on travaille à façon; (*b*) **glass is a brittle m.,** le verre est un matériau cassant. **materially** *adv.* **1.** matériellement, essentiellement. **2.** sensiblement; d'une manière appréciable.

materialism [məˈtiəriəlizm] *n. Phil:* matérialisme *m*.

materialist [məˈtiəriəlist] *a. & n.* matérialiste (*mf*).

materialistic [mətiəriəˈlistik] *a.* **1.** matérialiste. **2.** (*of pleasures, mind, etc.*) matériel.

materialize [məˈtiəriəlaiz] **1.** *v.tr.* (*a*) matérialiser (l'âme, qn); (*b*) *Psychics:* donner une forme matérielle à (un esprit). **2.** *v.i.* (*a*) (*of psychic ectoplasm*) se matérialiser; (*b*) (*of occurrence*) se réaliser, s'actualiser; (*of plans*) aboutir; se réaliser.

maternal [məˈtəːn(ə)l] *a.* maternel. **-ally** *adv.* maternellement.

maternity [məˈtəːniti] *n.* maternité *f*; **m. hospital,** maternité; clinique *f* d'accouchement; **m. ward,** salle *f* des accouchées; **m. dress,** robe *f* de grossesse; **m. benefit,** allocation *f* de maternité.

matey [ˈmeiti] *a. F:* copain-copain; **to be m.,** être à tu et à toi; être copains.

math [mæθ] *n. NAm: F:* = MATHS.

mathematical [mæθiˈmætik(ə)l] *a.* **1.** (science, calcul) mathématique. **2.** (connaissance) des mathématiques; (connaissances) en mathématiques; **he's a m. genius,** c'est un mathématicien de génie. **-ally** *adv.* mathématiquement.

mathematician [mæθiməˈtiʃ(ə)n] *n.* mathématicien, -ienne.

mathematics [mæθiˈmætiks] *n.pl.* (*usu. with sg. const.*) mathématiques *fpl*; **pure, applied, m.,** mathématiques pures, appliquées.

maths [mæθs] *n.pl. F:* math(s) *f*(*pl*).

matinée [ˈmætinei] *n.* (*a*) *Th:* (représentation *f* en) matinée (*f*); (*b*) **m. coat,** veste *f* (de bébé).

matiness [ˈmeitinis] *n. F:* camaraderie *f*.

matins [ˈmætinz] *n.pl.* (*a*) *R.C.Ch:* matines *fpl*; (*b*) *Ch. of Eng:* office *m* du matin.

matriarch [ˈmeitriɑːk] *n.f.* femme qui exerce une autorité matriarcale.

matriarchal [ˈmeitriɑːk(ə)l] *a.* matriarcal, -aux.

matric [məˈtrik] *n. F: A:* = MATRICULATION 2.

matricide¹ [ˈmeitrisaid] *n.* (*pers.*) matricide *mf*.

matricide² *n.* (crime *m* de) matricide *m*.

matriculate [məˈtrikjuleit] **1.** *v.tr.* immatriculer (un étudiant). **2.** *v.i. A:* passer l'examen d'entrée à l'université (et prendre ses inscriptions).

matriculation [mətrikjuˈleiʃ(ə)n] *n. Sch:* **1.** immatriculation *f*, inscription *f* (comme étudiant). **2.** *A:* examen *m* de fin d'études (qui admet à l'université).

matrimonial [matriˈmouniəl] *a.* matrimonial, -aux.

matrimony [ˈmætriməni] *n.* **1.** mariage *m*; *Ecc:* **joined in holy m.,** unis par les saints nœuds du mariage. **2.** *Cards:* mariage.

matrix, *pl.* **-ixes, -ices** [ˈmeitriks, ˈmeitriksiz, ˈmeitrisiːz] *n.* **1.** *Anat:* matrice *f*, utérus *m*. **2.** *Geol: Miner:* matrice, gangue *f*, gaine *f*. **3.** *Metall: Typ: etc:* matrice, moule *m*; *Art: Cer:* mère *f* (de moulages en plâtre, etc.). **4.** *Mth: etc:* matrice.

matron [ˈmeitrən] *n.f.* **1.** matrone; mère de famille; femme d'un certain âge; **m. of honour,** dame d'honneur. **2.** (*a*) intendante (d'une institution); (*b*) infirmière en chef (d'un hôpital); (*c*) intendante (d'un pensionnat).

matronly [ˈmeitrənli] *a.* matronal, -aux; de matrone.

matt [mæt] *a. & n.* = MAT³.

matter¹ [ˈmætər] *n.* **1.** matière *f*; substance *f*; (*a*) *Phil: etc:* **form and m.,** la forme et la matière; (*b*) **organic, inorganic, m.,** matière organique, inorganique; **vegetable m.,** matières végétales; *Anat:* **grey m.,** matière grise; *F:* **to have plenty of grey m.,** être très intelligent. **2.** *Med:* matière (purulente); pus *m*. **3.** (*a*) **(subject) m.,** matière, sujet *m* (d'un discours, d'un livre, etc.); **reading m.,** livres *mpl*, choses *fpl* à lire; **it is a m. for regret,** c'est à regretter; **it's no laughing m.,** il n'y a pas de quoi rire; (*b*) *Typ:* matière, copie *f*; (*c*) *Adm:* **printed m.,** imprimé *m*. **4. no m.!** n'importe! **no m. what he does, says,** quoi qu'il fasse, dise; **no m. how, when,** de n'importe quelle manière, à n'importe quel moment. **5.** affaire *f*; chose *f*; cas *m*; **let's come back to the m. in hand,** revenons à nos moutons; **it's an easy, no easy, m.,** c'est, ce n'est pas, facile; **it's no great m.,** ce n'est pas grand-chose; **that's quite another m.,** cela c'est tout autre chose; **as matters stand,** au point où en sont les choses; **money matters,** affaires d'argent; **business matters,** affaires; **in matters of religion,** en ce qui concerne la religion; **a m. of taste, of opinion,** une affaire, une question, de goût, d'opinion; **it's simply a m. of time,** c'est une simple question de temps; **it's just a m. of £100,** c'est une affaire de £100; **within a m. of hours,** en, au bout de, quelques heures; **for that m.,** quant à cela; **as a m. of fact,** (i) en réalité, à vrai dire; (ii) aussi bien; **what's the m.?** qu'est-ce qu'il y a? qu'y a-t-il? **what's the m. with you?** qu'est-ce que vous avez? qu'avez-vous? **there's something the m.,** il y a quelque chose; **I don't know what's the m. with me,** je ne sais pas ce que j'ai; **there's something the m. with his throat,** il a quelque chose à la gorge.

matter² *v.i.* importer (**to s.o.,** à qn); avoir de l'importance; **what really matters is that . . .,** ce qui est vraiment important, c'est que . . .; **it doesn't m.,** ce n'est pas important; cela ne fait rien; peu importe; **it doesn't m. a bit,** cela n'a pas la moindre importance; **what does it m. to you?** qu'est-ce que cela vous fait? **nothing else matters,** tout le reste n'est rien.

Matterhorn (the) [ðəˈmætəhɔːn] *Pr.n. Geog:* le (Mont) Cervin.

matter-of-fact [ˈmætərəvˈfækt] *a.* (*of pers., manner, statement, etc.*) pratique; terre-à-terre; prosaïque.

Matthew ['mæθju:] *Pr.n.m.* Mat(t)hieu.
mattins ['mætinz] *n.pl.* = MATINS.
mattock ['mætək] *n. Tls: Agr:* hoyau *m*; pioche *f*.
mattress ['mætris] *n.* matelas *m*; **inflatable, air, m.,** matelas pneumatique, de camping.
maturation [mætju'reiʃ(ə)n] *n.* maturation *f* (d'un fruit, d'un abcès, etc.); développement *m* (de l'intelligence, etc.).
mature¹ [mə'tjuər] *a.* **1.** (*of fruit, intelligence, person, etc.*) mûr; **of m. years,** (personne) d'âge mûr; **after m. consideration,** après mûre réflexion. **2.** *Fin:* (papier) échu. **-ly** *adv.* mûrement.
mature² **1.** *v.tr.* (*a*) mûrir (une plante); vieillir, affiner (le vin, le fromage); (*b*) **his plans were not yet matured,** ses projets n'étaient pas encore mûris, mûrs. **2.** *v.i.* (*a*) (*of plant, wine, etc.*) mûrir; (*b*) **to let a plan m.,** laisser mûrir un projet; (*c*) *Fin:* (*of bill*) échoir; arriver à échéance.
maturity [mə'tjuəriti] *n.* **1.** maturité *f* (d'un fruit, etc.); maturité (du vin); **to come to m.,** arriver à maturité; **the years of m.,** l'âge mûr (de qn). **2.** *Fin: Com:* **(date of) m.,** échéance *f* (d'une traite, d'un billet); **payable at m.,** payable à l'échéance.
maudlin ['mɔ:dlin] *a.* **1.** larmoyant, pleurard; **m. sentimentality,** sentimentalité larmoyante. **2.** dans un état d'ivresse larmoyante.
maul¹ [mɔ:l] *n. Tls:* maillet *m*, mailloche *f*.
maul² *v.tr.* (*a*) meurtrir, malmener (qn); **to be mauled by a tiger,** être mutilé, lacéré, par un tigre; **to m. s.o. about,** tirer qn de ci de là; tripatouiller (une femme); (*b*) éreinter (un auteur, une œuvre).
maunder ['mɔ:ndər] *v.i.* **1. to m. (along),** flâner, baguenauder. **2. to m. (on),** radoter.
maundy ['mɔ:ndi] *n.* **1.** *Ecc:* **M. Thursday,** le jeudi saint. **2. m. money,** pièces frappées pour les largesses du jeudi saint.
Mauritania [mɔri'teiniə] *Pr.n. Geog:* Mauritanie *f*.
Mauritian [mə'riʃ(ə)n] **1.** *a. Geog:* mauricien. **2.** *n.* Mauricien, -ienne.
Mauritius [mə'riʃəs] *Pr.n. Geog:* l'île *f* Maurice.
mausoleum [mɔ:sə'li:əm] *n.* mausolée *m*.
mauve [mouv] *a. & n.* (*colour*) mauve (*m*).
maverick ['mævərik] *n.* **1.** *NAm:* bouvillon *m* errant sans marque de propriétaire. **2.** *esp. U.S:* nonconformiste *mf*; politicien réfractaire, indépendant.
maw [mɔ:] *n.* **1.** (*a*) *Z:* quatrième poche *f* de l'estomac (d'un ruminant); (*b*) jabot *m* (d'oiseau); (*c*) *F:* estomac *m*, panse *f*. **2.** gueule *f* (du lion, du brochet).
mawkish ['mɔ:kiʃ] *a.* (*a*) fade, insipide; (*b*) d'une sensiblerie outrée.
mawkishness ['mɔ:kiʃnis] *n.* (*a*) fadeur *f*, insipidité *f*; (*b*) sensiblerie *f*; fausse sentimentalité.
maxi ['mæksi] *a. & n. Cost: F:* (jupe, manteau) maxi (*m or f*).
maxim ['mæksim] *n.* maxime *f*, dicton *m*.
maximize ['mæksimaiz] *v.tr.* maximaliser, maximiser; porter (qch.) au maximum.
maximum, *pl.* **-a** ['mæksiməm, -ə] **1.** *n.* maximum *m*, *pl.* -ums, -a; **to the m.,** au maximum; **to reach one's m.,** plafonner. **2.** *a.* maximum; *occ.* maximal, -aux; **m. efficiency,** maximum de rendement; **m. load,** charge *f* limite; **m. temperatures,** températures maximales.
may¹ [mei] *v.aux.* (*3rd pers. sing.* **he may;** *p.t.* **might** [mait]; *no pres. or past participle*) **1.** (*expressing possibility*) (*a*) **he m. return at any moment,** il peut revenir d'un moment à l'autre; **he m. not be hungry,** il n'a peut-être pas faim; **that m. or m. not be true,** cela est peut-être vrai ou peut-être pas; **he m. have lost it,** il a dû le perdre; peut-être qu'il l'a perdu; **he refused, as well he might,** rien d'étonnant à ce qu'il ait refusé; (*b*) **she might be thirty,** elle aurait peut-être trente ans; **and who might you be?** qui êtes-vous, sans indiscrétion? **and what might *you* be doing here?** peut-on savoir ce que vous faites là? **I wonder what I m. have done to offend him,** je me demande ce que j'ai bien pu faire pour le fâcher; (*c*) **it m., might, be that . . .,** il se peut, se pourrait, bien que + *sub.*; **be that as it m.,** quoi qu'il en soit; **that's as m. be,** c'est selon; **whatever faults he m. have he is never dull,** quels que soient ses défauts, il n'est jamais ennuyeux; (*d*) **he might have arrived in time if . . .,** il aurait pu arriver à temps si . . .; **you m. see him if you stay another hour,** vous le verrez peut-être si vous y restez encore une heure; **we m., might, as well stay where we are,** autant vaut rester où nous sommes; (*e*) **you might shut the door!** vous pourriez bien fermer la porte! **all the same, you might have made less noise,** tout de même vous auriez (bien) pu faire moins de bruit. **2.** (*asking or giving permission*) **m. I?** vous permettez? **m. I come in?** puis-je entrer? **you m. go,** (i) vous pouvez partir; (ii) (*at end of interview*) vous pouvez disposer; **if I m. be allowed to express an opinion,** si vous me permettez d'exprimer mon avis; **if I m. say so,** si j'ose dire. **3.** (*in clauses expressing purpose, fear, etc.*) **I only hope it m. last!** pourvu que cela, ça, dure! **I was afraid he might have done it,** j'avais peur qu'il ne l'eût fait. **4.** (*expressing a wish*) **m. he rest in peace!** qu'il repose en paix! **much good m. it do you!** grand bien vous fasse!
May² *n.* **1.** mai *m*; **in (the month of) M.,** en mai; au mois de mai; **(on) the first, the seventh, of M.,** le premier, le sept, mai; **M. queen,** reine *f* du premier mai. **2.** (*a*) *Bot:* **m. (tree),** aubépine *f*; (*b*) *Ent:* **M. bug, beetle,** hanneton *m*. **3.** *Sch:* (*Cambridge*) **M. week,** la semaine des courses à aviron (fin mai).
maybe ['meibi:] *adv.* peut-être; **m. yes, m. no,** peut-être bien que oui, peut-être bien que non.
Mayday ['meidei] **1.** *n.* (*also* **May Day**) le premier mai. **2.** *int.* (*signal of distress*) mayday!
mayfly ['meiflai] *n. Ent:* éphémère *m* vulgaire.
mayhem ['meihem] *n. Jur: A. & NAm:* (*a*) mutilation *f*; action *f* d'estropier qn; (*b*) *NAm:* **to commit m. on s.o.,** se livrer à des voies de fait contre qn.
mayonnaise [meiə'neiz, 'meiəniz] *n. Cu:* mayonnaise *f*.
mayor ['mɛər] *n.m.* maire.
mayoress ['mɛəres] *n.f.* femme du maire.
maypole ['meipoul] *n.* **1.** mai *m*. **2.** *F:* (*tall man*) échalas *m*; (*tall woman*) grande perche.
maze [meiz] *n.* labyrinthe *m*; dédale *m* (de rues, etc.).
me [*unstressed* mi, *stressed* mi:] *pers. pron., objective case.* **1.** (*unstressed*) (*a*) me, (*before vowel sound*) m'; **he told me so,** il me l'a dit; **listen to me,** écoutez-moi; **lend it (to) me,** prêtez-le-moi; **he wrote me a letter,** il m'a écrit une lettre; (*b*) (*refl.*) moi; **I'll take it with me,** je le prendrai avec moi. **2.** (*stressed*) moi; **you and me,** vous et moi; **he was thinking of me,** il pensait à moi; **that's for me,** ça c'est pour moi. **3.** (*complement of verb* **to be**) **it's me!** c'est moi! **he's younger than me,** il est plus jeune que moi. **4.** (*in int.*) **dear me!** mon Dieu!
mead [mi:d] *n.* hydromel *m*.
meadow ['medou] *n.* (*a*) pré *m*; prairie *f*; **m. grass,** pâturin *m*, herbe *f* des prés; (*b*) *Bot:* **m. saffron,** colchique *m* d'automne; safran *m* des prés; (*c*) *Orn:* **m. pipit,** pipit *m* des prés, farlouse *f*.
meadowland ['medoulænd] *n.* prairie(s) *f(pl)*.
meadowsweet ['medouswi:t] *n. Bot:* (spirée *f*) ulmaire (*f*); reine *f* des prés.
meagre, *NAm:* **meager** ['mi:gər] *a.* maigre, pauvre; peu copieux. **-ly** *adv.* maigrement; pauvrement.
meal¹ [mi:l] *n.* (*a*) farine *f* (d'avoine, de seigle, de maïs, etc.); (*b*) poudre *f* (de diverses substances).
meal² *n.* repas *m*; **light m.,** repas léger; **I've had a huge**

m., j'ai mangé comme quatre; *F:* **don't make a m. of it!** n'exagère pas!

mealtime ['mi:ltaim] *n.* heure *f* du repas.

mealworm ['mi:lwə:m] *n. Ent:* ver *m* de farine.

mealy ['mi:li] *a.* **1.** farineux; (fruit) cotonneux. **2.** saupoudré de blanc; poudreux.

mealymouthed [mi:li'mauðd] *a. F:* doucereux, mielleux, patelin; au parler onctueux.

mean¹ [mi:n] *n.* **1.** (*a*) milieu *m*; moyen terme; **the golden, happy, m.,** le juste milieu; (*b*) *Mth:* moyenne *f.* **2.** (*often with sg. const.*) **means,** moyen(s) *m(pl)*, voie(s) *f (pl)*; **to use every possible means to do sth.,** employer tous les moyens pour accomplir qch.; **there is no means of escape,** il n'y a aucun moyen de fuite; **by all means,** (i) par tous les moyens (possibles); (ii) mais certainement! mais oui! **may I come in?—by all means!** puis-je entrer?—je vous en prie; **by no means,** en aucune façon; aucunement; nullement; **she is not stupid by any means,** elle est loin d'être stupide; **by some means or other,** de manière ou d'autre; **by means of sth.,** au moyen, par le moyen, de qch.; **a means to an end,** un moyen d'arriver au but. **3. means,** moyens (de vivre); ressources *fpl*; fortune *f*; **according to our means,** selon nos moyens; **to live beyond one's means,** vivre au delà de ses moyens; **private means,** ressources personnelles; **to be without means,** être (i) sans ressources, (ii) sans fortune; *Adm:* **means test** = enquête *f* sur la situation (de fortune).

mean² *a.* moyen.

mean³ *a.* **1.** (*a*) misérable, pauvre; humble; minable; (*b*) (i) **he's no m. scholar,** c'est un grand érudit; (ii) *esp. NAm: F:* formidable; **he plays a m. guitar,** c'est un guitariste formidable; (*c*) *NAm:* **to feel m.,** se sentir mal en train. **2.** (*a*) (*of pers., character, action*) bas, méprisable, vil, mesquin; **a m. trick,** un vilain tour; *F:* un sale coup; **that's m. of him,** ce n'est pas chic de sa part; **I feel very m. about not going,** j'ai honte de ne pas y aller; (*b*) *esp. NAm:* difficile; méchant; vicieux. **3.** avare, radin; **he's very m. about tipping,** il n'aime pas donner de pourboires. **-ly** *adv.* **1.** misérablement, pauvrement. **2.** (agir, se conduire) peu loyalement, indignement. **3.** en lésinant.

mean⁴ *v.tr.* (*p.t. & p.p.* **meant** [ment]) **1.** (*purpose*) (*a*) avoir l'intention (**to do sth.,** de faire qch.); se proposer (de faire qch.); **what do you m. to do?** que comptez-vous faire? **I never meant to go,** je n'ai jamais eu l'intention d'y aller; **I m. him no harm,** je ne lui veux pas de mal; **he didn't m. (to do) it,** il ne l'a pas fait exprès; **without meaning it,** sans le vouloir, sans intention; (*b*) **to m. well by s.o.,** avoir de bonnes intentions à l'égard de qn; **he means well,** il a de bonnes intentions; (*c*) **I m. to be obeyed,** j'entends qu'on m'obéisse; **I m. to succeed,** je veux réussir; **I m. to have it,** je suis résolu à l'avoir. **2.** (*a*) **I meant this book for you,** je vous destinais ce livre; **the remark was meant for you,** la remarque s'adressait à vous; (*b*) **do you m. him?** est-ce de lui que vous parlez? est-ce lui à qui vous faites allusion? **this portrait is meant to be the duke,** ce portrait est censé représenter le duc. **3.** (*a*) (*of word, phrase*) vouloir dire; signifier; **what does that word m.?** que signifie ce mot? **the name means nothing to me,** ce nom ne me dit rien; **what is meant by . . .?** que veut dire . . .? **all this means nothing,** tout cela ne rime à rien; (*b*) (*of pers.*) vouloir dire; **what do you m.?** que voulez-vous dire? **what do you m. by that?** qu'entendez-vous par là? **do you think he meant what he said?** pensez-vous qu'il l'ait dit sérieusement? **I didn't m. that,** ce n'est pas cela que je voulais dire; **you don't m. it!** vous voulez rire! vous plaisantez! **I m. it,** je parle sérieusement; **when I say *no*, I m. *no*,** quand je dis non, c'est non; (*c*) **the price means nothing to him,** le prix n'est rien pour lui; **I cannot tell you what he has meant to me,** je ne saurais vous dire tout ce qu'il a été pour moi. **meaning 1.** *a.* (*a*) (*with adv. prefixed*) **well m.,** bien intentionné; (*b*) (regard) significatif; (sourire) d'intelligence. **2.** *n.* (*a*) signification *f*, sens *m*, acception *f* (d'un mot, etc.); **what is the m. of this word?** que signifie, que veut dire, ce mot? **figurative m. of a word,** acception figurée d'un mot; (*expressing indignation*) **what's the m. of this?** qu'est-ce que cela signifie? (*b*) **to understand s.o.'s m.,** comprendre ce que qn veut dire; (*c*) **look full of m.,** regard significatif.

meander¹ [mi'ændər] *n. Geog:* méandre *m* (d'un cours d'eau).

meander² *v.i.* **1.** (*of river*) serpenter, se replier; **the river meanders through the plain,** la rivière fait des méandres à travers la plaine. **2.** (*of pers.*) errer çà et là; errer à l'aventure. **meandering** *a.* **1.** (rivière) qui fait des méandres. **2.** (discours, etc.) sans plan, sans suite.

meanie ['mi:ni] *n. F:* (*a*) rapiat, -ate; pingre *mf*; (*b*) **what a m.!** quel chameau! qu'il est vache!

meaningful ['mi:niŋf(u)l] *a.* (*a*) plein de sens; (*b*) significatif; *esp. Pol:* **m. talks,** conversations constructives.

meaningless ['mi:niŋlis] *a.* dénué, vide, de sens; qui ne signifie rien; **a m. act, remark,** un non-sens.

meanness ['mi:nnis] *n.* **1.** médiocrité *f*, pauvreté *f*, petitesse *f* (de qch.); bassesse *f*, petitesse (d'esprit). **2.** (*a*) mesquinerie *f*, avarice *f*; (*b*) vilenie *f*.

meantime, meanwhile ['mi:ntaim, -(h)wail] *n. & adv.* **in the meantime, (in the) meanwhile,** dans l'intervalle; pendant ce temps-là; en attendant.

measles ['mi:z(ə)lz] *n.pl.* (*usu. with sg. const.*) *Med:* (*a*) rougeole *f*; (*b*) **German m.,** rubéole *f*.

measly ['mi:zli] *a. F:* insignifiant, misérable; minable; **a m. present,** un petit cadeau de rien du tout.

measurable ['meʒ(ə)rəbl] *a.* mesurable; *Ch: etc:* (constituent) dosable.

measure¹ ['meʒər] *n.* **1.** (*a*) mesure *f*; **linear m., m. of length,** mesure linéaire, de longueur; **cubic m.,** mesure de volume; **liquid, dry, m.,** mesure de capacité pour les liquides, les matières sèches; **weights and measures,** poids *mpl* et mesures; (*b*) *Tail: etc:* **made to m.,** fait sur mesure(s); *Fig:* **to take s.o.'s m.,** prendre la mesure d'un homme; jauger un homme; (*c*) *Typ:* **narrow m.,** petite justification. **2.** (*instrument*) (*a*) mesure (à grains, à lait, etc.); **half m.,** demi-mesure *f*, *pl.* demi-mesures; *F:* **there are no half measures with him,** avec lui il n'y a pas de demi-mesure; (*b*) **tape m.,** mètre *m* à ruban. **3.** (*limit* (*a*) mesure, limite *f*; **he annoys me beyond m.,** il m'irrite outre mesure; (*b*) **in some m.,** dans une certaine mesure; **a m. of independence,** une certaine indépendance. **4.** (*a*) mesure, démarche *f*; **security, safety, measures,** mesures de sécurité; **to take extreme measures,** employer les grands moyens; **as a m. of economy,** par mesure d'économie; (*b*) projet *m* de loi. **5.** *Min:* **coal measures,** gisements houillers. **6.** *Pros: etc:* mesure.

measure² **1.** *v.tr.* (*a*) mesurer (une distance, le temps, etc.); métrer (un mur, etc.); arpenter (un terrain); **to m. one's length (on the ground),** s'étaler par terre; tomber tout de son long; **to m. s.o. (with one's eye),** mesurer, toiser, qn (du regard); (*b*) *Dressm: Tail:* mesurer (qn); prendre la mesure de (qn); (*c*) **to m. one's strength, oneself, with s.o.,** mesurer ses forces avec qn; se mesurer avec, contre, qn; (*d*) mesurer, peser (ses paroles). **2.** *v.i.* mesurer; **column that measures 10 metres,** colonne *f* qui mesure 10 mètres. **measured** *a.* **1.** (*of time, distance, etc.*) mesuré, déterminé; *Nau:* **m. ton,** tonneau *m* d'encombrement. **2.** (*a*) (mouvement, pas) cadencé; **m. tread,**

marche scandée; (*b*) **with m. steps,** à pas mesurés, comptés. **3.** (langage) modéré; **to speak in m. tones,** parler sur un ton modéré. **4.** *Pros:* (vers, etc.) mesuré. **measure off** *v.tr.* mesurer (du tissu, etc.). **measure out** *v.tr.* répartir (qch.); mesurer (du blé, etc.); verser (qch.) dans une mesure. **measure up** **1.** *v.tr.* mesurer (du bois). **2.** *v.i.* **to m. up to one's job,** se montrer à la hauteur de sa tâche; **to m. up to s.o., to sth.,** être à la mesure de qn, de qch. **measuring** *n.* mesurage *m* (du drap, etc.); métrage *m*; arpentage *m* (d'un terrain); *Ch: etc:* dosage *m*; mesure *f* (du temps); **m. glass,** verre gradué; **m. tape,** mètre *m* à ruban; *Surv:* **m. chain,** chaîne *f* d'arpenteur, d'arpentage.

measurement ['meʒəmənt] *n.* **1.** mesure *f*; mesurage *m*; *Const: etc:* **inside, outside, m.,** mesure dans œuvre, hors œuvre. **2.** *Nau:* (*a*) jaugeage *m* (d'un bâtiment); (*b*) cubage *m*, encombrement *m* (du fret). **3.** (*of pers.*) **bust, waist, hip, measurements,** tour *m* de poitrine, de taille, de hanches; *Tail:* **to take a customer's measurements,** mesurer un client.

meat [mi:t] *n.* **1.** viande *f*; **fresh m.,** viande fraîche; *Cu:* **cold m.,** viande froide; **luncheon m.** = pâté *m* de viande; **minced,** *NAm:* **ground, m.,** hachis *m* (de viande); viande hachée; **dog's m.,** viande pour chiens; *Ecc:* **to abstain from m.,** faire maigre; **m. diet,** régime carné, gras; **m. broth,** bouillon gras; **m. hook,** croc *m* de boucherie. **2. m. and drink,** le manger et le boire; **it was m. and drink to them,** c'était leur plus grand plaisir; *Prov:* **one man's m. is another man's poison,** ce qui guérit l'un tue l'autre.

meatball ['mi:tbɔ:l] *n. Cu:* boulette *f* (de viande).

meathead ['mi:thed] *n. U.S: F:* crétin, -ine, imbécile *mf*.

meatpacking ['mi:tpækiŋ] *n. NAm:* abattage *m* et boucherie *f*.

meaty ['mi:ti] *a.* **1.** charnu. **2.** (odeur, etc.) de viande. **3.** (livre, etc.) plein de substance.

Mecca ['mekə] *Pr.n. Geog:* la Mecque.

mechanic [mi'kænik] *n.* mécanicien *m*; **motor m.,** mécanicien garagiste.

mechanical [mi'kænik(ə)l] *a.* **1.** *Mec:* mécanique; **m. efficiency,** rendement *m* mécanique. **2.** (*a*) **m. engineering,** constructions *fpl* mécaniques; **m. failure,** panne *f* mécanique; (*b*) **m. drawing,** dessin industriel, géométrique; **he has no m. skill,** il ne peut pas manier un outil. **3.** (*a*) (*of reply, smile, etc.*) machinal, -aux; automatique; (*b*) (*of pianist, etc.*) **his playing is very m.,** il joue d'une façon très mécanique. **-ally** *adv.* **1.** mécaniquement; **m. driven,** actionné mécaniquement. **2.** machinalement; par habitude.

mechanics [mi'kæniks] *n.pl.* **1.** (*usu. with sg. const.*) la mécanique. **2.** mécanisme *m* (du corps humain, etc.).

mechanism ['mekənizm] *n.* **1.** *Phil: Psy: etc:* mécanisme *m*; **defence m.,** (i) *Psy:* mécanisme de défense; (ii) *Z: etc:* système *m* de défense. **2.** appareil *m*; dispositif *m*; mécanisme; **a delicate piece of m.,** un mécanisme délicat; **safety m.,** mécanisme de sécurité; *Artil:* **firing m.,** mécanisme de détente.

mechanization [mekənai'zeiʃ(ə)n] *n.* mécanisation *f*.

mechanize ['mekənaiz] *v.tr.* mécaniser.

Med (the) [ðə'med] *Pr.n. F:* la Méditerranée.

medal ['med(ə)l] *n.* médaille *f*; **to award a m. to s.o.,** décerner une médaille, une décoration, à qn; **the reverse of the m.,** le revers de la médaille.

medallion [me'dæliən] *n.* médaillon *m*.

medallist, *NAm:* **medalist** ['medəlist] *n.* **1.** médailleur *m*; graveur *m* en médailles. **2.** médaillé, -ée; **gold m.,** titulaire *mf* d'une médaille d'or.

meddle ['medl] *v.i.* **to m. with, in, sth.,** se mêler de qch.; **to m. in other people's affairs,** se mêler des affaires d'autrui. **meddling 1.** *a.* = MEDDLESOME. **2.** *n.* (*a*) intervention *f* (**in, with,** dans); (*b*) manigances *fpl*, menées *fpl*.

meddler ['medlər] *n.* officieux, -euse; touche-à-tout *m inv*.

meddlesome ['med(ə)lsəm] *a.* officieux; qui se mêle de tout; qui touche à tout.

media. *see* MEDIUM.

medi(a)eval [medi'i:vəl] *a.* **1.** du moyen âge; médiéval, -aux. **2.** *F:* **you're positively m.!** tu es moyenâgeux! tu vis dans le passé!

medi(a)evalist [medi'i:vəlist] *n.* médiéviste *mf*.

medial ['mi:diəl] **1.** *a.* intermédiaire (**to,** entre); (*of letter*) médial. **2.** *n. Ling:* médiale *f*. **-ally** *adv.* médialement.

median ['mi:diən] **1.** *a.* médian; *NAm: Aut:* **m. strip,** terre-plein central; *Fr.C:* médiane *f*. **2.** *n.* (*a*) *Anat:* (i) nerf médian; (ii) veine médiane; (*b*) *Mth: Stat:* médiane *f*.

mediant ['mi:diənt] *n. Mus:* médiante *f*.

mediate ['mi:dieit] **1.** *v.i.* (*a*) (*of pers.*) s'entremettre, s'interposer; agir en, servir de, médiateur (**between,** entre); (*b*) (*of thg*) former un lien, un trait d'union (entre deux choses). **2.** *v.tr.* **to m. a peace,** intervenir en qualité de médiateur pour amener la paix.

mediation [mi:di'eiʃ(ə)n] *n.* médiation *f*; intervention (amicale); entremise *f*.

mediator ['mi:dieitər] *n.* médiateur, -trice.

medic ['medik] *n. F:* (*a*) étudiant, -ante, en médecine, carabin *m*; (*b*) médecin *m*, toubib *m*.

medical ['medik(ə)l] **1.** *a.* médical, -aux; (livre, etc.) de médecine; (étudiant) en médecine; **the m. profession,** (i) le corps médical; (ii) la profession de médecin; **m. practitioner,** médecin *m*; **you need m. attention,** il faut vous faire soigner par un médecin; *Adm:* **m. officer of health** = médecin départemental; **m. examination,** examen médical; **m. record,** dossier médical. **2.** *n. F:* examen médical. **-ally** *adv.* médicalement; **to be m. examined,** subir un examen médical.

medicament [me'dikəmənt] *n.* médicament *m*.

medicate ['medikeit] *v.tr.* **1.** donner un traitement médical à, traiter (un malade). **2.** rendre (qch.) médicamenteux. **medicated** *a.* (shampooing) médical, traitant; (savon) hygiénique.

medication [medi'keiʃ(ə)n] *n.* médication *f*; emploi *m* de médicaments; *U.S:* **it's time for the patient to have his m.,** il faut donner ses médicaments au malade.

medicinal [me'disin(ə)l] *a.* médicinal, -aux; médicamenteux; **m. plants,** plantes médicamenteuses. **-ally** *adv.* médicalement, comme médicament.

medicine ['med(i)sin] *n.* **1.** la médecine; **to study, practise, m.,** étudier, exercer, la médecine. **2.** (*a*) médicament *m*, remède *m*; **to give s.o. a dose of his own m.,** rendre la pareille à qn; **to take one's m.,** avaler la pilule; supporter les conséquences (de son action); **m. chest,** (coffre *m* à) pharmacie (*f*); (*b*) *Sp:* **m. ball,** medicine-ball *m*; (*c*) (*among NAm. Indians, etc.*) (i) sorcellerie *f*, magie *f*; (ii) charme *m*; **m. man, woman,** (sorcier *m*) guérisseur (*m*); (sorcière *f*) guérisseuse (*f*).

medico ['medikou] *n. F:* (*a*) médecin *m*, toubib *m*; (*b*) étudiant, -ante, en médecine; carabin *m*.

medieval [medi'i:v(ə)l] = MEDIAEVAL.

mediocre [mi:di'oukər] *a.* médiocre.

mediocrity [mi:di'ɔkriti] *n.* **1.** médiocrité *f* (de qn, de qch.). **2.** (*pers.*) **a m.,** une médiocrité.

meditate ['mediteit] **1.** *v.tr.* méditer (un projet, une entreprise). **2.** *v.i.* (*a*) méditer (**on, upon,** sur); réfléchir (**on, upon,** sur, à); (*b*) se livrer à la méditation; méditer; se recueillir.

meditation [medi'teiʃ(ə)n] *n.* **1.** méditation *f* (**upon,**

sur); recueillement *m.* **2.** *Lit:* **Meditations,** méditations.

meditative ['meditətiv] *a.* méditatif, recueilli. **-ly** *adv.* d'un air méditatif.

Mediterranean [meditə'reiniən] *a. Geog:* méditerranéen; **the M. Sea,** *n.* **the M.,** la (mer) Méditerranée.

medium¹, *pl.* **-a, -ums** ['mi:diəm, -ə, -əmz] *n.* **1.** milieu *m*; moyen terme (**between,** entre); **happy m.,** juste milieu. **2.** (*a*) *Ph:* milieu, véhicule *m*; (*b*) **(social) m.,** milieu, atmosphère *f*, ambiance *f*; (*c*) *Biol:* culture *m*, bouillon *m* de culture. **3.** (*a*) intermédiaire *m*, entremise *f*; **through the m. of the press,** par l'intermédiaire de la presse, par voie de presse; (*b*) moyen *m* (d'expression, de communication); agent *m*, organe *m*; **advertising m.,** organe *m* de publicité; **the (mass) media,** les (mass) média *mpl*; (*c*) moyen d'expression; **sculptor whose favourite m. is marble,** sculpteur *m* qui préfère travailler le marbre. **4.** *Psychics:* médium *m.*

medium² *a.* moyen; **of m. height,** de taille moyenne; **m. sized,** de grandeur moyenne, de taille moyenne; **m. dry wine,** vin demi-sec; *W.Tel:* **m. wave,** onde moyenne.

medlar ['medlər] *n. Bot:* (*a*) nèfle *f*; (*b*) **m.(-tree),** néflier *m.*

medley ['medli] *n.* mélange *m*, confusion *f*, méli-mélo *m*, *pl.* mélis-mélos, pêle-mêle *m inv* (de personnes, d'objets); *Mus:* pot pourri; *Swim:* **400 metres m. race,** 4 × 100 mètres quatre nages.

medulla [me'dʌlə] *n.* **1.** *Bot:* médulle *f*, moelle *f.* **2.** *Anat:* moelle (d'un os, d'un poil).

meek [mi:k] *a.* doux, *f.* douce; humble, soumis; *F:* **m. and mild,** doux comme un agneau. **-ly** *adv.* avec soumission; humblement.

meekness ['mi:knis] *n.* douceur *f* de caractère; soumission *f*, humilité *f.*

meerschaum ['miəʃəm] *n.* **1.** *Miner:* écume *f* (de mer). **2. m. (pipe),** pipe *f* en écume (de mer).

meet¹ [mi:t] *a. A: & Lit:* convenable; séant; **it is m. that . . .,** il convient que . . . .

meet² *n.* (*a*) *Ven:* rendez-vous *m* de chasse; rassemblement *m* de la meute; (*b*) *esp. NAm:* réunion *f.*

meet³ *v.* (*p.t. & p.p.* **met** [met]) **I.** *v.tr.* **1.** rencontrer (qn); se rencontrer avec (qn); **to m. s.o. on the stairs,** croiser qn dans l'escalier; **to m. another car,** croiser une autre voiture. **2.** (*a*) rencontrer (l'ennemi); (*b*) affronter (la mort, un danger); parer à (un danger); faire face à (une difficulté). **3.** rejoindre, (re)trouver (qn); se rencontrer avec (qn); **to go to m. s.o.,** aller au-devant de qn; aller à la rencontre de qn; **to m. s.o. at the station,** aller chercher qn à la gare; **the bus meets the train,** il y a une correspondance entre le train et l'autobus; **I arranged to m. him at three o'clock,** j'ai pris rendez-vous avec lui pour trois heures. **4.** faire la connaissance de (qn); **I met her at the Martins',** je l'ai rencontrée chez les Martin; **m. Mr Thomas,** je vous présente M. Thomas. **5. there's more in this than meets the eye,** on ne voit pas le dessous des cartes; **a strange sound met our ears,** un bruit étrange nous a frappé l'oreille. **6. here the road meets the railway,** c'est ici que la route rejoint, croise, le chemin de fer. **7.** (*a*) **to m. s.o.,** faire des concessions à qn; (*b*) satisfaire à, parer à, répondre à, remplir (un besoin); faire face à (une demande); satisfaire à, prévoir, prévenir (une objection); **to m. s.o.'s wishes,** remplir les désirs de qn; (*c*) *Com:* faire honneur à, faire bon accueil à, accueillir (un effet, une lettre de change); honorer (un chèque); **to m. one's commitments,** remplir ses engagements; (*d*) **to m. expenses,** supporter les dépenses; subvenir aux frais. **II.** *v.i.* (*a*) (*of pers.*) se rencontrer, se voir; **they met in 1960,** ils se sont connus en 1960; **when shall we m. again?** quand nous reverrons-nous? (*b*) (*of society, assembly*) se réunir (en session); s'assembler; (*c*) (*of thgs*) se rencontrer, se réunir, se joindre; **two rivers that m.,** deux rivières *fpl* qui confluent, qui se (re)joignent; **our eyes met,** nos regards se sont croisés; **to make (both) ends m.,** joindre les deux bouts; (*d*) **to m. with sth.,** rencontrer, trouver, découvrir, qch.; **to m. with difficulties,** éprouver des difficultés; **to m. with a refusal,** essuyer un refus; **he has met with an accident,** il lui est arrivé un accident; **we met up with him in Paris,** nous l'avons rencontré à Paris. **meeting** *n.* **1.** rencontre *f* (de personnes, de routes, etc.); **m. place,** lieu *m* de réunion; rendez-vous *m*; **m. point,** point *m* de jonction; *Mth:* point de rencontre. **2.** (*a*) assemblée *f*, réunion *f*, séance *f*; **to hold a m.,** tenir une réunion; **to call a m. of the shareholders,** convoquer les actionnaires; **to open the m.,** déclarer la séance ouverte; **to address the m.,** prendre la parole; (*b*) *Sp:* réunion, meeting *m*; *Turf:* (réunion de) courses *fpl*; (*c*) *Rel:* (*of Quakers*) **to go to m.,** aller au temple; **m. house,** temple.

megacycle ['megəsaikl] *n. El.Meas:* mégacycle *m.*

megadeath ['megədeθ] *n.* mort *f* d'un million de personnes.

megahertz ['megəhə:ts] *n. El.Meas:* mégahertz *m.*

megalith ['megəliθ] *n. Prehist:* mégalithe *m.*

megalithic [megə'liθik] *a.* mégalithique.

megalomania [megəlou'meiniə] *n.* mégalomanie *f.*

megalomaniac [megəlou'meiniæk] *a. & n.* mégalomane (*mf*).

megaphone ['megəfoun] *n.* mégaphone *m.*

megaton ['megətʌn] *n. Exp:* mégatonne *f.*

megavolt ['megəvoult] *n. El.Meas:* mégavolt *m.*

megawatt ['megəwɔt] *n. El.Meas:* mégawatt *m.*

meiosis [mai'ousis] *n.* **1.** *Rh:* litote *f.* **2.** *Biol:* méiose *f.*

melancholia [melən'kouliə] *n. Med:* mélancolie *f.*

melancholic [melən'kɔlik] *a.* mélancolique.

melancholy ['melənkəli] **1.** *n.* mélancolie *f.* **2.** *a.* (*a*) (*of pers.*) atrabilaire; (*b*) (*of pers.*) mélancolique; triste; (*c*) (*of news*) triste, attristant.

melee ['melei] *n.* mêlée *f.*

mellifluous [me'lifluəs] *a.* (*of words, etc.*) mielleux, doucereux.

mellow¹ ['melou] *a.* **1.** (fruit) fondant, mûr; (vin) moelleux, velouté. **2.** (terrain) meuble. **3.** (*of voice, light, sound*) moelleux; doux, *f.* douce; (*of colour*) doux, tendre, voilé. **4.** (esprit, caractère) mûr; **to grow m.,** mûrir; s'adoucir. **5.** (*of pers.*) (*a*) jovial, -aux, enjoué; (*b*) *F:* un peu gris.

mellow² **1.** *v.tr.* (*a*) (faire) mûrir (des fruits); donner du moelleux à (un vin, une couleur, un son); (*b*) ameublir (le sol); (*c*) mûrir, adoucir (le caractère de qn). **2.** *v.i.* (*a*) (*of fruit, wine*) mûrir; prendre du velouté; (*of sound, light*) prendre du moelleux; (*b*) (*of character*) s'adoucir. **mellowing** *n.* maturation *f*; adoucissement *m.*

mellowness ['melounis] *n.* **1.** maturité *f* (des fruits); moelleux *m* (du vin, d'un tableau); velouté *m* (du vin); velouté, moelleux (de la voix); douceur *f* (du caractère). **2.** maturité, richesse *f* (du sol).

melodic [mi'lɔdik] *a. Mus:* mélodique.

melodious [mi'loudiəs] *a.* mélodieux, harmonieux. **-ly** *adv.* mélodieusement.

melodrama ['melədrɑ:mə] *n.* mélodrame *m.*

melodramatic [melədrə'mætik] *a.* mélodramatique. **-ally** *adv.* d'un air, d'une manière, mélodramatique.

melody ['melədi] *n.* **1.** mélodie *f*, air *m*, chant *m.* **2.** *Mus:* (*a*) chant *m*, thème *m*; (*b*) (*as opposed to harmony*) mélodie.

melon ['melən] *n.* **1.** melon *m*; **water m.,** pastèque *f.* **2.** *NAm: F:* gros bénéfices (à distribuer); **to carve,**

cut up, the m., distribuer les bénéfices.

melt [melt] *v.* (*p.t. & p.p.* **melted**; *p.p. adj.* **molten** [ˈmoult(ə)n]) **1.** *v.i.* (*a*) fondre; se fondre; (*of jelly*) se déprendre; (*b*) (*of pers.*) s'attendrir; fléchir; (*c*) (i) (*of solid in liquid*) fondre, se dissoudre; **pear that melts in the mouth,** poire fondante; (ii) (*of colour, etc.*) **to m. into . . .,** se fondre dans . . ., se perdre dans . . .; **to m. into thin air,** disparaître. **2.** *v.tr.* (*a*) (faire) fondre (la glace, les métaux); **melted snow,** neige fondue; (*b*) attendrir, émouvoir (qn); (*c*) (faire) fondre, (faire) dissoudre (un sel, etc.). **melt away** *v.i.* (*a*) (*of snow, etc.*) fondre complètement; (*b*) (*of clouds, vapour*) se dissiper; (*of crowd*) se disperser; disparaître; (*of anger*) s'évaporer. **melt down** *v.tr.* fondre (de la ferraille, etc). **melting 1.** *a.* (*a*) (i) (neige, cire) qui (se) fond; (neige) fondante; (ii) (*of voice, etc.*) attendri; (iii) (fruit) fondant; (*b*) (*of words, scene, etc.*) attendrissant, émouvant. **2.** *n.* (*a*) fonte *f*, fusion *f* (de la neige, des métaux); **m. point, temperature,** point *m*, température *f*, de fusion; **everything's in the m. pot,** tout est à refaire; (*b*) attendrissement *m* (des cœurs).

member [ˈmembər] *n.* **1.** (*a*) *A:* membre *m* (du corps); (*b*) *Nat.Hist:* organe *m*; **male m.,** membre (viril). **2.** (*a*) *Arch:* membre (d'une façade, etc.); *Carp:* pièce *f*, élément *m* (d'une charpente); *Mec.E:* organe (d'une machine); (*b*) *Gram: Mth:* membre. **3.** (*a*) membre (d'une famille, d'un club, etc.); adhérent, -ente (d'un parti); **he's a m. of the family,** il fait partie de la famille; **the m. countries,** les pays *mpl* membres; (*b*) **m. of Parliament,** député *m*.

membership [ˈmembəʃip] *n.* **1.** qualité *f* de membre; sociétariat *m*; adhésion *f* (à un parti); **m. card,** carte *f* de membre, d'adhérent; **to pay one's m. (fee),** payer sa cotisation. **2.** (*a*) nombre *m* des membres, effectif *m* (d'une société, etc.); **club with a m. of a thousand,** club *m* de mille membres; (*b*) **the majority of our m.,** la majorité de nos membres.

membrane [ˈmembrein] *n. Nat.Hist: etc:* membrane *f*; **mucous m.,** (membrane) muqueuse *f*.

membranous [ˈmembrənəs] *a.* membraneux.

memento, *pl.* **-oes, -os** (miˈmentou, -ouz] *n.* mémento *m*; souvenir *m*.

memo [ˈmemou] *n. F:* mémo *m*; **m. pad,** bloc-notes *m, pl.* blocs-notes.

memoir [ˈmemwɑːr] *n.* (*a*) mémoire *m*, dissertation *f* (scientifique, etc.); (*b*) notice *f* biographique; (*c*) **memoirs,** mémoires.

memorable [ˈmem(ə)rəbl] *a.* mémorable. **-ably** *adv.* mémorablement.

memorandum, *pl.* **-da, -dums** [meməˈrændəm, -də, -dəmz] *n.* **1.** mémorandum *m*; note *f*. **2.** (*a*) mémoire *m* (d'un contrat, d'une vente, etc.); sommaire *m* des articles (d'un contrat); (*b*) *Jur:* **m. of association,** charte constitutive d'une société à responsabilité limitée; acte *m* de société. **3.** *Adm:* circulaire *f*; note *f*. **4.** *Com:* bordereau *m*; **m. book,** carnet *m*, calepin *m*, agenda *m*.

memorial [miˈmɔːriəl] **1.** *a.* (*of statue, festival, etc.*) commémoratif. **2.** *n.* (*a*) monument (commémoratif); **war m.,** monument aux morts; (*b*) **memorials,** mémoires *mpl*, mémorial *m*; (*c*) *Adm:* pétition *f*, demande *f*, requête *f*.

memorize [ˈmeməraiz] *v.tr.* **1.** rappeler (qn, qch.) au souvenir. **2.** apprendre (qch.) par cœur.

memory [ˈmeməri] *n.* **1.** (*a*) mémoire *f*; **to have a good, bad, m.,** avoir (une) bonne, mauvaise, mémoire; *F:* **m. like a sieve,** mémoire de lièvre; **loss of m.,** perte *f* de mémoire; amnésie *f*; **it slipped my m.,** cela m'est sorti de la mémoire, de l'esprit; **if my m. serves me right,** si j'ai bonne mémoire; **within living m.,** de mémoire d'homme; **from m.,** (jouer, réciter, peindre, qch.) de mémoire; (*b*) *Cmptr:* mémoire. **2.** mémoire, souvenir *m* (de qn, de qch.); **childhood memories,** souvenirs d'enfance; **I have very pleasant memories of your friend,** je garde un excellent souvenir de votre ami; **to keep s.o.'s m. alive,** garder le souvenir de qn; **in m. of . . .,** en mémoire de . . .; à la mémoire de . . .; en souvenir de . . .

menace¹ [ˈmenəs] *n.* menace *f*; **there was m. in his voice,** il parlait d'un ton menaçant; *F:* **he's an awful m.,** c'est une vraie plaie.

menace² *v.tr.* menacer (qn). **menacing** *a.* menaçant; **in a m. voice,** d'une voix menaçante. **menacingly** *adv.* d'un air, d'un ton, menaçant.

menagerie [miˈnædʒəri] *n.* ménagerie *f*.

mend¹ [mend] *n.* **1.** (*in fabric, etc.*) reprise *f*, raccommodage *m*. **2.** amélioration *f*; (*of pers.*) **to be on the m.,** être en voie de guérison.

mend² **1.** *v.tr.* (*a*) raccommoder (un vêtement, etc.) repriser (des bas); rem(m)ailler (un filet); réparer (un outil, une route, etc.); **to m. invisibly,** stopper (un vêtement); (*b*) rectifier, corriger; **to m. one's ways,** changer de conduite; se corriger; (*c*) (i) réparer (une faute, un mal); *Prov:* **least said soonest mended,** moins on parle, mieux cela vaut; (ii) **it does not m. matters to . . .,** cela n'arrange pas les choses de . . .. **2.** *v.i.* (*a*) (*of invalid, health, etc.*) se remettre; (*b*) (*of pers.*) se corriger; (*c*) (i) (*of fault*) se corriger; (ii) (*of condition*) s'améliorer; (*of broken bones*) se ressouder. **mending** *n.* **1.** raccommodage *m* (de vêtements, etc.); reprisage *m* (de bas); réparation (d'un mur, d'une route, etc.); **invisible m.,** (i) stoppage *m*; (ii) rem(m)aillage *m* (de bas). **2. pile of m.,** tas *m* de vêtements à raccommoder.

mendacious [menˈdeiʃəs] *a.* menteur, -euse; mensonger.

mendacity [menˈdæsiti] *n.* **1.** penchant *m* au mensonge; habitude *f* du mensonge. **2.** fausseté *f*. **3.** mensonge.

Mendelian [menˈdiːliən] *a. Biol:* mendélien.

mendicant [ˈmendikənt] **1.** *a.* mendiant, de mendiant. **2.** *n.* mendiant, -ante.

mendicity [menˈdisiti] *n.* mendicité *f*.

menfolk [ˈmenfouk] *n.m.pl.* les hommes (de la famille).

menial [ˈmiːniəl] **1.** *a.* (*of duties, offices*) de domestique; servile; bas, *f.* basse. **2.** *n. usu. Pej:* domestique *mf*; laquais *m*.

meningitis [meninˈdʒaitis] *n. Med:* méningite *f*.

menopausal [ˈmenoupɔːz(ə)l] *a.* ménopausique; (femme) à la ménopause.

menopause [ˈmenəpɔːz] *n. Physiol:* ménopause *f*.

menses [ˈmensiːz] *n.pl. Physiol:* menstrues *fpl*.

menstrual [ˈmenstruəl] *a. Physiol:* (cycle) menstruel.

menstruate [ˈmenstrueit] *v.i. Physiol:* avoir ses menstrues, ses règles.

menstruation [menstruˈeiʃ(ə)n] *n. Physiol:* menstruation *f*.

mensuration [mensjəˈreiʃ(ə)n] *n.* **1.** mesurage *m*, mesure *f*. **2.** *Mth:* mensuration *f*.

menswear [ˈmenzwɛər] *n. Com:* vêtements *mpl* d'hommes; habillement *m* pour hommes.

mental [ˈment(ə)l] *a.* (état, âge, etc.) mental, -aux; **m. reservation,** restriction mentale; arrière-pensée *f*, *pl.* arrière-pensées; **m. arithmetic,** calcul mental, de tête; **m. deficiency,** déficience, débilité, mentale; **m. defective,** déficient, -ente; débile intellectuel(le); **m. hospital, home,** hôpital *m*, clinique *f*, psychiatrique; *F:* **he's m.,** il est fou; il déménage. **-ally** *adv.* mentalement; **m. deficient, defective,** débile.

mentality [menˈtæliti] *n.* (*a*) mentalité *f*, état mental (de qn); (*b*) **the oriental m.,** la mentalité orientale.

menthol [ˈmenθɔl] *n. Ch:* menthol *m*.

mentholated ['menθəleitid] *a. Pharm:* mentholé.

mention¹ ['menʃ(ə)n] *n.* **1.** mention *f* (de qn, de qch.); **m. was made of . . .,** on a parlé de . . .; **to make no m. of sth.,** passer qch. sous silence. **2.** *Sch: etc:* **honourable m.,** mention (honorable); accessit *m.*

mention² *v.tr.* mentionner, citer, faire mention de, parler de (qn, qch.); relever (un fait); **the sum mentioned,** la somme indiquée; **I had forgotten to m. that . . .,** j'avais oublié de vous dire que . . .; **I shall m. it to him,** je lui en toucherai un mot; **too numerous to m.,** trop nombreux pour les citer; **I have no money worth mentioning,** je n'ai presque, pour ainsi dire, pas d'argent; **as mentioned above,** comme mentionné ci-dessus; **not to m. . . .,** sans parler de . . .; **I heard my name mentioned,** j'ai entendu prononcer mon nom; **to write mentioning s.o.'s name,** écrire en se recommandant de qn; **to m. s.o. in one's will,** coucher qn sur son testament; **don't m. it!** (i) ne m'en parlez pas! n'en parlez pas! (ii) *F:* il n'y a pas de quoi!

mentor ['mentɔːr] *n.* mentor *m*, guide *m.*

menu ['menju] *n.* menu *m*; **today's m.,** carte *f* du jour.

mercantile ['məːkəntail] *a.* (*a*) mercantile; commercial, -aux, commerçant; **m. nation,** nation commerçante; **m. marine,** marine marchande; **m. law,** droit commercial; code *m* de commerce; (*b*) *Pej:* mercantile, intéressé.

mercantilism ['məːkəntilizm] *n.* mercantilisme *m.*

mercantilist ['məːkəntilist] *a.* & *n.* mercantiliste (*m*).

mercenary ['məːsin(ə)ri] **1.** *a.* (âme, esprit) mercenaire, intéressé. **2.** *n.* (*soldier*) mercenaire *m.*

mercer ['məːsər] *n. A:* marchand, -ande, de tissus.

merchandise¹ ['məːtʃəndaiz] *n.* marchandise(s) *f*(*pl*).

merchandise² *v.i.* faire du commerce, du négoce. **merchandising** *n.* marchandisage *m.*

merchant ['məːtʃənt] **1.** *n.* (*a*) négociant, -ante; commerçant, -ante; marchand, -ande, en gros; **wine m.,** négociant en vins; (*b*) *Scot:* & *NAm:* marchand, -ande, boutiquier, -ière; (*c*) *Aut: F:* **speed m.,** chauffard *m.* **2.** *a.* marchand; de commerce; **m. bank,** banque *f* d'affaires; **m. navy,** marine marchande; **m. ship, vessel,** navire marchand.

merchantman, *pl.* **-men** ['məːtʃəntmən] *n.* navire marchand, navire de commerce.

merciful ['məːsif(u)l] *a.* miséricordieux (**to,** pour); clément (**to,** envers); pitoyable. **-fully** *adv.* (*a*) miséricordieusement; (*b*) heureusement.

merciless ['məːsilis] *a.* impitoyable; sans pitié, sans merci. **-ly** *adv.* impitoyablement; sans pitié.

mercurial [məː'kjuːriəl] **1.** *a.* (*a*) (*of pers.*) vif, éveillé; à l'esprit prompt; (*b*) (*of pers.*) inconstant; d'humeur changeante. **2.** *a. Med: Pharm:* (produit) mercuriel.

Mercury ['məːkjuri] **1.** *Pr.n.m. Myth: Astr:* Mercure. **2.** *n. Ch:* **m.,** mercure *m.*

mercy ['məːsi] *n.* miséricorde *f*; grâce *f*; merci *f*; pitié *f*; (*a*) *Ecc:* **Lord have m.!** Seigneur prends pitié! (*b*) **to show m. to s.o.,** faire miséricorde à qn; **to have m. on s.o.,** avoir pitié de qn; **to be without m.,** être impitoyable, sans pitié; **to call, beg, for m.,** demander grâce; **to throw oneself on s.o.'s m.,** s'abandonner à la merci de qn; **m.!** grâce! **m. killing,** euthanasie *f*; (*c*) **at the m. of s.o., of sth.,** à la discrétion, à la merci, de qn, de qch.; *Iron:* **I leave him to your tender mercies,** je le livre, je l'abandonne, à vos soins; (*d*) **to be thankful for small mercies,** être reconnaissant des moindres bienfaits; **what a m.!** quel bonheur! quelle chance! (*e*) **works of m.,** œuvres *fpl* de charité; **m. flight,** vol *m* pour transporter (i) un malade à l'hôpital, (ii) des médicaments d'urgence, (iii) un organe (pour une greffe).

mere ['miər] *a.* simple, pur, seul; rien que . . .; **a m. coincidence,** une pure et simple coïncidence; **it was only by the merest chance that . . .,** ce n'est que par le plus grand des hasards que . . .; **I shudder at the m. thought of it,** je frissonne rien que d'y penser; **he's a m. child,** ce n'est qu'un enfant. **-ly** *adv.* simplement, seulement; purement (et simplement); **he m. smiled,** il se contenta de sourire.

meretricious [meri'triʃəs] *a* (style, etc.) factice, d'un éclat criard.

merge [məːdʒ] **1.** *v.tr.* fondre, fusionner (deux systèmes, deux classes); **to m. sth. in, into, sth.,** fondre qch. dans qch.; amalgamer qch. avec qch. **2.** *v.i.* se fondre, se perdre (**in, into,** dans); se confondre (**in, into,** avec); (*of banks, etc.*) s'amalgamer, fusionner.

merger ['məːdʒər] *n.* **1.** *Fin:* fusion *f* (de plusieurs sociétés en une seule). **2.** *Jur:* extinction *f* par consolidation, par fusion.

meridian [mə'ridiən] **1.** *n.* (*a*) méridien *m*; **Greenwich m.,** méridien de Greenwich; (*b*) *Astr:* méridien, point culminant (d'un astre). **2.** *a.* (*a*) *Astr:* (*of altitude, angle, etc.*) méridien, -enne; **m. line,** (ligne) méridienne (*f*).

meridional [mə'ridiən(ə)l] *a.* & *n.* (*a*) méridional, -ale, -aux; du sud; (*b*) du midi de la France; méridional.

meringue [mə'ræŋ] *n. Cu:* meringue *f.*

merino [mə'riːnou] *n. Husb: Tex:* mérinos *m.*

merit¹ ['merit] *n.* **1.** mérite *m*; (*a*) *Rel:* **to acquire m.,** gagner du mérite; (*b*) **according to one's merits,** (être récompensé) selon ses mérites; (*c*) *Jur:* **the merits of a case,** le bien-fondé d'une cause; **to judge a proposal on its merits,** juger une proposition au fond, en considérant ses qualités intrinsèques. **2.** valeur *f*, mérite; **in order of m.,** par ordre de mérite.

merit² *v.tr.* mériter (une récompense, une punition).

meritocracy [meri'tɔkrəsi] *n.* aristocratie *f* du mérite.

meritorious [meri'tɔːriəs] *a.* (*of pers.*) méritant; (*of deed*) méritoire; (*of conduct*) digne, méritoire. **-ly** *adv.* méritoirement.

merlin ['məːlin] *n. Orn:* (faucon *m*) émerillon (*m*).

mermaid ['məːmeid] *n. Myth:* sirène *f.*

merman, *pl.* **-men** [məːmæn, -men] *n.m. Myth:* triton *m.*

Merovingian [merou'vin(d)ʒiən] *Hist:* **1.** *a.* mérovingien. **2.** *n.* Mérovingien, -ienne.

merriment ['merimənt] *n.* gaieté *f*, réjouissance *f*, divertissement(s) *m*(*pl*), amusement(s) *m*(*pl*).

merry ['meri] *a.* (**merrier, merriest**) **1.** (*a*) joyeux, gai; jovial, -aux; **to make m.,** se divertir, s'amuser, s'égayer, se réjouir; **(a) m. Christmas!** joyeux Noël! *Prov:* **the more the merrier,** plus on est de fous, plus on rit; (*b*) *F:* éméché; un peu parti, un peu gris. **2.** *A:* & *Lit:* (*a*) **m. England,** l'aimable Angleterre; **the m. month of May,** le gentil mois de mai; (*b*) **Robin Hood and his m. men,** Robin des Bois et ses joyeux, gais, lurons. **-ily** *adv.* gaiement, joyeusement.

merry-go-round ['merigouraund] *n.* manège *m* (de chevaux *mpl* de bois); *Belg:* carrousel *m.*

merrymaking ['merimeikiŋ] *n.* (*a*) réjouissances *fpl*, divertissement *m*; (*b*) réunion joyeuse, partie *f* de plaisir.

mescalin(e) ['meskəlin] *n. Pharm:* mescaline *f.*

mesh¹ [meʃ] *n.* **1.** (*a*) maille *f* (d'un filet, d'un tamis); **wire m.,** toile *f* métallique; (*b*) *Nat.Hist:* **meshes,** réseau *m* (vasculaire, etc.); (*c*) **m. stockings,** (i) bas *mpl* filet; (ii) bas indémaillables. **2.** *Mec.E:* prise *f*, engrènement *m*, engrenage *m*; **in m.,** en prise; *Fig:* **to be caught in the meshes,** être pris dans l'engrenage.

mesh² 1. *v.tr.* (*a*) prendre (des poissons) au filet; (*b*) *Mec.E:* endenter, engrener (des roues dentées); coordonner (qch. à qch.). 2. *v.i.* se coordonner; (*of teeth of wheel*) engrener, s'engrener; être, se mettre, en prise (**with,** avec). **meshing** *n.* 1. *Mec.E: etc:* (*a*) prise *f*; engrènement *m*, endentement; (*b*) mise *f* en prise. 2. (*a*) mailles *fpl* (d'un filet); (*b*) **wire m.,** treillis *m* métallique, en fil de fer.

mesmeric [mez'merik] *a.* magnétique, hypnotique.

mesmerize ['mezməraiz] *v.tr.* hypnotiser.

meson ['mezɔn] *n. Atom.Ph:* méson *m.*

Mesopotamia [mesəpə'teimiə] *Pr.n. Geog: Hist:* Mésopotamie *f.*

mess¹ [mes] *n.* 1. (*food*) *B:* **m. of pottage** = plat *m* de lentilles. 2. saleté *f*; **to make a m. of the tablecloth,** salir la nappe; **dog's m.,** crotte *f* de chien. 3. fouillis *m*, désordre *m*; gâchis *m*; **everything's in a m.,** tout est en désordre; **what a m.!** quel désordre! (*of pers.*) **to be in a m.,** être dans le pétrin, dans de beaux draps; **to make a m. of things,** tout gâcher; *F:* **after the fight his face was a terrible m.,** après la bagarre il avait le visage tout amoché. 4. *Mil: etc:* (i) mess *m*, table *f*, *F:* popote *f* (des officiers); ordinaire *m* (des hommes); *Navy:* plat *m*; (ii) (*room*) mess (des officiers); réfectoire *m* (des hommes); *Navy:* carré *m* (des officiers); *Navy:* **m. deck,** poste *m* des matelots, d'équipage; **m. kit,** ustensiles *mpl*, matériel *m*, d'ordinaire, de campement; **m. tin,** gamelle (individuelle); **m. jacket,** spencer *m.*

mess² 1. *v.tr.* salir, souiller (qch.). 2. *v.i. Mil: etc:* (*of officers*) faire table, (*of men*) faire plat; manger en commun, faire gamelle (**with,** avec); **to m. together,** manger à la même table; *F:* faire popote ensemble. **mess about** *F:* 1. *v.tr.* (*a*) houspiller (qn); tripoter (qch.); (ii) (*also* **mess around**) déranger qn; mettre la confusion dans les projets de (qn). 2. *v.i.* (*also* **mess around**) (i) bricoler; (ii) gaspiller son temps. **mess up** *v.tr. F:* (i) salir (qch.); (ii) gâcher, bousiller (un travail).

message ['mesidʒ] *n.* 1. (*a*) message *m*; communication *f* (téléphonique, etc.); **radio m.,** message radio; **telephone m.,** message téléphoné, téléphonique; **to send a m. to s.o.,** envoyer un message à qn; **to leave a m. for s.o.,** laisser un message, un mot, pour qn; (*b*) **the King's, the Queen's, m.,** discours télévisé et radiodiffusé du roi, de la reine, le jour de Noël; (*c*) *F:* **have you got the m.?** as-tu bien compris? tu as pigé? 2. (*errand*) commission *f*, course *f*. 3. (*a*) prédiction *f*, révélation *f*, évangile *m* (d'un prophète); (*b*) message, leçon (spirituelle); enseignement *m* (d'un livre, etc.).

messenger ['mesindʒər] *n.* (*a*) messager, -ère; coursier, -ière; (*b*) *Mil:* coureur *m*, estafette *f*; **motorcycle m.,** estafette motocycliste; **m. pigeon,** pigeon voyageur; (*c*) *Adm:* courrier *m* (diplomatique); **King's, Queen's, m.** = courrier d'État; (*d*) commissionnaire *m*; **by m.,** par porteur; **m. boy,** garçon *m* de courses.

Messiah [me'saiə] *Pr.n.* Messie *m.*

messianic [mesi'ænik] *a.* messianique.

messmate ['mesmeit] *n.* commensal, -ale, -aux; camarade *m* de table; *Navy:* camarade de plat.

Messrs ['mesəz] *n.m.pl. Com: etc:* Messieurs, *abbr.* MM.

mess-up ['mesʌp] *n. F:* 1. gâchis *m.* 2. embrouillement *m*; cafouillage *m.*

messy ['mesi] *a. F:* 1. (*a*) sale, malpropre; (*b*) en désordre. 2. qui salit; salissant; **oranges are a m. fruit (to eat),** les oranges vous poissent les doigts.

mestizo, *pl.* **-os** [mes'ti:zou, -ouz] *n.m.* métis.

met [met] *a. F:* météo; **the m. office,** la météo.

metabolic [metæ'bɔlik] *a. Biol:* métabolique.

metabolism [mi'tæbəlizm] *n. Biol:* métabolisme *m.*

metabolize [mi'tæbəlaiz] *v.tr.* transformer (un tissu, etc.) par métabolisme.

metacarpal [metə'kɑ:p(ə)l] *a. & n. Anat:* métacarpien (*m*).

metal¹ ['met(ə)l] *n.* 1. (*a*) métal, -aux; **precious m.,** métal précieux; **ferrous, non-ferrous, metals,** métaux ferreux, non ferreux; **m. engraver,** graveur *m* sur métaux; **m. polish,** nettoie-métaux *m inv*; (*b*) *Metall:* métal, fonte *f*; **molten m.,** métal en fusion; **sheet m.,** métal en feuilles; tôle *f*; (*c*) **bearing, white, m.,** métal à coussinets; (*d*) **m. casing,** enveloppe *f* métallique. 2. *Glassm:* verre *m* en fusion. 3. (*a*) *Min:* pierre *f* de mine; minerai; (*b*) *Min:* roc *m*; (*c*) *Civ.E:* (matériau *m* d') empierrement (*m*); ballast *m* (de voie ferrée); **road m.,** cailloutis *m*, pierraille *f*. 4. *Typ:* caractères *mpl*, métal, plomb *m*; **old m.,** vieille matière. 5. *Rail: etc:* **the metals,** les rails *mpl.*

metal² *v.tr.* (**metalled,** *NAm:* **metaled**) 1. empierrer, ferrer, caillouter (une route); **metalled road,** route empierrée. 2. (*a*) métalliser (le bois, etc.); (*b*) doubler de métal (une carène de navire, etc.). **metalling,** *NAm:* **metaling** *n.* (*a*) empierrement *m* (d'une route); (*b*) couche *f* d'empierrement.

metallic [mi'tælik] *a.* métallique; (*a*) *Ch:* (oxyde) métallique; (*b*) *El:* (arc) métallique; **m. circuit,** circuit *m* magnétique; (*c*) *Fin:* **m. currency,** monnaie *f* de métal, monnaie métallique; (*d*) (*brilliant*) **m. lustre,** éclat *m* métallique; **a m. blue, green,** un bleu, un vert, métallique; (*f*) (*harsh*) (son, voix) métallique; (*g*) (goût) de métal.

metallurgic(al) [metə'lə:dʒik(l)] *a.* métallurgique.

metallurgy [me'tælədʒi] *n.* métallurgie *f.*

metalwork ['met(ə)lwə:k] *n.* (*a*) travail *m* des métaux; **art m.,** ferronnerie *f*, serrurerie *f*, d'art; (*b*) métal ouvré; **open m.,** grillage *m.*

metalworker ['met(ə)lwə:kər] *n.* ouvrier *m* en métaux; **art m.,** ferronnier *m*, serrurier *m*, d'art.

metamorphic [metə'mɔ:fik] *a.* 1. *Geol:* métamorphique. 2. *Nat.Hist:* métamorphosique.

metamorphose [metə'mɔ:fouz] 1. *v.tr.* métamorphoser, transformer (**to, into,** en). 2. *v.i.* se métamorphoser (**into,** en).

metamorphosis, *pl.* **-oses** [metə'mɔ:fəsis, -əsi:z] *n.* métamorphose *f.*

metaphor ['metəfər] *n.* métaphore *f*; image *f*; **mixed m.,** métaphore disparate, incohérente.

metaphoric(al) [metə'fɔrik(l)] *a.* métaphorique. **-ally** *adv.* métaphoriquement.

metaphysical [metə'fizik(ə)l] *a.* métaphysique.

metaphysics [metə'fiziks] *n.pl.* (*usu. with sg. const.*) métaphysique *f.*

metatarsal [metə'tɑ:s(ə)l] *a. & n. Anat:* métatarsien (*m*).

mete [mi:t] *v.tr. Lit:* 1. mesurer. 2. **to m. out,** assigner (des punitions); distribuer, décerner (des récompenses).

meteor ['mi:tiər] *n.* météore *m.*

meteoric [mi:ti'ɔrik] *a.* 1. météorique; **m. rise,** montée *f* rapide (de l'échelle sociale). 2. atmosphérique.

meteorite ['mi:tiərait] *n.* météorite *f*, aérolithe *m.*

meteorological [mi:tiərə'lɔdʒik(ə)l] *a.* (bureau, bulletin, etc.) météorologique.

meteorologist [mi:tiə'rɔlədʒist] *n.* météorologiste *mf*, météorologue *mf.*

meteorology [mi:tiə'rɔlədʒi] *n.* météorologie *f.*

meter¹ ['mi:tər] *n.* appareil *m* de mesure, compteur *m*; **electric m.,** compteur électrique; **flow m.,** compteur de fluide, débitmètre *m*; **gas, water, m.,** compteur à gaz, à eau; **slot m.,** compteur à paiement préalable; *Aut:* **parking m.,** parc(o)mètre *m*, *Fr.C:* compteur de stationnement; *U.S: Aut:* **m. maid,** contractuelle *f*; **exposure m.,** (i) *Ph:* photomètre *m*;

actinomètre *m*; (ii) *Phot:* posemètre *m*; *Opt:* **light m.,** luxmètre *m*; **m. reading,** lecture *f* d'un appareil de mesure; relevé *m* (de(s) compteur(s); (*pers.*) **m. reader,** releveur, -euse, de(s) compteur(s).
meter[2] *n. NAm:* = METRE[1, 2].
methane ['mi:θein] *n. Ch:* méthane *m*; formène *m*.
methinks [mi'θiŋks] *v.impers.* (*p.t.* **methought** [mi:'θɔ:t]) *A: Lit:* il me semble.
method ['meθəd] *n.* (*a*) (*research, science*) méthode *f*; (*b*) méthode, manière *f* (**of doing sth.,** de faire qch.); procédé *m* (pour faire qch.); *Adm:* **m. of payment,** modalités *fpl* de paiement; *Ind:* **production m.,** procédé(s) de fabrication, de production; (*c*) *Ind:* **methods engineer,** ingénieur *m* des méthodes; **methods engineering,** étude *f* des méthodes; (*d*) **to work without m.,** travailler sans méthode; **there's m. in his madness,** il n'est pas si fou qu'il en a l'air.
methodical [mi'θɔdik(ə)l] *a.* méthodique; (homme) d'ordre; **to be m.,** avoir l'esprit méthodique, avoir de l'ordre. **-ally** *adv.* méthodiquement; avec méthode.
Methodism ['meθədizm] *n. Rel:* méthodisme *m*.
Methodist ['meθədist] *a. & n. Rel:* méthodiste (*mf*).
methodology [meθə'dɔlədʒi], *n.* méthodologie *f*.
meths [meθs] *n. F:* alcool *m* à brûler.
Methuselah [me'θju:zələ] *Pr.n.m. B:* Mathusalem; **as old as M.,** vieux comme Hérode.
methyl ['meθil] *n. Ch:* méthyle *m*; **m. alcohol,** alcool *m* méthylique.
methylated ['meθileitid] *a.* **m. spirit,** alcool dénaturé; alcool à brûler.
methylene ['meθili:n] *n. Ch:* méthylène *m*.
meticulous [me'tikjuləs] *a.* méticuleux; minutieux. **-ly** *adv.* méticuleusement; (habillé) avec un soin méticuleux.
meticulousness [me'tikjuləsnis] *n.* méticulosité *f*; soin méticuleux.
metre[1], *NAm:* **meter[1]** ['mi:tər] *n. Pros:* mètre *m*, mesure *f*; **in m.,** en vers.
metre[2], *NAm:* **meter[2]** *n. Meas:* mètre *m*; **square, cubic, m.,** mètre carré, cube.
metric ['metrik] *a. Meas:* (système) métrique; **m. area, volume,** métrage *m*; **m. ton,** tonne *f* (métrique); *F:* **to go m.,** adopter le système métrique.
metrical ['metrik(ə)l] *a.* métrique.
metrication [metri'keiʃ(ə)n] *n.* adoption *f*, introduction *f*, utilisation *f*, du système métrique.
metrics ['metriks] *n.pl. Pros:* métrique *f*.
metronome ['metrənoum] *n. Mus:* métronome *m*.
metropolis [mi'trɔpəlis] *n.* **1.** métropole *f*, capitale *f*. **2.** *Ecc:* siège métropolitain; métropole.
metropolitan [metrə'pɔlit(ə)n] **1.** *a.* métropolitain; **the m. area,** l'ensemble des communes de la ville de Londres. **2.** *n.* (*a*) habitant, -ante, de la métropole, de la capitale; (*b*) *Ecc:* métropolitain *m*.
mettle ['metl] *n.* **1.** (*of pers.*) ardeur *f*, courage *m*, feu *m*; (*of horse*) fougue *f*; **full of m.,** (*of pers.*) courageux, plein de courage, plein d'ardeur; (*of horse*) fougueux; **to be on one's m.,** se piquer d'honneur. **2.** caractère *m*, disposition *f*, tempérament *m*; **to show one's m.,** donner sa mesure.
mettlesome ['met(ə)lsəm] *a.* (*of pers.*) ardent, vif, plein de courage; (*of horse*) fougueux.
mew[1] [mju:] *n.* miaulement *m* (du chat).
mew[2] *v.i.* (*of cat*) miauler. **mewing** *n.* miaulement *m*.
mews [mju:z] *n.* (*originally pl., now used as sg.*) **1.** écuries *fpl*. **2.** impasse *f*, ruelle *f* (sur laquelle donnaient des écuries); **m. house,** maison aménagée dans une ancienne écurie.
Mexican ['meksik(ə)n] **1.** *a. Geog:* mexicain. **2.** *n. Geog:* Mexicain, -aine.
Mexico ['meksikou] *Pr.n. Geog:* **1.** Mexique *m*. **2.** **M. (City),** Mexico *f*.
mezzanine ['me(t)zəni:n] *n.* **1.** *Arch:* **m. (floor),** mezzanine *f*, entresol *m*. **2.** *Th:* premier dessous (de la scène).
mezzo ['metsou] *Mus:* **1.** *adv.* mezzo; **m. forte,** mezzo forte. **2.** *n.* **m. soprano,** *n.* **m.,** mezzo-soprano *m*, *pl.* mezzo-sopranos, -ni.
mezzotint ['metzoutint] *n. Engr:* **1.** mezzo-tinto *m inv*; gravure *f* à la manière noire. **2.** estampe *f* à la manière noire.
mi [mi:] *n. Mus:* **1.** (*fixed*) mi *m*. **2.** (*movable*) la médiante.
miaow[1] [mi(:)'au] *n.* miaulement *m*, miaou *m* (du chat).
miaow[2] *v.i.* (*of cat*) miauler.
mica ['maikə] *n. Miner:* mica *m*.
Michael ['maikl] *Pr.n.m.* Michel.
Michaelmas ['mikəlməs] *n.* **1.** la Saint-Michel; **M. term,** *Sch:* premier trimestre (de l'année scolaire); *Jur:* session *f* de la Saint-Michel. **2.** *Bot:* **m. daisy,** marguerite *f*, aster *m*, d'automne.
Michelangelo [maikəl'æn(d)ʒəlou] *Pr.n.m. Art:* Michel-Ange.
mickey ['miki] *n. F:* **1.** **m. (finn),** boisson droguée (secrètement). **2.** **to take the m. out of s.o.,** se payer la tête de qn; faire marcher qn.
microbe ['maikroub] *n.* microbe *m*.
microbiology [maikroubai'ɔlədʒi] *n.* microbiologie *f*.
microcamera [maikrou'kæmərə] *n.* appareil *m* de microphotographie.
microcard ['maikrouka:d] *n.* microfiche *f*.
microchip ['maikroutʃip] *n. Cmptr:* puce *f*, pastille *f*.
microcosm ['maikroukɔzm] *n.* microcosme *m*.
microdot ['maikroudɔt] *n.* micropoint *m*.
microfiche ['maikroufi:ʃ] *n.* microfiche *f*.
microfilm[1] ['maikroufilm] *n.* microfilm *m*.
microfilm[2] *v.tr.* microfilmer.
microgroove ['maikrougru:v] *n.* microsillon *m*.
micromesh ['maikroumeʃ] *a. Com:* (bas) à mailles très fines.
micrometer [mai'krɔmitər] *n.* micromètre *m*.
micron ['maikrɔn] *n. Meas:* micron *m*.
micro-organism [maikrou'ɔ:gənizm] *n.* micro-organisme *m*, *pl.* micro-organismes.
microphone ['maikrəfoun] *n.* microphone *m*.
microreader ['maikrouri:dər] *n.* microliseuse *f*.
microscope ['maikrəskoup] *n.* microscope *m*; **electron m.,** microscope électronique; **to examine an object under the m.,** examiner un objet au microscope.
microscopic [maikrə'skɔpik] *a.* **1.** (animalcule, etc.) microscopique. **2.** (examen, etc.) au microscope.
microscopy [mai'krɔskəpi] *n.* microscopie *f*.
microwave ['maikrouweiv] *n. Elcs: W.Tel:* micro-onde *f*, *pl.* micro-ondes; **m. oven,** four *m* à micro-ondes.
mid [mid] *a.* (*a*) mi-, du milieu; **in m. afternoon,** au milieu de l'après-midi; **in m. ocean,** en plein océan; **in m. air,** entre ciel et terre; **from m. June to m. August,** de la mi-juin à la mi-août; **m. season,** demi-saison *f*, *pl.* demi-saisons; (*b*) médian, moyen, central.
midday ['middei, 'mid'dei] *n.* midi *m*; **m. meal,** repas *m* de midi.
midden ['mid(ə)n] *n.* (tas *m* de) fumier (*m*).
middle ['midl] **1.** *a.* du milieu; central, -aux; moyen, intermédiaire; **the m. house,** la maison du milieu; **to take a m. course,** prendre un parti moyen, un entre-deux; **man of m. age,** homme d'âge mûr; **to be past m. age,** être sur le retour; *Hist:* **the M. Ages,** le

moyen âge; **the m. class(es),** la classe moyenne; la bourgeoisie; **m.-class prejudices,** préjugés bourgeois; **m. name,** second prénom; *Ling:* **M. English,** moyen anglais; *Geog:* **(the) M. East,** le Moyen-Orient; *Anat:* **m. ear,** l'oreille moyenne; barillet *m*; **m. finger,** médius *m*, doigt *m* du milieu; doigt majeur. **2.** *n.* (*a*) milieu, centre *m*; **in the m. of . . .,** au milieu de . . .; **in the m. of the summer,** en plein été; **about the m. of August,** à la mi-août; **in the m. of the night,** en pleine nuit; **I was in the m. of reading,** j'étais en train de lire; (*b*) *F:* taille *f*, ceinture *f*; **round his m.,** autour de sa taille; **the water came up to his m.,** l'eau lui venait à mi-corps.

middle-aged [mid(ə)l'eidʒd] *a.* (*of pers.*) entre deux âges; d'un certain âge.

middleman, *pl.* **-men** ['mid(ə)lmæn, -men] *n.m.* **1.** *Com:* intermédiaire, revendeur. **2.** *Pej:* entremetteur.

middlemost ['mid(ə)lmoust] *a.* le plus au milieu; central, -aux.

middle-of-the-road ['midləvðə'roud] *a.* (*of policy*) modéré, du juste milieu.

middle-roader ['mid(əl·roudər] *n.* *U.S:* *Pol:* modéré, -ée; partisan, -ane, du juste milieu.

middleweight ['mid(ə)lweit] *a.* & *n.* *Box:* (poids *m*) moyen (*m*).

middling ['midliŋ] **1.** *a.* (*a*) (i) médiocre; (ii) passable, assez bon; *F:* **how are you?—m.,** comment allez-vous?—comme ci comme ça; (*b*) *Com:* entrefin; bon ordinaire; de qualité moyenne. **2.** *adv.* *F:* assez bien; passablement; ni bien ni mal.

middy ['midi] *n.* *F:* *Nau:* aspirant *m* (de marine), *F:* midship *m*.

midge [midʒ] *n.* *Ent:* moucheron *m*.

midget ['midʒit] *n.* **1.** nain, *f.* naine; nabot, -ote. **2.** *attrib.* minuscule, miniature.

midi ['midi] *a.* & *n.* *Cost:* *F:* (jupe) de longueur moyenne; midi (*m*).

midland ['midlənd] **1.** *a.* (plaine, etc.) du centre (d'un pays). **2.** *n.pl.* **the Midlands,** les comtés *m* du centre (de l'Angleterre).

midmorning [mid'mɔ:niŋ] *a.* **m. coffee break,** pause-café *f* au milieu de la matinée.

midnight ['midnait] *n.* minuit *m*; **on the stroke of m.,** sur le coup de minuit; **m. mass,** messe *f* de minuit; **m. sun,** soleil *m* de minuit; **to burn the m. oil,** travailler, veiller, fort avant dans la nuit.

midriff ['midrif] *n.* *Anat:* diaphragme *m*; estomac *m*; **bare m.,** ventre nu; taille nue.

midshipman, *pl.* **-men** ['midʃipmən] *n.m.* *Nau:* aspirant (de marine); *F:* midship.

midships ['midʃips] *adv.* *Nau:* au milieu du navire; par le travers.

midst [midst] *n.* (*a*) **in the m. of sth.,** au milieu de qch.; **in the m. of winter,** en plein hiver; **in the m. of all this,** sur ces entrefaites; (*b*) **in our, your, their, m.,** parmi nous, vous, eux.

midstream [mid'stri:m] *n.* **in m.,** au milieu du courant.

midsummer ['midsʌmər] *n.* (*a*) milieu *m* de l'été; cœur *m* de l'été; (*b*) solstice *m* d'été; **m. day,** la Saint-Jean.

midway [mid'wei] *adv.* à mi-chemin; **m. up the hill,** à mi-côte; **m. between . . . and . . .,** à mi-distance, à mi-chemin, entre . . . et . . .; **a style m. between X's and Y's,** un style intermédiaire entre celui de X et celui de Y.

midweek [mid'wi:k] *n.* milieu *m* de la semaine.

midwife, *pl.* **-wives** ['midwaif, -waivz] *n.f.* sage-femme, *pl.* sages-femmes; accoucheuse.

midwifery ['midwif(ə)ri] *n.* **1.** profession *f* de sage-femme. **2.** obstétrique *f*.

midwinter ['mid'wintər] *n.* (*a*) milieu *m* de l'hiver, cœur *m* de l'hiver; (*b*) solstice *m* d'hiver.

mien [mi:n] *n.* *Lit:* mine *f*, air *m*, contenance *f*, (de qn).

miff¹ [mif] *n.* *F:* *O:* pique *f*, brouille *f* (entre deux personnes).

miff² *F:* *O:* **1.** *v.i.* se brouiller (**with s.o.,** avec qn). **2.** *v.tr.* **to be miffed,** être froissé, piqué, fâché.

might¹ [mait] *n.* puissance *f*, force(s) *f* (*pl*); **with all one's m.,** (travailler, pousser, etc.) de toute sa force, de toutes ses forces; *Prov:* **m. is right,** force passe droit.

might². *see* MAY¹.

might-have-been ['maitəvbi:n] *n.* *F:* **he's a m.-h.-b.,** c'est un raté.

mighty ['maiti] **1.** *a.* (*a*) puissant, fort; **a m. nation,** une grande nation; *b*) grand, grandiose; (*c*) *F:* grand, considérable; **you're in a m. hurry,** vous êtes diablement pressé. **2.** *adv.* *F:* fort, extrêmement, rudement; **you're making a m. big mistake,** vous commettez là une fameuse erreur. **-ily** *adv.* **1.** puissamment, fortement. **2.** *F:* extrêmement.

mignonette [minjə'net] *n.* *Bot:* réséda *m*.

migraine ['mi:grein] *n.* *Med:* migraine *f*.

migrant ['maigrənt] **1.** *a.* = MIGRATORY 1. **2.** *n.* (*pers., bird, etc.*) migrateur, -trice.

migrate [mai'greit] *v.i.* (*of birds, occ. pers.*) émigrer.

migration [mai'greiʃ(ə)n] *n.* (*a*) migration *f* (des oiseaux, etc.); (*b*) émigration *f*.

migratory ['maigrət(ə)ri, mai'greitəri] *a.* **1.** (peuple) migrateur, nomade; (travailleur) saisonnier; (oiseau) migrateur. **2.** (mouvement) migratoire.

mike¹ [maik] *n.* *F:* microphone *m*, micro *m*.

Mike² *Pr.n.m.* (*dim. of Michael*) Michel; *F:* **for the love of M.,** pour l'amour du ciel.

milch [miltʃ] *a.* **m. cow.** (vache) laitière (*f*).

mild [maild] *a.* **1.** (*of pers., remark*) doux, *f.* douce; (réponse) conciliatrice; (critique) anodine. **2.** (*of regulation, etc.*) doux, peu sévère, peu rigoureux; (punition) légère. **3.** (climat) doux, tempéré; (ciel) clément; (hiver) doux; **the weather is getting milder,** le temps s'adoucit. **4.** (*a*) (plat) peu relevé; (médicament) doux, bénin; (tabac, cigare) doux; **m. beer,** *n.* **mild,** bière brune (sous pression); (*b*) *Med:* bénin, *f.* bénigne; **a m. form of measles,** une forme bénigne de la rougeole. **5.** (exercice) modéré; (amusement) innocent, anodin; **the play was a m. success,** la pièce a obtenu un succès modéré. **6.** (acier) doux. **-ly** *adv.* **1.** doucement; avec douceur. **2.** modérément; **to put it m.,** pour ne pas en dire plus.

mildew¹ ['mildju:] *n.* **1.** (*a*) *Agr:* rouille *f* (sur le froment, etc.); (*b*) mildiou *m* (sur les vignes, etc.); oïdium *m* (des vignes); (*b*) chancissure *f* (sur le pain, etc.). **2.** moisissure *f*, taches *fpl* d'humidité, piqûres *fpl* (sur le papier, le cuir).

mildew² **1.** *v.tr.* (*a*) *Agr:* rouiller, moisir (une plante); frapper (une plante) de mildiou; (*b*) (*of damp, etc.*) piquer (le papier, etc.); chancir (le pain, etc.). **2.** *v.i.* (*a*) (*of plant*) se rouiller, moisir; (*b*) (*of paper, etc.*) se piquer.

mildness ['maildnis] *n.* **1.** douceur *f*, clémence *f* (de qn, du temps); caractère anodin (d'une critique); légèreté *f* (d'une punition). **2.** *Med:* bénignité *f* (d'une maladie).

mile [mail] *n.* *Meas:* mille *m*; **five miles,** cinq milles, = huit kilomètres; **nautical m.,** mille marin (= 1853 m 25); *Sp:* **four minute m.,** mille couru en quatre minutes; **square m.,** mille carré; **you don't see anyone for miles and miles,** on parcourt des kilomètres sans voir personne; **he lives miles away,** il habite loin d'ici; *F:* **to be miles away,** être dans la lune; *F:* **I feel miles better,** je me sens beaucoup mieux; *F:* **it sticks out a m.,** ça vous crève les yeux.

mileage ['mailidʒ] *n.* (*a*) distance *f* en milles; *Fr.C:* millage *m*; = kilométrage *m*; **car with a very small m.,** voiture *f* qui a très peu roulé; *Adm: Com: etc:* **m. (allowance),** indemnité *f* de déplacement.

milestone ['mailstoun] *n.* (*a*) borne routière, = borne kilométrique; (*b*) événement important; **this discovery is a m. in medical research,** cette découverte marque une étape importante dans les recherches médicales.

milieu ['mi:ljə:] *n.* milieu (social, géographique).

militant ['militənt] **1.** *a.* militant; **the Church m.,** l'Église militante. **2.** *n. Pol: etc:* **the militants,** les activistes *mfpl*; les militants, -antes.

militarism ['militərizm] *n.* militarisme *m*.

militarist ['militərist] *n.* militariste *mf*.

militaristic [militə'ristik] *a.* militariste.

militarize ['militəraiz] *v.tr.* militariser.

military ['milit(ə)ri] **1.** *a.* militaire; (*a*) **m. man,** militaire *m*; **m. service,** service *m* militaire; (*b*) *Jur:* **m. court, tribunal,** tribunal *m* militaire; **m. police,** police *f* militaire, police aux armées. **2.** *n.pl. coll.* **the m.,** les militaires *mpl*, les soldats *mpl*; l'armée *f*; **the m. were called in,** on fit venir la force armée. **-ily** *adv.* militairement.

militate ['militeit] *v.i.* (*of fact, reason, etc.*) militer **(against,** contre).

militia [mi'liʃə] *n.* milice *f*; = garde nationale.

militiaman, *pl.* **-men** [mi'liʃəmən] *n.m.* milicien, soldat de la milice; = garde nationale.

milk¹ [milk] *n.* **1.** (*a*) lait *m*; **m. fresh from the cow,** lait fraîchement trait; **whole m.,** lait entier; **m. diet,** régime lacté; **powdered m.,** lait en poudre; *Cu:* **m. pudding,** entremets sucré au lait; crème *f* (à la vanille, etc.); **chocolate m. shake,** frappé *m* au chocolat; **m. chocolate,** chocolat *m* au lait; **with m.,** au lait; **m. jug,** pot *m* à, au, lait; **m. bottle,** bouteille *f* à lait; **m. round,** tournée *f* de laitier; **m. train,** train *m* de nuit qui s'arrête à toutes les gares; **m. bar,** milk-bar *m*, *pl.* milk-bars; *Lit:* **land of m. and honey,** pays *m* de cocagne; **the m. of human kindness,** le lait de la tendresse humaine; *Prov:* **it's no use crying over spilt m.,** à chose faite point de remède; (*b*) *Anat:* **m. tooth,** dent *f* de lait; *Toil:* **cleansing m.,** lait démaquillant; (*c*) *Fung:* **m. cap,** lactaire *m;* (*d*) *Glassm:* **m. glass,** opaline *f*. **2.** lait, eau *f* (de noix de coco); **m. of almonds,** lait d'amandes.

milk² *v.tr.* **1.** traire (une vache, etc.). **2.** *F:* dépouiller, écorcher (qn); exploiter (qn). **milking** *n.* traite *f* (d'une vache); **m. machine,** trayeuse *f* mécanique.

milker ['milkər] *n.* **1.** (*pers.*) trayeur, -euse. **2.** (*cow, etc.*) **good, bad, m.,** bonne, mauvaise, laitière.

milkiness ['milkinis] *n.* couleur laiteuse, aspect laiteux (d'un liquide, etc.).

milkmaid ['milkmeid] *n.f.* trayeuse; fille de laiterie.

milkman, *pl.* **-men** ['milkmən] *n.m.* (*a*) laitier, crémier; (*b*) livreur de lait.

milksop ['milksɔp] *n. F:* poule mouillée.

milkweed ['milkwi:d] *n. Bot:* laiteron *m*, lait *m* d'âne.

milky ['milki] *a.* laiteux; lactescent; blanchâtre; (*of gem*) pâteux; *Astr:* **the M. Way,** la Voie lactée.

mill¹ [mil] *n.* **1.** (*a*) **(flour) m.,** moulin *m* (à farine); (*large*) minoterie *f*; **m. race,** bief *m* de moulin; **m. wheel,** roue *f* de moulin; *F:* **he's been through the m.,** il a passé par de rudes épreuves; *F:* **run of the m.,** ordinaire; quelconque; (*b*) **coffee, pepper, m.,** moulin à café, à poivre; (*c*) **(crushing) m.,** broyeur *m*, concasseur *m*. **2.** *Metalw:* **(rolling) m.,** laminoir *m*, train *m* (de laminage). **3.** *Tls:* fraise *f*, fraiseuse *f*; **end m.,** fraise en bout. **4.** (*a*) usine *f*, *esp.* usine textile; **spinning m.,** filature *f;* **cotton m.,** filature de coton; **m. hand,** ouvrier, -ière, textile; **m. owner,** industriel *m* de textile; (*b*) **sugar m.,** raffinerie *f* de sucre; **paper m.,** papeterie *f*, fabrique *f* de papier.

mill² **1.** *v.tr.* (*a*) moudre (le blé, la farine); (*b*) broyer; (*c*) *Tex:* fouler (le drap); (*d*) *Mec.E:* fraiser, tailler (des engrenages, etc.); (*e*) molet(t)er (une vis); créneler (une pièce de monnaie). **2.** *v.i.* **to m. (about, around),** (*of cattle, etc.*) tourner sur place, (*of crowd*) fourmiller; tourner en rond. **milled** *a.* **1.** (*a*) *Mec.E:* (écrou) moleté; (*b*) *Num:* crénelé; (*on coin*) **m. edge,** crénelage *m*, grènetis *m*. **2.** *Tex:* foulé. **milling** *n.* **1.** métier *m* de meunier, de minoterie; meunerie *f*, minoterie *f*. **2.** (*a*) mouture *f*, moulage *m* (du grain); (*b*) broyage *m*; (*c*) foulage *m* (du drap). **3.** *Metalw:* (*a*) fraisage *m*, fraisement *m*; **m. machine,** fraiseuse *f*; **m. cutter,** fraise *f*, fraiseuse; (*b*) moletage *m* (d'une vis, etc.); (*c*) cordonnage *m* (d'une pièce de monnaie). **4.** cordon *m*, grènetis, tranche cannelée (d'une pièce de monnaie).

mill³ *n. U.S:* millième *m* (de dollar).

millboard ['milbɔ:d] *n.* carton-pâte *m inv;* fort carton (pour reliure).

millennium [mi'leniəm] *n.* **1.** *Rel.H:* millénium *m*. **2.** millénaire *m*; mille ans *mpl*.

millepede ['milipi:d] *n.* = MILLIPEDE.

miller ['milər] *n.* meunier *m*; (*of mill*) minotier *m*.

millet ['milit] *n. Bot:* millet *m*, mil *m*; **African, Indian, black, m.,** sorgho *m*; millet d'Afrique, d'Inde.

milliard ['miliɑ:d] *n.* milliard *m* (10^9).

millibar ['miliba:r] *n. Meteor.Meas:* millibar *m*.

milligram(me) ['miligræm] *n. Meas.* milligramme *m*.

millilitre, *NAm:* **milliliter** ['milili:tər] *n. Meas:* millilitre *m*.

millimetre, *NAm:* **millimeter** ['milimi:tər] *n. Meas:* millimètre *m*.

milliner ['milinər] *n.* modiste *f*, chapelier, -ière.

millinery ['milin(ə)ri] *n.* (articles *mpl* de) modes (*fpl*).

million ['miliən] *n.* million *m*; **two m. men,** deux millions d'hommes; **half a m.** un demi-million; (*of pers.*) **worth millions,** riche à millions; *F:* **he's one in a m.,** c'est la perle des hommes; **thanks a m.!** merci mille fois! *U.S: F:* **I feel like a m. dollars,** je me sens en pleine forme.

millionaire ['miliə'nɛər] *a. & n.* millionnaire (*mf*).

millionth ['miliənθ] *a. & n.* millionième (*mf*).

millipede ['milipi:d] *n. Myr:* mille-pattes *m inv*.

millpond ['milpɔnd] *n.* réservoir *m* de moulin; retenue *f*; **as calm, as smooth, as a m.,** (mer) calme comme un lac; (mer) d'huile.

millrace ['milreis] *n.* bief *m* de moulin.

millstone ['milstoun] *n.* **1.** *Geol:* **m. (grit),** meulière *f*, grès meulier; **m. quarry,** meulière. **2.** meule *f* (de moulin); **it will be a m. round his neck all his life,** c'est un boulet qu'il traînera toute sa vie.

millstream ['milstri:m] *n.* **1.** courant *m* d'eau qui actionne la roue d'un moulin. **2.** = MILLRACE.

millwright ['milrait] *n.* constructeur *m* de moulins.

milometer [mai'lɔmi:tər] *n. Aut: etc:* compteur *m* de milles; = compteur kilométrique.

milt [milt] *n.* laitance *f*, laite *f* (des poissons).

mime¹ [maim] *n. Th:* (*performance, actor*) mime *m*.

mime² **1.** *v.tr.* mimer (une scène). **2.** *v.i.* jouer par gestes.

mimeograph¹ ['mimiougræf] *n.* **1.** autocopiste *m* (au stencil). **2.** polycopie *f*.

mimeograph² *v.tr.* polycopier.

mimic¹ ['mimik] **1.** *a.* (*a*) (*of gesture, etc.*) mimique; imitateur, -trice; (*b*) (*of warfare, etc.*) factice. **2.** *n.* (*a*) mime *m*; (*b*) imitateur, -trice; **he's a great m.,** c'est un grand imitateur, *F:* un vrai singe.

mimic² *v.tr.* **(mimicked) 1.** imiter, mimer, contrefaire; *F:* singer (qn). **2.** imiter, contrefaire (la nature, etc.).

mimicry ['mimikri] *n.* **1.** mimique *f*, imitation *f*. **2.**

Nat.Hist: mimétisme *m.*

mimosa [mi'mouzə] *n. Bot:* mimosa *m.*

minaret [minə'ret] *n.* minaret *m.*

mince¹ [mins] *n. Cu:* (*a*) hachis *m* (de viande); (*b*) **m. pie,** tarte fourrée au *mincemeat.*

mince² *v.tr.* **1.** hacher (menu) (de la viande, etc.); **minced meat,** hachis *m*; viande hachée. **2.** (*always in the neg.*) **not to m. one's words,** ne pas mâcher ses mots; parler carrément; **not to m. matters,** pour parler net, carrément. **3.** *v.i.* parler avec une élégance affectée, parler du bout des lèvres; (*of woman*) minauder; (*of man*) mignarder. **4.** *v.i.* marcher d'un air affecté. **mincing** *a.* (*of manner, tone*) affecté, minaudier.

mincemeat ['minsmi:t] *n. Cu:* compote de raisins secs, de pommes, de graisse de rognon, etc.; *F:* **to make m. of sth.,** pulvériser qch.; *F:* **to make m. of s.o.,** réduire qn en bouillie.

mincer ['minsər] *n. Dom.Ec:* hachoir *m.*

mind¹ [maind] *n.* **1. to bear, keep, sth. in m.,** (i) songer à qch.; ne pas oublier qch.; (ii) tenir compte de qch.; **we must bear in m. that she is only a child,** il ne faut pas oublier que ce n'est qu'une enfant; **to call sth. to m.,** se rappeler, se souvenir de, qch.; **to put s.o. in m. of s.o., of sth.,** rappeler qn, qch., à qn; **it went (completely, clean) out of my m.,** je l'ai (complètement) oublié. **2.** (*a*) (*opinion*) pensée *f*, avis *m*, idée *f*; *F:* **I gave him a piece of my m.,** je lui ai dit son fait, ses vérités; (*of several pers.*) **to be of one m., of the same m.,** être du même avis, être d'accord; **to my m.,** selon moi, à mon avis; (*b*) (*purpose, desire*) **to know one's own m.,** savoir ce qu'on veut; **to make up one's m.,** se décider; **make up your m.!** décidez-vous! **to be in two minds about sth.,** être indécis sur qch.; **to change one's m.,** changer d'avis, d'idée; se raviser; **I've a good m. to do it,** je suis bien tenté de le faire; (*c*) **to set one's m. on sth.,** vouloir absolument avoir qch.; se mettre en tête de faire qch.; **to give one's whole m. to sth.,** appliquer toute son attention à qch.; **to keep one's m. on sth.,** se concentrer sur qch.; **to have sth. in m.,** avoir qch. en vue; **the person I have in m.,** la personne à qui je pense. **3.** esprit *m*, âme *f*; **state of m.,** état *m* d'esprit; **turn of m.,** mentalité *f* (de qn); **attitude of m.,** manière *f* de penser; **peace of m.,** tranquillité *f* d'esprit; **he has no strength of m.,** c'est un homme sans volonté, sans caractère. **4.** (*a*) *Phil: Psy:* (*opposed to body*) âme; (*opposed to matter*) esprit; (*opposed to emotions*) intelligence *f*; (*b*) esprit; **such a thought had never entered his m.,** une telle pensée ne lui était jamais venue à l'esprit; **to have sth. on one's m.,** (i) avoir qch. qui vous préoccupe; (ii) avoir qch. sur la conscience; **in the mind's eye,** dans l'imagination; **a walk will take my m. off it,** une promenade me changera les idées; **to be easy, uneasy, in one's m.,** avoir, ne pas avoir, l'esprit tranquille; **that's a weight off my m.,** voilà qui me soulage l'esprit; **put it out of your m.,** n'y pensez plus; (*c*) *Prov:* **great minds think alike,** les grands esprits se rencontrent; (*d*) **m. reader,** liseur, -euse, de pensées. **5.** raison *f*; **to be out of one's m.,** avoir perdu la raison, la tête; **are you out of your m.? you must be out of your m.!** vous êtes fou! **to be in one's right m.,** avoir toute sa raison, toutes ses facultés.

mind² *v.tr.* **1.** (*a*) (*pay attention to*) faire attention à, prêter (son) attention à (qn, qch.); **never m. the money,** ne regardez pas à l'argent; **never m. the rest,** je vous tiens quitte du reste; *F:* **never you m.!** ça c'est mon affaire! **m. you, I've always thought that . . .,** notez bien, j'ai toujours pensé que . . .; (*b*) (*apply oneself to*) s'occuper de (qch.); **m. your own business!** occupez-vous, mêlez-vous, de ce qui vous regarde! (*c*) (*take care*) **m. you're not late!** prenez soin de ne pas être en retard! **m. you write to him!** ne manquez pas, n'oubliez pas, de lui écrire! **m. what you're doing!** faites attention à ce que vous faites! **m. you don't fall!** prenez garde de tomber! **m. the step!** attention à la marche! **m. your backs (please)!** dégagez (s'il vous plaît)! (*d*) *F:* **don't be late, m.!** surtout, ne sois pas en retard! **2.** (*a*) (*object to*) **would you m. if . . .?** cela vous gênerait-il que . . .? **if you don't m.,** si cela ne vous dérange pas; **I don't m.,** (i) cela m'est égal; (ii) je le veux bien; **if nobody minds,** si personne n'y voit d'inconvénient; **I don't m. trying,** je veux bien essayer; **do you m. my asking . . .?** puis-je vous demander sans indiscrétion . . .? **do you m. if I smoke?** cela ne vous dérange, gêne, pas que je fume? **I wouldn't m. a cup of tea,** je prendrais volontiers une tasse de thé; *P:* **another drop of wine?—I don't m. if I do,** encore un peu de vin?—ce n'est pas de refus; (*b*) (*trouble oneself about*) **don't m. them,** ne vous inquiétez pas d'eux; **never m.!** (i) ça ne fait rien! tant pis! (ii) ne vous inquiétez pas! **I don't m. the cold,** le froid ne me gêne pas. **3.** (*look after*) soigner (qn); surveiller (des enfants); garder (des animaux, etc.); garder, veiller sur (la maison); **to m. the shop,** s'occuper du magasin. **4.** *A: & Dial:* (*remember*) se souvenir de, se rappeler (qn, qch.). **minded** *a.* (*a*) disposé, enclin (à faire qch.); (*b*) (*with adv.*) **commercially m.,** commerçant; **he is mechanically m.,** il est bon mécanicien; (*c*) (*with n. or a. prefixed*) **feeble m.,** à l'esprit faible.

mind-blowing ['maindblouiŋ] *a. P:* hallucinant.

minder ['maindər] *n.* (*a*) gardeur, -euse (de bestiaux); surveillant, -ante (d'enfants); *esp. NAm:* **baby m.,** garde-bébé *mf*, *pl.* garde-bébés; (*b*) *Ind:* **(machine) m.,** surveillant, *Typ:* conducteur *m*, de machines.

mindful ['maindf(u)l] *a.* **1.** attentif (à sa santé, etc.); soigneux (de); **he is always m. of others,** il pense toujours aux autres. **2. to be m. of sth.,** se souvenir de qch.; ne pas oublier qch.

mindless ['maindlis] *a.* **1.** (*a*) sans esprit, sans intelligence; (*b*) (destruction) irresponsable. **2.** (*a*) insouciant **(of,** de); indifférent (à); (*b*) oublieux (de).

mine¹ [main] *n.* **1.** (*a*) mine *f*; **coal m.,** mine de houille, de charbon; **gold, salt, m.,** mine d'or, de sel; **opencast m.,** mine à ciel ouvert; (*b*) **a m. of information,** une mine d'information. **2.** *Mil: etc:* mine; **land m.,** mine terrestre; **m. detector,** détecteur *m* de mines; **to lay a m.,** poser, mouiller, une mine.

mine² *v.tr. & i.* **1.** (*a*) *Mil:* miner, saper (une muraille); (*b*) *Mil: etc:* miner (un port, etc.); **mined area,** zone semée de mines. **2.** *Min:* exploiter (une couche de houille, etc.); **to m. (for) coal, gold,** exploiter le charbon, l'or. **mining** *n.* **1.** exploitation minière, des mines; **opencast, surface, m.,** abattage *m*, exploitation, extraction *f*, au jour; **the m. industry,** l'industrie minière; **m. area, town,** région, ville, minière; **m. engineer,** ingénieur *m* des mines. **2.** (*a*) *Mil:* sape *f*; (*b*) *Mil: Navy:* pose *f* de mines, minage *m.*

mine³ **1.** *poss.pron.* le mien, la mienne, les miens, les miennes; (*a*) **your country and m.,** votre patrie et la mienne; **this letter is m.,** cette lettre est à moi; **this signature is not m.,** cette signature n'est pas de moi; **I took her hands in both of m.,** je pris ses mains dans les deux miennes; **a friend of m.,** un(e) de mes ami(e)s; un(e) ami(e) à moi; **it is no business of m.,** ce n'est pas mon affaire; (*b*) (*my family*) les miens; (*c*) (*my property*) **m. and thine,** le mien et le tien; *F:* **what's yours is mine,** ce qui est à toi est à moi. **2.** *poss.a. A: & Poet:* mon, *f.* ma, *pl.* mes; (*a*) (*before a noun or adj. beginning with a vowel or h*) *Hum:* **m. host,** l'aubergiste *m*; (*b*) (*after voc.*) **mistress m.!** ma (belle) maîtresse!

minefield ['mainfi:ld] *n. Mil: Navy:* champ *m* de mines.

minelayer ['mainleiər] *n. Navy:* mouilleur *m* de mines.
minelaying ['mainleiiŋ] *n. Mil: Navy:* pose *f*, mouillage *m*, de mines.
miner ['mainər] *n. Min:* mineur *m* (de fond); **miner's lamp,** lampe *f* de mineur.
mineral ['min(ə)rəl] **1.** *a.* minéral, -aux; **the m. kingdom,** le règne minéral; **m. spring,** source (d'eau) minérale; **m. water,** (i) eau minérale; (ii) *Com:* boisson gazeuse. **2.** *n.* (*a*) minéral *m*; *Min:* **m. deposits,** gisements miniers, minéraux; **the m. resources of a country,** les ressources minières d'un pays; (*b*) *Com: F:* **minerals,** boissons gazeuses.
mineralogist [minə'rælədʒist] *n.* minéralogiste *mf.*
mineralogy [minə'rælədʒi] *n.* minéralogie *f.*
mineshaft ['mainʃɑːft] *n.* puits *m* de mine.
minesweeper ['mainswiːpər] *n. Navy:* dragueur *m* de mines.
minesweeping ['mainswiːpiŋ] *n. Navy:* draguage *m* des mines.
mingle ['miŋgl] **1.** *v.tr.* mêler, mélanger (**sth. with sth.,** qch. avec qch.; **two things together,** deux choses ensemble). **2.** *v.i.* (*a*) (*of thg*) se mêler, se mélanger, se confondre (**with,** avec); (*b*) (*of pers.*) se mêler (**in, with, a company,** à une compagnie); **to m. with the crowd,** se mêler à, dans, la foule.
mingy ['mindʒi] *a. F:* **1.** mesquin; **don't be so m.!** ne sois pas si radin! **2.** misérable; **a m. helping,** une portion minuscule.
mini ['mini] *n.* **1.** *Cost: F:* mini *m or f.* **2.** *Aut: R.t.m:* mini *f.*
miniature ['miniətjər] **1.** *n.* (*a*) miniature *f*; **to paint in m.,** peindre en miniature; (*b*) (portrait *m* en) miniature; **m. painter,** miniaturiste *mf*; (*c*) *Com:* bouteille miniature (de cognac, etc.). **2.** *a.* en miniature, en raccourci; (jardin, bouteille, etc.) miniature; (livre, etc.) minuscule; *Phot:* (appareil) de petit format; *Breed:* **m. poodle,** caniche nain.
miniaturist ['miniətjərist] *n.* miniaturiste *mf.*
miniaturize ['miniətjəraiz] *v.tr.* miniaturiser.
minibus ['minibʌs] *n.* minibus *m*; microbus *m.*
minicab ['minikæb] *n.* radio-taxi *m, pl.* radio-taxis.
minim ['minim] *n. Mus:* blanche *f*; **m. rest,** demi-pause *f.*
minimal ['minim(ə)l] *a.* **1.** minime. **2.** minimal, -aux; minimum; **m. value,** valeur minimale, minimum.
minimization [minimai'zeiʃ(ə)n] *n.* minimisation *f.*
minimize ['minimaiz] *v.tr.* minimiser (qch., l'importance de qch.); restreindre (le bruit, le frottement, etc.) au minimum.
minimum, *pl.* **-a** ['miniməm, -ə] *n.* minimum *m, pl.* minimums, minima; **to reduce sth. to a m.,** réduire qch. au minimum; minimiser qch.; **m. speed,** minimum de vitesse.
minion ['miniən] *n. Pej:* (*a*) **the minions of the law,** les recors *mpl* de la justice; (*b*) *F: Iron:* subordonné, -ée.
miniskirt ['miniskəːt] *n. Cost:* minijupe *f.*
minister¹ ['ministər] *n.* **1.** (*a*) *Pol:* ministre *m* (d'État); (*b*) *Dipl:* **British m. in Paris,** ministre britannique à Paris. **2.** *Ecc:* (*a*) ministre, pasteur *m* (d'un culte réformé); (*b*) *R.C.Ch:* ministre (des Jésuites); **m. general,** ministre général.
minister² *v.i.* (*a*) **to m. to s.o., to s.o.'s needs,** soigner qn; pourvoir, subvenir, aux besoins de qn; (*b*) *Ecc:* **to m. to a parish,** desservir une paroisse. **ministering** *a.* (ange, etc.) secourable.
ministerial [minis'tiəriəl] *a.* **1.** exécutif; **m. functions,** fonctions exécutives. **2.** *Ecc:* sacerdotal, -aux. **3.** *Pol:* ministériel, gouvernemental, -aux.
ministration [minis'treiʃ(ə)n] *n.* **1.** ministère *m*, soins *mpl.* **2.** *Ecc:* (*a*) sacerdoce *m*; (*b*) **to receive the ministrations of a priest,** être administré par un prêtre.
ministry ['ministri] *n.* **1.** (*a*) *Pol:* ministère *m*, gouvernement *m*; **to form a m.,** former un ministère; (*b*) *Adm:* ministère, département *m*; **the M. of Defence,** le Ministère de la Défense. **2.** *Ecc:* **the m.,** le sacerdoce; **he was intended for the m.,** il fut destiné à l'Église. **3.** entremise *f* (**of,** de).
mink [miŋk] *n.* **1.** *Z:* **(American) m.,** vison *m*; martre *f* du Canada; **m. farm,** visonnière *f.* **2.** (*fur*) vison; **a m. coat,** *F:* **a m.,** un manteau de vison, un vison.
minnow ['minou] *n. Ich:* vairon *m*; (*also loosely*) épinoche *f.*
minor¹ ['mainər] **1.** *a.* (*a*) (*lesser*) petit, mineur; *Ecc:* **m. orders,** ordres mineurs; (*b*) (*unimportant*) petit, menu, peu important; **m. repairs,** petites réparations; **this drawback is of m. importance,** cet inconvénient est secondaire; **to play a m. part,** jouer un rôle subalterne, accessoire; **m. roads,** routes secondaires; *Med:* **m. operation,** opération *f* d'importance secondaire; (*c*) *Mus:* **m. key,** ton mineur; *Fig:* **in a m. key,** plutôt triste; (*e*) *Sch:* **Martin m.,** Martin junior. **2.** *n.* (*a*) *Jur:* mineur, -eure; (*b*) *Ecc:* **the Minors,** les frères mineurs; (*c*) *U.S: Sch:* matière *f* secondaire.
minor² *v.i. U.S: Sch:* **to m. in physics,** étudier la physique comme matière secondaire.
Minorca [mi'nɔːkə] *Pr.n. Geog:* Minorque *f.*
minority [mi'nɔriti, mai-] *n.* **1.** (*a*) minorité *f*; **to be in a, the, m.,** être en minorité; **to be in a m. of one,** être seul de son opinion; (*b*) **m. party,** parti minoritaire. **2.** *Jur:* minorité.
Minotaur ['m(a)inətɔːr] *Pr.n. Gr.Myth:* **the M.,** le Minotaure.
minster ['minstər] *n.* (*a*) église abbatiale; (*b*) grande église; **York M.,** la cathédrale d'York.
minstrel ['minstr(ə)l] *n.* (*a*) *Hist:* ménestrel *m*; (*b*) *Lit:* poète *m*, musicien *m*, chanteur *m.*
mint¹ [mint] *n.* **the** M., (l'Hôtel *m* de) la Monnaie; (*of medal, stamp, print, book, etc.*) **in m. condition,** à l'état (de) neuf; *F:* **to be worth a m.,** (i) (*of pers.*) rouler sur l'or; (ii) (*of thg*) valoir une somme fabuleuse, une fortune.
mint² *v.tr.* **1.** (*a*) **to m. money,** (i) frapper de la monnaie; (ii) *F:* amasser de l'argent à la pelle; (*b*) monnayer (de l'or, etc.). **2.** *Lit:* inventer, forger, créer (un mot, une expression).
mint³ *n.* (*a*) *Bot:* menthe *f*; (*b*) *Comest:* bonbon *m* à la menthe; **m. chocolate,** chocolat fourré de crème à la menthe; **m. sauce,** vinaigrette *f* à la menthe; **m. tea,** infusion *f* à la menthe; *esp U.S:* **m. julep,** boisson alcoolique parfumée à la menthe.
mintmark ['mintmɑːk] *n. Num:* marque *f* de l'atelier monétaire.
minuet [minju'et] *n. Mus: Danc:* menuet *m.*
minus ['mainəs] **1.** *prep.* moins; **ten m. eight leaves two,** dix moins huit égale deux; **he managed to escape, but m. his luggage,** il a réussi à s'échapper, mais sans (ses) bagages. **2.** *a. & n. Mth:* **m. (sign),** moins *m*; **m. quantity,** quantité négative.
minuscule ['minəskjuːl] *a.* minuscule.
minute¹ ['minit] *n.* **1.** (*a*) minute *f* (de temps); **it's ten minutes to,** *NAm:* **of, three, ten minutes past,** *NAm:* **after, three,** il est trois heures moins dix, trois heures dix; **m. hand,** grande aiguille (d'une montre, etc.); (*b*) **a minute's rest,** un moment de repos; **wait a m.!** attendez un instant! **he's come in this (very) m.,** il rentre à l'instant (même); **he'll be here any m.,** il va arriver d'une minute à l'autre; **in a few minutes,** dans quelques minutes; **I've just popped in for a m.,** je ne fais qu'entrer et sortir. **2.** *Mth: Astr:* minute (de degré). **3.** (*a*) note *f* (de service); **to take minutes of a conversation,** noter une conversation; (*b*) **minutes of a meeting,** compte rendu *m*, procès-verbal *m*, d'une séance.

minute² ['minit] *v.tr.* (*a*) prendre note (de qch.); (*b*) dresser le procès-verbal, le compte rendu (d'une séance).
minute³ [mai'nju:t] *a.* **1.** (*a*) tout petit; menu, minuscule, minime; (*b*) **the minutest details,** les moindres détails. **2.** minutieux; **m. examination,** inspection minutieuse. **-ly** *adv.* minutieusement; en détail.
minutiae [mai'nju:ʃii:] *n.pl.* minuties *fpl*; petits détails infimes.
minx [miŋks] *n.f. F:* friponne, coquine; **you little m.!** petite espiègle! petite polissonne!
miracle ['mirəkl] *n.* **1.** (*a*) miracle *m*; **by a m.,** par miracle; (*b*) miracle, prodige *m*; **it sounds like a m.,** cela tient du miracle; **it's a m. that . . .,** c'est (un) miracle que + *sub.* **2.** *Lit:* **m. play,** miracle.
miraculous [mi'rækjuləs] *a.* (*a*) miraculeux; (*b*) miraculeux, extraordinaire, merveilleux; **to have a m. escape,** échapper comme par miracle. **-ly** *adv.* (*a*) miraculeusement; (*b*) par miracle.
mirage ['mirɑ:ʒ] *n.* mirage *m.*
mire ['maiər] *n.* (*a*) bourbier *m*; fondrière *f*; (*b*) boue *f*, bourbe *f*, fange *f*.
mirror¹ ['mirər] *n.* miroir *m*; (*a*) *Opt: Ph:* **concave, convex, m.,** miroir concave, convexe; (*b*) miroir, glace *f*; **hand m.,** glace à main; **shaving m.,** miroir à raser; **m. writing,** écriture *f* en miroir, spéculaire; (*c*) *Aut:* **driving m., rear view m.,** rétroviseur *m*; *Tchn:* **m. finish, polish,** fini *m*, polissage *m*, spéculaire; (*d*) **the press is the m. of public opinion,** la presse est le miroir de l'opinion publique.
mirror² *v.tr.* refléter; **the steeple is mirrored in the lake,** le clocher se reflète, se mire, dans le lac.
mirth [mə:θ] *n.* gaieté *f*, allégresse *f*; réjouissance *f*.
mirthful ['mə:θf(u)l] *a.* **1.** gai, joyeux. **2.** amusant.
mirthless ['mə:θlis] *a.* sans gaieté; (rire) forcé.
miry ['maiəri] *a.* fangeux, bourbeux.
misadventure [misəd'ventjər] *n.* mésaventure *f*, contretemps *m*; avatar *m*.
misalliance [misə'laiəns] *n.* mésalliance *f*.
misanthrope ['miz(ə)nθroup] *n.* misanthrope *mf*.
misanthropic [miz(ə)n'θrɔpik] *a.* (personne) misanthrope; (humeur, etc.) misanthropique.
misanthropist [mi'zænθrəpist] *n.* misanthrope *mf*.
misanthropy [mi'zænθrəpi] *n.* misanthropie *f*.
misapply [misə'plai] *v.tr.* **1.** mal appliquer, mal employer (qch.); faire un mauvais usage (d'un remède). **2.** faire un emploi injustifié (d'une somme d'argent); détourner (des fonds).
misapprehend [misæpri'hend] *v.tr.* mal comprendre (qn, qch.); se méprendre sur (les paroles de qn).
misapprehension [misæpri'henʃ(ə)n] *n.* malentendu *m*, méprise *f*.
misappropriate [misə'prouprieit] *v.tr.* détourner (des fonds).
misappropriation ['misəproupri'eiʃ(ə)n] *n.* détournement *m* (de fonds).
misbegotten [misbi'gɔt(ə)n] *a.* **1.** (enfant) illégitime, bâtard. **2.** mal conçu; **another of his m. plans!** encore un de ses projets biscornus.
misbehave [misbi'heiv] *v.i.* se conduire mal; (*of child*) se tenir mal.
misbehaviour, *NAm:* **misbehavior** [misbi'heivjər] *n.* (*a*) mauvaise conduite; inconduite *f*; (*b*) faute *f*; écart *m* de conduite.
miscalculate [mis'kælkjuleit] **1.** *v.tr.* mal calculer (une somme, une distance, etc.). **2.** *v.i.* se tromper (sur qch).
miscalculation [miskælkju'leiʃ(ə)n] *n.* faux calcul; mécompte *m*; erreur *f* de calcul.
miscarriage [mis'kæridʒ] *n.* **1.** égarement *m*, perte *f* (d'une lettre, d'un colis). **2.** (*a*) insuccès *m*, échec *m*, (d'un projet); (*b*) *Jur:* **m. of justice,** erreur *f* judiciaire; déni *m* de justice. **3.** *Med:* fausse couche.
miscarry [mis'kæri] *v.i.* **1.** (*of letter*) (i) s'égarer, se perdre; (ii) parvenir à une fausse adresse. **2.** (*of scheme, enterprise*) échouer; ne pas réussir. **3.** *Med:* faire une fausse couche; avorter.
miscast [mis'kɑ:st] *v.tr. Th: Cin: etc:* donner une mauvaise distribution à (une pièce); **he was m. in the part,** il était mal choisi pour ce rôle.
miscellaneous [misə'leiniəs] *a.* varié, divers; **m. news,** nouvelles variées; *Journ:* **m. column,** avis *mpl* divers; **m. items,** (i) articles divers; (ii) faits divers.
miscellany [mi'seləni] *n.* **1.** mélange *m*; collection *f* d'objets variés. **2.** *Lit:* (*a*) **miscellanies,** miscellanées *fpl*, mélanges *mpl*; (*b*) recueil *m*; anthologie *f*; **prose m.,** mélanges en prose.
mischance [mis'tʃɑ:ns] *n.* malheur *m*, mésaventure *f*; **by m.,** par malchance.
mischief ['mistʃif] *n.* **1.** mal *m*, tort *m*; mauvais coup; **to make m.,** apporter le trouble (dans un ménage, etc.); semer la discorde. **2.** malice *f*; **out of pure m.,** (i) par pure espièglerie; (ii) par pure méchanceté; **he's full of m.,** il est très espiègle; **to keep s.o. out of m.,** empêcher qn de faire des sottises, des bêtises; **that'll keep him out of m.,** ça l'occupera; **I wonder what m. he's up to,** je me demande ce qu'il fricote. **3.** (*pers.*) fripon, -onne; malin, -igne; **little m.,** petit(e) espiègle, petit(e) coquin(e).
mischiefmaker ['mistʃifmeikər] *n.* brandon *m* de discorde; mauvaise langue.
mischievous ['mistʃivəs] *a.* **1.** (*a*) (*of pers.*) méchant, malfaisant; (*b*) (*of thg*) mauvais, malfaisant, nuisible. **2.** (enfant) espiègle, malicieux, coquin; **m. trick, prank,** espièglerie *f*; **as m. as a monkey,** malin comme un singe. **-ly** *adv.* **1.** (*a*) méchamment; (*b*) nuisiblement. **2.** malicieusement; par espièglerie.
mischievousness ['mistʃivəsnis] *n.* **1.** méchanceté *f*. **2.** malice *f*, espièglerie *f* (d'un enfant).
misconceive [miskən'si:v] *v.tr.* **to have a misconceived idea of sth.,** avoir une fausse idée de qch.
misconception [miskən'sepʃ(ə)n] *n.* **1.** conception erronée; idée fausse. **2.** malentendu *m*.
misconduct¹ [mis'kɔndʌkt] *n.* **1.** mauvaise administration, mauvaise gestion (d'une affaire). **2.** (*of pers.*) (*a*) inconduite *f*; (*b*) *Jur:* adultère *m*.
misconduct² [miskən'dʌkt] *v.tr.* **1.** mal diriger, gérer (une affaire). **2.** *O:* **to m. oneself,** se mal conduire.
misconstruction [miskən'strʌkʃ(ə)n] *n.* fausse interprétation.
misconstrue [miskən'stru:] *v.tr.* mal interpréter (qch.); interpréter (qch.) à contresens.
miscount¹ ['miskaunt] *n.* (*a*) faux calcul; (*b*) erreur *f* d'addition; *Pol:* erreur dans le dépouillement du scrutin.
miscount² [mis'kaunt] *v.tr. & i.* mal compter.
miscreant ['miskriənt] *a. & n.* scélérat (*m*), misérable (*m*).
misdeal¹ [mis'di:l] *n. Cards:* maldonne *f*.
misdeal² *v.tr. & i.* (**misdealt** [mis'delt]) *Cards:* **to m. (the cards),** faire maldonne.
misdeed [mis'di:d] *n.* méfait *m*; (*a*) mauvaise action; (*b*) crime *m*, délit *m*.
misdemeanour, *NAm:* **misdemeanor** [misdi'mi:nər] *n.* **1.** *Jur:* délit contraventionnel; acte délictueux (moins grave que *felony*). **2.** écart *m* de conduite; méfait *m*.
misdirect [misdi'rekt] *v.tr.* **1.** mal adresser (une lettre). **2.** mal diriger (un coup). **3.** mal diriger (une entreprise, etc.). **4.** mal renseigner, mal diriger (qn). **5.** *Jur:* (*of judge*) **to m. the jury,** mal instruire le jury.
misdirected *a.* **1.** (*of letter, parcel, etc.*) mal adressé. **2.** (coup) frappé à faux. **3.** (zèle) mal employé.
misdirection [misdi'rekʃ(ə)n] *n.* (*a*) (*on letter*)

erreur *f* d'adresse; (*b*) indication erronée, renseignement erroné.

miser ['maizər] *n.* avare *mf.*

miserable ['miz(ə)rəbl] *a.* **1.** (*of pers.*) malheureux, triste; **I feel m.,** j'ai le cafard; **to make s.o.'s life m.,** rendre la vie dure à qn. **2.** (*of event, condition*) misérable, déplorable; (*of journey*) pénible, désagréable. **3.** (*a*) misérable, pauvre, pitoyable; (somme) insignifiante; (salaire) dérisoire; (*b*) **I only want a m. £70 to get straight,** il ne me faudrait que soixante-dix misérables livres pour me remettre d'aplomb. **-ably** *adv.* (*a*) misérablement; malheureusement, lamentablement; (*b*) pauvrement; **to be m. paid,** avoir un salaire dérisoire.

miserere [mizə'riəri] *n. Ecc:* **1.** miséréré *m*, miserere *m.* **2. m. (seat)** = MISERICORD (*b*).

misericord [mi'zerikɔːd] *n. Ecc:* (*a*) miséricorde *f* (de monastère); (*b*) miséricorde, patience *f* (de stalle).

miserliness ['maizəlinis] *n.* avarice *f*, ladrerie *f.*

miserly ['maizəli] *a.* (*of pers.*) avare, pingre, ladre.

misery ['mizəri] *n.* **1.** souffrance(s) *f* (*pl*), supplice *m*; **to put s.o. out of his m.,** mettre fin aux souffrances de qn; **to put an animal out of its m.,** donner le coup de grâce à un animal. **2.** détresse *f*; **to make s.o.'s life a m.,** rendre la vie malheureuse à qn. **3.** (*pers.*) *F:* geignard, -arde; grincheux, -euse.

misfire¹ [mis'faiər] *n.* (*a*) *Sm.a: etc:* raté *m* (de percussion); (*b*) *Ball: I.C.E:* raté d'allumage.

misfire² *v.i.* **1.** (*a*) *Sm.a: etc:* rater, faire long feu; (*b*) *Ball:* (*of propulsive charge of rocket*) avoir un raté d'allumage; (*c*) *I.C.E:* (*of engine*) avoir des ratés; rater. **2.** (*of joke, etc.*) manquer son effet; foirer.

misfit ['misfit] *n.* (*a*) vêtement, etc., manqué, mal réussi; *Com:* laissé-pour-compte *m*, *pl.* laissés-pour-compte; (*b*) (*pers.*) inadapté, -ée.

misfortune [mis'fɔːtjuːn] *n.* infortune *f*, malheur *m*; **it is more his m. than his fault,** il est plus à plaindre qu'à blâmer.

misgiving [mis'giviŋ] *n.* doute *m*, crainte *f*, pressentiment *m*, inquiétude *f* (**about sth.,** sur qch.); **not without misgivings,** non sans hésitation.

misgovern [mis'gʌvən] *v.tr.* mal gouverner.

misgovernment [mis'gʌvənmənt] *n.* mauvais gouvernement; mauvaise administration.

misguided [mis'gaidid] *a.* **1.** (*of pers.*) qui manque de jugement; **these m. people,** ces malheureux. **2.** (*of conduct*) peu judicieux; (*of energy*) hors de propos; (*of attempt*) malencontreux. **-ly** *adv.* sans jugement.

mishandle [mis'hændl] *v.tr.* **1.** malmener, maltraiter (qn). **2.** mal manier, mal manœuvrer (une machine, un appareil); mal gérer, mal mener (une affaire, etc). **mishandling** *n.* **1.** mauvais traitements (à l'égard de qn.). **2.** maniement défectueux (d'un outil, etc.); mauvaise gestion (d'une affaire, etc.).

mishap ['mishæp] *n.* mésaventure *f*, contretemps *m*; accident *m*; **after many mishaps,** après bien des péripéties.

mishear [mis'hiər] *v.tr.* (**misheard** [mis'həːd]) mal entendre.

mishmash ['miʃmæʃ] *n. F:* méli-mélo *m*; salade *f.*

misinformed [misin'fɔːmd] *a.* mal informé; mal renseigné.

misinterpret [misin'təːprit] *v.tr.* mal interpréter (qn, les paroles de qn); mal traduire la pensée de (qn).

misinterpretation [misintəːpri'teiʃ(ə)n] *n.* **1.** fausse interprétation. **2.** (*in translating*) contresens *m.*

misjudge [mis'dʒʌdʒ] *v.tr.* mal juger (qn, qch.); se tromper sur le compte de (qn); mal juger de (qch.); se tromper dans l'estimation de (la distance).

misjudg(e)ment [mis'dʒʌdʒmənt] *n.* jugement erroné; fausse estimation (d'une distance).

mislay [mis'lei] *v.tr.* (*p.t. & p.p.* **mislaid** [mis'leid]) égarer, perdre (son parapluie, etc.).

mislead [mis'liːd] *v.tr.* (*p.t. & p.p.* **misled** [mis'led]) **1.** (*a*) induire (qn) en erreur; tromper (qn); (*b*) égarer, fourvoyer (qn). **2.** corrompre, dévoyer (qn). **misleading** *a.* trompeur, -euse; fallacieux.

mismanage [mis'mænidʒ] *v.tr.* mal conduire, mal diriger, mal gérer (une affaire, une entreprise).

mismanagement [mis'mænidʒmənt] *n.* (*a*) mauvaise administration, mauvaise gestion; (*b*) **there has been some m.,** l'affaire a été mal menée.

misnomer [mis'noumər] *n.* **1.** *Jur:* erreur *f* de nom. **2.** nom mal approprié; **changes which, by a great m., are called progress,** changements auxquels on donne fort mal à propos le nom de progrès.

misogynist [m(a)i'sɔdʒinist] *n.* misogyne *f.*

misogyny [m(a)i'sɔdʒini] *n.* misogynie *f.*

misplace [mis'pleis] *v.tr.* **1.** placer à faux (l'accent tonique, etc.). **2.** mal placer (ses affections, etc.); **misplaced remark,** remarque hors de propos. **3.** égarer (un livre, etc.).

misprint¹ ['misprint] *n. Typ:* faute *f* d'impression; erreur *f* typographique; *F:* coquille *f.*

misprint² [mis'print] *v.tr.* imprimer (un mot) incorrectement.

mispronounce [misprə'nauns] *v.tr.* mal prononcer (un mot).

mispronunciation [misprənʌnsi'eiʃ(ə)n] *n.* prononciation incorrecte; faute *f* de prononciation.

misquotation [miskwou'teiʃ(ə)n] *n.* citation inexacte.

misquote [mis'kwout] *v.tr.* citer (qch.) à faux, inexactement; citer (un auteur) incorrectement.

misread [mis'riːd] *v.tr.* (*p.t. & p.p.* **misread** [mis'red]) mal lire, mal interpréter (un texte, etc.).

misrepresent [misrepri'zent] *v.tr.* mal représenter; dénaturer, travestir (les faits); présenter (les faits) sous un faux jour.

misrepresentation [misreprizen'teiʃ(ə)n] *n.* faux rapport; présentation erronée (des faits, etc.); *Jur:* (i) fausse déclaration; (ii) réticence *f.*

misrule [mis'ruːl] *n.* mauvaise administration, mauvais gouvernement; désordre *m*, confusion *f.*

miss¹ [mis] *n.* coup manqué, coup perdu; *Bill:* manque *m* de touche; *F:* **it was a near m.,** il s'en est fallu de peu; c'était moins une; **we had a near m. with that car,** cette voiture a failli nous percuter; **to give (s.o., sth.) a m.,** passer le tour de (qn); ne pas aller voir, visiter (un monument); *Prov:* **a m. is as good as a mile,** manquer de près ou de loin, c'est toujours manquer.

miss² *v.tr.* **1.** (*fail to hit or to find*) (*a*) manquer; *F:* rater (le but); **to m. one's mark,** manquer son coup; *v.i.* **he never misses,** il ne manque jamais son coup; **missed!** manqué! *F:* raté!; **to m. the point (in one's answer),** répondre à côté; **you've missed the point,** vous n'avez pas compris; *Th:* (*of actor*) **to m. one's entrance,** louper son entrée; **to m. one's cue,** manquer la réplique; (*b*) **to m. one's way,** s'égarer; **he missed his footing,** le pied lui manqua; (*c*) ne pas trouver, rencontrer (qn); **I missed him (by two minutes),** je l'ai manqué, *F:* raté (de deux minutes); (*d*) manquer, *F:* rater (un train, etc.); (*e*) manquer, laisser échapper, *F:* rater (une occasion); **an opportunity not to be missed,** une occasion à saisir; **I've missed my turn,** j'ai perdu mon tour; *F:* **you haven't missed much!** vous n'avez pas raté grand-chose; *F:* **to m. the boat,** laisser échapper l'occasion; (*f*) **I missed my holiday this year,** je n'ai pas eu de vacances cette année; (*g*) manquer (un rendez-vous, un repas); *F:* sécher (un cours); **I never m. going there,** je ne manque jamais d'y aller; (*h*) **he narrowly, just, missed being killed,** il a failli se faire tuer; (*i*) ne pas saisir (une plaisanterie); **I missed that,** je n'ai pas (i) compris, (ii) entendu; **you can't m. the house,** vous ne pouvez pas manquer de reconnaître la maison. **2.** (*a*) (*omit*) **to m. (out) a word, a line,** omettre, sauter, un mot, une ligne; (*of bus, etc.*) **to m. (out) a stop,** brûler un arrêt; (*b*) *v.i. F:* **to m. out on sth.,** rater qch. **3.** (*a*) (*notice absence of*) remarquer l'absence de (qn, qch.); remarquer qu'il manque (qn, qch.); **we are sure to be missed,** on va sûrement remarquer notre absence; (*b*) (*feel lack of*) regretter (qn); regretter l'absence de (qn); **I m. you,** vous me manquez; **I am not allowed cigarettes, but I don't m. them,** on me défend les cigarettes, mais je n'en sens pas le besoin. **missing** *a.* (ami, etc.) absent; (objet) égaré; disparu; (argent) qui manque; **one man is m.,** un homme manque; *Mil: etc:* **to report s.o. m.,** porter qn disparu; *n.pl.* **the m.,** les disparus.

miss[3] *n.f.* **1. Miss Martin,** *pl.* **the Miss Martins, the Misses Martin,** mademoiselle, Mlle Martin; les demoiselles Martin; (*as address*) mademoiselle, Mesdemoiselles Martin; **thank you, Miss Martin,** merci mademoiselle; **Miss World,** Miss Monde. **2.** *P:* (*with omission of proper name*) **Yes, M., good morning, M.,** oui, mam'selle, bonjour mam'selle.

missal ['mis(ə)l] *n. Ecc:* missel *m.*

mis-shapen [mis'ʃeip(ə)n] *a.* (*of pers., limb, etc.*) difforme, contrefait; (*of hat, figure, etc.*) déformé.

missile ['misail, *NAm:* 'mis(ə)l] *n.* (*a*) projectile *m*; (*b*) *Mil:* missile *m*, engin *m*; **guided m.,** missile, engin, guidé; **anti-missile m.,** engin antimissile(s); **m. base,** base *f* de lancement de missiles; **m. launcher,** lance-missiles *m inv.*

mission ['miʃ(ə)n] *n.* mission *f.* **1.** (*task*) **to charge, entrust, s.o. with a m.,** charger qn d'une mission, confier une mission à qn; **m. accomplished,** mission accomplie; **minister on a special m.,** ministre *m* en mission spéciale; **she thinks her m. in life is to help lame dogs,** elle croit avoir mission de secourir les malheureux. **2.** (*body of persons*) *U.S:* ambassade *f*; représentation *f* diplomatique; (*b*) **military, trade, m.,** mission militaire, commerciale; *Ecc:* **foreign, home, missions,** missions étrangères, métropolitaines. **3.** (*place*) *Ecc:* **m. (station),** mission *f.*

missionary ['miʃən(ə)ri] **1.** *a.* (prêtre, œuvre, esprit) missionnaire; (vocation) de missionnaire; (tronc) des missions. **2.** *n.* missionnaire *mf.*

missis ['misiz] *n.f. P:* = MISSUS.

missive ['misiv] *n.* lettre *f*, missive *f.*

mis-spell ['mis'spel] *v.tr.* (*p.t. & p.p.* **mis-spelt** ['mis'spelt]) mal épeler, mal orthographier.

mis-spend ['mis'spend] *v.tr.* (*p.t. & p.p.* **mis-spent** ['mis'spent]) mal employer (son argent, son temps); gâcher (son argent); **a mis-spent youth,** une jeunesse (i) mal employée, (ii) passée dans la dissipation.

missus ['misis, 'misiz] *n.f. P:* (*corruption of mistress*) (*a*) madame; (*b*) (*wife*) femme; **the m., my m.,** ma femme, la patronne; **your m.,** votre dame.

mist[1] [mist] *n.* **1.** *Meteor:* brume *f*, *Nau:* brumaille *f*; **Scotch m.,** bruine *f*, crachin *m*; *Fig:* **lost in the mists of time,** perdu dans la nuit des temps. **2.** buée *f* (sur une glace, etc.); **to see things through a m.,** voir trouble.

mist[2] **1.** *v.tr.* couvrir (une glace, etc.) de buée. **2.** *v.i.* **to m. over,** (i) (*of landscape*) disparaître sous la brume; (ii) (*of mirror*) se couvrir de buée; (iii) (*of eyes*) se voiler; **misted-up windscreen,** pare-brise embué.

mistakable [mis'teikəbl] *a.* **1.** sujet à méprise. **2. easily m.,** facile à confondre (**for,** avec).

mistake[1] [mis'teik] *n.* erreur *f*, méprise *f*, faute *f*; **m. in calculation, in the date,** erreur de calcul, de date; **exercise full of mistakes,** exercice plein de fautes; **grammatical mistakes,** fautes de grammaire; **to make a m.,** faire, commettre, une faute, une erreur; se tromper (**about, over,** sur, au sujet de, quant à); **to make the m. of doing sth.,** avoir le tort de faire qch.; **by m.,** (faire qch.) par erreur, par méprise; **there is, can be, no m. about that,** il n'y a pas à s'y tromper; **make no m.,** que l'on ne s'y trompe pas; **it's warm and no m.!** il fait chaud, pas d'erreur!

mistake[2] *v.tr.* (*p.t.* **mistook** [mis'tuk]; *p.p.* **mistaken** [mis'teik(ə)n]) **1.** se méprendre sur (les paroles, les intentions, de qn); **I have mistaken the house,** je me suis trompé de maison; **if I'm not mistaken,** si je ne me trompe pas; **there's no mistaking it,** il n'y a pas à s'y méprendre. **2. to m. s.o., sth., for s.o., sth.,** confondre qn, qch., avec qn, qch.; **I mistook him for s.o. else,** je l'ai pris pour qn d'autre. **mistaken** *a.* **1.** (opinion) erronée; (idées) fausses; (bonté) mal placée. **2. m. identity,** erreur *f* sur la personne. **mistakenly** *adv.* **1.** par erreur, par méprise. **2.** peu judicieusement.

mister ['mistər] *n.* **1.** (*always abbreviated to* **Mr**) **Mr Thomas,** Monsieur Thomas; M. Thomas; (*on address*) Monsieur Thomas; **Mr Chairman,** monsieur le président; *Com:* **our Mr A,** notre représentant M. A. **2.** *P:* (*with omission of proper name*) m'sieur; **what's the time, m.?** quelle heure est-il, m'sieur?

mistime [mis'taim] *v.tr.* faire (qch.) mal à propos, à contretemps; mal calculer (un coup). **mistimed** *a.* inopportun, mal à propos; (coup) mal calculé.

mistiness ['mistinis] *n.* **1.** état brumeux, obscurité *f.* **2.** brouillard *m*, brume *f*; vapeurs *fpl.*

mistlethrush ['mislθrʌʃ] *n. Orn:* (grive *f*) draine (*f*).

mistletoe ['misltou] *n. Bot:* gui *m.*

mistranslate [mistræns'leit, -trɑː-] *v.tr.* mal traduire; interpréter (une phrase) à contresens.

mistranslation ['mistræns'leiʃ(ə)n, -trɑː-] *n.* mauvaise traduction; erreur *f* de traduction.

mistreat [mis'triːt] *v.tr.* maltraiter (qn, qch.).

mistress ['mistris] *n.f.* **1.** (*a*) maîtresse (qui exerce l'autorité); **to be one's own m.,** être indépendante; être sa propre maîtresse; **to be m. of oneself, of one's emotions,** être maîtresse de soi(-même); (*b*) maîtresse (de maison); (*c*) (*owner of pet*) maîtresse; (*d*) maîtresse (d'école), institutrice; professeur *m* (de lycée); **the French m.,** le professeur de français. **2.** maîtresse, concubine. **3.** (*in titles*) (*a*) *A:* Madame; (*b*) (*now always abbreviated to* **Mrs** ['misiz]) **Mrs Martin,** Madame Martin.

mistrial [mis'traiəl] *n. Jur:* (*a*) erreur *f* judiciaire; (*b*) jugement entaché d'un vice de procédure.

mistrust[1] [mis'trʌst] *n.* méfiance *f*, défiance *f* (**of,** de); manque *m* de confiance (**of,** en).

mistrust[2] *v.tr.* se méfier de, se défier de (qn, qch.); ne pas avoir confiance en (qn).

mistrustful [mis'trʌstf(u)l] *a.* méfiant; défiant. **-fully** *adv.* avec méfiance; avec défiance.

misty ['misti] *a.* (temps, lieu, etc.) brumeux, brumailleux, embrumé; (yeux) embués, troublés; (souvenir) vague, confus; (formes) estompées; **it's m.,** le temps est brumeux; **the windscreen is all m.,** le pare-brise est tout couvert de buée.

misunderstand [misʌndə'stænd] *v.tr.* (*p.t. & p.p.* **misunderstood** [misʌndə'stud]) **1.** mal comprendre (qch., qn); mal entendre, se méprendre sur (qch.); mal interpréter (une action); **if I have not misunderstood,** si j'ai bien compris; **we misunderstood each other,** il y a eu un malentendu. **2.** méconnaître (qn); se méprendre sur le compte de (qn). **misunderstanding** *n.* **1.** (*a*) conception erronée; (*b*) malentendu *m*; quiproquo *m.* **2.** mésintelligence *f*, malentente *f*; brouille *f*.

misuse[1] [mis'ju:s] *n.* abus *m*, mauvais usage, emploi abusif (de qch.); abus (d'autorité); emploi abusif (des mots); *Jur:* **fraudulent m. of funds,** détournement *m* de fonds.

misuse[2] [mis'ju:z] *v.tr.* faire (un) mauvais usage, (un) mauvais emploi, de (qch.); abuser de (qch.); employer (un mot) à tort, abusivement.

mite [mait] *n.* **1.** *A:* & *Lit:* (*a*) **the widow's m.,** le denier de la veuve; (*b*) **m. of consolation,** brin *m* de consolation. **2.** petit gosse, petite gosse; mioche *mf*; **poor little m.!** pauvre petit! **3.** *Arach:* acarien *m*; mite *f*; **cheese m.,** mite du fromage.

miter ['maitər] *n.* & *v.* *NAm:* = MITRE[1, 2, 3].

mitigate ['mitigeit] *v.tr.* **1.** adoucir (la colère de qn). **2.** adoucir, atténuer (la souffrance, le chagrin, etc.); apaiser (la douleur); mitiger, atténuer (une peine). **3.** tempérer (la chaleur); adoucir (le froid). **4.** atténuer (un crime, une faute); **mitigating circumstances,** circonstances atténuantes.

mitigation [miti'geiʃ(ə)n] *n.* **1.** adoucissement *m* (d'une douleur); mitigation *f*, réduction *f*, atténuation *f*, modération *f* (d'une peine). **2.** atténuation (d'une faute).

mitre[1], *NAm:* **miter**[1] ['maitər] *n.* (*a*) *Ecc. Cost:* mitre *f*; (*b*) *Moll:* **m. (shell),** mitre, mitra *m*.

mitre[2], *NAm:* **miter**[2] *n.* (*a*) *Carp:* **m. (joint),** (assemblage *m* à) onglet (*m*); **m. box,** boîte *f* à onglet(s); (*b*) *Tls:* **m. (square),** équerre *f* (à) onglet; onglet; angle *m* oblique.

mitre[3], *NAm:* **miter**[3] *v.tr.* **1.** *Carp: Metalw: etc:* tailler (une pièce) à onglet. **2.** assembler (deux pièces) à onglet.

mitt [mit] *n.* **1.** mitaine *f*. **2.** *F:* main *f*, patte *f*.

mitten ['mit(ə)n] *n.* **1.** mitaine *f*. **2.** moufle *f*. **3.** *Box:* *F:* **mittens,** gants *mpl*, les mitaines.

mix[1] [miks] *n.* **1.** (*a*) mélange *m* (de mortier, de plâtre, etc.); (*b*) *Com:* **cake, etc., m.,** préparation *f* pour gâteaux, etc. **2.** *Cin:* fondu enchaîné; enchaînement *m* (des images).

mix[2] **1.** *v.tr.* (*a*) mêler, mélanger (**several things together, sth. with sth.,** plusieurs choses ensemble, qch. à, avec, qch.); allier (des métaux); (*b*) préparer (un gâteau, une boisson); *Pharm:* mixtionner (des drogues); (*c*) gâcher (du mortier, du plâtre); *Cu:* retourner, fatiguer (la salade); *U.S: Cards:* battre, mélanger (les cartes); (*d*) *esp. U.S: P:* **to m. it (up),** en venir aux coups. **2.** *v.i.* se mêler, se mélanger (**with,** avec, à); (*of fluids*) s'allier; (*of colours, etc.*) **to m. well,** aller bien ensemble; s'accorder; (*of pers.*) **to m. with people,** s'associer à, avec, des gens; fréquenter les gens; **to m. with the crowd,** se mêler à la foule. **mixed** *a.* **1.** mêlé, mélangé; mixte; (*a*) **person of m. blood,** sang-mêlé *mf inv*; *Rel:* **m. marriage,** mariage *m* mixte; *Cu: etc:* **m. grill,** mixed-grill *m*, *pl.* mixed-grills; **m. sweets,** bonbons assortis; **m. vegetables,** jardinière *f*, macédoine *f*, de légumes; **m. feelings,** sentiments mêlés; (*b*) **m. company,** compagnie mêlée; milieu *m* hétéroclite; **m. society,** société hétérogène; *Nau:* **m. cargo,** cargaison *f* mixte, chargement *m* de divers; *F:* (*of pers. or thgs*) **they were a m. bag,** il y en avait de toutes sortes; *Mth:* **m. number,** nombre *m* fractionnaire. **2. m. school,** école *f* mixte; école pour garçons et filles; *Ten:* **m. doubles,** double *m* mixte. **mixing** *n.* **1.** mélange *m* (de qch. avec qch.). **2.** (*a*) barbotage *m* (des liquides); **m. bowl,** terrine *f*, bol *m* à mélanger; (*b*) gâchage *m* (du mortier, du plâtre); *Pharm:* mixtion *f* (d'une préparation, etc.); **m. drum,** mélangeur *m* (à tambour); *I.C.E:* **m. chamber,** chambre *f* de mélange, de carburation; (*c*) *Cin: etc:* mixage *m*. **mix up** *v.tr.* (*a*) mêler, mélanger (plusieurs substances, qch. à, avec, qch.); embrouiller (ses papiers, etc.); (*b*) confondre (**with,** avec); **I was mixing you up with your brother,** je faisais confusion avec vous et votre frère; (*c*) **to be mixed up in an affair,** être mêlé à une affaire, être compromis, être impliqué, dans une affaire; (*d*) embrouiller (qn); **I was getting all mixed up,** je ne savais plus où j'étais; **everything had got mixed up,** tout était en pagaille. **mixed-up** *a.* *F:* (*of pers.*) complexé.

mixer ['miksər] *n.* **1.** (*pers.*) (*a*) *Metall: Ind:* brasseur *m*; (*b*) *Cin:* opérateur *m* des sons. **2.** (*machine*) (*a*) *Ind: etc:* mélangeuse *f*; barboteur *m*; agitateur *m*; **concrete m.,** bétonnière *f*; (*b*) *Cin:* mélangeur *m* de sons; (*c*) *I.C.E:* diffuseur *m*; (*d*) *Dom.Ec:* **(electric) m.,** batteur *m* (électrique); **m. (tap),** (i) robinet mélangeur; (ii) mitigeur *m*. **3.** (*pers.*) **to be a good m.,** être très sociable.

mixture ['mikstʃər] *n.* **1.** (*a*) mélange *m* (de choses, de personnes); amalgame *m*; **cake, etc., m.,** préparation *f* pour gâteaux, etc.; (*b*) *Ch:* **homogeneous, heterogeneous, m.,** mélange homogène, hétérogène; (*c*) *I.C.E:* **fuel-air m.,** mélange air-carburant; **lean, weak, m.,** mélange pauvre. **2.** *Pharm:* mixtion *f*, mixture *f*; **cough m.,** sirop *m* pour, contre, la toux.

mix-up ['miksʌp] *n.* confusion *f*, embrouillement *m*; malentendu *m*; *F:* pagaïe *f*, pagaille *f*.

mizzen ['miz(ə)n] *n.* *Nau:* **m. (sail),** artimon *m*.

mizzenmast ['miz(ə)nmɑ:st] *n.* *Nau:* mât *m* d'artimon.

mnemonic [ni'mɔnik] **1.** *a.* mnémonique. **2.** *n.* aide-mémoire *m inv*; moyen *m* mnémotechnique.

mnemonics [ni'mɔniks] *n.pl.* (*usu. with sg. const.*) mnémonique *f*, mnémotechnie *f*.

mo [mou] *n.* *F:* instant *m*, minute *f*; **half a mo!** une petite seconde!

moan[1] [moun] *n.* (*a*) gémissement *m*, plainte *f*; *F:* **to have a (good) m.,** grogner, ronchonner; (*b*) gémissement *m* (du vent).

moan[2] **1.** *v.i.* gémir; pousser des gémissements; se lamenter; (*of wind*) gémir; **to m. about sth.,** se plaindre de qch.; **he's always moaning (and groaning),** ce sont des lamentations à n'en plus finir. **2.** *v.tr.* dire (qch.) en gémissant. **moaning** *n.* gémissement(s) *m(pl)*; **his constant m.,** ses plaintes continuelles.

moaner ['mounər] *n.* *F:* ronchonneur, -euse; râleur, -euse.

moat [mout] *n.* fossé(s) *m(pl)*, douves *f(pl)*.

mob[1] [mɔb] *n.* **1.** *Pej:* **the m.,** la populace; *F:* le populo; **m. rule,** voyoucratie *f*; **to join the m.,** descendre dans la rue. **2.** foule (agitée), cohue *f*, rassemblement *m*; attroupement *m*, ameutement *m*; (*of people in pursuit*) meute *f*. **3.** *F:* bande *f*, clique *f*.

mob[2] *v.* **(mobbed)** *v.tr.* (*a*) (*of angry crowd*) houspiller, attaquer, malmener (qn); (*b*) (*of admiring crowd*) assiéger (qn); faire foule autour de (qn).

mobile[1] ['moubail] *a.* **1.** (*of limb, component part, etc.*) mobile; **m. features,** physionomie changeante. **2.** (*a*) itinérant, mobile; **m. library,** bibliothèque itinérante, bibliobus *m*; **m. home,** grande caravane; *F:* **are you m.?** vous êtes motorisé? (*b*) *Mil:* (défense, unité, etc.) mobile; **m. warfare,** guerre *f* de mouvement.

mobile[2] ['moubail] *n.* *Art:* mobile *m*.

mobility [mou'biliti] *n.* mobilité *f*.

mobilization [moubilai'zeiʃ(ə)n] *n.* mobilisation *f* (des troupes, de capitaux, etc.); **m. order,** (i) (*public*) appel *m*, (ii) (*personal*) ordre *m*, de mobilisation.

mobilize ['moubilaiz] **1.** *v.tr.* mobiliser (des troupes, des capitaux) **2.** *v.i.* (*of army*) entrer en mobilisation.

mobster ['mɔbstər] *n.*(*a*) émeutier, -ière; (*b*) gangster *m*.

moccasin ['mɔkəsin] *n.* *Cost:* mocassin *m*.

mocha ['mɔkə] *n.* **m. (coffee),** (café *m*) moka (*m*).

mock¹ [mɔk] *n. O:* sujet *m* de moquerie; (*still so used in*) **to make a m. of s.o., of sth.,** se moquer de qn, de qch.
mock² *a.* d'imitation; feint, contrefait; faux, *f.* fausse; **m. tortoiseshell,** écaille *f* imitation; *Cu:* **m. turtle soup,** consommé *m* à la tête de veau; **to indulge in m. heroics,** jouer au, se prendre pour un, héros; **m. trial,** simulacre *m* de procès; **m. fight,** simulacre de combat; *Sch:* **m. examination,** examen blanc.
mock³ 1. *v.tr. & i.* **to m. (at) s.o., sth.,** se moquer de qn, de qch.; railler qn, qch.; bafouer qn. **2.** *v.tr.* (*a*) narguer (qn); (*b*) se jouer de, tromper (qn); (*c*) imiter, singer (qn). **mocking 1.** *a.* moqueur, -euse; railleur, -euse; (ironie) gouailleuse. **2.** *n.* moquerie *f*, raillerie *f.* **mockingly** *adv.* d'un ton moqueur, railleur; par moquerie.
mocker ['mɔkər] *n.* moqueur, -euse; railleur, -euse.
mockery ['mɔkəri] *n.* **1.** moquerie *f*, raillerie *f.* **2.** sujet *m* de moquerie, de raillerie; **this makes a m. of the whole thing,** cela tourne tout en dérision. **3.** semblant *m*, simulacre *m* (**of,** de); **his trial was a mere m.,** son procès n'a été qu'un simulacre.
mockingbird ['mɔkiŋbə:d] *n. Orn:* moqueur *m.*
mock-up ['mɔkʌp] *n.* maquette *f.*
mod [mɔd] *F:* **1.** *a.* (*a*) *O:* moderne, dans le vent; (*b*) **m. cons,** confort *m* moderne. **2.** *n.* **mods and rockers** = blousons noirs.
modal ['moud(ə)l] *a.* modal, -aux; *Gram:* (auxiliaire, etc.) de mode.
modality [mou'dæliti] *n.* modalité *f.*
mode [moud] *n.* **1.** (*manner*) mode *m*, méthode *f*, manière *f* (**of,** de); **m. of life,** train *m*, mode, de vie. **2.** (*fashion*) mode *f.* **3.** *Mus:* mode *m.* **4.** *Phil:* mode *m.*
model¹ ['mɔd(ə)l] *n.* **1.** (*a*) modèle *m*; maquette *f*; **working m.,** modèle pouvant fonctionner; **m. aircraft,** maquette, modèle (réduit) d'avion; **m. maker,** maquettiste *mf*; modéliste *m*; (*b*) *N.Arch: etc:* gabarit *m*; (*c*) *Surv:* plan *m* en relief. **2.** (*a*) *Art:* **to draw from, without, a m.,** dessiner d'après le modèle, de chic; **anatomical m.,** écorché *m*; (*b*) **to take s.o. as one's m.,** prendre modèle sur qn; prendre qn pour modèle; **to be a m. of virtue,** être un modèle, un exemple, de vertu; **m. pupil,** écolier, -ière, modèle; (*c*) *Dressm: etc:* modèle; **Paris models,** modèles de la haute couture parisienne; (*d*) *Pol.Ec:* **feasibility m.,** modèle probatoire. **3.** (*pers.*) (*a*) *Art:* modèle; (*b*) **(fashion) m.,** mannequin *m.*
model² *v.tr.* **(modelled,** *NAm:* **modeled) 1.** modeler (une figure, un groupe). **2. to m. sth. after, on, upon, sth.,** modeler qch. sur qch.; **to m. oneself on s.o.,** prendre exemple sur qn. **3.** (*a*) (*of mannequin*) présenter (une robe, etc.); (*b*) *v.i.* **she models.** elle travaille comme mannequin. **modelling,** *NAm:* **modeling** *n.* **1.** (*a*) modelage *m*; **m. clay,** pâte *f* à modeler; (*b*) facture *f* sur modèle. **2.** présentation *f* (d'une robe, etc.) par un mannequin.
modeller, *NAm:* **modeler** ['mɔdələr] *n.* modeleur, -euse (**of,** de).
moderate¹ ['mɔdərət] **1.** *a.* (*a*) modéré; moyen; (buveur) tempéré; (langage) mesuré; (prix) modéré, modique, moyen; **m. income,** revenu *m* modique; **of m. size,** de grandeur moyenne; **m. wind,** vent modéré; (*b*) *Ecc: Pol:* **m. opinions,** opinions modérées. **2.** *n.* (*pers.*) *Ecc: Pol:* modéré, -ée. **-ly** *adv.* modérément; avec modération; modiquement, moyennement; **m. priced,** de prix moyen.
moderate² ['mɔdəreit] **1.** *v.tr.* modérer (ses exigences, ses désirs); ralentir (son zèle); **a moderating influence,** une influence modérante, modératrice. **2.** *v.i.* (*of storm*) s'appaiser, se calmer. **3.** *Ecc: esp. Scot: v.i.* présider (une assemblée).
moderation [mɔdə'reiʃ(ə)n] *n.* **1.** modération *f*, mesure *f*; sobriété *f* (de langage); **in m.,** avec modération, modérément. **2.** *Sch:* (*at Oxford*) **Moderations,** premier examen pour le grade de *Bachelor of Arts.*
moderator ['mɔdəreitər] *n.* **1.** (*a*) président *m* (d'une assemblée); *Ecc: Scot:* **M. of the General Assembly,** modérateur *m*, président, de l'Assemblée générale (de l'Église d'Écosse). **2.** modérateur *m*, ralentisseur *m* (de réacteur, etc.).
modern ['mɔd(ə)n] **1.** *a.* moderne; **m. times,** les temps modernes; **m. languages,** langues vivantes. **2.** *n.* moderne *m.*
modernism ['mɔdənizm] *n.* **1.** (*a*) modernité *f*; (*b*) modernisme *m.* **2.** (*a*) usage nouveau; (*b*) *Ling:* néologisme *m.*
modernity [mɔ'də:niti] *n.* modernité *f.*
modernization [mɔdə(:)nai'zeiʃ(ə)n] *n.* modernisation *f.*
modernize ['mɔdənaiz] *v.tr.* moderniser.
modest ['mɔdist] *a.* (*a*) modeste; **to be m. about one's achievements,** ne pas se vanter de son succès; (*b*) *O:* (*of woman*) pudique; (*c*) modéré; (fortune) modeste; **to be m. in one's requirements,** être peu exigeant; (*d*) (*of style, etc.*) sans prétentions. **-ly** *adv.* **1.** modestement; avec modestie. **2.** pudiquement. **3.** modérément. **4.** sans prétentions.
modesty ['mɔdisti] *n.* **1.** modestie *f*; **let it be said with all due m.,** soit dit sans vanité. **2.** *O:* pudeur *f.* **3.** modération *f* (d'une demande); modicité *f* (d'une dépense). **4.** absence *f* de prétention.
modicum ['mɔdikəm] *n.* **a m. of . . .,** un minimum de . . .; **a m. of truth,** une petite part de vérité.
modification [mɔdifi'keiʃ(ə)n] *n.* modification *f.*
modify ['mɔdifai] *v.tr.* **1.** (*a*) modifier; apporter des modifications à (qch.); (*b*) mitiger, atténuer (une peine); rabattre de (ses prétentions). **2.** *Gram: Ling:* modifier (le verbe, une voyelle, etc.). **modifying** *a.* (*a*) modifiant; (*b*) mitigeant.
modish ['moudiʃ] *a.* (chapeau, etc.) à la mode. **-ly** (habillé) à la mode.
modiste [mɔ'di:st] *n.f.* modiste.
Mods [mɔdz] *n.pl. Sch: F:* (*at Oxford*) premier examen pour le grade de *Bachelor of Arts.*
modular ['mɔdjulər] *a. Arch: Mth: etc:* modulaire; (meubles) à éléments (composables).
modulate ['mɔdjuleit] **1.** *v.tr.* (*a*) moduler (sa voix, des sons); (*b*) *Ph:* moduler (l'amplitude, etc.); **modulating frequency,** fréquence *f* de modulation. **2.** *v.i. Mus:* moduler.
modulation [mɔdju'leiʃ(ə)n] *n.* **1.** modulation *f*, inflexion *f* (de la voix). **2.** *Mus:* modulation. **3.** *El: Elcs:* modulation.
modulator ['mɔdjuleitər] *n. El: Elcs:* modulateur *m.*
module ['mɔdju:l] *n.* **1.** *Arch: Hyd: etc:* module *m.* **2.** (*a*) *Civ.E: etc:* module; (*b*) *Space:* module; **lunar m.,** module lunaire; **command m.,** module de commande.
modulus, *pl.* **-i** ['mɔdjuləs, -ai] *n. Mth: Mec:* module *m*, coefficient *m.*
modus operandi ['moudəsɔpə'rændai, -di:] *n.* modus *m* operandi; façon *f*, manière *f*, d'opérer.
modus vivendi ['moudəsvi'vendai, -di:] *n.* modus *m* vivendi.
moggy ['mɔgi] *n. F:* chat *m.*
Mogul ['mougəl] *n.* **1.** *Hist:* mogol *m.* **2.** *F:* gros bonnet; **movie m.,** magnat *m* du cinéma.
mohair ['mouhɛər] *n.* mohair *m.*
Mohammed [mə'hæmid] *Pr.n.m.* **1.** Mohammed. **2.** *Rel.H:* Mahomet.
Mohammedan [mə'hæmid(ə)n] *a. & n. Rel:* musulman, -ane; mahométan, -ane.
moiré ['mwɑ:rei] **1.** *a. & n. Tex:* moiré (*m*). **2.** *n.*

Metalw: moiré *m*, moirure *f*; **m. effect,** moirage *m*.
moist [mɔist] *a.* (climat, région, chaleur, etc.) humide; (peau, main, chaleur) moite; **eyes m. with tears,** yeux mouillés de larmes; **to grow m.,** se mouiller, s'humecter.
moisten ['mɔis(ə)n] **1.** *v.tr.* (*a*) mouiller, humecter; moitir (la peau); arroser (la pâte, etc.); *Tchn:* humidifier, madéfier; (*b*) **to m. a cloth with . . .,** imbiber un chiffon de . . .. **2.** *v.i.* se mouiller, s'humecter.
moistness ['mɔistnis] *n.* humidité *f*; moiteur *f*.
moisture ['mɔistjər] *n.* humidité *f*; buée *f* (sur une glace, etc.).
moisturize ['mɔistjəraiz] *v.tr.* humidifier (qch.); *Toil:* hydrater (la peau).
moisturizer ['mɔistjəraizər] *n. Toil:* crème hydratante, hydratant *m*.
molar ['moulər] *a. & n.* (dent *f*) molaire (*f*).
molasses [mə'læsiz] *n.pl.* (*with sg. const.*) mélasse *f*.
mold [mould] *etc. NAm:* = MOULD, *etc.*
molder ['mouldər] *v.i. NAm:* = MOULDER [1].
mole[1] [moul] *n.* **1.** grain *m* de beauté (au visage). **2.** nævus *m*.
mole[2] *n.* (*a*) *Z:* taupe *f*; **m. trap,** taupière *f*; **m. catcher,** taupier *m*; (*b*) (*spy*) taupe.
mole[3] *n.* môle *m*; brise-lames *m inv*; digue *f*; jetée *f*.
molecular [mə'lekjulər] *a. Ph:* moléculaire.
molecule ['mɔlikju:l] *n. Ch: Ph:* molécule *f*.
molehill ['moulhil] *n.* taupinière *f*.
moleskin ['moulskin] *n.* **1.** (peau *f* de) taupe (*f*); **m. coat,** manteau *m* en taupe. **2.** *Tex:* velours *m* de coton.
molest [mou'lest] *v.tr.* **1.** molester, importuner (qn). **2.** attenter à la pudeur de (qn).
molestation [moules'teiʃ(ə)n] *n.* **1.** molestation *f*. **2.** attentat *m* à la pudeur.
Moll [mɔl] *n.f. P:* **(gangster's) m.,** poule, môme, d'un gangster.
mollify ['mɔlifai] *v.tr.* **to m. s.o.,** adoucir, apaiser, qn, la colère de qn.
mollusc, *NAm:* **mollusk** ['mɔləsk] *n.* mollusque *m*.
mollycoddle ['mɔlikɔdl] *v.tr. F:* dorloter, câliner (un enfant); élever (un enfant) dans du coton.
molt [moult] *n. & v. NAm:* = MOULT [1, 2].
molten ['moult(ə)n] *a. Metall:* fondu, en fusion; **m. lead,** plomb fondu.
mom [mɔm] *n. NAm: F:* maman *f*.
moment ['moumənt] *n.* **1.** moment *m*, instant *m*; **I haven't a m. to spare,** je n'ai pas un instant de libre; **wait a m.! just a m.! one m.!** une seconde! un moment! un instant! **he may return at any m.,** il peut revenir d'un instant à l'autre; **I have just, only, this m. heard about it,** je viens de l'apprendre, je l'apprends, à l'instant; **I saw him a m. ago,** je l'ai vu il y a un instant; **the m. he arrives,** dès son arrivée; **at this m., at the present m.,** en ce moment; actuellement; **at that m.,** à ce moment(-là); **at the last m.,** à la dernière minute; **I'll be with you in a m.,** je suis à vous dans une minute; **nothing else for the m.,** rien de plus pour l'instant; **not a moment's hesitation,** pas un moment d'hésitation; **the man of the m.,** l'homme du jour, du moment; **the m. of truth,** la minute de vérité; **on the spur of the m.,** sur le moment. **2.** *Mth: Mec: etc:* moment (d'une force); **m. of inertia,** moment d'inertie. **3.** (*of fact, event*) **of great, little, no, m.,** de grande, de petite, d'aucune, importance.
momentary ['moumənt(ə)ri] *a.* momentané, passager. **-ily** *adv.* momentanément.
momentous [mou'mentəs] *a.* important; (décision) capitale; **on this m. occasion,** en cette occasion mémorable.
momentousness [mou'mentəsnis] *n.* importance capitale.
momentum, *pl.* **-ta** [mou'mentəm, -tə] *n.* (*a*) *Mec: Ph:* force vive, force d'impulsion; quantité *f* de mouvement; *Atom.Ph:* impulsion *f* (d'une particule); (*b*) (*impetus*) vitesse acquise; élan *m*; *Fig:* force vive (d'une attaque, etc.); **carried away by my own m.,** emporté par mon (propre) élan; (*of movement*) **to gather m.,** acquérir de la force (vive), de la vitesse.
Monaco [mɔ'nɑ:kou] *Pr.n. Geog:* **(Principality of) M.,** (Principauté *f* de) Monaco.
monad ['mɔnæd] *n. Phil: Biol: Ch:* monade *f*.
Mona Lisa ['mounə'li:zə] *Pr.n.f. Art:* la Joconde.
monarch ['mɔnək] *n.* monarque *m*.
monarchic(al) [mɔ'nɑ:kik(l)] *a.* monarchique.
monarchist ['mɔnəkist] *n. Pol:* monarchiste *mf*.
monarchy ['mɔnəki] *n.* monarchie *f*.
monastery ['mɔnəst(ə)ri] *n.* monastère *m*.
monastic [mə'næstik] *a.* monastique; monacal, -aux; claustral, -aux.
monasticism [mə'næstisizm] *n.* **1.** vie *f* monastique. **2.** système *m* monastique; monachisme *m*.
monaural [mɔ'nɔ:r(ə)l] *a. Ac:* monaural, -aux.
Monday ['mʌndi] *n.* lundi *m*; **every M.,** tous les lundis; *F:* **that M. morning feeling,** le cafard du lundi; l'après-weekend *m*.
monetarist ['mʌnit(ə)rist] *n.* monétariste *mf*.
monetary ['mʌnit(ə)ri] *a.* monétaire; **m. unit,** unité *f* monétaire.
money ['mʌni] *n.* **1.** monnaie *f*, argent *m*; (*a*) **gold, silver, m.,** monnaie d'or, d'argent; **to coin, mint, m.,** frapper de la monnaie; *F:* **he's (just) coining m.,** il gagne un argent fou; *Pol.Ec:* **bank m.,** monnaie de banque; **paper m.,** billets *mpl* (de banque), papier-monnaie *m*; *Fin: Bank:* **cheap, easy, m.,** argent à bon marché; **m. market,** marché monétaire, financier; (*pers.*) **m. changer,** courtier *m* de change; *Com:* **ready m.,** argent comptant, liquide; **to pay in ready m.,** payer (au) comptant; **to throw good m. after bad,** s'enfoncer davantage dans une mauvaise affaire; **m. matters,** affaires *fpl* d'argent, questions financières; *Post:* **m. order,** mandat-poste *m*, *pl.* mandats-poste; **international m. order,** mandat international; (*b*) **my own m.,** mon argent personnel; **spending m.,** argent pour dépenses courantes; **to be worth a lot of m.,** (i) (*of thg*) avoir de la valeur; (ii) (*of pers.*) être riche; *F:* **I'm not made of m.,** je ne suis pas cousu d'or; **to be short of m.,** être à court d'argent; **your m. or your life!** la bourse ou la vie! **to earn, make, m.,** gagner, faire, de l'argent; **to do sth. for m.,** faire qch. pour l'argent; **m. makes m.,** l'argent va à l'argent; **you've had your money's worth,** vous en avez eu pour votre argent; **it's m. thrown away, down the drain,** c'est de l'argent gaspillé, jeté par la fenêtre; **m. belt,** ceinture *f* à porte-monnaie; *F:* (*of business, product, etc.*) **m. spinner,** mine *f* d'argent; *Arach:* **m. spider,** petite araignée rouge. **2.** (*a*) (*pl.* **moneys,** *occ.* **monies**) pièce *f* de monnaie; monnaie (particulière); (*b*) *A: & Jur:* **moneys, monies,** argent, fonds *mpl*; sommes *fpl* (d'argent); **public moneys,** deniers publics.
moneybag ['mʌnibæg] *n.* **1.** sac *m* à argent; sacoche *f* (d'une receveur d'autobus, etc.). **2.** *F: O:* (*pers.*) **moneybags,** richard, -arde; rupin, -ine.
moneybox ['mʌnibɔks] *n.* **1.** tirelire *f*. **2.** caisse *f*, cassette *f*.
moneyed ['mʌnid] *a.* **1.** riche; qui a de l'argent; **the m. classes,** les gens de fortune. **2. the m. interest,** les capitalistes *m*.
moneygrubber ['mʌnigrʌbər] *n.* grippe-sou *m*, *pl.* grippe-sous; pingre *m*.
moneylender ['mʌnilendər] *n.* prêteur *m* d'argent; maison *f* de prêt.
moneymaking ['mʌnimeikiŋ] **1.** *a.* (commerce, etc.) qui rapporte. **2.** *n.* acquisition *f* de l'argent.
Mongol ['mɔŋgəl] **1.** *a. Geog:* mongol. **2.** *n.* (*a*) *Geog:* Mongol, -ole; (*b*) *Ling:* mongol *m*. **3.** *a. & n. Med:*

m., mongolien, -ienne.
Mongolia [mɔŋ'gouliə] *Pr.n. Geog:* Mongolie *f.*
Mongolian [mɔŋ'gouliən] **1.** *a. Geog:* mongol. **2.** *n.* (*a*) *Geog:* Mongol, -ole; (*b*) *Ling:* mongol *m.*
mongolism ['mɔŋgəlizm] *n. Med:* mongolisme *m.*
mongoose, *pl.* **-ses** [mɔn'gu:s, -siz] *n. Z:* mangouste *f.*
mongrel ['mʌŋgr(ə)l] **1.** *n.* (*of dog, animal*) métis, -isse; (*of dog*) bâtard, -arde. **2.** *a.* (animal, *F:* peuple) métis.
moni(c)ker ['mɔnəkər] *n. NAm: F:* (*a*) nom *m*; (*b*) surnom *m*; (*c*) signature *f.*
monitor¹ ['mɔnitər] *n.* **1.** (*pers.*) (*a*) moniteur, -trice; (*b*) *Sch:* élève choisi (i) pour maintenir la discipline, (ii) pour aider le professeur dans les travaux pratiques, etc.; (*c*) *Tp:* opérateur *m* d'interception; (*d*) *Cin: T.V:* **m. (man),** ingénieur *m* du son. **2.** *W.Tel: etc:* appareil *m* de contrôle, de surveillance; moniteur *m*; *T.V:* **m. (screen),** écran *m* de contrôle.
monitor² *v.tr.* (*a*) *W.Tel: etc:* surveiller (des émissions); *Tp:* entrer en écoute (sur une conversation); surveiller (un circuit de transmissions); (*b*) *Cin:* contrôler (l'enregistrement sonore). **monitoring** *n.* (*a*) *W.Tel:* monitoring *m*, interception *f* (des émissions); **m. station,** station *f*, centre *m*, d'écoute; (*b*) *Tp:* (i) écoute (d'une conversation); (ii) surveillance *f* (d'un circuit de transmissions); (*c*) *Cin:* contrôle *m* (de l'enregistrement sonore); (*d*) *Med:* surveillance continue (de malades).
monk [mʌnk] *n.m.* moine, religieux.
monkey¹ ['mʌŋki] *n.* **1.** (*a*) *Z:* singe *m*; **female m., she-m.,** guenon *f*; **m. house,** pavillon *m* des singes; (*b*) *F:* **you little m.!** petit polisson! petit(e) espiègle! **little m. face,** petite frimousse espiègle; **to make a m. (out) of s.o.,** se payer la tête de qn; **m. business,** (i) fricotage *m*; combine *f*; (ii) conduite *f* malhonnête; **m. tricks,** espiègleries *fpl*; *P:* **I don't give a monkey's (toss),** je m'en fous éperdument; (*c*) *Bot:* **m. nut,** (i) *Bot:* arachide *f*; (ii) *Com:* cacah(o)uète *f*; **m. puzzle (tree),** araucaria *m*; (*d*) *Cost: O:* **m. jacket,** veste courte (de garçon de café, etc.). **2.** *Civ.E: etc:* mouton *m* (de sonnette); *Tls: NAm:* **m. wrench,** clef anglaise; clef à molette. **3.** *P:* billet *m*, faf(f)iot *m*, de cinq cents livres, *U.S:* de cinq cents dollars.
monkey² *v.i.* **to m. about, around,** faire des sottises, faire l'imbécile.
monkish ['mʌŋkiʃ] *a.* de moine; monacal, -aux.
monkshood ['mʌŋkshud] *n. Bot:* (aconit *m*) napel (*m*).
mono ['mɔnou] *a. Rec: F:* monaural, mono.
monochrome ['mɔnəkroum] **1.** *a.* monochrome; en camaïeu. **2.** *n.* camaïeu *m*; (peinture *f*) monochrome (*m*).
monocle ['mɔnəkl] *n.* monocle *m.*
monogamous [mə'nɔgəməs] *a.* monogame.
monogamy [mə'nɔgəmi] *n.* monogamie *f.*
monogram ['mɔnəgræm] *n.* monogramme *m.*
monogrammed ['mɔnəgræmd] *a.* (mouchoir) brodé d'initiales.
monograph ['mɔnəgræf] *n.* monographie *f.*
monolingual [mɔnou'liŋgw(ə)l] *a.* monolingue.
monolith ['mɔnəliθ] *n.* monolithe *m.*
monolithic [mɔnə'liθik] *a.* **1.** (monument) monolithe. **2.** *Pol: etc:* monolithique.
monologue ['mɔnəlɔg] *n.* monologue *m.*
monomania [mɔnou'meiniə] *n.* monomanie *f.*
mononucleosis [mɔnənju:kli'ousis] *n. Med:* mononucléose *f.*
monophonic [mɔnou'fɔnik] *a. Ac:* monophonique.
monoplane ['mɔnəplein] *n. Av:* monoplan *m.*
monopolist [mə'nɔpəlist] *n.* **1.** monopolisateur, -trice; accapareur, -euse. **2.** *Pol:* partisan, -ane, du monopole.
monopolization [mənɔpəlai'zeiʃ(ə)n] *n.* monopolisation *f.*
monopolize [mə'nɔpəlaiz] *v.tr.* **1.** *Com:* monopoliser, accaparer (une denrée, etc.). **2.** accaparer (qn, qch.); s'emparer de (la conversation).
monopoly [mə'nɔpəli] *n.* monopole *m*; **to have a m. of sth.,** *U.S:* **on sth.,** avoir, faire, le monopole de qch.; monopoliser qch.
monorail ['mɔnoureil] *n Rail: etc:* monorail *m.*
monosyllabic [mɔnousi'læbik] *a.* monosyllabe, monosyllabique.
monosyllable [mɔnou'siləbl] *n.* monosyllabe *m.*
monotheism [mɔnou'θi:izm] *n.* monothéisme *m.*
monotheistic [mɔnouθi:'istik] *a.* monothéiste.
monotone ['mɔnətoun] **1.** *a.* monotone. **2.** *n.* débit *m* monotone, uniforme, sans modulation; **to speak in a m.,** parler d'une voix uniforme, monotone.
monotonous [mə'nɔtənəs] *a.* **1.** monotone, dont le ton ne varie pas. **2.** monotone, sans variété. **-ly** *adv.* monotonement.
monotony [mə'nɔtəni] *n.* monotonie *f.*
monotype ['mɔnətaip] *n. Typ: R.t.m.* Monotype *f.*
monoxide [mɔ'nɔksaid] *n. Ch:* **carbon m.,** oxyde *m* de carbone.
monsignor ['mɔnsinjər] *n.m. Ecc:* monseigneur.
monsoon [mɔn'su:n] *n. Meteor:* mousson *f*; **wet, summer, m.,** mousson d'été.
monster ['mɔnstər] **1.** *n.* (*a*) monstre *m*; monstruosité *f*; *Fig:* **a m. of cruelty,** un monstre de cruauté; (*b*) colosse *m*; géant, -ante. **2.** *a. F:* monstre, monstrueux; colossal, -aux; énorme; immense.
monstrance ['mɔnstrəns] *n. Ecc:* ostensoir *m.*
monstrosity [mɔn'strɔsiti] *n.* monstruosité *f.*
monstrous ['mɔnstrəs] *a.* (*a*) (*of creature*) monstrueux; (*b*) odieux, monstrueux; **it is perfectly m. that such a thing should be allowed,** c'est monstrueux que cela soit permis; (*c*) monstrueux, énorme; colossal, -aux; immense. **-ly** *adv.* monstrueusement.
montage ['mɔntɑ:ʒ] *n. Cin:* montage *m.*
Monte Carlo [mɔnti'kɑ:lou] *Pr.n. Geog:* Monte-Carlo.
month [mʌnθ] *n.* mois *m*; **lunar m.,** mois lunaire; **calendar m.,** mois civil; **in the m. of August,** au mois d'août; **a m. ago today,** il y a aujourd'hui un mois; **a thirteen months' old baby,** un bébé de treize mois; **from m. to m.,** de mois en mois; **once a m.,** une fois par mois; *F:* **never in a m. of Sundays,** jamais de la vie.
monthly ['mʌnθli] **1.** *a.* (*a*) mensuel; *Physiol:* **m. periods,** règles *fpl*; *Com:* **m. payment, instalment,** mensualité *f*; (*b*) *Rail: etc:* **m. season ticket,** (billet *m* d')abonnement (*m*) valable pour un mois. **2.** *adv.* mensuellement; tous les mois. **3.** *n.* revue, publication, mensuelle.
Montreal [mɔntri'ɔ:l] *Pr.n. Geog:* Montréal.
monument ['mɔnjumənt] *n.* **1.** monument *m*; **ancient monuments,** monuments historiques. **2.** monument funéraire; pierre tombale.
monumental [mɔnju'ment(ə)l] *a.* **1.** (*a*) (*of statue, etc.*) monumental, -aux; (*b*) (*of literary work, etc.*) monumental; de grande envergure; (ignorance) prodigieuse. **2. m. mason,** marbrier *m.*
moo¹ [mu:] **1.** *n.* meuglement *m*, beuglement *m* (d'une vache, etc.). **2.** *int.* **m.!** meuh!
moo² *v.i.* **(mooed)** (*of cow, etc.*) meugler, beugler.
mooch [mu:tʃ] *F:* **1.** *v.i.* **to m. about,** flâner, traîner; se balader. **2.** *v.i. & tr. esp. NAm:* emprunter (qch. à qn); taper (qn de qch.).
moocow ['mu:kau] *n. F:* (*child's language*) vache *f*, meu-meu *f.*
mood¹ [mu:d] *n.* (*a*) *Log: Gram:* mode *m*; **the indicative m.,** l'indicatif *m*; (*b*) *esp. U.S: Mus:* mode.
mood² *n.* humeur *f*, disposition *f*; **to be in a good,**

bad, m., être bien, mal, disposé; être de bonne, de mauvaise, humeur; **to be in a generous m.,** être en veine de générosité; **to be in the m. for reading,** avoir envie de lire; **he's in no m. for laughing,** il n'est pas d'humeur à rire; **I'm not in the m.,** ça ne me dit rien.

moodiness ['mu:dinis] *n.* **1.** morosité *f*, maussaderie *f.* **2.** humeur changeante.

moody ['mu:di] *a.* **1.** chagrin, morose, maussade. **2.** d'humeur changeante. **-ily** *adv.* d'un air morose; maussadement.

moon[1] [mu:n] *n.* **1.** lune *f*; **new m.,** nouvelle lune; **full m.,** pleine lune; **to land on the m.,** atterrir, se poser, sur la lune; *F:* alunir; *Fig:* **to cry for the m.,** demander la lune; **to promise s.o. the m. (and stars),** promettre la lune à qn; **once in a blue m.,** tous les trente-six du mois; *F:* **to be over the m.,** être enchanté, ravi (**about,** de). **2.** (*month*) *Astr:* lunaison *f*; *Poet:* lune, mois *m.* **3.** lunule *f* (des ongles).

moon[2] *v.i.* **to m. about, around,** musarder, flâner; **to m. over s.o., sth.,** languir pour qn, qch.

moonbeam ['mu:nbi:m] *n.* rayon *m* de lune.

moonless ['mu:nlis] *a.* (nuit, etc.) sans lune.

moonlight[1] ['mu:nlait] *n.* clair *m* de lune; **in the m., by m.,** au clair de lune; à la clarté, la lumière, de la lune; *F:* **m. flit,** déménagement *m* à la cloche de bois.

moonlight[2] *v.i. F:* faire du travail noir, travailler au noir. **moonlighting** *n.* travail (au) noir.

moonlighter ['mu:nlaitər] *n. F:* travailleur *m* au noir.

moonlit ['mu:nlit] *a.* éclairé par la lune.

moonrise ['mu:nraiz] *n.* lever *m* de la lune.

moonshine ['mu:nʃain] *n.* **1.** clair *m* de lune. **2.** *F:* balivernes *fpl*, fariboles *fpl*, fadaises *fpl*; **that's all m.,** tout ça c'est de la blague. **3.** *NAm: F:* alcool (i) illicitement distillé, (ii) de contrebande.

moonstone ['mu:nstoun] *n. Lap:* adulaire *f*; feldspath nacré; pierre *f* de lune.

moonstruck ['mu:nstrʌk] *a.* à l'esprit dérangé; toqué.

moony ['mu:ni] *a.* (*of pers.*) (i) rêveur, -euse; musard; (ii) dans la lune.

moor[1] [muər] *n.* (*a*) lande *f*, bruyère *f*; (*b*) *Scot:* chasse réservée.

moor[2] [mɔ:r] *Nau:* **1.** *v.tr.* amarrer (un navire); mouiller (une bouée, une mine). **2.** *v.i.* s'amarrer. **mooring** *n.* **1.** (*a*) amarrage *m*; **m. pile, post,** pieu *m*, borne *f*, d'amarrage; **m. line,** câble *m* d'amarrage; (*b*) poste *m* d'amarrage; **ship at her moorings,** navire sur ses amarres.

Moor[3] [muər] *n.* Maure *m*, More *m*; Mauresque *f.*

moorfowl ['muəfaul] *n. Orn:* lagopède *m* rouge d'Écosse.

moorhen ['muəhen] *n. Orn:* **1.** poule *f* d'eau. **2.** lagopède *m* rouge d'Écosse (femelle).

Moorish ['muəriʃ] *a.* mauresque, maure.

moorland ['muələnd] *n.* lande *f*, bruyère *f.*

moose [mu:s] *n.* (*pl.* **moose**) *Z:* **American m.,** orignal *m*, élan *m* du Canada.

moot[1] [mu:t] *a.* (*of question, etc.*) sujet à controverse; discutable.

moot[2] *v.tr.* soulever (une question); mettre (une question) sur le tapis.

mop[1] [mɔp] *n.* **1.** (*a*) balai *m* à laver, balai-éponge *m*, *pl.* balais-éponges; balai à franges; lavette *f* (à vaisselle); (*b*) *Nau:* faubert *m*, vadrouille *f*, guipon *m.* **2. m. of hair,** tignasse *f*; toison *f.*

mop[2] *v.tr.* **(mopped)** éponger, essuyer (le parquet) avec un balai; *Nau:* fauberder, fauberter (le pont); **to m. one's brow,** s'éponger le front. **mopping** *n.* (*a*) **m. (up),** épongeage *m*, essuyage *m* (du parquet, etc.); (*b*) *Mil:* **m. up,** nettoyage *m* (d'une position, etc.); **m. up operations,** opérations *f* de nettoyage.

mop up *v.tr.* (*a*) éponger (de l'eau); **to take a piece of bread to m. up the sauce,** prendre un morceau de pain pour finir la sauce; (*b*) *Mil: etc:* liquider (les derniers résistants); nettoyer (une position, etc.).

mope [moup] *v.i.* être triste, mélancolique; broyer du noir.

moped ['mouped] *n. F:* vélomoteur *m*; mobylette *f* (*R.t.m.*)

moppet ['mɔpit] *n. F:* gamin, -ine, gosse *mf.*

moquette [mɔ'ket] *n. Tex:* moquette *f.*

moraine [mə'rein] *n. Geol:* moraine *f.*

moral ['mɔr(ə)l] **I.** *a.* moral, -aux; **m. standard,** sens moral; **m. life,** vie exemplaire; **m. courage,** courage moral; **m. victory,** victoire morale; **m. certainty,** certitude morale. **II.** *n.* **1.** morale *f*, moralité *f* (d'un conte); **story with a m.,** conte moral. **2. morals,** moralité, mœurs *fpl*; **man of loose morals,** homme de mœurs douteuses. **morally** *adv.* moralement; **m. bound to do sth.,** moralement obligé de faire qch.; **m. certain,** moralement certain.

morale [mɔ'rɑ:l] *n.* (*no pl.*) moral *m*; **to undermine the m. (of the army),** démoraliser (les troupes).

moralist ['mɔrəlist] *n.* moraliste *mf.*

morality [mə'ræliti] *n.* **1.** (*a*) moralité *f*, principes moraux; sens moral; (*b*) bonnes mœurs; conduite *f*; (*c*) **moralities,** principes moraux. **2.** réflexion morale; moralité. **3.** *Th:* **m. (play),** moralité.

moralize ['mɔrəlaiz] **1.** *v.i.* moraliser, faire de la morale (**on, upon, sth.,** sur qch.). **2.** *v.tr.* (*a*) donner une interprétation morale à (qch.); (*b*) élever le niveau moral de (qch.). **moralizing** *a.* moralisant; moralisateur, -trice.

morass [mə'ræs] *n.* marais *m*, fondrière *f.*

moratorium [mɔrə'tɔ:riəm] *n. Fin:* moratoire *m*; moratorium *m*, *pl.* moratoria.

morbid ['mɔ:bid] *a.* **1.** (symptôme, idée) morbide; (curiosité) morbide, malsaine. **2.** *Med:* (anatomie) pathologique. **-ly** *adv.* morbidement.

morbidness ['mɔ:bidnis] *n.* (*a*) morbidité *f*; (*b*) tristesse maladive (des pensées).

mordant ['mɔ:d(ə)nt] *a.* (acide, *Fig:* sarcasme) mordant, caustique.

more [mɔ:r] **1.** *a. & indef. pron.* plus (de); **he has m. patience than I (have),** il a plus de patience que moi; **one m.,** un de plus, encore un; **one or m.,** un ou plusieurs; **one m. hour,** une heure de plus; **there's only one m. problem to solve,** il n'y a plus qu'un problème à résoudre; **(some) m. bread, please!** encore du pain, s'il vous plaît! **to have some m. wine,** reprendre du vin; **do you want (any, some) m.?** en voulez-vous encore? **what m. can I say?** que puis-je dire de plus? **there is nothing m. to be said,** il n'y a plus rien à dire; **have you (got) any m. books?** avez-vous d'autres livres? **I need still m.,** il m'en faut encore davantage. **2.** *n. or indef.pron.* **I needn't say m.,** pas besoin d'en dire davantage; **that's m. than enough,** c'est plus qu'il n'en faut; **he knows m. about it than you,** il en sait plus (long) que vous; **he's m. than 30,** il a plus de 30 ans; **what is m.,** (et) qui plus est; de plus; **she's m. of an artist than her sister,** elle est plus artiste que sa sœur; **neither m. nor less,** ni plus ni moins. **3.** *adv.* (*a*) plus, davantage; **m. easily,** plus facilement; **this is far m. serious,** c'est bien, beaucoup, plus sérieux; **m. and m.,** de plus en plus; **he was m. surprised than annoyed,** il était plutôt surpris que fâché; **m. than satisfied,** plus que satisfait; **that's m. like it!** ça, c'est mieux! **m. or less,** plus ou moins; sensiblement; (*b*) **once m.,** encore une fois, une fois de plus. **4.** (*a*) *a.* **(the) more's the pity,** c'est d'autant plus malheureux, plus regrettable; (*b*) *n.* **the m. one has the m. one wants,** plus on a, plus on désire avoir; **the m. I read, the m. I learn,** plus je lis, plus j'apprends; (*c*) *adv.* **all the m. (reason),** à plus forte raison; raison de plus; **I am all the m. surprised as . . .,** j'en suis d'autant plus étonné que . . .; **it makes me all the m. proud,** je n'en suis que plus fier. **5.** (*a*) *a.* **I have no m. money,** je n'ai plus d'argent; **no m. soup, thank you,** plus de potage, merci; (*b*) *n.* **I have no m.,** je n'en ai plus; **I can do no m.,** je ne peux pas faire plus; **let us say no m. about it,** n'en parlons plus; **say no m.!** cela suffit! **he's just a good friend, nothing m.,** c'est un bon ami, rien de plus; (*c*) *adv.* (i) **I can't see her any m.,** je ne peux plus la voir; **he doesn't drink any m.,** il ne boit plus; **he doesn't know any m. about it,** il n'en sait pas davantage; *Lit:* **he is no m.,** il n'est plus, il est mort; (ii) (*just as little*) **he is no m. a lord than I am,** il n'est pas plus (un) lord que moi; **I can't make out how it happened—no m. can I,** je ne m'explique pas comment c'est arrivé—(ni) moi non plus.

more(-)ish ['mɔːriʃ] *a. F:* appétissant; **this cake is very m.,** ce gâteau a un goût de revenez-y.

morel [mɔ'rel] *n. Fung:* morille *f.*

morello [mə'relou] *n. Hort:* **m. (cherry),** griotte *f*; **m. (cherry) tree,** griottier *m.*

moreover [mɔː'rouvər] *adv.* d'ailleurs; du reste; et qui plus est; **and m.,** bien plus.

Moresque [mɔː'resk] *a. & n. Art: etc:* mauresque (*f*).

morganatic [mɔːgə'nætik] *a.* morganatique. **-ally** *adv.* morganatiquement.

morgue [mɔrg] *n.* **1.** morgue *f*; dépôt *m* mortuaire. **2.** *Journ: F:* archives *fpl.*

moribund ['mɔribʌnd] *a. & n.* moribond, -onde.

Mormon ['mɔːmən] *a. & n. Rel:* mormon, -one.

morn [mɔːn] *n. Lit:* matin *m.*

morning ['mɔːniŋ] *n.* **1.** (*a*) matin *m*; **to work from m. till night; to work m., noon and night,** travailler du matin au soir; **this m.,** ce matin; **tomorrow m.,** demain matin; **the next m., the m. after,** le lendemain matin; **the m. before,** la veille au matin; *F:* **the m. after the night before,** le lendemain de la cuite; **four o'clock in the m.,** quatre heures du matin; **early in the m.,** de grand matin; **good m.,** bonjour; (*b*) matinée *f*; **in the course of the m.,** dans la matinée; **m. off,** matinée de congé; **a morning's work,** une matinée de travail. **2.** *attrib.* (*of breeze, etc.*) matinal, -aux; du matin; **early m. tea,** tasse de thé prise au lit avant de se lever; *Bot:* **m. glory,** belle-de-jour *f*; liseron *m.*

Moroccan [mə'rɔkən] *Geog:* **1.** *a.* marocaine. **2.** *n.* Marocain, -aine.

Morocco [mə'rɔkou] **1.** *Pr.n. Geog:* Maroc *m.* **2.** *n.* **m.,** maroquin *m.*

moron ['mɔːrɔn] *n.* **1.** (homme, femme) faible d'esprit. **2.** *F:* idiot, -ote, crétin *m.*

moronic [mə'rɔnik] *a.* **1.** faible d'esprit. **2.** *F:* idiot, crétin.

morose [mə'rous] *a.* (*of pers., disposition*) chagrin, morose. **-ly** *adv.* d'un air chagrin, morose.

moroseness [mə'rousnis] *n.* morosité *f*; humeur chagrine, morose.

morpheme ['mɔːfiːm] *n. Ling:* morphème *m.*

Morpheus ['mɔːfiəs] *Pr.n.m. Myth:* Morphée.

morphia ['mɔːfiə], **morphine** ['mɔːfiːn] *n.* morphine *f*; **m. addict,** morphinomane *mf.*

morphological [mɔːfə'lɔdʒik(ə)l] *a.* morphologique.

morphology [mɔː'fɔlədʒi] *n.* morphologie *f.*

Morris ['mɔris] **M. dance,** (sorte de) danse *f* folklorique.

morrow ['mɔrou] *n. A: & Lit:* lendemain *m*; **on the m.,** le lendemain.

Morse [mɔːs] *Pr.n. Tg:* **M. alphabet, code,** (alphabet *m*, code *m*) Morse *m.*

morsel ['mɔːs(ə)l] *n.* (petit) morceau; **choice m., dainty m.,** morceau friand, de choix.

mortadella [mɔːtə'delə] *n.* **m. (sausage),** mortadelle *f.*

mortal ['mɔːt(ə)l] *a.* **1.** (*a*) mortel; **all men are m.,** tous les hommes sont mortels; **m. remains,** dépouille mortelle; (*b*) *n.* mortel *m*; **a m.,** un humain; (*c*) humain. **2.** mortel; funeste; fatal, -als (**to,** à); **m. blow,** coup mortel; **m. sin,** péché mortel. **3. m. enemy,** ennemi mortel; ennemi à mort; **m. combat,** combat *m* à mort; **to be in m. fear of . . .,** avoir une peur mortelle de . . .; *F:* **it's no m. use,** ça ne sert absolument à rien. **-ally** *adv.* mortellement; **m. wounded,** blessé à mort; **to be m. afraid,** avoir une peur mortelle.

mortality [mɔː'tæliti] *n.* **1.** mortalité *f* (de l'homme, etc.). **2.** *coll.* les mortels *mpl*, les humains *mpl.* **3.** mortalité; **infant m.,** mortalité infantile.

mortar¹ ['mɔːtər] *n.* **1.** (*a*) *Pharm: etc:* mortier *m* (pour piler); *Dom.Ec:* égrugeoir *m*; **pestle and m.,** pilon *m* et mortier; (*b*) *Artil:* mortier; lance-bombes *m inv.* **2.** *Const:* mortier; **cement m.,** mortier enduit *m*, de ciment; *F:* **to put one's money in bricks and m.,** placer son argent en immeubles.

mortar² *v.tr. Const:* lier (les pierres) avec du mortier.

mortarboard ['mɔːtəbɔːd] *n.* toque universitaire anglaise.

mortgage¹ ['mɔːgidʒ] *n.* hypothèque *f*; **first, prior, m.,** hypothèque de premier rang; **second m.,** seconde hypothèque; **to raise a m.,** contracter une hypothèque; **to buy a house on a m.,** prendre une hypothèque pour acheter une maison; **m. bond, debenture,** obligation *f* hypothécaire; **m. loan,** emprunt *m* hypothécaire.

mortgage² *v.tr.* hypothéquer, grever (une terre, un immeuble, etc.); engager, mettre en gage (des marchandises, des titres); **mortgaged estate,** domaine affecté d'hypothèques.

mortgagee [mɔːgi'dʒiː] *n.* créancier *m* hypothécaire.

mortgager, mortgagor ['mɔːgidʒər] *n.* débiteur *m* hypothécaire.

mortice ['mɔːtis] *n. & v.tr.* = MORTISE¹, ².

mortician [mɔː'tiʃ(ə)n] *n. U.S:* entrepreneur *m* de pompes funèbres.

mortification [mɔːtifi'keiʃ(ə)n] *n.* **1.** mortification *f* (du corps, des passions). **2.** mortification, humiliation *f.* **3.** *Med:* mortification, sphacélisme *m.*

mortify ['mɔːtifai] **1.** *v.tr.* (*a*) mortifier, châtier (son corps, ses passions); (*b*) mortifier, humilier (qn); (*c*) *Med:* mortifier, gangrener. **2.** *v.i. Med:* se gangrener, se mortifier. **mortifying** *a.* mortifiant, humiliant.

mortise¹ ['mɔːtis] *n. Carp:* mortaise *f*; **m. lock,** serrure encastrée.

mortise² *v.tr.* mortaiser; **to m. two beams together,** emmortaiser, emboîter, deux poutres.

mortuary ['mɔːtjəri] **1.** *a.* mortuaire. **2.** *n.* (*a*) dépôt *m* mortuaire; (*b*) morgue *f.*

mosaic¹ [mou'zeiik] *n.* (*a*) *Art: etc:* mosaïque *f*; **m. floor,** dallage *m* en mosaïque; (*b*) *T.V:* mosaïque (photoélectrique).

Mosaic² *a. B.Hist:* (loi, etc.) mosaïque, de Moïse.

Moscow ['mɔskou] *Pr.n. Geog:* Moscou.

Moses ['mouziz] *Pr.n.m. B.Hist:* Moïse; *int. F: O:* **Holy M.!** grand Dieu! **M. basket,** moïse *m.*

mosey ['mouzi] *v.i. U.S: P:* **to m. along,** aller son petit bonhomme de chemin.

Moslem ['mɔzlem] **1.** *a.* musulman. **2.** *n.* musulman, -ane.

mosque [mɔsk] *n.* mosquée *f.*

mosquito, *pl.* **-oes** [məs'kiːtou, -ouz] *n. Ent:* moustique *m*; **m. bite,** piqûre *f* de moustique; **m. net,** moustiquaire *f.*

moss [mɔs] *n.* **1.** *Dial:* **(peat) m.,** tourbière *f.* **2.** *Bot:* (*a*) mousse *f*; **tree m.,** usnée *f*; (*b*) *Algae: etc:* **Irish m., pearl m.,** carragheen *m*; mousse perlée (d'Irlande); (*c*) **m. rose,** rose moussue; *F:* rose mousseuse. **3.** *Miner:* **m. agate,** agate mousseuse. **4.** *Knit:* **m. stitch,** point *m* de riz.

mossy ['mɔsi] *a.* moussu.

most [moust] **1.** *a.* (*a*) le plus (de); **you have made (the) m. mistakes,** c'est vous qui avez fait le plus de fautes; (*b*) **m. men,** la plupart des hommes; **in m. cases,** dans la majorité des cas; **for the m. part,** (i) pour la plupart; (ii) le plus souvent. **2.** *n. & indef. pron.* (*a*) le plus; **do the m. you can,** faites le plus que vous pourrez; **at the (very) m.,** au maximum; (tout) au plus; **to make the m. (of sth.),** (i) tirer le meilleur parti possible (de qch.); faire valoir (son argent); bien employer (son temps); exploiter (son talent); ménager le plus possible (ses provisions, etc.); (ii) représenter (qch.) sous son plus beau jour ou sous son plus vilain jour; (*b*) la plupart; **m. of the work,** la plus grande partie du travail; **m. of the time,** la plupart du temps; (*c*) **he is more reliable than m.,** on peut compter sur lui plus que sur la plupart des hommes. **3.** *adv. as superlative of comparison* (*a*) (*with vb*) le plus; **what I want m.,** ce que je désire par-dessus tout; (*b*) (*with adj.*) **the m.,** le plus, la plus, les plus; **the m. beautiful woman,** la plus belle femme; (*c*) (*with adv.*) le plus; **those who have answered m. accurately,** ceux qui ont répondu le plus exactement. **4.** *adv.* (*intensive*) très, fort, bien; **m. unhappy,** bien malheureux; **m. likely, probably,** très probablement; **he has been m. rude,** il a été on ne peut plus impoli. **-ly** *adv.* **1.** pour la plupart; principalement; **they come m. from Scotland,** ils viennent surtout de l'Écosse. **2.** le plus souvent, (pour) la plupart du temps.

mote [mout] *n. Lit:* atome *m* de poussière; *B:* **the m. in thy brother's eye,** la paille dans l'œil de ton frère.

motel [mou'tel] *n.* motel *m.*

motet [mou'tet] *n. Mus:* motet *m.*

moth [mɔθ] *n. Ent:* (*a*) **(clothes) m.,** mite *f*; *F:* **the moths have been at my fur coat,** mon manteau de fourrure est tout mangé par les mites; (*b*) papillon *m* nocturne, de nuit; **gipsy m.,** zigzag *m*; **hawk m.,** sphinx *m*; crépusculaire *m*, smérinthe *m*; **tiger m.,** arctie *f.*

mothball ['mɔθbɔːl] *n.* boule *f* de naphtaline; *Fig:* **in mothballs,** en conserve; (*of plan*) en réserve.

motheaten ['mɔθiːt(ə)n] *a.* **1.** rongé, mangé, des mites; mangé aux mites; mité. **2.** *F: O:* (*of idea, etc.*) suranné. **3.** *F:* misérable; (hôtel) miteux.

mother[1] ['mʌðər] *n.f.* **1.** (*a*) mère; **yes m.!** oui, maman! **m. to be,** future maman; **m. of six,** mère de six enfants; **mother's day,** fête *f* des mères; (*b*) **m. hen,** mère poule; **m. country,** (i) mère-patrie *f*, *pl.* mères-patries; (ii) métropole *f* (d'une colonie); **m. tongue,** langue maternelle; **m. wit,** le bon sens inné; **m. church,** église mère; *Nau:* **m. ship,** ravitailleur *m.* **2.** *Ecc:* **reverend m.,** (i) (sœur) supérieure; (ii) (*form of address*) ma mère; **the M. Superior,** la Mère supérieure. **3.** (*a*) *Geol: etc:* **m. rock,** roche *f* mère; **m. of pearl,** nacre *f*; (*b*) *Ch:* **m. of vinegar,** mère de vinaigre.

mother[2] *v.tr.* (*a*) donner des soins maternels à (qn); servir de mère à (qn); (*b*) dorloter (qn). **mothering** *n.* **1.** soins maternels. **2. M. Sunday,** la fête des mères.

mothercraft ['mʌðəkrɑːft] *n.* puériculture *f.*

motherhood ['mʌðəhud] *n.* maternité *f.*

mother-in-law ['mʌðərinlɔː] *n.f.* belle-mère, *pl.* belles-mères.

motherland ['mʌðəlænd] *n.* patrie *f*; pays natal.

motherless ['mʌðəlis] *a.* sans mère; orphelin (de mère).

motherly ['mʌðəli] *a.* **1.** maternel, de mère. **2.** digne d'une mère.

moth-hole ['mɔθhoul] *n.* piqûre *f*, trou *m*, de mite.

mothproof[1] ['mɔθpruːf] *a.* traité à l'antimite; antimite(s).

mothproof[2] *v.tr.* traiter à l'antimite.

motif [mou'tiːf] *n.* motif *m.*

motion[1] ['mouʃ(ə)n] *n.* **1.** mouvement *m*, déplacement *m*; (*a*) *Mec: Ph:* **body in m.,** corps *m* en mouvement; **perpetual m.,** mouvement perpétuel; (*b*) *Mec.E: Mch:* **m. study,** analyse *f* du mouvement; chronophotographie *f*; (*c*) (*of vehicle, apparatus*) marche *f*, mouvement; **car in m.,** voiture *f* en marche; **to put, set, (sth.) in m.,** mettre (qch.) en mouvement, en marche, en jeu; embrayer (une machine); faire agir (la loi); (*d*) *esp. NAm: Cin:* **m. picture,** film *m.* **2.** (*a*) mouvement (du bras, etc.); *F:* **to go through the motions,** faire semblant d'agir selon les règles; (*b*) signe *m*, geste *m*; *Ind: etc:* **time and motion consultant,** organisateur-conseil *m*, *pl.* organisateurs-conseils. **3.** (*a*) motion *f*, proposition *f*; **to propose a m.,** faire une proposition; **to put the m.,** mettre la proposition aux voix; **the m. was carried,** la motion fut adoptée; (*b*) *Jur:* demande *f*, requête *f*. **4.** *Med:* **(bowel) m.,** évacuation *f*, selle *f*.

motion[2] *v.tr. & i.* **to m. (to) s.o. to do sth.,** faire signe à qn de faire qch.; **to m. s.o. away, in,** faire signe à qn de s'éloigner, d'entrer.

motionless ['mouʃ(ə)nlis] *a.* immobile; sans mouvement; **to remain m.,** ne pas bouger, rester immobile.

motivate ['moutiveit] *v.tr.* motiver (une action, etc.); pousser, inciter (qn).

motivation [mouti'veiʃ(ə)n] *n.* motifs *mpl*; *esp. Psy:* motivation *f.*

motive ['moutiv] **1.** *a.* moteur, -trice; **m. power,** force motrice. **2.** *n.* (*a*) motif *m* **(for doing sth.,** à, pour, faire qch.); (*b*) mobile *m* (d'une action); **interest is a powerful m.,** l'intérêt est un puissant ressort; **I wonder what his m. is,** je me demande pourquoi, pour quelle raison, il fait cela. **3.** *n. Art:* motif (d'un tableau, etc.).

motley ['mɔtli] **1.** *a.* (*a*) bariolé, bigarré; (*b*) divers, mêlé; **m. crowd,** foule hétéroclite. **2.** *n.* (*a*) mélange *m* hétéroclite; (*b*) *A:* livrée *f* de bouffon de cour.

motocross ['moutoukrɔs] *n. Sp:* moto-cross *m.*

motor[1] ['moutər] **1.** *a.* moteur, -trice; (*a*) *Anat:* (muscle, nerf, centre) moteur; *Med:* **m. paralysis,** paralysie *f* des centres moteurs; (*b*) *Mec:* **m. torque,** couple moteur. **2.** *n.* moteur *m*; (*a*) **starting m.,** moteur de démarrage; **m. vehicle,** voiture *f* automobile; **m. show,** salon *m* de l'automobile; (*b*) *El:* **electric m.,** moteur électrique; *Rail:* **(electric) m. carriage,** (voiture) motrice (*f*); (*c*) *P:* voiture *f.*

motor[2] **1.** *v.i.* voyager, circuler, en voiture. **2.** *v.tr. O:* conduire, transporter, (qn) en voiture. **motoring** *n.* automobilisme *m*; **school of m.,** auto-école *f*, *pl.* auto-écoles; **m. offence,** infraction *f* au code de la route.

motorail ['moutəreil] *n. Rail:* **m. (service),** train(s) *m*(*pl*) (à) auto-couchettes.

motor-assisted ['moutərə'sistid] *a.* (bicyclette) à moteur.

motorbike ['moutəbaik] *n. F:* = MOTORCYCLE.

motorboat ['moutəbout] *n.* vedette *f* automobile; canot *m* automobile, à moteur.

motorcade ['moutəkeid] *n.* défilé *m* de voitures.

motorcar ['moutəkɑːr] *n.* automobile *f*, voiture *f.*

motorcycle ['moutəsaikl] *n.* motocyclette *f*, *F:* moto *f*; **(lightweight) m.,** vélomoteur *m*; cyclomoteur *m.*

motorcycling ['moutəsaikliŋ] *n.* motocyclisme *m.*

motorcyclist ['moutəsaiklist] *n.* motocycliste *mf.*

motor-driven ['moutədriv(ə)n] *a.* actionné, commandé, par moteur; à (électro)moteur.

motorist ['moutərist] *n.* automobiliste *mf.*

motorization [moutərai'zeiʃ(ə)n] *n.* motorisation *f.*
motorize ['moutəraiz] *v.tr.* motoriser; **motorized,** motorisé; (bicyclette) à moteur.
motorman, *pl.* **-men** ['moutəmæn, -men] *n.m.* wattman (de tramway); conducteur (de tramway, de train de métro).
motorway ['moutəwei] *n.* autoroute *f.*
mottled ['mɔt(ə)ld] *a.* tacheté, moucheté, diapré; (peau) marbrée; (tissu) chiné; (bois) madré.
mottling ['mɔtliŋ] *n.* marbrure *f,* diaprure *f; Tex:* chinage *m,* chiné *m.*
motto, *pl.* **-oes** ['mɔtou, -ouz] *n.* **1.** devise *f.* **2.** *Her:* mot *m* (d'une devise). **3.** *Typ:* épigraphe *f* (en tête de chapitre). **4.** *Mus:* motif *m.* **5.** (*in Christmas cracker*) devinette *f;* phrase amusante.
mould¹, *NAm:* **mold¹** [mould] *n.* terre végétale, meuble; **vegetable m.,** terreau *m,* humus *m.*
mould², *NAm:* **mold²** *n.* **1.** *Const: etc:* (*template*) calibre *m,* profil *m; N.Arch: Av:* gabarit *m.* **2.** (*a*) *Art: Cer: etc:* moule *m; Dom.Ec:* **jelly m.,** moule à gelée; *Lit:* **to be cast in an heroic m.,** être de la trempe des héros; **characters cast in the same m.,** caractères jetés dans le même moule; (*b*) *Metall:* **casting m.,** moule à fonte; **box m.,** châssis *m* (de moule); (*c*) *Typ:* matrice *f* (de caractère); *Rec:* matrice (de disque). **3.** *Cu:* **rice m.,** gâteau *m* de riz. **4.** *Arch:* moulure *f.*
mould³, *NAm:* **mold³** *v.tr.* **1.** mouler, façonner; former, façonner (le caractère de qn); **moulded plastic,** plastique moulé. **2.** mettre (le pain) en forme. **moulding,** *NAm:* **molding** *n.* **1.** (*a*) *Metall: etc:* moulage *m;* **compression m.,** moulage sous pression; **m. box, flask,** châssis *m* (à mouler); (*b*) mise *f* en forme (du pain); (*c*) formation *f* (du caractère, etc.); manipulation *f,* mise *f* en condition (de l'opinion publique). **2.** moulure *f;* profilé *m;* (*a*) **drip, weather, m.,** rejéteau *m,* jet *m* d'eau (de fenêtre, de porte); larmier *m;* (*b*) *Arch:* baguette *f;* **plain m.,** listeau *m,* listel *m;* **grooved m.,** moulure à gorge.
mould⁴, *NAm:* **mold⁴** *n.* moisi *m,* moisissure *f.*
moulder, *NAm:* **molder** ['mouldər] *v.i.* tomber en poussière; s'effriter; (*of pers.*) moisir.
mouldy, *NAm:* **moldy** ['mouldi] *a.* (*a*) moisi; **to smell m.,** sentir le moisi; (*b*) *F: O:* moche.
moult¹, *NAm:* **molt¹** [moult] *n.* mue *f;* **bird in the m.,** oiseau *m* en mue.
moult², *NAm:* **molt²** **1.** *v.i.* (*of bird, reptile, etc.*) muer. **2.** *v.tr.* perdre (ses plumes, sa peau. **moulting,** *NAm:* **molting** **1.** *a.* en mue. **2.** *n.* **m. (season),** mue *f.*
mound [maund] *n.* (*a*) (*artificial*) tertre *m,* monticule *m,* butte *f; Civ.E: etc:* remblai *m;* **burial mound,** tumulus *m;* (*b*) monceau *m,* tas *m* (de pierres, etc.); (*c*) (*natural*) monticule.
mount¹ [maunt] *n.* **1.** mont *m,* montagne *f;* **M. Sinai,** le mont Sinaï. **2.** *Palmistry:* mont *m.*
mount² *n.* **1.** (*a*) montage *m;* support *m; Artil: etc:* affût *m;* trépied *m;* (*b*) monture (d'une lentille, d'un prisme); **lens m.,** porte-objectif *m inv* (d'un microscope); (*c*) *Art: etc:* carton *m* de montage (d'un tableau, etc.). **2.** (*a*) monture (d'un cavalier); cheval *m,* etc.; (*b*) *Turf:* monte *f.*
mount³ **I.** *v.i.* **1.** monter; **the blood mounted to his head,** le sang lui est monté à la tête. **2.** *Equit:* se mettre en selle; monter, sauter, à cheval. **II.** *v.tr. & i.* **1. to m. (on) the scaffold,** monter sur l'échafaud; (*of car, etc.*) **to m. the pavement,** monter sur le trottoir. **2. to m. (on) a horse, a bicycle,** monter sur, enfourcher, un cheval, une bicyclette. **3.** *Breed:* couvrir, monter (une femelle). **III.** *v.tr.* **1.** monter, gravir (l'escalier, une colline); monter à (une échelle); monter sur (un escabeau). **2. to m. s.o. (on a horse),** hisser qn sur un cheval; **to m. a squadron of cavalry,** monter un escadron de cavalerie; **the mounted police,** la police montée. **3.** (*a*) fixer (qch.) sur une monture; mettre (qch.) sur (son) pied, sur (son) socle; (*b*) *Artil: etc:* mettre (un canon, une pièce) sur (son) affût; (*c*) **to m. guard,** monter la garde. **4.** (*a*) monter, installer (une machine, un moteur, etc.); monter, sertir (une pierre précieuse); entoiler, monter (un tableau, une photographie); (*b*) *Th:* monter (une pièce); (*c*) *Mil: etc:* monter (une offensive, etc.). **mounting** *n.* **1.** (*a*) mise *f* (de qch.) sur (son) pied, sur (son) socle; fixation *f,* installation *f* (d'un télescope, etc.) sur sa monture; (*b*) *Artil: etc:* mise (d'un canon) sur (son affût); (*c*) *Mec.E:* montage *m,* assemblage *m,* installation (d'une machine, d'un moteur, etc.); (*d*) entoilage *m,* montage (d'une photographie, d'un tableau, etc.); (*e*) *Th:* montage *m* (d'une pièce); (*f*) *Equit:* **m. block,** montoir *m.* **2.** (*a*) support *m;* bâti *m,* socle *m* (d'une machine, d'un moteur); monture *f,* garniture *f* (de fusil, etc.); monture (d'une pierre précieuse); **engine mountings,** pièces *fpl* d'assemblage d'un moteur; (*b*) *Artil:* affût *m;* (*of machine-gun*) affût, trépied *m.* **mount up** *v.i.* croître, monter, augmenter; **the bill was mounting up,** la facture augmentait; **it all mounts up,** ça finit pas chiffrer.
mountain ['mauntin] *n.* (*a*) montagne *f;* **range of mountains, m. range,** chaîne *f* de montagnes; **the Rocky Mountains,** les montagnes Rocheuses; **to spend one's holidays in the mountains,** passer ses vacances à la montagne; **to make a m. out of a molehill,** se faire d'une mouche un éléphant; **m. scenery, stream,** paysage *m,* ruisseau *m,* de montagne; **m. tribe,** tribu montagnarde; **m. rescue,** secours *m* en montagne; **m. sickness,** mal *m* de montagne; (*b*) *Bot:* **m. pine,** pin *m* de montagne; **m. ash,** sorbier *m* commun, sauvage; (*c*) *Mil:* **m. troops,** troupes alpines, de montagne; (*d*) **a m. of work,** un travail monstre.
mountaineer¹ [maunti'niər] *n.* alpiniste *mf.*
mountaineer² *v.i.* faire de l'alpinisme. **mountaineering** *n.* alpinisme *m.*
mountainous ['mauntinəs] *a.* **1.** (pays, etc.) montagneux. **2. m. seas,** vagues gigantesques.
mountebank ['mauntibæŋk] *n.* charlatan *m.*
Mountie ['maunti] *n. F:* membre *m* de la police montée canadienne.
mourn ['mɔːn] *v.i. & tr.* pleurer, (se) lamenter, s'affliger; **to m. (for, over) sth.,** pleurer, déplorer, qch.; **to m. for s.o.,** pleurer (la mort de) qn. **mourning** *n.* **1.** affliction *f,* deuil *m.* **2.** (*a*) deuil; **house of m.,** maison endeuillée; (*b*) (habits *mpl* de) deuil; **to go into m.,** se mettre en deuil; prendre le deuil.
mourner ['mɔːnər] *n.* **1.** affligé, -ée; personne *f* qui porte le deuil. **2.** personne qui suit le cortège funèbre; **the mourners,** le convoi; le cortège funèbre.
mournful ['mɔːnful] *a.* triste, lugubre, mélancolique. **-fully** *adv.* tristement, lugubrement.
mouse¹, *pl.* **mice** [maus, mais] *n.* **1.** *Z:* souris *f;* **young m.,** souriceau *m;* **field m.,** mulot *m.* **2.** *a. & n.* **m. grey, m. colour(ed),** gris (*m*) (de) souris. **3.** *F:* personne *f* timide.
mouse² *v.i.* (*of cat, etc.*) chasser aux souris; chasser les souris.
mousehole ['maushoul] *n.* trou *m* de souris.
mouser ['mausər] *n.* (*cat, etc.*) souricier *m.*
mousetrap ['maustræp] *n.* souricière *f;* tapette *f; F:* **m. (cheese),** fromage ordinaire; *Fr. C:* fromage à souris.
mousse [muːs] *n. Cu:* mousse *f* (au chocolat, etc.).
moustache [məs'tɑːʃ], *NAm:* **mustache** ['mʌstæʃ] *n.* moustache(s) *f* (*pl*); **short m., clipped m.,** moustache courte, en brosse.

mousy ['mausi] *a.* **1.** (*a*) gris sale; gris pisseux; (*b*) *F:* (cheveux) queue-de-vache *inv.* **2.** (odeur, etc.) de souris. **3.** (*of pers.*) timide.

mouth¹ [mauθ] *n.* (*pl.* **mouths** [mauðz]) **1.** (*of pers.*) bouche *f*; *Med:* **m. to m. (resuscitation),** bouche-à-bouche *m*; **to have one's m. full,** avoir la bouche pleine; *F:* **big m.,** gueulard *m*, grande gueule; *P:* **to shoot one's m. off,** vendre la mèche; **shut your m.!** ta gueule! **the whole business left a nasty taste in my m.,** l'affaire *f* m'a laissé un arrière-goût désagréable; **to put words into s.o.'s m.,** attribuer des paroles à qn; **by word of m.,** de bouche à oreille; *F:* **to be down in the m.,** avoir le cafard; **to have seven mouths to feed,** avoir sept bouches à nourrir. **2.** bouche (de cheval, de bœuf, d'éléphant, etc.); gueule *f* (de chien, d'animaux carnassiers, etc.); *Equit:* **horse with a hard m.,** cheval fort en bouche, sans bouche; *F:* **it's straight from the horse's m.,** (i) ça vient de la source; je l'ai de première main; (ii) c'est un tuyau increvable. **3.** (*a*) bouche (de puits, de volcan); pavillon *m* (d'entonnoir); gueule (de sac, de canon, de four); ouverture *f*, entrée *f* (de tunnel, de caverne); entrée (de port, etc.); (*b*) embouchure *f* (de rivière).

mouth² [mauð] **1.** *v.tr.* (*a*) **to m. one's words,** déclamer ses phrases; (*b*) former (des mots) avec les lèvres (sans faire entendre de son). **2.** *v.i. esp. NAm:* grimacer; faire des grimaces.

mouthful ['mauθful] *n.* **1.** bouchée *f*; gorgée *f* (de potage, de vin); **to swallow sth. in, at, one m., to make one m. of sth.,** ne faire qu'une bouchée, qu'un morceau, de qch.; *Swim:* **I've swallowed, got, a m. (of water),** j'ai bu une tasse, un bouillon. **2.** *F:* mot qui vous remplit la bouche; nom à coucher dehors.

mouthorgan ['mauθɔ:g(ə)n] *n.* harmonica *m.*

mouthpiece ['mauθpi:s] *n.* **1.** (*a*) embouchure *f* (de chalumeau, etc.); embout *m* (de porte-voix); tuyau *m*, bout *m* (de pipe à tabac); (*b*) *Mus:* bec *m* (de clarinette, etc.); (embouchure en) bocal (*m*) (de cornet, etc.); (*c*) *Tp:* cornet *m*, microphone *m.* **2.** (*a*) porte-parole *m inv* (d'un parti, etc.); (*b*) *U.S:* *P:* avocat *m* (au criminel).

mouthwash ['mauθwɔʃ] *n. Pharm:* eau *f* dentifrice; bain *m* de bouche.

mouth-watering ['mauθwɔ:t(ə)riŋ] *a.* qui fait venir l'eau à la bouche.

mov(e)able ['mu:vəbl] **1.** *a.* (*a*) mobile; **m. feast,** fête *f* mobile; (*b*) *Jur:* mobilier, meuble; **m. property,** biens *mpl* meubles. **2.** *n.pl.* **movables,** (*a*) mobilier *m*; (*b*) *Jur:* biens meubles.

move¹ [mu:v] *n.* **1.** (*a*) *Chess: etc:* coup *m*; **mate in four moves,** (échec et) mat en quatre coups; **to have first m.,** avoir le trait; **to make a m.,** jouer; **your m.,** à vous de jouer; c'est votre tour *m*; (*b*) coup, démarche *f*; **smart m.,** coup habile; **what's the next m.?** qu'est-ce qu'il faut faire maintenant? **to make the first m.,** faire le premier pas. **2.** mouvement *m*; **to make a m. towards sth.,** faire un mouvement vers qch.; **we must make a m.,** il faut partir; **to be always on the m.,** ne jamais rester en place; **on the m.,** en marche; *F:* **to get a m. on,** se dépêcher; se grouiller; **get a m. on!** grouillez-vous! **3.** déménagement *m.*

move² I. *v.tr.* **1.** (*a*) déplacer (un meuble, des troupes, etc.); *Chess: etc:* jouer (une pièce); **to m. sth. from its place,** changer qch. de place; déranger qch.; **to m. one's position,** changer de place; **to m. one's chair near the fire,** approcher son fauteuil du feu; **he was moved to London,** on l'a envoyé (travailler) à Londres; *Sch:* **to be moved up,** passer dans la classe supérieure; (*b*) **to m. (house),** déménager; **to m. to the country,** aller s'installer à la campagne. **2.** (*a*) remuer, bouger (la tête, etc.); (*of wind, etc.*) agiter, remuer (les branches, etc.); **not to m. a muscle,** ne pas sourciller; (*b*) mouvoir, animer (qch.); mettre (qch.) en mouvement. **3.** (*a*) ébranler la résolution de (qn); **nothing will m. him,** il est inflexible; (*b*) **to m. s.o. to do sth.,** pousser, inciter, qn à faire qch.; (*c*) émouvoir, toucher, affecter (qn); **easily moved,** émotionnable; **to m. s.o. to anger,** provoquer la colère de qn; **to m. s.o. to tears,** émouvoir qn (jusqu')aux larmes; **to m. s.o. to pity,** exciter la pitié de qn. **4.** **to m. a resolution,** proposer une motion; déposer une résolution; **to m. that ...,** faire la proposition que ...; proposer que + *sub.* **II.** *v.i.* **1.** (*a*) se mouvoir, se déplacer; **the traffic was heavy but kept moving,** la circulation était intense mais fluide; **m. along (please)!** circulez! **to m. one step,** faire un pas, se déplacer d'un pas; **to m. to another seat,** changer de place; **moving train,** train *m* en marche; (*of pers.*) **to m. in high society,** fréquenter la haute société; (*b*) **to m. (about),** faire un mouvement; bouger, (se) remuer; **don't m.!** ne bougez pas! *Mec.E:* (*of part*) **to m. freely,** jouer librement; (*c*) marcher, aller; s'avancer; **the earth moves round the sun,** la terre tourne autour du soleil; **to m. towards a place,** se diriger, s'avancer, vers un endroit; **things are moving slowly,** les choses marchent, avancent, lentement; **it's time we were moving, we must be moving,** il est temps de partir. **2.** agir; **it is for him to m. first in the matter,** c'est à lui d'agir le premier dans l'affaire. **move away 1.** *v.tr.* écarter, éloigner (qch.). **2.** *v.i.* s'éloigner, s'écarter, s'en aller; **they've moved away from here,** ils ont déménagé. **move back 1.** *v.tr.* (faire) reculer. **2.** *v.i.* (*a*) (se) reculer; (*b*) **they have moved back to London,** ils sont revenus habiter à Londres. **move forward 1.** *v.tr.* avancer (la main, etc.); faire avancer (des troupes). **2.** *v.i.* (s')avancer. **move in 1.** *v.tr.* emménager (son mobilier). **2.** *v.i.* emménager. **move off** *v.i.* (*a*) s'éloigner, s'en aller; (*of army, train, etc.*) se mettre en marche, en branle; (*of car, etc.*) démarrer; (*b*) déboîter (d'une file d'hommes, de véhicules). **move on 1.** *v.tr.* faire circuler (la foule, etc.). **2.** *v.i.* (*a*) avancer; continuer son chemin; **m. on please!** circulez, s'il vous plaît! (*b*) (*of car, etc.*) se remettre en route. **move out 1.** *v.tr.* (*a*) sortir (qch.); faire sortir (qn); (*b*) déménager (ses meubles). **2.** *v.i.* déménager. **move over** *v.i.* se déplacer (vers le côté); se ranger; **m. over!** pousse-toi! **move up** *v.i.* se déplacer (pour faire place à qn); *Sch:* être transféré à une classe supérieure; *St.Exch:* (*of shares*) se relever. **moving 1.** *a.* (*a*) en mouvement, mouvant; (pièce, etc.) mobile; *Ph:* *Mec:* **m. body,** corps *m* en mouvement; mobile *m*; **m. pavement,** *U.S:* **m. sidewalk,** trottoir roulant; **m. staircase,** escalier mécanique; *Mil:* **m. target,** but *m*, cible *f*, mobile; *Cin:* **m. picture,** film *m*; (*b*) (*of force, etc.*) moteur, -trice; **the m. spirit,** l'âme *f* (d'une entreprise); (*c*) (*of story, etc.*) émouvant, touchant, attendrissant. **2.** *n.* (*a*) mouvement *m*, déplacement *m* (de qch.); (*b*) **m. (out),** déménagement *m*; **m. in,** emménagement *m*; *U.S:* **m. van,** camion *m* de déménagement. **movingly** *adv.* d'une manière émouvante, touchante.

movement ['mu:vmənt] *n.* **1.** mouvement *m*; déplacement *m*; (*a*) **there was a general m. towards the door,** tout le monde s'est dirigé vers la porte; **to watch s.o.'s movements,** surveiller les mouvements, les allées et venues, de qn; (*b*) mouvement, circulation *f* (des véhicules); mouvement, transport *m* (des marchandises); (*c*) *Mil: etc:* mouvement, manœuvre *f*; (*d*) circulation (des capitaux, etc.); mouvement (de baisse, de hausse) (des prix, etc.); **free m. of labour,** libre circulation de la main-d'œuvre. **2.** (*a*) mouvement, geste *m* (du bras, etc.); (*b*) *Physiol:* **(bowel) m.,** selle *f.* **3.** mouvement (politique, littéraire, etc.). **4.** mouvement, mécanisme *m* (d'horlogerie). **5.** *Mus:*

mouvement (d'une symphonie, etc.).

mover ['mu:vər] *n.* **1.** moteur *m*; **prime m.,** (i) *Mec:* moteur primaire; (ii) *Phil:* (*pers.*) premier moteur; inspirateur *m*, -trice (d'un projet, etc.). **2.** auteur *m* (d'une motion); motionnaire *m*.

movie ['mu:vi] *n. esp. NAm: Cin: F:* film *m*; **the movies,** le cinéma; **m. star,** vedette *f* de cinéma; **m. house,** cinéma.

mow [mou] *v.tr.* (*p.t.* **mowed** [moud]; *p.p.* **mown** [moun]) **1.** faucher, moissonner (le blé, un champ); **to m. down the enemy,** faucher l'ennemi. **2.** tondre (le gazon). **mowing** *n.* (*a*) fauchage *m*, moissonnage *m* (du foin, etc.); (*b*) tonte *f* (du gazon).

mower ['mouər] *n.* **1.** (*pers.*) faucheur, -euse. **2.** (*machine*) faucheuse *f*; **(lawn) m.,** tondeuse *f* (à gazon).

Mr ['mistər] (*form of address; not used without name*) **Mr Thomas,** Monsieur Thomas.

Mrs ['misiz] (*form of address; not used without name*) **Mrs Long,** Madame Long.

Ms [miz] (*form of address; not used without name*) **Ms Martin,** (i) Mademoiselle, (ii) Madame, Martin.

much [mʌtʃ] **1.** *a.* (*a*) beaucoup (de); bien (du, de la, des); **m. care,** beaucoup de soin; **I had m. difficulty in convincing her,** j'ai eu beaucoup de mal à la convaincre; *Iron:* **m. good may it do you!** grand bien vous fasse! (*b*) **how m. (money)?** combien (d'argent)? **how m. is it?** c'est combien? **2.** *adv.* beaucoup, bien; **(very) m. better,** beaucoup mieux; **m. worse,** bien pis; **it doesn't matter m.,** cela ne fait pas grand-chose; **m. more, less, pleasant,** beaucoup plus, moins, agréable; **m. the largest,** de beaucoup le plus grand; le plus grand de beaucoup; **thank you very m. (for . . .),** merci beaucoup (de . . .); **it's (pretty, very) m. the same thing,** c'est à peu près la même chose; **m. to my astonishment,** à mon grand étonnement; *P:* **not m. (he doesn't, etc.)!** et comment! **3.** *n.* (*a*) **m. remains to be done,** il reste beaucoup à faire; **m. has happened while you have been away,** il s'est passé bien des choses pendant votre absence; **there is not m. of it,** il n'y en a pas beaucoup; **it's not worth m.,** *F:* **not up to m.,** cela ne vaut pas grand-chose; (*b*) **this, that, m.,** autant que ceci, cela; **I'll say this m. for him,** je dirai ceci en sa faveur; **there's not (all) that m.,** il n'y en a pas tellement; (*c*) **to make m. of sth.,** (i) attacher beaucoup d'importance à qch.; faire grand cas de qch.; (ii) vanter qch.; **to make m. of (s.o.),** (i) être aux petits soins pour (qn), auprès de (qn); (ii) câliner, choyer (un enfant, etc.); (iii) flatter (qn); **I don't think m. of it,** j'en fais peu de cas. **4.** *adv.phrs.* (*a*) **m. as,** pour autant; **m. as I like him,** quelle que soit mon affection pour lui; (*b*) **as m.,** autant (de); **as m. again,** encore autant; **twice as m.,** deux fois autant; **I expected, thought, guessed, as m.,** je m'y attendais; je m'en doutais bien; (*c*) **as m. as,** autant que; **as m. as possible,** autant que possible; **quite as m. as . . .,** tout autant que . . .; **it is as m. your fault as mine,** c'est autant votre faute que la mienne; **it is as m. as he can do to read,** c'est tout juste s'il sait lire; **he looked at me as m. as to say . . .,** il me regarda avec l'air de (vouloir) dire . . .; (*d*) **as m. (as), so m. (as),** tant (que), autant (que); **as m. as that?** (au)tant que cela? **do you love her as m. as that?** vous l'aimez donc tant, à ce point-là? **he went away without so m. as saying goodbye,** il est parti sans même dire au revoir; **I would not so m. as raise a finger to help him,** je ne lèverais pas même le petit doigt pour l'aider; (*e*) **so m.,** tant (de), autant (de); **so m. money,** tant d'argent; **he has drunk so m. that . . .,** il a tellement bu que . . .; **so m. the better,** tant mieux; **so m. so that . . .,** au point que . . .; à tel point que . . .; **so m. for his friendship!** et voilà ce qu'il appelle l'amitié! (*f*) **so m. per cent,** tant pour cent; **so m. a kilo,** tant le kilo; (*g*) **too m.,** trop (de); **too m. bread,** trop de pain; **m. too m.,** beaucoup trop (de); **£10 too m.,** £10 de trop; **to cost too m.,** coûter trop cher; **this is (really) too m.!** *F:* **that's a bit m.!** c'est vraiment trop fort! **you can't have too m. of a good thing,** abondance de bien ne nuit pas.

muchness ['mʌtʃnis] *n. F:* (*of pictures, books, etc.*) **they're much of a m.,** ils se ressemblent beaucoup; ils sont tous les mêmes; **it's all much of a m.,** c'est toujours la même chose.

mucilage ['mju:silidʒ] *n.* **1.** mucilage (végétal, animal). **2.** *esp. NAm:* colle *f* (de bureau).

muck¹ [mʌk] *n.* **1.** (*a*) fumier *m*; *Agr:* **m. spreader,** épandeur *m*; (*b*) fange *f*; (*from the streets*) crotte *f*, ordures *fpl*. **2.** *F:* (i) saletés *fpl*, choses dégoûtantes; (ii) camelote *f*; **I must clear up all this m.,** il me faut me débarrasser de toutes ces saletés. **3.** *F:* **to make a m. of sth.,** faire un véritable gâchis de qch.

muck² *v.tr.* **to m. (out) a stable, etc.,** *v.i.* **to m. out,** nettoyer une écurie, etc. **muck about** *F:* **1.** *v.i.* (*a*) traîner, gaspiller son temps; (*b*) faire l'imbécile; (*c*) **to m. about with sth.,** tripoter qch. **2.** *v.tr.* **to m. s.o. about,** (i) houspiller qn; salir la robe de qn; (ii) déranger qn; mettre la confusion dans les projets de qn. **muck in** *v.i. F:* **to m. in with s.o.,** (i) chambrer avec qn; (ii) participer avec qn (à un travail, etc.). **muck up** *v.tr. F:* (i) salir, souiller (qch.); (ii) gâcher, bousiller (un travail); déranger (les projets de qn).

muckheap ['mʌkhi:p] *n.* tas *m* de fumier, d'ordures.

muckraker ['mʌkreikər] *n. F:* déterreur *m* de scandales; *P:* fouille-merde *m inv.*

muckraking ['mʌkreikiŋ] *n. F:* déterrement *m* de scandales.

mucky ['mʌki] *a.* sale, souillé; *F:* (*to child*) **you're a m. pup!** que tu es sale!

mucous ['mju:kəs] *a.* muqueux; **m. membrane,** muqueuse *f*.

mucus ['mju:kəs] *n.* **1.** *Physiol:* mucus *m*, mucosité *f*, glaire *f*. **2.** *Bot:* mucosité.

mud [mʌd] *n.* (*a*) boue *f*; bourbe *f*; **(river) m.,** vase *f*; **to get stuck, to sink, in the m.,** s'embourber; (*of ship*) s'envaser; **m. hut,** hutte *f* de terre; **to drag s.o.'s name in the m.,** traîner qn dans la boue; **to fling, sling, throw, m. at s.o.,** lancer des calomnies contre qn; *F:* **his name is m.,** sa réputation ne vaut pas cher; *P:* **here's m. in your eye!** à votre santé! à la vôtre! *F:* **as clear as m.,** clair comme de l'eau de boudin; (*b*) *Med:* **m. bath,** bain *m* de boue; illutation *f*; *Toil:* **m. pack,** emplâtre *m* de boues; (*c*) *Geog: etc:* **m. flat,** plaine boueuse; plage *f* de vase; *F:* **m. pie,** pâté de sable, de boue (fait par un enfant); (*d*) *Mch:* boue; tartres boueux; **m. hole,** trou *m* de sel (d'une chaudière); trou de vidange; vasière *f*.

mudbank ['mʌdbæŋk] *n.* (*in river*) banc vaseux.

muddle¹ ['mʌdl] *n.* confusion *f*, emmêlement *m*, embrouillement *m*; **to be in a m.,** (i) (*of thgs*) être en confusion, en désordre, en pagaille; (ii) (*of pers.*) avoir les idées brouillées; **to get into a m. (about sth.),** s'embrouiller (au sujet de qch.).

muddle² *v.tr.* (*a*) embrouiller, brouiller (qch.); emmêler (une histoire); brouiller, gâcher (une affaire); **to m. things (up),** embrouiller les choses; *F:* brouiller les fils; (*b*) brouiller l'esprit à (qn); embrouiller (qn). **muddle along** *v.i.* vivre au jour le jour; faire son chemin, se débrouiller, tant bien que mal. **muddled** *a.* **1.** (*of thgs*) brouillé; en désordre. **2.** (*of pers.*) confus, embrouillé. **muddle through** *v.i. F:* se débrouiller, s'en tirer, tant bien que mal. **muddling** *a.* (*of thg*) qui embrouille l'esprit.

muddleheaded [mʌdl'hedid] *a.* à l'esprit confus; brouillon; (idées) confuses, embrouillées.

muddler [ˈmʌdlər] *n.* brouillon, -onne; esprit brouillon.

muddy¹ [ˈmʌdi] *a.* **1.** (*a*) (chemin) boueux, fangeux, bourbeux; (cours d'eau) bourbeux, vaseux; (*b*) (vêtement, etc.) crotté, couvert de boue. **2.** (*a*) (liquide, vin, etc.) trouble; (encre) pâteuse, épaisse; (*b*) (couleur) sale, enfumée; (teint) brouillé, terreux. **3. to taste m.,** avoir un goût de vase.

muddy² *v.tr.* **1.** encrotter, crotter (ses habits, etc.). **2.** (*a*) troubler (l'eau); (*b*) brouiller (le teint).

mudflap [ˈmʌdflæp] *n.* pare-boue *m inv.*

mudguard [ˈmʌdgɑːd] *n.* garde-boue *m inv.*

mudlark [ˈmʌdlɑːk] *n. F:* gamin *m* des rues; loupiot *m.*

mudskipper [ˈmʌdskipər] *n. Ich:* gobie *m* des marais.

mudslinger [ˈmʌdsliŋər] *n. F:* calomniateur, -trice.

mudslinging [ˈmʌdsliŋiŋ] *n. F:* calomnies *fpl.*

mud-stained [ˈmʌdsteind] *a.* souillé de boue.

muezzin [muˈezin] *n.* muezzin *m.*

muff¹ [mʌf] *n.* **1.** *Cost:* manchon *m.* **2.** *Mec.E:* manchon d'accouplement (de tuyaux).

muff² *n. F: O:* **1.** (*pers.*) andouille *f*; nouille *f.* **2.** coup *m* raté.

muff³ *v.tr. F: O:* rater, louper; *Golf: etc:* manquer, rater (un coup).

muffin [ˈmʌfin] *n. Cu:* (*NAm:* **English m.**) muffin *m.*

muffle¹ [ˈmʌf(ə)l] *n. Metall: Cer:* moufle *m.*

muffle² *v.tr.* **1.** emmitoufler; **to m. oneself up,** s'emmitoufler. **2.** (*a*) envelopper (qch., pour amortir, assourdir, voiler, le son); assourdir (les avirons, une cloche); *Mus:* voiler, assourdir (un tambour); (*b*) **the carpet muffles every footstep,** le tapis éteint, étouffe, tout bruit de pas; (*c*) envelopper la tête, la bouche, de (qn, pour l'empêcher de crier); bâillonner (qn). **muffled** *a.* **1. m. up,** emmitouflé. **2.** (son) sourd; (aviron) assourdi; (voix) étouffée; **m. drums,** tambours voilés. **muffling** *n.* assourdissement *m* (d'un tambour, d'une cloche).

muffler [ˈmʌflər] *n.* **1.** cache-nez *m inv*; cache-col *m, pl.* cache-col(s). **2.** (*a*) *Mus:* étouffoir *m* (de piano); (*b*) *Mch:* **(exhaust) m.,** (i) gueule-de-loup *f, pl.* gueules-de-loup; (ii) *NAm: Aut:* silencieux *m.*

mufti [ˈmʌfti] *n.* **1.** *Moslem Rel:* mufti *m*, muphti *m.* **2.** *Mil: etc:* tenue civile; **in m.,** en civil.

mug¹ [mʌg] *n.* **1.** (*for beer*) chope *f*, pot *m*; (*for tea, etc.*) (grosse) tasse; gobelet *m*; (*made of metal*) timbale *f.* **2.** *F:* (*a*) visage *m*; *P:* **ugly m.,** vilain museau, gueule *f* d'empeigne; (*b*) *esp. NAm:* **m. (shot),** photo *f* (d'un criminel); (*c*) bouche *f*; *P:* **shut your (ugly) m.!** ta gueule! **3.** *F:* (*pers.*) (*a*) dupe *f*, poire *f*; **it's a mug's game,** c'est bon pour les poires; (*b*) idiot, -ote; nouille *f.*

mug² *v.tr. Sch: F:* **to m. up,** bûcher, potasser (un sujet).

mug³ *v.tr. F:* attaquer (qn) à main armée; agresser (qn). **mugging** *n.* (vol *m* avec) agression *f*; attaque *f* à main armée.

mugful [ˈmʌgful] *n.* chope *f*, pot *m* (de bière); timbale *f* (d'eau, etc.).

mugger [ˈmʌgər] *n. F:* voleur *m* à main armée; agresseur *m.*

muggins [ˈmʌginʒ] *n. F:* idiot, -ote, nouille *f*; **I suppose m. will have to do it!** sans doute ce sera à moi de le faire!

muggy [ˈmʌgi] *a.* (temps) mou, lourd; (temps) chaud et humide.

mugwump [ˈmʌgwʌmp] *n. Pol: F:* (*a*) dissident, -ente; (*b*) neutre *m.*

mulatto [mju(ː)ˈlætou] **1.** *a.* (*a*) mulâtre; (*b*) (teint) basané. **2.** *n.* mulâtre *mf*; mulâtresse *f.*

mulberry [ˈmʌlb(ə)ri] *n. Bot:* (*a*) mûre *f*; (*b*) **m. (bush, tree),** mûrier *m.*

mulch¹ [mʌl(t)ʃ] *n. Hort:* paillis *m*; litière *f* en décomposition.

mulch² *v.tr. Hort:* pailler.

mulct [mʌlkt] *v.tr.* **1.** *Jur:* frapper (qn) d'une amende. **2.** extorquer (qch. à qn).

mule¹ [mjuːl] *n.* **1.** (*a*) **(he) m.,** mulet *m*; **(she) m., m. mare,** mule *f*; **m. path,** sentier muletier; **m. driver,** muletier *m*; **as stubborn as a m.,** têtu comme une mule; (*b*) *F:* personne entêtée. **2.** *Tex:* **m. (jenny),** renvideur *m.*

mule² *n.* (*slipper*) mule *f.*

muleteer [mjuːliˈtiər] *n.* muletier *m.*

mulish [ˈmjuːliʃ] *a.* entêté, têtu (comme une mule).

mulishness [ˈmjuːliʃnis] *n.* entêtement *m.*

mull¹ [mʌl] *v.tr. F:* **to m. over an idea,** ruminer une idée.

mull² *v.tr.* chauffer (du vin, de la bière) avec des épices; **mulled wine,** vin chaud épicé.

mullet [ˈmʌlit] *n. Ich:* **1. grey m.,** muge *m* (capiton), mulet *m.* **2. red m.,** rouget(-barbet) *m.*

mulligatawny [mʌligəˈtɔːni] *n.* potage *m* au curry.

mullion [ˈmʌliən] *n. Arch:* meneau (vertical).

mullioned [ˈmʌliənd] *a. Arch:* (fenêtre) à meneau(x).

multicoloured [mʌltiˈkʌləd] *a.* multicolore.

multifarious [mʌltiˈfɛəriəs] *a.* varié, divers.

multiform [ˈmʌltifɔːm] *a.* multiforme.

multilateral [mʌltiˈlætərəl] *a.* multilatéral, -aux.

multilingual [mʌltiˈliŋgwəl] *a.* (*pers.*) polyglotte; (*country*) plurilingue.

multimillionaire [mʌltimiliəˈnɛər] *a. & n.* multimillionnaire (*mf*).

multinational [mʌltiˈnæʃ(ə)n(ə)l] *a.* multinational; **m. company,** multinationale *f.*

multiple [ˈmʌltipl] **1.** *a.* (*a*) multiple; **m. store,** magasin *m* à succursales (multiples); **m. ownership,** multipropriété *f* (d'un immeuble, etc.); *Psy:* **m. personality,** personnalité multiple, alternante; (*b*) *El:* **batteries in m.,** accus *mpl* en parallèle; (*c*) *Elcs: W.Tel: etc:* **m. reception,** réception *f* multiple; (*d*) *Tp:* **m. circuit,** circuit *m* multiple; **m. switchboard,** multiple *m* (téléphonique). **2.** *n.* (*a*) *Mth:* multiple; **lowest, least, common m.,** plus petit commun multiple; (*b*) *Tp:* multiplage *m.*

multiple-choice [ˈmʌltiplˈtʃɔis] *a. Sch:* (question) à choix multiples.

multiplication [mʌltipliˈkeiʃ(ə)n] *n. Mth: etc:* multiplication *f*; **m. table,** table *f* de multiplication.

multiplicity [mʌltiˈplisiti] *n.* multiplicité *f.*

multiplier [ˈmʌltiplaiər] *n.* **1.** *Mth: Cmptr:* multiplicateur *m.* **2.** *El:* résistance additionnelle en série; multiplicateur.

multiply [ˈmʌltiplai] **1.** *v.tr.* (*a*) multiplier (des difficultés, des erreurs, etc.); (*b*) *Mth:* **to m. two numbers,** multiplier deux nombres; **to m. 2 by 6,** multiplier 2 par 6. **2.** *v.i.* (*a*) (*of species, etc.*) se multiplier; (*b*) *Mth:* multiplier, faire une multiplication.

multipurpose [mʌltiˈpəːpəs] *a.* (outil) à usages multiples; (véhicule) (à) tous usages, toutes fins; (avion) polyvalent.

multiracial [mʌltiˈreiʃ(ə)l] *a.* multiracial, -aux.

multistage [ˈmʌltisteidʒ] *a. Elcs: Mec.E:* (amplificateur, compresseur) à plusieurs étages; **m. rocket,** fusée composite à étages multiples.

multistorey [mʌltiˈstɔːri] *a.* (*NAm: usu.* **multistory**) (immeuble, garage) à plusieurs étages.

multisyllabic [mʌltisiˈlæbik] *a.* polysyllabique.

multitude [ˈmʌltitjuːd] *n.* **1.** multitude *f*, multiplicité *f* (de raisons, etc.). **2.** multitude, foule *f.*

multitudinous [mʌltiˈtjuːdinəs] *a.* **1.** nombreux, innombrable. **2.** de toutes sortes; multiple. **3.** immense, vaste.

mum¹ [mʌm] *int. & a.* **mum's the word!** motus (et

bouche cousue)! **to keep m. (about sth.),** ne pas souffler mot (de qch.).

mum² [mʌm] *n. F:* maman *f.*

mumble¹ ['mʌmbl] *n.* marmonnement *m*, marmottement *m*.

mumble² *v.tr. & i.* (*a*) marmotter, marmonner; manger ses mots; **he mumbled a few words,** il a prononcé quelques mots entre ses dents.

mumbo-jumbo ['mʌmbou'dʒʌmbou] *n.* **1.** objet auquel on rend un culte ridicule. **2.** (*a*) culte superstitieux; (*b*) baragouin *m*, charabia *m*; galimatias *m.*

mummer ['mʌmər] *n.* mime *m.*

mummery ['mʌməri] *n.* momerie *f.*

mummification [mʌmifi'keiʃ(ə)n] *n.* momification *f.*

mummify ['mʌmifai] **1.** *v.tr.* momifier. **2.** *v.i.* se momifier.

mummy¹ ['mʌmi] *n.* momie *f.*

mummy² *n. F:* maman *f.*

mumps [mʌmps] *n.pl.* (*usu. with sg. const.*) *Med:* oreillons *mpl.*

munch [mʌn(t)ʃ] *v.tr.* mâcher, mâchonner; *v.i.* **to m. away,** mastiquer.

mundane ['mʌndein] *a.* (*a*) mondain; (*b*) banal, terre-à-terre.

municipal [mju:'nisip(ə)l] *a.* municipal, -aux; **m. loans,** emprunts *mpl* de ville; **m. buildings** = mairie *f*; hôtel *m* de ville; *Can: Austr:* **m. district** = municipalité *f.*

municipality [mjunisi'pæliti] *n.* municipalité *f.*

munificence [mju'nifisəns] *n.* munificence *f.*

munificent [mju'nifisənt] *a.* munificent, généreux.

munition [mju'niʃ(ə)n] *n.* **munition(s) of war,** munitions *fpl* de guerre; **m. factory,** fabrique *f*, usine *f*, de munitions.

mural ['mjuər(ə)l] **1.** *a.* mural, -aux; **m. paintings,** peintures murales. **2.** *n.* peinture murale.

murder¹ ['mə:dər] *n.* meurtre *m*; *Jur:* homicide *m* volontaire; **premeditated m.,** *U.S:* **m. in the first degree,** assassinat *m*; **to commit (a) m.,** commettre un meurtre, un assassinat; **the m. weapon,** l'arme *f* du crime; *F:* **it's (sheer, downright) m. in the rush hours,** c'est (absolument) épouvantable, impossible, aux heures de pointe; *F:* **to scream blue m.,** crier, gueuler, à tue-tête, comme un perdu; *F:* **he gets away with m.,** il s'en tire toujours à bon compte.

murder² *v.tr.* **1.** (*a*) assassiner; (*b*) *P:* **I'll m. you (for that)!** je vais te tabasser! **2.** *F:* massacrer, saboter, assassiner (une valse, une chanson).

murderer ['mə:d(ə)rər] *n.m.* meurtrier, assassin.

murderess ['mə:d(ə)res] *n.f.* meurtrière.

murderous ['mə:d(ə)rəs] *a.* meurtrier, assassin; **with m. intent,** dans une intention homicide.

murk [mə:k] *n.* obscurité *f*, ténèbres *fpl.*

murky ['mə:ki] *a.* obscur, ténébreux; (ciel) brouillé; **m. past,** passé obscur, ténébreux.

murmur¹ ['mə:mər] *n.* **1.** (*a*) murmure *m* (des vagues, d'un ruisseau, de la foule); bruissement *m*; (*b*) *Med:* **heart m.,** souffle *m* (au cœur). **2.** (*a*) murmure (d'approbation, etc.); **without a m.,** (faire qch.) sans murmurer, sans broncher; (*b*) **in murmurs,** à voix basse.

murmur² *v.i. & tr.* **1.** murmurer, susurrer; (*of brook*) bruire. **2.** murmurer, dire (qch.) à voix basse. **murmuring** *n.* **1.** murmure *m.* **2. murmurings,** murmures (**against,** contre).

muscatel [mʌskə'tel] *n.* muscat *m.*

muscle¹ ['mʌsl] *n.* muscle *m*; **he has plenty of m.,** il est bien musclé; **man of m.,** homme musculeux, musclé.

muscle² *v.i. F:* **to m. in,** s'immiscer (**on sth.,** dans une affaire); se pousser, jouer des coudes; s'injecter (dans une conversation).

Muscovite ['mʌskəvait] **1.** *a.* moscovite. **2.** *n.* Moscovite *mf.*

muscular ['mʌskjulər] *a.* **1.** (*of system, tissue, action*) musculaire. **2.** (homme) musculeux, musclé.

musculature ['mʌskjulətjər] *n. Anat:* musculature *f.*

Muse¹ [mju:z] *n.* **1.** *Myth:* Muse *f*; **the (nine) Muses,** les Muses. **2. the m.,** la muse (d'un poète).

muse² *v.i.* méditer, rêver, rêvasser; **to m. on, upon, sth.,** méditer sur qch.; réfléchir à qch.; **"that's queer," he mused,** "voilà qui est bien étrange," murmura-t-il d'un ton rêveur. **musing 1.** *a.* pensif; rêveur, -euse. **2.** rêverie *f* (**on,** à).

museum [mju(:)'ziəm] *n.* musée *m* (d'antiquités, etc.); **m. piece,** pièce *f* de musée.

mush [mʌʃ] *n.* **1.** *Cu: esp. U.S:* bouillie *f* de farine de maïs. **2.** *F:* bouillie, panade *f.* **3.** *F:* sentimentalité *f* (à l'eau de rose).

mushroom¹ ['mʌʃrum] *n.* **1.** *Fung:* champignon (blanc); **cultivated mushrooms,** champignons de couche, de Paris; **button m.,** champignon encore en bouton; **m. grower,** champignonnier *m*, champignonniste *m*; *Cu:* **m. soup,** potage *m* aux champignons. **2. m. town,** ville *f* champignon. **3.** (*a*) **m. cloud,** (i) nuage *m* en forme de champignon; (ii) champignon (atomique); (*b*) *Needlew:* boule *f* à repriser.

mushroom² *v.i.* **1.** ramasser, faire la cueillette, des champignons. **2.** (*a*) (*of bullet, etc.*) faire champignon; s'aplatir; (*b*) *F:* pousser comme un champignon; se multiplier, proliférer. **mushrooming** *n.* **1.** cueillette *f* des champignons; **to go m.,** aller aux champignons. **2.** multiplication *f* rapide; prolifération *f.*

mushy ['mʌʃi] *a.* **1.** (*of food, etc.*) en bouillie; (*of ground, etc.*) détrempé, bourbeux; (*of pear, etc.*) blet, *f.* blette. **2.** *F:* **m. sentimentality,** sensiblerie *f*, sentimentalité *f* (à l'eau de rose).

music ['mju:zik] *n.* (*a*) musique *f*; **to set words to m.,** mettre des paroles en musique; **chamber m.,** musique de chambre; **background m.,** musique d'ambiance, de fond; **m. lover,** mélomane *mf*; (*b*) **m. case,** porte-musique *m inv*; **m. centre,** combiné *m* stéréophonique; **m. stand,** pupitre *m* à musique; **m. paper,** papier *m* à, de, musique; (*c*) **m. hall,** music-hall *m*, *pl.* music-halls.

musical ['mju:zik(ə)l] **1.** *a.* (*a*) musical, -aux; (instrument) de musique; **m. evening,** soirée musicale; **m. box,** boîte *f* à musique; (*b*) (*pers.*) **to be m.,** aimer la musique; être (bon) musicien, (bonne) musicienne; (*c*) (*of sound, voice*) harmonieux, mélodieux. **2.** *n.* comédie musicale.

musician [mju'ziʃ(ə)n] *n.* musicien, -ienne.

musicianship [mju'ziʃ(ə)nʃip] *n.* sens *m* de la musique.

musicologist [mju:zi'kɔlədʒist] *n.* musicologue *mf.*

musicology [mju:zi'kɔlədʒi] *n.* musicologie *f.*

musk [mʌsk] *n.* (*a*) musc *m*; *Z:* **m. deer,** porte-musc *m inv*; musc; **m. cat,** civet *m*; (*b*) odeur *f* fauve (du corps); (*c*) *Bot:* **m. (plant),** musc; **m. rose,** rose musquée; (*bush*) rosier musqué.

musket ['mʌskit] *n. Sm.a: A:* mousquet *m.*

musketeer [mʌski'tiər] *n. A:* mousquetaire *m.*

muskrat ['mʌskræt] *n. Z:* **1.** rat musqué; ondatra *m.* **2.** desman musqué.

musky ['mʌski] *a.* musqué; qui sent le musc; **m. smell,** (i) odeur *f* de musc; (ii) odeur fauve.

Muslim ['mʌzlim] *a. & n.* = MOSLEM.

muslin ['mʌzlin] *n. Tex:* (*a*) mousseline *f*; (*b*) *NAm:* calicot *m.*

musquash ['mʌskwɔʃ] *n.* **1.** *Z:* rat musqué; ondatra *m.* **2.** *Com:* castor *m* du Canada.

muss [mʌs] *v.tr. NAm: F:* déranger (la coiffure de qn); froisser, chiffonner (une robe).

mussel ['mʌs(ə)l] *n. Moll:* moule *f*; **m. bank, bed,** banc *m* de moules; moulière *f*.
must¹ [mʌst] *n. Vit:* moût *m*; vin doux.
must² *n.* moisi *m*; moisissure *f*.
must³ *modal aux. v. inv.* (**must not** *is often contracted into* **mustn't**) (*finite tenses of*) falloir, devoir. **1.** (*a*) (*expressing obligation*) **you m. be ready at four o'clock,** vous devrez être prêt, il faut, faudra, que vous soyez prêt, à quatre heures; **you m. hurry up,** il faut vous dépêcher; **you mustn't tell anyone,** il ne faut le dire à personne; **plant that m. have continual attention,** plante *f* qui demande des soins continuels; **if you m.!** si vous l'exigez; **he is stupid, I m. say,** il est stupide, il faut l'avouer; (*b*) (*expressing probability*) **you m. be hungry after your walk,** vous devez avoir faim après votre promenade; **I m. have made a mistake,** j'ai dû me tromper; **if he says so it m. be true,** s'il le dit c'est que c'est vrai. **2.** (*past tense*) (*a*) **if he had looked he m. have seen it,** s'il avait regardé, il l'aurait sûrement vu; **I saw that he m. have suspected something,** j'ai bien vu qu'il avait dû se douter de quelque chose; (*b*) **just as I was at my busiest he m. come worrying me,** au moment où j'étais le plus occupé il a fallu qu'il vienne me tracasser.
must⁴ *n. F:* chose *f* à ne pas manquer, à faire à tout prix; **it's a m.,** c'est une nécessité; **this film's a m.,** ça, c'est un film à ne pas manquer.
mustache ['mʌstæʃ] *n. NAm:* = MOUSTACHE.
mustang ['mʌstæŋ] *n. Z:* mustang *m*.
mustard ['mʌstəd] *n.* **1.** (*a*) *Comest:* moutarde *f*; **French m.** = moutarde de Dijon; **m. pot,** moutardier *m*; pot *m* à moutarde; (*b*) *Med:* **m. plaster,** sinapisme *m*; (*c*) *Mil:* (*1914–18 war*) **m. gas,** ypérite *f*. **2.** *Bot:* (*a*) moutarde; **black m.,** moutarde noire; sénevé *m*; **white m.,** moutarde blanche; **m. seed,** graine *f* de moutarde; (*b*) **wild m.,** moutarde des champs; moutardin *m*, moutardon *m*; *Hort:* **m. and cress,** moutarde blanche et cresson alénois.
muster¹ ['mʌstər] *n.* **1.** (*a*) rassemblement *m* (de membres, etc., *esp. Austr:* des troupeaux); (*b*) *Mil:* revue *f*; **to pass m.,** passer, être passable; être à la hauteur; (*of work*) être acceptable; (*c*) *Nau: etc:* appel *m Mil:* contrôles *mpl*; *Nau:* rôle *m* de l'équipage; **m. roll,** feuille *f* d'appel; **to be on the m. roll,** figurer sur les cadres. **2.** assemblée *f*, réunion *f*.
muster² **1.** *v.tr.* (*a*) rassembler (ses partisans, etc.); **society that musters a hundred members,** association *f* qui compte cent membres; (*b*) *Mil:* passer (des troupes) en revue; (*c*) *Nau:* faire l'appel (des hommes); assembler (l'équipage); (*d*) rassembler (ses troupeaux, etc.); **to m. (up) one's courage,** prendre son courage à deux mains. **2.** *v.i.* s'assembler, se réunir, se rassembler.
musty ['mʌsti] *a.* (*a*) (goût, odeur) de moisi; **to smell m.,** sentir le moisi; (*of room, etc.*) sentir le renfermé; (*of food*) sentir l'évent; (*b*) (pain, etc.) moisi.
mutability [mju:tə'biliti] *n.* mutabilité *f*.
mutable ['mju:təbl] *a.* **1.** muable, changeant, variable. **2.** *Ling:* sujet à la mutation.
mutant ['mju:tənt] *a. & n.* mutant (*m*).
mutate [mju:'teit] *v.tr. & i.* (faire) subir une mutation.
mutation [mju:'teiʃ(ə)n] *n.* **1.** altération *f*, changement *m*; *Biol:* mutation *f*; **m. of type,** métatypie *f*. **2.** *Ling:* mutation (d'une consonne initiale, etc.).
mute¹ [mju:t] **I.** *a.* **1.** (*of pers., appeal, etc.*) muet; *F:* **she stood m. with wonder,** elle restait muette d'étonnement. **2.** *Ling:* (*a*) (lettre) muette; **h m.,** h muet; (*of sound*) **to become m.,** s'amuïr; (*b*) (consonne) sourde. **II.** *n.* **1.** (*pers.*) (*a*) muet, -ette; (*b*) pleureur *m*; (*c*) *Th:* personnage muet. **2.** *Ling:* consonne sourde. **3.** *Mus:* sourdine *f*. **mutely** *adv.* muettement; en silence.
mute² *v.tr.* **1.** amortir, étouffer, assourdir (un son). **2.** *Mus:* mettre une sourdine à, assourdir (un violon, etc.). **muted** *a.* (*of sound, voice, etc.*) assourdi, sourd; (*of colour*) sourd; (*of protest, etc.*) voilé; (*of violin, etc.*) en sourdine.
mutilate ['mju:tileit] *v.tr.* mutiler, estropier (qn); mutiler (une statue, une pièce de théâtre); tronquer (un passage, une citation).
mutilation [mju:ti'leiʃ(ə)n] *n.* mutilation *f*.
mutineer [mju:ti'niər] *n.* mutiné *m*, mutin *m*.
mutinous ['mju:tinəs] *a.* rebelle, mutiné, mutin; (équipage) en révolte.
mutiny¹ ['mju:tini] *n.* révolte *f*, mutinerie *f*.
mutiny² *v.i.* se révolter, se mutiner (**against,** contre).
mutism ['mju:tizm] *n.* mutisme *m*; mutité *f*.
mutt [mʌt] *n. F:* **1.** idiot, -ote; andouille *f*; **poor m.!** pauvre mec! **2.** *NAm:* chien *m* (sans race).
mutter¹ ['mʌtər] *n.* murmure *m* (entre les dents).
mutter² *v.tr. & i.* marmonner, marmotter, murmurer, grommeler. **muttering** *n.* marmottement *m*, grommellement *m*; murmures *mpl*.
mutton ['mʌt(ə)n] *n. Cu:* mouton *m*; **leg of m.,** gigot *m*; **m. chop, cutlet,** côtelette *f* de mouton; *F:* **m. -chop whiskers,** favoris *mpl* en côtelette; *F:* (*of woman*) **m. dressed (up) as lamb,** vieux tableau.
muttonhead ['mʌt(ə)nhed] *n. F:* idiot, -ote; andouille *f*, cornichon *m*.
mutual ['mju:tjuəl] *a.* **1.** (*a*) (*of feelings, etc.*) mutuel, réciproque; **m. benefit society,** société *f* de secours mutuels; (*b*) *El: Elcs:* (attraction, répulsion) mutuelle. **2.** commun; **our m. friends,** nos amis communs. **-ally** *adv.* mutuellement, réciproquement.
muzzle¹ ['mʌzl] *n.* **1.** museau *m* (d'un animal). **2.** bouche *f*, gueule *f* (d'une arme à feu); *Artil:* **m. loader,** pièce *f* se chargeant par la bouche; **m. velocity,** vitesse initiale. **3.** muselière *f* (pour chiens, etc.); bâillon *m* (pour chevaux).
muzzle² *v.tr.* museler (un chien, *F:* la presse, etc.); *F:* bâillonner (la presse, etc.).
muzzy ['mʌzi] *a.* (*a*) (*of pers.*) brouillé (dans ses idées); **I feel m.,** je me sens un peu abruti; (*b*) (*of ideas*) confus, vague; (*of outline*) flou, estompé; (*c*) (*of weather, place*) brumeux, embrumé.
my [mai] *poss.a.* mon, *f.* ma, *pl.* mes; (*in the fem. before a vowel sound*) mon; **my book and my pen,** mon livre et mon stylo; **in my opinion,** à mon avis; **one of my friends,** un de mes amis; un ami à moi; **my own son,** mon propre fils; **my hair is grey,** j'ai les cheveux gris; (*emphatic*) **my idea would be to . . .,** mon idée à moi serait de . . .; *Games: etc:* **my turn!** à moi! *int. F: O:* **(oh) my! my! my!** ça par exemple!
mycology [mai'kɔlədʒi] *n. Bot:* mycologie *f*.
myelitis [maiə'laitis] *n. Med:* myélite *f*.
myeloma [maiə'loumə] *n. Med:* myélome *m*.
myna(h) ['mainə] *n. Orn:* **m. (bird),** mainate *m*.
myopia [mai'oupiə] *n.* myopie *f*.
myopic [mai'ɔpik] *a.* **1.** (*suffering from myopia*) myope. **2.** (*relating to myopia*) myopique.
myriad ['miriəd] **1.** *n.* myriade *f*. **2.** *a. Lit:* innombrable.
myriapod ['miriəpɔd] *a. & n. Nat.Hist:* myriapode (*m*).
myrmidon ['mə:mid(ə)n] *n. F:* assassin *m* à gages; spadassin *m*.
myrrh [mə:r] *n.* myrrhe *f*.
myrtle ['mə:tl] *n. Bot:* **1.** myrte *m*. **2. bog m., Dutch m.,** myrte bâtard, des marais; trèfle *m* d'eau. **3.** *NAm:* pervenche grimpante.
myself [mai'self] *pers. pron.* (*a*) (*emphatic*) moi (-même); **I did it m.,** je l'ai fait moi-même; *F:* **I'm not quite m.,** je ne suis pas dans mon assiette; **I m. believe that . . .,** (quant à) moi, pour ma part, je crois que . . .; (*b*) (*reflexive*) me; **I've hurt m.,** je me suis

fait mal; **I was enjoying m. very much,** je m'amusais beaucoup; (*c*) (*after preposition*) **I live by m.,** je vis tout seul; **I was laughing to m.,** je riais tout seul; **I'll keep it for m.,** je le garderai pour moi.

mysterious [mis'tiəriəs] *a.* **1.** mystérieux; *n.* **the m.,** le mystérieux. **2.** (*of pers.*) mystérieux; qui aime le mystère. **-ly** *adv.* mystérieusement.

mysteriousness [mis'tiəriəsnis] *n.* caractère mystérieux (**of,** de); mystère *m.*

mystery ['mist(ə)ri] *n.* **1.** mystère *m*; **to make a m. of sth.,** faire mystère de qch.; **it's a m. to me,** pour moi c'est un mystère; **the key to the m.,** la clef du mystère. **2.** *A. Th:* **m. (play),** mystère.

mystic ['mistik] **1.** *a.* (*a*) (*of rites, arts*) ésotérique, cabalistique, mystique; (*b*) (*of power*) occulte; (*of formula*) magique; (*c*) surnaturel; (*d*) *Theol:* mystique. **2.** *n.* (*a*) magicien *m*, initié *m*; (*b*) *Theol:* mystique *mf.*

mystical ['mistik(ə)l] *a.* mystique.

mysticism ['mistisizm] *n.* mysticisme *m.*

mystification [mistifi'keiʃ(ə)n] *n.* **1.** mystification *f.* **2.** embrouillement *m*, désorientation *f*; complication *f.*

mystify ['mistifai] *v.tr.* **1.** mystifier (qn); **mystified by . . .,** intrigué par . . .. **2.** désorienter, dérouter.

mystique [mis'ti:k] *n.* mystique *f.*

myth [miθ] *n.* mythe *m.*

mythical ['miθik(ə)l] *a.* mythique.

mythological [miθə'lɔdʒik(ə)l] *a.* mythologique.

mythology [mi'θɔlədʒi] *n.* mythologie *f.*

myxomatosis [miksoumə'tousis] *n.* myxomatose *f.*

N

N, n [en] *n.* (*a*) (la lettre) N, n *f*; (*b*) *Mth:* **to the nth (power),** à la $n^{ième}$ puissance; *F:* **to the nth degree,** au suprême degré.

nab [næb] *v.tr.* **(nabbed)** *P:* **1.** (*a*) arrêter; *P:* pincer, choper (qn); **to get nabbed,** se faire pincer; (*b*) prendre (qn) sur le fait. **2.** escamoter, chiper (qch.); **he's nabbed my watch,** il m'a chipé, fauché, ma montre.

nabob ['neibɔb] *n.* nabab *m.*

nacelle [næ'sel] *n.* **1.** *Aer:* nacelle *f* (de dirigeable). **2.** *Av:* carlingue *f*, habitacle *m*; **(engine) n.,** fuseau-moteur *m*, *pl.* fuseaux-moteur.

nacre ['neikər] *n.* nacre *f.*

nadir ['neidiːər] *n. Astr:* nadir *m.*

naevus, *pl.* **-i** ['niːvəs, -ai] *n. Med:* nævus *m*, *pl.* nævi.

nag[1] [næg] *n. F:* bidet *m*, bourrin *m.*

nag[2] *v.tr. & i.* **(nagged)** quereller (qn); gronder (qn) sans cesse; criailler **(at s.o.,** contre qn); **to be always nagging (at) s.o.,** être toujours après qn, sur le dos de qn; harceler qn de plaintes. **nagging 1.** *a.* (*a*) (*of pers.*) grondeur, -euse; chamailleur, -euse; (*b*) (*of pain, etc.*) agaçant, énervant. **2.** *n.* chamaillerie *f.*

nagger ['nægər] *n.* grondeur, -euse; chamailleur, -euse; *F:* chipie *f.*

naiad, *pl.* **-ads, -ades** ['naiæd, -ædz, -ədiːz] *Myth:* naïade *f*; nymphe *f* des eaux.

nail[1] [neil] *n.* **1.** (*a*) (*of pers., occ. of animal, bird*) ongle *m* (de doigt, d'orteil); *Toil:* **n. brush,** brosse *f* à ongles; **n. file,** lime *f* à ongles; **n. scissors,** ciseaux *mpl* à ongles; **n. varnish, polish,** vernis *m* à ongles; **to bite one's (finger)nails,** se ronger les ongles; (*b*) lamelle *f* (du bec du canard, etc.). **2.** clou *m*, *pl.* clous; *Tls:* **n. claw, drawer, wrench,** arrache-clou *m*, *pl.* arrache-clous; pied-de-biche *m*, *pl.* pieds-de-biche; **n. set, punch,** chasse-clou *m*, chasse-pointe *m*, *pl.* chasse-clous, -pointes; **to drive in a n.,** enfoncer un clou; *F:* **to hit the n. (right) on the head,** tomber juste; mettre le doigt dessus. **3.** *F:* **to pay on the n.,** payer argent comptant; payer rubis sur l'ongle.

nail[2] *v.tr.* **1.** clouer **(on, to,** à); **he stood nailed to the spot,** il est resté cloué au sol. **2.** clouter (des chaussures, une porte, etc.); **nailed boots,** souliers cloutés. **3.** (*a*) *P:* attraper, saisir, coincer (qn); mettre la main sur (qn); (*b*) *F:* **to n. a lie,** exposer un mensonge. **nail down** *v.tr.* (*a*) clouer (le couvercle d'une boîte); (*b*) *F:* **to n. s.o. down (to his promise),** obliger qn à tenir sa promesse. **nailing** *n.* (*a*) clouage *m*; (*b*) cloutage *m*; (*c*) **n. up,** condamnation *f* (d'une porte). **nail up** *v.tr.* clouer (une caisse); condamner (une porte).

nailbiting ['neilbaitiŋ]. **1.** *a. F:* passionnant. **2.** *n.* habitude *f* de se ronger les ongles.

nailhead ['neilhed] *n.* **1.** tête *f* de clou. **2.** *Arch:* pointe *f* de diamant.

naïve, naive [nai'iːv] *a.* (*of pers., manner, etc.*) naïf, *f.* naïve; ingénu; *Art:* **n. art,** l'art naïf. **-ly** *adv.* naïvement.

naïvety [nai'iːvti] *n.* naïveté *f.*

naked ['neikid] *a.* **1.** (*a*) (*of pers.*) nu, *F:* à poil; **stark n.,** tout nu; **to strip (oneself) n.,** se mettre à nu, *F:* à poil; (*b*) (bras, dos, etc.) découvert, nu; (*c*) (mur, etc.) nu, dégarni; (pays, arbre) dénudé; *Nat.Hist:* (*of stalk, tail, etc.*) nu. **2.** (*a*) à découvert; (of *sword*) nu; **n. light,** feu nu, flamme nue; *Min:* lampe *f* à feu libre; (*b*) **visible to the n. eye,** visible à l'œil nu; (*c*) **the n. truth,** la pure vérité; **n. facts,** faits bruts.

nakedness ['neikidnis] *n.* nudité *f.*

namby-pamby ['næmbi'pæmbi] **1.** *a.* (*of style, etc.*) fade; (*of pers.*) (i) minaudier; (ii) sentimental, -aux. **2.** *n.* (i) personne (i) minaudière, (ii) sentimentale.

name[1] [neim] *n.* **1.** (*a*) nom *m*; devise *f*, nom (d'un navire); *Com:* raison sociale (d'une maison de commerce, d'une société); intitulé *m* (d'un compte); **full n.,** nom et prénoms *mpl*; **Christian n., first n.,** *esp. N.Am:* **given n.,** prénom; **family n., second n., last n.,** nom de famille; **maiden n.,** nom de jeune fille; **married n.,** nom de femme mariée; **n. day,** fête *f* (de qn); **n. tape, tab,** marque *f* à linge; **what's your n.?** quel est votre nom? comment vous appelez-vous? **my n. is . . .,** je m'appelle . . .; *Com:* **registered n., trade n.,** nom déposé; **brand n.,** marque de fabrique; **a man, X by n., by the n. of X,** un homme du nom de X; **to go by, under, the n. of . . .,** être connu sous le nom de . . .; (*of dog, etc.*) **he answers to his n.,** il répond à son nom; **to know s.o. (only) by n.,** (ne) connaître qn (que) de nom; **to mention s.o., sth., by n.,** nommer qn, qch.; (*to caller*) **what n. shall I say?** qui dois-je annoncer? **to send in one's n.,** (i) se faire inscrire (dans un concours, etc.); (ii) se faire annoncer; **to put one's n. down (for sth.),** (i) poser sa candidature; (ii) s'inscrire (pour qch.); **list of names,** liste nominative; **in the n. of . . .,** au nom de . . .; **in the n. of the law,** au nom de la loi; **in the n. of the king,** de par le roi; *F:* **what in the n. of goodness are you doing?** que diable faites-vous là? **to be master in n. only,** n'être maître que de nom; (*b*) terme *m*; **insulting n.,** appellation injurieuse; (*c*) nom (d'une plante, d'un objet, etc.); *Gram:* **proper n.,** nom propre; (*d*) titre *m* (d'une pièce de théâtre, d'un roman, etc.); **n. part,** rôle *m* qui donne le titre à une pièce, à un film, etc. **2.** réputation *f*, renommée *f*; **he has a good, a bad, n.,** il a (une) bonne, (une) mauvaise, réputation; **to get a bad n.,** se faire un mauvais renom; **he has several books to his n.,** il est l'auteur de plusieurs livres; **a big n. in the theatre,** un nom bien connu dans le monde du théâtre; **he has a n. for honesty,** il est connu, réputé, pour son honnêteté; **to make, achieve, a n. for oneself, to make one's n.,** se faire une réputation **(as,** de); **to lend one's n. to an undertaking,** prêter son nom pour une entreprise.

name[2] *v.tr.* **1.** nommer; donner un nom à (qn, qch.); dénommer (une nouvelle plante, etc.); **he was named Peter,** on lui a donné le nom de Pierre; **a person named Thomas,** un nommé Thomas; **to n. s.o. after s.o.,** *U.S:* **for s.o.,** donner à qn le nom de qn. **2. to n. s.o. to an office,** nommer qn à un poste. **3.** (*a*) désigner (qn, qch.) par son nom; mentionner, dénommer (qn); **n. the kings of England,** donnez les noms des rois d'Angleterre; (*b*) (*of the Speaker, in House of Commons*) **to n. a member,** signaler à la Chambre l'indiscipline d'un membre. **4.** (*a*) citer (un exemple, un fait); **naming no names,** sans nommer personne; *F:* **you n. it, he's done it, got it, etc.,** tout ce qu'on peut imaginer, il l'a fait, le possède, etc.; (*b*) fixer (le jour, une somme); **n. any price you like,** fixez le prix que vous voudrez. **named** *a.* (*a*) nommé; **on the n. day,** à jour nommé; (*b*) *a.* & *n.* *Jur:* **afore n.,** précité, -ée. **naming** *n.* **1.** attribution *f* d'un nom; baptême *m* (d'un navire). **2.** nomination *f* (d'un fonctionnaire). **3.** désignation *f*, dénommement *m* (de qn, qch.).

name-dropping ['neimdrɔpiŋ] *n.* *F:* habitude *f* de se dire ami(e) des gens connus.

nameless ['neimlis] *a.* **1.** (*of pers., etc.*) sans nom, inconnu, obscur. **2.** (écrivain, etc.) anonyme; (tombe) sans inscription; **s.o. who shall be, remain, n.,** qn dont je tairai le nom. **3.** (*a*) (*of dread, grief, etc.*) indéfinissable, indicible, inexprimable; (*b*) (vice, etc.) abominable.

namely ['neimli] *adv.* c'est-à-dire; (à) savoir.

nameplate ['neimpleit] *n.* plaque *f* (de porte, etc.); écusson *m*, médaillon *m* (avec le nom); (*on machine, etc.*) **manufacturer's n.,** plaque de constructeur.

namesake ['neimseik] *n.* **he's my n.,** il a le même nom que moi; il s'appelle comme moi; il porte mon nom.

nana ['nænə] *n.f.* *F:* grand-maman, mémé.

nancy ['nænsi] *n.* *P:* **n. (boy),** (i) homosexuel *m*, tapette *f*; (ii) femmelette *f*.

nanny ['næni] *n.f.* **1.** bonne d'enfant, nurse; (*child's speech*) nounou. **2. n. (goat),** chèvre; *F:* biquette.

nap¹ [næp] *n.* petit somme; **afternoon n.,** sieste *f*, méridienne *f*; **to take, have, a n.,** faire un petit somme; (*after lunch*) faire la sieste.

nap² *v.i.* **(napped)** faire un petit somme; sommeiller; **to be caught napping,** (i) être surpris en train de dormir; (ii) être pris au dépourvu; (iii) être pris en faute.

nap³ *n.* *Tex:* (*of velvet, cloth, felt*) poil *m*; (*of cloth*) duvet *m*, lainer *m*; **cloth with raised n.,** étoffe molletonnée, tirée à poil, garnie; **against the n.,** à contre-poil, à rebrousse-poil, à rebours.

nap⁴ *v.tr.* *Tex:* garnir, gratter, lainer (le drap, etc.); molletonner (la laine, le coton); faire la peluche (d'un tissu).

nap⁵ *n.* **1.** *Cards:* napoléon *m*; nap *m*; **to go n.,** demander les cinq levées; *F:* **to go n. on sth.,** être sûr et certain de qch.; **to hold a n. hand,** avoir en main toutes les cartes pour réussir. **2.** *Turf:* tuyau sûr.

nap⁶ *v.tr.* *Turf:* *F:* **to n. a winner,** donner un tuyau sûr.

napalm ['neipɑːm] *n.* napalm *m*.

nape [neip] *n.* **n. (of the neck),** nuque *f*.

naphtha ['næfθə] *n.* *Ind:* naphte *m*.

naphthalene ['næfθəliːn] *n.* *Ch:* *Com:* naphtaline *f*, naphtalène *m*.

napkin ['næpkin] *n.* **1. (table) n.,** serviette *f* (de table); **n. ring,** rond *m* de serviette. **2.** (*a*) **(baby's) n.,** couche *f* (de bébé); (*b*) *U.S:* **(sanitary) n.,** serviette hygiénique.

Napoleon [nə'pouliən] *Pr.n.m.* *Hist:* Napoléon.

Napoleonic [nəpouli'ɔnik] *a.* napoléonien.

nappy ['næpi] *n.* couche *f* (de bébé); **cotton n.,** lange *m*; **disposable n.,** couche à jeter.

narcissism ['nɑːsisizm] *n.* *Psy:* narcissisme *m*.

narcissistic [nɑːsi'sistik] *a.* *Psy:* narsissique.

narcissus [nɑː'sisəs] (*pl.* **narcissi, narcissuses** [nɑː'sisai, -'sisəsiz]) *n.* *Bot:* narcisse *m*.

narcosis [nɑː'kousis] *n.* *Med:* narcose *f*.

narcotic [nɑː'kɔtik] *a.* & *n.* narcotique (*m*), stupéfiant (*m*).

nark¹ [nɑːk] *n.* *P:* **(copper's) n.,** espion *m* de police; mouchard *m*; mouton *m*.

nark² *v.tr.* *P:* prendre (qn) à rebrousse-poil; fâcher, irriter (qn); **to get narked,** se mettre en colère.

narrate [nə'reit] *v.tr.* narrer, raconter, relater (qch.).

narration [nə'reiʃ(ə)n] *n.* **1.** narration *f* (d'une histoire, etc.). **2.** récit *m*, narration.

narrative¹ ['nærətiv] *n.* **1.** récit *m*, narration *f*; histoire *f*, conte *m*. **2.** (l'art *m* de) la narration.

narrative² *a.* (style, poème) narratif; **n. writer,** narrateur, -trice.

narrator [nə'reitər] *n.* (*a*) narrateur, -trice; (*b*) *Mus:* récitant, -ante.

narrow¹ ['nærou] **1.** *a.* (*a*) (chemin, etc.) étroit; (vallon, etc.) serré, resserré; (passage, chenal) étranglé; (jupe, etc.) étriquée; **the straight and n. way,** la voie étroite; **to grow, become, n.,** se rétrécir; *Rail:* **n. gauge (railway),** (chemin *m* de fer à) voie étroite; (*b*) restreint, étroit; de faibles dimensions; (esprit) étroit, borné; (existence) limitée, circonscrite; **within n. bounds,** dans des limites étroites; **in the narrowest sense,** dans le sens le plus exact; (*c*) (examen, etc.) minutieux, soigneux; (*d*) **a n. majority,** une faible majorité; **to have a n. escape,** l'échapper belle; *Sp:* **n. victory,** victoire *f* de justesse; (*e*) *Ling:* (voyelle) tendue. **2.** *n.pl.* **narrows,** passe étroite (entre deux terres); goulet *m* (d'un port); étranglement *m* (de rivière, de vallée); pertuis *m* (de fleuve). **-ly** *adv.* **1.** (interpréter qch.) strictement, étroitement. **2.** (enfermer qch.) étroitement, à l'étroit. **3.** tout juste; de justesse; **he n. missed being run over,** il a failli être écrasé.

narrow² **1.** *v.tr.* (*a*) resserrer, rétrécir (une rue, l'esprit, etc.); **narrowed eyelids,** paupières mi-closes; (*b*) restreindre, limiter, rétrécir (un espace, les idées, etc.). **2.** *v.i.* devenir plus étroit; se resserrer, se rétrécir. **narrow down** **1.** *v.tr.* limiter (qch.). **2.** *v.i.* se rétrécir.

narrow-minded [nærou'maindid] *a.* (d'un esprit) borné; à l'esprit étroit.

narrow-mindedness [nærou'maindidnis] *n.* étroitesse *f*, petitesse *f*, d'esprit; esprit borné, mesquin.

narrowness ['nærounis] *n.* **1.** (*a*) étroitesse *f* (d'un sentier, des épaules, etc.); rétrécissement *m* (d'un passage, etc.); (*b*) petitesse *f*, exiguïté *f* (d'un espace, etc.); limitation *f*, circonscription *f* (de la vie, de l'intelligence, etc.); **n. of mind,** étroitesse d'esprit. **2.** minutie *f*; caractère soigneux (d'un examen, des recherches).

narwhal ['nɑːwəl] *n.* *Z:* narval *m*, *pl.* narvals.

nasal ['neiz(ə)l] **1.** *a.* (*a*) *Anat:* nasal, -aux; **the n. fossae,** les fosses nasales; (*b*) (*of sound, letter, etc.*) nasal; **to have a n. voice,** parler du nez. **2.** *n.* *Ling:* nasale *f*. **-ally** *adv.* nasalement; **to speak n.,** parler du nez; nasiller.

nasalize ['neizəlaiz] *v.tr.* nasaliser (une syllabe, etc.).

nascent ['neisənt, 'næs-] *a.* (*of plant, society, etc.*) naissant; *Ch:* (corps, élément) à l'état naissant.

nastiness ['nɑːstinis] *n.* **1.** mauvais goût, odeur *f* désagréable. **2.** (*of pers.*) méchanceté *f*, rosserie *f*. **3.** (*a*) saleté *f*; (*b*) indécence *f*, obscénité *f*.

nasturtium [nə'stəːʃ(ə)m] *n.* *Bot:* capucine *f*.

nasty ['nɑːsti] *a.* **1.** (*a*) désagréable, dégoûtant; **his behaviour left (me with) a n. taste in the mouth,** sa conduite m'a laissé un mauvais souvenir; (*b*) **n. weather,** sale, mauvais, vilain, temps; **n. corner,** tournant dangereux; **n. wound,** vilaine blessure; **he's had a n. attack of bronchitis,** il a fait une mauvaise bronchite. **2.** (*of pers.*) méchant, déplaisant, *F:* rosse; **to turn n.,** prendre un air méchant; **don't be n.!** ne fais donc pas le méchant! **n. trick,** vilain tour; *F:* sale tour. **3.** (*a*) sale; *F:* **he's a n. piece of work,** c'est un sale individu, un sale type; (*b*) (*of language, book, etc.*) indécent, obscène; **n. word,** vilain mot. **-ily** *adv.* **1.**

désagréablement. **2.** méchamment. **3.** indécemment.

natal ['neit(ə)l] *a.* natal, -als; de naissance.

natality [nə'tæliti] *n.* natalité *f.*

nation ['neiʃ(ə)n] *n.* **1.** nation *f*; *Pol:* **United Nations (Organization),** (Organisation *f* des) Nations Unies. **2. the whole n. rose in arms,** tout le pays se souleva; **to serve the n.,** servir l'État *m.*

national ['næʃ(ə)n(ə)l] **1.** *a.* (*a*) national, -aux; de l'État; *Nau:* **n. flag,** pavillon *m* de nation; **n. service,** service *m* militaire; *Turf:* **n. hunt (racing),** courses *fpl* d'obstacles; (*b*) (costume) national; (coutume) du pays; **he's intensely n.,** il est d'un nationalisme extrême. **2.** *n.* ressortissant *m* (d'un pays); **a French n.,** un(e) Français(e). **-ally** *adv.* nationalement.

nationalism ['næʃ(ə)nəlizm] *n.* nationalisme *m.*

nationalist ['næʃ(ə)nəlist] **1.** *n.* nationaliste *mf.* **2.** *a.* nationaliste; **N. China,** la Chine nationaliste.

nationalistic [næʃ(ə)nə'listik] *a.* nationaliste.

nationality [næʃ(ə)'næliti] *n.* **1.** nationalité *f*; **to take British n.,** prendre la nationalité britannique; **dual n.,** double nationalité. **2.** nationalisme *m.*

nationalization [næʃ(ə)nəlai'zeiʃ(ə)n] *n.* **1.** nationalisation *f* (d'un peuple, etc.) **2.** naturalisation *f* (d'un étranger). **3.** nationalisation (d'une industrie).

nationalize ['næʃ(ə)nəlaiz] *v.tr.* **1.** nationaliser (un peuple, une industrie, etc.). **2.** naturaliser (un étranger, etc.).

nationwide ['neiʃ(ə)nwaid] *a.* répandu dans tout le pays.

native ['neitiv] **I.** *n.* **1.** (*a*) originaire *mf* (d'un pays, d'une ville); **n. of Australia,** Australien, -ienne, de naissance; **he speaks English like a n.,** il parle anglais comme un Anglais; (*b*) (*esp. of foreign country, of colony*) indigène *mf.* **2.** (*a*) (*of plant, animal*) indigène; (*b*) **natives,** huîtres anglaises (de Colchester). **II.** *a.* **1.** (*of qualities, etc.*) natif; naturel, inné; **n. wit,** esprit naturel. **2.** (*a*) (*of place*) natal, -als, de naissance; **n. country,** terre natale; patrie *f*, pays *m*; **n. language,** langue maternelle; **he returned to his n. London,** il est revenu à Londres, sa ville natale; (*b*) (costume, huîtres) du pays. **3.** (*a*) (*of metals, minerals*) (à l'état) natif. **4.** (*of plants, inhabitants, etc.*) indigène (**to,** de, à); originaire, aborigène (**to,** de); *Ling:* **n. word,** mot *m* indigène; **n. labour,** main-d'œuvre *f* indigène.

native-born ['neitivbɔːn] *a.* indigène, natif; **a. n.-b. German,** un(e) Allemand(e) de naissance.

nativity [nə'tiviti] *n.* **1.** nativité *f*, naissance *f* (du Christ, de la Vierge, de saint Jean-Baptiste); *Ecc:* **the (festival of the) N.,** la Nativité; **n. scene,** crèche *f*; *Th:* **n. play,** mystère *m* de la Nativité. **2.** *Astrol:* horoscope *m.*

Nato ['neitou] *n.* l'Otan *m.*

natter[1] ['nætər] *n. F:* causerie *f*; **to have a n.,** bavarder, jacter.

natter[2] *v.i. F:* bavarder, jacter.

natterjack ['nætədʒæk] *n. Amph:* **n. (toad),** crapaud *m* des roseaux; calamite *f.*

natty ['næti] *a.* **1.** (*of pers., dress, etc.*) pimpant; coquet, -ette; soigné. **2.** (*of gadget, etc.*) habilement exécuté; bien imaginé.

natural ['nætjərəl] **I.** *a.* **1.** (*a*) (droit, etc.) naturel; **n. law,** loi naturelle, de la nature; **n. size,** grandeur *f* nature; **for the rest of one's n. life,** pour le reste de sa vie; **death from n. causes,** mort naturelle; **be n.!** soyez naturel! **that'll look more n.,** ça fera plus nature; (*b*) **in the n. state,** à l'état naturel, primitif; à, dans, l'état de nature; **n. resources,** ressources naturelles (d'un pays); *Ph: Ch:* **n. gas,** gaz naturel; *Tex:* **cloth in n. colour,** tissu *m* beige; (*c*) *Mus:* **n. note,** (note) naturelle (*f*). **2.** (*a*) naturel, natif, inné; **n. gift,** don naturel; **n. inclination,** penchant naturel; **it comes n. to him,** c'est un don chez lui; *F:* **it comes n. to him to . . .,** il a une facilité innée pour . . .; **it comes, is, n. for a man to . . .,** il est dans, de, la nature de l'homme de . . .; **n.-born subject,** Anglais, Français, etc., de naissance; (*b*) *Ph:* **n. frequency,** fréquence *f* propre; **n. wavelength,** longueur *f* d'onde propre; (*c*) **it's n. (that) . . .,** il est (bien) naturel que + *sub.*; rien de surprenant à ce que + *sub.*; **it's only n. that . . .,** il est, c'est, tout à fait normal que + *sub.*; **as is n.,** comme de raison. **3.** (enfant) naturel, illégitime. **4. the n. world,** le monde physique; **n. history,** histoire naturelle. **II.** *n.* **1. as an actor, he's a n.,** c'est un acteur né. **2.** *Mus:* (*a*) (note) naturelle (*f*); (*b*) (*sign*) bécarre *m.* **naturally** *adv.* **1.** (*a*) naturellement; **n. curly hair,** cheveux *mpl* qui frisent naturellement; **he's n. shy,** il est timide de nature; **it comes n. to him to . . .,** il est dans sa nature de . . .; (*b*) (parler) naturellement, sans affectation; (se conduire) avec naturel; (*c*) (mourir) de mort naturelle, de sa belle mort. **2.** (= *of course*) naturellement.

naturalism ['nætjərəlizm] *n.* naturalisme *m.*

naturalist ['nætjərəlist] *a. & n.* naturaliste (*mf*).

naturalistic [nætjərə'listik] *a. Art: Lit: etc:* naturaliste.

naturalization [nætjərəlai'zeiʃ(ə)n] *n.* **1.** naturalisation *f* (d'un étranger, d'un mot étranger); **to take out (French) n. papers,** se faire naturaliser (français). **2.** acclimatation *f* (d'une plante, d'un animal).

naturalize ['nætjərəlaiz] **1.** *v.tr.* (*a*) naturaliser (un étranger, un mot); **to become naturalized,** se faire naturaliser; (*b*) acclimater (une plante, un animal); (*c*) rendre (l'art, etc.) conforme à la nature; donner du naturel à (son style, etc.). **2.** *v.i.* (*of plant, etc.*) s'acclimater.

naturalness ['nætjərəlnis] *n.* **1.** caractère naturel (d'une action, etc.). **2.** naturel *m.*

nature ['neitjər] *n.* **1.** (*a*) (*of thg*) nature *f*, essence *f*, caractère *m*; **it is in the n. of things that . . .,** il est dans l'ordre des choses que . . .; **in, by, from, the n. of things we cannot hope for more,** vu la nature de l'affaire nous ne pouvons espérer mieux; *Phil:* **the true n. of things,** l'être *m* véritable des choses; (*b*) (*of pers.*) nature; naturel *m*, tempérament *m*; **a jealous n.,** un caractère jaloux; **to have, to be of, a happy n.,** être d'un heureux naturel; **it's not in his n.,** ce n'est pas dans sa nature; **by n.,** par tempérament, de (sa) nature, naturellement; **he's shy by n.,** il est timide de nature; il est d'une nature timide; **it has become second n. to him,** il le fait presque par instinct; (*c*) **human n., divine n.,** nature humaine, divine. **2.** espèce *f*, sorte *f*, genre *m*; **things of this n.,** les choses *fpl* de ce genre; **something in the n. of a . . .,** une espèce, une sorte, de . . .; **n. of contents,** désignation *f* du contenu. **3.** (*a*) nature; **Mother N.,** la Nature; **the laws of n.,** les lois *fpl* de la nature; les lois naturelles; **n. study,** histoire naturelle; **n. lover,** ami, -e, amant, -ante, de la nature; **to draw, paint, from n.,** dessiner, peindre, d'après nature; **crime against n.,** crime *m* contre nature; **return to n.,** retour *m* à l'état de nature; (*b*) force vitale, fonctions vitales, naturelles (de l'homme).

naturism ['neitjərizm] *n.* naturisme *m.*

naturist ['neitjərist] *n.* naturiste *mf.*

naught [nɔːt] *n. A: & Lit:* rien *m*; (*of plans, etc.*) **to come to n.,** échouer; n'aboutir à rien; **to bring to n.,** confondre (les projets de qn).

naughtiness ['nɔːtinis] *n.* **1.** mauvaise conduite (de qn). **2.** *F:* caractère risqué, grivois (d'un conte, etc.).

naughty ['nɔːti] *a.* **1.** vilain, méchant; pas sage; **you n. child!** petit vilain! **he's been a n. boy,** il a été méchant; il n'a pas été sage. **2.** *F:* (*of tale*) risqué, grivois; (chanson) gaillarde; **to tell n. stories,** conter des gaillardises *fpl.* **-ily** *adv.* **to behave n.,** se mal conduire; ne pas être sage; être vilain.

nausea ['nɔːsiə] *n.* **1.** nausée *f*, envie *f* de vomir; **to be overcome with n.,** avoir mal au cœur; avoir des nausées. **2.** dégoût *m*, nausée, écœurement *m*.

nauseate ['nɔːsieit] *v.tr.* écœurer, dégoûter (qn); donner des nausées, donner mal au cœur, à (qn). **nauseating** *a.* **1.** *Med:* nauséeux. **2.** nauséabond; écœurant; *F:* **I find him n.,** il m'écœure. **nauseatingly** *adv.* d'une façon dégoûtante, écœurante.

nauseous ['nɔːsiəs] *a.* (*a*) *Med:* nauséeux; (*b*) nauséabond, écœurant; (*c*) *U.S: F:* **to feel n.** ['nɔːʃəs], avoir mal au cœur, des nausées.

nautical ['nɔːtik(ə)l] *a.* nautique, marin; naval, -als; (terme) de navigation, de marine; **n. almanac,** éphémérides *fpl* nautiques; **n. club,** club *m* nautique.

nautilus, *pl.* **-uses, -i** ['nɔːtiləs, -əsiz, -ai] *n.* *Moll:* nautile *m*; **paper n.,** argonaute *m*, voilier *m*.

naval ['neiv(ə)l] *a.* naval, -als; de marine (de guerre); (puissance) maritime; **n. war(fare),** guerre navale; **n. officer,** officier *m* de marine; **n. attaché,** attaché naval; **the N. College,** l'École navale; **n. base,** base navale; **n. dockyard,** arsenal *m* maritime; **n. stores,** approvisionnements *mpl*, matériel *m*; fournitures *fpl* de navires.

nave[1] [neiv] *n.* moyeu *m* (de roue).

nave[2] *n.* nef *f* (d'église); vaisseau *m* de la nef.

navel ['neiv(ə)l] *n.* (*a*) *Anat:* nombril *m*, ombilic *m*; (*b*) *Fig:* milieu *m*, centre *m* (d'un pays, etc.); *Hort:* **n. orange,** orange *f* navel *inv*.

navigability [nævigə'biliti] *n.* navigabilité *f* (d'un fleuve, d'un vaisseau); dirigeabilité *f* (d'un aérostat).

navigable ['nævigəbl] *a.* (fleuve, vaisseau) navigable; (aérostat) dirigeable; **n. waters,** eaux *fpl* navigables; **ship in n. condition,** vaisseau *m* en état de prendre la mer.

navigate ['nævigeit] **1.** *v.i.* naviguer. **2.** *v.tr.* (*a*) naviguer dans, sur (les mers, etc.); voyager (dans l'air); (*b*) naviguer (un navire, un avion, une voiture); gouverner (un navire); **navigating officer,** officier navigateur.

navigation [nævi'geiʃ(ə)n] *n.* navigation *f*; conduite *f* (d'un navire, d'un aérostat); **radio n.,** radionavigation *f*; **n. officer,** officier *m* de navigation; officier navigateur; **n. aids,** aides *fpl* à la navigation.

navigational [nævi'geiʃ(ə)nəl] *a.* (instrument, etc.) de navigation; (aides) à la navigation.

navigator ['nævigeitər] *n.* (*a*) *Nau: Av: Aut:* navigateur *m*; *Nau: Av:* officier navigateur; (*b*) navigateur, marin *m*.

navvy[1] ['nævi] *n.* **1.** (*pers.*) terrassier *m*. **2.** *Civ.E: etc:* **mechanical n.,** excavateur, -trice.

navvy[2] *v.i.* **(navvied)** travailler comme terrassier.

navy ['neivi] *n.* **1.** marine *f* de guerre, marine militaire; **to serve in the n.,** servir sur mer; **the Royal N.,** la Marine nationale britannique; **the merchant n.,** la marine marchande; **minister,** *U.S:* **secretary, for the N.** = ministre *m* de la Marine; *Com:* **n. cut,** carotte de tabac hachée. **2. n. (blue),** bleu *m* marine *inv*; bleu foncé *inv*.

nay [nei] **1.** *adv.* (*a*) *A: Lit: & Dial:* non; (*b*) *Lit:* (*introducing a more emphatic statement*) (et) même, qui plus est; voire; **I am astounded, n., disgusted,** j'en suis ahuri, voire révolté. **2.** *n. A: & Lit:* non *m*; (*in voting*) **ayes and nays,** voix *fpl* pour et contre.

Nazarene ['næzəriːn] *a. & n.* *B.Hist:* nazaréen, -éenne.

Nazi ['nɑːtsi] *a. & n.* *Hist: Pol:* nazi, -ie.

Nazism ['nɑːtsizm] *n.* *Hist: Pol:* nazisme *m*.

Neandert(h)al [niː'ændətɑːl] *Pr.n.* *Anthr:* **N. man,** l'homme de Néanderthal.

neap [niːp] *a. & n.* **n. (tide),** marée *f* de morte-eau; **n. tides, neaps,** (marées de) mortes-eaux (*fpl*).

Neapolitan [niːə'pɔlit(ə)n] *Geog:* **1.** *a.* napolitain; de Naples; **N. ice cream,** tranche napolitaine. **2.** *n.* Napolitain, -aine.

near[1] [niər] **I.** *adv.* **1.** (*a*) (*denoting proximity in space and time*) près, proche; **he lives quite n.,** il habite tout près; **to come, draw, n.,** (s')approcher (**to s.o., sth.,** de qn, qch.); **come nearer,** venez plus près; approchez-vous; **the time is drawing n.,** l'heure *f* approche; **to bring sth. nearer,** rapprocher qch. (**to,** de); **nearer and nearer,** de plus en plus proche; **n. at hand,** (*of thg*) tout près, à proximité; (*of event*) tout proche; **keep n. to me,** restez près de moi; **he was standing n. the table,** il se tenait auprès de la table; (*b*) (*closely connected by kinship or intimacy*) proche; **those n. and dear to him,** ceux qui lui touchent de près. **2.** (*a*) **as n. as I can remember,** autant que je puisse m'en souvenir; **as n. as makes no difference,** à peu de choses près; **I came n. to crying,** j'ai été sur le point de pleurer; (*b*) *A: & Lit:* (= NEARLY) presque, à peu près; (*c*) **he's nowhere n. so, as, strong as you,** il n'est pas à beaucoup près aussi fort que vous; **he's nowhere n. finished,** il est loin d'avoir fini. **II.** *prep.* **1.** près de, auprès de (qn, qch.); **n. the village,** près, auprès, du village; **situated n. the church,** situé près (de) l'église; **bring your chair near(er) the fire,** (r)approchez votre chaise du feu; **to come, draw, n. (to) s.o., sth.,** (s')approcher de qn, qch. **2.** près de, sur le point de; **n. death,** sur le point de mourir; **he came n. (to) being run over,** il a failli être écrasé. **3. to be, to come, n. s.o., sth.,** se rapprocher de qn, de qch. (par la ressemblance); ressembler à qn, à qch.; **language that is nearer Latin than Italian,** langue *f* qui est plus près du latin que de l'italien; **nobody can come anywhere n. her,** il n'y a personne à son niveau; **he's nowhere n. it!** il n'y est pas du tout! **4.** *Com:* **n. beer,** imitation *f* de bière; **she gave a n. smile,** elle a esquissé un sourire. **III.** *a.* **1.** (*of relative*) proche; (*of friend*) intime, cher; **our n. relations,** nos proches (parents). **2.** (*of horse, etc.*) **n. foreleg,** pied *m* du montoir; **n. rein,** rêne *f* du dedans. **3.** (*of place, time, event*) proche; **in the n. future,** dans un proche avenir; **the nearest hotel,** l'hôtel le plus proche; **go to the nearest chemist's,** allez à la prochaine pharmacie; **give the measurements to the nearest metre,** donnez les mesures à un mètre près. **4.** (*of road*) court, direct. **5.** qui touche, serre, de près; **n. resemblance,** grande ressemblance; **n. race,** course très disputée; **it was a n. thing,** nous l'avons échappé belle; il s'en est fallu de peu; il était moins cinq. **nearly** *adv.* **1.** (*a*) presque, à peu près, près de; **it's n. midnight,** il est bientôt minuit; **I've got n. all of them,** je les ai presque tous; **very n.,** peu s'en faut; **I n. fell,** j'ai failli tomber; **he very n. died,** il a frôlé la mort; (*b*) **she's not n. so, as, old as me,** elle est loin d'être aussi âgée que moi. **2.** (de) près; **we are n. related,** nous sommes proches parents; *Nat.Hist:* **n. allied species,** espèces voisines.

near[2] *v.tr. & i.* (s')approcher (de qn, de qch.); **as we were nearing Oxford,** comme nous approchions d'Oxford; **the road is nearing completion,** la route est près d'être achevée; **we are nearing our goal,** nous touchons au but.

nearby [niə'bai] **1.** *adv.* tout près, tout proche; **he lives n.,** il habite tout près. **2.** ['niəːbai] *a.* **he came out of a n. house,** il est sorti d'une maison avoisinante.

nearness ['niənis] *n.* (*a*) (*of time, place*) proximité *f*; (*of place*) voisinage *m*; (*b*) (*of translation*) fidélité *f*, exactitude *f*; (*c*) (*of friends*) intimité *f*.

nearside ['niəːsaid] *n.* (*a*) côté *m* gauche (d'un cheval); côté (du) montoir; (*b*) (*esp. in U.K.*) *Aut:* gauche *f* (de la route); côté gauche (d'une voiture); **keep to the n. lane,** serrez à gauche.

nearsighted [niəː'saitid] *a.* myope.

nearsightedness [niəː'saitidnis] *n.* myopie *f*.

neat [niːt] *a.* **1.** (*of spirits*) pur, sans eau; **to take,**

drink, one's whisky n., boire son whisky sec. **2.** (*a*) (*of clothes, etc.*) simple et de bon goût; (*of room, drawer, etc.*) bien rangé, en ordre; (*of exercise book, etc.*) bien tenu, propre; (*of garden, etc.*) bien tenu; *F:* propret; (*of attire*) soigné; **n. handwriting,** écriture soignée; **she has a n. figure,** elle est bien faite; **as n. as a new pin,** tiré à quatre épingles; (*b*) (*of style*) élégant, choisi; (*of phrase, answer, etc.*) bien tourné, adroit; **n. piece of work,** ouvrage bien exécuté. **3.** (*of pers.*) ordonné, qui a de l'ordre. **-ly** *adv.* **1.** (ranger, etc.) d'une manière soignée, ordonnée, avec ordre; **n. written,** écrit soigneusement. **2.** adroitement; **n. turned compliment,** compliment bien tourné; **that is n. put,** c'est joliment dit.

neaten ['niːt(ə)n] *v.tr.* ajuster (qch.); donner meilleure tournure à (qch.).

neatness ['niːtnis] *n.* **1.** simplicité *f*, bon goût (dans la mise); apparence soignée (d'un jardin); netteté *f* (d'écriture, de style); bon ordre (d'une chambre, etc.); propreté *f* (d'un cahier, etc.); tournure adroite (d'une phrase). **2.** (*of pers.*) (*a*) ordre *m*, propreté; (*b*) adresse *f*, habileté *f*.

nebula, *pl.* **-æ** ['nebjulə, -iː] *n. Astr:* nébuleuse *f*.

nebulous ['nebjuləs] *a. Astr: etc:* nébuleux.

necessary ['nesis(ə)ri] **1.** *a.* (*a*) nécessaire, indispensable (**to, for, s.o., sth.,** à qn, qch.); **it is n. to do sth.,** il est nécessaire de faire qch., il faut faire qch.; **it is n. for him to return,** il faut qu'il revienne; **I find it n. to . . .,** je juge nécessaire de . . .; **it is n. that . . .,** il est nécessaire, il faut, que + *sub.*; **to make all n. arrangements,** prendre toutes dispositions utiles; **to make it n. for s.o. to do sth.,** mettre qn dans la nécessité de faire qch.; **if n.,** si cela est nécessaire; s'il le faut; le cas échéant; au besoin; **to do what is n.,** faire le nécessaire; **not to do more than is absolutely n.,** ne faire que le strict nécessaire, que l'essentiel; (*b*) (résultat, conclusion, loi, etc.) nécessaire, inévitable, inéluctable. **2.** *n.* (*a*) *usu.pl.* = NECESSITY 2; (*b*) *F:* **the n.,** (i) le nécessaire; (ii) de l'argent *m*; **his father will provide the n.,** son père fournira les frais de l'entreprise; **to do the n.,** (i) faire le nécessaire; (ii) payer, casquer. **-ily** [nesi'serəli] *adv.* nécessairement; inévitablement; forcément.

necessitate [ni'sesiteit] *v.tr.* nécessiter (qch.), rendre (qch.) nécessaire.

necessitous [ni'sesitəs] *a.* nécessiteux, besogneux.

necessity [ni'sesiti] *n.* **1.** (*a*) nécessité *f*; obligation *f*, contrainte *f*, force *f*; **by, from, out of, n.,** par nécessité, par la force des choses; **of n.,** de (toute) nécessité; nécessairement, inévitablement; **case of absolute n.,** cas *m* de force majeure; *Prov:* **n. is the mother of invention,** nécessité est mère d'industrie, d'invention; (*b*) nécessité, besoin *m* (**of doing sth.,** de faire qch.); **the n. for sth.,** le besoin de qch.; **if the n. arose, should arise,** si le besoin s'en faisait sentir; **in case of n.,** au besoin, en cas de besoin. **2.** *usu.pl.* le nécessaire; **the bare necessities,** le strict nécessaire; **the necessities of life,** les nécessités de la vie; l'indispensable *m*.

neck¹ [nek] *n.* **1.** (*a*) cou *m* (d'une personne, d'un animal); **to have a stiff n.,** avoir un, le, torticolis; *F:* **to be up to one's n. in work,** avoir du travail pardessus la tête; être débordé de travail; **he's in it up to his n.,** il y est (mouillé) jusqu'au cou; **to throw, fling, one's arms round s.o.'s n.,** sauter, se jeter, au cou de qn; **to break one's n.,** se casser le cou; **to save one's n.,** sauver sa peau; *F:* **to get it in the n.,** écoper; en avoir pour son compte; *Rac:* **to win by a n.,** gagner par une encolure; **to finish n. and n.,** arriver à égalité; **to it's n. or nothing,** il faut risquer, jouer, le tout pour le tout; (*b*) *Cu:* collet *m* (d'agneau, etc.); collier *m* (de bœuf); (*c*) *Cost:* encolure (de robe, de chemise); **square, round, n.,** encolure carrée, ronde; **V n.,** encolure en pointe, en V; **high n.,** col montant; **low n.,** décolleté *m*. **2.** (*a*) orifice *m*, tubulure *f*; goulot *m*, col *m* (de bouteille); col (d'un vase); rétrécissement *m*, étranglement *m* (de tuyau); appendice *m*, manchon *m* (de ballon); *Anat:* col (de l'utérus); (*b*) langue *f* (de terre); collet (de ciseau, de vis, etc.); manche *m*, collet (d'un instrument à cordes); coude *m* (de baïonnette); gorge *f* (d'arme à feu); *Bot:* collet (de champignon, etc.).

neck² *v.i. P:* (*of couple*) se bécoter; se faire des papouilles, des mamours. **necking** *n.* papouilles *fpl*, pelotage *m*.

neckband ['nekbænd] *n.* tour-du-cou *m*, *pl.* tours-du-cou (de chemise); col *m*.

neckerchief ['nekətʃif] *n. A:* foulard *m*; mouchoir *m*, tour *m*, de cou.

necklace ['neklis] *n.* collier *m* (de diamants, etc.).

necklet ['neklit] *n.* collier *m* (de fourrure, etc.).

neckline ['neklain] *n. Cost:* encolure *f*, échancrure *f* (d'une robe de jour); (*low*) décolletage *m*, décolleté *m* (d'une robe de soir).

necktie ['nektai] *n. Cost:* cravate *f*.

neckwear ['nekwɛər] *n. Com:* cols *mpl*, cravates *fpl*, foulards *mpl*, etc.

necrological [nekrə'lɔdʒik(ə)l] *a.* nécrologique.

necrology [ne'krɔlədʒi] *n.* **1.** nécrologe *m* (d'une église, d'une année, etc.). **2.** nécrologie *f*.

necromancer ['nekroumænsər] *n.* nécromancien, -ienne.

necromancy ['nekrəmænsi] *n.* necromancie *f*.

necrophilia [nekrou'filiə], **necrophily** [ne'krɔfiliː] *n. Med:* nécrophilie *f*.

necropolis [ne'krɔpəlis] *n.* nécropole *f*.

necrosis [ne'krousis] *n. Med:* nécrose *f*.

nectar ['nektər] *n. Myth: Bot:* nectar *m*.

nectarine ['nektəri(ː)n] *n. Hort:* brugnon *m*; **n. tree,** brugnonier *m*.

nectary ['nektəri] *n. Bot:* nectaire *m*.

Ned [ned] *Pr.n.m.* (*dim of Edward*) Édouard.

Neddy ['nedi] **1.** *Pr.n.m.* = NED. **2.** *n. F:* bourricot *m*, âne *m*.

née [nei] *Fr. p.p.* née; **Mrs Thomas, née Long,** Mme Thomas, née Long.

need¹ [niːd] *n.* **1.** (*a*) besoin *m*; **to feel, satisfy, a n.,** éprouver, satisfaire, un besoin; **if need(s) be, in case of n.,** en cas de besoin, au besoin; s'il (en) est besoin, si besoin (en) est; **there is no n. to . . .,** il n'est pas nécessaire de . . ., il n'est pas besoin de . . .; **(there's) no n. to wait,** inutile d'attendre; (*b*) **to be in n., have n., of sth.,** avoir besoin de qch.; manquer de qch.; **premises badly in n. of repair,** local *m* qui a grand besoin de réparations; **she is in n. of a rest,** elle a besoin de se reposer, de repos. **2.** (*a*) adversité *f*, difficulté *f*; **in times, in the hour, of n.,** aux moments difficiles; (*b*) besoin, indigence *f*; **to be in n.,** être dans la nécessité, dans le besoin; **their n. is greater than mine,** ils en ont plus besoin que moi. **3. present needs,** besoins actuels; **to attend, minister, to s.o.'s needs,** pourvoir aux besoins de qn; **that will meet my needs,** cela fera mon affaire.

need² *v.* **1.** *v.tr.* (*3rd pers. sg. pr. ind.* **needs;** *p.t. & p.p.* **needed**) (*a*) (*of pers.*) avoir besoin de (qn, qch.); (*of thg*) réclamer, exiger, demander (qch.); **to n. rest,** avoir besoin de repos; **I work because I n. the money,** je travaille par besoin d'argent; **work that needs much care,** travail *m* qui exige, réclame, beaucoup de soin; **these facts n. no comment,** ces faits *mpl* se passent de commentaire; **a much needed lesson,** une leçon dont on avait grand besoin; **what he needs is a thrashing,** ce qu'il lui faudrait c'est une bonne raclée; (*b*) **to n. to do sth.,** être obligé, avoir besoin, de faire qch.; **they n. to be told everything,** il faut qu'on leur dise tout; **I didn't n. to be reminded of it,** je n'avais pas besoin qu'on me le rappelât; **he didn't n. to be told twice,** il ne se l'est pas fait dire deux fois; **you only needed to ask,** vous n'aviez qu'à demander. **2.** *modal aux.* (*3rd pers. sg. pr. ind.* **need;** *p.t.* **need;** *no pr.p.; no p.p.*) **adults only n. apply,** les adultes seuls peuvent postuler; **you needn't trouble yourself,** (vous n'avez) pas besoin de vous déranger; **you needn't wait,** inutile (pour vous) d'attendre; **I n. hardly tell you how grateful I am,** il n'est pas besoin de vous dire combien je vous suis reconnaissant. **3.** *impers.* **it needs a great deal of skill for this work,** il faut beaucoup d'habileté pour ce travail.

needful ['ni:df(u)l] *a.* nécessaire (**to, for,** à, pour).

neediness ['ni:dinis] *n.* indigence *f*, nécessité *f*.

needle¹ ['ni:dl] *n.* **1.** (*a*) aiguille *f* (à coudre, à tricoter, etc.); **n. threader,** filifère *m*; enfile-aiguilles *m inv*; **n. lace,** dentelle *f* à l'aiguille; **hypodermic n.,** aiguille pour injections hypodermiques; **n.(-)shaped,** en forme d'aiguille; (stylet, etc.) aiguillé; **to look for a n. in a haystack,** chercher une aiguille dans une botte de foin; (*b*) *Bot:* **(pine) n.,** aiguille (de pin); **n. gorse,** genêt épineux; (*c*) *P:* **to get the n.,** se froisser; se fâcher; **to give s.o. the n.,** taper sur les nerfs à qn; agacer qn. **2.** *Tchn:* (*a*) *O:* aiguille (de tourne-disque, etc.); (*on record player*) **n. noise, scratch,** bruit *m* d'aiguille; *Mec.E:* **n. valve,** soupape *f* à pointeau, à aiguille; *Art:* **engraving n.,** pointe *f* pour taille douce; pointe sèche; (*b*) aiguille (de boussole, d'indicateur de vitesse, etc.); aiguille, langue *f*, languette *f* (de balance); **compass n.,** aiguille aimantée. **3.** (*a*) *Arch:* obélisque *m*; (*b*) *Geol: Geog:* aiguille (rocheuse); (*c*) *Ch: Miner:* **crystalline needles,** aiguilles cristallines. **4.** *Civ.E:* cale *f* d'étayage.

needle² *v.tr. F:* irriter, exciter, agacer (qn).

needlecord ['ni:dlkɔ:d] *n. Tex:* velours *m* milleraies.

needlecraft ['ni:dlkrɑ:ft] *n.* travaux *mpl* à l'aiguille.

needlepoint ['ni:dlpɔint] *n.* **1.** (*a*) pointe *f* d'aiguille; (*b*) pointe sèche (de compas). **2. n. (lace),** dentelle *f* à l'aiguille.

needless ['ni:dlis] *a.* inutile, peu nécessaire, superflu; (remarque) déplacée; **n. to say we shall refund the money,** il va de soi que nous rembourserons l'argent. **-ly** *adv.* inutilement.

needlewoman, *pl.* **-women** ['ni:dlwumən, -wimin] *n.f.* **she's a good n.,** elle travaille adroitement à l'aiguille; **I'm no n.,** je ne sais pas coudre.

needlework ['ni:dlwə:k] *n.* travail *m* à l'aiguille; travaux à l'aiguille; (*school subject*) couture *f*.

needs [ni:dz] *adv. O:* (*used only with* **must**) (*a*) nécessairement, de toute nécessité; **if n. must . . .,** s'il le faut . . .; (*b*) *Pej:* **he had no money, but she must n. go and marry him,** il était sans le sou, mais la voilà qui commet la sottise de l'épouser.

needy ['ni:di] *a.* (*of pers.*) nécessiteux, besogneux, indigent; *n.pl.* **the n.,** les nécessiteux.

ne'er [nɛər] *adv. Poet:* (ne . . .) jamais; **ne'er the less,** néanmoins.

ne'er-do-well ['nɛə:du:wel] **1.** *a.* propre à rien. **2.** *n.* vaurien, -ienne; propre-à-rien *mf*.

nefarious [ni'fɛəriəs] *a.* (*of pers., purpose, etc.*) infâme, scélérat, vilain. **-ly** *adv.* d'une manière infâme.

negate [ni'geit] *v.tr.* **1.** *Lit:* nier. **2.** nullifier (la loi, etc.) **3.** *Gram:* mettre au négatif.

negation [ni'geiʃ(ə)n] *n.* négation *f* (d'un fait, etc.).

negative¹ ['negətiv] **I.** *a.* (*a*) (*of reply, result, virtue, etc.*) négatif; **to maintain a n. attitude,** se tenir sur la négative; (*b*) *Mth:* (*of quantity, etc.*) négatif; **n. sign,** (signe *m*) moins *m*; (*c*) *El:* (*of pole, electrode, etc.*) négatif; (*d*) *Phot:* (image) négatif. **II.** *n.* **1.** (*a*) négative *f*; *Gram:* négation *f*; **to answer in the n.,** répondre négativement, par la négative; (*b*) *Mth:* valeur, quantité, négative. **2.** (*a*) *Phot:* (cliché) négatif (*m*); épreuve négative; (*b*) *Rec:* **n. (record),** poinçon *m*; (*c*) *El:* plaque négative (de pile). **III.** *adv.* (*in answer to a question*) non. **negatively** *adv.* négativement.

negative² *v.tr.* **1.** s'opposer à, rejeter (un projet, etc.). **2.** réfuter (une hypothèse); contredire, nier (un rapport); *Nau: etc:* annuler (un signal). **3.** neutraliser (un effet, etc.).

neglect¹ [ni'glekt] *n.* **1.** (*a*) manque *m* d'égards (**of,** envers, pour); (*b*) manque de soin(s); **to die in total n.,** mourir complètement abandonné; (*c*) mauvais entretien (d'une machine, etc.). **2.** négligence *f*, inattention *f*; **out of n., from n., through n.,** par négligence; **n. of one's duties,** oubli *m* des devoirs.

neglect² *v.tr.* **1.** (*a*) manquer d'égards envers (qn); négliger (qn); (*b*) manquer de soins pour (qn); négliger (ses enfants, sa santé, etc.); **to n. oneself,** négliger sa personne; se négliger; **the garden looks neglected,** le jardin est mal tenu, à l'abandon. **2.** négliger, oublier (ses devoirs, un avis, etc.); laisser échapper (une occasion); **to n. to do sth.,** omettre de faire qch.

neglectful [ni'glektf(u)l] *a.* négligent; **to be n. of sth., of s.o.,** négliger qch., qn; être négligent de qch., de qn; **n. of one's duty,** oublieux de son devoir.

négligé(e) ['negliʒei] *n. Cost:* négligé *m*, déshabillé *m*.

negligence ['neglidʒəns] *n.* (*a*) négligence *f*; manque *m* de soins; **through n.,** par négligence; (*b*) nonchalance *f*, insouciance *f*; (*c*) *Jur:* négligence; **criminal n.,** négligence coupable, criminelle.

negligent ['neglidʒənt] *a.* **1.** négligent; **to be n. of sth.,** négliger qch.; être oublieux de (ses devoirs, etc.). **2.** (air, ton) nonchalant, insouciant. **-ly** *adv.* **1.** négligemment. **2.** nonchalamment.

negligible ['neglidʒibl] *a.* négligeable.

negotiable [ni'gouʃiəbl] *a.* **1.** *Fin: etc:* (effet, titre, etc.) négociable; bancable; **not n.,** non-négociable; (*of military pension, etc.*) incessible. **2.** (barrière, etc.) franchissable; (chemin, etc.) praticable.

negotiate [ni'gouʃieit] **1.** *v.tr.* (*a*) négocier, traiter (une affaire, u'gouʃiəbl] *a.* **1.** *Fin: etc:* (effet, titre, etc.) négociable; bancable; **not n.,** non-négociable; (*of military pension, etc.*) incessible. **2.** (barrière, etc.) franchissable; (chemin, etc.) praticable.

negotiate [ni'gouʃieit] **1.** *v.tr.* (*a*) négocier, traiter (une affaire, un mariage); négocier (un emprunt); **price to be negotiated,** prix *m* à débattre; (*b*) *Fin:* négocier, trafiquer (un effet); (*c*) franchir (une haie, etc.); surmonter (une difficulté); *Aut:* **to n. a bend,** négocier, prendre, un virage. **2.** *v.i.* (*a*) **to be negotiating with s.o. for . . .,** être en traité, en marché, avec qn pour . . .; **to n. for peace,** entreprendre des pourparlers de paix; (*b*) **they refuse to n.,** ils refusent de négocier.

negotiation [nigouʃi'eiʃ(ə)n] *n.* **1.** négociation *f* (d'un traité, d'un emprunt, etc.); **under n.,** en négociation; **to be in n. with s.o.,** être en pourparler(s) avec qn; **to break off, resume, negotiations,** rompre, reprendre, les négociations. **2.** franchissement *m* (d'un obstacle); prise *f* (d'un virage).

negotiator [ni'gouʃieitər] *n.* négociateur, -trice.

negress ['ni:gris] *n.f.* noire; *Anthr: & Pej:* négresse.

negro, *pl.* **-oes** ['ni:grou, -z] **1.** *a.* noir, nègre; **the n. race,** la race noire, nègre. **2.** *n.* noir *m*; *Anthr. & Pej:* nègre *m*.

negroid ['ni:grɔid] *a. & n. Anthr:* négroïde (*mf*).

neigh¹ [nei] *n.* hennissement *m*.

neigh² *v.i.* hennir. **neighing** *n.* hennissement(s) *m(pl).*

neighbour, *NAm:* **neighbor** [ˈneibər] *n.* **1.** voisin, -ine. **2.** *B: etc:* prochain *m;* **love thy n. as thyself,** aime ton prochain comme toi-même.

neighbourhood, *NAm:* **neighborhood** [ˈneibəhud] *n.* **1.** voisinage, proximité *f* **(of,** de); **to live in the (immediate) n. of . . .,** demeurer à proximité de . . .; *F:* **in the n. of £10,** environ £10, dans les £10. **2.** (*a*) alentours *mpl,* environs *mpl* (d'un lieu); (*b*) voisinage, quartier *m;* **the whole n. is talking about it,** tout le voisinage en parle.

neighbouring, *NAm:* **neighboring** [ˈneibəriŋ] *a.* avoisinant, voisin.

neighbourliness, *NAm:* **neighborliness** [ˈneibəlinis] *n.* (*of pers.*) (relations *fpl* de) bon voisinage; bons rapports entre voisins.

neighbourly, *NAm:* **neighborly** [ˈneibəli] *a.* (*of pers.*) obligeant; bon voisin; (*of action, etc.*) de bon voisin; (visite) de bon voisinage; **to be n. with s.o.,** voisiner avec qn.

neither [ˈnaiðər, *esp. NAm:* ˈniːðər] **1.** *adv.* & *conj.* (*a*) **n. . . . nor . . .,** ni . . . ni . . .; **he will n. eat nor drink,** il ne veut ni manger ni boire; **n. (the) one nor the other,** ni l'un ni l'autre; (*b*) non plus; **if you don't go n. shall I,** si vous n'y allez pas, je n'irai pas non plus; (*c*) **I haven't read it, n. do I intend to,** je ne l'ai pas lu et d'ailleurs je n'en ai pas l'intention. **2.** *a.* & *pron.* ni l'un(e) ni l'autre; aucun(e); **n. driver was injured,** ni l'un ni l'autre des conducteurs n'a été blessé; **on n. side,** ni d'un côté ni de l'autre.

nelly [ˈneli] *n. P:* **not on your n.!** jamais de la vie!

nelson [ˈnels(ə)n] *n. Wr:* nelson *m;* **double, full, n.,** double nelson.

nemesis [ˈnemisis] *n.* châtiment mérité.

neo-classic(al) [niːouˈklæsik(l)] *a.* néo-classique.

neo-classicism [niːouˈklæsisizm] *n.* néo-classicisme *m.*

neocolonialism [niːoukəˈlouniəlizm] *n. Pol:* néo-colonialisme *m.*

neofascism [niːouˈfæʃizm] *n. Pol:* néo-fascisme *m.*

neofascist [niouˈfæʃist] *a.* & *n.* néo-fasciste (*mf*).

neo-gothic [niːouˈgɔθik] *a.* & *n. Arch:* néo-gothique (*m*).

neolithic [niːouˈliθik] **1.** *a.* néolithique. **2.** *n.* **the N.,** l'âge *m* de la pierre polie, le néolithique.

neologism [niˈɔlədʒizm] *n.* néologisme *m.*

neon [ˈniːɔn] *n. Ch:* néon *m; El:* **n. tube,** tube fluorescent, *F:* au néon; **n. sign,** enseigne au néon.

neonatal [niːouˈneit(ə)l] *a. Med:* néo-natal.

neonazi [niːouˈnɑːtsi] *a.* & *n.* néo-nazi, -ie.

neophyte [ˈniːoufait] *n. Rel: etc:* néophyte *mf.*

neoplasm [ˈniːouplæzm] *n. Med:* néoplasme *m.*

Nepal [neˈpɔːl] *Pr.n. Geog:* Népal *m.*

Nepalese [nepəˈliːz], **Nepali** [neˈpɔːli] **1.** *a.* népalais. **2.** *n.* Népalais, -aise.

nephew [ˈnefju] *n.m.* neveu.

nephrite [ˈnefrait] *n. Miner:* néphrite *f;* jade *m.*

nephritic [neˈfritik] *a. Med:* néphrétique.

nephritis [neˈfraitis] *n. Med:* néphrite *f.*

nepotism [ˈnepətizm, ˈniː-] *n.* népotisme *m.*

nereid [ˈniəriid] *n. Myth: Ann:* néréide *f.*

Nero [ˈniərou] *Pr.n.m. Rom.Hist:* Néron.

nerve¹ [nəːv] *n.* **1.** (*a*) *Anat:* nerf *m;* **optic, auditory, n.,** nerf optique, auditif; **n. centre,** centre nerveux; **n. fibre,** fibre nerveuse; *Mil: etc:* **n. gas,** gaz *m* neurotoxique; *Med:* **n. specialist,** neurologue *mf; F:* **to be in a state of nerves,** être énervé, sur les nerfs; **(s)he's a bundle of nerves,** c'est un paquet de nerfs; **to get on s.o.'s nerves,** taper sur les nerfs à qn; énerver, agacer, qn; (*b*) courage *m;* sang-froid *m;* **to lose one's n.,** perdre son sang-froid; **his n. failed him, he lost his n.,** le courage lui a manqué; il s'est dégonflé; (*c*) *F:* audace *f;* **to have the n. to . . .,** avoir le toupet, le culot, de . . . **what a nerve!** quel culot! **you've got a n.!** tu es gonflé! **2.** *Bot: Ent: Arch:* nervure *f.* **3.** *Lit:* tendon *m,* nerf; **to strain every n. to do sth.,** mettre toute sa force à faire qch.

nerve² *v.tr.* (*a*) fortifier; donner du nerf, de la force, à (son bras, etc.); donner du courage à (qn); (*b*) **to n. oneself to do sth.,** s'armer de courage, de sang-froid, pour faire qch.

nerveless [ˈnəːvlis] *a.* (*of pers., limb, etc.*) inerte, faible; (style, etc.) sans vigueur, languissant.

nerveracking [ˈnəːvrækiŋ] *a.* énervant; éprouvant pour les nerfs.

nerviness [ˈnəːvinis] *n. F:* nervosité *f;* énervement *m.*

nervous [ˈnəːvəs] *a.* **1.** (*of pers.*) (*a*) excitable; irritable; (*b*) intimidé; timide, peureux, craintif; **to feel n.,** avoir peur; (*of singer, etc.*) avoir le trac; **to feel n. in s.o.'s presence,** se sentir intimidé en présence de qn; **to get n.,** s'intimider; **to be n. of (doing) sth.,** avoir peur de (faire) qch. **2.** (*a*) *Anat:* nerveux; **n. system,** système nerveux; (*b*) *Med:* **n. complaint,** maladie *f* de nerfs. **-ly** *adv.* (*a*) timidement; (*b*) craintivement.

nervousness [ˈnəːvəsnis] *n.* **1.** (*a*) nervosité *f;* état nerveux, d'agitation; (*b*) timidité *f; F:* trac *m.*

nervy [ˈnəːvi] *a. F:* (*a*) énervé, irritable; **to feel n.,** être dans un état d'énervement; avoir les nerfs en pelote; (*b*) (mouvement) nerveux.

nest¹ [nest] *n.* **1.** (*a*) nid *m* (d'oiseaux, de guêpes, etc.); *F:* **love n.,** nid d'amoureux; **n. egg,** (i) *Husb:* nichet *m;* œuf *m* en faïence; (ii) *F:* argent mis de côté, pécule *m;* (*b*) repaire *m,* nid (de brigands, etc.). **2.** nichée *f* (d'oiseaux, etc.). **3.** série *f,* jeu *m* (d'objets); **n. of tables,** table *f* gigogne.

nest² **1.** *v.i.* (*of birds, etc.*) (se) nicher; faire son nid. **2.** *v.tr.* emboîter (des tubes, etc.); (*with passive force*) s'emboîter. **nesting** **1.** *a.* (oiseau) nicheur. **2.** *n.* **n. time,** saison *f* de la ponte; **n. box,** pondoir *m,* nichoir *m.*

nestful [ˈnestful] *n.* nichée *f.*

nestle [nesl] *v.i.* & *tr.* se nicher, se pelotonner; **to n. close (up) to s.o.,** se serrer contre qn; **to n. (one's face) against s.o.'s shoulder,** se blottir contre l'épaule de qn; **village nestling in a valley,** village blotti, tapi, dans une vallée.

nestling [ˈnes(t)liŋ] *n.* oisillon *m.*

net¹ [net] *n.* **1.** filet *m;* (*a*) **fishing n.,** filet de pêche; **butterfly n.,** filet à papillons; **to haul in a n.,** relever un filet; (*b*) *Ven:* **(game) n.,** pan *m,* panneau *m;* **to be caught in the n.,** être pris au filet, au piège; (*c*) **hair n.,** filet, résille *f* (à cheveux); (*for horse*) **fly n.,** émouchette *f;* émouchette *f;* (*d*) *Ten: etc:* filet; **n. play,** jeu *m* au filet; (*e*) *Ind:* **guard n.,** filet de protection; *Mil:* **camouflage n.,** filet de camouflage; (*f*) (*at circus, etc.*) **safety n.,** filet; (*g*) *Aer:* filet (de ballon). **2.** *Tex:* tulle *m;* **Brussels n.,** tulle bruxelles; **foundation n.,** mousseline forte; **n. curtain,** rideau *m* de tulle. **3.** = NETWORK.

net² *v.* **(netted)** **1.** *v.tr.* (*a*) prendre (des poissons, des lièvres, etc.) au filet; (*b*) tendre des filets dans (une rivière); (*c*) *Sp:* envoyer (le ballon, la balle) dans le filet; (*d*) *Mil:* camoufler (un emplacement, etc.) avec un filet; (*e*) *Hort:* protéger (des petits pois, etc.) avec un filet; (*f*) faire (un hamac, etc.) au filet. **2.** *v.i.* faire du filet. **netting** *n.* **1.** fabrication *f* du filet; **n. needle,** navette *f.* **2.** pêche *f,* capture *f* du gibier, au(x) filet(s). **3.** (*a*) filet(s) (de protection, de camouflage); (*b*) grillage *m,* treillage *m,* treillis *m;* **wire n.,** treillis métallique, grillage en fil de fer; (*c*) *Tex:* tulle *m.*

net³ **1.** *a.* (*of weight, price, etc.*) net, *f.* nette; **n. proceeds of a sale,** (produit) net (*m*) d'une vente; **terms**

strictly n., sans déduction; payable au comptant. **2.** *n.* prix, poids, bénéfice, etc., net.

net⁴ *v.tr.* **(netted) 1.** (*of pers.*) toucher net, gagner net (tant de bénéfices, etc.). **2.** (*of enterprise, etc.*) rapporter net, produire net (une certaine somme).

netball ['netbɔːl] *n. Sp:* netball *m.*

nether ['neðər] *a.* inférieur, bas; *Lit:* **the n. regions,** l'enfer *m*; les régions infernales.

Netherlands (the) [ðə'neðələndz] *Pr.n.pl. Geog:* les Pays-Bas *mpl*; **in the N.,** dans les, aux, Pays-Bas.

nett [net] *a.* = NET³.

nettle¹ ['netl] *n. Bot:* ortie *f*; **stinging n.,** ortie brûlante; **dead n.,** ortie blanche; *Med:* **n. rash,** urticaire *f.*

nettle² *v.tr.* piquer, irriter (qn); faire monter la moutarde au nez de (qn).

network ['netwəːk] *n.* **1.** (*a*) réseau *m*, lacis *m* (de canaux, de rues, etc.); enchevêtrement *m* (de ronces, etc.); (*b*) **electric n.,** réseau électrique; (*c*) *T.V: W.Tel:* chaîne *f* (de télévision, de radiodiffusion); (*d*) *Cmptr:* réseau, graphe *m.* **2.** réseau (d'alliances, etc.); **spy n.,** réseau d'espionnage; *F:* **the old-boy n.** = la franc-maçonnerie des grandes écoles.

neural ['njuːr(ə)l] *a. Anat:* neural, -aux.

neuralgia [njuː'rældʒiə] *n. Med:* névralgie *f.*

neuralgic [njuː'rældʒik] *a. Med:* névralgique.

neurasthenia [njuːrəs'θiːniə] *n. Med:* neurasthénie *f.*

neurasthenic [njuːrəs'θiːnik] *a. & n. Med:* neurasthénique (*mf*).

neuritis [njuː'raitis] *n. Med:* névrite *f.*

neurological [njuːrə'lɔdʒik(ə)l] *a.* neurologique.

neurologist [njuː'rɔlədʒist] *n.* neurologue *mf.*

neurology [njuː'rɔlədʒi] *n.* neurologie *f.*

neuromuscular [njuːrou'mʌskjuːlər] *a.* neuromusculaire.

neuron ['njuːrɔn] *n. Physiol:* neurone *m.*

neuropathology [njuːroupə'θɔlədʒi] *n.* névropathologie *f*, neuropathologie *f.*

neurosis [njuː'rousis] *n. Med:* névrose *f.*

neurosurgeon [njuːrou'səːdʒən] *n.* neurochirurgien, -ienne.

neurosurgery [njuːrou'səːdʒəri] *n.* neurochirurgie *f.*

neurotic [nju'rɔtik] **1.** *a. Med.* (*a*) (*of pers.*) névrosé; *F:* **he's positively n. about it,** c'est une obsession chez lui; (*b*) (*relating to a neurosis*) névrotique. **2.** *n.* névrosé, -ée.

neuter¹ ['njuːtər] **1.** *a.* (*a*) *Gram:* (genre, verbe, etc.) neutre; (*b*) *Biol:* neutre, asexué; (*c*) *Pol: etc:* neutre; **to stand n.,** garder la neutralité. **2.** *n.* (*a*) *Gram:* (genre) neutre (*m*); (*b*) abeille asexuée, ouvrière; (*c*) animal châtré.

neuter² *v.tr. Vet:* châtrer (un chat, etc.).

neutral ['njuːtr(ə)l] **1.** *a.* (*a*) *Pol: etc:* neutre; **to remain n.,** rester neutre, garder la neutralité; (*b*) neutre, indéterminé, intermédiaire; *Ch: El: etc:* neutre; *Ph:* (équilibre) indifférent; (*c*) **in n. gear,** au point mort. **2.** *n.* (*a*) (État *m*, pays *m*) neutre (*m*); (*b*) ressortissant, -ante, d'un État neutre; (*c*) *Aut:* point mort.

neutralism ['njuːtrəlism] *n.* neutralisme *m.*

neutralist ['njuːtrəlist] *n.* neutraliste *mf.*

neutrality [nju(ː)'træliti] *n.* (*a*) *Pol: etc:* neutralité *f*; (*b*) *Ch:* neutralité, indifférence *f* (d'un sel).

neutralization [njuːtrəlai'zeiʃ(ə)n] *n.* neutralisation *f.*

neutralize ['njuːtrəlaiz] *v.tr.* neutraliser; **to n. one another,** (i) (*of chemical agents*) se neutraliser; (ii) (*of forces*) se détruire.

neutron ['njuːtrɔn] *n. Atom.Ph: El:* neutron *m*; **n. bomb,** bombe *f* à neutrons.

never ['nevər] *adv.* (*a*) (ne . . .) jamais; **I n. go there,** je n'y vais jamais; **n. again, n. more,** jamais plus; plus jamais (. . . ne); **he n. came back,** il n'est jamais revenu; **n. in (all) my life, n. in all my born days,** jamais de la vie; **that n. to be forgotten day,** ce jour inoubliable; (*b*) (*emphatic neg.*) **I n. expected him to come,** je ne m'attendais pas du tout à ce qu'il vînt; **he n. said a word,** il n'a pas dit un mot; **you (surely) n. left him all alone!** ne me dites pas que vous l'avez laissé tout seul! **he has eaten it all—n.!** il a tout mangé—pas possible! **well I n. (did)!** ça par exemple! (*c*) *A: Lit:* **be he n. so brave,** quelque courageux qu'il soit; si courageux soit-il.

never-ending ['nevər'endiŋ] *a.* perpétuel, éternel; sans fin; incessant; (tâche) interminable.

nevermore [nevə'mɔːər] *adv.* (ne . . .) plus jamais, (ne . . .) jamais plus; **n.!** jamais plus! plus jamais!

never-never ['nevə'nevər] *n. F:* **to buy sth. on the n.-n.,** acheter qch. à crédit, à tempérament.

nevertheless [nevəðə'les] *adv.* néanmoins, quand même, tout de même; pourtant; malgré tout.

new [njuː] **I.** *a.* **1.** (*a*) nouveau, -elle; (pays) neuf; (terre) vierge; **what's n.?** quoi de neuf? *F:* **that's nothing n.!** rien de nouveau à cela; **it's quite n. to me,** c'est tout nouveau pour moi; **it has made a n. man of him,** cela a fait de lui un autre homme; *Mil:* **the n. guard,** la garde montante; *Sch:* **the n. boys,** les nouveaux; (*b*) **he's n. to this work,** il est nouveau, novice, dans ce travail; (*c*) **I'm n. to this town,** je suis nouveau venu dans cette ville. **2.** (*a*) neuf, *f.* neuve; **to be dressed in n. clothes,** être habillé de neuf; *Com:* **in n. condition, as n.,** à l'état (de) neuf; **to do up sth. like n.,** remettre qch. à neuf; (*b*) **n. ideas,** idées neuves; **the subject is quite n.,** ce sujet n'a pas encore été traité. **3.** (pain) frais; (herbe) tendre; (pommes de terre) nouvelles; (vin) nouveau, jeune; **n. leaves,** jeunes feuilles *fpl.* **II.** *adv.* (*used to form compound adjs.*) nouvellement; **n. blown,** (fleur) fraîche épanouie; **n. mown hay,** foin fraîchement coupé. **III.** (*in geographical names*) **N. Caledonia,** Nouvelle-Calédonie; **N. Guinea,** Nouvelle-Guinée; **N. Mexico,** Nouveau-Mexique; **N. Orleans,** Nouvelle-Orléans; **N. York,** New York; **N. Yorker,** New yorkais, -aise; **N. Zealand,** Nouvelle-Zélande; **N. Zealander,** Néo-Zélandais, -aise. **newly** *adv.* (*usu. hyphenated when in conjunction with a.*) récemment, nouvellement, fraîchement; **he is n. arrived,** il est tout fraîchement arrivé; **he was n. shaven,** il était rasé de frais; **the n.-elected members,** les députés nouveaux élus; **n.-painted wall,** mur fraîchement peint.

newborn ['njuːbɔːn] *a.* **1.** nouveau-né; **n. baby,** nouveau-né *m.* **2.** *Theol:* régénéré.

newel ['njuːəl] *n. Const: etc:* **1.** noyáu *m* (d'escalier tournant). **2. n. (post),** pilastre *m* (de rampe d'escalier).

newfangled ['njuːfæŋg(ə)ld] *a. Pej:* (*of word, idea, etc.*) d'une modernité outrée; nouveau genre.

Newfoundland ['njuːfəndlænd, -lənd, -'faundlənd] **1.** *Pr.n. Geog:* Terre-Neuve. **2.** *n.* [njuː'faundlənd] **N. (dog),** chien *m* de Terre-Neuve; terre-neuve *m inv.*

Newfoundlander ['njuːfəndlændər, njuː'faundləndər] *n.* **1.** *Geog:* Terre-neuvien, -ienne. **2.** *Fish:* (*pers. or ship*) terre-neuvien, terre-neuvier *m.*

newlyweds ['njuːliwedz] *n.pl.* nouveaux mariés.

newness ['njuːnis] *n.* **1.** nouveauté *f* (d'une idée, etc.). **2.** état neuf (d'un vêtement, etc.). **3.** (*a*) fraîcheur *f* (du pain, etc.); (*b*) jeunesse *f* (du vin).

news [njuːz] *n.pl.* (*usu. with sg. const.*) **1.** nouvelle *f*; nouvelles; **what's the n.?** quelles nouvelles? quoi de nouveau, de neuf? **I've some n. for you,** j'ai une nouvelle à vous annoncer; **that's n. to me,** ça, c'est du nouveau; **a sad piece of n., sad n.,** une triste nouvelle; **no n. is good n.,** point de nouvelles, bonnes nouvelles. **2.** (*a*) *Journ: etc:* **official n.,** communiqué officiel; **financial n.,** chronique financière; **n. in brief,** faits divers; **to be in the n.,** faire vedette; défrayer la chronique; **n. agency,** agence *f* d'informations; **n. stand,** kiosque *m* (à journaux); (*b*) *W.Tel: T.V. etc:* **the n.,** informations *fpl*; téléjournal *m*; *Cin:* actualités *fpl*; **n. bulletin,** bulletin *m* d'informations; **n. theatre, cinema,** cinéma *m* d'actualités; (*c*) sujet *m* propre au reportage; **to make n.,** faire sensation.

newsagent ['nju:zeidʒənt] *n.* dépositaire *m* de journaux; marchand, -ande, de journaux.

newscaster ['nju:zkɑ:stər] *n. W.Tel: T.V:* speaker, speakerine.

newsdealer ['nju:zdi:lər] *n. NAm:* = NEWSAGENT.

newshawk, newshound ['njuzhɔ:k, -haund] *n. F:* reporter *m*, chasseur *m* de copie.

newsletter ['nju:zletər] *n.* bulletin *m* (d'informations); circulaire *f*.

newspaper ['nju:zpeipər] *n.* (*a*) journal, -aux *m*; **daily n.,** (journal) quotidien *m*; **weekly n.,** (journal) hebdomadaire (*m*); **n. report,** reportage *m*; **n. cuttings,** coupures *fpl* de journaux; **n. rack,** porte-journaux *m inv*; **n. man,** (i) journaliste *m*; (ii) marchand *m* de journaux; (*b*) papier *m* journal.

newsprint ['nju:zprint] *n.* papier *m* (de) journal.

newsreel ['nju:zri:l] *n. Cin:* actualités *fpl*.

newsroom ['nju:zru:m] *n.* **1.** *Journ:* salle *f* de rédaction des informations. **2.** (*in library*) salle des journaux.

newsvendor ['nju:zvendər] *n.* marchand, -ande, de journaux.

newsworthy ['nju:zwə:ði] *a. Journ:* propre au reportage; qui fera parler, qui fera sensation.

newsy ['nju:zi] *a. F:* (*of letter, etc.*) plein de nouvelles.

newt [nju:t] *n. Amph:* triton *m*.

next [nekst] **I.** *a.* **1.** (*of place*) prochain, le plus proche; **the n. room,** la chambre voisine; **her room is n. to mine,** sa chambre est à côté de la mienne; **seated n. to me,** assis à côté de moi; **I can't bear wool n. to my skin,** je ne peux pas supporter la laine à même la peau; **the n. house,** la maison d'à côté; **the girl (from) n. door,** la jeune fille d'à côté; **he lives n. door (to us),** il habite à côté (de chez nous); **n. door neighbours,** voisins d'à côté, immédiats. **2.** (*a*) (*of time*) prochain, suivant; **the n. day,** le lendemain, le jour (d')après; **the n. day but one,** le surlendemain; **(the) n. morning,** le lendemain matin; **from one moment to the n.,** d'un instant à l'autre; (*future time*) **n. year, n. week,** l'année prochaine, la semaine prochaine; **this time n. year,** dans un an d'ici; **the year after n.,** dans deux ans; **n. Friday, (on) Friday n.,** vendredi prochain; (*b*) (*of order*) **the n. chapter,** le chapitre suivant; **the n. time I see him,** la prochaine fois que je le verrai; **ask the n. person you meet,** demandez à la première personne que vous rencontrerez; **the n. thing is to . . .,** maintenant il s'agit de . . .; *F:* **what(ever) n.!** par exemple! et quoi encore! **n. (person), please!** au suivant! **who's n.? whose turn (is it) n.?** à qui le tour? c'est à qui? **I come n. to him,** je viens (immédiatement) après lui; (*c*) (*in shoes, etc.*) **the n. size (larger),** la pointure au-dessus; **the n. best thing would be to . . .,** à défaut de cela, le mieux serait de . . .; *F:* **I got it for n. to nothing,** je l'ai eu pour presque rien, pour une bouchée de pain; **there is n. to no evidence,** il n'y a pour ainsi dire pas de preuves. **3.** *Jur:* **n. friend,** ami le plus proche; représentant *m* ad litem. **4.** *esp. U.S: F:* **to get n. to s.o.,** se mettre bien avec qn. **II.** *adv.* **1.** ensuite, après; **what shall we do n.?** qu'est-ce que nous allons faire maintenant, après cela? **2.** la prochaine fois; **when I n. saw him,** quand je l'ai revu.

next-of-kin [nekstəv'kin] *n.* (i) parent le plus proche; (ii) *pl.* la famille; **to inform the n.-of-k.,** prévenir la famille.

Niagara [nai'æg(ə)rə] *Pr.n. Geog:* Niagara *m*; **the N. Falls,** les chutes *fpl* du Niagara.

nib [nib] *n.* **1.** (bec *m* de) plume (*f*); **broad n.,** grosse plume; plume à gros bec; **fine n.,** plume fine; plume à bec fin. **2.** pointe *f* (d'outil, etc.).

nibble¹ ['nibl] *n.* **1.** (*a*) grignotement *m*; **to have a n. at the cake,** grignoter le gâteau; (*b*) *Fish:* touche *f*; **I didn't get, have, a n. all day,** le poisson n'a pas mordu de toute la journée. **2.** juste de quoi grignoter; petit morceau (de biscuit). **3.** *F.* **nibbles,** amuse-gueules *mpl*.

nibble² *v.tr. & i.* grignoter, mordiller (qch.); **to n. (at) a biscuit,** grignoter un biscuit; (*of fish, F: of pers.*) **to n. (at the bait),** toucher; piquer; mordre à l'hameçon; *F:* **to n. at sth.,** chicaner sur qch.

nibbler ['niblər] *n.* grignoteur, -euse.

nibs [nibz] *n. F: Iron:* **his n.,** sa majesté.

Nicaragua [nikə'rægjuə] *Pr.n.* Nicaragua *m*.

Nicaraguan [nikə'rægjuən] **1.** *a.* nicaraguayen. **2.** *n.* Nicaraguayen, -enne.

nice [nais] *a.* **1.** *Lit:* (*a*) (*of pers.*) (i) difficile; exigeant; (ii) *O:* scrupuleux; **he is not too n. about the means,** il n'est pas trop scrupuleux quant aux moyens; (*b*) (*of experiment, question, etc.*) délicat; (*of taste, etc.*) subtil, fin, recherché. **2.** *F:* (*a*) (*of pers.*) gentil, *f.* gentille; agréable, aimable; **to be n. to s.o.,** se montrer gentil, aimable, pour, envers, qn; **it is n. of you to . . .,** vous êtes bien aimable de . . .; **it's not n. of you to make fun of him,** ce n'est pas bien de vous moquer de lui; **he's a n. chap,** c'est un gentil garçon; *Iron:* **you're a n. one to talk like that!** c'est du joli de parler comme ça! **she's a n.-looking woman,** c'est une jolie, belle, femme; (*b*) (*of thg*) joli, bon; (soirée) agréable; **the garden is beginning to look n.,** le jardin s'embellit; **to have a n. long chat,** faire une bonne petite causette; **a n. little sum,** une somme rondelette; (*c*) (*intensive*) *F:* **n. and handy,** bien commode; **it's n. and cool,** le temps est agréablement frais, d'une fraîcheur agréable; **it's n. and easy,** c'est très facile; (*d*) **n. people,** des gens bien; **not n.,** pas tout à fait convenable; **it's not a n. story,** c'est une histoire peu savoureuse; (*e*) *Iron:* **we *are* in a n. mess!** nous voilà dans de beaux draps! **that's a n. way to behave!** en voilà des manières! **-ly** *adv.* **1.** *Lit:* (*a*) minutieusement, scrupuleusement; (*b*) exactement; avec justesse. **2.** gentiment, bien; agréablement; **everything was n. done,** tout était bien fait; **those will do (very) n.,** ceux-là feront très bien l'affaire; **he spoke very n. about you,** il m'a parlé de vous en très bons termes.

niceness ['naisnis] *n.* **1.** *Lit:* (*a*) (*of pers.*) (i) délicatesse exagérée; (ii) scrupulosité *f*; (*b*) (*of experiment, etc.*) délicatesse *f*; (*of taste*) subtilité *f*, finesse *f*. **2.** gentillesse *f*, amabilité *f* (de qn); agrément *m*, caractère *m* agréable (de qch.).

nicety ['naisiti] *n.* **1.** = NICENESS 1 (*a*). **2.** (*a*) exactitude *f*, précision *f* (d'un calcul, etc.); **to a n.,** exactement, à la perfection; (*b*) subtilité *f*, délicatesse *f* (d'une question, etc.). **3.** *pl.* **niceties,** minuties *fpl*; finesses *fpl*.

niche [nitʃ, ni:ʃ] *n.* niche *f* (pour une statue, etc.); **to make a n. for oneself,** (trouver à) se caser.

Nicholas ['nikələs] *Pr.n.m.* Nicolas.

Nick¹ [nik] *Pr.n.m.* (*dim of Nicholas*) Nicolas; *F:* **Old N.,** le diable.

nick² *n.* **1.** (*a*) (*in plank, etc.*) entaille *f*, encoche *f*; (*in tally stick, etc.*) coche *f*, encoche; (*b*) brèche *f* (au tranchant d'une lame). **2.** (*in dice games*) coup gagnant. **3. in the n. of time,** fort à propos; juste à temps; **you've come just in the n. of time,** vous tombez bien. **4.** *P:* **in good n.,** en bon état. **5.** *P:* prison *f*, taule *f*.

nick³ **1.** *v.tr.* (*a*) entailler, encocher (un bâton, etc.); biseauter (les cartes); (*b*) anglaiser, niqueter (la queue d'un cheval, un cheval); (*c*) ébrécher (une lame, etc.); (*d*) **to n. oneself,** se couper. **2.** *v.tr. F:* (*a*) (*esp. of police*) pincer, choper qn; **to get nicked,** se faire pincer, épingler; (*b*) chiper, faucher (qch.). **3.** *v.tr. U.S: F:* **they've nicked me (for) £50,** je me suis fait avoir de £50.

nickel¹ ['nik(ə)l] *n.* **1.** *Metall:* nickel *m*; **n. plating,** nickelage *m.* **2.** (*a*) pièce *f* de monnaie en nickel; (*b*) *NAm:* pièce de cinq *cents.*

nickel² *v.tr.* (**nickelled,** *NAm:* **nickeled**) (*also* **nickel-plate**) nickeler (des objets en métal oxydable). **nickelling,** *NAm:* **nickeling** *n.* nickelage *m.*

nicker ['nikər] *n. P:* livre *f* sterling.

nick-nack ['niknæk] *n.* bibelot *m*, colifichet *m.*

nickname¹ ['nikneim] *n.* **1.** surnom *m.* **2.** (*a*) (*in derision*) sobriquet *m*; (*b*) (*shortened name*) diminutif *m.*

nickname² *v.tr.* **1.** surnommer (qn). **2.** (*a*) donner un sobriquet à (qn); (*b*) appeler (qn) par, de, son diminutif.

nicotine ['nikəti:n] *n. Ch:* nicotine *f*; **n. poisoning,** nicotinisme *m*, tabagisme *m.*

niece [ni:s] *n.f.* nièce.

niff [nif] *n. P:* puanteur *f*, mauvaise odeur.

niffy ['nifi] *a. P:* puant.

nifty ['nifti] *a.* **1.** *F:* (*a*) (*of pers.*) adroit, débrouillard; (*b*) (*of thg*) commode. **2.** *NAm: F:* coquet, pimpant.

Niger ['naidʒər] *Pr.n. Geog:* (*a*) (*river*) Niger *m*; (*b*) (République du) Niger.

Nigeria [nai'dʒiəriə] *Pr.n. Geog:* Nigeria *m.*

Nigerian [nai'dʒiəriən] *Geog:* **1.** (*in Niger*) (*a*) *a.* nigérien; (*b*) *n.* Nigérien, -ienne. **2.** (*in Nigeria*) (*a*) *a.* nigérian; (*b*) *n.* Nigérian, -ane.

niggard ['nigəd] *n.* grippe-sou *m*, *pl.* grippe-sou(s); pingre *m*, avare *mf.*

niggardly ['nigədli] **1.** *a.* (*of pers.*) ladre, pingre, parcimonieux, mesquin; (*of sum, portion*) mesquin. **2.** *adv.* chichement, mesquinement.

nigger ['nigər] *n.* (*a*) *P: Pej:* nègre *m*, *f.* négresse; (*b*) *F:* **there's a n. in the woodpile,** il y a anguille sous roche; **he's the n. in the woodpile,** c'est un empêcheur de tourner rond; (*c*) *a.* & *n.* (*colour*) **n. brown,** (tête-de-)nègre *inv.*

niggle ['nigl] *v.i.* vétiller; tatilloner; **to n. over trifles,** s'attarder à des vétilles. **niggling** *a.* (*of details, etc.*) insignifiant; de rien du tout; (*of work*) fignolé; léché; (*of pers.*) tatillon, -onne; (*of pain*) persistant; (*of doubt*) insinuant.

nigh [nai] *Poet: Dial:* **1.** *adv.* près, proche; **n. unto death,** près de mourir. **2.** *prep.* près de, auprès de (qn, qch.).

night [nait] *n.* **1.** (*a*) (i) nuit *f*; (ii) soir *m*; **last n.,** (i) la nuit dernière; cette nuit; (ii) hier (au) soir; **the n. before,** la veille (au soir); **tomorrow n.,** demain soir; **I saw him on Thursday n.,** je l'ai vu jeudi soir; **ten o'clock at n.,** dix heures du soir; **all n. long,** toute la nuit; **good n.!** bonsoir! bonne nuit! **to work day and n.,** travailler nuit et jour; **at n.,** (i) (à) la nuit; (ii) le soir; **in the n.,** (pendant) la nuit; **to travel by n., at n.,** voyager de nuit, la nuit; **we stayed the n. (there),** nous y avons passé la nuit; **n. clothes,** vêtements *mpl* de nuit; **n. boat, train,** bateau *m*, train *m*, de nuit; **n. work,** travail *m* de nuit; **n. shift,** équipe *f* de nuit; **he's on (the) n. shift,** il est de nuit; **n. watch,** (i) garde *f*, veille *f* (de nuit); (ii) *Nau:* quart *m* de nuit; **n. watchman,** veilleur *m* de nuit; garde *m*, gardien *m*, de nuit; *Av:* **n. flight,** vol *m* de nuit; **n. blindness,** héméralopie *f*; **n. lamp, light,** veilleuse *f*; *Nau:* **n. lights,** feux *npl* de position; *Orn:* **n. bird,** oiseau *m* de nuit, nocturne; (*b*) *Th: etc:* représentation *f*; **first n.,** première *f*; **Wagner n.,** soirée (consacrée à) Wagner. **2.** obscurité *f*, nuit, ténèbres *fpl*; **n. is falling,** la nuit tombe; il commence à faire nuit; il se fait nuit.

nightcap ['naitkæp] *n.* **1.** *A.Cost:* bonnet *m* de nuit. **2.** *F:* boisson (alcoolisée) prise avant de se coucher.

nightclub ['naitklʌb] *n.* boîte *f* de nuit; cabaret *m.*

nightdress ['naitdres] *n.* chemise *f* de nuit (de femme, d'enfant); *Fr.C:* jaquette *f.*

nightfall ['naitfɔ:l] *n.* tombée *f* du jour, de la nuit; **at n.,** à la nuit tombante.

nightgown ['naitgaun] *n.* chemise *f* de nuit (de femme).

nightie ['naiti] *n. F:* = NIGHTDRESS.

nightingale ['naitiŋgeil] *n. Orn:* rossignol *m.*

nightjar ['naitdʒɑ:r] *n. Orn:* engoulevent *m* (d'Europe).

nightlong ['naitlɔŋ] *n.* (veille, fête, etc.) qui dure toute la nuit.

nightly ['naitli] **1.** *a.* de toutes les nuits; de tous les *soirs;* **n. performance,** représentation *f* (de) tous les soirs; soirée quotidienne. **2.** *adv.* toutes les nuits; tous les soirs; **performances n.,** représentations tous les soirs.

nightmare ['naitmεər] *n.* cauchemar *m*; **the prospect was a n. to me,** cette perspective me donnait des cauchemars.

nightmarish ['naitmεəriʃ] *a.* qui donne des cauchemars; cauchemardesque.

nightshade ['naitʃeid] *n. Bot:* **(black) n.,** morelle noire; crève-chien *m inv*; **woody n.,** douce-amère *f*, *pl.* douces-amères; **deadly n.,** belladone *f.*

nightshirt ['naitʃə:t] *n. Cost:* chemise *f* de nuit (d'homme).

nightstick ['naitstik] *n. U.S:* casse-tête *m inv* (d'agent de police).

night(-)time ['naittaim] *n.* la nuit; **at n.,** la nuit.

nightwear ['naitwεər] *n.* vêtements *mpl* de nuit.

nihilism ['nai(h)ilizm] *n. Phil: Pol:* nihilisme *m.*

nihilist ['nai(h)ilist] *n.* nihiliste *mf.*

nihilistic [nai(h)i'listik] *a.* nihiliste.

nil [nil] *n.* rien *m*; (*on report sheet, etc.*) néant *m*; *Sp:* zéro *m*; **they won three n.,** ils ont gagné par trois (buts) à zéro.

Nile [nail] *Pr.n. Geog:* Nil *m.*

nimble ['nimbl] *a.* (*of pers., etc.*) agile, leste; (*of mind, etc.*) délié, subtil; **n.(-)fingered,** aux doigts agiles, souples, de fée; **n.(-)footed,** aux pieds agiles, lestes, légers. **-bly** *adv.* agilement; lestement; légèrement.

nimbleness ['nimb(ə)lnis] *n.* agilité *f*, souplesse *f* (de membres, etc.); subtilité *f*, vivacité *f* (d'esprit, etc.).

nimbus, *pl.* **i, -uses** ['nimbəs, -ai, -əsiz] *n.* **1.** nuage lumineux; halo *m.* **2.** (*a*) *Art:* nimbe *m*, auréole *f*; (*b*) *Meteor:* aréole *f* (autour de la lune). **3.** *Meteor:* nimbus *m.*

nincompoop ['niŋkəmpu:p] *n. F:* nigaud, -aude, niais, -aise.

nine [nain] *num.a.* & *n.* neuf (*m*); **n. times out of ten,** neuf fois sur dix; (*of cat, pers., etc.*) **to have n. lives,** avoir l'âme chevillée au corps; *Cards:* **the n. of diamonds,** le neuf de carreau; *F:* **dressed up to the nines,** sur son trente et un.

ninefold ['nainfould] **1.** *a.* (*a*) divisé en neuf parties; (*b*) neuf fois aussi grand. **2.** *adv.* neuf fois autant; **to increase n.,** (se) multiplier par neuf.

ninepence ['nainpəns] *n.* (somme *f* de) neuf pence *mpl.*

ninepin ['nainpin] *n.* **1.** *pl.* **ninepins,** (jeu *m* de) quilles (*fpl*). **2.** quille; *F:* **to go down like ninepins,** tomber comme des mouches.

nineteen [nain'ti:n] *num.a.* & *n.* dix-neuf (*m*); **she is n.,** elle a dix-neuf ans; *F:* **to talk n. to the dozen,** bavarder comme une pie.

nineteenth [nain'ti:nθ] **2.** *num.a.* & *n.* dix-neuvième (*mf*). **2.** *n.* (*fraction*) dix-neuvième *m.*

ninetieth ['naintiəθ] *num.a.* & *n.* quatre-vingt-dixième.

ninety ['nainti] *num.a.* & *n.* quatre-vingt-dix (*m*);

Belg: Sw.F: nonante; **n.-one, n.-nine,** quatre-vingt-onze, quatre-vingt-dix-neuf; **in the nineties,** dans les années quatre-vingt-dix; **he's in his nineties,** il est nonagénaire; *Jur:* **n.-nine years' lease,** bail *m* emphytéotique.

ninny ['nini] *n. F: O:* niais, -aise; nigaud, -aude.

ninth [nainθ] **1.** *num.a. & n.* neuvième (*mf*). **2.** *n.* (*fraction*) neuvième *m*. **3.** *n. Mus:* neuvième *f*.

nip¹ [nip] *n.* **1.** pincement *m*, pinçade *f*; **to give s.o. a n.,** pincer qn. **2.** (*a*) morsure *f* (de la gelée, du froid); *Hort:* coup *m* de gelée; (*b*) **the n. of the morning air,** le froid, le piquant, du petit jour; *F:* **there's a n. in the air,** ça pince; l'air est piquant.

nip² *v.* **(nipped) 1.** *v.tr.* (*a*) pincer; **he's nipped his finger,** il s'est pincé le doigt; (*b*) *Hort:* pincer, éborgner (des bourgeons, etc.); *F:* **to n. (sth.) in the bud,** écraser, détruire, étouffer, (qch.) dans l'œuf; étouffer (une rébellion) dans le germe; (*c*) (*of cold, frost*) (i) pincer, piquer (la figure, les doigts, etc.); (ii) brûler (les bourgeons, etc.); **nipped by the frost,** brûlé par la gelée. **2.** *v.i. F:* **just n. across, along, down, to the baker's,** cours vite chez le boulanger, fais donc un saut chez le boulanger; **to n. in and out of the traffic,** se faufiler adroitement parmi les voitures. **nip in** *v.i. F:* entrer lestement. **nip off 1.** *v.i. F:* filer, s'esquiver. **2.** *v.tr.* enlever, couper (qch.) en le pinçant. **nip out** *v.i. F:* sortir lestement.

nip³ *n. F:* goutte *f*, petit verre, doigt *m* (de cognac, etc.); **to have, take, a n.,** boire, prendre, une goutte.

nip⁴ *v.i.* **(nipped)** *F:* boire la goutte; siroter.

nipper ['nipər] *n.* **1.** *usu.pl.* **(pair of) nippers,** (*a*) pince(s) *f(pl)* (de serrage); pincette(s) *f(pl)*, tenaille(s) *f(pl)*; (*b*) cisaille(s) *f(pl)*. **2.** pince (d'un homard, etc.). **3.** *F:* gamin, -ine, gosse *mf*.

nipple ['nipl] *n.* **1.** (*a*) *Anat:* mamelon *m*; bout *m* de sein; (*b*) *esp. NAm:* tétine *f* (de biberon). **2.** (*a*) *Geog:* mamelon; (*b*) *Tchn:* raccord *m*, jonction *f* (d'une conduite de vapeur, etc.); *Mec.E:* graisseur *m*.

nippy ['nipi] *a. F:* **1.** vif; rapide; **look n.!** grouille-toi! **2.** (vent, etc.) froid, piquant.

nirvana [niə'vɑːnə, nəː-] *n. Rel:* nirvâna *m*.

nisi ['naisai] *Lt.conj. Jur:* (*of decree, order, etc.*) provisoire; (*of decision*) rendu sous condition.

Nissen ['nis(ə)n] *Pr.n.* **N. hut,** hutte préfabriquée (en tôle).

nit [nit] *n.* **1.** lente *f*. **2.** *F:* (*pers.*) nigaud, -aude; andouille *f*; **you silly n.!** crétin!

niter ['naitər] *n. NAm:* = NITRE.

nitery ['naitəri] *n. U.S: F:* boîte *f* de nuit.

nitrate ['naitreit] *n. Ch:* nitrate *m* (d'argent, *etc.*); **potassium n.,** nitrate de potassium; salpêtre *m*; *Agr:* **n. fertilizers,** *F:* **nitrates,** engrais azotés.

nitre, *NAm:* **niter** ['naitər] *n.* nitre *m*, salpêtre *m*.

nitric ['naitrik] *a. Ch:* (oxyde, etc.) nitrique; **n. acid,** acide *m* (trioxo)nitrique; *Com:* eau-forte *f*.

nitrogen ['naitredʒən] *n. Ch:* azote *m*.

nitroglycerin(e) [naitrou'glisəriːn] *n. Exp:* nitroglycérine *f*.

nitrous ['naitrəs] *a.* (oxyde, etc.) nitreux, d'azote.

nitty-gritty ['niti'griti] *n. F:* (fin) fond, tréfonds *m* (d'une affaire).

nitwit ['nitwit] *n. F:* idiot, -ote; imbécile *mf*.

nix¹ [niks] *F:* **1.** *n.* rien *m* (du tout); que dalle. **2.** *int.* rien à faire!

nix² *v.tr. U.S: F:* dire non; ne pas permettre (qch.).

no [nou] **I.** *a.* **1.** nul, pas de, point de, aucun (*with* ne *expressed or understood*); **no hope,** nul espoir; **he has no bread,** il n'a pas de pain; **this fact is of no importance whatever,** ce fait n'a aucune importance; **I have no intention of doing it,** je n'ai aucune intention de le faire; **no father was ever more indulgent,** jamais père ne fut plus indulgent; **it's no distance,** ce n'est pas loin; c'est tout près; **I am in no way surprised,** je n'en suis aucunement étonné; **no nonsense!** pas de bêtises! *P.N:* **no smoking,** défense de fumer; **no man's land,** (i) terrains *mpl* vagues; (ii) *Mil:* no man's land *m*, zone *f* neutre. **2.** (*a*) peu; ne . . . pas (du tout); **it's no easy job,** ce n'est pas une tâche facile; **no such thing,** pas du tout; nullement; (*b*) ne . . . pas; **he's no artist,** il n'est pas artiste; **he's no friend of mine,** il n'est pas de mes amis, tant s'en faut; *Cr: etc:* **no ball,** balle nulle; *esp. U.S: F:* **no way!** jamais de la vie! (*c*) (*with gerund*) ne . . . pas; **there's no pleasing him,** il n'y a pas moyen de le satisfaire; **there's no getting out of it,** impossible de s'en tirer. **3.** *pron.* **no(-)one** = NOBODY 1; **no one knew anyone else there,** personne ne se connaissait. **II.** *adv.* **1.** *A: Lit: & Scot:* **pleasant or no, it's true,** agréable ou non, c'est vrai; **whether or no,** que cela soit ou non. **2.** (*with comparatives*) ne . . . plus, ne . . . pas; **I'm no taller than he (is),** je ne suis pas plus grand que lui; **he's no longer here,** il n'est plus ici. **3.** non; **have you seen him?—no,** l'avez-vous vu?—non; **no, no, you're wrong!** mais non, mais non, vous vous trompez! **to say no,** (i) dire non; (ii) (*deny*) dire que non. **III.** *n.* (*pl.* **noes**) non *m inv*; **he won't take no for an answer,** il n'acceptera pas de refus; (*in voting*) **ayes and noes,** votes *mpl*, voix *fpl*, pour et contre.

Noah ['nouə] *Pr.n.m. B.Hist:* Noé; **Noah's ark,** l'arche *f* de Noé.

nob¹ [nɔb] *n. P:* tête *f*, coco *m*, caboche *f*.

nob² *n. P:* aristo *m*; **the nobs,** les rupins *mpl*.

nobble ['nɔbl] *v.tr. P:* **1.** *Turf:* (i) doper (un cheval), (ii) écloper (un cheval) (avant la course). **2.** soudoyer, acheter (qn, un journal, etc.). **3.** faucher, filouter, voler, qch. **4.** (*a*) pincer, choper, piger (un voleur); (*b*) attraper (qn) (au passage).

nobility [nou'biliti] *n.* **1.** noblesse *f* (de rang, de cœur, etc.); *Hist:* **patent of n.,** lettres *fpl* d'anoblissement. **2.** *coll.* noblesse; (la classe des) nobles *mpl*.

noble ['noubl] **1.** *a.* (*a*) (naissance, personne, etc.) noble; **to be of n. descent, of n. birth,** être de naissance noble; (*b*) (sentiment, etc.) noble, sublime; grand; **n. soul,** grande âme; (*c*) (*of monument, proportions, etc.*) empreint de grandeur; (montagne) altière, imposante; (édifice) aux dimensions impressionnantes; **n. wine,** grand vin; (*d*) (*of metals, stones*) noble, précieux; (*e*) *Ch:* **n. gas,** gaz *m* rare. **2.** *n.* noble *m*, aristocrate *mf*. **-bly** *adv.* **1.** noblement; **n. born,** noble de naissance. **2.** magnifiquement, superbement (proportionné, etc).

nobleman, *pl.* **-men** ['noub(ə)lmən] *n.m.* noble, aristocrate.

nobleminded ['noub(ə)l'maindid] *a.* (*of pers.*) magnanime; aux nobles sentiments.

nobleness ['noub(ə)lnis] *n.* **1.** noblesse *f* (de naissance, etc.). **2.** (*a*) noblesse, magnanimité *f* (d'esprit, d'une action, etc.); grandeur *f* (d'âme); (*b*) proportions *fpl* superbes, magnifiques (d'une statue, d'un cheval, etc.); dimensions impressionnantes (d'un édifice, etc.).

noblewoman, *pl.* **-women** ['noub(ə)lwumən, -wimin] *n.f.* (femme) noble; aristocrate.

nobody ['noubədi] **1.** *pron.* (*a*) personne *m*, nul *m*, aucun *m* (*with* ne *expressed or understood*); **n. spoke to me,** personne ne m'a parlé; **who's there?—n.,** qui est là?—personne; **n. knows it,** personne ne le sait; **n. is perfect,** nul n'est parfait; **n. was more surprised than me, than I was,** cela m'a étonné plus que personne; **n. who was there heard anything,** aucun de ceux, personne parmi tous ceux, qui étaient là n'a rien entendu; **there was n. there, n. about,** il n'y avait personne (là); **n. else,** personne d'autre; (*b*) **I knew him when he was n.,** j'ai été en relations avec lui alors qu'il était encore inconnu. **2.** *n.* (*pers.*) nullité *f*, zéro *m*; **they're (mere) nobodies,** ce sont des gens *mpl* de rien.

noctambulism [nɔk'tæmbjulizm] *n.* somnambulisme *m.*

nocturnal [nɔk'tə:n(ə)l] *a.* nocturne.

nocturne ['nɔktə:n] *n.* **1.** *Mus:* nocturne *m.* **2.** *Art:* effet *m* de nuit.

nod¹ [nɔd] *n.* **1.** (*a*) inclination *f* de la tête; signe *m* d'assentiment, signe de tête affirmatif; **to answer with a n.,** répondre d'une inclination de tête; *F:* **on the n.,** (i) *Com:* à crédit; (ii) *Parl: etc:* sans débats; (*b*) signe de tête (impératif). **2.** (*greeting*) signe de la tête; **he gave me a n.,** il m'a fait un petit signe de la tête. **3.** penchement *m* de tête (dû au sommeil); **the land of N.,** le pays des songes.

nod² *v.tr. & i.* **(nodded) 1. to n. (one's head),** faire un signe de tête (de haut en bas); incliner la tête; **to n. assent,** faire signe que oui; consentir d'un signe de tête. **2.** dodeliner (de) la tête; somnoler, sommeiller; *F:* **to n. off,** s'endormir; piquer un roupillon. **3.** (*of plumes, etc.*) ballotter, danser. **nodding** *n.* inclination *f* de tête; **I have a n. acquaintance with him,** nous nous saluons.

nodal ['noud(ə)l] *a. Opt: Ph:* nodal, -aux.

noddle ['nɔdl] *n. F:* tête *f*, boule *f*, caboche *f*.

node [noud] *n.* **1.** *Astr: Mth: Ph:* nœud *m*, point nodal (d'une orbite d'astre, d'une courbe, etc.). **2.** (*a*) *Bot:* nœud (d'un tronc d'arbre, etc.); (*b*) *Med:* nœud, nodosité *f*; **lymph n.,** ganglion *m* lymphatique.

nodular ['nɔdjulər] *a. Geol: Med: etc:* nodulaire.

nodule ['nɔdju:l] *n. Geol: Med: Bot:* nodule *m.*

Noël 1. *n.* [nou'el] Noël *m.* **2.** *Pr.n.m.* ['nouəl] Noël.

nog [nɔg] *n.* **egg n.** = lait *m* de poule.

noggin ['nɔgin] *n.* **1.** (*a*) (petit) pot; (*b*) son contenu. **2.** *F:* tête *f*, caboche *f*.

no-go ['nou'gou] *attrib.a. esp. Town P:* **no-go areas,** régions où l'autorité du gouvernement est impuissante, n'est pas reconnue.

no-good ['nougud] *F:* **1.** *a.* bon à rien. **2.** *n.* vaurien, -ienne.

nohow ['nouhau] *adv. P:* aucunement, en aucune façon.

noise [nɔiz] *n.* **1.** bruit *m*, tapage *m*, vacarme *m*; **n. abatement campaign,** campagne *f*, lutte *f*, contre le bruit; **to make a n.,** faire du bruit, du vacarme, du tapage; *F:* **to make a n. in the world,** faire du bruit dans le monde; faire parler de soi; *F:* **the big n.,** le grand manitou (de l'entreprise). **2.** (*a*) bruit; son *m*; **clicking n.,** cliquetis *m*; **tinkling n.,** tintement *m*; (*b*) *W.Tel: Elcs: etc:* bruit; parasite(s) *m(pl)*; **background n.,** bruit de fond; **n. level,** niveau *m* de bruit.

noiseless ['nɔizlis] *a.* sans bruit; (appareil) silencieux; **with n. tread,** à pas feutrés. **-ly** *adv.* sans bruit; silencieusement.

noiselessness ['nɔizlisnis] *n.* silence *f*, absence *f* de bruit.

noisiness ['nɔizinis] *n.* caractère bruyant, caractère tapageur (de qn, qch.); turbulence *f* (des enfants, etc.); tintamarre *m* (des rues).

noisome ['nɔisəm] *a.* **1.** (*of plant, germ, etc.*) nocif, nuisible. **2.** (*of smell, water, etc.*) puant, fétide. **3.** (tâche) désagréable.

noisy ['nɔizi] *a.* **1.** bruyant, tapageur; (enfant) turbulent; (*of crowd, street*) tumultueux; (*of pers.*) **to be n.,** faire du bruit, du tapage, du vacarme. **2.** (*of colours, etc.*) voyant, criard. **-ily** *adv.* bruyamment; avec grand bruit.

nomad ['noumæd] *a. & n.* nomade (*mf*).

nomadic [nou'mædik] *a.* nomade.

nom de plume ['nɔmdə'plu:m] (*pl.* **noms de plume**), *n.* pseudonyme *m* (d'un auteur).

nomenclature [nə'meŋklətjər] *n.* nomenclature *f*.

nominal ['nɔmin(ə)l] *a.* **1.** (*a*) nominal, -aux; **to be the n. head,** n'être chef que de nom; **n. rent,** loyer insignifiant; (*b*) **n. price,** prix fictif; **n. value,** valeur nominale. **2.** nominatif; **n. list,** liste nominative, état nominatif. **-ally** *adv.* **1.** nominativement; de nom. **2.** nommément; nominativement.

nominate ['nɔmineit] *v.tr.* **1.** *occ.* (*a*) nommer (qn, qch.); (*b*) fixer (un lieu de rendez-vous, etc.). **2.** (*a*) nommer, choisir, désigner (qn); **to n. s.o. to, for, a post,** nommer qn à un emploi; (*b*) proposer, présenter (un candidat); (*c*) présenter la candidature de (qn).

nomination [nɔmi'neiʃ(ə)n] *n.* **1.** (*a*) nomination *f* (de qn à un emploi, etc.); (*b*) droit *m* de nommer qn à un poste, de désigner qn pour un poste; (*c*) *Pol:* investiture *f* (d'un candidat). **2.** présentation *f* (d'un candidat).

nominative ['nɔminətiv] **1.** *Gram: a. & n.* nominatif (*m*); **in the n. (case),** au nominatif. **2.** *a.* (fonctionnaire, candidat, membre) désigné, nommé.

nominator ['nɔmineitər] *n.* présentateur, -trice.

nominee [nɔmi'ni:] *n.* candidat, -ate; désigné, -e.

non- [nɔn] *pref.* non-; in-; sans; peu.

non(-)acceptance [nɔnək'septəns] *n. Com: etc:* refus *m* d'acceptation (d'un effet, d'une traite).

nonagenarian [nounədʒi'nɛəriən] *a. & n.* nonagénaire (*mf*).

non(-)aggression [nɔnə'greʃ(ə)n] *n.* non-agression *f*; **n.(-)a. pact,** pacte *m* de non-agression.

non(-)alcoholic [nɔnælkə'hɔlik] *a.* (*of drinks*) non alcoolisé.

non(-)aligned [nɔnə'laind] *a. Pol:* (pays) non aligné.

non(-)arrival [nɔnə'raiv(ə)l] *n.* non-arrivée *f*.

non(-)attendance [nɔnə'tendəns] *n.* absence *f*.

nonce [nɔns] *n.* **for the n.,** pour la circonstance; pour l'occasion; **n. word,** mot créé pour l'occasion; mot de circonstance.

nonchalance ['nɔnʃələns] *n.* nonchalance *f*, indifférence *f*.

nonchalant ['nɔnʃələnt] *a.* nonchalant; indifférent. **-ly** *adv.* nonchalamment.

non(-)combattant [nɔn'kɔmbətənt] *a. & n. Mil:* non-combattant (*m*).

non(-)commissioned ['nɔnkə'miʃ(ə)nd] *a. Mil:* sans brevet; **n.(-)c. officer,** sous-officier *m*; gradé *m*.

noncommittal [nɔnkə'mit(ə)l] *a.* (*of answer, etc.*) qui n'engage à rien; diplomatique; (*in answering*) **to be n.,** observer, une prudente, réserve; être très réservé.

non(-)completion [nɔnkəm'pli:ʃ(ə)n] *n.* non-achèvement *m* (d'un travail); non-exécution *f* (d'un contrat).

non(-)compliance [nɔnkəm'plaiəns] *n.* refus *m* (de consentement); **n.(-)c. with an order,** refus d'obéissance à un ordre.

non(-)conductor [nɔnkən'dʌktər] *n. Ph:* non-conducteur *m*, mauvais conducteur; *El:* isolant *m*.

nonconformism [nɔnkən'fɔ:mizm] *n.* nonconformisme *m*.

nonconformist [nɔnkən'fɔ:mist] *a. & n.* nonconformiste (*mf*); dissident, -ente.

nonconformity [nɔnkən'fɔ:miti] *n.* non-conformité *f*.

non(-)contributory [nɔnkən'tribjut(ə)ri] *a.* (caisse de retraite, etc.) sans versements de la part des bénéficiaires.

nondescript ['nɔndiskript] *a. & n.* (personne, chose) indéfinissable; quelconque; (costume) hétéroclite.

non(-)directional [nɔndə'rekʃ(ə)n(ə)l, -di-] *a.* *Elcs: W.Tel:* non directionnel.

none [nʌn] **1.** *pron.* (*with* (i) *pl.*, (ii) *O: sg., verb*) (*a*) aucun; **n. of you can tell me,** personne, aucun, d'entre vous ne peut me dire; **n. of this concerns me,** rien de ceci ne me regarde; **no news today?—n.,** pas de nouvelles aujourd'hui?—aucune(s); **n. at all,** pas un(e) seul(e); **half a loaf is better than n.,** il vaut mieux avoir la moitié d'un pain que rien du tout; **n. of your impudence!** pas d'insolences de votre part! *F:* **n. of that!** pas de ça! (*b*) personne, nul; **n. can tell,** personne ne le sait; nul ne le sait; **he is aware, n. better, that . . .,** il sait mieux que personne que . . .; **the visitor was n. other than the king,** le visiteur n'était autre que le roi; (*c*) *Adm:* (*in schedules, etc.*) **n.,** néant. **2.** *a. A:* **money I had n.,** de l'argent je n'en avais point. **3.** *adv.* (*a*) **I like him n. the better, n. the worse, for that,** je ne l'en aime pas mieux, pas moins; (*b*) **he was n. too soon,** il est arrivé juste à temps; **he was n. too happy about it,** il n'en était pas trop content; **his position is n. too secure,** sa position n'est rien moins qu'assurée; (*c*) **n. the less,** néanmoins; **he continued n. the less,** il n'en continua pas moins.

nonentity [nɔn'entiti] *n.* **1.** non-être *m*, non-existence *f*; néant *m*. **2.** personne insignifiante, de peu d'importance; non-valeur *f*; nullité *f*.

non(-)essential [nɔni'senʃ(ə)l] *a.* non essentiel.

non-event [nɔni'vent] *n. F:* événement manqué.

non(-)existence [nɔnig'zistəns] *n.* non-existence *f*, non-être *m*; néant *m*.

non(-)existent [nɔnig'zistənt] *a.* non-existant; inexistant.

non(-)ferrous [nɔn'ferəs] *a.* non-ferreux.

non-fiction [nɔn'fikʃ(ə)n] *n.* **n.-f. (books),** ouvrages généraux.

non(-)flammable [nɔn'flæməbl] *a.* ininflammable, ignifuge.

non(-)inflammable [nɔnin'flæməbl] *a.* ininflammable, ignifuge.

non(-)intervention [nɔnintə'venʃ(ə)n] *n. Pol:* non-intervention *f*.

non-iron [nɔn'aiən] *a. Tex:* lavé-repassé *inv*.

non(-)malignant [nɔnmə'lignənt] *a. Med:* bénin.

non(-)member [nɔn'membər] *n.* (*at club, etc.*) invité, -ée; **open to n.-members,** ouvert au public.

non(-)negotiable [nɔnni'gouʃiəbl] *a.* (billet, etc.) non-négociable.

non(-)observance [nɔnəb'zəːvəns] *n.* inobservance *f* (des lois, du carême, etc.).

nonpareil ['nɔnpərel] (*a*) *a.* incomparable; sans égal; (*b*) *n.* personne, chose, sans pareille.

non(-)payment [nɔn'peimənt] *n.* non-paiement *m*.

non(-)performance [nɔnpə'fɔːməns] *n.* non-exécution *f*, inexécution *f* (d'un contrat, etc.).

nonplus [nɔn'plʌs] *v.tr.* **(nonplussed)** confondre, interdire, interloquer (qn); dérouter (qn); **to be nonplussed,** être désemparé.

non(-)poisonous [nɔn'pɔiz(ə)nəs] *a.* atoxique.

non(-)profit-making [nɔn'prɔfitmeikiŋ] *a.* (association) sans but lucratif.

non(-)recurring [nɔnri'kəːriŋ] *a.* exceptionnel, extraordinaire; **n.(-)r. expenditure,** frais *mpl*, dépenses *fpl*, extraordinaires.

non(-)resident [nɔn'rezidənt] *a. & n.* **1.** (*a*) (*of priest, etc.*) non-résident (*m*); (*b*) **n.(-)r. landowner,** propriétaire forain. **2.** *Sch: etc:* externe (*mf*); (*in hotel*) client, -ente, de passage.

non-returnable [nɔnri'təːnəbl] *a.* (emballage, etc.) perdu, non repris, non consigné.

non-scheduled [nɔn'ʃedjuːld] *a. Trans:* (service) spécial.

nonsense ['nɔns(ə)ns] *n.* **1.** non-sens *m*. **2.** (*a*) absurdité *f*, déraison *f*; **a piece of n.,** une bêtise, une absurdité; **to talk (a lot of) n.,** déraisonner; dire des bêtises, des sottises; **(what) n.!** quelle bêtise! **it's n. to think that . . .,** il est absurde de penser que . . .; (*b*) *Lit:* **n. verse,** vers *mpl* amphigouriques; **n. rhyme,** cliquette *f*; (*c*) *attrib.* (*of pers.*) **no-n.,** (i) (trop) sérieux; (ii) sévère.

nonsensical [nɔn'sensik(ə)l] *a.* **1.** (*of speech, reason, etc.*) absurde; qui n'a pas de sens. **2. don't be n.!** ne dites pas de bêtises, d'absurdités!

non sequitur [nɔn'sekwitər] *n.* fausse conclusion, conclusion illogique.

non(-)shrink [nɔn'ʃriŋk] *a.* irrétrécissable.

non(-)skid [nɔn'skid] *a.* antidérapant; **n.(-)skid tyre,** (pneu) antidérapant (*m*).

non(-)smoker [nɔn'smoukər] *n.* **1.** non-fumeur *m*; personne *f* qui ne fume pas. **2.** *Rail: Av:* compartiment *m* non-fumeurs.

non(-)smoking [nɔn'smoukiŋ] *a. Rail: Av:* (compartiment) non-fumeurs.

non(-)starter [nɔn'stɑːtər] *n.* (*a*) *Sp: etc:* non-partant *m*; (*b*) *F:* projet, etc., fichu d'avance.

non-stick ['nɔn'stik] *a.* (casserole) avec revêtement anti-adhésif, qui n'attache pas; (riz) décollable.

nonstop ['nɔnstɔp] **1.** *a.* (train) direct; (trajet) sans arrêt; *Av:* (vol) sans escale; *Cin:* (spectacle) permanent. **2.** *adv.* sans arrêt; **she talked for two hours n.,** elle a parlé sans arrêt, sans cesse, pendant deux heures.

non-taxable [nɔn'tæksəbl] *a. Adm:* (revenu, etc.) non imposable.

non(-)transferable [nɔn'trænsfərəbl] *a.* non transmissible, incessible; (*of shares*) nominatif.

non(-)union [nɔn'juːniən] *a.* (ouvrier) non syndiqué.

non(-)violence [nɔn'vaiələns] *n.* non-violence *f*.

non(-)violent [nɔn'vaiələnt] *a.* (mouvement, etc.) non-violent.

non-white [nɔn'w(h)ait] *a. & n.* (personne *f*) de couleur.

noodle ['nuːdl] *n.* **1.** *Cu:* (*usu.pl.*) nouilles *fpl.* **2.** *F:* niais, -aise, nigaud, -aude; nouille *f*.

nook [nuk] *n.* (*a*) coin *m*, recoin *m*; **nooks and crannies,** coins et recoins; (*b*) renfoncement *m* (dans une pièce).

noon [nuːn] *n.* midi *m*; **it is twelve n.,** il est midi; **to arrive about n.,** arriver vers, sur le, midi; **at high n.,** au milieu du jour.

noonday ['nuːndei], *O:* **noontide** ['nuːntaid] *n.* midi *m*.

no-one ['nouwʌn] *pron.* = NOBODY 1.

noose¹ [nuːs] *n.* (*a*) nœud coulant; (*for trapping animals*) lacet *m*, lacs *m*, collet *m*; (*b*) **hangman's n.,** corde *f* (de potence); (*c*) lasso *m*.

noose² *v.tr.* **1.** faire un nœud coulant à (une corde); **to n. a rope round s.o.'s neck,** mettre la corde au cou de qn. **2.** (*a*) prendre (un lièvre, etc.) au lacet, dans un lacs; (*b*) attraper (une bête) au lasso.

nope [noup] *adv. esp. U.S: P:* (= *no*) non.

nor [nɔːr] *conj.* **1.** (*continuing the force of a neg.*) (ne, ni . . .) ni; **he has neither father n. mother,** il n'a père ni mère, il n'a pas de père ni de mère; **he hasn't any, n. have I,** il n'en a pas, ni moi non plus. **2.** (*and not*) **I do not know, n. can I guess,** je n'en sais rien et je ne peux pas le deviner; **n. was this all,** et ce n'était pas tout.

Nordic ['nɔːdik] **1.** *a.* nordique, scandinave. **2.** *n.* Nordique *mf*, Scandinave *mf*.

norm [nɔːm] *n.* (*a*) norme *f*; **according to the n.,** selon la norme; normal, -aux; (*b*) règle *f*.

normal ['nɔːm(ə)l] **1.** *a.* (*a*) *Mth:* (*of line, etc.*) normal, -aux, perpendiculaire (**to,** à); (*b*) normal, de régime, régulier, ordinaire; **n. person,** personne normale; **n. working, running (of engine, etc.),** régime *m*; **n. temperature,** température moyenne, normale; (*c*) *Ch:* (*of solution, etc.*) normal, titré; **n. salt,** sel *m* neutre. **2.** *n.* (*a*) *Mth:* normale *f*, perpendiculaire *f*; (*b*) condition normale; **temperature above n.,** tempéature au-dessus de la normale. **-ally** *adv.* normalement.

normality [nɔːˈmæliti] *n.* normalité *f.*

normalization [nɔːməlaiˈzeiʃ(ə)n] *n.* normalisation *f.*

normalize [ˈnɔːməlaiz] **1.** *v.tr.* (*a*) ramener (qch.) à l'état normal, à la normale; normaliser, régulariser; (*b*) *Metall:* normaliser (un métal). **2.** *v.i.* se normaliser, redevenir normal.

Norman [ˈnɔːmən] **1.** *a.* normand; **N. architecture,** (i) l'architecture normande; (ii) l'architecture romane (anglaise); *Hist:* **the N. Conquest,** la conquête normande; *Ling: Hist:* **N. French,** normand *m.* **2.** *n.* Normand, -ande.

Normandy [ˈnɔːməndi] *Pr.n. Geog:* Normandie *f.*

Norse [nɔːs] **1.** *a.* norvégien; **N. mythology,** mythologie *f* scandinave. **2.** *n.* (*a*) *pl.* Scandinaves *mfpl, esp.* Norvégiens, -iennes; (*b*) *Ling:* (i) norvégien *m*; (ii) (*in Orkneys, Shetlands, etc.*) norse *m.*

Norseman, *pl.* **-men** [ˈnɔːsmən] *n.m. Hist:* Scandinave; Norvégien.

north [nɔːθ] **1.** *n.* (*a*) nord *m*; **true n.,** nord vrai, géographique; **magnetic n.,** nord magnétique; **house facing n.,** maison exposée au nord; **to the n. of,** au nord de; **in the n.,** au nord, dans le nord; (*b*) **to live in the n. of England,** habiter dans le nord de l'Angleterre; (*c*) *U.S: Hist:* **the N.,** les États *mpl* du nord (des États-Unis); les États anti-esclavagistes; (*d*) **the Canadian Far N.,** le Grand Nord Canadien. **2.** *adv.* au nord; (voyager) vers le nord; **it's n. of here,** c'est au nord d'ici; *F:* **I'm going up n.,** je vais dans le nord (de l'Angleterre); **n. by east, by west,** nord-quart-nord-est; nord-quart-nord-ouest. **3.** *a.* nord *inv*; (pays, vent) du nord; (mur, etc.) exposé au nord; **on the n. side,** du côté nord; **the N. Country,** le Nord (de l'Angleterre); **N. Africa,** Afrique *f* du Nord; **N. Africain,** (i) *a.* nord-africain; (ii) *n.* Nord-Africain, - aine; **the N. Sea,** la mer du Nord; **the N. Pole,** le Pôle Nord; *Arch:* (*in church*) **n. transept,** transept septentrional.

northbound [ˈnɔːθbaund] *a.* (train, etc.) allant vers le nord; (*on underground*) en direction de la banlieue nord; *Aut:* **the n. carriageway,** la voie nord (de l'autoroute).

northeast [nɔːθˈiːst], *Nau:* **nor'east** [nɔːˈriːst] **1.** *n.* nord-est *m*; *Nau:* nordé *m.* **2.** *a.* (du) nord-est *inv*; **n. wind,** nord-est. **3.** *adv.* vers le nord-est; **n. by east,** nord-est-quart-est; **n. by north,** nord-est-quart-nord.

northeasterly [nɔːθˈiːstəli], *Nau:* **nor'easterly** [nɔːˈriːstəli] **1.** *a.* (*of wind, etc.*) (du) nord-est *inv*; (*of district, etc.*) (au, du) nord-est; (*of direction*) vers le nord-est. **2.** *adv.* vers le nord-est.

northeastern [nɔːθˈiːstən], *Nau:* **nor'eastern** [nɔːˈriːstən] *a.* (du) nord-est *inv.*

northerly [ˈnɔːðəli] **1.** *a.* (*of wind, etc.*) du nord; (*of district, etc.*) (du, au) nord *inv*; (*of direction*) vers le nord; (*of house*) **n. aspect,** exposition *f* au nord. **2.** *adv.* vers le nord.

northern [ˈnɔːðən] *a.* (du) nord *inv*; septentrional, -aux; **N. Ireland,** l'Irlande *f* du Nord; **n. hemisphere,** hémisphère nord; **n. lights,** aurore boréale.

northerner [ˈnɔːðənər] *n.* **1.** habitant, -ante, du Nord (de l'Angleterre, etc.); **the Northerners,** les septentrionaux *mpl.* **2.** *U.S: Hist:* nordiste *m.*

north-northeast [nɔːθnɔːθˈiːst], *Nau:* **nor'nor'east** [nɔːnɔːˈriːst] **1.** *a. & n.* nord-nord-est (*m*) *inv.* **2.** *adv.* (vers le) nord-nord-est.

north-northwest [nɔːθnɔːθˈwest], *Nau:* **nor'nor'west** [nɔːnɔːˈwest] **1.** *a. & n.* nord-nord-ouest (*m*) *inv.* **2.** *adv.* (vers le) nord-nord-ouest.

northward [ˈnɔːθwəd] **1.** *n.* nord *m*; **to the n.,** au nord. **2.** *a.* au, du, nord; du côté du nord. **3.** *adv.* vers le nord.

northwards [ˈnɔːθwədz] *adv.* vers le nord.

northwest [nɔːθˈwest], *Nau:* **nor'west** [nɔːˈwest] **1.** *n.* nord-ouest *m.* **2.** *a.* (du) nord-ouest *inv*; **n. wind,** (vent *m* du) nord-ouest. **3.** *adv.* vers le nord-ouest; **n. by west, by north,** nord-ouest-quart-ouest; nord-ouest-quart-nord.

northwesterly [nɔːθˈwestəli], *Nau:* **nor'westerly** [nɔːˈwestəli] **1.** (*of wind, etc.*) du nord-ouest; (*of district, etc.*) (au, du) nord-ouest *inv*; (*of direction*) vers le nord-ouest. **2.** *adv.* vers le nord-ouest.

northwestern [nɔːθˈwestən], *Nau:* **nor'western** [nɔːˈwestən] *a.* (du) nord-ouest *inv.*

Norway [ˈnɔːwei] *Pr.n. Geog:* Norvège *f.*

Norwegian [nɔːˈwiːdʒən] **1.** *a.* norvégien. **2.** *n.* (*a*) Norvégien, -ienne; (*b*) *Ling:* norvégien *m.*

nose[1] [nouz] *n.* **1.** (*of pers.*) nez *m*; (*of many animals*) museau *m*; (*of horse*) museau, chanfrein *m*; (*of dog, etc.*) nez; **n. bag,** musette *f* (mangeoire); **n. ring,** (i) anneau nasal, nasière *f* (de taureau, etc.); (ii) (*of pers.*) anneau porté au nez; **his n. is bleeding,** il saigne du nez; **to blow one's n.,** se moucher; **to hold one's n.,** se boucher le nez; **to speak through one's n.,** parler du nez; nasiller; (*of fowl*) **the parson's, pope's, n.,** le croupion; *F:* **it's under your n.,** vous l'avez sous le nez; **I did it under his very n., right under his n.,** je l'ai fait sous son nez; **to poke one's n. into other people's business,** fourrer, mettre, son nez dans les affaires des autres; **to look down one's n. at s.o.,** regarder qn de haut en bas; **to cut off one's n. to spite one's face,** bouder contre son ventre; **to lead s.o. by the n.,** mener qn par le bout du nez. **2.** *F:* **to have a n. round,** faire le tour de la maison, etc., en furetant dans tous les recoins. **3.** (*a*) odorat *m*; **to have a good n.,** avoir bon nez, le nez fin, l'odorat fin; *F:* (*of pers.*) **to have a n. for sth.,** avoir un flair, du flair, pour qch.; (*b*) bouquet *m* (d'un vin, etc.); parfum *m* (du foin, etc.). **4.** *Tchn:* (*a*) nez, avant *m* (d'un véhicule, d'un avion, etc.); nez (du moteur, etc.); *Aut: etc:* **n. to tail,** pare-choc(s) à, contre, pare-choc(s); **n. cone,** (i) *Av:* cône *m* de nez (d'un avion); (ii) *Ball:* ogive *f* (d'une fusée); (*b*) *Tls:* bec *m*, nez (d'un outil); *Mch.Tls:* nez (d'un mandrin, etc.); (*c*) *Mec.E:* ajutage *m* (d'un tuyau); bec (d'un loquet); mentonnet *m* (d'une clavette); (*d*) *Ball:* pointe *f*, ogive (d'une balle, d'un missile); *Navy:* cône de choc (d'une torpille).

nose[2] **1.** (*a*) *v.tr.* (i) *O:* flairer, sentir (qch.); (ii) pousser du nez; (*b*) *v.i. F:* **to n. about, (a)round,** fouiller, fureter, fouiner; (*c*) *v.i. & tr.* **the ship nosed (her way) through the fog,** le navire s'avançait à l'aveuglette à travers le brouillard. **nose out** *v.tr.* (*a*) (*of dog*) flairer (le gibier); (*b*) *F:* découvrir, éventer (un secret); dépister, dénicher (qn).

noseband [ˈnouzbænd] *n. Harn:* muserolle *f.*

nosebleed [ˈnouzbliːd] *n.* saignement *m* de nez; **to have a n.,** saigner du nez.

nose-dive [ˈnouzdaiv] *Av:* **1.** *n.* (vol) piqué (*m*). **2.** *v.i.* piquer du nez; descendre en piqué.

nosegay [ˈnouzgei] *n.* petit bouquet (de fleurs).

nosey [ˈnouzi] *a.* = NOSY.

nosh[1] [nɔʃ] *n. F:* nourriture *f*, *F:* bouffe *f.*

nosh[2] *v.i. F:* manger; bouffer.

nosh-up [ˈnɔʃʌp] *n. P:* **a good n.-up,** une bonne boustifaille.

nostalgia [nɔsˈtældʒiə] *n.* nostalgie *f.*

nostalgic [nɔsˈtældʒik] *a.* nostalgique. **-ally** *adv.* nostalgiquement.

nostril [ˈnɔstril] *n.* (*of pers.*) narine *f*; (*of horse, ox, etc.*) naseau *m.*

nostrum [ˈnɔstrəm] *n.* panacée *f*, orviétan *m*; remède *m* de charlatan.

nosy [ˈnouzi] *a. F:* **1.** fouinard, fouineur, fureteur; **don't be so n.!** ne soyez pas si curieux! **n. parker,** fouinard *m*, fureteur, -euse; indiscret, -ète.

not [nɔt] *adv.* (ne) . . . pas, (ne) . . . point. **1.** *A: & Lit:* (*following the verb*) **I know n.,** je ne sais pas; **fear n.,** n'ayez pas peur. **2.** (*a*) (*following the aux. verb, usually affixed as* **n't**) **I don't, do n., know,** je ne sais pas; **he won't, will n., come,** il ne viendra pas; **is he coming?—no, he isn't, he's n.,** vient-il?—non; **don't move,** ne bougez pas; **I'm n. in the least surprised,** je ne suis nullement étonné; **you understand, don't you?** vous comprenez, n'est-ce pas? (*b*) (*stressed*) **she would n. wear an apron!** un tablier, elle n'en porterait pas! (*c*) (*elliptically, in answers, etc.*) **what's she like?—n. pretty,** comment est-elle?—pas jolie; **n. at all, n. a bit (of it),** pas du tout; **thank you so much!—n. at all!** merci beaucoup!—je vous en prie! **n. likely!** jamais de la vie! **why n.?** pourquoi pas? **whether he likes it or n.,** que cela lui plaise ou non; **little or n. at all,** peu ou pas, peu ou point; **I think, hope, n.,** je crois, j'espère, que non; **n. always,** pas toujours; **n. yet,** pas encore; **n. even in France,** (non) pas même en France; **n. negotiable,** non négociable; **n. guilty,** non coupable. **3.** (*with the verb infinite*) **n. wishing to be seen, I drew the curtain,** comme je ne désirais pas être vu j'ai tiré le rideau; **n. including . . ., n. to mention . . .,** sans compter . . .; *F:* **n. to worry!** ne vous en faites pas! **he asked me n. to do it,** il m'a demandé de ne pas le faire. **4. n. that . . .,** ce n'est pas que . . ., non (pas) que . . .; **n. that I can remember,** pas autant qu'il m'en souvienne. **5.** (*in contrasts*) **she's n. my mother but my aunt,** ce n'est pas ma mère, c'est ma tante; **he is respected but n. loved,** il est respecté mais non pas aimé; **n. only . . . but also . . .,** non seulement . . . mais encore . . . **6.** (*with pronoun*) **n. I,** pas moi; **n. one replied,** pas un(e) n'a répondu; **he'll never pay, n. he!** il ne paiera jamais, c'est sûr! **7.** (*understatement*) **I wasn't sorry to go,** j'étais bien content de partir; **n. a few . . .,** pas mal de . . .; **n. a beautiful town,** une ville pas belle; **n. far from the town,** non loin de la ville; **n. without reason,** non sans raison; *F:* **n. half!** et comment! tu parles! **8. n. a word was spoken,** on n'a pas dit un mot; **who will believe it?—n. a soul,** qui le croira?—pas un.

notability [noutə'biliti] *n.* **1.** (*pers.*) notabilité *f*, notable *mf*. **2.** prééminence *f*.

notable ['noutəbl] *a.* (*a*) (*of pers., thg*) notable, insigne, remarquable; (*of pers.*) éminent; (*b*) *n.* notable *m*. **-ably** *adv.* notamment, particulièrement.

notary ['noutəri] *n. Jur: Scot:* **n. (public),** notaire *m*.

notation [nou'teiʃ(ə)n] *n. Alg: Mus: etc:* notation *f*; *Mth:* numération *f*.

notch¹ [nɔtʃ] *n.* **1.** (*a*) entaille *f*, encoche *f*, cran *m*; hoche (faite sur une taille); enfourchement *m* (de tenon); trait *m* (de scie); cran, dent *f* (d'une roue); barbe *f* (de pêne); *Dressm:* cran; (*b*) brèche *f* (dans une lame, etc.); (*c*) échancrure *f*. **2.** *NAm:* défilé *m*, gorge *f* (de montagne).

notch² *v.tr.* **1.** (*a*) entailler, encocher, hocher (un bâton, etc.); denteler, créneler (une roue, etc.); (*b*) ébrécher (une lame, etc.). **2. to n. up,** marquer (un point, une victoire, etc.).

note¹ [nout] *n.* **1.** *Mus: etc:* (*a*) note *f*; (*b*) touche *f* (d'un piano, etc.); (*c*) note, son *m*; **to sing, play, a false n.,** faire une fausse note; (*d*) chant *m*, ramage *m* (d'oiseau); **there was a n. of impatience in his voice,** son ton indiquait une certaine impatience; **speech that strikes the right n.,** discours *m* dans la note voulue. **2.** marque *f*, signe *m*, indice *m* (d'un fait, d'une qualité, etc.). **3.** (*a*) note, mémorandum *m*, mémento *m*; *Sch:* **lecture notes,** notes de cours; **to make, take (down), notes,** prendre des notes; **to take, make, a n. of sth.,** prendre note de qch.; **I must make a n. of it,** il faut que je m'en souvienne; (*b*) note, commentaire *m*, annotation *f*, remarque *f* (sur un texte); **to write, make, notes on a text,** annoter un texte; (*at end of book*) **bibliographical n.,** souscription *f*; (*c*) billet *m*; petite lettre; **I wrote a n. to her at once,** je lui ai tout de suite écrit un mot; (*d*) **diplomatic n.,** note diplomatique, mémorandum. **4.** *Fin: Com:* (*a*) billet, bordereau *m*; **n. of hand,** reconnaissance *f* (de dette); billet simple; **promissory n.,** billet (simple); bon *m*; **credit, debit, n.,** note, bordereau, de crédit, de débit; **advice n.,** note, lettre, d'avis; (*b*) billet (de banque); **hundred-franc notes,** coupures *fpl* de cent francs. **5.** (*a*) distinction *f*, marque *f*, renom *m*; **a man of n.,** un homme de marque; (*b*) attention *f*, remarque *f*; **to take n. of sth.,** retenir qch. dans sa mémoire; remarquer qch.

note² *v.tr.* **1.** noter, remarquer, prendre note de (qch.); relever (une erreur); constater (un fait); **which fact is hereby duly noted,** dont acte; **it should be noted that . . .,** il est à noter que . . .; **we duly n. that . . .,** nous prenons bonne note (de ce) que . . . . **2. to n. sth. (down),** écrire, inscrire, prendre note de, qch. **noted** *a.* (*of pers.*) distingué, éminent; (*of thg*) fameux, remarquable (**for sth.,** par qch.).

notebook ['noutbuk] *n.* carnet *m*, calepin *m*, mémorandum *m*; (*for shorthand, etc.*) bloc-notes *m*, *pl.* blocs-notes; (*larger*) cahier *m*; **pocket n.,** carnet de poche.

notecase ['noutkeis] *n.* portefeuille *m*; porte-billets *m inv*.

notehead ['nouthed] *n. esp. U.S:* en-tête *m inv*.

notepad ['noutpæd] *n.* bloc-notes *m*, *pl.* blocs-notes.

notepaper ['noutpeipər] *n.* papier *m* à lettres, à écrire.

noteworthy ['noutwə:ði] *a.* (*of fact, etc.*) remarquable, mémorable; **it is n. that . . .,** il convient de noter que . . .

nothing ['nʌθiŋ] **I.** *pron.* rien (*with* ne *expressed or understood*) (*a*) **he does n.,** il ne fait rien; **I saw n.,** je n'ai rien vu; **what are you doing?—n.,** que faites-vous?—rien; **it's better than n.,** c'est mieux que rien; **n. could be simpler,** rien de plus simple; c'est tout ce qu'il y a de plus simple; **you can't live on n.,** on ne peut pas vivre de rien; **he let me have it for almost, next to, n.,** il me l'a cédé pour presque rien, pour une bouchée de pain; **it looks like n. (else) on earth,** cela ne ressemble à rien; **as if n. had happened,** comme si de rien n'était; **say n. about it,** n'en dites rien; **to say n. of . . .,** sans parler de . . .; **he gets angry about n.,** il se fâche pour un rien; **n. at all,** rien du tout; **there's n. in these rumours,** ces bruits sont sans fondement; *F:* **there's n. to it, in it,** c'est simple comme bonjour; **he was n. if not discreet,** il était surtout discret; il était discret avant tout; *Prov:* **n. venture, n. gain, win,** qui ne risque rien n'a rien; (*b*) (*followed by adj.*) **n. new,** rien de nouveau, rien de neuf; **that's n. unusual,** cela n'a rien d'anormal; **n. much,** pas grand-chose; **there is n. more to be said,** il n'y a plus rien à dire; (*c*) **I have n. to do,** je n'ai rien à faire; **to have n. to do with sth.,** n'avoir rien à faire avec qch.; **that's n. to do with you,** ce n'est pas votre affaire; cela ne vous regarde pas; **there is n. to cry about,** il n'y a pas de quoi pleurer; (*d*) **he has n. of his father in him,** il n'a rien de son père; (*e*) **n. else,** rien d'autre; **n. but . . .,** rien que . . .; **I have n. (else) to do but . . .,** je n'ai rien (d'autre) à faire que de . . .; **n. else matters,** tout le reste n'est rien; **n. but the truth,** rien que la vérité; **there's n. else for it,** c'est inévitable; (*f*) **to do sth. for n.,** (i) faire qch. en vain, inutilement; (ii) faire qch. gratuitement; **it's not for n. that . . .,** ce n'est pas sans raison que . . .; **all my efforts went for n.,** c'étaient des efforts perdus; **to count for n.,** ne compter pour rien; (*g*) **she is n. to him,** elle lui est indifférente; **£1000 is n. to him,** mille livres ne sont rien pour lui; **it's n. to me either way,**

cela m'est égal; (*h*) **to make, think, n. of sth.,** (i) n'attacher aucune importance à qch.; (ii) ne pas se faire scrupule de faire qch.; **he makes, thinks, n. of walking 10 km,** il se fait un jeu de faire 10 km à pied; (*i*) **I can make n., n. at all, of it,** je n'y comprends rien, rien du tout. **II.** *n.* **1.** *Mth:* zéro *m.* **2.** néant *m*; rien; **to come to n.,** ne pas aboutir; (*of hopes, etc.*) s'anéantir; (*of scheme, etc.*) s'effondrer. **3.** bagatelle *f*; vétille *f*; rien *m*; **a hundred francs? a mere n.!** cent francs? une bêtise! **in those days it was n. to see . . .,** en ce temps-là on voyait facilement . . . **III.** *adv.* aucunement, nullement; pas du tout; **n. like, near, so big, as big,** loin d'être aussi grand; **it is n. less than madness,** c'est de la folie ni plus ni moins.

nothingness ['nʌθiŋnis] *n.* néant *m.*

notice¹ ['noutis] *n.* **1.** (*a*) avis *m*, notification *f*, intimation *f*; **n. of delivery,** accusé *m* de réception; (*b*) préavis *m*, avertissement *m*; **to give s.o. n. of sth.,** prévenir, avertir, qn de qch.; **to give official n. that . . .,** donner acte que . . .; **without (prior) n.,** sans préavis; **n. is hereby given that . . .,** le public est avisé que . . .; on fait savoir que . . .; **public n.,** avis au public; **important n.,** avis important; *Ecc:* **the weekly notices,** les annonces *fpl* de la semaine; **until further n.,** jusqu'à nouvel ordre, nouvel avis; (*c*) avis formel, instructions formelles; (*served by bailiff, etc.*) exploit *m*; *Jur:* **n. of appeal,** intimation; **n. to pay,** avertissement; (*d*) **at short n.,** à court, à bref, délai; **to give s.o. short n.,** prendre qn de court; **at a moment's, a minute's, n.,** à la minute, à l'instant, sur-le-champ; **without a moment's n.,** sans crier gare; **to require three months' n.,** exiger un préavis de trois mois; (*e*) **n. (to quit),** (avis de) congé *m*; **to be under n. to quit,** avoir reçu son congé; **what n. do you require?** quel est le terme du congé? (*of landlord, employer*) **to give s.o. n.,** donner son congé à qn; (*of tenant, employee*) **to give n., to give, hand, in one's n.,** donner, demander, (son) congé; **to give s.o. a week's n.,** donner ses huit jours à qn. **2.** (*a*) affiche *f*; indication *f*; placard *m*; (*on a card*) écriteau *m*, pancarte *f*; **to stick up a n.,** placarder une affiche; **n. board,** (i) (*on house for sale, etc.*) écriteau; (*in schools, clubs, etc.*) tableau *m* d'affichage, d'annonces, de publicité; (ii) panneau *m* d'affichage; (*b*) (*in newspaper, etc.*) annonce *f*, note *f*; (*c*) revue *f* (d'un ouvrage). **3.** (*a*) attention *f*, connaissance *f*, observation *f*; **to take n. of s.o., sth.,** faire attention, prêter (son) attention, à qn, à qch.; tenir compte, prendre connaissance, de qn, de qch.; **to take no, not the least, n. of sth.,** ne pas prêter la moindre attention à qch.; **nobody took any n. of me,** personne ne s'est intéressé à moi; **I should take no n., I shouldn't take any n., of it,** je n'y prendrais pas garde; **the fact came to his n. that . . .,** son attention a été attirée par le fait que . . .; (*of author, etc.*) **to attract n.,** commencer à être connu, à percer; **to avoid n.,** se dérober aux regards; **to bring, call, sth., s.o., to s.o.'s n.,** appeler, porter, attirer, l'attention de qn sur qch., qn; (*b*) **the baby is beginning to take n.,** le bébé commence à avoir conscience des choses; *F:* **to sit up and take n.,** se réveiller; dresser l'oreille.

notice² *v.tr.* **1.** observer, remarquer, s'apercevoir de, prendre garde à (qn, qch.); relever (des fautes); **without his noticing it,** sans qu'il y prît garde; **to be noticed, to get oneself noticed, by s.o.,** attirer l'attention de qn (sur soi); *F:* (*with passive force*) **does it n.?** est-ce que ça se voit? **2.** donner congé, signifier son congé, à (un locataire, etc.).

noticeable ['noutisəbl] *a.* **1.** (*of fact, etc.*) digne d'attention, de remarque. **2.** perceptible; **the difference is very n.,** la différence est très sensible. **-ably** *adv.* perceptiblement, sensiblement.

notifiable ['noutifaiəbl] *a.* (maladie) dont la déclaration aux autorités est obligatoire.

notification [noutifi'keiʃ(ə)n] *n.* avis *m*, notification *f*, annonce *f* (d'un fait, etc.); déclaration *f* (de naissance); **letter of n.,** lettre notificative.

notify ['noutifai] *v.tr.* annoncer, notifier (qch.); déclarer (une naissance, etc.); **to n. s.o. of sth.,** avertir, aviser, qn de qch.; **to n. the authorities of a fact,** saisir l'administration d'un fait; **to n. the police of sth.,** signaler qch. à la police; **to be notified of sth.,** recevoir notification de qch.; être avisé de qch.

notion ['nouʃ(ə)n] *n.* **1.** *Phil:* notion *f*, concept *m.* **2.** (*a*) notion, idée *f*; **to have no n. of sth.,** n'avoir pas la moindre notion de qch.; **to have no n. of time,** n'avoir pas le sens de l'heure; **I haven't the first n. about it,** je n'en ai pas la moindre idée; (*b*) opinion *f*, pensée *f*, idée; **I have a n. that . . .,** j'ai dans l'idée que . . .; (*c*) caprice *m*; **as the n. takes him,** selon son caprice; **to have a n. to do sth.,** se mettre en tête de faire qch. **3.** *NAm:* **notions,** mercerie *f.*

notional ['nouʃ(ə)n(ə)l] *a.* **1.** (*of knowledge, etc.*) spéculatif. **2.** (*of thgs, relations, etc.*) imaginaire.

notoriety [noutə'raiəti] *n.* **1.** notoriété *f*; **to seek n.,** chercher à se faire remarquer; s'afficher. **2.** (*pers.*) notabilité *f*, notable *m.*

notorious [nou'tɔːriəs] *a.* d'une triste notoriété; (menteur, etc.) insigne; (malfaiteur) reconnu, notoire; (endroit) mal famé; (voleur) fieffé. **-ly** *adv.* notoirement; **n. cruel,** connu pour sa cruauté.

notwithstanding [nɔtwiθ'stændiŋ] **1.** *prep.* malgré, en dépit de, nonobstant. **2.** *adv.* quand même, tout de même; néanmoins.

nougat ['nuːgɑː] *n.* nougat *m.*

nought [nɔːt] *n.* **1.** = NAUGHT 1. **2.** *Mth:* zéro *m*; *Games:* **noughts and crosses** = morpion *m.*

noun [naun] *n.* *Gram:* substantif *m*, nom *m*; **proper n.,** nom propre.

nourish ['nʌriʃ] *v.tr.* **1.** (*a*) nourrir (qn, une plante, etc.); alimenter (qn); **to n. s.o. on, with, sth.,** nourrir qn de qch.; **to be well nourished,** être bien nourri; (*b*) *Ind:* nourrir (le bois); entretenir (le cuir). **2.** *O:* nourrir, entretenir (un sentiment, un espoir, etc.). **nourishing** *a.* nourrissant, nutritif.

nourishment ['nʌriʃmənt] *n.* **1.** (*a*) alimentation *f*, nourriture *f* (de qn, qch.); (*b*) *Leath:* entretien *m* (du cuir). **2.** nourriture, aliments *mpl*; **to take (some) n.,** prendre de la nourriture.

nous [naus] *n.* *F:* savoir-faire *m*; bons sens.

nova, *pl.* **-ae** ['nouvə, -iː] *n.* *Astr:* nova *f*, *pl.* novæ.

Nova Scotia ['nouvə'skouʃə] *Pr.n.* *Geog:* Nouvelle-Écosse *f.*

novel¹ ['nɔv(ə)l] *n.* *Lit:* roman *m*; **detective n.,** roman policier.

novel² *a.* nouveau, -elle; original, -aux; singulier; **that's a n. idea!** voilà qui est original!

novelette [nɔvə'let] *n.* *Lit:* (*a*) nouvelle *f*; (*b*) petit roman à l'eau de rose.

novelist ['nɔvəlist] *n.* *Lit:* romancier, -ière.

novella [nou'velə] *n.* *Lit:* nouvelle *f.*

novelty ['nɔvəlti] *n.* **1.** (*a*) chose nouvelle; innovation *f*; *Com:* (article *m* de) nouveauté (*f*); (*b*) *Com:* **novelties** = farces *fpl* et attrapes *fpl.* **2.** nouveauté, étrangeté *f* (de qch.).

November [nə'vembər, nou-) *n.* novembre *m*; **in N.,** au mois de novembre; en novembre; **(on) the first, the fifth, of N.,** le premier, le cinq, novembre.

novice ['nɔvis] *n.* **1.** *Ecc:* novice *mf.* **2.** novice, apprenti, -ie, débutant, -ante; **to be a n. in, at, sth.,** être novice dans, à, qch.

noviciate, novitiate [nou'viʃiet] *n.* *Ecc:* **1.** (temps *m* du) noviciat *m.* **2.** noviciat; maison *f* des novices.

now [nau] **I.** *adv.* **1.** (*a*) maintenant, à présent, actuellement, à l'heure actuelle; **what shall we do n.?**

qu'est-ce que nous allons faire maintenant? *F:* **it's (a case of) n. or never,** c'est le moment ou jamais; **n. or never!** allons-y! *F:* **goodbye for n.!** à bientôt! **that'll do for n.,** ça suffit pour le moment; (*b*) maintenant; **he won't be long n.,** il ne tardera plus guère; **even n., I don't understand,** même maintenant je ne comprends pas; (*c*) maintenant; tout de suite; **and n. I must go,** sur ce je vous quitte; **n. is the time to . . .,** c'est le bon moment pour . . .; **right n.,** tout de suite; (*d*) (*in narrative*) alors, à ce moment-là; **all was n. ready,** dès lors tout était prêt; **he was even n. on his way,** il était déjà en route; (*e*) **just n.,** (i) (*past*) tout à l'heure, il y a un instant; (ii) (*present*) en ce moment; **I can't do it just n.,** je ne puis pas le faire en ce moment; (*f*) **(every) n. and then, and again,** de temps en temps, de temps à autre; par intervalles, par moments; par-ci par-là; **n. . . ., n. . . ., n. . . . then . . ., n. . . . and again . . .,** tantôt . . . tantôt . . .; **n. here n. there,** tantôt ici tantôt là; **up to n.,** jusqu'ici; **from n. on,** dès maintenant; **it's two years (ago) n.,** ça fait déjà deux ans. **2.** (*without temporal significance*) (*a*) (*explanatory, or in development of an argument*) or; **n. to come back to what we were saying,** pour revenir à ce que nous disions; (*in story*) **n. it happened that . . .,** or il advint que . . .; (*b*) (*interjectional expletive*) **n. what's the matter with you?** qu'avez-vous donc? **come n.!** voyons! **n., n.! stop quarrelling!** voyons, voyons! assez de querelles! **well n.!** eh bien! **n. then!** (i) attention! (ii) voyons! allons! **II.** *conj.* maintenant que, à présent que; **n. (that) I'm older I think differently,** maintenant que je suis plus âgé je pense autrement. **III.** *n.* le présent, le temps actuel; **in three or four days from n.,** d'ici trois ou quatre jours; **he ought to be here by n., he ought to have been here before n.,** il devrait déjà être arrivé; **until n.,** jusqu'ici, jusqu'à présent; **from n. (on),** dès maintenant.

nowadays ['nauədeiz] *adv.* aujourd'hui; de nos jours; actuellement.

noway(s) ['nouwei(z)] *adv.* = NOWISE.

nowhere ['nou(h)wɛər] **1.** *adv.* nulle part; **he was n. to be found,** on ne le trouvait nulle part; **it's n. near enough,** c'est loin d'être suffisant; **flattery will get you n.,** la flatterie ne vous mènera à rien. **2.** *n.* le néant; **he seemed to come from n.,** il semblait apparaître tout d'un coup; **a small place in the middle of n.,** un petit trou perdu.

nowise ['nouwaiz] *adv.* *NAm:* en aucune façon; aucunement, nullement.

nowt [naut] *pron. & n.* *Dial: & P:* (ne . . .) rien (*m*); **I don't do owt for n.,** je ne fais rien pour rien.

noxious ['nɔkʃəs] *a.* nuisible, nocif; (*of plant, smell, etc.*) vireux; (*of gas, fumes, etc.*) délétère, nocif.

nozzle ['nɔzl] *n.* (*a*) ajutage *m*, jet *m* (de tuyau); lance *f* (de tuyau de pompe à incendie, etc.); canule *f* (de seringue); **petrol pump delivery n.,** pistolet *m* de distributeur d'essence; (*b*) bec, tuyau *m*, buse *f* (de soufflet); suceur *m* (d'aspirateur); tuyère *f*, ajutage (d'injecteur, de turbine, etc.).

nuance ['nju:ɑ̃(n)s] *n.* nuance *f*.

nub [nʌb] *n.* **1.** petit morceau (de charbon, etc.). **2.** bosse *f*, protubérance *f*. **3. the n. of the matter,** l'essentiel *m* de l'affaire.

nubile ['nju:bail] *a.* nubile.

nuclear ['nju:kliər] *a.* *Atom.Ph:* nucléaire; **n. physics,** physique *f* nucléaire; **n. power,** (i) énergie *f* nucléaire, atomique; (ii) électricité *f* d'origine nucléaire; **n. power station, plant,** centrale *f* (d'énergie) nucléaire; **n. weapon,** arme *f* nucléaire; **n. war(fare),** guerre *f* nucléaire; *Pol:* **the N. Powers,** les puissances *fpl* nucléaires.

nucleic [nju:'kli:ik] *a.* *Ch:* (acide) nucléique.

nucleus, *pl.* **-ei** ['nju:kliəs, -iai] *n.* (*a*) *Ph: Biol: Astr:* noyau *m*; *Ph:* **atomic n.,** noyau atomique; (*b*) noyau, embryon *m* (d'une organisation, etc.); **the n. of a library,** un commencement de bibliothèque; *Mil: etc:* **n. of resistance,** noyau de résistance.

nude [nju:d] **1.** *a.* (*of pers., limbs, etc.*) nu; *Art:* **n. figure,** figure nue; nu *m*, nudité *f*. **2.** *n.* (*a*) *Art:* **(the) n.,** (le) nu, (la) nudité, (la) figure nue; **to draw, paint, from the n.,** dessiner, peindre, d'après le nu; dessiner, peindre, des académies; (*b*) **to bathe in the n.,** se baigner tout nu.

nudge¹ [nʌdʒ] *n.* coup *m* de coude.

nudge² *v.tr.* pousser (qn) du coude; donner un coup de coude à (qn).

nudism ['nju:dizm] *n.* nudisme *m*, naturisme *m*.

nudist ['nju:dist] *n.* nudiste *mf*, naturiste *mf*; **n. camp, colony,** camp de nudistes.

nudity ['nju:diti] *n.* nudité *f*.

nugget ['nʌgit] *n.* pépite *f* (d'or).

nuisance ['nju:səns] *n.* **1.** *Jur:* dommage *m*; atteinte portée (i) aux droits du public, (ii) à la moralité publique, (iii) aux droits privés des voisins. **2.** *F:* (*a*) (*pers.*) casse-pieds *m inv*; peste *f*, fléau *m*; **go away, you('re a) n.!** va-t'en, tu m'embêtes! **to make a n. of oneself,** embêter le monde, les gens; (*b*) (*thg*) ennui *m*, incommodité *f*; embêtement *m*; **long skirts are a n.,** les jupes longues sont gênantes; **it's a n. for, to, me to . . .,** cela me gêne de . . .; **that's a n.!** voilà qui est bien ennuyeux! **what a n.!** quel ennui! que c'est embêtant, agaçant!

null [nʌl] *a.* (*a*) *Jur: etc:* (*of decree, act, etc.*) nul, *f.* nulle; (*of legacy*) caduc, *f.* caduque; **n. and void,** nul et de nul effet; **to declare a contract n. and void,** déclarer un contrat nul et non avenu; **to render n.,** annuler, infirmer, invalider (un décret, un testament); (*b*) (*of thg*) inefficace, sans valeur; (*of pers.*) nul, insignifiant.

nullification [nʌlifi'keiʃ(ə)n] *n.* annulation *f*, invalidation *f*.

nullify ['nʌlifai] *v.tr.* annuler, nullifier; infirmer (un acte); invalider; **his marriage was nullified,** son mariage a été déclaré nul.

nullity ['nʌliti] *n.* *Jur:* nullité *f*, invalidité *f* (d'un mariage, etc.); caducité *f* (d'un legs, etc.); *Jur:* **n. suit,** demande *f* en nullité de mariage.

numb¹ [nʌm] *a.* (*of limb, mind, etc.*) engourdi; (*of limb*) gourd; **hands n. with cold,** mains engourdies par le froid.

numb² *v.tr.* engourdir (les membres, l'esprit, etc.); **numbed with cold,** engourdi par le froid, transi; **numbed with horror,** glacé d'horreur.

number¹ ['nʌmbər] *n.* **1.** (*a*) *Mth:* nombre *m*; **three-figure n.,** nombre de trois chiffres; **even, odd, prime, n.,** nombre pair, impair, premier; (*b*) **the n. of people present,** le nombre des assistants; **we were in equal numbers,** nous étions en nombre égal; **to swell the number(s),** faire nombre; **they are few in n.,** ils sont peu nombreux; **without n.,** sans nombre; (*c*) **a n. of . . .,** (bon) nombre de . . ., un assez grand nombre de . . .; plusieurs . . .; **a large n. of men were killed,** nombre d'hommes ont été tués; **any n. of . . .,** un grand nombre de . . ., bon nombre de . . .; une quantité de . . .; (*d*) *pl.* **to be present in small numbers, in (great) numbers,** être présents en petit nombre, en grand nombre; **they are coming in ever increasing numbers,** ils viennent de plus en plus nombreux; (*e*) compagnie *f*, groupe *m* (de personnes); **one of their n.,** (l')un d'entre eux; (*f*) *B:* **(the Book of) Numbers,** le Livre des Nombres; les Nombres. **2.** chiffre *m*; **to write the n. on a page,** numéroter une page. **3.** numéro *m* (d'une maison, etc.); (numéro) matricule *m* (d'un soldat, d'un fusil, etc.); **I live at n. 40,** j'habite au numéro 40; *Navy:* **n. eight uniform,** *F:* **n. eights** = tenue de travail; bleu *m* de chauffe; *F:* (*child's language*) **to do n. one,** faire pipi, faire la petite commission; **to do number two,** faire la grosse commission; *F:* **to look after n. one,** penser à mézigue; tirer la couverture à soi; **running n.,** numéro de série, d'ordre; *Aut:* **registration n.,** numéro d'immatriculation, de police; **n. plate,** plaque *f* d'immatriculation; *F:* **to have s.o.'s n.,** en savoir long sur qn; *Com:* **reference n.,** numéro de commande; *Tp:* **telephone n.,** numéro d'appel; **subscriber's n.,** numéro d'abonné; (*at lottery, etc.*) **to draw a lucky n.,** tirer un bon numéro; *F:* **his number's up,** il a son compte; il est fichu. **4.** *Gram:* nombre. **5.** (*a*) *Th:* numéro (du programme); **vocal n.,** tour *m* de chant; (*b*) *Journ:* numéro (d'un journal, etc.); *Publ:* livraison *f*, fascicule *m* (d'un ouvrage qui paraît par fascicules); **current n.,** numéro du jour, de la semaine, du mois; dernier numéro; **back n.,** vieux numéro; *F:* (*of pers.*) **to be a back n.,** être vieux jeu. **6.** *F:* (*a*) **that's a pretty n.,** ça c'est une jolie robe, etc.; (*b*) fille *f*, nana *f*; **she's a good looking n.,** c'est une jolie nénette.

number² *v.tr.* **1.** (*a*) compter, dénombrer (les étoiles, etc.); **his days are numbered,** ses jours sont comptés; (*b*) **to n. s.o. among one's friends,** mettre, compter, qn au nombre de, parmi, ses amis; (*c*) **the town, the army, numbers thirty thousand,** la ville, l'armée, compte trente mille habitants, trente mille hommes. **2.** (*a*) numéroter (les maisons d'une rue, etc.); (*b*) *v.i. Mil:* **to n. (off),** se numéroter. **numbering** *n.* **1.** comptage *m*, compte *m*, dénombrement *m* (d'objets, de personnes). **2.** numérotage *m* (de maisons etc.).

numberless ['nʌmbəlis] *a.* innombrable; sans nombre.

numbness ['nʌmnis] *n.* engourdissement *m* (des doigts, etc.); torpeur *f* (de l'esprit).

numbskull ['nʌmskʌl] *n.* = NUMSKULL.

numeracy ['nju:m(ə)rəsi] *n.* degré *m* d'aptitude en calcul.

numeral ['nju:m(ə)r(ə)l] **1.** *a.* (*of word, letter, etc.*) numéral, -aux. **2.** *n.* (*a*) chiffre *m*, nombre *m*; **Roman numerals,** chiffres romains; (*b*) **the cardinal numerals,** les numéraux cardinaux.

numerate ['nju:mərət] *a.* qui a le sens de l'arithmétique.

numeration [nju:mə'reiʃ(ə)n] *n. Mth:* numération *f*; **binary n.,** numération binaire.

numerator ['nju:mərei̯tər] *n. Mth:* numérateur *m*.

numeric [nju:'merik] *Cmptr:* **1.** *a.* numérique; **n. coding,** codage *m* numérique. **2.** *n.pl.* **numerics,** chiffres *mpl*, caractères *mpl*, numériques.

numerical [nju:'merik(ə)l] *a.* (valeur, supériorité, ordre, etc.). **-ally** *adv.* numériquement.

numerous ['nju:m(ə)rəs] *a.* nombreux.

numismatic [nju:miz'mætik] *a.* numismatique.

numismatics [nju:miz'mætiks] *n.pl.* (*usu. with sg. const.*) la numismatique.

numismatist [nju:'mizmətist] *n.* numismate *mf*.

numskull ['nʌmskʌl] *n. F:* nigaud, -aude; bêta, -asse.

nun [nʌn] *n.f. Ecc:* religieuse; **to become a n.,** entrer en religion; se faire religieuse; prendre le voile.

nuncio ['nʌnʃiou] *n. Ecc:* nonce *m*; **papal n.,** nonce du Pape.

nunnery ['nʌnəri] *n.* couvent *m* (de religieuses).

nuptial ['nʌpʃəl] *Lit:* **1.** *a.* nuptial, -iaux. **2.** *n.pl.* **nuptials,** noces *fpl*.

nurse¹ [nə:s] *n.* **1.** (*a*) **(wet) n.,** nourrice *f*; **to put a baby out to n.,** mettre un bébé en nourrice; (*b*) nurse *f*, bonne *f* (d'enfants). **2.** infirmier, -ière; garde-malade *mf*, *pl.* gardes-malades; **night n.,** (i) (*in hospital*) infirmière de nuit, (ii) (*privately employed*) garde *f* de nuit; *O:* **district n.,** infirmière visiteuse; **nursery n.,** puéricultrice *f*. **3.** (*a*) *Ent:* (*of bees, ants*) ouvrière *f*; (*b*) *Z:* nourrice.

nurse² *v.tr.* **1.** nourrir (de son lait), allaiter (un enfant). **2.** (*a*) soigner (un malade); **she nursed him back to health,** elle lui a fait recouvrer la santé grâce à ses soins; *v.i.* **she wants to n.,** elle voudrait être infirmière; (*b*) soigner (un rhume). **3.** (*a*) soigner, abriter (des plantes, etc.); ménager (un cheval, une équipe, etc.) en vue du dernier effort à donner; *Pol:* **to n. a, one's, constituency,** chauffer ses électeurs; (*b*) nourrir, entretenir (un sentiment, un espoir, etc.); mitonner, mijoter (un projet); (*c*) *F: O:* **to n. the fire,** couver le feu; rester au coin du feu. **4.** bercer, dorloter (un enfant); tenir (qn, qch.) dans ses bras; **to n. one's knee,** tenir son genou dans ses mains. **nursing** **1.** *a.* (*a*) **n. mother,** mère qui allaite; (*b*) (*in hospital*) **the n. staff,** les infirmiers, -ières. **2.** *n.* (*a*) allaitement *m* (d'un enfant); (*b*) culture assidue (des plantes, d'une terre, etc.); ménagement *m*, soin *m* (d'une affaire); entretien *m* (d'un sentiment, etc.); (*c*) soins (d'une garde-malade); **n. home,** (i) clinique *f*; (ii) maison *f* de santé; (iii) maison de retraite; (*d*) profession *f* de garde-malade, d'infirmière; (*e*) bercement *m*, dorlotement *m* (d'un enfant) (dans les bras, etc.).

nursemaid ['nə:smeid] *n.f.* bonne d'enfants, nurse.

nursery ['nə:s(ə)ri] *n.* **1.** (*a*) chambre *f* des enfants; nursery *f*; **n. rhyme,** comptine *f*; (*b*) **(day) n.,** crèche *f*; garderie *f*; **resident n.,** pouponnière *f* ; **n. school,** maternelle *f*. **2.** (*a*) *For: Hort:* **n. (garden),** pépinière *f*; **n. gardener,** pépiniériste *mf*; (*b*) *Pisc:* vivier *m*; (*c*) *Ski:* **n. slopes,** pentes *fpl* des débutants.

nurseryman, *pl.* **-men** ['nə:s(ə)rimən] *n.m.* pépiniériste.

nursling ['nə:sliŋ] *n.* nourrisson *m*.

nurture¹ ['nə:tʃər] *n.* éducation *f*; soins *mpl*.

nurture² *v.tr.* **1.** nourrir (les enfants, etc.); nourrir, entretenir (des sentiments, etc.). **2.** élever, faire l'éducation de (qn); instruire (qn).

nut [nʌt] *n.* **1.** (*a*) (i) noix *f*; (ii) **hazel n.,** noisette *f*; aveline *f*; **n. tree,** noisetier *m*, coudrier *m*; *F:* **tough, hard, n. to crack,** (i) problème *m* difficile à résoudre; (ii) personne *f* difficile, peu commode; *F:* **to be nuts on s.o., on sth.,** raffoler de qn, de qch.; **he's nuts,** il est cinglé; **to go nuts,** perdre la boule; (*b*) *F:* tête *f*; caboche *f*; **to be off one's n.,** être timbré, toqué; avoir perdu la boule; **to do one's n.,** (i) être dans tous ses états; (ii) être en colère. **2.** *Mec.E:* écrou *m*; **butterfly, wing, n.,** écrou à oreilles; écrou (à) papillon; **n. wrench,** clé *f* à écrous. **3.** *Mus:* (*a*) sillet *m* (de violon); (*b*) hausse *f* (d'archet). **4.** *Com: Min:* **n. coal, nuts,** gailletin *m*; têtes *fpl* de moineau. **5.** *U.S: F:* **nuts!** des clous! zut!

nut-brown ['nʌtbraun] *a.* (couleur) noisette *inv.*

nutcase ['nŋtkeis] *n. F:* dingue *mf*, cinglé, -e.

nutcracker ['nʌtkrækər] *n.* **(pair of) nutcrackers,** casse-noisette(s) *m inv*, casse-noix *m inv*.

nuthatch ['nʌthætʃ] *n. Orn:* sittelle *f*.

nuthouse ['nʌthaus] *n. F:* asile *m* d'aliénés, maison *f* de fous.

nutmeg ['nʌtmeg] *n.* (noix *f*) muscade (*f*); **n. tree,** muscadier *m*; **n. grater,** râpe *f* à muscade.

nutrient ['nju:triənt] **1.** *a.* nutritif. **2.** *n.* substance nutritive; aliment *m*.

nutriment ['nju:trimənt] *n.* nourriture *f*; aliments *mpl*.

nutrition [nju'triʃ(ə)n] *n.* nutrition *f*; alimentation *f*.

nutritious [nju'triʃəs] *a.* nutritif, nourrissant.

nutritive ['nju:tritiv] *a.* nutritif.

nutshell ['nʌtʃel] *n.* coquille *f* de noix; **that's the whole thing in a n.,** voilà toute l'affaire (résumée) en un mot, en deux mots; **to put it in a n. . . .,** pour résumer . . .; bref. . ..

nutter ['nʌtər] *n. P:* fou, folle; toqué, -ée.

nutting ['nʌtiŋ] *n.* cueillette *f* des noisettes.

nutty ['nʌti] *a.* **1.** (goût) de noisette, de noix; au goût de noisette, de noix. **2.** *F:* **to be n. about s.o., sth.,** raffoler de qn, de qch. **3.** *F:* fou, timbré.

nuzzle ['nʌzl] *v.i. & tr.* **1. to n. (against) s.o.'s shoulder,** (*of dog, horse*) fourrer son nez sur l'épaule de qn; (*of pers.*) se blottir sur l'épaule de qn; **the dog nuzzled up to my leg,** le chien me reniflait la jambe.

nylon ['nailɔn] *n. Tex:* nylon *m*; **n. stockings, nylons,** bas *mpl* nylon.

nymph [nimf] *n.f. Myth:* nymphe; **tree, wood, n.,** hamadryade; **sea n.,** néréide; **water n.,** naïade.

nymphet ['nimfit] *n.f.* nymphette.

nympho ['nimfou] *a. & n.f. F:* = NYMPHOMANIAC.

nymphomania [nimfou'meiniə] *n. Med:* nymphomanie *f.*

nymphomaniac [nimfou'meiniæk] *a. & n.f.* nymphomane.

O

O¹, o, *pl.* **o's, oes, os** [ou, ouz] *n.* **1.** (la lettre) O, o *m*; *Sch:* **O-level (exam),** premier examen du *General Certificate of Education.* **2.** *Tp: etc:* (*nought*) zéro *m*; **for London numbers dial 01** [ˈouˈwʌn], pour Londres composez zéro un.

O² *int.* **1.** (*vocative*) O, ô. **2.** = OH.

oaf, *pl.* **-s,** *A:* **oaves** [ouf, -s, ouvz] *n.* lourdaud *m.*

oafish [ˈoufiʃ] *a.* lourdaud, rustre.

oak [ouk] *n.* **1.** (*a*) *Bot:* **o. (tree),** chêne *m*; **o. leaf,** feuille *f* de chêne; **o. grove, wood,** chênaie *f*; bois *m* de chênes; (*b*) **o. (wood),** (bois de) chêne; **o. furniture,** meubles *mpl* de, en, chêne; **dark o. (colour),** couleur *f* vieux chêne; (*c*) *Ent:* **o. moth,** tordeuse *f* des chênes; (*d*) porte extérieure (d'un appartement dans les universités d'Oxford et Cambridge); **to sport one's o.,** s'enfermer à double porte.

oakapple [ˈoukæpl] *n.* noix *f* de galle.

oaken [ˈouk(ə)n] *a.* de, en, chêne.

oakum [ˈoukəm] *n.* étoupe (noire), filasse *f*; **to pick o.,** démêler, tirer, l'étoupe; faire de la filasse.

oar [ɔːr] *n.* (*a*) aviron *m*, rame *f*; (*opposed to scull*) aviron de nage; *F:* **to put one's o. in,** intervenir (mal à propos); s'en mêler; (*b*) **good o.,** bon rameur.

oarlock [ˈɔːlɔk] *n. U.S:* tolet *m* (d'aviron).

oarsman, *pl.* **-men** [ˈɔːzmən] *n.m.* rameur; tireur d'aviron; *Nau:* nageur.

oasis, *pl.* **oases** [ouˈeisis, -iːz] *n. Geog:* oasis *f*; *Fig:* **an o. of calm,** une oasis de calme.

oast [oust] *n.* séchoir *m* (à houblon).

oasthouse [ˈousthaus] *n.* sécherie *f* (de houblon).

oat [out] *n.* (*a*) *Bot:* avoine (commune); *F:* **to sow one's wild oats,** faire des fredaines; jeter sa gourme; (*b*) **oats,** avoine; **(porridge) oats,** flocons *mpl* d'avoine.

oatcake [ˈoutkeik] *n. Cu:* galette *f* d'avoine.

oatmeal [ˈoutmiːl] *n.* farine *f* d'avoine; *Cu:* **o. porridge,** *NAm:* **o.,** bouillie *f* d'avoine, porridge *m.*

oath, *pl.* **oaths** [ouθ, ouðz] *n.* **1.** serment *m*; **o. of allegiance,** serment de fidélité; **to take an o.,** *Jur:* **to take the o.,** prêter serment; **witness on o.,** témoin assermenté. **2.** juron *m*; gros mot; **to let out an o.,** laisser échapper, lâcher, un juron.

obduracy [ˈɔbdjurəsi] *n.* **1.** (*a*) endurcissement *m* (de cœur); entêtement *m*; (*b*) inexorabilité *f*, inflexibilité *f*. **2.** *Theol:* impénitence *f.*

obdurate [ˈɔbdjurət] *a.* **1.** (*a*) endurci, obstiné, têtu; (*b*) inexorable; inflexible. **2.** *Theol:* impénitent. **-ly** *adv.* (*a*) avec entêtement; (*b*) inflexiblement.

obedience [əˈbiːdiəns] *n.* **1.** obéissance *f* **(to s.o., to the law,** à qn, à la loi). **2.** (*a*) *Ecc:* **the Roman o.,** l'obédience *f* de Rome; (*b*) *Pol:* **countries of the Communist o.,** pays *mpl* d'obédience communiste.

obedient [əˈbiːdiənt] *a.* obéissant, soumis; docile; **to be o. to s.o.,** être obéissant envers qn; obéir à qn. **-ly** *adv.* avec soumission; docilement.

obeisance [əˈbeisəns] *n. A: & Lit:* **1.** salut *m*, révérence *f*. **2.** obéissance *f*, hommage *m.*

obelisk [ˈɔbəlisk] *n.* **1.** obélisque *m.* **2.** *Typ:* croix *f*; obèle *m*; **double o.,** diésis *m.*

obese [ouˈbiːs] *a.* obèse.

obesity [ouˈbiːsiti], **obeseness** [ouˈbiːsnis] *n.* obésité *f.*

obey [əˈbei] *v.tr.* obéir à (qn, un ordre); être obéissant; **to o. the law,** obéir aux lois; **his legs refused to o. him,** ses jambes refusaient d'obéir; (*of ship*) **to o. the helm,** obéir à la barre.

obfuscate [ˈɔbfʌskeit] *v.tr.* obscurcir (le jugement).

obituary [əˈbitjuri] *a. & n.* **o. (list),** registre *m* des morts; nécrologe *m*; **o. notice,** notice *f* nécrologique; *Journ:* **the o. column, the obituaries,** la nécrologie.

object¹ [ˈɔbdʒikt] *n.* **1.** objet *m*; (*a*) objet, chose *f*; **o. lesson,** exemple *m*; (*of microscope*) **o. finder,** chercheur *m* d'objet; chariot *m* (à vernier, de centrage); (*b*) *Phil:* **formal, material, o.,** objet formel, matériel. **2.** objet, sujet *m;* **o. of, for, pity,** objet, sujet, de pitié; **to be an o. for ridicule,** être en butte au ridicule. **3.** (*a*) but *m*, objectif, fin *f*; **to have sth. for, as, an o.,** avoir qch. pour objectif, pour but; **with this o. (in view),** dans cette intention; à cette fin; **with the sole o. of doing sth.,** à seule fin de faire qch.; **what is the o. of all this?** à quoi vise tout cela? **to defeat one's o.,** manquer son but; **to attain, succeed in, one's o.,** atteindre son but; (*b*) *F:* **expense, distance, is no o.,** on ne regarde pas à la dépense; la longueur du trajet importe peu. **4.** *Gram:* **direct, indirect, o.,** complément direct, indirect.

object² [əbˈdʒekt] *v.i.* **to o. to sth.,** faire objection, s'opposer, à qch.; protester, réclamer, contre qch.; **to o. to s.o.,** avoir des objections à faire contre qn; *Jur:* **to o. to a witness,** récuser un témoin; **to o. to doing sth.,** se refuser à faire qch.; **he objects (to it),** il s'y oppose.

objection [əbˈdʒekʃ(ə)n] *n.* **1.** objection *f*; **to raise an o.,** dresser, soulever, une objection; *Jur:* **o. to a witness,** récusation *f* de témoin; **to make no o. to, against, sth.,** ne rien objecter contre qch.; **I have no o. to his doing so,** je ne m'oppose pas à ce qu'il le fasse; **I have no o. to him,** je n'ai rien à dire contre lui; **if you have no o.,** si cela ne vous fait rien; si vous le voulez bien. **2.** obstacle *m*, inconvénient *m*; **the chief o. to your plan is its cost,** le plus grand désavantage de votre projet, c'est le coût; **I see no o. (to it),** je n'y vois pas d'inconvénient.

objectionable [əbˈdʒekʃ(ə)nəbl] *a.* **1.** répréhensible; inacceptable. **2.** désagréable, répugnant; (*of language, etc.*) choquant.

objective [əbˈdʒektiv] **1.** *a.* (*a*) *Phil: Med:* objectif; **let's be o.,** voyons les choses objectivement; (*b*) *Gram:* **o. (case),** cas *m* régime; cas objectif. **2.** *n.* (*a*) but *m*, objectif; (*b*) *Opt:* objectif. **-ly** *adv.* (contempler qch.) objectivement, d'une manière objective.

objectivism [əbˈdʒektivizm] *n.* objectivisme *m.*

objectivity [ɔbdʒekˈtiviti] *n. Phil: etc:* objectivité *f.*

objector [əbˈdʒektər] *n.* **1.** protestataire *mf.* **2.** personne *f* qui soulève des objections.

oblate [ˈɔbleit] *a. Mth: etc:* (ellipsoïde) aplati (aux pôles), raccourci.

obligate [ˈɔbligeit] *v.tr.* **to o. s.o. to do sth.,** imposer à qn l'obligation de faire qch.; **to be obligated to do sth.,** avoir l'obligation de faire qch.

obligation [ɔbliˈgeiʃ(ə)n] *n.* (*a*) obligation *f*; **moral o.,** obligation morale; **to be under an o. to do sth.,** être dans l'obligation de faire qch.; **I am under no o. to go with them,** rien ne m'oblige à les accompagner; *Com:* **without o.,** sans engagement; (*b*) dette *f* de reconnaissance; **to be under an o. to s.o.,** avoir envers qn une dette de reconnaissance; **I am under a great**

o. to him, je lui suis redevable de beaucoup; (*c*) *Com:* **to meet one's obligations,** faire face à ses engagements.

obligatory [ə'bligət(ə)ri] *a.* obligatoire; **the wearing of a jacket is o.,** le port d'un veston est de rigueur.

oblige [ə'blaidʒ] *v.tr.* **1.** (*compel*) (*a*) *usu. Jur:* obliger, astreindre, assujettir (**s.o. to do sth.,** qn à faire qch.); (*b*) **to be obliged to do sth.,** être obligé, tenu, de faire qch.; *Adm:* être astreint à faire qch. **2.** (*a*) (*do s.o. a favour*) obliger (qn); rendre service à (qn); **he did it to o. (us),** il l'a fait par pure complaisance; **to be always willing to o.,** être très obligeant, très complaisant; *F:* **anything to o.,** tout ce que vous voudrez pour vous faire plaisir; (*b*) **to be obliged to s.o. (for sth.),** être reconnaissant à qn (pour qch.). **obliging** *a.* obligeant, complaisant. **obligingly** *adv.* obligeamment, complaisamment.

oblique [ə'bliːk] **1.** *a.* (*a*) (ligne, angle) oblique (**to,** à); **o. glance,** regard *m* en biais; (*b*) *Gram:* **o. case,** cas indirect, oblique. **2.** *n.* (*a*) (i) (ligne) oblique (*f*); (ii) *Mth:* figure *f* oblique; (*b*) *Anat:* (muscle) oblique (*m*); (*c*) *Typ:* barre transversale; (*d*) *Mil: etc:* (mouvement) oblique (*m*). **-ly** *adv.* (*a*) obliquement, de biais; (*b*) d'une façon indirecte; de biais.

obliqueness [ə'bliːknis], **obliquity** [ə'blikwiti] *n.* **1.** obliquité *f*, biais *m*. **2.** obliquité (de conduite); manque *m* de franchise.

obliterate [ə'blitəreit] *v.tr.* **1.** (*a*) faire disparaître, effacer (des chiffres, etc.); faire oublier, oblitérer (le passé); (*b*) oblitérer, composter (un timbre). **2.** *Anat: Med: etc:* oblitérer (un conduit, etc.).

obliteration [əblitə'reiʃ(ə)n] *n.* **1.** effaçage *m*; (*by crossing out*) rature *f*. **2.** oblitération *f* (d'un timbre). **3.** *Anat: Med:* oblitération (d'un conduit).

oblivion [ə'bliviən] *n.* (état *m* d')oubli (*m*); **to fall, sink, into o.,** tomber dans l'oubli.

oblivious [ə'bliviəs] *a.* oublieux (**of,** de); **o. of what was going on,** inconscient de ce qui se passait.

oblong ['ɔblɔŋ] **1.** *a.* oblong, -ongue; (sphéroïde) allongé; rectangulaire; *Typ: etc:* (format) oblong, à l'italienne. **2.** *n.* rectangle *m*.

obloquy ['ɔbləkwi] *n.* opprobre *m*.

obnoxious [əb'nɔkʃəs] *a.* (*a*) (*of pers., action, etc.*) odieux; (*of pers.*) antipathique (**to s.o.,** à qn); détesté (**to,** par); (*b*) (*of smell, etc.*) repoussant, désagréable.

oboe ['oubou] *n. Mus:* hautbois *m*; **o. (player),** hautboïste *mf*.

oboist ['oubouist] *n. Mus:* hautboïste *mf*.

obscene [əb'siːn] *a.* (*a*) (chanson, mot) obscène; (*b*) repoussant, révoltant. **-ly** *adv.* d'une manière obscène.

obscenity [əb'seniti, -'siːn-] *n.* obscénité *f*.

obscurantism [ɔbskju'ræntizm] *n.* obscurantisme *m*.

obscurantist [ɔbskju'ræntist] *a.* & *n.* obscurantiste (*mf*).

obscure¹ [əb'skjuər] *a.* **1.** (*a*) obscur, ténébreux; **to grow, become, o.,** s'obscurcir; (*b*) (sentiment) vague; (*c*) (village, etc.) inconnu, ignoré. **2.** (discours, livre, etc.) obscur; (style) obscur, ténébreux. **3.** (*undistinguished*) (naissance) obscure; (auteur) inconnu, peu connu, obscur. **-ly** *adv.* **1.** (*a*) (voir qch.) obscurément; (*b*) (sentir) vaguement. **2.** (parler) obscurément.

obscure² *v.tr.* **1.** (*a*) assombrir; (*b*) obscurcir, cacher; **to o. sth. from s.o.'s view,** cacher qch. à qn; (*c*) obscurcir (un argument, les faits). **2.** (*overshadow*) éclipser, surpasser.

obscurity [əb'skjuːriti] *n.* obscurité *f*.

obsequies ['ɔbsikwiz] *n.pl.* obsèques *fpl.*, funérailles *fpl*.

obsequious [əb'siːkwiəs] *a.* obséquieux. **-ly** *adv.* obséquieusement.

obsequiousness [əb'siːkwiəsnis] *n.* obséquiosité *f*.

observable [əb'zəːvəbl] *a.* **1.** (*discernible*) observable, visible; (changement) perceptible. **2.** remarquable; digne d'attention.

observance [əb'zəːvəns] *n.* **1.** (*a*) observation *f*, observance *f* (d'une loi, d'un usage, etc.); (*b*) *Ecc:* règle *f*, observance (d'un ordre religieux). **2. religious observances,** pratiques religieuses.

observant [əb'zəːvənt] *a.* (*a*) observateur, -trice (**of,** de); attentif (**of,** à); (*b*) attentif; **he is very o.,** rien ne lui échappe.

observation [ɔbzə(ː)'veiʃən] *n.* observation *f*. **1.** (*a*) **to put, keep, s.o., sth., under o.,** mettre, tenir, qn, qch., en observation; (*b*) *Mil:* surveillance *f* (du terrain, de l'ennemi); **aerial o.,** observation aérienne; (*c*) *Astr: Surv:* coup *m* de lunette; **to take an o.,** prendre, faire, une observation; *Nau:* faire le point; *Nau:* **position by o.,** point observé; (*d*) **o. aircraft,** avion *m* d'observation; *Rail:* **o. coach, car,** voiture *f* panoramique; *Mil:* **o. post, station,** poste *m* d'observation; *Med:* **o. ward,** salle *f* des malades en observation. **2.** remarque *f*; observation.

observatory [əb'zəːvət(ə)ri] *n.* observatoire *m*; poste *m* d'observation.

observe [əb'zəːv] *v.tr.* **1.** observer (la loi, les convenances, un jeûne); se conformer à (un ordre); **to o. silence,** garder un silence absolu; observer le silence; **to o. the Sabbath,** observer, respecter, (i) le sabbat, (ii) le dimanche. **2.** (*a*) observer, regarder (les étoiles, etc.); (*b*) **to o. the enemy's movements,** surveiller l'ennemi. **3.** apercevoir, remarquer, noter (un fait, etc.); *v.i.* **a man who observes keenly,** un homme qui observe attentivement, à qui rien n'échappe. **4.** dire; **'you are wrong', he observed,** 'vous avez tort', dit-il, fit-il.

observer [əb'zəːvər] *n.* **1.** observateur, -trice (des lois, des règles, etc.). **2.** (*a*) *Astr: Mil:* observateur, -trice; (*b*) **to send observers to a conference,** envoyer des observateurs à un congrès.

obsess [əb'ses] *v.tr.* (*a*) obséder (qn); (*b*) **to be obsessed with, by, an idea,** être obsédé d'une, par une, idée; être hanté par, en proie à, une idée.

obsession [əb'seʃ(ə)n] *n.* **1.** obsession *f*. **2.** obsession (**with,** de); hantise *f*.

obsessional [əb'seʃ(ə)n(ə)l] *a. Psy:* obsessionel.

obsessive [əb'sesiv] *a.* (*of idea, image*) obsédant.

obsolescence [ɔbsə'lesns] *n.* désuétude, *f*; vieillissement *m*; *Ind: etc:* obsolescence *f* (d'un outillage); *Ind:* **planned o.,** obsolescence prévue; *Ind: Com:* **built-in o.,** obsolescence prévue systématiquement.

obsolescent [ɔbsə'lesənt] *a.* qui tombe en désuétude; qui vieillit, qui a vieilli.

obsolete ['ɔbsəliːt] *a.* (*of word*) désuet, -ète; tombé en désuétude; (*of fashion*) suranné; (*of design, etc.*) démodé, dépassé; (*of ship*) déclassé; (*of institution*) aboli; **the word is o.,** ce mot n'est plus usité.

obsoleteness ['ɔbsəliːtnis] *n.* vétusté *f*, désuétude *f*.

obstacle ['ɔbstəkl] *n.* obstacle *m*; **to be an o. to sth.,** faire obstacle à qch.; **to put obstacles in s.o.'s way,** faire obstacle à qn; *Mil:* **o. course,** parcours *m*, piste *f*, d'obstacles; *Sp:* **o. race,** course *f* d'obstacles.

obstetric(al) [ɔb'stetrik(l)] *a.* obstétrical, -aux.

obstetrician [ɔbste'triʃ(ə)n] *n.* médecin accoucheur; obstétricien, -ienne.

obstetrics [ɔb'stetriks] *n.pl.* (*usu. with sg. const.*) obstétrique *f*.

obstinacy ['ɔbstinəsi] *n.* **1.** obstination *f*, entêtement *m*. **2.** *Med:* persistance *f* (d'une maladie).

obstinate ['ɔbstinət] *a.* **1.** obstiné (**in doing sth.,** à faire qch.); **to be o.,** s'entêter; **o. as a mule,** entêté, têtu, comme une mule. **2.** (fièvre) rebelle; (rhume) obstiné. **-ly** *adv.* obstinément; **to refuse o.,** s'obstiner à refuser.

obstreperous [əb'strep(ə)rəs] *a.* (*a*) bruyant, tapageur; (*b*) rebelle; **to be o.,** rouspéter. **-ly** *adv.* (*a*) bruyamment, tapageusement; (*b*) *F:* en rouspétant.

obstruct [əb'strʌkt] *v.tr.* (*a*) obstruer, encombrer (la rue, etc.); boucher (un tuyau, etc.); *Med:* oblitérer, obstruer (l'intestin); gêner (la vue); **to o. s.o.'s path,** barrer le chemin à qn; (*b*) gêner, entraver, empêcher (les mouvements de qn); **to o. s.o. in the execution of his duty,** gêner qn dans l'exercice de ses fonctions; *Sp:* **to o. another player,** *v.i.* **to o.,** faire de l'obstruction; *Parl:* **to o. a bill,** faire de l'obstruction; (*c*) gêner (la circulation, la navigation).

obstruction [əb'strʌkʃ(ə)n] *n.* **1.** (*a*) engorgement *m* (d'un tuyau, etc.); *Med:* obstruction *f*, oblitération (de l'intestin); (*b*) empêchement *m* (de qn dans ses affaires, de la circulation, etc.); *Sp: Pol:* obstruction. **2.** encombrement *m*, embarras *m* (dans la rue); gêne *f* (dans la circulation); entrave *f* (à la navigation); engorgement, stoppage *m* (dans un tuyau); *Rail:* **an o. on the line,** un obstacle sur la voie.

obstructionism [əb'strʌkʃənizm] *n. Pol:* obstructionnisme *m*.

obstructionist [əb'strʌkʃənist] *n. Pol:* obstructionniste *mf*.

obstructive [əb'strʌktiv] *a.* **1.** *Med:* obstructif, obstruant. **2.** (tactique) d'obstruction; *Parl: etc:* **to be o.,** faire obstruction; être obstructionniste.

obtain [əb'tein] **1.** *v.tr.* obtenir, se procurer, avoir (qch.); recueillir (des renseignements); se faire accorder (un congé); **to o. sugar from beet,** extraire du sucre de la betterave; **I obtained permission to see him,** j'ai obtenu la permission de le voir. **2.** *v.i. A:* (*of practice, etc.*) avoir cours; prévaloir.

obtainable [əb'teinəbl] *a.* procurable.

obtrude [əb'tru:d] **1.** *v.tr.* mettre (qch.) en avant; **to o. one's opinions on others,** imposer ses opinions à autrui; **to o. oneself,** s'imposer à l'attention. **2.** *v.i.* (*a*) (*of pers.*) s'imposer à l'attention (de qn); se montrer importun; (*b*) (*of thg*) être trop en évidence.

obtrusion [əb'tru:ʒ(ə)n] *n.* intrusion *f*; importunité *f*.

obtrusive [əb'tru:siv] *a.* **1.** (*of pers.*) importun, intrus; (*of behaviour*) indiscret. **2.** (*of smell, etc.*) pénétrant. **-ly** *adv.* inopportunément; importunément, indiscrètement.

obtrusiveness [əb'tru:sivnis] *n.* importunité *f*.

obtuse [əb'tju:s] *a.* **1.** obtus, émoussé; *Mth:* **o. angle,** angle obtus. **2.** (esprit) obtus, peu intelligent.

obtuseness [əb'tju:snis] *n.* **1.** manque *m* de (i) tranchant, (ii) pointe. **2.** stupidité *f*.

obverse ['ɔbvə:s] *a. & n.* (*a*) *Num:* **o. (side),** avers *m*, obvers *m*, face *f* (d'une médaille); (*b*) opposé *m* (d'une vérité).

obviate ['ɔbvieit] *v.tr.* prévenir, parer à, obvier à (une difficulté, etc.); aller au-devant (d'une objection).

obvious ['ɔbviəs] *a.* (*a*) évident, clair, manifeste; (*of fact, truth*) patent; **it's quite o. that he is lying,** il ment, cela saute aux yeux; **it was the o. thing to do,** c'était tout indiqué; cela s'imposait; **to state the o.,** enfoncer une porte ouverte; **to miss the o.,** ne pas voir l'essentiel; (*b*) (*of feature*) frappant; voyant; **his patriotism is a little (too) o.,** son patriotisme sonne faux. **-ly** *adv.* évidemment, manifestement; **she is o. wrong,** il est clair qu'elle a tort.

obviousness ['ɔbviəsnis] *n.* évidence *f*, clarté *f*.

ocarina [ɔkə'ri:nə] *n. Mus:* ocarina *m*.

occasion¹ [ə'keiʒ(ə)n] *n.* **1.** (*a*) sujet *m*, cause *f*, occasion *f*; **there's, you have, no o. to be alarmed,** il n'y a pas lieu de vous inquiéter; **should the o. arise,** s'il y a lieu; le cas échéant; (*b*) cause occasionnelle; cause immédiate. **2. occasions,** occupations *fpl*. **3.** occasion, occurrence *f*; **on this o.,** en cette occasion; **on the o. of his daughter's marriage,** à l'occasion du mariage de sa fille; **on one o.,** une fois; **on another o.,** une autre fois; **on several occasions,** à plusieurs reprises; **on rare occasions,** rarement; **on such an o.,** en pareille occasion; **on great occasions,** dans les grandes occasions; **words appropriate to the o.,** paroles de circonstance; **to be equal to the o.,** être à la hauteur de la situation; **to dress to suit the o.,** faire une toilette de circonstance; **we'll make this an o.,** nous allons fêter ça. **4.** (*opportunity*) **I'll speak to him on the first o.,** je lui parlerai à la prochaine occasion; **if you have o. to speak to him,** si vous avez l'occasion de lui parler.

occasion² *v.tr. O:* occasionner, entraîner (la mort, un incendie, etc.); donner lieu à (la peur, etc.).

occasional [ə'keiʒ(ə)n(ə)l] *a.* **1.** (*a*) (pièce, vers) de circonstance; (*b*) **o. table,** table volante; guéridon *m*; **o. chair,** chaise volante. **2.** (*of visits*) espacé; (*of incident*) qui se produit de temps en temps; **o. showers,** averses éparses. **-ally** *adv.* de temps en temps; parfois.

occident ['ɔksidənt] *n.* occident *m*, couchant *m*; *Pol: etc:* **the O.,** l'Occident.

occidental [ɔksi'dentl] *a.* occidental, -aux.

occipital [ɔk'sipitl] *a. & n. Anat:* occipital, -aux.

occiput ['ɔksipʌt] *n. Anat:* occiput *m*.

occlude [ɔ'klu:d] *v.tr.* (*a*) fermer, boucher (un orifice, etc.); occlure (les paupières); (*b*) *Ch:* (*of a metal*) absorber (et retenir) (un gaz); occlure (un gaz).

occlusion [ɔ'klu:ʒ(ə)n] *n.* **1.** (*a*) occlusion *f*, bouchage *m*, fermeture *f* (d'un conduit, etc.); (*b*) *Ch:* occlusion (d'un gaz). **2.** *Dent:* occlusion (molaire, etc.).

occlusive [ɔ'klu:siv] *a. & n. Ling:* **o. (consonant),** (consonne) occlusive (*f*).

occult [ɔ'kʌlt] **1.** *a.* occulte, secret, -ète; **the o. sciences,** les sciences *fpl* occultes. **2.** *n.* **the o.,** l'occulte *m*.

occultism ['ɔkəltizm] *n.* occultisme *m*.

occupancy ['ɔkjupənsi] *n.* **1.** *Jur:* possession *f* à titre de premier occupant. **2.** occupation *f*, habitation *f* (d'un immeuble).

occupant ['ɔkjupənt] *n.* **1.** (*a*) occupant, -ante (de terres); locataire *mf* (d'une maison); (*b*) *Jur:* premier occupant. **2.** voyageur *m*, passager *m* (d'une voiture, etc.). **3.** titulaire *mf* (d'un emploi).

occupation [ɔkju'peiʃ(ə)n] *n.* **1.** (*a*) occupation *f*; **to be in o. of a house,** occuper une maison; **house fit for o.,** maison habitable; (*b*) **army of o., o. troops,** armée *f*, troupes *fpl*, d'occupation; *Hist:* **the Roman o. of Britain,** l'occupation de la Grande-Bretagne par les Romains. **2.** (*a*) occupation; **to find s.o. (some) o.,** donner de l'occupation à qn; (*b*) métier *m*, emploi *m*, profession *f*.

occupational [ɔkju'peiʃ(ə)n(ə)l] *a.* **o. hazards,** risques *mpl* du métier; **o. disease,** maladie professionnelle; **o. therapy,** thérapeutique occupationnelle.

occupier ['ɔkjupaiər] *n.* occupant, -ante; locataire *mf*; habitant, -ante (d'une maison).

occupy ['ɔkjupai] *v.tr.* **1.** (*a*) occuper, habiter (une maison, etc.); (*b*) occuper, remplir (une fonction); (*c*) occuper (un pays ennemi); s'emparer (d'un point stratégique). **2.** (*a*) remplir (un espace); occuper (une place, l'attention); **this seat is occupied,** cette place est prise; (*b*) **to o. one's time (in, with,) doing sth.,** remplir, occuper, son temps à faire qch.; **his work occupies all his time,** son travail l'absorbe. **3.** occuper (qn); donner du travail à (qn); **to o. one's mind,** s'occuper l'esprit. **occupied** *a.* **1.** *Mil:* (territoire) occupé. **2. to be o. in, with, doing sth.,** être occupé à faire qch.; **gainfully o.,** salarié; **to keep one's mind o.,** s'occuper l'esprit.

occur [ə'kəːr] *v.i.* **(occurred) 1.** (*happen*) (*of event, etc.*) avoir lieu; survenir, arriver; se produire; (*of opportunity*) se présenter, s'offrir; (*of fire*) se déclarer; **this seldom occurs,** cela arrive rarement; **I hope it will not o. again,** j'espère que cela ne se répétera pas. **2.** (*to be met with*) (*of objects, types*) se rencontrer, se trouver, se présenter; **this word occurs twice in the letter,** ce mot se rencontre deux fois dans la lettre. **3.** (*of idea, etc.*) se présenter à l'esprit; **such an idea would never have occurred to me,** une pareille idée ne me serait jamais venue à l'esprit.

occurrence [ə'kʌrəns] *n.* **1. two hours before its o.,** deux heures avant que cela eût lieu; **to be of frequent o.,** arriver souvent; se produire fréquemment. **2.** événement *m*, fait *m*, occurrence *f*; **an everyday o.,** un fait journalier; **a singular o.,** un fait étrange.

ocean ['ouʃ(ə)n] *n.* océan *m.* **1. the Atlantic O.,** l'(océan) Atlantique (*m*); **o. floor,** fond sous-marin; **o. current,** courant *m* océanique. **2.** *Fig:* **an o. of sand,** une mer de sable.

ocean-going ['ouʃən'gouiŋ] *a.* (navire) au long cours, de haute mer.

Oceania [ouʃi'einiə] *Pr.n. Geog:* l'Océanie *f.*

oceanic [ouʃi'ænik] *a.* (voyage, climat) océanique.

oceanographer [ouʃə'nɔgrəfər] *n.* océanographe *mf.*

oceanography [ouʃə'nɔgrəfi] *n.* océanographie *f.*

ocelot ['ɔsəlɔt] *n. Z:* ocelot *m.*

ochre ['oukər] **1.** *n. Miner:* ocre *f*; **red o.,** ocre rouge; arcanne *f*; **yellow o.,** jaune *m* d'ocre; ocre jaune. **2.** *a.* **o.(-coloured),** ocre *inv*; ocreux.

o'clock [ə'klɔk] *adv.phr.* **one, two, o'c.,** une heure, deux heures; **the seven o'c. train,** le train de sept heures.

octagon ['ɔktəgən] *n. Mth:* octogone *m.*

octagonal [ɔk'tægən(ə)l] *a.* octogonal, -aux.

octahedral [ɔktə'hiːdrəl, -'hed-] *a.* octaédrique.

octahedron, *pl.* **-ons, -a** ['ɔktə'hiːdrən, -'hed-, -ənz, -ə] *n. Mth:* octaèdre *m.*

octane ['ɔktein] *n. Ch:* octane *m*; **o. number, rating,** indice *m* d'octane.

octave ['ɔktiv] *n. Ecc: Mus: Fenc:* octave *f*; *Pros:* huitain *m.*

octavo [ɔk'teivou] *a. & n. Typ:* in-octavo (*m*) *inv.*

octet [ɔk'tet] *n.* **1.** *Ch:* octet *m.* **2.** *Mus:* octuor *m.* **3.** *Pros:* huitain *m.*

October [ɔk'toubər] *n.* octobre *m*; **in O.,** au mois d'octobre; en octobre; **(on) the first, seventh, of O.,** le premier, le sept, octobre.

octogenarian ['ɔktədʒin'ɛəriən] *a. & n.* octogénaire (*mf*).

octopod ['ɔktəpɔd] *a. & n. Moll:* octopode (*m*).

octopus ['ɔktəpəs] *n. Moll:* poulpe *m*, pieuvre *f.*

octosyllabic [ɔktəsi'læbik] *a.* (vers, mot) octosyllabe, octosyllabique.

octuple [ɔk'tjuːpl] *a. & n.* octuple (*m*).

ocular ['ɔkjulər] **1.** *a.* (nerf, témoin, etc.) oculaire. **2.** *n. Opt:* oculaire *m* (de microscope, etc.).

oculist ['ɔkjulist] *n.* oculiste *mf.*

odalisk, odalisque ['oudəlisk] *n.* odalisque *f.*

odd [ɔd] *a.* **1.** (*a*) (nombre) impair; **to play at o. or even,** jouer à pair ou impair; (*b*) (i) (= *a slightly higher amount*) **a hundred o. sheep,** cent et quelques moutons; une centaine de moutons; **twenty pounds o., twenty o. pounds,** une vingtaine de livres; un peu plus de vingt livres; (ii) **a few o. grammes over,** quelques grammes de plus; **what shall we do with the o. six?** que ferons-nous avec les six qui restent? (*c*) **to be the o. man (out),** (i) être, rester, en surnombre; (ii) ne pas être du métier, de la partie; **to play at o.-man-out,** jouer à qui sera éliminé; **at o. moments,** dans mes, ses, moments perdus. **2.** (*a*) (*of one of a set*) dépareillé; (*of one of a pair*) déparié, disparate; **o. glove,** gant déparié, dépareillé; **o. stockings,** bas *mpl* qui ne vont pas ensemble; (*b*) quelconque; **any o. piece of cloth,** un bout d'étoffe quelconque; **at o. times,** par-ci par-là; **o. job man,** homme à tout faire; *Com:* **o. lot,** (i) solde *m*; (ii) *occ.* lot *m* d'appoint. **3.** (*a*) **o. size,** dimension spéciale, non courante; (*b*) singulier, drôle; (*of pers.*) excentrique, original; **o.-looking,** bizarre; **the o. thing about it is that . . .,** le curieux de l'affaire, ce qui est bizarre, c'est que . . .; **it's o. your not knowing about it,** il est curieux, singulier, que vous n'en sachiez rien; **how o. that he should have forgotten it!** comme c'est drôle qu'il l'ait oublié; **(well), that's o.!** voilà qui est singulier! c'est curieux! **-ly** *adv.* bizarrement, singulièrement; **o. enough nobody knew anything about it,** chose curieuse, personne n'en savait rien.

oddball ['ɔdbɔːl] *a. & n. NAm: P:* excentrique (*m*).

oddity ['ɔditi] *n.* **1.** (*a*) singularité *f*, bizarrerie *f*; (*b*) **he has some little oddities,** il a quelques petits travers. **2.** (*a*) personne excentrique; original, -ale; (*b*) chose *f* bizarre; curiosité *f.*

oddment ['ɔdmənt] *n.* article dépareillé; article en solde; coupon *m* d'étoffe; **oddments,** fins *fpl* de série, *Publ:* défets *mpl*; **remnants and oddments,** soldes *mpl* et occasions *fpl.*

oddness ['ɔdnis] *n.* singularité *f*, bizarrerie *f.*

odds [ɔdz] *n.pl.* (*occ. with sg. const.*) **1.** inégalité *f*; **to make o. evens,** égaliser les conditions, les avantages, etc.; répartir les choses également. **2.** (*a*) avantage *m*; chances *fpl*; **the o. are against him, in his favour,** les chances sont contre lui, pour lui; **to fight against great, long, o.,** lutter, combattre, contre des forces supérieures; avoir affaire à plus fort que soi; (*b*) différence *f*; **what's the o.?** qu'est-ce que ça fait? **it makes no o.,** ça ne fait rien; cela n'a pas d'importance; (*c*) *Turf:* **o. on, o. against, a horse,** cote *f* d'un cheval; **short, long, o.,** faible, forte, cote; **the o. are (at) ten to one,** la cote est à dix contre un; **odds-on-bet,** pari inégal; **odds-on favourite,** grand favori; **the o. are that he'll succeed,** il y a gros à parier qu'il réussira; (*d*) *Sp:* **to give s.o. o.,** donner l'avantage, donner de l'avance, à un concurrent. **3. to be at o. with s.o.,** (i) ne pas être d'accord avec qn; (ii) être brouillé avec qn. **4.** (*a*) **o. and ends,** petits bouts; chiffonneries *fpl.*

ode [oud] *n.* ode *f.*

odious ['oudiəs] *n.* odieux **(to,** à). **-ly** *adv.* odieusement.

odium ['oudiəm] *n.* **1.** réprobation *f*; détestation *f*; **to bring, cast, o. upon s.o.,** rendre qn odieux. **2.** caractère odieux; (l')odieux *m* (d'une action).

odometer [ou'dɔmitər] *n. Surv: etc:* odomètre *m.*

odontology [oudɔn'tɔlədʒi] *n.* odontologie *f.*

odor ['oudər] *n. NAm:* = ODOUR.

odoriferous [oudə'rifərəs] *a.* **1.** odoriférant; parfumé. **2.** *F:* malodorant.

odorous ['oudərəs] *a.* (*a*) odorant; qui exhale une odeur (agréable); (*b*) *F:* malodorant.

odour, *NAm:* **odor** ['oudər] *n.* **1.** (*a*) odeur *f*; **body o.,** odeur corporelle; (*b*) odeur (agréable); parfum *m*; (*c*) *F:* mauvaise odeur. **2. to be in good, bad, o. with s.o.,** être bien, mal, vu de qn; **to die in (the) o. of sanctity,** mourir en odeur de sainteté.

odourless, *NAm:* **odorless** ['oudəlis] *a.* inodore; sans odeur.

Odyssey ['ɔdisi] *n.* **the O.,** l'Odyssée *f*; **his journey was a real o.,** son voyage fut une véritable odyssée.

oedema, *NAm:* **edema** [i(ː)'diːmə] *n.* œdème *m.*

Oedipus ['iːdipəs] *Pr.n.m. Gr.Lit:* Œdipe; *Psy:* **O. complex,** complexe *m* d'Œdipe.

o'er [ɔːr, 'ouər] *prep.* = OVER 1.

oesophagus, *NAm:* **esophagus,** *pl.* **-gi, guses** [iː'sɔfəgəs, -gai, -gəsiz] *n. Anat:* œsophage *m.*

oestrogen ['iːstrədʒen] *n. Bio-Ch:* œstrogène *m.*

oestrous ['iːstrəs] *a.* (*of cycle, etc.*) œstral, -aux.

oestrus ['iːstrəs] *n.* œstrus *m.*

of [ɔv; *weak form*] *prep.* de. **1.** (*a*) (*indicating separation*) **south of,** au sud de; **within a mile of,** à moins d'un mille de; **free of,** libre de; **cured of,** guéri de; (*b*) (i) (*origin*) **of noble birth,** de naissance noble; **works of Shakespeare,** œuvres de Shakespeare; **to expect sth. of s.o.,** attendre, s'attendre à, qch. de qn; **to ask a favour of s.o.,** demander une faveur à qn; (ii) (*cause*) **of necessity,** par nécessité; **of one's own accord,** de soi-même; **of my own choice,** de mon propre choix; **she died of grief,** elle mourut de chagrin; **proud of sth.,** fier de qch; **I'm sick of it,** j'en ai assez. **2.** (*agency*) (*a*) *A:* **beloved of all,** aimé de tout le monde; (*b*) **it is very good, kind, of you,** c'est bien aimable de votre part, c'est très gentil à vous. **3.** (*a*) (*material*) **made of wood,** fait de, en, bois; **wall of stone,** mur en pierre; (*b*) **full of water,** plein d'eau. **4.** (*concerning, in respect of*) (*a*) (*introducing ind. obj. of verb*) **to think of s.o.,** penser à qn; **to warn s.o. of sth.,** avertir qn de qch.; **what do you think of him?** que pensez-vous de lui? (*b*) (*after adjs*) **guilty of,** coupable de; **capable of,** capable de; (*c*) **doctor of medicine,** docteur en médecine; (*d*) **well, what of** [ɔv] **it?** et bien, et après? **5.** (*a*) (i) **the city of Rome,** la cité de Rome; **man of genius,** homme de génie; **people of foreign appearance,** gens à l'air étranger; **child of ten,** enfant (âgé) de dix ans; *NAm:* **his wife of twenty years,** la femme qu'il a épousée il y a vingt ans; (ii) **to be of no account,** ne pas compter; **hard of hearing,** dur d'oreille; (*b*) **a fine figure of a woman,** une belle femme; **that fool of a sergeant,** cet imbécile de sergent; (*c*) **all of a tremble,** tout tremblant; **all of a sudden,** tout d'un coup, tout à coup. **6.** (*a*) **the love of a mother,** l'amour d'une mère; (*b*) **the fear of God,** la crainte de Dieu; **great drinker of whisky,** grand buveur de whisky. **7.** (*partitive*) (*a*) **three parts of the whole,** trois quarts du tout; *F:* **no more of that!** plus de cela! **how much of it do you want?** combien en voulez-vous? **many, several, of us,** beaucoup, plusieurs, d'entre nous; **there were two, several, of us,** nous étions deux, plusieurs; **he is one of us,** il est des nôtres; **one of the best,** un des meilleurs; **to give of one's best,** faire de son mieux; (*b*) **the best of men,** le meilleur des hommes; **the bravest of the brave,** le brave des braves; **first of all,** avant tout; (*c*) **he, of all men, of all people,** lui entre tous; **this day of all days,** ce jour entre tous; (*d*) **the Holy of Holies,** le saint des saints. **8.** (*a*) **the widow of a barrister,** la veuve d'un avocat; **citizen of London,** citoyen de Londres; **topic of conversation,** sujet de conversation; **the first of the month,** le premier du mois; (*b*) **he is a friend of mine,** c'est un de mes amis; **it's no business of yours,** cela ne vous regarde pas; ce n'est pas votre affaire. **9. of late years,** (pendant) ces dernières années; **of late,** dernièrement, récemment; depuis peu.

off¹ [ɔf] **I.** *adv.* **1.** (*away*) (*a*) **house a mile o.,** maison à un mille de distance; **some way o.,** à quelque distance; **far o.,** au loin; dans le lointain; (*b*) (*departure*) **to go o.,** *F:* **be o.,** s'en aller, partir; **I'm o. to London,** je pars pour Londres; **I must be o.,** (il faut que) je me sauve; **they're o.!** (i) les voilà partis! (ii) les voilà lancés! **to go o. (to sleep),** s'endormir; (*c*) *Nau:* au large; (*d*) *Th:* à la cantonade; **to speak o.,** parler à la cantonade. **2.** (*a*) **to take o. one's coat,** ôter son manteau; **a button has come o.,** un bouton a sauté; **to cut s.o.'s head o.,** décapiter qn; **to turn o. the gas,** fermer le gaz; (*at the main*) couper le gaz; *I.C.E:* **the ignition is o.,** l'allumage est coupé; (*in restaurant*) **this dish is o.,** ce plat est épuisé; **the deal is o.,** le marché est rompu, ne se fera pas; **it's all o., the whole thing is o.,** tout est rompu; *F:* l'affaire est tombée dans l'eau; (*b*) *F:* qui n'est plus frais; (*of meat*) avancé; **this beer's o.,** cette bière est éventée; **that's a bit o.!** ça c'est pas chic! (*c*) **to finish o. a piece of work,** achever un travail. **3. to be well, badly, o.,** être à l'aise, être pauvre; **to be badly o. for sth.,** être à court de qch.; **he is better o. where he is,** il est bien mieux où il est. **4.** *adv. phr.* **o. and on, on and o.,** par intervalles; à différentes reprises; de temps en temps; **right, straight, o.,** immédiatement, sur-le-champ, tout de suite. **II.** *prep.* **1.** (*a*) *usu.* de; **to fall o. sth.,** tomber de qch.; **to take a ring o. one's finger,** ôter une bague de son doigt; **to cut a slice o. sth.,** couper une tranche de qch.; **I dined o. a leg of lamb,** j'ai dîné d'une tranche de gigot; *El:* **to work o. the mains,** être branché sur le secteur; **a third o. everything,** rabais *m* d'un tiers sur tout; *adv.* **to allow 2% o.,** faire une réduction, une remise, de 2%; **to borrow money o. s.o.,** emprunter de l'argent à qn; (*b*) écarté de, éloigné de; **village o. the beaten track,** village éloigné, hors, du chemin battu; **street o. the main road,** rue qui donne sur la grande route; **to sing, play, o. key,** chanter, jouer, faux; *U.S: Mil:* **to put a public house o. limits,** consigner un café; **o. limits,** consigné à la troupe; (*c*) **to be o. one's food,** n'avoir pas d'appétit; **to have time o. (work),** avoir du temps de libre; **have you any time o. during the week?** avez-vous des heures libres, des loisirs, pendant la semaine? **to take some time o.,** prendre des loisirs; **day o.,** jour *m* de congé, de liberté; **to give the staff a day o.,** donner congé à son personnel pour la journée; **to arrange to take two days o.,** se libérer pour deux jours. **2.** *Nau:* (*a*) **o. the Cape,** à la hauteur du Cap; au large du Cap; (*b*) **to sail o. the wind,** naviguer vent largue. **3.** (*in compounds*) **o.-white,** blanc légèrement teinté, cassé. **III.** *a.* **1.** (*a*) *Equit:* **o. leg,** jambe *f* de dehors; (*b*) *Cr:* **o. drive,** coup *m* en avant à droite; (*c*) *Bookb:* **o. side, o. board,** verso *m*; plat inférieur. **2.** (*a*) **o. position,** position *f* de desserrage (des freins); *El:* position de rupture de circuit; position d'extinction (des lampes); position de repos; position "zéro", "fermé", "coupé"; (*b*) **o. day,** (i) jour *m* où l'on ne travaille pas; jour de chômage; (ii) jour où l'on n'est pas en train. **3.** *Adm:* **o. consumption,** consommation *f* (des boissons alcooliques) à domicile; **o. licence,** (i) licence *f* permettant exclusivement la vente de boissons alcoolisées à emporter; (ii) magasin *m*, bar *m*, où l'on peut acheter des boissons alcoolisées à emporter.

off² *n. F:* **the o.,** le départ.

offal ['ɔf(ə)l] *n.* **1.** (*a*) rebut *m*, déchets *mpl*; (*b*) immondices *fpl.* **2.** déchets d'abattage (de boucherie); (*edible*) abats *mpl*; (*inedible*) issues *fpl.*

offbeat ['ɔfbiːt] *a. F:* (*of pers., clothes, music*) original, excentrique..

off-centre, off-centred, *NAm:* **-center, -centered** [ɔf'sentər, -təd] *a.* décentré, décalé.

off-course ['ɔfkɔːs] *a.* (pari) effectué hors des champs de course.

offcut ['ɔfkʌt] *n.* découpure *f*; (*from wooden plank, length of cloth*) chute *f.*

offence, *NAm:* **offense** [ə'fens] *n.* **1.** (*a*) attaque *f*, agression *f*; (*b*) *NAm: Sp:* (i) attaque (d'une équipe); (ii) (l')attaque. **2.** blessure faite à la susceptibilité de qn; sujet *m* de mécontentement; **to cause o.,** déplaire; **to take o. (at sth.),** se froisser, se choquer (de qch.); **to take o. at the slightest thing,** s'offenser d'un rien; **to cause, to give, o. to s.o.,** offenser, blesser, froisser, qn; **I meant no o.,** je ne voulais offenser personne. **3.** (*a*) offense *f*, faute *f*; **minor, serious, o.,** faute légère, grave; **to commit an o. against the law,** commettre une infraction; (*b*) *Jur:* **indictable o.,** violation *f* de loi; crime ou délit; acte délictueux; **petty, minor, o.,** contravention *f* (de simple police); **capital o.,** crime capital; **second o.,** récidive *f*.

offend [ə'fend] **1.** *v.i.* (*a*) pécher; (*b*) **to o. against the law,** violer, enfreindre, la loi; **to o. against (the laws of) grammar,** offenser la grammaire. **2.** *v.tr.* (*a*) offenser, blesser, choquer (qn); **to be offended at, with, by, sth.,** se froisser, s'offenser, de qch.; **to be easily offended,** être très susceptible; se froisser facilement; (*b*) (*of thg*) **to o. the eye,** choquer les regards, la vue; **harsh sound that offends the ear,** son aigre qui offense l'oreille. **offended** *a.* **1.** fâché, froissé; **in an o. tone of voice,** d'une voix offensée. **2.** *Jur:* **the o. party,** l'offensé, -ée. **offending** *a.* offensant, fautif.

offender [ə'fendər] *n.* **1.** (*a*) pécheur, -eresse; (*b*) *Jur:* délinquant, -ante, malfaiteur, -trice; **a first o.,** un délinquant primaire. **2.** offenseur *m*; **she is the o.,** c'est elle qui est l'offenseur.

offense [ə'fens] *n. NAm:* = OFFENCE.

offensive [ə'fensiv] **1.** *a.* (*a*) *Mil: etc:* offensif; (*b*) (*of word, action*) offensant, blessant, choquant; (spectacle) repoussant; (odeur) nauséabonde; **book that is morally o.,** livre outrageant pour les bonnes mœurs; (*c*) (*of pers.*) **to be o. to s.o.,** insulter qn; injurier qn; **in an o. tone,** d'un ton injurieux. **2.** *n. Mil: Sp:* offensive *f*; **to take the o.,** prendre l'offensive. **-ly** *adv.* **1.** *Mil: Sp:* offensivement. **2.** (*a*) d'une manière offensante, choquante; (*b*) d'un ton injurieux.

offensiveness [ə'fensivnis] *n.* **1.** nature offensante (d'un spectacle, d'un son, d'une odeur). **2.** nature injurieuse (d'une réponse, etc.).

offer¹ ['ɔfər] *n.* (*a*) offre *f*, proposition *f*; *Com:* **to make an o. for sth.,** faire une offre pour qch.; **on o.,** en vente; **special o.,** article *m* (en) réclame; **bargain o.,** offre avantageuse; occasion *f*; *NAm:* **job offers,** offres d'emploi; (*b*) **o. of marriage,** demande *f* en mariage.

offer² **1.** *v.tr.* (*a*) offrir (qch., ses services); présenter (des excuses); tendre (la main); **to o. s.o. sth.,** offrir qch. à qn; **to o. up a sacrifice,** offrir un sacrifice; **he was offered a job,** on lui a offert un emploi; **house offered for sale,** maison mise en vente; **the conditions that we are able to o. you,** les conditions que nous sommes à même de vous faire; **to o. to do sth.,** faire l'offre, offrir, de faire qch.; (*b*) faire (une remarque); avancer (une opinion); proposer (une définition); *Jur:* **to o. a plea,** exciper d'une excuse; (*c*) (*of thg*) offrir, présenter (un beau spectacle); (*of scheme, etc.*) présenter (des difficultés, des avantages); (*d*) essayer, tenter; **to o. resistance,** offrir de la résistance. **2.** *v.i.* (*of occasion, etc.*) s'offrir, se présenter; **if a good occasion offers,** s'il s'offre une belle occasion. **offering** *n.* **1.** (*action*) offre *f*. **2.** (*thg offered*) offre; *Ecc:* offrande *f*; **burnt o.,** (i) holocauste *m*; (ii) *F:* viande brûlée, calcinée; plat brûlé.

offertory ['ɔfət(ə)ri] *n. Ecc:* **1.** offertoire *m* (de la messe). **2.** (*a*) quête *f* (de l'offrande); **o. box,** tronc *m*; (*b*) montant *m* de la quête.

offhand **1.** *adv.* [ɔf'hænd] (*a*) sur-le-champ; au premier abord; à première vue; (*b*) sans cérémonie, sans façon; brusquement. **2.** *a. before noun* ['ɔfhænd]; *following verb* [ɔf'hænd]; (*a*) spontané, improvisé; (*b*) brusque, cavalier; sans cérémonie, sans façon(s); **to be o. with s.o.,** se montrer désinvolte à l'égard de qn; **to treat s.o. in an o. manner,** traiter qn cavalièrement, avec désinvolture.

offhanded [ɔf'hændid] *a.* = OFFHAND 2 (*b*). **-ly** *adv.* = OFFHAND 1 (*b*).

offhandedness [ɔf'hændidnis] *n.* brusquerie *f*; désinvolture *f*.

office ['ɔfis] *n.* **1.** (*a*) office *m*, service *m*; **through, owing to, the good offices of a friend,** grâce aux bons offices, par les bons soins, d'un ami; (*b*) **last offices,** (i) derniers devoirs (rendus à un mort); (ii) obsèques *fpl*. **2.** (*a*) fonctions *fpl*, devoir; **to fill the o. of secretary,** faire office de secrétaire; (*b*) charge *f*, fonctions; **high o.,** fonctions élevées; haute charge; **public o.,** fonctions publiques; **to be in o., to hold o.,** (i) remplir un emploi; être en charge; (ii) (*of government*) être au pouvoir; **to take o., to come into o.,** (i) entrer en fonctions; (ii) (*of government*) prendre le pouvoir. **3.** *Ecc:* **o. of the day,** office du jour; **o. for the dead,** office des morts. **4.** (*a*) bureau *m*; (*lawyer's*) étude *f*; **business o.,** bureau commercial; **head o., registered offices (of company),** siège principal, social; **complaints o.,** bureau, service *m*, des réclamations; *Post: NAm: Tp:* **the central o.,** le central; **o. building, block,** immeuble *m* de bureaux; **o. equipment,** matériel *m* de bureau; **o. hours,** heures *fpl* de bureau; **for o. use only,** (cadre) réservé à l'administration; **o. work,** travail *m* de bureau; **o. worker,** employé, -ée, de bureau; (*b*) **private o.,** cabinet particulier; **the manager's o.,** le bureau du directeur; **the secretary's o.,** le secrétariat; (*c*) **government o.,** ministère *m* (d'État); **the Home O.** = le ministère de l'Intérieur; **the Foreign O.** = le ministère des Affaires étrangères; (*d*) **insurance o.,** compagnie *f* d'assurances; (*e*) *NAm:* cabinet *m* de consultation (d'un médecin, d'un dentiste); (*f*) **offices (of a house),** communs *mpl* et dépendances *fpl*.

office-holder ['ɔfishouldər] *n. NAm:* employé *m* de l'État; fonctionnaire *m*.

officer ['ɔfisər] *n.* **1.** (*a*) fonctionnaire *m*; officier *m*; **municipal o.,** officier municipal; *Adm:* **clerical o.,** secrétaire *m* d'administration; **administrative o.** = administrateur civil; **customs o.,** douanier *m*; **police o.,** *U.S:* **o.,** agent *m*, officier, de police; *Adm:* gardien *m* de la paix; (*b*) membre *m* du bureau (d'une société). **2.** *Mil: etc:* (*a*) officier; **army, naval, o.,** officier de l'armée de terre, officier de marine; **field o.,** officier supérieur; (*in Merchant Navy*) **first o.,** (commandant en) second (*m*); **radio o.,** radionavigant *m*; (*b*) officier, *f.* officière (de l'Armée du Salut). **3. high o.,** grand dignitaire (d'un ordre).

official [ə'fiʃ(ə)l] **1.** *a.* (*a*) officiel; (langage) administratif; (style) bureaucratique; **o. letter,** pli officiel, de service; *Post:* **o. paid,** en franchise postale; **to act in one's o. capacity,** agir dans l'exercice de ses fonctions; (*b*) (*of statement, etc.*) officiel; *Fin:* **o. quotation,** cote officielle; *Sp:* **o. record,** record homologué; (*c*) titulaire; **the o. organist,** le titulaire de l'orgue; (*d*) *Med:* officinal, -aux; autorisé par la pharmacopée. **2.** *n.* (*a*) fonctionnaire *m*; *Pej:* bureaucrate *m*; **minor officials,** petits fonctionnaires; **the o. at the entrance,** le préposé à l'entrée; **railway, post-office, o.,** employé *m* des chemins de fer, des Postes; (*b*) (i) (*at sports meeting, etc.*) commissaire *m*; (ii) *Sp: U.S:* arbitre *m*. **-ally** *adv.* officiellement.

officialdom [ə'fiʃ(ə)ldəm] *n.* **1.** l'administration *f*. **2.** bureaucratie *f*, fonctionnarisme *m*.

officialese [əfiʃə'li:z] *n. F:* jargon administratif.

officialism [ə'fiʃəlizm] *n.* bureaucratie *f*, fonctionnarisme *m*, chinoiseries *fpl* (de l'administration).

officiate [ə'fiʃieit] *v.i.* **1.** *Ecc:* **to o. at a service,** officier à un office; **to o. at a church,** desservir une église; **officiating minister,** (ministre) officiant (*m*). **2.** *O:* **to o. as host,** remplir, exercer, les fonctions d'hôte.

officious [ə'fiʃəs] *a.* **1.** empressé; trop zélé; officieux. **2.** (*unofficial*) officieux. **-ly** *adv.* **1.** avec trop de zèle; **to behave o.,** faire l'empressé. **2.** (*unofficially*) officieusement; à titre officieux.

offing ['ɔfiŋ] *n.* **in the o.,** au large; *Fig:* **a general election is in the o.,** une élection générale est en vue.

offload [ɔf'loud] *v.tr.* débarquer (un excédent de marchandises, etc.); *F:* **he offloads most of his work on his colleagues,** il se décharge de la plupart de son travail sur ses collègues.
offpeak ['ɔf'pi:k] *a.* **o. hours,** heures creuses, hors pointe; *El:* **o. tariff,** tarif *m* de nuit; *Rail:* **o. fare,** billet *m* à prix réduit.
offprint ['ɔfprint] *n.* tirage *m* à part; tiré *m* à part.
off-putting [ɔf'putiŋ] *a.* **1.** (événement) déconcertant, déroutant. **2.** (caractère) répugnant.
offscreen ['ɔfskri:n] *adv. & a. Cin:* **o., he's a modest man,** dans le privé c'est un type modeste.
offseason ['ɔfsi:z(ə)n] **1.** *n.* morte-saison *f, pl.* mortes-saisons. **2.** *adv.* pendant la morte-saison. **3.** *a.* (tarif, etc.) hors-saison.
offset¹ ['ɔfset] *n.* **1.** *Hort:* rejeton *m.* **2.** repoussoir *m.* **3.** (*a*) compensation *f,* dédommagement *m;* **as an o. to my losses,** en compensation de mes pertes; (*b*) *Book-k:* compensation (d'une écriture). **4.** (*a*) *Arch:* ressaut *m,* saillie *f;* retrait *m* (d'un mur); (*b*) *Mec.E: etc:* désaxage *m,* décalage *m,* décentrement *m;* (*c*) rebord *m* (de piston, etc.); bord biseauté (d'une roue); (*d*) double coude *m,* siphon *m* (d'un tuyau, etc.). **5.** *Surv:* perpendiculaire *f;* ordonnée *f.* **6.** (*a*) *Typ:* maculage *m;* (*b*) *Phot.Engr:* offset *m;* **printed in o.,** tiré en offset.
offset² *v.tr.* (*p.t. & p.p.* **offset;** *pr.p* **-setting**) (*a*) compenser (ses pertes); (*b*) *Mec.E:* désaxer, décentrer (une roue); déporter, décaler (un organe); (*c*) faire déborder (une pièce); (*d*) prévoir un dégagement, une courbure, à (un outil); faire un double coude à (un tuyau); (*e*) *Typ:* imprimer (un livre) en offset.
offshoot ['ɔfʃu:t] *n.* rejeton *m* (d'un arbre, d'une famille); *Fig:* ramifications *fpl.*
offshore ['ɔfʃɔ:r] **1.** *adv.* vers le large, au large. **2.** *a.* (*a*) **o. wind,** vent *m* de terre, d'aval; (*b*) (i) côtier, littoral; **o. fishing,** pêche côtière; (ii) éloigné de la côte; *Petr:* (prospection, forage) en mer; **o. installations,** installations pétrolières marines; (*c*) **o. purchases,** achats *mpl* à l'étranger.
offside 1. *n.* ['ɔfsaid] (i) *Equit:* côté *m* hors montoir; (ii) *Turf:* extérieur de la piste; (iii) *Aut:* (*in Britain*) côté droit; (*in France, U.S.*) côté gauche. **2.** *a.* ['ɔfsaid] *Sp:* hors jeu; **the o. rule,** la règle du hors jeu. **3.** *adv.* [ɔf'said] hors jeu.
offspring ['ɔfspriŋ] *n.* **1.** *coll.* (*a*) *Nat.Hist:* progéniture *f,* descendance *f,* descendants *mpl;* (*b*) enfants *mpl.* **2.** (*a*) descendant, rejeton *m;* (*b*) **the o. of much research,** le fruit de beaucoup de recherches.
offstage [ɔf'steidʒ] *adv. & a.* **1.** (parler, fracas, etc.) derrière la toile. **2.** (*of actor*) **his life o., his o. life,** sa vie privée. **3.** (*of work*) en secret.
offstreet ['ɔfstri:t] *a.* **o. parking,** (stationnement *m* dans un) parking.
oft [ɔft] *adv. Poet:* souvent; **many a time and o.,** maintes et maintes fois.
often ['ɔf(t)ən] *adv.* souvent, fréquemment; **I don't see him very o. now,** je ne le vois plus guère; **how o.?** (i) combien de fois? (ii) tous les combien? *F:* **how o. have I told you!** combien de fois ne vous l'ai-je pas dit! **as o. as I saw him,** toutes les fois, chaque fois, que je l'ai vu; **as o. as not, more o. than not,** assez souvent, le plus souvent; **every so o.,** de temps en temps; de temps à autre; **it cannot be too o. repeated,** on ne saurait trop le répéter; **once too o.,** une fois de trop.
ogee ['oudʒi:] *n. Arch:* **o. (moulding),** cimaise *f,* talon *m;* **o. arch,** arc *m* en accolade.
ogival [ou'dʒaiv(ə)l] *a. Arch:* ogival, -aux.
ogive ['oudʒaiv] *n. Arch:* ogive *f.*
ogle¹ ['ougl] *n.* œillade (amoureuse); lorgnade *f.*
ogle² 1. *v.tr.* lorgner, guigner (qn); lancer des œillades à (qn); faire les yeux doux à (qn). **2.** *v.i.* jouer de la prunelle; lancer des œillades.
ogre, *f.* **ogress** ['ougər, -gris] *n.* ogre, *f.* ogresse.
oh [ou] *int.* (*expressing surprise, etc.*) ô, oh; **oh how tired I am!** ah! que je suis fatigué!
ohm [oum] *n. El:* ohm *m.*
oil¹ [ɔil] *n.* huile *f.* **1.** (*a*) **vegetable o.,** huile végétale; **olive, groundnut, o.,** huile d'olive, d'arachide; **linseed o.,** huile (de graine) de lin; **edible o., cooking o.,** huile comestible, de cuisine; **to cook in, with, o.,** faire la cuisine à l'huile; **fried in o.,** frit à l'huile; (*b*) **o. paint,** peinture *f* à l'huile; **to paint in oils,** peindre à l'huile; **o. painting,** peinture *f* à l'huile; (*c*) *Ecc:* **holy o.,** les saintes huiles (pour l'extrême onction, etc.); (*d*) *Fig:* **to burn the midnight o.,** travailler fort avant dans la nuit; **it smells of the midnight o.,** cela sent l'huile; **to add o. to the flames,** jeter de l'huile sur le feu; **to pour o. on troubled waters,** calmer la tempête. **2.** **whale o.,** huile de baleine; **sperm o.,** huile de blanc de baleine; **cod-liver o.,** huile de foie de morue. **3.** (*a*) **mineral o.,** huile minérale; pétrole *m;* **crude o.,** pétrole brut; **fuel o.,** (i) pétrole; (ii) mazout *m;* **o. (-fired) heating,** chauffage au mazout; **o. refinery,** raffinerie *f* de pétrole; **o. rig,** derrick *m;* (*offshore*) plate-forme *f* de forage; **o. well,** puits *m* pétrolifère; **o. tanker,** pétrolier *m;* (*b*) *St.Exch:* **o. shares, oils,** valeurs *fpl* pétrolières; pétroles; (*c*) *Tchn:* **lubricating o.,** huile à graisser, de graissage; *Mec.E:* **motor o.,** huile à moteur; **o. cooling,** refroidissement *m* par huile. **4.** **essential o.,** huile essentielle; essence *f;* **o. of cloves, of lavender,** essence de girofle, de lavande.
oil² 1. *v.tr.* (*a*) huiler, graisser, lubrifier (une machine); **to o. the wheels,** graisser les roues; *F:* faciliter les choses; (*b*) huiler (la toile, etc.). **2.** *v.i.* (*a*) (*of butter*) devenir huileux; (*b*) *Nau:* faire le plein de mazout. **3.** **to o. up,** (*a*) *v.tr.* encrasser (d'huile); (*b*) *v.i.* (*of sparking plug, etc.*) s'encrasser (d'huile). **oiled** *a.* (*a*) huilé; graissé; *F:* **to be well o.,** être (un peu) éméché; (*b*) (papier) huilé; **o. silk,** taffetas *m* imperméable. **oiling** *n.* **1.** (*a*) graissage *m,* huilage *m* (d'un mécanisme, etc.); (*b*) enduisage *m* (d'un nageur, etc.) de graisse. **2.** **o. up,** encrassement *m* (d'une bougie d'allumage, etc.).
oil-bearing ['ɔilbɛəriŋ] *a. Geol:* pétrolifère.
oilcake ['ɔilkeik] *n.* (*a*) tourteau *m* de lin; (*b*) tourte *f* pour engrais.
oilcan ['ɔilkæn] *n.* **1.** (*a*) (i) bidon *m,* (ii) broc *m,* à huile; (*b*) estagnon *m* à huile. **2.** *Tls:* burette *f.*
oilcloth ['ɔilklɔθ] *n.* toile cirée.
oil-cooled ['ɔilku:ld] *a.* refroidi par l'huile.
oiler ['ɔilər] *n.* **1.** (*pers.*) graisseur *m.* **2.** (*a*) burette *f* à huile; (*b*) *Mec.E:* (i) graisseur; (ii) godet graisseur, de graissage. **3.** *Nau:* pétrolier *m.*
oilfield ['ɔilfi:ld] *n.* gisement *m,* champ *m,* pétrolifère.
oiliness ['ɔilinis] *n.* **1.** état graisseux; aspect graisseux. **2.** *Pej:* onctuosité (de qn).
oilpaper ['ɔilpeipər] *n.* papier huilé.
oil-producing ['ɔilprədju:siŋ] *a.* **1.** (*of plant*) oléifère; (*of substance, etc.*) oléifiant. **2.** (*of shale, etc.*) pétrolifère; (pays) producteur de pétrole.
oilskin ['ɔilskin] *n.* **1.** toile cirée. **2.** (*garment*) ciré *m.*
oilstone ['ɔilstoun] *n. Tls:* pierre *f* à huile (pour affûter); pierre à morfiler, à repasser; affiloir *m.*
oily ['ɔili] *a.* **1.** huileux; gras, *f.* grasse; graisseux; (papier) imprégné d'huile. **2.** (*of manner, etc.*) onctueux; (voix) grasse.
ointment ['ɔintmənt] *n.* onguent *m,* pommade *f;* *Fig:* **a fly in the o.,** un cheveu (dans la soupe).
O.K.¹, okay¹ ['ou'kei] *F:* **1.** *a.* correct, exact; **everything's O.K.,** tout est en règle; **that's O.K. by me,** d'accord! **O.K.!** bon! d'accord! (*on document*) **O.K.,** vu et approuvé. **2.** *n.* **to give one's O.K. to sth.,** approuver (une commande); contresigner, parafer (un ordre); **to give the O.K.,** donner le feu vert.

O.K.[2] **(O.K.'d), okay**[2] *v.tr. F:* passer, approuver (une commande); contresigner, parafer (un ordre).
okapi [ə'kɑːpi] *n. Z:* okapi *m.*
okey-doke, okey-dokey, okie-doke, okie-dokey [ouki'douk(i)] *int. P:* ça va! d'accord!
okra ['ɔkrə] *n. Bot:* okra *m.*
old [ould] *a.* **1.** (*a*) (*aged*) vieux; (*in sing. before a qualified noun beginning with a vowel or h "mute"*) vieil *or* vieux; *f.* vieille; *pl.* vieux, *f.* vieilles; âgé; **my o. friend,** mon vieil ami; **a man is as o. as he feels,** on a l'âge de ses artères; **to be growing, getting o.,** prendre de l'âge; vieillir; **to grow older,** vieillir; **an o. man,** un homme âgé, un vieillard; **an o. woman,** une vieille femme; *F:* une vieille; **o. people, old folk(s),** les vieux; *n.pl.* **o. and young,** grands et petits; **o. age,** la vieillesse; **to die at a good o. age,** mourir à un âge avancé; **he's saving for his o. age,** il économise pour ses vieux jours; (*b*) (*of thg*) **o. clothes,** vieux habits; **o. clothes man, woman,** fripier, -ière; **o. clothes shop,** friperie *f*; **o. wine,** vin vieux. **2. how o. are you?** quel âge avez-vous? **the oldest of the tribe,** l'aîné, -ée, de la tribu; **to be five years o.,** avoir cinq ans; être âgé de cinq ans; **he is older than I am,** il est plus âgé que moi; **at six years o.,** à (l'âge de) six ans; **a two-year-o. child,** *n.* **a two-year-o.,** un enfant (âgé) de deux ans; **to be o. enough to do sth.,** être d'âge à faire qch. **3.** (*a*) (*long-established*) vieux, ancien; (famille) de vieille souche; (dette) d'ancienne date; **he's an o. friend of mine,** c'est un de mes vieux amis; **an o. story,** une vieille histoire; **that's an o. dodge,** c'est un coup classique; (*b*) (*experienced*) vieux; **o. hand,** ouvrier expérimenté; *Nau:* vétéran *m*; **to be an o. hand at sth.,** avoir le coup pour faire qch.; (*c*) **to go over o. ground,** revenir sur un terrain déjà parcouru. **4.** (*former*) ancien; (*a*) **o. boy, girl, pupil,** ancien élève, ancienne élève; **the o.-boy net(work)** = la franc-maçonnerie des grandes écoles; **o. memories,** souvenirs *mpl* (i) du temps passé, (ii) de jeunesse; **in the o. days,** autrefois; dans le temps; (*b*) **the O. World,** l'ancien monde; **O. English, French,** l'ancien anglais, français; **the O. Testament,** l'Ancien Testament. **5.** *F:* (*a*) (*with* **any**) **any o. how,** n'importe comment; **any o. thing,** n'importe quoi; (*b*) **o. man, chap, fellow, boy,** mon vieux, mon pote; *F:* **the o. man,** (i) papa; (ii) le patron; (iii) *Nau:* le capitaine; (iv) *Mil:* le colonel; *P:* **my o. man,** mon homme; **the o. woman, lady,** ma femme; *P:* la bourgeoise; (*c*) *F:* **your o. book,** ton bouquin; **your o. bike,** ton clou. **6. of o.,** (*a*) *adj.phr.* ancien, d'autrefois; *Lit:* **in the days of o.,** autrefois, au temps jadis; (*b*) *adv.phr.* (i) jadis, autrefois; (ii) **I know him of o.,** je le connais depuis longtemps.
olden ['ould(ə)n] *a. Lit:* **in o. times,** au temps jadis.
old-established ['ouldis'tæbliʃt] *a.* ancien; établi depuis longtemps.
olde-worlde [ouldi'wəːldi] *a.* (maison, village, etc.) qui a un aspect factice d'antan.
oldfashioned [ould'fæʃ(ə)nd] **1.** *a.* (*a*) (*of dress, hat, etc.*) (i) vieille mode; (ii) démodé; passé de mode; **o. Christmas,** Noël à l'ancienne mode; (*b*) (i) (*of pers.*) partisan, -ane, des anciens usages; (*of manner*) de l'ancien temps; (ii) (*of ideas*) arriéré, vieillot, vieux jeu; (*c*) *F:* **o. look,** regard *m* de travers. **2.** *n.* cocktail composé de whisky, d'amers, de sucre et d'eau de seltz.
oldie ['ouldi] *n. F:* **1.** vieillard, -arde. **2.** vieillerie *f*, antiquaille *f*; *NAm:* ancienne chanson populaire.
oldish ['ouldiʃ] *a.* vieillot, -otte; assez vieux, vieille.
old-standing [ould'stændiŋ] *a.* ancien; (dette, etc.) d'ancienne date.
oldster ['ouldstər] *n. NAm:* vieillard *m*, vieille *f.*
old-style ['ould'stail] *a.* à l'ancienne mode; *Hist:* **the o.-s. calendar,** le calendrier ancien style.
old-time ['ouldtaim] *a.* du temps jadis; **o.-t. dancing,** danses *fpl* du bon vieux temps.
old-world [ould'wəːld] *a.* **1.** (*a*) des temps anciens; de l'ancien temps; (*b*) de l'ancien monde opposé (i) au monde moderne, (ii) à l'Amérique. **2.** (village) qui n'a pas changé au cours des siècles.
oleander [ouli'ændər] *n. Bot:* oléandre *m*; laurier-rose *m*, *pl.* lauriers-rose(s).
oleograph ['ouliougræf] *n. Lith:* oléographie *f.*
olfactory [ɔl'fæktəri] *a.* (bulbe, nerf, etc.) olfactif.
oligarchic(al) [ɔli'gɑːkik(l)] *a.* oligarchique.
oligarchy ['ɔligɑːki] *n.* oligarchie *f.*
olive ['ɔliv] *n.* **1. o. (tree),** olivier *m*; *B.Hist:* **the Mount of Olives,** le Mont, le Jardin, des Oliviers; **o. grove, plantation,** oliv(er)aie; **o. grower,** oléiculteur *m*; **o. branch,** rameau *m* d'olivier; **to hold out the o. branch,** présenter l'olivier. **2.** olive *f*; **o. oil,** huile *f* d'olive. **3. o. (wood),** (bois d')olivier. **4.** *Cu:* **meat o.,** paupiette *f.* **5.** *a.* (*a*) **o. (green),** (vert) olive *inv*; (*b*) (teint, etc.) olivâtre.
Oliver ['ɔlivər] *Pr.n.m.* Olivier.
olympiad [ə'limpiæd] *n. Gr.Ant: Sp:* olympiade *f.*
Olympian [ə'limpiən] **1.** *a.* (air, calme, etc.) olympien; (dieu) de l'Olympe. **2.** *n.* Olympien, -ienne.
Olympic [ə'limpik] **1.** *a. Gr.Ant: Sp:* (stade, etc.) olympique; **the O. Games,** les jeux *mpl* olympiques. **2.** *n.pl. F:* **the Olympics,** les Jeux olympiques.
Olympus [ə'limpəs] *Pr.n.* l'Olympe *m.*
ombudsman, *pl.* **-men** ['ɔmbudzmən] *n.* ombudsman *m*; *Belg:* commissaire *m* du Parlement.
omega ['oumigə] *n. Gr.Alph:* oméga *m.*
omelet(te) ['ɔmlit] *n. Cu:* omelette *f*; **ham o.,** omelette au jambon.
omen[1] ['oumen] *n.* présage *m*, augure *m*, pronostic *m*, auspice *m*; **to take sth. as a good o.,** prendre qch. à bon augure; **bird of ill o.,** oiseau *m* de mauvais augure; messager *m* de malheur.
omen[2] *v.tr.* augurer, présager.
ominous ['ɔminəs] *a.* de mauvais augure; sinistre; inquiétant; **o.-looking sky,** ciel menaçant; **an o. silence,** un silence lourd de menaces; **I heard an o. crack,** j'entendis un craquement qui ne présageait rien de bon. **-ly** *adv.* d'une façon menaçante, inquiétante.
omission [ə'miʃ(ə)n] *n.* **1.** omission *f* (d'un mot, etc.); *Com:* **errors and omissions excepted,** sauf erreur ou omission. **2.** négligence *f*, oubli *m*; *Theol:* omission; *Theol:* **sin of o.,** péché *m*, faute *f*, d'omission. **3.** *Typ:* bourdon *m.*
omit [ə'mit, ou'mit] *v.tr.* (**omitted**) **1.** (*a*) omettre (des détails); (*b*) *Typ:* bourdonner (un mot). **2. to o. to do sth.,** oublier, omettre, de faire qch.; manquer à faire qch.; **not to o. to do sth.,** ne pas manquer de faire qch.
omnibus, *pl.* **-uses** ['ɔmnibəs, -bəsiz] **1.** *n. A:* (*a*) **(horse) o.,** omnibus *m*; (*b*) **motor o.,** (*now usu.* **bus**), autobus *m.* **2.** *a. Publ:* **o. volume, edition,** gros recueil (de contes, de poèmes, etc.); publication *f* en un volume de plusieurs ouvrages d'un auteur; *n.* **detective o.,** recueil de romans policiers.
omnidirectional ['ɔmnidi'rekʃən(ə)l] *a. Rad: W.Tel:* (*of aerial*) omnidirectionnel.
omnipotence [ɔm'nipətəns] *n.* omnipotence *f*; toute-puissance *f.*
omnipotent [ɔm'nipətənt] **1.** *a.* omnipotent; tout-puissant, *pl.* tout-puissants. **2.** *n.* **the O.,** le Tout-Puissant.
omnipresence [ɔmni'prezəns] *n.* omniprésence *f.*
omnipresent [ɔmni'prezənt] *a.* omniprésent.
omniscience [ɔm'nisiəns] *n.* omniscience *f.*
omniscient [ɔm'nisiənt] *a.* omniscient.
omnivorous [ɔm'nivərəs] *a.* omnivore; *F:* (lecteur) insatiable, qui lit de tout.

on [ɔn] I. *prep.* **1.** (*a*) *usu.* sur; **on the table,** sur la table; **do not tread on it,** ne marchez pas dessus; **on the high seas,** en haute mer; **room on the second floor,** chambre du second; **on the train,** dans le train; (*b*) **on foot, horseback,** à pied, à cheval; **on a bicycle,** à bicyclette; **he had his rucksack on his back,** il portait le sac au dos; (*c*) (*member of*) **to be on the committee,** être membre du comité; **to be on a newspaper,** être attaché à la rédaction d'un journal; (*d*) **to swear sth. on the Bible,** jurer qch. sur la Bible. **2.** (*a*) **hanging on the wall,** pendu au mur; **on the ceiling,** au plafond; **he has a ring on his finger,** il a une bague au doigt; **have you any money on you?** avez-vous de l'argent sur vous? **dog on the lead,** chien en laisse; **to be on the phone,** (i) parler, être, au téléphone; (ii) avoir le téléphone; **he played it on his violin,** il l'a joué sur son violon; **on page four,** à la quatrième page, à la page quatre; (*b*) (*proximity*) **house on the main road,** maison sur la grande route; *NAm:* **he lives on Sixth Avenue,** il habite dans l'avenue VI; **just on a year ago,** il y a près d'un an; **just on £5,** tout près de cinq livres. **3.** (*direction*) (*a*) **on (to),** sur, à; **room that looks on (to) the street,** pièce qui donne sur la rue; (*b*) **on the right, left,** à droite, à gauche; **on this side,** de ce côté; (*c*) **to march on London,** avancer vers, sur, Londres; **to turn one's back on s.o.,** tourner le dos à qn; (*d*) **to hit s.o. on the head,** frapper qn sur la tête; **shame on you!** quelle honte! **4. based on a fact,** fondé sur un fait; **to have sth. on good authority,** savoir qch. de source certaine, de bonne part; **arrested on a charge of murder,** arrêté sous l'inculpation de meurtre; **on pain, penalty, of death,** sous peine de mort; **on (an) average,** en moyenne; **tax on tobacco,** impôt sur le tabac; **interest on capital,** intérêt du capital; **to retire on a pension of £x a year,** prendre sa retraite avec une pension de £x par an; **to be on half-pay,** être en demi-solde; **on condition that . . .,** à condition que + *sub.* **5.** (*in expressions of time*) (*a*) (*preposition omitted in French*) **on Sunday,** dimanche; **on Sundays,** le(s) dimanche(s); **on the day of my arrival,** le jour de mon arrivée; **on the following day,** le lendemain; **on April 3rd,** le trois avril; (*b*) **on a fine day in June,** par une belle journée de juin; **on and after the fifteenth,** à partir du quinze; **on or about the twelfth,** vers le douze; **on that occasion,** à, dans, cette occasion; **on the death of his mother,** à la mort de sa mère; **on my arrival,** à mon arrivée; **on application,** sur demande; **on examination,** après examen; **payable on sight,** payable à vue; (*c*) **on (my) entering the room,** quand j'entrai, en entrant, dans la pièce; à, dès, mon entrée dans la salle; (*d*) **on time, on the minute,** ponctuel, à l'heure, à la minute. **6.** (*manner*) **on the cheap,** à bon marché; **on the sly,** en sourdine, en catimini. **7.** (*state*) en; **on sale,** en vente; **on tap,** en perce. **8.** (*about, concerning*) **a book on France,** un livre sur la France; **a lecture on history,** une conférence d'histoire; **to congratulate s.o. on his success,** féliciter qn de son succès; **keen on sth.,** porté sur qch.; amateur de qch.; **mad on s.o.,** fou, entiché, de qn. **9. I am here on business,** je suis ici pour affaires; **on tour,** en tournée; **on holiday,** en vacances; **to be (working) on sth.,** travailler à qch.; **on the way,** en chemin. **10.** (*a*) **to have pity on s.o.,** avoir pitié de qn; **effect of sth. on s.o.,** effet de qch. sur qn; **attack on s.o.,** attaque contre qn; **decision binding on s.o.,** décision obligatoire pour qn; *F:* **this round (of drinks) is on me,** c'est moi qui paie cette tournée; **the police have nothing on him,** la police n'a rien contre lui; (*b*) **cheque on a bank,** chèque sur une banque. **11.** (*a*) **to live on one's private income,** vivre de ses rentes; **many live on less than that,** beaucoup vivent avec moins que ça; (*b*) **he's on insulin,** il a un traitement à l'insuline; *F:* **he's on drugs,** il se drogue; (*c*) **he travels on a British passport,** il voyage avec un passeport britannique. **12.** (*added to*) **disaster on disaster,** désastre sur désastre. **13.** *Turf: Games:* **to put money on a horse, on a colour,** parier sur un cheval; miser sur une couleur. **II.** *adv.* **1.** (*a*) **to put on the cloth,** mettre la nappe; **to put the kettle on,** mettre la bouilloire à chauffer; (*of actor*) **to be on,** être en scène; (*b*) **to put on one's clothes,** s'habiller; **to put on one's gloves,** se ganter; **what had he got on?** comment était-il vêtu? **to have nothing on,** être tout nu. **2.** (*expressing continuation*) **to go on, march on, work on,** continuer son chemin, sa marche, son travail; **to burn on, drive on, sail on, talk on,** continuer à brûler, à rouler, à naviguer, à parler; **sing on!** continuez à chanter! **go on!** allez toujours! **move on!** circulez! **and so on,** et ainsi de suite. **3. to be sideways on to sth.,** présenter le côté à qch. **4. later on,** plus tard; **from that day on,** à dater de ce jour; **well on in years,** d'un âge avancé. **5. to turn on the tap,** ouvrir le robinet; **on,** (i) (*of gas, etc.*) ouvert; (ii) *I.C.E:* marche, contact; (iii) *El:* (circuit) fermé; **the brakes are on,** les freins sont appliqués, serrés; **on with the show!** (i) que le spectacle commence! (ii) que le spectacle continue! **the play was on for weeks,** la pièce a tenu l'affiche pendant des semaines; **what's on tonight?** (i) qu'est-ce qui se passe ce soir? (ii) *W.Tel:* qu'est-ce qu'ils donnent, *TV:* qu'est-ce qui passe, ce soir? (iii) que fait-on ce soir? **have you anything on this evening?** avez-vous quelque chose en vue pour ce soir? **6.** *F:* (*a*) **I'm on!** je suis de la partie! **it's not on,** rien à faire! (*b*) **to be on to sth.,** comprendre, saisir, *P:* piger, qch.; **they were on to him at once,** ils ont tout de suite vu clair dans son jeu; (*c*) **to be on to a good thing,** (i) avoir un bon tuyau; (ii) être sur une bonne affaire; **the police are on to him,** la police est sur sa piste; (*d*) **I was on to him on the phone,** je lui ai parlé au téléphone; **I'll put you on to him,** je vais vous donner la communication; (*e*) **he's always on at, to, me,** il s'en prend toujours à moi; (*f*) **to have s.o. on,** en faire accroire à qn; faire marcher qn; (*g*) *Turf:* **to have a bit on,** (i) faire, (ii) avoir fait, un pari. **7. on and off** *see* OFF[1] I. 4. **III.** *a.* **1. on position,** position *f* de serrage (des freins); position de mise en marche (d'un moteur); *El:* position de fermeture (du circuit). **2.** *Cr:* **drive to the on side, on drive,** coup *m* avant à gauche. **3.** *F:* **it was not one of his on days,** il n'était pas dans un de ces meilleurs jours. **4.** *Adm:* **on licence,** licence *f* permettant la consommation de boissons alcoolisées sur les lieux.

once [wʌns] *adv.* **1.** (*a*) une fois; **o. only,** une seule fois; **more than o.,** plus d'une fois; **o. a week,** tous les huit jours; **o. or twice,** une ou deux fois, une fois ou deux; **o. more, o. again,** une fois de plus, encore une fois; **o. (and) for all,** une fois pour toutes; **you may do so this o., just for (this) o.,** je vous le permets pour une fois, pour cette fois(-ci); **for o. you are right,** pour une fois tu as raison; **o. a thief always a thief,** qui a volé volera; (*b*) **(if) o. you hesitate you're lost,** dès que vous hésitez, vous êtes fichu. **2.** autrefois; **o. upon a time there was a princess,** il était une fois une princesse; **I knew him o.,** je l'ai connu autrefois, dans le temps. **3. at o.,** (i) tout de suite; immédiatement; (ii) à la fois, en même temps; **to do several things at o.,** faire plusieurs choses à la fois.

once-over ['wʌnsouvər] *n. F:* **to give s.o., sth., the o.-o.,** jeter un coup d'œil (scrutateur) sur qn, qch.; **to give a room a o.-o.,** donner un coup de torchon à une chambre.

oncoming ['ɔnkʌmiŋ] *a.* (*a*) approchant, qui approche; **the o. traffic,** (i) (*for vehicle*) les véhicules venant en sens inverse; (*for pedestrian*) les véhicules qui approchent; (*b*) *Ind:* **o. shift,** poste entrant.

one [wʌn] **I.** *num.a.* **1.** (*a*) un; **twenty-o. apples,** vingt et une pommes; **fifty-o.,** cinquante et un; **seventy-o.,** soixante et onze; **eighty-o.,** quatre-vingt-un; **a hundred and o.,** cent un; **a thousand and o.,** mille un; **o. or two people saw it,** une ou deux personnes l'ont vu; (*b*) **o. day out of two,** un jour sur deux; **o. man in a hundred,** un homme entre, sur, cent; **I can't go; for o. thing I'm short of cash,** je ne pourrai pas y aller; entre autres raisons je suis à court d'argent. **2.** (*a*) seul, unique; **my o. and only suit,** mon seul et unique complet; **my o. and only son,** mon fils unique; **his o. care,** son seul, unique, souci; **no o. man can do it,** il n'y a pas d'homme qui puisse le faire à lui seul, tout seul; (*b*) **they cried out with o. voice, as o. man,** ils s'écrièrent d'une seule voix; (*c*) même; **all in o. direction,** tous dans la même direction; **o. and the same thought came into our minds,** une seule et même pensée nous est venue à l'esprit; *F:* **it's all o.,** cela revient au même. **II.** *n.* **1.** (*a*) un *m*; **chapter o.,** chapitre un, chapitre premier; **number o.,** numéro un; *F:* **to look after, take care of, number o.,** soigner sa petite personne; *Sp:* **o., two, three, go!** un(e), deux, trois, partez! (*b*) (*dominoes*) as; **double o.,** double-un *m, pl.* doubles-uns. **2.** (*a*) **there's only o. left,** il n'en reste qu'un; *F:* **there's o. born every minute,** on pend les andouilles sans les compter; **the top, bottom, stair but o.,** l'avant-dernière marche; **to arrive in ones and twos,** arriver par un et par deux, un ou deux à la fois; **two for the price of o.,** deux pour le prix d'un; **two volumes in o.,** deux volumes en un; **to be at o. with s.o.,** être d'accord avec qn; (*b*) **o. fifty,** (i) cent cinquante; (ii) une livre cinquante (pence); (iii) un dollar cinquante (cents); (iv) deux heures moins dix; une heure cinquante; **o. (o'clock),** une heure; **I landed him o.,** je lui ai flanqué un marron; **o. for the road,** le coup de l'étrier; **to have o. too many,** boire un verre de trop; *Sp:* **to be o. up on an opponent,** être en avance d'un point, d'un jeu, d'un but, etc., sur un concurrent; *F:* **to be o. up on s.o.,** avoir l'avantage sur qn; (*c*) *Knit:* **to make o.,** faire une augmentation; (*d*) *St.Exch:* unité *f*; unité de mille livres (au prix nominal des actions); *Turf:* **the odds are (at) ten to o.,** la cote est à dix contre un; *F:* **it's ten to o.,** *NAm:* **o. will get you ten, that he's at the office,** je parie (à) dix contre un qu'il est au bureau. **III.** *dem.pron.* (*a*) **this o.,** celui-ci, *f.* celle-ci; **that o.,** celui-là, *f.* celle-là; **which o. do you prefer?** lequel, laquelle, préférez-vous? **the o. I spoke of,** celui, celle, dont j'ai parlé; (*b*) **to pick the ripe plums and leave the green ones,** cueillir les prunes mûres et laisser les vertes; **the scheme was a good one on paper,** le plan était excellent en théorie; **that's a good o.!** celle-là est bonne! **have you heard the o. about . . .?** est-ce que tu as déjà entendu la blague du . . .? **our loved, dear, ones,** (i) ceux qui nous sont chers; (ii) nos chers disparus; **the little ones,** les petits enfants. **IV.** *indef.a.* **o. day,** un jour; **o. stormy evening in January,** par une soirée orageuse de janvier. **V.** *indef.pron.* **1.** (*pl.* **some, any**) **I haven't a pencil, have you got o.?** je n'ai pas de crayon, en avez-vous un? **this question is o. of extreme delicacy,** ce problème est délicat entre tous; **o. of them,** un d'entre eux; l'un d'eux; **he is o. of the family,** il fait partie de la famille; il est de la famille; **he is o. of us,** il est des nôtres; **o. of my friends,** un de mes amis; un ami à moi; **any o. of us,** n'importe lequel d'entre nous; **o. and all,** tous sans exception; **o. for all and all for o.,** un pour tous et tous pour un; **(the) o. . . . the other,** l'un . . . l'autre; **you can't have o. without the other,** l'un ne va pas sans l'autre; **o. after the other,** l'un après l'autre; **o. by o.,** un à un, une à une. **2. I want the opinion of o. better able to judge,** je voudrais avoir l'opinion de quelqu'un qui soit plus capable de juger; **o. Martin,** un certain M. Martin; **I, for o., do not believe it,** pour ma part je n'en crois rien; **I'm not o. to complain,** je ne suis point homme à me plaindre; **I'm not much of a o. for sweets,** je ne suis pas grand amateur de bonbons; *P:* **you *are* a o.!** vous êtes fameux, impayable, vous! **3.** (*a*) (*nom.*) on; **o. cannot always be right,** on ne peut pas toujours avoir raison; **if o. wanted to do it,** si l'on voulait le faire; (*b*) vous; **it is enough to kill o.,** il y a de quoi vous faire mourir. **4. one's,** son, *f.* sa, *pl.* ses; votre, *pl.* vos; **to give one's opinion,** donner son avis; **to cut one's finger,** se couper le doigt. **5. o. another,** l'un l'autre; les uns les autres; **to look at o. another,** se regarder.

one-armed ['wʌnɑːmd] *a.* à un seul bras; (*of pers.*) manchot, -ote; *F:* **o.-a. bandit,** machine *f* à sous; *F:* tire-pognon *m, pl.* tire-pognons.

one-eyed ['wʌnaid] *a.* (*a*) *Z:* unioculé; (*b*) (*of pers.*) borgne; **o.-e. man, woman,** borgne *mf*; (*c*) *F:* (*of outlook, etc.*) borné, étroit.

one-horse ['wʌnhɔːrs] *a. F:* **o.-h. town,** petite ville de rien du tout; trou perdu.

one-legged [wʌn'legid] *a.* **1.** (*a*) qui n'a qu'une jambe; **o.-l. man, woman,** unijambiste *mf*; (*b*) *Z:* monopode. **2.** *F:* (contrat, etc.) inégal, -aux.

one-liner [wʌn'lainər] *n.* courte plaisanterie; courte phrase bien tournée.

one-man ['wʌnmæn] *a.* (tâche, etc.) pour un seul homme; **o.-m. show,** (i) *Art:* exposition individuelle; (ii) *Th:* (spectacle *m*) solo (*m*); (iii) (*also* **o. -m. band**) entreprise individuelle; *Com:* **o.-m. company,** société *f* à une seule personne, à personne unique.

oneness ['wʌnnis] *n.* **1.** unité *f*; accord *m* (d'opinions). **2.** identité *f* dans le temps. **3.** caractère *m* unique.

one-off ['wʌnɔf] *a. Com:* (article) spécial, hors série; (film) en exclusivité; *Publ:* (livre) à tirage limité.

one-one, one-on-one ['wʌn'wʌn, wʌnɔn'wʌn] *NAm:* = ONE-TO-ONE.

one-piece ['wʌn'piːs] *n.* monobloc *inv*; d'une seule pièce; **o.-p. swimsuit,** maillot *m* une pièce.

onerous ['ɔnərəs, 'ou-] *a.* (devoir, impôt, etc.) onéreux; (tâche) pénible.

oneself [wʌn'self] *pron.* (*a*) (*emphatic*) soi-même; **one must do it o.,** il faut le faire soi-même; **to do sth. all by o.,** faire qch. tout seul; (*b*) (*reflexive*) se, soi(-même); **to flatter o.,** se flatter; **to look after o.,** se soigner; **to speak of o.,** parler de soi; **to keep o. to o.,** être peu sociable; **to feel o. again,** se sentir rétabli.

one-sided [wʌn'saidid] *a.* **1.** (*of contract*) unilatéral, -aux. **2.** (*of shape*) asymétrique. **3.** (*a*) (*of contract*) inégal, -aux; injuste; inéquitable; (*b*) (*of judgment*) partial, -aux; injuste.

onestep ['wʌnstep] *n. Danc:* one-step *m.*

one-time ['wʌntaim] *a.* (*also* **onetime**) **Mr Martin, o.-t. mayor,** M. Martin, ancien, autrefois, maire.

one-to-one ['wʌntə'wʌn] *a.* univoque; **o.-to-o. relationship,** tête-à-tête *m inv.*

one-track ['wʌntræk] *a.* **o.-t. mind,** esprit obsédé par une seule idée.

one-upmanship [wʌn'ʌpmənʃip] *n. F:* l'art *m* de se faire passer pour supérieur aux autres.

one-way ['wʌnwei] *a.* **1.** (*a*) (billet) simple; (*b*) *Com:* (emballage) perdu. **2.** (rue) à sens unique; (circulation) en sens unique.

ongoing ['ɔngouiŋ] *a. F:* progressif; continu.

onion ['ʌnjən] *n.* **1.** oignon *m*; **spring o.,** ciboule *f*; **string of onions,** chapelet *m*, corde *f*, d'oignons; **o. skin,** pelure *f* d'oignon; *Cu:* **o. soup,** soupe à l'oignon. **2.** *P:* (*a*) tête *f*, *P:* ciboulot *m*; (*b*) **she knows her onions,** elle connaît son affaire, elle s'y connaît.

oniony ['ʌnjəni] *a.* qui sent l'oignon, qui a un goût d'oignon.
onlooker ['ɔnlukər] *n.* spectateur, -trice.
only ['ounli] **I.** *a.* seul, unique; **o. son, child,** fils, enfant, unique; **his one and o. hope,** son seul et unique espoir; **his o. answer was to burst out laughing,** pour toute réponse il a éclaté de rire; **we are the o. people who know it,** nous sommes seuls à le savoir; **you are not the o. one,** vous n'êtes pas le seul; **the o. thing is that it's rather expensive,** seulement ça coûte cher. **II.** *adv.* seulement, ne . . . que, rien que; **he has o. one brother,** il n'a qu'un seul frère; **o. half an hour more,** plus qu'une demi-heure; **one man o.,** un seul homme; **(entrance for) season ticket holders o.,** entrée réservée aux abonnés; **o. an expert could advise us,** seul un expert pourrait nous conseiller; **I o. touched it,** je n'ai fait que le toucher; **he has o. to ask for it,** il n'a qu'à le demander; **I will o. say that I disagree,** je me bornerai à dire que je ne suis pas de cet avis; **I shall be o. too pleased to come,** je ne serai que trop heureux de venir; **o. think what pleasure it gave me,** imaginez un peu le plaisir que cela m'a fait; **if o. I knew where he is!** si seulement je savais où il est! **not o. useful but also decorative,** non seulement utile, mais aussi décoratif; **o. yesterday,** hier encore; pas plus tard qu'hier; **o. just,** à peine. **III.** *conj.* mais; **the book is interesting, o. rather too long,** le livre est intéressant, mais un peu long; *conj.phr.* **I would do it o. I can't spare the time,** je le ferais si ce n'était que le temps me fait défaut.
only-begotten [ounlibi'gɔt(ə)n] *a. & n.* **the o.-b. (Son) of the Father,** le Fils unique du Père.
onomatop(o)eia [ɔnəmætə'pi(:)ə] *n.* onomatopée *f.*
onomatop(o)eic [ɔnəmætə'pi:ik], *a.* onomatopéique.
onrush ['ɔnrʌʃ] *n.* ruée *f*, attaque *f.*
onset ['ɔnset] *n.* **1.** assaut *m*, attaque *f.* **2. at the o.,** d'emblée, de prime abord; **from the o.,** dès l'abord; **the o. of a disease,** la première attaque d'une maladie.
onshore ['ɔnʃɔ:r] *a.* **1.** (vent, etc.) du large. **2.** (installation pétrolière, etc.) à terre.
onslaught ['ɔnslɔ:t] *n.* assaut *m*, attaque *f.*
onstage ['ɔn'steidʒ] **1.** *adv.* (entrer, etc.) en scène. **2.** *a.* (manière de parler, style, etc.) sur la scène.
on-the-job ['ɔnðə'dʒɔb] *a.* **on-t.-j. training,** formation *f* sur le tas, par la pratique.
onto ['ɔntu(:), 'ɔntə] *prep.* = **on to,** *q.v. under* ON I.3.
ontological [ɔntou'lɔdʒik(ə)l] *a. Phil:* ontologique.
ontology [ɔn'tɔlədʒi] *n. Phil:* ontologie *f.*
onus ['ounəs] *n.* responsabilité *f*, charge *f*; **the o. lies on the government to compensate the victims,** il incombe au gouvernement d'indemniser les sinistrés; *Jur:* **o. of proof,** charge de la preuve.
onward ['ɔnwəd] **1.** *adv.* = ONWARDS. **2.** *a.* (*of motion, etc.*) en avant.
onwards ['ɔnwədz] *adv.* (*a*) en avant, plus loin; (*b*) **from tomorrow o.,** à partir de demain; **from this time o.,** désormais, dorénavant.
onyx ['ɔniks] *n. Miner:* onyx *m.*
oodles ['u:d(ə)lz] *n.pl. P:* **there's o. of it,** il y en a un tas, des tas, une tapée.
oolite ['ouəlait] *n. Geol:* oolithe *m.*
oomph [umf] *n. P:* (*a*) allant *m*; **to have plenty of o.,** être dynamique; (*b*) sex-appeal *m.*
oops [u:ps] *int.* **1.** (*to child who has fallen down*) (*also* **oops-a-daisy** ['u:psə'deizi]) houp-là! **2.** oh là là!
ooze¹ [u:z] *n.* **1.** (*a*) vase *f*, limon *m*; (*b*) marais *m*, fond bourbeux. **2.** suintement *m* (d'un liquide).
ooze² **1.** *v.i.* (*a*) suinter; s'infiltrer; **water that oozes out from the rock,** eau qui sourd du rocher; (*b*) **the walls were oozing with water,** les murs suintaient; l'eau suintait des murs. **2.** *v.tr.* suer, suinter, laisser dégoutter (l'eau); **to o. charm,** faire du charme.
op¹ [ɔp] *n. F: Med: etc:* opération *f.*
op² *a. Art:* (= OPTICAL) **o. art,** l'op art *m.*
opacity [ou'pæsiti] *n.* opacité *f* (d'un corps, etc.).
opal ['oup(ə)l] *n.* **1.** (*a*) opale *f*; (*b*) *a. & n.* (*colour*) opale (*m*) *inv.* **2. o. (glass),** verre opale; opaline *f.*
opalescence [oupə'lesəns] *n.* opalescence *f.*
opalescent [oupə'lesənt] *a.* opalescent; (*of hue*) opale *inv*; (*of haze, etc.*) opalisé.
opaline **1.** *a.* ['oupəlain] opalin. **2.** *n.* ['oupəli:n, -lain] *Glassm:* verre opalin; verre opale; opaline *f.*
opaque [ou'peik] *a.* opaque; **to become o.,** s'opacifier.
opaqueness [ou'peiknis] *n.* opacité *f* (d'un liquide, etc.).
open¹ ['oup(ə)n] *a.* **1.** (*a*) ouvert; **o. window,** fenêtre ouverte; **to fling, throw, the door wide o.,** ouvrir la porte toute grande; **the door flew o.,** la porte s'ouvrit brusquement; **half o.,** entrouvert, entrebâillé; **to keep o. house,** tenir table ouverte; (*b*) (*of box*) ouvert; (*of bottle*) débouché; (*of parcel*) défait; (*of envelope*) (i) non cacheté; (ii) décacheté; **to cut o.,** couper, ouvrir; **to read s.o. like an o. book,** lire à livre ouvert dans la pensée de qn; (*c*) **o. from ten to five,** ouvert de dix heures à cinq heures; (*of museum*) **o. to the public,** ouvert, accessible, au public; **o. all night,** ouvert la nuit; (*d*) **in (the) o. court,** en plein tribunal; **o. market,** marché public; (*e*) **career o. to very few,** carrière très fermée; *Sp:* **o. competition,** tournoi ouvert; *Golf:* **o. championship,** championnat open, ouvert; omnium *m*; *Ind:* **o. shop,** atelier qui admet les ouvriers non-syndiqués. **2.** (*a*) **o. country,** pays découvert; **in the o. air,** au grand air; à ciel ouvert; **to sleep in the o. air,** coucher à la belle étoile; **in the o. country,** en pleine, rase, campagne; **the o. sea,** la haute mer; le large; (*b*) *n.* **in the o.,** au grand air; à ciel ouvert; **to come out into the o.,** venir au grand jour; se dévoiler. **3.** (*a*) découvert, non couvert; **o. carriage,** voiture découverte; (*b*) (*of coast, position*) exposé **(to,** à); **o. to all the winds,** ouvert à tous les vents; *Fb:* **to leave the goal o.,** dégarnir ses buts; (*c*) **to lay oneself o. to (sth.),** prêter le flanc, donner prise, à (une accusation, la critique); s'exposer à (la calomnie); **o. to doubt,** douteux; **o. to ridicule,** qui prête au ridicule; (*d*) **to be o. to conviction,** être accessible à la conviction; **o. to any reasonable offer,** disposé à considérer toute offre raisonnable. **4.** (*a*) manifeste, public, -ique; **o. scandal,** scandale public; **o. secret,** secret *m* de Polichinelle; **o. letter,** lettre ouverte (dans la presse); **o. hostilities,** guerre ouverte; (*b*) ouvert; franc, *f.* franche; **o. enemy,** ennemi déclaré; **to be o. with s.o.,** parler franchement à qn; ne rien cacher à qn. **5.** (*a*) (*of flower, lips, hand*) ouvert; **with eyes o. wide,** les yeux écarquillés; **o. wound,** plaie (i) béante, (ii) non cicatrisée; *Cost:* **o. at the neck,** (i) (*of dress*) échancré; (ii) (*of shirt*) à col ouvert; (*b*) *Ling:* **o. vowel,** voyelle ouverte. **6.** *Fb:* (jeu) ouvert, dégagé. **7.** (*a*) libre, non obstrué; (*bowels*) libre; **road o. to traffic,** route ouverte à la circulation; **o. view,** vue dégagée; **to keep the bowels o.,** tenir le ventre libre; (*b*) **to keep a day o. for s.o.,** réserver un jour pour qn; **the job is still o.,** la place est toujours vacante; **two courses are o. to us,** deux moyens s'offrent à nous. **8.** non résolu; (question) discutable, pendante, indécise; **to keep an o. mind on sth.,** rester sans parti pris; se réserver; réserver son opinion sur qch.; **to leave the matter o.,** réserver la question. **9.** *Fin: Com:* **o. account,** compte ouvert; compte courant; **o. credit,** crédit à découvert; crédit en blanc; **o. cheque,** chèque ouvert, non barré. **-ly** *adv.* ouvertement; publiquement; au vu (et au su) de tous; (parler) sans réticence; **to act o.,** agir à découvert, cartes sur table; jouer franc jeu.

open² I. *v.tr.* **1.** (*a*) ouvrir (une porte, etc.); **to o. the door wide,** ouvrir la porte toute grande; (*b*) déboucher, entamer (une bouteille); écailler (une huître); décacheter (une lettre); ouvrir (un livre); défaire (un paquet); déplier (un journal); lâcher (une écluse); dépouiller (le courrier); *Med:* **to o. the bowels,** relâcher les intestins; (*c*) **to o. one's shop,** ouvrir son magasin; **to o. a new shop,** ouvrir, monter, un nouveau magasin; **to o. a park to the public,** ouvrir un parc au public; **to o. a road (to traffic),** livrer une route à la circulation; (*d*) présider à l'inauguration de, inaugurer (une institution, un établissement); **to o. Parliament,** ouvrir la session du Parlement. **2.** écarter (les jambes, etc.); ouvrir (la main, les yeux). **3.** découvrir, exposer, révéler; **to o. one's heart,** ouvrir son cœur, s'ouvrir (**to s.o.,** à qn); **that opens new prospects for me,** cela m'ouvre de nouveaux horizons. **4.** commencer; entamer, engager (des négociations, une conversation, un débat); ouvrir (le feu, les hostilités); défricher, défoncer (un terrain vierge); **to o. an account in s.o.'s name,** ouvrir un compte à qn, en faveur de qn; *Jur:* **to o. the case,** exposer les faits. **II.** *v.i.* s'ouvrir. **1.** (*a*) (*of door, etc.*) **to half o.,** s'entrebâiller, s'entrouvrir; **door that opens into the garden,** porte qui donne sur le jardin; (*b*) *El:* (*of cutout*) décoller; (*c*) (*of shop*) ouvrir; (*of bank, museum*) ouvrir ses portes; **as soon as the season opens,** dès l'ouverture *f* de la saison. **2.** (*a*) (*of view, prospects*) s'étendre; (*b*) (*of flower*) s'épanouir, s'ouvrir; (*c*) (*of bay*) s'ouvrir. **3.** commencer; **the play opens with a death scene,** la pièce s'ouvre sur une scène de mort; *St.Exch:* **coppers opened firm,** les valeurs cuprifères ont ouvert fermes. **opening** *n.* **1.** (*a*) ouverture *f* (de la porte, d'un magasin, de son cœur; d'un compte); débouchage *m* (d'une bouteille); décachetage *m* (d'une lettre); dépouillement *m* (de son courrier); *Com:* **late o. Friday** = nocturne *m* le vendredi; (*b*) **formal o.,** inauguration *f*; **the o. of Parliament,** l'ouverture du Parlement; (*c*) commencement *m* (d'une conversation); ouverture (de négociations); *Jur:* exposition *f* des faits. **2.** (*a*) épanouissement *m*, éclosion *f* (d'une fleur); **o. (out),** développement *m* (des ailes d'un oiseau); (*b*) commencement, début (d'une pièce de théâtre, d'une ère nouvelle). **3.** (*a*) trou *m*, percée *f* (à travers un mur); percée, éclaircie *f* (dans une forêt); (*b*) embrasure *f*, baie *f* (dans un mur); (*c*) échappée *f* (entre les arbres); (*d*) orifice *m*; embouchure *f* (d'un sac); *Min:* cloche *f* (d'une carrière); amorce *f* (d'une galerie). **4.** occasion *f* favorable; *Com:* débouché *m* (pour une marchandise). **5.** *attrib.* inaugural, -aux; de début; **o. ceremony,** cérémonie *f* d'inauguration; **o. day,** jour *m* d'ouverture; **o. address, speech,** discours *m* d'ouverture; *Com:* **o. hours,** heures *fpl* d'ouverture; *Cards:* **o. bid,** annonce *f* d'entrée, d'indication. **open out 1.** *v.tr.* (*a*) ouvrir, étendre, déplier (une feuille de papier); (*b*) développer (une entreprise); (*c*) élargir, aléser, agrandir (un trou); évaser, mandriner (la bouche d'un tuyau). **2.** *v.i.* (*of view, prospects*) s'ouvrir, s'étendre. **open up 1.** *v.tr.* ouvrir; éventer (une carrière); exposer, révéler (une perspective, etc.); frayer, pratiquer (un chemin); ouvrir (un pays au commerce). **2.** *v.i.* (*a*) (*of view, prospects*) s'ouvrir, s'étendre; (*b*) (*of pers.*) s'ouvrir (**to s.o.,** à qn); s'épancher.

open-air [oupən'ɛər] *a.* (*a*) (restaurant, marché, vie, etc.) en plein air; (*b*) **she's an o.-a. girl,** elle aime la vie, les occupations, en plein air.

open-armed [oup(ə)n'ɑːmd] *a.* (accueil) à bras ouverts.

opencast ['oup(ə)nkɑːst] *a.* (chantier, exploitation) à ciel ouvert.

open-ended ['oupən'endid] *a.* sans limites fixes; non déterminé; **o.-e. discussion,** libre discussion *f*.

opener ['oup(ə)nər] *n.* **1.** (*pers.*) ouvreur, -euse. **2.** (*thg*) **bottle o., crown cork o.,** décapsulateur *m*; **can, tin, o.,** ouvre-boîtes *m inv*. **3.** (*a*) *Th:* premier numéro; (*b*) *Cards:* **openers,** cartes *fpl* avec lesquelles on peut ouvrir (au poker).

open-eyed ['oupən'aid] *a.* **1.** qui a les yeux ouverts; qui voit clair. **2. to look at s.o. in o.-e. astonishment,** regarder qn les yeux écarquillés de surprise.

open-handed [oupən'hændid] *a.* libéral, -aux; **to be o.-h.,** avoir la main ouverte.

open-heart ['oupən'hɑːt] *a.* (chirurgie) à cœur ouvert.

openhearted [oupən'hɑːtid] *a.* **1.** ouvert; franc, *f.* franche; au cœur ouvert. **2.** au cœur tendre, compatissant.

openminded [oupən'maindid] *a.* qui a l'esprit ouvert, large; **to be o. on, about, sth.,** ne pas avoir de parti pris, d'idée préconçue, sur qch.

openmouthed [oupən'mauðd] *a.* **to stand o., in o. astonishment,** rester bouche bée.

openness ['oupənnis] *n.* **1.** situation exposée (d'une côte, etc.); aspect découvert (du terrain). **2.** (*a*) franchise *f*, candeur *f*; (*b*) largeur *f*, libéralité *f* (d'esprit).

openwork ['oupənwəːk] *n.* (*a*) ouvrage ajouré, à jour; (*b*) ajours *mpl*, jours *mpl*; **o. stockings,** bas ajourés, à jour.

opera ['ɔp(ə)rə] *n.* **1.** opéra *m*; **comic o., o. bouffe,** opéra bouffe; *T.V: F:* **soap o.,** feuilleton *m* à l'eau de rose. **2. o. (house),** (théâtre *m* de l')opéra. **3. o. (company),** (compagnie *f* d')opéra. **4. o. glasses,** jumelles *fpl* de théâtre; **o. goer,** amateur d'opéra; **o. singer,** chanteur, -euse, d'opéra.

operable ['ɔp(ə)rəbl] *a.* **1.** *Surg:* (malade, tumeur) opérable. **2.** (système, etc.) utilisable, praticable.

operate ['ɔpəreit] **I.** *v.i.* **1.** (*a*) (*of machine*) fonctionner; (*b*) (*of burglar, etc.*) opérer, travailler; (*c*) jouer; **the wage increase will o. from the first of January,** l'augmentation des salaires jouera à partir du premier janvier. **2.** *St.Exch:* faire des opérations. **3.** *Surg:* **to o. (on s.o.) for appendicitis,** opérer (qn) de l'appendicite; **to be operated on,** subir une opération, une intervention chirurgicale. **II.** *v.tr.* **1.** opérer, effectuer, accomplir (une guérison, un changement etc.). **2.** (*a*) (*of pers.*) manœuvrer (une machine); actionner (les freins); (*b*) (*of part of machine*) commander, actionner; **operated by electricity,** actionné par l'électricité. **3.** exploiter (un chemin de fer, une ligne d'autobus, etc.). **operating 1.** *a.* qui opère. **2.** *n.* (*a*) fonctionnement *m*; (*b*) manœuvre *f*, commande *f* (d'une machine); **o. instructions,** instructions *fpl*, règlements *mpl* de service; **o. lever,** levier *m* de commande; (*c*) exploitation *f* (d'une compagnie de chemins de fer); **o. costs,** frais *mpl* d'exploitation; (*d*) *Surg:* **o. table,** table *f* d'opération; *F:* (le) billard; **o. theatre,** salle *f* d'opération.

operatic [ɔpə'rætik] **1.** *a.* d'opéra; (chanteur) d'opéra; **o. society,** cercle *m* d'opéra d'amateurs. **2.** *n.pl. F:* **operatics,** opéra *m* d'amateurs.

operation [ɔpə'reiʃ(ə)n] *n.* opération *f*. **1.** fonctionnement *m*; marche *f* (d'un appareil, d'une machine); jeu *m* (d'un mécanisme); **in o.,** (i) (machine) en marche, en fonctionnement; (ii) (loi) en application, en vigueur; **to come into o.,** (i) (*of machine*) commencer à fonctionner; (ii) (*of law*) entrer en application, en vigueur. **2.** (*a*) commande *f* (d'une machine, etc.); (*b*) exploitation *f* (d'un réacteur, d'un navire, d'un réseau de transport). **3.** (*a*) **mathematical o.,** opération mathématique; (*b*) *Cmptr:* **computer o.,** opération machine; (*c*) travail *m*, -aux; unité *f* (de fabrication, etc.); **operations research,** recherche opérationnelle; (*d*) **a firm's operations,** les activités d'une entreprise; *St.Exch:* **credit**

o., opération à terme. **4.** *Mil:* **airborne o.,** opération aéroportée; **operations room,** salle *f* d'opérations (d'un état-major). **5. (surgical) o.,** opération, intervention (chirurgicale); **to perform an o. on s.o.,** opérer qn (**for,** de); **to undergo an o.,** se faire opérer, subir une opération (**for,** de).

operational [ɔpəˈreiʃən(ə)l] *a.* (*a*) opérationnel; *Mil:* **o. training,** instruction *f* tactique; entraînement *m* de guerre, au combat; (*b*) en état de marche, de fonctionnement, de service; **the new power station should be o. next year,** la nouvelle centrale électrique devrait être opérationnelle l'an prochain.

operative [ˈɔp(ə)rətiv] **1.** *a.* (*a*) opératif, actif; (*of law*) **to become o.,** entrer en vigueur; prendre effet; **to make a decree o.,** rendre un décret opérant; **the o. word,** le mot qui compte; (*b*) *Surg:* (méthode, champ) opératoire. **2.** *n.* (*a*) ouvrier, -ière; opérateur, -trice (d'une machine, etc.); (*b*) *NAm:* détective *m.*

operator [ˈɔpəreitər] *n.* **1.** (*pers.*) opérateur, -trice; (*a*) *Tg:* télégraphiste *mf*; *Tp:* téléphoniste *mf*; **radio, wireless, o.,** (opérateur de) radio (*m*); *Tp:* **switchboard o.,** standardiste *mf*; (*b*) opérateur (d'une machine); (*c*) *Com: Ind:* exploitant *m* (d'une entreprise); (*d*) *F:* brasseur *m* d'affaires. **2.** (*a*) *Mth:* opérateur (de logarithme); (*b*) *Mec.E:* appareil *m*, mécanisme *m*, de commande; opérateur (d'une machine-outil).

operetta [ɔpəˈretə] *n. Mus:* opérette *f.*

ophthalmic [ɔfˈθælmik] *a.* **1.** ophtalmique; **o. remedy,** ophtalmique *m.* **2.** (hôpital) ophtalmologique.

ophthalmologist [ɔfθælˈmɔlədʒist] *n. Med:* ophtalmologiste *mf*, ophtalmologue *mf.*

ophthalmology [ɔfθælˈmɔlədʒi] *n. Med:* ophtalmologie *f.*

opiate [ˈoupiət] *n. Pharm:* opiacé *m*, opiat *m*, narcotique *m.*

opine [ouˈpain] *v.tr. O: & U.S:* (*a*) être d'avis (**that,** que); (*b*) exprimer l'avis (**that,** que).

opinion [əˈpiniən] *n.* **1.** opinion *f*; (*a*) avis *m*; **in my o.,** selon mon avis; **in the o. of experts,** de l'avis, au dire, des experts; suivant, selon, l'opinion des experts; **to be of the o. that . . .,** être d'avis, estimer, que . . ., **to be of the same o. as s.o.,** être du même avis que qn; **to express, put forward, an o.,** exprimer une opinion; **to ask s.o.'s o.,** demander l'avis de qn; consulter qn; **to form an o. on s.o., sth.,** se faire une opinion sur, de, qn, qch.; **what is your o. of him?** que pensez-vous de lui? (*b*) estime *f*; **to have a high, low, o. of s.o.,** avoir une bonne, une mauvaise, opinion de qn; (*c*) **public o.,** l'opinion (publique); **o. poll, survey,** sondage *m* d'opinion publique. **2.** *Med:* **you ought to have a second o.,** vous devriez consulter un autre médecin.

opinionated [əˈpiniəneitid] *a.* opiniâtre; arrêté dans ses opinions.

opium [ˈoupiəm] *n.* opium *m*; **o. addict,** opiomane *mf*; **o. den,** fumerie *f* d'opium.

Oporto [əˈpɔːtou] *Pr.n. Geog:* Porto *m.*

opossum [əˈpɔsəm] *n. z:* opossum *m.*

opponent [əˈpounənt] *n.* adversaire *mf*, antagoniste *mf* (**of,** de), opposant, -ante (**of,** à).

opportune [ˈɔpətjuːn] *a.* (*of time*) opportun, convenable; (*of action*) à propos; **you have come at an o. moment,** vous arrivez à propos; vous tombez bien. **-ly** *adv.* opportunément; en temps opportun.

opportunism [ˈɔpətjuːnizm] *n.* opportunisme *m.*

opportunist [ˈɔpətjuːnist] *n.* opportuniste *mf.*

opportunity [ɔpəˈtjuːniti] *n.* occasion *f* (**for doing sth.,** de faire qch.); **golden o.,** affaire *f* d'or; **at the first, earliest, o.,** à la première occasion; **if I get an o.,** si l'occasion se présente; **to miss an o.,** laisser passer, perdre, une occasion; *Com:* **unique sales opportunities,** occasions exceptionnelles.

oppose [əˈpouz] *v.tr.* **1.** opposer; mettre (deux couleurs, etc.) en opposition, en contraste. **2.** s'opposer à (qn, qch.); mettre obstacle, mettre opposition, à (qch.); résister à (qn, qch.); **to be opposed to sth.,** être opposé à qch.; **as opposed to,** par contraste à, avec; *Jur:* **to o. an action, a marriage,** se rendre opposant à un acte, un mariage. **opposed** *a.* opposé; **directly o. evidence,** témoignages *mpl* en contradiction directe. **opposing** *a.* (*of armies, characters*) opposé; (*of party*) opposant; *Sp:* **o. team,** équipe *f* adverse.

opposite [ˈɔpəzit] **1.** *a.* (*a*) opposé (**to,** à); vis-à-vis (**to,** de); en face (**to,** de); **see the diagram on the o. page,** voir la figure ci-contre; **house o. the church,** maison en face de l'église, qui fait face à l'église; **the house o.,** la maison (d')en face; **o. number,** confrère *m*; homologue *m*; *Mil:* correspondant en grade; (*b*) contraire (**to, from,** à); **the o. sex,** l'autre sexe *m*; **in the o. direction,** en sens inverse, dans le sens opposé; **they went in o. directions,** ils prirent des directions opposées. **2.** *n.* opposé *m*; contre-pied; **he's the exact o. of his brother,** il est exactement le contraire de son frère. **3.** *adv.* vis-à-vis; en face. **4.** *prep.* en face de, vis-à-vis (de); **to stand, sit, o. s.o.,** faire vis-à-vis à qn; **we live o. them,** nous habitons en face de chez eux; *Th: Cin:* **he played o. many stars,** il a joué avec beaucoup de vedettes pour partenaire.

opposition [ɔpəˈziʃ(ə)n] *n.* (*a*) opposition *f*; *Astr:* **in o.,** en opposition; (*b*) **to act in o. to public opinion,** agir contrairement à l'opinion publique; (*c*) résistance *f*; **to break down all o.,** vaincre toutes les résistances; (*d*) **the o.,** le camp adverse; *Pol:* (le parti de) l'opposition; **member of the o.,** membre *m* de l'opposition; (*e*) *Com:* concurrence *f.*

oppress [əˈpres] *v.tr.* (*a*) opprimer (un peuple vaincu); (*b*) accabler (l'esprit). **oppressed** *a.* (peuple) opprimé; *n.pl.* **the o.,** les opprimés *mpl.*

oppression [əˈpreʃ(ə)n] *n.* **1.** oppression *f* (d'un peuple); *Jur:* abus *m* d'autorité. **2.** (*a*) accablement *m* (de l'esprit); (*b*) oppression de la poitrine.

oppressive [əˈpresiv] *a.* **1.** (*of law, regime*) oppressif, opprimant. **2.** (*a*) (*of atmosphere*) lourd, étouffant, alourdissant; (*b*) (*of mental burden*) accablant. **-ly** *adv.* **1.** d'une manière oppressive. **2.** d'une manière étouffante; **it was o. hot,** il faisait une chaleur accablante.

oppressiveness [əˈpresivnis] *n.* **1.** caractère oppressif. **2.** lourdeur *f* (du temps).

oppressor [əˈpresər] *n.* oppresseur *m*; **the oppressors and the oppressed,** les opprimants *mpl* et les opprimés *mpl.*

opprobrious [əˈproubriəs] *a.* injurieux, outrageant.

opprobrium [əˈproubriəm] *n.* opprobre *m.*

opt [ɔpt] *v.i.* **1.** opter (**for,** pour; **between,** entre). **2. to o. out of an association,** quitter une association; **to o. out of a competition,** abandonner un concours; **I'm opting out,** je ne veux pas participer.

optative [ˈɔptətiv] *a. & n. Gram:* optatif (*m*).

optic [ˈɔptik] **1.** *a.* (*a*) optique; *Anat:* **o. nerve,** nerf *m* optique; (*b*) **o. measure,** mesure transparente (utilisée dans les bars). **2.** *n. Opt:* (i) lentille *f*, (ii) miroir *m*, (iii) prisme *m* (d'un instrument d'optique).

optical [ˈɔptik(ə)l] *a.* (*a*) optique; **o. axis, centre,** axe *m*, centre *m*, optique (d'une lentille); (*b*) (instrument) d'optique; **o. illusion,** illusion *f* d'optique.

optician [ɔpˈtiʃ(ə)n] *n.* opticien, -ienne.

optics [ˈɔptiks] *n.pl.* (*usu. with sg. const.*) l'optique *f.*

optimal [ˈɔptim(ə)l] *a.* optimal, -aux; optimum, -ima.

optimism [ˈɔptimizm] *n.* optimisme *m.*

optimist [ˈɔptimist] *n.* optimiste *mf.*

optimistic [ɔptiˈmistik] *a.* optimiste; **to feel o. about the future,** augurer bien de l'avenir. **-ally** *adv.* d'une manière optimiste; avec optimisme.

optimum, *pl.* **-ima** ['ɔptiməm, -imə] **1.** *n.* optimum *m.* **2.** *a.* **o. conditions,** conditions les meilleure, optimum; **o. population density,** optimum de population.

option ['ɔpʃ(ə)n] *n.* **1.** option *f*, choix *m*; (*a*) **to make one's o.,** faire son option, son choix; opter (**between,** entre); (*b*) faculté *f*; **to have the o. of doing sth.,** avoir la faculté, le choix, de faire qch.; **we have no o. but to agree,** nous ne pouvons faire autrement que de consentir; *Jur:* **imprisonment without the o. of a fine,** emprisonnement *m* sans substitution d'amende; (*c*) **which of them is the best o.?** lequel est le meilleur choix? **there was no soft o.,** il n'y avait pas de solution facile. **2.** (*a*) option; **to take an o. on all the future works of an author,** prendre une option sur tous les ouvrages à paraître d'un auteur; (*b*) *St.Exch:* option; (marché à) prime *f*; **buyer's, seller's, o.,** prime acheteur, vendeur; **to take up an o.,** lever une prime; **o. deal,** opération à prime.

optional ['ɔpʃən(ə)l] *a.* facultatif; **evening dress is o.,** l'habit n'est pas de rigueur; **o. extras,** accessoires au choix (de l'acheteur); **o. retirement at sixty,** retraite *f* à soixante ans sur demande; *Sch:* **o. subjects,** matières *fpl* à option.

optometrist [ɔp'tɔmitrist] *n.* optométriste *mf.*

opulence ['ɔpjuləns] *n.* opulence *f*, richesse *f.*

opulent ['ɔpjulənt] *a.* (*a*) opulent, riche; (*b*) abondant. **-ly** *adv.* avec opulence.

opus ['oupəs, 'ɔp-] *n.* opus *m*; **magnum o.,** chef-d'œuvre *m*, *pl.* chefs-d'œuvre.

or [ɔːr; *unstressed* ər] *conj.* (*a*) ou; (*with neg.*) ni; **do you want beef or ham?** voulez-vous du bœuf ou du jambon? **either one or the other,** soit l'un soit l'autre; l'un ou l'autre; **either come in or (else) go out,** entrez ou (bien) sortez; **either you or he has done it,** c'est vous ou (c'est) lui qui l'a fait; **without money or luggage,** sans argent ni bagages; **in a day or two,** dans un ou deux jours; **a mile or so,** environ un mille; (*b*) **don't move, or I'll shoot,** ne bougez pas, sinon je tire.

oracle ['ɔrəkl] *n.* oracle *m*; (*a*) **the Delphic o.,** l'oracle de Delphes; (*b*) **to pronounce, utter, an o.,** rendre un oracle; (*c*) (prêtre, -esse, d')oracle; (*d*) *F:* **to work the o.,** (i) faire agir certaines influences; (ii) se procurer de l'argent.

oracular [ɔ'rækjulər] *a.* (*a*) (style, etc.) d'oracle, oraculaire; (*b*) (réponse, etc.) équivoque, obscur.

oral ['ɔːr(ə)l] *a.* oral, -aux; (*a*) *Sch:* **o. examination,** *n. F:* **oral,** (examen) oral (*m*); (*b*) (contraceptif) oral; (vaccin) buccal; (administration d'une drogue) par la bouche, par voie orale; *Anat:* **o. cavity,** cavité orale, buccale. **-ally** *adv.* **1.** oralement; de vive voix. **2.** *Med:* par la bouche; par voie orale.

orange¹ ['ɔrin(d)ʒ] *n.* **1.** orange *f*; **o. segment,** quartier *m*, tranche *f* (d'une orange); **bitter, Seville, o.,** orange amère; bigarade *f*; **blood o.,** (orange) sanguine (*f*); **o. peel,** peau *f*, écorce *f*, *Cu:* zeste *m*, d'orange; **o. marmalade,** confiture *f* d'orange(s). **2.** (*a*) **o. (tree),** oranger *m*; **o. blossom,** fleurs *fpl* d'oranger; **o. grove,** orangeraie *f*; **o. grower,** orangiste *mf*; *Toil:* **o. stick,** bâtonnet *m*; (*b*) **mock o.,** (i) seringa odorant; (ii) laurier-cerise *m*, *pl.* lauriers-cerises. **3.** *a.* & *n.* orangé (*m*), orange (*m*) *inv*; **o. red,** rouge orangé (*m*) *inv*; nacarat (*m*) *inv.*

Orange² *Pr.n.* **1.** *Geog:* **the O. (River),** l'Orange *m*; **the O. Free State,** l'État *m* libre d'Orange. **2.** *Hist:* **the Prince of O.,** le prince d'Orange.

orangeade [ɔrin'dʒeid] *n.* orangeade *f.*

Orangeman, *pl.* **-men** ['ɔrin(d)ʒmən] *n.m.* orangiste (du parti protestant de l'Irlande du Nord).

orangery ['ɔrin(d)ʒ(ə)ri] *n.* orangerie *f.*

orang-outang, -utan ['ɔːræŋ'uːtæŋ, -tæn] *n. Z:* orang-outan(g) *m*, *pl.* orangs-outan(g)s.

oration [ɔː'reiʃ(ə)n] *n.* allocution *f*, discours *m*; **funeral o.,** oraison *f* funèbre.

orator ['ɔrətər] *n.* orateur, -trice.

oratorical [ɔrə'tɔrik(ə)l] *a.* (style, talent) oratoire.

oratorio [ɔrə'tɔːriou] *n. Mus:* oratorio *m.*

oratory¹ ['ɔrət(ə)ri] *n.* art *m* oratoire; éloquence *f*; **a brilliant piece of o.,** un brillant spécimen d'art oratoire; **flight of o.,** envolée éloquente.

oratory² *n. Ecc:* oratoire *m*; chapelle privée.

orb [ɔːb] *n.* **1.** orbe *m*; (*a*) globe *m*, sphère *f*; **the o. of the sun,** le globe du soleil; (*b*) (*of regalia*) globe; **the o. and the sceptre,** l'orbe et le sceptre.

orbit¹ ['ɔːbit] *n.* **1.** orbite *f* (d'une planète, d'un véhicule spatial); **in o.,** en orbite; **to enter, go into, o.,** se mettre, se placer, en orbite. **2.** *Anat:* orbite (de l'œil); fosse *f* orbitaire.

orbit² **1.** *v.tr.* (*a*) mettre, placer (un satellite) en orbite; (*b*) (*of satellite*) **to o. the sun,** décrire une orbite, orbiter, autour du soleil. **2.** *v.i.* (*of satellite*) orbiter, décrire une orbite.

orbital ['ɔːbit(ə)l] *a.* **1.** *Astr: etc:* orbital, -aux. **2.** *Anat:* (cavité, etc.) orbitaire.

orchard ['ɔːtʃəd] *n.* verger *m*; **apple o.,** pommeraie *f.*

orchestra ['ɔːkistrə] *n.* **1.** *Th:* orchestre *m*; **the o. stalls,** *NAm:* **the o.,** les fauteuils *mpl* d'orchestre. **2.** *Mus:* orchestre; **string o.,** orchestre à cordes.

orchestral [ɔː'kestr(ə)l] *a.* orchestral, -aux.

orchestrate ['ɔːkistreit] *v.tr. Mus:* orchestrer (une symphonie, etc., *Fig:* une campagne de presse, etc.).

orchestration [ɔːkis'treiʃ(ə)n] *n.* orchestration *f.*

orchid ['ɔːkid] *n. Bot: Hort:* orchidée *f*; (*wild*) orchis *m*; **o. grower,** cultivateur, -trice, d'orchidées.

orchis ['ɔːkis] *n. Bot:* orchis *m.*

ordain [ɔː'dein] *v.tr.* **1.** *Ecc:* ordonner (un prêtre); **to be ordained,** recevoir les ordres. **2.** (*a*) destiner; ordonner, fixer; **fate ordained, it was ordained, that we should meet,** le sort a voulu que nous nous rencontrions; (*b*) décréter (une mesure).

ordeal [ɔː'diː(ə)l] *n.* **1.** *Hist:* épreuve *f* judiciaire; **o. by fire,** épreuve du feu. **2.** épreuve; danger *m* (qui éprouve la force et le courage); **to go through a terrible o.,** passer par une rude épreuve; **it is an o. for me to make a speech,** je suis au supplice quand je dois faire un discours.

order¹ ['ɔːdər] *n.* ordre *m.* **1.** (*a*) **the higher, lower, orders (of society),** les classes supérieures, inférieures; **workmanship of the highest o.,** travail de premier ordre; **population of, in,** *NAm:* **on, the o. of 100,000,** population de l'ordre de 100,000 habitants; (*b*) *Ecc:* **holy orders,** ordres sacrés; ordres majeurs; **minor orders,** ordres mineurs; **to be in holy orders,** être prêtre; (*c*) **monastic o.,** ordre religieux; communauté *f*; **o. of knighthood,** ordre de chevalerie; **the O. of the Garter,** l'Ordre de la Jarretière; (*d*) **to be wearing one's orders,** porter ses décorations; (*e*) *Arch:* **Ionic, Doric, o.,** ordre ionique, dorique; (*f*) *Nat.Hist:* ordre (d'un règne). **2.** succession *f*, suite *f*; **in alphabetical, chronological, o.,** en, par, ordre alphabétique, chronologique; **in o. of age,** par rang d'âge; **in ascending, descending, o.,** en, par, ordre croissant, décroissant. **3.** *Mil:* **in close o.,** en ordre serré; **o. of battle,** ordre de bataille. **4.** régime *m*; **the established o.,** l'ordre établi; **it's not in the natural o. of events,** ce n'est pas dans l'ordre des choses. **5.** (*a*) **to put things in o.,** mettre des choses en ordre; **to put, set, one's affairs in o.,** mettre ses affaires en ordre; régler ses affaires; **to set one's house in o.,** (i) remettre de l'ordre dans (i) son ménage, (ii) ses affaires; (*b*) *Adm:* (*of document*) **in o.,** en règle; conforme à la règle; (*c*) **machine in (good) working o.,** machine en (bon) état de fonctionnement, de marche; **out of o.,** (mécanisme) détraqué, dérangé; (compas) déréglé; (téléphone) en dérangement; (ascenseur, machine) en panne; (*d*) (*in meeting*) **o. of the day,** ordre du jour; *Parl:* **o. paper,** copie *f* de l'ordre du jour; **to rule a question out of o.,** statuer qu'une interpellation n'est pas dans les règles; **to call s.o. to o.,** rappeler qn à l'ordre; **o.! o.!** à l'ordre! (*e*) *Ecc:* **o. of service,** office *m*. **6. law and o.,** l'ordre public; **to keep o. in a town,** assurer, maintenir, l'ordre dans une ville; *Sch:* **to keep o. in class,** maintenir la discipline dans une classe; **to restore o.,** rétablir l'ordre. **7.** *Mil:* **arms at the o.,** l'arme au pied. **8.** *conj.phr.* **in o. to do sth.,** afin de, pour, faire qch.; **in o. that they understand,** afin qu'ils puissent comprendre. **9.** (*a*) commandement *m*, instruction *f*; *Mil:* consigne *f*; **verbal, written, o.,** ordre verbal, écrit; **standing orders,** ordres permanents; règlement(s) *m*(*pl*) (d'une assemblée, etc.); **I have orders to remain here,** j'ai ordre de rester ici; **to obey orders,** se conformer aux ordres; suivre la consigne; *F:* **I don't take (my) orders from him,** je ne dépends pas de lui; **until further o.,** jusqu'à nouvel avis; sauf avis contraire; **by o. of the King,** de par le roi; (*b*) *Fin:* **pay to the o. of J. Martin,** payez à l'ordre de J. Martin; **pay J. Martin or o.,** payez à J. Martin ou à son ordre; **cheque to o.,** chèque *m* à ordre; (*c*) *Com:* commande *f*, demande *f*; (*of representative*) **to call for orders,** passer prendre les commandes; **to place an o. with s.o., to give s.o. an o.,** (i) confier, passer, une commande à qn; (ii) commander qch. à qn; (*in restaurant*) **have you given your o.?** avez-vous commandé? **cash with o.,** payable à la commande; **o. form,** bon *m*, bulletin *m*, de commande; **o. book,** carnet *m* de commandes; **it's on o.,** c'est commandé; **made to o.,** fabriqué sur commande; (*of suit*) fait sur mesure; *F:* **that's a tall o.,** ce que vous demandez là n'est pas facile; (*d*) (i) (*goods ordered*) **to deliver an o.,** livrer une commande; (ii) *NAm:* (*in restaurant*) portion *f*. **10.** (*a*) **written o.,** ordre par écrit; **o. in council** = décret présidentiel; arrêté ministériel; décret-loi, *pl.* décrets-lois; **o. to pay, for payment,** ordonnance *f* de paiement; ordonnancement *m*; **o. to view,** permis *m* de visiter (une maison à vendre); *Jur:* **o. of the court,** injonction *f* de la cour; **deportation o.,** arrêté d'expulsion; (*b*) *Mil:* **daily orders,** décision journalière; **battle orders,** mémorandum *m* de combat; *Navy:* **sailing orders,** ordre d'appareiller, instructions pour l'appareillage; **sealed orders,** ordres cachetés, pli cacheté; (*c*) *Com: Adm:* bon *m*; **delivery o.,** bon de livraison; **purchase o.,** bon d'achat, de commande; (*d*) mandat *m*; **banker's o., standing o.,** ordre de transfert permanent; **postal o., money o.,** mandat de poste; mandat postal; mandat-poste *m*, *pl.* mandats-poste.

order² *v.tr.* **1.** (*a*) *O:* arranger, ranger, ordonner (des meubles, etc.); classer, ranger (des papiers); (*b*) *Mil:* **o. arms!** reposez armes! **2.** (*of fate, Deity*) destiner (qn à qch.). **3.** (*a*) **to o. s.o. to do sth.,** ordonner, commander, à qn de faire qch.; **he's been ordered to report tomorrow,** il a reçu l'ordre de se présenter demain; *Jur:* **to be ordered to pay costs,** être condamné aux dépens; (*b*) *Med:* prescrire, ordonner (un traitement à qn); **the doctor ordered him a change of air,** le médecin lui a ordonné un changement de climat; *F:* **that's just what the doctor ordered,** c'est tout à fait ce qu'il faut pour l'occasion; (*c*) *Com:* commander, demander, commissionner (qch.); **to o. goods from Paris,** commander des articles à Paris; **to o. a taxi,** (faire) demander un taxi; **what have you ordered for dinner?** qu'avez-vous commandé pour le dîner? **order about** *v.tr. F:* faire marcher, faire aller (qn); **he likes ordering people about,** il aime (à) commander les autres. **ordered** *a.* ordonné; en bon ordre; **an o. life,** une vie régulière, réglée. **order off** *v.tr. Fb:* **to o. a player off (the field),** faire sortir un joueur du terrain. **order out** *v.tr.* **to o. s.o. out (of the room, house),** mettre (qn) à la porte.

orderliness ['ɔːdəlinis] *n.* **1.** méthode *f*. **2.** habitudes *fpl* d'ordre. **3.** discipline *f*; bonne conduite (d'une foule, etc.).

orderly ['ɔːdəli] **1.** *a.* (*a*) (*of arrangement*) ordonné, méthodique; (*of life*) réglé, rangé, régulier; (*of pers.*) **to be very o.,** avoir beaucoup de méthode; (*b*) (*of crowd*) discipliné; (*c*) *Mil:* **o. room,** salle *f* des rapports; **o. officer,** officier *m* de service. **2.** *n.* (*a*) *Mil:* planton *m*; **to be on o. duty,** être de planton; (*b*) **hospital o., medical o.,** aide-infirmier, -ière; *Mil:* infirmier *m*, ambulancier *m*.

ordinal ['ɔːdin(ə)l] **1.** *a.* (nombre) ordinal, -aux. **2.** *n.* adjectif ordinal.

ordinance ['ɔːdinəns] *n.* **1.** ordonnance *f*, décret *m*, règlement *m*. **2.** *Ecc:* rite *m*, cérémonie *f* (du culte).

ordinary ['ɔːdin(ə)ri] *a.* & *n.* **I.** *a.* **1.** (*a*) ordinaire; (*of routine*) coutumier; normal, -aux; courant; *Fin:* **o. share,** action ordinaire; (*b*) **o. Englishman,** Anglais moyen, typique; **he was just an o. tourist,** c'était un touriste comme un autre. **2.** *Pej:* **a very o. kind of man,** un homme tout à fait quelconque. **II.** *n.* **1.** ordinaire *m*; **out of the o.,** exceptionnel; peu ordinaire; qui sort de l'ordinaire. **2.** *Her:* pièce *f* honorable. **3.** (*pers.*) (*a*) *Jur: Scot:* juge *m*; (*b*) *Ecc.Jur:* ordinaire (archevêque ou évêque). **4.** *Ecc:* **the O. (of the Mass),** l'Ordinaire (de la messe). **-ily** ['ɔːdin(ə)rili, *NAm:* ɔːdi'nɛərili] *adv.* ordinairement; d'ordinaire, d'habitude.

ordinate ['ɔːdinət] *n.* *Mth:* ordonnée *f*.

ordination [ɔːdi'neiʃ(ə)n] *n.* *Ecc:* ordination *f*.

ordnance ['ɔːdnəns] *n.* **1.** artillerie *f*; **piece of o.,** bouche *f* à feu; pièce *f* d'artillerie; **o. factory,** manufacture *f* d'artillerie. **2.** (*a*) *Mil:* (service *m* du) matériel; **Royal Army O. Corps,** *U.S:* **O. Service,** Service du Matériel; **o. and supplies,** les ravitaillements *mpl*; (*b*) *Adm: Mil:* **O. Survey,** (i) = Institut Géographique National; (ii) corps *m* des ingénieurs géographes; **o.(-survey) map,** (i) = carte *f* de l'Institut Géographique National; (ii) carte d'état-major.

ordure ['ɔːdjuər] *n.* ordure *f*.

ore [ɔːr] *n.* minerai *m*; **iron o.,** minerai de fer; **rich, high-grade, o.,** minerai à, de, haute teneur; **crude o.,** minerai brut; **o. deposit,** gisement *m* de minerai.

oregano [ɔri'gaːnou] *n.* *Bot:* origan *m*.

organ ['ɔːgən] *n.* **1.** *Mus:* (*a*) orgue *m*; *Ecc:* orgues *fpl*; **grand o.,** grand orgue, grandes orgues; **choir o.,** orgue du chœur; **to play the o.,** jouer, toucher, de l'orgue; **o. builder,** facteur *m* d'orgues; **o. loft, gallery,** tribune *f* d'orgues; **o. pipe,** tuyau *m* d'orgue; **o. stop,** jeu *m* d'orgue; (*b*) **American o.,** orgue de salon; (*c*) **street o.,** orgue de Barbarie; **o. grinder,** joueur, -euse, d'orgue de Barbarie. **2.** organe *m* (du corps humain, d'une plante); **o. of hearing,** organe de l'ouïe; **the vocal organs,** l'appareil vocal. **3.** (*a*) organe (de gouvernement); **an efficient o. of propaganda,** un organe de propagande efficace; (*b*) journal *m*, -aux, organe, porte-parole *m inv* (du gouvernement, d'un parti); **the official o.,** l'organe officiel.

organdi(e) ['ɔːgəndi] *n.* *Tex:* organdi *m*.

organic [ɔː'gænik] *a.* **1.** (maladie, fonction) organique. **2. o. beings,** êtres organisés; **the law of o. growth,** la loi de croissance organisée. **3.** (*a*) (dépôt, engrais) organique; **o. foods,** aliments produits à l'aide d'un engrais organique; (*b*) (chimie, acide, composé) organique; **o. chemist,** organicien, -ienne. **4.** systématisé; **an o. whole,** un ensemble systématique. **5.** organique, fondamental, -aux; **o. part of the whole,** partie essentielle de la totalité. **-ally** *adv.* **1.** organiquement; **o. grown foods,** aliments produits à l'aide d'un engrais organique. **2.** fondamentalement, foncièrement.

organism ['ɔ:gənizm] *n.* **1.** *Biol:* organisme *m*; **living o.,** organisme vivant. **2.** économie *f* (d'un corps, etc.).

organist ['ɔ:gənist] *n.* organiste *mf.*

organization [ɔ:gənai'zeiʃ(ə)n] *n.* organisation *f.* **1.** *Ind:* **o. of labour,** (i) régime *m* du travail; (ii) syndicalisme *m*; **o. and methods,** organisation scientifique du travail. **2.** organisation, organisme *m*; **charity o.,** organisation charitable; œuvre *f* de charité; **youth o.,** mouvement *m* de jeunesse; **national organizations,** collectivités nationales.

organizational [ɔ:gənai'zeiʃən(ə)l] *a.* (défaut, etc.) d'organisation, de structure.

organize ['ɔ:gənaiz] *v.tr.* **1.** organiser; **workmen organized into trade unions,** ouvriers organisés en syndicats. **2.** (*a*) organiser, arranger (un concert); (*b*) aménager (ses loisirs); (*c*) *F:* se faire accorder (un congé, etc.); **to o. a bottle of rum,** dénicher une bouteille de rhum. **organized** *a.* **1.** *Biol:* organisé. **2.** (*of society, crime*) organisé; **o. labour** = les organisations ouvrières; *Sch:* **o. games,** jeux dirigés. **organizing** *n.* **1.** organisation *f*; **o. ability,** qualités *fpl* d'organisation. **2.** aménagement *m* (de ses loisirs).

organizer ['ɔ:gənaizər] *n.* organisateur, -trice.

orgasm ['ɔ:gæz(ə)m] *n.* **1.** paroxysme *m* (de rage, etc.); excitation *f.* **2.** *Physiol:* orgasme *m.*

orgiastic [ɔ:dʒi'æstik] *a.* orgiastique.

orgy ['ɔ:dʒi] *n.* (*a*) *Gr: & Rom.Ant:* **orgies,** orgies *fpl*, bacchanales *fpl*; (*b*) orgie; débauche *f*; **drunken o.,** beuverie *f*; (*c*) **o. of colour,** orgie de couleurs.

oriel ['ɔ:riəl] *n.* *Arch:* **o. (window),** oriel *m*; fenêtre *f* (i) en saillie, (ii) en encorbellement.

orient¹ ['ɔ:riənt] *n.* orient *m*; **the O.,** l'Orient.

orient² ['ɔ:rient] *v.tr. & i.* = ORIENTATE. **oriented** *a.* **1.** orienté. **2. profit-o. undertaking,** entreprise *f* qui vise aux profits; *Cmptr:* **computer-o. language,** langage adapté au calculateur.

oriental [ɔ:ri'ent(ə)l] **1.** *a.* oriental, -aux; **o. rug,** tapis *m* d'Orient. **2.** *n.* Oriental, -ale.

orientalist [ɔ:ri'entəlist] *n.* orientaliste *mf.*

orientate ['ɔ:riənteit] **1.** *v.tr.* orienter (une carte, une église); **to o. oneself (physically, psychologically),** s'orienter. **2.** *v.i.* s'orienter.

orientation [ɔ:riən'teiʃ(ə)n] *n.* orientation *f.*

orienteering [ɔriən'tiəriŋ] *n.* *Sp:* exercice d'orientation (sur le terrain).

orifice ['ɔrifis] *n.* orifice *m*, ouverture *f.*

origami [ɔri'gɑ:mi] *n.* (art *m* du) pliage *m.*

origin ['ɔridʒin] *n.* origine *f.* **1. the o. of the universe,** la genèse des mondes; **to trace an event back to its o.,** remonter à l'origine d'un événement; *Arch:* **point of o.,** point *m* d'origine (d'une courbe, etc.). **2. word of Greek o.,** mot *m* d'origine grecque; **a man of humble o.,** un homme d'humble extraction *f*; *Com:* **country of o.,** pays *m* de provenance; *Cust:* **certificate of o.,** certificat *m* d'origine. **3.** *Anat:* attache *f* (d'un muscle).

original [ə'ridʒin(ə)l] **1.** *a.* (*a*) original, -aux; premier; primordial, -iaux; originaire; d'origine; **o. idea of a work,** idée *f* mère d'une œuvre; **o. meaning of a word,** sens premier d'un mot; *Com:* **o. packing,** emballage *m* d'origine; (*b*) originel, originaire; **o. defect,** vice *m* originaire; *Theol:* **o. sin,** péché originel; (*c*) (manuscrit, tableau) original; *Publ:* **o. edition,** édition princeps, originale; *Fin: Com:* **o. invoice,** facture originale; (*d*) (écrivain, style) original; (spectacle) inédit. **2.** *n.* original *m* (d'un tableau, d'une facture); *Fin:* primata *m* (d'une traite); **to copy sth. from the o.,** copier qch. sur l'original; **to read the classics in the o.,** lire les classiques dans l'original; *Lith:* matrice *f.* **3.** *n.* personne originale; original, -ale; *F:* type *m* (à part). **-ally** *adv.* **1.** (*a*) originairement; à l'origine; **he was o. English,** il est Anglais d'origine; (*b*) originellement; dès l'origine. **2.** originalement; d'une façon originale.

originality [əridʒi'næliti] *n.* originalité *f.*

originate [ə'ridʒineit] **1.** *v.tr.* donner naissance à, être l'auteur de (qch.); amorcer (une réforme, etc.). **2.** *v.i.* tirer son origine, dériver, provenir (**from, in,** de); avoir son origine, prendre sa source (**from, in,** dans); **the fire originated under the floor,** le feu a pris naissance sous le plancher; **the scheme originated with me,** je suis l'auteur de ce projet.

originator [ə'ridʒineitər] *n.* créateur, -trice; auteur *m*; initiateur, -trice; promoteur *m* (d'une industrie).

oriole ['ɔ:rioul] *n.* *Orn:* **1.** loriot *m*; **golden o.,** loriot (jaune d'Europe). **2.** *NAm:* troupiale *m*; *Fr.C:* oriole *m.*

Orkneys (the) [ði'ɔ:kniz] *Pr.n.pl.* les Orcades *fpl.*

ormolu ['ɔ:məlu:] *n.* or moulu.

ornament¹ ['ɔ:nəmənt] *n.* **1.** (*a*) ornement *m* (du style, d'architecture, etc.); agrément *m*, garniture *f* (sur une robe, etc.); **by way of o.,** pour ornement; (*b*) ornement; **vases and other ornaments,** vases et autres ornements; **he would be an o. to any circle,** il serait un ornement pour n'importe quelle société. **2.** *Mus:* **ornaments,** ornements.

ornament² ['ɔ:nəment] *v.tr.* orner, ornementer (une chambre, etc.); agrémenter, embellir (une robe, etc.); orner (son style) (**with,** de).

ornamental [ɔ:nə'ment(ə)l] *a.* ornemental, -aux; d'ornement, d'agrément; décoratif; **o. tree, plant,** *n.* **o.,** arbre *m*, plante *f*, d'ornement.

ornamentation [ɔ:nəmen'teiʃ(ə)n] *n.* ornementation *f*, embellissement *m.*

ornate [ɔ:'neit] *a.* orné; surchargé d'ornements; **o. style,** style orné, imagé, fleuri. **-ly** *adv.* avec une surabondance d'ornements; en style trop fleuri.

ornery ['ɔ:nəri] *a.* *NAm:* *F:* (*a*) désagréable; (*b*) d'humeur maussade; rouspéteur.

ornithological [ɔ:niθə'lɔdʒik(ə)l] *a.* ornithologique.

ornithologist [ɔ:ni'θɔlədʒist] *n.* ornithologue *mf*, ornithologiste *mf.*

ornithology [ɔ:ni'θɔlədʒi] *n.* ornithologie *f.*

orphan¹ ['ɔ:f(ə)n] **1.** *n.* orphelin, -ine; **to be left an o.,** rester, devenir, orphelin; **war o.,** pupille *mf* de la Nation. **2.** *a.* **an o. child,** un(e) orphelin(e).

orphan² *v.tr.* rendre (qn) orphelin, -ine; **orphaned of both parents,** orphelin de père et (de) mère.

orphanage ['ɔ:f(ə)nidʒ] *n.* orphelinat *m.*

Orpheus ['ɔ:fju:s] *Pr.n.m.* *Myth:* Orphée.

orris ['ɔris] *n.* *Pharm:* **o. root,** racine *f* d'iris.

orthodontics [ɔ:θə'dɔntiks] *n.pl.* (*usu. with sg. const.*) *Dent:* orthodontie *f.*

orthodox ['ɔ:θədɔks] *a.* **1.** *Ecc:* orthodoxe; **the O. Church,** l'Église *f* orthodoxe; *n.pl.* **the o.,** les orthodoxes *mpl.* **2.** (historien, etc.) traditionaliste; (méthode, opinion, etc.) orthodoxe; classique.

orthodoxy ['ɔ:θədɔksi] *n.* **1.** orthodoxie; conformisme *m* (d'une doctrine, des opinions de qn, etc.). **2.** *Jew.Rel:* judaïsme *m* rabbinique.

orthogonal [ɔ:'θɔgən(ə)l] *a.* *Mth:* orthogonal, -aux.

orthographic(al) [ɔ:θə'græfik(l)] *a.* *Gram:* orthographique. **-ally** *adv.* orthographiquement.

orthography [ɔ:θɔgrəfi] *n.* **1.** *Gram:* orthographe *f.* **2.** *Mth:* projection orthogonale.

orthop(a)edic [ɔ:θə'pi:dik] *a.* *Med:* (traitement, appareil) orthopédique; **o. surgeon,** (chirurgien *m*) orthopédiste *mf.*

orthop(a)edics [ɔ:θə'pi:diks] *n.pl.* (*usu. with sg. const.*) *Med:* orthopédie *f.*

orthop(a)edist [ɔ:θə'pi:dist] *n.* *Med:* orthopédiste *mf.*

ortolan ['ɔ:tələn] *n.* *Orn:* **o. bunting,** ortolan *m.*

oryx ['ɔriks] *n.* *Z:* oryx *m*; antilope *f* à sabre.

oscillate ['ɔsileit] **1.** *v.i.* (*a*) osciller; *Fig:* **to o. between two opinions,** osciller, balancer, hésiter, entre deux opinions; (*b*) *Ph:* *W.Tel:* osciller. **2.** *v.tr.* balancer, faire osciller. **oscillating** *a.* (*a*) oscillant, oscillatoire, d'oscillation; (électron) oscillateur.

oscillation [ɔsi'leiʃ(ə)n] *n.* oscillation *f* (d'un pendule, etc.).

oscillator ['ɔsileitər] *n.* oscillateur *m*; (bobine) oscillatrice (*f*); **o. valve, tube,** lampe oscillatrice.

oscillatory ['ɔsileit(ə)ri] *a.* oscillant, oscillatoire.

oscillogram [ɔ'siləgræm] *n.* oscillogramme *m.*

oscillograph [ɔ'siləgræf] *n.* oscillographe *m.*

oscilloscope [ɔ'siləskoup] *n. El:* oscilloscope *m.*

osculate ['ɔskjuleit] *v.i.* **1.** *Mth:* **curve that osculates with a line,** courbe osculatrice à, qui a un contact d'ordre supérieur avec, une ligne (**at a point,** en un point). **2.** *Nat.Hist:* avoir des traits en commun (**with,** avec).

osculation [ɔskju'leiʃ(ə)n] *n. Mth:* osculation *f*; **point of o.,** point *m* d'attouchement.

osier ['ouziər, 'ouʒər] *n.* osier *m*; **o. bed,** oseraie *f*; **o. basket,** panier *m* d'osier.

osmosis [ɔz'mousis] *n. Ch:* *Physiol:* osmose *f.*

osmotic [ɔz'mɔtik] *a. Ch:* *Physiol:* osmotique.

osprey ['ɔspri, -prei] *n.* **1.** *Orn:* balbuzard pêcheur, fluviatile; *Fr.C:* aigle pêcheur. **2.** *Cost:* aigrette *f.*

ossicle ['ɔsikl] *n. Anat:* osselet *m* (de l'oreille).

ossification [ɔsifi'keiʃ(ə)n] *n.* ossification *f.*

ossify ['ɔsifai] **1.** *v.i.* (*a*) (*of cartilage*) s'ossifier; (*b*) *Fig:* (*of pers.*) se fossiliser; (*of government*) se scléroser. **2.** *v.tr.* (*a*) ossifier (un cartilage); (*b*) *Fig:* amener, entraîner, la sclérose dans (le gouvernement). **ossified** *a.* **1.** (cartilage) ossifié. **2.** *Fig:* (esprit) sclérosé.

ossuary ['ɔsjuəri] *n.* ossuaire *m.*

Ostend [ɔs'tend] *Pr.n. Geog:* Ostende.

ostensible [ɔs'tensibl] *a.* prétendu; soi-disant; feint. **-ibly** *adv.* en apparence; censément; **he went out o. to buy some tobacco,** il sortit sous prétexte d'acheter du tabac, soi-disant pour acheter du tabac.

ostentation [ɔsten'teiʃ(ə)n] *n.* ostentation *f.*

ostentatious [ɔsten'teiʃəs] *a.* fastueux; plein d'ostentation; (luxe) affichant. **-ly** *adv.* avec ostentation; avec faste; **to display sth. o.,** faire ostentation de qch.

ostentatiousness [ɔsten'teiʃəsnis] *n.* ostentation *f.*

osteo-arthritis ['ɔstiouɑː'θraitis] *n. Med:* ostéoarthrite *f.*

osteomyelitis [ɔstioumaii'laitis] *n. Med:* ostéomyélite *f.*

osteopath ['ɔstiəpæθ], *NAm:* *also* **osteopathist** [ɔsti'ɔpəθist] *n. Med:* praticien manipulateur des os et des articulations; (médecin) ostéopathe *m.*

osteopathy [ɔsti'ɔpəθi] *n. Med:* traitement *m* des affections de la santé par la manipulation des os et des articulations.

ostler ['ɔslər] *n.m.* valet d'écurie; garçon d'écurie.

ostracism ['ɔstrəsiz(ə)m] *n.* ostracisme *m.*

ostracize ['ɔstrəsaiz] *v.tr.* ostraciser; frapper (qn) d'ostracisme; mettre (qn) au ban de la société.

ostrich [ɔ'stritʃ] *n.* autruche *f*; *Fig:* **o. policy,** politique *f* d'autruche.

other ['ʌðər] **1.** *a.* autre; (*a*) **the o. one,** l'autre; **every o. day, week,** un jour, une semaine, sur deux; tous les deux jours, semaines; **the o. day,** l'autre jour; (*b*) **the o. four,** les quatre autres; (*c*) **potatoes and (some) o. vegetables,** les pommes de terre et d'autres légumes; **o. people have seen it,** d'autres l'ont vu; **o. people's property,** le bien d'autrui; **any o. book,** tout autre livre; **no one o. than he knows it,** nul autre que lui, personne d'autre, ne le sait; il n'y a que lui qui le sache; **somebody o. than me, you, him,** quelqu'un d'autre; **all verbs o. than those in -er,** tous les verbes autres que ceux en -er; (*d*) (*different*) **to see things o. than as they are,** voir les choses autrement qu'elles ne le sont. **2.** *pron.* autre; (*a*) **one after the o.,** l'un après l'autre; (*b*) *pl.* **the others,** les autres, le reste; **all the others are there,** tous les autres sont là; (*c*) **some . . . others . . .,** les uns . . . les autres . . .; **have you any others?** (i) en avez-vous encore? (ii) en avez-vous d'autres? **I have no o.,** je n'en ai pas d'autre; **for this reason, if for no o.,** pour cette raison, à défaut d'une autre; **no o. than he,** nul autre que lui; **one or o. of us will see to it,** l'un de nous y veillera; **this day of all others,** ce jour entre tous; (*d*) (*of pers.*) **others,** d'autres; (*in oblique cases also*) autrui *m*; **they prefer you to all others,** ils vous préfèrent à tout autre. **3.** *adv.* autrement.

otherwise ['ʌðəwaiz] *adv.* & *a.* **1.** autrement (**than,** que); **he could not do o.,** il n'a pas pu faire autrement; **should it be o.,** dans le cas contraire; s'il en était autrement; **to think o.,** penser autrement; **if he's not o. engaged,** s'il n'est pas occupé à autre chose; **except where o. stated,** sauf indication contraire; **all people rich or o.,** tout le monde, riches et pauvres. **2.** autrement; sans quoi, sans cela; **do what I tell you, o. everything will go wrong,** faites ce que je vous dis, autrement, sans cela, tout ira de travers; **o. we will take legal proceedings against you,** faute de quoi nous vous poursuivrons en justice. **3.** sous d'autres rapports; **o. he is quite sane,** à part cela il est complètement sain d'esprit.

otherworldly [ʌðə'wəːldli] *a.* détaché de ce monde.

otic ['outik] *a. Anat:* (nerf, ganglion) otique.

otitis [ou'taitis] *n. Med:* otite *f.*

otter ['ɔtər] *n. Z:* loutre *f*; **sea o.,** loutre de mer, marine; **o. hound,** chien *m* pour la chasse aux loutres.

Ottoman[1] ['ɔtəmən] *Hist:* **1.** *a.* ottoman. **2.** *n.* Ottoman, -ane.

ottoman[2] *n. Furn:* ottomane *f.*

ouch [autʃ] *int.* (*expr. pain*) aïe!

ought[1] [ɔːt] *v.aux.* (*with present and past meaning*; *inv*; **o. not** *is frequently abbreviated to* **oughtn't**) (*parts of*) devoir, falloir. **1.** (*obligation*) **one o. never to be unkind,** il ne faut, on ne doit, jamais être malveillant; **this o. to have been done before,** on aurait dû, il aurait fallu, le faire auparavant; **to behave as one o.,** se conduire comme il convient; **to drink more than one o.,** boire plus que de raison; **I thought I o. to let you know about it,** j'ai cru devoir vous en faire part. **2.** (*vague desirability or advantage*) **you o. to go and see the Exhibition,** vous devriez aller voir l'Exposition; **you o. not to have waited,** vous n'auriez pas dû attendre; *F:* **I o. to be going,** il est temps que je parte; **you o. to have seen it!** il fallait voir ça! **3.** (*probability*) **your horse o. to win,** votre cheval a de grandes chances de gagner; *F:* **you o. to know,** vous êtes bien placé pour le savoir.

ought[2] *n. A:* & *Lit:* (= AUGHT) quelque chose *m.*

ouija ['wiːdʒɑː] *n. R.t.m:* **O. (board),** oui-ja *m.*

ounce[1] [auns] *n. Meas:* once *f*; (*a*) **avoirdupois o.** = 28,35 g.; **Troy o.** = 31,1035 g.; *Fig:* **he hasn't an o. of courage,** il n'a pas pour deux sous de courage; (*b*) **fluid o.** = 28,4 cm^3.

ounce[2] *n. Z:* once *f*; panthère *f* des neiges.

our ['auər] *poss.a.* notre, *pl.* nos; **o. friends,** nos ami(e)s; **o. father and mother,** notre père et notre mère; nos père et mère; **o. two,** les deux nôtres; *Com:* **o. Mr Martin,** M. Martin de notre maison.

ours ['auəz] *poss.pron.* le nôtre, la nôtre, les nôtres; **your house is larger than o.,** votre maison est plus grande que la nôtre; **this is o.,** ceci est à nous; ceci nous appartient; **o. is a nation of travellers,** nous sommes une nation de voyageurs; **a friend of o.,** un(e) de nos ami(e)s; un(e) ami(e) à nous; **it's no business of o.,** cela ne nous regarde pas.

ourself [auə'self] *pers.pron.* (*said by monarch, editor, etc.*) nous-même.

ourselves [auə'selvz] *pers.pron.pl.* (*a*) (*emphatic*) nous-mêmes; **we o. do not believe it,** nous, pour notre part, ne le croyons pas; (*b*) (*reflexive*) nous; **we are enjoying o. very much,** nous nous amusons bien; (*c*) (*after preposition*) nous, nous-mêmes; **we say to o.,** nous nous disons; **we shouldn't talk about o.,** on ne doit pas parler de soi; (*reciprocal*) **instead of fighting among o.,** au lieu de nous battre entre nous.

ousel ['u:z(ə)l] *n.* = OUZEL.

oust [aust] *v.tr.* **1.** (*a*) *Jur:* déposséder, évincer (qn) (**of,** de); (*b*) **to o. s.o. from his post,** déloger qn de son poste. **2.** évincer, supplanter, déplacer (qn).

out [aut] **I.** *adv.* **1.** dehors; (*a*) (*with motion*) **to go o., walk o.,** sortir; **to run o.,** sortir en courant; **where are you going?—o.,** où allez-vous?—dehors; je sors; **o. you go!** hors d'ici! allez, hop! **voyage o.,** voyage *m* d'aller; (*b*) (*without motion*) **my father is o.,** mon père est sorti; **I am dining o. this evening,** je dîne en ville, au restaurant, chez des amis, ce soir; **he is o. and about again,** il est de nouveau sur pied; *F:* **we had a night o. on Saturday,** nous sommes sortis samedi soir; **the mob was o.,** la populace était descendue dans la rue; **the men are o.,** les ouvriers sont en grève; **he does not live far o. (of the town),** il n'habite pas loin de la ville; **the jury was o. for two hours,** le jury s'est retiré pendant deux heures pour délibérer; **o. at sea,** en mer, au large; **four days o. from Liverpool,** à quatre jours de Liverpool; **o. there,** là-bas; **the tide is o.,** la marée est basse; (*c*) *F:* **way o.,** très avant-garde; **far o.!** fantastique! terrible! **2.** (*a*) en dehors; **to turn one's toes o.,** tourner les pieds en dehors; (*b*) au dehors; **to lean o. (of the window),** se pencher au dehors; (*of garment*) **to be o. at the elbow(s),** être troué, percé, aux coudes. **3.** (*a*) au clair; découvert, exposé; (*of secret*) échappé, éventé; **the sun is o.,** il fait du soleil; *F:* **the best game o.,** le meilleur jeu qui soit; **the book is o., is just o.,** le livre est paru, vient de paraître; **the secret is o.,** le secret est connu; (*b*) (*with motion*) **to whip o. a revolver,** tirer, sortir, vivement un revolver; *F:* **o. with it!** allons, dites-le! expliquez-vous! *Prov:* **murder will o.,** tôt ou tard la vérité se fait jour; (*c*) (*of sail*) déployé; (*of flower*) épanoui; **the may is o.,** l'aubépine *f* est en fleur; (*d*) *F:* **to be o. after s.o., sth.,** être à la recherche de qn, de qch.; **he's simply o. for money,** tout ce qui l'intéresse c'est l'argent; **I am not o. to reform the world,** je n'ai pas entrepris de réformer le monde; **to go all o. for sth.,** mettre toute son énergie pour faire aboutir qch.; se démener pour obtenir qch.; **I'm (going) o. for big results,** je vise aux grands résultats; (*e*) *Sp: etc:* **all o., flat o.,** à toute vitesse, à toute allure; *Aut:* **she does 80 (when she's going) flat o.,** elle fait du 130 quand on la laisse filer; (*f*) **o. loud,** tout haut, à haute voix; **to say sth. straight, right, o.,** dire qch. carrément, sans détours. **4. shoulder o. (of joint),** épaule luxée; **I'm o. of practice,** je n'ai plus la main; j'ai perdu le tour de main; *Pol:* **the party that's o.,** le parti qui n'est pas au pouvoir; **long skirts are o. this year,** les jupes longues sont hors de mode cette année; **the players who are o. (of the game),** les joueurs qui sont hors jeu, éliminés; *Cr:* **not o.,** encore au guichet (à la fin de l'innings, de la journée); (*of boxer*) **to be o. for seven seconds,** être sur le plancher pendant sept secondes; *F:* **to be o. on one's feet,** tomber de fatigue; **to be fifty pounds o. (of pocket),** être en perte de cinquante livres. **5.** dans l'erreur; **to be o. in one's calculations,** s'être trompé dans son calcul; **I was not far o.,** je ne me trompais pas de beaucoup; **the shot was only a centimetre o.,** le coup n'a manqué le but que d'un centimètre. **6. the fire, gas, is o.,** le feu, le gaz, est éteint; *Mil:* **lights o.,** extinction *f* des feux; *Nau:* **to steam with all lights o.,** naviguer avec tous les feux masqués. **7.** (*a*) à bout, achevé; **my pipe is smoked o.,** j'ai fini ma pipe; **before the week is o.,** avant la fin de la semaine; *W.Tel:* **o.!** terminé! (*b*) jusqu'au bout; **hear me o.,** entendez-moi jusqu'à la fin. **8.** (*a*) *adv.phr.* **this is o. and away the best,** c'est de beaucoup le meilleur; (*b*) **o. and o.,** (i) complètement, absolument; (ii) (*preceding noun*) (républicain, etc.) convaincu, intransigeant; (menteur) fieffé, achevé. **9.** *prep.phr.* **from o. (of) the open window came bursts of laughter,** par la fenêtre ouverte arrivaient des éclats de rire. **10.** *prep.phr.* **out of,** (*a*) hors de, en dehors de; **o. of danger,** (i) hors de danger; (ii) à l'abri du danger; **o. of sight,** hors de vue; **o. of doors** = OUTDOORS 1; **hardly were the words o. of my mouth,** à peine avais-je prononcé ces mots; *F:* **I'm glad I'm o. of the whole business,** je suis content d'en être quitte; **to feel o. of it,** se sentir dépaysé; se sentir de trop; (*b*) **o. of season,** hors de saison; **o. of date,** suranné, vieilli; passé de mode, démodé; (*of theory*) désuet; (*of passport*) périmé; **o. of fashion,** démodé, passé de mode; **to be o. of one's mind,** avoir perdu la raison; (*c*) (*with motion*) **to go o. of the house,** sortir de la maison; **is there a way o. of it?** y a-t-il (un) moyen d'en sortir? **to throw sth., to jump, o. of the window,** jeter qch., sauter, par la fenêtre; **to turn s.o. o. of the house,** mettre, flanquer, qn à la porte; **to get money o. of s.o.,** obtenir de l'argent de qn; **I got ten pounds o. of it,** j'y ai gagné dix livres; (*d*) *Breed:* **Gladiator by Monarch o. of Gladia,** Gladiateur par, issu de, Monarch et Gladia; (*e*) dans, à, par; **to drink o. of a glass,** boire dans un verre; **to drink o. of the bottle,** boire à (même) la bouteille; **to copy sth. o. of a book,** copier qch. dans un livre; **the firemen are paid o. of the rates,** on paie les pompiers sur le budget de la ville; (*f*) parmi, d'entre; **choose one o. of these ten,** choisissez-en un parmi les dix; **three days o. of four,** trois jours sur quatre; **one o. of every three,** un sur trois; (*g*) **hut made o. of a few old planks,** cabane faite de quelques vieilles planches; (*h*) **o. of respect for you,** par respect pour vous; **o. of friendship, curiosity,** par amitié, par curiosité; **to act o. of fear,** agir sous le coup de la peur; (*i*) **to be o. of tea,** ne plus avoir de thé; être à court de thé; **o. of cash,** démuni d'argent; *Com:* **I am o. of this article,** je suis démuni, désassorti, de cet article. **II.** *int.* **o. (with you)!** sortez! hors d'ici! **III.** *a.* (*preceding a noun*) **1.** extérieur, à l'extérieur. **2.** vers l'extérieur; (*a*) **the o. door,** la (porte de) sortie; (*b*) *Com:* **o. (tray),** (corbeille *f* à courrier) sorties *fpl*; (*c*) *Arch:* **o. thrust,** poussée *f* en dehors. **IV.** *n.* **1.** *Pol: etc: F:* **the outs,** ceux qui ne sont pas au pouvoir. **2.** *Ten:* balle *f* (qui tombe) en dehors des limites. **V.** *prep. F:* **to go o. the door,** sortir par la porte; **to look o. the window,** regarder par la fenêtre.

outback *a. & n. Austr:* **1.** *n.* ['autbæk] **the o.,** l'intérieur *m.* **2.** *adv.* [aut'bæk] à l'intérieur.

outbid [aut'bid] *v.tr.* (*p.t.* **outbid;** *p.p.* **outbid, -bidden** ['bidn]) **1.** (*at auction*) (r)enchérir, surenchérir, sur (qn). **2.** surpasser (**s.o. in sth.,** qn en qch.).

outboard ['autbɔ:d] **1.** *a. & n.* (*a*) *Nau:* (*of rigging, etc.*) extérieur, hors bord; **o. (motor),** moteur *m* hors bord; (*b*) *Av:* extérieur (au fuselage). **2.** *adv.* (*a*) *Nau:* (attaché, etc.) au dehors, hors bord; (jeter qch.) par-dessus bord; (*b*) *Av:* à l'extérieur (du fuselage).

outbound ['autbaund] *a.* en partance.

outbreak ['autbreik] *n.* **1.** éruption *f* (volcanique); début *m*, commencement *m* (des hostilités); première manifestation (d'une épidémie); **precautions against an o. of typhus,** précautions contre le typhus; **o. of fire,** incendie *m*; **at the o. of war,** quand la guerre a éclaté. **2.** révolte *f*, émeute *f*.

outbuilding ['autbildiŋ] *n.* bâtiment extérieur; annexe *f*; **outbuildings,** dépendances *fpl.*
outburst ['autbə:st] *n.* éruption *f*, explosion *f*; élan *m* (de générosité); déchaînement *m* (de la haine, etc.); **o. of temper,** accès *m*, bouffée *f*, éclat *m*, de colère.
outcast ['autkɑ:st] *a. & n.* expulsé, -ée; proscrit, -ite; **an o. of society,** un paria.
outclass [aut'klɑ:s] *v.tr.* surclasser (un concurrent).
outcome ['autkʌm] *n.* issue *f*, résultat *m*; **the o. of our labours,** le fruit de nos travaux; **I don't know what the o. will be,** je ne sais pas ce qui en résultera.
outcrop ['autkrɔp] *n.* **1.** *Geol: Min:* affleurement *m*, pointement *m*. **2.** éruption *f* (de crimes, etc.).
outcry ['autkrai] *n.* cri *m*, cris (de réprobation, d'indignation); clameur *f*; **to raise an o. against s.o.,** crier haro, tollé, sur qn.
outdated [aut'deitid] *a.* démodé, désuet, périmé.
outdistance [aut'distəns] *v.tr.* distancer, dépasser.
outdo [aut'du:] *v.tr.* (*p.t.* **outdid** [aut'did]; *p.p.* **outdone** [aut'dʌn]) surpasser (**s.o. in sth.,** qn en qch.); l'emporter, renchérir, sur (qn); **they are all anxious to o. each other,** c'est à qui fera le mieux; **not to be outdone,** pour ne pas être en reste.
outdoor ['autdɔ:*r*] *a.* (*a*) extérieur; à l'extérieur; au dehors; (vie, jeux) au grand air, en plein air, de plein air; **o. work,** travail (à l')extérieur, en plein air; *Cin:* **o. scenes, shots,** extérieurs *mpl*; *W.Tel:* **o. aerial,** antenne extérieure; (*b*) **o. clothes,** vêtements *mpl* de ville, de sortie.
outdoors [aut'dɔ:z] **1.** *adv.* dehors; au dehors; en plein air; **to sleep o.,** coucher à la belle étoile; *Hort:* **to sow o.,** semer en pleine terre. **2.** *n.* **the o.,** la vie en plein air; **the great o.,** la nature sauvage.
outer ['autə*r*] **1.** *a.* extérieur, externe; (*of boundary*) circonférentiel; **the o. world,** le monde extérieur; **the o. man,** (i) le corps; (ii) l'extérieur (d'un homme); **o. garments,** vêtements *mpl* de dessus; *Arch:* **o. door,** avant-portail *m*, *pl.* avant-portails; **o. space,** l'espace intersidéral. **2.** *n.* (*in range shooting*) (*a*) cercle extérieur (de la cible); (*b*) balle *f* dans le cercle extérieur.
outermost ['autəmoust] *a.* **1.** le plus à l'extérieur. **2.** le plus écarté; **to the o. parts of the earth,** jusqu'aux extrémités de la terre.
outface [aut'feis] *v.tr.* dévisager, décontenancer (qn).
outfit¹ ['autfit] *n.* **1.** appareil *m*, appareillage *m*, équipement *m*; *Nau:* armement *m* (d'un navire); **repair(ing) o.,** nécessaire *m*, trousse, de réparation. **2.** *Cost:* ensemble *m*; *Mil:* équipement *m*. **3.** (*a*) établissement *m*, organisation *f*; (*b*) *F:* équipe *f* d'ouvriers; *Mil:* (i) compagnie *f*; (ii) bataillon *m*.
outfit² *v.tr.* équiper (qn, qch.).
outfitter ['autfitə*r*] *n. Com:* confectionneur, -euse; **men's o.,** marchand *m* de confections et chemisier *m*.
outflank [aut'flæŋk] *v.tr.* **1.** *Mil:* déborder, tourner (une position adverse); **outflanking movement,** mouvement débordant, tournant. **2.** circonvenir (qn).
outflow ['autflou] *n.* (*a*) écoulement *m*, échappement *m* (d'un liquide); coulée *f* (de lave); décharge *f* (d'un égout); *Fin:* sortie (d'or, de devises); (*b*) **o. per hour,** débit *m* par heure.
outgoing ['autgouiŋ] **1.** *a.* (*a*) (i) (locataire, fonctionnaire) sortant; (ministère) démissionnaire; *Ind:* **o. shift,** équipe sortante, relevée; (ii) partant; (avion, navire, train) en partance; **o. mail,** courrier *m* à expédier; (iii) *Tp:* (communication) de sortie; (iv) **o. tide,** marée descendante; (*b*) (*of pers.*) sociable, qui se lie facilement; extraverti. **2.** *n.pl.* **outgoings,** dépenses *fpl*, débours *mpl*; sorties *fpl* de fonds.
outgrow [aut'grou] *v.tr.* (*p.t.* **outgrew** [aut'gru:]; *p.p.* **outgrown** [aut'groun]) **1.** croître plus vite que (qn, qch.), devenir plus grand que (qn, qch.) **2.** (*a*) devenir trop grand pour (ses vêtements, etc.); **to o. one's strength,** grandir trop vite; (*b*) perdre (une habitude) avec le temps, en vieillissant.
outgrowth ['autgrouθ] *n.* excroissance *f*; *Geol:* apophyse (éruptive).
outguess [aut'ges] *v.tr.* déjouer les intentions de (qn).
out-herod [aut'herəd] *v.tr.* **to o.-h. Herod,** se montrer plus violent qu'Hérode.
outhouse ['authaus] *n.* (*a*) bâtiment extérieur; dépendance *f*; (*b*) *NAm:* lieux *mpl* d'aisance.
outing ['autiŋ] *n.* (*a*) promenade *f*; (*b*) excursion *f*, sortie *f*, partie *f* de plaisir; **day's o. (in a car, etc.),** randonnée *f*; (*c*) *Sp:* match *m*, concours *m*.
outlandish [aut'lændiʃ] *a.* **1.** qui semble étranger. **2.** (*a*) (*of manner, dress*) incongru, bizarre; (*of language*) barbare; (*b*) (*of place*) retiré, écarté; **to live in an o. place,** habiter au bout du monde.
outlast [aut'lɑ:st] *v.tr.* durer plus longtemps que (qch.); survivre à (qn).
outlaw¹ ['autlɔ:] *n.* hors-la-loi *m inv*; proscrit, -e.
outlaw² *v.tr.* **1.** mettre (qn) hors la loi; proscrire (qn). **2.** proscrire, bannir (un usage, etc.).
outlay ['autlei] *n.* débours *mpl*, frais *mpl*, dépenses *fpl*; **to get back, recover, one's o.,** rentrer dans ses fonds, dans ses débours; **without any great o.,** (i) sans grande mise de fonds; (ii) à peu de frais.
outlet ['autlet] *n.* **1.** (*a*) orifice *m* d'émission; issue *f* (de tunnel); sortie *f*, départ *m* (d'air, de gaz); échappement *m* (de vapeur); débouché *m* (de tuyau); *Hyd.E:* **o. pipe, drain,** tuyau *m* d'écoulement; (*b*) **to find an o. for one's energy,** trouver une issue pour son trop-plein d'énergie; (*c*) *Com:* (i) débouché (pour marchandises); (ii) **retail o.,** magasin *m*. **2.** *NAm: El:* prise *f* de courant.
outlier ['autlaiə*r*] *n.* (*a*) *Geol:* massif détaché; butte témoin; (*b*) annexe *f* (d'une institution quelconque).
outline¹ ['autlain] *n.* (*a*) **outline(s),** contour(s) *m*(*pl*), profil *m* (d'une colline); configuration *f* (de la terre); silhouette *f* (de qn, d'un édifice); ligne *f* (d'une voiture); (*b*) dessin *m* au trait; tracé *m*; **drawn in o.,** dessiné au trait; **o. plan,** plan *m* schématique, d'ensemble; (*c*) argument *m*, canevas *m* (d'une pièce, d'un roman); **main, general, broad, outlines,** grandes lignes, données générales, aperçu *m* (d'un projet); **to give a general o. of sth.,** décrire qch. à grands traits; **an o. of French history,** un résumé de l'histoire de France; **outlines of astronomy,** éléments *mpl* d'astronomie; *Art: Lit:* **rough o.,** premier jet.
outline² *v.tr.* **1.** contourner, silhouetter (le profil de qch.). **2.** esquisser (un roman, un projet); tracer les grandes lignes (d'un projet); ébaucher, indiquer (un plan d'action). **3.** *Draw: etc:* esquisser (un dessin, etc.).
outlive [aut'liv] *v.tr.* survivre à (qn, une défaite); **he will o. us all,** il nous enterrera tous; (*of machine*) **to o. its usefulness,** ne plus servir (à rien).
outlook ['autluk] *n.* **1.** guet *m*; **to be on the o. for sth.,** guetter qch. **2.** (*a*) vue *f*, perspective *f*; **the political o.,** l'horizon *m* politique; (*b*) façon *f* de voir les choses; **o. on life,** conception *f* de la vie.
outlying ['autlaiiŋ] *a.* éloigné, écarté; (*of rock, island*) isolé; **o. areas,** régions *fpl* périphériques.
outmanoeuvre, *NAm:* **outmaneuver** [autmə'nu:və*r*] *v.tr.* **1.** l'emporter sur (l'ennemi) en tactique. **2.** déjouer (qn).
outmatch [aut'mætʃ] *v.tr.* se montrer supérieur à (qn).
outmoded [aut'moudid] *a.* démodé; passé de mode.
outnumber [aut'nʌmbə*r*] *v.tr.* l'emporter en nombre sur (l'ennemi, etc.).
out-of-doors [autəv'dɔ:z] *adv.* = OUTDOORS 1.
out-of-pocket [autəv'pɔkit] *a.* **o.-of-p. expenses,** menues dépenses; débours *mpl.*

out-of-the-way [autəvðə'wei] *a.* **1.** (*of place, etc.*) écarté; loin de tout et de tous. **2.** peu ordinaire, peu commun, insolite.

outpace [aut'peis] *v.tr.* dépasser, distancer (un concurrent, etc.); **the demand has outpaced production,** la demande a dépassé la production.

outpatient ['autpeiʃənt] *n.* malade *mf* qui vient consulter à l'hôpital; **outpatients' department,** service *m* des consultations externes.

outplay [aut'plei] *v.tr.* jouer mieux que (qn); *Sp:* **to o. the other side,** dominer la partie.

outpost ['autpoust] *n.* **1.** *Mil:* poste avancé. **2. o. of the Empire,** poste colonial éloigné.

outpouring ['autpɔːriŋ] *n.* épanchement *m* (de sentiments); **outpourings of the heart,** effusions de cœur.

output ['autput] *n.* **1.** (*a*) production *f*, rendement *m* (d'une exploitation, d'un travailleur); **literary o. of an author,** production littéraire d'un auteur; (*b*) débit *m*, rendement (d'une machine); débit, refoulement *m* (d'une pompe); *El:* débit (d'une génératrice). **2.** *Mec.E: etc:* puissance *f*, rendement (d'un moteur); *El:* **power o.,** puissance débitée, de sortie; **o. voltage,** tension *f* de sortie. **3.** *Cmptr:* (i) sortie *f* (de données, de renseignements); (ii) résultat(s) *m*(*pl*) (d'un traitement de données); **o. card,** carte sortie, carte résultat.

outrage¹ ['autreidʒ] *n.* **1.** (*a*) outrage *m*, atteinte *f*; **to commit an o. on, against, s.o., sth.,** faire outrage à qn, à qch.; **o. against humanity,** crime *m* de lèse-humanité; (*b*) **plastic bomb o.,** attentat au plastic. **2.** *NAm:* indignation *f* (**at,** de, contre).

outrage² *v.tr.* **1.** outrager, faire outrage à (la religion, etc.); violenter, faire outrage à (une femme). **2.** *NAm:* faire éclater l'indignation de (qn).

outrageous [aut'reidʒəs] *a.* (*a*) (*of cruelty*) immodéré; (*of price*) excessif, exorbitant; (*b*) (*of statement, accusation*) outrageant, outrageux; (*of conduct*) scandaleux; **o. injustice,** injustice flagrante, criante; **it's o.!** cela dépasse toutes les bornes! (*c*) *F:* **an o. get-up,** une toilette impossible. **-ly** *adv.* (*a*) immodérément, outre mesure; (*b*) d'une façon scandaleuse.

outrank [aut'ræŋk] *v.i.* **1.** être supérieur en grade à (qn). **2.** avoir, prendre, le pas sur (qch.).

outrider ['autraidər] *n.* (*a*) *Hist:* piqueur *m*, jockey *m* (de carrosse); (*b*) **motor-cycle o.,** motard *m* d'escorte.

outrigger ['autrigər] *n.* **1.** *Nau:* espar *m* en saillie. **2.** *Row:* (*a*) porte-nage *m inv* en dehors; porte-en-dehors *m inv*; (*b*) (*boat*) outrigger *m*. **3.** balancier *m* (d'un prao).

outright [aut'rait] **I.** *adv.* **1.** (*a*) complètement; **to buy sth. o.,** acheter qch. comptant, à forfait, à un prix forfaitaire; (*b*) du premier coup; sur le coup; **he was killed o.,** il fut tué net. **2.** sans ménagement; franchement, carrément; **to refuse o.,** refuser tout net. **II.** *a.* (*before noun* ['autrait]) **1.** (*a*) **o. sale,** vente *f* à forfait; **o. gift,** don pur et simple; (*b*) **it's o. wickedness,** c'est de la pure méchanceté. **2.** (*of manner*) carré.

outrival [aut'raiv(ə)l] *v.tr.* (**outrivalled,** *NAm:* **outrivaled**) surpasser, devancer, l'emporter sur, (qn).

outrun [aut'rʌn] *v.tr.* (*p.t.* **outran** [aut'ræn]; *p.p.* **outrun;** *pr.p.* **outrunning**) **1.** dépasser, gagner (qn) de vitesse. **2. his zeal outruns his discretion,** son ardeur l'emporte sur son jugement.

outrunner ['autrʌnər] *n.* *Hist:* piqueur *m*.

outsell [aut'sel] *v.tr.* (*p.t. & p.p.* **outsold** [aut'sould]) se vendre en plus grande quantité que (qch.).

outset ['autset] *n.* commencement *m*; **at the o.,** au départ, au début; **from the o.,** dès le début.

outshine [aut'ʃain] *v.tr.* (*p.t. & p.p.* **outshone** [aut'ʃɔn]) **1.** surpasser (qch.) en éclat. **2.** surpasser, éclipser, dépasser (qn, qch.).

outside 1. *n.* [aut'said, 'autsaid] (*a*) extérieur *m*, dehors *m* (d'une maison, d'un livre); **on the o. of sth.,** au dehors, en dehors, à l'extérieur, de qch.; **to open a door from the o.,** ouvrir une porte du dehors; **to turn a skin o.-in,** retourner une peau (de lapin, etc.); (*b*) **at the o.,** tout au plus; au maximum; (*c*) *Fb:* ailier *m*; **o. left, right,** ailier gauche, droit. **2.** *attrib.a.* ['autsaid] (*a*) du dehors, extérieur, -eure; **o. diameter,** diamètre extérieur (d'un tuyau, etc.); *Const:* **o. measurements,** dimensions *fpl* hors d'œuvre; (*b*) **o. work,** travail extérieur, à l'extérieur, au grand air, en plein air; *W.Tel:* **o. aerial,** antenne extérieure; **o. broadcast,** production extérieure; (*c*) **the o. world,** le monde extérieur; **o. interests,** intérêts en dehors de son travail, de sa famille; **o. worker,** ouvrier, -ière, à domicile; **to get an o. opinion,** obtenir un avis étranger; (*of theft*) **it was an o. job,** les voleurs étaient étrangers à la maison; *St.Exch:* **o. market,** coulisse *f*; **o. broker,** coulissier *m*; (*d*) **o. prices,** prix maximums, maxima; les plus hauts prix; (*e*) *F:* **it's an o. chance,** il y a tout juste une chance (de réussir). **3.** *adv.* [aut'said] (*a*) dehors, à l'extérieur, en dehors; **the taxi is o.,** le taxi vous attend à la porte; **seen from o.,** vu de dehors; **vase that is black o. and in,** vase qui est noir au dehors et au dedans; (*b*) *prep.phr. F:* **o. of,** (i) à l'extérieur de, en dehors de; **to get o. of a good dinner,** s'envoyer un bon dîner; (ii) **o. of a few friends nobody knows anything about it,** sauf quelques amis, personne n'en sait rien. **4.** *prep.* ['autsaid] en dehors de, hors de, à l'extérieur de; **o. my bedroom,** (i) à la porte, (ii) sous les fenêtres, de ma chambre; **I'll meet you o. the cinema,** je vous rencontrerai devant le cinéma; **o.,** *NAm:* **o. of, the town,** en dehors de la ville; **these questions lie o. the scope of my speech,** ces questions dépassent la portée de mon discours.

outsider [aut'saidər] *n.* *F:* **1.** étranger, -ère, profane *mf*; **a rank o.,** un intrus. **2.** *St.Exch:* coulissier *m*. **3.** *Turf: Sp:* outsider *m*.

outsize ['autsaiz] *n.* **1.** (i) dimension *f*, (ii) pointure *f*, hors série; taille exceptionnelle; (*in men's clothes*) très grand patron. **2.** *attrib.* (*a*) **o. dress,** robe en taille exceptionnelle; **o. shoes,** pointure hors série; (*b*) *F:* (paquet) géant, énorme. **3.** personne *f* de taille exceptionnelle; **for outsizes,** pour les grandes tailles.

outskirts ['autskəːts] *n.pl.* **1.** limites *fpl*, (a)bords *mpl*; lisière *f* (d'une forêt); faubourgs *mpl* (d'une ville); banlieue *f*, périphérie *f* (d'une grande ville). **2.** approches *fpl* (d'une ville, etc.).

outsmart [aut'smɑːt] *v.tr.* surpasser (qn) en finesse.

outspoken [aut'spouk(ə)n] *a.* (*of pers.*) franc, *f.* franche; carré; **to be o.,** parler franc; ne pas mâcher ses mots; **o. criticism,** critique franche. **-ly** *adv.* franchement, carrément, rondement.

outspokenness [aut'spoukənnis] *n.* franchise *f*; franc-parler *m*.

outspread [aut'spred] *a.* étendu, étalé, déployé; **with wings o., with o.** ['autspred] **wings,** les ailes déployées.

outstanding [aut'stændiŋ] *a.* **1.** (*a*) (*of detail, feature*) saillant; qui fait saillie; (*b*) (*of pers., incident*) marquant; (*of artist*) hors ligne, éminent; **man of o. personality, merit,** homme au-dessus du commun, de première valeur; **matter of o. importance,** affaire de la première importance. **2.** (*a*) (affaire) en suspens, en cours de règlement; (problème) pas encore résolu; (*b*) (compte) impayé, à recouvrer, à percevoir; (paiement) arriéré, en retard; (intérêt) échu, arriéré; **o. debts (due to us),** créances *fpl* à recouvrer, recouvrements *mpl*. **-ly** *adv.* éminemment; exceptionnellement.

outstay [aut'stei] *v.tr.* **1.** rester plus longtemps que (qn). **2. to o. one's welcome,** lasser l'amabilité de ses hôtes.

outstretched [aut'stretʃt] *a.* déployé, étendu; (bras) tendu; **with arms o., with o.** ['autstretʃt] **arms,** les bras étendus.

outstrip [aut'strip] *v.tr.* **(outstripped)** (*a*) devancer, dépasser (qn à la course); *Sp:* distancer (un concurrent); (*b*) surpasser (**s.o. in sth.,** qn en qch.).

outvote [aut'vout] *v.tr.* (*usu. in pass.*) **we were outvoted,** la majorité des voix a été contre nous.

outward ['autwəd] **1.** *a.* (*a*) (*of direction, etc.*) en dehors; *Nau:* pour l'étranger; **o. voyage,** voyage *m* d'aller; **o. half (of ticket),** billet *m* d'aller; (*b*) extérieur, de dehors; **o. form,** extérieur *m*, dehors *m*. **2.** *adv.* = OUTWARDS; *Nau:* **o.-bound,** (navire) (i) en partance; (ii) en route pour l'étranger; *Sch:* **o.-bound course,** école *f* d'endurcissement (en plein air). **3.** *n.* extérieur *m*, dehors *m*. **-ly** *adv.* **1.** à l'extérieur, extérieurement. **2.** en apparence.

outwards ['autwədz] *adv.* vers l'extérieur; **to turn one's feet o.,** tourner les pieds en dehors.

outwear [aut'wɛər] *v.tr.* (*p.t.* **outwore** [aut'wɔːr]; *p.p.* **outworn** [aut'wɔːn]) user complètement; **outworn doctrine,** doctrine désuète, périmée.

outweigh [aut'wei] *v.tr.* **1.** peser plus que (qch.). **2.** l'emporter sur (qch.).

outwit [aut'wit] *v.tr.* **(outwitted) 1.** circonvenir (qn); déjouer les intentions, les menées, de (qn); se montrer plus malin que (qn). **2.** (*of hunted animal or pers.*) dépister (les chiens, la police).

ouzel ['uːz(ə)l] *n. Orn:* **ring o.,** merle *m* à plastron, à collier; **water o.,** cincle plongeur, merle d'eau.

oval ['ouv(ə)l] **1.** *a.* ovale; en ovale; (bouton) à olive. **2.** *n.* ovale *m*.

ovarian [ou'vɛəriən] *a. Anat: Bot:* ovarien.

ovary ['ouvəri] *n. Anat: Bot:* ovaire *m*.

ovate ['ouveit] *a. Nat.Hist:* ové, ovale.

ovation [ou'veiʃ(ə)n] *n.* ovation *f*; **to give s.o. an o.,** faire une ovation, un triomphe, à qn.

oven ['ʌv(ə)n] *n.* **1.** *Dom.Ec:* four *m*; **electric o.,** four électrique; **to put sth. in the o.,** mettre qch. au four; **to cook sth. in a slow, quick, o.,** cuire qch. à four doux, vif; (*of poultry*) **o. ready,** prêt à rôtir; *F:* **it's like an o. in here,** il fait chaud comme dans un four. **2.** *Ind:* **drying o.,** étuve *f*, four de séchage.

ovenproof ['ʌv(ə)npruːf] *a.* (plat) allant au four.

ovenware ['ʌv(ə)nwɛər] *n.* vaisselle *f* allant au four.

over ['ouvər] **I.** *prep.* **1.** (*a*) sur, dessus, par-dessus; **to spill ink o. the table,** répandre de l'encre sur la table; **to spread a cloth o. sth.,** étendre une toile sur, par-dessus, qch.; (*b*) **all o. the north of England,** sur tout le nord de l'Angleterre; **famous all o. the world,** célèbre dans le monde entier; **to glance o. sth.,** parcourir qch. des yeux, du regard; **length o. all,** longueur totale; *F:* **to be all o. s.o.,** faire l'empressé auprès de qn; (*c*) **o. (the top of) sth.,** par-dessus (qch.); **to throw sth. o. the wall,** jeter qch. par-dessus le mur; **we're o. the worst,** le plus mauvais moment est passé; **to read o. s.o.'s shoulder,** lire par-dessus l'épaule de qn; **with his coat o. his shoulder,** le manteau sur l'épaule; **to stumble, trip, o. sth.,** buter contre qch. **2.** (*a*) **with his hat o. his eyes,** le chapeau enfoncé jusqu'aux yeux; *Mth: a* **o.** *b, a* divisé par *b*; (*b*) **to have an advantage o. s.o.,** avoir un avantage sur qn; **to reign o. a country,** régner sur un pays; (*c*) **bending o. his work,** courbé sur son travail; **to have a chat o. a glass of wine,** bavarder tout en prenant un verre de vin; **to go to sleep o. one's work,** s'endormir sur son travail; **to laugh o. sth.,** rire de qch.; **we had trouble o. the tickets,** nous avons eu des ennuis au sujet des billets. **3.** (*across*) (*a*) **to cross o. the road,** traverser la rue; **the house o. the way,** la maison d'en face; **o. the border,** au delà de la frontière; **to live o. the river,** demeurer de l'autre côté de la rivière; **from o. the seas,** de par delà les mers; (*b*) **the bridge o. the river,** le pont qui traverse, le pont sur, la rivière. **4.** (*in excess of*) **numbers o. a hundred,** numéros au-dessus de cent; **o. fifty pounds,** plus de cinquante livres; *Post:* **not o. 250 gr.,** jusqu'à 250 gr.; **children o. five (years of age), the o. fives,** les enfants au-dessus de cinq ans; **he's o. fifty,** il a (dé)passé la cinquantaine; **he spoke for o. an hour,** il a parlé pendant plus d'une heure; *prep.phr.* **he receives tips o. and above his wages,** il reçoit des pourboires en sus de son salaire. **5. o. the last three years,** au cours des trois dernières années. **II.** *adv.* **1.** (*a*) sur toute la surface; partout; **to search all o. Paris,** chercher par tout Paris; **famous the world o.,** célèbre dans le monde entier; **to ache all o.,** avoir mal partout; **he's French all o.,** il est français jusqu'au bout des ongles; **that's you all o.,** je vous reconnais bien là; (*b*) d'un bout à l'autre; **I've had to do it all o. again,** j'ai dû le faire de, à, nouveau, encore une fois; (*c*) (*repetition*) **ten times o.,** dix fois de suite; **twice o.,** à deux reprises; **o. and o. (again),** maintes et maintes fois; à n'en plus finir. **2.** par-dessus (qch.); **the milk boiled o.,** le lait s'est sauvé. **3.** (*a*) **to knock sth. o.,** renverser qch.; **and o. I went,** et me voilà par terre; (*b*) **please turn o.!** voir au dos! tournez s'il vous plaît! **to turn sth. o. and o.,** tourner et retourner qch.; **to bend sth. o.,** replier qch.; (*c*) *Nau:* **hard o.!** la barre toute! *Aut:* **to put the wheel hard o.,** braquer à fond. **4.** (*across*) **he led me o. to the window,** il m'a conduit à la fenêtre; **to cross o.,** (i) traverser (la rue); (ii) faire la traversée (de la Manche); **o. there,** là-bas; **o. here,** ici; de ce côté; **ask him o.,** demandez-lui de venir (chez nous); **our friends are coming o. tomorrow,** nos amis vont venir nous voir demain; **to deliver, hand, sth. o. to s.o.,** remettre qch. à qn, entre les mains de qn; **o. to you,** (i) *W.Tel:* (*usu.* **o.!**) répondez! à vous! (ii) c'est votre tour, c'est à vous. **5.** en plus, en excès; (*a*) **cook for an hour, but allow five minutes o.,** faire cuire pendant une heure, mais ajoutez-y cinq minutes; **children of fourteen and o.,** les enfants qui ont quatorze ans et au delà; **three into seven goes twice and one o.,** sept divisé par trois donne deux, et il reste un; (*b*) **you will keep what is (left) o.,** vous garderez l'excédent, le surplus; **I have one card left o.,** il me reste encore une carte; (*c*) **he didn't look o. cheerful,** il n'était pas d'une gaieté folle; **we're not o. busy,** nous n'avons pas trop à faire; (*d*) (*until later*) **to hold o.,** remettre (à plus tard) (une décision); **bills held o.,** effets en souffrance, en suspens. **6.** fini, achevé; **the danger is o.,** le danger est passé; **the rain is o.,** la pluie a cessé; **the game is o.,** la partie est finie; **the holidays are o.,** les vacances sont terminées; **the war was just o.,** la guerre venait de finir; **it is all o.,** c'est fini; **it is all o. with me,** c'en est fait de moi; **that's o. and done with,** voilà qui est fini et bien fini. **III.** *n.* **1.** *Cr:* **six-ball, eight-ball, o.,** série *f* de six, huit, balles. **2.** (*a*) *Com:* **shorts and overs,** déficits *mpl* et excédents *mpl*; (*b*) *Publ:* **overs,** exemplaires *mpl* de passe. **overly** *adv. esp. Scot: NAm:* trop, à l'excès, excessivement; **not o.,** pas trop.

overabundant [ouvərə'bʌndənt] *a.* surabondant.

overact [ouvər'ækt] **1.** *v.tr.* outrer, charger, exagérer (un rôle, etc.). **2.** *v.i.* exagérer; *F:* forcer la note.

overactive [ouvər'æktiv] *a.* trop actif.

overall ['ouvərɔːl] **1.** *a.* (*a*) hors tout; total, -aux; **o. length,** longueur totale, hors tout; (*b*) général, -aux, global, -aux, total; **o. efficiency,** (i) efficacité totale; (ii) rendement global; **o. plan,** plan *m* d'ensemble. **2.** *n.* (*a*) blouse *f*; (*child's*) tablier *m*, blouse; (*b*) **overalls,** combinaison *f* (de travail); salopette *f*; *F:* bleus *mpl* (de travail).

overanxious [ouvər'æŋ(k)ʃəs] *a.* **1.** extrêmement, trop, inquiet. **2.** qui fait des excès de zèle.
overarm ['ouvərɑːm] *a.* **1.** (*a*) *Swim:* **o. stroke,** brasse indienne, nage (à l')indienne; (*b*) *Cr:* **o. bowling,** *Ten:* **o. service,** service *m* au-dessus de la tête.
overawe [ouvə'rɔː] *v.tr.* intimider (qn).
overbalance [ouvə'bæləns] **1.** *v.tr.* (*a*) surpasser, l'emporter sur (qch.); (*b*) renverser (qch.). **2.** *v.i.* (*a*) (*of pers.*) perdre l'équilibre; *F:* faire la bascule; (*b*) (*of thg*) se renverser; tomber.
overbearing [ouvə'bɛəriŋ] *a.* arrogant, impérieux, autoritaire; **in an o. manner,** avec arrogance, autoritairement.
overboard ['ouvəbɔːd] *adv.* **1.** *Nau:* pardessus (le) bord; **to be washed o.,** être enlevé par une lame; **to throw sth., s.o., o.,** (i) jeter qch. pardessus (le) bord, à la mer; (ii) *F:* abandonner (un projet); (iii) abandonner, trahir (qn); **to fall o.,** tomber à la mer; **man o.!** un homme à la mer! **2.** *F:* **to go o.,** s'emballer (**for sth., s.o.,** pour qch., qn).
overbook [ouvə'buk] *v.tr. & i.* **to o. (a flight, etc.),** louer plus de places qu'il n'y en a de disponibles.
overboot ['ouvəbuːt] *n.* couvre-chaussure *m*, *pl.* couvre-chaussures.
overburden [ouvə'bəːd(ə)n] *v.tr.* surcharger, accabler (**with,** de); *Fig:* **not overburdened with principles,** peu encombré de principes.
overcapitalization [ouvəkæpitəlai'zeiʃ(ə)n] *n.* *Fin:* surcapitalisation *f*.
overcapitalize [ouvə'kæpitəlaiz] *v.tr.* *Fin:* surcapitaliser (une société).
overcast ['ouvəkɑːst] *a.* **1.** (*a*) (visage) assombri; (*b*) (ciel) couvert, sombre, nuageux; (temps) bouché.
overcharge¹ ['ouvətʃɑːdʒ] *n.* **1.** surcharge *f* (d'un accumulateur). **2.** (*a*) survente *f*; prix excessif; prix surfait; **to make an o. on sth.,** survendre qch.; (*b*) **o. on an account,** majoration *f* d'un compte.
overcharge² [ouvə'tʃɑːdʒ] *v.tr.* **1.** (*a*) surcharger (une batterie d'accus); (*b*) surcharger (un livre, un portrait, etc.) (**with details, etc.,** de détails, etc.). **2.** (*a*) survendre, surfaire (des marchandises); (*b*) faire payer trop cher un article à (qn); majorer (une facture).
overcoat ['ouvəkout] *n.* **1.** pardessus *m.* **2.** *Paint:* couche *f* de finition.
overcome [ouvə'kʌm] *v.tr.* (*p.t.* **overcame** [ouvə'keim]; *p.p.* **overcome**) **1.** triompher de, vaincre (ses adversaires, etc.); venir à bout de, avoir raison de (qn, qch.); dominer, maîtriser (son émotion); surmonter, vaincre (un obstacle). **2. to be o. with, by (sth.),** (*a*) être accablé de (douleur); être paralysé par (la peur); être transi de (peur); être gagné par (le sommeil, les larmes); succomber à (l'émotion); (*b*) être asphyxié par (des gaz); succomber à (la chaleur).
overcompensate [ouvə'kɔmpenseit] **1.** *v.tr.* surcompenser (une inégalité, etc.). **2.** *v.i.* *Psy:* présenter une surcompensation.
overconfidence [ouvə'kɔnfidəns] *n.* **1.** confiance exagérée (**in,** en). **2.** suffisance *f*, présomption *f*.
overconfident [ouvə'kɔnfidənt] *a.* **1.** trop confiant (**in s.o.,** en qn). **2.** suffisant, présomptueux.
overcook [ouvə'kuk] *v.tr.* trop cuire.
overcritical [ouvə'kritik(ə)l] *a.* **to be o.,** (i) chercher la petite bête; (ii) se montrer d'un rigorisme exagéré.
overcrowd [ouvə'kraud] *v.tr.* (*a*) trop remplir (un autobus, etc.); (*b*) surpeupler (une ville, etc.). **overcrowded** *a.* trop rempli (**with,** de); surchargé; bondé (de gens); (*of town, etc.*) surpeuplé. **overcrowding** *n.* **1.** remplissage excessif (d'un autobus); encombrement *m* (d'une pièce, etc.). **2.** surpeuplement *m* (d'une ville, d'une forêt).
overdeveloped [ouvədi'veləpt] *a.* *Phot: etc:* trop développé.
overdo [ouvə'duː] *v.tr.* (*p.t.* **overdid** [ouvə'did]; *p.p.* **overdone** [ouvə'dʌn]) **1.** outrer (les choses); charger (un rôle, etc.); *F:* **to o. it, things,** (i) forcer la note; exagérer; (ii) se surmener. **2.** *Cu:* trop cuire.
overdose¹ ['ouvədous] *n.* dose excessive; surdose *f*.
overdose² [ouvə'dous] *v.tr.* administrer à (qn) des remèdes à trop forte(s) dose(s); **to o. oneself,** *v.i.* **to o.,** prendre des médicaments, des drogues, à trop fortes doses.
overdraft ['ouvədrɑːft] *n.* *Bank:* découvert *m*, solde débiteur.
overdraw [ouvə'drɔː] *v.tr.* (*p.t.* **overdrew** [ouvə'druː]; *p.p.* **overdrawn** [ouvə'drɔːn]) **1.** charger (le portrait de qn); trop colorer (un récit). **2.** *Bank:* **to o. (one's account),** mettre son compte à découvert; **overdrawn account,** compte à découvert, compte désapprovisionné.
overdress [ouvə'dres] *v.tr. & i.* **to o. (oneself),** faire trop de toilette; **she's rather overdressed,** sa toilette manque de simplicité.
overdrive ['ouvədraiv] *n.* *Aut:* vitesse surmultipliée; **in o.,** en surmultipliée.
overdue [ouvə'djuː] *a.* (*a*) (*of account*) arriéré, échu; (intérêt) qui n'a pas été payé à l'échéance; (*b*) (*of pers., train, etc.*) en retard; **he's long o.,** il devrait être là depuis longtemps; (*c*) (bébé) tardif; (*d*) (*of reform, etc.*) qui tarde à être réalisé.
overeat [ouvər'iːt] *v.i.* (*p.t.* **overate** [ouvə'ret]; *p.p.* **overeaten** [ouvə'riːtn]) manger avec excès; trop manger. **overeating** *n.* excès *mpl* de table.
overemphasis [ouvər'emfəsis] *n.* accentuation excessive.
overemployment [ouvərim'plɔimənt] *n.* suremploi *m.*
overenthusiastic [ouvərinθjuzi'æstik] *a.* (par) trop enthousiaste.
overestimate [ouvər'estimeit] *v.tr.* surestimer, surévaluer (le coût de qch., les talents de qn); exagérer (le danger); trop présumer de (ses forces); *Com:* majorer (son actif); **to o. one's own importance,** s'en faire accroire.
overexcite [ouvərek'sait] *v.tr.* surexciter.
overexcitement [ouvərek'saitmənt] *n.* surexcitation *f*.
overexert [ouvəreg'zəːt] *v.tr.* surmener, fatiguer outre mesure; **to o. oneself,** se fatiguer; se surmener.
overexertion [ouvəreg'zəːʃ(ə)n] *n.* surmenage *m.*
overexpose [ouvəreks'pouz] *v.tr.* *Phot:* surexposer.
overexposure [ouvəreks'pouʒər] *n.* *Phot:* surexposition *f*.
overfamiliar [ouvəfə'miliər] *a.* **to be o. with s.o.,** se montrer trop familier, prendre des libertés, avec qn.
overfeed [ouvə'fiːd] **1.** *v.tr.* suralimenter. **2.** *v.i.* se suralimenter, trop manger.
overflow¹ ['ouvəflou] *n.* **1.** (*a*) débordement *m* (d'un liquide); (*b*) eau débordée; inondation *f*. **2.** (*a*) trop-plein *m inv*; **o. pipe,** (tuyau *m* de) trop-plein; déversoir *m* (d'une citerne); (*b*) surplus *m* (de population); (*c*) **o. meeting,** réunion *f* supplémentaire (pour ceux qui ont trouvé salle comble).
overflow² [ouvə'flou] **1.** *v.tr.* (*a*) (*of liquid*) déborder de (la coupe); (*b*) (*of river*) inonder (un champ); (*of river*) **to o. its banks,** sortir de son lit. **2.** *v.i.* (*a*) (*of cup, heart*) déborder; **room overflowing with people,** salle qui regorge de monde; (*b*) (*of liquid*) déborder, s'épancher; (*of gutter, stream*) dégorger; **the guests overflowed into the other rooms,** les invités se répandaient dans les autres pièces. **overflowing 1.** *a.* débordant; plein à déborder; (*of kindness*) surabondant. **2.** *n.* débordement *m*; **full to o.,** plein à déborder.
overfond ['ouvəfɔnd] *a.* trop attaché (**of,** à); **I'm not o. of oranges,** je n'aime pas trop les oranges.

overfull [ouvə'ful] *a.* trop plein (**of, with,** de).
overgrown [ouvə'groun] *a.* **1.** couvert (**with sth.,** de qch.); **o. with weeds,** (jardin) envahi, par les mauvaises herbes; **o. with ivy,** tapissé de lierre. **2.** (*of child*) trop grand pour son âge; **he's like an o. schoolboy,** il est resté très écolier.
overgrowth ['ouvəgrouθ] *n.* **1.** croissance excessive. **2.** couverture *f* (d'herbes, etc.).
overhang¹ ['ouvəhæŋ] *n.* surplomb *m*; porte-à-faux *m inv*; saillie *f*; *Const:* **to have an o.,** porter à faux.
overhang² [ouvə'hæŋ] *v.* (*p.t. & p.p.* **overhung** [ouvə'hʌŋ]) **1.** *v.tr.* surplomber; faire saillie au-dessus de (qch.); avancer, déborder, sur (qch.). **2.** *v.i.* surplomber, faire saillie; être en porte-à-faux. **overhanging** *a.* surplombant, en surplomb, en porte-à-faux; (mur) déversé; **the o. threat,** la menace suspendue sur nos, leurs, têtes.
overhaul¹ ['ouvəhɔːl] *n.* **1.** révision *f* (d'une machine etc.); **complete o.,** révision complète. **2.** remise *f* en état (d'un véhicule, d'une machine).
overhaul² [ouvə'hɔːl] *v.tr.* **1.** (*a*) examiner en détail, réviser; vérifier (les machines, contacts); *Nau:* repasser (le gréement); (*b*) remettre en état, au point, réviser (une machine). **2.** *Nau:* rattraper, dépasser (un autre navire).
overhead [ouvə'hed] **1.** *adv.* au-dessus (de la tête); en haut, en l'air. **2.** *a.* (*a*) (câble, etc.) aérien; **o. railway,** chemin de fer aérien; (*b*) *Civ.E: Rail:* **o. crossing,** croisement supérieur; (*c*) *I.C.E:* **o. valves,** soupapes *fpl* en dessus, en tête; (*d*) *Art: Phot:* **o. lighting,** éclairage vertical; (*e*) *Ten:* **o. volley,** volley pris au-dessus de la tête. **3.** ['ouvəhed] *a. & n. Com:* **o. expenses, charges, overhead(s),** frais généraux.
overhear [ouvə'hiər] *v.tr.* (*p.t. & p.p.* **overheard** [ouvə'həːd]) surprendre (une conversation, etc.).
overheat [ouvə'hiːt] **1.** *v.tr.* (*a*) surchauffer, trop chauffer (un four, etc.); (*b*) **to get overheated,** (i) (*of pers.*) s'échauffer (trop); (ii) (*of engine, brakes, etc.*) chauffer. **2.** *v.i.* (*with passive force*) (*of engine, etc.*) chauffer. **overheating** *n.* **1.** surchauffe *f*, surchauffage *m*. **2.** *Mec.E:* échauffement (anormal).
overindulge [ouvərin'dʌldʒ] **1.** *v.tr.* montrer trop d'indulgence envers (qn); gâter (qn). **2.** *v.i.* **to o. (in sth.),** abuser (de qch.); trop manger, trop boire.
overindulgence [ouvərin'dʌldʒəns] *n.* **1.** indulgence excessive (**of s.o.,** envers qn). **2.** abus *m*.
overjoyed [ouvə'dʒɔid] *a.* transporté, rempli, de joie.
overkill ['ouvəkil] *n.* surcapacité *f* de tuer.
overland **1.** *adv.* [ouvə'lænd] par voie de terre. **2.** *a.* ['ouvəlænd] **o. route,** (i) voie *f* de terre; (ii) *Av:* trajet survolant la terre.
overlap¹ ['ouvəlæp] *n.* **1.** recouvrement *m*; (*a*) *Const:* chevauchement *m*, imbrication *f* (des tuiles, etc.); (*b*) empiètement *m*, chevauchement (d'une opération sur une autre). **2.** partie chevauchante, débordante.
overlap² [ouvə'læp] *v.tr. & i.* (**overlapped** [ouvə'læpt]) **1.** recouvrir (partiellement); (*of tiles, slates*) **to o. (one another),** chevaucher. **2.** dépasser, outrepasser (l'extrémité de qch.); déborder. **3.** (*of categories, etc.*) se chevaucher.
overlay¹ ['ouvəlei] *n.* (*a*) matelas *m* (de lit); (*b*) (i) couvre-lit *m*, *pl.* couvre-lits; (ii) napperon *m*.
overlay² [ouvə'lei] *v.tr.* (*p.t. & p.p.* **overlaid** [ouvə'leid]) recouvrir, couvrir (**with,** de).
overleaf [ouvə'liːf] *adv.* au dos (de la page); **see o.,** voir au verso.
overlie [ouvə'lai] *v.tr.* (*p.t.* **overlay** [ouvə'lei]; *p.p.* **overlain** [ouvə'lein]) recouvrir, couvrir. **overlying** *a.* superposé; (*of stratum*) surjacent.
overload¹ ['ouvəloud] *n.* **1.** (poids *m* en) surcharge (*f*). **2.** (*a*) *Mch: etc:* **o. running,** marche *f* en surcharge; (*b*) *El:* surcharge; surélévation *f* d'intensité. **3.** *I.C.E:* excès *m* d'injection, de richesse.
overload² [ouvə'loud] *v.tr.* **1.** surcharger (un véhicule, etc.). **2.** surcharger, surmener (une machine).
overlong [ouvə'lɔŋ] **1.** *adv.* trop longtemps. **2.** *a.* trop long, *f.* longue.
overlook [ouvə'luk] *v.tr.* **1.** avoir vue sur (qch.); (*of building*) dominer, commander (un vallon); (*of window*) donner sur (la rue); **we are overlooked by our neighbours,** nos voisins ont vue sur nous. **2.** (*a*) oublier, laisser passer (l'heure); négliger, laisser échapper (une occasion); **I overlooked the fact,** ce fait m'a échappé; (*b*) fermer les yeux sur (qch.), laisser passer (une erreur). **3.** surveiller (un travail); avoir l'œil sur (qn).
overlord ['ouvəlɔːd] *n.m.* suzerain.
overman [ouvə'mæn] *v.tr.* **to be overmanned,** avoir un personnel trop nombreux; *Ind:* avoir du superflu de main-d'œuvre. **overmanning** *n. Ind:* superflu *m* de main-d'œuvre.
overmuch [ouvə'mʌtʃ] *adv.* (par) trop; à l'excès: outre mesure.
overnight **1.** *adv.* [ouvə'nait] (*a*) la veille (au soir); (*b*) (pendant) la nuit; **to stay o.,** rester jusqu'au lendemain; passer la nuit; (*c*) (changer, etc.) du jour au lendemain; **he became famous o.,** il est devenu célèbre du jour au lendemain. **2.** *a.* ['ouvənait] (*a*) d'une nuit (de durée); **o. guest,** ami(e) qui passe la nuit (chez qn); client(e) qui passe la nuit (à un hôtel); **o. bag, case,** sac *m* de voyage; mallette *f*; **o. stay,** séjour *m* d'une nuit, (*in hotel*) nuitée *f*; **o. stop,** arrêt *m* pour la nuit; (*b*) (succès) soudain.
overoptimism [ouvər'ɔptimizm] *n.* excès *m* d'optimisme.
overoptimistic [ouvərɔpti'mistik] *a.* excessivement, par trop, optimiste.
overparticular [ouvəpə'tikjulər] *a.* (par) trop exigeant, trop méticuleux.
overpass ['ouvəpɑːs] *n. Civ.E:* passage supérieur.
overpay [ouvə'pei] *v.tr.* (*p.t. & p.p.* **overpaid** [ouvə'peid]) surpayer; trop payer (qn).
overpayment [ouvə'peimənt] *n.* **1.** surpaie *f*; paiement *m* en trop; (*of taxes*) trop-perçu *m*, *pl.* trop-perçus. **2.** remunération excessive (d'un employé).
overplay [ouvə'plei] *v.tr.* **to o. one's hand,** (i) *Cards:* annoncer au-dessus de ses moyens; (ii) *Fig:* essayer de faire quelque chose au-dessus de ses moyens.
overpolite [ouvəpə'lait] *a.* trop poli.
overpopulated [ouvə'pɔpjuleitid] *a.* surpeuplé.
overpopulation [ouvəpɔpju'leiʃ(ə)n] *n.* surpeuplement *m*, surpopulation *f*.
overpower [ouvə'pauər] *v.tr.* maîtriser, dominer, subjuguer (un bandit, ses passions); **to be overpowered by superior numbers,** succomber, être écrasé, sous le nombre. **overpowering** *a.* (*of emotion, heat, etc.*) accablant; (*of desire, etc.*) tout-puissant, irrésistible; **I find her o.,** c'est une femme par trop imposante.
overprint¹ ['ouvəprint] *n.* **1.** (*a*) *Typ:* impression *f* en surcharge; surcharge *f* (sur un timbre-poste, etc.); (*b*) *Phot:* surimpression *f*. **2.** timbre-poste surchargé.
overprint² [ouvə'print] *v.tr.* (*a*) *Typ:* imprimer (une rectification) en surcharge; surcharger (un timbre-poste); (*b*) *Phot:* tirer en surimpression. **overprinting** *n.* (*a*) *Typ:* impression *f* en surcharge; (*b*) *Phot:* (tirage *m* en) surimpression *f*.
overproduce [ouvəprə'djuːs] *v.tr. & i.* surproduire.
overproduction [ouvəprə'dʌkʃ(ə)n] *n.* surproduction *f*.
overrate [ouvə'reit] *v.tr.* surévaluer, surestimer (qn, qch.); faire trop de cas de (qch.); exagérer (les qualités de qn); **to o. one's strength,** trop présumer de ses forces; **overrated restaurant,** restaurant surfait.

overreach [ouvə'ri:tʃ] *v.tr.* **1.** tromper, duper (qn). **2. to o. oneself,** trop présumer de ses forces. **3.** *v.i.* (*of horse*) (s')attraper.

overreact [ouvəri'ækt] *v.i.* réagir trop vivement (**to,** à; **against,** contre).

overreaction [ouvəri'ækʃ(ə)n] *n.* réaction trop forte, excessive.

override [ouvə'raid] *v.tr.* (*p.t.* **overrode** [ouvə'roud]; *p.p.* **overridden** [ouvə'rid(ə)n]) **1.** (*of mounted troops*) ravager (une région ennemie). **2.** (*a*) outrepasser (ses ordres); passer outre à (la loi); fouler aux pieds (les droits de qn); (*b*) avoir plus d'importance que, avoir la priorité sur (qch.); **decision that overrides a former decision,** arrêt qui annule, casse, un arrêt antérieur. **3.** surmener (un cheval). **4.** *v.i.* (*of ends of fractured bone*) chevaucher. **overriding** *a.* principal, -aux; (principe) premier.

overripe [ouvə'raip] *a.* trop mûr; (*of cheese*) trop fait; (*of fruit*) blet, *f.* blette.

overrule [ouvə'ru:l] *v.tr.* **1.** (*a*) décider contre (qn, l'avis de qn); (*b*) *Jur:* annuler, casser (un arrêt); rejeter (une réclamation); (*c*) passer à l'ordre du jour sur (une objection). **2.** être plus fort que (qn, qch.); l'emporter sur (qn).

overrun[1] ['ouvərʌn] *n.* **1.** *Typ:* (*at end of line*) chasse *f*; (*at end of page*) report *m*; ligne(s) *f*(*pl*) à reporter. **2.** *NAm:* **o. (costs),** dépassement *m* du coût estimé.

overrun[2] [ouvə'rʌn] *v.tr.* (*p.t.* **overran** [ouvə'ræn]; *p.p.* **overrun**; *pr.p.* **overrunning**) **1.** (*a*) (*of invaders*) (i) se répandre sur, envahir (un pays); (ii) dévaster, ravager (un pays); (*b*) **garden o. with weeds,** jardin envahi par les mauvaises herbes; **house o. with mice,** maison infestée de souris. **2.** dépasser (la limite, le temps prévu); *Rail:* brûler (un signal). **3.** *Typ:* reporter (un mot) à la ligne ou à la page suivante; **words that o. the line,** *v.i.* **words that o. (into the margin),** mots qui chassent.

overseas 1. *a.* ['ouvəsi:z] (colonie, commerce) d'outre-mer; (dette) extérieure. **2.** *adv.* [ouvə'si:z] par delà les mers; **from o.,** d'outre-mer.

oversee [ouvə'si:] *v.tr.* (*p.t.* **oversaw** [ouvə'sɔ:]; *p.p.* **overseen** [ouvə'si:n]) surveiller (un atelier).

overseer ['ouvəsiər] *n.* surveillant, -ante; *Ind:* contremaître, -tresse; *Civ.E:* brigadier *m*; *Typ:* prote *m.*

oversell [ouvə'sel] *v.tr.* **1.** vendre trop de (qch.). **2.** exagérer les mérites de, surfaire (qch.).

oversensitive [ouvə'sensitiv] *a.* hypersensible.

oversew ['ouvəsou] *v.tr.* (*p.t.* & *p.p.* **oversewn** ['ouvəsoun]) *Needlew:* surjeter; surfiler (un bord).

oversexed [ouvə'sekst] *a.* à tendances sexuelles exagérées.

overshadow [ouvə'ʃædou] *v.tr.* **1.** ombrager; couvrir de son ombre. **2.** éclipser (qn); surpasser (qch., qn) en éclat.

overshoe ['ouvəʃu:] *n.* couvre-chaussure *m*, *pl.* couvre-chaussures; galoche *f*; **rubber overshoes,** caoutchoucs *mpl.*

overshoot [ouvə'ʃu:t] *v.tr.* (*p.t.* & *p.p.* **overshot** [ouvə'ʃɔt]) dépasser, outrepasser (le point d'arrêt); (*of shot, gun*) porter au delà de (qch.); **to o. the mark,** (i) dépasser le but; (ii) *Fig:* dépasser les bornes; *Av:* **to o. the runway,** *v.i.* **to o.,** (i) atterrir, se présenter, trop long (sur la piste); (ii) remettre les gaz (au lieu d'atterrir). **overshot** *a.* *Hyd.E:* (roue) en dessus.

oversight ['ouvəsait] *n.* **1.** oubli *m*, omission *f*, inadvertance *f*; **through, by, an o.,** par mégarde; par inadvertance; par oubli. **2.** surveillance *f.*

oversimplification [ouvəsimplifi'keiʃ(ə)n] *n.* simplification excessive.

oversimplify [ouvə'simplifai] *v.tr.* trop simplifier.

oversized ['ouvəsaizd] *a.* au-dessus des dimensions normales.

oversleep [ouvə'sli:p] *v.i.* (*p.t.* & *p.p.* **overslept** [ouvə'slept]) dormir trop longtemps; s'éveiller après l'heure.

oversleeve ['ouvəsli:v] *n.* manchette *f.*

overspend [ouvə'spend] *v.tr.* & *i.* (*p.t.* & *p.p.* **overspent** [ouvə'spent]) dépenser trop; dépenser au delà de (ses moyens, etc.).

overspill ['ouvəspil] *n.* surplus *m*, déversement *m*, de population; **o. town,** ville servant à décongestionner une agglomération surpeuplée.

overstaffed [ouvə'stɑ:ft] *a.* qui a un personnel trop nombreux.

overstate [ouvə'steit] *v.tr.* exagérer (les faits, etc.); **I am neither overstating nor understating the case,** je n'exagère ni dans un sens ni dans l'autre.

overstay [ouvə'stei] *v.tr.* dépasser (son congé, etc.); **to o. one's welcome,** lasser l'amabilité de ses hôtes.

oversteer [ouvə'stiər] *v.i.* *Aut:* survirer.

overstep [ouvə'step] *v.tr.* (*p.t.* & *p.p.* **overstepped** [ouvə'stept]) outrepasser, dépasser (les bornes de qch.); *F:* **don't o. the mark,** n'y allez pas trop fort.

overstock [ouvə'stɔk] *v.tr.* (*a*) encombrer (le marché, etc.) (**with,** de); (*b*) trop meubler (une ferme) de bétail; surcharger (un étang) de poissons.

oversubscribe [ouvəsəb'skraib] *v.tr.* *Fin:* surpasser, sursouscrire (une émission).

overt [ou'və:t] *a.* patent, évident, manifeste; *Jur:* **o. act,** acte *m* manifeste. **-ly** *adv.* ouvertement.

overtake [ouvə'teik] *v.tr.* (*p.t.* **overtook** [ouvə'tuk]; *p.p.* **overtaken** [ouvə'teik(ə)n]) **1.** (*a*) rattraper (qn); **demand has overtaken supply,** la demande a rattrapé l'offre; (*b*) doubler, dépasser, devancer (un concurrent, une voiture). **2.** (*of accident*) arriver à (qn); (*of fate, etc.*) s'abattre sur (qn); **darkness overtook us,** la nuit nous gagna. **overtaking** *n.* dépassement *m*; *Aut:* **o. lane,** piste *f* de doublage; *P.N:* **no o.,** défense de doubler.

overtax [ouvə'tæks] *v.tr.* **1.** (*a*) accabler (la nation) sous les impôts; (*b*) surcharger (qn); **to o. one's strength,** se surmener; abuser de ses forces. **2.** *Adm:* surtaxer, surimposer (qn).

over-the-counter ['ouvəðə'kauntər] *a.* (ventes) au comptant; (médicaments) vendus sans ordonnance.

overthrow[1] ['ouvəθrou] *n.* subversion *f*, renversement *m* (d'un empire); défaite *f* (de qn, d'un projet).

overthrow[2] [ouvə'θrou] *v.tr.* (*p.t.* **overthrew** [ouvə'θru:]; *p.p.* **overthrown** [ouvə'θroun]) **1.** abattre (un adversaire). **2.** défaire, vaincre (qn); abattre, mettre à bas (un empire); renverser (un ministère, etc.); réduire à néant (les projets de qn).

overtime ['ouvətaim] **1.** *n.* *Ind:* (*a*) heures *fpl* supplémentaires; (*b*) **wages, including o.,** le salaire, y compris le paiement d'heures supplémentaires. **2.** *adv.* **to work o.,** faire des heures supplémentaires.

overtire [ouvə'taiər] *v.tr.* surmener (qn); **to o. oneself,** se fatiguer outre mesure; se surmener.

overtness [ou'və:tnis] *n.* franchise *f.*

overtone ['ouvətoun] *n.* **1.** *Mus:* harmonique *m.* **2.** *Fig:* nuance *f*, soupçon *m* (de tristesse, d'amertume); **the phrase bears an o. of disparagement,** la phrase comporte un soupçon, un rien, de dénigrement.

overtop [ouvə'tɔp] *v.tr.* (*p.t.* & *p.p.* **overtopped** [ouvə'tɔpt]) **1.** dépasser (qn, qch.) en hauteur; dominer (qch.). **2.** l'emporter sur (qn).

overture ['ouvətjər] *n.* *Mus:* ouverture *f*; *Fig:* **to make overtures to s.o.,** faire des avances *f* à qn,

overturn [ouvə'tə:n] **1.** *v.tr.* (*a*) renverser (une table); faire verser (une voiture); faire chavirer (un canot); (*b*) abattre, mettre à bas (un empire); ruiner, réduire à néant (les projets de qn). **2.** *v.i.* (*a*) se renverser; (*of vehicle*) verser; (*of boat*) chavirer; (*b*) (*turn turtle*) *Aut:* *Av:* *Nau:* capoter; faire capot(age).

overuse [ouvə'ju:s] *n.* emploi excessif (**of,** de).

overvalue [ouvə'vælju:] *v.tr.* **1.** *Com:* surestimer, majorer (l'actif); estimer (un objet) au-dessus de sa valeur. **2.** faire trop de cas de (la capacité de qn).
overwater [ouvə'wɔ:tər] *v.tr.* arroser à l'excès.
overweening [ouvə'wi:niŋ] *a.* (*of pers.*) outrecuidant, présomptueux; (ambition) sans bornes.
overweight 1. *n.* ['ouvəweit] (*a*) surpoids *m*; poids *m* en excès; (*b*) excédent *m* (de bagages); (*c*) (*of pers.*) embonpoint *m*. **2.** *a.* [ouvə'weit] (*a*) au-dessus du poids réglementaire; (*b*) au-dessus du poids normal; **he's o.,** il pèse trop.
overwhelm [ouvə'(h)welm] *v.tr.* **1.** ensevelir (une ville dans la lave). **2.** (*a*) écraser, accabler (l'ennemi); (*b*) **to be overwhelmed with work,** être accablé, débordé, de travail; (*c*) combler (qn de bontés); confondre (qn de honte); **I am overwhelmed by your kindness,** je suis confus de vos bontés; **overwhelmed with joy,** au comble de la joie. **overwhelming** *a.* irrésistible; accablant; **o. majority,** majorité écrasante. **overwhelmingly** *adv.* irrésistiblement.
overwind [ouvə'waind] *v.tr.* (*p.t. & p.p.* **overwound** [ouvə'waund]) trop remonter (une montre, etc.).
overwork¹ [ouvə'wə:k] *n.* surmenage *m*; travail *m* outre mesure; **suffering from o.,** surmené.
overwork² 1. *v.tr.* (*a*) surmener (qn); surcharger (qn) de travail; **he doesn't o. himself,** *F:* il ne se foule pas la rate; (*b*) abuser (d'un truc, d'une idée, etc.). **2.** *v.i.* se surmener; travailler outre mesure. **overworking** *n.* surmenage *m*.
overwrought [ouvə'rɔ:t] *a.* (*of pers.*) excédé (de fatigue); surmené.
overzealous [ouvə'zeləs] *a.* trop zélé.
Ovid ['ɔvid] *Pr.n.m. Lt.Lit:* Ovide.
oviduct ['ouvidʌkt] *n. Nat.Hist:* oviducte *m*.
ovine ['ouvain] *a.* (animal, etc.) ovin.
oviparous [ou'vipərəs] *a. Nat.Hist:* ovipare.
ovoid ['ouvɔid] **1.** *a.* ovoïde. **2.** *n.* figure *f* ovoïde.
ovulate ['ouvjuleit] *v.i. Biol:* pondre des ovules.
ovulation [ouvju'leiʃ(ə)n] *n. Biol:* ovulation *f*.
ovule ['ouvju:l] *n. Biol:* ovule *m*.
ovum, *pl.* **ova** ['ouvəm, 'ouvə] *n. Biol:* ovule *m*.
ow [au] *int.* aïe!
owe [ou] *v.tr.* (*p.p. & p.t.* **owed** [oud]) devoir. **1.** (*a*) **to o. s.o. sth., to o. sth. to s.o.,** devoir qch. à qn; **the sum owed (to) her by her brother,** la somme qui lui est due par son frère; **I still o. you for the petrol,** je vous dois encore l'essence; *v.i.* **he owes for three months' rent,** il doit trois mois de loyer; **all the money owing to me,** tout l'argent qui m'est dû; (*b*) devoir (du respect, de l'obéissance, etc.) (**to s.o.,** à qn); **I o. you an apology,** je vous dois mes excuses; **you o. it to yourself to do your best,** vous vous devez à vous-même de faire de votre mieux; (*c*) *Sp:* rendre (tant de points à son adversaire). **2. I o. my life to you,** je vous dois la vie; **to whom, to what, do I o. this honour?** qu'est-ce qui me vaut cet honneur? **owing** *prep.phr.* **o. to,** à cause de, en raison de; **o. to a recent bereavement,** en raison d'un deuil récent.
owl [aul] *n.* (*a*) *Orn:* hibou *m*, -oux; **tawny o.,** chouette *f* hulotte; **barn o.,** (chouette) effraie *f*; **eagle o.,** grand-duc *m* (d'Europe); (*b*) **a wise old o.,** un vieux sage; (*c*) *Scout:* **Brown O.,** cheftaine *f* (de ronde, de Jeannettes).
owlet ['aulit] *n. Orn:* jeune hibou *m*.
owlish ['auliʃ] *a.* de hibou; **o. look,** air de faux sage.
own¹ [oun] *v.tr.* **1.** posséder; être propriétaire d'(une terre, une maison, etc.); **who owns this land?** qui est le propriétaire de cette terre? **he behaves as if he owned the place,** il se conduit comme en pays conquis; **state-owned company,** compagnie qui appartient à l'état. **2.** reconnaître; (*a*) avouer (un enfant); **dog nobody will o.,** chien que personne ne réclame; (*b*) avouer (qch.); convenir de (qch.); **I o. I was wrong,** j'ai eu tort, je l'avoue, je le reconnais; **to o. oneself beaten,** se reconnaître vaincu; (*c*) reconnaître l'autorité, la suzeraineté, de (qn). **3.** *v.ind.tr.* **to o. to a mistake,** reconnaître, avouer, une erreur; **she owns to being thirty,** (i) elle admet qu'elle a trente ans; (ii) elle se donne trente ans; **to o. up to a crime,** faire l'aveu d'un crime; **to o. up to having done sth.,** avouer avoir fait qch.; *v.i. F:* **to o. up,** faire des aveux.
own² 1. *a.* (*a*) *attrib.* propre; **her o. money,** son propre argent; son argent à elle; **I saw it with my o. eyes,** je l'ai vu de mes propres yeux; **o. brother, sister,** frère germain, sœur germaine; **I had my o. table,** j'avais ma table à part; **I do my o. cooking,** je fais la cuisine moi-même; je fais ma propre cuisine; **to roll one's o. cigarettes,** *F:* **one's o.,** rouler ses cigarettes; (*b*) le mien, le tien, etc.; à moi, à toi, etc.; **the house is my o.,** la maison est à moi; la maison m'appartient; **to make sth. one's o.,** s'approprier qch.; **his ideas are his o.,** ses idées lui sont propres; **my time is my o.,** mon temps est à moi, m'appartient; je suis libre de mon temps. **2.** *n.* **my o., his o., one's o., etc.,** (*a*) le mien, le sien, etc.; **to look after one's o.,** soigner son bien; **I have money of my o.,** j'ai de l'argent à moi; **a child of his o.,** un enfant à lui; **a small thing, but my o.,** une bagatelle, mais qui est de moi; **he has a copy of his o.,** il a un exemplaire à lui, en propre; **for reasons of his o.,** pour des raisons particulières, à lui connues; **a style of one's o., all one's o.,** un style original; **the landscape has a wild beauty of its o.,** le paysage a une beauté sauvage qui lui est propre; **may I have it for my (very) o.?** est-ce que je peux l'avoir pour moi seul? **there's not a thing here that I can call my o.,** il n'y a pas ici un objet qui m'appartienne en propre; **to come into one's o.,** (i) entrer en possession de son bien; (ii) recevoir sa récompense; (*b*) *coll.* les miens, les siens, etc.; (*c*) **my o. (sweetheart)!** ma chérie! (*d*) *adv.phr.* **to do sth. on one's o.,** faire qch. (i) de sa propre initiative, de son chef, (ii) tout seul; **to be, work, on one's o.,** (i) être établi à son propre compte; (ii) travailler (tout) seul; **I am (all) on my o.,** je suis seul.
owner ['ounər] *n.* **1.** propriétaire *mf*; patron, -onne (d'une maison de commerce); **rightful o.,** possesseur légitime; *Jur:* ayant *m* droit; **cars parked here at the owner's risk,** parc *m* pour voitures aux risques et périls de leurs propriétaires; *Aut:* **o. driver,** conducteur *m* propriétaire; **o. occupier,** propriétaire-occupant *m*, *pl.* propriétaires-occupants. **2.** *Nau:* **the owners (of a ship),** les armateurs *mpl*, l'armement *m*.
ownerless ['ounəlis] *a.* sans propriétaire; (chien) sans maître.
ownership ['ounəʃip] *n.* **1.** (droit *m* de) propriété (*f*); **change of o.,** mutation *f*; *Com:* changement *m* de propriétaire. **2. during his o. of the property,** pendant qu'il possédait la propriété.
owt [aut] *n. Dial: P:* n'importe quoi; quelque chose.
ox, *pl.* **oxen** [ɔks, 'ɔks(ə)n] *n.* bœuf *m*; **humped ox,** zébu *m*; *Cu:* **o. heart, tongue,** cœur *m*, langue *f*, de bœuf; **ox cart,** char *m* à bœufs.
oxalic [ɔk'sælik] *a. Ch:* oxalique.
oxblood ['ɔksblʌd] *a. & n.* rouge sang (*m*) *inv*.
oxbow ['ɔksbou] *n. Geog:* **o. (lake),** bras mort (d'un cours d'eau).
Oxbridge ['ɔksbridʒ] *Pr.n. F:* les universités d'Oxford et de Cambridge.
oxeye ['ɔksai] *n.* **1.** œil *m* de bœuf. **2.** *Bot:* **o. daisy, white o.,** marguerite *f* des champs.
Oxford ['ɔksfəd] *Pr.n.* **O. blue,** bleu foncé *inv*; *Sch:* **O. man, woman,** membre *m* de l'Université d'Oxford; **O. shoes, oxfords,** souliers *mpl* richelieu; *Tail: F:* **O. bags,** pantalon *m* très large.
oxherd ['ɔkshə:d] *n.* bouvier, -ière.
oxhide ['ɔkshaid] *n.* cuir *m* de bœuf.

oxidation [ɔksi'deiʃ(ə)n] *n. Ch:* oxydation *f.*
oxide ['ɔksaid] *n. Ch:* oxyde *m.*
oxidization [ɔksidai'zeiʃ(ə)n] *n. Ch:* oxydation *f.*
oxidize ['ɔksidaiz] *Ch:* **1.** *v.tr.* oxyder. **2.** *v.i.* s'oxyder.
Oxonian [ɔk'souniən] **1.** *a. Geog:* oxfordien, -ienne; oxonien, -ienne. **2.** *n.* membre *m* de l'Université d'Oxford.
oxtail ['ɔkstail] *n. Cu:* queue *f* de bœuf; **o. soup,** soupe *f* de queue de bœuf.
oxyacetylene [ɔksiə'setili:n] *a.* oxyacétylénique; **o. cutting,** découpage *m* au chalumeau; **o. torch,** chalumeau *m* oxyacétylénique de découpage.
oxygen ['ɔksidʒən] *n. Ch:* oxygène *m*; **o. bottle, cylinder,** bouteille *f* d'oxygène; **o. mask, tent,** masque *m*, tente *f*, à oxygène.
oxygenate ['ɔksidʒineit, ɔk'si-] *v.tr.* oxygéner.
oxygenation [ɔksidʒi'neiʃ(ə)n] *n.* oxygénation *f.*
oxygenize ['ɔksidʒinaiz] *v.tr.* oxygéner.
oyez! oyez! [ou'jes] *int.* oyez! (interjection par laquelle le crieur public réclame le silence).
oyster ['ɔistər] *n. Moll:* huître *f*; **pearl o.,** (huître) perlière (*f*); **o. bed, bank,** huîtrière *f*; (i) banc *m* d'huîtres; (ii) parc *m* à huîtres; **o. breeder, farmer,** ostréiculteur, -trice; **o. farm, park,** parc *m* à huîtres; **o. shell,** écaille *f* d'huître; *F:* **he shut up like an o.,** il est resté muet comme une carpe.
oystercatcher ['ɔistəkætʃər] *n. Orn:* huîtrier *m.*
ozone ['ouzoun] *n. Ch:* ozone *m*; *Meteor:* **o. layer,** ozonosphère *f.*

P

P, p [pi:] *n.* **1.** (la lettre) P, p *m*; *F:* **to mind one's P's and Q's,** (i) se surveiller; (ii) faire bien attention aux détails. **2.** *F:* penny *m*, *pl.* pence; **a 10p stamp,** un timbre de 10 pence; **a half p,** un demi-penny.

pa [pɑ:] *n.m. F: O:* papa.

pace¹ [peis] *n.* **1.** pas *m*; **ten paces off,** à dix pas de distance; *Mil: etc:* **one p. forward!** un pas en avant! **2.** (*a*) (*gait*) allure *f*; **to put a horse through its paces,** faire passer un cheval à la montre; **to put s.o. through his paces,** mettre qn à l'épreuve; (*b*) amble *m* (d'un cheval, etc.). **3.** (*speed*) vitesse *f*, train *m*, allure; **at a smart p.,** à vive allure; **at a slow p.,** au petit pas; **at a walking p.,** au pas; **to keep p. with s.o.,** marcher du même pas que qn; **supply is keeping p. with demand,** l'offre suit la demande; **to force, slacken, the p.,** forcer, ralentir, le pas, l'allure; **to set the p.,** donner le pas (à qn); *Sp:* donner, régler, l'allure; mener le train.

pace² **1.** *v.i.* (*a*) aller au pas; marcher à pas mesurés; **to p. up and down,** faire les cent pas; (*b*) (*of horse, etc.*) aller l'amble. **2.** *v.tr.* (*a*) arpenter (une rue, une pièce, etc.); (*b*) **to p. off, out,** mesurer (une distance) au pas; (*c*) *Sp:* entraîner (qn).

pacemaker ['peismeikər] *n.* **1.** *Sp:* (i) meneur, -euse, de train; (ii) entraîneur *m* (d'un coureur). **2.** (*a*) *Anat:* nœud sinusal cardiaque; (*b*) *Med:* (*device*) stimulateur *m* (cardiaque), pacemaker *m*.

pachyderm ['pækidə:m] *n. Z:* pachyderme *m*.

pacific [pə'sifik] *a.* **1.** (*a*) pacifique; (*b*) paisible. **2.** *Geog:* **the P. (Ocean),** l'océan *m* Pacifique; le Pacifique; **-ally** *adv.* pacifiquement.

pacification [pæsifi'keiʃ(ə)n] *n.* pacification *f* (d'un pays, etc.); apaisement *m* (de qn).

pacifier ['pæsifaiər] *n.* **1.** (*pers.*) pacificateur, -trice. **2.** *esp. NAm:* (*for babies*) sucette *f*, tétine *f*.

pacifism ['pæsifizm] *n. Pol:* pacifisme *m*.

pacifist ['pæsifist] *n. & a.* pacifiste (*mf*).

pacify ['pæsifai] *v.tr.* pacifier (une foule, un pays, etc.); apaiser, adoucir, calmer (qn, la colère de qn).

pack¹ [pæk] *n.* **1.** (*a*) paquet *m*, ballot *m* (de linge, de marchandises, etc.); ballot (de colporteur); (*b*) *Mil:* (i) sac *m* (porté sur le dos); (ii) paquetage *m*; **p. drill,** exercice *m* en tenue de campagne (à titre de punition), *P:* le bal; (*c*) bât *m* (de bête de somme); **p. animal,** animal *m* de bât, de charge; bête *f* de somme; **p. train,** convoi *m* de bêtes de somme; (*d*) *Av:* **parachute p.,** (i) parachute (plié et prêt à servir); (ii) enveloppe *f*, sac, de parachute; (*e*) **a p. of lies,** un tissu de mensonges. **2.** (*a*) bande *f* (de loups, de voleurs); volée *f* (de gibier); presse *f* (de gens); **p. of fools,** tas d'imbéciles; (*b*) *Ven:* (*of foxhounds*) meute *f*; (*of staghounds*) équipage *m*; **to lay on the p.,** laisser courre; (*c*) *Scout:* meute (de Louveteaux, de Louvettes); ronde *f* (de Jeannettes); (*d*) *Rugby: Fb:* **the p.,** le pack. **3.** jeu *m* (de cartes, de dominos); paquet (de cartes); *esp. U.S:* paquet (de cigarettes). **4.** *Oc:* **(ice) p.,** banquise *f*; **p. ice,** pack *m*. **5.** *Med:* **wet, cold, p.,** enveloppement humide, froid.

pack² **I.** *v.tr.* **1.** (*a*) emballer, empaqueter (des objets); mettre (ses effets) dans sa valise, sa malle; **packed lunch,** panier-repas *m*, *pl.* paniers-repas; pique-nique *m*, *pl.* pique-niques; (*with passive force*) **tent that packs easily,** tente *f* facile à emballer; *F:* **I've decided to p. it in,** j'y renonce! *P:* **p. it in!** assez! *U.S: F:* **to p. a pistol,** porter un revolver; *P:* **to p. a punch,** cogner dur; (*b*) *Com:* conserver (de la viande) en boîtes; embariller (des harengs, etc.); baguer (des marchandises périssables); (*c*) *Med:* faire un enveloppement froid à (un malade). **2.** (*a*) tasser (de la terre dans un trou, etc.); entasser, serrer (des voyageurs dans une voiture, etc.); **we were packed (in) like sardines,** nous étions serrés, pressés, comme des harengs (en caque), comme des sardines; (*b*) *Nau:* **to p. on all sail,** mettre toutes voiles dehors. **3.** remplir, bourrer **(sth. with sth.,** qch. de qch.); *Civ.E: Min: etc:* remblayer (un fossé, etc.); **to p. one's case,** faire sa valise; **the train was packed,** le train était bondé; **the hall was packed,** *F:* **packed out,** la salle était comble; **book packed with information,** livre bourré de faits. **4.** *Mec.E: Mch:* garnir, étouper (un gland, etc.); fourrer (un assemblage); garnir (un piston). **5.** bâter (un mulet, etc.). **6.** (*a*) **to p. a jury,** se composer un jury favorable; **to p. a meeting, the house,** faire la salle; s'assurer un nombre prépondérant de partisans à une réunion; (*b*) *Cards:* **to p. the cards,** apprêter les cartes. **7. to p. a child off to bed,** envoyer un enfant au lit; **his father packed him off to America,** son père l'a embarqué pour l'Amérique. **II.** *v.i.* **1.** faire sa valise, ses valises; *F:* **to send s.o. packing,** envoyer promener qn. **2.** (*of earth, etc.*) se tasser; (*of snow, etc.*) **to p. down hard,** se tasser dur. **3.** (*a*) (*of wolves*) s'assembler en bande; (*b*) (*of people*) s'attrouper; se presser (ensemble); (*c*) (*of runners, etc.*) se former en peloton; (*d*) *Rugby.Fb:* former le pack. **packing** *n.* **1.** (*action of wrapping*) (*a*) *Com: etc:* emballage *m*; empaquetage *m*; colisage *m*; **p. case,** caisse *f*, boîte *f*, d'emballage; (*b*) *Nau:* arrimage *m* (de la cargaison); (*c*) **to do one's p.,** faire sa valise, ses valises; (*d*) embarillage *m* (des harengs, etc.); mise *f* en conserve (de la viande, etc.); (*e*) *Med:* enveloppement *m* (dans un drap mouillé). **2.** (*material used*) (*a*) matériel *m* d'emballage; **non-returnable p.,** emballage perdu; (*b*) *Med:* pansement *m*. **3.** (*action of insertion, of pressing down*) (*a*) *Civ.E: etc:* remblayage *m* (d'un fossé, etc.); (*b*) tassement *m* (de la terre, etc.); (*c*) *Atom.Ph:* tassement (des particules); (*d*) *Mch: etc:* bourrage *m*, étoupage *m*, garnissage *m* (d'un joint, etc.); *Mch:* **p. box,** presse-étoupe *m inv*; **p. ring,** (i) *Mec.E:* rondelle, bague, de garniture; bague de fond (d'un cylindre); (ii) *Mch:* segment *m*, bague, garniture (de piston); (*e*) *Med:* tamponnement *m*; (*f*) *Pej:* manipulation *f* (du choix des membres d'un jury, etc.). **4.** (*material object, added or inserted*) (*a*) *Civ.E: etc:* remblai *m* (pour combler un fossé, etc.); (*b*) *Atom.Ph:* masse (spécifique apparente); (*c*) *Mec.E: etc:* garniture (d'un joint, d'un piston, etc.); joint *m* (d'un gland, etc.); (*d*) *Med:* tampon *m*. **pack up** *v.tr. & i.* (*a*) emballer (ses effets); ranger (ses livres, etc.); faire ses valises; (*b*) *F:* (*at end of day*) cesser le travail; (*c*) *F:* (*of machine, etc.*) tomber en panne; **my car's packed up,** ma voiture ne marche plus! (*d*) *P:* **p. it up!** assez!

package¹ ['pækidʒ] *n.* **1.** empaquetage *m*, emballage *m*. **2.** (*a*) paquet *m*, colis *m*; (*b*) *Cmptr:* progiciel *m*. **3.** matériel d'emballage. **4. p. deal,** (i) compromis *m*; (ii) *Com: etc:* contrat global; **p. tour, holiday,** voyage *m*, vacances *fpl*, à prix forfaitaire. **5.** *U.S:* **p. store,** magasin *m* qui vend des boissons alcoolisées (à emporter).

package² *v.tr. Com: etc:* empaqueter; emballer; conditionner. **packaging** *n.* empaquetage *m*; emballage *m*; conditionnement *m*.

packer ['pækər] *n.* **1.** *(pers.) Com: etc:* emballeur, -euse; empaqueteur, -euse. **2.** *(device)* *(a)* machine *f* à emballer, à empaqueter; *(b)* bourroir *m*.

packet ['pækit] *n.* **1.** *(a)* paquet *m* (de thé, de cigarettes, etc.); pochette *f* (de papier, etc.); sachet *m* (d'aiguilles); **p. soup,** bouillon *m*, potage *m*, en sachet; **pay, wage, p.,** paie *f*; salaire *m*; *(b)* **(postal) p.,** colis (postal), paquet poste; *(c) F:* **to make a p.,** gagner un argent fou; **that'll cost a p.,** ça va coûter les yeux de la tête. **2.** *O:* **p. (boat),** paquebot *m*.

packhorse ['pækhɔːs] *n.* cheval *m* de somme.

packsaddle ['pæksædl] *n.* bât *m*.

pact [pækt] *n.* pacte *m*, convention *f*, contrat *m*; **to make a p. with s.o.,** signer un pacte avec qn.

pad¹ [pæd] *n.* bruit sourd des pas d'une bête (chien, loup, etc.); bruit de pas feutrés.

pad² *v.tr. & i.* **(padded)** *(of dog, etc.)* **to p. (along),** trotter à pas sourds; *(of pers.)* **to p. about the room,** aller et venir à pas feutrés.

pad³ *n.* **1.** *(a)* bourrelet *m*, coussinet *m*; *Sp:* **shin pads,** *Cr:* **pads,** jambières *fpl*; *(b)* tampon *m* (d'ouate, etc.); *Med:* tampon, compresse *f*; **inking p.,** tampon encreur; **stamp p.,** tampon à timbrer; *(c) Harn:* (i) sellette *f* (de cheval de trait); (ii) coussinet (de selle, de collier); *(d) Fenc:* plastron *m*. **2.** *(a)* pelote digitale (de certains animaux); pulpe *f* (du doigt, de l'orteil); *(b)* patte *f* (de renard, de lièvre, etc.). **3.** bloc *m* (de papier à écrire, etc.); sous-main *m inv*; **memo, scribbling, p.,** bloc-notes *m*, *pl.* blocs-notes. **4.** *Tls:* *(a)* mandrin *m* (de vilebrequin); *(b)* manche *m* porte-outils. **5.** *Mec.E:* *(a)* semelle *f*, support *m* (de moteur, etc.); patin *m* (d'appui); *(b)* patin (de butée), amortisseur *m*; *(c)* bride *f*, patte *f*; **mounting p.,** bride de fixation, de montage. **6.** *(a)* aire *f* de décollage et d'atterrissage (pour hélicoptères); *(b)* **launching p.,** aire, plateforme *f*, de lancement (d'une fusée). **7.** *W.Tel:* atténuateur *m* (d'amplitude) non réglable. **8.** *P:* *(a)* logement *m*, piaule *f*; *(b)* lit *m*, pieu *m*; **to hit the p.,** se coucher, se pieuter.

pad⁴ *v.tr.* **(padded) 1.** bourrer, rembourrer (un coussin, etc.); matelasser (une porte, etc.); capitonner (un fauteuil); ouater (un vêtement); *Tail:* garnir (les épaules d'un manteau); **padded cell,** cabanon *m*. **2.** *F:* délayer (un discours, etc.); cheviller (un vers); **to p. (out) a book,** ajouter des pages de remplissage dans un livre. **padding** *n.* **1.** remplissage *m*, rembourrage *m*; garnissage *m* (avec de la bourre, etc.); ouatage *m*, ouatinage *m*. **2.** *(a)* bourre *f*, ouate *f*, rembourrage (d'un coussin, etc.); *(b)* matelassure (d'un siège, etc.). **3.** *F:* délayage *m* (d'un discours).

paddle¹ ['pædl] *n.* **1.** pagaie *f*; **double p.,** pagaie à double pale. **2.** *(a)* aube *f*, pale *f*, palette *f* (de roue hydraulique, de bateau à roues); *O:* **p. boat, steamer,** bateau *m*, vapeur *m*, à aubes, à roues; *(b)* **p. wheel,** roue *f* à aubes, à palettes; *(c)* vannelle *f* (de porte d'écluse). **3.** *Z: etc:* nageoire *f* (de cétacé, de manchot, de tortue); patte *f* (de canard).

paddle² **1.** *v.tr.* pagayer; **to p. one's own canoe,** arriver par soi-même; se débrouiller (tout seul). **2.** *v.i.* *Row:* tirer en douce.

paddle³ *n.* barbotage *m*; *(of child)* **to go for a p.,** aller barboter dans l'eau.

paddle⁴ *v.i.* **1.** barboter (dans l'eau, etc.); patauger, patouiller (dans la boue, etc.); **paddling pool,** bassin *m* à patauger. **2.** *O:* *(toddle)* trottiner.

paddock ['pædək] *n.* *(a)* parc *m*, enclos *m*, pré *m* (pour chevaux); paddock *m*; **to put a horse in the p.,** parquer un cheval; *(b) Turf:* pesage *m*, paddock; *(c) Austr:* champ *m*.

Paddy¹ ['pædi] **1.** *Pr.n. m.* *(a)* *(dim.)* Patrice, Patrick; *(b)* *(nickname)* Irlandais; *(c) n. F: NAm:* **p. wagon,** panier *m* à salade. **2.** *n. F:* **to be, get, in a p.,** être, se mettre, en colère.

paddy² *n. Com:* paddy *m* (riz non décortiqué); **p. field,** rizière *f*.

padlock¹ ['pædlɔk] *n.* cadenas *m*.

padlock² *v.tr.* **(padlocked)** cadenasser; fermer (une porte, etc.) au cadenas.

padre ['pɑːdrei] *n.m.* prêtre, *esp.* aumônier (militaire).

paean ['piːən] *n.* péan *m*, pæn *m*.

paederast ['pedəræst, 'piː-] *etc.* = PEDERAST, etc.

paediatric [piːdi'ætrik] *a.* (hôpital, etc.) de pédiatrie; (spécialiste) en pédiatrie.

paediatrician [piːdiə'triʃ(ə)n] *n.* pédiatre *mf*.

paediatrics [piːdi'ætriks] *n.* pédiatrie *f*.

pagan ['peigən] *a. & n.* païen, -ïenne.

paganism ['peigənizm] *n.* paganisme *m*.

page¹ [peidʒ] *n.* **1.** *(attending person of rank)* page *m*; *(at wedding)* page (d'honneur). **2.** jeune chasseur (d'hôtel).

page² *v.tr.* **to p. s.o., to have s.o. paged,** envoyer chercher qn par un chasseur; appeler qn par haut-parleur, par radio portative.

page³ *n.* page *f*; **front p.,** (i) recto *m* (d'une feuille de papier); (ii) la une (d'un journal); **at the back of the p.,** au dos, au verso, de la page, de la feuille; **on p. 6,** à la page 6; *Journ: etc:* **continued on p. 6, on back p.,** suite *f* (en) page 6, en dernière page; *Typ:* **p. setting,** mise *f* en pages; **p. proofs,** épreuves *fpl* en pages.

page⁴ *v.tr.* numéroter (les feuilles); paginer, folioter (un livre); chiffrer les pages (d'un registre, etc.).

pageant ['pædʒ(ə)nt] *n.* **1.** spectacle pompeux. **2.** cortège *m*, cavalcade *f*, historique.

pageantry ['pædʒəntri] *n.* apparat *m*, pompe *f*.

pageboy ['peidʒbɔi] *n.* **1.** petit chasseur (d'hôtel). **2.** *Hairdr:* **p. style,** coiffure *f* à la page.

paginate ['pædʒineit] *v.tr.* paginer (un livre).

pagination [pædʒi'neiʃ(ə)n] *n.* pagination *f*.

pagoda [pə'goudə] *n. Arch:* pagode *f*.

pah [pɑː] *int.* pouah!

pail [peil] *n.* **1.** seau *m*; **milking p.,** seille *f* à traire. **2. a p. of water,** un seau d'eau.

pain¹ [pein] *n.* **1.** *(a)* douleur *f*, souffrance *f*; *(mental)* peine *f*; **to give s.o. p.,** (i) *(of tooth)* faire mal à qn, faire souffrir qn; (ii) *(of incident, etc.)* faire de la peine à qn; **to be in (great) p.,** souffrir beaucoup; **is he in p.?** souffre-t-il? **to put a wounded animal out of its p.,** achever un animal blessé; *(b)* **shooting pains,** élancements *mpl*, douleurs lancinantes; *F:* **he's a p. in the neck,** il me tape sur le système. **2. pains,** *(a)* peine; **to take pains, be at great pains, to do sth.,** se donner de la peine, du mal, pour faire qch.; **to take pains over sth.,** s'appliquer à qch.; **to have nothing for one's pains,** en être pour sa peine; *(b)* **labour pains,** douleurs *fpl* de l'accouchement. **3.** *A: still used in:* **on, under, pain of (death, etc.),** sous peine de (mort, etc.).

pain² *v.tr.* faire souffrir (qn); faire mal à (qn); *(mentally)* faire de la peine à (qn), peiner, affliger (qn). **pained** *a.* *(a)* attristé, peiné **(at,** de); *(b)* **p. expression,** air affligé, peiné.

painful ['peinf(u)l] *a.* **1.** *(of wound, part of the body)* douloureux; **I find walking p.,** je souffre à marcher; *(of limb, etc.)* **to become p.,** s'endolorir. **2.** *(of spectacle, effort)* pénible; **p. subject,** sujet *m* pénible. **3.** *A:* (travail) laborieux, pénible. **-fully** *adv.* **1.** douloureusement, péniblement. **2.** *A:* laborieusement.

painkiller ['peinkilər] *n.* calmant *m*, analgésique *m*.

painkilling ['peinkiliŋ] *a.* calmant.

painless ['peinlis] *a.* **1.** indolore; (extraction, etc.) sans douleur. **2.** (tumeur) indolente, indolore. **-ly** *adv.* sans douleur.

painstaking ['peinzteikiŋ] *a.* soigneux, assidu; (travail) soigné. **-ly** *adv.* avec (grand) soin.

paint¹ [peint] *n.* **1.** (*a*) peinture *f*; **coat of p.,** couche de peinture; **glossy p.,** peinture brillante, laquée; **oil p.,** peinture, couleur, à l'huile; **pot of p.,** pot *m* de peinture; **p. pot,** pot à peinture; **p. gun, roller,** pistolet *m*, rouleau *m*, à peindre, à peinture; **p. shop,** (i) magasin *m* de couleurs; (ii) *Ind:* atelier *m* de peinture; *P.N:* **wet p.! mind the p.!** attention, peinture fraîche! (*b*) *Art:* couleur; **box of paints,** boîte *f* de couleurs; **tube of p.,** tube *m* de peinture, de couleurs; (*c*) *Med:* badigeon *m*; (*d*) *F:* fard *m*.

paint² *v.tr.* peindre. **1.** (*a*) **to p. a portrait in oils,** peindre un portrait à l'huile; **to p. everything in rosy colours,** peindre tout en rose; (*b*) *v.i.* faire de la peinture; **to p. in water-colours,** faire de l'aquarelle. **2.** dépeindre; **what words can p. the scene?** comment dépeindre cette scène? **3.** (*a*) peindre (une pièce, une porte, etc.) (**green,** en vert); **the kitchen needs painting,** il faut faire repeindre la cuisine; *Th:* **to p. the scenery for a play,** brosser les décors d'une pièce; *F:* **to p. the town red,** faire la noce, la bringue; (*b*) *F:* **to p. one's face,** se farder; (*c*) *Med:* badigeonner (la gorge, etc.). **painting** *n.* **1.** peinture *f*; (*a*) **to study p.,** étudier la peinture; (*b*) **(house) p.,** peinture (de bâtiments, etc.). **2.** tableau *m*.

paintbox ['peintbɔks] *n.* boîte *f* de couleurs.

paintbrush ['peintbrʌʃ] *n.* pinceau *m*.

painter¹ ['peintər] *n.* **1.** (*a*) *Art:* peintre *m*; **she was a famous p.,** elle fut un peintre célèbre; **landscape p.,** paysagiste *m*; (*b*) coloriste *mf* (de jouets, etc.). **2.** **(house) p.,** peintre en bâtiments; peintre décorateur.

painter² *n. Nau:* bosse *f* (d'embarcation, de lof); **to cut the p.,** couper l'amarre.

paintwork ['peintwəːk] *n.* les peintures *fpl*.

pair¹ [pɛər] *n.* **1.** (*a*) paire *f* (de chaussures, de vases, de ciseaux, de jambes, etc.); **in pairs,** deux par deux, par paires, par couples; **the p. of you,** vous deux; (*b*) **a p. of trousers,** un pantalon; *O:* **a p. of scales,** une balance; (*c*) attelage *m* (de deux chevaux); **carriage and p.,** voiture *f* à deux chevaux; (*d*) (*man and wife*) couple *m*; (*e*) (*match*) **these two pictures are a p.,** ces deux tableaux se font pendant; **stockings that are not a p.,** bas *mpl* disparates, qui ne vont pas ensemble; (*f*) **where is the p. of this glove?** où se trouve l'autre gant de cette paire? (*g*) *Row:* deux *m*; (*h*) **p. royal,** (i) *Cards:* brelan *m*; (ii) (*dice*) rafle *f*; *Atom.Ph:* **electron, ion, p.,** paire d'électrons, d'ions. **2.** **p. of steps,** marchepied (volant), escabeau *m*. **3.** *Parl:* (*a*) paire de membres de partis adverses qui se sont pairés (pour un vote); (*b*) membre *m* du parti adverse avec qui on puis se pairer.

pair² **1.** *v.tr.* (*a*) appareiller, apparier, assortir (des gants, etc.); (*b*) accoupler, apparier (des oiseaux, etc.). **2.** *v.i.* (*a*) faire la paire (**with s.o., sth.,** avec qn, qch.); (*b*) (*of birds, etc.*) s'accoupler, s'apparier (**with,** avec); (*c*) *Parl:* **to p.,** se pairer (**with s.o.,** avec qn). **paired** *a.* (*a*) deux par deux, par paires, par couples; (organe, etc.) pair; (*of guns*) jumelés, conjugués; *I.C.E:* (cylindres) accouplés; (*b*) *Tp:* (câbles) à paires. **pair off** **1.** *v.tr.* arranger (des personnes, des objets) deux par deux. **2.** *v.i.* s'en aller, se disperser, deux par deux, en couples.

pair³ *n.* **au p.,** au pair; **au p. (student),** étudiant(e) au pair; **she's staying with them au p.,** elle est chez eux au pair.

Paisley ['peizli] *Pr.n. Tex:* **P. pattern,** (dessin *m*) cachemire (*m*).

pajamas [pə'dʒæməz] *n.pl. NAm:* pyjama *m*.

Paki ['pæki] *n. F:* = Pakistani.

Pakistan [pæki'stɑːn] *Pr.n. Geog:* Pakistan *m*.

Pakistani [pæki'stɑːni] *Geog:* **1.** *a.* pakistanais. **2.** *n.* Pakistanais, -aise.

pal¹ [pæl] *n. F:* camarade *mf*; copain, *f.* copine.

pal² *v.i. F:* **(palled) to p. up with s.o.,** se lier (d'amitié) avec qn; devenir copain avec qn.

palace ['pælis] *n.* **1.** palais *m*; **Bishop's, Archbishop's, p.,** palais épiscopal, archiépiscopal; *Pol:* **p. revolution,** révolution *f* de palais. **2.** (*hotel, etc.*) palace *m*; *O:* **picture p.,** cinéma *m*.

paladin ['pælədin] *n.* paladin *m*.

palatable ['pælətəbl] *a.* (*a*) d'un goût agréable; agréable au palais, au goût; (vin) qui se laisse boire; (*b*) (*of doctrine, etc.*) agréable (**to,** à).

palatal ['pælət(ə)l] **1.** *a. Anat: Ling:* palatal, -aux. **2.** *n. Ling:* palatale *f*.

palatalize ['pælətəlaiz] *v.tr. Ling:* palataliser; mouiller (un *l*, la combinaison *gn*).

palate ['pælət] *n.* (*a*) *Anat:* palais *m*; **hard p.,** palais (dur), voûte *f* du palais, voûte palatine; **soft p.,** voile *m* du palais; **cleft p.,** palais fendu; (*b*) **to have a delicate p.,** avoir le palais fin.

palatial [pə'leiʃ(ə)l] *a.* (édifice) magnifique, grandiose.

palatinate [pə'lætineit] *n.* palatinat *m*.

palaver¹ [pə'lɑːvər] *n.* **1.** palabre *f*; **after a long p.,** après de longues palabres. **2.** *F:* embarras *mpl*; **what's all the p. about?** qu'est-ce qu'il y a qui cloche?

palaver² *v.i.* palabrer.

pale¹ [peil] *n.* **1.** pieu *m* (de clôture); pal *m*, *pl.* pals. **2.** *A:* bornes *fpl*; *still used in:* **beyond the p.,** au ban de la société; pas fréquentable.

pale² *a.* (*a*) pâle, blême; (*of complexion*) délavé; **p. as death, deadly p.,** pâle comme un mort; d'une pâleur mortelle; **to grow, become, p.,** pâlir; **to turn p. with fright,** pâlir de terreur; (*b*) (*of colour*) pâle, clair; **p. blue dress,** robe *f* bleu pâle; (*c*) **by the p. light of the moon,** à la lumière blafarde de la lune.

pale³ *v.i.* (*a*) pâlir, blêmir; (*b*) **my adventures p. beside yours,** mes aventures *fpl* pâlissent auprès des vôtres.

paleface ['peilfeis] *n.* visage *m* pâle.

pale-faced ['peilfeist] *a.* au visage, au teint, pâle.

paleness ['peilnis] *n.* pâleur *f*.

paleographer [pæli'ɔgrəfər] *n.* paléographe *mf*.

paleography [pæli'ɔgrəfi] *n.* paléographie *f*.

paleolithic [pæliou'liθik] *a.* paléolithique; **the P. age,** le paléolithique, l'âge *m* de la pierre taillée.

paleontologist [pælion'tɔlədʒist] *n.* paléontologiste *mf*, paléontologue *mf*.

paleontology [pælion'tɔlədʒi] *n.* paléontologie *f*.

Palestine ['pælistain] *Pr.n.* Palestine *f*.

Palestinian [pælis'tiniən]. **1.** *a.* palestinien. **2.** *n.* Palestinien, -ienne.

palette ['pælit] *n. Art:* palette *f*; **p. knife,** couteau *m* à palette.

palfrey ['pɔːlfri] *n. A: & Lit:* palefroi *m*.

palimpsest ['pælimpsest] *a. & n.* palimpseste (*m*).

palindrome ['pælindroum] *n.* palindrome *m*.

paling ['peiliŋ] *n.* palissade *f*, palis *m*.

palisade [pæli'seid] *n.* palissade *f*.

pall¹ [pɔːl] *n.* **1.** *Ecc:* poêle *m*; drap *m* mortuaire; **p. bearer,** porteur *m* (d'un cordon du poêle). **2.** manteau *m* (de neige, etc.); voile *m* (de fumée, etc.).

pall² *v.tr.* couvrir d'un poêle; voiler.

pall³ **1.** *v.i.* s'affadir; devenir fade, insipide (**on s.o.,** pour qn); **it never palls,** on ne s'en dégoûte jamais. **2.** *v.tr.* blaser, émousser (les sens).

pallet¹ ['pælit] *n.* (*a*) paillasse *f*; (*b*) grabat *m*.

pallet² *n.* **1.** palette *f* (de doreur, de potier, etc.). **2.** *Art:* palette *f*. **3.** *Com:* palette (de manutention).

palliasse [pæl'jæs] *n.* paillasse *f*.

palliate ['pælieit] *v.tr.* pallier (la misère, une faute, une maladie, etc.); lénifier (une maladie); pallier, atténuer (un vice, etc.).

palliative ['pæliətiv] *a. & n.* palliatif (*m*).

pallid ['pælid] *a.* (*a*) pâle, décoloré; (*b*) (*of light, moon, etc.*) blafard; (*c*) (*of face*) blême.
pallidness ['pælidnis] *n.* pâleur *f.*
pallor ['pælər] *n.* pâleur *f.*
pally ['pæli] *a. F: O:* **to be p. with s.o.,** être lié, être copain, avec qn.
palm¹ [pɑːm] *n.* **1.** (*a*) **p. (tree),** palmier *m;* **date p.,** dattier *m;* **p. grove, plantation,** palmeraie *f;* **p. leaf,** feuille *f* de palmier; *Arch:* **p. leaf (moulding),** palmette; (*b*) **p. oil,** huile *f* de palme, de palmier; pumicin *m;* (*c*) **p. cabbage,** (chou *m*) palmiste *m.* **2.** (*branch*) palme *f; Ecc:* rameau *m,* buis (béni); **P. Sunday,** le Dimanche des Rameaux, *F:* les Rameaux; *Fig:* **to bear, win, the p.,** remporter la palme.
palm² *n.* (*a*) paume *f* (de la main); *F:* **to grease s.o.'s p.,** graisser la patte à qn; *F:* **to hold s.o. in the p. of one's hand,** avoir qn sous sa coupe; (*b*) empaumure *f* (d'un gant).
palm³ *v.tr.* **1.** tripoter (qch., qn). **2. to p. a card,** empalmer, escamoter, une carte; filer la carte. **palm off** *v.tr.* faire passer, *F:* refiler (**sth. on s.o.,** qch. à qn); (*conjuring*) **to p. off a card,** filer la carte; **to p. off a bad coin on s.o.,** refiler une fausse pièce à qn.
palmist ['pɑːmist] *n.* chiromancien, -ienne.
palmistry ['pɑːmistri] *n.* chiromancie *f.*
palmy ['pɑːmi] *a.* **p. days,** époque florissante (d'une nation, etc.); **in his p. days,** dans ses beaux jours.
palpable ['pælpəbl] *a.* **1.** palpable; que l'on peut toucher. **2.** palpable, manifeste; (mensonge) évident; (différence) sensible. **-ably** *adv.* manifestement.
palpitate ['pælpiteit] *v.tr. & i.* palpiter. **palpating** *a.* palpitant.
palpitation [pælpi'teiʃ(ə)n] *n.* palpitation *f.*
palsy ['pɔːlzi] *n. Med:* paralysie *f;* **cerebral p.,** paralysie cérébrale.
paltry ['pɔːltri] *a.* misérable, mesquin; **p. excuses,** piètres excuses.
pampa ['pæmpə] *n. Geog:* pampa *f;* **the Pampa(s),** la Pampa; **pampas grass,** herbe *f* des pampas.
pamper ['pæmpər] *v.tr.* **1.** choyer, dorloter (un enfant); flatter, charmer, délecter (l'esprit, la vanité de qn); **pampered tastes,** goûts difficiles, exigeants.
pamphlet ['pæmflit] *n.* brochure *f;* (*literary, scientific*) opuscule *m;* (*libellous, scurrilous*) pamphlet *m.*
pamphleteer [pæmfli'tiər] *n.* auteur *m* de brochures; (*scurrilous*) pamphlétaire *m.*
pan¹ [pæn] *n.* **1.** (*a*) *Dom.Ec:* casserole *f;* **frying p.,** poêle *f;* **roasting p.,** plat *m* à rôtir; **pots and pans,** batterie *f* de cuisine; (*b*) *NAm:* visage *m.* **2.** (*a*) (i) plateau *m,* plat, (ii) bassin *m* (d'une balance); (*b*) **lavatory p.,** cuvette *f* de W.C.; (*c*) *Min:* (*gold*) batée *f.* **3. (priming) p.,** bassinet *m* (d'un fusil). **4.** *Geol: etc:* cuvette; bassin *m* de déposition, de sédimentation; **salt p.,** marais salant; saline *f,* salin *m.*
pan² *v.* **(panned) 1.** *v.tr. Min:* **to p. (out),** laver (le gravier, etc.) à la batée. **2.** *v.i.* **it didn't p. out well,** cela n'a pas réussi. **panning** *n. Min:* lavage *m.*
pan³ *v.tr.* **(panned)** *F:* décrier, éreinter (qn, qch.).
Pan⁴ *Pr.n.m. Myth:* (le dieu) Pan; *Mus:* **p.-pipes,** flûte *f* de Pan.
pan⁵ *v.tr.* **(panned)** *Cin: F:* panoramiquer (une vue). **panning** *n.* panoramique *m.*
panacea [pænə'siə] *n.* panacée *f;* remède universel.
panache [pə'næʃ] *n.* **1.** panache *m* (de casque). **2.** panache, ostentation *f.*
pan-African [pæn'æfrikən] *a.* panafricain.
Panama [pænə'mɑː] **1.** *Pr.n. Geog:* Panama *m.* **2.** *n.* **p. (hat),** panama.
Panamanian [pænə'meiniən] *Geog:* **1.** *a.* panaméen. **2.** *n.* Panaméen, -éenne.
pan-American [pænə'merikən] *a.* panaméricain.
pan-Americanism [pænə'merikənizm] *n.* Panaméricanisme *m.*
pancake¹ ['pænkeik] *n.* **1.** *Cu:* crêpe *f;* **p. day,** mardi gras. **2.** *Nau:* **p. ice,** gâteaux *mpl* de glace; glace *f* en fragments. **3.** *Av:* **p. (landing),** atterrissage brutal.
pancake² *v.i. Av:* faire un atterrisage brutal.
panchromatic [pænkrou'mætik] *a. Phot:* (plaque) panchromatique.
pancreas ['pæŋkriæs] *n. Anat:* pancréas *m.*
pancreatic [pæŋkri'ætik] *a.* pancréatique.
panda ['pændə] *n. Z:* panda *m;* **giant p.,** panda géant; **p. car,** voiture *f* pie (de la police).
pandemic [pæn'demik] *Med:* **1.** *a.* pandémique. **2.** *n.* pandémie *f.*
pandemonium [pændi'mouniəm] *n.* pandémonium *m;* **it's p.,** c'est un désordre indescriptible.
pander ['pændər] *v.i.* **to p. to s.o.,** encourager bassement qn; **to p. to a vice,** se prêter à un vice.
Pandora [pæn'dɔːrə] *Pr.n.f.Gr.Hist:* Pandore; **Pandora's box,** la boîte de Pandore.
pandowdy [pæn'daudi] *n. U.S: Cu:* (genre *m* de) tourte *f* aux pommes.
pane¹ [pein] *n.* **1.** vitre *f,* carreau *m* (de fenêtre); *Glassm:* plat *m* (de verre). **2.** carreau (d'un tissu à carreaux).
pane² *n. Tls:* panne *f* (d'un marteau).
panegyric [pæni'dʒirik] *a. & n.* panégyrique (*m*).
panel¹ ['pæn(ə)l] *n.* **1.** (*a*) panneau *m* (de lambris, etc.); placard *m* (de porte); caisson *m* (de plafond); **sunk p.,** panneau en retrait; arrière-corps *m inv;* **sliding p.,** panneau mobile; *Mec.E: etc:* **access, inspection, p.,** panneau d'accès, de visite; *Aut: etc:* **p. beater,** tôlier *m;* (*b*) *Dressm:* panneau; (*shaped*) volant *m;* (*c*) *Arch: Civ.E:* entre-deux *m inv;* (*d*) *Aut: Av:* **instrument p.,** tableau *m* de bord; **p. light,** lampe *f,* éclairage *m,* de tableau de bord; *Tp:* **distribution p.,** tableau de distribution; *Cmptr:* **control p.,** pupitre *m,* tableau, de commande; *Com:* **advertisement p.,** panneau d'affichage, de publicité; panneau-réclame *m, pl.* panneaux-réclame. **2.** (*a*) *Jur:* (i) tableau, liste *f,* du jury; (ii) **the p.,** le jury; (iii) *Scot:* l'accusé; les accusés; (*b*) (i) liste des membres d'un comité, d'une commission; (ii) comité, commission (d'enquête, etc.); groupe *m* de travail; table ronde; **p. of experts,** comité, commission, d'experts; **p. game,** jeu télévisé, radiophonique, par équipes.
panel² *v.tr.* **(panelled,** *NAm:* **paneled)** (*a*) diviser (un mur, etc.) en panneaux; (*b*) recouvrir de panneaux; lambrisser (une paroi); plaquer (une surface); **panelled,** (*of room*) boisé, lambrissé; (*of wall*) revêtu de boiseries. **panelling,** *NAm:* **paneling** *n.* **1.** (*a*) division *f* (d'un mur) en panneaux; panneautage *m* (d'une surface); (*b*) lambrissage *m* (d'une pièce). **2.** (*a*) lambris *m,* boiserie *f;* placage *m;* **oak p.,** lambris *mpl* de chêne; (*b*) (*wood for panelling*) aubage *m.*
pang [pæŋ] *n.* angoisse *f,* douleur *f;* serrement *m* de cœur; **pangs of jealousy,** tourments *mpl* de la jalousie; **to feel a p.,** sentir une petite pointe au cœur; **pangs of hunger,** tiraillements *mpl* d'estomac.
panhandle ['pænhændl] *v.i. NAm: F:* mendier.
panhandler [pæn'hændlər] *n. NAm: F:* mendiant, -ante.
panic¹ ['pænik] *a. & n.* **p. (terror),** (terreur *f*) panique (*f*); affolement *m;* **to create a p.,** causer une panique; **to throw the crowd into a p.,** affoler la foule; **in a p.,** pris de panique; **p. measures,** mesures dictées par la panique.
panic² *v.* **(panicked) 1.** *v.tr.* remplir de panique; affoler (la foule, etc.); F: paniquer (qn). **2.** *v.i.* être pris de panique; perdre la tête; s'affoler.
panic³ *n. Bot:* **p. (grass),** panic *m* (d'Italie); panis *m.*
panicky ['pæniki] *a. F:* (*of feelings*) panique; (*of pers.*) sujet à la panique; (*of market, etc.*) enclin à la panique; **don't get p.,** ne vous affolez pas.
panicstricken ['pænikstrik(ə)n] *a.* pris de panique; affolé.

panjandrum [pən'dʒændrəm] *n. F: O:* gros bonnet.
pannier ['pæniər] *n.* (*a*) (*basket*) panier *m*; (*b*) panier de bât (d'une bête de somme).
panoply ['pænəpli] *n.* panoplie *f.*
panorama [pænə'rɑːmə] *n.* panorama *n.*
panoramic [pænə'ræmik] *a.* (vue, etc.) panoramique; *Aut:* **p. mirror,** rétroviseur *m* panoramique.
pansy ['pænzi] *n.* **1.** *Bot:* pensée *f.* **2.** *F:* (*a*) pédéraste *m*, pédale *f*, tante *f*; (*b*) homme efféminé.
pant[1] [pænt] *n.* souffle pantelant, haletant; halètement *m.*
pant[2] *v.i.* **1.** (*a*) panteler; (*of animal*) battre du flanc; (*of heart*) palpiter; (*b*) haleter; **to p. for breath,** chercher à reprendre haleine; (*c*) *v.tr.* **he panted out a few words,** il a dit quelques mots en haletant. **2.** *F:* **he's panting to do it,** il a tellement envie de le faire. **panting** *n.* essoufflement *m*, halètement *m*; palpitation *f.*
pantechnicon [pæn'teknikən] *n. O:* camion *m* de déménagement.
pantheism ['pænθiizm] *n.* panthéisme *m.*
pantheist ['pænθiist] *a.* & *n.* panthéiste (*mf*).
pantheistic [pænθi'istik] *a.* panthéiste.
pantheon ['pænθiən] *n.* panthéon *m.*
panther ['pænθər] *n. Z:* **1.** panthère *f*; **black p.,** panthère noire. **2.** *U.S:* couguar *m*, puma *m.*
pantie ['pænti] *n. Cost:* **panties,** culotte *f*, slip *m* (de femme); **p. girdle,** gaine-culotte, *pl.* gaines-culottes; **p. hose,** collant *m.*
panto ['pæntou] *n. Th: F:* = PANTOMIME (*b*).
pantograph ['pæntəgræf] *n.* **1.** *Draw:* pantographe *m*, singe *m.* **2.** *El:* pantographe (de locomotive électrique, etc.).
pantomime ['pæntəmaim] *n. Th:* (*a*) (*dumb show*) pantomime *f*; (*b*) revue-féerie à grand spectacle (représentée aux environs de Noël).
pantry ['pæntri] *n.* (*a*) dépense *f*; (grand) placard à provisions; **(butler's) p.,** office *f* or *m*; (*b*) *Av:* bar *m.*
pants [pænts] *n. pl.* (*a*) caleçon *m* (d'homme); slip *m* (de femme); (*b*) *NAm:* pantalon *m*; (*c*) *F:* **a kick in the p.,** un coup de pied au derrière, au cul; **to be caught with one's p. down,** être pris dans une situation fort embarrassante.
panty ['pænti] *n. U.S:* = PANTIE.
pap [pæp] *n.* (*a*) bouillie *f*; (*b*) pulpe *f*, pâte *f* (très liquide).
papa [pə'pɑː] *n.m. F: O:* papa.
papacy ['peipəsi] *n.* papauté *f.*
papal ['peip(ə)l] *a.* papal, -aux.
papaw [pə'pɔː] *n. Bot:* **1.** (*a*) papaye *f*; (*b*) **p.(-tree),** papayer *m.* **2.** (*in USA*) (*a*) asimine *f*; (*b*) asiminier *m.*
paper[1] ['peipər] *n.* **1.** papier *m*; (*a*) **rice p.,** papier de Chine, de riz; **India p.,** papier bible, papier pelure; **blotting p.,** (papier) buvard *m*; **carbon p.,** papier carbone; **emery p.,** papier émeri; **glass p.,** papier de verre; **brown p., wrapping p.,** papier gris; **cigarette p.,** papier à cigarettes; *Phot:* **sensitized p.,** papier sensible; **tracing p.,** papier-calque, à calquer; **writing p.,** papier à écrire; **drawing p.,** papier à dessin; **rough p.,** papier brouillon; **toilet,** *F:* **loo, p.,** papier hygiénique; (*b*) **a sheet, a piece, of p.,** une feuille, un morceau, de papier; **p. bag,** sac *m*, en papier; (*c*) papier peint; (*d*) **the p. industry,** l'industrie papetière; la papeterie; **p. mill,** papeterie, moulin *m* à papier, fabrique *f* de papier; **p. knife,** coupe-papier *m inv*; (*e*) **to put sth. down on p.,** mettre qch. sur papier; **it's a good plan on p.,** ce projet est excellent en théorie; **p. profits,** profits fictifs. **2.** (*a*) écrit *m*, document *m*, pièce *f*; **p. clip, fastener,** trombone *m*; **private, personal, papers,** papiers personnels; **identity papers,** papiers d'identité; *Mil: etc:* **call-up papers,** ordre *m* d'appel (sous les drapeaux); **to send, hand, in one's papers,** donner sa démission; (*b*) *Fin: etc:* papier valeur; **long, short, p.,** papier à long terme, à court terme; **negotiable p.,** papier négociable; **p. securities,** papiers valeurs, titres *mpl* fiduciaires; (*c*) billets *mpl* (de banque); **p. money, currency,** papier-monnaie *m*, *pl.* papiers-monnaie; (*d*) **voting p.,** bulletin *m* de vote; (*e*) *Parl:* papiers, documents communiqués à la Chambre. **3.** *Sch:* **(examination) p.,** (i) questions *fpl* d'examen; (ii) copie *f*; **to correct, mark, papers,** corriger l'écrit. **4.** étude *f*, mémoire *m* (sur un sujet scientifique, etc.); **to read a p.,** (i) faire une communication (à une société savante, etc.); (ii) faire une conférence, un exposé, *F:* lire un papier. **5.** journal, -aux *m*; **daily, weekly, p.,** quotidien *m*; hebdomadaire *m*; **p. boy,** (i) vendeur *m*, (ii) livreur *m*, de journaux.
paper[2] *v.tr.* (*a*) doubler (une boîte) de papier; (*b*) tapisser (une chambre); *F:* **to p. over the cracks,** déguiser (i) les défauts (de qch.), (ii) les mésententes (entre deux personnes).
paperback ['peipəbæk] *n. Publ:* livre *m* de poche.
paperweight ['peipəweit] *n.* presse-papiers *m inv.*
paperwork ['peipəwəːk] *n.* paperasseries *fpl.*
papery ['peipəri] *a.* semblable au papier; mince comme du papier.
papier mâché ['pæpjei'mæʃei] *n.* carton-pâte *m.*
papist ['peipist] *n.* papiste *mf.*
papistry ['peipistri] *n. Pej:* papisme *m.*
paprika ['pæprikə, pə'priːkə] *n.* paprika *m.*
Papua ['pæpjuə] *Pr.n. Geog:* Papouasie *f.*
Papuan ['pæpjuən] **1.** *a.* papou. **2.** *n.* Papou, -oue.
papyrus, *pl.* **-ri** [pə'paiərəs, -rai] *n.* papyrus *m.*
par [pɑːr] *n.* pair *m*, égalité *f*; (*a*) **to be on a p. with s.o., sth.,** être au niveau de, aller de pair avec, qn, qch.; (*b*) *Fin:* **p. of exchange,** pair du change; **above, below, p.,** au-dessus, au-dessous, du pair; **at p.,** au pair; (*c*) moyenne *f*; **above, below, p.,** au-dessus, au-dessous, de la moyenne; *F:* **to feel below p.,** ne pas être dans son assiette; (*d*) *Golf:* par *m.*
parable ['pærəbl] *n.* parabole *f.*
parabola [pə'ræbələ] *n. Mth:* parabole *f.*
parabolic [pærə'bɔlik] *a.* **1.** (enseignement) parabolique, en paraboles. **2.** *Mth: etc:* (courbe, miroir, etc.) parabolique.
parachute[1] ['pærəʃuːt] *n.* (*a*) parachute *m*; **p. harness,** ceinture *f*, harnais *m*, de parachute; **p. jump, descent,** saut *m*, descente *f*, en parachute; **to make a p. jump,** sauter en parachute; **to drop s.o., sth., by p.,** larguer qn, qch., par parachute; parachuter qn, qch.; (*b*) **brake, tail, p.,** parachute de freinage (à l'atterrissage); **p. flare,** fusée (éclairante) à parachute.
parachute[2] **1.** *v.i.* **to p. (down),** descendre en parachute. **2.** *v.tr.* parachuter (qn, qch.); larguer (qn. qch.) par parachute. **parachuting** *n.* **1.** le parachutisme. **2.** parachutage *m* (de qn, de qch.).
parachutist ['pærəʃuːtist] *n.* parachutiste *mf.*
parade[1] [pə'reid] *n.* **1.** parade *f.* **2.** *Mil:* (*a*) rassemblement *m*; **church p.,** rassemblement (du bataillon, etc.) pour assister à l'office du dimanche; (*b*) exercice *m*; **on p.,** à l'exercice; **to go on p.,** parader; **p. ground,** terrain *m* de manœuvres; place *f* d'armes; (*c*) *Fenc:* parade. **3.** (*a*) procession *f*, défilé *m*; (*b*) **fashion p.,** défilé de mannequins; présentation *f* de collections. **4.** esplanade *f*; boulevard *m* (le long d'une plage).
parade[2] **1.** *v.tr.* (*a*) faire parade, ostentation, étalage, de (ses richesses, ses connaissances, etc.); (*b*) *Mil:* faire l'inspection (des troupes); rassembler (un bataillon); faire parader, faire défiler (les troupes). **2.** *v.i.* (*a*) *Mil:* se rassembler; faire la parade; parader (pour l'exercice, pour l'inspection); (*b*) **to p. (through) the streets,** défiler dans les rues.
paradigm ['pærədaim] *n. Gram:* paradigme *m*; modèle *m* (de conjugaison, etc.).
paradise ['pærədais] *n.* **1.** paradis *m*; **an earthly p.,** un paradis sur terre; **to go to p.,** aller en paradis. **2.**

Orn: (*a*) **bird of p.,** paradisier *m*, oiseau de paradis; (*b*) **p. crane,** grue *f* de paradis.
paradisiac [pærə'diziæk], **paradisiacal** [pærədi'zaiək(ə)l] paradisiaque.
paradox ['pærədɔks] *n.* paradoxe *m*; antinomie *f*.
paradoxical [pærə'dɔksik(ə)l] *a.* paradoxal, -aux. **-ally** *adv.* paradoxalement.
paraffin ['pærəfin] *n.* paraffine *f*; **p. wax,** paraffine solide; **to coat with p.,** paraffiner; **p. (oil),** pétrole (lampant), kérosène *m*; **p. lamp,** lampe *f* à pétrole; *Pharm:* **liquid p.,** huile *f* de vaseline, vaseline liquide.
paragon ['pærəgən] *n.* modèle *m* (de beauté, de vertu, etc.); phénix *m*.
paragraph¹ [pærəgræf] *n.* **1.** paragraphe *m*, alinéa *m*; (*when dictating*) **new p.,** à la ligne; *Typ:* **p. (mark),** pied *m* de mouche. **2.** *Journ:* entrefilet *m*.
paragraph² *v.tr.* **1.** diviser en paragraphes. **2.** *Journ:* écrire un entrefilet sur (qn, qch.).
Paraguay ['pærəgwai] *Pr.n. Geog:* Paraguay *m*.
Paraguayan [pærə'gwaiən] *Geog:* **1.** *a.* paraguayen. **2.** *n.* Paraguayen, -enne.
parakeet ['pærəki:t] *n. Orn:* perruche *f*.
parallel¹ ['pærəlel] **I.** *a.* parallèle (**to, with, sth.,** à qch.). **1.** (*a*) *Mth: etc:* **p. lines,** lignes *fpl* parallèles; **to be, run, p. to sth.,** être parallèle à qch.; **p. rule(r),** règle *f* à (tracer des) parallèles; parallèle *m*; (*b*) *Gym:* **p. bars,** barres *fpl* parallèles; (*c*) **p. motion,** (i) *Mec:* parallélogramme *m* de Watt; (ii) *Mch:* parallélogramme (articulé); (*d*) *El:* **p. circuits,** circuits *m* parallèles; **p. connection,** couplage *m*, montage *m*, en parallèle, en dérivation. **2.** pareil, semblable; (cas) analogue (**to, with, sth.,** à qch.). **II.** *n.* **1.** (*a*) (ligne *f*) parallèle *f*; (*b*) *Geog: Astr:* parallèle *m* (de latitude, de déclinaison); (*c*) *Fort:* (tranchée *f*) parallèle (*f*); (*d*) *Typ:* **parallels,** barres *fpl*. **2.** *El:* (*of dynamo*) **out of p.,** déphasé, hors de phase, hors de synchronisme. **3.** parallèle *m*, comparaison *f*; **to draw a p. between two things,** établir un parallèle, une comparaison, entre deux choses; **without p.,** sans pareil.
parallel² *v.tr.* **(paralleled) 1.** (*a*) placer parallèlement (des objets); (*b*) *El:* mettre (deux circuits, deux piles, etc.) en parallèle; (*c*) *NAm:* être parallèle à (qch.). **2.** mettre (deux choses) en parallèle; comparer (deux choses). **3.** (*a*) trouver un parallèle à (qch.); (*b*) égaler (qch.); être égal, pareil, à (qch.).
parallelism ['pærəlelizm] *n.* parallélisme *m*.
parallelogram [pærə'leləgræm] *n.* parallélogramme *m*.
paralyse, *NAm:* **paralyze** ['pærəlaiz] *v.tr.* paralyser; (*a*) **paralysed in one leg,** paralysé d'une jambe; (*b*) **laws that p. industry,** lois qui paralysent l'industrie; **paralysed with fear,** paralysé par l'effroi; glacé d'effroi. **paralysing,** *NAm:* **paralyzing** *a.* (*of poison, fear, etc.*) paralysant.
paralysis [pə'ræləsis] *n.* **1.** *Med:* paralysie *f*. **2.** paralysie, impuissance *f*.
paralytic [pærə'litik] **1.** *a.* (*a*) *Med:* paralytique; **p. stroke,** attaque *f* de paralysie; (*b*) *F:* **he's p.,** il est ivre mort. **2.** *n.* paralytique *mf*.
paralyze ['pærəlaiz] *v.tr. NAm:* = PARALYSE.
paramedic [pærə'medik] *n.* auxiliaire médical.
parameter [pə'ræmitər] *n. Mth: etc:* paramètre *m*.
paramilitary [pærə'milit(ə)ri] *a.* paramilitaire.
paramount ['pærəmaunt] *a.* **1.** éminent, souverain. **2.** suprême; de la plus haute importance; (nécessité) de toute première urgence.
paramour ['pærəmuər] *n. A:* amant *m*, amante *f*.
paranoia [pærə'nɔiə] *n. Med:* paranoïa *f*.
paranoiac [pærə'nɔiæk] *a. & n.* paranoïque (*mf*).
paranoid ['pærənɔid] *a. Med:* paranoïde.
parapet ['pærəpet] *n.* (*a*) *Fort:* parapet *m*; berge *f* (de tranchée); (*b*) parapet; garde-fou *m*, *pl.* garde-fous; garde-corps *m inv* (d'un pont, etc.).
paraphernalia [pærəfə'neiliə] *n.pl.* (*a*) effets *mpl*; affaires *fpl*; **all the p.,** *F:* tout le bazar; (*b*) attirail *m*, accessoires *mpl*.
paraphrase¹ ['pærəfreiz] *n.* paraphrase *f*.
paraphrase² *v.tr.* paraphraser.
paraplegia [pærə'pli:dʒiə] *n. Med:* paraplégie *f*.
paraplegic [pærə'pli:dʒik] *a. & n. Med:* paraplégique (*mf*).
parapsychology [pærəsai'kɔlədʒi] *n.* parapsychologie *f*; parapsychisme *m*; métapsychique *f*.
parasite ['pærəsait] *n.* parasite *m*.
parasitic [pærə'sitik] *a.* (insecte, plante) parasite (**on,** de); *Elcs: etc:* **p. noise,** bruit *m* parasite.
parasitism ['pærəsaitizm] *n.* parasitisme *m*.
parasitize ['pærəsitaiz] *v.tr.* vivre en parasite.
parasitology [pærəsai'tɔlədʒi] *n.* parasitologie *f*.
parasol ['pærəsɔl] *n.* (*a*) ombrelle *f*; (*b*) **p. pine,** pin *m* parasol; **p. mushroom,** coulemelle *f*.
paratrooper ['pærətru:pər] *n.* parachutiste *m*.
paratroops ['pærətru:ps] *n.pl.* (soldats) parachutistes (*mpl*).
paratyphoid [pærə'taifɔid] *n.* paratyphoïde *f*.
parboil ['pɑ:bɔil] *v.tr. Cu:* faire cuire à demi (dans l'eau); blanchir (des légumes, etc.).
parcel¹ ['pɑ:s(ə)l] *n.* **1.** (*a*) *A:* partie *f*; (*b*) pièce *f*, parcelle *f* (de terrain); (*c*) *St.Exch:* paquet *m* (de titres); (i) lot *m*, (ii) envoi *m* (de marchandises). **2.** paquet *m*, colis *m*; **to do up goods into parcels,** empaqueter des marchandises; **to send sth. by p. post,** envoyer qch. comme, par, colis postal; **parcel(s) office,** bureau *m* des messageries; messageries *fpl*.
parcel² *v.tr.* (**parcelled,** *NAm:* **parceled**) (*a*) **to p. (out),** parceller, partager (un héritage); morceler (**into,** en); lotir (des terres, etc.); répartir (des vivres, etc.); (*b*) empaqueter (du thé, etc.); **to p. up,** mettre en paquets, emballer (des livres, etc.).
parch [pɑ:tʃ] *v.tr.* (*a*) rôtir, griller, sécher (des céréales); (*b*) (*of fever*) brûler (qn); (*of sun*) dessécher (l'herbe, etc.); **to be parched with thirst,** avoir une soif dévorante; **I'm parched,** je meurs de soif.
parchment ['pɑ:tʃmənt] *n.* (*a*) parchemin *m*; (*b*) **p. paper,** papier parchemin; papier parcheminé.
pardon¹ ['pɑ:d(ə)n] *n.* **1.** pardon *m*; **I beg your p.!** je vous demande pardon! **I beg your p.?** plaît-il? comment? **2.** *Ecc:* indulgence *f*. **3.** *Jur:* (*a*) **free p.,** grâce *f*; (*of monarch*) **to grant s.o. a free p.,** faire grâce à qn; **to receive the King's, Queen's, p.,** être gracié; **general p.,** amnistie *f*; (*b*) lettre *f* de grâce.
pardon² *v.tr.* **1.** pardonner, excuser, passer (une faute, etc.); **p. my contradicting you, p. me for contradicting you,** pardonnez(-moi) si je vous contredis. **2.** (*a*) **to p. s.o.,** pardonner à qn; *P:* **p. me!** faites excuse! (*b*) **to p. s.o. sth.,** absoudre qn de qch. **3.** *Jur:* faire grâce à (qn); gracier, amnistier (qn).
pardonable ['pɑ:dənəbl] *a.* **1.** pardonnable, excusable. **2.** *Jur:* graciable. **-ably** *adv.* excusablement.
pare [pɛər] *v.tr.* **1.** rogner (ses ongles, etc.); *Farr:* parer (le sabot d'un cheval). **2.** éplucher (un légume, etc.) **3. pare down,** réduire (les dépenses, etc.) **paring** *n.* **1.** (*a*) rognage *m* (des ongles, etc.); (*b*) épluchage *m* (de légumes, etc.). **2. parings,** (*a*) rognures *fpl*; (*of metal*) cisaille *f*; (*b*) épluchures *fpl* (de légumes, etc.). **3. p. knife,** (*a*) rognoir *m*; (*b*) couteau *m* de cuisine.
parent ['pɛərənt] *n.* **1.** père *m*, mère *f*; *pl.* parents *mpl*; *Sch:* **p.-teacher association,** association *f* de parents d'élèves. **2.** origine *f* (d'un événement, etc.); souche *f* (d'une famille); *Com:* **p. company,** société mère, maison mère.
parentage ['pɛərəntidʒ] *n.* origine *f*; **of unknown p.,** parents inconnus.
parental [pə'rent(ə)l] *a.* (autorité, etc.) des parents, des père et mère; (pouvoir) paternel.

parenthesis, *pl.* **-theses** [pə'renθəsis, -i:z] *n.* **1.** parenthèse *f*; **in parentheses,** entre parenthèses. **2.** intermède *m*.

parenthesize [pə'renθəsaiz] *v.tr.* (*a*) mettre (des mots) entre parenthèses; (*b*) mentionner (qch.) par parenthèse.

parenthetic(al) [pæren'θetik(l)] *a.* **1.** entre parenthèses. **2.** *Gram:* **p. clause,** incidente *f*. **-ally** *adv.* par parenthèse.

parenthood ['pɛərənthud] *n.* paternité *f*, maternité *f*.

pariah ['pæriə] *n.* (*a*) paria *m*; (*b*) **p. dog,** chien pariah, chien métis des Indes.

pari passu [pæri'pæsu] *Lt. phr.* **to go p. p. with . . .,** marcher de pair avec . . ..

Paris ['pæris] *Pr.n. Geog:* Paris *m*; **the P. basin,** le bassin parisien.

parish ['pæriʃ] *n.* (*a*) *Ecc:* paroisse *f*; **p. church,** église paroissiale; **p. hall,** salle *f* d'œuvres (de la paroisse); **p. register,** registre paroissial; (*b*) **civil p.,** commune *f*; **p. council** = conseil municipal (d'une petite commune); **p. school,** école communale.

parishioner [pə'riʃənər] *n.* (*a*) paroissien, -ienne; (*b*) habitant, -ante, de la commune.

Parisian [pə'riziən] **1.** *a.* parisien. **2.** *n.* Parisien, -ienne.

parity ['pæriti] *n.* **1.** (*a*) égalité *f* (de rang, etc.); parité *f*; (*b*) analogie *f*, comparaison *f*; **p. of reasoning,** raisonnement *m* analogue; analogie de raisonnement. **2.** *Fin:* **exchange at p.,** change *m* à (la) parité, au pair; **exchange parities,** parités de change; **p. value,** valeur *f* au pair.

park¹ [pɑ:k] *n.* **1.** (*a*) parc (clôturé); *Ven:* réserve *f*; **deer p.,** parc (clôturé) réservé à cerfs; **national p.,** parc national; (*b*) parc (d'un château, etc.); **public p.,** jardin public; parc; **p. keeper, officer,** gardien *m* de parc. **2.** (*a*) **car p.,** parc de stationnement pour voitures, parking *m*; garage *m* pour voitures; (*b*) *Mil: O:* **ammunition p.,** parc à munitions.

park² *v.tr.* **1.** (*a*) parquer (des moutons); (*b*) mettre (de l'artillerie, etc.) en parc. **2.** (*a*) parquer, garer (une voiture); (*b*) *v.i.* (*of car, aircraft, etc.*) stationner, être en stationnement, se garer; (*c*) *F:* **to p. oneself,** s'installer, se planquer (chez qn, dans un fauteuil, etc.). **parked** *a.* (avion, voiture, etc.) en stationnement. **parking** *n.* **1.** parcage *m* (d'animaux, etc.). **2.** (mise *f* en) stationnement (*m*) (de véhicules, d'avions, etc.); **p. area,** aire *f* de stationnement, parking *m*; *Aut:* **p. lights,** feux *mpl* de position; **p. meter,** parc(o)mètre *m*; **p. attendant,** gardien *m* de parking, de voitures; **no p., p. prohibited,** défense *f* de stationner; stationnement interdit; **p. place,** créneau *m*, lieu *m*, de stationnement; **double p.,** stationnement en double file; **p. fees,** tarif *m* de stationnement; **p. lot,** parcage, parking. **3.** *Space:* **p. orbit,** orbite *f* d'attente.

parka ['pɑ:kə] *n. Cost:* parka *f*.

parkway ['pɑ:kwei] *n. NAm:* = route *f* touristique.

parky ['pɑ:ki] *a. F:* (*of weather*) frisquet; un peu froid.

parlance ['pɑ:ləns] *n.* langage *m*, parler *m*; **in common p.,** dans la langue familière, en langage courant; **in legal p.,** en termes de pratique.

parley¹ ['pɑ:li] *n.* conférence *f*, parlementage *m*; *Mil:* pourparlers *mpl* (avec l'ennemi); **to hold a p.,** parlementer (**with,** avec).

parley² *v.i.* être, entrer, en pourparlers; parlementer (**with the enemy,** avec l'ennemi).

parliament ['pɑ:ləment] *n.* le Parlement; **the Houses of P.,** le palais, les chambres, du Parlement; **in p.,** au parlement.

parliamentarian [pɑ:ləmen'tɛəriən] *n.* (*a*) parlementaire *m*, membre *m* du Parlement; (*b*) député rompu aux débats de la Chambre.

parliamentary [pɑ:lə'ment(ə)ri] *a.* (régime, gouvernement) parlementaire; **p. election,** élection législative; **p. candidate,** candidat *m* à la Chambre des communes; (*in Fr.*) candidat à la députation.

parlour, *NAm:* **parlor** ['pɑ:lər] *n.* (*a*) parloir *m* (d'un couvent); (*b*) *O: & NAm:* salon *m*; **p. games,** petits jeux de salon, de société; (*c*) **beauty p.,** salon de beauté; *NAm:* **beer p.,** bar *m* (où on sert la bière); *U.S:* **funeral p.,** bureau *m* d'un entrepreneur de pompes funèbres.

parlourmaid ['pɑ:ləmeid] *n.f.* bonne (affectée au service de table).

parlous ['pɑ:ləs] *a. Lit:* périlleux, précaire.

Parma ['pɑ:mə] *Pr.n. Geog:* Parme; **P. ham,** jambon *m* de Parme.

Parmesan [pɑ:mi'zæn] *n.* **P. (cheese),** parmesan *m*.

Parnassus [pɑ:'næsəs] *Pr.n.* le Parnasse.

parochial [pə'roukiəl] *a.* (*a*) *Ecc:* paroissial, -aux; (*b*) (*of civil parish*) communal, -aux; (*c*) *Pej:* provincial, -aux; **p. outlook,** esprit *m* de clocher; (*d*) *NAm:* **p. school,** école religieuse.

parochialism [pə'roukiəlizm] *n.* esprit *m* de clocher; patriotisme *m* de clocher.

parodist ['pærədist] *n.* parodiste *m*.

parody¹ ['pærədi] *n.* parodie *f*, pastiche *m*; travestissement *m* (de la justice).

parody² *v.tr.* parodier, pasticher; travestir (la justice, etc.).

parole¹ [pə'roul] *n.* parole *f* (d'honneur); **prisoner on p.,** (i) *Mil:* prisonnier *m* sur parole, sur sa foi; (ii) *Jur:* prisonnier (de droit commun) libéré conditionnellement; **to be put on p.,** être libéré sur parole; **to break one's p.,** manquer à sa parole.

parole² *v.tr.* libérer (un prisonnier) (i) sur parole, (ii) conditionnellement.

paroxysm ['pærəksizm] *n.* (*a*) *Med:* paroxysme *m* (d'une fièvre, etc.); (*b*) crise *f* (de fou rire, etc.).

parquet ['pɑ:kei] *n.* **1. p. (floor),** parquet *m*; **p. flooring,** parquetage *m*. **2.** *Th: U.S:* premiers rangs du parterre.

parricide¹ ['pærisaid] *n.* (*pers.*) parricide *mf*.

parricide² *n.* (crime *m* de) parricide (*m*).

parrot ['pærət] *n.* **1.** (*a*) *Orn:* perroquet *m*; **to repeat sth. p. fashion,** répéter qch. comme un perroquet; (*b*) *Fig:* (*pers.*) perroquet *m*. **2.** *Ich:* **p. fish,** scare *m*; poisson *m* perroquet.

parry¹ ['pæri] *n. Fenc: Box:* parade *f*.

parry² **1.** *v.tr.* (*a*) *Box: Fenc: etc:* parer (un coup); (*b*) détourner, éviter (un danger); parer (une question). **2.** *v.i.* **to p. and thrust,** (i) *Fenc:* parer et tirer; (ii) *Fig:* riposter, répondre du tac au tac.

parse [pɑ:z] *v.tr.* faire l'analyse (grammaticale) (d'un mot); analyser (grammaticalement) (une phrase). **parsing** *n.* analyse grammaticale.

Parsee ['pɑ:si:, pɑ:'si:] *a. & n.* Parsi, -ie.

parsimonious [pɑ:si'mouniəs] *a.* parcimonieux; économe; *Pej:* pingre. **-ly** *adv.* parcimonieusement.

parsimony ['pɑ:siməni] *n.* parcimonie *f*; épargne *f*.

parsley ['pɑ:sli] *n. Bot:* persil *m*; *Cu:* **p. sauce,** sauce *f* au persil, sauce persillée.

parsnip ['pɑ:snip] *n.* panais *m*.

parson ['pɑ:s(ə)n] *n. Ecc:* **1.** titulaire *m* d'un bénéfice. **2.** ecclésiastique *m*; prêtre *m*; pasteur *m*.

parsonage ['pɑ:sənidʒ] *n.* = presbytère *m*; cure *f*.

part¹ [pɑ:t] **I.** *n.* **1.** partie *f*; (*a*) **p. of the house is to let,** une portion de la maison est à louer; **good in parts,** bon en partie; **it's not bad in parts,** il y a des parties qui ne sont pas mal; **the funny, odd, p. about it is that . . .,** ce qu'il y a de comique, d'étrange, c'est que . . .; **in the early p. of the week,** dans les premiers jours de la semaine; **the greater p. of the population,** la plus grande partie de la population;

to be, form, p. of sth., faire partie de qch.; **it is p. and parcel of . . .,** c'est une partie intégrante, essentielle, de . . .; **to contribute in p. to the expenses,** contribuer pour partie aux frais; **for the most p.,** pour la plupart; (*b*) **ten parts of water to one of milk,** dix parties d'eau pour une partie de lait; (*c*) **the parts of the body,** les parties du corps; (*d*) *Ind: etc:* pièce *f*, organe *m*, élément *m*; **moving parts,** organes, parties, en mouvement; **spare parts,** pièces détachées, de rechange; (*e*) *Cmptr:* exemplaire *m* (de liasse); (*f*) *Gram:* **parts of speech,** parties du discours; **principal parts,** temps principaux (d'un verbe); (*g*) *Publ:* fascicule *m*, livraison *f* (d'un ouvrage); **to buy a work in parts,** acheter un ouvrage par fascicules; (*h*) **in that p. of the world, in those parts,** dans cette partie du monde; dans cette région; **they are not from our p. of the world,** ils ne sont pas de chez nous; **what are you doing in these parts?** qu'est-ce que vous faites ici, dans ces parages? (*i*) **p. owner,** copropriétaire *mf*; *Nau:* coarmateur *m*; **to work p. time, to have a p.-time job,** travailler à mi-temps; **p.-time worker, p. timer,** ouvrier, -ière, employé, -ée, qui travaille à temps partiel, à mi-temps. **2.** part *f*; (*a*) **to take (a) p. in sth.,** prendre part à, participer à, qch.; **to take p. in the conversation,** prendre part à, se mêler à, la conversation; *T.V: etc:* **those taking p. were . . .,** avec le concours de . . .; **to take no p. in sth.,** se désintéresser de qch.; **I had no p. in it,** je n'y suis pour rien; (*b*) *Th: etc:* rôle *m*; personnage *m*; **supporting p.,** second rôle; **small p., bit p.,** petit rôle; *pl.* utilités *f*; **to play one's p.,** jouer, remplir, son rôle; **in all this imagination plays a large p.,** dans tout ceci l'imagination entre pour beaucoup; (*c*) *Mus:* **orchestral parts,** parties d'orchestre; **p. music,** musique *f* d'ensemble; **p. song,** chanson *f* à plusieurs voix; **p. singing,** chant à plusieurs voix. **3.** (*a*) côté *m*; *O:* **on the one p. . . ., on the other p. . . .,** d'un côté . . ., de l'autre . . .; d'une part . . ., d'autre part . . .; (*b*) parti *m*; **to take s.o.'s p.,** prendre parti pour qn; prendre fait et cause pour qn; (*c*) **an indiscretion on the p. of . . .,** une indiscrétion de la part de . . .; **for my p.,** quant à moi; en ce qui me concerne. **4. to take sth. in good p., in bad p.,** prendre qch. en bonne part, en mauvaise part; prendre qch, du bon, du mauvais, côté. **5. parts,** moyens *mpl*, facultés *fpl*; **man of many parts,** homme à facettes. **6.** *NAm:* raie *f* (dans les cheveux). **II.** *adv.* partiellement; en partie; **p. silk p. cotton,** mi-soie mi-coton; **p. one and p. the other,** moitié l'un moitié l'autre.

part² **1.** *v.tr.* (*a*) séparer en deux; (*of island*) diviser (un cours d'eau); (*of pers.*) fendre (la foule); **to p. one's hair,** se faire une raie (dans les cheveux); **to p. one's hair in the middle, at the side,** faire, porter, la raie au milieu, sur le côté; (*c*) séparer (**sth. from sth.,** qch. de qch.); (*c*) rompre (une amarre, etc.). **2.** *v.i.* (*a*) (*of crowd, etc.*) se diviser; se ranger de part et d'autre; (*b*) (*of two pers.*) se quitter, se séparer; (*of two thgs*) se séparer; (*of roads*) diverger; **to p. good friends,** se quitter bons amis; **to p. from s.o.,** quitter qn; se séparer de, d'avec, qn; **to p. with (sth.),** céder (qch.); se dessaisir, se défaire, de (qch.); *Jur:* aliéner (un droit, un bien); **he hates to p. with his money,** il n'aime pas à débourser; (*c*) (*of cable, etc.*) rompre, se rompre, partir, céder. **parting** *n.* **1.** (*a*) séparation *f*; (*of waters*) partage *m*; **to be at the p. of the ways,** (i) se trouver là où deux routes se séparent; (ii) être au carrefour, à la croisée des chemins; (*b*) départ *m*; séparation *f*; **p. kiss,** baiser *m* d'adieu; **p. shot,** riposte (lancée en partant). **2.** rompement *m*, rupture *f* (d'un câble, etc.) **3.** (*of hair*) raie *f*; **centre p.,** raie médiane.

partake [pɑː'teik] *v.* (**partook** [pɑː'tuk]; **partaken** [pɑː'teikən]) *v.i.* **to p. in, of, sth.,** participer à qch. (**with s.o.,** avec qn); *O:* **to p. of a meal,** prendre un repas; *Ecc:* **to p. of the Sacrament,** s'approcher des sacrements.

parthenogenesis [pɑːθənou'dʒenisis] *n. Biol:* parthénogénèse *f*.

partial ['pɑːʃ(ə)l] *a.* **1.** (*a*) partial, -aux (envers qn); injuste; (*b*) *F:* **to be p. to s.o., sth.,** avoir un faible, une prédilection, pour qn, qch.; avoir un penchant pour qn; **I am p. to a pipe after dinner,** je fume volontiers une pipe après dîner. **2.** partiel, -ielle; en partie; **p. eclipse,** éclipse partielle; **p. loss,** perte partielle, sinistre partiel; (*of pers.*) **p. disability,** incapacité partielle. **-ally** *adv.* **1.** avec partialité. **2.** partiellement; en partie.

partiality [pɑːʃi'æliti] *n.* **1.** (*a*) partialité *f* (**for, to,** pour, envers); injustice *f*; (*b*) favoritisme *m*. **2.** prédilection *f*, préférence marquée, faible *m* (**for,** pour); penchant *m* (**for,** pour).

participant [pɑː'tisipənt] *a. & n.* participant (**in,** à).

participate [pɑː'tisipeit] *v.i.* (*a*) **to p. in sth.,** prendre part, participer, s'associer, à qch.; **to p. in s.o.'s joy, work,** s'associer à la joie, aux travaux, de qn; (*b*) (*of thg*) participer, tenir (**of sth.,** de qch.).

participation [pɑːtisi'peiʃ(ə)n] *n.* participation *f* (**in sth.,** à qch.).

participator [pɑː'tisipeitər] *n.* participant, -ante (**in,** de); **to be a p. in a crime,** (i) s'associer à un crime; (ii) avoir participé à un crime.

participial [pɑːti'sipiəl] *a. Gram:* participial, -aux.

participle ['pɑːtisipl] *n. Gram:* participe *m*; **present, past, p.,** participe présent, passé.

particle ['pɑːtikl] *n.* **1.** (*a*) particule *f*, parcelle *f* (de matière); paillette *f* (de métal); grain *m* (de sable); **there's not a p. of truth in this story,** il n'y a pas l'ombre de vérité dans ce récit; (*b*) *Atom.Ph:* particule, corpuscule *m*. **2.** *Gram:* particule.

parti-coloured, *NAm:* **-colored** ['pɑːtikʌled] *a.* **1.** mi-parti. **2.** bigarré, bariolé.

particular [pə'tikjulər] **I.** *a.* **1.** (*a*) particulier; spécial, -aux; (objet) déterminé; **that p. book,** ce livre-là; ce livre en particulier; (*of a service*) **p. branch,** spécialité *f*; **my own p. feelings,** mes sentiments particuliers, personnels; (*b*) **to take p. care over doing sth.,** faire qch. avec un soin particulier; **I left for no p. reason,** je suis parti sans raison précise; **I didn't notice anything p.,** je n'ai rien remarqué de particulier; (*c*) *adv.phr.* **in p.,** en particulier; notamment. **2.** (*of account, etc.*) détaillé, circonstancié. **3.** (*of pers.*) méticuleux, minutieux, soigneux; pointilleux; **to be p. about one's food,** être difficile, exigeant, sur la nourriture; **to be p. about one's dress,** soigner sa mise, sa tenue; **he is p. in his choice of friends,** il est difficile dans le choix de ses relations; **don't be too p.,** ne vous montrez pas trop exigeant. **4.** *P:* **I'm not p. (about it),** je n'y tiens pas plus que ça. **II.** *n.* détail *m*, particularité *f*; **alike in every p.,** semblables en tout point; **to give particulars of sth.,** donner les détails de qch.; **to ask for fuller particulars about sth.,** demander des précisions *fpl*, des indications *fpl* supplémentaires, sur qch.; **for further particulars apply to . . .,** pour plus amples détails, renseignements, s'adresser à . . .. **-ly** *adv.* particulièrement, spécialement; en particulier; **note p. that . . .,** notez en particulier que . . .; **I asked him to be p. careful,** je lui ai demandé de prendre particulièrement soin; **not p.,** pas particulièrement, spécialement; **he's not p. rich,** il n'est pas tellement riche.

particularity [pətikju'læriti] *n.* **1.** particularité *f*. **2.** méticulosité *f*; minutie *f* (d'une description, etc.).

particularization [pətikjulərai'zeiʃ(ə)n] *n.* particularisation *f*.

particularize [pə'tikjuləraiz] **1.** *v.tr.* particulariser, spécifier. **2.** *v.i.* entrer dans les détails; préciser.

partisan [pɑːti'zæn] *n.* **1.** partisan, -ane; **to act in a p. spirit,** faire preuve (i) d'esprit de parti, (ii) de parti pris. **2.** partisan; soldat *m*, officier *m*, d'une troupe irrégulière.

partisanship [pɑːti'zænʃip] *n.* partialité *f*; esprit *m* de parti.

partition¹ [pɑː'tiʃ(ə)n] *n.* **1.** partage *m* (d'un pays vaincu, d'un héritage, etc.); division *f*, découpage *m* (en plusieurs parties). **2.** (*a*) cloison *f*, cloisonnage *m*; paroi *m*; *Const:* **internal p., p. wall,** mur *m* de refend, de séparation; **wooden p.,** pan *m* de bois; **glass p.,** vitrage *m*; (*in vehicle*) glace *f* de séparation; (*b*) compartiment *m* (de cale, etc.); section *f*.

partition² *v.tr.* **1.** partager (un héritage, etc.); démembrer (un pays vaincu); diviser (qch. en plusieurs parties). **2. to p. (off),** cloisonner (une pièce); séparer (une partie d'une pièce) par une cloison.

partitive ['pɑːtitiv] *a.* & *n.* *Gram:* partitif (*m*).

partly ['pɑːtli] *adv.* partiellement; en partie; **wholly or p.,** en tout ou en partie; **p. by force p. by persuasion,** moitié de force moitié par persuasion.

partner¹ ['pɑːtnər] *n.* (*a*) associé, -ée (**with s.o. in sth.,** de qn dans qch.); **to be s.o.'s p. in a crime,** être associé à qn dans un crime; *Com:* **senior p.,** associé principal; **full p.,** associé à part entière; **sleeping p., silent p.,** (associé) commanditaire (*m*); bailleur *m* de fonds; (*b*) partenaire *mf* (au tennis, etc.); *Cards:* **to cut, draw, for partners** = faire les rois; (*c*) *Danc:* cavalier, -ière; **my p.,** mon danseur, ma danseuse.

partner² *v.tr.* (*a*) être associé, s'associer, à, avec (qn); (*b*) *Games:* être le partenaire de (qn).

partnership ['pɑːtnəʃip] *n.* **1.** (*a*) association *f* (**in sth. with s.o.,** avec qn dans qch.); **p. in crime,** association dans le crime; (*b*) *Com: etc:* **to enter, go into, p. with s.o.,** entrer en association avec qn; s'associer avec qn; **to take s.o. into p.,** prendre qn comme associé. **2.** *Com: etc:* société *f*; **general p.,** société commerciale en nom collectif; **sleeping p.,** (société en) commandite *f* (simple).

partridge ['pɑːtridʒ] *n.* *Orn:* (*pl.* **partridges,** *Ven: Cu:* **partridge**) perdrix *f*; *Cu:* perdreau *m*; **a brace of p.,** un couple de perdrix.

party ['pɑːti] *n.* **1.** (*faction*) parti *m*; *Pol:* **the Labour P.,** le parti travailliste; **p. leader, man,** chef *m*, homme, de parti; **p. quarrels,** querelles partisanes; **p. politics, spirit,** politique *f*, esprit *m*, de parti; **to follow,** *F:* **toe, the p. line,** obéir aux directives du parti. **2.** (*a*) **pleasure, shooting, p.,** partie *f* de plaisir, de chasse; **will you join our p.?** voulez-vous être des nôtres? **we're a small p.,** nous sommes peu nombreux; **I was one of the p.,** j'étais de la partie; (*b*) réunion (privée, intime); réception *f*; soirée *f*; **dinner p.,** dîner *m*; **children's tea p.,** goûter *m* d'enfants; (*of child*) **may I wear my p. dress?** puis-je mettre ma belle robe? *F:* **he's caught the p. spirit,** il s'est abandonné aux joies de la fête; *U.S:* **p. pooper,** trouble-fête *mf inv.* **3.** (*a*) groupe *m*, bande *f* (de touristes, etc.); **the official p.,** le groupe des officiels, les officiels *mpl*; **p. ticket,** billet collectif; (*b*) brigade *f*, équipe *f*, groupe (de mineurs, etc.); atelier *m* (d'ouvriers, etc.); **rescue p.,** équipe de secours; *Adm: etc:* **working p.,** comité *m* d'étude; (*c*) *Mil: etc:* détachement *m*; **the advance p.,** les éléments *mpl* d'avant-garde; **firing p.,** peloton *m* d'exécution; **landing p.,** compagnie *f* de débarquement; (*d*) *Mil:* parti (détaché pour battre la campagne). **4.** (*a*) *Jur:* **p. (to a suit, to a dispute),** partie; **the parties to the case,** les parties en cause; **to be p. to a suit,** être en cause; (*b*) *Com: etc:* **parties to a bill of exchange,** intéressé(e)s à une lettre de change; **a third p.,** un tiers, une tierce personne; **third p. insurance,** assurance *f* au tiers; (*c*) **to be, to become, (a) p. to a crime,** être, se rendre, complice d'un crime; **I would never be (a) p. to such a thing,** je ne donnerais jamais mon consentement, je ne m'associerais jamais, à chose pareille; (*d*) *P:* individu *m*, type *m*.

paschal ['pæsk(ə)l] *a.* pascal, -aux.

pass¹ [pɑːs] *n.* col *m*, défilé *m* (de montagne).

pass² **1.** (*a*) *A: & Lit:* **to come to p.,** arriver, avoir lieu; **it came to p. that . . .,** or il arriva, il advint, que . . .; (*b*) **things have come to a pretty p.!** voilà donc où en sont les choses! **things came to such a p. that . . .,** les choses en vinrent à ce point, à tel point, que . . .. **2.** *Sch:* (*in examination*) **to obtain, get, a p.,** être reçu; **p. mark,** moyenne *f*. **3.** (*a*) passe *f* (de magnétiseur, de prestidigitateur); (*b*) *Fenc:* passe, passade, *f*, botte *f*; *F:* **to make a p. at s.o.,** essayer d'embrasser, de peloter, qn. **4.** *Metalw:* passe, passage *m* (du métal dans le laminoir). **5.** permis *m*, passe, permission *f*, laissez-passer *m inv*; **(free) p.,** (i) *Rail: etc:* titre *m*, carte *f*, de circulation; (ii) *Th: etc:* billet gratuit, de faveur; carte d'entrée; **p. key,** (clef *f*) passe-partout (*m inv*); **p. book,** carnet *m*, livret *m*, de banque. **6.** (*a*) *Fb: etc:* passe; **back p.,** passe en arrière; (*b*) **the aircraft made two low passes over the village,** l'avion a effectué deux passages à basse altitude au-dessus du village.

pass³ **I.** *v.i.* passer. **1.** (*a*) **as we were passing,** comme nous passions; **the tourists passed into the dining hall,** les touristes ont défilé dans le réfectoire; **words passed between them,** il y a eu un échange d'injures; (*b*) **to p. along a street,** passer par une rue; **the procession passed slowly by,** le cortège passa, défila, lentement; **everyone smiles as he passes,** tout le monde sourit à son passage; **the motorway passes close to the village,** l'autoroute passe tout près du village; **to let s.o. pass, allow s.o. to p.,** laisser passer qn; *Rail: etc:* **p. along, down, the car!** avancez! dégagez la portière! **to p. unobserved,** passer inaperçu; **let it p.!** passe pour cela! **I'd like to say in passing,** soit dit en passant; (*c*) *Aut:* doubler; **no passing,** défense de doubler; (*d*) *Cards:* passer, renoncer, passer parole; (*at dominoes*) bouder; *Cards:* **p.!** parole! **2.** (*of time*) **to p. (by),** (se) passer, s'écouler; **when five minutes had passed,** au bout de cinq minutes; **how time passes!** comme le temps passe vite! **he let the opportunity p.,** il a laissé passer l'occasion. **3. water passes from a liquid to a solid state when it freezes,** l'eau se transforme de liquide en solide quand il gèle. **4.** disparaître; (*of clouds, etc.*) se dissiper. **5.** *O:* avoir lieu, se passer; **I don't know what passed between them,** je ne sais pas ce qui s'est passé entre eux. **6. it would p. in certain circles,** cela passerait dans certains milieux; *F:* **you'd p. in a crowd!** tu n'es pas si mal que ça! **II.** *v.tr.* **1.** (*a*) passer devant, près de (qn, la fenêtre, etc.); **to p. s.o. on the stairs, in the street,** croiser qn dans l'escalier, dans la rue; (*b*) passer (sans s'arrêter); dépasser (le but); outrepasser (les bornes de qch.); (*c*) *Com:* **to p. a dividend,** conclure un exercice sans payer de dividende; (*d*) passer, franchir (une frontière, etc.); *Nau:* dépasser, doubler (un cap); (*e*) surpasser (qn); gagner (qn) de vitesse; dépasser, rattraper (qn, un autre navire, etc.); doubler (une autre voiture); *Sp: etc:* devancer (un concurrent); (*f*) etre reçu, admis, à (un examen); **to p. a test,** subir une épreuve avec succès; (*g*) **bill that has passed the House of Commons,** projet *m* de loi qui a été voté par la Chambre des Communes; (*h*) **to p. the censor, the customs,** être accepté par la censure, par la douane. **2.** (*a*) approuver, admettre, apurer (une facture); allouer (une dépense); (*of company*) **to p. a dividend of 5%,** approuver un dividende de 5%; **the censor has passed the play,** le censeur a accordé le visa; (*b*) *Sch:* **to p. a candidate,** recevoir un candidat; admettre un candidat (à un examen); (*c*) *Parl: etc:*

passer, voter, adopter (un projet de loi, une résolution); (*d*) *Mil: etc:* **to be passed fit,** être reconnu apte. **3.** (*a*) transmettre; donner; **to p. sth. from hand to hand,** passer qch. de main en main; **to p. sth. up, down,** monter, descendre, qch.; **p. me the salt, please,** donnez-moi le sel, s'il vous plaît; **p. the cakes round,** faites passer les gâteaux; *Fb: etc:* **to p. the ball,** passer le ballon; faire une passe, des passes; (*b*) *Book-k:* **to p. an item to current account,** passer, porter, un article en compte courant; (*c*) (faire) passer, écouler, *F:* refiler (un faux billet de banque, etc.). **4.** mettre; glisser; **to p. one's hand between the bars,** glisser sa main à travers les barreaux; **to p. a rope round sth.,** passer une corde autour de qch.; **to p. vegetables through a sieve,** passer des légumes; **to p. a sponge over sth.,** passer l'éponge sur qch. **5.** *Mil:* **to p. troops in review,** passer des troupes en revue. **6. to p. the time,** passer le temps; **it passes the time,** cela fait passer le temps. **7.** (*a*) *Jur:* **to p. sentence,** prononcer le jugement; (*b*) **to p. criticism on sth.,** faire la critique de qch.; **to p. remarks (on sth.),** faire des commentaires, des observations (sur qch.). **8.** *Physiol:* **to p. water,** uriner; *Med:* **to p. blood,** être affecté d'hématurie, *F:* pisser du sang. **pass away** *v.i.* (*a*) disparaître; (*b*) mourir. **passing 1.** *a.* (*a*) passant; qui passe; (remarque) en passant; *Ten:* **p. shot,** passing-shot *m*; (*b*) passager, éphémère; (désir, etc.) fugitif; **the p. hour,** l'heure fugitive. **2.** *adv. A: & Lit:* **p. fair,** de toute beauté. **3.** *n.* (*a*) (i) passage *m* (d'un train, d'oiseaux, etc.); (ii) (*overtaking*) dépassement *m*, doublement *m* (d'une autre voiture); **p. place,** (*on road*) garage *m*; *Rail:* voie *f* d'évitement, de dédoublement; (iii) *adv.phr.* **in p.,** à propos; entre parenthèses; (*b*) (i) écoulement *m* (du temps); *O:* disparition *f* (de la beauté de qn, etc.); (ii) mort *f* (de qn); **p. bell,** glas *m*; (*c*) (i) *Sch: etc:* admission *f* (d'un candidat); (ii) *Pol: etc:* adoption *f* (d'une résolution, etc.); vote *m* (d'une loi); (iii) *Fin: Com:* approbation *f* (des comptes); passation *f* (d'un dividende); (*d*) *Jur:* prononcé *m* (du jugement); (*e*) (i) **p. (on),** transmission *f* (d'un message, etc.); (ii) *Fb: etc:* passe *f* (du ballon). **pass off 1.** *v.i.* (*a*) (*of pain, etc.*) disparaître; (*b*) **everything passed off well,** tout s'est bien passé. **2.** *v.tr.* (*a*) **to p. sth. off on s.o.,** repasser, refiler, qch. à qn; **to p. off one's goods as those of another make,** faire passer ses propres produits pour ceux d'une autre marque; (*b*) **to p. oneself off as an artist,** se faire passer pour artiste; (*c*) **to p. sth. off as a joke,** (i) prendre qch. en riant; (ii) dire qu'on a fait qch. comme plaisanterie. **pass on 1.** *v.i.* (*a*) continuer son chemin, sa route; **to p. on to another subject,** passer à un nouveau sujet; (*b*) mourir, passer à la vie éternelle. **2.** *v.tr.* faire circuler (qch.); (faire) passer qch. à qn; **read this and p. it on,** lisez ceci et faites circuler. **pass out** *v.i.* (*a*) sortir (d'une salle, etc.); (*b*) **don't let this document p. out of your hands,** gardez soigneusement ce document; (*c*) *Sch: etc:* (*after final examination*) sortir; **cadets passing out,** élèves sortants; **passing-out list,** classement *m* de sortie; (*d*) s'évanouir. **pass over 1.** *v.i.* (*a*) traverser, franchir (une rivière, etc.); franchir, passer sur (un obstacle); passer (qch.) sous silence; passer sur, glisser sur (une difficulté, etc.); (*b*) **to p. over to the enemy,** passer à l'ennemi; (*c*) (*of storm*) se dissiper, finir. **2.** *v.tr.* (*in making a promotion*) **to p. s.o. over,** passer par-dessus le dos à qn; faire un passe-droit. **pass through** *v.i.* (*a*) traverser (un pays, etc.); **he was (only) passing through Paris,** il était de passage à Paris; (*b*) traverser (une crise).

passable ['pɑːsəbl] *a.* **1.** (rivière, bois, etc.) traversable, franchissable; (route) praticable. **2.** passable, assez bon; **it's p.,** ce n'est pas si mauvais, trop mal. **-ably** *adv.* passablement, assez.

passage ['pæsidʒ] *n.* **1.** (*a*) passage *m*; trajet *m*; **bird of p.,** oiseau *m* de passage; (*b*) *esp. Nau:* traversée *f*; **to have a bad, rough, p.,** avoir, faire, une mauvaise traversée; **to work one's p.,** gagner son passage (en travaillant à bord); (*c*) **to force a p.,** se forcer un passage; *Jur:* **right of p.,** droit *m* de passage; (*d*) *Pol:* adoption *f* (d'un projet de loi). **2.** (*a*) couloir *m*, corridor *m*; **underground p.,** passage souterrain; (*b*) passage, ruelle *f*; (*at end of street*) échappée *f*; (*c*) **the North-West, North-East, p.,** le passage Nord-Ouest, Nord-Est. **3.** (*a*) *Mec.E:* canalisation *f*, conduit *m*, conduite *f*; **air p.,** conduit d'aérage, conduit(e) à air; (*b*) *Anat:* **air passages,** voies aériennes, aérifères; *F:* **the back p.,** le rectum. **4. p. of arms,** passe *f* d'armes; échange de mots vifs; *F:* prise *f* de bec. **5.** passage (d'un livre); **selected passages,** morceaux choisis.

passageway ['pæsidʒwei] *n.* **1.** passage *m*; **to leave a p.,** laisser le passage libre. **2.** (*a*) passage, ruelle *f*; (*b*) (*in house*) couloir *m*, corridor *m*.

passé ['pɑːsei] *a.* (*a*) qui n'est plus à la mode; (*b*) défraîchi; fané; (femme) qui a perdu sa beauté.

passel ['pæs(ə)l] *n. U.S: F:* grand nombre (de personnes).

passenger ['pæsəndʒər] *n.* (*a*) voyageur, -euse; (*on ship, aircraft*) passager, -ère; **p. train,** train *m* de voyageurs; **p. coach, carriage,** *NAm:* **car,** voiture *f*, wagon *m*, à voyageurs; *Aut:* **p. seat,** le siège à côté du conducteur; (*b*) *F:* non-valeur *f*, *pl.* non-valeurs; poids mort; **we can't take passengers,** on ne peut pas embarquer des poids morts; (*c*) *Orn: A:* **p. pigeon,** pigeon migrateur.

passe-partout [pɑːspɑː'tuː] *n.* **1.** (clef) passe-partout (*m*) *inv.* **2.** ruban *m* de bordure (de photographie sous verre, etc.); **p.-p. framing,** encadrement *m* sous verre.

passer-by ['pɑːsə'bai] *n.* (*pl.* **passers-by**) passant.

passion ['pæʃ(ə)n] *n.* **1.** (*a*) **the P. (of Christ),** la Passion (de Jésus-Christ); **P. Sunday, week,** le dimanche, la semaine, de la Passion; *Mus:* **the Saint Matthew P.,** la Passion selon saint Matthieu; (*b*) *Lit:* **p. play,** mystère *m* de la Passion. **2.** passion; **to have a p. for music, for painting,** avoir la passion de la musique, de la peinture. **3.** accès *m* de colère; colère *f*, emportement *m*; **to fly into a p.,** s'emporter. **4.** amour *m*, passion; **to have a p. for s.o.,** aimer qn passionnément, à la folie.

passionate ['pæʃənət] *a.* **1.** emporté, irascible; (discours) véhément. **2.** passionné, ardent. **-ly** *adv.* passionnément; ardemment; avec passion; **to be p. in love with s.o.,** aimer qn passionnément, à la folie; **to be p. fond of (doing) sth.,** être passionné de qch.; avoir la passion de faire qch.

passionflower ['pæʃənflauər] *n. Bot:* passiflore *f*.

passionfruit ['pæʃənfruːt] *n.* fruit *m* de la passiflore.

passionless ['pæʃənlis] *a.* sans passion; impassible.

passive ['pæsiv] **1.** *a.* passif; (*a*) **p. resistance,** résistance passive, inerte; (*b*) *Com:* (dettes) ne portant pas d'intérêt; (*c*) *Metall: El:* (*of iron, electrode, etc.*) passif. **2.** *a. & n. Gram:* **the p. (voice),** la voix passive, le passif; **verb in the p.,** verbe *m* au passif. **-ly** *adv.* passivement.

passiveness ['pæsivnis], **passivity** [pæ'siviti] *n.* passivité *f* (de l'esprit, d'un métal, etc.); inertie *f*.

Passover ['pɑːsouvər] *n.* la Pâque.

passport ['pɑːspɔːt] *n.* (*a*) passeport *m*; **ship's p.,** permis *m* de navigation; (*b*) **money is a p. to anything,** l'argent est un bon passe-partout.

password ['pɑːswəːd] *n.* mot *m* de passe; mot d'ordre.

past[1] [pɑːst] **1.** *a.* (*a*) passé; ancien; **those days are p.,** ces jours sont passés; **in p. times., in times p.,** autrefois, *Lit:* au temps jadis; **p. chairman,** (i) président sortant; (ii) ancien président; **he's a p. master at (doing) it,** il est expert dans la matière; il est passé maître dans l'art de le faire; (*b*) *Gram:* **p. participle,** participe passé; *a. & n.* **in the p. (tense),** au passé; (*c*) (*of the immediate past*) passé, dernier; **the p. week,** la semaine dernière, passée; **for some time p.,** depuis quelque temps. **2.** *n.* (*a*) **the p.,** le passé; **in the p.,** autrefois; **this plan is a thing of the p.,** ce projet (i) n'existe plus, (ii) est périmé; **to live in the p.,** vivre dans le passé; (*b*) **town with a p.,** ville *f* historique; (*c*) (*of pers.*) antécédents *mpl*; **woman with a p.,** femme qui a eu des aventures, avec un passé.

past² **1.** *prep.* au delà de; (*a*) **a little p. the bridge,** un peu plus loin que le pont; **to walk p. the house,** passer (devant) la maison; (*b*) plus de; **it is p. four (o'clock),** il est passé quatre heures; il est quatre heures passées; **half, a quarter, p. four,** quatre heures et demie, et quart; **ten (minutes) p. four,** quatre heures dix; **it is half p.,** il est la demie; (*c*) **p. all understanding,** hors de toute compréhension; **p. endurance,** insupportable; **that's p. all belief,** cela est incroyable; **I'm p. work,** je ne suis plus d'âge à travailler; **to be p. caring for sth.,** être revenu de qch.; *F:* **he's p. it,** il est trop vieux (pour travailler, pour jouer au tennis, etc.); *F:* **I wouldn't put it p. him,** il en est bien capable. **2.** *adv.* **to walk p., go p.,** passer; **to run p.,** passer en courant; **to march p.,** défiler.

pasta ['pæstə] *n. Cu:* pâtes *fpl* (alimentaires).

paste¹ [peist] *n.* **1.** *Cu:* pâte *f* (à pâtisserie). **2.** pâte; (*a*) *Cer:* **hard, soft, p.,** pâte dure, tendre; (*b*) *Comest:* **anchovy p.,** beurre *m* d'anchois; **fish p.** = mousse *f* de poisson. **3.** colle *f* (de pâte); **p. pot,** pot *m* à colle. **4.** *Jewel:* stras(s) *m*; **it's only p.,** c'est en toc.

paste² *v.tr.* **1.** coller; (*a*) **to p. (up),** coller (une affiche); afficher (un avis); (*b*) **to p. a screen with pictures,** coller des images sur un écran. **2.** *F:* battre, rosser (qn). **pasting** *n.* **1.** collage *m* (d'affiches, etc.). **2.** *F:* rossée *f*, raclée *f*; *Sp:* **to get a p.,** être battu à plate(s) couture(s).

pasteboard ['peistbɔːd] *n.* carton *m*.

pastel ['pæst(ə)l] *n.* (*a*) *Art:* (crayon *m*) pastel (*m*); **p. drawing, drawing in p.,** (dessin *m* au) pastel; (*b*) **p. blue,** bleu pastel; **p. shades,** tons pastels.

paste-up ['peistʌp] *n. Publ:* maquette *f*.

pasteurization [pæst(j)ərai'zeiʃ(ə)n] *n.* pasteurisation *f*.

pasteurize ['pæst(j)əraiz] *v.tr.* pasteuriser; **pasteurized milk,** lait pasteurisé.

pastiche [pæs'tiːʃ] *n.* pastiche *m*.

pastille ['pæstil] *n.* (*a*) pastille *f*; **fruit pastilles** = pâtes *fpl* de fruits; (*b*) pastille à brûler.

pastime ['pɑːstaim] *n.* passe-temps *m inv*, distraction *f*, divertissement *m*.

pastiness ['peistinis] *n.* **1.** consistance pâteuse (du pain, etc.). **2.** (*of face*) teint terreux.

pastor ['pɑːstər] *n. Ecc:* pasteur *m*.

pastoral ['pɑːstərəl] **1.** *a.* pastoral, -aux; (*a*) **p. land,** (terre *f* en) pâturages (*mpl*); (*b*) *Ecc:* **p. letter,** *n.* **pastoral,** (lettre) pastorale; mandement *m* (de l'évêque). **2.** *n. Lit: Mus: Art: Th:* pastorale *f*.

pastry ['peistri] *n.* (*a*) pâte *f*; **short p.,** pâte brisée; **flaky, puff, p.,** pâte feuilletée; **choux p.,** pâte à choux; **p. board,** planche *f* à pâtisserie; **p. wheel,** rouleau *m*; **p. cutter,** emporte-pièce *m inv*; (*b*) (*cake*) pâtisserie *f*.

pastrycook ['peistrikuk] *n.* pâtissier, -ière.

pasturage ['pɑːstjuridʒ] *n.* **1.** (droit *m* de) pâturage (*m*), pacage *m*. **2.** = PASTURE¹.

pasture¹ ['pɑːstjər] *n.* **p. (ground, land),** (lieu *m* de) pâture (*f*); pâturage *m*, pâtis *m*, herbage *m*; *F:* **to be put out to p.,** être mis à la retraite, au vert.

pasture² **1.** *v.i.* paître, pâturer, pacager. **2.** *v.tr.* (*a*) (*of shepherd*) (faire) paître (les bêtes); (*b*) (*of animals*) pâturer (un pré).

pasty¹ ['peisti] *a.* **1.** empâté; pâteux. **2.** (teint) terreux, brouillé.

pasty² ['pæsti] *n. Cu:* = (petit) pâté en croûte (cuit sans moule); **Cornish p.,** pâté (en croûte) qui contient du bœuf, des pommes de terre et autres légumes.

pat¹ [pæt] *n.* **1.** (*a*) coup *m* de patte; petite tape; (*b*) caresse *f*; **to give s.o. a p. on the back,** (i) donner une tape à qn dans le dos; (ii) féliciter qn. **2.** bruit sourd (de pas, etc.). **3.** (*a*) rondelle *f*, médaillon *m* (de beurre); (*b*) **cow p.,** bouse *f* de vache.

pat² *v.tr.* **(patted)** (*a*) taper, tapoter; **to p. one's hair,** se tapoter les cheveux; (*b*) caresser (un animal, etc.); flatter (qn, un animal, etc.) de la main; **to p. s.o. on the back,** (i) donner une tape à qn dans le dos; (ii) féliciter qn; **to p. oneself on the back,** se féliciter.

pat³ *adv.* à propos; à point; **his answer came p.,** il a répondu du tac au tac; **to know sth. off p.,** savoir qch. par cœur; **to stand p.,** (i) *Cards:* jouer d'autorité; (ii) refuser de bouger.

patch¹ [pætʃ] *n.* **1.** (*a*) pièce *f* (pour raccommoder un vêtement); **to put a p. on a garment,** rapiécer un vêtement; *F:* **his last novel isn't a p. on the others,** son dernier roman est loin de valoir les autres; (*b*) pièce rapportée; *Nau:* placard *m*; *Tail: etc:* **p. pocket,** poche rapportée, appliquée; (*c*) *El: Tp:* **p. board,** tableau *m* de commutation (à cordon); **p. cord,** cordon *m* de commutation; (*d*) *Aut: etc:* **(rubber) p.,** (i) (*for inner tube*) pastille *f*; (ii) (*for outer cover*) emplâtre, guêtre *f*; (*e*) **eye p.,** couvre-œil *m*, *pl.* couvre-œils. **2.** (*a*) tache *f* (de couleur, de lumière, etc.); bouchon *m* (de brume); flaque *f* (d'huile); plaque *f* (de verglas); **p. of blue sky,** pan *m*, coin *m*, échappée *f*, de ciel bleu; (*on wood, metal, etc.*) **rough patches,** aspérités *fpl*; **book that is good in patches,** livre *m* qui contient de bons passages; *F:* **to strike a bad p.,** être en guigne, en déveine; (*b*) morceau *m*, coin; lopin *m*, parcelle *f* (de terre); carré *m*, plant *m* (de légumes); (*c*) *F:* (*of police*) secteur *m*; (*of criminal, etc.*) **keep off my p.!** ça c'est mon territoire (à moi)!

patch² *v.tr.* (*a*) mettre une pièce à, rapiécer (un vêtement, etc.); poser une pastille à (une chambre à air); (*b*) placarder (une voile); (*c*) **to p. together,** réunir (les fragments de qch.). **patching** *n.* **1.** rapiéçage *m*, rapiècement *m* (d'un vêtement). **2. p. up,** rafistolage *m*. **patch up** *v.tr.* rafistoler (qch.); arranger (une querelle); *Med: F:* retaper (qn).

patchwork ['pætʃwəːk] *n.* (*a*) ouvrage fait de pièces et de morceaux, de pièces disparates; **p. of fields,** campagne bigarrée; (*b*) patchwork *m*; **p. quilt,** couverture *f* en patchwork.

patchy ['pætʃi] *a.* (*a*) qui offre des taches; inégal, -aux; (*b*) inégal; qui manque d'unité.

pate [peit] *n. A: & F:* tête *f*, *F:* caboche *f*.

pâté ['pætei] *n. Cu:* pâté *m*; **liver p.,** pâté de foie.

patella, *pl.* **-ae, -as** [pə'telə, -iː, -əs] *n. Anat:* rotule *f*.

paten ['pæt(ə)n] *n. Ecc:* patène *f*.

patent¹ ['peitənt, 'pæt-] **I.** *a.* **1.** *Jur:* **letters p.,** (i) lettres patentes, de nobilité; (ii) lettres patentes, brevet *m* d'invention, d'inventeur. **2.** breveté; **p. medicine,** spécialité pharmaceutique, médicale; **p. food,** spécialité alimentaire; **p. leather,** cuir verni; **p.-leather shoes,** chaussures vernies. **3.** (fait, etc.) manifeste, clair, évident; **how can we deny p. facts?** comment nier l'évidence même? **II.** *n.* **1.** lettres patentes; **p. of nobility,** lettres d'anoblissement, de noblesse. **2.** (*a*) brevet *m* d'invention; **to take out a p. for an invention,** faire breveter une invention; **p. applied for,** une demande de brevet a été déposée; **infringement of a p.,** contrefaçon *f*; **p. agent,** agent *m* en brevets (d'invention); **p. office,** bureau *m* des brevets; office national de la propriété industrielle; **p. rights,**

propriété industrielle; (*b*) invention, fabrication, brevetée. **patently** *adv.* manifestement; clairement.

patent[2] *v.tr.* protéger par un brevet, faire breveter (une invention); prendre un brevet pour (une invention); **patented,** (*of invention, etc.*) breveté.

patentee [peitən'ti:] *n.* possesseur *m* d'un brevet.

pater ['peitər] *n.m. F: O:* papa, le paternel.

paterfamilias [peitəfə'miliæs] *n.m. F:* père de famille; chef de maison.

paternal [pə'tə:n(ə)l] *a.* paternel; **the p. roof,** la maison paternelle; **the p. side,** le côté paternel. **-ally** *adv.* paternellement.

paternalism [pə'tə:nəlizm] *n.* paternalisme *m.*

paternity [pə'tə:niti] *n.* paternité *f.*

path, *pl.* **paths** [pɑ:θ, pɑ:ðz] *n.* **1.** chemin *m*, sentier *m*; (*in garden*) allée *f*; **mule p.,** sentier muletier; **the p. of glory,** le chemin de la gloire. **2.** cours *m*, trajet *m*, course (d'un corps en mouvement); trajectoire *f* (d'un projectile, d'une particule, d'une planète, etc.); passage, trajet (d'un rayon de lumière); route *f* (du soleil); **p. of a bullet,** (i) (*through the air*) trajectoire, (ii) (*through the body*) trajet, sillon *m*, d'une balle; *Av:* **flight p.,** ligne *f* de vol; **glide p.,** axe *m* de descente, trajectoire d'atterrissage.

pathfinder ['pɑ:θfaindər] *n.* **1.** pionnier *m.* **2.** avion éclaireur.

pathetic [pə'θetik] **1.** *a.* pathétique, touchant, attendrissant; **she's a p. creature,** c'est une créature pitoyable; **you're p.!** tu me fais pitié! **how p.! it's p.! isn't it p.?** c'est malheureux, pitoyable! **2.** *n.* **the p.,** le pathétique; pathétisme *m.* **-ally** *adv.* pathétiquement.

pathological [pæθə'lɔdʒik(ə)l] *a.* pathologique. **-ally** *adv.* pathologiquement.

pathologist [pə'θɔlədzist] *n.* pathologiste *mf*; **(forensic) p.,** médecin *m* légiste.

pathology [pə'θɔlədʒi] *n.* pathologie *f.*

pathos ['peiθɔs] *n.* pathétique *m.*

pathway ['pɑ:θwei] *n.* sentier *m.*

patience ['peiʃəns] *n.* **1.** patience *f*; **to try, tax, s.o.'s p.,** éprouver la patience de qn; **my p. is exhausted, is at an end,** ma patience est à bout; je suis à bout de patience; **(have) p.!** (prenez) patience! **to lose p.,** perdre patience; **I've no p. with him,** il m'impatiente. **2.** *Cards:* réussite *f*; **to play p.,** faire des réussites.

patient ['peiʃənt] **1.** *a.* patient, endurant; **to be p.,** patienter; prendre patience. **2.** *n.* malade *mf*; patient, -ente; opéré, -ée; **a doctor and his patients,** un médecin et ses clients. **-ly** *adv.* patiemment; **to wait p.,** attendre patiemment, avec patience; patienter.

patina ['pætinə] *n.* patine *f*; (*of bronze*) **to take on a p.,** se patiner.

patio ['pætiou] *n. Arch:* patio *m.*

patriarch ['peitriɑ:k] *n.* (*a*) *Anthr: Ecc: etc:* patriarche *m*; (*b*) fondateur *m* (d'une organisation, etc.).

patriarchal [peitri'ɑ:k(ə)l] *a.* patriarcal, -aux.

patriarchy ['peitriɑ:ki] *n.* patriarcat *m*, système patriarcal.

patrician [pə'triʃ(ə)n] *a. & n. Rom.Hist: etc:* patricien, -ienne.

patrimony ['pætriməni] **1.** patrimoine *m.* **2.** biens-fonds *mpl*, revenu *m*, d'une église.

patriot ['peitriət, 'pæ-] *n.* patriote *mf.*

patriotic [peitri'ɔtik, pæ-] *a.* **1.** (*of pers.*) patriote. **2.** (*of speech, etc.*) patriotique. **-ally** *adv.* patriotiquement; en patriote.

patriotism ['peitriətizm, 'pæ-] *n.* patriotisme *m.*

patrol[1] [pə'troul] *n.* patrouille *f*; (*a*) *Mil:* **p. leader,** chef *m* de patrouille; **security p.,** patrouille de sûreté, de protection; **to be on p.,** être en patrouille; patrouiller; (*b*) *Av:* **fighter p.,** patrouille de chasse; **p. bomber,** patrouilleur de bombardement, bombardier *m* patrouilleur; *Navy:* **p. craft, vessel,** patrouilleur; vedette *f* de surveillance; (*c*) (*of police*) patrouille (de surveillance); ronde *f*; **traffic p.,** patrouille de la circulation (routière); **p. car,** voiture *f* de reconnaissance, de liaison policière; (*d*) **A.A. p.,** (i) patrouilleur, (ii) voiture de patrouille, de l'Automobile Association; (*e*) *Scout:* patrouille.

patrol[2] *v.* **(patrolled) 1.** *v.i.* patrouiller, aller en patrouille. **2.** *v.tr.* faire la patrouille dans (un quartier).

patrolman, *pl.* **-men** [pə'troulmən] *n.m.* (*a*) patrouilleur; (*b*) *NAm:* agent de police (en service de ronde).

patron ['peitrən] *n.* **1.** (*a*) protecteur *m*, mécène *m* (des artistes, des arts, etc.); patron *m* (d'une œuvre de charité, etc.); (*b*) *Ecc:* **p. saint,** patron, -onne; saint patronal, sainte patronale (d'une église, de qn); (*c*) *Ecc:* patron, collateur *m* (d'un bénéfice). **2.** *Com:* client, -ente (d'un magasin); habitué, -ée.

patronage ['pætrənidʒ] *n.* **1.** (*a*) protection *f*; mécénat *m*; patronage *m*; **concert under the p. of . . .,** concert honoré d'une souscription de . . .; (*b*) *Pej:* air protecteur (envers qn). **2.** clientèle *f* (d'un hôtel, etc.). **3.** *Ecc:* droit *m* de présentation (à un bénéfice).

patroness ['peitrənis] *n.f.* protectrice (des arts, etc.); (dame) patronnesse (d'une œuvre de charité).

patronize ['pætrənaiz] *v.tr.* **1.** (*a*) patronner, protéger (un artiste, etc.); encourager (un art); subventionner (un hôpital, etc.); souscrire pour, à (une œuvre de bienfaisance); (*b*) traiter (qn) d'un air protecteur, avec condescendance. **2.** accorder sa clientèle à (une maison); être un habitué (d'un cinéma, d'un restaurant, etc.). **patronizing** *a.* (ton, air) de condescendance. **patronizingly** *adv.* d'un air, d'un ton, de condescendance.

patronymic [pætrə'nimik] **1.** *a.* patronymique. **2.** *n.* patronyme *m*, nom *m* patronymique.

patsy ['pætsi] *n. U.S: F:* dupe *f*, jobard *m.*

patten ['pæt(ə)n] *n.* claque *f*, socque *m* (pour protéger les chaussures contre la boue).

patter[1] ['pætər] *n.* bavardage *m*, baratin *m*; boniment *m*, bagout *m.*

patter[2] *v.* **1.** *v.tr.* marmotter, expédier (ses prières, etc.) **2.** *v.i.* bavarder sans arrêt; jaser, caqueter.

patter[3] *n.* petit bruit (de pas précipités, etc.); trottinement *m*; fouettement *m* (de la pluie).

patter[4] *v.i.* (*a*) trottiner, marcher à petits pas rapides; (*of rain*) fouetter; (*b*) **to p. about,** trottiner çà et là.

pattern[1] ['pæt(ə)n] *n.* **1.** modèle *m*, exemple *m*; **to be a p. of virtue,** être un exemple, un modèle, de vertu. **2.** (*a*) modèle, dessin *m*, maquette *f*; **machines all built to one p.,** machines construites, fabriquées, toutes sur le même modèle; *Ind:* **p. designer,** dessinateur, -trice, de modèles; **p. shop,** atelier *m* de modelage; atelier des modèles; (*b*) *Dressm: etc:* patron *m* (en papier, etc.); **to cut out a shirt to, from, a p.,** tailler une chemise sur un patron; (*c*) *Metall:* modèle, gabarit *m*, calibre *m* (de fonderie). **3.** *Com:* échantillon *m*; **p. book, card,** livre *m*, carte *f*, d'échantillons. **4.** (*a*) dessin, motif *m* (de papier peint, etc.); *Tex:* broché *m* (d'un tissu); (*b*) grille *f* (de mots croisés); (*c*) **streets arranged in an orderly p.,** rues établies suivant un plan ordonné; **the normal p. of trade,** la tendance normale du marché; (*d*) *Ball:* groupement (des points d'impact de projectiles sur une cible, sur le sol, etc.); gerbe *f* (d'un fusil tirant des cartouches à plombs); *Mil: Av:* **p. bombing,** bombardement *m* systématique; (*e*) *Cmptr:* combinaison *f* (de perforations).

pattern[2] *v.tr.* **1. to p. sth. after, (up)on, sth.,** modeler qch. sur qch. **2.** tracer des dessins, des motifs, sur (qch.); orner (qch.) de motifs; **patterned fabrics,** tissus imprimés, à dessins.

patty ['pæti] *n. Cu:* pâté (en croûte).

paucity ['pɔːsiti] *n.* manque *m*, disette *f*; rareté *f*.
paunch [pɔːnʃ] *n.* (*a*) panse *f*, ventre *m*, *F:* bedaine *f* (de qn); (*b*) panse, rumen *m* (des ruminants).
paunchy ['pɔːnʃi] *a.* ventru; corpulent.
pauper ['pɔːpər] *n.* indigent, -ente; pauvre, -esse; *A:* **pauper's grave,** fosse commune.
pause[1] [pɔːz] *n.* **1.** (*a*) pause *f*, arrêt *m*; **to make a p.,** faire une pause; (*b*) *Rec:* blanc *m* sonore; silence *m*. **2.** *Pros:* repos *m*; césure *f*. **3.** *Mus:* point *m* d'orgue; (*over a rest*) point d'arrêt.
pause[2] *v.i.* **1.** faire une pause; marquer un temps; **he paused at the door to say to me . . .,** il s'est arrêté à la porte pour me dire . . .. **2.** hésiter; **to make s.o. p.,** faire hésiter qn; donner à réfléchir à qn. **3. to p. on a word,** s'arrêter sur un mot; *Mus:* **to p. on a note,** tenir une note.
pave [peiv] *v.tr.* paver (une rue, etc.); carreler (une cour, etc.); **to p. the way,** préparer le terrain. **paving** *n.* **1.** pavage *m*; carrelage *m*; **p. stone,** pierre *f* à paver; pavé *m*; **p. tile,** carreau *m* (de pavage). **2.** pavé, dalles *fpl*.
pavement ['peivmənt] *n.* (*a*) pavé *m*; carrelage *m*; **wood(-block) p.,** pavé en bois; **cobblestone, cobbled, p.,** empierrement *m* en cailloux; (*b*) trottoir *m*; **p. artist,** artiste *mf* de trottoir; (*c*) *NAm:* chaussée *f*.
pavilion [pə'viliən] *n.* **1.** (*a*) *Sp: etc:* pavillon *m*; (*b*) *Mus:* **Chinese p.,** chapeau chinois. **2.** *Arch:* pavillon.
paw[1] [pɔː] *n.* *F:* (*a*) patte *f* (d'animal onguiculé); (*b*) *F:* main *f*, patte (de qn); **paws off!** bas les pattes!
paw[2] *v.tr.* **1.** (*a*) (*of animal*) donner des coups de patte, de griffe, à (qn, qch.); (*b*) (*of horse*) **to p. the ground,** *v.i.* **to p.,** gratter (la terre) du pied; battre la poussière. **2.** (*of pers.*) *F:* tripoter, peloter (qn).
pawky ['pɔːki] *a.* *Scot:* rusé; finaud, narquois.
pawl [pɔːl] *n.* *Mec.E: etc:* linguet *m*, ginguet *m* (de cabestan, etc.); cliquet *m* (d'arrêt); **p. and ratchet wheel,** roue *f*, encliquetage *m*, à rochet.
pawn[1] [pɔːn] *n.* **1.** gage *m*, nantissement *m*. **2. in p.,** en gage; **to put one's watch in p.,** mettre sa montre en gage, au mont-de-piété, *F:* au clou; **p. ticket,** reconnaissance *f* (de dépôt de gage).
pawn[2] *v.tr.* (*a*) mettre (qch.) en gage; engager (qch.); (*b*) engager (sa vie, son honneur).
pawn[3] *n.* *Chess:* pion *m*; **to be s.o.'s p.,** être le jouet de qn.
pawnbroker ['pɔːnbroukər] *n.* prêteur, -euse, sur gage(s).
pawnbroking ['pɔːnbroukiŋ] *n.* prêt *m* sur gage(s).
pawnshop ['pɔːnʃɔp] *n.* bureau *m* de prêt sur gage(s); maison *f* de prêt; = crédit municipal.
pawpaw ['pɔːpɔː] *n.* *Bot:* = PAPAW.
pax [pæks] *n.* **1.** *Ecc:* paix *f*. **2.** *int.* *Sch:* *F:* pouce!
pay[1] [pei] *n.* **1.** paie *f*; salaire *m* (d'un ouvrier, etc.); appointements *mpl*; gages *mpl* (d'un domestique); traitement *m* (d'un fonctionnaire); indemnité *f* (d'un parlementaire); *Mil:* solde *f*; **basic p.,** salaire, traitement, de base; **take-home p.,** salaire reçu (moins impôt retenu à la source); **back p.,** arrérages *mpl*, rappel *m*, de traitement, de salaire; **p. day,** jour *m* de paie; **p. slip,** bulletin *m*, feuille *f*, de paie; **p. cheque,** chèque *m* de règlement de traitement, de salaire; **p. packet,** paie; salaire; *Mil:* **p. book,** livret *m* de solde; **to be in s.o.'s p.,** (i) être dans l'emploi de qn; (ii) être à la solde, aux gages, de qn. **2. p. desk,** caisse *f*; **p. bed,** lit *m* pour malade payant (dans un hôpital); *NAm:* **p. station, p. phone** = cabine *f* téléphonique; téléphone public; taxiphone *m*; **p. TV,** télévision *f* à péage.
pay[2] *v.tr.* & *i.* (*p.t.* & *p.p.* **paid** [peid]) payer; (*a*) **to p. s.o. £100,** payer £100 à qn; **how much do you p. for tea?** combien payez-vous le thé? *F:* **to make s.o. p. through the nose,** écorcher qn; **his uncle paid for his schooling,** son oncle a subvenu aux frais de ses études; **to be paid in four instalments,** payable en quatre termes; **p. at the gate, at the door,** entrée payante; **to p. cash (down), ready money,** payer (argent) comptant, payer au comptant; **p. as you earn,** *NAm:* **as you go,** retenue *f* (de l'impôt sur le revenu) à la base, à la source; **to p. back a loan,** rembourser, restituer, un emprunt; **could you lend me £5? I'll p. you back tomorrow,** peux-tu me prêter £5? je te rembourserai demain; **to p. s.o. back in his own coin,** rendre la pareille à qn; **to p. sth. down, on account,** verser une (somme à titre de) provision; (*b*) *Com: Fin: etc:* **to p. on demand,** payer à vue, à présentation; **p. to the order of . . .,** payez à l'ordre de . . .; (*on cheque*) **p. self, p. cash,** payez (à l'ordre de) moi-même; **to p. in a cheque,** encaisser un chèque; **to p. money into s.o.'s account,** verser de l'argent au compte de qn; (*c*) payer (ses employés, etc.); **to be paid by the hour, by the week,** être payé à l'heure, à la semaine; **badly paid job,** situation mal payée; **to p. s.o. to do sth.,** payer qn pour faire qch.; **I wouldn't do it if you paid me,** je ne le ferais pas même si on me payait; (*d*) payer, régler, acquitter (un compte, une facture); payer (une amende); payer, liquider, régler, acquitter (une dette); rembourser (un créancier); purger (une hypothèque); (*on receipted bill*) **paid,** pour acquit; *F:* **to put paid to (sth.),** anéantir (un espoir, un projet); **carriage paid,** port payé; (*e*) **to p. tribute, homage, to s.o.,** rendre hommage à qn; **to p. one's respects to s.o.,** présenter ses respects à qn; **to p. a visit to s.o.,** rendre visite à qn; **p. attention to what you are doing,** faites attention à ce que vous faites; (*f*) *F:* **he'll p. for this! I'll make him p. for this!** il me le payera! (*g*) **it will p. you to do it,** c'est dans votre intérêt de le faire; **business that doesn't p.,** affaire *f* qui ne rapporte pas, qui ne paie pas, qui n'est pas rentable; **it wouldn't p.,** cela ne rapporterait pas; **it will p. for itself,** cela s'amortira tout seul; **it pays to advertise,** la publicité rapporte; pas d'affaires sans réclame. **paid** *a.* **1.** (*of pers., work*) rétribué, rémunéré; **p. holidays,** congés payés; **p. worker,** travailleur salarié. **2.** (*a*) *Com:* (*of goods, bill, etc.*) payé; (*b*) **p. up,** (i) *Fin:* (*of capital*) versé; (*of shares*) libéré; (ii) **(fully) paid up member,** membre *m* (d'un parti, etc.) qui a payé sa cotisation. **paying** **1.** *a.* (*a*) (élève, etc.) payant; **p. guest,** pensionnaire *mf*; (*b*) (*business, etc.*) rémunérateur, -trice, profitable; qui rapporte. **2.** *n.* (*a*) paiement *m*, versement *m* (d'argent); (*b*) **p. back,** remboursement *m*, restitution *f* (d'un emprunt); (*c*) versement *m* (d'argent à la banque, etc.); **p.-in book,** carnet *m* de versements; (*d*) **p. off,** (i) liquidation *f*, règlement *m* (d'une dette); purge *f* (d'une hypothèque); (ii) congédiement *m* (des ouvriers, etc.); licencement *m* (de troupes); débarquement *m* (de marins); (*e*) **p. out,** (i) (*also* **p. up**) déboursement *m*; (ii) *Nau:* filage *m* (d'un câble, etc.). **pay off** *v.tr.* & *i.* (*a*) liquider, régler (une dette, etc.); rembourser (un créancier); purger (une hypothèque); (*b*) congédier (des ouvriers, etc.); licencier (des troupes); débarquer (des marins); (*c*) (*of deal, etc.*) être payant, rentable, fructueux; (*of efforts, etc.*) porter fruit; **all these years of work have paid off at last,** nous sommes enfin récompensés aprés toutes ces années de travail. **pay out** *v.tr.* & *i.* (*a*) payer, verser, débourser; (*b*) *F:* se venger (de qn, sur qn); rendre (à qn) la pareille; (*c*) (*p.t.* **payed**) *Nau:* (laisser) filer (un câble). **pay up** *v.tr.* & *i.* payer, *F:* s'exécuter; se libérer (de ses dettes, etc.); **I finally made him p. up,** j'ai finalement réussi à le faire payer, débourser.
payable ['peiəbl] *a.* **1.** payable, acquittable; **rates p. by the tenant** = impôts *mpl* à la charge du locataire; *Com:* **p. at sight, to order, to bearer,** payable à vue, à ordre, au porteur; **to make a bill p. to s.o.,** faire un

billet à l'ordre de qn; **cheque p. to bearer,** chèque *m* au porteur; **bonds made p. in francs,** bons libellés en francs; **bills p.,** *n.pl. US:* **payables,** factures *fpl* à payer. **2.** *Min:* (*of seam, etc.*) exploitable.

paycheck ['peitʃek] *n. NAm:* chèque *m* de règlement de traitement, de salaire.

payee [pei'i:] *n.* (*a*) bénéficiaire *mf* (d'un bon de poste, etc.); (*b*) *Com:* porteur *m* (d'un effet).

payer ['peiər] *n.* payeur, -euse, payant, -ante; **he's a good, bad, p.,** c'est un bon, mauvais, payeur.

payload ['peiloud] *n.* charge payante, utile (d'un véhicule); charge utile (d'un missile); *Av:* poids *m* utile.

paymaster ['peimɑ:stər] *n.* (*a*) intendant *m*, caissier *m*, payeur *m*; (*b*) *Mil: etc:* trésorier *m*; *Navy:* commissaire *m*.

payment ['peimənt] *n.* **1.** (*act or fact of paying*) paiement *m*, versement *m* (d'argent); paiement, règlement *m*, acquittement *m* (d'une dette, etc.); remboursement *m* (d'un créancier); **without p.,** à titre gracieux; à titre bénévole; **terms of p.,** conditions *fpl* de paiement; **cash p.,** paiement (au) comptant; **p. by cheque,** paiement par chèque; **to stop p. on a cheque,** faire opposition sur un chèque; **p. by instalments,** paiement par acomptes, paiement échelonné; **(hire purchase) p.,** traite *f*; **down p.,** premier versement; arrhes *fpl*; **on p. of £100,** contre paiement de £100; **non p.,** défaut *m* de paiement; **to present a bill for p.,** présenter un effet au paiement, à l'encaissement. **2.** paiement *m*, rémunération *f*; rétribution *f*; **as (a) p. for your services,** en rémunération de vos services.

payoff ['peiɔf] *n. NAm:* (*a*) paiement *m*, règlement *m*; (*b*) bénéfice *m*; pot-de-vin, *pl.* pots-de-vin; (*c*) *F:* dénouement *m* (de l'histoire).

payroll ['peiroul] *n.* feuille *f* des appointements, des salaires; *Mil: etc:* feuille, état *m*, de solde; **to be on the p.,** émarger au budget.

pea [pi:] *n.* (*a*) pois *m*; **p. pod,** cosse *f* de pois; (*b*) *Cu:* **(green) peas,** petits pois; **split peas,** pois cassés; **p. soup,** soupe *f* aux pois (cassés); (*thick*) purée *f* de pois; *F:* **p. souper,** purée de pois, brouillard *m* (jaune) à couper au couteau; (*c*) **sweet p.,** pois de senteur; (*d*) *a. & n.* **p. green,** vert feuille (*m*) *inv*.

peace [pi:s] *n.* **1.** (*a*) paix *f*; **at p.,** en paix (**with,** avec); **in time of p.,** en temps de paix; **to make (one's) p. with s.o.,** faire la paix, se réconcilier, avec qn; **p. treaty,** traité *m* de paix; **p. offering,** cadeau *m* de réconciliation; (*b*) traité *m* de paix; **the P. of Amiens,** la Paix d'Amiens. **2. p. and order,** la paix et l'ordre public; le repos public; **to keep the p.,** (i) ne pas troubler l'ordre public; (ii) veiller à l'ordre public; **to break, disturb, the p.,** troubler, violer, l'ordre public; (*at night*) faire du tapage nocturne; **justice of the p.** = juge *m* de paix. **3.** (*a*) tranquillité *f* (de l'âme, du soir, etc.); **to live in p.,** vivre en paix; **for the sake of p. and quiet,** pour avoir la paix; **to leave s.o. in p.,** laisser qn tranquille; **he gave me no p. until . . .,** il ne m'a pas laissé la paix tant que . . .; **go in p.!** allez en paix! (*b*) *A:* **to hold one's p.,** se taire.

peaceable ['pi:səbl] *a.* **1.** pacifique; qui aime la paix; **p. man,** homme de paix. **2.** = PEACEFUL 2. **-ably** *adv.* pacifiquement.

peaceful ['pi:sf(u)l] *a.* **1.** paisible, calme, tranquille; (mort) tranquille. **2.** pacifique; qui porte la paix; qui ne trouble pas la paix; **p. settlement of a dispute,** règlement *m* pacifique d'un litige; règlement à l'amiable. **-fully** *adv.* **1.** paisiblement; tranquillement. **2.** pacifiquement.

peacefulness ['pi:sfulnis] *n.* tranquillité *f*, paix *f*.

peacekeeping ['pi:ski:piŋ] *n.* maintien *m* de la paix.

peace-loving ['pi:slʌviŋ] *a.* (nation) pacifique, qui aime la paix.

peach¹ [pi:tʃ] *n.* (*a*) pêche *f*; (*b*) **p. (tree),** pêcher *m*; (*c*) *n. & a.* **p. (colour),** (couleur *f*) fleur de pêcher *inv*; (*d*) *F:* **she's a p.,** c'est une jolie pépée; **it's a p.,** c'est magnifique.

peach² *v.i. P: O:* **to p. on s.o.,** moucharder qn.

peacock ['pi:kɔk] *n.* (*a*) *Orn:* paon *m*; **as proud as a p.,** fier comme un paon; (*b*) **p. (blue),** bleu paon *m inv*; (*c*) *Ent:* **p. butterfly,** paon (du jour).

peahen ['pi:hen] *n.* paonne *f*.

peajacket ['pi:dʒækit] *n. Nau:* caban *m*.

peak¹ [pi:k] *n.* **1.** (*a*) visière *f* (de casquette, etc.); (*b*) bec *m* (d'une selle de bicyclette, d'une ancre, etc.); (*c*) pointe *f* (de barbe, de toit, etc.); **widow's p.,** pointe de cheveux sur le front. **2.** *Nau:* (*a*) coqueron *m* (de la cale); (*b*) pic *m*, corne *f*, empointure *f* (de voile). **3.** (*a*) pic, cime *f*, sommet *m* (de montagne); **the highest peaks,** les plus hauts sommets; (*b*) pointe, apogée *f* (d'une courbe, d'une charge); *Med:* pointe, poussée (d'une fièvre); *Ph:* crête *f* (d'une onde); **p. load,** charge maximum; débit *m* maximum (d'un générateur); **prosperity was at its p.,** la prospérité était à son apogée, à son maximum; *El: Trans: T.V: etc:* **p. hours, period,** heures *fpl* de pointe; heures d'affluence; **off-p. hours, time,** heures creuses; temps mort (dans l'utilisation d'un matériel, etc.); **off-p. fare, tariff,** tarif *m* hors pointe, en dehors des périodes d'affluence.

peak² **1.** *v.tr. Nau:* apiquer (une vergue). **2.** *v.i.* (*of whale*) plonger (à pic). **3.** *v.i.* (*of curve, etc.*) passer par son apogée. **peaked** *a.* (casquette) à visière.

peak³ *v.i.* **to p. and pine,** tomber en langueur.

peaky ['pi:ki] *a. F:* pâlot, malingre, souffreteux; **to look p.,** avoir les traits tirés.

peal¹ [pi:l] *n.* (*a*) **p. of bells,** carillon *m*; **to ring a p.,** sonner un carillon; carillonner; (*b*) retentissement *m*; grondement *m* (du tonnerre, de l'orgue); coup *m* (de tonnerre); (*c*) **peals of laughter,** éclats *mpl* de rire.

peal² **1.** *v.i.* (*a*) (*of bells*) (i) carillonner; (ii) sonner à toute volée; (*b*) (*of thunder, of the organ*) retentir, gronder; (*of laughter*) résonner. **2.** *v.tr.* (*a*) sonner (les cloches) à toute volée; (*b*) carillonner (un air).

peanut ['pi:nʌt] *n.* (*a*) arachide *f*; *Com:* cacah(o)uète *f*, cacahouette *f*; **p. oil, butter,** huile *f*, beurre *m*, d'arachide; (*b*) *F:* **peanuts,** deux fois rien; une bagatelle.

pear ['pɛər] *n.* (*a*) poire *f*; **butter p.,** beurré *m*; (*b*) **p. (tree),** poirier *m*; (*c*) **avocado p.,** poire d'avocat; (*tree*) avocatier *m*; **prickly p.,** figue *f*, figuier *m*, de Barbarie; (*d*) *El:* **p. switch,** (interrupteur *m* à) poire.

peardrop ['pɛədrɔp] *n.* bonbon parfumé à la poire.

pearl¹ [pə:l] *n.* **1.** perle *f*; **cultured p.,** perle cultiveé, de culture; perle japonaise; **p. necklace,** collier *m* de perles; **p. diver,** pêcheur *m* de perles; **p. oyster,** huître perlière; **p. grey,** gris *m* de perle *inv*; gris perle *inv*; **to cast pearls before swine,** jeter des perles devant les, aux, pourceaux; *F:* **she's a p.,** c'est une perle, un trésor. **2.** (*a*) **mother of p.,** nacre *f* (de perle); **p. button,** bouton *m* de nacre; (*b*) *El:* **p. lamp,** ampoule opale. **3.** (*a*) **p. barley, tapioca,** orge, tapioca, perlé; (*b*) *Pharm:* perle, globule; (*c*) **pearls of dew,** perles de rosée; *Algae:* **p. moss,** mousse perlée, d'Irlande.

pearl² **1.** *v.i.* (*a*) (*of moisture, etc.*) perler; former des gouttelettes; (*b*) pêcher des perles. **2.** *v.tr.* perler (de l'orge); *Cu:* cuire (le sucre) au perlé.

pearl³ *n. Lacem:* picot *m*, engrêlure *f* (de dentelle).

pearly ['pə:li] **1.** *a.* (*a*) perlé; nacré; **p. (white) teeth,** dents perlées, de perle; *Moll:* **p. nautilus,** nautile *m*, nautilus *m*; (*b*) **p. king,** marchand *m* des quatre saisons de Londres (qui porte les jours de fête un costume couvert de boutons de nacre). **2.** *n.* (*a*) bouton *m* de nacre; (*b*) membre *m* d'une famille de *pearly kings*.

peasant ['pezənt] *n.* paysan, -anne; campagnard, -arde; *Pej:* rustre *mf*.

pease [piːz] *n.* **p. pudding,** purée *f* de pois (cassés).
peashooter ['piːʃuːtər] *n.* petite sarbacane.
peat [piːt] *n.* (*a*) tourbe *f*; **p. bog,** tourbière *f*; **p. cutting, digging,** tourbage *m*; **p. cutter,** tourbier *m*; (*b*) **(turf, sod, block, of) p.,** motte *f* de tourbe.
peaty ['piːti] *a.* (*a*) (sol) tourbeux; (*b*) (goût) de fumée de tourbe.
pebble [pebl] *n.* **1.** (*a*) caillou, -oux *m*; **p. beach,** plage *f* de galets; *F:* **you're not the only p. on the beach,** il n'y a pas que toi sur la terre; (*b*) *Const:* **p. dash,** crépi (moucheté); cailloutage *m*; **p.-dash finish,** crépissure *f*. **2.** *Opt:* (*a*) cristal *m* de roche; (*b*) lentille *f* en cristal de roche.
pebble-dash ['pebldæʃ] *v.tr. Const:* crépir (un mur).
pebbly ['pebli] *a.* caillouteux; (plage) à galets.
pecan ['piːkən, 'pe-, pi'kæn] *n. Bot:* (*a*) **p. (nut),** pacane *f*, (noix) pecan *m*; (*b*) **p. (tree),** pacanier *m*.
peccadillo [pekə'dilou] *n.* peccadille *f*; faute légère.
peccary ['pekəri] *n. Z:* pécari *m*.
peck¹ [pek] *n.* (*a*) coup *m* de bec; (*b*) *F:* (*kiss*) bécot *m*; **to give s.o. a p.,** bécoter qn.
peck² **1.** *v.tr.* (*a*) (*of bird*) picoter, becqueter (qch., qn); donner un coup de bec à (qn); (*b*) *F:* (*kiss*) bécoter, baisoter (qn). **2.** *v.i. & ind.tr.* **to p. (at sth.),** picoter (qch.); donner des coups de bec (à qch.); **to p. at one's food,** pignocher, mangeotter, son repas. **pecking** *n.* becquetage *m*; **p. order,** (i) *Orn:* hiérarchie *f* du becquetage; (ii) *Fig:* hiérarchie sociale.
peck³ *n.* picotin *m* (d'avoine, etc.); *Fig:* **she's had a p. of trouble,** elle a eu bien des malheurs.
pecker ['pekər] *n.* **1.** *Orn: F:* pic vert. **2.** *Tls:* pioche *f*. **3.** (*a*) *P:* nez *m*, bec *m*; (*b*) *F:* courage *m*; cran *m*; **keep your p. up!** (du) courage!
peckish ['pekiʃ] *a. F:* **to be, feel, p.,** se sentir le ventre creux.
pectin ['pektin] *n. Ch:* pectine *f*.
pectoral ['pektər(ə)l] **1.** *a. Anat: Med: etc:* pectoral, -aux; **p. cross,** croix pectorale (d'évêque); *Ich:* **p. fin,** nageoire pectorale. **2.** *n.* (*a*) *Jew. Rel:* pectoral *m*; (*b*) *Anat:* (muscle) pectoral.
peculate ['pekjuleit] **1.** *v.i.* détourner des fonds. **2.** *v.tr.* détourner (des fonds).
peculation [pekju'leiʃ(ə)n] *n.* malversation *f*; détournement *m* de fonds.
peculiar [pi'kjuːliər] *a.* (*a*) particulier; **this gait is p. to him,** cette façon de marcher lui est particulière, lui est propre; **smell p. to an animal,** odeur *f* spécifique d'un animal; (*b*) spécial, -aux; particulier; **of p. interest,** d'un intérêt tout particulier; (*c*) (*of thg*) étrange; (*of pers.*) bizarre, singulier; original, -aux; (goût) insolite; **well, that's p.,** voilà qui est singulier; bizarre! **he, she, is a little p.,** c'est un(e) excentrique. **-ly** *adv.* (*a*) particulièrement; (*b*) singulièrement, bizarrement.
peculiarity [pikjuːli'æriti] *n.* **1.** trait distinctif; particularité *f*. **2.** bizarrerie *f*, singularité *f*; originalité *f*, excentricité *f*.
pecuniary [pi'kjuːniəri] *a.* pécuniaire; **p. difficulties,** embarras financiers; ennuis *mpl* d'argent.
pedagogic(al) [pedə'gɔdʒik(l)] *a.* pédagogique.
pedagogue ['pedəgɔg] *n. Pej:* pédagogue *m*, pédant, -ante.
pedagogy ['pedəgɔdʒi] *n.* pédagogie *f*.
pedal¹ ['ped(ə)l] *n.* **1.** pédale *f* (de machine, de véhicule, de bicyclette, d'instrument de musique, etc.); (*of piano*) **soft, loud, p.,** petite, grande, pédale; (*of organ*) **p. keyboard,** pédalier *m*; *Aut: Mch: etc:* **accelerator p.,** pédale d'accélérateur; **clutch p.,** pédale de débrayage, d'embrayage; **gear(-change) p.,** pédale de changement de vitesse; **brake p.,** pédale de frein; *Dom.Ec:* **p. bin,** poubelle *f* à pédale. **2.** *Mus:* **p. (note),** (note) fondamentale *f*; pédale.
pedal² *v.i.* **(pedalled,** *NAm:* **pedaled) 1.** *Cy: etc:* pédaler. **2.** *Mus:* (*a*) (*organ*) jouer sur le pédalier; (*b*) (*piano*) mettre la pédale.
pedalboat ['ped(ə)lbout] *n.* pédalo *m*.
pedalcar ['ped(ə)lkɑːr] *n.* **1.** vélocar *m*. **2.** voiture *f* à pédales.
pedal-operated ['pedəlɔpəreitid] *a. Mec.E: etc:* commandé par pédale(s).
pedant ['pedənt] *n.* pédant, -ante.
pedantic [pi'dæntik] *a.* pédant; pédantesque. **-ally** *adv.* en pédant.
pedantry ['pedəntri] *n.* pédantisme *m*, pédanterie *f*.
peddle [pedl] **1.** *v.i.* faire le colportage. **2.** *v.tr.* (*a*) colporter (des marchandises); **to p. drugs,** trafiquer en stupéfiants; faire le trafic des stupéfiants.
peddler ['pedlər] *n.* (*a*) *NAm: n.* colporteur *m*; (*b*) **drug p.,** trafiquant *m* en stupéfiants.
pederast ['pedəræst, 'piː-] *n.m.* pédéraste.
pederasty ['pedəræsti, 'piː-] *n.* pédérastie *f*.
pedestal ['pedist(ə)l] *n.* **1.** *Arch: Sculp: etc:* piédestal *m*, -aux; socle *m*; **to put s.o. on a p.,** mettre qn sur un piédestal, sur le chandelier. **2.** socle *m* (de pompe, etc.); suppot *m*, colonne *f* (de projecteur, etc.); *Furn:* **p. table,** guéridon *m*; *Dom.Ec:* **p. washbasin,** lavabo *m* à pied.
pedestrian [pi'destriən] **1.** *a.* (*a*) pédestre; (*b*) (style, etc.) prosaïque, terre à terre. **2.** *n.* piéton *m*; **p. crossing,** passage pour piétons, passage clouté.
pediatric [piːdi'ætrik] *NAm:* = PAEDIATRIC.
pedicure¹ ['pedikjuər] *n.* **1.** (*pers.*) pédicure *mf*. **2.** soins *mpl*, traitement *m*, pédicure.
pedicure² *v.tr.* pédicurer.
pedigree ['pedigriː] *n.* **1.** arbre *m* généalogique. **2.** (*a*) ascendance *f*, généalogie *f* (de qn); (*b*) *Breed:* certificat *m* d'origine, pedigree *m* (d'un chien, etc.); **p. dog, bull,** chien, taureau *m*, de (pure) race, de bonne lignée.
pediment ['pedimənt] *n. Arch:* fronton *m*; (*small*) fronteau *m*.
pedlar ['pedlər] *n.* colporteur *m*; marchard ambulant, (marchand) forain (*m*).
pedometer [pe'dɔmitər] *n.* podomètre *m*.
pee¹ [piː] *v.i. F:* faire pipi, pisser.
pee² *n. F:* pipi *m*; **to go and have a p.,** aller pisser.
peek¹ [piːk] *n.* regard furtif; coup d'œil (furtif).
peek² *v.i.* jeter un regard furtif, un coup d'œil furtif (sur qn, qch.); risquer un coup d'œil.
peekaboo ['piːkəbuː] **1.** *int.* coucou! **2.** *attrib. Cost:* (corsage, etc.) (i) d'un tissu transparent, (ii) avec, en, broderie(s) ajourée(s).
peel¹ [piːl] *n.* pelure *f* (de pomme, etc.); écorce *f*, peau *f*, *Cu:* zeste *m* (de citron, d'orange); **candied p.,** zeste confit; (*of orange*) orangeat *m*; (*of lemon*) citronnat *m*.
peel² **1.** *v.tr.* (*a*) peler (un fruit); éplucher (des pommes de terre, etc.); décortiquer (un chêne, des amandes); écorcer (un bâton, etc.); **to p. (off) the bark, the skin,** enlever l'écorce, la peau; **to p. off one's clothes,** se déshabiller. **2.** *v.i.* (*a*) **to peel (off),** (*of paint, etc.*) s'écailler; (*of skin*) peler; *Med:* se desquamer; (*b*) (*of the nose, etc.*) peler; (*of tree*) se décortiquer; (*of wall*) se décrépir; (*c*) *Av:* **to p. off,** se détacher (de la formation). **peeling** *n.* **1.** (*a*) épluchage *m*; écorçage *m*; (*b*) **p. (off),** écaillement *m*; *Med:* desquamation *f* (de l'épiderme). **2. peelings,** épluchures *fpl* (de pommes de terre, etc.).
peeler ['piːlər] *n. Dom.Ec:* éplucheur *m*.
peep¹ [piːp] *n.* piaulement *m*, pépiement *m* (d'oiseau); cri *m* (de souris); *F:* **if I hear so much as a p. out of you,** si vous faites le moindre bruit.
peep² *v.i.* (*of bird*) piauler, pépier; (*of mouse*) crier.
peep³ *v.i.* **1. to p. at s.o., sth.,** regarder qn, qch., à la dérobée; jeter un coup d'œil furtif sur qn, qch.; **to p.**

through the door, glisser un œil par la porte; **I saw you peeping through the keyhole,** je vous ai vu regarder par le trou de la serrure; **a Peeping Tom,** (i) un curieux, un indiscret; (ii) un voyeur. **2. to p. (out),** se laisser entrevoir, se montrer; (*of flower*) percer, pointer; **violets peeping (up) from the grass,** violettes *fpl* qui émergent au milieu de l'herbe.

peep⁴ *n.* **1.** coup d'œil furtif; **to have, take, a p. at sth.,** jeter un regard furtif sur qch.; **to get a p. at sth.,** entrevoir qch. **2.** filtrée *f* (de lumière).

peep-bo ['pi:pbou] **1.** *int.* coucou! **2.** *n.* **to play at p.-bo,** jouer à cache-cache (avec un enfant).

peephole ['pi:phoul] *n.* **1.** judas *m.* **2.** *Mec.E: etc:* (trou *m* de) regard (*m*); regard, orifice *m*, de visite.

peepshow ['pi:pʃou] *n.* vues *fpl* stéréoscopiques.

peer¹ [piər] *n.* **1.** pair *m*; égal, -ale; **you will not find his p.,** vous ne trouveriez pas son pareil. **2. p. of the realm,** pair du Royaume-Uni; **life p.,** pair à vie.

peer² *v.i.* (*a*) **to peer at s.o., sth.,** scruter qn, qch., du regard; **he peered (out) into the night,** il cherchait à percer l'obscurité; (*b*) **to p. round the corner,** risquer un coup d'œil au coin de la rue.

peerage ['piəridʒ] *n.* **1.** pairie *f*; **life p.,** pairie personnelle; **to confer a p. on s.o., to raise s.o. to the p.,** élever qn à la pairie. **2.** *coll.* **the p.,** les pairs *mpl.* **3. p. (book),** (almanach *m*) nobiliaire (*m*).

peeress ['piəres] *n.f.* pairesse.

peerless ['piəlis] *a. Lit:* sans pareil, sans pair; hors de pair; incomparable.

peeve [pi:v] *v.tr. F:* fâcher, irriter (qn); **to be peeved,** être fâché, irrité.

peevish ['pi:viʃ] *a.* maussade; irritable; (enfant) pleurnicheur. **-ly** *adv.* maussadement; avec humeur.

peevishness ['pi:viʃnis] *n.* maussaderie *f*, mauvaise humeur; hargne *f*.

peewit ['pi:wit] *n. Orn:* **1.** vanneau (huppé). **2. p. (gull),** mouette rieuse.

peg¹ [peg] *n.* **1.** (*a*) cheville *f* (en bois), fiche *f*; fausset *m*, fosset *m* (d'un tonneau); *Mec.E:* (i) cheville, clavette *f*, goupille *f*; (ii) goujon *m*, ergot *m*; *Games*; **cribbage p.,** fiche; (*b*) ranche *f*, enture *f* (d'échelier); (*c*) **hat, coat, p.,** patère *f*; **clothes off the p.,** vêtements *mpl* de confection; (*d*) **clothes p.,** pince *f* à linge; (*e*) piquet *m* (de tente, etc.); (*f*) *Mus:* cheville (de violon, etc.); bouton *m* (de corde de harpe); (*g*) *F:* **he's a square p. in a round hole,** il n'est pas à sa place; **to take s.o. down a p. (or two),** remettre qn à sa place; **that's a p. to hang a grievance on,** voilà un prétexte de plainte. **2.** (*a*) pointe *f*, fer *m* (de toupie); pied *m*, pique *f* (de violoncelle); **p. top,** toupie *f*; (*b*) *O:* **p. leg,** jambe de bois, pilon *m.* **3.** doigt *m* (de whisky, etc.).

peg² *v.tr.* **(pegged) 1.** cheviller (un assemblage, etc.); brocher (des peaux); **to p. clothes on the line,** accrocher du linge sur la corde (avec des pinces). **2.** *Games:* marquer (des points). **3.** *St. Exch: Fin:* stabiliser (les prix); **to p. the market,** stabiliser le marché; maintenir le marché ferme. **peg away** *v.i. F:* **to p. away (at sth.),** travailler assidûment, bosser (à qch.); piocher, bûcher (un sujet). **peg down** *v.tr.* fixer, assujettir, (un filet, etc.) avec des piquets; **pegged down by regulations,** entravé par des règlements. **peg out 1.** *v.tr.* (*a*) piqueter, jalonner, (a)borner (une concession); jalonner (une ligne); *Const:* **to p. out the ground plan,** implanter le tracé des fondations; (*b*) **to p. out clothes on the line,** accrocher du linge sur la corde (avec des pinces). **2.** *v.i.* (*a*) (*croquet*) toucher le piquet final (et se retirer de la partie); (*b*) *P:* mourir; casser sa pipe. **pegging** *n.* **1.** chevillage *m.* **2.** *Sp:* **it's still level p.,** ils sont encore à égalité. **3.** *St. Exch: Fin:* stabilisation *f* (du marché, etc.).

pegboard ['pegbɔ:d] *n.* (*a*) panneau alvéolé; (*b*) *U.S:* table *f* à trous (de solitaire, etc).

pejorative [pe'dʒɔrətiv, pi-; 'pi:dʒ-] **1.** *a.* péjoratif. **2.** *n.* (mot) péjoratif (*m*). **-ly** *adv.* péjorativement.

peke [pi:k] *n. F:* (chien) pékinois (*m*).

Pekinese, Pekingese [pi:ki'ni:z, -ki'ŋi:z] **1.** *a. Geog:* pékinois. **2.** (*a*) *Geog:* Pékinois, -oise; (*b*) (chien) pékinois (*m*).

Peking [pi'kiŋ] *Pr.n. Geog:* Pékin.

pelagic [pi'lædʒik] *a. Oc:* pélagien, pélagique.

pelargonium [pelɑ:'gouniəm] *n. Bot:* pélargonium *m*, *F:* géranium *m*; *Hort:* **trailing p.,** géranium lierre.

pelican ['pelikən] *n.* **1.** *Orn:* pélican *m.* **2. p. crossing,** passage clouté avec feux opérés par les piétons.

pellagra [pe'lægrə, -'lei-] *n. Med:* pellagre *f*.

pellet ['pelit] *n.* (*a*) boulette *f* (de papier, etc.); pelote *f* (d'argile, etc.); pastille *f* (de matière plastique); (*b*) *Sm.a: etc:* grain *m* de plomb; (*c*) *Pharm:* pilule *f*, grain *m*, bol *m*; *Med:* pellet *m*; (*d*) *Orn:* boulette d'aliments regurgités (par les hiboux, etc.); (*e*) *Husb:* granulé *m*; (*f*) *Metall: Ch:* boulette.

pell-mell ['pel'mel] **1.** *adv.* pêle-mêle; (courir, etc.) à la débandade. **2.** *a.* mis pêle-mêle; en confusion. **3.** *n.* pêle-mêle *m*, confusion *f*.

pellucid [pe'lju:sid] *a. Lit:* (*a*) pellucide, transparent; (*b*) (style, esprit, etc.) lucide.

pelmet ['pelmit] *n. Furn:* lambrequin *m.*

pelota [pə'loutə] *n. Games:* pelote *f* basque.

pelt¹ [pelt] *n.* **1.** peau *f*, fourrure *f* (de mouton ou de chèvre). **2.** *Tan:* (i) (*with hair on*) peau verte; (ii) (*without hair*) peau en tripe.

pelt² *n.* grêle *f* (de pierres); fracas *m* (de la pluie). *adv.phr.* **(at) full p.,** (courir, s'enfuir) à toute vitesse, ventre à terre.

pelt³ 1. *v.tr.* **to p. s.o. with stones, snowballs,** lancer des pierres, des boules de neige, à qn; **he pelted abuse at them,** il les a criblés d'injures. **2.** *v.i.* (*of rain, etc.*) **to p. (down),** tomber à verse; **pelting rain,** pluie battante.

pelvic ['pelvik] *a. Anat:* pelvien; **p. girdle,** ceinture pelvienne; **p. bone,** os *m* du bassin; *Ich:* **p. fins,** pelviennes *fpl.*

pelvis ['pelvis] *n. Anat:* (*a*) bassin *m*; (*b*) bassinet *m* (du rein).

pen¹ [pen] *n.* **1.** (*a*) parc *m*, enclos *m* (à moutons, etc.); **bull p.,** toril *m*; **pig p.,** *U.S:* **hog p.,** porcherie *f*; (*b*) *Nau:* cage *f*. **2.** *Navy:* abri *m* (de sous-marins).

pen² *v.tr.* **(penned) to p. (up, in),** parquer (des moutons, etc.); **house in which one feels penned up,** maison *f* où on se sent à l'étroit.

pen³ *n.* (*a*) plume *f* (pour écrire); **fountain p.,** stylo *m*; **ball(point) p.,** stylo à bille, stylo-bille *m*; **felt p.,** crayon *m* feutre; **quill p.,** plume (d'oie); **drawing, mapping, p.,** plume à dessin; **p. (-and-ink) drawing,** dessin *m* à la plume, à l'encre; **stroke of the p.,** trait *m* de plume; **to put p. to paper,** prendre la plume (en main); écrire; **p. friend,** *U.S:* **p. pal,** correspondant, -ante; **to earn one's living by one's p.,** vivre de sa plume; **p. name,** nom *m* de plume; (*of journalist*) nom de guerre; *F: Pej:* **p. pusher,** gratte-papier *m inv*; scribouillard, -arde; (*b*) **p. (nib),** plume; **p. compass,** compas *m* à tire-ligne.

pen⁴ *v.tr.* **(penned)** écrire, rédiger (une lettre, un article, etc.).

pen⁵ *n. Orn:* cygne *m* femelle.

penal ['pi:n(ə)l] *a.* (*of laws, code*) pénal, -aux; (*of offence*) qui comporte, entraîne, une pénalité; **p. servitude,** travaux forcés (d'une durée minimum de trois ans); *A:* **p. colony, settlement,** colonie *f* pénitentiaire; colonie de déportation.

penalization [pi:nəlai'zeiʃ(ə)n] *n.* infliction *f* d'une peine (**of s.o.,** à qn); *Sp:* pénalisation *f*.

penalize ['pi:nəlaiz] *v.tr.* **1.** sanctionner (un délit) d'une peine, d'une pénalité; attacher une peine à (un délit). **2.** (*a*) infliger une peine à (qn); *Sp:* pénaliser (un concurrent, un joueur); déclasser (un coureur); (*b*) *Sp:* handicaper.

penalty ['penəlti] *n.* **1.** (*a*) peine *f*, pénalité *f*; *Com:* amende *f* (pour retard de livraison, etc.); *Adm:* sanction (pénale); **to impose penalties,** prendre des sanctions; (*in contract*) **p. clause,** clause pénale (de dommages-intérêts); **the death p.,** la peine de mort; **on, upon, under, p. of death,** sous peine de mort; sous peine de la vie; **to pay the p. of one's foolishness,** subir les conséquences, être puni, de sa sottise; (*b*) désavantage *m*; **to pay the p. of fame,** payer la rançon de la gloire. **2.** *Sp:* (*a*) pénalisation *f*, pénalité; *Golf:* **p. stroke,** coup *m* d'amende; *Fb:* **p. (kick),** penalty *m*; **p. area, spot,** surface *f*, point *m*, de réparation; (*b*) handicap *m*.

penance ['penəns] *n.* (*a*) *Theol:* **the sacrament of p.,** le sacrement de la pénitence; (*b*) **to do p.,** faire pénitence (**for,** de, pour); **to do sth. as a p.,** faire qch. par pénitence.

pence [pens] *n.pl. see* PENNY.

pencil ['pens(ə)l] *n.* **1.** crayon *m*; (*a*) **lead p.,** crayon à mine de plomb; **coloured p.,** crayon de couleur; **indelible p.,** crayon (à encre) indélébile; **propelling p.,** porte-mine *m inv* réglable, à vis; stylomine *m*; **p. case,** plumier *m*; **p. sharpener,** taille-crayon(s) *m inv*; **p. mark,** trait *m*, marque *f*, au crayon; **to mark, write, sth. in p., with a p.,** marquer, écrire, qch. au crayon; **p. sketch,** croquis *m*; **drawing in p., p. drawing,** (dessin *m* au) crayon; crayonnage *m*; (*b*) **slate p.,** crayon d'ardoise; (*c*) *Toil:* **eyebrow p.,** crayon à sourcils. **2.** (*a*) *Opt:* **p. of light rays, light p.,** faisceau lumineux; faisceau de lumière, de rayons; (*b*) *Mth:* faisceau (de courbes, etc.).

pencil² *v.tr.* (**pencilled,** *NAm:* **penciled**) **1.** (*a*) marquer (qch.) au crayon; (*b*) dessiner, esquisser, (une figure) au crayon; (*c*) **to p. one's eyebrows,** se faire les sourcils (au crayon); **pencilled eyebrows,** sourcils tracés au crayon. **2.** crayonner (un billet); **a pencilled note,** un billet écrit au crayon.

pendant ['pendənt] *n.* **1.** (*a*) pendentif *m* (de collier); breloque *f* (de bracelet); pendeloque *f* (de lustre); **ear p.,** pendant *m* d'oreille; (*b*) *Arch:* clef pendante; cul-de-lampe *m*, *pl.* culs-de-lampe; (*c*) **electric light p.,** (lampe *f* à) suspension (*f*). **2.** *Nau:* (*a*) (*rope*) pantoire *f*; (*b*) ['penənt] (*flag*) flamme *f*, guidon *m*.

pendent ['pendənt] *a.* **1.** (*of plants, etc.*) pendant; (*of draperies, etc.*) retombant; (*of rocks, etc.*) surplombant, en surplomb. **2.** *Jur:* (procès) pendant, en instance; (négociations) en cours.

pending ['pendiŋ] **1.** *a.* (procès) pendant, en instance; (négociations) en cours; *Adm: Com:* (documents) en attendant, en attente. **2.** *prep.* en attendant (le retour de qn, etc.); **p. further news,** en attendant de plus amples nouvelles.

pendulous ['pendjuləs] *a.* (*of branch, lip, etc.*) pendant; **dog with p. ears,** chien *m* aux oreilles pendantes.

pendulum ['pendjuləm] *n. Ph: Clockm:* pendule *m*; balancier *m*; **p. clock,** horloge *f* à pendule, à balancier; **p. ball, bob,** lentille *f* de pendule, de balancier.

penetrable ['penitrəbl] *a.* pénétrable.

penetrate ['penitreit] **1.** *v.tr.* (*a*) pénétrer, percer; **darkness that the eye could not p.,** ténèbres *fpl* que l'œil ne pouvait percer; (*b*) pénétrer, percer (un secret); **to p. s.o.'s mind,** voir clair dans l'esprit de qn; (*c*) *Lit:* **to p. s.o. with a feeling,** pénétrer qn d'un sentiment. **2.** *v.i.* pénétrer; **the water is penetrating everywhere,** l'eau s'introduit partout; **to p. through sth.,** passer à travers qch.; **to p. into a forest,** pénétrer dans une forêt. **penetrating** *a.* (*a*) (vent, froid) pénétrant; (*of sound, voice*) mordant; (*of bullet, shell*) perforant; **to have a p. eye,** avoir des yeux perçants; (*b*) (esprit) pénétrant.

penetration [peni'treiʃ(ə)n] *n.* (*a*) pénétration *f* (de qch., des marchés étrangers, etc.); (*b*) pénétration (de l'esprit).

penguin ['peŋgwin] *n. Orn:* manchot *m*, gorfou *m*.

penholder ['penhouldər] *n.* porte-plume *m inv*.

penicillin [peni'silin] *n.* pénicilline *f*.

peninsula [pi'ninsjulə] *n. Geog:* péninsule *f*; presqu'île *f*; **the Iberian P.,** la péninsule Ibérique.

peninsular [pi'ninsjulər] *a.* péninsulaire.

penis, *pl.* **-nes** ['pi:nis, -ni:z] *n. Anat:* pénis *m*, verge *f*.

penitence ['penitəns] *n.* pénitence *f*, repentir *m*, contrition *f*.

penitent ['penitənt] **1.** *a.* pénitent, repentant, contrit. **2.** *n.* (*a*) (*pers. doing penance*) pénitent, -ente; (*b*) *R.C.Ch:* (*member of a Penitent order*) pénitent, -ente. **-ly** *adv.* d'un air contrit.

penitential [peni'tenʃ(ə)l] **1.** *a.* pénitentiel; (psaumes) de la pénitence. **2.** *n.* (*book*) pénitentiel *m*.

penitentiary [peni'tenʃəri] **1.** *a.* (*a*) (maison) pénitentiaire; (*b*) *U.S:* (délit) puni de réclusion dans une maison pénitentiaire. **2.** *n.* (*a*) *R.C.Ch:* (*pers.*) pénitencier; (*b*) *R.C.Ch:* (*tribunal*) pénitencerie *f*; (*c*) *NAm:* prison *f*.

penknife ['pennaif] *n.* canif *m*.

penman, *pl.* **-men** ['penmən] *n.m.* **1.** homme de plume. **2. good, expert, p.,** calligraphe.

penmanship ['penmənʃip] *n.* **1.** l'art *m* d'écrire. **2.** calligraphie *f*.

pennant ['penənt] *n.* **1.** *Nau:* flamme *f*, guidon *m*. **2.** = PENNON.

penniless ['penilis] *a.* sans le sou; sans ressources; **to be p.,** n'avoir pas le sou, pas un sou vaillant; **to leave s.o. p.,** laisser qn sans le sou; *n.pl.* **the p.,** les sans-le-sou *mpl*.

pennine ['penain] *a. Geog:* **the P. Chain,** *n.pl.* **the Pennines,** la chaîne Pennine.

pennon ['penən] *n.* flamme *f*, banderole *f*.

Pennsylvania [pensil'veiniə] *Pr.n. Geog:* Pen(n)sylvanie *f*.

penny ['peni] *n.* **1.** (*coin*) (*pl. usu.* **pennies**) penny *m*; **a ten pence, fifty pence, piece,** une pièce de dix pence, de cinquante pence; **they haven't a p. (to their name, to bless themselves with),** ils sont sans le sou, sans un sou vaillant; **pennies from heaven,** une aubaine; **to count every p.,** compter ses sous; *F:* **the penny's dropped,** j'y suis, ça y est, etc.; *F:* **to spend a p.,** aller faire pipi. **2.** (*pl.* **pence** [pens]) (*a*) (*value*) **I paid 60 pence for it,** je l'ai payé 60 pence; **they're two a p. nowadays,** c'est monnaie courante à l'heure actuelle; **a p. for your thoughts,** *F:* **for them,** à quoi rêvez-vous, pensez-vous? *Prov:* **in for a p. in for a pound,** quand le vin est tiré il faut boire; *F:* **p. dreadful,** roman *m* à deux sous, à sensation; *Prov:* **take care of the pence and the pounds will take care of themselves,** les petites économies font les bonnes maisons; **to be p. wise and pound foolish,** économiser les sous et prodiguer les louis; (*b*) **that'll cost a pretty p.,** cela coûtera cher; **to make a pretty p. out of sth.,** tirer une petite fortune de qch.; **to earn, turn, an honest p.,** gagner honnêtement sa vie. **3.** (*a*) *B:* denier *m*; (*b*) *NAm:* cent *m*.

penny-in-the-slot [peniinðə'slɔt] *attrib.* (machine) à sous.

penny-pinching ['penipintʃiŋ] **1.** *a.* parcimonieux; pingre. **2.** *n.* parcimonie *f*; pingrerie *f*.

pennyworth ['peniwə:θ] *n.* (*a*) **to buy ten p. of sweets,** acheter pour dix pence de bonbons; (*b*) **not a p.,** rien du tout.

penology [pi:'nɔlədʒi] *n.* pénologie *f*.

pension¹ *n.* **1.** ['penʃ(ə)n] pension *f*; retraite *f*; **government p.,** pension sur l'État; **retirement, old age, p.,** pension de retraite; **p. fund,** caisse *f* de retraite; **to**

retire on a p., prendre sa retraite. **2.** ['pɑ̃sjɔ̃] pension de famille; (*at hotel*) **en p.**, en pension.

pension² ['penʃ(ə)n] *v.tr.* pensionner (qn); faire une rente à (qn); **to p. s.o. off,** mettre qn à la retraite.

pensionable ['penʃənəbl] *a.* **1.** (*of pers.*) qui a droit à une pension, à sa retraite. **2.** (*of injury, etc.*) qui donne droit à une pension; **p. age,** âge *m* de la mise à la retraite. **3.** (emploi) donnant droit à une pension.

pensioner ['penʃənər] *n.* titulaire *mf* d'une pension; pensionné, -ée; **old-age p.,** retraité, -ée.

pensive ['pensiv] *a.* pensif, méditatif, rêveur. **-ly** *adv.* pensivement; d'un air pensif.

pent [pent] *a.* **1. p. (in, up),** enfermé. **2.** (émotion) refoulée, contenue; **to be p. up,** être sous pression.

pentagon ['pentəgən] *n.* **1.** *Mth:* pentagone *m.* **2.** *Mil:* **the P.,** le Pentagone.

pentagonal [pen'tægən(ə)l] *a.* pentagonal.

pentameter [pen'tæmitər] *n. Pros:* pentamètre.

Pentateuch (the) [ðə'pentətju(:)k] *n. B:* le Pentateuque.

pentathlon [pen'tæθlən] *n. Sp:* pentathlon *m.*

Pentecost ['pentikɔst] *n. Ecc:* la Pentecôte.

pentecostal [penti'kɔst(ə)l] *a. Ecc:* de la Pentecôte.

penthouse ['penthaus] *n. Const:* **1.** (*a*) appentis *m*; abrivent *m*; hangar *m*; (*b*) (*over door, window*) auvent *m*; abat-vent *m inv.* **2.** appartement *m* (de) terrasse, construit sur le toit d'un immeuble.

penultimate [pe'nʌltimət] **1.** *a.* pénultième; avant-dernier. **2.** *n.* pénultième *f*; avant-dernière syllabe.

penumbra [pe'nʌmbrə] *n.* pénombre *f.*

penurious [pe'nju:riəs] *a.* pauvre.

penury ['penjuri] *n.* pénurie *f.* **1.** indigence *f.* **2.** manque *m*, disette *f* (**of,** de).

peony ['pi:əni] *n. Bot:* pivoine *f.*

people¹ ['pi:pl] *n.* (*coll. with pl. const. except for* **1.** *where pl. is usu.* **peoples**) **1.** peuple *m*, nation *f*; **the French p.,** les Français; **English-speaking people(s),** peuple, nations, de langue anglaise. **2.** (*a*) peuple, habitants *mpl*; **country p.,** les populations rurales; (*b*) **a king and his p.,** un roi et ses sujets; **I'll get one of my p. to do it,** un de mes employés, de mes ouvriers, le fera; (*c*) parents *mpl*; famille *f*; **how are your p.?** comment va votre famille? (*d*) *Ecc:* ouailles *fpl*; fidèles *mpl.* **3.** (*a*) citoyens *mpl* (d'un État); **people's republic,** république *f* populaire; **the will of the p.,** la volonté du peuple; (*b*) **the (common) p.,** le peuple; la populace; **a man of the p.,** un homme sorti du peuple. **4.** (*a*) gens *mpl*; **young p.,** jeunes gens; **old p.,** les vieux; **old people's home,** maison *f* de retraite pour personnes âgées; **thousands of p.,** des milliers de gens; **there were not many p.,** il n'y avait pas beaucoup de monde; **most p.,** la plupart des gens; **he's one of those p. who . . .,** il est de ceux qui . . .; c'est un homme qui . . .; (*b*) personnes *fpl*; **there were five p. in the room,** il y avait cinq personnes dans la pièce; **it's a question of knowing the right p.,** il faut avoir des relations; **we're having p. to dinner tonight,** nous aurons des invités, du monde, à dîner ce soir; (*c*) (*indefinite*) on; **p. say that . . .,** on dit que . . .; (*d*) *Myth:* **the little p., the good p.,** les fées *fpl.*

people² *v.tr.* peupler (**with,** de).

pep¹ [pep] *n. F:* entrain *m*, fougue *f*; **full of p.,** plein de sève, d'allant; **p. talk,** petit discours d'encouragement; **p. pill,** excitant *m*, stimulant *m.*

pep² *v.tr.* (**pepped**) *F:* **to p. s.o. up,** ragaillardir qn; **to p. up a business,** remonter une affaire.

pepper¹ ['pepər] *n.* (*a*) poivre *m*; **p. (plant),** poivrier *m*; *Cu:* **black, white, p.,** poivre noir, gris; **p. mill,** moulin *m* à poivre; **p. pot,** poivrière *f*; (*b*) **long p.,** poivre long; **Cayenne p.,** poivre de Cayenne; **Jamaica p.,** poivre de la Jamaïque, piment *m*; **sweet p.,** piment doux, poivron *m.*

pepper² *v.tr.* **1.** poivrer (de la viande, etc.). **2.** cribler (l'ennemi, etc.) de balles.

pepper-and-salt ['pepərən(d)'sɔ:lt] *attrib.* (*of hair, etc.*) poivre et sel.

peppercorn ['pepəkɔ:n] *n.* **1.** grain *m* de poivre. **2.** *Jur:* **p. rent,** loyer nominal, insignifiant.

peppermint ['pepəmint] *n.* **1.** menthe poivrée; menthe anglaise. **2. p. drop, lozenge,** bonbon *m*, pastille *f*, à la menthe.

peppery ['pepəri] *a.* **1.** (*of dish, etc.*) poivré. **2.** *F:* (*of pers.*) irascible, coléreux, colérique.

peppy ['pepi] *a. F:* (*of pers.*) plein de sève, d'allant.

pepsin ['pepsin] *n. Ch: Physiol:* pepsine *f.*

peptic ['peptik] *a. Physiol:* peptique; **p. ulcer,** ulcère *m* de l'estomac, gastro-duodénal.

peptone ['peptoun] *n. Bio-Ch:* peptone *f.*

per [pə:r] *prep. Com: etc:* (*a*) par; **sent p. carrier,** envoyé par messageries; (*b*) **as p. invoice,** suivant facture; **as p. sample,** conformément à l'échantillon; *O:* **as p. usual,** comme d'habitude; (*c*) **p. cent,** pour cent; **ten francs p. kilo,** dix francs le kilo; **100 km p. hour,** cent kilomètres par heure; (*e*) **p. annum,** par an; **p. day,** par jour.

peradventure [pə:rəd'ventjər] *adv. A:* **1.** paraventure, par hasard. **2.** peut-être.

perambulate [pə'ræmbjuleit] *v.tr.* parcourir, se promener dans (son jardin, etc.).

perambulator [pə'ræmbjuleitər] *n. A: & Lit:* voiture *f* d'enfant; landau *m.*

perceive [pə'si:v] *v.tr. esp. Lit:* **1.** percevoir (la vérité, etc.). **2.** percevoir (un son, une odeur); s'apercevoir de (qch.); **he perceived that he was being watched,** il s'aperçut qu'on l'observait. **3.** apercevoir (qn).

percentage [pə'sentidʒ] *n.* **1.** pourcentage *m*; **to allow a p. on all transactions,** allouer un tant pour cent, un tantième, sur toutes opérations. **2. p. of acid, of alcohol, etc.,** teneur *f* en acide, en alcool, etc.

perceptibility [pəsepti'biliti] *n.* perceptibilité *f.*

perceptible [pə'septibl] *a.* (*a*) perceptible (à l'esprit); *Phil:* cognoscible; (différence) sensible; (*b*) **p. to the eye,** apercevable; visible; **p. to the ear,** perceptible à l'oreille; audible. **-ibly** *adv.* perceptiblement, sensiblement.

perception [pə'sepʃ(ə)n] *n.* (*a*) perception *f*; **organs of p.,** organes percepteurs; (*b*) sensibilité *f* (aux impressions extérieures); faculté perceptive.

perceptive [pə'septiv] *a.* **1.** perceptif; **p. faculties,** facultés perceptives. **2.** perspicace; sensible.

perceptiveness [pə'septivnis] *n.* perceptivité *f*; faculté perceptive.

perch¹ [pə:tʃ] *n.* **1.** perchoir *m*; (*in cage*) bâton *m*; *F:* **to knock s.o. off his p.,** (i) détrôner qn; (ii) rabattre le caquet à qn. **2.** *A. Meas:* perche *f* (de $5\frac{1}{2}$ yards, *approx.* = 5 m.).

perch² **1.** (*a*) *v.i.* (*of bird, F: of pers.*) percher, se percher (**on,** sur); giter; (*of poultry*) jucher; **perching bird,** oiseau percheur; (*b*) *v.pr.* se percher, se jucher (**on,** sur). **2.** *v.tr.* **castle perched on a hill,** château perché sur (le sommet d')une colline.

perch³ *n. Ich:* perche *f.*

perchance [pə'tʃɑ:ns] *adv. A:* peut-être.

percipient [pə'sipiənt] **1.** *a.* percepteur, -trice (de sensations, etc.). **2.** *n.* sujet *m* télépathique.

percolate ['pə:kəleit] **1.** *v.i.* s'infiltrer; (*of coffee, etc.*) filtrer, passer. **2.** *v.tr.* (*a*) (*of liquid*) filtrer à travers, s'infiltrer dans (le sable); (*b*) (*of pers., filter, etc.*) filtrer (un liquide); passer (le café).

percolator ['pə:kəleitər] *n.* (*a*) filtre *m*; percolateur *m*; (*b*) cafetière à pression.

percussion [pə:'kʌʃ(ə)n] *n.* percussion *f*; (*a*) **p. gun,** fusil *m* à percussion; *Artil:* **p. pin,** rugueux *m* (de fusée); (*b*) *Mus:* (i) **p. instruments,** instruments *mpl* de, à, percussion; **p. player,** percussionniste *mf*; (ii) **p. (section),** la batterie.

percussive [pə'kʌsiv] *a.* percutant.
perdition [pəː'diʃ(ə)n] *n.* perte *f*, ruine *f*, *Theol:* perdition *f*.
peregrination [perigri'neiʃ(ə)n] *n.* pérégrination *f*; voyage *m*.
peregrine ['perigrin] *a.* & *n.* *Orn:* **p. (falcon),** (faucon) pèlerin (*m*).
peremptory [pə'rem(p)təri] *a.* péremptoire; (*a*) *Jur:* **p. writ,** mandat *m* de comparaître en personne; (*b*) (*of refusal*) absolu, décisif; (*c*) (*of tone*) dogmatique, impératif; (*of pers.*) impérieux, autoritaire. **-ily** *adv.* (*a*) péremptoirement; (*b*) dictatorialement.
perennial [pə'reniəl] **1.** *a.* (*a*) éternel, perpétuel; (*b*) *Bot:* vivace, persistant. **2.** *n.* plante *f* vivace. **-ally** *adv.* à perpétuité; éternellement.
perfect[1] ['pəːfikt] *a.* **1.** parfait; (*a*) **God alone is p.,** Dieu seul est parfait; (*b*) **p. example,** exemple parfait; **a p. piece of work,** un travail achevé; **his English is p.,** son anglais est impeccable; **to be p.,** (i) avoir toutes les perfections; (ii) (*also* **to be in p. condition**) être intact, sans défaut; **p.!** parfait! (*c*) **in p. sincerity,** en toute sincérité; **he's a p. stranger to me,** il m'est tout à fait inconnu; *F:* **he's a p. idiot,** c'est un parfait imbécile. **2.** (*a*) *Mth:* (nombre, carré) parfait; (*b*) *Mus:* (intervalle) juste; (accord) parfait; **p. cadence,** cadence parfaite; (*c*) (*of flower, insect*) parfait; (*d*) *Bookb:* (reliure) arraphique, sans couture. **3.** *a.* & *n.* *Gram:* **the p. (tense),** le parfait, le passé composé; **future p.,** futur antérieur; **verb in the p.,** verbe au parfait. **-ly** *adv.* parfaitement; (savoir qch.) à fond; (faire qch.) à la perfection; **she's p. right,** elle a parfaitement raison.
perfect[2] [pəː'fekt] *v.tr.* **1.** achever, accomplir (un travail, etc.). **2.** rendre parfait, perfectionner, parfaire (une méthode, etc.); mettre (une invention, un dessin) au point. **3.** *Typ:* imprimer, mettre, (une feuille) en retiration. **perfecting** *n.* **1.** achèvement *m*, accomplissement *m*. **2.** perfectionnement *m*; mise *f* au point (d'un dessin, d'un projet, etc.). **3.** *Typ:* (impression *f* en) retiration (*f*); **p. machine,** presse *f* à retiration.
perfection [pəː'fekʃ(ə)n] *n.* **1.** *O:* perfection *f*; (*a*) achèvement *m*, accomplissement *m* (d'une tâche); (*b*) perfectionnement *m* (d'un travail, etc.). **2.** (*a*) perfection; **p. itself,** la perfection même; **to attain p.,** toucher, arriver, à la perfection; **to do sth. to p.,** faire qch. à la perfection; (*b*) développement complet (d'une plante, d'un insecte).
perfectionism [pəː'fekʃənizm] *n.* perfectionnisme *m*.
perfectionist [pəː'fekʃənist] *n.* perfectionniste *mf*.
perfidious [pəː'fidiəs] *a.* perfide; *Lit:* **p. Albion,** la perfide Albion. **-ly** *adv.* perfidement.
perfidiouness [pəː'fidiəsnis], **perfidy** ['pəːfidiː] *n.* perfidie *f*.
perforate ['pəːfəreit] **1.** *v.tr.* (*a*) perforer, percer, transpercer; (*b*) poinçonner (une tôle, un billet, etc.); (*c*) grillager (une plaque, etc.); (*d*) *Tchn:* perforer (un papier, etc.) en pointillé. **2.** *v.i.* (*a*) pénétrer (**into,** dans); **to p. through sth.,** perforer qch.; (*b*) *Med:* (*of ulcer*) déterminer une perforation.
perforation [pəːfə'reiʃ(ə)n] *n.* **1.** perforation *f*; perforage *m*, perçage *m*. **2.** (*a*) petit trou; *Anat:* orifice *m*; *Med:* perforation; (*b*) *coll.* trous *mpl*, ajours *mpl*, perforation(s); (*for counterfoils, etc.*) (perforation(s) en) pointillé (*m*); (*of postage stamp*) dentelure *f*.
perforce [pəː'fɔːs] *adv. Lit:* forcément.
perform [pəː'fɔːm] *v.tr.* **1.** célébrer (un rite); remplir (son devoir); *Surg:* **to p. an operation on s.o.,** opérer qn. **2.** *Th: etc:* (*a*) jouer, représenter (une pièce); exécuter (une danse); exécuter, jouer (un morceau de musique); tenir, remplir (un rôle); (*b*) *v.i.* **to p. in a play,** tenir un rôle, jouer, dans une pièce; **to p. on the flute,** jouer de la flûte. **performing 1.** *a.* (chien) savant. **2.** *n.* (*a*) accomplissement *m*, exécution *f* (**of,** de); (*b*) représentation *f* (d'une pièce); **p. rights,** droits *mpl* (i) *Th:* de représentation, (ii) *Mus:* d'exécution.
performance [pəː'fɔːməns] *n.* **1.** exécution *f* (d'un contrat, d'un opéra); accomplissement *m* (d'une tâche); célébration *f* (d'un rite). **2.** (*a*) acte *m*, exploit *m*; **to make a great p. of doing sth.,** faire qch. avec beaucoup de brio; *F:* **what a p.!** quelle histoire! (*b*) *Sp:* performance *f*; **to put up a good p.,** accomplir une performance; (*c*) *Ind:* cadence *f* (de travail d'un ouvrier); (*d*) *Mec.E:* (i) fonctionnement *m*, marche *f* (d'une machine); (ii) rendement *m*, performance (d'un avion, d'un appareil, d'un moteur, etc.); (iii) comportement *m*, tenue *f* (d'un matériel). **3.** *Th: etc:* représentation *f* (d'une pièce); séance *f* (de cinéma); **first p.,** première *f*; *Cin:* **continuous p.,** spectacle permanent; **there is no p. tonight,** il y a relâche ce soir.
performer [pəː'fɔːmər] *n.* **1.** *Mus:* exécutant, -ante; artiste *mf*. **2.** *Th:* acteur, -trice; artiste *mf*.
perfume[1] ['pəːfjuːm] *n.* parfum *m*; (*a*) odeur *f* agréable; (*b*) **bottle of p.,** flacon *m* de parfum.
perfume [pə'fjuːm] *v.tr.* parfumer.
perfumery [pə'fjuːməri] *n.* parfumerie *f*.
perfunctory [pə'fʌŋkt(ə)ri] *a.* **1.** (*of inquiry, etc.*) fait pour la forme; superficiel; **the examination was p.,** l'examen a été une pure formalité; **p. inquiry,** (i) enquête peu poussée; (ii) renseignements pris par manière d'acquit. **2.** (*of pers.*) négligent; peu zélé. **-ily** *adv.* par manière d'acquit; superficiellement.
pergola ['pəːgələ] *n.* pergola *f*.
perhaps [pəː'hæps, præps] *adv.* peut-être; **p. so, p. not,** peut-être (bien) que oui, que non; **p. we shall come back tomorrow,** peut-être reviendrons-nous demain; **p. you would like to try it on,** voulez-vous l'essayer?
perigee ['peridʒiː] *n.* *Astr:* périgée *m*.
perihelion [peri'hiːliən] *n.* *Astr:* périhélie *m*.
peril ['peril] *n.* péril *m*, danger *m*; **in p.,** en danger, en péril; **in p. of one's life,** en danger de mort; **to do sth. at one's (own) p.,** faire qch. à ses risques et périls; *M.Ins:* **peril(s) of the sea,** fortune *f* de mer; risque(s) *m*(*pl*) de mer.
perilous ['periləs] *a.* périlleux, dangereux. **-ly** *adv.* dangereusement.
perimeter [pə'rimitər] *n.* périmètre *m*.
period ['piəriəd] *n.* **1.** (*a*) période *f*; durée *f*, délai *m*; **for a p. of three months,** pendant une période de trois mois; **within the agreed p.,** dans les délais convenus; *Bank:* **deposit for a fixed p.,** dépôt *m* à terme fixe; (*b*) *Sch:* heure *f* de cours; *Meteor:* **clear periods,** éclaircies *fpl*; *Med:* **incubation p.,** période d'incubation; *Physiol:* **(monthly) period(s),** règles *fpl*; (*c*) *Astr:* cycle *m*, période (de la révolution d'une planète); *Ph:* période (d'une onde, d'un courant alternatif); (*d*) *Atom.Ph:* période (d'un corps radioactif, etc.). **2.** (*a*) époque *f*, âge *m*; ère *f*; **attitude typical of the p.,** attitude *f* caractéristique (i) de l'époque (en question), (ii) de notre époque; **p. play, novel,** comédie *f*, roman *m*, historique; **p. dress,** robe *f* de style; **p. costume,** toilette *f* d'époque; **p. furniture,** meubles *mpl* de style, d'époque; (*b*) *Com: etc:* **accounting p.,** exercice *m*. **3.** (*a*) *Lit:* phrase *f*; (*b*) *Mus:* phrase complète. **4.** *Gram: Typ:* point *m* (de ponctuation); *F:* **he's no good at maths!–he's no good, p.!** il est nul en math!—il est nul, un point, c'est tout!
periodic [piəri'ɔdik] *a.* **1.** périodique. **2.** *Lit:* (style) périodique, riche en périodes.
periodical [piəri'ɔdik(ə)l] **1.** *a.* périodique. **2.** *n.* (publication *f*) périodique (*m*); journal *m*. **-ally** *adv.* périodiquement.
peripatetic [peripə'tetik] *a.* ambulant, itinérant.
peripheral [pə'rifərəl] **1.** *a.* (région, *Opt:* vision,

etc.) périphérique. **2.** *a. & n. Cmptr:* périphérique (*m*); **p. equipment,** matériel *m* périphérique; périphériques *mpl.*

periphery [pə'rifəri] *n.* périphérie *f*, circonférence *f*; pourtour *m*; **on the p. of . . .,** en bordure de . . ..

periphrasis, *pl.* **-es** [pə'rifrəsis, -i:z] *n.* périphrase *f*; circonlocution *f.*

periscope ['periskoup] *n.* périscope *m.*

perish ['periʃ] **1.** *v.i.* (*a*) (*of pers.*) périr, mourir; **p. the thought!** loin de nous cette pensée! *F:* **I'm perishing, I'm perished,** je meurs de froid; (*b*) (*of rubber*) se détériorer, se gâter, s'altérer; (*of leather*) s'avachir. **2.** *v.tr.* (*a*) détériorer, altérer; (*b*) (*of frost*) brûler, griller (la végétation). **perishing** *a.* (*a*) (effet) destructif; (*b*) *F:* très froid; **it's p.,** il fait un froid de loup; (*c*) sacré; **p. idiot,** sacré idiot.

perishable ['periʃəbl] **1.** *a.* périssable; *Nau:* **p. cargo,** chargement *m* périssable. **2.** *n.pl.* **perishables,** marchandises *fpl* périssables.

perisher ['periʃər] *n. P:* saligaud *m*; *F:* **little p.,** petit coquin.

peristyle ['peristail] *n. Arch:* péristyle *m.*

peritoneum [peritə'ni:əm] *n. Anat:* péritoine *m.*

peritonitis [peritə'naitis] *n. Med:* péritonite *f.*

periwig ['periwig] *n. A:* perruque *f.*

periwinkle¹ ['periwiŋkl] *n. Bot:* (*genus*) vinca *f*; (petite) pervenche; **p. (blue),** bleu pervenche *inv.*

periwinkle² *n. Moll:* bigorneau *m.*

perjure ['pə:dʒər] *v.pr.* **to p. oneself,** (i) se parjurer; *Jur:* porter faux témoignage; (ii) commettre un parjure; violer son serment.

perjurer ['pə:dʒərər] *n.* parjure *mf.*

perjury ['pə:dʒəri] *n.* **1.** (*as a moral offence*) parjure *m.* **2.** *Jur:* (*a*) faux serment; **to commit p.,** faire un faux serment; (*b*) faux témoignage.

perk¹ [pə:k] **1.** *v.i. F:* (*a*) **to p. (up),** (i) redresser la tête; (ii) se raviver; se ranimer; (iii) (*after illness*) se ravigoter. **2.** *v.tr.* (*a*) **to p. up one's head,** redresser la tête (d'un air crâneur ou guilleret); (*of dog*) **to p. up its ears,** dresser les oreilles; (*b*) *F:* **to p. s.o. up,** (i) requinquer qn; (ii) (*of drink, etc.*) ravigoter qn.

perk² [pə:k] *n. F:* à-côté *m*; **perks,** petits profits.

perky ['pə:ki] *a.* (*a*) éveillé; guilleret; (*b*) suffisant; (ton) dégagé, désinvolte. **-ily** *adv.* (*a*) d'un air éveillé; (*b*) d'un air dégagé.

perm¹ [pə:m] *n. Hairdr: F:* permanente *f.*

perm² *v.tr. Hairdr: F:* **to have one's hair permed,** se faire faire une permanente.

perm³ *n.* (*in football pool*) permutation *f.*

permafrost ['pə:məfrɔst] *n. Geol:* permafrost *m.*

permanence ['pə:mənəns] *n.* permanence *f.*

permanency ['pə:mənənsi] *n.* **1.** permanence. **2.** emploi permanent.

permanent ['pə:mənənt] *a.* permanent; (établissement) à demeure; (assemblée) en permanence; (résidence, adresse) fixe; **p. job,** situation permanente; *Rail:* **p. way,** voie (ferrée); superstructure *f*; *a. & n. Hairdr:* **p. (wave),** permanente *f.* **-ly** *adv.* d'une façon permanente; en permanence; à demeure.

permanganate [pə:'mæŋgəneit] *n. Ch:* permanganate *m.*

permeability [pə:miə'biliti] *n.* perméabilité *f*; pénétrabilité *f.*

permeable ['pə:miəbl] *a.* perméable; pénétrable.

permeate ['pə:mieit] *v.tr. & ind.tr.* **to p. (through) sth.,** filtrer, passer, à travers qch.; **water permeates everywhere,** l'eau s'insinue partout; **the soil was permeated with water,** le sol était saturé d'eau.

permissible [pə:'misibl] *a.* admissible, acceptable.

permission [pə:'miʃ(ə)n] *n.* permission *f*; autorisation *f*; **to ask, give, s.o. p. to do sth.,** demander, donner, à qn la permission, l'autorisation, de faire qch.; **with your p.,** avec votre permission.

permissive [pə:'misiv] *a.* **1.** (législation) facultative. **2.** permis, toléré; **p. morals,** morale *f* commode; **p. society,** société *f* à la morale commode, qui se croit tout permis. **-ly** *adv.* peu strictement.

permissiveness [pə:'misivnis] *n.* **1.** légalité *f* (d'une action). **2.** tolérance *f*; laxisme *m.*

permit¹ ['pə:mit] *n.* **1.** (*a*) permis *m*; permission *f*, autorisation *f*; **work p.,** permis de travail; (*b*) permis de circuler; laissez-passer *m inv.* **2.** *Cust:* acquit-à-caution *m*, *pl.* acquits-à-caution; passavant *m*; **export p.,** autorisation d'exporter.

permit² [pə:'mit] *v.* **(permitted) 1.** *v.tr.* permettre; **to p. s.o. to do sth.,** permettre à qn de faire qch.; autoriser qn à faire qch.; **if I may be permitted,** si vous me le permettez; (*angrily*) **p. me to tell you . . .!** laissez-moi vous dire . . .! *Adm:* **permitted hours,** heures légales de la vente des boissons alcooliques. **2.** *v. ind. tr.* **to p. of sth.,** permettre, admettre, qch. **3.** *v.i.* **if time permits,** si j'ai, nous avons, le temps; **weather permitting,** si le temps le permet.

permutation [pə:mju'teiʃ(ə)n] *n.* permutation *f.*

permute [pə:'mju:t] *v.tr. Ling: Mth:* permuter.

pernicious [pə:'niʃəs] *a.* pernicieux; (*of doctrine, etc.*) malsain, délétère. **-ly** *adv.* pernicieusement.

pernickety [pə:'nikiti] *a. F:* (*a*) tatillon, vétilleux, pointilleux; **to be p. about one's food,** être difficile sur sa nourriture; (*b*) (*of job*) délicat, minutieux.

perorate ['perəreit] *v.i.* **1.** faire la péroraison. **2.** pérorer; discourir longuement.

peroration [perə'reiʃ(ə)n] *n.* **1.** péroraison *f.* **2.** discours prolongé, de longue haleine.

peroxide¹ [pə'rɔksaid] *n. Ch:* peroxyde *m*; *F:* **p. blonde,** fausse blonde.

peroxide² *v.tr.* faire blondir (ses cheveux) à l'eau oxygénée.

perpendicular [pə:pən'dikjulər] **1.** *a.* (*a*) perpendiculaire; (*of wall, cliff, etc.*) vertical, -aux; à plomb; (*of cliff*) à pic; **line p. to another,** ligne perpendiculaire à, sur, une autre; (*b*) *Eng.Arch:* **p. style,** style *m* (gothique) perpendiculaire. **2.** *n.* (*a*) fil *m* à plomb; **out of (the) p.,** hors d'aplomb; hors d'équerre; (*b*) *Mth:* perpendiculaire *f.* **-ly** *adv.* perpendiculairement; verticalement; d'aplomb.

perpetrate ['pə:pitreit] *v.tr.* commettre, perpétrer (un crime); être l'auteur (d'une gaffe, une farce).

perpetration [pə:pi'treiʃ(ə)n] *n.* perpétration *f* (d'un crime, etc.).

perpetrator ['pə:pitreitər] *n.* auteur *m* (d'un crime, etc.).

perpetual [pə:'petjuəl] *a.* (*a*) perpétuel, éternel; **p. motion,** mouvement perpétuel; (*b*) sans fin, continuel, incessant. **-ally** *adv.* (*a*) perpétuellement, éternellement; (*b*) sans cesse; continuellement.

perpetuation [pə:petju'eiʃ(ə)n] *n.* perpétuation *f*, éternisation *f*; préservation *f* de l'oubli.

perpetuate [pə:'petjueit] *v.tr.* (*a*) perpétuer, éterniser; (*b*) **to p. s.o.'s memory,** préserver le nom de qn de l'oubli.

perpetuity [pə:pe'tju:iti] *n.* **1.** perpétuité *f*; **in, to, for, p.,** à perpétuité. **2.** *Jur:* (*a*) jouissance *f* (d'un bien) à perpétuité; (*b*) **(rent in) p.,** rente constituée en perpétuel; rente perpétuelle.

perplex [pə:'pleks] *v.tr.* embarrasser (qn); **to be perplexed,** être perplexe, embarrassé. **perplexing** *a.* (*of problem, etc.*) embarrassant, troublant; (*of book, pers., etc.*) difficile (à comprendre); **it's very p.,** on n'y comprend rien.

perplexity [pə:'pleksiti] *n.* perplexité *f*, embarras *m.*

perquisite ['pə:kwizit] *n.* (*a*) bénéfice *m*; casuel *m*; revenant-bon *m*, *pl.* revenants-bons; (*b*) **perquisites,** (i) avantages *mpl* en nature; (ii) petits profits, *esp.* pourboires *mpl.*

persecute ['pə:sikju:t] *v.tr.* (*a*) persécuter (des hérétiques, etc.); (*b*) tourmenter, harceler (qn); brimer (des recrues, des nouveaux élèves, etc.).

persecution [pə:si'kju:ʃ(ə)n] *n.* persécution *f*; **p. mania,** délire *m*, manie *f*, de la persécution.

persecutor ['pə:sikju:tər] *n.* persécuteur, -trice.

perseverance [pə:si'viərəns] *n.* persévérance *f*; constance *f* (dans le travail).

persevere [pə:si'viər] *v.i.* persévérer (dans son travail, à faire qch.). **persevering** *a.* persévérant; assidu.

Persia ['pə:ʃə] *Pr.n. Geog:* Perse *f.*

Persian ['pə:ʃən] **1.** *a.* persan; *A.Hist:* perse; (chat, cheval) persan; (tapis) de Perse; **the P. Gulf,** le Golfe persique. **2.** *n.* (*a*) (*pers.*) Persan, -ane; *A.Hist:* Perse *mf*; (*b*) chat persan; (*c*) *Ling:* perse *m.*

persimmon [pə:'simən] *n. Bot:* (*a*) (i) plaquemine *f*; (ii) kaki *m*; (*b*) **p. (tree),** plaqueminier *m.*

persist [pə:'sist] *v.i.* **1. to p. in one's opinion,** persister, s'obstiner, dans son opinion; **to p. in doing sth.,** persister, s'obstiner, à faire qch. **2.** (*of fog, fever, etc.*) persister, continuer.

persistence [pə:'sistəns] *n.* **1.** persistance *f* **(in doing sth.,** à faire qch.); ténacité *f*, obstination *f.* **2.** persistance; continuité *f.*

persistent [pə:'sistənt] *a.* **1.** persistant, opiniâtre, tenace; (pluie) qui s'obstine. **2.** persistant; continu; *Com:* **p. demand for . . .,** demande suivie pour . . .. **3.** *Bot:* (feuillage) persistant. **-ly** *adv.* avec persistance.

person ['pə:s(ə)n] *n.* **1.** (*a*) personne *f*, individu *m*; **private p.,** (simple) particulier *m*; **to act through a third p.,** passer par une tierce personne; **there is no p. of that name here,** il n'y a ici personne de ce nom; *Jur:* **some p. or persons unknown,** un certain quidam; (*b*) *Pej:* individu, type *m*; **who is this p.?** quel est cet individu? (*c*) **in (one's own) p.,** en (propre) personne; **he came in p.,** il est venu en personne; **to be delivered in p.,** à remettre en main(s) propre(s); **to carry weapons on one's p.,** porter des armes sur soi; (*d*) *Jur:* **natural p.,** personne physique, naturelle; **artificial p.,** personne, personnalité, morale, civile, juridique; (*e*) personnage *m* (d'un roman, etc.). **2. (one) God in three Persons,** un (seul) Dieu en trois personnes. **3.** *Gram:* **verb in the first p.,** verbe à la première personne; **the second p. plural,** la deuxième personne du pluriel.

personable ['pə:sənəbl] *a.* bien (fait) de sa personne; **he's very p.,** il présente bien.

personage ['pə:sənidʒ] *n.* (*a*) personnage *m*; personnalité *f*; (*b*) *Th: O:* personnage.

personal ['pə:sən(ə)l] *a.* personnel. **1.** (*a*) **p. liberty,** liberté individuelle; **p. friend,** ami(e) personnel(le); **to give a p. touch to sth.,** personnaliser qch.; **it's a p. matter,** c'est une affaire privée, personnelle; **I want it for my p. use,** j'en ai besoin pour mon usage personnel; *Cust:* **articles for p. use,** effets usagers; *Adm:* **p. income,** revenu *m* des personnes physiques; **to be careless about one's p. appearance,** négliger sa tenue; (*on letter*) **personal,** personnelle; *Journ:* **p. column,** petites annonces; (*b*) **don't be p., don't make p. remarks,** ne faites pas des allusions personnelles; (*c*) **to make a p. appearance,** venir, paraître, en personne. **2.** *Jur:* **p. estate, property,** biens personnels, biens meubles, biens mobiliers; **p. effects,** effets personnels; **p. action,** action mobilière. **3.** *Gram:* (pronom) personnel. **-ally** *adv.* personnellement; (intervenir) en personne; **p. I think . . .,** pour ma part, pour moi, je pense . . .; **that belongs to me p.,** cela m'appartient en propre; **to deliver sth. to s.o. p.,** remettre qch. à qn en main(s) propre(s).

personality [pə:sə'næliti] *n.* **1.** (*a*) personnalité *f*; personnage *m*; (*b*) caractère *m* propre (de qn); **he's got no p.,** il manque de personnalité. **2.** (*a*) caractère personnel (d'une remarque, etc.); (*b*) **to indulge in personalities,** faire des remarques personnelles.

personalize ['pə:sənəlaiz] *v.tr.* (*a*) personnaliser; personnifier; (*b*) **a personalized shirt, etc.,** une chemise, etc., personnalisée, avec vos initiales; **personalized letter,** lettre personnelle.

personalty ['pə:sənəlti] *n. Jur:* biens meubles, biens mobiliers.

personification [pə:sɔnifi'keiʃ(ə)n] *n.* personnification *f.*

personify [pə:'sɔnifai] *v.tr.* personnifier; **he's meanness personified,** il est, c'est, l'avarice même, l'avarice en personne.

personnel [pə:sə'nel] *n.* personnel *m*; **p. department, manager,** service, directeur, du personnel; *Mil:* **armoured p. carrier,** véhicule blindé de transport de personnel; **anti-p. mine,** mine *f* anti-personnel.

perspective [pə:'spektiv] **1.** *n.* (*a*) *Mth: Art:* perspective *f*; **drawing in p.,** dessin en perspective; **picture out of p.,** tableau qui manque de perspective; **to see a matter in its true p.,** voir une affaire sous son vrai jour; (*b*) vue *f*; **a fine p. opened out before his eyes,** une belle perspective s'ouvrit devant ses yeux; (*c*) **with a long p. of happy days before us,** avec devant nous une longue perspective de jours heureux. **2.** *a.* (dessin, etc.) perspectif, en perspective; **p. lines of a picture,** fuyants *mpl* d'un tableau.

perspicacious [pə:spi'keiʃəs] *a.* perspicace; fin; pénétrant. **-ly** *adv.* avec perspicacité.

perspicacity [pə:spi'kæsiti] *n.* perspicacité *f*; pénétration *f*, discernement *m.*

perspicuity [pə:spi'kju:iti] *n.* perspicuité *f*; clarté *f*, netteté *f*, lucidité *f* (du style, etc.).

perspicuous [pə:'spikjuəs] *a.* clair, net, lucide. **-ly** *adv.* clairement, nettement.

perspiration [pə:spə'reiʃ(ə)n] *n.* (*a*) transpiration *f*; (*b*) sueur *f*; **beads of p.,** gouttes *f* de sueur; **bathed in, dripping with, p.,** trempé de sueur; en nage.

perspire [pə:'spaiər] *v.i.* transpirer; suer.

persuade [pə:'sweid] *v.tr.* persuader, convaincre (qn); **to p. s.o. not to do sth.,** déconseiller à qn, dissuader qn, de faire qch.

persuasion [pə:'sweiʒ(ə)n] *n.* **1.** persuasion *f*; **power of p.,** force *f* de persuasion; **the art of p.,** l'art *m* de persuader. **2.** (*a*) *O:* conviction *f*; **it's my p. that,** je suis persuadé, convaincu, que . . .; (*b*) **(religious) p.,** (i) religion *f*, foi *f*, confession *f*; (ii) secte *f*, communion *f*; (*c*) **(political) p.,** opinions *fpl* en matière de politique; idéologie *f.*

persuasive [pə:'sweiziv, -siv] *a.* persuasif; persuadant. **-ly** *adv.* d'un ton persuasif.

persuasiveness [pə:'sweizivnis, -siv-] *n.* force persuasive; persuasion *f.*

pert [pə:t] *a.* **1.** effronté, hardi. **2.** *NAm:* guilleret; gaillard. **-ly** *adv.* **1.** d'un ton effronté. **2.** *NAm:* d'un air guilleret.

pertain [pə:'tein] *v.i.* appartenir (à qch.); regarder (qch.); **the house and the land pertaining to it,** la maison et le terrain qui fait partie de la propriété.

pertinacious [pə:ti'neiʃəs] *n.* obstiné, opiniâtre. **-ly** *adv.* obstinément, opiniâtrement.

pertinence ['pə:tinəns] *n.* pertinence *f* (d'une raison); à-propos *m*, justesse *f* (d'une remarque).

pertinent ['pə:tinənt] *a.* (*a*) pertinent; à propos, juste; (*b*) **to be p. to (sth.),** avoir rapport à (une question); relever (d'une affaire, etc.). **-ly** *adv.* d'une manière pertinente; à propos.

pertness ['pə:tnis] *n.* **1.** effronterie *f.* **2.** *NAm:* air guilleret.

perturb [pə:'tə:b] *v.tr.* **1.** jeter le désordre, la perturbation, dans (un royaume, etc.). **2.** (*a*) *Astr:* dévier (un astre); (*b*) *Ph:* affoler (l'aiguille d'une boussole). **3.** troubler, inquiéter, agiter; **to be perturbed,** être agité, troublé, inquiet.

perturbation [pəːtəː'beiʃ(ə)n] *n.* **1.** perturbation *f*, désordre *m.* **2.** affolement *m* (de l'aiguille aimantée). **3.** agitation *f*, inquiétude *f*, trouble *m* (de l'esprit).

Peru [pə'ruː] *Pr.n. Geog:* Pérou *m.*

perusal [pə'ruːz(ə)l] *n.* lecture *f*; (*of document*) **for p.,** en communication.

peruse [pə'ruːz] *v.tr.* lire attentivement, prendre connaissance de (qch.).

Peruvian [pəː'ruːviən] *Geog:* **1.** *a.* péruvien. **2.** *n.* Péruvien, -ienne.

pervade [pəː'veid] *v.tr.* s'infiltrer dans, se répandre dans (qch.); **the scent of pine trees pervaded the air,** l'air était embaumé de l'odeur des pins. **pervading** *a.* (*of smell*) pénétrant; **(all-) p.,** qui se répand partout; (*of influence, etc.*) régnant, dominant.

pervasive [pəː'veisiv] *a.* qui se répand partout; pénétrant; (parfum, etc.) subtil.

perverse [pə'vəːs] *a.* (*a*) pervers, perverti; (*b*) opiniâtre dans l'erreur; (*c*) contrariant, désobligeant; (*d*) revêche, acariâtre: **-ly** *adv.* (*a*) perversement, avec perversité; (*b*) d'une manière contrariante.

perverseness, perversity [pə'vəːsnis, -'vəːsiti] *n.* (*a*) perversité *f*; (*b*) esprit contraire, contrariant; (*c*) caractère *m* revêche; acariâtreté *f.*

perversion [pə'vəːʃ(ə)n] *n.* **1.** action *f* de pervertir; pervertissement *m.* **2.** perversion *f*; **a p. of the truth,** un travestissement de la vérité; **sexual perversions,** perversions sexuelles.

pervert¹ ['pəvəːt] *n.* **1.** (*a*) perverti, -ie; (*b*) apostat *m.* **2.** *Psy:* **sexual p.,** perverti(e) sexuel(le).

pervert² [pə'vəːt] *v.tr.* **1.** détourner (qch. de son but); **to p. the course of justice,** égarer la justice. **2.** pervertir (qn); dépraver (le goût). **3.** altérer, dénaturer (les faits, les mots de qn).

pervious ['pəːviəs] *a.* perméable (à l'eau, etc.).

pesky ['peski] *a. NAm: F:* maudit, sacré.

pessary ['pesəri] *n. Med:* pessaire *m.*

pessimism ['pesimizm] *n.* pessimisme *m.*

pessimist ['pesimist] *n.* pessimiste *mf.*

pessimistic [pesi'mistik] *a.* pessimiste. **-ally** *adv.* d'une manière pessimiste; avec pessimisme.

pest [pest] *n.* **1.** (*a*) *Med: A:* peste *f*; (*b*) *F:* **to avoid s.o. like the p.,** fuir qn comme un pestiféré. **2.** (*a*) insecte *m*, plante *f*, nuisible; **rabbits are a p. here,** ici les lapins sont un fléau; **p. control,** (service de) dératisation, désinsectisation, etc.; (*b*) **he's a perfect p.!** c'est un vrai casse-pieds!

pester ['pestər] *v.tr. F:* tourmenter, importuner (qn); **to p. s.o. with questions,** importuner, assommer, harceler, qn de (ses) questions; **to p. s.o. for money,** harceler qn pour obtenir de l'argent.

pesticide ['pestisaid] *n.* pesticide *m.*

pestiferous [pes'tifərəs] *a.* (*a*) (*of air*) pestilentiel; (*b*) (*of insects*) nuisible; (*c*) (*of doctrine*) pernicieux.

pestilence ['pestiləns] *n.* peste *f*, *esp.* peste bubonique.

pestilential [pesti'lenʃ(ə)l] *a.* (*a*) (*of disease*) pestilentiel, pestifère; (*b*) (*of smell*) infect; (*c*) *F:* assommant, empoisonnant.

pestle ['pesl] *n.* pilon *m* (pour mortier).

pet¹ [pet] *n.* (*a*) animal familier; oiseau *m*, chien *m*, etc., d'appartement; **p. shop,** boutique *f* où l'on vend des animaux familiers; **p. food,** nourriture *f* pour chiens, chats, etc.; (*b*) mignon, -onne; enfant gâté; **mother's, teacher's, p.,** le chouchou de sa maman, du professeur; **my p.!** mon chéri! mon petit chou! (*c*) **p. subject,** sujet *m* de prédilection; **p. name,** (i) diminutif *m*; (ii) nom *m* d'amitié; **my p. hate,** ma bête noire.

pet² *v.tr.* **(petted)** (*a*) choyer, chouchouter (qn); (*b*) caresser, caliner (qn, un chien, etc.); (*c*) peloter (qn). **petting** *n.* pelotage *m.*

pet³ *n. F: O:* **to be in a p.,** bouder; être de mauvaise humeur.

petal [pet(ə)l] *n. Bot:* pétale *m.*

petard [pe'tɑːd] *n.* **1.** *Mil.A:* pétard *m.* **2.** *Pyr:* pétard.

Pete [piːt] *Pr.n.m.* (*dim. of* **Peter**) Pierrot; *F:* **for Pete's sake!** pour l'amour du ciel!

Peter ['piːtər] **1.** *Pr.n.m.* Pierre. **2.** *n. Nau:* **Blue P.,** pavillon *m* de partance, de départ.

peter ['piːtər] *v.i. F:* **to p. out,** (*a*) (*of flame, etc.*) mourir; (*b*) (*of stream, path*) disparaître; (*c*) (*of scheme*) venir à rien; (*of conversation*) tarir.

petersham ['piːtəʃəm] *n. Tex:* gros-grain *m.*

petite [pə'tiːt] *a.* (*of woman*) menue (et svelte).

petition¹ [pi'tiʃ(ə)n] *n.* (*a*) prière *f* (à Dieu); (*b*) pétition *f*, supplique *f*, requête *f*; **to grant a p.,** faire droit à une pétition; (*c*) *Jur:* **p. for mercy,** recours en grâce; **p. for a divorce,** demande *f* en divorce; **p. in bankruptcy,** (i) requête des créanciers; (ii) requête du négociant insolvable.

petition² **1.** *v.tr.* adresser, présenter, une pétition, une requête, à (la cour, un souverain, etc.); supplier (le souverain) (**to do sth.,** de faire qch.) **2.** *v.i.* pétitionner; **to p. for sth.,** demander, requérir, solliciter, qch.; **to p. for mercy,** se pourvoir, recourir, en grâce.

petitioner [pi'tiʃənər] *n.* pétitionnaire *mf*; *Jur:* requérant, -ante.

petrel ['petrəl] *n. Orn:* pétrel *m*; **storm(y) p.,** pétrel tempête.

petrifaction [petri'fækʃ(ə)n] *n.* pétrification *f.*

petrify ['petrifai] **1.** *v.tr.* (*a*) pétrifier (le bois, etc.); (*b*) pétrifier, méduser, paralyser (qn). **2.** v.i. se pétrifier. **petrified** *a.* (*a*) (bois, etc.) pétrifié; (*b*) **p. with fear,** petrifié, paralysé, de terreur. **petrifying** *a.* (*a*) pétrifiant; (*b*) paralysant.

petrochemical [petrou'kemik(ə)l] **1.** *a.* (industrie, etc.) pétrochimique. **2.** *n.pl.* **petrochemicals,** produits *mpl* pétrochimiques.

petrodollar ['petroudɔlər] *n.* pétrodollar *m.*

petrol ['petrəl] *n. Ch:* essence (minérale); *Aut:* essence, *Sw. Fr:* benzine *f*; *I.C.E:* **anti-knock p.,** essence antidétonante; **high-grade, four-star, p.** = supercarburant *m*, *F:* super *m*; **p. tank,** réservoir *m* à essence; **p. pump,** (i) (*in car*) pompe *f* à essence; (ii) distributeur *m* d'essence; **p. can,** bidon *m* à essence.

petroleum [pi'trouljəm] *n.* pétrole *m*; huile minérale (naturelle); huile de roche; **crude p.,** pétrole brut; **p. jelly,** gelée *f* de pétrole, vaseline *f.*

petrology [pi'trɔlədʒi] *n.* pétrologie *f.*

petticoat ['petikout] *n.* (*a*) jupon *m*, combinaison *f*; (*b*) *F:* **p. government,** régime *m* de cotillons.

pettifogging ['petifɔgiŋ] *a.* **1.** procédurier; **p. lawyer,** avocassier *m.* **2.** chicanier; (objections) de pure chicane.

pettiness ['petinis] *n.* petitesse *f*; (i) insignifiance *f*, (ii) mesquinerie *f.*

pettish ['petiʃ] *a.* de mauvaise humeur; maussade; irritable. **-ly** *adv.* avec humeur.

petty ['peti] *a.* **1.** (*a*) petit, insignifiant; **these are only p. differences,** ce ne sont que des différences insignifiantes, sans importance; **p. annoyances,** (i) coups *mpl* d'épingle; (ii) petits ennuis (de la vie journalière); (*b*) *Jur:* **p. offences,** contraventions *fpl*; **p. larceny,** vol *m* simple; (*c*) *Com:* **p. cash,** petite caisse; (*d*) **p.(-minded),** mesquin. **2.** *Navy:* **p. officer,** officier marinier; sous-officier *m*, *pl.* sous-officiers; gradé *m*; **chief p.-officer,** (i) maître principal; (ii) premier maître; (iii) maître.

petty-mindedness [peti'maindidnis] *n.* petitesse *f* (d'esprit); mesquinerie *f.*

petulance ['petjuləns] *n.* irritabilité *f*; **an outburst of p.,** un accès de mauvaise humeur.

petulant ['petjulənt] *a.* irritable; susceptible. **-ly** *adv.* avec irritation; d'un ton irrité; avec humeur.

petunia [pi'tjuːniə] *n. Bot:* pétunia *m.*

pew [pjuː] *n.* banc *m* d'église; *F:* **take a p.!** assieds-toi!

pewter [ˈpjuːtər] *n.* étain *m*; **p. (ware),** poterie *f* d'étain; vaisselle *f* d'étain.

phalanx [ˈfælæŋks] *n.* **1.** (*pl. usu.* **phalanxes** [ˈfælæŋksiz]) *A.Mil:* phalange *f.* **2.** *Anat: Bot:* (*pl. usu.* **phalanges** [fæˈlændʒiːz]) phalange.

phallic [ˈfælik] *a.* phallique; **p. symbol,** emblème *m* phallique.

phallus [ˈfæləs] *n.* phallus *m*.

phantasm [ˈfæntæzm] *n.* (*a*) illusion *f*; (*b*) apparition *f*.

phantasmagoria [fæntæzmæˈgɔriə] *n.* fantasmagorie *f*.

phantasy [ˈfæntəsi] *n.* = FANTASY.

phantom [ˈfæntəm] *n.* fantôme *m*, spectre *m*; **p. ship,** vaisseau *m* fantôme; *Tp: Tel:* **p. circuit,** circuit *m* fantôme; *Med:* **p. limb,** membre *f* fantôme.

Pharaoh [ˈfɛərou] *n. A.Hist:* pharaon *m*.

pharisee [ˈfærisiː] *n.* pharisien *m*.

pharmaceutical [fɑːməˈsjuːtikl] *a.* pharmaceutique.

pharmacist [ˈfɑːməsist] *n.* pharmacien, -ienne.

pharmacological [fɑːməkəˈlɔdʒikl] *a.* pharmacologique.

pharmacologist [fɑːməˈkɔlədʒist] *n.* pharmacologiste *mf*, pharmacologue *mf*.

pharmacology [fɑːməˈkɔlədʒi] *n.* pharmacologie *f*.

pharmacopoeia [fɑːməkouˈpiːə] *n.* (*a*) pharmacopée *f*; (*b*) (*collection of drugs*) pharmacie *f*.

pharmacy [ˈfɑːməsi] *n.* (*a*) pharmacie *f*; pharmaceutique *f*; (*b*) (*shop*) pharmacie.

pharyngitis [færinˈdʒaitis] *n. Med:* pharyngite *f*.

pharynx [ˈfæriŋks] *n. Anat:* pharynx *m*.

phase[1] [feiz] *n.* **1.** phase *f* (d'un phénomène, d'un processus, etc.); **initial, final, p.,** phase initiale, finale; **to enter upon a new p.,** entrer dans une nouvelle phase. **2.** (*a*) *Ph: Mec:* **in p.,** en phase; **out of p.,** hors de phase; déphasé, décalé; (*b*) *El:* **single-p., two-p., three-p., current,** courant monophasé, diphasé, triphasé.

phase[2] *v.tr.* **1.** faire (qch.) progressivement; développer (un projet) en phases successives; échelonner (un programme de fabrication, etc.). **2.** *El: etc:* mettre en phases; caler en phase. **phased** *a.* **1.** par phases, par stades; progressif; échelonné; (évacuation) par échelons, par étapes. **2.** *El:* phasé; (lumière) cohérente. **phase in** *v.tr.* adopter, introduire, progressivement (de nouvelles méthodes, etc.); mettre en place progressivement (de nouvelles installations, etc.). **phase out** *v.tr.* éliminer progressivement (de vieilles méthodes, de vieux équipements, etc.). **phasing** *n.* **1.** exécution par phases, par stades, progressive (de qch.); échelonnement (d'un programme de fabrication, etc.); **p. in,** adoption, introduction, progressive (de nouvelles méthodes, etc.); mise en place progressive (de nouvelles installations, etc.); **p. out,** élimination progressive (de vieilles méthodes, de vieux équipements, etc.). **2.** *El: etc:* mise *f* en phase; calage *m* en phase.

pheasant [ˈfez(ə)nt] *n.* (*a*) faisan *m*; **cock p.,** (coq *m*) faisan; **hen p.,** (poule) faisane (*f*); **young p., p. poult,** faisandeau *m*; (*b*) **golden p.,** faisan doré; (*c*) **p. shoot,** faisanderie *f*; **p. shooting,** chasse *f* au faisan.

phenobarbitone [fiːnouˈbɑːbitoun] *n. Pharm:* phénobarbital *m*.

phenol [ˈfiːnɔl] *n. Ch:* phénol *m*; acide *m* phénique.

phenomenal [fiˈnɔmin(ə)l] *a.* **1.** *Phil:* phénoménal, -aux. **2.** phénoménal, prodigieux. **-ally** *adv.* phénoménalement, prodigieusement.

phenomenon, *pl.* **-mena** [fiˈnɔminən, -minə] *n.* phénomène *m*.

phew [fjuː] *int.* **1.** pffft! pouf! **2.** (*disgust*) pouah!

phial [ˈfaiəl] *n.* fiole *f*, flacon *m*, ampoule *f*.

philander [fiˈlændər] *v.i. O:* flirter.

philanderer [fiˈlændərər] *n.* flirteur *m*; coureur *m* de jupons.

philanthropic [filənˈθrɔpik] *a.* philanthropique; (*pers.*) philanthrope.

philanthropist [fiˈlænθrəpist] *n.* philanthrope *mf*.

philanthropy [fiˈlænθrəpi] *n.* philanthropie *f*.

philatelic [filəˈtelik] *a.* philatélique, philatéliste.

philatelist [fiˈlætəlist] *n.* philatéliste *mf*.

philately [fiˈlætəli] philatélie *f*, philatélisme *m*.

philharmonic [fil(h)əˈmɔnik] **1.** *a.* philharmonique. **2.** *n.* philharmonique *f*.

Philippine [ˈfilipiːn] *Geog:* **1.** *a.* philippin. **2.** *Pr.n.* **the Philippines,** les (îles) Philippines *fpl*.

Philistine [ˈfilistain] **1.** *n.pl. B:* **the Philistines,** les Philistins *mpl.* **2.** *a. & n. Art: Lit:* philistin (*m*).

philological [filəˈlɔdʒik(ə)l] *a.* philologique.

philologist [fiˈlɔlədʒist] *n.* philologue *mf*.

philology [fiˈlɔlədʒi] *n.* philologie *f*.

philosopher [fiˈlɔsəfər] *n.* (*a*) philosophe *mf*; (*b*) **the philosopher's stone,** la pierre philosophale.

philosophic(al) [filəˈsɔfik(l)] *a.* **1.** philosophique. **2.** (*of pers.*) philosophe, calme, modéré. **-ally** *adv.* philosophiquement; en philosophe.

philosophize [fiˈlɔsəfaiz] *v.i.* philosopher.

philosophy [fiˈlɔsəfi] *n.* (*a*) philosophie *f*; **moral p.,** philosophie morale; **natural p.,** sciences *fpl* de la nature; (*b*) **a personal p.,** une philosophie personnelle; **one's own p. about sth.,** sa conception personnelle d'une chose; (*c*) **with p.,** (supporter des malheurs) avec philosophie, en philosophe.

philtre, *NAm:* **philter** [ˈfiltər] *n.* philtre *m*.

phiz [fiz], **phizog** [ˈfizɔg] *n. F:* visage *m*, binette *f*.

phlebitis [fliˈbaitis] *n. Med:* phlébite *f*.

phlegm [flem] *n.* **1.** flegme *m*; pituite (bronchiale); **to cough up p.,** tousser gras. **2.** flegme, calme *m*.

phlegmatic [flegˈmætik] *a.* flegmatique. **-ally** *adv.* flegmatiquement.

phlox [flɔks] *n. Bot:* phlox *m*.

phobia [ˈfoubiə] *n.* phobie *f*.

phobic [ˈfoubik] *a. & n. Med:* phobique (*mf*).

Phoenician [fiˈniːʃ(ə)n] *A. Geog:* **1.** *a.* phénicien. **2.** *n.* (*a*) Phénicien, -ienne; (*b*) *Ling:* le phénicien.

phoenix [ˈfiːniks] *n. Myth:* phénix *m*.

phone[1] [foun] *n. Ling:* phonème *m*.

phone[2] *n. F:* téléphone *m*; **to be on the p.,** (i) être au téléphone; (ii) être abonné au téléphone; **p. call,** coup *m* de téléphone; **to speak to s.o. on the p.,** parler à qn au téléphone; **p. book,** annuaire *m* (du téléphone); **p. box,** cabine *f* téléphonique; *W.Tel: T.V:* **p.-in (programme),** programme *m* à ligne ouverte.

phone[3] *v.tr. & i.* **to p. s.o.,** téléphoner à qn; appeler qn au téléphone; donner un coup de téléphone à qn; **to p. a piece of news,** téléphoner une nouvelle.

phoneme [ˈfouniːm] *n. Ling:* phonème *m*.

phonetic [fəˈnetik] *a.* phonétique; **p. alphabet,** alphabet *m* phonétique. **-ally** *adv.* phonétiquement.

phonetician [founəˈtiʃ(ə)n] *n.* phonéticien, -ienne; phonétiste *mf*.

phonetics [fəˈnetiks] *n.pl.* phonétique *f*.

phoney [ˈfouni] *F:* **1.** *a.* **(phonier, phoniest)** faux, *f.* fausse; factice; (*of story, etc.*) bidon; **he's p.,** il est faux comme un jeton. **2.** *n.* imposteur *m*; fumiste *m*.

phonic [ˈfɔnik, ˈfounik] *a.* phonique.

phonograph [ˈfounəgræf] *n. NAm:* phonographe *m*.

phonology [fəˈnɔlədʒi] *n.* phonologie *f*; phonétique *f* historique.

phony [ˈfouni] *a. & n.* = PHONEY.

phooey [ˈfuːi] *int.* peuh!

phosgene [ˈfɔzdʒiːn] *n. Ch:* phosgène *m*.

phosphate[1] [ˈfɔsfeit] *n. Ch:* phosphate *m*; **p. of lime, calcium p.,** phosphate de chaux; **p. mine, works,** phosphaterie *f*.

phosphate² *v.tr. Agr: Metalw:* phosphater.
phosphoresce [fɔsfə'res] *v.i.* être phosphorescent; luire par phosphorescence.
phosphorescence [fɔsfə'resəns] *n.* phosphorescence *f.*
phosphorescent [fɔsfə'resənt] *a.* phosphorescent.
phosphoric [fɔs'fɔrik] *a. Ch:* phosphorique.
phosphorous ['fɔsfərəs] *a.* phosphoreux.
phosphorus ['fɔsfərəs] *n. Ch:* phosphore *m.*
photo ['foutou] *n. F:* photo *f*; *Sp:* **p. finish,** photo-finish *f inv.*
photocopier ['foutoukɔpiər] *n.* photocopieur *m.*
photocopy¹ ['foutoukɔpi] *n.* photocopie *f.*
photocopy² *v.tr.* photocopier.
photoelectric [foutoui'lektrik] *a.* photoélectrique; **p. cell,** cellule *f* photoélectrique.
photoengraving [foutouin'greiviŋ] *n.* photogravure *f.*
photogenic [foutou'dzenik] *a.* photogénique.
photograph¹ ['foutəgræf] *n.* photographie *f*; **to take s.o.'s p.,** prendre une photographie de qn; **he had his p. taken,** il s'est fait photographier.
photograph² *v.tr.* **1.** photographier; prendre une photographie de (qn, qch.). **2.** (*with passive force*) (*of pers.*) **to p. well,** être photogénique.
photographer [fə'tɔgrəfər] *n.* photographe *mf*; *Journ:* **press p.,** reporter *m* photographe, photographe de presse.
photographic [foutə'græfik] *a.* (procédé, papier, description, etc.) photographique. **-ally** *adv.* photographiquement.
photography [fə'tɔgrəfi] *n.* photographie *f*; **aerial p.,** photographie aérienne; **colour p.,** photographie en couleurs.
photogravure [foutougrə'vjuər] *n.* photogravure *f.*
photolithography [foutouli'θɔgrəfi] *n.* photolithographie *f.*
photometer [fou'tɔmitər] *n. Ph:* photomètre *m.*
photometry [fou'tɔmitri] *n. Ph:* photométrie *f.*
photon ['foutɔn] *n. Opt: Meas:* photon *m.*
photosensitive [foutou'sensitiv] *a.* photosensible.
photostat¹ ['foutoustæt] *n.* photostat *m.*
photostat² *v.tr. & i.* faire des photostats.
photosynthesis [foutou'sinθisis] *n.* photosynthèse *f.*
phototropism [foutou'trɔpizm] *n. Nat.Hist:* phototropisme *m.*
phrase¹ [freiz] *n.* **1.** (*a*) locution *f*, expression *f*; tournure *f* de phrase; **p. book,** recueil *m* de locutions, d'idiotismes; (*b*) *Gram:* locution (adverbiale, etc.); membre *m* de phrase. **2.** *Mus:* phrase.
phrase² *v.tr.* **1.** exprimer (sa pensée, etc.); donner un tour à (sa pensée); **that is how he phrased it,** voilà comment il s'est exprimé; voilà l'expression qu'il a employée. **2.** *Mus:* phraser. **phrasing** *n. Mus:* phrasé *m.*
phraseology [freizi'ɔlədʒi] *n.* phraséologie *f.*
phrenology [fre'nɔlədʒi] *n.* phrénologie *f.*
phthisis ['θaisis] *n. Med:* phtisie *f.*
phut [fʌt] *F:* **1.** *n.* bruit sourd (de deux objets qui se heurtent, etc.). **2.** *adv. F:* (*of business, engine, etc.*) **to go p.,** claquer; (*of rope, etc.*) se casser; **the light went p.,** nous avons eu une panne d'électricité.
phylloxera [filɔk'siərə] *n. Ent: Vit:* phylloxéra *m.*
phylum, *pl.* **-la** ['failəm, -lə] *n. Nat.Hist:* phylum *m.*
physic ['fizik] *n. O:* médecine *f*, médicament *m.*
physical ['fizik(ə)l] *a.* physique. **1. p. body,** corps matériel; **p. impossibility,** impossibilité physique; **p. geography,** géographie physique; **p. features,** topographie *f.* **2. p. sciences,** sciences *fpl* physiques; **p. chemistry,** chimie *f* physique; **p. property,** propriété *f* physique. **3.** (*a*) *Med:* (*of symptoms*) somatique; (*b*) **p. strength,** force *f* physique; **p. fitness,** bonne santé; aptitude *f* physique; **p. education,** culture *f*, éducation *f*, physique; **p. exercises, training,** *F:* **jerks,** exercices physiques, d'assouplissement. **-ally** *adv.* physiquement; matériellement; **p. fit,** en bonne santé.
physician [fi'ziʃ(ə)n] *n.* médecin *m.*
physicist ['fizisist] *n.* physicien, -ienne.
physics ['fiziks] *n.pl.* (*usu. with sg. const.*) la physique; **nuclear p.,** physique nucléaire.
physiognomy [fizi'ɔnəmi] *n.* **1.** physionomie *f.* **2.** physiognomonie *f.*
physiological [fiziə'lɔdʒik(ə)l] *a.* physiologique. **-ally** *adv.* physiologiquement.
physiologist [fizi'ɔlədʒist] *n.* physiologiste *mf*, physiologue *mf.*
physiology [fizi'ɔlədʒi] *n.* physiologie *f*; **plant p.,** physiologie végétale.
physiotherapist [fiziou'θerəpist] *n.* physiothérapiste *mf*, physiothérapeute *mf.*
physiotherapy [fiziou'θerəpi] *n.* physiothérapie *f.*
physique [fi'ziːk] *n.* (*a*) physique *m* (de qn); structure *f* du corps; **fine p.,** beau physique; **he hasn't the p. for it,** il manque les aptitudes physiques à faire cela; (*b*) plastique *f* (d'une actrice, d'une danseuse).
pi [pai] *n. Gr.Alph:* pi *m.*
piaffe [pi'æf] *n. Equit:* piaffé *m.*
pianissimo [piə'nisimou] *adv. & n.* pianissimo (*m*).
pianist ['piənist] *n.* pianiste *mf.*
piano¹ [pi'ɑːnou] *adv. & n.* piano *m*; doucement.
piano² [pi'ænou], **pianoforte** [piænou'fɔːrti] *n.* piano *m*; **grand p.,** piano à queue; **upright p.,** piano droit; **to play the p.,** jouer du piano; **sonata for p. and violin,** sonate *f* pour piano et violon; **p. key,** touche *f* de piano; **p. stool,** tabouret *m* de piano.
piastre [pi'æstər] *n. Num:* piastre *f.*
piazza [pi'ætsɑː] *n.* (*a*) (*esp. in Italy*) place (publique); (*b*) *NAm:* véranda *f*; terrasse *f.*
pica ['paikə] *n. Typ:* pica *m*, cicéro *m*, corps *m* 12.
picador ['pikədɔr] *n.* picador *m.*
Picardy ['pikədi] *Pr.n. Geog:* Picardie *f.*
picaresque [pikə'resk] *a.* (roman) picaresque.
piccalilli [pikə'lili] *n. Comest:* pickles *mpl* à la moutarde.
piccaninny [pikə'nini] *n. F:* négrillon, -onne.
piccolo ['pikəlou] *n. Mus:* piccolo *m.*
pick¹ [pik] *n.* (*a*) pic *m*, pioche *f*; **miner's p.,** pic à main; **p. and shovel man,** terrassier *m*; (*b*) **lobster p.,** fourchette *f* à homard.
pick² *n.* choix *m*, élite *f*; **the p. of the bunch,** le dessus du panier; *F:* le gratin (du gratin); **take your p.,** choisissez.
pick³ *v.tr.* **1.** (*a*) piocher (la terre, etc.); (*b*) **to p. a hole in sth.,** faire un trou dans qch., à qch. (avec une pioche, ses ongles, etc.); *F:* **to p. holes in sth.,** critiquer, trouver à redire à, qch.; chercher la petite bête; (*c*) *F:* **to p. on s.o.,** chercher querelle à qn. **2.** (*a*) **to p. one's nose, one's teeth,** se curer le nez, les dents; **to p. a spot,** gratter un bouton (du bout de l'ongle); (*b*) *NAm:* **to p. a guitar,** pincer de la guitare. **3.** épailler, échardonner (de la laine); époutier (un tissu); démêler (l'étoupe); **to p. a bone,** (i) ôter, enlever, la chair d'un os; (ii) ronger un os; *F:* **to have a bone to p. with s.o.,** avoir un compte à régler avec qn. **4.** (*of birds*) picoter, becqueter (le blé, etc.); *F:* (*of pers.*) **to p. at one's food,** manger du bout des dents. **5.** (*a*) choisir; sélectionner; **(hand-)picked men,** hommes *mpl* d'élite; **to p. one's words,** choisir ses mots; **to p. the winners,** repérer les gagnants; **to p. and choose,** se montrer difficile; faire le, la, difficile; (*b*) trier (du minerai, etc.). **6.** cueillir (des fleurs, des fruits, etc.). **7.** (*a*) **to p. s.o.'s pocket,** prendre, voler, qch. dans la poche de qn; (*b*) crocheter (une serrure); **to p. s.o.'s brains,** exploiter l'intelligence, les connaissances, de qn. **8.** mettre (qch.) en pièces; défaire, détisser, effi-

locher (des chiffons etc.). **picking** *n.* **1.** (*a*) échardonnage *m*, épaillage *m* (de la laine, etc.); époutiage *m* (des étoffes); (*b*) triage *m* (du minerai, etc.); **hand p.,** triage à la main; (*c*) cueillette *f*, cueillage *m* (de fruits, de fleurs, etc.); **p. season,** cueillette; (*d*) crochetage *m* (d'une serrure); (*e*) démêlage *m*, démêlement *m* (de l'étoupe). **2. pickings,** (i) épluchures *fpl*; rognures *fpl*; (ii) bénéfices *mpl*, gratte *f*. **pick off** *v.tr.* (*a*) enlever, ôter (les fleurs mortes d'une plante, etc.); (*b*) descendre, abattre un à un (des soldat ennemis, etc.). **pick out** *v.tr.* (*a*) extirper, enlever (qch.); ôter (qch.) (avec les doigts, etc.); (*b*) désigner, choisir (qch.); **he picked out the best peaches,** il a choisi les meilleures pêches; (*in identification parade*) **to p. out a criminal,** identifier un criminel; **can you p. out the tune?** pouvez-vous distinguer la mélodie? (*c*) **picked out in gold,** à filets d'or. **pick over** *v.tr.* trier (des fruits, etc.). **pick up 1.** *v.tr.* (*a*) prendre; ramasser, relever (qch. par terre); décrocher (le téléphone); *Knit:* relever (une maille); *Nau:* recueillir (des naufragés); **to p. up the odd pound or two,** gagner un peu d'argent; **to p. up a child,** (i) prendre un enfant dans les bras; (ii) relever un enfant (qui est tombé); **to p. up the pieces,** repartir à zéro; **I'll p. you up at the station,** je viendrai vous chercher à la gare; **the train stops to p. up passengers,** le train s'arrête pour prendre des voyageurs; (*b*) apprendre (un tour, un fait, etc.); recueillir (des nouvelles, des informations); s'initier à (une langue); (*c*) trouver, retrouver, relever (une erreur); **to p. (sth.) up again,** reprendre (le fil de la conversation, etc.); **we soon picked up the road again,** nous avons vite retrouvé notre chemin; **to p. sth. up cheap,** acheter qch. bon marché; **she's good at picking up bargains,** elle a du flair pour les bonnes affaires; (*d*) *F:* faire la connaissance de (qn); ramasser (qn); (*of prostitute*) raccrocher (un client); (*e*) *El:* prendre, capter (le courant); accrocher (un poste); capter, recevoir (un message); (*of searchlight*) repérer (un avion); (*f*) **to p. s.o. up sharply,** reprendre qn vertement; (*g*) *Aut: etc:* **to p. up speed,** reprendre de la vitesse; **this engine picks up well,** ce moteur a de bonnes reprises; (*h*) (*of pers.*) **to p. up strength,** reprendre des forces; **that will p. you up,** voilà qui vous remettra. **2.** *v.i.* (*a*) (*of pers.*) retrouver la santé, ses forces; se rétablir; **business is picking up,** les affaires reprennent; **the weather looks like picking up,** le temps a l'air de s'arranger; (*b*) *Sp: etc:* **to p. up on s.o.,** gagner de l'avance sur qn; rattraper qn.

pick-a-back ['pikəbæk] **1.** *adv.* sur le dos; sur les épaules; **to ride p.-a-b. on s.o.,** monter à dos sur qn. **2.** *n.* **to give s.o. a p.-a-b.,** porter qn sur le dos.

pickaninny [pikə'nini] *n.* = PICCANINNY.

pickaxe¹ ['pikæks] *n. Tls:* pioche *f*, pic *m*.

pickaxe² *v.tr. & i.* piocher.

picker ['pikər] *n.* (*a*) éplucheur, -euse (de laine, etc.); démêleur, -euse (de coton, etc.); (*b*) cueilleur, -euse (de fleurs, de fruits, etc.).

picket¹ ['pikit] *n.* **1.** (*a*) piquet *m*; *Surv:* jalon *m*; (*b*) *Surv:* repère *m*; (*c*) pieu *m* (d'une clôture, etc.); **p. fence,** palis *m*, palissade *f*; (*d*) piquet d'attache (pour chevaux, etc.). **2.** (*a*) *Mil: etc:* (i) piquet (d'hommes); (ii) poste *m* de surveillance; **to be on p.,** être de piquet; (*b*) *Ind: etc:* (i) piquet (de grévistes); (ii) gréviste *m* en faction; **strike p., p. line,** piquet de grève. **picketing** *n.* constitution *f* de piquets de grève.

picket² *v.tr.* **(picketed) 1.** mettre (des chevaux) au(x) piquet(s); attacher (une chèvre). **2.** entourer (un terrain) de piquets, de pieux; palissader (un terrain). **3.** *Mil:* détacher (des soldats) en grand'garde. **4. to p. a factory,** mettre un piquet de grève aux portes d'une usine (pour en interdire l'accès).

pickle¹ [pikl] *n.* **1.** marinade *f*, saumure *f*. **2. pickles,** pickles *mpl*; conserves *fpl* au vinaigre; **mixed pickles,** variantes *fpl*. **3.** *F:* (*a*) **to be in a fine p.,** être dans de beaux draps, dans le pétrin; (*b*) enfant *mf* terrible; petit diable.

pickle² *v.tr.* mariner, saumurer; conserver (au vinaigre, à la saumure). **pickled** *a.* (*a*) mariné, saumuré; **p. cabbage,** chou *m* rouge au vinaigre; (*b*) *F:* (*of pers.*) ivre, gris. **pickling** *n.* marinage *m*, saumurage *m*; conservation *f* au vinaigre; **p. onions,** petits oignons.

picklock ['piklɔk] *n.* **1.** (*pers.*) crocheteur *m* (de serrures). **2.** (*key*) crochet *m*, rossignol *m*.

pick-me-up ['pikmiʌp] *n. F:* remontant *m*; **that's a good p.-me-up!** voilà qui vous remonte!

pickpocket ['pikpɔkit] *n.* voleur, -euse, à la tire; pickpocket *m*.

pickup ['pikʌp] *n.* **1.** ramassage *m*, ramassement *m* (de qch.); *Elcs: W.Tel:* captage *m* (des ondes, d'un signal). **2.** (*a*) *Rec:* lecteur *m* (phonographique); pick-up *m inv*; **p.-up arm,** bras *m* de pick-up; (*b*) *Elcs: etc:* capteur *m*, détecteur *m* (d'ondes, de vibrations). **3.** *Veh:* pick-up; camionnette *f* à ridelles basses, à plateau. **4.** *F:* partenaire *mf* de rencontre.

picky ['piki] *a. F:* difficile, délicat; maniaque.

picnic¹ ['piknik] *n.* (*a*) pique-nique *m*, *pl.* pique-niques; **p. basket,** panier garni (pour pique-niques); mallette *f* de camping; (*b*) **we'll take a p. (meal) with us,** nous emporterons un pique-nique; (*c*) *F:* **it was no p.,** cela n'a guère été une partie de plaisir.

picnic² *v.i.* **(picnicked)** pique-niquer; faire un pique-nique.

picknicker ['piknikər] *n.* pique-niqueur, -euse.

pics [piks] *n.pl. F:* cinéma *m*, ciné *m*.

Pict [pikt] *n. Ethn: Hist:* Picte *mf*.

Pictish ['piktiʃ] *a.* picte, pictique.

pictograph ['piktəgræf] *n.* pictographe *m*.

pictorial [pik'tɔːriəl] **1.** *a.* (*a*) (talent, etc.) pictural, -aux; (*b*) (écriture) en images; (représentation) par une image, par images; (*c*) (périodique, etc.) illustré; (*d*) graphique. **2.** *n.* périodique illustré; journal illustré. **-ally** *adv.* par images.

picture¹ ['piktjər] *n.* (*a*) tableau *m*, peinture *f*; **to paint a p.,** faire, peindre, un tableau; **p. rail,** rail *m*, moulure *f*, pour accrocher les tableaux; **p. dealer,** marchand *m* de tableaux; **p. gallery,** musée *m* de peinture; **p. hat,** chapeau *m* gainsborough; **she's a perfect p.,** elle est à peindre; *F:* **to be in the p.,** être au courant, au fait, à la page; **put me in the p.,** mets-moi au courant; **it doesn't come into the p.,** cela n'entre pas en ligne de compte; (*b*) (*in book, etc.*) image *f*; illustration *f*; **p. book,** livre *m* d'images, album *m*; **p. postcard,** carte postale illustrée; **p. puzzle,** rébus *m*; **p. writing,** pictographie *f*; *Cards:* **p. card,** figure *f*; *Jur:* **identikit p.,** portrait robot; (*c*) (i) image, portrait *m*; **he's the p. of health,** il respire la santé; (ii) **this book gives a more accurate p. of the general,** ce livre offre un portrait plus fidèle du général; **to get a mental p. of sth.,** se représenter qch.; (*d*) *Med:* **clinical p.,** facies *m*, tableau *m*, clinique; (*e*) *T.V:* image; (*f*) *Cin: O:* film *m*; **to go to the pictures,** aller au cinéma.

picture² *v.tr.* peindre, dépeindre, représenter (qn, qch.); (*b*) **to p. (to oneself),** s'imaginer, se figurer, se représenter (qch.).

picturesque [piktjə'resk] *a.* pittoresque; (expressions) qui font image. **-ly** *adv.* pittoresquement.

picturesqueness [piktjə'resknis] *n.* pittoresque *m*.

piddle ['pidl] *v.i. F:* faire pipi. **piddling** *a. F:* insignifiant; futile.

pidgin ['pidʒin] *n.* **1.** pidgin *m*; **p. (English, etc.)** = petit nègre. **2. that's my p.,** ça c'est mon affaire.

pie¹ [pai] *n.* (*a*) **(veal and ham, etc.) p.** = pâté *m* en croûte; **chicken p.** = croustade *f* de volaille; **cottage**

p., shepherd's p., hachis parmentier; **fish p.** = timbale *f* de poissons; **(apple, etc.) p.** = (i) tourte *f*, (ii) *esp. NAm:* tarte *f* (aux pommes); **custard p.** = tarte à la crème; *F:* **p. in the sky,** le miel de l'autre monde; (*b*) *F:* **as easy as p.,** simple comme bonjour.

pie² *n. Typ:* (composition tombée en) pâte (*f*); pâté *m.*

piebald ['paibɔːld] **1.** *a.* (*a*) (cheval, etc.) pie; (*b*) bigarré, disparate. **2.** *n.* (cheval) pie (*m*).

piece¹ [piːs] *n.* pièce *f.* **1.** (*a*) morceau *m* (de papier, de pain, etc.); bout *m* (de ruban, de ficelle, etc.); parcelle *f* (de terrain); tranche *f* (de gâteau); coupon *m* (de drap); **p. by p.,** pièce à pièce; (*b*) fragment *m*, éclat *m* (de verre, etc.); **to break sth. in, to, pieces,** briser qch.; mettre qch. en morceaux; **to fall to pieces,** tomber en morceaux; (*of house, etc.*) se délabrer; crouler; **my coat is falling to pieces,** mon manteau ne tient plus (ensemble); *F:* **to go (all) to pieces,** (i) (*of pers.*) perdre tout empire sur soi-même; (ii) *Sp:* (*of team, etc.*) s'effondrer; **to pick sth. to pieces,** mettre qch. en pièces, en miettes *fpl*; *F:* **to pick s.o. to pieces,** déchirer qn à belles dents; **to tear to pieces,** déchirer (qch.); mettre, réduire, (qch.) en pièces; déchirer (du papier) en morceaux; mettre (de l'étoffe) en lambeaux; déchirer (une proie) à belles dents; démolir (un argument); *F:* **they'll tear you to pieces,** vous allez vous faire écharper; *F:* **to pull s.o., a play, to pieces,** critiquer qn, une pièce, sévèrement. **2.** partie *f*, pièce (d'une machine, etc.); **to take a machine to pieces,** démonter une machine. **3.** *Com:* pièce (de drap, etc.); **to sell sth. by the p.,** vendre qch. à la pièce; *Tex:* **p. goods,** marchandises *fpl*, tissus *mpl*, à la pièce; **p. dyeing,** teinture *f* en pièces; *Ind:* **p. work, rate,** travail *m*, salaire *m*, à la tâche, à la pièce. **4. all in one p.,** tout d'une pièce; d'une seule pièce; *F:* (*of pers.*) **they are all of a p.,** ils sont tous du même acabit; *Metall:* **to cast cylinders in one p.,** couler des cylindres d'un seul jet, en bloc; **cast, pressed, made, in one p.,** monobloc *inv.* **5.** (*a*) **a p. of work,** un travail; un ouvrage; **a p. of my work,** un échantillon de mon travail; **p. out of a book,** passage *m* d'un livre; (*b*) **p. of bravery, of folly,** acte *m* de bravoure, de folie; **p. of good luck,** coup *m* de chance; (*c*) **what a p. of luck!** quelle chance! **a p. of advice,** un conseil; **a p. of carelessness,** une étourderie; **a p. of cruelty,** une cruauté; **a p. of (bad) news,** une (mauvaise) nouvelle; **a p. of luggage,** une valise; **a p. of furniture,** un meuble; **a p. of clothing,** un vêtement; *F:* **she's a pretty p.,** c'est un beau brin de fille. **6.** (*a*) (i) *Artil:* pièce (d'artillerie); (ii) **fowling p.,** fusil de chasse; (*b*) *Metall:* **punched, shaped, p.,** pièce estampée, profilée; (*c*) pièce (de monnaie); **five-pence p.,** pièce de cinq pence. **7.** (*a*) morceau *m* (de musique, de poésie); *Journ:* article *m*, papier *m*; **to say one's p.,** prononcer son discours; (*b*) instrument *m* de musique; **three-p. ensemble,** trio *m.* **8.** (*a*) (*backgammon*) dame *f*; (*dominoes*) domino *m*, dé *m*; *Draughts:* pion *m*; (*b*) *Chess:* **pieces and pawns,** pièces et pions.

piece² *v.tr.* **1.** rapiécer, raccommoder; mettre une pièce à (un habit, etc.). **2.** joindre, unir (**one thing to another,** une chose à une autre); **to p. together,** joindre, assembler (des cordages, etc.); coordonner (des faits, etc.). **3.** *Tex:* rattacher (les fils cassés).

piecemeal ['piːsmiːl] **1.** *adv.* par morceaux, pièce à pièce; peu à peu; **the collection was sold p.,** les pièces de la collection ont été vendues séparément. **2.** *a.* (*a*) fragmentaire; (*b*) (travail, etc.) fait pièce à pièce.

piecrust ['paikrʌst] *n.* croûte *f* de pâté (en croûte).

pied [paid] *a.* mi-parti; bigarré, panaché; *Lit:* **the P. Piper of Hamelin,** le Joueur de flûte d'Hamelin.

pied-à-terre [pjeda'tɛːr] *n.* pied-à-terre *m inv.*

piedish ['paidiʃ] *n.* (*a*) terrine *f* (pour pâtés à croûte); (*b*) tourtière *f.*

Piedmont ['piːdmɔnt] *Pr.n. Geog:* Piémont *m.*

pier [piər] *n.* **1.** (*a*) (*of stone*) jetée *f*, môle *m*, digue *f*; (*b*) (*on piles*) estacade *f*; **landing p.,** embarcadère *m*, débarcadère *m*; (*c*) **floating p.,** ponton *m*; (*d*) (*at seaside resort*) jetée. **2.** *Civ.E:* pilier *m* (de maçonnerie).

pierce [piəs] **1.** *v.tr.* (*a*) percer, transpercer (qch.); percer (un trou); **to have one's ears pierced,** se faire percer les oreilles; (*of light*) **to p. the darkness,** percer les ténèbres; **to p. the air with one's cries,** percer l'air de ses cris; (*b*) *Metall:* épingler (un moule, l'âme). **2.** *v.i.* **to p. through the enemy's lines,** pénétrer les lignes de l'ennemi. **piercing** *a.* (outil, regard, cri, etc.) aigu, perçant, pénétrant; (froid, vent) pénétrant.

pierhead ['piəhed] *n.* musoir *m.*

pierrot ['piərou] *n.m. Th:* pierrot.

piety ['paiəti] *n.* piété *f.*

piffle ['pifl] *n. F:* futilités *fpl*, bêtises *fpl*, niaiseries *fpl*; **to talk p.,** dire des futilités.

piffling ['pifliŋ] *a. F:* futile; (discours, etc) creux.

pig¹ [pig] *n.* **1.** (*a*) porc *m*, cochon *m*; pourceau *m*; *NAm:* cochonnet *m*, porcelet *m:* **suck(l)ing p.,** cochon de lait; **roast p.,** rôti *m* de porc; **p. farm,** porcherie *f*; *F:* **to buy a p. in a poke,** acheter chat en poche; **when pigs begin to fly,** à, dans, la semaine des quatre jeudis; **to eat like a p., to make a p. of oneself,** manger comme un goinfre; (*b*) **wild p.,** sanglier *m*; *NAm:* marcassin *m*, jeune sanglier; (*c*) (*pers.*) (i) *F:* goinfre *m*, glouton *m*; (ii) *F:* sale type *m*; vache *f*; (iii) *P:* agent *m* de police, flic *m*; **you dirty little p.!** petit cochon! **he's a greedy p.,** c'est un goinfre; **what a selfish p.!** quel égoïste! **2.** *Metall:* gueuse *f* (de fonte); saumon *m* (de plomb, d'étain, etc.); **p. iron,** fer *m* de première coulée; fonte brute, en gueuses.

pig² *v.i.* **(pigged) 1.** (*of sow*) mettre bas, cochonner. **2.** *F:* (*of pers.*) (*a*) manger comme un cochon; (*b*) **to p. it,** vivre comme un cochon.

pigeon ['pidʒin] *n.* **1.** *Orn:* pigeon *m*; (*a*) **fantail p.,** pigeon paon; **homing, racing, carrier, p.,** pigeon voyageur; **p. fancier,** colombophile *mf*; **p. loft,** colombier *m*, pigeonnier *m*; **p. post,** transport *m* de dépêches par pigeons voyageurs; *Sp:* **clay p.,** pigeon (d'argile); **clay p. shooting,** ball-trap *m*; (*b*) **wood p.,** (pigeon) ramier *m.* **2.** (= PIDGIN) **that's my p.,** ça c'est mon affaire.

pidgeon-chested [pidʒin'tʃestid] *a.* qui a la poitrine en saillie.

pigeonhole¹ ['pidʒinhoul] *n.* **1.** boulin *m* (de colombier). **2.** case *f*, casier *m* (de bureau, etc.).

pigeonhole² *v.tr.* (*a*) caser, classer (des papiers, etc.); (*b*) classer (une réclamation, etc.); (*c*) reléguer (qch.) dans sa mémoire.

pigeon-toed [pidʒin'toud] *a.* qui marche les pieds tournés en dedans.

piggery ['pigəri] *n.* porcherie *f.*

piggish ['pigiʃ] *a. F:* (*of pers.*) (*a*) sale, malpropre; (*b*) goinfre; (*c*) égoïste; désagréable.

piggy ['pigi] *F:* **1.** *n.* (*a*) cochonnet *m*, petit cochon; (*b*) **p. bank,** (cochon) tirelire (*f*). **2.** *a.* (*of pers.*) goinfre.

piggyback ['pigibæk] *adv. & n.* = PICK-A-BACK.

pigheaded [pig'hedid] *a.* obstiné, entêté. **-ly** *adv.* obstinément.

pigheadedness [pig'hedidnis] *n.* obstination *f*; entêtement *m.*

piglet, pigling ['piglit, -liŋ] *n.* cochonnet *m.*

pigment¹ ['pigmənt] *n.* **1.** *Art: Paint:* couleur *f*, colorant *m*, pigment *m.* **2.** *Physiol:* pigment; **p. cell,** cellule *f* pigmentaire.

pigment² *v.tr. & i.* (se) colorer; (se) pigmenter; **pigmented,** pigmenté.

pigmentation [pigmən'teiʃ(ə)n] *n.* pigmentation *f.*

pigmy ['pigmi] *n.* = PYGMY.
pigskin ['pigskin] *n. Leath:* peau *f* de porc, de truie; **p. purse,** bourse *f* en peau de porc.
pigsty ['pigstai] *n.* **1.** porcherie *f.* **2.** *F:* (sale) taudis *m*, porcherie.
pigswill ['pigswil] *n.* pâtée *f* pour les porcs; eaux grasses (de cuisine).
pigtail ['pigteil] *n.* natte *f* (de cheveux).
pigwash ['pigwɔʃ] *n.* = PIGSWILL.
pike[1] [paik] *n.* **1.** *A.Arms:* pique *f*; **p. bearer,** piquier *m.* **2.** *Geog:* (*in the Lake District*) pic (de montagne).
pike[2] *n. Ich:* brochet *m.*
pike[3] *n. NAm:* (*a*) barrière *f* de péage; (*b*) péage *m*; (*c*) route *f* à péage.
pikestaff ['paikstɑːf] *n.* **1.** bois *m*, hampe *f*, de pique. **2.** bâton *m* à pointe de fer.
pilaf(f) ['piːlæf] *n. Cu:* pilaf *m*, pilau *m*, pilaw *m.*
pilaster [pi'læstər] *n. Arch:* pilastre *m.*
Pilate ['pailət] *Pr.n.m.* **Pontius P.,** Ponce Pilate.
pilau, pilaw ['piːlau, -lou, -lɔː] *n.* = PILAF(F).
pilchard ['piltʃəd] *n. Ich:* pilchard *m.*
pile[1] [pail] *n. Civ.E: Const:* pieu *m*, pilot *m*; **to drive piles,** enfoncer des pieux, piloter; **built on piles,** bâti sur pilotis; **p. driver,** (i) *Civ.E:* sonnette *f*; (ii) *F:* coup *m* d'assommoir; *Fb:* shot vigoureux; *Prehist:* **p. dwelling,** habitation *f* lacustre.
pile[2] *v.tr. Civ.E: Const:* (*a*) soutenir (un édifice) au moyen de pilots; (*b*) piloter (un terrain).
pile[3] *n.* **1.** (*a*) (*heap*) tas *m* (de bois, de pierres, etc.); monceau *m* (d'or, de détritus, etc.); amas *m*, amoncellement *m* (d'objets, de marchandises, etc.); pile *f* d'assiettes, de linge, etc.); **funeral p.,** bûcher *m* (funéraire); **to put in(to) a p., to make a p.,** mettre en tas, empiler; (*b*) *Mil:* faisceau *m* (d'armes); (*c*) *F:* fortune *f*, magot *m.* **2.** (*a*) *El:* **(electric) p.,** pile (électrique); (*b*) *Atom.Ph:* **(atomic) p.,** pile, réacteur *m* (atomique). **3.** (*a*) masse *f* (d'un édifice); (*b*) édifice.
pile[4] *v.tr.* (*a*) **to p. (up),** (i) entasser, amonceler (de la terre, etc.); mettre (des objets) en tas; (ii) empiler (du bois, des livres, etc.), mettre (des objets) en pile; **to p. up money,** amasser de l'argent; **ship piled up on the rocks,** navire échoué sur les rochers; **to p. on the agony,** dramatiser (qch.); *F:* **to p. it on,** exagérer, charrier; (*b*) *Mil:* **to p. arms,** former les faisceaux; (*c*) *F:* **to p. up one's plane, a car,** bousiller son appareil, une voiture; (*d*) **to p. a table with dishes,** charger une table de plats. **2.** *v.i.* (*a*) **to p. up,** s'amonceler, s'entasser, s'empiler; (*of cars*) caramboler; **the clouds are piling up,** les nuages s'amoncellent; (*b*) **seven of them piled into the car,** sept d'entre eux se sont empilés dans la voiture; **fifteen piled out of the compartment,** ils sont descendus quinze du compartiment. **piled** *a.* **p. (up),** entassé; en tas, en pile.
pile[5] *n.* **1.** poil *m* (de chameau, etc.); laine *f* (de mouton). **2.** *Tex:* poil (d'un tapis, etc.); **p. fabrics,** tissus *mpl* à poil.
piles [pailz] *n.pl. Med: F:* hémorroïdes *fpl.*
pile-up ['pailʌp] *n. Aut: F:* carambolage *m*, emboutissage *m*; téléscopage *m* en série.
pilfer ['pilfər] *v.tr. & i.* chaparder, marauder **(sth. from s.o.,** qch. à qn). **pilfering** *n.* = PILFERAGE.
pilferage ['pilfəridʒ] *n.* petits vols; larcins *mpl.*
pilferer ['pilfərər] *n.* chapardeur, -euse.
pilgrim ['pilgrim] *n.* **1.** pèlerin, -ine. **2.** *Hist:* **the P. Fathers,** les (pères) Pèlerins.
pilgrimage ['pilgrimidʒ] *n.* pèlerinage *m*; **to go on (a) p.,** aller en pèlerinage; faire un pèlerinage.
pill [pil] *Pharm:* pilule *f*; *F:* **the p.,** la pilule; **she's on the p.,** elle prend la pilule; **(sugar coated) p.,** dragée *f*; **sleeping p.,** cachet *m* pour dormir; somnifère *m*; **to swallow the (bitter) p.,** avaler la pilule; **to sugar the p.,** dorer la pilule.
pillage[1] ['pilidʒ] *n.* pillage *m.*
pillage[2] **1.** *v.tr.* piller, saccager; mettre (une ville) au pillage, à sac. **2.** *v.i.* se livrer au pillage; piller.
pillager ['pilidʒər] *n.* pilleur, -euse; pillard, -arde.
pillar ['pilər] *n.* **1.** (*a*) pilier *m*, colonne *f*; (*of pers.*) **a p. of the Church,** un pilier, une colonne, de l'Église; **to drive s.o. from p. to post,** envoyer qn de droite à gauche, d'un endroit à l'autre; (*b*) *Min:* pillier, stappe *m*; **p. and stall system,** méthode *f* de piliers et galeries; (*c*) *Furn:* pied central (d'une table, d'un guéridon); *Surv: etc:* borne *f*, colonne (de démarcation, de signalisation, etc.); (*in street*) **p. box,** boîte *f* aux lettres; **p. box red** = rouge-drapeau *m*; (*d*) **p. of fire, of smoke,** colonne de feu, de fumée. **2.** (*a*) *Mec.E:* colonne, montant *m* (d'une machine-outil); (*small and round*) chandelle *f*; (*b*) *Aut:* **door p.,** montant de porte.
pillared ['piləd] *a.* à piliers, à colonnes.
pillbox ['pilbɔks] *n.* **1.** boîte *f* à pilules, pilulier *m.* **2.** *Cost:* **p. (hat),** petit chapeau rond sans bord. **3.** *Mil:* blockhaus *m.*
pillion ['piljən] *n.* (*on motor cycle*) **p. (seat),** siège *m* arrière; selle tandem; tan-sad *m*, *pl.* tan-sads; **to ride p.,** monter derrière; **p. rider, passenger,** passager, -ère (de derrière).
pillory[1] ['piləri] *n.* pilori *m.*
pillory[2] *v.tr.* **(pilloried)** dénoncer (un abus).
pillow[1] ['pilou] *n.* (*a*) oreiller *m*; **p. fight,** bataille *f* d'oreillers, de polochon(s); (*b*) *Lacem:* **(lace) p.,** carreau *m*, coussin *m* (pour dentelle); oreiller (pour dentelle aux fuseaux).
pillow[2] *v.tr.* **to p. one's head on one's arms,** reposer sa tête sur ses bras; se faire un oreiller de ses bras.
pillowcase, pillowslip [piloukeis, -slip] *n.* taie *f* d'oreiller.
pilot[1] ['pailət] *n.* **1.** (*a*) *Nau:* pilote *m*; **p. waters,** zone *f* de pilotage; **p. boat, cutter,** bateau-pilote *m*, *pl.* bateaux-pilotes; **p. flag,** pavillon *m* de, du, pilote; (*b*) *Av:* **(air, aircraft) p.,** pilote (aviateur, d'avion); **airline p.,** pilote de ligne; **test p.,** pilote d'essais; *Mil.Av:* **fighter p.,** pilote de chasse; **p. officer,** sous-lieutenant *m* (aviateur); (*c*) guide *m*, mentor *m.* **2.** *Av: etc:* **automatic p.,** pilote automatique; *Rail:* **p. (engine),** locomotive *f* estafette; locomotive pilote. **3.** (*a*) *Mec.E:* guide *m*; axe-guide *m*, *pl.* axes-guides; (*b*) **p. light, flame, jet, burner,** veilleuse *f* (de bec de gaz, etc.); *El: etc:* **p. light, lamp,** lampe *f* témoin, lampe pilote; témoin *m* de contrôle; *Av: etc:* **p. parachute,** parachute extracteur; *Meteor:* **p. balloon,** ballon-sonde *m*, *pl.* ballons-sondes; (*c*) **p. factory,** usine *f* pilote; *Ind: Com:* **p. run, series,** présérie *f*; *Cin: T.V:* **p. film,** film *m* d'essai; (*d*) **p. scheme,** projet *m* d'essai.
pilot[2] *v.tr.* **1.** (*a*) piloter (un navire, un avion, une auto de course, etc.); (*b*) mener, conduire (qn à travers des obstacles, etc.). **2.** *Mec.E: etc:* guider (la mèche).
pilothouse ['pailəthaus] *n.* *Nau:* (kiosque *m* de) timonerie (*f*).
pimento [pi'mentou] *n.* **1.** *Bot:* piment *m.* **2.** *Cu:* (i) poivron; (ii) piment.
pimp[1] [pimp] *n.* souteneur *m*; proxénète *m*; *P:* maquereau *m.*
pimp[2] *v.i.* exercer le métier de proxénète.
pimpernel ['pimpənel] *n. Bot:* **scarlet p.,** mouron *m* rouge.
pimple ['pimp(ə)l] *n.* bouton *m*, (sur la peau); **come out in pimples,** boutonner, bourgeonner.
pimply ['pimpli] *a.* boutonneux, couvert de boutons.
pin[1] [pin] *n.* **1.** (*a*) épingle *f*; **safety p.,** épingle de nourrice; **p. money,** somme prévue pour les dépenses personnelles d'une femme; argent de poche (d'une femme); **you could have heard a p. drop,** on aurait

entendu voler une mouche; **for two pins I'd punch his face,** pour un rien je lui casserais la figure; (*b*) **pins and needles,** fourmillements *mpl*; (*c*) *Hairdr:* épingle (à cheveux); (*d*) **drawing p.,** punaise *f*. **2.** (*a*) *Mec.E:* axe *m* (de fixation, etc.); goupille *f*, clavette *f*; **split p.,** goupille fendue; (*b*) pivot *m* (d'une grue, etc.); axe, verge *f* (de girouette); (*c*) broche *f* (de clef, de serrure); gond *m* (de penture, de paumelle); tourillon *m* (de porte); *El:* broche (de fiche mâle); **firing p.,** percuteur *m* (d'une arme à feu); (*d*) *Surg:* broche, clou *m* (pour fracture). **3.** *Cu:* **rolling p.,** rouleau *m* à pâtisserie, à pâte. **4.** *Golf:* drapeau *m* de trou. **5.** (*a*) (*at ninepins*) quille *f*; **p. table,** billard chinois, japonais; (*b*) *O:* **p. leg,** jambe *f* de bois, pilon *m*; (*c*) *F:* **pins,** jambes; quilles.

pin² *v.tr.* **(pinned) 1.** (*a*) épingler; attacher, assujettir, fixer, avec une épingle, des épingles; **to p. a map to, on, the wall,** fixer une carte au mur (avec des punaises); **to p. up one's hair, a hem,** épingler ses cheveux, rabattre un ourlet, avec des épingles; (*b*) *Mec.E: etc:* cheviller, goupiller; mettre une goupille à (qch.); (*with a cotter*) claveter. **2.** fixer, clouer; **to p. s.o. against a wall,** clouer, plaquer, qn contre un mur; **to p. s.o.'s arms to his sides,** coller, plaquer, les bras de qn au corps; **to be pinned (down) under a fallen tree,** se trouver pris, coincé, sous un arbre déraciné; *Mil:* **to p. down the enemy,** clouer l'ennemi (au sol); **to p. s.o. down to do sth.,** obliger, contraindre, qn à faire qch.; **without pinning himself down to anything,** sans s'engager à rien; sans rien préciser; **to p. sth. on s.o.,** rendre qn responsable de qch.; **to p. one's hopes on s.o., sth.,** mettre tous ses espoirs en qn, dans qch. **3.** étayer, étançonner (un mur, etc.).

pinafore ['pinəfɔːr] *n.* **1.** tablier *m* (d'enfant, etc.). **2. p. dress,** robe *f* à bretelles, robe chasuble.

pinball ['pinbɔːl] *n.* billard *m* électrique; flipper *m*; **p. machine, game, table,** billard chinois, japonais.

pincers ['pinsəz] *n.pl.* **1.** *Tls:* **(pair of) p.,** pince *f*, tenaille(s) *f*(*pl*). **2.** *Nat.Hist:* pince (de crustacé, d'insecte). **3.** *Mil:* **pincer(s) movement,** mouvement *m*, manœuvre *f*, en tenailles.

pinch¹ [pintʃ] *n.* **1.** (*a*) action *f* de pincer; pincement *m*, pinçure *f*, pinçade *f*; **to give s.o. a p.,** pincer qn; (*b*) **the p. of hunger,** la morsure de la faim; *F:* **to feel the p.,** tirer le diable par la queue; (*c*) **at a p.,** à la rigueur. **2.** pincée *f* (de sel, etc.); prise *f* (de tabac).

pinch² *v.tr.* **1.** (*nip*) pincer (qn, la joue de qn, etc.); **to p. sth. off,** enlever qch. en le pinçant (avec les ongles, etc.); *Hort:* **to p. off a bud,** épincer un bourgeon; **shoe that pinches,** chaussure qui blesse, qui serre; **that's where the shoe pinches,** c'est là que le bât (le) blesse. **2.** (*restrict*) serrer, gêner (qn); **to p. and scrape,** faire de petites économies. **3.** *F:* (*a*) chiper, faucher (qch.) **(from s.o.,** à qn); **I've had my purse pinched,** on m'a piqué mon porte-monnaie; (*b*) arrêter, pincer, choper (un voleur, etc.); **to get pinched,** se faire pincer, épingler. **pinched** *a.* **1.** (*of face, etc.*) tiré, hâve; **to be p. with hunger,** être tenaillé par la faim. **2.** étroit; **to be (a bit) p. for money, time, etc.,** être à court d'argent, de temps, etc.

pinchbeck ['pintʃbek] **1.** *n.* toc *m*. **2.** *a.* simili, en toc.

pincushion ['pinkuʃ(ə)n] *n.* pelote *f* à épingles.

pine¹ [pain] *n.* (*a*) *Bot:* **p. (tree),** pin *m*; **Norway p.,** pin sylvestre, suisse; pinasse *f*; **Scotch p.,** sapin *m* du Nord, de l'Écosse; **pitch p.,** pitchpin *m*; **p. forest,** forêt de pins, pinède *f*; **p. needle,** aiguille *f* de pin; (*b*) (bois *m* de) pin.

pine² *v.i.* **1. to p. (away),** languir, se consumer; tomber en langueur; **to p. with grief,** languir de tristesse. **2. to p. for s.o., sth.,** languir pour, après, qn, qch.; **he's pining for home,** il a la nostalgie du foyer. **pining** *n.* **1.** langueur *f*, languissement *m*. **2.** (i) désir ardent, (ii) nostalgie *f* **(for sth.,** de qch.).

pineapple ['painæpl] *n.* ananas *m*.

pinecone ['paincoun] *n.* pomme *f*, cône *m*, de pin; pigne *f*.

pinewood ['painwud] *n.* **1.** (bois *m* de) pin (*m*). **2.** pinède *f*.

ping¹ [piŋ] *n.* cinglement *m*, fouettement *m* (d'une balle de fusil, etc.).

ping² *v.i.* (*of bullet, etc.*) cingler, fouetter.

pinger ['piŋər] *n.* *F:* compte-minutes *m inv*.

ping-pong ['piŋpɔŋ] *n.* *R.t.m:* ping-pong *m*; **p.-p. table, ball,** table *f*, balle *f*, de ping-pong.

pinhead ['pinhed] *n.* tête *f* d'épingle.

pinhole ['pinhoul] *n.* **1.** trou *m* de cheville, de goujon. **2.** (*a*) trou d'épingle; (*b*) *Opt:* très petite ouverture (dans un écran, etc.); *Phot:* sténopé *m*; **p. source of light,** source *f* de lumière punctiforme, ponctuelle.

pinion¹ ['piniən] *n.* *Orn:* (*a*) bout *m* d'aile; (*b*) penne *f*, rémige *f*.

pinion² *v.tr.* **1.** rogner les ailes à (un oiseau). **2.** (*a*) lier les bras à, ligoter (qn); **to p. s.o.'s arms,** lier les bras de qn; (*b*) lier **(s.o. to a tree,** qn à un arbre).

pinion³ *n.* *Mec. E:* pignon *m*; (*mounted on shaft*) tympan *m*; **rack and p.,** crémaillère *f* et pignon; **p. wheel,** roue *f* à pignon.

pink¹ [piŋk] **1.** *n.* (*a*) *Bot:* œillet *m*; **garden p.,** (œillet) mignardise (*f*); (*b*) **in the p. of condition,** en excellente, parfaite, santé; (*of racehorse, etc.*) entraîné à fond; *O:* (*of pers.*) **to be in the p.,** se porter à merveille. **2.** *a.* & *n.* (couleur *f* de) rose (*m*); **salmon p.,** rose saumon *inv*; **shocking p.,** rose bonbon; (*of albino rabbit, etc.*) **p. eyes,** yeux rouges; (*b*) **(hunting) p.,** rouge (*m*), écarlate (*m*).

pink² *v.tr.* **1.** percer, toucher (son adversaire). **2.** *Dressm: etc:* (i) denteler, hocher, découper, les bords (de qch.); (ii) travailler à jour, évider (le cuir, etc.). **pinking** *n.* *Dressm: etc:* découpage *m*, découpure *f*; **p. shears, scissors,** ciseaux *mpl* à cranter, à denteler; **p. iron,** emporte-pièce *m inv*.

pink³ *v.i.* *I.C.E:* (*of engine*) cliqueter. **pinking** *n.* cliquetis *m* (produit par les auto-allumages).

pinkeye ['piŋkai] *n.* *Med:* conjonctivite aiguë contagieuse.

pinkish ['piŋkiʃ] *a.* rosâtre; rosé.

pinky ['piŋki] *a.* *F:* rosâtre; **p. grey,** gris rosâtre *inv*.

pinnace ['pinəs] *n.* *Nau:* chaloupe *f*; grand canot.

pinnacle ['pinəkl] *n.* **1.** *Arch:* (*a*) pinacle *m*, clocheton *m*; (*b*) couronnement *m* (de faîte, etc.). **2.** cime *f* (d'une montagne, etc.). **3. on the highest p. of fame,** à l'apogée, au sommet, de la gloire.

pinny ['pini] *n.* *F:* tablier *m*.

pinpoint¹ ['pinpɔint] *n.* (*a*) pointe *f* d'épingle; (*b*) point infime, infinitésimal; (*c*) (i) point repéré, point désigné (au sol, etc.); (ii) point de repère; (ii) *Mil:* objectif ponctuel; **p. accuracy,** haute précision; *Mil:* **p. bombing, firing,** bombardement *m*, tir *m*, de précision; **p. target,** objectif ponctuel.

pinpoint² *v.tr.* (*a*) indiquer exactement, mettre le doigt sur (qch.); localiser, repérer (qch.) avec exactitude, avec précision; souligner (un fait); (*b*) *Mil:* viser (un objectif) avec précision; effectuer un tir, un bombardement de précision, sur (un objectif).

pinprick ['pinprik] *n.* (*a*) piqûre *f* d'épingle; (*b*) *F:* **pinpricks,** picoterie(s) *f* (*pl*), tracasseries *fpl*; coups *mpl* d'épingle.

pinstripe ['pinstraip] *n.* *Tex:* rayure fine (de couleur); **p. suit,** costume rayé.

pint [paint] *n.* *Meas:* pinte *f* (= 0,568 litre; *U.S:* = 0,473 litre); *F:* **p.-size(d),** minuscule.

pinta ['paintə] *n.* *F:* une pinte de lait.

pintail ['pinteil] *n. Orn:* **1.** pilet *m.* **2.** tétras *m* à longue queue, *Fr.C:* gelinotte *f* à queue fine.
pinto ['pintou] *a. & n. U.S:* (cheval) pie (*m*).
pinup ['pinʌp] *a. & n. F:* **p. (girl),** pin-up *f inv.*
pioneer¹ [paiə'niər] *n.* pionnier *m.*
pioneer² **1.** *v.t.r.* (*a*) frayer (un chemin) en pionnier; (*b*) servir de guide, de pionnier à (qn); **to p. a new method,** être le premier, l'un des premiers, à utiliser une nouvelle méthode. **2.** *v.i.* faire œuvre de pionnier; frayer le chemin; **to do pioneering work in a science,** défricher le terrain d'une science.
pious ['paiəs] *a.* pieux; **p. fraud,** (i) pieux mensonge; (ii) *F:* (*pers.*) hypocrite *mf.* **-ly** *adv.* pieusement; avec piété.
piousness ['paiəsnis] *n.* piété *f.*
pip¹ [pip] *n.* **1.** *Husb:* pépie *f* (de la volaille). **2.** *F:* **to give s.o. the p.,** embêter qn.
pip² *n.* **1.** point *m* (d'une carte, d'un dé, etc.). **2.** *Mil: F:* **to get one's third p.** = recevoir sa troisième ficelle. **3.** *W. Tel:* top *m*; *Rad:* top d'écho; *W. Tel:* **the pips,** le signal horaire (par points musicaux).
pip³ *v.tr.* **(pipped)** *F:* **1.** blackbouler (qn). **2.** *O:* vaincre, battre (qn); *F:* **to be pipped at the post,** se faire coiffer, battre, sur le poteau.
pip⁴ *n.* pépin *m* (de fruit).
pipe¹ [paip] *n.* **1.** tuyau *m*, tube *m*; conduit *m*, conduite *f*; **water, gas, p.,** tuyau, conduite, d'eau, de gaz; **pipes and fittings,** tuyauterie *f* et accessoires *mpl* de tuyauterie; **connecting p.,** tuyau de communication; raccord *m*; **elbow p.,** coude *m*; raccord coudé. **2.** (*a*) *Mus:* (i) chalumeau *m*; **the pipes,** la cornemuse; *Mil:* **p. major,** cornemuse-chef *m*; (ii) **organ p.,** tuyau d'orgue; **reed p.,** tuyau à anche; (*b*) *Nau:* sifflet *m* (du maître d'équipage); (*c*) (filet *m* de) voix (*f*); chant *m* (d'oiseau). **3.** pipe *f*; **to smoke a p.,** fumer une pipe; **p. of peace, peace p.,** calumet *m* de (la) paix; *F:* **put that in your p. and smoke it!** mettez ça dans votre poche et votre mouchoir par-dessus! **p. cleaner,** cure-pipe *m*, *pl.* cure-pipes; **p. rack,** porte-pipes *m inv*; **p. dream,** rêve *m* (chimérique); projet *m* illusoire.
pipe² **I.** *v.i.* (*a*) jouer (i) *A:* du chalumeau, (ii) de la cornemuse; (*b*) (*of bird, etc.*) siffler; (*of pers.*) parler d'une voix flûtée; (*c*) *Navy:* donner un coup de sifflet. **II.** *v.tr.* **1.** (*a*) installer, poser, des canalisations dans (une maison, etc.); canaliser (l'eau, le pétrole, etc.); **piped water,** eau courante; **to p. oil to a refinery,** amener le pétrole à une raffinerie par oléoduc, par pipeline; (*b*) *F:* **piped music,** musique (de fond) enregistrée. **2.** (*a*) jouer (un air) (i) *A:* au chalumeau, (ii) sur la cornemuse; (*in Scot.*) **to p. in the guests,** jouer de la cornemuse en tête de la procession (lors de l'entrée solonelle des invités); (*b*) chanter (un air) d'une voix flûtée; (*c*) *Navy:* siffler (un commandement); **to p. s.o. aboard,** rendre les honneurs du sifflet à qn. **3.** (*a*) *Dressm: etc:* passepoiler (une robe, etc.); (*b*) *Cu:* décorer (un gâteau avec une douille). **pipe down** *v.i. F:* se taire; **p. down!** boucle-la! **pipe up** *v.i.* (i) se mettre à jouer sur la cornemuse, etc.; (ii) *F:* se mettre à chanter, à parler; **a little voice piped up,** une petite voix s'est fait entendre. **piping** **1.** (*a*) *a.* (son) aigu, sifflant; (voix) flûtée; (*b*) *adv.* **p. hot,** tout chaud, tout bouillant. **2.** *n.* (*a*) (i) installation *f*, pose *f*, de tuyaux, de canalisations (dans un immeuble, etc.); (ii) canalisation *f* (de l'eau, du gaz, etc.); (iii) *coll.* conduites *fpl*, tuyaux *mpl*, tuyauterie *f*; (*b*) (i) son *m* du chalumeau, de la cornemuse; (ii) gazouillement *m*, gazouillis *m* (d'oiseaux); (iii) *Navy:* commandement *m* au sifflet; (*c*) *Dressm: etc:* passepoil *m*; *Cu:* décoration (d'un gâteau, etc.) faite avec une douille; **p. bag,** poche *f* à douilles.
pipeclay ['paipklei] *n.* terre *f* de pipe; blanc *m* de terre à pipe (pour astiquage).
pipeline ['paiplain] *n.* **1.** canalisation *f*, conduite *f*; (*for gas*) conduite de gaz naturel, gazoduc *m*; (*for petrol*) oléoduc *m*, pipeline *m.* **2.** canal *m*, voie *f*, d'acheminement (des nouvelles, du matériel, etc.); *F:* **it's in the p.,** ce sera bientôt prêt; c'est en route.
piper ['paipər] *n.* joueur *m* de chalumeau, de cornemuse; cornemuseur *m*; **he who pays the p. calls the tune,** qui paye a bien le droit de choisir.
pipette [pi'pet] *n. Ch: etc:* pipette *f*; compte-gouttes *m inv.*
pipit ['pipit] *n. Orn:* pipit *m.*
pippin ['pipin] *n. Hort:* (pomme *f*) reinette (*f*).
pipsqueak ['pipskwi:k] *n. F:* (*pers.*) petit bonhomme de rien du tout; gringalet *m.*
piquancy ['pi:kənsi] *n.* **1.** goût piquant (d'un mets). **2.** sel *m*, piquant *m* (d'un conte, d'une affaire, etc.).
piquant ['pi:kənt] *a.* (*of flavour, story, etc.*) piquant. **-ly** *adv.* d'une manière piquante; avec du piquant.
pique¹ [pi:k] *n.* pique *f*, ressentiment *m*; **in a fit of p.,** dans un accès de dépit.
pique² *v.tr.* **1.** piquer, dépiter (qn); **to p. s.o.'s pride,** piquer, blesser, qn dans son orgueil. **2.** piquer, exciter (la curiosité de qn).
piquet [pi'ket] *n. Cards:* piquet *m.*
piracy ['pairəsi] *n.* **1.** piraterie *f*, flibusterie *f*; **air p.,** piraterie de l'air. **2.** atteinte *f* au droit d'auteur; pillage *m*, vol *m* (des idées, etc.); **film p.,** piratage *m* de films.
piranha [pi'rɑ:n(j)ə] *n. Ich:* piranha *m*, piraya *m.*
pirate¹ ['pairət] *n.* **1.** (*a*) pirate *m*; flibustier *m*; (*b*) navire *m* pirate; (*c*) *W. Tel:* **p. station,** poste *m*, émetteur *m*, pirate. **2.** contrefacteur *m* (d'un ouvrage littéraire, etc.); voleur, -euse (d'idées, etc.).
pirate² *v.tr.* (*a*) saisir (un navire) en pirate, en flibustier; (*b*) s'approprier, voler (une invention, etc.); contrefaire (une marque de fabrique); **to p. a book,** (i) republier un livre sans autorisation; (ii) contrefaire, démarquer, un livre.
piratical [pai'rætik(ə)l] *a.* **1.** de pirate, de flibustier. **2.** de contrefacteur; de contrefaçon.
pirouette¹ [piru'et] *n. Danc:* pirouette *f.*
pirouette² *v.i.* pirouetter.
Pisa ['pi:zə] *Pr.n. Geog:* Pise *f.*
pisces ['paisi:z] *Pr.n.pl. Astr:* les Poissons *mpl.*
piss¹ [pis] *n. P:* pisse *f.*
piss² *P:* **1.** *v.i.* (*a*) pisser; (*b*) **p. off!** fous le camp! **2.** *v.tr.* pisser (du sang, etc.). **pissed** *a.* (*a*) soûl; (*b*) **to be p. off,** en avoir marre, plein le dos.
pistachio [pis'tɑ:ʃiou] *n. Bot:* (*a*) **p. (nut),** pistache *f*; (*b*) **p. (tree),** pistachier *m.*
pistil ['pistil] *n. Bot:* pistil *m.*
pistol ['pist(ə)l] *n.* **1.** *Sm.a:* pistolet *m*; **cap p.,** pistolet à amorces; **p. shot,** coup *m* de pistolet; **to hold a p. to s.o.'s head,** (i) tenir un pistolet braqué contre la tempe de qn; (ii) *Fig:* mettre à qn le pistolet sous la gorge. **2.** pistolet (d'un outil pneumatique, etc.); **p. grip,** poignée pistolet (d'un outil).
piston ['pistən] *n.* (*a*) *Mec.E: Mch: etc:* piston *m*; **p. engine,** moteur *m* à pistons; **p. head,** tête *f*, fond *m*, du piston; (*b*) *Mus:* piston (d'instrument à vent en cuivre).
pit¹ [pit] *n. NAm:* noyau *m* (de cerise, etc.).
pit² *v.tr.* **(pitted)** *NAm:* dénoyauter (des cerises, etc.).
pit³ *n.* **1.** (*a*) fosse *f*; (*roughly dug*) fouille *f*; **to dig a p.,** creuser une fosse; *Metall:* **casting p.,** fosse de coulée (de fonderie); **tan p.,** cuve *f*, fosse, à tanner; *Aut: etc:* **inspection p.,** fosse de visite; (*b*) *Lit:* **the (bottomless) p.,** l'enfer *m*, les enfers; (*c*) piège *m*, fosse (à attraper les animaux); (*d*) *Min:* (i) puits *m* (de mine); (ii) mine *f* (de houille); **chalk p.,** carrière *f* à chaux; **p. prop,** poteau *m*, étai *m*, de mine; étançon *m*; **p. pony,** cheval *m* de mine; **to work in the pits,** être mineur (de fond). **2.** (*a*) arène *f* (de combat de

coqs); fosse (à ours); (*b*) *Th:* parterre *m*; **orchestra p.,** fosse d'orchestre; (*c*) *NAm:* marché *m* (à la Bourse); **wheat p.,** Bourse des blés; (*d*) *Rac:* **the pits,** les stands *mpl* de ravitaillement. **3.** (*a*) piqûre *f*, alvéole *m or f* (dans un métal, etc.); (*b*) *Med:* cicatrice *f*, marque *f* (de la petite vérole). **4.** *Anat:* **the p. of the stomach,** le creux de l'estomac.

pit⁴ *v.tr.* **(pitted) 1. to p. s.o. against s.o.,** mettre qn aux prises avec qn; opposer qn à qn; **to pit oneself against s.o.,** se mesurer contre qn. **2.** (*a*) (*of acids, etc.*) piquer, trouer (le métal, etc.); (*b*) *Med:* (*of smallpox*) grêler, marquer (le visage). **pitted** *a.* (*a*) (*of metal, etc.*) piqué, alvéolé (par un acide, etc.); (*b*) (*of pers.*) grêlé (par la petite vérole).

pit-a-pat ['pitə'pæt] **1.** *adv.* **to go p.-a-p.,** (*of rain, etc.*) crépiter; (*of feet*) trottiner; (*of the heart*) faire toc-toc. **2.** *n.* crépitement *m* (de la pluie); battement *m* (du cœur).

pitch¹ [pitʃ] *n.* poix *f*; (*from coal tar*) brai *m*; **p. dark, p. black,** noir comme poix; **it's p. dark, black,** il fait nuit noire.

pitch² *v.tr.* brayer; enduire (qch.) de poix, de brai.

pitch³ *n.* **1.** lancement *m* (d'une pierre, d'une balle, etc.). **2.** (*a*) place *f*, emplacement *m* (dans un marché, etc.); place habituelle (d'un marchand forain, d'un mendiant, etc.); (*b*) terrain *m* (de football, etc.); *Cr:* terrain entre les guichets. **3.** (*a*) *Arch:* hauteur *f* (du plafond); (*b*) *Mus:* hauteur (d'un son); **p. pipe,** diapason *m* à bouche; **he has perfect p.,** il a l'oreille absolue; **to give the orchestra the p.,** donner l'accord à un orchestre; **to rise in p.,** monter de ton; (*c*) degré *m* (d'insolence, etc.); **to such a p. that . . .,** à tel point que . . .; à ce point que . . .; au point que . . .; **to the highest p.,** au plus haut degré; au dernier point; **expectation had reached fever p.,** l'attente était fébrile. **4.** (*a*) pente, rampant *m* (d'un toit, d'un comble, d'un escalier); chute *f*, inclinaison *f* (d'un toit, d'un comble); *Min:* plongement *m* (d'un filon); (*b*) *Tls:* inclinaison, basile *f* (d'un fer de rabot). **5.** (i) tangage *m*, (ii) coup *m* de tangage (d'un navire, d'un avion); **angle of p., p. angle,** angle *m* de tangage. **6.** (*a*) espacement *m*, écartement *m* (des rivets, des trous); (*b*) pas *m* (d'une roue dentée, d'une scie, d'un engrenage); **p. circle,** cercle primitif; ligne *f* d'engrènement (d'une roue); (*c*) pas (d'une vis, d'un boulon); (*d*) pas (d'une hélice, etc.).

pitch⁴ **I.** *v.tr.* **1.** (*a*) dresser (une tente); établir (un camp); (*b*) *Cr:* planter, dresser (les guichets). **2.** *Civ.E:* (*a*) (i) empierrer, (ii) paver (une chaussée); (*b*) établir la fondation (d'une route). **3.** (*a*) *Mus:* jouer (un morceau) dans une clef donnée; **to p. one's voice higher, lower,** hausser, baisser, le ton de sa voix; (*b*) **to p. an estimate too low,** arrêter trop bas un devis estimatif; **to p. one's aspirations too high,** viser trop haut. **4.** jeter, lancer (une balle); (*at baseball*) lancer; **to p. the hay onto the cart,** jeter le foin sur la charrette; charger le foin. **7.** *F:* raconter (une histoire). **II.** *v.i.* **1.** tomber; **to p. forward,** être projeté en avant; piquer du nez; **the ball pitched on a stone,** le ballon a rebondi sur une pierre. **2.** (*of ship, aircraft*) tanguer. **3.** (*a*) **to p. on sth., s.o.,** se décider pour qch., qn; choisir qch., qn; (*b*) *F:* **to p. in,** (i) se mettre à la besogne; (ii) *U.S:* payer son écot. **pitched** *a.* **p. battle,** bataille rangée. **pitching** *n.* **1.** dressage *m* (d'une tente); établissement *m* (d'un camp). **2.** (*a*) (*action*) (i) pavage *m*; (ii) empierrement *m*; (*b*) (*result*) (i) pavage, pavé *m*; (ii) empierrement, perré *m*. **3.** lancement *m*, jet *m* (d'une pierre, etc.). **4.** tangage *m* (d'un navire, d'un avion). **pitch into** *v.i.* *F:* (*a*) (i) taper sur (qn); s'attaquer à (qn); (ii) dire son fait à (qn); (*b*) tomber la tête la première dans (une mare, etc.). **pitch over** *v.i.* *F:* (*of pers.*) tomber à la renverse; faire la culbute.

pitcher¹ ['pitʃər] *n.* (*a*) cruche *f* (de grès); broc *m*, pichet *m*; (*b*) *esp. NAm:* pot *m* (à lait, etc.).

pitcher² *n.* (*pers.*) (*baseball*) lanceur *m*.

pitchfork¹ ['pitʃfɔːk] *n.* *Agr:* fourche *f*, fouine *f* (à foin); (*two-pronged*) bident *m*.

pitchfork² *v.tr.* **1.** lancer (une gerbe, etc.) avec la fourche. **2.** *F:* bombarder (qn dans un poste).

piteous ['pitiəs] *a.* pitoyable, piteux. **-ly** *adv.* pitoyablement, piteusement.

pitfall ['pitfɔːl] *n.* trappe *f*, fosse *f*; piège *m*; **the pitfalls of the English language,** les traquenards *mpl* de l'anglais.

pith [piθ] *n.* **1.** (*a*) *Bot:* mœlle *f*; **p. helmet,** casque (colonial) en sola; (*b*) peau blanche (d'une orange, etc.). **2.** (*a*) vigueur *f*, force *f*; (*b*) mœlle, essence *f* (d'un livre, etc.); piquant *m* (d'une histoire).

pithead ['pithed] *n.* bouche *f* de puits; carreau *m* (de mine); **p. baths,** bains *mpl*, douches *fpl*, de la mine.

pithiness ['piθinis] *n.* concision *f*.

pithy ['piθi] *a.* **1.** (*of stem, etc.*) mœlleux; (*of orange, etc.*) couvert de peau blanche. **2.** (*of style, etc.*) (i) concis; vigoureux; (ii) (phrase) lapidaire.

pitiable ['pitiəbl] *a.* pitoyable, piteux; (*of appearance, object*) minable, lamentable; **he was in a p. state,** il était dans un état à faire pitié.

pitiful ['pitif(u)l] *a.* (*a*) pitoyable, apitoyant; **it's p. to see him,** il fait pitié; (*b*) *Pej:* lamentable; à faire pitié. **-fully** *adv.* pitoyablement; **she was p. thin,** elle était d'une maigreur pitoyable.

pitiless ['pitilis] *a.* impitoyable; (vent, froid) cruel. **-ly** *adv.* impitoyablement; sans pitié.

piton ['piːtɔ̃] *n.* *Mount:* piton *m*.

pittance ['pitəns] *n.* maigre salaire *m*; **to work for a p.,** travailler pour un salaire dérisoire.

pitter-patter¹, ² ['pitəpætər] *n.* & *v.i* = PATTER³, ⁴.

pituitary [pi'tjuːit(ə)ri] *a.* & *n.* *Anat:* **p. (gland),** hypophyse *f*; glande *f* pituitaire.

pity¹ ['piti] *n.* pitié *f*; (*a*) compassion *f*, apitoiement *m*; attendrissement *m*; **to take p. on s.o.,** prendre pitié de qn; **out of p. for s.o.,** (faire qch.) par pitié pour qn; **for pity's sake,** par pitié; de grâce; (*b*) dommage *m*; **what a p.!** quel dommage! **it's a great p. that . . .,** il est bien malheureux, dommage, que . . ..

pity² *v.tr.* plaindre (qn); avoir pitié de, s'apitoyer sur (qn); **he is to be pitied,** il est à plaindre; il fait pitié. **pitying** *a.* compatissant; (regard) de pitié. **pityingly** *adv.* avec pitié.

Pius ['paiəs] *Pr.n.m.* Pie.

pivot¹ ['pivət] *n.* **1.** *Mec.E: etc:* pivot *m*, axe *m* (de rotation); pivot (d'une grue, etc.); tourillon *m*. **2.** (*pers.*) pivot, cheville ouvrière (d'une entreprise, etc.); *Mil:* **p. (man),** pivot, guide *m*, homme de base (d'un mouvement d'ordre serré).

pivot² *v.* **(pivoted) 1.** *v.tr.* monter (une pièce) sur pivot. **2.** *v.i.* pivoter, tourner (**on sth.,** sur qch.).

pivotal ['pivət(ə)l] *a.* (*a*) pivotal, -aux; (*b*) (point) cardinal; (position) clef.

pix [piks] *n.* *F:* (*a*) cinéma *m*, ciné *m*; (*b*) photo(s) *f*(*pl*).

pizza ['piːtsə] *n.* *Cu:* pizza *f*.

pizzeria [pitsə'riə] *n.* pizzeria *f*.

pixie, pixy ['piksi] *n.* (*a*) lutin *m*; (*b*) fée *f*.

placard¹ ['plækɑːd] *n.* écriteau *m*; affiche *f*.

placard² *v.tr.* **1.** placarder (un mur). **2.** placarder; afficher (une annonce, etc.).

placate [plə'keit] *v.tr.* apaiser, calmer, concilier.

place¹ [pleis] *n.* **1.** (*a*) lieu *m*, endroit *m*; **this would be an ideal p. for a picnic,** voilà un endroit idéal pour piqueniquer; **this is the p.!** nous voilà (arrivés)! **to move from one p. to another,** se déplacer d'un lieu, d'un endroit, à un autre; *F:* **to go places,** réussir (dans la vie); *Sch:* *F:* **the other p.,** (i) (*at Oxford*)

Cambridge; (ii) (*at Cambridge*) Oxford; **p. of refuge,** lieu de refuge; **in its proper time and p.,** en temps et lieu; **all over the p.,** partout; de tous les côtés; (*b*) **p. of amusement,** lieu de divertissement; **p. of worship,** église *f*, temple *m*, etc.; **my p. of work,** l'endroit *m* où je travaille; mon bureau, etc.; **market p.,** place *f* du marché; **meeting p.,** (lieu de) rendez-vous (*m inv*); (*c*) localité *f*; ville *f*, village *m*, etc.; **p. name,** nom *m* de lieu; (*d*) maison *f*, etc.; **p. of residence,** résidence *f*; demeure *f*; domicile (réel); **a little p. in the country,** une petite maison à la campagne; *F:* **come round to my p.,** venez chez moi; **this is no p. for you,** vous n'avez que faire ici; *Mil:* **fortified p.,** place forte, place de guerre; (*e*) (*in street names*) cour *f*, passage *m*, rue *f*, ruelle *f*; (*f*) *Fin: Bank:* place; **p. of payment,** lieu de paiement. **2.** place; (*a*) **everything in its p.,** chaque chose à sa place; **to find a p. for sth.,** trouver une place pour qch.; caser qch.; **to hold sth. in p.,** tenir qch. en place; assujettir qch.; **this remark is out of p.,** cette observation est déplacée, est hors de propos, mal à propos; (*of pers.*) **to look out of p.,** avoir l'air dépaysé; (*b*) **to book a p.,** réserver une place; **if I get there first I'll keep a p. for you,** si j'y arrive le premier je te garderai une place; **to change places with s.o.,** changer de place avec qn; **his anger gave p. to pity,** sa colère a fait place à un sentiment de pitié; (*c*) (*at table*) **p. (setting),** couvert *m*; **p. mat** = napperon (individuel); **p. card,** carte portant le nom du convive; (*d*) (*situation*) **put yourself in my p.,** mettez-vous à ma place; **if I were in your p. I should go,** à votre place, j'irais; (*e*) **to take p.,** avoir lieu; se passer; se produire; se faire; **the marriage will not take p.,** le mariage ne se fera pas; **many changes have taken p.,** il y a eu beaucoup de changements; **while this was taking p.,** tandis que cela se passait. **3.** (*a*) place, rang *m*; **to hold the first p.,** tenir, occuper, le premier rang; **to keep s.o. in his p.,** garder les distances avec qn; *O:* **to know one's p.,** observer les distances; *F:* **to put s.o. in his p.,** remettre qn à sa place; (*b*) **in the first, second, p.,** en premier, second, lieu; *Turf:* **to back a horse for a p.,** jouer un cheval placé; (*c*) *Mth:* **to three places of decimals,** à trois décimales. **4.** (*a*) *A:* place, emploi *m*; (*b*) **to take s.o.'s p.,** remplacer qn; prendre la place de qn; **it's not my p. to do it,** ce n'est pas à moi de le faire. **5.** (*a*) endroit; **in places,** par endroits; (*b*) *Rugby: Fb:* **p. kick,** coup de pied placé; (*c*) (*in a book*) **to lose, find, one's p.,** perdre, retrouver, la page.

place² *v.tr.* **1.** (*a*) placer, mettre; **to p. a book back on a shelf,** remettre un livre (en place) sur un rayon; **strategically placed airfields,** des champs d'aviation stratégiquement situés; (*b*) (*of pers.*) **to be awkwardly placed,** être dans une situation délicate; (*c*) *Com: Fin:* placer, vendre (des marchandises, des actions); passer (une commande); placer, négocier (un emprunt); adjuger, concéder (un contrat); faire (un pari); **to p. a book with a publisher,** faire accepter un livre par un éditeur; (*d*) confier; **to p. a matter in s.o.'s hands,** mettre une affaire dans les mains de qn; **I p. myself at your disposal,** je me mets à votre disposition; **to p. a child in s.o.'s care,** confier un enfant à la garde de qn. **2.** placer, donner un emploi à (qn). **3. I would p. him among the outstanding biographers of the century,** je le classerais parmi les meilleurs biographes du siècle; *Sch: Sp: etc:* **to be placed third,** se classer troisième. **4.** (*a*) *Archeol: etc:* assigner une date à, dater (un tombeau, etc.); (*b*) localiser (un son); (*c*) **I know his face but I can't p. him,** je le reconnais mais je ne peux pas le remettre. **placing** *n.* (*a*) placement *m* (de qch.); (*b*) *Com: Fin:* placement, vente *f* (de marchandises, d'actions); (*c*) *Sp: etc:* classement *m*.

placebo [plæ'si:bou] *n. Med:* placebo *m*.

placenta [plə'sentə] *n. Anat: Bot:* placenta *m*.

placid ['plæsid] *a.* placide, calme, tranquille. **-ly** *adv.* placidement; tranquillement.

placidity [plæ'siditi], **placidness** ['plæsidnis] *n.* placidité *f*, calme *m*, tranquillité *f*.

plagiarism ['pleidʒiərizm] *n.* **1.** (habitude *f* du) plagiat; démarquage *m*. **2.** plagiat; larcin *m* littéraire.

plagiarist ['pleidʒiərist] *n.* plagiaire *mf*.

plagiarize ['pleidʒiəraiz] *v.tr.* plagier (une œuvre, un auteur); faire un plagiat à, contrefaire (une œuvre); *v.i.* se livrer à des plagiats.

plague¹ [pleig] *n.* **1.** fléau *m*, plaie *f*. **2.** *Med:* peste *f*; *Vet:* **cattle p.,** peste bovine; *F:* **to avoid s.o. like the p.,** fuir qn comme la peste.

plague² *v.tr. F:* tourmenter, harceler, embêter (qn); **to p. s.o.'s life,** empoisonner l'existence de qn; **to p. s.o. with questions,** harceler qn de questions.

plaice [pleis] *n. Ich:* carrelet *m*; plie (franche).

plaid [plæd, *Scot:* pleid] *n.* **1.** (*a*) *Scot: Cost:* plaid *m*; couverture *f* servant de manteau; (*b*) couverture de voyage en tartan. **2.** *Tex:* tartan *m*, écossais *m*.

plain¹ [plein] **I.** *a.* **1.** (*a*) clair, évident, distinct; **to make sth. p. to s.o.,** faire comprendre qch. à qn; **it's as p. as (p.) can be, as p. as a pikestaff,** *F:* **as the nose on your face,** c'est on ne peut plus clair; c'est clair comme le jour; **in p. English,** en bon anglais; *Com:* **marked in p. figures,** marqué en chiffres connus; (*b*) (*not in code*) **p. text,** texte *m* en clair; *n.* **in p.,** en clair. **2.** (*a*) (style) simple, uni; (mobilier, robe) simple; (cigarettes) sans filtre; **p. (post)card,** carte *f* de correspondance; **under p. cover,** sous pli discret; **in p. clothes,** en civil; **p.-clothes policeman,** agent *m* en civil; *Knit:* **one p. one purl,** une maille à l'endroit, une maille à l'envers; **p. knitting,** (i) point *m* jersey; (ii) point mousse; (*b*) uni; lisse; (papier) non réglé; *Tex:* **p. material,** tissu (i) uni, (ii) (de teinte) uni(e); (*c*) (couture) simple; **p. cooking,** cuisine simple, bourgeoise; **p. chocolate,** chocolat *m* à croquer; **p. living,** vie simple; (*d*) **the p. truth,** la franche, pure, simple, vérité; **I'll be quite p. with you,** je vais vous parler franchement; **p. answer,** réponse carrée; **p. speech, p. speaking,** le franc-parler; **to be p. spoken,** être franc, carré; **I'm a p. man,** je ne fais pas de cérémonies; (*e*) **p. country people,** de simples campagnards. **3.** (*esp. of woman*) sans beauté; **to be p.,** manquer de beauté; **a p. Jane,** une jeune fille plutôt laide. **II.** *adv. F:* **1.** clairement, distinctement. **2.** franchement; **to speak p.,** parler franc, sans détours. **plainly** *adv.* **1.** (voir) distinctement, nettement; (parler) distinctement, clairement; **I can see p. that . . .,** il est évident que . . .; **p. I was not wanted,** il était clair que j'étais de trop. **2.** (*a*) (vivre) simplement; (s'habiller) simplement, sans recherche; (*b*) **to speak p.,** parler carrément; user de franchise.

plain² *n. Geog:* (i) plaine *f*; (ii) prairie *f*; **alluvial p.,** plaine alluviale; **the Great Plains,** la Prairie (américaine).

plainchant ['pleintʃɑ:nt] *n.* = PLAINSONG.

plainness ['pleinnis] *n.* **1.** clarté *f* (de langage); netteté *f* (des objets lointains); évidence *f* (des preuves). **2.** (*a*) simplicité *f* (de vie, etc.); (*b*) franchise *f*, rondeur *f* (de langage). **3.** manque *m* de beauté.

plainsong ['pleinsɔŋ] *n. Mus:* plain-chant *m*.

plaint [pleint] *n. Jur:* plainte *f*.

plaintiff ['pleintif] *n. Jur:* demandeur, -eresse; plaignant, -ante.

plaintive ['pleintiv] *a.* plaintif. **-ly** *adv.* plaintivement.

plaintiveness ['pleintivnis] *n.* ton plaintif.

plait¹ [plæt] *n.* natte *f*, tresse *f* (de cheveux, etc.).

plait² *v.tr.* natter, tresser (les cheveux, etc.).

plan¹ [plæn] *n.* **1.** (*a*) plan *m* (d'un bâtiment, etc.); **ground p.,** plan géométral; **sketch p.,** plan sommaire;

croquis *m*; **to draw a p.,** tracer, dessiner, un plan; (*b*) *Surv:* plan, levé *m* (d'un terrain); (*c*) cadre *m*, plan (d'un roman, etc.). **2.** projet *m*, dessein *m*, plan; **p. of battle,** plan de bataille; *Fin:* **investment p.,** plan d'investissement; *Pol.Ec:* **five year p.,** plan quinquennal; *Av:* **flight p.,** plan de vol; **to change one's plans,** changer de dessein; **to have no fixed plan(s),** ne pas avoir de projet bien déterminé; **everything went according to p.,** tout a marché comme prévu; **the best p. would be to . . .,** le mieux serait de . . .; **it would be a good p. to . . .,** ce serait une bonne idée, on ferait bien, de . . .; **what are your plans for the summer?** quels sont vos projets pour cet été?

plan² *v.* **(planned) 1.** *v.tr.* (*a*) faire, dessiner, le plan de (qch.); **the school was planned for 500 pupils,** l'école a été prévue pour 500 élèves; (*b*) faire, établir, élaborer, le plan de (son nouveau roman, etc.); (*c*) *Pol.Ec:* planifier (la production, etc.). **2.** *v.tr.* projeter (un voyage, etc.); combiner (une attaque, etc.); comploter, tramer (un crime); **to p. to do sth.,** former le projet de faire qch.; **he had planned it all (out),** il en avait établi tous les détails; **they were planning to rob a bank,** ils faisaient des plans pour voler une banque. **3.** *v.i.* faire des projets; **to p. for the future,** (i) faire des projets pour l'avenir; (ii) songer à l'avenir. **planned** *a.* (*a*) conçu, projeté; organisé; **well, badly, p.,** bien, mal, conçu; (complot, crime) bien, mal, concerté, organisé; (*b*) *Pol.Ec: etc:* planifié; **p. economy,** économie dirigée. **planning** *n.* **1.** tracé *m* (d'un plan); **town p.,** architecture urbaine; urbanisme *m*. **2.** conception *f*, organisation *f* (d'un projet, d'un complot, etc.). **3.** *Pol.Ec: etc:* dirigisme *m*, planification *f*; *F:* planning *m*; **economic p.,** planification économique. **4. family p.,** planning familial.

plane¹ [plein] *a.* (*a*) plan, uni; égal, -aux; **p. surface,** surface plane; (*b*) *Mth: etc:* (*of angle, geometry, etc.*) plan; **p. trigonometry,** trigonométrie *f* rectiligne.

plane² *n.* **1.** (*a*) *Mth: etc:* plan *m*; **horizontal, vertical, p.,** plan horizontal, vertical; *Opt:* **focal p.,** plan focal; (*b*) *Geol:* **bedding p., p. of stratification,** plan de stratification; **fault p.,** plan de faille; (*c*) **on the economic p.,** sur le plan économique; **a higher p. of intelligence,** un niveau intellectuel supérieur. **2.** *Mec:* **inclined p.,** plan incliné. **3.** *Av:* (*a*) plan; **tail p.,** plan fixe horizontal; (*b*) avion *m*; **I came by p.,** je suis venu en avion.

plane³ *v.i.* **1.** (*a*) (*of bird, aircraft*) planer; **to p. down,** descendre en vol plané, en planant; (*b*) (*of hydroplane*) **to p. along the water,** courir le redan.

plane⁴ *n. Tls:* rabot *m*.

plane⁵ *v.tr.* raboter (le bois); aplanir, planer (le bois, le métal); dégauchir (le bois). **planing** *n.* rabotage *m*; planage *m*, aplanissage *m*; **p. machine,** raboteuse *f*.

plane⁶ *n. Bot:* **p. (tree),** platane *m*.

planer ['pleinər] *n.* **1.** (*pers.*) raboteur *m*. **2.** *Tls:* raboteuse *f*, planeuse *f*.

planet ['plænit] *n. Astr:* planète *f*; **to be born under a lucky p.,** être né sous une bonne étoile.

planetarium [plæni'tɛəriəm] *n.* planétarium *m*.

planetary ['plænit(ə)ri] *a. Astr:* (système, heure, mouvement) planétaire.

planisphere ['plænisfiər] *n.* planisphère *m* céleste.

plank¹ [plæŋk] *n.* **1.** planche (épaisse); madrier *m*; *A:* **to walk the p.,** passer à la planche. **2.** *Pol:* **p. in the party platform,** article *m* du programme du parti.

plank² *v.tr.* **1.** planchéier (un plancher, etc.). **2.** *F:* **to p. sth. down,** déposer qch. (brusquement). **planking** *n.* **1.** *Const:* planchéiage *m*. **2.** *coll.* planches *fpl*, madriers *mpl*.

plankton ['plæŋktən] *n.* plancton *m*.

planner ['plænər] *n.* planificateur, -trice; **town p.,** urbaniste *mf*.

plant¹ [plɑːnt] *n.* **1.** (*a*) plante *f*; **flowering p.,** plante à fleurs; **(indoor) pot p., house p.,** plante d'appartement; **bedding p.,** plant *m* à repiquer; (*b*) **ice p.,** ficoïde cristalline, glaciaire; **tobacco p.,** tabac *m*; (*c*) **p. physiology,** physiologie végétale; **p. biology,** phytobiologie *f*; **p. life,** (i) vie végétale; (ii) flore *f* (d'une région). **2.** *Ind:* (*a*) appareil(s) *m*(*pl*), appareillage *m*; équipement *m*, matériel *m* (industriel); **cooling p.,** appareil de refroidissement; (*b*) installation (industrielle); usine *f*; **(electric) power p., generating p.,** centrale électrique. **3.** *P:* coup monté. **4.** *P:* (*a*) agent *m* de la police secrète; mouchard *m*; (*b*) fabrication *f* de faux témoignage.

plant² *v.tr.* **1.** planter (un arbre, etc.); **to p. a field with wheat,** mettre une terre en blé; **to p. out,** repiquer (des semis). **2.** (*a*) planter (un piquet dans la terre, etc.); *Nau:* mouiller (une mine); *Mil:* poser, déposer (une bombe); **to p. an idea in s.o.'s mind,** implanter une idée dans l'esprit de qn; (*b*) *F:* **a well planted blow,** un coup bien asséné, bien appliqué; (*c*) *F:* **to p. oneself in front of s.o.,** se planter devant qn. **3.** *F:* (*a*) planter (un espion chez qn); (*b*) **to p. incriminating evidence on s.o.,** fabriquer de faux témoignages contre qn.

plantain¹ ['plæntin] *n. Bot:* plantain *m*.

plantain² *n. Bot:* **1.** banane *f* des Antilles. **2. p. (tree),** bananier *m* du paradis.

plantation [plæn'teiʃ(ə)n] *n.* (*a*) *For:* plantation *f*, pépinière *f* (d'arbres); (*b*) plantation (de coton, etc.); **p. song,** chanson *f* de noirs (des plantations).

planter ['plɑːntər] *n.* **1.** (*a*) planteur *m* (de choux, etc.); (*b*) planteur; propriétaire *m* d'une plantation; **coffee p.,** planteur de café. **2.** *Tls:* planteuse *f*.

plaque [plɑːk] *n.* **1.** plaque *f* (de bronze, de marbre, etc.). **2.** plaque dentaire.

plash¹ [plæʃ] *n.* (*a*) clapotement *m*, clapotis *m* (des vagues); babillement *m* (d'un ruisseau, etc.); (*b*) flac *m* (d'un corps qui tombe dans l'eau).

plash² **1.** *v.tr.* plonger (qch. dans l'eau) avec un flac. **2.** *v.i.* (*a*) (*of liquids*) clapoter, faire un clapotis; (*of stream*) babiller; (*b*) faire flac (sur l'eau).

plasm [plæzm] *n.* protoplasme *m*.

plasma ['plæzmə] *n.* plasma *m*.

plaster¹ ['plɑːstər] *n.* **1.** *Med:* emplâtre *m*; **sticking p.,** pansement adhésif, sparadrap *m*; **corn p.,** emplâtre, pansement, cor(r)icide. **2.** *Const: etc:* plâtre *m*; **p. cast,** (i) *Surg:* plâtre; (ii) *Art:* (moulage *m* en) plâtre; empreinte *f* en plâtre; **there was p. falling from the ceiling,** le plafond se déplâtrait; **p. of Paris,** plâtre de Paris, plâtre de moulage; **to put a leg in p.,** plâtrer une jambe, mettre une jambe dans un plâtre.

plaster² *v.tr.* **1.** *Med:* mettre un emplâtre sur (une plaie, etc.). **2.** (*a*) plâtrer, ravaler (un mur), enduire (un mur) de plâtre; **wall plastered with advertisements,** mur tapissé d'affiches; (*of pers.*) **plastered with mud,** plâtré, tout couvert, de boue; (*b*) *F:* **to p. the enemy,** bombarder l'ennemi; (*c*) *P:* **to get plastered,** se soûler; **he's plastered,** il est soûl.

plasterer ['plɑːstərər] *n.* plâtrier *m*.

plasterwork ['plɑːstəwəːk] *n.* plâtrage *m*; (*esp. on walls and ceilings*) les plâtres *mpl*.

plastic ['plæstik] **1.** *a.* (*a*) plastique; **the p. arts,** les arts plastiques; **p. surgery,** chirurgie *f* (i) plastique, (ii) esthétique; **p. surgeon,** plasticien; chirurgien esthétique; (*b*) (*qui se laisse mouler*) (matière) plastique; *Fig:* **p. nature,** caractère *m* malléable; (*c*) *Ph: etc:* (déformation, stabilité) plastique; (*d*) **p. explosive,** explosif *m* plastique; plastic *m*; **to attack a house with a p. bomb,** plastiquer une maison. **2.** *n.* plastique *m*; matière plastique; **laminated p.,** (plastique) stratifié (*m*), lamifié (*m*); **moulded p.,** plastique moulé; **a p. cup,** une tasse en (matière) plastique; **the plastics industry,** l'industrie *f* des plastiques.

plasticine ['plæstisiːn] *n.* pâte *f* à modeler.

plasticity [plæs'tisiti] *n.* (*a*) plasticité *f*; (*b*) *Art: Cin:* effet *m* plastique.

plate¹ [pleit] *n.* **1.** (*a*) (petite) plaque, lamelle *f* (de métal, de verre, de matière plastique, etc.); (*b*) **(dental) p.,** (i) appareil *m* (dentaire); (ii) dentier *m*. **2.** (*a*) *Metall:* plaque; (grande) feuille (de métal); tôle *f*; *Mil: Navy:* **p. armour,** blindage *m*; (*b*) *Hist:* plaque, plate *f* (d'armure); (*c*) *N.Arch:* **bilge p.,** tôle de bouchain; **bulkhead p.,** tôle de cloison; (*d*) *Mec.E: etc:* plaque (de montage, etc.); (*e*) plateau *m* (de balance, etc.); platine *f*, palastre *m* (de serrure); paumelle *f* (de gond de porte); *Aut:* **p. clutch,** embrayage *m* à disque, à plateau; *Dom.Ec:* **hot p.,** (i) plaque chauffante (de cuisinière); (ii) réchaud *m* (électrique, à gaz); (iii) chauffe-assiettes *m inv*; (*f*) **name p.,** (i) plaque de porte; (ii) plaque indicatrice (de rue); (iii) plaque d'identification, de série (d'une machine); *Aut: etc:* **number p.,** plaque d'immatriculation; plaque minéralogique. **3.** (*a*) *El:* plaque, lame (de batterie, etc.); **accumulator p.,** plaque d'accumulateur; (*b*) *Elcs:* plaque, anode *f* (de tube éléctronique). **4.** (*a*) *Phot:* **(photographic) p.,** plaque (photographique); **dry p.,** plaque sèche; (*b*) *Engr: Typ:* plaque; **p. cylinder,** cylindre *m* de plaque; (*c*) *Engr: Phot: etc:* cliché *m* (photographique, imprimant); cliché (de photogravure); **half-tone p.,** cliché de similigravure; (*d*) *Engr:* planche, gravure *f*, estampe *f*; **full-page p.,** hors-texte *m inv*. **5.** *Const:* (poutre *f*) sablière (*f*); panne *f*; **wall p.,** plaque d'assise (de poutre); lambourde *f* (pour les solives du plancher). **6.** (*a*) orfèvrerie *f*; **silver p.,** argenterie *f*; (*b*) **it's (only) p.,** c'est de l'argenté, du plaqué; (*c*) *Rac:* coupe (d'or, d'argent) (donnée en prix). **7.** (*a*) assiette *f*; **dinner, soup, p.,** assiette plate, creuse; *F:* **to have enough, a lot, on one's p.,** avoir du pain sur la planche; *F:* **to hand s.o. sth. on a p.,** le servir sur un plateau; **p. warmer,** chauffe-assiettes *m inv*; **p. rack,** égouttoir *m*; (*b*) *Ecc: etc:* **(collection) p.,** plateau de quête; **to pass round the p.,** faire la quête.

plate² *v.tr.* **1.** blinder; recouvrir, garnir, (qch.) de plaques. **2.** métalliser; plaquer en or, en argent; étamer (une glace). **3.** *Typ:* clicher (les pages). **plated** *a.* **1.** recouvert, garni, de plaques; **armour p.,** blindé. **2.** plaqué; **gold p.,** doublé d'or; **silver p.,** argenté; **chromium p.,** chromé. **plating** *n.* **1.** (*a*) revêtement *m* en tôle; armature *f* (de four, etc.); **steel, armour, p.,** blindage *m*; (*b*) (*plates*) tôles *fpl*; **deck p.,** bordé *m* de pont. **2.** placage *m*; **copper p.,** cuivrage *m*; **silver p.,** argentage *m*, argenture *f*; **gold p.,** dorage *m*, dorure *f*. **3.** *Typ:* clichage *m*.

plateau, *pl.* **-eaux, -eaus** ['plætou, -ouz], *n.* *Geog:* plateau *m*.

plateful ['pleitful] *n.* assiettée *f*, assiette *f*.

platelayer ['pleitleiər] *n. Rail:* poseur *m* de rails.

platform ['plætfɔ:m] *n.* **1.** terrasse *f*. **2.** (*a*) plate-forme; tablier *m* (de bascule, de pont, etc.); passerelle *f* (de grue); **launching, firing, p.,** plate-forme de lancement, de tir (de missiles); *Rail: NAm:* **p. car,** (wagon *m*) plate-forme; (*b*) *Nau:* parquet *m*, plancher *m*; plate-forme (de cale, de soute); (*c*) *Rail:* quai *m*; **arrival, departure, p.,** quai d'arrivée, de départ. **3.** (*a*) estrade *f*, tribune *f* (de réunion publique); (*b*) *Pol:* plate-forme, programme *m* (d'un parti). **4. p. shoes,** chaussures *f* à semelles compensées.

platinum ['plætinəm] *n.* platine *m*; **p. blond hair,** cheveux platinés; **she's a p. blonde,** c'est une blonde platinée.

platitude ['plætitju:d] *n.* **1.** platitude *f*, insipidité *f* (d'un discours, etc.) **2.** platitude; lieu commun; banalité *f*.

platitudinize [plæti'tju:dinaiz] *v.i.* débiter des platitudes, des banalités.

platitudinous [plæti'tju:dinəs] *a.* (style) plat, banal.

Plato ['pleitou] *Pr.n.* Platon.

Platonic [plə'tɔnik] *a.* (*a*) (philosophie, etc.) platonicien; (*b*) (amour) platonique.

platoon [plə'tu:n] *n. Mil:* (i) section *f* (dans l'infanterie); (ii) peloton *m* (dans les blindés, le train); **p. commander,** chef *m* de section, de peloton.

platter ['plætər] *n.* plat *m* (de bois); écuelle *f*.

platypus ['plætipəs] *n. Z:* ornithor(h)ynque *m*.

plaudits ['plɔ:dits] *n.pl. esp. Lit:* (salve *f* d') applaudissements (*mpl*).

plausibility [plɔ:zi'biliti] *n.* plausibilité *f*.

plausible ['plɔ:zibl] *a.* **1.** (*a*) (*of argument, excuse, etc.*) plausible, vraisemblable; (*b*) (prétexte, etc.) spécieux. **2.** (*of pers.*) captieux; enjôleur; aux belles paroles. **-ibly** *adv.* plausiblement.

play¹ [plei] *n.* **1.** (*a*) jeu *m*, reflets *mpl* (de lumière); chatoiement *m*, reflets (de couleurs); (*b*) maniement *m*, manipulation *f* (d'une arme); jeu (d'un escrimeur); (*c*) jeu, mouvement *m*, activité *f*; **to come into p.,** entrer en jeu; intervenir; **to bring, call, put, sth. into p.,** mettre qch. en jeu, en œuvre; exercer (ses facultés); *U.S:* **to make a p. for sth.,** jouer le grand jeu pour obtenir qch.; **to give, allow, full p. to one's imagination,** donner libre cours à son imagination; (*d*) *Mch:* course *f*, jeu (du piston d'un moteur, etc.); (*e*) *Mec.E: etc:* jeu (d'un boulon, etc., dans son logement). **2.** (*a*) jeu, amusement *m*; **to be at p.,** être en train de jouer; (*b*) **to say sth. in p.,** dire qch. en plaisantant, pour rire; **p. on words,** calembour *m*, jeu de mots; (*c*) échange *m* de caresses, flirt *m*. **3.** (*a*) jeu (de hasard); **to lose at p.,** perdre au jeu; **high, low, p.,** gros jeu, petit jeu; (*b*) *Games:* **p. began at one o'clock,** la partie a commencé à une heure; **ball in, out of, p.,** ballon *m* en jeu; ballon hors-jeu; (*c*) *Pol.Ec: etc:* jeu (des hypothèses, des combinaisons). **4.** pièce *f* (de théâtre); **Shakespeare's plays,** le théâtre de Shakespeare.

play² **I.** *v.i.* **1.** se mouvoir vivement; (*of animals*) folâtrer, gambader; (*of light, colour*) se jouer, chatoyer; **the sun is playing on the water,** le soleil se joue sur l'eau. **2.** (*a*) (*of fountain*) jouer; (*b*) *Mus:* (*of instrument, band, etc.*) jouer; (*c*) (*of part of mechanism, etc.*) jouer, se mouvoir (librement); (*of bolt, etc.*) avoir du jeu. **3.** (*a*) jouer, s'amuser; **to p. (at) soldiers,** jouer aux soldats; **to p. at keeping shop,** jouer à la marchande; **to p. at doing sth.,** faire qch. en amateur; **to p. with a doll,** jouer, s'amuser, avec une poupée; (*b*) **to p. with one's glasses,** jouer (distraitement) avec ses lunettes; (*c*) **to p. with fire,** jouer avec le feu; **to p. with s.o.'s affections,** jouer avec l'affection de qn; (*d*) **to p. on words,** jouer sur les mots, équivoquer; (*e*) (*of man and woman*) flirter; se peloter. **II.** *v.tr. or ind.tr.* **1. to p. football, chess,** jouer au football, aux échecs; **to p. ball,** jouer au ballon; *F:* **what d'you think you're playing at?** que diable fais-tu là? **to p. fair,** jouer franc jeu; **to p. for money,** jouer pour de l'argent; **to p. high, for high stakes,** jouer gros (jeu); *F:* **to p. into s.o.'s hands,** fournir à qn des armes contre soi. **2.** (*a*) **to p. the piano, the flute,** jouer du piano, de la flûte; **to p. a piece,** jouer un morceau; (*b*) faire marcher (un tourne-disques); **to p. a record, a tape,** passer un disque, une bande. **III.** *v.tr.* **1.** *Th: Cin:* (*a*) jouer (un rôle); **to p. Macbeth,** jouer, tenir, le rôle de Macbeth; **to p. an important part,** jouer un rôle important; *v.i.* (*of actor*) **to p. on the stage,** jouer, se produire, sur la scène; **to p. in a film,** jouer, tourner, dans un film; *F:* **to p. the fool,** faire l'idiot, l'imbécile; (*b*) jouer, représenter (une tragédie); **production, film, now playing at . . .,** pièce, film, qui passe actuellement à . . .. **2. to p. a joke, a trick, on s.o.,** jouer un tour à qn. **3.** (*a*) *Cards:* jouer (une carte); **to p. clubs, spades,** jouer trèfle, pique; *v.i.* **to p. high, low,** jouer une forte, basse, carte; *Turf:* **to p. the**

favourite, jouer le favori; *F:* **to p. a hunch,** jouer, agir, par intuition; (*b*) *Games:* jouer (un coup, une balle, etc.); *v.i.* **who plays first?** à qui de commencer? (*at bowling*) à qui la boule? *Golf:* à qui l'honneur? **4.** (*a*) jouer (une partie de tennis); disputer (un match); (*b*) **to p. s.o. at chess,** faire une partie d'échecs avec qn; **I'll p. you for the drinks,** je vous joue les consommations; (*c*) *Fb: etc:* **to p. left back,** jouer arrière *m* gauche; (*d*) *Sp:* inclure (qn) dans son équipe; **the team was playing two reserves,** l'équipe jouait avec deux réserves. **5.** *esp. Lit:* **to p. s.o. false,** trahir qn. **6.** manier avec dextérité, avec habileté (un bâton, une arme, etc.). **7.** diriger (**upon, over,** sur); **to p. a hose on the fire,** diriger la lance sur le feu; *v.i.* **to p. on s.o.'s feelings,** agir, faire pression, sur les sentiments de qn. **play back** *v.tr. Rec:* (faire) repasser (une bande). **play down** *v.tr.* minimiser (l'importance de qch.). **play in** *v.pr. Sp:* **to p. oneself in,** s'accoutumer, se faire, au jeu. **playing** *n.* jeu *m*; **p. card,** carte *f* à jouer; **p. field,** terrain *m* de jeux, de sports. **play off** *v.tr.* (*a*) montrer (qn) sous un jour désavantageux; **to p. s.o. off against s.o.,** opposer qn à qn; to p. **sth. off as sth. (else),** faire passer qch. pour qch.; (*b*) *Sp:* rejouer (un match nul). **play out** *v.tr.* (*a*) jouer (une pièce de théâtre) jusqu'au bout; (*b*) *Cr:* **to p. out time,** faire durer la partie pour obtenir match nul; (*c*) *F:* **played out,** (i) (*of pers., horse, etc.*) très fatigué, vanné, éreinté; (ii) (*of idea, etc.*) vieux jeu, démodé. **play up 1.** *v.i.* (*a*) *Sp:* jouer de son mieux; (*b*) **to p. up to s.o.,** (i) soutenir qn; donner la réplique à qn; (ii) *F:* flatter, aduler, qn; (*c*) (*of child, horse, etc.*) faire des siennes. **2.** *v.tr. F:* (*a*) agacer, enquiquiner (qn); faire marcher (qn); **my rheumatism is playing me up,** mon rhumatisme me fait mal; (*b*) faire ressortir (qch.); exploiter (un incident, un scandale).

playact ['pleiækt] *v.i.* jouer la comédie. **play-acting** *n.* **it's just p.,** c'est de la comédie; c'est une comédie qu'il nous joue.

playback ['pleibæk] *n. Rec: etc:* réécoute *f.*

playbill ['pleibil] *n.* (*a*) affiche *f* (de théâtre); (*b*) *NAm:* programme *m.*

playboy ['pleibɔi] *n.* playboy *m.*

player ['pleiər] *n.* **1.** joueur, -euse; *Mus:* musicien, -ienne; artiste *mf*; **p. piano,** piano *m* mécanique. **2.** *Th:* acteur, -trice; interprète *mf* (d'un rôle). **3.** *Sp:* (*a*) équipier, -ière; (*b*) joueur professionnel. **4. card, billiards, p.,** joueur aux cartes, au billard. **5.** *Rec:* **record p.,** tourne-disques *m*; **cassette p.,** magnétophone *m* à cassettes.

playfellow ['pleifelou] *n. O:* = PLAYMATE.

playful ['pleif(u)l] *a.* enjoué, espiègle, taquin. **-fully** *adv.* gaiement; en badinant.

playfulness ['pleif(u)lnis] *n.* enjouement *m*, badinage *m*, espièglerie *f.*

playgoer ['pleigouər] *n.* habitué, -ée, du théâtre.

playground ['pleigraund] *n.* **1.** *Sch:* cour *f* (de récréation); **covered p.,** préau *m.* **2.** lieu *m* de divertissement.

playhouse ['pleihaus] *n.* théâtre *m.*

playmate ['pleimeit] *n.* camarade *mf* (de jeu); copain, copine.

play-off ['pleiɔf] *n. Sp:* second match nécessité par un match nul; match de barrage.

playpen ['pleipen] *n.* parc *m* à bébé, pour enfants.

playroom ['pleiru:m] *n.* salle *f* de jeux.

playschool ['pleiskul] *n.* = (école) maternelle (*f*).

plaything ['pleiθiŋ] *n.* jouet *m*, joujou *m*; **the children treat the dog like a p.,** le chien sert de jouet aux enfants.

playtime ['pleitaim] *n. Sch:* récréation *f.*

playwright ['pleirait] *n.* auteur *m* dramatique; dramaturge *m.*

plea [pli:] *n.* **1.** *Jur:* (*a*) moyens *mpl* (de défense); défense *f*; (*b*) **incidental p.,** exception *f*; **special p.,** exception péremptoire; (*of counsel*) **to put forward a p. of insanity,** plaider la folie. **2.** (*a*) excuse *f*, prétexte *m*, justification *f* (**for doing sth.,** pour faire qch.); (*b*) **p. for mercy,** appel *m* à la clémence.

plead [pli:d] *v.tr. & i.* (**pleaded,** *occ. NAm:* **pled** [pled]) **1.** *v.i.* (*a*) *Jur:* plaider (**for,** pour; **against,** contre); (*b*) **to p. with s.o. for s.o., sth.,** intervenir, intercéder, plaider, auprès de qn pour qn, qch.; **they were pleading with him to stop,** ils le suppliaient de s'arrêter; (*c*) *Jur:* **to p. guilty, not guilty,** plaider coupable, non coupable. **2.** *v.tr.* (*a*) *Jur:* plaider (une cause); **to p. s.o.'s cause with s.o.,** intercéder pour qn auprès de qn; plaider la cause de qn auprès de qn; (*b*) *Jur:* (*of counsel*) **to p. insanity,** plaider la folie; (*c*) invoquer, alléguer (une excuse); prétexter (l'ignorance, etc.). **pleading 1.** *a.* suppliant, implorant; (regard, ton) de prière. **2.** *n.* (*a*) l'art *m* de plaider; (*b*) *Jur:* plaidoyer *m*; plaidoirie *f*; (*c*) prières *fpl*, intercession *f* (**for,** en faveur de). **pleadingly** *adv.* d'un ton, d'un regard, suppliant.

pleasant ['plezənt] *a.* **1.** agréable, charmant, aimable; **story that makes p. reading,** histoire *f* agréable à lire; **p. breeze,** brise douce; **to keep a p. memory of s.o.,** garder un doux souvenir de qn; **it's a p. day,** il fait bon aujourd'hui; **to have a p. day,** passer agréablement la journée; **goodnight, p. dreams,** bonne nuit, faites de beaux rêves. **2.** (*of pers.*) plaisant; **a man p. to deal with,** un homme d'humeur facile; **to make oneself p., to be p., (to s.o.),** faire l'agréable (auprès de qn), faire l'aimable (avec qn); **he was very p.,** il s'est montré très affable, très gentil. **-ly** *adv.* **1.** agréablement. **2.** d'une manière agréable.

pleasantness ['plezəntnis] *n.* **1.** agrément *m*, charme *m* (d'un endroit, etc.). **2.** (*of pers., manner, etc.*) affabilité *f.*

pleasantry ['plezəntri] *n.* **1.** plaisanterie *f.* **2.** *pl.* **pleasantries,** civilités *fpl.*

please [pli:z] *v.tr.* **1.** (i) plaire à (qn); faire plaisir à (qn); (ii) contenter (qn); **you can't p. everybody,** on ne peut plaire à tout le monde; **he's hard to p.,** il est difficile (à contenter); **music that pleases the ear,** musique qui flatte l'oreille; **p. yourself! do as you p.!** faites comme il vous plaira, comme vous voudrez; **to set out to p. s.o.,** chercher à plaire à qn; **anything to p.!** à tes ordres! **2.** (*a*) *impers. A: & Lit:* **may it p. your Majesty,** plaise, n'en déplaise, à votre Majesté; **p. God!** plaise à Dieu! Dieu le veuille! (*b*) **(if you) p.,** s'il vous plaît; s'il te plaît; **come in, p.,** entrez, s'il vous plaît; entrez, je vous prie; **p. don't cry,** ne pleurez pas, je vous en supplie; **p. tell me . . .,** veuillez me dire . . .; **may I?—p. do!** vous permettez?—je vous en prie! **p. sit down, p. take a seat,** veuillez vous asseoir; **p. don't interrupt!** veuillez bien ne pas nous interrompre; *P.N:* **p. do not walk on the grass,** prière de ne pas marcher sur le gazon; *Sch:* **p., sir!** pardon, monsieur! *Iron:* **and then if you p. he blamed me for it!** et puis il a dit que c'était de ma faute! **3.** *v.i.* **to do as one pleases,** agir à sa guise, à son gré; **do as you p.,** faites comme vous voudrez; **he will only do as he pleases,** il n'en fera qu'à sa tête; *F:* **just as you p.,** c'est, ce sera, comme vous voudrez. **pleased** *a.* **1.** satisfait, content; heureux; (sourire) de satisfaction; **to be p. with sth.,** être satisfait de qch.; approuver qch.; **he's very, highly, p., with himself,** il est très content, fort satisfait, de sa petite personne; **I'm very p. he's coming,** cela me fait grand plaisir, je suis très content, qu'il vienne; *F:* **he's as p. as Punch,** (i) il est heureux comme un roi; (ii) il en est fier comme Artaban; **to be p. to do sth.,** faire qch. avec plaisir; **I'll be p. to come,** je viendrai avec plaisir; **I'm very p. to see you,** je suis très content, cela me fait grand plaisir, de vous voir; **I'm p. to say that . . .,** je suis heureux de pouvoir vous dire que . . .; *Com:* **I am p. to inform you that . . .,** je m'empresse de vous aviser que . . .. **2. His Majesty has been graciously p. to . . .,** il a plu à sa gracieuse Majesté de . . .. **pleasing** *a.* agréable; sympathique; **p. manner,** abord *m* agréable; prévenance *f.* **pleasingly** *adv.* agréablement.

pleasurable ['pleʒərəbl] *a.* agréable. **-ably** *adv.* agréablement.

pleasure[1] ['pleʒər] *n.* **1.** plaisir *m*; **to take, find, (a) p. in doing sth.,** éprouver du plaisir, prendre, avoir (du) plaisir à faire qch.; **I have p. in informing you that . . .,** je suis heureux de vous apprendre que . . .; **it gave me great p.,** cela m'a fait grand plaisir; **it's a real p. to see you looking so cheerful,** cela me fait (infiniment de) plaisir de vous voir si gai; **it is a p. to listen to him,** on a plaisir à l'écouter; **I haven't the p. of knowing him, of his acquaintance,** je n'ai pas le plaisir de le connaître; **Mr X requests the p. of the company of Miss Y at . . .,** M. X prie Mlle Y de lui faire le plaisir d'assister à . . .; **with p.,** avec plaisir; volontiers; de grand cœur; **with the greatest (of) p.,** avec le plus grand plaisir. **2.** (*a*) plaisir(s), jouissances *fpl*; **life given up to p., life of p.,** vie adonnée au plaisir; **to take one's p.,** s'amuser, se divertir; **to travel for p.,** voyager pour son plaisir; **p. seeker,** jouisseur, -euse; **p. seeking,** recherche *f* des plaisirs; **p. trip,** partie *f* de plaisir; **p. boat,** bateau *m* de plaisance; (*b*) **sensual p.,** volupté *f*, débauche *f.* **3.** volonté *f*; bon plaisir; **at s.o.'s p.,** au gré de qn; au bon plaisir de qn; **during the King's p.,** pendant le bon plaisir du roi.

pleasure[2] *v.* **1.** *v.tr.* faire plaisir à (qn). **2.** *v.i.* se plaire, prendre plaisir (**in sth., in doing sth.,** à qch., à faire qch.).

pleat[1] [pli:t] *n. Dressm: etc:* pli *m*; **inverted p.,** pli creux, rentré, inverti; **box p.,** double pli.

pleat[2] *v.tr.* plisser, faire des plis à (une jupe, etc.). **pleated** *a.* (*of skirt, etc.*) plissé. **pleating** *n.* **1.** plissage *m.* **2.** *coll.* plissé(s) *m(pl).*

pleb [pleb] *n.* (*a*) *F:* plébéien, -ienne; prolétaire *mf*; (*b*) *F:* **the plebs,** le prolétariat.

plebeian [pli'bi:ən] **1.** *n.* plébéien; prolétaire *mf.* **2.** *a.* plébéien, vulgaire.

plebiscite ['plebisit] *n.* plébiscite *m*; **to vote for (s.o., sth.) by p.,** plébisciter (qn, qch.).

plectrum ['plektrəm] *n. Mus:* médiator *m.*

pledge[1] [pledʒ] *n.* **1.** gage *m*, nantissement *m*; **p. holder,** détenteur, -trice, de gage(s); (créancier *m*) gagiste (*m*); **unredeemed p.,** gage non retiré; **to hold in p.,** (dé)tenir en gage, en nantissement; **to redeem a p.,** retirer un gage; **to take sth. out of p.,** dégager qch. **2. p. of good faith,** garantie *f* de bonne foi. **3.** (*a*) promesse *f*, vœu *m*; **I am under a p. of secrecy,** j'ai fait vœu de garder le secret; (*b*) **to take, sign, the p.,** promettre de s'abstenir d'alcool.

pledge[2] *v.tr.* **1.** donner, mettre (qch.) en gage; déposer (qch.) en gage, en nantissement; donner (qch.) en garantie; engager, gager (qch.). **2.** engager (sa parole, etc.); **to p. oneself, one's word, to do sth.,** s'engager à faire qch.; **to be pledged to do sth.,** avoir pris l'engagement de faire qch.; **to p. one's honour,** donner sa parole d'honneur; s'engager d'honneur (**to do sth.,** à faire qch.); **to p. one's allegiance to the king,** vouer obéissance au roi.

pleiad *pl.* **-ads, -ades** ['plaiæd, -ædz, -ədi:z] *n.* **1.** *Lit:* pléiade *f.* **2.** *Myth: Astr:* **the Pleiads, the Pleiades,** les Pléiades.

plenary ['pli:nəri] *a.* complet, -ète, entier; **p. power,** pouvoir absolu; plein pouvoir; **p. assembly,** assemblée plénière.

plenipotentiary [plenipə'tenʃ(ə)ri] *a.* & *n.* plénipotentiaire (*m*).

plenitude ['plenitju:d] *n.* plénitude *f.*

plentiful ['plentif(u)l] *a.* abondant, copieux, ample; **to be p.,** abonder, affluer. **-fully** *adv.* abondamment; copieusement.

plenty ['plenti] **1.** *n.* (*a*) abondance *f*; **p. of money, money in p.,** une ample provision d'argent; de l'argent en abondance; **to have p. of courage,** ne pas manquer de courage; **you've got p. of time,** vous avez largement le temps; **to arrive in p. of time,** arriver de bonne heure; **to have p. to live on,** avoir grandement de quoi vivre; (*b*) **to live in p.,** vivre à l'aise; vivre dans l'abondance; **land of p.,** pays *m* de cocagne; **year of p.,** année *f* d'abondance. **2.** *adv. F:* **it's p. big enough,** c'est bien assez gros. **3.** *a. A: & U.S:* abondant, ample; **money is p.,** l'argent abonde.

pleonasm ['pli:ənæzm] *n.* pléonasme *m.*

pleonastic [pli:ə'næstik] *a.* pléonastique, redondant; (*of word*) **to be p.,** faire pléonasme.

plethora ['pleθərə] *n.* **1.** *Med:* pléthore *f.* **2.** pléthore, surabondance *f* (de bien, etc.).

pleurisy ['pluərisi] *n. Med:* pleurésie *f.*

plexus ['pleksəs] *n.* **1.** *Anat:* plexus *m*; **solar p.,** plexus solaire. **2.** enchevêtrement *m* (de rues, etc.).

pliability [plaiə'biliti] *n.* (*a*) flexibilité *f*, souplesse *f* (d'une tige); (*b*) docilité *f*, souplesse (de caractère).

pliable ['plaiəbl] *a.* **1.** pliable, pliant, flexible; (cuir) souple. **2.** (caractère, etc.) docile, malléable, souple.

pliers ['plaiəz] *n.pl. Tls:* pince(s) *f(pl)*, tenaille(s) *f(pl)*; **universal p.,** pinces universelles; **surgical p.,** pince(s) chirurgicale(s).

plight[1] [plait] *n.* condition *f*, état *m*; **to be in a sorry, sad, p.,** (i) être en mauvaise passe; (ii) être dans un triste état; **what a p. you're in!** comme vous voilà fait!

plight[2] *v.tr. Lit:* engager, promettre (sa foi, etc.); **to p. one's troth to s.o.,** (i) donner sa foi à qn; (ii) *A:* se fiancer à qn.

Plimsoll ['plimsəl] **1.** *Pr.n. Nau:* **P. line, mark,** ligne *f* de Plimsoll. **2.** *n.pl.* **plimsolls,** chaussures *fpl* de gymnastique, de tennis, etc.

plinth [plinθ] *n. Arch:* plinthe *f*; socle *m* (d'une statue, d'une colonne).

Pliny ['plini] *Pr.n.m. Lt. Lit:* **P. the Elder, the Younger,** Pline l'Ancien, le Jeune.

plod[1] [plɔd] *n.* **1.** (*a*) marche lourde, pénible; (*b*) pas pesant. **2.** travail *m* pénible, rebutant; travail assidu.

plod[2] *v.i.* **(plodded) 1.** marcher lourdement, péniblement; **to p. along, to p. one's way,** cheminer, avancer, aller, marcher, d'un pas pesant; **to p. on,** continuer sa marche pénible. **2. to p. (away),** travailler laborieusement; peiner, trimer (**at,** à). **plodding 1.** *a.* (*a*) (par) pesant, lourd; (*b*) qui travaille laborieusement. **2.** *n.* (*a*) marche lourde; (*b*) labeur assidu.

plodder ['plɔdər] *n.* travailleur, -euse, persévérant, -ante; **he's a p.,** il est courageux au travail.

plonk[1] [plɔŋk] *n.* bruit sourd.

plonk[2] *v.tr. F:* poser (qch.) lourdement et sans façons; **to p. oneself down in an armchair,** se laisser tomber dans un fauteuil.

plonk[3] *n. F:* vin *m* ordinaire; pinard *m.*

plop[1] [plɔp] *n., adv.* **1.** flac (*m*), plouf (*m*) (de qch. tombant dans l'eau). **2.** (bruit sourd de) pouf (*m*).

plop[2] *v.i.* **(plopped). 1.** faire flac; tomber (dans l'eau) en faisant flac, plouf. **2.** tomber en faisant pouf.

plosive ['plousiv] *a.* & *n. Ling:* (consonne) explosive.

plot[1] [plɔt] *n.* **1.** (parcelle *f*, lot *m*, de) terrain (*m*); coin *m*, lopin *m*, quartier *m* (de terre); **building p.,** terrain à bâtir, lotissement *m*; (*in garden*) **vegetable p.,** coin des légumes. **2.** intrigue *f*, action *f* (d'une pièce de théâtre, d'un roman, etc.); **the p. thickens,** l'affaire *f* se corse. **3.** *Mth: etc:* tracé *m*; graphe *m*, graphique *m*; courbe *f* (d'un point mobile, etc.); *Surv:* relèvement *m*; point *m*; *Av: Nau:* tracé, graphe (de la route d'un avion, d'un navire, etc.); *Rad:* pointé *m*. **4.** complot *m*, conspiration *f*; **to hatch a p.,** tramer, ourdir, un complot.

plot² *v.* **(plotted) I.** *v.tr.* **1.** *Surv: etc:* (*a*) dresser, lever, le plan de, faire le levé de, lever (un terrain, etc.); (*b*) tracer, rapporter (une figure géométrique, un levé topographique); (*c*) marquer, tracer, repérer (un point) (sur une carte); *Rad:* marquer, relever (un pointé de radar); **to p. a course,** relever, tracer, une route (d'avion, de navire, etc.); *Av: Nau:* **to p. the position,** faire le point. **2.** *Mth: Ph:* tracer, faire le graphe, le graphique (d'une courbe, etc.); tracer, relever (un diagramme, un graphe). **3.** comploter, combiner (la ruine de qn); ourdir, tramer (un complot). **II.** *v.i.* comploter, conspirer (**against s.o.,** contre qn). **plotting** *n.* **1.** *Surv: etc:* (*a*) report *m* (d'un point repéré sur le terrain); levé *m* (d'un terrain); **p. of details,** levé des détails; (*b*) pointage *m* (d'une carte); (*c*) report (des cotes relevés sur un appareil enregistreur, etc.); (*d*) *Rad:* report, marquage *m* (des pointés de radar); plotting *m*. **2.** représentation *f* graphique; tracé *m* (d'une courbe); *Av: Nau:* tracé (de la route). **3.** complots *mpl*.

plotter ['plɔtər] *n.* **1.** (*a*) (*pers.*) traceur, -euse; *Rad:* marqueur, -euse, plotteur *m* (de pointés de radar); (*b*) (*device*) abaque *m*; appareil *m* à tracer; traceur (de courbes). **2.** conspirateur, -trice; comploteur *m*.

plough¹, *NAm:* **plow¹** [plau] *n.* **1.** (*a*) charrue *f*; **to put one's hand to the p.,** mettre la main à la charrue; **to follow the p.,** être laboureur; (*b*) *F:* terres *fpl* de labour; labours *mpl*. **2.** *Astr:* **the P.,** la Grande Ourse. **3.** *Sch: F: O:* échec *m* (à un examen).

plough², *NAm:* **plow² I.** *v.tr.* **1.** (*a*) labourer (un champ, etc.); tracer, creuser (un sillon); **to p. the soil,** retourner la terre (à la charrue); *v.i.* **to p.,** labourer la terre; **ploughed land,** terres *fpl* de labour; labours *mpl*; **to p. (one's way) through the snow,** avancer péniblement dans la neige; **to p. through a book,** lire laborieusement un livre jusqu'au bout; (*b*) (*of ship*) fendre, sillonner (les flots); (*c*) **as negotiations p. on,** pendant que les négociations continuent avec difficulté. **2.** *Sch: F: O:* **to p. an exam, to be, get, ploughed in an exam,** échouer, être recalé, collé, à un examen. **3.** *Com: Fin:* **profits ploughed back into the business,** bénéfices reversés dans l'affaire; **ploughing back of profits,** autofinancement *m*. **plough in,** *NAm:* **plow in** *v.tr.* enterrer, enfouir (le fumier, etc.) dans le sol en labourant. **ploughing,** *NAm:* **plowing** *n.* labourage *m*, labour *m*. **plough up,** *NAm:* **plow up** *v.tr.* (*a*) (i) faire passer la charrue dans, sur (un champ); (ii) (*of shells, etc.*) effondrer, défoncer (le terrain); (*b*) déraciner, arracher, (des mauvaises herbes, etc.) avec la charrue.

ploughland, *NAm:* **plowland** ['plaulænd] *n.* (*a*) terre labourée, cultivée; terres *fpl* de labour; labours *mpl*; (*b*) terre arable, labourable; labourage *m*.

ploughman, *NAm:* **plowman,** *pl.* **-men** ['plaumən] *n.m.* (*a*) laboureur; (*b*) **ploughman's lunch,** déjeuner *m* de pain, de beurre et de fromage arrosé de bière.

ploughshare, *NAm:* **plowshare** ['plauʃɛər] *n.* soc *m* de charrue.

plover ['plʌvər] *n.* **1.** *Orn:* pluvier *m*; **golden p.,** pluvier doré. **2.** *Cu:* **plovers' eggs,** œufs *mpl* de vanneau.

plow¹, ² [plau] *n.* & *v.* *NAm:* = PLOUGH¹, ².

ploy [plɔi] *n.* stratagème *m*, *F:* truc *m*.

pluck¹ [plʌk] *n.* courage *m*, cran *m*; **he's got plenty of p.,** il a du cran; il a du cœur au ventre.

pluck² *v.tr.* **1.** arracher (des cheveux, des plumes, etc.); cueillir (une fleur). **2.** (*a*) **to p. (at) s.o.'s sleeve,** tirer qn par la manche; (*b*) **to p. a guitar,** pincer de la guitare. **3.** (*a*) plumer (une volaille); (*b*) **to p. one's eyebrows,** s'épiler les sourcils. **pluck up** *v.tr.* **to p. up (one's) courage to do sth.,** s'armer de courage pour faire qch.

pluckiness ['plʌkinis] *n.* *O:* courage *m*.

plucky ['plʌki] *a.* courageux; **to be p.,** avoir du courage, du cran. **-ily** *adv.* courageusement, avec courage.

plug¹ [plʌg] *n.* **1.** (*a*) bouchon *m*, tampon *m*; bonde *f*, crapaudine *f* (de bassin, de réservoir, etc.); **waste p.,** tampon, soupape *f* (de baignoire, de lavabo); bouchon (d'évier); (*b*) *Surg: Dent:* tampon (d'ouate, de coton); (*c*) *Geol:* culot *m* volcanique. **2.** (*a*) fiche *f*; *El:* fiche (mâle); prise *f* de courant; broche *f* (de lampe, etc.); **two-pin, three-pin, p.,** fiche à deux, à trois, broches; **wall p.,** prise de courant (murale); **p. socket,** prise de courant (femelle); (*b*) (*for nail, screw, in wall*) fiche; tampon (de scellement); scellement *m*; (*c*) *Rail:* cale *f*, coin (pour coussinet de rail); (*e*) *I.C.E:* **spark(ing) p.,** bougie. **3.** (*a*) **fire hydrant p.,** bouche *f* d'incendie; (*b*) chasse *f* d'eau (de w.c.); **to pull the p.,** tirer la chaîne. **4.** *O:* **p. of tobacco,** chique *f* de tabac; carotte *f*. **5.** *F: Com:* réclame; battage *m*.

plug² *v.* **(plugged) I.** *v.tr.* **1.** **to p. (up),** boucher, obturer (une ouverture, un tuyau); tamponner (une ouverture, une plaie); *Nau:* taper (un écubier, etc.); *Dent:* obstruer (une cavité dentaire); (*of pipe, etc.*) **to get plugged (up),** se boucher, s'obstruer. **2.** (*a*) enfoncer des chevilles dans (un mur, etc.); (*b*) **to p. in,** (i) *v.tr. El:* brancher (une lampe, etc.); connecter; (ii) *v.i.* mettre une fiche dans une prise de courant. **3.** *P:* (*a*) fusiller, flinguer (qn); (*b*) flanquer un coup à (qn); **p. him one in the earhole,** donne-lui une beigne. **4.** *F:* faire de la réclame, du battage, pour (un produit, etc.). **II.** *v.i.* (*a*) se boucher, s'obstruer; (*b*) *F:* **to p. away,** persévérer, s'acharner.

plughole ['plʌghoul] *n.* bonde *f*; trou *m* d'écoulement (d'évier, de baignoire).

plum [plʌm] *n.* **1.** (*a*) prune *f*; **p. jam,** confiture *f* de prunes; (*b*) **p. (tree),** prunier *m*. **2.** *Cu:* **p. cake,** cake *m*, gâteau *m* aux raisins; **p. pudding,** pudding de Noël. **3.** **p.(-coloured),** (de couleur) prune *inv.* **4.** *F:* (*a*) travail bien rétribué; **to have a p. job,** avoir une place en or; (*b*) fin morceau, morceau de choix.

plumage ['plu:midʒ] *n.* plumage *m*.

plumb¹ [plʌm] *n.* **1.** **p. (bob),** plomb *m* (d'un fil à plomb). **2.** aplomb *m*; **out of p.,** hors d'aplomb; dévoyé; (mur) qui porte à faux; **p. line,** (i) fil à plomb; (ii) verticale *f*. **3.** *Nau:* **p. (line)** (ligne *f* de) sonde (*f*).

plumb² *v.tr.* **1.** sonder (la mer, etc.); *Lit:* **to p. the depths,** toucher le fond du désespoir. **2.** vérifier l'aplomb de (qch.); plomber (un mur, etc.). **3.** **to p. in a washing machine,** raccorder une machine à laver. **plumbing** *n.* **1.** plomberie *f*, plombage *m*. **2.** *coll.* tuyauterie *f*; tuyaux *mpl*. **3.** *F:* installations *fpl* sanitaires; **to have a look at the p.,** aller faire pipi.

plumb³ 1. *a.* (*a*) droit; vertical, -aux; d'aplomb; (*b*) *NAm: F:* (*intensive*) **p. nonsense,** pure sottise. **2.** *adv.* perpendiculairement (**with sth.,** à qch.); à la verticale, à l'aplomb (**with sth.,** de qch.); *F:* **p. in the centre,** en plein milieu, au beau milieu; *F:* **p. crazy,** complètement fou.

plumbago [plʌm'beigou] *n.* *Miner:* plombagine *f*.

plumber ['plʌmər] *n.* plombier *m*.

plume¹ [plu:m] *n.* **1.** *A:* & *Lit:* plume *f*; *Fig:* **in borrowed plumes,** paré des plumes du paon. **2.** panache *m*, aigrette *f*; plumet *m* (de casque).

plume² 1. *v.tr.* (*a*) orner, garnir, de plumes; **black-plumed,** aux plumes noires; (*b*) **plumed helmet,** casque empanaché. **2.** *v.pr.* (*a*) (*of bird*) **to p. itself,** se lisser les plumes; (*b*) (*of pers.*) *O:* **to p. oneself on sth.,** se glorifier de qch.

plummet¹ ['plʌmit] *n.* **1.** plomb *m* (de fil à plomb, de sonde, de ligne de pêche). **2.** (*a*) fil *m* à plomb; (*b*) *Nau:* sonde *f.*

plummet² **1.** *v.tr. Nau:* sonder. **2.** *v.i.* (*a*) plonger, tomber, verticalement; **the aircraft plummeted to the ground,** l'avion s'est écrasé au sol; (*b*) (*of prices, etc.*) s'effondrer; (*of blood pressure, etc.*) tomber soudainement.

plummy ['plʌmi] *a.* **1.** *F:* (travail) agréable, bien payé. **2.** (*of voice*) de la haute, snob.

plump¹ [plʌmp] *a.* (*of pers.*) rebondi, grassouillet, dodu, boulot; (*of fowl*) dodu; (*of chicken or pers.*) bien en chair; (*of hands*) potelé.

plump² **1.** *v.tr.* engraisser; rendre dodu; (*b*) **to p. up,** secouer, brasser (un oreiller). **2.** *v.i.* **to p. (out, up),** devenir dodu; engraisser.

plump³ **1.** *n.* bruit sourd (de chute); floc *m,* plouf *m.* **2.** *adv.* (*a*) **to fall p. into the mud,** tomber dans la boue avec un floc; (*b*) (dire qch.) brusquement, carrément, tout net. **3.** *a.* (dénégation) catégorique.

plump⁴ **1.** *v.tr.* jeter brusquement, flanquer; **to p. down,** déposer brusquement (une valise, etc.); **to p. oneself into an armchair,** s'affaler dans un fauteuil. **2.** *v.i.* (*a*) tomber lourdement; faire plouf; (*b*) **to p. for sth.,** choisir qch.

plumpness ['plʌmpnis] *n.* embonpoint *m,* rondeur *f.*

plunder¹ ['plʌndər] *n.* (*a*) butin *m*; (*b*) *F:* petits bénéfices; gratte *f.*

plunder² **1.** *v.tr.* piller, mettre à sac, dépouiller (un pays, etc.); dépouiller (qn). **2.** *v.i. F:* brigander. **plundering** **1.** *a.* pillard. **2.** *n.* pillage *m.*

plunge¹ [plʌndʒ] *n.* plongeon *m*; **to take a p.,** faire un plongeon, plonger (**into,** dans); *F:* **to take the p.,** (i) prendre le taureau par les cornes; (ii) se marier.

plunge² **1.** *v.tr.* plonger, immerger (le linge dans la lessive, etc.); **to p. a dagger into s.o.'s back,** plonger un poignard dans le dos de qn; **plunged in darkness,** plongé dans l'obscurité; **to p. s.o. into despair,** plonger qn dans le désespoir. **2.** *v.i.* (*a*) plonger, se jeter (la tête la première) (dans l'eau, etc.); s'enfoncer, s'engouffrer (dans un bois, etc.); se jeter (à corps perdu) (dans une affaire, etc.); **the lorry plunged over the cliff,** le camion plongea par-dessus la falaise; **she plunged to her death,** elle fit une chute mortelle; (*b*) **to p. forward,** s'élancer en avant; (*c*) (*of ship*) tanguer, piquer du nez; (*d*) *Gaming:* jouer sans compter, gros jeu. **plunging** **1.** *a.* **p. neckline,** décolleté plongeant. **2.** *n.* (*a*) plongement *m*; immersion *f*; (*b*) tangage *m* (d'un bateau).

plunger ['plʌndʒər] *n.* **1.** (*pers.*) (*a*) plongeur, -euse; (*b*) *F:* joueur, -euse, effréné(e). **2.** (*device*) (*a*) plongeur (de pompe, etc.); heuse *f,* chopine *f* (de pompe); (*b*) *Dom.Ec:* **(rubber) p.,** ventouse *f.*

plunk [plʌŋk] *v.tr.* (*a*) pincer les cordes (d'un banjo, etc.); *F:* (*b*) laisser tomber lourdement (qch.); **to p. down,** déposer (qch.) lourdement.

pluperfect [plu'pəːfikt] *a.* & *n. Gram:* plus-que-parfait (*m*).

plural ['pluər(ə)l] **1.** *a.* & *n. Gram:* pluriel (*m*); **in the p.,** au pluriel. **2.** *a. Pol:* **p. vote,** vote plural.

pluralism ['pluərəlizm] *n.* **1.** cumul *m* de fonctions, *Ecc:* de bénéfices. **2.** *Phil: etc:* pluralisme *m.*

plurality [pluə'ræliti] *n.* **1.** pluralité *f.* **2.** cumul *m* (de fonctions, *Ecc:* de bénéfices). **3.** *Ecc:* bénéfice détenu par cumul. **4.** majorité *f* (des voix).

plus [plʌs] **1.** *prep.* plus; **seven p. nine,** sept plus neuf; **two floors p. an attic,** deux étages plus un grenier. **2.** *a.* (*a*) (*of quantity, number, electric charge, etc.*) positif; (*b*) **on the p. side of the account,** à l'actif du compte; (*c*) *Cost:* **p. fours,** culotte (bouffante) de golf; (*d*) *F:* **fifteen p.,** au-dessus de quinze ans. **3.** *n.* (*pl.* **plusses** ['plʌsiz]) (*a*) plus *m*; signe *m* de l'addition; (*b*) quantité positive; (*c*) avantage *m*; atout *m.*

plush¹ [plʌʃ] *n. Tex:* peluche *f,* panne *f.*

plush² *a.* **1.** en peluche. **2.** *F:* (appartement, etc.) somptueux, luxueux.

plushy ['plʌʃi] *a.* peluché; rupin.

Plutarch ['pluːtɑːk] *Pr.n.m. Gr.Lit:* Plutarque.

Pluto ['pluːtou] *Pr.n.m. Myth: Astr:* Pluton.

plutocracy [pluː'tɔkrəsi] *n.* ploutocratie *f.*

plutocrat ['pluːtəkræt] *n.* ploutocrate *m.*

plutocratic [pluːtə'krætik] *a.* ploutocratique.

plutonium [pluː'touniəm] *n. Ch:* plutonium *m.*

pluviometer [pluːvi'ɔmitər] *n.* pluviomètre *m.*

ply¹ [plai] *n.* **1.** (*a*) pli *m* (de tissu appliqué en plusieurs plis); (*b*) placage *m,* épaisseur *f* (de contreplaqué); pli (d'un pneu). **2.** brin *m,* fil *m* (de corde, de laine); toron *m* (de corde); **three-p. wool,** laine *f* trois fils.

ply² **1.** *v.tr.* (*a*) manier vigoureusement (un outil, etc.); faire courir (l'aiguille); (*b*) exercer (un métier); (*c*) **to p. s.o. with questions,** presser, harceler, qn de questions; **to p. s.o. with drink,** verser force rasades à qn; arroser (un client); **to p. s.o. with food,** bourrer qn de nourriture. **2.** *v.i.* (*of ship, bus, etc.*) faire le service, la navette, le va-et-vient (**between . . . and . . .,** entre . . . et . . .); (*of taxi, etc.*) **to p. for hire,** prendre des voyageurs.

plywood ['plaiwud] *n.* (bois) contre-plaqué (*m*).

pneumatic [njuː'mætik] *a.* (machine, outil) pneumatique; **p. drill,** marteau *m* pneumatique; **p. tyre,** pneumatique *m,* pneu *m.* **-ally** *adv.* **p. operated,** (appareil) à marche pneumatique, à air comprimé.

pneumatics [njuː'mætiks] *n.pl. Ph:* (*usu. with sg. const.*) pneumatique *f.*

pneumonia [njuː'mouniə] *n. Med:* pneumonie *f*; congestion *f* pulmonaire.

po [pou] *n. F:* pot *m* de chambre, Jules *m*; **po-faced,** avec une figure d'enterrement.

poach¹ [poutʃ] *v.tr. Cu:* pocher (des œufs); **poached egg,** œuf poché.

poach² **1.** *v.tr.* (*a*) braconner dans (un bois, etc.); (*b*) braconner (le gibier, etc.). **2.** *v.i.* braconner; **to p. on s.o.'s preserves,** (i) braconner sur la chasse réservée de qn; (ii) *Fig:* empiéter sur les prérogatives de qn. **poaching** *n.* braconnage *m.*

poacher¹ ['poutʃər] *n.* pocheuse *f* (à œufs).

poacher² *n.* braconnier *m.*

pock [pɔk] *n. Med:* pustule *f* (de la petite vérole).

pocket¹ ['pɔkit] *n.* **1.** (*a*) poche *f* (de vêtement); **waistcoat p.,** gousset *m*; **small p.,** pochette *f*; **p. comb, handkerchief,** peigne *m,* mouchoir *m,* de poche; *F:* **to line one's pockets,** faire sa pelote; **to put one's hands in one's pockets,** mettre les mains dans ses poches; **to go through s.o.'s pockets,** faire les poches à qn; *F:* **to have s.o. in one's p.,** faire marcher qn comme on veut; **p. money,** argent *m* de poche; **p. dictionary,** dictionnaire *m* de poche; *Bookb:* **p. size,** format *m* de poche; *Navy:* **p. battleship,** cuirassé *m* de poche; (*b*) **prices to suit every p.,** des prix à la portée de tout le monde; *F:* **to suffer in one's p.,** en être de sa poche; **he's always got his hand in his p.,** il a toujours la main à la poche; il est toujours à débourser; **to be in p.,** être en bénéfice, en gain; **to be out of p. (over a transaction),** être en perte; ne pas rentrer dans ses fonds. **2.** (*a*) sac *m* (de houblon, de laine); (*b*) *Bill:* blouse *f*; (*c*) *Aut:* (*in door, etc.*) **car p.,** poche intérieure; (*d*) **pockets under the eyes,** poches sous les yeux. **3.** *Mec.E:* retrait *m* (pour recevoir un organe, etc.); *I.C.E:* chambre *f* (de soupape). **4.** (*a*) *Min:* poche, nid *m,* sac (de minerai); (*b*) poche (d'eau, de gaz); nid (de grisou); (*c*) **air p.,** (i) *Av:* trou *m* d'air; (ii) *Hyd.E: etc:* cantonnement *m,* poche, d'air (dans une canalisation); (iii) collecteur *m* à air; poche à air. **5.** *Fig:* poche (de résistance, de rébellion, etc.).

pocket² *v.tr.* **(pocketed) 1.** (*a*) empocher (qch.); mettre (qch.) dans sa poche; (*b*) *Pej:* soustraire (de l'argent); chiper (qch.). **2.** avaler, empocher, encaisser (un affront, une insulte, etc.). **3.** faire taire (ses sentiments); **to p. one's pride,** mettre son amour-propre dans sa poche. **4.** *Bill:* blouser (la bille).

pocketbook ['pɔkitbuk] *n.* (*a*) carnet *m*; (*b*) *Nam:* (i) portefeuille *m*; (ii) sac *m* à main; (*c*) *NAm:* livre *m* de poche.

pocketful ['pɔkitful] *n.* pleine poche; **pocketfuls of sweets,** des poches pleines de bonbons.

pocketknife ['pɔkitnaif] *n.* couteau *m* de poche, canif *m.*

pockmark ['pɔkmɑːk] *n.* marque *f* de la petite vérole.

pockmarked ['pɔkmɑːkt] *a.* marqué, picoté, de la petite vérole; (visage) grêlé.

pod¹ [pɔd] *n.* **1.** (*a*) cosse *f*, gousse *f* (de fèves, de pois, etc.); (*b*) **senna pods,** follicules *mpl* de séné. **2.** cocon *m* (de ver à soie). **3.** *Fish:* nasse *f* (pour anguilles). **4.** *Av:* nacelle *f*, fuseau *m* (de réacteur, etc.); **engine p.,** nacelle-moteur *f*, *pl.* nacelles-moteur.

pod² *v.* **(podded) 1.** *v.i.* (*of plant*) former des cosses, des gousses. **2.** *v.tr.* écosser, écaler (des pois, etc.).

podgy ['pɔdʒi] *a.* boulot, -otte, replet, -ète; (doigts) boudinés, rondelets.

podium, *pl.* **-ia** ['poudiəm, -iə] *n.* podium *m.*

poem ['pouim] *n.* poème *m*; poésie *f.*

poet ['pouit] *n.* poète *m.*

poetaster [poui'tæstər] *n.* mauvais poète; rimailleur *m.*

poetess ['pouitis] *n.f.* femme poète; poétesse.

poetic(al) [pou'etik(l)] *a.* poétique. **-ally** *adv.* poétiquement.

poetry ['pouitri] *n.* poésie *f*; **to write p.,** écrire des vers; **the art of p.,** l'art *m* poétique.

pogrom ['pɔgrəm] *n.* pogrom(e) *m.*

poignancy ['pɔinjənsi] *n.* caractère poignant (d'une émotion, etc.).

poignant ['pɔinjənt] *a.* (*of feeling*) poignant, vif; (*of regret, etc.*) amer. **-ly** *adv.* d'une façon poignante.

poinsettia [pɔin'setiə] *n.* *Bot:* poinsettia *f.*

point¹ [pɔint] *n.* **I.** point *m.* **1.** (*a*) *Gram:* **full p.,** point (de ponctuation); (*b*) *Mth:* **decimal p.,** virgule (décimale); **three p. five (3.5)** = trois virgule cinq (3,5). **2.** (*point in space*) (*a*) **p. of arrival, of departure,** point d'arrivée, de départ; **assembly p.,** lieu *m* de rassemblement; **observation p.,** point d'observation; *Rac:* **p.-to-p. (race),** course *f* au clocher; *Mil:* **key points,** points vitaux; points d'importance stratégique, tactique; (*b*) **p. of view,** point de vue; **to consider sth. from all points of view,** considérer qch. sous tous ses aspects. **3.** (*a*) point, détail *m* (d'un raisonnement, etc.); **the chief p. of an argument,** l'important, l'essentiel, d'un raisonnement; **figures that give p. to his argument,** chiffres qui ajoutent du poids à sa thèse; **on that p. we disagree,** là-dessus nous ne sommes pas d'accord; **I see, take, your p.,** je vois ce que vous voulez dire; **p. taken!** très juste! **to make a p.,** faire ressortir un argument; **points to be reed,** considérations *fpl* à se rappeler; **to make a p. of doing sth.,** se faire un devoir de faire qch.; ne pas manquer de faire qch.; **p. of grammar, of law,** question de grammaire, de droit; **in p. of fact,** en fait; à vrai dire; **p. of honour,** point d'honneur; (*b*) **the p.,** le sujet, la question; **the p. is (that) . . .,** c'est que . . .; **that's the p.,** justement; **that's not the p.,** il ne s'agit pas de cela; **beside, off, the p.,** à côté de la question; hors de propos; **on this p.,** à cet égard; à ce propos; **this is very much to the p.,** c'est bien parlé, bien dit; (*c*) **what would be the p. of (doing sth.)?** à quoi bon (faire qch.)? **there is no p. in (doing) it,** cela ne servirait à rien; **I don't see the p. of the story,** je ne vois pas où cette histoire veut en venir; (*d*) caractère *m*; trait distinctif; **p. of interest,** détail intéressant; **to have its good points,** avoir ses bons côtés. **4.** (*a*) (*precise moment*) **to be on the p. of doing sth.,** être sur le point de faire qch.; **at, on, the p. of death,** sur le point de mourir; à l'article de la mort; **to be on the p. of departure,** être sur le point de partir; **p. of no return,** point de non-retour; **critical p.,** point critique; (*b*) **to come to the p.,** arriver au fait; **when it came to the p.,** quand le moment critique est arrivé; **up to a (certain) p.,** jusqu'à un certain point; **severe to the p. of cruelty,** sévère jusqu'à la cruauté. **5.** *Games:* **to score so many points,** marquer, faire, tant de points; *Cards: etc:* **to play ten pence a p.,** jouer à dix pence le point; *Box:* **to win on points,** gagner aux points; **beaten on points,** battu aux points; *Ten:* **match p., set p.,** balle de match, de set. **6.** (*measure*) (*a*) **the thermometer went up, down, two points,** le thermomètre a monté, a baissé, de deux degrés, divisions; **freezing, melting, boiling, p.,** point de congélation, de fusion, d'ébullition; *St. Exch:* (*of price*) **rise, fall, of one p.,** hausse *f*, baisse *f*, d'un point; (*b*) *Typ:* point. **II.** pointe *f.* **1.** (*a*) pointe (d'une aiguille, d'un clou, d'une épée, d'un outil, etc.); mouche *f* (d'un foret); bec *m* (d'une plume à écrire); *Danc:* **to dance on points,** faire des pointes; **on (full) p.,** sur la pointe; **on demi-p.,** sur la demi-pointe; **p. work,** pointes; **to end in a p.,** aller, se terminer, en pointe; **to give a p. to a pencil,** tailler un crayon en pointe; **p. of a joke,** piquant *m*, sel *m*, d'une plaisanterie; (*b*) **points,** extrémités *fpl* (d'un cheval, etc.); *Ven:* cors *mpl* (du cerf); (*c*) *Geog:* pointe, promontoire *m.* **2.** *Tls:* pointe, poinçon *m.* **3.** *El:* (*a*) (point de) prise *f* de courant (sur le secteur); **power p.,** prise de courant (force); (*b*) *I.C.E:* **eight-p. distributor,** distributeur *m* (d'allumage) à huit plots. **4.** (*a*) *Rail:* **points,** aiguillage *m*; (*b*) **p. duty,** service *m* de la circulation; **policeman on p. duty,** agent *m* de circulation. **5. the points of the compass,** les aires *fpl* du vent; **p. of the compass,** quart *m* (de vent); **to alter course 16 points,** venir de 16 quarts. **6.** *Games:* (*backgammon*) flèche *f*, pointe, case *f.* **7.** (*a*) *Lacem:* **p. (lace),** dentelle *f* à l'aiguille; point *m*; guipure *f*; (*b*) *Tex:* **p. paper,** carte *f.*

point² **I.** *v.tr.* **1.** (*a*) marquer (qch.) de points; (*b*) *Gram:* ponctuer (une phrase); (*c*) *Mth:* **to p. off,** séparer (les décimales) par une virgule. **2.** (*a*) tailler en pointe (un bâton, etc.); appointer (un outil, un clou, etc.); (*b*) *Danc: etc:* **to p. the toe, the foot,** pointer le pied; (*c*) donner du piquant à (des remarques, etc.). **3.** pointer, braquer (un canon); diriger, orienter, braquer (une longue-vue) **(at,** sur); **to p. a rifle at s.o.,** coucher qn en joue. **4. to p. the way,** indiquer, montrer, le chemin **(to s.o.,** à qn; **to a place,** vers un endroit). **5.** *Const:* jointoyer (un mur). **6.** *Ven:* (*of hound*) arrêter (le gibier); *v.i.* tomber en arrêt. **II.** *v.i.* **1. to p. at s.o.,** montrer, désigner, qn du doigt, etc. **2.** (*a*) **to p. s.o. to a direction,** désigner à qn le chemin à prendre; **the magnetic needle always points north,** l'aiguille aimantée est toujours tournée vers le nord; (*b*) **this points to the fact that . . .,** cette circonstance (i) laisse supposer, (ii) fait ressortir, que . . .; **everything seems to p. to success,** tout semble indiquer le succès. **pointed** *a.* **1.** pointu; à pointe; (barbe) en pointe; *Tchn:* alené. **2.** (*a*) (réflexion) sarcastique, mordante; (*b*) (allusion) peu équivoque, peu voilée. **pointedly** *adv.* (*a*) sarcastiquement; d'un ton mordant; (*b*) explicitement, nettement; (*c*) d'une manière marquée; **not too p.,** sans y appuyer. **pointing** *n.* **1.** ponctuation *f* (d'une phrase). **2.** appointage *m*, taillage *m* en pointe; affûtage *m.* **3.** pointage *m*, braquage *m* (d'un canon, etc.). **4.** *Const:* (*a*) jointoiement *m* (d'un mur); (*b*) (*cement*) gobetis *m.* **point out** *v.tr.* (*a*) **to p. out sth. to s.o. (with one's finger),** désigner, montrer, qch. du doigt à qn; (*b*) signaler, relever (une erreur, etc.); faire ressortir, faire valoir (un fait, etc.); **to p. out sth. to s.o.,** attirer l'attention de qn sur qch.; signaler, faire remarquer, qch. à qn; **to p. out to s.o. that he is wrong,** remontrer à qn qu'il a tort; **to p. out to s.o. the advantages of sth.,** représenter à qn les avantages de qch.; **might I p. out that . . .,** permettez-moi de vous faire observer que . . .; **he has been pointed out to me as a capable man,** on me l'a signalé comme un homme capable.

point-blank ['pɔint'blæŋk] **1.** *a.* (*a*) *Artil: etc:* (tir) direct, à bout portant; (*b*) *F:* (question) faite de but en blanc; (refus) net, catégorique. **2.** *adv.* **to fire p.-b. at s.o.,** tirer sur qn à bout portant, de but en blanc; **he asked me p.-b. whether . . .,** il m'a demandé de but en blanc si . . .; **to refuse p.-b.,** refuser catégoriquement, carrément, (tout) net.

pointedness ['pɔintidnis] *n.* **1.** mordant *m* (d'une remarque). **2.** caractère *m* explicite (d'une allusion).

pointer ['pɔintər] *n.* **1.** *Z:* chien *m* d'arrêt; pointer *m.* **2.** (*a*) aiguille *f* (d'horloge); aiguille, languette *f* (d'une balance); (*b*) *Sch:* baguette *f* (du tableau noir); (*c*) (*for slides*) **optical, illuminated, p.,** flèche lumineuse. **3.** *Tls:* pointe *f* (de maçon, etc.). **4.** *F:* renseignement *m*, conseil *m*; tuyau *m.*

pointillism ['pwæntilizm] *n. Art:* pointillisme *m.*

pointless ['pɔintlis] *a.* (*a*) (*of story, etc.*) qui ne rime à rien; (plaisanterie) fade, sans sel; (*b*) (observation, etc.) qui n'a rien à voir à la question; (démarche) inutile; **it would be p.,** ce serait inutile, cela ne servirait à rien (**to,** de). **-ly** *adv.* inutilement, vainement.

pointlessness ['pɔintlisnis] *n.* **1.** fadeur *f* (d'une plaisanterie, etc.). **2.** manque *m* d'à-propos (d'une observation, etc.); inutilité *f* (d'une démarche).

poise¹ [pɔiz] *n.* **1.** (*a*) **(equal, even, just) p.,** équilibre *m*, aplomb *m*; (*b*) (*of pers.*) **to have p.,** (i) avoir de la prestance; (ii) avoir l'esprit bien équilibré; **a man of p.,** un homme pondéré. **2.** port *m* (de la tête, du corps).

poise² *v.tr.* (*a*) équilibrer; (*b*) tenir (qch.) en équilibre; **to be poised,** être en équilibre; **the cat was poised ready to spring,** le chat se tenait prêt à bondir.

poison¹ ['poizən] *n.* (*a*) poison *m*, toxique *m*; **to take p.,** s'empoisonner; *F:* **what's your p.?** qu'est-ce que tu veux boire? **p. pen letter,** lettre malicieuse anonyme; (*b*) *Bot:* **p. ivy,** sumac vénéneux; *Z:* **p. gland,** glande *f* à venin; **p. gas,** gaz toxique.

poison² *v.tr.* (*a*) empoisonner (qn, qch.); intoxiquer (qn); (*b*) corrompre, pervertir (l'esprit); empoisonner (la vie de qn); **to p. s.o.'s mind against s.o.,** empoisonner l'esprit de qn contre qn. **poisoning** *n.* (*a*) empoisonnement *m*; intoxication *f*; **food p.,** intoxication alimentaire; (*b*) corruption *f* (de l'esprit).

poisoner ['pɔizənər] *n.* empoisonneur, -euse.

poisonous ['pɔizənəs] *a.* (*a*) toxique, intoxicant; (gaz) asphyxiant, toxique; (*of animal*) venimeux; (*of plant*) vénéneux, vireux; (*b*) (doctrine) pernicieuse, empoisonnée.

poke¹ [pouk] *n. Dial:* sac *m*, poche *f*; *F:* **to buy a pig in a p.,** acheter chat en poche.

poke² *n.* **1.** poussée *f*; (*nudge*) coup *m* de coude; (*with the finger*) coup du bout du doigt; **to give s.o. a p. in the ribs,** cogner qn du coude. **2.** *P:* coït *m*, bourre *f.*

poke³ **I.** *v.tr.* **1.** (*a*) pousser (qn, qch.) du bras, du coude; piquer (qch.) du bout (d'un bâton); **to p. s.o. in the ribs,** donner une bourrade (amicale) à qn; (*b*) **to p. a hole in sth.,** faire un trou dans qch.; crever qch. (avec le doigt, etc.). **2.** tisonner, attiser (le feu). **3.** mettre, fourrer (qch.) **(into,** dans); **to p. one's head through the window,** passer la tête par la fenêtre; *F:* **to p. one's nose into other people's business,** fourrer son nez dans les affaires d'autrui. **4. to p. fun at s.o., sth.,** se moquer de qn, qch. **5.** *P:* coïter avec, bourrer (qn). **II.** *v.i.* **to p. at sth.,** tâter qch. du bout du doigt, d'un bâton, etc. **2.** (*a*) **to p. (about) in every corner,** fouiller, fureter, dans tous les coins; (*b*) **to p. into other people's business,** fourrer son nez dans les affaires d'autrui. **poke out** *v.tr.* (*a*) **to p. s.o.'s eye out,** éborgner qn; (*b*) **to p. one's head out (of the window),** passer, sortir, la tête par la fenêtre.

poker¹ ['poukər] *n.* **1.** tisonnier *m*; *Ind:* fourgon *m*; (*for furnace*) ringard *m.* **2.** pointe *f* métallique (pour pyrogravure); **p. work,** pyrogravure *f.*

poker² *n. Cards:* poker *m*; **p. dice,** poker dice; *F:* **p. face,** visage impassible; **p.-faced,** au visage impassible.

poky ['pouki] *a.* (*of room*) exigu; sombre; **to live in a p. little place,** être logé à l'étroit, étroitement.

Poland ['poulənd] *Pr.n. Geog:* Pologne *f.*

polar ['poulər] *a.* (*a*) *Astr: Geog: Z:* **p. bear,** ours blanc; (*b*) *Mth: Ph:* (axe, courbe, etc.) polaire.

polarimeter [poulə'rimitər] *n. Opt:* polarimètre *m.*

polarity [pou'læriti] *n. Ph:* polarité *f.*

polarization [poulərai'zeiʃ(ə)n] *n. Ph:* polarisation *f.*

polarize ['pouləraiz] *v.tr.* **1.** (*a*) polariser (la lumière, une barre de fer, etc.); (*b*) (*with passive force*) se polariser. **2.** donner une direction unique à (des efforts, l'opinion, etc.).

Polaroid ['poulərɔid] *n. Opt: R.t.m:* Polaroid *m.*

pole¹ [poul] *n.* **1.** (*a*) perche *f* (à houblon); échalas *m*, rame *f*; mât *m* (d'échafaudage); hampe *f* (d'un drapeau); **tent p.,** mât de tente; **telegraph p.,** poteau *m* télégraphique; *Sp:* **p. vault(ing),** saut *m* à la perche; **to p.-vault,** sauter à la perche; **p. vaulter,** sauteur, -euse, à la perche; perchiste *m*; *F:* **to be up the p.,** être timbré, toqué; (*b*) bras *m* (de civière); barre *f* (d'écurie); (*c*) *Nau:* flèche *f* (de mât). **2.** *A. Meas:* (*a*) perche; (*b*) perche carrée.

pole² *n.* pôle *m*; (*a*) *Geog:* **North p.,** pôle nord, arctique, boréal; **South p.,** pôle sud, antarctique, austral; **magnetic, true, p.,** pôle magnétique, géographique; **to be poles apart,** être aux antipodes l'un de l'autre; (*of views, etc.*) être diamétralement opposé; (*b*) *Magn:* pôle (d'un aimant); **opposite poles,** pôles de nom contraire; (*c*) *El:* pôle.

Pole³ *n. Geog:* Polonais, -aise.

poleax(e)¹ ['poulæks] *n.* merlin *m.*

poleax(e)² *v.tr.* assommer; abattre (un animal) avec un merlin.

polecat ['poulkæt] *n. Z:* putois *m.*

polemic [pə'lemik] **1.** *a.* polémique. **2.** *n.* (*a*) polémique *f*; (*b*) (*pers.*) polémiste *mf.*

polemics [pə'lemiks] *n.pl. Theol:* polémique *f.*

police¹ [pə'li:s] *n.inv.* (*a*) (*usu. with sg. const.*) police *f*; **p. inspector,** (i) inspecteur *m* de police; (ii) (*in the C.I.D.*) commissaire *m* de police; **p. constable,** agent *m* de police; **p. station,** poste *m* de police; commissariat *m*; **p. car,** voiture *f* de police; **p. van,** (i) voiture *f* cellulaire; panier *m* à salade; (ii) car *m* de police; **p. dog,** chien policier; **p. state,** état policier; (*b*) (*with pl. const.*) **the p. (force),** la police; **twenty p. were on duty,** vingt agents étaient de service; **military p.,** police militaire; **traffic p.,** police de la circulation, de la route; **to be a member of the p. force, to be in the p.,** être de, dans, la police.

police² *v.tr.* policer; assurer la police de (l'État, etc.); maintenir l'ordre dans (le pays, etc.).

policeman, *pl.* **-men** [p(ə)'li:smən] *n.m.* agent (de police); (*in town*) gardien de la paix; **traffic p.,** agent de la circulation; **motor cycle p.,** agent motocycliste; motard.

policewoman, *pl.* **-women** [p(ə)'li:swumən, -wimin] *n.f.* femme-agent (de police), *pl.* femmes-agents; auxiliaire féminine (de la police).

policy¹ ['pɔlisi] *n.* politique *f*; ligne *f* de conduite;

tactique *f*; **foreign p.,** politique étrangère, extérieure; **economic, agricultural, p.,** politique économique, agricole; **prices and incomes p.,** politique des prix et des salaires; **to adopt a p.,** adopter une ligne de conduite, un plan; **sales p.,** méthodes *fpl* de vente.

policy² *n.* **(insurance) p.,** police *f* (d'assurance); **(fully) comprehensive, all-risks, p.,** (police) omnium (*m*), police tous risques; **life insurance, assurance, p.,** police d'assurance (sur la) vie; **fire insurance p.,** police d'assurance (contre l')incendie; **p. holder,** assuré, -ée.

polio ['pouliou] *n. Med: F:* polio *f.*

poliomyelitis [poulioumaiə'laitis] *n. Med:* poliomyélite *f.*

polish¹ ['pɔliʃ] *n.* **1.** poli *m*, brillant *m*, lustre *m* (d'une surface, etc.); brunissure *f* (des métaux); **high p.,** poli brillant; **to lose its p.,** se dépolir; **to take the p. off sth.,** dépolir, ternir, qch. **2.** crème *f*, pâte *f*, à polir; **boot, shoe, p.,** cirage *m*, crème, pour chaussures; **floor p.,** encaustique *f*, cire *f*, à parquet; **metal p.,** nettoie-métaux *m inv*; **nail p.,** vernis *m* à ongles. **3.** belles manières, savoir-vivre *m inv*, vernis; **to have a certain p.,** avoir un certain vernis; **he lacks p.,** il manque d'éducation, de savoir-vivre.

polish² *v.tr.* **1.** polir (le bois, le fer, etc.); brunir (l'or, l'argent); cirer (des chaussures); astiquer (le cuir, etc.); lisser (une pierre, etc.); encaustiquer (les meubles, les dalles); cirer (le parquet); glacer, polir (le riz). **2.** polir, dégrossir (qn, les mœurs). **polished** *a.* **1.** poli; (bois) ciré. **2.** (*of manners, etc.*) poli, distingué. **3.** (*of style, etc.*) châtié, raffiné. **polishing** *n.* (*a*) polissage *m*, brunissage *m*; (*b*) cirage *m* (des chaussures, etc.); encaustiquage *m* (des meubles, des parquets); astiquage *m* (des cuirs, etc.). **polish off** *v.tr.* (*a*) (i) expédier, dépêcher (un travail); (ii) vider (un verre); achever (un plat); expédier (un repas); (iii) régler le compte de, en finir avec (qn); (*b*) donner le coup de fion à, mettre la dernière main à (un travail). **polish up** *v.tr.* (*a*) faire reluire (qch.); astiquer, brunir, lustrer (des objets en cuivre); (*b*) dérouiller (son français); polir (son style).

Polish³ ['pouliʃ] **1.** *a. Geog:* polonais. **2.** *n. Ling:* polonais *m.*

polisher ['pɔliʃər] *n.* **1.** (*pers.*) polisseur, -euse, brunisseur, -euse (de métaux, etc.); astiqueur, -euse (de cuivre, etc.). **2.** *Tls:* instrument *m* à polir, polissoir *m*; brunissoir *m* (pour métaux); **electric floor p.,** cireuse électrique à parquet.

polite [pə'lait] *a.* **1. p. society,** (i) le beau monde; (ii) les gens instruits, cultivés. **2.** poli, courtois (**to s.o.,** envers, avec, qn); **p. refusal,** refus poli; **to be p.,** être poli. **-ly** *adv.* poliment; avec politesse.

politeness [pə'laitnis] *n.* politesse *f*, courtoisie *f.*

politic ['pɔlitik] *a.* **1.** (*of pers., conduct*) (*a*) politique, avisé; (*b*) *Pej:* rusé, astucieux. **2. the body p.,** le corps politique; l'État *m.*

political [pə'litik(ə)l] *a.* (parti, etc.) politique; **p. science,** sciences *fpl* politiques. **-ally** *adv.* politiquement.

politician [pɔli'tiʃ(ə)n] *n.* **1.** (homme) politique (*m*). **2.** *esp. NAm: Pej:* politicien *m*, politicard *m.*

politicize [pə'litisaiz] **1.** *v.tr.* faire de la politique; parler politique. **2.** *v.tr.* politiser.

politico-economical [pə'litikoui:kə'nɔmik(ə)l] *a.* politico-économique.

politics ['pɔlitiks] *n.pl.* (*usu. with sg. const.*) la politique; **to talk p.,** parler politique; **foreign p.,** politique étrangère.

polity ['pɔliti] *n.* **1.** administration *f* politique. **2.** (*a*) constitution *f* politique; régime *m*; (*b*) État *m.*

polka ['pɔlkə] *n. Danc: Mus:* polka *f*; *Tex:* **blue p. dot tie,** cravate bleue à pois (blancs).

poll¹ [poul] *n.* (i) votation *f* par tête; (ii) vote *m* (par bulletins); scrutin *m*; **public opinion p.,** sondage *m* d'opinion; **to go to the polls,** aller aux urnes; **to head the p.,** arriver en tête de scrutin; **heavy, light, p.,** forte, faible, participation électorale.

poll² [poul] **I.** *v.tr.* **1.** (*a*) *Arb:* étêter, écimer (un arbre); (*b*) décorner (un taureau, etc.). **2.** (*a*) (*of polling clerk*) recueillir le bulletin de vote de (qn); (*b*) (*of candidate*) réunir (tant de voix); (*c*) **to p. a vote for s.o.,** donner sa voix, voter, pour qn. **II.** *v.i.* voter (à une élection); aller aux urnes. **polling** *n.* vote *m*; élections *fpl*; **p. station,** bureau *m* de vote; **p. booth,** isoloir *m.*

poll³ [poul] *n.* (vache *f*, etc.) sans cornes.

pollard¹ ['pɔləd] *n.* (*a*) *Arb:* têtard *m*; arbre étêté; (*b*) *Husb:* animal *m* sans cornes.

pollard² *v.tr. Arb:* étêter, écimer (un arbre).

pollen ['pɔlən] *n. Bot:* pollen *m*; **p. sac,** sac *m* pollinique; **p. count,** taux *m* du pollen.

pollinate ['pɔlineit] *v.tr. Bot:* transporter, émettre, du pollen sur les stigmates (d'une fleur); polliniser.

pollination [pɔli'neiʃ(ə)n] *n. Bot:* pollinisation *f*, fécondation *f*; **self p.,** pollinisation directe; **cross p.,** pollinisation croisée.

polliwog ['pɔliwɔg] *n. NAm:* = POLLYWOG.

pollster ['poulstər] *n. NAm:* enquêteur, -euse, organisateur, -trice, d'un sondage Gallup.

pollutant [pə'lu:tənt] *n.* polluant *m.*

pollute [pə'lu:t] *v.tr.* **1.** polluer (une rivière, etc.). **2.** profaner, violer (un lieu saint, etc.).

pollution [pə'lu:ʃ(ə)n] *n.* (*a*) pollution *f*, souillure *f*; **atmospheric p., p. of the atmosphere,** pollution atmosphérique, de l'air; (*b*) profanation *f.*

Polly ['pɔli] *F: Pr.n.f.* (*dim. of Mary*) (*a*) Marie, Mariette; (*b*) (*parrot*) **(pretty) P.,** Jacquot *m.*

pollywog ['pɔliwɔg] *n. NAm:* têtard *m.*

polo ['poulou] *n. Sp:* polo *m*; **p. stick,** maillet *m*; *Cost:* **p. neck,** col roulé.

polonaise [pɔlə'neiz] *n. Mus: Danc:* polonaise *f.*

poltergeist ['pɔltəgaist] *n.* esprit frappeur.

poly ['pɔli] *n. F:* École professionnelle d'enseignement technique.

polyandrous [pɔli'ændrəs] *a. Bot: etc:* polyandre.

polyanthus [pɔli'ænθəs] *n. Bot:* primevère *f* des jardins.

polychrom(at)ic [pɔlikrou'mætik, -'kroumik] *a.* polychrome.

polychrome ['pɔlikroum] **1.** *a.* polychrome. **2.** *n.* polychromie *f.*

polyclinic [pɔli'klinik] *n. Med:* polyclinique *f.*

polyester [pɔli'estər] *n. Ch:* polyester *m.*

polyethylene [pɔli'eθili:n] *n. Ch:* polyéthylène *m*, polythène *m.*

polygamist [pə'ligəmist] *n.* polygame *mf.*

polygamous [pə'ligəməs] *a.* polygame.

polygamy [pə'ligəmi] *n.* polygamie *f.*

polyglot ['pɔliglɔt] *a. & n.* polyglotte (*mf*).

polygon ['pɔligən] *n. Mth:* polygone *m.*

polygonal [pə'ligən(ə)l] *a. Mth: etc:* polygonal, -aux.

polyhedron [pɔli'hi:drən] *n. Mth:* polyèdre *m.*

polymer ['pɔlimər] *n. Ch:* polymère *m.*

polymerization [pɔlimərai'zeiʃ(ə)n] *n. Ch:* polymérisation *f.*

polymorphic, polymorphous [pɔli'mɔ:fik, -'mɔ:fəs] *a. Biol: Ch:* polymorphe, polymorphique.

polymorphism [pɔli'mɔ:fizm] *n. Biol: Ch:* polymorphisme *m*, polymorphie *f.*

Polynesia [pɔli'ni:ziə] *Pr.n. Geog:* Polynésie *f.*

Polynesian [pɔli'ni:ziən] *Geog:* **1.** *a.* polynésien. **2.** *n.* Polynésien, -ienne.

polyneuritis [pɔlinjuə'raitis] *n. Med:* polynévrite *f.*

polynomial [pɔli'noumiəl] *n. Mth:* polynôme *m.*

polyp ['pɔlip] *n. Cœl: Med:* polype *m.*

polyphase ['pɔlifeiz] *a. El:* polyphasé.

polyphonic [pɔli'fɔnik] *a. Mus: Ling:* polyphone, polyphonique.
polyphony [pə'lifəni] *n. Mus: Ling:* polyphonie *f.*
polypus ['pɔlipəs] *n. Med:* polype *m.*
polystyrene [pɔli'stairi:n] *n. Ch:* polystyrène *m.*
polysyllabic [pɔlisi'læbik] *a.* polysyllabe, polysyllabique.
polysyllable ['pɔlisiləbl] *n.* polysyllable *m.*
polytechnic [pɔli'teknik] **1.** *a.* polytechnique. **2.** *n.* École professionnelle d'enseignement technique.
polytheism ['pɔliθi:izm] *n.* polythéisme *m.*
polytheistic [pɔliθi:'istik] *a.* polythéiste.
polythene ['pɔliθi:n] *n.* polyéthylène *m,* polythène *m.*
polyunsaturated [pɔliʌn'sætjureitid] *a. Ch:* polyinsaturé.
polyurethane [pɔli'juəriθein] *n. Ch: etc:* polyuréthane *m.*
polyvalent [pɔli'veilənt] *a. Ch:* polyvalent.
polyvinyl [pɔli'vainil] *n. Ch:* polyvinyle *m.*
pom¹ [pɔm] *n. Z: F:* loulou *m* de Poméranie.
Pom² *n. Austr: F:* Anglais, -aise.
pomegranate ['pɔm(i)grænit] *n. Bot:* **1.** grenade *f.* **2. p. (tree),** grenadier *m.*
Pomerania [pɔmə'reiniə] *Pr.n. Geog:* Poméranie *f.*
Pomeranian [pɔmə'reiniən] *a. & n.* **P. (dog),** loulou *m* (de Poméranie).
pommel¹ ['pɔm(ə)l] *n.* **1.** pommeau *m* (d'épée). **2.** *Harn:* pommeau (de selle). **3.** *Gym:* **p. horse,** cheval *m* d'arçons.
pommel² *v.tr.* **(pommelled,** *NAm:* **pommeled)** battre, rosser, gourmer (qn); bourrer (qn) de coups.
pommie, pommy ['pɔmi] *n. Austr: F:* Anglais, -aise.
pomp [pɔmp] *n.* pompe *f,* éclat *m,* faste *m;* **p. and circumstance,** (grand) apparat; parade *f.*
Pompeii [pɔm'peii] *Pr.n. Geog:* Pompéi.
pom-pom ['pɔmpɔm] *n. Artil:* canon-mitrailleuse *m, pl.* canons-mitrailleuses (système Maxim).
pompom, pompon ['pɔmpɔm, -pɔn] *n. Cost: etc:* pompon *m.*
pomposity [pɔm'pɔsiti] *n.* emphase *f,* suffisance *f.*
pompous ['pɔmpəs] *a.* **1.** pompeux, fastueux. **2.** (*a*) (homme) suffisant, qui fait l'important; (*b*) (style) emphatique, pompeux. **-ly** *adv.* pompeusement; avec suffisance; avec emphase.
pompousness ['pɔmpəsnis] *n.* **1.** pompe *f,* faste *m.* **2.** emphase *f,* suffisance *f.*
ponce¹ [pɔns] *n. P:* souteneur *m,* maquereau *m.*
ponce² *P: v.i.* être souteneur.
poncho, *pl.* **-os** ['pɔn(t)ʃou, -ouz] *n.* poncho *m.*
pond [pɔnd] *n.* étang *m;* bassin *m,* pièce *f* d'eau (de parc); mare *f* (de village); vivier *m,* réservoir *m* (pour le poisson); réservoir (de moulin).
ponder ['pɔndər] **1.** *v.tr.* réfléchir sur (une question); considérer, peser (un avis); méditer (sur) (la situation); ruminer (une idée). **2.** *v.i.* méditer; **to p. on, over, sth.,** réfléchir à, méditer sur, spéculer sur, qch.
ponderable ['pɔnd(ə)rəbl] *a.* pondérable.
ponderous ['pɔnd(ə)rəs] *a.* **1.** massif, lourd, pesant. **2.** (travail) laborieux. **3.** (style) lourd, pesant. **-ly** *adv.* lourdement.
pondlife ['pɔndlaif] *n.* vie animale des eaux stagnantes.
pondweed ['pɔndwi:d] *n. Bot:* épi *m* d'eau.
pone [poun] *n. U.S:* **(corn) p.,** pain *m* de maïs.
pong¹ [pɔŋ] *n. P:* puanteur *f;* **what a p.!** comme ça pue!
pong² *v.i. P:* puer, schlinguer.
pontiff ['pɔntif] *n. Ecc:* pontife *m; esp.* **the sovereign p.,** le souverain pontife.
pontifical [pɔn'tifik(ə)l] **1.** *a.* pontifical, -aux; **2.** *n.* (*book*) pontifical *m.*
pontificate¹ [pɔn'tifikeit] *n.* pontificat *m.*
pontificate² *v.i.* **1.** pontifier; officier en qualité de pontife ou d'évêque. **2.** *Pej:* pontifier; faire l'important.
Pontius Pilate ['pɔnʃəs'pailət] *Pr.n.m. B.Hist:* Ponce Pilate.
pontoon¹ [pɔn'tu:n] *n.* **1.** ponton *m,* bac *m.* **2.** (*a*) *Mil:* bateau *m* (d'un pont de bateaux); **p. bridge,** pont de bateaux, pont flottant; (*b*) flotteur *m* (d'hydravion).
pontoon² *n. Cards:* vingt-et-un *m.*
pony ['pouni] *n.* **1.** (*a*) poney *m;* **p. trekking,** randonnées *fpl* à dos de poney; (*b*) *U.S:* petit cheval, *esp.* mustang *m;* **cow p.,** cheval de ranch. **2.** *P:* vingt-cinq livres sterling. **3.** *U.S: Sch: F:* traduction *f* (juxtalinéaire). **4.** petit verre (sans pied). **5. p. engine,** *Rail: O:* locomotive *f* de manœuvre.
ponytail ['pouniteil] *n. Hairdr:* queue *f* de cheval.
pooch [pu:tʃ] *n. P:* chien *m,* cabot *m.*
poodle ['pu:dl] *n.* caniche *mf,* barbet, -ette.
poof [pu:f] *n. P:* pédéraste *m,* tante *f.*
pooh [pu:] *int.* bah! peuh!
pooh-pooh ['pu:'pu:] *v.tr.* traiter légèrement, ridiculiser (une idée, une théorie, etc.); se moquer, faire peu de cas (d'une idée, d'un avertissement); repousser (un conseil) avec mépris.
pool¹ [pu:l] *n.* (*a*) calme *m* (dans une rivière); (*b*) mare *f;* (*ornamental*) pièce *f* d'eau; (*left on beach by tide*) bâche *f;* (*c*) **swimming-p.,** piscine *f;* **paddling p.,** bassin *m* à patauger; (*d*) flaque *f* (d'eau, etc.); **lying in a p. of blood,** baignant dans son sang.
pool² *n.* **1.** (*a*) *Games:* poule *f,* cagnotte *f;* (*b*) *Bill: Fenc:* poule; (*c*) **football p. (competitions),** *F:* **the pools,** concours *m* de pronostics de matchs de football. **2.** (*a*) groupe *m* (de travail); pool *m;* **typing p.,** central *m* dactylographique; pool de dactylos; (*b*) *Com:* groupement *m* (pour opérations en commun); syndicat *m* de placement (de marchandises, etc.); (*c*) *Pol.Ec:* fonds commun, *F:* pool.
pool³ *v.tr.* mettre en commun (ses capitaux, ses bénéfices, etc.); grouper (ses moyens); **we pooled our resources,** nous avons fait bourse commune; (*b*) *Com: etc:* grouper (les commandes).
poop [pu:p] *n. Nau:* **1.** poupe *f.* **2. p. (deck),** (pont *m* de) dunette *f,* gaillard *m* d'arrière.
pooped [pu:pt] *a. P:* épuisé, vanné.
poor [puər] *a.* pauvre. **1.** (*a*) indigent; **a p. man,** un pauvre; **as p. as a church mouse,** *U.S:* **as Job's cat,** pauvre comme Job; **I'm poorer by a thousand francs,** j'en suis pour mille francs; (*b*) *n.pl.* **the p.,** les pauvres; *Ecc:* **p. box,** tronc *m* pour les pauvres. **2.** de mauvaise qualité; mauvais; médiocre; (qualité) inférieure; (santé) débile; (sol) maigre, peu fertile; **p. harvest,** mauvaise récolte; **p. excuse,** piètre excuse; **I've a p. memory,** je n'ai pas de mémoire; **to cut a p. figure,** faire piètre figure; **the patient's had a p. night,** le malade a passé une mauvaise nuit; **p. reception,** (i) mauvais accueil; (ii) *W.Tel: etc:* mauvaise transmission; **he's p. at maths,** il est faible en math(s). **3.** (*a*) (*to be pitied*) **p. creature! p. thing!** pauvre petit! pauvre petite! **I'm so sorry for the p. man,** je le plains bien, le pauvre homme; (*b*) (*of pers. who has died*) **when p. Alice was alive,** du vivant de la pauvre Alice. **-ly 1.** *adv.* pauvrement; **p. dressed,** pauvrement vêtu; **p. lit,** mal éclairé; **he did p. in his exams,** il a eu de mauvais résultats aux examens. **2.** *a.* (*of pers.*) souffrant, indisposé; **he's looking p.,** il a mauvaise mine; **I'm feeling p.,** je ne me sens pas bien; *F:* je ne suis pas dans mon assiette.
poorhouse ['puəhaus] *n. A:* asile *m* des pauvres.
poorness ['puənis] *n.* **1.** pauvreté *f* (du sol). **2.** infériorité *f;* mauvaise qualité.
pop¹ [pɔp] **1.** *int.* crac! pan! **to go p.,** éclater, crever;

p. goes the cork! paf! le bouchon saute. **2.** *n.* (*a*) bruit sec (de bouchon qui saute, etc.); (*b*) *F:* (i) boisson gazeuse; (ii) champagne; vin pétillant.

pop² *v.* **(popped) 1.** *v.i.* (*a*) faire entendre une petite explosion; éclater, péter; (*of cork*) sauter, péter; (*of balloon*) crever; (*b*) *F:* **to p. over, across, down, to the grocer's,** faire un saut (jusque) chez l'épicier; **I'm going to p. into town,** je vais faire un saut en ville; **to p. into bed,** se glisser dans son lit; **this question has popped up again,** cette question est revenue sur le tapis. **2.** *v.tr.* (*a*) crever (un ballon); faire sauter (un bouchon); (*b*) *P: O:* mettre (sa montre, etc.) en gage, au clou; (*c*) *F:* **to p. sth. into a drawer,** mettre, fourrer, qch. dans un tiroir; **to p. one's head out of the window,** sortir (tout à coup) sa tête par la fenêtre; (*d*) *F:* **then he popped the question,** alors il lui a demandé de l'épouser. **pop in** *v.i.* *F:* entrer à l'improviste; entrer en passant, pour un instant (chez qn); **I've just popped in,** je ne fais qu'entrer et sortir. **pop off** *v.i.* (*a*) *F:* filer, partir; (*b*) *P:* mourir (subitement). **pop out** *v.i.* *F:* sortir; **his eyes were popping out of his head,** les yeux lui sortaient de la tête.

pop³ *n. esp. NAm: F:* papa *m.*

pop⁴ (*abbr. for* popular) *F:* **1.** *a.* (*a*) **p. song,** chanson *f* pop; **p. singer,** chanteur, -euse, de pop; **p. music,** musique *f* pop; (*b*) **p. art,** pop'art *m*, pop *m.* **2.** *n.* musique, chanson, pop.

popcorn ['pɔpkɔːn] *n.* maïs grillé et éclaté, *F:* popcorn *m.*

pope¹ [poup] *n.* pape *m*; le Saint-Père.

pope² *n.* pope *m* (de l'Église orthodoxe).

popery ['poupəri] *n. Pej:* papisme *m*; romanisme *m.*

popeyed ['pɔpaid] *a. F:* (*a*) aux yeux protubérants; (*b*) aux yeux en boules de loto.

popgun ['pɔpgʌn] *n. Toys:* canonnière *f*, pétoire *f.*

popinjay ['pɔpindʒei] *n. A:* fat *m*, freluquet *m.*

popish ['poupiʃ] *a. Pej:* papiste; (*of thg*) de papiste.

poplar ['pɔplər] *n. Bot:* peuplier *m.*

poplin ['pɔplin] *n. Tex:* popeline *f.*

popover ['pɔpouvər] *n.* **1.** *Cu:* (genre *m* de) beignet soufflé. **2.** *Cost:* robe *f* jumper (pour enfant).

popper ['pɔpər] *n. F:* bouton-pression *m*, *pl.* boutons-pression.

poppet ['pɔpit] *n. F:* **she's a p.,** elle est charmante; **my p.,** mon chéri; ma chérie; mon petit chou.

poppy ['pɔpi] *n. Bot:* pavot *m*; **corn p., field p.,** coquelicot *m*, pavot rouge; **opium p.,** pavot somnifère; **p. (coloured), p. red,** rouge coquelicot *inv*; *F:* **P. Day,** anniversaire *m* (du jour) de l'Armistice.

poppycock ['pɔpikɔk] *n. F:* bêtises *fpl*, inepties *fpl.*

poppyhead ['pɔpihed] *n.* tête *f* de pavot.

poppyseed ['pɔpisiːd] *n.* graine(s) *f(pl)* de pavot.

popsicle ['pɔpsikl] *n. NAm: Comest:* glace parfumée (servie sur un bâton).

popsy ['pɔpsi] *n. F:* pépée *f*, nana *f.*

populace ['pɔpjuləs] *n.* **the p.,** (i) le peuple; (ii) *Pej:* la populace.

popular ['pɔpjulər] *a.* (*a*) populaire; du peuple; (*b*) populaire; à la mode, en vogue; (musique, chanson) populaire; **to make oneself p.,** se rendre populaire; (*c*) **p. work, treatise,** ouvrage *m* de vulgarisation; **with a p. appeal,** qui plaît au grand public; **p. prices,** prix *mpl* à la portée de tous; (*d*) **p. error,** erreur courante. **-ly** *adv.* populairement; **it is p. believed that . . .,** les gens croient que . . . .

popularity [pɔpju'læriti] *n.* popularité *f*; succès *m* (d'un produit, etc.) auprès du (grand) public.

popularization [pɔpjulərai'zeiʃ(ə)n] *n.* popularisation *f*; vulgarisation *f* (d'une science, etc.).

popularize ['pɔpjuləraiz] *v.tr.* (*a*) populariser (une idée, une science); vulgariser (des connaissances, etc.); propager (une méthode, etc.); (*b*) rendre (qn) populaire; (*c*) mettre (une mode, etc.) en vogue.

populate ['pɔpjuleit] *v.tr.* peupler; **densely, thickly, populated country,** pays très peuplé; **sparsely populated,** (région) à faible peuplement, population.

population [pɔpju'leiʃ(ə)n] *n.* population *f*; **p. explosion,** explosion *f* démographique; **p. statistics,** statistique(s) *f(pl)* démographique(s); **working p.,** (i) population active; (ii) classes laborieuses.

populous ['pɔpjuləs] *a.* populeux; très peuplé.

pop-up [pɔp'ʌp] *a. Dom.Ec:* (grille-pain) automatique.

porcelain ['pɔːslin] *n.* (*a*) porcelaine *f*; **p. manufacturer,** porcelainier *m*; (*b*) *Moll:* **p. shell,** porcelaine *f*, cyprée *f*; *F:* coquille *f* de Vénus.

porch [pɔːtʃ] *n.* **1.** (*a*) porche *m*, portique *m*; (*b*) **(glass) p.,** marquise *f* (d'hôtel, etc.); (*c*) **p. roof,** auvent *m.* **2.** *NAm:* véranda *f.*

porcine ['pɔːsain] *a.* porcin; de porc.

porcupine ['pɔːkjupain] *n. Z:* porc-épic *m*, *pl.* porcs-épics.

pore¹ [pɔːr] *n. Anat: Bot: etc:* pore *m.*

pore² *v.i.* **to p. over a book,** s'absorber dans la lecture, dans l'étude, d'un livre; être plongé dans un livre; **to p. over a problem,** méditer longuement un problème.

pork [pɔːk] *n.* **1.** (viande *f* de) porc (*m*); **salt p.,** porc salé; **roast p.,** rôti *m* de porc; **p. chop,** côtelette *f* de porc; **p. pie,** pâté *m* de porc en croûte; **p.-pie hat,** chapeau de feutre rond à forme aplatie. **2.** *U.S: F:* **the p. barrel** = l'assiette *f* au beurre.

porker ['pɔːkər] *n.* **1.** jeune porc engraissé, destiné à la boucherie. **2.** *F:* cochon *m.*

porn [pɔːn] *n. F:* pornographie *f*; **soft, hard, p.,** (livre, etc.) légèrement, grossement, obscène.

pornographic [pɔːnə'græfik] *a.* pornographique.

pornography [pɔː'nɔgrəfi] *n.* pornographie *f.*

porosity [pɔː'rɔsiti] *n.* porosité *f.*

porous ['pɔːrəs] *a.* poreux, perméable; **non-p.,** non-poreux; anti-poreux.

porousness ['pɔːrəsnis] *n.* porosité *f.*

porphyry ['pɔːfiri] *n. Miner:* porphyre *m.*

porpoise ['pɔːpəs] *n. Z:* marsouin *m.*

porridge ['pɔridʒ] *n.* **1.** bouillie *f* d'avoine, porridge *m.* **2.** *P:* **to do p.,** purger sa peine en prison.

porringer ['pɔrindʒər] *n. A:* écuelle *f.*

port¹ [pɔːt] *n.* port *m*; (*a*) **the p. of London,** le port de Londres; **river p.,** port fluvial; **in p.,** au port; **to put into p.,** relâcher; **to call at a p.,** faire escale à un port; **p. of call,** port d'escale, de relâche; **p. of refuge,** port de refuge; **p. charges, dues,** droits *mpl* de port; (*b*) **fishing p.,** port de pêche; *Com:* **free p.,** port franc; **naval p.,** port de guerre, port militaire.

port² *n.* **1.** *Nau:* (i) sabord *m*; (ii) **p.(-lid),** mantelet *m*, panneau *m*, volet *m*, de sabord; contre-sabord *m*, *pl.* contre-sabords; **air, ventilation, p.,** sabord d'aération; **gangway p.,** sabord de coupée. **2.** *Mch:* orifice *m*, lumière *f* (d'un cylindre, etc.); *I.C.E:* **admission, inlet, p.,** orifice *m*, pipe *f*, d'admission.

port³ *n. Nau:* **p. (side),** bâbord *m*; **land to p.!** la terre par bâbord! **on the p. bow,** par bâbord devant.

port⁴ *n.* vin *m* de Porto; porto *m.*

portable ['pɔːtəbl] *a.* portatif; transportable; mobile.

portage ['pɔːtidʒ] *n.* **1.** transport *m*, port *m* (de marchandises). **2.** frais *mpl* de port, de transport.

portal ['pɔːt(ə)l] *n. Arch:* portail *m* (de cathédrale).

portcullis [pɔːt'kʌlis] *n. A.Fort:* herse *f*; sarrasine *f.*

portend [pɔː'tend] *v.tr.* présager, augurer, faire pressentir (qch.).

portent ['pɔːtent] *n.* présage *m*; prodige *m.*

portentous [pɔː'tentəs] *a.* **1.** de mauvais présage, augure. **2.** prodigieux. **3.** solennel.

porter¹ ['pɔːtər] *n.* (*a*) portier *m*, concierge *m* (de musée, etc.); concierge (d'un immeuble); **porter's lodge,** (i) loge *f* de concierge; (ii) maisonnette *f* du portier (à l'entrée d'une grande propriété); (*b*) *Rail: NAm:* garçon *m* (de wagon-lit, etc.).

porter² *n.* **1.** porteur *m* (de bagages, etc.); chasseur *m,* garçon *m* (d'hôtel). **2.** bière brune (anglaise); porter *m.*

porterage ['pɔːtəridʒ] *n.* **1.** transport *m,* factage *m* (de marchandises, de colis). **2.** prix *m* de transport; factage.

porterhouse ['pɔːtəhaus] *n. Cu:* **p. steak** = châteaubriant *m.*

portfolio [pɔːt'fouliou] *n.* **1.** (*a*) serviette *f* (pour documents, etc.); (*b*) chemise *f* de carton; garde-notes *m inv*; carton *m* (à dessins, à estampes); (*c*) **minister's p.,** portefeuille *m* de ministre; **minister without p.,** ministre *m* sans portefeuille. **2.** *Fin:* **securities in p.,** valeurs *fpl* en portefeuille.

porthole ['pɔːthoul] *n. Nau:* sabord *m,* hublot *m.*

portico, *pl.* **-o(e)s** ['pɔːtikou, -ouz] *n. Arch:* portique *m.*

portion¹ ['pɔːʃ(ə)n] *n.* **1.** (*a*) partie *f*; part *f* (dans un partage); (*on ticket*) **this p. to be given up,** côté *m* à détacher; (*b*) portion *f,* ration *f* (de viande, etc.); (*c*) *Jur:* **p. (of inheritance),** (i) part d'héritage (d'un enfant); (ii) avancement *m* d'hoirie; (*d*) **(marriage) p.,** dot *f*; (*e*) *Rail:* rame *f,* tranche *f* (de wagons, de voitures). **2.** *A: & Lit:* destinée *f,* sort *m.*

portion² *v.tr.* **to p. (out),** partager (un bien, etc.); répartir (une somme); distribuer (les parts).

portliness ['pɔːtlinis] *n.* corpulence *f,* embonpoint *m.*

portly ['pɔːtli] *a.* corpulent, ventru.

portmanteau, *pl.* **-eaus, -eaux** [pɔːt'mæntou, -ouz] *n.* valise *f*; **p. word,** mot-valise *m.*

portrait ['pɔːtreit] *n.* portrait *m*; **p. painter,** portraitiste *mf*; **p. bust,** (portrait en) buste (*m*); **to have one's p. painted, to sit for one's p.,** se faire peindre.

portraitist ['pɔːtrətist] *n.* portraitiste *mf.*

portraiture ['pɔːtrətjər] *n.* **1.** portrait *m.* **2.** art *m* du portrait.

portray [pɔː'trei] *v.tr.* **1.** *A: & Lit:* faire le portrait de (qn). **2.** dépeindre, décrire (une scène, etc.).

portrayal [pɔː'treiəl] *n.* **1.** portrait *m.* **2.** peinture *f,* description *f* (d'une scène, des mœurs d'une époque).

Portugal ['pɔːtjug(ə)l] *Pr.n. Geog:* Portugal *m.*

Portuguese [pɔːtju'giːz] **1.** *a. Geog:* portugais. **2.** *n.* (*a*) Portugais, -aise; (*b*) *Ling:* portugais *m.*

pose¹ [pouz] *n.* **1.** pose *f,* attitude *f* (du corps); pose (d'un modèle). **2.** pose, affectation *f.*

pose² **1.** *v.tr.* (*a*) (i) poser (un problème); (ii) émettre, énoncer (une opinion); (*b*) *Art:* faire prendre une pose à (qn) (pour son portrait); poser (un modèle). **2.** *v.i.* (*a*) (i) poser (pour son portrait); poser (comme modèle); (ii) *F:* poser; se donner des airs (affectés); (*b*) **to p. as a Frenchman,** se faire passer pour Français; **to p. as a socialist,** faire profession de socialisme.

poser ['pouzər] *n. F:* question difficile; colle *f*; **to give s.o. a p.,** poser une colle à qn.

poseur, *f,* **-euse** [pou'zəːr. -əːz] *n.* poseur, -euse.

posh¹ [pɔʃ] *a. F:* chic; **it looks p.,** ça fait bien.

posh² *v.tr. F:* **to p. oneself up,** se faire beau, belle; s'attifer; **all poshed up,** sur son trente et un.

posit ['pɔzit] *v.tr. Phil: etc:* avancer (une proposition); poser en principe **(that,** que).

position¹ [pə'ziʃ(ə)n] *n.* **1.** (*a*) position *f*; posture *f,* attitude *f* (du corps); **horizontal, vertical, p.,** position horizontale, verticale; **prone p.,** position couchée; (*b*) position; attitude, disposition *f* (de l'esprit); **to take up an uncompromising p. (about sth.),** prendre une attitude intransigeante (à l'égard de qch.). **2.** (*a*) position; place *f* (d'un objet); situation *f* (d'une ville, etc.); **in p.,** en place; **out of p.,** déplacé; **to put sth. in p., to get sth. into p.,** mettre qch. en place; *Nau:* **to take up p. ahead, astern,** prendre poste en tête, derrière; (*b*) *Post: Bank:* guichet *m*; **p. closed,** guichet fermé; (*c*) *Av: Nau:* position (d'un avion, d'un navire); **estimated p.,** point estimé; **to fix, work out, one's p.,** faire le point; **p. finding,** (i) orientation *f*; (ii) *Artil:* goniométrie *f*; (*d*) *Mil:* emplacement *m,* position; **to move into p.,** se mettre en place, en position; **to bring guns into p.,** mettre des pièces en batterie, en position; **p. warfare,** guerre *f* de position; **defensive p.,** position défensive, de défense. **3.** (*a*) état *m,* situation *f*; **to be in an awkward p.,** se trouver dans une situation difficile; **to be in a strong p.,** être bien placé; **put yourself in my p.,** mettez-vous à ma place; **to be in a p. to do sth.,** être à même, en mesure, en état, de faire qch.; **financial p.,** situation financière; **what is the p. of the firm?** quelle est la situation (financière) de cette maison? (*b*) condition *f,* état, rang social; **to keep up one's p.,** tenir son rang. **4.** (*a*) *O:* emploi *m,* situation; (*b*) **to work one's way up to a good p.,** se faire une belle situation; **key p.,** position clef; **p. of trust,** poste *m* de confiance. **5.** *Phil: etc:* (*a*) énonciation *f* (d'une proposition); (*b*) proposition *f.*

position² *v.tr.* **1.** mettre (qch., des troupes) en place, en position; mettre, placer, (qch.) dans une position (déterminée). **2.** déterminer la position de (qch.)

positioning *n.* mise *f* en place, en position.

positive ['pɔzitiv] **1.** *a.* (*a*) positif; affirmatif; **p. proof,** preuve positive, manifeste; *Med: etc:* **p. reaction,** réaction positive; (*b*) (fait, etc.) authentique, indiscutable; **a p. miracle,** un véritable miracle; *F:* **it's a p. shame,** c'est une véritable honte. **2.** *a.* convaincu, certain, sûr **(of,** de); **I'm p. on that point,** je n'ai aucun doute à ce sujet; **I'm p. (that) I saw him,** je suis certain que je l'ai vu. **3.** (*a*) *a.* (*of pers., philosophy*) positif; (*b*) *a.* (proposition, aide) constructive; (*c*) *n.* le positif, la réalité. **4.** *a.* (*a*) *Mth: El:* positif; (*b*) *a. & n. Phot:* **p. (print),** positif; épreuve positive. **5.** *a. & n. Gram:* **p. (degree),** (degré) positif (d'un adjectif, d'un adverbe). **-ly** *adv.* **1.** (*a*) positivement; affirmativement; (*b*) *F:* **p. not,** absolument pas. **2.** assurément, certainement, sûrement. **3.** (*a*) *El:* **p. charged,** à charge positive; (*b*) *Mec.E:* **p. driven,** à commande directe.

positivism ['pɔzitivizm] *n. Phil:* positivisime *m.*

positivist ['pɔzitivist] *a. & n. Phil:* positiviste (*mf*).

posse ['pɔsi] *n.* (*a*) détachement *m* (d'agents de police); (*b*) troupe *f,* bande *f* (de personnes).

possess [pə'zes] *v.tr.* **1.** (*a*) posséder (un bien); être en possession de (qch.); **all I p.,** tout mon avoir; (*b*) avoir, posséder (une qualité, une faculté). **2.** *Lit:* **to be possessed of a property,** posséder un bien. **3.** *Lit:* **to p. oneself in patience,** se munir de patience. **4.** (*of evil spirit*) posséder (qn); **possessed by fear,** sous le coup de l'effroi; **what possessed you to do that?** qu'est-ce qui vous a pris de faire cela? **to be possessed with an idea,** être obsédé d'une idée; **to scream like one possessed,** crier comme un possédé.

possession [pə'zeʃ(ə)n] *n.* **1.** possession *f,* jouissance *f* **(of,** de); **to have sth. in one's p.,** avoir qch. en sa possession; **to take p., to come, enter, into p., of an estate,** entrer en possession, en jouissance, d'un bien; **to take, get, p. of sth.,** s'emparer de qch.; **the information in my p.,** les renseignements dont je dispose; **in full p. of his faculties,** en, dans la, pleine possession de toutes ses facultés; **vacant p.,** libre possession (d'un immeuble). **2.** possession (par le démon). **3.** (*a*) objet possédé; possession; (*b*) **possessions,** (i) possessions, biens, avoir *m*; (ii) possessions, colonies *fpl*; **overseas possessions,** possessions d'outre-mer.

possessive [pə'zesiv] *a.* **1.** possessif; **a p. mother,**

une mère abusive. **2.** *Gram:* **p. adjective, pronoun,** adjectif, pronom, possessif; *a. & n.* **the p. (case),** le (cas) possessif.

possessiveness [pə'zesivnis] *n.* possessivité *f.*

possessor [pə'zesər] *n.* possesseur *m.*

possibility [pɔsi'biliti] *n.* **1.** possibilité *f*, éventualité *f* (d'un événement); **have you considered the p. of his being dead?** avez-vous envisagé la possibilité qu'il soit mort? **within the range, the bounds, of p.,** dans la limite du possible. **2.** (*a*) événement *m* possible; éventualité *f*; **to allow for all possibilities,** parer à toute éventualité; (*b*) **possibilities,** possibilités de succès; **the plan has possibilities,** ce projet offre des chances de succès.

possible ['pɔsibl] **1.** *a.* (*a*) possible; **it's p.,** c'est possible; **that's quite p.,** c'est très, fort, possible; **it is p. that he will come,** il se peut qu'il vienne; **is it p. to see him?** y a-t-il moyen de le voir? **to give as many details as p.,** donner le plus de détails possible, tous les détails possibles; **what p. interest can you have in it?** quel diable d'intérêt cela peut-il avoir pour vous? **if p.,** (i) (*if feasible*) si possible; (ii) (*if imaginable*) si c'est possible; **as far as p.,** dans la mesure du possible; **as early as p.,** le plut tôt possible; (*b*) **the p. nomination of . . .,** la nomination éventuelle de . . .; **to insure against p. accidents,** s'assurer contre des accidents éventuels; (*c*) *F:* (*of pers.*) tolérable, supportable. **2.** *n.* (*a*) **to do one's p.,** faire son possible (**to,** pour); (*b*) (*pers.*) candidat *m* possible, acceptable. **-ibly** *adv.* **1. I can't p. do it,** il ne m'est pas possible de le faire; **I'll do all I p. can,** je ferai tout mon possible. **2.** peut-être (bien); **he has p. heard of you,** il se peut qu'il ait entendu parler de vous; **p.!** c'est possible; cela se peut.

possum ['pɔsəm] *n.* *F:* (*a*) *Z:* opossum *m*; (*b*) **to play p.,** faire le mort; se tenir coi.

post¹ [poust] *n.* **1.** (*a*) poteau *m*; pieu *m*; montant *m*; **telegraph p.,** poteau télégraphique; (*b*) *Const: etc:* poteau, pilier *m*; (*of door, window*) montant, jambage *m*; (*c*) **bed p.,** colonne *f* de lit; (*d*) arbre *m*, fût *m* (de grue). **2.** *Min:* pilier (de houille). **3.** *Nau:* **(stern) p.,** étambot *m.* **4.** *Turf: etc:* **starting p.,** (poteau de) départ (*m*); barrière *f*; **winning p.,** (poteau d')arrivée (*f*); **to be left at the p.,** manquer au départ; **to be beaten,** *F:* **pipped, at the p.,** se faire coiffer, battre, sur le poteau.

post² *v.tr.* **1.** (*a*) **to p. (up),** placarder, coller (des affiches, etc.); afficher (un avis, etc.); *P.N:* **p. no bills,** défense d'afficher; (*b*) **to p. (up),** placarder (un mur). **2.** inscrire, porter (qn) sur une liste; *M.Ins:* porter (un navire) disparu; **to be posted for night duty,** être sur la liste (du personnel) de service de nuit; **to be posted missing,** (*of ship*) être porté disparu; (*of pers.*) être porté manquant.

post³ *n.* **1.** *A:* **p. (coach),** (malle-)poste *f*, *pl.* malles-poste(s); **p. chaise,** chaise *f* de poste. **2.** (*a*) courrier *m*; **by return of p.,** par retour du courrier; **when does the next p. go?** à quelle heure est la prochaine levée? **to miss the p.,** manquer la levée; **the first p.,** la première distribution; **there's no p. today,** pas de courrier, pas de lettres, aujourd'hui; (*b*) la poste; **the P. Office** = les Postes et Télécommunications; **to send sth. by p.,** envoyer qch. par la poste; (*c*) **p. (office),** (bureau *m* de) poste; **to take a letter to the p.,** porter une lettre à la poste; **p.-office box,** boîte postale.

post⁴ *v.tr.* (*a*) mettre (une lettre) à la poste, à la boîte; poster (une lettre); **I'll p. it to you,** je vous l'enverrai par la poste; (*b*) *Book-k:* passer écriture (d'un article); *F:* **I'll keep you posted,** je vous tiendrai au courant. **posting** *n.* (*a*) envoi *m* (d'une lettre) par la poste; (*b*) *Book-k:* passation *f* (d'écritures).

post⁵ *n.* **1.** *Mil: etc:* (*a*) poste *m* (de combat, etc.); **to be, die, at one's p.,** être, mourir, à son poste; (*b*) (*group of men, or the place where they are stationed*) poste; **advanced, outlying p.,** poste avancé; **lookout p.,** poste de guet, d'observation; **frontier p.,** poste frontière; (*c*) *U.S:* camp *m*, fort *m* (servant de lieu de garnison); garnison *f.* **2.** (*a*) *Hist:* **trading p.,** comptoir *m*, établissement *m* (aux Indes, au Canada, etc.); (*b*) *Av:* **staging p.,** escale aérienne. **3.** poste, emploi *m*; **to take up a p.,** entrer en fonction.

post⁶ *v.tr.* **1.** poster, placer (qn à un endroit); poster, placer, mettre en faction (une sentinelle); aposter (un espion); **she posted herself at the window,** elle s'est postée à la fenêtre. **2.** *Mil: etc:* désigner (qn) à un commandement; **to be posted to a unit, a ship,** être affecté à une unité, un navire. **posting** *n.* *Mil: etc:* **1.** mise *f* en faction (de sentinelles, etc.). **2.** affectation *f* (à un poste, etc.).

post⁷ *n.* *Mil:* **first p.,** première partie (de la sonnerie) de la retraite; **last p.,** (i) dernière partie (de la sonnerie); (ii) (la) sonnerie aux morts; **to sound the last p. (over the grave),** rendre les honneurs par la sonnerie aux morts.

postage ['poustidʒ] *n.* affranchissement *m*, port *m* (d'une lettre, etc.); **p. stamp,** timbre(-poste) *m*; **p. rates,** tarifs postaux; (*on insufficiently stamped letter*) **additional p.,** surtaxe (postale); **p. paid,** port payé.

postal ['poust(ə)l] *a.* postal, -aux; **p. charges,** frais *mpl* d'envoi, port *m* (d'une lettre, etc.); **p. services,** les services postaux, les Postes *fpl* et Télécommunications; les postes; *U.S:* **p. card,** *n.* **postal,** carte postale.

postbag ['poustbæg] *n.* sac postal, de dépêches.

postbox ['poustbɔks] *n.* boîte *f* aux lettres.

postcard ['poustkɑːd] *n.* carte postale.

postcode ['poustkoud] *n.* code postal.

postdate¹ ['poustdeit] *n.* postdate *f.*

postdate² [poust'deit] *v.tr.* postdater.

poster ['poustər] *n.* affiche murale; placard *m* (de publicité).

poste restante [poust'restɑ̃nt] *n.* poste restante.

posterior [pɔs'tiəriər] **1.** *a.* postérieur (**to,** à). **2.** *n.* *F:* le postérieur, le derrière (de qn).

posterity [pɔs'teriti] *n.* postérité *f.*

postern ['poustəːn] *n.* *Fort:* poterne *f.*

postgraduate [poust'grædjuət] *a.* post-universitaire; **p. student** = licencié(e) qui continue ses études; **p. studies** = études supérieures (après la licence).

posthaste [poust'heist] *adv.* en toute hâte.

posthumous ['pɔstjuməs] *a.* (œuvre) posthume. **-ly** *adv.* posthumement.

postil(l)ion [pɔs'tiliən] *n.* postillon *m.*

post-impressionism [poustim'preʃənizm] *n.* *Art:* post-impressionnisme *m.*

post-impressionist [poustim'preʃənist] *a. & n.* *Art:* post-impressionniste (*mf*).

postman, *pl.* **-men** ['poustmən] *n.m.* facteur *m*; *Adm:* préposé (des postes); *Games:* **postman's knock** = mariage chinois.

postmark¹ ['poustmɑːk] *n.* cachet *m* de la poste; (cachet d')oblitération (*f*); timbre *m* (i) de départ, (ii) d'arrivée.

postmark² *v.tr.* timbrer (une lettre); **the letter was postmarked London,** la lettre était timbrée (au départ) de Londres; **date as p.,** date *f* de la poste (faisant foi).

postmaster ['poustmɑːstər] *n.m.* receveur (des postes); *A: & Can:* **P. General** = ministre *m* des Postes et Télécommunications.

post meridiem [poustmə'ridiəm] *Lt.phr.* (*usu* **p.m.**) de l'après-midi, du soir.

postmistress ['poustmistris] *n.f.* receveuse des postes.

postmortem [poust'mɔːtəm] (*a*) *a. & n.* **p. (ex-**

amination), autopsie *f* (d'un cadavre); **to hold a p. (examination),** faire une autopsie; (*b*) *n. Fig:* autopsie; analyse rétrospective, après coup.

postnatal [poust'neit(ə)l] *a.* postérieur à la naissance; (*of medical case, etc.*) postnatal, -als.

postoperative [poust'ɔpərətiv] *a. Med:* (choc, etc.) postopératoire.

postpaid [poust'peid] *a.* affranchi; port payé.

postpone [poust'poun] *v.tr.* remettre, ajourner, renvoyer à plus tard, reculer (un départ, un projet, etc.); différer, arriérer (un paiement); **to p. a matter for a week,** remettre, renvoyer, une affaire à huitaine; **postponed action, trial,** cause remise.

postponement [poust'pounmənt] *n.* remise *f* à plus tard; ajournement *m* (d'une réunion, d'une cause); renvoi *m* (d'une cause); sursis *m.*

postposition [poustpə'ziʃ(ə)n] *n. Gram:* postposition *f.*

postprandial [poust'prændiəl] *a. usu. Hum:* postprandial, -aux; après le repas.

postscript ['pous(t)skript] *n.* post-scriptum *m inv*; **by way of p.,** en post-scriptum.

postulant ['pɔstjulənt] *n. Ecc:* postulant, -ante.

postulate¹ ['pɔstjulət] *n. Mth: Log:* postulat *m.*

postulate² ['pɔstjuleit] **1.** *v.tr. & i.* **to p. (for) sth.,** postuler, demander, réclamer, qch. **2.** *v.tr. Mth: Log:* postuler (qch.); poser (qch.) en postulat.

posture¹ ['pɔstjər] *n.* (*a*) posture *f*, pose *f*, attitude *f* (du corps); (*b*) position, situation *f*, état *m* (des choses).

posture² *v.i.* prendre une pose; prendre une attitude (affectée).

postwar [poust'wɔːr] *a.* d'après-guerre; **the p. period,** l'après-guerre *m inv.*

posy ['pouzi] *n.* petit bouquet (de fleurs).

pot¹ [pɔt] *n.* **1.** (*a*) pot *m*; **flower p.,** pot à fleurs; **coffee p.,** cafetière *f*; **a p. of tea,** un thé; **chamber p.,** pot de chambre; (*b*) marmite *f*; **pots and pans,** batterie *f* de cuisine; **p. roast,** morceau de viande cuit à l'étouffé; **to take p. luck,** manger à la fortune du pot; *F:* **to go to p.,** aller à la ruine; *F:* **to take a p. shot at sth.,** (i) lâcher à l'aveuglette un coup de fusil à qch.; (ii) faire qch. au petit bonheur; (*c*) *Ind:* **melting p.,** creuset *m*; *Fig:* **to be in the melting p.,** (i) être en pleine réorganisation; (ii) être en pleine révolution sociale; (*d*) *Sp: F:* coupe *f* (remportée en prix). **2.** *F:* **pots of money,** des tas *mpl* d'argent; **to have pots of money,** rouler sur l'or; **we have pots of time,** nous avons tout le temps. **4.** herbe *f*; *P:* (i) marijuana *f*; (ii) hachisch *m.*

pot² *v.tr.* **(potted) 1.** (*a*) mettre en pot (le beurre, la viande salée, etc.); (*b*) *Hort:* mettre en pot, empoter (une plante); (*c*) mettre (un bébé) sur son pot (de chambre); (*d*) *Bill:* blouser (une bille). **2.** *F:* (*a*) abattre (du gibier, etc.); (*b*) *v.i.* **to p. at,** lâcher un coup de fusil à (une pièce de gibier). **potted** *a.* (*a*) (conservé) en pot, en terrine; **p. meat,** terrine *f* de porc, etc.; **p. shrimps,** crevettes en conserve cuites dans du beurre; (*b*) *F:* abrégé, condensé. **potting** *n.* **1.** mise *f* en pot (des plantes, etc.); *Hort:* **p. shed,** serre *f* de bouturages. **2.** *Bill:* mise en blouse.

potable ['poutəbl] *a.* potable, buvable.

potash ['pɔtæʃ] *n.* potasse *f.*

potassium [pə'tæsiəm] *n. Ch:* potassium *m*; **p. chloride,** chlorure *m* de potassium.

potation [pou'teiʃ(ə)n] *n.* action de boire; *pl.* libations *fpl.*

potato, *pl.* **-oes** [p(ə)'teitou, -ouz] *n.* **1.** (*a*) pomme *f* de terre; **to dig up, lift, potatoes,** arracher des pommes de terre; *Cu:* **roast potatoes,** pommes de terre rôties au four; **boiled potatoes,** pommes de terre à l'eau, à l'anglaise; **chipped potatoes, French fried potatoes,** pommes (de terre) frites, *F:* frites *fpl*; **p. crisps,** *U.S:* **p. chips,** pommes chips; **mashed potatoes,** purée *f* (de pommes de terre); pommes mousseline; **jacket potatoes,** pommes de terre en robe de chambre, en robe des champs; (*b*) *F:* **hot p.,** affaire épineuse; **to drop s.o. like a hot p.,** laisser tomber qn; **2. sweet p.,** patate *f.*

potbellied [pɔt'belid] *a. F:* ventru, bedonnant.

potbelly ['pɔtbeli] *n. F:* gros ventre, bedon *m.*

potboiler ['pɔtbɔilər] *n. F:* œuvre *f* alimentaire.

poteen [pɔ'tiːn] *n.* whisky irlandais distillé en fraude.

potency ['poutənsi] *n.* force *f*, puissance (d'un argument); efficacité *f*, activité *f* (d'un médicament); force, degré *m* (d'une boisson alcoolique).

potent ['poutənt] *a.* **1.** *Lit: Poet:* puissant. **2.** (*of drug, etc.*) efficace, puissant, actif; (*of motive, etc.*) convaincant, décisif; (boisson) très forte; (poison) violent.

potentate ['poutənteit] *n.* potentat *m.*

potential [pə'tenʃəl] **1.** *a.* (*a*) (danger) possible, latent; (ennemi, criminel) en puissance; (client) éventuel; (*b*) potentiel; **p. value of a mineral deposit,** valeur virtuelle d'un gîte métallifère; (*c*) *Mth: etc:* potentiel; **p. energy,** énergie potentielle. **2.** *a. & n. Gram:* **the p. (mood),** le potentiel. **3.** *n.* (*a*) **human p.,** potentiel humain; **to reach one's p.,** atteindre son maximum; (*b*) *Ph:* potentiel (électrique); (*c*) *El:* tension *f*, potentiel; **operating p.,** tension de fonctionnement. **-ally** *adv.* potentiellement.

potentiality [pətenʃi'æliti] *n.* potentialité *f*; virtualité *f*; **situation full of potentialities,** situation *f* (i) où tout devient possible, (ii) qui promet.

pother ['pɔðər] *n.* (*a*) agitation *f*, confusion *f*; (*b*) tapage *m*, vacarme *m.*

pothole ['pɔthoul] *n.* (*a*) *Geol:* marmite torrentielle, de géants; (*b*) (*in road*) trou *m.*

potholer ['pɔthoulər] *n.* spéléologue *mf.*

potholing ['pɔthouliŋ] *n.* spéléologie *f.*

pothook ['pɔthuk] *n.* crémaillère *f* (de foyer).

pothunter ['pɔthʌntər] *n. F: Sp:* coureur, -euse, de prix.

potion ['pouʃ(ə)n] *n.* potion *f*; dose *f*; **love p.,** philtre *m* d'amour.

potpourri [pou'puːriː] *n.* (*a*) fleurs séchées; (*b*) *Mus:* pot-pourri *m*, *pl.* pots-pourris.

pottage ['pɔtidʒ] *n. A:* potage (épais); potée *f* (de viande et de légumes); *B:* **mess of p.** = plat *m* de lentilles.

potter¹ ['pɔtər] *n.* potier *m*; **potter's clay,** terre *f* de potier, à potier; terre glaise; **potter's wheel,** tour *m* de potier.

potter² *v.i.* **1.** s'occuper de bagatelles; **to p. about (at odd jobs),** bricoler. **2.** traîner, traînasser; *Aut: etc:* **to p. along,** aller doucement; **to p. about the house,** faire des petits travaux dans la maison.

pottery ['pɔtəri] *n.* (*a*) poterie *f*; **p. industry,** industries *fpl* céramiques; (*b*) (*works, studio*) poterie; faïencerie *f*; (*c*) vaisselle *f* de terre; faïence *f*; **a piece of p.,** (i) une poterie; (ii) une céramique.

potty¹ ['pɔti] *a. F:* **1.** insignifiant, **a p. little state,** un petit état de rien du tout. **2.** (*a*) toqué, timbré; **to go p.,** devenir fou, maboule; (*b*) **to be p. about, over, s.o., sth.,** être mordu pour, toqué de, qn, qch.

potty² *n. F:* pot *m* de chambre (d'enfant).

pouch [pautʃ] *n.* **1.** (*a*) (petit) sac; bourse *f*; **tobacco p.,** blague *f* à tabac; (*b*) *Dipl:* valise *f* diplomatique. **2.** *Nat.Hist:* poche ventrale.

pouf(fe) [puːf] *n. Furn:* pouf *m.*

poult [poult] *n.* (*a*) dindonneau *m*; (*b*) pouillard *m*; (i) faisandeau *m*; (ii) perdreau *m*; (*c*) (jeune) poulet *m.*

poulterer ['poultərər] *n.* marchand, -ande, de volaille.

reprimand¹ ['reprimɑːnd] *n.* (*a*) réprimande *f*; (*b*) *Adm: & Jur:* blâme *m.*
reprimand² *v.tr.* (*a*) réprimander; (*b*) *Adm: & Jur:* blâmer publiquement (qn).
reprint¹ ['riːprint] *n.* réimpression *f*; nouveau tirage; **separate r. (of magazine article),** tirage à part.
reprint² [riː'print] *v.tr.* réimprimer; faire un nouveau tirage (d'un livre); reproduire (un article); **this book is being reprinted,** ce livre est en réimpression.
reprisal [ri'praiz(ə)l] *n.* représailles *fpl*; **to make reprisal(s),** exercer des représailles; user de représailles.
reproach¹ [ri'proutʃ] *n.* **1.** (*a*) motif *m* de honte, d'opprobre; **to be a r. to . . .,** être la honte de . . .; (*b*) honte; **things that have brought r. upon him,** choses qui ont jeté le discrédit sur lui. **2.** reproche *m*; **she heaped reproaches on him,** elle l'a accablé de reproches; **beyond, above, r.,** irréprochable; **look of r.,** regard de reproche, réprobateur.
reproach² *v.tr.* faire, adresser, des reproches à (qn); blâmer (qn); **to r. oneself,** se faire des reproches; **to r. s.o. with sth.,** reprocher qch. à qn; **I have nothing to r. myself with,** je n'ai rien à me reprocher.
reproachful [ri'proutʃf(u)l] *a.* réprobateur, -trice; (ton, air) de reproche. **-fully** *adv.* d'un air, d'un ton, de reproche.
reprobate¹ ['reprəbeit] *a. & n.* réprouvé (*m*).
reprobate² *v.tr.* (*a*) réprouver (un crime); blâmer, critiquer (qn); (*b*) *Theol:* (*of God*) réprouver.
reprobation [reprə'beiʃ(ə)n] *n.* réprobation *f.*
reprocess [riː'prouses] *v.tr. Ind: etc:* recycler.
reproduce [riːprə'djuːs] **1.** *v.tr.* (*a*) reproduire (un tableau, etc.); copier (un texte, etc.); (*b*) *Nat. Hist:* reproduire, régénérer (une queue, etc.). **2.** *v.i.* (*a*) se reproduire, se multiplier; (*b*) **this print will r. well,** cette estampe se prêtera à la reproduction.
reproduction [riːprə'dʌkʃ(ə)n] *n.* **1.** (*a*) *Biol: etc:* reproduction *f*; **(a)sexual r.,** reproduction (a)sexuée; (*b*) reproduction (d'un tableau, d'un document, etc.); **thousands of reproductions have been made of this picture,** ce tableau a été reproduit à des milliers d'exemplaires. **2.** reproduction; copie *f*, imitation *f.*
reproductive [riːprə'duktiv] *a.* reproducteur, -trice; **the r. organs,** les organes de la reproduction.
reproof¹ [ri'pruːf] *n.* **1.** reproche *m*, blâme *m*, réprobation *f*; **word, look, of r.,** mot, regard, de reproche. **2.** réprimande *f.*
reproof² [riː'pruːf] *v.tr.* réimperméabiliser.
reprove [ri'pruːv] *v.tr.* (*a*) reprendre, réprimander (qn); (*b*) condamner (une action). **reproving** *a.* réprobateur, -trice; (ton, air) de reproche. **reprovingly** *adv.* d'un ton, d'un air, de reproche.
reptile ['reptail] *a. & n.* reptile (*m*).
reptilian [rep'tiliən] **1.** *a.* reptilien, reptile. **2.** *n.* reptile *m.*
republic [ri'pʌblik] *n.* république *f.*
republican [ri'pʌblikən] *a. & n.* républicain, -aine.
republicanism [ri'pʌblikənizm] *n.* républicanisme *m.*
republication [riːpʌbli'keiʃ(ə)n] *n.* (*a*) nouvelle édition, réédition *f* (d'un livre); (*b*) nouvelle publication (d'une loi, etc.).
republish [riː'pʌbliʃ] *v.tr.* (*a*) rééditer (un livre); (*b*) republier (une loi, etc.).
repudiate [ri'pjuːdieit] *v.tr.* répudier (une épouse); répudier, désavouer (un ami, une opinion); repousser (une accusation); nier (une dette); **to r. the authorship of a book,** désavouer la paternité d'un livre.
repudiation [ripjuːdi'eiʃ(ə)n] *n.* répudiation *f* (d'une épouse); répudiation, désaveu *m* (de qn, d'une opinion); reniement *m* (d'une dette).
repugnance [ri'pʌgnəns] *n.* **1.** incompatibilité *f* (**of, between, ideas,** d'idées). **2.** répugnance *f*, antipathie *f* (**to, against,** pour); **to feel r. to sth., to doing sth.,** avoir de la répugnance pour qch., à faire qch.
repugnant [ri'pʌgnənt] *a.* **1.** incompatible (**to, with,** avec). **2.** répugnant (**to,** à); **to be r. to s.o.,** répugner à qn.
repulse¹ [ri'pʌls] *n.* rebuffade *f*, refus *m*; échec *m*; **to meet with a r.,** essuyer un refus.
repulse² *v.tr.* **1.** repousser, refouler (un assaut, un ennemi). **2.** repousser (les avances de qn, une demande); refuser, rebuter (qn).
repulsion [ri'pʌlʃ(ə)n] *n.* **1.** *Ph:* répulsion *f.* **2.** répulsion, aversion *f.*
repulsive [ri'pʌlsiv] *a.* **1.** *Ph:* répulsif. **2.** (*of thg*) répulsif, repoussant; (*of pers.*) répugnant. **-ly** *adv.* **r. ugly,** d'une laideur repoussante.
repulsiveness [ri'pʌlsivnis] *n.* **1.** *Ph:* farce répulsive. **2.** caractère repoussant; aspect répugnant.
reputable ['repjutəbl] *a.* **1.** (*of pers.*) honorable, de bonne réputation; réputé. **2.** (emploi) honorable.
reputation [repju(ː)'teiʃ(ə)n] *n.* réputation *f*, renom *m*; **to make a r. (for oneself),** se faire une réputation; **to have the r. of being, of doing, sth.,** avoir la réputation d'être, de faire, qch.; **to have a good, bad, r.,** avoir (une) bonne, (une) mauvaise, réputation.
repute¹ [ri'pjuːt] *n.* réputation *f*, renom *m*; **to know s.o. by r.,** connaître qn de réputation; *O:* **to be held in high r.,** avoir une haute réputation; **doctor of r.,** médecin réputé; **house of ill r.,** maison de passe.
repute² *v.tr.* (*usu. passive*) **to be reputed wealthy,** avoir la réputation d'être riche; **he is reputed to be a good doctor,** il a la réputation d'être (un) bon médecin. **reputedly** *adv.* censément; **he is r. the best heart specialist,** il passe pour le meilleur cardiologue.
request¹ [ri'kwest] *n.* **1.** demande *f*, prière *f*, requête *f*; **r. for money,** demande d'argent; **at the r. of s.o., at s.o.'s r.,** à, sur, la demande, à la requête, de qn; **samples sent on r.,** échantillons sur demande; **to make a r.,** faire, formuler, une demande; **by (popular) r.,** à la demande générale; **r. (bus) stop,** arrêt facultatif; *W.Tel:* **r. programme, show,** programme des auditeurs. **2.** recherche *f*, demande; **to be in r.,** être recherché; être en vogue.
request² *v.tr.* **1. to r. sth. of s.o.,** demander qch. à qn; solliciter qch. de qn. **2. to r. s.o. to do sth.,** demander à qn de faire qch.; prier qn de faire qch.; *Com:* **as requested,** conformément à vos instructions. **3. to r. (permission) to do sth.,** demander à faire qch.
requiem ['rekwiəm] *n. Ecc:* **r. (mass),** (messe *f* de) requiem (*m*); messe des morts; *Mus:* requiem.
require [ri'kwaiər] *v.tr.* **1. to r. sth. of s.o.,** demander, réclamer, qch. à qn; **to r. s.o. to do sth.,** demander à qn de faire qch.; **he had done all that was required by law,** il s'était conformé à toutes les exigences de la loi. **2.** exiger, demander; **this plant requires plenty of water,** il faut beaucoup d'eau à cette plante; **have you everything you r.?** avez-vous tout ce qu'il vous faut? **I shall do whatever is required,** je ferai tout ce qu'il faudra; **if required,** s'il le faut; si besoin est; **when required,** au besoin; **in the required time,** dans le délai prescrit; en temps voulu; **the qualifications required for this job,** les qualités requises pour ce poste.
requirement [ri'kwaiəmənt] *n.* **1.** demande *f*, réclamation *f.* **2.** exigence *f*, nécessité *f*, besoin *m*; **to meet s.o.'s requirements,** répondre aux désirs de qn; satisfaire les exigences, aux exigences, de qn. **3.** *usu.pl.* condition(s) requise(s); qualité voulue; spécifications *fpl* (d'une machine).
requisite ['rekwizit] **1.** *a.* requis (**to,** pour); nécessaire (**to,** à); indispensable (**to,** pour). **2.** *n.* (*a*) condition requise (**for,** pour); (*b*) chose *f* nécessaire; **toilet requisites,** articles *mpl*, accessoires *mpl*, de toilette.
requisition¹ [rekwi'ziʃ(ə)n] *n.* **1.** demande *f*; *Com:*

etc: **r. for supplies,** commande *f* pour fournitures; **r. number,** numéro de référence. **2.** (*a*) *Mil:* réquisition *f*; (*b*) **his services were in constant r.,** on avait constamment recours à ses services.

requisition² *v.tr.* **1.** réquisitionner (des vivres, etc.); recourir, avoir recours (aux services de qn). **2.** faire des réquisitions dans (une ville).

requital [ri'kwait(ə)l] *n.* **1.** récompense *f*, retour *m*; **in r. of, for, sth.,** en récompense, retour, de qch. **2.** revanche *f*.

requite [ri'kwait] *v.tr.* récompenser, payer de retour (un service); se venger d'(une injure); venger (une injure); **to r. s.o.'s love,** répondre à l'amour de qn.

reread [riː'riːd] *v.tr.* relire.

reredos ['riədɔs] *n. Ecc:* retable *m*.

re(-)route [riː'ruːt] *v.tr.* dérouter (un navire, etc.).

rerun¹ ['riːrʌn] *n.* reprise *f*, rediffusion *f* (d'un film, etc.).

rerun² [riː'rʌn] *v.tr.* repasser, rediffuser (un film, etc.).

resale [riː'seil] *n.* revente *f*.

rescind [ri'sind] *v.tr.* rescinder, abroger (une loi); annuler, résilier (un contrat).

rescission [ri'siʒ(ə)n] *n.* rescision *f*, abrogation *f* (d'un acte); annulation *f*, résiliation *f* (d'un contrat).

rescue¹ ['reskjuː] *n.* **1.** délivrance *f*; (*from shipwreck, fire, etc.*) sauvetage *m*; **to come, go, to s.o.'s r.,** venir, aller, au secours de qn; **r. party,** équipe de sauvetage, de sauveteurs; **air-sea r.,** sauvetage aérien en mer; sauvetage aéromaritime; **mountain r.,** secours en montagne. **2.** délivrance illégale (d'un prisonnier).

rescue² *v.tr.* **1.** sauver, délivrer, secourir; **to r. s.o. from danger,** arracher qn à un danger; **to r. s.o. from drowning,** sauver qn qui se noie; **the rescued,** les rescapés. **2.** arracher (un prisonnier) aux mains de la justice; délivrer (un prisonnier) par force.

rescuer ['reskjuər] *n.* **1.** libérateur, -trice. **2.** (*from fire, etc.*) secouriste *mf*; sauveteur *m*.

research¹ [ri'səːtʃ] *n.* recherche *f*; **scientific, medical, r.,** recherche(s) scientifique(s), médicale(s); **to do, be engaged in, r. (on, into, sth.),** faire des recherches (sur qch.); **r. work,** recherches; travaux de recherche; **r. worker, assistant,** (i) chercheur, -euse (de laboratoire); (ii) documentaliste *mf*; **r. scientist,** maître de recherche; **market r.,** étude *f* de marché.

research² *v.i. & tr.* faire des recherches (scientifiques, etc.) (sur qch.).

researcher [ri'səːtʃər] *n.* chercheur, -euse.

reseat [riː'siːt] *v.tr.* **1.** rasseoir (qn); **to r. oneself,** se rasseoir. **2.** remettre un fond à (un pantalon, une chaise). **3.** *I.C.E: etc:* roder le siège d'(une soupape).

resection [ri'sekʃ(ə)n] *n. Surg:* résection *f*.

resell [riː'sel] *v.tr.* (*p.t. & p.p.* **resold** [riː'sould]) revendre.

resemblance [ri'zembləns] *n.* ressemblance *f* (**to,** à, avec; **between,** entre); **to bear a r. to s.o., sth.,** ressembler à qn, qch.

resemble [ri'zembl] *v.tr.* ressembler à, approcher de (qn, qch.); **to r. one another,** se ressembler.

resent [ri'zent] *v.tr.* **1.** être offensé, froissé, de (qch.); **you r. my being here,** ma présence vous déplaît. **2.** s'offenser, se froisser, se fâcher, de (qch.).

resentful [ri'zentf(u)l] *a.* **1.** plein de ressentiment; rancunier. **2.** froissé, irrité (**of,** de). **-fully** *adv.* avec ressentiment; d'un ton, d'un air, rancunier.

resentment [ri'zentmənt] *n.* ressentiment *m*; rancœur *f*, rancune *f*; **to feel, bear, r. against s.o.,** garder rancune à qn, avoir de la rancune contre qn.

reservation [rezə'veiʃ(ə)n] *n.* **1.** (*a*) réservation *f* (de places, etc.); (*b*) place retenue. **2.** réserve *f*, restriction *f*; **without r.,** sans réserve; sans arrière-pensée; **not without r., with some r.,** non sans réserves; **with this r.,** à cette restriction près; sous le bénéfice de cette observation. **3.** *Ecc:* **the R. (of the Sacrament),** la sainte Réserve. **4.** *Jur:* réservation (d'un droit). **5.** (*a*) *Aut:* **central r.,** terreplein central; (*b*) *NAm:* terrain réservé; **Indian r.,** réserve indienne.

reserve¹ [ri'zəːv] *n.* **1.** (*a*) réserve *f* (d'argent, d'énergie); *Fin:* **bank reserves,** réserves bancaires; **to draw on the reserves,** puiser dans les réserves; **to have great reserves of energy,** avoir beaucoup d'énergie, en réserve; *Mch:* **r. power, energy,** réserve de puissance, d'énergie; *Aut:* **r. (petrol) tank,** réservoir *m* de réserve, nourrice *f*; *Min:* **known reserves,** réserves prouvées; (*b*) **to have, keep, sth. in r.,** tenir qch. en réserve. **2.** (*a*) *Mil: etc:* **the reserves,** (i) les réserves; (ii) les réservistes *mpl*; **r. officer,** officier de réserve; (*b*) *Sp:* remplaçant, -ante. **3.** terrain réservé; *For: Ven:* réserve; **nature r.,** réserve naturelle. **4.** (*a*) réserve, restriction *f*; **without r.,** sans réserve; sans restriction; (*b*) (*at sale*) **r. price,** prix minimum; mise *f* à prix. **5.** réserve, retenue *f*; **when he breaks through his r.,** quand il sort de sa réserve.

reserve² *v.tr.* réserver (**sth. for s.o.,** qch. pour, qn); mettre (qch.) en réserve; **to r. a seat for s.o.,** réserver, retenir, une place à qn; **reserved seat,** place réservée, louée; **to r. the right to do sth.,** se réserver le droit de faire qch.; *Publ:* **all rights reserved,** tous droits (de reproduction, etc.) réservés. **reserved** *a.* (*of pers.*) réservé, renfermé; peu communicatif; **to be r. with s.o.,** être réservé, se tenir sur la réserve, avec qn.

reservedly [ri'zəːvidli] *adv.* avec réserve.

reservist [ri'zəːvist] *n. Mil: etc:* réserviste *m*.

reservoir ['rezəvwɑːr] *n.* **1.** *Hyd.E:* réservoir *m*; bassin *m* de retenue. **2.** *Mec.E:* réservoir (à huile).

reset [riː'set] *v.tr.* (*p.t. & p.p.* **reset;** *pr.p.* **resetting**) **1.** remonter (des pierres précieuses, etc.); **to r. the table,** remettre le couvert. **2.** retendre, rebander (un ressort); **to r. one's watch,** remettre sa montre à l'heure. **3.** *Surg:* remettre, remboîter (un membre luxé). **4.** *Typ:* recomposer (un texte).

resettle [riː'setl] **1.** *v.tr.* rétablir (**s.o. in a country,** qn dans un pays); réinstaller (qn). **2.** *v.i.* se fixer de nouveau (dans un endroit); se réinstaller.

resettlement [riː'set(ə)lmənt] *n.* transfert *m* de population.

reshape [riː'ʃeip] *v.tr.* reformer, refaçonner.

reshuffle¹ [riː'ʃʌfl] *n.* **Cabinet r.,** remaniement ministériel.

reshuffle² *v.tr.* (*a*) mêler de nouveau (les cartes); (*b*) remanier (un personnel, etc.).

reside [ri'zaid] *v.i.* **1.** (*of pers.*) résider (**at, in,** à, dans). **2.** (*of quality*) résider (dans qn, qch.).

residence ['rezidəns] *n.* **1.** résidence *f*, demeure *f*, séjour *m*; **to take up r. in a country,** se fixer, s'établir, dans un pays; **r. permit,** permis de séjour; **place of r.,** lieu de résidence; **to be in r.,** être en résidence. **2.** demeure, maison *f*; **desirable r. for sale,** belle propriété à vendre.

residency ['rezidənsi] *n.* **1.** *Hist:* (*a*) résidence *f* (d'un protectorat); (*b*) résidence officielle (du résident). **2.** *U.S: Med:* internat *m*.

resident ['rezidənt] **1.** *a.* (*a*) résidant, qui réside; **to be r. in a place,** résider dans un endroit; **the r. population,** la population fixe; (*b*) **r. teacher,** professeur à demeure; professeur résident. **2.** *n.* (*a*) habitant, -ante (d'un pays, d'une rue, etc.); pensionnaire *mf* (dans un hôtel, etc.); **residents' parking bay, place,** emplacement réservé aux riverains; (*b*) *Adm:* (*pers. living in a foreign country*) résident, -ente; (*c*) *Hist:* (ministre) résident; (*d*) *U.S: Med:* interne *mf*.

residential [rezi'denʃ(ə)l] *a.* **1.** résidentiel; **r. area, district,** quartier résidentiel. **2.** (cours) à temps complet; **r. qualification,** (i) quotité d'imposition nécessaire pour être électeur; (ii) droit de vote en tant que propriétaire ou locataire.

residual [ri'zidjuəl] *a.* (*a*) *Ph: etc:* résiduel; **r. magnetism,** magnétisme rémanent, résiduel; rémanence *f*; (*b*) (*of objection, mistake, etc.*) qui reste; restant.

residuary [ri'zidjuəri] *a. Jur:* **r. legatee,** légataire *m* à titre universel.

residue ['rezidjuː] *n.* **1.** *Ch: Ind: etc:* résidu *m*; reliquat *m.* **2.** reste(s) *m(pl)* (d'une armée, etc.).

residuum, *pl.* **-a** [ri'zidjuəm, -ə] *n. Ch:* résidu *m.*

resign [ri'zain] *v.tr. & i.* **1.** (*a*) résigner (une fonction); démissionner; donner sa démission; *Parl:* **r.! r.!** démission! démission! (*b*) abandonner (un droit, tout espoir); (*c*) **to r. sth. to s.o.,** abandonner, céder, qch. à qn. **2.** (*a*) **to r. oneself to s.o., sth.,** se livrer à qn, qch.; (*b*) **to r. oneself, to be resigned, to one's fate, to doing sth.,** se résigner, être résigné, à son sort, à faire qch.

resignedly [ri'zainidli] *adv.* avec résignation; d'un air, d'un ton, résigné.

resignation [rezig'neiʃ(ə)n] *n.* **1.** (*a*) démission *f*; **to give (in), send in, tender, one's r.,** donner sa démission; (*b*) abandon *m* (d'un droit). **2.** résignation; **to accept one's fate with r.,** se résigner à son sort.

resilience [ri'ziliəns] *n.* (*a*) *Mec:* résilience *f*; résistance vive; (*b*) (*of pers.*) élasticité *f* de caractère, de tempérament; **to have r.,** avoir du ressort.

resilient [ri'ziliənt] *a.* élastique; (*of pers.*) **to be r.,** avoir du ressort; **children are more r. than adults,** les enfants se remettent plus vite que les adultes.

resin ['rezin] *n.* résine *f*; **polyvinyl r.,** résine polyvinylique; **to tap trees for r.,** gemmer des arbres.

resinous ['rezinəs] *a.* résineux.

resist [ri'zist] *v.tr.* **1.** (*a*) résister à (une attaque, la chaleur, une tentation); (*b*) **I couldn't r. telling him,** je n'ai pas pu m'empêcher, me retenir, m'abstenir, de le lui dire; **I can't r. chocolates,** je ne peux pas résister aux chocolats. **2.** (*a*) résister à, s'opposer à (un projet, etc.); refuser d'obéir à (un ordre); s'opposer à (une influence); **to r. arrest,** résister à l'arrestation; **it's best not to r.,** mieux vaut ne pas offrir de résistance, ne pas résister; (*b*) repousser (une suggestion, etc.); se refuser à (l'évidence).

resistance [ri'zistəns] *n.* **1.** (*a*) résistance *f*; **to offer r.,** résister (à qn, à qch.); **to offer no r.,** n'offrir, n'opposer, aucune résistance; ne pas résister; **she made no r.,** elle s'est laissé faire; **to meet with no r.,** ne rencontrer aucune résistance; **passive r.,** résistance passive; (*b*) *Pol: etc:* **r. (movement),** résistance; (*c*) **r. to disease,** résistance à la maladie. **2.** (*a*) *Ph: etc:* résistance; *Fig:* **to take the line of least r.,** aller au plus facile; suivre la loi du moindre effort; (*b*) *El:* résistance (électrique); (*c*) *Tex:* **crease r.,** infroissabilité *f*.

resistant, resistent [ri'zistənt] *a.* résistant.

resit [riː'sit] *v.tr.* (*p.t. & p.p.* **resat** [riː'sæt]; *pr.p.* **resitting**) *Sch:* passer de nouveau (un examen).

resolute ['rezəl(j)uːt] *a.* résolu, déterminé; (ton) résolu, ferme; (homme) résolu; **to be r. for, against, sth.,** avoir résolu de, être décidé à, faire, ne pas faire, qch. **-ly** *adv.* résolument.

resoluteness ['rezəl(j)uːtnis] *n.* fermeté *f*.

resolution [rezə'l(j)uːʃ(ə)n] *n.* **1.** (*a*) résolution *f* (d'une tumeur, d'une dissonance, etc.); *T.V:* définition *f* (d'une image); (*b*) résolution (d'une difficulté). **2.** résolution, délibération *f* (d'une assemblée); **to put a r. to the meeting,** soumettre, proposer, une résolution; **to pass, carry, adopt, a r.,** adopter une résolution. **3.** résolution, détermination *f*; **to make a r.,** prendre la résolution de, se résoudre à, faire qch. **4.** résolution, fermeté *f*.

resolve¹ [ri'zɔlv] *n.* **1.** résolution *f*, détermination *f*; **to keep one's r.,** tenir sa résolution. **2.** *Lit:* résolution, fermeté *f*; **deeds of high r.,** nobles élans *mpl.*

resolve² **I.** *v.tr.* **1.** (*a*) résoudre (qch. en ses éléments); (*of substance*) **to r. itself,** se résoudre; (*b*) **the House resolved itself into a committee,** la Chambre s'est constituée en commission. **2.** résoudre (un problème, une difficulté); dissiper (un doute). **3.** (*a*) (*of committee, etc.*) résoudre, adopter la résolution (de faire qch.); (*b*) (*of individual*) se résoudre à, prendre la résolution de (faire qch.); **to be resolved to do sth.,** être résolu, décidé, à faire qch. **II.** *v.i.* **1.** se résoudre (en ses éléments); *Med:* (*of tumour*) se résoudre; se résorber. **2.** (*of pers.*) se résoudre (à faire qch.); prendre la résolution (de faire qch.).

resonance ['rez(ə)nəns] *n.* (*a*) *Mus:* résonance *f* (d'un instrument); vibration *f* (de la voix); (*b*) *Elcs: etc:* résonance; **r. curve,** courbe de résonance.

resonant ['rezənənt] *a.* (*a*) (*of sound, room, etc.*) résonnant; (voix) sonore; (*b*) *Elcs: etc:* (circuit) résonnant; (fréquence) de résonance.

resonate ['rezəneit] *v.i.* résonner, retentir (**with,** de).

resonator ['rezəneitər] *n. Elcs: etc:* résonateur *m.*

resorption [ri'sɔːpʃ(ə)n] *n.* (*a*) réabsorption *f* (de qch.); (*b*) *Med:* résorption *f* (d'une tumeur, etc.).

resort¹ [ri'zɔːt] *n.* **1.** ressource *f*; recours *m*; **in the, as a, last r.,** en dernière ressource, en dernier ressort; en désespoir de cause. **2. health r.,** station climatique, thermale; **seaside r.,** station balnéaire; plage *f*; **holiday r.,** centre *m* de villégiature; **winter, ski, r.,** station d'hiver, de ski.

resort² *v.i.* **1.** avoir recours, recourir (**to,** à); user (**to,** de); **to r. to violence,** avoir recours à la violence. **2. to r. to s.o. (for help),** avoir recours, faire appel, recourir, à qn.

resound [ri'zaund] *v.i.* (*a*) (*of place*) résonner, retentir (**with cries,** de cris); (*b*) (*of voice*) résonner; (*c*) (*of event*) avoir du retentissement. **resounding** *a.* résonnant, retentissant; (rire) sonore; (succès) éclatant, retentissant. **resoundingly** *adv.* d'une manière retentissante; (*of play*) **to be r. successful,** avoir un succès retentissant.

resource [ri'sɔːs, -'zɔːs] *n.* **1.** (*a*) ressource *f*; **person of r.,** personne de ressource(s); (*b*) ressource, expédient *m.* **2. resources,** (*a*) ressources (**in,** en); **to be at the end of one's resources,** être au bout de ses ressources, à bout de ressources; **he was left to his own resources,** il a dû se débrouiller tout seul; (*b*) *NAm: Fin:* actif disponible, liquide.

resourceful [ri'sɔːsf(u)l, -'zɔːs-] *a.* habile; ingénieux; **a r. man,** un homme de ressources. **-fully** *adv.* habilement.

resourcefulness [ri'sɔːsf(u)lnis, -'zɔːs-] *n.* ressource *f*.

respect¹ [ri'spekt] *n.* **1.** (*a*) *esp. Com:* (*reference*) rapport *m*, égard *m*; **with r. to . . .,** en ce qui concerne . . .; concernant . . .; (*b*) rapport, égard, point *m* de vue; **in some, certain, respects,** à certains égards; **in all respects, in every r.,** sous tous les rapports; à tous (les) égards; **in this r.,** à cet égard, sous ce rapport; **in other respects,** sous d'autres rapports; à d'autres égards. **2.** égard; **without r. of persons,** sans acceptation de personnes. **3.** respect *m*; (**for the truth,** pour la vérité); respect, considération *f* (**for s.o.,** pour, envers, qn); **to have r. for s.o.,** avoir, témoigner, du respect à, envers, pour, qn; **he shows little r. for his parents,** il ne se montre guère respectueux envers ses parents; **he can command r.,** il sait se faire respecter; **out of r. for . . .,** par respect, par égard, par considération, pour . . .; **with all due r. (to you),** sauf votre respect. **4. respects,** respects; hommages *mpl*; **to pay one's respects to s.o.,** présenter (i) ses respects, (ii) ses hommages, à qn.

respect² *v.tr.* **1.** respecter, honorer (qn); avoir, témoigner, du respect à, envers, pour (qn); **to be universally respected,** être respecté de tous. **2.** respecter (qch.); (*a*) **he respected my wish to be alone,** il a respecté mon désir d'être seul; **to r. s.o.'s opinion,** respecter l'opinion de qn; (*b*) **I r. myself too much to do that,** je me respecte trop pour faire cela. **respecting** *prep.* concernant; relatif à.

respectability [rispektə'biliti] *n.* respectabilité *f.*

respectable [ri'spectəbl] *a.* **1.** respectable, digne de respect. **2.** respectable; convenable; comme il faut; **r. clothes,** vêtements convenables. **3.** (*a*) respectable, passable; **a r. number of people,** un bon nombre de gens; (*b*) **a r. sum,** une somme respectable, rondelette. **-ably** *adv.* respectablement; convenablement.

respecter [ri'spektər] *n.* **to be no r. of the law,** ne pas respecter les lois; **to be no r. of persons,** ne faire acception de personne.

respectful [ri'spektf(u)l] *a.* respectueux **(to,** envers, pour); **to stand at a r. distance,** se tenir à distance respectueuse. **-fully** *adv.* respectueusement, avec respect; *Corr: O:* **(I remain) yours r.,** veuillez agréer l'expression de mes sentiments respectueux.

respectfulness [ri'spektf(u)lnis] *n.* respect *m*; caractère respectueux.

respective [ri'spektiv] *a.* respectif; **our r. homes,** nos demeures respectives. **-ly** *adv.* respectivement.

respiration [respi'reiʃ(ə)n] *n.* respiration *f*; **artificial r.,** respiration artificielle.

respirator ['respireitər] *n.* respirateur *m.*

respiratory [ri'spaiərət(ə)ri, ri'spirit(ə)ri] *a.* (appareil, système) respiratoire.

respire [ri'spaiər] *v.tr. & i.* respirer.

respite ['respait] *n.* **1.** *Jur:* sursis *m*, délai *m*; **to get a r.,** obtenir un délai. **2.** répit *m*, relâche *m & f*; **to work without r.,** travailler sans relâche.

resplendence [ri'splendəns] *n.* splendeur *f*, resplendissement *m.*

resplendent [ri'splendənt] *a.* resplendissant, éblouissant.

respond [ri'spɔnd] *v.i.* **1.** (*a*) répondre, faire une réponse **(to,** à); (*b*) *Ecc:* réciter, chanter, les répons. **2.** (*a*) répondre, être sensible (à l'affection, à la bonté); se prêter (à une proposition); **to fail to r. to s.o.'s advances,** ne pas répondre aux avances de qn; (*of aircraft*) **to r. to the controls,** obéir aux commandes; (*b*) (*of nerves, etc.*) réagir **(to,** contre).

respondent [ri'spɔndənt] *n.* (*a*) (i) (*esp. in divorce case*) défendeur, -eresse; (ii) (*in appeal case*) intimé, -ée; (*b*) *U.S:* personne interrogée, sondée.

response [ri'spɔns] *n.* **1.** (*a*) réponse *f*, réplique *f*; **he made no r.,** il n'a fait aucune réponse; (*b*) *Ecc:* répons *m*; **to make the responses at mass,** répondre la messe. **2.** (*a*) réponse; **the appeal met with a generous r.,** on a répondu largement à l'appel; (*b*) *Physiol:* réponse, réaction *f*; **motor r.,** réponse, réaction, motrice; (*c*) *Ph: Elcs:* **frequency r.,** réponse de, en, fréquence; **r. curve,** courbe *f* de réponse.

responsibility [rispɔnsi'biliti] *n.* (*a*) responsabilité *f*; **sense of r.,** sens des responsabilités; **to assume, accept, a r.,** accepter une responsabilité; **to take the r. of sth., to accept r. for sth.,** prendre la responsabilité de qch.; **to do sth. on one's own r.,** faire qch. sous sa (propre) responsabilité, de son (propre) chef; (*b*) responsabilité (d'une faute); **to refuse to accept any r. for the accident,** décliner toute responsabilité au sujet de l'accident; (*c*) **his new responsabilities give him no time for leisure,** ses nouvelles fonctions ne lui laissent pas de loisirs.

responsible [ri'spɔnsibl] *a.* **1.** chargé **(for sth.,** d'un devoir, etc.); **I am r. for s.o., sth.,** j'ai la responsabilité de qn, qch.; **I will be r. for his safety,** je me porte garant qu'il ne lui sera fait aucun mal; **r. to s.o.,** responsable devant qn, envers qn; **to be r. to s.o. for sth.,** être comptable à qn de qch.; (*b*) responsable (d'un accident, etc.); **to hold s.o. r. (for sth.),** tenir qn (pour) responsable (de qch.); *Jur:* **to be r. for s.o.'s actions,** être solidaire des actes de qn; **he is not r. for his actions,** il n'est pas maître de ses actes. **2.** (*a*) compétent; digne de confiance, sur qui on peut compter; **a r. man,** un homme sérieux; (*b*) **r. job,** poste qui entraîne des responsabilités; responsabilité. **-ibly** *adv.* de façon responsable; avec sérieux.

responsive [ri'spɔnsiv] *a.* impressionnable; sensible **(to,** à); **to be r. to sth.,** répondre, être sensible, à qch.

responsiveness [ri'spɔnsivnis] *n.* sensibilité *f.*

respray [ri:'sprei] *v.tr.* repeindre qch. (au pistolet).

rest¹ [rest] *n.* **1.** (*a*) repos *m*; **to have a good night's r.,** passer une bonne nuit; **at r.,** au, en, repos; **to be laid to r.,** être enterré; **to set s.o.'s mind at r.,** calmer, tranquilliser, l'esprit de qn; dissiper les craintes, les inquiétudes, de qn; (*b*) **to have, take, a r.,** prendre du repos; se reposer; **to give s.o. a r. from sth.,** permettre à qn de se reposer de qch.; **a day of r., a day's r., a r. day,** un jour de repos; **the day of r.,** le jour du Seigneur; le repos dominical; (*c*) (*of moving body*) **to come to r.,** s'arrêter, s'immobiliser. **2.** (*a*) *Mus:* pause, silence *m*; **semibreve r.,** pause; **minim r.,** demi-pause *f*, *pl.* demi-pauses: **crotchet r.,** soupir *m*; (*b*) (*in elocution, verse*) repos. **3. r. centre,** centre *m* d'accueil; **r. home,** maison *f* de repos (pour convalescents, personnes âgées); (*in factory, etc.*) **r. room,** (i) salle *f* de repos; (ii) toilettes *fpl*; **r. cure,** cure *f* de repos. **4.** (*a*) (*of chair*) **arm r.,** accoudoir *m*; (*b*) *Bill:* chevalet *m*; *Mil:* **rifle r.,** chevalet de pointage; *Tp:* **receiver r.,** étrier *m* du récepteur; *Dom.Ec:* **knife r.,** porte-couteau *m*, *pl.* porte-couteaux.

rest² **I.** *v.i.* **1.** (*a*) se reposer; **to r. in the Lord,** s'en remettre à Dieu; **may they r. in peace!** qu'ils reposent en paix! (*b*) se reposer, prendre du repos; **you need to r. (up),** il vous faut le repos complet; **to r. from one's work,** se reposer de son travail; **to feel rested,** se sentir (bien) reposé, rafraîchi; *Th: F:* (*of actor*) **to be resting,** se trouver sans engagement; chômer; (*c*) **there the matter rests,** l'affaire en reste là, en est là; **I won't let it r. at that,** cela ne se passera pas ainsi; **let it r.!** n'en parlons plus! **2.** (*a*) se poser, être posé, s'appuyer; **his hand resting on the table,** sa main posée, appuyée, sur la table; **to let one's eyes r. on sth.,** poser ses regards sur qch.; **a heavy responsibility rests upon them,** une lourde responsabilité pèse sur eux; (*b*) **his fame rests on his novels,** sa gloire repose sur ses romans. **II.** *v.tr.* **1.** (*a*) reposer, faire reposer (qn); **to r. one's men,** faire, laisser, reposer ses hommes; **(God) r. his soul!** Dieu donne le repos à son âme! (*b*) appuyer (ses coudes sur la table); poser, déposer (un fardeau par terre); **to r. one's head on a cushion,** reposer la tête sur un coussin. **2.** *esp. NAm: Jur:* **to r. the case,** conclure son plaidoyer. **resting** *n.* repos *m*; **r. place,** (lieu *m* de) repos; **last r. place,** dernière demeure.

rest³ *n.* **1.** reste *m*, restant *m* (de la journée, d'une somme d'argent, etc.); **(as) for the r.,** quant au reste, pour le reste; **and all the r. of it,** et tout le reste. **2.** (*with pl. const.*) **the r.,** les autres *mfpl*; **the r. of us,** nous autres; les autres (d'entre nous).

rest⁴ *v.i.* **1. r. assured that . . .,** soyez assuré que . . .. **2. it rests with you (to do sth.),** il dépend de vous, il ne tient qu'à vous (de faire qch.); **the responsibility rests with the author,** la responsabilité incombe à l'auteur.

restart [ri:'stɑ:t] **1.** *v.tr.* (*a*) recommencer, reprendre (un travail); (*b*) (re)mettre (une machine) en marche; relancer (un moteur). **2.** *v.i.* (*a*) recommencer, reprendre; (*b*) (*of machine, etc.*) se remettre en marche.

restate [ri:'steit] *v.tr.* (*a*) exposer de nouveau (une théorie, un point de vue); (*b*) répéter (une question).

restaurant ['rest(ə)rɔ̃, -rɔ(:)nt] *n.* restaurant *m*; *Rail:* **r. car,** wagon-restaurant *m*, *pl.* wagons-restaurants.

restaurateur [restərə'tə:r] *n.* restaurateur *m.*

restful ['restf(u)l] *a.* qui repose; paisible, tranquille; **r. to the eyes,** qui repose les yeux, reposant pour la vue. **-fully** *adv.* paisiblement.

restitution [resti'tju:ʃ(ə)n] *n.* restitution *f*; **to make r. of sth.,** restituer qch.; *Jur:* **r. of conjugal rights,** réintégration *f* du domicile conjugal.

restive ['restiv] *a.* **1.** (*of horse*) rétif, vicieux; (*of pers.*) rétif, indocile, récalcitrant. **2.** nerveux, agité.

restless ['restlis] *a.* **1.** (*a*) agité; **to be r. in one's sleep,** avoir le sommeil agité, troublé; **I've had a r. night,** j'ai passé une nuit agitée; (*b*) (enfant) agité, remuant. **2.** nerveux, agité; **r. mind,** esprit agité; **the audience was getting r.,** l'auditoire s'impatientait. **-ly** *adv.* **1.** avec agitation. **2.** nerveusement, fiévreusement.

restlessness ['restlisnis] *n.* **1.** (*a*) inquiétude *f*, agitation *f*; (*b*) turbulence *f*; mouvement incessant (de la mer). **2.** nervosité *f*; état fiévreux (des esprits).

restock [ri:'stɔk] *v.tr.* **1.** (*a*) repeupler (un étang); (*b*) reboiser (un terrain). **2.** remonter (un magasin); réapprovisionner (**with food,** en comestibles).

restoration [restə'reiʃ(ə)n] *n.* **1.** restitution *f* (de biens); remise *f* (d'objets trouvés). **2.** restauration *f* (d'un monument, d'un bâtiment, d'un meuble, etc.); restitution *f* (d'un texte); rétablissement *m* (de l'ordre, de la paix, des communications, etc.); rénovation *f* (d'un bâtiment, etc.). **3.** (*a*) réintégration *f* (d'un fonctionnaire); (*b*) rétablissement (de la santé); (*c*) relèvement *m* (d'une fortune). **4.** (*a*) restauration (d'une dynastie); (*b*) rétablissement sur le trône; *Hist:* **the R.,** la Restauration.

restorative [ri'stɔ(:)rətiv] *a.* & *n. Med:* (*a*) fortifiant (*m*); reconstituant (*m*); (*b*) cordial (*m*), -aux.

restore [ri'stɔ:r] *v.tr.* **1.** restituer, rendre (qch.); **to r. sth. to s.o.,** rendre qch. à qn. **2.** (*a*) restaurer (un monument, un bâtiment, etc.); rénover (un meuble); **to r. one's reputation,** se refaire une réputation; (*b*) reconstituer, restituer (un texte). **3.** (*a*) **to r. sth. to its place, to its former condition,** remettre qch. en place, en état; (*b*) rétablir, réintégrer (qn dans ses droits, etc.); restaurer (une dynastie); (*c*) **to r. s.o. to health,** rétablir la santé de qn; **to r. s.o. to life,** ramener qn à la vie. **4.** (*a*) rétablir (la confiance, l'ordre, etc.); faire renaître (le calme, la confiance); restaurer (la paix, la discipline); **order is being restored,** l'ordre se rétablit; (*b*) **to r. s.o.'s strength,** redonner des forces à qn; **to r. the circulation,** réactiver la circulation.

restorer [ri'stɔ:rər] *n.* **1.** (*a*) restaurateur, -trice (d'un tableau, d'une église); (*b*) restituteur *m* (d'un texte). **2.** *Toil:* **hair r.,** régénérateur *m* des cheveux.

restrain [ri'strein] *v.tr.* **1.** retenir, empêcher (qn) (**from,** de). **2.** détenir (qn). **3.** refréner (ses passions); contenir, refouler (sa colère, ses larmes); retenir (ses larmes, sa curiosité); **to r. oneself,** se contraindre; **in restrained terms,** en termes mesurés; **to r. s.o.'s activities,** mettre un frein aux activités de qn. **restraining** *a.* qui retient; restrictif.

restraint [ri'streint] *n.* **1.** (*a*) contrainte *f*, restriction *f*; **to put a r. on s.o.,** contraindre qn; **to break loose from all r.,** se donner libre cours; **to be under no r.,** avoir ses coudées franches; **wage r.,** limitation *f* des salaires; **without r.,** sans contrainte; (*b*) contrainte; réserve *f*, gêne *f*; **lack of r.,** abandon *m*; manque *m* de réserve; **to throw aside all r.,** ne garder aucune mesure; (*c*) sobriété *f* (de style); mesure *f*. **2.** contrainte par corps; interdiction *f* (d'un aliéné); emprisonnement *m*; **to keep s.o. under r.,** tenir qn emprisonné.

restrict [ri'strikt] *v.tr.* restreindre; limiter; **in a restricted sense,** dans un sens restreint; **to r. oneself to . . .,** se limiter à . . .; **he is restricted to one glass of wine a day,** on ne lui permet qu'un verre de vin par jour; **restricted diet,** régime sévère; **restricted area,** (i) *Aut:* zone à vitesse limitée; (ii) *Adm: Mil:* zone interdite; *Adm:* **restricted document,** document secret.

restriction [ri'strikʃ(ə)n] *n.* restriction *f*; (*a*) réduction *f* (des dépenses); (*b*) *Aut:* **r. of speed, speed r.,** limitation *f* de vitesse; (*c*) **to place, set, restrictions on sth.,** apporter des restrictions à qch.

restrictive [ri'striktiv] *a.* restrictif.

restring [ri:'striŋ] *v.tr.* (*p.t.* & *p.p.* **restrung** [ri:'strʌŋ]) **1.** enfiler de nouveau (des perles). **2.** remonter (un violon); recorder (une raquette).

result[1] [ri'zʌlt] *n.* **1.** résultat *m* (**of,** de); aboutissement *m* (des efforts de qn); **the r. is that . . .,** il en résulte que . . .; **to yield results,** donner des résultats; **as a r. of . . .,** par suite de . . .; **without r.,** sans résultat; **results,** résultats (d'un examen, etc.). **2.** *Mth:* résultat.

result[2] *v.i.* **1.** résulter, provenir, découler (**from,** de); **it results from this that . . .,** il s'ensuit que . . .; **consequences resulting from . . .,** conséquences découlant de . . .. **2.** aboutir (à un échec); **to r. in . . .,** avoir pour résultat de . . .; **this will r. in unpleasantness,** cela entraînera des désagréments.

resultant [ri'zʌltənt] *a.* & *n.* résultant; **the r. economic benefits,** les avantages économiques qui en résultent; *Mec:* **r. (force),** (force) résultante (*f*).

resume [ri'zju:m] *v.tr.* **1.** reprendre, regagner (sa vigueur, etc.); **to r. one's seat,** reprendre sa place; se rasseoir. **2.** (*a*) reprendre; renouer (des relations); continuer, poursuivre (un discours); **to r. work,** se remettre au travail; **to r. one's duties,** reprendre son service, ses fonctions; **she resumed her maiden name,** elle a repris son nom de jeune fille; (*b*) **this was a great mistake, he resumed,** c'était une grosse erreur, continua-t-il, reprit-il.

résumé [rei'zju(:)mei] *n.* résumé *m*, abrégé *m.*

resumption [ri'zʌmpʃ(ə)n] *n.* reprise *f* (de négociations, etc.).

resurface [ri:'sə:fis] **1.** *v.tr.* refaire le revêtement (d'une route). **2.** *v.i. Nau:* revenir à la surface.

resurgence [ri'sə:dʒəns] *n. Lit:* résurrection *f* (d'une idée, etc.); *Pol.Ec:* reprise *f*, renouveau *m.*

resurgent [ri'sə:dʒənt] *a. Lit:* renaissant.

resurrect [rezə'rekt] *v.tr.* ressusciter, faire revivre.

resurrection [rezə'rekʃ(ə)n] *n.* **1.** (*a*) résurrection *f* (des morts); (*b*) **the R.,** la résurrection du Christ. **2.** *F:* résurrection, reprise *f* (d'une coutume, etc.).

resuscitate [ri'sʌsiteit] *v.tr.* ressusciter (qn, qch); rappeler (qn) à la vie; ranimer, réanimer.

resuscitation [risʌsi'teiʃ(ə)n] *n.* ressuscitation *f*, réanimation *f*, ranimation *f* (d'un asphyxié, etc.).

retail[1] ['ri:teil] *n. Com:* (vente *f* au) détail (*m*); **to sell goods r.,** *NAm:* **at r.,** vendre des marchandises au détail; **wholesale and r. business,** commerce *m* en gros et au détail; **r. trade,** commerce de détail; **r. price,** prix *m* de détail.

retail[2] ['ri:teil, ri:'teil] **1.** *v.tr.* détailler, vendre au détail (des marchandises). **2.** *v.i.* (*of goods*) se vendre au détail, se détailler (**at, for,** à).

retailer ['ri:teilər, ri:'teilər] *n.* détaillant, -ante; marchand, -ande, au détail.

retain [ri'tein] *v.tr.* **1.** retenir, maintenir (qch. dans une position); *Const:* **retaining wall,** mur *m* de soutènement, de retenue. **2.** (*a*) *O:* prendre (qn) à son service; **to r. s.o.'s services,** retenir les services de qn; (*b*) **to r. a barrister, a counsel,** retenir un avocat (à l'avance); **retaining fee,** avance *f*; provision *f*. **3.** conserver, garder (un bien, etc.); conserver (une coutume, la chaleur, etc.); **to r. the power to . . .,** se réserver le droit de . . .. **4.** garder (qch.) en mémoire; conserver (le souvenir de qch.).

retainer [ri'teinər] *n.* **1.** (*a*) *Hist:* (*pers.*) serviteur *m*, suivant *m*; (*b*) **an old (family) r.,** un vieux domestique. **2.** *Jur:* (*a*) (droit *m* de) rétention (*f*) (de qch.); (*b*) mandat donné à un avocat; (*c*) **(general) r.,** avance *f*; provision *f*.

retake¹ ['ri:teik] *n.* *Cin:* reprise *f* (d'une prise de vues).

retake² [ri:'teik] *v.tr.* (*p.t.* **retook** [ri:'tuk]; *p.p.* **retaken** [ri:'teik(ə)n]) **1.** reprendre (une place forte, etc.); rattraper (un prisonnier qui s'est sauvé, etc.). **2.** *Cin: T.V:* retourner (un plan).

retaliate [ri'tælieit] *v.i.* **to r. (on s.o.),** rendre la pareille (à qn); user de représailles (envers qn).

retaliation [ritæli'eiʃ(ə)n] *n.* revanche *f*, représailles *fpl*; **in r.,** en revanche; par mesure de représailles; **the law of r.,** la loi du talion.

retaliatory [ri'tæliət(ə)ri] *a.* **r. measures,** représailles *fpl*.

retard¹ [ri'tɑ:d] *n.* retard *m*.

retard² *v.tr.* (*a*) retarder (qch.; *I.C.E:* l'allumage); (*b*) retarder (qn); **mentally retarded person,** personne attardée, arriérée; attardé, -ée.

retardation [ri:tɑ:'deiʃ(ə)n] *n.* **1.** retard *m*. **2.** *Mec: Ph:* retardation *f*. **3.** *Psy:* arriération *f*.

retch [retʃ, ri:tʃ] *v.i.* faire des efforts pour vomir; avoir des haut-le-cœur. **retching** *n.* efforts *mpl* pour vomir; haut-le-cœur *mpl*.

retell [ri:'tel] *v.tr.* (*p.t.* & *p.p.* **retold** [ri:'tould]) (*a*) redire, répéter; (*b*) raconter de nouveau.

retention [ri'tenʃ(ə)n] *n.* **1.** *Med:* rétention *f* (d'urine, etc.). **2.** conservation *f* (d'un usage, etc.); maintien *m* (d'une autorité). **3.** *Psy:* mémorisation *f*, mémoire *f*.

retentive [ri'tentiv] *a.* **1.** (*a*) (*of memory*) tenace, fidèle; (*b*) **r. soil,** sol qui retient l'eau.

retentiveness [ri'tentivnis] *n.* **1.** pouvoir *m*, faculté *f*, de retenir; fidélité *f*, ténacité *f* (de mémoire).

rethink¹ [ri:'θiŋk] *v.tr.* (*p.t.* & *p.p.* **rethought** [-'θɔ:t]) repenser, reconsidérer (une question).

rethink² *n.* **to have a r. on sth.,** repenser, reconsidérer, qch.

reticence ['retisəns] *n.* **1.** réticence *f*; **without any r.,** sans aucune réserve. **2.** caractère peu communicatif; taciturnité *f*.

reticent ['retisənt] *a.* peu communicatif; taciturne; **to be very r. about, on, sth.,** faire (grand) mystère de qch. **-ly** *adv.* avec réticence, avec réserve.

reticle ['retikl] *n.* *Opt:* réticule *m*.

reticulate¹ [ri'tikjulət] *a.* réticulé; rétiforme.

reticulate² [ri'tikjuleit] **1.** *v.tr.* diviser (une surface) en réseau; *Arch:* **reticulated (masonry) work,** appareil réticulé. **2.** *v.i.* former un réseau.

reticule ['retikju:l] *n.* *Opt:* réticule *m*.

retina, *pl.* **-as, -ae** ['retinə, -əz, -i:] *n.* *Anat:* rétine *f* (de l'œil); *Med:* **detached r.,** rétine décollée.

retinue ['retinju:] *n.* suite *f* (d'un prince, etc.).

retire [ri'taiər] **I.** *v.i.* **1.** (*a*) se retirer (dans un endroit); **to r. from the world,** se retirer du monde; **to r. into oneself,** rentrer en soi-même; (*b*) **to r. from the room,** quitter la pièce; **to r. (to bed, for the night),** (aller) se coucher. **2. to r. (from business),** se retirer des affaires; **to r. (on a pension),** prendre sa retraite; **to have retired,** être à la retraite. **3.** (*a*) *Mil: etc:* reculer; se replier; (*b*) *Sp: etc:* se retirer du match; abandonner. **II.** *v.tr.* **1.** mettre (qn) à la retraite. **2.** *Mil:* replier (les troupes). **retired** *a.* **1.** (*a*) (*of life, etc.*) retiré; **to live a r. life,** mener une vie retirée; (*b*) (endroit, etc.) retiré, écarté. **2.** (*a*) (négociant, etc.) retiré des affaires; (officier, fonctionnaire) retraité, à la retraite; (*b*) *Mil:* **r. pay,** retraite des cadres; **to put, place, s.o. on the r. list,** mettre qn à la retraite. **retiring 1.** *a.* (*a*) (*of pers.*) renfermé, réservé; timide; (*b*) (président, administrateur) sortant. **2.** *n.* (*a*) action *f* de se retirer; (*b*) mise *f* à la retraite (d'un officier, etc.); **r. age,** âge de la retraite.

retiree [ritai'ri:] *n.* *U.S:* retraité, -ée.

retirement [ri'taiəmənt] *n.* **1.** (*a*) *Adm: Mil: etc:* retraite *f*; **compulsory r.,** retraite d'office; **r. pension,** (pension *f* de) retraite; (*b*) **to live in r.,** vivre retiré du monde. **2.** (*a*) *Mil:* retraite, repli *m* (des troupes); (*b*) *Sp:* abandon *m* (du match) (par un concurrent).

retort¹ [ri'tɔ:t] *n.* réplique *f* (**to,** à); riposte *f*.

retort² *v.tr.* (*a*) renvoyer, rendre, retourner (une injure); (*b*) *v.tr.* & *i.* répliquer, riposter.

retort³ *n.* *Ch: Ind:* cornue *f*.

retouch [ri:'tʌtʃ] *v.tr.* retoucher (une photographie, etc.). **retouching** *n.* retouche *f*.

retrace [ri'treis] *v.tr.* **1.** remonter à l'origine de (qch.). **2.** reconstituer, retracer (le passé). **3. to r. one's steps,** revenir sur ses pas; rebrousser chemin.

retract [ri'trækt] **1.** *v.tr.* (*a*) rétracter; *Av:* escamoter (le train d'atterrissage); **the cat retracts its claws,** le chat rentre ses griffes; (*b*) rétracter (ce qu'on a dit); reprendre, revenir sur (sa parole, etc.); désavouer, rétracter (une opinion, etc.); *v.i.* **to r.,** se rétracter; se dédire. **2.** *v.i.* se rétracter; (*of cat's claws*) rentrer.

retractable [ri'træktəbl] *a.* (*a*) *Nat.Hist:* rétractile; (*b*) (*of handle, etc.*) escamotable; (stylo à bille) à cartouche rétractable; *Av:* (train d'atterrissage) rentrant, escamotable.

retraction [ri:'trækʃən] *n.* **1.** rétractation *f* (de sa parole); désaveu *m*, reniement *m* (d'une opinion). **2.** rétraction *f* (des griffes, etc.).

retrain [ri:'trein] *v.tr.* (*a*) *Med:* rééduquer (un muscle); (*b*) recycler (qn). **retraining** *n.* (*a*) *Med:* rééducation *f* (d'un muscle); (*b*) recyclage *m* (de qn).

retread ['ri:tred] *n.* *Aut:* (pneu) rechapé.

retreat¹ [ri'tri:t] *n.* **1.** *Mil:* retraite *f*; **to sound, beat, the r.,** sonner, battre, la retraite; **to beat a r.,** battre en retraite. **2.** (*a*) retrait *m*, recul *m* (des eaux, etc.); recul (d'un glacier); (*b*) *Ecc:* retraite. **3.** (*a*) abri *m*; retraite; (*b*) repaire *m* (de brigands, etc.).

retreat² **1.** *v.i.* (*a*) se retirer, s'éloigner; (*b*) *Box:* rompre; *Mil:* battre en retraite; (*c*) (*of glacier*) reculer. **2.** *v.tr.* *Chess:* ramener (une pièce en danger).

retrench [ri'tren(t)ʃ] **1.** *v.tr.* (*a*) restreindre (ses dépenses); (*b*) réduire (les privilèges, etc., de qn); faire des coupures dans (une œuvre littéraire). **2.** *v.i.* restreindre ses dépenses; faire des économies.

retrenchment [ri'tren(t)ʃmənt] *n.* **1.** réduction *f* (des dépenses); **policy of r.,** politique d'économies, de redressement. **2.** suppression *f*, retranchement *m* (d'un passage littéraire, etc.).

retrial [ri:'trai(ə)l] *n.* *Jur:* nouveau procès.

retribution [retri'bju:ʃ(ə)n] *n.* **1.** châtiment *m*; vengeance *f*; **the Day of R.,** le jour du jugement; **just r. of, for, a crime,** juste récompense *f* d'un crime.

retrievable [ri'tri:vəbl] *a.* **1.** (somme) recouvrable. **2.** (perte, erreur) réparable. **3.** *Cmptr:* accessible.

retrieval [ri'tri:v(ə)l] *n.* **1.** recouvrement *m* (de biens). **2.** rétablissement *m* (de sa fortune, sa réputation). **3.** (*a*) réparation *f* (d'une erreur, etc.); (*b*) **beyond, past, r.,** (erreur, etc.) irréparable. **4.** *Cmptr:* extraction *f*, recherche *f* (d'une instruction); **information r. system,** système *m* de recherche documentaire.

retrieve *v.tr.* **1.** (*a*) *Ven:* (*of dog*) rapporter (le gibier); (*b*) recouvrer (des biens); retrouver (un objet perdu, sa liberté). **2.** (*a*) rétablir (sa fortune, sa réputation); (*b*) **to r. s.o. from ruin,** arracher qn à la ruine. **3.** réparer (une perte, une erreur, etc.); remédier à (une situation); *Gaming: etc:* **to r. one's losses,** se racquitter, se refaire. **4.** *Cmptr:* retrouver, extraire (une instruction).

retriever [ri'tri:vər] *n. Breed:* retriever *m.*
retroactive [retrou'æktiv] *a.* rétroactif. **-ly** *adv.* rétroactivement.
retrograde¹ ['retrəgreid] *a.* (*a*) rétrograde; (mouvement) en arrière, à reculons; (*b*) décadent.
retrograde² *v.i.* rétrograder; revenir en arrière.
retrogress [retrə'gres] *v.i.* = RETROGRADE².
retrogression [retrə'greʃ(ə)n] *n.* rétrogradation *f.*
retrogressive [retrə'gresiv] *a.* rétrogressif; régressif.
retrorocket ['retrourɔkit] *n. Space:* rétrofusée *f.*
retrospect ['retrəspekt] *n.* coup d'œil rétrospectif; examen rétrospectif; vue rétrospective; **when I consider these events in r.,** quand je jette un coup d'œil rétrospectif sur ces événements.
retrospection [retrə'spekʃ(ə)n] *n.* rétrospection *f*; examen rétrospectif (des événements, etc.).
retrospective [retrə'spektiv] *a.* **1.** (examen) rétrospectif. **2.** (loi) avec effet rétrospectif. **3.** *Art: a. & n.* **r. (exhibition),** rétrospective *f.* **-ly** *adv.* **1.** rétrospectivement. **2.** rétroactivement.
retry [ri:'trai] *v.tr. Jur:* juger à nouveau.
retsina [ret'si:nə] *n.* (vin) résiné *m.*
return¹ [ri'tə:n] *n.* **1.** (*a*) retour *m*; rentrée *f* (à la maison); **on my r.,** dès, à, mon retour; **on his r. to France,** à sa rentrée en France; **by r. (of post),** par retour (du courrier); **many happy returns (of the day)!** bon anniversaire! **r. journey,** (voyage de) retour; *Rail: etc:* **r. ticket,** *n.* **r.,** billet *m* de retour; aller *m* (et) retour; **point of no r.,** point *m* de non-retour; (*b*) **r. stroke,** course *f* de retour (d'un piston); **r. angle,** retour d'angle; (*c*) *Arch:* **r. wall,** mur *m* en retour; (*d*) *El:* circuit *m* de retour; **r. current,** courant *m* de retour. **2.** *Com:* (*a*) **returns,** recettes *fpl*; rentrées; **quick returns,** un prompt débit; une vente rapide; (*b*) gain *m*, profit *m*; rendement *m*; **to bring (in) a fair r.,** rapporter un bénéfice raisonnable; *Pol.Ec:* **law of diminishing returns,** loi *f* du rendement non proportionnel. **3.** (*a*) renvoi *m*, retour (de marchandises); **on sale or r.,** (marchandises) vendues avec faculté de retour, à condition; *Post:* **r. address,** adresse *f* de l'expéditeur; (*b*) restitution *f* (d'un objet volé, etc.); ristourne *f* (d'une somme payée en trop); remise *f* (d'un objet à sa place); rentrée (d'un livre); (*c*) échange *m*; **to give sth. in r. for sth.,** donner qch. en échange de qch.; **in r. for which . . .,** moyennant quoi . . .; **if you will do sth. in r.,** si vous voulez bien faire qch. en retour; (*d*) *Com:* **returns,** rendus *mpl*; (*of books, newspapers*) invendus *mpl*, *F:* bouillons *mpl.* **4.** (*a*) renvoi, répercussion *f* (d'un son); *Av: Radar:* **ground r.,** écho *m* de sol; *Typewr:* **carriage r.,** retour, rappel *m*, de chariot; (*b*) *Ten: etc:* renvoi (de la balle); riposte *f.* **5.** (*a*) récompense *f*; **in r. for this service . . .,** en récompense, en retour, de ce service . . .; **you must expect the same treatment in r.,** il faut vous attendre à la pareille; (*b*) *Sp:* **r. match, game,** match retour; revanche *f.* **6.** (*a*) rapport officiel; *Adm:* recensement *m* (de la population, etc.); **the official returns,** les relevés officiels; **sales returns,** statistique *f* des ventes; (*b*) **income tax r.,** déclaration *f* de revenu. **7.** *Pol:* élection *f* (d'un député); **to announce the returns of the election,** annoncer les résultats du scrutin.
return² **I.** *v.i.* **1.** (*come back*) revenir; (*go back*) retourner; **I was returning from a journey,** je rentrais de voyage; **to r. home,** rentrer (chez soi); **he has returned,** il est de retour; **to r. from the dead,** ressusciter d'entre les morts; **her colour returned,** elle a repris des couleurs; *Nau:* **to r. to port,** rentrer au port. **2. to r. to a task,** reprendre une tâche; **I shall r. to this subject later,** je reviendrai plus tard à ce sujet; **to r. to one's old habits,** retomber dans ses vieilles habitudes. **3.** *B:* **unto dust shalt thou r.,** tu retourneras en poussière. **II.** *v.tr.* **1.** (*a*) rendre (un livre emprunté, un dépôt, etc.); restituer (un objet volé, etc.); renvoyer (un cadeau, etc.); rembourser (un emprunt); *Post:* **returned letter,** lettre renvoyée à l'expéditeur; (*b*) **to r. a book to its place,** remettre un livre à sa place. **2.** renvoyer (la lumière, un son, une balle, etc.); *Ten:* **to r. the service, a stroke,** relancer la balle. **3.** (*a*) rendre (une visite, un compliment); rendre (un coup); renvoyer (une accusation); *Mil:* **to r. fire,** riposter (au feu adverse); **to r. s.o.'s greeting,** rendre un salut à qn; **to r. good for evil,** rendre le bien pour le mal; **to r. s.o.'s love,** aimer qn en retour; *Cards:* **to r. clubs,** rejouer du trèfle (après son partenaire); (*b*) répondre, répliquer. **4.** *Com: Fin:* rapporter, donner (un bénéfice). **5.** (*a*) déclarer, rapporter; rendre compte de (qch.); (*b*) *Jur:* rendre (un verdict); **the jury returned a verdict of guilty, not guilty,** le jury a déclaré l'accusé coupable, non coupable; (*c*) *Sp:* **returned time,** temps contrôlé, temps officiel. **6.** *Parl:* (*a*) **to r. the result of the poll,** faire son rapport sur les résultats du scrutin; (*b*) élire (un député); **returning officer,** directeur, -trice, du scrutin.
returnable [ri'tə:nəbl] *a.* qui peut être rendu, renvoyé; **r. bottle,** bouteille consignée; **empties are not r.,** on ne reprend pas les bouteilles.
reunification [ri:ju:nifi'keiʃ(ə)n] *n. Pol:* réunification *f.*
reunify [ri:'ju:nifai] *v.tr. Pol:* réunifier.
reunion [ri:'ju:niən] *n.* réunion *f*, assemblée *f.*
reunite [ri:ju'nait] **1.** *v.tr.* (*a*) unir de nouveau; réunir (des fragments, etc.); (*b*) réunir, rassembler (ses partisans, etc.); (*after quarrel*) réconcilier (une famille, etc.). **2.** *v.i.* se réunir.
reusable [re:'ju:zəbl] *a.* remployable.
reuse¹ [ri:'ju:s] *n.* réutilisation *f*; remploi *m.*
reuse² [ri:'ju:z] *v.tr.* remployer.
rev¹ [rev] *n. Aut: F:* (*abbr. of* **revolution) four thousand revs a minute,** quatre mille tours *mpl* à la minute.
rev² *v.* **(revved)** *Aut:* **1.** *v.tr.* **to r. up,** (faire) emballer (le moteur). **2.** *v.i.* **the engine began to r. up,** le moteur s'est emballé.
revaluation [ri:valju'eiʃ(ə)n] *n.* réévaluation *f*; réestimation *f*; *Fin:* revalorisation *f* (du franc, etc.).
revalue [ri:'vælju:] *v.tr.* réestimer; réévaluer (une propriété, etc.); *Fin:* revaloriser (le franc, etc.).
revamp [ri:'væmp] *v.tr.* **1.** remplacer l'empeigne d'(une chaussure). **2.** réparer. **3.** modifier, améliorer.
reveal [ri'vi:l] *v.tr.* (*a*) révéler, découvrir (son jeu); faire connaître (un fait); **to r. one's identity,** se faire connaître; (*b*) laisser voir (une qualité, etc.); (*c*) révéler, découvrir (un objet caché); dévoiler (un mystère); faire voir, mettre à jour (qch.). **revealing** *a.* révélateur, -trice; **r. dress,** robe décolletée.
reveille [ri'væli, ri'veli] *n. Mil:* le réveil; la diane.
revel¹ ['rev(ə)l] *n. often pl.* (*a*) divertissement(s) *m(pl)*; réjouissances *fpl*; (*b*) bacchanale *f*, orgie *f.*
revel² *v.* **(revelled,** *NAm:* **reveled; revelling,** *NAm:* **reveling) 1.** *v.i.* (*a*) se réjouir, se divertir; (*b*) festoyer; *F:* faire la noce; (*c*) **to r. in sth., in doing sth.,** se délecter à qch., à faire qch.; **to r. in one's freedom,** se réjouir de sa liberté. **2.** *v.tr.* **to r. away the time,** passer tout son temps à s'amuser.
revelation [revi'leiʃ(ə)n] *n.* **1.** révélation *f*; **it was a r. to me,** cela a été une révélation pour moi. **2.** *B:* **the R., (the Book of) Revelations,** l'Apocalypse *f.*
reveller, *NAm:* **reveler** ['rev(ə)lər] *n.* (*a*) joyeux convive; (*b*) viveur, -euse, noceur, -euse.
revelry ['revəlri] *n.* (*a*) divertissements *mpl*, réjouissances *fpl*; ébats *mpl*; (*b*) bacchanale *f*, orgie *f.*
revenge¹ [ri'vendʒ] *n.* **1.** vengeance *f*; **to take r. on s.o. for sth.,** se venger de qch. sur qn; **to have one's**

r., se venger **(for,** de). **2.** (*esp. in games*) revanche *f*; contre-partie *f*.

revenge² *v.tr.* **1. to r. oneself,** se venger **(on s.o.,** sur qn; **for sth.,** de qch.). **2.** venger (une injure) **(on, upon s.o.,** sur qn).

revengeful [ri'vendʒf(u)l] *a.* vindicatif; porté à la vengeance. **-fully** *adv.* par vengeance.

revenger [ri'vendʒər] *n.* vengeur, -eresse **(of,** de).

revenue ['revənju:] *n.* **1.** revenu *m*, rentes *fpl.* **2. the Inland R.,** (i) le Trésor public; (ii) *Adm:* le fisc.

revenuer ['revənju:ər] *n. U.S:* percepteur *m*.

reverberate [ri'və:bəreit] **1.** *v.tr.* renvoyer, répercuter (le son); réverbérer, réfléchir (la lumière, la chaleur); **to be reverberated,** réverbérer. **2.** *v.i.* (*of sound*) retentir, résonner; (*of light, heat*) réverbérer.

reverberation [rivə:bə'reiʃ(ə)n] *n.* renvoi *m*, répercussion *f* (d'un son); réverbération *f* (de la lumière, de la chaleur).

revere [ri'viər] *v.tr.* révérer, vénérer.

reverence¹ ['rev(ə)rəns] *n.* **1.** respect religieux; vénération *f*; **to hold s.o. in r.,** révérer qn. **2.** (*esp. in Ireland*) **your R., his R.,** monsieur l'abbé.

reverence² *v.tr.* révérer.

reverend ['rev(ə)rənd] *a.* **1.** vénérable. **2.** *Ecc:* (*a*) **the r. gentleman,** le révérend abbé, père, ou pasteur; (*b*) (*as title*) **the Rev. Father Martin,** le révérend père Martin; **the R. Mother Superior,** la révérende mère supérieure; (*of bishop*) **Right R.,** très révérend.

reverent ['rev(ə)rənt] *a.* respectueux; plein de vénération. **-ly** *adv.* avec respect, avec vénération.

reverential [revə'renʃ(ə)l] *a.* révérenciel.

reverie ['revəri] *n.* rêverie *f*; **in a r.,** rêveur, -euse.

revers [ri'viəz] *n.pl. Cost:* revers *mpl* (d'une veste).

reversal [ri'və:s(ə)l] *n.* **1.** *Jur:* réforme *f*, annulation *f* (d'un jugement). **2.** (*a*) renversement *m*; inversion *f*, changement *m*; revirement *m* (d'opinion); (*b*) *Phot:* **r. film,** film *m* inversible; (*c*) *Typ:* **offset r. process,** procédé *m* d'inversion.

reverse¹ [ri'və:s] *a.* inverse, contraire **(to,** à); **in (the) r. order,** en ordre inverse; **r. side,** revers *m*, envers *m* (d'une médaille); dos *m* (d'un tableau); *Tp:* **r. charge call,** communication *f* en P.C.V.; *Mec:* **r. motion,** marche *f* arrière; **r. thrust,** inversion *f* de la poussée.

reverse² *n.* **1.** (*a*) inverse *m*, contraire *m*, opposé *m*; **to be quite the r. of sth.,** être tout le contraire, tout l'opposé, de qch.; **quite the r.!** bien au contraire! (*b*) *Aut:* **in r.,** en marche arrière. **2.** (*a*) revers *m* (d'une médaille, d'une monnaie); (*b*) verso *m* (d'un feuillet). **3.** (*defeat*) revers; échec *m*.

reverse³ *v.tr.* **1.** renverser; *Mil:* **to r. arms,** renverser les fusils. **2.** (*a*) retourner (un habit, un tableau); (*b*) renverser (un mouvement); intervertir, renverser (l'ordre de qch.); *Tp:* **to r. the charge(s),** demander une communication en P.C.V.; **to r. one's decision,** revenir sur sa décision; *Pol: etc:* **to r. one's policy,** faire volte-face; **their roles are reversed,** les rôles sont intervertis; (*c*) *El: Mch:* renverser (le courant, la vapeur); **to r. the engine,** *abs.* **to r.,** (i) renverser la marche de la machine; (ii) *Nau: Rail:* marcher en arrière; *Aut:* **to r. (one's car),** faire marche arrière; **to r. (the car) out of the garage,** sortir du garage en marche arrière. **3.** *Jur:* révoquer (une sentence); réformer (un jugement). **reversed** *a.* **1.** renversé. **2.** inverse, contraire, opposé; *El:* **r. current,** renverse *f* de courant; *Mch:* **r. steam,** contre-vapeur *f*; *Tp:* **r. charge call,** communication *f* en P.C.V. **reversing** *n.* **1.** renversement *m*. **2.** (*a*) inversion *f*; changement complet; (*b*) *Mch: Aut: etc:* changement de marche; marche *f* (en) arrière; **r. light,** phare *m* de recul.

reversible [ri'və:səbl] *a.* **1.** renversable. **2.** (tissu, vêtement) réversible, à double face. **3.** (*a*) (procédé, *Ch:* réaction, etc.) réversible; (*b*) **r. gear,** engrenage *m* réciproque. **4.** *Phot:* (film) inversible. **5.** (*of decree, judgment, sentence*) révocable, réformable.

reversion [ri'və:ʃ(ə)n] *n.* **1.** *Jur:* (*a*) retour *m* (d'un bien); réversion *f*; (*b*) substitution *f*; (*c*) **right of r.,** réversion; droit *m* de retour (d'une donation); **estate in r.,** bien grevé (i) d'une réversion, (ii) de substitution. **2.** retour (à un état antérieur).

reversionary [ri'və:ʃən(ə)ri] *a.* **1.** (droit) de réversion; réversible. **2.** *Biol:* atavique.

revert [ri'və:t] *v.i.* (*a*) *Jur:* (*of property*) revenir, retourner **(to,** à); (*b*) retourner (à l'état sauvage); (*c*) revenir **(to a subject,** à un sujet); **we shall r. to this matter,** nous reviendrons sur cette question.

revetment [ri'vetmənt] *n. Const: Fort:* revêtement *m*; **r. wall,** mur *m* de revêtement; épaulement *m*.

review¹ [ri'vju:] *n.* **1.** (*a*) *Jur:* révision *f* (d'un procès); (*b*) **to keep a question under r.,** suivre une question de très près. **2.** *Mil:* revue *f*; **to hold a r.,** passer une revue; **to pass troops in r.,** passer en revue des troupes. **3.** examen *m*, revue (du passé, etc.); **a r. of the year,** recensement *m* des événements de l'année. **4.** critique *f*, compte rendu (d'un livre); **r. copy,** exemplaire fourni au critique. **5.** *Publ:* revue.

review² *v.tr.* **1.** revoir, réviser (un procès, etc.). **2.** revoir, examiner (des événements passés); passer (des faits, etc.) en revue. **3.** passer (les troupes) en revue; (*of troops*) **to be reviewed,** passer en revue. **4.** faire la critique, le compte rendu (d'un livre).

reviewer [ri'vju:ər] *n.* critique *m*.

revile [ri'vail] **1.** *v.tr.* injurier (qn). **2.** *v.i.* se répandre en injures; **to r. against s.o.,** invectiver (contre) qn.

revilement [ri'vailmənt] *n.* **1.** injures *fpl.* **2.** discours injurieux.

revise¹ [ri'vaiz] *n. Typ:* épreuve *f* de révision; seconde *f*; **second r., final r.,** troisième épreuve; tierce *f*.

revise² *v.tr.* **1.** (*a*) revoir, réviser (un texte); corriger, réviser (des épreuves); (*b*) *Sch:* repasser, revoir, réviser (une leçon); *v.i.* **to r.,** réviser, faire des révisions. **2.** (*a*) réviser (les lois, la constitution); (*b*) revenir sur (une décision). **revised** *a.* revu, révisé; **the R. Version,** la traduction de la Bible de 1884.

reviser [ri'vaizər] *n.* réviseur *m*.

revision [ri'viʒ(ə)n] *n.* révision *f*; **for r.,** à revoir.

revisionism [ri'viʒənizm] *n. Pol:* révisionnisme *m*.

revisionist [ri'viʒənist] *a. & n.* révisionniste (*mf*).

revisit [ri:'vizit] *v.tr.* visiter de nouveau; revisiter.

revitalize [ri:'vaitəlaiz] *v.tr.* ranimer, revigorer.

revival [ri'vaiv(ə)l] *n.* **1.** renaissance *f*, renouvellement *m* (des arts, de l'industrie); réapparition *f* (d'un usage); reprise (d'une pièce de théâtre); remise en vigueur (d'une loi); réveil *m*, renouvellement (de la nature); **the r. of trade,** la reprise des affaires. **2.** (*a*) retour *m* à la vie; retour des forces; (*b*) reprise des sens. **3.** *Rel:* réveil; **religious r.,** renouveau religieux; revival *m*, *pl.* revivals; **r. meeting,** réunion *f* dans le but de ranimer la foi (dans une ville).

revivalist [ri'vaivəlist] *n. Rel:* revivaliste *mf*.

revive [ri'vaiv] **1.** *v.i.* (*a*) (*of pers.*) ressusciter, revenir à la vie; reprendre connaissance; reprendre ses sens; (*b*) (*of feelings*) se ranimer; renaître; **his spirits revived,** son courage s'est ranimé; **to feel one's hopes reviving,** sentir renaître l'espoir; (*c*) (*of custom*) se renouveler; reprendre; (*of fashion*) rentrer en vogue; (*of arts*) renaître; (*of business, commerce*) reprendre, se relever. **2.** *v.tr.* (*a*) faire revivre (qn); rappeler (qn) à la vie; ressusciter (qn); **that will r. you,** voilà qui vous remontera; (*b*) ranimer, faire renaître (les espérances); ranimer (le commerce, les forces de qn); remonter (le courage de qn); rallumer (la colère de qn); raviver (la douleur, l'intérêt); rappeler (un souvenir); renouveler (un usage); remettre en vogue (une mode); remettre en vigueur (une loi); (*c*) ressusciter (un périodique); *Th:* remonter (une pièce); (*d*) rafraîchir (la peinture).

revivify [ri(:)ˈvivifai] *v.tr.* revivifier.
revocation [revəˈkeiʃ(ə)n] *n.* révocation *f* (d'un décret, d'un ordre, d'une donation); annulation *f.*
revoke¹ [riˈvouk] *n. Cards:* fausse renonce.
revoke² **1.** *v.tr.* (*a*) révoquer (un ordre, un décret); annuler, contremander (un ordre); rétracter (une promesse); (*b*) retirer (un permis de conduire). **2.** *v.i. Cards:* faire une fausse renonce.
revolt¹ [riˈvoult] *n.* révolte *f;* **to rise in r.,** se soulever, se révolter (**against,** contre); **to be in r.,** être en sédition, en révolte.
revolt² **1.** *v.i.* (*a*) se révolter, s'insurger, se soulever (**against,** contre); (*b*) se révolter (**at, against, sth.,** contre qch.). **2.** *v.tr.* (*of action*) révolter, dégoûter (qn). **revolting** *a.* **1.** (*of action*) révoltant, dégoûtant. **2.** (troupes) insurgées, en révolte. **revoltingly** *adv.* d'une facon révoltante, dégoûtante.
revolution [revəˈlu:ʃ(ə)n] *n.* **1.** *Astr:* révolution *f.* **2.** (*a*) rotation *f* (autour d'un axe); (*b*) tour *m,* révolution (d'une roue); tour (d'hélice); **the engine runs at two thousand revolutions a minute,** la machine fait deux mille tours à la minute; **r. counter,** compte-tours *m inv.* **3.** (*a*) *Pol:* révolution; *Hist:* **the French R.,** la Révolution française; (*b*) **industrial r.,** révolution industrielle; (*c*) **this process has brought about a complete r. of the industry,** ce procédé a complètement transformé l'industrie.
revolutionary [revəˈlu:ʃən(ə)ri] (*a*) *a. & n.* révolutionnaire (*mf*); (*b*) *a.* (invention) qui fait révolution.
revolutionize [revəˈlu:ʃənaiz] *v.tr.* révolutionner.
revolve [riˈvɔlv] **1.** *v.tr.* (*a*) retourner, repasser (**a problem in one's mind,** un problème dans son esprit); (*b*) faire tourner (les roues, etc.). **2.** *v.i.* (*a*) (*of wheel, etc.*) tourner; (*b*) **the earth revolves round the sun,** la terre tourne autour du soleil; (*c*) **our life revolves around the children,** toute notre vie tourne autour des enfants; (*d*) **the seasons, years, r.,** les saisons, les années, font leur révolution, reviennent. **revolving** *a.* **1.** *Bank:* **r. credit,** accréditif *m* automatiquement renouvelable. **2.** (corps, planète) en rotation, qui accomplit sa révolution. **3.** (fauteuil, etc.) tournant, pivotant; (grue) à pivot; **r. door,** tambour *m.*
revolver [riˈvɔlvər] *n.* revolver *m.*
revue [riˈvju:] *n. Th:* revue *f.*
revulsion [riˈvʌlʃ(ə)n] *n.* (*a*) revirement *m* (de sentiments, etc.); **r. from s.o.,** réaction *f* contre qn; (*b*) répugnance *f;* écœurement *m.*
reward¹ [riˈwɔ:d] *n.* récompense *f;* **to offer a r.,** offrir une récompense; **as a r. for . . .,** en récompense de . . .; **to get a fair r. for, from, one's labour,** tirer de son travail une récompense légitime.
reward² *v.tr.* récompenser, rémunérer (**sth., s.o. for sth.,** qch., qn de qch.); **that's how he rewards me for my loyalty,** voilà comment il reconnaît mon dévouement. **rewarding** *a.* (*a*) **(financially) r.,** rémunerateur, -trice; (*b*) **a r. job,** un travail qui donne (de la) satisfaction.
rewind [ri:ˈwaind] *v.tr.* (*p.t. & p.p.* **rewound** [ri:ˈwaund]) **1.** (*a*) rebobiner (la soie, un induit); (*b*) réembobiner (le film). **2.** remonter (une montre).
rewire [ri:ˈwaiər] *v.tr.* **to r. a house,** remettre à neuf, refaire, la canalisation électrique d'une maison.
reword [ri:ˈwə:d] *v.tr.* recomposer, rédiger à nouveau (un paragraphe, etc.).
rewrite [ri:ˈrait] *v.tr.* (*p.t.* **rewrote** [ri:ˈrout]; *p.p.* **rewritten** [ri:ˈrit(ə)n]) récrire; remanier (un article).
rhapsodic(al) [ræpˈsɔdik(l)] *a.* rhapsodique.
rhapsodize [ˈræpsədaiz] *v.i.* **to r. over sth.,** s'extasier sur qch.
rhapsody [ˈræpsədi] *n.* **1.** *Lit: Mus:* rhapsodie *f.* **2.** transports *mpl;* dithyrambe *m.*
rhea [ˈri:ə] *n. Orn:* nandou *m.*
Rhenish [ˈreniʃ, ri:niʃ] *a. Geog:* rhénan; du Rhin; **R. wine,** vin *m* du Rhin.
rheostat [ˈri:oustæt] *n. El:* rhéostat *m.*
rhesus [ˈri:səs] *n.* **1.** *Z:* **r. (monkey),** (macaque *m*) rhésus (*m*). **2.** *Physiol:* **R. factor,** facteur *m* rhésus.
rhetoric [ˈretərik] *n.* **1.** rhétorique *f,* éloquence *f.* **2.** *Pej:* rhétorique, emphase *f.*
rhetorical [riˈtɔrik(ə)l] *a.* (*a*) (terme, etc.) de rhétorique; **r. question,** question *f* pour la forme; (*b*) *Pej:* (style) emphatique, ampoulé. **-ally** *adv.* **1.** (poser une question) pour la forme. **2.** avec emphase.
rheumatic [ru(:)ˈmætik] *a. Med:* (*of pain, etc.*) rhumatismal, -aux; **r. person,** *n.* **r.,** rhumatisant, -ante; **r. fever,** rhumatisme articulaire aigu.
rheumatics [ru(:)ˈmætiks] *n.pl. F:* rhumatisme *m.*
rheumatism [ˈru(:)mətizm] *n.* rhumatisme *m;* **to suffer from r.,** avoir des rhumatismes.
rheumatoid [ˈru(:)mətɔid] *a.* rhumatoïde; **r. arthritis,** rhumatisme *m* articulaire.
rheumy [ˈru:mi] *a.* **r. eyes,** yeux chassieux.
Rhine (the) [ðəˈrain] *Pr.n.m. Geog:* le Rhin; **R. wines,** vins *mpl* du Rhin.
Rhineland (the) [ðəˈrainlənd] *Pr.n. Geog:* les pays rhénans; la Rhénanie.
rhinestone [ˈrainstoun] *n. Lap:* **1.** caillou *m* du Rhin (en cristal de roche). **2.** faux diamant; strass *m.*
rhino [ˈrainou] *n. F:* rhinocéros *m.*
rhinoceros [raiˈnɔsərəs] *n.* **1.** *Z:* rhinocéros *m.* **2.** *Ent:* **r. beetle,** rhinocéros.
rhizome [ˈraizoum] *n. Bot:* rhizome *m.*
Rhodes [roudz] *Pr.n. Geog:* (l'île *f* de) Rhodes *f.*
Rhodesia [rouˈdi:siə, -ziə] *Pr.n. Geog: Hist:* Rhodésie *f.*
Rhodesian [rouˈdi:siən, -ziən] *Hist:* **1.** *a.* rhodésien; de Rhodésie. **2.** *n.* Rhodésien, -ienne.
rhododendron, *pl.* **-ons, -a** [roudəˈdendrən, -ənz, -ə] *n. Bot:* rhododendron *m.*
rhomb [rɔm(b)] *n.* **1.** *Geom:* losange *m;* rhombe *m.* **2.** *Cryst:* rhomboèdre *m.*
rhombic [ˈrɔmbik] *a.* rhombique, rhombe.
rhomboid [ˈrɔmbɔid] *a. & n. Mth:* rhomboïde (*m*).
rhombus, *pl.* **-uses, -i** [ˈrɔmbəs, -əsiz, -ai] *n. Mth:* losange *m,* rhombe *m.*
Rhone (the) [ðəˈroun] *Pr.n.* le Rhône; **the R. valley,** la vallée du Rhône; **R. wines,** côtes *mpl* du Rhône.
rhubarb [ˈru:bɑ:b] *n. Bot: Pharm:* rhubarbe *f.*
rhumb [rʌm(b)] *n. Nau:* r(h)umb *m.*
rhyme¹ [raim] *n.* **1.** (*a*) *Pros:* rime *f;* (*b*) **without r. or reason,** sans rime ni raison; à tort et à travers; **there's neither r. nor reason about it,** cela ne rime à rien; cela n'a ni rime ni raison. **2.** *usu. pl.* vers (rimés); poésie *f;* **in r.,** en vers.
rhyme² **1.** *v.i.* (*a*) rimer; rimailler; faire des vers; (*b*) se servir de la rime; (*c*) (*of words*) rimer (**with,** avec); **2.** *v.tr.* (*a*) **to r. a word with another,** faire rimer un mot avec un autre; (*b*) mettre en vers (un récit, ses pensées). **rhymed** *a.* rimé; en vers (rimés).
rhymester [ˈraimstər] *n. Pej:* rimailleur *m.*
rhythm [ˈrið(ə)m] *n.* rythme *m;* cadence *f;* **r. of work,** cadence de travail; *Mus:* **r. section,** section *f* rythmique (d'un orchestre de jazz, etc.).
rhythmic(al) [ˈriðmik(l)] *a.* rythmique, cadencé; **r. tread,** marche scandée. **-ally** *adv.* avec rhythme.
rib¹ [rib] *n.* **1.** *Anat:* côte *f;* **r. cage,** cage *f* thoracique; *Cu:* **r. of beef,** côte de bœuf; **spare ribs,** côtes découvertes (de porc); *F:* **his ribs stick out,** on lui voit, on lui compterait, les côtes. **2.** (*a*) *Nat. Hist:* nervure *f* (d'une feuille, d'une aile d'insecte); (*b*) nervure (d'une voûte, etc.); *Bookb:* nervure; *Arch:* ogive *f;* *I.C.E:* **cooling ribs,** ailettes (de radiateur, de piston, etc.); (*c*) **the ribs left on the sand,** les rides laissées sur le sable (de la plage); (*d*) *Knit: Tex:* côte. **3.** (*a*) étançon *m,* entretoise *f* (d'un échafaudage); baleine

f (de parapluie); *Av:* nervure (d'une aile); (*b*) *N.Arch:* membre *m*, membrure *f*.
rib² *v.tr.* **(ribbed) 1.** garnir (qch.) de côtes, de nervures. **2.** *F:* taquiner (qn). **ribbed** *a.* **1.** (verre) à côtes, cannelé; (sable) ridé; *Arch:* **r. vault,** voûte *f* d'ogives. **2.** (bas, velours) à côtes, côtelé. **ribbing** *n.* **1.** *Ind: Mec.E:* nervurage *m.* **2.** *coll.* côtes *fpl* (d'un bas, etc.). **3.** *F:* taquinage *m*.
ribald ['r(a)ibəld] **1.** *a.* licencieux, impudique, paillard; (rire) gras; **r. song,** chanson paillarde, grivoise; **r. joke,** paillardise *f*. **2.** *n.* homme grossier.
ribaldry ['r(a)ibəldri] *n.* paillardises *fpl*; langage licencieux; grivoiserie *f*.
riband ['ribənd] *n. A:* ruban *m*.
ribbon ['ribən] *n.* **1.** ruban *m*; *Typewr:* **(inking) r.,** ruban (encreur); **r. industry, trade,** rubanerie; industrie rubanière. **2.** (*a*) ruban (d'une décoration); cordon *m* (d'un ordre); **blue r.,** ruban bleu; (*b*) *Navy:* **cap r.,** ruban légendé (du béret). **3.** *Equit: A: F:* **ribbons,** guides *fpl*. **4.** bande *f*, ruban (de terre, de route, etc.); lambeau *m* (de ciel); **r. development,** extension urbaine en bordure de route. **5. to tear sth. to ribbons,** mettre qch. en lambeaux; déchiqueter qch.
riboflavin(e) [raibou'fleivi(:)n] *n. Ch:* riboflavine *f*.
ribonucleic [raibounju:'kli:ik] *a. Ch:* (acide) ribonucléique.
rice¹ [rais] *n.* (*a*) *Bot:* riz *m*; **r. straw,** paille *f* de riz; **r. grower,** riziculteur *m*; **r. growing,** riziculture *f*; (*b*) **long grain, short grain, r.,** riz à grains longs, courts; **ground r.,** farine *f* de riz; *Cu:* **r. pudding,** riz au lait; **r. water,** eau *f* de riz; **r. paper,** papier *m* de riz.
rice² *v.tr. U.S:* passer (des légumes) au presse-purée.
ricer ['raisər] *n. U.S:* presse-purée *m inv*.
rich [ritʃ] *a.* **1.** (personne, société) riche; **r. people,** *n.* **the r.,** les riches *mpl*; **r. man, woman,** richard, -arde; **extremely r.,** richissime; **the new, newly, r.,** les nouveaux riches; les parvenus *mpl*; **to grow r.,** s'enrichir. **2.** (*of country*) riche; (*of soil*) riche, fertile; (*of harvest, supply*) abondant; (*of pasture*) gras; **r. vegetation,** végétation luxuriante; **r. clay,** argile grasse; **r. in . . .,** riche en . . .; abondant en . . .. **3.** (toilette) magnifique; (meubles) luxueux; (festin) somptueux. **4.** (*a*) (gâteau) riche en beurre et en œufs; **r. dish,** (i) plat gras; (ii) plat composé d'ingrédients de choix; **I can't eat r. food,** je ne digère pas les plats gras; (*b*) *I.C.E:* **r. mixture,** mélange *m* riche. **5. r. colour,** couleur chaude; **r. green,** vert intense; **r. voice,** voix étoffée, ample, pleine. **6.** *F:* (*of incident, situation*) très divertissant; impayable. **-ly** *adv.* **1.** richement; somptueusement. **2.** (*a*) richement; abondamment; (*b*) **r. deserved,** bien mérité.
riches ['ritʃiz] *n.pl.* richesse(s) *f*(*pl*).
richness ['ritʃnis] *n.* **1.** richesse *f*, abondance *f*. **2.** richesse (du sol); fertilité *f*. **3.** somptuosité *f*, magnificence *f*. **4.** (*a*) richesse (en principes nutritifs) (d'un aliment); (*b*) *I.C.E:* richesse (du mélange). **5.** ampleur *f* (de la voix); richesse, coloris *m* (du style); **r. of colour,** chaleur *f* des tons.
rick¹ [rik] *n.* meule *f* (de foin).
rick² *v.tr.* mettre (le foin) en meule(s).
rick³,⁴ *n.* & *v.tr.* = WRICK¹,².
rickets ['rikits] *n.pl. Med:* rachitisme *m*; **to have r.,** être rachitique.
rickety ['rikiti] *a.* **1.** *Med:* rachitique, *F:* noué. **2.** *F:* (escalier) branlant, délabré; (pont) branlant; (meubles) bancaux; **r. table,** table boiteuse, branlante; **to be in a r. state,** ne tenir ni à fer ni à clou.
rickrack ['rikræk] *n. NAm:* soutache *f*, galon *m* (en forme de zigzag).
rickshaw ['rikʃɔ:] *n.* pousse-pousse *m inv*.
ricochet¹ ['rikəʃei, *occ.* -ʃet] *n. Artil:* ricochet *m*.
ricochet² *v.i.* **(ricochetted** ['rikəʃeid, -ʃetid] **ricochetting** ['rikəʃeiiŋ, -ʃetiŋ]) ricocher.
rid [rid] *v.tr.* (*p.t.* **ridded, rid;** *p.p.* **rid;** *pr.p.* **ridding)** débarrasser, délivrer (**s.o. of sth.,** qn de qch.); débarrasser (**a place of sth.,** un endroit de qch.); purger (un pays de bandits), **to r. s.o. of his enemies,** délivrer qn de ses ennemis; **to get r. of sth., to r. oneself of sth.,** se débarrasser, se défaire, de qch.; **I've got r. of my car,** j'ai bazardé ma voiture; *Cards:* **to get r. of a card,** se défausser d'une carte; **to get r. of s.o.,** (i) se débarrasser de qn; (*politely*) éconduire qn; (ii) renvoyer (un domestique); *F:* balayer, débarquer (un ministre, etc.); (iii) supprimer qn; se défaire (d'un ennemi).
riddance ['ridəns] *n.* (*a*) débarras *m*; **good r.!** bon débarras! (*b*) délivrance *f* **(from,** de).
ridden. *see* RIDE².
riddle¹ ['ridl] *n.* énigme *f*, devinette *f*; **to speak in riddles,** parler par énigmes.
riddle² *n.* (*a*) crible *m*, claie *f*; (*b*) *Ind:* cribleuse *f*.
riddle³ *v.tr.* **1.** cribler (le grain); passer à la claie. **2. to r. s.o. with bullets,** cribler qn de balles; **riddled with corruption,** criblé de corruption.
ride¹ [raid] *n.* **1.** (*a*) course *f*, promenade (à cheval, à bicyclette); **to go for a r., to take a r.,** faire une promenade à cheval; **to give a child a r. on one's back,** porter un enfant sur son dos; (*b*) promenade, voyage *m* (en voiture, etc.); **to go for a r. in a car, for a car r.,** aller se promener en voiture; **r. on a roundabout,** tour *m* de chevaux de bois; **it's a 20p r. on the bus,** c'est un trajet de 20p en autobus; **it's a quarter of an hour's r. on a bicycle,** il y en a pour un quart d'heure à bicyclette; **to take s.o. for a r.,** (i) emmener qn faire une promenade (à cheval, en voiture); (ii) *F:* faire marcher qn, duper qn; **he's been taken for a r.,** on l'a eu. **2.** (*in forest*) allée cavalière; piste *f*; laie *f*.
ride² *v.* (*p.t.* **rode** [roud]; *p.p.* **ridden** ['rid(ə)n], *Nau:* **rode) I.** *v.i.* **1.** (*a*) chevaucher; aller, se promener, monter, être monté, à cheval; être à cheval; **to r. side-saddle,** monter en amazone; **can you r.?** montez-vous à cheval? **he rides well,** il monte bien (à cheval); il est bon cavalier; (*b*) **to r. on an elephant,** aller à dos d'éléphant; **to r. on s.o.'s shoulders,** être monté sur les épaules de qn; (*of child*) **to r. on s.o.'s knee,** être à califourchon sur le genou de qn; (*c*) (*on horseback, on a bicycle, etc.*) **to r. to a place,** se rendre à un endroit (à cheval, à bicyclette, etc.); **to r. up, down (in a lift),** monter, descendre (en ascenseur); (*d*) **to r. 50 kilometres,** aller, faire, 50 kilomètres (à cheval, en voiture, etc.). **2.** *Equit: Turf:* **he rides 76 kilos,** il pèse 76 kilos en selle. **3.** aller, se promener, en voiture; aller, venir, être, en autobus; (*with passive force*) **this car rides very smoothly,** cette voiture est bien suspendue. **4.** (*a*) **the ship was riding over the waves,** le navire flottait, voguait, sur les eaux; **the moon was riding high in the heavens,** la lune voguait haut dans le ciel; (*b*) *Nau:* (*of ship*) **to r. at anchor,** mouiller; être à l'ancre. **5.** (*of skirt, etc.*) **to r. (up),** remonter. **II.** *v.tr.* **1.** (*a*) courir (une course); (*b*) traverser (le pays) à cheval; parcourir (les rues) à cheval. **2.** (*a*) monter, être monté sur (un cheval); *Turf:* **Comet ridden by Martin,** Comet monté par Martin; **to r. an ass, an elephant,** être monté à dos d'âne, d'éléphant; *F:* **to r. s.o.,** persécuter qn; **to r. a bicycle,** aller à, en, bicyclette; **witches r. broomsticks,** les sorcières chevauchent des manches à balai; (*b*) **to r. one's horse at a fence,** diriger son cheval sur une barrière; **to r. an idea to death,** être féru d'une idée; **he rides this theory to death,** cette théorie est son cheval de bataille; (*c*) opprimer, dominer; oppresser (qn); (*esp. in the passive*) **ridden by fear,** sous le coup de la peur; dominé, hanté, par la peur. **3.** (*a*) **the ship rides the waves,** le navire vogue sur les flots; **to r. the storm,** soutenir le choc de la tempête, le déchaînement de l'indignation publique; (*b*) **to r. out**

the storm, (i) *Nau:* étaler la tempête; (ii) surmonter la crise. **4.** *U.S:* (*of elevator, elevator boy*) **to r. s.o. up, down,** faire monter, faire descendre, qn. **ridden** *a.* (*with noun prefixed*) **gangster-r.,** infesté de gangsters; **cliché-r. language,** langage plein de clichés. **riding** *n.* **1.** équitation *f*; **r. costume,** habit *m* de cavalier; **r. habit,** amazone *f*; **r. boots,** bottes *fpl* à l'écuyère; **r. breeches,** culotte *f* de cheval; **r. whip,** stick *m*; cravache *f*; **Litte Red R. Hood,** le petit Chaperon rouge; **r. school,** école *f* d'équitation; manège *m*; **r. instructor,** professeur *m* d'équitation; maître *m* de manège. **2.** *Aut:* **smooth r.,** suspension douce. **3.** allée cavalière.

rider ['raidər] *n.* **1.** cavalier, -ière; (*in circus*) écuyer, -ère; (*on cycle*) cycliste *mf*; (*on motorcycle*) motocycliste *mf*; *Mil:* **dispatch r.,** estafette *f*; **to be a good r.,** monter bien à cheval; être bon cavalier, bonne cavalière. **2.** ajouté *m*, annexe *f*, papillon *m* (d'un document); avenant *m* (d'un verdict); clause additionnelle (d'un projet de loi).

riderless ['raidərlis] *a.* sans cavalier; (motocyclette) sans conducteur; *Rac:* **r. horse,** cheval *m* sauvage.

ridge¹ [ridʒ] *n.* **1.** (*a*) arête *f*, crête *f* (d'une chaîne de montagnes); (*b*) faîte *m*, faîtage *m*, crête (d'un comble); *Const:* **r. pole,** poutre *f* de faîte; **r. roof,** toit en dos d'âne; **r. tile,** (tuile) faîtière; (*c*) arête (du nez); **r. of the back,** épine dorsale; (*d*) *Nau:* banc *m* (de rochers, de récifs); (*e*) *Meteor:* **r. of high pressure,** dorsale *f* barométrique. **2.** chaîne *f* (de coteaux). **3.** *Agr:* butte *f*; **r. plough,** buttoir *m*. **4.** strie *f* (sur une surface); ride *f* (sur le sable).

ridge² *v.tr.* (*a*) *Agr:* disposer (le terrain) en sillons; (*b*) *Hort:* **to r. (out),** butter (des plantes); (*c*) sillonner, canneler, strier (une surface); (*of tide, etc.*) rider (le sable). **ridging** *n.* **1.** *Const:* enfaîtement *m* (d'un comble). **2.** *Hort:* buttage *m*; **r. plough,** buttoir *m*.

ridicule¹ ['ridikju:l] *n.* moquerie *f*, raillerie *f*, dérision *f*; **to hold s.o., sth., up to r.,** tourner qn, qch., en ridicule, en dérision; **to lay oneself open to r.,** s'exposer au ridicule; **to be an object of r.,** *F:* être en butte au ridicule.

ridicule² *v.tr.* se moquer de, railler, ridiculiser (qn, qch.); tourner (qn, qch.) en ridicule, en dérision.

ridiculous [ri'dikjuləs] *a.* ridicule; **to make s.o., sth., r.,** rendre qn, qch., ridicule; ridiculiser qn, qch.; **to make oneself r.,** se rendre ridicule; prêter à rire; *n.* **from the sublime to the r.,** du sublime au ridicule. **-ly** *adv.* ridiculement; d'une façon ridicule.

ridiculousness [ri'dikjuləsnis] *n.* ridicule *m*.

riding ['raidiŋ] *n. Adm:* **1.** *Hist:* **the East, West, North Riding,** les divisions est, ouest, nord, du comté d'York. **2.** (*in Canada*) circonscription électorale.

rife [raif] *a.* **to be r.,** (*of disease, etc.*) régner, sévir; (*of rumour*) courir (les rues).

riffle [rifl] **1.** *v.tr.* (*a*) troubler (la surface de l'eau); (*b*) battre (les cartes). **2.** *v.i.* **to r. through,** feuilleter.

riff-raff ['rifræf] *n. coll.* canaille *f*, racaille *f*, gueusaille *f*; **all the r.-r.,** tout le rebut de la société.

rifle¹ ['raifl] *v.tr.* piller (un endroit); (fouiller et) vider (les poches de qn); violer, spolier (un tombeau); **to r. a cupboard,** vider une armoire de son contenu.

rifle² *n.* (*a*) fusil (rayé); carabine *f* (de chasse); **r. club,** société *f* de tir; **r. practice,** (exercice *m* de) tir *m* au fusil; **r. range,** (i) portée *f* de, du, fusil; (ii) champ *m*, stand *m*, de tir (au fusil); **r. shot,** (i) coup *m* de fusil; (ii) tireur *m* (au fusil); (*b*) *Mil:* **rifles,** fantassins (armés de fusils); fusiliers *mpl*; **R. Corps,** corps *m* des fusiliers, des chasseurs à pied.

rifle³ *v.tr.* rayer (l'âme d'une arme à feu). **rifling** *n.* **1.** rayage *m* (de l'âme d'une arme à feu). **2.** *coll.* rayure(s) *f(pl)* (d'une arme à feu).

rifleman, *pl.* **-men** ['raiflmən] *n.m. Mil:* (*a*) fantassin (armé du fusil); fusilier; (*b*) chasseur à pied.

rift [rift] *n.* (*a*) fente *f*; fissure *f* (dans la terre, dans une roche, etc.); crevasse *f*; *Geol:* **r. valley,** rift *m*; fossé *m* (tectonique); (*b*) éclaircie (dans la fumée, dans la brume); (*c*) rupture *f* (entre deux personnes).

rig¹ [rig] *n.* **1.** *Nau:* gréement *m* (d'un navire). **2.** *F:* **r.(-out),** (i) toilette *f*, tenue *f*; (ii) *Pej:* accoutrement *m*; **to be in full r.,** être en grande tenue. **3.** *Mec.E:* (*a*) équipement *m*, installation *f*, accessoires *mpl*; (*b*) *Min:* **oil(-drilling) r.,** appareil *m* de forage pétrolier, derrick *m*.

rig² *v.tr.* **(rigged)** *Nau:* gréer, équiper (un navire); **to r. up,** monter, installer (un appareil, etc.); mâter (un mât de charge, etc.); *F:* **to r. s.o. out,** attifer, accoutrer, qn; *F:* **to r. sth. up,** faire une installation de fortune. **rigged** *a. Nau:* (navire) gréé. **rigging** *n.* **1.** (*a*) *Nau:* gréage *m* (d'un navire); (*b*) *Mec.E:* montage *m* (d'une machine). **2.** (*a*) *Nau:* gréement *m* (d'un navire); (*b*) *Av:* gréement, câblage *m*; (*c*) *Mec.E:* mécanisme *m* de manœuvre; timonerie *f*.

rig³ *v.tr.* truquer (une élection); *Fin: St.Exch:* **to r. the market,** agir sur le marché; provoquer (i) une hausse, (ii) une baisse, factice. **rigging** *n. St.Exch:* **r. the market,** agiotage *m*.

rigger ['rigər] *n.* **1.** (*pers.*) (*a*) *Nau:* gréeur *m*, mâteur *m*; (*b*) *Av:* monteur-régleur *m*, *pl.* monteurs-régleurs. **2.** *Nau:* **square r.,** navire gréé en carré.

right¹ [rait] **I.** *a.* **1.** *Mth:* **r. angle,** angle droit; **at r. angles to . . ., with . . .,** à angle droit avec . . .; perpendiculaire à . . .; **r. angled,** rectangle, rectangulaire; à angle droit. **2.** (*morally good*) bon; juste; honnête; droit; **to know what is r. and wrong,** savoir ce qui est bien et ce qui est mal; **to be r. minded,** avoir l'esprit droit; **it's only r.,** ce n'est que justice; **I thought it r. to go,** j'ai jugé bon, à propos, d'y aller; **to do the r. thing,** se conduire honnêtement, honorablement. **3.** (*a*) correct, juste, exact; **to give the r. answer,** répondre juste; donner la bonne réponse; **to put a mistake r.,** redresser, corriger, rectifier, une erreur; **what's the r. time?** quelle heure est-il (exactement)? quelle est l'heure juste? **my watch is r.,** ma montre est à l'heure; **to put one's watch r.,** régler sa montre; (*b*) (*of pers.*) **to be r.,** avoir raison; **you're quite r.!** vous avez bien raison! (*c*) **the r. word,** le mot propre, juste; le mot qu'il faut; **the r. side of the material,** l'endroit *m* du tissu; **r. side, r. way, up,** à l'endroit; **have you the r. amount?** avez-vous (i) votre compte? (ii) la monnaie exacte? **is this the r. house?** est-ce bien la maison? **to know the r. people,** (i) avoir des relations; (ii) avoir d'utiles relations; **we're on the r. road,** nous sommes dans le bon chemin; **to put s.o. r.,** (i) mettre qn sur la voie; (ii) détromper, désabuser, qn; (*d*) (*most appropriate*) **in the r. place,** (i) bien placé; (ii) à sa place; **the r. man in the r. place,** l'homme qu'il faut pour la tâche; **you came at the r. time,** vous êtes venu au bon moment; **to wait for the r. moment,** attendre le moment opportun; **the r. thing to do,** ce qu'il faut faire; **that's r.!** parfaitement! c'est ça! **r. (you are)!** entendu! d'accord! *F:* **r.?** d'acc.? (*e*) **he's on the r. side of forty,** il n'a pas encore quarante ans; **to get on the r. side of s.o.,** s'insinuer dans les bonnes grâces de qn. **4.** (*in good condition*) (*a*) **to be in one's r. mind,** avoir toute sa raison; être en possession de toutes ses facultés; **I'm not feeling quite r.,** je ne suis pas d'aplomb, *F:* pas dans mon assiette; **as r. as rain,** en parfaite santé; **that'll put you r.,** voilà qui vous remontera; **to put things r.,** rétablir les choses; arranger une affaire; (*b*) **everything's all r.,** tout est, va, très bien; **it's all r.,** (i) tout va bien; ne vous inquiétez pas; (ii) (*to pers. apologizing*) je vous en prie! **all r.!** bien! entendu! **are you all r.?** (i) est-ce que vous allez bien? (ii) vous ne vous êtes pas blessé? (iii) *Iron:* tu ne te sens pas bien? **I'm all r. again now,** je suis tout à fait remis maintenant; **it's all r. for** *you* **to laugh!** vous avez beau rire! **he's all r.,** c'est un bon type; *P:* **she's a bit of all r.!** voilà une jolie pépée! **5.** (*genuine*) (*a*) **r. whale,** baleine franche; (*b*) *F:* **a r.,** *esp. U.S:* **r.-down, swindle,** une vraie escroquerie. **6.** (côté, etc.) droit; **on the r. side,** à droite, sur la droite; **r. hand,** main droite; **on my r. hand,** sur ma droite; **he's my r. hand,** il est mon bras droit; **r. wing,** (i) *Mil: Fb: etc:* aile droite; (ii) *Pol:* la droite; *Pol:* **r.-wing policy,** politique conservatrice, de droite. **II.** *n.* **1.** le droit; la justice; le bien; **might and r.,** la force et le droit; **r. and wrong,** le bien et le mal; **to be in the r.,** avoir raison; être dans son droit. **2.** (*a*) droit, titre *m*; **divine r.,** droit divin; **to have a r., the r., to sth.,** avoir droit à qch.; **r. of way,** (i) *Jur:* servitude *f*, droit, jouissance *f*, de passage; (ii) *Aut:* priorité *f* de passage; (iii) *NAm:* la voie ferrée; **to have a, the, r. to do sth.,** avoir le droit de faire qch.; être en droit de faire qch.; **what r. have you to do that?** de quel droit, à quel titre, faites-vous cela? **r. to vote,** droit de vote; **by what r.?** de quel droit? à quel titre? **it belongs to him by r.,** cela lui appartient de droit; **to possess sth. in one's own r.,** avoir qch. en propre; (*b*) **the rights of man, human rights,** les droits de l'homme; **to be within one's rights,** être dans son droit; **by rights,** en toute justice. **3.** (*a*) **to put, set, sth. to rights,** arranger qch.; mettre qch. en ordre, en règle; (*b*) **to know the rights and wrongs of a case,** connaître tous les détails d'une affaire. **4.** (*a*) droite *f*; côté droit; **on the r.,** à droite; **on your r.,** à votre droite; **to keep to the r.,** tenir la droite; (*b*) *Pol:* **the r.,** la droite; les conservateurs *mpl*; (*c*) *Box:* coup *m* du droit. **III.** *adv.* **1.** (*a*) (*straight*) **go r. on,** continuez tout droit; **he went r. at him,** il est allé droit vers lui; (*b*) **to do sth. r. away, r. off,** faire qch. (i) sur-le-champ, immédiatement, (ii) du premier coup; **I'll be r. back,** je reviens tout de suite. **2.** (*a*) (*completely*) **a wall r. round the house,** un mur tout autour de la maison; **he turned r. round,** il a fait un tour complet; (*b*) (*exactly*) **r. at the top,** tout en haut; **r. in the middle,** au beau milieu; en plein milieu; **r. in the middle of the harvest,** en pleine moisson; **the wind was r. behind us,** nous avions le vent juste dans le dos; *F:* **I'll be waiting r. here,** j'attendrai ici même. **3.** (*to the full*) **I know r. well that . . .,** je sais fort bien que . . .; *F: O:* **I was r. glad to hear it,** j'étais fort heureux de l'apprendre; *Ecc:* **r. reverend,** très révérend. **4.** (*a*) (*justly*) **you did r. to wait,** vous avez bien fait d'attendre; **to act r.,** agir bien; (*b*) (répondre, etc.) correctement; (deviner) juste; **if I remember r.,** si je me souviens bien; **nothing goes r. with me,** rien ne me réussit; **I got your letter all r.,** j'ai bien reçu votre lettre; **he's to blame r. enough,** c'est bien de sa faute (à lui). **5.** à droite; **turn r.,** tournez à droite; **he looked neither r. nor left,** il n'a regardé ni à droite ni à gauche; **he owes money r. and left,** il doit de l'argent de tous les côtés; *F:* **he cheated us r., left and centre,** il nous a eus jusqu'à la gauche. **rightly** *adv.* **1. to act, judge, r.,** bien agir, juger. **2.** correctement; à juste titre; **r. or wrongly,** à tort ou à raison; **I cannot r. say,** je ne saurais dire au juste.

right² *v.tr.* **1.** (*a*) redresser (un canot, une voiture, etc.); relever (un canot); (*of boat*) **to r. itself,** se redresser, se relever; (*b*) *Nau:* redresser, mettre droite (la barre). **2.** (*a*) redresser, réparer (un tort); (*b*) rendre justice à (qn). **3.** corriger, rectifier (une erreur). **righting** *n.* redressement *m.*

righteous ['raitjəs] *a.* **1.** droite, juste; verteux; *n.pl.* **the r.,** les bons; les justes. **2.** juste, justifié; **r. anger,** juste colère *f*. **-ly** *adv.* vertueusement.

righteousness ['raitjəsnis] *n.* droiture *f*, vertu *f*; rectitude *f*.

rightful ['raitf(u)l] *a.* **1.** (héritier, roi) légitime. **2.** (*of claim*) légitime, juste. **3.** (héritage) auquel on a droit; **to have one's r. share,** avoir sa juste part. **-fully** *adv.* légitimement; à juste titre.

right-hand ['raithænd] *a.* **1.** (gant, etc.) de la main droite; (*b*) (tiroir, etc.) de droite; **on the r.-h. side,** à droite; **r.-h. man,** (i) *Mil:* homme de droite; (ii) bras droit (de qn); homme de confiance. **2.** (vis, serrure) à droite; *Av:* (hélice) à pas à droite.

right-handed [rait'hændid] *a.* **1.** (*of pers.*) droitier. **2.** *Box:* **r.-h. blow,** coup *m* du droit. **3.** (*a*) = RIGHT-HAND 2; (*b*) (outil) pour la main droite.

right-hander [rait'hændər] *n.* **1.** (*pers.*) droitier, -ière. **2.** *Box:* coup *m* du droit.

rightist ['raitist] *a. & n.* droitiste (*mf*); *a.* de droite.

rightness ['raitnis] *n.* (*a*) justesse *f* (d'une décision); (*b*) justesse, exactitude *f* (d'une réponse).

righto [rai'tou] *int. F:* entendu! d'accord!

rightyho [raiti'ou] *int. P:* = RIGHTO.

rigid ['ridʒid] *a.* **1.** (*of bar, etc.*) rigide, raide. **2.** (*of discipline, etc.*) sévère, strict; (*of etiquette*) rigide. **-ly** *adv.* **1.** rigidement. **2.** sévèrement, strictement.

rigidity [ri'dʒiditi] *n.* **1.** rigidité *f*, raideur *f*. **2.** sévérité *f*; intransigeance *f*.

rigmarole ['rigməroul] *n. F:* galimatias *m*; litanie *f*.

rigor ['raigɔːr, 'ri-] *n. Med:* **r. mortis** ['mɔːtis], rigidité *f* cadavérique.

rigorous ['rigərəs] *a.* rigoureux; (mesures) de rigueur. **-ly** *adv.* rigoureusement.

rigour, *NAm:* **rigor** ['rigər] *n.* **1.** (*a*) rigueur *f*, sévérité *f*; **the r. of the law,** la rigueur de la loi; (*b*) **the rigours of prison life,** les rigueurs de la vie de prison. **2.** rigueur, âpreté *f* (du temps). **3.** exactitude *f*.

rig-out ['rigaut] *n. see* RIG¹ 2.

rile [rail] *v.tr. F:* agacer, exaspérer (qn).

rill [ril] *n.* ruisselet *m*; petit ruisseau.

rim¹ [rim] *n.* **1.** (*a*) jante *f* (de roue); couronne *f* (de roue d'engrenage); (*b*) cercle *m* (d'un tamis). **2.** bord *m* (d'un vase, etc.); cordon *m*, carnèle *f* (d'une pièce de monnaie); rebord, ourlet *m* (de l'oreille); **spectacle rims,** monture *f* de lunettes.

rim² *v.tr.* **(rimmed) 1.** janter (une roue). **2.** border, cercler.

rime¹ [raim] *n.* givre *m*; gelée blanche.

rime² *n. & v.* = RHYME¹·².

rimless ['rimlis] *a.* (lunettes) sans monture.

rind [raind] *n.* peau, pelure *f* (de légume, de fruit); pelure, croûte *f* (de fromage); couenne *f* (de lard).

ring¹ [riŋ] *n.* **1.** (*a*) anneau *m*; (*jewelled*) bague *f*; **wedding r.,** alliance *f*; **diamond r.,** bague de diamants; **signet r.,** chevalière *f*; **r. finger,** annulaire *m*; (*b*) **nose r.,** (i) anneau porté au nez; (ii) anneau nasal; **arm r.,** bracelet *m*; (*c*) (*for marking birds*) bague. **2.** (*a*) anneau, bague, rond *m*; rondelle *f* (de métal, etc.); rondelle (de bâton de ski); **curtain r.,** anneau de rideau; **napkin r.,** rond de serviette; **key r.,** porte-clés *m inv*; *Gym:* **the rings,** les anneaux; *Sp:* **tilting at the r.,** jeu *m* de bagues; *Tchn:* **r. bolt,** anneau à fiche; piton *m* à boucle; **r. gauge,** calibre *m* à bague; **r. spanner,** clef fermée, clef à œil; (*b*) *Mec.E:* anneau, bague, frette *f*; virole *f*; (*c*) *Mch: I.C.E:* **(piston) r.,** segment *m* (de piston); **packing r.,** garniture *f*; (*d*) *Mch:* couronne *f* (de turbine). **3.** (*a*) anneau (d'une planète); halo *m* (autour du soleil, de la lune); cerne *m* (des yeux); rond (de fumée); **he has rings round his eyes,** il a les yeux cernés; *F:* **to make, run, rings round s.o.,** surpasser qn; l'emporter sur qn; (*b*) (*of tree*) anneau, cercle, annuel; (*c*) *Orn:* collier *m* (d'un pigeon, etc.); **r.-necked,** à collier; **r. dove,** pigeon ramier; palombe *f*. **4.** cercle *m* (de personnes, etc.); **sitting in a r.,** assis en rond, en cercle. **5.** (*a*) groupe *m*; petit cercle (de personnes); (*b*) *Com:* syndicat *m*; cartel *m*; (*c*) **spy r.,** réseau *m* d'espionnage; (*d*) *St.Exch:* **the R.,** le Parquet. **6.** (*a*) arène *f*, piste *f* (de cirque, etc.); (*b*) **the r.**, le cirque. **7.** *Box: Wr:* enceinte *f*, ring *m*. **8.** *Turf:* **the R.**, (i) l'enceinte *f* (du pesage); (ii) les bookmakers *mpl*.

ring² *v.tr.* **1.** (*a*) baguer (un oiseau); (*b*) boucler (un taureau); (*c*) *Tchn:* baguer, fretter (un pieu, etc.). **2.** (*a*) **to r. (s.o., sth.) round, about, in,** encercler, entourer, cerner (qn, qch.); (*b*) *Ven:* rabattre, cerner (le gros gibier). **3.** *Arb:* baguer (un arbre). **4.** couper en rondelles. **ringed** *a.* **1.** bagué. **2.** (*a*) **blade-r. eyes,** yeux cernés de noir; (*b*) (oiseau) à collier. **ringing** *n.* **1.** (*a*) baguage *m* (d'un oiseau); bouclement *m* (d'un taureau); (*b*) *Tchn:* baguage (d'un tube, etc.). **2.** *Arb:* baguage.

ring³ *n.* **1.** son (clair, métallique); sonnerie *f* (de cloches); tintement *m* (de cloches, de pièces de monnaie); timbre *m*, intonation *f* (de la voix); *Tchn:* son, voix (d'une pièce de monnaie); **it has a hollow r.,** cela sonne creux; **the r. of truth,** l'accent *m* de la vérité. **2.** (*a*) coup *m* de sonnette, de timbre; (*b*) *Tp:* appel *m* téléphonique; coup de téléphone; **I'll give you a r.,** je vous donnerai un coup de téléphone, de fil.

ring⁴ *v.* (*p.t.* **rang** [ræŋ]; *p.p.* **rung** [rʌŋ]) **1.** *v.i.* (*a*) (*of bell*) sonner, tinter; (*of telephone*) sonner; **the bell is ringing for dinner,** on sonne pour le dîner; (*b*) (*of coin*) **to r. true, false,** sonner clair, faux; **his answer did not r. true,** sa réponse a sonné faux; (*c*) résonner, retentir (**with,** de); **the air rang with their cries,** l'air résonnait de leurs cris; (*d*) **his words still r. in my ears,** ses paroles sonnent encore à mes oreilles; **my ears are ringing,** mes oreilles bourdonnent. **2.** *v.tr.* (*a*) (faire) sonner (une cloche); **to r. the (door) bell, to r. (at the door),** sonner à la porte; *v.ind.tr.* **to r. for some coffee,** sonner pour demander du café; (*b*) faire sonner (une pièce de monnaie); (*c*) *F: O:* **to r. the bell,** réussir le coup; (*d*) *F:* **does that r. a bell?** est-ce que cela vous rappelle, dit, quelque chose? **3.** *v.tr. Tp:* **I'll r. you,** je vous téléphonerai. **ring down** *v.tr. Th:* **to r. down the curtain,** sonner pour la chute du rideau. **ring in** *v.tr.* **to r. in the New Year,** célébrer la nouvelle année par une volée de cloches. **ring off** *v.i. Tp:* raccrocher (l'appareil). **ring out 1.** *v.tr.* **to r. out the Old Year,** sonner, carillonner, la fin de l'année. **2.** *v.i.* sonner; retentir; **the bells were ringing out,** les cloches sonnaient à toute volée; **a shot rang out,** un coup de fusil a retenti. **ring up** *v.tr.* (*a*) *Th:* **to r. up the curtain,** sonner pour faire lever le rideau; (*in Fr.*) frapper les trois coups; (*b*) *Tp:* **to r. s.o. up,** donner un coup de téléphone, de fil, à qn; (*c*) enregister (une somme) (sur une caisse enregistreuse). **ringing 1.** *a.* (*a*) (*of bell*) qui tinte, qui sonne; (*b*) (*of voice, etc.*) sonore, retentissant; **in r. tones,** d'une voix vibrante. **2.** *n.* (*a*) son *m*, sonnerie *f*, tintement *m* (de cloches); bruit *m* de sonnette; (*b*) *Tp:* appel *m*, sonnerie; (*c*) bourdonnement *m* (dans les oreilles).

ringer ['riŋər] *n.* **1.** (*a*) sonneur *m*; carillonneur *m*; (*b*) *Tp:* machine *f* d'appel. **2.** (*a*) *F:* **to be a dead r. for s.o.,** être le sosie de qn; (*b*) *Turf: F:* cheval substitué pour un autre.

ringleader ['riŋliːdər] *n.* chef *m* de bande, d'émeute; organisateur, -trice, de troubles.

ringlet ['riŋlit] *n.* **1.** petit anneau. **2.** boucle *f* (de cheveux); anglaise *f*; **to wear one's hair in ringlets,** porter les cheveux en boucles; porter des anglaises.

ringmaster ['riŋmɑːstər] *n.* maître *m* de manège (d'un cirque); chef *m* de piste.

ringneck ['riŋnek] *n. Orn:* oiseau *m* à collier.

ringnecked ['riŋnekt] *a. Orn:* (pluvier) à collier.

ringside ['riŋsaid] *n.* **to have a r. seat,** (i) (*at circus, boxing match*) avoir une place au premier rang; (ii) *Fig:* être aux premières loges.

ringwall ['riŋwɔːl] *n.* mur *m* de clôture; clôture *f*.

ringworm ['riŋwəːm] *n. Med:* teigne *f*.

rink [riŋk] *n.* **skating, ice, r.,** patinoire *f*; **rollerskating r.,** skating *m*.

rinkydink [rinki'dink] *a. U.S. F:* de mauvaise qualité.

rinse¹ [rins] *n.* (*a*) rinçage *m*; **to give a bottle a r.,** rincer une bouteille; (*b*) *Hairdr:* **colour r.,** rinçage.

rinse² *v.tr.* **1.** (*a*) **to r. (out),** rincer (une bouteille, etc.); **to r. one's mouth,** se rincer la bouche; (*b*) **to r. one's hands,** se rincer les mains. **2.** rincer (le linge). **rinsing** *n.* rinçage *m*.

riot¹ ['raiət] *n.* **1.** émeute *f*; manifestion violente; **to call out the r. squad** = appeler police secours; **the R. Act,** la loi contre des attroupements; *F:* **to read s.o. the R. Act,** semoncer, tancer, qn. **2.** orgie *f* (de couleurs, etc.). **3.** (*a*) **to run r.,** (*of pers., etc.*) se déchaîner; (*of plants*) pulluler; (*b*) **the play was a r.,** la pièce a fait fureur; (*c*) *F:* **it's, he's, a r.,** c'est rigolo; c'est un rigolo.

riot² *v.i.* **(rioted)** (*a*) s'ameuter; faire une manifestation violente; (*b*) faire du vacarme. **rioting 1.** *a.* qui fait émeute; **r. mob,** bande *f* d'émeutiers. **2.** *n.* émeutes *fpl*; troubles *mpl*; manifestations violentes.

rioter ['raiətər] *n.* émeutier, -ière.

riotous ['raiətəs] *a.* **1.** (*of assembly*) séditieux. **2.** tapageur, -euse, bruyant; **r. students,** étudiants qui font des manifestations violentes. **-ly** *adv.* **1.** séditieusement. **2.** tapageusement.

rip¹ [rip] *n.* déchirure *f*; fente *f*.

rip² *v.* **(ripped) 1.** *v.tr.* (*a*) **to r. (up),** fendre; déchirer; **to r. open,** ouvrir (un paquet) en le déchirant; **to r. up, open,** éventrer (qn); découdre (un vêtement, le ventre); (*b*) **to r. (up),** refendre (le bois, l'ardoise); scier de long; (*c*) **to r. sth. off, away,** arracher, déchirer, qch.; *F:* **to r. s.o. off,** voler, rouler, qn. **2.** *v.i.* (*a*) se déchirer, se fendre; se découdre; (*b*) *F:* **to r. into s.o.,** attaquer qn; **to r. (along),** aller, avancer, à toute vitesse, à fond de train; (*of car*) **let her r.!** mettez tous les gaz! laissez-la filer! (*c*) *F: O:* **to let r.,** (i) faire une noce à tout casser; (ii) éclater de colère. **ripping 1.** *a. F: O:* épatant, formidable. **2.** *n.* (*a*) déchirement *m*; (*b*) sciage *m* en long; refente *f* (du bois).

riparian [rai'pɛəriən] *a.* & *n.* riverain, -aine.

ripcord ['ripkɔːd] *n.* (*a*) corde *f* de déchirure (d'un ballon); (*b*) corde d'ouverture, cordelette *f* de déclenchement (d'un parachute).

ripe [raip] *a.* **1.** (*a*) mûr; (fromage) bien fait, bien à point; **to grow r.,** mûrir; (*b*) (jugement) mûr; **a r. old age,** un bel âge. **2. the plan is r. for execution,** le projet est mûr; **time is r. for speaking the truth,** le temps est venu où on devrait dire la vérité; **r. for mischief,** prêt à faire le mal.

ripen ['raip(ə)n] **1.** *v.tr.* (faire) mûrir; affiner (le vin, le fromage). **2.** *v.i.* (*a*) (*of fruit, abscess, plan, etc.*) mûrir; (*b*) **to r. into manhood,** atteindre l'âge d'homme. **ripening 1.** *a.* (*a*) qui fait mûrir; (*b*) (*of fruit*) mûrissant, qui mûrit. **2.** *n.* maturation *f*; mûrissage *m*, mûrissement *m*; affinage *m* (du fromage, du vin); mise *f* à point (d'un projet, etc.).

ripeness ['raipnis] *n.* maturité *f*.

rip-off ['ripɔf] *n. F:* escroquerie *f*; **it's a rip-off!** c'est du vol manifeste!

riposte¹ [ri'pɔst] *n. Box: Fenc: etc:* riposte *f*.

riposte² *v.i. Box: Fenc: etc:* riposter.

ripple¹ [ripl] *n.* **1.** (*a*) ride *f* (sur l'eau); ondulation *f*; *Geog:* **r. mark,** ride de sable; (*b*) (*in hair*) ondulation. **2.** (*a*) gazouillement *m* (d'un ruisseau); léger clapotis (de l'eau); (*b*) murmure(s) *m(pl)* (de conversation); **a r. of laughter,** une vague de rires.

ripple² **1.** *v.i.* (*a*) (*of lake*) se rider; (*b*) (*of corn, hair*) onduler, ondoyer; (*c*) (*of stream*) murmurer; (*of tide*) clapoter; (*of laughter*) perler. **2.** *v.tr.* (*of wind*) rider (l'eau, le sable.).

rip(-)roaring ['riprɔːriŋ] *a. F:* (*a*) tumultueux; (*b*) **a r. success,** un succès fulgurant.

ripsaw ['ripsɔː] *n. Tls:* scie *f* à refendre.

riptide ['riptaid] *n.* courant *m* de retour.

rise¹ [raiz] *n.* **1.** (*a*) *Lit:* **r. of day,** l'aube *f*; *Th:* **r. of the curtain,** lever *m* du rideau; (*b*) *Fish:* (*of fish*) montée *f*; **I haven't had a r. all day,** ça n'a pas mordu de toute la journée; *F:* **to take, get, a r. out of s.o.,** mettre qn en colère. **2.** (*a*) montée, côte *f*; rampe *f*; **r. in the ground,** exhaussement *m* du terrain; (*sharp*) ressaut *m* de terrain; (*b*) éminence *f*, élévation *f*; hauteur *f*. **3.** (*a*) *Arch:* flèche *f*, hauteur sous clef (d'un arc, d'une voûte); hauteur (d'une marche); (*b*) *Metalw:* volée *f* (du marteau). **4.** (*a*) crue *f* (des eaux); hausse *f* (du baromètre); élévation *f*, relèvement (de température); augmentation *f* (de pression); **r. of the tide,** montée de l'eau; **r. and fall of the sea,** flot et jusant *m*, flux et reflux *m*, de la mer; (*b*) augmentation, hausse (de prix, de salaire); **food prices are on the r.,** le prix des denrées est en hausse; *St.Exch:* **to speculate on, operate for, a r.,** jouer à la hausse; **to ask (one's employer) for a r.,** demander une augmentation. **5.** avancement *m*; élévation (en rang); essor *m*; **r. to power,** montée au pouvoir. **6.** source *f*, naissance *f*, origine *f*; **to give r. to sth.,** faire naître, engendrer, susciter, qch.; provoquer qch.; **it would give r. to misunderstandings,** cela donnerait lieu à des malentendus.

rise² *v.i.* (*p.t.* **rose** [rouz]; *p.p.* **risen** ['riz(ə)n]) **1.** (*a*) **to r. (to one's feet),** se lever; se mettre debout; (*after kneeling, after a fall*) se relever; **to r. from table,** se lever de table; (*of horse*) **to r. on its hind legs,** se cabrer; (*b*) (*of parliament*) (i) lever la séance; (ii) entrer en vacances; (*c*) **to r. early, late,** se lever tôt, tard; *F:* **r. and shine!** debout les morts! (*d*) **to r. from the dead,** ressusciter des morts; **Christ is risen,** le Christ est ressuscité. **2. to r. (in revolt),** se soulever, se révolter (**against,** contre); **to r. (up) in arms,** prendre les armes; **to r. in protest against sth.,** se soulever, se révolter, contre qch. **3.** (*a*) (*of sun, star*) se lever; (*of smoke, balloon*) monter, s'élever; **I saw the sun r.,** j'ai vu le lever du soleil; (*b*) **to r. off the ground,** quitter le sol; **to r. in the saddle,** faire du trot enlevé; **to r. to the surface,** monter à la surface; (*c*) (*of fish*) **to r. to the bait,** mordre; *F:* (*of pers.*) **to r. to it,** se laisser provoquer; (*d*) *Ven:* (*of game*) se lever, partir, s'envoler; (*e*) **a murmur rose from the crowd,** une rumeur s'est dégagée de la foule. **4.** (*a*) (*of ground, road, etc.*) monter, s'élever; (*of ground*) se relever; (*of tide, barometer*) monter; (*of dough*) lever; (*of river*) être en crue; (*of wind*) se lever; **the boat rose and fell on the water,** le bateau se balançait sur l'eau; **it makes my stomach r.,** cela me soulève le cœur; (*b*) **trees rising a hundred feet above the plain,** arbres *mpl* qui s'élèvent à cent pieds au-dessus de la plaine; (*c*) **a picture rose in my mind,** une image s'est présentée à mon esprit; (*d*) (*of wind*) (i) se lever; (ii) croître, forcer; (*of voice*) s'élever; (*of spirits, hope*) remonter; **her colour rose,** ses joues s'empourpraient; **his voice rose above the noise of the crowd,** sa voix se faisait entendre au-dessus du bruit de la foule; (*e*) (*of prices*) monter; **prices are rising,** les prix sont à la hausse, en hausse; **everything has risen (in price),** tout a augmenté de prix, tout a renchéri. **5.** (*a*) être au-dessus de; **to r. above events,** se montrer supérieur aux événements; (*b*) **to r. to the occasion,** se montrer à la hauteur de la situation. **6. to r. in the world,** faire son chemin; parvenir; **to r. to the rank of colonel,** monter au grade de colonel; **to r. in s.o.'s esteem,** monter dans l'estime de qn; **he rose from nothing,** il est parti de rien. **7.** (*of river*) prendre sa source (**at,** à; **in,** dans); (*of difficulty, quarrel*) provenir, naître (**from,** de). **rising 1.** *a.* (*a*) (i) (soleil) levant; (brume) qui s'élève; (ii) **r. trot,** trot enlevé; (iii) (route) qui monte; (baromètre, température) en hausse; **r. ground,** élévation *f* du terrain; éminence *f*; **r. tide,** marée montante; *Const:* **r. damp,** humidité *f* qui monte du sol; (iv) *Arch:* **r. arch,** voûte rampante; (v) *Plumb: El:* **r. main,** conduite montante; (*b*) (i) (vent) qui se lève; (colère) qui croît, qui monte; (colère, importance) croissante; (ii) (prix) en hausse; (marché) orienté à la hausse; (*c*) **r. man,** homme *m* d'avenir; **the r. generation,** la nouvelle, la jeune, génération; (*d*) (*used adverbially*) **he's r. sixty,** il va sur (ses) soixante ans. **2.** *n.* (*a*) lever *m* (du rideau); levée *f*, clôture *f* (d'une assemblée); **I don't like early r.,** je n'aime pas me lever tôt; **r. from the dead,** résurrection *f*; (*b*) ameutement *m*, insurrection *f*, révolte *f*, soulèvement *m*; (*c*) lever, ascension *f* (d'un astre); (*d*) crue *f* (des eaux); montée *f* (de la sève); **r. and falling,** mouvement *m* de montée et de descente; (*e*) élévation *f*, avancement *m* (en rang).

riser ['raizər] *n.* **1. early r.,** personne matinale; **to be an early r.,** être matinal; (avoir l'habitude de) se lever de bonne heure. **2.** *Const:* contremarche *f*. **3.** *Ind:* tuyau *m* de montée.

risibility [rizi'biliti] *n.* caractère *m* ridicule.

risible ['rizibl] *a.* risible, ridicule; (offre) dérisoire.

risk¹ [risk] *n.* (*a*) risque *m*; **to be full of risks,** comporter beaucoup de risques; **to run the r. of losing everything,** courir le risque, risquer, de tout perdre; **to take risks,** courir, prendre, des risques; **I'm not taking any risks,** je ne veux rien risquer; **to be at r.,** être en danger; être menacé; **with no r. of . . .,** sans risque de . . .; **at the r. of his life,** au risque, au péril, de sa vie; **at one's own r.,** à ses risques et périls; **calculated r.,** risque calculé; (*b*) *Ins:* risque; **fire r.,** risque d'incendie; **risks and perils at sea,** fortune *f* de mer; **comprehensive, all risk, policy,** police *f* tous risques; **third-party r.,** risque du recours du tiers; (*pers., thg*) **a good, bad, r.,** un bon, mauvais, risque.

risk² *v.tr.* risquer; (*a*) aventurer, hasarder (qch.); **to r. one's skin,** risquer sa peau; (*b*) **I wouldn't r. a crossing in such weather,** je ne me risquerais pas à tenter la traversée par un temps pareil; **I'll r. it,** je vais risquer le coup; (*c*) **to r. defeat,** courir les chances d'une défaite; **to r. breaking one's leg,** risquer, courir le risque, de se casser une jambe.

riskiness ['riskinis] *n.* nature hasardeuse, aléatoire (d'une entreprise, etc.).

risky ['riski] *a.* **1.** hasardeux. **2.** (*of story*) risqué.

risqué ['ri(:)skei] *a.* risqué, osé.

rissole ['risoul] *n. Cu:* croquette *f*.

rite [rait] *n.* rite *m*; cérémonie *f*; **the Roman r.,** le rite romain; **the rites of the Church,** les sacrements de l'Église; **funeral rites,** rites funèbres.

ritual ['ritjuəl] **1.** *a.* rituel; selon les rites. **2.** *n.* (*a*) rites, cérémonies *fpl*, cérémonial *m*; (*b*) (*book*) rituel *m*; (*c*) *Parl: etc:* rituel; *F:* **to make a r. of sth.,** faire qch. selon des rites. **-ally** *adv.* rituellement.

ritualism ['ritjuəlizm] *n. Ecc:* ritualisme *m*.

ritualist ['ritjuəlist] *a.* & *n.* ritualiste (*mf*).

ritualistic [ritjuə'listik] *a.* ritualiste.

ritzy ['ritsi] *a. F:* (*a*) tape-à-l'œil, voyant; (*b*) ultra-chic *inv*.

rival¹ ['raiv(ə)l] *a.* & *n.* (*a*) rival, -ale, *pl.* -aux, -ales; concurrent, -ente; (*b*) **as a harpist she has no r.,** comme harpiste elle n'a pas d'égal.

rival² *v.* (**rivalled,** *NAm:* **rivaled**) **1.** *v.tr.* rivaliser avec (qn, qch.). **2.** *v.i.* rivaliser (**with,** avec).

rivalry ['raivəlri] *n.* (*a*) rivalité *f*; **in r. with s.o.,** en concurrence avec qn; en rivalité avec qn; (*b*) émulation *f*.

rive [raiv] *v.* (*p.t.* **rived** [raivd]; *p.p.* **riven** ['riv(ə)n]) **1.** *v.tr.* fendre (le bois, la roche, etc.); *Lit:* **riven heart,** cœur déchiré. **2.** *v.i.* se fendre.

river ['rivər] *n.* **1.** cours *m* d'eau; (*entering sea*) fleuve *m*; (*tributary*) rivière *f*; **the r. Thames,** la Tamise; **on the r. bank,** au bord de la rivière; **r. port,** port fluvial; *F:* **to sell s.o. down the r.,** trahir, vendre, qn; *U.S: F:* **he's up (the) r.,** il est en prison. **2.** coulée *f* (de lave, etc.); flot *m*, fleuve (de sang).

riverside ['rivəsaid] *n.* bord *m* de l'eau; rive *f*; **r. inn,** auberge située au bord de la rivière; **r. properties,** propriétés riveraines.

rivet¹ ['rivit] *n.* rivet *m*; **r. head, hole,** tête *f*, trou *m*, de rivet; *Tls:* **r. gun,** pistolet *m* à river.

rivet² *v.tr.* **(rivet(t)ed)** (*a*) river (un clou, etc.); (*b*) assembler avec des rivets; river, riveter; **rivet(t)ed together,** assemblés à rivets; **rivet(t)ed joint,** rivure *f*; (*c*) **his eyes were riveted on the speaker,** il avait les yeux fixés sur l'orateur; **I stood riveted to the spot,** je restais cloué sur place. **rivet(t)ing** *n.* *Metalw:* rivetage *m*; **r. machine,** riv(et)euse *f*.

riveter ['rivitər] *n.* **1.** (*pers.*) riveur *m*. **2.** (*machine*) machine *f*, presse *f*, à river.

Riviera (the) [ðərivi'ɛərə] *Pr.n. Geog:* **the (French) R.,** la Côte d'Azur.

rivulet ['rivjulit] *n.* ruisseau *m*; petit cours d'eau.

roach [routʃ] *n.* *Ich:* gardon *m*.

road [roud] *n.* **1.** route *f*; chemin *m*; voie *f*; (*a*) **r. works, r. repairs,** travaux *mpl* de voirie; *P.N:* *Aut:* **r. works,** travaux; **r. roller,** rouleau compresseur; **major r., main r., A r.** = route nationale; grande route; **secondary r., B r.** = route secondaire, route départementale; **through r.,** route directe; *P.N:* **no through r.,** voie sans issue; **ring r.,** route de ceinture; boulevard *m* périphérique; **toll r.,** route à péage; **approach r.,** route d'accès; **r. conditions,** état *m* des routes; **r. transport,** transports routiers; **r. accidents,** accidents *mpl* de la circulation; **r. users,** usagers *mpl* de la route; **r. map,** carte routière; *Aut:* **r. fund licence** = vignette *f*; *Ind:* **r. test,** essai(s) *m(pl)* (d'une voiture) sur route; (*b*) rue *f*; **Church R.,** rue de l'Église; **they live in the same road as you,** ils habitent la même rue que vous; (*c*) **the r. to London,** la route de Londres; **to take the r. for London,** prendre la route de Londres; **to be on the r.,** (i) être en route, en chemin, en voyage; (ii) *Com:* être représentant; (iii) *Com:* (*of rep.*) être en tournée; **to be on the right r.,** être dans la bonne voie; **the r. to success,** le chemin du succès; **to be on the r. to recovery,** être en voie de guérison; (*d*) voie, chemin; **it's your r.,** vous avez la priorité; *P:* **get out of my r.!** allez, ouste! (*e*) tablier *m* (d'un pont). **2.** chaussée *f*; **in the r.,** sur la chaussée; **to step into the r.,** quitter le trottoir; **car that holds the r. well,** voiture qui tient bien la route. **3.** *Min:* galerie *f*, voie; **air r.,** voie d'aérage. **4.** *Nau:* **road(s),** rade *f*. **5.** *NAm:* chemin de fer; voie ferrée.

roadbed ['roudbed] *n.* (*a*) encaissement *m* (de la route); (*b*) *Rail:* terre-plein *m*, *pl.* terre-pleins.

roadblock ['roudblɔk] *n.* barrage routier.

roadhog ['roudhɔg] *n.* *F:* écraseur *m*, chauffard *m*.

roadhouse ['roudhaus] *n.* hôtellerie *f* en bord de route.

roadside ['roudsaid] *n.* bord *m*, bas-côté *m*, accotement *m*, de la route, de la chaussée; **r. inn,** auberge, café, situé(e) au bord de la route; *Aut:* **r. repairs,** réparations *fpl* de fortune; dépannage *m*.

roadstead ['roudsted] *n.* *Nau:* rade *f*.

roadster ['roudstər] *n.* (*a*) bicyclette routière; (*b*) *Aut:* *O:* torpédo *m*.

roadway ['roudwei] *n.* **1.** chaussée *f*. **2.** (*a*) passage *m* carrossable; (*b*) tablier *m*, plancher *m* (de pont).

roadworthy ['roudwəːði] *a.* (*of vehicle*) en état de rouler; en état de marche.

roam [roum] **1.** *v.i.* errer, rôder; **to r. about,** (i) battre du pays; (ii) se promener de-ci de-là; **to r. about the world,** courir le monde; *F:* rouler sa bosse. **2.** *v.tr.* parcourir (les rues); sillonner (les mers). **roaming** **1.** *a.* errant, vagabond. **2.** *n.* course *f* à l'aventure.

roan [roun] **1.** *a.* rouan. **2.** *n.* (cheval) rouan (*m*); vache rouanne; **red r.,** (cheval) aubère (*m*).

roar¹ [rɔːr] *n.* **1.** (*a*) (*of pers.*) hurlement *m*; rugissement *m*, vocifération *f*; **roars of laughter,** grands éclats de rire; (*b*) rugissement (du lion); mugissement *m* (du taureau). **2.** grondement *m* (de tonnerre, etc.); mugissement (de la mer); clameurs *fpl* (de la foule); ronflement *m* (d'un fourneau).

roar² **1.** *v.i.* (*a*) (*of pers.*) hurler, rugir, vociférer; **to r. with anger,** rugir de colère; **to r. with laughter,** éclater de rire; (*b*) (*of lion*) rugir; (*of bull*) mugir; (*c*) (*of thunder, storm*) gronder; (*of sea*) mugir; (*of fire*) ronfler; **a car roared by,** une voiture a passé en ronflant. **2.** *v.tr.* **to r. (out) an order,** hurler, vociférer, un ordre. **roaring** *a.* (*a*) (homme) hurlant; (lion) rugissant; (taureau) mugissant; (*b*) (tonnerre) grondant; (vent) mugissant; **a r. fire,** (i) une belle flambée; (ii) un feu d'enfer; **the r. forties,** les parages océaniques situés entre les 40° et 50° degrés de latitude; (*b*) *F:* **to do a r. trade,** faire un gros commerce; **r. success,** succès fou. **2.** *n.* = ROAR¹.

roast¹ [roust] *n.* *Cu:* rôti *m*; **a r. of pork,** un rôti de porc; **pot r.,** rôti *m* à la cocotte.

roast² **1.** *v.tr.* (*a*) (faire) rôtir (la viande); cuire (la viande) au four; rôtir (des marrons); **to r. oneself in front of the fire,** se rôtir, se griller, devant le feu; (*b*) torréfier, griller (le café). **2.** *v.i.* (*a*) (*of meat, etc.*) rôtir; (*b*) *F:* **I was roasting in the sun,** je grillais au soleil. **roasting** **1.** *a.* (feu, etc.) brûlant; torréfiant. **2.** *n.* (*a*) rotissage *m* (de la viande); **r. meat,** viande *f* à rôtir; **r. jack,** tournebroche *m*; (*b*) torréfaction *f* (du café); (*c*) *F:* *O:* semonce *f*; **to give s.o. a r.,** flanquer un savon à qn.

roast³ *a.* **r. meat,** viande rôtie; **r. pork,** porc rôti; rôti *m* de porc; **r. beef,** rôti de bœuf; rosbif *m*; **r. potatoes,** pommes de terre rôties (au four).

roaster ['roustər] *n.* **1.** (*pers.*) rôtisseur, -euse. **2.** (*a*) rôtissoire *f*; (*b*) *Metall:* four *m* à griller; (*c*) brûloir *n*, torréfacteur *m* (à café). **3.** volaille *f* à rôtir.

rob [rɔb] *v.tr.* **(robbed)** voler (qn); dévaliser (qn); piller (un verger); **to r. s.o. of sth.,** (i) voler, dérober, qch. à qn; (ii) escroquer qch. à qn; **to r. the till,** voler la caisse; **to r. Peter to pay Paul,** faire un trou pour en boucher un autre; déshabiller saint Pierre pour habiller saint Paul; *Sp:* **he was robbed of victory,** on lui arracha la victoire.

robber ['rɔbər] *n.* voleur, -euse.

robbery ['rɔbəri] *n.* vol; **armed r.,** vol à main armée; **highway r.,** vol de grand chemin; brigandage *m*; **it's highway r., daylight r.!** c'est de l'escroquerie pure et simple! c'est du vol manifeste!

robe¹ [roub] *n.* **1.** (*a*) robe longue; **(baby's) christening r.,** robe de baptême; (*b*) *NAm:* (i) robe de chambre; (ii) sortie *f* de bain; (*c*) robe (d'office, de cérémonie); **magistrate in his robes,** magistrat *m* en robe. **2.** *NAm:* couverture *f* (de voyage, etc.).

robe² **1.** *v.tr.* revêtir (qn) d'une robe d'office, de cérémonie. **2.** *v.i.* revêtir sa robe, sa toge, etc. **robing** *n.* revêtissement *m* des robes de cérémonie; **r. room,** vestiaire *m* (d'un juge, etc.).

Robin ['rɔbin] **1.** *Pr.n.m.* (*dim.*) Robert, Bob. **2.** *n.* (*a*) *Orn:* rouge-gorge *m*, *pl.* rouges-gorges; (*b*) *Bot:* **ragged R.,** lychnide *f* des prés; fleur *f* de coucou; (*c*) **round r.,** *see* ROUND I. 2.

robot ['roubɔt] *n.* robot *m*; automate *m*.

robust [rou'bʌst] *a.* **1.** (*of pers. faith*) robuste, vigoureux, solide; **r. appetite,** appétit *m* robuste; rude appétit. **2.** (*a*) (*of machinery*) solide; (*b*) (*of wine*) corsé.

robustness [rou'bʌstnis] *n.* (*a*) nature *f* robuste; vigueur *f*; (*b*) bonne santé.

roc [rɔk] *n. Myth:* rock *m.*

rock¹ [rɔk] *n.* **1.** (*a*) rocher *m*; roc *m*; **cut in(to) the r.,** creusé dans le roc; **r. face,** paroi *f*; *Mount:* varappe *f*; **r. climber,** varappeur *m*; **r. bottom,** (i) fond rocheux; (ii) *F:* le fin fond; le comble; **r.-bottom price,** prix le plus bas; **prices have reached r. bottom,** les prix sont au plus bas; *Miner:* **r. crystal,** cristal *m* de roche; quartz hyalin; **r. salt,** sel *m* gemme; **r. dove, r. pigeon,** (pigeon *m*) biset (*m*); *Com:* **r. salmon,** roussette *f*; (*b*) *Geol:* roche *f.* **2.** (*a*) **a r.,** (i) un rocher, une roche; (ii) *NAm:* (*also*) une pierre; **as firm as a r.,** ferme comme un roc; *Geog:* **the R. of Gibraltar,** *F:* **the R.,** le Rocher de Gibraltar; *Nau:* **to run on, strike, the rocks,** se jeter sur des roches; donner sur les écueils; *F:* **to be on the rocks,** (i) (*of pers.*) être sans le sou, fauché, à sec; (ii) (*of marriage*) crouler; *NAm:* **whisky on the rocks,** whisky *m* aux glaçons, *Fr.C:* sur glace; *Cu:* **r. cake,** rocher; *Hort:* **r. garden,** (jardin *m* de) rocaille *f*; (*b*) **the R. of Ages,** Jésus-Christ; (*c*) *esp. U.S:* **rocks,** diamants *mpl.* **3.** *Comest:* **a stick of r.,** un bâton de sucrerie.

rock² *n.* **1.** bercement *m*; balancement *m.* **2.** *Mus: Danc:* rock *m*; **r. 'n roll,** rock-and-roll *m.*

rock³ *v.tr. & i.* (*a*) bercer (un enfant); balancer (un berceau); *Tchn: Mec.E:* basculer (un levier); **to r. a child on one's knees,** balancer un enfant sur ses genoux; **rocked gently by the waves,** bercés par les flots; **to r. (backwards and forwards) in one's chair,** se balancer sur sa chaise; **the house was rocked by the earthquake,** le tremblement de terre a secoué, a ébranlé, la maison; (*b*) *F:* secouer, ébranler (qn); **that'll r. him,** voilà qui va le secouer; **to r. the boat,** secouer la barque; (*c*) danser le rock. **rocking 1.** *a.* (*a*) oscillant; à bascule; **r. motion,** (i) *Mec: etc:* mouvement *m* de bascule; (ii) *Rail:* mouvement de lacet (d'un wagon); (*b*) branlant. **2.** *n.* balancement *m,* bercement *m*; oscillation *f*; *Mec.E:* basculage *m*; *Rail: etc:* mouvement *m* de lacet; **r. chair,** fauteuil *m* à bascule; berceuse *f*; **r. horse,** cheval *m* à bascule.

rocker ['rɔkər] *n.* **1.** bascule *f* (de berceau, de fauteuil à bascule, etc.); *F:* **to be off one's r.,** être un peu fou, timbré. **2.** (*a*) *Min:* (*gold*) berceau *m*; sas *m* mobile; (*b*) *Phot:* balance-cuvette *m, pl.* balance-cuvettes; (*c*) *esp. NAm: F:* fauteuil *m* à bascule. **3.** *I.C.E:* culbuteur *m*; *Mec.E:* basculeur *m.*

rockery ['rɔkəri] *n.* rochers artificiels; rocaille *f.*

rocket² ['rɔkit] *n.* **1.** (*a*) *Pyr:* fusée *f*; **signal r.,** fusée de signalisation; **tracer r.,** fusée traçante; **r. gun,** (i) *Pyr:* lance-fusée(s) *m*; (ii) *Nau:* lance-amarre *m*; **to fire a r.,** lancer, tirer, une fusée; (*b*) *F:* **he's just had a r. from the boss,** il vient de se faire engueuler par le patron. **2.** (*a*) *Space: etc:* fusée; **r. propulsion,** propulsion *f* par fusée(s); **to launch a r.,** lancer une fusée; **r. launcher,** (i) lance-fusée(s) *m*; (ii) *Mil:* lance-roquettes *m*; **r. base,** base *f* de lancement de fusées; (*b*) *Ball:* roquette *f*; **r.(-firing) aircraft,** avion (armé, équipé, de) lance-roquettes.

rocket³ *v.i.* (*a*) (*of horse*) se lancer comme un éclair; (*b*) (*of partridge, aircraft*) monter en chandelle; (*c*) (*of prices*) monter en flèche.

rocketry ['rɔkitri] *n.* **1.** l'étude *f,* la technologie, la technique, des fusées. **2.** l'arsenal *m* des fusées.

rockfall ['rɔkfɔːl] *n.* éboulement *m.*

Rockies (the) [ðə'rɔkiz] *Pr.n.pl. Geog:* les (Montagnes) Rocheuses.

rockslide ['rɔkslaid] *n.* (*a*) avalanche *f* de rochers; (*b*) traînée *f* d'éboulis.

rocky¹ ['rɔki] *a.* **1.** rocailleux; rocheux, plein de rochers. **2.** rocheux; (terrain, fond) de roche; *Geog:* **the R. Mountains,** les Montagnes Rocheuses.

rocky² *a. F:* (*a*) instable, branlant; **his business is in a r. condition,** ses affaires vont mal; (*b*) **I feel a bit r.,** je ne suis pas dans mon assiette.

rococo [rə'koukou] *a. & n. Art: etc:* rococo (*m*).

rod [rɔd] *n.* **1.** baguette *f,* canne *f.* **2.** verge *f*; **to make, pickle, a r. for one's own back,** se préparer des ennuis; **to have a r. in pickle for s.o.,** garder à qn un chien de sa chienne; la garder bonne à qn; *Prov:* **spare the r. and spoil the child,** qui aime bien châtie bien. **3.** verge (d'huissier, de bedeau); **to rule s.o. with a r. of iron,** gouverner qn avec une main de fer. **4.** (*a*) **(fishing) r.,** canne à pêche; **r. and line,** ligne *f* de pêche; **to fish with r. and line,** pêcher à la ligne; **r. fishing,** pêche *f* à la ligne; (*b*) pêcheur *m* à la ligne. **5.** *Meas:* perche *f* (= approx. 5 m). **6.** (*a*) tringle *f* (de rideau, d'escalier); (*b*) **iron r.,** barre *f* de fer; *Atom.Ph:* **fuel r.,** barreau *m* de combustible; (*c*) *Mec.E: etc:* tige *f*; **control r.,** tringle de manœuvre; **(system, series, of) rods,** tringlerie *f*; (*d*) *NAm: P:* revolver *m,* basset *m.* **7.** *Anat: etc:* **retinal rods,** bâtonnets rétiniens; **r. bacterium,** bâtonnet. **8.** *P:* verge; membre viril. **9.** *Surv:* mire *f*; jalon *m.*

rodent ['roudənt] **1.** *a.* rongeur. **2.** *n. Z:* rongeur *m.*

rodeo ['roudiou, rou'deiou] *n.* rodéo *m.*

Roderick ['rɔd(ə)rik] *Pr.n.m.* Rodrigue, Roderic.

roe¹ [rou] *n. Z:* **r. (deer),** chevreuil *m*; **r. calf,** faon *m* (de chevreuil); **r. doe,** chevrette *f.*

roe² *n.* (*a*) **(hard) r.,** œufs *mpl* (de poisson); (*b*) **soft r.,** laite *f,* laitance *f.*

roebuck ['roubʌk] *n.* chevreuil *m* (mâle).

roed [roud] *a.* (hareng) rogué; **hard-r.,** œuvé; **soft-r.,** laité.

Roentgen ['rəːntjən, -gən] *Pr.n.* Röntgen, Roentgen.

rogation [rou'geiʃ(ə)n] *n. Ecc:* Rogations *fpl*; **R. Week,** la semaine des Rogations; **R. Sunday,** le dimanche avant l'Ascension.

Roger ['rɔdʒər] *Pr.n.m.* **1.** Roger; *Nau: F: A:* **the Jolly R.,** le pavillon noir (des pirates). **2.** *int.* **R.!** (i) *W.Tel:* = reçu et compris! (ii) d'accord!

rogue [roug] *n.* **1.** escroc *m,* filou *m*; **rogues' gallery,** collection *f* de portraits de criminels. **2.** espiègle *mf*; **she's a little r.,** c'est une petite coquine, friponne. **3.** **r. (elephant, buffalo),** (éléphant *m,* buffle *m*) solitaire (*m*).

roguery ['rougəri], **roguishness** ['rougiʃnis] *n.* **1.** coquinerie *f,* friponnerie *f*; **a piece of r.,** une coquinerie, friponnerie. **2.** espièglerie *f* (d'enfant).

roguish ['rougiʃ] *a.* **1.** (tour) de filou; (air) coquin, fripon. **2.** espiègle. **-ly** *adv.* avec espièglerie.

roisterer ['rɔistərər] *n.* tapageur, -euse; fêtard, -arde.

rôle [roul] *n. Th: & Fig:* rôle *m*; **to play an important r. in sth.,** jouer un rôle important dans qch.

roll¹ [roul] *n.* **1.** (*a*) rouleau *m* (de papier, de musique, de tissu, etc.); pièce *f* (de tissu); bobine *f* (de film, de papier); *Cost:* **r.-neck sweater,** chandail *m* à col roulé; *Furn:* **r.-top desk,** bureau *m* à cylindre; **r. shutter,** rideau (de classeur, etc.); (*b*) *Arch:* volute *f* (de chapiteau ionique); (*c*) *Cu:* **jam r.,** pudding (en forme de bûche) rempli de confiture; **Swiss r.** = bûche *f*; biscuit roulé; *Bak:* **(bread) r.,** petit pain; **bridge r.,** petit pain mollet; **ham r.** = sandwich *m* au jambon; (*d*) *NAm:* liasse *f* (de billets de banque). **2.** *Adm: etc:* rôle *m,* contrôle *m,* liste *f*; **r. call,** appel (nominal); **to call the r.,** faire l'appel; **death r.,** liste des morts; **the r. of honour,** la liste de ceux qui sont morts pour la patrie; *Jur:* **to strike s.o. off the rolls,** rayer qn du tableau, du barreau. **3.** bâton *m* (de cannelle); rouleau, torquette *f,* boudin *m* (de tabac); **r. tobacco,** tabac roulé. **4.** (*roller*) (*a*) rouleau, cylindre *m* (de laminoir, etc.); *Tex:* rouleau, ensouple *f* (d'un métier); (*b*) *Metalw:* **rolls,** train *m* (de laminoir). **5.** *Aut:* **r. bar,** arceau *m* de sécurité.

roll² *n.* **1.** (*a*) *Nau: Av:* roulis *m*; **r. axis,** axe *m* de roulis; **to walk with a r.,** se balancer, se dandiner, en marchant; (*b*) **the r. of the sea,** la houle. **2.** (*a*) roulement *m* (d'une balle, etc.); (*b*) (*of horse, etc.*) **to have a r. on the ground,** se rouler par terre; (*c*) *Av:* (vol *m* en) tonneau (*m*); (*d*) *Sp:* (i) (*high jump*) **western r.,** rouleau costal; **to do a r.,** sauter en rouleau; (ii) (*canoeing*) esquimautage *m*. **3.** roulement *m* (d'un véhicule). **4.** roulement (de tambour, de tonnerre); **r. on the side drum,** batterie *f*.

roll[3] **I.** *v.tr.* **1.** (*a*) rouler (une bille, etc.); (*b*) **to r. one's eyes,** rouler les yeux; (*c*) **to r. string into a ball,** rouler de la ficelle en pelote; **to r. a snowball,** faire une boule de neige; (*d*) *Cin:* **r. it!** tournez! **2. to r. one's r's,** rouler les r; grasseyer. **3.** (*a*) rouler, passer au rouleau (le gazon); cylindrer (une route); (*b*) laminer (les métaux); planer (l'or); calandrer (les peaux); (*c*) *Cu:* **to r. (out),** étendre (la pâte) au rouleau. **4.** (*a*) **to r. (up) paper,** rouler, enrouler (du papier, etc.); rouler (des cigarettes); *Cu:* **loin of mutton boned and rolled,** carré de mouton roulé; **the hedgehog rolls itself into a ball,** le hérisson se roule en boule; (*b*) **chauffeur and gardener rolled into one,** chauffeur et jardinier en une seule personne. **5.** *NAm: P:* **to r. a drunk,** dévaliser un ivrogne. **II.** *v.i.* rouler. **1.** (*a*) **the ball rolled under the table,** la balle a roulé sous la table; *Fig:* **some heads will r. in the government,** quelques ministres vont être limogés; (*b*) *Av:* voler en tonneau. **2.** *v.i. & pr.* **to r. (oneself) from side to side,** se retourner, se rouler, de côté et d'autre; **to r. in the mud,** se rouler dans la boue; *F:* **to be rolling in money,** rouler sur l'or; nager dans l'opulence. **3.** (*of thunder*) gronder, rouler; **to hear the drums rolling,** entendre le roulement des tambours. **4.** (*of ship, aircraft*) rouler; avoir du roulis; **to r. (in one's walk),** se dandiner, se balancer, en marchant. **roll about 1.** *v.tr.* rouler (qch.) çà et là. **2.** *v.i.* rouler çà et là. **roll along 1.** *v.tr.* rouler (qch.) le long de la route, etc. **2.** *v.i.* (*a*) rouler; (*of car*) avancer (en roulant); **to r. along in one's car,** rouler dans sa voiture; (*b*) *F:* arriver, se pointer. **roll away 1.** *v.tr.* éloigner, faire rouler (qch.). **2.** *v.i.* s'éloigner (en roulant); **the mist is rolling away,** la brume se retire. **roll back 1.** *v.tr.* (*a*) rouler (qch.) en arrière; *Mil:* **to r. back the enemy,** faire reculer l'ennemi; (*b*) *NAm:* (*of government*) **to r. back prices,** baisser les prix. **2.** *v.i.* (*a*) rouler en arrière; reculer (en roulant); (*of car*) reculer en dérive; (*b*) (*of eyes*) chavirer. **roll by** *v.i.* passer (en roulant); (*of time*) s'écouler. **roll down 1.** *v.tr.* rouler (qch.) de haut en bas; descendre (qch.) (en le roulant). **2.** descendre (en roulant); **to r. down the hill,** débouler la pente; **the tears rolled down his cheeks,** les larmes coulaient sur ses joues. **rolled** *a.* **1.** (papier) en rouleau; (paquet) roulé; **r. (up) leaf,** feuille enroulée. **2.** *Metalw:* (fer, etc.) laminé. **3. r. gold,** doublé *m*; **r.-gold watch,** montre en plaqué or. **4.** (gazon) passé au rouleau, roulé. **roll in 1.** *v.tr.* (*a*) faire entrer (qch.) (en le roulant); (*b*) (*at hockey*) remettre (la balle) en jeu. **2.** *v.i.* (*a*) entrer en roulant; (*of waves*) déferler; *Com: F:* **orders are rolling in,** les commandes affluent; (*b*) *F:* **he rolled in at midnight,** il a rappliqué à minuit. **rolling 1.** *a.* (*a*) (i) roulant, qui roule; *Prov:* **a r. stone gathers no moss,** pierre qui roule n'amasse pas mousse; *Fig:* **he's a r. stone,** il a roulé sa bosse; (ii) (brouillard) qui avance; (fumée) qui s'élève en volutes; (*b*) (bateau) qui roule, a du roulis; (*of pers.*) **to have a r. gait,** se balancer, se dandiner, en marchant; (*c*) (i) **r. sea,** mer grosse, houleuse; (ii) **r. country,** pays ondulant, ondulé. **2.** *n.* (*a*) roulement *m* (d'une bille, etc.); (*b*) (i) roulades *fpl* (dans la poussière, etc.); (ii) rotation *f* (du corps); *Sp:* (*canoeing*) esquimautage *m*; (*c*) *Ind:* cylindrage *m*; *Metalw:* laminage *m*; **r. press,** presse *f* à cylindres; *Cu:* **r. pin,** rouleau *m* (à pâtisserie); (*d*) roulis *m* (d'un navire, avion, véhicule); (*e*) roulement *m* (du tambour, tonnerre); (*f*) **r. stock,** parc *m* (d'une entreprise de transports); *Rail:* matériel roulant. **roll off 1.** *v.i.* tomber (en roulant). **2.** *v.tr.* (i) sortir (qch.), (ii) faire tomber (qch.) (en le roulant). **roll on 1.** *v.i.* continuer de rouler; (*of time*) s'écouler; *F:* **r. on the holidays!** vivement les vacances! **2.** *v.tr.* (*a*) étendre (de la peinture, etc.) au rouleau; (*b*) passer (un vêtement) en le faisant rouler sur le corps. **roll out 1.** *v.tr.* (*a*) faire sortir (qch.) en le roulant; *F:* **to r. out the red carpet for s.o.,** recevoir qn avec la croix et la bannière; (*b*) débiter (des vers) d'une voix ronflante; (*c*) faire disparaître (des inégalités) au rouleau; (*d*) *Cu:* étendre (la pâte) (au rouleau). **2.** *v.i.* (*a*) (*of pers.*) sortir (d'un café, etc.) en roulant, en titubant; (*b*) (*of ball, etc.*) rouler (dehors); *F:* (*of pers.*) **to r. out of bed,** se dépagnoter. **roll over 1.** *v.tr.* **to r. sth. over,** retourner qch.; **to r. s.o. over,** culbuter qn. **2.** *v.i.* se retourner (en roulant); (*of car, etc.*) capoter; **to r. over on the ground,** rouler sur le sol; **to r. over (and over),** rouler sur soi-même (plusieurs fois). **roll up 1.** *v.tr.* (*a*) rouler, enrouler (une carte, etc.); relever, retrousser (ses manches); (*b*) envelopper (qch.); **to r. oneself up in a blanket,** s'enrouler dans une couverture. **2.** *v.i.* (*a*) (*of smoke*) s'élever en volutes; (*b*) (*of blind*) s'enrouler; (*of hedgehog*) **to r. up into a ball,** se mettre, se rouler, en boule; (*c*) *F:* (*of guests*) arriver, se pointer.

rollaway ['roulǝwei] *a. & n. NAm:* **r. (bed),** lit *m* pliable sur roulettes.

rollback ['roulbæk] *n. U.S:* baisse *f* des prix; réduction *f*.

roller ['roulǝr] *n.* **1.** (*a*) rouleau *m*; **paint r.,** rouleau à peinture; (*b*) rouleau, cylindre *m*; (*c*) **road r.,** rouleau compresseur; *Agr:* **toothed r.,** rouleau à dents; (*d*) *Paperm: Tex:* calendre *f*; (*e*) *Mec.E:* galet *m*, rouleau; *Furn:* roulette *f* (de fauteuil, etc.); *Mec.E:* **r. bearing,** roulement *m* à rouleaux; (*f*) (*for moving heavy objects*) rouleau transporteur; **r. conveyor,** transporteur *m* à rouleaux. **2.** (*a*) enrouleur *m*, rouleau (de store, carte géographique, etc.); **r. blind,** store *m* sur rouleau; **r. map,** carte *f* (géographique) sur rouleau; (*b*) *Hairdr:* bigoudi *m*, rouleau. **3.** *Nau:* lame *f* de houle.

roller(-)coaster ['roulǝ'koustǝr] *n. NAm:* montagnes *fpl* russes.

rollick ['rɔlik] *v.i.* faire la fête, la noce, la bombe. **rollicking** *a.* joyeux; d'une gaieté exubérante; **r. laughter,** rires bruyants.

rollmops ['roulmɔps] *n. Cu:* rollmops *m*.

roll-on ['roulɔn] *n.* **1.** *Cost:* gaine *f* (élastique). **2.** *Toil:* flacon *m* à bille. **3.** *attrib.* **r.-on roll-off ferry-boat,** navire *m* roulier.

roll-up ['roulʌp] *a.* (carte, etc.) à enrouler.

roly-poly ['rouli'pouli] *n.* **1.** *Cu:* **r.-p. (pudding),** pudding (en forme de bûche) rempli de confiture. **2.** *F:* (*of child*) boulot, -otte; grassouillet, -ette.

Roman ['roumǝn] **1.** *a.* (*a*) (droit, chiffre, etc.) romain; (nez) busqué, aquilin; **R. architecture,** architecture romaine; (*b*) **the Holy R. Empire,** le Saint Empire romain (germanique); *Ecc:* **R. Catholic,** catholique; **R. Catholicism,** catholicisme *m*; (*c*) *Typ:* **r. (type),** (caractère) romain. **2.** *n.* Romain, -aine.

romance[1] [rou'mæns] *n.* **1.** *Ling:* **Romance,** le roman; la langue romane; **R. languages,** langues romanes; **student of R. languages,** romaniste *m*. **2.** (*a*) *Lit:* roman *m* de chevalerie, d'aventures, etc.; **the age of r.,** les temps chevaleresques; (*b*) histoire *f* romanesque; fable *f*, roman; aventure *f* romanesque; (*c*) idylle *f* (entre deux jeunes gens); (*d*) **the r. of the sea,** la poésie de la mer. **3.** *Mus:* romance *f*.

romance[2] *v.i.* (*a*) exagérer; (*b*) inventer à plaisir. **romancing** *n.* (*a*) exagération *f*; (*b*) invention.

Romanesque [roumǝ'nesk] *a. & n. Arch:* roman (*m*).

Romania [rou'meiniə] *Pr.n. Geog:* Roumanie *f.*
Romanian [rou'meiniən] **1.** *a. Geog:* roumain. **2.** *n.* (*a*) Roumain, -aine; (*b*) *Ling:* roumain *m.*
romanize ['roumənaiz] *v.tr.* (*a*) romaniser (un peuple vaincu, etc.); (*b*) convertir (un pays, etc.) au catholicisme; (*c*) *Typ:* transcrire (un texte) en caractères romains.
Romansh [rou'mænʃ] *a. & n. Ling:* romanche (*m*).
romantic [rə'mæntik] **1.** *a.* (*a*) romanesque; **r. adventure,** aventure *f* romanesque; **r. young woman,** jeune fille sentimentale; (*b*) **r. landscape,** paysage *m* romantique; (*c*) *Art: Lit: Mus:* romantique. **2.** *n.* (*a*) *Art: Lit: Mus:* romantique *mf*; (*b*) **romantics,** idées romanesques, exaltées. **-ally** *adv.* **1.** romanesquement, pittoresquement. **2.** romantiquement, en romantique.
romanticism [rou'mæntisizm] *n.* **1.** idées *fpl* romanesques. **2.** *Art: Lit: Mus:* romantisme *m.*
romanticist [rou'mæntisist] *n.* romantique *mf.*
romanticize [rou'mæntisaiz] **1.** *v.tr.* romancer (une idée, un incident, etc.); faire tout un roman de (qch.). **2.** *v.i.* donner dans le romanesque.
Romany ['rɔməni] **1.** *n.* (*a*) romanichel, -elle; (*b*) *Ling:* le romanichel. **2.** *a.* (vie, etc.) de romanichel.
Rome [roum] *Pr.n.* **1.** Rome *f*; *Prov:* **R. was not built in a day** = Paris n'a pas été fait, bâti, en un jour; **when in R. you must do as the Romans do,** à Rome il faut vivre comme les Romains; **all roads lead to R.,** tous les chemins mènent à Rome. **2.** *Ecc:* **(the Church of) R.,** l'Église romaine; le catholicisme.
romp¹ [rɔmp] *n.* **1.** enfant turbulent(e). **2.** gambades *fpl*; ébats *mpl.*
romp² *v.i.* **1.** s'ébattre (bruyamment); gambader. **2.** **to r. away with a race,** gagner une course haut la main; **to r. home,** arriver dans un fauteuil; **to r. through an examination,** passer un examen sans effort.
romper ['rɔmpər] *n.* **r. suit, rompers,** barboteuse *f.*
rondo ['rɔndou] *n. Mus:* rondeau *m.*
roneo ['rouniou] *v.tr. R.t.m.* ronéotyper, ronéoter.
roo [ru:] *n. Austr: F:* kangourou *m.*
rood [ru:d] *n.* **1.** *Ecc:* crucifix *m* (au centre du jubé); **r. arch,** arche *f* du jubé; **r. loft,** (galerie *f* du) jubé; **r. screen,** jubé. **2.** *Meas:* rood *m*; quart *m* d'arpent.
roof¹ [ru:f] *n.* **1.** toit *m*; (*a*) **thatched, tiled, r.,** toit de chaume, de tuiles; **r. timbering, timbers,** les combles *mpl*; **r. light,** lucarne *f*; *F:* **to raise the r.,** (i) applaudir à tout casser; (ii) faire du vacarme; **to hit, go through, the r.,** sortir de ses gonds; (*b*) **to be without a r. over one's head,** se trouver sans logement; **under the same, under one, r.,** (habiter) sous le même toit, dans le même bâtiment. **2.** (*a*) voûte *f* (de tunnel); **the r. of heaven,** la voûte des cieux; (*b*) *Anat:* **r. of the mouth,** (voûte du) palais. **3.** *Aut:* toit, pavillon *m*; **sunshine r.,** toit ouvrant; **r. light,** plafonnier *m.* **4.** ciel *m*, plafond *m*, toit (d'une mine). **5.** *Av:* plafond (opérationnel, etc.).
roof² *v.tr.* (*a*) *Const:* couvrir (une maison, etc.); **house roofed with tiles,** maison couverte de tuiles; (*b*) **to r. sth. (in, over),** recouvrir qch. d'un toit. **roofing** *n.* **1.** pose *f* de la toiture; **r. strip,** volige *f*; latte *f* volige. **2.** (*a*) **r. (materials),** (matériaux *m* de) couverture *f* pour toitures; (*b*) toiture d'ardoises.
roofer ['ru:fər] *n. Const:* couvreur *m* (de maisons).
roofless ['ru:flis] *a.* **1.** sans toit; à ciel ouvert. **2.** (*of pers.*) sans abri, sans asile.
rooftop ['ru:ftɔp] *n.* toit *m*; **to shout sth. from the rooftops,** crier, publier, qch. sur les toits.
rooftree ['ru:ftri:] *n.* poutre *f* de faîte; faîtage *m.*
rook¹ [ruk] *n.* **1.** *Orn:* freux *m.* **2.** *F: O:* escroc *m.*
rook² *v.tr. F:* refaire, rouler, (qn).
rook³ *n. Chess:* tour *f.*
rookery ['rukəri] *n.* **1.** colonie *f* de freux. **2.** colonie (de phoques, de manchots); rookerie *f.*
rookie ['ruki] *n. P:* **1.** *Mil:* recrue *f*, bleu *m.* **2.** *Sp:* (i) novice *m*; (ii) nouveau membre (d'une équipe).
room¹ [ru(:)m] *n.* **1.** place *f*, espace *m*; **to take up a great deal of r.,** occuper beaucoup de place; **there is plenty of r.,** il y a amplement de la place; **there is no r.,** il n'y a pas de place; **to be cramped for r.,** être à l'étroit; **to give oneself r. to move,** se donner de l'air; **to make r. for s.o.,** faire place à qn; laisser le champ libre à qn. **2.** lieu *m*; **there's r. for uneasiness,** il y lieu d'être inquiet (**at,** de); **that leaves no r. for doubt,** cela ne laisse place à aucun doute; **there is r. for improvement,** cela laisse à désirer; on peut faire mieux encore. **3.** (*a*) (*in house*) pièce *f*; (*public room*) salle *f*; **(bed)r.,** chambre *f* (à coucher); **double, single, r.,** chambre à deux personnes, à une personne; **r. with twin beds,** chambre à deux lits; **spare r.,** chambre d'ami; **dining r.,** salle à manger; **sitting r.,** salon *m*; *F:* **the smallest r. in the house,** les cabinets *mpl*; le petit coin; (*of wine*) **serve at r. temperature,** servir chambré; (*at hotel*) **r. service,** repas servis dans les chambres; **r. and board,** chambre et pension; (*b*) **the whole r. burst out laughing,** toute la salle éclata de rire; (*c*) **(furnished) rooms to let,** chambres garnies à louer; **(set of) rooms,** appartement *m*, logement *m*; **I have rooms in town,** j'ai un appartement en ville. **4.** (*a*) *Ind:* salle, hall *m* (des chaudières); (*b*) *Nau:* **store r.,** soute *f.*
room² *v.i.* (*a*) vivre en garni; (*b*) partager un logement (**with s.o.,** avec qn); **to r. together,** vivre ensemble dans le même logement. **rooming** *n.* vie *f* en garni; *NAm:* **r. house,** maison *f* de rapport.
roomed [ru(:)md] *a.* (*with num. or adj. prefixed*) **three-r., four-r., flat,** appartement *m* de trois, quatre, pièces.
roomer ['ru:mər] *n. NAm:* locataire *mf* en garni.
roomful ['ru(:)mf(u)l] *n.* salle pleine, chambrée *f.*
roominess ['ru:minis] *n.* ample espace *m*, dimensions spacieuses, généreuses (d'une maison, etc.).
roommate ['ru(:)m'meit] *n.* compagnon *m*, compagne *f*, de chambre.
roomy ['ru:mi] *a.* spacieux; où l'on a de la place; (vêtement) ample.
roost¹ [ru:st] *n.* (*a*) juchoir *m*, perchoir *m*; **to go to r.,** (i) (*of hens*) se jucher; (ii) *F:* (*of pers.*) aller se coucher; *F:* **to rule the r.,** être le maître chez soi; (*of crime, mistake, etc.*) **to come home to r.,** retourner sur son auteur; (*b*) *F:* logement *m*, gîte *m.*
roost² *v.i.* se percher (pour la nuit), se jucher.
rooster ['ru:stər] *n.* coq *m.*
root¹ [ru:t] **1.** *Bot:* (*a*) racine *f*; **tap r.,** racine pivotante; **to pull up a plant by the roots,** déraciner une plante; **to take, strike, r.,** prendre racine; prendre pied; **to put down roots,** s'enraciner; **to strike at the r. of an evil,** aller à la source d'un mal; **to destroy abuses r. and branch,** extirper des abus; **a r. and branch revision,** une révision complète, à fond; (*b*) **edible roots,** racines alimentaires; *Agr:* **r. crops,** (cultures *fpl* de) racines alimentaires; *NAm:* **r. beer,** boisson gazeuse (faite avec les racines de certaines plantes). **2.** racine (d'une dent, d'un ongle, d'un cheveu). **3.** source *f*, souche *f*; **money is the r. of all evil,** l'argent est la source de tous les maux; **to get to the r. of things,** aller au fond des choses; **r. cause,** cause première. **4.** *Mth:* racine (d'une équation, d'un nombre); **square, cube, r.,** racine carrée, cubique; **r. sign,** (signe) radical (*m*). **5.** *Ling:* racine (d'un mot); **r. word,** mot racine, mot souche; **r. syllable,** syllabe radicale. **6.** *Mus:* **r. (note),** base *f*, son fondamental (d'un accord).
root² **1.** *v.tr.* enraciner (des plantes); **to remain rooted to the spot, ground,** rester cloué, figé, sur place. **2.** *v.i.* (*of plants*) s'enraciner, prendre racine. **rooted** *a.* **1.** (*of plant*) enraciné; (bouture) qui a des racines.

2. (préjugé) enraciné, invétéré. **rooting** *n.* **1.** enracinement *m.* **2. r. out,** déracinement *m*; extirpation *f*, éradication *f*. **root out** *v.tr.* (*a*) (*also* **root up**) déraciner (une plante); (*b*) déraciner, extirper (un abus).

root³ **1.** *v.i.* (*a*) (*of swine*) fouiller avec le groin; (*b*) *F:* **to r. among, in, papers,** fouiller dans des paperasses; (*c*) *esp. NAm: F:* **to r. for one's team,** encourager son équipe (de ses applaudissements); **to r. for a candidate,** appuyer un candidat (aux élections). **2.** *v.tr.* (*of boar*) fouiller (la terre); *F:* **to r. sth. out, up,** trouver qch. (en fouillant); dénicher qch.

rootless ['ru:tlis] *a.* sans racines.

rootstock ['ru:tstɔk] *n.* **1.** *Bot:* rhizome *m*, souche *f* (d'iris, etc.). **2.** *Fig:* souche, origine *f*.

rope¹ [roup] *n.* **1.** (*a*) corde *f*, cordage *m*; *Nau:* filin *m*; **wire r.,** câble *m* métallique; **r. yarn,** (i) fil *m* de caret; (ii) *U.S: F:* bagatelle *f*; **r. ladder,** échelle *f* de corde; **r. yard,** corderie *f*; **r. maker,** cordier *m*; (*b*) **(piece of) r.,** corde; **bell r.,** (i) cordon *m* de sonnette; (ii) corde d'une cloche; *Mount:* **(climbing) r.,** corde (d'assurance, d'attache); **to put on the r.,** s'encorder; **(climbers on the) r.,** (alpinistes en) cordée *f*; *F:* **to know the ropes,** connaître son affaire; **to show s.o. the ropes,** (i) mettre qn au courant; (ii) dresser, former, qn; **crime worthy of the r.,** crime pendable, qui mérite la corde; (*c*) *Box: etc:* **the ropes,** les cordes, *F:* les ficelles *fpl*; (*d*) corde tendue, raide; (*e*) *Mec.E: etc:* **r. drive,** commande *f* par câble; **r. brake,** frein *m* à corde. **2.** glane *f*, chapelet *m* (d'oignons); rangée *f*, grand collier (de perles). **3.** (*in beer, etc.*) graisse *f*.

rope² *v.tr.* **1.** corder (un paquet). **2.** (*a*) attacher avec une corde; **to r. s.o. to a tree,** lier qn à un arbre; **to r. climbers (together),** encorder des alpinistes; **climbers roped together,** (alpinistes en) cordée *f*; (*b*) *NAm:* prendre (un animal) au lasso. **rope in** *v.tr.* (*a*) entourer (un terrain) de cordes; (*b*) *F:* **to r. s.o. in,** entraîner qn dans un projet; s'assurer le concours de qn. **rope off** *v.tr.* réserver (une partie de la salle, etc.) au moyen d'une corde tendue.

ropedancer ['roupdɑ:nsər] *n.* danseur, -euse, de corde; funambule *mf*; équilibriste *mf*.

rope-soled ['roupsould] *a.* (espadrilles, etc.) à semelles de corde.

ropewalker ['roupwɔ:kər] *n.* = ROPEDANCER.

rop(e)y ['roupi] *a.* **1.** visqueux; (*of beer, etc.*) graisseux; (*of wine*) **to become r.,** tourner à la graisse; graisser. **2.** *P:* (*usu.* **ropey**) (*of goods*) de mauvaise qualité; (*of excuse, etc.*) de mauvaise foi.

ropiness ['roupinis] *n.* **1.** viscosité *f*; (*in beer, wine*) graisse *f*. **2.** *P:* mauvaise qualité (d'une marchandise).

rosary ['rouzəri] *n.* rosaire *m*; chapelet *m*.

rose [rouz] *n.* **1.** *Bot:* (*a*) rose *f*; **wild, briar, r.,** églantine *f*; *Fig:* **life is not a bed of roses, not all roses,** tout n'est pas rose dans la vie; **her life wasn't a bed of roses,** elle n'avait pas la vie bien rose; *Prov:* **there is no r. without a thorn,** il n'y a pas de rose sans épine; *Hist:* **the Wars of the Roses,** la guerre des Deux-Roses; (*b*) rosier *m*; **wild r.,** rosier sauvage, églantier *m*; *Hort:* **bush r.,** rosier buisson; **standard r., r. tree,** *NAm:* **tree r.,** rosier sur tige; **r. bed,** parterre *m* de rosiers; **r. garden,** roseraie *f*; **r. grower,** rosiériste *mf*; (*c*) **Alpine r.,** rhododendron *m* alpestre. **2.** (*colour*) (couleur *f* de) rose (*m*); **r. red,** (i) *a.* vermeil; (ii) *n.* vermillon *m*; **r. pink,** (i) *a.* (couleur de) rose (*m*); rosé, incarnat; (ii) *n.* (*colour*) rose *m.* **3.** (*on hat, etc.*) rosette *f*. **4.** pomme *f* (d'arrosoir). **5. (ceiling) r.,** rosace *f* de plafond. **6. compass card r.,** rose des vents. **7.** *Arch:* **r. window,** rosace; rose. **8.** *Lap:* **r.(-cut) diamond,** diamant (taillé) en rose.

rosé ['rouzei] *n.* (vin) rosé (*m*).

rosebay ['rouzbei] *n.* *Bot:* laurier-rose *m*, *pl.* lauriers-rose(s).

rosebud ['rouzbʌd] *n.* bouton *m* de rose; **r. mouth,** bouche *f* en cerise.

rose-coloured ['rouzkʌləd] *a.* rose, rosé; couleur de rose *inv*; **to see things through r.-c. spectacles,** voir tout en rose, en beau.

rosemary ['rouzməri] *n.* romarin *m*, encensier *m*.

roseola [rou'zi:ələ] *n.* *Med:* roséole *f*.

rosette [rə'zet] *n.* (*a*) chou *m*, -oux (de ruban); (*as prize*) cocarde *f*; rosette *f* (de la Légion d'honneur, etc.); (*b*) *Sculp: Arch:* rosette.

rosewater ['rouzwɔ:tər] *n.* eau *f* de rose.

rosewood ['rouzwud] *n.* *Com:* bois *m* de rose.

rosin ['rɔzin] *n.* colophane *f*.

rosiness ['rouzinis] *n.* couleur *f* rose; **the r. of her cheeks,** le rose de ses joues.

roster ['rɔstər] *n.* *Mil: etc:* (*a*) **duty r.,** tableau *m*, contrôle *m*, de service; **by r.,** à tour de rôle; (*b*) liste *f*, rôle *m*, feuille *f*; *Adm:* **promotion, advancement, r.,** tableau d'avancement.

rostrum, *pl.* **-a, -ums** ['rɔstrəm, -ə, -əmz] *n.* estrade *f*, tribune *f*; *Sp:* podium *m*.

rosy ['rouzi] *a.* rose, rosé; **r. cheeks,** joues vermeilles; **her r. complexion,** son teint de rose; *Fig:* **to paint everything in r. colours,** peindre tout en rose; **a r. prospect,** une perspective attrayante.

rot¹ [rɔt] *n.* **1.** pourriture *f*, putréfaction *f*; *Agr: Hort:* rot *m.* **2.** *Vet:* (*of sheep, etc.*) **liver r., the r.,** distomatose *f*. **3.** *F:* bêtises *fpl*; **to talk (utter) r.,** dire des imbécillités; **what r.!** quelle idiotie! **4.** (*in sport, war, etc.*) démoralisation *f*; **to stop the r.,** parer à la démoralisation.

rot² *v.* **(rotted) 1.** *v.i.* (*a*) (se) pourrir; se décomposer, se putréfier; **they let him r. in prison,** on le laissait pourrir dans un cachot; (*b*) *F:* dire des bêtises. **2.** *v.tr.* (faire) pourrir, décomposer, putréfier; *Agr:* **rotted manure,** fumier décomposé; **oil rots rubber,** l'huile désagrège le caoutchouc. **rotting 1.** *a.* qui pourrit; en pourriture. **2.** *n.* pourriture *f*; putréfaction *f*.

rota ['routə] *n.* **1.** *R.C. Ch:* **the R. (Romana),** la Rote. **2.** liste *f* de roulement; liste, tableau *m*, contrôle *m*, de service; **according to a r.,** à tour de rôle.

Rotarian [rə'tɛəriən] *n.* rotarien *m*.

rotary ['routəri] *a.* **1.** (*a*) (mouvement) rotatif, de rotation; *a. & n. NAm:* **r. (intersection),** rond-point *m*, *pl.* ronds-points; croisement *m* à circulation giratoire; (*b*) (bouton) tournant; *Typ:* **r. printing press,** (machine) rotative (*f*); *F:* roto *f*. **2. R. Club,** Rotary Club *m*.

rotate [rou'teit] **1.** *v.i.* (*a*) tourner; pivoter; (*b*) remplir ses fonctions à tour de rôle. **2.** *v.tr.* (*a*) (faire) tourner; (*b*) remplir (des fonctions) à tour de rôle; (*c*) *Agr:* alterner (les cultures). **rotating 1.** *a.* tournant; rotatif; en rotation. **2.** *n.* rotation *f*.

rotation [rou'teiʃ(ə)n] *n.* **1.** rotation *f*. **2.** (*a*) succession *f* tour à tour; rotation, roulement *m*; **by, in, r.,** par roulement; à tour de rôle; (*b*) *Agr:* **r. of crops,** rotation des cultures; assolement *m*. **3.** rotation, tour *m*; **rotations per minute,** tours-minute *mpl*.

rotative ['routətiv, rou'teitiv] *a.* rotatif.

rotator [rou'teitər] *n.* **1.** *Anat:* (muscle) rotateur (*m*). **2.** appareil rotateur.

rotatory [rou'teitəri] *a.* rotatoire, de rotation.

rote [rout] *n.* (*used only in* **by r.**) **to say, learn, sth. by r.,** dire, apprendre, qch. mécaniquement, par cœur; **to know sth. by r.,** savoir qch. par cœur.

rotgut ['rɔtgʌt] *n.* *F:* (*spirits*) tord-boyau *m*.

rotogravure ['routougrəvjuər] *n.* rotogravure *f*.

rotor ['routər] *n.* (*a*) *Mec.E: El:* rotor *m* (de turbine, compresseur, etc.); (*b*) rotor (d'un hélicoptère).

rotten ['rɔt(ə)n] *a.* **1.** pourri, putréfié; (œuf, fruit) gâté; **to smell r.,** sentir le pourri; *F:* **he's r. to the core,** il est corrompu jusqu'à la moelle des os. **2.** *F:*

lamentable; moche; **r. weather,** temps *m* de chien; **r. job,** sale besogne *f*; **he played a r. game,** il a joué abominablement; **I'm feeling r.,** je me sens mal fichu; **r. luck!** quelle guigne!

rottenness ['rɔt(ə)nnis] *n.* **1.** état *m* de pourriture, de décomposition. **2.** *F:* caractère *m* lamentable, abominable (de qch.).

rotter ['rɔtər] *n.* **1.** sale type *m.* **2.** propre *m* à rien.

rotund [rə'tʌnd] *a.* **1.** rond, arrondi; **his r. figure,** ses formes arrondies. **2.** (discours, style) grandiloquent.

rotunda [rə'tʌndə] *n. Arch:* rotonde *f.*

rotundity [rə'tʌnditi] *n.* **1.** (*a*) rondeur *f*, rotondité *f* (d'une courbe, etc.); (*b*) rotondité (de qn); embonpoint *m.* **2.** grandiloquence *f* (de style).

rouble, *NAm:* **ruble** ['ru:bl] *n. Num:* rouble *m.*

roué ['ru:ei] *n.* vieux roué, vieux débauché.

rouge¹ [ru:ʒ] *n.* **1.** *Toil:* rouge *m* (à joues). **2.** *Cards:* **r. et noir** ['rouʒei'nwɑ:r] trente et quarante *m.*

rouge² *v.tr. & i.* **to r. (one's cheeks),** se mettre du rouge aux joues; se farder.

rough¹ [rʌf] **I.** *a.* **1.** (*a*) (*to the touch*) rude, rugueux, raboteux; (*of surface, skin*) rêche, rugueux; *F:* **to give s.o. the r. edge of one's tongue,** passer un savon à qn; (*b*) (*uneven*) (*of road*) raboteux; (*of coast, etc.*) accidenté; (*of ground*) inégal, raboteux; (*c*) (*unrefined, etc.*) brut; **in the r. state,** à l'état brut; *Const:* **to r.-coat,** ravaler (une façade); **r. coat(ing),** ravalement *m*; (*d*) *F:* **to feel r.,** se sentir patraque. **2.** (*violent*) grossier; brutal; rude, dur; (*of wind*) violent; **r. sea,** mer grosse, houleuse; **to have a r. crossing,** faire une mauvaise traversée; *F:* **he's had a r. deal, ride, a r. time of it,** il en a bavé; il a mangé de la vache enragée; **r. handling,** *F:* **r. stuff,** brutalités *fpl*; **to be r. with s.o.,** brutaliser, rudoyer, qn; *F:* **it was r. on him,** c'était dur pour lui; **r. and ready,** (i) exécuté grossièrement; (ii) (*of pers.*) cavalier, sans façon; **r. and ready installation,** installation *f* de fortune; **r. and tumble,** mêlée *f*, bousculade *f.* **3.** (*of manners*) grossier, fruste; (*of speech*) bourru, rude; (*of style*) fruste; *F:* **r. customer,** mauvais coucheur; *F:* **to give s.o. a r. time,** traiter qn avec sévérité; être vache avec qn; *Dom.Ec:* **r. work,** le gros ouvrage, *F:* le plus gros; **r. justice,** justice *f* sommaire. **4.** approximatif; **r. sketch,** (i) ébauche *f*, esquisse *f*; (ii) plan *m* en croquis; premier jet; **r. draft,** *Sch:* **r. work,** brouillon *m*; **r. guess,** approximation *f*; **at a r. guess, estimate,** approximativement. **5.** (*a*) (*of voice*) rude, rauque, âpre; (*b*) (*of wine*) gros, grossier, âpre, rude. **II.** *adv.* (*a*) rudement, grossièrement; **to play r.,** jouer brutalement; (*b*) *F:* **to sleep r.,** coucher sur la dure. **III.** *n.* **1.** (*a*) terrain accidenté; (*b*) *Golf:* **to be in the r.,** être dans l'herbe longue. **2.** (le) côté désagréable des choses; **to take the r. with the smooth,** prendre le bien avec le mal. **3.** (*pers.*) vaurien *m*, voyou *m.* **4.** (*a*) état brut; **wood in the r.,** bois (à l'état) brut; bois en grume; (*b*) ébauche *f* (d'un tableau, etc.). **roughly** *adv.* **1.** rudement, brutalement; **to treat s.o. r.,** maltraiter, malmener, rudoyer, qn. **2.** grossièrement; **r. made table,** table grossière; **to sketch sth. r.,** faire un croquis sommaire de qch. **3.** approximativement; en gros; **r. speaking,** en général; généralement parlant; **to estimate sth. r.,** estimer qch. approximativement.

rough² *v.tr.* **1. to r. (up),** ébouriffer (les cheveux); faire hérisser (le poil). **2.** *F:* (*a*) **to r. it,** (i) vivre à la dure; (ii) en voir de dures; **we've, you've, got to r. it,** à la guerre comme à la guerre; (*b*) **to r. s.o. up,** rudoyer, malmener, maltraiter, qn. **3. to r. (down),** dégrossir (une lentille, etc.); *Sculp:* **to r. in,** ébaucher (un bloc de marbre); **to r. out,** ébaucher (un plan); dégrossir (une pièce, une statue); concevoir (un projet) dans ses grandes lignes. **roughing** *n.* **1. r. (down, out),** dégrossissage *m*, dégrossissement *m*; ébauchage *m*; **r. tool,** ciseau *m* à dégrossir; ébauchoir *m.* **2.** *Const:* crépissage *m*, ravalement *m* (d'un mur).

roughage ['rʌfidʒ] *n. Physiol:* ballast *m.*

roughcast¹ ['rʌfkɑ:st] *Const:* crépi *m*, ravalement *m.*

roughcast² *v.tr.* (*p.t. & p.p.* **roughcast**) **1.** *Const:* crépir, hourder (un mur, etc.); ravaler (une façade). **2.** ébaucher (un plan, etc.).

rough-coated ['rʌfkoutid] *a.* (cheval) à long poil; (chien) à poil dur.

roughen ['rʌf(ə)n] **1.** *v.tr.* rendre rude, rugueux, âpre. **2.** *v.i.* (*a*) devenir rude, rugueux, âpre; (*b*) (*of the sea*) grossir; devenir houleuse.

roughhew [rʌf'hju:] *v.tr.* (*p.t.* **roughhewed**; *p.p.* **roughhewn**) ébaucher, dégrossir (une statue, etc.); dégrossir, bûcher (du bois d'œuvre).

roughhouse¹ ['rʌfhaus] *n. F:* boucan *m.*

roughhouse² **1.** *v.i.* chahuter. **2.** *v.tr.* malmener (qn).

roughneck ['rʌfnek] *n. F:* vaurien *m*, voyou *m.*

roughness ['rʌfnis] *n.* **1.** (*a*) rudesse *f*, aspérité *f*, rugosité *f*; (*b*) rugosité, inégalité *f* (du sol, du chemin). **2.** (*a*) grossièreté *f*, brusquerie *f*; (*b*) agitation *f* (de la mer). **3.** âpreté *f*, rudesse (de la voix).

roughrider ['rʌfraidər] *n.* dresseur *m* de chevaux.

roughshod ['rʌfʃɔd] *a. Fig:* **to ride r. over s.o.,** fouler qn aux pieds; traiter qn cavalièrement.

rough-spoken [rʌf'spouk(ə)n] *a.* au langage grossier.

roulette [ru:'let] *n. Gaming:* roulette *f*; **Russian r.,** roulette russe.

Roumania [ru(:)'meiniə] *Pr.n. Geog:* Roumanie *f.*

Roumanian [ru(:)'meiniən] **1.** *a. Geog:* roumain. **2.** *n.* (*a*) Roumain, -aine; (*b*) *Ling:* roumain *m.*

round¹ [raund] **I.** *a.* **1.** rond, circulaire; *Lit:* **the R. Table,** la Table ronde; *Pol: Ind: etc:* **r. table conference,** table ronde; **to become r.,** s'arrondir; **to listen in r.-eyed amazement,** écouter les yeux ronds; **r. shoulders,** épaules voûtées; **r. cheeks,** joues rebondies; **to be r.-shouldered,** avoir les dos voûté; **r. hand,** (écriture) ronde *f*; écriture grosse. **2. r. dance,** ronde; **r. trip,** voyage aller *m* et retour; **r. robin,** (i) pétition revêtue de signatures en cercle; (ii) *NAm: Sp:* poule *f.* **3.** (*a*) (chiffre, nombre) rond; **in r. figures,** en chiffres ronds; **r. sum,** compte rond; **a r. dozen,** une bonne douzaine; (*b*) **good r. sum,** somme rondelette. **II.** *n.* **1.** (*a*) cercle *m*, rond *m*; (*b*) *Art:* **sculpture in the r.,** ronde(-)bosse *f*; (*c*) **theatre in the r.,** théâtre en rond. **2.** (*a*) barreau *m*, échelon *m* (d'une échelle, etc.); (*b*) *Arch:* rond (de moulure); (*c*) *Cu:* **r. of beef,** gîte *m* à la noix; **r. (of bread),** tranche *f* (de pain). **3. the daily r.,** la routine de tous les jours; **one continual r. of pleasure,** une succession perpétuelle de plaisirs. **4.** (*a*) tour *m*; **a r. of golf,** une tournée de golf; **the story went the r. (of the village, etc.),** l'histoire a fait le tour (du village, etc.); (*b*) tournée *f* (d'un facteur, d'un inspecteur, etc.); **to make, do, one's rounds,** faire sa tournée; **to do a hospital r.,** (i) faire sa visite à l'hôpital; (ii) faire une clinique; (*c*) *Mil:* ronde *f* (d'inspection); (*of officer*) **to go the rounds,** faire sa, la, ronde. **5.** (*a*) *Box:* round *m*, reprise *f*; (*b*) *Ten:* tour, série (d'un tournoi); (*c*) *Sp:* manche *f* (d'une compétition); (*d*) *Equit:* **clear r.,** sans-faute *m inv.* **6.** (*a*) **to stand a r. of drinks,** payer une tournée (générale); (*b*) *Cards:* tour; levée *f*; (*c*) *Mil:* **r. of ten shots,** salve *f* de dix coups; **r. of applause,** salve d'applaudissements; (*d*) *Mil:* **r. (of ammunition),** cartouche *f*; (*of company*) **to fire a r.,** tirer un coup (chacun). **7.** *Mus:* canon *m*; fugue *f* (pour voix égales); *Danc:* ronde. **roundly** *adv.* (parler, etc.) rondement, carrément.

round² **I.** *adv.* **1.** (*a*) **to go r. (in a circle),** tourner (en rond); décrire un cercle; *Fig:* **to go r. in circles,** tourner en rond; **the wheels go r.,** les roues tournent; **my head's going r.,** la tête me tourne; **there's a rumour going r. that . . .,** le bruit court, circule, que . . .; **to turn r. and r.,** tournoyer; **to turn, look, r.,** se retourner; (*b*) **all the year r.,** (pendant) toute l'année; **winter came r.,** l'hiver est revenu; (*c*) **to bring s.o. r. (after fainting),** ranimer qn; **to come r.,** revenir à soi; **to come r. to s.o.'s opinion,** se ranger à l'opinion de qn; (*d*) **it's the other way r.,** c'est (tout) le contraire. **2.** (*a*) autour; **garden with a wall right r., all r.,** jardin avec un mur tout autour; **to show s.o. r.,** faire faire à qn le tour de la maison, du jardin, etc.; **taking it, taken, all r.,** dans l'ensemble; en général; (*b*) **the villages r. about,** les villages à l'entour. **3. to hand, pass, r. the cakes,** faire passer, faire circuler, les gâteaux; **there's not enough to go r.,** il n'y en a pas assez pour tout le monde; **will the meat go r.?** est-ce qu'il y aura assez de viande? **4.** (*a*) (*at obstacle, etc.*) **to go r.,** faire le tour; **it's a long way r.,** cela fait un grand détour; **to go, take, the long way r.,** prendre le chemin le plus long; (*b*) **to order the car r.,** demander qu'on amène la voiture; **to ask s.o. r. for the evening,** inviter qn à venir passer la soirée; **he brought his friend r. (with him),** il a amené son ami (avec lui); **if you are r. this way next week,** si vous passez par ici la semaine prochaine. **II.** *prep.* **1.** (*a*) (*position*) autour de; **sitting r. the table,** assis autour de la table; **he's 95 cm r. the chest,** il a un tour de poitrine de 95 cm; **shells were exploding r. (about) him,** des obus éclataient autour de lui; **r. (about) midday,** vers midi; (*b*) (*motion*) **to travel r. the world,** faire le tour du monde; **to take, show, s.o. r. the garden,** faire faire à qn le tour du jardin; **to look r. the room,** jeter un coup d'œil autour de la pièce; **the earth moves r. the sun,** la terre tourne autour du soleil; **to go r. (and r.) sth.,** tourner autour de qch. **2. to go r. an obstacle,** contourner un obstacle; **to sail r. a cape,** doubler, franchir, un cap; **to go r. the corner,** (*of pers.*) tourner le coin; (*of vehicle*) prendre le virage; **the grocer r. the corner,** l'épicier du coin; *F:* **to be, go, r. the bend,** être, devenir, fou.

round³ 1. *v.tr.* (*a*) arrondir (qch.); rendre (qch.) rond; *Ling:* arrondir (une voyelle); (*b*) contourner (un obstacle); *Nau:* doubler, franchir (un cap); contourner (une île); *Aut:* prendre (un virage). **2.** *v.i.* (*a*) s'arrondir; devenir rond; (*b*) **to r. on one's heel,** faire demi-tour; *F:* **to r. on s.o.,** (i) dénoncer, vendre, qn; (ii) tomber sur qn; se retourner contre qn. **rounded** *a.* arrondi; **r. cheeks,** joues rebondies. **rounding** *n.* **1.** (*a*) *Tchn:* arrondissage *m*; *Bookb:* endossure *f* (d'un livre); (*b*) **r. off,** arrondissement *m* (d'un domaine, d'une phrase, etc.); *Com: etc:* **r. off, up, down, of a sum,** arrondissement d'une somme. **2. r. up,** rassemblage *m* (du bétail); rafle *f* (de filous). **round off** *v.tr.* arrondir (un angle, un domaine, une phrase, etc.); achever (des négociations, etc.); **to r. off one's speech,** achever son discours. **round up** *v.tr.* (*a*) rassembler (du bétail); faire une rafle de (filous); (*b*) arrondir (une somme).

roundabout ['raundəbaut] **1.** *n.* (*a*) (manège *m* de) chevaux *mpl* de bois; carrousel *m*; *F:* **what you gain on the swings you lose on the roundabouts,** à tout prendre on ne gagne ni ne perd; (*b*) *Aut:* rond-point *m, pl.* ronds-points; *Adm:* carrefour *m* à sens giratoire. **2.** *a.* (chemin) détourné, indirect; **to take a r. way,** faire un détour; *F:* prendre le chemin des écoliers; **to hear of sth. in a r. way,** apprendre qch. indirectement; **to lead up to a question in a r. way,** aborder de biais une question.

roundel ['raund(ə)l] *n.* (*a*) *Arch:* œil-de-bœuf *m, pl.* œils-de-bœuf; (*b*) *Av:* cocarde *f.*

roundelay ['raundilei] *n. Mus: A:* rondeau *m.*

rounder ['raundər] *n. Sp:* **rounders,** balle *f* au camp.

roundhouse ['raundhaus] *n. NAm: Rail:* rotonde *f.*

roundness ['raundnis] *n.* rondeur *f.*

roundsman, *pl.* **-men** ['raundzmən] *n.m. Com:* livreur.

roundup ['raundʌp] *n.* rassemblement *m* (du bétail, etc.); rafle *f* (de filous).

rouse [rauz] **I.** *v.tr.* **1. to r. s.o.,** (i) (*from sleep*) (r)éveiller qn; (ii) tirer qn de sa torpeur; (iii) remuer, activer, qn; **to r. the camp,** donner l'alerte au camp; **to r. oneself,** se secouer; **to r. s.o. to action,** inciter qn à agir; (*c*) mettre (qn) en colère; **he is terrible when roused,** il est terrible quand il est monté. **2.** soulever (l'indignation, etc.); susciter (l'admiration, etc.); *Lit:* **to r. the passions,** éveiller les passions. **II.** *v.i. O:* **to r. (up),** (i) se réveiller; (ii) se secouer; sortir de sa torpeur. **rousing** *a.* qui (r)éveille; qui excite; (discours) entraînant; **r. cheers,** applaudissements chaleureux.

roustabout ['raustəbaut] *n. F:* **1.** *NAm:* débardeur *m.* **2.** *Austr:* homme *m* à tout faire; manœuvre *m.*

rout¹ [raut] *n. Mil:* déroute *f*; **to put troops to r.,** mettre des troupes en déroute.

rout² *v.tr. Mil:* mettre (une armée) en déroute; mettre (l'ennemi) en fuite.

rout³ *v.i.* **to r. out,** dénicher (qn); faire sortir (qn).

route¹ [ru:t, *NAm: also* raut] *n.* **1.** itinéraire *m*; route *f*, voie *f*; parcours *m* (d'un défilé); *Mount:* course *f*; **to map out a r.,** tracer un itinéraire; **shipping r.,** route de navigation; **sea, overland, r.,** route maritime, terrestre; **bus r.,** (i) ligne *f* d'autobus; (ii) itinéraire, parcours *m*, d'un autobus; *Aut: P.N:* **all routes,** toutes directions; **r. map,** (i) levé *m* d'itinéraire; (ii) carte routière. **2.** *Mil:* (*often* [raut]) **column of r.,** colonne de route; **r. march,** marche *f* d'entraînement (au pas de route). **3.** *NAm:* tournée *f* (du facteur).

route² *v.tr.* router, acheminer (un colis, etc.).

routine [ru:'ti:n] *n.* **1.** routine *f*; **to do sth. as a matter of r.,** faire qch. d'office; **the daily r.,** le train-train quotidien; **it's just r.,** c'est une simple formalité; **r. examination,** examen de routine; **r. work,** travail *m* de routine, travail routinier; **r. enquiries,** constatations *fpl* d'usage. **2.** *Th:* enchaînement *m* (de pas de danse); numéro *m* (d'un comique, etc.). **3.** *Cmptr:* programme *m.*

rove [rouv] **1.** *v.i.* (*a*) rôder; vagabonder; **his eyes roved from one to the other,** ses yeux erraient de l'un à l'autre. **2.** *v.tr.* parcourir (la campagne, un pays); (*of pirate*) écumer (les mers). **roving 1.** *a.* vagabond; (ambassadeur, journaliste) itinérant; *F:* **to have a r. eye,** avoir l'œil égrillard. **2.** *n.* vagabondage *m*; **r. life,** vie nomade.

rover ['rouvər] *n.* (*a*) rôdeur, -euse; vagabond, -onde; (*b*) *Scout:* routier *m.*

row¹ [rou] *n.* **1.** (*a*) rang *m*, rangée *f*; ligne *f*; file *f*; brochette *f* (de décorations); **r. of trees,** rangée d'arbres; **r. of figures,** (i) (*horizontal*) ligne, (ii) (*vertical*) colonne *f*, de chiffres; **r. of lights,** rampe *f* (de lumières); **r. of knitting,** rang de tricot; **in a r.,** en rang, en ligne; **to put things in a r.,** mettre des objets en rang; aligner des objets; **in rows,** par rangs; **in two rows,** sur deux rangs; **two Sundays in a r.,** deux dimanches de suite; (*b*) rang, rayon *m* (d'oignons, de laitues); **in rows,** en lignes, en rayons. **2.** (*a*) rang (de chaises); **in the front, third, r.,** au premier, au troisième, rang; (*b*) ligne, rangée, de maisons; (*c*) (*in street names*) rue *f.*

row² [rou] *n.* promenade *f* en canot.

row³ [rou] **1.** *v.i.* (*a*) ramer; *Nau:* nager; **to r. hard,** faire force de rames; (*with cogn. acc.*) **to r. a race,** faire une course d'aviron; **to r. stroke,** être chef de nage; (*b*) faire du canotage; faire de l'aviron. **2.** *v.tr.* (*a*) conduire (un bateau) à l'aviron; (*b*) conduire (qn) dans une embarcation à rames. **rowing** *n.* conduite *f* (d'un bateau) à l'aviron; *Nau:* nage *f*; *Sp:* aviron *m*, canotage *m*; **r. boat,** bateau, canot, à rames; *Gym:* **r. machine,** machine *f* à ramer.

row⁴ [rau] *n.* **1.** chahut *m*, tapage *m*, vacarme *m*; **to make, kick up, a r.,** (i) faire du chahut; faire du tapage; (ii) *F:* faire une scène. **2.** querelle *f*, dispute *f*; scène *f*; **family r.,** querelle de famille; **to have a r. with s.o.,** se quereller, se disputer, avec qn. **3.** *F:* **to get into a r.,** se faire attraper; se faire laver la tête.

row⁵ [rau] *F:* **1.** *v.tr. A:* semoncer (qn). **2.** *v.i.* se quereller, se disputer **(with s.o.,** avec qn). **rowing** *n.* querelle *f*, dispute *f*.

rowan ['rauən, 'rou-] *n.* **1. r. (tree),** sorbier *m* (domestique), cormier *m*. **2. r. (berry),** sorbe *f*; corme *f*.

rowboat ['roubout] *n. esp. NAm:* bateau *m*, canot *m*, à rames.

rowdiness ['raudinis] *n.* tapage *m*; chahut *m*.

rowdy ['raudi] **1.** *a.* tapageur, chahuteur; **to be r.,** chahuter. **2.** *n.* (*a*) chahuteur, -euse; (*b*) voyou *m*.

rowdyism ['raudiizm] *n.* tapage *m*; chahut *m*.

rowel ['rauəl] *n.* molette *f* (d'éperon).

rower ['rouər] *n.* rameur, -euse; *Nau:* nageur.

rowlock ['rɔlək] *n. Nau:* tolet *m* (d'aviron).

royal ['rɔiəl] **1.** *a.* (*a*) royal, -aux; du roi, de la reine; **His, Her, R. Highness,** son Altesse royale; **r. charter,** acte *m* du souverain; **r. blue,** bleu *inv* (de) roi, (de) France; (*b*) royal, princier; magnifique; (*c*) *Ap:* **r. jelly,** gelée royale; (*d*) *Nau:* **r. (sail),** cacatois *m*; **r. mast,** (mât *m* de) cacatois; (*e*) *Cards:* **r. flush,** quinte royale. **2.** *n.* (*a*) cerf *m* à douze andouillers; (*b*) *Paperm:* = grand raisin; (*c*) *F:* membre *m* de la famille royale. **-ally** *adv.* royalement.

royalism ['rɔiəlizm] *n.* royalisme *m*.

royalist ['rɔiəlist] *a. & n.* royaliste (*mf*).

royalty ['rɔiəlti] *n.* **1.** royauté *f*. **2.** *coll.* **hotel patronized by r.,** hôtel fréquenté par les personnages royaux. **3. royalties,** (*a*) (i) redevance (due à un inventeur, au détenteur de la propriété littéraire ou artistique d'une œuvre); (ii) *Publ:* droits *mpl* d'auteur; (*b*) *Petr:* royalties *fpl*.

rozzer ['rɔzər] *n. P:* agent *m* de police; flic *m*.

rub¹ [rʌb] *n.* **1.** frottement *m*; friction *f*; **to give sth. a r.,** (i) donner un coup de torchon à qch.; (ii) frotter, astiquer (des cuivres); **to give s.o. a r. down,** faire une friction à, frictionner, qn. **2.** *Fig:* **there's the r.!** c'est là la difficulté!

rub² *v.* **(rubbed) 1.** *v.tr.* (*a*) frotter; **to r. one's leg with liniment,** se frotter, se frictionner, la jambe avec de l'embrocation; **to r. one's hands (together),** se frotter les mains; **to r. one's eyes,** se frotter les yeux; *F:* **to r. s.o. up the wrong way,** prendre qn à rebrousse-poil; énerver, irriter, qn; (*b*) **to r. sth. dry,** sécher qch. en le frottant; (*c*) **to r. a horse down,** bouchonner un cheval; **to r. s.o., oneself, down,** frictionner qn, se frictionner (après un bain, etc.); **to r. down a wall, paintwork,** regratter un mur, poncer de la peinture; **to r. sth. off, away,** enlever qch. par le frottement; **to r. sth. in,** faire pénétrer qch. par des frictions, en frottant; *F:* **don't r. it in!** n'insistez pas davantage (sur ma gaffe, etc.)! *Cu:* **to r. the butter into the flour,** mélanger (avec les doigts) le beurre et la farine; **to r. out a word,** effacer, gommer, un mot; **to r. sth. through a sieve,** passer qch. au tamis; (*d*) **to r. a brass,** prendre un frottis d'un cuivre. **2.** *v.i.* (*a*) frotter **(against,** contre); (*of pers.*) **to r. (up) against s.o., sth.,** se frotter contre qn, qch.; **these shoes r.,** ces chaussures me font mal; **this colour rubs off easily,** cette couleur s'enlève facilement; *F:* **it rubs off on them,** cela déteint sur eux; *F:* **to r. along,** se débrouiller; **we r. along (together) very well,** nous nous accordons très bien. **rubbing** *n.* **1.** (*a*) frottage *m* (de qch. avec qch.); *Med: etc:* friction *f*; **r. surface,** frottoir *m* (d'une boîte d'allumettes, etc.); **r. down,** (i) bouchonnement *m*, bouchonnage *m* (d'un cheval); (ii) regrattage *m* (d'un mur); ponçage *m* (de la peinture); *U.S;* **r. alcohol,** alcool à 90 (degrés); (*b*) frottement *m*; friction. **2.** calque *m* par frottement; frottis *m*; **to take a r. of an inscription,** prendre un frottis d'une inscription.

rub-a-dub ['rʌbədʌb] *n.* ra(n)ta(n)plan *m*.

rubber¹ ['rʌbər] *n.* **1.** frottoir *m*; **blackboard r.,** effaceur *m*. **2.** (*pers.*) frotteur, -euse. **3.** (*a*) caoutchouc *m*; gomme *f* élastique; **crêpe r.,** crêpe *m* de latex; **foam r.,** caoutchouc mousse; **r. ball,** balle *f* en caoutchouc; **r. band,** élastique *m*; **r. gloves,** gants *mpl* en caoutchouc; **r. overshoes,** *NAm:* **rubbers,** caoutchoucs; *F:* **r. cheque,** chèque *m* sans provision; **r. stamp,** (i) timbre *m* (de, en) caoutchouc; tampon *m*; (ii) légende *f* du tampon de caoutchouc; (iii) *F:* (*pers.*) béni-oui-oui *m inv*; **r. stamp parliament,** parlement ratificateur; **to r.-stamp sth.,** (i) apposer un cachet sur qch., estampiller qch.; (ii) *F:* approuver (une décision) sans discussion; (*b*) gomme (à effacer); (*c*) *Bot:* **r. tree,** arbre *m* à gomme; **r. plant,** caoutchouc, caoutchoutier *m*; (*d*) *F:* rondelle *f* de caoutchouc (d'une pompe); (*e*) *Hyg: P:* préservatif *m*; capote anglaise; **r. goods,** préservatifs.

rubber² *n. Cards:* rob(re) *m*; **to play a r.,** faire un robre; **the r. (game),** la belle.

rubberize ['rʌbəraiz] *v.tr.* caoutchouter; **rubberized material,** tissu caoutchouté.

rubberneck¹ ['rʌbənek] *n. F:* (*a*) badaud, -aude; curieux, -euse; (*b*) touriste *mf*.

rubberneck² *v.i. F:* (*a*) badauder, faire le badaud; (*b*) excursionner; visiter (des monuments, etc.).

rubbery ['rʌbəri] *a.* (*a*) caoutchouteux; (*b*) coriace.

rubbish ['rʌbiʃ] *n.* **1.** (*a*) ordures *fpl*; immondices *fpl*, détritus *mpl*; **r. bin,** boîte *f* à ordures; poubelle *f*; (*indoors*) seau *m* à ordures; **r. chute,** vide-ordures *m inv*; **r. dump,** dépotoir *m*; décharge publique; (*b*) choses *fpl* sans valeur; **old r.,** vieilleries *fpl*; *F:* **good riddance to bad r.,** (un) bon débarras; (*c*) camelote *f*; **never buy r.,** achetez toujours de la bonne qualité. **2.** bêtises *fpl*, sottises *fpl*; **to talk r.,** dire des bêtises; **(what) r.! what a load of (old) r.!** quelle fichaise, foutaise!

rubbishy ['rʌbiʃi] *a.* sans valeur; (marchandises) (i) de rebut; (ii) de mauvaise qualité.

rubble ['rʌbl] *n.* **1.** *Const:* **r. (stone),** moellon (brut); (ii) *coll.* (*for roads, etc.*) blocaille *f*; **to fill up the empty spaces with r.,** bloquer les vides; **r. wall,** mur sans assises; **r. work,** moellon(n)age *m*. **2.** (*after demolition, etc.*) décombres *mpl*, déblai *m*.

rube [ru:b] *n. NAm: F:* paysan *m*, rustaud *m*.

rubella [ru:'belə] *n. Med:* rubéole *f*.

rubicund ['ru:bikənd] *a.* rubicond, rougeaud.

Rubicon ['ru:bikən] *Pr.n. Geog:* Rubicon *m*; *Fig:* **to cross the R.,** franchir le Rubicon; sauter le pas.

ruble ['ru:bl] *n. NAm: Num:* rouble *m*.

rubric ['ru:brik] *n. Ecc: Typ: etc:* rubrique *f*.

rubstone ['rʌbstoun] *n.* pierre *f* à aiguiser.

ruby ['ru:bi] *n.* **1.** *Miner: Lap:* (*a*) rubis *m*; (*b*) *Clockm:* rubis. **2.** *a. & n.* (*a*) **r. (red),** rouge (*m*), *Lit:* rubis *inv*; **r. port,** porto *m* rouge; **r. lips,** lèvres vermeilles; (*b*) **r. wedding,** noces *fpl* de vermeil.

ruck¹ [rʌk] *n.* **1.** *Rac:* peloton *m* (des coureurs). **2. the (common) r.,** le commun (du peuple); **to get out of the r.,** sortir du rang.

ruck² *n.* (*in cloth*) faux pli; (*in garment*) godet *m*.

ruck³ **to r. (up)** (*a*) *v.tr.* froisser (des vêtements); (*b*) *v.i.* (*of sheet*) se froisser; (*of garment*) goder.

rucksack ['rʌksæk, 'ruk-] *n.* sac *m* à dos.

ruckus ['rʌkəs] *n. F:* (*a*) chahut *m*, vacarme *m*; (*b*) dispute *f*, bagarre *f*.

ruction [ˈrʌkʃ(ə)n] *n. F:* dispute *f*; **there'll be ructions,** il va y avoir du grabuge, de la casse.
rudder [ˈrʌdər] *n.* **1.** *Nau:* gouvernail *m.* **2.** *Av:* gouverne *f*; **rudders,** empennage *m.* **3.** queue *f* (d'un moulin à vent).
rudderless [ˈrʌdəlis] *a.* (navire) sans gouvernail, à la dérive.
ruddiness [ˈrʌdinis] *n.* teint coloré.
ruddy [ˈrʌdi] **1.** *a.* (*a*) (teint) coloré, haut en couleur; (*b*) rougeâtre; **r. glow,** lueur rouge (d'un feu); (*c*) (oiseau) roux, *f.* rousse; (*d*) *P:* **you r. fool!** espèce d'imbécile! **2.** *adv. P:* **it's r. cold,** il fait bigrement froid.
rude [ru:d] *a.* **1.** (*a*) primitif, rude; grossier; (style) fruste; (*b*) (outil) grossier; rudimentaire; (dessin) primitif, sans art; **r. beginnings,** commencements *mpl* informes. **2.** brusque; rude; (choc) violent. **3. r. health,** santé robuste. **4.** (*a*) (*of pers.*) impoli, grossier; mal élevé; **to be r. to s.o.,** être impoli avec qn; dire des grossièretés *f* à qn; **r. remark,** indiscrétion *f*; (*b*) (*of story*) scabreux, licencieux; obscène. **-ly** *adv.* **1.** primitivement, grossièrement. **2.** violemment; **r. awakened,** brusquement éveillé. **3.** (parler) impoliment, grossièrement.
rudeness [ˈru:dnis] *n.* **1.** (*a*) caractère primitif (des coutumes); manque *m* d'art; (*b*) violence *f* (des passions). **2.** (*of pers.*) impolitesse *f*, grossièreté *f*.
rudiment [ˈru:dimənt] *n.* **1.** *Anat:* rudiment *m* (d'une queue, etc.). **2. rudiments,** rudiments, premières notions (de grammaire, etc.).
rudimentary [ru:diˈment(ə)ri] *a.* rudimentaire.
rue¹ [ru:] *v.tr.* regretter amèrement (une action); **to r. the day when . . .,** regretter le jour où . . ..
rue² *n. Bot:* rue *f*.
rueful [ˈru:f(u)l] *a.* triste, lugubre. **-fully** *adv.* tristement, lugubrement.
ruff¹ [rʌf] *n.* **1.** *Cost:* fraise *f*, collerette *f*. **2.** *Z: Orn:* collier *m*, cravate *f*. **3.** *Orn:* pigeon *m* à cravate.
ruff² *n. Orn:* (chevalier) combattant *m*.
ruff³ *n. Cards:* coupe *f* (avec un atout).
ruff⁴ *v.tr. Cards:* couper (avec un atout).
ruffian [ˈrʌfiən] *n.* (*a*) brute *f*; bandit *m*; (*b*) *F:* **young ruffians,** petits polissons.
ruffle¹ [ˈrʌfl] *n.* **1.** rides *fpl* (sur l'eau). **2.** (*a*) *Cost:* (*at wrist*) manchette *f* (en dentelle); (*at breast*) jabot plissé; (*b*) collier *m*; cravate *f* (d'un oiseau).
ruffle² **1.** *v.tr.* (*a*) troubler, rider (la surface de l'eau); ébouriffer (les cheveux de qn); **hair ruffled by the breeze,** cheveux agités par la brise; (*of bird*) **to r. (up) its feathers,** hérisser ses plumes; **to r. s.o., s.o.'s feelings,** *F:* **s.o.'s feathers,** (i) froisser, (ii) irriter, contrarier, (iii) troubler, qn; **to be ruffled,** être (i) froissé, (ii) énervé; (*b*) rucher (des manchettes, etc.); plisser (un jabot, etc.). **2.** *v.i.* (*of hair*) s'ébouriffer; (*of feathers*) se hérisser; (*of sea*) s'agiter, se rider.
rug [rʌg] *n.* **1.** couverture *f*; **travelling r.,** couverture de voyage; plaid *m.* **2.** (petit) tapis, carpette *f*; *NAm:* tapis; **bedside r.,** descente *f* de lit.
rugby [ˈrʌgbi] *n.* **r. (football),** rugby *m*; **r. player,** rugbyman *m*, *pl.* rugbymen.
rugged [ˈrʌgid] *a.* **1.** (*of ground, country*) accidenté; (*of rock*) déchiqueté; (*of road*) raboteux. **2. r. features,** traits rudes, irréguliers. **3.** *O:* (*of character*) bourru, rude; **r. life,** vie rude, dure; **r. independence,** indépendance *f* farouche. **4.** vigoureux, robuste.
ruggedness [ˈrʌgidnis] *n.* **1.** rugosité *f*, aspérité *f*; caractère déchiqueté (d'un rocher, etc.). **2.** rudesse *f* (de caractère, etc.). **3.** robustesse *f*, rigueur *f*.
rugger [ˈrʌgər] *n. F:* rugby *m*.
ruin¹ [ˈruin] *n.* **1.** ruine *f*; **to fall, lie, in ruin(s),** tomber, être, en ruine; **to go to r.,** tomber en ruine; **he's on the road to r.,** il va, court, à la ruine. **2.** (*often pl.*) ruine(s); **the castle is a r.,** le château est en ruines. **3. to be the r. of s.o.,** ruiner, perdre, qn; **it will be the r. of him,** ce sera sa ruine; **gambling has led to his r.,** le jeu a fait son malheur; *P:* **mother's r.,** gin *m*.
ruin² *v.tr.* ruiner. **1.** (*a*) abîmer (la récolte, une robe); (*b*) gâcher (sa vie, son avenir); **to r. one's eyes,** user la vue, les yeux; **to r. one's health,** se ruiner la santé; (*c*) **ruined castle,** château en ruines, ruiné. **2. her extravagance ruined him,** ses folles dépenses l'ont ruiné; **to r. oneself gambling,** se ruiner au jeu.
ruination [ru:iˈneiʃ(ə)n] *n.* ruine *f*, perte *f*; **to be the r. of s.o.,** faire la ruine de qn.
ruinous [ˈru:inəs] *a.* **1.** (tombé) en ruines. **2.** ruineux; **r. expense,** dépenses ruineuses. **-ly** *adv.* ruineusement; **r. expensive,** ruineux.
rule¹ [ru:l] *n.* **1.** règle *f*; (*a*) **to lay, set, sth. down as a r.,** établir qch. en règle générale; **as a (general) r.,** en règle générale; **the exception proves the r.,** sans règle il n'y aurait pas d'exceptions; **r. of thumb,** méthode *f*, procédé *m* empirique; (*b*) **he makes it a r. to go to bed early,** il se fait une règle de se coucher de bonne heure; **rules of conduct,** règles, normes *fpl*, de conduite; *Ecc:* **r. of an order,** règle d'un ordre; (*c*) **rules and regulations,** statuts *mpl* et règlements *mpl*; *Ind:* **work(ing) to r.,** grève *f* du zèle; **to work to r.,** faire la grève du zèle; **to observe, play according to, the rules (of the game),** jouer selon les règles; entrer dans les règles du jeu; **it's against the rules,** c'est contre les règles; **the r. of the road,** (i) *Aut:* le code de la route; (ii) *Nau:* les règles de route. **2.** empire *m*, autorité *f*; administration *f*; **under his r.,** sous son administration; **under British r.,** sous l'autorité britannique; **majority r.,** règle majoritaire. **3.** *Jur:* décision *f*; **r. of court,** décision du tribunal. **4.** (*a*) *Carp: Mec.E:* règle (graduée); **pocket r.,** règle, mètre *m*, de poche; **folding r.,** mètre pliant; (*b*) *Surv:* **sight r.,** règle de visée. **5.** *Typ:* (*a*) **(brass) r.,** filet *m*; (*b*) **em r.,** tiret *m*, moins *m*; **en r.,** tiret sur demicadratin.
rule² *v.tr.* **1.** gouverner (un état; un peuple); maîtriser, commander à (ses passions); **to r. (over) a nation,** régner sur une nation; **to r. the waves,** tenir la mer; être maître, maîtresse, des mers. **2.** (*a*) décider **(that,** que); **to r. sth. out of order,** déclarer que qch. n'est pas en règle; (*b*) **a possibility that can't be ruled out,** une possibilité que l'on ne saurait écarter, éliminer. **3.** régler, rayer (du papier); tracer (une ligne) à la règle; **ruled paper,** papier réglé; *Com:* **to r. off an account,** clore, arrêter, un compte. **ruling 1.** *a.* (*a*) souverain, dominant; **the r. classes,** les classes dirigeantes; **r. passion,** passion dominante; (*b*) **r. price,** cours actuel; cours, prix *m*, du jour. **2.** *n.* (*a*) gouvernement *m*; (*b*) décision *f* (d'un juge, etc.) (sur un point de droit); **to give a r. in favour of s.o.,** décider en faveur de qn; (*c*) réglage *m*, réglure *f* (d'une feuille de papier).
ruler [ˈru:lər] *n.* **1.** souverain, -aine **(of, over,** de). **2.** règle *f* (pour tirer des lignes).
rum¹ [rʌm] *n.* **1.** *Dist:* rhum *m.* **2.** *NAm: F:* boisson *f* alcoolique.
rum² *a.* **(rummer)** *F:* drôle, bizarre; **a r. 'un,** un drôle de type, de numéro.
Rumania [ru(:)ˈmeiniə] *Pr.n. Geog:* Roumanie *f*.
Rumanian [ru(:)ˈmeiniən] **1.** *a. Geog:* roumain. **2.** *n.* (*a*) Roumain, -aine; (*b*) *Ling:* roumain *m*.
rumba [ˈrʌmbə] *n Danc: Mus:* rumba *f*.
rumble¹ [ˈrʌmbl] *n.* grondement *m* (du tonnerre); roulement *m* (d'une charrette); borborygmes *mpl.*
rumble² *v.i.* (*of thunder, etc.*) gronder (sourdement), rouler; (*of stomach*) gargouiller; **a cart rumbled along the street,** une charrette a passé avec bruit dans la rue. **rumbling** *n.* **r. (sound),** grondement *m* (de tonnerre); roulement *m* (d'une charrette); **stomach rumblings,** borborygmes *mpl.*
rumble³ *v.tr. F:* flairer, se douter de, subodorer

(qch.); voir venir (qn, qch.); **I soon rumbled him,** j'ai bien vite deviné son jeu.

rumbustious [rʌm'bʌstʃəs, -iəs] *a. F:* turbulent; tapageur, chahuteur, -trice.

ruminant ['ru:minənt] *a. & n. Z:* ruminant (*m*).

ruminate ['ru:mineit] **1.** *v.i.* (*of animal*) ruminer. **2.** *v.i. & tr.* ruminer, méditer; **to r. (on, over, about) a plan,** ruminer, remâcher, un projet.

rumination [ru:mi'neiʃ(ə)n] *n.* **1.** *Z:* rumination *f.* **2.** (*of pers.*) rumination, méditation *f.*

ruminative ['ru:minətiv] *a.* méditatif.

rummage¹ ['rʌmidʒ] *n.* **1.** fouille *f* (dans de vieux documents). **2.** vieilleries *fpl*; choses *fpl* de rebut; **r. sale,** vente *f* de charité, de bienfaisance.

rummage² **1.** *v.tr.* (*a*) fouiller (une armoire); **to r. sth. out, up,** dénicher qch.; (*b*) *Cust:* visiter (un navire). **2.** *v.i.* **to r. in one's pockets,** fouiller dans ses poches; **to r. about among old papers,** fouiller, fourrager, dans de vieux documents.

rummy¹ ['rʌmi] *a. F: O:* bizarre, drôle.

rummy² *n. Cards:* rami *m.*

rumour¹, *NAm:* **rumor¹** ['ru:mər] *n.* rumeur *f*, bruit *m* (qui court); on-dit *m inv*; **r. has it, there's a r. going round, that . . .,** le bruit court que . . ..

rumour², *NAm:* **rumor²** *v.tr.* **it is rumoured that . . .,** le bruit court que . . .; **he is rumoured to be . . .,** le bruit court, on dit, qu'il est . . ..

rump [rʌmp] *n.* **1.** croupe *f* (d'un quadrupède); croupion *m* (d'un oiseau); *F:* postérieur *m* (d'une personne); *Cu:* culotte *f* (de bœuf); **r. steak,** romsteck *m.* **2.** *F:* restant *m* (d'un parti politique).

rumple ['rʌmpl] *v.tr.* chiffonner, friper, froisser (une robe, etc.); ébouriffer (les cheveux).

rumpus ['rʌmpəs] *n. F:* (i) chahut *m*, vacarme *m*; (ii) bagarre *f*; **to kick up, make, a r.,** (i) faire un chahut à tout casser; (ii) faire une scène; (iii) se bagarrer.

run¹ [rʌn] *n.* **1.** (*a*) **at a r.,** en courant; **to break into a r.,** se mettre à courir; **we've got them on the r.,** nous les avons mis en déroute; **criminal on the r.,** malfaiteur recherché par la police; **to make a r. for it,** s'enfuir, se sauver; (*b*) course *f*; **to have a (good) r. for one's money,** en avoir pour son argent; (*c*) élan *m*; **he took a short r. and cleared the gate,** après un court élan il a franchi la barrière; (*d*) *Cr:* **to make ten runs,** marquer dix points; (*e*) remonte *f* (de saumons, etc.). **2.** (*a*) promenade *f*; **to go for a r. (in the car),** faire une promenade (en voiture); **trial r.,** (i) course d'essai (d'une voiture, d'une locomotive); voyage *m* d'essai (d'un navire); (ii) *Aut:* essai *m* (que l'on fait faire à un client); (*b*) trajet *m*; parcours *m*; **our town is two hours' r. from London,** notre ville est à deux heures (de chemin de fer, de voiture) de Londres; (*c*) *Av:* roulement *m* (au décollage, à l'atterrissage); (*d*) marche *f* (d'une machine); **trial r.,** marche d'essai (d'une machine, etc.); *Typ:* **r. of ten thousand (copies),** tirage *m* à dix mille. **3.** (*a*) *Min:* direction *f*, cours *m* (d'un filon); (*b*) cours, marche (des événements); **the ordinary r. of things,** la routine de tous les jours. **4.** (*a*) **a r. of bad luck,** une suite de malheurs; **we had a r. of good luck last week,** la semaine dernière la chance nous a souri; *Cards:* **r. of three,** séquence *f* de trois; **to have a long r.,** (i) (*of fashion*) rester longtemps en vogue; (ii) (*of play*) tenir longtemps l'affiche; **in the long r.,** à la longue; en fin de compte; (*b*) *Tchn:* suite, ligne *f* (de tuyaux); (*c*) *Gaming:* **r. on the red,** série *f* à la rouge. **5.** descente *f* (sur une banque); ruée *f* (sur des valeurs en bourse); **a r. on the banks,** un retrait massif de dépôts bancaires. **6.** (*a*) généralité *f*, commun *m* (des hommes); **the ordinary r. of mankind,** le commun des mortels; (*b*) **it's just r. of the mill,** c'est ce qu'il y a de plus ordinaire. **7.** libre accès *m*; **to give s.o. the r. of one's library,** mettre sa bibliothèque à la disposition de qn; **to have the r. of the house,** être libre d'aller partout dans la maison. **8.** (*a*) galerie *f* (de la taupe); coulée *f* (d'un lapin); **sheep r.,** pâturage *m* de moutons; **chicken r.,** parcours *m* de poulailler; (*b*) **ski r.,** piste *f* de ski; (*c*) *Rail:* **level r.,** palier *m.* **9.** maille *f* qui file, échelle *f* (dans un bas). **10.** *Mus:* roulade *f.*

run² *v.* (*p.t.* **ran** [ræn]; *p.p.* **run;** *pr.p.* **running) I.** *v.i.* **1.** (*a*) courir; **to r. towards s.o.,** courir à, vers, qn; **to come running towards s.o.,** accourir vers qn; **to r. up, down, the street,** monter, descendre, la rue en courant; **I'll just r. across, round, over, to the grocer's,** je vais faire un saut chez l'épicier; **to r. after s.o.,** courir après qn; **to r. into, across, up against, s.o.,** rencontrer qn par hasard; **r. along!** allez-vous-en! (*b*) **to r. a race,** courir, disputer, une course; (*c*) **to r. a kilometre,** courir, faire, un kilomètre; **to r. an errand, a message,** faire une course; **to r. the blockade,** forcer le blocus. **2.** fuir, s'enfuir, se sauver; **r. for it!** sauve qui peut! **3. to r. in a race,** courir, disputer, une course; **to r. for Parliament,** se présenter à la députation; **to r. for office,** se porter candidat. **4.** (*of salmon*) remonter les rivières; faire la montaison. **5.** *Nau:* courir, filer, faire route; **to r. before the wind,** courir vent arrière; **to r. on the rocks,** donner sur les rochers; **to r. aground,** échouer. **6.** (*a*) aller, marcher; **the table runs on wheels,** la table peut se rouler; **trains running to Paris,** trains à destination de Paris; (*b*) circuler; **trains running between London and the coast,** trains qui font le service, le trajet, entre Londres et la côte; **this train is not running today,** ce train est supprimé aujourd'hui; **the buses stop running at midnight,** après minuit il n'y a plus d'autobus. **7.** (*a*) **a murmur ran through the crowd,** un murmure a parcouru la foule; **that song keeps running through my head,** cette chanson me trotte dans la tête; **it runs in the family,** cela tient de la famille; (*b*) **the conversation ran something like this,** la conversation suivait à peu près ces lignes; **things must r. their course,** il faut que les choses suivent leur cours; **the lease has only a year to r.,** le bail n'a plus qu'un an à courir; *Th:* **the play has been running for a year,** la pièce tient l'affiche depuis un an; (*c*) (*of amount, number*) **to r. to . . .,** monter, s'élever, à . . .; **this paper runs to 32 pages,** ce journal est publié sur 32 pages; (*d*) **I can't, my money won't, r. to a car,** je n'ai pas assez d'argent pour (i) acheter, (ii) avoir, entretenir, une voiture. **8.** (*of engine*) fonctionner, marcher; (*of wheel, spindle*) tourner; **the engine's running,** le moteur marche, tourne, est en marche; **the engine is running smoothly,** le moteur tourne rond; *El:* **this machine runs off the mains,** cet appareil se branche sur le secteur. **9.** (*a*) (*of colour in fabric*) déteindre; (*of ink*) s'étendre; (*of dye*) couler (au lavage); **colour that runs in the wash,** couleur qui déteint au lavage; (*b*) (*of stocking*) filer, se démailler. **10.** (*a*) (*of liquid*) couler; **the river runs into a lake,** la rivière débouche, se jette, dans un lac; **there was a heavy sea running,** la mer était grosse; **his funds are running low,** ses fonds baissent; **our stores are running low,** nos provisions s'épuisent, tirent à leur fin; (*b*) **the floor was running with water,** le parquet ruisselait; **my nose is running,** j'ai le nez qui coule; (*c*) **the ice cream is beginning to r.,** la glace commence à fondre; **money runs through his fingers like water,** l'argent lui fond entre les mains; c'est un panier percé. **11.** (*a*) s'étendre; **the road runs alongside the river,** la route suit, longe, la rivière; **to r. north and south,** être orienté du nord au sud; **the line runs from . . . to . . .,** la ligne s'étend depuis . . . jusqu'à . . .; **the road runs quite close to the village,** la route passe tout près du village; (*b*) **to r. to extremes,** pousser les choses à l'extrême; (*of plant*) **to r. to seed,** monter en graine; (*of pers.*) **to r. to fat,** prendre de l'embonpoint; (*c*) **prices are running high,** en général les prix sont élevés. **II.** *v.tr.* **1.** (*a*) chasser, courre (le renard); **to r. a fox to earth,** chasser un renard jusqu'à son terrier; (*b*) **to r. s.o. hard, close,** presser qn; serrer qn de près; *F:* **I'm r. off my feet,** je suis éreinté. **2.** mettre (du bétail) au vert. **3.** (*a*) **to r. the car into the garage,** rentrer la voiture dans le garage; **to r. s.o. to town, back home,** conduire qn en ville, reconduire qn chez lui; **to r. logs,** flotter des bois; (*b*) **to r. trains between X and Y,** établir un service de trains entre X et Y; **they are running an extra train,** il y aura un train supplémentaire; (*c*) faire la contrebande (de l'alcool, des armes). **4.** faire fonctionner, faire travailler (une machine); **I can't afford to r. a car,** je n'ai pas les moyens d'entretenir une voiture; *Av:* (*for checking*) **to r. the engines,** faire le point fixe. **5.** (*a*) diriger (une affaire); tenir (un magasin, un hôtel); exploiter (une ferme); diriger (un théâtre); éditer, gérer (un journal, une revue); (*b*) **to r. a (high) temperature,** faire de la température; avoir (de) la fièvre. **6.** *Turf:* faire courir (un cheval); *Pol:* **to r. a candidate,** mettre en avant, un candidat. **7.** (faire) passer; **to r. pipes through a wall,** faire passer des tuyaux à travers un mur; **to r. a needle into one's finger,** s'enfoncer une aiguille dans le doigt; **to r. one's fingers over sth.,** promener ses doigts sur qch.; **he ran his hand through his hair,** il a passé sa main dans ses cheveux; *Cmptr:* **to r. a programme,** passer un programme. **8.** (faire) couler (de l'eau, etc.) (**into sth.,** dans qch.); **to r. a bath,** faire couler un bain. **9.** tracer (une ligne). **10.** *Needlew:* coudre (un tissu) au point devant. **run away** *v.i.* (*a*) (*of pers.*) s'enfuir, se sauver; s'échapper; faire une fugue; **to r. away from the facts,** se refuser à l'évidence des faits; (*b*) (*of horse*) s'emballer, s'emporter; (*c*) **to r. away with sth.,** emporter, enlever, qch.; **to r. away with the idea that . . .,** se mettre dans la tête que . . .; **his imagination runs away with him,** son imagination prend la galopade. **run down 1.** *v.i.* (*a*) descendre en courant; (*b*) (*of clockwork*) se décharger; (*of clock*) s'arrêter (faute d'être remontée). **2.** *v.tr.* (*a*) (aborder et) couler (un navire); *F:* **to r. s.o. down,** heurter, renverser, qn; (*of motorist*) écraser qn; (*b*) découvrir, dénicher (qn, qch.); (*c*) rabaisser, dénigrer (qn, qch.); (*d*) diminuer (les effectifs); laisser épuiser (les stocks); restreindre la production (d'une industrie, d'une usine). **run in 1.** *v.i.* entrer en courant. **2.** *v.tr.* (*a*) *F:* **to r. s.o. in,** arrêter qn; **to be, get, r. in,** se faire ramasser; (*b*) *I.C.E:* roder (un moteur); **running in,** en rodage. **run into 1.** *v.i.* (*a*) **to r. into debt,** faire des dettes; s'endetter; (*b*) **to r. into sth.,** entrer en collision avec (une voiture, un arbre); (*of vehicle*) heurter, entrer dans (un autre, etc.); (*of pers.*) **to r. into s.o.,** (i) se heurter contre qn; (ii) rencontrer qn par hasard; **to r. into difficulties,** rencontrer des difficultés; **takings r. into five figures,** la recette atteint les cinq chiffres. **2.** *v.tr.* **to r. one's car into a wall,** rentrer dans un mur avec sa voiture. **running 1.** *a.* (*a*) (i) (*of pers.*) courant; (ii) *Sp:* **r. jump,** saut *m* avec élan; *P:* **go and take a r. jump at yourself!** va te faire foutre! **to keep up a r. battle,** (i) se battre en retraite; (ii) *Fig:* lutter continuellement (**with,** avec); (*b*) **r. water,** eau courante; (*in hotel*) **room with r. water,** chambre *f* avec eau courante; **r. stream,** ruisseau coulant; *Med:* **r. sore,** plaie *f* qui suppure; (*c*) **r. hand,** écriture cursive; (*d*) (i) continu; **r. pattern,** dessin continu; *Mil:* **r. fire,** feu roulant; *Typ:* **r. title,** titre courant (d'un volume); (ii) **r. account,** compte courant; **r. expenses,** dépenses courantes; (iii) *A:* **r. board,** *Aut:* marchepied *m*; *Rail:* tablier *m*; (*e*) *Needlew:* **r. stitch,** point devant, point droit. **2.** *n.* (*a*) course(s) *f(pl)*; **r. race,** course *f* à pied; **r. track,** piste *f*; **to make the r.,** mener la course; **to be in the r.,** avoir des chances d'arriver; **he's out of the r.,** il n'a aucune chance (d'être nommé, d'arriver); (*b*) (i) marche *f*, fonctionnement *m* (d'une machine); roulement *m* (d'une voiture); marche, circulation *f* (de trains); **in r. order,** en bon état (de marche); **r. costs,** frais *mpl* d'entretien; (ii) direction *f* (d'un hôtel, etc.); exploitation *f* (des chemins de fer); (iii) introduction *f* (de l'alcool) en contrebande; (*c*) écoulement *m* (des eaux); ruissellement *m* (de l'eau); (*d*) **r. in,** rodage *m* (d'un moteur); (*e*) **r. down,** (i) déchargement *m* (d'un accu); (ii) ravalement *m*, dénigrement *m* (de qn, de qch.); (iii) diminution *f* (des effectifs); restriction de la production (d'une industrie, d'une usine). **run off 1.** *v.i.* (*a*) fuir, s'enfuir, se sauver; **to r. off with the cash,** filer avec l'argent; (*b*) (*of liquid*) s'écouler. **2.** *v.tr.* (*a*) écrire, rédiger, (un article) rapidement; *Typ:* **machine that runs off x copies a minute,** machine qui imprime x feuilles par minute; (*b*) faire écouler (un liquide); *Metall:* couler (le métal). **run on 1.** *v.i.* (*a*) continuer à courir; (*b*) (*of verse*) enjamber; *Typ:* (*of words*) se rejoindre; être liés; (*of text*) suivre sans alinéa; (*as instruction*) **r. on,** alinéa à supprimer. **2.** *v.tr. Typ:* **to r. on the matter,** faire suivre sans alinéa. **run out 1.** *v.i.* (*a*) sortir en courant; *F:* **to r. out on s.o.,** abandonner qn; **the tide is running out,** la mer se retire; (*b*) (*of lease*) expirer; **we're running out of time, time is running out,** il nous reste peu de temps; **to r. out of provisions,** épuiser ses provisions; **I've r. out of cigarettes,** je n'ai plus de cigarettes; (*c*) (*of rope*) filer, se dérouler. **2.** *v.tr.* (*a*) *Cr:* mettre (un batteur) hors jeu pendant sa course; (*b*) (laisser) filer (une corde); élonger (une amarre). **run over** *v.i.* (*a*) parcourir (un document); *Mus:* **to r. one's fingers over the keys,** passer les doigts sur les touches (du piano); (*b*) *Aut:* écraser (qn); **the car ran over his legs,** la voiture lui a passé sur les jambes; (*c*) (*of vessel or contents*) déborder. **run through 1.** *v.i.* (*a*) traverser, passer, en courant; (*b*) parcourir (un document); feuilleter (un livre); *Th:* **to r. through one's part,** répéter son rôle; (*c*) gaspiller, dissiper (une fortune); (*d*) rayer (un mot). **2.** *v.tr.* transpercer (qn) (**with a sword,** d'une epée). **run up 1.** *v.i.* (*a*) monter en courant; (*b*) **to r. up to s.o.,** courir vers qn; **to r. up against s.o.,** rencontrer qn par hasard; **to r. up against difficulties,** buter contre, se heurter à, des difficultés. **2.** *v.tr.* (*a*) laisser grossir (un compte); laisser accumuler (des dettes); (*b*) hisser (un drapeau); (*c*) confectionner (une robe) (à la hâte).

runabout ['rʌnəbaut] *n. Aut:* petite voiture.

runaround ['rʌnəraund] *n.* **to give s.o. the r.,** éviter de donner une réponse directe à qn.

runaway ['rʌnəwei] **1.** *a. & n.* (*a*) fuyard, -arde; fugitif, -ive; fugueur, -euse; (*b*) **r. (horse),** cheval emballé, échappé; (*c*) **r. lorry, train,** camion, train, fou. **2.** *a.* (*a*) (mariage) à la suite d'un enlèvement; (*b*) (*of victory*) remporté haut la main.

run(-)down[1] [rʌn'daun] *a.* **1.** (*of clock*) au bas; (*of battery*) à plat, épuisé. **2.** *F:* (*a*) (*of pers.*) **to be, feel, r. d.,** être, se sentir, affaibli; (*b*) (*of building*) délabré.

rundown[2] ['rʌndaun] *n.* **1.** recensement minutieux. **2.** diminution *f* (des effectifs); restriction *f* (de la production).

rune [ru:n] *n.* rune *f*.

rung [rʌŋ] *n.* échelon *m*, barreau *m* (d'une échelle); bâton *m* (d'une chaise).

runic ['ru:nik] *a.* (*of letters, verse*) runique.

runnel ['rʌn(ə)l] *n.* (*a*) ruisseau *m*; filet *m* d'eau; (*b*) ruisseau (de rue); caniveau *m*.

runner ['rʌnər] *n.* **1.** (*a*) (*pers., horse*) coureur, -euse; *Turf:* **five runners,** cinq partants *mpl*; **non r.,** non partant; (*b*) messager *m*, courrier *m*; *esp. U.S:* **bank r.,** garçon *m* de recette; (*c*) contrebandier *m*; **block-**

ade r., forceur *m* de blocus; (*d*) **r.-up,** (bon) second. **2.** *Hort:* (*a*) coulant *m*, stolon *m*, marcotte *f* (de fraisier); (*b*) **scarlet r., r. bean,** haricot *m* d'Espagne; haricot à rames. **3.** patin *m* (de traîneau); lame *f* (de patin). **4.** (*a*) *Nau:* chaîne *f* de charge; **r. and tackle,** palan *m* sur itague; (*b*) anneau *m* mobile. **5.** (*a*) chariot *m* de roulement; trolley *m*; (*b*) galet *m* (de roulement); (*c*) roue *f* parasite, intermédiaire; (*d*) roue mobile, couronne *f* mobile (d'une turbine); (*e*) coulisseau *m* (de lit, de tiroir). **6.** (*of carpet*) chemin *m* (d'escalier, de couloir); **table r.,** jeté *m* de table.

runny [ˈrʌni] *a. F:* (*a*) (trop) liquide; (*b*) (nez) qui coule.

runoff [ˈrʌnɔf] *n. Sp:* (course) finale *f*.

run-proof, run-resist [ˈrʌnˈpruːf, -rəˈzist] *a.* (bas, etc.) indémaillable.

runt [rʌnt] *n.* **1.** (*a*) bœuf *m*, vache *f*, de race petite; (*b*) petit dernier (d'une portée de porcs). **2.** *F:* (*a*) nabot *m*; (*b*) avorton *m*.

run-through [ˈrʌnθruː] *n.* **1.** *Bill:* coulé *m*. **2.** *Fb:* percée *f*. **3.** (*a*) lecture *f* rapide; (*b*) *Th:* répétition *f* rapide.

run-up [ˈrʌnʌp] *n.* (*a*) *Golf:* coup roulé d'approche; (*b*) *Sp:* élan *m* (pris avant un saut, etc.); *Av:* **the pilot was making his r.-u. to the target,** le pilote fonçait sur l'objectif; (*c*) période *f* préparatoire (avant une élection, etc.).

runway [ˈrʌnwei] *n. Av:* piste *f* d'envol.

rupee [ruːˈpiː] *n. Num:* roupie *f*.

rupture¹ [ˈrʌptjər] *n.* **1.** rupture *f* (de négociations); brouille *f* (entre amis, entre époux). **2.** *Med:* (*a*) éclatement *m*, rupture (d'une veine, etc.); (*b*) hernie *f*.

rupture² **1.** *v.tr.* **to r. a ligament, a blood vessel,** se rompre un tendon, un vaisseau sanguin; **to r. oneself,** se donner une hernie. **2.** *v.i.* (*of membrane*), se rompre. **ruptured** *a.* **1.** rompu. **2.** *Med:* (intestin) hernié; (*of pers.*) **to be r.,** avoir une hernie.

rural [ˈruər(ə)l] *a.* rural, -aux; *Ecc:* **r. dean,** doyen -rural.

ruse [ruːz] *n.* ruse *f*, stratagème *m*, subterfuge *m*.

rush¹ [rʌʃ] *n.* **1.** *Bot:* jonc *m*; **r. bed,** jonchaie *f*. **2.** paille *f* (pour fonds de chaises); **r.-bottomed chair,** chaise à fond de paille; **r. mat,** natte *f* de jonc.

rush² *v.tr.* pailler (une chaise).

rush³ *n.* **1.** (*a*) course précipitée; mouvement *m* rapide; **to make a r. at s.o.,** s'élancer, se jeter, se précipiter, sur qn; (*b*) **general r.,** ruée générale; bousculade *f*; **gold r.,** ruée vers l'or; **there was a r. for the papers,** on s'arrachait les journaux; **the r. hours,** les heures d'affluence, de pointe; (*c*) *Rugby Fb:* charge *f* à fond. **2.** hâte *f*, empressement *m*; **life is too much of a r. in London,** la vie à Londres est trop enfiévrée; **to be in a r.,** être pressé; **r. order,** commande urgente; **r. work,** travail *m* de première urgence. **3. a r. of cold air,** une bouffée d'air glacé; **r. of water,** coup *m* d'eau; **r. of blood to the head,** un coup de sang. **4.** *Cin:* **rushes,** épreuves *fpl*.

rush⁴ **I.** *v.i.* **1.** (*a*) se précipiter; **to r. about,** courir çà et là; **to r. into a room,** entrer précipitamment; faire irruption dans une pièce; **to r. into things,** agir sans réfléchir, à la hâte, étourdiment; **to r. to conclusions,** conclure trop hâtivement, à la légère; (*b*) **to r. out,** sortir précipitamment; **he came rushing down the stairs,** il a dégringolé l'escalier; **stream that rushes down the mountain side,** ruisseau qui dévale de la montagne; **to r. upstairs,** monter l'escalier à la hâte; **to r. back,** revenir en toute hâte, en vitesse; (*c*) **to r. at, on, s.o.,** se ruer, se jeter, sur qn; fondre sur qn. **2. the wind was rushing through the tunnel,** le vent s'engouffrait dans le tunnel; **the blood rushed to his cheeks, to his head,** le sang lui est monté au visage, à la tête. **II.** *v.tr.* **1.** (*a*) pousser, entraîner, violemment; **he was rushed to hospital,** on l'a transporté d'urgence à l'hôpital; **to r. s.o. into an undertaking,** entraîner qn dans une entreprise sans lui donner le temps de réfléchir; **I don't want to r. you,** je ne voudrais pas vous bousculer; **don't r. me,** laissez-moi le temps de souffler; **to be rushed,** être (i) pressé, (ii) débordé de travail; **to r. a bill through (the House),** faire passer un projet de loi à la hâte; (*b*) *Mil:* **to r. up reinforcements,** amener, envoyer, des renforts en toute hâte. **2.** dépêcher (un travail); expédier (un travail) à toute vitesse; exécuter (une commande) d'urgence; **you needn't r. it,** ce n'est pas pressé. **3.** (*a*) **horse that rushes his fences,** cheval qui se précipite sur l'obstacle avec trop d'impétuosité; *F:* **don't r. your fences!** réfléchissez donc! (*b*) *Mil:* prendre d'assaut (une position); s'emparer (d'une tranchée) par surprise; **the audience rushed the platform,** le public a envahi l'estrade. **rushing** *a.* (vent, fleuve) impétueux.

rusk [ˈrʌsk] *n. Comest:* = biscotte *f*.

russet [ˈrʌsit] **1.** *n. Hort:* reinette grise. **2.** *a. & n.* (couleur *f*) roussâtre; roux, *f.* rousse; feuille-morte (*m*) *inv*.

Russia [ˈrʌʃə] *Pr.n. Geog:* Russie *f*.

Russian [ˈrʌʃən] **1.** *a.* russe; de Russie. **2.** *n.* (*a*) Russe *mf*; (*b*) *Ling:* russe *m*.

Russianize [ˈrʌʃənaiz] *v.tr.* russifier.

Russophil(e) [ˈrʌsouf(a)il] *a. & n.* russophile (*mf*).

rust¹ [rʌst] *n.* **1.** rouille *f*; **to get covered with r.,** se couvrir de rouille; **r. preventer,** antirouille *m inv*; **r.-resistant,** antirouille; **r. (coloured), r. red,** roux, *f.* rousse; roussâtre. **2.** *Agr:* rouille; **black r.,** nielle *f*.

rust² **1.** *v.i.* se rouiller; s'oxyder. **2.** *v.tr.* rouiller (le fer, etc.). **rusting** *n.* rouillement, *m*, rouillage *m*.

rustic [ˈrʌstik] **1.** *a.* rustique; *Cons:* **r. work,** ouvrage *m* rustique; **r. seat,** banc *m* rustique. **2.** *n.* (*a*) paysan, -anne; campagnard, -arde; (*b*) rustaud, -aude.

rusticate [ˈrʌstikeit] **1.** *v.i.* habiter la campagne. **2.** *v.tr.* (*a*) *Const:* rustiquer (un mur, etc.); (*b*) *Sch:* renvoyer temporairement (un(e) étudiant(e)).

rustication [rʌstiˈkeiʃ(ə)n] *n.* **1.** vie *f* à la campagne. **2.** *Arch:* ouvrage *m* rustique. **3.** *Sch:* renvoi *m* temporaire (d'un(e) étudiant(e)).

rustiness [ˈrʌstinis] *n.* rouillure *f*, rouille *f*.

rustle¹ [ˈrʌsl] *n.* bruissement *m*, frémissement *m* (des feuilles); frou-frou *m* (de la soie, d'une robe); froissement *m* (de papiers).

rustle² **1.** *v.i.* (*of leaves, paper*) produire un bruissement; (*of leaves*) bruire, frémir; (*of garment*) faire frou-frou; froufrouter. **2.** *v.tr.* faire bruire, faire frémir (les feuilles); faire froufrouter (la soie); froisser (le papier). **3.** *v.tr. F:* (*a*) voler (du bétail, etc.); (*b*) **to r. up support,** rassembler des partisans; **she can always r. up a good meal,** elle peut toujours confectionner un bon repas. **rustling** **1.** *a.* bruissant; (jupon) froufroutant; **r. leaves,** feuilles frémissantes. **2.** *n.* (*a*) = RUSTLE¹; (*b*) *F:* vol *m* de bétail.

rustler [ˈrʌslər] *n. F:* voleur, -euse (de bétail).

rustproof¹ [ˈrʌstpruːf] *a.* antirouille *inv*.

rustproof² *v.tr.* protéger (qch.) contre la rouille.

rusty [ˈrʌsti] **1.** (*a*) rouillé; **to get r.,** se rouiller; **my French is getting r.,** mon français se rouille. **2.** couleur de rouille; rouilleux. **3.** *Agr:* (blé) rouillé.

rut¹ [rʌt] *n.* ornière *f*; *Fig:* **to get into a r.,** s'encroûter; s'enliser dans la routine.

rut² *v.tr.* **(rutted)** sillonner (un chemin) d'ornières; **deeply rutted,** (chemin) coupé d'ornières.

rut³ *n.* (*of stag, etc.*) rut *m*.

rut⁴ *v.i.* **(rutted)** (*of stag, etc.*) être en rut. **rutting** *n.* rut *m*; **r. season,** saison *f* du rut.

rutabaga [ruːtəˈbeigə] *n. NAm:* rutabaga *m*.

ruthless [ˈruːθlis] *a.* impitoyable; sans pitié; (*of act*) brutal, -aux. **-ly** *adv.* impitoyablement.

ruthlessness [ˈruːθlisnis] *n.* nature *f* impitoyable.

rye [rai] *n.* **1.** (*a*) seigle *m*; **r. bread,** pain *m* de seigle; (*b*) **r. grass,** ivraie *f* vivace. **2.** *NAm:* whisky *m* (de seigle).

S

S, s [es] *n.* **1.** (la lettre) S, s *m.* **2.** (courbe *f* en) S; esse *f*; **S(-shaped) hook,** crochet *m* en S; *Aut:* **S bend,** virage *m* en S. **3.** *A:* (*abbr. for Lt.* **solidus**) shilling *m.*
's [s, z] **1.** (*shortened form of*) (*a*) **is: it's raining,** il pleut; (*b*) **has: he's found a knife,** il a trouvé un couteau; (*c*) **us: let's go!** partons! **2.** (*genitive case*) (*for pl. nouns and some polysyllabic sing. nouns ending in s,* **s'**) (*a*) (*possessive*) **the pupil's books,** les livres de l'élève; **the pupils' books,** les livres des élèves; (*b*) (*genitive of nouns of measure*) **in an hour's time,** dans une heure. **3. the Thomas's,** les Thomas, la famille Thomas; **a series of o's,** une série d'o.
Saar [sɑːr] *Pr.n. Geog:* **the S.,** la Sarre.
sabbath ['sæbəθ] *n.* **1. s. (day),** (i) (jour du) sabbat *m* (des Juifs); (ii) dimanche *m* (des chrétiens); **s. day observance,** observation *f* du dimanche; **to keep, break, the s.,** observer, violer, (i) le sabbat, (ii) le dimanche. **2. witches' s.,** sabbat.
sabbatical [sə'bætik(ə)l] *a. Jew.Rel:* sabbatique; *Sch: etc:* **s. year, term,** *n.* **sabbatical,** année *f*, trimestre *m*, de congé (accordé(e) à un professeur, etc., pour faire des recherches, etc.).
sable¹ ['seibl] *n.* **1.** *Z:* zibeline *f.* **2. s. (fur),** zibeline; **s. coat,** manteau *m* de zibeline. **3.** *Art:* **s. (brush),** pinceau *m* en poil de martre.
sable² **1.** *Her:* (*a*) *n.* sable *m*; (*b*) *a.* (écusson, etc.) de sable. **2.** *a. & n.* (*a*) *A: & Lit:* noir (*m*); (*b*) *a. Z:* **s. antelope,** antilope noire.
sabot ['sæbou] *n. Cost:* sabot *m.*
sabotage¹ ['sæbətɑːʒ] *n.* sabotage *m.*
saboteur [sæbə'təːr] *n.* saboteur, -euse.
sabre, *NAm:* **saber** ['seibər] *n. Mil:* sabre *m*; **s. cut,** (i) coup *m* de sabre; (ii) (*scar*) balafre *f.*
sac [sæk] *n. Nat.Hist:* sac *m*; **yolk s.,** membrane vitelline; *Moll:* **ink s.,** poche *f* du noir.
saccharin ['sækərin] *n. Ch: etc:* saccharine *f.*
saccharine ['sækəriːn] *a. Ch:* saccharin.
sacerdotal [sæsə'dout(ə)l] *a.* sacerdotal, -aux.
sachet ['sæʃei] *n.* sachet *m.*
sack¹ [sæk] *n.* **1.** (*a*) (grand) sac; **s. of coal, of flour,** sac de charbon, de farine; *Sp:* **s. race,** course *f* en sac; (*b*) *F:* **to hit the s.,** se coucher, se pieuter. **2.** *F:* **to give s.o. the s.,** congédier, sa(c)quer, qn; mettre, flanquer, qn à la porte; **to get the s.,** être congédié, sa(c)qué.
sack² *v.tr.* **1.** ensacher, mettre en sac (du charbon, etc.). **2.** *F:* congédier, sa(c)quer, qn; mettre, flanquer, qn à la porte. **sacking** *n.* **1.** mise *f* en sac (du charbon, etc.). **2.** *F:* congédiement *m* (d'un employé). **3.** = SACKCLOTH ¹.
sack³ *n. Mil: etc:* sac *m*, pillage *m* (d'une ville, etc.).
sack⁴ *v.tr. Mil: etc:* saccager, piller, mettre à sac. (une ville, etc.). **sacking** *n.* sac *m* (d'une ville, etc.).
sackcloth ['sækklɔθ] *n.* **1.** *Tex:* toile *f* à sacs; grosse toile; toile d'emballage. **2.** *B: etc:* sac *m*; **s. and ashes,** le sac et la cendre.
sackful ['sækful] *n.* sachée *f*, plein sac (de farine, etc.).
sacrament ['sækrəmənt] *n. Ecc:* sacrement *m*; **the (Most) Holy S., the Blessed S.,** le saint Sacrement (de l'autel); **the last sacraments** les derniers sacrements.
sacramental [sækrə'mentəl] **1.** *a.* sacramentel. **2.** *n.pl. Ecc:* **the sacramentals,** les sacramentaux *mpl.*
sacred ['seikrid] *a.* **1.** (*a*) (lieu, etc.) sacré; (*b*) **s. to the memory of . . .,** consacré à la mémoire de . . .. **2.** (*a*) *Ecc:* sacré, saint; **s. books,** (i) livres *mpl* d'Église; (ii) livres saints; **the S. Heart,** le Sacré-Cœur; (*b*) (musique, procession) religieuse. **3.** (*of promise, duty, etc.*) sacré, inviolable; **nothing was s. to him,** il ne respectait rien.
sacredness ['seikridnis] *n.* **1.** caractère sacré (d'un lieu, etc.). **2.** inviolabilité *f* (d'un serment, etc.).
sacrifice¹ ['sækrifais] *n.* **1.** (*a*) sacrifice *m*, immolation *f* (d'une victime); **to offer (up) sth. as a s.,** offrir qch. en sacrifice (**to,** à); (*b*) victime; offrande *f.* **2.** *Theol:* sacrifice (du Christ). **3.** (*a*) sacrifice, abnégation *f* (de qch.); renoncement *m* (à qch.); **to make great sacrifices,** faire de grands sacrifices; **he succeeded at the s. of his health,** il a réussi en sacrifiant sa santé; (*b*) *Com:* mévente *f*; vente *f* à perte.
sacrifice² *v.tr.* sacrifier, immoler (une victime); *v.i.* **to s. to idols,** sacrifier aux idoles. **2.** (*a*) sacrifier, renoncer à (qch.); **to s. oneself,** se sacrifier (**for,** pour); (*b*) *Com:* mévendre, vendre à perte (des marchandises).
sacrificial [sækri'fiʃ(ə)l] *a.* sacrificatoire.
sacrilege ['sækrilidʒ] *n.* sacrilège *m.*
sacrilegious [sækri'lidʒəs] *a.* sacrilège; **s. person,** sacrilège *mf.*
sacristy ['sækristi] *n. Ecc:* sacristie *f.*
sacristan ['sækristən] *n. Ecc:* sacristain *m.*
sacrosanct ['sækrousæŋkt] *a.* (*usu. iron.*) sacro-saint, *pl.* sacro-saint(e)s.
sacrum ['seikrəm, 'sæk-] *n. Anat:* sacrum *m.*
sad [sæd] *a.* **(sadder, saddest) 1.** (*a*) triste; **to become s.,** s'attrister; **to look s.,** avoir l'air triste; **to make s.o. s.,** attrister, affliger, qn; **we were very s. to hear of our friend's death,** nous étions désolés d'apprendre la mort de notre ami; **to be s. at heart,** avoir le cœur gros, serré; (*b*) déplorable; (*of news, etc.*) affligeant, désolant; (*of place, etc.*) morne, lugubre; **he came to a s. end,** il a eu, fait, une triste fin. **2.** *Cu:* (*of cake, etc.*) pâteux, lourd, mal levé. **-ly** *adv.* **1.** tristement; d'un air triste. **2.** déplorablement. **3.** très; beaucoup; **he is s. missed,** il nous manque beaucoup.
sadden ['sæd(ə)n] **1.** *v.tr.* attrister, affliger (qn). **2.** *v.i.* s'affliger, s'attrister.
saddle¹ ['sædl] *n.* **1.** (*a*) selle *f* (de cheval); **hunting s.,** selle anglaise; **s. horse,** cheval *m* de selle; monture *f*; **s. room,** sellerie *f*; **to rise in the s.,** faire du trot enlevé; **in the s.,** (i) en selle, monté; (ii) en plein exercice (de ses fonctions); en selle; (*b*) selle (de bicyclette, etc.). **2.** *Geog:* col *m* (de montagne). **3.** *Cu:* selle (de mouton, de chevreuil). **4.** *Tchn:* support *m* (d'un cric, etc.); *I.C.E:* selle, assiette *f* (de cylindre).
saddle² *v.tr.* (*a*) seller (un cheval); (*b*) *F:* **to s. s.o. with sth.,** charger, encombrer, qn de qch.; mettre qch. sur le dos de qn; **she's saddled with five children,** elle a cinq enfants sur les bras, sur le dos. **saddling** *n.* sellage *m* (d'un cheval).
saddleback ['sædlbæk] *n.* (*a*) *Arch:* toit *m* en bâtière; (*b*) (*of hill*) ensellement *m*; (*c*) cochon noir avec une ceinture blanche.
saddlebag ['sædlbæg] *n. Equit: Cy: etc:* sacoche *f* (de selle).

saddlecloth ['sædlklɔθ] *n.* couverture *f,* tapis *m,* de selle.
saddler ['sædlər] *n.* sellier *m;* bourrelier *m.*
saddlery ['sædləri] *n.* **1.** (*trade*) sellerie *f,* bourrellerie *f.* **2.** sellerie, harnachement *m* de selle.
Sadducee ['sædjusi:] *n.* Saducéen, -éenne.
sadism ['seidizm] *n.* sadisme *m.*
sadist ['seidist] *n.* sadique *mf.*
sadistic [sə'distik] *a.* sadique. **-ally** *adv.* sadiquement, avec sadisme.
sadness ['sædnis] *n.* tristesse *f,* mélancolie *f.*
sadomasochism [seidou'mæsəkizm] *n. Psy:* sadomasochisme *m.*
sadomasochist [seidou'mæsəkist] *n. Psy:* sadomasochiste *mf.*
safari [sə'fɑ:ri] *n.* safari *m;* **on s.,** en safari; **s. park,** réserve *f* d'animaux sauvages.
safe[1] [seif] *n.* **1.** coffre-fort *m, pl.* coffres-forts; *Bank:* **night, deposit, s.,** coffret *m* de nuit; **s. deposit,** dépôt *m* en coffre-fort. **2. (meat) s.,** garde-manger *m inv.* **3. rifle (set) at s.,** carabine *f* au cran de sûreté.
safe[2] *a.* **1.** (*a*) en sûreté, à l'abri; **s. from sth.,** à l'abri de qch.; **at last we are s.,** enfin nous voilà saufs, hors de danger; **to be s. from recognition,** ne pas risquer d'être reconnu; (*b*) (sain et) sauf; **s. and sound,** sain et sauf; **to come home s.,** rentrer sans accident. **2.** (*a*) (*of place, thg*) sans danger, sûr; **s. retreat,** asile assuré, sûr; **to put s.o., sth., in a s. place,** mettre qn, qch., en lieu sûr; **s. beach for children,** plage *f* où les enfants sont en sécurité; **at a s. distance,** à distance respectueuse; *Med:* **s. dose,** dose inoffensive; (*b*) (*of building, bridge, etc.*) solide; (*c*) **not s.,** dangereux; **these toys aren't s.,** ces jouets sont dangereux; **is it s. to leave him alone?** est-ce qu'il n'y a pas de danger à le laisser seul? *Tchn:* **s. load,** charge *f* admissible; charge de sécurité; (*d*) **(in order) to be on the s. side,** pour plus de sûreté, pour être plus sûr; **s. investment,** placement sûr, de tout repos; **in s. keeping,** en lieu sûr, en sûreté; **it's as s. as the Bank of England, as s. as houses,** c'est de l'or en barres; **it is s. to say that . . .,** on peut dire à coup sûr que . . .. **3.** *adv.* **to play (it) s.,** ne rien risquer; jouer serré. **-ly** *adv.* **1. to arrive s.,** arriver sain et sauf, sans accident; (*of parcel*) sans dommage; (*of ship, etc.*) arriver à bon port; **to put sth. s. away,** mettre qch. en lieu sûr, en sûreté. **2.** sûrement; sans danger; **I can s. say that . . .,** je puis dire à coup sûr que . . ..
safebreaker ['seifbreikər] *n.* perceur *m* de coffres-forts.
safeguard[1] ['seifgɑ:d] *n.* sauvegarde, garantie *f* (**against,** contre).
safeguard[2] *v.tr.* sauvegarder, protéger (les intérêts, les droits, de qn); mettre (ses intérêts) à couvert.
safeness ['seifnis] *n.* **1. a feeling of s.,** un sentiment de sécurité *f,* de sûreté *f.* **2.** solidité *f* (d'un pont). **3.** sûreté (d'une affaire, d'un placement, etc.).
safety ['seifti] *n.* sûreté *f,* sécurité *f* (de qch., de qn); salut *m* (de qn); **to seek s. in flight,** chercher son salut dans la fuite; **for safety's sake,** pour plus de sûreté; **in a place of s.,** en lieu sûr; **road s.,** prévention routière; **s. first!** la sécurité d'abord! soyez prudents! *Sm.a:* **s. catch,** cran *m* de sûreté; *Min:* **s. lamp,** lampe *f* de sûreté; **s. measures,** mesures *fpl* de sécurité; **s. net,** filet *m;* **s. pin,** épingle *f* de nourrice, de sûreté; *Aut: etc:* **s. glass,** verre *m* de sécurité; **s. belt,** ceinture *f* de sécurité; **s. chain,** (i) (*of door*) chaîne *f* de sûreté, de porte; (ii) (*of bracelet, etc.*) chaînette *f* de sûreté; **s. valve,** (i) *Mch:* soupape *f* de sûreté; (ii) *Fig:* soupape.
saffron ['sæfrən] *n.* **1.** (*a*) *Cu: Pharm:* safran *m;* (*b*) *Bot:* **s. (crocus),** safran; **wild, meadow, s.,** colchique *m* d'automne; safran des prés. **2.** *a. & n.* (*colour*) safran *inv;* jaune safran *inv.*
sag[1] [sæg] *n.* **1.** (*a*) affaissement *m,* fléchissement *m* (du sol, d'un toit, etc.); (*b*) *Com:* baisse *f* (des valeurs, etc.). **2.** flèche *f,* ventre *m* (d'une ligne, d'un cordage, etc.).
sag[2] *v.i.* **(sagged) 1.** (*a*) (*of platform, roof, etc.*) s'affaisser, fléchir (sous un poids, etc.); (*b*) (*of gate, etc.*) pencher d'un côté; (*c*) (*of cheek, etc.*) pendre; (*d*) (*of cable, etc.*) se relâcher, se détendre; (*of curtain, rope, etc.*) fléchir au milieu; faire ventre; faire flèche. **2.** *Com:* (*of prices*) baisser, fléchir. **sagging** *a.* (*a*) (*of roof, etc.*) affaissé, fléchi; (*b*) (*of gate, etc.*) penché d'un côté; (*c*) (*of cheek, etc.*) flasque, tombant, pendant; (*d*) (*of line, etc.*) courbe; (*of rope*) lâche; (*e*) *Com: Fin:* (*of market*) creux, en baisse.
saga ['sɑ:gə] *n. Lit:* (*a*) saga *f;* (*b*) **s. (novel),** roman-cycle *m,* roman-fleuve *m, pl.* romans-cycles, -fleuves; roman *m* cyclique.
sagacious [sə'geiʃəs] *a.* (*of pers., mind*) sagace, avisé; (*of action, remark*) plein de sagesse. **-ly** *adv.* avec sagacité.
sagacity [sə'gæsiti] *n.* sagacité *f,* perspicacité *f;* sagesse *f* (d'une remarque, etc.).
sage[1] [seidʒ] **1.** *a. Lit:* (*of pers., conduct, etc.*) sage, prudent, judicieux. **2.** *n.* philosophe *m,* sage *m.* **-ly** *adv.* sagement, prudemment.
sage[2] *n. Bot: Cu:* sauge *f;* **s. tea,** infusion *f* de sauge; *a. & n.* **s. green,** vert cendré *inv.*
Sagittarius [sædʒi'tɛəriəs] *Pr.n. Astr:* le Sagittaire.
sago ['seigou] *n.* (*a*) *Bot:* **s. palm,** sagoutier *m;* (*b*) *Cu:* sagou *m;* **s. pudding,** sagou au lait.
Sahara [sə'hɑ:rə] *Pr.n.* **the S. (Desert),** le Sahara.
sahib ['sɑ:ib] *n.m.* sahib.
sail[1] [seil] *n.* **1.** *Nau:* (*a*) voile *f;* **square s.,** voile carrée; **to hoist, lower, a s.,** hisser, amener, une voile; *Fig:* **to haul in one's sails,** (i) rabattre de ses prétentions; en rabattre; (ii) réduire ses dépenses; (*b*) *coll.* voile(s), voilure *f,* toile *f;* **to make s.,** faire (de la) voile, de la toile; (*of ship*) **under s.,** sous voile(s); à la voile; **under full s.,** toutes voiles dehors; **to get under s.,** mettre à la voile; faire voile; appareiller; (*c*) (*ship*) **s. ho!** voilier en vue! **a fleet of twenty s.,** une flotte de vingt voiles, de vingt voiliers. **2.** (*a*) aile *f,* volant *m,* toile (de moulin); (*b*) *Ich:* nageoire dorsale (du pèlerin).
sail[2] *n.* **1.** sortie *f* à voile. **2. it will be a three hours' s.,** la traversée prendra trois heures sous voile.
sail[3] **1.** *v.i.* (*a*) (*of sailing ship*) faire voile; (*of any ship*) naviguer; faire route; **to s. round a cape,** contourner un promontoire; (*b*) partir; prendre la mer; (*c*) *F:* **to s. into a room,** entrer majestueusement dans une pièce. **2.** *v.tr. & i.* (*a*) **to s. (on, over) the seas,** parcourir les mers; naviguer (sur) les mers; (*b*) planer (dans l'air, etc.); *Aer:* voler; **there were clouds sailing by,** des nuages voguaient dans le ciel; **to s. through an examination,** passer un examen sans le moindre effort. **3.** *v.tr.* (*a*) manœuvrer (un voilier); naviguer (un navire); (*b*) **to s. a toy boat on a pond,** faire naviguer un petit bateau sur un bassin. **sailing** *n.* **1.** (*a*) navigation *f;* **it's (all) plane, plain, s.,** cela va tout seul; (*b*) *Sp:* nautisme *m;* (*c*) navigation à voile; **s. ship,** voilier *m;* (*d*) marche *f,* allure *f* (d'un voilier, d'un navire); **s. before the wind,** allure du vent arrière. **2.** départ *m,* appareillage *m.*
sailboat ['seilbout] *n. NAm:* voilier *m;* bateau *m* à voiles.
sailcloth ['seilklɔθ] *n. Tex:* toile *f* à voile(s); canevas *m.*
sailmaker ['seilmeikər] *n.* (*pers.*) voilier *m.*
sailor ['seilər] *n.* (*a*) marin *m* (officier ou matelot); (*b*) **to be a good s.,** avoir le pied marin; **to be a bad s.,** être sujet au mal de mer; (*c*) *Cost: A:* **s. suit,** costume marin (d'enfant); **s. hat,** (i) canotier *m* (pour femmes); (ii) Jean-Bart *m* en paille (de petit garçon).
sainfoin ['seinfɔin] *n. Bot: Agr:* sainfoin *m.*

saint [seint] *n.* **1.** (*a*) saint, -e; **saint's day,** fête *f* de saint; fête patronale; **All Saints' (Day),** la Toussaint; *F:* **to try the patience of a s.,** lasser la patience d'un saint; (*b*) [sənt] *with Pr.n.* (*abbr. usu.* **St.** *or* **S.**) **St. George,** Saint Georges; **St. George's Day,** la Saint-Georges; **St. Bernard,** (i) Saint Bernard; (ii) (chien *m*) saint-bernard *inv*; *Geog:* **St. Helena,** Sainte-Hélène *f*; **St. John the Baptist,** Saint Jean-Baptiste; *Geog:* **St. Lawrence,** le (fleuve) Saint-Laurent; **St. Peter's,** (la cathédrale, l'église) Saint-Pierre. **2. the Communion of Saints,** la Communion des Saints.
sainthood ['seinthud] *n.* sainteté *f.*
saintliness ['seintlinis] *n.* sainteté *f.*
saintly ['seintli] *a.* (*of life, action, etc.*) (de) saint; *Iron:* **to put on a s. air,** prendre un air de petit saint.
sake¹ [seik] *n.* **1. to do sth. for the s. of s.o., for s.o.'s s.,** faire qch. dans l'intérêt de qn, par égard pour qn, en considération de qn; **I forgive you for her s.,** je vous pardonne par égard pour elle; **do it for the s. of your family,** faites-le pour (l'amour de) votre famille; **do it for my s.,** faites-le pour moi, pour me faire plaisir; **for God's s., for goodness' s.,** pour l'amour de Dieu; **for old times' s.,** en souvenir du passé; **for economy's s.,** par économie; **art for art's s.,** l'art pour l'art. **2.** *U.S: F:* **sakes alive! sakes!** grand Dieu! par exemple!
sake² ['sɑːki] *n.* saké *m.*
sal [sæl] *n.* **s. ammoniac,** sel ammoniac; **s. volatile** [və'lætili], (solution *f* de) sels volatils anglais.
salaam¹ [sə'lɑːm] *n. F:* salamalec *m*; **salaams to David,** meilleurs vœux à David.
salaam² *v.tr. & i.* faire des salamalecs (à qn).
salacious [sə'leiʃəs] *a.* (*of pers., story, etc.*) salace, lubrique.
salaciousness [sə'leiʃəsnis] *n.* salacité *f*, lubricité *f.*
salad ['sæləd] *n.* salade *f*; **green s.,** salade (verte); **fruit s.,** macédoine *f*, salade, de fruits; **s. bowl,** saladier *m*; **s. dressing,** (i) vinaigrette *f*; (ii) sauce *f* genre mayonnaise; **s. oil,** huile *f* comestible, de table; *F:* **s. days,** années *f* de jeunesse, d'inexpérience.
salamander ['sæləmændər] *n. Amph:* salamandre *f.*
salami [sə'lɑːmi] *n. Comest:* salami *m.*
salaried ['sælərid] *a. Ind: Com:* **1.** (personnel) aux appointements; **s. staff** = cadres *mpl.* **2.** (emploi) rétribué.
salary ['sæləri] *n.* traitement *m*, appointements *mpl.*
sale [seil] *n.* **1.** vente *f*; (*a*) débit *m*, mise *f* en vente (de marchandises); **cash, credit, s.,** vente au comptant, à crédit; **article for which there is no s.,** article qui n'a pas de marché; **house for s.,** maison à vendre; **business for s.,** fonds *m* à céder; **to put sth. up for s.,** offrir, mettre, qch. en vente; **on s.,** en vente; **bill of s.,** acte *m* de vente; *Ind:* **sales department,** service commercial, service ventes; (*b*) **s. by auction, auction s.,** vente à l'enchère, aux enchères; **s. ring,** cercle *m* d'acheteurs; *Jur:* **compulsory s.,** adjudication forcée; (*c*) **s. of work,** vente de charité. **2.** *Com:* **(clearance) s.,** soldes *mpl*; vente; **s. price,** prix *m* de solde.
saleability [seilə'biliti] *n. Com:* qualité marchande (d'un article); facilité *f* d'écoulement.
saleable ['seiləbl] *a.* (*of goods, etc.*) vendable, marchand; de vente facile.
saleroom ['seilruːm] *n.* salle *f* de(s) vente(s).
salesclerk ['seilzkləːk] *n. NAm:* vendeur, -euse.
salesgirl ['seilzgəːl] *n.f.* vendeuse.
salesman, *pl.* **-men** ['seilzmən] *n.m. Com:* **1.** vendeur. **2.** représentant de commerce; courtier.
salesmanship ['seilzmənʃip] *n.* l'art *m* de vendre.
saleswoman, *pl.* **-women** ['seilzwumən, -wimin] *n.f.* vendeuse.
Salic ['seilik] *a. Hist:* **S. law,** loi *f* salique.
salient ['seiliənt] *a.* **1.** (*a*) (*of angle, etc.*) saillant; en saillie; (*b*) *n. Fort:* saillant *m.* **2.** (trait) saillant, frappant.
saline ['seilain] **1.** *a.* (*a*) (*of spring, water, etc.*) salin, salé; (*b*) (purgatif) salin; (*c*) **normal s. solution,** solution *f* physiologique. **2.** *n.* (*a*) purgatif salin; sel purgatif; (*b*) sérum *m* physiologique.
salinity [sə'liniti] *n.* salinité *f.*
saliva [sə'laivə] *n.* salive *f.*
salivary [sə'laivəri] *a.* (*of glands, etc.*) salivaire.
salivate ['sæliveit] *v.i.* saliver.
salivation [sæli'veiʃ(ə)n] *n.* salivation *f.*
sallow¹ ['sælou] *n. Bot:* saule *m.*
sallow² *a.* (teint) jaunâtre, olivâtre.
sallowness ['sælounis] *n.* ton *m* jaunâtre (du teint).
sally¹ ['sæli] *n.* **1.** *Mil:* sortie *f* (des assiégés). **2.** excursion *f*, sortie. **3.** (*a*) saillie *f*, élan *m* (d'activite, etc.); (*b*) **s. (of wit),** saillie (d'esprit); boutade *f*; trait *m* d'esprit.
sally² *v.i.* **1.** *Mil:* **to s. (out),** faire une sortie. **2.** *O:* **to s. forth, out,** sortir; partir en promenade.
salmon ['sæmən] **1.** *n.* (*usu. inv. in pl.*) *Ich:* (*a*) saumon *m*; **young s.,** saumoneau *m*; **s. ladder, leap, pass,** échelle *f* à poissons, à saumon(s); (*b*) **s. trout,** truite saumonée, truite de mer; (*c*) *Com:* **rock s.,** roussette *f.* **2.** *a. & n.* (*colour*) **s. (pink),** saumon *inv.*
salmonella [sælmə'nelə] *n. Bac:* salmonella *f inv;* salmonelle *f.*
salon ['sælɔ̃] *n.* **1.** salon *m.* **2.** (*a*) salon d'exposition (d'une modiste, etc.); (*b*) *Art:* **the S.,** le Salon; (*c*) **beauty s.,** institut *m* de beauté; **hairdressing s.,** salon de coiffure.
saloon [sə'luːn] *n.* **1.** (*a*) salle *f*, salon *m*; **billiard s.,** salle de billard; **hairdressing s.,** salon de coiffure; **dancing s.,** dancing *m*; (*b*) *NAm:* café *m*; bar *m*; débit *m* de boissons; **s. keeper,** cafetier *m*; (*c*) **s. bar** = bar *m.* **2.** *Nau:* salon (de paquebot); la cabine. **3.** (*a*) *Rail:* **s. (coach, carriage),** wagon-salon *m*, *pl.* wagons-salons; voiture-salon *f*, *pl.* voitures-salons; (*b*) *Aut:* **s. (car),** conduite intérieure; **two-door s.,** coach *m*; **four-door s.,** berline *f.*
salsify ['sælsifi] *n. Bot:* salsifis *m.*
salt¹ [sɔlt] **I.** *n.* **1.** (*a*) *Cu:* sel *m*; **cake of s.,** salignon *m*; **rock s.,** sel gemme; **sea s.,** sel marin; sel de mer; **s. marsh,** marais salant; **s. pan,** (i) marais salant; (ii) vase *m* de saunage; **s. mine,** mine *f* de sel; **s. spring,** source *f* saumâtre, saline; **s. lake,** lac salé; *Geog:* **the Great S. Lake,** le Grand Lac Salé; **kitchen s.** = gros sel; **table s.,** sel de table; *Hist:* **s. tax,** gabelle *f*; **to take a story with a grain, pinch, of s.,** prendre une histoire avec un grain de sel; **he's not worth his s.,** il ne gagne pas sa nourriture; (*b*) *Hist:* **to sit (at table) above, below, the s.,** être assis au haut bout, au bas bout, de la table; (*c*) *F:* **old s.,** loup *m* de mer; vieux matelot. **2.** (*a*) *Ch:* sel; (*b*) **bath salts,** sels de bain. **II.** *a.* **1.** (*a*) **s. water,** eau salée; eau saline; **s. beef,** bœuf *m* de conserve; (*b*) (*of food*) **too s.,** trop salé. **2.** (*of concretion, etc.*) salin; (*of rocks, ground*) salifère, saliférien.
salt² *v.tr.* **1.** (*a*) **to s. (down),** saler (de la viande, du beurre); **to s. away (money, etc.),** économiser, mettre en lieu sûr (de l'argent, etc.); (*b*) saler (un mets); assaisonner (un mets, etc.) de sel. **2.** *F: O:* cuisiner, truquer (des livres de compte, etc.). **salted** *a.* **1.** (beurre, etc.) salé. **2.** *F: O:* (*of campaigner, etc.*) aguerri, endurci. **salting** *n.* salaison *f*, salage *m* (de la viande, etc.).
saltbox ['sɔltbɔks] *n.* (*a*) boîte à sel; (*b*) *U.S:* maison *f* à toit penchant (avec deux étages à l'avant et un étage à l'arrière).
saltcellar ['sɔltselər] *n.* **1.** salière *f* (de table). **2.** *F:* salière (derrière la clavicule).
salt-free ['sɔltfriː] *a.* (régime) sans sel.
saltine ['sɔltiːn] *n. NAm: Comest:* biscuit salé; craquelin *m.*

saltiness [ˈsɔltinis] *n.* salure *f*, salinité *f.*
saltmill [ˈsɔltmil] *n.* égrugeoir *m* de table.
saltpetre, *NAm:* **saltpeter** [sɔltˈpiːtər] *n.* salpêtre *m*; nitrate *m* de potassium.
saltspoon [ˈsɔltspuːn] *n.* cuiller *f* à sel; pelle *f* à sel.
saltwater [ˈsɔltwɔːtər] *a.* **s. fish,** poisson *m* de mer.
saltworks [ˈsɔltwəːks] *n.* (*a*) saunerie *f*, saline *f*; (*b*) raffinerie *f* de sel.
saltwort [ˈsɔltwəːt] *n. Bot:* **1.** soude *f*; **prickly s.,** kali *m.* **2.** salicorne *f.*
salty [ˈsɔlti] *a.* **1.** (*of taste, sauce, etc.*) salé, saumâtre. **2.** *F:* (*of anecdote, book*) (i) piquant; (ii) salé, corsé.
salubrious [səˈluːbriəs] *n.* salubre, sain.
salubrity [səˈluːbriti] *n.* salubrité *f.*
saluki [səˈluːki] *n. Z:* sloughi *m.*
salutary [ˈsæljut(ə)ri] *a.* salutaire (**to,** à).
salutation [sæljuˈteiʃ(ə)n] *n.* salutation *f.*
salute¹ [səˈluːt] *n.* (*a*) salut *m*, salutation *f*; (*b*) *Mil: Navy:* salut; (*at march past*) **to take the s.,** passer les troupes en revue; (*c*) *Mil: Navy:* **to fire a s.,** tirer une salve; **to fire a s. of ten guns,** saluer de dix coups.
salute² **1.** *v.tr.* saluer (qn). **2.** *v.tr. & i. Mil:* faire un salut, faire le salut militaire.
salvage¹ [ˈsælvidʒ] *n.* **1.** indemnité *f*, prime *f*, de sauvetage; (*paid to salvage tug*) indemnité de remorquage. **2.** sauvetage *m* (d'un navire, etc.); **s. tug,** remorqueur *m* de sauvetage; **s. vessel,** navire *m* de relevage. **3.** objets sauvés (d'un naufrage, d'un incendie). **4.** récupération *f* (de matières pour l'industrie).
salvage² *v.tr.* (*a*) sauver, relever (un navire, etc.); sauver, récupérer (des objets dans un incendie, etc.); (*b*) récupérer (une voiture, etc.); *F:* rattraper (une mayonnaise); **salvaged goods,** matériel récupéré.
salvation [sælˈveiʃ(ə)n] *n.* salut *m*; (*a*) **to work out one's own s.,** travailler à son (propre) salut; **S. Army,** Armée *f* du Salut; (*b*) **you've been my s.,** vous m'avez sauvé.
salvationist [sælˈveiʃ(ə)nist] *n.* salutiste *mf.*
salve¹ [sælv, sɑːv] *n. Pharm:* onguent *m*, pommade *f* (pour les lèvres, etc.).
salve² [sælv] *v.tr.* adoucir, apaiser (les sentiments, l'amour-propre, etc., de qn); **to do sth. to s. one's conscience,** faire qch. par acquit de conscience.
salve³ [ˈsælvi] *n. R.C.Ch:* salvé *m.*
salver [ˈsælvər] *n.* plateau *m* (d'argent, etc.).
salvia [ˈsælviə] *n. Hort:* sauge (ornementale).
salvo [ˈsælvou] *n. Mil: Navy:* salve *f*; **to fire a s.,** tirer une salve; **s. of applause,** salve d'applaudissements.
Sam [sæm] *Pr.n.m.* (*dim.*) Samuel; *F:* **Uncle S.,** l'oncle Sam; les États-Unis.
Samaritan [səˈmærit(ə)n] **1.** *a.* samaritain. **2.** *n.* Samaritain, -aine; *B:* **the good S.,** le bon Samaritain; **to be a good s.,** être charitable; (*telephone service*) **the Samaritans** = S.O.S. Amitié.
samba [ˈsæmbə] *n. Danc:* samba *f.*
same [seim] **1.** *a. & pron.* (*a*) (le, la) même; (les) mêmes; **to repeat the s. words,** répéter les mêmes mots; **at the s. time that . . .,** au moment même où . . .; **he's the s. age as me,** il est du même âge que moi; **in the s. way,** de même, de la même façon; **we are going the s. way,** nous allons dans la même direction; **a Happy New Year to you!—the s. to you!** je vous souhaite une bonne année!—à vous de même! **I should have done the s.,** j'aurais fait de même; j'aurais agi de la même façon; **the very s. thing, one and the s. thing,** une seule et même chose; tout à fait la même chose; **at the s. time,** (i) en même temps; (ii) à la fois; du même coup; **it's the s. everywhere,** il en est de même partout; **it is always, it is no longer, the s. (thing),** c'est toujours, ce n'est plus, la même chose; **it, all that, amounts, comes, to the s. thing,** tout cela revient au même; **it's all the s., it's just the s.,** c'est tout un; *F:* c'est tout comme; **if it's all the s. to you,** si cela ne vous fait rien; si ça vous est égal; **it's much the s.,** c'est à peu près la même chose; (*b*) (*he, she, it, etc.*) **the s.,** celui-là, celle-là; *pl.* ceux-là, celles-là; (*nom.*) il, elle; lui, *pl.* eux; **that s. man is now a millionaire,** ce même homme est maintenant millionnaire; *F:* **the s. again?** encore un (verre de whisky, etc.)? **the s. again!** remettez ça! *P:* **s. here!** et moi aussi! et moi de même! **2.** *adv.* de même; **to think, feel, act, the s.,** penser, sentir, agir, de même; **all the s.,** quand même; tout de même; **when I am away things go on just the s.,** quand je suis absent tout marche comme d'habitude.
sameness [ˈseimnis] *n.* **1.** (*a*) identité *f* (**with,** avec); (*b*) ressemblance *f* (**with,** à). **2.** monotonie *f.*
samovar [ˈsæməvɑːr] *n.* samovar *m.*
sampan [ˈsæmpæn] *n. Nau:* sampan(g) *m.*
sample¹ [ˈsɑːmpl] *n. Com: etc:* échantillon *m* (de tissu, de blé, etc.); prise *f*, prélèvement *m* (de minerai, de sang, etc.); essai *m* (de vin); **up to s.,** pareil, conforme, à l'échantillon; **to take a s. (test),** faire un sondage; **s. book, card,** collection *f*, carte *f*, d'échantillons.
sample² *v.tr.* (*a*) *Com:* prendre, prélever, des échantillons; goûter à, déguster (un vin); (*b*) goûter (un mets, etc.); essayer (un nouveau restaurant, etc.). **sampling** *n.* prise *f* d'échantillons; gustation *f* (d'un mets, etc.); *Com: Ind:* **random s.,** prélèvement *m* d'échantillons au hasard.
sampler [ˈsɑːmplər] *n. Needlew:* modèle *m* de broderie (sur canevas).
samurai [ˈsæmurai] *n. inv.* sam(o)uraï *m.*
sanatorium, *pl.* **-iums, -ia** [sænəˈtɔːriəm, -iəmz, -iə] *n.* **1.** sanatorium *m.* **2.** *Sch:* infirmerie *f.*
sanctification [sæn(k)tifiˈkeiʃ(ə)n] *n.* sanctification *f.*
sanctify [ˈsæŋ(k)tifai] *v.tr.* **1.** sanctifier (qn, qch.); consacrer (un jour, un terrain, etc.). **2. sanctified by time,** consacré par le temps. **sanctified** *a.* (*a*) (*of pers.*) sanctifié, saint; (*of thg*) consacré; (*b*) **s. air,** air confit (en dévotion).
sanctimonious [sæŋ(k)tiˈmouniəs] *a.* d'une piété suffisante; (air) de petit saint. **-ly** *adv.* d'un air de petit saint.
sanction¹ [ˈsæŋ(k)ʃ(ə)n] *n.* **1.** *Jur:* **punitive s.,** sanction pénale; *Pol:* **to impose sanctions on a country,** prendre des sanctions contre un pays. **2.** sanction, autorisation *f*, consentement *m*; **without their s.,** sans leur consentement. **3.** *Hist:* sanction, décret *m.*
sanction² *v.tr.* **1.** *Jur:* sanctionner; attacher des sanctions (pénales) à (une loi, etc.). **2.** (*a*) *Jur:* ratifier (une loi, etc.); (*b*) sanctionner, autoriser (qch.); **sanctioned by usage,** consacré par l'usage.
sanctity [ˈsæŋ(k)titi] *n.* **1.** sainteté *f* (d'une personne, d'une vie, etc.). **2.** caractère sacré (d'un terrain, d'un serment, etc.); inviolabilité *f* (de la vie privée, etc.).
sanctuary [ˈsæŋ(k)tj(u)əri] *n.* **1.** (*a*) sanctuaire *m*, temple *m*; (*b*) sanctuaire, Saint *m* des Saints. **2.** asile (sacré); refuge *m*; **to take s.,** chercher asile. **3.** refuge (d'oiseaux); **wild life s.,** réserve *f* zoologique.
sanctum [ˈsæŋ(k)təm] *n.* **1.** *Rel:* sanctuaire *m.* **2.** sanctuaire; cabinet privé.
sanctus [ˈsæŋ(k)təs] *n. Ecc: Mus:* sanctus *m.*
sand¹ [sænd] *n.* (*a*) sable *m*; **to build on s.,** bâtir sur le sable; **s. castle,** château fort en sable (construit par les enfants sur la plage); **s. dune,** dune *f*; *Meteor:* **s. spout,** trombe *f* de sable; (*b*) **on the sand(s),** (i) sur la plage; (ii) sur un banc de sable; (*d*) *Med:* **urinary s.,** sable, gravier *m*; (*e*) *Ich:* **s. eel,** lançon *m*, ammodyte *f*; **s. flea,** (i) *Ent:* puce pénétrante, chique *f*; (ii) *Crust:*

(*also* **s. hopper**) puce de mer; *Orn:* **s. martin,** hirondelle *f* de rivage.

sand² **1.** *v.tr.* sabler (une allée, etc.); répandre du sable sur (le plancher). **2.** *v.i.* (*of river mouth, etc.*) **to s. up,** s'ensabler. **3.** *v.tr.* sabler, sablonner; *Metalw:* **to s. down,** poncer, sabler (une tôle). **sanding** *n.* **1.** sablage *m* (d'une allée, etc.). **2. s. up,** ensablement *m* (d'un port, etc.). **3.** sablage, sablonnage *m*; nettoyage *m* au sable; **s. down,** ponçage *m*.

sandal ['sænd(ə)l] *n.* sandale *f*.

sandal(wood) ['sænd(ə)l(wud)] *n.* (bois *m* de) santal *m*.

sandbag¹ ['sændbæg] *n.* (*a*) *Fort: etc:* sac *m* à terre; *Aer: Nau:* sac de lest; (*b*) *F:* assommoir *m*; boudin *m*.

sandbag² *v.tr.* **(sandbagged)** (*a*) protéger (un bâtiment, etc.) avec des sacs de terre, de sable; (*b*) assommer (qn) (d'un coup de boudin sur la nuque).

sandbank ['sændbæŋk] *n.* banc *m* de sable.

sandbar ['sændbɑ:r] *n.* ensablement *m* (à l'embouchure d'un fleuve).

sandblast¹ ['sændblɑ:st] *n. Glassm: Metalw: etc:* jet *m* de sable.

sandblast² *v.tr.* passer (une surface) au jet de sable; décaper (une surface); sabler (une surface). **sandblasting** *n.* décapage *m*, décapement *m*, au (jet de) sable; sablage *m* (d'une surface).

sandboy ['sændbɔi] *n.m.* **as jolly, as happy, as a s.,** gai comme un pinson.

sander ['sændər] *n. Tls:* ponceuse *f*.

sandglass ['sændglɑ:s] *n.* sablier *m*.

sandman, *pl.* **-men** ['sændmæn, -men] *n.m.* marchand de sable.

sandpaper¹ ['sændpeipər] *n.* papier *m* de verre.

sandpaper² *v.tr.* poncer, dresser (une surface) au papier de verre.

sandpiper ['sændpaipər] *n. Orn:* bécasseau *m*; chevalier *m*.

sandpit ['sændpit] *n.* (*a*) sablière *f*, sablonnière *f*, carrière *f* à sable; (*b*) tas *m* de sable (pour enfants).

sandshoes ['sændʃu:z] *n.pl. O:* = espadrilles *fpl*.

sandstone ['sændstoun] *n. Geol:* grès *m*.

sandstorm ['sændstɔ:m] *n.* tempête *f* de sable.

sandwich¹ ['sændwitʃ] *n.* **1.** (*a*) sandwich *m*, *pl.* sandwichs, sandwiches; **ham sandwiches,** sandwichs au jambon; **open s.,** canapé *m*, tranche de pain garnie; *U.S:* **hero, submarine, s.,** gros sandwich coupé dans une baguette; (*b*) *Sch:* **s. course,** cours intercalaire; (*c*) **s. man,** homme-sandwich, *pl.* hommes-sandwiches; **s. board,** panneau *m* publicitaire (que porte l'homme-sandwich). **2. the S. Islands,** les îles *fpl* Sandwich.

sandwich² *v.tr.* serrer, intercaler (**between,** entre); **to be sandwiched between two people,** être (pris) en sandwich entre deux personnes.

sandy ['sændi] *a.* **1.** (*of earth, etc.*) sableux, sablonneux; (*of path*) sablé; *Nau:* **s. bottom,** fond *m* de sable. **2.** (*of hair, etc.*) roux pâle *inv*; blond roux *inv*.

sane [sein] *a.* (*of pers.*) sain d'esprit; (*of views, speech, etc.*) raisonnable; sensé; **to be s.,** avoir toute sa raison. **-ly** *adv.* raisonnablement.

sangfroid [sɑ̃:(ŋ)'frwɑ:] *n.* sang-froid *m*.

sanguinary ['sæŋgwinəri] *a.* sanguinaire; (bataille) sanglante.

sanguine ['sæŋgwin] **1.** *a.* (*a*) (*of complexion, etc.*) d'un rouge sanguin; rubicond; (*b*) (*of temperament*) sanguin; (*c*) (*of pers., disposition, etc.*). confiant, optimiste; **to be of a s. disposition,** être porté à l'optimisme. **2.** *n. Art:* (*crayon or drawing*) sanguine *f*. **-ly** *adv.* avec confiance; avec optimisme.

sanitarium [sæni'tɛəriəm] *n. NAm:* = SANATORIUM.

sanitary ['sænit(ə)ri] *a.* hygiénique, sanitaire; **s. inspector,** inspecteur *m* de la salubrité publique; **s. engineer,** technicien *m* en équipement sanitaire.

sanitation [sæni'teiʃ(ə)n] *n.* système *m* sanitaire.

sanity ['sæniti] *n.* **1.** santé *f* d'esprit. **2.** modération *f*; bon sens.

Sanskrit ['sænskrit] *a. & n. Ling:* sanscrit, sanskrit (*m*).

Santa (Claus) ['sæntə(klɔ:z)] *Pr.n.m.* le Père Noël.

Santa Cruz [sæntə'kru:z] *Pr.n. Geog:* **S.C. Island,** l'île *f* Sainte-Croix.

Santo Domingo [sæntoudɔ'miŋgou] *Pr.n. Geog:* Saint-Domingue *m*; la République Dominicaine.

sap¹ [sæp] *n.* **1.** (*a*) *Bot:* sève *f*; (*b*) *Fig:* vigueur *f*, sève. **2.** *F:* niais, -aise; andouille *f*.

sap² *n. Mil: etc:* sape *f*.

sap³ *v.* **(sapped) 1.** *v.tr. & i. Mil: Civ.E:* saper, miner (des fondations, etc.); approcher (d'un endroit) à la sape. **2.** *v.tr.* saper, miner (les fondements d'une doctrine, etc.); **the fever has sapped his strength,** la fièvre l'a miné.

sapless ['sæplis] *a.* (*of plant, wood*) sans sève; desséché; (*of pers., character*) sans vigueur; (*of saying, idea*) insipide, fade.

sapling ['sæpliŋ] *n.* **1.** jeune arbre *m*; plant *m*. **2.** (*a*) jeune homme *m*; (*b*) jeune lévrier *m*.

sapper ['sæpər] *n. Mil:* sapeur *m*; mineur *m*; *F:* **the sappers,** le génie.

sapphic ['sæfik] *a.* (*a*) *Pros:* saphique; (*b*) saphique, lesbien; **s. vice,** saphisme *m*.

sapphire ['sæfaiər] *n.* **1.** *Miner: Lap: Rec:* saphir *m*. **2.** *a. & n.* (couleur de) saphir *inv*.

sappiness ['sæpinis] *n.* **1.** abondance *f* de sève; teneur *f* en sève (du bois). **2.** *F: O:* stupidité *f*, bêtise *f*.

sappy ['sæpi] *a.* **1.** (*a*) (*of tree, etc.*) plein de sève; (*b*) (*of timber*) vert. **2.** *F: O:* bête, stupide.

saraband ['særəbænd] *n. Danc: Mus:* sarabande *f*.

Saracen ['særəs(ə)n] *Hist:* **1.** *a.* sarrasin. **2.** *n.* Sarrasin, -ine.

sarcasm ['sɑ:kæzm] *n.* **1.** langage *m*, ton *m*, sarcastique; esprit *m* sarcastique. **2. (piece of) s.,** sarcasme *m*.

sarcastic [sɑ:'kæstik] *a.* sarcastique; **s. remark,** sarcasme *m*. **-ally** *adv.* d'une manière sarcastique; avec sarcasme.

sarcoma [sɑ:'koumə] *n. Med:* sarcome *m*.

sarcophagus, *pl.* **-phagi** [sɑ:'kɔfəgəs, -fədʒai] *n.* sarcophage *m*.

sardine [sɑ:'di:n] *n. Ich:* sardine *f*; **s. boat,** sardinier *m*.

Sardinia [sɑ:'diniə] *Pr.n. Geog:* Sardaigne *f*.

Sardinian [sɑ:'diniən] **1.** *a. Geog:* sarde. **2.** *n.* (*a*) Sarde *mf*; (*b*) *Ling:* sarde *m*.

sardonic [sɑ:'dɔnik] *a.* (*a*) *Med:* (rire) sardonien; (*b*) (expression, rire) sardonique. **-ally** *adv.* d'une manière sardonique; sardoniquement.

sarge [sɑ:dʒ] *n. F: Mil: Av:* sergent *m*.

sari ['sɑ:ri] *n. Cost:* sari *m*.

sarong [sə'rɔŋ] *n. Cost:* sarong *m*.

sarsaparilla [sɑ:səpə'rilə] *n.* salsepareille *f*.

sartorial [sɑ:'tɔ:riəl] *a.* de tailleur; **s. elegance,** élégance *f* de mise.

sash¹ [sæʃ] *n. Cost:* (*a*) écharpe *f*, ceinture *f* (d'étoffe) (portée par les officiers); (*b*) large ceinture à nœud bouffant.

sash² *n. Const:* châssis *m* mobile, cadre *m* (d'une fenêtre à guillotine); **s. window,** fenêtre *f* à guillotine.

sashay ['sæʃei] *v.i. NAm: F:* flâner, se balader.

sashcord ['sæʃkɔ:d] *n.* corde *f* (d'une fenêtre à guillotine).

sass [sæs] *v.tr. U.S: P:* se payer la tête de (qn); faire l'insolent avec (qn).

Sassenach ['sæsənæk] *n. Scot:* Anglais, -aise.
sassy ['sæsi] *a. U.S: P:* effronté, qui a du culot.
Satan ['seit(ə)n] *Pr.n.m.* Satan.
satanic [sə'tænik] *a.* satanique, diabolique. **-ally** *adv.* sataniquement, diaboliquement.
satanism ['seitənizm] *n.* satanisme *m.*
satanist ['seitənist] *n.* démonolâtre *mf*; sataniste *mf.*
satchel ['sætʃ(ə)l] *n.* sacoche *f*; *Sch:* cartable *m.*
sate [seit] *v.tr.* **1.** assouvir (sa faim, ses passions, etc.); rassasier (qn, la faim). **2.** = SATIATE 1.
sateen [sə'ti:n] *n. Tex:* satinette *f*; satin *m* de coton.
satellite ['sætəlait] *n.* (*a*) *Astr: etc:* satellite *m*; **artificial s.,** satellite artificiel; **manned, unmanned, s.,** satellite habité, non habité; **(tele)communications s.,** satellite de télécommunications; **meteorological, weather, s.,** satellite météorologique; (*b*) **s. (state),** (état *m*) satellite; **s. town,** ville *f* satellite.
satiate ['seiʃieit] *v.tr.* rassasier (qn) jusqu'au dégoût (**with,** de). **satiated** *a.* rassasié (de manger, etc.); gorgé (de plaisirs, etc.).
satiation [seiʃi'eiʃ(ə)n] *n.* **1.** rassasiement *m.* **2.** satiété *f.*
satiety [sə'taiəti] *n.* satiété *f*; **to s.,** (manger) jusqu'à plus faim; (goûter un plaisir) jusqu'à satiété.
satin ['sætin] *n.* **1.** *Tex:* satin *m.* **2.** *Bot:* **s. flower,** (i) lunaire *f*; monnaie *f* du pape; (ii) stellaire *f.* **3. s. finish,** apprêt satiné (du papier, etc.); **s. paper,** papier satiné.
satinette [sæti'net] *n. Tex:* satinette *f.*
satinwood ['sætinwud] *n.* (bois) satiné *m*; bois de satin.
satire ['sætaiər] *n.* satire *f.*
satiric(al) [sə'tirik(l)] *a.* **1.** satirique. **2. satirical,** sarcastique, ironique. **-ally** *adv.* satiriquement.
satirist ['sætirist] *n.* (auteur, écrivain) satirique *m.*
satirize ['sætiraiz] *v.tr.* satiriser; faire la satire de (qch.).
satisfaction [sætis'fækʃ(ə)n] *n.* **1.** (*a*) acquittement *m*, paiement *m* (d'une dette); désintéressement *m* (d'un créancier); accomplissement *m* (d'une condition); (*b*) réparation *f*, expiation *f* (d'une offense); **to demand s. for an insult,** demander raison d'un affront; (*c*) assouvissement *m* (de la faim, d'une passion). **2.** (*a*) satisfaction *f*, contentement *m* (**at, with,** de); **to have the s. of doing sth.,** avoir la satisfaction de faire qch.; (*b*) **it gives me great s. to know that . . .,** je suis heureux d'apprendre que . . ..
satisfactory [sætis'fækt(ə)ri] *a.* **1.** satisfaisant; (élève) qui donne satisfaction; **the result is not very s.,** le résultat laisse à désirer; **to bring negotiations to a s. conclusion,** mener à bien des négociations. **2.** *Theol:* satisfactoire, expiatoire. **-ily** *adv.* d'une manière, de façon, satisfaisante.
satisfy ['sætisfai] *v.tr.* **1.** (*a*) payer, liquider (une dette); exécuter (une promesse); faire droit à (une réclamation); remplir (une condition); désintéresser (ses créanciers); *Mth:* satisfaire à (une équation); (*b*) satisfaire (qn); faire réparation à, satisfaire à (l'honneur). **2.** (*a*) satisfaire, contenter (qn); **to be satisfied with sth.,** (i) être content, satisfait, de qch.; (ii) se contenter de qch.; *Sch:* **to s. the examiners,** être reçu à un examen; (*b*) satisfaire, donner satisfaction à (un désir, un appétit, etc.); **(in order) to s. your curiosity,** pour satisfaire votre curiosité. **3.** convaincre, assurer, satisfaire (qn); **I am satisfied that he was telling the truth,** je suis convaincu qu'il disait la vérité. **satisfied** *a.* (client, etc.) content, satisfait. **satisfying** *a.* satisfaisant; (*of food*) nourrissant; (*of job*) qui donne de la satisfaction.
satsuma [sæt'su:mə] *n.* **s. (orange),** satsuma *f.*
saturate ['sætjəreit] *v.tr.* **1.** imprégner, saturer, tremper (**with,** de); **to become saturated with sth.,** s'imprégner de qch. **2.** *Ch: Ph:* saturer (une solution, etc.). **saturated** *a.* **1.** (terrain, vêtement, etc.) trempé. **2.** *Ch: Ph:* (*of solution, compound, etc.*) saturé. **3.** (*of colour*) riche; non combiné avec le blanc.
saturation [sætjə'reiʃ(ə)n] *n.* **1.** imprégnation *f*; trempage *m.* **2.** *Ch: Ph:* saturation *f*; **s. point,** point *m* de saturation; *Com:* **the market has reached s. point,** le marché est saturé; *Mil:* **s. bombing,** bombardement *m* en masse.
Saturday ['sætədi] *n.* samedi *m*; **he's coming on S.,** il viendra samedi; **he comes on Saturdays,** il vient le samedi; **he comes every S.,** il vient tous les samedis.
Saturn ['sætən] *Pr.n. Astr: Myth:* Saturne *m.*
saturnine ['sætənain] *a.* **1.** (*of pers.*) taciturne, sombre. **2.** saturnin.
satyr ['sætər] *n. Myth: etc:* satyre *m.*
sauce [sɔ:s] *n.* **1.** (*a*) *Cu:* sauce *f*; **tomato s.,** sauce tomate; **white s.,** sauce béchamel; **caper s.,** sauce aux câpres; (*b*) assaisonnement *m*; condiment *m*; *Prov:* **what's s. for the goose is s. for the gander,** ce qui est bon pour l'un l'est aussi pour l'autre. **2.** *F:* impertinence *f*; **what s.! you've got a s.!** quel toupet! quel culot!
sauceboat ['sɔ:sbout] *n.* saucière *f.*
saucepan ['sɔ:spən] *n.* casserole *f*; **double s.,** bain-marie *m*, *pl.* bains-marie.
saucer ['sɔ:sər] *n.* soucoupe *f*; *F:* **flying s.,** soucoupe volante; *F:* **eyes like saucers,** yeux en soucoupe.
sauciness ['sɔ:sinis] *n. F:* (*a*) impertinence *f*; toupet *m*; (*b*) *O:* élégance *f*; chic *m.*
saucy ['sɔ:si] *a. F:* (*a*) impertinent, effronté. (*b*) *O:* **s. little hat,** petit chapeau coquet. **-ily** *adv.* impertinemment; d'un ton, air, effronté.
Saudi ['saudi] **1.** *a.* séoudite, saoudite; **S. Arabia,** Arabie *f* séoudite, saoudite; **S. Arabian,** arabe séoudite, saoudite. **2.** *n.* **S. (Arabian),** Arabe *mf* séoudite, saoudite.
sauerkraut ['sauəkraut] *n. Cu:* choucroute *f.*
sauna ['saunə, 'sɔ:-] *n.* sauna *m.*
saunter[1] ['sɔ:ntər] *n.* **1.** flânerie *f.* **2. at a s.,** (arriver) tout doucement.
saunter[2] *v.i.* **to s. (along),** flâner; se balader; **to s. along, down, the street,** descendre la rue en flânant.
saurian ['sɔ:riən] *a. & n. Rept:* saurien (*m*).
sausage ['sɔsidʒ] *n.* **1.** (*a*) *Cu:* (*fresh*) saucisse *f*; **s. skin,** peau *f* à saucisses; boyau *m*; **s. roll** = friand *m*; (*b*) (*preserved, hard, dry*) saucisson *m*; (*c*) *P:* **not a s.,** nib de nib; que dalle. **2.** *F:* **s. dog,** teckel *m.*
sausagemeat ['sɔsidʒmi:t] *n.* chair *f* à saucisse.
sauté[1] ['souti] *a. & n. Cu:* sauté (*m*).
sauté[2] *v.tr. Cu:* (faire) sauter (des pommes de terre).
savage[1] ['sævidʒ] **1.** *a.* (*a*) (*of race, custom, etc.*) sauvage, barbare; (*b*) (animal, coup) féroce; (coup) brutal, -aux; (*c*) *F:* (*of pers.*) en rage, en colère; **to make a s. attack on s.o.,** s'attaquer férocement à qn. **2.** *n.* sauvage *mf.* **-ly** *adv.* sauvagement, férocement.
savage[2] *v.tr.* (*a*) (*of animal*) attaquer, mordre (qn, les autres bêtes); (*b*) *F:* (*of pers.*) attaquer (qn) du bec et des ongles.
savageness ['sævidʒnis], **savagery** ['sævidʒ(ə)ri] *n.* **1.** sauvagerie *f*, barbarie *f* (d'une race, d'une coutume, etc.). **2.** férocité *f* (d'un animal, d'un coup); brutalité *f* (d'un coup).
savanna(h) [sə'vænə] *n. Geog:* savane *f.*
save[1] [seiv] *n.* **1.** *F:* économie *f*; **a great s. in heating,** une grande économie de chauffage. **2.** *Fb:* arrêt *m* (du ballon) (par le gardien).
save[2] *v.tr.* **1.** (*a*) sauver (qn, une bête); **to s. s.o.'s life;** sauver la vie à, de, qn; **the doctors could not s. him,** les médecins étaient incapables de le sauver; **to s. s.o. from falling,** empêcher qn de tomber; *Fb: etc:* **to s. a goal,** arrêter le ballon; *Sp:* **to s. the game,** éviter la défaite; (*b*) *Theol:* **to s. one's soul,** sauver son âme;

(*c*) **to s. the situation,** se montrer à la hauteur des circonstances; **(God) s. me from my friends!** Dieu me protège contre mes amis! **God save the King, the Queen!** Dieu sauve le Roi, la Reine! **2.** (*a*) mettre (qch.) de côté; **s. a dance for me,** réservez-moi une danse; (*b*) économiser, épargner, mettre de côté (de l'argent); **to s. on sth.,** économiser sur qch; *v.i.* **to s. (up),** faire des économies; épargner son argent. **3.** ménager (ses vêtements, etc.); économiser (le travail, etc.); éviter (une dépense, de la peine, etc.); ménager (de l'espace); **to s. time,** gagner du temps; **I am saving my strength,** je me ménage; je ménage mes forces; **I might as well have saved my breath,** j'avais beau parler; **to s. oneself for sth.,** se réserver pour qch. **4.** (*a*) **to s. s.o. sth.,** éviter, épargner, qch. à qn; **this has saved him a great deal of expense, of trouble,** cela lui a évité beaucoup de dépense, de peine; **to s. s.o. the trouble of doing sth.,** épargner à qn la peine de faire qch.; (*b*) **to s. s.o. from sth., from doing sth.,** épargner qch. à qn; épargner à qn la peine de faire qch. **saving 1.** *a.* (*a*) (i) qui sauve; qui protège; (ii) (qualité, etc.) qui rachète des défauts; (*b*) (i) (*of pers.*) économe, ménager (**of,** de); (*of system, etc.*) économique; (*c*) **s. clause,** clause *f* de sauvegarde; réservation *f.* **2.** *A:* (*a*) *prep. & conj.* = SAVE³; (*b*) *prep.* sauf; **s. your presence,** sauf votre respect. **3.** *n.* (*a*) (i) délivrance *f*; salut *m* (de qn, des âmes, des vies); **this was the s. of him,** cela a été son salut; (ii) sauvetage *m*; (iii) protection *f* (de qn, qch.); (*b*) (i) économie *f*, épargne *f*; (ii) **savings,** économies; *Pol.Ec:* dépôts *mpl* d'épargne; **to live on one's savings,** vivre de ses épargnes; **savings account,** compte *m* de dépôt; **(National) Savings Bank** = Caisse (Nationale) d'Épargne; **(National) savings certificate** = bon *m* d'Épargne.

save³ 1. *prep. A: & Lit:* sauf, excepté; à l'exception de. **2.** *conj.phr.* **s. that . . .,** sauf que . . ., excepté que . . ..

saveloy ['sævəlɔi] *n. Comest:* cervelas *m.*

saver ['seivər] *n.* **1.** (*a*) sauveur *m*, libérateur, -trice (de sa patrie, etc.); (*b*) sauveteur *m* (de vie, de biens). **2.** appareil économiseur. **3.** épargnant, -ante.

saviour, *NAm:* **savior** ['seivjər] *n.* sauveur *m*; *Theol:* **Our S.,** Notre Sauveur.

savory ['seivəri] *n. Bot: Cu:* sarriette *f.*

savour¹, *NAm:* **savor¹** ['seivər] *n.* saveur *f*, goût *m* (d'un mets, etc.).

savour², *NAm:* **savor². 1.** *v.tr.* (*of pers.*) savourer (un mets, etc.). **2.** *v.i.* (*of thg*) **to s. of sth.,** sentir qch.; tenir de qch.

savoury, *NAm:* **savory** ['seivəri] **1.** *a.* (*a*) (goût, mets) savoureux, appétissant; *F:* **he looked even less s. than the majority of tramps,** il avait l'air encore plus répugnant que la plupart des chemineaux; (*b*) (mets) piquant ou salé; **s. omelette,** omelette *f* aux fine herbes, etc. **2.** *n.* entremets non sucré.

Savoy [sə'vɔi] **1.** *Pr.n. Geog:* Savoie *f.* **2.** *n.* **s. (cabbage),** chou, *pl.* choux, frisé de Milan.

savvy¹ ['sævi] *n. P:* jugeotte *f.*

savvy² *v.tr. P: O:* comprendre; **savvy?** tu piges?

saw¹ [sɔː] *n. Tls:* scie *f*; **metal s.,** scie à métaux; **circular s.,** scie circulaire; **s. blade,** lame *f*, de scie; **s. cut,** trait *m* de scie; **s. tooth,** dent *f* de scie; **s.-tooth(ed) roof,** (toit *m* en) shed (*m*).

saw² *v.tr.* (*p.t.* **sawed;** *p.p.* **sawn; sawed)** scier (le bois, etc.); sciotter (la pierre, le marbre); **to s. off,** comper, enlever, (un morceau) à la scie; **to s. up wood,** débiter du bois; **sawn-off shotgun,** carabine *f* à canon tronçonné. **sawing** *n.* sciage *m* (du bois); **s. (up),** débitage *m* (du bois).

saw³ *n.* adage *m*; proverbe *m*; dicton *m.*

sawbones ['sɔːbounz] *n. F: O:* chirurgien *m*, carabin *m.*

sawbuck ['sɔːbʌk] *n. NAm:* **1.** = SAWHORSE. **2.** *F:* billet *m* de dix dollars.

sawdust ['sɔːdʌst] *n.* sciure *f* (de bois).

sawfish ['sɔːfiʃ] *n. Ich:* (posisson *m*) scie (*f*).

sawhorse ['sɔːhɔːs] *n.* chevalet *m* de sciage, chèvre *f.*

sawmill ['sɔːmil] *b.* scierie *f.*

sawyer ['sɔːjər] *n.* scieur *m* (de long).

sax [sæks] *n. Mus: F:* saxo(phone) *m.*

saxe [sæks] *a. & n.* **s. blue,** bleu (*m*) de Saxe.

saxifrage ['sæksifreidʒ] *n. Bot:* saxifrage *f.*

Saxon ['sæks(ə)n] **1.** *a. Geog: etc:* saxon; saxonique; **S. architecture,** architecture anglaise préromane. **2.** *n.* (*a*) Saxon, -onne; (*b*) *Ling:* saxon *m.*

Saxony ['sæksəni] *Pr.n. Geog:* Saxe *f.*

saxophone ['sæksəfoun] *n. Mus:* saxophone *m.*

saxophonist [sæk'sɔfənist] *n. Mus:* saxophoniste *mf.*

say¹ [sei] *n.* dire *m*, parole *f*, mot *m*; **to have one's s.,** dire ce qu'on a à dire; son mot; **let me have my s.,** laissez-moi parler; **I have no s. in the matter,** je n'ai pas voix au chapitre.

say² *v.tr.* (*p.t. & p.p.* **said** [sed] *3rd sg. pr. ind.* **says** [sez]) dire. **1.** (*a*) (*utter*) **to s. a word,** dire un mot; **you have only to s. the word,** vous n'avez qu'à le dire; **it's for him, not for him, to s.,** c'est, ce n'est pas, à lui de décider; *Tp:* **who shall I s. called, rang?** c'est de la part de qui? **to s. sth. again,** répéter, redire, qch.; **I'm not saying,** je ne dis rien; **I can't, couldn't, s.,** je ne sais pas; je n'en sais rien; **it goes without saying that . . .,** il va de soi, cela va sans dire, que . . .; **what d'you s. to that?** qu'en dites-vous, pensez-vous? **what did you s.?** (i) qu'avez-vous dit? (ii) pardon? **whatever he may s.,** quoi qu'il en ait; quoi qu'il dise; **to s. yes, no,** dire (que) oui, (que) non; *F:* **I wouldn't s. no to a glass of beer,** je boirais bien, volontiers, un verre de bière; **what do you s. to a drink?** si on prenait un verre? *P:* **says you!** que tu dis! (*b*) **he said that you were here,** il a dit que vous étiez ici; **as I said in my letter,** comme je vous l'ai dit dans ma lettre; **the Bible says, it says in the Bible, that . . .,** comme on lit dans la Bible . . .; **the church clock says ten,** le cadran de l'église marque dix heures; **let it be said,** soit dit en passant; **you don't mean to s. he's 86,** vous n'allez pas me dire qu'il a 86 ans; **I mean to s.!** tout de même! quand même! **as they s., as people s.,** comme on dit; **as one might s.,** comme qui dirait; **one might as well s. . . .,** autant dire . . .; **I must s. . . .,** j'avoue . . ., je dois dire . . .; **that is to s.,** c'est-à-dire; **have you said anything about it to him?** lui en avez-vous parlé? **the less said the better, least said soonest mended,** moins nous parlerons, mieux cela vaudra; **he knows no English, to s. nothing of French,** il ne sait pas l'anglais, sans parler du français; **he has very little to s. for himself,** il est peu communicatif; **what have you to s. for yourself?** eh bien, expliquez-vous! **there is much to be said for beginning now,** il y a de bonnes raisons pour s'y mettre dès maintenant; *F:* **you don't s. (so)!** pas possible! vraiment? ça alors! **you can s. that again! you've said it!** vous l'avez dit! bien vrai! (*c*) (*report*) **they s. that . . ., it is said that . . .,** on dit que . . .; on prétend que . . .; **I've heard it said that . . .,** j'ai entendu dire que . . .; **he is said to be rich,** on le dit riche; on dit qu'il est riche; (*d*) (*hold an opinion*) **anyone would s. that he was asleep,** on dirait qu'il dort; **I should s. not,** je ne crois pas; je crois que non; **it is difficult to s. (when, where, which, etc.),** il est difficile de dire, on ne sait pas (quand, où, quel, etc.); **didn't I s. so!** je vous l'avais bien dit! (*e*) **let us, shall we, shall I, s.,** disons; **if I had, s., £10,000 a year,** si j'avais, mettons £10,000 par an: (*f*) (*exclamatory*) **I s.,** *NAm:* **s.!** dites donc! **s., I've got an idea,** écoutez donc, j'ai une idée; (*expressing surprise*)

I s.! pas possible! fichtre! **I'll s.! I should s. so!** et comment donc! **I should s. not!** jamais de la vie! **2.** dire, réciter (une prière, etc.); faire (ses prières); **to s. mass,** dire la messe; **to s. grace,** dire le bénédicité. **saying** *n.* (*a*) dit *m* (de qn); (*b*) (*popular*) **s.,** adage *m*, proverbe *m*; diction *m*; **as the s. goes,** comme dit le proverbe; comme on dit.

scab¹ [skæb] *n.* **1.** *Vet:* gale *f.* **2.** (*on wound*) croûte *f*, escarre *f.* **3.** *Ind: P:* (*pers.*) renard *m*, jaune *m.*

scab², *v.i.* **(scabbed) 1.** (*of wound*) **to s. (over),** former une croûte. **2.** *P:* supplanter les grévistes; trahir ses camarades.

scabbard ['skæbəd] *n.* fourreau *m* (d'une épée); gaine *f* (d'un poignard, etc.).

scabby ['skæbi] *a.* **1.** *Vet:* (*of sheep, etc.*) galeux. **2.** (*of sore, etc.*) croûteux, scabieux.

scabies ['skeib(i)i:z] *n. Med:* gale *f.*

scabious ['skeibiəs] *n. Bot:* scabieuse *f.*

scabrous ['skeibrəs] *a.* **1.** (*of surface, etc.*) rugueux, raboteux. **2.** (*of topic, tale, etc.*) scabreux, risqué.

scads [skædz] *n.pl. NAm: F:* grande quantité **(of,** de).

scaffold ['skæf(ə)ld] *n.* **1.** échafaud *m* (pour exécutions); **to go to the s.,** monter à, sur, l'échafaud. **2.** *Const:* échafaudage *m.*

scaffolding ['skæʃəldiŋ] *n.* échafaudage *m.*

scalawag ['skæləwæg] *n. esp. NAm:* = SCALLYWAG.

scald¹ [skɔ:ld] *n.* échaudure *f* (sur la main, etc.).

scald² *v.tr.* **1.** échauder, ébouillanter (la main, etc.). **2.** (*a*) échauder (un porc, etc.); blanchir (un chou, etc.); échauder, ébouillanter (des fruits, etc., pour les peler); (*b*) faire chauffer (le lait, etc.) juste au-dessous du point d'ébullition; (*c*) échauder, ébouillanter (un récipient). **scalding 1.** *a.* (*of liquid*) **s. (hot),** brûlant, tout bouillant; *Lit:* **s. tears,** larmes brûlantes. **2.** (*a*) échaudage *m*, ébouillantage *m*; (*b*) *Cu:* (i) blanchiment *m* (de la viande, etc.); ébouillantage (de légumes, etc.); (ii) cuisson *f* (du lait, etc.) juste au-dessous du point d'ébullition.

scale¹ [skeil] *n.* **1.** (*on fish, reptile, bud, etc.*) écaille *f*; *Med:* (*on skin*) écaille, squame *f.* **2.** *Metalw:* (*a*) barbure *f* (de pièce coulée); (*b*) *coll.* **scale(s),** écailles de fer; battitures *fpl.* **3.** incrustation *f*, dépôt *m*; tartre *m* (des dents); (*on copper, iron, etc.*) oxyde *m*; **boiler s.,** tartre; **s. remover,** détartrant *m.*

scale² **1.** *v.tr.* (*a*) écailler (un poisson); (*b*) détartrer, (les dents); désincruster, détartrer (une chaudière, un tube). **2.** *v.i.* (*a*) **to s. (off),** écailler; (*of skin*) se desquamer; (*of paint*) s'effeuiller; (*of wall, ceiling, etc.*) se déplâtrer; (*b*) (*of boiler, etc.*) s'entartrer, s'incruster. **scaling** *n.* **1.** (*a*) écaillage *m* (d'un poisson, etc.); (*b*) détartrage *m* (des dents); désincrustation *f*, détartrage (d'une chaudière, des tubes). **2.** *Mch:* formation *f* du tartre; entartrage *m* (d'une chaudière).

scale³ *n.* (*a*) **s. (pan),** plateau *m*, plat *m* (de balance); (*deep*) bassin *m*; **to tip, turn, the scale(s) at 100 kilos,** peser un peu plus de 100 kilos; **to turn the scale(s),** emporter, faire pencher, la balance; (*b*) **(pair of) scales,** balance; **platform scales,** bascule *f*; **letter scales,** pèse-lettres *m inv*; **bathroom scales,** pèse-personne *m*, *pl.* pèse-personnes; **baby scales,** pèse-bébé *m*, *pl.* pèse-bébés; (*c*) *Astr:* **the Scales,** la Balance.

scale⁴ *v.i.* **to s. six kilos,** peser six kilos.

scale⁵ *n.* (*a*) échelle (de thermomètre, de baromètre, etc.); graduation(s) *f*(*pl*) (d'un thermomètre, d'un système numérique, etc.); série *f* (de nombres, etc.); échelle, barème *m* (de traitements); échelle, gamme *f* (de prix); **sliding s.,** échelle mobile (des salaires, des prix); **sliding s. tariff,** tarif dégressif; **at the top of the (social) s.,** en haut, au sommet, de l'échelle (sociale); (*b*) cadran gradué; (*c*) règle (divisée); (*d*) échelle (d'une carte, etc.); **small-s., large-s., map,** carte à petite, à grande, échelle; **to draw sth. to scale,** dessiner qch. à l'échelle; **s. model,** maquette *f*, modèle réduit; **on a national s.,** à l'échelle nationale; **the s. of the disaster,** l'étendue *f* du sinistre; (*e*) *Mus:* gamme *f*; **major, minor, s.,** gamme majeure, mineure; **to practise scales,** faire des gammes; (*f*) échelle, gamme (de couleurs).

scale⁶ *v.tr.* **1.** escalader (un mur, etc.); faire l'ascension (d'une montagne). **2. to s. down,** établir (un dessin) à une échelle réduite; **to s. up, down,** augmenter, réduire (des prix, etc.) selon une échelle mobile; **to s. down production,** ralentir la production. **scaling** *n.* **1.** escalade *f.* **2.** graduation *f* (des prix, des salaires, etc.); **s. up, down,** augmentation *f*, réduction *f*, à l'échelle.

scallion ['skælyən] *n. Bot:* échalote *f.*

scallop¹ ['skɔləp] *n.* **1.** (*a*) *Moll:* **s. (shell),** peigne *m*, coquille *f* Saint-Jacques; (*b*) *Cu:* coquille Saint-Jacques; (*c*) *Cu:* escalope *f* (de veau, etc.). **2.** *Needlew: etc:* feston *m*, dentelure *f.*

scallop² *v.tr.* **1.** *Cu:* faire cuire (du poisson, etc.) en coquille(s). **2.** *Needlew:* festonner; découper, denteler; **scalloped handkerchief,** mouchoir échancré.

scallywag ['skæliwæg] *n. F:* propre à rien *m*; (*of child*) **little s.,** petit coquin.

scalp¹ [skælp] *n.* **1.** *Anat:* cuir chevelu (de la tête). **2.** *NAm:* scalp(e) *m*; **to be out for scalps,** (i) partir en guerre; (ii) *F:* chercher qui démolir, qui éreinter.

scalp² *v.tr.* (*a*) (*of NAm: Indians*) scalper (un ennemi); (*b*) *F: O:* (*of critic*) éreinter (un auteur, un livre).

scalpel ['skælp(ə)l] *n. Surg:* scalpel *m.*

scaly ['skeili] *a.* (*a*) (*of fish, skins, etc.*) écailleux, squameux; (*b*) (*of slate, etc.*) écailleux; (*of metal*) paillé, lamelleux, lamellé; (*of boiler*) tartreux.

scamp¹ [skæmp] *n.* **(a)** vaurien, -ienne; fripouille *f*; (*b*) *F:* (*of child*) **little s.,** petit coquin.

scamp² *v.t. F:* bâcler, bousiller (un travail).

scamper¹ ['skæmpər] *n.* course *f* (i) folâtre, allègre, (ii) rapide.

scamper² *v.i.* (*a*) courir allégrement, d'une manière folâtre; (*b*) **to s. away, off,** détaler, décamper.

scampi ['skæmpi] *n.pl. Cu:* grosses crevettes.

scan¹ [skæn] *n.* **1.** regard scrutateur. **2.** *Rad: Elcs: etc:* balayage *m.*

scan² *v.tr.* **(scanned) 1.** *Pros:* scander, mesurer (des vers); **this line doesn't s.,** ce vers est faux. **2.** (*a*) examiner minutieusement; sonder, scruter (l'horizon); (*b*) jeter un coup d'œil sur (qch.); feuilleter, parcourir (un livre, etc.); (*c*) *Rad: Elcs: etc:* balayer, explorer (l'image à transmettre, la piste sonore). **scanning** *n.* **1.** scansion *f* (de vers). **2.** (*a*) examen minutieux; (*b*) *T.V: etc:* balayage *m*, exploration *f* (de l'image à transmettre, de la piste sonore); **radar s.,** exploration, balayage, radar; (*c*) *Cmptr:* analyse *f*, scrutation *f.*

scandal ['skænd(ə)l] *n.* **1.** scandale *m*; **it's a s.,** c'est un scandale; **to create a s.,** faire un scandale; causer du scandale. **2.** médisance *f.* **3.** *Jur:* allégations *fpl* diffamatoires.

scandalize ['skændəlaiz] *v.tr.* scandaliser, choquer, offusquer (qn).

scandalmonger ['skænd(ə)lmʌŋgər] *n.* cancanier, -ière; colporteur, -euse, d'histoires scandaleuses.

scandalous ['skændələs] *a.* **1.** (*of conduct, event, etc.*) scandaleux; **it's s.!** c'est scandaleux! **2.** *Jur:* (*of statement, writing*) diffamatoire, calomnieux. **-ly** *adv.* scandaleusement.

Scandinavia [skændi'neiviə] *Pr.n.* Scandinavie *f.*

Scandinavian [skændi'neiviən] **1.** *a.* scandinave. **2.** *n.* Scandinave *mf.*

scanner ['skænər] *n.* (*a*) **radar s.,** explorateur *m*, balayeur *m*, radar; antenne *f* (de) radar; (*b*) *Cmptr:*

visual, optical, s., lecteur *m*, liseur *m*, optique.
scansion [ˈskænʃ(ə)n] *n. Pros:* scansion *f*.
scant [skænt] *a.* insuffisant, peu abondant; (végétation) pauvre.
scantiness [ˈskæntinis] *n.* insuffisance *f* (de provisions, etc.); pauvreté *f* (de la végétation); étroitesse *f* (d'un vêtement).
scanty [ˈskænti] *a.* (*of supply, etc.*) insuffisant, à peine suffisant; peu abondant; (*of garment, etc.*) étriqué; **s. meal,** maigre repas. **-ily** *adv.* insuffisamment; peu abondamment; **s. dressed,** à peine vêtu.
scapegoat [ˈskeipgout] *n.* bouc *m* émissaire; souffre-douleur *m inv*.
scapegrace [ˈskeipgreis] *n. O:* **1.** vaurien, -ienne; garnement *m*. **2.** (*child*) petit garnement.
scapula, *pl.* **-ae** [ˈskæpjulə, -iː] *n. Anat:* scapula *f*.
scapular [ˈskæpjulər] *a. Anat: etc:* scapulaire.
scar¹ [skɑːr] *n.* **1.** cicatrice *f*; (*on face*) balafre *f*; **s. tissue,** tissu cicatriciel. **2.** *Bot:* cicatrice, hile *m*.
scar² *v.tr.* (**scarred**) marquer (le visage, etc.) d'une cicatrice; balafrer (le visage); **to be scarred,** porter des cicatrices; (*of country, etc.*) **war-scarred,** dévasté par la guerre.
scar³ *n.* (*in mountain range, etc.*) rocher escarpé.
scarab [ˈskærəb] *n. Ent: Lap:* scarabée *m*.
scarce [ˈskɛəs] **1.** *a.* (*of commodities*) rare, peu abondant; *F:* **to make oneself s.,** s'éclipser, s'esquiver. **2.** *adv. A: & Lit:* à peine; guère. **-ly** *adv.* **1.** à peine; guère; **I have s. any left,** il ne m'en reste presque plus; **she could s. speak,** c'est à peine si elle pouvait parler; **s. ever,** presque jamais; **he had s. come in when the telephone rang,** à peine était-il rentré que le téléphone a sonné. **2.** (*expressing incredulity*) sûrement pas!
scarceness [ˈskɛəsnis], **scarcity** [ˈskɛəsiti] *n.* rareté *f*; manque *m*, disette *f* (de qch.).
scare¹ [ˈskɛər] *n.* panique *f*, alarme *f*; *F:* **you gave me an awful s.,** vous m'avez fait rudement peur.
scare² **1.** *v.tr.* effrayer, effarer, alarmer; faire peur à (qn); **to s. away,** effaroucher (le gibier). **2.** *v.i.* s'effrayer, s'alarmer; **I don't s. easily,** je ne m'effraie pas facilement, pour rien. **scared** *a.* apeuré, épeuré; (regard) effaré; (air) épouvanté; **to be s. to death, out of one's wits,** *F:* **to be s. stiff,** avoir une peur bleue.
scarecrow [ˈskɛəkrou] *Agr:* épouvantail *m*; *F:* (*of pers.*) (i) épouvantail; (ii) grand escogriffe; **to be dressed like a s.,** être mis à faire peur.
scaremonger [ˈskɛəmʌŋgər] *n.* alarmiste *mf*.
scarf¹, *pl.* **scarfs, scarves** [skɑːf(s), skɑːvz] *n.* écharpe *f*; cache-col *m*, *pl.* cache-col(s); cache-nez *m inv.*; (*in silk*) foulard *m*.
scarf² *n.* **s. (joint),** assemblage *m* à mi-bois; enture *f*, empatture *f*.
scarface [ˈskɑːfeis] *n.* balafré *m*.
scarification [skærifiˈkeiʃ(ə)n] *n.* scarification *f*.
scarify [ˈskærifai] *v.tr.* scarifier (la peau, le sol).
scarlatina [skɑːləˈtiːnə] *n. Med:* scarlatine *f*.
scarlet [ˈskɑːlət] *a. & n.* écarlate (*f*); **to blush, go, s.,** devenir cramoisi; *Bot:* **s. pimpernel,** mouron *m* rouge; **s. runner,** haricot *m* d'Espagne; *Med:* **s. fever,** scarlatine *f*; *R.C.Ch:* **s. hat,** chapeau *m* de cardinal.
scarp [skɑːp] *n.* **1.** *Fort:* escarpe *f*. **2.** escarpement *m* (d'une colline).
scarper [ˈskɑːpə] *v.i. P:* se tirer, déguerpir.
scary [ˈskɛəri] *a. U.S: F:* **1.** redoutable. **2.** timide.
scat [skæt] *int. F:* filez! fichez le camp!
scathing [ˈskeiðiŋ] *a.* (*of remark, sarcasm, etc.*) acerbe, mordant, cinglant, caustique. **-ly** *adv.* d'une manière acerbe, caustique; d'un ton cinglant.
scatological [skætəˈlɔdʒik(ə)l] *a.* scatologique.
scatology [skəˈtɔlədʒi] *n.* scatologie *f*.
scatter¹ [ˈskætər] *n.* (*of shot, etc.*) éparpillement *m*; dispersion *f*; **s. cushions,** petits coussins placés çà et là dans une pièce; **s. rug,** petit tapis; descente *f* de lit.
scatter² **1.** *v.tr.* (*a*) disperser (une armée, etc.); dissiper (des nuages, etc.); égailler, faire envoler (des oiseaux); (*b*) éparpiller (des feuilles, des papiers, etc.); semer (des graines) à la volée; *Ph:* (*of surface*) diffuser (la lumiére); **scattered light,** lumière diffuse; **scattered over the floor,** éparpillés sur le plancher. **2.** *v.i.* (*of crowd, etc.*) se disperser; (*of birds, etc.*) s'égailler; (*of army*) se débander; (*of clouds, etc.*) se dissiper; (*of shot*) s'éparpiller. **scattering** *n.* **1.** dispersion *f* (d'une armée, etc.); éparpillement *m* (de feuilles, etc.); diffusion *f* (de la lumière). **2.** petit nombre; petite quantité; **he only has a s. of followers,** ses adhérents sont peu nombreux.
scatterbrain [ˈskætəbrein], *n. F:* étourdi, -ie; écervelé, -ée.
scatterbrained [ˈskætəbreind] *a. F:* étourdi, écervelé.
scattiness [ˈskætinis] *n.* (*a*) étourderie *f*; (*b*) loufoquerie *f*.
scatty [ˈskæti] *a. F:* (*a*) étourdi, écervelé; (*b*) farfelu, loufoque.
scavenge [ˈskævindʒ] **1.** *v.tr.* (*a*) *A:* ébouer (les rues, etc.); (*b*) *I.C.E:* balayer, refouler (les gaz brûlés). **2.** *v.i.* fouiller dans les ordures. **scavenging** *n.* **1.** *A:* ébouage *m* (des rues). **2.** fouillage *m* (dans les ordures).
scavenger [ˈskævindʒər] *n.* **1.** (*a*) *A:* boueur *m*; (*b*) (*pers., animal*) fouilleur, -euse, d'ordures; animal *m* nécrophage.
scenario [siˈnɑːriou] *n. Th: etc:* scénario *m*.
scene [siːn] *n.* **1.** (*a*) *Th:* (*place of action*) scène; **change of s.,** changement *m* de décor; **the s. is set in London,** l'action *f* se passe à Londres; (*b*) théâtre *m*, lieu *m* (d'un événement); **the political s.,** la scène politique; **a change of s. would do him good,** un changement d'air lui ferait du bien; **the s. of the crime,** le(s) lieu(x) du crime; *F:* **it's not my s.,** ce n'est pas mon genre. **2.** (*a*) *Th:* (*subdivision of play*) scène; **act three, s. two,** deuxième scène du troisième acte; (*b*) scène, spectacle *m*; **it was a painful s.,** c'était une scène pénible. **3.** (*a*) *Th:* **(set) s.,** décor *m*; **scenes painted by . . .,** décors par . . .; **behind the scenes,** (i) dans les coulisses; (ii) *Fig:* dans la coulisse; (*b*) vue *f*; **the s. from the window,** la vue de la fenêtre. **4.** *F:* **now don't make a s.!** ne fais pas une scène!
scenery [ˈsiːnəri] *n.* **1.** (*a*) *Th:* decors *mpl*; (mise *f* en) scène *f*; (*b*) *F:* **you need a change of s.,** il vous faut du changement. **2.** paysage *m*; vue *f*.
sceneshifter [ˈsiːnʃiftər] *n. Th:* machiniste *m*.
scenic [ˈsiːnik] *a.* **1.** (*of performance, etc.*) scénique; théâtral, -aux. **2.** (*a*) (paysage) pittoresque; *U.S:* **s. road,** route *f* touristique; **area of great s. beauty,** région *f* qui offre de très beaux panoramas; (*b*) *O:* (*at fair*) **s. railway,** montagnes *fpl* russes.
scent¹ [sent] *n.* **1.** (*a*) parfum *m*, senteur *f*; odeur *f* agréable (des fleurs, etc.); (*b*) **bottles of s.,** flacon *m* de parfum. **2.** (*a*) *Ven:* fumet *m*, vent *m* (de la bête); **s. gland, organ,** glande *f* à sécrétion odoriférante; (*b*) *Ven:* piste *f*, voie *f*, trace *f*; (*of pack*) **to pick up the s.,** empaumer, assentir, la voie; **to be on the right s.,** être sur la piste; **to lose, be thrown off, the s.,** perdre la trace; **to throw the police off the s.,** dérouter la police. **3.** odorat *m*, flair *m* (d'un chien).
scent² *v.tr.* **1.** (*of hounds, etc.*) **to s. (out) game,** flairer, sentir, le gibier; **keen-scented dog,** chien *m* au nez fin. **2.** (*a*) (*of flower, etc.*) parfumer, embaumer (l'air, etc); (*b*) **to s. sth. with sth.,** parfumer, imprégner, qch. de qch.; **scented soap,** savon parfumé.
scentless [ˈsentlis] *a.* (fleur) inodore, sans odeur.
sceptic, *NAm:* **skeptic** [ˈskeptik] *n.* sceptique *mf*.

sceptical, *NAm:* **skeptical** ['skeptik(ə)l] *a.* sceptique. **-ally** *adv.* sceptiquement.
scepticism, *NAm:* **skepticism** ['skeptisizm] *n.* scepticisme *m.*
sceptre, *NAm:* **scepter** ['septər] *n.* sceptre *m.*
schedule¹ ['ʃedju:l, *NAm:* 'skedju:l] *n.* **1.** *Jur:* annexe *f* (à une loi, aux statuts d'une société, etc.). **2.** (*a*) *Com:* nomenclature *f* (des pièces, etc.); inventaire *m* (des machines); barème *m* (des prix); (*b*) *Adm:* cédule *f* (d'impôts). **3.** (*a*) plan *m* (d'exécution d'un travail); **to be behind, ahead of, s.,** être en retard, en avance, sur les prévisions; **everything went off according to s.,** tout a marché selon les prévisions; **I work to a very tight s.,** mon temps est très minuté; (*b*) *Rail: etc:* horaire *m;* **on s.,** (train) à l'heure.
schedule² *v.tr.* **1.** *Jur:* ajouter (un article) comme annexe (à une loi, etc.). **2.** inscrire (un article, etc.) sur une liste, sur l'inventaire; **scheduled prices,** prix selon le tarif. **3.** (*a*) dresser un plan, un programme, de (qch.); **the mayor is scheduled to make a speech,** le maire doit prononcer un discours; (*b*) inscrire (un train) à l'horaire; **to arrive at the scheduled time,** arriver à l'heure indiquée; **scheduled services,** services réguliers. **4. to s. as an ancient monument,** classer (comme) monument historique.
schema, *pl.* **-ata** ['ski:mə, -ətə] *n.* schéma *m.*
schematic [ski'mætik] *a.* schématique.
scheme¹ [ski:m] *n.* **1.** (*a*) arrangement *m,* combinaison *f;* **colour s.,** combinaison de(s) couleurs; coloris *m;* (*b*) système *m.* **2.** résumé *m,* exposé *m* (d'un sujet d'étude); plan *m* (d'un ouvrage littéraire). **3.** (*a*) plan, projet *m;* étude *f;* (*b*) *Pej:* machination *f,* intrigue *f;* **the best laid schemes,** les combinaisons les mieux étudiées.
scheme² **1.** *v.i.* intriguer. **2.** *v.tr. O:* machiner, combiner (une conspiration). **scheming 1.** *a.* intrigant, tripoteur. **2.** *n.* machinations *fpl,* intrigues *fpl.*
schemer ['ski:mər] *n. Pej:* intrigant, -ante; tripoteur, -euse.
scherzo ['skɛətsou], *s. Mus:* scherzo *m.*
schism ['s(k)izm] *n.* schisme *m.*
schismatic [s(k)iz'mætik] *a. & n.* schismatique (*mf*).
schist [ʃist] *n. Miner:* schiste *m;* **mica s.,** micaschiste *m.*
schizo ['skitsou] *a. & n. F:* schizophrène (*mf*).
schizoid ['skitsɔid] *a. & n. Psy:* schizoïde (*mf*).
schizophrenia [skitsou'fri:niə] *n. Psy:* schizophrénie *f.*
schizophrenic [skitsou'fri:nik] *a. & n. Psy:* schizophrène (*mf*), schizophrénique (*mf*).
schmal(t)z [ʃmɔ(:)lts] *n. F:* sensiblerie *f,* sentimentalité doucereuse.
scholar ['skɔlər] *n.* **1.** *A:* élève *mf,* écolier, -ière. **2.** savant, -ante; érudit, -ite; **Latin s.,** latiniste *mf.* **3.** *Sch:* boursier, -ière.
scholarly ['skɔləli] *a.* savant, érudit.
scholarship ['skɔləʃip] *n.* **1.** savoir *m;* érudition *f.* **2.** *Sch:* bourse *f* (d'études).
scholastic [skə'læstik] **1.** *a.* (*a*) (philosophie, théologie) scolastique; (*b*) (*of schools, etc.*) scolaire. **2.** *n. Phil: Theol:* scolastique *m.*
school¹ [sku:l] *n.* **1.** (*a*) école *f;* **nursery s.,** école maternelle, maternelle *f;* **primary,** *A:* **elementary, s.,** école primaire; **comprehensive s.** = centre *m* d'études secondaires; **grammar s., high s.** = lycée *m;* **independent, private s.** = école, collège, libre; **public s.,** (i) collège privé (de niveau supérieur) (avec internat); (ii) *U.S:* = **state s.; state s.,** école d'État, établissement national; **approved s.,** centre d'éducation surveillée; **Sunday s.,** école du dimanche; **s. book,** livre *m* de classe; livre scolaire; (*b*) (les éléves d'une) école; **the whole s. knew it,** tous, toutes, les élèves le savaient; toute l'école le savait; **the upper, lower, s.,** les grandes, petites, classes. **2.** (*schooling*) **to go to s.,** aller en classe; **s. attendance,** scolarisation *f;* **s. leaving age,** âge *m* de fin de scolarité; **(of) s. age,** (d')âge scolaire; **s. year,** année *f* scolaire; **s. report,** livret *m* scolaire; bulletin (trimestriel). **3.** école, académie *f,* institut *m* (d'enseignement technique, industriel, etc.); **art s., s. of art,** école des beaux-arts; **s. of dancing,** académie, école, de danse; **fencing s.,** académie, salle *f,* d'escrime; **driving s., s. of motoring,** auto-école *f, pl.* auto-écoles; **summer s.,** cours de vacances. **4.** (*a*) *Art: etc:* école; **the Flemish s.,** l'école flamande; **the Platonic s.,** l'école de Platon; (*b*) **s. of thought,** école (de pensée); **one of the old s.,** un homme de la vieille école; (*c*) disciples *mpl* (d'un maître).
school² *v.tr.* **1.** instruire (qn); faire l'éducation de (qn). **2.** former (un enfant, l'esprit de qn, etc.); discipliner (sa voix, son geste, etc.); dresser (un cheval). **to s. oneself,** se discipliner. **schooling** *n.* instruction *f,* éducation *f;* dressage *m* (d'un cheval); **he paid for his nephew's s.,** il a subvenu aux frais d'études de son neveu.
school³ *n.* banc voyageur (de poissons); bande *f* (de marsouins).
schoolboy ['sku:lbɔi] *n.m.* écolier; élève; **s. slang,** argot *m* scolaire.
schoolchild, *pl.* **-children** ['sku:ltʃaild, -tʃildrən] *n.* écolier, -ière.
schoolday ['sku:ldei] *n.* **1.** jour *m* de classe. **2. schooldays,** vie *f* scolaire; années *fpl* de classe, d'école.
schoolfellow ['sku:lfelou] *n. O:* camarade *mf* de classe.
schoolgirl ['sku:lgə:l] *n.f.* écolière; élève.
schoolhouse ['sku:lhaus] *n.* **1.** (bâtiment *m,* maison *f,* d')école *f.* **2.** maison du directeur, de la directrice (faisant corps avec l'école).
schoolma'am, schoolmarm ['sku:lmɑ:m] *n.f. F:* institutrice; **she's a real s.,** c'est une pédante.
schoolmaster ['sku:lmɑ:stər] *n.m.* (*in primary school*) instituteur; maître (d'école); (*in secondary school*) professeur.
schoolmate ['sku:lmeit] *n.* camarade *mf* de classe.
schoolmistress ['sku:lmistris] *n.f.* (*in primary school*) institutrice; maîtresse (d'école); (*in secondary school*) professeur *m.*
schoolroom ['sku:lru:m] *n.* salle *f* de classe.
schoolteacher ['sku:lti:tʃər] *n.* (*in primary school*) instituteur, -trice; maître *m,* maîtresse *f* (d'école); (*in secondary school*) professeur *m.*
schooltime ['sku:ltaim] *n.* **1.** heures *fpl* de classe. **2.** vie *f* scolaire; années *fpl* de classe, d'école.
schooner¹ ['sku:nər] *n. Nau:* schooner *m;* goélette *f;* **s.-rigged,** gréé en goélette.
schooner² *n.* grand verre (à bière, à vin de Xérès).
sciatic [sai'ætik] *a. Anat:* (nerf, etc.) sciatique.
sciatica [sai'ætikə] *n. Med:* sciatique *f.*
science ['saiəns] *n.* science; **pure, applied, s.,** science pure, sciences appliquées; **natural s.,** sciences naturelles; **social s.,** sciences sociales; **s. master, mistress,** professeur *m* de sciences; **s. fiction,** science-fiction *f.*
scientific [saiən'tifik] *n.* scientifique; **s. research,** recherches scientifiques. **-ally** *adv.* scientifiquement.
scientist ['saiəntist] *n.* **1.** scientifique *mf;* homme *m* de science. **2. Christian S.,** scientiste chrétien(ne).
sci-fi ['saifai] *n. F:* science-fiction *f.*
Scilly ['sili] *Pr.n. Geog:* **the S. Isles, the Scillies,** les Sorlingues *fpl.*
scimitar ['simitər] *n.* cimeterre *m.*
scintillate ['sintileit] *v.i.* scintiller, étinceler; **scintillating with wit,** qui scintille, qui pétille, d'esprit. **scintillating** *a.* scintillant, étincelant, pétillant.
scintillation [sinti'leiʃ(ə)n] *n.* scintillation *f,* scintillement *m* (des étoiles, de l'esprit, etc.).
scion ['saiən] *n.* **1.** *Hort:* scion *m,* greffon *m.* **2.** de-

scendant *m*, rejeton *m* (d'une famille noble, etc.).

scissor[1] ['sizər] *n.* **1.** (*a*) **(pair of) scissors,** ciseaux *mpl*; **nail scissors,** ciseaux à ongles; (*b*) *Gym: Wr: etc:* **scissors,** ciseaux; *Swim:* **scissors kick,** les ciseaux. **2.** *Orn:* **s. bill,** bec-en-ciseaux *m, pl.* becs-en-ciseaux.

scissor[2] *v.tr.* (dé)couper (qch.) avec des ciseaux.

sclerosis, *pl.* **-oses** [skliə'rousis, -ousi:z] *n. Med:* sclérose *f*; **multiple, disseminated, s.,** sclérose en plaques.

scoff[1] [skɔf] *n.* moquerie *f*, raillerie *f*.

scoff[2] *v.i.* se moquer; **to s. at,** railler (qn); se moquer de (qn, qch.); mépriser (un danger). **scoffing** *a.* moqueur, -euse.

scoff[3] *n. P:* nourriture *f*; boustifaille *f*, bouffe *f*.

scoff[4] *v.tr. P:* bouffer, bâfrer (de la nourriture).

scold[1] [skould] *n.f.* mégère; grondeuse, bougonne.

scold[2] **1.** *v.i.* gronder, criailler (**at s.o.,** contre qn). **2.** *v.tr.* gronder, réprimander, attraper (qn). **scolding 1.** *a.* grondeur, -euse. **2.** *n.* (*a*) gronderie *f*; réprimande *f*, semonce *f*; **to give s.o. a good s.,** laver la tête à qn; (*b*) **constant s.,** des criailleries *fpl* sans fin.

scollop[1, 2] ['skɔləp] *n. & v.* = SCALLOP[1, 2].

sconce [skɔns] *n.* **1.** bougeoir *m*. **2.** applique *f*.

scone [skɔn, skoun] *n.* petit pain au lait.

scoop[1] [sku:p] *n.* **1.** (*a*) *Nau:* épuisette *f*, écope *f*; (*b*) pelle *f* à main; **grocer's s.,** main *f*; (*c*) *Dom. Ec:* **ice cream s.,** portionneur *m* à glace. **2.** (*a*) *Civ. E:* cuiller *f*, godet *m* (de drague); *Fish:* **s. net,** drague *f*; (*b*) *I.C.E:* cuiller de graissage.

scoop[2] *n.* (*a*) coup *m* de pelle; **at one s.,** d'un seul coup (de pelle); (*b*) *F:* coup de chance; **to make a s.,** réussir un coup; (*c*) *Journ: F:* nouvelle sensationnelle; reportage *m* exclusif, à sensation; scoop *m*; (*d*) *Dressm:* **s. neck,** décolleté (arrondi).

scoop[3] *v.tr.* **1. to s. (out),** écoper (l'eau) (d'un bateau); excaver (la terre); évider (du bois. etc.); vider (une tomate, etc.); **to s. up,** (i) ramasser (du charbon, de la farine, etc.) avec la pelle; (ii) épuiser, écoper (l'eau, etc.). **2.** *F:* (*a*) réussir un beau coup; (*b*) *Journ:* **to s. the other papers,** publier (une nouvelle, etc.) avant les autres journaux; faire un scoop.

scoot [sku:t] *v.i. F:* **to s. (off, away),** détaler, filer, déguerpir.

scooter ['sku:tər] *n.* (*a*) (*for child*) trottinette *f*, patinette *f*; (*b*) **(motor) s.,** scooter *m*.

scope [skoup] *n.* (*a*) portée *f*, étendue *f* (d'une action, etc.); domaine *m* (d'une science, etc.); envergure *f* (d'une entreprise); **it's beyond, outside, my s.,** cela n'est pas de, ne rentre pas dans, ma compétence; (*b*) espace *m*, place *f* (pour les mouvements de qn, etc.); **to give full, free, s. to s.o., one's imagination, etc.,** donner libre carrière à, laisser le champ libre à qn, son imagination, etc.

scorch[1] [skɔ:tʃ] *n.* **s. (mark),** roussissement *m*; brûlure superficielle.

scorch[2]. **1.** *v.tr.* (*of fire, etc.*) roussir, brûler légèrement (le linge, etc.); (*of sun*) rôtir, dessécher (l'herbe, etc.); **scorched earth policy,** tactique *f*, politique *f*, de la terre brûlée. **2.** *v.i.* (*of material, etc.*) roussir. **2.** *v.i. Aut: etc: F: O:* **to s. (along),** brûler le pavé; filer à toute vitesse. **scorching 1.** *a.* (*of sun, wind, etc.*) brûlant, ardent; (chaleur) torride. **2.** *adv. F:* **it's s. hot here,** on rôtit ici. **3.** *n.* roussissement *m* (du linge, etc.); dessèchement *m* (de l'herbe, etc.).

scorcher ['skɔ:tʃər] *n. F:* journée *f* torride.

score[1] [skɔ:r] *n.* **1.** incision *f*; éraflure *f*; entaille *f*; (*on rock, etc.*) strie *f*; (*on cylinder, etc.*) rayure *f*. **2.** (trait *m* de) repère (*m*). **3.** (*a*) (en)coche *f*; (*b*) (i) *O:* (*at a pub, etc.*) ardoise *f*; **to pay one's s.,** régler son compte; (ii) **to pay off, settle, old scores,** régler de vieux comptes. **4.** (*a*) *Sp: Games:* marque *f*, score *m*; **what's the s.?** quel est le score, la marque? où en est le jeu? **to keep the s.,** marquer, compter, les points; *Cards:* tenir la marque; (*b*) *F:* (i) réponse bien envoyée; (ii) coup *m* de fortune; **to make a s.,** toucher son adversaire (au vif); (*c*) *F:* **to know the s.,** être au courant; *F:* connaître la musique. **5.** *Mus:* partition *f*; **full s.,** partition d'orchestre. **6.** (*a*) (*pl.* **score)** vingt; une vingtaine; **a s. of people,** une vingtaine de gens; *F:* **you can find them by the s.,** on les ramasse à la pelle; (*b*) *F:* **scores,** un grand nombre; **scores of people,** une foule de gens. **7.** point *m*, compte *m*, question *f*, sujet *m*; **don't worry on that s.,** n'ayez aucune crainte sur ce point.

score[2] *v.tr.* **1.** (*a*) érafler, couturer (qch.); inciser (le cuir, etc.); strier (un rocher, etc.); rayer (un cylindre, la terre, le papier, etc.); **mountainside scored by torrents,** flanc de montagne sillonné par les torrents; (*b*) faire un trait de plume au-dessous de (qch.); **to s. a passage in a book,** souligner un passage dans un livre. **2.** (*a*) entailler, (en)cocher (une latte de bois, etc.); (*b*) *F: O:* **to score (up),** porter (une dette) en compte. **3.** *v.tr. & i. Sp: Games:* (*a*) compter, marquer, les points; (*b*) faire, marquer (trente points, etc.); **to fail to s.,** ne marquer aucun point; *Fb: etc:* **to s. a goal,** marquer, enregistrer, un but; (*c*) réussir; **to s. a success,** remporter, enregistrer, un succès; **that's where he scores,** c'est par là qu'il l'emporte; *F:* **to s. (points) off s.o.,** river son clou à qn. **4.** *Mus:* (*a*) noter (un air); (*b*) orchestrer (une composition). **scoring** *n.* **1.** éraflement *m* (de la peau, etc.); striation *f* (d'un rocher); rayage *m* (d'un cylindre, etc.). **2.** (*a*) entaillage *m*, encochage *m* (d'un bâton, etc.); (*b*) **s. (up),** inscription *f*, enregistrement *m* (d'une dette). **3.** *Games:* marque *f* (des points); **to open the s.,** ouvrir la marque. **4.** *Mus:* (*a*) notation *f* (d'un air); (*b*) orchestration *f* (d'une composition), arrangement *m* (pour divers instruments). **scored for piano, violin and flute,** arrangé pour piano, violon et flûte.

scoreboard ['skɔ:bɔ:d] *n.* tableau *m* (des points, etc.).

scorecard ['skɔ:kɑ:d] *n. Games:* carte *f*, fiche *f*, de score; *Golf:* carte du parcours; (*at shooting range*) carton *m*.

scorer ['skɔ:rər] *n. Games:* **1.** marqueur, -euse (des points). **2.** celui, celle, qui marque des points; *Fb: etc:* marqueur, -euse, de but.

scorn[1] [skɔ:n] *n.* (*a*) dédain *m*, mépris *m*; **to pour s. on sth.,** rejeter qch. d'un ton de mépris.

scorn[2] *v.tr.* **1.** dédaigner, mépriser (qn, qch.). **2. to s. to do sth.,** dédaigner de faire qch.

scornful ['skɔ:nf(u)l] *a.* (*of pers., smile, etc.*) dédaigneux, méprisant; **to be s. of s.o., sth.,** dédaigner, mépriser, qn, qch.; traiter qn, qch., avec mépris. **-fully** *adv.* dédaigneusement; avec mépris.

Scorpio ['skɔ:piou] *Pr.n. Astr:* le Scorpion.

scorpion ['skɔ:piən] *n. Arach:* scorpion *m*; *Astr:* **the S.,** le Scorpion.

Scot [skɔt] *n.* **1.** Écossais, -aise. **2.** *Hist:* **the Scots,** les Scots *mpl*.

scotch[1] [skɔtʃ] *v.tr.* mettre fin à, faire échouer (un projet, etc.).

Scotch[2] **1.** (*not used of persons in Scotland*) (*a*) *a.* écossais; d'Écosse; **S. terrier,** scottish-terrier *m*; **S. pine, fir,** pin *m* d'Écosse; **S. mist,** bruine *f*, crachin *m*; (*b*) *n. F:* **the S.,** les Écossais. **2.** *n.* (*a*) *Ling:* l'anglais *m* d'Écosse; (*b*) *F:* whisky écossais, scotch *m*; **a (glass of) S.,** un whisky, un scotch.

Scotchman *pl.* **-men** ['skɔtʃmən] *n.* (*not used in Scotland*) Écossais *m*.

scot-free ['skɔt'fri:] *a.* **to get off s.-f.,** s'en tirer. (i) indemne, (ii) sans être puni.

Scotland ['skɔtlənd] *Pr.n.* **1.** *Geog:* l'Écosse *f*. **2. S. Yard** = la Sûreté.

Scots [skɔts] **1.** *a.* écossais; **the S. Guards,** la Garde écossaise; les Écossais. **2.** *n. Ling:* écossais *m*.

Scotsman, *pl.* **-men** ['skɔtsmən] *n.m.* Écossais.

Scotswoman, *pl.* **-women** ['skɔtswumən, -wimin] *n.f.* Écossaise.

Scott [skɔt] *int.* **Great S.!** Grand Dieu!

Scottie ['skɔti] *n. F:* scottish-terrier *m.*

Scottish ['skɔtiʃ] *a.* écossais.

scoundrel ['skaundr(ə)l] *n.* scélérat *m*; canaille *f.*

scour¹ ['skauər] *v.tr.* **1.** (*a*) lessiver, frotter (le plancher, etc.); **to s. (out) a saucepan,** récurer une casserole; (*b*) *Metalw:* décaper (une surface métallique). **2.** (*a*) donner une chasse d'eau à (un égout, etc.); (*b*) (*of river*) affouiller, dégrader (les rives). **scouring** *n.* **1.** (*a*) récurage *m*, frottage *m*; (*b*) *Metalw:* décapage *m.* **2.** nettoyage à grande eau (d'un fossé).

scour **1.** *v.i.* **to s. (about),** battre la campagne. **2.** *v.tr.* parcourir, battre (la campagne); (*of pirates*) balayer, écumer (la mer); fouiller (un bois); **to s. the country for s.o.,** battre la campagne à la recherche de qn.

scourer ['skauərər] *n.* **1.** (*pers.*) nettoyeur, -euse; (r)écureur, -euse. **2.** *Dom.Ec:* **(pot) s.,** cure-casseroles *m inv*; éponge *f* métallique, en nylon, etc.

scourge¹ [skəːdʒ] *n.* **1.** *A: & Lit:* fouet *m*; *Ecc:* (*for self flagellation*) discipline *f.* **2.** fléau *m.*

scourge² *v.tr.* **1.** *A: & Lit:* fouetter, flageller (qn); *Ecc:* **to s. oneself,** se donner la discipline. **2.** affliger, opprimer, (un peuple, etc.).

scouse [skaus] *F:* **1.** *a. & n.* (habitant, -ante) de Liverpool. **2.** *n. Ling:* l'anglais *m* de Liverpool.

scout¹ [skaut] *n.* **1.** (*a*) *Mil:* éclaireur *m*, avant-coureur *m*; (*b*) **(boy) s.,** (*Catholic*) scout *m*; (*non Catholic*) éclaireur *m*; *U.S:* **(girl) s.,** guide *f*, éclaireuse *f*; (*c*) *Aut:* dépanneur *m* (employé par les associations automobiles); (*d*) *Cin: Sp: etc:* **talent s.,** recruteur *m* de talent (*e*) *NAm: F:* **a good s.,** un bon type. **2.** (*a*) *Navy:* **s. (ship),** vedette *f*; (croiseur-) éclaireur *m*, *pl.* (croiseurs-)éclaireurs; (*b*) *Av:* avion *m* de reconnaissance; (*c*) **s. car,** voiture *f* de reconnaissance.

scout² *v.i.* (*a*) *Mil: etc:* aller en reconnaissance; (*b*) **to s. (about, around) for sth.,** aller à la recherche de qch.; (*c*) *Cin: Sp: etc:* **to s. for talent,** se mettre à la recherche de futures vedettes. **scouting** *n.* **1.** *Mil: etc:* reconnaissance *f.* **2.** *Scout:* scoutisme *m.*

scout³ *n. Sch:* garçon *m* de service (à Oxford, etc.).

scoutmaster ['skautmɑːstər] *n. Scout:* chef *m* de troupe.

scow [skau] *n. Nau:* chaland *m.*

scowl¹ [skaul] *n.* air menaçant, renfrogné; froncement *m* de(s) sourcils; **to look at s.o. with a s.,** menacer qn du regard.

scowl² *v.i.* (*of pers.*) se renfrogner; froncer les sourcils; **to s. at s.o.,** menacer qn du regard; regarder qn d'un air menaçant. **scowling** *a.* renfrogné, menaçant.

scrabble ['skræbl] *v.i.* **to s. about,** gratter (çà et là); jouer des pieds et des mains **(for sth.,** pour attraper qch.).

scrag¹ [skræg] *n.* (*a*) **the s. of the neck,** la nuque; (*b*) *Cu:* **s. (end) of mutton,** collet *m* de mouton.

scrag² *v.tr.* **(scragged)** *F:* **1.** tordre le cou à (qn). **2.** *Rugby.Fb:* saisir (un adversaire) autour du cou.

scraggy ['skrægi] *a.* (*of pers., etc.*) décharné, maigre.

scram [skræm] *v.i.* **(scrammed)** *F:* filer, décamper; ficher le camp; **s.!** (allez) ouste! fiche le camp!

scramble¹ ['skræmbl] *n.* **1.** ascension *f* difficile; escalade *f* à quatre pattes; *Sp:* **(motorcycle) s.,** motocross *m.* **2.** (*a*) mêlée *f*, lutte *f*; (*b*) *Av: F:* décollage immédiat (en cas d'alerte, etc.).

scramble² **1.** *v.i.* (*a*) monter, descendre, entrer, sortir, etc., à quatre pattes; jouer des pieds et des mains; **to s. up a hill,** grimper une colline à quatre pattes; (*b*) **to s. for sth.,** se battre, se bousculer, pour avoir qch.; se disputer qch.; (*c*) *Av: F:* décoller rapidement (en cas d'alerte, etc.); (*d*) *Sp:* faire du motocross. **2.** *v.tr.* (*a*) brouiller (des œufs); **scrambled egg,** œuf brouillé; (*b*) *Tp: Elcs: etc:* brouiller (un message). **scrambling** *n.* **1.** *Tp: Elcs: etc:* brouillage *m* (d'un message). **2. (motorcycle) s.,** moto-cross *m.*

scrambler ['skræmblər] *n. Tp: etc:* (circuit *m*) brouilleur (*m*).

scrap¹ [skræp] *n.* **1.** (*a*) petit morceau; bout *m*, brin *m* (de papier); parcelle *f* (de terrain, etc.); bout (de ruban); bribe *f* (de pain, etc.); **not a s. of evidence,** pas une parcelle de preuve; **to catch scraps of a conversation,** saisir des bouts, des bribes, de conversation; **s. paper,** (papier *m*) brouillon (*m*): (*b*) découpure *f* (pour album); coupure *f* (de journal). **2.** (*a*) **scraps (left over),** restes *mpl*, (d'un repas); déchets *mpl* (de papeterie, d'usine, etc.); bouts, bribes (de tissu); (*b*) **s. (metal),** bocage *m*; **s. iron,** ferraille *f*; **s. merchant,** marchand *m* de ferraille; **to sell (sth.) for s.,** vendre (qch.) à la casse.

scrap² *v.tr.* **(scrapped)** **1.** mettre (qch.) au rebut; mettre hors service (une machine); envoyer, mettre, (qch.) à la ferraille, à la casse. **2.** mettre au rancart (un projet).

scrap³ *n. F:* querelle *f*, rixe *f*; bagarre *f*; **to have a s.,** se quereller.

scrap⁴ *v.i.* **(scrapped)** *F:* se quereller, se bagarrer.

scrapbook ['skræpbuk] *n.* album *m* (de découpures).

scrape¹ [skreip] *n.* **1.** (*a*) coup *m* de grattoir, de racloir; (*b*) *F:* mince couche *f* (de beurre, etc.); (*c*) grincement *m* (d'un violon, etc.). **2.** *F:* embarras *m*, mauvais pas; **to get into a s.,** se mettre dans le pétrin, dans l'embarras: s'attirer des ennuis; **to get out of a s.,** se tirer d'affaire, d'embarras.

scrape² *v.tr.* **I.** érafler, écorcher (la peau, une surface polie, etc.); **to s. one's shins,** s'érafler les tibias; (*of ship*) **to s. the bottom,** sillonner le fond; talonner. **2.** (*a*) (*clean*) racler, gratter (qch.); regratter, ravaler (un mur); *Cu:* gratter (des carottes, etc.); *Tan:* racler, dépiler (une peau); **to s. off the paint,** racler, enlever, la peinture; **to s. one's shoes,** se décrotter les pieds; **to s. one's plate,** gratter le fond de son assiette; *Nau:* **to s. a ship's bottom,** nettoyer la carène d'un navire; *Fig:* **to s. the (bottom of the) barrel,** racler les fonds de tiroir; (*b*) (*smooth*) riper (une sculpture, etc.); racler, raturer (le parchemin); (*c*) **with her hair scraped back,** aux cheveux tirés. **3.** *v.i.* **to s. (on the fiddle),** racler, gratter, du violon. **4.** (*laboriously*) (*a*) **to s. (an) acquaintance with s.o.,** trouver moyen de lier connaissance avec qn; (*b*) **to s. (together, up) a sum of money,** amasser petit à petit, peu à peu, sou par sou, une somme d'argent. **II.** *v.i.* **1.** (*a*) gratter; **branches that s. against the shutters,** branches *fpl* qui frottent les volets; (*b*) (*of wheel, pen, violin, etc.*) grincer. **2.** (*a*) *F:* **to s. along,** vivoter, s'en tirer péniblement; **to s. through (an examination),** être reçu tout juste (à un examen); (*b*) *F:* **to s. home,** gagner tout juste la partie. **scraping** *n.* **1.** éraflement *m* (d'un doigt, etc.). **2.** (*a*) raclage *m*, grattage *m* (de qch.); regrattement *m*, ravalement *m* (d'un mur); décrottage *m* (des souliers, etc.); *Cu:* grattage (des carottes); *Tan:* dépilage *m*, drayage *m* (d'une peau); (*b*) ripage (d'une sculpture); raturage *m* (du parchemin). **3.** grincement *m* (d'une plume, d'une scie, d'un violon, etc.); grattement *m.* **4. bowing and s.,** salamalecs *mpl*; courbettes *fpl.* **5.** mince couche *f* (de beurre, etc.).

scraper ['skreipər] *n.* (*a*) racloir *m*, grattoir *m*; racle *f*, raclette *f*; *Aut: etc:* **ice s.,** grattoir (pour pare-brise, etc.); (*b*) (*cleaner*) curette *f*; **door, shoe, s.,** décrottoir *m*; gratte-pieds *m inv.*

scrapheap ['skræphiːp] *n.* tas *m* de ferraille; **to throw sth. on the s.,** mettre qch. à la ferraille, au rebut.

scrapman, *pl.* **-men** ['skræpmən] *n. esp. U.S:* marchand *m* de ferraille; ferrailleur *m.*

scrapple ['skræpl] *n. NAm: Cu:* (genre *m* de) friand

m fait de farine de maïs et de morceaux de porc que l'on frit à la poêle.

scrappy ['skræpi] *a.* **1.** (*of collection, etc.*) hétérogène, hétéroclite; (*of speech, etc.*) décousu. **2. s. knowledge,** bribes *fpl* de connaissances. **3. s. meal,** (i) maigre repas; (ii) repas composé de restes.

scratch¹ [skrætʃ] *n.* **1.** (*a*) coup *m* d'ongle, de griffe; (*b*) égratignure *f*, éraflure *f* (sur la peau); griffure *f*; **he came out of it without a s.,** il s'en est sorti indemne; (*c*) rayure *f*, frottis *m* (sur une surface polie); égratignure (sur un film, etc.); (*d*) *NAm:* **s. pad,** bloc-notes *m, pl.* blocs-notes; **s. paper,** brouillon *m.* **2.** (*a*) grattement *m* (de la peau); **to give one's head a s.,** se gratter la tête; (*b*) grincement *m* (d'une plume). **3.** *Sp:* **s. (line),** scratch *m*; ligne *f* de départ (d'une course); **s. race,** course *f* scratch; **s. player,** scratch *m*; joueur, -euse, classé(e) à zéro (dans un tournoi); **to start (at) s.,** partir scratch; *F:* **to start from s.,** partir de zéro; *F:* **to come up to s.,** se montrer a la hauteur (de l'occasion); s'exécuter; **to bring s.o. up to s.,** (i) amener qn à se décider, à s'exécuter; (ii) chauffer qn (pour un examen); **he's not up to s.,** il ne fait pas le poids.

scratch². **I.** *v.tr.* **1.** (*a*) (*of cat, etc.*) égratigner, griffer (qn); (*b*) (*of thorn, etc.*) écorcher, érafler (la peau); **to s. oneself,** s'égratigner; (*c*) rayer (le verre, etc.); strier (la roche, etc.); *Cin:* **scratched film,** film rayé, égratigné; (*d*) **to s. s.o.'s eyes out,** arracher les yeux à qn. **2.** (*a*) gratter (le métal, la peau qui démange); **to s. one's head,** se gratter la tête; **you s. my back and I'll s. yours,** passez-moi la casse et je vous passerai le séné; (*b*) **to s. the surface,** effleurer (le problème, etc.). **3.** (*of bird, animal*) gratter (le sol); creuser (un trou) avec les griffes; **to s. up a bone,** déterrer un os (en grattant); **to s. together, s. up, a few pounds,** ramasser quelques livres. **4. to s. out,** rayer, biffer, raturer (un mot); (*with penknife*) gratter, effacer; **to s. s.o. off, from, a list,** rayer, biffer, qn d'une liste; *Turf:* **to s. a horse,** (i) déclarer forfait pour un cheval; (ii) (*of stewards*) scratcher un cheval. **5.** griffonner, écrire (quelques mots). **II.** *v.i.* **1.** (*a*) **cat that scratches,** chat qui griffe; (*b*) (*of pers., animal*) se gratter; (*of bird, animal*) gratter (dans la terre, etc.); **to s. about, around, for evidence,** dénicher des preuves; **to s. at the door,** gratter à la porte. **2.** (*of pen, etc.*) grincer, gratter. **3.** *Sp:* (*of entrant*) déclarer forfait. **scratching** *n.* **1.** (*a*) coups *mpl* d'ongle, de griffe; (*b*) écorchement *m*, éraflement *m* (de la peau); (*c*) rayage *m*, striation *f* (d'une surface). **2.** grattement *m* (de la tête, etc.). **3.** rayage (d'un concurrent). **4.** grattement *m*; grincement *m* (d'une plume); bruit *m* de surface, de fond (d'un disque).

scratch³ *a.* (repas, etc.) improvisé, sommaire; *Sp:* **s. team,** équipe improvisée.

scratcher ['skrætʃər] *n.* **1.** gratteur, -euse; chat, etc., qui griffe. **2.** *Tls:* grattoir *m*, gratteau *m*; **back s.,** gratte-dos *m inv.*

scratchy ['skrætʃi] *a.* **1.** (*of drawing*) au trait maigre, peu assuré; **s. writing,** pattes *fpl* d'araignée; pattes de mouche. **2.** (*a*) (*of pen, etc.*) (i) qui gratte; (ii) qui grince (sur le papier); (*b*) (*of material, etc.*) rugueux, grossier; qui gratte la peau.

scrawl¹ [skrɔːl] *n.* (*a*) griffonnage *m*, gribouillage *m*, *F:* grimoire *m*; (*b*) petit mot écrit à la hâte.

scrawl² *v.tr. & i.* griffonner, gribouiller (une lettre, etc.); écrire comme un chat.

scrawny ['skrɔːni] *a. F:* maigre, décharné.

scream¹ [skriːm] *n.* **1.** (*a*) cri perçant, aigu; (*b*) **screams of laughter,** de grands éclats de rire. **2.** *F: O:* **it was a perfect s.,** c'était à se tordre (de rire); **he's a s.,** il est tordant.

scream² **1.** *v.i.* (*a*) pousser un cri perçant, aigu; pousser des cris aigus; (*of rabbit, hare*) couiner; **to s. with pain,** crier, hurler, de douleur; (*b*) **to s. with laughter,** rire à gorge déployée, aux éclats. **2.** *v.tr.* (*a*) **to s. oneself hoarse,** s'enrouer à (force de) crier; (*b*) **to s. abuse,** hurler des injures. **screaming** **1.** *a.* (*of pers.*) criard, brailleur. **2.** *n.* (*a*) cris *mpl* (de terreur, etc.); hurlements *mpl*; (*b*) cris perçants (d'oiseaux, etc.). **screamingly** *adv. F:* **s. funny,** tordant.

scree [skriː] *n. Geol:* éboulis *m.*

screech¹ [skriːtʃ] *n.* (*a*) cri perçant; cri aigu; (*b*) crissement *m* (de pneus, etc.); (*c*) *Orn:* **s. owl,** effraie *f.*

screech² *v.i.* (*a*) (*of pers., parrot, etc.*) pousser des cris perçants, aigus; (*b*) (*of tyres*) crisser. **screeching,** *n.* (*a*) cris perçants, aigus; (*b*) crissement *m* (de pneus, etc.).

screed [skriːd] *n.* **1.** *Const:* **(floating) s.,** cueillie *f*; guide *m* (pour plâtrage). **2.** (*a*) harangue *f*; (*b*) longue liste (de réclamations, etc.); (*c*) longue lettre.

screen¹ [skriːn] *n.* **1.** (*a*) *Furn:* écran *m*; (*against draught*) paravent *m*; (*b*) cloison *f*; grille *f* (en fer forgé, etc.); *Ecc.Arch:* **choir s.,** grille de chœur; **rood s.,** jubé *m*; (*c*) rideau (protecteur); **s. of trees,** rideau d'arbres; **under s. of night,** sous le couvert, à la faveur, de la nuit; **to act as a s. for a criminal,** couvrir un criminel; **smoke s.,** nuage artificiel; rideau de fumée; (*d*) **protective, safety, s.,** écran de protection, de sécurité; **fire s.,** écran ignifuge; **(camouflage) s.,** écran (de camouflage); masque *m.* **2.** *Cin: etc:* écran (de projection); *coll.* **the s.,** le cinéma, l'écran; **television s.,** écran de télévision; *F:* **the small s.,** la télé, le petit écran; **s. rights,** droits *mpl* d'adaptation à l'écran; **s. test,** bande *f*, bout *m*, d' essai. **3.** *El: Elcs:* écran (de tube cathodique, etc.); **fluorescent s.,** écran fluorescent. **4.** (*for camera*) filtre *m*; (*for dark room work*) écran; (*for colour photography*) réseau *m* mosaïque polychrome; *Phot.Engr:* trame *f.* **5.** (*a*) *Civ.E: Min: etc:* crible *m*, tamis *m*, sas *m*; (*b*) *Mec.E: etc:* tamis filtrant, filtre, crépine *f*; (*c*) *NAm:* grille de ventilation (dans une porte, etc.).

screen² *v.tr.* **1.** (*a*) cacher (qch.) derrière un écran, un paravent; (*b*) **to s. sth. from view,** cacher, masquer, dérober, qch. aux regards, à la vue; (*c*) *Mil:* jalonner (l'avance de l'ennemi). **2.** (*a*) abriter, protéger (qn, qch.); mettre (qn, qch.) à l'abri, à couvert; (*b*) *El: Elcs:* blinder (un câble, une antenne, etc.). **3.** *Cin: etc:* (*a*) projeter, passer (un film); (*b*) mettre, porter (une pièce, un roman) à l'écran. **4.** *Phot:* munir (l'objectif) d'un filtre correcteur. **5.** (*a*) cribler, passer au crible (du gravier, du charbon, du minerai, du grain, etc.); sasser (le grain); (*b*) (i) trier, sélectionner (du personnel); filtrer (des immigrants, etc.); *Med:* soumettre (qn) à une visite de dépistage; (ii) filtrer, passer au crible (des nouvelles, etc.). **screening** *n.* **1.** (*a*) mise à l'abri; dissimulation *f* aux regards; (*b*) *Mil: etc:* jalonnement *m* (de l'avance ennemie). **2.** *El: Elcs:* blindage *m* (d'un câble, d'une antenne, etc.). **3.** (*a*) criblage *m* (du gravier, du charbon, etc.); sassement *m* (du grain); **screenings,** criblure *f*; déchets *mpl* de criblage; (*b*) triage *m*, sélection *f* (du personnel); filtrage *m* (des immigrants, des nouvelles, etc.); examen sélectif (de demandes d'emploi, etc.); *Med:* triage, dépistage *m* (des contagieux).

screenplay ['skriːnplei] *n. Cin:* scénario *m.*

screenwriter ['skriːnraitər] *n.* scénariste *mf.*

screw¹ [skruː] *n.* **1.** vis *f*; (*a*) **thumb s.,** vis à molette, à tête moletée; **wing, butterfly, s.,** vis à oreilles, à ailettes; (écrou *m*) papillon *m*; (*b*) **s. cap, top,** couvercle, bouchon, vissant (d'un bocal, d'une bouteille); *El:* **s. base, cap,** culot *m* à vis, culot Edison; (*c*) *Ind:* **s. conveyor,** vis de transport, vis transporteuse; transporteur *m* à vis; *Hyd.E:* **Archimedes, Archimedean, s.,** vis d'Archimède; (*d*) **loose s.,** (i) écrou desserré; (ii) (*loosely fitting*) écrou gai; *F:* **to**

have a s. loose, être toqué; avoir une araignée au plafond; (*e*) *A:* **the screws,** les poucettes *fpl*; *F:* **to put the screws on s.o., to tighten the s.,** serrer la vis à qn. **2.** *Av: Nau:* **s. (propeller),** hélice *f* (d'avion, de bateau); **twin s.,** helice double. **3.** (*a*) coup *m* de tournevis; tour *m* de vis; **give it another s.,** serrez-le encore un peu; (*b*) *Bill: Ten: etc:* effet *m*; **to put (a) s. on the ball,** donner de l'effet (de côté); (*c*) cornet *m*; papillote *f* (de tabac, etc.); cornet, morceau chiffonné (de papier); (*d*) *F: O:* avare *m*, pingre *m*, ladre *m*; (*e*) *P:* gardien *m* de prison, gaffe *m*; (*f*) *V:* coït *m*. **4.** *F:* salaire *m*, paye *f*.

screw² **I.** *v.tr.* **1.** (*a*) visser (qch.); **to s. sth. (on) to sth.,** visser qch. à, sur, qch.; *F:* **his head's screwed on the right way,** il a la tête solide, la tête sur les épaules; (*with passive force*) **the knobs s. into the drawer,** les boutons se vissent sur le tiroir; (*b*) **to s. sth. (down),** fixer, assujettir, qch. avec des vis; **screwed together,** assemblé(s) à vis; **to s. off,** dévisser (un écrou, un couvercle); (*with passive force*) **the end screws off,** le bout se dévisse. **2.** (*a*) **to s. (up),** visser; serrer (un écrou); (res)serrer (un tourniquet, les chevilles d'un violon, etc.); **to s. sth. (up) tight,** visser qch. à bloc; **to s. up a piece of paper,** tortiller du papier; **to s. up one's eyes,** plisser les yeux; **to s. up one's courage,** prendre son courage à deux mains; *P:* **to s. up a piece of work,** gâcher, bousiller, un travail; (*b*) **to s. one's head round to see sth.,** se tordre la tête pour voir qch.; (*c*) **to s. money from, out of, s.o.,** extorquer de l'argent à qn; (*d*) *Bill:* donner de l'effet à (une bille); (*e*) *V:* s'envoyer, culbuter (une fille). **3.** *Tchn:* **to s. (cut),** fileter (une vis, un boulon); tarauder (un tuyau, etc.). **II.** *v.i.* **1.** (*of tap, etc.*) tourner (à gauche, à droite). **2.** *Bill:* (*of ball*) rebondir de travers; dévier; **to s. back,** (i) (*of player*) faire de l'effet rétrograde; faire un rétro; (ii) (*of ball*) revenir en arrière. **screwed** *a. F:* ivre, soûl.

screwball ['skru:bɔ:l] *a. & n. esp. U.S: F:* loufoque (*mf*).

screwdriver ['skrudraivər] *n.* tournevis *m*; **cross-headed s.,** tournevis cruciforme.

screw-on ['skru:ɔn] *a.* (boucles d'oreilles) à vis; (objectif) détachable, mobile.

screwy ['skru:i] *a. F:* fou, cinglé, loufoque.

scribble¹ ['skribl] *n.* **1.** griffonnage *m*, gribouillage *m*. **2.** écriture *f* illisible; pattes *fpl* de mouche.

scribble² **1.** *v.tr.* griffonner, gribouiller (quelques mots à qn, une note dans son carnet, etc.). **2.** *v.i.* barbouiller du papier. **scribbling** *n.* griffonnage *m*, gribouillage *m*; **s. paper,** (papier *m*) brouillon (*m*); **s. pad,** bloc *m* mémmento.

scribbler ['skriblər] *n.* **1.** griffonneur, -euse; *F:* gribouilleur, -euse. **2.** *F:* écrivailleur, -euse.

scribe¹ [skraib] *n. Hist:* (*pers.*) scribe *m*.

scribe² *n. Tls:* **s. (awl),** pointe *f* à tracer.

scribe³ *v.tr. Carp: Const:* tracer (une ligne).

scrimmage¹ ['skrimidʒ] *n.* **1.** mêlée *f*; bagarre *f*, bousculade *f*. **2.** *U.S: Fb:* mêlée.

scrimmage². **1.** *v.i.* se quereller; se bousculer. **2.** *v.tr. U.S: Fb:* mettre (le ballon) en mêlée.

scrimshank ['skrimʃæŋk] *v.i. Mil: P:* tirer au flanc.

scrimshanker ['skrimʃæŋkər] *n. Mil: P:* tire-au-flanc *m inv*.

scrip [skrip] *n. Fin:* (*a*) **s. (certificate),** certificat *m* d'actions provisoire; (*b*) *coll.* valeurs *fpl*, titres *mpl*, actions *fpl*; (*c*) **s. (issue),** titres attribués à un actionnaire (au lieu de dividende, etc.).

script [skript] *n.* **1.** (*a*) manuscrit *m*; (*b*) *Sch:* copie *f* (d'examen); (*c*) *Jur:* (document) original *m*, -aux; (*d*) *Cin:* scénario *m*; *Cin: T.V:* **s. girl,** script-girl *f*, *pl.* script-girls. **2.** (*a*) (*as opposed to print*) écriture *f*; **Gothic s.,** écriture gothique; (*b*) *Typ:* **s. (type),** cursive *f*.

scriptural ['skriptjərəl] *a.* scriptural, -aux; biblique.

scripture ['skriptjər] *n.* (*a*) **Holy S., the Scriptures,** l'Écriture sainte, les (saintes) Écritures; (*b*) *Sch:* **s. (lesson),** histoire sainte.

scriptwriter ['skriptraitər] *n. Cin:* scénariste *mf*.

scrofula ['skrɔfjulə] *n. Med:* scrofule *f*; écrouelles *fpl*.

scrofulous ['skrɔfjuləs] *a. Med:* scrofuleux.

scroll [skroul] *n.* **1.** rouleau *m* (de parchemin, de papier); **the Dead Sea scrolls,** les manuscrits *mpl* de la Mer morte. **2.** (*a*) *Art: etc:* banderole *f* à inscription; (*b*) *Her:* listel *m*. **3.** (*a*) *Arch: etc:* spirale *f*; volute *f* (de chapiteau ionique); (*b*) (*in writing*) enjolivement *m*, arabesque *f*; (*c*) *Engr: etc:* cartouche *m* (encadrant un titre); (*d*) crosse *f* (de violon).

scrotal ['skroutəl] *a. Anat:* scrotal, -aux.

scrotum ['skroutəm] *n. Anat:* scrotum *m*.

scrounge [skraundʒ] *F:* **1.** *v.tr.* (*a*) (*steal*) chiper, chaparder (qch.); (*b*) (*sponge*) écornifler (un diner, du tabac). **2.** *v.i.* (*a*) **to s. round for sth.,** aller à la recherche de qch.; (*b*) **to s. on s.o.,** vivre aux crochets de qn. **scrounging** *n. F:* (*a*) chipage *m*, chapardage *m*; (*b*) écorniflerie *f*, écorniflage *m*.

scrounger ['skraundʒər] *n. F:* (*a*) chipeur, -euse; chapardeur, -euse; (*b*) écornifleur, -euse.

scrub¹ [skrʌb] **1.** (*a*) arbuste rabougri; (*b*) broussailles *fpl;* brousse *f*; garrigue *f*. **2.** brosse *f* à soies courtes; **deck s.,** lave-pont *m*, *pl.* lave-ponts.

scrub² *n.* **1.** friction *f* (à la brosse); **to give the table a good s.,** frotter la table à la brosse; *U.S:* **s. brush,** brosse dure, de chiendent. **2.** *U.S:* **s. team,** équipe *f* de deuxiéme ordre.

scrub³ *v.tr. & i.* (**scrubbed**) **1.** (*a*) récurer (une casserole); laver, frotter, (le plancher) avec une brosse, à la brosse; (*of surgeon*) **to s. up,** se brosser les mains, etc. (avant d'opérer); (*b*) *Nau:* (i) goreter, (ii) briquer (le pont, etc.). **2.** (*a*) *Rec:* démagnétiser (une bande); (*b*) *F:* annuler (qch.). **scrubbing** *n.* **1.** récurage *m*; nettoyage *m*, lavage *m*, avec une brosse dure; **s. brush,** brosse dure, de chiendent. **2.** = SCRUB² 1.

scrubber ['skrʌbər] *n.* **1.** (*pers.*) (*a*) laveur, -euse (à la brosse); (*b*) *P:* putain *f*. **2. pan s.,** tampon *m* à récurer.

scrubland ['skrʌblænd] *n.* terrain broussailleux; brousse *f*.

scruff [skrʌf] *n.* nuque *f*; peau *f* de la nuque; **to take, seize, an animal by the s. of the, its, neck,** saisir un animal par la peau du cou.

scruffy ['skrʌfi] *a. F:* mal soigné; mal fichu; (hôtel) minable. **-ily** *adv.* **s. dressed,** (individu) débraillé.

scrum [skrʌm] *n.* (*a*) *Rugby.Fb:* mêlée *f*; **s. cap,** protège-oreilles *m inv*. (*b*) *F:* mêlée, bousculade *f*.

scrummage ['skrʌmidʒ] *n.* = SCRUM.

scrumptious ['skrʌm(p)ʃəs] *a. F:* épatant, fameux.

scrunch¹ [skrʌn(t)ʃ] *n.* crissement; grincement *m*.

scrunch² **1.** *v.tr.* croquer (qch. avec les dents). **2.** *v.i.* craquer, grincer, crisser.

scruple¹ ['skru:pl] *n.* scrupule *m* (de conscience); **to have scrupules about sth., about doing sth.,** avoir des scrupules au sujet de qch.; se faire (un) scrupule de faire qch.

scruple² *v.i.* **to s. to do sth.,** avoir des scrupules à faire qch.; se faire (un) scrupule de faire qch.

scrupulous ['skru:pjuləs] *a.* **1.** (*of pers., conscience, etc.*) scrupuleux. **2.** (*of care, work*) scrupuleux; minutieux. **-ly** *adv.* **1.** scrupuleusement. **2.** méticuleusement, minutieusement.

scrupulousness ['skru:pjuləsnis] *n.* **1.** scrupulosité *f* (**in doing sth.,** à faire qch.). **2.** esprit scrupuleux.

scrutineer [skru:ti'niər] *n.* scrutateur, -trice (des votes).

scrutinize ['skru:tinaiz] *v.tr.* (*a*) scruter, sonder (qch.); examiner (qch.) à fond; (*b*) vérifier (des suffrages). **scrutinizing** *a.* scrutateur, -trice; **s. look,** regard pénétrant, scrutateur.

scrutiny ['skru:tini] *n.* (*a*) examen minutieux, attentif; investigation, recherche, minutieuse; (*b*) *Pol:* vérification *f* (des bulletins de vote).

scuba ['skju:bə] *n.* scaphandre *m* autonome; **s. diving,** plongée sous-marine autonome.

scud¹ [skʌd] *n.* **1.** course précipitée, rapide. **2.** rafale *f.*

scud² *v.i.* **(scudded)** (*of pers., animal, etc.*) filer comme le vent; **the clouds were scudding across the sky,** les nuages galopaient à travers le ciel.

scuff [skʌf]. **1.** *v.tr.* (*a*) frotter, racler, user (avec les pieds); (*b*) érafler (le cuir, etc.); (*with passive force*) (*of leather*) s'érafler; (*c*) **to s. up.** soulever (la neige, la poussière) (en traînant le pas). **2.** *v.i.* traîner les pieds.

scuffle¹ ['skʌfl] *n.* mêlée *f,* échauffourée *f;* bagarre *f.*

scuffle² *v.i.* se battre, se bousculer; se bagarrer.

scull¹ [skʌl] *n.* **1.** *Row:* aviron *m* de couple. **2.** godille *f.*

scull² **1.** *v.i.* (*a*) ramer, nager, à couple; (*b*) godiller. **2.** *v.tr.* faire avancer (un bateau) (i) à couple, (ii) à la godille. **sculling** *n.* nage *f* (i) à couple, (ii) à la godille.

sculler ['sknlər] *n.* **1.** (*a*) rameur *m* de couple; (*b*) godilleur *m.* **2.** (*boat*) **double s.,** double-scull *m, pl.* doubles-sculls.

scullery ['skʌləri] *n.* arrière-cuisine *f, pl.* arrière-cuisines; souillarde *f;* **s. maid,** laveuse *f* de vaisselle.

sculp(t) [skʌlp(t)] **1.** *v.tr.* sculpter (une statue). **2.** *v.i.* faire de la sculpture.

sculptor ['skʌlptər] *n.* sculpteur *m.*

sculptress ['skʌlptris] *n.f.* femme sculpteur.

sculptural ['skʌlptjərəl] *a.* (art) sculptural, -aux.

sculpture¹ ['skʌlptjər] *n.* (*art or object*) sculpture *f.*

sculpture² *v.tr.* **1.** sculpter (une statue, la pierre, etc.); *v.i.* faire de la sculpture. **2.** orner (un fronton, etc.) de sculptures, de bas-reliefs.

scum¹ [skʌm] *n.* **1.** (*a*) écume *f,* mousse *f;* (*on wine*) chapeau *m;* **to take the s. off,** écumer (le pot, etc.); (*b*) *Metall:* scories *fpl,* crasse(s) *f(pl).* **2. the s. of society,** le rebut de la société; **s. of the earth!** excrément de la terre!

scum² *v.* **(scummed) 1.** *v.tr.* écumer (le bouillon, etc.). **2.** *v.i.* écumer; se couvrir d'écume.

scunner ['skʌnər] *n.* dégoût *m;* **to take a s. at, against, sth., s.o.,** prendre qch., qn, en dégoût.

scupper¹ ['skʌpər] *n. Nau:* dalot *m* (de pont).

scupper² *v.tr. F:* couler à fond (un navire, un projet, etc.); saborder (un navire).

scurf [skə:f] *n.* pellicules *fpl* (du cuir chevelu).

scurfy ['skə:fi] *a.* (*of head, etc.*) pelliculeux.

scurrilous ['skʌriləs] *a.* (*of language, etc.*) grossier, injurieux; (*of pers.*) ignoble, vil; **to make a s. attack on s.o.,** se répandre en injures contre qn. **-ly** *adv.* grossièrement; injurieusement.

scurry¹ ['skʌri] *n.* **1.** course *f* précipitée; débandade *f.* **2.** tourbillon *m* (de neige, de poussière, etc.).

scurry² *v.i.* aller, courir, à pas précipités; **to s. off, away,** détaler, décamper.

scurvy ['skə:vi] *n. Med:* scorbut *m.*

scutcheon ['skʌtʃ(ə)n] *n. Her:* écu *m,* écusson *m.*

scuttle¹ ['skʌtl] *n.* **(coal) s.,** seau *m* à charbon.

scuttle² *n.* (*a*) *Nau:* écoutille *f;* (*b*) *NAm:* (*in ceiling*) trappe *f.*

scuttle³ *v.tr. Nau:* saborder (un navire); **to s. one's ship,** s'envoyer par le fond. **scuttling** *n.* sabordement *m.*

scuttle⁴ *n.* fuite *f;* course précipitée; débandade *f.*

scuttle⁵ *v.i.* courir à pas précipités; **to s. (off, away),** déguerpir, détaler; (*of rabbit, etc.*) débouler.

scythe¹ [saið] *n. Agr:* faux *f.*

scythe² *v.tr.* faucher (le blé, etc.).

sea [si:] *n.* **1.** mer *f;* (*a*) **at the bottom of the s.,** au fond de la mer; **s. level,** niveau (moyen) de la mer; **by the s.,** au bord de la mer; **by s.,** par (voie de) mer; **beyond, over, the sea(s),** outre-mer; au delà des mers; **to go to s.,** se faire marin; **s. voyage,** voyage *m* en mer; **s. air,** air marin; **s. breeze,** brise *f* de mer; **room with a s. view,** chambre avec vue sur la mer; **s. battle,** bataille navale; **s. green,** vert *m* de mer; vert d'eau; *Nau:* **s. chest,** coffre *m* de marin, de bord; (*b*) **the open s., the high seas,** le large, la haute mer, la grande mer; **on the high seas, out at s.,** en haute mer, en pleine mer, au grand large; (*of ship*) **to put (out) to s.,** prendre la mer, le large; *F:* **to be all at s.,** être tout dérouté, désorienté, désemparé; *F:* (*of pers.*) **to find, get, one's s. legs,** s'amariner; **he hasn't found his s. legs,** il n'a pas encore le pied marin; (*c*) **inland, enclosed, s.,** mer intérieure; **the seven seas,** toutes les mers du monde; (*d*) **S. Lord,** lord *m* de l'Amirauté; **s. scout,** scout marin; *Myth:* **s. god,** dieu marin, de la mer; triton *m;* (*e*) **s. fish,** poisson *m* de mer; **s. fishery, fishing,** pêche *f* maritime; *Ich:* **s. trout,** truite *f* de mer; *Orn:* **s. eagle,** pygargue *m,* orfraie *f; Z:* **s. cow,** vache marine; **s. elephant,** éléphant *m* de mer; **s. otter,** loutre marine, de mer; **s. serpent,** (i) serpent *m* de mer; (ii) (*also* **s. monster**) monstre marin; *Coel:* **s. anemone,** actinie *f;* anémone *f* de mer. **2.** (*a*) (*state of the sea*) **heavy, strong, s.,** grosse mer; mer grosse, houleuse; **there's a heavy s.,** il y a de la mer; (*b*) lame *f,* houle *f;* **to run before the s.,** avoir la mer de l'arrière; **head s.,** mer debout; mer contraire; (*c*) coup *m* de mer; paquet *m* de mer; (grosse) vague. **3.** océan *m,* multitude *f;* **a s. of faces,** un océan de visages; **a s. of blood,** une mer de sang; *Lit:* **a s. of troubles,** une multitude de soucis.

seabird ['si:bə:d] *n.* oiseau *m* de mer.

seaboard ['si:bɔ:d] *n.* littoral *m,* -aux; bord *m* de la mer.

seaboots ['si:bu:ts] *n. pl.* bottes *fpl* de marin, de mer.

seaborne ['si:bɔ:n] a. (*of trade*) maritime; (*of goods*) transporté par mer.

seadog ['si:dɔg] *n. F:* **old s.,** vieux loup de mer.

seafarer ['si:fεərər] *n.* homme *m* de mer; marin *m.*

seafaring ['si:fεəriŋ] *a.* (gens, etc.) de mer, qui naviguent; **s. man,** marin *m.*

seafood ['si:fu:d] *n. coll.* fruits *mpl* de mer.

seafront ['si:frʌnt] *n.* **1.** bord *m* de la mer; **(house) on the s.,** (maison) qui donne sur la mer. **2.** esplanade *f;* front *m* de mer.

seagoing ['si:gouiŋ] *a.* (navire, etc.) de mer; (commerce) maritime; (personnel) navigant.

seagull ['si:gʌl] *n. Orn:* mouette *f,* goéland *m.*

seakale ['si:keil] *n. Bot:* crambe *m;* chou marin.

seal¹ [si:l] *n.* **1.** (*a*) *Z:* phoque *m; F:* veau marin; **elephant s.,** éléphant *m* de mer; **grey s.,** phoque gris; **eared s.,** otarie *f;* **fur s.,** otarie à fourrure; (*b*) **s. oil,** huile *f* de phoque. **2.** *Leath:* (peau *f* de) phoque.

seal² *v.i.* chasser, pêcher, le phoque. **sealing** *n.* chasse *f* au phoque; **s. fleet,** flotte phoquière.

seal³ *n.* **1.** (*a*) (*on deed, etc.*) sceau *m;* (*on letter*) cachet *m; Jur:* **given under my hand and s.,** signé et scellé par moi; **under the s. of silence, of secrecy,** sous le sceau du silence, du secret; **to set one's s. to sth.,** autoriser, confirmer, qch.; donner son approbation à qch.; (*b*) cachet (de bouteille de vin, etc.); *Jur:* (*affixed to property, etc.*) **official s.,** scellé *m;* **under s.,** sous scellés; *Com: etc:* **lead s.,** (i) plomb *m* (pour sceller une caisse, etc.); (ii) capsule *f* (de bouteille de vin). **2.** (*instrument*) sceau, cachet; *Adm:* **the Great S.,** le grand sceau (employé pour les actes publics). **3.** *Tchn:* dispositif *m* d'étanchéité; joint *m* étanche.

seal⁴ *v.tr.* **1.** (*a*) sceller (un acte, etc.); cacheter (une lettre); **his fate is sealed,** son sort est décidé, réglé; (*b*) cacheter (une bouteille, etc.); *Cust:* (faire) plomber (des marchandises, etc.); *Jur:* apposer les scellés sur (une porte, etc.). **2.** (*a*) **to s. (up),** fermer (une lettre, etc.); **the frontier has been sealed,** la frontière est fermée; **the area was sealed off by the police,** le quartier a été isolé, cerné, par la police; (*b*) rendre (qch.) étanche, étancher (qch.); obturer, boucher (un puits de mine, un tuyau); (*c*) **my lips are sealed,** il m'est défendu de parler; (*d*) assurer l'étanchéité (d'un joint, etc.); (*e*) *Cu:* saisir (de la viande). **sealing** *n.* **1.** (*a*) scellage *m* (d'un acte, etc.); cachetage *m* (d'une lettre, etc.); **s. wax,** cire *f* à cacheter; (*b*) *Cust:* plombage *m* (des marchandises, etc.). **2. s. (up),** fermeture *f* (de qch.); obturation *f* (d'un d'un tuyau, etc.). **3. s. compound,** (i) lut *m*, mastic *m*; *Aut:* anti-fuite *m inv* (de radiateur); (ii) vernis *m* hermétique.

sealer ['siːlər] *n.* **1.** (*ship*) phoquier *m.* **2.** (*pers.*) chasseur *m* de phoques.

sealion ['siːlaiən] *n. Z:* otarie *f.*

sealskin ['siːlskin] *n.* (peau *f* de) phoque (*m*).

seam¹ [siːm] *n.* **1.** (*a*) *Needlew:* couture *f*; **flat s.,** couture rabattue, plate; **French s.,** couture double, anglaise; (*b*) (*in metal pipe, between boards, etc.*) couture, joint *m*; **welded s.,** soudure *f*; *N.Arch:* **ship's seams,** coutures d'un navire; (*c*) *F:* **room bursting at the seams,** salle pleine à craquer. **2.** (*a*) (*on face, etc.*) ride *f*; (*b*) fissure *f*, gerçure *f.* **3.** *Min: etc:* veine *f* (de houille).

seam² *v.tr.* **1.** *Needlew:* faire une couture à (un vêtement, etc.). **2. face seamed with scars,** visage couturé de cicatrices.

seaman, *pl.* **-men** ['siːmən] *n.m.* **1.** marin; matelot; **ordinary s.,** matelot de troisième classe, de pont; **able(-bodied) s.,** matelot de deuxième classe: **leading s.,** matelot (breveté) de première classe; quartier-maître, *pl.* quartier(s)-maîtres. **2. a good s.,** un bon (i) manœuvrier, (ii) navigateur.

seamanship ['siːmənʃip] *n.* manœuvre *f* et matelotage *m*; la manœuvre; expertise *f* du marin.

seamless ['siːmlis] *a.* **1.** (bas, tapis, etc.) sans couture. **2.** *Metalw:* (*of tube, etc.*) sans soudure.

seamstress ['semstris] *n.f.* couturière.

seamy ['siːmi] *a.* **the s. side of life,** l'envers *m*, les dessous *mpl*, de la vie; **the s. side of politics,** le vilain côté. les dessous, de la politique.

seance ['seiɑ̃ːs] *n.* séance *f* de spiritisme.

seaplane ['siːplein] *n. Av:* hydravion *m.*

seaport ['siːpɔːt] *n.* port *m* maritime, de mer.

sear¹ [siər]. *Lit:* flétri, desséché.

sear² *v.tr.* (*a*) cautériser (une blessure); (*b*) *Lit:* endurcir (la conscience, etc.); dessécher (le cœur); (*c*) marquer au fer rouge. **searing** *a.* (*of pain*) fulgurant.

search¹ [səːtʃ] *n.* **1.** recherche(s) *f*(*pl*); **to make a s.,** (i) faire des recherches; (ii) (*in property transactions*) faire une enquête de commodo et incommodo; **in s. of sth.,** à la recherche de qch.; **to be in s. of sth.,** être en quête de qch.; être à la recherche de qch.; **s. party,** expédition *f* de secours. **2.** (*a*) *Cust:* visite *f*; **right of s.,** droit *m* de visite; (*at sea*) droit de recherche; (*b*) *Jur:* perquisition *f* (à domicile); **s. warrant,** mandat *m*. ordre *m*, de perquisition; (*c*) fouille *f* (dans un tiroir, etc.).

search² **1.** *v.tr.* inspecter (un endroit); chercher dans (un endroit, une boîte); fouiller dans (un tiroir); fouiller (un suspect, les poches de qn); scruter (un visage, *Lit:* sa mémoire); *Cust:* visiter (un navire, la valise de qn); *Jur:* **to s. a house,** faire une perquisition, une visite domiciliaire; *F:* **s. me!** je n'ai pas la moindre idée! **2.** *v.i.* faire des recherches; **to s. after truth,** rechercher la vérité; **to s. for s.o., sth.,** (re)chercher qn, qch. **searching** **1.** *a.* (examen) minutieux; (regard) scrutateur; **s. questions,** questions *fpl* qui vont au fond des choses. **2.** *n.* (*a*) inspection *f* (d'un endroit, etc.); fouille *f* (d'un suspect, etc.); *Cust:* visite *f*; *Jur:* perquisition *f*; (*b*) recherche *f* (**for,** de).

searcher ['səːtʃər] *n.* (re)chercheur, -euse.

searchlight ['səːtʃlait] *n.* (*a*) projecteur *m*; (*b*) (*beam*) projection *f*; **to turn a s. on sth.,** donner un coup de projecteur sur qch.

seascape ['siːskeip] *n.* **1.** panorama marin. **2.** *Art:* marine *f.*

seashell ['siːʃel] *n.* coquille *f* de mer; coquillage *m.*

seashore ['siːʃɔːr] *n.* (*a*) bord *m* de la mer; côte *f*, littoral *m*; (*b*) plage *f.*

seasick ['siːsik] *a.* **to be s.,** avoir le mal de mer.

seasickness ['siːsiknis] *n.* mal *m* de mer.

seaside ['siːsaid] *n.* bord *m* de la mer; **at the s.,** au bord de la mer; **s. resort,** plage *f*; station *f* balnéaire.

season¹ ['siːz(ə)n] *n.* **1.** saison *f*; (*a*) **the four seasons,** les quatre saisons; **the rainy s.,** la saison des pluies; (*b*) **hunting s.,** saison de la chasse; *Ven:* **close, open, s.,** chasse (ou pêche) fermée, ouverte; **the tourist s.,** la saison touristique; **the high s.,** la haute saison; **the slack s., the off s.,** la morte-saison; (*of oysters, etc.*) **to be in, out of, s.,** être de saison, hors de saison; **strawberries are in s.,** c'est la saison des fraises; (*of animal*) **in s.,** en rut; en chaleur; (*c*) *O:* **the (London) s.,** la saison londonienne. **2.** période *f*, temps *m*; **in due s.,** en temps voulu, en temps et saison; **word in s.,** mot dit à propos; **in s. and out of s.,** à tout propos et hors de propos; à tout bout de champ. **3. s. ticket,** *F:* **s.,** carte *f* d'abonnement; **s. ticket holder,** abonné, -ée.

season² **1.** *v.tr.* (*a*) assaisonner, apprêter, relever (un mets); (*b*) dessécher, étuver, conditionner (le bois); aviner (un tonneau); mûrir (le vin); (*c*) acclimater, endurcir (qn); aguerrir (un soldat). **2.** *v.i.* (*of wood*) se sécher; (*of wine, etc.*) mûrir, se faire. **seasoned** *a.* **1.** (*of dish*) assaisonné; **highly s. dish,** plat relevé, épicé. **2.** (*a*) (*of wood, cigar, etc.*) sec, *f.* sèche; (*of wine*) mûr, fait; (*b*) (*of pers.*) acclimaté, endurci; (soldat) aguerri. **seasoning** *n.* **1.** (*a*) *Cu:* assaisonnement *m*, apprêt *m* (d'un mets); (*b*) dessiccation *f*, séchage *m* (du bois, etc.); avinage *m* (d'un tonneau); maturation *f* (du vin, etc.); (*c*) acclimatement *m*, endurcissement *m* (de qn); aguerrissement *m* (des troupes, etc.). **2.** *Cu:* assaisonnement, condiment *m.*

seasonable ['siːzənəbl] *a.* **1. s. weather,** un temps de saison. **2.** (*of help, advice*) opportun, à propos.

seasonal ['siːzən(ə)l] *a.* (changements, etc.) des saisons; (commerce) saisonnier; **s. worker,** (ouvrier) saisonnier (*m*).

seat¹ [siːt] *n.* **1.** (*a*) siège *m*; banc *m*; banquette *f* (d'autobus, de train, etc.); gradin *m* (d'amphithéâtre); lunette *f* (de W.C.); *Av:* **ejection, ejector, s.,** siège éjectable; *F:* **to be in the hot s.,** être sur la sellette; *Aut: Th: etc:* **flap, folding, s.,** strapontin *m*; (*b*) **to take a s.,** s'asseoir; **to keep one's s.,** rester assis; (*c*) *Trans: Th: etc:* place *f*; **keep a s. for me,** gardez une place pour moi; (*d*) *Parl: etc:* siège; **to have a s. in the House,** être député; **to have a s. on the Council,** être conseiller (municipal). **2.** (*a*) siège, fond *m* (d'une chaise); (*b*) *F:* (*of pers.*) derrière *m*; fesses *fpl*; (*c*) fond *m* (de pantalon). **3.** (*a*) siège, centre *m* (du gouvernement, d'une industrie); chef-lieu *m* (judiciaire); centre (intellectuel); foyer *m* (de science, d'une maladie, etc.); *Med:* **the s. of the trouble,** le siège du mal; (*b*) **country s., s. in the country,** château *m*; manoir *m*. **4.** *Equit:* assiette *f*; **to have a good s.,** avoir une bonne assiette. **5.** *Tchn:* siège (d'une soupape); chaise (d'un coussinet); embase *f*, assiette (d'une machine, etc.); *I.C.E:* selle, assiette (de cylindre).

seat^{2} *v.tr.* **1.** (faire) asseoir (un enfant, etc.); **to remain seated,** rester assis. **2.** (*a*) placer (qn); disposer, placer (les invités); (*b*) **bus to s. thirty,** autobus *m* à trente places (assises); **this table seats twelve,** on tient douze à cette table. **3.** (*a*) (re)mettre le siège à (une chaise); (*b*) remettre un fond à (une culotte). **4.** fournir (une salle, etc.) de chaises, de sièges. **5.** asseoir, poser (une machine, etc.); *Mec.E: etc:* faire reposer, caler, (une pièce) sur son siège; *I.C.E:* assurer, ajuster, l'assise (d'une soupape). **6.** *v.i.* (*of skirt, etc.*) faire des poches. **seating** *n.* **1.** (*a*) allocation *f* des sièges, des places; disposition *f* (des invités); (*b*) sièges *mpl* (dans une salle, etc.); **s. capacity,** nombre *m* de places (assises) (dans une salle, etc.). **2.** matériaux *mpl* pour sièges de chaises. **3.** *Tchn:* portage *m*; siège (de soupape, etc.); embase *f*, lit *m* de pose (d'une machine); assiette *f*, logement *m* (d'un organe de machine). **4.** montage *m* (d'une piece, d'une soupape, etc.).

seatbelt ['si:tbelt] *n. Aut: Av:* ceinture *f* (de sécurité); *Aut:* **inertia reel s.,** ceinture à enrouleur (automatique); **fasten your seatbelts,** attachez vos ceintures.

seawall ['si:wɔ:l] *n.* digue *f*.

seaward ['si:wəd] **1.** *adv.* (*also* **seawards**) vers la mer; du côté du large. **2.** *a.* **s. breeze,** brise *f* du large **3.** *n.* **to s.,** du côté du large; vers le large.

seawater ['si:wɔ:tər] *n.* eau *f* de mer.

seaway ['si:wei] *n. Nau:* **1.** route *f*, sillage *m* (d'un navire). **2.** mer dure; levée *f* (de la mer). **3. the St. Lawrence S.,** la voie maritime du Saint-Laurent.

seaweed ['si:wi:d] *n.* algue *f*; varech *m*, goémon *m*.

seaworthiness ['si:wə:ðinis] *n.* (bon état de) navigabilité *f*.

seaworthy ['si:wə:ði] *a.* (*of ship*) en (bon) état de navigabilité; qui tient la mer.

sebaceous [si'beiʃəs] *a.* (*of gland, cyst, etc.*) sébacé.

sebum ['si:bəm] *n. Physiol:* sébum *m*.

sec [sek] *n. F:* **half a s.! just a s.!** un instant! une seconde!

secant ['sekənt, 'si:-] *Mth:* **1.** *a.* sécant. **2.** *n.* sécante *f*.

secateurs ['sekətə(:)z] *n.pl. Tls: Hort:* sécateur *m*.

secede [si'si:d] *v.i.* faire scission, faire sécession (**from,** de); se séparer (d'un parti).

secession [si'seʃ(ə)n] *n.* sécession *f*; *U.S: Hist:* **the War of S.,** la Guerre de Sécession.

secessionist [si'seʃənist] *a. & n.* (*a*) scissionniste (*mf*); (*b*) *U.S: Hist:* sécessionniste (*mf*).

seclude [si'klu:d] *v.tr.* tenir (qn, qch.) retiré, éloigné, écarté (**from,** de); **to s. oneself,** se reclure; se retirer du monde. **secluded** *a.* (endroit) écarté, retiré; **s. life,** vie retirée, cloîtrée; **to live as s. life,** vivre dans la solitude.

seclusion [si'klu:ʒ(ə)n] *n.* solitude *f*, retraite *f*; **in s.,** retiré du monde; **to live in s.,** vivre dans la solitude.

second^{1} ['sekənd] *n.* **1.** seconde *f* (de temps); *Clockm:* **second(s) hand,** trotteuse *f*; **in a split s.,** en moins d'une seconde; en un rien de temps; **wait a s.!** attendez une seconde, un instant! **2.** *Mth: Astr:* seconde (de degré).

second^{2} **I.** *a.* **1.** second; deuxième; (*a*) **the s. of March,** le deux mars; **twenty-s., thirty-s.,** vingt-deuxième, trente-deuxième; **ninety-s.,** quatre-vingt-douzième; **to live on the s. floor,** habiter (i) au deuxième, au second (étage), (ii) *NAm:* au troisième; **Charles the S.,** Charles Deux; **in (the) s. place,** deuxièmement, en second lieu; **to marry for the s. time,** se marier en secondes noces; (*at meal*) **to take a s. helping,** reprendre; **to get one's s. wind,** (i) reprendre haleine; (ii) se remettre; *Sch:* **s. form** = classe *f* de cinquième; *Aut:* **s. gear,** deuxième vitesse *f*; *n.* **to start in s.,** démarrer en deuxième; *Gram:* **s. person,** deuxième personne; (*b*) **the s. largest city in the world,** la deuxième ville du monde (en importance); **to take s. place,** passer second; **he is s. to none in intelligence,** pour l'intelligence il ne le cède à personne; **to be s. in command,** commander en second; *Mus:* **the s. violins,** les seconds violons; (*c*) **s. best,** deuxième; **it's only a s. best,** ce n'est qu'un pis-aller; *Rail:* **to travel s. class,** voyager en seconde; *Post:* **s.-class mail,** courrier *m* à tarif réduit; *F:* **s.-class citizen,** citoyen, -enne, de seconde zone; **s. rate,** médiocre, inférieur; (artiste) de second ordre. **2.** second; autre; nouveau; **s. nature,** seconde nature; **s. childhood,** deuxième enfance *f*; **s. sight,** clairvoyance *f*, seconde vue. **II.** *n.* **1.** (le) second, (la) seconde; (le, la) deuxième; *Sp: etc:* **to come in a good s.,** arriver bon second; *Mil: etc:* **s. in command,** commandant *m* en second; *Sch:* **to get a s.** = être reçu à la licence avec mention assez bien; *F:* (*at meal*) **anyone for seconds?** qui est-ce qui va reprendre? **2.** *Mus:* **major, minor, s.,** seconde majeure, mineure. **3.** *Com:* **seconds,** articles *mpl* de deuxième qualité. **4.** (*a*) (*in duel*) témoin *m*; (*b*) *Box:* second; soigneur *m*. **secondly** *adv.* deuxièmement; en second lieu.

second^{3} *v.tr.* **1.** ['sekənd] (*a*) seconder (qn); **to be seconded by s.o.,** être secondé de, par, qn; (*b*) (*in debate, etc.*) appuyer (une proposition). **2.** [si'kɔnd] mettre (un officier) en disponibilité, hors cadre (pour fonctions spéciales, etc.); (*esp. in passive*) **to be seconded,** être mis hors cadre; être détaché (**to,** à; **from,** de).

secondary ['sekənd(ə)ri] *a.* **1.** secondaire; (*of evidence*) indirect; **s. meaning of a word,** sens dérivé d'un mot; *Sch:* **s. education,** enseignement *m* secondaire, du second degré; *Astr:* **s. planet,** *n.* **s.,** planète *f* secondaire. **2.** (rôle, etc.) peu important, accessoire; **of s. importance,** d'importance secondaire; **s. road** = route secondaire, départementale.

seconder ['sekəndər] *n.* **to be the s. of a proposal,** appuyer une proposition.

secondhand [sekənd'hænd] **1.** *adv.* de seconde main; d'occasion; **to hear news s.,** recevoir des nouvelles de seconde main, d'un tiers. **2.** *a.* (nouvelle, etc.) de seconde main; (voiture, livre, meubles, etc.) d'occasion; **s. dealer,** revendeur, -euse; (*in clothes*) fripier *m*; (*in books*) bouquiniste *m*; **s. bookshop,** librairie *f* d'occasion; **s. clothes shop,** friperie *f*.

secondment [si'kɔndmənt] *n. Mil: etc:* détachement *m* (**to,** à; **from,** de).

secrecy ['si:krisi] *n.* **1.** discrétion *f*; **to bind, swear, s.o. to s.,** faire jurer le silence à qn. **2. in s.,** en secret.

secret ['si:krit] **1.** *a.* (*a*) secret, -ète; caché; **to keep sth. s.,** tenir, garder, qch. secret; cacher, taire, qch.; **s. meeting, assembly,** conciliabule *m*; **s. agent,** (i) agent secret; (ii) affidé(e); *F:* **the S. Service** = le Deuxième Bureau; **s. door,** porte cachée, dérobée; **desk with a s. compartment,** bureau *m* à secret; (*b*) *O:* (*of pers.*) discret; peu communicatif; (*c*) (*of place*) secret, caché. **2.** (*a*) secret *m*; **I make no s. of it,** je n'en fais pas mystère; **to let s.o. into the s.,** mettre qn dans le secret; **an open s.,** le secret de tout le monde, de Polichinelle; (*b*) **in s.,** en secret. **-ly** *adv.* secrètement; en secret.

secretarial [sekrə'tɛəriəl] a. (travail) de secrétaire; **s. college, course,** école *f* cours *m*, de secrétariat.

secretariat [sekrə'tɛəriət] *n.* secrétariat *m*.

secretary ['sekrət(ə)ri] *n.* **1.** (*a*) secrétaire *mf*; **private s.,** secrétaire particulier, -ière; **company s.,** secrétaire de direction; (*b*) **S. of State,** ministre *m* (à portefeuille), secrétaire d'État; **Foreign S.,** *U.S:* **S. of State** = ministre des Affaires étrangères; (*c*) *Dipl:* **(1st, 2nd, 3rd) s.** = secrétaire d'ambassade. **2.** *Orn:* **s. (bird),** serpentaire *m*, secrétaire *m*.

secrete¹ [si'kri:t] *v.tr.* (*of gland, etc.*) sécréter.
secrete² *v.tr.* cacher (qn, qch.).
secretion [si'kri:ʃ(ə)n] *n. Physiol:* sécrétion *f.*
secretive ['si:krətiv] *a.* (*of pers.*) réservé, dissimulé; cachottier.
secretiveness [si'kri:tivnis] *n.* (*of pers.*) réserve *f*; cachotterie *f.*
sect [sekt] *n.* secte *f.*
sectarian [sek'tεəriən] **1.** *a.* (esprit, culte) sectaire; **s. quarrels,** querelles partisanes. **2.** *n.* sectaire *mf.*
sectarianism [sek'tεəriənizm] *n.* sectarisme *m*; esprit *m* sectaire.
section¹ ['sekʃ(ə)n] *n.* **1.** sectionnement *m*, section *f* (de qch.); *Surg:* section (d'un nerf). **2.** (*a*) tranche *f*, lamelle *f*; **microscopic s.,** mince lame, plaque *f* (pour examen au microscope); (*b*) *Mth:* section; **conic, plane, s.,** section conique, plane; (*c*) *Arch: Const: etc:* coupe *f*, profil *m*, section; **horizontal s.,** coupe, section, horizontale; (*d*) *Metalw: Civ.E: etc:* profilé *m* (en métal). **3.** (*a*) section, portion *f* (de qch.); partie *f*, division *f* (d'une structure, etc.); tronçon *m* (de tube, de voie ferrée, etc.); section, tronçon (de circuit, etc.); quartier *m* (d'orange, etc.); *Com:* rayon *m* (d'un magasin); *U.S: Rail:* compartiment *m* (d'un wagon-lit); *Cmptr:* **input, output, s.,** zone *f* d'entrée, de sortie (des données); *Rail:* **block s.,** section de block; *Av:* **nose s.,** section avant, nez *m* (de l'appareil); (*b*) élément (constitutif, préfabriqué); (*c*) *Bookb:* cahier *m*; (*d*) *Ap:* cadre *m* (dans une ruche); (*e*) *U.S:* lotissement *m* (d'un mille carré); (*f*) division *f* (d'un document, etc.); article *m* (d'une loi, etc.); *Typ:* section, paragraphe *m*, alinéa *m*; (*g*) *Journ:* rubrique *f*; **sports s.,** rubrique sport; (*h*) *St. Exch:* rubrique, compartiment; (*i*) *Mus:* (*in orchestra*) groupe *m* (de cuivres, etc.); (*j*) **all sections of the population,** toutes les couches de la population, toutes les catégories sociales; (*k*) *Mil:* (i) section (d'un service); (ii) (*fighting unit*) groupe de combat (d'une section d'infanterie); équipe *f* (de fusiliers, de grenadiers).
section² *v.tr.* couper, diviser (qch.) en sections; sectionner (un pays, etc.).
sectional ['sekʃən(ə)l] *a.* appartenant à une classe, à un parti. **2.** (dessin, etc.) en coupe, en profil; (surface) de section.
sectionalism ['sekʃənəlizm] *n. U.S:* régionalisme *m*; esprit *m* de clocher.
sector ['sektər] *n.* **1.** (*a*) *Mth: Astr:* secteur *m*; **s. of a circle,** secteur circulaire; (*b*) *Mil:* secteur; *Adm:* **public, private, s.,** secteur public, privé. **2.** *Mec.E:* secteur, couronne *f.* **3.** *Mth:* compas *m* de proportion.
secular ['sekjulər] *a.* **1.** (*a*) *Ecc:* **s. priest,** *n.* **s.,** (prêtre) séculier (*m*); (*b*) (*of history, art, etc.*) séculier, laïque; (*of music*) profane. **2.** (fête, etc.) séculaire.
secularism ['sekjulərizm] *n.* **1.** *Phil:* sécularisme *m*; **2.** laïcisme *m.*
secularization [sekjulərai'zeiʃ(ə)n] *n.* sécularisation *f* (de biens ecclésiastiques, etc.); désaffectation *f* (d'une église); laïcisation *f* (d'une école, etc.).
secularize ['sekjuləraiz] *v.tr.* séculariser (un domaine, etc.); laïciser (une école, etc.); **secularized church,** église désaffectée.
secure¹ [si'kjuər] *a.* **1.** (*a*) (*free from anxiety*) sûr; (avenir) assuré; *Fin:* (placement) sûr, de tout repos; (*b*) **to feel s. of victory,** être assuré, certain, de la victoire. **2.** (*a*) (*safe*) en sûreté; à l'abri; sauf; (*b*) **the prisoner is s.,** le prisonnier est en lieu sûr. **3.** (*of door, plank, etc.*) fixe, assujetti; (*of foundations*) solide; (*of foothold, grasp*) ferme, sûr; **to make the boat s.,** bien amarrer le canot. **-ly** *adv.* **1.** sûrement; sans danger. **2.** solidement.
secure² *v.tr.* **1.** (*a*) mettre (qn, qch.) en sûreté, à l'abri (du danger); **to s. a pass,** garder un défilé; (*b*) mettre (un prisonnier) en lieu sûr; (*c*) *Mil:* **to s. arms,** mettre l'arme sous le bras gauche. **2.** immobiliser; assurer, assujettir (qch. qui a du jeu); fixer (un volet qui bat, etc.); retenir (qch. à sa place); accorer (un tonneau, etc.); arrimer (une cargaison); *Nau:* saisir (les canots, l'ancre). **3.** *Jur: Com:* nantir (un prêteur) (par une hypothèque, d'un titre, etc.); **to s. a debt by mortgage,** hypothéquer une créance. **4.** obtenir, acquérir; se procurer (qch.); atteindre (son but); **to s. sth. for s.o.,** procurer qch. à qn. **secured** *a.* **1.** (avenir, etc.) sûr, assuré. **2.** *Jur:* (emprunt) garanti, gagé; (créancier) garanti, nanti.
security [si'kjuəriti] *n.* **1.** (*a*) sécurité *f*, sûreté *f*; **to live in s.,** vivre en sûreté, en sécurité; **s. device,** dispositif *m* de sûreté; *Adm:* **social s.,** sécurité sociale; *Adm: Mil: etc:* **s. clearance,** (i) contrôle *m* de sécurité (sur qn); (ii) certificat *m* de sécurité; **he's, it's, a s. risk,** il, cela, constitue un danger, un risque, pour la securité; (*b*) stabilité *f*; solidité *f* (d'une fermeture, etc.); (*c*) *Adm:* organes *mpl* de renseignements et de sécurité. **2.** (moyen *m* de) sécurité; sauvegarde *f.* **3.** *Com: Jur:* (*a*) caution *f*, cautionnment *m*; gage *m*, garantie *f*; (*collateral*) nantissement *m*; **s. for a debt,** garantie d'une créance; **to give sth. as (a) s.,** donner qch. en gage, en cautionnement; **to lend money on s., without s.,** prêter de l'argent sur nantissement, sur gage, à découvert; (*b*) (*pers.*) (donneur, -euse, de) caution; garant, -ante; (*c*) *Fin:* **securities,** (i) titres *mpl*, valeurs *fpl*, fonds *mpl*; (ii) portefeuille *m* titres; *F:* portefeuille; **government securities,** fonds d'État; **the s. market,** le marché des valeurs; la Bourse.
sedan [si'dæn] *n.* **1.** *A:* **s. (chair),** chaise *f* à porteurs. **2.** *Aut: NAm:* voiture *f* à conduite intérieure; **four-door s.,** berline *f.*
sedate¹ [si'deit] *a.* (*of pers.*) posé, reposé; (maintien) composé, calme; (esprit) rassis. **-ly** *adv.* posément.
sedate² *v.tr. Med:* donner un sédatif à (qn).
sedation [si'deiʃ(ə)n] *n. Med:* sédation *f.*
sedative ['sedətiv] *a.* & *n. Med:* sédatif (*m*); calmant (*m*).
sedentary ['sedənt(ə)ri] *a.* (*a*) (*of posture*) assis; (*b*) (emploi, etc.) sédentaire; **s. life,** vie *f* sédentaire.
sedge [sedʒ] *n.* **1.** *Bot:* (*a*) carex *m*; laîche *f*; (*b*) joncs *mpl*, roseaux *mpl.* **2.** *Orn:* **s. warbler,** phragmite *m* des joncs.
sediment ['sedimənt] *n.* sédiment *m*, dépôt *m*; boue *f* (d'un accu, etc.); lie *f* (du vin); *Ch:* résidu *m.*
sedimentary [sedi'ment(ə)ri] *a. Geol:* (couche, roche) sédimentaire.
sedimentation [sedimen'teiʃ(ə)n] *n.* sédimentation *f.*
sedition [si'diʃ(ə)n] *n.* sédition *f.*
seditious [si'diʃəs] *a.* séditieux.
seduce [si'dju:s] *v.tr.* **1.** séduire, corrompre (qn). **2.** séduire (une femme).
seducer [si'dju:sər] *n.* **1.** séducteur, -trice; corrupteur, -trice. **2.** séducteur (d'une femme).
seduction [si'dʌkʃ(ə)n] *n.* **1.** (*a*) séduction *f*, corruption *f* (de qn); (*b*) séduction (d'une femme). **2.** attrait *m*, charme *m*, séduction (de qch.); allèchement *m* (de la volupté, etc.).
seductive [si'dʌktiv] *a.* **1.** séduisant, attrayant; (sourire) aguichant; **s. offer,** offre séduisante, alléchante. **2.** (discours, etc.) suborneur. **-ly** *adv.* d'une manière séduisante.
seductiveness [si'dʌktivnis] *n.* caractère séduisant, attrayant (d'une offre, etc.); attraits *mpl*, charmes *mpl* (d'une femme); séduction *f* (du style).
see¹ [si:] *v.tr.* (*p.t.* **saw** [sɔ:]; *p.p.* **seen** [si:n]) **1.** voir; (*a*) **I saw it with my own eyes,** je l'ai vu de mes (propres) yeux; **the cathedral can be seen from a long way off,** la cathédrale se voit, est visible, de loin; **to**

s. the sights of the town, visiter les monuments de la ville; **there's nothing to s.,** il n'y a rien à voir; **the moment I saw him,** dès que je l'ai aperçu, vu; **s. what a mess you've made!** regardez-moi ce gâchis! **s. page 50,** voir page 50; **s. above,** se reporter plus haut; **s. (on) the back,** voir au verso; **I'm not fit to be seen,** je ne suis pas présentable; *F:* **to s. things,** avoir des hallucinations, des visions; (*b*) **as far as the eye can s.,** à perte de vue; **cats can s. in the dark,** les chats y voient clair la nuit; (*c*) **to s. s.o. do, doing, sth.,** voir qn faire qch.; **I saw him fall,** je l'ai vu tomber; **to s. s.o. coming,** voir venir qn; **I can't s. myself doing this,** je ne me vois pas dans ce rôle; *F:* **I'll s. you damned, in hell, first!** va-t-en au diable! va te faire pendre! (*d*) **to s. s.o. home,** reconduire qn, accompagner qn, jusque chez lui; **I saw him to the station,** je l'ai accompagné jusqu'à la gare; (*e*) **he has seen a great deal of the world,** (i) il a beaucoup voyagé; (ii) il a une vaste expérience du monde; il connaît bien la vie; *Mil:* **the first time he saw action,** quand il a reçu le baptême du feu. **2.** (*a*) comprendre, saisir (une pensée, etc.); reconnaître (ses erreurs, etc.); **they cannot s. the truth,** la vérité leur échappe; **I don't s. the point,** je ne saisis pas la nuance; **he can't s. a joke,** il n'entend pas la plaisanterie; **as far as I can s.,** à ce que je vois; autant que j'en puis juger; **I s.!** je comprends! **(d'you) s.?** vous comprenez? vous y êtes? **you s., I never liked them,** c'est que je ne les ai jamais aimés; (*b*) observer, remarquer (qch.); s'apercevoir de (qch.); **s. for yourself,** voyez pour vous-même; **to s. oneself in one's children,** se reconnaître dans ses enfants; **I don't know what you can s. in her,** je ne sais pas pourquoi vous l'admirez; **it remains to be seen whether . . .,** reste à savoir si . . .; **it remains to be seen, wait and s., we shall s.,** qui vivra verra; nous verrons bien; (*c*) voir, juger, apprécier (qch. d'une certaine manière); **I s. things differently now,** aujourd'hui je vois les choses autrement; **this is how I s. it,** voici comme j'envisage la chose. **3.** examiner (qch.); regarder (qch.) avec attention; **let me s. that letter again,** repassez-moi cette lettre (pour que je la relise); **I'll s. what I can do,** je vais voir ce que je peux faire; *v.ind.tr.* **I'll s. about it,** je m'en occuperai; je verrai; **let's s. (it)!** faites voir! **let me s.!** (i) faites voir! (ii) attendez un moment! *F:* **s. here!** dites donc! voyons! **4. to s. (to it) that everything is in order,** s'assurer que tout est en ordre; **I shall s. (to it) that he comes,** je me charge de le faire venir; **s. that you don't miss the train!** faites attention de ne pas manquer le train! **5.** (*a*) fréquenter, avoir des rapports avec, voir (qn); **he sees a great deal of the Longs,** il fréquente beaucoup les Long; **we don't s. much of each other,** nous ne nous voyons pas souvent; **when shall I s. you again?** quand est-ce que je vais vous revoir? *F:* **s. you soon! (I'll) be seeing you!** à bientôt! **(I'll) s. you Thursday!** a jeudi! (*b*) **to go to, and, s. s.o.,** aller voir qn; **I'd like to s. you on business,** je voudrais vous parler d'affaires; **to s. a doctor,** consulter un médecin; (*c*) recevoir (un visiteur); **I can't s. him today,** je ne peux pas le recevoir aujourd'hui. **see in** *v.tr.* faire entrer (qn); **to s. the new year in,** faire le réveillon du nouvel an. **seeing 1.** *a.* voyant; qui voit. **2.** *conj.* **s. (that) . . .,** vu que . . .; puisque . . .; étant donné que . . . **3.** *n.* vue *f*; vision *f*; **s. is believing,** voir c'est croire. **see in, see into** *v.tr.* voir, pénétrer, dans (l'avenir, etc.). **see off** *v.tr.* (*a*) **to s. s.o. off at the station,** accompagner qn jusqu'à la gare (pour lui dire au revoir); (*b*) **to s. s.o. off (the premises),** s'assurer du départ de qn; se débarrasser de qn. **see out** *v.tr.* (*a*) accompagner (qn) jusqu'à la porte; (*b*) voir la fin de (qch.); mener (une entreprise, etc.) à bonne fin; (*c*) survivre à (qn); **he'll s. us all out!** il nous enterrera tous. **see over, see round** *v.tr.* visiter, voir (une maison, etc.). **see through 1.** *v.tr.* pénétrer les intentions de (qn); pénétrer, percer à jour (un mystère); **I'm beginning to s. through it,** je commence à y voir clair. **2.** *v.tr.* assister à (un spectacle, etc.) jusqu'au bout; mener (une affaire) à bonne fin, jusqu'au bout; **I'll s. it through,** je vais tenir jusqu'au bout. **see to** *v.tr.* s'occuper de (qn, qch.); **I'll s. to it,** je vais m'en occuper; je m'en charge.

see² *s. Ecc:* siège épiscopal; (*of bishop*) évêché *m*; (*of archbishop*) archevêché *m*; métropole *f*; **the Holy S.,** le Saint-Siège.

seed¹ [siːd] *n.* **1.** (*a*) *Bot:* graine *f*, grain *m* (d'un fruit); **mustard s.,** grain de moutarde; **s. vessel,** péricarpe *m*; (*b*) *Agr: Hort:* **seed(s),** semence *f*; graine(s); semis *m*; **to go, run, to s.,** (i) (*of plant*) monter en graine; (ii) (*of land*) s'affricher; (iii) (*of pers.*) se laisser aller; **s. corn,** grain de semence; **s. potatoes,** pommes *f* de terre à semence; **s. bed,** (couche *f* de) semis; germoir *m*; **s. box, tray,** boîte *f*, terrine *f*, à semis; **s. merchant,** grainetier, -ière; (*c*) **the seeds of discord,** les semences, les germes *mpl*, de discorde; **to sow (the) seeds of discord,** semer la discorde; (*d*) frai *m* (d'huître); **s. oysters,** naissain *m*; (*e*) **s. pearls,** semence de perles; (*f*) *Ten:* tête *f* de série. **2.** (*a*) = SEMEN; (*b*) *B: Lit:* descendance *f*, lignée *f*; **the s. of Abraham,** la semence d'Abraham.

seed² **1.** *v.i.* (*of plant*) (*a*) monter en graine; porter semence; (*b*) (*of cereals*) grener; venir à graine; (*c*) s'égrener. **2.** *v.tr.* (*a*) semer (un champ, etc.); (*b*) enlever la graine (d'un fruit); épépiner (des melons, etc.); égruger (des raisins, etc.); (*c*) *Ten:* **to s. the players,** trier les joueurs; **seeded players,** têtes *f* de série.

seedcake [ˈsiːdkeik] *n.* gâteau parfumé au carvi.

seediness [ˈsiːdinis] *n. F:* **1.** état *m* minable; tenue *f* minable. **2.** indisposition *f*.

seedless [ˈsiːdlis] *a.* (*a*) *Bot:* asperme; (*b*) (fruit) sans pépins.

seedling [ˈsiːdliŋ] *n. Hort:* (jeune) plant *m*; *Arb:* sauvageon *m*; **seedlings,** semis *m*.

seedsman, *pl.* **-men** [ˈsiːdzmən] *n.m.* grainetier.

seedy [ˈsiːdi] *a.* **1.** (*of plant*) plein de graines; (épi) grenu. **2.** *F:* (*a*) (*of pers.*) miteux; (*b*) (*of hotel, etc.*) moche. **3.** *F:* (*of pers.*) mal en train, patraque; **to feel s.,** ne pas être dans son assiette.

seek [siːk] *v.tr.* (*p.t. & p.p.* **sought** [sɔːt]) **1.** chercher (un objet perdu, etc.); rechercher, quêter (l'amitié de qn, de l'avancement, etc.); **to s. s.o. (out),** chercher (et trouver) qn; **to s. shelter,** chercher un abri; se réfugier (sous qch.); **to s. s.o.'s help,** rechercher, demander, l'aide de qn. **2.** (*a*) **to s. sth. from, of, s.o.,** demander qch. à qn; **to s. advice,** demander conseil; (*b*) **to be much sought after,** être très recherché.

seeker [ˈsiːkər] *n.* chercheur, -euse; **a s. after truth,** un chercheur de vérité; **pleasure seekers,** gens *m* en quête de plaisirs.

seem [siːm] *v.i.* sembler, paraître. **1.** (*a*) **to s. tired,** paraître fatigué; avoir l'air fatigué; **how does it s. to you?** qu'en pensez-vous? **it seems like a dream,** on croirait rêver; (*b*) **I s. to have heard his name,** il me semble avoir entendu son nom; **I seemed to be floating on a cloud,** j'avais l'impression de flotter sur un nuage. **2.** *impers.* **it seems (that) . . ., it would s. that . . .,** il paraît, il semble, que . . .; **it seemed to me (that) I was dreaming,** il me semblait, on aurait dit, que je rêvais; **it seemed as though, as if . . .,** il semblait que + *sub.*; on aurait dit que + *ind.*; **it seems so, it would s. so,** à ce qu'il paraît; **it seems not, it wouldn't s. so,** il paraît que non. **seemingly** *adv.* apparemment; en apparence.

seemliness [ˈsiːmlinis] *n. O:* bienséance *f*.

seemly [ˈsiːmli] *a. O:* convenable, bienséant.

seep [si:p] *v.i.* (*a*) suinter; s'infiltrer; **the water was seeping through the earth,** l'eau filtrait à travers la terre; (*b*) **information was seeping out,** des renseignements filtraient.

seepage ['si:pidʒ] *n.* **1.** suintement *m.* **2.** fuite *f*, déperdition *f* (par infiltration).

seer ['si(:)ər] *n. Lit:* prophète *m.*

seersucker ['si(:)əsʌkər] *n. Tex:* coton gaufré, crépon *m* de coton.

seesaw¹ ['si:sɔ:] **1.** *n.* bascule *f.* **2.** *a.* (mouvement) (i) de bascule, (ii) de va-et-vient.

seesaw² *v.i.* **1.** jouer à la bascule. **2.** (*of machine part, etc.*) basculer; osciller.

seethe [si:ð] *v.i.* (*a*) (*of liquid*) bouillonner; s'agiter; (*b*) (*of crowd, etc.*) s'agiter; **the street is seething with people,** la rue grouille de monde; **to be seething with anger,** bouillir de colère. **seething** *a.* (*of liquid*) bouillonnant, agité; **a s. mass of worms,** une masse grouillante, foisonnante, de vers.

see-through ['si:θru:] *a.* transparent.

segment¹ ['segmənt] *n.* (*a*) *Mth:* segment *m* (d'une sphère, d'un cercle, etc.); **s. of a line,** segment linéaire; (*b*) quartier *m* (d'une orange); (*c*) *Ann:* segment (d'un ver).

segment² [seg'ment] **1.** *v.tr.* couper, partager (qch.) en segments; segmenter. **2.** *v.i. Biol:* se segmenter.

segmentation [segmen'teiʃ(ə)n] *n. Biol:* segmentation *f.*

segregate ['segrigeit] **1.** *v.tr.* isoler, mettre à part (qch.); séparer (deux espèces, etc.) l'un(e) de l'autre; ségréger (des races). **2.** *v.i.* (*a*) se diviser; se désunir **(from,** de); (*b*) se grouper à part **(from,** de).

segregation [segri'geiʃ(ə)n] *n.* ségrégation *f*; séparation *f*, isolement *m*; **policy of s.,** ségrégationnisme *m.*

segregationist [segri'geiʃənist] *a.* & *n. Pol:* ségrégationniste (*mf*).

seism [saizm] *n.* séisme *m.*

seismic ['saizmik] *a.* s(é)ismique.

seismograph ['saizməgræf] *n.* s(é)ismographe *m.*

seismologist [saiz'mɔlədʒist] *n.* s(é)ismologiste *mf*, s(é)ismologue *mf.*

seismology [saiz'mɔlədʒi] *n.* s(é)ismologie *f.*

seize [si:z] **I.** *v.tr.* **1.** (*a*) *Jur:* confisquer, arrêter; saisir (qch.); opérer la saisie de (qch.); (*b*) **to s. s.o.,** arrêter qn; appréhender qn (au corps). **2.** (*a*) saisir; se saisir, s'emparer, de qch.; prendre (une forteresse); capturer (un navire ennemi); (*b*) **to s. (hold of) s.o., sth.,** saisir, empoigner qn, qch.; saisir (une idée); **to s. s.o. by the throat,** prendre qn à la gorge; (*c*) **to be seized with fright,** être saisi, frappé, d'effroi; **to s. the opportunity of doing sth.,** saisir, empoigner, l'occasion de faire qch.; **to s. the meaning of sth.,** prendre, saisir, le sens de qch.; (*d*) *v.ind.tr.* **to s. on a pretext for leaving,** saisir un prétexte, se saisir d'un prétexte, pour partir. **II.** *v.i. Mec.E:* (*of part*) **to s. (up),** (se) gripper, coincer; se coller; (se) caler; **the brake is seizing,** le frein prend, mord, brutalement. **seizing** *n.* **1.** (*a*) saisie *f* (d'une propriété, de marchandises, etc.); prise *f* (d'une forteresse, etc.); capture *f* (d'un navire ennemi, etc.); (*b*) empoignement *m* (de qn, de qch.). **2.** *Mec.E: etc:* grippage *m*, grippement *m*; calage *m* (d'un piston, etc.).

seizure ['si:ʒər] *n.* **1.** (*a*) *Jur:* appréhension *f* au corps **(of s.o.,** de qn); mainmise *f* **(of s.o.,** sur qn); (*b*) *Jur:* saisie *f* (de marchandises); (*c*) prise *f* (d'une ville, etc.); capture *f* (d'un navire ennemi, etc.). **2.** *Med:* crise *f*, attaque *f*; **(apoplectic) s.,** attaque d'apoplexie. **3.** *Mec.E:* grippage *m*, grippement *m*, calage *m.*

seldom ['seldəm] *adv.* rarement; peu souvent; **he is s. seen,** on le voit rarement; **such things are s. seen now,** de telles choses se font rares.

select¹ [si'lekt] *a.* **1.** choisi; *Parl:* **s. committee,** commission *f* d'enquête. **2.** de (premier) choix; d'élite; (club) très fermé, select; (public) choisi.

select² *v.tr.* choisir (des objets); sélectionner (des joueurs, etc.); **to s. from . . .,** choisir parmi . . . **selected** *a.* (*a*) choisi; *Lit:* **s. passages,** morceaux choisis; (*b*) *Com:* de choix.

selection [si'lekʃ(ə)n] *n.* **1.** choix *m*, sélection *f*; **natural s.,** sélection naturelle. **2. a good s. of wines,** un bon choix de vins; **to make a s.,** faire un choix; **selections from Byron,** morceaux choisis de Byron; *Turf:* **our selections,** nos pronostics *mpl.*

selective [si'lektiv] *a.* sélectif; sélecteur, -trice; **s. breeding,** élevage *m* à base de sélection; (*of pers.*) **to be s.,** savoir choisir; choisir avec discernement.

selectivity [selek'tiviti] *n.* sélectivité *f.*

selectman [si'lektmən] *n. U.S:* (*in New England*) = conseiller municipal.

selector [si'lektər] *n.* **1.** celui, celle, qui choisit, qui sélectionne; *Sp:* sélectionneur, -euse (d'une équipe etc.). **2.** (*a*) *Aut:* (*automatic gearbox*) **s. lever,** levier *m* de sélection; (*b*) *W. Tel: Tp:* sélecteur *m*; *El:* **s. switch,** combinateur *m*; (*c*) *Rec:* tête chercheuse.

self, *pl.* **selves** [self, selvz] **1.** *n.* (*a*) le moi; la personnalité; la personne; **he's quite his old, former, s., again,** (i) il est complètement rétabli; (ii) il est tout à fait comme auparavant; *Com:* **your good selves,** vous-mêmes; vous; (*b*) *Hort:* fleur *f* de couleur uniforme. **2.** *pron.* (*on cheque*) **pay s.,** payez à moi-même.

self- [self] *comb.fm.* automatique; auto-; de soi-même.

self-absorbed [-əb'sɔ:bd] *a.* égoïste.

self-addressed [-ə'drest] *a.* (enveloppe) adressée à soi-même.

self-adhesive [-əd'hi:ziv] *a.* autocollant.

self-adjusting [-ə'dʒʌstiŋ] *a. Tchn:* à autoréglage.

self-apparent [-ə'pærənt] *a.* évident; de toute évidence.

self-appointed [-ə'pɔintid] *a.* (*of pers.*) qui a pris sur lui, sur elle, de (faire qch.).

self-assertive [-ə'sə:tiv] *a.* autoritaire; impérieux; dominateur, -trice; outrecuidant.

self-assured [-ə'ʃu:əd] *a.* sûr de soi; plein d'assurance.

selfcentred ['-sentəd] *a.* égocentrique.

self-cleaning ['-kli:niŋ] *a.* (four) autonettoyant.

self-composed [-kəm'pouzd] *a.* (*of pers.*) posé, calme.

self-confessed [-kən'fest] *a.* qui s'accuse soi-même; (maoïste, etc.) avéré.

self(-)confidence [-'kɔnfidəns] *n.* (*a*) confiance *f* en soi; assurance *f*; sûreté de soi; aplomb *m*; **to lack s.(-)c.,** se défier de soi-même; (*b*) présomption *f.*

self-confident [-'kɔnfidənt] *a.* (*a*) sûr de soi; plein d'assurance; (*b*) présomptueux.

selfconscious [-'kɔnʃəs] *a.* **1.** *Phil:* conscient. **2.** (*a*) (*of pers.*) embarrassé, gêné; (sourire) contraint; (*b*) poseur; (style, etc.) affecté.

selfconsciousness [-'kɔnʃəsnis] *n.* **1.** *Phil:* conscience *f.* **2.** (*a*) contrainte *f*, embarras *m*, gêne *f*; (*b*) pose *f*, affectation *f.*

self-contained [-kən'teind] *a.* **1.** (*of pers.*) réservé; peu communicatif. **2.** (appareil, etc.) independant, complet par lui-même; autonome; (appartement) indépendant, avec entrée particuliére.

self(-)control [-kən'troul] *n.* empire *m* sur soi-même; maîtrise *f* de soi; **to exercise s.-c.,** faire un effort sur soi-méme; **to have no s.-c.,** ne savoir pas se maîtriser; **to lose one's s.-c.,** perdre tout empire sur soi-même; ne plus se maîtriser; **to regain one's s.-c.,** se ressaisir.

self-criticism [-'kritisizm] *n.* autocritique *f.*

self(-)defence, *NAm:* **-defense** [-di'fens] *n.* défense personnelle; autodéfense *f*; *Jur:* légitime défense; **to kill s.o. in s.(-)d.**, tuer qn en légitime défense.

self(-)denial [-di'naiəl] *n.* (*a*) abnégation *f* de soi; renoncement(s) *m(pl)*; privations *fpl*; (*b*) frugalité *f*.

self-denying [-di'naiiŋ] *a.* (*a*) qui fait abnégation de soi; qui s'impose des privations; (*b*) frugal, -aux.

self-destruction [-dis'trʌkʃ(ə)n] *n.* autodestruction *f*; suicide *m*.

self-determination [-ditə:mi'neiʃ(ə)n] *n. Pol:* autodétermination *f*.

self-drive ['draiv] *n.* **s.-d. cars for hire,** location *f* de voitures sans chauffeur.

self-educated [-'edjukeitid] *a.* autodidacte.

self-effacing [-i'feisiŋ] *n.* qui aime à s'effacer.

self-employed [-im'plɔid] *a.* qui travaille à von (propre) compte.

self-esteem [-i'sti:m] *n.* estime *f*, respect, *m*, de soi; amour-propre *m*.

self-evident [-'evid(ə)nt] *a.* évident en soi; qui saute aux yeux.

self-explanatory [-ik'splænət(ə)ri] *a.* qui s'explique de soi-même.

self(-)expression [-ik'spreʃ(ə)n] *n.* libre expression *f*.

self(-)fertilization [-fə:tilai'zeiʃ(ə)n] *n. Nat.Hist:* autofécondation *f*.

self-financing [-fai'nænsiŋ] **1.** *a.* (entreprise) qui se finance par ses propres ressources. **2.** *n.* autofinancement *m*.

self-governing [-'gʌvəniŋ], *a.* autonome.

self(-)government [-'gʌvənmənt] *n.* autonomie *f*.

self(-)help [-'help] *n.* efforts personnels.

self(-)importance [-im'pɔ:təns] *n.* suffisance *f*, présomption *f*; **eaten up with s.(-)i.**, pourri d'orgueil.

self-important [-im'pɔ:tənt] *a.* suffisant, presomptueux.

selfimposed [-im'pouzd] *a.* (tâche, etc.) dont on a pris de soi-même la responsabilité; (exil) volontaire.

self(-)induction [-in'dʌkʃən] *n. El:* self-induction *f*, auto-induction *f*; **s.-i. coil,** bobine *f* de self-induction, *F:* self *f*.

self(-)indulgence [-in'dʌldʒəns] *n.* sybaritisme *m*; habitude *f* de ne rien se refuser.

self(-)indulgent [-in'dʌldʒənt] *a.* sybarite; qui ne se refuse rien.

self-inflicted [-in'fliktid] *a.* (*of penance, etc.*) que l'on s'inflige à soi-même; **s.-i. wound,** mutilation *f* volontaire.

self(-)interest [-'int(ə)rest] *n.* intérêt (personnel); **to act from s.(-)i.**, agir dans un but intéressé.

selfish ['selfiʃ] *a.* égoïste, intéressé. **-ly** *adv.* égoïstement, d'une manière intéressée; **to act s.,** agir en égoïste.

selfishness ['selfiʃnis] *n.* égoïsme *m*.

selfless ['selflis] *a.* désintéressé; altruiste.

selflessness ['selflisnis] *n.* désintéressement *m*; altruisme *m*.

self-locking [-'lɔkiŋ] *a.* **1.** *Mec.E:* à blocage automatique; auto-bloqueur; (écrou) indesserrable. **2.** (porte, etc.) à verrouillage, fermeture, automatique.

selfmade ['selfmeid] *a.* (homme) qui est (le) fils de ses œuvres, qui est l'artisan de sa fortune, qui est arrivé par lui-même.

self-pity [-'piti] *n.* attendrissement *m* sur soi-même; **full of s.-p.,** attendri sur soi-même.

self-pollination [-pɔli'neiʃ(ə)n] *n. Bot;* autopollinisation *f*.

self-portrait [-'pɔ:treit] *n.* portrait *m* de l'artiste par lui-même; auto-portrait *m*.

self-possessed [-pə'zest] *a.* maître de soi; qui a beaucoup d'aplomb, de sang-froid; qui a de l'empire sur soi-même; **to remain entirely s.-p.,** rester entièrement maître de soi.

self(-)possession [-pə'zeʃ(ə)n] *n.* aplomb *m*, sang-froid *m*; empire *m* sur soi-même.

self(-)preservation [-prezə'veiʃ(ə)n] *n.* (instinct *m* de) conservation *f* (de soi-même).

self-propelled [-prə'peld, -'peliŋ] *a.* (*of vehicle*) automoteur, -trice; autopropulsé.

selfraising, *U.S:* **selfrising** ['selfreiziŋ, -raisiŋ] *a. Cu:* (farine) contenant de la levure chimique.

self-regulating [-'regjuleitiŋ] *a. Mec.E:* autorégulateur, -trice; à autoréglage.

self-reliant [-ri'laiənt] *a.* indépendant; qui a confiance en soi.

self-respect [-ri'spekt] *n.* respect *m* de soi; amour-propre *m*; **to lose all s.-r.,** tomber dans la dégradation.

self-respecting [-ri'spektiŋ] *a.* qui se respecte, qui a de l'amour-propre.

self-restraint [-ris'treint] *n.* retenue *f*; modération *f*; **to exercise s.-r.,** se contenir; se retenir.

selfrighteous [-'raitjəs] *a.* pharisaïque.

selfrighteousness [-'raitjəsnis] *n.* pharisaïsme *m*.

self-righting [-'raitiŋ] *a.* (*of lifeboat, etc.*) à redressement automatique; inchavirable.

self-sacrifice [-'sækrifais] *s.* abnégation *f* (de soi); immolation *f* du moi.

selfsame ['selfseim] *a.* identique; absolument le même.

self-satisfaction [-sætis'fækʃ(ə)n] *n.* contentement *m* de soi; fatuité *f*, suffisance *f*.

self-satisfied [-'sætisfaid] *a.* content de soi; suffisant.

self-service [-'sə:vis] *n. Com:* libre-service *m*.

self-starter [-'stɑ:tər] *n. Aut:* démarreur *m* (automatique).

selfstyled ['selfstaild] *a.* soi-disant *inv.* prétendu.

self(-)sufficiency [(-)sə'fiʃənsi] *n.* **1.** indépendance *f*; *Pol.Ec:* **national s.(-)s.,** autarcie *f*. **2.** vanité *f*, suffisance *f*.

self-sufficient [-sə'fiʃənt] *a.* **1.** (*of pers., thg*) indépendant; autosuffisant. **2.** (*of pers.*) suffisant.

self-supporting [-sə'pɔ:tiŋ] *a.* indépendant; (*of pers.*) qui suffit à ses besoins; (*of business*) qui fait, couvre, ses frais; *Arch:* (*of vault*) autoportant.

self-taught [-'tɔ:t] *a.* **1.** (*of pers.*) autodidacte. **2.** (*of knowledge*) que l'on a appris tout seul.

selfwilled [-'wild] *a.* opiniâtre, obstiné, volontaire.

self-winding [-'waindiŋ] *a.* (pendule) à remontage automatique.

sell¹ [sel] *n. F:* **1.** vente *f*; **hard s.,** vente au sabot; **soft s.,** vente facile, à publicité discrète. **2.** déception *f*; attrape *f*; **what a s.!** on s'est fait avoir!

sell² *v.tr.* (*p.t. & p.p.* **sold** [sould]) **1.** (*a*) vendre (qch.); vendre, placer (des marchandises); **difficult to s.,** de vente, d'écoulement, difficile; **to s. sth. by auction,** vendre qch. aux enchères; **to s. sth. at a loss,** vendre qch. à perte; **to sell sth. dear, cheap,** vendre qch. cher, (à) bon marché; **he sold it to me for £10,** il me l'a vendu (pour) £10; **to s. oneself,** se faire accepter, se faire valoir; *F:* **I couldn't s. my father the idea,** je n'ai pas pu faire accepter l'idée à mon père; **to be sold on an idea,** être entiché d'une idée; (*b*) (*with passive force*) **goods that s. well,** marchandises d'écoulement facile, qui se vendent bien; **certain to s.,** d'un débit assuré; **what are plums selling at?** combien valent, à combien se vendent, les prunes? **2.** (*a*) vendre, trahir (un secret, son pays, etc.); **to s. oneself,** se vendre; (*b*) *F:* duper, refaire (qn); **you've been sold!** on vous a refait! **selling** *n.* vente *f*, écoulement *m*, placement *m* (de marchandises, etc.); **s. price,** prix *m* de vente; prix marchand, fort; **s. off, out,** liquidation *f* (des stocks); *Fin:* (re)vente *f*, réalisation *f* (de titres, etc.). **sell off** *v.tr.* solder (des marchandises); se défaire de (ses marchandises); liquider (son stock, etc.). **sell out** *v.tr.* (*a*) *Fin:* réaliser (tout un portefeuille d'actions); *Com:* vendre tout son stock de (qch.); se défaire de (ses marchandises); **the edition is sold out,** l'édition est épuisée; **I'm sold out,** j'ai tout vendu; (*b*) vendre, trahir (qn). **sell up,** *v.tr. & i.* vendre ses effets; *Com:* vendre son fonds; vendre, faire saisir (un failli); **he sold up and went to Canada,** il a tout vendu et est parti au Canada.

seller [ˈselər] *n.* **1.** (*pers.*) (*a*) vendeur, -euse; *Fin:* réalisateur *m* (de titres); *St.Exch:* **seller's market,** marché *m* à la hausse; (*b*) marchand, -ande; débitant, -ante (**of,** de). **2.** (*of thg*) **good, bad, s.,** article de bonne, mauvaise, vente. **3.** *Turf:* course *f* à réclamer.

sellotape [ˈselouteip] *n. R.t.m.* ruban adhésif, scotch *m* (*R.t.m.*).

sellout [ˈselaut] *n. F:* **1.** trahison *f.* **2.** (*a*) **this play's a s.,** cette pièce a fait salle comble; (*b*) *Com:* **this line has been a s.,** cet article s'est vendu à merveille (et il ne nous en reste plus).

selvage, selvedge [ˈselvidʒ] *n. Tex:* lisière *f*; cordeau *m* (de lainages épais).

semantic [siˈmæntik] *a. Ling:* sémantique. **-ally** *adv.* du point de vue sémantique.

semantics [siˈmæntiks] *n.pl. Ling:* sémantique *f.*

semaphore¹ [ˈseməfɔːr] *n.* sémaphore *m*; *Rail: etc:* **s. signal,** signal *m* à bras.

semaphore² *v.tr.* transmettre (une communication) par sémaphore.

semblance [ˈsembləns] *n.* apparence *f*, semblant *m*; simulacre *m*; **a (mere) s. of friendship,** un semblant d'amitié.

semen [ˈsiːmen] *n. Physiol:* sperme *m*, semence *f.*

semester [siˈmestər] *n. NAm:* semestre *m.*

semi [ˈsemi] *n. F:* maison jumelée.

semi- [ˈsemi] *pref.* semi-; demi-.

semibreve [ˈsemibriːv] *n. Mus:* ronde *f.*

semicircle [ˈsemisəːkl] *n.* demicercle *m, pl.* demicercles.

semicircular [-ˈsəːkjulər] *n.* demi-circulaire, semicirculaire.

semicolon [-ˈkoulən] *n.* point-virgule *m, pl.* points-virgules.

semiconscious [-ˈkɔnʃəs] *a.* à demi conscient.

semiconsonant [-ˈkɔːsənənt] *n.* semi-consonne *f, pl.* semi-consonnes.

semidetached [-diˈtætʃt] *a.* (maison) jumelée, jumelle.

semifinal [-ˈfain(ə)l] *Sp:* **1.** *a.* demi-final, -als. **2.** *n.* demi-finale *f, pl.* demi-finales.

semifinalist [-ˈfainəlist] *n. Sp;* joueur, -euse, de la demi-finale.

semi-invalid [-ˈinvəlid] *n.* maladif, -ive.

seminal [ˈsiːminəl, ˈsem-] *a. Physiol: Bot:* séminal, -aux; **s. fluid,** sperme *m*; liquide séminal.

seminar [ˈseminɑːr] *n. Sch:* (*a*) séminaire *m*; (*b*) *U.S:* cycle *m* d'études.

seminarist [ˈseminərist] *n. R.C.Ch:* séminariste *m.*

seminary [ˈseminəri] *n. R.C.Ch:* séminaire *m.* **2.** *A:* pensionnat *m* de jeunes filles.

semi-obscurity [-əbˈskjuəriti] *n.* pénombre *m.*

semi-official [-əˈfiʃ(ə)l] *a.* semi-officiel; officieux.

semi-precious [-ˈpreʃəs] *a. Lap:* semi-précieux; fin.

semiquaver [ˈsemikweivər] *n. Mus:* double croche *f.*

semi-skilled [-ˈskild] *a.* (ouvrier) spécialisé.

Semite [ˈsemait] *n. Ethn:* Sémite *mf.*

Semitic [siˈmitik] *a. Ethn:* sémitique.

semitone [ˈsemitoun] *n. Mus:* demi-ton *m.*

semivowel [-ˈvauəl] *n.* semi-voyelle *f, pl.* semi-voyelles.

semolina [seməˈliːnə] *n.* semoule *f.*

senate [ˈsenət] *n.* (*a*) *Pol:* sénat *m*; **s. house,** sénat; (*b*) *Sch:* conseil *m* de l'université.

senator [ˈsenətər] *n. Pol:* sénateur *m.*

senatorial [senəˈtɔːriəl] *a.* sénatorial, -aux.

send [send] *v.tr.* (*p.t. & p.p.* **sent** [sent]) **1.** (*a*) envoyer (qn); **to s. a child to school,** envoyer un enfant à l'école; **to s. s.o. on an errand,** envoyer qn faire une commission; **to s. s.o. for sth.,** envoyer qn chercher qch., à la recherche de qch.; **to s. s.o. away,** renvoyer, congédier, qn; **to s. s.o. back,** renvoyer qn; **s. him along!** envoyez-le me voir; dites-lui de venir me voir; (*b*) envoyer, faire parvenir (qch.); expédier (une lettre, etc.); remettre (de l'argent, etc.); **to s. word to s.o.,** envoyer un mot à qn; faire savoir qch. à qn; **to s. one's love to s.o.,** envoyer, (faire) faire, ses amitiés à qn; **to s. clothes to the laundry,** donner du linge à blanchir; *F:* **to s. round the hat,** faire la quête. **2. force that sends sth. in a certain direction,** force *f* qui fait marcher, qui pousse, qch. dans une certaine direction; **it sent a shiver down my spine,** cela m'a fait passer un frisson dans le dos; **the blow sent him sprawling,** le coup l'a renversé. **3.** *A:* accorder, envoyer (qch.); **s. him, her, victorious,** que Dieu lui donne, lui accorde, la victoire; **what fortune sends us,** ce que la fortune nous envoie. **4.** *v.ind.tr.* **to s. for s.o., sth.,** envoyer chercher qn, qch.; **we sent for a barrel of beer,** nous avons fait venir un tonneau de bière; **we sent for the doctor,** (i) nous avons appelé, envoyé chercher, (ii) nous avons fait venir, le médecin. **5.** (*a*) **you'll s. me mad,** vous allez me rendre fou; (*b*) *F: O:* **it sends me,** ça me transporte. **send down** *v.tr.* (*a*) faire descendre (qch.); (*b*) faire descendre (les prix, la température, etc.); (*c*) renvoyer, expulser (un étudiant de l'université); (*d*) *F:* envoyer (qn) en prison; coffrer (qn). **send in** *v.tr.* (*a*) faire (r)entrer (qn); (faire) servir (le diner); **to s. in one's name,** se faire annoncer; (*b*) livrer, rendre (un compte); remettre (une demande, etc.); **he has sent in his bill,** il nous a envoyé sa note. **send off** *v.tr.* (*a*) expédier (une lettre, etc.); (*b*) *Sp:* renvoyer, expulser (un joueur) du terrain. **send on** *v.tr.* (*a*) faire suivre (une lettre); (*b*) transmettre (un ordre); (*c*) expédier à l'avance (des bagages). **send out** *v.tr.* (*a*) envoyer (qn) dehors; mettre (un élève) à la porte; (*b*) lancer, expédier (des prospectus); (*c*) vomir (des nuages de fumée, etc.); émettre (des signaux, de la chaleur, etc.). **send up** *v.tr.* (*a*) faire monter (qn, qch.); lancer (une fusée); (*b*) faire monter (les prix, la température, etc.); (*c*) *F:* se moquer de, parodier (qn. qch.); *Th:* prendre (une pièce, son rôle) à la rigolade; (*d*) *F:* envoyer (qn) en prison; coffrer (qn).

sender [ˈsendər] *n.* **1.** (*pers.*) envoyeur, -euse; expéditeur, -trice (d'une lettre, des marchandises). **2.** *Tg: Tp:* (*device*) manipulateur *m*, transmetteur *m.*

send-off [ˈsendɔf] *n. F:* (*a*) fête *f* d'adieu; **to give s.o. a good s.-o.,** assister en nombre au départ de qn (pour lui souhaiter bon voyage); (*b*) inauguration réussie; **the press has given the book a good s.-o.,** le livre a eu d'excellentes critiques dans les journaux; (*c*) enterrement *m.*

send-up [ˈsendʌp] *n. F:* satire *f*, parodie *f.*

Senegal [seniˈgɔːl] *Pr.n. Geog:* (République *f* du) Sénégal.

Senegalese [senigəˈliːz] **1.** *a. Geog:* sénégalais. **2.** *n.* Sénégalais, -aise.

senile [ˈsiːnail] *a.* sénile; **s. decay,** dégénérescence *f* sénile; sénilité *f*; **s. dementia,** démence *f* sénile.

senility [siˈniliti] *n.* sénilité *f.*

senior [ˈsiːnjiər] **1.** *a.* (*a*) aîné, doyen; **Bernard Long s.,** Bernard Long père; **he's two years s. to me,** il est mon aîné de deux ans; (*b*) (le plus) ancien, (la plus) ancienne; *Mil: etc:* (officier, commandement, etc.) supérieur; **s. in rank,** de grade supérieur; **the s. Service,** la marine; **the s. boys, girls, of a school,** les grands, grandes (élèves); **s. citizens,** retraité(e)s; personnes âgées; **s. partner,** associé principal; **the s.**

officer, le doyen des officiers; *Sch:* **s. master, mistress,** professeur *m* en premier; **s. French master, mistress,** premier professeur de français. **2.** *n.* (*a*) aîné, -ée; doyen, -enne (d'âge); **she is his s. by three years,** elle est son aînée de trois ans; (*b*) (le plus) ancien, (la plus) ancienne; supérieur, -eure; doyen, -enne; **to be s.o.'s s.,** être l'ancien, le doyen, de qn; **he is my s. by two years,** il est mon ancien de deux ans; (*of pupils*) **the seniors,** les grand(e)s; (*c*) *Sch: U.S:* étudiant(e) de quatrième (et dernière) année.

seniority [siːni'ɔriti] *n.* **1.** priorité *f* d'âge; supériorité *f* d'âge; doyenneté *f*; **chairman by s.,** président d'âge. **2.** ancienneté *f* (de grade); **to be promoted by s.,** avancer (de grade), être promu, à l'ancienneté.

senna ['senə] *n. Bot:Pharm:* séné *m.*

sensation [sen'seiʃ(ə)n] *n.* **1.** sensation *f*; sentiment *m,* impression *f* (de malaise, de bien-être, etc.); **I had the s. of falling,** j'avais l'impression que je tombais. **2.** sensation; effet sensationnel; (*of event, etc.*) **to create, make, cause, a s.,** faire sensation.

sensational [sen'seiʃənəl] *a.* sensationnel; à sensation; **s. novel,** roman *m* à sensation, à gros effets. **-ally** *adv.* d'une manière sensationnelle.

sensationalism [sen'seiʃənəlizm] *n.* **1.** recherche *f* du sensationnel. **2.** *Phil:* sensualisme *m,* sensationnisme *m.*

sensationalist [sen'seiʃənəlist] *n.* (*a*) colporteur *m* de nouvelles à sensation; dramatiseur, -euse; (*b*) auteur *m* de romans à sensation.

sensationalize [sen'seiʃənəlaiz] *v.tr.* exagérer (un incident, etc.).

sense¹ [sens] *n.* **1.** (*a*) sens *m*; **the five senses,** les cinq sens; **the sixth s.,** le sixième sens; l'instinct *m*; l'intuition *f*; **to have a keen s. of smell, of hearing,** avoir l'odorat fin, l'ouïe fine; **to be in possession of all one's senses,** jouir de toutes ses facultés; **pleasures of the senses,** plaisirs sensuels, des sens; (*b*) les sens; **s. organs,** organes *m* des sens; **s. impression,** sensation *f.* **2.** (*a*) **to be in one's senses,** être sain d'esprit; **have you taken leave of your senses?** avez-vous perdu l'esprit? avez-vous votre raison? **to come to one's senses (again),** rentrer dans son bon sens; revenir á la raison; **to bring s.o. to his senses,** ramener qn à la raison; dégriser qn; (*b*) **to lose one's senses,** perdre connaissance; **to come to one's senses,** (i) revenir à soi; reprendre ses sens; (ii) sortir d'un rêve; reprendre le sentiment de la réalité des faits. **3.** (*a*) sensation *f,* sens; **a s. of pleasure, of warmth,** une sensation de plaisir, de chaleur; **s. of injustice,** sentiment *m* d'injustice; (*b*) sentiment, conscience *f*; **s. of colour, of beauty,** sentiment des couleurs, de la beauté; **to lose all s. of reality,** perdre la notion de la réalité. **4.** bon sens; jugement *m*; **common s., good s.,** sens commun; bon sens; **to talk s.,** parler raison; **there's no s. in that, that doesn't make s.,** cela n'a pas de sens; cela ne rime à rien; **to have the (good) s. to do sth.,** avoir l'intelligence de faire qch.; **to have more s. than to do sth.,** avoir trop de bon sens pour faire qch. **5.** sens, signification *f* (d'un mot); **these words don't make s.,** ces mots n'ont pas de sens, sont incompréhensibles; **I can't make s. of it,** je n'arrive pas à le comprendre; **in the literal, figurative, s.,** au sens propre, figuré; **in every s. of the word,** dans toute l'acception du mot; **in a s.,** d'une certaine façon; dans un (certain) sens; **in the s. that . . .,** en ce sens que . . .. **6.** *Ph: etc:* direction *f,* sens; **s. of rotation,** sens de rotation. **7.** *Cmptr:* lecture *f* (par exploration).

sense² *v.tr.* **1.** sentir (qch.) intuitivement; pressentir (qch.). **2.** comprendre (qch.). **3.** *Phil:* percevoir (qch.) par le sens. **4.** *Elcs: etc:* (*a*) explorer; palper, sonder; (*b*) *Cmptr:* lire (par exploration).

senseless ['senslis] *a.* **1.** (*of pers.*) sans connaissance, inanimé; **to fall s.,** tomber sans connaissance; **to knock s.o. s.,** assommer qn. **2.** (*of pers., thg, conduct, etc.*) qui n'a pas le sens commun; insensé; stupide; déraisonnable; **a s. remark,** une bêtise. **3.** dépourvu des facultés des sens; insensible. **-ly** *adv.* stupidement.

senselessness ['senslisnis] *n.* **1.** manque *m* de bon sens; stupidité *f.* **2.** insensibilité *f.*

sensibility [sensi'biliti] *n.* **1.** sensibilité *f* (d'un organe, etc.). **2.** (*emotional*) sensibilité, émotivité *f,* susceptibilité *f.*

sensible ['sensəbl] *a.* **1.** sensible, perceptible. **2.** (*of quantity, difference, etc.*) sensible, appréciable. **3.** *A: & Lit:* (*aware*) (*of pers.*) conscient **(of,** de); sensible **(of,** à); **to be s. of the fact that . . .,** apprécier le fait que . . .. **4.** sensé, raisonnable, judicieux; **s. person,** personne sensée, pleine de bon sens; **s. choice,** choix judicieux; **be s.,** soyez raisonnable; **s. clothes,** vêtements *mpl* commodes, pratiques; **s. shoes,** chaussures rationnelles. **-ibly** *adv.* **1.** sensiblement, perceptiblement. **2.** raisonnablement, judicieusement; **to be s. dressed,** porter des vêtements pratiques.

sensitive ['sensitiv] *a.* (*a*) sensible, sensitif; **s. to sth.,** sensible à qch.; (*of pers.*) **to be s. to cold,** être frileux, -euse; (*b*) (*of pers.*) susceptible; impressionnable; sensible, chatouilleux (sur l'honneur); (*c*) (balance, machine) sensible; *Com: Fin:* (marché) instable, prompt à réagir; *Phot:* (plaque) impressionnable, sensible à la lumière; (papier) sensible, sensibilisé; (*d*) (*of question, issue, etc.*) délicat. **-ly** *adv.* sensiblement; d'une manière sensible; (écrire, etc.) avec sensibilité.

sensitiveness ['sensitivnis], **sensitivity** [sensi'tiviti] *n.* (*a*) sensibilité *f,* sensitivité *f*; (*b*) susceptibilité *f*; (*c*) sensibilité (d'une machine, etc.); *Phot:* impressionnabilité *f,* rapidité *f* (d'une émulsion); (*d*) caractère *m* délicat (d'une question, etc.).

sensitization [sensitai'zeiʃ(ə)n] *n. Med: Phot:* sensibilisation *f.*

sensitize ['sensitaiz] *v.tr.* sensibiliser, rendre sensible; *Phot:* **sensitized paper,** papier sensible.

sensitizer ['sensitaizər] *n. Phot:* sensibilisateur *m.*

sensor ['sensər] *n. Elcs: etc:* (*a*) détecteur *m*; (*b*) *Space:* (*in satellite, etc.*) détecteur, capteur *m*; (*c*) sonde *f,* jauge *f*; (*d*) *Elcs: Ph:* analyseur *m.*

sensory ['sensəri] *a.* (nerf, etc.) sensoriel; **s. organs,** organes *mpl* des sens.

sensual ['sensjuəl] *a.* **1.** sensuel; (instinct) animal; **s. pleasures,** plaisirs *mpl* des sens. **2.** sensuel, voluptueux; libidineux.

sensualism ['sensjuəlizm] *n.* **1.** *Phil:* sensualisme *m.* **2.** sensualité *f.*

sensualist ['sensjuəlist] *n.* **1.** *Phil:* sensualiste *mf.* **2.** sensualiste; voluptueux, -euse.

sensuality [sensju'æliti] *n.* sensualité *f.*

sensuous ['sensjuəs] *a.* (*of pleasure, life, etc.*) sybaritique, voluptueux; (*of charm, etc.*) capiteux. **-ly** *adv* voluptueusement; avec volupté.

sensuousness ['sensjuəsnis] *n.* sybaritisme *m*; volupté *f.*

sentence¹ ['sentəns] *n.* **1.** *Jur:* (*a*) jugement *m*; sentence *f,* condamnation *f*; **life s.,** condamnation à vie; **s. of death, death s.,** arrêt *m,* sentence, de mort; **under s. of death,** condamné à mort; **to pass (a) s.,** prononcer une condamnation, une sentence; (*b*) peine *f*; **while he was serving his s.,** pendant qu'il purgeait sa peine. **2.** *Gram:* phrase *f.*

sentence² *v.tr. Jur:* condamner (qn); prononcer une condamnation, une sentence, contre (qn); **to s. s.o. to a month's imprisonment, to death,** condamner qn à un mois de prison, à mort.

sententious [sen'tenʃəs] *a.* (*of pers., speech, etc.*) sentencieux. **-ly** *adv.* sentencieusement.

sententiousness [sen'tenʃəsnis] *n.* (i) caractère, (ii) ton, sentencieux.

sentient ['senʃənt] *a.* sentant, sensible.

sentiment ['sentimənt] *n.* **1.** (*a*) *A: & Lit:* sentiment *m*, mouvement *m* de l'âme; **noble sentiments,** sentiments nobles; (*b*) sentiment, opinion *f*, avis *m*; **these are my sentiments,** voilà mon sentiment, mon opinion. **2.** sentimentalité *f*; (*mawkish*) sensiblerie *f*; **one cannot mix s. and business,** on ne fait pas de sentiment en affaires.

sentimental [senti'ment(ə)l] *a.* (*a*) sentimental, -aux; **s. value,** valeur sentimentale; (*b*) (roman) sentimental, d'une sensiblerie romanesque; **don't be so s.!** pas tant de sentiment! **-ally** *adv.* sentimentalement; avec sensiblerie.

sentimentalism [senti'mentəlizm] *n.* sentimentalisme *m*; sensiblerie *f*.

sentimentalist [senti'mentəlist] *n.* personne sentimentale; **he's, she's, a s.,** c'est un(e) sentimental(e).

sentimentality [sentimen'tæliti] *n.* sentimentalité *f*; sensiblerie *f*.

sentimentalize [senti'mentəlaiz] **1.** *v.i.* faire du sentiment. **2.** *v.tr.* apporter du sentiment dans (une œuvre).

sentinel ['sentin(ə)l] *n.* factionnaire *m*; sentinelle *f*; **to stand s.,** monter la garde; être de garde.

sentry ['sentri] *n. Mil:* factionnaire *m*, sentinelle *f*; **s. box,** guérite *f*; **to be on, to do, s. duty, to stand s.,** être en sentinelle, de faction; monter la garde; **to relieve a s.,** relever une sentinelle.

sepal ['sep(ə)l] *n. Bot:* sépale *m.*

separable ['sep(ə)rəbl] *a.* séparable.

separate¹ ['sep(ə)rət] **1.** *a.* (*a*) (*of parts*) séparé, détaché (**from,** de); (*b*) distinct; indépendant; (*of room, entrance*) particulier; **entered in a s. column,** inscrit dans une colonne particulière; (*of married couple*) **to sleep in s. rooms,** faire chambre à part. **2.** *n.pl. Com:* **separates,** coordonnés *mpl.* **-ly** *adv.* séparément; à part.

separate² ['sepəreit] **1.** *v.tr.* (*a*) séparer, dégager, détacher (**from,** de); départir (les métaux); dédoubler (un brin de fil, etc.); écrémer (le lait); **to s. two boxers,** séparer deux boxeurs; (*b*) désunir (les membres d'une famille, etc.); détacher (qn de sa famille, etc.); **he is separated (from his wife),** il est séparé (de sa femme); (*c*) **the Channel separates England from France,** la Manche sépare la France et l'Angleterre; **the gulf that separates him from his colleagues,** l'abîme (qui s'ouvre) entre lui et ses collègues. **2.** *v.i.* (*a*) (*of thg*) se séparer, se détacher, se décoller (**from,** de); *Ch:* **to s. out,** se séparer (par précipitation); (*b*) (*of pers.*) **when we separated for the night,** quand nous nous sommes quittés pour la nuit; **to s. from s.o.,** se séparer de, rompre avec, qn; (*c*) (*of man and wife*) se séparer (de corps et de biens).

separation [sepə'reiʃ(ə)n] *n.* **1.** (*a*) séparation *f*; écrémage *m* (du lait); *Min:* classement *m* (du minerai); (*b*) séparation (**from s.o.,** d'avec qn); *Mil:* **s. allowance,** allocation faite à la femme (d'un soldat); (*c*) **judicial s.,** séparation judiciaire, séparation de corps (et de biens). **2.** écart *m*; écartement *m.*

separatism ['sepərətizm] *n.* séparatisme *m.*

separatist ['sepərətist] *n.* séparatiste *mf.*

separator ['sepəreitər] *n. Tchn:* séparateur *m.*

sepia ['si:piə] *n.* **1.** *Moll:* seiche *f.* **2.** *Art:* sépia; **s. (drawing),** (dessin *m* à la) sépia.

sepoy ['si:pɔi] *n. Mil:* cipaye *m.*

sepsis ['sepsis] *n. Med:* septicité *f*; état *m* septique.

September [sep'tembər] *n.* septembre *m*; **in S.,** au mois de septembre, en septembre; **(on) the first, the seventh, of S.,** le premier, le sept, septembre.

septet [sep'tet] *n. Mus:* septuor *m.*

septic ['septik] *a. Med:* septique; **s. poisoning,** septicémie *f*; **to become, go, s.,** s'infecter; *Hyg:* **s. tank,** fosse *f* septique.

septicaemia, *NAm:* **septicemia** [septi'si:miə] *n. Med:* septicémie *f.*

septuagenarian [septjuədʒi'nɛəriən] *n. & a.* septuagénaire (*mf*).

Septuagesima [septjuə'dʒesimə] *n. Ecc:* **S. (Sunday),** (le dimanche de) la Septuagésime.

Septuagint ['septjuədʒint] *n.* version *f* (de la Bible) des Septante; la Septante.

septum *pl.* **-a** ['septəm, -ə] *n.* (*a*) *Anat:* septum *m* (du nez, etc.); (*b*) *Bot:* cloison *f* (d'une spore).

sepulchral [si'pʌlkr(ə)l] *a.* sépulcral, -aux; **s. voice,** voix sépulcrale, caverneuse.

sepulchre, *NAm:* **sepulcher** ['sepəlkər] *n.* sépulcre *m*, tombeau *m*; **the Holy S.,** le Saint Sépulcre.

sequel ['si:kw(ə)l] *n.* suite *f* (d'un roman, etc.); **as a s. to these events,** comme suite à ces événements; **action that had an unfortunate s.,** acte *m* qui a entraîné des suites malheureuses.

sequence ['si:kwəns] *n.* **1.** (*a*) succession *f*; ordre naturel; **in s.,** en série; en succession; **logical s.,** enchaînement *m* logique; (*b*) suite *f*, série *f*, chaîne *f* (d'événements, etc.); (*c*) *Cin:* (i) séquence *f* (de liaison); (ii) scène *f* (de film); *Cmptr:* **s. check(ing),** contrôle *m* de séquence; (*d*) *Mus:* **s. of chords,** (i) marche *f* des accords; (ii) séquence; (*e*) *Gram:* **s. of tenses,** concordance *f* des temps; (*f*) *Cards:* séquence. **2.** *Ecc:* séquence (chantée avant l'Évangile).

sequential [si'kwenʃ(ə)l] *a.* (*a*) séquentiel; consécutif; *Cmptr:* **s. computer,** calculateur séquentiel; (*b*) (*of teaching, history, etc.*) continu. **-ally** *adv.* sequentiellement.

sequester [si'kwestər] **1.** *v.pr. Lit:* **to s. oneself (from the world),** se retirer (du monde). **2.** *v.tr.* (*a*) confisquer (qch.); (*b*) *Jur:* séquestrer (les biens d'un débiteur); mettre (un bien) sous séquestre.

sequestrate [si'kwestreit] *v.tr.* (*a*) confisquer (qch.); (*b*) *Jur:* séquestrer (les biens du débiteur, etc.); mettre (un bien) sous, séquestre.

sequestration [si:kwes'treiʃ(ə)n] *n.* (*a*) confiscation *f*; appropriation *f*; (*b*) *Jur:* séquestration; mise *f* sous séquestre.

sequin ['si:kwin] *n.* paillette *f* (de robe, etc.).

sequoia [si'kwɔiə] *n. Bot:* sequoia *m*, wellingtonia *m.*

seraglio [se'rɑ:liou] *n.* sérail, -ails *m.*

seraph, *pl.* **seraphs, seraphim** ['serəf, əfs, əfim] *n.* séraphin *m.*

seraphic [se'ræfik] *a.* séraphique.

Serb [sə:b] *n.* Serbe *mf.*

Serbia ['sə:biə] *Pr.n. Geog:* Serbie *f.*

Serbian ['sə:biən] **1.** *a. Geog: Ethn:* serbe. **2.** *n. Ling:* serbe *m.*

Serbo-Croat [sə:bou'krouæt], **Serbo-Croatian** [sə:boukrou'eiʃən] **1.** *a. Geog:* serbo-croate. **2.** *n.* (*a*) Serbo-croate *mf*; *Ling:* serbo-croate *m.*

sere [siər] *a. Lit:* flétri, desséché.

serenade¹ [serə'neid] *n.* sérénade *f.*

serenade² *v.tr.* donner une sérénade à (qn).

serendipity [seren'dipiti] *n.* découverte heureuse et inattendue; don *m* de faire des trouvailles.

serene [si'ri:n] *a.* **1.** (*of sky, sea, pers.*) serein, calme, tranquille; (*of sky*) clair; **her face wore a s. look,** son visage exprimait le calme. **2.** (*title*) sérénissime; **His S. Highness,** son Altesse sérénissime. **-ly** *adv.* tranquillement; avec sérénité.

serenity [si'reniti] *n.* sérénité *f*, calme *m.*

serf [sə:f] *n.* serf, *f.* serve.

serfdom ['sə:fdəm] *n.* servage *m.*

serge [sə:dʒ] *n. Tex:* serge *f*; **cotton s.,** sergé *m.*

sergeant ['sɑːdʒənt] *n.* (*a*) (*infantry, air force*) sergent *m*; (*artillery, armoured corps, cavalry*) maréchal *m* des logis; (*in all arms*) sous-officier *m, pl.* sous-officiers; **quartermaster s.,** *U.S:* **staff s.,** sergent fourrier, comptable; maréchal des logis fourrier, comptable; (*b*) **police s.,** brigadier *m*.

sergeant-major [sɑːdʒənt'meidʒər] *n. Mil:* adjudant *m*; **regimental s.-m.,** adjudant-chef *m, pl.* adjudants-chefs.

serial ['siəriəl] **1.** *a.* qui appartient à la série; *Mus:* sériel; **s. number,** numéro *m* de série; *Ind:* numéro matricule (d'un moteur). **2.** (*a*) *a.* en série; formant série; **s. story,** roman-feuilleton *m, pl.* romans-feuilletons; **s. rights,** droit *m* de reproduction en feuilleton; (*b*) *n.* roman-feuilleton; *W.Tel:* radioroman *m*; *T.V:* téléroman *m*. **-ally** *adv.* **1.** en, par, série. **2.** *Journ:* en feuilleton.

serialize ['siəriəlaiz] *v.tr. Journ:* publier, *T.V:* diffuser (un roman, etc.) en feuilleton.

sericulture ['serikʌltjər] *n.* sériciculture *f*.

series ['siəriːz] *n.* **1.** série *f*; échelle *f*, gamme *f* (de couleurs, etc.); *Publ:* collection *f*. **2.** *adv.phr.* **in s.,** en série, en succession; *El:* **connection in s., s. connection,** montage *m* en série.

seriocomic [siəriou'kɔmik] *a.* moitié sérieux moitié comique; (*of poem*) héroï-comique.

serious ['siəriəs] *a.* **1.** sérieux, grave; **s. mistake,** grosse faute; **things are becoming s.,** cela prend un aspect sérieux. **2.** (*a*) **s. artist,** artiste sérieux; **s. promise,** promesse sérieuse, sincère; (*b*) (*of pers.*) réfléchi, sérieux; **I have never given the subject s. thought,** je n'y ai jamais pensé sérieusement; **s. mood,** humeur sérieuse; **I'm s.,** je ne plaisante pas. **-ly** *adv.* sérieusement. **1. s. ill,** gravement malade; **s. wounded,** grièvement blessé; *Mil:* **the s. wounded,** les grands blessés. **2.** (parler) sérieusement; (prendre qch.) au sérieux; **to take oneself s.,** se prendre au sérieux; **but s., what will you do?** plaisanterie à part, qu'allez-vous faire?

serious-minded [siəriəs'maindid] *a.* (*of pers.*) réfléchi, sérieux; **s.-m. people,** les esprits sérieux.

seriousness ['siəriəsnis] *n.* **1.** gravité *f* (d'une situation, d'une maladie, etc.). **2.** sérieux *m* (de maintien, etc.). **3. in all s.,** sérieusement.

serjeant ['sɑːdʒənt] *n.* **S. at Arms,** (i) *A:* huissier *m* d'armes; (ii) commandant *m* militaire du Parlement.

sermon ['səːmən] *n.* **1.** *Ecc:* sermon *m*; homilie *f*; (*Protestant Ch:*) prêche *m*; **collection of sermons,** sermonnaire *m*; *B:* **the S. on the Mount,** le Sermon sur la montagne. **2.** *F:* sermon, semonce *f*.

sermonize ['səːmənaiz] **1.** *v.i. Pej:* sermonner, prêcher. **2.** *v.tr.* sermonner (qn). **sermonizing** *n. Pej:* **1.** prêcherie *f*; **no s.!** pas de sermons! **2.** moralisation *f*.

serous ['siərəs] *a. Anat: etc:* (fluide, etc.) séreux.

serpent ['səːpənt] *n.* serpent *m*.

serpentine¹ ['səːpəntain] *n. Miner:* serpentine *f*; **s. (marble),** marbre serpentin.

serpentine² *a. Lit:* serpentin; (sentier) sinueux, tortueux, serpentant; **s. windings,** sinuosités *f*.

serrate ['sereit] *a.* denté en scie; *Bot:* **s.-leaved,** serratifolié.

serrated [se'reitid] *a.* denté en scie; **s. edge,** denture *f*; **knife with a s. edge,** couteau *m* à scie.

serried ['serid] *a. Lit:* serré; **in s. ranks,** en rangs serrés.

serum, *pl.* **-ums, -a** ['siərəm, -əmz, -ə] *n. Physiol:* sérum *m*; **blood s.,** sérum sanguin.

servant ['səːvənt] *n.* **1.** (*a*) **(domestic) s.,** domestique *mf*; servante *f*, bonne *f*; **a large staff of servants,** une nombreuse domesticité; (*b*) serviteur, servante (de Dieu, etc.); (*c*) *Corr: esp. Dipl:* **your most humble and obedient s.,** votre très humble et très obéissant serviteur. **2.** employé, -ée; **public servants,** employés d'un service public; **civil s.,** fonctionnaire *m*.

serve¹ [səːv] *n. Ten: F:* service *m*; **(it's) your s.!** à vous de servir!

serve² *v.tr. & i.* **1.** (*a*) (*of pers.*) servir (un maître, une cause, etc.); **to s. God, one's country,** servir Dieu, sa patrie; **to have served one's country well,** bien mériter de la patrie; **to s. one's own interests,** servir ses propres intérêts; (*b*) **to s. in the army,** servir dans l'armée; **to s. with s.o.,** faire la guerre avec qn; **to have served ten years,** (i) avoir dix ans de service(s); (ii) avoir fait dix ans de prison; *Jur:* **to s. on the jury,** être du jury; **to s. one's apprenticeship,** faire son apprentissage; **to s. one's sentence,** *F:* **one's time,** subir, purger, sa peine; **he served a sentence of five years' imprisonment,** il a fait cinq ans de prison. **2.** (*a*) (*of thg*) être utile à (qn); suffire à (qn); **to s. the purpose,** remplir le but; faire l'affaire; **tool that serves several purposes,** outil *m* qui sert à plusieurs usages; **the desks s. as tables,** les bureaux tiennent lieu de tables; **to s. as a pretext, as an example,** servir de prétexte, d'exemple; (*b*) **if my memory serves me right,** si j'ai bonne mémoire. **3.** desservir. **4.** (*a*) (*in shop*) **to s. s.o. with a pound of butter,** servir une livre de beurre à qn; **are you being served?** est-ce qu'on s'occupe de vous? (*b*) **tradesman who has served us for ten years,** marchand qui fournit chez nous depuis dix ans; (*c*) **to s. in a shop,** être vendeur, -euse. **5.** (*a*) *Ecc:* **to s. (at) (mass),** servir la messe; (*b*) **to s. (at table),** servir à table; **to s. s.o. with soup, with vegetables,** servir du potage, des légumes, à qn; **to s. a dish,** servir un mets; **dinner is served, madam,** le dîner est servi, madame; *O:* madame est servie; **s. chilled,** servir très frais. **6.** *Ten:* **to s. (the ball),** servir (la balle). **7.** *Jur:* **to s. a writ, a summons, on s.o., to s. s.o. with a writ, a summons,** délivrer, signifier, notifier, une assignation, une citation, à qn. **8.** traiter (qn) (bien, mal); **he served me very badly,** il a très mal agi envers moi; **it serves you right!** vous n'avez que ce que vous méritez! **9.** (*of stallion*) saillir, couvrir (la jument). **serving. 1.** *a.* (soldat) au service. **2.** *n.* (*a*) (i) service *m* (d'un maître); (ii) service (du dîner, *Ten:* d'une balle); **s. hatch,** guichet *m*; (iii) *Jur:* signification *f*, notification *f* (d'une citation); (*b*) portion *f* (d'un mets).

server ['səːvər] *n.* **1.** (*a*) (*at table*) serveur, -euse; (*b*) *Ten:* serveur, -euse; servant *m*; (*c*) *Ecc:* (*at mass*) acolyte *m*, répondant *m*. **2.** (*a*) plateau *m* (de service); (*b*) **(set of) salad, fish, servers,** service *m* à salade, à poisson; (*c*) *U.S:* = service (à café, à thé).

service¹ ['səːvis] *n.* service *m*. **1.** (*a*) **in the s. of God, of one's country,** au service de Dieu, de son pays, sa patrie; **to die in the King's, Queen's, s.,** mourir au service du roi, de la reine; **I am (entirely) at your s.,** je suis à votre (entière) disposition; **promotion according to length of s.,** avancement *m* selon l'ancienneté *f*; (*b*) *Mil:* **military, national, s.,** service militaire, national; **when I was doing my military s.,** quand j'étais au régiment; **active s.,** (i) service actif; (ii) service en campagne; **fit, unfit, for s.,** apte, inapte, au service; *Navy:* **s. afloat,** service à bord; **s. ashore,** service à terre; (*c*) **domestic s.,** service domestique; **to be in s.,** être en service; **to go into s.,** entrer en service; (*d*) service; **ten per cent s. charge,** service dix pour cent; **s. lift, hoist,** monte-plats *m inv*; **s. hatch,** guichet *m*; **s. flat,** appartement *m* avec service compris (et repas à volonté); **rent plus s. charge,** loyer *m* plus charges; (*e*) *Adm: Ind:* **s. agreement,** contrat *m* de service; **24-hour s.,** service permanent, de 24 heures sur 24; (*f*) **to bring, put, into s.,** mettre (un appareil, un véhicule) en service; **s. life,** durée, potentiel *m*, d'utilisation; **this pen has given me good s.,** ce stylo m'a bien servi; (*g*) *Av:* **s.**

ceiling, plafond *m* pratique (d'un appareil); *Mch: El:* **s. test,** essai *m* en charge. **2.** (*a*) **to do s.o. a s.,** rendre (un) service à qn; **to offer one's services,** offrir ses services; **his services to education,** les services qu'il a rendus à l'enseignement; **services rendered,** services rendus; *Pol.Ec:* **goods and services,** biens *m* et services; (*b*) utilité *f*; **to be of some s.,** servir à quelque chose; **to be of s. to s.o.,** être utile à qn; **can I be of any s. to you?** puis-je vous être utile, vous aider en aucune manière? **3.** (*a*) **the civil s.,** l'administration *f*, la fonction publique; **to be in the civil s.,** être fonctionnaire; **the Foreign, Diplomatic, S.,** le service diplomatique, la diplomatie, *F:* la carrière; *F:* **the Secret S.** = le Deuxième Bureau; (*b*) *Mil: etc:* **the s.,** (i) l'armée *f*; (ii) la marine; (iii) l'armée de l'air; **the (armed) services,** les forces armées; l'armée, la marine et l'armée de l'air; **the Senior S.,** la Marine; **Joint Services Staff College** = École *f* d'État-major interarmes; **s. rifle,** fusil *m* réglementaire, de l'armée; **s. vehicle,** véhicule *m* militaire, de l'armée; **s. personnel,** personnel *m* militaire. **4.** (*a*) **public services,** services publics; **postal, telephone, services,** services postaux, téléphoniques; **social, medical, services,** services sociaux, médicaux; (*b*) *Trans:* service (aérien, ferroviaire); **bus s.,** service d'autobus, de cars; *Austr: N.Z:* **s. bus, car,** autocar *m*; **we have a good bus, train, s.,** notre ville est bien desservie par les autobus, par le chemin de fer; **goods, freight, s.,** service de marchandises; **passenger s.,** service de voyageurs; (*c*) distribution *f* (d'eau, de gaz, d'électricité); **s. area,** zone *f* de desserte; région desservie. **5.** (*a*) (i) entretien *m*; (ii) dépannage *m* (d'un appareil ménager, etc.); **my car needs a complete s.,** ma voiture a besoin d'une révision générale; *Aut:* **s. station,** station-service *f*, *pl.* stations-service; **s. area,** *NAm:* **s. centre,** aire *f* de services (au bord d'une autoroute); *P.N:* **services, 10 km,** essence, 10 km; **after-sales s.,** service après vente; **s. manual, handbook,** manuel *m* d'entretien; (*b*) *Artil:* service (de la pièce). **6.** *Ecc:* office *m*; culte *m*; **morning, evening, s.,** office du matin, du soir; **the communion s.,** la sainte communion; **open-air s.,** *Mil:* **drumhead s.,** office en plein air; **to attend s.,** assister à l'office, au culte. **7.** *Jur:* délivrance *f*, signification *f* (d'un acte, d'une assignation). **8.** *Breed:* service (par l'etalon, etc.). **9. tea, dinner, s.,** service à thé; service de table. **10.** *Ten:* service; **s. line,** ligne *f* de fond; **s. court,** rectangle *m* de service.

service² *v.tr.* **1.** faire la révision (d'une voiture); faire l'entretien (d'un appareil ménager). **2.** *Husb:* (*of bull, stallion*) couvrir (la femelle). **servicing** *n.* entretien *m.*

service³ *n. Bot:* **s. (tree),** sorbier *m*, cormier *m*; **s. apple, berry,** corme *f*, sorbe *f*.

serviceable ['sɜːvisəbl] *a.* (*of thg*) (*a*) en état de fonctionner; utilisable; (*b*) utile; de bon usage; (vêtement) pratique; (*c*) pratique, commode.

serviceman, *pl.* **-men** ['sɜːvismən, -men] *n.m.* **1.** soldat; mobilisé; *Hist:* **national s.,** appelé *m*; **ex-s.,** ancien combattant; **disabled ex-s.,** mutilé de guerre. **2.** *NAm:* technicien d'entretien; dépanneur.

servicewoman, *pl.* **-women** ['sɜːviswumən, -wimin] *n.f.* soldate, femme soldat.

serviette [sɜːvi'et] *n.* serviette *f* de table.

servile ['sɜːvail] *a.* **1.** (*of race, condition*) servile; d'esclave. **2.** (*of pers., behaviour*) servile.

servility [sɜː'viliti] *n.* servilité *f.*

servitude ['sɜːvitjuːd] *n.* **1.** servitude *f*, esclavage *m.* **2.** *Jur:* **penal s. for life,** travaux forcés à perpétuité. **3.** *Jur:* servitude (réelle ou personnelle).

servo ['sɜːvou] *n.* **1.** servomoteur *m.* **2.** servomécanisme *m.*

servobrake ['sɜːvoubreik] *n. Aut:* servofrein *m.*

servocontrol [sɜːvoukən'troul] *n.* servocommande *f.*

servomechanism [sɜːvou'mekənizm] *n.* servomécanisme *m.*

servomotor ['sɜːvoumoutər] *n.* servomoteur *m.*

sesame ['sesəmi] *n.* **1.** *Bot:* sésame *m.* **2.** (*magic formula*) **open s.!** sésame, ouvre-toi!

session ['seʃ(ə)n] *n.* **1.** session *f*; séance *f*; **to have a long s.,** faire une longue séance; **to go into secret s.,** se former en comité secret. **2.** (*a*) session; *Parl:* **the autumn s.,** la session d'automne; **the House is now in s.,** la Chambre siège actuellement; (*b*) *U.S:* trimestre *m* scolaire, universitaire; (*c*) *U.S: & Scot:* année *f* universitaire.

set¹ [set] *n.* **1.** (*a*) jeu *m* (d'outils, de boîtes, de dominos, d'aiguilles, etc.); équipage *m*, assortiment *m*, attirail *m* (d'outils); série *f* (de poids, de casseroles, *Nau:* de pavillons); train *m* (de pneus, de roues); batterie *f* (de turbines, d'ustensiles de cuisine); suite *f* (d'estampes); collection complète (des œuvres de qn); service *m* (de porcelaine); parure *f* (de lingerie, de boutons, de pierres précieuses); **s. of teeth,** (i) denture *f*; (ii) (*artificial*) dentier *m*; *Mth:* **theory of sets,** théorie *f* des ensembles; **s. of golf clubs,** jeu de crosses; **s. of bells,** sonnerie *f* (d'église, etc.); **toilet s.,** *O:* **dressing-table s.,** garniture *f* de toilette; **construction s.,** jeu de construction; **chairs, the s. of six, £200,** chaises, £200 les six; (*b*) **television s.,** téléviseur *m*; poste *m* de télévision; (*c*) *Cmptr:* (i) jeu, ensemble *m* (de caractères, d'instructions, etc.); (ii) liasse *f* (de papier sur imprimante, etc.); (iii) positionnement *m*, mise *f* à 1; (*d*) *Ten:* manche *f*, set *m*; **s. point,** balle *f* de set; (*e*) groupe *m* (de personnes); **literary, political, s.,** coterie *f* littéraire, politique; **the smart s.,** le monde élégant. **2.** (*a*) *Poet:* **at s. of sun,** au coucher du soleil; (*b*) couvée *f* (d'œufs); (*c*) *Ven:* **(dead) s.,** arrêt *m* (d'un chien); *F:* **to make a dead s. at s.o.,** (i) attaquer furieusement qn; (ii) (*of woman*) se jeter à la tête d'un homme. **3.** (*a*) conformation *f* (d'une chaîne de montagnes, etc.); attitude *f*, posture *f* (du corps); disposition *f* des plis (d'une draperie); **s. of the features,** modelé *m* des traits; physionomie *f*; **I knew him by the s. of his head,** je l'ai reconnu à son port de tête; *Tls:* **s. of a saw,** voie *f*, chasse *f*, d'une scie; (*b*) direction *f* (du courant, de la marée); tendances *fpl* (de l'opinion publique); (*c*) *Mec.E:* déviation *f*; déformation *f* (d'une pièce); (*d*) *Typ:* approche *f*; (*e*) *Hairdr:* mise *f* en plis. **4.** (*a*) *Hort:* plant *m* à repiquer; (*b*) *Civ.E:* **(paving) s.,** pavé *m* d'échantillon; (*c*) *Th:* décor *m*; **rehearsal on the s., répétition** *f* sur le plateau. **5.** *Tls:* (*a*) **saw s.,** tourne-à-gauche *m inv*; (*b*) **nail s.,** chasse-clou(s) *m inv.* **6.** *Const:* dernière couche (appliquée à une paroi, etc.). **7.** terrier *m* (du blaireau).

set² *v.* (*p.t. & p.p.* **set;** *pr.p.* **setting**) **I.** *v.tr.* **1.** (*a*) asseoir, placer (qn sur le trône); (*b*) mettre (une poule, des œufs) à couver. **2.** (*a*) mettre, poser (qch. sur, contre, qch., devant qch., qn); **to s. one's glass (down) on the table,** poser son verre sur la table; **to s. a dish in front of s.o.,** servir un plat (à qn); **to s. one's hand, seal, to a document,** apposer sa signature, son sceau, à un acte; **to s. money by,** mettre de l'argent de côté, en réserve; (*b*) **to s. s.o. on his feet again,** remettre qn sur pied; (*c*) **to s. one's heart on sth.,** avoir qch. au cœur; vouloir absolument (faire, avoir) qch.; (*d*) **the house is set in the heart of the woods,** la maison est située au milieu des bois. **3. to s. the table,** mettre le couvert, la table; **to s. the table for two,** mettre deux couverts. **4.** (*a*) **to s. a melody half a tone higher, lower,** hausser, baisser, un air d'un demi-ton; (*b*) **to set words to music,** mettre des paroles en musique. **5.** (*a*) **to s. a stake in the ground,** enfoncer, planter, un pieu dans la terre; (*b*) planter (des graines); mettre (une plante) en terre. **6.** (*a*) régler (une montre, etc.); mettre (une montre, etc.) à l'heure; **to s. one's watch by the town clock,** prendre l'heure à l'horloge de la ville; **to s. the alarm (clock) for, at, five o'clock,** mettre le réveille-matin sur cinq heures; **to s. the speedometer to zero,** ramener le compteur à zéro; (*b*) *Mch: etc:* régler, caler; *Phot:* caler (l'obturateur); (*c*) régler, ajuster (le fer d'un rabot); donner de la voie à (une scie); (*d*) **to s. one's hat straight,** ajuster son chapeau; **to have one's hair set,** se faire faire une mise en plis. **7.** (*a*) monter (un papillon) (en spécimen); (*b*) *Th:* **to s. a scene,** monter un décor; **the second act is set in a street,** le second acte se passe dans une rue; (*c*) monter, sertir (une pierre); **set with diamonds,** orné, incrusté, de diamants; (*d*) *Mec.E:* loger, mettre en place (une pièce); (*e*) *Nau:* déployer (une voile); mettre dehors (une voile); **to s. the sails,** déferler les voiles; **(with) all sails set,** toutes voiles dehors. **8.** (*a*) dresser, tendre (un piège); **to s. a trap for s.o.,** tendre un piège à qn; (*b*) armer (un piège à loups, *Phot:* un obturateur). **9.** affiler (un rasoir); aiguiser, affûter (un ciseau); affûter (une scie). **10.** *Typ:* **to s. type,** composer; **to s. a page,** composer une page. **11.** fixer, désigner, arrêter (une date, un jour); **to s. limits to sth.,** assigner des limites à qch. **12. to s. the fashion,** fixer, mener, la mode; donner le ton, la note; **to s. a fashion,** lancer une mode. **13.** *Surg:* remettre (un os, un membre); réduire (une fracture). **14. to s. one's teeth,** serrer les dents; **lips firmly set,** lèvres fortement serrées. **15. to s. s.o. on his way,** mettre qn dans le bon chemin; **to s. s.o. on the wrong track,** aiguiller qn sur une fausse piste; **to s. the police on the tracks of a thief,** mettre la police aux trousses d'un voleur; **to s. a dog on, at, s.o.,** lâcher un chien contre qn. **16.** (*a*) **to s. s.o. to do sth.,** mettre qn à faire qch.; **to s. a man to work,** mettre un homme au travail; (*b*) **that set me thinking,** cela m'a fait réfléchir, m'a donné à réfléchir; **to s. the dog barking,** faire aboyer le chien; **to s. people talking,** (i) déclancher la conversation; (ii) provoquer des commentaires; (*c*) **to s. (sth.) going,** mettre (qch.) en train; mettre (un mécanisme) en marche. **17. to s. a good example,** donner un bon exemple; **to s. oneself a task,** s'imposer, entreprendre, une tâche; **to s. s.o. a question, problem,** poser une question, un problème, à qn; *Sch:* **to s. an essay,** donner un sujet de dissertation (à une classe); **to s. a book,** mettre (un livre) au programme (d'études); **to s. an exam(ination) paper,** choisir les questions d'une épreuve écrite. **II.** *v.i.* **1.** (*a*) (*of sun, moon*) se coucher; **we saw the sun set(ting),** nous avons vu le coucher du soleil; (*b*) *Lit:* (*of fame, etc.*) s'éteindre, pâlir. **2.** (*a*) (*of character*) se former, s'affermir; (*of foundations*) se tasser; (*b*) **this sleeve doesn't s. well,** la manche ne tombe pas bien. **3.** (*a*) (*of the face, eyes*) s'immobiliser; (*of the features*) se figer; (*b*) (*of broken bone*) se ressouder; (*c*) (*of blossom, fruit*) se former; (*d*) (*of tree*) reprendre racine. **4.** (*a*) (*of white of egg, blood*) se coaguler; (*of blood*) se figer; (*of jelly*) prendre; (*b*) (*of cement*) prendre, durcir. **5.** *Ven:* (*of dog*) tomber en arrêt. **6.** (*of current, etc.*) **to s. southwards,** porter au sud; **the tide is setting in, out,** la marée commence à monter, à descendre, à se retirer. **7. to s. to work,** se mettre au travail, à l'œuvre. **set** *a.* **1.** (*a*) (visage) immobile, aux traits rigides; (regard) fixe; (sourire) figé; (*b*) (ressort) bandé, tendu; *Sp:* **(get) s.!** en position! attention! *F:* **to be all s.,** être prêt(s) à commencer; (*c*) **(hard) s.,** ferme, figé; (ciment) bien pris; (*d*) **the fruit is s.,** le fruit est formé, noué (*e*) **well s. person,** personne à la taille cambrée. **2.** (*a*) **s. price,** prix *m* fixe; **s. time,** heure fixée, prescrite; **at s. hours,** à des heures réglées; **s. purpose,** ferme intention *f*; **s. ideas,** idées arrêtées; (*b*) **s. phrase,** cliché *m*; expression consacrée; **s. forms,** les formes prescrites; **s. form of prayer,** prière *f* liturgique; **s. dinner,** (dîner *m* de) table *f* d'hôte; dîner à prix fixe; **s. speech,** discours composé à l'avance, préparé; (*c*) **s. piece,** (i) *Cu:* pièce montée; (ii) *Pyr:* pièce montée, pièce d'artifice; (iii) *Th:* ferme *f*; *Th:* **s. scene,** décor (monté); (*d*) **s. task,** tâche assignée; *Sch:* **s. subject,** sujet imposé aux candidats; **s. books,** les auteurs *m* au programme. **3. to be s. on sth.,** être résolu, déterminé, à qch.; tenir beaucoup à ce que qch. se fasse; **to be (dead) s. on doing sth.,** être résolu, déterminé, à faire qch.; **to be dead s. against s.o.,** s'acharner après, contre, sur, qn. **set about** *v.i.* (*a*) **to s. about a piece of work,** se mettre à, entreprendre, un travail; **to s. about doing sth.,** se mettre à faire qch.; **I don't know how to s. about it,** je ne sais pas comment m'y prendre; (*b*) *F:* **to s. about s.o.,** attaquer qn. **set against** *v.tr.* (*a*) **to s. s.o. against s.o.,** indisposer qn contre qn; monter (la tête à) qn contre qn; **he's trying to s. you against me,** il cherche à me nuire auprès de vous; (*b*) **to s. oneself, one's face, against sth.,** s'opposer résolument à qch.; (*c*) opposer (qch. à qch.); contre-balancer (qch. par qch.). **set apart** *v.tr.* isoler (qn); **they s. themselves apart,** ils faisaient bande à part. **set aside** *v.tr.* (*a*) rejeter; laisser (qch.) de côté; (*b*) mettre (qch.) de côté, en réserve; (*c*) écarter (une proposition, etc.); ne tenir aucun compte (d'un ordre); **to s. aside one's personal feelings,** mettre de côté tout sentiment personnel; (*d*) *Jur:* casser, infirmer (un jugement, etc.); rejeter (une réclamation); annuler (un testament). **set back** *v.tr.* (*a*) *Const: etc:* renfoncer (une façade); **house s. back (from the road),** maison en retrait (de la route); (*of horse*) **to s. back its ears,** coucher les oreilles; (*b*) retarder le progrès de (qn, qch.); **this will s. him back,** cela retardera sa guérison; *F:* **it s. me back £5000,** ça m'a coûté £5000. **set down** *v.tr.* (*a*) déposer (qch., qn); **the train stops to s. down passengers only,** le train ne s'arrête que pour déposer des voyageurs; (*b*) **to s. sth. down in writing,** coucher qch. par écrit; **condition s. down in the contract,** condition énoncée dans le contrat. **set forth** *v.i. A:* se mettre en route; partir. **set in 1.** *v.i.* commencer; **before winter sets in,** avant la venue de l'hiver; **night was setting in,** la nuit se faisait; **rain is setting in,** le temps se met à la pluie. **2.** *v.tr.* encastrer, entabler (une pierre, une poutre); poser (une vitre); *Dressm:* monter (une manche, des fronces). **set off 1.** *v.tr.* (*a*) compenser (une dette); **to s. off a gain against a loss,** compenser une perte par un gain; (*b*) faire ressortir, faire valoir, rehausser (les charmes de qn, une couleur); mettre (qch.) en relief, en valeur; (*c*) rapporter (un angle); (*d*) faire partir (une fusée, etc.); **this answer s. them off laughing,** cette réponse a déclenché les rires. **2.** *v.i.* (*a*) se mettre en route; partir; **to s. off on a journey,** se mettre en voyage; **to s. off again,** se remettre en route; **to s. off running,** partir en courant; (*b*) *Typ:* (*of wet ink*) maculer. **set out 1.** *v.tr.* (*a*) arranger, disposer (qch.); étaler (des marchandises); exposer (ses idées); **his work is well set out,** son travail est bien présenté; (*b*) *Mth: Surv: etc:* faire le tracé d'(une courbe); (*c*) *Typ:* espacer (les caractères, les mots). **2.** *v.i.* (*a*) se mettre en route; partir (en voyage); **just as he was setting out,** au moment de son départ; **to s. out for school,** partir pour l'école; **to s. out again,** repartir; **to s. out in pursuit, in search, of s.o.,** se mettre à la poursuite, à la recherche, de qn; (*b*) **I didn't s. out to attack the government,** je n'avais aucune intention d'attaquer le gouvernement. **setting 1.** *a.* (*a*) (soleil, astre) couchant; (astre, gloire) sur son déclin; (*b*) **slow-s., quick-s., cement,** ciment *m* à prise lente, rapide. **2.** *n.* (*a*) (i) mise *f*, pose *f* (de qch.); (ii) disposition *f*, arrangement *m*; **s. to music,** mise en musique; (iii) réglage *m*; mise à l'heure (d'une horloge); (iv) *Ent:* montage *m* (d'un spécimen); (v) montage, sertissage *m* (d'une pierre); dressage *m* (d'un piège); *Hairdr:* mise en plis; **s. lotion,** lotion *f* pour mise en plis; (vi) *Typ:* **s. (up),** composition *f*; **page s.,** mise en page; **s. stick,** composteur *m*; (vii) fixation *f*, désignation *f* (d'une date, etc.); (viii) *Surg:* réduction *f* (d'une fracture); (ix) imposition *f* (d'une tâche); (*b*) (i) coucher *m* (du soleil, etc.); (ii) tassement *m* (de fondations, etc.); (iii) recollement *m* (d'un os brisé); (iv) nouure *f*, formation *f* (du fruit); (v) affermissement *m*; prise *f* (du ciment); coagulation *f* (de l'albumine); (*c*) (i) cadre *m* (d'un récit, d'une fête, etc.); *Th:* mise en scène; (ii) monture *f* (d'un diamant); (iii) *Mus:* **s. for violin,** arrangement pour violon; (iv) *Dom.Ec:* **place s.,** couvert *m*; (*d*) **s. apart, aside,** mise à part; **s. aside,** rejet *m* (d'une demande); *Jur:* annulation *f*, cassation *f* (d'un jugement, etc.); (*e*) **s. off, s. out,** départ *m*; (*f*) **s. up,** (i) montage *m*; installation *f*; (ii) établissement *m*, création *f*, fondation *f*. **set to** *v.i.* (*a*) se mettre (résolument) au travail, à l'œuvre; (*b*) *F:* (*of two pers.*) avoir une prise de bec; en venir aux coups. **set up 1.** *v.tr.* (*a*) dresser (un mât, une statue, etc.); élever, ériger (une statue); élever (une barrière); planter (un drapeau); installer (une batterie); monter (une machine, etc.); armer (un appareil); **to s. sth. up again,** relever qch.; (*b*) *Typ:* composer (un MS); (*c*) exalter, élever (qn); (*d*) *U.S:* arranger (un déjeuner, etc.); tramer (un complot); agencer (qch.); (*e*) *P:* **I've been s. up good and proper,** on m'a monté le coup; on m'a bien eu; (*f*) établir (une agence, etc.); instituer, constituer (un comité, un tribunal); créer, fonder (une maison de commerce); monter (un magasin); **to s. up house,** s'installer dans une maison; (*g*) *Med: etc:* occasionner, causer (une infection, une irritation); (*h*) **to s. s.o. up in business,** établir qn, lancer qn, dans un commerce; (*i*) **to s. up a howl,** se mettre à hurler; (*j*) donner, rendre, de la vigueur à (qn); **a fortnight in the country will s. you up,** une quinzaine à la campagne va vous remettre d'aplomb. **2.** *v.i.* (*a*) **to s. up as a chemist,** s'établir pharmacien(ne); **he has s. up for himself,** il s'est établi à son (propre) compte; (*b*) **to s. up as a critic,** se poser en critique. **set upon** *v.tr.* attaquer (qn); **to be s. upon by s.o.,** être attaqué par qn.

setback ['setbæk] *n.* **1.** (*a*) recul *m* (dans les affaires, etc.); *Fin: St. Exch:* tassement *m*, repli *m*; (*b*) rechute *f* (d'une maladie); (*c*) déconvenue *f*, déception *f*; revers *m* de fortune. **2.** *Arch:* décrochement *m*.

set-in ['setin] *a.* (*a*) encastré; (*b*) *Dressm:* **s.-in sleeve,** manche rapportée.

set-off ['setɔf] *n.* **1.** contraste *m*; **as a s.-o.,** par contraste. **2.** compensation *f* (d'une dette); *Book-k:* écriture *f* inverse; **as a s.-o. against (sth.),** en compensation de (qch.); en contrepartie de, à (qch.).

set-square ['setskwɛər] *n.* équerre *f* (à dessin).

sett [set] *n. Civ.E:* **(paving) s.,** pavé *m* d'échantillon.

settee [se'ti:] *n. Furn:* canapé *m*; **bed s., s. bed,** lit-canapé *m*, *pl.* lits-canapés.

setter ['setər] *n.* **1.** (*pers.*) (*a*) *Mec.E:* ajusteur *m*; (*b*) *Typ:* **type s.,** compositeur, -trice; (*c*) *Th:* **stage s.,** chef *m* machiniste; (*d*) sertisseur *m* (de diamants, etc.). **2.** (*dog*) setter *m*; **Irish s.,** setter irlandais.

settle[1] ['setl] *n.* banc *m* à dossier.

settle[2] **I.** *v.tr.* **1.** (*a*) établir, installer (qn, un peuple, etc.) (dans un pays); (*b*) coloniser, peupler (un pays); (*c*) rendre stable; (*d*) mettre bien en place; **to s. one's feet in the stirrups,** assurer ses pieds dans les étriers. **2.** (*a*) **to s. an invalid for the night,** arranger un malade pour la nuit; (*b*) établir (ses enfants); marier, caser (sa fille); (*c*) régler, mettre ordre à (ses affaires). **3.** (*a*) laisser se déposer (un liquide); (*b*) **to s. s.o.'s doubts,** dissiper les doutes de qn. **4.** apaiser, calmer (qn, les nerfs, etc.); **give me something to s. my stomach,** donnez-moi quelque chose pour me remettre l'estomac. **5.** fixer, déterminer (un jour, un endroit, etc.); **it's as good as settled,** l'affaire est dans le sac; **everything is settled, it's settled,** c'est une affaire faite, tout est d'accord; **that's settled then,** alors c'est dit; c'est convenu; **to s. to do sth.,** décider de faire qch. **6.** (*a*) résoudre, décider (une question); trancher, arranger (un différend); vider (une querelle); arranger, liquider (une affaire); **questions not yet settled,** questions *f* en suspens; **that settles it!** voilà qui tranche la question! voilà qui décide tout! **s. it among yourselves,** arrangez cela entre vous; **to s. (sth.) amicably,** régler (une question) à l'amiable; *Jur:* arranger (un procès); **to s. out of court,** transiger avant jugement; (*b*) conclure, terminer (une affaire); régler, solder (un compte); payer (une dette, etc.); **to s. one's bills,** payer ses comptes; *F:* **that settled him,** (i) ça lui a réglé son compte; (ii) ça lui a rabattu le caquet. **7. to s. an annuity on s.o.,** constituer une annuité à qn; **to s. all one's property on one's wife,** mettre tous ses biens sur la tête de sa femme. **II.** *v.i.* **1.** (*a*) élire domicile, s'établir, se fixer **(in a place,** dans un lieu); (*b*) **to s. in an armchair,** s'installer dans un fauteuil; **she had settled (herself) in a corner,** elle s'était installée dans un coin; (*c*) (*of bird, insect, etc.*) se percher, se poser (sur un arbre, etc.); (*d*) **the snow is settling,** la neige ne fond pas; (*e*) **the wind is settling in the north,** le vent souffle ferme du nord; (*f*) **to s. to work, to do sth.,** se mettre sérieusement au travail, à faire qch.; **he can't s. to anything,** il ne se décide pas à choisir une occupation. **2.** (*of liquid*) se clarifier, déposer; (*of sediment*) se déposer; **to let (sth.) s.,** laisser déposer (un précipité); laisser rasseoir (le vin); laisser reposer (une solution). **3.** (*a*) (*of ground, pillar, etc.*) prendre son assiette, s'asseoir; (*of foundation, etc.*) se déniveler, s'affaisser; (*b*) (*of ship*) couler, (s')enfoncer. **4.** (*of excitement*) s'apaiser, se calmer; **the weather is settling,** le temps se calme. **5. I settled for £100,** j'ai décidé d'accepter £100; **as there's no meat I'll s. for fish,** comme il n'y a pas de viande, je prends du poisson. **6. to s. with s.o.,** (i) régler ses comptes avec qn; (ii) *F:* régler son compte à qn. **settled** *a.* **1.** (*a*) (*of state*) invariable, sûr; (*of idea, habit*) fixe, enraciné; (intention) bien arrêtée; **s. weather,** temps fixe, sûr; beau *m* fixe; **I am a man of s. habits,** je suis un homme d'habitude; (*b*) (*of pers., character*) rassis, réfléchi; (*of bearing, etc.*) tranquille, calme; (*c*) (*of pers.*) rangé; *esp.* marié. **2.** (*a*) (*of affair, etc.*) arrangé, décidé; (*b*) (*of bill, etc.*) réglé. **3.** (*of pers.*) domicilié, établi. **4.** (*of ground*) tassé. **5.** (*of country*) colonisé. **settle down** *v.i.* (*a*) (i) s'établir, se fixer (dans un lieu); (ii) s'installer (dans un fauteuil, etc.); **to s. down to sleep,** se disposer à dormir; (iii) **to s. down to work,** se mettre sérieusement au travail; **to s. down to a job,** attaquer, se mettre à, une tâche; (*b*) (i) (*of pers.*) se ranger, s'assagir; **to s. down (for life),** (i) se marier; (ii) se caser; se fixer; **he's beginning to s. down at school,** il commence à s'habituer à l'école; (ii) (*of situation*) s'arranger; redevenir normal; (*of excitement*) se calmer; **things are settling down,** (i) les choses commencent à prendre tournure; (ii) l'ordre se rétablit; **as soon as the market settles down,** aussitôt que le marché reprend son train (ordinaire). **settle in** *v.i.* s'installer, s'établir (dans une nouvelle maison, etc.). **settle up** *v.i.* payer ses comptes; **to s. up with s.o.,** régler ses comptes avec qn. **settling** *n.* **1.** = SETTLEMENT[1]. **2.** (*a*) apaisement *m* (d'une agitation, des nerfs, etc.); (*b*) clarification *f* (d'un liquide); (*c*) précipitation *f*, dépôt *m* (du sédiment); (*d*) tassement *m*; affaissement *m* (du terrain); dénivellement *m* (d'un pilier, etc.); (*e*) **settlings,** dépôt, sédiment *m*. **3.** = SETTLEMENT³ (*a*). **4.** (*a*) conclusion *f*, terminaison *f* (d'une affaire); **s. (up),** règlement *m* (d'un compte); (*b*) *St. Exch:* **s. day,** jour *m* de (la) liquidation, du règlement. **5. s. (down, in),** installation *f* (dans une nouvelle maison, etc.).

settlement ['setəlmənt] *n.* **1.** (*a*) établissement *m* (d'un peuple dans un pays, etc.); installation *f* (de qn dans une maison, etc.); (*b*) colonisation *f* (d'un pays). **2.** (*a*) tassement *m*, affaissement *m* (des terres); (*b*) clarification *f* (d'un liquide). **3.** (*a*) règlement *m* (d'une affaire); arrangement *m* (d'un différend, etc.); résolution *f*, décision *f* (d'une question); détermination *f* (d'une date, etc.); conclusion *f* (d'un traité, etc.); (*b*) *Com:* règlement, paiement *m* (d'un compte); **in (full) s.,** pour règlement de tout compte; (*c*) *St.Exch:* liquidation *f*; **the s.,** le terme; **s. day,** jour *m* de (la) liquidation, du règlement; (*d*) accord *m* (entre deux puissances, etc.); **they have reached a s.,** ils sont arrivés à un accord; (*e*) *Jur:* **s. of an annuity,** constitution *f* de rente (**on**, en faveur de); **family s.,** pacte *m* de famille; **marriage s.,** (i) contrat *m* de mariage; (ii) (*in favour of daughter*) dot *f*; (*in favour of wife*) douaire *m*. **4.** *Jur:* domicile légal. **5.** colonie *f*; **penal s.,** colonie pénitentiaire. **6.** *U.S:* petit village.

settler ['setlər] *n.* **1.** colon *m*, immigrant, -ante (dans un pays nouvellement découvert). **2.** *F:* coup décisif.

set-to ['settu:] *n. F:* (*a*) bagarre *f*; (*b*) prise *f* de bec.

set-up ['setʌp] *n. F:* **1.** organisation *f*; **it's an odd s.-up,** c'est une drôle de boîte, d'affaire. **2.** installation *f*; **you've got a nice s.-up here,** vous êtes bien installé ici. **3.** machination *f*, coup monté.

seven ['sev(ə)n] *num.a. & n.* sept (*m*); **two sevens are fourteen,** deux fois sept font quatorze; **s.-league boots,** bottes *fpl* de sept lieues (du Petit Poucet); *Cards:* **s. of hearts,** le sept de cœur.

sevenfold ['sev(ə)nfould] **1.** *a.* septuple. **2.** *adv.* sept fois autant; **to increase s.,** septupler.

seventeen [sev(ə)n'ti:n] *num.a. & n.* dix-sept (*m*); **she's s.,** elle a dix-sept ans.

seventeenth [sev(ə)n'ti:nθ] **1.** *num.a. & n.* dix-septième (*mf*); **(on) the s. of May,** le dix-sept mai. **2.** *n.* (*fractional*) dix-septième *m*.

seventh ['sev(ə)nθ] **1.** *num.a. & n.* septième (*mf*); **to be in the s. heaven (of delight),** être aux anges, au septième ciel; **Edward the S.,** Edouard Sept; **the s. of May,** le sept mai; *Rel:* **S.-day Adventist,** adventiste *mf* du septième jour. **2.** *n.* (*a*) (*fractional*) septième *m*; (*b*) *Mus:* septième *f*; (note) sensible (*f*).

seventieth ['sev(ə)ntiiθ] **1.** *num.a. & n.* soixante-dixième (*mf*); *Belg: Sw. Fr:* septantième (*mf*). **2.** *n.* (*fractional*) soixante-dixième *m*.

seventy ['sev(ə)nti] *num.a. & n.* soixante-dix (*m*); *Belg: Sw.Fr:* septante (*mf*); **s.-one, s.-nine, s.-five,** soixante et onze, soixante-dix neuf, soixante-quinze; **to be in one's seventies,** être septuagénaire.

sever ['sevər] **1.** *v.tr.* (*a*) désunir, disjoindre (les parties d'un tout); rompre (l'amitié, une liaison, etc.); **to s. one's connections with s.o.,** se désassocier de qn, d'avec qn; (*b*) **to s. sth. from sth.,** séparer qch. de qch. **2.** *v.i.* (*of rope, etc.*) (se) rompre.

several ['sev(ə)r(ə)l] *a.* **1.** (*a*) *O:* séparé; **on three s. occasions,** à trois occasions (différentes); (*b*) respectif; *Lit:* **each went his s. way,** ils s'en allèrent, chacun de son côté. **2.** (*a*) plusieurs; divers; quelques; **I've been there s. times,** j'y suis allé plusieurs fois; **he and s. others,** lui et plusieurs autres; (*b*) (*with noun function*) **s. of us, of them,** plusieurs d'entre nous, d'entre eux; **s. of our party heard it,** plusieurs membres de notre groupe l'ont entendu. **-ally** *adv.* séparément, individuellement.

severance ['sevərəns] *n.* séparation *f*, désunion *f*, disjonction *f* (**from,** de); rupture *f* (des relations, etc.); **s. pay,** compensation *f* pour perte d'emploi.

severe [si'viər] *a.* **1.** (*of pers.*) sévère, strict, rigoureux (**with,** envers); (mesures) de rigueur; **a s. reprimand,** une verte réprimande. **2.** (*a*) (temps) rigoureux; (hiver, climat) rigoureux, rude, dur; (*of illness, wound*) grave; **s. blow,** coup *m* rude; **s. loss,** grosse, forte, perte; **s. pain,** douleur violente, vive. **3.** (style, etc.) sévère, austère. **-ly** *adv.* **1.** sévèrement, strictement; avec sévérité. **2.** grièvement (blessé); gravement (malade); **s. tried,** durement éprouvé. **3.** sévèrement, austèrement.

severity [si'veriti] *n.* **1.** sévérité *f*, dureté *f*, rigueur *f* (de qn, d'une punition, etc.). **2.** (*a*) rigueur (du temps, du climat, etc.); rudesse *f* (du temps); (*b*) gravité *f* (d'une maladie, d'une perte); violence *f* (d'une douleur); (*c*) rigueur, caractère rigoureux (d'un examen, etc.). **3.** sévérité, austérité *f* (de style).

Seville ['sevil] *Pr.n. Geog:* Séville *f*; **S. orange,** orange amère.

sew [sou] *v.tr. & i.* (*p.t.* **sewed** [soud]; *p.p.* **sewn** [soun], *occ.* **sewed**) (*a*) coudre; (*with awl*) piquer; **to s. on a button,** (re)coudre un bouton; **hand, machine, sewn,** cousu (à la) main, à la machine; (*b*) *F:* **it's all sewn up,** tout est arrangé. **sewing** *n.* **1.** couture *f*; **s. needle,** aiguille *f* à coudre; **s. cotton, thread,** fil *m* à coudre; **s. machine,** machine *f* à coudre. **2.** ouvrage *m* (à l'aiguille).

sewage ['s(j)u:idʒ] *n.* eau(x) *f* (*pl*) d'égout(s); effluent *m*; **s. system,** système *m* du tout-à-l'égout; **s. farm,** champs *mpl* d'épandage.

sewer¹ ['souər] *n.* couseur, -euse.

sewer² ['s(j)u:ər] *n. Civ.E:* égout *m*; **main s.,** égout collecteur; *Fig:* **s. of vice, etc.,** cloaque *m* de vice.

sewerage ['s(j)u:əridʒ] *n.* **1.** système *m* d'égouts. **2.** *F:* = SEWAGE.

sex¹ [seks] *n.* sexe *m*; (*a*) *Biol:* **s. determination,** détermination *f* du sexe; *Psy:* **the s. urge,** le désir sexuel; **s. organs,** organes sexuels; **the s. act,** l'acte sexuel; *F:* **to have s. with s.o.,** faire l'amour avec qn; **s. appeal,** attrait sexuel, sex-appeal *m*; (*b*) *O:* **the fair s.,** le beau sexe; **the sterner s.,** le sexe fort.

sex² *v.tr.* **1.** déterminer le sexe de (qn, un animal). **2.** *F:* **to s. up,** introduire du sexe (dans un roman, etc.). **sexed** *a.* **1.** *Nat.Hist:* sexué. **2.** *Psy:* **highly s.,** à tendances sexuelles très prononcées; **over-s.,** hypersexué; **under-s.,** frigide, froid.

sexagenarian [seksədʒi'nɛəriən] *a. & n.* sexagénaire (*mf*).

sexiness ['seksinis] *n.* charme, caractère, provocant; airs provocants; tendances sexuelles prononcées.

sexless ['sekslis] *a.* (*a*) asexué; *Bot:* (fleur) neutre; (*b*) *F:* froid, frigide.

sexologist [sek'sɔlɔdʒist] *n.* sexologue *mf*.

sexology [sek'sɔlədʒi] *n.* sexologie *f*.

sexpot ['sekspɔt] *n.f. F:* femme très sexy; allumeuse.

sextant ['sekstənt] *n. Mth: Nau:* sextant *m*.

sextet [seks'tet] *Mus:* sextuor *m*; (*jazz*) sextette *f*.

sexton ['sekst(ə)n] *n. Ecc:* sacristain *m* et sonneur *m* de cloches (et fossoyeur *m*).

sextuple ['sekstjupl] *a. & n.* sextuple (*m*).

sextuplet ['sekstjuplet] *n.* **1.** *Mus:* sextolet *m*, sixain *m*. **2.** (*child*) sextuplé, -ée.

sexual ['seksjuəl] *a.* sexuel; **s. intercourse,** rapports sexuels; **the s. organs,** les organes sexuels. **-ally** *adv.* d'une manière sexuelle; sexuellement.

sexuality [seksju'æliti] *n.* **1.** sexualité *f*. **2.** tendances sexuelles prononcées.

sexy ['seksi] *a. F:* qui excite les instincts sexuels; (*of pers.*) sensuel, sexy; (sexuellement) provocant.

sez you [sez'ju:] *int. P:* (=*says you*) tu parles! et ta sœur!

sh [ʃ] *int.* chut!

shabbiness ['ʃæbinis] *n.* **1.** état râpé, usé (d'un vêtement, etc.); piètre état (d'un meuble, etc.); apparence pauvre, *F:* miteuse (de qn). **2.** mesquinerie *f*, petitesse *f* (de conduite, etc.).

shabby ['ʃæbi] *a.* **1.** (vêtement, etc.) râpé, usé, élimé; (mobilier, pièce, etc.) pauvre, minable; **s. house,** maison délabrée, minable; (*of pers.*) **to look s.,** avoir l'air minable, miteux; **to be s. genteel,** s'efforcer de sauver les apparences; (*of material*) **to become s.,** se délustrer, s'élimer. **2.** (*of pers., conduct*) mesquin, vilain, petit; **s. trick,** mesquinerie *f*; **s. excuse,** prétexte mesquin. **-ily** *adv.* **1.** pauvrement, piètrement (meublé, vêtu, etc.); **s. dressed,** miteux, râpé. **2.** (se conduire) mesquinement.

shack[1] [ʃæk] *n.* cabane *f*, hutte *f*; bicoque *f*.

shack[2] *v.i. P:* **to s. up (with s.o.),** se coller (avec qn).

shackle[1] ['ʃækl] *n.* **1. shackles,** fers *m* (d'un prisonnier, etc.); **the shackles of convention,** les entraves *f* des conventions sociales. **2.** maillon *m* de liaison, manille *f* d'assemblage (d'une chaîne); anse *f* (d'un cadenas); cigale *f* (d'une ancre).

shackle[2] *v.tr.* mettre les fers à, entraver (un prisonnier); **shackled by conventions,** entravé par les conventions.

shacktown ['ʃæktaun] *n. NAm: F:* bidonville *f*.

shade[1] [ʃeid] *n.* **1.** (*a*) ombre *f*; **in the s. of a tree,** à l'ombre d'un arbre; **temperature in the s.,** température *f* à l'ombre; **to put s.o. in the s.,** éclipser qn; faire ombre à qn; **a s. of annoyance on his face,** une ombre de contrariété sur son visage; *Lit:* **the Shades,** les Enfers *mpl*; (*b*) *Art:* ombre (dans un tableau). **2.** (*a*) nuance *f* (de couleur, d'opinion); teinte *f*; **different shades of blue,** différentes nuances de bleu; (*b*) nuance; petit peu; tantinet *m*; **a s. longer,** un tantinet plus long; **he is a s. better,** il va un tout petit peu mieux; **a s. of regret,** une nuance de regret. **3.** (*a*) pâle reflet *m*, ombre (de qch.); (*b*) *O:* ombre, fantôme *m* (d'un mort). **4.** (*a*) **(eye) s.,** visière *f*; **lamp s.,** abat-jour *m inv*; (*b*) *NAm:* (i) store *m* (de fenêtre); (ii) **shades,** lunettes *fpl* de soleil.

shade[2] **I.** *v.tr.* **1.** (*a*) ombrager (qch.); couvrir (qch.) d'ombre; **to s. (sth.) from the sun,** abriter (qch.) du soleil; **to s. one's eyes with one's hand,** s'abriter les yeux de la main; **to s. a light,** (i) voiler, atténuer, une lumière; (ii) masquer une lumière; (*b*) obscurcir, assombrir (le visage, etc.). **2.** *Art:* ombrer, mettre des ombres à (un dessin). **3.** nuancer (un tissu, etc.); **to s. away, off,** dégrader (des couleurs). **II.** *v.i.* **blue that shades (off) into green,** bleu qui se fond en vert; **these categories shade into one another,** ces catégories se confondent. **shaded** *a.* **1.** (*a*) (chemin, etc.) ombragé; (*b*) (lampe, etc.) à abat-jour. **2.** (*a*) *Art:* (dessin) ombré; (*b*) *Mapm: etc:* hachuré. **3.** nuancé. **shading** *n.* **1.** projection *f* d'une ombre (sur qch.); protection *f* (de qch.) contre la lumière, contre le soleil. **2.** (*a*) *Art:* dessin *m* des ombres; *Mapm:* **hill s.,** modelé *m*; (*b*) ombres (d'un dessin). **3.** nuancement *m* (de couleurs); **s. (away, off),** dégradation *f* (d'une couleur); estompage *m*.

shadeless ['ʃeidlis] *a.* (*a*) sans ombre; (*b*) qui ne donne pas d'ombre.

shadiness ['ʃeidinis] *n.* **1.** ombre *f*, ombrage *m* (d'un sentier, etc.). **2.** *F:* aspect *m* louche (d'une affaire, etc.); réputation suspecte (de qn).

shadow[1] ['ʃædou] *n.* ombre *f*. **1.** (*a*) obscurité *f*; **in the s.,** à, dans, l'ombre; dans l'obscurité; **the s. of death,** les ombres de la mort; **under the s. of a terrible accusation,** sous le coup d'une accusation terrible; (*b*) noir *m* (d'un tableau, d'une photographie); *X-Rays:* **a s. on the right lung,** un voile au poumon droit; **to have (dark) shadows round, under, one's eyes,** avoir les yeux cernés; *Toil:* **eye s.,** ombre à paupières; (*c*) *F:* **five o'clock s.,** la barbe du soir. **2.** (*a*) **to cast a s.,** projeter une ombre; faire ombre; **this cast a s. over the festivities,** cela a jeté une ombre sur la fête; **coming events cast their shadows,** les événements *m* à venir se font pressentir; **to catch at shadows, to run after a s.,** courir après une ombre; **town nestling in the s. of a mountain,** ville nichée à l'ombre d'une montagne; **to be afraid of one's own s.,** avoir peur de son ombre; **not the s. of a doubt,** pas l'ombre d'un doute; (*b*) **s. boxing,** (i) boxe simulée; (ii) *Fig:* attaque rituelle, de pure forme. **3.** (*a*) compagnon, *f.* compagne, inséparable (de qn); (*b*) ombre (d'un mort); **he's worn to a s., he's a mere s. of his former self,** il n'est plus qu'une ombre, que l'ombre de lui-même; (*d*) personne qui prend qn en filature. **4. s. government,** gouvernement *m* fantôme; **s. cabinet,** cabinet *m* fantôme.

shadow[2] *v.tr.* **1.** (*a*) ombrager (qch.); couvrir (qch.) de son ombre; (*b*) *Tex:* chiner (un tissu). **2.** filer, pister (qn); prendre (un suspect) en filature. **shadowing** *n.* filature *f*, pistage *m* (d'un suspect, etc.).

shadowy ['ʃædoui] *a.* **1.** (chemin, etc.) ombragé, ombreux. **2.** (projet) indécis, vague; (contour) vague, indistinct; **a s. form,** une silhouette vague.

shady ['ʃeidi] *a.* **1.** (*a*) qui donne de l'ombre; ombreux; (*b*) ombragé; couvert d'ombre. **2.** *F:* (*of pers., transaction, etc.*) louche; (financier) véreux; **s. business,** (i) commerce *m* interlope; (ii) affaire véreuse; **the s. side of politics,** les dessous *m* de la politique.

shaft[1] [ʃɑːft] *n.* **1.** (*a*) hampe *f*, bois *m* (d'une lance, etc.); (*b*) manche *m* (de club de golf, d'un outil à long manche). **2.** flèche *f*, trait *m*; **the shafts of satire,** les traits de la satire. **3.** rayon *m* (de lumière); éclair *m* (de foudre). **4.** (*a*) tige *f* (de plume d'oiseau, de candélabre, etc.); (*b*) fût *m* (d'une colonne); souche *f* (de cheminée d'usine). **5.** *Mec. E:* arbre *m*; (*stationary*) axe *m*; **connecting, coupling, s.,** arbre de liaison, d'accouplement; **driving s.,** arbre moteur; **transmission s.,** arbre de transmission; **propeller s.,** arbre porte-hélice, arbre d'hélice. **6.** *Veh:* brancard *m*; **s. horse,** cheval *m* de brancard.

shaft[2] *n.* **1.** *Min:* puits *m*; **air, ventilation, s.,** puits d'aérage, conduit *m* d'air; **to sink a s.,** foncer, creuser, un puits; **s. sinking,** fonçage *m*, foncement *m*, creusage *m*, d'un puits. **2.** cage *f* (d'un ascenseur).

shag[1] [ʃæg] *n.* **1.** *Tex:* peluche *f*; long poil (d'un tissu, tapis, etc.). **2.** tabac fort (coupé fin).

shag[2] *n. Orn:* cormoran huppé.

shagged [ʃægd] *a. P:* **s. (out),** fourbu, claqué.

shagginess ['ʃæginis] *n.* rudesse *f*, longueur *f* de poil (d'un poney, etc.); état ébouriffé (des cheveux).

shaggy ['ʃægi] *a.* poilu; (poney, etc.) à longs poils, à poils rudes; (cheveux) ébouriffés; (barbe) hirsute, touffue; (sourcils) en broussailles; (terrain) couvert de broussailles; *Tex:* (drap) poilu, à long poil; **s. dog story** = histoire farfelue.

shagreen [ʃæ'griːn] *n.* **1.** *Leath:* (peau de) chagrin (*m*).

shah ['ʃɑː] *n.* s(c)hah *m* (de Perse).

shake[1] [ʃeik] *n.* **1.** (*a*) secousse *f*; **to give sth. a good s.,** bien secouer, bien agiter, qch.; **to give oneself a s.,** se secouer; **a s. of the head,** un hochement de tête; **in two shakes of a lamb's tail,** en un rien de temps; en moins de rien; (*b*) tremblement *m* (de la main, etc.); *U.S: N.Z:* tremblement de terre; *F:* **to be all of a s.,** trembler dans tous ses membres; **to have the shakes,** (i) avoir la tremblote; (ii) avoir le délirium tremens; (*c*) *Mus:* trille *m*; (*d*) **with a s. in his voice,** d'une voix tremblotante, mal assurée. **2.** *Comest:* **milk s.,** milk-shake *m*. **3.** (*in wood*) gerçure *f*, crevasse *f*. **4.** *F:* **to be no great shakes,** être médiocre; ne pas valoir grand-chose.

shake[2] *v.* (*p.t.* **shook** [ʃuk]; *p.p.* **shaken** ['ʃeik(ə)n]) **1.** *v.tr.* (*a*) secouer (qn, qch.); agiter (un liquide); **s. the bottle,** agiter le flacon; **to s. one's head,** (i) secouer, hocher, la tête; (ii) faire non de la tête; **to s. one's fist at s.o.,** menacer qn du poing; **to s. hands with s.o.,** serrer la main à, de, qn; donner une poignée de main à qn; **they shook hands on it,** ils ont topé; *F:* **s.!** (i) félicitations! (ii) (*to seal bargain*) touchez là! tope (là)! **to s. oneself free (from sth.),** se dégager (de qch.) d'une secousse; (*b*) ébranler, secouer (un bâtiment, etc.); ébranler (une opinion, la foi de qn, etc.); **that has shaken my faith in him,** cela m'a fait douter de sa bonne foi; **event that shook the country,** événement *m* qui a bouleversé le pays; **he was badly shaken by the accident,** il a été très bouleversé par l'accident; **to feel shaken after a fall,** se ressentir d'une chute; *F:* **that'll s. him!** cela le fera tiquer! **voice shaking with emotion,** voix émue; (*c*) *Mus:* triller (un passage); (*d*) *Austr: P:* voler, cambrioler (qn). **2.** *v.i.* trembler; chanceler; branler; (*of door, window*) branler; (*of voice*) trembloter, chevroter; **his hand was shaking,** la main lui tremblait; **to s. with fright, with rage,** trembler, frémir, de crainte, de colère; *F:* **to s. in one's shoes,** trembler dans sa peau; grelotter de peur. **shake down 1.** *v.tr.* secouer, hocher (des fruits); *NAm: F:* (i) **to s. s.o. down for ten dollars,** faire casquer qn de dix dollars; (ii) fouiller (qn, un appartement, etc.). **2.** *v.i.* (*a*) s'installer; **to s. down for the night,** se coucher, s'installer pour la nuit; (*b*) s'habituer (à une routine, à un travail). **shake off** *v.tr.* (*a*) **to s. the dust off sth.,** secouer la poussière de qch.; *Fig:* **to s. off the dust from one's feet,** secouer la poussière de ses pieds, de ses souliers; **to s. s.o. off,** se dégager des mains de qn; **to s. off a cold,** venir à bout d'un rhume; (*b*) *F:* se débarrasser, se défaire, de (qn); semer (un importun, *Sp:* un concurrent); **I can't s. him off,** il ne me lâche pas d'un cran. **shake out** *v.tr.* (*a*) secouer; faire sortir (la poussière, etc.); vider (un sac) en le secouant; (*b*) déferler (une voile, un drapeau). **shake up** *v.tr.* (*a*) secouer, brasser (un oreiller, etc.); (*b*) *F:* éveiller, secouer (qn); secouer l'indifférence, l'inertie, de (qn). **shaking 1.** *a.* tremblant, branlant; (voix) tremblotante, chevrotante. **2.** *n.* (*a*) ballottement *m* (pendant le transport, etc.); **to give (s.o., sth.) a good s.,** bien secouer (un tapis, un enfant, etc.); (*in car, etc.*) **we got a good s. (up),** nous avons été pas mal cahotés; (*b*) ébranlement *m* (d'une maison, etc.); tremblement *m* (du sol, des vitres, etc.); tremblotement *m* (de la voix).

shakedown ['ʃeikdaun] *n.* (*a*) *F:* lit improvisé; lit de fortune (installé par terre); (*b*) *NAm: F:* (i) chantage *m*, extorsion *f*; (ii) fouille *f*.

shaker ['ʃeikər] *n.* (*a*) secoueur, -euse; (*b*) (appareil *m*) secoueur; **salad s.,** panier *m* à salade; **cocktail s.,** shaker *m*.

Shakespearian [ʃeiks'piəriən] *a.* shakespearien; de Shakespeare.

shake-up ['ʃeikʌp] *n. F:* **1.** remaniement *m* (du personnel). **2.** commotion *f*, bouleversement *m*.

shakiness ['ʃeikinis] *n.* manque *m* de stabilité, de fermeté, de solidité (d'un bâtiment, d'une chaise, etc.); faiblesse *f* (de qn, de la santé, des connaissances); tremblement *m* (de la main); chevrotement *m* (de la voix); instabilité *f* (du crédit, d'une position).

shako ['ʃækou] *n. Mil.Cost:* s(c)hako *m*.

shaky ['ʃeiki] *a.* (meuble, etc.) branlant, peu solide; (santé) faible, chancelante; (position) mal affermie; (main) tremblante, vacillante; (écriture) tremblée; (voix) mal assurée; **to be s. on one's legs,** *F:* **one's pins,** ne pas tenir sur ses quilles; **I feel very s.,** (i) je suis tout tremblant; (ii) je ne me sens pas bien solide; (iii) je suis tout patraque; **his English is s.,** il est faible en anglais. **-ily** *adv.* peu solidement; faiblement; (marcher) à pas chancelants; (écrire) d'une main tremblante; (parler) d'une voix chevrotante.

shale [ʃeil] *n.* schiste (argileux, ardoisier); argile schisteuse; **s. oil,** huile *f* de schiste.

shall [*stressed* ʃæl, *unstressed* ʃ(ə)l] *modal aux. v.* (*pr.* **shall,** *A: & B:* **shalt** [ʃælt]; **shall;** *p.t. & condit.* **should** [*stressed* ʃud, *unstressed* ʃ(ə)d]; *A:* **shouldst** [ʃudst]; *no other parts*; **shall not** *and* **should not** *are often contracted into* **shan't** [ʃɑːnt], **shouldn't** ['ʃud(ə)nt]) **I. 1.** (*with full meaning, denotes duty or command*) (*a*) (*in general precepts*) (*second and third pers.*) **thou shalt not kill,** tu ne tueras point; **ships s. carry three lights,** les navires sont tenus de porter trois feux; **which is as it should be,** ce qui n'est que justice; (*b*) (*in particular cases*) (*second and third pers.*) **he s. do it if I order it,** il devra le faire si je l'ordonne; **he shall not do it,** je défends qu'il le fasse; **he says he won't do it—he s.!** il dit qu'il ne le fera pas—je l'ordonne! **you *shall* do it!** vous le ferez, je le veux! (*c*) (*advice, remonstrance, etc.*) (*all three persons*) **you should do it at once,** vous devriez le faire tout de suite; **you should have come earlier,** vous auriez dû arriver plus tôt; **you, he, she, they, should not have gone,** il ne fallait pas y aller; **it was an accident that should have been foreseen,** c'était un accident à prévoir; **you should have seen him!** il fallait le voir! si vous l'aviez vu! **you shouldn't laugh at him,** vous avez tort de vous moquer de lui; (*d*) (*expression of opinion*) **he should have arrived by this time,** il devrait être arrivé à l'heure qu'il est; **that should suit you!** voilà qui fera sans doute votre affaire! **this weather should be ideal for anglers,** ce temps doit être ce que les pêcheurs peuvent désirer de mieux; *Iron:* **I should worry!** (i) ce n'est pas mon affaire! (ii) ne te tracasse pas pour ça! **2.** (*in deference to another*) **s. I open the window?** voulez-vous que j'ouvre la fenêtre? **let's go in, s. we?** rentrons, voulez-vous? **what should I have said?** qu'est-ce que j'aurais dû dire? **3.** (*with weakened force*) (*a*) (*exclamatory, in rhetorical questions*) **why should you suspect me?** pourquoi me soupçonner (, moi)? **how should I not be happy?** comment ne serais-je pas heureux? **whom should I meet but Martin!** voilà que je rencontre Martin! **who s. describe their surprise?** comment décrire leur surprise! (*b*) (*in subordinate clauses*) **he ordered that they should be released,** il ordonna qu'on les relâchât; **she insisted that he should wear his hair short,** elle exigeait qu'il porte les cheveux courts; **they recommend that classes should be smaller,** ils proposent de réduire le nombre des élèves dans les classes; (*c*) (*in conditional clauses*) **if he should come, should he come, let me know,** si par hasard il vient, s'il vient, faites-le-moi savoir; **should I be free I shall come,** si je suis libre je viendrai; **should the occasion arise, should it (so) happen,** le cas échéant; **in case he should not be there,** au cas, en cas, où il n'y soit pas, dans le cas où il n'y serait pas. **II.** (*used as an auxiliary verb forming the future tenses*) **1.** (*still expressing something of the speaker's will, assurance, promise, menace, etc. Used in the 2nd and 3rd persons; for the 1st pers. see* WILL[3]) **you shan't have any!** tu n'en auras pas! **you shall pay for this!** vous me le payerez! **2.** (*simple future*) (*a*) (*used in the 1st pers: for the 2nd and 3rd pers. see* WILL[3]) (i) **tomorrow I s. go and he will arrive,** demain, moi je partirai et lui arrivera; **my holiday was over; the next day I should be far away,** mon congé était fini; le lendemain je serais bien loin; **will you be there?—I shall,** y serez-vous?—oui (, j'y serai); **no, I s. not, I shan't,** non (, je n'y serai pas); (ii) (*immediate future*) **I shall explain the situation to you and you will listen,** je vais vous expliquer la situation et vous allez m'écouter; (*b*) (*used in the second pers. in interrogation*) **s. you come tomorrow?** vous viendrez demain? **3.** (*in the main clause of conditional sentences*) **if he comes I shall speak to him,** s'il vient je lui parlerai; **we should come if we were invited,** nous viendrions si on nous invitait; **had you written to me I should have answered you,** si vous m'aviez écrit je vous aurais répondu. **4.** (*in softened affirmation*) **I should like a drink,** je prendrais bien quelque chose; **I should have thought that you would have known better,** j'aurais pensé que vous auriez été plus avisé; **I shouldn't be surprised (if . . .),** cela ne me surprendrait pas (que + *pr. sub.*).

shallot [ʃə'lɔt] *n.* échalote *f.*

shallow ['ʃælou] **1.** *a.* (*a*) (*of water, dish, etc.*) peu profond; (*b*) (*of soil*) superficiel; **s.-rooted,** (arbre) à enracinement superficiel; (*c*) (*of pers., mind, etc.*) superficiel, qui manque de fond; (amitié) de surface. **2.** *n.* (*in sea, etc.*) (*often in pl.*) bas-fond *m*, *pl.* bas-fonds; haut-fond *m*, *pl.* hauts-fonds.

shallowness ['ʃælounis] *n.* (*a*) (le) peu de profondeur (de l'eau, d'un plat, etc.); (*b*) caractère superficiel; superficialité *f* (de qn, de l'esprit).

shaly ['ʃeili] *a.* schisteux.

sham¹ [ʃæm] **1.** *a.* faux; truqué; (*of illness, etc.*) simulé, feint; (piété) apparente; **s. peace,** paix fourrée. **2.** *n.* (*a*) feinte *f*, trompe-l'œil *m inv*, *P:* chiqué *m*; **that's all s.,** tout ça c'est de la frime; (*b*) **he's a s.,** c'est un imposteur.

sham² *v.tr.* **(shammed)** feindre, simuler; **to s. sickness,** faire semblant d'être malade; **he's only shamming,** c'est une comédie qu'il nous joue; il fait semblant; **he shammed dead,** il fit le mort.

shamateur ['ʃæmətɔːr] *n. Sp: F:* amateur marron.

shamble ['ʃæmbəl] *v.i.* **to s. (along),** aller à pas traînants; **to s. up to s.o.,** approcher qn d'un pas traînant.

shambles ['ʃæmb(ə)lz] *n.pl.* (*usu. with sg. const.*) (*a*) scène *f* de carnage; (*b*) *F:* désordre *m*, fouillis *m*; **what a s.!** quelle pagaille!

shambolic [ʃæm'bɔlik] *a. F:* chaotique; en pagaille.

shame¹ [ʃeim] *n.* (*a*) honte *f*; **to put s.o. to s.,** (i) faire honte à qn; faire rougir qn; (ii) l'emporter sur qn; **to my s.,** à ma honte; **s. (up)on you!** quelle honte! **for s.!** vous n'avez pas honte! **to blush for, with, s.,** rougir (i) de honte, (ii) de pudeur; **without s.,** effronté; éhonté; **to be past, lost to all, s.,** avoir perdu toute honte; (*b*) **it would be a s. to . . .,** il serait dommage de . . .; **what a s.!** quel dommage!

shame² *v.tr.* faire honte à, mortifier (qn); couvrir (qn) de honte; **to be shamed into doing sth.,** faire qch. par amour-propre. **shaming** *a.* mortifiant.

shamefaced ['ʃeimfeist] *a.* **1.** (à l'air) honteux; embarrassé, décontenancé. **2.** *Lit:* timide; modeste. **-ly** [-feisidli] *adv.* **1.** d'un air honteux, embarrassé. **2.** timidement.

shameful ['ʃeimf(u)l] *a.* honteux, scandaleux, indigne. **-fully** *adv.* honteusement; scandaleusement.

shamefulness ['ʃeimf(u)lnis] *n.* honte *f*, infamie *f.*

shameless ['ʃeimlis] *a.* **1.** (*a*) (*of pers., conduct*) éhonté, effronté; impudent; sans honte; (*b*) (*of pers.*) sans pudeur; dévergondé; (*of conduct*) impudique. **2.** (*of action*) honteux, scandaleux, indigne. **-ly** *adv.* (*a*) effrontément; impudemment; (*b*) impudiquement.

shamelessness ['ʃeimlisnis] *n.* **1.** (*a*) impudeur *f*; (*b*) impudicité *f.* **2.** effronterie *f*, impudence *f*; absence *f* de tout sentiment de honte.

shammy ['ʃæmi] *n.* **s. (leather),** peau *f* de chamois.

shampoo¹ [ʃæm'puː] *n.* **1.** (*action*) shampooing *m*; **to give s.o. a s.,** faire un shampooing à qn; **s. and set,** shampooing et mise en plis. **2.** (*product*) shampooing; **liquid, dry, s.,** shampooing liquide, sec; **carpet s.,** shampooing pour tapis.

shampoo² *v.tr.* (*a*) **to s. one's hair,** se faire un shampooing; se laver la tête; **to s. s.o., s.o.'s hair,** faire un shampooing à qn; (*b*) nettoyer (une moquette, etc.).

shamrock ['ʃæmrɔk] *n. Bot:* trèfle *m.*

shandy ['ʃændi], **shandygaff** ['ʃændigæf] *n.* mélange *m* de bière et de limonade; panaché *m.*

Shanghai¹ [ʃaŋ'hai] *Pr.n.* Shanghaï *m*, Changhaï *m.*

shanghai² *v.tr. Nau: F:* (*a*) embarquer (un homme) de force sur un navire à court d'equipage; (*b*) forcer (**s.o. into doing sth.,** qn à faire qch.).

Shangri-La [ʃæŋgri'lɑː] *n.* paradis *m* terrestre.

shank [ʃæŋk] *n.* **1.** (*a*) **shanks,** jambes *fpl*, *F:* quilles *fpl*; *F:* **to go, ride, on Shanks' mare, pony,** prendre le train onze; (*b*) (i) **s. (bone),** tibia *m*; (ii) *Farr:* canon *m* (du membre antérieur); (*c*) *Cu:* jarret *m* (de bœuf); (*d*) jambe (d'un bas). **2.** (*a*) fût *m* (d'une colonne); tige *f*, branche *f* (de clef, de rivet); hampe *f* (d'hameçon); *Typ:* corps *m*, tige (de lettre); *Nau:* verge *f* (d'ancre); *Bot:* pédoncule *m*; (*b*) queue *f* (d'un bouton).

shan't *see* SHALL.

Shantung [ʃæ'tʌŋ] *n. Tex:* shant(o)ung *m.*

shanty¹ [ʃænti] *n.* hutte *f*, cabane *f*; baraque *f*, bicoque *f*; **s. town,** bidonville *m.*

shanty² *n.* **(sea) s.,** chanson *f* de bord.

shape¹ [ʃeip] *n.* **1.** (*a*) forme *f* (de la terre, etc.); **spherical in s., of spherical s.,** de forme sphérique; **trees of all shapes,** des arbres de toutes les formes; **my hat was knocked out of s.,** mon chapeau a été déformé; **to get out of s., to lose (its) s.,** se déformer; *Journ: etc:* **to put,** *F:* **get, knock, an article into s.,** mettre un article au point; **to keep in s.,** garder sa forme; (*of pers. etc.*) **to be in good, poor, s.,** être en bonne forme, en petite forme; (*b*) taille *f*, tournure *f*; (*c*) forme indistincte; **two shapes loomed up in the darkness,** deux formes surgirent dans l'obscurité. **2. to give s. to a plan,** faire prendre corps à un projet; **to take s.,** prendre forme; prendre tournure; **our plans are taking s.,** nos projets se dessinent. **3.** forme, sorte *f*, espèce *f*; **no communication in any s. or form,** aucune communication de n'importe quelle sorte; **something in the s. of . . .,** une espèce, une sorte, de . . .. **4.** (i) forme (pour chapeau); (ii) carcasse *f* (de chapeau). **5.** (*of iron, etc.*) profil *m.*

shape² *v.tr.* (*a*) façonner, modeler (de l'argile, etc.); tailler (un bloc de pierre, etc.); **to s. sth. out of sth.,** façonner qch. avec qch.; **to s. the clay into an urn,** donner à l'argile la forme d'une urne; **to s. s.o.'s character,** pétrir le caractère de qn; **to s. the destiny of man,** diriger, régler, la destinée de l'homme; (*b*) former (un plan); (*c*) *Lit:* **to s. one's course,** diriger ses pas, se diriger **(towards,** vers); **to s. the course of public opinion,** imprimer une direction à l'opinion publique. **2.** *v.i.* (*a*) se développer; **to s. (up) well,** promettre; (*of affair, etc.*) prendre bonne tournure; **let's see how he shapes (up) in his new job,** voyons comment il va se tirer de son nouvel emploi; **things are shaping badly,** l'affaire prend une mauvaise tournure; (*b*) **to s. up to s.o.,** avancer sur qn en posture de combat. **shaped** *a.* **1.** façonné, taillé; *Metalw:* (pièce) profilée, emboutie. **2. well, badly, s.,** bien, mal, formé; **egg-s., s. like an egg,** en forme d'œuf; **heart-s., wedge-s.,** en forme de cœur, de coin. **shaping** *n.* **1.** façonnement *m*, façonnage *m* (d'un bloc de pierre, etc.); **s. of character,** développement *m*, formation *f*, du caractère. **2.** invention *f*, formation, (d'un projet); mise *f* au point.

shapeless ['ʃeiplis] *a.* informe; difforme.

shapelessness ['ʃeiplisnis] *n.* **1.** manque *m* de forme. **2.** difformité *f.*

shapeliness ['ʃeiplinis] *n.* beauté *f* de forme; belles proportions; galbe *m.*

shapely ['ʃeipli] *a.* bien fait; **a s. leg,** une belle jambe; (*of woman*) **to be s.,** être bien faite, bien roulée.

shard [ʃɑːd] *n.* tesson *m* (de poterie).
share¹ [ʃɛər] *n. Agr:* soc *m* (de charrue).
share² *n.* **1.** (*a*) part *f*, portion *f*; **in equal shares,** par portions égales; **to have a s. in sth.,** avoir part à qch.; **the lion's s.,** la part du lion; **s. in profits,** participation *f* aux bénéfices; tantième *m* (des bénéfices); **to give s.o. a s. in the profits,** mettre qn de part; **to go shares,** partager (**with,** avec); **to go half shares with s.o.,** mettre qn de part à demi; **to come in for a s. of sth.,** avoir sa part de qch.; (*b*) **(fair) s.,** portion juste; lot *m*; *Jur:* **legal s.,** réserve légale (d'une succession); **to come in for one's full s. of sth.,** avoir sa bonne part de qch.; **I've had my s. of worries,** j'ai eu ma bonne part, mon lot, de soucis; (*c*) *Agr:* **s. cropping,** métayage *m*; **s. cropper,** métayer, -ère. **2.** contribution *f*, écot *m*, cotisation *f*, quote-part *f*; **to pay one's s.,** payer sa (quote-)part; **to take, bear, one's s. of the burden,** prendre, avoir, sa part du fardeau; **he doesn't do his s.,** il n'y met pas du sien; **you had a s. in this,** (i) vous y êtes pour quelque chose; (ii) vous y avez mis du vôtre; **to have a s. in an undertaking,** avoir un intérêt, être intéressé, dans une entreprise. **3.** *Fin:* action *f*, titre *m*; **registered s., personal s.,** action nominative; **fully paid(-up) s.,** action (entièrement) libérée; **ordinary, deferred, s.,** action ordinaire, différée; **to hold shares,** détenir des actions; être actionnaire; **s. certificate,** certificat *m* d'action(s), de titre(s).
share³ **I.** *v.tr.* (*a*) partager; **to s. sth. with s.o.,** partager qch. avec qn; (*b*) avoir part à (qch.); **to s. s.o.'s opinion,** partager l'avis de qn; **I s. all his secrets,** il me met dans tous ses secrets; **to s. and s. alike,** partager entre tous également. **2.** *v.tr. & ind.tr.* (*a*) **to s. (in) sth.,** prendre part à, avoir part à, participer à, qch.; **to s. in the profits,** participer, avoir part, aux bénéfices; **to s. (in) s.o.'s grief,** partager la douleur de qn; **I want you to s. in my happiness,** je veux vous associer à mon bonheur; (*b*) **to s. out,** partager, distribuer, répartir (le butin, etc.); répartir, distribuer (le travail). **sharing** *n.* **1.** partage *m* (du butin, de ses biens, etc.). **2.** participation *f*, partage; **profit s.,** participation aux bénéfices.
shareholder [ˈʃɛəhouldər] *n. Fin:* actionnaire *mf*, sociétaire *mf* (d'une société anonyme).
shareholding [ˈʃɛəhouldiŋ] *n. Fin:* **1.** possession *f* d'actions, de titres. **2. shareholdings,** actions *fpl*.
share-out [ˈʃɛəraut] *n.* partage *m*; répartition *f*.
shark [ʃɑːk] *n.* **1.** *Ich:* requin *m*. **2.** *F:* requin; accapareur, -euse; (*esp. of lawyer*) brigandeau *m*. **3.** *NAm: F:* as *m*; **to be a s. at maths,** être calé en math.
sharkskin [ˈʃɑːkskin] *n.* peau *f* de requin.
sharp [ʃɑːp] **I.** *a.* **1.** (*a*) (*of knife, edge*) tranchant, affilé; (*of spear, tooth, point*) aigu, pointu; (*b*) (*of features, etc.*) anguleux, tiré; (*of peak, etc.*) pointu; (*of angle*) saillant, aigu; (*of curve*) prononcé; (*of ascent, descent*) raide; (toit) pointu, en pointe; (tournant) brusque; **s. rise, drop, in prices,** forte hausse, baisse, des prix; (*c*) (*of outline, Phot: of image*) net, *f.* nette; **s. contrast,** contraste marqué. **2.** (*a*) (*of sight*) perçant; (*of hearing*) fin, subtil; (*of glance, wit*) pénétrant; (*of pers.*) **s. (witted),** fin, éveillé; **a s. mind,** un esprit délié; **he's as s. as a needle,** il est malin comme un singe; (*b*) (*of pers., etc.*) rusé, malin; peu scrupuleux; **s. practice(s),** procédés indélicats, peu honnêtes. **3.** (*a*) (combat) vif, acharné; (*b*) (orage) violent; **s. shower,** forte averse; **s. frost,** forte gelée; **s. appetite,** vif appétit; (*c*) (hiver) rigoureux; (air, vent) vif, perçant; (froid) pénétrant, piquant; **s. pain,** douleur vive; **it's a bit s. this morning,** il fait frisquet ce matin; (*d*) rapide; (trot) vif; (*e*) **in a s. voice,** d'une voix coupante, cinglante; **to make a s. retort,** (i) répondre d'une voix cassante; (ii) faire une réplique cinglante; **in a s. tone,** d'un ton brusque; **s. reproof,** verte réprimande; **s. tongue,** langue acérée, caustique. **4.** (*of taste, sauce*) piquant; (*of apple, etc.*) aigre, acide; (*of wine*) vert. **5.** (*a*) (*of sound*) perçant, aigu; (*b*) *Mus:* (fa, etc.) dièse; (*of singer, violinist, etc.*) **you're s.!** vous chantez, jouez, faux (en haussant le ton). **II.** *n.* **1.** *Mus:* dièse *m*; **double s.,** double dièse. **2. sharps,** (i) *Mill:* issues *fpl* de blé; recoupe *f*; (ii) aiguilles longues et fines. **3.** (*a*) = SHARPER; (*b*) *NAm: F:* expert, -erte; connaisseur *m*. **III.** *adv.* **1. s. cut outline,** profil nettement découpé; **s. pointed pencil,** crayon taillé fin; **s. edged,** (i) (*of knife, etc.*) tranchant, affilé; (ii) (*of beam, roof, etc.*) aux arêtes vives. **2.** (s'arrêter, tourner) brusquement, court; **turn s. right,** prenez à angle droit. **3.** ponctuellement, exactement; **at four o'clock s.,** à quatre heures sonnantes, précises, *F:* tapantes. **4.** *F:* **look s.!** dépêchez-vous! remuez-vous! **5.** *Mus:* **to sing s.,** chanter faux (en haussant le ton). **sharply** *adv.* **1.** (*a*) (*of pencil, etc.*) **s. pointed,** à pointe fine, taillé fin; (*b*) (qui se détache) nettement; **to bring sth. s. home,** mettre qch. en relief d'une façon saisissante. **2.** raidement, brusquement; **he turned s.,** il a tourné brusquement, court. **3.** (*a*) (marcher) vivement, à vive allure; (geler) fort; (frapper qn) raide; (*b*) (regarder, écouter) attentivement; **he looked s. at her,** il l'a regardée d'un œil pénétrant; (*c*) (réprimander) sévèrement; (répondre) d'un ton brusque. **4.** (sonner) sec.
sharpen [ˈʃɑːp(ə)n] **I.** *v.tr.* **1.** (*a*) affiler, aiguiser (un couteau, un outil, etc.); (*b*) tailler en pointe, aiguiser (un bâton, etc.); tailler (un crayon); (*of cat, etc.*) **to s. its claws,** faire ses griffes; (*c*) rendre (un angle) plus saillant; aviver (une arête); (*d*) accentuer (un trait, un contraste). **2. to s. s.o.'s wits,** éveiller l'esprit de qn; *F:* dégourdir qn. **3.** (*a*) aviver (la douleur, l'animosité); exciter (une passion, un désir); (*of walk, etc.*) aiguiser, ouvrir (l'appétit); (*b*) rendre plus sévère (une loi, etc.); **to s. one's voice,** prendre un ton plus acerbe, plus âpre. **4.** *Cu:* donner du piquant à (une sauce). **5.** *Mus:* diéser (une note). **II.** *v.i.* **1.** (*of faculties, etc.*) s'aiguiser. **2.** (*of the voice*) devenir plus acerbe, plus âpre. **3.** (*of sound*) devenir plus perçant, plus aigu. **sharpening** *n.* **1.** (*a*) affilage *m*, aiguisage *m* (d'un outil, etc.); (*b*) accentuation *f* (d'un contraste). **2.** affinage *m* (de l'intelligence). **3.** aggravation *f* (d'une douleur, etc.). **4.** relèvement *m* (d'une sauce). **5.** *Mus:* haussement *m* (d'une note) d'un demi-ton.
sharpener [ˈʃɑːp(ə)nər] *n.* **1.** (*pers.*) aiguiseur *m*; affileur *m*. **2.** aiguisoir *m*; **knife s.,** aiguiseur *m* (pour couteaux); **pencil s.,** taille-crayon(s) *m*.
sharper [ˈʃɑːpər] *n.* escroc *m*; *Cards:* tricheur, -euse.
sharp-eyed [ˈʃɑːpaid] *a.* aux yeux perçants; à la vue perçante.
sharpness [ˈʃɑːpnis] *n.* **1.** (*a*) acuité *f*, finesse *f* (du tranchant d'un couteau, etc.); acuité (d'une pointe, etc.); (*b*) *Aut: etc:* **s. of the turn,** raccourci *m* du virage; (*c*) netteté *f* (des contours, d'une image photographique); (*d*) caractère marqué (d'un contraste). **2.** (*a*) finesse (de l'esprit, de l'ouïe); **s. of sight,** acuité visuelle; (*b*) intelligence *f* (d'un enfant). **3.** (*a*) acuité (de la douleur, etc.); (*b*) **there's a s. in the air,** il fait frisquet; (*c*) sévérité *f*, âpreté *f* (du ton, d'une réprimande); brusquerie *f* (du ton); aspérité *f* (du caractère, de la voix). **4.** (goût) piquant *m* (d'une sauce); acidité *f* (d'une pomme, etc.). **5.** acuité, qualité perçante (d'un son).
sharpshooter [ˈʃɑːpʃuːtər] *n. Mil:* tireur *m* d'élite.
sharp-sighted [ʃɑːpˈsaitid] *a.* **1.** à la vue perçante. **2.** perspicace.
sharp-tongued [ʃɑːpˈtʌŋd] *a.* qui a la langue acérée, caustique.
shatter [ˈʃætər] **1.** *v.tr.* (*a*) fracasser; briser en éclats; (*b*) briser, renverser (des espérances); rompre (le

silence); (*c*) détraquer (la santé, les nerfs); *F:* **I was absolutely shattered!** j'étais complètement (i) bouleversé(e), (ii) éreinté(e)! **2.** *v.i.* se briser (en éclats); se fracasser. **shattering** *a.* (coup) écrasant; **s. news,** des nouvelles renversantes.

shave¹ [ʃeiv] *n. Tls:* plane *f*, racloir *m*.

shave² *n.* **1.** rasage *m*; **to have a s.,** (i) se raser; (ii) *O:* se faire raser; **this razor gives you a really close s.,** avec ce rasoir vous pouvez vraiment vous raser de près. **2.** coup affleurant; *F:* **that was a close s.!** vous l'avez échappé belle! il était moins cinq!

shave³ *v.tr.* **1.** (*a*) raser; faire la barbe à (qn); **to s. s.o.'s head,** raser la tête à qn; **to s. off one's moustache,** se raser la moustache; (*b*) *v.tr. & i.* **to s. (oneself),** se raser, se faire la barbe. **2.** planer (le bois, etc.); rogner; **to s. off a slice of sth.,** couper une mince tranche de qch. **3.** friser, effleurer (qch.). **shaving** *n.* **1.** rasage *m*; **s. brush,** blaireau *m*; **s. cream,** crème *f* à raser; **s. soap, stick,** savon *m* à barbe; bâton *m* de savon pour la barbe. **2.** copeau *m*; rognure *f*; (*for scrubbing floors*) **iron shavings,** paille *f* de fer.

shaven ['ʃeiv(ə)n] *a.* (*of monk*) tonsuré; (*of head, chin*) rasé; **clean s.,** (homme) sans barbe ni moustache; (visage) glabre.

shaver ['ʃeivər] *n.* **1.** (*a*) barbier *m*; (*b*) *F:* **young s.,** gosse *m*, gamin *m*. **2. electric s.,** rasoir *m* électrique.

shawl [ʃɔːl] *n.* châle *m*.

she [ʃi, ʃiː] *pers. pron. nom. f.* **1.** (*a*) (*of pers., female animal*) elle; **s. was running,** elle courait; **what's s. doing?** qu'est-ce qu'elle fait? **here s. comes!** la voici (qui vient)! (*b*) (*of thing personified as female*) (i) (*of a motor vehicle, Lit: the moon, nature, a nation, etc.*) elle; (ii) (*of a ship*) il; **s. sails at ten o'clock,** il part à dix heures. **2.** (*stressed*) (*a*) elle; **s. and I,** elle et moi; ***she* knows nothing about it,** elle n'en sait rien, elle; **if I were s.,** si j'étais à sa place; (*b*) (*antecedent to a rel. pron.*) *A.Lit:* **s. of whom you speak,** celle dont vous parlez. **3.** (*substantive*) (*a*) *F:* femelle; **it's a s.,** (*of animal*) c'est une femelle; (*b*) **s. ass,** ânesse *f*; **s. bear,** ours *m* femelle; ourse *f*; **s. cat,** chatte *f*; **s. devil,** diablesse *f*; **s. monkey,** singe *m* femelle; guenon *f*.

sheaf *pl.* **-ves** [ʃiːf, -vz] *n.* **1.** (*a*) gerbe *f* (de blé, etc.); (*b*) gerbe (de fleurs). **2.** faisceau *m*, botte *f* (de branchages); liasse *f* (de papiers); **I had a whole s. of letters this morning,** j'ai reçu toute une pile de lettres ce matin.

shear¹ [ʃiər] *n.* (*a*) **(pair of) shears,** cisaille(s) *f(pl)*; (grands) ciseaux; **garden shears,** cisaille à haie; *Dressm: etc:* **pinking shears,** ciseaux à denteler; (*b*) **shears,** tondeuse *f* (à moutons).

shear² *n.* tonte *f* (de laine).

shear³ *v.tr.* (*p.t.* **sheared;** *p.p.* **shorn** [ʃɔːn], **sheared) 1.** (*a*) **to s. (off),** couper (une branche, etc.); **to s. through sth.,** trancher qch.; (*b*) *Metalw:* cisailler (une tôle, etc.); (*c*) *Tex:* ciseler (le velours). **2.** tondre (un mouton, etc.); **to be shorn of sth.,** être dépouillé, privé, de qch. **3.** *Mec:* cisailler (qch.). **4.** *v.i. Mec:* (*of material*) céder sous le cisaillement; se cisailler; **to s. off,** se détacher. **shearing** *n.* **1.** taille *f* (d'une haie, etc.), cisaillement *m* (d'une tôle); tonte *f* (des moutons); tondage *m* (du drap); **s. machine,** tondeuse *f* (pour moutons). **2. shearings,** tontes (de laine); tontisse *f*, tonture (du drap). **shorn** *a.* **1.** (*of head*) rasé. **2.** (mouton) tondu.

shearer ['ʃiərər] *n.* **1.** (*pers.*) (*a*) tondeur, -euse (de moutons); (*b*) *Metalw:* cisailleur *m*. **2.** (*machine*) (*a*) *Metalw:* cisailleuse *f*; (*b*) tondeuse (pour moutons).

sheath *n.* [ʃiːθ] *n.* (*pl.* [ʃiːðz, ʃiːθs]) (*a*) manchon protecteur; fourreau *m* (d'épée, de parapluie, etc.); étui *m* (de ciseaux, etc.); gaine *f* (de couteau, *El:* d'un câble); *Cost:* **s. dress,** fourreau; (*b*) *Anat:* enveloppe *f* (d'un organe); fourreau (du cheval, du taureau, etc.); gaine (de muscle, etc.); *Bot:* gaine; (*c*) **(contraceptive) s.,** préservatif *m*, condom *m*.

sheathe [ʃiːð] *v.tr.* **1.** (re)mettre au fourreau, rengainer (une épée, etc.); engainer (un couteau, etc.). **2.** (*a*) *Nat. Hist:* envelopper (qch.) dans une gaine; (*b*) *El:* gainer (un câble). **sheathing** *n.* **1.** mise *f* au fourreau (d'une épée); mise dans sa gaine (d'un couteau, etc.). **2.** (*a*) revêtement *m* (de, en, métal); (*b*) *Mec.E: etc:* garniture *f*; chemise *f* (d'un cylindre, etc.); (*c*) gaine *f* (d'un câble).

sheathknife ['ʃiːθnaif] *n.* couteau *m* à gaine.

sheave¹ [ʃiːv] *n.* réa *m*, rouet *m* (de poulie).

sheave² *v.tr.* gerber, engerber (le blé, etc.).

Sheba ['ʃiːbə] *Pr.n. A. Geog:* Saba *f*; **the Queen of S.,** la reine de Saba.

shebang [ʃi'bæŋ] *n. esp. NAm: P:* **the whole s.,** tout le bataclan.

shebeen [ʃi'biːn] *n. Dial:* (*Irish*) débit *m* de boissons clandestin.

shed¹ [ʃed] *n.* (*a*) hangar *m*; resserre *f*; remise *f*; **lean-to s.,** appentis *m*; *Rail:* **engine s.,** remise *f* de locomotives; (*b*) baraque *f*; (*c*) *Const:* **s. roof,** toit *m* en appentis.

shed² *v.tr.* (*p.t. & p.p.* **shed;** *pr.p.* **shedding) 1.** (*a*) perdre (ses dents, ses feuilles, etc.); (*of animal*) jeter (sa peau, ses cornes, etc.); (*of crab, etc.*) dépouiller (sa carapace); (*of plant*) **to shed its leaves,** s'effeuiller; (*b*) **to s. labour,** licencier de la main-d'œuvre; (*c*) (*of lorry, etc.*) déverser (sa charge); *El:* **to s. the load,** délester; *O:* **to s. one's clothes,** se dépouiller de ses vêtements. **2.** répandre, verser (des larmes, le sang); (r)épandre (de la lumière); déverser (de l'eau); **to s. light on sth.,** éclairer une affaire. **shedding** *n.* **1.** (*a*) perte *f*, chute *f* (des feuilles, des dents, etc.); (*b*) *El:* **load s.,** délestage *m*. **2.** effusion *f* (de sang, etc.).

she'd = (i) **she had;** *see* HAVE²; (ii) **she would;** *see* WILL³.

sheen [ʃiːn] *n.* luisant *m*; lustre *m*, reflet *m*; brillant *m*, chatoiement *m* (d'un tissu, d'un bijou, etc.); **hair with a s. like gold,** cheveux *mpl* à reflets d'or.

sheep [ʃiːp] *n. inv. in pl.* (*a*) mouton *m*; **black s.,** brebis noire; **the black s. (of the family, etc.),** la brebis galeuse; **lost, stray, s.,** brebis perdue, égarée; **they follow one another like s.,** ce sont les moutons de Panurge; **to separate the s. from the goats, the s. and the goats,** séparer les brebis d'avec les boucs; (*b*) **s. farmer,** éleveur *m* de moutons; **s. farming,** élevage *m* de moutons; **s. pen,** parc *m* à moutons; bercail *m*; **s. shearer,** (i) (*pers.*) tondeur, -euse (de moutons); (ii) tondeuse *f* mécanique; **s. shearing,** tonte *f*.

sheepdog ['ʃiːpdɔg] *n.* chien *m* de berger; berger *m*; **Old English s.,** berger anglais sans queue; bobtail *m*.

sheepfold ['ʃiːpfould] *n.* parc *m* à moutons; bercail *m*.

sheepish ['ʃiːpiʃ] *a.* **1.** penaud; interdit, décontenancé; **to look s.,** rester penaud. **2.** embarrassé, gauche. **-ly** *adv.* d'un air (i) penaud, (ii) embarrassé.

sheepishness ['ʃiːpiʃnis] *n.* timidité *f*; air penaud.

sheepskin ['ʃiːpskin] *n.* **1.** peau *f* de mouton. **2.** *Leath:* basane *f*. **3.** parchemin *m*; *esp. U.S:* diplôme *m* (sur parchemin).

sheer¹ [ʃiər] *n. Nau:* embardée *f*.

sheer² *v.i. Nau:* **1.** embarder; faire une embardée. **2. to s. off,** (i) *Nau:* alarguer; prendre le large; (ii) *F:* (*of pers.*) partir, prendre le large; **to s. off, away from, a subject,** éviter un sujet.

sheer³ 1. *a.* (*a*) pur, véritable, vrai; **it's s. madness,** c'est de la folie pure (et simple); c'est de la pure folie; **a s. waste of time,** une simple perte de temps; **out of s. malice,** par pure méchanceté; **it was s. stupidity,** c'était franchement stupide; **in s. desperation she wrote to him,** en désespoir de cause elle lui écrivit; (*b*) perpendiculaire; (rocher, chemin, etc.) à pic, abrupt, escarpé; (*c*) *Tex:* (*of linen, etc.*) fin, transparent, diaphane; **s. silk stockings,** bas de soie extra-fins. **2.** *adv.* (*a*) tout à fait; complètement; **the tree was torn s. out by the roots,** l'arbre fut bel et bien déraciné; (*b*) (tomber, etc.) perpendiculairement, à pic, à plomb.

sheet¹ [ʃiːt] *n.* **1.** drap *m* (de lit); **fitted s.,** drap-housse *m*; *F:* **to get between the sheets,** se mettre au lit; se pieuter. **2.** (*a*) feuille *f*, feuillet *m* (de papier); **loose s., fly s.,** feuille volante; *Com:* **order s.,** bulletin *m* de commande; *Ind:* **time, work, job, s.,** feuille de présence; (*b*) *F: O:* journal *m*, -aux; feuille. **3.** (*a*) feuille (de verre, de plomb, etc.); feuille, tôle *f*, plaque *f* (de métal); **s. copper,** cuivre *m* en tôles; **s. mill,** laminoir *m* à tôles; tôlerie *f*; **s. glass,** verre *m* à vitres; *Cu:* **baking s.,** plaque *f* à pâtisserie; (*b*) *Civ.E: Min:* **s. piles,** palplanches *f*. **4.** (*a*) nappe *f* (d'eau, d'écume, de feu, etc.); couche *f* (de glace); (*b*) **s. lightning,** éclairs *mpl* diffus; éclairs en nappe(s).

sheet² *v.tr.* **1.** couvrir, garnir (qch.) d'un drap, d'une bâche. **2. the town was sheeted over with snow,** la ville était recouverte de neige. **sheeting** *n.* **1.** *Tex:* toile *f* pour draps. **2.** *Civ.E: Min:* blindage *m*. **3.** *coll.* tôlerie *f*; tôles *fpl*.

sheet³ *n. Nau:* écoute *f*; **s. bend,** nœud *m* d'écoute; *F:* **to be three sheets in the wind,** être aux trois quarts ivre.

sheet⁴ *n.* **s. (anchor),** ancre *f* de veille; *Fig:* **our s. anchor,** notre ancre de salut.

sheik(h) [ʃeik, ʃiːk] *n.m.* cheik, s(c)heik.

shekel ['ʃek(ə)l] *n.* **1.** *A.Meas: & Num:* sicle *m*. **2.** *F:* **shekels,** argent *m*, galette *f*.

shelf, *pl.* **shelves** [ʃelf, ʃelvz] *n.* **1.** (*a*) tablette *f* (de rayonnage); planche *f* (d'armoire); rayon *m* (d'armoire, de bibliothèque); étagère *f* (de buffet, etc.); plateau *m* (de four, etc.); **set of shelves,** étagère; **s. space,** rayonnage *m*; *Aut:* **window s.,** plage *f* arrière; (*b*) (*pers.*) (*in supermarket, etc.*) **s. filler,** réassortisseur, -euse; **s. life,** durée *f* de conservation avant vente (d'une denrée, etc.); (*of goods*) **to stay on the shelves,** être de vente difficile; *F:* **to be on the s.,** (i) être laissé pour compte; (ii) (*of woman*) être en passe de devenir vieille fille. **2.** (*a*) rebord *m*, saillie *f* (d'un rocher, d'un précipice, etc.); (*b*) *Geog: Oc:* terrasse *f*; plate-forme *f*; banc *m* (de roche, de sable); **continental s.,** plate-forme continentale; plateau continental.

shell¹ [ʃel] *n.* **1.** (*a*) coquille *f* (de mollusque, d'escargot); carapace *f* (de homard, de tortue); écaille *f* *f* (d'huître, de moule, de tortue); **(empty) shells,** coquillages *m*; **to come out of, retire into, one's s.,** sortir de, rentrer dans, sa coquille; *a. & n.* **s. pink,** rose pâle (*m*) *inv*; (*b*) coquille (d'œuf, de noix); écale *f* (de noix); gousse *f*, cosse *f* (de pois, etc.); *Ent:* enveloppe *f* (de nymphe); (*c*) forme *f* vide; simple apparence *f*; **his knowledge is a mere s.,** son savoir est tout en surface. **2.** (*a*) *Mch:* paroi *f*, coque (de chaudière); (*b*) caisse *f*, chape *f* (de poulie); caisse (de tambour); (*c*) enveloppe extérieure; *Metall:* manteau *m* (de moule). **3.** carcasse *f*, squelette *m*, coque (de navire, etc.); carcasse, cage *f* (d'un édifice). **4.** *Row:* canot *m* de course. **5.** *Artil:* obus *m*; **incendiary s.,** obus incendiaire; **live, spent, s.,** obus armé, mort.

shell² *v.tr.* **1.** (*a*) écaler, décortiquer (des noix, etc.); écosser, égrener (des pois, etc.); écailler (des huîtres, des moules); éplucher (des crevettes); (*b*) (*with passive force*) **nuts, peas, that s. easily,** noix *fpl* qui se laissent écaler, pois *mpl* qui se laissent écosser. **2.** *Mil:* bombarder. **shelled** *a.* **1.** *Moll: Rept: etc:* à coquille, à écaille, à carapace. **2.** (*of nuts, etc.*) écalé; (*of peas, etc.*) écossé, égrené. **shelling** *n.* **1.** égrenage *m* (de pois, etc.); décorticage *m* (d'amandes, etc.); épluchage *m* (de crevettes); écaillage *m* (d'huîtres). **2.** *Mil:* bombardement *m*. **3.** *F:* **s. out,** déboursement *m*. **shell out** *v.tr. & i. F:* **to s. out (one's money),** payer la note; débourser; casquer.

she'll = **she will;** *see* WILL³.

shellac¹ [ʃe'læk] *n.* gomme-laque *f*; *Ch:* shellac *m*.

shellac² *v.tr.* **(shellacked) 1.** traiter à la gomme-laque. **2.** *U.S: Sp:* battre (qn) à plate(s) couture(s).

shellfire ['ʃelfaiər] *n.* tir *m* à obus; **to be under s.,** subir un bombardement.

shellfish ['ʃelfiʃ] *n.* **1.** (*a*) mollusque *m* (comestible); coquillage *m*; (*b*) crustacé *m*. **2.** *coll.* mollusques et crustacés; *Cu:* fruits *mpl* de mer.

shell-shaped ['ʃelʃeipt] *a.* conchiforme.

shellshock ['ʃelʃɔk] *n. Med: Mil:* psychose *f* traumatique; syndrome commotionnel.

shellshocked ['ʃelʃɔkt] *a. Med: Mil:* (invalide) commotionné; **s. soldier,** commotionné de guerre.

shellwork ['ʃelwəːk] *n.* (décoration en) coquillages *mpl*.

shelter¹ ['ʃeltər] **1.** (*a*) lieu *m* de refuge; abri *m* (contre la pluie, à un arrêt d'autobus, etc.); asile *m*, refuge *m* (pour indigents, etc.); abrivent *m* (pour sentinelles, etc.); (*b*) *Mil:* **air raid s.,** abri contre les attaques aériennes, abri de défense passive. **2. under s.,** à l'abri, à couvert; **to take s. under sth., from sth.,** s'abriter, se mettre à l'abri, sous qch., de qch.; **to seek s. under a tree,** chercher l'abri d'un arbre; **to find s.,** trouver un abri; trouver asile; **to give s. to s.o.,** abriter qn; offrir un asile, un refuge, à qn.

shelter² **1.** *v.tr.* (*a*) abriter; **to s. s.o., sth., from the rain,** abriter qn, qch., de la pluie; (*b*) donner asile à, recueillir (un malheureux, etc.). **2.** *v.i.* s'abriter, se mettre à l'abri, à couvert (**from,** de); **to s. under a tree, from the wind,** s'abriter sous un arbre; s'abriter du vent; **to s. from the rain,** se mettre à couvert (de la pluie). **sheltered** *a.* abrité, protégé (**against, from,** de); *Pol.Ec:* **s. industry,** industrie garantie contre la concurrence étrangère; **s. workshop,** atelier *m* pour les handicapés qui ont besoin de conditions spéciales.

shelve [ʃelv] **1.** *v.tr.* munir, garnir, (une bibliothèque, etc.) de rayons. **2.** *v.tr.* mettre (des livres, etc.) sur les rayons. **3.** *v.tr. F:* accrocher, ajourner, enterrer (une question, etc.); mettre (un projet) en veilleuse; mettre au rancart. **4.** *v.i.* aller en pente. **shelving** **1.** *a.* en pente; incliné. **2.** *n.* (*a*) *F:* enterrement *m*, ajournement *m* (d'une question, etc.); mise *f* au rancart (de qn); (*b*) (ensemble *m* de) rayons *mpl*; rayonnage *m*; **adjustable s.,** rayons mobiles.

shemozzle [ʃi'mɔzl] *n. F:* (*a*) chahut *m*; (*b*) bagarre *f*.

shenanigans [ʃi'nænigənz] *n.pl. esp. NAm: F:* (*a*) ruses *fpl*; supercheries *fpl*; (*b*) histoires *fpl*.

shepherd¹ ['ʃepəd] *n.m.* (*a*) berger, pâtre; (*b*) *Ecc:* **the Good S.,** le bon Pasteur; *B:* **the Lord is my S.,** l'Éternel *m* est mon berger; *U.S: Z:* **German s.,** berger allemand; **s. dog,** chien *m* de berger; (*c*) *Bot:* **shepherd's purse,** capselle *f*; bourse-à-pasteur *f*.

shepherd² *v.tr.* **1.** (*a*) surveiller, garder (les moutons); (*b*) (*of priest*) soigner, guider (ses ouailles). **2.** conduire, piloter (des touristes, etc.).

shepherdess [ʃepə'des] *n.f.* bergère.

sherbet ['ʃəːbət] *n.* **1.** sorbet *m* (du Levant, etc.). **2. s. (powder),** limonade sèche (pour préparer une boisson gazeuse). **3.** (*water ice*) sorbet.

sheriff ['ʃerif] *n.* **1.** *Adm:* shérif(f) *m* (représentant de la Couronne dans un comté). **2.** *Jur: Scot:* premier président (d'un comté). **3.** *U.S.* chef de la police (d'un comté); shérif; **deputy s.,** citoyen assermenté faisant fonction d'agent de police.

sherry ['ʃeri] *n.* vin *m* de Xérès; xérès *m*; **s. glass** = verre *m* à madère.

she's = (i) **she is;** *see* BE; (ii) **she has;** *see* HAVE².

Shetland ['ʃetlənd] **1.** *Pr.n. Geog:* **the S. Islands, the Shetlands,** les îles *fpl* Shetland; **S. pony,** poney shetlandais, de Shetland. **2.** *n. Tex:* shetland *m.*

shew [ʃou] *v.* (*p.t.* **shewed** [ʃoud]; *p.p.* **shewn** [ʃoun]) *A: & Lit:* = SHOW².

shibboleth ['ʃibəleθ] *n.* (*a*) *B.Hist:* s(c)hibboleth *m;* (*b*) mot *m* d'ordre (d'un parti, etc.); **outworn shibboleths,** doctrines vieux-jeu, désuètes.

shield¹ [ʃi:ld] *n.* **1.** (*a*) *Arm:* bouclier *m;* **s. bearer,** écuyer *m;* (*b*) *Her:* écu *m,* écusson *m;* (*c*) *Geol:* **the Laurentian s.,** le bouclier canadien. **2.** *Tchn:* tôle protectrice; écran protecteur; bouclier; *Aut:* **sun s.,** pare-soleil *m inv.* **3.** (*in spray painting*) masque, cache *m.* **4.** (*a*) *Hort:* **s. bud,** écusson *m;* **s. grafting,** écussonnage *m;* greffe *f* en écusson; (*b*) *Bot:* **s. fern,** aspidie *f.* **5.** *U.S:* plaque *f,* médaille *f,* de policier.

shield² *v.tr.* **1.** protéger (**from, against,** contre); **to s. s.o. from (sth.),** soustraire qn à (la censure); faire échapper qn à (la punition); protéger qn contre (le danger); **to s. s.o. with one's (own) body,** faire un bouclier de son corps à qn. **2.** (*a*) **to s. one's eyes,** se protéger les yeux; (*b*) (*in spray painting*) masquer (les surfaces); (*c*) *El: W.Tel:* blinder.

shieling ['ʃi:liŋ] *n. Scot:* **1.** pâturage *m.* **2.** abri *m* (pour moutons, chasseurs, etc.).

shift¹ [ʃift] *n.* **1.** (*a*) changement *m* (de position, etc.); renverse *f* (de la marée, du courant); décalage *m* (des joints d'un mur, etc.); saute *f,* renversement *m* (du vent); *Typew:* **s. key,** touche *f* des majuscules, de manœuvre; **s. lock,** (i) dispositif *m* de blocage; (ii) (*key*) touche *f* de blocage; fixe-majuscules *m inv;* *NAm: Aut:* **(gear) s.,** changement de vitesse; *Ling:* **consonant s.,** mutation *f* consonantique; **s. in meaning,** glissement *m* de sens; (*b*) *Astr:* **red s.,** décalage *m* vers le rouge. **2.** *Ind: etc:* (*a*) équipe *f,* brigade *f,* relais *m* (d'ouvriers); **day, night, s.,** équipe de jour, de nuit; **to work in shifts,** travailler par équipes; se relayer; (*b*) journée *f* de travail; poste *m;* **to work eight-hour shifts,** se relayer toutes les huit heures; **to be on night s.,** être de nuit. **3.** *Cost:* (*a*) *A:* chemise *f* (de femme); (*b*) robe *f* fourreau. **4.** (*a*) expédient *m,* ressource *f;* **to make s.,** s'arranger; se débrouiller; (*b*) échappatoire *f;* faux-fuyant *m, pl.* faux-fuyants.

shift² **1.** *v.tr.* (*a*) changer (qch.) de place; remuer, bouger, déplacer (qch.); *Nau:* désarrimer, déplacer (la cargaison); **I can't s. it,** je ne peux pas le bouger; **to s. the responsibility onto s.o.,** rejeter la responsabilité sur (le dos de) qn; (*b*) changer; *Th:* **to s. the scenery,** changer le décor; (*c*) *NAm: Aut:* **to s. (the gears),** changer de vitesse; **to s. up,** passer à une vitesse supérieure; (*d*) *v.tr. & i. Cmptr:* décaler; **to s. in, out,** introduire, éliminer, par décalage. **2.** *v.i.* (*a*) changer de place; remuer, bouger, se déplacer; *Nau:* (*of cargo*) se désarrimer, se déplacer; (*b*) changer; *Th:* **the scene shifts,** la scène change; **the wind has shifted (round),** le vent a tourné, viré; (*c*) *F:* **to s. (for oneself),** se débrouiller; se suffire; **he can s. for himself,** il est débrouillard. **shifting** **1.** *a.* (*a*) qui se déplace; (*b*) (*of relationship, scene, etc.*) changeant; (*of wind, etc.*) inégal, -aux. **2.** *n.* (*a*) (i) déplacement *m* (de qch. par qn); *Th:* **scene s.,** changement *m* des décors; (ii) *NAm: Aut:* **(gear) s.,** changement de vitesse; (*b*) changement (de place, de direction, etc.); mouvement *m,* déplacement (de qch.); (*of cargo*) désarrimage *m.*

shifter ['ʃiftər] *n. Th:* **scene s.,** machiniste *m.*

shiftiness ['ʃiftinis] *n.* sournoiserie *f;* manque *m* de franchise; fausseté *f.*

shiftless ['ʃiftlis] *a.* (*of pers.*) **1.** paresseux; sans énergie. **2.** peu débrouillard; qui manque d'initiative; de ressource; (*of action*) inefficace, futile.

shiftlessness ['ʃiftlisnis] *n.* **1.** paresse *f;* manque *m* d'énergie. **2.** manque de ressource, d'initiative; futilité *f* (d'une action).

shiftwork ['ʃiftwə:k] *n. Ind:* travail *m* par équipes, par roulement.

shifty ['ʃifti] *a.* (individu) roublard, retors; (regard) faux, sournois; (conduite) ambiguë; **s. eyes,** yeux fuyants. **-ily** *adv.* sournoisement.

shillelagh [ʃi'leilə] *n.* gourdin irlandais.

shilling ['ʃiliŋ] *n. A.Num:* shilling *m;* **to cut s.o. off with a s.,** déshériter qn.

shillyshally ['ʃiliʃæli] *v.i. F:* tergiverser; vaciller. **shillyshallying** *n.* tergiversation *f;* vacillement *m.*

shimmer¹ ['ʃimər] *n.* lueur *f;* faible miroitement *m,* chatoiement *m;* **the s. of the moon on the lake,** les reflets *mpl* de la lune sur le lac.

shimmer² *v.i.* miroiter, luire; chatoyer. **shimmering** *a.* miroitant, luisant; chatoyant.

shimmy¹ ['ʃimi] *n.* **1.** *U.S:* chemise *f* (de femme). **2.** flottement *m* des roues avant; shimmy *m.* **3.** *Danc:* (genre *m* de) fox-trot *m;* shimmy.

shimmy² *v.i.* osciller.

shin¹ [ʃin] *n.* (*a*) *Anat:* le devant de la jambe; *Sp:* **s. guard, pad,** jambière *f;* (*b*) *Cu:* jarret *m* (de veau).

shin² *v.i.* **(shinned)** *F:* **to s. up a tree,** grimper à un arbre; **to s. down,** dégringoler.

shinbone ['ʃinboun] *n. Anat:* tibia *m.*

shindig ['ʃindig] *n. esp. NAm:* **1.** réunion (bruyante); fête *f.* **2.** = SHINDY 1.

shindy ['ʃindi] *n. F:* **1.** (*a*) tapage *m,* chahut *m;* **to kick up a s.,** (i) chahuter; faire du chahut, du tapage; (ii) élever des protestations énergiques (**about sth.,** contre qch.). **2.** *U.S:* = SHINDIG 1.

shine¹ [ʃain] *n.* **1.** éclat *m,* lumière *f;* **rain or s.,** par tous les temps. **2.** (*on shoes, etc.*) brillant *m;* (*on textiles, etc.*) luisant; **to give the brass a s.,** astiquer les cuivres; **to take the s. off sth.,** défraîchir, délustrer, qch.; *F:* **to take the s. out of s.o.,** éclipser, surpasser, qn. **3.** *U.S: F:* **to take a s. to s.o.,** s'éprendre, s'enticher, de qn.

shine² *v.* (*p.t. & p.p.* **shone** [ʃɔn]) **1.** *v.i.* (*a*) (*of sun, etc.*) briller; (*of polished article*) (re)luire; **the moon, the sun, is shining,** il fait clair de lune, il fait du soleil; **his face was shining with joy,** sa figure rayonnait de joie; *F:* **he doesn't s. in conversation,** il ne brille pas dans la conversation; (*b*) **to s. on,** éclairer, illuminer (qch.). **2.** *v.tr.* **to s. a light on sth.,** éclairer qch. (avec une lampe, etc.); braquer une lampe sur qch. **3.** *v.tr.* (*p.t. & p.p.* **shined**) *esp. NAm:* polir, cirer (les chaussures, etc.); astiquer (les cuivres, etc.). **shining** *a.* brillant; (re)luisant; **a s. example,** un exemple brillant, insigne (**of sth.,** de qch.).

shiner ['ʃainər] *n. F:* **1.** œil poché, *F:* œil au beurre noir. **2.** (*pers.*) **(shoe) s.,** cireur, -euse (de chaussures).

shingle¹ ['ʃiŋgl] *n.* **1.** *Const:* bardeau *m,* aisseau *m.* **2.** *NAm:* plaque *f* (de cuivre) (de médecin, d'avocat, etc.). **3.** *Hairdr: A:* coupe *f* à la garçonne.

shingle² *v.tr.* **1.** *Const:* couvrir (un toit) de bardeaux. **2.** *A:* **to s. s.o., s.o.'s hair,** couper les cheveux de qn à la garçonne.

shingle³ *n.* galets *mpl;* (gros) cailloux *mpl.*

shingles ['ʃiŋg(ə)lz] *n. Med:* zona *m.*

shingly ['ʃiŋgli] *a.* couvert de galets; caillouteux; (plage) de galets.

shininess ['ʃaininis] *n.* luisance *f;* (*due to wear*) lustrage *m.*

shinny ['ʃini] *v.i. NAm: F:* **to s. up a tree,** grimper à un arbre.

Shintoism ['ʃintouizm] *n.* shintoïsme *m,* shintô *m.*

shiny ['ʃaini] *a.* (*a*) brillant, luisant; (*b*) **clothes made s. by long wear,** vêtements lustrés par l'usage.

ship¹ [ʃip] *n.* **1.** (*a*) navire *m*; **sailing s.,** voilier *m*, navire à voiles; **passenger s.,** paquebot *m*; **merchant s.,** navire marchand; cargo *m*; **container s.,** navire porte-conteneurs; **depot, supply, s.,** (navire) ravitailleur *m*; **training s.,** navire-école *m*, *pl.* navires-écoles; **to lay down a s.,** mettre un navire en chantier, sur cale; **the ship's company,** l'équipage *f*; **ship's carpenter,** charpentier *m* du bord; **ship's boy,** mousse *m*; **s. to shore telephone,** téléphone *m* bâtiment-terre; (*b*) *Fig:* **the s. of State,** le char de l'État: **the s. of the desert,** le chameau; **when my s. comes home,** dès que j'aurai fait fortune. **2.** *F:* avion *m*.

ship² *v.* **(shipped) 1.** *v.tr.* (*a*) embarquer (une cargaison, etc.); enrôler (l'équipage); (*b*) *Com:* (i) mettre (des marchandises) à bord; (ii) envoyer, expédier (des marchandises, etc., par voie de mer, *esp. NAm:* par chemin de fer, etc.); (*c*) (*of ship*) **to s. water,** embarquer de l'eau; **to s. a sea,** embarquer une lame, un coup de mer; (*d*) **to s. oars,** (i) armer, (ii) rentrer, border, les avirons. **2.** *v.i.* (*a*) (*of passenger*) s'embarquer; (*b*) (*of sailor*) armer sur un navire; **to s. as cook,** embarquer comme cuisinier. **shipping** *n.* **1.** (*a*) embarquement *m*, mise *f* à bord (d'une cargaison, etc.); enrôlement *m* (d'un équipage); **s. bill,** connaissement *m*; **s. agent,** agent *m* maritime; (*for goods*) expéditeur *m*; commissionnaire chargeur; (*b*) expédition *f*, envoi *m* (de marchandises par voie de mer, *esp. NAm:* par chemin de fer, etc.). **2.** *coll.* navires *mpl* (d'un pays, d'un port); marine marchande; **s. intelligence,** nouvelles *fpl* maritimes. **3.** navigation *f*; **dangerous to, for, s.,** dangereux pour la navigation; **s. routes,** routes *fpl* de navigation.

shipboard [ˈʃipbɔːd] *n.* **on s.,** à bord d'un navire.

shipbroker [ˈʃipbroukər] *n.* courtier *m* maritime.

shipbuilder [ˈʃipbildər] *n.* constructeur *m* de navires.

shipbuilding [ˈʃipbildiŋ] *n.* construction navale; architecture navale.

shipload [ˈʃiploud] *n.* chargement *m*; cargaison *f*.

shipmate [ˈʃipmeit] *n.* compagnon *m*, camarade *m*, de bord.

shipment [ˈʃipmənt] *n.* **1.** (*a*) embarquement *m*, mise *f* à bord (de marchandises, etc.); (*b*) expédition *f*, envoi *m* (de marchandises) par mer, *esp. NAm:* par chemin de fer, etc. **2.** (*goods shipped*) chargement *m*.

shipowner [ˈʃipounər] *n.* propriétaire *m* de navire; armateur *m*.

shipper [ˈʃipər] *n.* (*a*) chargeur *m*, expéditeur *m* (de marchandises par mer); (*b*) affréteur *m*.

shipshape [ˈʃipʃeip] **1.** *a.* bien tenu, bien arrangé; en bon ordre; fin prêt; **everything's s.,** tout est à sa place. **2.** *adv.* comme à bord; comme il faut.

shipwreck¹ [ˈʃiprek] *n.* naufrage *m*; (*of ship*) **to suffer s.,** faire naufrage; **the s. of one's fortune,** le naufrage, la ruine, de sa fortune.

shipwreck² *v.tr.* (*usu. in passive*) **to be shipwrecked,** faire naufrage. **shipwrecked** *a.* naufragé.

shipwright [ˈʃiprait] *n.* (*a*) constructeur *m* de navires; (*b*) charpentier *m* du bord.

shipyard [ˈʃipjɑːd] *n.* atelier *m*, chantier *m*, de constructions navales; chantier maritime, naval.

shire [ˈʃaiər] *n.* comté *m*; **s. horse,** (type de) cheval anglais de gros trait.

shirk [ʃəːk] *v.tr. & i.* manquer à, se soustraire à (une obligation, etc.); renâcler à (une besogne); esquiver (un devoir); négliger son devoir; *Mil:* (i) tirer au flanc; (ii) s'embusquer; **to s. the question,** esquiver, éluder, la question.

shirker [ˈʃəːkər] *n.* renâcleur *m*; *Mil:* (i) tireur *m* au flanc; (ii) embusqué *m*.

shirr [ʃəːr] *v.tr. Dressm:* bouillonner. **shirring** *n.* bouillonné *m*.

shirt [ʃəːt] *n.* (*a*) chemise *f* (d'homme); **sports s.,** chemise sport; (*with short sleeves*) chemisette *f*; *F:* (*pers.*) **stuffed s.,** pédant *m*; prétentieux *m*; crâneur *m*; **to change one's s., to put on a clean s.,** changer de chemise; **to be in one's s. sleeves,** être en bras, en manches, de chemise; **s. collar,** col *m* de chemise; **s. front,** plastron *m*, devant *m*, de chemise; *Turf: F:* **to put one's s. on a horse,** parier tout ce qu'on possède sur un cheval; *F:* **to lose one's s.,** (i) tout perdre, être lessivé; (ii) *U.S:* s'emporter, prendre la chèvre; *F:* **keep your s. on!** ne vous emballez pas! calmez-vous! (*b*) *Arm:* **s. of mail,** chemise de mailles; (*c*) *Hist:* **Red, Black, Brown, Shirts,** Chemises rouges, noires, brunes; (*d*) **s. (blouse, waist),** chemisier *m* (de femme).

shirting [ˈʃəːtiŋ] *n.* toile *f* pour chemises; shirting *m*.

shirtmaker [ˈʃəːtmeikər] *n.* chemisier, -ière.

shirtwaister [ˈʃəːtweistər] *n. Cost:* robe *f* chemisier.

shirty [ˈʃəːti] *a. F:* irritable; en rogne; **to get s.,** se fâcher.

shit¹ [ʃit] *n. V:* **1.** merde *f*. **2.** (*pers.*) salaud *m*, merdeux *m*. **3.** *int.* merde!

shit² *v.i. V:* chier.

shiver¹ [ˈʃivər] *n.* éclat *m*, fragment *m*; **to break sth. into shivers,** briser qch. en éclats.

shiver² **1.** *v.tr.* fracasser (qch.); briser (qch.) en morceaux. **2.** *v.i.* se fracasser; se briser en morceaux.

shiver³ *n.* frisson *m*; **it sent cold shivers down my back,** cela m'a donné un frisson; *F:* **to have the shivers,** avoir la tremblote; **it gives me the shivers to think of it,** ça me donne le frisson quand j'y pense.

shiver⁴ **1.** *v.i.* frissonner, trembler (**with cold, fear,** de froid, de peur); grelotter (de froid); **to s. like a leaf, a jelly,** trembler comme une feuille. **2.** *Nau:* (*a*) *v.i.* (*of sail*) faseyer, ralinguer; (*b*) *v.tr.* faire faseyer, faire ralinguer (les voiles). **shivering** *a.* **1.** tremblant, grelotant, frissonnant. **2.** *n.* tremblement *m*, frissonnement *m*; **to have a s. fit,** être pris de frissons.

shivery [ˈʃivəri] *a.* **1.** = SHIVERING 1. **2. to feel s.,** avoir des frissons; se sentir fiévreux; **it gives you a s. feeling,** cela donne le frisson.

shoal¹ [ʃoul] **1.** *a.* (eau) peu profonde. **2.** *n.* haut-fond *m*, *pl.* hauts-fonds; banc *m*.

shoal² *n.* banc voyageur (de poissons); bande *f* (de marsouins); *F:* foule *f*, multitude *f* (de personnes); grande quantité, tas *m* (de lettres, etc.).

shock¹ [ʃɔk] *n.* **s. of hair,** tignasse *f*.

shock² *n.* **1.** (*a*) choc *m*, heurt *m*; impact *m* (d'une collision, etc.); secousse *f*; à-coup *m*, *pl.* à-coups; **to stand the s.,** résister au choc; *Aut: etc:* **s. absorber,** amortisseur *m* (de chocs); (*b*) *Geol:* séisme *m*; **slight (earthquake) shocks were felt,** on a senti de petites secousses sismiques; (*c*) **s. wave,** onde *f* de choc; **acoustic s.,** choc acoustique; (*d*) *Mil:* **s. tactics, action,** tactique *f*, action *f*, de choc; **s. troops,** troupes *fpl* d'assaut, de choc; force *f* de choc. **2.** (*a*) coup *m*; choc (porté par une mauvaise nouvelle, etc.); **the s. killed him, he died of the s.,** il est mort de saisissement; **be prepared for a s.,** attendez-vous à encaisser un choc; (*b*) *Med:* choc; traumatisme *m*; **post-operative s.,** choc post-opératoire; **in a state of s.,** en état de choc; (*c*) **electric s.,** commotion *f* électrique; décharge *f*; **to get an electric s.,** recevoir une décharge; (*d*) *Med:* **s. therapy,** thérapeutique *f* du choc; **electric s. treatment,** traitement *m* par électrochocs.

shock³ *v.tr.* **1.** (*a*) choquer, scandaliser (qn); **book that shocked the public,** livre *m* qui a fait scandale; **easily, not easily, shocked,** choquable; peu choquable; **to be shocked at, by, sth.,** être choqué de, scandalisé par, qch.; (*b*) bouleverser (qn); frapper (qn) d'indignation, d'horreur; **I was shocked to hear that . . .,** j'ai été bouleversé, atterré, choqué, d'apprendre que . . .; (*c*) blesser (l'oreille); (*d*) *Med:* **to be shocked,**

être en état de choc; être commotionné. **shockable** ['ʃɔkəbl] *a.* **he's easily, not easily, s.,** il est choquable, peu choquable. **shocked** *a.* (*a*) (*of pers., voice, etc.*) choqué, scandalisé; (*b*) bouleversé; atterré. **shocker** ['ʃɔkər] *n. F:* **1.** (*a*) chose affreuse; (*b*) **he really is a s.!** il est vraiment impossible! **2.** *Publ: O:* roman *m* à gros effets, sensationnel. **3. that was a real s.,** ç'a été un rude coup. **shocking 1.** *a.* (*a*) (*of spectacle, etc.*) (i) choquant; (ii) révoltant, affreux; (nouvelle) atterrante, bouleversante; (conduite) indigne; **how s.!** quelle horreur! (*b*) (*of weather*) abominable, exécrable; (douleur, etc.) atroce. **2.** *adv. P:* **he carried on something s.!** il nous a fait une scène abominable! **shockingly** *adv.* **1.** abominablement, affreusement. **2.** excessivement, extrêmement; **s. dear,** excessivement cher; **in s. bad taste,** du dernier mauvais goût.

shockproof ['ʃɔkpru:f] *a.* **1.** (*of scientific instrument, etc.*) antichoc *inv*; protégé contre les chocs. **2.** (*of pers.*) (*a*) inébranlable; (*b*) *F:* peu choquable.

shod *see* SHOE².

shoddiness ['ʃɔdinis] *n.* mauvaise qualité.

shoddy¹ ['ʃɔdi] *n. Tex:* drap *m* de laine d'effilochage; laine *f*, tissu *m*, de renaissance.

shoddy² *a.* **1.** *Tex:* (*of cloth*) d'effilochage, de renaissance. **2.** (*a*) (marchandises, etc.) de camelote, de pacotille; **s. goods,** de la camelote; (*b*) (*of conduct*) mesquin. **-ily** *adv.* (*a*) **s. made,** mal fait; (*b*) (se conduire) mesquinement.

shoe¹ [ʃu:] *n.* **1.** (*a*) chaussure *f*, soulier *m*; **a pair of shoes,** une paire de chaussures; **lace-up shoes,** richelieus *m*; **high-heeled shoes,** chaussures à talons hauts; **s. polish,** cirage *m*; **s. tree,** embauchoir *m* (pour chaussures); **s. rack,** porte-chaussures *m inv*; **to put on, take off, one's shoes,** se chausser, se déchausser; mettre, enlever, ses chaussures; (*b*) **to put the s. on the right foot,** s'en prendre à celui qui le mérite; **to step into s.o.'s shoes,** prendre la place de qn; succéder à qn; **I shouldn't like to be in his shoes,** je ne voudrais pas être à sa place; **to be waiting for dead men's shoes,** attendre la mort de qn (pour le remplacer). **2.** fer *m* (de cheval); **to cast, throw, a s.,** perdre un fer; se déferrer. **3.** *Tchn:* sabot *m* (d'un pieu, de frein, etc.); patin (de traîneau, etc.).

shoe² *v.tr.* (*p.t. & p.p.* **shod** [ʃɔd]; *pr.p.* **shoeing**) **1.** chausser (qn); **to be well shod,** être bien chaussé. **2.** (*p.t. & p.p. also* **shoed**) ferrer; mettre un fer à (un cheval). **3.** garnir d'une ferrure, d'une semelle, d'un patin, etc.; saboter, armer (un pieu, etc.); embattre, ferrer (une roue); **ironshod stick,** bâton ferré. **shoeing** *n.* **1.** ferrage *m*, ferrure *f* (d'un cheval); **s. smith,** maréchal-ferrant *m*, *pl.* maréchaux-ferrants. **2.** pose *f* d'une ferrure, d'un patin, etc.; mise *f* d'un sabot (à un pieu, etc.); embattage *m*, ferrage (d'une roue).

shoeblack ['ʃu:blæk] *n.* cireur *m* (de chaussures).

shoebrush ['ʃu:brʌʃ] *n.* brosse *f* à chaussures, à souliers.

shoehorn ['ʃu:hɔ:n] *n.* chausse-pied *m*, *pl.* chausse-pieds.

shoelace ['ʃu:leis] *n.* lacet *m* (de soulier); cordon *m* de soulier; **he's not fit to tie your shoelaces,** il n'est pas digne de vous déchausser.

shoeleather ['ʃu:leðər] *n.* cuir *m* pour chaussures; **you might as well save your s.,** c'est inutile que vous y alliez.

shoemaker ['ʃu:meikər] *n.* **1.** fabricant *m* de chaussures; chausseur *m*. **2.** cordonnier *m*.

shoemender ['ʃu:mendər] *n.* cordonnier *m*.

shoeshine ['ʃu:ʃain] *n. NAm:* **1.** (*action*) cirage *m* de chaussures. **2.** cireur *m* de chaussures.

shoestring ['ʃu:striŋ] *n.* lacet *m* de chaussure; *F:* **on a s.,** à peu de frais; **they're doing it on a s.,** ils tirent sur la corde.

shoo¹ [ʃu:] *int.* (*a*) (*to chickens*) ch-ch! (*b*) (*to children, etc.*) allez! filez!

shoo² *v.tr.* **to s. (away, off),** chasser (les poules, etc.).

shoot¹ [ʃu:t] *n.* **1.** *Bot:* pousse *f* (d'une plante); rejet *m*, rejeton *m*, scion *m*; *Vit:* sarment *m*, pampre *m*; **young, tender, shoot,** tendrille *f*, tendron *m*. **2.** (*in river*) rapide *m*. **3.** = CHUTE 2. **4.** (*a*) (i) partie *f* de chasse; (ii) gibier (tué); (*b*) *Mil: etc:* **to carry out a s.,** effectuer un tir; (*c*) concours *m* de tir. **5.** chasse gardée. **6.** *F:* **the whole (bang) s.,** tout le bataclan.

shoot² *v.* (*p.t. & p.p.* **shot** [ʃɔt]) **I.** *v.i.* **1.** se précipiter; se lancer; s'élancer; (*of star*) filer; **he shot into the room,** il est entré dans la pièce en éclair, en trombe; **to s. forward,** foncer, s'élancer, à toute allure; **to s. ahead,** devancer les autres (concurrents). **2.** (*of pain*) lanciner, élancer; **I've got pains shooting through my shoulder,** j'ai des élancements *m* dans l'épaule. **3.** (*of tree, bud, etc.*) pousser, bourgeonner; (*of plant*) germer. **II. 1.** *v.tr.* franchir (un rapide); passer rapidement sous (un pont); *Aut:* **to s. the (traffic) lights,** griller, brûler, le feu rouge. **2.** *v.tr.* (*a*) précipiter, lancer (qch.); pousser vivement (un verrou); **we were shot out of the car,** nous avons été précipités hors de la voiture; (*b*) déverser, décharger (du charbon dans la cave); (*c*) *Fish:* jeter (un filet); *F:* **to s. a line,** (i) exagérer son importance; (ii) baratiner. **3.** *v.tr.* darder, faire jaillir (des rayons, etc.). **4.** *v.tr. & i.* (*a*) décocher (une flèche); lancer, tirer (un projectile, une balle, etc.); **to s. a glance at s.o.,** lancer, décocher, un regard à qn; (*b*) décharger (un fusil, etc.); **don't s.!** ne tirez pas! **to s. straight,** bien viser; **to s. at s.o., at sth.,** tirer, faire feu, sur qn, sur qch.; **to be shot at,** essuyer un coup de feu; (*c*) atteindre, blesser (qn) d'un coup de feu; **to be shot in the arm,** être atteint (d'un coup de feu) au bras; *F: O:* **I'll be shot if . . .,** le diable m'emporte si . . .; (*d*) tuer (qn) d'un coup de feu; fusiller (un espion); **to s. s.o. dead,** *U.S:* **to death,** tuer qn net, raide; **to s. oneself through the head,** se tirer une balle dans la tête; se brûler la cervelle; *Mil:* **to be (court-martialled and) shot,** être passé par les armes; (*e*) chasser (le gibier); tirer (une perdrix); **to s. over an estate,** chasser dans un domaine. **5.** *v.tr. & i. Cin:* tourner (un film); filmer; *F:* **s.!** (i) allez-y! (ii) allons, accouche! **6.** *v.tr. & i. Games:* (*a*) **to s. a marble,** caler une bille; *Fb: etc:* **to s. (the ball),** shooter; (*b*) **to s. a goal,** marquer un but; (*c*) *Golf:* **to s. a 64,** faire le parcours en 64 coups. **shoot down** *v.tr.* (*a*) abattre (qn) à coups de fusil, d'un coup de fusil; (*b*) abattre, descendre (un avion). **shooting 1.** *a.* qui s'élance; (*of water, flame*) jaillissant; **s. star,** étoile filante; **s. pains,** douleurs lancinantes. **2.** *n.* (*a*) franchissement *m* (d'un rapide); course *f* rapide (sous un pont, etc.); (*b*) déchargement *m* (de charbon, etc.); *Fish:* jet *m* (d'un filet); (*c*) (i) décochement *m* (d'une flèche); coups de feu; *F:* **s. war,** guerre chaude; (ii) tir *m* (avec une arme à feu); **s. range,** champ *m* de tir; **s. match,** concours *m* de tir; *F:* **the whole s. match,** tout le bataclan; **s. gallery,** tir; stand *m*; (iii) coup de feu (porté à qn); fusillade *f* (d'un espion, etc.); meurtre *m* (de qn) (avec une arme à feu); (iv) la chasse; **pigeon s.,** tir aux pigeons; **the s. season,** la saison de la chasse; **s. party,** partie *f* de chasse; **s. stick,** canne-siège *f*, *pl.* cannes-sièges; *Aut:* **s. brake,** break *m* de chasse, canadienne *f*; (*d*) *Cin:* tournage *m* (d'un film). **shoot off 1.** *v.i.* partir comme une flèche. **2.** *v.tr.* (*a*) emporter (qch.) par une balle, par un obus; **he had a foot shot off,** il a eu un pied fauché par un obus; (*b*) *P:* **to s. one's mouth off,** (i) bavarder (indiscrètement); (ii) révéler un secret; vendre la mèche. **shoot out 1.** *v.i.* (*of water, flames*) jaillir; **to s. out of a side street,** déboucher brusquement d'une rue latérale. **2.** *v.tr.* (*a*) lancer (des étincelles, etc.); **the**

snake shot out its tongue, le serpent a dardé sa langue; (*b*) *F:* **to s. it out,** avoir un règlement de comptes. **shoot up 1.** *v.i.* (*a*) (*of flame, etc.*) jaillir; (*of aircraft, etc.*) **to s. up (like a rocket),** monter en chandelle; (*b*) (*of prices*) augmenter rapidement; monter en flèche; (*c*) (*of plant*) pousser rapidement; (*of child*) grandir rapidement. **2.** *v.tr. F:* terroriser (une ville, etc.) (en tirant des coups de feu). **shot** *a.* **1.** *Tex:* changeant, chatoyant; **s. silk,** taffetas changeant. **2.** *F:* (*a*) **to be all s. up,** être (i) fini, (ii) à bout de nerfs, (iii) éreinté; (*b*) **to be, get, s. of s.o., sth.,** être débarrassé, se débarrasser, de qn, qch.

shooter ['ʃuːtər] *n.* **1.** (*a*) *esp. U.S:* chasseur, -euse; tireur, -euse; (*b*) *Games:* marqueur *m* de but. **2.** *P:* arme *f* à feu; revolver *m*.

shoot-out ['ʃuːtaut] *n. F:* échange *m* de coups de feu; règlement *m* de comptes.

shop¹ [ʃɔp] *n.* **1.** (*a*) magasin *m*; (*small*) boutique *f*; **grocer's s.,** épicerie *f*; **baker's s.,** boulangerie *f*; **shoe s.,** magasin de chaussures; **duty-free s.,** boutique hors taxes; **mobile s.,** camionnette-boutique *f*, *pl.* camionnettes-boutiques; *O:* **s.!** il y a quelqu'un (pour servir)? **to set up s.,** ouvrir un magasin; s'établir comme commerçant, -ante; **to keep (a) s.,** tenir un magasin; **to shut up s.,** fermer boutique; suspendre ses activités; *F:* **you've come to the wrong s.,** vous tombez mal; vous vous trompez de porte; **all over the s.,** (i) dans la confusion; en désordre; (ii) partout; dans tous les coins; **s. front,** devanture *f* de magasin; **s. window,** vitrine *f*; devanture (de magasin); étalage *m*; **in the s. window,** dans la, en, vitrine, en étalage; **s. assistant,** vendeur, -euse (de magasin); employé(e) de magasin; (*b*) (*as name*) maison *f*; **the Pen S.,** la Maison du Porte-Plume. **2.** *Ind: etc:* atelier *m*; **assembly s.,** atelier de montage; **pattern s.,** atelier de modelage; **machine s.,** (i) atelier de construction, de réparation, de machines; (ii) atelier d'usinage; (iii) atelier des machines; **repair s.,** atelier de réparations; **carpenter's s.,** atelier de menuiserie; **the s. floor,** (i) l'atelier; (ii) *coll.* les ouvriers *mpl*; **s. foreman,** chef *m* d'atelier; **closed s.,** entreprise *f* qui n'admet que du personnel appartenant à un certain syndicat. **3.** *F:* bureau *m*, maison, où on travaille; la boîte; **to talk s.,** parler métier, parler affaires.

shop² *v.* **(shopped) 1.** *v.i.* **to s., to go shopping,** (aller) faire ses courses; (*for food*) aller faire son marché; aller aux provisions; *Fr.C:* magasiner; **to s. around,** chercher des occasions. **2.** *v.tr. P:* (*a*) (faire) coffrer (qn); (*b*) dénoncer (qn). **shopping** *n.* achats *mpl*; courses *fpl*; **to do one's s.,** faire ses courses; (*for food*) faire son marché, aller aux provisions; **window s.,** lèche-vitrine(s) *m*; **s. street,** rue commerçante; **s. centre,** quartier commerçant; centre commercial; **s. precinct,** *Can:* **s. plaza,** centre commercial; **s. bag, basket,** sac *m*, panier *m*, à provisions.

shopfitter ['ʃɔpfitər] *n.* installateur *m*, agenceur *m*, de magasins.

shopgirl ['ʃɔpgəːl] *n.f.* vendeuse; employée de magasin.

shopkeeper ['ʃɔpkiːpər] *n.* commerçant, -ante; boutiquier, -ière.

shoplifter ['ʃɔpliftər] *n.* voleur, -euse, à l'étalage.

shoplifting ['ʃɔpliftiŋ] *n.* vol *m* à l'étalage.

shopman, *pl.* **-men** ['ʃɔpmən] *n.m. U.S:* mécanicien (dans un atelier de réparations).

shopper ['ʃɔpər] *n.* **1.** acheteur, -euse. **2.** *F:* sac *m* à provisions.

shopsoiled, shopworn ['ʃɔpsɔild, -wɔːn] *a.* (article) défraîchi, qui a fait l'étalage.

shopwalker ['ʃɔpwɔːkər] *n.* (*a*) chef *m* de rayon; (*b*) inspecteur, -trice, surveillant, -ante (de magasin).

shore¹ [ʃɔːr] *n.* (*a*) rivage *m*, littoral *m*, côte *f*; bord *m* (de la mer, d'un lac, d'un fleuve); **on the s.,** sur le rivage; au bord de la mer; (*b*) *Nau:* **on s.,** à terre; **to go on s.,** se rendre à terre; débarquer; **off s.,** au large; **in shore,** près de la côte; (*c*) *Lit:* **distant shores,** de lointains rivages.

shore² *n. Const: etc:* étai *m*, étançon *m*, *N.Arch:* accore *m*; béquille *f*; épontille *f*.

shore³ *v.tr.* **to s. (up),** étayer, étançonner (une maison, un mur); épontiller (un navire).

shoreline ['ʃɔːlain] *n.* rivage *m*; bord *m* de mer.

shoreward(s) ['ʃɔːwəd(z)] *adv.* vers la terre.

shorn *see* SHEAR³.

short¹ [ʃɔːt] **I.** *a.* **1.** (*a*) (*in space*) court; **to go by the shortest road, to go the shortest way,** prendre par le plus court, au plus court; **a s. distance from the station,** à une petite distance de la gare; **at s. range,** à courte portée; **a s. man,** un homme de petite taille; un petit homme; **to be s. in the arm, in the leg,** avoir les bras courts, les jambes courtes; **hair cut s.,** cheveux coupés court; (*b*) *Turf:* **s. price,** faible cote *f*. **2.** (*a*) court, bref; **at s. intervals,** à de courts intervalles; **of s. duration,** de peu de durée; **the days are getting shorter,** les jours raccourcissent; **for a s. time,** pour peu de temps; **in a s. time,** sous peu; bientôt; *U.S:* **in s. order,** peu de temps après; **a s. time ago,** il y a peu de temps; **s. and sweet,** court et bon; **to have a s. memory,** avoir la mémoire courte; *Ling:* **s. vowel,** voyelle brève; *Pros:* **s. syllable,** syllabe brève; *Fin:* **s. bills, bills at s. date,** billets *mpl*, traites *fpl*, à courte échéance; **deposit, loan, at s. notice,** dépôt *m*, prêt *m*, à court terme; **to make s. work of (sth.),** expédier (qch.); trancher (un problème, une difficulté); **to make s. work of it,** ne pas y aller par quatre chemins; (*b*) **s. story,** nouvelle *f*, conte *m*; **s. history of France,** précis *m* d'histoire de France; **s. list,** liste choisie (d'aspirants à un poste, etc.); **in s.,** bref; en un mot; en résumé; en somme; **Bill is s. for William,** Bill est un diminutif de William; **a s. drink,** un whisky, un apéritif, etc. (plutôt qu'une bière); *F:* du court; (*c*) (pouls) rapide; (haleine) courte; (*d*) (style) concis, serré; (*e*) (*of reply, tone, etc.*) brusque; sec, *f.* sèche; tranchant, abrupt; **to be s. with s.o.,** être cassant avec qn; **he was very s. with me,** il s'est montré très brusque; **s. temper,** caractère emporté. **3.** (*a*) (*of weight, measure, etc.*) insuffisant; **to give s. weight,** ne pas donner le poids; tricher sur le poids; **it is two francs s.,** il s'en faut de deux francs; **I am twenty francs s.,** il me manque vingt francs; **water in s. supply,** approvisionnement d'eau réduit; *Ind:* **to be on s. time,** être en chômage partiel; **little, not far, s. of it,** peu s'en faut; **he is not far s. of thirty,** il n'a guère moins de trente ans; **it is little s. of folly,** cela tient de la folie; **it was nothing s. of a masterpiece,** ce n'était rien moins qu'un chef-d'œuvre; **nothing s. of violence would compel him,** la violence seule le contraindrait; (*b*) (*of pers.*) **to be s. of sth.,** être à court de qch.; manquer de qch.; **to be s. of work,** chômer de besogne; *Cards:* **to be s. of, in, spades,** avoir une renonce à pique; **to go s. of sth.,** se priver de qch.; **to run s. of sth.,** venir à bout de (ses provisions, etc.); **we are running s. of provisions, our provisions are running s.,** les vivres *m* commencent à manquer, à s'épuiser. **4.** (*a*) *Cu:* **s. pastry,** pâte brisée; (*b*) (*of metal, clay*) aigre, cassant; *Cer:* (pâte) courte. **II.** *n.* **1.** (*a*) **the long and the s. of it,** le fin mot de l'affaire; **he knows the long and the s. of it,** il connaît l'affaire à fond; (*b*) *Cost:* **shorts,** (i) short *m*; (ii) *NAm:* caleçon *m*. **2.** (*a*) *Pros:* (syllabe) brève (*f*); (*b*) *Ling:* voyelle brève. **3.** *El:* *F:* court-circuit *m*, *pl.* courts-circuits. **5.** *Cin:* court métrage. **III.** *adv.* **1.** brusquement; court; **to stop s.,** s'arrêter (tout) court, net; *F:* s'arrêter pile; **to cut s.o. s.,** couper la parole à qn; **to be taken s.,** (i) être pris de court; être pris au dépourvu; (ii) *F:* être pris d'un besoin pressant. **2. to**

fall s. of (sth.), (i) (*of arrow, etc.*) ne pas atteindre (le but); tomber court; (ii) être, rester, au-dessous de (l'attente de qn); **to fall s. of one's duty,** manquer à son devoir; **s. of a miracle we are ruined,** à moins d'un miracle nous sommes perdus; **to stop s. of crime,** s'arrêter au seuil du crime. **3.** (*a*) *St.Exch:* (i) (vendre) à découvert; (ii) (emprunter) à courte échéance; (*b*) *Fig:* **to sell s.o. s.,** (i) duper, *F:* avoir, qn; (ii) rabaisser qn; dénigrer qn. **shortly** *adv.* **1.** (raconter qch., etc.) brièvement, en peu de mots. **2.** (répondre, etc.) brusquement, sèchement. **3.** bientôt, prochainement; sous peu; **s. after(wards),** peu (de temps) après; bientôt après.

short² *v.i. El: F:* = SHORT-CIRCUIT².

shortage [ˈʃɔːtidʒ] *n.* **1.** (*a*) insuffisance *f*, manque *m* (de poids, etc.); **s. in the cash,** tare *f* de caisse; **to make up, make good, the s.,** combler le déficit; (*b*) *Com:* **shortages,** manquants *mpl.* **2.** crise *f*, disette *f*; **food s.,** disette; **the paper s.,** la crise du papier.

shortbread, shortcake [ˈʃɔːtbred, -keik] *n. Cu:* = sablé *m.*

shortchange [ˈʃɔːt(t)ʃeindʒ] *v.tr. F:* (*a*) voler (qn) (en lui rendant la monnaie); (*b*) rouler (qn).

short-circuit¹ [ʃɔːtˈsəːkit] *n. El:* court-circuit *m*, *pl.* courts-circuits.

short-circuit² **1.** *v.tr. El: & Fig:* court-circuiter. **2.** *v.i. El:* (*of current*) se mettre en court-circuit.

shortcoming [ˈʃɔːtkʌmiŋ] *n.* **1.** *usu. pl.* **shortcomings,** défauts *mpl*; imperfections *fpl*; points *mpl* faibles (chez qn). **2.** manque *m*, déficit *m.*

short-dated [ʃɔːtˈdeitid] *a. Fin:* (billet) à courte échéance; (papier) court.

shorten [ˈʃɔːt(ə)n] **1.** *v.tr.* (*a*) raccourcir, rapetisser (une jupe, etc.); abréger (un texte, une tâche); écourter (un séjour); **Albert is often shortened to Bert,** le diminutif d'Albert est Bert. **2.** *v.i.* (*of days, etc.*) raccourcir. **3.** *v.tr. Cu:* **to s. pastry,** travailler la pâte avec une matière grasse. **shortening** *n.* **1.** raccourcissement *m* (des jours). **2.** *Cu:* matière grasse.

shortfall [ˈʃɔːtfɔːl] *n.* déficit *m*, manque *m.*

shorthaired [ˈʃɔːthɛəd] *a.* (homme) à cheveux courts; (chat) à poil court.

shorthand [ˈʃɔːthænd] *n.* sténographie *f*; **s. writing,** écriture *f* sténographique; **to take a speech down in s.,** sténographier un discours; (*pers.*) **s. typist,** sténodactylographe *mf*; *F:* sténodactylo *mf*; **s. writer, reporter,** sténographe *mf.*

shorthanded [ʃɔːtˈhændid] *a.* à court de personnel, de main-d'œuvre; **to be s.,** manquer de personnel.

short-haul [ˈʃɔːthɔːl] *a. Av:* **s.-h. transport aircraft,** (avion *m*) court-courrier (*m*).

shorthorn [ˈʃɔːthɔːn] *n.* (*a*) race bovine shorthorn; (*b*) shorthorn *m.*

shortish [ˈʃɔːtiʃ] *a.* assez, plutôt, court; (*of pers.*) courtaud.

short-legged [ʃɔːtˈleg(i)d] *a.* à jambes courtes.

shortlist [ˈʃɔːtlist] *v.tr.* **to s. a candidate,** retenir une candidature.

short-lived [ʃɔːtˈlivd] *a.* (*of pers., animal*) qui ne vit que peu de temps; (*of joy, triumph, etc.*) bref, éphémère, de courte durée.

shortness [ˈʃɔːtnis] *n.* **1.** (*a*) peu *m* de longueur (du bras, d'une jupe); (*b*) brièveté *f*, courte durée (de la vie); **s. of memory,** manque *m* de mémoire; (*c*) brusquerie *f* (d'humeur). **2.** manque, insuffisance *f* (de vivres, etc.). **3.** friabilité *f.*

short-range [ʃɔːtˈreindʒ] *a.* (tir, missile, etc.) à courte portée; (prévision) à court terme.

shortsheet [ˈʃɔːtʃiːt] *v.tr. U.S:* mettre (un lit) en portefeuille.

shortsighted [ʃɔːtˈsaitid] *a.* **1.** myope; à la vue basse; **I am getting s.,** ma vue baisse. **2.** imprévoyant.

shortsightedness [ʃɔːtˈsaitidnis] *n.* **1.** myopie *f.* **2.** imprévoyance *f*; manque *m* de perspicacité.

short-staffed [ʃɔːtˈstɑːft] *a.* **to be s.-s.,** manquer de personnel, de main-d'œuvre.

short-tempered [ʃɔːtˈtempəd] *a.* vif; d'un caractère emporté.

short-term [ˈʃɔːttəːm] *a.* **1.** (détenu) qui subit un emprisonnement de courte durée. **2.** *Fin:* (placement, etc.) à court terme.

short-time [ˈʃɔːttaim] *a.* **1.** (contrat, etc.) à court terme. **2. s.-t. worker, working,** chômeur, chômage, partiel.

short-winded [ʃɔːtˈwindid] *a.* au souffle court; **to be s.-w.,** manquer de souffle.

shorty [ˈʃɔːti] *n. F:* homme, femme, de petite taille.

shot [ʃɔt] *n.* **1.** (*a*) *Artil:* (i) *A:* boulet(s) *m(pl)*; **round s.,** boulet(s) rond(s); *Fig:* **I've still got a s. in the locker,** il me reste encore quelques ressources, une ressource; (ii) *coll.* projectiles *mpl*; (*b*) *Ven:* plomb *m*; **small s.,** menu plomb, petit plomb; **bird s.,** cendrée *f*; *F:* **like a s.,** (partir) comme une flèche; (accepter) d'emblée, sans hésitation; (*c*) *Metall:* grenaille *f*; **lead s.,** grenaille de plomb; (*d*) *Sp:* poids *m*; **to put the s.,** lancer le poids. **2.** (*a*) coup *m* (de feu); **pistol s.,** coup de pistolet; **warning s.,** coup d'avertissement; *Navy:* coup de semonce; **to fire a s.,** tirer un coup de feu; **without firing a s.,** sans tirer un (seul) coup de feu; **parting s.,** remarque *f*, réplique *f*, qu'on lance en partant; (*b*) (*pers.*) tireur, -euse; *Ven:* chasseur *m*; **he's a good s.,** il est bon tireur, bon chasseur; (*c*) *F:* **a big s.,** un type important, un gros manitou, *P:* une grosse légume. **3.** coup; (*a*) *Games:* **it's your s.,** à vous de jouer; **good s.!** bien joué! *Ten: etc:* **drop s.,** amortie *f*; **passing s.,** passing-shot *m*; *Fig:* **I'll have a s. at it,** je vais essayer, tenter le coup; **it's worth having a s. at,** cela vaut le coup; **he made a good s. at it,** (i) il est arrivé fort près du but; (ii) il s'est très bien acquitté; **to make a long s.,** (i) viser de loin; (ii) (*also* **a s. in the dark**) deviner au hasard; (iii) prendre un (gros) risque; **not by a long s.,** il s'en faut de beaucoup; (*b*) *Fb: etc:* **s. (at the goal),** shot *m*, shoot *m*; (*c*) *Fish:* (i) coup de filet; (*d*) *Phot:* photo *f*; *Cin:* (i) prise *f* de vue; (ii) section *f* de film; (iii) plan *m*; **high angle s.,** plongée *f*; **pan s.,** panoramique *f*; (*e*) *Med: F:* piqûre *f*; *P:* (*drugs*) piquouse *f*; **s. in the arm,** (i) piqûre au bras; (ii) remontant *m*, coup de fouet; (*f*) petit verre (d'eau de vie).

shotgun [ˈʃɔtgʌn] *n.* fusil *m* de chasse; *F:* **s. wedding,** mariage forcé.

should *see* SHALL.

shoulder¹ [ˈʃouldər] *n.* **1.** (*a*) épaule *f*; **s. blade,** (i) *Anat:* omoplate *f*; (ii) paleron *m* (de cheval, etc.); **round shoulders,** dos rond, voûté; **he's got broad shoulders,** (i) il est large d'épaules; (ii) *Fig:* il a bon dos; **coat too tight across the shoulders,** manteau trop étroit de carrure; **off-the-s. dress,** robe dégageant les épaules; **slung across, over, the s.,** en bandoulière; **s. bag,** sac *m* en, à, bandoulière; **s. belt,** baudrier *m*; **s. strap,** (i) bretelle *f*, bandoulière *f* (d'un sac, etc.); (ii) (*on clothes*) épaulette *f*, patte *f* d'épaules; (*on underwear*) bretelle; *Mil: etc:* **s. strap,** *U.S:* **loop,** patte d'épaule; épaulette; **s. braid,** fourragère *f*; **s. knot,** aiguillette *f*; *Av:* **s. harness,** bretelles; **to bring the gun to the s.,** épauler le fusil; **to tell s.o. sth. straight from the s.,** dire qch. carrément, brutalement, à qn; **to have a good head on one's shoulders,** avoir de la tête, du bon sens; **to stand head and shoulders above the rest,** (i) dépasser les autres d'une tête; (ii) surpasser tous les autres; **s. high,** à la hauteur des épaules; **to carry s.o. s. high,** porter qn en triomphe; **s. to s.,** côte à côte; épaule contre épaule; **to lay the blame on s.o.'s shoulders,** rejeter la faute sur qn; **to put one's s. to the wheel,** pousser à la roue; se mettre à l'œuvre (avec énergie); (*b*) *Cu:* épaule (de mouton, etc.); *Nau:* **s. of mutton sail,** (voile *f* à) houari *m*; (*c*) épaulement *m* (de colline, etc.); contrefort *m* (de montagne); **hard s.,** bas-côté *m* (d'une route); **soft s.,** accotement non stabilisé. **2.** (i) collet *m* (de raquette, de bouteille); (ii) *Typ:* épaule (d'une lettre).

shoulder² *v.tr.* **1.** pousser (qn, qch.) avec l'épaule; **to s. one's way through the crowd,** se frayer un passage à travers la foule; **to s. s.o. out of the way, aside,** écarter, repousser, qn d'un coup d'épaule. **2.** mettre (qch.) sur l'épaule; **to s. one's gun,** mettre son fusil sur l'épaule; **to s. the responsibility,** endosser la responsabilité. **3.** *Mil:* **to s. arms,** se mettre au port d'armes; **s. arms!** portez armes!

shout¹ [ʃaut] *n.* (*a*) cri *m* (de joie, de douleur, etc.); **shouts of laughter,** éclats *mpl* de rire; (*b*) clameur *f*.

shout² **1.** *v.i.* **to s. (out),** crier; pousser un cri, des cris; **to s. for s.o.,** appeler qn de toutes ses forces; **to s. for help,** crier, appeler, au secours; **to s. at s.o.,** crier contre, après, qn; *v.pr.* **to s. oneself hoarse,** s'enrouer à force de crier. **2.** *v.tr.* (*a*) crier (qch.); vociférer (des injures, etc.); **to s. out,** crier; **to s. to s.o. to do sth.,** crier à qn de faire qch.; (*b*) **the speaker was shouted down,** l'orateur a été hué. **shouting** *n.* cris *mpl*; clameur *f*; **it's all over bar the s.,** c'est dans le sac, les applaudissements suivront.

shove¹ [ʃʌv] *n.* *F:* coup *m* (d'épaule, etc.); poussée *f*; **to give sth., s.o., a s.,** pousser qch., qn; donner une poussée à qch., à qn.

shove² *F:* **1.** *v.tr.* pousser (qn, un objet); **to s. off,** pousser (une embarcation) au large; **to s. s.o. around,** (i) bousculer qn; (ii) faire marcher qn; **to s. s.o., sth., along, forward,** pousser qn, qch., en avant; faire avancer qn, qch.; **to s. s.o., sth., aside, away,** écarter qn, qch., d'une poussée; **to s. sth. into a drawer,** fourrer qch. dans un tiroir. **2.** *v.i.* (*a*) *F:* **to s. along, on,** se frayer un chemin; (*b*) *F:* **to s. off,** partir; décamper; *P:* **s. off!** fiche le camp!

shove-halfpenny, -ha'penny ['ʃʌvheipni] *n.* = (jeu *m* de) galet (*m*).

shovel¹ ['ʃʌv(ə)l] *n.* pelle *f*; **coal s.,** pelle à charbon, à feu; *Civ.E: etc:* **power, steam, s.,** pelle mécanique, à vapeur.

shovel² *v.tr.* **(shovelled)** pelleter (le charbon, etc.); prendre, jeter (le charbon, etc.) à la pelle; **to s. away,** déblayer (la neige, etc.); **to s. up,** ramasser, entasser, (le grain, etc.) à la pelle; *F:* **to s. food into one's mouth,** bâfrer sa mangeaille.

shovelful ['ʃʌvəlful] *n.* pelletée *f* (de sable, etc.).

shovel(l)er ['ʃʌvələr] *n.* *Orn:* (canard) souchet (*m*).

show¹ [ʃou] *n.* **1.** mise *f* en vue; étalage *m*, exposition *f* (de qch.); **to vote by s. of hands,** voter à mains levées; **to be on s.,** être exposé; **s. house, flat,** maison *f*, appartement *m*, témoin; **s. window,** vitrine *f*, devanture *f* (de magasin); étalage. **2.** (*a*) exposition (d'horticulture, etc.); exhibition *f* (de bêtes sauvages, etc.); concours *m*, comice *m* (agricole, etc.); **motor, air, s.,** salon *m* de l'automobile, de l'aviation; **fashion s.,** présentation *f* de collections; **dog s.,** exposition canine; **s. animal,** bête *f* à concours; *Equit:* **s. jumping,** jumping *m*; **s. jumper,** (cheval) sauteur (*m*); (*b*) spectacle *m*; (*at a fair*) **travelling s.,** spectacle forain; *F:* **to make a s. of oneself,** se donner en spectacle; se rendre ridicule; (*c*) spectacle, concert *m*; émission *f* (de radio, de télévision); **to go to a s.,** aller au spectacle; **to stop the s.,** être applaudi avec enthousiasme par les spectateurs; **to steal the s.,** (r)emporter la vedette; **film s.,** séance *f* de cinéma; *W.Tel: T.V:* **talk, chat, s.,** émission de bavardages; talk-show *m*; **one-man s.,** solo *m*; **s. business,** industrie *f*, monde *m*, du spectacle; **s. bill,** affiche *f* (de spectacle); **s. girl,** girl *f*; (*d*) étalage; **wonderful s. of flowers,** étalage merveilleux de fleurs; **to put up a good s.,** se bien acquitter; *F:* **good s.!** très bien! bravo! **it was a poor, bad, s.!** c'était plutôt manqué! (*e*) *F:* occasion *f*, chance *f*; **to give s.o. a (fair) s.,** laisser franc jeu à qn. **3.** (*a*) (i) apparence *f*; (ii) semblant *m*, simulacre *m*; **s. of generosity,** affectation *f* de générosité; **s. of strength,** démonstration *f* de force; **to make a s. of resistance, of being angry,** faire un semblant de résistance, faire semblant, faire mine, d'être fâché; **to make a great s. of friendship,** faire de grandes démonstrations d'amitié; (*b*) parade *f*, ostentation *f*, étalage, apparat *m*; **to be fond of s.,** aimer l'éclat *m*, la parade; **to make a s. of learning,** faire parade d'érudition; **to do sth. for s.,** faire qch. pour les apparences. **4.** *F:* affaire *f*; **to run the s.,** être à la tête de, diriger, l'affaire.

show² *v.* (*p.t.* **showed** [ʃoud]; *p.p.* **shown** [ʃoun]) **I.** *v.tr.* **1.** (*a*) montrer; faire voir, laisser voir (qch.); exposer, exhiber (qch.); présenter (son passeport); (*of cinema*) passer, présenter (un film); **to s. sth. to s.o., to s. s.o. sth.,** montrer, faire voir, qch. à qn; **to s. one's wares,** déployer, étaler, ses marchandises; **we're going to s. some films this evening,** nous allons passer des films ce soir; *T.V:* **this programme will be shown tomorrow,** cette émission passera sur l'écran demain; **to s. one's cards, one's hand,** (i) jouer cartes sur table; (ii) découvrir son jeu; **to have sth. to s. for one's money,** en avoir pour son argent; **to s. one's legs,** exposer ses jambes; **he won't s. his face here again,** il ne se montrera plus ici; **colour that doesn't s. the dirt,** couleur qui n'est pas salissante; **to s. oneself,** se montrer, se faire voir; (*for inspection, etc.*) se présenter, s'exhiber; (*at a reception, etc.*) faire acte de présence; (*of thg*) **to s. itself,** devenir visible, se montrer, se manifester, se révéler; (*b*) représenter, figurer (qch. par la peinture, par le discours, etc.); **the picture shows three figures,** le tableau représente trois personnes; (*c*) indiquer; **place shown on a map,** lieu indiqué sur une carte; (*of watch, thermometer, etc.*) **to s. the time, the temperature,** indiquer, marquer, l'heure, la température; **to s. a profit, a loss,** faire ressortir un bénéfice, une perte; **to s. great improvement,** montrer, accuser, une grande amélioration. **2.** (*a*) **to s. s.o. the way,** indiquer, montrer, tracer, le chemin à qn; (*b*) **to s. s.o. to his room,** conduire qn à sa chambre; **to s. s.o. round the town,** faire visiter, faire voir, la ville à qn; **we were shown over the house,** on nous a fait visiter la maison; **to s. s.o. into a room,** introduire, faire entrer, qn dans une pièce; **to s. s.o. in,** faire entrer qn; **to s. s.o. out,** reconduire qn; accompagner qn jusqu'à la porte. **3.** (*a*) montrer (des qualités); manifester (ses sentiments, etc.); témoigner (sa reconnaissance, etc.); laisser voir, laisser paraître (ses sentiments); faire preuve de (courage, zèle); **to s. a taste for sth.,** témoigner d'un goût pour qch.; **his face showed his delight,** son visage annonçait sa joie; **he showed no sign of having heard anything,** il n'a manifesté en aucune façon avoir rien entendu; **he shows his age,** il accuse, il fait (bien), son âge; **to s. oneself (to be) a coward,** se montrer lâche; **time will s.,** qui vivra verra; (*b*) révéler, montrer, accuser, faire ressortir (qch.); **his round shoulders s. his age,** son dos voûté accuse, révèle, son âge; (*c*) prouver, démontrer; **a mere glance will s. that . . .,** il suffit d'un coup d'œil pour se rendre compte que . . .; **it only, all, goes to s. that . . .,** ce qui prouve que . . .; *F:* **I'll s. you!** je vous apprendrai! **to s. cause, reason,** exposer ses raisons; offrir des raisons valables. **II.** *v.i.* se montrer, (ap)paraître, se (laisser) voir; **the buds are beginning to s.,** les bourgeons *mpl* commencent à se montrer, à paraître; **your slip's showing,** votre jupon *m* dépasse; **it shows in your face,** cela se voit, se lit, sur votre visage; **to s. to advantage,** faire bonne figure; *F:* **to s. willing,** faire preuve de bonne volonté. **showing** *n.* **1.** exposition *f*, mise *f* en vue (de qch.); **on this s.,** si l'on envisage ainsi les faits; **on your own s.,** à ce que vous dites, faites, vous-même; *Cin:* **first s.,** en première vision. **2.** manifestation *f*, témoignage *m* (de ses sentiments, etc.). **show off 1.** *v.tr.* (*a*) faire valoir, mettre en valeur (qch.); **coat that shows off the figure well,** manteau *m* qui marque, dessine, bien la taille; (*b*) faire parade, montre, étalage, de (qch.). **2.** *v.i.* parader, poser; se pavaner; se donner des airs; s'afficher; **to s. off in front of s.o.,** chercher à épater qn; **stop showing off!** cessez de faire l'important, de vous donner des airs! **show up 1.** *v.tr.* (*a*) démasquer, dénoncer (un imposteur, etc.); dévoiler (une imposture); révéler (un défaut, etc.); (*b*) attirer l'attention sur (qn); **he's been shown up,** le voilà grillé. **2.** *v.i.* (*a*) se dessiner, se détacher, ressortir (sur un fond); (*b*) *F:* se présenter, être présent; faire acte de présence; **they'll s. up at twelve,** ils s'amèneront à midi.

showbiz ['ʃoubiz] *n. F:* industrie *f*, monde *m*, du spectacle.

showboat ['ʃoubout] *n. U.S: A:* bateau-théâtre *m*, *pl.* bateaux-théâtres (sur le Mississipi).

showcase ['ʃoukeis] *n. Com:* vitrine *f*, montre *f*.

showdown ['ʃoudaun] *n.* **1.** *Cards:* étalement *m* de son jeu (sur la table). **2.** (*a*) révélation *f*, mise *f* au point, à jour, de ses projets, de ses capacités, de ses exploits, etc.; (*b*) *F:* confrontation *f*, déballage *m*.

shower¹ ['ʃouər] *n.* exposant, -ante (à une exposition, etc.); exhibiteur, -trice; montreur, -euse.

shower² ['ʃauər] *n.* **1.** (*a*) averse *f*; giboulée *f*; **(heavy) s.,** ondée *f*; (*b*) volée *f* (de coups, de pierres); gerbe *f* (d'étincelles); avalanche *f* (d'injures). **2.** *Toil:* douche *f*; **to have, take, a s.,** prendre une douche, se doucher; **s. unit,** bloc-douche *m*, *pl.* blocs-douches; **s. cabinet,** cabine *f* de douche; **s. attachment,** douchette *f*; *O:* **s. bath,** bain-douche *m*, *pl.* bains-douches. **3.** *Astr:* essaim *m* (de météores). **4.** *NAm: F:* réception *f* où chacun apporte un cadeau (de noce, etc.). **5.** *F:* **what a s.!** quelle bande, quel tas, de crétins!

shower³ ['ʃauər] **1.** *v.tr.* (*a*) verser; faire tomber (de l'eau, etc.) par ondées; (*b*) **to s. (sth.) on s.o.,** faire pleuvoir (des coups) sur qn, combler qn (de cadeaux, d'honneurs); assaillir qn (de questions); **to s. invitations on s.o., to s. s.o. with invitations,** accabler qn d'invitations. **2.** *v.i.* (*a*) pleuvoir; (*of rain*) tomber par ondées; (*b*) prendre une douche, se doucher.

showerproof ['ʃauəpru:f] *a. Tex:* imperméabilisé.

showery ['ʃauəri] *a.* (temps) pluvieux; **it's s. (weather),** le temps est à l'averse.

showground ['ʃougraund] *n.* (*a*) champ *m* de foire; (*b*) terrain *m* de concours hippique, etc.

showiness ['ʃouinis] *n.* prétention *f*, clinquant *m*, faste *m*; luxe criard, tapageur; ostentation *f*.

showman *pl.* **-men** ['ʃoumən] *n.m.* (*a*) (*at fair*) forain; (*b*) homme qui a le sens de la mise en scène.

showmanship ['ʃoumənʃip] *n.* art *m* de la mise en scène.

show-off ['ʃouɔf] *n. F:* (*pers.*) poseur, -euse, m'as-tu-vu(e).

showpiece ['ʃoupi:s] article *m* d'exposition, de vitrine; objet *m*, monument *m*, etc., de grand intérêt.

showplace ['ʃoupleis] *n.* endroit *m* pittoresque; monument *m* d'intérêt architectural, touristique.

showring ['ʃouriŋ] *n.* arène *f* (i) d'exposition, (ii) de vente (de chevaux, etc.), (iii) de concours hippique.

showroom ['ʃouru(:)m] *n.* salle *f*, salon *m*, magasin *m*, d'exposition (d'une maison de commerce); salle de démonstration (de voitures, etc.).

showstopper ['ʃoustɔpər] *n. F:* acteur, -trice, chanteur, -euse, numéro *m*, etc., applaudi(e) avec enthousiasme par les spectateurs.

showy ['ʃoui] *a.* (*of appearance, dress, decoration, etc.*) prétentieux, voyant; tapageur; tape-à-l'œil *inv.*

shrapnel ['ʃræpn(ə)l] *n. Artil:* **1.** shrapnel *m*; obus *m* à balles, à mitraille. **2.** éclats *mpl* d'obus.

shred¹ [ʃred] *n.* brin *m*; lambeau *m*, fragment *m* (de tissu, etc.); petit morceau (de viande, etc.); **to tear sth. (in)to shreds,** déchiqueter qch.; mettre qch. en lambeaux; **to tear s.o.'s reputation, s.o., to shreds,** déchirer qn à belles dents; **her dress was all in shreds,** sa robe était tout en lambeaux; **there isn't a s. of evidence,** il n'y a pas la moindre preuve; **not a s. of truth,** pas un grain de vérité.

shred² *v.tr.* **(shredded)** déchirer (qch.) en lambeaux; déchiqueter; *Cu:* râper (des légumes); *Paperm:* effilocher (des chiffons). **shredding** *n.* déchiquetage *m* (du tissu, etc.); *Cu:* râpage *m* (de légumes); *Paperm:* effilochage *m* (de chiffons).

shredder ['ʃredər] *n.* (*device*) (*a*) *Dom. Ec:* **vegetable s.,** coupe-légumes *m inv*; râpe *f* à légumes; (*b*) (*for papers, etc.*) effilocheuse *f*.

shrew¹ [ʃru:] *n. Z:* musaraigne *f*.

shrew² *n.f.* femme criarde; mégère, chipie.

shrewd [ʃru:d] *a.* **1.** (*of pers., etc.*) sagace, perspicace, fin; (homme d'affaires) d'une grande acuité; **he's a s. man,** c'est une fine mouche; **s. answer,** réponse adroite. **2.** (*intensive*) **I've got a s. idea that . . .,** je suis porté à croire que . . .; **to make a s. guess,** avoir de fortes raisons pour deviner. **-ly** *adv.* sagacement, finement; avec finesse; avec perspicacité.

shrewdness ['ʃru:dnis] *n.* sagacité *f*, perspicacité *f*; acuité *f*, finesse *f*.

shrewish ['ʃru:iʃ] *a.* (femme) acariâtre, querelleuse.

shriek¹ ['ʃri:k] *n.* cri aigu, perçant (d'une personne, d'un animal); **shrieks of laughter,** grands éclats de rire.

shriek² 1. *v.i.* pousser un cri aigu, des cris aigus; **to s. with laughter,** rire aux éclats; s'esclaffer, pouffer (de rire). **2.** *v.tr.* **to s. (out) a warning,** pousser un cri d'avertissement. **shrieking** *n.* cris aigus, perçants.

shrift [ʃrift] *n. A:* confession *f* et absolution *f*; *Fig:* **to give s.o. short s.,** expédier vite qn; envoyer promener qn.

shrike [ʃraik] *n. Orn:* pie-grièche *f*, *pl.* pies-grièches.

shrill¹ [ʃril] *a.* (*of voice, sound, etc.*) aigu, strident, perçant; **in a s. voice,** d'une voix perçante; **s. whistle,** coup de sifflet strident. **shrilly** *adv.* d'un ton aigu.

shrill² *v.i. Lit:* pousser, avoir, un son aigu, strident; **a whistle shrilled,** un coup de sifflet déchira l'air.

shrillness ['ʃrilnis] *n.* acuité *f* stridence *f*, (d'un son).

shrimp¹ [ʃrimp] *n.* (*a*) *Crust:* crevette (grise); **s. boat,** crevettier *m*; (*b*) *F:* (*pers.*) nabot, -ote.

shrimp² *v.i.* **to go shrimping, to s.,** pêcher la crevette, faire la pêche à la crevette.

shrine [ʃrain] *n.* **1.** châsse *f*, reliquaire *m*. **2.** tombeau *m* de saint(e). **3.** lieu de pèlerinage.

shrink¹ [ʃriŋk] *n.* **1.** rétrécissement *m* (d'un tissu); retrait *m* (du bois, etc.). **2.** *F:* psychiatre *mf*, psychanalyste *mf*.

shrink² *v.* (*p.t.* **shrank** [ʃræŋk]; *p.p.* **shrunk** [ʃrʌŋk], *as adj.* **shrunken** ['ʃrʌŋk(ə)n]) **1.** *v.i.* (*a*) se contracter; (se) rétrécir; rapetisser; (*of material, etc.*) rétrécir; **he is beginning to s. (with age),** il commence à se tasser; **to s. in the wash,** rétrécir au lavage; **my income has shrunk,** mon revenu s'est amoindri, a diminué; (*b*) reculer; se retirer, se dérober; **he shrank back,** il a eu un mouvement de recul; **to s. (away, back) from sth.,** reculer devant, se dérober à, qch.; **to s. (back) in horror,** reculer d'horreur; **to s. from doing sth.,** reculer, répugner, à faire qch.; (*c*) **to s. into oneself,** rentrer en soi-même; (*d*) se faire tout petit (par timidité, etc.). **2.** *v.tr.* contracter (du métal); (faire) rétrécir (un tissu); **fully shrunk material,** tissu irrétrécissable. **shrinking** *n.* = SHRINKAGE; **s. (away),**

rétrécissement *m*, rapetissement *m*. **2. s. (away, back) from sth.,** reculement *m* devant qch.; répugnance *f* à une action. **shrunk(en)** *a.* contracté; *Tex:* rétréci; (*of features, etc.*) ratatiné; **s. with age,** tassé par l'âge; *Anthr:* **shrunken heads,** têtes réduites.

shrinkage ['ʃriŋkidʒ] *n.* contraction *f*; retrait *m* (du bois); *Tex: etc:* rétrécissement *m*.

shrinker ['ʃriŋkər] *n.* **head s.,** (i) *Anthr:* réducteur *m* de têtes; (ii) *F:* psychiatre *mf*, psychanalyste *mf*.

shrive ['ʃraiv] *v.tr.* (*p.t.* **shrove** ['ʃrouv]; *p.p.* **shriven** ['ʃriv(ə)n]) *A:* confesser, absoudre (un pénitent).

shrivel ['ʃriv(ə)l] *v.* (**shrivelled,** *NAm:* **shriveled**) **1.** *v.tr.* **to s. (up),** rider, ratatiner, recroqueviller (la peau, une pomme, etc.); (*of sun*) brûler, hâler (les plantes); **the old man's shrivelled face,** le visage ratatiné, ridé, du vieillard. **2.** *v.i.* **to s. (up),** se rider, se ratatiner; se recroqueviller.

shroud¹ [ʃraud] *n.* **1.** linceul *m*, suaire *m*; **in a s. of mystery,** enveloppé de mystère; *Lit:* **under a s. of darkness,** sous les voiles *mpl* de la nuit; à l'abri *m* de la nuit. **2.** *Mec.E: etc:* bouclier *m*, blindage *m*.

shroud² *n.* (*a*) *Nau:* hauban *m*; (*b*) (*of parachute*) **s. (lines),** suspentes *fpl*.

shroud³ *v.tr.* (*a*) ensevelir (un cadavre) (d'un linceul); (*b*) envelopper, voiler (qch.) (**in,** de); *Lit:* **shrouded in mist, in mystery,** enveloppé de brume, de mystère; **shrouded in gloom,** (i) (*of place*) enténébré; (ii) (*of pers.*) plongé dans la tristesse.

shrove [ʃrouv] **1.** *see* SHRIVE. **2. S. Tuesday,** Mardi gras.

Shrovetide ['ʃrouvtaid] *n. Ecc:* les jours gras.

shrub [ʃrʌb] *n. Bot:* arbrisseau *m*, arbuste *m*.

shrubbery ['ʃrʌbəri] *n.* bosquet *m*; massif *m* d'arbustes.

shrubby ['ʃrʌbi] *a.* **1.** qui ressemble à un arbuste, un arbrisseau; **s. tree,** arbrisseau. **2.** couvert d'arbustes.

shrug¹ [ʃrʌg] *n.* **s. (of the shoulders),** haussement *m* d'épaules.

shrug² *v.tr.* & *i.* (**shrugged**) **to s. (one's, the, shoulders),** hausser les épaules; **s. sth. off,** écarter (un avis, un problème, etc.); dédaigner, mépriser (un danger).

shuck¹ [ʃʌk] *NAm:* **1.** *n.* cosse *f*, gousse *f* (de petits pois, etc.); spathe *f* (de maïs); écale *f* (de noix, etc.); coquille *f* (d'huître, de palourde). **2.** *F: int.* **shucks!** mince (alors)! flûte (alors)!

shuck² *v.tr. NAm:* (*a*) écosser (des petits pois, etc.); écaler (des noix); éplucher (du maïs); écailler (des huîtres); (*b*) **to s. off,** ôter (un vêtement); se défaire (d'une habitude).

shudder¹ ['ʃʌdər] *n.* frisson *m*, frémissement *m*, frissonnement *m*; *F:* **it gives me the shudders,** j'en ai le frisson.

shudder² *v.i.* (*a*) frissonner (**with cold, horror,** de froid, d'horreur); **I s. to think of it, at the thought of it,** j'ai le frisson rien que d'y penser; (*b*) (*of ship*) vibrer. **shuddering** *n.* (*a*) frisson *m*, frémissement *m*, frissonnement *m*; (*b*) vibration *f*.

shuffle¹ ['ʃʌfl] *n.* **1.** (*a*) mouvement traînant des pieds; marche traînante; (*b*) *Danc:* frottement *m* de pieds; **soft shoe s.,** danse de music-hall (exécutée en chaussons). **2.** battement *m*, mélange *m* (des cartes). **3.** (*a*) atermoiement *m*, tervigersations *fpl*; (*b*) faux-fuyant *m*, *pl.* faux-fuyants. **4.** *F:* **Cabinet s.,** remaniement ministériel.

shuffle² **1.** *v.tr.* & *i.* **to s. (one's feet),** traîner les pieds; **to s. (along),** avancer lentement en traînant les pieds; **to s. off,** s'en aller en traînant le pas. **2.** *v.tr.* (*a*) mêler (des papiers, etc.); (*b*) *Cards:* battre, mêler (les cartes); (*c*) brasser (les dominos); (*d*) **to s. off,** se débarrasser (d'une responsabilité), ôter (ses vêtements) à la hâte; **3.** *v.i.* atermoyer; tergiverser. **shuffling** *a.* **1.** (*of pers.*) qui traîne les pieds; (*of gait*) traînant. **2.** *F:* (*of conduct, speech*) équivoque, évasif; (politicien) fuyant, évasif.

shun¹ [ʃʌn] *v.tr.* (**shunned**) fuir, éviter (qn, qch.); **to s. society,** fuir le monde; **to s. everybody,** s'éloigner de tout le monde.

'shun² *int. Mil: etc: F:* (= *attention!*) garde à vous!

shunt¹ [ʃʌnt] *n.* **1.** *Rail:* garage *m*, manœuvre *f* (d'un train). **2.** *El:* shunt *m*, dérivation *f*.

shunt² **1.** *Rail:* (*a*) *v.tr.* garer, manœuvrer (un train, des wagons); **to s. a train onto a siding,** aiguiller, dériver, un train sur une voie de garage; *F:* **to s. (s.o., sth.),** mettre (qn, qch.) au rancart; ajourner (un projet); (*b*) *v.i.* (*of train*) se garer. **2.** *v.tr. El:* shunter, dériver (un circuit, etc.); monter (un condensateur) en dérivation. **shunting** *n.* **1.** (*a*) *Rail:* garage *m*, manœuvre *f*; changement *m* de voie; **s. operations,** manœuvres de triage; **s. engine,** locomotive *f*, machine *f*, de manœuvre; locotracteur *m*; **s. yard,** gare *f* de triage; (*b*) *F:* ajournement *m* (d'un projet); mise *f* au rancart (de qn, de qch.). **2.** *El:* dérivation *f*, shuntage *m*.

shush [ʃʌʃ] **1.** *v.tr.* faire taire (qn). **2.** *int.* chut!

shut [ʃʌt] *v.* (*p.t.* & *p.p.* **shut;** *pr.p.* **shutting**) **1.** *v.tr.* (*a*) fermer (une porte, un magasin, une boîte, un livre, etc.); **to s. the door on s.o., in s.o.'s face,** fermer la porte au nez de qn; **to find the door s.,** trouver la porte fermée, trouver porte close; **to s. one's eyes,** fermer les yeux; *F:* **to keep one's mouth s.,** avoir la bouche cousue; **to s. s.o.'s mouth (for him),** faire taire qn; *P:* **s. your mouth!** la ferme! ta gueule! (*b*) **to s. s.o., sth., in,** enfermer qn, qch.; **to s. one's finger in the door,** se pincer le doigt dans la porte; **we're s. in by hills,** nous sommes entourés de collines. **2.** *v.i.* (*of door*) (se) fermer; (*of shop*) fermer; **the door won't s.,** la porte ne ferme pas; **the door s. to,** la porte s'est fermée (toute seule). **shut down** **1.** *v.tr. Ind:* fermer (une usine, etc.); *Tchn:* couper (la vapeur); *Av:* arrêter (le moteur). **2.** *v.i.* (*of factory, etc.*) (i) chômer; (ii) fermer ses portes. **shut off** *v.tr.* (*a*) couper, interrompre, intercepter (la vapeur); fermer (l'eau); *Aut:* couper, arrêter (le moteur); (*b*) séparer, isoler (**from,** de); **to be s. off from society,** être exclu du monde. **shut out** *v.tr.* (*a*) exclure (qn, l'air, la lumière); chasser (un souvenir, etc.); **the trees s. out the view,** les arbres bouchent la vue; **to s. s.o. out (from sth.),** exclure qn (de qch.); (*b*) **to s. s.o. out (of doors),** fermer la porte à qn. **shutting** *n.* fermeture *f* (d'une porte, d'une boîte, etc.); **s. down,** (i) fermeture, (ii) chômage *m* (d'une usine); **s. off,** interruption *f* (de la vapeur); fermeture (de l'eau); **s. out,** exclusion *f* (de qn, de l'air). **shut up** **1.** *v.tr.* enfermer (qn, qch.); **to s. oneself up,** s'enfermer chez soi; (*b*) **to s. s.o. up (in prison),** emprisonner qn; (*c*) fermer (une porte); **to s. up shop,** (i) fermer le magasin, la boutique; (ii) fermer boutique; suspendre ses activités; (*d*) condamner (une porte, une pièce); obstruer (un orifice, etc.); (*e*) *F:* faire taire qn; réduire (qn) au silence. **2.** *v.i. F:* se taire; **s. up!** taisez-vous! *P:* la ferme! ta gueule!

shutdown ['ʃʌtdaun] *n.* (i) fermeture *f*, (ii) chômage *m* (d'une usine).

shut-eye ['ʃʌtai] *n. F:* somme *m*, roupillon *m*; **to have a bit of s.-e.,** faire un (petit) somme.

shut-out ['ʃʌtaut] *n.* **1.** *Ind:* lock-out *m inv.* **2.** *Cards:* **s.o. bid,** ouverture préventive. **3.** *NAm: Sp:* défaite *f* à zéro.

shutter¹ ['ʃʌtər] *n.* **1.** volet *m*; *Ecc:* guichet *m* (de confessional); **slatted shutters,** persiennes *f*; **folding shutters,** volets pliants, brisés; **to open, close, the shutters,** ouvrir, fermer, les volets; **to put up the shutters,** (i) mettre les volets (d'un magasin); fermer la, les, devanture(s); (ii) *Fig:* fermer boutique. **2.** *Phot:* obturateur *m*; **s. speed,** vitesse *f* d'obturation; **to set, release, the s.,** armer, déclencher, l'obturateur. **3.** (*a*) *Metall:* écluse *f*; (*b*) *Hyd.E:* hausse *f* (de vanne). **4.** *Civ.E:* banche *f* (pour béton).

shutter² *v.tr.* mettre les volets à (une fenêtre, une maison); fermer les volets d('une maison, etc.); **shuttered window,** fenêtre aux volets fermés, clos.

shuttle¹ ['ʃʌtl] *n.* **1.** *Tex: Needlew: etc:* navette *f.* **2.** (*a*) *Trans:* navette; **s. service,** service *m* de navettes; navette; *Rail:* **s. train,** (train *m* qui fait la) navette; *Space:* **space s.,** navette spatiale; (*b*) *Mec.E:* **s. (movement),** (mouvement *m* de) va-et-vient *m inv.*

shuttle² **1.** *v.i.* faire la navette; aller et venir; (**between,** entre). **2.** *v.tr.* **to s. s.o. back and forth, to and fro,** faire aller et venir qn, envoyer qn à droite et à gauche.

shuttlecock ['ʃʌtlkɔk] *n. Games:* volant *m.*

shy¹ [ʃai] *n.* écart *m,* faux bond (d'un cheval).

shy² *v.i.* **(shied; shying)** (*of horse*) avoir, faire, un écart; broncher; (*of horse, pers.*) **to s. at sth.,** prendre ombrage de qch.; *Fig:* (*of pers.*) tiquer sur qch.

shy³ *a.* **(shyer, shyest;** *occ.* **shier, shiest) 1.** (*of bird, child, etc.*) sauvage, farouche; (*of horse, etc.*) ombrageux; (*of pers.*) timide, modeste; **to make s.o. s.,** intimider qn; **to be s. of people,** être gêné, mal à l'aise, parmi les gens; **to fight s. of (sth.),** se défier, se méfier, de (qch.); renâcler à (une besogne); **to be s. of doing sth.,** hésiter à faire qch. **2.** *NAm:* **to be s. of sth.,** manquer de qch.; être à court (d'argent). **-ly** *adv.* timidement, modestement.

shy⁴ *n. F:* **1.** jet *m,* lancement *m* (d'une pierre, etc.); (*at fairs*) **5p a s.,** 5p le coup. **2.** *O:* essai *m,* tentative *f* (pour atteindre qch.); **to have a s. at doing sth.,** s'essayer à faire qch.

shy⁵ *v.* **(shied; shying)** *F:* **1.** *v.i.* lancer, jeter, qch. (**at,** à). **2.** *v.tr.* lancer (une pierre) (**at s.o.,** à qn).

Shylock ['ʃailɔk] *n.* usurier *m.*

shyness ['ʃainis] *n.* timidité *f,* réserve *f,* modestie *f* (de qn); sauvagerie *f* (d'un animal, de qn); **to lose one's s.,** s'enhardir.

shyster ['ʃaistər] *n. esp. NAm: F:* (*a*) avocassier *m;* procédurier, -ière; (*b*) homme d'affaires véreux.

si [si:] *n. Mus:* **1.** (*fixed*) si *m.* **2.** (*movable*) la (note) sensible.

Siam [sai'æm] *Pr.n.* Siam *m.*

Siamese [saiə'mi:z] **1.** *a. Geog:* siamois; **S. twins,** frères siamois, sœurs siamoises; **S. cat** *n.* **S.,** (chat) siamois (*m*). **2.** *n.* (*a*) *Geog:* Siamois, -oise; (*b*) *Ling:* siamois.

Siberia [sai'biəriə] *Pr.n. Geog:* Sibérie *f.*

Siberian [sai'biəriən] *Geog:* **1.** *a.* sibérien. **2.** *n.* Sibérien, -ienne.

sibilant ['sibilənt] **1.** *a.* sifflant. **2.** *n. Ling:* (lettre, consonne) sifflante (*f*).

sibling ['sibliŋ] *n.* l'un(e) de deux, de plusieurs, enfants qui ont (i) les mêmes parents, (ii) le même père ou la même mère.

sibyl ['sibil] **1.** *n.* sibylle *f.* **2.** *Pr.n.f.* **S.,** Sibylle.

sibylline ['sibilain] *a.* (livre, etc.) sibyllin.

sic [sik] *Lt.adv.* sic, ainsi.

siccative ['sikətiv] *a. & n.* siccatif (*m*).

Sicilian [si'siliən] *Geog:* **1.** *a.* sicilien. **2.** *n.* Sicilien, -ienne.

Sicily ['sisili] *Pr.n. Geog:* Sicile *f.*

sick¹ [sik] *a.* **1.** (*a*) malade; **the s.,** les malades; **to report s.,** se faire porter malade; **s. list,** rôle *m,* état *m,* des malades; *Mil: etc:* **s. call, parade,** visite *f* des malades; **s. leave,** congé *m* (i) de maladie, (ii) *Mil: etc:* de réforme; **s. pay,** allocation *f* de maladie; **s. benefit,** prestations en cas de maladie; assurance *f* maladie; **s. bay,** infirmerie *f*; *Navy:* poste *m* des malades; **s. bed,** lit *m* de malade, de douleur; (*b*) *F:* (humour) noir; (plaisanterie) macabre. **2. to be s.,** (i) vomir, rendre; (ii) *NAm:* être malade; **to feel s.,** avoir mal au cœur; avoir des nausées; **s. feeling,** malaise *m*; **s. headache,** migraine *f*; **he was as s. as a cat, a dog,** il a été malade comme un chien; *F:* **it makes me s.,** cela m'écœure; c'est à vomir; *P:* **you make me s.!** tu m'écœures! *NAm:* **to be s. at, to, in, on, one's stomach,** avoir mal au cœur. **3.** (*a*) *Lit:* **to be s. at heart,** avoir le cœur navré; (*b*) *F:* **he was very s. at, about, failing his exam,** son échec l'a tout retourné; **to grow s. of sth.,** se dégoûter de qch.; **to be s. of sth.,** être las de qch.; **I'm s. and tired, I'm s. to death, of it,** j'en ai assez, j'en ai plein le dos; j'en ai marre.

sick² *v.tr. F:* **to s. sth. up,** vomir, dégobiller, qch.

sicken ['sik(ə)n] **1.** *v.i.* (*a*) *O:* tomber malade (**of, with,** de); (*of plants*) languir, dépérir; (*b*) **to be sickening for an illness,** *F:* **for sth.,** couver une maladie, qch.; (*c*) **to s. of sth.,** se lasser, se dégoûter, de qch. **2.** *v.tr.* (*a*) rendre (qn) malade; donner mal au cœur à (qn); *F:* **his business methods s. me,** ses procédés me révoltent; (*b*) **to s. s.o. of sth.,** dégoûter, écœurer, qn de qch. **sickening** *a.* écœurant, dégoûtant; (odeur) nauséabonde; (peur) qui serre le cœur; (spectacle) révoltant; *F:* **how perfectly s.!** c'est vraiment écœurant! **sickeningly** *adv.* de façon à vous soulever le cœur, à vous écœurer.

sickle ['sikl] *n. Agr:* faucille *f*; *Pol:* **the hammer and s.,** la faucille et le marteau.

sickliness ['siklinis] *n.* **1.** état maladif (de qn). **2.** pâleur *f* (de teint). **3.** goût écœurant (d'un gâteau).

sickly ['sikli] *a.* **1.** (*a*) (*of child*) maladif, souffreteux, malingre; (*of plant*) étiolé; (*b*) (*of colour, light*) faible, pâle; (*of complexion*) terreux; (pâleur) maladive; (soleil) blafard; (*c*) (sourire) pâle. **2.** (*of climate*) malsain, insalubre. **3.** (*a*) (*of taste, etc.*) fade; (*of smell*) écœurant, nauséabond; **s. sweet,** douceâtre; (*b*) (*of sentiment*) qui écœure, qui dégoûte; *F:* (*of story, tune*) d'une sentimentalité outrée.

sickness ['siknis] *n.* **1.** maladie *f*; **sleeping s.,** maladie du sommeil; **s. benefit,** prestations en cas de maladie; assurance *f* maladie. **2.** (*a*) mal *m* (de cœur); malaise *m*; **mountain s.,** mal des montagnes; **(bouts of) s.,** (i) nausée(s) *f(pl)*; (ii) vomissement(s) *m(pl)*; **morning s.,** nausées matinales.

sickroom ['sikru(:)m] *n.* chambre *f* de malade.

side¹ [said] *n.* **1.** (*a*) côté *m,* flanc *m*; **to be lying on one's s.,** être couché sur le côté; **right, left, s.,** côté droit, gauche; **by the s. of s.o.,** à côté de qn; **by, at, my s.,** à côté de moi; à mes côtés; **s. by s. (with s.o.),** l'un à côté de l'autre; côte à côte (avec qn); *F:* **to split, burst, one's sides (with laughing),** se tordre (de rire); (*b*) **s. of beef,** demi-carcasse *f* de bœuf; **s. of bacon,** flèche *f* de lard. **2.** côté (d'une maison, d'une boîte, d'un triangle); pan *m* (d'un objet taillé, d'un comble); flanc, versant *m* (d'une montagne); paroi *f* (d'un fossé, d'un vase); bande *f,* bord *m,* côté (d'un navire); *Mth:* membre *m* (d'une équation); *Opt:* branche *f* (de lunettes). **3.** (*surface*) (*a*) côté; *Rec:* face *f* (d'un disque); **the right, wrong, s. (of sth.),** le bon, mauvais, côté (de qch.); l'endroit *m,* l'envers *m* (d'un tissu); **the under, upper, s., of sth.,** le dessous, le dessus, de qch.; **printed on one s. only,** imprimé d'un seul côté; (*b*) **the good, bad, s. of the business,** le bon, mauvais, côté de l'affaire; **the other s. of the picture,** le revers de la médaille; **to look on the bright s. (of things),** voir les choses du bon côté, prendre les choses par le bon côté; **he always looks on the gloomy s. of things,** il voit tout en noir; **to be, to get, on the right s. of s.o.,** être, se mettre, dans les petits papiers de qn; **to get on the wrong s. of s.o.,** prendre qn à rebrousse-poil; **to hear, look at, both sides (of a question),** considérer les deux aspects d'une question; entendre, envisager, le pour et le contre; **there are many sides to his character,** son caractère est très complexe; **his good s.,** ses bons côtés; **his speech was a bit on the long, short, s.,** son discours était plutôt long, court; **the weather's on the cool s.,** il fait plutôt froid. **4.** (*a*) **on this s.,** de ce côté(-ci); **on that s.,** de ce côté-là; par(-)delà; **on this s. of sth.,** de ce côté(-ci), en deçà, de qch.; **on that s. of sth.,** de ce côté-là, au delà, de qch.; **on the other s. (of sth.),** de l'autre côté (de qch.); **with a dog on either s.,** flanqué de deux chiens; **on both sides,** des deux côtés, de part et d'autre; **on all sides, on every s.,** de tous (les) côtés; partout; **on the left hand, right hand, s.,** à (main) gauche, droite; **on the south s.,** du côté sud; **to be on the wrong s. of forty,** avoir quarante ans sonnés; **the tower leans on, to, one s.,** la tour penche d'un côté; **to put sth. on, to, one s.,** mettre, laisser, qch. de côté; mettre qch. à l'écart; **to take s.o. on, to, one s.,** prendre qn à part, en particulier; **to stand on, to, one s.,** se tenir à l'écart, à part; **from all sides, from every s.,** de tous (les) côtés, de toutes parts; **from s. to s.,** d'un côté à l'autre, de-ci de-là; (*b*) *Bill:* **running s.,** effet *m* en tête, en avant; (*c*) *F:* **to put on s.,** se donner des airs; poser; (*d*) **to do a bit of gardening on the s.,** faire un peu de jardinage (pour qn) dans ses heures libres; *F:* **to make sth., a bit, on the s.,** se faire des petits à-côtés; **profits on the s.,** de la gratte; *P:* **to have a bit on the s.,** avoir une petite amie. **5.** (*a*) parti *m*; **to be on the right s.,** être du bon parti; **to take sides,** se ranger d'un côté; **to take sides with s.o., to take the s. of s.o.,** se ranger avec qn, du côté de qn; **he's on our s.,** il est avec nous, de notre parti, de notre côté; **to change sides,** changer de camp, virer de bord; *Pol: etc:* faire volte-face; **time's on our s.,** le temps travaille pour nous; *Jur:* **the other s.,** la partie adverse; (*b*) *Games:* équipe *f*, camp *m*; **to pick sides,** tirer les camps; **to let the s. down,** trahir, décevoir, ses amis, etc.; (*c*) (*lineage*) côté; **on his mother's s.,** du côté maternel, de sa mère. **6.** *attrib.* latéral, -aux; de côté; **s. entry, entrance,** entrée de côté; entrée latérale; **s. door,** porte latérale: *F:* **to enter a profession by the s. door,** entrer dans une profession par la petite porte; **s. street,** rue latérale, transversale; **s. road,** chemin latéral; route *f* secondaire; **s. view,** vue *f* de profil, de côté; **with a s. glance at her,** en la regardant de côté, du coin de l'œil; **s. face,** profil *m*; **s. issue,** question *f* d'importance, d'intérêt, secondaire; **the s. issues of a question,** les à-côtés d'une question; **s. effect,** effet *m*, réaction *f*, secondaire (d'un médicament, etc.); *O:* **s. dish,** entremets *m*, hors-d'œuvre *m inv*; **s. salad,** salade *f* (pour accompagner un bifteck, etc.); **s. drum,** tambour *m*; **s. pocket,** poche *f* de côté; **s. table,** petite table; desserte *f*; *NAm:* **s. chair,** chaise *f* (de salle à manger, etc.); *Ecc.Arch:* **s. chapel,** chapelle latérale; **s. aisle,** (i) *Ecc.Arch:* nef latérale; bas-côté *m*; (ii) *Th: etc:* passage latéral, de côté; **s. rail,** rambarde *f* (de navire); garde-fou *m* (de pont); *Gym:* **s. horse,** cheval *m* d'arçons; **s. whiskers,** favoris *mpl.*

side² *v.i.* **to s. with s.o.,** se ranger du côté de qn; faire cause commune avec qn; **to s. against s.o.,** prendre parti contre qn, se tourner contre qn.

sideboard ['saidbɔːd] *n.* **1.** *Furn:* buffet *m.* **2.** *F:* **sideboards,** favoris *mpl.*

sideburns ['saidbəːnz] *n.pl. F:* = SIDEBOARD 2.

sidecar ['saidkɑːr] *n.* **1.** side-car *m*, *pl.* side-cars (de motocyclette). **2.** *esp. NAm:* cocktail composé de cointreau, de cognac et de jus de citron.

sidekick ['saidkik] *n. F:* associé, -ée; camarade *mf*; copain, copine.

sidelight ['saidlait] *n.* **1.** *Phot: etc:* lumière *f* oblique, qui vient de côté; *Fig:* **to throw a s. on a subject,** (i) éclairer fortuitement un sujet; (ii) donner un aperçu indirect sur un sujet. **2.** *Const:* fenêtre latérale. **3. sidelights,** (i) *Aut:* feux *mpl* de position; (ii) *Nau: etc:* feux de côté.

sideline¹ ['saidlain] *n.* **1.** ligne latérale; *Fb: etc:* ligne de touche; **to be on the sidelines,** ne pas se mêler à une affaire; rester sur la touche. **2.** (*a*) occupation *f* secondaire; (*b*) *Com:* article *m* à côté.

sideline² *v.tr. NAm:* (*usu. passive*) **to be sidelined,** être mis, rester, sur la touche.

sidelong ['saidlɔŋ] **1.** *adv.* (se mouvoir) obliquement, de côté; (regarder qn) de côté, du coin de l'œil. **2.** *a.* (regard) oblique, de côté; **to give s.o. a s. glance,** regarder qn de côté, du coin de l'œil.

sidereal [sai'diəriəl] *a. Astr:* sidéral, -aux.

side-saddle ['saidsædl] **1.** *n.* selle *f* de dame, de femme. **2.** *adv.* **to ride s.-s.,** monter en amazone.

sideshow ['saidʃou] *n.* **1.** spectacle forain (à une foire). **2.** *F:* affaire *f* d'importance secondaire.

sideslip¹ ['saidslip] *n.* **1.** *Aut: Cy: Ski:* dérapage *m.* **2.** *Av:* glissade *f* (sur l'aile); glissement latéral.

sideslip² *v.i.* **1.** *Aut: Cy: Ski:* déraper. **2.** *Av:* glisser sur l'aile.

sidesman *pl.* **-men** ['saidzmən] *n.m. Ecc:* = marguillier adjoint.

side-splitting ['saidsplitiŋ] *a. F:* (*of joke*) tordant.

sidestep ['saidstep] **1.** *v.i.* faire un pas de côté; *Box: etc:* esquiver. **2.** *v.tr. F:* éviter (une question).

sidestroke ['saidstrouk] *n. Swim:* nage *f* sur le côté; marinière *f.*

sideswipe¹ ['saidswaip] *n. NAm:* coup *m* dans, sur, le côté (d'une voiture, etc.).

sideswipe² *v.tr. NAm:* donner un coup dans, cogner (le côté d'une voiture, etc.).

sidetrack¹ ['saidtræk] *n. Rail:* voie *f* de garage; voie secondaire.

sidetrack² *v.tr.* (*a*) garer (un train); aiguiller (un train) sur une voie de garage; (*b*) *Fig:* (i) détourner l'attention de (qn); (ii) remettre à plus tard (un projet, etc.); **to be, get, sidetracked,** (i) se détourner de son but; (ii) s'écarter de son sujet.

sidewalk ['saidwɔːk] *n. esp. NAm:* trottoir *m.*

sideways ['saidweiz] **1.** *adv.* de côté; de profil; latéralement; **to walk s.,** marcher en crabe. **2.** *a.* latéral, -aux; de côté; **s. motion,** mouvement latéral.

sidewinder ['saidwaindər] *n. Rept: U.S:* serpent à sonnettes cornu.

siding ['saidiŋ] *n. Rail:* (*a*) voie *f* de garage, d'évitement; (*b*) embranchement *m*; voie de raccordement (d'usine); **goods s.,** voie de chargement.

sidle ['saidl] *v.i.* **to s. along,** s'avancer de côté, de guingois; **to s. up to s.o.,** se couler auprès de qn.

siege [siːdʒ] *n. Mil:* siège *m*; **to lay s. to a town,** assiéger une ville; mettre le siège devant une ville; **to raise the s.,** lever le siège; **to declare a state of s.,** déclarer l'état de siège; *Hist:* **s. gun,** pièce *f* de siège.

Siena [si'enə] *Pr.n. Geog:* Sienne *f.*

sienna [si'enə] *n.* **1.** terre *f* de Sienne; **raw, burnt, s.,** terre de Sienne naturelle, brûlée. **2.** *a.* (*colour*) **s. (brown),** terre de Sienne *inv.*

sierra [si'erə] *n. Geog:* sierra *f.*

siesta [si'estə] *n.* sieste *f*; **to take a s.,** faire la sieste.

sieve¹ [siv] *n.* (*with coarse mesh*) crible *m*; (*with fine mesh*) tamis *m*; (*for grain*) van *m*; sas *m*; **to pass sth. through a s.,** passer qch. au tamis, au crible; *F:* **he's got a memory like a s.,** il a une mémoire de lièvre.

sieve² *v.tr.* = SIFT 1.

sift [sift] **1.** *v.tr.* (*a*) passer (qch.) au tamis, au crible, au sas; tamiser, bluter (la farine); escarbiller (des cendres); vanner (le blé); cribler (du sable, etc.); **to s. sugar over a cake,** saupoudrer un gâteau de sucre; (*b*) examiner minutieusement, passer par l'étamine (des preuves); approfondir, éplucher (une question); **to s. (out) the facts,** passer les faits au crible. **2.** *v.i.* (*of dust, etc.*) filtrer (**through,** à travers). **sifting** *n.* (*a*) tamisage *m*, criblage *m*, sassement *m*, blutage *m* (de qch.); (*b*) examen minutieux (des preuves, etc.); démêlement *m* (du vrai et du faux).

sifter ['siftər] *n.* **1.** (*sieve*) tamis *m*, crible *m*; sas *m.*

2. saupoudroir *m* (à sucre).

sigh¹ [sai] *n.* soupir *m*; **heavy, deep, long(-drawn), s.,** gros, profond, long, soupir; **he breathed, heaved, a s. of relief,** il a poussé un soupir de soulagement; **with a s.,** en soupirant.

sigh² **1.** *v.i.* (*a*) soupirer, pousser un soupir; **to s. with relief,** pousser un soupir de soulagement; (*b*) *O:* **to s. for (sth., s.o.),** soupirer pour, après (qch.). **2.** *v.tr.* *Lit:* **to s. out,** prononcer (qch.) en soupirant. **sighing** *n.* soupirs *mpl*; *Lit:* plainte *f* (du vent).

sight¹ [sait] *n.* **1.** (*faculty*) vue *f*; (*a*) **to have good, bad, s.,** avoir la vue bonne, mauvaise; **to have long s.,** avoir la vue longue; être presbyte; **short s.,** myopie *f*; **s. testing,** examen *m* de la vue; **to lose one's s.,** perdre la vue; devenir aveugle; (*b*) **to catch s., get a s., of s.o., sth.,** apercevoir, entrevoir, qn, qch.; **to lose s. of s.o.,** perdre qn de vue; **to lose s. of the fact that . . .,** perdre de vue que . . .; **I can't bear the s. of him, I hate the very s. of him,** je ne peux pas le sentir, le voir; **to translate at s.,** traduire à première vue, à livre ouvert; **to shoot s.o. at, on, s.,** faire feu, tirer, sur qn à première vue; *Mus:* **to play at s.,** jouer à vue, déchiffrer; *Com: Fin:* **bill payable at s.,** effet *m* payable à vue; **at first s.,** à première vue; à, dès, l'abord; au premier abord; **to fall in love at first s.,** tomber amoureux à première vue (**with,** de); **it was a case of love at first s.,** c'était le coup de foudre; **to know s.o. by s.,** connaître qn de vue; *Tchn:* **s. check, control,** contrôle à vue, contrôle visuel; mirage *m*; (*c*) **to find favour in s.o.'s s.,** trouver grâce devant qn. **2.** (*range of vision*) **to come into s.,** (ap)paraître; **to be within s.,** être à portée de la vue; être en vue; **to be (with)in s. of land,** être en vue de (la) terre; **land in s.!** terre! **keep him in s.,** ne le perdez pas de vue; **out of s.,** caché aux regards; **to vanish out of s.,** disparaître; **to put sth. out of s.,** faire disparaître qch.; éloigner, cacher, qch.; **to keep out of s.,** se cacher, se dérober; **out of my s.!** hors de ma vue! hors d'ici! *Prov:* **out of s. out of mind,** loin des yeux, loin du cœur. **3.** *Opt:* (*a*) visée *f* (avec un instrument d'optique, une arme à feu, etc.); *Surv:* coup *m* de lunette; **angle of s.,** angle *m* de visée, de site; **line of s.,** (i) ligne *f* de visée (d'un instrument d'optique); (ii) ligne de mire, de tir (d'une arme à feu); **to take a s. on sth.,** viser, mirer, qch.; (*b*) appareil *m* de visée, de pointage (d'un instrument, d'une arme à feu); œilleton *m* (de viseur); lumière *f* (de sextant); *Artil: Sm.a:* **back, rear, s.,** hausse *f*; cran *m* de mire; **fore, front, s.,** guidon *m*; bouton *m* de mire; **telescopic s.,** hausse téléscopique, hausse à lunette; **to adjust sights,** prendre, régler, la hausse; *Fig:* **to lower one's sights,** viser moins haut, baisser ses prétentions. **4. s. (hole),** (i) *Opt:* lumière *f* (de pinnule, etc.); (ii) regard *m* (d'inspection, d'égout, etc.). **5.** (*a*) spectacle *m*; **sad s.,** spectacle navrant; **it's a s. to see,** cela vaut la peine d'être vu; **it was a s. for sore eyes,** c'était réjouissant à voir; (*b*) *F:* **his face was a s.,** si vous aviez vu son visage! **to make a s. of oneself,** se rendre ridicule; *esp.* se fagoter, s'affubler; **what a s. you are! you do look a s.!** comme vous voilà fait! de quoi avez-vous l'air! (*c*) chose digne d'être vue; **the sights,** (i) les sites *m* pittoresques; (ii) les monuments *m*, les curiosités *f* (de la ville, etc.). **6.** *F:* **not by a long s.,** loin de là; *P:* **he's a damn s. better,** il est de beaucoup mieux.

sight² *v.tr.* **1.** apercevoir (qn, qch.). **2.** viser, observer (un astre, etc.). **3.** pointer (un fusil); **to s. a gun,** viser. **sighted** *a.* **1.** qui voit; **the s.,** les voyants *mpl.* **2.** (*with adj. prefixed*) **long-s.,** presbyte; à la vue longue; **short-s.,** myope; **to be long-s.,** avoir la vue longue; **far-s.,** sagace, prévoyant. **sighting** *n.* **1.** vue *f*; *Ven:* **several sightings of teal have been reported,** on a vu des sarcelles à plusieurs reprises. **2.** visée *f* (avec un instrument d'optique, avec une arme à feu); pointage *m* (d'une arme à feu, etc.).

sightless ['saitlis] *a.* aveugle; (yeux) éteints.

sightlessness ['saitlisnis] *n.* cécité *f*.

sightly ['saitli] *a.* agréable à voir; **not very s.,** pas très beau à voir.

sight-read ['saitri:d] *v.tr. & i. Mus:* déchiffrer. **sight-reading** *n.* déchiffrage *m*.

sight(-)see ['saitsi:] *v.i.* visiter des sites pittoresques, les curiosités (d'une ville). **sightseeing** *n.* tourisme *m*; **we spent the day s.,** nous avons passé la journée à visiter le pays, les monuments.

sightseer ['saitsi:ər] *n.* touriste *mf*.

sign¹ [sain] *n.* **1.** signe *m*; (*a*) **to make a s., signs, to s.o.,** faire (un) signe, des signes, à qn; **s. of the cross,** signe de la croix; **to make the s. of the cross,** se signer; **s. language,** (langage *m*) mimique *f*; (*of the deaf*) langage par signes; (*b*) **s. of recognition,** signe de reconnaissance; *Mil:* **the s. and the countersign,** le mot d'ordre et le mot de ralliement; (*c*) *Tg:* **call s.,** indicatif *m* d'appel. **2.** (*a*) indice *m*, indication *f*; **sure s.,** indice certain; **it's a good, bad, s.,** c'est bon, mauvais, signe; **s. of the times,** marque *f*, signe, des temps; **as a s. of . . .,** en signe de . . .; **he gave no s. of having heard anything,** il n'a manifesté en aucune façon avoir rien entendu; (*b*) trace *f*; **no s. of . . .,** nulle, aucune, trace de . . .; **there is little s. of progress,** les progrès se font attendre; **the room showed signs of having been recently occupied,** la pièce révélait une occupation récente; **to show no s. of life,** ne donner aucun signe de vie, ne pas donner signe de vie; **there was no s. of him,** (i) on ne l'a pas aperçu; (ii) il restait invisible. **3.** (*a*) (*of pub, inn, etc.*) enseigne *f*; **at the s. of the Golden Lion,** à l'enseigne du Lion d'Or; **s. writer, painter,** peintre en lettres; peintre d'enseignes; (*b*) **(shop) s.,** enseigne, écriteau *m*; **illuminated, neon, s.,** enseigne, réclame *f*, au néon; (*c*) **road signs,** signalisation routière; **road s.,** panneau indicateur (de route); signal *m* de route; **traffic s.,** panneau de signalisation (routière); **advance warning s.,** panneau de présignalisation; (*d*) **s. of the zodiac,** signe du zodiaque; **lucky s.,** signe de chance. **4.** (*a*) symbole *m*; **positive, plus, s.,** signe positif; (signe) plus (*m*); **negative, minus, s.,** signe négatif; (signe) moins (*m*); (*b*) *Cmptr:* **s. digit,** chiffre *m* de signe.

sign² *v.tr.* **1.** (*a*) *A:* signer (qn, qch.); marquer (qn, qch.) d'un signe; (*b*) signer (son nom, un document, un chèque, etc.); viser (un compte); accepter (une traite); signer, passer (un contrat); **the letter was signed by the president,** la lettre portait la signature du président; *Jur:* **signed, sealed and delivered in presence of . . .,** fait et signé en présence de . . .; **s. here,** signez là! **to s. sth. away, over, to s.o.,** céder qch. par écrit à qn. **2.** *O:* **to s. assent,** faire signe que oui; **to s. (to, for) s.o. to do sth.,** faire signe à qn de faire qch. **signing** *n.* signature *f* (d'un document, etc.); passation *f* (d'un acte); acceptation *f* (d'une traite). **sign off** *v.i.* (*a*) (*of workers in factories*) se pointer au départ; (*b*) *W.Tel:* terminer l'émission (en jouant l'indicatif). **sign on** **1.** *v.tr.* embaucher (un ouvrier); engager (qn). **2.** *v.i.* (*a*) (*of workers*) s'embaucher; (*of soldier*) s'engager; (*b*) (*of workers in factories, etc.*) se pointer à l'arrivée; (*c*) *W.Tel:* commencer l'émission (en jouant l'indicatif); (*d*) *F:* s'inscrire au chômage. **sign up** **1.** *v.i.* s'inscrire à (un cours, etc.); (*of soldier*) s'engager. **2.** *v.tr. Sp: Th: etc:* donner un contrat à, engager (qn).

signal¹ ['sign(ə)l] *n.* **1.** (*sign*) signal, -aux *m*; signe *m*; **warning s.,** signal avertisseur, d'avertissement; **alarm s.,** signal d'alarme, d'alerte; **all clear s.,** signal de fin d'alerte; **time s.,** signal horaire; *Sp: etc:* **starting s.,** signal de, du, départ; *Tp:* **calling,** *U.S:* **line, s.,** indicatif *m* d'appel; **line engaged,** *U.S:* **busy, s.,** signal de ligne occupée; signal *pas libre*; **s. communications,** télécommunications *fpl*, transmissions *fpl*; **to give, send, receive, a s.,** faire, envoyer, recevoir, un signal. **2.** (*a*) **traffic signals,** feux *mpl* de circulation; *NAm:* **s. red,** vermillon chinois; **light s.,** signal lumineux; *Nau:* **flashing (light) s.,** signal à éclats, par scott; **s. light,** (i) *Nau:* fanal, -aux *m*; (ii) (lampe) témoin (*m*); **s. lamp,** (i) lampe *f*, projecteur *m*, de signalisation; (ii) (lampe) témoin; voyant (lumineux); **arm, hand, s.,** signal à bras; **semaphore s.,** signal sémaphorique, *Navy:* à bras; **flag s.,** signal (i) *Mil:* par fanion(s), (ii) *Nau:* à pavillon, (iii) *Rail:* par drapeau; **s. flag,** (i) *Mil:* fanion *m* de signalisation; (ii) *Nau:* pavillon *m* pour signaux; (iii) *Rail:* drapeau *m* (de signalisation); **Morse signals,** signaux Morse; **s. flare,** (i) fusée éclairante; (ii) bengale *m*; **s. rocket,** fusée de signalisation; fusée-signal *f*, *pl.* fusées-signaux; *Nau:* **s. book,** livre *m* des signaux; (*b*) *Rail:* **disc s.,** disque *m*; **distant s.,** signal à distance, signal avancé; **home s.,** signal rapproché; **stop s.,** signal d'arrêt immédiat; **s. box,** poste *m* d'aiguillage. **3.** *Elcs: W.Tel: etc:* **input, output, s.,** signal d'entrée, de sortie. **4.** (*a*) *Mil:* **s. officer,** officier *m* des transmissions; (*b*) *Navy:* **yeoman of signals,** maître-timonier *m*, *pl.* maîtres-timoniers.

signal² *v.* **(signalled,** *NAm:* **signaled) 1.** *v.i.* donner un signal, faire des signaux **(to,** à); **I signalled to him (to stop),** je lui ai fait signe (de s'arrêter); *Aut:* **to s. before stopping,** prévenir, avertir, avant de s'arrêter. **2.** *v.tr.* (*a*) signaler (un train, un navire); (*b*) transmettre (un ordre); *Aut:* **to s. that one is turning,** signaler un changement de direction. **signalling** *NAm:* **signaling** *n.* (*a*) signalisation *f*; avertissement *m*; transmission *f* de signaux; *Nau:* timonerie *f*; **s. flag,** (i) *Mil:* fanion *m* de signalisation; (ii) *Nau:* pavillon *m* pour signaux; (iii) *Rail:* drapeau *m* (de signalisation); (*b*) balisage *m* (d'une route, etc.); (*c*) *coll.* signaux *mpl*.

signal³ *a.* (service) signalé, insigne; (succès) éclatant, remarquable; (faveur) insigne; (échec) notoire. **-ally** *adv.* remarquablement; d'un façon éclatante.

signalize ['signəlaiz] *v.tr.* signaler, marquer (une victoire, un succès).

signaller ['signələr] *n.* signaleur *m*.

signalman *pl.* **-men** ['signəlmən] *n.m.* signaleur; sémaphoriste; *Navy:* timonier; *Rail:* bloqueur.

signatory ['signət(ə)ri] *a.* & *n.* signataire (*mf*) **(to a treaty,** d'un traité).

signature ['signətjər] *n.* **1.** signature *f*; *Adm:* visa *m*; **to put one's s. to a letter,** apposer sa signature à une lettre; **his s. was on the letter,** la lettre portait sa signature; *Com: etc:* **for s.,** pour signature; *W.Tel: T.V:* **s. tune,** indicatif (musical) (d'une émission). **2.** *Typ:* (*a*) signature (d'un cahier); (*b*) cahier (d'imprimerie). **3.** *Mus:* **key s.,** armature *f* (de la clef).

signboard ['sainbɔːd] *n.* enseigne *f* (d'auberge).

signet ['signit] *n.* cachet *m*; **s. ring,** (i) (*for sealing*) anneau *m* sigillaire, (ii) (bague) chevalière (*f*).

significance [sig'nifikəns] *n.* **1.** signification *f* (d'un mot, d'un geste, etc.); **what is the s. of this ceremony?** que signifie cette cérémonie? **look of deep s.,** regard très significatif. **2.** importance *f*, portée *f*; **event of no, of great, s.,** événement sans importance, de la plus haute importance.

significant [sig'nifikənt] *a.* **1.** (mot, geste, regard) significatif. **2.** *Mth:* **s. figure,** chiffre significatif. **3.** (événement, etc.) important, de grande portée. **-ly** *adv.* (*a*) (regarder, etc.) d'une manière significative; (*b*) **s. cheaper,** sensiblement moins cher.

signification [signifi'keiʃ(ə)n] *n.* signification *f*, sens *m* (d'un mot, etc.); *Ling:* signifié *m*.

significative [sig'nifikətiv] *a.* significatif **(of,** de).

signify ['signifai] **1.** *v.tr.* (*a*) signifier; être (le) signe de (qch.); **a broad forehead signifies intelligence,** un front large est (un) signe d'intelligence; (*b*) signifier, vouloir dire; (*c*) signifier, faire connaître (ses intentions, etc.). **2.** *v.i.* importer; **it doesn't s.,** cela n'a aucune importance; peu importe.

signpost¹ ['sainpoust] *n.* (*a*) poteau indicateur; (*b*) *Fig:* indication *f*.

signpost² *v.tr.* marquer de poteaux indicateurs; **well, badly, signposted road,** route dont la signalisation est bonne, mauvaise. **signposting** *n.* signalisation *f* des routes.

Sikh [siːk] *a.* & *n.* *Rel:* sikh, -e.

silage ['sailidʒ] *n.* *Agr:* fourrage ensilé.

silence¹ ['sailəns] *n.* silence *m*; (*a*) **there was a sudden s.,** il s'est fait un silence subit; **to keep s.,** garder le silence; se taire; **to break (the) s.,** rompre le silence; **to reduce s.o. to s.,** réduire qn au silence; faire taire qn; **to suffer in s.,** souffrir en silence; **s.!** (du) silence! (*notice in library, etc.*) défense *f* de parler; *Prov:* **s. is golden,** le silence est d'or; (*b*) **to write to s.o. after five years' s.,** écrire à qn après un silence de cinq ans; **to pass over sth. in s.,** passer qch. sous silence; (*c*) **the s. of the night,** le silence de la nuit.

silence² *v.tr.* (*a*) réduire (qn) au silence; imposer silence à (qn); faire taire (qn, sa conscience); étouffer (les plaintes); faire cesser, faire taire (le feu de l'ennemi); (*b*) amortir, étouffer (un bruit); *I.C.E:* assourdir (l'échappement).

silencer ['sailənsər] *n.* *Sm.a:* silencieux *m*; *I.C.E:* silencieux, pot *m* d'échappement.

silent ['sailənt] *a.* **1.** silencieux; (*a*) **to keep s.,** (i) observer le silence; (ii) garder le silence, se taire **(about,** sur); se tenir coi, coite; **to remain s.,** rester muet; **be s.!** taisez-vous! **s. as the grave,** muet comme la tombe; *Ecc:* **s. orders,** ordres (religieux) qui gardent le silence; **s. majority,** majorité silencieuse; **s. sorrow,** douleur muette; (*b*) (homme) silencieux, taciturne, peu loquace; (*c*) *Com:* **s. partner,** (associé *m*) commanditaire *m*; bailleur *m* de fonds. **2.** (*a*) silencieux, insonore; **s. footsteps,** des pas silencieux; (*b*) *Ling:* (lettre) muette; **the k is s.,** le k ne se prononce pas, le k est muet. **-ly** *adv.* silencieusement, en silence.

silex ['saileks] *n.* *Miner:* silex *m*.

silhouette¹ [silu(:)'et] *n.* (*a*) silhouette *f*; **in s.,** (voir qn) en silhouette; (*b*) ombre chinoise.

silhouette² *v.tr.* silhouetter, projeter en silhouette; **to be silhouetted against a light background,** se détacher (en silhouette), sur un fond clair.

silica ['silikə] *n.* *Ch:* silice *f*.

silicate ['silikət] *n.* *Ch:* silicate *m*.

siliceous [si'liʃəs] *a.* *Ch:* siliceux.

silicon ['silikən] *n.* *Ch:* silicium *m*; **s. chip,** puce *f*, pastille *f*, de silicium.

silicone ['silikoun] *n.* *Ch:* silicone *f*.

silicosis [sili'kousis] *n.* *Med:* silicose *f*.

silk [silk] *n.* **1.** soie *f*; (*a*) **raw s.,** soie grège, écrue; **s. waste, waste s.,** bourre *f* de soie; (fils de) schappe *m or f*; **s. yarn,** fil *m* de soie; **sewing s.,** soie à coudre; **s. stockings,** bas *mpl* de, en, soie; **a black s. dress,** une robe de soie noire; **s. culture,** sériciculture *f*; (*b*) *Tex:* **wild s.,** soie sauvage; **artificial s.,** rayonne *f*; **s. fabric(s), silk(s),** soierie *f*; **s. finish,** similisage *m*; **s. screen printing, process,** sérigraphie *f*. **2.** (*a*) *Turf:* **silks,** casaque *f* (de jockey); (*b*) *Jur:* **to take s.,** être nommé conseiller du roi, de la reine; (*c*) *Jur: F:* (i) conseiller *m* du roi, de la reine; (ii) *coll.* les conseillers du roi, de la reine.

silken ['silk(ə)n] *a.* *Lit:* **1.** soyeux; (boucles) de soie. **2.** (*of voice, words*) doucereux, mielleux.

silkiness ['silkinis] *n.* **1.** nature soyeuse (d'un tissu). **2.** moelleux *m* (de la voix, des paroles).

silkworm ['silkwəːm] *n.* ver *m* à soie; **s. moth,**

bombyx *m* (mori, du mûrier); **s. breeder,** séricículteur *m*, magnanier, -ière; **s. breeding,** sériciculture *f*, magnanerie *f*; **s. nursery, farm,** magnanerie.

silky ['silki] *a.* (*a*) soyeux; (*b*) **s. voice,** voix moelleuse; (*c*) *Pej:* doucereux, mielleux.

sill [sil] *n.* (*a*) *Const: etc:* sole *f*, semelle *f* (de cadre); seuil *m* (de porte); (*b*) rebord *m*, appui *m*, tablette *f* (de fenêtre); (*c*) *Hyd.E:* seuil, radier *m* (d'écluse).

sillabub ['siləbʌb] *n. Cu:* entremets sucré semblable au sabayon.

silliness ['silinis] *n.* sottise *f*, bêtise *f*, niaiserie *f*.

silly ['sili] **1.** *a.* (*a*) (*of pers.*) sot, *f.* sotte; stupide, bête; **don't be so s.!** ne sois pas si bête, si stupide! ne fais pas le sot, la sotte! **(you) s. fool, ass!** imbécile! idiot(e)! **it would make me look s.,** j'aurais l'air bien bête, stupide, ridicule; (*b*) (question, réponse) stupide, ridicule; **that was a s. thing to do!** ça, ce, n'était pas très intelligent! **to say sth. s.,** dire une bêtise; *Journ: F:* **the s. season,** l'époque des vacances (dépourvue de nouvelles sérieuses); (*c*) **to knock s.o. s.,** étourdir, assommer, qn. **2.** *n. F:* sot, sotte; idiot, -ote; niais, -aise.

sillybilly ['sili'bili] *n. F:* (*to child*) idiot, -ote, imbécile *mf*.

silo ['sailou] *n.* (*a*) *Agr:* silo *m*; (*b*) *Ball:* **launching s.,** puits *m*, silo, de lancement.

silt[1] [silt] *n.* dépôt (vaseux), vase *f*, limon *m* (dans un chenal, etc.); (apports *mpl* de) boue *f*.

silt[2] *v.* **to s. (up). 1.** *v.tr.* envaser (un port, un canal). **2.** *v.i.* (*of harbour, etc.*) s'envaser; se combler. **silting** *n.* (*a*) *Min: Petr:* embouage *m* (d'une galerie, etc.); (*b*) **s. (up),** envasement *m*.

silver[1] ['silvər] *n.* **1.** argent *m*. **2.** *attrib.* (*a*) (médaille, cuillère) d'argent; (encrier) en argent; **he was born with a s. spoon in his mouth,** il est né coiffé; **s. plate,** doublé *m* d'argent; plaqué *m* (d')argent; **to s.-plate sth.,** argenter qch.; **s.-plated,** argenté; (en) doublé, (en) plaqué, d'argent; **s. plating,** argenture *f*; **s. gilt,** vermeil *m*; **s. paper,** papier d'étain; papier argenté, d'argent; *Ch:* **s. bromide,** bromure *m* d'argent; (*b*) argenté; **s. haired,** aux cheveux argentés; **s. grey,** gris argenté *inv*; *Lit:* (*of voice, etc.*) **s.-toned,** argentin; **s. wedding,** noces *fpl* d'argent; *Z:* **s. fox,** renard argenté. **3. s. (money),** argent monnayé; **s. coin,** (i) pièce *f* d'argent; (ii) *coll.* (pièces d')argent; **a pound in s.,** une livre en argent, en pièces, en monnaie, d'argent. **4.** *coll.* argenterie *f* (de table).

silver[2] *v.tr.* (*a*) argenter (des couverts, etc.); (*b*) étamer (un miroir); (*c*) *Lit:* argenter (les flots, etc.).

silverfish ['silvəfiʃ] *n.* **1.** *Ich:* argentine *f*. **2.** *Ent:* lépisme *m*; poisson *m* d'argent.

silverside ['silvəsaid] *n. Cu:* gîte *f* à la noix.

silversmith ['silvəsmiθ] *n.* orfèvre *m*.

silverware ['silvəwɛər] *n.* argenterie *f* (de table).

silverwork ['silvəwəːk] *n.* orfèvrerie *f*.

silvery ['silvəri] *a.* (*a*) (nuage, flot) argenté; (écailles, etc.) d'argent; (*b*) (rire, timbre) argentin.

simian ['simiən] **1.** *a.* simiesque, simien. **2.** *n. Z:* anthropoïde *m*; **the simians,** les simiens *mpl*.

similar ['similər] *a.* (*a*) semblable, pareil, ressemblant, analogue (**to,** à); similaire; **your case is s. to mine,** votre cas est semblable au mien; (*b*) *Mth:* (triangles) semblables. **-ly** *adv.* pareillement, semblablement.

similarity [simi'læriti] *n.* ressemblance *f*, similitude *f*, similarité *f*; *Mth:* similitude (de triangles).

simile ['simili] *n.* comparaison *f*; similitude *f*.

similitude [si'militju(ː)d] *n.* **1.** ressemblance *f*, similitude *f*. **2.** (*a*) comparaison *f*; (*b*) allégorie *f*.

simmer[1] ['simər] *n. Cu: O:* **to keep sth. at a s., on the s.,** (faire) mijoter qch.

simmer[2] **1.** *v.i.* (*a*) (*of liquid*) frémir, mitonner; (*of food in pot*) mijoter, cuire à petit feu, à feu doux; (*b*) (*of revolt, etc.*) fermenter; **he was simmering with rage,** il était prêt à éclater de colère; (*of pers.*) **to s. down,** s'apaiser peu à peu; se calmer. **2.** *v.tr.* (faire) mijoter (un ragoût, etc.). **simmering** *n.* **1.** frémissement *m* (d'un liquide); cuisson *f* à petit feu, à feu doux. **2.** ferment *m* (de révolte, etc.).

simnel ['simn(ə)l] *n.* **s. (cake),** gâteau *m* de Pâques, de la mi-carême.

simony ['saiməni] *n. Ecc:* simonie *f*.

simper[1] ['simpər] *n.* sourire affecté, minaudier.

simper[2] *v.i.* minauder, mignarder; sourire avec affectation. **simpering 1.** *a.* minaudier, mignard, affecté. **2.** *n.* minauderie *f*.

simple ['simpl] **1.** *a.* (*a*) simple, naturel (de caractère); **to have s. tastes,** avoir des goûts simples; **the s. life,** la vie simple; (*b*) (i) simple, naïf, crédule; (ii) bête, niais; **s. hearted,** simple, ingénu, candide; **s.-minded,** simple (d'esprit); naïf, candide; **s.-mindedness,** simplicité *f* (d'esprit, de caractère); naïveté *f*, candeur *f*; **she's a s. soul,** elle est candide, naïve; **I'm not so s. as to believe that,** je ne suis pas assez simple pour croire cela; je n'ai pas la naïveté de croire cela; (*c*) (méthode, etc.) simple, élémentaire; **to become s., simpler,** se simplifier; **it's as s. as ABC, as falling off a log,** c'est simple comme bonjour; (*d*) (fleur, *Med:* fracture) simple; *Com:* **s. interest,** intérêts simples; *Gram:* **s. sentence,** proposition indépendante; **that's the plain and s. truth,** c'est la vérité pure et simple. **2.** *n. Bot: A:* simple *m*, herbe médicinale. **-ply** *adv.* **1.** (parler, agir) simplement; (vêtu) avec simplicité. **2.** (*a*) absolument; **I s. won't do it,** je refuse absolument de le faire; **I was s. amazed by it,** j'en étais tout à fait abasourdi; (*b*) uniquement; tout simplement; **purely and s.,** purement et simplement; **it's s. a matter of time,** c'est une simple question de temps.

simpleness ['simpəlnis] *n.* (*a*) candeur *f*, simplicité *f* (d'un enfant, etc.); (*b*) bêtise *f*, niaiserie *f*.

simpleton ['simp(ə)ltən] *n.* nigaud, -aude, niais, -aise.

simplicity [sim'plisiti] *n.* **1.** (*a*) candeur *f*, simplicité *f* (d'un enfant, etc.); (*b*) bêtise *f*, sottise *f*. **2.** (*a*) simplicité (d'un problème, etc.); **it's s. itself,** c'est simple comme bonjour; (*b*) absence *f* de recherche, simplicité (dans la tenue).

simplification [simplifi'keiʃ(ə)n] *n.* simplification *f*.

simplify ['simplifai] *v.tr.* simplifier (un raisonnement, un calcul, etc.); apporter des simplifications à (un procédé).

simplistic [sim'plistik] *a.* simpliste.

simulacrum *pl.* **-a** [simju'leikrəm, -ə] *n.* simulacre *m*, semblant *m*.

simulate ['simjuleit] *v.tr.* simuler, feindre (une maladie, etc.); affecter (de l'enthousiasme, etc.); imiter l'apparence de (qn, qch.); prendre l'aspect de (qn, qch.).

simulation [simju'leiʃ(ə)n] *n.* (*a*) simulation *f*, feinte *f*; (*b*) *Tchn:* simulation; **flight s.,** simulation de vol.

simulator ['simjuleitər] *n.* (*a*) simulateur, -trice; (*b*) *Tchn:* simulateur; **flight s.,** simulateur de vol.

simultaneity [siməltə'niːiti] *n.* simultanéité *f*.

simultaneous [siməl'teiniəs] *a.* (*a*) simultané; **s. translation,** traduction simultanée; (*b*) **s. with . . .,** qui a lieu en même temps que . . .. **-ly** *adv.* simultanément; en même temps (**with,** que).

sin[1] [sin] *n.* (*a*) péché *m*; **original s.,** péché originel; **the seven deadly sins,** les sept péchés capitaux; **the forgiveness of sins,** le pardon des offenses *fpl*; **to live in s.,** vivre en concubinage; **to die in s.,** mourir dans le péché; *F:* **for my sins, I was appointed . . .,** pour mes péchés j'ai été nommé . . .; *F:* **like s.,** furieusement, violemment; (*b*) *F:* offense (contre le goût, etc.).

sin[2] *v.i.* **(sinned)** (*a*) pécher; commettre un péché, des péchés; (*b*) **to s. against,** pécher contre, blesser (les convenances); manquer à (une règle, etc.); (*c*) (*of* *pers.*) **more sinned against than sinning,** plus à plaindre qu'à blâmer. **sinning** *n.* le péché.

Sinai ['sainai] *Pr.n. Geog:* Sinaï *m*; **the S. Peninsula,** la presqu'île de Sinaï; **Mount S.,** le mont Sinaï.

since [sins] **1.** *adv.* depuis; (*a*) **I've not seen him s.,** je ne l'ai pas revu depuis; **he's been in perfect health ever s.,** depuis (lors), sa santé a été parfaite; (*b*) *O:* (*ago*) **many years s.,** il y a bien des années; **long s.,** (i) depuis longtemps; (ii) il y a longtemps; **not long s.,** il n'y a pas très longtemps; **how long s.?** depuis combien? **2.** *prep.* depuis; **s. his death,** depuis sa mort; **s. early June,** dès les premiers jours de juin; **I've been here (ever) s. lunch,** je suis là depuis le déjeuner; **s. then, s. that time,** depuis ce temps-là, depuis lors; **s. when?** depuis quand? *F:* **s. when do you come into a room without knocking?** depuis quand est-il permis d'entrer sans frapper? **s. seeing you,** depuis que je vous ai vu. **3.** *conj.* (*a*) depuis que; que; **s. I've been here,** depuis que je suis ici; **it's a long time s. I saw her,** il y a longtemps que je ne l'ai vue; je ne l'ai pas vue depuis longtemps; **(ever) s. I have lived in London,** depuis que j'habite Londres; (*b*) puisque; **I'll do it s. I must,** je le ferai puisqu'il le faut.

sincere [sin'siər] *a.* (*a*) sincère; franc, *f.* franche; **he is completely s.,** il est de bonne foi; (*b*) (sentiment) sincère. **-ly** *adv.* sincèrement; *Corr:* **yours s.,** veuillez agréer, Monsieur, etc., l'expression de mes sentiments distingués, les meilleurs.

sincerity [sin'seriti] *n.* sincérité *f*; bonne foi; **in all s.,** de la meilleure foi du monde; en toute sincérité.

sine [sain] *n. Mth:* sinus *m* (d'un angle).

sinecure ['sainikjuər] *n.* sinécure *f.*

sinew ['sinju:] *n.* **1.** *Anat:* tendon *m*; *Cu:* (*in meat*) croquant *m*, tirant *m*. **2. sinews,** nerf *m*, force *f*, vigueur *f*; **the sinews of war,** le nerf de la guerre.

sinewy ['sinju(:)i] *a.* **1.** (*of meat*) tendineux. **2.** (bras, etc.) musclé, nerveux, vigoureux.

sinful ['sinf(u)l] *a.* (*a*) (plaisir) coupable; **s. person,** pécheur, *f.* pécheresse; **it is s. to . . .,** c'est un péché de . . .; **s. world,** monde de pécheurs; (*b*) (acte) criminel; (gaspillage) scandaleux. **-fully** *adv.* (*a*) d'une façon coupable; (*b*) scandaleusement.

sinfulness ['sinf(u)lnis] *n.* **1.** caractère criminel (d'un acte); culpabilité *f*. **2.** le péché.

sing [siŋ] *v.* (*p.t.* **sang** [sæŋ]; *p.p.* **sung** [sʌŋ]) **1.** *v.tr. & i.* (*a*) chanter (un air, une chanson); **to s. up,** chanter plus fort; **s. me a song!** chante-moi une chanson! **to s. in tune,** chanter juste; **to s. out of tune,** chanter faux; détonner; *F:* **to s. small,** (i) déchanter; rabattre de ses prétentions; (ii) filer doux; **to s. another, a different, tune,** changer de ton; **to s. s.o. to sleep,** endormir qn en chantant; chanter pour endormir qn; **to s. out an order,** crier un ordre; (*b*) **to s. s.o.'s praises,** chanter les louanges de qn. **2.** *v.i.* (*a*) (*of the wind, etc.*) siffler; (*of the ears*) tinter, bourdonner; **the kettle is singing,** la bouilloire chante; (*b*) *F:* informer contre qn; moucharder; (*c*) *F:* **s. out if you need me,** appelez si vous avez besoin de moi. **singing 1.** *a.* qui chante; (oiseau, etc.) chanteur. **2.** *n.* (*a*) chant *m* (de qn, d'un oiseau, etc.); **s. lesson,** leçon *f* de chant; (*b*) sifflement *m* (du vent, etc.).

singable ['siŋəbl] *a.* chantable.

Singapore [siŋə'pɔ:r] *Pr.n. Geog:* Singapour *m.*

singe¹ [sindʒ] *n.* **s. (mark),** légère brûlure; roussissement *m*, roussissure *f* (sur le linge, etc.).

singe² *v.tr.* **1.** brûler (qch.) légèrement; roussir (du linge, etc.); **to s. one's wings,** se brûler les doigts. **2.** flamber (une volaille, les cheveux); *Tex:* **to s. (off) cloth,** griller l'étoffe. **singeing** *n.* flambage *m* (d'une volaille, etc.); roussissement *m* (du linge); *Tex:* grillage *m* (d'un tissu).

singer ['siŋər] *n.* **1.** chanteur, *f.* chanteuse, (*operatic, etc.*) cantatrice.

Singhalese [siŋgə'li:z] *a. & n.* = SINHALESE.

single¹ ['siŋgl] *n.* **1.** *Ten: etc:* simple *m*, single *m*; **men's, women's, singles,** simple messieurs, dames. **2.** (*a*) *Rec:* disque *m* 45 tours; (*b*) billet *m* simple; aller *m* (simple); (*c*) billet (de banque) d'une livre, *NAm:* d'un dollar; (*d*) *U.S:* maison *f*, appartement *m*, pour une seule personne, pour une seule famille.

single² *a.* **1.** seul, unique; **not a s. one,** pas un seul; pas un; **(one) s. case,** un cas unique; **I haven't seen a s. soul,** je n'ai pas vu âme qui vive; **don't say a s. word,** ne dites pas un seul mot, un traître mot; **s. sum,** somme payée en une fois; **s.-track railway, s. line,** chemin de fer à voie unique; *Aut:* **s.-line traffic only,** circulation *f* à sens unique (alterné); **I did it s. handed,** je l'ai fait tout seul, à moi seul; **to sail s. handed,** naviguer seul; **s.-breasted jacket,** veston droit; *Aut: etc:* **s.-cylinder engine,** moteur *m* monocylindrique; **s.-engined aircraft,** (avion *m*) monomoteur *m*; **s.-deck bus, s.-decker (bus),** autobus *m* sans impériale; *El:* **s.-phase current,** courant uniphasé, monophasé; (*b*) individuel, particulier; **s. parts,** pièces détachées (d'une machine); **every s. day,** tous les jours. **2.** (*a*) (lit) à une place, pour une personne; (chambre) à un lit, pour une personne; *Nau:* (cabine) individuelle; **s. seater,** (i) (voiture *f*) monoplace *f*; (ii) (avion *m*) monoplace *m*; **in s. rank,** sur un rang; *Bot:* **s. flower,** fleur simple; (*b*) (*of pers.*) célibataire; non marié(e); **a s. man, woman,** un, une, célibataire; **s. parent,** père *m*, mère *f*, célibataire; **he, she, is s.,** il, elle, ne s'est pas marié(e); **he remained s.,** il est resté célibataire, garçon; **she remained s.,** elle est restée célibataire, demoiselle. **3.** (*a*) **s. hearted,** sincère, honnête; (*b*) **s. minded,** constant (dans la poursuite d'un but); immuable (dans ses convictions, etc.); obstiné, résolu; **s. mindedness,** constance *f*; obstination *f*; résolution *f*; **s. mindedly,** avec constance; obstinément; résolument. **-gly** *adv.* **1.** séparément; un à un; **articles sold s.,** articles qui se vendent séparément, à la pièce. **2.** *O:* seul, sans aide.

single³ *v.tr. & ind.tr.* **to s. out s.o., sth.,** (i) choisir qn, qch.; (ii) remarquer, distinguer, qn, qch.

singleness ['siŋg(ə)lnis] *n.* **1.** sincérité *f*, probité *f* (du cœur, de l'esprit). **2.** (*a*) unicité *f*, unification *f* (d'une idée); (*b*) **with s. of purpose,** avec un seul but en vue.

singlet ['siŋglit] *n. Cost:* (*a*) maillot *m* de corps; gilet *m* (de coton, de flanelle); (*b*) *Sp:* maillot.

singleton ['siŋg(ə)ltən] *n. Cards: Mth:* singleton *m.*

singsong ['siŋsɔŋ] *n.* **1.** chant *m* monotone; ton chantant; psalmodie *f*; **to recite sth. in a s. (manner),** psalmodier qch.; **in a s. voice,** d'un ton traînant. **2.** *F:* concert improvisé (entre amis).

singular ['siŋgjulər] *a.* **1.** *Gram:* (nombre) singulier; *n.* **in the s.,** au singulier. **2.** (*a*) rare, remarquable; (*b*) singulier, bizarre. **-ly** *adv.* singulièrement; (*a*) remarquablement; (*b*) bizarrement.

singularity [siŋgju'læriti] *n.* singularité *f.* **1.** particularité *f.* **2.** bizarrerie *f.* **3.** exemple *m* unique, remarquable.

singularize ['siŋgjuləraiz] *v.tr.* singulariser.

Sinhalese [sin(h)ə'li:z] *Geog:* **1.** *a.* cing(h)alais. **2.** *n.* Cing(h)alais, -aise; (*b*) *Ling:* cing(h)alais *m.*

sinister ['sinistər] *a.* **1.** (*a*) (influence, présage, événement) sinistre; (*b*) (sourire) sinistre; (air) menaçant; **a man of s. appearance,** un homme de mauvaise mine. **2.** *Her:* senestre, sénestre.

sink¹ [siŋk] *n.* **1.** (*a*) évier *m* (de cuisine); **s. unit,** bloc-évier *m*, *pl.* blocs-éviers; **to pour (sth.) down the s.,** jeter (qch.) à l'égout; (*b*) *Fig:* **s. of iniquity,** cloaque *m*, sentine *f*, de tous les vices. **2.** *Geol: etc:* bétoire *f.*

sink² *v.* (*p.t.* **sank** [sæŋk]; *p.p.* **sunk** [sʌŋk], *A: & as adj.* **sunken** ['sʌŋkən]) **I.** *v.i.* **1.** aller au fond (des eaux); (*of ship*) sombrer, couler; (*of pers.*) **to s. like a stone,** couler à pic; **here goes! s. or swim!** allons-y! il faut risquer le tout pour le tout! *F:* **we're sunk,** nous sommes ruinés, fichus. **2.** (*a*) **to s. into (sth.),** (i) s'enfoncer dans (la boue, la neige); s'enliser dans (des sables mouvants); (ii) (*of words*) entrer dans (la mémoire); **his words are beginning to s. in,** ses paroles commencent à faire impression; **the lesson hasn't sunk in,** la leçon n'a pas été (i) apprise, (ii) (bien) comprise; (*b*) **to s. into oblivion,** tomber dans l'oubli; **sunk in thought,** plongé dans ses pensées; **to s. deep(er) into crime,** s'enfoncer dans le crime; **to s. into a deep sleep,** s'endormir profondément. **3.** (*subside*) (*a*) **to s. (down),** s'affaisser; (*of wall, building, etc.*) s'affaisser, se tasser, (*b*) (*of pers.*) **to s. (down) into an armchair,** se laisser tomber, s'effondrer, dans un fauteuil; **to s. to the ground,** (se laisser) tomber à terre; **his heart sank at the news,** à cette nouvelle son cœur s'est serré; **his spirits sank,** son courage s'est abattu. **4.** (*of ground, etc.*) descendre; s'abaisser; **the sun is sinking,** le soleil baisse. **5.** baisser (en valeur, en puissance); s'affaiblir, décliner; **prices are sinking,** les cours baissent, sont en baisse; **the patient is sinking fast,** le malade baisse, décline, rapidement; **his voice sank to a whisper,** sa voix s'est réduite à un murmure; **he has sunk in my estimation,** il a baissé, diminué, dans mon estime. **II.** *v.tr.* **1.** (*a*) couler, faire sombrer (un navire); envoyer (un navire) au fond; (*b*) mouiller (une mine). **2.** (faire) baisser (qch. à un niveau inférieur); enfoncer (un pieu, etc.); **stone sunk into the wall,** pierre encastrée dans le mur; **to s. one's teeth into sth.,** enfoncer ses dents dans qch.; *F:* **to s. a drink, a pint,** vider un pot; s'envoyer un demi. **3.** creuser, forer (un puits). **4.** supprimer (une objection, etc.); laisser de côté (son opinion, etc.); **they sank their differences,** ils ont fait table rase de leurs différends. **5.** *Fin:* éteindre, amortir (une dette). **6. to s. money in an undertaking,** (i) placer, (ii) engloutir, de l'argent dans une entreprise. **7. to s. the ball,** (i) *Bill:* mettre la bille dans la blouse; (ii) *Golf:* envoyer la balle dans le trou. **sinking 1.** *a.* qui s'enfonce, qui s'affaisse; (mur, etc.) qui se tasse; (navire) qui coule; **with a s. heart,** avec un serrement de cœur. **2.** *n.* (*a*) (i) enfoncement *m*; enlisement *m* (dans une fondrière, etc.); engloutissement *m* (d'un navire); (ii) (*in war*) torpillage *m* (d'un navire); (*b*) affaissement *m* (du sol, etc.); tassement *m* (d'un édifice, etc.); serrement *m* (du cœur); abattement *m* (des esprits); **that s. feeling,** ce sentiment de défaillance; (*c*) affaiblissement *m*, déclin *m* (des forces, etc.); abaissement (de la voix, etc.); (*d*) creusage *m*, forage *m* (d'un puits); (*e*) (i) amortissement *m*, extinction *f* (d'une dette); **s. fund,** fonds *m*, caisse *f*, d'amortissement; (ii) placement *m* (d'une somme) à fonds perdu. **sunken** *a.* (*a*) (rocher) submergé; (épave) sous-marine; (*b*) (*of cheeks*) creux; **s. eyes,** yeux creux, enfoncés; (*c*) (jardin, etc.) encaissé, en contrebas.

sinker ['siŋkər] *n.* **1.** (*pers.*) **well s.,** *Min:* **shaft s.,** foreur *m*; puisatier *m.* **2.** (*a*) *Navy:* crapaud *m* d'amarrage (d'une mine); (*b*) plomb *m* (d'une ligne de pêche); (*c*) *NAm: Cu: F:* beignet soufflé.

sinless ['sinlis] *a.* sans péché; innocent, pur.

sinner ['sinər] *n.* pécheur, *f*, pécheresse.

sinologist [s(a)i'nɔlədʒist] *n.* sinologue *mf.*

sinology [s(a)i'nɔlədʒi] *n.* sinologie *f.*

sinuosity [sinju'ɔsiti] *n.* sinuosité *f.*

sinuous ['sinjuəs] *a.* **1.** sinueux, tortueux. **2.** (*of pers.*) souple, agile.

sinus ['sainəs] *n. Anat:* sinus *m.*

sinusitis [sainə'saitis] *n. Med:* sinusite *f.*

Sioux [su:] *Ethn:* **1.** *a.* sioux *inv.* **2.** *n.* (*a*) Sioux *mf*; (*b*) *Ling:* sioux *m.*

sip¹ [sip] *n.* petite gorgée; petit coup; **to drink sth. in sips,** siroter, buvoter, qch.

sip² *v.tr. & i.* **(sipped)** boire à petites gorgées, à petits coups; siroter (qch.).

siphon¹ ['saif(ə)n] *n.* siphon *m.*

siphon² *v.tr.* siphonner (un liquide); *Fin:* **to s. off,** éponger, résorber (un excédent).

sir [sə:r, sər] *n.* **1.** (*a*) (*as form of address to a superior, esp. NAm: to an equal*) Monsieur *m*; **yes, s.,** (i) oui, monsieur; (ii) *Mil: etc:* (*to superior officer*) oui, mon capitaine, mon colonel, etc.; *Navy:* oui, commandant, amiral; **dinner is served, s.,** Monsieur est servi; (*b*) *Corr:* **Dear S.,** Monsieur; (*less formal*) Cher Monsieur; **Dear Sirs,** Messieurs; (*c*) *Sch: P:* **s. told me,** le maître me l'a dit. **2.** sir (titre d'un *baronet* et d'un *knight*; ne s'emploie jamais sans le prénom, ainsi Sir Walter Scott, Sir Walter).

sire¹ [saiər] *n.* **1.** (*a*) *A: & Lit:* père *m*; aïeul *m*; (*b*) *Breed:* père (en parlant des quadrupèdes); *esp.* étalon *m.* **2.** *A:* (*address to sovereign*) sire *m.*

sire² *v.tr.* (*of stallion, etc.*) engendrer, procréer (un poulain, etc.); être le père (d'un poulain, etc.).

siren ['saiərən] *n.* **1.** (*a*) *Myth:* sirène *f*; **s. song,** chant *m* de sirène; (*b*) *O:* tentatrice *f*; sirène. **2.** *Ind: Nau: etc:* sirène (d'usine, de navire, d'alarme).

sirloin ['sə:lɔin] *n. Cu:* aloyau *m* (de bœuf); faux-filet *m.*

sirocco [si'rɔkou] *n. Meteor:* siroc(c)o *m.*

sirup ['sirəp] *n. NAm:* sirop *m.*

sis [sis] *n.f. F:* (*sister*) sœurette; (petite) sœur.

sisal ['sais(ə)l] *n.* (*plant or fibre*) sisal *m.*

sissy ['sisi] *n. Pej:* (*a*) homme, garçon, efféminé; (*b*) enfant, etc., peureux; poule mouillée.

sister ['sistər] *n.f.* **1.** sœur; **s.-in-law,** belle-sœur. **2.** (*a*) *Ecc:* religieuse; sœur; **S. of Mercy,** sœur de la Charité; **come in, S.,** entrez, ma sœur; (*b*) (*in hospital*) **(ward) s.,** infirmière-major; **theatre s.,** infirmière-major qui fait le service de la salle d'opération. **3. s. nations,** nations sœurs; **s. company,** société sœur; **s. ships,** bâtiments *mpl* identiques; sister-ship *m.*

sisterhood ['sistəhud] *n.* communauté religieuse (de sœurs).

sisterly ['sistəli] *a.* de sœur; **in a s. fashion,** en sœur.

Sistine ['sisti:n, -tain] *a.* **the S. chapel,** la chapelle Sixtine.

sit¹ [sit] *n.* **come and have a s. down,** venez vous asseoir; **s.-down meal,** repas servi à table; *Ind:* **s.-down strike,** grève *f* sur le tas; **s.-in,** sit-in *m*; (grève avec) occupation *f* des locaux.

sit² *v.* (*p.t. & p.p.* **sat** [sæt]; *pr.p.* **sitting) I.** *v.i.* **1.** (*a*) (*of pers.*) s'asseoir; être assis, rester assis (dans un fauteuil, par terre, etc.); **we usually s. in the living room,** nous nous tenons d'ordinaire dans le salon; **where would you like me to s.? where shall I s.?** où dois-je me mettre, m'asseoir? **he was sitting reading,** il était assis à lire, en train de lire; **to s. at home,** se tenir chez soi; **to s. at (the) table,** s'asseoir, se mettre, à (la) table; s'attabler; **they were sitting at (the) table,** ils étaient (assis) à (la) table; ils étaient attablés; **we were sitting at lunch, dinner,** nous étions en train de déjeuner, de dîner; **he sits for hours over his books,** il passe des heures penché sur ses livres; **he sat through the whole play,** il est resté jusqu'à la fin de la pièce; *F:* **to s. tight,** (i) ne pas bouger de sa place; ne pas céder; (ii) avoir les pieds nickelés; *F:* **to s. on s.o.,** rabrouer qn; remettre qn à sa place; (*b*) **to s. for one's portrait,** poser pour son portrait; (*c*) **to s. for an examination,** passer, subir, un examen; (*d*) **to s. on the committee,** être du comité; **to s. in Parliament** = être député. **2.** (*of assemblies*) siéger; être en séance; **the court is sitting,** la séance est ouverte; *Jur:* (*of judge*) **to s. on a case,** juger une affaire; *F:* **to s. on a project,** laisser dormir un projet. **3.** (*a*) (*of bird*) (se) percher; être perché; (*b*) (*of hen*) **to s. (on eggs),** couver (des œufs). **4.** (*a*) (*of responsibility, etc.*) **to s.**

heavy on s.o., peser sur qn; **sorrow sits lightly on him,** la douleur ne l'accable pas, ne lui pèse pas; (*b*) *O:* (*of garment*) tomber (bien, mal). **II.** *v.tr.* **1. to s. a horse well, badly,** se tenir bien, mal, à cheval; avoir une bonne, mauvaise, assiette. **2. to s. a child on the table,** asseoir un enfant sur la table; **to s. a hen (on eggs),** mettre une poule à couver. **3.** passer (un examen). **sit back** *v.i.* (*a*) **to s. back in one's chair,** s'appuyer sur le dossier de sa chaise, son fauteuil; (*b*) *F:* se reposer, se relaxer; **to s. back and let the others do the work,** regarder les autres travailler. **sit down 1.** *v.i.* s'asseoir; prendre un siège; **please s. down,** asseyez-vous, je vous en prie; veuillez vous asseoir; **to s. down again,** se rasseoir; (*at table*) se remettre à (la) table; **to s. down at (the) table,** se mettre à table, s'attabler; **to s. down to a game of bridge,** s'installer pour faire une partie de bridge. **2.** *v.tr.* asseoir (un enfant, etc.); *F:* **s. yourself down!** asseyez-vous donc! **sit in** *v.i.* (*a*) faire grève avec occupation des locaux; (*b*) **to s. in on a rehearsal, a meeting,** assister à une répétition, une réunion (sans y participer). **sit out 1.** *v.i.* s'asseoir dehors; être assis dehors. **2.** *v.tr.* (*a*) ne pas prendre part à (un jeu, etc.); **to s. out a dance,** sauter une danse; manquer une danse; (*b*) rester (patiemment) jusqu'à la fin d'(une conférence, etc.). **sitting 1.** *a.* (*a*) assis; *Art:* **s. figure,** figure assise; (*b*) (*of tribunal, etc.*) siégeant; **s. tenant,** locataire *mf* en possession des lieux; *Parl:* **our s. member,** le député qui nous représente actuellement; (*c*) (i) (animal) au repos; (lièvre) au gîte; (faisan) au perché; (ii) **s. hen,** poule en train de couver. **2.** *n.* (*a*) (i) posture assise; **s. still,** immobilité *f*; **s. and standing room,** places assises et places debout; **s. up (late),** veille *f*; (*in house*) **s. room,** salon *m*; salle *f* de séjour; (ii) pose *f* (pour son portrait, etc.); **to paint a portrait in three sittings,** faire un portrait en trois séances *fpl*; (*b*) (i) (*for meals*) **first, second, s.,** premier, deuxième, service; **to serve 500 people in, at, one s.,** servir 500 personnes à la fois; **to write two chapters at one s.,** écrire deux chapitres d'un trait, d'un (seul) jet; (ii) séance, réunion *f* (d'une commission, etc.); **s. of a court,** audience *f*; **the sittings,** les (quatre) sessions *fpl* de l'année judiciaire; (*c*) *Husb:* (i) (*of hen*) couvaison *f*, incubation *f*; (ii) couvée *f* (d'œufs). **sit up 1.** *v.i.* (*a*) se tenir droit; se redresser (sur sa chaise); **s. up straight!** tiens-toi droit! *F:* **to make s.o. s. up,** étonner, épater, qn; (*b*) **to s. up,** se dresser, se mettre, sur son séant; (*of convalescent*) **he's beginning to s. up and take notice,** il est en train de se remettre; (*c*) (*of dog*) **to s. up (and beg),** faire le beau; (*d*) **to s. up (late),** veiller tard; **to s. up for s.o.,** (rester levé à) attendre qn; veiller en attendant le retour de qn; **to s. up with someone who is ill,** garder, veiller, un malade; (*e*) **to s. up to (the) table,** approcher sa chaise de la table. **2.** *v.tr.* **to s. s.o. up,** soulever qn pour l'asseoir.

site[1] [sait] *n.* **1.** emplacement *m*, situation *f* (d'un édifice, etc.); site *m* (archéologique, etc.); **camp(ing) s.,** (terrain *m* de) camping *m*; **launching s.,** aire *f* de lancement. **2. building s.,** (i) terrain à bâtir; (ii) chantier *m* (de construction); **on s.,** sur place; sur le tas; **to be on s.,** être à pied d'œuvre.

site[2] *v.tr.* placer, situer (un bâtiment, etc.).

sitter ['sitər] *n.* **1.** personne assise. **2.** personne qui pose (chez un artiste). **3.** *F:* **s.(-in),** gardien, -ienne, d'enfants. **4.** (*a*) (poule) couveuse *f*; (*b*) *Sp: F:* **to miss a s.,** rater un but tout fait.

situate ['sitjueit] *v.tr.* **1.** situer (une maison, etc.); **pleasantly situated house,** maison bien située. **2. awkwardly situated,** dans une situation, une position, embarrassante.

situation [sitju'eiʃ(ə)n] *n.* **1.** situation *f*, emplacement *m* (d'un édifice, d'une ville). **2.** situation (politique, etc.); **to explain the s.,** exposer la situation; **to find oneself in an unfortunate s.,** se trouver dans une déplorable conjoncture; *F:* **what's, how's, the coffee s.?** combien nous reste-t-il de café? **3.** *Th:* situation (dramatique); **s. comedy,** comédie de situation. **4.** emploi *m*, position *f*; **to get a s.,** obtenir un emploi; (*in advertisements*) **situations vacant, wanted,** offres *fpl*, demandes *fpl*, d'emplois.

sit-upon ['sitəpɔn] *n. F:* derrière *m*, postérieur *m*.

six [siks] **1.** *num. a & n.* (*a*) six (*m*); **number s.,** (le) numéro six; **twenty-s.,** vingt-six; **s. fours, four sixes, are twenty-four,** six fois quatre, quatre fois six, font vingt-quatre; **s. and a half,** six et demi; **at s. (o'clock),** à six heures; **at s. thirty,** à six heures et demie; **to be s. (years old),** avoir six ans; (*at dominoes, etc.*) **double s.,** double-six *m*, *pl.* doubles-six; *Cards:* **the s. of hearts,** le six de cœur; *F:* **it's s. of one and half a dozen of the other,** c'est blanc bonnet et bonnet blanc; c'est kif-kif; **we're all, everything's, at sixes and sevens,** tout est désorganisé, en pagaille; *F:* **to be s. feet under,** être enterré; (*b*) **s.-cylinder car,** une six cylindres; **s.-seater (car),** voiture *f* à six places; **s. day bicycle race,** les six jours *mpl.* **2.** *n. Cr:* six points (marqués par le batteur); *F:* **to knock s.o. for s.,** (i) étendre qn; (ii) abasourdir qn.

sixfold ['siksfould] **1.** *a.* sextuple. **2.** *adv.* six fois autant; au sextuple; **to increase s.,** sextupler.

six-foot ['siksfut] *a.* (poutre, etc.) de six pieds.

six-footer [siks'futər] *n.* homme (haut) de six pieds.

sixpence ['sikspəns] *n.* **1.** six pence. **2.** *A:* pièce *f* de six pence; **two and s.,** deux shillings et six pence.

sixpenny ['sikspəni] *attrib.a.* (*a*) (bonbon, etc.) qui coûte, qui vaut, six pence; (timbre) de six pence; (*b*) *A:* **s. piece, bit,** pièce *f* de six pence.

sixpennyworth [siks'peniwəθ] *n. O:* **to buy s. of chocolate,** acheter pour six pence de chocolat.

six-shooter [siks'ʃu:tər] *n.* revolver *m* à six coups.

six-sided [siks'saidid] *a.* qui a six côtés; hexagone.

sixteen ['siks(')ti:n] *num. a. & n.* seize (*m*); **she is s.,** elle a seize ans.

sixteenth ['siks(')ti:nθ] **1.** *num. a. & n.* seizième (*mf*); **Louis the S.,** Louis Seize; **(on) the s. (of August),** le seize (août); *Mus: NAm:* **s. note,** double croche *f*. **2.** *n.* (*fraction*) seizième *m*.

sixth [siksθ] **1.** *num. a. & n.* sixième (*mf*); **Henry the S.,** Henri Six; **(on) the s. (of December),** le six (décembre); *Sch:* **the s. form** = les classes terminales; **s. former** = élève *mf* des classes terminales; élève de la (classe de) première. **2.** *n.* (*a*) (*fraction*) sixième *m*; (*b*) *Mus:* sixte (majeure, mineure).

sixthly ['siksθli] *adv.* sixièmement; en sixième lieu.

sixtieth ['sikstiəθ] *num. a. & n.* soixantième (*mf*).

sixty ['siksti] *num. a. & n.* soixante (*m*); **s.-one,** soixante et un; **s.-third,** soixante-troisième; **about, some, s. books,** une soixantaine de livres; **he's in his sixties,** il a passé la soixantaine; **in the sixties,** pendant les années soixante (de notre siècle).

sixty-four [siksti'fɔ:r] *num. a. & n.* soixante-quatre (*m*); *F:* **the s.-f. (thousand) dollar question,** la question du gros lot; la question cruciale.

sizable ['saizəbl] *a.* = SIZEABLE.

size[1] [saiz] *n.* **1.** (*a*) grandeur *f*, dimension *f*, mesure *f*; étendue *f*; grosseur *f*, volume *m*; **of equal, the same, s., of a s.,** de (la) même grandeur, taille; **(in) all shapes and sizes,** (de) toutes (les) grandeurs; (de) toutes les grosseurs; **books arranged according to s.,** livres disposés par rang de taille; **the s. of an egg,** grand comme un œuf; **full s.,** grandeur naturelle; grandeur nature; **a town of that s.,** une ville de cette importance; *F:* **that's about the s. of it,** c'est à peu près cela; (*b*) *Ind:* cote *f*, dimensions; **standard s.,** cote d'origine; **to cut a piece to s.,** tailler une pièce à la dimension, à la cote; *F:* **to cut s.o. down to s.,**

rabaisser le caquet à qn; remettre qn à sa place. **2.** (*a*) taille *f*; **a boy half, twice, his s.**, un garçon deux fois moins grand, deux fois plus grand, que lui; (*b*) *Com:* taille (de vêtements); encolure *f* (de chemise); pointure *f* (de chaussures, de gants, de coiffures); **a s. larger, smaller,** une pointure au-dessus, au-dessous; **what s. do you take? what's your s.? what s. are you?** (*in dresses, etc.*) quelle est votre taille? (*in shoes*) quelle pointure chaussez-vous? **I've nothing in your s.,** je n'ai rien à votre taille, à votre pointure; **to try sth. for s.,** essayer qch. (pour voir si cela vous convient); (*c*) format *m* (d'un livre, de papier); (*d*) calibre *m* (d'un fusil, d'une cartouche).

size² *v.tr.* **1.** classer (des objets) par grosseur, par dimension. **2.** *Ind: etc:* (*a*) (*to gauge*) calibrer (une pièce); (*b*) (*to finish to size*) mettre (un trou, une pièce) à la cote, à dimensions; (*c*) **to s. sth. up,** jauger, prendre les dimensions de, qch.; *F:* **to s. s.o. up,** évaluer, jauger, qn. **sized** *a.* **1.** classé par ordre de grandeur, de taille. **2.** (*with adj. or adv. prefixed*) **fair s.,** assez grand; d'une grandeur raisonnable; **large, small, s.,** de grande, petite, taille; (livre, papier, etc.) de grand, petit, format; **medium s.,** de grandeur moyenne; de taille moyenne. **sizing** *n.* **1.** classement *m* par ordre de grandeur, de grosseur, de taille. **2.** (*a*) calibrage *m*; (*b*) (i) mise *f* à la cote, (ii) vérification *f* des dimensions (d'une pièce).

size³ *n. Tchn:* apprêt *m*; (*a*) colle *f*, encollage *m*; **animal s.,** colle animale; (*b*) *Tex:* empois *m*.

size⁴ *v.tr.* apprêter, coller, encoller (le papier, etc.); *Tex:* parer. **sizing** *n.* **1.** apprêtage *m*; collage *m*, encollage *m* (du papier, etc.); *Tex:* parage *m*. **2.** colle *f*; *Paint:* apprêt *m*.

sizeable ['saizəbl] *a.* d'une belle taille; assez grand, plutôt grand.

sizzle¹ ['sizl] *n.* grésillement *m* (de la friture, etc.).

sizzle² *v.i.* (*of frying pan, sausages, etc.*) grésiller. **sizzling 1.** *a.* grésillant. **2.** *adv.* **s. hot,** tout chaud; *F:* (jour) torride. **3.** *n.* grésillement *m*.

skate¹ [skeit] *n. Ich:* raie *f*; pocheteau *m*.

skate² *n.* patin *m*; **ice s.,** patin à glace; **roller s.,** patin à roulettes; *F:* **to get one's skates on,** se dépêcher.

skate³ *v.i.* patiner, faire du patin (sur glace); **to roller s.,** faire du skating; *F:* **to s. round sth.,** tourner autour du pot; **to s. over sth.,** effleurer un sujet. **skating** *n.* patinage *m* (sur glace); **roller s.,** skating *m*; **s. rink,** patinoire *f*; (*for roller skating*) skating.

skateboard¹ ['skeitbɔːd] *n. Sp:* planche *f* à roulettes; *F:* skate(board) *m*; *Fr.C: R.t.m:* rouli-roulant *m*.

skateboard² *v.i. Sp:* faire de la planche à roulettes, *F:* du skate, *Fr.C:* du rouli-roulant.

skater ['skeitər] *n.* patineur, -euse (sur glace); **roller s.,** qui fait du skating.

skedaddle¹ [ski'dædl] *n. F:* fuite (i) précipitée, (ii) en débandade.

skedaddle² *v.i. F:* (*a*) se sauver à toutes jambes; décamper, déguerpir; (*b*) s'enfuir à la débandade.

skeet [skiːt] *n. Sp:* **s. (shooting),** tir *m* au pigeon (d'argile); (genre de) ball-trap *m*.

skein [skein, skiːn] *n.* **1.** écheveau *m* (de soie, de laine); *Fig:* **(tangled) s.,** confusion *f*, embrouillamini *m*. **2.** vol *m* (d'oies sauvages).

skeletal ['skelit(ə)l] *a.* squelettique.

skeleton ['skelit(ə)n] *n.* **1.** squelette *m*, ossature *f* (d'homme, d'animal, de feuille, etc.); carcasse *f* (d'animal); *Fig:* **s. in the cupboard,** *NAm:* **in the closet,** secret honteux de la famille; **s. at the feast,** rabat-joie *m inv*, trouble-fête *m inv*; **he's a living s.,** c'est un vrai squelette; il n'a plus que la peau et les os. **2.** (*d*) charpente *f*, carcasse, squelette (d'un bâtiment, etc.); **s. key,** (clef *f* à) crochet *m* (de serrurier); fausse clef; rossignol *m*; (*b*) canevas *m*, esquisse *f* (d'un roman, etc.); *Surv:* **s. map,** carte muette; (*c*) **s. staff, crew,** personnel, équipage, réduit.

skeptic ['skeptik], *etc. n. NAm:* = SCEPTIC, *etc.*

sketch¹ [sketʃ] *n.* **1.** (*a*) *Art: Lit:* croquis *m*, esquisse *f*; **character s.,** portrait *m* littéraire; **first s.,** premier jet; **to make a s. of sth.,** faire le croquis de qch.; croquer qch.; **s. block,** bloc *m* à croquis; **s. map,** croquis; plan *m* sommaire (d'un terrain); (*b*) *Surv:* levé *m* (topographique). **2.** (*a*) exposé *m*, ébauche *f* (d'un projet); (*b*) *Th: T.V:* sketch *m*, saynète *f*.

sketch² *v.tr.* **1.** esquisser, dessiner à grands traits, croquer (un paysage, etc.); faire un, le, croquis de (qch.); **to s. in,** dessiner sommairement (des détails); **to s. out,** faire le canevas, l'esquisse, d'(un roman). **2. to s. (out),** esquisser, tracer (un projet, etc.); donner un exposé (d'un projet, etc.). **sketching** *n.* action *f* de croquer, d'esquisser; dessin *m* rapide, à main levée; **s. block, pad,** bloc *m* à croquis.

sketchbook ['sketʃbuk] *n.* cahier *m* de croquis.

sketchy ['sketʃi] *a.* (ouvrage) qui manque de fini; (dessin) qui manque de détails; (connaissances) superficielles, sommaires; (idées) plutôt vagues. **-ily** *adv.* d'une manière incomplète, vague, sans détails.

skew¹ [skjuː] *n.* biais *m*, obliquité *f* (d'un pont, etc.); **on the s.,** de, en, biais; obliquement.

skew² 1. *a.* en biais; oblique. **2.** *adv.* de, en, biais; de travers; *F:* **s.-whiff,** de travers, *F:* de traviole.

skew³ 1. *v.i.* biaiser, obliquer. **2.** *v.tr.* couper en sifflet, en biseau.

skewbald ['skjuːbɔːld] *a.* (cheval) blanc à taches alezanes; (cheval) blanc et roux.

skewer¹ ['skju(ː)ər] *n. Cu:* brochette *f*, broche *f*.

skewer² *v.tr. Cu:* brocheter, embrocher (de la viande, etc.).

ski¹, *pl.* **ski, skis** [skiː(z)] *n.* ski *m*; **s. binding,** fixation(s) *f(pl)*; **s. boots,** chaussures *fpl* de ski; **s. stick,** *U.S:* **s. pole,** bâton *m* de ski; **s. lift,** remonte-pente *m*, *pl.* remonte-pentes; téléski *m*; **s. run, slope,** piste *f* de ski; **s. jump,** saut *m* de ski; tremplin *m*; **s. jump(ing),** saut en, à, ski(s).

ski² *v.i.* (*p.t. & p.p.* **skied**) skier; faire du ski; aller à, en, skis; **to s. down the slope,** descendre la piste à, en, skis. **ski(-)ing** *n.* ski *m*; **to go s.,** faire du ski.

skid¹ [skid] *n.* **1.** (*a*) *Com:* palette *f* sur patins; (*b*) *Av:* patin (d'atterrissage, etc.); **tail s.,** béquille *f* (arrière); (*c*) *NAm: F:* **s. row,** quartier mal famé; bas-fonds *mpl*; (*d*) **s.-mounted,** à glissière; sur patins; (*e*) *F:* **to put the skids under s.o.,** (i) faire se dépêcher qn; presser qn; (ii) faire échouer qn. **2.** *Aut:* dérapage *m*; **to go into a s.,** déraper, faire un dérapage; *F:* **s. lid,** casque *m* de moto.

skid² *v.* **(skidded) 1.** *v.tr.* faire faire un dérapage à (une voiture). **2.** *v.i.* (*a*) (*of car, tyre, etc.*) déraper; (*of wheel*) patiner; (*b*) *Av:* glisser sur l'aile. **skidding** *n.* **1.** ensabotement *m*, enrayage *m*. **2.** (*a*) dérapage *m* (d'un pneu, d'une voiture); patinage *m* (d'une roue); (*b*) *Av:* glissement *m* (sur l'aile).

skidpan ['skidpæn] *n. Aut:* piste savonnée.

skier ['skiːər] *n.* skieur, -euse.

skiff [skif] *n.* (*a*) esquif *m*; yole *f*; (*b*) *Row:* skiff *m*.

skiffle ['skifl] *n. Mus:* skiffle *m*; **s. group,** skiffle-group *m inv*.

skilful, *NAm:* **skillful** ['skilf(u)l] *a.* adroit, habile; **to be s. at, in, doing sth.,** être habile, adroit, à (faire) qch. **-fully** *adv.* habilement, adroitement.

skilfulness, *NAm:* **skillfulness** ['skilf(u)lnis] *n.* habileté *f*, adresse *f*.

skill [skil] *n.* **1.** habileté *f*, adresse *f*, dextérité *f*; **technical s.,** habileté, aptitude *f*, technique; compétence *f* technique; **s. in doing sth.,** (i) talent *m*, habileté, pour faire qch.; (ii) art *m* de faire qch.; **lack of s.,** maladresse *f*, inhabileté *f*. **2.** *NAm:* métier *m*; art *m* pratique.

skilled [skild] *a.* habile; (travail) de spécialiste; **s. worker,** ouvrier, -ière, qualifié(e); **s. labour,** main-d'œuvre qualifiée; **to be s. in doing sth.,** être habile, adroit, à faire qch.

skillet ['skilit] *n. NAm:* poêle *f* (à frire).

skillful ['skilful] *a. NAm:* = SKILFUL.

skim¹ *n.* **1.** vol plané (d'un oiseau, d'un avion). **2. s. milk,** lait écrémé; **s. (milk) cheese,** fromage maigre.

skim² *v.tr. & i.* **(skimmed) 1.** écumer (le bouillon, etc.); écrémer (le lait, le verre en fusion, etc.); **to s. off,** enlever, prélever (la crème, etc.); *Fig:* **to s. the cream off sth.,** prendre la meilleure partie de qch. **2.** effleurer, raser (une surface); **to s. over sth.,** glisser, passer à la hâte, sur qch.; **to s. (along, over) the ground,** voler au ras du sol; raser le sol; **to s. (over) the water,** raser l'eau; voler à fleur d'eau; **to s. through a novel,** parcourir rapidement un roman.

skimmer ['skimər] *n.* (*for soup, metals*) écumoire *f*; (*for milk*) écrémeuse *f*; (*for glass*) casse *f*.

skimp [skimp] **1.** *v.tr.* lésiner sur (la nourriture, le tissu d'une robe); **skimped coat,** manteau étriqué; (*c*) *F:* bâcler (son travail). **2.** *v.i.* lésiner sur tout; vivre avec parcimonie. **skimping** *n.* **1.** lésine(rie) *f*; parcimonie *f*. **2.** *F:* bâclage *m* (d'un travail).

skimpiness ['skimpinis] *n.* insuffisance *f*; aspect étriqué (d'un vêtement).

skimpy ['skimpi] *a.* insuffisant; **s. skirt,** jupe étriquée; **s. meal,** maigre repas. **-ily** *adv.* parcimonieusement (meublé, etc.); **s. made,** (robe) étriquée; **s. dressed,** légèrement vêtu.

skin¹ [skin] *n.* **1.** (*a*) peau *f*; **outer s.,** épiderme *m*; *Fig:* **to have a thin s.,** être susceptible; **to have a thick s.,** avoir la peau dure; (*of snake, etc.*) **to cast, throw, its s.,** se dépouiller; muer; **he cannot change his s.,** il mourra dans sa peau; **I always wear cotton next to my s.,** je porte toujours du coton sur la peau; **to strip to the s.,** se mettre tout nu; **wet to the s.,** mouillé jusqu'aux os; (*of wound, emotions*) **s. deep,** à fleur de peau; superficiel; **beauty is but s. deep,** la beauté n'est qu'à fleur de peau; *Toil:* **s. care,** soins *mpl* de la peau; **s. cream,** crème *f* de beauté; *Med:* **s. graft(ing),** greffe cutanée; **s. test,** cuti-réaction *f*, *pl.* cuti-réactions; *F:* **he's nothing but, he's all, s. and bone,** il n'a que la peau et les os; **to sell one's s. dearly,** vendre (bien) cher sa peau; **I nearly jumped out of my s.,** cela m'a fait sursauter; **to escape by, with, the s. of one's teeth,** s'échapper de justesse; **to save one's (own) s.,** sauver sa peau; se tirer d'affaire; *F:* **to get under s.o.'s s.,** ennuyer qn; donner, taper, sur les nerfs de qn; énerver qn; *F:* **I've got her under my s.,** je l'ai dans la peau; *F:* **it's no s. off my nose,** (i) ce n'est pas mon affaire; (ii) ça ne me fait, coûte, rien; *F:* **s. game,** escroquerie *f*, filouterie *f*; (*b*) **s. diving,** plongée sous-marine autonome; **s. diver,** plongeur, -euse, sous-marin(e) autonome. **2.** (*a*) dépouille *f*, peau (d'un animal); **skins,** peausserie(s) *f(pl)*; **fur skins,** pelleterie(s) *f(pl)*; **s. dressing,** peausserie; (*b*) (*for wine, etc.*) outre *f*. **3.** (*a*) *Bot:* tunique *f* (d'une graine); pellicule *f* (d'un grain de café, etc.); (*b*) peau (de fruit, de saucisse); pelure, robe *f* (d'oignon); *Cu:* **potatoes (cooked) in their skins,** pommes *fpl* de terre en robe de chambre. **4.** *Nau:* bordé extérieur (d'un navire, d'un canot); enveloppe *f*, coque *f* (d'un navire); *Av:* revêtement *m* (du fuselage, de la coque); *El:* **s. effect,** effet *m* pelliculaire. **5.** (*a*) peau, pellicule (sur le lait, etc.); (*b*) *Metall:* croûte *f* (de la fonte).

skin² *v.* **(skinned) 1.** *v.tr.* (*a*) écorcher, dépouiller (un lapin, etc.); **to s. one's knees,** s'écorcher les genoux; *F:* **to s. s.o.,** écorcher, estamper, qn; (*b*) peler, éplucher (un fruit, etc.). **2.** *v.i. Med:* (*of wound*) **to s. over,** se recouvrir de peau; se cicatriser. **skinning** *n.* **1.** (*a*) écorchement *m* (d'un lapin, etc.); (*b*) épluchage *m* (d'un fruit). **2.** *Med:* **s. over,** cicatrisation *f*.

skinflint ['skinflint] *n. F:* avare *mf*, pingre *mf*; grippe-sou *m*, *pl.* grippe-sous.

skinful ['skinful] *n.* **1.** (pleine) outre (de vin, etc.). **2.** *P:* **he's had, got, a s.,** il a pris une (bonne) cuite.

skinless ['skinlis] *a.* (saucisse, etc.) sans peau.

skinny ['skini] *a. F:* (*of pers.*) maigre; efflanqué.

skinny-dip¹ [skini'dip] *n. U.S: F:* baignade *f* tout nu, à poil.

skinny-dip² *v.i. U.S: F:* nager, se baigner, tout nu, à poil.

skint [skint] *a. P:* **to be s.,** être sans le sou, fauché.

skintight ['skintait] *a.* (vêtement) collant.

skip¹ [skip] *n.* (petit) saut; gambade *f*; *NAm:* **s. rope,** corde *f* à sauter.

skip² *v.* **(skipped) 1.** *v.i.* (*a*) (*of lambs, children*) sauter, sautiller, gambader; (*b*) **to s.,** *NAm:* **to s. rope,** sauter à la corde; (*c*) **to s. from one subject to another,** sauter d'un sujet à un autre; (*d*) *F:* **to s. (off),** filer; décamper; *v.tr. F:* **to s. bail,** se dérober à la justice (alors qu'on jouit de la liberté provisoire). **2.** *v.tr. & i.* omettre (qch.); sauter (un repas, etc.); *Sch:* sauter (une classe); **to s. (over),** omettre, sauter (pardessus), passer (un mot, etc.); **to read without skipping,** lire sans rien sauter; *F:* **s. it!** (i) ça suffit! (ii) passons! laisse courir! **skipping** *n.* **1.** gambades *fpl*, sauts *mpl*. **2.** saut à la corde; **s. rope,** corde à sauter. **3.** omission *f* (de qch.).

skip³ *n. Const: Min: etc:* benne *f*; caisse guidée.

skipper¹ ['skipər] *n.* **1.** (*a*) *Nau:* capitaine *m*, patron *m* (d'un navire); *Av:* commandant *m* de bord; (*b*) *Nau: F:* **the s.,** le capiston. **2.** *Nau: F:* **skipper's daughters,** vagues *f* à crêtes d'écume. **3.** *Games:* capitaine, chef *m* (d'une équipe sportive).

skipper² *v.tr. F:* être le commandant (d'un navire), le commandant à bord (d'un avion), le chef (d'une équipe sportive).

skirl [skərl] *n. Scot:* son aigu (de la cornemuse).

skirmish¹ ['skə:miʃ] *n. Mil:* escarmouche *f*, échauffourée *f*; *Fig:* escarmouche (verbale); **s. of wit,** assaut *m* d'esprit.

skirmish² *v.i. Mil: etc:* combattre par escarmouches.

skirmisher ['skə:miʃər] *n. Mil:* tirailleur *m*.

skirt¹ [skə:t] *n.* **1.** *Cost:* (*a*) jupe *f*; **divided s.,** jupe-culotte *f*, *pl.* jupes-culottes; (*b*) pan *m*, basque *f* (de pardessus, etc.); (*c*) *P:* **(bit of) s.,** nana *f*; poupée *f*; poule *f*; (*d*) *Cu:* **s. of beef,** flanchet *m* de bœuf. **2.** (*a*) *Harn:* **(saddle) s.,** petit quartier (de la selle); (*b*) (*of hovercraft*) jupe. **3.** *I.C.E:* jupe (du piston).

skirt² *v.tr. & i.* contourner (un village, une colline); (*of pers.*) longer, serrer (le mur, etc.); (*of ship*) côtoyer (le rivage); **the path skirts (along, round) the wood,** le sentier côtoie, contourne, le bois. **skirting** *n.* (*a*) bord *m*, bordure *f*; (*b*) *Const:* **s. (board),** plinthe *f*; socle *m* de lambris.

skit [skit] *n. Lit: Mus: Th:* pièce *f* satirique; satire *f*.

skittish ['skitiʃ] *a.* **1.** (*of horse*) ombrageux. **2.** (femme) (i) capricieuse; (ii) évaporée. **-ly** *adv.* (*a*) capricieusement; (*b*) en faisant la coquette.

skittishness ['skitiʃnis] *n.* **1.** ombrage *m* (d'un cheval). **2.** (i) inconstance *f*, (ii) pétulance *f*, frivolité *f* (d'une femme).

skittle ['skitl] *n.* **1. s. (pin),** quille *f*. **2. (game of) skittles,** jeu *m* de quilles; **to play (at) skittles,** jouer aux quilles; **s. alley,** (terrain *m* de) jeu de quilles; *F:* **life isn't all beer and skittles,** tout n'est pas rose dans ce monde.

skive [skaiv] *v.i. F:* **to s. (off),** tirer au flanc; s'esquiver. **skiving** *n.* tirage *m* au flanc.

skiver ['skaivər] *n. F:* tire(-)au(-)flanc *m inv.* tire(-)au(-)cul *m inv.*

skivvy ['skivi] *n. Pej: O:* domestique *f*; bonne *f* à tout faire.

skua ['skju(:)ə] *n. Orn:* stercoraire *m*.

skulduggery [skʌl'dʌgəri] *n.* procédés *mpl* peu honnêtes; tripotage *m.*

skulk [skʌlk] *v.i.* **1.** se cacher; se tenir caché. **2.** rôder furtivement; **to s. in, out,** entrer, sortir, furtivement. **3.** (*a*) paresser, fainéanter; (*b*) tirer au flanc.

skull [skʌl] *n.* crâne *m*; **s. and crossbones,** tête *f* de mort et tibias; **he's got a thick s.,** il a la tête dure.

skullcap ['skʌlkæp] *n.* calotte *f* (de prêtre, etc.).

skunk [skʌŋk] *n.* **1.** *Z:* mouffette *f.* **2.** (*fur*) sconse *m*, skunks *m.* **3.** *F:* mufle *m*, salaud *m.*

sky¹ [skai] *n.* **1.** ciel *m*, *pl.* cieux, *Art: Tchn:* ciels; **under the open s.,** au grand air; (dormir) à la belle étoile; **s. blue,** bleu *m* (de) ciel; azur *m*; **the sky's the limit,** tout va! **to praise s.o. to the skies,** porter qn aux nues; **the bridge was blown s. high,** le pont a sauté jusqu'aux cieux; **prices are s. high,** les prix sont astronomiques; *Prov:* **red s. at night (is the) shepherd's delight,** rouge le soir, espoir; *Aer: Sp:* **s. diving,** parachutisme *m* en chute libre; **s. diver,** parachutiste *mf* qui pratique la chute libre. **2.** (*climate*) **the sunny skies of Italy,** le climat ensoleillé d'Italie; les ciels bleus d'Italie.

sky² *v.tr.* **(skied)** *Cr: Ten: etc:* lancer (la balle) en chandelle.

Skye [skai] *Pr.n. Geog:* (l'île *f* de) Skye; **S. terrier,** skye-terrier *m*, *pl.* skye-terriers.

skyjack¹ ['skaidʒæk] *n. F:* piraterie aérienne.

skyjack² *v.tr. F:* pirater un avion; détourner un avion. **skyjacking** *n.* piraterie aérienne.

skyjacker ['skaidʒækər] *n. F:* pirate *m* de l'air.

skylark¹ ['skailɑːk] *n. Orn:* alouette *f* des champs.

skylark² *v.i. F:* rigoler, batifoler; faire des farces. **skylarking** *n. F:* rigolade *f*; farces *fpl.*

skylight ['skailait] *n.* jour *m* (dans le toit, le plafond); (*in attic*) (lucarne) faîtière *f*; (*hinged*) (châssis, fenêtre *f*, lucarne, à) tabatière *f.*

skyline ['skailain] *n.* (ligne *f* d')horizon *m*; profil *m* de l'horizon; le profil, la silhouette (d'une ville).

skyrocket¹ ['skairɔkit] *n.* fusée blanche, éclairante.

skyrocket² *v.i.* (*of prices, etc.*) monter en flèche.

skyscape ['skaiskeip] *n. Art:* tableau *m* représentant des nuages, une partie du ciel.

skyscraper ['skaiskreipər] *n.* gratte-ciel *m inv.*

skyward(s) ['skaiwəd(z)] *adv.* vers le ciel.

skyway ['skaiwei] *n.* **1.** *Av:* route aérienne. **2.** *NAm:* saut-de-mouton *m*; route surélevée.

sky(-)writing ['skairaitiŋ] *n.* publicité aérienne.

slab [slæb] *n.* **1.** (*a*) *Tchn:* plaque *f*, dalle *f* (de pierre, marbre, etc.); (*b*) (*of timber*) dosse *f*; (*c*) pavé *m* (de pain d'épice); (grosse) tranche (de gâteau); darne *f*, dalle (de poisson); plaque, tablette *f* (de chocolat). **2.** *Typ:* marbre *m* (pour broyer les couleurs).

slabstone ['slæbstoun] *n.* dalle *f*, plaque *f* (de pierre).

slack¹ [slæk] *n.* (i) menu charbon; charbonnaille *f*; (ii) poussier *m.*

slack² *n.* **1.** (*a*) mou *m* (d'un câble, d'une courroie); **to take up the s. in a cable,** mettre un câble au raide; (*b*) *Mec.E:* jeu *m* (nuisible). **2.** *Nau:* mer *f* étale; étale *m* de la marée. **3.** ralentissement *m* d'activité (dans les affaires); morte-saison *f.* **4.** *Cost:* **slacks,** pantalon *m* (de dame, *NAm:* d'homme).

slack³ *a.* **1.** (*a*) (cordage, etc.) mou, lâche, flasque; (écrou) desserré; (*of rope*) **to be, hang, s.,** avoir du mou; **(acrobat's) s. rope,** corde *f* lâche; voltige *f*; (*b*) (main, prise) faible; *Fig:* **to have a s. rein on sth.,** gouverner qch. sans fermeté, mollement. **2.** (*of pers.*) négligent; mou, *f.* molle; *F:* flemmard; **to get, become, s.,** se relâcher; se laisser aller; **to be s. in, about, doing sth.,** être lent, paresseux, à faire qch. **3.** (*a*) peu vif; faible; (commerce) stagnant; **business is s.,** les affaires ne marchent pas fort; **s. periods,** moments *mpl* de creux; **s. time,** (période d')accalmie *f*; **the s. season,** la morte-saison, la saison creuse; **s. sea, s. water,** mer étale; (*b*) **we're s. this afternoon,** nous ne sommes pas très occupés cet après-midi. **4.** *adv.* (*a*) mollement; (*b*) imparfaitement. **-ly** *adv.* **1.** (lier qch.) lâchement. **2.** (agir) négligemment.

slack⁴ **1.** *v.tr.* (*a*) ralentir (l'allure, l'activité); (*b*) détendre, relâcher (un cordage); donner du mou à (une courroie, une voile); desserrer (un écrou); *Mch:* **to s. off the pressure,** relâcher la pression; (*c*) éteindre (la chaux). **2.** *v.i* (*a*) (*of train*) **to s. up,** ralentir; (*b*) *F:* (*of pers.*) **to s. (off),** se relâcher; paresser, fainéanter; **your pupils are slacking,** vos élèves se relâchent. **slacking** *n.* **1.** (*a*) ralentissement *m* (de l'allure); (*b*) relâchement *m* (d'un cordage). **2.** manque *m* d'application au travail; paresse *f*, flemme *f.*

slacken ['slæk(ə)n] **1.** *v.tr.* (*a*) ralentir (le pas, ses efforts, son ardeur); **to s. speed,** diminuer de vitesse; ralentir (la marche); (*b*) détendre, relâcher (un cordage); donner du mou à (un cordage, une voile); **to s. the reins,** lâcher la bride, les rênes; (*c*) affaiblir (l'opposition); adoucir (la sévérité). **2.** *v.i.* (*a*) (*of pers.*) **to s. (off, up),** se relâcher; devenir négligent, diminuer d'efforts; (*b*) (*of rope*) prendre du mou; (*c*) (*of speed*) ralentir; (*of storm*) se calmer; (*of energy, mind, etc.*) diminuer (de force, d'ardeur); **business is slackening,** les affaires deviennent stagnantes; (*d*) (*of the tide*) mollir; (*e*) (*of lime*) s'éteindre, s'amortir. **slackening** *n.* ralentissement *m* (de zèle); diminution *f* (de force, de zèle, de vitesse); relâchement *m* (d'un cordage, d'ardeur, d'efforts); **s. of speed,** ralentissement.

slacker ['slækər] *n.* paresseux, -euse; flemmard, -arde.

slackness ['slæknis] *n.* **1.** (*a*) manque *m* d'énergie; négligence *f*; mollesse *f*; paresse *f*, *F:* flemme *f*; (*b*) désœuvrement *m*; (*c*) relâchement *m* (de la discipline). **2.** détente *f* (des muscles, etc.); mou *m* (d'un cordage). **3.** *Com:* stagnation *f* (des affaires).

slag [slæg] *n. Metall:* scorie(s) *f(pl)* (de métal); crasse *f*, laitier(s) *m(pl)* (de haut fourneau); *Geol:* **volcanic s.,** scories volcaniques.

slagheap ['slæghiːp] *n.* crassier *m.*

slake [sleik] *v.tr.* (*a*) **to s. one's thirst,** étancher, apaiser, éteindre, sa soif; se désaltérer; (*b*) éteindre (la chaux); **slaked lime,** chaux éteinte. **slaking** *n.* **1.** étanchement *m*, assouvissement *m* (de la soif). **2.** extinction *f* (de la chaux).

slalom ['slɑːləm] *n. Ski:* slalom *m.*

slam¹ [slæm] **1.** *n.* claquement *m* (d'une porte, etc.). **2.** *adv.* **s. (bang) in the middle of . . .,** en plein dans . . .; *int.* **s.!** v'lan!

slam² *v.* **(slammed) 1.** *v.tr.* (*a*) (faire) claquer (une porte); envoyer, lancer, violemment, *F:* flanquer (**against,** contre; **into,** dans); **to s. the door in s.o.'s face,** claquer la porte au nez de qn; **she slammed the book (down) on the table,** elle a flanqué le livre sur la table; **to s. on the brakes,** bloquer les freins; (*b*) critiquer, éreinter (qn, qch.). **2.** *v.i.* (*a*) (*of door, etc.*) se fermer avec bruit; claquer; (*b*) (*of pers.*) **to s. out of the house,** sortir furieusement de la maison.

slam³ *n.* (*a*) *Cards:* (*at bridge*) chelem *m*, schelem *m*; **grand s.,** grand chelem; **to make a s.,** faire (le) chelem; (*b*) *Sp:* **the grand s.,** le grand chelem.

slander¹ ['slɑːndər] *n.* calomnie *f*; *Jur:* diffamation verbale.

slander² *v.tr.* calomnier, *Jur:* diffamer (qn).

slanderer ['slɑːndərər] *n.* calomniateur, -trice; *Jur:* diffamateur, -trice.

slanderous ['slɑːndərəs] *a.* (propos) calomnieux, calomniateur; *Jur:* diffamatoire. **-ly** *adv.* calomnieusement.

slang¹ [slæŋ] *n.* argot *m*; **theatrical, stage, s.,** argot des coulisses; **s. phrase, expression,** expression *f* argotique; argotisme *m.*

slang² *v.tr. F:* (*a*) injurier, engueuler (qn); (*b*) réprimander sévèrement (qn). **slanging** *n. F:* (*a*) pluie *f* d'injures; **s. match,** prise *f* de bec, engueulade *f*; (*b*) verte réprimande.

slangy ['slæŋi] *a.* **1.** (*of pers.*) qui aime à s'exprimer en argot; argotier. **2.** (style, langage) argotique; (terme) populaire, d'argot. **-ily** *adv.* (s'exprimer) en termes d'argot.

slant¹ [slɑ:nt] *n.* **1.** pente *f*, inclinaison *f*. **2.** biais *m*; biseau *m*; **on the, at a, s.,** de biais, obliquement. **3.** *F:* (*a*) point *m* de vue; (*b*) **information with a s. on it,** informations tendancieuses, faussées.

slant² *a.* oblique; **s.-eyed,** aux yeux bridés.

slant³ **1.** *v.i.* (*a*) être en pente; (s')incliner; (*b*) être oblique. **2.** *v.tr.* (*a*) incliner (qch.); mettre en pente; (*b*) *F:* fausser; **slanted news,** informations tendancieuses, faussées. **slanting** *a.* (*a*) (toit) en pente, incliné; (*b*) (direction) oblique; (écriture) couchée.

slantwise, slantways ['slɑ:ntwaiz, -weiz] *adv.* obliquement; en, de, biais.

slap¹ [slæp] **I.** *n.* coup *m*, claque *f*, tape *f*; **s. in the face,** (i) gifle *f*; (ii) *Fig:* affront *m*, soufflet *m*; *Fig:* **s. on the back,** félicitations *fpl*. **II.** *adv.* **the car went s. into the wall,** la voiture est rentrée en plein dans le mur; *F:* **s. bang,** brusquement; de but en blanc; **they ran s. (bang) into each other,** ils se sont rentrés en plein dedans.

slap² *v.* (**slapped** [slæpt]) *v.tr.* frapper avec la main (ouverte); donner une claque, une tape, à (qn); donner une fessée; **to s. s.o.'s face,** gifler qn; **to s. s.o. on the back,** (i) donner à qn une tape sur le dos; (ii) féliciter qn; *F:* **t. s. s.o. down,** réprimander qn; (re)mettre qn à sa place; **he slapped the money (down) on the table,** il a jeté, flanqué, l'argent sur la table. **slapping** *n.* (*a*) claques *fpl*, gifles *fpl*; (*b*) fessée *f*.

slapdash ['slæpdæʃ] *a. & adv.* sans soin(s); (travail) à la six-quatre-deux; **s. worker,** sabreur *m* de besogne; **to do sth. s., in a s. manner,** faire qch, à la va-vite, à la six-quatre-deux.

slap(-)happy [slæp'hæpi] *a. F:* **1.** (*a*) plein d'entrain; (*b*) insouciant; **he's s.,** il fait les choses au petit bonheur. **2.** *F:* groggy, abruti de coups.

slapstick ['slæpstik] *n.* **1.** batte *f* d'Arlequin. **2.** **s. (comedy),** comédie bouffonne, farce *f*.

slap-up ['slæpʌp] *a. F:* (restaurant, etc.) soigné, chic; **s. meal,** festin *m*, repas somptueux.

slash¹ [slæʃ] *n.* **1.** estafilade *f*, entaille *f*, taillade *f*; (*on the face*) balafre *f*. **2.** *A. Cost:* crevé *m*. **3.** *NAm: For:* (*a*) déchets *mpl* (d'abattage); (*b*) clairière *f*. **4.** *P:* **to have a s.,** uriner.

slash² **1.** *v.tr.* (*a*) taillader (la chair); balafrer (le visage); couper, trancher, net (un cordage, etc.); (*b*) cingler (un cheval, etc.) (d'un coup de fouet); (*c*) éreinter (un ouvrage littéraire, etc.); (*d*) faire de fortes réductions (de prix, de salaires); couper (un texte, etc.); **all prices slashed,** tous prix réduits; (*e*) *A. Cost:* **slashed sleeve,** manche *f* à crevés. **2.** *v.i.* frapper à droite et à gauche; sabrer; **to s. at sth.,** (i) couper, taillader, (ii) cingler, fouetter, qch. **slashing** *a.* (*of criticism*) mordant, cinglant.

slat [slæt] *n.* lame *f*, lamelle *f*, planchette *f* (de jalousie, etc.); traverse *f* (de lit).

slate¹ [sleit] *n.* **1.** (*a*) *Geol:* ardoise *f*; **s. colour(ed), s. grey,** ardoisé; (gris) ardoise *inv*; **s. blue,** bleu ardoise *inv*; **s. worker, quarryman,** ardoisier *m*; **s. quarry,** ardoisière *f*; (*b*) *Const:* (feuille *f* d')ardoise; **s. roof,** toit *m* d'ardoises. **2.** **(writing) s.,** ardoise (pour, à, écrire); **s. pencil,** crayon *m* d'ardoise; *F:* **on the s.,** sur la note, sur le compte; **to wipe the s. clean,** faire table rase (du passé); **I have a clean s.,** (i) je n'ai pas de dettes; (ii) mon casier judiciaire est vierge.

slate² *v.tr.* **1.** *Const:* couvrir (un toit) d'ardoises, en ardoise; **slated roof,** toit *m* d'ardoises. **2.** *NAm: Pol:* inscrire (un candidat) sur la liste.

slate³ *v.tr. F:* **1.** réprimander vertement (qn). **2.** critiquer, éreinter (un auteur, un livre, etc.). **slating** *n. F:* **1.** verte réprimande; savon *m*. **2.** *Lit: etc:* critique *f* acerbe; éreintement *m*.

slater ['sleitər] *n.* **1.** (*pers.*) couvreur *m* (en ardoises). **2.** *Crust:* cloporte *m*.

slatted ['slætid] *a.* (*of shutters, etc.*) à lames, à planchettes.

slattern ['slætə(:)n] *n.f.* femme mal soignée; souillon.

slatternly ['slætənli] *a.* (*of woman*) mal soignée; qui manque de propreté.

slaty ['sleiti] *a.* **1.** *Geol:* ardoisier, schisteux. **2.** (*of colour*) ardoisé.

slaughter¹ ['slɔ:tər] *n.* **1.** abattage *m* (d'animaux de boucherie). **2.** tuerie *f*, carnage *m*, massacre *m*.

slaughter² *v.tr.* **1.** abattre (des animaux de boucherie). **2.** (*a*) tuer, massacrer (des gens); (*b*) *F:* battre (un adversaire) à plate(s) couture(s). **slaughtering** *n.* **1.** abattage *m* (d'animaux de boucherie). **2.** tuerie *f*, carnage *m*, massacre *m* (de gens).

slaughterer ['slɔ:tərər] *n.* **1.** abatteur *m*, tueur *m* (d'animaux). **2.** tueur, -euse (de gens).

slaughterhouse ['slɔ:təhaus] *n.* abattoir *m*.

Slav [slɑ:v] *Ethn:* **1.** *a.* slave. **2.** *n.* Slave *mf*.

slave¹ [sleiv] *n.* esclave *mf*; **to be s.o.'s s.,** être l'esclave de qn; **to be the s. of, a s. to, a passion,** être l'esclave d'une passion; **to be a s. to duty,** ne connaître que son devoir; **to be a s. to one's work,** être esclave de son travail; **s. trade,** traite *f* des noirs; commerce *m*, traffic *m*, des esclaves; **white s. trade,** traite des blanches; **s. trader,** marchand *m* d'esclaves; **s. driver,** (i) *A:* surveillant *m* des esclaves; (ii) *F:* garde-chiourme *m*, *pl.* garde(s)-chiourme(s); **s. labour,** travail *m* d'esclave.

slave² *v.i.* travailler comme un nègre; peiner, bûcher; **to s. away at sth.,** s'échiner, s'éreinter, à qch.

slaver¹ ['slævər] *n.* bave *f*, salive *f*.

slaver² ['slævər] *v.i.* baver (**over,** sur).

slaver³ ['sleivər] **1.** *Nau:* (bâtiment) négrier *m*. **2.** (*pers.*) marchand *m* d'esclaves; **black s.,** négrier *m*; **white s.,** courtier *m* de chair humaine.

slavery ['sleivəri] *n.* **1.** esclavage *m*; **to sell s.o. into s.,** vendre qn comme esclave; **to reduce to s.,** réduire (qn) en esclavage; asservir (un peuple); **white s.,** traite *f* des blanches. **2.** asservissement *m* (**to a passion,** à une passion). **3.** *F:* travail tuant; **this work is sheer s.,** ce travail est un véritable esclavage.

Slavic ['slɑ:vik] *a. & n. Ethn: Ling:* slave (*m*).

slavish ['sleiviʃ] *a.* (soumission) d'esclave; (imitation) servile. **-ly** *adv.* servilement.

slavishness ['sleiviʃnis] *n.* servilité *f*.

Slavonic [slə'vɔnik] **1.** *a. Ethn:* slave; **student of S. languages,** slavisant, -ante. **2.** *n. Ling:* slave *m*; **Church S., Old S.,** slavon *m*.

slaw [slɔ:] *n. esp. NAm: Cu:* salade *f* de chou cru.

slay [slei] *v.tr.* (*p.t.* **slew** [slu:]; *p.p.* **slain** [slein]) *Lit:* tuer; assassiner; **the slain,** les morts *mpl*. **slaying** *n.* meurtre *m*; massacre *m*.

slayer ['sleiər] *n.* tueur, -euse; assassin *m* (**of,** de).

sleaziness ['sli:zinis] *n. F:* apparence *f* louche, aspect *m* sordide (d'un endroit, etc.).

sleazy ['sli:zi] *a. F:* (*a*) (quartier, etc.) louche, sordide; (*b*) (*of pers.*) dégueulasse.

sled¹,² [sled] *n. & v. N.Am:* = SLEDGE¹,².

sledge¹ [sledʒ] *n.* traîneau *m*.

sledge² **1.** *v.i.* aller en traîneau; **to go sledging,** se promener en traîneau; faire une promenade en traîneau. **2.** *v.tr.* transporter (qch.) en traîneau.

sledge³ *n.* = SLEDGEHAMMER.

sledgehammer ['sledʒhæmər] *n. Tls:* marteau *m* à

deux mains, à frapper devant; *F:* **s. arguments,** arguments *mpl* massue.

sleek¹ [sli:k] *a.* **1.** (*a*) lisse; luisant; **s. hair,** cheveux lisses; **s. horse,** cheval *m* d'un beau poil; (*b*) (*of pers.*) luisant de santé. **2.** (*of manner*) mielleux; onctueux. **-ly** *adv.* **1.** avec une apparence lisse. **2.** mielleusement; onctueusement.

sleek² *v.tr.* lisser (les cheveux, le poil d'un cheval).

sleekness ['sli:knis] *n.* **1.** luisant *m* (d'une peau, du satin, etc.). **2.** onctuosité *f* (de manières).

sleep¹ [sli:p] *n.* **1.** sommeil *m*; **short s.,** somme *m*; **deep, sound, s.,** sommeil profond; **beauty s.,** sommeil avant minuit (considéré comme le plus réparateur); **to go, drop off, to s.,** s'endormir, s'assoupir; **to go, drop off, to s. again,** se rendormir; **to put, send, lull, s.o. to s.,** endormir qn; *Med:* **to put s.o. to s.,** endormir qn; *Vet: F:* **to put an animal to s.,** piquer un animal; **to read oneself to s.,** lire pour s'endormir; **he's ready to drop with s.,** il tombe de sommeil; **to rouse s.o. from his s.,** réveiller qn; arracher qn au sommeil; **to have a good (night's) s.,** bien dormir; **I didn't get a wink of s. all night,** je n'ai pas dormi, je n'ai pas fermé l'œil, de la nuit; j'ai passé une nuit blanche; **in my s.,** pendant que je dors, que je dormais; **to walk in one's s.,** être somnambule; **to talk in one's s.,** rêver tout haut. **2. my foot's gone to s.,** j'ai des fourmis dans le pied; j'ai le pied engourdi.

sleep² *v.i. & tr.* (*p.t. & p.p.* **slept** [slept]) **1.** dormir; (*a*) **to s. like a log, a top,** dormir à poings fermés; dormir comme un sabot, comme une marmotte; **to s. soundly,** dormir profondément; **to s. the night through,** dormir toute la nuit; **to s. through a noise,** ne pas être réveillé par un bruit; **I haven't slept a wink all night,** je n'ai pas dormi, je n'ai pas fermé l'œil, de (toute) la nuit; j'ai passé une nuit blanche; **to try to s.,** chercher le sommeil; **he can't s. for thinking about it,** il n'en dort pas; **to s. on a question,** *F:* **to s. on it,** prendre conseil de son oreiller; **s. on it,** la nuit porte conseil; (*b*) *Lit:* **to s. the sleep of the just,** dormir du sommeil du juste. **2.** coucher; (*a*) **to s. at an hotel,** coucher à un hôtel; **to s. rough,** coucher sur la dure; (*of servant*) **to s. in,** coucher à la maison; **to s. late, in,** (i) faire la grasse matinée; (ii) ne pas se réveiller à l'heure; **the bed had not been slept in,** le lit n'avait pas été défait; **to s. out,** (i) découcher; (ii) (*of servant*) coucher à son domicile; venir en journée; (*b*) **to s. with s.o.,** coucher avec qn; **to s. together,** coucher ensemble; *F:* **to s. around,** coucher avec n'importe qui. **3.** *v.tr.* (*a*) **house that sleeps ten people,** maison *f* où dix personnes peuvent coucher; **this room sleeps four,** on peut coucher à quatre dans cette chambre; (*b*) **to s. off,** faire passer (un mal de tête) en dormant; **to s. off a hangover,** *F:* **to s. it off** = cuver son vin; **to s. the day, the hours, away,** passer la journée, les heures, à dormir, en dormant. **sleeping 1.** *a.* (*a*) dormant, endormi; *Prov:* **let s. dogs lie,** ne réveillez pas le chat qui dort; (*b*) *Com:* **s. partner,** (associé *m*) commanditaire *m*; bailleur *m* de fonds. **2.** *n.* sommeil *m*; **s. pill,** (comprimé *m*) somnifère (*m*); **s. accommodation,** logement *m*; **the house has s. accommodation for ten,** c'est une maison où dix personnes peuvent coucher; **s. quarters,** chambres *fpl*; dortoir(s) *m(pl)*; *Rail:* **s. car(riage),** wagon-lit *m*, *pl.* wagons-lits; **s. bag,** sac *m* de couchage; **s. suit,** pyjama *m* (d'enfant); *Med:* **s. sickness,** maladie *f* du sommeil.

sleeper ['sli:pər] *n.* **1.** dormeur, -euse; **to be a light, a heavy, s.,** avoir le sommeil léger, profond. **2.** *Const: etc:* (*a*) poutre horizontale; sole *f*; lambourde *f* (de parquet, etc.); gîte *m* (de plancher); (*b*) *Rail:* **(cross) s.,** traverse *f*. **3.** *Rail:* wagon-lit *m*, *pl.* wagons-lits. **4.** *NAm:* **sleeper(s),** pyjama *m* d'enfant.

sleepiness ['sli:pinis] *n.* **1.** envie *f* de dormir; somnolence *f*. **2.** apathie *f*, indolence *f*, léthargie *f*.

sleepless ['sli:plis] *a.* **1.** (*a*) sans sommeil; (nuit) d'insomnie; **to have a s. night,** passer une nuit blanche; (*b*) (*of pers.*) insomnieux. **2.** *Lit:* (*of mind*) sans cesse en éveil; (énergie) inlassable. **-ly** *adv.* sans dormir.

sleeplessness ['sli:plisnis] *n.* insomnie *f*.

sleepwalker ['sli:pwɔ:kər] *n.* somnambule *mf*.

leepwalking ['sli:pwɔ:kiŋ] *n.* somnambulisme *m*.

sleepy ['sli:pi] *a.* **1.** (*a*) somnolent; **to be, feel, s.,** avoir envie de dormir; avoir sommeil; **to make s.o. s.,** assoupir qn; (*b*) **s. look,** air endormi; **s. little town,** petite ville endormie. **2.** apathique; indolent; léthargique. **3.** (*of fruit*) blet, *f.* blette. **-ily** *adv.* (répondre) d'un air endormi, somnolent.

sleepyhead ['sli:pihed] *n. F:* endormi, -ie.

sleet¹ [sli:t] *n.* **1.** pluie mêlée de neige. **2.** *NAm:* verglas *m*.

sleet² *v.impers.* **it's sleeting,** il tombe de la neige fondue; la pluie tourne à la neige.

sleeve [sli:v] *n.* **1.** manche *f*; **short s.,** manche courte, mancheron *m*; **s. hole,** emmanchure *f* (de robe, etc.); *F:* **to have something up one's s.,** avoir un expédient en réserve; **to have more than one trick up one's s.,** avoir plus d'un tour dans son sac. **2.** (*a*) *Mec.E:* chemise *f*, fourreau *m*, gaine *f* (souple); douille *f*; **s. nut,** manchon fileté, taraudé; (*b*) *Rec:* pochette *f* (de disque). **3.** *Av:* **air s.,** manche (à air).

sleeveboard ['sli:vbɔ:d] *n. Dom.Ec:* jeannette *f*.

sleeved [sli:vd] *a.* (vêtement) à manches; **long-s., short-s., dress,** robe *f* à manches longues, courtes.

sleeveless ['sli:vlis] *a.* (robe, etc.) sans manches.

sleigh [slei] *n.* traîneau *m*; **s. bell,** grelot *m*, clochette *f*; **s. ride,** promenade *f* en traîneau.

sleight [slait] *n.* **s. of hand,** prestidigitation *f*; escamotage *m*; tour *m* de passe-passe.

slender ['slendər] *a.* **1.** mince, ténu; (fil) délié; (*of figure*) svelte, fluet; **s. waist,** taille fine, fluette. **2.** (*of intelligence, hope, etc.*) faible; (*of income, etc.*) modique, maigre, modeste; **s. means,** ressources médiocres, exiguës; **of s. means,** peu fortuné; pauvre. **-ly** *adv.* **1. s. built,** d'une taille svelte. **2.** maigrement, faiblement.

slenderize ['slendəraiz] *v.tr. NAm:* amincir.

slenderness ['slendənis] *n.* **1.** minceur *f*, ténuité *f*; sveltesse *f* (de qn, de la taille). **2.** modicité *f* (d'une fortune); exiguïté *f*, faiblesse *f* (des ressources).

sleuth¹ ['slu:θ] *n. F:* limier *m*, détective *m*.

sleuth² *v.i. F:* faire le détective.

sleuthhound ['slu:θhaund] *n.* (*a*) limier *m*; (*b*) *F:* limier, détective *m*.

slew¹ [slu:] *n.* virage *m*; *Aut:* tête(-)à(-)queue *m inv*.

slew² **1.** *v.tr.* **to s. sth. round,** faire pivoter qch. **2.** *v.i.* pivoter; (*of car*) faire un tête(-)à(-)queue.

slew³ *n. NAm: F:* grande quantité.

slice¹ [slais] *n.* **1.** (*a*) tranche *f* (de pain, etc.); côte *f*, tranche (de melon); darne *f* (de gros poisson); (*thin*) lèche *f* (de pain, viande, etc.); **(round) s.,** rond *m*, rondelle *f* (de citron, saucisse, etc.); **s. of bread and butter,** tartine *f* beurrée; (*b*) **to take a large s. of the credit for sth.,** s'attribuer une large part du mérite de qch.; **a s. of life,** une tranche de vie. **2.** *Dom.Ec:* **fish s.,** truelle *f* (à poisson). **3.** *Golf:* coup *m* qui fait dévier la balle à droite.

slice² *v.tr.* **1. to s. (up),** couper, découper (qch.) en tranches; **to s. off,** trancher, couper, détacher (un morceau); **to s. thinly,** émincer (la viande, etc.). **2.** *Lit:* fendre (l'air, les vagues, etc.). **3.** (*a*) *Ten:* couper (la balle); (*b*) *Golf:* faire dévier la balle à droite.

slicer ['slaisər] *n. Dom.Ec:* éminceur *m*; **bacon s.,** coupe-jambon *m inv*.

slick¹ [slik] *a. F:* (*a*) habile, adroit; (*b*) en bon ordre; lisse; (*c*) malin, rusé. **-ly** *adv.* habilement.

slick² *n.* (*a*) **(oil) s.,** nappe *f* d'huile; (*b*) plaque *f* de neige.

slick³ **1.** *v.tr.* **to s. one's hair down,** lisser ses cheveux. **2.** *U.S:* (*a*) *v.tr.* mettre (une chambre) en ordre; (*b*) *v.i.* **to s. up,** s'attifer.

slicker ['slikər] *n.* **1.** *NAm:* imperméable *m*; ciré *m*. **2.** *NAm: F:* (*a*) escroc adroit; combinard *m*; (*b*) **(city) s.,** homme du milieu.

slickness ['sliknis] *n. F:* (*a*) habileté *f*, adresse *f*; (*b*) ruse *f*.

slide¹ [slaid] *n.* **1.** (*a*) glissade *f*, glissement *m*; (*of pers.*) **to have a s.,** faire une glissade; (*b*) éboulement *m*, glissement (de terrain); (*c*) *Mus:* (i) (*ornament*) coulé *m*; (ii) (*in violin playing, etc.*) glissade. **2.** (*a*) (*on snow or ice*) glissoire *f*; (*in playground*) toboggan *m*; (*b*) plan *m* de glissement; piste *f* en pente; *For:* **timber s.,** glissoir *m*; (*c*) *Av:* **escape s.,** toboggan d'évacuation. **3.** *Mec.E:* glissière *f*, coulisse *f*. **4.** (*a*) pièce *f* qui glisse, qui coulisse; curseur *m* (d'une règle, d'un compas, etc.); coulisseau *m*, réglette *f* (d'une règle à calcul); *Row:* glissière; **s. rule,** règle à calcul; *esp. NAm:* **s. fastener,** fermeture *f* éclair, à glissière; (*b*) *Mus:* coulisse (de trombone, etc.). **5.** (*a*) (*microscopy*) **(object) s.,** (plaque *f*, lame *f*) porte-objet *m*, *pl.* porte-objet(s); (*b*) *Phot:* **(colour) s.,** diapositive *f* (en couleur); **lecture illustrated with slides,** conférence *f* avec projections. **6.** *Phot:* **dark s.,** châssis porte-plaques; châssis négatif. **7. (hair) s.,** barrette *f*.

slide² *v.* (*p.t. & p.p.* **slid** [slid]) **1.** *v.i.* (*a*) glisser, coulisser; **mechanism that slides between runners,** mécanisme qui glisse, coulisse, entre des guides; (*b*) (*of pers.*) **to s. (on ice),** glisser (sur la glace); faire une glissade, des glissades; (*c*) **he slid on the floor,** il a glissé sur le parquet; **the dish slid off the table,** le plat a glissé de sur la table; (*d*) **to s. over a delicate subject,** glisser sur un sujet délicat; (*e*) se glisser (dans une pièce, derrière un rideau, etc.); (*f*) **to let things, everything, s.,** laisser tout aller à la dérive, à vau-l'eau; se désintéresser de tout. **2.** *v.tr.* (faire) glisser; **to s. sth. into one's pocket,** glisser qch. dans sa poche. **slide down** *v.i.* descendre en glissant; **to s. down a rope,** se laisser couler, se laisser glisser, le long d'une corde; **to s. down the banisters,** glisser le long de la rampe. **slide off** *v.i. F:* décamper; filer. **slide out** *v.i. F:* se glisser dehors; se défiler. **sliding 1.** *a.* glissant; (panneau) coulissant, mobile; *Aut:* (toit) ouvrant; **s. door,** porte coulissante, glissante; porte à coulisse, à glissières; **s. seat,** (i) *Row:* banc *m* à coulisses, à glissières; (ii) *Aut:* siège *m* réglable, mobile; *Mec.E:* **s. parts,** organes *mpl* mobiles; *Pol.Ec:* **s. scale,** échelle *f* mobile (des prix, etc.). **2.** *n.* glissement *m*; coulissement *m*.

slight¹ [slait] *a.* **1.** (*thin*) mince, ténu; (*of figure*) frêle; maigrelet. **2.** (*small*) (*of pain, mistake, etc.*) léger, petit; (*of intelligence, difference, etc.*) faible; (*of occasion, etc.*) de peu d'importance; (*of damage*) peu considérable; (*of wound*) sans gravité; **a s. accident,** un petit accident; **a s. improvement,** un léger mieux; **not the slightest danger,** pas le moindre danger; **to take offence at the slightest thing,** se piquer d'un rien; **on the slightest pretext,** sous un prétexte quelconque; **I haven't the slightest idea,** je n'en ai pas la moindre idée; **not in the slightest,** pas du tout, pas le moins du monde. **-ly** *adv.* **1. s. built,** (i) au corps frêle; (ii) à la taille mince. **2.** légèrement; peu; **s. better,** un petit peu mieux; **I know him s.,** je le connais un peu.

slight² *n.* manque *m* de considération, d'égards; affront *m*; **to put a s. on s.o.,** traiter qn sans considération; manquer d'égards pour, à, qn; faire un affront à qn.

slight³ *v.tr.* traiter (qn) sans considération; manquer d'égards pour, à (qn); faire un affront à (qn); **to feel slighted,** éprouver un froissement. **slighting** *a.* (air) de mépris, de dédain. **slightingly** *adv.* dédaigneusement.

slightness ['slaitnis] *n.* **1.** minceur *f* (d'une pièce de bois, du corps). **2.** légèreté *f* (d'une faute, etc.); faiblesse *f* (de l'intelligence, d'une différence); peu *m* d'importance, insignifiance *f* (des dégâts).

slim¹ [slim] *a.* **(slimmer; slimmest) 1.** (*a*) (*of pers.*) svelte, élancé, fluet; (*of fingers, etc.*) fuselé, menu; (*of book, etc.*) mince; (*b*) (*of chance, hope, etc.*) mince, léger. **-ly** *adv.* **s. built,** à la taille svelte.

slim² *v.* **(slimmed) 1.** *v.tr.* (*a*) amincir; **dress that is slimming,** robe amincissante; (*b*) *Fig:* **to s. down,** réduire (la main-d'œuvre). **2.** *v.i.* **to s. (down),** maigrir; **to be slimming,** suivre un régime amaigrissant. **slimming** *n.* amincissement *m*; **s. diet,** régime amaigrissant; **s. course,** cure d'amaigrissement.

slime [slaim] *n.* **1.** limon *m*, vase *f*; (*gold mining*) boue *f*, poussier *m*, de minerai. **2.** (*a*) humeur visqueuse (sur les poissons, etc.); bave *f* (de limace).

sliminess ['slaiminis] *n.* **1.** état vaseux, gluant; viscosité *f*. **2.** *F:* servilité *f*, obséquiosité *f*.

slimmer ['slimər] *n.* personne *f* qui suit un régime amaigrissant.

slimness ['slimnis] *n.* (*a*) taille *f* mince; sveltesse *f*; (*b*) minceur *f* (d'un livre, etc.)

slimy ['slaimi] *a.* **1.** (*a*) limoneux, vaseux; (boue) grasse; (*b*) (*of paste, etc.*) visqueux, gluant. **2.** (*a*) couvert de vase, de limon; (*b*) (*of fish*) couvert d'une sécrétion visqueuse; (*of slug, etc.*) couvert de bave. **3.** *F:* (*of pers.*) servile, obséquieux.

sling¹ [sliŋ] *n.* **1.** fronde *f*. **2.** (*a*) *Med:* écharpe *f*; **to have one's arm in a s.,** avoir, porter, le bras en écharpe; (*b*) bandoulière *f* (de harpe, etc.); bretelle *f* (de fusil, etc.); (*c*) (*for hoisting*) *Nau: etc:* élingue *f*; (*for animals*) ventrière *f*; **boat slings,** pattes *f* d'embarcation; *Const:* **(rope) s.,** brayer *m* (de maçon); (*d*) (*for hoisting s.o.*) agui *m*, chaise *f* (pour charpentier, etc.); **rescue s.,** bridage *m* (de sauvetage); (*e*) *Vet:* travail *m* (pour chevaux), *pl.* travails.

sling² *v.tr.* (*p.t. & p.p.* **slung** [slʌŋ]) **1.** lancer, jeter ((i) avec une fronde, (ii) *F:* avec la main); **to s. s.o. out,** flanquer qn dehors. **2.** suspendre; **to s. sth. over one's shoulder,** jeter qch. sur l'épaule; mettre qch. en bandoulière; **slung rifle,** fusil *m* à la grenadière. **3.** élinguer (un fardeau); **to s. up,** hisser (avec une grue).

slingback ['sliŋbæk] *a. & n.* (chaussure *f*) à talon découvert; sandale *f*.

slingshot ['sliŋʃɔt] *n. NAm:* fronde *f*.

slink [sliŋk] *v.i.* (*p.t. & p.p.* **slunk** [slʌŋk]) **to s. off, away,** partir furtivement, en catimini; s'éclipser; **to s. in,** entrer furtivement. **slinking** *a.* furtif.

slinky ['sliŋki] *a. F:* (*a*) (*of figure*) svelte, mince; (*b*) (*of clothing*) collant, ajusté.

slip¹ [slip] *n.* **1.** (*a*) glissade *f*, glissement *m*, faux pas; **it was only a s. of the hand,** sa main a glissé; (*b*) **to give s.o. the s.,** se dérober à qn; fausser compagnie à qn; (*c*) faute *f*, erreur *f*, d'inattention; faute d'étourderie; lapsus *m*; **to make a s.,** faire un lapsus; **s. of the pen,** petite erreur d'orthographe; **he made a s. of the tongue,** la langue lui a fourché; (*d*) écart *m* (de conduite); peccadille *f*; (*e*) *Geol:* glissement *m*, éboulement *m* (de terrain). **2.** (*a*) glissement; patinage *m* (d'une courroie, *Aut:* de l'embrayage); **s. stitch,** (i) *Knit:* maille glissée; (ii) *Needlew:* point perdu; (*b*) *Av: Nau:* recul *m* (de l'hélice). **3.** laisse *f*, slip *m* (de chien de chasse). **4.** *Rail:* **s. carriage, coach,** voiture *f*, rame *f*, à décrocher en cours de route. **5.** (*a*) *Cost:* combinaison *f* (de femme); **half, waist, s.,** jupon *m*; **your slip's showing,** (i) votre jupon dépasse; (ii) *F:* vous cherchez une belle-mère? *O:* **gym s.,** tunique *f* (d'écolière); (*b*) **(pillow) s.,** taie *f* d'oreiller. **6.** (*a*) cale *f* de chargement (d'un bac); (*b*) *N.Arch:* **building s.,** cale, chantier *m*, de construction; **ship on the slips,** navire *m* sur cale(s), en construction. **7.** *Th:* **the slips,** les coulisses *fpl.* **8.** *Cr:* (*a*) chasseur posté à droite du garde-guichet; (*b*) **the slips,** station *f* à droite du garde-guichet.

slip² *v.* **(slipped** [slipt]) **I.** *v.i.* **1.** (*a*) glisser; (*of knot*) couler, courir; (*of earth, etc.*) s'ébouler; *Mec.E: etc:* (*of belt, etc.*) patiner, glisser; *El: etc:* (*of frequency, etc.*) se décaler; **his foot slipped,** son pied a glissé; **I slipped on a banana skin,** j'ai glissé sur une peau de banane; *F:* **you're slipping,** tu perds les pédales; (*of vase, etc.*) **to s. from s.o.'s hands, grasp,** glisser des mains, des doigts, de qn; **to s. through s.o.'s fingers,** glisser entre les doigts de qn; (*b*) se glisser, se couler; **to s. into bed,** se glisser, se couler, dans son lit; **to s. into one's dressing gown,** passer, enfiler, sa robe de chambre; **to s. into bad habits,** se laisser aller à, prendre, de mauvaises habitudes; **error that has slipped into the text,** faute qui s'est glissée dans le texte; **the patient slipped into a coma,** le malade est entré dans le coma; (*c*) *F:* aller (vivement); **just s. round, over, to the post,** faites un saut jusqu'au bureau de poste; (*d*) (*of bolt*) **to s. home,** fermer à fond. **2.** faire une (faute d')étourderie, une bévue; se fourvoyer, se tromper. **3. to let s.,** lâcher (un lévrier, etc.); laisser échapper (une belle occasion, un mot, un secret). **II.** *v.tr.* **1.** (*a*) se dégager de (qch.); (*of animal*) **to s. its chain, leash, lead,** se détacher; **the dog has slipped its collar,** le chien s'est dégagé de son collier; (*b*) **his name has slipped my mind,** son nom m'échappe; **to s. s.o.'s attention,** échapper à l'attention de qn. **2.** (*a*) *Ven:* **to s. the hounds,** lâcher, découpler, les chiens; (*b*) *Nau:* **to s. a cable,** larguer, filer, une amarre par le bout; **to s. one's moorings,** filer le corps-mort; (*c*) *Rail:* décrocher (une voiture en cours de route); (*d*) (*of animal*) **to s. its young,** mettre bas avant terme. **3.** (*a*) couler, glisser (qch. dans la main de qn, une lettre à la poste); **to s. the bolt (home),** pousser le verrou à fond; **I slipped my arm round her waist,** je lui ai passé mon bras autour de la taille; (*b*) *Med:* **to s. a disc,** se faire une hernie discale; (*c*) *Knit:* glisser (une maille); (*d*) *F:* **to s. sth., one, over on s.o.,** donner le change à qn; duper qn. **4.** *Aut:* **to s. the clutch,** laisser patiner l'embrayage. **slip away** *v.i.* (*a*) (*of pers.*) filer; s'esquiver, s'éclipser; (*b*) (*of time*) s'écouler, (se) passer, fuir. **slip by** *v.i.* = SLIP AWAY (*b*). **slip down** *v.i.* (*a*) descendre en glissant; (*b*) (*of socks, etc.*) tomber; glisser. **slip in** *v.i.* entrer (en passant); se glisser dans une pièce, une maison, etc. **slip off 1.** *v.tr.* enlever, ôter (un vêtement). **2.** *v.i.* (*a*) filer; s'esquiver, s'éclipser; (*b*) se détacher; tomber. **slip on** *v.tr.* enfiler, passer (un vêtement). **slip out** *v.i.* (*a*) s'échapper; **to let sth. s. out,** laisser échapper qch.; **the secret has slipped out,** le secret a transpiré; (*b*) sortir (à la dérobée); **I'm just slipping out for a few minutes,** je sors pour quelques moments. **slipping 1.** *a.* glissant; qui glisse. **2.** *n.* (*a*) glissement *m*; patinage *m*; (*b*) glissade *f.* **slip up** *v.i.* (*a*) se tromper; faire une gaffe; (*b*) échouer.

slip³ *n.* **1.** (*a*) *Hort:* bouture *f*; (*for grafting*) scion *m*; (*b*) *F:* **s. of a girl,** jeune fille fluette, élancée. **2.** (*a*) bande étroite (de terre, etc.); fiche *f*; bout *m* (de papier); **pay s.,** bulletin *m* de paie; **sales s.,** récépissé *m*; (*b*) *Typ:* **(proof) s.,** placard *m*. **3.** *Th:* **slips,** couloir *m* du balcon.

slip⁴ *n.* *Cer:* barbotine *f*, engobe *m*.

slipcase ['slipkeis] *n.* *esp. Publ:* étui *m*.

slipcover ['slipkʌvər] *n.* *Furn:* housse *f*; *esp. Publ:* étui *m*.

slipknot ['slipnɔt] *n.* nœud coulant.

slip-on ['slipɔn] *n.* *F:* (*a*) **s.-ons,** *a.* **s.-on shoes,** mocassins *mpl*; (*b*) *NAm:* pull-over *m*, *pl.* pull-overs.

slipover ['slipouvər] *n.* pull-over *m* (sans manches).

slipper ['slipər] *n.* **1. (bedroom) s.,** chausson *m*; (*backless*) pantoufle *f*; (*ladies'*) mule *f*. **2.** *Mec.E:* patin *m* (de frein).

slipperiness ['slipərinis] *n.* **1.** nature glissante (d'une surface). **2.** caractère rusé.

slippery ['slipəri] *a.* **1.** (*of pavement, fish, etc.*) glissant; **it's s. (underfoot),** le pavé est glissant; ça glisse. **2.** (*a*) instable, incertain; **to be on a s. slope, on s. ground,** être sur un terrain glissant, une pente glissante; (*b*) (sujet) délicat, scabreux. **3.** fin, rusé; retors; **he's as s. as an eel,** il glisse, échappe, comme une anguille; **a s. customer,** une fine mouche.

slippy ['slipi] *a.* *F:* (*a*) glissant; (*b*) **look s.!** grouille-toi!

sliproad ['sliproud] *n.* bretelle *f* (d'une autoroute).

slipshod ['slipʃɔd] *a.* (personne) (i) mal soignée, (ii) négligente; (travail) négligé, bâclé; (style) débraillé; **book written in a s. manner,** livre écrit sans soin.

slipstream ['slipstriːm] *n.* (*a*) sillage *m*, remous *mpl* (d'air, d'eau); (*b*) *Av:* souffle *m*, vent *m*, de l'hélice.

slip(-)up ['slipʌp] *n.* **1.** gaffe *f*, bévue *f*. **2.** échec *m*.

slipway ['slipwei] *n.* *N.Arch:* cale *f*, chantier *m*, de construction; slip *m* (de halage, de carénage).

slit¹ [slit] *n.* (*a*) fente *f*; fissure *f*, rainure *f*; (*between curtains, etc.*) entrebâillement *m*; (*in wall, for shooting through, etc.*) taillade *f*; guichet *m* (d'une boîte aux lettres); **s. eyed,** aux yeux bridés; (*b*) *Tail:* **s. pocket,** fente verticale donnant accès aux vêtements de dessous; fausse poche.

slit² *v.tr.* (*p.t. & p.p.* **slit;** *pr.p.* **slitting**) (*a*) fendre; **to s. s.o.'s throat,** couper la gorge à qn; **to s. open a sack,** éventrer un sac; **s. skirt,** jupe fendue; (*b*) *Surg:* faire une incision dans (la chair); **the blow s. his cheek,** le coup lui a déchiré la joue; (*c*) refendre (le cuir, le bois, etc.).

slither¹ ['sliðər] *n.* glissement *m*, glissade *f*.

slither² *v.i.* (*a*) glisser; **to s. down a hill,** dégringoler une pente; (*b*) (*of snake, worm*) ramper.

sliver¹ ['sl(a)ivər] *n.* **1.** (*a*) tranche (fine); (*b*) éclat *m* (de bois, d'obus). **2.** *Tex:* ruban *m* (de lin cardé).

sliver² **1.** *v.tr.* couper (qch.) en tranches (fines). **2.** *v.i.* (*of wood, shell*) voler en éclats.

slob [slɔb] *n.* *F:* rustaud *m*; **big fat s.,** gros lard.

slobber¹ ['slɔbər] *n.* *F:* (*a*) bave *f*, salive *f*; (*b*) sentimentalité larmoyante.

slobber² *F:* *v.i.* (*a*) baver; (*b*) larmoyer; **to s. (all) over s.o.,** témoigner une tendresse exagérée envers qn; s'attendrir sur qn.

sloe [slou] *n.* *Bot:* **1.** prunelle *f*; **s. gin** = (alcool *m* de) prunelle. **2. s. bush, tree,** prunellier *m*; épine noire.

slog¹ [slɔg] *n.* *F:* **1.** coup (violent). **2.** corvée *f*; boulot *m*; **a hard s.,** un gros effort.

slog² *v.* **(slogged)** *F:* **1.** *v.tr.* (*a*) cogner, battre (qch., qn); (*b*) *Cr:* frapper fort sur (la balle). **2.** *v.i.* (*a*) *Box:* cogner dur (au hasard); *Cr:* donner de grands coups de batte; (*b*) turbiner, trimer; **to s. away at sth.,** travailler avec acharnement à qch.; (*c*) **to s. on, along,** marcher d'un pas lourd, péniblement.

slogan ['slougən] *n.* (*a*) cri *m* de guerre, de bataille; mot *m* d'ordre; (*b*) *Com:* devise *f*; slogan *m*.

slogger ['slɔgər] *n.* *F:* **1.** *Box:* *Cr:* cogneur *m* (qui frappe au hasard). **2.** travailleur acharné, abatteur *m* de besogne, bûcheur *m*.

sloop [sluːp] *n.* *Nau:* sloop *m*.

slop¹ [slɔp] *n.* **1. slops,** (*a*) boissons renversées (sur la table, etc.); (*b*) *Pej:* (*drink*) lavasse *f*; (*c*) *O:* aliments *mpl* liquides; bouillons *mpl*; (*d*) eaux ménagères; eaux sales; **s. pail,** seau *m* de toilette, hygiénique; (*e*) fonds *m* de tasse; **s. basin,** vide-tasses *m inv.* **2.** *F:* sentimentalité excessive.

slop² *v.* **(slopped)** **1.** *v.tr.* renverser, répandre (un liquide) (**over the table,** sur la table). **2.** *v.i.* (*a*) (*of liquids*) **to s. (over),** déborder; *F: O:* **to s. over s.o.,** témoigner une tendresse exagérée envers qn; s'attendrir sur qn; (*b*) **to s. about in the mud,** patauger, barboter, dans la boue; (*c*) (*in prison*) **to s. out,** vider les seaux hygiéniques.

slop³ *n. Nau:* **slops,** effets *mpl,* frusques *fpl* (d'un matelot); **s. room,** magasin *m* d'habillement.

slope¹ [sloup] *n.* **1.** pente *f,* inclinaison *f;* **steep, gentle, s.,** pente raide, douce; *Mil:* **with rifle at the s.,** l'arme sur l'épaule. **2.** pente; talus *m;* versant *m* (de montagne); (*in road, railway*) rampe *f; Ski:* piste *f;* **half way down, up, the s.,** à mi-pente.

slope² **1.** *v.i.* (*a*) être en pente; incliner, pencher; (*of writing*) **to s. forward, backward,** pencher à droite, à gauche; (*b*) aller en pente; aller en descendant; s'abaisser; **the garden slopes down to the river,** le jardin dévale vers la rivière. **2.** *v.tr.* (*a*) couper (qch.) en pente; déverser (un mur); (*b*) *Mil:* **to s. arms,** mettre l'arme sur l'épaule; **s. arms!** arme sur l'épaule! **sloping** *a.* en pente; incliné; (jardin, etc.) en talus; (terrain) déclive; **s. shoulders,** épaules tombantes; **s. (hand)writing,** écriture couchée.

slope³ *v.i. F:* **to s. off,** décamper, filer.

sloppiness ['slɔpinis] *n.* (*a*) (*of pers.*) mollesse *f;* avachissement *m;* (*b*) manque *m* de soin (dans un travail); négligence *f* (de style); (*c*) ampleur *f* (d'une robe mal coupée); (*d*) *F:* sentimentalité excessive.

sloppy ['slɔpi] *a.* **1.** (plancher) mouillé; (table) qui n'a pas été essuyée. **2.** (*a*) *F:* (*of pers.*) mou, *f.* molle; **to become s.,** s'avachir; (*b*) *F:* (travail) fait sans soin; (style) négligé, débraillé; (*c*) (vêtement) mal ajusté, trop large; *F:* **s. joe,** pull-over *m* très ample; (*d*) *F:* (roman, etc.) larmoyant; **s. sentimentality,** sensiblerie *f.* **-ily** *adv.* **1.** sans soin. **2.** *F:* avec sensiblerie.

slosh [slɔʃ] **1.** *v.i.* (*a*) (*of liquid*) **to s. (around),** clapoter; (*b*) (*of pers., animal*) **to s. about,** patauger. **2.** *v.tr. F:* (*a*) flanquer (de la peinture sur un mur, etc.); (*b*) flanquer un coup à (qn), tabasser (qn). **sloshed** *a. P:* ivre, soûl.

slot¹ [slɔt] *n.* (*a*) entaille *f,* encoche *f,* rainure *f;* fente *f* (de la tête d'une vis, d'une tirelire); **to put a coin in the s.,** introduire pièce de monnaie dans la fente (d'un distributeur, etc.); **s. machine,** (i) distributeur (automatique); (ii) *esp. NAm:* machine *f,* appareil *m,* à sous; **s. meter,** compteur *m* (à gaz) à paiement préalable; (*b*) *W.Tel: T.V: etc:* portion délimitée de l'horaire de diffusion; créneau *m* (horaire); **prime time s.,** créneau de pointe.

slot² *v.* **(slotted) 1.** *v.tr. Mec.E: etc:* tailler une fente, une rainure, dans (qch.); rain(ur)er (qch.); **to s. sth. into sth.,** insérer, mettre, qch. dans qch. **2.** *v.i.* s'introduire, se glisser (**into sth.,** dans qch.).

slot³ *n. Ven:* foulées *fpl,* voies *fpl* (d'une bête).

sloth [slouθ] *n.* **1.** paresse *f,* fainéantise *f;* indolence *f.* **2.** *Z:* (*a*) paresseux *m;* (*b*) **s. monkey,** loris lent; **s. bear,** ours jongleur.

slothful ['slouθf(u)l] *a.* paresseux, fainéant; indolent. **-fully** *adv.* paresseusement; avec indolence.

slothfulness ['slouθf(u)lnis] *n.* = SLOTH 1.

slouch¹ [slautʃ] *n.* **1.** démarche *f* mollasse; mollesse *f,* lourdeur *f,* d'allure; **s. of the shoulders,** épaules arrondies. **2. s. hat,** (grand) chapeau mou, rabattu. **3.** *esp. NAm: F:* **he's no s.,** il n'est pas empoté.

slouch² *v.i.* se tenir d'une façon négligée; avoir une allure lourde; **don't s.!** tenez-vous droit! **to s. about,** traîner le pas.

slough¹ [slau] *n.* (*a*) bourbier *m,* fondrière *f;* (*b*) terrain marécageux.

slough² [slʌf] *n.* **1.** (*of reptile, insect*) dépouille *f,* mue *f;* (*of snake*) **to cast its s.,** se dépouiller; muer. **2.** *Med:* croûte *f* (sur une plaie).

slough³ [slʌf] **1.** *v.i.* (*a*) (*of reptile, etc.*) se dépouiller; muer; (*b*) (*of scab, etc.*) **to s. off, away,** se détacher. **2.** *v.tr.* (*of reptile, insect*) **to s. its skin,** se dépouiller; muer; *Lit:* **to s. (off) a bad habit,** se dépouiller d'une mauvaise habitude.

Slovak, Slovakian ['slouvæk, slou'vækiən] **1.** *a. Ethn:* slovaque. **2.** *n.* (*a*) *Ethn:* Slovaque *mf;* (*b*) *Ling:* slovaque *m.*

Slovakia [slou'vækiə] *Pr.n. Geog:* Slovaquie *f.*

sloven ['slʌv(ə)n] *n.* **1.** mal soigné, -ée; souillon *f.* **2.** bousilleur, -euse.

Slovene, Slovenian ['slouviːn, -'viːniən] **1.** *a. Ethn:* slovène. **2.** *n.* (*a*) *Ethn:* Slovène *mf;* (*b*) *Ling:* slovène *m.*

slovenliness ['slʌv(ə)nlinis] *n.* **1.** négligence *f* (de mise); débraillé *m* (de la tenue). **2.** négligence; manque *m* de soin.

slovenly ['slʌv(ə)nli] *a.* **1.** (*of pers.*) mal soigné; (tenue) débraillée. **2.** (*a*) (*of pers.*) négligent; qui manque de soin; (*b*) (travail) négligé, bousillé; (style) débraillé; **done in a s. way,** fait sans soin.

slow¹ [slou] **I.** *a.* **1.** (*a*) lent; **s. steps,** pas lents; *Cin: etc:* **(in) s. motion,** (au) ralenti; *Mch:* **s. running,** ralenti; **to be s. over (doing) sth.,** mettre longtemps à faire qch.; **it's s. work,** ça ne va pas vite; *Cu:* **to cook sth. in a s. oven,** faire cuire qch. à four doux; *Rail:* **s. train,** (train *m*) omnibus *m;* (*b*) (*of pers.*) **to be s. to do sth.,** être lent à faire qch.; **s. to act, to take action, s. in action,** lent à agir; (*c*) **s. (of intellect),** lent d'esprit, à l'esprit lourd; **s. child,** enfant attardé, arriéré; (*d*) (spectacle, etc.) ennuyeux, qui manque d'entrain; **business is s.,** les affaires traînent; (*e*) *Games:* (terrain, billard, etc.) qui ne rend pas. **2.** (*of clock, watch*) en retard; **my watch is five minutes s.,** ma montre retarde de cinq minutes. **II.** *adv.* (*a*) lentement; **to go s.,** (i) aller lentement; (ii) *Ind:* faire la grève perlée; (*of engine*) **to run s.,** tourner au ralenti; *P.N:* **s.!** ralentir! *Nau:* **s. ahead, astern!** en avant, en arrière, doucement! (*b*) **s. moving, going,** qui se meut lentement; à marche lente; **s. spoken,** à la parole lente; **s. burning,** qui brûle lentement; à combustion lente; *Exp:* (poudre) lente. **slowly** *adv.* lentement; **running s.,** (moteur) au ralenti; **to cook sth. s.,** faire cuire qch. à feu doux.

slow² **1.** *v.i.* (*a*) **to s. down, up,** ralentir (son allure, sa marche); ralentir le pas; diminuer de vitesse; *Aut:* (*of engine*) prendre le ralenti; (*b*) **to s. down, up (to a stop),** s'arrêter. **2.** *v.tr.* **to s. sth. down, up,** ralentir qch.; *Ind:* **to s. down production,** marcher au ralenti. **slowing** *n.* **s. down,** ralentissement *m.*

slowcoach ['sloukoutʃ] *n. F:* lambin, -ine; traînard, -arde.

slowdown ['sloudaun] *n.* (*a*) ralentissement *m* (des affaires, etc.); (*b*) travail *m* au ralenti.

slowness ['slounis] *n.* **1.** (*a*) lenteur *f;* (*b*) lourdeur *f,* lenteur (d'esprit); (*c*) manque *m* d'entrain (d'un spectacle, etc.). **2.** retard *m* (d'une pendule, etc.).

slowpoke ['sloupouk] *n. NAm: F:* = SLOWCOACH.

slow-worm ['slouwəːm] *n. Rept:* orvet *m* (fragile); serpent *m* de verre.

sludge [slʌdʒ] *n.* (*a*) vase *f,* fange *f;* neige à moitié fondue; (*b*) **sewage s.,** vidanges *fpl;* (*c*) *Ind:* boue *f.*

sludgy ['slʌdʒi] *a.* (*a*) vaseux; (*b*) *Ind:* boueux.

slug¹ [slʌg] *n. Moll:* limace *f.*

slug² *n.* **1.** balle *f,* plomb *m* (d'une arme à feu). **2.** *esp. NAm: F:* goutte *f,* coup *m* (d'eau-de vie, etc.).

slug³ *n. NAm: F:* coup violent.

slug⁴ *v.tr. NAm: F:* (*a*) battre, tabasser (qn); **to s. it out,** se rentrer dedans; (*b*) (*in baseball*) frapper fort.

sluggard ['slʌgəd] *a. & n.* paresseux, -euse; fainéant, -ante.

sluggish ['slʌgiʃ] *a.* **1.** paresseux; léthargique; *F:* flemmard; (esprit) lourd, engourdi. **2.** (*of river, pulse, etc.*) lent, paresseux; *Aut:* (moteur) mou; (*of market*) stagnant; (*of sales*) difficile, qui ne va pas fort. **-ly** *adv.* **1.** paresseusement. **2.** lentement.

sluggishness ['slʌgiʃnis] *n.* **1.** (*a*) paresse *f*; *F:* flemme *f*; (*b*) lourdeur *f* (de l'esprit). **2.** lenteur *f* (d'une rivière, etc.); paresse (du foie, de l'intestin); *Aut:* mollesse *f* (du moteur).

sluice¹ [slu:s] *n.* **1.** (*a*) écluse *f*; **s. (gate),** porte *f* d'écluse; vanne *f*; *Lit:* **the s. gates of heaven have opened,** les écluses du ciel sont ouvertes; (*b*) canal *m*, -aux, de décharge (du trop-plein d'un réservoir); (*c*) **put it down the s.,** versez-le aux égouts. **2.** *F:* **to give sth. a s. down,** laver qch. à grande eau.

sluice² **1.** *v.tr.* (*a*) *Hyd.E:* vanner (un cours d'eau); (*b*) **to s. out,** laisser échapper (l'eau d'un réservoir) (par les vannes); (*c*) laver à grande eau; débourber (un égout, *Min:* le minerai); **to s. oneself down with cold water,** s'inonder d'eau fraîche. **2.** *v.i.* (*of water, etc.*) **to s. out,** couler à flots.

sluiceway ['slu:swei] *n.* canal *m*, -aux, à vannes.

slum¹ [slʌm] *n.* (*a*) rue *f*, impasse *f*, sordide; (*b*) bas quartier, quartier pauvre; (*c*) taudis *m*; **s. clearance,** suppression *f* des taudis.

slum² *v.i.* **(slummed)** *F:* **to s. it,** vivre pauvrement; manger de la vache enragée.

slumber¹ ['slʌmbər] *n.* (*a*) *Lit:* sommeil *m*; assoupissement *m*; (*b*) *Com:* **s. wear,** vêtements *mpl* de nuit.

slumber² *v.i. Lit:* sommeiller; dormir (paisiblement).

slummy ['slʌmi] *a.* (rue, etc.) sordide; **s. district,** bas quartier; quartier de taudis.

slump¹ [slʌmp] *n. Com:* baisse soudaine, chute *f*, effondrement *m* (des cours, etc.); crise *f*; **s. in the pound,** dégringolade *f* de la livre; **the s.,** la crise, la dépression, économique.

slump² *v.i.* **1.** tomber lourdement; s'affaisser (**into a chair,** dans un fauteuil). **2.** *Com: Ind: etc:* (*of prices, etc.*) baisser tout à coup; s'effondrer, dégringoler.

slur¹ [slə:r] *n.* **1.** (*a*) insulte *f*; (*b*) tache *f*, flétrissure *f*; souillure *f*; **to cast a s. on s.o.'s reputation,** ternir, porter atteinte à, la réputation de qn. **2.** *Typ:* macule *f*, maculage *m*. **3.** *Mus:* (*a*) (*sign*) liaison *f*; (*b*) (*passage*) coulé *m*. **4.** (*in speech*) mauvaise articulation.

slur² *v.tr. & i.* **(slurred)** (*a*) mal articuler (ses mots); **to s. (over),** bredouiller, escamoter (un mot); **to s. over a fact,** passer légèrement, glisser, sur un fait; **his speech was slurred,** il articulait mal; ses paroles étaient indistinctes; (*b*) *Mus:* lier (deux notes); couler (un passage); **slurred passage,** passage coulé; **slurred notes,** notes liées coulant.

slurp [slə:p] *v.tr. & i.* boire (qch.) avec bruit.

slush [slʌʃ] *n.* **1.** (*a*) neige à moitié fondue; (*b*) fange *f*, bourbe *f*. **2.** *F:* sensiblerie *f*. **3.** *F:* **s. fund,** caisse noire; **s. (money) payments,** graissage *m* de patte.

slushy ['slʌʃi] *a.* (*a*) (i) détrempé par la neige; (ii) bourbeux, fangeux; (*b*) *F:* (roman, etc.) d'une sentimentalité excessive, fadasse.

slut [slʌt] *n.f.* **1.** sagouine; saligaude. **2.** coureuse; salope.

sluttish ['slʌtiʃ] *a.* (*of woman*) malpropre, sale; (*of behaviour, etc.*) de salope.

sluttishness ['slʌtiʃnis] *n.* malpropreté *f*; saloperie *f*.

sly [slai] *a.* **(slyer, slyest) 1.** (*a*) rusé; **s. dog,** fin matois; (*b*) sournois; *n. F:* **on the s.,** faire qch. furtivement, à la dérobée, en cachette. **2.** malin, -igne, espiègle. **-ly** *adv.* **1.** (*a*) avec finesse; (*b*) sournoisement. **2.** d'une manière espiègle.

slyboots ['slaibu:ts] *n. F:* **1.** (*a*) sournois, -oise; (*b*) petit(e) rusé(e). **2.** espiègle *mf*; petit(e) coquin(e).

slyness ['slainis] *n.* **1.** (*a*) finesse *f*; (*b*) sournoiserie *f*. **2.** espièglerie *f*.

smack¹ [smæk] *n. O:* léger goût; soupçon *m* (d'ail, *Fig:* de malice, etc.).

smack² *v.i.* **to s. of sth.,** avoir un léger goût de qch.; **opinions that s. of heresy,** opinions *fpl* qui sentent, qui fleurent, l'hérésie.

smack³ **I.** *n.* **1.** claquement *m*, clic-clac *m* (d'un fouet, etc.); **with a s. of his tongue,** avec un claquement de langue. **2.** claque *f*; **s. in the face,** (i) gifle *f*; (ii) *F:* (*also* **s. in the eye**) affront *m*, rebuffade *f*; **to give a child a s. on the bottom,** donner une fessée à un enfant; **he gave the ball a hard s.,** il frappa vigoureusement la balle; *F:* **to have a s. at sth.,** essayer de faire qch. **3.** *F:* gros baiser retentissant; grosse bise. **II.** *adv.* **1. to go s.,** faire clic-clac; claquer. **2. to bump s. into a tree,** donner en plein contre un arbre; **s. in the middle,** en plein milieu.

smack⁴ **1.** *v.tr.* (*a*) faire claquer (un fouet); *F:* **to s. one's lips,** se lécher les babines; (*b*) frapper, taper (avec le plat de la main); donner une claque à (qn); **to s. s.o.'s face,** donner une gifle à qn; gifler qn; **to s. a child's bottom,** donner une fessée à un enfant. **2.** *v.i.* claquer. **smacking 1.** *a.* (baiser) retentissant. **2.** *n.* (*a*) claquement *m* (d'un fouet); (*b*) fessée *f*.

smack⁵ *n. Nau:* **(fishing) s.,** bateau de pêche.

smacker ['smækər] *n.* **1.** (*a*) *F:* gifle retentissante; (*b*) *F:* gros baiser, grosse bise. **2.** *P:* (*a*) livre *f* sterling; (*b*) dollar *m*.

small [smɔ:l] **I.** *a.* petit. **1.** (*a*) menu (caillou, etc.); faible (dose, etc.); **s. man,** petit homme; homme de petite taille; **s. child,** enfant en bas âge; petit enfant; **to make sth. smaller,** rapetisser qch.; **of s. dimensions,** de petites dimensions; **s. stature,** petite taille; **to make oneself s.,** se faire tout petit; **a s. coffee,** une demi-tasse (de café); **he's a s. eater,** il n'est pas gros mangeur; **s. arms,** armes portatives; *Typ:* **s. letters,** minuscules *fpl*; **s. capitals, s. caps,** petites majuscules; *F:* (*in contract, etc.*) **the s. print,** le texte en petits caractères; (*b*) **in s. numbers,** en petit nombre; **s. party,** (i) parti peu nombreux; (ii) réunion peu nombreuse. **2. s. voice,** (i) voix fluette; (ii) petite voix (que l'on entend à peine). **3. s. income,** revenu *m* modique; **not the smallest difference,** pas la moindre différence; **it's s. wonder that . . .,** ce n'est guère étonnant que + *sub.*; **it was no s. surprise to me,** à ma grande surprise; **of no s. consequence,** de très grande importance. **4.** (*a*) peu important; peu considérable; **a s. matter,** une bagatelle; *F:* (*of s.o., sth.*) **to be s. beer,** être insignifiant; **s. change,** petite monnaie; **s. details,** menus détails; **the smallest details,** les moindres détails; **a s. hotel,** un hôtel modeste; **the smaller industries,** la petite industrie; **s. shopkeeper,** petit commerçant; **in a s. way,** en petit; modestement; *Journ: F:* **s. ads,** petites annonces; (*b*) **the smallest possible number of people,** le moins de gens possible. **5.** mesquin, chétif; **s. mind,** petit esprit; **only a s. man could behave like that,** il n'y a qu'un petit esprit pour agir de la sorte; **I felt very s.,** je n'étais pas fier; **to make s.o. look s.,** humilier qn; ravaler qn. **II.** *n.* **1. s. of the back,** creux *m*, chute *f*, des reins. **2.** menu *m* du charbon; menus; charbonnaille *f*. **3.** *F:* **smalls,** lingerie *f*, sous-vêtements *mpl*; **to wash one's smalls,** faire sa petite lessive. **III.** *adv.* **1.** (hacher, etc.) menu, en petits morceaux. **2.** (écrire) fin.

smallholder ['smɔ:lhouldər] *n.* petit cultivateur.

smallholding ['smɔ:lhouldiŋ] *n. Agr:* petite ferme.

smallish ['smɔ:liʃ] *a.* assez, plutôt, petit.

small-minded [smɔ:l'maindid] *a.* à l'esprit mesquin, étroit; **a s.-m. man,** un petit esprit.

smallness ['smɔ:lnis] *n.* **1.** petitesse *f*; modicité *f* (de revenus); faiblesse *f* (d'une somme). **2. the s. of his mind,** sa petitesse d'esprit; sa mesquinerie.

smallpox ['smɔ:lpɔks] *n. Med:* petite vérole; variole *f*; **s. pustules,** pustules *f* varioliques; **s. patient,** varioleux, -euse.

small-scale ['smɔːlskeil] *a.* **1.** (modèle) réduit; (carte) à petite échelle. **2.** (entreprise) peu importante, de peu d'étendue.

small-time ['smɔːltaim] *a.* *F:* insignifiant, médiocre; **s.-t. crook,** petit escroc.

small-town ['smɔːltaun] *a.* *F:* provincial, de province.

smarm [smɑːm] *v.tr.* & *i.* *F:* **to s. (up to, over) s.o.,** flatter, flagorner, qn; lécher les bottes à qn.

smarmy ['smɑːmi] *a.* *F:* *Pej:* doucereux, flatteur.

smart¹ [smɑːt] *n.* douleur cuisante.

smart² *v.i.* (*a*) (*of wound, etc.*) cuire, brûler; picoter; **my eyes are smarting,** les yeux me brûlent, me picotent; (*b*) (*of pers.*) souffrir; **to s. under an insult,** souffrir sous le coup d'une insulte; **he'll make you s. for it,** il vous le fera payer cher. **smarting 1.** *a.* (*of pain, eyes*) cuisant, brûlant. **2.** *n.* douleur cuisante.

smart³ *a.* **1.** (coup de fouet) cuisant, cinglant; **s. box on the ear,** bonne gifle; **s. reprimand,** verte réprimande. **2.** vif; prompt; alerte; **s. pace,** allure vive, leste; **that's s. work!** vous allez vite en besogne! *adv.* **look s. (about it)!** dépêchez-vous! remuez-vous! **3.** (*a*) habile, adroit; à l'esprit éveillé; dégourdi, débrouillard; **s. lad wanted,** on demande un jeune homme intelligent; **s. business man,** homme d'affaires habile; **s. answer,** réponse adroite; *F:* **he's a s. one,** c'est une fine mouche; **s. trick,** (i) truc ingénieux; (ii) bon tour; (*b*) *Pej:* malin, *f.* maligne; **to be too s. for s.o.,** être trop malin pour qn; **trying to be s., eh?** tu essaies de faire le malin, hein? **4.** (*of dress, pers., etc.*) élégant, chic; coquet, pimpant; **to make oneself s.,** se faire beau, belle; **you do look s.!** comme vous voilà beau! **the s. set,** le monde élégant; les gens chics. **-ly** *adv.* **1.** promptement, vivement; (marcher) d'une vive allure; (se retourner) brusquement; **to answer s.,** riposter du tac au tac; **to pull s.o. up s.,** réprimander qn vertement. **2.** habilement, adroitement. **3.** (s'habiller, etc.) élégamment.

smarten ['smɑːt(ə)n] *v.tr.* & *i.* **to s. up,** donner du chic à (qch.); **to s. (oneself) up,** se faire beau.

smartness ['smɑːtnis] *n.* **1.** (*a*) vivacité *f* (d'esprit); intelligence *f*; esprit débrouillard, débrouillardise *f*; (*b*) à-propos *m.* **2.** finesse *f.* **3.** élégance *f*; chic *m.*

smash¹ [smæʃ] **I.** *n.* **1.** (*a*) coup dur, écrasant; (*b*) *Ten:* smash *m.* **2.** (*a*) mise *f* en morceaux, en miettes; fracassement *m*; (*b*) désastre *m*, sinistre *m* (de chemin de fer); collision *f*, tamponnement *m* (de trains, de voitures). **3.** (*a*) débâcle *f*; faillite (commerciale); (*b*) déroute *f*; défaite complète. **4.** *U.S:* **(brandy) s.,** cognac *m* à la glace et à la menthe. **5. s. (hit),** gros succès, succès fou. **II.** *adv.* **1. to go s.,** (*of firm*) faire faillite, tomber en faillite; (*of bank*) sauter. **2. to run s. into sth.,** se heurter de front contre qch.; (*of car*) s'emboutir contre (un mur, etc.).

smash² **I.** *v.tr.* **1.** (*a*) **to s. sth. on, against, sth.,** heurter, choquer, lancer, qch. contre qch. avec violence; (*b*) *Ten:* écraser, smasher (la balle). **2.** (*a*) **to s. sth. to pieces,** briser qch. en morceaux; fracasser qch.; **to s. the door open,** enfoncer la porte; (*b*) détruire (qn, qch.); écraser, démolir (une armée, etc.); *Sp:* pulvériser (un record); (*c*) ruiner (qn); faire faire faillite à (qn); faire échouer (un projet). **II.** *v.i.* **1.** se heurter violemment (contre qch.); **the car smashed into the wall,** la voiture s'est écrasée, est allée s'emboutir, contre le mur. **2. to s. (in pieces),** éclater en morceaux, en pièces. **3.** (*of firm, etc.*) faire faillite. **smashed** *a.* *P:* ivre, soûl; **to get s.,** se soûler. **smash in** *v.tr.* enfoncer, défoncer (une boîte, etc.); enfoncer (une porte); *F:* **to s. s.o.'s face in,** casser la figure, *F:* la gueule, à qn. **smashing** *a.* (*a*) (coup) écrasant, assommant; (*b*) *F:* formidable; épatant; **she's s.!** ce qu'elle est belle! **smash up** *v.tr.* briser (qch.) en morceaux; démolir (une voiture, etc.).

smash-and-grab [smæʃənd'græb] *a.* **s.-a.-g. raid,** rafle *f* (de bijoux, etc.) après bris de devanture.

smasher ['smæʃər] *n.* **1.** briseur, -euse. **2.** *F:* coup écrasant, assommant. **3.** *F:* **what a s.!** ce qu'elle est belle! **that's a s.!** c'est épatant!

smash-up ['smæʃʌp] *n.* *F:* (*a*) destruction complète; *Aut: Rail: etc:* grave collision *f*; (*b*) débâcle *f.*

smattering ['smæt(ə)riŋ] *n.* légère connaissance (d'une langue, etc.); **to have a s. of sth.,** savoir un peu, quelques bribes (d'anglais, etc.); avoir des notions de (chimie, etc.).

smear¹ ['smiər] *n.* **1.** (*a*) tache *f*, macule *f*, souillure *f*; (*b*) **s. campaign,** campagne *f* de calomnies. **2.** (*for microscope*) frottis *m* (vaginal, etc.).

smear² *v.tr.* **1.** (*a*) barbouiller, salir **(with,** de); salir (la réputation de qn); (*b*) enduire **(with,** de). **2.** maculer, barbouiller (une page écrite, etc.); (*of outline*) **to get smeared,** s'estomper. **3.** calomnier (qn); porter atteinte à (la réputation de qn, etc.).

smeary ['smiəri] *a.* **1.** taché, barbouillé; aux contours brouillés. **2.** graisseux.

smell¹ [smel] *n.* **1. (sense of) s.,** odorat *m*; flair *m* (d'un chien); **to have a keen sense of s.,** avoir l'odorat fin. **2.** (*a*) odeur *f*, senteur *f*, parfum *m* (des fleurs, etc.); **there's a bad s.,** ça sent mauvais; **stale s.,** relent *m* (de bière, etc.); **(pleasant) s. of cooking,** fumet *m* de cuisine; (*b*) mauvaise odeur. **3. to take a s. at sth.,** flairer qch.; respirer (un flacon de sels, etc.).

smell² *v.* (*p.t.* & *p.p.* **smelt,** *occ.* **smelled**) **1.** *v.tr.* & *ind.tr.* (*a*) flairer (qch.); sentir (une fleur); respirer l'odeur (d'un bouquet); (*of dog*) **to s. (at) sth.,** flairer, renifler, qch.; (*b*) avoir de l'odorat; **he can't s.,** il n'a pas d'odorat; il ne sent rien; (*c*) sentir l'odeur de (qch.); sentir, percevoir (une odeur); **I can s. something burning,** je sens quelque chose qui brûle; (*d*) sentir, flairer, pressentir (le danger, etc.). **2.** *v.i.* (*a*) (*of flower, etc.*) sentir; **to s. good, bad, strong(ly),** sentir bon, mauvais, fort; **to s. of violets,** sentir, fleurer, la violette; **these flowers don't s.,** ces fleurs n'ont pas d'odeur; (*b*) sentir (mauvais); avoir une forte odeur; **his breath smells,** il a une mauvaise haleine. **smelling 1.** *a.* odoriférant, odorant; **sweet s.,** qui sent bon. **2.** *n.* *O:* **s. salts,** sels (volatils) anglais, sel de vinaigre; **s. bottle,** flacon *m* de sels. **smell out** *v.tr.* (*of dog*) flairer, dépister (le gibier); (*of pers.*) flairer, découvrir (un secret).

smelliness ['smelinis] *n.* *F:* mauvaise odeur; puanteur *f.*

smelly ['smeli] *a.* *F:* malodorant, puant.

smelt¹ [smelt] *v.tr.* (*a*) fondre (le minerai); (*b*) extraire (le métal) par fusion. **smelting** *n.* (*a*) fonte *f*, fusion *f* (d'un minerai, d'un métal); (*b*) extraction *f* (du métal) par fusion; **s. works,** fonderie *f.*

smelt² *n.* *Ich:* éperlan *m.*

smidgen['smidʒən] *n.* *NAm:* *F:* (très) petite quantité.

smile¹ [smail] *n.* sourire *m*; **with a s.,** en souriant, avec un sourire; **with a s. on his lips,** le sourire aux lèvres; **to give s.o. a s.,** adresser un sourire à qn; **she was all smiles,** elle était toute souriante.

smile² **1.** *v.i.* sourire; **to s. at s.o.,** sourire à qn; adresser un sourire à qn; **Fortune smiles on him,** la fortune lui sourit; **to keep smiling,** *Lit:* **to s., in the face of adversity,** garder le sourire; **he always comes up smiling,** il garde toujours le sourire. **2.** *v.tr.* (*a*) *with cogn. acc.* **to s. a bitter smile,** sourire amèrement; avoir un sourire amer; (*b*) **to s. a welcome to s.o.,** accueillir qn avec, par, un sourire; **to s. one's gratitude,** exprimer sa gratitude par un sourire. **smiling** *a.* souriant; **to look s.,** être tout souriant. **smilingly** *adv.* en souriant; avec un sourire.

smirch¹ [smɔːtʃ] *n.* tache *f*; salissure *f*, souillure *f.*

smirch² *v.tr.* salir, souiller; **smirched reputation,** réputation souillée, salie.

smirk¹ [smə:k] *n.* sourire affecté; minauderie *f.*

smirk² *v.i.* sourire d'un air affecté; minauder, mignarder.

smite [smait] *v.tr.* (*p.t.* **smote** [smout]; *p.p.* **smitten** ['smitən]) **1.** *A: & Lit:* frapper, battre (l'ennemi); **to s. s.o. down,** abattre qn; **my conscience smote me,** je fus frappé de remords. **2. to be smitten with (sth.),** être frappé de (cécité); être pris de (remords); **to be smitten with a desire to do sth.,** être pris de désir de faire qch.; *F:* **to be smitten with a girl,** être épris, amouraché, d'une jeune fille.

smith [smiθ] *n.* forgeron *m*; **shoeing s.,** maréchal ferrant.

smithereens [smiðə'ri:nz] *n.pl. F:* morceaux *mpl*; miettes *fpl*; **the ship was blown to s.,** l'explosion a réduit le navire en miettes; **to smash sth. to s.,** briser, réduire, qch. en éclats, en mille morceaux.

smithy ['smiði] *n.* forge *f*; **shoeing s.,** (atelier *m* de) maréchalerie *f.*

smock¹ [smɔk] *n. Cost:* blouse *f*, sarrau *m.*

smock² *v.tr. Needlw:* orner (une robe, etc.) de smocks. **smocking** *n.* smocks *mpl.*

smog [smɔg] *n. F:* brouillard fumeux, smog *m.*

smoke¹ [smouk] *n.* **1.** fumée *f*; **s. bomb,** bombe *f* fumigène; **s. signals,** signaux *mpl* de fumée; **s. brown, grey,** brun, gris, fumée (*inv*); *F:* (*of project, etc.*) **to end in, go up in, s.,** s'en aller en fumée; n'aboutir à rien; *Prov:* **there's no s. without fire,** il n'y a pas de fumée sans feu. **2.** (*a*) **let's have a s.,** si on fumait une cigarette, une pipe, un cigare? **s. room,** fumoir *m*; (*b*) *F: O:* cigare *m*, cigarette *f*; **pass round the smokes,** faites circuler les cigares, les cigarettes.

smoke² **1.** *v.i.* (*emit smoke, vapour*) fumer; (*of lamp*) fumer, filer; **the horses' flanks were smoking,** les flancs des chevaux fumaient; les chevaux étaient tout fumants. **2.** *v.tr.* (*a*) (i) fumer (du jambon, des harengs, etc.); boucaner (la viande, le poisson); (ii) enfumer (une plante, les pucerons, etc.); (iii) **to s. out,** enfumer, faire déguerpir (un renard, etc.); (*b*) noircir de fumée, enfumer (le plafond, etc.); (*c*) *v.tr. & i.* fumer (du tabac); **do you s.?** fumez-vous? **do you mind if I s.?** la fumée vous gêne-t-elle? **smoked** *a.* (*a*) (jambon, etc.) fumé; (*b*) (plafond, etc.) enfumé; (*c*) **s. glass,** (i) verre fumé, noirci à la fumée; (ii) verre à teinte fumée. **smoking** **1.** *a.* fumant, qui fume. **2.** *n.* (*a*) émission *f* de fumée; (*b*) fumage *m* (de jambon, etc.); (*c*) (*tobacco*) **no s. (allowed),** défense *f* de fumer; *Rail:* **s. compartment,** compartiment *m* fumeurs; **s. room,** fumoir *m.*

smokeless ['smouklis] *a.* (houille) sans fumée; **s. zone,** zone *f* où il est interdit de rejeter de la fumée.

smoker ['smoukər] *n.* **1.** (*pers.*) (*a*) *Ind:* fumeur, -euse (de jambon, etc.); (*b*) fumeur, -euse (de tabac); **heavy s.,** grand fumeur. **2.** *F: Rail: etc:* compartiment *m* fumeurs.

smokescreen ['smoukskri:n] *n.* rideau *m*, écran *m*, de fumée.

smokestack ['smoukstæk] *n.* cheminée *f* (de locomotive, d'usine, etc.).

smoky ['smouki] *a.* **1.** (*of atmosphere*) fumeux; fuligineux; (*of room, town*) enfumé. **2.** (*a*) (plafond, etc.) noirci par la fumée; (*b*) *Geol:* **s. quartz,** quartz enfumé. **3.** (feu) qui fume; **s. lamp,** lampe qui fume, qui file. **4.** (goût) de fumée.

smolder ['smouldər] *v.i. NAm:* = SMOULDER.

smooch [smu:tʃ] *v.i. P:* se bécoter; se peloter.

smooth¹ [smu:ð] *a.* **1.** (*a*) (surface, pâte, papier) lisse; (chemin, etc.) uni, égal; (front) sans rides; **to make s.,** lisser (ses cheveux); aplanir (une route, etc.); **s. skin,** peau douce, satinée; (*of sea*) **as s. as a millpond,** calme, plate, comme un lac; (*b*) (tige, menton) glabre; (drap) à poil ras. **2.** (*a*) doux, *f.* douce; (voyage, vol, etc.) (i) confortable, (ii) sans anicroches; **s. running,** fonctionnement doux, régulier (d'une machine); (*b*) (vin) moelleux; (style) uni, coulant; (*c*) **s. temper,** humeur égale, facile; (*d*) doucereux, mielleux; **s. tongue,** langue doucereuse; *F:* **s. type, character,** personne mielleuse; beau parleur; **s.-spoken,** aux paroles doucereuses, mielleuses. **-ly** *adv.* **1.** uniment; sans inégalités. **2.** (marcher, travailler) doucement; (*of machine*) **to work, go, s.,** marcher sans à-coups; **everything's going s.,** tout va comme sur des roulettes.

smooth² *n.* **1. to give one's hair a s. (down),** lisser ses cheveux; se lisser les cheveux. **2.** (*a*) partie *f* lisse (de qch.); (*b*) terrain uni.

smooth³ *v.tr.* **1.** (*a*) **to s. (down),** lisser (ses plumes, ses cheveux, etc.); (*b*) aplanir (une planche); égaliser (le terrain); (*c*) défroisser (un vêtement); **to s. out,** faire disparaître (un faux pli); **to s. out, over, away, difficulties,** aplanir des difficultés; (*d*) **to s. one's brow,** dérider son front; **to s. the way for s.o.,** aplanir la voie pour qn. **2. to s. off,** adoucir (un angle). **smoothing** *n.* lissage *m*; aplanissement *m*, aplanissage *m* (du bois); égalisation *f* (du terrain); *Carp:* **s. plane,** rabot *m* à repasser.

smoothbore ['smu:ðbɔər] *n. Sm.a:* à canon lisse.

smoothie ['smu:ði] *n. F:* personne mielleuse.

smoothness ['smu:ðnis] *n.* **1.** (*a*) égalité *f* (d'une surface); douceur *f*, satiné *m* (de la peau); (*b*) calme *m* (de la mer). **2.** douceur (de la marche d'une machine); bon fonctionnement (d'une machine, d'une administration, etc.); coulant *m* (du style). **3.** (*of pers.*) air doucereux.

smooth-running [smu:ð'rʌniŋ] *a.* (*of machine, etc.*) à marche douce, régulière.

smother ['smʌðər] **1.** *v.tr.* (*a*) étouffer (qn, le feu, ses sentiments); suffoquer (qn); éteindre, étouffer (un son); retenir (un cri); réprimer (un juron); faire taire (son orgueil); *F:* **to smother s.o. with kisses,** étouffer qn de caresses; **to s. (up) a scandal,** cacher, couvrir, un scandale; (*b*) recouvrir; **strawberries smothered in, with, cream,** fraises enrobées de crème; **to be smothered in furs,** être emmitouflé de fourrures. **2.** *v.i.* suffoquer. **smothered** *a.* (cri) sourd.

smoulder, *NAm:* smolder [smouldər] *v.i.* (*a*) (*of coal, etc.*) brûler lentement, sans flamme; (*b*) (*of fire, rebellion, etc.*) couver (sous la cendre). **smouldering, *NAm:* smoldering** *a.* (*a*) (charbon, etc.) qui brûle sans fumée; (*b*) (feu, etc.) qui couve (sous la cendre). **2.** *n.* combustion lente.

smudge¹ [smʌdʒ] *n.* tache *f*; salissure *f*; bavure *f* de plume; **you've got a s. on your nose,** vous avez une tache (de suie, d'encre, etc.) sur le nez.

smudge² *v.tr.* salir, souiller; barbouiller, maculer (son écriture); *Typ:* mâchurer (une épreuve).

smudgy ['smʌdʒi] *a.* **1.** taché, souillé; (*of writing*) barbouillé, maculé. **2.** (contour, etc.) estompé.

smug [smʌg] *a.* (ton, air) suffisant, satisfait de soi-même; **he has a s. look,** il a l'air suffisant. **-ly** *adv.* d'un air suffisant.

smuggle [smʌgl] *v.tr. & i.* (faire) passer (des marchandises, etc.) en contrebande, en fraude; **to s. sth. into, out of, a country,** entrer, sortir, qch. en contrebande; **to s. sth. into a room,** apporter qch. subrepticement dans une pièce. **smuggling** *n.* contrebande *f*; fraude *f* (aux droits de douane).

smuggler ['smʌglər] *n.* contrebandier, -ière; fraudeur, -euse (à la douane).

smugness ['smʌgnis] *n.* suffisance *f.*

smut [smʌt] *n.* **1.** (*a*) parcelle *f* de suie; (*b*) tache *f* de suie (**on the face,** au visage). **2.** *coll.* saletés *fpl*, grivoiseries *fpl*, indécences *fpl*; **to talk s.,** dire des malpropretés, des saletés. **3.** *Agr:* charbon *m* (des céréales).

smuttiness ['smʌtinis] *n.* **1.** noirceur *f*, saleté *f*. **2.** grivoiserie *f*, grossièreté *f* (d'une remarque, etc.).

smutty ['smʌti] *a.* (*a*) noirci, noir; sali (de suie); (*b*) (*of conversation, etc.*) malpropre, grossier, grivois.

snack [snæk] *n.* léger repas; casse-croûte *m inv*; collation *f*; **to have a s.,** casser la croûte; manger un morceau sur le pouce; **s. bar,** snack(-bar) *m*.

snaffle ['snæfl] *n. Harn:* **s. (bit),** mors *m* de filet, mors brisé; **s. (bridle),** bridon *m*.

snafu [snæ'fu:] *a. NAm: P:* en (grand) désordre; chaotique.

snag¹ [snæg] *n.* **1.** (*a*) chicot *m* (d'arbre, de dent); (*b*) chicot, souche *f*, au ras d'eau ou formant écueil; (*c*) écueil *m*, obstacle caché; accroc *m*; **to strike, hit, come across, a s.,** se heurter à un obstacle, à une anicroche; **that's the s.!** voilà le hic! **2.** accroc (dans un vêtement).

snag² *v.tr.* **(snagged)** *F:* faire un accroc à (sa robe, etc.); accrocher (un bas, etc.).

snail [sneil] *n.* escargot *m*; colimaçon *m*, limaçon *m*; **edible s.,** escargot comestible; **at a snail's pace,** à pas de tortue.

snake¹ [sneik] *n.* (*a*) *Rept:* serpent *m*; **common s., grass s.,** couleuvre *f* à collier; **s. charmer,** charmeur, -euse, de serpents; *Fig:* **to nourish a s. in one's bosom,** réchauffer un serpent dans son sein; **a s. in the grass,** (i) un danger caché; une anguille sous roche; (ii) un faux jeton, un individu louche; *F:* **snakes alive!** grand Dieu! (*b*) *Games:* **snakes and ladders** = le jeu de l'oie; (*c*) *Fin:* serpent (monétaire).

snake² *v.i.* (*of road, etc.*) **to s. (along),** serpenter.

snakebite ['sneikbait] *n.* morsure *f* de serpent.

snake(-)like ['sneiklaik] *a.* anguiforme, ophidien.

snakeskin ['sneikskin] *n.* peau *f* de serpent.

snaky ['sneiki] *a.* **1.** (*a*) couleuvrin; de serpent; (*b*) (langue, etc.) de vipère; (homme) perfide. **2.** (*of road, etc.*) serpentant, sinueux. **3.** infesté de serpents.

snap¹ [snæp] **I.** *n.* **1.** (*a*) coup *m* de dents; **to make a s. at sth.,** tâcher de happer qch.; (*b*) coup de ciseaux; (*c*) coup sec, claquement *m* (des dents, d'un fouet, etc.); bruit *m* d'un bouton pression qui se ferme; **with a s. of the fingers,** en faisant claquer ses doigts. **2.** cassure *f*, rupture soudaine; **there was a s.,** quelque chose a cassé. **3. cold s.,** courte période de temps froid; coup de froid. **4.** *F:* énergie *f*, vivacité *f*. **5.** *Cu:* **ginger s.,** croquet *m* au gingembre. **6. s. fastener,** bouton-pression *m*; **s. lock,** serrure *f* à ressort. **7.** *Tls: Metalw:* **(rivet) s., s. tool,** bouterolle, chasse-rivet(s) *m inv.* **8.** *Phot:* = SNAPSHOT. **9.** *Cards:* = (jeu *m* de) bataille *f*. **10.** *U.S: F:* **soft s.,** chose *f* facile. **II.** *a.* instantané, imprévu; **s. decision,** décision *f* rapide; *Parl:* **s. division,** vote *m* de surprise. **III. adv. to go s.,** faire crac; se casser net; **s. went my stick!** crac! voilà ma canne cassée!

snap² *v.* **(snapped** [snæpt]) **I.** *v.i.* **1.** (*a*) (*of dog, etc.*) **to s. at s.o., sth.,** chercher à mordre, à happer, qn, qch.; (*of trigger, etc.*) **to s. back,** revenir brusquement; (*b*) *F:* **to s. at s.o.,** s'adresser à qn d'un ton sec, cassant; rembarrer qn. **2.** (*of teeth, whip, etc.*) claquer; faire un bruit sec; (*of fastener, door, etc.*) **to s. (shut),** se fermer avec un bruit sec. **3.** (*of stick, rope, etc.*) **to s. (in two),** se casser net; se rompre avec un bruit sec. **4.** *F:* **to s. out of it,** se secouer. **II.** *v.tr.* **1.** (*of dog, etc.*) saisir (qch.) d'un coup de dents; happer (qch.). **2.** (*a*) faire claquer (un fouet, etc.); **to s. one's fingers,** faire claquer ses doigts; **to s. one's fingers at s.o., in s.o.'s face,** narguer qn; faire la nique à qn; (*b*) *Phot: F:* prendre un instantané de qn, de qch. **3.** casser, rompre (une canne, etc.); **to s. sth. in two,** casser qch. net. **4. to s. (out),** jeter (des mots) d'un ton cassant; donner (un ordre) d'un ton sec. **snap off 1.** *v.tr.* (*a*) enlever (qch.) d'un coup de dents; *F:* **to s. s.o.'s head off,** rembarrer vivement qn; (*b*) casser (le bout d'une canne, etc.). **2.** *v.i.* se détacher avec un bruit sec; se casser. **snap to** *v.i.* (*of lid, door, etc.*) se (re)fermer avec un bruit sec. **snap up** *v.tr.* saisir, happer (qch.); **to s. up a bargain,** saisir, sauter sur, une occasion; **the tickets are being snapped up like hot cakes,** les billets s'enlèvent comme des petits pains.

snapdragon ['snæpdræg(ə)n] *n. Bot:* muflier *m*, gueule-de-loup *f*, *pl.* gueules-de-loup.

snappish ['snæpiʃ] *a.* (*of pers., dog*) hargneux.

snappishness ['snæpiʃnis] *n.* humeur hargneuse, ton hargneux.

snappy ['snæpi] *a.* **1.** (*of pers., dog*) hargneux. **2.** (*a*) (style, etc.) vif, plein d'allant; (*b*) *F:* **make it s.!** dépêche-toi! grouille-toi!

snapshot ['snæpʃɔt] *n. Phot: F:* instantané *m*.

snare¹ ['snɛər] *n.* **1.** (*a*) *Ven:* lacet *m*, lacs *m*; filet *m*; collet *m*; **to lay, set, a s.,** dresser, tendre, un filet, un lacet; **to be caught in a s.,** être pris au lacet; (*b*) piège *f*; (*of pers.*) **to be caught in a, the, s.,** être pris au piège. **2.** *Mus:* **s. drum,** caisse claire.

snare² *v.tr.* (*a*) prendre (un oiseau) au filet; prendre (un lapin) au collet, au lacet; (*b*) prendre (qn) au piège.

snarl¹ [snɑ:l] *n.* (*of dog, pers.*) grondement *m*, grognement *m*; (*of tiger*) feulement *m*.

snarl² *v.i.* **1.** (*of animal*) montrer les dents; grogner, gronder; (*of tiger*) feuler. **2.** (*of pers.*) **to s. at s.o.,** grogner, gronder, contre qn. **snarling 1.** *a.* grondant, grognant. **2.** *n.* grondement *m*, grognement *m*.

snarl³ *n.* (*a*) enchevêtrement *m*, emmêlement *m*, entortillement *m*; (*b*) **(traffic) s.(-up),** embouteillage *m*.

snarl⁴ 1. *v.i.* s'emmêler, s'enchevêtrer. **2.** *v.tr.* (*a*) emmêler, enchevêtrer; (*b*) **to s. up the traffic,** provoquer des embouteillages.

snatch¹ [snætʃ] *n.* **1.** (*a*) mouvement vif (pour saisir qch.); **to make a s. at sth.,** chercher à saisir qch.; (*b*) *F:* kidnapping *m*, enlèvement *m* (de qn); vol *m* à l'arraché (de bijoux, d'argent, etc.); (*c*) *Sp:* (*weight-lifting*) arraché *m*. **2.** (*a*) courte période; **s. of sheep,** petit somme; **in, by, snatches,** (dormir) par intervalles; (travailler) à bâtons rompus; (*b*) fragment *m*; **to overhear snatches of conversation,** surprendre des bouts *mpl*, des bribes *fpl*, de conversation.

snatch² *v.tr. & i.* **1.** (*a*) saisir, empoigner (qch.); s'emparer brusquement, se saisir, de (qch.); **to s. at sth.,** tâcher de saisir qch.; **to s. sth. up,** ramasser vivement qch.; **to s. an opportunity,** saisir une occasion; **to s. a meal,** manger un morceau sur le pouce; **to s. a bit of sleep,** faire un petit somme; (*b*) *Sp:* (*weight-lifting*) arracher (un poids). **2.** (*a*) **to s. sth. (away) from s.o.,** arracher, enlever, qch. à qn; **to s. sth. out of s.o.'s hands,** arracher qch. des mains de qn; (*b*) *F:* voler (de l'argent, un sac à main); kidnapper (un bébé).

snazzy ['snæzi] *a. F:* élégant, chic.

sneak¹ [sni:k] *n.* **1.** (*pers.*) pleutre *m*. **2.** *Sch: F:* cafard, -arde; mouchard *m*. **3.** *F:* **s. thief,** chipeur, -euse; chapardeur, -euse.

sneak² 1. *v.i.* (*a*) **to s. off, away,** partir furtivement; se défiler; **to s. in, out,** se glisser furtivement, se faufiler, dans un endroit, hors d'un endroit; (*b*) *Sch: F:* **to s. on s.o.,** moucharder, cafarder, qn. **2.** *v.tr.* (*a*) *P:* voler, chiper (qch.); (*b*) **to s. a glance at s.o.,** glisser un œil vers qn. **sneaking** *a.* (*a*) furtif; **to have a s. liking for sth.,** avoir un penchant caché, inavoué, pour qch.; (*b*) sournois, dissimulé.

sneakers ['sni:kəz] *n.pl. NAm:* espadrilles *fpl*.

sneaky ['sni:ki] *a.* (*a*) furtif; (*b*) sournois.

sneer¹ ['sniər] *n.* **1.** sourire *m* de mépris; ricanement *m*. **2.** sarcasme *m*.

sneer² *v.i.* sourire, rire, d'un air moqueur; ricaner;

to s. at s.o., (i) se moquer de qn; (ii) lancer des sarcasmes à qn. **sneering** 1. *a.* ricaneur, -euse; sarcastique. 2. *n.* (*a*) ricanerie *f*; (*b*) sarcasmes *mpl.* **sneeringly** *adv.* d'un air (i) de mépris, (ii) sarcastique; en ricanant.

sneeze¹ [sni:z] *n.* éternuement *m.*

sneeze² *v.i.* éternuer; *F:* **that's not to be sneezed at,** cela n'est pas à dédaigner; il ne faut pas cracher dessus. **sneezing** *n.* éternuement *m*; *Med:* sternutation *f*; **s. powder,** poudre *f* sternutatoire.

snick¹ [snik] *n.* 1. entaille *f*, encoche *f*. 2. coup *m* de ciseaux; entaille (dans l'étoffe).

snick² *v.tr.* 1. entailler, encocher; faire une entaille dans (le drap). 2. *Cr:* couper légèrement (la balle).

snicker¹ ['snikər] *n.* 1 = SNIGGER¹. 2. (*of horse*) hennissement *m.*

snicker² *v.i.* 1. = SNIGGER². 2. (*of horse*) hennir.

snide [snaid] *a. F:* (*a*) faux, *f.* fausse; factice; (*b*) **s. remarks,** remarques insidieuses.

sniff¹ [snif] *n.* reniflement *m*; **to take a s. at sth.,** renifler qch.; **with a s. of disgust,** en reniflant d'un air dégoûté.

sniff² *v.tr. & i.* 1. (*a*) renifler; (*b*) *F:* **the offer is not to be sniffed at,** l'offre n'est pas à dédaigner. 2. (*a*) flairer (un bon diner, un danger, etc.); (*b*) **to s. (at) sth.,** flairer, renifler, qch.; **the dog sniffed (at) my hand,** le chien m'a flairé la main; (*c*) **to s. out,** déterrer (un scandale, etc.); (*of dog*) détecter, flairer. 3. humer, renifler (une prise de tabac, etc.); aspirer (la cocaïne); *Med:* **to be sniffed up the nostrils,** pour être aspiré par les narines.

sniffle¹ ['snifl] *n.* petit rhume (de cerveau).

sniffle² *v.i. F:* 1. renifler. 2. pleurnicher. **sniffling** *a.* 1. enrhumé. 2. pleurnicheur, -euse.

sniffy ['snifi] *a. F:* 1. (*a*) dédaigneux; **to be s. about sth.,** (i) prendre qch. en mauvaise part; (ii) regarder qch. avec mépris. 2. *O:* malodorant.

snifter ['sniftər] *n. F:* goutte *f*, petit verre (d'alcool).

snigger¹ ['snigər] *n.* (*a*) rire *m* en dessous; petit rire contenu; (*b*) petit rire grivois.

snigger² *v.i.* rire sous cape; ricaner tout bas. **sniggering** *n.* rires *mpl* (i) en dessous, (ii) grivois.

snip¹ [snip] *n.* 1. morceau coupé; bout *m*, petit morceau (de papier, de toile). 2. (*a*) petite entaille; (*b*) coup *m* de ciseaux. 3. *F:* (*a*) affaire certaine; (*b*) affaire avantageuse; occasion *f*.

snip² *v.tr.* **(snipped** [snipt]**)** couper (du papier, du tissu) avec des ciseaux; **to s. sth. off,** enlever, détacher (qch.) d'un coup de ciseaux. **snipping** *n.* morceau coupé; petit coupon (de tissu).

snipe¹ [snaip] *n.* 1. *Orn:* (*pl.* **snipe**) (*a*) bécassine *f*; **to go s. shooting,** chasser la bécassine. 2. *F:* **(gutter) s.,** gamin, -ine.

snipe² *v.tr. & i.* (*a*) *Mil:* **to s. (at) the enemy,** canarder l'ennemi; tirer à l'affût, en embuscade, sur l'ennemi; **to be sniped at,** se faire canarder; (*b*) *Fig:* **to s. at s.o.,** critiquer qn sournoisement. **sniping** *n.* (*a*) tir *m* d'embuscade; (*b*) *Fig:* critique sournoise **(at s.o.,** de qn).

sniper ['snaipər] *n.* tireur embusqué.

snippet ['snipit] *n.* 1. bout *m*, morceau (coupé). 2. court extrait (d'un livre, etc.).

snitch [snitʃ] *P:* 1. *v.i.* vendre la mèche; **to s. on s.o.,** dénoncer, moucharder, qn. 2. *v.tr.* voler, chaparder (qch.).

snivel¹ ['sniv(ə)l] *n.* reniflement larmoyant; (*b*) pleurnicherie *f*.

snivel² *v.i.* **(snivelled,** *NAm:* **sniveled)** 1. renifler. 2. pleurnicher, larmoyer. **snivelling,** *NAm:* **sniveling** 1. *a.* (*a*) (*of pers.*) enchifrené; **s. cold,** rhume *m* de cerveau. 2. pleurnicheur, -euse. 2. *n.* (*a*) reniflement *m*; (*b*) pleurnicherie *f*.

sniveller, *NAm:* **sniveler** ['sniv(ə)lər] *n.* pleurnicheur, -euse.

snob ['snɔb] *n.* snob *mf*; **he's, she's, a bit of a s.,** c'est un(e) snobinard(e).

snobbery ['snɔbəri] *n.* snobisme *m;* **inverted s.,** snobisme à rebours; **intellectual s.,** snobisme intellectuel.

snobbish ['snɔbiʃ] *a.* snob.

snobbishness ['snɔbiʃnis] *n.* snobisme *m.*

snog [snɔg] *v.i. F:* (*of couple*) se caresser; se peloter. **snogging** *n.* pelotage *m.*

snood [snu:d] *n. Cost:* résille *f* pour cheveux.

snook [snu:k] *n. P:* pied *m* de nez; **to cock a s. at s.o.,** faire un pied de nez à qn; faire la nique à qn.

snooker¹ ['snu:kər] *n.* (sorte de) jeu *m* de billard.

snooker² *v.tr.* **to be snookered,** (i) *Bill:* se trouver dans l'impossibilité de frapper directement la bille; (ii) *F:* se trouver en mauvaise posture; *F:* **to s. s.o.,** mettre qn dans une impasse.

snoop [snu:p] *v.i. F:* **to s. (around),** fourrer le nez partout; fureter, fouiner; **to s. on s.o.,** espionner qn.

snooper ['snu:pər] *n. F:* fureteur *m*; inquisiteur *m.*

snooty ['snu:ti] *a. F:* arrogant, orgueilleux.

snooze¹ [snu:z] *n. F:* petit somme; **to have a s.,** faire un petit somme.

snooze² *v.i. F:* sommeiller; faire un petit somme.

snore¹ [snɔ:r] *n.* ronflement *m* (d'un dormeur).

snore² *v.i.* ronfler; **to s. gently,** ronflot(t)er. **snoring** 1. *a.* ronflant. 2. *n.* ronflement *m.*

snorer ['snɔ:rər] *n.* ronfleur, -euse.

snorkel ['snɔ:k(ə)l] *n.* (*a*) schnorchel *m*, schnorkel *m* (de sous-marin); (*b*) *Swim:* tuba *m.*

snort¹ [snɔ:t] *n.* 1. reniflement *m*; ébrouement *m* (d'un cheval, etc.). 2. (*a*) haut-le-corps *m inv* de dédain, de colère, d'impatience; reniflement de dégoût; (*b*) **s. of laughter,** court éclat de rire.

snort² 1. *v.i.* renifler fortement; (*of horse*) s'ébrouer; **to s. with laughter,** rire par courts éclats; **to s. at sth.,** dédaigner qch. 2. *v.tr.* **to s. out,** grogner (une réponse). **snorting** *n.* reniflement *m*; ébrouement *m* (d'un cheval).

snorter ['snɔ:tər] *n. F:* (*a*) chose épatante; (*b*) **he wrote me back a s.,** il m'a (r)envoyé une lettre carabinée; (*of problem*) **that's a real s.,** ça va nous donner du fil à retordre; (*c*) goutte *f*, petit verre (d'alcool).

snot [snɔt] *n. P:* morve *f*; **s. rag,** mouchoir *m.*

snotty ['snɔti] *a. P:* (*a*) **s. (nosed),** morveux; (*b*) sale, dégoûtant; (*c*) arrogant.

snout [snaut] *n.* (*a*) museau *m*; groin *m* (de porc, de hérisson); boutoir *m* (de sanglier); (*b*) *F:* nez *m*, pif *m*; (*c*) *P:* tabac *m.*

snow¹ [snou] *n.* 1. (*a*) neige *f*; **driven s.,** neige vierge; **eternal s.,** neiges éternelles; **the s. line,** la limite des neiges (éternelles); (*on road*) **s. fence,** paraneige *m*; **s. tyres,** *NAm:* **tires,** pneus *mpl* neige; **s. goggles,** lunettes *fpl* d'alpiniste; **s. blindness,** cécité *f* des neiges; (*b*) *Orn:* **s. goose,** oie *f* des neiges; *Z:* **s. leopard,** léopard *m* des neiges; once *f*. 2. (*a*) *Ind:* **carbonic acid s.,** neige carbonique; (*b*) *Cu:* **apple s.,** pommes meringuées; (*c*) *T.V: Rad:* neige; (*d*) *P:* cocaïne *f*, neige.

snow² 1. *v.i. impers.* neiger; **it's snowing,** il neige, il tombe de la neige. 2. *v.tr.* **to be snowed in, up,** être retenu, bloqué, pris, par la neige; **snowed under with work,** débordé de travail.

snowball¹ ['snoubɔ:l] *n.* 1. boule *f* de neige; *P:* **he hasn't a snowball's chance in hell,** il n'a pas l'ombre d'une chance. 2. *Bot:* **s. (tree, bush),** boule-de-neige *f*, *pl.* boules-de neige; rose *f* de Gueldre.

snowball² 1. *v.tr. & i.* lancer des boules de neige (à qn); se bettre à coups de boules de neige. 2. *v.i.* (*of story, debts, etc.*) faire boule de neige.

snowboot ['snoubu:t] *n.* après-ski *m inv.*

snowbound ['snoubaund] *a.* retenu, pris, bloqué, par la neige.
snowcapped ['snoukæpt] *a.* couronné de neige.
snowdrift ['snoudrift] *n.* congère *f.*
snowdrop ['snoudrɔp] *n. Bot:* perce-neige *m inv.*
snowfall ['snoufɔ:l] *n.* chute *f* de neige.
snowfield ['snoufi:ld] *n.* champ *m* de neige.
snowflake ['snoufleik] *n.* flocon *m* de neige.
snowman, *pl.* **-men** ['snoumæn, -men] *n.m.* (*a*) bonhomme de neige; (*b*) **the abominable s.,** l'abominable homme des neiges.
snowmobile ['snoumoubi:l] *n.* motoneige *m*; autoneige *f.*
snowplough, *NAm:* **-plow** ['snouplau] *n.* **1.** *Trans: Rail:* chasse-neige *m inv.* **2.** *Ski:* chasse-neige.
snowshoe ['snouʃu:] *n.* raquette *f.*
snowstorm ['snoustɔ:m] *n.* tempête *f* de neige.
snowsuit ['snous(j)u:t] *n.* = ensemble *m* ski.
snow(-)white ['snou(h)wait] **1.** *a.* (*a*) blanc comme la neige; (*b*) *O: Lit:* pur, innocent. **2.** *Pr.n.f.* **S.W.,** Blanche-Neige.
snowy ['snoui] *a.* neigeux; de neige; (la saison) des neiges; **s. (white) hair,** cheveux blancs (comme la neige).
snub¹ [snʌb] *n.* rebuffade *f*, affront *m*, *F:* soufflet *m.*
snub² *v.tr.* **(snubbed)** rabrouer, rebuffer (qn); faire un affront à (qn).
snub³ *a.* (nez) camard, camus, retroussé.
snub-nosed ['snʌbnouzd] *a.* au nez retroussé.
snuff¹ [snʌf] *n.* tabac *m* à priser; **to take s.,** priser; **a pinch of s.,** une prise; **s. taker,** priseur, -euse; *a.* **s. (coloured),** (couleur) tabac *inv*; cachou *inv.*
snuff² *v.i.* priser (du tabac).
snuff³ 1. *v.tr.* (*a*) **to s. (out),** moucher (une chandelle); (*b*) éteindre (un espoir, etc.). **2.** *v.tr. & i. P:* **to s. it, to s. out,** mourir, lâcher la rampe, éteindre sa lampe.
snuffbox ['snʌfbɔks] *n.* tabatière *f.*
snuffer ['snʌfər] *n.* **snuffers,** mouchettes *fpl.*
snuffle¹ ['snʌfl] *n.* **1.** (*a*) reniflement *m*; (*b*) **snuffles,** enchifrènement *m.* **2.** ton nasillard.
snuffle² *v.i.* **1.** (*a*) renifler; (*b*) être enchifrené. **2.** nasiller.
snug [snʌg] **1.** *a.* (*a*) (*of house, etc.*) confortable, où l'on est bien; (*of pers.*) bien abrité; bien au chaud; (lit) douillet; (gilet) bien chaud; *F:* **s. little job,** emploi pépère; **s. little fortune,** fortune rondelette; **to make oneself s.,** se mettre à son aise; **to lie s. in bed,** être bien au chaud dans son lit; *F:* **as s. as a bug in a rug,** tranquille comme Baptiste; (*b*) **to lie s.,** se tenir caché; être tapi (dans un trou). **2.** *n. O:* = SNUGGERY 2. **-ly** *adv.* confortablement; (bien chaud) à l'aise; **s. wrapped,** douillettement enveloppé (dans une couverture, etc.); **garment that fits s.,** vêtement bien ajusté à la taille.
snuggery ['snʌgəri] *n.* petite pièce intime (et confortable); petite arrière-salle (dans un café).
snuggle ['snʌgl] **1.** *v.i.* **to s. up to s.o.,** se pelotonner, se blottir, contre qn; **to s. down in bed,** se blottir dans son lit; **village snuggling in the valley,** village niché dans la vallée. **2.** *v.tr.* **to s. a child close to one,** serrer un enfant dans ses bras.
so [sou] **I.** *adv.* **1.** si, tellement; **it's so easy,** c'est si, tellement, facile; **she isn't so very old,** elle n'est pas tellement vieille; **the young and the not so young,** les jeunes et les moins jeunes; **I'm not so sure of that,** je n'en suis pas bien sûr; **so serious a wound,** une blessure aussi grave; **he's not so clever as she is,** il est moins intelligent qu'elle; **he wouldn't be so stupid as to do that,** il ne serait pas si bête que de faire cela; **would you be so kind as to . . .?** voudriez-vous avoir la gentillesse de . . .? **he's so rich that he doesn't know what he's worth,** il est riche au point d'ignorer sa fortune; **I loved him so much,** je l'aimais tant; **we enjoyed ourselves so much,** nous nous sommes tellement amusés. **2.** (*a*) ainsi; de cette façon; de cette manière; **stand just so,** tenez-vous ainsi, comme ça; **while he was so occupied,** pendant qu'il était ainsi occupé; **as X is to Y, so Y is to Z,** comme X est à Y, Y est à Z; **she so arranged things that . . .,** elle a fait en sorte que + *sub.*; **I have been so informed,** c'est ce que l'on m'a dit; **it so happened that I was there,** le hasard a voulu que je fusse là; **and so on, and so forth,** et ainsi de suite; **so to say, so to speak,** pour ainsi dire; comme qui dirait; (*b*) **has the train gone?—I think so,** est-ce que le train est parti?—je crois, je pense, que oui; **he's clever!—you think so?** il est intelligent!—vous le croyez? **I suppose so, I expect so,** je le suppose; **I hope so,** je l'espère bien; **I'm afraid so,** j'en ai bien peur; **I didn't say so,** moi, je n'ai pas dit cela; **is she really ill?—so it seems,** elle est donc vraiment malade?—à ce qu'il paraît; **so I told him,** c'est ce que je lui ai dit; **I told you so!** je vous l'avais bien dit! **so much so that . . .,** à tel point que . . .; tellement que . . .; **much more so,** bien plus encore; **that's so,** c'est bien vrai; **is that so?** vraiment? **that being so,** puisqu'il en est ainsi; dans ces conditions; **so be it!** soit! qu'il en soit ainsi! (*c*) **if so,** s'il en est ainsi; **why so?** pourquoi cela? **how so?** comment cela? **perhaps so,** cela se peut; **quite so,** parfaitement; absolument; **a hundred pounds or so,** une centaine de livres; **a week or so,** une huitaine de jours; (*d*) **a little girl** ***so*** **high,** une petite pas plus haute que ça; (*e*) **he's right and so are you,** il a raison et vous aussi; **and so am I, are we,** et moi, et nous, aussi; **he thinks he can do it—so he can,** il pense qu'il peut le faire—mais oui, en effet, il le peut; (*f*) **you're late!—so I am!** vous êtes en retard!—c'est vrai! **3.** *conj. phrs.* **so that, so as to** (*a*) (*purpose*) **he stood up so as to, so that he could, see better,** il s'est levé afin de mieux voir; **we hurried so as not to, so that we shouldn't, be late,** nous nous sommes dépêchés pour ne pas être en retard; (*b*) (*consequence*) **he tied me up so that I couldn't move,** il m'a ligoté de sorte que je ne pouvais pas bouger. **4.** (*used adverbially & adjectivally*) **so so,** médiocre(ment), passable(ment); comme ci comme ça; **how are you?—so so,** comment vas-tu?—comme ci comme ça; **the cooking is only so so,** la cuisine est médiocre, quelconque. **II.** *conj.* **1.** donc, c'est pourquoi; **he has a bad temper, so be careful,** il a mauvais caractère, par conséquent faites attention; **he wasn't there, so I came back again,** il n'était pas là, donc je suis revenu. **2. so there you are!** vous voilà donc! **so that's what it is!** ah! c'est comme ça! **so you're not coming?** vous ne venez donc pas?
soak¹ [souk] *n.* **1.** (*a*) **to put (sth.) in s.,** (mettre à) tremper (le linge sale, etc.); (*b*) **I intend to have a good s. (in the bath),** je vais prendre un bon bain. **2.** *P:* (*a*) ribote *f*, cuite *f*; (*b*) ivrogne *m*, soûlard *m.*
soak² 1. *v.tr.* (*a*) (*of liquid*) tremper, détremper; **the rain soaked me to the skin,** la pluie m'a trempé jusqu'aux os; (*b*) tremper qch. **(in sth.,** dans qch.); imbiber (une éponge); (*c*) *F:* écorcher (un client); **to s. the rich,** faire payer les riches. **2.** *v.i.* (*a*) baigner, tremper **(in sth.,** dans qch.); (*b*) (*of liquid*) s'infiltrer, s'imbiber **(into sth.,** dans qch.); (*c*) *P:* boire comme une éponge. **soaked** *a.* trempé; (sol) détrempé; **s. to the skin, s. through,** trempé jusqu'aux os. **soak in 1.** *v.i.* (*of liquid*) pénétrer. **2.** *v.tr.* **to s. in water,** s'imprégner d'eau, absorber de l'eau. **soaking 1.** *a.* trempé, mouillé. **2.** *adv.* **s. wet,** trempé. **3.** *n.* trempage *m;* **to get a s.,** se faire tremper. **soak through** *v.i.* (*a*) s'infiltrer à travers (qch.); (*b*) pénétrer, s'infiltrer. **soak up** *v.tr.* absorber, boire, imbiber (un liquide); **to s. up water,** s'imprégner d'eau; absorber de l'eau.
so-and-so ['sou(ə)n(d)sou] *n. F:* (*a*) **Mr. So-and-so, Mrs. So-and-so,** Monsieur un tel, Untel; Madame

une telle; (*b*) *Pej:* type *m*; **a crafty so-and-so,** une fine mouche; **the old so-and-so!** quel sale type!

soap¹ [soup] *n.* (*a*) savon *m;* **toilet s.,** savon de toilette; (*small*) savonnette *f*; **shaving s.,** savon à barbe; **soft s.,** (i) savon noir, vert, mou; (ii) *F:* flatterie *f*; eau bénite; **to wash with s.,** savonner (qch.); **s. powder,** lessive *f* en poudre; *T.V: F:* **s. opera,** feuilleton sentimental, à l'eau de rose; (*b*) *P:* **no s.,** rien à faire; je ne marche pas.

soap² *v.tr.* **1.** savonner (le linge, etc.). **2.** *F:* **to (soft-) s. s.o.,** flatter qn; flagorner qn.

soapbox ['soupbɔks] *n.* caisse *f* à savon; *F:* **s. orator,** orateur *m* de carrefour; harangueur *m.*

soapdish ['soupdiʃ] *n.* porte-savon *m inv.*

soapflakes ['soupfleiks] *n.pl.* savon *m* en paillettes.

soapiness ['soupinis] *n.* (*a*) caractère savonneux (de qch.); (*b*) *F:* (*of pers.*) onctuosité *f.*

soapstone ['soupstoun] *n. Miner:* stéatite *f.*

soapsuds ['soupsʌdz] *n.pl.* (*a*) mousse *f* de savon; (*b*) eau *f* de savon; lessive *f.*

soapy ['soupi] *a.* **1.** savonneux; (goût) de savon. **2.** *F:* (*of pers., voice*) doucereux, onctueux.

soar [sɔːr] *v.i. esp. Lit:* (*a*) prendre son essor; monter, s'élever (dans les airs); **rents have soared,** les loyers ont fait un bond; (*b*) planer (dans les airs); (*of the mind*) voler. **soaring 1.** *a.* (*a*) (i) (oiseau, flèche) qui monte, s'élève, dans les airs; (clocher) élancé; (ii) **s. flight,** vol plané (d'un oiseau); (*b*) (*of prices, etc.*) qui montent en flèche. **2.** *n.* (*a*) essor *m*; (*b*) hausse *f* (des prix); (*c*) vol plané (d'un oiseau).

sob¹ [sɔb] *n.* sanglot *m*; F: **s. stuff,** sensiblerie *f,* mélo *m*; **to tell s.o. a s. story,** raconter une histoire pour apitoyer qn.

sob² *v.* **(sobbed) 1.** *v.i.* sangloter. **2.** *v.tr.* (*a*) **to s. (out) sth.,** dire qch. en sanglotant; (*b*) **she was sobbing her heart out,** elle pleurait à gros sanglots; (*c*) **she sobbed herself to sleep,** elle s'est endormie en sanglotant. **sobbing** *a.* **in a s. voice,** d'une voix sanglotante, brisée de sanglots. **2.** *n.* sanglots *mpl.*

sober¹ ['soubər] *a.* **1.** (*a*) sobre, modéré, tempéré; (*b*) calme; rassis, posé; (visage) grave; **s. opinion,** opinion réfléchie; (*c*) **s. truth,** la simple vérité; (*d*) **s. colours,** couleurs sobres, peu voyantes; **s. dress,** vêtement discret. **2.** (*a*) qui n'est pas ivre; qui n'a pas bu; **as s. as a judge,** sobre comme un chameau; **when he's s. (again),** quand il sera dégrisé; (*b*) qui ne s'enivre jamais. **sobering** *a.* **s. thought,** réflexion sérieuse. **-ly,** *adv.* (*a*) sobrement, modérément; (*b*) avec calme; sérieusement; (*c*) (vêtu) discrètement.

sober² **1.** *v.tr.* **to s. (down),** assagir, dégriser (un déréglé, etc.); **to s. (up),** dégriser (un homme ivre); **this news sobered him,** cette nouvelle l'a dégrisé. **2.** *v.i.* (*a*) (*of reckless pers., enthusiast*) **to s. down,** s'assagir, se dégriser; (*b*) (*of intoxicated pers.*) **to s. up,** se dégriser.

sober-minded [soubə'maindid] *a.* sérieux; de caractère sobre; pondéré.

soberness ['soubənis] *n.* (*a*) sobriété *f,* modération *f,* tempérance *f*; **s. of speech,** sobriété de parole; (*b*) calme *m,* tranquillité *f*; sérieux *m.*

so-called [sou'kɔːld] *a.* (*a*) appelé ainsi; ainsi nommé; **the so-c. temperate zone,** la zone dite tempérée; (*b*) **a so-c. doctor,** un soi-disant, un prétendu, docteur; **so-c. improvements,** prétendus progrès.

soccer ['sɔkər] *n. F:* football(-association) *m.*

sociability [souʃə'biliti] *n.* sociabilité *f.*

sociable ['souʃəbl] *a.* (*a*) sociable; (*of pers.*) **to become more s.,** s'apprivoiser; (*b*) *Z:* **s. animals,** (animaux) sociétaires *mpl*; (*c*) *U.S:* **s. evening,** *n.* **sociable,** soirée amicale; réunion *f.* **-ably** *adv.* sociablement.

social ['souʃ(ə)l] *a.* **1.** social, -aux; (*a*) **s. sciences,** sciences humaines; **s. reformer,** réformateur, -trice, de la société; **the s. order,** l'ordre social; **s. work,** œuvres sociales; **the s. services,** les services sociaux, d'assistance sociale; **s. worker,** assistant(e) social(e); *Adm:* **s. security,** sécurité sociale; (*b*) mondain; **the s. ladder,** l'échelle sociale; **s. position,** rang *m* dans la société; **to have a busy s. life,** voir beaucoup de monde; sortir beaucoup; **s. evening,** *n.* **s.,** (i) soirée *f*; (ii) réunion *f*; (*c*) *Pol:* **s. democrat,** social-démocrate *mf.* **2.** *Nat.Hist:* social; **man is an essentially s. animal,** l'homme est essentiellement sociable. **-ally** *adv.* socialement.

socialism ['souʃəlizm] *n.* socialisme *m.*

socialist ['souʃəlist] *a.* & *n.* socialiste (*mf*).

socialite ['souʃəlait] *n. F:* membre *m* de la haute société; homme, femme, du monde; mondain, -aine.

socialize ['souʃəlaiz] **1.** *v.tr. Pol.Ec: O:* nationaliser (la propriété); *U.S:* **socialized medicine,** médecine *f* d'État. **2.** *v.i. U.S:* **to s. with s.o.,** frayer avec qn; **he won't s.,** il n'accepte jamais une invitation.

society [sə'saiəti] *n.* **1.** société *f*; (*a*) **to avoid the s. of one's colleagues,** éviter la société de ses collègues; (*b*) la haute société, le (grand) monde; **fashionable s.,** le beau monde; **s. people,** gens du monde; *Journ:* **s. news, column,** mondanités *fpl*; échos mondains; (*c*) **consumer s.,** société de consommation; **alternative s.,** société alternative. **2.** société; association *f*; **charitable s.,** œuvre *f* de bienfaisance, de charité.

sociocultural [sousiou'kʌltjər(ə)l] *a.* socioculturel.

socioeconomic [sousiouiːkə'nɔmik] *a.* socioéconomique.

sociological [sousiou'lɔdʒik(ə)l] *a.* sociologique.

sociologist [sousi'ɔlədʒist] *n.* sociologiste *mf,* sociologue *mf.*

sociology [sousi'ɔlədʒi] *n.* sociologie *f.*

sociometry [sousi'ɔmitri] *n.* sociométrie *f.*

sock¹ [sɔk] *n.* (*NAm: pl. also* **sox**) **1.** chaussette *f*; **(ankle) socks,** socquettes *fpl,* mi-chaussettes *fpl.* **2.** semelle intérieure (d'une chaussure).

sock² *n. P:* coup *m,* gnon *m,* beigne *f*; (*in the eye*) pochon *m*; **to give s.o. a s. on the jaw,** flanquer une beigne à qn.

sock³ *v.tr.* & *i. P:* **1. to s. a brick at s.o.,** lancer un briqueton à qn. **2. to s. (into) s.o., to s. it to s.o.,** flanquer une beigne à qn.

socket ['sɔkit] *n.* (*a*) orbite *f* (de l'œil); alvéole *m or f* (de dent, de diamant); cavité *f* articulaire, glène *f* (d'un os); **ball and s. joint,** emboîtement *m* réciproque; énarthrose *f*; (*b*) *Plumb:* emboîtement, manchon *m* (de tuyau); (*c*) *El:* (i) douille *f* (de lampe); (ii) prise (de courant) femelle; **wall s.,** prise de courant murale; **microphone s.,** prise microphone.

Socrates ['sɔkrətiːz] *Pr.n.m.* Socrate.

Socratic [sɔ'krætik] *a.* socratique.

sod¹ [sɔd] *n.* **1.** gazon *m*; **under the s.,** enterré. **2.** motte *f* de gazon; **to cut, turn, the first s.,** donner le premier coup de bêche.

sod² *n. P:* (*not in polite use*) (*a*) bougre *m*; **poor s.!** pauvre con! (*b*) **odds and sods,** petits bouts, bribes *fpl* et morceaux *mpl.*

sod³ *v. P:* (*not in polite use*) **1.** *v.tr.* **s. you!** va te faire foutre! **s. it!** merde, alors! **2.** *v.i.* **to s. off,** foutre le camp.

soda ['soudə] *n.* (*a*) *Ch: etc:* soude *f*; **caustic s.,** soude caustique; **washing s.,** carbonate *m* de soude; **bicarbonate of s., baking s.,** bicarbonate *m* de soude; **s. bread,** pain *m* qu'on fait lever au bicarbonate de soude; *NAm:* **s. cracker,** biscuit *m* au bicarbonate de soude; (*b*) **s. (water),** eau *f* de Seltz; soda *m*; **s. fountain,** bar *m* pour glaces et boissons (non alcoolisées).

sodden¹ ['sɔd(ə)n] *a.* **1.** (*a*) (*of field*) (dé)trempé; (*b*) mal cuit; pâteux. **2. s. with drink,** abruti par l'alcool.
sodium ['soudiəm] *n. Ch:* sodium *m*; **s. chloride,** chlorure *m* de sodium.
Sodom ['sɔdəm] *Pr.n. B. Geog:* Sodome *f.*
sodomite ['sɔdəmait] *n.* sodomite *m.*
sodomy ['sɔdəmi] *n.* sodomie *f.*
sofa ['soufə] *n. Furn:* sofa *m*, canapé *m*; **s. bed,** canapé-lit *m*, *pl.* canapés-lits.
soft [sɔft] **I.** *a.* **1.** (*a*) (substance, terrain, fromage, etc.) mou, *f.* molle; (roche, crayon, etc.) tendre; (houille) grasse; **as s. as butter, as wax,** mou comme le beurre, comme la cire; (*b*) (oreiller, etc.) mou, doux, douillet; (tissu, etc.) moelleux; (chapeau) mou; (cuir) souple; **s. skin,** peau douce, veloutée; **s. to the touch,** doux au toucher; **as s. as silk,** doux comme du satin; *Com:* **s. furnishings,** (i) tissus *mpl* d'ameublement; (ii) tapis *mpl* et rideaux *mpl*; (*c*) (*of pers.*) (i) mou, qui manque de vigueur; (ii) doux, malléable; **s. muscles,** muscles flasques; (*of horse*) **s. mouth,** bouche tendre, sensible; **to become s.,** s'amollir; **you mustn't be so s. with them,** il faut les traiter plus sévèrement. **2.** (*a*) (*of voice, music, colour, rain, wind, etc.*) doux, *f.* douce; **s. water,** eau douce, non calcaire; **s. light,** lumière douce, atténuée; **s. outline,** contour flou; *Phot:* **s. focus,** flou *m*; *Cin: Th:* **s. lighting,** éclairage *m* donnant des ombres à contours flous; **s. step,** pas feutré; *Av: Space:* **s. landing,** atterrissage *m* en douceur; *Com:* **s. sell,** publicité *f* discrète; *Ling:* **s. consonant,** consonne douce; (*b*) **s. drinks,** boissons *fpl* non alcoolisées; **s. drugs,** drogues (toxiques) mineures; (*c*) **s. life,** vie douce; *F:* **a s. job,** un emploi pépère, un filon; (*d*) **s. words,** mots doux, tendres; **s. heart,** cœur *m* tendre; **to have a s. spot for s.o.,** avoir un faible pour qn; *F:* **to be s. on s.o.,** être amoureux, entiché, de qn. **3.** *F:* stupide, bête; **don't be s.!** ne fais pas l'imbécile! **he's gone s. in the head!** il a perdu la boule! **II.** *adv.* (*a*) *F:* doucement; (*b*) *P:* **don't talk s.!** ne dis pas de bêtises! **softly** *adv.* **1.** (*a*) doucement; (marcher) sans bruit; (*b*) tendrement. **2.** mollement.
soft-boiled ['sɔftbɔild] *a.* (œuf) mollet.
softback, soft-cover ['sɔftbæk, -kʌvər] *n. esp. U.S:* livre *m* de poche.
softball ['sɔftbɔ:l] *n. NAm:* genre *m* de baseball (joué avec une balle plus grande et plus molle).
soften ['sɔf(ə)n] **1.** *v.tr.* (*a*) amollir, ramollir (la cire, etc.); (*b*) adoucir (la peau); assouplir (le cuir); détremper, adoucir (l'acier); (*c*) affaiblir, énerver (qn); **to s. up,** réduire la résistance de (qn); **troops softened by idleness,** troupes amollies par l'oisiveté; (*d*) adoucir (une couleur, sa voix, l'eau, etc.); atténuer (une couleur, une lumière, un contraste, etc.); radoucir (le ton, la colère de qn); (*e*) attendrir, émouvoir (qn); **to s. s.o. up,** amadouer qn. **2.** *v.i.* (*a*) s'amollir, se ramollir; (*b*) s'adoucir, se radoucir; (*c*) s'attendrir. **softening** *n.* (*a*) amollissement *m*, ramollissement *m*; **s. of the brain,** ramollissement du cerveau; (*b*) assouplissement *m* (du cuir); *Metalw:* détrempe *f*, adoucissage *m* (de l'acier); (*c*) adoucissement *m* (du caractère); (*d*) adoucissement (de l'eau); atténuation *f* (de la lumière, des contrastes, des contours); (*e*) attendrissement *m.*
softener ['sɔf(ə)nər] *n.* **water s.,** adoucisseur *m* d'eau; **fabric s.,** adoucissant *m.*
softheaded [sɔft'hedid] *a. F:* bête, niais.
softhearted [sɔft'hɑ:tid] *a.* au cœur tendre; compatissant; **he's too s.,** il a trop de cœur.
softie ['sɔfti] *n. F:* = SOFTY.
softness ['sɔftnis] *n.* **1.** douceur *f* (de la peau, d'un tissu, du climat, etc.). **2.** (*a*) mollesse *f* (de caractère); manque *m* d'énergie, de caractère; (*b*) flou *m* (des contours). **3.** *F:* niaiserie *f*; simplicité *f.*
soft(-)pedal [sɔft'ped(ə)l] **1.** *v.i. Mus:* appuyer sur la pédale douce (d'un piano). **2.** *v.i. & tr. F:* y aller doucement, ne pas trop insister; atténuer, amoindrir (l'importance d'un incident).
soft-soap [sɔft'soup] *v.tr. F:* flatter, passer la pommade à (qn).
soft-spoken [sɔft'spouk(ə)n] *a.* (*of pers.*) (*a*) à voix douce; (*b*) mielleux, doucereux.
software ['sɔftwɛər] *n. Cmptr:* logiciel *m*; software *m.*
softwood ['sɔftwud] *n. Carp: etc:* bois *m* tendre.
softy ['sɔfti] *n. F:* **1.** (*a*) **a s.,** un mou, une molle; (*b*) couard, -arde; (*c*) **to be a terrible s.,** être sentimental à l'excès. **2.** niais, -aise.
soggy ['sɔgi] *a.* **1.** détrempé; saturé d'eau. **2.** (*of bread*) pâteux; lourd. **3.** (*of heat, atmosphere*) lourd; saturé d'humidité.
soh [sou] *n. Mus:* **1.** (*fixed*) sol *m inv.* **2.** (*movable*) la dominante.
soil¹ [sɔil] *n.* (*a*) sol *m*, terrain *m*, terre *f*; **to cultivate the s.,** cultiver la terre; **alluvial s.,** terrain d'alluvion(s); (*b*) *Lit:* **one's native s.,** le sol natal.
soil² *n.* **1.** souillure *f*, salissure *f.* **2.** *Hyg: O:* **night s.,** vidanges *fpl*; gadoue *f.*
soil³ *v.tr.* (*a*) souiller, salir; encrasser (ses habits); maculer (son linge); (*b*) (*with passive force*) **fabric that soils easily,** tissu salissant, qui se salit facilement. **soiled** *a.* souillé, sali; **s. linen,** linge *m* sale.
sojourn ['sɔdʒə(:)n] *v.i. A: & Lit:* séjourner.
sol [sɔl] *n. Mus:* **1.** (*fixed*) sol *m inv.* **2.** (*movable*) la dominante.
solace¹ ['sɔləs] *n. Lit:* consolation *f*, soulagement *m*; **to find s. in sth.,** trouver une consolation dans qch.
solace² *v.tr. Lit:* consoler (qn); **I solaced myself with this thought,** j'ai trouvé une consolation dans cette pensée.
solar ['soulər] *a.* (système, énergie, etc.) solaire; *Anat:* **s. plexus,** plexus *m* solaire.
solarium, *pl.* **-ia** [sou'lɛəriəm, -iə] *n.* solarium *m.*
solder¹ ['sɔldər, 'souldər] *n.* soudure *f*; **hard, brazing, s.,** soudure forte; brasure *f*; **soft s.,** soudure tendre.
solder² *v.tr. Metalw:* souder. **soldering** *n.* soudure *f* (hétérogène); **s. iron,** fer à souder.
solderer ['sɔldərər] *n.* soudeur, -euse.
soldier¹ ['souldʒər] *n.* **1.** (*a*) soldat *m*; militaire *m*; **private s.,** simple soldat; (soldat de) deuxième classe *m*; **an old s.,** un ancien soldat, un vétéran; **s. of fortune,** soldat, officier *m*, de fortune; aventurier *m*; **tin s.,** soldat de plomb; (*b*) tacticien *m*, stratégiste *m.* **2.** *Ent:* **s. (ant),** (fourmi *f*) soldat.
soldier² *v.i.* **1.** faire le métier de soldat; **to s. on,** (i) rester au service; (ii) *F:* persévérer. **2.** *U.S: & Nau: F:* tirer au flanc. **soldiering** *n.* le métier, la carrière, militaire, des armes; **to go s.,** se faire soldat.
soldierlike, soldierly ['souldʒəlaik, -li] *a.* de soldat; (allure) martiale, militaire.
soldiery ['souldʒəri] *n. coll. O:* soldats *mpl*, militaires *mpl.*
sole¹ [soul] *n.* **1.** plante *f* (du pied); (*of horse, etc.*) sole *f.* **2.** semelle *f* (de chaussure). **3.** semelle (de rabot, de crosse de golf, etc.).
sole² *v.tr.* (i) mettre une semelle à, (ii) ressemeler (une chaussure). **soling** *n.* (i) mise *f* d'une semelle; (ii) ressemelage *m.*
sole³ *n. Ich:* sole *f*; **Dover s.,** (vraie) sole; **lemon s.,** plie *f* sole; limande *f* sole.
sole⁴ *a.* seul, unique; (légataire) universel; **his s. reason,** son unique raison; **s. right,** droit exclusif. **-ly** *adv.* seulement, uniquement; **I went there s. to see it,** j'y suis allé dans le seul but de le voir.
solecism ['sɔlisizm] *n.* solécisme *m.*
solemn ['sɔləm] *a.* **1.** (*of oath, etc.*) solennel; (devoir) sacré; (question) grave; **s. fact,** réalité sérieuse; **s. warning,** avertissement formel; **s. ceremony,** solen-

nité *f*; *Jur* **s. agreement,** contrat solennel. **2.** (*of pers.*) grave, sérieux; (ton) solennel; **as s. as a judge,** sérieux comme un évêque. **-ly** *adv.* **1.** solennellement. **2.** gravement; (parler) avec solennité.

solemness ['sɔləmnis] *n.* = SOLEMNITY 1.

solemnity [sə'lemniti] *n.* **1.** (*a*) solennité *f*; **with all s.,** en toute solennité; (*b*) gravité *f*, sérieux *m* (de maintien). **2.** *Lit:* fête solennelle; solennité.

solemnization [sɔləmnai'zeiʃ(ə)n] *n.* solennisation *f*; célébration *f* (d'un mariage).

solemnize ['sɔləmnaiz] *v.tr.* solenniser (une fête); célébrer, bénir (un mariage).

solenoid ['sɔlənɔid] *n. El:* solénoïde *m.*

solfa ['sɔlfɑː] *n. Mus:* **1.** (*a*) solmisation *f*; (*b*) solfège *m.* **2. tonic s.,** système de solmisation dans lequel le do est mobile et représente toujours la tonique.

solicit [sə'lisit] *v.* (*a*) *v.tr.* solliciter (qch. de qn); solliciter, briguer (des suffrages); (*b*) *v.tr. & i.* (*of prostitute*) racoler. **soliciting** *n.* **1.** sollicitation *f.* **2.** (*of prostitute*) racolage *m.*

solicitation [səlisi'teiʃ(ə)n] *n.* sollicitation *f.*

solicitor [sə'lisitər] *n.* **1.** *Jur:* = avocat, -ate; **S. General,** conseiller *m* juridique de la Couronne. **2.** *U.S: Com:* placier, -ière.

solicitous [sə'lisitəs] *a. esp. Lit:* soucieux, désireux (**of sth.,** de qch.); préoccupé (de qch.); **s. attention to detail,** soin méticuleux des détails. **-ly** *adv.* avec sollicitude.

solicitousness, solicitude [sə'lisitəsnis, -tjuːd] *n.* sollicitude *f*, souci *m*, préoccupation *f.*

solid ['sɔlid] **1.** *a.* solide; ferme; (*a*) **s. food,** nourriture *f* solide; (*of fluid*) **to become s.,** se solidifier; (*b*) **to build on s. foundations,** bâtir sur le solide; **on s. ground,** sur un terrain ferme; (*c*) **man of s. build,** homme bien charpenté; **s. common sense,** solide bon sens; **to have s. reasons for believing sth.,** avoir des raisons solides pour croire qch.; (*d*) (or, argent) massif; (pneu) plein; (mur) plein, sans ouvertures; **s. mahogany table,** table *f* en acajou massif; **pond frozen s.,** étang gelé jusqu'au fond; *Mth:* **s. angle,** angle *m* solide; **to sleep for nine s. hours,** *adv.* **to sleep for nine hours s.,** dormir neuf heures d'affilée; **three days' s. rain,** trois jours de pluie continue; **s. vote,** vote *m* unanime; (*e*) en une seule pièce; *adv.* **parts cast s.,** parties coulées monobloc. **2.** *n.* (*a*) solide *m*; (*b*) **milk solids,** extrait *m* du lait; **non-fat solids,** solides non gras; (*c*) **solids,** aliments *mpl* solides. **-ly** *adv.* **1.** (*a*) solidement; **s. held,** tenu fermement, solidement; **s. built man.** homme bien charpenté; (*b*) sans interruption, sans s'arrêter. **2.** (voter) à l'unanimité.

solidarity [sɔli'dæriti] *n.* solidarité *f.*

solidification [səlidifi'keiʃ(ə)n] *n.* solidification *f*; congélation *f.*

solidify [sə'lidifai] **1.** *v.tr.* (*a*) solidifier; (*b*) consolider. **2.** *v.i.* (*a*) se solidifier; (*b*) se figer; se congeler; (*c*) se consolider.

solidity [sə'liditi] *n.* solidité *f.*

solid-state [sɔlid'steit] *a.* (physique) des solides.

soliloquize [sə'liləkwaiz] *v.i.* faire un soliloque, soliloquer; monologuer.

soliloquy [sə'liləkwi] *n.* soliloque *m*; monologue *m.*

solitaire [sɔli'tɛər] *n.* **1. s. (diamond),** solitaire *m.* **2.** *Games:* (*a*) solitaire; (*b*) *Cards:* (jeu *m* de) patience *f.*

solitary ['sɔlit(ə)ri] *a.* (*a*) solitaire; seul, isolé; **not a s. one,** pas un seul; (*in prison*) **s. confinement,** *F:* **s.,** régime *m* cellulaire; (*b*) *Lit:* (lieu) solitaire, isolé.

solitude ['sɔlitjuːd] *n.* solitude *f*, isolement *m*; **to live in s.,** vivre dans la solitude.

solo ['soulou] *n.* **1.** *Mus:* solo *m*; **violin s.,** solo de violon; **to play s.,** jouer en solo. **2.** *Cards:* **s. (whist),** whist *m* de Gand; **to go s.,** jouer solo. **3.** *Av:* **s. flight,** vol *m* solo *inv*; **to fly s.,** voler seul.

soloist ['soulouist] *n. Mus:* soliste *mf.*

solstice ['sɔlstis] *n. Astr:* solstice *m.*

solubility [sɔlju'biliti] *n.* solubilité *f* (d'un sel, etc.).

soluble ['sɔljubl] *a.* **1.** soluble (**in water,** dans l'eau). **2.** (problème) (ré)soluble.

solution [sə'luːʃ(ə)n] *n.* **1.** (*a*) *Ch: etc:* solution *f*; **salt in s.,** sel *m* en solution; (*b*) solution; liqueur *f*; (*c*) *Engr: etc:* solution, bain *m.* **2.** (*a*) (*solving*) résolution *f*, solution (d'une difficulté, d'une équation); (*b*) (*answer*) solution; résultat *m* (d'un problème de mathématique); **there is no real s. to this,** ce cas ne comporte aucune solution.

solvable ['sɔlvəbl] *a.* (problème) (ré)soluble.

solve [sɔlv] *v.tr.* résoudre (un problème, une équation); éclaircir (un mystère); **this question has not yet been solved,** cette question reste toujours en suspens; **to s. a riddle,** trouver le mot de l'énigme.

solvency ['sɔlvənsi] *n. Com: Jur:* solvabilité *f.*

solvent ['sɔlvənt] **1.** *a. Com: Jur:* solvable. **2.** *a. & n.* **s. (agent),** dissolvant *m*, solvant *m.*

Somali [sou'mɑːli] **1.** *a. Geog:* somali; somalien. **2.** *n.* (*a*) Somali, -ie; **the Somali,** les Somalis; (*b*) *Ling:* somali *m.*

Somalia [sou'mɑːliə] *Pr.n. Geog:* (République démocratique de) Somalie *f.*

Somaliland [sou'mɑːlilænd] *Pr.n. Geog: Hist:* Somalie *f*; **French S.,** Côte française des Somalis.

somatic [sou'mætik] *a. Biol:* somatique.

sombre, *NAm:* **somber** ['sɔmbər] *a.* (*a*) (couleur, etc.) sombre; (*b*) (*of pers., mood, etc.*) sombre, morne. **-ly** *adv.* sombrement; d'un air sombre, morne.

some [sʌm] **I.** *a.* **1.** (*a*) **s. (sort of an) excuse,** une excuse quelconque; **he'll come s. day,** il arrivera un de ces jours; **s. days he is better,** certains jours il va mieux; **s. books are difficult to read,** il y a des livres qui sont difficiles à lire; **s. people say . . .,** il y en a qui disent . . .; (*b*) **s. book or other,** un livre quelconque. **2.** de; **to drink s. water,** boire de l'eau; **I ate s. fruit,** j'ai mangé des fruits. **3.** (*certain quantity, number*) **I felt s. uneasiness,** je ressentais quelque inquiétude; **that would be s. help,** cela faciliterait un peu les choses; **in s. measure,** jusqu'à un certain point; **s. distance away,** à quelque distance; **s. days ago,** il y a quelques jours; **for s. time,** pendant quelque temps; **he has been waiting for s. time,** il attend depuis quelque temps; **at s. length,** assez longuement. **4.** *F:* (*intensive*) **(that was) s. storm!** quelle tempête! **she's s. girl!** c'est une fille formidable! **that was s. meal!** ce que nous avons bien mangé! **5. s. hope!** quelle illusion! **II.** *pron.* **1.** *pl.* (*pers.*) certains; **s. or all of them,** tous ou certains d'entre eux; **s. believe that . . .,** il y en a qui croient que . . .; certains croient que . . .; **they went off, s. one way, s. another,** ils se sont dispersés, qui d'un côté, qui de l'autre; **s. of my friends,** certains de mes amis. **2.** (*thg*) **I have s.,** j'en ai; **give me s.,** donnez-m'en; **I've s. more,** (i) j'en ai encore; (ii) j'en ai d'autres; **s. of the time,** une partie du temps; **s. of the most beautiful scenery in the world,** un des plus beaux paysages du monde. **III.** *adv.* **1.** environ, quelque *inv*; **s. thirty pounds,** une trentaine de livres; **s. fifteen minutes,** un bon petit quart d'heure; **s. few minutes,** quelques minutes. **2.** *esp. NAm: F:* (*intensive*) **to go it s.,** y aller en plein; **it annoyed him s.,** il en était pas mal fâché.

somebody ['sʌmbədi] *pron. & n.* **1.** *pron.* **s. told me so,** quelqu'un, on, me l'a dit; **somebody's knocking,** on frappe; **s. is missing,** il manque quelqu'un; **s. (or other) has told him,** je ne sais qui lui a dit; **Mr S. (or other),** Monsieur Chose; **s. else,** quelqu'un d'autre; un autre. **2.** *pron. & n.* (*pl.* **somebodies** ['sʌmbədiz]) **he's (a) s.,** c'est un personnage; ce n'est pas le premier venu; **he thinks he's s.,** il se croit quelqu'un.

somehow ['sʌmhau] *adv.* **1.** de façon ou d'autre, d'une manière ou d'une autre; **we shall manage it s.**

(or other), tant bien que mal nous y parviendrons. **2. I never liked him s.,** je ne sais pourquoi mais il ne m'a jamais été sympathique; **s. (or other) it's different,** il y a pourtant une différence.

someone [ˈsʌmwʌn] *pron.* = SOMEBODY 1.

someplace [ˈsʌmpleis] *adv. NAm:* = SOMEWHERE.

somersault¹ [ˈsʌməsɔːlt] *n.* (i) *Gym:* saut périlleux; culbute *f*; (ii) (*accidental*) culbute; **to turn a s.,** faire (i) le saut périlleux, (ii) la culbute.

somersault² *v.tr.* (i) *Gym:* faire le saut périlleux, des sauts périlleux; (ii) faire la culbute.

something [ˈsʌmθiŋ] **I.** *n. or pron.* quelque chose *m.* **1.** (*a*) **say s.,** dites quelque chose; **s. or other,** une chose ou une autre; **Jim s. (or other),** Jacques je ne sais plus quoi; **there's s. about him I don't like,** il y a en lui je ne sais quoi qui me déplaît; **s. tells me he'll come,** quelque chose me dit qu'il viendra; **s. to drink,** de quoi boire; quelque chose à boire; **to ask for s. to drink,** demander (quelque chose) à boire; **can I get you s.?** qu'est-ce que je puis vous offrir (à manger, à boire)? **let's have s. to eat,** mangeons quelque chose; **s. to live for,** une raison de vivre; **to have s. to be annoyed about,** avoir de quoi se fâcher; **s. new,** quelque chose de nouveau, de neuf; **I've s. else to do,** j'ai autre chose à faire; **he's s. in a bank,** il travaille dans une banque; **in the year eleven hundred and s.,** en l'an onze cent et quelque chose; (*b*) **an indefinable s.,** un je ne sais quoi d'indéfinissable. **2.** (*a*) **there's s. of an improvement,** il y a une certaine amélioration; **he's s. of a miser,** il est un peu, quelque peu, avare; **he has seen s. of the world,** (i) il a voyagé; (ii) il a l'expérience du monde; (*b*) **his plan has s. in it, there's s. in his plan,** son projet mérite considération; **there's s. in what you say,** il y a de la vérité dans ce que vous dites; **there's s. in him,** il a du fond; il a de l'étoffe; **he has s. to do with it,** il y est pour quelque chose; **well, that's s.!** c'est déjà quelque chose! **that was quite s.!** c'était vraiment quelque chose! **II.** *adv.* (*a*) quelque peu, tant soit peu; **s. like a guinea pig,** qui ressemble à un cochon d'Inde; (*b*) *P:* **he treated me s. shocking,** il m'a traité d'une façon abominable.

sometime [ˈsʌmtaim] *adv.* **1.** *occ.* = SOMETIMES. **2.** (*a*) autrefois, jadis; **s. priest of this parish,** autrefois prêtre de cette paroisse; (*b*) *adj.* **Mr Martin, my s. tutor,** M. Martin, autrefois mon professeur. **3.** (*often written in two words*) **s. (or other),** tôt ou tard; un jour ou l'autre; **s. last year,** au cours de l'année dernière; **s. in August,** pendant le mois d'août; **s. soon,** bientôt; un de ces jours; *F:* **see you s.!** à bientôt!

sometimes [ˈsʌmtaimz] *adv.* quelquefois, parfois; **s. one, s. the other,** tantôt l'un, tantôt l'autre.

someway [ˈsʌmwei] *adv. F:* **s. (or other),** de façon ou d'autre.

somewhat [ˈsʌm(h)wɔt] **1.** *adv.* quelque peu; tant soit peu; **it's s. difficult,** c'est assez difficile; **s. disappointed,** quelque peu, légèrement, déçu; **s. complicated,** assez compliqué. **2.** *n.* **he was s. of a coward,** il était quelque peu poltron; **this was s. of a relief,** c'était en quelque sorte un soulagement.

somewhere [ˈsʌm(h)wɛər] *adv.* **1.** quelque part; **it's s. in the Bible,** cela se trouve quelque part dans la Bible; **s. near us,** pas bien loin de chez nous; **s. in the world,** de par le monde; **s. in France,** quelque part en France; **s. else,** ailleurs; autre part; **s. or other,** je ne sais où; **he lives s. near Oxford,** il habite dans les environs d'Oxford. **2. he is s. around fifty,** il a à peu près cinquante ans.

somnambulism [sɔmˈnæmbjulizm] *n.* somnambulisme *m.*

somnambulist [sɔmˈnæmbjulist] *n.* somnambule *mf.*

somnolence [ˈsɔmnələns] *n.* somnolence *f.*

somnolent [ˈsɔmnələnt] *a.* somnolent.

son [sʌn] *n.m.* fils; **how is your s.?** comment va votre fils? **the S. of God,** le fils de Dieu.

sonar [ˈsounɑːr] *n. Nau:* sonar *m.*

sonata [səˈnɑːtə] *n. Mus:* sonate *f.*

sonatina [sɔnəˈtiːnə] *n. Mus* sonatine *f.*

sonde [sɔnd] *n. Meteor: etc:* sonde *f.*

song [sɔŋ] *n.* **1.** chant *m*; **to burst, break, into s.,** se mettre à chanter; **the s. of the birds,** le chant, le ramage, des oiseaux. **2.** (*a*) chanson *f*; **s. book,** recueil *m* de chansons; chansonnier *m*; **s. writer,** compositeur, -trice, de chansons; **marching s.,** chanson de route; *F:* **to buy sth. for a s.,** acheter qch. pour rien, pour une bouchée de pain; **it went for a s.,** cela s'est vendu pour rien; *F:* **he made a great s. and dance about it,** il en faisait un tas d'histoires; (*b*) *Lit:* chant; **s. of victory,** chant de victoire; (*c*) *Ecc:* cantique *m*; **the S. of Songs, the S. of Solomon,** le Cantique des Cantiques.

songbird [ˈsɔŋbəːd] *n.* oiseau chanteur.

songster [ˈsɔŋstər] *n.m.* **1.** chanteur. **2.** poète, chantre. **3.** oiseau chanteur.

songstress [ˈsɔŋstris] *n.f.* chanteuse *f.*

sonic [ˈsɔnik] *a. Ph:* acoustique, audible; *Av:* (vitesse) sonique; **s. barrier,** mur *m* du son; **s. boom,** bang *m.*

son-in-law [ˈsʌninlɔː] *n.m.* gendre, beau-fils, *pl.* beaux-fils.

sonnet [ˈsɔnit] *n. Pros:* sonnet *m.*

sonny [ˈsʌni] *n.m. F: O:* mon petit; fiston *m.*

sonority [səˈnɔriti] *n.* sonorité *f.*

sonorous [ˈsɔnərəs] *a.* sonore; **s. voice,** voix sonore, timbrée. **-ly** *adv.* d'un ton sonore.

sonorousness [ˈsɔnərəsnis] *n.* sonorité *f.*

soon [suːn] *adv.* **1.** (*a*) bientôt, tôt; **s. after,** bientôt après; peu après; **s. after four,** un peu après quatre heures; **it will s. be three years since . . .,** voici bientôt trois ans que . . .; **he'll be here very s.,** il sera ici sous peu; **must you leave so s.?** vous faut-il partir si tôt? **too s.,** trop tôt; avant l'heure; **an hour too s.,** (arriver, etc.) avec une heure d'avance; **it ended all too s.,** cela a fini bien trop vite; **none too s.,** juste à temps; (*b*) **as s. as,** aussitôt que, dès que; **I'll see him as s. as he comes,** je le verrai aussitôt, dès, qu'il arrivera; **as s. as I arrived in London,** dès mon arrivée à Londres; **as s. as he saw them,** du moment qu'il les a vus; **as s. as possible,** le plus tôt possible; aussitôt que possible; (*c*) **I would just as s. stay,** j'aime autant rester. **2. sooner,** (*a*) plus tôt; **the sooner you begin the sooner you will have finished,** plus tôt vous commencerez plus vite vous aurez fini; **the sooner the better,** le plus tôt sera le mieux; **sooner or later,** tôt ou tard; **no sooner said than done,** aussitôt dit, aussitôt fait; **no sooner had he finished than he was arrested,** à peine eut-il fini qu'il fut arrêté; (*b*) plutôt; **sooner than give in I would die,** je mourrais plutôt que de céder; **I would sooner die,** j'aimerais mieux mourir. **3.** *Journ: F:* **soonest,** (faire qch.) aussitôt que possible; **it will be next week at soonest,** ce sera la semaine prochaine au plus tôt; *Prov:* **least said soonest mended,** trop gratter cuit, trop parler nuit.

soot¹ [sut] *n.* suie *f.*

soot² *v.tr.* enduire, couvrir, (qch.) de suie.

sooth [suːθ] *n. A:* vérité *f*; **in (good) s.,** en vérité.

soothe [suːð] *v.tr.* calmer, apaiser (la douleur, etc.); tranquilliser (l'esprit); apaiser (qn); **to s. s.o.'s, anger,** apaiser la colère de qn. **soothing** *a.* calmant, apaisant; *Med:* lénitif; **in a s. voice,** d'une voix calmante. **soothingly** *adv.* (d'un ton) calmant.

soothsayer [ˈsuːθseiər] *n.* devin *m, f.* devineresse.

soothsaying [ˈsuːθseiiŋ] *n.* divination *f.*

sooty [ˈsuti] *a.* **1.** couvert de suie; noir de suie. **2.** (dépôt) de suie; fuligineux.

sop¹ [sɔp] *n.* **1.** morceau de pain trempé. **2.** don *m* propitiatoire; concession *f*; *Lit:* **to throw a s. to Cerberus,** jeter le gâteau à Cerbère.

sop² *v.tr.* **(sopped) 1.** tremper, faire tremper (le pain). **2. to s. up,** éponger (un liquide). **sopping** *a.* trempé; **s. wet,** tout trempé; monillé à tordre; (*of pers.*) trempé jusqu'aux os.

sophism ['sɔfizm] *n.* sophisme *m.*

sophist ['sɔfist] *n.* sophiste *mf.*

sophistical [sə'fistik(ə)l] *a.* sophistique; captieux.

sophisticated [sə'fistikeitid] *a.* (*of pers.*) sophistiqué; aux goûts raffinés; (*of style*) recherché; (*of machinery*) (très) perfectionné, raffiné; sophistiqué.

sophistication [səfisti'keiʃ(ə)n] *n.* **1.** raisonnements sophistiques. **2.** (*a*) (*of pers.*) sophistication; goûts compliqués; intérêts intellectuels; (*b*) (*of style*) recherche *f.* (*c*) (*of machinery*) perfectionnement *m.*

sophistry ['sɔfistri] *n.* **1.** sophistique *f*; **to indulge in s.,** sophistiquer. **2.** sophisme *m.*

Sophocles ['sɔfəkli:z] *Pr.n.m. Gr.Lit:* Sophocle.

sophomore ['sɔfəmɔ:r] *n. Sch: NAm:* étudiant, -ante, de seconde année.

soporific [sɔpə'rifik] *a. & n.* somnifère (*m*), soporifique (*m*).

soppiness ['sɔpinis] *n. F:* mollesse *f*; fadasserie *f.*

soppy ['sɔpi] *a.* **1.** (terrain, etc.) détrempé. **2.** *F:* (*a*) (*of pers.*) mou, *f.* molle; (*of sentiment*) fadasse; (*of story, etc.*) larmoyant; (*b*) stupide, bête; **don't be s.!** ne sois pas si bête!

soprano, *pl.* **-os, -i** [sə'prɑ:nou, -ouz, -i:] *n. Mus:* soprano *mf*, *pl.* soprani, sopranos; **s. voice,** voix *f* de soprano.

sorb [sɔ:b] *n. Bot:* **1. s. (apple),** (i) sorbe *f*; (ii) alise *f.* **2. s. (tree),** (i) sorbier *m*, cormier *m*; (ii) alisier *m.*

sorbet ['sɔ:bei] *n. Cu:* sorbet *m.*

sorcerer ['sɔ:s(ə)rər] *n.m.* sorcier; magicien.

sorceress ['sɔ:s(ə)ris] *n.f.* sorcière; magicienne.

sorcery ['sɔ:s(ə)ri] *n.* sorcellerie *f.*

sordid ['sɔ:did] *a.* sordide; (*a*) sale, crasseux; (*b*) bas, vil. **-ly** *adv.* sordidement.

sordidness ['sɔ:didnis] *n.* sordidité *f*; (*a*) saleté *f*; (*b*) bassesse *f.*

sore¹ [sɔ:r] *a.* **1.** (*a*) douloureux, endolori; **s. to the touch,** douloureux au toucher; (*b*) enflammé; irrité; **s. eyes,** yeux enflammés; **s. throat,** mal *m* de gorge; **I've (got) a s. throat,** j'ai mal à la gorge; (*c*) **to have a s. finger,** avoir une (petite) plaie, une écorchure, au doigt; **it's a s. point, subject, with him,** il est très sensible sur ce point. **2.** (*of pers.*) (*a*) chagriné; **to be, feel, s. about sth.,** être chagriné, dépité, de qch.; (*b*) *NAm: F:* fâché; **to be, get s.,** se fâcher. **3.** *Lit:* **to be in s. need of sth.,** avoir grandement besoin de qch.; **s. trial,** cruelle épreuve; **s. temptation,** tentation *f* difficile à vaincre. **-ly** *adv. Lit:* gravement; grandement; **s. wounded,** gravement, grièvement, blessé; **s. tried,** cruellement éprouvé; **s. distressed,** dans une grande détresse; **s. needed,** dont on a grandement besoin; **s. tempted,** soumis à une grande tentation.

sore² *n.* (*a*) plaie *f*; écorchure *f*; **to (re)open an old s.,** raviver une ancienne plaie; (*b*) **(running) s.,** ulcère *m.*

sorehead ['sɔ:hed] *n. esp. NAm:* rancunier, -ière.

soreness ['sɔ:nis] *n.* **1.** endolorissement *m*; douleur *f.* **2.** (*a*) chagrin *m*; peine *f*; (*b*) *esp. NAm:* rancune *f.*

sorghum ['sɔ:gəm] *n. Bot:* sorg(h)o *m.*

sorrel¹ ['sɔrəl] *n. Bot:* oseille *f.*

sorrel² **1.** *a.* (cheval) saure, alezan. **2.** *n.* alezan *m*; **chestnut s.,** alezan châtain.

sorrow¹ ['sɔrou] *n.* douleur *f*, chagrin *m*, tristesse *f*; **to my s.,** à mon (grand) regret; **more in s. than in anger,** avec plus de compassion que de colère; *B:* **Man of Sorrows,** l'Homme de douleur.

sorrow² *v.i. esp. Lit:* s'affliger, être affligé (**over, at, about, sth.,** de qch.); **to s. for, after, s.o., sth.,** pleurer qn, qch. **sorrowing** *a.* affligé.

sorrowful ['sɔrəf(u)l] *a.* (*of pers.*) affligé, chagriné; triste; (*of news, etc.*) attristant, pénible; **s. look,** regard attristé, désolé. **-fully** *adv.* tristement; d'un air affligé, désolé.

sorry ['sɔri] *a.* **1.** (*a*) fâché, chagriné, désolé (**about sth.,** de qch.); **he's s. he did it, for having done it,** il est fâché, il se repent, il regrette, de l'avoir fait; **to be s. not to have done sth.,** avoir du regret de ne pas avoir fait qch.; *F:* **you'll be s. for it,** il vous en cuira; **I'm (very) s. to hear that . . .,** je regrette (infiniment), je suis désolé, d'apprendre que . . .; **I'm s. to say that . . .,** je regrette d'avoir à vous dire que . . .; **I'm so s. to keep you waiting,** excusez-moi de vous faire attendre; **(I'm) s.!** pardon! excusez-moi! (*b*) **I'm s. for him,** je le plains; il me fait pitié; **to look s. for oneself,** avoir l'air piteux; faire piteuse mine. **2.** *O:* pauvre, misérable, piteux; **to be in a s. plight,** (i) être en mauvaise passe; (ii) être dans un état piteux; **to cut a s. figure,** faire piètre figure.

sort¹ [sɔ:t] *n.* **1.** (*a*) sorte *f*, genre *m*, espèce *f*; **all sorts of people,** des gens de toutes sortes; **what s. of a man is he?** comment est-il? **he's a good s.,** c'est un brave type; **this,** *F:* **these, s. of people,** les gens de cette espèce; ces gens-là; **what s. of tree is it?** quelle sorte d'arbre est-ce? **what s. of day was it?** (i) quel temps faisait-il? (ii) vous avez passé une journée agréable? **I've heard all sorts of things about him,** j'en ai entendu de toutes les couleurs sur son compte; **I can't stand that s. of thing,** je ne peux pas souffrir des choses comme ça; **something of the s., of that s.,** quelque chose de pareil, de semblable, dans ce genre-là; **nothing of the s.,** (i) rien de semblable, de la sorte; (ii) pas du tout! **I've a s. of feeling that . . .,** *F:* **I s. of feel that . . .,** j'ai un peu l'idée que . . .; *F:* **I s. of expected it,** je m'en doutais presque; **the trees formed a s. of arch,** les arbres formaient comme une arche; (*b*) *Pej:* **coffee of a s.,** un soi-disant café; **a peace of sorts,** une paix telle quelle; **some s. of writer, a writer of sorts,** quelque vague écrivain; **to make some s. of (a) reply,** répondre d'une façon quelconque, tant bien que mal; (*c*) **to be out of sorts,** (i) être mal en train; ne pas être dans son assiette; (ii) être de mauvaise humeur, *F:* mal fichu. **2.** *Lit:* manière *f*, façon *f*; **in some s.,** à un certain degré; jusqu'à un certain point. **3.** *Typ:* sorte; **sorts,** assortiment *m.*

sort² *v.tr.* trier, faire le tri de (qch); assortir; classer (des papiers, etc.); **to s. out,** (i) éliminer (par tri); (ii) arranger, débrouiller (une affaire); (iii) *F:* régler son compte à (qn), arranger (qn); *Post:* **to s. the letters,** (i) trier, (ii) router, les lettres. **sorting** *n.* triage *m*, tri *m*; classement *m*; *Post:* **s. office,** bureau *m* de tri.

sorter ['sɔ:tər] *n.* (*a*) (*pers.*) trieur, -euse; classeur, -euse; *Post:* **(letter) s.,** trieur de lettres; (*b*) (*device*) trieur (de minerai, etc.); trieuse (de laine, etc.).

sortie ['sɔ:ti:] *n. Mil: Av: etc:* sortie *f.*

sot [sɔt] *n.* ivrogne *m*; soûlard, -arde.

sottish ['sɔtiʃ] *a.* abruti par l'alcool; d'ivrogne.

sotto voce [sɔtou'voutʃi] *adv.* (parler, etc.) tout bas.

soufflé ['su:flei] *n. Cu:* soufflé *m*; **cheese s.,** soufflé au fromage.

sough¹ [sau, sʌf] *n. Lit:* murmure *m*, susurration *f* (du vent, etc.).

sough² *v.i. Lit:* (*of wind, etc.*) murmurer, susurrer.

sought *see* SEEK.

soul [soul] *n.* âme *f.* **1.** (*a*) **to throw oneself body and s., heart and s., into sth.,** se donner corps et âme à qch.; se jeter de tout son cœur dans (une entreprise, etc.); *O:* **upon my s.!** sur mon âme! (*b*) **he's the s. of discretion,** il est la discrétion même. **2. departed souls,** les âmes des trépassés; **to pray for s.o.'s s.,** prier pour l'âme de qn; **God rest his s.!** que Dieu ait son âme! **All Souls' Day,** la Fête des Morts. **3.** (*a*) **population of two thousand souls,** population *f* de deux mille âmes; **without meeting a living s.,** sans recontrer âme qui vive; **there wasn't a s. in the street,** il n'y avait pas un chat dans la rue; (*b*) **he's a good s.,** c'est une bonne âme; **poor s.!** le, la, pauvre! **poor little s.!** pauvre petit(e)! **4. s. (music),** (sorte de) blues *m* (élaboré par les Noirs d'Amérique du Nord); *F:* soul *m*; *esp. U.S:* **s. brother, sister,** frère, sœur; **s. food,** nourriture traditionnelle des Noirs américains.

soul-destroying ['souldistrɔiŋ] *a.* (emploi, etc.) abrutissant, d'une monotonie mortelle.

soulful ['soulf(u)l] *a.* (*a*) plein d'âme; (musique) qui émeut l'âme; **s. eyes,** yeux expressifs; (*b*) sentimental, -aux. **-fully** *adv.* (*a*) (chanter) avec âme, avec expression; (*b*) sentimentalement.

soulless ['soullis] *a.* **1.** sans âme; terre à terre. **2.** (emploi) abrutissant.

soulmate ['soulmeit] *n.* âme *f* sœur.

soul-searching ['soulsəːtʃiŋ] *n.* examen *m* de conscience; **after a lot of s.-s.,** après mûre réflexion.

soul-stirring ['soulstəːriŋ] *a.* émouvant.

sound¹ [saund] *n.* (*a*) son *m*; bruit *m*; **there was not a s. to be heard,** on n'entendait pas le moindre bruit; **the s. of a dog barking,** le bruit d'un chien qui aboie; **musical s.,** son musical; **vowel s.,** son vocalique; **within (the) s. of . . .,** à portée du son de . . .; *T.V: etc:* **to turn up, turn down, the s.,** augmenter, diminuer, le volume; **I don't like the s. of it,** cela ne me dit rien qui vaille; **he's angry by the s. of it,** il est fâché, ça en a tout l'air, à ce qu'il paraît; (*b*) *Ph: Mus: etc:* son; *Ph:* **s. wave,** onde *f* sonore; *Av:* **s. barrier,** mur *m* du son; **s. recording,** enregistrement *m* du son; *Cin:* **s. track,** bande *f*, piste *f*, sonore; **s. effects,** effets *mpl* sonores; bruitage *m*; **s. effects man,** bruiteur *m*; **s. board,** (i) table *f* d'harmonie (de piano); tamis *m* (d'orgue); (ii) abat-voix *m inv* (de chaire, etc.); **s. box,** (i) caisse *f* de résonance (d'un instrument à cordes); (ii) diaphragme *m* (de phonographe); **s. hole,** ouïe *f* (de violon, de guitare); esse *f* (de violon); (*c*) *Ph:* l'acoustique *f*.

sound² **I.** *v.i.* **1.** (*a*) sonner, résonner; retentir; **the trumpet was sounding,** la trompette sonnait; **there are notes on this piano that don't s.,** ce piano a des notes qui ne sonnent pas; (*b*) *F:* **to s. off about sth.,** faire de grands laïus sur qch.; **to s. off at s.o.,** engueuler qn. **2.** (*a*) **it sounds hollow,** cela sonne creux; **it doesn't s. right,** cela sonne faux; (*b*) paraître, sembler; **name that sounds French,** nom qui a une consonance française; **that sounds odd!** voilà que paraît étrange, bizarre! **the noise sounded a long way off,** le bruit semblait venir de loin; **it sounds like Mozart,** on dirait du Mozart; **he doesn't s. like a man to . . .,** d'après ce que vous dites il ne serait pas homme à . . .. **II.** *v.tr.* **1.** (*a*) sonner (le tocsin, etc.); donner (l'alerte); **to s. the trumpet,** sonner de la trompette; *Aut:* **to s. one's horn,** appuyer sur l'avertisseur; *Mil:* **to s. the retreat,** sonner la retraite; (*b*) *Lit:* **to s. s.o.'s praises,** chanter les louanges de qn. **2.** prononcer (une lettre); **the h is not sounded,** l'h ne se prononce pas, est muet. **3.** (*a*) *Med:* ausculter (qn, la poitrine); (*by percussion*) percuter (la poitrine); **he sounded my chest,** il m'a ausculté; (*b*) *Rail: etc:* vérifier (une roue) au marteau. **sounding** *n.* **1.** résonnement *m*; retentissement *m* (d'un tambour, etc.); *Mil:* **the s. of the retreat,** le signal de la retraite; **s. board,** (i) abat-voix *m inv* (de chaire, etc.); (ii) table *f* d'harmonie (de piano); tamis *m* (d'orgue). **2.** *Med:* auscultation *f*; percussion *f*.

sound³ *n. Med:* sonde *f*.

sound⁴ **1.** (*a*) *v.tr. & i. Nau:* sonder; prendre, trouver, le fond; (*b*) *v.tr. Med:* sonder (une plaie); (*c*) *v.tr.* **to s. s.o. (out),** sonder qn (**about sth.,** à propos de qch.); tâter qn (à propos de qch.); **to s. public opinion,** sonder l'opinion. **2.** *v.i.* (*of whale*) plonger au fond. **sounding** *n.* **1.** (*a*) *Nau:* sondage *m*; **echo s.,** sondage par ultra-sons; **s. line,** (ligne *f* de) sonde *f*; **s. lead** [led], (plomb *m* de) sonde; (*b*) *Meteor:* sondage. **2.** *Nau:* **soundings,** les sondes; les fonds *mpl*; **to take soundings,** sonder; prendre le fond.

sound⁵ *n.* (i) détroit *m*; goulet *m*; (ii) bras *m* de mer; *Geog:* **the S.,** le Sund.

sound⁶ **I.** *a.* **1.** (*a*) (*of pers., animal*) sain; (cheval) sans tare; **s. in body and mind,** sain de corps et d'esprit; **of s. mind,** sain d'esprit; *F:* (*of pers.*) **to be s. in wind and limb,** avoir bon pied bon œil; **I'm as s. as a bell,** je suis en parfaite santé; (*b*) (*of thg*) en bon état; non endommagé; solide; (bois) sans tare; (fruit) sain. **2.** sain, solide; (*a*) **s. financial position,** situation financière solide; **s. business,** entreprise saine, solide; (*b*) (argument) valide, irréfutable; (raisonnement) juste; **s. doctrines,** doctrines (i) saines, (ii) orthodoxes; **s. piece of advice,** bon conseil; *Jur:* **s. title,** titre *m* valable, valide, légal. **3. s. sleep,** sommeil profond; sommeil de plomb; **I'm a s. sleeper,** je dors bien; **to give s.o. a s. thrashing,** administrer une bonne correction à qn. **II.** *adv.* **to be s. asleep,** être profondément endormi; dormir à poings fermés. **soundly** *adv.* **1.** sainement; judicieusement; solidement. **2.** (*a*) (dormir) profondément; (*b*) **to thrash s.o. s.,** administrer une bonne correction à qn.

sounder ['saundər] *n. Nau:* sondeur *m*.

soundless ['saundlis] *a.* muet; silencieux. **-ly** *adv.* silencieusement, sans bruit.

soundness ['saundnis] *n.* **1.** (*a*) état sain (de l'esprit); (*b*) bon état, bonne condition (des marchandises, etc.). **2.** solidité *f* (d'une entreprise); solvabilité *f*. **3.** (*a*) solidité (d'un argument, etc.); justesse *f* (d'un jugement); (*b*) orthodoxie *f* (d'une doctrine).

soundproof¹ ['saundpruːf] *a.* (*of room, etc.*) insonorisé; insonore.

soundproof² *v.tr.* insonoriser (une pièce, etc.). **soundproofing** *n.* insonorisation *f*.

soup¹ [suːp] *n.* (*a*) soupe *f*; (*thinner*) potage *m*; **cream s.,** velouté *m*; **onion s.,** soupe à l'oignon; **s. plate,** assiette creuse; **s. spoon,** cuillère *f* à soupe; **s. tureen,** soupière *f*; **s. ladle,** louche *f*; *F:* **to be in the s.,** être dans le pétrin; (*b*) *F:* brouillard (épais).

soup² *v.tr. F:* **to s. up,** gonfler (un moteur).

soupçon ['suːpsɔn] *n.* soupçon *m*, pointe *f* (d'ail).

souper ['suːpər] *n. F:* **pea s.,** brouillard épais, purée *f* de pois.

soupy ['supi] *a. F:* (*of weather*) très brumeux.

sour¹ ['sauər] *a.* **1.** (*a*) (fruit, etc.) aigre, acide; (*b*) (lait, crème, pain, etc.) aigre; (vin) suret, verjuté; **to turn s.,** tourner à l'aigre; (s')aigrir; surir; **to turn sth. s.,** (faire) aigrir qch.; **to smell s.,** sentir l'aigre; **the plan went s. on him,** le projet (i) a perdu son charme, (ii) a mal tourné, pour lui; (*c*) (*of soil*) trop humide. **2.** (*of pers.*) revêche; aigre. **-ly** *adv.* (répondre) aigrement; (regarder qn) d'un air revêche.

sour² **1.** *v.i.* (*a*) surir; (s')aigrir; **soured cream,** crème aigre; (*b*) **her temper has soured,** son caractère a aigri, s'est aigri. **2.** *v.tr.* (*a*) aigrir (le lait, etc., le caractère); **soured by misfortune,** aigri par le malheur.

source [sɔːs] *n.* source *f* (d'un fleuve, de malheurs, etc.); foyer *m* (de chaleur, d'infection, etc.); **light s.,** source lumineuse; **the Rhone has its s. in the Alps,** le Rhône prend sa source dans les Alpes; *Prov:* **idleness is the s. of all evil,** l'oisiveté est la mère de tous les vices; **I have it from a good s.,** je le sais, tiens, de bonne source; **s. materials,** matériaux *mpl* (d'un livre, etc.).

sourface ['sauəfeis] *n. F:* = SOURPUSS.

sourfaced ['sauəfeist] *a.* au visage morose, revêche.

sourness ['sauənis] *n.* **1.** aigreur *f*, acidité *f* (d'un fruit, etc.); aigreur (du lait). **2.** aigreur (de qn).

sourpuss ['sauəpus] *n. F:* personne morose, revêche; rabat-joie *m inv*.

souse¹ [saus] *n. Cu:* saumure *f*, marinade.
souse² *v.tr.* (*a*) *Cu:* faire mariner (le poisson); (*b*) plonger, immerger (**in,** dans). **soused** *a.* **1.** *Cu:* mariné; **s. herrings,** harengs marinés. **2.** *P:* ivre, soûl.
south [sauθ] **1.** *n.* (*a*) sud *m*, midi *m*; **house facing (the) s.,** maison (exposée) au sud, au midi; **to the s. (of sth.),** au sud (de qch.); du côté du sud; (*b*) le sud, le midi (d'un pays); **the S. of France,** le Midi (de la France); (*c*) *U.S: Hist:* **the S.,** les États *mpl* du sud (des États-Unis). **2.** *adv.* (*a*) au sud; (voyager) vers le sud; **s. of a place,** (être situé) au sud d'un endroit; (*of wind*) **to blow s.,** venir, souffler, du sud; **s. by east,** sud-quart-sud-est; **s. by west,** sud-quart-sud-ouest; (*b*) **to go s.,** aller dans le sud, dans le midi. **3.** *a.* (*a*) sud *inv*; (vent) du sud; (pays) du sud, méridional, -aux; (mur, fenêtre) qui fait face au sud; **s. side,** côté *m* sud; **on the s. side (of sth.),** au sud (de qch.); du côté du sud; **the s. coast,** la côte sud; (*b*) **S. Africa,** l'Afrique *f* du Sud; **S. African,** (i) *a.* sud-africain; (ii) *n.* Sud-africain, -aine; **S. America,** Amérique *f* du Sud; **S. American,** (i) *a.* sud-américain; de l'Amérique du Sud; (ii) *n.* Sud-américain, -aine; Américain, -aine, du Sud; **the S. Pole,** le pôle sud; **the S. Pacific,** le Pacifique sud; **the S. Seas,** les mers *fpl* du Sud; **the S. Sea Islands,** l'Océanie *f*.
southbound [ˈsauθbaund] *a.* (train, etc.) allant vers le sud; en direction de la banlieue sud.
southeast [sauθˈiːst] **1.** *n.* sud-est *m*; *Nau:* suet *m*. **2.** *adv.* vers le sud-est; **s. by east,** sud-est-quart-est; **s. by south,** sud-est-quart-sud. **3.** *a.* du sud-est.
southeasterly [sauθˈiːstəli] **1.** *a.* (vent, etc.) du sud-est; (quartier, etc.) (du, au) sud-est; (direction) vers le sud-est. **2.** *adv.* vers le sud-est.
southeastern [sauθˈiːstən] *a.* du, au, sud-est.
southerly [ˈsʌðəli] **1.** *a.* (*a*) (i) (vent) du sud, qui vient du sud; (ii) (direction) vers le sud; (courant) qui se dirige vers le sud; (*b*) **s. point,** point situé au sud, vers le sud; (*of house*) **s. aspect,** exposition *f* au midi, au sud; *Nau:* **to steer a s. course,** faire route au sud; mettre le cap au sud. **2.** *adv.* (*a*) vers le sud; (*b*) **the wind blows s.,** le vent souffle du sud.
southern [ˈsʌðən] *a.* **1.** (du) sud; du midi; méridional, -aux; austral, -aux; **s. Italy,** l'Italie *f* du sud; **the countries of s. Europe,** les pays méridionaux; **the s. hemisphere,** l'hémisphère sud, austral; **s. lights,** aurore australe; *Astr:* **the S. Cross,** la Croix du Sud. **2.** *U.S: Hist:* (armée, etc.) sudiste.
southerner [ˈsʌðənər] *s.* **1.** habitant, -ante, du sud; méridional, -ale. **2.** *U.S: Hist:* sudiste *mf*.
southpaw [ˈsauθpɔː] *n. Box: etc:* gaucher, -ère.
south-south-east, *Nau:* **sou'sou'east** [sau(θ)sau(θ)ˈiːst] **1.** *a. & n.* sud-sud-est (*m.*) **2.** *adv.* (vers le) sud-sud-est.
south-south-west, *Nau:* **sou'sou'west** [sau(θ)sau(θ)ˈwest] **1.** *a. & n.* sud-sud-ouest (*m*); *Nau:* susuroît *m*. **2.** *adv.* (vers le) sud-sud-ouest.
southward [ˈsauθwəd] **1.** *n.* sud *m*; **to the s.,** vers le sud. **2.** *a.* au, du, sud; du côté du sud. **3.** *adv.* **s. bound,** allant vers le sud.
southwards [ˈsauθwədz] *adv.* vers le sud.
southwest, *Nau:* **sou'west** [sau(θ)ˈwest] **1.** *n.* sud-ouest *m*; *Nau:* suroît *m*. **2.** *adv.* vers le sud-ouest; **s. by west,** sud-ouest-quart-ouest; **s. by south,** sud-ouest-quart-sud. **3.** *a.* du sud-ouest; **s. wind,** (vent *m* du) sud-ouest.
southwesterly, *Nau:* **sou'westerly** [sau(θ)ˈwestəli] **1.** *a.* (vent, etc.) du sud-ouest; (quartier, etc.) (du, au) sud-ouest; (direction) vers le sud-ouest. **2.** *adv.* vers le sud-ouest.
southwestern [sau(θ)ˈwestən] *a.* au, du, sud-ouest.
souvenir [suːvəˈniər] *n.* souvenir *m*.
sou'wester [sauˈwestər] *s.* **1.** *Nau:* (vent *m* du) sud-ouest *m*. **2.** *Cost:* suroît *m*, ciré *m*.
sovereign [ˈsɔvrin] **1.** *a.* souverain, suprême; **s. rights,** droits *mpl* de souveraineté; **the s. good,** le souverain bien; **s. remedy,** remède infaillible. **2.** *n.* (*a*) souverain, -aine; monarque *m*; (*b*) *Num: A:* souverain *m* (pièce d'or de la valeur d'une livre).
sovereignty [ˈsɔvrənti] *n.* souveraineté *f*.
soviet [ˈsouviet] **1.** *n.* soviet *m*; **Supreme S.,** soviet suprême. **2.** *a.* soviétique; **the Union of Socialist S. Republics, the S. Union,** l'Union *f* des Républiques socialistes soviétiques, l'Union soviétique.
sovietization [souvietaiˈzeiʃ(ə)n] *n.* soviétisation *f*.
sow¹ [sou] *v.tr. & i.* (*p.t.* **sowed** [soud]; *p.p.* **sown** [soun], **sowed**) semer (des graines, un champ); **to s. a field with wheat,** ensemencer un champ de blé; **to s. (the seeds of) discord,** semer la discorde. **sowing** *n.* semailles *fpl*, semis *m*; ensemencement *m*; **s. time, season,** la saison des semailles.
sow² [sau] *n. Z:* truie *f*; (*wild*) laie *f*.
sower [ˈsouər] *n.* **1.** (*pers.*) semeur, -euse. **2.** (*device*) semoir *m*.
sox [sɔks] *n.pl. NAm:* = **socks,** *see* SOCK¹.
soy(a) [ˈsɔi(ə)] *n.* (*a*) **s. (bean),** soya *m*, soja *m*; (*b*) **s. sauce,** sauce de soya.
sozzled [ˈsɔz(ə)ld] *a. P:* ivre, soûl; **to get s.,** se soûler.
spa [spɑː] *n.* (*a*) source thermale; (*b*) station thermale.
space¹ [speis] *n.* **1.** espace *m*, intervalle *m* (de temps); **in the s. of a year,** dans l'espace d'un an; **after a short s. of time,** après un court intervalle. **2.** (*a*) espace; **he sat staring into s.,** il était assis le regard perdu dans le vide, dans l'espace; **the conquest of s.,** la conquête de l'espace; **outer s.,** espace extra-atmosphérique; **s. flight,** vol, voyage, spatial; **s. travel,** voyages dans l'espace; astronautique *f*; **s. rocket,** fusée spatiale, interplanétaire; **s. suit,** scaphandre *m* d'astronaute; **s. station,** station spatiale; (*b*) *Mth: Ph:* espace; **s.-time,** espace-temps *m*; (*c*) espace; étendue *f*; place *f*; **open spaces,** espaces verts; étendues non bâties; **wide open spaces,** vastes paysages; **living s.,** espace vital; **in a confined s.,** dans un espace restreint; **to take up a lot of s.,** prendre, occuper, beaucoup de place; être encombrant; *F:* **s. saver,** gagne-place *m*, *pl.* gagne-places; **s.-saving,** qui permet de gagner de la place; (meuble, etc.) compact. **3.** (*a*) espace libre; espacement *m*, intervalle; (*between lines of writing, etc.*) interligne *m*; entre-ligne *m*; **blank s.,** (endroit *m* en) blanc *m*; *Typewr:* **s. between letters,** intervalle; **s. bar,** barre *f* d'espacement; (*b*) *Typ:* espace *f* (en métal); blanc; **s. rule,** filet *m* maigre.
space² *v.tr.* **to s. (out),** espacer (des arbres, des mots, des visites); échelonner (des troupes, des paiements, etc.); **the posts are spaced ten feet apart,** les poteaux sont plantés à dix pieds d'intervalle. **spacing** *n.* (*a*) espacement *m*, écartement *m* (des arbres, etc.); (*b*) *Typ:* espacement (des lettres, des lignes); *Typew:* **in single, double s.,** à simple, double, interligne.
spacecraft [ˈspeiskrɑːft] *n.* véhicule, vaisseau, spatial; astronef *m*.
spaceman, *pl.* **-men** [ˈspeismæn, -men] *n.m.* **1.** astronaute, cosmonaute. **2.** (*in science fiction*) habitant de l'espace.
spacer [ˈspeisər] *n.* **1.** *Typ:* espace *f*. **2.** *Typewr:* barre *f* d'espacement; **back s.,** rappel *m* de chariot; rappel arrière. **3.** *Mec.E:* pièce *f* d'écartement, écarteur *m*.
spaceship [ˈspeisʃip] *n.* = SPACECRAFT.
spacious [ˈspeiʃəs] *a.* (*a*) spacieux, vaste; (*b*) ample.
spaciousness [ˈspeiʃəsnis] *n.* vaste étendue *f*; dimensions spacieuses (d'une maison, etc.).
spade¹ [speid] *n. Tls:* bêche *f*; (*child's*) pelle *f*; **to call a s. a s.,** appeler les choses par leur nom.
spade² *v.tr.* bêcher (la terre, etc.).

spade³ *n. Cards:* pique *m*; **ace of spades,** as *m* de pique; **to play a s., to play spades,** jouer pique.
spadeful ['speidful] *n.* pleine bêche; pelletée *f*.
spadework ['speidwɔːk] *n.* **1.** travaux *mpl* à la bêche. **2.** travaux préliminaires (en vue d'une enquête).
spaghetti [spə'geti] *n. Cu:* spaghetti *mpl*; *Cin:* **s. western,** western de production italienne.
Spain [spein] *Pr.n. Geog:* Espagne *f*.
span¹ [spæn] *n.* **1.** (*a*) empan *m* (de la main); (*b*) (*of bird, aircraft*) **wing s.,** envergure *f*. **2.** (*a*) portée *f* (entre deux appuis); largeur *f* (d'une arche); écartement *m* (de deux piliers); volant *m* (d'une poutre); (*b*) travée *f* (d'un pont, d'un comble); **single s. bridge,** pont *m* à travée unique. **3.** (*a*) petite étendue (de terre); (*b*) *Lit:* court espace de temps.
span² *v.tr.* **(spanned) 1.** (*a*) mesurer (à l'empan); (*b*) encercler (le poignet) avec la main. **2.** (*a*) (*of bridge, etc.*) franchir, traverser, enjamber (une rivière, etc.); (*b*) **his life spans nearly the whole century,** sa vie embrasse presque tout le siècle.
span³ *n.* (*a*) *esp. NAm:* paire *f*, couple *m* (de chevaux, de bœufs); (*b*) (*S. Africa*) attelage *m* (de bœufs).
spangle¹ ['spæŋgl] *n. Tex: etc:* paillette *f*; (*large*) paillon *m*; **gold spangles,** paillettes d'or.
spangle² *v.tr.* pailleter (**with,** de); **spangled with silver,** pailleté d'argent.
Spaniard ['spæniəd] *n.* Espagnol, -ole.
spaniel ['spænjəl] *n.* épagneul *m*; **cocker, springer, s.,** épagneul cocker, springer.
Spanish ['spæniʃ] **1.** *a.* espagnol; **S. American,** hispano-américain; *Bot:* **S. onion,** oignon *m* d'Espagne. **2.** *n.* (*a*) *Ling:* espagnol *m*; (*b*) *pl.* **the S.,** les Espagnols *mpl.*
spank¹ [spæŋk] *n.* claque *f* sur le derrière; fessée *f*.
spank² *v.tr.* fesser (un enfant); administrer une fessée à (un enfant). **2.** *v.i.* (*of horse, etc.*) **to s. along,** aller bon train. **spanking 1.** *a.* (*a*) *F:* épatant; (*b*) **to go at a s. pace,** aller bon train. **2.** *n.* fessée *f*.
spanner ['spænər] *n. Tls:* clef *f*; **adjustable s.,** (i) clef anglaise; clef à molette; (ii) clef universelle; **box s.,** clef à douille, à tire-fonds; *F:* **to throw a s. in the works,** mettre des bâtons dans les roues.
spar¹ [spɑːr] *n.* **1.** perche *f*, poteau *m*. **2.** *Nau:* espar(t) *m*. **3.** *Av:* **wing s.,** poutrelle *f*; bras *m* d'aile.
spar² *n. Miner:* spath *m*.
spar³ *n.* **1.** combat *m* de coqs. **2.** (*a*) *Box:* combat d'entraînement; (*b*) escarmouche *f*; *F:* prise *f* de bec.
spar⁴ *v.tr.* **(sparred) 1.** (*of cocks*) se battre. **2.** (*of pers.*) **to s. with s.o.,** (i) *Box:* s'entraîner avec qn; (ii) argumenter avec qn. **sparring** *n.* boxe *f* d'entraînement; (ii) *F:* prise *f* de bec; **s. partner,** (i) sparring-partner *m*; (ii) *F:* adversaire *m*.
spare¹ ['spɛər] **I.** *a.* **1.** (*a*) frugal, -aux; **s. diet,** régime frugal; (*b*) (*of pers.*) sec, *f.* sèche; maigre, fluet; **he was tall and s.,** c'était un grand mince. **2.** de trop, de reste; disponible; **s. time,** (i) temps *m* disponible; (ii) moments perdus; loisirs *mpl*; **in my s. time,** à mes heures perdues; **s. capital,** fonds *mpl* disponibles; **s. room,** chambre *f* d'ami(s); **we have a s. bed,** on peut vous offrir un lit (pour la nuit); **to go s.,** (i) être de reste, en surplus; (ii) *P:* (*of pers.*) sortir de ses gonds. **3.** (accessoires, vêtements) de rechange; **s. parts,** pièces *fpl* de rechange; pièces détachées; **have you a s. handkerchief?** as-tu un mouchoir à me prêter? *Aut:* **s. wheel,** roue *f* de secours; **s. tyre,** *NAm;* **tire,** (i) pneu de rechange; (ii) *F:* bourrelet *m* de graisse. **II.** *n.* **1. to take up the s. in a rope,** raidir un cordage. **2. spares,** pièces de rechange; pièces détachées; **I've lost my pencil; have you a s.?** j'ai perdu mon crayon; en as-tu un à me prêter?
spare² *v.tr.* **1.** épargner, ménager; **to s. no expense,** ne pas regarder à la dépense; **to s. no pains,** se donner beaucoup de mal; **he spared no pains to please me,** il n'a rien épargné pour me contenter. **2.** (*a*) se passer de (qch.); se priver de (qch.); **can you s. it?** pouvez-vous vous en passer? **we can't s. him,** il nous est indispensable; **to have nothing to s.,** n'avoir que le strict nécessaire; **to have enough and to s. (of sth.),** avoir plus qu'il n'en faut (de qch.); **there is room and to s.** la place ne manque pas; (*b*) **I cannot s. the time to finish it,** je n'ai pas le temps de le finir; **to have no time to s.,** ne pas avoir de temps de libre; **when I have time to s.,** quand j'ai des loisirs *mpl*; **I have a minute to s.,** je peux disposer d'un instant; **to catch a train with five minutes to s.,** prendre un train avec cinq minutes de battement; (*c*) **to s. s.o. sth.,** donner, céder, qch. à qn; **can you s. me a hundred francs?** pouvez-vous me prêter cent francs? **can you s. me a few moments?** voulez-vous m'accorder quelques minutes? **3.** (*a*) faire grâce à (qn); **to s. s.o.'s life,** épargner la vie de qn; **s. me!** grâce! épargnez-moi! **if he is spared,** s'il vit; **death spares no one,** la mort n'épargne personne; **to s. s.o.'s feelings,** ménager qn; épargner qn; **s. my blushes!** ne me faites pas rougir! **I'll s. you the rest,** je vous fais grâce du reste; (*b*) ménager (qn, son cheval); **he doesn't s. himself,** il ne se ménage pas; **to s. s.o. the trouble of doing sth.,** éviter à qn la peine de faire qch. **sparing** *a.* frugal; ménager; économe; **to be s. with the butter,** ménager le beurre; *Lit:* **he is s. of praise,** il est avare de louanges. **sparingly** *adv.* **1.** frugalement; (manger) sobrement; **to use sth. s.,** ménager qch. **2.** modérément.
spark¹ [spɑːk] *n.* (*a*) étincelle *f*; (*from fire*) flammèche *f*; **the s. of life,** l'étincelle de la vie; **s. of wit,** étincelle, lueur *f*, d'esprit; **he hasn't a s. of generosity in him,** il n'a pas la moindre parcelle de générosité; (*b*) *El: etc:* étincelle; **s. discharge,** décharge disruptive; **s. gap,** (i) *El:* distance explosive, d'éclatement; (ii) *I.C.E:* pont *m* d'allumage; (*c*) *I.C.E:* **s. ignition,** allumage *m* par bougies; **s. plug,** bougie *f* (d'allumage); (*d*) *Nau: Av: F:* **sparks,** le radio.
spark² *v.i.* (*a*) émettre des étincelles; (*of dynamo, etc.*) cracher; (*b*) (*of current*) **to s. across the terminals,** jaillir entre les bornes. **2.** *v.ind.tr.* **to s. off an idea,** provoquer (une idée, etc.); **to s. off a revolution,** déclencher une révolution. **sparking** *n.* **1.** émission *f* d'étincelles; (*accidental*) jaillissement *m* d'étincelles; **2.** *I.C.E:* **s. plug,** bougie *f* (d'allumage).
spark³ *n.* **gay s.,** gaillard *m*; noceur *m*.
sparkle¹ ['spɑːkl] *n.* **1.** étincelle *f*; brève lueur; **not a s. of wit,** pas la moindre parcelle d'esprit. **2.** (*a*) étincellement *m*; éclat *m*, pétillement *m* (des yeux); feux *mpl* (d'un diamant); (*b*) **wine that has lost its s.,** vin *m* qui ne pétille plus. **3.** vivacité *f* d'esprit.
sparkle² *v.i.* **1.** (*a*) étinceler, scintiller; miroiter; **her eyes sparkled (with joy),** ses yeux étincelaient, brillaient (de joie); **sparkling with wit,** (livre) qui pétille d'esprit; (*b*) (*of wine*) pétiller, mousser. **2.** (*of fire*) émettre des étincelles; pétiller. **sparkling 1.** *a.* (*a*) étincelant, brillant, miroitant; (conversation) brillante; (*b*) (vin) mousseux; (limonade) gazeuse. **2.** *n.* (*a*) étincellement *m*; scintillement *m*; (*b*) pétillement *m*.
sparkler ['spɑːklər] *n.* **1.** *Pyr:* allumette japonaise. **2.** *P:* diamant *m*.
sparrow ['spærou] *n. Orn:* (*a*) moineau *m*; (*b*) *NAm:* pinson *m* (*Fr.C.*); (*c*) **hedge s.,** fauvette *f* d'hiver.
sparrowhawk ['spærouhɔːk] *n. Orn:* épervier *m*.
sparse [spɑːs] *a.* (*of trees, population, etc.*) clairsemé, épars; peu dense; **s. hair,** cheveux rares, clairsemés; **s. vegetation,** végétation éparse. **-ly** *adv.* peu abondamment; **s. populated,** peu peuplé; **s. covered with trees,** aux arbres clairsemés.
sparseness ['spɑːsnis] *n.* faible densité *f* (de la population); manque *m* (de végétation).
Sparta ['spɑːtə] *Pr.n. Geog:* Sparte *f*.
Spartan ['spɑːtən] **1.** *a.* (*a*) *Geog:* spartiate; (*b*) **to**

lead a s. life, vivre en spartiate; mener une vie austère. **2.** *n.* (*a*) *Geog:* Spartiate *mf;* (*b*) spartiate, homme austère.

spasm ['spæzm] *n.* **1.** *Med:* spasme *m.* **2.** accès *m* (de toux, de jalousie); **to work in spasms,** travailler par à-coups.

spasmodic [spæz'mɔdik] *a.* **1.** *Med:* spasmodique. **2.** irrégulier; intermittent; **s. work,** travail fait par à-coups. **-ally** *adv.* **1.** *Med:* spasmodiquement. **2.** irrégulièrement; (travailler) par à-coups.

spastic ['spæstik] **1.** *a.* (paralysie, etc.) spasmodique. **2.** *n.* (*pers.*) paralysé(e) spasmodique; handicapé(e) moteur.

spasticity [spæs'tisiti] *n.* spasticité *f.*

spat¹ [spæt] *n.* frai *m,* naissain *m* (d'huîtres, etc.).

spat² *n. Cost:* demi-guêtre *f, pl.* demi-guêtres.

spat³ *n. NAm: F:* querelle *f.*

spat⁴ *v.i.* **(spatted)** *NAm: F:* se quereller avec qn.

spate [speit] *n.* cure *f; Fig:* avalanche *f* (de lettres, etc.); **river in s.,** rivière *f* en crue.

spatial ['speiʃ(ə)l] *a. Mth: Ph: etc:* spatial, -aux.

spatter¹ ['spætər] *n.* éclaboussure *f; Ind:* projection *f* (de soudure).

spatter² **1.** *v.tr.* **to s. s.o. with mud, to s. mud over s.o.,** éclabousser qn de boue. **2.** *v.i.* (*of liquid*) jaillir, gicler; **the rain spattering down on the pavement,** la pluie qui gicle sur le trottoir.

spatula ['spætjulə] *n. Pharm: Surg: etc:* spatule *f.*

spatulate ['spætjuleit] *a. Nat.Hist:* spatulé.

spavin ['spævin] *n. Vet:* éparvin *m.*

spawn¹ [spɔːn] *n.* **1.** frai *m,* œufs *mpl* (de grenouille, poisson, etc.). **2.** *F:* progéniture *f.* **3. mushroom s.,** blanc *m* de champignon.

spawn² **1.** *v.i.* (*a*) (*of fish, etc.*) frayer; (*b*) *F:* (*of pers.*) se multiplier. **2.** *v.tr.* (*a*) (*of fish, frog, etc.*) déposer (son frai, ses œufs); (*b*) *F:* engendrer, donner naissance à (qch.). **spawning** *n.* (le moment du) frai *m;* **s. season,** fraie *f,* fraieson *f;* **s. ground,** frayère *f.*

spay [spei] *v.tr. Vet:* châtrer (une femelle). **spaying** *n.* castration *f* (d'une femelle).

speak [spiːk] *v.* (*p.t.* **spoke** [spouk]; *p.p.* **spoken** ['spouk(ə)n]) **I.** *v.i.* **1.** (*a*) parler; **without speaking,** sans parler; sans rien dire; (*b*) **to s. to s.o.,** (i) parler à qn; (**about sth.,** de qch.); adresser la parole à qn; s'adresser à qn; (ii) réprimander qn; **I'll s. to him about it,** je lui en toucherai un mot; **I know him to s. to,** nous nous disons bonjour; **speaking for myself,** pour ma part; en ce qui me concerne; *F:* **s. for yourself!** parle pour toi! **honestly speaking,** franchement; **roughly speaking,** approximativement; **so to s.,** pour ainsi dire; *Tp:* **who's speaking?** c'est de la part de qui? **Mr Thomas?—yes, speaking,** M. Thomas?—lui-même; (*c*) **the facts s. for themselves,** ces faits n'ont pas besoin de commentaires, parlent d'eux-mêmes; **that speaks well for his courage,** cela fait honneur à son courage; (*d*) (*of gun, organ, etc.*) parler; (*e*) *Ven:* (*of dog*) donner de la voix; (*f*) (*of deaf-mute, etc.*) **to s. by signs,** parler par gestes. **2.** faire un discours; **he spoke on the subject of . . .,** il a parlé, traité, de . . .; **to have the right to s.,** avoir le droit de se faire entendre; avoir droit à la parole. **II.** *v.tr.* **1.** (*a*) dire (un mot, la vérité); **not to s. a word,** ne pas dire un mot; **he has never spoken a word to me,** il ne m'a jamais adressé la parole; (*b*) **to s. one's mind,** dire ce qu'on pense. **2.** indiquer (qch.); témoigner de (qch.); **eyes that s. affection,** yeux *mpl* qui témoignent de l'amitié. **3.** parler (une langue); **do you s. French?** parlez-vous français? **English is spoken everywhere,** l'anglais se parle partout: *P.N:* **English spoken,** on parle anglais. **speak for** *v.i.* (*a*) **to s. for s.o.,** (i) parler, (ii) plaider, pour qn; (*b*) retenir, réserver (des places, etc.); **to be spoken for,** être réservé. **speaking** **1.** *a.* (*a*) (i) (*of doll, etc.*) parlant; (ii) (*of eyes, etc.*) expressif, éloquent; (*b*) **slow-s.,** qui a la parole lente; **English-s.,** de langue anglaise, anglophone; **French-s.,** francophone. **2.** *n.* (*a*) (i) parler *m,* discours *m,* parole *f;* **plain s.,** franchise *f,* franc-parler *m;* **we're no longer on s. terms,** nous sommes brouillés; nous ne nous parlons plus; (ii) **s. tube,** tube *m* acoustique, *Nau: etc:* porte-voix *m inv; Av:* aviophone *m;* (*b*) **public s.,** l'art *m* oratoire; *F:* **unaccustomed as I am to public s.,** n'ayant pas l'habitude de parler en public. **speak of** *v.i.* (*a*) parler de (qch.); **speaking of . . .,** à propos de . . .; **it's nothing to s. of,** ce n'est rien; cela ne vaut pas la peine d'en parler; **to s. well, highly, of s.o., sth.,** dire du bien, beaucoup de bien, de qn; **he is well spoken of,** il a une bonne réputation; **to s. ill of s.o.,** dire du mal de qn; médire de qn; (*b*) être significatif de (qch.). **speak out** *v.i.* (*a*) parler fort, à haute voix; (*b*) parler franchement. **speak up** *v.i.* (*a*) parler plus fort, plus haut; (*b*) **to s. up for s.o.,** parler en faveur de qn. **spoken** *a.* **1. the s. word,** la parole; **s. language,** langue parlée. **2. to be well s. of,** avoir une bonne réputation. **3. a well-s. man,** un homme (i) à la parole courtoise, (ii) qui parle bien.

speakeasy ['spiːkiːzi] *n. U.S:* débit, bar, clandestin.

speaker ['spiːkər] *n.* **1.** parleur, -euse; (*in dialogue*) interlocuteur, -trice; **I'm a plain s.,** j'appelle les choses par leur nom. **2.** (*in public*) orateur *m;* **to be a fluent, good, s.,** avoir la parole facile, avoir le don de la parole. **3.** *Parl:* **the S.** = le Président (des Communes). **4.** haut-parleur *m, pl.* haut-parleurs.

spear¹ ['spiər] *n.* **1.** lance *f; Ven:* épieu *m;* (*for throwing*) javelot *m.* **2.** *Fish:* harpon *m;* **s. gun,** fusil *m* à harpon; **s. fishing,** pêche, chasse, (sous-marine) au harpon.

spear² *v.tr.* (*a*) (trans)percer, tuer (qn) d'un coup de lance; (*b*) harponner (un poisson); (*c*) piquer (une olive, etc., avec une fourchette, etc.).

spear³ *n.* brin *m* (d'herbe); jet *m,* tige *f* (d'osier).

spearhead¹ ['spiəhed] *n.* (*a*) fer *m,* pointe *f,* de lance; (*b*) *Mil:* pointe *f;* **to launch a s. against . . .,** pousser une pointe sur . . ..

spearhead² *v.tr.* (*a*) *Mil:* **they spearheaded the crossing of the river,** ils ont forcé les premiers le passage du fleuve; (*b*) **to s. a movement,** être à l'avant-garde d'un mouvement.

spearmint ['spiəmint] *n. Bot:* menthe verte; baume vert.

spec [spek] *n. F:* **to buy sth. on s.,** acheter qch. à tout hasard.

special ['speʃ(ə)l] **1.** *a.* (*a*) spécial, -aux, particulier (to, à); *Journ:* **our s. correspondent,** notre envoyé spécial; **s. mission,** mission particulière; **s. feature, characteristic,** particularité *f; Com:* **s. price,** prix *m* de faveur; *Post: U.S:* **s. delivery,** envoi *m* par exprès; (*b*) particulier; (ami) intime; **nothing s.,** rien de particulier; **for s. occasions,** pour les jours de fête; (*c*) *Com: Ind:* (article) hors série; (*d*) *Cin: T.V: etc:* **s. effects,** trucages *mpl.* **2.** (*a*) *a.* & *n.* **s. (constable),** citoyen assermenté faisant fonction d'agent de police; (*b*) train spécial; (*c*) édition spéciale (d'un journal); (*d*) **today's s.,** plat *m* du jour. **-ally** *adv.* spécialement, particulièrement; surtout; **I went there s. to see them,** j'y ai été dans le seul but de les voir; **it's not s. good,** ce n'est pas particulièrement bon.

specialist ['speʃ(ə)list] *n.* spécialiste *mf;* **to become a s. in electronics, an electronics s.,** se spécialiser dans l'électronique; *Med:* **heart s.,** cardiologue *mf.*

speciality [speʃi'æliti] *n.* **1.** spécialité *f* (d'un magasin, etc.); objet spécial d'étude, de recherches; **that's my s.,** ça c'est mon fort, c'est ma spécialité. **2.** qualité particulière; particularité *f.* **3.** *Jur* = SPECIALTY 1.

specialization [speʃəlai'zeiʃ(ə)n] *n.* spécialisation *f.*

specialize ['speʃəlaiz] **1.** *v.tr.* désigner, adapter, à un but spécial. **2.** *v.i.* (*a*) se spécialiser; **to s. in historical research,** se spécialiser dans les recherches historiques; *Iron:* **she specializes in that sort of blunder,** elle est spécialiste de ce genre de gaffes; (*b*) *Biol:* se différencier.

specialty ['speʃəlti] *n.* **1.** *Jur:* contrat formel sous seing privé. **2.** *esp. NAm:* = SPECIALITY 1.

specie ['spi:ʃi:] *n.* (*no pl.*) espèces (monnayées).

species ['spi:ʃi(:)z] *n. inv.* **1.** (*a*) *Nat.Hist:* espèce *f*; **the human s.,** l'espèce humaine; **the origin of s.,** l'origine *f* des espèces; (*b*) *For:* essence *f*. **2.** espèce, sorte *f*. **3.** *Theol:* **(Eucharistic) s.,** les (saintes) espèces.

specific [spi'sifik] **1.** *a.* (*a*) spécifique; *Ph:* **s. gravity,** poids *m* spécifique; (*b*) (*of statement, etc.*) précis; (*of order, etc.*) explicite; **s. aim,** but déterminé. **2.** *n.* (*a*) *Med:* spécifique *m* **(for,** contre); (*b*) *U.S: Ind:* **specifics,** description précise; caractéristiques *fpl*. **-ally** *adv.* (*a*) spécifiquement; (*b*) précisément.

specification [spesifi'keiʃ(ə)n] *n.* **1.** spécification *f* (des détails, etc.). **2.** (*a*) description précise; devis descriptif; caractéristiques *fpl* (d'une voiture); prescriptions *fpl* (des travaux à exécuter); (*b*) *Const: Ind:* **specifications,** cahier *m* des charges.

specify ['spesifai] *v.tr.* spécifier, désigner, déterminer; préciser (des conditions, etc.); **specified load,** charge prévue, prescrite; **unless otherwise specified,** sauf indication contraire.

specimen ['spesimin] *n.* (*a*) spécimen *m*; **the finest specimens in his collection,** les plus belles pièces de sa collection; (*b*) spécimen, exemple *m*, échantillon *m*, exemplaire *m*; **s. page,** page *f* spécimen; page type; *Publ:* **s. copy,** livre *m* à l'examen; *Med:* **to take a s. of s.o.'s blood, a blood s. from s.o.,** faire une prise de sang à qn; *F:* **a s.,** un échantillon d'urine; (*c*) *F:* (*of pers.*) **odd s.,** drôle *m* de type.

specious ['spi:ʃəs] *a.* (*of appearance*) spécieux, trompeur; (*of argument, etc.*) captieux, spécieux.

speciousness ['spi:ʃəsnis] *n.* spéciosité *f*; apparence trompeuse.

speck [spek] *n.* **1.** petite tache; point *m* (de couleur, d'encre); *Med:* **floating specks (in front of the eyes),** mouches volantes. **2.** (*a*) grain *m*, atome *m* (de poussière); **the ship was only a s. on the horizon,** le navire n'était qu'un point noir à l'horizon; (*b*) brin *m* (de consolation, de générosité, etc.). **3.** (*a*) défaut *m*; (*b*) tavelure *f* (sur un fruit).

specked [spekt] *a.* tacheté, moucheté; (fruit) tavelé.

speckle¹ ['spekl] *n.* petite tache; point *m* (de couleur); moucheture *f*, tacheture *f*.

speckle² *v.tr.* tacheter, moucheter. **speckled** *a.* tacheté, moucheté; (*of plumage*) grivelé; (*of hen*) bariolé; **bird s. with white,** oiseau tacheté de blanc.

specs [speks] *n.pl. F:* lunettes *fpl*.

spectacle ['spektəkl] *n.* **1.** spectacle *m*; **to make a s. of oneself,** se donner en spectacle. **2.** **(pair of) spectacles,** lunettes *fpl*; **to put on one's spectacles,** mettre, chausser, ses lunettes; **s. case,** étui *m* à lunettes.

spectacled ['spektəkld] *a.* à lunettes.

spectacular [spek'tækjulər] **1.** *a.* spectaculaire; **s. play,** pièce *f* à spectacle. **2.** *a.* & *n.* *Cin:* **s. (film),** superproduction *f*.

spectator [spek'teitər] *n.* spectateur, -trice; assistant, -ante; **the spectators,** l'assistance *f*.

spectral ['spektr(ə)l] *a.* (*a*) *Ph: Ch:* spectral, -aux; **s. colours,** couleurs spectrales; (*b*) spectral.

spectre, *NAm:* **specter** ['spektər] *n.* spectre *m*, fantôme *m*, apparition *f*; **the s. of war,** le spectre de la guerre.

spectrogram ['spektrougræm] *n.* *Ph: Opt:* spectrogramme *m*.

spectrograph ['spektrougræf] *n.* spectrographe *m*.

spectrometer [spek'trɔmitər] *n.* spectromètre *m*.

spectroscope ['spektrɔskoup] *n.* spectroscope *m*.

spectroscopy [spek'trɔskəpi] *n.* spectroscopie *f*.

spectrum *pl.* **-tra** ['spektrəm, -trə] *n.* (*a*) *Ph: etc:* spectre *m*; **the colours of the s.,** les couleurs spectrales, du spectre; **s. analysis,** analyse spectrale; (*b*) **a wide s. of opinions,** toute une gamme d'opinions.

speculate ['spekjuleit] *v.i.* **1.** **to s. on, about, sth.,** (i) spéculer, méditer, sur qch.; (ii) faire des conjectures sur qch. **2.** spéculer; **to s. on the Stock Exchange,** jouer à la Bourse. **speculating** *n.* spéculation *f*.

speculation [spekju'leiʃ(ə)n] *n.* **1.** (*a*) spéculation *f*, méditation *f* **(on,** sur); (*b*) conjecture *f*; **it was pure s. on his part,** c'était (une) pure conjecture de sa part. **2.** (*a*) *Fin:* spéculation; *St.Exch:* **to buy sth. on s.,** acheter qch. (i) à titre de spéculation, (ii) (*F:* **on spec**) à tout hasard; (*b*) entreprise spéculative; *St.Exch:* coup *m* de Bourse.

speculative ['spekjulətiv] *a.* **1.** (*a*) spéculatif, contemplatif; (*b*) conjectural, -aux; théorique; **there are merely s. assumptions,** ce sont là de pures hypothèses, de pures conjectures. **2.** *Fin:* spéculatif.

speculator ['spekjuleitər] *n.* spéculateur, -trice; *St. Exch:* joueur, -euse, à la Bourse; agioteur *m*.

speculum, *pl.* **-ums, -a** ['spekjuləm, -əmz, -ə] *n.* **1.** *Med:* spéculum *m*. **2.** miroir *m* (d'un télescope).

speech [spi:tʃ] *n.* **1.** (*a*) **(faculty of) s.,** la parole; **to lose the power of s.,** perdre la parole; (*b*) **(manner of) s.,** articulation *f*; élocution *f*; façon *f* de parler, de s'exprimer; **to be slow of s.,** parler lentement; **to be abrupt in one's s.,** parler d'une manière brusque; **s. therapy,** orthophonie *f*; **s. therapist,** orthophoniste *mf*. **2.** paroles, propos *mpl*; **without further s.,** sans plus rien dire. **3.** langue *f* (d'un peuple); parler *m* (d'une région, etc.). **4.** discours *m*; allocution *f*; **to make a s.,** faire, prononcer, un discours; **s. making,** l'art *m* oratoire; *Sch:* **s. day** = distribution *f* des prix. **5.** *Gram:* **parts of s.,** parties *fpl* du discours; **direct, indirect, s.,** discours, style, direct, indirect; **figure of s.,** figure *f* de rhétorique.

speechify ['spi:tʃifai] *v.i. F: Pej:* discourir; pérorer. **speechifying** *n.* beaux discours; laïus *m*.

speechless ['spi:tʃlis] *a.* **1.** incapable de parler; aphone. **2.** interdit, interloqué, muet **(with surprise, fright,** de surprise, d'épouvante); **emotion left him s.,** l'émotion lui a coupé la parole.

speechwriter ['spi:tʃraitər] *n.* discourier *m*.

speed¹ [spi:d] *n.* **1.** (*a*) vitesse *f*, rapidité *f*; *Lit:* **to make all s.,** faire diligence; se hâter; **with all possible s.,** aussi rapidement, aussi vite, que possible; *Art: etc:* **at s.,** (rouler) à grande vitesse; **at top, full, s.,** à toute vitesse; au plus vite; (*of runners*) à toutes jambes; (*of motorist*) **to drive at top s.,** rouler à toute vitesse, à toute allure; *Nau:* **full s. ahead, astern!** en avant, en arrière, toute! (*b*) *Mch: Veh:* vitesse, régime *m*; **maximum, top, s.,** vitesse maximale, maximum; vitesse limite; **car with a maximum s. of 150 km an hour,** voiture avec un plafond de 150 km à l'heure; **cruising s.,** vitesse, régime, de croisière; *Av:* **take-off s.,** vitesse de décollage; **to gather, lose, s.,** prendre, perdre, de la vitesse; **to reduce (the) s.,** ralentir; **to pick up s.,** (*of train, etc.*) prendre de la vitesse, gagner en vitesse; (*of car*) reprendre; **s. indicator,** indicateur *m* de vitesse; *Av:* badin *m*; **s. limit,** (i) *Mch:* vitesse maximale, maximum; régime maximal, maximum; (ii) *Aut:* limitation *f* de vitesse; **to exceed the s. limit,** dépasser la vitesse autorisée; **exceeding the s. limit,** excès *m* de vitesse; *F:* **s. cop,** motard *m*; *F:* **s. merchant,** chauffard *m*; fou *m* du volant; (*c*) *Phot:* rapidité *f* (d'une émulsion); rapidité, luminosité *f* (d'un objectif). **2.** *I.C.E:* (*gear*) vitesse; **three-s. gearbox,** boîte *f* à trois vitesses. **3.** *A:* **to wish s.o. good s.,** souhaiter bonne chance à qn. **4.** *P:* amphétamine *f*, speed *m*.

speed² **I.** (*p.t. & p.p.* **sped**) **1.** *v.i.* se hâter, se presser; aller vite; **to s. along,** foncer; **to s. off,** partir à toute vitesse. **2.** *v.tr.* (*a*) *A: & Lit:* **s. the parting guest,** (i) souhaiter bon voyage à un invité qui part; (ii) *F:* encourager, presser, un invité à partir plus vite; (*b*) *A:* **God s.!** = bon voyage! **II.** (*p.t. & p.p.* **speeded**) **1.** *v.tr.* (*a*) régler la vitesse (d'une machine); (*b*) **to s. up,** accélérer (le travail, etc.); **that will s. things up a bit!** comme ça nous irons plus vite! **2.** *v.i. Aut: etc:* (i) faire de la vitesse; (ii) dépasser la vitesse autorisée; **I was caught speeding,** j'ai eu une contravention (pour excès) de vitesse. **speeding** *n.* **1.** grande vitesse; excès *m* de vitesse. **2. s. up,** accélération *f.*

speedboat ['spi:dbout] *n.* canot *m* automobile; vedette *f*; hors-bord *m inv.*

speediness ['spi:dinis] *n.* rapidité *f*; célérité *f.*

speedometer [spi:'dɔmitər] *n.* (*a*) indicateur *m* de vitesse; compteur *m* (de vitesse); (*b*) tachymètre *m.*

speedster ['spi:dstər] *n. esp. U.S: F:* chauffard *m*; fou *m* du volant.

speed(-)up ['spi:dʌp] *n.* accélération *f.*

speedway ['spi:dwei] *n.* **1.** piste *f* (d'autodrome); circuit *m* de vitesse. **2.** *NAm:* = autoroute *f.*

speedwell ['spi:dwel] *n. Bot:* véronique *f.*

speedy ['spi:di] *a.* rapide, prompt; **s. revenge,** prompte vengeance. **-ily** *adv.* rapidement.

speleologist [spili'ɔlədʒist] *n.* spéléologue *mf.*

speleology [spili:'ɔlədʒi] *n.* spéléologie *f.*

spell¹ [spel] *n.* **1.** charme *m*, incantation *f*; formule *f* magique. **2.** charme, sort *m*, maléfice *m*; **to cast a s. over s.o., to put a s. on s.o.,** jeter un sort à, sur, qn; ensorceler, envoûter, qn; **to break the s.,** rompre le charme; **under a spell,** sous un charme; ensorcelé.

spell² *v.tr.* (*p.t. & p.p.* **spelt, spelled** [spelt, speld]) **1.** épeler; (*in writing*) orthographier (un mot); **he can't spell,** il ne sait pas l'orthographe; **to s. out sth.,** déchiffrer qch. péniblement; **do I have to s. it out for you?** faut-il que je te l'explique davantage, que je mette les points sur les i? **how is it spelt?** comment cela s'écrit-il? **2. what do these letters s.?** quel mot forment ces lettres? **3.** signifier; **it would s. disaster,** cela précipiterait un désastre. **spelling** *n.* (*a*) épellation *f*; orthographe *f*; **s. mistake,** faute *f* d'orthographe; **s. book,** alphabet *m*; (*b*) **s. reform,** réforme *f* orthographique; **another s. of the same word,** une autre orthographe du même mot.

spell³ *n.* **1.** relais *m*, relève *f.* **2.** (*a*) tour *m* (de travail, etc.); **to do a s. of duty,** faire un tour de service; **to take spells at the pumps,** se relayer aux pompes; (*b*) **to have another s. of prison,** retâter de la prison. **3.** période; temps *m*; (*a*) **to rest for a (short) s.,** se reposer pendant quelque temps; (*b*) **a long s. of cold weather,** une longue période de froid; **during the cold s.,** pendant le coup de froid; **we're in for a s. of wet weather,** le temps se met à la pluie; (*c*) **to suffer from dizzy spells,** être sujet à des vertiges; (*d*) *Austr:* repos *m.*

spell⁴ *v.tr.* **1.** *NAm: F:* relayer, relever (qn) (dans son travail). **2.** *Austr:* laisser reposer (un cheval).

spellbinder ['spelbaindər] *n.* orateur entraînant (qui tient ses auditeurs).

spellbound ['spelbaund] *a.* (*a*) retenu par un charme; (*b*) fasciné, magnétisé; envoûté; **to hold s.o. s.,** fasciner qn; envoûter qn.

speller ['spelər] *n.* **1. to be a good, a bad, s.,** être fort, faible, en orthographe; savoir, ne pas savoir, l'orthographe. **2.** alphabet *m.*

spend [spend] *v.tr.* (*p.t. & p.p.* **spent** [spent]) **1.** dépenser (de l'argent); **to s. one's money on cigarettes,** dépenser son argent en cigarettes; **her father has spent a great deal on her education,** son père a dépensé beaucoup pour son éducation; **to s. money on s.o.,** faire des dépenses pour qn; **he spends money like water,** l'argent lui fond entre les mains; *F:* **to s. a penny,** aller faire une petite commission, aller faire pipi. **2. to s. time on (doing) sth.,** consacrer, employer, du temps à (faire) qch. **3.** passer, employer (son temps); **to s. Sunday in the country,** passer le dimanche à la campagne. **4.** épuiser (ses forces); consumer (son énergie); **our ammunition was all spent,** nos munitions étaient épuisées. **spending** *n.* dépense *f*; **s. power,** pouvoir *m* d'achat; **s. money,** argent *m* de poche; argent pour ses dépenses courantes. **spent** *a.* (*a*) épuisé (de fatigue); (*b*) **s. bullet,** balle morte.

spender ['spendər] *n.* **to be a big s.,** dépenser beaucoup.

spendthrift ['spendθrift] *n.* dépensier, -ière; prodigue *mf*; dissipateur, -trice; **s. habits,** habitudes dépensières.

sperm¹ [spə:m] *n. Physiol:* sperme *m.*

sperm² *n.* **1.** *Z:* **s. whale,** cachalot *m*; **2. s. oil,** huile *f* de spermaceti.

spermaceti [spə:mə'seti] *n.* spermaceti *m*; blanc *m* de baleine.

spermatozoon, *pl.* **-oa** [spə:mətou'zouən, -ouə] *n. Biol:* spermatozoïde *m.*

spermicidal [spə:mi'said(ə)l] *a.* spermicide.

spermicide ['spə:misaid] *n.* spermicide *m.*

spew [spju:] *v.tr. & i.* vomir; *Fig:* **to s. out, forth,** vomir, rejeter (de la fumée, etc.).

sphagnum, *pl.* **-a** ['sfægnəm, -ə] *n. Moss:* sphaigne *f.*

sphere [sfiər] *n.* **1.** *Astr: Mth:* sphère *f*; **the celestial s.,** la sphère céleste. **2.** (*a*) milieu *m*, sphère; **to be out of one's s.,** être hors de sa sphère; se sentir dépaysé; (*b*) domaine *m*, sphère; **to extend one's s. of activity,** étendre sa sphère d'activité; **that is not within my s.,** cela n'est pas de mon domaine, de mon ressort; **in the political s.,** sur le plan politique; **s. of influence,** sphère, zone *f*, d'influence.

spherical ['sferik(ə)l] *a.* sphérique.

spheroid ['sfiərɔid] *n.* sphéroïde *m.*

sphincter ['sfiŋ(k)tər] *n. Anat:* sphincter *m.*

sphinx, *pl.* **sphinxes** [sfiŋks, 'sfiŋksiz] *n. Myth: Ent:* sphinx *m.*

spice¹ [spais] *n.* **1.** épice *f*, aromate *m*; **mixed spice(s),** épices mélangées. **2. to give s. to a story,** pimenter, épicer, un récit; **the s. of life,** le sel, le piquant, de la vie; **the s. of adventure,** le piment de l'aventure.

spice² *v.tr.* **1.** épicer (un gâteau, une boisson, etc.). **2.** pimenter, épicer (un récit, etc.).

spiciness ['spaisinis] *n.* **1.** goût épicé. **2.** piquant *m*, sel *m* (d'un récit).

spick and span ['spik(ə)n'spæn] *adj.phr.* reluisant de propreté; propre comme un sou neuf; (*of pers.*) tiré à quatre épingles.

spicy ['spaisi] *a.* **1.** épicé; (goût) relevé. **2.** aromatique, parfumé. **3.** (*of story, conversation, etc.*) (i) piquant, croustillant; (ii) salé, épicé, poivré; **to tell s. stories,** en dire de vertes.

spider ['spaidər] *n.* (*a*) *Arach:* araignée *f*; **spider's web,** *NAm:* **s. web,** toile *f* d'araignée; (*b*) *Crust:* **s. crab,** araignée de mer; *Z:* **s. monkey,** atèle *m.*

spiderman, *pl.* **-men** ['spaidəmæn, -men] *n.m.* ouvrier qui travaille au sommet des édifices; homme-mouche, *pl.* hommes-mouches.

spidery ['spaidəri] *a.* **1.** d'araignée; qui ressemble à une araignée; **s. handwriting,** pattes *fpl* d'araignée. **2.** (grenier, etc.) infesté d'araignées.

spiel¹ [ʃpi:l, spi:l] *n. F:* boniment *m*, baratin *m.*

spiel² *v.i. F:* baratiner; faire du baratin.

spieler ['spi:lər] *n. F:* **1.** beau parleur; baratineur; -euse. **2.** *esp. Austr:* (*a*) tricheur, -euse, aux cartes; (*b*) chevalier *m* d'industrie; escroc *m.*

spiffing ['spifiŋ] *a. F: O:* épatant.

spigot ['spigət] *n.* **1.** fausset *m*, broche *f* (de tonneau). **2.** (*a*) clef *f* (de robinet); (*b*) robinet *m.*

spike¹ [spaik] *n.* **1.** pointe *f* (de fer); piquant *m* (de fil de fer barbelé, etc); (*on railing, etc.*) lance *f*; (*on woman's shoes*) **s. heel,** talon *m* aiguille. **2.** (*a*) **s. (nail),** clou *m* à large tête, à tête de diamant; broche *f*; clou barbelé; (*b*) *Rail: etc:* crampon *m* (d'attache); chevillette *f*; (*c*) **bill s., s. file,** pique-notes *m inv*; (*d*) *Sp: F:* **spikes,** chaussures *fpl* à pointes. **3.** *Bot:* (*a*) épi *m*; (*b*) **s. (lavender),** (lavande) aspic *m*.

spike² *v.tr.* (*a*) *Civ: E: etc:* clouer, cheviller; (*b*) armer (qch.) de pointes; **spiked gate,** grille *f* à pointes, garnie de pointes; *Sp:* **spiked shoes,** chaussures *fpl* à pointes; (*c*) *Fig:* **to s. s.o.'s guns,** priver qn de ses moyens d'action; contrarier les projets de qn; (*d*) corser (une boisson); (*e*) *NAm:* faire avorter (une affaire); contrecarrer, entraver (des projets).

spikenard ['spaikna:d] *n. A.Toil:* nard (indien).

spiky ['spaiki] *a.* **1.** à pointe(s) aiguë(s); **s. hair,** cheveux hérissés. **2.** armé de pointes.

spill¹ [spil] *n.* culbute *f*, chute *f* (de cheval, de voiture); **to have a s.,** culbuter; (*from bicycle, horse*) *F:* ramasser une pelle.

spill² *v.* (*p.t. & p.p.* **spilt, spilled** [spilt, spild]) **1.** *v.tr.* (*a*) répandre, renverser (un liquide, du sel); verser (du sang); **without spilling a drop,** sans laisser tomber une goutte; *F:* **to s. the beans,** vendre la mèche; (*b*) *U.S:* dire, débiter (des paroles); (*c*) désarçonner (un cavalier); verser (les occupants d'une voiture). **2.** *v.i.* (*of liquid*) se répandre; s'écouler.

spill³ *n.* allumette *f* (de papier, etc.); allume-feu *m inv*.

spillage ['spilidʒ] *n.* (*a*) action *f* de répandre un liquide; (*b*) quantité (de liquide) répandue.

spillover ['spilouvər] *n.* surplus *m*, déversement *m*, de population.

spillway ['spilwei] *n. Hyd.E:* déversoir *m*.

spin¹ [spin] *n.* **1.** (*a*) tournoiement *m*; (mouvement de) rotation *f* (d'une balle, etc.); *Games:* **to put s. on a ball,** donner de l'effet à une balle; *Cr:* **s. bowler,** lanceur *m* qui donne de l'effet à la balle; *Dom.Ec:* **s. drier,** essoreuse *f* (centrifuge); **s. drying,** essorage *m*; (*b*) *Atom.Ph:* spin *m* (de l'électron, etc.); (*c*) *Av:* vrille *f*; **flat s.,** vrille à plat; tonneau *m*; *Fig:* **to be in a flat s.,** ne pas savoir où donner de la tête. **2.** tour *m*, promenade *f* (en voiture, etc.); **to go for a s.,** aller faire un tour (en voiture, etc.). **3.** *Austr: F:* (i) coup *m* de chance; (ii) malchance *f*.

spin² *v.* (*p.t. & p.p.* **spun** [spʌn]; *pr.p.* **spinning**) **1.** *v.tr.* (*a*) filer (la laine, le coton, etc.); (*of spider*) **to s. its web,** filer sa toile; (*b*) **to s. a top,** lancer, fouetter, une toupie; **to s. a coin,** jouer à pile ou face; **to s. s.o. round,** faire tourner, faire tournoyer, qn; *Dom.Ec:* **to s. dry,** (faire) essorer (du linge); (*c*) *Fish:* pêcher à la cuillère; *v.i.* **to s. for fish,** pêcher au lancer. **2.** *v.i.* (*a*) (*of top, etc.*) tourner; (*of suspended object*) tournoyer; (*of compass*) être affolé, s'affoler; **to s. round and round,** tournoyer, tourbillonner; **my head's spinning,** la tête me tourne; **to s. round,** (*of car*) faire un tête-à-queue; (*of pers.*) (i) pivoter, virevolter; (ii) se retourner vivement; faire un demi-tour; **the blow sent him spinning,** le coup l'a envoyé rouler; (*b*) *Veh:* (*of wheel*) patiner (sur place). **spinning 1.** *a.* tournant; (*of suspended object*) tournoyant. **2.** *n.* (*a*) filage *m* (au rouet); *Ind:* filature *f*; **s. wheel,** rouet *m*; **s. mill, factory,** filature; *Ent:* **s. gland,** filière *f* (de l'araignée, du ver à soie); (*b*) (i) tournoiement *m*; rotation *f*; affolement *m* (de l'aiguille magnétique); *Av:* vrille *f*; **s. motion, movement,** mouvement rotatif, de rotation; **s. top,** toupie *f*. **spin out** *v.tr.* délayer (un discours); faire durer, prolonger (une discussion); faire traîner (une affaire, un récit) en longueur; **to s. out one's money,** *v.i.* **to make one's money s. out,** ménager son argent. **spun** *a. Tex:* câblé; **s. silk,** soie filée.

spina bifida [spainə'bifidə] *n. Med:* spina-bifida *m*.

spinach ['spinitʃ] *n.* épinard *m*; *Cu:* épinards *mpl*.

spinal ['spain(ə)l] *a. Anat:* spinal, -aux; vertébral, -aux; **s. column,** colonne vertébrale; **s. cord,** moëlle épinière; **s. curvature,** déviation *f* de la colonne vertébrale.

spindle ['spindl] *n.* **1.** *Tex:* fuseau *m*; **s.-shaped,** fusiforme; fuselé. **2.** *Mec.E: etc:* arbre *m*, axe *m*, mandrin *m*; (*of potter's wheel, etc.*) pivot *m*; (*of axle, shaft*) fusée *f*.

spindleshanks ['spindlʃæŋks] *n. pl. F:* **1.** jambes *fpl* en fuseau. **2.** (*with sg. const.*) type grand et maigre; manche *m* à balai.

spindly ['spindli] *a.* (*a*) (*of pers.*) maigrelet, maigrichon; (*of legs*) fuselé; (*b*) (*of furniture, etc.*) peu solide, peu robuste.

spindrift ['spindrift] *n.* embrun(s) *m(pl)*; poudrin *m*.

spine [spain] *n.* **1.** *Nat.Hist:* piquant *m*, épine *f* (d'une plante, d'un poisson, d'un hérisson, etc.). **2.** *Anat:* épine dorsale; colonne vertébrale; **s. chiller,** histoire *f* à vous glacer le sang; roman *m*, film *m*, d'épouvante. **3.** *Bookb:* dos *m* (d'un livre). **4.** *Geog:* arête *f*.

spineless ['spainlis] *a.* **1.** sans épines, sans piquants. **2.** *Fig:* (*of pers.*) faible; mou, *f.* molle; qui manque de caractère.

spinet [spi'net] *n. Mus:* épinette *f*.

spinnaker ['spinəkər] *n. Nau:* spinnaker *m*.

spinner ['spinər] *n.* **1.** (*a*) *Tex:* fileur, -euse; (*b*) **s. of tales, yarns,** conteur, -euse, d'histoires. **2.** *Nat.Hist:* filière *f* (de ver à soie, etc.). **3.** *Fish:* cuillère *f*.

spinneret ['spinəret] *n.* filière *f* (d'araignée, etc.).

spinney ['spini] *n.* petit bois; bosquet *m*; breuil *m*.

spin(-)off ['spinɔf] *n.* (*a*) avantage *m*, bénéfice *m*, supplémentaire; (*b*) sous-produit *m*, *pl.* sous-produits; produit *m* secondaire; (produit) dérivé *m*.

spinster ['spinstər] *n.* (*a*) célibataire *f*; femme, fille, non mariée; (*b*) *Pej:* vieille fille.

spiny ['spaini] *a.* (*a*) *Nat.Hist:* épineux; couvert d'épines, de piquants; **s. lobster,** langouste *f*; (*b*) (problème) épineux.

spiracle ['spaiərəkl] *n.* (*a*) évent (d'un cétacé); (*b*) *Ent:* stigmate *m*.

spiral¹ ['spaiər(ə)l] **1.** *n.* (*a*) spirale *f*; **in a s.,** en spirale; (*b*) spire *f*; tour *m* (de spirale); (*c*) *Av:* **s. (climb, dive),** montée *f*, descente *f*, en spirale; (*d*) **wage-price s.,** course *f*, spirale, des prix et des salaires. **2.** *a.* spiral, -aux; en spirale; ressort spiral; *Bookb:* **s. binding,** reliure spirale; **s.-bound notebook,** bloc-notes *m* à reliure spirale. **-ally** *adv.* en spirale.

spiral² *v.i.* **(spiralled,** *NAm:* **spiraled)** former une spirale; tourner, monter, en spirale; (*of steam, smoke*) tire(-)bouchonner; *Av:* (*of aircraft*) **to s. up, down,** monter, descendre, en spirale.

spire ['spaiər] *n. Arch:* aiguille *f*, flèche *f* (d'église).

spirit¹ ['spirit] *n.* **1.** esprit *m*, âme *f*; **I'll be with you in s.,** je serai avec vous de cœur; *B:* **the poor in s.,** les pauvres d'esprit. **2.** (*incorporeal being*) esprit; (*a*) **the Holy S.,** le Saint-Esprit; l'Esprit saint; **evil s.,** esprit malin, mauvais génie; **the s. of liberty,** le génie de la Liberté; (*b*) **to raise a s.,** évoquer un esprit; **to believe in spirits,** croire aux esprits, aux revenants; **s. writing,** psychogramme *m*. **3.** (*pers.*) esprit; **the leading s.,** (i) l'âme, le chef (d'une entreprise); (ii) le meneur, la meneuse (d'une révolte). **4.** esprit, disposition *f*; **the s. of the age,** l'esprit du siècle; **to have the party s.,** participer dans la gaieté de la réunion; **to enter into the s. of sth., of the thing,** entrer dans l'esprit de qch.; entrer de bon cœur dans (la partie); *F:* **that's the s.!** à la bonne heure! **5.** (*a*) caractère *m*, cœur *m*, courage *m*; **man of unbending s.,** homme d'un caractère inflexible; **man of s.,** homme de caractère; homme courageux; **to show s.,** montrer du caractère, du courage; (*b*) ardeur *f*, feu *m*, entrain *m*; **to have s.,**

avoir de l'allant; (*c*) **to be in good spirits,** être gai, dispos; être de bonne humeur; **to be in high spirits,** être en train, en verve; être d'une gaieté folle; **to be in low spirits,** être abattu, accablé; se sentir tout triste; **to keep up one's spirits,** ne pas perdre courage; **to raise, revive, s.o.'s spirits,** relever, remonter, le courage, le moral, de qn; **their spirits rose,** ils reprenaient courage. **6.** (*a*) **spirits,** spiritueux *mpl*; alcools *mpl*; **wines and spirits,** vins *mpl* et spiritueux; (*b*) *Ch:* **(volatile) s.,** esprit; **methylated spirits,** alcool dénaturé, à brûler; **surgical s.** = alcool à 90°; **s. lamp, stove,** lampe *f*, réchaud *m*, à alcool; *Th: etc:* **s. gum,** gomme arabique (pour coller de faux cheveux); **spirit(s) of salt,** esprit-de-sel *m*.

spirit² *v.tr.* **(spirited) to s. away, off,** faire disparaître, enlever, (qn) comme par enchantement; subtiliser, escamoter (qch.). **spirited** *a.* **1.** (*of pers.*) vif, animé; plein de fougue, de verve; intrépide; (*of horse*) fougueux. **2.** (*of style, reply, etc.*) chaleureux, plein de verve; **s. discussion,** vive discussion; **s. attack,** attaque fougueuse; **to give a s. performance,** jouer avec brio, avec verve.

spiritless ['spiritlis] *a.* (*a*) (style) sans vie, qui manque de verve; (conversation, etc.) qui manque d'entrain; (*b*) sans courage, sans caractère; lâche; (*c*) abattu; déprimé; (*d*) sans vigueur, sans ardeur; mou, *f.* molle.

spiritual ['spiritjuəl] **1.** *a.* (*a*) spirituel; (tribunal) ecclésiastique; **s. life,** vie spirituelle; **s. father,** père, directeur, spirituel; (*b*) **s. features,** traits purs, raffinés; (*c*) spirituel, immatériel. **2.** *n.* **negro s.,** (negro-)spiritual *m*, *pl.* (negro-)spirituals. **-ally** *adv.* spirituellement.

spiritualism ['spiritjuəlizm] *n.* **1.** *Psychics:* spiritisme *m*. **2.** *Phil:* spiritualisme *m*.

spiritualist ['spiritjuəlist] *n.* & *a.* **1.** *Psychics:* spirite (*mf*). **2.** *Phil:* spiritualiste (*mf*).

spirituality [spiritju'æliti] *n.* spiritualité *f* (de l'âme).

spirituous ['spiritjuəs] *a.* spiritueux, alcoolique.

spirt¹˒² [spəːt] *n.* & *v.* = SPURT¹˒².

spit¹ [spit] *n.* **1.** *Cu:* broche *f*. **2.** *Geog:* langue *f* de sable; flèche (littorale).

spit² *v.tr.* **(spitted)** (*a*) embrocher, mettre à la broche (un rôti, etc.); (*b*) *Lit:* embrocher (qn).

spit³ *n.* **1.** (*a*) crachat *m*, salive *f*; *F:* **he's the dead s. of his father,** c'est son père tout craché; *F:* **s. and polish,** astiquage *m*, fourbissage *m*; (*b*) crachement *m*. **2.** crachin *m* (de pluie).

spit⁴ *v.* (*p.t.* & *p.p.* **spat** [spæt]; *pr.p.* **spitting) 1.** *v.i.* (*a*) cracher; **to s. in s.o.'s face, to s. at s.o.,** cracher au visage à qn; (*b*) (*of cat*) cracher; félir; (*of pen*) cracher, crachoter; (*of fire*) crépiter, pétiller; (*of hot fat*) pétiller, grésiller; (*c*) crachiner; **it's spitting (with rain),** il crachine, il fait du crachin; (*d*) *El:* (*of collector, etc.*) cracher; (*e*) *I.C.E:* (*of engine*) **to s. back,** avoir des retours *mpl* de flamme (au carburateur). **2.** *v.tr.* cracher (de la salive, du sang, des injures); **to s. sth. out,** cracher qch.; recracher qch. (de mauvais); *F:* **s. it out!** accouche! vide ton sac! **spitting** *n.* (*a*) crachement *m*; *P.N:* **no s.,** défense de cracher; *F:* **he's the s. image of his father,** c'est son père tout craché; (*b*) *I.C.E:* crachotement *m* (du moteur); **s. back,** retour *m* de flamme (au carburateur).

spit⁵ *n.* profondeur *f* de fer de bêche; **to dig the ground two spits deep,** labourer la terre à deux fers de bêche.

spite¹ [spait] *n.* **1.** (i) rancune *f*; (ii) malveillance *f*; (iii) pique *f*, dépit *m*; **from, out of, s.,** (i) par rancune; (ii) par dépit; (iii) par malveillance, par méchanceté *f*; par animosité *f*; **to have a s. against s.o.,** garder rancune à qn; avoir de la rancune contre qn. **2.** *prep.phr.* **in s. of . . .,** en dépit de . . .; malgré . . .; **in s. of everything,** malgré tout.

spite² *v.tr.* vexer, contrarier (qn); **he does it to s. me,** il le fait pour me tracasser, m'ennuyer.

spiteful ['spaitf(u)l] *a.* rancunier, vindicatif; méchant, malveillant; **s. tongue,** langue venimeuse; **s. remark,** observation méchante. **-fully** *adv.* **1.** par dépit; par malveillance. **2.** méchamment.

spitefulness ['spaitf(u)lnis] *n.* méchanceté *f*; rancœur *f*; malveillance *f*.

spitfire ['spitfaiər] *n.* rageur, -euse.

spitter ['spitər] *n.* cracheur, -euse.

spittle ['spitl] *n.* salive *f*, crachat *m*; bave *f* (du crapaud).

spittoon [spi'tuːn] *n.* crachoir *m*.

spitz [spits] *n.* (*dog*) loulou *m*.

spiv [spiv] *n.* profiteur *m*, trafiquant *m* du marché noir.

splash¹ [splæʃ] *n.* **1.** éclaboussement *m* (de l'eau, du métal fondu); clapotement *m*, clapotis *m* (des vagues); **to fall into the water with a s.,** tomber dans l'eau en faisant floc, flac; *F:* **to make a (big) s.,** faire sensation; faire de l'épate; *Journ:* **s. headline,** grosse manchette; **s. back,** panneau protecteur (d'évier, etc.). **2.** (*a*) éclaboussure *f* (de boue, d'encre, etc.); (*b*) tache *f* (de couleur, de lumière); (*c*) *F:* **a whisky and s.,** un whisky soda; **just a s., please,** très peu, juste un soupçon, (d'eau, etc.), s'il vous plaît; (*d*) **water s.,** gué (peu profond). **3.** *int.* floc! flac! ploc!

splash² **1.** *v.tr.* (*a*) éclabousser (**s.o. with water,** qn d'eau); (*b*) **to s. water about,** faire jaillir, faire gicler, de l'eau; **to s. water at one another,** se jeter de l'eau; *F:* **to s. one's money about,** prodiguer son argent; dépenser sans compter; **I've splashed out on a new hat,** je me suis payé un nouveau chapeau; *Journ:* **to s. a piece of news,** mettre une nouvelle en manchette; (*c*) **to s. one's way across a field,** traverser un champ en pataugeant; (*d*) **to s. oneself,** s'éclabousser (d'eau, etc.); se tacher (de peinture, etc.); **to s. oneself, one's face, with water,** s'asperger, s'asperger la figure, d'eau. **2.** *v.i.* (*a*) (*of liquid*) jaillir en éclaboussures; (*of waves*) clapoter; (*of tap*) cracher; **to s. up,** gicler; (*b*) (*of pers., animal*) barboter; patauger; (*of space capsule*) **to s. down,** amerrir; **to s. about in the water,** barboter, patauger, dans l'eau.

splashdown ['splæʃdaun] *n.* amerrissage *m* (d'un engin spatial).

splatter¹ ['splætər] *n.* éclaboussure *f*.

splatter² **1.** *v.tr.* **to s. s.o. with mud, to s. mud over s.o.,** éclabousser qn de boue. **2.** *v.i.* (*of liquid*) jaillir, gicler.

splay¹ [splei] **1.** *v.tr.* (*a*) **to s. (out),** étendre (ses mains); (*b*) *Arch: etc:* **to s. the sides of a window,** ébraser, évaser, une fenêtre; **splayed opening,** ouverture ébrasée, évasée. **2.** *v.i.* **to s. out,** s'évaser.

splay² *a.* (*of knees, etc*) tourné en dehors.

splayfooted [splei'futid] *a.* (*of pers.*) aux pieds plats tournés en dehors.

spleen [spliːn] *a.* **1.** *Anat:* rate *f*. **2.** (*a*) *Lit:* spleen *m*; humeur noire; (*b*) mauvaise humeur; bile *f*; **to vent one's s. (up)on s.o.,** décharger sa bile sur qn.

splendid ['splendid] *a.* splendide; superbe; (palais, dîner, etc.) magnifique; **that's s.!** à la bonne heure! **-ly** *adv.* splendidement; magnifiquement.

splendiferous [splen'difərəs] *a.* *F: O:* magnifique.

splendour, *NAm:* **splendor** ['splendər] *n.* splendeur *f*; magnificence *f*.

splice¹ [splais] *n.* **1.** (*in rope, cable, etc.*) épissure *f*. **2.** (*a*) *Carp:* enture *f*; (*b*) (point *m* de) collage *m* (d'un film); (*in magnetic tape*) raccord *m*.

splice² *v.tr.* **1.** *Nau: etc:* épisser (un cordage, un câble). **2.** *Carp:* enter (deux pièces de bois). **3.** *Cin: etc:* coller (un film); raccorder, faire un raccord à (une bande magnétique). **4.** *F:* **to get spliced,** se marier. **splicing** *n.* **1.** épissage *m* (d'un cordage, d'un câble). **2.** *Carp:* enture *f* (de deux pièces de bois). **3.** *Cin: etc:* collage *m* (d'un film, d'une bande magnétique); raccordement *m* (d'une bande magnétique).

splint¹ [splint] *n. Med:* attelle *f*, éclisse *f*; clisse *f*; **to put a limb in splints,** éclisser, clisser, un membre.

splint² *v.tr. Med:* éclisser, clisser (un membre fracturé).

splinter¹ ['splintər] *n.* éclat *m* (de bois, d'obus, etc.); picot *m* (de bois); *Surg:* esquille *f* (d'os fracturé); **I've got a s. in my finger,** j'ai une écharde dans le doigt; *Pol:* **s. group,** groupe séparatiste.

splinter² **1.** *v.tr.* (*a*) briser (qch.) en éclats; faire voler (qch.) en éclats; (*b*) craquer (un aviron, un mât, etc.). **2.** *v.i.* (*a*) voler en éclats; éclater; (*b*) craquer, éclater.

splinterproof ['splintəpru:f] *a.* **1.** (abri) à l'épreuve des éclats d'obus. **2.** (verre) se brisant sans éclats.

split¹ [split] *n.* **1.** fente *f* (dans un mur, etc.); fissure *f*, crevasse *f* (dans une roche, etc.); déchirure *f* (dans une robe, etc.); gerçure *f* (de la peau). **2.** division *f*; scission *f* (dans un groupe). **3.** *F:* demi(-bouteille) *f* (d'eau de Vichy, etc.). **4.** *Cu:* **Devonshire s.,** brioche fourrée à la crème; **banana s.,** banane *f* à la crème. **5.** *Gym:* **to do the splits,** faire le grand écart.

split² *v.* (*p.t. & p.p.* **split;** *pr.p.* **splitting**) **1.** *v.tr.* (*a*) fendre (du bois, etc.); (re)fendre (de l'ardoise); cliver (la roche, etc.); déliter (la pierre); **to s. sth. in two, in half,** couper qch. en deux; *Atom.Ph:* **to s. the atom,** fissionner l'atome; **to s. sth. off,** détacher, séparer, enlever, qch. (par clivage); (*b*) déchirer; **I've s. my skirt,** j'ai déchiré ma jupe; (*c*) diviser, partager (une somme, etc.) (**into equal shares,** en parts égales); **to s. a bottle,** partager une bouteille (de vin); **to s. sth. up,** fragmenter, diviser, qch.; *Ch:* **to s. up a compound into its elements,** dédoubler un composé en ses éléments; *F:* **can you s. a pound for me?** pouvez-vous me donner la monnaie d'une livre? (*d*) *Pol:* **to s. the party,** provoquer une scission dans le parti; **to s. the vote,** partager les voix (dans un parti); **to s. one's vote,** *esp. U.S:* **to s. the ticket,** partager ses votes entre plusieurs candidats. **2.** *v.i.* (*a*) (*of wood, etc.*) se fendre; éclater; (*of stone*) se déliter; (*of rock*) se cliver; (*of the skin, etc.*) se gercer; **to s. open,** se fendre, s'ouvrir; **to s. off,** se séparer, se détacher (par clivage); (*b*) (*of dress, etc.*) se déchirer; (*of seam in dress, etc.*) craquer; (*c*) *F:* **my head's splitting,** j'ai un mal de tête fou; (*d*) (*of party, etc.*) se scinder; **to s. up,** se fractionner; **the party s. up into three groups,** le parti s'est divisé en trois groupes; **Paul and Anne have s. up,** Paul et Anne se sont séparés, ont rompu; (*e*) *F:* **to s. on s.o.,** dénoncer qn; vendre (un complice, un camarade); (*f*) *F:* s'en aller, partir; **let's s.!** fichons le camp! **split** *a.* **1.** fendu; **s. peas,** pois cassés; **s. ends,** cheveux fourchus; *Psy:* **s. personality,** dédoublement *m* de personnalité; **splitting 1.** *a.* qui (se) fend; *F:* **to have a s. headache,** avoir un mal de tête fou. **2.** *n.* (*a*) fendage *m* (de peaux, etc.); refendage *m* (de bois, d'ardoises, etc.); délitement *m*, délitage *m* (de la pierre); *Atom.Ph:* **s. of the atom,** fission *f* de l'atome; **s. up,** fragmentation *f*, division *f*, fractionnement *m* (de qch.); (*b*) **s. (up),** division, morcellement *m* (d'une terre, etc.); séparation *f* (de deux personnes, etc.); scission *f* (d'un parti politique, etc.).

splodge [splɔdʒ] *n. F:* = SPLOTCH¹.

splotch¹ [splɔtʃ] *n. F:* tache *f* (de couleur, d'encre).

splotch² *v.tr. F:* tacher, barbouiller (**with,** de).

splurge¹ [splə:dʒ] *n. F:* (*a*) esbrouffe *f*; épate *f*; (*b*) folles dépenses; folie *f*.

splurge² *v.i. F:* faire de l'esbrouffe, de l'épate; **to s. out,** faire des dépenses extravagantes.

splutter¹ ['splʌtər] *n.* **1.** bredouillement *m*. **2.** crachement *m* (d'un stylo, *El:* d'un collecteur, etc.); bafouillage *m* (d'un moteur).

splutter² **1.** *v.tr.* **to s. (out),** bredouiller (une excuse, une menace). **2.** *v.i.* (*a*) (*of pers.*) envoyer des postillons en parlant; *F:* crachoter; (*b*) (*of pers.*) bredouiller; (*c*) (*of pen, El: of collector*) cracher; *I.C.E:* (*of engine*) bafouiller.

spoil¹ [spɔil] *n.* **1.** (*usu.pl.*) dépouilles *fpl*; butin *m*; **to claim one's share of the spoil(s),** demander sa part du gâteau. **2.** *Min: etc:* **s. (earth),** déblai(s) *m(pl)*; décombres *mpl*; **s. bank,** talus *m* de déblai; **s. heap,** halde *f* (de déblais); terri(l) *m*; crassier *m*.

spoil² *v.* (*p.t. & p.p.* **spoiled, spoilt** [spɔild, spɔilt]) **1.** *v.tr.* (*a*) gâter, abîmer, gâcher (qch.); avarier (des marchandises); altérer, gâter (la viande, le vin); **this book was spoilt by the rain,** ce livre a été abîmé par la pluie; **to get spoilt, spoiled,** s'abîmer; **to s. s.o.'s fun,** gâter, gâcher, le plaisir de qn; **to s. the beauty of sth., s.o.,** défigurer qch.; *F:* **it spoils her,** ça lui fait tort; **to s. s.o.'s appetite,** couper l'appétit, la faim, à qn; *Pol:* **spoilt paper,** bulletin (de vote) nul; (*b*) gâter (un enfant, etc.); **her husband spoils her,** son mari la gâte; **a spoilt child,** un enfant gâté. **2.** *v.i.* (*of fruit, fish, etc.*) se gâter, s'abîmer; s'avarier; **to be spoiling for a fight,** brûler du désir de se battre.

spoilage ['spɔilidʒ] *n. Typ:* déchets *mpl* de tirage.

spoilsport ['spɔilspɔ:t] *n. F:* trouble-fête *mf inv*, rabat-joie *mf inv*.

spoke [spouk] *n.* **1.** (*a*) rayon *m*, rai *m* (de roue); (*b*) *Nau:* poignée *f*, manette *f* (de roue de gouvernail). **2.** (*a*) échelon *m* (d'échelle); (*b*) bâton *m* (à enrayer); **to put a s. in s.o.'s wheel,** mettre des bâtons dans les roues de, à, qn.

spokeshave ['spoukʃeiv] *n. Tls: Carp:* vastringue *f*.

spokesman, *pl.* **-men** ['spouksmən] *n.* porte-parole *m inv* (d'un parti, etc.); **to act as s. for s.o.,** être le porte-parole de, prendre la parole pour, qn.

spokeswoman, *pl.* **-women** ['spoukswumən, -wimin] *n.* (femme) porte-parole.

spoliation [spouli'eiʃ(ə)n] *n.* **1.** (*a*) spoliation *f*, dépouillement *m*; (*b*) pillage *m*. **2.** *Jur:* destruction *f*, altération *f* (de documents probants).

spondaic [spɔn'deiik] *a. Pros:* spondaïque.

spondee ['spɔndi:] *n. Pros:* spondée *m*.

sponge¹ [spʌn(d)ʒ] *n.* **1.** (*a*) éponge *f*; *Toil:* **s. bag,** trousse *f* de toilette, de voyage; *Tex:* **s. cloth,** tissu éponge; **to throw up, in, the s.,** (i) *Box:* jeter l'éponge; abandonner; (ii) *Fig:* s'avouer vaincu; abandonner la partie; **s. fisher,** pêcheur, -euse, d'éponges; (*b*) coup *m* d'éponge; **to give sth. a s.,** passer l'éponge sur, donner un coup d'éponge à, qch. **2.** *Cu:* gâteau *m* mousseline; **s. biscuit** = madeleine *f*. **3.** *F:* (*a*) gros buveur; (*b*) parasite *m*; écornifleur, -euse.

sponge² **1.** *v.tr.* (*a*) éponger (qch.); passer l'éponge sur (qch.); laver à l'éponge; **to s. up,** éponger, étancher (qch.); **to s. down,** doucher (qn) avec une éponge; éponger (un cheval); **to s. off, out,** enlever, effacer, (une tache) à l'éponge; (*b*) *Med:* lotionner (une plaie); (*c*) *F:* écornifler, grappiller (un repas, etc.). **2.** *v.i.* (*a*) pêcher les éponges; (*b*) *F:* faire le parasite; **to s. on s.o.,** vivre aux crochets, aux dépens, de qn. **sponging 1.** *a. F:* (*of pers.*) parasite. **2.** *n.* (*a*) (i) nettoyage *m* à l'éponge; (ii) *Med:* lavage *m* (d'une plaie) avec une lotion; (*b*) pêche *f* des éponges.

sponger ['spʌn(d)ʒər] *n.* **1.** pêcheur, -euse, d'éponges. **2.** *F:* parasite *m*; écornifleur, -euse.

sponginess ['spʌn(d)ʒinis] *n.* spongiosité *f*.

spongy ['spʌn(d)ʒi] *a.* spongieux.

sponsor¹ ['spɔnsər] *n.* **1.** *Jur:* garant *m*, répondant *m* (**for s.o.,** de qn); caution *f*. **2.** (*a*) (*at baptism*) parrain *m*, marraine *f*; **to stand s. to a child,** tenir un enfant sur les fonts (baptismaux); (*b*) (*introducing* *new member to club, etc.*) parrain; (*c*) *W.Tel: T.V: Sp:* personne *f* qui assure le patronage.

sponsor² *v.tr.* **1.** être le garant de, répondre pour, se porter caution pour (qn); parrainer (qn); **2.** *W.Tel: T.V: Sp:* patronner; **sponsored walk,** marche *f* pour aider une œuvre de charité.

sponsorship [ˈspɔnsəʃip] *n.* (*a*) *Jur:* garantie *f*, caution *f*; (*b*) parrainage *m*.

spontaneity [spɔntəˈniːiti, -ˈnei-] *n.* spontanéité *f*.

spontaneous [spɔnˈteiniəs] *a.* spontané, primesautier; (i) (mouvement) automatique; (ii) (acte, aveu) volontaire. **-ly** *adv.* spontanément; (i) automatiquement; (ii) volontairement; de bonne volonté.

spoof¹ [spuːf] *n. F:* attrape *f*; duperie *f*; blague *f*.

spoof² *v.tr. F:* mystifier, attraper, duper (qn).

spook [spuːk] *n.* spectre *m*, fantôme *m*, apparition *f*.

spooky [ˈspuːki] *a. F:* (histoire, etc.) de spectres, de revenants; (endroit) hanté.

spool¹ [spuːl] *n.* **1.** (*a*) *Tex:* bobine *f*, can(n)ette *f*; (*of sewing machine*) can(n)ette; (*b*) *esp. U.S:* **s. of thread,** bobine de coton (à coudre). **2.** *Fish:* tambour *m* (de moulinet). **3.** (*a*) *El:* (corps *m* de) bobine; (*b*) *Phot: Cin:* bobine (de film); **take-up s.,** bobine enrouleuse; (*c*) *Typew:* **(ribbon) s.,** bobine du ruban.

spool² *v.tr. Tex: etc:* bobiner; **to s. off,** débobiner, dévider.

spoon¹ [spuːn] *n.* **1.** cuillère *f*, cuiller *f*; **soup s.,** cuillère à soupe; **serving s.,** cuillère de service, à service; **wooden s.,** cuillère de, en, bois. **2.** (*a*) *Fish:* **s. (bait), trolling s.,** cuillère; **s. net,** épuisette *f*; (*b*) *Tls:* **s. drill,** cuillère; (*c*) *Golf:* bois *m* numéro 3; spoon *m*.

spoon² **1.** *v.tr.* (*a*) **to s. (up) one's soup,** manger sa soupe (avec une cuillère); **to s. out the sauce,** servir la sauce (avec une cuillère); (*b*) *Fish:* pêcher à la cuillère; (*c*) *Sp:* prendre (la balle) en, à la, cuillère. **2.** *v.i. F:* (*of couples*) se faire des mamours.

spoonbill [ˈspuːnbil] *n. Orn:* spatule (blanche).

spoonerism [ˈspuːnərizm] *n.* contrepèterie *f*.

spoonfeed [ˈspuːnfiːd] *v.tr.* (*p.t. & p.p.* **-fed** [-fed]) (*a*) nourrir (qn) à la cuillère; (*b*) mâcher (le travail) (à qn).

spoonful [ˈspuːnf(u)l] *a.* cuillerée *f*.

spoor [ˈspuər] *n. Ven:* foulées *fpl*, piste *f* (d'un cerf).

sporadic [spəˈrædik] *a.* sporadique. **-ally** *adv.* sporadiquement.

spore [spɔːr] *n.* spore *f*.

sporran [ˈspɔrən] *n. Scot:* aumônière en cuir brut (pendue sur le devant du kilt).

sport¹ [spɔːt] *n.* **1.** (*a*) jeu *m*, divertissement *m*, amusement *m*; **in s.,** pour rire; par plaisanterie; **to make s. of sth.,** s'amuser, se moquer, de qch.; (*b*) **to have good s.,** (i) (*in hunting*) faire bonne chasse; (ii) (*in fishing*) faire bonne pêche, bonne prise. **2.** sport *m*; **aquatic, winter, sports,** sports nautiques, d'hiver; **sports day,** fête sportive; **sports ground,** terrain *m* de sport, de jeux; **sports jacket, coat,** veston *m* sport; **sports car,** voiture *f* de sport; *Journ:* **sports page,** rubrique sportive; *T.V: etc:* **sports results,** résultats sportifs. **3.** *Lit:* **to be the s. of fortune,** être le jouet, le jeu, de la fortune. **4.** *Biol:* variété anormale, type anormal. **5.** *F:* **a (good, real) s.,** (i) un beau joueur; (ii) un chic type; **come on, be a s.!** voyons, sois chic! *esp. Austr:* **hello, (old) s.!** salut, mon vieux!

sport² **1.** *v.i.* (*a*) *O:* se divertir, s'amuser; (*b*) *Biol:* (*of plants, animals*) produire une variété anormale. **2.** *v.tr.* porter, arborer (qch. de très voyant); exhiber (un manteau de fourrure, etc.). **sporting** *a.* **1.** amateur de chasse, de pêche. **2.** de sport; sportif; **s. man,** (i) amateur de sport; (ii) turfiste; **in a s. spirit,** animé de l'esprit sportif, sportivement; *F:* **it's very s. of him,** c'est très chic de sa part; **you've a s. chance,** il vaut la peine d'essayer le coup; **I'll make you a s. offer,** je vais vous faire une offre à laquelle vous ne perdrez rien. **sportingly** *adv.* sportivement.

sportive [ˈspɔːtiv] *a. O:* badin; folâtre.

sportscast [ˈspɔːtskɑːst] *n. W.Tel: T.V:* émission sportive.

sportscaster [ˈspɔːtskɑːstər] *n. W.Tel: T.V:* reporter sportif.

sportsman *pl.* **-men** [ˈspɔːtsmən] *n.m.* **1.** chasseur, pêcheur. **2.** amateur de sport(s); sportif; **a keen s.,** un ardent sportif. **3. he's a real s.,** il est animé de l'esprit sportif; c'est un beau joueur.

sportsmanlike [ˈspɔːtsmənlaik] *a.* animé de l'esprit sportif.

sportsmanship [ˈspɔːtsmənʃip] *n.* **1.** habileté *f*, qualités *fpl*, de sportif; pratique *f* des sports, de la chasse, de la pêche, etc. **2.** esprit sportif; sportivité *f*.

sportswear [ˈspɔːtswɛər] *n.* vêtements *mpl* (de) sport.

sportswoman *pl.* **-women** [ˈspɔːtswumən, -wimin] *n.* **1.** femme amateur de chasse, de pêche, etc. **2.** (femme) sportive; femme amateur du sport.

sporty [ˈspɔːti] *a.* **1.** *F:* (*a*) sportif; (*b*) *O:* **it's awfully s. of you to . . .,** c'est très chic de votre part de . . .. **2.** *F:* (veston, etc.) de couleurs criardes.

spot¹ [spɔt] *n.* **1.** (*a*) endroit *m*, lieu *m*; **remote s.,** endroit écarté, isolé; **X marks the s.,** la croix indique le lieu (du crime, etc.); **the police are on the s.,** la police est sur les lieux; **rely on the man on the s.,** remettez-vous en à la personne qui est sur place; *F:* **to put s.o. on the s.,** (i) mettre qn dans une situation difficile; (ii) *esp. NAm:* décider d'assassiner qn; *F:* **to be on the s.,** (i) être alerte, vif, éveillé; être sur le qui-vive; (ii) se montrer à la hauteur de la situation; (iii) *esp. NAm:* être dans une situation dangereuse; *F:* **to hit the high spots,** faire la noce: *F:* **to be in a (tight) s.,** (i) être dans le pétrin; (ii) avoir des ennuis pécuniaires; **night s.,** boîte *f* de nuit; **s. check,** (i) vérification *f* sur place; (ii) contrôle-surprise *m*; **to s.-check sth.,** contrôler, vérifier, qch. à l'improviste; *F:* **s. on,** exact, au point; **to be s. on,** mettre dans le mille; *Journ:* **s. news,** (édition *f* de) dernière heure; (*b*) *adv.phr.* **on the s.,** sur-le-champ, sur le coup; **to be killed on the s.,** être tué sur le coup; être tué net, raide; **to do sth. on the s.,** faire qch. sur place, sur-le-champ; (*c*) place *f*, position *f* (dans une organisation, dans une hiérarchie); (*d*) *T.V: W.Tel:* créneau (réservé à la publicité, à une personne); spot *m* publicitaire; **s. announcement,** bref message publicitaire; (*e*) *Com:* **s. cash,** (argent) comptant *m*; *St.Exch:* **s. transaction, deal,** opération *f* au comptant; **s. market,** marché *m* du disponible, du comptant; (*f*) **weak s.,** point faible; **to find s.o.'s weak s.,** trouver le défaut dans la cuirasse de qn; **the sore s.,** l'endroit sensible. **2.** (*a*) tache *f*, macule *f*; (*on fruit, etc.*) tavelure *f*; **s. remover,** détachant *m*; (*b*) (*on face, etc.*) bouton *m*. **3.** (*a*) pois *m* (de couleur, de broderie); **blue tie with red spots,** cravate bleue à pois rouges; **a panther's spots,** la tacheture, la moucheture, d'une panthère; *F:* **to knock spots off s.o.,** battre qn à plate(s) couture(s); (*b*) **blind s.,** (i) *Anat:* point *m* aveugle; (ii) *Aut:* angle *m* aveugle; *F:* **that's your blind s.,** c'est là où vous refusez de voir clair; (*c*) point (sur une carte à jouer, etc.); *Bill:* mouche *f*; (*d*) *Med:* (*radiography*) **a s. on the lung,** un voile au poumon; (*e*) *Th: Cin:* projecteur (orientable, intensif); (*f*) *Elcs: T.V:* spot; **flying s.,** spot mobile; (*g*) **s. welding,** soudure *f* par points. **4.** (*a*) goutte *f* (de pluie, de vin); (*b*) *F:* **a s. of whisky,** deux doigts *mpl* de whisky; **what about a s. of lunch?** si nous allions déjeuner? **to do a s. of work,** faire un peu de travail; **a s. of bother, of trouble,** un petit ennui.

spot² *v.tr.* **(spotted) 1.** (*a*) tacher, souiller (qch.); (*with passive force*) **material that spots easily,** tissu qui se tache facilement; (*b*) tacheter, moucheter (qch.);

Phot: repiquer (une épreuve); **it's spotting (with rain),** il commence à pleuvoir; (*c*) *Bill:* mettre (la bille) sur la mouche. **2.** *F:* (*a*) repérer, apercevoir (qn, qch.); **I spotted him in the crowd,** je l'ai repéré au milieu de la foule; (*b*) reconnaître; **I spotted him as a German,** je l'ai reconnu pour, comme, allemand; (*c*) *Turf: etc:* prédire, repérer (le gagnant); (*d*) *Mil:* repérer, observer (des emplacements ennemis, etc.); (*e*) repérer (des différents modèles de trains, etc.); (*f*) dénicher (du talent). **3.** *Metalw: Mec.E:* marquer, centrer (un trou). **spotted** *a.* tacheté, moucheté; (cravate, etc.) à pois; (fruit, etc.) tavelé; *F:* **s. Dick,** *Cu:* pudding *m* aux raisins secs. **spotting** *n.* **1.** taches *fpl*; tachetures *fpl.* **2.** *Phot:* repiquage *m*, repiquement *m* (des épreuves). **3.** (*a*) repérage *m* (de trains, d'avions, etc.); (*b*) *Mil: Av:* observation *f*, repérage (d'emplacements ennemis, etc.). **4.** *Mec.E:* centrage *m* (d'un trou).

spotless ['spɔtlis] *a.* sans tache; immaculé; (maison, cuisine) d'une propreté irréprochable. **-ly** *adv.* **s. white,** d'une blancheur immaculée, parfaite; **s. clean,** d'une propreté irréprochable.

spotlessness ['spɔtlisnis] *n.* propreté *f.*

spotlight¹ ['spɔtlait] *n.* (*a*) *Th: Cin:* lumière *f* de projecteur; (*b*) *Th: Cin:* projecteur (orientable, intensif); projecteur directif; spot *m*; **to hold the s.,** (i) *Th:* occuper le centre de la scène (dans la lumière du projecteur); (ii) avoir, tenir, la vedette; être en vedette; (*c*) *Aut:* projecteur auxiliaire orientable.

spotlight² *v.tr.* (*a*) *Th:* diriger les projecteurs sur (qn, qch.); (*b*) mettre (qn, qch.) en vedette. **spotlighting** *n. Th: Cin:* éclairage *m* à effet.

spotter ['spɔtər] *n.* **1.** *Mil: Av:* (*a*) observateur *m*; (*b*) avion *m* d'observation. **2.** (*a*) **train s.,** personne *f* qui regarde passer des trains (pour repérer les différents modèles); (*b*) **talent s.,** dénicheur, -euse, de talent.

spotty ['spɔti] *a.* **1.** moucheté, tacheté; couvert de taches; (visage) couvert de boutons, boutonneux. **2.** *F:* (travail) qui manque d'ensemble, inégal.

spouse [spauz] *n.* (*a*) *A: & Lit:* époux, *f.* épouse; (*b*) *Adm: Jur:* conjoint, -ointe.

spout¹ [spaut] *n.* **1.** (*a*) *Const:* **rainwater s.,** (i) tuyau *m* de décharge; (ii) gargouille *f*, chantepleure *f* (de gouttière); (*b*) bec *m* (de théière, de bouilloire, etc.); canon, goulot *m* (d'arrosoir); jet *m* (de pompe). **2.** *F:* **up, down, the s.,** perdu, fichu, foutu.

spout² **1.** *v.i.* (*a*) (*of liquid*) jaillir, rejaillir; gicler; (*b*) (*of whale*) lancer un jet d'eau, d'air; souffler; (*c*) *F:* (*of pers.*) parler à jet continu, dégoiser. **2.** *v.tr.* (*a*) faire jaillir, lancer (de l'eau, etc.); (*b*) *F:* dégoiser, débiter à jet continu (des discours, des sottises).

sprain¹ [sprein] *n.* entorse *f*, foulure *f.*

sprain² *v.tr.* se fouler (la cheville, le poignet); se donner, se faire, une entorse (au pied, au poignet); **sprained ankle,** foulure *f* au pied, entorse.

sprat [spræt] *n. Ich:* sprat *m*, harenguet *m.*

sprawl [sprɔːl] *v.i.* **1.** (*a*) s'étendre, s'étaler; *F:* faire le veau; **to s. on a sofa,** s'étaler, se vautrer, sur un divan; (*b*) **to send s.o. sprawling,** envoyer rouler qn de tout son long; **to go sprawling,** s'étaler par terre; tomber les quatre fers en l'air. **2.** (*of town, etc.*) s'étendre de tous les côtés. **sprawling** *a.* **1.** (*a*) vautré; (*b*) étendu les quatre fers en l'air. **2.** (ville) informe, tentaculaire; **s. handwriting,** écriture informe.

spray¹ [sprei] *n.* brin *m*, ramille *f*; **s. of flowers,** (i) branche *f* de fleurs; rameau fleuri; (ii) *Arch: Needlew: etc:* chute *f* de fleurs; **s. of diamonds,** aigrette *f* de diamants.

spray² *n.* **1.** embrun *m*, poudrin *m*; écume *f.* **2.** (*a*) poussière *f* d'eau, eau vaporisée; *Ind:* **s. drying,** séchage *m* (du lait, etc.) par atomisation; (*b*) jet pulvérisé (de parfum, d'essence, etc.); **s. gun,** pistolet *m*, pulvérisateur *m* (à peinture, etc.); *I.C.E:* **s. nozzle,** gicleur *m*. **3.** (*a*) liquide *m* pour vaporisation; **hair s.,** laque *f*; **s. deodorant, deodorant s.,** désodorisant *m* en atomiseur; (*b*) coup *m* de vaporisateur; jet (de peinture, de parfum, etc.); (*c*) (*atomizer*) atomiseur *m*, vaporisateur *m*; **perfume s.,** atomiseur à parfum; *Med:* **nasal s.,** nébuliseur *m.*

spray³ *v.tr.* **1.** atomiser, pulvériser, vaporiser (un liquide); **to s. a solution up one's nostrils,** se vaporiser un liquide dans le nez; *Ind:* **to s. dry,** sécher par atomisation. **2.** asperger, arroser; bassiner (des plants, etc.); peindre (qch.) au pistolet; *Hort:* passer (un arbre) au vaporisateur; **to s. sth. with machine-gun fire,** arroser qch. à la mitrailleuse. **spraying** *n.* **1.** pulvérisation *f*, vaporisation *f*, atomisation *f* (d'un liquide). **2.** arrosage *m*; bassinage *m* (de semis).

sprayer ['spreiər] *n.* **1.** (*a*) vaporisateur *m*, pulvérisateur *m*; atomiseur *m*; (*b*) pistolet *m* (à peinture); (*c*) **foam s.,** extincteur *m* à mousse. **2.** arroseuse *f.*

spread¹ [spred] *n.* **1.** (*a*) étendue *f* (de pays, etc.); (*b*) (*of wings, of sails, etc.*) envergure *f*; *F:* **middle-age(d) s.,** embonpoint *m* de la maturité; (*c*) *Com:* différence *f* (entre le prix de fabrique et le prix de vente, entre deux tarifs); (*d*) *NAm:* ranch *m*. **2.** (*a*) diffusion *f* (de l'éducation); propagation *f* (d'une doctrine, d'une maladie); expansion *f*, dissémination *f* (des idées); (*b*) dispersion latérale (d'un phare); *Ball:* dispersion (du tir). **3. bed s.,** dessus-de-lit *m inv*; couvre-lit *m*, *pl.* couvre-lits. **4.** *F:* festin *m*, repas somptueux; **cold s.,** repas froid. **5.** *Journ: etc:* **double page s.,** annonce *f*, article *m*, sur deux pages. **6.** fromage *m*, pâte *f* de viande, etc., à tartiner.

spread² *v.* (*p.t. & p.p.* **spread**) **I.** *v.tr.* **1.** (*a*) étendre (les bras, etc.); tendre (un filet); déployer (les voiles); écarter (les doigts); **to s. out,** déployer, étaler (une carte, etc.); **a bird with its wings s. (out),** un oiseau aux ailes déployées; **to s. (oneself) out,** s'étendre, s'allonger (sur un divan, etc.); **to s. oneself,** (i) faire le généreux; (ii) s'étendre (**on a subject,** sur un sujet); (*b*) **s. eagle,** (i) *Her:* aigle éployée; (ii) (*skating*) grand aigle; **sunbathers lying s.-eagled on the sand,** baigneurs vautrés sur la plage. **2.** (*a*) répandre (du sable, de la paille); épandre (du fumier); semer (la terreur); répandre, colporter, rapporter (des nouvelles); propager (une maladie); **to s. s.o.'s fame (abroad),** faire connaître la réputation de qn; (*b*) **the payments are s. over several months,** les paiements sont échelonnés, étalés, répartis, sur plusieurs mois. **3. to s. butter on a slice of bread,** étendre, étaler, du beurre sur une tranche de pain; tartiner une tranche de pain; **to s. ointment on a burn,** appliquer de l'onguent *m* sur une brûlure. **4.** (*a*) **to s. a surface with sth.,** recouvrir, enduire, une surface de qch;. (*b*) *O: & NAm:* **to s. the table,** dresser, mettre, la table; mettre le couvert. **II.** *v.i.* **1.** s'étendre, s'étaler. **2.** (*of rumour, news, ideas, etc.*) se répandre, se propager; (*of disease, fire, theory, etc.*) se propager; (*of smell, smoke, sound*) se répandre; (*of evil, epidemic, fame*) s'étendre; (*of evil, cancer*) se généraliser; **the fire is spreading,** l'incendie gagne (du terrain); **his ideas are spreading,** ses idées font tache d'huile; **the rumour was spreading,** la rumeur grandissait. **3.** (*of group of people, of small shot*) se disperser. **spreading** **1.** *a.* qui s'étend, qui se répand, étendu; (arbre) rameux. **2.** *n.* (*a*) (i) déploiement *m*, développement *m*; (ii) colportage *m* (de nouvelles); propagation *f* (d'une maladie, d'une doctrine); dissémination *f* (d'idées); diffusion *f* (de l'éducation); (iii) étendage *m* (de la peinture, etc.); répandage *m* (du goudron sur la chaussée, etc.); (*b*) (i) extension *f* (de territoire, d'une industrie); (ii) disperson *f* (d'un groupe, etc.).

spreader ['spredər] *n.* **1.** propagateur, -trice (d'une idée, d'un bruit); colporteur, -euse, rapporteur, -euse (de nouvelles, d'un bruit); semeur, -euse (de discordes, etc.). **2.** (*a*) arrosoir *m* (d'une machine à arroser); éventail *m* (d'une lance d'arrosage); (*b*) *Agr: Civ.E:* épandeur *m*, épandeuse *f*.

spree [spri:] *n. F:* partie *f* de plaisir; bombe *f*, bamboche *f*; **to have a s., to go (out) on a s.,** faire la noce, la bombe; **to go on a shopping, spending, s.,** faire des achats extravagants.

sprig [sprig] *n.* brin *m*, brindille *f*.

sprightliness ['spraitlinis] *n.* vivacité *f*, enjouement *m*; pétillement *m* (de l'esprit).

sprightly ['spraitli] *a.* éveillé, enjoué, vif; (esprit) pétillant; **to be as s. as a two-year-old,** avoir des jambes de vingt ans.

spring¹ [spriŋ] *n.* **1.** (*a*) source *f* (d'eau); fontaine *f*; **hot, thermal, spring(s),** source thermale; eaux thermales; **mineral s.,** source d'eau minérale; (*b*) source, origine *f* (d'une coutume, etc.). **2.** (*a*) printemps *m*; **in (the) s.,** au printemps; **a lovely s. evening,** une belle soirée de printemps; **to have s. fever,** être amoureux; *Fr.C:* avoir la fièvre du printemps; **s. flowers,** fleurs printanières; **s. vegetables,** primeurs *mpl*; *Cu:* **s. chicken,** poussin *m*; *F:* **she's no s. chicken,** elle n'est plus jeune; **to s.-clean,** nettoyer à fond (une maison) (au printemps); *Fr.C:* faire le grand ménage; **s.-cleaning,** grand nettoyage (fait au printemps); *Fr.C:* grand ménage; (*b*) **s. tide,** (marée *f* de) vives-eaux *fpl*. **3.** saut *m*, bond *m*; **to take a s.,** prendre son élan; faire un bond. **4.** élasticité *f*; **the s. of a bow,** la force, la souplesse, d'un arc. **5.** (*a*) ressort *m*; **(interior) s. mattress,** matelas *m* à ressorts; *Mec.E:* **spiral s.,** ressort à, en, boudin; **s.-loaded, -driven,** à ressort; actionné par ressort; **s. balance,** balance *f* à ressort; **s. gun,** piège *m* à fusil; (*b*) **springs, s. suspension,** suspension *f* à ressort(s) (d'une voiture, etc.).

spring² *v.* (*p.t.* **sprang** [spræŋ], *p.p.* **sprung** [sprʌŋ]) **I.** *v.i.* **1.** (*a*) bondir, sauter; **to s. up, to s. to one's feet,** se lever vivement, d'un bond; **the branch sprang back,** la branche s'est redressée; **to s. forward,** s'élancer, se précipiter, en avant; (*b*) se mouvoir sous l'action (subite) d'un ressort; **the lid sprang open,** le couvercle a sauté. **2.** (*a*) (*of water, etc.*) jaillir, filtrer, sourdre; (*b*) **hope springs eternal,** l'espérance *f* reste toujours vivace; **to s. into existence,** naître, surgir; *F:* **where did you s. from?** d'où sortez-vous? (*c*) (*of plant, etc.*) **(to begin to) s. (up),** (commencer à) pousser, poindre; (*d*) **a breeze sprang up,** une brise s'est levée; **an intimacy sprang up between them,** l'intimité s'est établie entre eux; **a doubt sprang up in his mind,** un doute a germé dans son esprit. **3.** (*a*) (*of wood*) gauchir; se déformer, se déjeter; (*b*) (*of mast, pole*) craquer; se fendre. **II.** *v.tr.* **1.** (*a*) fendre (une raquette); faire craquer (un mât, un aviron); gauchir, déformer (une planche, etc.); (*b*) *Nau:* **to s. a leak,** faire une voie d'eau. **2.** (faire) lever (une perdrix, etc.). **3.** (*a*) faire jouer (un piège); faire sauter (une mine); (*b*) **to s. a question on s.o.,** poser à qn une question inattendue; demander qch. à brûle-pourpoint; **to s. a surprise on s.o.,** faire une surprise à qn. **4.** munir (une voiture) de ressorts; **sprung carriage,** voiture suspendue. **5.** *F:* faire échapper (qn) de prison; larguer (qn). **springing** *n.* **1.** bonds *mpl*, sauts *mpl*. **2.** (*a*) jaillissement *m* (d'une source); (*b*) germination *f* (de plantes). **3.** (*a*) craquement *m* (d'un mât, etc.); (*b*) gauchissement *m* (d'une planche, etc.). **4.** suspension *f* (d'une voiture, d'un lit, etc.).

springboard ['spriŋbɔ:d] *n.* (*a*) *Gym: Swim:* tremplin *m*; (*b*) *Fig:* source *f*.

springbok ['spriŋbɔk] *n. Z:* springbok *m*.

springe [sprin(d)ʒ] *n.* (*for rabbits*) lacet *m*, collet *m*.

springer ['spriŋər] *n.* **1.** (*pers.*) sauteur, -euse. **2. S. (spaniel),** épagneul springer.

springiness ['spriŋinis] *n.* élasticité *f* (d'un matelas, etc.); effet *m* de ressort.

springless ['spriŋlis] *a.* sans ressort(s); **s. step,** démarche lourde.

springlike ['spriŋlaik] *a.* printanier; de printemps.

springtide, springtime ['spriŋtaid, -taim] *n.* printemps *m*.

springwater ['spriŋwɔ:tər] *n.* eau *f* de source; eau vive.

springy ['spriŋi] *a.* **1.** élastique, qui fait ressort; flexible; (corps) à ressort; (tapis) moelleux. **2. with a s. step,** (marcher) d'un pas leste, léger.

sprinkle¹ ['spriŋkl] *n.* (*a*) **a s. of rain,** quelques gouttes *fpl* de pluie; (*b*) **a s. of salt,** quelques grains *mpl* de sel; une pincée de sel.

sprinkle² *v.tr.* (*a*) répandre, jeter (de l'eau, du sel, du gravier); (*b*) asperger, arroser, bassiner **(with water,** d'eau); saupoudrer **(with sugar,** de sucre); **to s. the floor with sand,** répandre du sable par terre. **sprinkling** *n.* **1.** aspersion *f*, arrosage *m*; (*with sugar, etc.*) saupoudrage *m*; *U.S:* **s. can,** arrosoir *m*; *Ecc:* **s. of holy water,** aspergès *m*, aspersion. **2.** (*a*) **a s. of gravel,** une légère couche de gravier; (*b*) **a s. of knowledge,** quelques connaissances.

sprinkler ['spriŋklər] *n.* **1.** (*for lawns, etc.*) appareil *m* d'arrosage; rampe *f* d'arrosage; **(rotary) s.,** arroseur (rotatif); tourniquet *m* hydraulique, de jardinier; (*extinguisher*) **(automatic) fire s.,** extincteur *m* (automatique) d'incendie; **s. system,** noyage *m* en pluie. **2.** *Ecc:* goupillon *m*, aspersoir *m*.

sprint¹ [sprint] *n.* (*a*) **s. (race),** course *f* de vitesse; (*b*) pointe *f* de vitesse; sprint *m*.

sprint² *v.i.* faire une course de vitesse; sprinter; **to s. past one's opponent,** dépasser son adversaire.

sprinter ['sprintər] *n.* coureur, -euse, de vitesse; sprinter *m*.

sprit [sprit] *n. Nau:* livarde *f*.

sprite [sprait] *n.* lutin *m*; esprit (follet); farfadet *m*.

sprocket ['sprɔkit] *n. Mec.E:* **1.** dent *f* (de pignon). **2. s. (wheel),** pignon *m* de chaîne.

sprout¹ [spraut] *n. Bot:* **1.** (*a*) jet *m*, rejeton *m*, pousse *f*; (*b*) germe *m*, bourgeon *m*. **2. Brussels sprouts,** *F:* **sprouts,** choux *m* de Bruxelles.

sprout² **1.** *v.i.* (*a*) (*of plant*) pousser, pointer; (*b*) (*of branch, shrub*) bourgeonner; (*c*) (*of seed*) germer. **2.** *v.tr.* (*of animal*) **to s. horns,** pousser des cornes; *F:* (*of pers.*) **to s. a moustache,** laisser pousser sa moustache. **sprouting** *n. Bot:* (*a*) germination *f*, bourgeonnement *m*; (*b*) **s. broccoli,** brocoli *m*.

spruce¹ [spru:s] *a.* pimpant; soigné; tiré à quatre épingles.

spruce² *v.tr.* **to s. oneself up,** se parer; se faire beau, belle; **all spruced up,** sur son trente et un.

spruce³ *n. Bot:* **s. (fir),** (sapin *m*) épicéa *m*; **Norway s.,** sapin de Norvège.

spruceness ['spru:snis] *n.* mise pimpante; soignée.

spry [sprai] *a.* **(spryer, spryest)** vif, actif; (plein d')allant.

spud [spʌd] *n.* **1.** *Agr: Hort:* petite bêche; sarcloir *m*. **2.** *F:* pomme *f* de terre; patate *f*; *Mil:* **s. bashing,** corvée *f* de patates, (corvée de) pluches *fpl*.

spue [spju:] *v. tr. & i.* = SPEW.

spume [spju:m] *n. A: & Lit:* écume *f* (de la mer).

spunk [spʌŋk] *n.* **1.** amadou *m*. **2.** *F:* (*a*) courage *m*, cran *m*; **to have plenty of s.,** avoir du cran; (*b*) *U.S:* colère *f*.

spunky ['spʌŋki] *a. F:* (*a*) courageux; qui a du cran; (*b*) *U.S:* coléreux.

spur¹ [spə:r] *n.* **1.** éperon *m*; *Fig:* **to win one's spurs,** faire ses preuves; **the s. of Italy,** l'éperon de la botte (de l'Italie). **2.** coup *m* d'éperon; stimulant *m*; **to do sth. on the s. of the moment,** faire qch. sous l'impulsion, sous l'inspiration, du moment; faire qch. par coup de tête, à l'improviste. **3.** (*a*) ergot *m* (de coq); (*b*) éperon (d'un coq de combat). **4.** (*a*) éperon, contrefort *m* (d'une chaîne de montagnes); (*b*) épi *m* (de chemin de fer). **5. climbing spurs,** grappins *m*, crampons *m*. **6.** *Bot:* éperon; *Hort:* **fruit s.,** dard *m*. **7.** *Mec.E: etc:* **s. gear, wheel,** (roue d')engrenage cylindrique, droit; roue droite, dentée.

spur² *v.tr.* **(spurred) 1. to s. (on),** éperonner, talonner (un cheval). **2. to s. s.o. on,** aiguillonner, stimuler, qn; **spurred on by the wish to . . .,** fouetté par le désir de . . .. **3.** éperonner (un cavalier, un coq de combat); **booted and spurred,** botté et éperonné.

spurge [spəːdʒ] *n. Bot:* euphorbe *f*, épurge *f*; **s. laurel,** (daphné *m*) lauréole *f*; laurier *m* des bois.

spurious [ˈspjuəriəs] *a.* **1.** faux, *f.* fausse; controuvé; falsifié; **s. coin,** pièce de monnaie fausse. **2.** (*of writings*) apocryphe; (*of edition*) de contrefaçon. **3.** *Nat. Hist:* (*of limb, etc.*) faux. **-ly** *adv.* faussement.

spuriousness [ˈspjuəriəsnis] *n.* **1.** fausseté *f* **(of,** de). **2.** caractère *m* apocryphe (d'un texte).

spurn [spəːn] *v.tr.* **1.** repousser, écarter, (qch.) du pied. **2.** rejeter (une offre) avec mépris; repousser (qn, les avances de qn) avec mépris; traiter (qn) avec mépris.

spurt¹ [spəːt] *n.* **1.** jaillissement *m*; jet *m*; giclée *f*. **2.** (*a*) effort soudain; coup *m* de collier; poussée *f* d'énergie; (*b*) *Sp:* effort de vitesse; pointe *f* de vitesse; emballage *m*; **to put on a s.,** démarrer, emballer; **final s.,** pointe finale; rush *m*.

spurt² **1.** *v.i.* **to s. (up, out),** jaillir; gicler. **2.** *v.tr.* (*a*) **to s. (out),** faire jaillir, faire gicler (un liquide); (*b*) (*of pen*) cracher, gicler (de l'encre). **3.** *v.i. Sp:* démarrer, faire un effort de vitesse.

sputnik [ˈsputnik] *n. Space:* spoutnik *m*.

sputter [ˈspʌtər] **1.** *v.tr.* dire (qch.) (i) en bredouillant, (ii) en lançant des postillons. **2.** *v.i.* (*a*) (i) lancer des postillons en parlant; (ii) bredouiller; (*b*) (*of pen, El: of electric arc*) cracher; (*of kindling wood*) pétiller; (*of meat on grill*) grésiller; (*of flame*) grésiller, crépiter; **the candle sputtered out,** la bougie s'est éteinte en grésillant. **sputtering** *n.* (*a*) bredouillement *m*; (*b*) crachement *m* (d'un stylo); crachement, crépitement *m* (d'un arc électrique); pétillement *m* (du bois); grésillement *m* (de la friture, d'une bougie).

sputum *pl.* **-a** [ˈspjuːtəm, -ə] *n. Med:* crachat *m*.

spy¹ *pl.* **spies** [spai, spaiz] *n.* espion, -onne; *F:* mouchard, -arde.

spy² *v.* **(spied; spying) 1.** *v.tr.* apercevoir, voir; reconnaître; **to s. out the land,** explorer le terrain. **2.** *v.i.* espionner; *F:* moucharder; **to s. on s.o.,** épier, espionner, qn. **spying** *n.* espionnage *m*.

spyglass [ˈspaiglɑːs] *n.* lunette *f* d'approche; longue-vue *f*, *pl.* longues-vues.

spyhole [ˈspaihoul] *n.* (*a*) trou *m* (dans un rideau, etc.); (*b*) judas *m*, guichet *m* (de porte).

squab [skwɔb] *n.* **1.** pigeonneau *m* sans plumes. **2.** (*a*) coussin capitonné; (*b*) *Aut:* coussin (de siège).

squabble¹ [ˈskwɔbl] *n.* querelle *f*, altercation *f*, chamaillerie *f*; prise *f* de bec.

squabble² **1.** *v.i.* se quereller, se chamailler **(with,** avec). **squabbling** *n.* querelles *fpl*; chamaillerie *f*.

squabbler [ˈskwɔblər] *n.* querelleur, -euse; chamailleur, -euse.

squad [skwɔd] *n.* **1.** (i) escouade *f*; (ii) peloton *m*; **firing s.,** peloton d'exécution. **2.** (*a*) brigade *f*, équipe *f* (de cheminots, etc.); **rescue s.,** équipe de secours; (*b*) **the Flying S. (of Scotland Yard),** l'équipe volante; **the Vice S.** = la police mondaine, des mœurs; la mondaine; **s. car,** voiture *f* de police; (*c*) *Sp:* équipe.

squadron [ˈskwɔdren] *n.* **1.** (*a*) *Mil:* escadron *m*; **armoured s.,** escadron de chars; (*b*) *Mil.Av:* escadron, escadrille *f*; groupe *m* d'aviation (d'avions de transport); **fighter s.,** escadron de chasse; (*rank*) **s. leader** = commandant *m*. **2.** *Navy:* escadre *f*.

squalid [ˈskwɔlid] *a.* sale; misérable, sordide. **-ly** *adv.* misérablement, sordidement.

squalidness [ˈskwɔlidnis] *n.* = SQUALOR.

squall¹ [skwɔːl] *n.* cri *m* (rauque, discordant).

squall² **1.** *v.i.* crier, brailler, piailler. **2.** *v.tr.* **to s. (out),** brailler, crier (qch.). **squalling 1.** *a.* criard, piaillard. **2.** *n.* criaillerie *f*, piaillerie *f*.

squall³ *n. Nau:* grain *m*; coup *m* de vent; bourrasque *f*; rafale *f*; *Fig:* **look out for squalls!** veille, pare, au grain! il va y avoir du grabuge!

squally [ˈskwɔːli] *a.* (temps) à grains, à rafales.

squalor [ˈskwɔlər] *n.* saleté *f*; misère *f*; **to die in s.,** mourir dans la misère.

squander [ˈskwɔndər] *v.tr.* gaspiller (de l'argent, son temps); dissiper, dilapider, *F:* claquer (une fortune). **squandering** *n.* gaspillage *m* (d'argent, de temps); dissipation *f*, dilapidation *f* (d'une fortune).

square¹ [ˈskwɛər] **I.** *n.* **1.** (*a*) *Mth: etc:* carré *m*; **magic s.,** carré magique; (*b*) *Mil.Hist:* (formation *f* en) carré. **2.** (*a*) carreau *m* (de figure quadrillée, etc.); case *f*, compartiment *m* (d'échiquier, etc.); **to divide a map into squares,** quadriller une carte; (*for enlargement, etc., of maps and plans*) **framework of squares,** graticule *m*; (*on map*) **(reference) s.,** carreau-module *m*, *pl.* carreaux-modules; **to be back at s. one,** revenir à son point de départ; repartir à zéro; (*b*) **(silk) s.,** carré, foulard *m* (de soie). **3.** (*a*) (*of town, village*) place *f*; (*with garden*) square *m*; (*in front of church*) parvis *m*; (*b*) *Mil:* terrain *m* de manœuvre(s); *F:* **s. bashing** = l'exercice *m*; (*c*) *NAm:* block *m*, pâté *m*, de maisons (entre quatre rues). **4.** équerre *f*; **set s.,** équerre à dessin; **T s.,** équerre en T; té *m* (à dessin); **to cut sth. on the s.,** couper qch. à angles droits; **out of s.,** hors d'équerre; hors d'aplomb; *F:* **to be on the s.,** jouer franc jeu; être honnête. **5.** *Mth:* carré (d'un nombre, etc.). **6.** *F:* **he's a s.,** il est tout à fait vieux jeu. **II.** *a.* **1.** carré; (*a*) **s. table,** table carrée; **s. ruler,** carrelet *m*; règle *f* quadrangulaire; **s. dance,** danse *f* à quatre; *Nau:* **s. sail,** voile carrée; **s. measure,** mesure *f* de surface, de superficie; **s. metre, centimetre,** mètre, centimètre, carré; **nine metres s.,** de neuf mètres carrés; (*b*) (*of chin, shoulders, etc.*) carré; **s.-shouldered,** aux épaules carrées; **s.-built,** (i) bâti en carré; (ii) (*of pers.*) aux épaules carrées; de belle carrure; **s.-toed shoes,** chaussures *fpl* à bouts carrés; *Cost:* **s. neck,** encolure carrée; décolleté (en) carré; (*c*) plat; *Carp:* **s. joint,** assemblage *m* à plat. **2.** (*a*) **line s. with another,** ligne à angle droit avec une autre; **s. corner,** coin *m* en angle droit; (*b*) (*of screw*) **s. thread,** filet carré; **s.-headed,** à tête carrée; (*c*) *Elcs: etc:* **s. wave,** onde carrée, rectangulaire. **3.** *Mth:* **s. root, number,** racine carrée; nombre carré. **4.** (*a*) **to get things s.,** (i) arranger les choses; (ii) mettre tout en ordre; **to make an account s.,** régler un compte; (*b*) (refus) net, catégorique; (repas) copieux; (*c*) **a s. deal,** une affaire honnête; **he always gives you a s. deal,** il est toujours loyal en affaires; (*d*) **to be s. with s.o.,** être quitte envers qn; **to be (all) s.,** (i) être à égalité; (ii) (*of two people*) être quittes; **let's call it s.,** je vous tiens quitte; **to get s. with s.o.,** (i) régler son compte à qn; (ii) être quitte envers qn. **III.** *adv.* **1.** à angles droits **(to, with,** avec); d'équerre **(to, with,** avec); **set s. upon its base,** d'aplomb sur sa base; **he hit him (fair and) s. on the jaw,** il l'a frappé en plein menton. **2.** (agir) honnêtement; **fair and s.,** loyalement, carrément. **squarely** *adv.* **1.** carrément; **s. built,** (i) bâti en carré; (ii) (*of pers.*) aux épaules carrées. **2.** carrément, honnêtement; (agir) loyalement.

square² **I.** *v.tr.* **1.** (*a*) carrer, équarrir (un bloc de marbre, du bois); **to s. off, up,** mettre d'équerre, équarrir (le bout d'une planche); (*b*) **to s. one's shoulders,** (i) se carrer (en face de qn); (ii) raidir sa volonté. **2.** (*a*) **to s. one's practice with one's principles,** accorder ses actions avec ses principes; **how do you s. it with your conscience?** comment arrangez-vous cela avec votre conscience? (*b*) balancer, régler (un compte); *F:* **to s. accounts with s.o.,** (i) régler ses comptes avec qn; (ii) se venger de qn; régler son compte à qn; **to s. matters,** arranger les choses; (*c*) *F:* acheter, soudoyer (qn); graisser la patte à (qn); (*d*) *NAm:* **to s. away,** ranger (des livres); arranger (une chambre). **3. to s. the circle,** s'efforcer de faire, tenter, l'impossible. **4.** *Mth:* élever, mettre, porter, (un nombre, une expression) au carré; **four squared,** quatre au carré. **5. to s. (off),** quadriller (une feuille de papier); **squared paper,** papier quadrillé, à carreaux. **II.** *v.i.* **1.** (*a*) **the end and the side should s. with each other,** le bout et le côté doivent se raccorder; (*b*) **to s. up to s.o.,** *NAm:* **to s. (off, away) to s.o.,** s'avancer vers qn, se mettre, en posture de combat; **to s. up to the difficulties,** faire face aux difficultés. **2.** s'accorder avec; **the theory does not s. with the facts,** la théorie ne correspond pas aux faits. **3.** (*a*) *v.tr. Golf: etc:* **to s. the match,** égaliser la marque; (*b*) **to s. (up) with s.o.,** (i) régler ses comptes avec qn; (ii) se venger de qn; régler son compte à qn. **squaring** *n.* **1.** équarrissage *m* (d'un bloc de pierre, etc.). **2.** quadrillage *m* (d'une carte, etc.). **3.** règlement *m* (d'un compte).

squareness ['skwɛənis] *n.* **1.** forme carrée. **2.** honnêteté *f*, loyauté *f* (dans les affaires). **3.** *F:* conservatisme *m* (d'une personne vieux jeu).

squash¹ [skwɔʃ] *n.* **1.** écrasement *m*, aplatissement *m*; *O:* **s. hat,** chapeau mou. **2.** cohue *f*; foule *f*; **there was a dreadful s. at the doors,** la foule s'écrasait aux portes. **3.** (*a*) pulpe *f*; (*b*) **orange, lemon, s.,** (i) sirop *m* d'orange, de citron; (ii) orangeade, limonade, non gazeuse. **4.** *Sp:* **s. (rackets),** squash(-rackets) *m*; **s. court,** terrain *m* de squash.

squash² **1.** *v.tr.* (*a*) écraser, aplatir (qch.); (*b*) écraser, étouffer (une révolte, etc.); (*c*) *F:* remettre (qn) à sa place; rembarrer (qn). **2.** *v.i.* (*a*) s'écraser, s'aplatir; (*b*) **to s. (up),** se serrer, se presser.

squash³ *n. Hort:* (*a*) gourde *f*; (*b*) *esp. NAm:* courge *f* (calebasse); gourde *f*.

squashy ['skwɔʃi] *a.* mou et humide; qui s'écrase facilement; (fruit) à pulpe molle; (terrain) bourbeux, détrempé.

squat¹ [skwɔt] *n.* **1.** accroupissement *m*; posture accroupie. **2.** *F:* terrain, etc., occupé par un squatter.

squat² *v.i.* **(squatted) 1.** (*a*) **to s. (down),** s'accroupir; **she was squatting by the fire,** elle était accroupie au coin du feu; (*b*) *Ven:* (*of game*) se tapir. **2.** (*a*) *NAm:* **to s. upon a piece of land,** s'établir sur un terrain commun (avec titre légal de propriété); (*b*) s'établir comme squatter dans une maison inoccupée. **squatting** *n.* **1.** accroupissement *m*. **2.** occupation *f* d'un terrain, d'une maison, en qualité de squatter; squatting *m*.

squat³ *a.* **1.** accroupi. **2.** (*a*) (*of pers.*) ramassé, trapu; (*b*) (*of object, building, etc.*) écrasé; (arc) surbaissé.

squatter ['skwɔtər] *n.* squatter *mf*.

squaw [skwɔ:] *n.f.* squaw; femme peau-rouge.

squawk¹ [skwɔ:k] *n.* **1.** cri *m* rauque, couic *m* (d'un oiseau, *F:* de qn). **2.** *esp: NAm: F:* rouspétance *f*.

squawk² *v.i.* **1.** (*of bird, F: of pers.*) pousser des cris rauques; faire couac. **2.** *esp. NAm: F:* rouspéter.

squeak¹ [skwi:k] *n.* **1.** petit cri aigu; couinement *m*; couic *m* (d'un animal); crissement *m*, grincement *m* (de choses mal huilées); *F:* **I don't want to hear another s. out of you,** je ne veux pas entendre le moindre murmure. **2.** *F:* **that was a near s.,** nous l'avons échappé belle; il était moins cinq!

squeak² **1.** *v.i.* (*a*) (*of pers.*) pousser des cris aigus; couiner; (*of animal*) faire couic; (*of mouse*) guiorer; (*of machine part, etc.*) crier, grincer; (*of shoes*) craquer, couiner; (*b*) *F:* vendre la mèche; moucharder. **2.** *v.tr.* **to s. (out),** crier (qch.) d'une petite voix aiguë. **squeaking** *n.* couics *mpl*; couinements *mpl*; grincement *m* (de porte).

squeaky ['skwi:ki] *a.* criard, qui crie; (chaussures) qui craquent **s. voice,** petite voix aiguë.

squeal¹ [skwi:l] *n.* (*a*) cri aigu; cri perçant (d'un animal); (*b*) grincement *m* (de freins); crissement *m* (de pneus).

squeal² **1.** *v.i.* (*a*) pousser des cris aigus; couiner; (*of tyres, brakes*) grincer, crisser; **to s. like a pig,** crier comme un porc qu'on égorge; (*b*) *F:* protester; jeter les hauts cris; (*c*) *F:* vendre la mèche; moucharder; **to s. on s.o.,** dénoncer qn. **2.** *v.tr.* **to s. (out),** crier (qch.) d'une voix aiguë, perçante. **squealing** **1.** *a.* qui crie, qui piaille. **2.** *n.* (*a*) cris aigus; hauts cris; (*b*) crissement *m*; grincement *m*.

squealer ['skwi:lər] *n.* **1.** personne criarde. **2.** *F:* dénonciateur, -trice; mouchard, -arde.

squeamish ['skwi:miʃ] *a.* **1.** sujet aux nausées; (estomac) délicat; **to feel s.,** avoir des nausées; avoir mal au cœur; **I'm s. about seeing blood,** ça me donne mal au cœur de voir du sang. **2.** (*a*) difficile, exigeant; (*b*) scrupuleux à l'excès; (*c*) pudique à l'excès; **don't be so s.!** pas tant de délicatesses! ne faites pas le dégoûté!

squeamishness ['skwi:miʃnis] *n.* **1.** disposition *f* à avoir des nausées. **2.** délicatesse exagérée; goût *m* difficile.

squeegee ['skwi:dʒi:] *n.* **1.** balai *m* en caoutchouc; racloir *m*; *Nau:* râteau *m* de pont. **2.** *Phot: etc:* raclette *f*; **roller s.,** rouleau *m* en caoutchouc.

squeeze¹ [skwi:z] *n.* **1.** (*a*) compression *f*; serrage *m*; serrement *m* (de main); (*b*) étreinte *f*; **to give s.o. a s.,** serrer qn dans ses bras; (*c*) *Pol.Ec:* mesures *fpl* d'austérité; **credit s.,** restriction *f* du crédit. **2.** foule *f*, cohue *f*; **it was a tight s.,** on tenait tout juste. **3. a. s. of lemon,** quelques gouttes *fpl* de citron. **4.** exaction *f*; **to put the s. on s.o.,** forcer la main à qn.

squeeze² *v.tr.* **1.** (*a*) presser (une éponge, un citron); **to s. s.o.'s hand,** serrer la main à qn; (*b*) embrasser, étreindre (qn). **2.** (*a*) **to s. sth. into a box,** faire entrer qch. de force dans une boîte; **to s. the juice out of a lemon,** extraire le jus d'un citron; **to s. out a tear,** y aller de sa (petite) larme; verser un pleur; (*b*) *v.i.* **to s. into a crowded train,** entrer de force dans un train bondé; **to s. up (together),** se serrer (les uns contre les autres). **3.** (*a*) exercer une pression sur (qn, etc.); forcer la main à (qn); (*b*) **to s. money out of s.o.,** extorquer de l'argent à qn.

squeezebox ['skwi:zbɔks] *n. F:* accordéon *m*, concertina *m*.

squeezer ['skwi:zər] *n.* presse *f*; **lemon s.,** presse-citrons *m inv.*

squelch¹ [skwel(t)ʃ] *n.* **1.** giclement *m* (de boue); gargouillement *m*, gargouillis *m* (de chaussures détrempées, etc.). **2.** lourde chute (sur qch. de mou).

squelch² **1.** *v.tr.* (*a*) écraser (qch.) (en le faisant gicler); (*b*) *F:* faire taire (qn); réprimer, étouffer (une rébellion, etc.). **2.** *v.i.* (*a*) **to s. through the mud,** patauger dans la boue; (*b*) **the water squelched in his shoes,** l'eau gargouillait dans ses chaussures.

squib [skwib] *n.* **1.** *Pyr:* pétard *m*, serpenteau *m*; *Fig:* **damp s.,** affaire ratée. **2.** satire *f*, brocard *m*.

squid [skwid] *n. Moll:* calmar *m*.

squiffy ['skwifi] *a. F: O:* un peu ivre; gris, éméché.

squiggle ['skwigl] *n. F:* (*a*) trait *m*, ligne *f*, en paraphe; (*b*) écriture *f* illisible.

squiggly ['skwigli] *a. F:* tortueux, sinueux.

squint¹ [skwint] *n.* **1.** strabisme *m*; **he has a slight s.,** il louche légèrement. **2.** regard *m* de côté, de travers;

I had a s. at his paper, j'ai jeté un coup d'œil oblique sur son journal. **3.** *F:* regard; coup d'œil; **let's have a s. at it!** faites voir! **4.** inclination *f*, penchant *m* (**to, towards,** vers).

squint² *v.i.* **1.** loucher. **2. to s. at sth., at s.o.,** regarder qch., qn, de côté, de travers, furtivement. **squinting** *n.* strabisme *m.*

squint³ *a.* **s. eyes,** yeux louches; **s.-eyed,** (i) au regard louche, (ii) malveillant.

squire¹ ['skwaiər] *n.m.* **1.** *Hist:* écuyer (attaché à un chevalier). **2.** *A:* (*a*) propriétaire foncier; (*b*) châtelain; seigneur du village. **3.** *U.S:* juge de paix.

squire² *v.tr.* servir de cavalier à, escorter (une dame).

squirm¹ [skwə:m] *n.* tortillement *m* (de douleur, etc.).

squirm² *v.i.* (*a*) (*of worm, etc.*) se tordre, se tortiller; (*b*) éprouver de l'embarras; être mal à l'aise; être au supplice; **to make s.o. s.,** mettre qn au supplice.

squirrel ['skwir(ə)l] *n.* **1.** (*a*) *Z:* écureuil *m*; **Siberian s.,** petit-gris *m*, *pl.* petits-gris, de Sibérie; (*b*) **s. cage,** (i) cage *f* d'écureuil; tournette *f*; (ii) *El:* cage d'écureuil. **2.** *Com:* **s. (fur),** petit-gris.

squirt¹ [skwə:t] *n.* **1.** seringue *f.* **2.** jet *m*, giclée *f* (de liquide). **3.** *F:* (*pers.*) merdaillon *m.*

squirt² **1.** *v.tr.* faire (re)jaillir, faire gicler (un liquide, etc.); injecter (un liquide, etc.) avec une seringue; **to s. soda water into a glass,** faire gicler du soda dans un verre. **2.** *v.i.* (*of liquid, etc.*) (re)jaillir, gicler.

squishy ['skwiʃi] *a. F:* détrempé; mou; **the ground's s. under foot,** le sol gargouille sous les pas.

stab¹ [stæb] *n.* **1.** (*a*) coup *m* de poignard, de couteau; **s. in the back** = coup de Jarnac; attaque déloyale; **s. of pain,** élancement *m*; (*b*) *F:* **to have a s. at sth.,** essayer de faire qch. **2.** *Games:* **s. shot,** coup sec.

stab² *v.* (**stabbed**) **1.** *v.tr.* poignarder (qn); donner un coup de couteau à (qn); **to s. s.o. to death,** tuer qn d'un coup de poignard; **to s. s.o. in the back,** (i) poignarder qn dans le dos; (ii) calomnier qn. **2.** *v.i.* **to s. at s.o.,** porter un coup de couteau, de poignard, à qn. **stabbing** **1.** *a.* **s. pain,** élancement *m*, douleur lancinante. **2.** *n.* (*a*) coups de poignard, de couteau; (*b*) assassinat *m* à coups (de couteau, etc.).

stability [stə'biliti] *n.* (*a*) stabilité *f*, solidité *f* (d'une construction); (*b*) stabilité (d'un avion, d'un composé chimique, etc.); (*c*) stabilité (économique, etc.).

stabilization [steibilai'zeiʃ(ə)n] *n.* (*a*) stabilisation *f* (du sol, d'un avion, *Ph: El:* de phase, etc.); (*b*) *Fin:* stabilisation, valorisation *f* (des cours, etc.).

stabilize ['steibilaiz] **1.** *v.tr.* stabiliser (le sol, un navire, le cours du change). **2.** *v.i.* se stabiliser. **stabilizing** **1.** *a.* (*a*) stabilisateur, -trice; **to have, exert, a s. effect on prices,** exercer une action stabilisatrice sur les prix; (*b*) **s. agent,** agent stabilisant (pour produits alimentaires, etc.). **2.** *n.* = STABILIZATION.

stabilizer ['steibilaizər] *n.* **1.** *Nau: Av:* stabilisateur *m*; *Av:* empennage *m.* **2.** stabilisant *m* (de produits alimentaires, d'explosifs, etc.).

stable¹ ['steibl] *n.* **1.** écurie *f*; **to lock the s. door after the horse has bolted,** fermer la cage quand les oiseaux se sont envolés. **2.** chevaux *mpl* (d'une certaine écurie); *Turf: Aut: etc:* écurie; **racing s.,** écurie de courses; **s. companion, mate,** (i) cheval *m* de la même écurie; (ii) *F:* membre *m* de la même entreprise, etc.

stable² *v.tr.* loger (un cheval) dans une écurie; **we can s. three horses,** nous avons de la place pour trois chevaux. **stabling** *n.* **1.** logement *m* (de chevaux) dans une écurie. **2.** *coll.* écuries *fpl*; **we have plenty of s.,** nous ne manquons pas de place aux écuries.

stable³ *a.* **1.** stable; solide, fixe; *Ch: Ph:* stable; **s. state,** état *m* stable, état de stabilité; **s. currency,** monnaie *f* stable; **the government is becoming more s.,** le gouvernement se consolide; **s. job,** emploi stable, permanent. **2.** (*of pers.*) constant, ferme: *F:* **he's perfectly s.,** il est parfaitement sain d'esprit.

stableboy ['steiblboi] *n.m.* palefrenier.

stablelad ['steibllæd] *n.m.* lad.

staccato [stə'kɑ:tou] *a. adv.* & *n.* (*a*) *Mus:* staccato (*m*); **s. note,** note piquée; **to play the notes s.,** détacher les notes; (*b*) (style) haché; (voix) saccadée.

stack¹ [stæk] *n.* **1.** (*a*) meule *f* (de foin, etc.); (*b*) pile *f*, tas *m* (de bois, de charbon, d'assiettes); *F:* **I've stacks of work to do,** j'ai de quoi faire; **to make stacks of money,** ramasser l'argent à la pelle; **I've got stacks of it,** j'en ai des tas; (*c*) (*in library*) **stacks,** rayonnages *mpl*; **s. room,** réserve *f*; (*d*) faisceau *m* (d'armes). **2.** (*a*) souche *f*, corps *m* (de cheminée); (*b*) cheminée *f* (d'une locomotive, etc.); (*c*) **s. (pipe),** tuyau *m* de descente, descente *f* d'eau (d'une gouttière). **3.** *Geog:* haut rocher (au large d'une côte). **4.** *Av:* (*a*) circuit *m* d'attente; (*b*) avions en attente (échelonnés en altitude).

stack² *v.tr.* **1.** mettre (le foin) en meule(s). **2. to s. (up),** empiler, entasser (du bois, du charbon, des assiettes, etc.). **3.** mettre (les armes) en faisceaux. **4.** *NAm:* **to s. the cards,** tricher aux cartes. **5.** *Av:* échelonner en altitude (les avions en attente). **stacking** *n.* **1.** mise *f* en meule (du foin). **2. s. (up),** empilement *m*, entassement *m* (du bois, du charbon, etc.); *Furn:* **s. chairs,** chaises *fpl* superposables. **3.** mise *f* en faisceaux (des armes). **4.** *Av:* échelonnement *m* en altitude (des avions en attente).

stadium, *pl.* **-iums, -ia** ['steidiəm, -iəmz, -iə] *n. Sp: etc:* stade *m.*

staff¹ [stɑ:f] *n.* **1.** (*a*) bâton *m*; **pilgrim's s.,** bourdon *m* de pèlerin; (*b*) *Ecc:* **pastoral s.,** bâton pastoral; (*c*) hampe *f* (de bannière, de lance); *Nau:* mât *m* (de pavillon); *U.S:* (*of flag*) **at half s.,** en berne; (*d*) *Tls:* crochet *m*, ringard *m*; (*e*) *Surv:* jalon *m*, mire *f.* **2.** (*a*) *Mil:* état-major *m*, *pl.* état-majors; **general s.,** état-major général; **chief of s.,** chef d'état-major; **joint chiefs of s.,** état-major interarmées; **s. officer,** officier d'état-major; **S. College** = École supérieure de guerre; (*b*) personnel *m*; **domestic s.,** les domestiques; *Journ:* **editorial s.,** la rédaction; **teaching s.,** personnel enseignant; **s. room,** salle des professeurs; **nursing s.,** les infirmiers, les infirmières; **office s.,** personnel de bureau; **senior, managerial, s.,** les cadres supérieurs; **s. management,** direction *f* du personnel; (*c*) *Med:* **s. nurse,** *F:* **s.,** = infirmière diplômée. **3.** *Mus:* (*pl.* **staves** [steivz]) portée *f.*

staff² *v.tr.* (*a*) fournir (un bureau, etc.) de personnel, d'employés; (*b*) **army staffed with brilliant generals,** armée dont l'état-major se compose de généraux remarquables.

staffer ['stɑ:fər] *n. U.S:* membre *m* du personnel.

stag [stæg] *n.* **1.** *Z:* (*a*) cerf *m*; (*b*) *Ent:* **s. beetle,** lucane *m*; cerf-volant *m*, *pl.* cerfs-volants. **2.** *St.Exch:* *F:* (*premium hunter*) loup *m.* **3. s. party, dinner,** réunion *f* pour hommes seulement, *F:* un P.H.S.

stage¹ [steidʒ] *n.* **1.** (*a*) estrade *f*, échafaud *m*, échafaudage *m*; *Const: etc:* **hanging s.,** échafaud volant; **landing s.,** débarcadère *m*; embarcadère *f*; (*b*) platine *f* (d'un microscope); (*c*) étage *m* (d'un fusée, d'un engin spatial). **2.** (*a*) *Th:* scène *f*; tréteaux *mpl* (de saltimbanque); **front of the s.,** avant-scène *f*; **revolving s.,** plateau tournant; **to come on (the) s.,** entrer en scène; **to set the s.,** (i) monter les décors; (ii) *Fig:* exposer la situation; **s. directions,** indications *fpl* scéniques; **s. effects,** effets *mpl* scéniques; **s. manager,** régisseur *m*; **s. name,** nom *m* de théâtre; **s. whisper,** aparté *m*; **s. fright,** trac *m*; **s. door,** entrée *f* des artistes; (*b*) **the s.,** le théâtre; **to go on the s.,** devenir acteur, actrice; **s. rights,** droits *mpl* de production (d'une pièce); (*c*) *Fig:* théâtre, champ *m.* **3.** phase *f*, période *f*; stade *m*, étape *f*; étage; **the stages**

of an evolution, les étapes, les stades, d'une évolution; *Elcs: etc:* **input s.,** étage d'entrée; **to reach a critical s.,** arriver à une phase, période, critique; **at this s.,** à ce point, à ce moment; **in the larval s.,** à l'état de larve; **to do sth. in (successive) stages,** faire qch. par reprises; **at what s. in its development?** à quel moment de son développement? **4.** (*a*) étape; **s. by s.,** d'étape en étape; **we did the journey in easy stages,** nous avons fait le voyage en petites étapes; (*b*) *A:* relais *m*; **s. (coach),** diligence *f*; (*c*) **fare s.,** (changement *m* de) section *f* (de l'itinéraire d'un autobus).

stage² *v.tr.* (*a*) monter (une pièce), mettre (une pièce) sur la scène; (*b*) organiser, faire (une manifestation, etc.); monter (un coup); (*c*) **carefully staged reduction of nuclear weapons,** réduction soigneusement étagée des armes nucléaires. **staging** *n.* **1.** mise *f* à la scène (d'une pièce). **2.** *A:* **s. post,** relais *m* (de diligences).

stagecraft ['steidʒkrɑːft] *n. Th:* technique *f* de la scène.

stagehand ['steidʒhænd] *n. Th:* machiniste *m.*

stager ['steidʒər] *n.* **old s.,** vieux routier.

stagestruck ['steidʒstrʌk] *a.* épris, féru, du théâtre.

stagger¹ ['stægər] *n.* **1.** (*a*) chancellement *m*; (*b*) allure chancelante. **2.** *Vet:* **staggers,** vertigo *m.*

stagger² **1.** *v.i.* chanceler, tituber; **to s. along,** marcher en chancelant, en titubant; **to s. to one's feet,** se relever en chancelant, avec difficulté. **2.** *v.tr.* confondre, consterner, renverser (qn); **to be staggered,** être saisi d'étonnement. **3.** *v.tr.* (*a*) *Av:* décaler (les ailes); (*b*) *Mec.E:* disposer (des rivets, des joints, etc.) en quinconce, en zigzag; alterner, étager (des rivets); (*c*) *El:* échelonner (les balais); (*d*) échelonner (les heures de travail, les vacances). **staggering** *a.* (*a*) **s. blow,** coup *m* de massue, d'assommoir; (*b*) (*of news*) renversant, atterrant; **s. increase in prices,** hausse vertigineuse des prix. **2.** *n.* (*a*) chancellement *m*; (*b*) (i) *Av:* décalage *m* (des ailes); (ii) *Mec.E: etc:* disposition *f* en quinconce; (iii) *El:* échelonnage *m* (des balais); (iv) échelonnement *m* (des vacances, des heures de travail).

staghorn ['stæghɔːn] *n.* corne *f* de cerf.

staghunt(ing) [stæghʌnt(iŋ)] *n.* chasse *f* au cerf.

stagnant ['stægnənt] *a.* stagnant; (*of trade, business*) en stagnation; dans le marasme.

stagnate [stæg'neit] *v.i.* (*of water, trade*) être, devenir, stagnant; être dans un état de stagnation. **stagnating** *a.* stagnant; dans un état de stagnation.

stagnation [stæg'neiʃ(ə)n] *n.* stagnation *f*; marasme *m* (des affaires).

stagy ['steidʒi] *a.* théâtral, -aux; histrionique.

staid [steid] *a.* posé, sérieux, sage.

staidness ['steidnis] *n.* caractère posé, sérieux, sage.

stain¹ [stein] *n.* **1.** (*a*) tache *f*, souillure *f*; **to remove a s.,** enlever une tache (**from,** de); **s. remover,** détachant *m*; (*b*) **without a s. on his character,** sans atteinte à sa réputation. **2.** colorant *m*; **(wood) s.,** teinture *f* (pour bois).

stain² *v.tr.* **1.** (*a*) tacher; souiller, salir (**with,** de); **hands stained with blood,** mains tachées, souillées, de sang; (*with passive force*) **material that stains easily,** tissu *m* qui se tache facilement; (*b*) entacher, souiller, ternir (la réputation de qn). **2.** teindre, teinter (le bois); peindre (le verre). **staining** *n.* **1.** souillure *f.* **2.** teinture *f*; coloration *f.*

stainless ['steinlis] *a.* **1.** sans tache; immaculé, pur. **2. s. steel,** acier *m* inoxydable.

stair [stɛər] *n.* **1.** marche *f*, degré *m* (d'un escalier). **2. (flight of) stairs,** escalier; **spiral stairs,** escalier tournant, en vis; **back stairs,** escalier de service.

staircarpet ['stɛəkɑːpit] *n.* tapis *m* d'escalier.

staircase ['stɛəkeis] *n.* (i) cage *f* d'escalier; (ii) escalier *m*; **spiral s.,** escalier tournant, en colimaçon; **secret s.,** escalier dérobé.

stairway ['stɛəwei] *n.* = STAIRCASE.

stairwell ['stɛəwel] *n.* cage *f* d'escalier.

stake¹ [steik] *n.* **1.** (*a*) pieu *m*, poteau *m*; jalon *m*, fiche *f*; piquet *m*; *Hort:* tuteur *m*; échalas *m* (de vigne); (*b*) *Surv:* jalon, piquet; *Row:* **s. boat,** bateau *m* de ligne de départ; (*c*) *NAm: F:* **to pull up stakes,** partir; déménager. **2.** (poteau du) bûcher; **to die, be burned, at the s.,** mourir sur le bûcher. **3.** (*a*) *Gaming:* mise *f*, enjeu *m*; **the stakes are down,** les jeux sont faits; **to play for high stakes,** jouer gros jeu; **our honour is at s.,** il y va de notre honneur; notre honneur est en jeu; **to have large sums at s. in an enterprise,** avoir de fortes sommes engagées dans une entreprise; **to have a s. in sth.,** avoir des intérêts dans une affaire; (*b*) *Turf:* **stakes,** prix *m.*

stake² *v.tr.* **1. to stake (off, out),** (i) jalonner, piqueter (une concession, etc.); (ii) *Surv:* jalonner (une ligne, une route, etc.); **to s. a claim,** (i) *Min:* jalonner une concession; (ii) *Fig:* établir, faire valoir, ses droits. **2.** soutenir (qch.) avec des pieux; échalasser (une vigne, etc.); tuteurer (des tomates). **3.** mettre (une somme) en jeu; jouer, risquer (une somme); **to s. twenty francs,** miser vingt francs; **to s. everything, one's all,** jouer son va-tout; mettre tout en jeu; **I'd s. my life on it,** j'y mettrais, j'en gagerais, ma tête à couper. **6.** *NAm: F:* fournir (qn) d'argent; fournir aux besoins de (qn). **staking** *n.* **1. s. (off, out),** jalonnement *m*, piquetage *m* (d'une concession, etc.). **2.** échalassage *m* (d'une vigne); tuteurage *m* (des tomates). **3.** mise *f* (en jeu) (d'une somme).

stalactite ['stæləktait, *NAm: also* stə'læktait] *n. Geol:* stalactite *f.*

stalagmite ['stæləgmait, *NAm: also* stə'lægmait] *n. Geol:* stalagmite *f.*

stale¹ [steil] *a.* **1.** (*a*) (pain, gâteau) rassis; (*b*) (œuf, etc.) qui n'est pas frais; (vin) éventé; (*c*) (air) vicié, croupi; **s. smell,** odeur *f* de renfermé. **2.** (*a*) vieux, *f.* vieille; vieilli, passé; **s. joke,** vieille plaisanterie; **s. news,** nouvelle défraîchie; **s. cheque,** chèque périmé; (*b*) *Fin:* (marché) lourd, plat. **3.** fatigué, éreinté; (*of athlete, etc.*) **to go s.,** se surentraîner; **I'm s.,** je n'ai plus d'enthousiasme; *F:* **it's gone s. on me,** ça ne me plaît plus; je n'arrive plus à m'y mettre.

stale² *v.i.* (*a*) (*of beer, etc.*) s'éventer; (*b*) (*of news, etc.*) perdre son intérêt; **pleasure that never stales,** plaisir toujours nouveau.

stalemate¹ ['steilmeit] *n.* (*a*) *Chess:* pat *m*; (*b*) **negotiations have reached a s.,** les négociations sont arrivées, ont abouti, à une impasse.

stalement² *v.tr. Chess:* faire pat (son adversaire).

staleness ['steilnis] *n.* **1.** (*a*) état rassis (du pain); (*b*) évent *m* (de la bière, etc.); (*c*) relent *m* (d'un aliment, d'une pièce); odeur *f* de renfermé. **2.** manque *m* de fraîcheur (d'une nouvelle).

Stalinism ['stɑːlinizm] *n.* stalinisme *m.*

Stalinist ['stɑːlinist] *a. & n.* stalinien, -ienne.

stalk¹ [stɔːk] *n.* **1.** démarche majestueuse, dédaigneuse. **2.** *Ven:* chasse *f* à l'approche.

stalk² **1.** *v.i.* **to s. (along),** marcher, s'avancer, d'un pas majestueux; **to s. out of a room,** sortir d'une pièce d'un air dédaigneux. **2.** *v.tr.* (*a*) *Ven:* chasser (le daim) à l'approche; (*b*) suivre furtivement (qn); filer (qn). **stalking** *n. Ven:* chasse *f* à l'approche; **s. horse,** (i) *Ven:* cheval *m* d'abri; (ii) prétexte *m.*

stalk³ *n.* **1.** tige *f* (de plante, de fleur); queue *f* (de fruit, de fleur); chaume *m* (de blé); rafle *f*, râpe *f* (de grappe de raisins); trognon *m* (de chou); *Nat.Hist:* pédoncule *m*; **s.-eyed,** aux yeux pédonculés. **2.** pied *m* (de verre à vin).

stalk⁴ *v.tr.* égrapper (des raisins); équeuter (des

cerises, etc.). **stalked** *a.* (*a*) *Bot:* (feuille) pétiolée; (champignon) stipité; (*b*) *Nat.Hist:* pédonculé.

stalker ['stɔːkər] *n.* (*a*) *Ven:* chasseur *m* à l'approche; (*b*) (*pers. following s.o.*) fileur, -euse.

stall¹ [stɔːl] *n.* **1.** stalle *f* (d'écurie); case *f* (d'étable); loge *f*, box *m* (de porcherie). **2.** étalage *m* (en plein vent); échoppe *f*, éventaire *m*; étal, -aux *m* (de boucher); (*at exhibition, etc.*) stand *m*; **(market) s.,** place *f*, emplacement *m* (au marché); **newspaper s.,** kiosque *m*. **3.** (*a*) *Ecc.Arch:* **choir s.,** stalle; (*b*) *Th:* **(orchestra) stalls,** fauteuils *mpl* d'orchestre. **4.** *Min:* taille *f*. **5. finger s.,** doigtier *m*. **6.** *Aut:* calage *m* (du moteur).

stall² **1.** *v.tr.* mettre à l'étable (du bétail). **2.** *v.tr. & i.* *Aut:* caler (le moteur); (*of engine*) (se) caler; *Av:* mettre l'appareil, se mettre, en perte de vitesse. **3.** *v.i.* s'embourber; s'enfoncer dans la boue, *NAm:* dans la neige. **stalling** *n. Aut:* arrêt *m* (du moteur).

stall³ **1.** *v.tr.* **to s. sth. off,** repousser, écarter, qch.; **to s. s.o. off,** repousser, faire attendre, qn. **2.** *v.i.* **to s. (for time),** chercher à gagner du temps.

stall-feed ['stɔːlfiːd] *v.tr.* (**stall-fed** [-fed]) nourrir, engraisser (du bétail) à l'étable.

stallholder ['stɔːlhouldər] *n.* **1.** étalagiste *mf*; hallier *m*; marchand, -ande, en plein vent. **2.** (*at charity bazaar*) vendeuse *f*.

stallion ['stæliən] *n.* étalon *m*.

stalwart ['stɔːlwət] *a.* **1.** robuste, vigoureux. **2.** vaillant, résolu.

stamen ['steimen] *n. Bot:* étamine *f*.

stamina ['stæminə] *n.* force vitale; vigueur *f*, résistance *f*; **to lack s.,** manquer de résistance, de nerf.

stammer¹ ['stæmər] *n.* (i) bégaiement *m*; (ii) balbutiement *m*; **man with a s.,** homme *m* qui bégaie; homme bègue.

stammer² **1.** *v.i.* (i) bégayer; (ii) balbutier. **2.** *v.tr.* bégayer, balbutier (qch.); **to s. (out) an excuse,** bégayer une excuse. **stammering** *n.* (i) bégaiement *m*; (ii) balbutiement *m*.

stammerer ['stæmərər] *n.* bègue *mf*.

stamp¹ [stæmp] *n.* **1.** (*a*) battement *m* de pied (d'impatience, de colère); **with a s. of the foot,** en frappant du pied; (*b*) **ceaseless s. of feet,** piétinement perpétuel; bruit continuel de pas. **2.** (*a*) timbre *m*, empreinte *f*; **signature s.,** griffe *f*; **date s.,** (timbre) dateur *m*; **rubber s.,** timbre de caoutchouc; (*b*) estampe *f*, étampe *f*, poinçon *m*; (*c*) (*minting*) coin *m*. **3.** (*a*) timbre; marque (apposée); *Ind:* estampille *f*, marque, de contrôle; **(hallmark) s.,** poinçon (de contrôle) (marquant l'or, l'argent); **customs s.,** marque de la douane; (*b*) **to bear the s. of genius,** porter la marque du génie. **4. (postage) s.,** timbre(-poste) *m*, *pl.* timbres(-poste); **s. album,** album *m* de timbres-poste (de collectionneur); **s. collector,** philatéliste *mf*; **s. machine,** distributeur *m* automatique de timbres-poste; **s. duty,** impôt *m* du timbre; droit *m* de timbre. **5.** *Metalw:* étampeuse *f*, estampeuse *f*.

stamp² *v.tr. & i.* **1.** (*a*) **to s. one's foot,** frapper du pied; **to s. one's feet,** *v.i.* **to s. about,** (i) trépigner, piétiner; (ii) (*for warmth*) battre la semelle; (*b*) *v.i.* **to s. on sth.,** piétiner qch.; fouler qch. aux pieds; **to s. upstairs,** monter l'escalier à pas bruyants. **2.** frapper, imprimer, une marque sur (qch.); marquer (du beurre, du papier, etc.); contrôler, poinçonner (l'or, l'argent); frapper, estamper (la monnaie, le cuir, etc.); gaufrer (le cuir). **3.** timbrer (un document, etc.); viser (un passeport); timbrer, affranchir (une lettre); estampiller (un document, des marchandises); **the letter is insufficiently stamped,** l'affranchissement est insuffisant. **4.** *Metalw:* étamper, estamper (des objets en métal). **5.** *O:* **to s. s.o., sth., (as) . . .,** donner à qn, qch., le caractère de . . .. **stamped** *a.* **1.** (*a*) broyé, concassé; (*b*) **s. earth,** terre piétinée, battue. **2.** (*a*) (document, etc.) timbré; (*b*) estampillé, marqué, poinçonné; (or, argent) contrôlé. **3.** (*a*) *Metalw:* étampé, estampé; (*b*) (cuir) gaufré. **stamping** *n.* **1.** (*a*) piétinement *m*; trépignement *m*; *F:* **it's our favourite s. ground,** c'est notre endroit préféré; (*b*) **s. out,** écrasement *m* (d'une rébellion, etc.); enraiement *m* (d'un abus, etc.); éradication *f* (d'une maladie). **2.** (*a*) timbrage *m* (des documents, etc.); estampillage *m* (des marchandises, etc.); affranchissement *m* (des lettres); (*b*) poinçonnage *m* (de l'or, etc.); (*c*) *Metalw:* estampage *m*, étampage *m*; **s. press,** estampeuse *f*, étampeuse *f*; (*d*) **s. (out),** découpage *m* à la presse, à l'emporte-pièce. **3.** *Metalw:* pièce estampée; *Aut:* **body s.,** embouti *m*, pièce emboutie, pour carrosserie. **stamp out** *v.tr.* **1.** *Metalw:* découper (des tôles) à la presse, à l'emporte-pièce. **2.** (*a*) éteindre (un feu) en piétinant dessus; (*b*) écraser (une rébellion, etc.); enrayer (un abus, etc.); étouffer, écraser (une épidémie, etc.).

stampede¹ [stæm'piːd] *n.* **1.** (*a*) fuite précipitée; panique *f*; (*b*) débandade *f* (de troupes, de chevaux, etc.). **2.** ruée *f*; **there was a s. for the door,** on s'est précipité vers la porte.

stampede² **1.** *v.i.* (*a*) fuir en désordre, à la débandade; (*b*) se ruer, se précipiter (**for, towards,** vers, sur). **2.** *v.tr.* (*a*) jeter la panique parmi (des bêtes, des personnes); (*b*) **to s. a nation into war,** précipiter un peuple dans la guerre.

stance [stæns] *n. Golf: Cr:* posture *f* (du joueur); **to take up one's s.,** se mettre en posture (pour jouer).

stanch [stɑːn(t)ʃ] *v.tr.* = STAUNCH².

stanchion ['stɑːnʃ(ə)n] *n.* étançon *m*; étai *m*.

stand¹ [stænd] *n.* **1.** (*a*) manière *f* de se tenir (debout); **to take a firm s.,** ne pas transiger; (*b*) arrêt *m*, halte *f*, pause *f*; (*c*) *Th:* arrêt (dans une ville); **one-night s.,** soirée *f*, représentation *f*, unique. **2.** résistance *f*; **to make a s. against (s.o., sth.),** résister à (qn, l'ennemi); s'opposer résolument à (un abus). **3.** (*a*) situation *f*; place *f*, position *f*; **to take one's s. near the door,** se placer, se poster, prendre position, près de la porte; (*b*) **to take one's s. on a principle,** s'en tenir à, se fonder sur, un principe. **4.** station *f* (de taxis). **5.** support *m*, pied *m* (de lampe, etc.); affût *m* (de télescope); râtelier *m* (pour bouteilles, etc.); (*for books, postcards, etc.*) **revolving s.,** tourniquet *m*. **6.** étalage *m*, étal *m*, boutique *f* (en plein air); (*at exhibition, etc.*) stand *m*. **7.** (*a*) *Sp: Rac: etc:* tribune *f*; **the stands,** les tribunes; (*b*) estrade *f*. **8.** (*a*) *Agr:* récolte *f* sur pied; (*b*) *For:* peuplement *m*. **9.** *U.S: Jur:* barre *f* des témoins; **to take the s.,** paraître à la barre.

stand² *v.* (*p.t. & p.p.* **stood** [stud]) **I.** *v.i.* **1.** (*a*) (*have, maintain, upright position*) être debout; se tenir debout; rester debout; **table that stands firm,** table qui pose bien sur ses pieds; **to be, keep, standing,** être, rester, debout; **I was too weak to s.,** j'étais trop faible pour me tenir debout; **I could hardly s.,** je pouvais à peine me tenir; **to s. on one's own legs, feet,** ne dépendre que de soi; *F:* **he hasn't a leg to s. on,** il est entièrement dans son tort; **I've lost everything but what I s. up in,** j'ai tout perdu sauf ce que j'ai sur le dos; (*b*) **to s. six feet high,** avoir six pieds de haut; mesurer six pieds; (*c*) (*assume upright position*) se lever; *Sch:* **stand!** levez-vous! **2.** (*a*) (*be situated; be*) se trouver; être; s'élever; **a chapel stands at the top of the hill,** une chapelle se dresse au sommet de la colline; **a car was standing at the door,** il y avait une voiture à la porte; **I found the door standing open,** j'ai trouvé la porte ouverte; **as it stands,** tel quel; **nothing stands between you and success,** rien ne s'oppose à votre succès; (*b*) **a man stood in the doorway,** un homme se tenait à la porte; **I stood and looked at him, I stood looking at him,** je suis resté à le regarder; **to s. talking,** rester à parler; **don't s. there arguing!** ne restez pas là à discuter! **don't s. in the passage!**

n'encombrez pas le couloir! **to leave s.o. standing (there),** laisser qn planté (là); *Sp: etc:* **to be left standing,** être laissé sur place; *Rac:* **to leave a competitor standing,** brûler, griller, un concurrent. **3.** (*take up a stationary position*) s'arrêter; faire halte; **stand!** halte (là)! **s. and deliver!** la bourse ou la vie! **to s. still,** rester immobile, sans bouger. **4.** (*maintain position*) rester, durer; **to s. fast, firm,** tenir ferme; tenir bon; tenir; **we s. or fall together,** nous sommes solidaires (les uns des autres); **I shall s. or fall by the issue,** je suis prêt à engager ma fortune sur le résultat. **5.** (*remain valid*) tenir, se maintenir; **the passage must stand,** le passage doit rester comme il est, sans modification; **the bet stands,** le pari tient; **the objection stands,** cette objection subsiste. **6.** (*a*) (*be in certain position*) être, se trouver; **to s. convicted of . . .,** être déclaré coupable de . . .; être convaincu de . . .; **to s. in need of . . .,** avoir besoin de . . .; **you s. in danger of getting killed,** vous risquez de vous faire tuer; **to s. to lose £100,** risquer de perdre £100; (*b*) **to s. as security for a debt,** assurer une créance; **to s. (as candidate) for Parliament,** se présenter, se porter candidat, à la députation; (*c*) **the thermometer stood at 30°,** le thermomètre marquait 30°; (*d*) **the house does not s. in his name,** la maison n'est pas portée à son nom; (*e*) **the balance stands at £50,** le reliquat de compte est de cinquante livres; **the amount standing to your credit,** votre solde créditeur; **how do we s.?** où en sont nos comptes? **as matters s., as it stands,** au point où en sont les choses; dans l'état actuel des choses; **to know how things s.,** être au fait de la question; **I don't know where I s.,** j'ignore quelle est ma situation, ma position; **how do you s. with him?** quelle est votre position vis-à-vis de lui? **7.** (*move to and remain in certain position*) se tenir, se mettre; **I'll s. at, by, the window,** je me mettrai à la fenêtre; **I didn't know where to s.,** je ne savais où me mettre; *Nau:* **to s. to the south,** avoir, mettre, le cap au sud; **to s. inshore,** rallier la terre. **8.** (*remain motionless*) **to allow a liquid to s.,** laisser reposer, laisser déposer, un liquide. **II.** *v.tr.* **1.** (*place upright*) mettre, poser, placer; **to s. sth. on the table,** mettre, poser, qch. sur la table; **to s. sth. against the wall,** dresser qch. contre le mur; **to s. sth. upright,** mettre qch. debout. **2. to s. one's ground,** tenir bon, ferme; **stand your ground!** ne reculez pas d'une semelle! **3.** (*endure*) supporter, soutenir, subir; **to s. cold,** supporter le froid; **to s. a shock,** soutenir un choc; **we had to s. the loss,** la perte a porté sur nous; **argument that does not s. investigation,** argument qui ne supporte pas l'examen; **he can't stand her,** il peut pas la souffrir, la sentir; **I won't stand such behaviour,** je ne supporterai pas une pareille conduite; **I can't s. it any longer,** je n'y tiens plus; j'en ai assez. **4.** *F:* payer, offrir; **to s. s.o. a drink,** payer à boire à qn; **to s. s.o. a dinner,** payer un dîner à qn. **stand aside** *v.i.* (*a*) se tenir à l'écart; (*b*) se ranger; **to s. aside to let s.o. pass,** s'effacer pour laisser passer qn; (*c*) **to s. aside in favour of s.o.,** se désister en faveur de qn. **stand away** *v.i.* s'éloigner (**from,** de); *Nau:* **to s. away from shore,** s'éloigner de la côte; prendre le large. **stand back** *v.i.* (i) se tenir en arrière; (ii) (se) reculer; (iii) être situé en retrait; **house standing back from the road,** maison en retrait (de la route). **stand by** *v.i.* (*a*) (i) se tenir prêt; *Mil:* **the troops are standing by,** les troupes sont en état d'alerte; (ii) *Nau:* se tenir paré; veiller; **s. by!** paré! attention! (iii) se tenir là (sans intervenir); (*b*) (i) se tenir près de, à coté de (qn); (ii) soutenir, défendre (qn); se ranger du côté de (qn); (iii) rester fidèle à (sa promesse); **I s. by what I said,** je m'en tiens à ce que j'ai dit. **stand down** *v.i.* (*a*) (*of witness*) quitter la barre; (*b*) se retirer (d'une équipe, d'un poste, etc.); (*of candidate*) retirer sa candidature (**in favour of,** en faveur de); (*c*) *Mil:* quitter son service; descendre de garde. **stand for** *v.ind.tr.* (*a*) défendre, soutenir (qn, une cause); (*b*) remplacer, tenir lieu de (qn, qch.); *Jur: Pol:* représenter (qn); (*c*) signifier, vouloir dire (qch.); (*d*) supporter, tolérer (qch.); **I won't s. for it,** je ne supporterai pas cela. **stand in** *v.i.* (*a*) *Nau:* **to s. in to land, for (the) land,** courir, porter, à terre; (*b*) **to s. in for s.o.,** remplacer qn; *Cin:* doubler (un acteur). **standing 1.** *a.* (*a*) (i) (qui se tient) debout; **s. passengers,** voyageurs *mpl* debout; *Prehist:* **s. stone,** menhir *m*; (ii) **s. crops,** récoltes *fpl* sur pied; **to sell a crop s.,** vendre une récolte sur pied; (iii) *Sp:* **s. start,** départ *m* debout; **s. jump,** saut *m* sans élan; **s. water,** eau stagnante, dormante; (*c*) (i) (prix) fixe; *Com:* **s. expenses,** frais généraux; *Bank:* **s. order,** ordre de transfert permanent; (ii) **s. rule,** règle fixe; **s. joke,** plaisanterie courante, traditionnelle; **I have a s. invitation,** j'ai mes entrées libres (dans cette famille). **2.** *n.* (*a*) (i) station *f* debout; (ii) *Rail: Th: etc:* **s. room,** place(s) *f(pl)* debout; **s. (room) only!** debout seulement! **no s.!** défense de voyager debout; (*b*) durée *f*; **of long s.,** (amis) de longue date; **friend of twenty years' s.,** ami *m* de vingt ans; (*c*) rang *m*, position *f*; standing *m*; **social s.,** position sociale; **the firm's s.,** l'importance *f* de la maison; **financial s.,** situation financière; **firm of recognized s.,** entreprise *f* d'une solidité reconnue. **stand off 1.** *v.i.* (*a*) se tenir éloigné, à l'écart; (*b*) s'éloigner; *Nau:* courir au large. **2.** *v.tr.* (*of employer*) congédier (des ouvriers). **stand out** *v.i.* (*a*) résister (**against,** à); tenir bon, ferme (**against,** contre); (*b*) **to s. out for sth.,** insister sur qch.; (*c*) faire saillie; être en saillie; avancer; **to s. out in relief,** ressortir, se détacher; **to s. out against sth.,** faire contraste avec qch.; **mountains that s. out against the horizon,** montagnes *fpl* qui se dessinent, à l'horizon, sur l'horizon; **the qualities that s. out in his work,** les qualités marquantes de son œuvre; **characteristics that make him s. out in the crowd,** traits *mpl* qui le détachent de la foule; (*d*) *Nau:* **to s. out to sea,** (i) gagner le large; (ii) se tenir au large. **stand over** *v.i.* (*a*) rester en suspens; **to let a question s. over, to allow a question to s. over,** remettre une question à plus tard; laisser une question en suspens; (*b*) **to s. over s.o.,** (i) se pencher sur qn, (ii) surveiller qn de près; **if I don't s. over him he does nothing,** si je ne suis pas toujours sur son dos il ne fait rien. **stand to** *v.i.* (*a*) *Nau:* **to s. to the south,** avoir le cap au sud; (*b*) *Mil: etc:* être prêt, être en état d'alerte; **s. to!** aux armes! **stand up 1.** *v.i.* (*a*) se lever; se mettre debout; **s. up!** levez-vous! debout! **to s. up and be counted,** se déclarer publiquement pour, contre, une question discutable; (*b*) **to s. up to s.o., sth.,** résister à qn, qch.; tenir tête à qn; **to s. up for s.o.,** défendre, soutenir, qn; prendre le parti de qn. **2.** *v.tr.* (*a*) **to s. sth. up,** mettre qch. debout; **to s. a child up (again),** (re)mettre un enfant sur ses pieds; (*b*) *F:* **to s. s.o. up,** lâcher, planter là, qn.

standard ['stændəd] *n.* **1.** bannière *f*; *Mil:* étendard *m*; *Nau:* pavillon *m*; **the Royal S.,** la bannière royale; *Mil:* **s. bearer,** porte-étendard *m inv.* **2.** *Meas: etc:* étalon *m*; **the metre is the s. of length,** le mètre est le module des longueurs; *Fin:* **gold, silver, s.,** étalon (d')or, d'argent; **s. measure,** mesure *f* étalon; **s. weight,** (i) poids *m* étalon; (ii) poids normal; **s. thickness,** épaisseur type, courante (du fer, etc.); (*of car*) **s. model,** voiture *f* de série; **headrests are s. (equipment),** les appuis-tête sont montés en série; *Rail:* **s. gauge,** voie normale; **British s. time,** heure légale anglaise. **3.** (*a*) modèle *m*, type, niveau *m*, norme *f;* **s. of living,** niveau de vie; **everyone has his own standards,** tout homme a sa manière de voir; (*b*) qualité *f*; aloi *m*; niveau; **to aim at, reach, a high s.,**

viser à, atteindre, un niveau élevé; **not to come up to s.,** ne pas atteindre le niveau exigé; (*c*) **s. authors,** auteurs *mpl* classiques; **s. edition,** édition courante (d'un auteur); **a s. French dictionary,** un dictionnaire général de la langue française; **s. English,** l'anglais *m* des gens cultivés; **one of his s. jokes,** une de ses plaisanteries habituelles. **4.** *Sch: A:* classe *f* (dans une école primaire). **5.** (*a*) *Tchn:* pied *m*, support *m* (d'un instrument scientifique, etc.); montant *m* (d'une machine, etc.); (*b*) pylône *m* d'éclairage; réverbère *m* électrique; (*c*) *Furn:* **s. lamp,** lampadaire *m*. **6.** (*a*) *Hort:* **s. (tree),** arbre *m* de plein vent; **s. rose (tree),** rosier *m* sur tige; (*b*) *For:* baliveau *m*.

standardization [stændədai'zeiʃ(ə)n] *n.* étalonnage *m*, étalonnement *m* (des poids, etc.); uniformisation *f* (des méthodes, etc.); *Ind:* standardisation *f*.

standardize ['stændədaiz] *v.tr.* étalonner; uniformiser (des méthodes, des objets de commerce); normaliser (une condition); *Ind:* standardiser.

standby ['stændbai] *n.* **1.** personne sur qui l'on peut compter. **2.** réserve *f*; ressource *f*; **to have a sum in reserve as a s.,** avoir une somme en réserve comme en-cas. **3. s. engine,** locomotive *f* de réserve. **4.** (*a*) *Mil: etc:* (état *m* d')alerte *f*; (*b*) *Av: etc:* (*of pers.*) **to be on s.,** attendre une place libre; **s. passenger, ticket,** voyageur, -euse, billet, sans garantie, standby.

standee [stæn'di:] *n. esp. NAm:* (*in bus*) voyageur, -euse, debout; *Th:* spectateur, -trice, debout.

stand-in ['stændin] *n.* (*pers.*) remplaçant, -ante; *Th: etc:* doublure *f*.

stand-offish [stænd'ɔfiʃ] *a. F:* (*of pers.*) peu accessible; distant, réservé; **to be s.-o.,** se mettre, se tenir, sur son quant-à-soi.

stand-offishness [stænd'ɔfiʃnis] *n. F:* raideur *f*, réserve *f*.

standpoint ['stændpɔint] *n.* point de vue; position *f*.

standstill ['stændstil] *n.* arrêt *m*, immobilisation *f*; **to come to a s.,** s'arrêter, s'immobiliser; **to bring sth. to a s.,** arrêter qch.; **many factories are at a s.,** beaucoup d'usines chôment.

stand-up ['stændʌp] *a.* **1.** *Cost:* (col) droit, montant. **2.** (repas) pris debout. **3. s.-up fight,** combat *m* en règle.

stannic ['stænik] *a. Ch:* stannique.

stanza, *pl.* **-as** ['stænzə, -əz] *n. Pros:* stance *f*, strophe *f*.

staphylococcus, *pl.* **-cocci** [stæfilou'kɔkəs, -'kɔksai] *n. Bac:* staphylocoque *m*.

staple¹ ['steipl] *n.* crampon *m* (à deux pointes); agrafe *f*; **s. gun,** agrafeuse *f*; **wire s.,** (clou) cavalier *m*.

staple² *v.tr.* **1.** *Const: etc:* fixer, attacher (qch.) avec un crampon, une agrafe; agrafer; cramponner. **2.** *Bookb:* brocher (des feuilles). **stapling** *n.* (i) fixage *m* à l'aide de crampons, d'agrafes; agrafage *m*; (ii) *Bookb:* brochage; **s. machine,** (i) agrafeuse *f*; (ii) *Bookb:* brocheuse *f* mécanique.

staple³ *n.* (*a*) produit principal (d'un pays); **s. commodities,** produits de première nécessité; **s. diet,** régime *m* de base; (*b*) matière première, matière brute.

staple⁴ *n. Tex:* brin *m*, fibre *f* (de laine, de lin).

stapler ['steiplər] *n.* (*device*) agrafeuse *f*.

star¹ [sta:r] *n.* **1.** *Astr:* étoile *f*; astre *m*; **shooting s.,** étoile filante; **the morning s.,** l'étoile du matin; **the pole s.,** l'étoile polaire; la polaire; **to be born under a lucky s.,** naître sous une bonne étoile; **to reach for the stars,** demander la lune; *F:* **to see stars,** voir les étoiles en plein midi; voir trente-six chandelles; *Bot:* **s. of Bethlehem,** ornithogale *m* (à ombelle); *F:* dame *f* d'onze heures. **2.** (*a*) plaque *f* (d'un ordre); (*b*) *Mil:* étoile (sur l'épaule); (*c*) **S. of David,** étoile de David; (*d*) **three s. brandy,** cognac *m* trois étoiles; **three s. hotel,** hôtel *m* trois étoiles. **3.** (*a*) *U.S:* **the stars and stripes,** la bannière étoilée; (*b*) (*on horse's forehead*) étoile; (*c*) *Typ:* astérisque *m*; (*d*) *Mec.E:* étoile, croix *f*. **4.** *Cin: etc:* étoile, vedette *f*, star *f*; **s. part,** rôle *m* de vedette; **s. turn,** (i) numéro *m* de premier ordre; (ii) *F:* clou *m* (d'une fête).

star² *v.* **(starred) 1.** *v.tr.* (*a*) étoiler (qch.); (par)semer (qch.) d'étoiles; (*b*) étoiler, fêler (une glace, une vitre); (*c*) *Typ: etc:* marquer (un mot) d'un astérisque; (*d*) *Th: etc:* présenter (qn) dans un rôle de vedette, avoir (qn) pour vedette. **2.** *v.i.* (*a*) (*of glass*) se fêler, s'étoiler; (*b*) *Th: etc:* être en vedette; **to have a starring role,** avoir un rôle de vedette. **starred** *a.* **1.** étoilé; parsemé d'étoiles. **2. ill-s.,** né sous une mauvaise étoile. **3.** *Typ:* marqué d'un astérisque.

starboard ['sta:bəd] *n. Nau:* tribord *m*; **on the s. side, to s.,** à tribord; **on the s. bow,** par tribord devant; **hard a-s.!** tribord toute!

starch¹ [sta:tʃ] *n.* (*a*) amidon *m*; **laundry s.,** empois *m* (d'amidon); (*b*) fécule *f* (de pommes de terre); amidon (de riz, etc.).

starch² *v.tr. Laund:* empeser, amidonner (le linge). **starched** *a.* empesé, amidonné. **starching** *n.* empesage *m*, amidonnage *m*.

starchy ['sta:tʃi] *a.* **1.** *Ch:* amylacé, amyloïde; féculent; **s. foods,** féculents *mpl*. **2.** *F:* (*of pers., manner*) empesé, guindé; raide.

stardom ['sta:dəm] *n. Cin: etc:* célébrité *f*; vedettariat *m;* **to rise to s.,** devenir une vedette.

stardust ['sta:dʌst] *n. Astr:* amas *m* stellaire.

stare¹ ['stɛər] *n.* regard *m* fixe; **glassy, stony, s.,** regard terne, dur; **vacant s.,** regard vague.

stare² **1.** *v.i.* (*a*) regarder fixement; **to s. into the distance,** regarder au loin; (*b*) ouvrir de grands yeux. **2.** *v.ind.tr.* **to s. at s.o., sth.,** (i) regarder qn, qch., fixement; appuyer son regard sur qn; fixer qn; (ii) regarder qn effrontément; dévisager qn; (iii) regarder qn d'un air hébété. **3.** *v.tr.* **to s. s.o. in the face,** dévisager qn; *F:* **it's staring you in the face,** ça vous saute aux yeux. **staring** *a.* **1. s. eyes,** (i) yeux *mpl* fixes; (ii) yeux grands ouverts. **2.** (*a*) criard; (*b*) **stark s. mad,** complètement fou.

starfish ['sta:fiʃ] *n. Echin:* astérie *f*, étoile *f* de mer.

stargaze ['sta:geiz] *v.i. F:* **1.** faire de l'astronomie. **2.** bayer aux corneilles; rêvasser. **stargazing** *n.* **1.** astronomie *f*. **2.** rêvasserie(s) *f*(*pl*).

stargazer ['sta:geizər] *n. F:* (*a*) astronome *mf*; (*b*) rêveur, -euse; rêvasseur, -euse.

stark [sta:k] **1.** *a. esp. Lit:* (*a*) raide, rigide; **he lay s. in death,** il gisait dans la rigidité de la mort; (*b*) **s. madness,** folie pure; **the s. desolation of the region,** l'absolue désolation de la région; (*c*) **the s. towns of the North,** les mornes villes du Nord; (*d*) (lumière) crue. **2.** *adv.* **s. naked,** tout nu; à poil.

starkers ['sta:kəz] *a. & adv. F:* tout nu.

starkness ['sta:knis] *n.* **1.** raideur *f*; rigidité *f*. **2.** nudité *f*; aspect morne (des montagnes, etc.).

starless ['sta:lis] *a.* sans étoiles.

starlet ['sta:lit] *n. Cin: etc:* starlette *f*, starlet *f*.

starlight ['sta:lait] *n.* **1.** lumière *f* des étoiles; **in the, by, s.,** à la lumière des étoiles. **2. s. night,** nuit étoilée.

starling ['sta:liŋ] *n. Orn:* étourneau *m*.

starlit ['sta:lit] *a.* (ciel) étoilé; **s. night,** nuit étoilée.

starry ['sta:ri] *a.* **1.** (ciel) étoilé, (par)semé d'étoiles; **s. night,** nuit étoilée. **2.** *Lit:* étincelant, brillant.

starry-eyed [sta:ri'aid] *a.* (*a*) extasié, qui voit les choses en rose; (*b*) visionnaire; **a s.-e. scheme,** un projet utopique.

starshell ['sta:ʃel] *n. Mil:* obus éclairant, à étoiles.

star-spangled ['sta:spæŋg(ə)ld] *a.* étoilé; (par)semé d'étoiles; **the s.-s. banner,** la bannière étoilée (des États-Unis).

start¹ [sta:t] *n.* **1.** (*a*) tressaillement *m*, sursaut *m*, soubresaut *m*; **to wake with a s.,** se réveiller en sursaut; **he gave a s.,** il a tressailli, a sursauté; **to give s.o. a s.,** faire tressaillir qn; (*b*) saut *m*; mouvement brusque. **2.** (*a*) commencement *m*, début *m*; **for a s.,** pour débuter, pour commencer; **at the s.,** au début; **at the very s.,** de prime abord; **from s. to finish,** du commencement (jusqu')à la fin; **he had a good s. in life,** il a bien débuté dans la vie; **to give s.o. a s.,** lancer qn (dans les affaires, etc.); **to make a good s.,** bien commencer; **to make a fresh s.,** recommencer (sa carrière, sa vie); (*b*) départ *m*; *Aut:* démarrage *m*; *Av:* envol *m*; *Rac:* **false s.,** faux départ; (*c*) *Sp:* **to give s.o. a s.,** laisser qn partir le premier; donner un peu d'avance à qn; **to give s.o. a 60 metre(s) s.,** donner à qn 60 mètres d'avance.

start² **I.** *v.i.* **1.** (*a*) tressaillir, tressauter, sursauter; avoir un haut-le-corps; **he started at the sound of my voice,** il a tressailli au son de ma voix; **he started with surprise,** il a eu un mouvement de surprise; **to s. out of one's sleep,** se réveiller en sursaut; (*b*) se déplacer brusquement; **to s. to one's feet,** se lever d'un bond; **tears started from his eyes,** les larmes ont jailli de ses yeux. **2.** (*of timber*) se déjeter; (*of planks*) se disjoindre; (*of rivets*) se détacher. **3.** (*a*) commencer; débuter; **starting Monday,** à partir de lundi; **to s. again,** (i) recommencer; (ii) se ranger; refaire sa vie; **he had started as a doctor,** il avait commencé par être médecin; **to s. in business,** se mettre, se lancer, dans les affaires; **there were only six members to s. with,** il n'y avait que six membres au début; **to s. with,** en premier lieu, tout d'abord; **to s. on a job,** commencer, entamer, un travail; (*b*) **to s. (off, out, on one's way),** partir; se mettre en route; **to s. (off, out) on a journey,** commencer un voyage; **we s. tomorrow,** nous partons demain; **to s. again,** repartir; se remettre en route; **he started out to write a novel,** il a eu (d'abord) l'idée d'écrire un roman; (*c*) **to s. (off),** (*of car*) démarrer; se mettre en route; (*of train*) partir, s'ébranler; (*d*) **to s. (up),** (*of engine*) démarrer; se mettre en marche; (*of injector, dynamo*) s'amorcer; **the engine won't, refuses to, s.,** le moteur refuse de partir, de démarrer. **II** *v.tr.* **1.** commencer (un travail, etc.); amorcer (un sujet, etc.); entamer (une conversation, des négociations, etc.); **you started it,** c'est vous qui avez commencé; **to s. doing sth., to s. to do sth.,** commencer, se mettre, à faire qch.; **to s. crying again,** se remettre à pleurer; **it's just started raining,** voilà qu'il commence à pleuvoir. **2.** (*a*) **to s. a horse at a gallop,** faire partir un cheval au galop; (*b*) *Rac:* donner le signal du départ à (des coureurs, etc.); (*c*) *Ven:* lancer (un cerf); lever (un lièvre); faire partir (une perdrix, etc.). **3.** (*a*) lancer (une entreprise); fonder (un commerce); lancer (un journal); ouvrir (une école); *F:* **now you've started something!** en voilà une affaire! (*b*) **to s. a fire,** provoquer un incendie. **4.** (*a*) mettre en marche (une horloge); (*b*) **to s. (up),** mettre (un moteur) en marche; lancer (une machine); amorcer (un injecteur, une pompe). **5. if you s. him on this subject he will never stop,** si vous le lancez sur ce sujet il ne tarira pas; **to s. s.o. in business,** lancer qn dans les affaires. **starting** *n.* **1.** tressaillement *m*; sursaut *m*. **2.** (*a*) commencement *m*, début *m*; **s. salary,** traitement initial, de début; (*b*) départ *m*; **s. point, place,** point *m* de départ; **s. signal,** signal *m* de, du, départ; *Sp:* **s. line, block,** ligne *f*, bloc *m*, de départ; **s. pistol,** pistolet *m* de starter; *Turf:* **s. price,** dernière cote avant le départ. **3.** (*a*) mise *f* en route, en train (d'une entreprise, etc.); (*b*) **s. (up),** mise en marche, démarrage *m* (d'un moteur, etc.); lancement *m* (d'une machine); déclenchement *m* (d'un mécanisme); amorçage *m* (d'une dynamo, etc.); *Aut: O:* **s. handle,** manivelle *f*; (*c*) *Ven:* lancer *m* (du gibier).

starter ['stɑːtər] *n.* **1.** (*a*) **to be an early s.,** partir, commencer son travail, de bonne heure; (*b*) *Sp:* partant *m*. **2.** *Sp: etc:* starter *m*; **under starter's orders,** sous les ordres du starter. **3.** (*device*) (*a*) *Mec.E: I.C.E:* démarreur *m*; dispositif *m* de mise en marche; **s. motor,** moteur *m* auxiliaire de démarrage; (*b*) *El:* (rhéostat *m*) démarreur; rhéostat de démarrage. **4.** *F:* (*a*) = hors-d'œuvre *m inv* (ou potage *m*); entrée *f*; **what will you have for a s.?** qu'est-ce que vous prendrez pour commencer? (*b*) **for starters,** pour commencer; (tout) d'abord.

startle ['stɑːtl] *v.tr.* effrayer, alarmer (qn); faire sursauter (qn); **she was startled to see him so pale,** elle a été saisie de le voir si pâle. **startled** *a.* effrayé; (cri) d'alarme, d'effroi; **she was quite s.,** elle est restée toute saisie. **startling** *a.* (*of noise, etc.*) effrayant; (*of news, etc.*) renversant; (événement) sensationnel; **s. resemblance,** ressemblance saisissante.

starvation [stɑː'veiʃ(ə)n] *n.* privation *f*, manque *m*, de nourriture; famine *f*; **to die of s.,** mourir de faim.

starve [stɑːv] **1.** *v.i.* (*a*) **to s. (to death),** mourir de faim; (*b*) manquer de nourriture; endurer la faim; *F:* **I'm starving,** je meurs, je crève, de faim; (*c*) (*of tree, plant*) dépérir; s'étioler. **2.** *v.tr.* (*a*) faire mourir (qn) de faim; **to s. out,** affamer (une ville, une garnison); **to s. a garrison into surrender,** réduire une garnison par la faim; (*b*) priver (qn) de nourriture; *Med:* soumettre (un malade) à un régime affamant. **starved** *a.* (*a*) affamé; famélique; **he looks half s.,** il a l'air famélique; (*b*) **s. of affection,** privé d'affection. **starving** **1.** *a.* affamé. **2.** *n.* privation *f* de nourriture; *Med*: régime affamant.

stash [stæʃ] *v.tr. F:* cacher, planquer (qch.); **to s. sth. away,** mettre qch. à l'abri; planquer qch.

state¹ [steit] *n.* **1.** (*a*) état *m*, condition *f*; situation *f*; **in a good s.,** en bon état; en bonne condition; **here's a nice, a pretty, s. of affairs,** nous voilà bien! c'est du joli, du propre! (*b*) état; **body in a s. of rest,** corps *m* à l'état de repos, au repos; **s. of health,** état de santé; **I am not in a fit s. to travel,** je ne suis pas en état de voyager; **the married s.,** le mariage; **the single s.,** le célibat; **s. of mind,** disposition *f* d'esprit; *F:* **to be in a a terrible s.,** être dans tous ses états. **2.** (*a*) rang *m*, dignité *f*; **he lived in a style befitting his s.,** il vivait sur un pied digne de son rang; (*b*) pompe *f*, parade *f*, apparat *m*; *Adm:* représentation *f* (d'un ambassadeur, etc.); **to live in s.,** mener grand train; **to travel in s.,** voyager en grand apparat; **to dine in s.,** dîner en grand gala; (*of body*) **to lie in s.,** être exposé (sur un lit de parade); **lying in s.,** exposition *f* (d'un corps); **he was in his robes of s.,** il était en costume d'apparat; (*c*) **s. carriage, s. coach,** voiture *f* d'apparat; **s. ball,** grand bal officiel; **s. apartments,** grands appartements; salons *m* d'apparat. **3.** (*a*) *Fr.Hist:* **the States General,** les États généraux; (*b*) (*Channel Islands*) **the States,** l'Assemblée législative. **4.** (*a*) *Pol:* **the S.,** l'État; **Church and S.,** l'Église et l'État; **Secretary of S.,** (i) secrétaire *m* d'État; (ii) *U.S:* = Ministre *m* des Affaires étrangères; *U.S:* **S. Department** = Ministère *m* des Affaires étrangères; **affairs of S.,** affaires *fpl* d'État; **s. documents, papers,** documents officiels; papiers *mpl* d'État; **s. church,** église *f* d'État; **s. control,** étatisme; **to bring an industry under s. control,** étatiser une industrie; **s.-aided industry,** industrie subventionnée par l'État; *U.S:* **S. university,** université subventionnée et contrôlée par l'État; (*b*) état, nation *f*; **the United States of America,** *F:* **the States,** les États-Unis (d'Amérique).

state² *v.tr.* **1.** (*a*) énoncer, déclarer, affirmer (qch.); **this condition was expressly stated,** cette condition était expressément énoncée; **the receipt should s. the source of payment,** la quittance doit énoncer l'origine de l'argent; **please s. below . . .,** veuillez noter en bas . . .; **I have stated my opinion,** j'ai donné mon opinion; (*b*) exposer (une réclamation, etc.); *Jur:* **to s. the case,** faire l'exposé des faits; (*c*) *Mth:* poser, énoncer (un problème). **2.** arrêter, fixer (une heure, une date); **at stated intervals,** à intervalles réglés.

stateless ['steitlis] *a.* apatride; **s. person,** apatride *mf.*

stateliness ['steitlinis] *n.* majesté *f*; aspect imposant; grandeur *f*; dignité *f.*

stately ['steitli] *a.* **1.** majestueux; imposant; **the s. homes of England,** les châteaux historiques de l'Angleterre. **2.** plein de dignité; noble, élevé; **s. bearing,** allure pleine de majesté.

statement ['steitmənt] *n.* **1.** (*a*) exposition *f*, exposé *m*, énoncé *m* (des faits, de la situation, etc.); rapport *m*, compte rendu, relation *f*; **official s. (to the press),** communiqué *m*; **he made the following s. . . .,** il a déclaré que . . .; **bare s. of the facts,** simple énoncé des faits; **according to his own s.,** suivant sa propre déclaration; *Jur:* **the statements made by the witnesses,** les dépositions *f* des témoins; (*b*) assertion *f*, affirmation *f*; **a s. appeared in the press to the effect that . . .,** il fut affirmé dans la presse que . . .. **2.** *Com:* **s. of account,** état *m* de compte; relevé *m* de compte; bordereau *m* de compte; **monthly s.,** fin *f* de mois; **bank s.,** relevé de compte; (*in bankruptcy*) **s. of affairs,** bilan *m* de liquidation.

stateroom ['steitru:m] *n.* **1.** chambre *f* d'apparat; grand appartement. **2.** (*a*) *Nau:* cabine *f* de luxe; (*b*) *NAm: Rail: O:* (compartiment *m* de) wagon-lit *m.*

statesman, *pl.* **-men** ['steitsmən] *n.* **1.** homme d'État. **2.** *NAm:* homme politique; = député *m.*

statesmanlike ['steitsmənlaik] *a.* (*of attitude, etc.*) d'homme d'État; diplomatique.

statesmanship ['steitsmənʃip] *n.* l'art *m* de gouverner.

static ['stætik] *a.* **1.** (électricité, etc.) statique. **2.** statique; immuable; **the situation remains s.,** la situation n'a pas changé.

statics ['stætiks] *n.pl.* **1.** *Mec:* (*usu. with sg. const.*) la statique. **2.** *W.Tel:* parasites *mpl.*

station¹ ['steiʃ(ə)n] *n.* **1.** (*a*) position *f*, place *f*; poste *m*; emplacement *m*; **to take up one's s.,** prendre sa place; se rendre à son poste; **fire s.,** poste d'incendie; *Mil: etc:* **action stations,** postes de combat; (*b*) station *f*, poste; **naval s.,** station navale; port de guerre; **military s.,** poste militaire; garnison *f*; **field dressing s.,** poste de secours; *Av:* **air s.,** base aérienne, d'aviation; *Nau:* **lifeboat s.,** station de sauvetage; *Meteor:* **weather s.,** station météo(rologique); (*c*) **police s.,** *F:* **the s.,** commissariat *m*, poste, de police; **fire s.,** poste, caserne *f*, de pompiers; (*d*) **power s.,** centrale *f* électrique; **atomic power s.,** centrale atomique; *W. Tel: etc:* **broadcasting s.,** poste émetteur, d'émission, de radiodiffusion; (*e*) *Aut:* **petrol, filling, service, s.,** *NAm:* **gas s.,** poste d'essence; station-service *f*, *pl.* stations-service; (*f*) *Nat. Hist:* habitat *m* (d'un animal, d'une plante); (*g*) *Ecc:* **the stations of the Cross,** le chemin de la Croix. **2.** *Austr: N.Z:* ferme *f* (et ses dépendances); **sheep s.,** élevage *m* de moutons. **3.** position, condition *f*; rang *m*; **s. in life,** situation sociale; *O:* **to marry below one's s.,** faire une mésalliance; se mésallier. **4.** (*a*) **(railway) s.,** gare *f*; **underground s.,** station de métro; **passenger, goods, s.,** gare de voyageurs, de marchandises; **s. hotel,** hôtel *m* de la gare; (*b*) **bus, coach, s.,** gare routière; (*c*) *Aut:* **s. wagon,** break *m.*

station² *v.tr.* (*a*) placer, mettre (qn dans un endroit); **he stationed himself behind a door,** il s'est posté derrière une porte; (*b*) désigner son poste à (un soldat); poster (des troupes); (*c*) **to be stationed at . . .,** (i) *Mil:* être stationné, être en garnison, à . . .; (ii) *Navy:* être en station à . . ..

stationary ['steiʃən(ə)ri] *a.* **1.** stationnaire; immobile; (voiture) en stationnement; **to remain s.,** rester stationnaire, immobile; *Mil:* **s. target,** cible *f* fixe. **2.** (*a*) fixe; installé à demeure; *Mec.E:* **s. shaft,** arbre *m* fixe; (*b*) *Mil:* **s. troops,** troupes *fpl* sédentaires.

stationer ['steiʃənər] *n.* papetier *m*; **stationer's shop,** papeterie *f.*

stationery ['steiʃən(ə)ri] *n.* papeterie *f*; **office s.,** fournitures *fpl* de bureau; *Adm:* **the S. Office,** le Service des fournitures et des publications de l'Administration.

stationman, -woman, *pl.* **-men, -women** ['steiʃənmæn, -wumən; -men, -wimin] *n.* employé(e) de station de métro.

station-master ['steiʃənmɑ:stər] *n.m.* chef de gare.

statistic [stə'tistik] *n.* **1.** élément *m* d'un tableau statistique; **statistics for 1980,** statistiques *fpl* pour 1980; **vital statistics,** (i) statistiques démographiques; (ii) *F:* mensurations *fpl* (d'une femme). **2.** (*usu. with sg. const.*) **statistics,** la statistique.

statistical [stə'tistik(ə)l] *a.* statistique; **s. tables,** statistiques *fpl.* **-ally** *adv.* statistiquement.

statistician [stætis'tiʃ(ə)n] *n.* statisticien, -ienne.

stator ['steitər] *n. Mch: El:* stator *m* (d'une turbine).

statuary ['stætjuəri] **1.** *a.* (art, marbre, etc.) statuaire. **2.** *n.* (*pers.*) statuaire *mf.* **3.** *n.* (*a*) la statuaire; l'art *m* statuaire; (*b*) *coll.* statues *fpl.*

statue ['stætju:] *n.* statue *f*; **don't stand there like a s.!** ne reste pas là comme une souche!

statuesque [stætju(:)'esk] *a.* sculptural, -aux; (beauté, etc.) plastique.

statuette [stætju(:)'et] *n.* statuette *f.*

stature ['stætjər] *n.* stature *f*; taille *f*; **to be short of s.,** (être) de petite taille; (*of author, etc.*) **it will increase his s.,** sa réputation y gagnera.

status ['steitəs] *n.* (*a*) statut légal (de qn); **personal s.,** statut personnel; (*b*) *Adm:* **civil s.,** état civil; (*c*) condition *f*, position *f*, rang *m*; **social s.,** rang social; **s. symbol,** signe extérieur de prestige, *F:* de standing; **with no official s.,** sans titre officiel.

status quo ['steitəs'kwou] *n.* statu quo *m inv.*

statute ['stætju:t] *n.* **1.** (*a*) *Jur:* acte *m* du Parlement; loi *f*, ordonnance *f*; **s. law,** droit écrit; jurisprudence *f*; **s. book,** code *m* (des lois); (*b*) **the statutes of God,** les ordonnances de Dieu **2. statutes,** statuts *mpl*, règlements *mpl* (d'une société).

statutory ['stætjut(ə)ri] *a.* **1.** établi, fixé, imposé, par la loi; réglementaire; (*of offence*) prévu par la loi; **s. holiday,** fête légale; **s. declaration,** (i) attestation *f* (en lieu de serment); (ii) acte *m* de notoriété; **s. regulations,** règlements *mpl* statutaires. **2.** statutaire; conforme aux statuts.

staunch¹ [stɔ:n(t)ʃ] *a.* **1.** (*of pers.*) sûr, dévoué; (courage) inébranlable; **s. friend,** ami à toute épreuve; **s. socialist,** socialiste convaincu(e). **2.** (*of ship*) étanche. **-ly** *adv.* avec fermeté; avec résolution.

staunch² [stɔ:n(t)ʃ, stɑ:n(t)ʃ] *v.tr.* **1.** étancher (le sang). **2. to s. a wound,** étancher le sang d'une blessure.

staunchness ['stɔ:n(t)ʃnis] *n.* **1.** fermeté *f*; dévouement *m.* **2.** (*a*) étanchéité *f.*

stave¹ [steiv] *n.* **1.** (*a*) *Coop:* **barrel staves,** douves *fpl* pour tonneaux; (*b*) bâton *m*; (*c*) échelon *m* (d'une échelle). **2.** *Pros:* stance *f*, strophe *f* (d'un poème). **3.** *Mus:* portée *f.*

stave² *v.tr.* (*p.t.* **staved;** *p.p.* **staved,** *esp. Nau:* **stove** [stouv]) **1.** *Coop:* garnir (un tonneau) de douves. **2. to s. in,** défoncer, enfoncer (une barrique, un bateau, etc.). **stave off** *v.tr.* détourner, écarter (un ennui, etc.); prévenir, parer à (un danger); conjurer (un désastre); **to s. off hunger,** tromper la faim.

stay¹ [stei] *n.* **1.** séjour *m* (dans une ville, etc.); visite *f* (chez un ami); **fortnight's s.,** séjour de quinze jours. **2.** (*a*) *A: & Lit:* retard *m*; (*b*) *Jur:* **s. of proceedings,** suspension *f* d'instances; **s. of execution,** sursis *m*.

stay² **I** *v.i.* **1.** (*a*) *A:* s'arrêter; (*b*) (*in imper.*) **s.!** attendez! **2.** (*a*) rester; demeurer sur les lieux; **s. there!** tenez-vous là! *F:* **to s. put,** (i) rester en place; refuser de bouger; (ii) ne plus changer; **I shall s. put,** j'y suis, j'y reste; **to s. at home,** rester à la maison, chez soi; **to s. in bed,** rester au lit; garder le lit; **to s. to, for, dinner,** rester (à) dîner; **he has come to s.,** il est venu (i) passer quelques jours chez nous, (ii) habiter chez nous; **this word is here to s.,** ce mot est entré dans la langue; (*b*) séjourner, demeurer quelque temps (**in a place,** dans un endroit); **to s. at a hotel,** (i) descendre, (ii) être installé, à un hôtel; **to s. with s.o.,** faire une visite à qn; passer quelque temps, quelques jours, chez qn; **we are staying with relations,** nous sommes chez des parents. **3.** *Rac:* **he can s. five kilometres,** il peut fournir une course de cinq kilomètres; **horse that can s.,** cheval qui a du fond. **II** *v.tr.* **1.** *A: & Lit:* arrêter (le progrès de qn); enrayer (une épidémie); **to s. the course of events,** endiguer la marche des événements; **to s. s.o.'s arm, hand,** retenir le bras de qn; **to s. one's hand,** se retenir. **2.** *Jur: etc:* remettre, ajourner (une décision, etc.); suspendre (son jugement, etc.); **to s. judgment,** surseoir à un jugement. **stay away** *v.i.* ne pas venir; s'absenter. **stay down** *v.i. Sch:* redoubler (une classe). **stay in** *v.i.* (*a*) ne pas sortir; rester à la maison; (*b*) *Sch:* être en retenue. **staying** *n.* **1. s. power,** résistance *f*; endurance *f*; (*of horse*) **to have good s. power,** avoir du fond. **2.** (*a*) *A: & Lit:* arrêt *m* (du progrès de qch., etc.); enraiement *m* (d'une épidémie, etc.); (*b*) *Jur: etc:* ajournement *m* (d'une décision, etc.). **stay on** *v.i.* rester encore quelque temps. **stay out** *v.i.* (*a*) rester dehors; ne pas rentrer; **to s. out all night,** découcher; (*b*) *Ind:* **it was decided to s. out,** on a décidé que la grève continuerait. **stay up** *v.i.* (i) ne pas se coucher; veiller; **to s. up late,** veiller tard; (ii) (*of child*) se coucher plus tard que d'habitude.

stay³ *n.* **1.** (*a*) support *m*, soutien *m*; *Arb:* tuteur *m;* (*b*) *Const: Mec.E: etc:* support, étai *m*, étançon *m*. **2.** *Cost: O:* **stays,** corset *m*.

stay⁴ *v.tr. Const: etc:* **to s. (up),** étayer, étançonner, accorer (un mur, une maison).

stay⁵ *n.* **1.** *Nau:* étai *m* (de mât). **2.** *Nau:* (*of ship*) **to be in stays,** être pris vent devant.

stay⁶ **1.** *v.tr.* hauban(n)er (un mât, un poteau, etc.). **2.** *Nau:* (*a*) *v.tr.* faire virer de bord (un navire) vent devant; (*b*) *v.i.* (*of ship*) virer de bord vent devant.

stay-at-home ['steiət(h)oum] *a. & n.* casanier, -ière.

stayer ['steiər] *n. Sp:* (*a*) coureur *m* de fond; stayer *m*; (*b*) cheval *m* qui a du fond.

stead [sted] *n. Lit:* **1. to stand s.o. in good s.,** être fort utile à qn. **2. in s.o.'s s.,** à la place, au lieu, de qn.

steadfast ['stedfɑːst] *a.* ferme, stable; inébranlable; **s. in love, in adversity,** constant en amour, dans l'adversité. **-ly** *adv.* fermement; avec constance.

steadfastness ['stedfɑːstnis] *n.* fermeté *f* (d'esprit); constance *f*; ténacité *f* (de caractère).

steadiness ['stedinis] *n.* **1.** fermeté *f*, sûreté *f*; **s. of hand,** sûreté de main. **2.** fermeté (d'esprit); assiduité *f*, persévérance *f*, application *f*. **3.** (*a*) régularité *f* (de mouvement, d'action); (*b*) stabilité *f*; *St.Exch:* **s. of prices,** tenue *f* des prix; (*c*) fixité *f*, rigidité *f*. **4.** (*of pers.*) conduite rangée, posée; sagesse *f*.

steady¹ ['stedi] **1.** *a.* (*a*) ferme, solide; fixe, rigide; **to make a table s.,** mettre une table en bon équilibre; **to keep s.,** ne pas bouger; **to have a s. hand,** avoir la main sûre; **with a s. hand,** d'une main assurée, ferme; **to be s. on one's legs,** être d'aplomb sur ses jambes; **s. horse,** cheval *m* calme; (*b*) continu, soutenu; persistant; régulier; (pouls) égal; *Com:* (marché) soutenu; *Sp:* **to play a s. game,** avoir un jeu régulier; **s. progress,** progrès ininterrompus; **s. pace,** allure modérée; **s. weather,** temps établi; **s. breeze,** brise étale, franche; **s. rain,** pluie persistante; *Com:* **s. demand for . . .,** demande suivie pour . . .; **s. prices,** prix *mpl* fixes; (*c*) (*of pers.*) ferme, constant; assidu; **s. worker,** travailleur appliqué, assidu; (*d*) (*of pers.*) rangé, posé; sage. **2.** *adv. & int.* (*a*) **s.!** (i) ne bougez pas! (ii) attention (de ne pas tomber)! *F:* **s. (on)!** doucement! (*b*) *adv. P:* (*of young man and woman*) **to go s. with s.o.,** sortir avec qn. **3.** *n.* (*a*) support *m* (pour la main, etc.); (*b*) *Mec.E:* **s. (rest),** lunette *f* (d'un tour, etc.); (*c*) *F:* **my s.,** mon petit, ma petite, ami(e). **-ily** *adv.* **1.** solidement, fermement; **to walk s.,** marcher d'un pas ferme. **2.** (*a*) régulièrement; sans arrêt; **s. increasing output,** rendement *m* augmentant de façon soutenue; **his health grows s. worse,** sa santé va (en) empirant; (*b*) sans à-coups. **3.** fermement; avec fermeté; assidûment; **to work s. at sth.,** travailler fermement, assidûment, à qch.; **to refuse s. to do sth.,** refuser fermement de faire qch. **4.** (se conduire) d'une manière rangée, posée.

steady² **1.** *v.tr.* (*a*) raffermir, affermir; **to s. one's hand,** assurer sa main; **to s. oneself against sth.,** s'étayer contre qch.; **to s. the nerves,** calmer, détendre, les nerfs; (*b*) **marriage has steadied him,** le mariage l'a rangé. **2.** *v.i.* **to s. (down),** reprendre son aplomb; (*of boat, etc.*) retrouver son équilibre; **prices are steadying,** les prix *mpl* se raffermissent.

steak [steik] *n. Cu:* (*a*) tranche *f* (de viande, de poisson); darne *f* (de saumon); (*b*) bifteck *m*, steak *m*; (*cut from the ribs*) entrecôte *f*; **fillet s.,** tournedos *m*; **s. and chips,** steak frites; (*c*) **s. tartare,** steak tartare; *NAm:* **Salisbury s.,** côtelette *f* de viande hachée accompagnée d'une sauce.

steal [stiːl] *v.* (*p.t.* **stole** [stoul]; *p.p.* **stolen** ['stoul(ə)n]) **1.** *v.tr.* (*a*) voler, dérober, soustraire (**sth. from s.o.,** qch. à qn); **stolen goods,** objets volés; **I've had my purse stolen,** on m'a volé mon porte-monnaie; *B:* **thou shalt not s.,** tu ne déroberas point; (*b*) dérober (un baiser); **to s. s.o.'s heart,** séduire le cœur de qn; **to s. a few hours from one's studies,** dérober quelques heures à ses études; (*c*) **to s. a glance at s.o.,** jeter un coup d'œil furtif à qn; regarder qn à la dérobée, d'un œil furtif; (*d*) **to s. a march on s.o.,** prendre les devants sur qn; devancer qn. **2.** *v.i.* **to s. away, in, out,** s'en aller, entrer, sortir, à la dérobée, furtivement; **he stole into the room,** il s'est faufilé, glissé, dans la pièce. **stealing** *n.* vol *m*.

stealer ['stiːlər] *n.* voleur, -euse (**of,** de).

stealth [stelθ] *n.* (*only in the phr.*) **by s.,** à la dérobée; furtivement; (faire qch.) sous main, en cachette.

stealthiness ['stelθinis] *n.* caractère furtif (d'une action, etc.).

stealthy ['stelθi] *a.* furtif; (regard) dérobé, à la dérobée; **with a s. step,** d'un pas furtif; à pas de loup, à pas feutrés. **-ily** *adv.* furtivement; à la dérobée.

steam¹ [stiːm] *n.* (*a*) vapeur *f* (d'eau); buée *f*; **s. cooking,** cuisson *f* à la vapeur; **s. iron,** fer *m* à vapeur; **s. bath,** bain *m* de vapeur; (*b*) *Ph: Mch:* vapeur; **dry s.,** vapeur sèche; **s. power,** la vapeur (en tant qu'énergie); **s. engine,** machine *f* à vapeur; *Mch: etc:* **to get up, to raise, s.,** mettre (une chaudière) sous pression; (*of pers.*) **to get up s.,** rassembler toutes ses forces, toute son énergie; *Nau:* **engine under s.,** machine *f* sous pression, en pression; **at full s.,** à toute vapeur; *Nau:* **full s. ahead!** en avant toute! **to keep up s.,** (i) tenir (de) la pression; (ii) *F:* (*of pers.*) ne pas se relâcher; **to run out of s.,** (i) *Mch:* ne plus être sous pression; (ii) *F:* (*of pers.*) être épuisé; **to let off, blow off, s.,** (i) *Mch:* lâcher, laisser échapper, (de) la vapeur; (ii) *F:* (*of pers.*) dépenser son trop-plein d'énergie; (iii) *F:* (*of pers.*) donner libre cours à ses sentiments; (*of damaged ship*) **to proceed under its own s.,** marcher par ses seuls moyens; **I can do it under my own s.,** je puis le faire tout seul, sans aide.

steam² **1.** *v.tr.* (*a*) *Cu:* cuire (des légumes, etc.) à la vapeur, à l'étuvée; **steamed potatoes,** pommes *fpl* vapeur; (*b*) passer (qch.) à la vapeur, étuver (qch.); **to s. open an envelope,** décacheter une lettre à la vapeur. **2.** *v.i.* (*a*) jeter, exhaler, de la vapeur; fumer; **horses steaming with sweat,** chevaux *m* fumants (de sueur); (*b*) marcher (à la vapeur); **to s. ahead,** (i) avancer (à la vapeur); (ii) *F:* faire des progrès rapides; **the train steamed out of the station,** le train a quitté la gare; (*c*) *Mch:* **to s. up,** mettre la vapeur; *F:* (*of pers.*) **to get (all) steamed up,** perdre son sang-froid; se laisser emporter (par la colère); (*d*) (*of window, windscreen, etc.*) **to s. up,** s'embuer. **steaming 1.** *a.* fumant; *a. phr.* **s. hot,** tout chaud. **2.** *n.* (*a*) *Cu:* cuisson *f* à la vapeur, à l'étuvée; (*b*) étuvage *m*, injection *f* de vapeur.

steamboat ['stiːmbout] *n.* (bateau *m* à) vapeur *m*.

steamer ['stiːmər] *n.* **1.** *Nau:* vapeur *m*. **2.** *Dom.Ec:* marmite *f* à vapeur.

steamroller¹ [stiːm'roulər] *n.* (*a*) *Civ.E:* rouleau *m* compresseur; (*b*) *F:* force *f* irrésistible, qui écrase toute opposition.

steamroller² *v.tr.* (*a*) *Civ.E:* *A:* cylindrer (une route); (*b*) *F:* écraser (l'opposition).

steamship ['stiːmʃip] *n.* (bateau *m* à) vapeur *m*.

steamy ['stiːmi] *a.* plein de vapeur; couvert de buée.

steed [stiːd] *n. Lit:* coursier *m*, destrier *m*.

steel¹ [stiːl] *n.* **1.** *Metall:* acier *m*; **rolled s.,** acier laminé; **s. plated,** cuirassé; **the iron and s. industry,** l'industrie *f* sidérurgique; la sidérurgie; **a grip, a will, of s.,** une poigne, une volonté, de fer; **nerves of s.,** nerfs *mpl* d'acier. **2.** *A: & Lit:* fer *m*, épée *f*; lame *f*. **3.** (*for sharpening knives*) affiloir *m*; fusil *m*.

steel² *v.tr.* **to s. oneself, one's heart, to do sth.,** (i) s'endurcir à faire qch.; (ii) s'armer de courage pour faire qch.; **to s. oneself against sth.,** se cuirasser contre qch.

steelclad ['stiːlklæd] *a.* couvert, revêtu, d'acier; (*of ancient knight*) bardé de fer.

steelwork ['stiːlwəːk] *n.* **1.** (*a*) **constructional s.,** profilés *mpl* pour constructions; (*b*) *Aut: etc:* tôleries *fpl*. **2.** (*usu. with sg. const.*) **steelworks,** aciérie *f*.

steely ['stiːli] *a.* **1.** d'acier. **2.** dur, inflexible; (regard, etc.) d'acier. **3.** (bleu) acier.

steelyard ['stiːljɑːd, 'stiljəd] *n.* (balance) romaine *f*.

steep¹ [stiːp] **1.** *a.* (*a*) escarpé; à pic; raide; (pente) rapide; (chemin) à forte pente; **s. gradient,** forte pente; pente raide, rapide; **s. climb,** rude montée *f*; montée rude, raide; **s. rise in prices,** hausse considérable des prix; (*b*) *F:* fort, raide; **that's a bit s.!** c'est un peu fort! **s. price,** prix exorbitant. **2.** *n. Lit:* pente rapide; escarpement *m*. **-ly** *adv.* en pente rapide; à pic; **road that climbs s.,** route à forte pente; (*of prices*) **to rise s.,** monter en flèche.

steep² *n. Ind:* **1.** = STEEPING; **to put sth. in s.,** mettre qch. en trempe. **2.** bain *m* (de macération).

steep³ **1.** *v.tr.* (*a*) *Ind: etc:* baigner, tremper; mouiller (le linge); rouir (le lin); *Tan:* tremper, (les peaux); (*b*) saturer, imbiber (qch. de qch.); **terrace steeped in sunshine,** terrasse baignée de soleil; **steeped in prejudice,** imbibé de préjugés; **to s. oneself in the atmosphere of the Middle Ages,** se tremper, se plonger, dans l'atmosphère du moyen âge. **2.** *v.i.* tremper; (*of flax*) rouir. **steeping** *n. Ind: etc:* trempage *m*, macération *f*, trempe *f*; mouillage *m* (du linge); rouissage *m* (du chanvre).

steepen ['stiːp(ə)n] *v.t.* (*a*) (*of slope, etc.*) devenir plus raide; s'escarper; (*b*) (*of prices*) augmenter.

steeple ['stiːpl] *n.* (*a*) clocher *m*; (*b*) flèche *f* (de clocher).

steeplechase ['stiːpltʃeis] *n. Turf:* steeple-chase *m*, *pl.* steeple-chases; steeple *m*.

steeplechaser ['stiːpltʃeisər] *n.* **1.** cavalier *m* qui monte en steeple-chases. **2.** (*horse*) steeple-chaser *m*.

steeplechasing ['stiːpltʃeisiŋ] *n. Turf:* steeple-chases *mpl*.

steeplejack ['stiːpldʒæk] *n.* réparateur *m* de clochers, de cheminées d'usines.

steepness ['stiːpnis] *n.* raideur *f*, escarpement *m* (d'une pente).

steer¹ ['stiər] *v.tr. & i.* (*a*) *Nau:* gouverner (un navire); barrer (un yacht); *Aut:* conduire, diriger (une voiture); **to s. a northerly course, to s. north,** faire route au nord; mettre le cap sur le nord; **to s. clear of sth., s.o.,** éviter qch., qn; (*with passive force*) **ship that steers well,** navire qui gouverne bien; (*b*) diriger (qn) (**towards,** vers); **to s. the conversation away from a subject,** détourner la conversation d'un sujet; **to s. the conversation round to another subject,** faire tourner, aiguiller, la conversation vers un autre sujet. **steering** *n.* **1.** (*a*) direction *f*, conduite *f* (d'un bateau, d'une voiture); (*b*) **s. (gear),** organes *mpl* de transmission d'un moteur; *Aut:* (i) timonerie *f*; (ii) boîte *f* de direction; *Nau:* appareil *m* à gouverner; *Av:* direction; **s. wheel,** (i) *Nau:* roue *f* du gouvernail; (ii) *Aut:* volant *m*; *Aut:* **s. column,** colonne *f* de direction; (*c*) **s. committee,** comité *m* d'organisation. **2.** *Nau:* manœuvre *f* de la barre.

steer² *n.* (*a*) jeune bœuf *m*; bouvillon *m*; (*b*) bœuf.

steerage ['stiəridʒ] *n. Nau: A:* emménagements *mpl* pour passagers de troisième classe; entrepont *m*.

steerageway ['stiəridʒwei] *n.* vitesse *f* nécessaire pour gouverner; erre *f* (pour gouverner).

steersman, *pl.* **-men** ['stiəzmən] *n.m. Nau:* homme de barre; timonier.

stellar ['stelər] *a.* stellaire.

stellate ['steleit] *a. Nat.Hist:* étoilé; en étoile; radié.

stem¹ [stem] *n.* **1.** *Bot:* tige *f* (de plante, de fleur); queue *f* (de fruit, de feuille); pétiole *m*, pédoncule *m* (de fleur); tronc *m*, souche *f* (d'arbre). **2.** (*a*) pied *m*, patte *f* (de verre à boire); tige (de soupape, de clef); tuyau *m* (de pipe); (*b*) *Mus:* queue (d'une note). **3.** (*a*) souche (de famille); (*b*) *Ling:* thème *m* (étymologique), radical *m* (d'un mot). **4.** *N.Arch:* étrave *f*, avant *m*; **from s. to stern,** de l'avant à l'arrière.

stem² *v.* **(stemmed) 1.** *v.tr.* égrapper (des raisins). **2.** *v.i.* **to s. from sth.,** être issu de, provenir de, qch.; **much harm stemmed from this,** il en est résulté beaucoup de mal. **stemmed** *a.* **1.** (fleur, etc.) à tige, à queue; (verre) à pied, à patte. **2.** *Bot:* **long-s.,** longicaule; **thick-s.,** crassicaule.

stem³ **1.** *v.tr.* (*a*) contenir, endiguer (un cours d'eau); enrayer (une épidémie); (*b*) lutter contre (la marée); remonter (le courant); résister à (une attaque); **to s. the tide of . . .,** arrêter le flot de . . . . **2.** *v.i. Ski:* faire un stem.

stench [sten(t)ʃ] *n.* odeur infecte; puanteur *f*.

stencil¹ ['stens(ə)l] *n.* **1.** (*a*) patron (ajouré); poncif *m*, pochoir *m*; **s. plate,** pochoir; **coloured by s.,** colorié au patron; (*b*) **cipher s.,** grille *f*. **2.** peinture *f*, travail *m*, au poncif, au pochoir; tracé *m*. **3.** *Typewr: etc:* cliché *m*; stencil *m*; **s. paper,** papier *m* stencil.

stencil² *v.tr.* **(stencilled,** *NAm:* **stenciled)** (*a*) peindre, marquer, (qch.) au poncif, au patron, au pochoir; poncer, pocher, patronner (qch.); *Ind: Com:* marquer (une caisse, un ballot); (*b*) polycopier (une circulaire, etc.); tirer (une circulaire) au stencil.

sten-gun ['stengʌn] *n.* mitraillette *f* sten.

stenographer, *US:* **stenographist** [stə'nɔgrəfər, -fist] *n.* sténographe *mf*; *F:* sténo *mf*.

stenography [stə'nɔgrəfi] *n.* sténographie *f*.

stentorian [sten'tɔːriən] *a.* (voix) de stentor.

step¹ [step] *n.* **1.** pas *m*; **to take a s.,** faire un pas

(back, forward, en arrière, en avant); **to turn one's steps towards a place,** se diriger, diriger ses pas, vers un lieu; **at every s.,** à chaque pas; **s. by s.,** pas à pas; petit à petit; graduellement; **within a few steps of, from, the house,** à deux pas de la maison; **that's a great s. forward,** c'est déjà un grand pas de fait; **with a quick s.,** d'un pas rapide; **to tread in s.o.'s steps,** marcher sur les traces de qn. **2.** (*a*) pas, cadence *f*; *Mil: Mus:* **quick s.,** pas redoublé; pas accéléré, cadencé; **marching s.,** pas ordinaire; **to keep s., to be in s.,** marcher au pas; être au pas; **to fall into s.,** se mettre au pas; **to change s.,** changer de pas; **to break s.,** rompre le pas; **to be out of s.,** marcher à contre-pas de qn; (*b*) *El:* **alternators in s.,** alternateurs synchronisés; **alternators out of s.,** alternateurs déphasés; (*c*) **waltz s.,** pas de valse. **3.** (*a*) démarche *f*, mesure *f*; **a s. in the right direction,** un pas dans la bonne voie; **false s.,** fausse démarche; **to take the necessary steps,** faire, entreprendre, les démarches nécessaires; **to take steps to do sth.,** prendre des mesures pour faire qch.; **the first s. will be to . . .,** la première chose à faire, ce sera de . . .; (*b*) *F:* **to go up a s.,** avancer en grade. **4.** (*a*) marche *f*, degré *m* (d'un escalier); échelon *m*, marche (d'une échelle); marchepied *m* (d'un véhicule); **flight of steps,** (i) escalier; (ii) perron *m*; (*b*) *Geol:* **rock s.,** ressaut *m*; *Mount:* **to cut steps,** tailler. **5. (pair of) steps,** escabeau *m*, échelle double; *Av:* **steps,** passerelle *f*. **6.** cran *m*; **steps of a key,** dents *f* d'une clef.

step² *v.* **(stepped** [stept]) **1.** *v.i.* (*a*) faire un pas, des pas; marcher, aller; **to s. on s.o.'s foot,** marcher sur le pied de qn; **s. this way,** venez par ici; (*b*) **to s. back, forward,** faire un pas en arrière, en avant; **to s. aside to let s.o. pass,** s'écarter pour laisser passer qn; **s. in(side) for a moment,** entrez pour un moment. **2.** *v.tr.* (*a*) **to s. (off, out),** mesurer (une distance) au pas; (*b*) *F:* **to s. it with s.o.,** danser avec qn; (*c*) disposer en échelons; échelonner; recouper (un mur, un parapet); (*d*) *Nau:* dresser, arborer (un mât). **step down 1.** *v.tr. El:* dévolter (le courant); *Mec.E:* **to s. down the gear,** démultiplier la transmission. **2.** *v.i.* démissionner. **step in** *v.i.* intervenir; s'interposer. **step on** *v.i.* marcher sur (qch.); *F:* **to s. on the gas, to s. on it,** (i) *Aut:* appuyer sur l'accélérateur, *F:* sur le champignon; (ii) se dépêcher, se grouiller; **to s. on the brakes,** donner un coup de frein brusque. **step out** *v.i.* (*a*) sortir (de la maison, etc.); (*b*) allonger, forcer, le pas; **to s. out briskly,** marcher rapidement. **stepped** *a.* à gradins, en gradins; à étages; (engrenage) échelonné, en échelon; *Arch:* **s. gable,** pignon *m* à redans. **stepping** *n.* **1.** marche *f*, pas *mpl.* **2.** échelonnement *m*; **s. down,** (i) *El:* dévoltage *m*, (ii) *Mec.E:* démultiplication *f* (de la transmission); **s. up,** (i) *El:* survoltage *m*; (ii) *Mec.E:* multiplication *f* (d'un engrenage); (iii) augmentation *f* (de production, etc.); intensification *f* (d'une campagne, etc.). **step up** *v.tr.* (*a*) *El:* survolter (le courant); (*b*) augmenter (la production, etc.); intensifier (une campagne, etc.).

stepbrother ['stepbrʌðər] *n.m.* demi-frère, *pl.* demi-frères.

stepchild, *pl.* **-children** ['steptʃaild, -tʃildrən] *n.* beau-fils *m*, belle-fille *f*, *pl.* beaux-fils, belles-filles.

stepdaughter ['stepdɔːtər] *n.f.* belle-fille, *pl.* belles-filles.

stepfather ['stepfɑːðər] *n.m.* beau-père (second mari de la mère), *pl.* beaux-pères.

Stephen ['stiːvən] *Pr.n.m.* Étienne.

stepladder ['steplædər] *n.* escabeau *m.*

stepmother ['stepmʌðər] *n.f.* belle-mère (seconde femme du père), *pl.* belles-mères.

steppe [step] *n. Geog:* steppe *f.*

stepsister ['stepsistər] *n.f.* demi-sœur, *pl.* demi-sœurs.

stepson ['stepsʌn] *n.m.* beau-fils, *pl.* beaux-fils.

stereo, *pl.* **-os** ['steriou, -ouz; 'stiə-] *n. F:* **1.** = STEREOTYPE 1. **2.** = STEREOSCOPE. **3.** *Rec:* (*a*) *a.* stéréo *inv*; (*b*) *n.* (appareil *m*) stéréo *f.*

stereograph ['stiəriougræf, 'ster-] *n.* **1.** stéréographe *m.* **2.** stéréogramme *m*, vue *f* stéréographique.

stereophonic [steriə'fɔnik, stiə-] *a.* stéréophonique.

stereoscope ['steriəskoup, 'stiər-] *n. Opt:* stéréoscope *m.*

stereoscopic [steriou'skɔpik, 'stiə-] *a.* stéréoscopique.

stereotype¹ ['steriətaip, 'stiə-] *n.* (*a*) *Typ:* cliché *m*; (*b*) *Fig:* stéréotype *m.*

stereotype² *v.tr.* (*a*) *Typ:* stéréotyper, clicher; (*b*) *Fig:* stéréotyper. **stereotyped** *a.* (*a*) *Typ:* stéréotypé; (*b*) **s. phrase,** stéréotype *m*; cliché *m.*

sterile ['sterail] *a.* stérile.

sterility [ste'riliti] *n.* stérilité *f.*

sterilization [sterilai'zeiʃ(ə)n] *n.* stérilisation *f.*

sterilize ['sterilaiz] *v.tr.* stériliser; **sterilized milk,** lait stérilisé. **sterilizing** *n.* stérilisation *f.*

sterilizer ['sterilaizər] *n.* stérilisateur *m.*

sterling ['stəːliŋ] **1.** *a.* (*a*) (monnaie, or, argent) de bon aloi, d'aloi; (*b*) de bon aloi, vrai, solide; **s. qualities,** qualités *fpl* solides; **man of s. worth,** homme de valeur. **2.** *n.* (livre *f*) sterling *m*; **to pay in s.,** payer en livres sterling.

stern¹ [stəːn] *a.* sévère, dur. **-ly** *adv.* sévèrement, durement.

stern² *n.* **1.** *Nau:* arrière *m*; **s. light,** feu *m* d'arrière, de poupe. **2.** (*a*) *F:* (*of pers.*) postérieur *m*, derrière *m*; (*b*) *Ven:* queue *f* (d'un chien courant).

sternness ['stəːnnis] *n.* sévérité *f*; austérité *f*; dureté *f.*

sternum, *pl.* **-a, -ums** ['stəːnəm, -ə, -əmz] *n. Anat:* sternum *m.*

steroid ['stiərɔid] *n. Bio-Ch:* stéroïde *m.*

stertorous ['stəːtərəs] *a. Med:* stertoreux, ronflant.

stet¹ [stet] *Lt.imper. Typ:* bon; à maintenir.

stet² *v.tr.* **(stetted)** maintenir (un mot sur l'épreuve).

stethoscope ['steθəskoup] *n. Med:* stéthoscope *m.*

stetson ['stets(ə)n] *n. Cost:* chapeau mou à larges bords; stetson *m.*

stevedore ['stiːv(ə)dɔːr] *n.* docker *m*; arrimeur *m.*

Steven ['stiːvən] *Pr.n.m.* Étienne.

stew¹ [stjuː] *n.* (*a*) *Cu:* ragoût *m*; **Irish s.,** ragoût de mouton à l'irlandaise; (*b*) *F:* trouble *m* (de qn); **to be in a s.,** être dans tous ses états.

stew² **1.** *v.tr. Cu:* faire cuire (la viande) en ragoût, faire un ragoût de (qch.); **to s. fruit,** faire une compote de fruits. **2.** *v.i. Cu:* (*of meat*) mijoter; *F:* **to let s.o. s. in his own juice,** laisser qn cuire, mijoter, dans son jus; laisser mariner qn. **stewed** *a.* **1.** *Cu:* (*a*) **s. beef,** ragoût *m* de bœuf; bœuf *m* (à la) mode; **s. fruit,** compote *f* de fruits; (*b*) (thé) trop infusé. **2.** *F:* ivre. **stewing** *n.* **s. beef,** bœuf *m* pour ragoût; **s. pears,** poires *fpl* à cuire; **s. pan** = STEWPAN.

steward ['stjuəd] *n.* **1.** économe *m*, régisseur *m*, intendant *m* (d'une propriété). **2.** (*a*) économe (d'un collège); maître *m* d'hôtel (d'un cercle, etc.); (*b*) *Nau:* distributeur *m*; commis *m*, agent *m*, aux vivres; **steward's mate,** cambusier *m*; (*c*) *Nau: Av:* garçon *m* (de bord, de cabine); steward *m.* **3.** commissaire *m* (d'une réunion sportive, d'un bal). **4.** *Ind:* **shop s.,** délégué *m* d'atelier, d'usine, du personnel.

stewardess [stjuə'des] *n.f. Nau:* femme de chambre (de bord); stewardess; *Av:* **air s.,** hôtesse de l'air.

stewardship ['stjuədʃip] *n.* économat *m*, intendance *f.*

stewpan ['stjuːpæn] *n.* (grande) casserole.

stewpot ['stju:pɔt] *n.* cocotte *f*, fait-tout *m inv.*

stick¹ [stik] *n.* **1.** (*a*) bâton *m*; **in a cleft s.**, dans une impasse; **you're giving him a s. to beat you with,** vous lui donnez des verges *fpl* pour vous fouetter; **to take a lot of s,** être critiqué, éreinté; **the big s.**, la manière forte; (la politique de) la force; *Hort:* **pea sticks,** rames *fpl*; **hop sticks, vine sticks,** échalas *mpl*; (*b*) **(walking) s.**, canne *f*; (*c*) manche *m* (à balai, de parapluie); *F:* levier *m* (de changement de vitesse); baguette (de chef d'orchestre); *Av:* **control s.**, *F:* **joy s.**, manche à balai; (*d*) *Sp:* **(hockey, etc.) s.**, crosse *f*; **to give sticks,** couper; donner des crosses; (*e*) morceau *m* de bois; **to gather sticks,** ramasser du bois sec, du petit bois; **cocktail, cherry, s.**, bâtonnet *m* (pour cerise de cocktail); **swizzle s.**, agitateur *m* (pour cocktails, etc.); **not a s. was left standing,** tout était rasé; **my few sticks of furniture,** mes quelques meubles; **s. figure,** bonhomme dessiné, composé de bâtonnets; *Ent:* **s. insect,** phasme *m*, insecte-brindille *m*; (*f*) *Typ:* **(setting, composing) s.**, composteur *m*; (*g*) *F:* **he lives out in the sticks,** il habite un trou perdu, il vit dans la brousse. **2.** *F: O:* (*of pers.*) (*a*) **rum, queer, s.**, drôle de type, drôle de paroissien; **old s.**, vieille perruque; (*b*) personne *f* sans entrain; acteur *m* au jeu raide. **3.** bâton (de sucre d'orge, de cire à cacheter, etc.); bâton, canon *m* (de soufre); *El:* baguette *f* (de charbon); bâtonnet *m* (de dynamite). **4.** *Cu:* **s. of celery,** branche *f* de céleri; **s. of rhubarb,** tige *f* de rhubarbe; **s. of asparagus,** asperge *f*. **5.** *Mil: Av:* **s. of bombs,** chapelet *m* de bombes; **s. of parachutists,** stick *m* (de parachutistes).

stick² *v.* (*p.t. & p.p.* **stuck** [stʌk]) **I.** *v.tr.* **1.** (*a*) piquer, enfoncer (**sth. into sth.**, qch. dans qch.); **to s. a pin into sth.**, ficher une épingle dans qch.; **he stuck the spade into the ground,** il a planté la bêche dans le sol; **to get stuck in,** se mettre (i) à travailler, (ii) à manger; (*b*) **to s. pigs,** (i) (*of butcher*) égorger, saigner, les porcs; (ii) *Ven:* chasser le sanglier à l'épieu; (*c*) planter, fixer (**sth. on a spike,** qch sur une pointe). **2.** *F:* (*put*) **to s. one's hat on one's head,** mettre, planter, *F:* camper, son chapeau sur sa tête; **s. it in your pocket,** fourrez-le dans votre poche; **s. it in the corner, on the table,** collez ça dans le coin, mettez ça sur la table. **3.** coller, attacher; **to s. sth. on(to) sth.**, coller qch. à, sur, qch.; **trunk stuck all over with labels,** malle bardée d'étiquettes. **4.** *F:* supporter, endurer, souffrir (qn, qch.); **to s. it,** tenir le coup; tenir; **I can't s. it any longer,** je n'en peux plus; **I can't s. him,** je ne peux pas le sentir. **5.** *Hort:* ramer (des pois, etc.); mettre des tuteurs à (des plantes). **II.** *v.i.* **1. sewing left with a needle sticking in it,** ouvrage laissé avec une aiguille piquée dedans. **2.** (*a*) (se) coller, s'attacher, tenir (**to,** à); *Cu:* (*of rice, etc.*) **to s. (to the pan),** attacher; **the stamp won't s.**, le timbre ne colle pas; **his shirt stuck to his back,** il avait la chemise collée au dos; **the name stuck (to him),** ce nom lui est resté; **to s. by, to, a friend,** ne pas abandonner un ami; **friends should s. together,** les amis doivent se serrer les coudes; **to s. like a limpet, a leech, like glue, to s.o.**, se cramponner, s'accrocher, à qn; **to s. to one's post,** rester à son poste; **to s. to one's promise,** tenir sa promesse; **s. to it!** persévérez! ne lâchez pas! *F:* **to s. to one's guns,** ne pas en démordre; **to s. to an opinion,** maintenir une opinion, ne pas démordre d'une opinion; **to s. to (the) facts,** s'en tenir, s'attacher, aux faits; **to s. to the point,** ne pas s'écarter de la question; **to s. to the text,** serrer le texte de près; **I s. to what I said,** j'en suis pour ce que j'ai dit; **to stick with,** (i) se contenter de; (ii) rester fidèle à; (*b*) **to s. to sth.**, garder qch. pour soi; **s. to what you've got!** gardez vos biens! ne lâchez pas ce que vous avez; (*c*) *F:* rester; **he sticks to his room,** il ne sort pas de sa chambre; (*d*) *F:* **I'm stuck with it, him,** je ne peux pas m'en débarrasser; je l'ai sur le dos; **we're stuck with it,** il faut s'y résigner; (*e*) *F: O:* **he's stuck on her,** il est entiché d'elle. **3.** (*a*) **to s., to be stuck, to become stuck,** être pris, être engagé; (*in mud, etc.*) s'embourber, être embourbé; **to get stuck in a bog,** s'embourber dans un marécage; *F:* **he's an old s.-in-the-mud,** c'est un vieux plumeau; il retarde sur son siècle; (*of boat*) **to s. fast,** s'enliser (sur un banc de sable, dans la vase); **here I am stuck in hospital for six weeks,** me voilà cloué à l'hôpital pour six semaines; **I'm stuck,** je n'avance plus; je suis en panne; **the book's finished but I'm stuck for a title,** le livre est fini mais je ne trouve pas de titre; **stuck for money,** en panne d'argent; **to s., to be stuck (in a speech),** *F:* rester en carafe, en panne; (*b*) (*to be caught, jammed*) être pris, rester pris; s'enfoncer; s'empêtrer; (*of machine parts*) (se) coincer, gommer; *Aut:* (*of valve, cut-out*) rester collé; **the words stuck in his throat,** les mots lui restèrent dans la gorge; **it sticks in my throat,** je ne peux pas avaler, digérer, ça; **the lift has stuck,** l'ascenseur est coincé, en panne.
stick around *v.i. F:* attendre; **s. a.!** restez (si vous voulez)! **stick at** *v.tr.* (*a*) **to s. at a difficulty,** s'arrêter devant, *F:* rester en panne devant, une difficulté; **to s. at doing sth.**, se faire scrupule de faire qch.; **to s. at nothing,** ne reculer devant rien; (*b*) **to s. at sth.**, s'acharner à (faire) qch.; travailler à qch.; **s. at it!** persévérez! **stick down** *v.tr. F:* (*a*) **s. it down anywhere,** mettez-le, collez-le, n'importe où; **to s. sth. down in a notebook,** inscrire qch. sur un carnet; (*b*) fermer, coller (une enveloppe). **sticking 1.** *a.* collant, adhésif. **2.** *n.* (*a*) adhérence *f*, adhésion *f* (**to,** à); **s. plaster,** pansement adhésif, sparadrap *m*; (*b*) arrêt *m*, coincement *m*; bloquage *m* (d'une soupape). **stick on 1.** *v.tr.* (*a*) coller, fixer (un timbre, etc.); (*b*) *F:* **to s. it on,** exagérer. **2.** *v.i.* rester collé; adhérer. **stick out 1.** *v.tr.* (*a*) faire dépasser (qch.); sortir (qch.); **to s. out one's tongue,** tirer la langue; **to s. out one's chest,** bomber la poitrine; *F:* **to s. one's neck out,** prendre des risques; **it sticks out a mile,** c'est clair comme le jour; (*b*) *F:* **to s. it out,** tenir jusqu'au bout. **2.** *v.i.* (*a*) faire saillie, ressortir; **to s. out (beyond sth.),** dépasser (qch.); **his ears s. out,** il a les oreilles décollées; **her teeth s. out,** elle a les dents saillantes; (*b*) *F:* **to s. out for sth.**, s'obstiner à demander qch. **stick up 1.** *v.tr.* (*a*) *F:* dresser (une cible, etc.); *P:* **s. 'em up!** haut les mains! (*b*) *U.S: P:* **to s. up a bank,** attaquer une banque à main armée; (*c*) afficher (un avis, etc.). **2.** *v.i.* (*a*) se dresser; se tenir debout; **his hair sticks straight up,** il a les cheveux récalcitrants; (*b*) *F:* **to s. up for s.o.**, prendre la défense de qn.

sticker ['stikər] *n.* **1.** (*a*) couteau *m* de boucher; (*b*) couteau de chasse. **2.** colleur, -euse (d'affiches). **3.** *F:* rude travailleur. **4.** (*a*) *U.S: F:* affiche *f*; placard électoral; (*b*) étiquette gommée.

stickiness ['stikinis] *n.* nature gluante, collante (d'un produit); adhésivité *f*.

stickleback ['stiklbæk] *n. Ich:* épinoche *f*.

stickler ['stiklər] *n.* rigoriste *mf* (**for sth.**, à l'égard de qch.); **to be a s. for etiquette,** être à cheval sur l'étiquette; être très cérémonieux.

stick-on ['stikɔn] *a.* (étiquette) adhésive; *Bootm:* **s.-on soles,** semelles autocollantes.

stick-up ['stikʌp] *n. esp. U.S: F:* attaque *f* à main armée; braquage *m*.

sticky ['stiki] *a.* **1.** collant, gluant; adhésif; (*of substance, hands*) poisseux; **s. tape,** ruban adhésif; *F:* **to have s. fingers,** être voleur; **s. weather,** temps lourd; **to be on a s. wicket,** être dans une situation difficile. **2.** *F:* (*a*) peu accommodant; difficile; **he will come to a s. end,** il finira mal; (*b*) (problème) difficile.

stiff [stif] **I.** *a.* **1.** (*a*) raide, rigide, dur, inflexible; (brosse) dure, rude; **s. shirt front,** plastron empesé;

book bound in s. cover, livre relié en carton; (*b*) **s. joint,** articulation ankylosée; (*of joint*) **to grow s.,** s'ankyloser; **s. neck,** torticolis *m*; *Fig:* **s. necked,** obstiné, entêté; **to be quite s.,** (i) (*with sitting still*) être engourdi; (ii) (*after exercise*) être tout courbaturé; *F:* (*of pers.*) **s. as a poker,** raide, droit, comme un piquet; *F:* **exams scare me s.,** j'ai une peur bleue des examens; (*c*) (*of pers., manner*) raide, contraint, guindé; **s. bow,** salut contraint, froid; **he is very s.,** il est d'un abord difficile; *Lit:* **s. style,** style guindé, empesé; (*d*) (*of pers.*) inflexible, obstiné; **to offer a s. resistance,** (*of pers.*) résister opiniâtrement; (*of thg*) tenir ferme; (*e*) *Fin:* (*of market, commodity*) ferme, raffermi. **2.** (*a*) (*of door-handle, hinge, etc.*) qui fonctionne mal; **the handle is s.,** le bouton est dur; (*b*) (*of paste, batter*) épais, *f.* épaisse; ferme; (*of soil, clay*) tenace; (*c*) *Nau:* **s. wind,** forte brise. **3.** (*a*) raide, pénible; (examen) difficile; **I had a s. job to get it,** j'ai eu fort à faire pour l'obtenir; (*b*) *F:* **s. price,** prix élevé; **s. bill,** note salée; **s. sentence,** dure peine; *F:* **pour me out a s. one, a s. drink,** versez-moi quelque chose de fort. **II.** *n. P:* **1.** lettre *f* de change, billet *m* à ordre. **2.** cadavre *m*; macchabée *m*. **3. big s.,** grand nigaud; grand bêta. **stiffly** *adv.* **1.** raidement, avec raideur. **2.** d'un air guindé. **3.** (résister, etc.) obstinément. **4.** sévèrement.

stiffen [ˈstif(ə)n] **I.** *v.tr.* **1.** (*a*) raidir, renforcer (une plaque, un mur, une poutre, etc.); *Laund:* empeser (un plastron); (*b*) **age has stiffened his joints,** l'âge lui a noué les membres; (*c*) raidir, rendre obstiné (qn). **2.** (*a*) rendre ferme, donner de la consistance à (une pâte); (*b*) corser (une boisson). **3.** rendre (un examen) plus difficile. **II.** *v.i.* **1.** (*a*) (se) raidir, devenir raide; (*b*) (*of pers.*) se raidir; se guinder; **opposition is stiffening,** l'opposition se montre de plus en plus intransigeante. **2.** (*a*) (*of paste, etc.*) devenir ferme; prendre de la consistance; (*b*) *Nau:* (*of wind*) fraîchir. **2.** (*of examination*) devenir plus difficile. **stiffening** *n.* **1.** raidissement *m*, renforcement *m* (de qch.); durcissement *m* (de la résistance); **s. of the joints,** ankylose *f*. **2.** (*a*) empois *m*; (*for cloth*) cati *m*; (*b*) *Tail:* entoilage *m* (du col d'un habit).

stiffener [ˈstif(ə)nər] *n.* **1.** (pièce *f* de) renfort; entretoise *f*. **2.** *F:* verre *m* d'eau-de-vie; remontant *m*.

stiffness [ˈstifnis] *n.* **1.** (*a*) raideur *f*, rigidité *f* (d'une poutre, des membres, etc.); dureté *f* (d'un ressort, etc.); **s. of the legs,** (*after exercise*) courbatures *fpl* dans les jambes; (*after sitting*) engourdissement *m* des jambes; (*b*) **s. of manner,** raideur, contrainte *f*; air guindé; (*c*) obstination *f*; (*d*) fermeté *f* (du marché). **2.** fermeté, consistance *f* (d'une pâte); ténacité *f* (du sol). **3.** (*a*) raideur (d'une pente); (*b*) difficulté *f* (d'un examen).

stifle[1] [ˈstaifl] **1.** *v.tr.* (*a*) étouffer, suffoquer (qn); **to s. a revolt at birth,** étouffer une révolte dans son germe; (*b*) étouffer (les cris de qn, etc.); **to s. a scandal,** étouffer un scandale; (*c*) réprimer (une émotion); étouffer (un bâillement, un rire); retenir (un cri). **2.** *v.i.* suffoquer, étouffer. **stifled** *a.* (cri, etc.) étouffé; **with a s. voice,** d'une voix éteinte. **stifling** *a.* **1.** étouffant, suffocant; **it's s. here!** on étouffe ici! **2.** (sensation) d'étouffement.

stifle[2] *n.* **s. (joint),** grasset *m* (du cheval, etc.).

stigma, *pl.* **-as, -ata** [ˈstigmə, -əz, ˈstigmətə, stigˈmɑːtə] *n.* **1.** (*pl. usu.* **stigmas**) (*a*) *A:* flétrissure *f* (au fer rouge); (*b*) stigmate *m*, tache *f*; flétrissure (morale). **2.** (*pl.* **stigmata**) (*a*) *Nat.Hist:* stigmate (d'un insecte, etc.); (*b*) **stigmata,** stigmates (d'un saint). **3.** *Bot:* (*pl.* **stigmas**) stigmate (du pistil).

stigmatism [ˈstigmətizm] *n. Opt:* stigmatisme *m*.

stigmatize [ˈstigmətaiz] *v.tr.* **1.** marquer de stigmates. **2.** stigmatiser, flétrir (qn); **stigmatized as a coward, as illegitimate,** marqué comme lâche; entaché de bâtardise.

stile[1] [stail] *n.* (*a*) échalier *m*, échalis *m*; (*b*) tourniquet *m*, moulinet *m*.

stile[2] *n.* montant *m* (de porte, etc.).

stiletto, *pl.* **-os, -oes** [stiˈletou, -ouz] *n.* **1.** (*dagger*) stylet *m*; **s. heels,** talons *m* aiguille. **2.** *Needlew: etc:* poinçon *m*.

still[1] [stil] **1.** *a.* (*a*) immobile; **to keep s.,** ne pas bouger; se tenir, rester, tranquille; **sit s.!** restez tranquille! **to stand s.,** (i) ne pas bouger; se tenir tranquille; (ii) s'arrêter, s'immobiliser; (*of science, etc.*) rester stationnaire; **his heart stood s.,** son cœur cessa de battre; (*b*) silencieux; (*c*) calme; **s. water,** eau dormante; (*d*) (vin) non mousseux; (champagne) nature; (eau) plate; (*e*) *Art:* **s. life,** *pl.* **s. lifes,** nature morte. **2.** *n.* (*a*) **in the s. of the night,** dans le calme de la nuit; (*b*) *Cin:* photo (empruntée au film).

still[2] **1.** *v.tr.* tranquilliser, calmer, apaiser; **to s. s.o.'s fears,** calmer les craintes de qn. **2.** *v.i. Lit:* se calmer.

still[3] **1.** *adv.* (*a*) encore; **he is s. here,** il est encore, toujours, ici; **I s. have 500 francs,** il me reste 500 francs; **I have s. to thank you,** il me reste à vous remercier; **in spite of his faults, I love him s.,** malgré ses fautes je l'aime toujours; (*b*) **s. more, s. less,** encore plus, encore moins; **if you can reduce the price s. further,** si vous pouvez réduire encore le prix. **2.** *conj.* cependant, pourtant, néanmoins, toutefois; **s. the fact remains that . . .,** toujours est-il que . . .; **but s., if he *did* accept!** mais enfin, s'il acceptait!

still[4] *n.* alambic *m*; **water s.,** appareil *m* à eau distillée.

stillbirth [ˈstilbəːθ] *n.* mortinatalité *f*; mort *f* à la naissance.

stillborn [ˈstilbɔːn] *a.* mort-né, -ée, *pl.* mort-nés, -ées; *Fig:* (projet, etc.) avorté, mort-né.

stillness [ˈstilnis] *n.* tranquillité *f*, calme *m*, repos *m*; silence *m*, paix *f*.

stilt [stilt] *n.* **1.** échasse *f*. **2.** *Civ.E:* pilotis *m*, pieu *m*.

stilted [ˈstiltid] *a.* **1.** *Arch:* (arc) surhaussé, surélevé. **2.** (*of style, manner, etc.*) guindé.

Stilton [ˈstilt(ə)n] *n.* fromage *m* de Stilton; stilton *m*.

stimulant [ˈstimjulənt] **1.** *a.* & *n. Med:* stimulant (*m*); remontant (*m*); **heart s.,** tonicardiaque *m*. **2.** *n.* surexcitant *m*.

stimulate [ˈstimjuleit] *v.tr.* (*a*) stimuler (qn, le zèle de qn); aiguillonner, activer, exciter (**to,** à); aiguiser (l'esprit, l'appétit, etc.); *Ind:* encourager, activer (la production); (*b*) *Med:* stimuler (le foie, etc.). **stimulating** *a.* **1.** stimulant; (désir) aiguillonnant; (musique) entraînante; (livre) qui donne à penser. **2.** *Med:* (régime, etc.) stimulant, remontant.

stimulation [stimjuˈleiʃ(ə)n] *n.* stimulation *f*.

stimulative [ˈstimulətiv] *a.* stimulateur, -trice.

stimulus, *pl.* **-i** [ˈstimjuləs, -ai] *n.* (*a*) stimulant *m*; aiguillon *m*; **to give a stimulus to trade,** donner de l'impulsion *f* au commerce; (*b*) *Physiol:* stimulus *m inv*; **to apply a s. to a muscle,** exciter un muscle.

sting[1] [stiŋ] *n.* **1.** (*a*) dard *m*, aiguillon *m* (d'abeille); (*b*) dard; poil piquant (d'ortie); (*c*) crochet venimeux (d'un serpent). **2.** (*a*) piqûre *f* (de guêpe, etc.); (*b*) pointe *f* (d'une épigramme); mordant *m*; **joke with a s. in it,** plaisanterie mordante, piquante; *Lit:* **the s. of remorse,** l'aiguillon du remords; (*c*) douleur cuisante (d'une blessure); (*d*) vigueur *f*, mordant (d'une attaque).

sting[2] *v.* (*p.t. & p.p.* **stung** [stʌŋ]) **1.** *v.tr.* (*a*) (*of bees, nettles, etc.*) piquer; **a bee stung his finger, stung him on the finger,** une abeille lui a piqué le doigt; **the blow stung him,** le coup le cingla; **that reply stung him (to the quick),** cette réponse l'a piqué (au vif); **smoke that stings the eyes,** fumée qui picote les yeux; (*b*) *F:* **to s. s.o. for £50,** estamper, avoir, qn en le faisant payer £50; **to be stung,** essuyer le coup de fusil. **2.** *v.i.* (*of parts of the body*) cuire; sentir des élancements; **my eyes were stinging,** les yeux me cuisaient. **stinging** ['stiŋiŋ] *a.* (*of pain, etc.*) cuisant; (*of blow, answer*) cinglant; **s. plant,** plante piquante; **s. remark,** remarque blessante, offensante.

stinginess ['stindʒinis] *n.* mesquinerie *f,* ladrerie *f;* pingrerie *f.*

stingray ['stiŋrei] *n. Ich:* pastenague *f.*

stingy ['stindʒi] *a.* mesquin, chiche, ladre; **he, she, is s.,** il, elle, est pingre. **-ily** *adv.* mesquinement, chichement.

stink[1] ['stiŋk] *n.* (*a*) puanteur *f;* odeur *f* fétide; **what a s.!** c'est une infection ici! (*b*) *P:* grabuge *m;* **to raise, kick up, a s.,** faire de l'esclandre, du grabuge.

stink[2] *v.* (*p.t.* **stank** [stæŋk], **stunk** [stʌŋk]; *p.p.* **stunk**) **1.** *v.i.* puer, sentir mauvais; *F:* empester; **it stinks in here,** c'est une infection ici; **to s. of garlic,** puer l'ail; *P:* **to s. of money,** avoir un argent fou; *P:* **what do you think of it?—it stinks!** qu'en dis-tu?—c'est moche! **2.** *v.tr.* **to s. s.o. out,** chasser qn par la mauvaise odeur. **stinking 1.** *a.* (*a*) puant; empesté, infect; (*b*) *P:* dégoûtant, dégueulasse; **a s. cold,** un gros rhume. **2.** *adv. F:* **to be s. rich,** avoir un argent fou.

stinkbomb ['stiŋkbɔm] *n. F:* boule puante.

stinker ['stiŋkər] *n. F:* **1.** individu *m* méprisable; salaud *m.* **2.** (*a*) **to write s.o. a s.,** écrire une lettre carabinée à qn; (*b*) **the algebra paper was a s.,** on a eu une sale composition d'algèbre.

stinkhorn ['stiŋkhɔːn] *n.* phallus *m* impudique.

stinkpot ['stiŋkpɔt] *n. F:* type *m* dégueulasse.

stint[1] [stint] *n.* **1.** restriction *f;* **without s.,** sans limite; (dépenser) sans compter. **2.** besogne assignée; **to do one's daily s.,** accomplir sa tâche quotidienne. **3.** temps *m,* période *f;* **he had a two-year s. in the army,** il a fait ses deux ans dans l'armée.

stint[2] *v.tr.* **1.** imposer des restrictions à (qn); **to s. oneself,** se refuser le nécessaire; **to s. s.o. of sth.,** priver qn de qch., refuser qch. à qn. **2.** réduire (la nourriture); épargner (l'argent, la peine); lésiner sur (qch.); **to give without stinting,** donner sans compter.

stipend ['staipend] *n.* traitement *m,* appointements *mpl* (d'un ecclésiastique, d'un magistrat).

stipendiary [stai'pendjəri] *a.* appointé; qui reçoit des appointements fixes; **s. magistrate,** *n.* **s.,** juge *m* d'un tribunal d'instance (à Londres et dans les grandes villes).

stipple ['stipl] *v.tr.* (*a*) figurer (un dessin) en pointillé; pointiller; (*b*) *Engr:* graver (un dessin) au pointillé.

stipulate ['stipjuleit] **1.** *v.i.* **to s. for sth.,** stipuler, énoncer, expressément (une condition obligatoire); convenir de (certaines conditions). **2.** *v.tr.* **to s. (in writing) that . . .,** stipuler (par écrit) que . . .; **within the period stipulated,** dans le délai prescrit.

stipulation [stipju'leiʃ(ə)n] *n.* (*a*) *Jur:* stipulation *f* (d'une condition); (*b*) condition *f;* **the only s. I make is that . . .,** la seule condition que je pose c'est que . . .; **on the s. that . . .,** à condition que . . ..

stir[1] [stəːr] *n.* **1.** remuement *m;* **to give (sth.) a stir,** remuer (son café); tisonner (le feu). **2.** (*a*) mouvement *m;* **there was a great s.,** il y eut un grand remue-ménage; (*b*) agitation *f,* émoi *m;* **to make a s.,** faire du bruit; faire sensation; **the news caused a s. in the town,** la nouvelle a mis la ville en émoi.

stir[2] *v.* **(stirred) 1.** *v.tr.* (*a*) remuer, mouvoir; (*usu. neg.*) **not a breath stirs the leaves,** pas un souffle ne remue, ne fait trembler, les feuilles; (*b*) activer, attiser, tisonner (le feu); agiter (un mélange); *Cu:* tourner (une crème); **to s. one's tea,** remuer son thé; (*c*) émouvoir, remuer, troubler (qn); agiter, emouvoir (les passions de qn); **stirred,** agité, troublé; ému; **to s. s.o. to pity,** émouvoir la compassion de qn; **events that s. the soul,** événements qui remuent l'âme; *F:* **to s. it,** fomenter la discorde. **2.** *v.i.* bouger, remuer; **don't s.!** ne bougez pas! **don't s. from here,** ne bougez pas d'ici; **he did not s. out of the house,** il n'est pas sorti de la maison; **he is not stirring yet,** il n'est pas encore levé; *P:* **s. yourself, your stumps!** remue-toi! **3.** *v.tr.* **to s. up,** (*a*) remuer, agiter (un liquide); ranimer, activer (le feu); (*b*) fomenter (une sédition, les dissensions); remuer, ameuter (le peuple); exciter, animer (la curiosité); *F:* travailler (des ouvriers); **to s. up hatred,** attiser les haines; **to s. up trouble,** fomenter la discorde; **stirred up,** agité, troublé; en émoi; **he wants stirring up,** il a besoin d'être secoué. **stirring 1.** *a.* (*a*) actif, remuant; **s. times,** époque mouvementée; (*b*) émouvant; (discours) vibrant, entraînant. **2.** *n.* (*a*) remuement *m;* agitation *f;* (*b*) **s. up,** excitation *f* (des émotions); mise *f* en émoi (du peuple); fomentation *f* (de la discorde).

stir[3] *n. P:* prison *f,* taule *f.*

stir-crazy [stəː'kreizi] *a. esp. NAm: F:* fou, *f.* folle, détraqué (à cause d'une longue période de détention).

stirrer ['stəːrər] *n.* **1.** (*pers.*) **s.(-up),** incitateur, -trice. **2.** (*device*) *Ch: Phot:* agitateur *m.*

stirrup ['stirəp] *n. Harn:* étrier *m;* **to put one's feet in the stirrups,** chausser les étriers; **s. leather, strap,** étrivière *f;* **s. cup,** coup *m* de l'étrier.

stitch[1] [stitʃ] *n.* **1.** (*a*) *Needlew:* point *m;* **(machine) s.,** piqûre *f* (à la machine); *Knit:* **moss s.,** point de riz; **to put a few stitches in a garment,** faire un point à un vêtement; *Prov:* **a s. in time saves nine,** un point à temps en épargne cent; un point fait à temps en vaut mille; *Nau:* **with every s. of canvas set,** toutes voiles dehors; *F:* **he has not a dry s. on him,** il est complètement trempé; **without a s. on,** complètement nu; (*b*) (*in knitting, crochet*) maille *f;* **to drop a s.,** sauter une maille; **dropped s.,** maille coulée; **to make a s.,** faire une augmentation; (*c*) *Surg:* (point de) suture *f;* **to put stitches in a wound,** suturer, faire une suture à, une plaie. **2. s. (in the side),** point de côté; **I've got a s., the s.,** j'ai un point; *F:* **we were in stitches,** on se tordait de rire.

stitch[2] *v.tr.* **1.** (*a*) coudre (un vêtement); **to (machine) s.,** piquer (à la machine); **to s. sth. on to sth.,** coudre qch. sur qch.; **to s. up,** recoudre (une déchirure); (*b*) piquer (le cuir). **2.** *Surg:* **to s. (up),** suturer (une plaie). **3.** *Bookb:* brocher (un livre). **stitching** *n.* **1.** (*a*) *Needlew:* couture *f; Leath:* piqûre *f; Dressm:* **line of s.,** piqûre; (*b*) *Surg:* suture *f;* (*c*) *Bookb:* brochage *m,* brochure *f.* **2.** points *mpl,* piqûres; **ornamental s.,** broderie *f.*

stoat [stout] *n. Z:* hermine *f* (d'été).

stock[1] [stɔk] *n.* **1.** (*a*) *Bot:* tronc *m* (d'arbre); (*b*) souche *f* (d'arbre, d'iris); bûche *f,* bloc *m;* billot (d'enclume); (*c*) *Hort:* sujet *m,* ente *f;* porte-greffe *m inv; Vit:* cep *m* (de vigne); (*d*) race *f,* lignée *f;* **true to s.,** fortement racé; **he comes of good s.,** il descend d'une bonne famille; il vient de bonne souche. **2.** (*a*) fût *m,* bois *m,* monture *f* (de fusil); manche *m* (de fouet); mancheron *m* (de charrue); sommier *m,* mouton *m* (de cloche); boîte *f* de bois (enfermant une serrure); *Nau:* jas *m* (d'ancre); (*b*) **die s.,** porte-filière *m, pl.* porte-filières. **3.** *A:* **stocks,** ceps *mpl* (en place publique). **4.** *N.Arch:* **stocks,** (i) chantier *m;* cale *f* de construction; (ii) (*on slips*) tins *mpl;* **ship on the stocks,** navire *m* en construction, sur cales. **5.** (*a*) provision *f,* approvisionnement *m;* **s. of wood,** provision de bois; **s. of plays,** répertoire *m;* **to lay in a s. of food,** faire (une) provision, s'approvisionner, de vivres; (*b*) *Com:* **s. (in trade),** marchandises *fpl* (en magasin); stock *m;* **new, fresh, s.,** rassortiment *m;* **old s.,** fonds *mpl* de boutique; **surplus s.,** soldes *mpl;* **s. in hand,** marchandises en magasin; stock, existences *fpl* (en magasin); **to take s.,** faire, dresser, l'inventaire; *Fig:* **to take s. of s.o.,** scruter, toiser, qn; **to take s. of the situation,** faire le bilan de la situation; faire le point; **s. control,** gestion *f* des stocks; **s. keeper,** magasinier *m*; **s. list,** inventaire *m*; **in s.,** en magasin, en stock; (*of goods*) **to be out of s.,** manquer en magasin; *Publ:* **book temporarily out of s.,** livre qui est temporairement épuisé; (*c*) (*at cards, dominoes*) talon *m*; (*d*) *Husb:* (*livestock*) **grazing s.,** bétail *m*; animaux *m* sur pied; **fat s.,** bétail de boucherie; **s. farm,** élevage *m*; **s. farmer, breeder,** éleveur *m*; **s. farming, breeding,** élevage; **s. mare,** jument *f* de haras; *Austr:* **s. rider,** cowboy *m*; (*e*) *For:* peuplement *m*; (*f*) *Ind:* dotation *f*; *Rail:* **locomotive s.,** effectif *m*, dotation, en locomotives; (*g*) *Cin:* **(film) s.,** film *m* vierge; films, bandes *fpl*, vierges. **6.** (*a*) *Ind:* matières premières (de pâte à papier, de savon); (*b*) *Cu:* **soup s.,** consommé *m*; **meat s.,** bouillon (concentré); **s. cube,** bouillon-cube *m*. **7.** *Fin:* fonds *mpl*, valeurs *fpl*, actions *fpl*; **government s.,** fonds d'État; fonds, effets, publics; rentes *fpl* (sur l'État); **s. exchange,** bourse *f* (des valeurs); **the S. Exchange,** la Bourse (de Londres); **stocks and shares,** valeurs mobilières; valeurs de bourse; titres *mpl*; *St. Exch:* **s. list,** bulletin *m* de la cote; **s. market,** marché des titres, de valeurs; *Fig:* **his s. is going up, down,** ses actions sont en hausse, en baisse. **8.** *Bot:* matthiole *f*; giroflée des jardins. **9.** *Cost:* (*a*) col-cravate *m* (d'équitation), *pl.* cols-cravates; (*b*) plastron *m* en soie noire (des ecclésiastiques anglais). **10.** *a.* (*a*) normal; **s. sizes,** tailles courantes; *Aut:* **s. car,** stock-car *m*, *pl.* stock-cars; **s.-car racing,** courses *fpl* de stock-cars; (*b*) *Th:* **s. play, piece,** pièce *f* de, du, répertoire; **s. company,** troupe *f* à demeure (dans une ville); (*c*) **he has three s. speeches,** il a un répertoire de trois discours; **s. phrase,** phrase toute faite; expression consacrée; **s. answer,** réponse régulière.

stock² *v.tr.* **1.** (*a*) monter (un fusil); (*b*) *Nau:* jaler, enjaler (une ancre). **2.** monter, assortir, stocker (un magasin) (**with,** de); meubler (une ferme) (**with,** de); monter (une ferme) de bétail; approvisionner (une maison) (**with,** de); empoissonner (un étang); peupler (une forêt) (**with,** de); **this shop is well stocked,** ce magasin est bien approvisionné; **to have a well-stocked cellar,** avoir une cave bien montée. **3.** avoir, tenir, garder (des marchandises) en magasin, en dépôt; stocker (des marchandises); **I don't s. this article,** je ne tiens pas cet article. **4.** *v.i.* **to s. up with sth.,** bien s'approvisionner en, de, qch.

stockade¹ [stɔ'keid] *n.* palissade *f*, palanque *f*.

stockade² *v.tr.* palissader, palanquer.

stockbroker ['stɔkbroukər] *n.* agent *m* de change; courtier *m* de bourse.

stockfish ['stɔkfiʃ] *n.* stockfisch *m*, merluche *f*.

stockholder ['stɔkhouldər] *n.* actionnaire *mf*; porteur *m*, détenteur *m*, de titres.

stockiness ['stɔkinis] *n.* air trapu, costaud.

stockinet(te) [stɔki'net] *n.* *Tex:* **wool, cotton, s.,** jersey *m* de laine, coton.

stocking ['stɔkiŋ] *n.* **1.** *Cost:* bas *m*; *Med:* **elastic s.,** bas pour varices; **to stand six feet in one's stockings,** mesurer six pieds sans chaussures; **body s.,** combinaison *f* (une pièce); **s. filler,** petit cadeau de Noël supplémentaire (pour enfant); **s. mask,** bas utilisé comme masque par les bandits; *Knit:* **s. stitch,** point *m* (de) jersey. **2.** (*of horse*) **white s.,** balzane *f*.

stockinged ['stɔkiŋd] *a.* **in one's s. feet,** sans chaussures.

stockist ['stɔkist] *n.* *Com:* stockiste *m*.

stockman, *pl.* **-men** ['stɔkmən] *n.m.* **1.** *Austr:* gardeur de bestiaux; bouvier. **2.** *NAm:* magasinier.

stockpile¹ ['stɔkpail] *n.* (*a*) tas *m* (de matériaux); (*b*) stocks *mpl* de réserve, de sécurité.

stockpile² *v.tr.* (*a*) stocker (des marchandises); (*b*) entasser, accumuler (le matériel de guerre). **stockpiling** *n.* stockage *m*, constitution *f* de réserves.

stockpot ['stɔkpɔt] *n.* *Cu:* pot *m* à bouillon; pot-au-feu *m inv*.

stockroom ['stɔkrum] *n.* magazin *m*, réserve *f*, resserre *f*.

stock-still ['stɔk'stil] *adv.* **to stand s.-s.,** rester (complètement) immobile, sans bouger.

stocktaking ['stɔkteikiŋ] *n.* *Com:* *Ind:* (établissement *m*, levée *f* d')inventaire *m*.

stocky ['stɔki] *a.* trapu, courtaud; (cheval) ragot. **-ily** *adv.* **s. built,** trapu.

stockyard ['stɔkjɑːd] *n.* parc *m* à bétail, à bestiaux.

stodge [stɔdʒ] *n.* *F:* **1.** (*a*) aliment bourrant; (*b*) *esp. Sch:* littérature *f* indigeste. **2.** personne *f* à l'esprit lourd.

stodgy ['stɔdʒi] *a.* **1.** (repas) lourd; (pain) pâteux; (aliment) qui bourre. **2.** (*a*) (livre) indigeste; (style) lourd; (*b*) (*of pers.*) à l'esprit lourd; lourdaud.

stoic ['stouik] *a.* & *n.* stoïque (*mf*), stoïcien, -ienne.

stoical ['stouik(ə)l] *a.* stoïque. **-ally** *adv.* stoïquement.

stoicism ['stouisizm] *n.* stoïcisme *m*.

stoke ['stouk] **1.** *v.tr.* **to s. (up),** charger (un foyer); entretenir le feu (d'un four); chauffer le foyer (d'une machine à vapeur). **2.** *v.i.* **to s. up,** (i) pousser les feux; (ii) *F:* manger, bouffer, bâfrer.

stokehole ['stoukhoul] *n.* (*a*) ouverture *f* de foyer; (*b*) *Nau:* enfer *m* (devant la chaudière).

stoker ['stoukər] *n.* **1.** (*pers.*) chauffeur *m*; chargeur *m* (d'un foyer). **2. mechanical s.,** chauffeur automatique; chargeur mécanique.

stole [stoul] *n.* **1.** *Ecc:* étole *f*. **2.** *Cost:* étole (de vison).

stolid ['stɔlid] *a.* lent, flegmatique, impassible. **-ly** *adv.* flégmatiquement.

stolidity [stɔ'liditi], **stolidness** ['stɔlidnis] *n.* flegme *m*.

stoma, *pl.* **-ata,** ['stoumə, -ətə] *n.* stomate *m*.

stomach¹ ['stʌmək] *n.* **1.** (*a*) estomac *m*; **pain in the s.,** mal *m* d'estomac; **upset s., s. upset,** troubles *mpl* de digestion; *Pharm:* **to be taken on an empty s.,** à prendre à jeun; **to turn s.o.'s s.,** soulever le cœur à qn; écœurer qn; **to have a cast iron s.,** avoir un estomac d'autruche; *Z:* (*of ruminants*) **first s.,** panse *f*; **second s.,** bonnet *m*; **third s.,** feuillet *m*, mellier *m*; **fourth, true, s.,** caillette *f*; (*b*) ventre *m*; **to have a large s.,** être pansu, ventru; (*c*) **s. ache,** (i) douleurs d'estomac; (ii) *F:* mal de ventre; **to have s. ache,** avoir mal au ventre; **s. pump,** pompe stomacale. **2.** (*a*) appétit *m*; **to have no s. for one's food,** ne pas avoir d'appétit; (*b*) *O:* cœur *m*, courage *m* (pour faire qch.); **he had no s. for a fight,** il ne se sentait pas d'humeur à se battre.

stomach² *v.tr.* **1.** manger avec appétit; bien digérer (qch.); **I can't s. oysters,** je n'aime pas les huîtres. **2.** endurer, supporter, tolérer (qch.); *F:* avaler, digérer (une insulte); **I can't s. it any longer,** j'en ai plein le dos.

stomp [stɔmp] *v.i.* frapper du pied; **to s. out of the room,** quitter la pièce d'un pas lourd.

stone¹ [stoun] *n.* **1.** (*a*) pierre *f*; caillou, -oux *m*; **to leave no stone unturned,** mettre tout en œuvre, en jeu, remuer ciel et terre (**to do sth.,** pour accomplir qch.); **to throw, cast, stones at s.o.,** (i) lancer des pierres sur, à, qn; (ii) *Fig:* jeter des pierres dans le jardin de qn; **a stone's throw from here,** à deux pas d'ici; (*b*) *Const:* mœllon *m*, pierre de taille; **not to leave a s. standing,** ne pas laisser pierre sur pierre; (*c*) (*flagstone*) dalle *f*; (*gravestone*) pierre tombale; (*d*) *Typ:* **(imposing, press) s.,** marbre *m*; (*e*) **scouring s.,** brique anglaise: (*f*) meule *f* (à repasser, de moulin); **honing s.**, pierre à huile. **2.** (*a*) **precious stones,** pierres précieuses; pierreries *fpl*; (*b*) *Com: F:* diamant *m*; (*c*) *Clockm:* rubis *m*. **3.** (*material*) pierre (à bâtir, etc.); grès *m*; **broken s.,** pierraille *f*, cailloutis *m*. **4.** *Med:* calcul *m*. **5.** (*a*) noyau *m* (de fruit); pépin *m* (de raisin); **s. fruit,** fruit *m* à noyau; drupe *m or f*; (*b*) (*domino*) dé *m*. **6.** *inv. Meas:* stone *m* (= 6·348 kg); **he weighs 12 s.,** il pèse 76 kilos. **7. s. cold,** froid comme (le) marbre; **the tea is s. cold,** le thé est complètement froid; *P:* **I've got him s. cold,** je l'ai à ma merci; **s. dead,** raide mort; **s. blind,** complètement aveugle; **s. deaf,** complètement sourd; *F:* sourd comme un pot. **8.** (*a*) **s. axe,** (i) hache *f* de pierre; (ii) *Const:* marteau *m* à dresser; **s.-coloured,** (de) couleur pierre *inv*; **s. cutter,** tailleur *m*, équarrisseur *m*, de pierres; **s. saw,** scie *f* à pierre, de carrier; (*b*) **s. jug,** cruche *f* de grès.

stone² *v.tr.* **1.** lapider (qn); assaillir (qn) à coups de pierres; *P:* **s. the crows!** ça alors! **2.** dénoyauter (les fruits); épépiner (les raisins secs). **stoned** *a.* **1.** (chemin) pavé, revêtu, de pierres. **2.** (*of fruit*) dénoyauté; (*of raisins*) épépiné. **3.** *P:* **to be s.,** être (i) soûl, (ii) drogué. **stoning** *n.* **1.** lapidation *f*. **2.** dénoyautage *m* (d'un fruit); épépinage *m* (des raisins secs).

stonechat ['stounʃæt] *n. Orn:* traquet *m* pâtre.

stonecrop ['stounkrɔp] *n. Bot:* orpin *m*.

stoneless ['stounlis] *a.* (raisins secs) sans pépins.

stonemason ['stounmeis(ə)n] *n.* maçon *m*.

stonewall [stoun'wɔ:l] *v.i.* **1.** *Cr:* jouer un jeu prudent pour tenir jusqu'à la fin. **2.** *Parl:* faire de l'obstruction. **stonewalling** *n.* **1.** *Cr:* jeu prudent. **2.** *Parl:* obstructionnisme *m*.

stoneware ['stounwɛər] *n. Cer:* poterie *f* de grès.

stonework ['stounwə:k] *n.* maçonnerie *f*.

stoniness ['stouninis] *n.* **1.** nature pierreuse (du sol). **2.** dureté *f* (de cœur); froideur *f* (du regard).

stony ['stouni] *a.* **1.** pierreux; rocailleux. **2.** (*a*) de, en, pierre; (*b*) dur comme la pierre; **s. concretion,** concrétion pierreuse. **3.** froid, dur; (regard) glacial, -ials; **s. heart,** cœur de marbre; **s. politeness,** politesse glacée. **4.** *F:* **s. (broke),** sans le sou; à sec; **I'm s. (broke),** je n'ai pas le sou. **-ily** *adv.* froidement; (regarder qn) d'un air glacial.

stony-hearted [stouni'hɑ:tid] *a.* au cœur de marbre.

stooge¹ [stu:dʒ] *n. F:* (*a*) *Th:* faire-valoir *m inv* (d'un comique); (*b*) souffre-douleur *mf inv*; (*c*) (i) subalterne *m*, nègre *m*; (ii) pantin *m*.

stooge² *v.i. F:* **to s. for s.o.,** (i) *Th:* servir de faire-valoir à (un comique); (ii) faire le nègre de qn.

stook¹ [stu:k] *n. Agr:* tas *m* de gerbes; moyette *f*.

stook² *v.tr. Agr:* mettre (les gerbes) en moyettes.

stool [stu:l] *n.* **1.** (*a*) tabouret *m*; (*wooden*) escabeau *m*; **folding s.,** pliant *m*; **piano s.,** tabouret de piano: *Fig:* **to fall between two stools,** demeurer entre deux selles (le cul à terre); (*b*) **prayer s.,** prie-Dieu *m inv*. **2.** (*a*) **to go to s.,** aller à la selle; (*b*) *Med:* **stools,** selles, fèces *f*. **3.** *Hort: Agr:* pied *m* mère, plante *f* mère. **4. s. pigeon,** mouchard *m*, indicateur, -trice (de police). **5.** *Const:* tablette *f*, rebord *m* (de fenêtre).

stoop¹ [stu:p] *n.* **1.** inclination *f* en avant (du corps), penchement *m* en avant. **2.** dos rond; épaules voûtées; **to walk with a s.,** marcher le dos voûté.

stoop² **1.** *v.i.* (*a*) se pencher, se baisser; **he stooped to pick up the pin,** il s'est baissé pour ramasser l'épingle; (*b*) (i) s'abaisser, s'avilir, descendre (**to do sth.,** à, jusqu'à, faire qch.); (ii) daigner (**to do sth.,** faire qch.); **man who would s. to anything,** homme prêt à toutes les bassesses; *Lit:* **to s. to conquer,** s'abaisser pour triompher; (*c*) avoir le dos rond; être voûté; **to begin to s.,** se voûter. **2.** *v.tr.* pencher, incliner (la tête); courber, arrondir (le dos). **stooping** *a.* penché (en avant); courbé, voûté.

stoop³ *n. NAm:* porche *m* (avec perron); terrasse surélevée (devant une maison).

stop¹ [stɔp] *n.* **1.** (*a*) arrêt *m*, interruption *f*; **to put a s. to sth.,** arrêter, faire cesser, qch.; mettre fin à qch.; (*b*) arrêt, halte *f*, pause *f*; **ten minutes' s.,** dix minutes d'arrêt; **to come to a s.,** s'arrêter; faire halte; faire une pause; (*of car*) stopper; **to bring sth. to a s.,** arrêter qch.; (*c*) **bus s.,** arrêt d'autobus; **regular s.,** arrêt fixe; **request s.,** arrêt facultatif; (*d*) *Av:* (*in flight*) escale *f*. **2.** signe *m* de ponctuation; point *m*; (*in telegram*) **s.,** stop *m*. **3.** *Mus:* jeu *m*, registre *m* (d'orgue); **s. (key, knob),** bouton *m* d'appel; **to pull out a s.,** tirer un registre; *F:* **to pull out all the stops,** y aller à plein. **4.** *Carp: Mec.E: etc:* dispositif *m* de blocage; arrêt, taquet *m*, butée *f*; heurtoir *m* (d'une porte); arrêtoir *m* (de vis, de boulon); (*on moving part of machine*) mentonnet *m*; *Mec.E:* butoir *m* (de bout de course); *Carp:* **bench s.,** crochet *m*, griffe *f*, d'établi; *Typew:* **margin(al) s.,** margeur *m* (réglable). **5.** (*a*) *Cards:* (carte *f* d')arrêt; (*b*) *Box:* coup bloqué. **6.** *Opt: Phot:* diaphragme *m* (d'objectif). **7.** *Ling:* plosive *f*, explosive *f*. **8.** *Z:* cassure *f* du nez (d'un chien). **9.** *Phot: etc:* **s. bath,** bain *m* d'arrêt; **s. signal,** *Aut:* stop; *Rail:* signal *m* d'arrêt; *NAm:* **s. street,** rue *f* avec un stop au débouché; *Mch:* **s. valve,** soupape *f*, robinet *m*, d'arrêt.

stop² *v.* **(stopped) I.** *v.tr.* **1.** boucher, étancher, tamponner (une voie d'eau); plomber, obturer (une dent); **to s. (up),** boucher, fermer (un trou); obstruer, obturer (un tuyau); (*of pipe*) **to get stopped (up),** super, s'obstruer; **to s. one's ears,** se boucher les oreilles; **to s. a gap,** boucher, combler, un trou. **2.** (*a*) arrêter (un cheval qui court, une balle qui roule); interrompre (la circulation); **to s. s.o. short,** arrêter qn (tout) court; **s. thief!** au voleur! **to s. an opponent,** *Fb:* arrêter un adversaire; *Box:* mettre son adversaire knock-out; **to s. a blow,** parer un coup; *Box:* bloquer; *Mil: P:* **to s. a bullet,** être atteint d'une balle; **curtains that s. the light,** rideaux qui interceptent la lumière; (*b*) **to s. s.o.'s doing sth., s.o. (from) doing sth.,** empêcher qn de faire qch.; **to s. sth. being done,** empêcher que qch. (ne) se fasse; **nothing will s. him,** rien ne l'arrêtera; **what's stopping you?** qu'est-ce qui vous retient? *Com:* **to s. (payment of) a cheque,** arrêter le paiement d'un chèque; bloquer un chèque; (*c*) arrêter (une pendule); arrêter, stopper (une machine); (*d*) mettre fin à (qch.); enrayer (un abus, une grève); **it ought to be stopped,** il faudrait y mettre fin. **3.** (*a*) cesser (ses efforts, ses visites, son travail); *Com:* **to s. payment,** cesser ses paiements; **to s. doing sth.,** s'arrêter de faire qch.; **to s. playing,** cesser de jouer; **she never stops talking,** elle n'arrête pas de parler; elle parle sans cesse; **s. that noise!** assez de bruit! **s. it!** assez! finissez! (*b*) *impers.* **it has stopped raining,** il a cessé de pleuvoir; la pluie a cessé. **4. to s. s.o.'s wages,** retenir le salaire de qn; **to s. so much out of s.o.'s wages,** faire une retenue de tant sur le salaire de qn; **to s. s.o.'s pension,** rayer, supprimer, la pension de qn; *Mil:* **all leave is stopped,** toutes les troupes sont consignées; toutes les permissions sont suspendues. **5.** *Hort:* pincer (une plante). **6.** *Mus:* (*a*) **to s. (down) a string,** presser une corde; (*b*) **to s. a flute,** boucher les trous d'une flûte. **II.** *v.i.* **1.** (*a*) s'arrêter; (*of ship, car*) stopper; **to s. short, dead,** s'arrêter (tout) court, s'arrêter net, *F:* pile; **to do a hundred kilometres without stopping,** faire cent kilomètres sans s'arrêter, sans arrêt, tout d'une traite; **all buses s. here,** arrêt fixe; **buses s. by request,** arrêt facultatif; **to pass a station without stopping,** brûler une gare; *Nau:* **to s. at a port,** faire escale à un port; (*to engine room*) **s.!** stop! stoppez!

(*b*) cesser (de parler, fonctionner); **my watch has stopped,** ma montre (s')est arrêtée; **to work fifteen hours without stopping,** travailler pendant quinze heures d'arrache-pied, de suite; **he stopped in the middle of a sentence,** il s'arrêta au milieu d'une phrase; **he never stops to think,** il ne prend jamais le temps de réfléchir; **he did not s. at that,** il ne s'en tint pas là; **he'll s. at nothing,** rien ne l'arrêtera; **s. a moment!** arrêtez un instant! **the matter will not s. there,** l'affaire n'en demeurera pas là; (*c*) cesser; **the rain has stopped,** la pluie a cessé. **2.** (*stay*) rester; **to s. at home,** rester à la maison; **he's stopping with us for a few days,** il est venu passer quelques jours chez nous; **to s. at a hotel,** descendre, séjourner, à un hôtel. **stop away** *v.i.* ne pas venir; ne pas y aller. **stop by** *v.i. NAm: F:* faire une petite visite chez qn. **stop off** *v.i. NAm:* faire étape (**at London,** à Londres). **stop out 1.** *v.tr. Engr:* recouvrir de vernis (un faux trait); réserver (certaines parties de la planche). **2.** *v.i.* **to s. out all night,** ne pas rentrer de toute la nuit. **stopping 1.** *a.* qui s'arrête; *Rail:* **s. train,** train *m* omnibus. **2.** *n.* (*a*) (i) arrêt *m*; **s. place,** (point *m* d')arrêt; halte *f*; (ii) suspension *f*; cessation *f*; suppression *f* (d'un service); (iii) arrêt de paiement (d'un chèque); (iv) **s. (up),** obturation *f*, bouchage *m*, obstruction *f* (d'une voie d'eau); plombage *m* (d'une dent); (*b*) (i) bouchon *m*, tampon *m*; (ii) mastic *m* (à reboucher); *Dent:* plombage *m*, mastic. **stop up 1.** *v.tr.* boucher (un trou); obstruer, obturer (un tuyau). **2.** *v.i.* **to s. up late,** veiller tard.

stop-(and-)go [ˈstɔp((ə)n)ˈgou] *a.* (politique) de coups de frein et d'accélérateur alternés.

stopcock [ˈstɔpkɔk] *n.* robinet *m* d'arrêt.

stopgap [ˈstɔpgæp] *n.* bouche-trou *m*, *pl.* bouche-trous.

stoplight [stɔplait] *n.* **1.** (*in street*) feu *m* rouge. **2.** (*on car*) stop *m*.

stopoff [ˈstɔpɔf] *n.* escale *f*, arrêt *m*.

stopover [ˈstɔpouvər] *n.* **1.** *Rail: NAm:* (*a*) faculté *f* d'arrêt; **s. ticket,** billet *m* avec (faculté d')arrêt; (*b*) étape *f*. **2.** *Av:* escale *f*.

stoppage [ˈstɔpidʒ] *n.* **1.** (*a*) arrêt *m*; suspension *f*; *Mil: etc:* suppression *f* (de solde, des permissions); (*b*) retenue *f* (sur les appointements); (*c*) (i) arrêt, halte *f*, interruption *f* (du travail); (ii) (*by discontented employees*) débrayage *m*. **2.** obstruction *f*, engorgement *m* (d'un tuyau); *Med:* occlusion *f*.

stopper¹ [ˈstɔpər] *n.* **1.** (*a*) bouchon *m* (*esp.* en verre); **(ground) glass s.,** bouchon à l'émeri; (*b*) obturateur *m* (de tuyau). **2.** *Mec.E:* taquet *m* (d'arrêt de mouvement); *Fig:* **to put a s. on s.o.'s activities,** enrayer les activités de qn.

stopper² *v.tr.* boucher (un flacon, etc.).

stop-press [ˈstɔppres] *a. Journ:* **s.-p. news,** informations de dernière heure.

stopwatch [ˈstɔpwɔtʃ] *n.* chronomètre *m* (à déclic).

storage [ˈstɔːridʒ] *n.* **1.** (*a*) emmagasinage *m*, emmagasinement *m*; **the kitchen has plenty of s. space,** la cuisine a un grand volume de rangement; *Furn:* **s. unit,** meuble *m*, élément *m*, de rangement; **s. tank,** réservoir *m* de magasinage, de stockage; (*b*) accumulation *f*; *El:* emmagasinage, emmagasinement; *El:* **s. cell,** élément *m* d'accumulateur; **(night) s. heater,** radiateur à accumulation (chauffé pendant la nuit). **2.** espace *m* disponible (en magasin, pour rangement); caves *fpl*, greniers *mpl* (d'une maison particulière); entrepôts *mpl*, magasins *mpl* (d'une maison de commerce). **3.** frais *mpl* d'entrepôt; magasinage *m*.

store¹ [stɔːr] *n.* **1.** (*a*) provision *f*, approvisionnement *m*; **to have (a) good s. of wine,** avoir une bonne provision de vin; **to lay in a s. of sth.,** faire une provision de qch.; s'approvisionner de qch.; **to lay in stores,** s'approvisionner; (*b*) **to hold, keep, sth. in s.,** tenir, garder, qch. en réserve; **what the future holds in s. for us,** ce que l'avenir nous réserve; **I have a surprise in s. for him,** je lui ménage une surprise; (*c*) **to set great, little, s. by sth.,** faire grand, peu de, cas de qch.; (*d*) **s. cattle,** bétail *m* à l'engraissage. **2. stores,** provisions, approvisionnements; vivres *mpl*; **marine stores,** (i) approvisionnements, matériel *m*, de navires; (ii) magasin *m*, maison *f*, d'approvisionnements de navires. **3.** (*a*) *Com: Ind:* entrepôt *m*, magasin; (*for furniture*) garde-meuble *m*, *pl.* garde-meubles; *Mil: Navy:* (*in barracks*) magasin; (*b*) (i) **(small) general s.,** épicerie *f*; **the village s.,** l'épicerie, l'alimentation *f*, du village; (ii) *esp. NAm:* boutique *f*, magasin; **toy s.,** magasin de jouets; (*c*) **(department, big) store,** grand magasin; **chain s.,** (i) magasin à succursales (multiples); (ii) succursale *f* (de grand magasin). **4.** *Cmptr:* mémoire *f*.

store² *v.tr.* **1.** pourvoir, munir, approvisionner (**with,** de). **2. to s. (sth.) (up),** amasser, accumuler (qch.); mettre (qch.) en réserve; emmagasiner (l'électricité, la chaleur). **3.** (*a*) (em)magasiner (le foin, le blé); mettre en silo (des betteraves, etc.); **squirrels s. food for the winter,** les écureuils organisent des réserves de vivres pour l'hiver; *v.i.* **goods that don't s. well,** marchandises qui ne se conservent, ne se gardent, pas bien; *Fig:* **dates stored away in the memory,** dates emmagasinées dans la mémoire; (*b*) (i) prendre, (ii) mettre (des meubles) en dépôt; **stored furniture,** mobilier *m* au garde-meuble. **4.** *Cmptr:* mettre (des données) en réserve. **storing** *n.* **1.** approvisionnement *m* (**with,** en). **2. s. (up),** accumulation *f* (**of,** de). **3.** emmagasinage *m*, emmagasinement *m* (**of,** de).

storefront [ˈstɔːfrʌnt] *n. NAm:* devanture *f* de magasin.

storehouse [ˈstɔːhaus] *n.* magasin *m*, entrepôt *m*, dépôt *m*; *Fig:* **a s. of information,** une mine de renseignements.

storekeeper [ˈstɔːkiːpər] *n.* **1.** (*a*) magasinier *m*; (*b*) (*in hospital*) dépensier, -ière. **2.** *NAm:* marchand, -ande; boutiquier, -ière.

storeroom [ˈstɔːru(ː)m] *n.* **1.** (*a*) (*in private house*) office *f*, dépense *f*; (*b*) *Ind:* halle *f* de dépôt; (*c*) *Nau:* (i) soute *f* aux vivres, à provisions, magasin *m*; (ii) cambuse *f*. **2.** *NAm:* (chambre *f* de) débarras *m*.

storey, *NAm:* **story** [ˈstɔːri] *n.* étage *m* (d'un bâtiment); **on the third s.,** *NAm:* **on the fourth s.,** au troisième étage; **single, one, s. house,** maison *f* sans étage, de plain-pied.

storeyed, *NAm:* **storied** [ˈstɔːrid] *a.* **two-s. house,** maison *f* à un étage; **one-s., single-s., house,** maison sans étage.

stork [stɔːk] *n. Orn:* cigogne *f*.

storm¹ [stɔːm] *n.* **1.** orage *m*; (*wind*) tempête *f*; (*a*) **rain s.,** tempête de pluie; **there's a s. coming,** le temps est à l'orage; *Fig:* **a s. in a teacup,** une tempête dans un verre d'eau; **political s.,** ouragan *m*, tourmente *f*, politique; **to bring a s. about one's ears,** s'attirer une véritable tempête d'indignation; soulever un tollé général; (*b*) **s. cone,** cône *m* de tempête; **s. damage,** dommage causé par l'orage, la tempête; **s. lantern,** lampe-tempête *f*, *pl.* lampes-tempêtes; **s. centre,** (i) centre *m* de la tempête, du cyclone; (ii) *Fig:* foyer *m* d'agitation; **s. cloud,** (i) nuée *f* d'orage; (ii) *Fig:* nuage à l'horizon, menaçant; *Civ.E:* **s. drain** *U.S:* **s. sewer,** égout pluvial; *NAm:* **s. cellar,** abri cyclonique. **2.** pluie (de projectiles); bordée *f* (d'injures); tempête (d'applaudissements, de protestations); **to raise a s. of laughter,** déchaîner l'hilarité générale. **3.** *Mil:* assaut *m*; **to take a**

stronghold by s., prendre d'assaut une place forte; *Fig:* **to take the audience by s.,** emporter, soulever, l'auditoire; **s. troops,** (i) troupes *fpl* d'assaut; (ii) *German Hist:* sections *fpl* d'assaut.

storm² **1.** *v.i.* (*a*) (*of wind, rain*) se déchaîner; faire rage; (*b*) (*of pers.*) tempêter, pester; **to s. at s.o.,** s'emporter contre qn; **to s. into, out of, the room,** entrer dans, quitter, la pièce violemment. **2.** *v.tr. Mil:* (i) donner, livrer, l'assaut à (une place forte); (ii) prendre d'assaut, emporter d'assaut, enlever (une place forte). **storming** *n.* **1.** violence *f*, emportements *mpl*. **2.** *Mil:* (i) assaut *m*; (ii) prise *f* d'assaut.

stormbound ['stɔːmbaund] *a.* retenu par une tempête.

stormy ['stɔːmi] *a.* (temps, ciel) orageux, d'orage; (mer) démontée; **the weather is s.,** le temps est à l'orage; *Fig:* **s. discussion,** discussion orageuse; **s. meeting,** réunion houleuse; **s. life,** vie tumultueuse, orageuse; *Orn:* **s. petrel,** pétrel *m* tempête.

story¹ ['stɔːri] *n.* **1.** (*a*) histoire *f*, récit *m*, conte *m*; **to tell a s.,** raconter, conter, une histoire; **there is a s. that . . .,** on raconte que . . .; **as the s. goes,** à ce que l'on raconte; *F:* **that is quite another s.,** ça c'est une autre histoire; **it's the (same) old s., the old, old s.,** c'est toujours la même histoire; **it's a long s.,** c'est toute une histoire; **these bruises tell their own s.,** ces meurtrissures en disent long; (*b*) anecdote *f*; **funny, good, s.,** bonne histoire; **he can tell a good s.,** il en sait de bonnes; (*c*) histoire (de qn, qch.). **2. short s.,** nouvelle *f*, conte; **short s. writer,** nouvelliste *mf*. **3.** intrigue *f* (d'un roman, d'une pièce de théâtre). **4.** *Journ: F:* article *m*. **5.** *F:* conte; mensonge *m*; **to tell stories,** dire des mensonges. **6.** *A:* l'histoire, la légende.

story² *n. esp. NAm:* = STOREY.

storybook ['stɔːribuk] *n.* livre *m* de contes; livre d'histoires; *attrib.* **it looks like a s. castle,** cela ressemble au château d'un conte de fées.

storyteller ['stɔːritelər] *n.* **1.** conteur, -euse. **2.** *F: O:* (*esp. said to children*) menteur, -euse.

storytelling ['stɔːriteliŋ] *n.* **1.** l'art *m* de conter; **to be good at s.,** avoir le talent de raconter des histoires. **2.** *F: O:* mensonges *mpl*.

stoup ['stuːp] *n. Ecc:* bénitier *m*.

stout¹ [staut] *a.* **1.** (i) fort, vigoureux; (ii) brave, vaillant; (iii) ferme, résolu; **s. fellow,** (i) homme vaillant, courageux; (ii) gaillard *m* solide; **to put up a s. resistance,** se défendre vaillamment; **s. heart,** cœur vaillant. **2.** (*of thg*) fort, solide; (*of cloth*) renforcé; (*of material*) résistant. **3.** gros, *f.* grosse; corpulent, fort; **to grow s.,** engraisser; prendre de l'embonpoint, du ventre. **-ly** *adv.* **1.** fortement, vigoureusement; (nier qch.) (fort et) ferme; **he s. maintained that . . .,** il affirmait énergiquement que . . .. **2.** (bâti) solidement.

stout² *n.* stout *m*; bière brune forte.

stouthearted [staut'hɑːtid] *a.* courageux, intrépide.

stoutness ['stautnis] *n.* **1.** fermeté *f*, vigueur *f* (de la résistance, etc.). **2.** solidité *f*. **3.** embonpoint *m*.

stove [stouv] *n.* **1.** (*a*) poêle *m*, fourneau *m*; **oil s.,** (i) poêle à pétrole; (ii) calorifère *m* à mazout; (*b*) fourneau de cuisine; cuisinière *f*; (*small, portable*) réchaud *m*; **electric, gas, s.,** cuisinière électrique, à gaz. **2.** *Ch: Ind:* étuve *f*, four *m*.

stove-enamelled ['stouvinæm(ə)ld] *a.* émaillé au four.

stovepipe ['stouvpaip] *n.* **1.** tuyau *m* de poêle. **2.** *F: O:* **s. hat,** chapeau tuyau de poêle.

stow [stou] *v.tr.* **1. to s. (away),** mettre en place, ranger, serrer (des objets); **to s. away a huge meal,** bouffer un repas énorme; *P:* **s. it!** (i) la ferme! (ii) ça suffit! **2.** *Nau:* arrimer (des marchandises); saisir (l'ancre, les canots). **3.** *v.i.* **to s. away,** s'embarquer clandestinement (à bord d'un navire, d'un avion). **4. to s. sth. full of sth.,** remplir qch. de qch. **stowing** *n.* **1. s. (away),** rangement *m*, mise *f* en place. **2.** *Nau:* arrimage *m* (de la cargaison). **3. s. away,** voyage clandestin.

stowage ['stouidʒ] *n. Nau:* (*a*) arrimage *m*; (*b*) capacité *f* utilisable pour marchandises; espace *m* utile; (*c*) frais *mpl* d'arrimage.

stowaway ['stouəwei] *n. Nau: Av:* passager, voyageur, clandestin.

stower ['stouər] *n.* **1.** *Nau:* arrimeur *m*. **2.** *Min:* remblayeur *m*.

strabismus [stræ'bizməs] *n. Med:* strabisme *m*.

straddle ['strædl] **1.** *v.i.* (*a*) écarter, écarquiller, les jambes; (*b*) éviter de se compromettre, de se prononcer; (*c*) *Artil:* tirer à la fourchette. **2.** *v.tr.* (*a*) enfourcher (un cheval); se mettre à califourchon sur (une chaise); chevaucher (un mur); (*b*) *NAm:* refuser de se compromettre sur (une question).

strafe [strɑːf, *NAm:* streif] *v.tr.* **1.** *Mil:* (i) faire subir à (l'ennemi) un bombardement en règle; (ii) mitrailler (l'ennemi) en rase-mottes. **2.** (*a*) rosser (qn); (*b*) semoncer (qn).

straggle ['strægl] *v.i.* **1. to s. (along),** marcher sans ordre, à la débandade; *Mil:* rester en arrière; traîner. **2. his hair straggled over his collar,** ses cheveux traînaient en désordre sur le col de son veston. **straggling** *a.* **a few s. houses,** quelques maisons eparpillées; **s. hairs,** cheveux épars, mal plantés.

straggler ['stræglər] *n.* traînard, -arde; *Nau:* (*ship, sailor*) retardataire *m*.

straggly ['strægli] *a.* (*of branches, hair*) épars.

straight [streit] **I.** *a.* **1.** (*a*) droit, rectiligne; **s. line,** (ligne) droite (*f*); (*of figure*) **s. up and down,** tout d'une venue; **s. back, legs,** dos droit, jambes droites; **s. hair,** cheveux (i) raides, (ii) plats; *Tls:* **s. edge,** règle *f* (à araser); (*b*) (mouvement) en ligne droite; **to fly s. as a dart, an arrow,** voler droit comme une flèche; *Box:* **s. right, left,** direct *m* du droit, gauche; (*c*) *Turf: Fin:* **s. tip,** tuyau sûr, de la source; (*d*) de suite; *Ten:* **to win in three s. sets,** gagner par trois sets de suite. **2.** (*a*) honnête; loyal, -aux; franc, *f.* franche; (réponse) sans équivoque; **s. as a die,** d'une droiture absolue; **s. dealings,** procédés *mpl* honnêtes; **to be s. with s.o.,** agir loyalement avec qn, envers qn; **to play a s. game,** jouer bon jeu bon argent; (*b*) *F:* normal, hétérosexuel. **2.** net, *f.* nette; tout simple; *Th:* **s. part,** rôle sérieux; **s. actor,** comédien *m* dramatique; (*comedian's*) **s. man,** faire-valoir *m inv*; *Pol:* **s. fight,** campagne électorale à deux candidats; *U.S:* **s. ticket,** (i) programme *m* (du parti) sans modification aucune; (ii) voix donnée à tous les candidats d'un parti; *F:* **s. whisky,** whisky sec; **to drink one's whisky s.,** boire son whisky sec. **4.** (*a*) droit; d'aplomb; **to put sth. s.,** redresser, ajuster, qch.; **your tie isn't s.,** votre cravate est (tout) de travers; (*b*) en ordre; **to put the room s.,** remettre de l'ordre dans la pièce; **to put things, matters, s.,** arranger les choses; débrouiller l'affaire; **let's try to get things s.,** essayons d'y voir clair; *F:* **get this s.!** comprends-moi bien! **I need five hundred pounds to get me s.,** il me faut cinq cents livres pour me remettre d'aplomb. **5. s.-edged,** à tranchant droit; **s.-faced,** (personne) qui ne sourit pas; impassible; **s.-haired,** aux cheveux (i) plats, (ii) raides. **II.** *n.* **1.** (*a*) aplomb *m*; **to be out of (the) s.,** n'être pas d'aplomb; être de travers; **to cut a material on the s.,** couper une étoffe de droit fil; (*b*) **the s. and narrow,** le droit chemin; *F:* **to be on the s.,** vivre honnêtement; **to act on the s.,** agir loyalement. **2.** (*a*) *Rac:* **the s.,** la ligne droite; (*b*) *Rail:* alignement (droit). **3.** *P:* (*a*) personne honnête (et vieux jeu); (*b*) personne normale, hétérosexuelle. **III.** *adv.* **1.** droit; **to shoot**

s., tirer juste; **to go s.,** (i) aller droit; (ii) vivre honnêtement; (iii) (*of drug addict*) se désintoxiquer; **keep s. on,** continuez tout droit; **to read a book s. through,** lire un livre d'un bout à l'autre. **2.** directement; **it comes s. from Paris,** ça vient directement, tout droit, de Paris; **I'll come s. back,** je ne ferai qu'aller et (re)venir; **to come, go, s. to the point,** aller, venir, droit au fait; **to drink s. from the bottle,** boire à même la bouteille; **to walk s. in,** entrer sans frapper; **s. away,** immédiatement, aussitôt; tout de suite; **s. off,** sur-le-champ; tout de suite; **I can't tell you s. off,** je ne peux pas vous le dire tout de suite. **3.** tout droit; directement; **it is s. across the road,** c'est juste en face; **s. above sth.,** juste au-dessus de qch.; **to look s.o. s. in the face,** regarder qn bien en face; *F:* **to let s.o. have it s.,** dire son fait à qn; **I told him s. (out) what I thought of it,** je lui ai dit carrément, franchement, tout net, ce que j'en pensais. **4.** (*a*) honnêtement; **to deal s. with people,** être loyal en affaires; **to play s.,** jouer beau jeu; *F:* **s.!** vrai de vrai! sans blague! (*b*) *Th:* **to play a part s.,** jouer un rôle sans complications.

straightaway ['streitəwei] *NAm:* **1.** *a.* (*a*) en ligne droite; (*b*) (*of line*) droit; (*c*) (*of style, language*) simple, sans détours; (*d*) (*of result*) immédiat. **2.** *adv.* immédiatement; tout de suite.

straighten ['streit(ə)n] **1.** *v.tr.* (*a*) rendre (qch.) droit; (re)dresser (qch.); **to s. one's back,** se redresser; **to s. (out),** défausser (une barre); *F:* **to s. out the traffic,** canaliser les véhicules; (*b*) **to s. (up),** ranger, mettre en ordre; **to s. one's tie,** arranger sa cravate; **to s. (out) one's affairs,** arranger ses affaires; mettre ses affaires en ordre; **I will try to s. things out,** je vais essayer d'arranger les choses. **2.** *v.i.* se redresser; devenir droit; (*of pers.*) **to s. up,** se redresser; **I expect things will s. out,** je pense que ça se rangera.

straightforward [streit'fɔːwəd] *a.* **1.** (*of movement*) droit, direct. **2.** (*of pers., conduct*) loyal, -aux; franc, *f.* franche; sans détours; **to give a s. answer to a question,** répondre sans détours à une question; **to be quite s. about it,** y aller de franc jeu. **-ly** *adv.* (agir) avec droiture, loyalement; (parler) carrément, franchement, sans détours.

straightforwardness [streit'fɔːwədnis] *n.* droiture *f,* honnêteté *f,* franchise *f.*

straightness ['streitnis] *n.* **1.** rectitude *f* (d'une ligne). **2.** droiture *f,* rectitude (de conduite).

strain¹ [strein] *n.* **1.** (*a*) (i) tension *f,* surtension *f;* effort *m,* contrainte *f;* (ii) *Ph:* rapport *m* de la déformation, allongement *m* unitaire; **the s. on the rope,** la tension de la corde; **to relieve the s. on, take the s. off, a beam,** soulager une poutre; *Mec.E:* **breaking s.,** force *f,* contrainte, à la rupture; effort de rupture; (*of beam*) **to take the s.,** (i) être soumis à, (ii) supporter, la tension; (*b*) **it would be, put, too great a s. on my purse,** ce serait trop demander à ma bourse; **the s. of modern life,** la tension de la vie moderne; **the s. of business,** la fatigue des affaires; **mental s.,** surmenage *m;* **eye s.,** fatigue *f* des yeux. **2.** (*a*) *Med:* entorse *f,* foulure *f;* **s. in the back,** tour *m,* effort, de reins; (*b*) déformation. **3.** *Poet:* (*usu. pl.*) accents *mpl;* **sweet strains,** doux accords. **4.** ton *m* (d'un discours, etc.); **he said much more in the same s.,** il s'est étendu longuement dans ce sens.

strain² **I.** *v.tr.* **1.** tendre, surtendre (un câble); **to s. one's ears,** tendre l'oreille; **to s. one's eyes,** (i) se fatiguer, s'abîmer, les yeux, la vue (**doing sth.,** à faire qch.); (ii) s'efforcer (**to see sth.,** pour voir qch.); **to s. one's voice,** se fatiguer la voix; forcer sa voix; **to s. one's powers,** pousser trop loin l'exercice de ses pouvoirs; **to s. relations,** tendre les rapports (**between,** entre); **to s. one's resources,** grever ses ressources jusqu'à la limite. **2.** (*a*) fouler, forcer (un membre); **to s. one's back,** se donner un tour, un effort, de reins; **to s. one's heart,** se forcer le cœur; **to s. a muscle,** se froisser un muscle; (*b*) forcer (un mât, une poutre); *Mec.E:* déformer (une pièce); (*c*) **to s. oneself,** (i) se surmener, *F:* s'éreinter (**doing sth.,** à faire qch.); (ii) faire un faux mouvement; se donner un effort; **he doesn't (exactly) s. himself,** il ne se foule pas la rate. **3.** (*a*) filtrer, passer (un liquide) (à travers un linge); tamiser; passer (le bouillon); (*b*) faire égoutter (les légumes); **to s. sth. out (of a liquid),** enlever, ôter, extraire, qch. d'un liquide (en se servant d'une passoire). **II.** *v.i.* **1.** faire un (grand) effort; peiner; **to s. at a rope, at the oars,** tirer sur une corde, sur les rames; **the author doesn't s. after effect,** l'auteur ne s'évertue pas à produire de l'effet; (*of dog*) **to s. at the leash,** tirer sur la laisse. **2.** (*of beam*) fatiguer, travailler; (*of rope*) être trop tendu. **3.** *Mec.E:* (*of machine part*) se déformer; gauchir; se fausser. **4.** **to s. at (doing) sth.,** se faire scrupule de (faire) qch. **5.** (*of liquid*) filtrer (**through,** à travers). **strained** *a.* **1.** (*a*) (*of rope, etc.*) tendu; trop tendu; **s. nerves,** nerfs tendus; **s. relations,** rapports tendus; (*b*) **s. ankle,** cheville foulée; **s. heart,** cœur forcé. **2.** (*a*) (rire) forcé, contraint; (*b*) (*of language, interpretation*) forcé, exagéré; poussé trop loin. **3.** (*of liquid*) filtré.

strain³ *n.* **1.** qualité héritée, inhérente; **a s. of weakness,** un fond de faiblesse. **2.** (*a*) race *f,* lignée *f;* (*b*) *Biol:* souche *f* (d'un virus); variété *f* (de graine).

strainer ['streinər] *n.* (*a*) (i) filtre *m;* (ii) tamis *m;* *Cu:* passoire *f;* **tea s.,** passe-thé *m inv;* **milk s.,** passe-lait *m inv;* (*b*) *Ind: etc:* épurateur *m* (d'air, etc.).

strait [streit] **1.** *a.* (*a*) *A:* étroit; (*b*) **s. jacket, waistcoat,** camisole *f* de force. **2.** *n.pl.* (*a*) *Geog:* (*with proper name*) détroit *m;* **the Straits of Gibraltar,** le détroit de Gibraltar; **the Straits of Dover,** le Pas de Calais; (*b*) **to be in dire, desperate, straits,** être dans (i) une situation désespérée, (ii) la plus grande gêne.

straitlaced ['streit'leist] *a.* prude; collet monté *inv.*

strand¹ [strænd] *n. Lit:* rive *f,* plage *f,* grève *f.*

strand² **1.** *v.tr.* échouer (un navire). **2.** *v.i.* (*of ship, whale*) (s')échouer. **stranded** *a.* **1.** (navire) échoué; **s. whale,** baleine échouée à la côte. **2.** (*a*) (*of pers.*) à bout de ressources; (*b*) laissé en arrière; abandonné; **to leave s.o. s.,** laisser qn en plan; **to be s.,** être, rester, en panne.

strand³ *n.* **1.** (*a*) brin *m,* toron *m* (de cordage); *Needlew:* brin (de fil à coudre); (*b*) brin, corde *f;* (*c*) fil *m* (d'un tissu); *Fig:* **to unravel the strands of a complicated affair,** démêler les fils d'une affaire compliquée. **2.** fil (de perles); tresse *f* (de cheveux).

strand⁴ *v.tr.* (*a*) toronner (un cordage); (*b*) **to s. a coloured thread into a piece of cloth,** introduire un fil de couleur dans la trame d'une étoffe. **stranded** *a.* **three-s. rope,** corde à trois torons.

strange [strein(d)ʒ] *a.* **1.** (*a*) *A:* étranger; **in a s. land,** dans un pays étranger; **a s. man,** un étranger; (*b*) **s. faces,** des visages nouveaux, inconnus; **I can't work with s. tools,** je ne peux pas travailler avec des outils qui ne sont pas les miens; **this handwriting is s. to me,** je ne connais pas cette écriture; **I felt s. in those surroundings,** je me sentais dépaysé dans ce milieu. **2.** étrange; singulier, bizarre; **s. beasts,** bêtes curieuses; **she wears the strangest clothes,** elle porte les vêtements les plus bizarres; **it's a s. thing,** c'est une chose étrange, curieuse; **s. to say, I've never met him,** chose étrange (à dire), je ne l'ai jamais rencontré; **it's s. that you should not have, haven't, heard of it,** il est étonnant que vous ne l'ayez pas appris. **-ly** *adv.* étrangement, singulièrement; **s. enough, he felt nothing,** chose étrange, il n'a rien senti.

strangeness ['strein(d)ʒnis] *n.* **1.** étrangeté *f;* singularité *f,* bizarrerie *f.* **2.** étrangeté, nouveauté *f.*

stranger ['strein(d)ʒər] *n.* **1.** (*a*) étranger, -ère; inconnu, -ue; **I'm a s. here,** je suis étranger ici, je ne suis pas d'ici; **they're strangers (to us),** nous ne les connaissons pas; **he's a complete s. to me,** il m'est tout à fait inconnu; **you're quite a s.,** vous vous faites rare; **to become a s. to s.o., sth.,** s'aliéner de qn, qch.; **he's a s., no s., to fear,** il ne connaît pas, il connaît bien, la peur; (*in House of Commons*) **I spy strangers!** je demande le huis clos! (*b*) *Jur:* celui qui n'est pas partie (**to an act,** à un fait); tiers *m.* **2.** *F:* (*in cup of tea*) chinois *m.*

strangle ['stræŋgl] **1.** *v.tr.* étrangler (qn); étouffer (un rire); réprimer (un éternuement); **to s. the press,** étrangler la presse; **strangled voice,** voix étranglée, strangulée. **2.** *v.i.* s'étrangler. **strangling** *n.* étranglement *m.*

stranglehold ['stræŋglhould] *n.* **1.** *Wr:* étranglement *m.* **2. to have a s. on s.o.,** tenir qn à la gorge; **economic s.,** mainmise *f* économique.

strangler ['stræŋglər] *n.* (*pers.*) étrangleur, -euse.

strangulate ['strængjuleit] *Med:* **1.** *v.tr.* étrangler (l'intestin). **2.** *v.i.* (*of hernia, intestine*) devenir étranglé; **strangulated hernia,** hernie étranglée.

strangulation [stræŋgju'leiʃ(ə)n] *n.* strangulation *f*; *Fig:* **economic s.,** asphyxie *f* économique.

strap¹ [stræp] *n.* **1.** (*a*) courroie *f*; **watch s.,** bracelet *m* (en cuir) pour montre; *Harn:* **stirrup s.,** étrivière *f*; (*b*) martinet *m.* **2.** (*a*) bande *f*, sangle (de cuir, de toile); (*b*) *Veh:* **window s.,** tirant *m* de fenêtre, de vitre; (*in tube*) **(standing passengers') s.,** poignée *f* d'appui; (*c*) *Cost:* bande, patte *f* (d'étoffe); bretelle *f*; *Bootm:* barrette *f* (de soulier); **trouser s.,** sous-pied *m*, *pl.* sous-pieds (de pantalon). **3.** *Tchn:* (*a*) attache *f*, lien *m* (en métal); armature *f*, étrier *m* (de renfort); (*b*) *Mch:* chape *f*, bride *f* (de bielle); collier *m*, bague *f* (d'excentrique); (*c*) *Mec.E:* bande, ruban *m.*

strap² *v.tr.* (**strapped** [stræpt]) **1. to s. sth. (up),** attacher, lier, fixer, qch. avec une courroie; boucler (une malle); ceinturer (une caisse); sangler (un paquet). **2.** administrer une correction à (un enfant) avec le bout d'une courroie. **3.** *Med:* (*a*) mettre des bandelettes, un pansement adhésif, sur (une blessure); (*b*) maintenir (un membre cassé) au moyen de bandages. **strapping 1.** *a.* solide, robuste; **s. fellow,** grand gaillard; **tall s. girl,** fille grande et bien faite. **2.** *n. coll.* courroies *fpl*; liens *mpl.*

straphang ['stræphæŋ] *v.i.* voyager debout (en se tenant à la courroie, à la poignée).

straphanger ['stræphæŋər] *n.* voyageur, -euse, debout (dans le métro, etc.).

strapless ['stræplis] *a.* sans bretelles; **s. bra,** bustier *m*; soutien-gorge *m* sans bretelles.

stratagem ['strætədʒəm] *n.* ruse *f*; stratagème *m.*

strategic [strə'tiːdʒik] *a.* stratégique. **-ally** *adv.* stratégiquement.

strategist ['strætədʒist] *n.* stratège *m.*

strategy ['strætidʒi] *n.* stratégie *f.*

stratification [strætifi'keiʃ(ə)n] *n.* stratification *f.*

stratify ['strætifai] **1.** *v.tr.* stratifier. **2.** *v.i.* se stratifier. **stratified** *a.* (formation) en couches.

stratocruiser ['strætoukruːzər] *n.* avion *m* (de ligne) stratosphérique.

stratosphere ['strætəsfiər] *n.* stratosphère *f.*

stratum *pl.* **-a** ['strɑːtəm, -ə] *n.* (*a*) *Geol:* strate *f*, couche *f*; (*b*) couche (d'air, etc.); **the various strata of society,** les différentes couches sociales.

straw [strɔː] *n.* **1.** paille *f*; **loose s.,** paille de litière; **rice s.,** paille de riz; *Fig:* **man of s.,** *NAm:* **s. man,** (i) homme de paille, de carton; (ii) prête-nom *m*, *pl.* prête-noms; **s. mattress,** paillasse *f*; **s. mat,** paillasson *m*; **s. hat,** chapeau *m* de paille; *Agr:* **s. cutter,** hache-paille *m inv*; **s.-coloured,** (jaune) paille *inv*; **s.-bottomed,** (chaise) de paille, paillée. **2. to drink lemonade through a s.,** boire de la limonade avec une paille; **it's not worth a s.,** cela ne vaut pas quatre sous; *Fig:* **to clutch at any s.,** se raccrocher à n'importe quoi; **straws in the wind,** indications *fpl* de l'opinion publique; **s. vote,** sondage *m* d'opinion publique (à un meeting, etc.); *Prov:* **it's the last s. that breaks the camel's back,** une goutte d'eau suffit pour faire déborder le vase; **it's the last s.!** ça c'est le comble! il ne manquait plus que cela!

strawberry ['strɔːb(ə)ri] *n.* (*a*) *Bot:* fraise *f*; **wild s.,** *NAm:* **field s.,** (petite) fraise des bois; **s. jam,** confiture *f* de fraises; **s. ice,** glace *f* à la fraise; (*b*) **s. (plant),** fraisier *m*; **s. bed,** planche *f*, plant *m*, de fraisiers; **s. field,** plantation *f* de fraisiers, fraiseraie *f*; (*c*) **s. colour,** fraise *inv*; **s. blond,** blond ardent; **s. mark,** fraise (sur la peau).

stray¹ [strei] **I.** *n.* **1.** (*a*) animal égaré; *Jur:* bête épave; (*b*) **waifs and strays,** enfants abandonnés. **2.** *W.Tel:* **strays,** bruissements *mpl* parasites; (bruits *mpl* de) friture *f.* **II.** *a.* **1.** (*of animal*) égaré, perdu; *Jur:* épave. **2.** égaré; (exemple, specimen) isolé; **s. bullets,** balles perdues; **s. thoughts,** pensées détachées.

stray² *v.i.* s'égarer, errer; (*of sheep*) s'écarter du troupeau; **to s. from the right path,** s'écarter du bon chemin; **to let one's thoughts s.,** laisser vaguer, errer, ses pensées; **to s. from the point,** sortir du sujet.

streak¹ [striːk] *n.* **1.** raie *f*, rayure *f*; bande *f*, strie *f*; traînée *f* (de brume, de vapeur); trait *m*, filet *m*, filtrée *f* (de lumière); **s. of sunlight,** coulée *f* de soleil; **the first s. of dawn,** la première lueur du jour; **like a s. of lightning,** comme un éclair; *F:* **to do a s.,** courir nu (en public). **2.** filon *m* (de minerai); *F:* **I've had a s. of luck,** je tiens le filon; **winning s.,** suite *f* de victoires; **to hit a winning s.,** être en veine; **there's a s. of Irish blood in him,** il y a en lui une trace de sang irlandais; **there was a s. of cowardice in him,** il y avait de la lâcheté dans sa nature.

streak² **1.** *v.tr.* rayer, strier; zébrer; **fur streaked with black,** pelage rayé de bandes sombres; **wall streaked with damp,** mur couturé d'humidité; **white marble streaked with red,** marbre blanc veiné de rouge. **2.** *v.i.* *F:* (*a*) **to s. along, past,** aller, passer, comme un éclair; **to s. off,** se sauver à toutes jambes; (*b*) courir nu (en public). **streaking** *n.* **1.** raies *fpl*, rayures *fpl*, bandes; *Hairdr:* effet de rayure (obtenu en colorant une mèche). **2.** *F:* course *f* de nudiste (devant le public).

streaker ['striːkər] *n.* *F:* coureur, -euse, nu(e) (en public).

streaky ['striːki] *a.* **1.** (nuage, etc.) en raies, en bandes. **2.** rayé, strié; zébré. **3.** (*of bacon*) entrelardé.

stream¹ [striːm] *n.* **1.** (*a*) cours *m* d'eau; fleuve *m*, rivière *f*; (*b*) ruisseau *m*; **mountain s.,** torrent *m*; *Prov:* **little streams make great rivers,** les petits ruisseaux font les grandes rivières; (*c*) flot *m* (d'eau); **in a thin s.,** en mince filet; (*d*) *Sch:* **three-s. school,** école où les classes sont réparties sur trois niveaux différents. **2.** coulée *f* (de lave); flot(s) *m(pl)*, jet *m* (de lumière, de sang); flux *m*, torrent (de larmes, de paroles); flots (de gens); averse *f* (de félicitations); **s. of cars,** défilé ininterrompu de voitures; **to hold up the s. of traffic,** arrêter le flot de voitures; **in one continuous s.,** à jet continu. **3.** courant *m*; **with the s.,** dans le sens du courant; au fil de l'eau; **against the s.,** contre le courant, à contre-courant; *Fig:* **to go with the s.,** suivre le courant; suivre le mouvement; **the main s. of public opinion,** le courant de l'opinion publique; *Lit:* **s. of consciousness,** monologue intérieur.

stream² **1.** *v.i.* (*a*) (*of liquid*) couler à flots; ruisseler; **people were streaming over the bridge,** les gens traversaient le pont à flot continu; **the sunlight streams in(to the room),** le soleil pénètre à flots (dans la chambre); (*b*) (*of surface*) ruisseler (**with,** de); **her**

eyes were streaming with tears, ses larmes coulaient à flots; (*c*) (*of hair, garment, banner*) flotter (au vent). **2.** *v.tr.* (*a*) verser, laisser couler, (un liquide) à flots; **the river streamed blood,** la rivière coulait rouge; (*b*) *Sch:* répartir (les élèves) en sections de force homogène. **streaming 1.** *a.* (*a*) (i) (liquide) qui coule; *F:* **to have a s. cold,** avoir un gros rhume; (ii) (*of surface, umbrella*) ruisselant; (*b*) (drapeau) flottant au vent. **2.** *n. Sch:* répartition *f* (des élèves) en sections de force homogène.

streamer ['stri:mər] *n.* **1.** (*a*) banderole *f*; *Nau:* flamme *f*; **(paper) streamers,** serpentins *mpl* (de carnaval); (*b*) *Journ:* titre flamboyant. **2.** *Meteor:* **streamers,** lumière *f* polaire; aurore boréale.

streamline¹ ['stri:mlain] *n.* **1.** *Ph:* courant naturel (d'un fluide). **2.** *Aut: Av:* ligne fuyante.

streamline² *v.tr.* **1.** caréner (une voiture). **2.** simplifier, rationaliser (une méthode); réduire (l'économie) à l'essentiel. **streamlined** *a.* **1.** (*a*) *Aut: Av:* caréné; (fuselage) aérodynamique; (*b*) (*of fish, ship's hull*) hydrodynamique. **2.** (*of system*) rationalisé; (économie) réduite à l'essentiel. **streamlining** *n.* **1.** carénage *m*, profilage *m* (de la carrosserie). **2.** simplification *f*, rationalisation *f* (d'un système); réduction *f* (de l'économie) à l'essentiel.

street [stri:t] *n.* (*a*) rue *f*; **back s.,** (i) petite rue écartée; (ii) *Pej:* rue pauvre, mal fréquentée; **the High S.,** la Grand-rue; **to turn, throw, s.o. (out) into the s.,** jeter qn à la rue, mettre qn sur le pavé; **to walk the streets,** (i) courir les rues, battre le pavé; (ii) (*of prostitute*) (*also* **to be on the streets**), faire le trottoir; **s. walker,** fille *f* de trottoir; racoleuse *f*; **the man in the s.,** Monsieur Tout-le-Monde; **he's streets ahead of his competitors,** il a devancé de beaucoup, dépassé de tout en tout, ses concurrents; **that's right up my s.,** c'est mon rayon, dans ma ligne; **s. guide,** indicateur *m* des rues; **s. lamp, light,** réverbère *m*; **s. level,** rez-de-chaussée *m inv;* **s. market,** (i) marché *m* en plein air (dans une rue); (ii) *St. Exch:* marché après Bourse; **s. musician,** musicien, -ienne, des rues, de carrefour; (*b*) (habitants *mpl* de la) rue; **the whole s. heard the row,** toute la rue a entendu le chahut; *F:* **the S.,** (i) *Journ:* **(Fleet S.),** le monde des journalistes; (ii) *U.S:* **(Wall S.),** le monde financier.

streetcar ['stri:tka:r] *n. NAm:* tramway *m*.

strength [streŋθ] *n.* **1.** (*a*) force *f* (d'un homme, d'un acide); *Ch:* titre *m*, teneur *f* (d'une solution); *El:* intensité *f* (d'un courant); **solution at full s., full-s. solution,** solution concentrée; **s. of mind,** force de caractère; **s. of will,** résolution *f*; **by sheer s.,** de vive force; à force de bras; **to recover, regain, s.,** se rétablir, se remonter; reprendre des forces; **you must keep up your s.,** il faut vous sustenter; **to build up one's s. again,** se reconstituer; **to lose s.,** s'affaiblir; **to do sth. on the s. of what one has been told,** faire qch. en se fiant à, en s'appuyant sur, ce qu'on vous a dit; **he got a good job on the s. of his qualifications,** il a obtenu un bon emploi grâce à ses diplômes; (*b*) solidité *f*, résistance *f* (d'une poutre, d'une corde); ténacité *f* (du papier); robustesse *f* (d'un meuble); **s. of a friendship,** solidité d'une amitié; *Mec:* **s. of materials,** résistance des matériaux; (*c*) force (d'un joueur, d'une équipe); **to go from s. to s.,** aller de mieux en mieux; avancer à pas de géant. **2. to be present in great s.,** être présents en grand nombre; **to be there in full s.,** assister (à la cérémonie) au grand complet. **3.** *Mil:* effectif(s) *m(pl)* (d'un régiment); **war, peace, s.,** effectif de guerre, de paix; **under s.,** à effectif insuffisant; **to bring a battalion up to s.,** compléter, recruter, un bataillon; **to be on the s.,** figurer sur les contrôles.

strengthen ['streŋθ(ə)n] **1.** *v.tr.* consolider (un mur, une maison); renforcer (une poutre, une loi); fortifier (qn, le corps); (r)affermir (l'autorité de qn); *Ch:* augmenter la concentration d'(une solution); *Typ:* charger (une couleur); **it would s. my hand, position,** cela raffermirait ma position. **2.** *v.i.* (*a*) se fortifier, se renforcer, s'affermir; (*b*) prendre, reprendre, des forces. **strengthening 1.** *a.* fortifiant; (*of drink*) réconfortant. **2.** *n.* renforcement *m*, renforçage *m*; consolidation *f*, (r)affermissement *m*; armement *m* (d'une poutre); **s. piece,** renfort *m*.

strenuous ['strenjuəs] *n.* **1.** (*of pers.*) actif, énergique; zélé. **2.** (*of opposition*) acharné; (*of effort*) tendu; (*of work*) ardu; **s. life,** vie toute d'effort; **to make s. efforts to get sth. done,** tendre tous ses efforts vers l'accomplissement de qch. **-ly** *adv.* vigoureusement; énergiquement.

strenuousness ['strenjuəsnis] *n.* (*of pers.*) ardeur *f*, vigueur *f*, zèle *m*; (*of work*) dureté *f*; (*of opposition*) acharnement *m*.

streptococcal [streptou'kɔk(ə)l] *a.* streptococcique.

streptococcus, *pl.* **-cocci** [streptou'kɔkəs, -'kɔk(s)ai] *n. Med:* streptocoque *m*.

streptomycin [streptou'maisin] *n. Med:* streptomycine *f*.

stress¹ [stres] *n.* **1.** force *f*, contrainte *f*; **s. of weather,** gros temps. **2.** (*a*) *Mec.E: Mec:* tension *f*, travail *m*, contrainte; (*of beam*) **to be in s.,** travailler; **subjected to great s.,** assujetti à des efforts considérables; **s. limit,** limite *f* de travail, de fatigue; (*b*) **times of slackness and times of s.,** temps *mpl* de relâchement et temps d'effort; **period of storm and s.,** période *f* de trouble et d'agitation; (*c*) état tendu des nerfs; *Med:* stress *m*; tension nerveuse. **3.** (*a*) insistance *f*; **to lay s. on (sth.),** insister sur, faire ressortir (un fait); insister, peser, sur (un mot); appuyer sur (une syllabe); (*b*) *Ling:* accent *m* (d'intensité); accent tonique; *Pros:* temps marqué; **the s. falls on the last syllable,** l'accent tonique tombe sur la dernière syllabe; **s. mark,** accent écrit.

stress² *v.tr.* **1.** *Mec.E:* charger, fatiguer, faire travailler (une poutre); (*of beam*) **to be stressed,** travailler. **2.** insister sur (qch.); faire ressortir (un fait); souligner, peser sur (un mot); appuyer sur (une syllabe); **stressed syllable,** syllabe accentuée.

stressful ['stresful] *a.* (*of situation*) qui provoque de la tension nerveuse.

stretch¹ [stretʃ] *n.* **1.** (*a*) allongement *m*, extension *f*; déploiement *m* (des ailes); **with a yawn and a s.,** en bâillant et en s'étirant; *F:* **to have a s.,** se dégourdir; *Rac:* **at full s.,** à toute allure, ventre à terre; (*b*) allongement, élargissement *m*, par traction; **by no s. of the imagination could I conceive that . . .,** il me serait absolument impossible de croire que . . .; (*c*) étendue *f*, portée *f* (du bras, du sens d'un mot); **s. of wing,** envergure *f*; *Mus:* **s. of the fingers,** écart *m* des doigts (au piano); (*d*) élasticité *f*; (*of elastic fabric*) **with two-way s.,** extensible dans les deux sens; *Obst:* **s. mark,** vergeture *f*; (*e*) **s. fabric,** tissu extensible. **2.** (*a*) étendue (de pays, d'eau); bande *f* (de terrain); section *f* (de route); (*b*) **for a long s. of time,** longtemps; *F:* **at a s., at one s.,** (tout) d'un trait; d'arrache-pied, d'affilée; **he has been working for hours at a s.,** voilà des heures qu'il travaille sans désemparer; *P:* **to do a five-year s.,** faire cinq ans de prison.

stretch² **I.** *v.tr.* (*a*) tendre (de l'élastique); tendre, tirer, bander (une courroie, un câble, un ressort); étendre, élargir (des souliers, des gants); détirer (le linge); *Art:* **to s. the canvas on the frame,** tendre la toile sur le châssis; **how far can I s. this dish?** pour combien de portions ce plat suffira-t-il au besoin? (*b*) **to s. oneself,** *v.i.* **to s.,** s'étirer; se détirer; **to s. (out),** allonger (le bras); tendre, avancer (la main);

to s. one's neck to see sth., allonger le cou pour voir qch.; **to s. one's legs,** (i) allonger les jambes; (ii) se dégourdir les jambes; **to lie stretched (out) on the ground,** être étendu par terre de tout son long; (*of bird*) **to s. its wings,** déployer ses ailes; (*c*) éprouver, exercer (la patience de qn); demander le maximum effort de (qn); grever (les ressources) jusqu'à la limite; **to be fully stretched,** (i) (*of pers.*) donner son plein; (ii) (*of resources, services*) être poussé à bout; (*d*) forcer (le sens d'un mot); **to s. the truth,** outrepasser les bornes de la vérité; **to s. a point,** faire une concession, une exception (**for s.o.,** en faveur de qn); *F:* **that's stretching it a bit!** c'est le tirer par les cheveux; (*e*) **to s. a rope across a room,** tendre une corde à travers une pièce; **to s. an awning over the deck,** établir une tente sur le pont. **II.** *v.i.* **1.** (*a*) s'étirer; (*of elastic*) s'étendre, s'allonger; (*of rope*) rendre; (*of gloves, etc.*) s'étendre, s'élargir; **material that stretches,** étoffe qui prête; (*b*) être susceptible d'extension. **2.** (*a*) s'étendre; **the road stretches away into the distance,** la route se déroule au loin; (*b*) **to s. out,** (i) (*of line of runners*) s'étirer; (ii) (*of racehorse*) aller ventre à terre; (iii) *Row:* souquer sur les avirons. **3. my resources won't s. to that,** mes moyens (pécuniaires) ne vont pas jusque-là; **the dish will s. to six helpings,** au besoin on peut faire six portions de ce plat.

stretcher ['stretʃər] *n.* **1.** (*a*) tendeur *m*; tenseur *m* (de hauban); **shoe stretchers,** tendeurs (pour chaussures); conformateurs *mpl*; (*b*) *Art:* **canvas s.,** châssis *m* (de toile d'artiste). **2.** (*a*) bois *m* d'écartement (de hamac); traverse *f* (de tente); baleine *f* (d'un parapluie); (*b*) barreau *m*, bâton *m* (de chaise). **3.** brancard *m*, civière *f*; **s. bearer,** brancardier *m*, ambulancier *m*; **s. party,** détachement *m*, équipe *f*, de brancardiers. **4.** *Nau:* barre *f* des pieds, traversin *m* (d'une embarcation).

stretchy ['stretʃi] *a. F:* élastique.

strew [stru:] *v.tr.* (*p.p.* **strewed** [stru:d] *or* **strewn** [stru:n]) **1. to s. sand over the floor,** jeter, répandre, du sable sur le plancher; **toys were strewn over, around, on, the floor,** des jouets étaient éparpillés sur le plancher. **2. to s. the floor with sand, with flowers,** couvrir le plancher de sable; joncher le plancher de fleurs; **the ground was strewn with rushes,** une jonchée de roseaux recouvrait le sol.

strewth [stru:θ] *int. P:* ça alors!

striated [strai'eitid] *a.* strié; **striated muscle,** muscle strié.

strict [strikt] *a.* **1.** exact, strict; (*a*) précis; **the s. minimum,** le strict minimum; **in the s. sense of the word,** au sens précis, rigoureux, du mot; (*b*) rigoureux; **to observe s. neutrality,** observer une neutralité rigoureuse; **in strictest confidence,** à titre tout à fait confidentiel. **2.** (règlement) étroit, rigide; *Jur:* (délai) péremptoire; (obligation) stricte; (discipline) sévère; (étiquette) rigide; (régime) exact; (jeûne) austère; **s. morals,** morale stricte, rigide; mœurs *fpl* sévères; **s. Moslem,** musulman de stricte obédience; **he gave s. orders,** il a donné des ordres formels; **to keep a s. watch over s.o.,** exercer sur qn une surveillance rigoureuse. **3.** (*of pers.*) sévère; **to be s. with s.o.,** être sévère avec, envers, pour, qn; traiter qn avec beaucoup de rigueur. **-ly** *adv.* **1.** exactement, rigoureusement; **s. speaking,** à proprement parler. **2.** étroitement, strictement; **smoking (is) s. prohibited,** défense formelle, expresse, de fumer; **it is s. forbidden,** c'est absolument défendu; **to guard s.o. s.,** surveiller étroitement qn. **3.** sévèrement; (traité, élevé) avec rigueur.

strictness ['striktnis] *n.* **1.** exactitude rigoureuse, précision *f* (d'une traduction). **2.** rigueur *f* (des règles). **3.** sévérité *f* (de la discipline).

stricture ['striktjər] *n.* **1.** (*a*) *Med:* rétrécissement *m* (du canal de l'urètre); étranglement *m* (de l'intestin); (*b*) *NAm:* restriction *f*. **2.** (*usu. pl.*) **to pass strictures (up)on s.o., sth.,** diriger ses critiques *fpl* contre qn, qch.

stride[1] [straid] *n.* (grand) pas; enjambée *f*; *Sp:* foulée *f*; **to shorten, lengthen, one's s.,** raccourcir, allonger, le pas, *Sp:* la foulée; **to make great strides,** faire de grands progrès, des progrès rapides; **to take sth. in one's s.,** *U.S:* **in s.,** faire qch. sans le moindre effort; **to get into one's s.,** prendre son allure normale; attraper la cadence (d'un travail, etc.).

stride[2] *v.* (*p.t.* **strode** [stroud]; *p.p.* **stridden** ['stridn]) **1.** *v.i.* (*a*) marcher à grands pas, à grandes enjambées; **to s. along, away,** avancer, s'éloigner, à grands pas; **science is striding further ahead each year,** la science avance, progresse, à pas de géant d'année en année; (*b*) **to s. over sth.,** enjamber qch. **2.** *v.tr. Lit:* enjamber (un fossé, etc.).

stridency ['straidənsi] *n.* stridence *f*.

strident ['straidənt] *a.* strident. **-ly** *adv.* stridemment.

strife [straif] *n.* lutte *f*, contestation *f*, différends *mpl*; **domestic s.,** querelles *fpl* de ménage; *Lit:* **to be at s.,** être en conflit, en lutte (**with,** avec).

strike[1] [straik] *n.* **1.** (*a*) coup *m*; sonnerie *f* (d'horloge); (*b*) *Fish:* (i) (*by angler*) ferrage *m*; (ii) (*by fish*) mordage *m*; (*c*) *Games:* (i) (*baseball*) balle manquée (par le batteur); (ii) (*tenpin bowling*) honneur *m* double; (*d*) *Mil:* attaque *f*; **air s.,** raid *m*, intervention aérienne; **s. aircraft,** avions *mpl* d'assaut. **2.** grève *f*; **lightning s.,** grève surprise; **sit-down s.,** grève sur le tas; **sympathy s.,** grève de solidarité; **to go, come out, on s.,** se mettre en grève; *F:* débrayer; (*of prisoner*) **to go on hunger s.,** faire la grève de la faim; **s. breaker,** briseur, -euse, de grève; *F:* renard *m*, jaune *m*; **s. pay,** allocation *f* de grève. **3.** *Min:* rencontre *f* (de minerai, pétrole); découverte *f* (d'un gisement); *F:* **lucky s.,** coup de veine.

strike[2] *v.* (*p.t.* **struck** [strʌk]. *p.p.* **struck,** *A:* **stricken** ['strik(ə)n]) **I.** *v.tr. & ind. tr.* **1.** (*a*) frapper (qn, qch.); **to s. s.o. in the face,** frapper qn à la figure; **to s. s.o. a blow,** porter, assener, un coup à qn; **without striking a blow,** sans coup férir; **ready to s. a blow for freedom of speech,** prêt à se battre pour défendre la liberté de parole; **to be struck by a stone,** être frappé d'une pierre; (*of ship*) **to be struck by a heavy sea,** essuyer un coup de mer; *v.i.* **to s. home,** frapper juste; *Prov:* **s. while the iron is hot,** il faut battre le fer tant il est chaud; (*b*) frapper (une monnaie, une médaille); (*c*) *Mus:* frapper (les touches du piano); toucher de (la harpe); **to s. a chord,** plaquer un accord; **that strikes a familiar note,** cela fait l'effet du déjà vu, du déjà entendu; (*d*) **to s. a bargain,** faire, conclure, un marché. **2.** (*a*) allumer, frotter (une allumette); faire jaillir (des étincelles); *Fig:* **to s. a spark out of s.o.,** tirer de qn un peu d'animation; (*b*) *El:* **to s. the arc,** produire l'arc (entre les charbons). **3. to s. terror into s.o.,** frapper qn de terreur; **the plant strikes root,** la plante prend (racine). **4.** (*a*) **struck by lightning,** (maison) frappée par la foudre; (arbre) foudroyé; **lightning had struck the house,** la foudre était tombée sur la maison; (*b*) **to s. s.o. with surprise,** frapper qn d'étonnement; **struck with terror, panic,** saisi d'effroi, pris de panique. **5.** (*a*) **to s. (against) sth.,** frapper, heurter, donner, contre qch.; buter contre qch.; **his head struck (against) the pavement,** sa tête a porté sur le trottoir; (*of ship*) **to s. (the) bottom,** *v.i.* **to s.,** toucher (le fond); talonner; **to s. an obstruction,** rencontrer un obstacle; (*of ship*) **to s. a mine,** heurter une mine; (*of car*) **to s. a pedestrian,** heurter, tamponner, un piéton; **a sound struck**

my ear, un bruit frappa mon oreille; **the thought struck me that . . .,** l'idée m'est venue, il m'est venu à l'idée, que . .; (*b*) faire une impression (quelconque) sur (qn); **how does, did, she s. you?** quelle impression vous a-t-elle faite? **he strikes me as (being) sincere,** il me paraît sincère; **the place struck him as familiar,** l'endroit lui paraissait familier; **that is how it struck me,** voilà l'effet que cela m'a fait; **did it never s. you that you weren't wanted there?** ne vous est-il jamais venu à l'esprit que vous étiez de trop? (*c*) faire impression à (qn); impressionner (qn); frapper (l'œil, l'imagination); **what struck me was his brazen impudence,** ce qui m'a frappé, c'est son effronterie cynique. **6.** tomber sur, découvrir (une piste); découvrir (un filon d'or); **to s. oil,** (i) atteindre une nappe pétrolifère; rencontrer, toucher, le pétrole; (ii) avoir du succès; trouver le filon; *F:* **he has struck it rich,** il tient le filon. **7.** (*a*) *Nau:* amener, caler (une voile); abaisser, dépasser (un mât); **to s. one's flag, one's colours,** (i) *Nau:* amener, *Navy:* rentrer, son pavillon; mettre pavillon bas; (ii) *Fig:* se rendre; (*b*) démonter (une tente); **to s. camp,** lever le camp. **8. to s. an attitude,** prendre une attitude dramatique; poser. **9.** (*a*) tirer (une ligne), décrire (un cercle); (*b*) **to s. an average,** établir, prendre, une moyenne. **II.** *v.i.* **1.** (*a*) attaquer; **don't wait for the enemy to s.,** n'attendez pas que l'ennemi attaque; (*b*) **to s. at sth.,** menacer qch.; (*c*) (*of serpent*) foncer. **2.** (*of clock*) sonner; (*with cogn. acc.*) **to s. the hour,** sonner l'heure; **it has struck ten,** dix heures viennent de sonner; **his hour has struck,** son heure est sonnée, a sonné. **3.** *Ind:* se mettre en grève; *F:* débrayer. **4.** prendre (une certaine direction); **to s. across country,** prendre à travers champs. **5.** (*of roots*) s'enfoncer (**into sth.,** dans qch.); (*of cutting*) prendre (racine). **stricken** *a. Lit:* **1.** *Ven:* (daim) blessé. **2.** (*a*) (*of pers.*) affligé; éprouvé; **s. with grief,** accablé de douleur; **s. by a disease,** frappé d'une maladie; (*b*) **the s. city,** la ville sinistrée; **the s. vessel,** le vaisseau en détresse, naufragé. **strike back 1.** *v.tr.* **to s. s.o. back,** répondre au coup de qn; **if anyone strikes me I s. (him) back,** si quelqu'un me frappe je rends le coup. **2.** *v.i.* rebrousser chemin. **strike down** *v.tr.* abattre, renverser (qch., qn) (d'un coup de poing); **struck down by disease,** terrassé par la maladie. **strike off 1.** *v.tr.* (*a*) trancher (la tête de qn); (*b*) **to s. off a name from a list, to s. a name off a list,** biffer, rayer, un nom d'une liste; **to s. off a solicitor, doctor,** radier un avoué, médecin; (*c*) *Com:* (*deduct*) **to s. off 5%,** déduire, faire une réduction de, 5%; (*d*) *Typ:* tirer (tant d'exemplaires). **2.** *v.i.* prendre (une certaine direction); **to s. off to the left,** (*of pers.*) prendre à gauche; (*of road*) tourner à gauche. **strike out 1.** *v.tr.* rayer, biffer, raturer, barrer (un mot). **2.** *v.i.* (*a*) **to s. out at s.o.,** allonger, porter, un coup à qn; **to s. out right and left,** frapper à droite et à gauche; (*b*) **I struck out for the shore,** j'ai commencé à nager dans la direction du rivage; (*c*) *Fig:* **to s. out for oneself,** voler de ses propres ailes. **strike up** *v.tr.* (*a*) entonner (une chanson); commencer de jouer (un morceau); *v.i.* **on his arrival the band struck up,** à son arrivée la fanfare attaqua un morceau; (*b*) conclure, nouer (une alliance); contracter (une amitié); **to s. up an acquaintance, a friendship, with s.o.,** lier connaissance avec qn; se lier, se prendre, d'amitié avec qn; **to s. up a conversation with s.o.,** entrer en conversation avec qn. **striking 1.** *a.* (*a*) **s. clock,** pendule *f* à sonnerie; (*b*) (spectacle) frappant, saisissant; (trait) saillant; (situation) dramatique; **he was a s. figure,** il était impressionnant. **2.** *n.* (*a*) (i) frappement *m*; coups *mpl*; **within s. distance,** à portée de la main; *Mil:* frappe *f*; **s. power,** puissance *f* de frappe; (iii) frappe (de la monnaie); (iv) frottement *m* (d'une allumette); **s. surface,** frottoir *m*; (v) *El:* amorçage *m* (de l'arc); (*b*) *Hort:* **s. (root),** reprise *f* (d'une bouture); *Nau:* calage *m* (d'une voile); *Mil:* **s. camp,** levée *f* du camp; (*d*) établissement *m* (d'une moyenne); (*e*) sonnerie *f* (d'une horloge); **s. mechanism,** sonnerie; (*f*) *Ind:* grèves *fpl*; (*g*) (i) **s. down,** abattage *m*, renversement *m*; (ii) **s. off,** rayure *f* (d'un nom); radiation (d'un avoué, d'un médecin); (iii) **s. out,** rayure, biffage *m* (d'un mot). **strikingly** *adv.* d'une manière frappante, saisissante; **s. beautiful,** d'une beauté frappante.

strikebound ['straikbaund] *a.* paralysé par une grève.

striker ['straikər] *n.* **1.** (*pers.*) (*a*) *Metalw:* frappeur, -euse; (*b*) *Sp:* (i) *Ten:* relanceur, -euse; (ii) *Baseball:* batteur *m.* **2.** *Ind:* gréviste *mf.* **3.** (*device*) frappeur; (*of clock*) marteau *m*; (*of firearm*) percuteur *m.*

string[1] [striŋ] *n.* **1.** (*a*) (i) ficelle *f*; (ii) corde *f*, cordon *m*; **ball of s.,** pelote *f* de ficelle; *F:* **to have s.o. on a s.,** (i) tenir qn en lisière; (ii) mener qn par le bout du nez; **to keep s.o. on a s.,** tenir qn en suspens; **with no strings (attached),** sans conditions, sans condition aucune; **s. bag,** filet *m* (à provisions); (*b*) **the strings of a marionette,** les fils *mpl* d'une marionnette; *Fig:* **to pull the strings,** tenir les fils, tirer les ficelles; **to pull strings,** faire jouer ses relations, *F:* le piston. **2.** fibre *f*, filament *m* (de plante); **strings in beans,** fils des haricots; **s. bean,** haricot vert. **3.** (*a*) *Mus:* corde (de violon, piano); **the strings of a violin,** la monture d'un violon; (*in orchestra*) **the strings,** les (instruments, joueurs des instruments, à) cordes; **s. orchestra, s. band,** orchestre *m* à cordes; **s. quartet,** quatuor *m* à cordes; *NAm:* **s. bass,** contrebasse *f*; *Fig:* **to touch a s. in s.o.'s heart,** faire vibrer une corde dans le cœur de qn; **to have more than one s. to one's bow,** avoir plusieurs cordes, plus d'une corde, à son arc; (*b*) corde (d'un arc); cordes, cordage *m* (d'une raquette de tennis); (*c*) *Sp:* **first s.,** meilleur athlète (sélectionné pour une épreuve); *Turf:* premier champion (d'une écurie); **second s.,** second athlète sélectionné; *Turf:* second champion. **4.** (*a*) chapelet *m*, rang *m* (d'oignons); chapelet (d'îles); brochette *f* (de décorations); file *f* (de véhicules); rame *f* (de wagons); train *m* (de péniches); suite *f*, série *f* (de mots); **s. of beads,** (i) collier *m*; (ii) *Ecc:* chapelet; **a whole s. of children, of names,** toute une kyrielle d'enfants, de noms; (*b*) *Turf:* **Lord Derby's s. (of horses),** l'écurie *f* de Lord Derby. **5.** (*a*) *Arch:* **s. course, moulding,** bandeau *m*, cordon *m*; (*b*) *Const:* **s. (board),** limon *m* (d'escalier); **s. piece,** longeron *m*, longrine *f.*

string[2] *v.tr.* (*p.p.* & *p.t.* **strung** [strʌŋ]) **1.** (*a*) mettre une ficelle, une corde, à (qch.); ficeler (un paquet); (*b*) garnir, munir (qch.) de cordes; corder (une raquette de tennis, etc.); mettre les cordes à, monter (un violon). **2.** bander (un arc); (*of pers.*) **to be highly strung,** être nerveux, impressionnable. **3.** enfiler (des perles); **to s. fairy lamps across a garden,** accrocher des guirlandes de lampions dans un jardin; *Fig:* **to s. sentences together,** enfiler des phrases. **4.** *Cu:* **to s. beans,** ôter les fils des haricots. **5.** *NAm:* *F:* (i) tenir (qn) en suspens; (ii) duper, tromper (qn). **string along** *F:* **1.** *v.tr.* (i) tenir (qn) en suspens; (ii) duper, tromper (qn). **2.** *v.i.* **to s. along with s.o.,** (i) accompagner, faire route avec, qn; (ii) être copain avec qn. **stringed** *a. Mus:* (instrument) à cordes. **stringing** *n.* **1.** (*a*) montage *m* (d'un violon); cordage *m* (d'une raquette); (*b*) bandage *m* (d'un arc); (*c*) enfilement *m* (de perles). **2.** cordage, cordes *fpl* (d'une raquette). **string out 1.** *v.i.* s'espacer (à la file); **the field strung out behind,** le peloton des coureurs s'égrenait, s'allongeait, derrière. **2.** *v.tr.* faire traîner (qch.) en longueur. **string up** *v.tr.* (*a*) pendre (qn) haut et court; (*b*) *F:* **to get (oneself) strung up,** s'en faire, s'énerver (**about sth.,** à propos de qch.).

stringency ['strin(d)ʒənsi] *n.* **1.** rigueur *f,* sévérité *f* (des règles). **2.** *Fin:* resserrement *m* (de l'argent).

stringent ['strin(d)ʒənt] *a.* **1.** (règlement) rigoureux, strict. **2.** *Fin:* (argent) serré; (marché) tendu. **-ly** *adv.* rigoureusement, strictement.

stringer ['striŋər] *n.* **1.** (*pers.*) (*a*) monteur *m* de cordes (de piano); (*b*) *Journ:* reporter local. **2.** *Const:* longrine *f,* longeron *m* (d'une charpente); *Aut: Av:* longeron (du châssis, de l'aile).

stringy ['striŋi] *a.* (*of vegetables*) fibreux, filandreux; **s. meat,** viande filandreuse.

strip¹ [strip] *n.* **1.** bande *f* (de tissu, de papier); lambeau *m* (de tissu); lame *f,* lamelle *f* (de métal); bande, langue *f* (de terrain); *F:* **to tear s.o. off a s.,** laver la tête à qn; donner, passer, un savon à qn; **narrow s.,** bandelette *f; Med:* **dressing s.,** bande à pansement; **s. mill,** (i) usine *f* de laminage; (ii) laminoir *m;* (*of machine gun*) **feeding, loading, s.,** bande-chargeur *f, pl.* bandes-chargeurs; **s. light,** rampe *f* au néon fluorescente; **s. lighting,** éclairage *m* au néon, fluorescent; *Journ:* **s. cartoon, comic s.,** bande dessinée; *Av:* **landing s.,** bande (d'atterrissage); piste *f* (de fortune); **take-off s.,** bande d'envol. **2.** *Sp: F:* tenue *f,* couleurs *fpl* (d'une équipe de football).

strip² *n.* **to do a s.,** se déshabiller (en public); **s. show,** (spectacle *m* de) strip-tease *m; Cards:* **s. poker,** poker *m* dans lequel celui qui perd le jeu est obligé d'enlever un vêtement; strip-tease-poker *m.*

strip³ *v.* **(stripped) I.** *v.tr.* **1.** mettre (qn) tout nu; déshabiller, dévêtir (qn); **to s. s.o. to the skin,** mettre qn à poil; **stripped to the waist,** nu jusqu'à la ceinture; torse nu. **2.** (*a*) **to s. s.o. of sth.,** dépouiller, déposséder, qn de qch.; **to s. s.o. of his clothes,** dépouiller qn de ses vêtements; **trees stripped of their leaves,** arbres dépouillés de leurs feuilles; **stripped of all his worldly goods,** dépouillé de tous ses biens; (*b*) défaire (un lit); *Nau:* déshabiller, décapeler (un mât, une vergue); *El:* dénuder, dépouiller (un câble); *Metall:* démouler, décocher (une pièce coulée); *Phot:* pelliculer (un cliché); **to s. a tree,** (i) effeuiller, (ii) écorcer, (iii) ébrancher, (iv) défruiter, un arbre; **to s. a wall,** arracher le papier d'un mur; **thieves have stripped the house,** des cambrioleurs ont complètement vidé, dévalisé, la maison; *Mil: F:* **to s. an N.C.O.,** dégrader un sous-officier; **to s. (down) an engine, a gun,** démonter un moteur, un fusil; *Aut:* **stripped chassis,** châssis nu; *Cmptr:* **stripped down version,** version réduite. **3. to s. sth. off, from, sth.,** enlever, ôter, qch. à, de, qch.; **to s. the paint off a wall,** enlever, gratter, la peinture d'un mur. **II.** *v.i.* **1.** (*of pers.*) **to s. (off),** se déshabiller; se dévêtir; **to s. to the skin,** se mettre tout nu; se mettre à poil; **to s. to the waist,** se mettre nu jusqu'à la ceinture. **2.** (*of bark, negative, film*) **to s. (off),** s'enlever, se détacher. **stripping** *n.* **1.** (*of pers.*) déshabillage *m,* déshabillement *m.* **2.** (*a*) dégarnissement *m* (d'un lit); dénudation *f,* dépouillement *m* (d'un câble); effeuillage *m* (d'un arbre); **s. (down),** démontage *m* (d'un moteur, d'un fusil); *Com:* **asset s.,** réalisation *f* (d'une partie) de l'actif d'une société; (*b*) *Ch:* grattage *m,* décapage *m* (d'une surface); (*c*) *Nau:* décapelage *m,* déshabillage (d'un mât, d'une vergue); (*d*) *Metall:* démoulage *m,* décochage *m* (d'une pièce coulée); (*e*) *Phot:* pelliculage *m* (d'une cliché).

stripclub ['stripklʌb] *n.* strip-tease *m, pl.* strip-teases.

stripe¹ [straip] *n.* **1.** (*a*) raie *f,* barre *f* (d'un tissu); raie, rayure *f,* zébrure *f* (du pelage); **black with a red s.,** noir à raie rouge; **to mark sth. with stripes,** rayer, zébrer, qch.; (*b*) bande (de pantalon); (*c*) *Mil:* galon *m, F:* ficelle *f;* **long service s.,** chevron *m;* **to get, lose, a s.,** être promu, dégradé. **2.** *NAm:* **a man of that s.,** un homme de ce genre.

stripe² *v.tr.* rayer, barrer (un tissu). **striped** *a.* (*a*) (chaussettes) à raies, à rayures; (tigre, pelage) rayé; *Nat.Hist:* zébré; **red and blue s. jacket,** veston rayé rouge et bleu; (*b*) *Anat:* (muscle) strié.

stripling ['stripliŋ] *n.* tout jeune homme; adolescent *m.*

stripper ['stripər] *n.* **1.** (*pers.*) (*a*) *Tex:* teilleur, -euse (de lin, de chanvre); (*b*) *Metall:* démouleur *m;* (*c*) strip-teaseuse *f;* (*d*) *Com:* **asset s.,** personne *f* qui achète une société pour profiter de la réalisation de l'actif. **2. (paint) s.,** décapant *m.*

striptease ['stripti:z] *n.* (spectacle *m* de) strip-tease *m;* **s. artist,** strip-teaseuse *f.*

stripy ['straipi] *a.* rayé; zébré; à rayures.

strive [straiv] *v.i.* (*p.t.* **strove** [strouv]; *p.p.* **striven** ['striv(ə)n]) **1. to s. to do sth.,** s'efforcer de faire qch.; faire des efforts pour faire qch.; **to s. for sth.,** essayer d'obtenir qch.; **to s. after effect,** rechercher (de) l'effet. **2. to s. against s.o.,** lutter contre qn.

strobe [stroub] *n. Ph: etc: F:* stroboscope *m.*

stroboscope ['stroubouskoup] *n.* stroboscope *m.*

stroke¹ [strouk] *n.* coup *m.* **1.** (*a*) **to receive twenty strokes,** recevoir vingt coups (de férule); **to fell a tree at a s.,** abattre un arbre d'un seul coup; **to abolish a practice at a s.,** abolir un usage d'un seul coup; (*b*) **s. of lightning,** coup de foudre. **2.** (*a*) coup (d'aile, d'aviron); coup, trait *m* (de lime); (*at billiards*) **whose s. is it?** à qui de jouer? *Golf:* **s. play competition,** concours *m* par coups; *Row:* **to lengthen the s.,** allonger la nage; **to keep s.,** nager ensemble; garder la cadence; *F:* **to be off one's s.,** être mal en train; **to put s.o. off his s.,** déconcerter qn; (*b*) *Swim:* brassée *f;* **the swimming strokes,** les nages *fpl;* **stroke's length,** nagée *f;* **arm s.,** brassée; (*c*) *Mec.E:* mouvement *m,* course *f* (du piston); **two-s., four-s., engine,** moteur *m* à deux, à quatre, temps; (*d*) *F:* **not to do a s. of work,** ne rien faire; (*e*) **s. of good luck,** coup de bonheur, de fortune; aubaine *f;* **s. of wit, of genius,** trait d'esprit, de génie; **bold s.,** coup hardi. **3.** coup (d'horloge, etc.); **on the s. of nine,** sur le coup de neuf heures; à neuf heures sonnant(es); **to arrive on the s. (of time),** arriver à l'heure juste. **4.** *Med:* **(apoplectic) s.,** attaque *f* d'apoplexie; **to have a s.,** tomber en apoplexie; avoir une attaque. **5.** trait; *Typ:* barre *f;* coup de crayon, de pinceau; trait de plume; **oblique s.,** barre transversale; *Fig:* **to give the finishing strokes to one's work,** faire les dernières retouches, mettre la dernière main, à son travail. **6.** *Row:* (*a*) (*pers.*) chef *m* de nage; (*b*) **to row s.,** donner la nage; être chef de nage; **s. oar,** (i) aviron *m* du chef de nage; (ii) chef de nage.

stroke² *Row: v.tr. & i.* **to s. (a boat),** être chef de nage (d'un canot); donner la nage.

stroke³ *n.* caresse *f* de la main.

stroke⁴ *v.tr.* passer la main sur, lisser avec la main, caresser de la main (une fourrure, les cheveux de qn); **to s. one's chin,** se flatter le menton de la main; *Fig:* **to s. s.o. (up) the wrong way,** prendre qn à rebrousse-poil; **to s. s.o. down,** (i) apaiser la colère de qn; (ii) câliner, cajoler, qn. **stroking** *n.* caresses *fpl* (de la main).

stroll¹ [stroul] *n.* petit tour, flânerie *f; F:* balade *f;* **to take, go for, a s.,** (aller) faire un tour.

stroll² *v.i.* flâner; déambuler; *F:* se balader. **strolling** *a.* vagabond, errant; **s. player,** comédien ambulant; **s. players,** troupe ambulante.

stroller ['stroulər] *n.* **1.** flâneur, -euse; promeneur, -euse. **2.** *NAm:* poussette *f* (d'enfant).

strong [strɔŋ] *a.* **(stronger** ['strɔŋgər] **strongest** ['strɔŋgist]) fort. **1.** (*a*) (bâtiment) solide, résistant, ferme, robuste; (drap) fort, solide, résistant; (chaussures) de fatigue; *Com:* (marché) ferme; **s. conviction,** ferme conviction; **s. faith,** foi solide, robuste; **s. character,** caractère fort, ferme; (*of faith*) **to get stronger,** s'affermir; (*b*) **s. constitution,** forte constitution; **s. nerves,** nerfs bien équilibrés; **he is not very s.,** il est peu robuste; **to grow stronger,** reprendre des forces. **2.** (*a*) (homme) fort; (cheval) vigoureux; (candidat) sérieux; (argument, attrait) puissant; *El:* (courant) intense; **s. fellow,** gars solide; *F:* costaud *m*; **he's as s. as a horse, an ox,** il est fort comme un cheval; **s. voice,** voix forte, puissante; **the s. arm of the law,** l'autorité publique; **to be s. in the arm,** avoir le bras fort; **s. measures,** mesures énergiques; **he is a s. man,** c'est un homme à poigne, de poigne; *n.pl.* **the s.,** les forts, les puissants; **politeness is not his s. point,** la politesse n'est pas son fort; **strong in numbers,** en grand nombre; **to give s. support to s.o., a measure,** donner un grand appui à, appuyer fortement, qch., une mesure; *Cards:* **s. suit,** (couleur) longue *f*; **company two hundred s.,** compagnie forte de deux cents hommes; **s. evidence,** preuves convaincantes; **s. reason,** raison majeure; **s. likeness,** grande ressemblance; **to write in s. terms to s.o.,** écrire une lettre énergique à qn; **s. wind,** grand vent; **the wind is growing stronger,** le vent renforce; *Nau:* **s. gale,** gros vent; **s. tide,** grande marée, forte marée; *Mus:* **s. beat,** temps fort; (*b*) **s. drink,** boisson(s) forte(s); **s. wine,** vin corsé; **s. solution,** solution forte, concentrée; **s. light,** lumière forte, vive lumière; **s. colour,** couleur forte; (*c*) (fromage) qui pique; (*of food*) **to have a s. smell,** sentir fort; *Fig:* **I found the book rather s. meat,** j'ai trouvé ce livre assez corsé. **3.** *Gram:* **s. verb,** verbe fort. **4.** *adv. F:* **things are going s.,** les choses avancent, tout marche à merveille; **he's going s.,** il est toujours d'attaque, solide au poste; **how's grandfather?—still going s.,** comment va le grand-père?—toujours solide. **-ly** *adv.* **1.** fortement, solidement, fermement; **s. built bicycle,** bicyclette robuste. **2.** fortement, vigoureusement, énergiquement; **to be s. in favour of sth.,** être chaud partisan de qch.; **s. worded letter,** lettre en termes énergiques; **I don't feel s. about it,** je n'y attache pas une grande importance.

strong-arm[1] ['strɔŋɑːm] *a.* **to use s.-a. tactics,** se fier à la main forte; **by s.-a. methods,** de vive force.

strong-arm[2] *v.tr. NAm: F:* (i) rouer (qn) de coups; (ii) voler (qn) avec violence.

strong-box ['strɔŋbɔks] *n.* coffre-fort *m*, *pl.* coffres-forts.

stronghold ['strɔŋhould] *n.* forteresse *f*; place forte; redoute *f*; **s. of trade unionism,** citadelle *f* du syndicalisme.

strong-minded [strɔŋ'maindid] *a.* à l'esprit solide, résolu, décidé; **s.-m. person,** forte tête. **-ly** *adv.* avec décision, avec résolution.

strong-mindedness [strɔŋ'maindidnis] *n.* force *f* de caractère; résolution *f*.

strong-room ['strɔŋru(ː)m] *n.* chambre forte.

strong-willed [strɔŋ'wild] *a.* = STRONG-MINDED.

strontium ['strɔnʃiəm] *n. Ch:* strontium *m*.

strop[1] [strɔp] *n.* **(razor) s.,** cuir *m* (à repasser, à rasoir); affiloir *m*.

strop[2] *v.tr.* (**stropped** [strɔpt]) affiler, repasser, (un rasoir) sur le cuir.

strophe ['stroufi, strɔf] *n. Pros: Lit:* strophe *f*.

stroppy ['strɔpi] *a. P:* maussade; difficile.

structural ['strʌktjər(ə)l] *a.* **1.** de construction; **s. iron, steel,** fer, acier, de construction; charpentes *fpl* métalliques; **s. engineer,** (ingénieur) constructeur. **2.** structural, -aux; structurel. **-ally** *adv.* structuralement, structurellement.

structuralism ['strʌktjər(ə)lizm] *n. Psy: Ling:* structuralisme *m*.

structure[1] ['strʌktjər] *n.* **1.** structure *f*; agencement *m* (de vers, d'un récit); construction *f* (d'un bâtiment). **2.** (*a*) construction, édifice *m*; bâtiment; **the social s.,** l'édifice social; (*b*) *Civ.E:* ouvrage *m*, travail *m*, d'art: (*c*) *Pol.Ec:* **price s.,** structure des prix.

structure[2] *v.tr.* (*a*) structurer (une organisation, une situation); (*b*) architecturer (une œuvre d'art). **structured** *a.* à structure; structuré.

struggle[1] ['strʌgl] *n.* lutte *f* (**for, against,** pour, contre); **fierce, desperate, s.,** lutte acharnée, désespérée; **he gave in without a s.,** il n'a fait aucune résistance; **the class s.,** la lutte des classes; **s. for freedom,** lutte pour la liberté; **the s. for life, for existence,** la lutte pour la vie, pour l'existence.

struggle[2] *v.i.* (*a*) lutter (**with, against, for,** avec, contre, pour); se débattre, se démener; **the child struggled and kicked,** l'enfant se débattait des pieds et des mains; **he was struggling with his umbrella,** il se debattait pour ouvrir, fermer, son parapluie; **he struggled to his feet,** il s'est levé avec difficulté; **to s. along,** marcher, avancer, péniblement; **we are struggling along,** on se défend; **we struggled through,** nous avons surmonté tous les obstacles; (*b*) *Lit:* **to s. against circumstances,** nager contre le courant; **to s. with death,** lutter contre la mort. **struggling** *a.* (artiste, etc.) qui vit péniblement.

strum[1] [strʌm] *n.* son *m*, bruit *m* (d'une guitare, etc.).

strum[2] *v.tr. & i.* **(strummed) to s. (on) a guitar,** pincer (distraitement) les cordes d'une guitare; pincer, gratter, de la guitare; **to s. a tune,** (i) jouer un air (à la guitare); (ii) tapoter un air (au piano); **his fingers strummed on the table,** ses doigts pianotaient, tapotaient, sur la table.

strumpet ['strʌmpit] *n.f. A: & Lit:* prostituée.

strut[1] [strʌt] *n.* démarche affectée.

strut[2] *v.i.* **(strutted) to s. (about),** se pavaner, parader; se rengorger; **to s. in, out,** entrer, sortir, d'un air important.

strut[3] *n.* entretoise *f*, étrésillon *m*; étai *m*; traverse *f*; (*spur*) arc-boutant *m*, *pl.* arcs-boutants; jambe *f* de force; (*of roof truss*) contrefiche *f*; *Av:* pilier *m*, mât *m*.

strut[4] *v.tr.* **(strutted)** *Const: etc:* entretoiser, étrésillonner; moiser (une charpente).

strychnine ['strikniːn] *n.* strychnine *f*.

stub[1] [stʌb] *n.* **1.** souche *f* (d'arbre); chicot *m* (d'arbre, de dent); bout *m* (de crayon, de cigarette); tronçon *m* (de mât, de queue de chien); *F:* mégot *m* (de cigarette, de cigare). **2.** *Com:* talon, souche (de chèque).

stub[2] *v.tr.* **(stubbed) 1. to s. out one's cigarette,** éteindre sa cigarette en l'écrasant (par le bout). **2. to s. one's toe against sth.,** heurter, se cogner, le pied contre qch.; buter contre qch.

stubble ['stʌbl] *n.* **1.** (*a*) chaume *m*, éteule *f*; **to clear a field of s.,** (dé)chaumer un champ; (*b*) **s. field,** chaume. **2.** barbe piquante (de plusieurs jours).

stubbly ['stʌbli] *a.* **1.** (champ) couvert de chaume, d'éteule; **s. field,** chaume *m*. **2. s. beard,** barbe piquante (de plusieurs jours).

stubborn ['stʌbən] *a.* **1.** obstiné, opiniâtre; entêté, têtu; (volonté) tenace; (caractère) buté; *F:* **as s. as a mule,** têtu, entêté, comme un mulet, une mule. **2.** (*of thg*) réfractaire, rebelle; **s. fever,** fièvre rebelle. **-ly** *adv.* obstinément; avec entêtement.

stubbornness ['stʌbənnis] *n.* entêtement *m*, obstination *f*, opiniâtreté *f*; ténacité *f* (de volonté).

stubby ['stʌbi] *a.* (*of plant*) tronqué; (*of pers.*) trapu; **s. fingers,** doigts boudinés.

stucco[1] ['stʌkou] *n.* stuc *m*; **s. work,** stucage *m*.

stucco[2] *v.tr.* **(stuccoed; stuccoing)** stuquer.

stuck-up ['stʌk'ʌp] *a. F:* prétentieux, guindé.

stud¹ [stʌd] *n.* **1.** (*a*) clou *m* à grosse tête; clou doré (pour ornement); (*b*) (*on football boots*) **studs,** crampons *mpl*; (*c*) clou (de passage clouté). **2.** bouton *m* (double) (de chemise de soirée); **collar s.,** bouton de col. **3.** *Tchn:* (*a*) (*short pin*) goujon *m*; tourillon *m*; (*b*) **s. (bolt),** goujon; (*c*) *Nau:* étai *m* (d'un maillon de chaîne). **4.** *Const:* poteau *m*, montant *m*.

stud² *v.tr.* **(studded) 1.** garnir de clous; clouter; **studded door,** porte garnie de clous, cloutée. **2. studded with stars, star-studded,** (ciel) criblé, (par)semé, d'étoiles; **her dress was studded with jewels,** sa robe était constellée de pierreries. **3.** *Const:* établir la charpente (d'une cloison).

stud³ *n.* **1.** écurie *f* (de chasse). **2. s. (farm),** haras *m* (de pur-sang); **to be at s.,** (i) (*of horse*) être en haras; (ii) (*of dog*) faire saillies; **s. book,** livre d'origines, généalogique; registre *m* (d'un haras, des chevaux); stud-book *m*, *pl.* stud-books; **s. mare,** (jument) poulinière *f*. **3.** étalon *m*.

student ['stju:dənt] *n.* **1.** étudiant, -ante; **law, medical, arts, s.,** étudiant en droit, en médecine, en lettres; **s. life,** la vie d'étudiant; **the s. body,** les étudiants. **2.** (*a*) investigateur, -trice (d'un phénomène); (*b*) **he is a great s.,** il est très studieux.

studhorse ['stʌdhɔ:s] *n.* étalon *m*.

studio ['stju:diou] *n.* atelier *m*, studio *m* (d'artiste, de photographe); **film s.,** studio de cinéma; **recording s.,** studio d'enregistrement; auditorium *m*; **s. flat,** studio; **s. couch,** lit *m* canapé.

studious ['stju:diəs] *a.* **1.** (*of pers.*) studieux; **person of s. habits,** personne adonnée à l'étude. **2. with s. attention,** avec une attention réfléchie. **-ly** *adv.* **1.** studieusement. **2.** attentivement; avec empressement; **he s. avoided me,** il s'ingéniait à m'éviter. **3. he was s. polite,** il était d'une politesse étudiée.

studiousness ['stju:diəsnis] *n.* **1.** amour *m* de l'étude; attachement *m* à l'étude. **2.** *O:* empressement *m*, zèle *m* (**to do sth., in doing sth.,** à faire qch.).

study¹ ['stʌdi] *n.* **1.** *A:* soin(s) *m(pl)*, attention *f*. **2. (brown) s.,** rêverie *f*; **to be (lost) in a brown s.,** être plongé, absorbé, dans ses réflexions, dans de vagues rêveries. **3.** (*a*) étude *f* (**of,** de); **to make a s. of sth.,** s'appliquer à l'étude de qch.; étudier qch.; **feasibility s.,** étude de faisabilité; **field s.,** étude(s) sur le terrain; **home s. course,** programme *m* d'études chez soi; **s. group,** groupe de travail; (*b*) **studies,** études; **to finish one's studies,** achever ses études; (*c*) **his face was a s.!** il fallait voir son visage! **4.** *Art: Mus:* étude. **5.** *Th:* (*of pers.*) **to be a good, a slow, s.,** apprendre vite, lentement, ses rôles. **6.** (*a*) cabinet *m* de travail; bureau *m*; (*b*) *Sch:* salle *f* d'étude.

study² *v.* **(studied; studying) 1.** *v.tr.* (*a*) étudier (une langue, la musique, un rôle); observer (le terrain, les astres); faire des études de (français, droit); examiner, étudier (des plans); mettre (une question) à l'étude; (*b*) *O:* s'occuper de, être soigneux de (qn, qch.). **2.** *v.i.* faire ses études; étudier; **he's studying,** (i) il fait ses études; (ii) il travaille; **he's studying to be a doctor,** il fait des études de médecine; **to s. for an examination,** préparer, se préparer à, un examen. **studied** *a.* étudié, recherché; prémédité, calculé; (négligence) voulue; **s. elegance,** élégance recherchée. **studying** *n.* études *fpl*.

stuff¹ [stʌf] *n.* **1.** (*a*) matière(s) *f*(pl), matériaux *mpl*, substance *f*, étoffe *f*; *Paperm:* pâte *f* (à papier); **he is of the s. that heroes are made of,** il est du bois dont sont faits les héros; *F:* **he writes good s.,** il écrit bien; (*b*) *F:* **this wine is good s.,** ce vin est excellent; **I don't like that s. you gave me,** je n'aime pas ce que vous m'avez donné là; **come on, do your s.!** allons, montrenous ce que tu sais faire! **he knows his s.,** il s'y connaît; **that's the s.!** voilà ce qu'il faut! (*c*) *P:* (i) héroïne *f*, jus *m*; (ii) came *f*; (*d*) fatras *m*; **old s.,** vieilleries *fpl*; **silly s.,** sottises *fpl*, balivernes *fpl*; *O:* **s. and nonsense!** ça c'est de la bêtise! **2.** *Tex:* étoffe, tissu *m* (de laine).

stuff² *v.tr.* **1.** (*a*) bourrer (**with,** de); rembourrer (un meuble, un coussin) (**with,** de); **his pockets are stuffed with sweets,** il a des bonbons plein les poches; **to s. oneself,** se bourrer; s'empiffrer; **head stuffed with romantic ideas,** tête bourrée, farcie, d'idées romanesques; (*b*) *Cu:* farcir (un poulet); *F:* **stuffed shirt,** individu suffisant, prétentieux; (*c*) empailler, naturaliser (un spécimen zoologique); (*d*) *P:* **get stuffed! you can s. it!** va te faire foutre! **s. the job!** merde pour le boulot! **2. to s. up,** boucher (un trou, etc.); **to s. (up) one's ears with cotton wool,** se boucher les oreilles avec de l'ouate; **my nose is stuffed up,** je suis enchifrené. **3. to s. sth. into sth.,** fourrer, serrer, qch. dans qch.; **to s. one's fingers in one's ears,** se boucher les oreilles (avec les doigts). **stuffing** *n.* **1.** (*a*) bourrage *m*, rembourrage *m*; empaillage *m* (d'animaux); (*b*) *F:* gavage *m*, bâfrerie *f*. **2.** (*a*) bourre *f*; rembourrage; **horsehair s.,** matelassure *f* de crin; *F:* **to knock the s. out of s.o.,** (i) battre qn à plate(s) couture(s); (ii) désarçonner, dégonfler, qn; (iii) épuiser qn; affaiblir qn; (*b*) *Cu:* farce *f*.

stuffy ['stʌfi] *a.* **1.** mal ventilé, mal aéré; **to smell s.,** sentir le renfermé; **it's a bit s. in here,** cela manque d'air ici. **2.** *F:* fâché; en rogne. **3.** *F:* collet monté; aux préjugés vieillots; **don't be so s.,** il n'y a a pas de quoi te scandaliser. **4. to feel s.,** se sentir enchifrené.

stultify ['stʌltifai] *v.i.* **1.** enlever toute valeur à (un argument, un témoignage); invalider, infirmer (un décret); (*of work*) abrutir, assommer (qn). **2.** ridiculiser (qn, qch.); faire ressortir l'absurdité (d'une action). **stultifying** *a.* (travail) abrutissant.

stumble¹ ['stʌmbl] *n.* trébuchement *m*, faux pas; bronchement *m* (d'un cheval).

stumble² *v.i.* **1.** trébucher; faire un faux pas; (*of horse*) broncher; **to s. along,** avancer en trébuchant. **2. to s. in one's speech,** (i) hésiter en parlant; (ii) s'embrouiller en prononçant son discours. **3. to s. across, on, s.o., sth.,** rencontrer qn, qch., par hasard; tomber sur qn, qch. **stumbling 1.** *a.* qui trébuche; (*of horse*) qui bronche; (*of speech*) hésitant. **2.** *n.* (*a*) trébuchement *m*, faux pas; bronchement *m* (d'un cheval); **s. block,** pierre *f* d'achoppement; (*b*) hésitation *f*.

stump¹ [stʌmp] *n.* **1.** tronçon *m*, souche *f*, chicot *m* (d'arbre); chicot (de dent); moignon *m* (de bras, de jambe); bout *m* (de cigare, de crayon); *F:* mégot *m* (de cigare); tronçon (de queue, de colonne, de mât); trognon *m* (de chou). **2.** *F:* **stumps,** jambes *fpl*, quilles *fpl;* **stir your stumps!** remuez-vous! grouillezvous! **3.** *Pol: F:* **to be on the s.,** faire des harangues politiques; **s. orator,** *NAm:* **s. speaker,** orateur *m* de carrefour. **4.** *Cr:* piquet *m* (du guichet); **to draw stumps,** enlever les piquets; cesser le match.

stump² **1.** *v.i.* (*a*) **to s. along,** marcher, avancer, en clopinant; (*b*) *Pol: F:* faire des harangues politiques; (*c*) *F:* **to s. up,** payer, casquer. **2.** *v.tr.* (*a*) *F:* coller (un candidat); faire sécher (qn) (sur un sujet); **to be stumped,** ne savoir plus que faire; sécher, piquer une sèche; **it stumped me,** cela m'a désarçonné; (*b*) *F:* **to s. up the money,** payer, casquer; (*c*) *Cr:* mettre hors jeu (un batteur qui est sorti de son camp).

stumpy ['stʌmpi] *a.* (*of pers.*) trapu, ragot, ramassé; **s. pencil,** petit bout de crayon.

stun [stʌn] *v.tr.* **(stunned) 1.** étourdir, assommer. **2.** renverser, abasourdir; **the news stunned us,** c'était un coup de massue; **stunned with surprise,** stupéfié; frappé de stupeur. **stunning** *a.* **1.** (*a*) (coup) étourdissant, abrutissant; (*b*) (malheur) accablant, bouleversant. **2.** *F:* renversant; formidable, épatant;

she's really s., elle est ravissante. **stunningly** *adv. F:* **s. beautiful,** d'une beauté ravissante.
stunner ['stʌnər] *n. F:* **1.** type épatant; **she's a s.,** elle est (i) épatante, (ii) ravissante. **2.** chose épatante.
stunt[1] [stʌnt] *v.tr.* arrêter (qn, qch.) dans sa croissance; rabougrir; **stunted,** (arbre) rabougri; (esprit) noué; **to become stunted,** se rabougrir.
stunt[2] *n.* **1.** coup *m* d'épate; affaire *f* de publicité, de pure réclame. **2.** (*a*) tour *m* de force; *Av:* **s. flying,** vol *m* de virtuosité; **s. pilot,** pilote *m* de voltige; **to perform stunts,** faire des acrobaties (en vol); (*b*) *Cin:* acrobatie *f*; **s. man,** cascadeur *m*.
stupefaction [stju:pi'fækʃ(ə)n] *n.* stupeur *f*.
stupefy ['stju:pifai] *v.tr.* **1.** (*a*) *Med:* stupéfier, engourdir; (*b*) hébéter, abrutir. **2.** abasourdir, stupéfier; **I'm absolutely stupefied (by what has happened),** je n'en reviens pas; j'en reste stupéfait, stupéfié. **stupefying** *a.* stupéfiant.
stupendous [stju(:)'pendəs] *a.* prodigieux; *F:* formidable. **-ly** *adv.* prodigieusement.
stupid ['stju:pid] *a.* (*a*) stupide, sot, *f.* sotte; bête; **I did a s. thing,** j'ai fait une bêtise, une chose stupide; **don't be s.!** ne faites pas l'idiot! **how s. of me!** que je suis bête! **what a s. place to put it in!** c'est idiot de l'avoir mis là! (*b*) ennuyeux. **-ly** *adv.* stupidement, bêtement.
stupidity [stju:'piditi] *n.* stupidité *f*; bêtise *f*.
stupor ['stju:pər] *n.* stupeur *f*; **in a drunken s.,** abruti par la boisson.
sturdiness ['stə:dinis] *n.* **1.** vigueur *f*, robustesse *f*. **2.** hardiesse *f*, résolution *f*, fermeté *f*.
sturdy ['stə:di] *a.* (*a*) vigoureux, robuste, fort; **s. fellow,** gaillard robuste; (*b*) (*of opposition, resistance*) hardi, résolu, ferme. **-ily** *adv.* (*a*) fortement; **s. built,** solide; robuste; (*b*) hardiment, résolument.
sturgeon ['stə:dʒ(ə)n] *n. Ich:* esturgeon *m*.
stutter[1] ['stʌtər] *n.* bégaiement *m*; **he has a s.,** il est bègue.
stutter[2] **1.** *v.i.* bégayer. **2.** *v.tr.* bégayer (qch.). **stuttering 1.** *a.* bègue. **2.** *n.* bégaiement *m*.
stutterer ['stʌtərər] *n.* bègue *mf*.
sty[1] *pl.* **sties** [stai, staiz] *n.* (*a*) étable *f* (à porcs); porcherie *f*; (*b*) taudis *m*.
sty[2], **stye** [stai] *n. Med:* orgelet *m*.
Stygian ['stidʒiən] *a. Lit:* **S. gloom,** (i) nuit noire; (ii) humeur noire, comme le Styx.
style[1] [stail] *n.* **1.** (*a*) *Engr:* burin *m*; (*b*) (*of sundial*) style *m*, gnomon *m*; (*c*) *Bot:* style. **2.** (*a*) style, manière *f*, façon *f*; **s. of living,** manière de vivre; genre *m*, train *m*, de vie; **to live in (grand, great) s.,** mener grand train; **they arrived in s.,** ils ont fait leur entrée en grande pompe; **let's do things in s.,** faisons bien les choses; **that's the s.!** c'est cela! bravo! (*b*) **Gothic, Byzantine, s.,** style gothique, byzantin; **building in the classical s.,** bâtiment de style classique; (*c*) style, genre; type *m*, modèle *m* (d'une voiture); (*d*) **that's not my s.,** ce n'est pas mon genre; **something in that s.,** quelque chose de, dans, ce genre; (*e*) mode *f*; **in the latest s.,** à la mode; *F:* dernier cri. **3.** (*a*) style, ton *m*; manière d'écrire; **written in a humorous s.,** écrit sur un ton de plaisanterie; (*b*) (*good style*) **this writer lacks s.,** cet écrivain n'a pas de style. **4.** chic *m*, cachet *m*, ton; **she has s.,** elle a de l'allure, du genre. **5.** (*of calendar*) **old, new, s.,** vieux, nouveau, style.
style[2] *v.tr.* **1.** *O:* dénommer; appeler; **to s. oneself doctor,** se donner le titre de docteur. **2.** *Cost:* créer; **dress styled by X,** robe créée par X; **hair styled by X,** coiffé(e) par X. **styling** *n.* façon *f*; ligne *f* (d'une voiture); **hair s.,** coiffure *f*.
stylish ['stailiʃ] *a.* élégant, chic; qui a du cachet. **-ly** *adv.* élégamment; avec chic.
stylishness ['stailiʃnis] *n.* élégance *f*, chic *m*.
stylist ['stailist] *n.* styliste *mf*; **hair s.,** (i) coiffeur, -euse (d'art); (ii) (*shop sign*) = coiffure *f* (d'art).
stylistic [stai'listik] *a.* stylistique; du, de, style.
stylistics [stai'listiks] *n.pl.* (*usu. with sg. const.*) stylistique *f*.
stylization [stailai'zeiʃ(ə)n] *n.* stylisation *f*.
stylize ['stailaiz] *v.tr. Art:* styliser; **stylized flowers,** fleurs stylisées.
stylus, *pl.* **-i, -uses** ['stailəs, -ai, -əsiz] *n. Engr: etc:* style *m*; *Rec:* pointe *f* de lecture; saphir *m*.
stymie ['staimi] *v.tr. F:* **to be stymied,** être dans une impasse.
styptic ['stiptik] *a. & n. Med:* styptique (*m*), astringent (*m*); **s. pencil,** pierre *f* d'alun.
suasion ['sweiʒ(ə)n] *n. A:* persuasion *f*; **to subject s.o. to moral s.,** agir sur la conscience de qn.
suave [swɑ:v] *a. Pej:* doucereux, mielleux. **-ly** *adv.* doucereusement.
suaveness ['swɑ:vnis] **suavity** ['swɑ:viti] *n. Pej:* manières mieleuses.
sub[1] [sʌb] *n. F:* **1.** = SUBALTERN 2. **2.** cotisation *f* (à un club). **3.** *Sp:* remplaçant *m*. **4.** sous-marin *m*. **5.** = SUBEDITOR.
sub[2] *v.* **(subbed)** *F:* **1.** *v.i.* (= *substitute*) **to s. for s.o.,** remplacer qn. **2.** *v.tr. & i.* (= *subedit*) *Journ:* mettre (un article) au point.
subagent [sʌb'eidʒənt] *n.* sous-agent *m*.
subalpine [sʌb'ælpain] *a.* subalpin.
subaltern ['sʌbəltə:n] **1.** *a.* subalterne, subordonné. **2.** *n.* (*a*) subalterne *m*, subordonné *m*; (*b*) *Mil:* lieutenant *m*; sous-lieutenant *m*; subalterne *m*.
subaqua [sʌb'ækwə] *a.* (sport) subaquatique.
subatomic [sʌbə'tɔmik] *a.* subatomique.
subclass ['sʌbklɑ:s] *n. Nat.Hist:* sous-classe *f*.
subclause ['sʌbklɔ:z] *n. esp. Jur:* paragraphe *m* (d'un contrat).
subcommittee ['sʌbkəmiti] *n.* sous-comité *m*; sous-commission *f*.
subconscious [sʌb'kɔnʃəs] *a. & n. Psy:* subconscient (*m*). **-ly** *adv.* subconsciemment.
subcontinent [sʌb'kɔntinənt] *n.* sous-continent *m*; **the Indian s.,** le sous-continent indien.
subcontract[1] [sʌb'kɔntrækt] *n.* sous-traité *m*.
subcontract[2] [sʌbkən'trækt] *v.tr.* sous-traiter (une affaire).
subcontractor [sʌbkən'træktər] *n.* sous-entrepreneur *m*, sous-traitant *m*; *Const: etc:* tâcheron *m*.
subculture [sʌb'kʌltʃər] *n.* **1.** *Bac:* repiquage *m*; culture *f* secondaire. **2.** groupe culturel secondaire.
subcutaneous [sʌbkju(:)'teiniəs] *a.* sous-cutané.
subdeacon [sʌb'di:kən] *n. Ecc:* sous-diacre *m*.
subdivide [sʌbdi'vaid] **1.** *v.tr.* subdiviser, sous-diviser. **2.** *v.i.* se subdiviser.
subdivision [sʌbdi'viʒ(ə)n] *n.* subdivision *f*, sous-division *f*.
subdominant [sʌb'dɔminənt] *n. Mus:* sous-dominante *f*.
subdue [səb'dju:] *v.tr.* **1.** subjuguer, soumettre, assujettir (une tribu); maîtriser (un incendie); dompter, réprimer (un mouvement de colère); asservir (ses passions). **2.** adoucir (la lumière, la chaleur, la voix); amortir, atténuer (la lumière, la douleur). **subdued** *a.* **1.** (*of pers.*) préoccupé; déprimé. **2.** (*of heat, light, sound*) adouci; **s. light,** demi-jour *m*; lumière tamisée; **s. colours,** couleurs sobres; **s. conversation,** conversation *f* à voix basse; **in a s. tone, voice,** à voix basse; à mi-voix.
subedit [sʌb'edit] *v.tr. & i. Journ:* mettre au point (un article); *Publ:* être secrétaire à la rédaction.
subeditor [sʌb'editər] *n.* (*a*) *Journ:* secrétaire *m* de la rédaction; **assistant s.,** secrétaire adjoint; (*b*) *Publ:* rédacteur, -trice.
subfamily ['sʌbfæmili] *n. Nat.Hist:* sous-famille *f*.

subfusc [sʌb'fʌsk] *a.* (*of clothing, etc.*) sombre.
subgenus *pl.* **-genera** ['sʌbdʒi:nəs, -dʒenərə] *n. Nat.Hist:* sous-genre *m.*
subgroup ['sʌbgru:p] *n.* sous-groupe *m.*
subheading ['sʌbhediŋ] *n.* sous-titre *m.*
subhuman [sʌb'hju:mən] *a.* pas tout à fait humain; *F:* **he's positively s.,** il est bête comme ses pieds.
subject¹ ['sʌbdʒikt] *n.* **1.** sujet, -ette (d'un souverain); **British s.,** sujet britannique. **2.** *Gram:* sujet (du verbe). **3.** (*a*) sujet (de conversation, d'un livre); objet *m* (d'un litige, de méditation); **this will be the s. of my next lecture,** cela fera l'objet de ma prochaine conférence; **s. matter,** contenu *m* (d'une lettre); sujet (d'un livre); objet *m* (d'un contrat réel); **to wander from the s.,** sortir de la question; **while we are on the s.,** à ce propos; pendant que nous sommes sur ce sujet; **on the s. of,** au sujet de; **to change the s.,** parler d'autre chose; changer de sujet; (*b*) *Mus:* sujet (d'une fugue); (*c*) *Sch:* matière *f*; **what subjects do you teach?** quelles matières enseignez-vous? **4.** (*a*) sujet (d'une expérience); **to be a s. of experiment,** servir de sujet d'expérience; **to be a s. for pity,** être un objet de pitié; (*b*) *Med:* sujet, malade *mf* (que l'on traite).
subject² *a.* **1.** (état, pays) assujetti, soumis (**to,** à); sous la dépendance (**to,** de); **s. to military laws,** justiciable des tribunaux militaires. **2.** (*liable*) (*a*) sujet (au rhumatisme); porté (à l'envie); (*b*) **prices s. to 5% discount,** prix bénéficiant d'une remise de 5%; **s. to stamp duty,** soumis au timbre; **the plan is s. to modifications,** ce projet pourra subir des modifications. **3.** (*conditional*) **s. to . . .,** sauf . . .; sous réserve de . . .; **s. to your consent,** sauf votre consentement; **s. to alteration,** sauf nouvel avis.
subject³ [səb'dʒekt] *v.tr.* **1.** soumettre, assujettir, subjuguer (un peuple). **2.** soumettre, exposer (**s.o., sth., to sth.,** qn, qch., à qch.); **to s. s.o. to torture,** mettre qn à la torture; **to s. s.o., sth., to an examination,** faire subir un examen à qn; soumettre qch. à un examen; **to be subjected to much criticism,** être en butte à de nombreuses critiques; **metal subjected to great heat,** métal exposé à une grande chaleur.
subjection [səb'dʒekʃ(ə)n] *n.* soumission *f*, assujettissement *m* (**to,** à); **in a state of s.,** dans la sujétion.
subjective [səb'dʒektiv] *a.* subjectif. **-ly** *adv.* subjectivement.
subjectivism [səb'dʒektivizm] *n.* subjectivisme *m.*
subjectivity [sʌbdʒek'tiviti] *n.* subjectivité *f.*
subjoin [sʌb'dʒɔin] *v.tr.* ajouter, adjoindre (une liste).
sub judice ['sʌb'dʒu:disi] *Lt.phr. Jur:* **the case is s. j.,** l'affaire n'est pas encore jugée.
subjugate ['sʌbdʒugeit] *v.tr.* subjuguer, soumettre, assujettir (un peuple); dompter (un animal).
subjugation [sʌbdʒu'geiʃ(ə)n] *n.* subjugation *f*, assujettissement *m.*
subjunctive [səb'dʒʌŋktiv] *a. & n. Gram:* subjonctif (*m*); **in the s. (mood),** au subjonctif.
sublease¹ ['sʌbli:s] *n.* sous-bail *m*, *pl.* sous-baux; sous-location *f*; *Husb:* sous-ferme *f.*
sublease² [sʌb'li:s] *v.tr.* sous-louer (un appartement); sous-affermer (une terre).
sub-lessee [sʌble'si:] *n.* sous-locataire *mf* (à bail).
sub-lessor [sʌb'lesər] *n.* sous-bailleur, -bailleresse.
sublet [sʌb'let] *v.tr.* (*p.t. & p.p.* **-let;** *pr.p.* **-letting**) sous-louer (un appartement); sous-affermer (une terre). **sub-letting** *n.* sous-location *f.*
sub-lieutenant [sʌblef'tenənt] *n. Navy:* enseigne *m* (de vaisseau) première classe.
sublimate¹ ['sʌblimeit] *n. Ch:* sublimé *m.*
sublimate² *v.tr.* **1.** *Ch:* sublimer (un solide). **2.** raffiner, idéaliser (un sentiment); *Psy:* (*of instinct*) **to become sublimated,** se sublimiser.
sublimation [sʌbli'meiʃ(ə)n] *n.* sublimation *f.*
sublime¹ [sə'blaim] **1.** *a.* (*a*) (pensée, poète) sublime; (*b*) **s. indifference,** suprême indifférence *f.* **2.** *n.* **the s.,** le sublime; **to from the s. to the ridiculous,** passer du sublime au terre à terre. **-ly** *adv.* **1.** sublimement. **2.** suprêmement; **to be s. unconscious of . . .,** être dans une ignorance absolue de . . ..
sublime² **1.** *v.tr.* (*a*) *Ch:* sublimer (un solide); (*b*) idéaliser (une idée). **2.** *v.i. Ch:* (*of solid*) se sublimer.
subliminal [sʌb'limin(ə)l] *a. Psy:* subliminal, -aux, subliminaire; **s. advertising,** publicité *f* subliminaire.
sublimity [sʌb'limiti] *n.* sublimité *f.*
submachine gun [sʌbmə'ʃi:ngʌn] *n.* mitraillette *f.*
submarine [sʌbmə'ri:n] **1.** *a.* (câble, volcan) sous-marin. **2.** *n.* sous-marin *m*; **midget, pocket, s.,** sous-marin de poche.
submediant [sʌb'mi:diənt] *n.* sus-dominante *f.*
submerge [səb'mə:dʒ] *v.tr.* (*a*) submerger, immerger; plonger, enfoncer, (qch.) sous l'eau; (*b*) inonder, noyer (un champ). **2.** *v.i.* plonger; (*of submarine*) effectuer sa plongée. **submerged** *a.* **1.** (*a*) submergé; noyé; **wreck s. at high tide,** épave submergée à (la) haute marée; (*b*) (sous-marin) en plongée; (*c*) (écueil) sous-marin.
submergence [səb'mə:dʒəns] *n.* submersion *f.*
submersible [səb'mə:sibl] *a. & n.* (bateau *m*) submersible (*m*); sous-marin (*m*).
submersion [səb'mə:ʃ(ə)n] *n.* submersion *f.*
submission [səb'miʃ(ə)n] *n.* **1.** (*a*) soumission *f* (à la volonté de qn, à une autorité); résignation *f* (à une défaite); *Wr:* abandon *m*; **to starve s.o. into s.,** réduire qn par la famine; (*b*) docilité *f*; humilité *f.* **2.** soumission (d'une question à un arbitre); présentation *f* (de pièces d'identité). **3.** *Jur:* plaidoirie *f*; **in my submission . . .,** selon ma thèse . . ..
submissive [səb'misiv] *a.* (ton, air) soumis, humble; (personne) docile. **-ly** *adv.* avec soumission; humblement.
submissiveness [səb'misivnis] *n.* soumission *f*, docilité *f*, humilité *f.*
submit [səb'mit] *v.* **(submitted) 1.** *v.i. & pr.* se soumettre (à qn, à la volonté de qn, à une force supérieure); se plier (à une nécessité); s'astreindre (à la discipline); se résigner (à un malheur); *Wr:* abandonner; **to s. to authority,** se subordonner. **2.** *v.tr.* (*a*) soumettre; **to s. sth. for s.o.'s approval, to s.o.'s inspection,** soumettre, présenter, qch. à l'approbation, à l'inspection, de qn; **to s. proofs of identify,** présenter des pièces d'identité; (*b*) **to s. that . . .,** représenter, alléguer, que . . .; *Jur:* **I s. that there is no case against my client,** je plaide le non-lieu.
subnormal [sʌb'nɔ:məl] *a.* subnormal, -aux; (température) au-dessous de la normale; (*of pers.*) faible d'esprit; **educationally s.,** arriéré.
suborder ['sʌbɔ:dər] *n. Nat. Hist:* sous-ordre *m.*
subordinate¹ [sə'bɔ:dinət] **1.** *a.* (*a*) (rang) inférieur, subalterne; (rôle) accessoire; (*b*) subordonné (**to,** à); *Gram:* **s. clause,** proposition subordonnée. **2.** *n.* subordonné, -ée.
subordinate² [sə'bɔ:dineit] *v.tr.* subordonner (**to,** à).
subordination [səbɔ:di'neiʃ(ə)n] *n.* **1.** subordination *f* (**to,** à). **2.** soumission *f* (**to,** à).
suborn [sʌ'bɔ:n] *v.tr. Jur:* suborner (un témoin).
subplot ['sʌbplɔt] *n. Lit: Th:* intrigue *f* secondaire.
subpoena¹ [sʌb'pi:nə, sə'pi:nə] *n. Jur:* citation *f*, assignation *f* (de témoins) (sous peine d'amende).
subpoena² *v.tr.* **(subpoenaed) to s. s.o. to appear,** citer qn à comparaître (sous peine d'amende); **to s. s.o. as witness,** assigner qn comme témoin; **to s. a witness,** signifier une assignation à un témoin.
sub post office [sʌb'poustɔfis] *n.* petit bureau de poste (dans un village).
sub-prefect [sʌb'pri:fekt] *n. Fr.Adm:* sous-préfet *m.*

subroutine [sʌbruː'tiːn] *n.* sous-programme *m.*

subscribe [səb'skraib] *v.tr. & i.* **1.** (*a*) souscrire (son nom); signer (un document); **to s. one's name to a document,** apposer sa signature à un document; (*b*) **to s. to an opinion,** souscrire à une opinion; **I cannot s. to that,** je ne peux pas consentir à cela. **2.** (*a*) **to s. ten pounds,** souscrire pour (la somme de) dix livres; **to s. a thousand francs to a charity,** souscrire mille francs pour une œuvre de charité; *Fin:* **to s. shares,** souscrire des actions; **to s. to a loan,** souscrire à un emprunt; **subscribed capital,** capital souscrit; (*b*) **to s. to a newspaper,** (i) s'abonner, (ii) être abonné, à un journal; (*c*) *Publ:* **to s. a book,** (i) (*of publisher*) offrir un livre en souscription; (ii) (*of bookseller*) acheter un livre en souscription.

subscriber [səb'skraibər] *n.* **1.** signataire *mf*, souscripteur *m* (d'un document); **the s.,** (i) le soussigné; (ii) le contractant. **2.** souscripteur *m* (à une œuvre de charité). **3.** abonné, -ée (à un journal); **telephone s.,** abonné du téléphone; **s. trunk dialling,** (téléphone) automatique *m.*

subscription [sʌb'skripʃ(ə)n] *n.* **1.** (*a*) souscription *f* (de son nom); signature *f*; (*b*) adhésion *f* (**to,** à); approbation *f* (**to,** de). **2. s. to a charity,** souscription à une œuvre de bienfaisance; **to pay a s.,** verser une cotisation; **to get up a s.,** se cotiser; **monument erected by public s.,** monument élevé par souscription publique; *Fin:* **s. to a loan,** souscription à un emprunt; **s. list,** liste *f* de souscription, des souscripteurs. **3.** abonnement *m* (à un journal); **to take out a s. to a paper,** s'abonner à un journal; **s. to a club,** cotisation (annuelle) à un club; **to pay one's s.,** payer sa cotisation (**to,** à). **4.** *Publ:* souscription.

subsection ['sʌbsekʃ(ə)n] *n.* subdivision *f*; paragraphe *m.*

subsequent ['sʌbsikwənt] *a.* subséquent; **at a s. meeting,** dans une séance ultérieure; **s. to . . .,** postérieur, consécutif, à . . .. **-ly** *adv.* plus tard; dans, par, la suite; postérieurement (**to,** à).

subservience [sʌb'səːviəns] *n.* **1.** utilité *f* (**to,** à). **2.** soumission *f*, servilité *f*; assujettissement *m* (à la mode).

subservient [sʌb'səːviənt] *a.* **1.** utile, qui aide (**to,** à); **to make sth. s. to sth.,** faire servir qch. à qch. **2.** subordonné (**to,** à). **3.** obséquieux; servile.

subside [səb'said] *v.i.* **1.** (*a*) (*of ground, building*) s'affaisser, se tasser, se déniveler; (*b*) *F:* **to s. into an armchair,** s'affaler dans un fauteuil. **2.** (*of water*) baisser, diminuer; (*of blister*) se dégonfler; **the flood is subsiding,** la crue diminue. **3.** (*a*) (*of storm, excitement, fever*) s'apaiser, se calmer; (*b*) *F:* (*of pers.*) se taire.

subsidence ['sʌbsidəns, səb'saidəns] *n.* **1.** (*a*) subsidence *f*; affaissement *m* (d'un édifice); dénivellation *f*, dénivellement *m* (d'un pont); abaissement *m* (du terrain); tassement *m* (du terrain, des fondations); (*b*) décrue *f*, baisse *f* (d'une rivière); (*c*) *Med:* délitescence *f* (d'une tumeur); (*d*) apaisement *m* (d'une fièvre). **2.** *Geol:* effondrement *m.*

subsidiary [sʌb'sidiəri] *a.* subsidiaire, auxiliaire; **s. account,** sous-compte *m*; *Fin:* **s. company,** *n.* **subsidiary,** filiale *f*; *Mil:* **s. troops,** *n.* **subsidiaries,** auxiliaires *mpl.*

subsidize ['sʌbsidaiz] *v.tr.* subventionner; primer (une industrie); **to be subsidized by the State, the government,** recevoir une subvention de, être subventionné par, l'État; **subsidized industry,** industrie primée.

subsidy ['sʌbsidi] *n.* subvention *f*; *Ind:* prime *f.*

subsist [səb'sist] *v.i.* (*a*) subsister; **custom that still subsists,** coutume qui existe encore; (*b*) s'entretenir, vivre (**on,** de).

subsistence [səb'sistəns] *n.* **1.** existence *f.* **2.** subsistance *f*; **means of s.,** moyens *m* de subsistance; **a bare s. wage,** un salaire à peine suffisant pour vivre; **to live at s. level,** avoir tout juste de quoi vivre; **s. farming,** autoconsommation *f*; **s. (allowance),** frais *mpl* de subsistance.

subsoil ['sʌbsɔil] *n.* *Geol: etc:* sous-sol *m.*

subsonic [sʌb'sɔnik] *a.* *Av:* subsonique.

subspecies [sʌb'spiːʃiːz] *n.* *Nat.Hist:* sous-espèce *f.*

substance ['sʌbstəns] *n.* **1.** (*a*) substance *f*, matière *f*; *Ch:* **stable s.,** corps *m* stable; (*b*) *Theol:* substance (spirituelle, corporelle). **2.** substance, fond *m*, essentiel *m* (d'un article, d'un argument); **I agree in s.,** en substance, je suis d'accord. **3.** solidité *f*; **book of s.,** livre *m* solide; **his argument has little s.,** son argument n'a rien de solide. **4.** bien *m*, fortune *f*; **he's a man of s.,** il a du bien.

substandard [sʌb'stændəd] *a.* de qualité inférieure.

substantial [səb'stænʃ(ə)l] *a.* **1.** substantiel, réel. **2.** (point) important; (progrès, *Com:* réduction) considérable; (différence) appréciable; **s. proof,** preuve concluante, valable. **3.** (*a*) (repas) substantiel, copieux, solide; (*b*) (construction, livre) solide; (drap) résistant. **4.** (bourgeois) qui a de quoi, qui a des écus; (maison de commerce) solide, bien assise; **s. landlord,** gros propriétaire. **-ally** *adv.* **1.** substantiellement, réellement; en substance. **2.** solidement, substantiellement. **3.** fortement, considérablement; **this contributed s. to our success,** cela a contribué pour une grande part à notre succès.

substantiate [səb'stænʃieit] *v.tr.* établir, prouver, justifier (une affirmation, etc.); prouver, établir, le bien-fondé d'(une réclamation).

substantiation [səbstænʃi'eiʃ(ə)n] *n.* justification *f* (d'une affirmation); énumération *f* des faits à l'appui (d'une accusation).

substantival [sʌbstən'taiv(ə)l] *a.* *Gram:* qui fait fonction de substantif. **-ally** *adv.* substantivement.

substantive ['sʌbstəntiv] **1.** *a.* (*a*) *Gram:* substantif; (*b*) réel, indépendant; *Jur:* **s. law,** droit positif. **2.** *n.* *Gram:* substantif *m* **-ly** *adv.* substantivement.

substation ['sʌbsteiʃ(ə)n] *n.* *El: etc:* sous-station *f.*

substitute¹ ['sʌbstitjuːt] *n.* **1.** (*pers.*) remplaçant, -ante, suppléant, -ante; *Sp:* remplaçant; *Jur: Ecc:* substitut *m*; **as a s. for . . .,** en remplacement de . . ., pour remplacer . . .; **to act as a s. for s.o., sth.,** remplacer qn, se substituer à qn, à qch. **2.** (*a*) (*of foodstuffs, drugs*) succédané *m*; **as a s. for . . .,** comme succédané de . . .; **coffee s.,** ersatz *m* de café; (*b*) (*imitation*) contrefaçon *f*; **beware of substitutes,** se méfier des contrefaçons.

substitute² **1.** *v.tr.* substituer; **to s. margarine for butter,** remplacer le beurre par la margarine. **2.** *v.i.* **to substitute for s.o.,** remplacer, suppléer, qn.

substitution [sʌbsti'tjuːʃ(ə)n] *n.* substitution *f*; remplacement *m.*

substratum *pl.* **-a, -ums** [sʌb'streitəm, -ə, -əmz] *n.* couche inférieure; *Geol:* substrat(um) *m.*

substructure ['sʌbstrʌktjər] *n.* *Const:* fondement *m* (d'un édifice); *Civ.E:* infrastructure *f* (d'une route).

subtenancy [sʌb'tenənsi] *n.* sous-location *f.*

subtenant [sʌb'tenənt] *n.* sous-locataire *mf.*

subtend [səb'tend] *v.tr.* *Mth:* sous-tendre (un arc).

subterfuge ['sʌbtəfjuːdʒ] *n.* subterfuge *m*; faux-fuyant *m*, *pl.* faux-fuyants; **to resort to s.,** user de subterfuge.

subterranean [sʌbtə'reiniən] *a.* souterrain.

subtilize ['sʌtilaiz] **1.** *v.tr.* subtiliser; donner de la subtilité à (une pensée). **2.** *v.i.* subtiliser.

subtitle¹ ['sʌbtaitl] *n.* *Typ: Cin:* sous-titre *m*; **film with English subtitles,** film sous-titré en anglais.

subtitle² *v.tr. Cin: etc:* sous-titrer. **subtitling** *n.* sous-titrage *m.*
subtle [sʌtl] *a.* **1.** (parfum, charme) subtil; **s. distinction,** distinction ténue, subtile. **2.** (*a*) (esprit, raisonnement) subtil, fin; **s. remark,** observation subtile; **s. irony,** fine ironie; **you are being too s.,** vous raffinez; (*b*) rusé, astucieux. **subtly** *adv.* subtilement; avec finesse; **s. different,** avec une différence à peine perceptible.
subtlety ['sʌt(ə)lti] *n.* **1.** (*a*) subtilité *f* (de l'esprit, d'un raisonnement); raffinement *m,* finesse *f* (d'une politique); (*b*) subtilité; distinction subtile. **2.** subtilité, ténuité *f* (d'une distinction).
subtonic [sʌb'tɔnik] *n. Mus:* note *f* sensible; la sensible.
subtotal [sʌb'toutl] *n.* total partiel.
subtract [sʌb'trækt] *v.tr. Mth:* soustraire, retrancher (**from,** de).
subtraction [səb'trækʃ(ə)n] *n. Mth:* soustraction *f* (**from,** de).
subtropical [sʌb'trɔpik(ə)l] *a.* subtropical, -aux.
suburb ['sʌbəːb] *n.* banlieue *f*; **in the suburbs,** dans la, en, banlieue; **garden s.,** cité-jardin *f, pl.* cités-jardins.
suburban [sə'bəːbən] *a.* (*a*) suburbain; (maison, train) de banlieue; (*b*) *Pej:* (*of pers.*) à l'esprit étroit.
suburbanite [sə'bəːbənait] *n. F:* banlieusard, -arde.
suburbia [sə'bəːbiə] *n. F:* la banlieue.
subvention [sʌb'venʃən] *n.* subvention *f.*
subversion [səb'vəːʃ(ə)n] *n. Pol: etc:* subversion *f.*
subversive [səb'vəːsiv] **1.** *a.* subversif (**of,** de). **2.** *n.* individu subversif.
subvert [səb'vəːt] *v.tr.* renverser, subvertir.
subway ['sʌbwei] *n.* **1.** passage, couloir, souterrain; souterrain *m.* **2.** *esp. NAm:* chemin de fer souterrain; métro *m.*
sub-zero [sʌb'ziərou] *a.* au-dessous de zéro.
succeed [sək'siːd] *v.* **1.** (*a*) *v.tr.* succéder à (qn); **George III was succeeded by George IV,** George IV succéda à, fut le successeur de, George III; (*b*) *v.i.* **to s. to the throne, the Crown,** succéder à la couronne; **to s. to an office, estate,** hériter d'une fonction, d'une propriété; *Jur:* **right to s.,** droits successifs; (*c*) *v.tr.* **day succeeds day,** un jour suit l'autre. **2.** *v.i.* réussir; atteindre son but; venir à bien; **hard workers always s.,** les grands travailleurs arrivent toujours; *Prov:* **nothing succeeds like success,** rien ne réussit comme le succès; **how to s.,** le moyen de parvenir; **young man who will s.,** jeune homme qui ira loin; **to s. in doing sth.,** réussir, arriver, à faire qch. **succeeding** *a.* **1.** suivant, subséquent. **2.** futur; à venir. **3.** successif; **each s. year,** chaque année successive.
success [sək'ses] *n.* **1.** *A:* succès *m,* issue *f* (d'une affaire); **a second attempt met with no better s.,** une seconde tentative n'a pas eu plus de succès. **2.** (*a*) succès, réussite *f*; **we wish you s.,** bonne chance! **to meet with, to achieve, s.,** avoir, remporter, du succès; réussir; **without s.,** sans succès; sans y parvenir; **to score a s.,** remporter, avoir, un succès; (*b*) **to be, turn out, a s.,** réussir; avoir du succès; **the evening was a great s.,** la soirée a été très réussie; **it was a huge, great, s.,** c'était un succès fou; **he was the s. of the evening,** il a été le clou de la soirée; **to make a s. of sth.,** réussir qch.; **s. story,** histoire d'une réussite.
successful [sək'sesf(u)l] *a.* (projet) couronné de succès; (résultat) heureux; (portrait) réussi; (pièce) qui a du succès; **to bring an operation to a s. conclusion,** mener une opération à bonne fin, à bien; **to be s. in doing sth.,** réussir à faire qch.; **he is s. in everything,** tout lui réussit; **a s. businessman,** un homme d'affaires réussi, arrivé; **to be s. at the polls,** sortir victorieux du scrutin; **s. candidates,** (i) candidats élus; (ii) *Sch:* candidats reçus. **-fully** *adv.* avec succès.
succession [sək'seʃ(ə)n] *n.* succession *f.* **1.** (*a*) suite *f*; **in s.,** consécutivement, successivement; **for two years in s.,** pendant deux années successives, consécutives, de suite; **in close s.,** se succédant de près; **in rapid s.,** coup sur coup; (*b*) série *f,* suite ininterrompue (de victoires); **long s. of kings,** longue suite de rois. **2.** (*a*) succession (à la couronne); **to settle the s.,** régler la succession; **at the time of his s. to the throne,** au moment de son avènement *m*; *Hist:* **the Wars of S.,** les guerres *fpl* de succession; (*b*) *Jur:* succession; **law of s.,** droit successif; **right of s.,** droits successifs; (*c*) héritage *m*; (*d*) lignée *f*; descendance *f,* descendants *mpl.*
successive [sək'sesiv] *a.* successif, consécutif. **-ly** *adv.* successivement.
successor [sək'sesər] *n.* successeur *m* (**to,** à); **my first car and its successors,** ma première voiture et celles qui lui ont succédé, qui sont venues ensuite.
succinct [sʌk'siŋ(k)t] *a.* (récit, écrivain) succinct. **-ly** *adv.* succinctement.
succinctness [sʌk'siŋ(k)tnis] *n.* concision *f.*
succour¹, *NAm:* **succor¹** ['sʌkər] *n. Lit:* secours *m,* aide *f.*
succour², *NAm:* **succor²** *v.tr. Lit:* secourir (les pauvres); venir en aide à, venir à l'aide de (qn).
succulence ['sʌkjuləns] *n.* succulence *f.*
succulent ['sʌkjulənt] **1.** *a.* (*a*) (*of food*) succulent; (*b*) *Bot:* **s. leaf,** feuille charnue. **2.** *n. Bot:* plante grasse.
succumb [sə'kʌm] *v.i.* succomber (**to temptation,** à la tentation); céder (**to sleep,** au sommeil); **to s. to odds,** succomber sous le nombre; **to s. to one's injuries,** succomber à, mourir de, ses blessures; **we have all succumbed to her charm,** son charme nous a tous conquis.
such [sʌtʃ] **I.** *a.* tel, pareil, semblable. **1.** (*a*) **beasts of prey s. as the lion or the tiger,** des bêtes fauves telles que le lion ou le tigre; **s. books as these are always useful,** les livres de ce genre sont toujours utiles; **s. a man,** un tel homme; **s. things,** de telles choses; **in s. cases,** en pareils cas; **on s. an occasion,** en semblable occasion; **in s. weather,** (i) par un temps pareil; (ii) par le temps qu'il fait; **why do you ask s. a question!** pourquoi me demander une chose pareille! **how can you tell s. lies?** comment pouvez-vous mentir de la sorte? **did you ever see s. a thing!** a-t-on jamais vu chose pareille! **some s. plan was in my mind,** j'avais dans l'esprit un projet de ce genre; **there is no s. thing,** cela n'existe pas; **if there were no s. thing as money,** si l'argent n'existait pas; **I said no s. thing,** je n'ai rien dit de semblable, de la sorte; **no s. thing!** pas du tout! *Jur:* **persons guilty of s. offences,** personnes coupables des délits susmentionnés; (*b*) **s. is not my intention,** ce n'est pas là mon intention; **if s. were the case,** s'il en était ainsi; **the village boasts a bus, s. as it is,** le village a un autobus, si l'on peut dire. **2.** **on s. (and s.) a day in s. (and s.) a place,** tel jour en tel endroit; **your letter of s. and s. a date,** votre lettre de tant; **s. a one,** un tel, une telle. **3.** **he arranges things in s. a way that he is free on Saturdays,** il s'arrange de manière à être libre les samedis; **her kindness was s. as to make us feel ashamed,** sa bonté était telle que nous en étions confus; **to take s. steps as shall be considered necessary,** prendre toutes mesures qui paraîtront nécessaires; **until s. time as is convenient to me,** jusqu'à ce que cela me convienne. **4.** (*intensive*) **s. large houses,** de si grandes maisons; **I had never heard s. good music,** je n'avais jamais entendu d'aussi bonne musique; **s. a clever man,** un homme si habile; **s. courage,** tant de courage; **it was s. a long time ago,** il y a si longtemps de cela; **he is s. a liar,** il est si, tellement, menteur; **s. an enjoyable day,** une journée si agréable; **we had s. a**

good time, on s'est si bien amusé(s); **don't be in s. a hurry,** ne soyez pas si pressé; **you gave me s. a fright!** vous m'avez fait une peur! **he has s. ideas!** il a de ces idées! **II.** *pron.* **1. he enjoys cakes, ices and s.,** il mange avec plaisir des gâteaux, des glaces et autres choses de ce genre. **2.** (*a*) **that's not for s. as you,** cela n'est pas pour quelqu'un comme toi; **I haven't many, but I will send you s. as I have,** je n'en ai pas beaucoup, mais je vous enverrai ce que j'ai. **3. he was a very gallant man and well known as s.** il était très crâne et connu pour tel; **history as s. is too often neglected,** l'histoire en tant que telle est trop souvent négligée.

suchlike ['sʌtʃlaik] *F:* **1.** *a.* semblable, pareil. **2.** *pron.* **beggars, tramps, and s.,** mendiants, chemineaux et autres gens de la sorte; **concerts, theatres, and s.,** concerts, théâtres, et autres choses de ce genre.

suck¹ [sʌk] *n.* **1.** (*a*) action *f* de sucer; **to have, take, a s. at a sweet,** sucer un bonbon; (*b*) *Hyd.E:* succion *f*, aspiration *f* (d'un déversoir, d'une pompe). **2. to give a child s.,** donner à téter, la tétée, à un enfant.

suck² **1.** *v.tr.* (*a*) sucer (le lait, etc.); (*of horse*) **to s. wind,** avaler de l'air; (*b*) sucer; suçoter (une orange, des bonbons); mordiller (le coin de son mouchoir); tirer sur (sa pipe); **to s. one's fingers,** se sucer les doigts; **to s. one's thumb,** sucer son pouce; *Fig:* **to s. s.o. dry,** sucer qn jusqu'à la moelle; *F:* **you can't teach your grandmother to s. eggs,** ce n'est pas aux vieux singes qu'on apprend à faire des grimaces; (*c*) **the dust is sucked into the bag,** la poussière est aspirée dans le sac; *Fig:* **to get sucked into a conspiracy,** être entraîné dans une conspiration. **2.** *v.i.* (*a*) (*of child, etc.*) sucer le lait; téter (le lait); **the child won't s.,** l'enfant ne prend pas le sein; (*b*) **to s. at sth.,** sucer, suçoter (un bonbon); sucer, tirer sur (sa pipe); (*c*) (*of pump*) super. **suck down** *v.tr.* engloutir; entraîner au fond. **suck in** *v.tr.* (*a*) sucer; absorber; aspirer; absorber (des connaissances); (*of air pump*) aspirer (l'air); (*b*) engloutir (dans un tourbillon); (*c*) faire rentrer (ses joues). **sucking 1.** *a.* **s. pig,** cochon *m* de lait. **2.** *n.* (*a*) succion *f*; aspiration *f*; (*b*) **s. up,** (i) aspiration (d'un liquide); (ii) *P:* flagornerie *f*. **suck out** *v.tr.* sucer (du jus); **to s. out the poison from the wound,** aspirer, sucer, le poison de la blessure. **suck up 1.** *v.tr.* sucer, aspirer, pomper (un liquide, de l'air). **2.** *P: v.i.* **to s. up to s.o.,** faire (de) la lèche à qn; lécher les bottines à qn.

sucker¹ ['sʌkər] *n.* **1.** suceur, -euse. **2.** niais *m*, blanc-bec *m*, *pl.* blancs-becs; **to be a s. for sth.,** raffoler de qch. **3.** suçoir *m* (de pou); ventouse *f* (de sangsue, sur une machine). **4.** *F:* bonbon *m*. **5.** *Hort:* rejeton *m*, rejet *m* (d'une plante); drageon *m*, surgeon *m* (d'arbre); (*of tree*) **to throw out suckers,** drageonner, surgeonner.

sucker² **1.** *v.tr. Hort:* enlever les drageons (d'un arbre). **2.** *v.i.* (*of tree*) drageonner.

suckle ['sʌkl] **1.** *v.tr.* allaiter (un enfant, un petit); donner le sein, donner à téter, à (un enfant). **2.** *v.i.* (*of baby, etc.*) téter. **suckling** *n.* **1.** allaitement *m*. **2.** (*a*) nourrisson, -onne; enfant *mf* au sein; (*b*) jeune animal *m* qui tette encore; **s. pig,** cochon *m* de lait.

sucrose ['s(j)u:krous] *n. Ch:* saccharose *m*.

suction ['sʌkʃ(ə)n] *n.* succion *f*; aspiration *f* (de l'eau dans une pompe); aspiration, appel *m* (d'air); **to adhere by s.,** faire ventouse; **s. pump,** pompe aspirante; **s. stroke,** temps *m* de l'aspiration; *Aut: etc:* **s. cup,** ventouse *f*.

Sudan (the) [ðəsu:'dæn] *Pr.n.* le Soudan.

Sudanese [su:də'ni:z] *Geog:* **1.** *a.* soudanais, soudanien. **2.** *n.* Soudanais, -aise; Soudanien, -ienne.

sudden ['sʌdn] **1.** *a.* (*a*) soudain, subit; **s. shower,** averse inopinée, intempestive; **s. death,** (i) mort soudaine; (ii) *Sp: etc:* jeu pour décider d'un match nul (dans lequel celui qui marque le premier point est le gagnant); **this is rather s.,** je ne m'y attendais pas; (*b*) (mouvement, tournant) brusque; **he's very s. in his movements,** ses mouvements sont très brusques. **2.** *adv.phr.* **all of a s.,** soudain; tout à coup. **-ly** *adv.* (*a*) soudain, soudainement; tout à coup; **he died s.,** il est mort soudainement; (*b*) brusquement.

suddenness ['sʌdənnis] *n.* (*a*) soudaineté *f*; **with startling s.,** en coup de théâtre; (*b*) brusquerie *f*.

suds [sʌdz] *n.pl.* **(soap) s.,** (*a*) mousse *f* de savon; (*b*) eau *f* de savon; lessive *f*.

sue [s(j)u:] **1.** *v.tr. Jur:* **to s. s.o. at law,** intenter un procès à qn; poursuivre qn en justice; **to s. s.o. for damages,** poursuivre qn en dommages-intérêts. **2.** *v.i.* (*a*) **to s. for a separation,** plaider en séparation; **to s. for libel,** attaquer en diffamation; (*b*) **to s. for peace,** demander la paix.

suede, suède [sweid] *n. Leath:* (*for shoes*) daim *m*; (*for gloves, etc.*) (peau *f* de) suède; **s. gloves,** gants *m* de suède; **s. shoes,** chaussures *f* en daim; **s. cloth,** suédine *f*.

suet ['s(j)u:it] *n. Cu:* graisse *f* de rognon; **beef s.,** graisse (de rognon) de bœuf; **s. pudding,** pouding fait avec de la farine et de la graisse de bœuf,

Suez ['sju(:)iz, 'su(:)iz] *Pr.n. Geog:* Suez; **the S. Canal,** le canal de Suez.

suffer ['sʌfər] **1.** *v.tr.* (*a*) éprouver, subir, souffrir (une perte); endurer, ressentir (une douleur); subir (une peine); **to s. hunger,** souffrir la faim; **to s. defeat,** essuyer, subir, une défaite; (*b*) permettre, supporter, tolérer; **he does not s. fools gladly,** il ne peut pas supporter les imbéciles. **2.** *v.i.* (*a*) (*of pers.*) souffrir; **to s. from rheumatism,** souffrir de rhumatismes; **to s. for one's misdeeds,** supporter la conséquence de ses méfaits; **you'll s. for it,** il vous en cuira; (*b*) **to s. from neglect,** pâtir d'un manque de soins; **country suffering from labour troubles,** pays *m* en proie à l'agitation ouvrière; **his good name has suffered,** il a souffert dans sa réputation; (*c*) subir une perte, un dommage; **the vines have suffered from the frost,** les vignes ont souffert de la gelée. **suffering 1.** *a.* souffrant; qui souffre. **2.** *n.* souffrance *f*; **cheerful in spite of his s.,** gai malgré ses souffrances.

sufferance ['sʌf(ə)rəns] *n.* tolérance *f* (**of,** de); **children are admitted on s.,** l'entrée des enfants est tolérée.

sufferer ['sʌfərər] *n.* **to be a s. from ill health,** souffrir d'une mauvaise santé; **sufferers from asthma,** personnes sujettes à l'asthme.

suffice [sə'fais] **1.** *v.i.* suffire; **that will s. for me,** cela me suffira; **s. it to say that I got nothing out of it,** suffit que je n'en ai rien obtenu. **2.** *v.tr.* suffire à (qn); être suffisant pour (qn).

sufficiency [sə'fiʃənsi] *n.* (*a*) suffisance *f*; **to have a s. of sth.,** avoir assez de qch.; (*b*) fortune suffisante; aisance *f*; **to have no more than a bare s.,** avoir tout juste de quoi vivre.

sufficient [sə'fiʃənt] **1.** *a.* assez, suffisant; **lack of s. food,** insuffisance *f* d'alimentation; **this is s. to feed them,** cela suffit pour les nourrir; **a hundred francs will be s.,** j'aurai assez de cent francs; **one light will be s.,** il suffira d'une lampe. **2.** *n.* assez; **have you had s. (to eat)?** avez-vous mangé à votre faim? êtes-vous rassasié? **-ly** *adv.* suffisamment, assez.

suffix¹ ['sʌfiks] *n. Gram:* suffixe *m*.

suffix² ['sʌfiks, sʌ'fiks] *v.tr. Gram:* suffixer. **suffixed** *a.* (lettre, particule) suffixe.

suffocate ['sʌfəkeit] **1.** *v.tr.* (*a*) (*to death*) étouffer (qn); (*b*) (*of smell*) suffoquer (qn); (*c*) *Fig:* **all signs of initiative were suffocated,** toute indication d'initiative était étouffée. **2.** *v.i.* étouffer, suffoquer (**with rage, etc.,** de colère). **suffocating** *a.* suffocant, étouffant; **it's s. (in) here,** on étouffe ici.

suffocation [sʌfə'keiʃ(ə)n] *n.* suffocation *f*, étouffement *m*.

suffragan ['sʌfrəgən] *a. & n. Ecc:* **s. (bishop), bishop s.,** (évêque) suffragant (*m*).

suffrage ['sʌfridʒ] *n. Pol:* suffrage *m*; (*a*) vote *m*, voix *f*; (*b*) droit *m* de vote; **women's, s.,** droit de vote pour les femmes; **universal s.,** suffrage universel.

suffragette [sʌfrə'dʒet] *n.f. Pol. Hist:* suffragette.

suffuse [sə'fju:z] *v.tr.* se répandre sur (qch.); **a blush suffused her cheeks,** une rougeur s'est répandue sur ses joues; *Lit:* ses joues s'empourprèrent; **eyes suffused with tears,** yeux noyés, baignés, de larmes; **suffused with light,** inondé de lumière.

sugar¹ ['ʃugər] *n.* **1.** sucre *m*; **granulated s.,** sucre cristallisé; **lump s.,** sucre en morceaux; **lump, cube, of s.,** morceau *m*, *Fr.Can:* cube *m*, de sucre; **caster s.,** sucre en poudre; sucre semoule; **icing s.,** sucre glace; **brown s.,** cassonade *f*; **help yourself to s.,** prenez du sucre. **2.** (*a*) **s. mouse,** souris *f* en sucre; **s. almond,** dragée *f*; **s. basin, bowl,** sucrier *m*; **s. shaker,** saupoudroir *m* à sucre; **(pair of) s. tongs,** pince *f* à sucre; **s. refinery,** raffinerie *f* (de sucre); sucrerie *f*; *F:* **s. daddy,** protecteur âgé; papa gâteau; (*b*) **s. beet,** betterave *f* à sucre; **s. cane,** canne *f* à sucre; **s. maple,** érable *m* à sucre; (*c*) *Hort:* **s. pea,** mange-tout *m inv*. **3. milk s.,** sucre de lait; lactose *f*; *Physiol:* **blood s.,** glucose sanguin. **4.** douceur affectée. **5.** *NAm: P:* (*a*) (*money*) galette *f*, pognon *m*; (*b*) belle fille; (*c*) drogue *f*, narcotique *m*.

sugar² **1.** *v.tr.* sucrer (son café, etc.); recouvrir (une pilule) de sucre; **sugared almond,** dragée *f*; *Fig:* **to s. the pill,** dorer la pilule.

sugar-coated [ʃugə'koutid] *a.* recouvert de sucre; (*of almond*) lissé; **s.-c. pill,** pilule dragéifiée.

sugarloaf ['ʃugəlouf] *n.* pain *m* de sucre; **s. mountain,** montagne *f* en pain de sucre.

sugarplum ['ʃugəplʌm] *n. A:* bonbon *m*.

sugary ['ʃugəri] *a.* **1.** (*a*) sucré; saupoudré de sucre; (*b*) trop sucré; (*c*) (*of jam*) **to go s.,** se cristalliser. **2.** (sourire, ton) mielleux, sucré; (ton) doucereux.

suggest [sə'dʒest] *v.tr.* **1.** (*a*) suggérer, proposer (qch. à qn); **he suggested going for a walk,** il a suggéré de faire une promenade; **I shall do as you s.,** je ferai comme vous le suggérez; **a solution suggested itself to me,** une solution m'est venue à l'esprit; (*b*) *Med: Psy:* suggérer (une idée, une action). **2.** inspirer, faire naître (une idée); **prudence suggests a retreat,** la prudence conseille la retraite. **3.** insinuer; **are you suggesting that I am lying?** est-ce que vous insinuez que je mens? **are eggs as scarce as the price would s.?** les œufs sont-ils aussi rares que le prix le laisse supposer? *Jur:* **I s. that . . .,** n'est-il pas vrai que . . .? **4.** évoquer; **his nose and ears s. a rabbit,** son nez et ses oreilles donnent l'idée d'un lapin.

suggestible [sə'dʒestibl] *a.* (sujet) influençable par la suggestion (hypnotique); (sujet) suggestible.

suggestion [sə'dʒestʃ(ə)n] *n.* **1.** suggestion *f*; (*a*) **to be open to s.,** être prêt à accueillir des suggestions; **at his s. I stayed at home,** suivant son conseil je suis resté chez moi; **hypnotic s.,** suggestion hypnotique; (*b*) **to make a s.,** faire une suggestion, proposition; **practical s.,** conseil *m* pratique; **suggestions for improvement,** propositions en vue d'une amélioration; **to be full of suggestions,** être fécond en idées, en conseils; (*c*) *Jur:* **my s. is that you were not there at the time,** n'est-il pas vrai que vous étiez absent à ce moment-là? **2. to speak with just a s. of a foreign accent,** parler avec une pointe d'accent étranger; **s. of regret,** nuance *f* de regret.

suggestive [sə'dʒestiv] *a.* suggestif; (*a*) évocateur, -trice; **s. of sth.,** qui évoque qch.; (*b*) **s. joke,** plaisanterie grivoise. **-ly** *adv.* d'une façon suggestive.

suggestiveness [sə'dʒestivnis] *n.* caractère suggestif (d'un dessin, etc.).

suicidal [s(j)u:i'said(ə)l] *a.* (malade) suicidaire; **s. tendencies,** tendances *fpl* au suicide; **it would be s. (to do it),** ce serait un véritable suicide d'agir de la sorte.

suicide¹ ['s(j)u:isaid] *n.* (*pers.*) suicidé, -ée.

suicide² *n.* (crime *m* du) suicide; **to commit s.,** se suicider; **attempted s.,** tentative *f* de suicide; **to commit political s.,** se suicider politiquement; **it would be s. to go there,** ce serait un véritable suicide d'y aller.

suit¹ [s(j)u:t] *n.* **1.** *Jur:* **s. at law,** procès (civil); poursuites *fpl* (en justice); **criminal s.,** action *f*, procès, au criminel; **to be a party in a s.,** être en cause. **2.** *O:* prière *f*, demande *f*. **3.** *O:* demande en mariage; **to press one's s. with a girl,** faire une cour assidue à une jeune fille. **4.** *Cost:* (*a*) ensemble *m*; (i) (*man's*) complet *m*, costume *m*; **two-piece, three-piece, s.,** complet en deux, trois, pièces; **lounge s.,** complet veston; (ii) (*woman's*) tailleur *m*; (*b*) *Av: Space:* **flying, flight, s.,** combinaison *f* de vol; **pressure s.,** combinaison pressurisée. **5.** *Nau:* **s. of sails,** jeu *m* de voiles. **6.** *Cards:* **the four suits,** les quatre couleurs; **politeness is not his long s.,** la politesse n'est pas son fort; **to follow s.,** (i) fournir à la couleur (demandée); (ii) *Fig:* en faire autant, faire de même.

suit² **1.** *v.tr.* (*a*) accommoder, adapter (**sth. to sth.,** qch. à qch.); **to be suited to, for, sth.,** être adapté à qch.; être fait pour qch.; **the premises are not suited for display purposes,** le local ne se prête pas à l'étalage; **he is not suited for, to be, a doctor,** il n'est pas fait pour être médecin; **they are suited to each other,** ils sont faits l'un pour l'autre; (*b*) convenir à, aller à (qn); **a small job in the country would s. me very well,** un petit emploi en province m'irait, me conviendrait, très bien; **he found a house that suited him,** il a trouvé une maison à son gré; **marriage suits you,** le mariage vous réussit; **that suits me best,** c'est ce qui m'arrange le mieux; **that suits me (just) fine,** *F:* **down to the ground,** ça me va à merveille; **I shall do it when it suits me,** je le ferai quand cela me conviendra; **would that s. you?** cela ferait-il votre affaire? **s. yourself,** faites comme vous voudrez; **this climate, this food, does not s. me,** ce climat, cette nourriture, ne me va pas; **this hat suits you,** ce chapeau vous va (bien); (*c*) *NAm:* habiller (qn) d'un costume. **2.** *v.i.* **that date does not s.,** cette date ne convient pas. **suiting** *n.* **1.** adaptation *f*, appropriation *f* (**of sth. to sth.,** de qch. à qch.). **2.** *Com:* tissu *m* de confection; **men's suitings,** tissus *mpl* pour complets.

suitability [s(j)u:tə'biliti] *n.* convenance *f* (d'une date); à-propos *m* (d'une remarque); accord *m*, rapport *m* (de caractères); **s. of a candidate for a post,** aptitude *f* d'un candidat à un poste.

suitable ['s(j)u:təbl] *a.* **1.** (sujet, travail) convenable, qui convient; (exemple) apte; **s. expression,** expression pertinente, appropriée; **s. marriage,** union bien assortie; **we have found nothing s.,** nous n'avons rien trouvé à notre convenance; **the most s. date,** la date qui conviendrait le mieux; **wherever you think s.,** où bon vous semblera. **2. s. to, for, sth.,** bon à qch.; propre, approprié, à qch.; **is it a book s. for children?** est-ce un livre pour les enfants? **to make sth. s. for sth.,** adapter qch. à qch. **-ably** *adv.* convenablement; à propos; **s. matched,** bien assortis.

suitcase ['s(j)u:tkeis] *n.* valise *f*.

suite [swi:t] *n.* **1.** suite *f* (d'un prince). **2.** (*a*) **s. (of rooms),** appartement *m*; (*b*) **three-piece s.,** canapé *m* avec deux fauteuils assortis; salon *m* (en) trois pièces; **bedroom s.,** chambre *f* à coucher; **bathroom s.,** salle *f* de bains. **3.** *Mus:* suite; **orchestral s.,** suite d'orchestre.

suitor ['s(j)u:tər] *n.* **1.** *Jur:* plaideur, -euse. **2.** soupirant *m*; **her suitors,** les aspirants *mpl* à sa main.

sulfa, sulfur, etc. *see* SULPHA, SULPHUR, *etc.*
sulk¹ ['sʌlk] *n. usu. pl.* bouderie *f*; **to have (a fit of) the sulks,** bouder; faire la mine.
sulk² *v.i.* bouder; faire la mine.
sulkiness ['sʌlkinis] *n.* bouderie *f.*
sulky ['sʌlki] *a.* boudeur; **to be s.,** bouder; **to look s.,** avoir un air boudeur; faire la mine. **-ily** *adv.* en boudant; d'un ton, d'un air, boudeur.
sullen ['sʌlən] *n.* (*of pers.*) maussade, renfrogné, morose; (*of outlook*) sombre, morne; (silence) obstiné, buté. **-ly** *adv.* d'un air maussade, renfrogné; (obéir) de mauvaise grâce.
sullenness ['sʌlənnis] *n.* maussaderie *f*; air renfrogné.
sully ['sʌli] *v.tr.* souiller, ternir; tacher (sa réputation). **sullied** *a.* souillé, terni.
sulpha, sulfa ['sʌlfə] *n.* **s. drug,** sulfamide *f.*
sulphate, sulf- ['sʌlfeit] *n.* **1.** *Ch:* sulfate *m*; **iron s., ferrous s.,** sulfate de fer; **copper s.,** sulfate de cuivre. **2.** *Com:* sulfate de soude.
sulphide, sulf- ['sʌlfaid] *n. Ch:* sulfure *m*; **hydrogen s.,** hydrogène sulfuré; acide *m* sulfhydrique.
sulphonamide, sulf- [sʌl'fɔnəmaid] *n. Pharm:* sulfamide *m.*
sulphur, sulf- ['sʌlfər] *n.* soufre *m*; **flowers of s.,** fleur(s) *f(pl)* de soufre; **s. dioxide,** anhydride sulfureux; *Geol:* **s. spring,** source sulfureuse; **s. mine,** soufrière *f.*
sulphureous, sulf- [sʌl'fju:riəs] *a.* (*a*) sulfureux; (*b*) couleur de soufre *inv*; soufré.
sulphuric, sulf- [sʌl'fju:rik] *a.* (acide) sulfurique.
sulphurous, sulf- ['sʌlfərəs, -fjur-] *a.* **1.** = SULPHUREOUS. **2.** *Ch:* (acide) sulfureux.
sultan ['sʌltən] *n.* sultan *m.*
sultana [sʌl'tɑ:nə] *n.* **1.** sultane *f.* **2.** *Cu:* raisin sec de Smyrne.
sultanate ['sʌltəneit] *n.* sultanat *m.*
sultriness ['sʌltrinis] *n.* chaleur étouffante; lourdeur *f* (de l'atmosphère).
sultry ['sʌltri] *a.* **1.** étouffant, suffocant; (temps) lourd, orageux; **it is s.,** il fait très lourd. **2.** (*a*) (*of voice*) chaud; (*b*) sensuel, aguichant.
sum¹ [sʌm] *n.* **1.** (*a*) somme *f*, total *m*; montant *m* (d'un compte); **s. total,** somme totale, montant total; (*b*) **the s. and substance of the matter,** la substance, l'essence *f*, de l'affaire; **in s.,** en somme, somme toute; (*c*) **s. (of money),** somme (d'argent); **large s.,** grosse somme; **nice little s.,** somme rondelette. **2.** problème *m*, exercice *m* (d'arithmétique); **to do a s. in one's head,** faire un calcul de tête; **to do sums,** faire du calcul, de l'arithmétique.
sum² *v.* **(summed) 1.** *v.tr.* additionner (des nombres); *Mth:* sommer (une série). **2.** *v.tr. & i.* **to s. up** (*a*) faire la somme de, totaliser (des nombres); (*b*) résumer, faire un résumé (des faits); **to s. up I will say that . . .,** en résumé je dirai que . . .; **to s. up (what one has said before),** se résumer; résumer les faits; (*c*) *Jur:* (*of judge*) **to s. up (the case, the evidence),** résumer les débats (avant la délibération du jury); (*d*) **to s. up the situation at a glance,** se rendre compte de la situation d'un coup d'œil; **to s. s.o. up,** juger, classer, qn. **summing** *n.* **1.** *Mth:* **s. (up),** addition *f*, sommation *f.* **2. s. up,** (*a*) *Jur:* résumé *m* des débats (par le juge); (*b*) évaluation *f* (de la situation).
sumac(h) ['s(j)u:mæk, 'ʃu:] *n. Bot:* sumac *m.*
summarize ['sʌməraiz] *v.tr.* résumer sommairement (un ouvrage, etc.); récapituler (les débats, etc.).
summary ['sʌməri] **1.** *a.* sommaire; **s. account,** (i) récit sommaire, succinct; (ii) récit récapitulatif; *Jur:* référé *m*; **s. proceedings,** affaire *f* sommaire; **s. offences,** délits qui peuvent être jugés en procédure sommaire. **2.** *n.* sommaire *m*, résumé *m*, aperçu *m*; argument *m* (d'un livre); récapitulation *f*, relevé *m* (d'opérations commerciales); **s. of the news,** nouvelles *fpl* en bref. **-ily** *adv.* sommairement.
summation [sʌ'meiʃ(ə)n] *n.* **1.** sommation *f*, addition *f.* **2.** somme *f*, total *m.* **3.** *NAm: Jur:* résumé *m* des débats (par le juge).
summer¹ ['sʌmər] *n.* été *m*; **in s.,** en été; **a summer('s) day,** un jour d'été; **winter and s. alike, I live in the country,** hiver comme été j'habite la campagne; **next s.,** l'été prochain; **Indian s.,** été de la Saint-Martin; **s. clothes,** habits, vêtements, d'été; **s. resort,** station estivale; **s. visitor,** estivant(e); **the s. holidays,** les grandes vacances; *Adm:* **s. time,** heure *f* d'été.
summer² **1.** *v.i.* passer l'été (au bord de la mer); (*b*) (*of cattle*) estiver. **2.** *v.tr.* estiver (le bétail).
summerhouse ['sʌməhaus] *n.* pavillon *m.*
summertime ['sʌmətaim] *n.* (saison *f* d')été *m.*
summery ['sʌməri] *a.* estival, -aux; d'été.
summit ['sʌmit] *n.* sommet *m*, cime *f*, faîte *m* (d'une montagne); **the s. of greatness,** le faîte, sommet, des grandeurs; **the s. of happiness,** le summum de la félicité; **to be at the s. of power, fame,** être au pinacle; *Pol:* **s. conference, talks,** *F:* **s.,** conférence *f* au sommet.
summon ['sʌmən] *v.tr.* **1.** (*a*) appeler, faire venir (un domestique); convoquer (une assemblée, qn à une réunion); **business summoned him back to London,** les affaires l'ont rappelé à Londres; **to s. help,** appeler au secours; (*b*) *Jur:* sommer (qn) de comparaître; **to s. a defendant, a witness, to appear,** citer, assigner, un défendeur, un témoin. **2.** sommer, requérir. **3. to s. up,** faire appel à (son courage, etc.); **to s. up all one's strength,** rassembler toutes ses forces.
summons¹, *pl.* **-ses** ['sʌmənz, -ziz] *n.* **1.** appel (fait d'autorité); convocation urgente. **2.** *Jur:* (i) citation *f* (à comparaître); assignation *f*; sommation *f*; (ii) mandat *m* de comparution; **to issue a s.,** lancer une assignation; **to serve a s. on s.o.,** signifier une citation à qn; assigner qn; **to take out a s. against s.o.,** faire assigner qn.
summons² *v.tr. Jur:* citer (qn) à comparaître; assigner (qn); appeler (qn) en justice.
sump [sʌmp] *n.* **1.** (*a*) *Min: etc:* puisard *m*; (*b*) fosse *f* d'aisance. **2.** *Mec.E: I.C.E:* **(oil) s.,** carter *m* à huile; fond *m* de carter; cuvette *f* d'égouttage; *Aut:* **to drain the s.,** faire la vidange.
sumptuous ['sʌm(p)tjuəs] *a.* somptueux. **-ly** *adv.* somptueusement.
sumptuousness ['sʌm(p)tjuəsnis] *n.* somptuosité *f.*
sun¹ [sʌn] *n.* (*a*) soleil *m*; **the s. is shining,** il fait (du) soleil; **the s. rises, sets,** le soleil se lève, se couche; **rising, setting, s.,** soleil levant, couchant; **against the s.,** dans le soleil; (*b*) **to have a place in the s.,** avoir une place au soleil; **(full) in the s.,** au (grand) soleil; en plein soleil; **to take the s., to bask in the s.,** prendre le soleil; **to get a touch of the s.,** prendre, attraper, un coup de soleil; (*c*) *Pyr:* **fixed s.,** gloire *f*; (*d*) **s. hat,** chapeau *m* de soleil; **s. helmet,** casque (colonial) (à couvre-nuque); *Aut:* **s. visor,** pare-soleil *m inv.*; **s. awning,** store *m*; **s. oil, lotion,** huile *f*, lotion *f*, solaire; **s. lamp,** (i) *Cin:* grand projecteur; sunlight *m*; (ii) lampe ultra(-)violette (pour le bronzage); **s. trap,** coin très ensoleillé; **s. lounge,** *NAm:* **s. parlor, porch,** solarium *m*; *Nau:* **s. deck,** pont-promenade *m*, *pl.* ponts-promenades; **s. worship,** culte *m* du soleil.
sun² *v.tr.* **(sunned)** exposer au soleil; **to s. oneself,** prendre le soleil; *F:* faire le lézard.
sunbaked ['sʌnbeikt] *a.* brûlé par le soleil; cuit au soleil.
sunbathe ['sʌnbeið] *v.i.* prendre un bain de soleil;

se faire bronzer. **sunbathing** *n.* bains *mpl* de soleil.
sunbather ['sʌnbeiðər] *n.* personne *f* qui prend un bain, des bains, de soleil.
sunbeam ['sʌnbi:m] *n.* rayon *m* de soleil.
sunblind ['sʌnblaind] *n.* store *m.*
sunburn ['sʌnbə:n] *n.* **1.** *Med:* coup *m* de soleil. **2.** hâle *m*, bronzage *m*, teint *m* bronzé.
sunburnt, sunburned ['sʌnbə:nt, -bə:nd] *a.* (i) brûlé par le soleil; (ii) bronzé, hâlé; **to get s.,** (i) attraper, prendre, un coup de soleil; (ii) (se) bronzer, se hâler.
sunburst ['sʌnbə:st] *n.* (*a*) échappée *f* de soleil; (*b*) bijou *m* (en forme de) soleil.
sundae ['sʌndei] *n.* glace aux fruits recouverte de noix, de crème Chantilly, etc.
Sunday ['sʌnd(e)i] *n.* dimanche *m*; **I expect him on S., this (coming) S.,** je l'attends dimanche; **he comes on Sundays,** il vient le dimanche; **he comes every S.,** il vient tous les dimanches; **S. paper,** journal *m* du dimanche; **in one's S. clothes, one's S. best,** dans ses habits *mpl* du dimanche; **to put on one's S. best,** s'habiller en dimanche, s'endimancher.
sundial ['sʌndaiəl] *n.* cadran *m* solaire; gnomon *m.*
sundown ['sʌndaun] *n.* coucher *m* du soleil.
sundried ['sʌndraid] *a.* séché au soleil.
sundry ['sʌndri] **1.** *a.* divers; **s. expenses,** frais divers; **on s. occasions,** à différentes occasions. **2.** *n.* (*a*) **all and s.,** tous sans exception; tout le monde et son père; **for all and s.,** pour chacun et pour tous; (*b*) **sundries,** (i) articles divers; (ii) frais divers.
sunfish ['sʌnfiʃ] *n.* *Ich:* môle *f*; poisson-lune *m*, *pl.* poissons-lunes.
sunflower ['sʌnflauər] *n.* *Bot:* hélianthe *m*, soleil *m*, tournesol *m*; **s. (seed) oil,** huile *f* de tournesol.
sunglasses ['sʌnglɑ:siz] *n.pl.* lunettes *fpl* de soleil.
sunless ['sʌnlis] *a.* sans soleil.
sunlight ['sʌnlait] *n.* lumière *f* du soleil; **in the s.,** au (grand) soleil, en plein soleil.
sunlit ['sʌnlit] *a.* éclairé par le soleil; ensoleillé.
sunniness ['sʌninis] *n.* situation ensoleillée.
sunny ['sʌni] *a.* **1.** (journée) de soleil; (endroit) ensoleillé; (bâtiment) rempli de soleil; (côté) exposé au soleil; **it's s.,** il fait (du) soleil; *esp. NAm:* **s. side up,** (œuf sur le plat) cuit d'un seul côté. **2.** (visage) radieux, rayonnant; (caractère) heureux.
sunray ['sʌnrei] *n.* rayon *m* de soleil; rayon solaire; *Med:* **s. treatment,** héliothérapie *f*; **s. lamp,** lampe ultra(-)violette (pour le bronzage).
sunrise ['sʌnraiz] *n.* lever *m* du soleil; **at s.,** au soleil levant, au lever du soleil.
sunroof ['sʌnru:f] *n.* *Aut:* toit ouvrant.
sunset ['sʌnset] *n.* coucher *m* du soleil; **at s.,** au soleil couchant; au coucher du soleil.
sunshade ['sʌnʃeid] *n.* **1.** ombrelle *f*; (*for table, etc.*) parasol *m.* **2.** parasoleil *m*, pare-soleil *m inv.*
sunshine ['sʌnʃain] *n.* (clarté *f*, lumière *f*, du) soleil; **in the s.,** au soleil; **in the bright, brilliant, s.,** au grand soleil; **period of s.,** période d'ensoleillement; *Aut:* **s. roof,** toit ouvrant; **hello s.!** bonjour ma jolie!
sunspot ['sʌnspɔt] *n.* tache *f* solaire, tache du soleil.
sunstroke ['sʌnstrouk] *n.* *Med:* insolation *f*; **to get s.,** attraper un coup de soleil.
sunsuit ['sʌns(j)u:t] *n.* costume *m* bain de soleil.
suntan ['sʌntæn] *n.* bronzage *m*, hâle *m*; **s. lotion, oil,** lotion *f*, huile *f*, solaire.
suntanned ['sʌntænd] *a.* bronzé, hâlé.
sunup ['sʌnʌp] *n.* *NAm:* lever *m* du soleil.
sup¹ [sʌp] *n.* *esp. Scot:* petite gorgée; **to take a s. of soup,** prendre une goutte de bouillon.
sup² *v.* (**supped** [sʌpt]) **1.** *v.tr. esp. Scot:* boire à petites gorgées. **2.** *v.i. O:* souper (**off, on,** de).
super ['s(j)u:pər] **1.** *n. F:* surnuméraire *m*; (*a*) employé *m* supplémentaire; (*b*) *Th: Cin:* figurant, -ante. **2.** *n. F:* (*a*) surveillant, -ante; chef *m* (des travaux, etc.); surintendant *m*; (*b*) = commissaire *m* (de police). **3.** *a.* (*a*) *Com:* superfin, surfin; (*b*) *F:* superbe, formidable, magnifique.
superabundance [s(j)u:pərə'bʌndəns] *n.* surabondance *f* (**of,** de).
superabundant [s(j)u:pərə'bʌndənt] *a.* surabondant. **-ly** *adv.* surabondamment.
superannuate [s(j)u:pər'ænjueit] *v.tr.* (*a*) mettre (qn) à la retraite; retraiter (qn); (*b*) mettre au rancart, remiser. **superannuated** *a.* **1.** suranné; (*of car*) démodé. **2.** (mis) en, à la, retraite; retraité.
superannuation [s(j)u:pərænju'eiʃ(ə)n] *n.* retraite *f* par limite d'âge; **s. fund,** caisse *f* des retraites.
superb [s(j)u:'pə:b] *a.* superbe. **-ly** *adv.* superbement.
supercargo ['s(j)u:pəkɑ:gou] *n.* subrécargue *m.*
supercharge ['s(j)u:pətʃɑ:dʒ] *v.tr.* *I.C.E:* suralimenter, surcomprimer (un moteur, etc.); **supercharged engine,** moteur suralimenté, surcomprimé, à compresseur.
supercharger ['s(j)u:pətʃɑ:dʒər] *n.* *I.C.E:* compresseur *m*, surpresseur *m.*
supercilious [s(j)u:pə'siliəs] *a.* sourcilleux, hautain; (air) dédaigneux. **-ly** *adv.* avec hauteur.
superciliousness [s(j)u:pə'siliəsnis] *n.* hauteur *m.*
superconductor [s(j)u:pəkən'dʌktər] *n.* *Ph: El:* supraconducteur *m.*
supercooling ['s(j)u:pə'ku:liŋ] *n.* sous-refroidissement *m.*
supercritical [s(j)u:pə'kritik(ə)l] *a.* *Atom.Ph:* supercritique, surcritique.
superelevation [s(j)u:pəreli'veiʃ(ə)n] *n.* *Civ.E:* surhaussement *m*; dévers *m* (de la voie).
supererogation [s(j)u:pərerou'geiʃ(ə)n] *n.* surérogation *f.*
superficial [s(j)u:pə'fiʃ(ə)l] *a.* superficiel. **1. s. measurement,** mesure *f* de superficie; **s. foot,** pied carré. **2.** (*a*) **s. wound,** blessure superficielle; (*b*) **s. learning,** science *f* d'emprunt; teinture *f* de science; **to have a s. knowledge of sth.,** avoir des connaissances superficielles de qch.; **she has a s. mind,** elle manque de profondeur. **-ally** *adv.* superficiellement.
superficiality [s(j)u:pəfiʃi'æliti] *n.* superficialité *f.*
superfine ['s(j)u:pəfain] *a.* **1.** *Com: etc:* superfin, surfin. **2.** (esprit, etc.) raffiné.
superfluity [su:pə'flu:iti] *n.* superfluité *f*; **s. of good things,** embarras *m* de richesses; **s. of words,** superfétation *f* de paroles.
superfluous [su:'pə:fluəs] *a.* superflu; superfétatoire. **-ly** *adv.* d'une manière superflue.
superfluousness [su:'pə:fluəsnis] *n.* superfluité *f.*
superhighway ['su:pəhaiwei] *n.* *NAm:* autoroute *f.*
superhuman [s(j)u:pə'hju:mən] *a.* surhumain.
superimpose [s(j)u:pərim'pouz] *v.tr.* superposer; *Phot: Cin:* faire une surimpression; surimprimer.
superimposition [s(j)u:pərimpə'ziʃ(ə)n] *n.* superposition *f*; (*b*) *Phot: Cin:* surimpression *f.*
superintend [s(j)u:pərin'tend] *v.tr.* diriger, surveiller; **to s. an election,** présider au scrutin.
superintendence [s(j)u:pərin'tendəns] *n.* direction *f*, surveillance *f*, contrôle *m*; surintendance *f.*
superintendent [s(j)u:pərin'tendənt] *n.* **1.** (*a*) directeur, -trice; surveillant, -ante; chef *m* (des travaux, etc.); surintendant *m*; (*b*) *U.S: F:* **sidewalk s.,** passant, -ante, qui regarde les travaux de construction. **2. (police) s.** = commissaire *m* (de police).
superior [s(j)u:'piəriər] **1.** *a.* (*a*) (*of position, officer, quality*) supérieur; **to be s. in numbers to the enemy,** être supérieur en nombre à l'ennemi; avoir la supériorité du nombre sur l'ennemi; **they were overcome by s. numbers,** ils ont été vaincus par le nombre;

Com: **article of s. quality,** article *m* de qualité supérieure; (*b*) (*of pers.*) orgueilleux; (air) de supériorité; **with a s. smile,** avec un sourire condescendant; (*c*) *Astr:* **the s. planets,** les planètes supérieures; (*d*) *Bot:* (ovaire) supère; (*e*) *Typ:* **s. letter,** lettre supérieure; **s. number,** chiffre supérieur; (*f*) *Geog:* **Lake S.,** le lac Supérieur. **2.** *n.* (*a*) supérieur, -eure; **he is your s.,** il est votre supérieur; **to be s.o.'s s. in courage,** être supérieur en courage à qn; (*b*) supérieur, -eure (d'une communauté religieuse); **Father, Mother, S.,** père supérieur; mère supérieure.

superiority [s(j)u:piəri'ɔriti] *n.* supériorité *f*; **s. in men and materials,** supériorité en hommes et en matériel.

superlative [s(j)u:'pə:lətiv] **1.** *a.* suprême; superlatif. **2.** *a.* & *n.* *Gram:* superlatif (*m*); **to speak in superlatives,** se répandre en éloges dithyrambiques. **-ly** *adv.* superlativement; au suprême degré.

superman, *pl.* **-men** ['s(j)u:pəmæn, -men] *n.m.* surhomme.

supermarket ['s(j)u:pəmɑ:kit] *n.* supermarché *m.*

supernatural [s(j)u:pə'nætjərəl] *a.* & *n.* surnaturel (*m*). **-ally** *adv.* surnaturellement.

supernova [s(j)u:pə'nouvə] *n.* *Astr:* supernova *f.*

supernumerary [s(j)u:pə'nju:m(ə)rəri] **1.** *a.* surnuméraire; en surnombre. **2.** *n.* (*a*) surnuméraire *m*; (*b*) *Th:* *Cin:* figurant, -ante.

superphosphate [s(j)u:pə'fɔsfeit] *n.* superphosphate *m.*

superpose [s(j)u:pə'pouz] *v.tr.* superposer (**upon, on,** à); étager (des planches, etc.).

superposition [s(j)u:pəpə'ziʃ(ə)n] *n.* superposition *f*; application *f* (**of sth. on sth.,** de qch. à, sur, qch.).

superpower ['su:pəpauər] *n.* superpuissance *f.*

superscribe ['s(j)u:pəskraib] *v.tr.* marquer (qch.) d'une inscription, d'une suscription.

superscription [s(j)u:pə'skripʃ(ə)n] *n.* (*on coin*) inscription *f*; (*on letter*) adresse *f*, suscription *f.*

supersede [s(j)u:pə'si:d] *v.tr.* (*a*) remplacer (qch., qn); **this catalogue supersedes previous issues,** ce catalogue annule les précédents; **method now superseded,** méthode périmée; (*b*) prendre la place de (qn); supplanter (qn); **to be superseded by s.o.,** être évincé par qn.

supersensitive [s(j)u:pə'sensitiv] *a.* hypersensible.

supersonic [s(j)u:pə'sɔnik] *a.* **1.** ultrasonore, ultrasonique. **2.** (avion, vitesse) supersonique; **s. boom, bang,** bang *m.*

superstar ['s(j)u:pəstɑ:r] *n.* *Cin:* super vedette *f.*

superstition [s(j)u:pə'stiʃ(ə)n] *n.* superstition *f.*

superstitious [s(j)u:pə'stiʃəs] *a.* superstitieux. **-ly** *adv.* superstitieusement.

superstructure ['s(j)u:pəstrʌktjər] *n.* superstructure *f*; tablier *m* (d'un pont).

supertanker ['s(j)u:pətæŋkər] *n.* *Nau:* pétrolier géant; supertanker *m.*

supertonic [s(j)u:pə'tɔnik] *n.* *Mus:* sus-tonique *f.*

supervene [s(j)u:pə'vi:n] *v.i.* survenir; **if no complications s.,** s'il ne survient pas de complications.

supervise ['s(j)u:pəvaiz] *v.tr.* **1.** surveiller (une entreprise). **2.** diriger, conduire (une entreprise).

supervision [s(j)u:pə'viʒ(ə)n] *n.* **1.** surveillance *f*; **to be under police s.,** être sous la surveillance de la police; **to keep s.o. under strict s.,** surveiller qn de très près. **2.** direction *f* (d'une entreprise).

supervisor ['s(j)u:pəvaizər] *n.* **1.** surveillant, -ante; directeur, -trice. **2.** *U.S:* **(chief) s.,** président *m* du conseil d'administration (d'une commune).

supervisory [s(j)u:pə'vaiz(ə)ri] *a.* (comité, etc.) de surveillance.

supine¹ ['s(j)u:pain] *a.* **1.** (*of pers.*) couché, étendu, sur le dos; *Med:* en supination. **2.** (*of pers., life*) mou, *f.* molle; indolent, inerte.

supine² *n.* *Lt. Gram:* supin *m*; **in the s.,** au supin.

supineness ['s(j)u:painnis] *n.* indolence *f.*

supper ['sʌpər] *n.* souper *m*; dîner *m*; **to have s.,** souper; dîner; **the Last S.,** la (Sainte) Cène; *Ecc:* **the Lord's S.,** la communion, la cène, l'eucharistie *f.*

suppertime ['sʌpətaim] *n.* heure *f* du souper.

supplant [sə'plɑ:nt] *v.tr.* supplanter; prendre la place de (qn); remplacer (qn, qch.); évincer (qn).

supple ['sʌpl] *a.* **1.** souple, pliable, flexible; (cordage) maniable; **s. figure,** taille souple, déliée; **to become s.,** s'assouplir; **s. limbed,** aux membres souples. **2.** complaisant, souple; **s. minded,** à l'esprit souple. **supply** *adv.* souplement.

supplement¹ ['sʌplimənt] *n.* supplément *m* (d'un journal); *Mth:* supplément (d'un angle).

supplement² [sʌpli'ment] *v.tr.* ajouter un supplément à (un livre); **to s. one's income by writing articles,** augmenter ses revenus en écrivant des articles.

supplementary [sʌpli'ment(ə)ri] *a.* supplémentaire (**to,** de); additionnel (**to,** à); **s. income,** revenus annexes; *Mth:* **s. angle,** angle *m* supplémentaire.

suppleness ['sʌp(ə)lnis] *n.* **1.** souplesse *f*, flexibilité *f* (du corps, etc.). **2.** complaisance *f.*

suppliant ['sʌpliənt] **1.** *a.* suppliant; de supplication. **2.** *n.* suppliant, -ante.

supplicant ['sʌplikənt] *n.* suppliant, -ante.

supplicate ['sʌplikeit] *v.tr.* & *i.* (*a*) supplier (qn) (**to do sth.,** de faire qch.); (*b*) solliciter humblement (la protection de qn). **supplicating** *a.* suppliant.

supplication [sʌpli'keiʃ(ə)n] *n.* **1.** supplication *f.* **2.** supplique *f.*

supplier [sə'plaiər] *n.* *Com:* fournisseur, -euse.

supply¹ [sə'plai] *n.* **1.** (*a*) approvisionnement *m*, fourniture *f*; **s. column,** convoi de ravitaillement; *Navy:* **s. ship,** (transport) ravitailleur *m*; *Ind:* **power s.,** cession *f* de force motrice; (*b*) *Parl:* **bill of s.,** projet *m* de crédit supplémentaire; **committee of s.,** commission *f* du budget; (*c*) **s. (post),** occupation *f* (d'une place) par intérim; suppléance *f*; **to be in s.,** occuper une place par intérim; suppléer à un poste. **2.** (*a*) provision *f*; **to get (in) a fresh s. of sth.,** se remonter en qch.; *Pol.Ec:* **s. and demand,** l'offre *f* et la demande; (*b*) **supplies,** fournitures (de photographie, de bureau); **supplies of money,** fonds *mpl*, ressources *fpl*; **food supplies,** vivres *mpl*; **to cut off, stop, the enemy's supplies,** couper les vivres à l'ennemi; (*c*) **s. teacher,** suppléant, -ante; remplaçant, -ante.

supply² *v.tr.* **(supplied) 1.** (*a*) fournir, pourvoir, munir, approvisionner (**s.o. with sth.,** qn de qch.); alimenter (un marché); **to s. oneself with sth.,** s'approvisionner en qch.; **the tradesmen who s. us,** nos fournisseurs *mpl*; *El:* **to s. a factory with current,** alimenter une usine en courant; **the arteries that s. the brain,** les artères qui amènent le sang au cerveau; (*b*) **to s. sth.,** fournir, apporter, qch.; amener (l'eau, le gaz, etc.); **to s. proof,** fournir des épreuves. **2.** (*a*) réparer (une omission); répondre à (un besoin); **to s. s.o.'s needs,** fournir, pourvoir, subvenir, aux besoins de qn; (*b*) **to s. for s.o.,** faire une suppléance; assurer l'intérim.

support¹ [sə'pɔ:t] *n.* **1.** (*a*) appui *m*, soutien *m*; **moral s.,** appui, soutien, moral; **to give s. to the proposal,** venir à l'appui de, appuyer, la proposition; **to produce documents in s. of an allegation,** produire des pièces à l'appui d'une allégation, pour appuyer une allégation; *Jur:* fournir les pièces au soutien; **in s. of this theory,** en appui à, pour corroborer, cette théorie; *Mil:* **air s.,** appui, soutien, aérien; **s. unit,** unité *f* de soutien; (*b*) soutènement *m* (d'une voûte); (*c*) **insufficient air for the s. of life,** air insuffisant pour entretenir la vie; **they depended on their son for**

s., ils n'avaient que leur fils pour les faire vivre; **to be without means of s.,** être sans ressources *fpl.* **2.** (*a*) soutien; **he is the s. of the family,** c'est lui le soutien de la famille; (*b*) appui, support, soutien (d'une voûte); pied *m* (de sustentation); console *f*, soupente *f* (de treuil de poulie); assiette *f* (d'une poutre); *Phot: Cin:* support (de la couche sensible); *Hort:* tuteur *m*; (*c*) *Cost:* **(athletic) s.,** slip *m* de soutien (pour sportifs); support athlétique; **s. stockings,** bas *mpl* à varices; (*d*) *U.S:* **price supports,** subventions *fpl.*

support² *v.tr.* **1.** (*a*) supporter, soutenir, appuyer, maintenir, buter (une voûte); *Hort:* tuteurer (un arbuste); **I supported him with my arm,** je lui ai prêté l'appui de mon bras; (*b*) *Mec.E:* supporter, résister à (un effort, une charge). **2.** appuyer (qn, une pétition); soutenir, corroborer (une théorie); apporter son soutien à (un gouvernement); seconder les efforts de (qn); patronner (qn, un bal de charité); faire une donation à (une œuvre de charité); *Sp:* supporter (une équipe); *Mil:* soutenir (des troupes); **proofs that s. a case,** preuves à l'appui d'une cause; **theory supported by facts,** théorie appuyée sur, corroborée par, des faits; *Parl:* **to s. the motion,** soutenir la motion; **to be supported by s.o. (in a proposal),** être secondé par qn; **the mayor, supported by the clergy and the officers of the garrison,** monsieur le maire, entouré du clergé et des officiers de la garnison. **3.** entretenir (la vie, la combustion); subvenir à l'entretien de (qn); faire vivre, faire subsister (qn); **to have a wife and three children to s.,** avoir une femme et trois enfants à nourrir; **hospital supported by voluntary contributions,** hôpital entretenu par souscriptions volontaires; **to s. oneself,** se suffire (à soi-même); gagner sa vie. **4.** supporter, tolérer, endurer (une injure). **supporting** *a.* (mur, point) d'appui, de soutènement; *Mil:* (troupes) de soutien; *Cin:* (film, programme) supplémentaire; *Th:* **the s. cast,** la troupe qui seconde les premiers rôles.

supportable [sə'pɔːtəbl] *a.* **1.** supportable, tolérable. **2.** (*of theory, etc.*) soutenable.

supporter [sə'pɔːtər] *n.* **1.** (*device*) soutien *m*, support *m*; *Cost:* **athletic s.,** slip *m* de soutien (pour sportifs); support athlétique. **2.** (*pers.*) défenseur *m*, tenant, -ante (d'une opinion); adhérent, -ente (d'un parti); partisan, -ane (d'un homme politique); *Sp:* supporter *m* (d'une équipe). **3.** *Her:* (i) (*animal*) support, (ii) (*human*) tenant (de l'écu).

supportive [sə'pɔːtiv] *a.* soutenant; (*of pers.*) **to be s.,** prêter son appui; être un soutien.

suppose [sə'pouz] *v.tr.* supposer; (*a*) **s. ABC an equilateral triangle,** soit ABC un triangle équilatéral; **supposing, (let us) s., (that) you're right,** supposons, supposé, mettons, que vous ayez raison; **s., supposing, you were ill,** supposez que vous soyez malade; **supposing, s., he came back,** si par supposition il revenait; **yes, but s. I were to die,** oui, mais si je venais à mourir; *F:* **s. we change the subject,** si nous changions de sujet; (*b*) (*postulate*) **the creation supposes the creator,** la création suppose le créateur; (*c*) s'imaginer; croire, penser; **you mustn't s. that . . .,** il ne faut pas vous imaginer que . . .; **I don't s. he'll do it,** je ne crois pas qu'il le fera; **will you go?—I s. so,** irez-vous?—probablement; **I don't think he'll come—no, I s. not, I don't s. so,** je ne crois pas qu'il viendra—non, sans doute; probablement pas; **I don't s. you remember me,** vous ne vous souvenez pas de moi sans doute; **he is supposed to be wealthy, in London,** il est censé être riche, être à Londres; **there is supposed to be a well in the garden,** on dit qu'il y a un puits dans le jardin; (*d*) **to be supposed to do sth.,** être censé faire qch.; **I'm not supposed to do it,** je ne suis pas censé le faire; **I'm supposed not to know,** je suis censé ne pas le savoir. **supposed** *a.* supposé, prétendu; soi-disant; **the s. culprit,** le présumé coupable. **supposedly** [sə'pouzidli] *adv.* par supposition; censément; **he went away, s. to fetch help,** il est parti soi-disant pour chercher de l'aide.

supposition [sʌpə'ziʃ(ə)n] *n.* supposition *f*, hypothèse *f*; (*a*) **unfounded s.,** supposition gratuite; **on the s. that . . .,** supposé que + *sub.*; (*b*) **on s.,** par supposition, par conjecture; **on the s. that . . .,** dans l'hypothèse que . . . .

supposititious [səpɔzi'tiʃəs] *a.* **1.** faux, *f.* fausse. **2.** *Jur:* (enfant, testament) supposé.

suppository [sə'pɔzit(ə)ri] *n. Pharm:* suppositoire *m.*

suppress [sə'pres] *v.tr.* **1.** (*a*) réprimer, étouffer (une révolte); (*b*) supprimer (un journal, une association); faire disparaître (un abus). **2.** étouffer (une toux, un scandale); étouffer, ravaler (un sanglot); réprimer, refouler (ses sentiments); dominer (une émotion); **to s. one's feelings,** se contenir. **3.** cacher, dissimuler (qch.); passer (qch.) sous silence; ne pas révéler (un fait); taire, ne pas donner (un nom); *Jur:* supprimer (un fait, une circonstance). **4.** *W.Tel: El:* antiparasiter (un appareil). **suppressed** *a.* étouffé, réprimé; **s. anger,** colère refoulée; **s. excitement,** agitation contenue.

suppression [sə'preʃ(ə)n] *n.* **1.** répression *f* (d'une émeute, d'un abus); suppression *f* (d'un livre). **2.** (*a*) étouffement *m* (d'un scandale); refoulement *m* (des émotions); (*b*) *Med:* suppression (de transpiration, d'urine). **3.** suppression (d'un fait); dissimulation *f* (de la vérité). **4.** *W.Tel:* antiparasitage *m.*

suppressor [sə'presər] *n.* **1.** (*a*) étouffeur, -euse (d'une émeute); (*b*) dissimulateur, -trice (d'un fait). **2.** *W. Tel:* (dispositif *m*, appareil *m*) antiparasite *m*; *W.Tel:* **s. grid,** grille *f* de freinage.

suppurate ['sʌpjureit] *v.i.* (*of wound, sore*) suppurer. **suppurating** *a.* (abcès, etc.) suppurant.

suppuration [sʌpju'reiʃ(ə)n] *n.* suppuration *f.*

supranational [s(j)uːprə'næʃən(ə)l] *a.* supranational, -aux.

supremacy [s(j)u(ː)'preməsi] *n.* suprématie *f.*

supreme¹ [s(j)u(ː)'priːm] *a.* suprême; **the S. Being,** l'Être suprême; **to reign s.,** régner en maître, en souverain absolu; *Jur:* **S. Court (of Judicature),** cour souveraine, suprême; **s. happiness,** bonheur suprême; souverain bonheur; **to hold s.o. in s. contempt,** avoir un souverain mépris pour qn. **-ly** *adv.* suprêmement; **we are s. happy,** nous jouissons d'un bonheur suprême.

supreme² *n. Cu:* (i) sauce suprême, veloutée; (ii) (*dish*) suprême *m* (de volaille, etc.).

supremo *pl.* **-s** [s(j)u(ː)'priːmou, -mouz] *n.* commandant *m*, chef *m*, suprême.

surcharge¹ ['səːtʃɑːdʒ] *n.* **1.** (*overload*) surcharge *f*; charge excessive. **2.** (*a*) prix excessif; (*b*) droit *m* supplémentaire; majoration *f* d'impôt (par pénalisation); **s. on a letter,** surtaxe *f* d'une lettre; taxe *f* supplémentaire. **3.** *Post:* surcharge (sur un timbre).

surcharge² *v.tr.* **1.** (*overload*) surcharger (**with,** de). **2.** (*a*) faire payer (qn) trop cher; surimposer (les contribuables); (*b*) majorer (un impôt); (*c*) (sur)taxer (une lettre). **3.** *Post:* surcharger (un timbre).

surd [səːd] *n.* (*a*) *Mth:* quantité *f* incommensurable; racine irrationnelle; (*b*) *Ling:* (consonne) sourde *f.*

sure ['ʃuər] **1.** *a.* sûr, certain; (*a*) **to be s. of, about, sth.,** être sûr, certain, de qch.; **I'm s. of it,** j'en suis sûr, certain; **I'm not so s. of, about, that,** je n'en suis pas bien sûr, certain; **I'm s. you're mistaken,** je suis sûr que vous vous trompez; **are you quite s. he hasn't left yet?** êtes-vous bien sûr qu'il n'est pas encore parti? **I'm s. you don't know the answer,** vous ne savez assurément pas la réponse; **to be s. of oneself,** être sûr de soi(-même); **I don't know, I'm sure,** ma foi, je ne sais pas; **to make s. of sth.,** s'assurer de qch.; **make s. (that) the door is shut,** assurez-vous que la porte est fermée; **to make s. of a seat,** s'assurer une place; **don't be too, so, s.!** vous êtes trop sûr de vous! (*b*) infaillible; (jugement, tireur) sûr; (asile) assuré; (remède) sûr, infaillible; **with a s. hand,** d'une main assurée; **there is only one s. way of doing it,** il n'y a qu'un moyen sûr de le faire; (*c*) indubitable; (bénéfice, succès) sûr, assuré; **(it's a) s. thing,** c'est une certitude, c'est une chose certaine; *NAm: F:* **s. thing!** bien sûr! pour sûr! **I don't know for s.,** je n'en suis pas bien sûr; **tomorrow for s.,** demain sans faute; **he won't come, that's for s.,** il ne viendra certainement pas; (*d*) **it's s. to be fine,** il fera sûrement beau; **he's s. to come,** il viendra sûrement, à coup sûr; **be s. to come early,** ne manquez pas d'arriver de bonne heure; **be s. not to lose it,** prenez garde de le perdre. **2.** *adv.* (*a*) *A:* vraiment; certainement; *NAm: F:* **it s. is cold,** il fait vraiment froid; (*b*) **as s. as fate, as s. as eggs are,** *F:* **is, eggs,** aussi vrai qu'il fait jour; aussi sûr que deux et deux font quatre; **s. enough he was there,** il était bien là; **he will come s. enough,** il viendra à coup sûr; *F:* **for s.!** *esp. NAm:* **s.!** mais oui! bien sûr! **-ly** *adv.* **1.** sûrement; **slowly but s.,** lentement mais sûrement. **2.** (*a*) assurément; sans doute; **he will s. come,** il viendra sûrement; (*b*) **s. you don't believe that!** vous ne croyez pas cela, voyons! **s. you're not going to leave us?** vous n'allez pourtant pas nous quitter? (*c*) *O:* **will you help me?—s.!** voulez-vous m'aider?—bien sûr!

surefooted [ʃuə'futid] *a.* au pied sûr, aux pieds sûrs; **to be s.,** avoir le pied sûr.

sureness ['ʃuənis] *n.* **1.** sûreté *f* (de main, etc.). **2.** certitude *f.*

surety ['ʃuəti] *n. Jur:* (*pers.*) caution *f*; garant, -ante; *Com:* donneur *m* d'aval; **to stand s. for s.o.,** se porter caution pour qn; se rendre, se porter, garant de qn; **s. for a debt,** garant d'une dette.

surf [sə:f] *n.* barre *f* de plage; ressac *m*; **s. riding,** surfing *m*, surf *m.*

surface¹ ['sə:fis] *n.* **1.** surface *f*; (*a*) **the earth's s.,** la surface, la superficie, de la terre; **to rise to the s. of the water,** remonter, revenir, sur l'eau; (*of submarine*) **to rise, come, to the s.,** revenir en surface; **to break s.,** faire surface; **s. speed,** vitesse *f* en surface (d'un sous-marin); *Min:* **s. work,** travail *m* au jour; **s. worker,** ouvrier *m* du jour; *Post:* **to send a letter by s. mail,** envoyer une lettre par voie de terre, de mer; **s. water,** eau superficielle, eaux de surface; (*b*) **smooth, even, s.,** surface lisse, unie; *Rec:* **s. scratching, noise,** bruit *m* de surface; *Ph:* **s. tension,** tension superficielle, de surface; (*c*) extérieur *m*, dehors *m*; **his politeness is only on the s.,** sa politesse est toute de surface, toute en superficie; **meaning that lies below the s.,** signification cachée. **2.** (*a*) *Mth:* **s. of revolution,** surface de révolution, de rotation; (*b*) aire *f*, étendue *f*, superficie *f*; **working s.,** plan *m* de travail; surface utile (d'un bureau); *Av:* **lifting s.,** surface portante, de sustentation. **3.** revêtement *m* (d'une route); **temporary s.,** chaussée *f* provisoire.

surface² **1.** *v.tr.* (*a*) apprêter la surface de (qch.); (*b*) *Paperm:* calandrer (le papier); (*c*) *Civ.E:* revêtir (une route) (**with,** de). **2.** *v.i. Navy:* (*of submarine*) faire surface; revenir en surface; *F:* (*of pers.*) (i) réapparaître; (ii) reprendre connaissance. **surfacing** ['sə:fisiŋ] *n.* **1.** apprêtage *m* de la surface (de qch.); surfaçage *m*; *Paperm:* calandrage *m*. **2.** *Civ.E:* revêtement *m* (d'une route).

surfboard ['səfbɔ:d] *n. Sp:* planche *f* de surfing.

surfboarder, surfboarding = SURFER, SURFING.

surfeit¹ ['sə:fit] *n.* **1.** surabondance *f*. **2.** (*a*) réplétion *f* (d'aliments); **to have a s. of oysters, of music,** être rassasié d'huîtres, de musique; (*b*) dégoût *m*; nausée *f.*

surfeit² **1.** *v.i.* se gorger; se repaître. **2.** *v.tr.* gorger, rassasier (qn de qch.); **to s. oneself with sth.,** se gorger de qch. jusqu'à s'en dégoûter; **surfeited with pleasure,** blasé de plaisirs; écœuré par les plaisirs.

surfer ['sə:fər] *n.* surfeur, -euse.

surfing ['sə:fiŋ] *n. Sp:* surfing *m*, surf *m.*

surfrider, surfriding = SURFER, SURFING.

surge¹ [sə:dʒ] *n.* (*a*) *Nau:* levée *f* de la lame; houle *f*; *Fig:* **the s. of the crowd,** les remous *mpl* de la foule; (*b*) poussée *f* (d'activité); accès *m* (d'enthousiasme, colère); **a s. of anger,** un flot, une vague, de colère; (*c*) irrégularité *f* (dans la marche d'une machine); *El:* **s. of current,** vague, à-coup *m*, impulsion *f*, de courant; surintensité *f*; **s. of voltage,** surtension *f.*

surge² *v.i.* **1.** (*a*) (*of sea*) être houleux; (*of waters*) se soulever; (*b*) **the crowd surged along the street, onto the pitch,** la foule s'est répandue en flots dans la rue, a inondé le terrain; **the crowd surged back,** la foule a reflué; **anger surged (up) within her,** un flot de colère est monté en elle. **2.** *El:* **the current surges,** il y a des à-coups de courant. **3.** *Nau:* (*of cable*) choquer brusquement. **surging** *a.* **s. sea,** mer houleuse; **a s. mass of people,** un flot pressé d'êtres humains.

surgeon ['sə:dʒ(ə)n] *n.* chirugien, -ienne.

surgery ['sə:dʒəri] *n.* **1.** chirurgie *f*; **major, minor, s.,** grande, petite, chirurgie; **heart s.,** chirurgie du cœur. **2.** cabinet *m* de consultation (chez un médecin); cabinet (de dentiste); **s. (hours),** heures *fpl* de consultation.

surgical ['sə:dʒik(ə)l] *a.* chirurgical, -aux; **s. instruments,** instruments de chirurgie; **s. appliances,** appareils (i) chirurgicaux, (ii) orthopédiques; **s. boot,** chaussure *f* orthopédique; **s. spirit,** alcool *m* à 90°.

surliness ['sə:linis] *n.* (*a*) air bourru; caractère *m*, humeur *f*, maussade; (*b*) ton bourru.

surly ['sə:li] *a.* (*a*) (ton, air) bourru; (*b*) hargneux, maussade, revêche; **s. disposition,** humeur rébarbative.

surmise¹ [sə:'maiz] *n.* conjecture *f*, supposition *f.*

surmise² [sə:'maiz] *v.tr.* conjecturer, soupçonner, deviner.

surmount [sə(:)'maunt] *v.tr.* **1.** surmonter; **column surmounted by a cross,** colonne surmontée d'une croix. **2.** surmonter (un obstacle, une difficulté, etc.); triompher (d'une passion, d'une difficulté).

surmountable [sə(:)'mauntəbl] *a.* surmontable.

surname ['sə:neim] *n.* nom *m* de famille; **s. and Christian, first, names,** nom et prénoms *mpl.*

surpass [sə(:)'pɑ:s] *v.tr.* **1.** surpasser (qn); devancer (ses rivaux); **to s. s.o. in kindness,** renchérir sur la bonté de qn; **he has surpassed himself,** il s'est surpassé. **2.** dépasser, excéder; **the result surpassed my hopes,** le résultat a excédé mes espérances, a dépassé mon attente. **surpassing** *a.* sans égal, sans pareil; **of s. beauty,** d'une beauté incomparable.

surplice ['sə:plis] *n. Ecc:* surplis *m.*

surplus ['sə:pləs] *n.* surplus *m*, excédent *m*; **to have a s. of sth.,** avoir qch. en excès; avoir (des livres) en surnombre; **s. population, products,** surplus, excédent, de la population, des produits; *Com:* **s. stock,** surstock *m*; **government s. (stock),** les surplus du gouvernement.

surprise¹ [sə'praiz] *n.* surprise *f*. **1. to take s.o. by s.,** prendre qn à l'improviste, au dépourvu; surprendre qn; *Mil:* **to take a town by s.,** enlever une ville par (un coup de) surprise; **s. visit,** visite *f* à l'improviste; **to pay s.o. a s. visit,** aller surprendre qn chez lui. **2. to give s.o. a s.,** faire une surprise à qn; **what a s. to see you here!** je m'étonne de vous rencontrer ici; **what a pleasant s.!** quelle bonne surprise! **he's in for a bit of a s.!** s'il savait ce qu'on lui prépare! (*at fete*) **s. packet,** surprise. **3.** étonnement *m*; **struck**

with s., saisi d'étonnement; **to my great s., much to my s.,** à ma grande surprise.

surprise² *v.tr.* **1.** (*a*) surprendre (une armée, etc.); prendre (une place) par surprise; (*b*) **to s. s.o. in the act,** suprendre qn en flagrant délit; prendre qn sur le fait. **2.** (*a*) surprendre, étonner (qn); **nothing surprises him,** il ne s'épate de rien; (*b*) **to be surprised at sth.,** être surpris de qch.; **I am surprised to see you, at seeing you,** je m'étonne de vous voir; **I should be surprised if he came back,** cela m'étonnerait qu'il revienne; **it doesn't s. me in the least,** ça ne m'étonne pas du tout; **I was agreeably surprised,** j'ai été agréablement surpris; **I'm surprised at you!** vous m'étonnez! **surprised** *a.* (regard) étonné, surpris; (air) de surprise. **surprising** *a.* surprenant, étonnant; **it wouldn't be s. if he was in the plot,** rien de surprenant s'il était du complot; **that's s. coming from him,** cela surprend de sa part. **surprisingly** *adv.* étonnamment; **I found him s. young,** j'ai été surpris de lui trouver l'air si jeune.

surrealism [sə:'riəlizm] *n. Lit: Art:* surréalisme *m.*

surrealist [sə:'riəlist] *a. & n.* surréaliste (*mf*).

surrealistic [sə:riə'listik] *a. Lit: Art:* surréaliste.

surrender¹ [sə'rendər] *n.* **1.** (*a*) *Mil:* reddition *f* (d'une forteresse); (*b*) action *f* de se rendre; **no s.!** on ne se rend pas! (*c*) *Jur:* **s. of a defendant to his bail,** décharge *f* de ses cautions par un accusé (libéré sous caution). **2.** abandon *m*, cession *f* (de biens, de droits); restitution *f* (d'un droit de propriété); abdication *f* (de droits, de l'autorité); **to make a s. of principle,** transiger avec ses principes. **3.** *Ins:* rachat *m* (d'une police).

surrender² **1.** *v.tr.* (*a*) *Mil:* rendre, livrer (une forteresse); (*b*) *Jur:* abandonner, céder (un droit, ses biens); abdiquer (un droit); **to s. all hope of sth.,** abandonner, renoncer à, tout espoir de qch.; (*c*) *Ins:* racheter (une police d'assurances). **2.** *v.i.* se rendre; *Mil:* faire (sa) soumission; rendre les armes; **to s. to the police,** se constituer prisonnier; **to s. to one's bail,** décharger ses cautions; comparaître en jugement.

surreptitious [sʌrəp'tiʃəs] *a.* subreptice, clandestin. **-ly** *adv.* subrepticement, clandestinement.

surreptitiousness [sʌrəp'tiʃəsnis] *n.* caractère *m*, nature *f*, subreptice; clandestinité *f*.

surrogate ['sʌrəgəit] *n.* **1.** (*pers.*) suppléant, -ante; substitut *m*; *Ecc: Jur:* subrogé, -ée. **2.** succédané *m* **(for, of, sth.,** de qch.).

surround¹ [sə'raund] *n.* encadrement *m*, bordure *f*.

surround² *v.tr.* entourer. (*a*) **to s. a town with walls,** entourer, ceinturer, une ville de murs; **the crowd surrounded the car,** la foule assiégeait la voiture; **surrounded by, with, dangers,** entouré de dangers; (*b*) *Mil:* entourer, cerner (l'ennemi); investir (une ville). **surrounding** *a.* entourant, environnant; **the s. country,** le pays d'alentour.

surroundings [sə'raundiŋz] *n.pl.* **1.** entourage *m*, milieu *m*, ambiance *f*; cadre *m*, environnement *m*; **to be in familiar s.,** être en pays de connaissance. **2.** environs *mpl*, alentours *mpl* (d'une ville, etc.).

surtax¹ ['sə:tæks] *n. Adm:* surtaxe *f*; *esp.* surtaxe progressive sur le revenu.

surtax² *v.tr.* surtaxer.

surveillance [sə(:)'veiləns] *n. Adm:* surveillance *f*, contrôle *m*; **to be under s.,** être en surveillance.

survey¹ ['sə:vei] *n.* **1.** (*a*) aperçu *m*, exposé *m* sommaire (d'un sujet); (*b*) examen attentif; étude *f* (de la situation); **to make a s. of sth.,** (i) jeter un coup d'œil sur qch.; (ii) étudier (une question). **2.** *Surv:* (*a*) levé *m* des plans; relevé *m*; *Const:* métrage *m* des travaux; (*b*) plan *m*, levé (du terrain, d'un édifice); *Civ.E:* étude; **aerial s.,** levé aérophotogrammétrique; **to make a s. of an estate,** relever un domaine; (*c*) **quantity s.,** métrage *m*; métré *m*; toisé *m*. **3.** inspection *f*, visite *f*.

survey² [sə(:)'vei] *v.tr.* **1.** (*a*) regarder, contempler, promener ses regards sur (le paysage, etc.); (*b*) examiner attentivement; mettre (une question) à l'étude; **to s. the situation,** procéder à l'etude de la situation; passer la situation en revue; (*of politician*) faire un tour d'horizon. **2.** *Surv:* relever, faire le (re)levé de, lever le(s) plan(s) de (la ville, la propriété); hydrographier, faire l'hydrographie (d'une côte); **to s. for work done,** métrer, toiser, le travail accompli. **3.** inspecter; visiter; faire l'expertise de l'état (d'un navire, d'un immeuble); **to have a house surveyed,** faire inspecter un immeuble par un (architecte) expert. **surveying** *n.* **1.** (*a*) *Surv:* levé *m* de plans; géodésie *f*; topographie *f*; **s. instruments,** instruments *mpl* topographiques; (*b*) **quantity s.,** métrage *m*, métré *m*, toisé *m*. **2.** inspection *f*, visite *f*.

surveyor [sə(:)'veiər] *n.* **1. (land) s.,** géomètre expert; **naval s.,** (ingénieur) hydrographe *m*; **surveyor's table,** planchette *f*; *Adm:* **land s. and valuer, district s.,** cadastreur *m*; (*b*) **quantity s.,** métreur vérificateur. **2.** (*a*) *Adm:* surveillant, -ante; inspecteur, -trice; (*b*) *Nau:* **ship s.,** visiteur *m*, inspecteur, de navires; expert *m*; (*c*) **property s.,** (architecte) expert.

survival [sə(:)'vaiv(ə)l] *n.* **1.** (*a*) survivance *f*; *Nat. Hist:* **the s. of the** fittest, la survivance des mieux adaptés, du plus apte; (*b*) survie *f* (d'un accidenté); **s. kit,** équipement *m* de survie. **2.** restant *m* (d'une ancienne coutume); **a s. of times past,** une survivance des temps passés.

survive [sə(:)'vaiv] **1.** *v.i.* survivre; (*of custom*) subsister; **those who survived,** les survivants *mpl.* **2.** *v.tr.* (*a*) survivre à (qn); **he will s. us all,** il nous enterrera tous; (*b*) **to s. an injury,** survivre à une blessure; **to s. an illness,** réchapper d'une maladie. **surviving** *a.* survivant.

survivor [sə(:)'vaivər] *n.* survivant, -ante; **he is the sole s. of his family,** il est le seul qui reste de sa famille; **the survivors of the disaster,** les rescapé(s).

Susan ['su:z(ə)n] *Pr.n.f.* Suzanne.

susceptibility [səsepti'biliti] *n.* **1.** (*a*) susceptibilité *f*; (*b*) **s. to a disease,** prédisposition *f* à une maladie; **s. to pain,** sensibilité *f* à la douleur. **2.** sensibilité, susceptibilité; **words that wound susceptibilities,** mots qui blessent les susceptibilités; mots blessants.

susceptible [sə'septibl] *a.* **1.** susceptible; (*a*) **s. of proof,** susceptible d'être prouvé; (*b*) **s. to a disease,** prédisposé à une maladie. **2.** (*a*) sensible **(to,** à); **to be s.,** avoir la fibre sensible; **s. to cold,** frileux; (*b*) qui se froisse facilement; susceptible.

suspect¹ ['sʌspekt] *a. & n.* suspect, -e.

suspect² [sə'spekt] *v.tr.* (*a*) **to s. s.o. of a crime,** soupçonner qn d'un crime; suspecter qn; **to be suspected by s.o. of sth., of doing sth.,** être suspect à qn de qch., de faire qch.; (*b*) **to s. the authenticity of a work,** suspecter l'authenticité d'une œuvre; (*c*) soupçonner, s'imaginer (qch.); se douter de (qch.); flairer, subodorer (un danger); **I suspected as much,** je m'en doutais; **he suspects nothing,** il ne se doute de rien; **I never suspected it for a moment,** je n'en avais pas le moindre soupçon; **I s. you're right,** je crois bien que vous avez raison. **suspected** *a.* **a s. person,** un(e) suspect(e); *Med:* **s. case of typhoid,** cas présumé de typhoïde; **s. fracture,** crainte *f* de fracture.

suspend [sə'spend] *v.tr.* **1.** suspendre, pendre (qch.); **to s. sth. from the ceiling,** suspendre, pendre, qch. au plafond. **2.** suspendre (un service d'autobus, le travail); *Jur:* **to s. judgment,** surseoir au jugement; **to s. proceedings,** suspendre les poursuites; *Com:* **to s. payment,** suspendre ses paiements **3.** (*a*) suspendre **(s.o. from his office,** qn de ses fonctions); interdire (qn); mettre (un officier) en non-activité; mettre (un jockey) à pied; **to s. a pupil (from school),** renvoyer un élève (provisoirement); *Adm:* **suspended on full pay,** suspendu sans suppression de traitement, *Mil:* de solde; (*b*) suspendre (un journal). **suspended** *a.* suspendu; (*a*) (particules) en suspension; (*b*) *Jur:* en suspens; suspendu; **he was given a s. prison sentence of six months,** il a été condamné à six mois de prison avec sursis; **the scheme is in a state of s. animation,** le projet est en suspens.

suspender [sə'spendər] *n.* (*a*) suspensoir *m*; (*b*) (*women's*) jarretelles *fpl*; (*men's*) supports-chaussettes *mpl*; (*c*) *NAm:* **(pair of) suspenders,** (paire *f* de) bretelles *fpl.*

suspense [sə'spens] *n.* **1.** suspens *m*; **to keep, hold, s.o. in s.,** tenir, garder, qn en suspens, en haleine; **the question remains in s.,** la question reste pendante; *Book-k:* **s. account,** compte *m* d'ordre. **2.** *Lit:* suspens, suspense *m*; **author who has used s. to good effect,** auteur qui s'est bien servi du suspens(e).

suspension [sə'spenʃ(ə)n] *n.* **1.** (*a*) suspension *f*; *Mec.E:* **s. chain, hook,** chaîne *f*, croc *m*, de suspension; **s. cable,** câble porteur; **spring s.,** suspension par ressorts; *Civ.E:* **s. bridge,** pont suspendu; (*b*) *Ch:* **(substance in) s.,** (substance *f* en) suspension. **2.** (*a*) suspension (de la circulation, des hostilités); *Jur:* surséance *f* (de jugement); (*b*) *Com:* suspension de paiements; (*c*) *Gram:* **points of s.,** points de suspension. **3.** suspension (d'un fonctionnaire); mise *f* en non-activité (d'un officier); mise à pied (d'un jockey).

suspensory [sə'spensəri] *a.* (*a*) *Anat:* (*of ligament*); suspenseur; (*b*) *Med:* **s. bandage,** suspensoir *m.*

suspicion [sə'spiʃ(ə)n] *n.* **1.** soupçon *m*; *Jur:* suspicion *f*; **not the shadow, ghost, of a s.,** pas l'ombre d'un soupçon; **to look at s.o. with s.,** regarder qn avec défiance; **to have (one's) suspicions about s.o.,** avoir des doutes sur qn; soupçonner qn; **to arouse s.,** éveiller, faire naître, les soupçons; **to arouse, awaken, s.o.'s suspicions,** éveiller la défiance de qn; **above s.,** au-dessus de tout soupçon; **praise free from any s. of flattery,** louanges aucunement suspects de flatterie; **to be right in one's suspicions,** soupçonner juste; *Jur:* **to arrest, detain, s.o. on s.,** arrêter, détenir, qn préventivement; **detention on s.,** détention préventive; prévention *f.* **2. I had my suspicions about it,** je m'en doutais; **I had no s. of it,** je n'en avais pas le moindre soupçon. **3.** très petite quantité, soupçon **(of,** de); pointe *f* (d'ironie, de malice).

suspicious [sə'spiʃəs] *a.* **1.** soupçonnable, suspect; (*of conduct*) louche, équivoque; **it looks s.,** cela me paraît louche; **s. character,** (i) individu *m* louche; (ii) *Adm:* sujet noté; **he died in s. circumstances,** il est mort dans des circonstances équivoques. **2.** méfiant, soupçonneux; **to be, feel, s. about s.o., sth., of s.o., sth.,** avoir des soupçons à l'endroit, à l'égard, de qn, sur qch.; **his behaviour made me s.,** sa conduite a éveillé ma défiance. **-ly** *adv.* **1.** (*a*) d'une manière suspecte, louche; (*b*) **it looks s. like measles (to me),** cela ressemble étrangement à la rougeole. **2.** d'un air méfiant; (regarder qn) avec méfiance.

suspiciousness [sə'spiʃəsnis] *n.* **1.** caractère suspect, louche. **2.** caractère soupçonneux; méfiance *f.*

suss [sʌs] *v.tr. P:* **to s. s.o. out,** savoir ce que vaut qn, *P:* cataloguer qn.

sustain [sə'stein] *v.tr.* soutenir, supporter. **1.** (*a*) **enough to s. life,** de quoi entretenir la vie; de quoi vivre; **to s. the body,** soutenir, sustenter, le corps; **evidence to s. an assertion,** témoignages pour soutenir, appuyer, une affirmation; *Mus:* **to s. a note,** soutenir, prolonger, une note; (*b*) *Jur:* (*of court*) **to s. an objection,** admettre une réclamation; **objection sustained,** réclamation admise. **2.** (*a*) *Mil:* soutenir (une attaque); (*b*) éprouver, essuyer, subir (une perte); **to s. an injury,** recevoir une blessure; être blessé. **sustained** *a.* soutenu; **s. applause,** applaudissements prolongés; *Mil:* **s. fire,** feu soutenu, nourri; *Mus:* **s. note,** tenue *f.* **sustaining** *a.* (*of power*) soutenant; (nourriture) qui soutient (bien).

sustenance ['sʌstinəns] *n.* (*a*) **necessary for the s. of our bodies,** nécessaire à notre subsistance *f*; **means of s.,** moyens de subsistance; moyens de vivre; (*b*) aliments *mpl*, nourriture *f.*

suttee [sʌ'ti:] *n. Hindu Rel:* **1.** (*practice*) satî *m.* **2.** (*widow*) satî *f.*

suture¹ ['su:tjər] *n.* **1.** *Anat: Bot:* suture *f.* **2.** *Surg:* (*a*) (*action*) suture; (*b*) (*stitch*) point *m* de suture; (*c*) fil *m* pour sutures.

suture² *v.tr. Surg:* suturer (une plaie).

suzerain ['su:zərein] *n.m.* suzerain.

suzerainty ['su:zəreinti] *n.* suzeraineté *f.*

svelte [svelt] *a.* svelte.

swab¹ [swɔb] *n.* (*a*) *Dom.Ec:* torchon *m*; serpillière *f*; *Nau:* vadrouille *f*; (*b*) *Artil:* écouvillon *m*; (*c*) *Med:* **s. of cotton wool,** tampon *m* d'ouate; **to take a s. of s.o.'s throat,** faire un prélèvement dans la gorge de qn.

swab² *v.tr.* **(swabbed) 1.** nettoyer, essuyer (avec un torchon); *Nau:* essarder (le pont). **2.** *Artil:* **to s. (out),** écouvillonner (une pièce); *Med:* nettoyer avec un tampon. **3. to s. (down),** laver (la cour) à grande eau.

swaddle ['swɔdl] *v.tr.* emmailloter **(with,** de). **swaddling** *n. A:* **s. clothes,** maillot *m*, langes *mpl.*

swag [swæg] *n. F:* (*a*) rafle *f*, butin *m* (d'un cambrioleur); (*b*) *Austr:* baluchon *m* (de chemineau).

swagger¹ ['swægər] *n.* **1.** (*a*) air important; **to walk with a s.,** marcher avec un air avantageux; se pavaner; (*b*) air cavalier, désinvolte; (*c*) *Mil:* **s. stick, cane,** jonc *m*, stick *m*; (*short*) badine *f.* **2.** rodomontades *fpl*; crâneries *fpl*; fanfaronnades *fpl.*

swagger² *v.i.* (*a*) crâner, se pavaner; **to s. about,** se promener d'un air conquérant, en se rengorgeant; **to s. in, out,** entrer, sortir, d'un air important; (*b*) faire de l'esbrouffe; **to s. about sth.,** se vanter de qch. **swaggering 1.** *a.* (air) important, crâneur. **2.** *n.* (*a*) air important; (*b*) rodomontades *fpl.*

swagman *pl.* **-men** ['swægmən] *n.m. Austr: F:* (*a*) chemineau (qui porte son baluchon); (*b*) colporteur; (*c*) homme de peine ambulant.

Swahili [swɑ'hi:li] **1.** *a. Ethn:* souahéli, swahéli. **2.** *n.* (*a*) (*pl.* **Swahili(s)),** Souahéli, -ie, Swahéli, -ie; *pl.* -i(s); (*b*) *Ling:* le souahéli, swahéli.

swain [swein] *n.m.* (*a*) *A: & Poet:* jeune berger; (*b*) *Hum: O:* soupirant.

swallow¹ ['swɔlou] *n.* **1.** gorge *f.* **2.** gorgée *f* (d'eau); **at one s.,** d'un seul coup, d'un seul trait. **3.** *Geol:* **s. hole,** aven *m.*

swallow² 1. *v.tr.* (*a*) (i) avaler, ingurgiter, *Physiol:* déglutir (qch.); gober (une huître); (ii) gober, avaler (une histoire); avaler (un affront); (r)avaler (ses larmes); retenir (sa colère); mettre (son orgueil) dans sa poche; **to s. the bait,** (i) (*of fish*) avaler l'appât; (ii) *F:* (*of pers.*) se laisser prendre à l'appât; **I told her a lie and she swallowed it,** je lui ai raconté un mensonge et elle a marché; **he swallowed it hook, line and sinker,** il a gobé le morceau; **story hard to s.,** histoire invraisemblable; **to s. one's words,** (i) parler vite et indistinctement; (ii) se dédire; ravaler ses paroles; (*b*) **to s. sth. (up),** dévorer, avaler, qch.; (*of the sea*) engloutir, engouffrer, qch. **2.** *v.i.* avaler: **to s. hard,** avaler sa salive (pour faire passer une émotion). **swallowing** *n.* **1.** avalement; *Physiol:* déglutition *f.* **2. s. (up),** engloutissement *m*, engouffrement *m.*

swallow³ *n.* **1.** *Orn:* hirondelle *f*; *Prov:* **one s. doesn't make a summer,** une hirondelle ne fait pas le printemps. **2.** *Swim:* **s. dive,** saut *m* de l'ange.

swallow-dive ['swɔloudaiv] *v.i. Swim:* faire un saut de l'ange.

swallowtail ['swɔlouteil] *n.* **1.** queue fourchue; queue d'hirondelle. **2.** *Cost: F: O:* (*often pl.*) queue-de-morue *f, pl.* queues-de-morue. **3.** *Ent:* **s. (butterfly),** machaon *m.*

swallow-tailed ['swɔlouteild] *a.* **1.** à queue fourchue. **2. s.-t. coat** = SWALLOWTAIL 2.

swamp¹ [swɔmp] *n.* marais *m,* marécage *m.*

swamp² *v.tr.* (*a*) inonder; submerger (un pré); (*b*) remplir d'eau (une embarcation); (*c*) *F:* **to be swamped with work,** être débordé de travail.

swampy ['swɔmpi] *a.* (terrain) marécageux.

swan¹ [swɔn] *n.* **1.** cygne *m;* **mute s.,** cygne commun, muet; **black s.,** cygne noir. **2.** (*a*) **s. song,** chant *m* du cygne; (*b*) *NAm: Swim:* **s. dive,** saut *m* de l'ange; (*c*) *Mec.E:* **s. neck,** cou *m,* col *m,* de cygne.

swan² *v.i.* **(swanned) to s. around,** se pavaner.

swank¹ [swæŋk] *F:* **1.** *n.* (*a*) épate *f;* (*b*) épateur, -euse; crâneur, -euse. **2.** *a.* élégant; chic.

swank² *v.i. F:* se donner des airs; faire de l'épate.

swanky ['swæŋki] *a. F:* (*a*) (*of pers.*) prétentieux, poseur; (*b*) (restaurant) élégant; (dîner) chic.

swan-necked ['swɔnnekt] *a.* au cou de cygne.

swansdown ['swɔnzdaun] *n.* **1.** duvet *m* de cygne (pour garnitures); cygne *m.* **2.** *Tex:* molleton *m.*

swap¹ [swɔp] *n.* (*a*) troc *m,* échange *m;* **to do a s.,** faire un troc; (*b*) objet *m,* article *m,* à échanger, qu'on a échangé; **he took my old car as a s. for this one,** il a pris ma vieille voiture en échange de celle-ci; (*in stamp collecting, etc.*) **swaps,** doubles *mpl.*

swap² *v.* **(swapped) 1.** *v.tr. F:* **to s. sth. for sth.,** échanger, troquer, qch. contre, pour, qch.; **to s. places with s.o.,** changer de place avec qn; **to s. stories,** échanger ses impressions. **2.** *v.i. F:* faire du troc; **shall we s.?** si nous faisons un échange? **swapping** *n. F:* échange *m,* troc *m;* **wife s.,** échange de femmes entre maris.

sward [swɔːd] *n. Lit:* gazon *m;* pelouse *f.*

swarm¹ [swɔːm] *n.* essaim *m* (d'abeilles, de gens); vol *m* (de sauterelles); nuée *f* (de moucherons); fourmillement *m* (de petits bateaux); essaim, troupe *f* (d'enfants).

swarm² *v.* **1.** *v.i.* (*a*) (*of bees*) essaimer; faire l'essaim; (*b*) (*of pers.*) accourir en foule, se presser (**round, in,** autour de, dans); **the crowd swarmed over the pitch,** la foule a inondé, a fait irruption, sur le terrain; (*c*) pulluler, grouiller; **children s. in these districts,** dans ces quartiers les enfants pullulent. **2.** *v.i.* fourmiller, grouiller (**with,** de); **the roads were swarming with people,** les rues grouillaient, regorgeaient, fourmillaient, de monde. **swarming** *n. Ap:* essaimage *m.*

swarm³ *v.tr. & i.* **to s. (up) a tree, mast,** grimper à un arbre, à un mât.

swarthiness ['swɔːðinis] *n.* teint basané, bistré.

swarthy ['swɔːði] *a.* (*of complexion*) basané, bistré, (*of pers.*) noiraud.

swash¹ [swɔʃ] *n.* clapotis *m* (des vagues).

swash² *v.i.* (*of water*) clapoter.

swashbuckler ['swɔʃbʌklər] *n.* bravache *m.*

swashbuckling ['swɔʃbʌkliŋ] **1.** *a.* fanfaron, bravache; **s. fellow,** fanfaron *m.* **2.** *n.* rodomontades *fpl.*

swastika ['swɔstikə] *n.* svastika *m,* croix gammée.

swat¹ [swɔt] *n.* (*a*) tape *f;* (*b*) **fly s.,** tapette *f* tue-mouches.

swat² *v.* **(swatted)** *F: v.tr.* frapper, taper (qn, qch.); **s. that fly!** écrasez donc cette mouche!

swath [swɔːθ] *n. Agr:* andain *m.*

swathe¹ [sweið] *n.* bandage *m,* bandelette *f.*

swathe² *v.tr.* emmailloter, envelopper; **head swathed in bandages,** tête enveloppée de bandages.

swatter ['swɔtər] *n.* **fly s.,** tapette *f* tue-mouches.

sway¹ [swei] *n.* **1.** balancement *m,* oscillation *f;* mouvement *m* de va-et-vient; *Rail:* mouvement de lacet (des wagons); *Aut:* roulis *m* (de la voiture). **2.** empire *m,* domination *f;* **under his s.,** sous son empire; sous son influence; **to have, hold, s. over a people,** régner sur un peuple; **to hold s. over a country,** tenir un pays en souveraineté.

sway² **1.** *v.i.* (*a*) se balancer; osciller; (*of drunkard*) vaciller; (*of trees*) **to s. in the wind,** se balancer au vent; (*b*) rester indécis, vaciller. **2.** *v.tr.* (*a*) faire osciller; balancer, agiter (les arbres); (*b*) gouverner, diriger; **considerations that s. our opinions,** considérations *fpl* qui influencent nos opinions; (*c*) **to s. s.o. from his course,** détourner qn de ses projets; **to refuse to be swayed,** rester inflexible. **swaying 1.** *a.* qui se balance de-ci de-là; oscillant; **s. motion,** balancement *m;* mouvement *m* de va-et-vient. **2.** *n.* balancement, oscillation *f;* mouvement de va-et-vient; *Rail:* mouvement de lacet (des wagons); *Aut:* roulis *m* (de la voiture).

Swazi ['swɑːzi] **1.** *a. Geog:* souazi. **2.** *n.* (*a*) Souazi(e); (*b*) *Ling:* le dialecte souazi.

Swaziland ['swɑːzilænd] *Pr.n. Geog:* le Souaziland.

swear ['swεər] *v.* (*p.t.* **swore** [swɔːr] *p.p.* **sworn** [swɔːn]) **1.** *v.tr.* (*a*) jurer; **to s. an oath,** faire un serment; jurer; **to s. sth. on the Bible,** jurer qch. sur la Bible; **to s. to do sth.,** jurer de faire qch.; **I could have sworn I heard a shout,** j'aurais juré entendre un cri; **to s. revenge,** jurer, faire serment, de se venger; (*b*) **to s. (in),** faire prêter serment à, assermenter (un témoin, un jury); (*of juryman*) **to be sworn (in),** prêter serment; **to s. s.o. to secrecy,** faire jurer le secret à qn; (*c*) déclarer (qch.) sous (la foi du) serment. **2.** *v.i.* jurer; proférer, lâcher, un juron, des jurons; **to s. at s.o.,** injurier qn; **to s. like a trooper, bargee,** jurer comme un charretier. **swear by** *v.tr. & i.* (*a*) jurer par (qn, qch.); **to s. by one's honour,** jurer sa foi; **to s. by all that one holds sacred,** jurer ses grands dieux; (*b*) se fier à (qn, qch.); **he swears by his boss,** il ne jure que par son patron. **swearing** *n.* **1.** (*a*) attestation *f* sous serment; (*b*) prestation *f* de serment. **2. s. (in),** assermentation *f* (du jury). **3.** jurons *mpl;* gros mots. **swear off** *v. ind.tr.* jurer de renoncer à (l'alcool, etc.). **swear to** *v. ind.tr.* attester, certifier, (qch.) sous serment; **I s. to it,** j'en lève la main; **I would s. to it,** j'en jurerais; *F:* j'en mettrais la main au feu. **sworn** *a.* (*a*) (agent) assermenté; **s. enemies,** ennemis jurés, acharnés; (*b*) (déclaration) sous serment; (témoin) qui a prêté serment.

swearword ['swεəwəːd] *n.* gros mot; juron *m.*

sweat¹ [swet] *n.* **1.** (*a*) sueur *f,* transpiration *f;* **by the s. of one's brow,** à la sueur de son front; **to be in a s.,** *F:* **all of a s.,** (i) être trempé de sueur; être tout en nage; (ii) être tout en émoi; **to be in a s. about sth.,** s'inquiéter de qch.; **to work oneself (up) into a s.,** s'énerver (**about sth.,** de qch.); **to be in a cold s.,** avoir des sueurs froides; *Anat:* **s. duct,** conduit *m* sudorifère; **s. gland,** glande *f* sudoripare; *Sp:* **s. shirt,** sweat-shirt *m, pl.* sweat-shirts; (*b*) *Med: Vet:* suerie *f,* suée *f;* (*c*) *F:* corvée *f,* travail *m* pénible; **it's an awful s.,** c'est une suée, un drôle de travail; *NAm:* **no s.,** il n'y a pas de difficulté; (*d*) *Mil: P:* **old s.** vieux troupier. **2.** condensation *f;* suintement *m* (d'un mur, etc.).

sweat² **1.** *v.i.* (*a*) suer, transpirer; **to s. profusely,** suer à grosses gouttes; *F:* être (tout) en nage; (*b*) (*of worker*) peiner; turbiner; **schoolboy sweating over his lessons,** élève qui bûche, potasse, ses devoirs; (*c*) *F:* s'inquiéter; se faire de la bile; (*d*) (*of walls*) suinter. **2.** *v.tr.* (*a*) suer; **to s. blood,** suer sang et eau; *P:* **to s. one's guts out,** s'échiner; (*b*) faire suer (qn, un cheval); exploiter (la main-d'œuvre); (*c*) *NAm: F:* cuisiner (un suspect). **sweated** *a.* **s. labour,** travail exténuant et mal rétribué; travail d'esclave; **s. goods,** articles produits par des ouvriers exploités. **sweating 1.** *a.* (*a*) en sueur; suant; (*b*) (mur) suintant. **2.** *n.* (*a*) transpiration *f*; suintement *m* (d'un mur); (*b*) *Med:* suée *f*; **s. room,** étuve *f*; salle *f* de sudation (d'un hammam); (*c*) exploitation *f* (de la main-d'œuvre); **the s. system,** l'exploitation patronale; (*d*) *NAm: F:* cuisinage *m* (d'un prisonnier). **sweat out** *v.tr.* (*a*) chasser, guérir (un rhume) en transpirant; (*b*) *F:* **to s. it out,** endurer jusqu'à la fin; tenir jusqu'an bout.

sweatband [ˈswetbænd] *n. Hatm:* cuir intérieur (d'un chapeau); *Sp:* bandeau *m.*

sweater [ˈswetər] *n. Cost:* pullover *m*, chandail *m.*

sweatiness [ˈswetinis] *n.* moiteur *f* (du corps).

sweatshop [ˈswetʃɔp] *n.* atelier *m* où les ouvriers sont exploités.

sweaty [ˈsweti] *a.* **1.** couvert de sueur; en sueur; **s. hands,** mains moites. **2.** (travail) qui fait transpirer; **s. afternoon,** après-midi d'une chaleur humide. **3.** (vêtement) imprégné de sueur; (odeur) de sueur.

Swede [swi:d] *n.* **1.** *Geog:* Suédois, -oise. **2.** *Agr:* **s.,** rutabaga *m.*

Sweden [ˈswi:d(ə)n] *Pr.n. Geog:* Suède *f.*

Swedish [ˈswi:diʃ] **1.** *a.* suédois. **2.** *n.* le suédois.

sweep¹ [swi:p] *n.* **1.** (*a*) coup *m* de balai, de pinceau, de faux; **at one s.,** d'un seul coup; (*b*) balayage *m*; **to give a room a good s. (out),** balayer une chambre à fond; **to make a clean s.,** (i) faire table rase (**of,** de); (ii) *Gaming:* faire rafle, rafler le tout; **the thieves made a clean s.,** les voleurs ont tout enlevé, tout raflé. **2.** (*a*) mouvement *m* circulaire (du bras); **with a wide s. of the arm,** d'un geste large; **s. of the eye,** regard *m* circulaire; *Fish:* **within the s. of the net,** dans le cercle du filet; (*b*) *Mil: Av:* balayage; opération offensive de chasse en territoire ennemi. **3.** (*a*) zone *f* de jeu (d'une manivelle); (*b*) *Artil:* (i) battage *m*, (ii) portée *f* (d'une pièce); portée (d'un phare); (*c*) envergure *f* (des ailes, d'un génie). **4.** *Rad: Elcs:* **scan(ning) s.,** balayage. **5.** course *f* rapide (d'un fleuve). **6.** (*a*) courbe *f*, courbure *f*; boucle *f* (d'une rivière); *Arch:* courbure (d'un arc); **to make a wide s. to take a bend,** prendre du champ pour effectuer un virage; **s. of a car's lines,** galbe *f* d'une voiture; (*b*) *Av:* **s. (back),** flèche *f*; (*c*) **a fine s. of grass, of country,** une belle étendue de gazon, de pays. **7.** (*a*) aviron *m* de queue (d'une embarcation); (*b*) bascule *f* (pour tirer l'eau d'un puits). **8.** *Clockm:* **s. second hand,** trotteuse centrale. **9.** *Nau:* câble balayeur; drague *f* (pour mines). **10.** (*pers.*) **(chimney) s.,** ramoneur *m.* **11.** *F:* sweepstake *m.*

sweep² *v.* (*p.t. & p.p.* **swept** [swept]) **1.** *v.tr.* (*a*) balayer (une pièce, etc.); ramoner (une cheminée); ébouer (les rues); **dress that sweeps the ground,** robe qui balaie le sol; **a storm swept the town,** un orage ravagea la ville; **the deck was swept by a sea,** une grosse vague balaya le pont; **to s. the horizon with a telescope,** parcourir, scruter, l'horizon avec une lunette; **to s. the seas,** parcourir, balayer, les mers; **to s. the board,** (i) *Gaming:* faire rafle; rafler le tout; (ii) *F:* remporter un succès complet; **the latest craze to s. the country,** la dernière chose qui fait fureur partout dans le pays; (*b*) *Nau:* draguer (un chenal); *v.i.* **to s. for mines,** draguer des mines; (*c*) balayer (la poussière): *Fig:* **to s. (sth.) under the carpet,** enterrer (une question); (*d*) emporter, entraîner; **a wave swept him overboard,** une lame le jeta à la mer; *F:* **to be swept off one's feet by s.o.,** s'emballer, être emballé, pour qn. **2.** *v.i.* (*a*) (*extend widely*) s'étendre, s'étaler; (*b*) **to s. (along),** avancer rapidement; avancer avec un mouvement rapide et uni; **she swept into, out of, the room,** elle est entrée dans, sortie de, la salle d'un air majestueux; (*of car*) **to s. round the corner,** tourner le coin de la rue en faisant un large virage; **the plague swept over Europe,** la peste parcourut toute l'Europe; **the beam swept across the sea,** le faisceau lumineux balaya la mer; **the road sweeps round the lake,** la route décrit une courbe autour du lac. **sweep along** *v.tr.* (*of current, etc.*) entraîner, emporter (qch.). **sweep aside** *v.tr.* écarter d'un geste large; **to s. aside opposition,** écarter brusquement l'opposition. **sweep away** *v.tr.* balayer (la neige, les nuages); supprimer, détruire (un abus); **bridge swept away by the torrent,** pont emporté, entraîné, par le torrent. **sweep by** *v.i.* (*of traffic*) passer avec vitesse; (*of pers.*) passer (i) majestueusement, (ii) dédaigneusement. **sweep down 1.** *v.tr.* **the current sweeps the logs down with it,** le courant emporte, entraîne, le bois. **2.** *v.i.* (*a*) **the enemy swept down upon us,** l'ennemi s'abattit, fonça, sur nous; (*b*) **hills sweeping down to the sea,** collines qui descendent, qui dévalent, vers la mer. **sweep in** *v.i.* **the wind sweeps in,** le vent s'engouffre par la porte; **she swept in,** elle est entrée (dans la pièce) d'un air majestueux. **sweeping 1.** *a.* (*a*) (*of stream*) rapide, impétueux; (*b*) (geste) large; (mouvement) circulaire; (regard) qui embrasse toute l'assemblée; **s. plain,** vaste plaine; **s. curtsy,** révérence profonde; *Art:* **s. line,** ligne allongée, élancée; *Veh:* **low s. lines,** lignes basses et allongées; (*c*) **s. statement, s. generalization,** déclaration par trop générale; généralisation par trop absolue; **s. reform,** réforme complète, radicale; **s. changes,** changement *m* de fond en comble. **2.** *n.* (*a*) balayage *m* (d'une chambre); ramonage *m* (d'une cheminée); ébouage *m* (d'une rue); **s. machine,** balayeuse *f*; (*for roads*) ébouseuse *f*; (*b*) balayage (d'un projecteur); *Mil:* fauchage *m* (d'une arme à feu); (*c*) **sweepings,** balayures *fpl*, ordures *fpl*; (*d*) **s. away,** balayage (de la neige); **s. up,** balayage, ramassement *m.* **sweepingly** *adv.* **1.** rapidement. **2.** sans distinction; d'une façon par trop générale. **sweep off** *v.tr.* enlever, emporter, avec violence; **the plague swept off thousands,** la peste emporta des milliers de personnes. **sweep on** *v.i.* (*of flood*) avancer d'un flot régulier; continuer d'avancer (irrésistiblement). **sweep out 1.** *v.tr.* balayer (une pièce) (à fond). **2.** *v.i.* **she swept out (of the room),** elle est sortie (de la pièce) d'un air majestueux. **sweep past** *v.i.* = SWEEP BY. **sweep up 1.** *v.tr.* balayer, ramasser (la poussière); ramasser (la poussière) en tas. **2.** *v.i.* **the car swept up to the door,** la voiture a roulé jusqu'à la porte.

sweepback [ˈswi:pbæk] *n. Av:* (angle *m* de) flèche *f.*

sweeper [ˈswi:pər] *n.* **1.** (*pers.*) balayeur, -euse. **2.** (*machine*) balayeuse; balai *m* (mécanique).

sweepstake [ˈswi:psteik] *n. Turf:* sweepstake *m.*

sweet [swi:t] **I.** *a.* doux, *f.* douce. **1.** sucré; (vin) doux; **as s. as honey,** doux comme (le) miel; **to taste s.,** avoir une saveur douce; **to have a s. tooth,** aimer les douceurs, les sucreries; *Cu:* **s. corn,** maïs doux; *Cu:* **s. and sour sauce,** sauce aigre-douce. **2.** (*of flower*) parfumé, odorant; **s. violet,** violette odorante; **to smell s.,** avoir une douce odeur; (*of rose*) embaumer. **3.** *Bot:* **s. cherry,** merisier *m*; **s. william,** œillet *m* de(s) poète(s); **s. pea,** pois *m* de senteur. **4. s. breath,** haleine saine, pure, fraîche. **5.** (son) doux, mélodieux; (chanteur) à la voix douce; **flattery that sounds s., is s. to hear,** flatteries douces aux oreilles. **6.** (*a*) agréable; **s. repose,** doux repos; **s. temper,** caractère doux, aimable; **revenge is s.,** la vengeance est douce; *F:* **to keep s.o. s.,** cultiver la bienveillance de qn; (*b*) charmant, gentil, -ille; (sourire) doux; **s. old lady,** vieille dame charmante; **s. girl,** gentille jeune fille; **what a s. kitten!** quel petit chat adorable! **my s.!** ma chérie! **that's very s. of you,** c'est bien gentil à vous; **a s. little dress,** une gentille petite robe; une petite robe exquise; **to say s. nothings to**

s.o., conter fleurette à qn; *NAm: F:* **s. talk,** flatterie *f*; boniment *m*. **7.** *F:* **to be s. on s.o.,** être amoureux de qn; avoir un béguin pour qn. **8. s. running,** fonctionnement doux, sans à-coups (d'une machine). **II.** *n.* (*a*) bonbon *m*; **sweets,** sucreries *fpl*, confiserie *f*; friandises *fpl*; (*b*) (*at dinner*) entremets sucré. **sweetly** *adv.* **1.** (*a*) doucement; avec douceur; (*b*) (chanter) mélodieusement. **2.** agréablement, *F:* gentiment.

sweetbread ['swi:tbred] *n. Cu:* ris *m* (de veau, d'agneau).

sweeten ['swi:t(ə)n] *v.tr.* (*a*) sucrer (un plat, une boisson); (*b*) épurer (l'eau); déodoriser (l'air, l'haleine, etc.); (*c*) adoucir, rendre plus agréable (un son, la vie); (*d*) *F:* **to s. s.o. (up),** (i) flatter, pommader, qn; (ii) graisser la patte à qn. **sweetening** *n.* **1.** (*a*) adoucissement *m*; sucrage *m*; (*b*) assainissement *m* (de l'air); déodorisation *f* (de l'air, de l'haleine); (*c*) adoucissement (du travail, de l'humeur de qn). **2.** substance *f* pour sucrer; **what s. did you use?** avec quoi (l')avez-vous sucré?

sweetener ['swi:t(ə)nər] *n.* **1.** *Cu:* édulcorant *m*. **2.** *F:* pot-de-vin *m*; **to give s.o. a s.,** graisser la patte à qn.

sweetheart ['swi:thɑ:t] *n.* amoureux, -euse; **(my) s.!** mon amour! mon cœur! **they have been sweethearts since childhood,** ils s'aiment depuis leur enfance.

sweetie ['swi:ti] *n. F:* **1.** bonbon *m*. **2. s. (pie),** chéri, -e.

sweetish ['swi:tiʃ] *a.* assez doux; douceâtre.

sweetmeat ['swi:tmi:t] *n.* bonbon *m*; **sweetmeats,** sucreries *fpl*, confiserie *f*, douceurs *fpl*.

sweetness ['swi:tnis] *n.* **1.** douceur *f* (du miel). **2.** (*a*) gentillesse *f*, charme *m*; (*b*) **she's all s. when you are there,** elle fait la sucrée quand vous êtes là; (*c*) **s. and light,** amabilité *f* et raison *f*.

sweet-scented, -smelling [swi:t'sentid, -'smeliŋ] *a.* qui sent bon; odorant.

sweetshop ['swi:tʃɔp] *n.* confiserie *f*.

sweet-talk ['swi:tɔk] *v.tr. NAm: F:* flagorner, flatter (qn).

sweet-tempered [swi:t'tempəd] *a.* doux, *f*, douce; au caractère doux.

swell¹ [swel] **I.** *n.* **1.** (*a*) bosse *f*; bombement *m*; renflement *m* (d'une colonne); gros *m* (de l'avant-bras); saillie *f* (du mollet); (*b*) augmentation *f* (d'un son); *Lit:* **the majestic s. of the organ,** les accents majestueux du grand orgue. **2.** *Nau:* houle *f*; levée *f* (de la lame); **ground s.,** houle de fond. **3.** *Mus:* soufflet *m* (d'un orgue); **s. box,** boîte expressive; récit *m*; **s. organ,** (jeux *mpl* de) récit. **4.** *F: O:* (*a*) élégant *m*; (*b*) aristo *m*. **II.** *a. F:* (*a*) *O:* chic *inv*, élégant; (*b*) *NAm: O:* épatant; **a s. guy,** un chic type.

swell² *v.* (*p.t.* **swelled;** *p.p.* **swollen** ['swoul(ə)n], *occ.* **swelled) 1.** *v.tr.* (*a*) (r)enfler, gonfler; **river swollen by the rain,** rivière grossie, enflée, par la pluie; **eyes swollen with tears,** yeux gonflés de larmes; **all this has helped to s. the ranks of the unemployed,** tout cela a augmenté le nombre de chômeurs; (*b*) *Mus:* enfler (une note). **2.** *v.i.* (*a*) **to s. (up),** (s')enfler, se gonfler; (*of part of the body*) se tuméfier; (*of earth, lime*) foisonner; (*of number, crowd*) augmenter, grossir; **his arm is swelling (up),** son bras enfle; **his heart swelled with pride,** son cœur se gonflait d'orgueil; (*b*) (*of sea*) se soulever; **hate swelled up within him,** la haine montait en lui; (*c*) **to s. out,** être bombé; bomber; **the sails s. (out),** les voiles *mpl* se gonflent. **swelling 1.** *a.* qui s'enfle, se gonfle; (*of sail*) gonflé; *Med:* tumescent; (*of pers.*) **s. with importance,** gonflé d'importance. **2.** *n.* (*a*) enflement *m*, gonflement *m* (d'un fleuve); crue *f* (d'un fleuve); gonflement, bombement *m* (des voiles); augmentation *f* (d'un nombre); renflement *m* (d'une colonne); (*b*) *Med:* tuméfaction *f*, gonflement (du visage); (*c*) bosse *f*, enflure *f* (au front); tumescence *f*, tumeur *f*. **swollen** *a.* (*a*) enflé, gonflé; (visage) bouffi; **the river is s.,** la rivière est en crue; (*b*) (*also* **swelled**) *F:* **to suffer from, to have, a s. head,** être bouffi d'orgueil.

swellheaded [swel'hedid] *a.* vaniteux, suffisant.

swelter ['sweltər] *v.i.* étouffer, être accablé, de chaleur. **sweltering** *a.* (chaleur) étouffante, accablante; **s. (hot) day,** journée embrasée.

swerve¹ [swə:v] *n.* écart *m*, déviation *f*; *Fb:* crochet *m*; *Aut:* embardée *f*; *Sp* courbe latérale (décrite par la balle).

swerve² 1. *v.i.* faire un écart, un crochet; (*of horse*) se dérober; (*of car*) embarder, faire une embardée; (*of footballer*) crocheter; *Fig:* **he never swerves from his duty,** il ne s'écarte, s'éloigne, jamais de son devoir. **2.** *v.tr.* faire dévier (une balle); faire faire une embardée à (une voiture).

swift [swift] **1.** *a.* (*a*) rapide; *Sp:* (coureur, cheval) vite; **as s. as an arrow,** vif comme l'éclair; *Lit:* **s. of foot,** rapide à la course; (*b*) prompt; **s. to anger,** toujours prêt à s'emporter; irascible. **2.** *adv.* (*forming compound adjs.*) **s.-flowing,** (rivière) au cours rapide; **s.-footed,** au pied léger. **3.** *n. Orn:* **(black) s.,** martinet (noir). **-ly** *adv.* (*a*) vite, rapidement; (*b*) promptement.

swiftness ['swiftnis] *n.* **1.** rapidité *f*, vitesse *f*. **2.** promptitude *f* (d'une réplique, etc.).

swig¹ [swig] *n. P:* grand trait, lampée *f*; **to take a s. at the bottle,** boire un grand coup à la bouteille.

swig² *v.tr. & i.* **(swigged)** *P:* boire à grands traits, à grands coups; **to s. off a glass,** boire un verre d'un seul coup, d'un trait.

swill¹ [swil] *n.* **1.** lavage *m* à grande eau; **to give a pail a s. out,** laver, rincer, un seau à grande eau. **2.** pâtée *f* pour les porcs; eaux grasses.

swill² *v.tr.* **1.** laver (le plancher) à grande eau; **to s. out a basin,** rincer une cuvette. **2.** *P:* (*a*) boire avidement (qch.); (*b*) *v.i.* boire comme une éponge.

swim¹ [swim] *n.* **1. to have, take, a s.,** nager; **to go for a s.,** aller se baigner; *Ich:* **s. bladder,** vessie *f* natatoire. **2.** *F:* **to be in the s.,** être dans le mouvement, dans le train, à la page.

swim² *v.* (*p.t.* **swam** [swæm]; *p.p.* **swum** [swʌm] *pr.p.* **swimming) 1.** *v.i.* nager; (*a*) *F:* **to s. like a fish,** nager comme un poisson; **to s. to the shore,** gagner le rivage à la nage; **to s. over, across, a stream,** traverser une rivière à la nage; **to s. with the tide,** suivre le courant, le mouvement; *with cogn. acc.* **to s. a stroke,** faire une brasse; **to s. the breast stroke,** nager (à) la brasse; **to s. a race,** faire une course de natation **(with s.o.,** contre qn); (*b*) **meat swimming in gravy,** viande nageant dans la sauce; (*c*) surnager, flotter; (*d*) être inondé **(in, with,** de); **eyes swimming with tears,** yeux noyés de larmes; (*e*) (*of head*) tourner; (*of eyes, vision*) se brouiller; **to make s.o.'s head s.,** faire tourner la tête à qn; **my head is swimming,** la tête me tourne; **everything swam before my eyes,** tout semblait tourner autour de moi. **2.** *v.tr.* traverser, passer (une rivière) à la nage. **swimming 1.** *a.* (*a*) (animal) nageant, qui nage; (*b*) **s. eyes,** yeux noyés de larmes; **s. head,** tête qui tourne. **2.** *n.* (*a*) nage *f*, natation *f*; **s. pool,** piscine *f*; **s. match,** concours *m* de natation; *Ich:* **s. bladder,** vessie *f* natatoire; (*b*) **s. of the head,** vertige *m*, étourdissement *m*. **swimmingly** *adv. F:* au mieux, à merveille; **everything is going s.,** tout va comme sur des roulettes.

swimmer ['swimər] *n.* (*pers.*) nageur, -euse.

swimsuit ['swims(j)u:t] *n.* maillot *m* de bain(s).

swindle¹ [ˈswindl] *n.* **1.** escroquerie *f*, filouterie *f*. **2.** duperie *f*.

swindle² *v.tr.* escroquer, filouter (qn); *P:* rouler (qn); **to s. s.o. out of sth.,** escroquer qch. à qn.

swindler [ˈswindlər] *n.* filou *m*, escroc *m*.

swine [swain] *n. inv. in pl.* **1.** cochon *m*, porc *m*; pourceau *m*; *Vet:* **s. fever,** peste porcine. **2.** *P:* salaud *m*; **dirty s.!** sale cochon!

swineherd [ˈswainhəːd] *n.m. A: & Lit:* porcher; gardeur de cochons.

swing¹ [swiŋ] *n.* **1.** (*a*) balancement *m*; **to give a child a s.,** pousser un enfant sur une balançoire; (*b*) tour *m* (de manivelle); (*c*) coup balancé; *Box: Golf:* swing *m*; *F:* **to take a s. at s.o.,** lancer un coup de poing à qn. **2.** (*a*) oscillation *f*, va-et-vient *m* (d'un pendule); *Pol:* **the s. of the pendulum,** le jeu de bascule (entre les partis); *Fig:* **to give full s. to one's imagination,** donner libre cours à son imagination; **to be in full s.,** (*of fete*) battre son plein; (*of organization*) être en pleine activité; **when the season is in full s.,** quand la saison bat son plein; (*b*) **single s. of a pendulum,** oscillation simple, battement *m*, d'un pendule; *Fig:* **sudden s. of public opinion,** revirement inattendu de l'opinion publique; *Pol:* **s. to the left,** glissement *m* à gauche, vers la gauche; *Pol.E:* **seasonal swings,** variations saisonnières. **3.** (*a*) amplitude *f* (d'une oscillation); **s. of a door,** ouverture *f* d'une porte; (*b*) *Nau:* évitage *m* (d'un navire à l'ancre). **4.** (*a*) mouvement rythmé; **to walk with a s.,** marcher d'un pas rythmé, d'un pas dégagé; **song that goes with a s.,** chanson très rythmée; *F:* **everything went with a s.,** tout a très bien marché; *F:* **to get into the s. of things,** se mettre au courant, dans le bain; (*b*) *Mus:* **s. (music),** swing *m*. **5.** balançoire *f*. **6.** (*a*) (*at fair*) **s. boat,** (bateau *m*) balançoire; **s. bridge,** pont tournant, pivotant; **s. door,** porte battante; **s. glass, mirror,** miroir *m* à bascule, (*full length*) psyché *f*; *Av:* **s.-wing aircraft,** avion *m* à géométrie variable; (*b*) *NAm: Ind:* **s. shift,** (i) équipe *f* (d'ouvriers) assurant la relève (*esp.* entre celle de jour et celle de nuit); (ii) journée *f* de travail mi-jour mi-nuit.

swing² *v.* (*p.t. & p.p.* **swung** [swʌŋ]) **1.** *v.i.* (*a*) **to s. to and fro,** se balancer; (*of bell*) brimbaler; (*of pendulum*) osciller; **shop sign that swings to and fro in the wind,** enseigne de magasin qui ballotte au vent; *P:* **to s. for a crime,** être pendu pour un crime; (*b*) **to s. on, round, an axis,** tourner, pivoter, sur un axe; (*of mirror*) basculer; **the door swings on its hinges,** la porte tourne sur ses gonds; (*of door*) **to s. open,** s'ouvrir; **to s. to,** se refermer; (*c*) (*of ship*) **to s. (at anchor),** éviter (sur l'ancre); (*d*) se balancer (sur la balançoire); (*e*) faire un mouvement de conversion; changer de direction; (*f*) **to s. round,** se retourner vivement; faire volte-face; (*of car*) virer; faire un virage; **the car swung right round,** la voiture a fait un tête-à-queue; (*g*) *Mil:* **the whole line swung to the left,** toute la ligne fit une conversion vers la gauche; (*h*) **to s. along,** marcher d'un pas rythmé; scander le pas; (*i*) *Mus:* jouer le swing; (*j*) *F:* être dans le mouvement; être dynamique, être swing. **2.** *v.tr.* (*a*) (faire) balancer (qch.); faire osciller (un pendule, etc.); **to s. one's arms,** balancer les bras (en marchant); **to s. the hips (in walking),** se dandiner; *Box:* **to s. a blow,** balancer un coup; (*b*) (i) *Nau:* **boat swung out,** embarcation parée au dehors; (ii) **to s. a car round,** faire faire un brusque virage à une auto; **to s. a car right round,** faire faire un tête-à-queue à une auto; (iii) *Cr:* **to s. the ball,** faire dévier la balle en l'air; (*c*) faire tourner (qch.); *Av:* lancer, brasser (l'hélice); (*d*) **to s. the voting in favour of s.o.,** faire balancer les votes en faveur de qn; *NAm: F:* **to s. a deal,** mener une affaire à bien; (*e*) suspendre (qch.); pendre, (ac)crocher (un hamac); (*f*) *v.pr. & i.* **to s. (oneself) into the saddle,** monter vivement à cheval, en selle; **to s. from branch to branch,** se balancer d'une branche à une autre; **to s. into action,** passer (vivement) à l'action; (*g*) *Mus:* interpréter (une mélodie, etc.) en swing. **swing back** *v.i.* (*a*) (*of door*) basculer; se rabattre; (*b*) (*of pendulum*) revenir; **public opinion swung back,** il y eut un revirement d'opinion. **swinging 1.** *a.* (*a*) (i) balançant; oscillant; **with s. arms,** les bras ballants; (ii) (miroir) à bascule; **s. door,** porte battante; (*b*) (i) **s. stride,** allure rythmée, cadencée, dégagée; **s. blow,** coup balancé; **s. tune,** air enlevant, entraînant; (*c*) *F:* (*of pers.*) dans le vent, avant-garde *inv*, swing; **s. London,** le Londres d'avant-garde. **2.** *n.* (*a*) balancement *m*, oscillation *f*; **s. motion,** mouvement *m* pendulaire; balancement *m*; (*b*) mouvement de bascule, de rotation; (*of door*) **s. open,** ouverture *f*; **s. to,** rabattement *m*; (*c*) *Nau:* évitage *m*; (*d*) **s. round,** (i) virage *m*, (ii) tête-à-queue *m inv* (d'une voiture); (*e*) *Av:* lancement *m* (de l'hélice). **swingingly** *adv.* avec rythme; avec entrain.

swingeing [ˈswin(d)ʒiŋ] *a.* **1. s. blow,** coup bien envoyé. **2.** énorme; **s. majority,** majorité écrasante; **s. damages,** forts dommages-intérêts.

swinish [ˈswainiʃ] *a.* (i) sale (ii) glouton, -onne.

swingle¹ [ˈswiŋgl] *n.* **1.** *Tex:* écang *m*. **2.** *Husb:* battoir *m* (d'un fléau). **3.** *Veh:* **s. tree, bar,** palonnier *m*.

swingle² *v.tr. Tex:* teiller, écanguer (le lin).

swipe¹ [swaip] *n.* (*a*) *Cr: Golf:* coup *m* à toute volée; (*b*) *F:* **to take a s. at s.o.,** (i) lâcher un coup (de poing) à qn; (ii) *Fig:* lâcher un coup de patte à qn.

swipe² 1. *v.i.* **to s. at the ball,** lancer un coup à la balle à toute volée. **2.** *v.tr.* (*a*) frapper (la balle) à toute volée; (*b*) *F:* donner un coup de poing, de bâton, à (qn); (*c*) *F:* chiper, faucher (qch.).

swirl¹ [swəːl] *n.* remous *m* (de l'eau); tourbillonnement *m* (d'un mélange gazeux); **a s. of dust,** un tourbillon de poussière.

swirl² 1. *v.i.* tournoyer, tourbillonner; (*of dust*) **to s. up,** monter en tourbillons. **2.** *v.tr.* faire tournoyer (qch.). **swirling 1.** *a.* tourbillonnant. **2.** *n.* tourbillonnement *m*.

swish¹ [swiʃ] *n.* **1.** bruissement *m* (de l'eau); froufrou *m* (d'une robe); sifflement *m* (d'un fouet); crissement *m* (d'une faux). **2.** coup *m* de fouet.

swish² 1. *v.i.* (*of water*) bruire; susurrer; (*of silk*) froufrouter; (*of whip*) siffler. **2.** *v.tr.* (*a*) fouetter (qn, qch.); (*b*) faire siffler (sa canne, une badine); (*c*) (*of animal*) **to s. its tail,** battre l'air de sa queue.

swish³ *a. F:* élégant, chic, rupin.

Swiss [swis] **1.** *a.* suisse; **the S. government,** le gouvernement helvétique. **2.** *n. inv. in pl.* Suisse *m*; Suissesse *f*.

switch¹ [switʃ] *n.* **1.** (*a*) baguette *f*, badine *f*; (*for caning pupil*) canne *f*; **riding s.,** petite cravache; (*b*) coup *m* de baguette. **2.** (*a*) *Rail:* aiguille *f* (de changement de voie); (*b*) *U.S: Rail:* voie *f* de raccordement, de garage; (*c*) changement *m* (d'une chose à une autre); (*d*) *Cmptr:* aiguillage *m* (des éléments d'un programme). **3.** *El:* commutateur *m*, interrupteur *m*; **two-way s.,** commutateur à deux directions; interrupteur d'escalier; **s. gear,** appareillage *m* de commutation, de distribution. **4.** postiche *m*.

switch² I. *v.tr.* **1.** (*a*) donner un coup de badine à (qn, qch.); (*b*) (*of cow*) **to s. its tail,** battre l'air de sa queue. **2.** faire mouvoir brusquement. **3.** (*a*) *Rail:* aiguiller (un train); **to s. a train onto a branch line,** aiguiller un train sur un embranchement; (*b*) *U.S:* manœuvrer (un train); (*c*) **to s. the conversation to another subject,** faire tourner la conversation sur une autre voie; (*d*) changer la position (d'une manette, d'un levier). **4.** *El:* commuter (le courant). **switching** *n. Rail:* (*a*) aiguillage *m*; *U.S:* **s. tower,** cabine *f* d'aiguillage; (*b*) *U.S:* triage *m*; **s. yard,** gare *f*, centre *m*, de triage. **switch off** *v.tr. & i.* (*a*) *El:* interrompre, couper (le courant); arrêter (la radio, la télévision); **s. (the light) off when you go out!** éteignez l'électricité quand vous sortez! *I.C.E:* **to s. off the ignition, the engine,** couper l'allumage; *F:* (*of pers.*) **to s. off (completely),** cesser d'écouter. **switch on** *v.tr. & i. El:* mettre (une lampe, etc.) en circuit; donner (du courant); établir, mettre (le contact); allumer (l'électricité); mettre (la radio, la télévision) en marche; *I.C.E:* **to s. on the ignition, the engine,** mettre le contact (d'allumage); (*of pers.*) **to be switched on,** (i) *F:* être bien au courant de ce qui se passe; (ii) *P:* être chargé (par des drogues). **switch over** *v.tr. & i. El:* commuter (le courant); *W. Tel: T.V:* **to s. over to another channel,** changer de réglage; **to s. over to modern languages,** réorienter ses études vers les langues vivantes.

switchback ['switʃbæk] *n.* (*at fair*) montagnes *fpl* russes; **s. road,** route *f* qui monte et descend.

switchboard ['switʃbɔːd] *n. Tp: El:* tableau (commutateur, de distribution); (*in office*) standard *m*; **s. operator,** standardiste *mf*.

switchman *pl.* **-men** ['switʃmən, -men] *n.m. U.S: Rail:* aiguilleur.

Switzerland ['switsələnd] *Pr.n.* la Suisse; **German S.,** la Suisse alémanique; **French(-speaking) S.,** la Suisse romande; **Italian(-speaking) S.,** la Suisse italienne.

swivel¹ ['swivl] *n.* **1.** (*a*) émerillon *m*, maillon tournant (de câble-chaîne); (*b*) pivot *m*; rotule *f*. **2.** *attrib.* pivotant, tournant; à pivot; **s. chair, seat,** siège tournant; **s. joint,** (joint *m* à) rotule.

swivel² *v.* **(swivelled,** *NAm:* **swiveled) 1.** *v.i.* pivoter, tourner; **to s. round on one's heels,** pivoter sur ses talons. **2.** *v.tr.* faire pivoter (une mitrailleuse); **to s. one's eyes round,** tourner les yeux de côté. **swivelling** *NAm:* **swiveling** *a.* pivotant, tournant; à pivot.

swiz(z) [swiz] *n. Sch: P:* **1.** duperie *f*. **2.** déception *f*.

swizzle ['swizl] *n.* **1.** *NAm: F:* cocktail *m*; **s. stick,** fouet *m*, marteau *m*, à champagne. **2.** *P:* = SWIZ(Z).

swollen-headed [swoulən'hedid] *a.* vaniteux.

swoon¹ [swuːn] *n. O:* évanouissement *m*, défaillance *f*; **to fall into a s.,** s'évanouir, se pâmer.

swoon² *v.i. O:* s'évanouir, se pâmer; défaillir.

swoop¹ [swuːp] *n.* abat(t)ée *f* (d'un avion) (**upon,** sur); descente *f* (du faucon qui fond sur sa proie); **police s.,** descente de police (sur une boîte de nuit); *F:* **at one (fell) s.,** d'un seul coup.

swoop² *v.i.* (*of hawk, pers.*) **to s. (down) on sth.,** s'abattre, foncer, sur qch.; **the police swooped on the district,** la police a fait une descente sur le quartier.

swop [swɔp] *n. & v.tr.* = SWAP[1,2].

sword [sɔːd] *n.* (*a*) épée *f*; *A: & Poet:* glaive *m*; **to draw one's s.,** tirer son épée; dégainer; **to cross swords with s.o.,** (i) croiser l'épée, le fer, avec qn; (ii) mesurer ses forces avec qn; **to put the inhabitants to the s.,** passer les habitants au fil de l'épée; *Lit:* **the S. of Justice,** le glaive de la Justice; (*b*) *Mil: Navy:* sabre *m*; **to draw one's s.,** tirer sabre au clair; dégainer; (*c*) **s. arm,** bras droit; **s. bearer,** officier (*esp.* municipal) qui porte le glaive; **s. stick,** canne *f* à épée; **s. cut,** (i) coup *m* de sabre; (ii) blessure faite avec le sabre; (*on face*) balafre *f*; **s. dance,** danse *f* du sabre.

swordbelt ['sɔːdbelt] *n.* ceinturon *m*.

swordfish ['sɔːdfiʃ] *n. Ich:* espadon *m*.

swordplay ['sɔːdplei] *n.* **1.** maniement *m* de l'épée; escrime *f* (à l'épée). **2. verbal s.,** joute *f* oratoire.

swordsman *pl.* **-men** ['sɔːdzmən] *n.m.* épéiste, tireur d'épée; **fine s.,** fine lame, bonne épée.

swot¹ [swɔt] *n. F:* **1.** (*a*) *Sch:* travail *m* intense; (*b*) travail de chien; corvée *f*. **2.** (*pers.*) bûcheur, -euse.

swot² *v.tr. & i.* **(swotted)** *Sch: F:* bûcher; **to s. up one's maths,** potasser, piocher, bûcher, les math.

sybarite ['sibərait] *a. & n.* sybarite (*mf*).

sybaritic [sibə'ritik] *a.* sybaritique, sybarite.

sycamore ['sikəmɔːr] *n. Bot:* (*a*) (érable *m*) sycomore *m*, faux platane; (*b*) *NAm:* platane.

sycophancy ['sikəfənsi] *n.* flagornerie *f*.

sycophant ['sikəfənt] *n.* flagorneur *m*.

sycophantic [sikə'fæntik] *a.* adulateur, -trice.

syllabic [si'læbik] *a.* syllabique.

syllabi(fi)cation [silæbi(fi)'keiʃ(ə)n] *n.* syllabisation *f*.

syllabify [si'læbifai] *v.tr.* syllabiser (un mot).

syllable ['siləbl] *n.* syllabe *f*; *Pros:* **short s.,** brève *f*; **long s.,** longue *f*; **to explain sth. in words of one s.,** expliquer qch. en termes très simples.

syllabub ['siləbʌb] *n. Cu:* = sabayon *m*.

syllabus, *pl.* **-i, -uses** ['siləbəs, -ai, -əsiz] *n.* programme *m*, sommaire *m* (d'un cours).

syllogism ['silədʒizm] *n. Log:* syllogisme *m*.

syllogistic [silə'dʒistik] *a. Log:* syllogistique.

sylph [silf] *n.* **1.** sylphe *m*, sylphide *f*. **2.** (*of woman*) sylphide; *F:* **she's no s.,** elle prend de la place. **3.** *NAm: Orn:* (espèce *f* de) colibri *m*.

sylph-like ['silflaik] *a.* (taille, etc.) de sylphide.

sylvan [silvən] *a.* sylvestre.

symbiosis *pl.* **-ses** [simb(a)i'ousis, -iːz] *n. Biol:* symbiose *f*.

symbiotic [simb(a)i'ɔtik] *a. Biol:* symbiotique.

symbol¹ ['simb(ə)l] *n.* symbole *m*, emblème *m*; attribut *m* (de la puissance souveraine, etc.); *NAm:* **road symbols,** pictogrammes routiers.

symbol² *v.tr.* **(symboled)** *NAm:* = SYMBOLIZE.

symbolic [sim'bɔlik] *a.* symbolique. **-ally** *adv.* symboliquement.

symbolism ['simbəlizm] *n.* symbolisme *m*.

symbolist ['simbəlist] *a. & n.* symboliste (*mf*).

symbolization [simbəlai'zeiʃn] *n.* symbolisation *f*.

symbolize ['simbəlaiz] *v.tr.* symboliser.

symmetrical [si'metrik(ə)l] *a.* symétrique (**about sth.,** par rapport à qch.) **-ally** *adv.* symétriquement.

symmetry ['simitri] *n.* symétrie *f*.

sympathetic [simpə'θetik] *a.* **1.** (*of pain*) sympathique; **the s. nerve,** le grand sympathique; (*b*) *Ph:* (vibration) due à la résonance; **s. string,** corde *f* qui vibre par résonance; (*c*) **s. landscape,** paysage évocateur. **2.** (*a*) qui marque la sympathie; (regard, sourire) de sympathie; (*b*) **s. audience,** auditoire bien disposé; **he's always very s.,** il est toujours prêt à vous écouter; **to be s. to a proposal,** être en sympathie avec une proposition; (*c*) compatissant; (lettre) de sympathie. **3.** (*of pers., face*) qui évoque la sympathie; sympathique. **-ally** *adv.* **1.** sympathiquement; avec sympathie; par sympathie; *Ph:* (vibrer) par résonance. **2.** d'une manière compatissante.

sympathize ['simpəθaiz] *v.i.* **1. to s. with s.o. (in his loss),** (i) sympathiser avec qn; (ii) avoir de la compassion pour qn. **2.** (*a*) **to s. with s.o.'s point of view,** comprendre le point de vue de qn; (*b*) **to s. with s.o.,** s'associer (de cœur) aux sentiments de qn.

sympathizer ['simpəθaizər] *n.* **1. to be a s. with s.o.,** (i) sympathiser avec qn; (ii) ressentir de la compassion pour qn; **to be a s. in s.o.'s grief,** compatir au chagrin de qn. **2.** sympathisant, -ante (**with a cause,** d'une cause).

sympathy ['simpəθi] *n.* **1.** compassion *f*; condoléances *fpl*; **accept my deep s.,** agréez mes condoléances. **2.** (*a*) sympathie *f* (**for s.o.,** pour qn); **to feel a s. for s.o.,** se sentir de l'attrait *m* pour qn; **popular sympathies are on his side,** il a l'opinion pour lui; **to view a proposal with s.,** regarder une proposition d'un bon œil; **to be in s. with s.o.'s ideas,** être en sympathie avec les, sympathique aux, idées de qn; **my s. is, my sympathies are, with the opposition,** je partage les opinions de l'opposition; **to strike, come**

out (on strike), in s., se mettre en grève de solidarité (**with,** avec); (*b*) **prices went up in s.,** les prix sont montés par contrecoup; (*c*) *Ph:* **string that vibrates in s.,** corde qui vibre par résonance.

symphonic [sim'fɔnik] *a. Mus:* symphonique.

symphony ['simfəni] *n. Mus:* **1.** symphonie *f*; **s. orchestra,** orchestre *m* symphonique; **s. concert,** concert *m* symphonique. **2.** *NAm:* orchestre symphonique.

symposium *pl.* **-ia -iums** [sim'pouziəm, iə, -iəmz] *n.* (*a*) conférence *f* (académique); colloque *m*, symposium; (*b*) recueil *m* d'articles (sur un sujet du jour).

symptom ['sim(p)təm] *n.* symptôme *m.*

symptomatic [sim(p)tə'mætik] *a.* symptomatique **-ally** *adv.* symptomatiquement.

synagogue ['sinəgɔg] *n.* synagogue *f.*

synchromesh ['siŋkroumeʃ] *n. Aut:* synchronisation *f*; **s. (gear),** (boîte *f* de vitesses) avec les rapports synchronisés.

synchronism ['siŋkrənizm] *n.* synchronisme *m.*

synchronization [siŋkrənai'zeiʃ(ə)n] *n.* synchronisation *f.*

synchronize ['siŋkrənaiz] **1.** *v.tr.* (*a*) synchroniser (deux montres; **sth. with sth.,** qch. avec qch.); *El:* coupler (deux générateurs) en phase; (*b*) établir le synchronisme de (différents événements). **2.** *v.i.* (*a*) (*of events*) arriver, avoir lieu, simultanément; (*b*) **clocks that s.,** horloges qui marquent la même heure. **synchronized** *a.* synchronisé; *El:* **s. generators,** générateurs synchronisés, en phase. **synchronizer** ['siŋkrənaizər] *n.* synchronisateur *m.* **synchronizing** *n.* synchronisation *f.*

synchronous ['siŋkrənəs] *a.* synchrone (**with,** de).

syncline ['siŋklain] *n. Geol:* synclinal *m.*

syncopate ['siŋkəpeit] *v.tr.* syncoper; **syncopated music,** musique syncopée.

syncopation [siŋkə'peiʃ(ə)n] *n. Mus:* syncope *f.*

syncope ['siŋkəpi] *n. Med: Gram:* syncope *f.*

syndic ['sindik] *n.* syndic *m.*

syndicalism ['sindikəlizm] *n.* syndicalisme *m.*

syndicalist ['sindikəlist] *n. & a.* syndicaliste (*mf*).

syndicate¹ ['sindikət] *n.* **1.** (*a*) *Com: Fin:* syndicat *m*, consortium *m*; **financial s.,** syndicat financier; **member of a s.,** syndicataire *m*; (*b*) *NAm:* association *f* de malfaiteurs; (*c*) *NAm:* agence *f* de presse spécialisée; (*d*) *U.S:* chaîne *f* de journaux. **2.** conseil *m* de syndics.

syndicate² ['sindikeit] **1.** *v.tr.* publier (un article) simultanément dans plusieurs journaux. **2.** *v.i.* se syndiquer.

syndication [sindi'keiʃ(ə)n] *n.* publication simultanée (d'un article) dans plusieurs journaux.

syndrome ['sindroum] *n. Med:* syndrome *m.*

synod ['sinəd] *n.* (*a*) *Ecc:* synode *m*, concile *m*; **the General S.,** le conseil d'administration de l'Église anglicane; (*b*) assemblée *f*, convention *f.*

synodic [si'nɔdik] *a.* (*a*) *Ecc:* synodique, synodal, -aux; (*b*) *Astr:* (période, etc.) synodique.

synonym ['sinənim] *n.* synonyme *m.*

synonymous [si'nɔniməs] *a.* synonyme (**with,** de). **-ly** *adv.* (employer un mot) comme synonyme (**with,** de).

synopsis *pl.* **-pses** [si'nɔpsis, -psi:z] *n.* résumé *m*, sommaire *m*; synopsis *f* (d'une science); *Cin:* **brief s. of a film,** résumé du scénario; synopsis.

synoptic [si'nɔptik] *a.* synoptique.

synovia [si'nouviə, sai-] *n. Physiol: Anat:* synovie *f.*

syntactic(al) [sin'tæktik(l)] *a. Gram: etc:* syntactique, syntaxique.

syntax ['sintæks] *n. Gram:* syntaxe *f.*

synthesis *pl.* **-es** ['sinθisis, -i:z] *n.* synthèse *f.*

synthesize ['sinθəsaiz] *v.tr.* synthétiser (des éléments); faire la synthèse (d'un produit).

synthesizer ['sinθəsaizər] *n.* synthétiseur *m.*

synthetic [sin'θetik] **1.** *a.* (produit, fibre) synthétique; **s. rubber,** caoutchouc *m* synthétique; *F:* **s. smile,** sourire factice. **2.** *n. usu.pl.* **synthetics,** (matières) plastiques *fpl.* **-ally** *adv.* synthétiquement.

syphilis ['sifilis] *n. Med:* syphilis *f.*

syphilitic [sifi'litik] *a. & n. Med:* syphilitique (*mf*).

syphon ['saif(ə)n] *n. & v.* = SIPHON[1, 2].

Syria ['siriə] *Pr.n. Geog:* Syrie *f.*

Syrian ['siriən] **1.** *a.* syrien. **2.** *n.* Syrien, -ienne.

syringe¹ ['sirindʒ, si'rindʒ] *n.* seringue *f.*

syringe² *v.tr.* seringuer (une plaie, etc.); **to s. (out) the ears,** laver les oreilles avec une seringue.

syrup ['sirəp] *n.* **1.** sirop *m*; **red currant s.,** sirop de groseilles; *Med:* **cough s.,** sirop pectoral; sirop pour, contre, la toux. **2. (golden) s.,** mélasse raffinée; sirop de sucre. **3.** douceur affectée.

syrupy ['sirəpi] *a.* **1.** sirupeux. **2.** (ton) mielleux.

system ['sistəm] *n.* **1.** (*a*) système *m* (de philosophie); **the feudal s.,** le régime féodal; *F:* **the s.,** l'ordre établi; **systems analysis,** analyse fonctionnelle; **systems analyst,** analyste-programmeur *m*; *Sch:* **block s.,** enseignement groupé; (*b*) *Astr:* **the solar s.,** le système solaire; (*c*) *Anat:* **nervous, muscular, s.,** système nerveux, musculaire; **the digestive s.,** l'appareil digestif; **bad for the s.,** mauvais pour l'organisme; *F:* **to get sth. out of one's s.,** se libérer, se purger, de qch. **2.** (*a*) réseau *m* (télégraphique); réseau ferré (d'un chemin de fer); **road, river, s.,** réseau routier, fluvial; (*b*) **s. of pulleys,** système de poulies; **central heating s.,** installation *f* de chauffage central. **3.** méthode *f* (de travail); **to lack s.,** manquer de méthode, d'organisation.

systematic [sistə'mætik] *a.* systématique, méthodique; **he's very s.,** il a de l'ordre, de la méthode. **-ally** *adv.* systématiquement; avec méthode.

system(at)ization [sistəm(ət)ai'zeiʃ(ə)n] *n.* systématisation *f.*

system(at)ize ['sistəm(ət)aiz] *v.tr.* réduire en système, systématiser.

systemic [si'stemik] *a.* (insecticide) systémique.

T

T, t [ti:] *n.* **1.** (la lettre) T, t, té *m*; **to cross one's t's,** (i) barrer ses t; (ii) *F:* mettre les points sur les i; *adv.phr.* **to a T,** exactement; à la perfection; **that's you to a T,** c'est absolument vous; **that suits me to a T,** cela me va à merveille. **2. T-shaped,** en (forme de) T; **T square,** té, équerre *f* en T; (*of roads*) **T junction,** tête *f* de carrefour; **T shirt,** T-shirt *m*, tee-shirt *m; Cu:* **T-bone steak,** bifteck *m* d'aloyau.

ta [tɑ:] *n. & int. P:* merci (*m*).

tab [tæb] *n.* **1.** (*a*) patte *f* (de vêtement, etc.); *Mil:* patte du collet; écusson *m* (d'officier d'état-major); (*b*) ferret *m* (de lacet); (*c*) attache *f*; tirant *m* (de botte); (*d*) patte *f* (de carton de classement); onglet *m* (de dictionnaire, etc.). **2.** étiquette *f* (pour bagages); *Fig:* **to keep tabs on s.o., sth.,** tenir qn, qch., à l'œil; ne pas perdre qn, qch., de vue; contrôler (les dépenses). **3.** *NAm:* facture *f*, note *f*.

tabard ['tæbəd] *n. Cost:* tabar(d) *m* (de héraut).

tabby ['tæbi] *n.* **t. (cat),** (i) chat tigré, moucheté; (ii) *F:* chatte *f*.

tabernacle ['tæbənækl] *n.* tabernacle *m*.

table¹ ['teibl] *n.* table *f*. **1.** (*a*) guéridon *m*; **card, gaming, t.,** table de jeu; **nest of tables,** table gigogne; *Parl:* **to lay a measure on the t.,** (i) déposer un projet de loi sur le bureau; (ii) ajourner un projet de loi; *Psychics:* **t. turning,** (phénomène *m* des) tables tournantes; (*b*) **the (breakfast, dinner) t.,** la table; **to lay, set, the t.,** mettre la table, le couvert; **to clear the t.,** desservir; **to sit down to t.,** se mettre à table; **to be at t.,** être à table, être attablé; (*at banquet, etc.*) **high t.,** *F:* **top t.,** table d'honneur; *F:* **to drink s.o. under the t.,** mettre qn sous la table; **he has awful t. manners,** il se tient très mal à table; **t. knife,** couteau *m* de table; **t. wine,** vin *m* de table; **t. linen,** linge *m* de table; **t. mat,** (i) dessous *m* d'assiette; (ii) napperon individuel; *Ecc:* **the Lord's T., the communion t.,** la Sainte Table; (*c*) *Geog:* **T. Mountain,** la Montagne de la Table. **2.** *Fig:* **to turn the tables on s.o.,** retourner un argument contre qn; retourner la situation; **the tables are turned,** les rôles sont renversés. **3.** *Tchn:* console *f*, plateau *m* (de machine-outil); banc *m*, table (de machine à percer). **4.** plaque *f*, tablette *f* (de marbre, d'ivoire); *B.Hist:* **the Tables of the Law,** les Tables de la loi. **5.** *Geog:* plateau *m*. **6.** (*list*) table, tableau *m*, répertoire *m*; **t. of contents,** table des matières; *Mth:* **multiplication t.,** table de multiplication; *Nau:* **tide t.,** annuaire *m*, indicateur *m*, des marées; *Rail: etc:* **t. of fares, of charges,** barème *m* des prix.

table² *v.tr.* **1.** (*a*) *Parl:* présenter (une motion); **to t. a bill,** (i) déposer un projet de loi sur le bureau; (ii) *NAm:* ajourner (indéfiniment) un projet de loi; **to t. a motion of confidence,** poser la question de confiance; (*b*) *Cards:* jouer (une carte). **2.** dresser une liste; classifier (des résultats).

tableau, *pl.* **-eaux** ['tæblou, -ouz] *n. Th:* tableau *m*; **t. vivant** [vi'vɑ̃:], tableau vivant.

tablecloth ['teiblklɔθ] *n.* nappe *f*.

table d'hôte ['tɑ:bl'dout] *n.* table *f* d'hôte; **t. d'h. dinner,** dîner *m* à prix fixe.

tableland ['teibllænd] *n. Geog:* plateau *m*.

tablespoon ['teiblspu:n] *n.* cuiller *f*, cuillère *f*, à servir.

tablespoonful ['teiblspu:nful] *n.* cuillerée *f* à soupe.

tablet ['tæblit] *n.* **1.** plaque commémorative; *Ecc:* **votive t.,** ex-voto *m inv.* **2.** *Pharm:* comprimé *m*, cachet *m*. **3.** pain *m* (de savon); tablette *f* (de chocolat).

tableware ['teiblwεər] *n.* articles *mpl* de table.

tabloid ['tæblɔid] *n. Journ:* (*a*) **news in t. form,** nouvelles *fpl* en condensé; (*b*) **t. (newspaper),** tabloïd *m*.

taboo¹ [tə'bu:] *Anthr: etc:* **1.** *n.* tabou *m*, *pl.* -ous. **2.** *a.* tabou (*often inv. in pl.*); **to declare s.o., sth., t.,** déclarer qn, qch., tabou; tabou(is)er qn, qch.; *Fig:* **these subjects are t.,** ces sujets sont tabou(s).

taboo² *v.tr. Anthr: etc:* tabou(is)er (qn, qch.); déclarer (qn, qch.) tabou.

tabu [tə'bu:] *a. & n. Anthr:* = TABOU.

tabular ['tæbjulər] *a.* **1.** disposé en table(s), en tableau(x); **statistics in t. form,** statistique sous forme de tableau. **2.** (*of surface, crystal*) tabulaire.

tabulate ['tæbjuleit] *v.tr.* disposer (des chiffres, des faits) en forme de table(s), de tableau(x); classifier (des résultats); cataloguer (des marchandises).

tabulation [tæbju'leiʃ(ə)n] *n.* arrangement *m*, disposition *f* (de chiffres, etc.) en tables, en tableau(x); classification *f* (de résultats); tabulation *f*.

tabulator ['tæbjuleitər] *n. Typewr:* tabulateur *m*; *Cmptr:* tabulatrice *f*.

tachograph ['tækougræf] *n. Aut:* tachygraphe *m*.

tachometer [tæ'kɔmitər] *n.* tachymètre *m*.

tachymeter [tæ'kimitər] n. *Surv:* tachéomètre *m*.

tacit ['tæsit] *a.* (aveu) tacite. **-ly** *adv.* tacitement.

taciturn ['tæsitə:n] *a.* taciturne.

taciturnity [tæsi'tə:niti] *n.* taciturnité *f*.

tack¹ [tæk] *n.* **1.** (*a*) petit clou; pointe *f*; broquette *f*; semence *f* (de tapissier); *F:* **to get down to brass tacks,** en venir au fait; arriver à la réalité; (*b*) *NAm:* punaise *f*. **2.** *Needlew:* point *m* de bâti. **3.** *Nau:* (*a*) (i) amure *f*, (ii) point *m* d'amure (d'une voile); (*b*) bord *m*, bordée *f*; **to be, sail, run, on the starboard, port, t.,** être, courir, faire route, tribord amures, bâbord amures; *F:* **to be on the right t.,** être sur la bonne voie; **to be on the wrong t.,** faire fausse route; **let's try another t.,** essayons une autre tactique.

tack² **1.** *v.tr.* (*a*) **to t. sth. (down),** clouer qch. avec des broquettes; *F:* **to t. sth. (on) to sth.,** attacher, joindre, qch. à qch.; (*b*) *Needlew:* faufiler, bâtir; pointer. **2.** *v.i. Nau:* (*a*) virer de bord vent devant; **to t. to port,** virer (de bord) sur bâbord; (*b*) tirer des bordées; louvoyer. **3.** *v.i. F:* (*of pers.*) **to t. on to s.o.,** se coller à qn. **tacking** *n.* **1.** (*a*) clouage *m*; (*b*) *Needlew:* bâti *m*; faufilure *f*. **2.** *Nau:* virement *m* de bord; **t. (about),** louvoiement *m*.

tack³ *n. F:* nourriture *f*, aliment *m*; **hard t.,** biscuit *m* de mer.

tack⁴ *n. Equit:* sellerie *f*; **t. room,** sellerie.

tackiness ['tækinis] *n.* adhésivité *f*.

tackle¹ ['tækl] *n.* **1.** (*a*) attirail *m*, appareil *m*; **fishing t.,** articles *mpl* de pêche. **2.** *Nau: etc:* palan *m*; **single t.,** palan simple. **3.** *Fb:* arrêt *m*; *Rugby Fb:* plaquage *m*; (*hockey, etc.*) interception *f*; accrochage *m*.

tackle² *v.tr.* (*a*) empoigner; saisir (qn) à bras-le-corps; *Sp:* intercepter, *Rugby Fb:* plaquer; *Fig:* **to t. s.o. about sth.,** entreprendre qn sur qch.; (*b*) attaquer, s'attaquer à (sa nourriture, une question); aborder (un problème, etc.); **I don't know how to t. it,** je ne sais pas comment m'y prendre. **tackling** *n.* (*a*) *Sp:* arrêt *m* sur un homme; *Rugby Fb:* plaquage *m*; (*b*) entreprise *f* (d'une besogne).

tackler ['tæklər] *n. Sp:* (*hockey, etc.*) intercepteur, -trice; *Rugby Fb:* plaqueur *m*.

tacky¹ ['tæki] *a.* collant; (vernis) presque sec.

tacky² *a. NAm: F:* piteux, minable; (*of pers.*) mal fagoté.

tact [tækt] *n.* tact *m*; doigté *m*, savoir-faire *m*; **a matter requiring t.,** une question de doigté.

tactful ['tæktf(u)l] *a.* (homme) de tact; **to be t.,** avoir du tact; **I'll drop him a t. hint,** je vais lui en toucher quelques mots délicats. **-fully** *adv.* avec tact.

tactfulness ['tæktf(u)lnis] *n.* (*of pers.*) tact *m*.

tactic ['tæktik] *n.* tactique *f*, manœuvre *f*.

tactical ['tæktik(ə)l] *a.* **1.** tactique; *Mil etc:* **t. mistake,** erreur *f* (de) tactique. **2.** (*of pers., conduct*) adroit. **-ally** *adv.* du point de vue de la tactique.

tactician [tæk'tiʃ(ə)n] *n. Mil: etc:* tacticien, -ienne.

tactics ['tæktiks] *n.pl. Mil: etc:* tactique *f*; **to resort to new t.,** avoir recours à une tactique nouvelle.

tactile ['tæktail] *a. Biol:* tactile.

tactless ['tæktlis] *a.* (*a*) (*of pers.*) qui manque de tact, de savoir-faire, de doigté; (*b*) **t. question,** question indiscrète. **-ly** *adv.* sans tact.

tadpole ['tædpoul] *n. Amph:* têtard *m*.

taffeta ['tæfitə] *n. Tex:* taffetas *m*.

taffrail ['tæfreil] *n. N.Arch:* lisse *f* de couronnement (de la poupe).

taffy¹ ['tæfi] *n. NAm:* **1.** (pâte à) berlingot(s) *m(pl)*. **2.** *P:* flagornerie *f*.

Taffy² *n. F:* Gallois *m*.

tag¹ [tæg] *n.* **1.** (*a*) morceau *m* (de ruban, d'étoffe) qui pend; (*b*) tirant *m* (de botte); (*c*) étiquette *f*; *U.S: Aut:* **license t.,** plaque *f* d'immatriculation; (*d*) *NAm:* insigne *m*, cocarde *f*; **t. day,** jour *m* de quête (pour une œuvre de bienfaisance); (*e*) ferret *m* (de lacet, etc.); (*f*) (bout *m* de la) queue (d'un animal). **2.** (*a*) *Th:* (i) discours adressé au public après la représentation; (ii) *F:* **t. (line),** mot *m* de la fin; (*b*) *Lit:* cheville (ajoutée à un vers.). **3.** (*a*) cliché *m*; **old t.,** vieille rengaine; (*b*) refrain *m* (d'une chanson). **4. t. end,** bout (d'un morceau d'étoffe); queue (d'une affaire, etc.); bribes *fpl* (d'une conversation).

tag² *v.* **(tagged) 1.** *v.tr.* (*a*) aiguilleter, ferrer (un lacet); (*b*) étiqueter (des marchandises, etc.); *U.S:* attacher une contravention, *F:* un papillon, à (une voiture); (*c*) *F:* **to t. sth. on to sth.,** attacher qch. à qch. **2.** *v.i.* **to t. along,** traîner (**behind s.o.,** derrière qn); **to t. after s.o.,** suivre qn (de près); **to t. on to s.o.,** s'attacher, *F:* coller, à qn.

tag³ *n.* (jeu *m* de) chat *m*.

tag⁴ *v.tr.* **(tagged)** toucher (qn) au jeu de chat; *Baseball:* éliminer (un coureur) en le touchant avec la balle.

Tahitian [tɑː'hiːʃən] **1.** *a. Geog:* tahitien. **2.** *n.* (*a*) Tahitien, -ienne; (*b*) *Ling:* tahitien *m*.

taiga ['taigɑː] *n. Geog:* taïga *f*.

tail¹ [teil] *n.* **1.** (*a*) queue *f* (d'animal, etc.); (*of peacock*) **to spread its t.,** faire la roue; *F:* **the tail's wagging the dog,** les subordonnés l'emportent sur les chefs; **with his t. between his legs,** (i) (*of dog*) la queue entre les jambes; (ii) (*of pers.*) l'oreille basse; *F:* (*of pers.*) **sitting on his t.,** assis sur son derrière; **to keep one's t. up,** ne pas se laisser abattre; **to turn t.,** montrer les talons; **story with a sting in the t.,** histoire avec une méchanceté finale; *Orn:* **t. feather,** (penne) rectrice *f*; (*b*) queue (de cerf-volant, etc.); natte *f* (de cheveux); *Cost:* traîne *f* (d'une jupe); pan *m* (de chemise); **coat tails,** queue, basques *fpl*, pans, d'un habit; **to wear tails,** porter l'habit à queue; (*c*) *Av:* queue (d'un avion); **t. spin,** (descente *f* en) vrille *f*; *F:* (*of pers.*) **to go, get, into a t. spin,** s'affoler, paniquer; **t. fin,** (plan *m* de) dérive *f*; (*d*) arrière *m* (d'une voiture, d'un ski, etc.); **to be on s.o.'s t.,** suivre qn de près; (*of detective*) filer qn; **t. end,** bout *m*; queue (d'un défilé, etc.); fin (d'un orage); **t. wind,** vent *m* arrière; **t. light, lamp,** *Aut:* feu *m* arrière; *Rail:* fanal *m* de queue; (*e*) pied *m* (d'une page, etc.); (*f*) **to look at s.o. out of the t. of one's eye,** regarder qn de côté: (*g*) *Hyd.E:* aval *m* (d'une écluse); **t. gate,** porte *f* d'aval; (*h*) suite *f*, escorte *f* (d'un chef de clan); adhérents *mpl* (d'un chef politique); (*i*) **the t. of the class,** la queue de la classe. **2.** *F:* fileur *m*; **we've got a t.,** quelqu'un nous file. **3.** (*of coin*) pile *f*, revers *m*.

tail² **1.** *v.tr.* (*a*) mettre une queue à (un cerf-volant, etc.); **to t. sth. on to sth.,** attacher qch. derrière qch.; (*b*) couper la queue à (un agneau); enlever les queues, équeuter (des cerises, etc.); (*c*) *F:* (*of detective, etc.*) filer (qn). **2.** *v.i.* **to t. after s.o.,** (i) suivre qn de près; (ii) (*of several persons*) suivre qn à la queue leu leu. **tail away** *v.i.* (*a*) (*of competitors in a race, etc.*) s'espacer, s'égrener; (*of column on the march*) s'allonger; (*b*) diminuer, décroître; (*c*) finir en queue de poisson. **tailed** *a.* (*a*) à queue; (*b*) **long-t.,** à longue queue. **tail off** *v.i.* = TAIL AWAY.

tailback ['teilbæk] *n. Aut:* bouchon *m*; **3-mile t.,** bouchon de 5 kilomètres.

tailboard ['teilbɔːd] *n.* hayon *m* arrière.

tailgate¹ ['teilgeit] *n.* (a) porte *f* à rabattement arrière (d'un camion); (*b*) hayon *m* arrière (d'une voiture).

tailgate², *v.tr. NAm: F:* suivre (une voiture) de (trop) près; *F:* coller (une voiture).

tailless ['teillis] *a.* sans queue.

tailor¹ ['teilər] *n.* tailleur *m* (d'habits); **tailor's chalk,** craie *f* de tailleur, de Meudon.

tailor² *v.tr.* (*a*) faire, façonner (un complet, etc.); **(woman's) tailored suit,** (costume *m*) tailleur *m*; **tailored shirt,** chemise cintrée; (*b*) **to t. sth. for a special purpose,** faire qch. pour un usage spécial. **tailoring** *n.* **1.** métier *m* de tailleur. **2.** ouvrage *m* de tailleur; **to do dressmaking and t.,** faire le flou et le tailleur.

tailormade ['teiləmeid] *a.* (*a*) (*of suit, etc.*) fait sur mesure; (*b*) adapté aux besoins particuliers de l'utilisateur; (outil) spécial; **it's t. for me,** c'est fait pour moi; c'est juste ce qu'il me faut.

tailpiece ['teilpiːs] *n.* **1.** queue *f*; contre-tige *f*, *pl.* contre-tiges (de piston). **2.** *Mus:* cordier *m* (de violon, etc.). **3.** *Typ:* cul-de-lampe *m*, *pl.* culs-de-lampe.

tailrace ['teilreis] *n.* bief *m* d'aval (d'un moulin).

taint¹ [teint] *n.* **1.** (*a*) corruption *f*, infection *f*; (*b*) **the t. of sin,** la tache, la souillure, du péché. **2.** tare *f* héréditaire. **3.** trace *f* (d'infection, etc.); **book with no t. of bias,** livre *m* sans trace de préjugés.

taint² **1.** *v.tr.* infecter (l'air); infecter, vicier, corrompre (les esprits, les mœurs); gâter (la nourriture). **2.** *v.i.* se corrompre; se gâter. **tainted** *a.* (*a*) infecté, corrompu; **t. heredity,** hérédité chargée; *Jur:* **t. with fraud,** entaché de dol; (*b*) (*of meat*) qui a un mauvais goût.

take¹ [teik] *n.* **1.** *Cin:* prise *f* de vue(s); *Rec:* enregistrement *m*. **2.** (*a*) prise (de gibier, poisson); (*b*) *NAm:* recette *f*, produit *m* (d'un magasin, etc.); (*c*) *F:* **to be on the t.,** être corruptible, vénal.

take² *v.* (*p.t.* **took** [tuk]; *p.p.* **taken** ['teik(ə)n]) prendre. **I.** *v.tr.* **1.** (*a*) **to t. sth. in one's hand,** prendre qch. dans la main; **to t. sth. again,** reprendre qch.; (*b*) **to t. sth. from s.o.,** enlever, prendre, ôter, qch. à qn; **to t. one number from another,** soustraire un nombre d'un autre; **to t. sth. from the table, out of a drawer,** prendre qch. sur la table, dans un tiroir; **to t. a saucepan off the heat,** retirer une casserole du feu; (*c*) **to t. (hold of) s.o., sth.,** saisir, empoigner, se saisir de, s'emparer de, qn, qch.; **she took my arm,** elle m'a pris le bras; **he took her in his arms,** il l'a prise dans ses bras; *F:* **to t. a woman,** prendre une femme; **to t. the opportunity to do sth., of doing sth.,** profiter de l'occasion pour faire qch.; **to t. a chance,** risquer le coup; (*d*) prendre (une ville); prendre, attraper (un poisson); **to t. s.o. prisoner,** faire qn prisonnier; **to t. s.o. by surprise,** prendre qn à l'improviste, surprendre qn; **the devil t. him!** que le diable l'emporte! *Chess: etc:* **to t. a piece,** prendre une pièce; **to be taken ill,** tomber malade; **he was very much taken with the idea,** l'idée l'enchantait; **I was not taken with him,** il ne m'a pas fait bonne impression; (*e*) **to t. a passage from a book,** emprunter un passage à un livre; **word taken from the Latin,** mot emprunté du latin. **2.** (*a*) louer (une maison); prendre, louer (une voiture); (*b*) prendre (un billet, etc.); **all the seats are taken,** toutes les places sont prises; (*of seat, table*) **taken,** occupé; **what paper do you t.?** quel journal lisez-vous? (*c*) **to t. a seat,** s'asseoir; **t. your seats!** prenez vos places! (*d*) **he took the road to London,** il a pris la route de Londres; **t. the turning on the left,** prenez à gauche; *Sp:* **to t. an obstacle,** franchir, sauter, un obstacle; **to t. a corner at full speed,** prendre un virage à toute vitesse; (*e*) **to t. legal advice,** consulter un avocat; (*f*) **to t. holy orders,** recevoir les ordres. **3.** (*a*) gagner, remporter (le prix); **to t. the first prize in Latin,** obtenir le premier prix de latin; *Cards:* **to t. a trick,** faire une levée; (*b*) passer, se présenter à (un examen); **to t., be taking, law,** faire son droit; **I didn't t. Latin at school,** je n'ai pas fait de latin au lycée; (*c*) *Com: etc:* **to t. so much a week,** faire (une recette de) tant par semaine. **4.** prendre (de la nourriture, un médicament, etc.); (*of fish*) **to t. the hook, the bait,** mordre à l'hameçon; **to t. something to drink,** prendre quelque chose à boire; **do you t. sugar?** prenez-vous du sucre? **not to be taken internally,** médicament pour usage externe. **5.** (*a*) faire (une promenade, un voyage); prendre (un bain, un congé); **to t. a nap,** faire un petit somme; **to t. a few steps,** faire quelques pas; *Fb:* **penalty shot taken by X,** penalty botté par X; **to t. a print from a negative,** tirer une épreuve d'un cliché; **to t. notes,** prendre des notes; (*b*) prendre (une photo); **to have one's photograph taken,** se faire photographier; (*c*) **to t. sth. apart, to pieces,** démonter qch. **6.** *Ecc:* **to t. a service,** célébrer un office; *Sch:* **he takes them in English,** il fait la classe d'anglais. **7.** (*a*) prendre, accepter, recevoir; **t. it or leave it!** c'est à prendre ou à laisser; **to take a beating,** recevoir une rossée; **t. that (and that)!** attrape (ça et ça)! **what will you t. for it?** combien en voulez-vous? **to t. a bet,** tenir un pari; **to t. all responsibility,** assumer toute la responsabilité; **we must t. things as we find them, as they come,** il faut prendre les choses comme elles sont; **t. it from me!** croyez-moi! **to t. s.o. seriously,** prendre qn au sérieux; **to t. s.o., sth., the wrong way,** mal comprendre qn, qch.; **I wonder how he'll t. it,** je me demande quelle tête il fera; **he can't t. a joke,** il n'entend pas la plaisanterie; **I can't t. any more,** je n'en peux plus; **I can't t. any more of him,** je ne peux plus le supporter; (*b*) **cotton does not t. dyes well,** le coton est réfractaire à la teinture; **surface that will t. a high polish,** surface qui prend un beau poli; (*c*) (*of mare*) **to t. the stallion,** souffrir l'étalon; (*d*) **bus that takes twenty passengers,** autobus qui tient vingt voyageurs; **the petrol tank takes 40 litres,** le réservoir à essence a une capacité de 40 litres; (*of crane, engine, etc.*) **to t. heavy loads,** supporter de fortes charges. **8. to t. a dislike to s.o.,** prendre qn en aversion, en grippe; **to t. a decision about sth.,** prendre une décision touchant, quant à, qch. **9.** (*a*) **t. (for example) the pensioners,** prenez (par exemple) les, le cas des, retraités; **to t. the news as, to be, true,** tenir la nouvelle pour vraie; **how old do you t. him to be?** quel âge lui donnez-vous? **I t. it that you agree,** je suppose que vous êtes d'accord; (*b*) **to t. one person, one thing, for another,** prendre une personne, une chose, pour une autre; **I took you for an Englishman,** je vous croyais anglais; *F:* **what do you t. me for?** pour qui me prenez-vous? **10.** (*a*) (*of journey, etc.*) prendre (du temps); (*of engine, etc.*) user, consommer (du charbon, etc.); **that will t. some explaining,** voilà qui va demander des explications; **the work took some doing,** le travail a été difficile; **it will t. him two hours,** il en aura pour deux heures; **how long does it t. to go there?** combien de temps faut-il pour y aller? **it would t. hours to relate,** il faudrait des heures pour le raconter; **it took me, I took, two years to do it,** cela m'a pris, il m'a fallu, deux ans pour le faire; **it takes a clever man to do that,** bien habile qui peut le faire; *F:* **he hasn't got what it takes to be a leader,** il lui manque ce qu'il faut pour être un chef; **she's got what it takes,** elle a du sex-appeal; (*b*) *Gram:* **verb that takes a preposition,** verbe qui veut la préposition; **noun that takes an "s" in the plural,** nom qui prend un "s" au pluriel; (*c*) **to t. tens in shoes,** chausser du dix. **11.** (*a*) (*lead*) conduire, mener, emmener; prendre (qn avec soi); **to t. oneself to bed,** aller se coucher; **to t. the dog for a walk,** promener le chien; **to t. s.o. (along) with one,** emmener qn avec soi; **to t. s.o. round a museum,** faire faire la visite d'un musée à qn; **to t. s.o. across the road,** conduire qn de l'autre côté de la rue; (*b*) (*carry*) **to t. sth. to s.o.,** porter qch. à qn; **t. some food with you,** emportez des provisions; **to t. s.o. to hospital,** transporter qn à l'hôpital; *F:* **you can't t. it with you,** vous n'emporterez pas votre fortune avec vous; (*c*) **his father took a stick to him,** son père lui a donné des coups de bâton. **II.** *v.i.* (*a*) avoir du succès; réussir; prendre; **this play won't t.,** cette pièce ne passera pas la rampe; (*b*) (*of vaccine, graft*) prendre; (*c*) **the fire took at once,** le feu a pris tout de suite. **take after** *v.i.* **to t. after s.o.,** ressembler à qn, tenir de qn. **take away** *v.tr.* (*a*) enlever, emporter (qch.); emmener (qn); **sandwiches to t. away,** sandwichs à emporter; (*on book in library*) **not to be taken away,** exclu du prêt; (*b*) **to t. away a knife from a child,** ôter un couteau à un enfant; (*c*) **to t. away sth. from sth.,** ôter, retrancher, qch. de qch.; *Mth:* soustraire (un nombre d'un autre); (*d*) **to t. a child away from school,** retirer un enfant de l'école. **take back** *v.tr.* (*a*) reconduire, remmener (qn, un cheval, etc.); **that takes me back to my childhood,** cela me rappelle mon enfance; (*b*) **to take a book back to s.o.,** reporter un livre à qn; (*c*) *Typ:* transférer (un mot) à la ligne précédente; (*d*) reprendre (un ancien employé, *Com:* les invendus); (*e*) **I t. back what I said,** je retire ce que j'ai dit; **I t. it all back,** mettons que je n'aie rien dit. **take down** *v.tr.* (*a*) descendre, décrocher (un tableau, etc.); (*b*) démolir (un mur); démonter (une machine); (*c*) *F:* **to t. s.o. down (a peg or two),** remettre qn à sa place, rabattre le caquet à qn; (*d*) noter, inscrire (un nom, etc.); prendre (des notes); **to t. down a letter in shorthand,** prendre une lettre en sténo. **take in** *v.tr.* (*a*) faire entrer (qn); (*b*) rentrer (les chaises, le linge, etc.); rentrer (la moisson); *Nau:* **to t. in water,** (*of boat*) faire eau; avoir une voie d'eau; (*c*) (*admit, receive*) recueillir, donner asile à (un réfugié, etc.); héberger, loger (qn); prendre (des locataires); **to t. in washing,** faire des lessives; (*d*) *A: & NAm:* **to t. in a paper,** prendre (régulièrement) un journal; (*of yearly subscriber, etc.*) être abonné à un journal; (*e*) rentrer, reprendre (une couture); serrer (une manche); (*f*) *Nau:* carguer (une voile); **to t. in sail,** diminuer de voile(s); (*g*) comprendre, inclure, englober; **tour which takes in all the important towns,** excursion qui passe par toutes les villes importantes; (*h*) comprendre, se rendre compte de (qch.); **to t. in the situation,** juger la situation; **to t. in everything at a glance,** tout embrasser d'un coup d'œil; (*i*) *F:* (*believe*) **he takes it all in,** il prend tout ça pour argent comptant; il gobe tout ce qu'on lui dit; (*j*) **to be taken in,** se laisser attraper; **I've been taken in,** on m'a eu, roulé; **to allow oneself to be taken in,** se laisser duper, tromper. **take off 1.** *v.tr.* (*prep. use*) **to t. s.o.'s attention off sth.,** distraire l'attention de qn; **he never took his eyes off us,** il ne nous quittait pas de yeux; **to t. s.o. off a list,** rayer qn (d'une liste). **2.** *v.tr.* (*adv. use*) (*a*) enlever, ôter, emporter, retirer (qch.); *Surg:* amputer (une jambe, etc.); **to t. off one's clothes,** se déshabiller; **to t. off one's gloves,** se déganter; **to t. off one's coat,** enlever son manteau; *Tp:* **to t. off the receiver,** décrocher le récepteur; *Aut: etc:* **to t. off the brake,** desserrer le frein; (*b*) emmener (qn); **to t. oneself off,** s'en aller, *F:* décamper; (*c*) **to t. off £10 from the total,** défalquer dix livres du total; **to t. so much off (the price of sth.),** rabattre tant (sur le prix de qch.); (*d*) supprimer (un train, un malaise, etc.); (*e*) imiter, singer (qn); copier les gestes, les manières, de (qn); (*f*) **to t. three days off,** prendre trois jours de congé. **3.** *v.i.* (*a*) (*of athlete, etc.*) prendre son élan, s'élancer (**from,** de); (*b*) *Av:* décoller, s'envoler; (*c*) *F:* (*of pers.*) s'en aller, décamper, filer. **take on 1.** *v.tr.* (*a*) se charger de, entreprendre (un travail); assumer (une responsabilité); (*b*) accepter le défi de (qn); **to t. s.o. on at tennis,** engager une partie de tennis avec qn; (*c*) engager, embaucher (un ouvrier); (*d*) prendre, revêtir, affecter (une couleur, l'apparence de qch.); **the word takes on another meaning,** le mot prend une autre signification; (*e*) (*of train, etc.*) **to t. on passengers,** prendre des voyageurs; (*f*) mener (qn) plus loin; mener (qn) au delà de sa destination. **2.** *v.i.* *F:* laisser éclater son chagrin; **don't t. on so!** ne vous désolez pas comme ça! **take out** *v.tr.* (*a*) **to t. sth. out,** sortir qch. (**of,** de); arracher (une dent); ôter, enlever (une tache); (*b*) *F:* **to t. it out of s.o.,** épuiser, éreinter, qn; **don't t. it out on me,** ne vous en prenez pas à moi; (*c*) **to t. s.o. out of himself,** faire oublier soi-même à qn; (*d*) *NAm:* **sandwiches to t. out,** sandwichs à emporter; (*e*) faire sortir (qn); promener, sortir (le chien); **he's going to t. me out to dinner,** il va m'emmener dîner; (*f*) prendre, obtenir (un brevet, permis, etc.); souscrire (une police d'assurance). **take over** *v.tr.* (*a*) prendre possession de (qch.); **to t. over a business,** prendre la suite des affaires; **to rent a flat and t. over the furniture,** louer un appartement avec une reprise de meubles; **to t. over power,** prendre possession du pouvoir; *v.i.* **to t. over from s.o.,** relever, remplacer, qn (dans ses fonctions); (*b*) (i) transporter (qn, qch.); (ii) transborder (des marchandises); (iii) *Typ:* transférer (un mot) à la ligne suivante. **take to** *v.i.* (*a*) **to t. to flight,** prendre la fuite; **to t. to the mountains,** se réfugier dans les montagnes; **to t. to the bush,** prendre le maquis; **to t. to the road again,** reprendre la route; (*b*) (i) **to t. to bad habits,** prendre de mauvaises habitudes; **to t. to drink, to drinking,** se mettre à boire; (ii) **to t. to writing,** se mettre à écrire; se faire écrivain; (*c*) **to t. to s.o.,** éprouver de la sympathie pour qn; **I took to him at once,** il me fut sympathique dès l'abord; **I didn't t. to him,** il ne m'était pas sympathique; **to t. to a game,** prendre goût à un jeu. **take up 1.** *v.tr.* (*a*) relever, ramasser (qch.); **to t. up a book from the table,** prendre un livre sur la table; (*b*) enlever, déclouer (un tapis); enlever (des pavés, des rails); dépaver, défoncer (une rue); (*c*) faire monter (qn) (dans sa chambre); **there's a lift to t. you up,** vous pouvez monter en ascenseur; (*d*) *Rail: etc:* **to stop to t. up passengers,** s'arrêter pour prendre des voyageurs; (*e*) *Dressm:* raccourcir (une jupe); (*f*) **to t. up the slack in a cable,** retendre un câble; *Cin:* **to t. up the film,** enrouler la bande; (*g*) absorber (de l'eau). **2.** *v.tr.* (*a*) *Com:* honorer (un effet); *St.Exch:* souscrire à (des actions); **to t. up an option,** lever une prime; (*b*) relever (un défi); **to t. up a bet,** tenir un pari; (*c*) adopter (une idée); suivre (un conseil); **to t. up an attitude on sth.,** prendre, adopter, une attitude à l'égard de qch.; (*d*) aborder la discussion (d'une question); **I will not t. up the matter,** je ne veux pas entrer dans l'affaire; (*e*) embrasser, suivre (une carrière); s'adonner à (une occupation); adopter (une méthode); épouser (une querelle); **he has taken up photography,** il fait de la photographie; **to t. up one's duties again,** reprendre ses fonctions; (*f*) prendre (qn) sous sa protection; (*g*) **to t. s.o. up on sth.,** prendre qn au mot; **I'll t. you up on that,** (i) je vous prendrai au mot sur cela; (ii) je vous défie de prouver, justifier, cela; **to t. s.o. up sharply,** reprendre qn vertement; **to t. s.o. up short,** couper la parole à qn; (*h*) (i) **to t. up too much room,** occuper trop de place; être encombrant; (ii) **to t. up all s.o.'s attention, time,** absorber l'attention, le temps, de qn; (iii) (*in the passive*) **he is entirely taken up with his business,** il est entièrement absorbé dans son commerce. **3.** *v.i.* **to t. up with s.o.,** se mettre à fréquenter qn. **taking 1.** *a.* (style, titre) attrayant; (visage) séduisant; **t. manners, ways,** manières engageantes. **2.** *n.* (*a*) prise *f* (d'une ville, etc.); arrestation *f* (d'un voleur); *Med:* prélèvement *m* (de sang, etc.); (*b*) *Com:* **takings,** recette *f*.

takeaway [ˈteikəwei] *n.* *F:* (*a*) magasin *m* qui vend des sandwichs, mets, repas, à emporter; (*b*) sandwich *m*, mets *m*, repas *m*, etc., à emporter.

take-home [ˈteikhoum] *a.* **t.-h. pay,** salaire reçu (moins impôt retenu à la source, etc.).

take-in [ˈteikin] *n.* *F:* attrape *f*, duperie *f*.

takeoff [ˈteikɔf] *n.* **1.** imitation *f*, caricature *f*, charge *f* (de qn). **2.** (*a*) élan *m*; **to step back to get a better t.,** reculer pour mieux sauter; (*b*) *Av:* décollage *m*, envol *m*. **3.** *Sp:* point *m*, ligne *f*, de départ; appel *m*.

takeover [ˈteikouvər] *n.* (*a*) **t. (of power),** prise *f* de possession du pouvoir; (*b*) prise de contrôle, achat *m* (d'une société); **t. bid,** offre publique d'achat.

taker [ˈteikər] *n.* (*a*) preneur, -euse (d'un bail); acceptant, -ante (d'une offre); **at that price there were no takers,** à ce prix on n'a pas trouvé d'acheteurs; **any takers?** est-ce qu'il y a des amateurs? (*b*) *St.Exch:* preneur (d'une lettre de change); **t. (in),** reporteur *m* (de titres); **t. of an option,** optant *m*.

take-up [ˈteikʌp] *n.* (*a*) *Mec.E:* rattrapage *m* (du jeu); compensation *f*; (*b*) *Cin: Cmptr:* enroulement *m*; **t.-up spool, reel,** bobine réceptrice; enrouleuse *f*.

talc [tælk] *n.* (*a*) talc *m*; (*b*) *Toil:* (poudre *f* de) talc.

talcum [ˈtælkəm] *n.* **t. (powder),** (poudre *f* de) talc.

tale [teil] *n.* **1.** (*a*) conte *m*, récit *m*; **old wives' tales,** contes de bonne femme; **thereby hangs a t.,** il y a là-dessus toute une histoire; **his drawn face told the t. of his sufferings,** ses traits tirés en disaient long sur ses souffrances; **he lived to tell the t.,** il a survécu; (*b*) *Lit:* nouvelle *f*, conte. **2.** *Pej:* (*a*) racontar *m*, potin *m*, on-dit *m inv*; **this is the t. that is going about,** voilà ce qu'on raconte; (*b*) rapport *m*, cafardage *m*; **to tell tales,** rapporter, cafarder.

talebearer [ˈteilbɛərər] *n.* rapporteur, -euse; cafard, -e.

talebearing [ˈteilbɛəriŋ] *n.* = TALETELLING.

talent [ˈtælənt] *n.* **1.** *Ant:* talent *m*; **gold, silver, t.,** talent d'or, d'argent. **2.** talent; aptitude *f*; **to have a t. for doing the right thing,** avoir le don d'agir à propos; **he has no t. for business,** il manque de talent pour les affaires. **3.** (*a*) personne bien douée; *Pol: etc:* **to call upon all the talents,** faire appel à tous les talents; (*b*) *coll.* gens *mpl* de talent; *F:* **t. scout, spotter,** dénicheur, -euse, de talent(s), de vedettes.

talented ['tæləntid] *a.* qui a du talent; (enfant, etc.) (bien) doué; (écrivain, etc.) de talent, de valeur.

taleteller ['teiltelər] *n.* **1.** conteur, -euse, d'histoires. **2.** rapporteur, -euse.

taletelling ['teiltelìŋ] *n.* rapportage *m*, cafardage *m.*

talisman ['tælizmən] *n.* talisman *m.*

talk[1] [tɔːk] *n.* **1.** (*a*) paroles *fpl*; **he's all t.,** ce n'est qu'un bavard; (*b*) bruit *m*, dires *mpl*, racontages *mpl*; **there is some t. of his returning,** il est question qu'il revienne; le bruit court qu'il va revenir; **there has been t. of it,** on en a parlé; il en a été question; **it's all t.,** tout ça c'est des racontars; (*c*) propos *mpl*; bavardage *m*; **idle t.,** paroles en l'air; balivernes *fpl*; **small t.,** conversation banale; banalités *fpl*; **to indulge, engage, in small t.,** causer de choses et d'autres; **double t.,** propos (i) ambigus, (ii) insincères; (*d*) langage *m* (des marins, etc.); **baby t.,** babil enfantin. **2.** (*a*) entretien *m*, conversation *f*; causerie *f*; **to have a t. with s.o.,** s'entretenir avec qn; (*b*) *Pol: etc:* **talks,** dialogue *m*, pourparlers *mpl*; **to start talks,** engager le dialogue; entrer en pourparlers; (*c*) causerie; **to give a t. on, about, sth.,** faire une causerie sur qch.; *T.V:* **t. show,** émission *f* de bavardages; talk-show *m.* **3. it's the t. of the town,** c'est la fable, le bruit, de la ville; **she's the t. of the town,** elle défraie la chronique.

talk[2] **1.** *v.i.* (*a*) parler; **to learn to t.,** apprendre à parler; (*b*) parler, discourir; **to t. and t.,** parler sans arrêt; *F:* **that's no way to t.!** (i) en voilà un langage! (ii) il ne faut pas dire des choses pareilles! **he likes to hear himself t.,** il aime à s'entendre parler; **to t. through one's hat,** dire, débiter, des sottises; *do* **t. sense!** tu radotes! **now you're talking! that's the way to t.!** à la bonne heure! *you* **can, can't, t.!** c'est bien à vous de parler! **to t. of, about, sth.,** parler de qch.; **to t. of one thing and another, of this and that,** parler de choses et d'autres; **what are you talking about?** (i) de quoi parlez-vous? (ii) *F:* qu'est-ce que vous racontez? **he knows what he is talking about,** il s'y connaît; il sait ce qu'il dit; *F:* **t. about luck!** tu parles d'une chance! (*c*) **to t. of, about, doing sth.,** parler de faire qch.; (*d*) **to t. on the radio,** parler, faire un discours, à la radio; (*e*) **to make a prisoner t.,** faire avouer, confesser, un prisonnier; **his accomplices are afraid he'll t.,** ses complices craignent qu'il ne vende la mèche; (*f*) **to t. to, with, s.o.,** s'entretenir avec qn; parler à, avec, qn; **he never talked to me the whole evening,** il ne m'a pas dit un mot de la soirée; **to t. to oneself,** parler tout seul; monologuer; *F:* **who do you think you are talking to!** à qui croyez-vous donc parler? **to t. (severely) to s.o.,** réprimander, gronder, qn; *I'll* **t. to him!** je vais lui dire son fait! (*g*) **money talks,** l'argent veut tout dire; (*h*) jaser, bavarder, babiller; **she is always talking,** elle bavarde sans cesse; (*i*) cancaner; **people will t.,** (i) cela fera scandale; (ii) le monde est cancanier; **to get oneself talked about,** faire parler de soi; **the whole town was talking about it,** toute la ville en parlait. **2.** *v.tr.* (*a*) **to t. French,** parler français; (*b*) **to t. politics,** parler politique; **to t. (common) sense,** parler raison; **there is a great deal of nonsense talked about this matter,** on a dit beaucoup de sottises à ce sujet; (*c*) **to t. oneself hoarse,** s'enrouer à force de parler; **he talked himself into trouble,** ses discours imprudents finirent par le mettre dans le pétrin; (*d*) **to t. s.o. into, out of, doing sth.,** persuader, dissuader, qn de faire qch. **talk away** *v.tr.* (*a*) passer (le temps, la nuit, etc.) à parler, à bavarder; (*b*) **to t. a child's fears away,** chasser les craintes d'un enfant avec des paroles réconfortantes. **talk back** *v.i.* (*a*) *W.Tel:* (*on two-way radio*) répondre; (*b*) *NAm:* répondre d'une manière impertinente; répliquer. **talk down** **1.** *v.i.* **to t. down to one's audience,** se mettre à la portée de son auditoire (avec condescendance). **2.** *v.i.* (*a*) faire taire (qn), réduire (qn) au silence; (*b*) *Av:* donner des instructions d'atterrissage à (un avion). **talking** **1.** *a.* parlant; **t. doll,** poupée parlante; *Cin:* **t. film,** film parlant, parlé. **2.** *n.* (*a*) discours *mpl*, propos *mpl*, paroles *fpl*; **that's enough of t.,** c'est assez parlé; **t. point,** (i) bonne matière de discussion; (ii) bon argument; (*b*) (i) conversation *f*; (ii) bavardage *m*; **to do all the t.,** faire tous les frais de la conversation; **no t., please!** pas de bavardage! (*c*) **t.-to,** réprimande *f*, semonce *f*; **to give s.o. a good t.-to,** donner à qn une verte semonce. **talk out** *v.tr.* (*a*) **I want to t. things out with you,** je voudrais discuter la chose à fond; (*b*) *Parl:* **to t. a bill out,** prolonger les débats de façon qu'un projet de loi ne puisse être voté avant la clôture. **talk over** *v.tr.* discuter, débattre (une question); **let's t. it over,** discutons la chose. **talk round** *v.tr.* enjôler (qn); amener (qn) à changer d'avis; **I talked them round at last,** j'ai fini par les persuader.

talkative ['tɔːkətiv] *a.* causeur; jaseur, bavard, loquace; **she's very t.,** elle a la langue déliée.

talkativeness ['tɔːkətivnis] *n.* loquacité *f.*

talk-back ['tɔːkbæk] *n.* *W.Tel:* émetteur-récepteur *m*, *pl.* émetteurs-récepteurs.

talkdown ['tɔːkdaun] *n.* *Av:* atterrissage *m* par contrôle au sol.

talker ['tɔːkər] *n.* **1.** parleur, -euse; **brilliant t.,** personne *f* qui brille dans la conversation. **2.** bavard, -arde; **to be a great t.,** être bavard, avoir la langue bien pendue. **3.** fanfaron, -onne; vantard, -arde.

talkie ['tɔːki] *n.* *Cin: F: O:* film parlant, parlé.

tall [tɔːl] *a.* **1.** (*of pers.*) (*a*) grand; de haute taille; (*b*) **how t. are you?** quelle est votre taille? **she's taller than I am,** elle est plus grande que moi; **he was taller by a head, stood a (whole) head taller, than I,** il me dépassait de la tête; **she's growing taller,** elle se fait grande; **he has grown t.,** il a, est, grandi. **2.** (*of thg*) haut, élevé; **how t. is that mast?** quelle hauteur a ce mât? **tree fifty metres t.,** arbre qui a cinquante mètres de hauteur. **3.** *F:* (*a*) (histoire) incroyable, invraisemblable; **that's a t. story,** celle-là est raide, vous m'en contez de belles; **to tell t. stories,** *NAm:* **tales,** raconter des histoires invraisemblables; (*b*) **t. talk,** hâblerie *f*, vantardises *fpl*; (*c*) **that's a t. order,** voilà qui va être difficile, compliqué. **4.** *adv. F: O:* **to talk t.,** se vanter; hâbler; **to walk t.,** être fier.

tallboy ['tɔːlbɔi] *n.* *Furn:* commode *f* haute.

tallness ['tɔːlnis] *n.* (*a*) (*of pers.*) grande taille; (*b*) hauteur *f* (d'un édifice, etc.).

tallow ['tælou] *n.* (*a*) suif *m*; **t. candle,** chandelle *f*; (*b*) **vegetable t.,** suif végétal.

tally[1] ['tæli] *n.* **1.** pointage *m*; **to keep t. of goods, names,** pointer des marchandises, des noms (sur une liste); **t. clerk,** pointeur *m*, contrôleur *m* (de marchandises, etc.). **2.** (*a*) compte *m*; (*b*) *NAm:* (nombre *m* de) points *mpl* (dans un match). **3.** (*a*) étiquette *f*; (*b*) jeton *m* (de présence). **4.** pendant *m*, contrepartie *f* (d'un document).

tally[2] **1.** *v.tr.* pointer (des marchandises). **2.** *v.i.* correspondre (**with,** à); s'accorder (**with,** avec); **these accounts do not t.,** ces comptes ne s'accordent pas.

tally-ho [tæli'hou] *int. & n.* *Ven:* taïaut (*m*).

talon ['tælən] *n.* **1.** serre *f* (d'oiseau de proie); griffe *f* (de lion, etc.). **2.** *Arch:* talon *m*, doucine *f.* **3.** *Com:* **t. of a sheet of coupons,** talon de souche. **4.** *Games:* (*at cards, dominoes*) talon.

tamable ['teiməbl] *a.* = TAMEABLE.

tamarind ['tæmərind] *n. Bot:* **1.** tamarin *m.* **2. t. (tree),** tamarinier *m.*

tamarisk ['tæmərisk] *n. Bot:* tamaris *m.*

tambour ['tæmbu:r] *n.* **1.** *Mus:* caisse *f, esp.* grosse caisse. **2.** (*a*) *Needlew:* **t. (frame),** tambour à broder; **t. lace,** dentelle (brodée) sur tulle; (*b*) tambour (de vestibule, *Arch:* de colonne).

tambourine [tæmbə'ri:n] *n. Mus:* tambourin *m.*

tame¹ [teim] *a.* **1.** (*a*) (i) (animal) apprivoisé, domestiqué, (ii) domestique; **to grow, become, t.,** s'apprivoiser; (*b*) *NAm:* (*of plant, land*) cultivé. **2.** *F:* (*a*) (*of pers.*) soumis, docile; **we have a t. builder,** nous disposons d'un entrepreneur complaisant; (*b*) anodin, insipide; **the story has a t. ending,** l'histoire se termine sur une note banale. **-ly** *adv.* **1.** (se soumettre) sans résistance, docilement. **2.** fadement.

tame² *v.tr.* (*a*) apprivoiser; (*b*) domestiquer (une bête); *NAm:* cultiver (une plante, un terrain); (*c*) mater (qn, une passion); dompter (un lion). **taming** *n.* **1.** (*a*) apprivoisement *m*; (*b*) domestication *f.* **2.** domptage *m* (d'un lion, *Fig:* de qn).

tameable ['teiməbl] *a.* (animal, etc.) (i) apprivoisable, (ii) domptable.

tamer ['teimər] *n.* apprivoiseur, -euse (d'oiseaux, etc.); dompteur, -euse (de lions, etc.).

Tamil ['tæmil] **1.** *a. Ethn:* tamoul; tamil (*no f.*) **2.** *n.* (*a*) Tamoul, -e; Tamil *m*; (*b*) *Ling:* tamoul *m*, tamil *m.*

tammy ['tæmi] *n. F:* béret écossais.

tam-o'-shanter [tæmə'ʃæntər] *n.* béret écossais.

tamp [tæmp] *v.tr.* **1.** *Civ.E:* damer, pilonner (la terre, etc.). **2.** bourrer (un fourneau de mine). **tamping** *n.* **1.** *Civ.E:* damage *m*, pilonnage *m.* **2.** (i) bourrage *m*, (ii) bourre *f* (d'un fourneau de mine).

tamper ['tæmpər] *v.i.* (*a*) **to t. with (sth.),** (i) toucher à, *F:* trifouiller (un mécanisme, etc.); (ii) altérer (un document, etc.); falsifier (un registre); fausser, brouiller (une serrure); tripatouiller (des comptes, etc.); *Post:* spolier (une lettre, un colis); *Turf:* **to t. with a horse,** doper un cheval; (*b*) **to t. with a witness,** suborner un témoin. **tampering** *n.* (*a*) **t. with (sth.),** altération *f*, adultération *f* (de documents); falsification *f* (de registres); tripatouillage *m* (de comptes, etc.); spoliation *f* (de colis, etc.); (*b*) **t. with witnesses,** subornation *f* de témoins.

tampon ['tæmpən] *n.* (*a*) *Surg:* tampon *m* (d'ouate, de gaze); (*b*) *Hyg:* tampon périodique.

tan¹ [tæn] **1.** *n.* (*a*) *Tan:* tan *m*; **t. bark,** écorce *f* à tan; **spent t. (bark),** tannée *f*; (*b*) couleur *f* du tan; (i) tanné *m*; **leather goods in t.,** maroquinerie *f* en havane; (ii) hâle *m*, teint hâlé (de la peau); **to lose one's t.,** débronzer. **2.** *a.* tanné; tan *inv*; (souliers) en cuir jaune; (gants) en tanné ; **black and t. dog,** chien noir et feu *inv.*

tan² **(tanned) 1.** *v.tr.* (*a*) tanner (les peaux); *F:* **to t. s.o., s.o.'s hide,** tanner le cuir à qn; (*b*) (*of sun*) hâler, bronzer (la peau). **2.** *v.i.* (*of complexion*) se hâler, se bronzer; **I t. easily,** je bronze facilement. **tanned** *a.* (*a*) (cuir) tanné; (*b*) (teint, visage) basané, halé, bronzé. **tanning** *n.* **1.** (*a*) tannage *m*; (*b*) **t. (trade),** tannerie *f.* **2.** *F:* raclée *f.*

tandem ['tændəm] **1.** *n.* (*a*) *Veh:* tandem *m*; (*b*) *Cy:* **t. (bicycle),** tandem (de tourisme); (*c*) **to harness two horses in t.,** atteler deux chevaux en tandem, en flèche; (*d*) *Mch:* **t. engine,** machine *f* à cylindres en tandem; **t. working,** fonctionnement *m* en tandem. **2.** *adv.* **to drive t.,** conduire en flèche, en tandem.

tang [tæŋ] *n.* **1.** soie *f* (d'un couteau); queue *f* (d'une lime). **2.** (*a*) saveur *f* piquante; montant *m*; **a t. of irony,** une pointe d'ironie; (*b*) **the t. of the morning air,** le piquant de l'air matinal.

tangent ['tændʒənt] **1.** *a.* tangent, tangentiel (**to,** à); *Mth:* **t. line,** ligne tangentielle; tangente *f.* **2.** *n. Mth:* tangente *f*; **at a t. to a curve,** tangentiellement à une courbe; *F:* **to fly, go, off at a t.,** changer de sujet.

tangential [tæn'dʒenʃ(ə)l] *a. Mth: etc:* tangentiel.

tangerine [tændʒə'ri:n, 'tænd-] *n.* mandarine *f.*

tangibility [tæn(d)ʒi'biliti] *n.* tangibilité *f.*

tangible ['tæn(d)ʒibl] *a.* **1.** tangible, palpable; **the t. world,** le monde sensible; *Jur:* **t. assets,** valeurs matérielles. **2.** réel; **t. difference,** différence *f* sensible. **-ibly** *adv.* **1.** tangiblement. **2.** sensiblement.

Tangier(s) [tæn'dʒiər, -'dʒiəz] *Pr.n. Geog:* Tanger *m.*

tangle¹, tangleweed ['tæŋgl, -wi:d] *n. Algae:* laminaire *f.*

tangle² *n.* embrouillement *m* (de fils, d'affaires); emmêlement *m* (de fils, cheveux); fouillis *m* (de broussailles); enchevêtrement *m* (de branches, de barbelés); entrelacs *m* (de ronces); **to be (all) in a t.,** (*of string, etc.*) être (tout) embrouillé; (*of wool, hair*) être (tout) enchevêtré; *Fig:* (*of pers.*) ne savoir plus où on en est; **to get into a t.,** (*of string, business*) s'embrouiller; (*of wool, hair*) s'enchevêtrer.

tangle³ **1.** *v.tr.* **to t. sth. (up),** embrouiller, (em)mêler (des fils, des cheveux); embrouiller (une affaire); **to get tangled (up),** (*of thgs*) s'emmêler; (*of thgs, pers.*) s'embrouiller. **2.** *v.i.* s'embrouiller, s'emmêler, s'enchevêtrer; *F: O:* **to t. with s.o.,** se brouiller avec qn. **tangled** *a.* embrouillé, emmêlé.

tango¹ ['tæŋgou] *n. Danc:* tango *m.*

tango² *v.i.* danser le tango.

tangy ['tæŋi] *a.* qui a un goût piquant.

tank¹ [tæŋk] *n.* **1.** réservoir *m*; (*a*) **water t.,** réservoir à eau, d'eau; *Nau:* caisse *f* à eau; *Rail:* caisse à eau, soute *f* (à eau); (*along track*) château *m* d'eau; *Fish:* **(live) fish t.,** vivier *m*; **storage t.,** réservoir de stockage; (*b*) *Aut: Av:* **fuel, petrol,** *NAm:* **gas(oline), t.,** réservoir de carburant, d'essence; (*c*) **t. lorry,** *NAm:* **truck,** camion-citerne *m*, *pl.* camions-citernes; *Rail:* **t. wagon,** *NAm:* **car,** wagon-citerne *m*, *pl.* wagons-citernes. **2.** (*a*) *Ind: etc:* cuve *f*, bac *m*; *Phot:* **developing t.,** cuve pour développement; (*b*) *Pol:* **think t.,** comité *m*, groupe *m*, d'experts; (*c*) compartiment *m* (d'un réservoir, etc.); *Nau:* **(water) ballast t.,** ballast *m*; (*on lifeboat, etc.*) **air, buoyancy, t.,** caisson *m* à air, de flottabilité; (*d*) bassin *m.* **3.** (*a*) *Mil:* char *m*; **the tanks,** les blindés *mpl;* **t. trap,** obstacle *m* antichar; (*b*) *Cost:* **t. top,** débardeur *m.*

tank² *v.i.* **to t. up,** (i) *Aut:* faire le plein (d'essence); (ii) *P:* (*also* **to get tanked up**), se soûler.

tankard ['tæŋkəd] *n.* pot *m*, chope *f*, en étain; **a t. of ale,** un pot de bière.

tanker ['tæŋkər] *n.* **1.** navire-citerne *m*, *pl.* navires-citernes; **oil t.,** (navire) pétrolier (*m*). **2.** (*a*) **t. (lorry,** *NAm:* **truck),** camion-citerne *m*, *pl.* camions-citernes; (*b*) *Rail:* wagon-citerne *m*, *pl.* wagons-citernes; (*c*) **t. (aircraft),** avion *m* de ravitaillement; avion-citerne *m*, *pl.* avions-citernes.

tanner¹ ['tænər] *n.* tanneur *m.*

tanner² *n. P: A:* (pièce *f* de) six anciens pence.

tannery ['tænəri] *n.* tannerie *f.*

tannic ['tænik] *a. Ch:* (acide) tannique.

tannin ['tænin] *n. Ch:* tan(n)in *m.*

tannoy ['tænɔi] *n.* (*R.t.m.*) système *m* de haut-parleurs.

tansy ['tænzi] *n. Bot:* tanaisie *f.*

tantalize ['tæntəlaiz] *v.tr.* infliger le supplice de Tantale à (qn); tourmenter, taquiner, torturer (qn). **tantalizing** *a.* tentant (mais hors de portée); **it's t.,** c'est un vrai supplice de Tantale. **tantalizingly** *adv.* (*a*) cruellement; (*b*) d'un air provocant.

tantamount ['tæntəmaunt] *a.* équivalent (**to,** à); **to be t. to sth.,** équivaloir à qch.; **that's t. to saying I'm a liar,** cela revient à dire que je mens.

tantrum ['tæntrəm] *n.* accès *m* de colère; **to get into a t.,** se mettre en colère; piquer une colère.

Tanzania [tænzə'niə] *Pr.n. Geog:* Tanzanie *f.*
Tanzanian [tænzə'niən] **1.** *a.* tanzanien. **2.** *n.* Tanzanien, -ienne.
Taoism ['tɑːouizm] *n. Rel: H:* taôisme *m.*
Taoist ['tɑːouist] *n. Rel.H:* taôiste *mf.*
tap[1] [tæp] *n.* **1.** (*a*) robinet *m*; (*of cask*) cannelle *f*, cannette *f*; **to turn on, turn off, the t.,** ouvrir, fermer, le robinet; *F:* **to turn on the t.,** pleurer; **t. water,** eau du robinet; (*b*) (*of beer, etc.*) **on t.,** (i) en perce, en vidange; (ii) au tonneau; (*of pers., thg*) **to be on t.,** être (toujours) disponible. **2.** (*a*) boisson *f*, *esp.* bière *f* (sous pression); **an excellent t.,** une bière excellente; (*b*) = TAPROOM. **3.** (*a*) *El:* prise *f* (intermédiaire); (*b*) *Tp:* (i) *U.S:* branchement *m*; (ii) captage (clandestin) (d'une communication téléphonique). **4.** *Tls:* (*a*) **(screw) t.,** taraud *m*; (*b*) *Coop: etc:* **t. auger, borer,** (tarière *f*) bondonnière *f*; foret *m.*
tap[2] *v.tr.* **(tapped) 1.** (*a*) percer, mettre en perce (un fût); (*b*) inciser, entailler (un arbre); gemmer (un pin); tirer (du vin); exploiter (des ressources naturelles, etc.); capter (un cours d'eau); faire un branchement sur (une conduite de gaz, d'eau); **to t. a telephone conversation,** capter une communication téléphonique; *F:* **to t. s.o. for fifty francs,** taper qn de cinquante francs. **2.** tarauder, fileter (un écrou). **tapping** *n.* **1.** (*a*) perçage *m* (d'un tonneau); incision *f*, gemmage *m* (d'un arbre); (*b*) tirage *m* (du vin); (*c*) prise *f* d'eau (sur une rivière); branchement *m* (sur une conduite d'eau); (*d*) prise, branchement (de gaz, d'électricité); (*e*) *Tp: Tg:* branchement d'écoute; **telephone t.,** captage (clandestin) de communications téléphoniques; (*f*) exploitation *f* (des ressources naturelles). **2.** *Mec.E: Tls:* taraudage *m.*
tap[3] *n.* **1.** tape *f*; petit coup; **t. at the door,** coup léger, discret, à la porte. **2.** *U.S: Mil:* **taps,** (sonnerie *f* de) l'extinction *f* des feux. **3. t. dance, dancing,** danse *f* à claquettes; **t. dancer,** danseur, -euse, à claquettes; **to do t.,** faire des claquettes.
tap[4] **(tapped) 1.** (*a*) *v.tr.* frapper légèrement; taper, tapoter; **she tapped me on the shoulder,** elle m'a tapé sur l'épaule; (*b*) *v.i.* **to t. at, on, the door,** frapper doucement à la porte; **to t. out a message,** émettre un message (en morse); **to t. out one's pipe,** débourrer sa pipe. **2.** *v.i.* **to t. (dance),** faire des claquettes. **tapping** *n.* petits coups; tapotement *m.*
tape[1] [teip] *n.* **1.** (*a*) ruban *m* (de coton); bande *f* (de toile, de papier); **masking t.,** ruban-cache *m*; **(self-)adhesive t.,** ruban adhésif; *Pharm:* **adhesive t.,** sparadrap *m*; *El:* **insulating t.,** ruban isolant; chatterton *m*; (*b*) *Sp:* bande d'arrivée; **to breast the t.,** arriver le premier; *Turf:* (*at start*) **the tapes,** les rubans. **2. t. (measure),** mètre *m* (ruban); centimètre *m* (de couturière). **3.** (*a*) *Tg:* bande, ruban, du récepteur; **ticker t.,** bande de téléimprimeur; (*b*) **magnetic, recording, t.,** bande magnétique; **pre-recorded t.,** bande enregistrée; **t. recorder,** magnétophone *m*; **t. recording,** enregistrement *m* sur bande.
tape[2] *v.tr.* **1.** (*a*) attacher (un paquet) avec un ruban adhésif; (*b*) *Dressm: etc:* border (un vêtement); (*c*) guiper (un fil électrique). **2.** mesurer (un terrain, etc.) au cordeau; (*of pers.*) **I've got him taped,** j'ai pris sa mesure; je sais ce qu'il vaut. **3.** enregistrer (qch.) sur bande; **taped music,** musique enregistrée sur bande. **taping** *n.* **1.** (*a*) bordage *m* (d'une robe, etc.); (*b*) *El:* guipage *m* (de câbles, etc.). **2.** *Rec:* enregistrement *m* sur bande.
taper[1] ['teipər] *n.* bougie filée; *Ecc:* cierge *m.*
taper[2] *n. Arch: Const: etc:* conicité *f*, cône *m.*
taper[3] **1.** *v.tr.* effiler; tailler en pointe, en cône; *Mec.E:* ajuster en cône, côner (une fusée, etc.); *Arch:* fuseler, diminuer (une colonne). **2.** *v.i.* **to t. (off, away),** s'effiler, s'amincir, aller en diminuant; se terminer en pointe; **column that tapers upwards,** colonne qui diminue vers le haut. **tapered** *a.* effilé; **t. trousers,** fuseaux *mpl*; pantalon étroit du bas. **tapering 1.** *a.* en pointe; (doigt) effilé, fuselé; *Arch:* (colonne) diminuée. **2.** *n.* (*a*) taille *f* en pointe; effilement *m*; (*b*) *Hairdr:* technique *f* du dégradé.
tape-record ['teiprikɔːd] *v.tr.* enregistrer sur bande.
tapestry ['tæpistri] *n.* tapisserie *f*; **t. maker, weaver,** tapissier, -ière.
tapeworm ['teipwəːm] *n.* ténia *m*; ver *m* solitaire.
tapioca [tæpi'oukə] *n.* tapioca *m.*
tapir ['teipər] *n.* (*often inv. in pl.*) *Z:* tapir *m.*
tappet ['tæpit] *n. Mec:* taquet *m*; poussoir *m*; came *f*; **t. guide,** guide *m* de poussoir; **t. rod,** tige-poussoir *f*, *pl.* tiges-poussoirs; **t. lever,** basculeur *m.*
taproom ['tæpruːm] *n.* bar *m.*
taproot ['tæpruːt] *n. Bot:* racine pivotante; pivot *m.*
tar[1] [tɑːr] *n.* **1.** goudron *m*; *F:* **to spoil the ship for a ha'porth of t.,** faire des économies de bouts de chandelle; **t. paper,** papier goudronné. **2.** *Nau: F:* **(Jack) t.,** marin *m*; loup *m* de mer.
tar[2] *v.tr.* **(tarred)** goudronner (une route, le bois, etc.) bitumer (un trottoir, du carton); *Nau:* goudronner, brayer (un navire). **tarring** *n.* goudronnage *m*; bituminage *m.*
tarantella [tærən'telə] *n. Danc: Mus:* tarentelle *f.*
tarantula [tə'ræntjulə] *n. Arach:* tarentule *f.*
tardiness ['tɑːdinis] *n.* **1.** *esp. Lit:* lenteur *f*, nonchalance *f* (**in doing sth.,** à faire qch.). **2.** (*a*) tardiveté *f* (d'un fruit, etc.); (*b*) *esp. U.S:* retard *m.*
tardy ['tɑːdi] *a.* **1.** *esp. Lit:* (*a*) lent; nonchalant; (*b*) peu empressé. **2.** (*a*) tardif; (*b*) *esp. U.S:* en retard. **-ily** *adv.* **1.** lentement. **2.** (*a*) tardivement; (*b*) *esp. U.S:* en retard.
tare[1] ['tɛər] *n. Bot:* **1.** vesce *f.* **2.** *B:* **tares,** ivraie *f.*
tare[2] *n.* (*a*) *Com:* tare *f*; (*b*) poids net (d'un camion).
target ['tɑːgit] *n.* **1.** (*a*) *Mil: etc:* cible *f*, but *m*, objectif *m*; **moving t.,** objectif mobile, mouvant; **t. practice,** exercices *mpl* de tir; **t. area,** zone *f* des objectifs; **sitting t.,** cible facile; *Com: etc:* **t. date,** date *f* limite (de livraison, etc.); **t. figure,** objectif; (*b*) **t. language,** langue d'arrivée. **2.** (*a*) *Surv:* voyant *m*; (*over a bench mark*) signal *m*, -aux; (*b*) *Rail: U.S:* disque *m*; **position t.,** signal de position.
tariff[1] ['tærif] *n.* **1.** *Cust: Rail: etc:* tarif *m*; **reduced, full, t.,** tarif réduit, plein tarif; **t. wall,** barrière douanière. **2.** *Rail: Post: etc:* tableau *m*, liste *f*, des prix.
tariff[2] *v.tr.* tarifer (des marchandises, etc.).
tarmac[1] ['tɑːmæk] *n.* **1.** *Civ.E: R.t.m:* macadam goudronné. **2.** *Av:* piste *f*; aire *f* de stationnement.
tarmac[2] *v.tr.* macadamiser (une route, etc.).
tarmacadam [tɑːmə'kædəm] *n. Civ.E:* macadam goudronné, macadam *m.*
tarn [tɑːn] *n.* petit lac (de montagne).
tarnish[1] ['tɑːniʃ] *n.* ternissure *f.*
tarnish[2] **1.** *v.tr.* ternir (la surface d'un métal, la réputation de qn). **2.** *v.i.* (*of metal, etc.*) se ternir. **tarnishing** *n.* ternissure *f* (d'un métal).
tarot ['tærou] *n. Cards:* tarot *m*; **t. cards,** tarots.
tarpaulin [tɑː'pɔːlin] *n.* (*a*) toile goudronnée; (*b*) bâche *f*; prélart *m*; banne *f.*
tarragon ['tærəgən] *n. Bot: Cu:* estragon *m.*
tarry[1] ['tɑːri] *a.* **1.** goudronneux, bitumineux. **2.** couvert, souillé, de goudron.
tarry[2] ['tæri] *v.i. A. & Lit:* **1.** rester, demeurer (**at, in, a place,** dans un endroit); **2.** tarder, s'attarder.
tarsus, *pl.* **-i** ['tɑːsəs, -ai] *n. Anat:* tarse *m.*
tart[1] [tɑːt] *n.* **1.** *Cu:* tarte *f*; (*small*) tartelette *f* aux confitures. **2.** *P:* prostituée *f*, poule *f.*
tart[2] *v.tr. P:* **to t. oneself up,** s'affubler, s'attifer; **to t. sth. up,** décorer qch. (avec du tape-à-l'œil).
tart[3] *a.* (*a*) au goût âpre, aigrelet; (*b*) (*tone*) acerbe, aigre. **-ly** *adv.* avec aigreur; d'un ton acerbe.

tartan ['tɑːt(ə)n] *n. Tex: Cost:* (*cloth or plaid*) tartan *m*, écossais *m*; **t. shirt,** chemise *f* écossaise.
tartar¹ ['tɑːtər] *n. Ch: Dent:* tartre *m*.
Tartar² **1.** (*a*) *a.* tatar, tartare; (*b*) *n.* Tatar, Tartare. **2.** *n.* homme *m* intraitable; (*of woman*) mégère *f*.
tartaric [tɑː'tærik] *a. Ch:* (acide, etc.) tartrique.
tartness ['tɑːtnis] *n.* acerbité *f*; goût *m* âpre (d'un fruit); verdeur *f* (d'un vin); aigreur *f* (du ton).
tarty ['tɑːti] *a. P:* (*a*) (*of woman*) **to look t.,** avoir l'air d'une prostituée, d'une poule; (*b*) (*of clothes, etc.*) qui font du tape-à-l'œil.
task [tɑːsk] *n.* **1.** tâche *f*; (*a*) *Sch:* devoir *m*; (*b*) travail, -aux *m*; ouvrage *m*, besogne *f*; **it's an endless t.,** c'est un travail sans fin; **to set s.o. a t.,** imposer une tâche à qn. **2. to take s.o. to t. for (doing) sth.,** prendre qn à partie, réprimander qn, pour avoir fait qch. **3.** *Mil: etc:* **t. force,** corps *m* expéditionnaire.
taskmaster, taskmistress ['tɑːskmɑːstər, -mistris] *n.* chef *m* de corvée, surveillant, -ante; **hard t.,** véritable tyran *m*.
Tasmania [tæz'meiniə] *Pr.n. Geog:* Tasmanie *f*.
Tasmanian [tæz'meiniən] **1.** *a.* tasmanien. **2.** *n.* Tasmanien, -ienne.
tassel ['tæs(ə)l] *n.* **1.** (*a*) *Const: Furn: etc:* gland *m*; (*b*) *Bookb:* signet *m*. **2.** *Bot:* épi *m* mâle (du maïs).
tasselled ['tæs(ə)ld] *a.* à glands; orné de glands.
taste¹ [teist] *n.* **1.** (*a*) **(sense of) taste,** goût *m*; **t. bud,** papille gustative; (*b*) saveur *f*, goût; **it has a burnt t.,** cela a un goût de brûlé; **this drink has no t.,** cette boisson n'a pas de goût, est insipide; (*c*) **a t. of sth.,** un petit peu (de fromage, etc.); une petite gorgée (de vin, etc.); **have a t. of this claret,** goûtez donc à ce bordeaux; (*d*) **he gave us a t. of his bad temper,** il nous a donné un échantillon de sa mauvaise humeur; **he's already had a t. of prison,** il a déjà tâté de la prison. **2.** goût, penchant particulier, prédilection *f* (**for,** pour); **to have a t. for sth.,** avoir du goût pour qch., avoir le goût de (la musique, etc.); **to have expensive tastes,** avoir des goûts de luxe; **to acquire, develop, a t. for sth.,** prendre goût à qch.; **to find sth. to one's t.,** trouver qch. à son goût; *Cu:* **add sugar to t.,** on ajoute du sucre à volonté; **it's a matter of t.,** c'est (une) affaire de goût; *Prov:* **everyone to his t.,** des goûts et des couleurs on ne discute pas; chacun (à) son goût. **3.** (*a*) **she has excellent t. in dress,** elle s'habille avec (beaucoup de) goût; (*b*) **in perfect t.,** d'un goût parfait; **in bad t.,** de mauvais goût; **it would be bad t. to refuse,** il serait de mauvais goût de refuser.
taste² **1.** *v.tr.* percevoir la saveur de (qch.); sentir (qch.); **I can't t. anything when I have a cold,** je n'ai pas de goût quand je suis enrhumé. **2.** (*a*) (*of cook*) goûter (un mets); (*b*) déguster (des vins, des thés, etc.); sonder (un fromage). **3.** (*a*) goûter de, à (qch.); tâter de (qch.); boire une petite gorgée (d'un liquide); **I haven't even tasted it,** je n'y ai pas même goûté; **he had not tasted food for three days,** il n'avait pas mangé depuis trois jours; (*b*) **to t. happiness,** connaître le bonheur. **2.** *v.i.* **the meat tasted of garlic,** la viande avait un goût d'ail. **tasting** *n.* **1.** *Physiol:* gustation *f*. **2.** dégustation *f* (de vins).
tasteful ['teistf(u)l] *a.* **1.** de bon goût; fait avec goût. **2.** (personne) de goût. **-fully** *adv.* avec goût.
tastefulness ['teistf(u)lnis] *n.* bon goût.
tasteless ['teistlis] *a.* **1.** (mets, etc.) sans goût, sans saveur; fade, insipide. **2.** (vêtement, etc.) qui manque de goût. **-ly** *adv.* (s'habiller, etc.) sans goût.
tastelessness ['teistlisnis] *n.* **1.** insipidité *f*, fadeur *f* (d'un mets, etc.). **2.** manque *m* de goût.
taster ['teistər] *n.* (*pers.*) dégustateur, -trice, tâteur, -euse (de vins, de thés, etc.).
tastiness ['teistinis] *n.* saveur *f*, goût *m* agréable.
tasty ['teisti] *a.* (mets, repas) savoureux; **t. morsel,** morceau succulent.
tat¹ [tæt] *n. in the phr.* **tit for t.,** un prêté pour un rendu; à bon chat bon rat; donnant donnant.
tat² *n. F:* camelote *f*.
ta-ta [tæ'tɑː] *int. P: & child's language:* au revoir!
Tatar ['tɑːtər] **1.** *a.* tatar, tartare; **T. Republic,** République *f* de Tatarie. **2.** *n.* Tatar *m*, Tartare *m*.
Tatary ['tɑːtəri] *Pr.n. Geog:* Tatarie *f*.
tater ['teitər] *n. P:* pomme *f* de terre, patate *f*.
tatter ['tætər] *n.* lambeau *m*, loque *f*; **in tatters,** en lambeaux, en loques; **to tear s.o.'s reputation to tatters,** éreinter qn; déchirer qn à belles dents.
tattered ['tætəd] *a.* (vêtement) en loques, en lambeaux; (homme) déguenillé, loqueteux.
tattle¹ ['tætl] *n.* **1.** bavardage *m*, commérage *m*. **2.** cancans *mpl*, potins *mpl*.
tattle² *v.i.* (*a*) bavarder; commérer; (*b*) cancaner; faire des cancans.
tattler ['tætlər] *n.* **1.** bavard. **2.** cancanier, -ière.
tattoo¹ [tə'tuː] *n. Mil:* **1.** retraite *f* (du soir); **to beat, sound, the t.,** battre, sonner, la retraite; *F:* **to beat the devil's t.,** tambouriner, pianoter (sur la table, etc.). **2.** (*a*) **torchlight t.,** retraite aux flambeaux; (*b*) carrousel *m* militaire.
tattoo² *n.* (*design*) tatouage *m*.
tattoo³ *v.tr.* tatouer. **tattooing** *n.* tatouage *m*.
tattooist [-'tuːist] *n.* tatoueur *m*.
tatty ['tæti] *a. F:* défraîchi; miteux; moche.
taught *see* TEACH.
taunt¹ [tɔːnt] *n.* reproche méprisant; injure *f* (en paroles); sarcasme *m*, brocard *m*.
taunt² *v.tr.* (*a*) accabler de sarcasmes; (*b*) **to t. s.o. with sth.,** reprocher qch. à qn (avec mépris); **to t. s.o. with cowardice,** traiter qn de lâche. **taunting** *a.* sarcastique. **tauntingly** *adv.* d'un ton sarcastique.
Taurus ['tɔːrəs] *Pr.n. Astr:* le Taureau.
taut [tɔːt] *a. Nau: etc:* (cordage, câble) tendu, raide, raidi; **t. situation,** situation tendue.
tauten ['tɔːt(ə)n] *v.tr.* raidir, tendre (un câble).
tautness ['tɔːtnis] *n.* raideur *f* (d'un câble).
tautological [tɔːtə'lɔdʒik(ə)l] *a.* tautologique.
tautology [tɔː'tɔlədʒi] *n.* tautologie *f*.
tavern ['tæv(ə)n] *n. A:* taverne *f*, cabaret *m*.
tawdriness ['tɔːdrinis] *n.* clinquant *m*; faux brillant (d'un bijou); misère parée (de l'existence de qn).
tawdry ['tɔːdri] *a.* (vêtement, ornement) d'un mauvais goût criard; **t. jewellery,** clinquant *m*, toc *m*; **t. existence,** misère dorée.
tawny ['tɔːni] *a.* (*a*) fauve; tirant sur le roux; **old t. port,** porto *m* qui a jauni dans le fût; (*b*) *Orn:* **t. eagle,** aigle ravisseur; **t. owl,** chouette *f* hulotte.
tax¹ [tæks] *n.* **1.** impôt *m*; contribution *f*; taxe *f*; **direct, indirect, t.,** impôt direct, indirect; **income t.,** impôt sur le revenu; **inspector of taxes,** inspecteur des contributions directes; **t. collector,** percepteur d'impôt; **t. office,** (bureau de) perception *f*; **t. year,** année *f* d'imposition; **capital gains t.,** impôt sur les plus-values; **value added t.,** *U.S:* **processing t.,** taxe à la valeur ajoutée; **t. avoidance,** évasion fiscale; **t. evasion,** fraude fiscale; **to levy a t. on sth.,** frapper qch. d'un droit; **t. free,** exempt d'impôts; **t. paid,** net d'impôt. **2.** charge *f*; fardeau (imposé à qn).
tax² *v.tr.* **1.** *Adm:* (*a*) taxer (les objets de luxe, etc.); frapper (qch.) d'un impôt; **to t. income,** imposer (des droits sur) le revenu; (*b*) imposer (qn); **to be heavily taxed,** être lourdement imposé; (*c*) mettre à l'épreuve; **to t. s.o.'s patience to the limit,** pousser à bout la patience de qn. **2. to t. s.o. with sth., with doing sth.,** taxer, accuser, qn de qch., d'avoir fait qch.
taxable ['tæksəbl] *a.* **1.** (revenu, terrain, etc.) imposa-

ble; **to make sth. t.,** imposer qch. **2.** *Jur:* **costs t. to s.o.,** frais *mpl* à la charge de qn.

taxation [tæk'seiʃ(ə)n] *n.* (*a*) imposition *f* (de la propriété); **the t. authorities,** l'administration fiscale, *F:* le fisc; (*b*) charges fiscales; prélèvement fiscal; (*c*) revenu réalisé par les impôts; les impôts *mpl.*

taxi¹ ['tæksi] *n.* taxi *m*; **t. rank,** *esp. NAm:* **stand,** station *f* de taxis; **t. driver,** chauffeur *m* de taxi.

taxi² *v.i.* **(taxied; taxying) 1.** aller en taxi. **2.** *Av:* (*of aircraft*) (*a*) rouler au sol; (*b*) **to t. along the water,** hydroplaner. **taxiing, taxying** *n. Av:* roulement *m* (au sol).

taxicab ['tæksikæb] *n.* taxi *m.*

taxidermist ['tæksidə:mist] *n.* empailleur, -euse; naturaliste *mf*; taxidermiste *m.*

taxidermy ['tæksidə:mi] *n.* taxidermie *f*; naturalisation *f* des animaux.

taximeter ['tæksimi:tər] *n.* taximètre *m*; compteur *m* (de taxi).

taxonomic [tæksə'nɔmik] *a.* taxonomique.

taxonomy [tæk'sɔnəmi] *n.* taxonomie *f.*

taxpayer ['tækspeiər] *n.* contribuable *mf.*

tea [ti:] *n.* **1.** *Bot:* (*a*) thé *m*; **t. plant,** arbre *m* à thé, théier *m*; **t. plantation,** plantation *f* de thé; **t. planter,** planteur *m* de thé; (*b*) **t. rose,** rose *f* thé. **2.** (*a*) thé; **China t.,** thé de Chine; **black, green, t.,** thé noir, vert; **t. blending,** mélange *m* des thés; **t. chest,** caisse *f* à thé; **t. caddy,** boîte *f* à thé; **t. strainer,** passe-thé *m inv*; **to drink t.,** boire, prendre, du thé; **a cup of t.,** une tasse de thé; (*b*) (*as meal*) **(afternoon) t.,** thé; = goûter *m*; **(high) t.,** repas *m* du soir (arrosé de thé); **to ask s.o. to t.,** inviter qn à (venir) prendre le thé; **t. break,** la pause-thé, = pause-café *f*; **to give a t. party,** (i) donner un thé; (ii) organiser un goûter d'enfants; **t. table,** table *f* à thé; **t. service, set,** service *m* à thé. **3.** tisane *f*, infusion *f*; **mint t.,** infusion de menthe. **4.** *P:* marijuana *f*, thé.

teabag ['ti:bæg] *n.* sachet *m* de thé.

teacake ['ti:keik] *n. Cu:* (genre de) brioche plate.

teach [ti:tʃ] *v.tr.* (*p.t. & p.p.* **taught** [tɔ:t]) (*a*) enseigner, instruire (qn); enseigner (qch.); **to t. s.o. sth.,** enseigner, apprendre, qch. à qn; **she teaches the young pupils,** elle fait la classe, l'école, aux petits; **she teaches the piano,** elle est professeur de piano; **he teaches French,** il enseigne le français, il est professeur de français; *v.i.* **to t.,** *NAm:* **to t. school,** enseigner; être dans l'enseignement; **to t. s.o. (how) to do sth.,** apprendre à qn à faire qch.; **to t. oneself sth.,** apprendre qch. tout seul; (*b*) *F:* **to t. s.o. a lesson,** donner à qn une leçon; **that'll t. him!** ça lui apprendra! **to t. s.o. a thing or two,** dégourdir qn; **I'll t. you to speak to me like that!** je vous apprendrai à me parler de la sorte! **teaching** *n.* **1.** enseignement *m*, instruction *f*; **the t. profession,** (i) le corps enseignant; (ii) l'enseignement; **the t. staff,** les professeurs, les instituteurs (d'un lycée, d'une école); **t. aids,** matériel *m*, équipement *m*, pédagogique; **t. method,** méthode *f* d'enseignement. **2.** enseignement; leçons *fpl*; **the teachings of experience,** les leçons de l'expérience. **3.** (*a*) doctrine *f*; (*b*) **teachings,** préceptes *mpl.*

teachable ['ti:tʃəbl] *a.* **1.** (*of pers.*) qui apprend facilement. **2.** (sujet) enseignable.

teacher ['ti:tʃər] *n.* (i) instituteur, -trice; maître, *f.* maîtresse (d'école); (ii) professeur *m*; (iii) enseignant, -ante; **history t.,** professeur d'histoire; **to become a t.,** entrer dans l'enseignement.

teach-in ['ti:tʃin] *n.* colloque *m.*

teacloth ['ti:klɔθ] *n.* **1.** nappe *f* à thé; napperon *m.* **2.** torchon *m* (à vaisselle).

teacup ['ti:kʌp] *n.* tasse *f* à thé.

teacupful ['ti:kʌpful] *n.* (*measure*) tasse *f* **(of,** de).

teak [ti:k] *n. Com:* teck *m*, tek *m.*

teal [ti:l] *n.* (*pl. usu.* **teal**) *Orn:* sarcelle *f.*

tealeaf, *pl.* **-leaves** ['ti:li:f, -li:vz] *n.* feuille *f* de thé; **used tealeaves,** marc *m* de thé.

team¹ [ti:m] *n.* **1.** attelage *m* (de chevaux, de bœufs). **2.** équipe *f* (de joueurs, d'ouvriers); **football t.,** équipe de football; **member of a t., t. member, one of the t.,** équipier *m*; **t. mate,** coéquipier *m*; **t. games,** jeux *m* d'équipe; **the t. spirit,** l'esprit *m* d'équipe.

team² **1.** *v.tr.* **to t. (up),** associer (qch.) **(with,** avec); mettre (qn) en collaboration **(with,** avec). **2.** *v.i.* s'associer; entrer en collaboration; **to t. up with s.o.,** se joindre à qn (pour faire qch.).

teamster ['ti:mstər] *n.* **1.** conducteur *m* (d'attelage); charretier *m.* **2.** *U.S:* camionneur *m*; routier *m.*

teamwork ['ti:mwə:k] *n.* travail d'équipe; collaboration *f*; *Sp:* jeu *m* d'ensemble.

teapot ['ti:pɔt] *n.* théière *f.*

tear¹ ['tiər] *n.* **1.** larme *f*; **to shed bitter tears, tears of joy,** verser des larmes amères, des larmes de joie; **on the verge of tears,** au bord des larmes; **to burst into tears,** fondre en larmes; **to bring tears to s.o.'s eyes,** faire venir des larmes aux yeux de qn; **she was in tears,** elle était (tout) en larmes; **crocodile tears,** larmes de crocodile; *Anat:* **t. duct,** conduit lacrymal; **t. gas,** gaz *m* lacrymogène; **t. (gas) bomb,** bombe *f* lacrymogène. **2.** larme (de résine, etc.).

tear² ['tɛər] *n.* déchirure *f*; accroc *m.*

tear³ ['tɛər] (*p.t.* **tore** [tɔ:r]; *p.p.* **torn** [tɔ:n]) **1.** *v.tr.* (*a*) déchirer; **I've torn my dress,** j'ai déchiré ma robe; **to t. sth. in two, in half,** déchirer qch. en deux; **to t. (sth.) open,** ouvrir (qch.) en le déchirant; **to t. s.o.'s character to shreds,** déchirer qn à belles dents; **to t. a hole in sth.,** faire un trou, un accroc, à (un vêtement, etc.); (*with passive force*) **material that tears easily,** tissu *m* qui se déchire facilement; (*of pers.*) **to t. a muscle,** se déchirer un muscle; **torn tendon,** tendon déchiré; *F:* **that's torn it,** il ne manquait plus que ça; **country torn by civil war,** pays déchiré par la guerre civile; **torn between two feelings,** tiraillé entre deux émotions; (*b*) **to t. sth. down, away, off, out,** arracher qch. (de qch.); **he tore down the poster from the wall,** il a arraché l'affiche du mur; **to t. s.o.'s eyes out,** arracher les yeux à qn; **to t. a page out of a book,** arracher une page d'un livre; *F:* **to t. one's hair,** s'arracher les cheveux. **2.** *v.i.* (*a*) **to t. at sth.,** déchirer, arracher, qch. avec des doigts impatients; (*b*) **to t. along,** aller à toute vitesse, à fond de train; (*of horseman*) aller à bride abattue; (*of horse*) aller ventre à terre; **he was tearing along (the road),** il dévorait la route; **to t. about,** courir de tous côtés; **to t. back,** revenir en toute hâte. **tear away 1.** *v.tr.* (*a*) arracher (qch.) **(from,** de); (*b*) **to t. oneself away,** se décider à partir; **I couldn't t. myself away from the place,** je ne pouvais pas m'arracher de, à, cet endroit. **2.** *v.i. F:* partir à toute vitesse; (*of car*) démarrer en trombe. **tearing** *n.* déchirement *m* (d'un tissu, etc.); rupture *f* (d'un muscle); **t. (up),** déchirement (d'un morceau de papier, etc.); **t. away, off, out,** arrachage *m*; *F:* **t. rage,** rage *f* à tout casser; **to be in a t. hurry,** être terriblement pressé. **tear off 1.** *v.tr.* arracher (qch.) **(from,** de); *F:* **to t. s.o. off a strip,** donner, passer, un savon à qn. **2.** *v.i. F:* = TEAR AWAY 2. **tear up 1.** *v.tr.* (*a*) déchirer (une lettre, etc.); (*b*) **to t. up a plant by the roots,** déraciner une plante. **2.** *v.i. F:* **to t. up the stairs,** monter l'escalier quatre à quatre.

tearaway ['tɛərəwei] *F:* **1.** *n.* casse-cou *m.* **2.** *a.* impulsif.

teardrop ['tiədrɔp] *n.* (*a*) larme *f*; (*b*) pendeloque *f.*

tearful ['tiəf(u)l] *a.* tout en pleurs; **in a t. voice,** (i) avec des larmes dans la voix; (ii) *Pej:* d'un ton pleurnicheur. **-fully** *adv.* en pleurant; les larmes aux yeux.

tearjerker ['tɪədʒəːkər] *n. F:* histoire larmoyante, film larmoyant.

tearless ['tɪəlis] *a.* **t. eyes,** yeux secs; **t. grief,** chagrin *m* sans larmes.

tear-off ['tɛərɔf] *a.* (*of label, etc.*) perforé; **t.-o. calendar,** calendrier *m* éphéméride.

tearoom ['tiːruːm] *n.* salon *m* de thé.

tearstained ['tɪəsteind] *a.* (visage) portant des traces de larmes, barbouillé de larmes.

tease¹ [tiːz] *n.* taquin, -ine; **he's a t.,** il est taquin.

tease² *v.tr.* **1.** (*a*) **to t. (out),** effiler, effilocher (un tissu, etc.); démêler (de la laine); (*b*) = TEASEL². **2.** taquiner, tourmenter (qn); exciter (un chien, etc.); **don't t. the cat,** ne tourmente pas le chat. **teasing 1.** *a.* (ton, etc.) railleur. **2.** *n.* (*a*) (i) **t. (out),** effilage *m*, effilochage *m* (d'un tissu); démêlage *m* (de la laine); (*b*) taquinerie *f*. **teasingly** *adv.* d'un ton railleur; pour taquiner.

teasel¹ ['tiːzl] *n.* **1.** *Bot:* cardère *f*. **2.** *Tex:* carde *f*.

teasel² *v.tr.* **(teaseled)** *Tex:* lainer, chardonner.

teaser ['tiːzər] *n.* **1.** = TEASE¹. **2.** *F:* problème *m* difficile; colle *f*; **that really was a t.!** ça m'a donné du fil à retordre!

teashop ['tiːʃɔp] *n.* salon *m* de thé.

teaspoon ['tiːspuːn] *n.* cuillère *f*, cuiller *f*, à thé.

teaspoonful ['tiːspuːnf(u)l] *n.* cuillerée *f* à thé.

teat [tiːt] *n.* (*a*) mamelon *m*; bout *m* de sein; tétin *m* (de femme); tette *f*, trayon *m* (de vache, etc.); (*b*) tétine *f* (de biberon).

teatime ['tiːtaim] *n.* l'heure *f* du thé.

teazel, teazle ['tiːzl] *n.* & *v.tr.* = TEASEL¹˒ ².

technical ['teknik(ə)l] *a.* **1.** (collège, etc.) technique; (difficulté *f*) d'ordre technique; **t. hitch,** incident *m* technique. **2.** *Jur:* **t. offence,** quasi-délit *m*, *pl.* quasi-délits; *Box:* **t. knockout,** victoire *f* sur un adversaire qui ne peut pas continuer. **-ally** *adv.* techniquement; (s'exprimer) en termes techiques.

technicality [tekni'kæliti] *n.* **1.** technicité *f* (d'un terme). **2.** détail *m* technique; terme *m* technique.

technician [tek'niʃ(ə)n] *n.* technicien, -ienne.

Technicolor ['teknikʌlər] *a.* & *n.* *R.t.m:* *Cin:* Technicolor (*m*).

technique [tek'niːk] *n.* technique *f* (d'un art, d'un artiste, etc.); **his t. is poor,** il manque de technique.

technocracy [tek'nɔkrəsi] *n.* technocratie *f*.

technocrat ['teknəkræt] *n.* technocrate *mf*.

technological [teknə'lɔdʒik(ə)l] *a.* technologique.

technologist [tek'nɔlədʒist] *n.* technologue *mf*, technologiste *mf*.

technology [tek'nɔlədʒi] *n.* technologie *f*.

techy ['tetʃi] *a.* = TETCHY.

ted¹ [ted] *v.tr.* **(tedded)** *Agr:* faner (le foin). **tedding** *n.* fanage *m*; **t. machine,** faneuse *f*.

Ted² 1. *Pr.n.m.* = TEDDY 1. (*a*). **2.** *n. F: O:* = blouson noir.

tedder ['tedər] *n.* *Agr:* (*machine*) faneuse *f*.

Teddy ['tedi] (*a*) *Pr.n.m.* (*dim. of Edward, Theodore*) Édouard, Théodore; (*b*) *n. F: O:* **t. boy** = blouson noir; (*c*) *n. Toys:* **t. bear,** ours *m* en peluche.

tedious ['tiːdiəs] *a.* (*of work, etc.*) fatigant, pénible; (*of speech, etc.*) ennuyeux, fastidieux. **-ly** *adv.* d'une manière ennuyeuse.

tediousness, tedium ['tiːdiəsnis, -diəm] *n.* ennui *m*; manque *m* d'intérêt (d'un travail, de l'existence).

tee¹ [tiː] *n.* **1.** (la lettre) té *m*. **2.** *Const:* **t. iron,** (fer *m* en) té; (*of pipes*) **t. piece union,** raccord *m* à T.

tee² *n. Golf:* (*a*) tee *m*; (*b*) tertre *m*, point *m*, de départ.

tee³ *v.tr.* & *i.* *Golf:* surélever (la balle); **to t. up,** placer la balle sur le tee; **to t. off,** jouer sa balle (du tertre de départ).

tee⁴ *n. Games:* (*curling*) but *m*.

teem [tiːm] *v.i.* abonder (**with,** en); foisonner, fourmiller (**with,** de). **teeming** *a.* grouillant.

teenage ['tiːneidʒ] *a.* adolescent; (de) jeune.

teenager ['tiːneidʒər] *n.* adolescent(e).

teens [tiːnz] *n.pl. F:* l'âge de 13 à 19 ans; l'adolescence *f*; **to be in one's t.,** être adolescent(e).

teen(s)y(-ween(s)y) ['tiːn(z)i('wiːn(z)i)] *a. F:* minuscule; tout petit.

teeny-bopper ['tiːnibɔpər] *n.* minet, minette.

teeshirt ['tiːʃəːt] *n. Cost:* tee-shirt *m*, T-shirt *m*.

teeter¹ ['tiːtər] *n. esp. U.S:* bascule *f*, balançoire *f*.

teeter² *v.i.* (*a*) *U.S:* se balancer; (*b*) chanceler; **to t. on the brink of ruin,** être à deux doigts de la ruine.

teethe [tiːð] *v.i.* (*used only in pr.p. and progressive tenses*) faire ses (premières) dents. **teething** *n.* dentition *f*; poussée *f* dentaire; **t. ring,** anneau *m* de dentition; *Fig:* **t. troubles,** difficultés initiales.

teetotal [tiː'tout(ə)l] *a.* antialcoolique; qui ne prend pas de boissons alcooliques.

teetotalism [tiː'toutəlizm] *n.* abstention *f* des boissons alcooliques; antialcoolisme *m*.

teetotaller, *NAm:* **teetotaler** [tiː'tout(ə)lər] *n.* membre *m* de la ligue antialcoolique; abstinent, -ente.

tegument ['tegjumənt] *n. Nat.Hist:* tégument *m*.

telecast¹ ['telikɑːst] *n.* émission *f* de télévision; programme télédiffusé.

telecast² *v.tr.* (*p.t.* & *p.p.* **telecast**) téléviser.

telecommunication [telikəmjuːni'keiʃ(ə)n] *n.* télécommunication *f*; **telecommunications engineer,** télémécanicien *m*.

telecontrol [telikən'troul] *n.* télécommande *f*, téléguidage *m*; commande *f*, réglage *m*, à distance.

telefilm ['telifilm] *n.* téléfilm *m*, film télévisé.

telegenic [teli'dʒenik] *a.* télégénique.

telegram ['teligræm] *n.* télégramme *m*; dépêche *f* (télégraphique); **greetings t.,** télégramme de luxe; **radio t.,** radiotélégramme *m*.

telegraph¹ ['teligræf] *n.* **1.** télégraphe *m*; *F:* **bush t.,** téléphone *m* arabe; **t. pole, wire,** poteau *m*, fil *m*, télégraphique. **2.** *Sp:* **t. (board),** tableau *m* d'affichage (des résultats).

telegraph² *v.tr.* & *i.* télégraphier (une nouvelle).

telegrapher [ti'legrəfər] *n. U.S:* télégraphiste *mf*.

telegraphese [teligræ'fiːz] *n.* langage *m*, style *m*, télégraphique.

telegraphic [teli'græfik] *a.* télégraphique. **-ally** *adv.* **1.** télégraphiquement. **2.** en style télégraphique.

telegraphist [ti'legrəfist] *n.* télégraphiste *mf*.

telegraphy [ti'legrəfi] *n.* télégraphie *f*.

telekinesis [telikai'niːsis] *n. Psychics:* télékinésie *f*.

telemeter¹ ['telimiːtər] *n.* (*a*) *Surv: Artil: etc:* télémètre *m*; (*b*) appareil *m* de télémesure.

telemeter² *v.tr.* (*a*) télémétrer; (*b*) télémesurer.

teleology [teli'ɔlədʒi] *n. Phil:* téléologie *f*.

telepathic [teli'pæθik] *a.* télépathique; (personne) télépathe. **-ally** *adv.* télépathiquement.

telepathy [ti'lepəθi] *n.* télépathie *f*.

telephone¹ ['telifoun] *n.* téléphone *m*; **t. subscriber,** abonné *m* du téléphone; **public t., coin-operated t.** = taxiphone *m*; **t. box,** cabine *f* téléphonique; *Mil:* **field t.,** téléphone de campagne; *Nau:* **ship-to-shore t.,** téléphone bâtiment-terre; **t. line, network,** ligne *f*, réseau *m*, téléphonique; **t. operator,** téléphoniste *mf*; standardiste *mf*; **t. directory, book,** annuaire *m* (du téléphone); **to be on the t.,** être abonné au téléphone; **what's your t. number?** quel est votre numéro de téléphone? **to speak to s.o. on the t.,** parler à qn au téléphone; **t. call,** appel *m* téléphonique; **you're wanted on the t.,** on vous demande au téléphone.

telephone² **1.** *v.i.* téléphoner (**to,** à); **to t. for a taxi,** appeler un taxi (par téléphone). **2.** *v.tr.* (*a*) téléphoner (un message); (*b*) téléphoner à (qn).

telephonic [teli'fɔnik] *a.* téléphonique.

telephonist [ti'lefənist] *n.* téléphoniste *mf*.

telephony [ti'lefəni] *n.* téléphonie *f*; **radio, wireless, t.,** téléphone sans fil; radiotéléphonie *f*.
telephoto [teli'foutou] *a.* téléphotographique; **t. lens,** téléobjectif *m*.
telephotograph [teli'foutəgræf] *n.* téléphotographie *f*.
telephotography [telifə'tɔgrəfi] *n.* téléphotographie *f*.
teleprinter ['teliprintər] *n.* téléimprimeur *m*, téléscripteur *m*, télétype *m*; **t. operator,** télétypiste *mf*.
teleprompter ['teliprɔm(p)tər] *n. T.V: R.t.m:* télésouffleur *m*.
telescope¹ ['teliskoup] *n.* (*a*) **(reflecting) t.,** télescope *m* (à réflexion, à miroir); **radio t.,** radiotélescope *m*; (*b*) **(refracting) t.,** lunette *f* (d'approche); longue-vue *f*, *pl.* longues-vues; *Astr:* réfracteur *m*.
telescope² **1.** *v.tr.* télescoper (un train, etc.). **2.** *v.i.* (*a*) (*of trains, etc.*) (se) télescoper; (*b*) **parts made to t.,** pièces qui s'emboîtent.
telescopic [telis'kɔpik] *a.* **1.** (*a*) télescopique; *Phot:* **t. lens,** téléobjectif *m*; (*of firearm*) **t. sight,** appareil *m* de visée à lunette; hausse *f* télescopique; (*b*) visible au télescope. **2.** télescopique; coulissant; **t. tripod,** trépied *m* téléscopique; **t. ladder,** échelle à coulisse.
telethon ['teliθɔn] *n. NAm: T.V:* programme *m* de télévision très long généralement au profit d'une œuvre de charité.
teletype¹ ['telitaip] *n.* télétype *m*, téléscripteur *m*; **t. operator,** télétypiste *mf*.
teletype² *v.tr.* envoyer (un message) par télétype, par téléscripteur.
teletypewriter [teli'taipraitər] *n. U.S:* **1.** télétype *m*, téléscripteur *m*. **2.** (*pers.*) télétypiste *mf*.
televiewer ['telivjuər] *n.* téléspectateur, -trice.
televise ['telivaiz] *v.tr.* téléviser; **televised programme,** programme télédiffusé.
television [teli'viʒ(ə)n] *n.* télévision *f*; (*a*) **closed-circuit t.,** télévision à, en, circuit fermé; **colour t.,** télévision (en) couleur; **pay t.,** télévision à péage; (*b*) **t. (set), t. receiver,** téléviseur *m*, (poste *m* de) télévision; **colour t. (set),** téléviseur couleur; **t. screen,** écran *m* de télévision; **to watch t.,** regarder la télévision; **I saw it on t.,** je l'ai vu à la télévision; (*c*) **t. programme,** émission *f* de télévision; **t. film,** téléfilm *m*; **t. news,** journal télévisé; **t. commentary,** téléreportage.
Telex¹ ['teleks] *n. R.t.m:* Telex *m*; **T. operator,** télexiste *mf*; **T. subscriber,** abonné *m* du Télex; **to send by T.,** télexer (qch.).
telex² *v.tr.* télexer (un message).
tell [tel] *v.* (*p.t. & p.p.* **told** [tould]) **I.** *v.tr.* **1.** (*a*) dire; **to t. the truth,** dire la vérité; **to t. a lie,** dire, faire, un mensonge; (*b*) **to t. s.o. sth.,** dire, apprendre, qch. à qn; faire savoir qch. à qn; **can you t. me the way to the station?** pouvez-vous m'indiquer le chemin de la gare? **I can't t. you how pleased I am,** je ne saurais vous dire combien je suis content; **we are told that . . .,** on nous informe, dit, que . . .; **I t. you no!** je vous dis que non! **it's just as I told you,** c'est tout comme je vous l'ai dit; **I told you so! didn't I tell you!** je vous l'avais bien dit! **you're telling me!** à qui le dites-vous? **t. me another!** à d'autres! *esp. U.S: F:* **t. him goodbye (for me)!** dites lui au revoir de ma part! (*c*) raconter (une histoire, etc.); **I'll t. you what happened,** je vais vous raconter ce qui est arrivé; **t. me something about yourself,** parlez-moi un peu de vous(-même); (*d*) *Dial: F:* **to hear t. of . . .,** entendre parler de . . .; **to hear t. that . . .,** entendre dire que . . .; (*e*) annoncer, proclamer (un fait, etc.); révéler (un secret); *F:* **that would be telling!** ça c'est mon secret! (*f*) (*of clock*) **to t. the time,** marquer l'heure. **2.** (*a*) **to t. s.o. about s.o.,** parler de qn à qn; **he wrote to t. me of his father's death,** il m'a écrit pour m'annoncer la mort de son père; **t. me what you know about it,** dites-moi ce que vous en savez; (*b*) **let me t. you . . .,** permettez-moi de vous dire . . .; **it's not so easy, let me t. you!** ce n'est pas si facile, je vous assure! (*c*) **to t. s.o. to do sth.,** dire à qn de faire qch.; **t. him to come,** dites-lui de venir; **do as you are told,** faites comme on vous dit; **he'll do as he's told,** il marchera; (*d*) **to t. good from bad, right from wrong,** discerner le bien du mal; **you can hardly t. him from his brother,** c'est à peine si on peut le distinguer de son frère; **one can t. him by his voice,** on le reconnaît à sa voix; **he can't t. the time,** il ne sait pas lire l'heure; (*e*) **one can t. that she's intelligent,** on voit bien qu'elle est intelligente; **I can t. it from the look in your eyes,** je le lis dans vos yeux; (*f*) savoir; **nobody can t. what the future has in store for him,** l'homme est ignorant de sa destinée. **3.** (*a*) *A:* compter, énumérer (les voix); *Ecc:* **to t. one's beads,** égrener son chapelet; (*b*) **all told,** tout compris; somme toute; **I made £100 out of it all told,** tout compte fait j'en ai retiré £100. **II.** *v.i.* (*a*) produire son effet; porter (coup); **breeding will t.,** bon sang ne peut mentir; **his age is beginning to t. on him,** il commence à accuser son âge; (*b*) **time will t.,** qui vivra verra; **who can t.? there's no telling!** qui sait? **you never can t.,** on ne sait jamais; **more than words can t.,** plus qu'on ne saurait dire; (*c*) **it will t. against you,** cela vous nuira; (*d*) **to t. of sth.,** annoncer, accuser, révéler, qch.; (*e*) *P:* **to t. on s.o.,** rapporter sur le compte de qn. **telling 1.** *a.* fort, efficace; qui fait de l'effet; **t. blow,** coup bien asséné, qui porte; **with t. effect,** avec un effet marqué. **2.** *n.* (*a*) récit *m*; relation *f*; narration *f* (d'une histoire); (*b*) divulgation *f*, révélation *f* (d'un secret, etc.); (*c*) *A:* énumération *f* (des votes, etc.); (*d*) *F:* **t. off,** réprimande *f*. **tell off** *v.tr.* (*a*) *Mil: etc:* désigner (qn pour une corvée); (*b*) *F:* dire son fait à (qn); **he told them off in no uncertain terms,** il leur a dit leurs quatre vérités.
teller ['telər] *n.* **1.** raconteur, -euse; narrateur, -trice. **2.** (*a*) caissier, -ière, guichetier, -ière (de banque); (*b*) *Parl:* scrutateur *m*; recenseur *m*.
telltale ['telteil] *n.* (*pers.*) rapporteur, -euse; cafard, -arde; *attrib.* **t. sign,** signe révélateur.
telly ['teli] *n. T.V: F:* télé *f*.
telpher ['telfər] *n.* **t. (line, railway),** (ligne *f*) téléphérique *m*; **t. car, carrier,** télébenne *f*, télécabine *f*.
temerity [ti'meriti] *n.* témérité *f*, audace *f*.
temp¹ [temp] *n. F:* secrétaire *mf*, dactylo *mf*, qui fait des remplacements; **to do t. work,** faire des remplacements.
temp² *v.i. F:* travailler comme remplaçant(e) (surtout comme secrétaire).
temper¹ ['tempər] *n.* **1.** coefficient *m* de dureté (de l'acier); trempe *f*; **soft t.,** trempe douce. **2.** sang-froid *m*, calme *m*; **to keep one's t.,** rester calme; garder son sang-froid; **to lose one's t.,** se mettre en colère; s'emporter; **to be out of t.,** être de mauvaise humeur. **3.** humeur *f*; (*a*) caractère *m*, tempérament *m*; **(habitual) good t.,** placidité *f*; **fiery, even, t.,** caractère fougueux, égal; (*b*) état *m* d'esprit; **to be in a good, bad, t.,** être de bonne, mauvaise, humeur; (*c*) colère *f*, irritation *f*; mauvaise humeur; **in an outburst of t.,** d'un mouvement d'humeur; **to be in a t.,** être en colère; **to put s.o. in a t.,** mettre qn en colère.
temper² *v.tr.* **1.** *Tchn:* (*a*) délayer (le mortier, etc.); broyer (les couleurs, etc.); (*b*) (i) donner la trempe à (l'acier, une lame); (ii) recuire, adoucir (un métal). **2.** tempérer; (*a*) modérer, adoucir (une action, etc.); (*b*) retenir, maîtriser (son chagrin, etc.); modérer (son ardeur, etc.). **3.** accorder (un piano) par tempérament. **tempered** *a.* **1.** (acier) trempé, recuit. **2.** *Mus:* **equally t. scale,** gamme tempérée. **3. good-t.,** d'une humeur égale; **to be bad-t.,** (i) avoir le caractère mal fait; (ii) être de mauvaise humeur.

tempera ['tempərə] *n. Art:* **t. painting,** peinture *f* a tempera; **to paint in t.,** peindre a tempera.

temperament ['temp(ə)rəmənt] *n.* **1.** (*of pers.*) (*a*) *A:* (*physical*) tempérament *m*, constitution *f*; (*b*) (*mental*) caractère *m*, tempérament; (*c*) caractère fantasque; caractère émotif. **2.** *Mus:* tempérament; **equal, even, t.,** tempérament égal.

temperamental [temp(ə)rə'ment(ə)l] *a.* **1.** du tempérament; constitutionnel. **2.** (*of pers.*) (*a*) capricieux, fantasque; (*b*) qui s'emballe, se déprime, facilement; (*c*) instable; (*machine*) qui fonctionne irrégulièrement; (joueur, coureur) inconstant.

temperance ['temp(ə)rəns] *n.* **1.** tempérance *f*; modération *f*, retenue *f* (dans les plaisirs, etc.). **2.** (*a*) tempérance, sobriété *f* (à table); (*b*) abstention *f* des boissons alcooliques; antialcoolisme *m*; **t. society,** société *f* de tempérance; ligue *f* antialcoolique.

temperate ['temp(ə)rət] *a.* **1.** (*a*) (*of pers., etc.*) tempérant, sobre; modéré; (*b*) (*of language, etc.*) modéré, mesuré. **2.** (*of climate, zone, etc.*) tempéré.

temperature ['temp(ə)rətjər] *n.* température *f*; (*a*) **fall in t., t. drop,** chute *f* de température; **room t.,** température ambiante; (*of wine*) **at room t.,** chambré; **the t. was in the thirties,** le thermomètre marquait plus de trente degrés; (*b*) *Med:* **to take s.o.'s t.,** prendre la température de qn; **to have a raised t.,** *F:* **to have, to run, a t.,** avoir de la température, de la fièvre; **he's got a t. of forty,** il a quarante de fièvre; (*c*) **to judge the t. of the meeting,** estimer la réaction des auditeurs.

tempest ['tempist] *n.* tempête *f*, tourmente *f*.

tempestuous [tem'pestjuəs] *a.* **1.** (*of weather, etc.*) tempétueux. **2.** (*of meeting, etc.*) orageux; (*of pers., mood, etc.*) turbulent, agité, violent. **-ly** *adv.* **1.** tempétueusement. **2.** violemment.

tempestuousness [tem'pestjuəsnis] *n.* **1.** violence *f* (du temps). **2.** caractère orageux (d'une réunion); turbulence *f*, agitation *f* (de la foule).

Templar ['templər] *n. Hist:* **(Knight) T.,** Templier *m*; chevalier *m* du Temple.

template ['templit] *n.* **1.** *Metalw: Carp: etc:* gabarit *m*, calibre *m*, patron *m*. **2.** *Const:* sablière *f*.

temple¹ ['templ] *n.* **1.** temple (grec, etc.). **2.** *Hist:* **the Knights of the T.,** les chevaliers *mpl* du Temple, les Templiers *mpl*.

temple² *n. Anat:* (*a*) tempe *f*; (*b*) larmier *m* (du cheval).

templet ['templit] *n.* = TEMPLATE.

tempo, *pl.* **-i** ['tempou, -i:] *n.* (*a*) *Mus:* tempo *m*; (*b*) *Fig:* **strikes that upset the t. of production,** grèves *fpl* qui interrompent le rythme de la production.

temporal¹ ['tempər(ə)l] *a.* (os, etc.) temporal, -aux.

temporal² *a.* **1.** (pouvoir, etc.) temporel. **2.** *Gram:* (argument, etc.) temporel.

temporary ['temp(ə)rəri] *a.* (*a*) provisoire; **to exercise t. command,** commander par intérim; **on a t. basis,** par intérim; provisoirement; **t. appointment,** emploi *m* (à titre) temporaire; *Adm:* emploi *m* amovible; (*b*) **the improvement is only t.,** l'amélioration n'est que passagère, momentanée; **this will at least give you t. relief,** cela vous soulagera pour le moment. **-ily** *adv.* (*a*) temporairement; provisoirement; par intérim; (*b*) momentanément; pour le moment.

temporize ['tempəraiz] *v.i.* **1.** temporiser; chercher à gagner du temps. **2.** se plier aux circonstances.

tempt [tem(p)t] *v.tr.* tenter. **1. to t. s.o. to do sth.,** tenter qn pour lui faire faire qch.; **to let oneself be tempted,** se laisser tenter; céder à la tentation; **I'm tempted to try,** je suis tenté, j'ai envie, d'essayer; **the fine weather tempts us to go out,** le beau temps nous invite à sortir. **2. to t. providence, fate,** tenter la providence, le sort. **tempting** *a.* tentant, alléchant; (*of offer*) séduisant, attrayant; (*of meal*) appétissant. **temptingly** *adv.* d'une manière tentante.

temptation [tem(p)'teiʃ(ə)n] *n.* tentation *f*; **to throw t. in s.o.'s way,** exposer qn à la tentation; **to yield to t.,** succomber, céder, à la tentation; se laisser tenter.

tempter ['tem(p)tər] *n.* tentateur *m*.

temptress ['tem(p)tris] *n.f.* tentatrice.

ten [ten] *num.a. & n.* dix (*m*); **number t.,** le numéro dix; **some, about, t. years ago,** il y a une dizaine d'années; **three tens are thirty,** trois fois dix font trente; **t. to one he'll find out,** je vous parie qu'il le découvrira; *Rec: etc:* **the top t.,** palmarès *m* des dix.

tenable ['tenəbl] *a.* **1.** (position, forteresse) tenable; (théorie) soutenable. **2. appointment t. for three years,** poste auquel on est nommé pour trois ans.

tenacious [te'neiʃəs] *a.* (*a*) tenace; **t. memory,** mémoire sûre; (*of pers.*) **to be t. in, of, one's opinion,** adhérer à, tenir à, son opinion; (*b*) opiniâtre, obstiné; **to be t.,** s'opiniâtrer (dans un projet, etc.). **-ly** *adv.* obstinément; avec ténacité.

tenaciousness, tenacity [te'neiʃəsnis, -'næsiti] *n.* (*a*) ténacité *f*; sûreté *f* (de la mémoire); attachement *m* (à ses idées); (*b*) obstination *f*, opiniâtreté *f*.

tenancy ['tenənsi] *n.* (*a*) location *f*; **expiration of t.,** expiration *f* de bail; échéance *f* de location; (*b*) **during my t.,** pendant la période de ma location; (*c*) **to hold a life t. of a house,** jouir viagèrement d'une maison.

tenant¹ ['tenənt] *n.* locataire *mf*; **t. in possession, sitting t.,** occupant(e); **t. farmer,** cultivateur *m* à bail.

tenant² *v.tr.* habiter, occuper (une maison, etc.) comme locataire.

tenantry ['tenəntri] *n. coll.* (*a*) locataires *mpl*; (*b*) fermiers *mpl* et tenanciers *mpl* (d'un domaine).

tench [tenʃ] *n. Ich:* tanche *f*.

tend¹ [tend] *v.tr.* soigner (un malade, etc.); surveiller (une machine, etc.); garder (les moutons, etc.); entretenir (un jardin); soigner (le feu).

tend² *v.i.* **1.** (*a*) tendre, se diriger, aller (**towards,** vers); **doctrine that tends towards socialism,** doctrine socialisante; doctrine qui penche vers le socialisme; **blue tending to green,** bleu tirant sur le vert; (*b*) **examples that t. to undermine morality,** exemples *mpl* qui tendent à ébranler les mœurs. **2. to t. to do sth.,** être susceptible de, être sujet à, faire qch.; (*of car*) **to t. to skid,** être sujet à déraper; déraper facilement.

tendency ['tendənsi] *n.* tendance *f*, inclination *f*, disposition *f*, penchant *m* (**to,** à); **t. to drink,** penchant à la boisson; **to have a t. to (do) sth.,** avoir (une) tendance à (faire) qch.; **a growing t.,** une tendance de plus en plus marquée; *Fin:* **tendencies of the market,** tendances du marché.

tendentious [ten'denʃəs] *a.* tendancieux. **-ly** *adv.* tendancieusement; dans un but tendancieux.

tendentiousness [ten'denʃəsnis] *n.* caractère tendancieux.

tender¹ ['tendər] *n.* **1.** (*pers.*) (*a*) machiniste *m*; (*b*) garde *m*, gardien *m*; (*c*) **bar t.,** barman *m*. **2.** (*a*) *Nau:* navire annexe; ravitailleur *m*; (*b*) *Rail:* tender *m*.

tender² *a.* **1.** tendre; *Cu:* **t. meat,** viande tendre; **to make meat t.,** amortir, attendrir, la viande. **2.** tendre, sensible; (*a*) **t. to the touch,** sensible, douloureux, au toucher; **to touch s.o. on a t. spot,** toucher qn à l'endroit sensible; (*b*) **t. heart,** cœur tendre, sensible; **t. conscience,** conscience délicate, susceptible. **3.** (*a*) (*of plant, etc.*) délicat, fragile; (*b*) jeune, tendre; **t. youth,** la tendre, verte, jeunesse; **child of t. years,** enfant en bas âge. **4.** (*of light, etc.*) tendre, doux; **the t. green of the first leaves,** le vert tendre des premières feuilles. **5.** (*of pers., sentiment, etc.*) tendre, affectueux; **t. look,** regard doux. **6.** soigneux, soucieux, jaloux (**of,** de). **-ly** *adv.* **1.** (toucher, tenir, qch.) doucement, délicatement. **2.** tendrement; avec tendresse.

tender³ *n.* **1.** *Jur:* **t. of payment,** offre de paiement. **2.** *Com:* soumission *f*, offre; **to invite tenders for a piece of work, to put a piece of work out to t.,** mettre un travail en adjudication; **to make, put in, a t. for sth.,** soumissionner, faire une soumission, pour qch.; **by t.,** par voie d'adjudication. **3.** *Jur: Com:* **legal t.,** cours légal; monnaie *f* libératoire; (*of money*) **to be legal t.,** avoir cours; avoir force libératoire.

tender⁴ **1.** *v.tr.* (*a*) *Jur:* **to t. money in discharge of debt,** faire une offre réelle; (*b*) *Jur:* **to t. an oath to s.o.,** déférer le serment à qn; (*c*) offrir (ses services, une somme, etc.); **to t. one's resignation,** offrir de démissionner; **to t. one's apologies,** faire, présenter, ses excuses. **2.** *v.i. Com:* **to t. for sth.,** soumissionner (pour) qch.; faire une soumission pour qch.; **to t. for a contract,** soumissionner à une adjudication.

tenderfoot, *pl.* **-foots, -feet** ['tendəfut(s), -fi:t] *n.* (*a*) *U.S:* nouveau venu (dans un lieu sauvage); (*b*) novice *mf*.

tenderhearted [tendə'hɑ:tid] *a.* au cœur tendre, sensible; **to be too t.,** avoir trop de cœur.

tenderheartedness [tendə'hɑ:tidnis] *n.* sensibilité *f*; compassion *f*.

tenderize ['tendəraiz] *v.tr.* attendrir (la viande).

tenderizer ['tendəraizər] *n.* attendrisseur *m*.

tenderloin ['tendəlɔin] *n. Cu:* filet *m* (de bœuf, etc.).

tenderness ['tendənis] *n.* **1.** tendreté *f* (de la viande). **2.** délicatesse *f*, fragilité *f* (d'une plante); délicatesse (de conscience). **3.** douceur *f* (de la lumière, etc.). **4.** tendresse *f*; affection *f* (**for,** pour).

tendon ['tendən] *n. Anat:* tendon *m*.

tendril ['tendril] *n. Bot:* vrille *f*, cirre *m*.

tenement ['tenimənt] *n.* **1.** *Jur:* fonds *m* de terre. **2.** (i) **t. (house),** bâtiment *m*; (ii) = HLM.

tenet ['tenet, 'ti:-] *n.* (*a*) doctrine *f*, dogme *m*; (*b*) opinion *f*; croyance *f*.

tenfold ['tenfould] **1.** *a.* décuple. **2.** *adv.* dix fois autant; au décuple; **to increase t.,** décupler.

tenner ['tenər] *n. F:* billet *m* de dix (i) livres, (ii) dollars.

tennis ['tenis] *n.* **1.** (*a*) **(lawn) t.,** (lawn-)tennis *m*; **t. court,** tennis, court *m*; **to play t.,** jouer au tennis; **t. player,** joueur, -euse, de tennis; **t. ball,** balle *f* de tennis; *Med:* **t. elbow,** synovite *f* du coude; (*b*) **table t.,** tennis de table; **deck t.,** deck-tennis *m*. **2. (real, royal) t.,** (jeu *m* de) paume *f*; **t. court,** jeu de paume.

tenon ['tenən] *n. Carp:* tenon *m*.

tenor ['tenər] *n.* **1.** (*a*) *Jur:* copie *f* conforme; (*b*) contenu *m*, sens général (d'une lettre, etc.); (*c*) cours *m*, marche *f*, progrès *m* (des affaires, de la vie, etc.). **2.** *Mus:* (*a*) (*voice or singer*) ténor *m*; **t. voice,** voix *f* de ténor; **t. clef,** clé *f* d'ut quatrième ligne; (*b*) **t. sax(ophone),** saxo(phone) *m* ténor; ténor.

tenpence ['tenpəns, -pens] *n.* (pièce de) dix pence *m*.

tenpenny ['tenpəni] *a.* de, à, dix pence; **t. stamp,** timbre *m* de dix pence.

tenpin ['tenpin] *n.* quille *f*; **tenpins, t. bowling,** jeu *m* de quilles, bowling *m*.

tense¹ [tens] *n. Gram:* temps *m*; **verb in the present, the future, t.,** verbe au (temps) présent, futur.

tense² *a.* **1.** (*of cord, etc.*) tendu, raide. **2.** (*of nerves, situation, etc.*) tendu; **t. moment,** moment *m* de forte tension; **t. silence,** silence émotionnant, impressionnant; **t. voice,** voix étranglée (par l'émotion); (*of pers.*) **to be t.,** être contracté, tendu. **-ly** *adv.* **1.** raidement. **2.** (avec) les nerfs tendus, l'esprit tendu.

tense³ **1.** *v.tr.* tendre. **2.** *v.i.* **to t. up,** se raidir.

tenseness ['tensnis] *n.* **1.** rigidité *f*; (état *m* de) tension *f* (des muscles, etc.). **2.** tension, état tendu (des nerfs, d'une situation, etc.).

tensile ['tensail] *a.* **1.** extensible, élastique; (*of metal*) ductile. **2.** *Mec: etc:* (effort, force) de traction; **t. strength,** limite *f* élastique à la traction.

tension ['tenʃən] *n.* **1.** (*a*) tension *f* (d'une corde, etc.); **muscular t.,** tension musculaire; (*b*) tension (de l'esprit, des nerfs); (*c*) *Ph:* tension, force *f* élastique (d'un fluide); *Mch:* pression *f* (de la vapeur); **surface t.,** tension superficielle; (*d*) *El:* tension, voltage *m*; **cable under t.,** câble sous tension. **2.** (force de) traction *f*; tension (d'un ressort); **to be in t.,** être en traction. **3.** (*of sewing machine, etc.*) tendeur *m*.

tent [tent] *n.* (*a*) tente *f*; **bell t.,** tente conique; **to pitch, strike, tents,** monter, démonter, les tentes; **t. peg,** piquet *m* de tente; (*b*) **oxygen t.,** tente à oxygène.

tentacle ['tentək(ə)l] *n. Nat.Hist:* tentacule *m*.

tentative ['tentətiv] **1.** *a.* (*a*) d'essai; **t. move,** démarche expérimentale; **t. offer,** offre *f* préliminaire, d'essai; (*b*) hésitant, indécis. **2.** *n.* tentative *f*; essai *m*. **-ly** *adv.* à titre d'essai; avec hésitation.

tenterhook ['tentəhuk] *n.* **to be on tenterhooks,** être au supplice, sur le gril, sur des charbons ardents; **to keep s.o. on tenterhooks,** faire languir qn.

tenth [tenθ] **1.** *num.a. & n.* dixième (*mf*); **in the t. place,** en dixième lieu; dixièmement. **2.** *n.* (*fractional*) dixième *m*. **3.** *n. Mus:* (intervalle de) dixième *f*.

tenthly ['tenθli] *adv.* dixièmement; en dixième lieu.

tenting ['tentiŋ] *n.* toile *f* à tentes.

tenuity [te'nju:iti] *n.* ténuité *f*, finesse *f*.

tenuous ['tenjuəs] *a.* **1.** ténu; très fin.

tenure ['tenjər] *n.* **1.** *Hist: Jur:* tenure *f*; **system of land t.,** régime foncier. **2.** *Jur:* (période *f* de) jouissance *f*, (d')occupation *f* (d'un office, d'une propriété, etc.); **during his t. of office,** pendant qu'il exerçait ses fonctions.

tepee ['ti:pi(:)] *n.* tente *f* (des Amérindiens).

tepid ['tepid] *a.* (*of water, etc.*) tiède; (*of feeling, etc.*) tiède, qui manque d'ardeur.

tepidness ['tepidnis] *n.* tiédeur *f*.

tercentenary [tə:sen'ti:nəri], **tercentennial** [tə:sen'teniəl] *a. & n.* tricentenaire (*m*).

tercet ['tə:sit] *n. Pros:* tercet *m*.

term¹ [tə:m] *n.* **1.** (*a*) *A: & Lit:* terme *m*, fin *f*, limite *f*; **to set, put, a t. to sth.,** fixer une limite à qch.; (*b*) (*of pregnancy*) **to have reached (full) t.,** être à terme; (*c*) *Com:* (terme d')échéance *f* (d'une lettre de change). **2.** (*a*) terme, période *f*, durée *f*; **to serve a t. of five years (in prison),** faire cinq ans de prison; **during his t. of office,** pendant qu'il exerçait ses fonctions; *Com:* **long t., short t., transaction,** opération *f* à long, court, terme; **a long-t. policy,** une politique à longue échéance; **in the long t.,** à la longue; **in the short t.,** dans l'immédiat; (*b*) *Sch:* trimestre *m*; **in t. time, during t.,** pendant le trimestre; **half t. (holiday),** congé *m* de mi-trimestre; *U.S:* **t. paper,** dissertation trimestrielle; (*c*) *Jur:* session *f*; (*d*) *Jur: Scot:* **t. day,** (jour *m* de) terme. **3.** (*a*) *Com: etc:* **terms,** conditions *fpl*; clauses *fpl*, termes (d'un contrat); *Fin:* **terms and conditions of an issue,** modalités *fpl* d'une émission; **on these terms I accept,** à ces conditions j'accepte; **make, name, your own terms,** faites vos conditions vous-même; **under the terms of the clause,** sous le bénéfice de la clause; **to dictate terms,** imposer des conditions; **to come to terms, make terms,** s'arranger, s'accorder, prendre un arrangement (**with,** avec); **terms of reference,** attributions *fpl*, mandat *m* (d'une commission, etc.); (*b*) **terms of payment,** conditions de paiement; **terms strictly cash,** payable au comptant; (*in hotel, etc.*) **weekly terms £x,** pension £x par semaine; **on easy terms,** avec facilités de paiement; **not on any terms,** à aucun prix. **4. friendly terms,** relations amicales; relations d'amitié; **to be on good, bad, terms with s.o.,** être bien, mal, être en bonne, mauvaise, intelligence, avec qn; **to be on the best of terms with s.o.,** être au mieux, dans les meilleurs termes, avec qn. **5.** (*a*) *Mth: Log:* terme; **to express one quantity in terms of another,** exprimer une quantité en fonction d'une autre; **in terms of financial risk,** en ce qui concerne les risques financiers; (*b*) **terms of a problem,** énoncé *m* d'un problème. **6.** (*a*) terme, expression *f*; **technical, scientific, t.,** terme, expression, technique, scientifique; (*b*) **he spoke of him in the most flattering terms,** il a parlé de lui en termes les plus flatteurs; **I told him in no uncertain terms,** je le lui ai dit carrément, sans mâcher mes mots.

term² *v.tr.* appeler; désigner; **that is what I would t. a stupid answer,** voilà ce que j'appelle une sotte réponse.

termagent ['tə:məgənt] *n.f.* mégère, virago.

terminal ['tə:min(ə)l] **I.** *a.* **1.** (*of line, mark*) qui borne, qui termine (une région, etc.). **2.** (*a*) *Nat.Hist:* terminal, -aux; distal, -aux; (*b*) *Geol:* **t. moraine,** moraine frontale; (*c*) *Rail: etc:* (gare, etc.) terminus, de tête de ligne; **t. point,** terminus *m*; (*d*) (*of word, market, etc.*) final, -als; dernier; (*e*) *Med:* (maladie) en phase terminale; **t. case,** malade, cas, condamné. **3.** *Sch: etc:* trimestriel. **II.** *n.* **1.** *El:* borne *f* (de prise de courant); borne d'attache; cosse *f* (d'un conducteur); tête *f*, extrémité *f* (de câble); **t. voltage,** tension *f* aux bornes. **2.** *Gram:* terminaison *f*. **3.** (*a*) *NAm: Rail: etc:* terminus *m*; gare *f* terminus; (*b*) *Av:* **air t.,** aérogare *f*; (*c*) *Cmptr:* (poste) terminal *m*. **-ally** *adv.* *Med:* **to be t. ill,** être en phase terminale; **the t. ill,** les malades incurables, condamnés.

terminate ['tə:mineit] **1.** *v.tr.* terminer; (*a*) (*of boundary, line, etc.*) délimiter (une région, etc.); (*b*) résoudre, résilier (un contrat, etc.); mettre fin à (un engagement, etc.); (*c*) être à la fin de (qch.); (*d*) **to have one's pregnancy terminated,** se faire avorter. **2.** *v.i.* (*a*) (*of word, etc.*) se terminer, finir (**in,** en, par); (*b*) (*of line, etc.*) se terminer; aboutir (**in, at,** à).

termination [tə:mi'neiʃ(ə)n] *n.* **1.** (*a*) terminaison *f*, fin *f* (d'un procès, etc.); cessation *f* (de relations d'affaires, etc.); *Jur:* résolution *f*, résiliation *f* (d'une obligation, etc.); (*b*) **t. of pregnancy,** avortement provoqué. **2.** *Gram:* terminaison, désinence *f*.

terminological [tə:minə'lɔdʒik(ə)l] *a.* terminologique.

terminology [tə:mi'nɔlədʒi] *n.* terminologie *f*.

terminus, *pl.* **-i, -uses** ['tə:minəs, -ai, -əsiz] *n.* (gare *f*) terminus *m*; (gare de) tête *f* de ligne.

termite ['tə:mait] *n.* *Ent:* termite *m*; fourmi blanche.

tern [tə:n] *n.* *Orn:* sterne *f*; **arctic t.,** sterne arctique.

ternary ['tə:nəri] *a.* *Ch: Mth: etc:* ternaire.

terra ['terə] *Lt.n.* terre *f*; *used in* **t. firma** ['fə:mə], terre ferme, *F:* le plancher des vaches.

terrace¹ ['teris] *n.* **1.** (*a*) *Const: Geol: Agr:* terrasse *f*; (*b*) *Fb: etc:* **the terraces,** les gradins *mpl*. **2. t. (of houses),** rangée *f* de maisons (attenantes).

terrace² *v.tr.* (*a*) disposer (un jardin, etc.) en terrasse(s); (*b*) terrasser (un flanc de colline, etc.). **terraced** *a.* **1.** (jardin) en terrasse; **t. hillsides,** collines cultivées en terrasses. **2. t. houses,** rangée *f* de maisons (attenantes.)

terracotta ['terə'kɔtə] *n.* terre cuite; terra-cotta *f*; *Art:* **a t.,** une terre cuite.

terrain [tə'rein] *n.* *Mil: Geog:* terrain *m*.

terrapin ['terəpin] *n.* *Rept:* tortue *f* d'eau douce.

terrarium, *pl.* **-ia, -iums** [te'rɛəriəm, -iə, -iəmz] *n.* terrarium *m*.

terrestrial [ti'restriəl] *a.* (*a*) (*of globe, plant, etc.*) terrestre; (*b*) (*of life, etc.*) terrestre; de ce monde.

terrible ['teribl] *a.* terrible; affreux, épouvantable; **he's a t. talker,** c'est un terrible bavard; **I'm t. at maths,** je suis nul en math. **-bly** *adv.* terriblement, affreusement, atrocement; **t. busy,** terriblement occupé; **t. important,** de la dernière importance; **that's t. kind of you,** vous êtes vraiment trop aimable.

terrier ['teriər] *n.* **1.** (chien *m*) terrier *m*; **bull t.,** bull-terrier *m*, *pl.* bull-terriers. **2.** *Mil:* = TERRITORIAL 2.

terrific [tə'rifik] *a.* **1.** terrifiant, épouvantable. **2.** *F:* terrible; énorme; **t. pace,** allure vertigineuse; **t.!** magnifique! **-ally** *adv.* **1.** d'une manière terrifiante. **2.** *F:* **it was t. hot,** il faisait terriblement chaud.

terrify ['terifai] *v.tr.* terrifier, effrayer, affoler (qn); frapper (qn) de terreur; **to be terrified of s.o.,** avoir une peur bleue de qn. **terrifying** *a.* terrifiant, terrible, épouvantable. **terrifyingly** *adv.* épouvantablement; d'une manière terrifiante.

terrine [te'ri:n] *n.* terrine *f*.

territorial [teri'tɔ:riəl] **1.** *a.* (*a*) (*of possessions, tax, etc.*) territorial, -aux; **t. waters,** eaux territoriales; **the T. Army,** l'armée territoriale, la territoriale; (*b*) terrien, foncier. **2.** *n.* *Mil:* territorial *m*.

territoriality [teritɔ:ri'æliti] *n.* territorialité *f*.

territory ['terit(ə)ri] *n.* territoire *m* (d'un état, d'un animal); région assignée (à un représentant); **the Northern T.,** le Territoire du Nord (de l'Australie).

terror ['terər] *n.* **1.** terreur *f*, effroi *m*, épouvante *f*; **to be in (a state of) t.,** être dans la terreur; **to be in t. of one's life,** craindre pour sa vie; **to go in t. of s.o.,** avoir une peur bleue de qn; *F:* **to have a holy t. of sth.,** craindre qch. comme le feu. **2.** (*a*) **he was the t. of the countryside,** c'était la terreur du pays; (*b*) *F:* **he's a little, a holy, t.,** c'est un enfant terrible, un petit diable; **he's a t. for being late,** il est d'une inexactitude désespérante.

terrorism ['terərizm] *n.* terrorisme *m*.

terrorist ['terərist] *a. & n.* terroriste (*mf*); **there have been several t. attacks,** les terroristes ont monté plusieurs attaques; **t. bombing,** attentat *m* à la bombe.

terrorize ['terəraiz] *v.tr.* terroriser.

terrorstricken, terrorstruck ['terəstrik(ə)n, -strʌk] *a.* saisi de terreur; sous le coup de la terreur.

terry ['teri] *a. & n.* *Tex:* **t. (cloth),** tissu *m* éponge; **t. towel,** serviette *f* éponge.

terse [tə:s] *a.* (*a*) (*of style, language*) concis, net; (*b*) abrupt, brusque. **-ly** *adv.* (*a*) d'une façon concise; avec concision; (*b*) abruptement, brusquement.

terseness ['tə:snis] *n.* (*a*) concision *f* (du style, du langage); netteté *f* (de style); (*b*) brusquerie *f*.

tertiary ['tə:ʃiəri] *a. & n.* tertiaire (*m*).

terylene ['terili:n] *n.* *Tex:* *R.t.m:* térylène *m*.

tessellated ['tesileitid] *a.* *Const:* en mosaïque.

tessellation [tesi'leiʃ(ə)n] *n.* mosaïque *f*.

test¹ [test] *n.* **1.** (*a*) épreuve *f*; **to put s.o., sth., to the t.,** mettre qn, qch., à l'épreuve, à l'essai; éprouver qn, qch.; **to undergo a t.,** subir une épreuve; **to pass, stand, the t.,** soutenir, supporter, l'épreuve; **method that has stood the t. of time,** méthode éprouvée; **the acid t.,** l'épreuve concluante; (*b*) essai *m*, épreuve; *Ind: etc:* **endurance t.,** épreuve d'endurance; **t. bench, bed,** banc *m* d'essai; **field t.,** essai sur le terrain; *Aut: etc:* **road t.,** essai sur route; **t. drive, run,** course *f* d'essai; **to t. drive a car,** faire l'essai d'une voiture; *Av:* **t. flight,** vol *m* d'essai; **t. pilot,** pilote *m* d'essai; (*c*) *Ch: etc:* **t. paper,** papier réactif; **t. tube,** éprouvette *f*; tube *m* à essai(s); *F:* **t.-tube baby,** bébé-éprouvette *m*, *pl.* bébés-éprouvette; *Atom.Ph:* **nuclear t.,** test *m* nucléaire; (*d*) *Med: etc:* **blood t.,** examen *m* du sang, *F:* prise *f* de sang; **Wassermann t.,** réaction *f* de Wassermann; (*e*) *Jur:* **t. case,** précédent *m*; (*f*) *Cmptr:* **t. run,** essai de programme; passage *m* d'essai; *T.V:* **t. pattern, t. card,** mire *f*. **2.** (*a*) examen; **eye t.,** examen des yeux; *Aut:* **driving t.,** (examen du) permis de conduire; (*b*) *Sch:* **t. (paper)** = composition *f*; **oral t.,** épreuve orale; *Mus:* **t. piece,** morceau imposé (dans un concours, etc.); *Cin:*

etc: **screen t.,** bout *m* d'essai; (*c*) *Cr:* **t. (match),** match international.

test² *v.tr. & i.* **1.** (*a*) éprouver (qn, qch.); mettre (qn, qch.) à l'épreuve, à l'essai; (*b*) essayer (un ciment, une machine, etc.); contrôler, vérifier (des poids et mesures, etc.); examiner (la vue de qn, etc.); expérimenter (un procédé); sonder (une poutre, etc.); analyser (l'eau, etc.); *v.ind.tr.* **to t. out a scheme,** essayer un projet; (*c*) *Sch:* **to t. a class in algebra,** examiner une classe en algèbre. **2.** (*a*) coupeller (l'or); (*b*) *Ch:* déterminer la nature (d'un corps) au moyen d'un réactif; **to t. for alkaloids,** faire la réaction des alcaloïdes. **testing 1.** *a.* (problème, etc.) difficile. **2.** *n.* essai *m*, épreuve *f* (d'une machine, d'un pont, etc.); contrôle *m*, vérification *f* (des poids et mesures, etc.); examen *m* (de la vue de qn, etc.).

testament ['testəmənt] *n.* **1. to make one's (last will and) t.,** tester; faire son testament. **2.** *B:* **the Old, the New, T.,** l'Ancien, le Nouveau, Testament.

testamentary [testə'ment(ə)ri] *a.* (*a*) testamentaire; (*b*) **t. capacity,** habilité *f* à tester.

testate ['testeit] *a. & n.* (personne) qui a testé, qui est morte en laissant un testament valable.

testator, *f.* **testatrix,** *pl.* **-trices, -trixes** [tes'teitər; -'teitriks, -trisi:z, -triksiz] *n.* testateur, -trice.

tester¹ ['testər] *n.* baldaquin *m*, ciel *m* (de lit).

tester² *n.* **1.** essayeur, -euse; vérificateur, -trice; contrôleur, -euse. **2.** (*a*) appareil de contrôle; (appareil) vérificateur; (*b*) échantillon *m* (de cosmétique).

testicle ['testikl] *n.* *Anat:* testicule *m*.

testify ['testifai] **1.** *v.tr.* témoigner (son regret, sa foi, etc.). **2.** *Jur:* (*a*) *v.tr.* déclarer, affirmer (qch.) (sous serment); (*b*) *v.i.* **to t. in s.o.'s favour,** rendre témoignage en faveur de qn; **to t. against s.o.,** déposer contre qn; (*c*) *v.ind.tr.* **to testify to a fact,** attester, affirmer, un fait; se porter garant d'un fait; témoigner d'un fait.

testimonial [testi'mouniəl] *n.* **1.** certificat (délivré par une maison, un chef); (lettre de) recommandation *f*; attestation *f*. **2.** témoignage *m* d'estime, cadeau (offert en reconnaissance de services).

testimony ['testiməni] *n.* témoignage *m* (des sens, etc.); *Jur:* attestation *f*; déposition *f* (d'un témoin); **to bear t. to sth.,** témoigner de qch.; rendre témoignage de qch.; **in t. whereof,** en foi de quoi.

testis, *pl.* **testes** ['testis, 'testi:z] *n.* testicule *m*.

testy ['testi] *a.* irritable. **-ily** *adv.* d'un air irrité; avec humeur.

tetanus ['tetənəs] *n.* *Med:* tétanos *m*; **t. injection,** piqûre *f* antitétanique.

tetchiness ['tetʃinis] *n.* maussaderie *f*; mauvaise humeur.

tetchy ['tetʃi] *a.* irritable; maussade. **-ily** *adv.* d'un air maussade.

tête-à-tête ['teitɑ:'teit] **1.** *adv.* tête-à-tête. **2.** *n.* (*pl.* **tête-à-têtes**) tête-à-tête *m inv*; **t.-à-t. dinner,** dîner *m* en tête-à-tête.

tether¹ ['teðər] *n.* *Harn:* longe *f*, attache *f* (d'un cheval, etc.); (*of pers.*) **to be at the end of one's t.,** (i) être à bout de forces; (ii) être à bout de ressources, *F:* au bout de son rouleau.

tether² *v.tr.* attacher (un cheval, etc.).

tetrachloride [tetrə'klɔ:raid] *n.* tétrachlorure *m*.

tetragon ['tetrəgən] *n.* *Mth: etc:* quadrilatère *m*.

tetragonal [te'trægənəl] *a.* *Mth:* quadrilatère.

tetrahedron [tetrə'hi:drən, -'hed-] *n.* tétraèdre *m*.

tetrameter [te'træmitər] *n.* *Pros:* tétramètre *m*.

tetrasyllable [tetrə'siləbl] *n.* mot *m* tétrasyllabe.

Teutonic [tju:'tɔnik] **1.** *a.* teuton, teutonique; *Hist:* **the T. Order (of Knights),** l'ordre Teutonique. **2.** *n.* *Ling.* teuton *m*.

Texan ['teks(ə)n] **1.** *a.* texan. **2.** *n.* Texan, -ane.

text [tekst] *n.* **1.** texte *m* (d'un manuscrit, d'un auteur). **2.** citation tirée de l'Écriture sainte.

textbook ['tekstbuk] *n.* *Sch: etc:* manuel *m*; **t. on physics, on algebra,** physique *f*, algèbre *f*; **t. definitions,** définitions exactes, exemplaires; **a t. example,** un exemple classique, modèle (**of,** de).

textile ['tekstail] **1.** *a.* textile. **2.** *n.* (i) tissu *m*; (ii) textile *m*; **the t. industries,** l'industrie textile; le textile.

textual ['tekstjuəl] *a.* (*a*) textuel; (*b*) **t. error,** erreur *f* de texte. **-ally** *adv.* textuellement.

texture ['tekstʃər] *n.* tissage *m* (d'un tissu); texture *f*, grain *m* (de la peau, du bois, etc.); contexture *f* (des muscles); **close, loose, t.,** tissage serré, lâche.

Thai [tai] **1.** *a.* thaïlandais; *Ling:* thaï. **2.** *n.* (*a*) *Geog:* Thaïlandais, -aise; (*b*) *Ling:* thaï *m*.

Thailand ['tailænd] *Pr.n.* *Geog:* Thaïlande *f*.

thalidomide [θə'lidəmaid] *n.* *Pharm:* thalidomide *f*; **t. baby,** victime *f* de la thalidomide.

Thames [temz] *Pr.n.* *Geog:* **the T.,** la Tamise; **he'll never set the T. on fire,** il n'a pas inventé le fil à couper le beurre.

than [ðæn; *unstressed* ð(ə)n] *conj.* (*a*) (*in comparison of inequality*) que; (*with numbers*) de; **I have more, less, t. you,** j'en ai plus, moins, que vous; **more t. twenty,** plus de vingt; **more t. once,** plus d'une fois; **he's taller t. I (am),** *F:* **t. me,** il est plus grand que moi; **she would do anything rather t. let him suffer,** elle ferait n'importe quoi plutôt que de le laisser souffrir; **no sooner had we entered t. the music began,** nous étions à peine entrés que la musique a commencé; (*b*) **any person other t. himself,** tout autre que lui; **it was none other t. his old friend,** ce n'était nul autre que son vieil ami.

thane [θein] *n.* *Eng: & Scot.Hist:* = baron *m*.

thank [θæŋk] *v.tr.* **1.** (*a*) remercier (qn); faire des remerciements, dire merci, à (qn); rendre grâce(s) à (Dieu); **to t. s.o. for sth.,** remercier qn de, pour, qch.; **t. God! t. heaven(s)! t. goodness!** Dieu merci! grâce au ciel! (*b*) **t. you,** *F:* **thanking you,** je vous remercie; merci; **will you have some tea?—no, t. you,** prenez-vous, voulez-vous, du thé?—(non) merci! (non) je vous remercie! **(yes,) t. you,** (i) oui, merci; (ii) s'il vous plaît; **t. you very much,** merci bien, merci beaucoup; **t. you for coming,** merci d'être venu; *F:* **t. you for nothing!** merci de rien! **t. you note,** mot *m* de remerciement. **2.** *often Iron:* *O:* **I'll t. you to mind your own business!** occupez-vous donc de ce qui vous regarde! **3. to have s.o. to t. for sth.,** devoir qch. à qn; **you have only yourself to t. for it,** c'est à vous seul qu'il faut vous en prendre.

thankful ['θæŋkf(u)l] *a.* reconnaissant; **to be t. to s.o. for sth.,** être reconnaissant à qn de qch.; savoir gré à qn de qch.; **to be t. that . . .,** être bien content que . . .; **it's something to be t. for,** il y a de quoi nous féliciter. **-fully** *adv.* avec reconnaissance; avec gratitude.

thankfulness ['θæŋkf(u)lnis] *n.* reconnaissance *f*, gratitude *f*.

thankless ['θæŋklis] *a.* **1.** (*of pers.*) ingrat. **2.** (travail, etc.) mal récompensé, ingrat.

thankoffering ['θæŋkɔf(ə)riŋ] *n.* (*a*) cadeau *m* de reconnaissance; (*b*) sacrifice *m* d'action de grâces.

thanks [θæŋks] *n.pl.* remerciement(s) *m*(*pl*); **give him my t.,** remerciez-le de ma part; **(very) many t.!** *F:* **t. very much! t. awfully!** merci bien! merci beaucoup! **t.!** merci! *F:* **t. for your letter, for coming,** merci de, pour, votre lettre; merci d'être venu; *F:* **no t.,** (non,) merci; **to give t. to s.o. for sth.,** remercier qn de, pour, qch.; **to offer, give, t. to God,** rendre grâce à Dieu; **to propose a vote of t. to s.o.,** voter des remerciements à qn; **t. be to God!** (rendons) grâce à Dieu! **t. to him, to his help,** grâce à lui, à son aide; **that's all the t. I get!** voilà comme on me remercie!

thanksgiving [θæŋks'giviŋ] *n.* action *f* de grâce(s); **T. Day,** fête célébrée (i) *U.S:* le 4e jeudi de novembre; (ii) *Can:* le 2e lundi d'octobre, *Fr.C:* le jour de l'action de grâces.

that¹ [ðæt] **I.** *dem.pron., pl.* **those** [ðouz]. **1.** cela; ce; *F:* ça; (*a*) **give me t.,** donnez-moi cela, ça; **what's t.?** qu'est-ce (que c'est) que cela, que ça? **who's t.?** qui est-ce? **that's Mr Thomas,** c'est M. Thomas; **is t. you, Anne?** est-ce vous, c'est vous, Anne? **those are my things,** ce sont mes affaires; **those are my orders,** voilà mes ordres; **is t. all the luggage you're taking?** c'est tout ce que vous emportez comme bagages? **that's where he lives,** c'est là qu'il habite; **after, before, t.,** après, avant, cela; **t. was two years ago,** il y a deux ans de cela; **with t. she took out her handkerchief,** là-dessus, elle a sorti son mouchoir; **what do you mean by t.?** qu'entendez-vous par là? **t. is, that's, to say,** c'est-à-dire; (*b*) (*stressed*) **so** *that's* **settled,** alors, c'est décidé; **it needs a good actor and an experienced one at t.,** cela demande un bon acteur et de plus, un acteur expérimenté; **that's right! that's it!** c'est cela! ça y est! **that's all,** voilà tout; **that's strange!** voilà qui est curieux! *F:* **good stuff, t.!** ça c'est du bon! voilà du bon! **and that's t.! so that's t.!** et voilà! alors voilà qui est fini! **t. will do,** cela, ça, suffit; **that's enough of t.!** en voilà assez! **2.** (*opposed to* **this, these**) celui-là, *f.* celle-là; *pl.* ceux-là, *f.* celles-là; **this is new and that's old,** celui-ci est neuf et celui-là est vieux. **3.** (*indefinite, as antecedent to a relative*) celui, *f.* celle; *pl.* ceux, *f.* celles; **what's t. (that) you're holding?** qu'est-ce que (c'est que) vous avez dans la main? **all those that I saw,** tous ceux que j'ai vus; **one of those who were present,** (l')un de ceux qui étaient présents; **I'm not one of those who . . .,** je ne suis pas de ceux qui . . .; (*with relative understood*) **all those present at the wedding,** tous ceux qui ont assisté au mariage. **II.** *dem.a., pl.* **those** (*a*) ce, (*before vowel or h mute*) cet; *f.* cette; *pl.* ces; (*for emphasis and in opposition to* **this, these**) ce . . . -là, cet . . .-là, cette . . .-là, ces . . .-là; **t. book, those books,** ce livre(-là), ces livres(-là); **compare t. edition with these two,** comparez cette édition-là avec ces deux-ci; **t. one,** celui-là, celle-là; **at t. time, in those days,** en ce temps-là; à cette époque; **everybody is agreed on t. point,** tout le monde est d'accord là-dessus; **t. fool of a gardener,** cet imbécile de jardinier; *P:* **t. there table,** cette table-là; (*b*) *F:* **well, how's t. leg of yours?** eh bien, et cette jambe? **it's t. wife of his who's to blame,** c'est la faute de sa femme; (*c*) **all those flowers that you have there,** toutes ces fleurs que vous avez là; (*d*) **I don't have t. much confidence in him to believe all he says,** je n'ai pas assez de foi en lui pour croire tout ce qu'il dit; (*e*) (**that** *with pl. noun;* **those** *with noun sg. coll.*) **what about t., those, five pounds you owe me?** et ces cinq livres que vous me devez? **III.** *dem.adv.* **1.** (*with adj. or adv. of quantity*) aussi . . . que cela; **t. high,** aussi haut que ça; **can you run t. far, as far as t.?** peux-tu courir aussi loin (que ça)? **2.** tellement; si; **is he t. tall?** est-il si grand (que ça)?

that² [ðət] *rel.pron.sg. & pl., standing for pers. or thg to introduce a defining clause (sometimes omitted in rapid speech)* **1.** (*for subject*) qui; (*for object*) que; **the letter t. came yesterday,** la lettre qui est arrivée hier; **the letter t. I sent you,** la lettre que je vous ai envoyée; **you're the only person t. can help me,** vous êtes la seule personne qui puisse m'aider; **miser t. he was, he would not pay,** avare comme il était, il n'a pas voulu payer. **2.** (*governed by prep., which always follows* **that**) lequel, *f.* laquelle; *pl.* lesquels, *f.* lesquelles; **the envelope t. I put it in,** l'enveloppe dans laquelle je l'ai mis; **the man t. we're talking about,** l'homme dont nous parlons; **the person t. I gave it to,** la personne à laquelle, à qui, je l'ai donné; **no one has come t. I know of,** personne n'est venu que je sache. **3.** (*after expression of time*) où; que; **the time t. I saw him,** la fois, le jour, où je l'ai vu; **during the years t. he had spent in prison,** pendant les années qu'il avait passées en prison.

that³ [ðæt; *unstressed* ðət] *conj.* **1.** (*introducing subordinate clause; often omitted in rapid speech*) que; (*a*) (*of statement, result, reason*) **she said t. she would come,** elle a dit qu'elle viendrait; **I'll see to it t. everything is ready,** je veillerai à ce que tout soit prêt; **he's so ill t. he can't work,** il est si malade qu'il est incapable de travailler; (*b*) (*of wish + sub. or ind.*) **I wish t. it had never happened,** j'aurai voulu que cela ne soit jamais arrivé; **I hope t. you'll come,** j'espère que vous viendrez; (*c*) (*of purpose + sub.*) (afin) que, pour que, +*sub.*; **they kept quiet so t. he might sleep,** ils ont gardé le silence pour, afin, qu'il puisse dormir; **come nearer so t. I can see you,** approchez, que je vous voie; **put it there so t. it won't be forgotten,** mettez-le là pour qu'on ne l'oublie pas. **2.** *esp. Lit:* (*exclamatory*) (*a*) (*expressing sorrow, indignation, etc.*) **t. he should behave like this!** dire qu'il se conduit comme cela! (*b*) (*expressing desire +sub.*) **oh t. it were possible!** oh, si c'était possible!

thatch¹ [θætʃ] *n.* (*a*) chaume *m* (de toiture); (*b*) *F:* cheveux *mpl*, crinière *f*.

thatch² *v.tr.* couvrir (un toit) de, en, chaume; **thatched roof,** toit de chaume; **thatched cottage,** chaumière *f*.

thatcher ['θætʃər] *n.* couvreur *m* en chaume.

thaw¹ [θɔ:] *n.* dégel *m*; fonte *f* des neiges; **the t. is setting in,** le temps est, se met, au dégel.

thaw² **1.** *v.tr.* (*a*) dégeler (la neige, etc.); **to t. (out),** décongeler (des aliments congelés); (*b*) **to t. s.o., s.o's reserve,** dégeler qn; tirer qn de sa réserve. **2.** *v.i.* (*a*) (*of snow, ice*) fondre; (*of frozen food, etc.*) **to t. (out),** se décongeler; dégeler; (*b*) *impers.* **it's thawing,** il dégèle; (*c*) (*of pers.*) se dégeler; *F:* **come in and t. out,** entrez et réchauffez-vous. **thawing** *n.* **1.** dégel *m* (d'un cours d'eau, etc.); fonte *f* (des neiges). **2.** décongélation *f* (d'aliments congelés).

the¹ [ði:; *unstressed before consonant* ðə; *unstressed before vowel* ði] *def.art.* **1.** le, *f.* la; (*before vowel or h mute*) l'; *pl.* les; (*a*) (*particularizing*) **t. father and (t.) mother,** le père et la mère; **I spoke to t. driver,** j'ai parlé au chauffeur; **give it to t. maid,** donnez-le à la bonne; **t. roof of t. house,** le toit de la maison; **t. arrival of t. guests,** l'arrivée des invités; **at t. corner,** au coin; **on t. other side,** de l'autre côté; **on t. Monday he fell ill,** le lundi il est tombé malade; **(in) t. year 1939,** (en) l'an 1939; **t. Greeks,** les Grecs; **t. Martins,** les Martin; **Edward t. Seventh,** Édouard Sept; **t. England of today,** l'Angleterre de nos jours; **she's t. most beautiful woman I know,** c'est la femme la plus belle que je connaisse; *F:* **well, how's t. throat then?** eh bien, et cette gorge? *P:* **t. wife,** ma femme; (*b*) (*with noun in apposition: omitted in Fr.*) **Mr Long, t. manager of the firm,** M. Long, directeur de la maison; (*c*) **t. impudence of it!** quelle audace! **I didn't have t. heart to tell him,** je n'ai pas eu le courage de le lui dire; (*d*) (*used in forming nouns from adjs.*) **t. beautiful,** le beau; **words borrowed from t. French,** mots empruntés au français; **t. poor,** les pauvres; (*e*) *F:* **he's got t. measles,** il a la rougeole; (*f*) (*generalizing*) **t. owl sees well at night,** le hibou voit bien la nuit; **who invented t. wheel?** qui a inventé la roue? (*g*) (*distributive*) **to be paid by t. hour,** être payé à l'heure; **eight apples to t. kilo,** huit pommes au kilo; **thirty miles to t. gallon** = dix litres aux cent kilomètres. **2.** (*demonstrative in Fr.*) ce, (*before vowel or h mute*) cet, *f.* cette, *pl.* ces; **I was absent at t. time,** j'étais absent à cette époque, à ce moment-là; **I'll see**

him in t. summer, je le verrai cet été; **do leave t. child alone!** mais laissez-la donc, cette enfant! **3.** (*stressed*) [ði:] **her father is Professor X,** *t.* **Professor X,** son père est le professeur X, le grand, le célèbre, professeur X; **Maurice's is** *t.* **shop for furniture,** la maison Maurice est la meilleure pour les meubles.

the² *adv.* (*preceding an adj. or adv. in the comparative degree*) (*a*) **I am all t. more, the less, surprised that . . .,** j'en suis d'autant plus, d'autant moins, surpris que . . .; **he ran all t. faster,** il a couru d'autant plus vite; (*b*) **t. sharper the point t. better the needle,** les aiguilles sont d'autant meilleures que leur pointe est fine; **t. sooner t. better,** le plus tôt sera le mieux; **t. less said about it t. better,** moins on en parlera mieux cela vaudra; **t. more he drinks the thirstier he gets,** plus il boit, plus il a soif.

theatre, *NAm:* **theater** ['θiətər] *n.* **1.** (*a*) théâtre *m*; salle *f* de spectacle(s); **open air t.,** théâtre de verdure; **to go to the t.,** aller au théâtre, au spectacle; **t. bill,** affiche *f* de théâtre; (*b*) **news t.,** cinéma où l'on passe des actualités; (*c*) **the t.,** l'art dramatique; le théâtre; **the English t.,** le théâtre anglais. **2.** (*a*) **(lecture) t.,** amphithéâtre *m*; (*b*) **(operating) t.,** salle d'opération. **3. the t. of war,** le théâtre de la guerre.

theatre(-)goer, *NAm:* **theater-** ['θiətəgouər] *n.* amateur, -trice, du théâtre.

theatre(-)going, *NAm:* **theater-** ['θiətəgouiŋ] *n.* fréquentation *f* des théâtres; **the t.(-)g. public,** ceux qui vont au théâtre.

theatrical [θi'ætrik(ə)l] *a.* **1.** théâtral, -aux; **t. company,** troupe d'acteurs. **2.** (*of attitude, etc.*) théâtral, histrionique. **-ally** *adv.* **1.** théâtralement. **2.** théâtralement, avec affectation.

theatricals [θi'ætrikəlz] *n.pl.* **amateur t.,** théâtre *m* d'amateurs.

thee [ði:] *pers.pron., objective case A: & Poet:* **1.** (*unstressed*) (*a*) te; (*before a vowel or h mute*) t'; **we beseech t.,** nous te supplions; (*b*) (*refl.*) **sit t. down,** assieds-toi. **2.** (*stressed*) **he thinks of t.,** il pense à toi.

theft [θeft] *n.* vol *m*; *Jur:* **petty t.,** larcin *m.*

theftproof ['θeftpru:f] *a.* (véhicule, etc.) muni d'un dispositif antivol; (serrure, etc.) antivol, de sécurité.

their ['ðεər] *poss.a.* **1.** (*a*) leur, *f.* leur; *pl.* leurs; **t. neighbour(s),** leur(s) voisin(s); **t. father and mother,** leur père et leur mère; leurs père et mère; **t. eyes are blue,** ils ont les yeux bleus; **they have a car of t. own,** ils ont leur propre voiture (à eux); (*b*) **T. Majesties,** leurs Majestés. **2.** (*after indef. pron.*) *F:* **nobody in t. right mind . . .,** personne jouissant de bon sens . . .

theirs ['ðεəz] *poss.pron.* (*a*) le leur, la leur, les leurs; **this house is t.,** cette maison est la leur, est à eux, à elles, leur appartient; **a friend of t.,** un ami à eux, à elles; un de leurs amis; (*b*) (*their family*) **I'm interested in them and (in) t.,** je m'intéresse à eux et aux leurs.

theism ['θi:izm] *n. Theol:* théisme *m.*

theistic(al) [θi:'istik(l)] *a. Theol:* théiste.

them [ðem, ðəm] *pers. pron. pl., objective case.* **1.** (*unstressed*) (*a*) (*direct*) les *mf*; (*indirect*) leur *mf*; **I like t.,** je les aime; **have you seen t.?** les avez-vous vu(e)s? **give t. some,** donnez-leur-en; **speak to t.,** parlez-leur; **look at t.,** regardez-les; (*b*) **they took the keys away with t.,** ils ont emporté les clefs avec eux. **2.** (*stressed*) eux, *f.* elles; **I'm thinking of t.,** c'est à eux, à elles, que je pense. **3.** (*other prep. combinations*) **every one of t. was killed,** ils ont été tous tués; **there were three of t.,** ils, elles, étaient trois; il y en avait trois; **give me half of t.,** donnez-m'en la moitié; **several, many, most, of t.,** plusieurs, la plupart, d'entre eux; **neither of t.,** ni l'un ni l'autre; **none of t.,** aucun d'eux. **4.** (*disjunctive nom.*) **it's t.!** c'est eux, elles! ce sont eux, elles! les voilà! **we're not as rich as t.,** nous ne sommes pas si riches qu'eux. **5.** (*after indef. pron.*) *F:* **when anyone comes she says to t. . . .,** quand quelqu'un vient elle lui dit . . ..

thematic [θi:'mætik] *a. Mus: etc:* thématique.

theme [θi:m] *n.* **1.** sujet *m*, thème *m* (d'un discours, etc.). **2.** *Sch: & NAm:* dissertation; exercice *m* littéraire. **3.** *Mus:* thème, motif *m*; **t. with variations,** air varié; **t. song,** mélodie principale, chanson *f* leitmotiv.

themselves [ðəm'selvz, *stressed* ðem-] *pers.pron.pl.* (*a*) (*emphatic*) eux-mêmes, *f.* elles-mêmes; **they did it t.,** ils l'ont fait eux-mêmes; **they t. are resigned to it,** eux, pour leur part, s'y sont résignés; (*b*) (*refl.*) **they've hurt t.,** ils se sont fait mal; (*c*) (*after prep.*) **they were standing in a corner by t.,** ils étaient tout seuls dans un coin; **they were whispering among t.,** ils chuchotaient entre eux.

then [ðen] **I.** *adv.* **1.** (*a*) alors; en ce temps-là; à cette époque; **what were you doing t.?** que faisiez-vous alors? **the t. existing system,** le système qui existait à cette époque, à ce moment-là; **there and t.,** séance tenante; sur-le-champ; (*b*) (*in space*) puis; **on the left the church, t. a few old houses,** à gauche l'église, puis quelques vieilles maisons. **2.** puis, ensuite, alors; **we'll have soup first (and) t. some fish,** on prendra d'abord du potage (et) ensuite du poisson; **what t.?** et puis (quoi)? et (puis) après? **3.** d'ailleurs; aussi (bien); et puis; **and t. there are the children to be considered,** et puis, et aussi, il faut penser aux enfants; **it's beautiful material, but t. it is expensive,** c'est une belle étoffe, mais aussi elle coûte cher. **II.** *conj.* en ce cas, donc, alors; **if you want to go, well t. go!** si vous voulez partir, eh bien (alors) partez! **well t., you're coming?** alors vous viendrez? **(but) t. you should have told him so,** en ce cas vous auriez dû le lui dire; **you knew all the time t.?** vous le saviez donc d'avance? **III.** *quasi n.* ce temps-là; cette époque-là; **before t.,** avant cela; **will you have finished by t.?** est-ce que vous aurez fini d'ici là? **until t.,** (i) jusqu'alors; (ii) jusque-là; **(ever) since t., from t. on,** dès lors; depuis ce temps-là; **between now and t.,** d'ici là; **every now and t.,** de temps en temps; de temps à autre.

thence [ðens] *adv. A: & Lit:* **I.** de là; **we went to Paris and (from) t. to Rome,** nous sommes allés à Paris et de là à Rome. **2.** pour cette raison; par conséquent.

thenceforth, thenceforward ['ðens'fɔ:θ, -'fɔ:wəd] *adv. A: & Lit:* **(from) t.,** dès lors; désormais.

theocracy [θi:'ɔkrəsi] *n.* théocratie *f.*

theocratic [θi:ə'krætik] *a.* théocratique.

theodolite [θi:'ɔdəlait] *n. Surv:* théodolite *m.*

theologian [θi:ə'loudʒ(i)ən] *n.* théologien *m.*

theological [θi:ə'lɔdʒik(ə)l] *a.* théologique; **t. college,** séminaire *m.* **-ally** *adv.* théologiquement.

theology [θi:'ɔlədʒi] *n.* théologie *f.*

theorem ['θiərəm] *n. Mth: Ph: etc:* théorème *m.*

theoretical [θi:ə'retik(ə)l] *a.* (raisonnement, etc.) théorique; (doctrine, etc.) théorétique; **it's only t.,** ce n'est que de la théorie. **-ally** *adv.* théoriquement.

theoretician [θi:əri'tiʃ(ə)n] *n.* théoricien, -ienne.

theorist ['θi:ərist] *n.* théoricien, -ienne.

theorize ['θi:əraiz] *v.i.* théoriser; faire de la théorie, se lancer dans des théories. **theorizing** *n.* théorisation *f*; création *f* de théories.

theory ['θi:əri] *n.* théorie *f*; **in t.,** en théorie.

theosophical [θi:ə'sɔfik(ə)l] *a.* théosophique.

theosophist [θi:'ɔsəfist] *n.* théosophe *mf.*

theosophy [θi:'ɔsəfi] *n.* théosophie *f.*

therapeutic [θerə'pju:tik] *a. Med:* thérapeutique. **-ally** *adv.* thérapeutiquement.

therapeutics [θerə'pju:tiks] *n.pl.* (*usu. with sg. const.*) *Med:* thérapeutique *f.*

therapist ['θerəpist] *n.* thérapeute *mf*; **occupational t.,** spécialiste *mf* de thérapie rééducative.

therapy ['θerəpi] *n. Med:* thérapie *f*; **occupational t.,** thérapeutique occupationnelle; thérapie rééducative; **speech t.,** orthophonie *f*; *Psy:* **group t.,** sociatrie *f*.

there [ðɛər, *unstressed* ðər] **I.** *adv.* **1.** (*stressed*) (*a*) là, y; **the keys aren't t.,** les clefs ne sont pas là, n'y sont pas; **put it t.,** mettez-le là; **he's still t.,** il est encore là; il y est toujours; **does he work t.?** c'est là qu'il travaille? **we're t.!** nous voilà arrivés! **who's t.?** qui est là? *F:* **to be all t.,** (i) être malin, avisé, dégourdi; (ii) avoir toute sa raison; **he's not all t.,** (i) il a un (petit) grain; il est marteau; (ii) c'est un crétin; (*b*) **I'm going t.,** j'y vais; **t. and back,** aller et retour; (*c*) *F:* (*emphatic*) (*when appended to noun or pron.*) -là; **give me that book t.,** donnez-moi ce livre-là; **that man t.,** cet homme-là; **your friend t.,** votre ami que voilà; **hey! you t.!** hé, vous là-bas! **move along t., please!** circulez, s'il vous plaît (*d*) (*calling attention to s.o., sth.*) **there is, are,** voilà; **there's the bell ringing,** voilà la cloche qui sonne; **t. they are!** les voilà! **t. she comes!** la voilà qui vient! **there's a dear!** tu seras bien gentil! **t. you are!** (et) voilà! **just press the button and t. you are!** vous n'avez qu'à appuyer sur le bouton et ça y est! **2.** (*a*) **t. is, are,** il y a, il est; **t. was,** il y avait, il était; **t. will be,** il y aura; **t. was once a king,** il était, il y avait, une fois un roi; **t. was singing and dancing,** on a chanté et dansé; **there's a page missing,** il manque une page; **t. is only one,** il n'y en a qu'un; **there's one slice left,** il en reste une tranche; **t. isn't any,** il n'y en a pas; **there's someone at the door,** il y a quelqu'un à la porte; (*b*) **t. comes a time when . . .,** il arrive un moment où . . .. **3.** (*stressed*) quant à cela; en cela; sur ce sujet; **there's the difficulty,** voilà la difficulté; c'est là qu'est la difficulté; *F:* **t. you have me! you've got me t.!** ça, ça me dépasse. **II.** *int.* (*stressed*) voilà! **t. now!** (i) voilà! (ii) là, voyez-vous! allons bon! **t. now, that's done!** là! voilà qui est fait! **t. (you are), I told you so,** là! je vous l'avais bien dit! **t.! t.! (now) don't worry!** là là, ne vous inquiétez pas! **I'll do as I like, so t.!** je ferai comme il me plaira, na! **III.** *quasi n.* (*that place*) **we go to Paris and from t. to Rome,** nous allons à Paris et de là à Rome; **somewhere round t., near t.,** quelque part par là; **put it over t.,** mettez-le là-bas; **down t., up t.,** en bas, là-haut; **in t.,** là-dedans; **under t.,** là-dessous.

thereabouts ['ðɛərə'bauts] *adv.* **1.** près de là; dans le voisinage; **in Brighton or t.,** à Brighton ou quelque part par là. **2.** à peu près; environ; **the parcel weighs two kilos or t.,** le colis pèse environ deux kilos.

thereafter [ðɛər'ɑːftər] *adv. A: & Lit:* après (cela); par la suite.

thereby [ðɛə'bai *when at the end of clause*; 'ðɛəbai *when preceding verb*] *adv.* par ce moyen; de ce fait; de cette façon.

therefore ['ðɛəfɔːr] *adv.* donc; par conséquent; aussi; **I think, t. I am,** je pense, donc je suis; **I should t. be grateful if you would . . .,** par conséquent je vous serais reconnaissant de vouloir bien . . ..

therefrom [ðɛə'frɔm] *adv. A: & Lit:* de là; **it follows t. that . . .,** il suit de là que . . ..

therein [ðɛər'in] *adv. A: & Lit:* **1.** en cela; à cet égard; **t. you are mistaken,** en cela vous vous trompez. **2.** (là-)dedans.

thereof [ðɛər'ɔv] *adv. A: & Lit:* de cela; en; **in lieu t.,** au lieu de cela.

thereto [ðɛə'tuː] *adv. A: & Lit: & Jur:* à cela; y; **the house and the garden pertaining t.,** la maison et le jardin qui y appartient.

theretofore ['ðɛətuː'fɔːr] *adv. A: & Lit:* jusqu'alors; avant cela.

thereupon ['ðɛərə'pɔn] *adv.* **1.** sur ce; sur quoi; là-dessus; **t. he left,** sur quoi il est parti. **2.** *Lit:* **there is much to be said t.,** il y aurait beaucoup à dire là-dessus, à ce sujet.

therewith [ðɛə'wið, -'wiθ] *adv. A: & Lit:* **1.** avec cela. **2.** = THEREUPON 1.

therm [θəːm] *n. Ph: etc:* (*a*) *A:* petite calorie; (*b*) (*in gas industry*) 100 000 Btu (unités britanniques de chaleur).

thermal¹ ['θəːm(ə)l] *a.* **1.** thermal, -aux; **t. springs,** eaux, sources, thermales. **2.** *Ph:* thermal, thermique, calorifique; **t. energy,** énergie *f* thermique, calorifique; **t. unit,** unité *f* thermique, de chaleur; **t. reactor,** pile *f*, réacteur *m*, à neutrons thermiques.

thermal² *n. Meteor: Av:* thermique *m*; ascendance *f*.

thermic ['θəːmik] *a. Ph: etc:* thermique; calorifique.

thermionic [θəːmi'ɔnik] *a. Elcs:* thermoélectronique, thermionique.

thermocouple ['θəːmoukʌpl] *n. El:* couple *m* thermoélectrique; thermocouple *m*.

thermodynamic [θəːmoudai'næmik] *a.* thermodynamique.

thermoelectric [θəːmoui'lektrik] *a.* thermoélectrique; électrothermique.

thermometer [θə'mɔmitər] *n.* thermomètre *m*.

thermonuclear [θəːmou'njuːkliər] *a. Atom. Ph:* thermonucléaire.

thermopile ['θəːmoupail] *n. El:* pile *f* thermoélectrique; thermopile *f*.

thermoplastic [θəːmou'plæstik] *a. & n.* thermoplastique (*m*).

Thermos ['θəːmɔs] *n. R.t.m.* (*marque déposée désignant les articles fabriqués par Thermos (1925) Limited*) **T. (flask),** (bouteille *f*) Thermos *m or f inv.*

thermostat ['θəːməstæt] *n.* thermostat *m*.

thermostatic [θəːmə'stætik] *a.* thermostatique; **t. control,** réglage *m* (de la température) par thermostat. **-ally** *adv.* **t. controlled,** réglé par thermostat.

thesaurus, *pl.* **-i** [θi'sɔːrəs, -ai] *n.* (*a*) thesaurus *m*; trésor *m* (de la langue grecque, etc.); recueil *m* de connaissances; (*b*) dictionnaire *m* de synonymes.

these *see* THIS.

thesis, *pl.* **theses** ['θiːsis, -iːz] *n.* **1.** *Pros:* thésis *f*. **2.** (*a*) *Sch: Log: etc:* thèse *f*; **to uphold, defend, a t.,** soutenir, défendre, une thèse; (*b*) *Sch:* dissertation *f*.

Thespian ['θespiən] **1.** *a.* tragique, dramatique. **2.** *n.* acteur, -trice.

thew [θjuː] *n.* (*a*) tendon *m*, muscle *m*; (*b*) *Fig:* **thews,** ardeur *f*, vigueur *f*.

they [ðei] **1.** *pers. pron. nom. pl.* (*a*) (*unstressed*) ils, *f.* elles; **t. are dancing,** ils, elles, dansent; **here t. come,** les voici (qui arrivent); **what are t. doing?** que font-ils, -elles? (*b*) (*stressed*) eux, *f.* elles; **t. alone can . . .,** eux seuls, elles seules, peuvent . . .; **we are as rich as t. are,** nous sommes aussi riches qu'eux, qu'elles; (*c*) (*with dem. force*) ceux, *f.* celles; *Lit:* **t. who believe,** ceux, celles, qui croient. **2.** (*a*) *indef. pron.* on; **t. say that . . .,** on dit que . . .; (*b*) (*after indef. pron.*) *F:* **nobody ever admits they're wrong,** on ne veut jamais reconnaître ses torts.

they'd = (i) **they had,** *see* HAVE²; (ii) **they would,** *see* WILL³.

they'll = **they will,** *see* WILL³.

they're = **they are,** *see* BE.

they've = **they have,** *see* HAVE³.

thiamine ['θaiəm(a)in] *n. Bio-Ch:* thiamine *f*.

thick [θik] **I.** *a.* **1.** (*of walls, material, etc.*) épais, *f.* épaisse; (*of book, thread, lips, etc.*) gros, *f.* grosse; **wall one metre t.,** mur qui a un mètre d'épaisseur; **the t. end of a stick,** le gros bout d'un bâton; **t. lipped,** lippu; à grosses lèvres; **t. skinned,** (i) à la peau épaisse; (ii) *Fig:* (*of pers.*) peu sensible; qui est peu susceptible; *Typ:* **t. stroke,** plein *m*. **2.** (*of wheat, forest*) épais, dru, serré, touffu; (*of hair*) abondant, épais; (*of crowd*) compact, serré; **t. eyebrows,** sourcils touffus, épais. **3.** (*a*) (*of liquid*) épais, visqueux; (*of mist*) dense, épais; (*of weather*) couvert, bouché; (*of darkness*) profond; **t. mud,** boue grasse; **air t. with smoke,** air épaissi par la fumée; (*b*) (*of voice*) étouffé; (*c*) *F:* (*of pers.*) obtus; borné. **4.** *F:* **to be very t. with s.o.,** être très lié, être à tu et à toi, avec qn; **they're as t. as thieves,** ils s'entendent comme larrons en foire. **5.** *F:* excessif, fort; **that's a bit t.!** ça c'est un peu raide, un peu fort! **II.** *n.* **1.** (*a*) partie charnue, gras *m* (de la jambe, etc.); (*b*) **in the t. of the forest,** au beau milieu de la forêt; **in the t. of it, of things,** en plein dedans; **in the t. of the fight,** au (plus) fort, au vif, de la mêlée. **2. to go through t. and thin for s.o.,** courir tous les risques, aller contre vent et marée, pour qn; **to follow s.o., stick to s.o., through t. and thin,** rester fidèle à qn à travers toutes les épreuves. **III.** *adv.* **1.** en couche épaisse; **snow lay t. on the ground,** une neige épaisse, une épaisse couche de neige, couvrait le sol; **to cut the bread t.,** couper le pain en tranches épaisses; *F:* **to lay it on a bit t.,** exagérer. **2. his blows fell t. and fast,** il frappait à coups redoublés; les coups pleuvaient dru. **thickly** *adv.* **1.** en couche(s) épaisse(s); (couper qch.) en tranches épaisses. **2.** épais; dru; **the snow fell t.,** la neige tombait dru. **3. to speak t.,** parler d'une voix étouffée; (*when drunk*) avoir la langue pâteuse.

thicken ['θik(ə)n] **1.** *v.tr.* (*a*) épaissir (un mur, etc.); (*b*) épaissir, lier (une sauce). **2.** *v.i.* (*a*) (*of tree trunk, figure, air, etc.*) (s')épaissir; (*b*) (*of sauce*) épaissir; (*c*) (*of plot*) se compliquer, se corser. **thickening** *n.* (*a*) épaississement *m* (d'un mur, de la taille, d'un liquide); (*b*) complication *f* (d'une intrigue).

thicket ['θikit] *n.* bosquet *m*, hallier *m*, fourré *m*.

thickhead ['θikhed] *n.* bêta, *f.* bêtasse; andouille *f.*

thickheaded [θik'hedid] *a.* *F:* bête, stupide; obtus.

thickness ['θiknis] *n.* **1.** (*a*) épaisseur *f* (d'un mur, etc.); grosseur *f* (des lèvres, etc.); (*b*) épaisseur (d'une forêt, etc.); abondance *f* (de la chevelure, etc.); (*c*) consistance *f* (d'un liquide); épaisseur (du brouillard); (*d*) étouffement *m* (de la voix). **2.** couche *f* (de papier, etc.).

thickset ['θik'set] *a.* **1.** (*of forest*) épais, *f.* épaisse; touffu; (*of beard*) fourni. **2.** (*of pers.*) trapu.

thief, *pl.* **thieves** [θi:f, θi:vz] *n.* voleur, -euse; **stop t.!** au voleur! *Prov:* **set a t. to catch a t.,** à fripon, fripon et demi.

thieve [θi:v] **1.** *v.i.* être voleur, -euse. **2.** *v.tr.* voler. **thieving 1.** *a.* voleur. **2.** *n.* vol *m*; **petty t.,** larcin *m*.

thievish ['θi:viʃ] *a.* voleur.

thigh [θai] *n.* cuisse *f*; **t. boots,** (bottes) cuissardes *fpl.*

thighbone ['θaiboun] *n.* *Anat:* fémur *m*.

thimble ['θimbl] *n.* *Needlew:* dé *m* (à coudre); *Games:* **hunt the t.** = cache-tampon *m inv.*

thimbleful ['θimb(ə)lful] *n.* doigt *m* (de cognac, etc.).

thin¹ [θin] **(thinner; thinnest) I.** *a.* **1.** (*a*) (*of paper, etc.*) mince, fin; (*of thread, etc.*) ténu, fin; (*of material*) fin, mince, léger; *Typ:* **t. stroke,** délié *m*; (*b*) (*of pers.*) maigre, mince; **long t. fingers,** doigts effilés; **t. lipped,** aux lèvres minces; **t. skinned,** (i) à la peau mince; (ii) *Fig:* (*of pers.*) susceptible; trop sensible; **to grow, become, thinner,** maigrir; s'amaigrir; **as t. as a lath, a rake,** maigre comme un clou. **2.** (*of wheat, hair, etc.*) clairsemé, rare; (*of population, audience*) clairsemé; **t. beard,** barbe peu fournie; **his hair was getting t.,** ses cheveux s'éclaircissaient; **t. on the ground,** peu nombreux. **3.** (*a*) (*of liquid*) clair; peu consistant; (*of blood*) appauvri; **t. soup,** potage clair; (*b*) **t. voice,** voix fluette, grêle. **4. t. excuse,** pauvre excuse; **my patience is wearing t.,** je suis presque à bout de patience; **to have a t. time (of it),** (i) s'ennuyer, s'embêter; (ii) manger de la vache enragée. **II.** *adv.* **1. to cut t.,** couper en tranches minces. **2.** (*of wheat, etc.*) **t. sown,** clairsemé. **III.** *n. see* THICK II. 2. **-ly** *adv.* **1.** (*a*) en couche(s) mince(s); en tranches minces; (*b*) clair; **t. sown wheat,** blé clairsemé; **t. populated,** (pays) de population peu dense. **2.** à peine; **t. clad,** vêtu (i) légèrement, (ii) insuffisamment; **t. veiled allusion,** allusion à peine voilée.

thin² **(thinned) 1.** *v.tr.* (*a*) **to t. (down),** amincir (qch.); (*b*) **to t. (down),** diluer, délayer (la peinture); allonger, éclaircir (une sauce); (*c*) **to t. (out),** éclaircir (les arbres, etc.); **to t. out seedlings,** éclaircir, démarier, des jeunes plants. **2.** *v.i.* s'amincir, s'effiler; (*of trees, crowd, hair, etc.*) s'éclaircir; (*of liquid*) devenir clair; **his hair is thinning,** il perd ses cheveux. **thinning** *n.* (*a*) **t. (down),** (i) amincissement *m*; (ii) délayage *m* (de la peinture, etc.); dilution *f*; **t. agent,** dissolvant *m*, diluant *m*; (*b*) **t. (out),** éclaircissement *m*; démariage *m* (des jeunes plants).

thine [ðain] *A: & Lit:* **1.** *poss.pron.* (*a*) le tien, la tienne; *pl.* les tiens, les tiennes; (*b*) **for thee and t.,** pour toi et les tiens; (*c*) **what is mine is t.,** ce qui est à moi est à toi. **2.** *poss.a.* (*used instead of* THY *before a noun or adj. beginning with a vowel or h mute*) **when I look into t. eyes,** quand je regarde dans tes yeux.

thing [θiŋ] *n.* **1.** chose *f*; (*a*) objet *m*, article *m*; **a t. of beauty,** une belle chose; **the things of this world,** les choses de ce monde; **to go the way of all things,** mourir; aller où va toute chose; **things to be washed,** du linge à laver; **chocolate, sweets, and things (like that),** le chocolat, les bonbons, et autres sucreries; (*b*) *F:* **what's that t.?** qu'est-ce que c'est que ce machin-là? (*c*) *usu. pl.* (*implements*) **tea things,** service *m* à thé; (*d*) *pl.* vêtements *m*, effets *m*; **winter things,** vêtements d'hiver; **bring along your swimming things,** apportez votre maillot de bain; (*e*) *pl.* affaires *f*, effets; **I forbid you to touch my things,** je vous défends de toucher à mes affaires; **to pack (up) one's things,** faire ses malles, ses valises; (*f*) *Jur:* **things personal, real,** biens *mpl* meubles, immeubles. **2.** *F:* (*pers.*) (*with adj. expressing pity, contempt, etc.*) être *m*, créature *f*; **poor t.!** le, la, pauvre! **you silly t.!** sot, sotte, que tu es! **poor little things!** pauvres petits! **she's a dear old t.,** c'est une bonne vieille très sympathique. **3.** (*a*) (*action, fact, etc.*) **that was a silly t. to do,** quelle bêtise! **how could you do such a t.?** comment avez-vous pu faire une chose pareille? **did you ever hear of such a t.?** on n'a pas idée d'une chose pareille! **you take things too seriously,** vous prenez les choses trop au sérieux; **he gets things done,** il fait marcher les choses; **to think things over,** réfléchir; étudier la question; **it's just one of those things,** ce sont des choses qui arrivent; **to talk of one t. and another,** parler de choses et d'autres; **that's the very t.,** c'est juste ce qu'il faut; **the t. is this,** voici ce dont il s'agit; **the t. is, I haven't got any money,** le problème c'est que je n'ai pas d'argent; **the only t. left is to . . .,** il ne reste plus qu'à . . .; **the important t. is that . . .,** l'important c'est que . . .; **that's quite another t.,** ça c'est tout autre chose; **neither one t. nor another,** ni l'un ni l'autre; **and another t.,** en plus; *F:* **he's on to a good t.,** il est sur un bon filon; **I don't know a t. about algebra,** je ne comprends, n'entends, rien à l'algèbre; **it doesn't mean a t. to me,** (i) je n'y comprends (absolument) rien; (ii) je ne m'en souviens pas; (iii) ça ne me concerne pas; **to know a t. or two,** (i) avoir plus d'un tour dans son sac; (ii) être bien renseigné; *F:* **he's got a t. about that, it's a t. with him,** c'est son idée fixe; **do your (own) t.!** fais comme il te plaira! (*b*) **things are going badly,** les affaires vont mal; **as things are,** les choses étant comme elles sont; *F:* **how are things? how's things?** (i) comment vont les affaires? (ii) comment ça va? **4.**

the latest t. in shoes, chaussure(s) dernier cri; **it's the (very) latest t.,** c'est tout ce qu'il y a de plus moderne. **5. the t. (to do),** l'usage *m*, l'étiquette *f*; **it's not the done t.,** cela ne se fait pas.

thingummy, thingamy, thingumajig, thingumabob ['θiŋəmi, -dʒig, -bɔb] *n. F:* chose *m*, machin *m*, truc *m*.

think¹ [θiŋk] *n.* **to have a (quiet) t.,** réfléchir; *F:* **you've got another t. coming!** tu peux toujours courir!

think² *v. tr. & i.* (*p.t. & p.p.* **thought** [θɔːt]) **1.** penser, réfléchir; **to t. aloud,** penser tout haut; **to t. hard,** réfléchir profondément; se creuser la tête; *F:* **to t. big,** être ambitieux; **what are you thinking?** à quoi pensez-vous? **I did it without thinking,** je l'ai fait sans réfléchir, sans y penser; **t. before you speak,** pesez vos paroles; **just t. a minute!** réfléchissez un peu! **give me time to t. (and remember),** laissez-moi me reprendre; **to t. again,** se raviser; **you can (just) t. again!** tu peux toujours courir! **2.** songer, s'imaginer, se figurer; **I (really) can't t. why, what, where . . .,** je me demande bien pourquoi, ce que, où . . .; **I can't t. what you mean,** je ne peux pas m'imaginer ce que vous voulez dire; **what will people t.?** qu'en dira-t-on? **he thinks he knows everything,** il s'imagine tout savoir; **one would have thought that . . .,** c'était à croire que . . .; **anyone would t. he was asleep,** on dirait qu'il dort; **who'd have thought it!** qui l'aurait dit? **just t.!** songez donc! **to t. that he's only twenty!** et dire qu'il n'a que vingt ans! **3.** (*a*) (*conceive the notion of*) **I have been thinking that . . .,** l'idée m'est venue que . . .; **I only thought to help you,** ma seule pensée était de vous aider; (*b*) **did you t. to bring any money?** avez-vous pensé, songé, à apporter de l'argent? **4.** (*a*) **do you t. you could do it?—I t. I could,** pensez-vous que cela vous serait possible?—je pense que oui; **it's better, don't you t., to get it over with?** il vaut mieux, n'est-ce pas, en finir? **I thought I heard him,** j'ai cru l'entendre; **I thought it was all over,** je croyais que tout était fini; **everyone asked him what he thought,** chacun lui a demandé son avis; **I t. she's pretty,** je la trouve jolie; **everyone thought he was mad,** on le tenait pour fou; **I rather t. it's going to rain,** j'ai dans l'idée qu'il va pleuvoir; **it is thought that . . .,** on suppose que +*ind.*; **I t. so,** c'est ce qui me semble; je pense que oui; **I t. not, I don't t. so,** je pense que non; **so I thought, I thought so, I thought as much,** je le pensais bien; **I (should) hardly t. so,** c'est peu probable; **I should t. so!** je crois bien! **I shouldn't t. so,** je ne crois pas; *F:* **that's what you t.!** tu penses! (*b*) juger, considérer, croire, trouver, penser; **if you t. it necessary to . . .,** si vous jugez nécessaire de . . .; **I hardly t. it likely that . . .,** il n'est guère probable que +*sub.*; **you thought her (to be) a fool,** vous l'avez prise pour une sotte; **they were thought to be rich,** on les disait, supposait, riches; ils passaient pour (être) riches. **5.** s'attendre à (qch.); **I little thought I would see him again,** je ne m'attendais guère à le revoir. **think about, of** *v.ind.tr.* (*a*) penser à (qn, qch.); songer à (qch.); **we're thinking of you,** nous pensons à vous; **I have thought about your proposal,** j'ai réfléchi à votre proposition; **one can't t. of everything,** on ne saurait penser à tout; **I never thought of it, about it,** je n'y ai pas pensé; je n'y ai jamais songé; **I can't t. of his name,** son nom ne me revient pas; **I can't t. of the right word,** le mot propre m'échappe; **(when you) come to t. of it,** à la réflexion; **he can't sleep for thinking about it,** il perd le sommeil à force d'y penser; *F:* il n'en dort pas; **that's worth thinking about,** cela mérite réflexion; **what am I thinking of?** où ai-je la tête? (*b*) s'imaginer, se figurer; **t. of a number,** pensez à un chiffre; **I thought of him as being tall,** je le voyais grand; *F:* **(just) t. of that! to t. of it!** qui l'aurait cru? **t. of it, he's in love with her!** il l'aime, figure-toi! **when I t. of what might have happened!** quand je pense à ce qui aurait pu arriver! (*c*) considérer (qn); avoir égard à (qn); songer à (qch.); (*d*) **to t. of, about, doing sth.,** méditer, projeter, de faire qch.; penser à faire qch.; **I couldn't t. of it!** c'est impossible! (*e*) penser (qch.) de (qch., qn); **what do you t. of it, about it?** qu'en pensez-vous? **what do you t. of this picture?** que dites-vous de ce tableau? **to t. a great deal of oneself, to t. too much of oneself,** avoir une haute idée de sa personne; **to t. too much of sth.,** attacher trop d'importance à qch.; **I told him what I thought of him,** je lui ai dit son fait; (*f*) **to t. well, badly, of s.o.,** avoir une bonne, mauvaise, opinion de qn; **he is well thought of,** il est bien vu, bien considéré. **thinking 1.** *a.* pensant; qui pense. **2.** *n.* (*a*) pensée(s) *f*(*pl*), méditation(s) *f*(*pl*), réflexion(s) *f*(*pl*); **he did some hard t.,** il a réfléchi profondément; **to put on one's t. cap,** méditer une question; (*b*) pensée, opinion *f*, avis *m*; **to my (way of) t.,** à mon avis; **I hope to bring you round to my way of t.,** j'espère vous amener à mon opinion, à mon point de vue. **think of** *v.ind.tr. see* THINK ABOUT. **think out** *v.tr.* (*a*) imaginer, méditer (qch.); combiner (un plan); **well thought out plan,** projet bien étudié; **carefully thought out answer,** réponse bien pesée; (*b*) arriver à la solution de (qch.); **he thinks things out for himself,** il juge des choses par lui-même. **think over** *v.tr.* réfléchir sur, aviser à (une question, etc.); délibérer de (qch.); **I'll t. it over,** j'y réfléchirai; **t. it over (carefully),** réfléchissez-y, songez-y, bien; **on thinking it over . . .,** après réflexion . . .. **think up** *v.tr. F:* imaginer (un projet, une méthode).

thinkable ['θiŋkəbl] *a.* (projet) concevable, imaginable; **is it t. that . . .?** peut-on imaginer que +*sub.*

thinker ['θiŋkər] *n.* penseur, -euse.

thinner ['θinər] *n.* (*occ.* **thinners**) diluant *m*, dissolvant *m* (pour peinture, etc.).

thinness ['θinnis] *n.* **1.** (*a*) minceur *f* (d'une feuille de papier, etc.); légèreté *f* (d'un tissu, etc.); (*b*) maigreur *f*, minceur (d'une personne). **2.** état clairsemé (du blé, etc.); rareté *f* (des cheveux, etc.). **3.** fluidité *f* (d'un liquide); raréfaction *f*, légèreté (de l'air); caractère grêle, fluet (d'une voix).

third [θəːd] **1.** (*a*) *num.a.* troisième (jour, étage, etc.); tiers (état, etc.); **t. person,** (i) *Jur:* tierce personne; tiers *m*; (ii) *Gram:* troisième personne; *Sch:* **t. form, year,** *approx.* = classe *f* de quatrième; **Edward the T.,** Édouard Trois; **the T. World,** le tiers monde; **(on) the t. (of May),** le trois (mai); **in (the) t. place,** en troisième lieu; troisièmement; **every t. day,** tous les trois jours; **a t. rate pianist,** un joueur de piano de troisième ordre; (*b*) *n.* (*pers.*) tiers. **2.** *n.* (*a*) *Mus:* tierce *f*; (*b*) *Sch:* **to get a t. (class honours degree) in history,** obtenir la mention *passable* en histoire; (*c*) *Aut:* **to go into t.,** passer en troisième *f*. **3.** *n.* (*fraction*) tiers; **to lose a t., two thirds, of one's money,** perdre le tiers, les deux tiers, de son argent.

thirdly ['θəːdli] *adv.* troisièmement; en troisième lieu.

thirst¹ [θəːst] *n.* **1.** soif *f*. **2.** *Lit:* **the t. for, after, knowledge,** la soif de connaître, de la science; **to satisfy one's t. for adventure,** apaiser sa soif d'aventures.

thirst² *v.i.* **1.** *A: & Lit:* avoir soif; être altéré. **2. to t. for blood, revenge,** être altéré de sang, de vengeance.

thirsty ['θəːsti] *a.* **1.** (*a*) altéré; assoiffé; **to be, feel, t.,** avoir soif; *F:* **all this talking is t. work,** de tant parler, cela donne soif, cela vous sèche le gosier; (*b*) *Lit:* **t. for blood, for riches,** assoiffé, altéré, avide, de sang, de richesses. **2.** (*of earth, etc.*) desséché, sec, *f.* sèche. **-ily** *adv.* avidement.

thirteen [θəː'tiːn, 'θəːtiːn] *num. a. & n.* treize (*m*);

she's t. (years old), elle a treize ans; **at t. hundred hours,** à treize heures.

thirteenth [θɔːˈtiːnθ] **1.** *num.a. & n.* treizième (*mf*); **(on) the t. (of May),** le treize (mai). **2.** *n.* (*fraction*) treizième *m.*

thirtieth [ˈθɔːtiiθ] *num.a. & n.* trentième (*mf*); **(on) the t. (of June),** le trente (juin).

thirty [ˈθɔːti] *num.a. & n.* trente (*m*); **t.-three,** trente-trois; **t.-first, t.-second,** trente et unième, trente-deuxième; **(on) the t.-first (of May),** le trente et un (mai); **about t. guests,** une trentaine d'invités; **to be t. (years old),** avoir trente ans; **the thirties,** les années trente; **he leaves at two-t.,** il part à deux heures trente.

this [ðis] **I.** *dem.pron.pl.* **these** [ðiːz] **1.** ceci; ce; **what's t.? what are these?** qu'est-ce que c'est (que ceci, *F:* que ça)? **who's t.?** qui est-ce? *Tp:* **who is t.?** qui est à l'appareil? **you'll be sorry for t.,** vous le regretterez; **at, upon, t.,** sur ce; là-dessus; **it ought to have come before t.,** cela devrait être déjà arrivé; **after t.,** après cela; ensuite; **t. is curious,** voilà qui est curieux; **t. is what he told me,** voici ce qu'il m'a dit; **t. is Mr Thomas,** je vous présente M. Thomas; **these are my children,** voici mes enfants; **t. is where he lives,** c'est ici qu'il habite; **these are things we cannot do without,** ce sont des choses dont on ne peut se passer; **listen to t.,** écoutez bien ceci; **what's t. (that) I hear?** qu'est-ce que j'entends? **do it like t.,** fais comme ceci; **what's all t.?** qu'est-ce qu'il y a? qu'est-ce qui se passe? **2.** (*opposed to* **that**) **will you have t. or that?** voulez-vous ceci ou cela? *F:* **they were talking about t. and that,** ils parlaient de choses et d'autres. **3.** (*referring to sth. already mentioned*) celui-ci, *f.* celle-ci, *pl.* ceux-ci, *f.* celles-ci; **I prefer these to those,** je préfère ceux-ci à ceux-là. **II.** *dem.a., pl.* **these** (*a*) ce, (*before vowel or h mute*) cet, *f.* cette, *pl.* ces; (*for emphasis and in opposition to* **that, those**) ce . . .-ci, cet . . .-ci, cette . . .-ci, ces . . .-ci; **t. book, these books,** ce livre(-ci), ces livres(-ci); **t. morning, t. afternoon, t. week,** ce matin, cet après-midi, cette semaine; **one of these days,** un de ces jours; **(in) these days, in t. day and age,** de nos jours; **by t. time,** à l'heure qu'il est; **to run t. way and that,** courir de-ci, de-là; **he will tell you that in t. or that case you should . . .,** il vous dira qu'en tel ou tel cas il faut . . .; **for t. reason,** voilà pourquoi; pour cette raison; *P:* **t. here house,** cette maison(-ci); (*b*) *Pej:* **he's one of these artist chaps,** c'est un de ces artistes; (*c*) **I've known him these three years,** je le connais depuis trois ans. **III.** *dem.adv.* aussi . . . que ceci; **t. high, as high as t.,** aussi haut que ceci, que cela, que ça; **t. far,** jusqu'ici; jusque-là.

thistle [ˈθisl] *n. Bot:* chardon *m.*

thistledown [ˈθis(ə)ldaun] *n.* duvet *m* de chardon.

thither [ˈðiðər] *adv. A: & Lit:* (*expressing motion*) là; y; **to run hither and t.,** courir çà et là.

tho' [ðou] *conj. & adv. F:* = THOUGH.

thole, tholepin [ˈθoul(pin)] *n. Nau:* tolet *m.*

thong [θɔŋ] *n.* (*a*) lanière *f* de cuir; (*b*) lanière, longe *f* (de fouet).

thoracic [θɔːˈræsik] *a.* thoracique.

thorax, *pl.* **thoraces** [ˈθɔːræks, θɔːˈreisiːz] *n. Anat: Ent:* thorax *m.*

thorn [θɔːn] *n.* (*a*) *Bot:* épine *f*; *Fig:* **a t. in one's, the, flesh, in one's side,** une épine au pied; **to be a t. in s.o.'s flesh, side,** être un sujet continuel d'irritation à qn; (*b*) *Bot:* épine; **t. apple,** pomme épineuse.

thornback [ˈθɔːnbæk] *n. Ich:* raie bouclée.

thornbush [ˈθɔːnbuʃ] *n.* (arbrisseau) épineux *m*; épine *f.*

thornless [ˈθɔːnlis] *a.* sans épines.

thorny [ˈθɔːni] *a.* épineux; *Rept:* **t. devil,** moloch *m*; *Fig:* **t. question,** question épineuse.

thorough [ˈθʌrə] *a.* (*a*) (*of search, etc.*) minutieux; (*of knowledge*) profond; (*of work*) consciencieux; **to give a room a t. cleaning,** nettoyer une pièce à fond; **to be t. in one's work,** travailler consciencieusement; (*b*) **a t. musician,** un musicien consommé; **a t. scoundrel,** un coquin fieffé. **-ly** *adv.* tout à fait; (savoir une langue, etc.) parfaitement; (renouveler) entièrement; (nettoyer, savoir qch.) à fond; **t. honest,** d'une honnêteté à toute épreuve.

thoroughbred [ˈθʌrəbred] **1.** *a.* (cheval) pur sang *inv*; (chien, etc.) de race; (*of pers.*) qui a de la race. **2.** *n.* (*a*) (*horse*) pur-sang *m inv*; (*b*) animal, -aux *m,* de race; (*of pers.*) **she's a real t.,** elle est très racée.

thoroughfare [ˈθʌrəfɛər] *n.* voie *f* de communication; **public t.,** voie publique; **one of the main throughfares of the town,** une des rues principales, une des artères, de la ville; **busy t.,** rue très passante; route *f* à grande circulation, à circulation intense; *P.N:* **no t.,** rue barrée; passage interdit (au public).

thoroughgoing [ˈθʌrəgouiŋ] *a.* (*a*) (*of search, inspection, etc.*) minutieux; (*of knowledge, etc.*) profond; (*of work, etc.*) consciencieux; (*b*) (travailleur, etc.) consciencieux; (moraliste, etc.) intransigeant.

thoroughness [ˈθʌrənis] *n.* perfection *f,* minutie *f* (du travail).

those *see* THAT[1].

thou [ðau] *pers.pron. A: & B:* (*a*) (*unstressed*) tu; **t. seest,** tu vois; **t. art,** tu es; **hearest t.?** entends-tu? (*b*) (*stressed*) toi; **t. and I,** toi et moi.

though [ðou] **I.** *conj.* **1.** quoique, bien que +*sub. or occ. ind.*; **t. he is poor he is generous,** quoiqu'il soit pauvre il est généreux; **I respect him t. I don't like him,** je le respecte, bien qu'il ne me soit pas sympathique; **t. I am a father,** tout père que je suis; **t. not beautiful, she was attractive,** sans être belle elle plaisait. **2.** *A: & Lit:* (*with sub.*) **this statement, terrible t. it be,** cette déclaration, pour terrible qu'elle soit; **strange t. it may seem,** si étrange que cela semble; **even t. you'll laugh at me,** quand vous devriez vous moquer de moi. **3. as t.,** comme si; **it looks as t. he's gone,** il semble qu'il soit parti; **as t. nothing had happened,** comme si de rien n'était. **II.** *adv.* (*a*) cependant, pourtant; **he had promised to go; he didn't t.,** il avait promis d'y aller; cependant il n'en a rien fait; (*b*) (*exclamatory*) **did he t.!** il a dit, fait, cela?

thought[1] [θɔːt] *n.* **1.** pensée *f*; **t. is free,** la pensée est libre; **capable of t.,** capable de penser. **2.** (*a*) pensée, idée *f*; **he hasn't a t. in his head,** il n'a pas une idée dans la tête; **happy t.,** heureuse idée; **dark, gloomy, thoughts,** idées, pensées, sombres; *F:* **a penny for your thoughts,** à quoi pensez-vous? **to read s.o.'s thoughts,** lire dans la pensée de qn; **t. reading,** lecture *f* de la pensée; **t. reader,** liseur, -euse, de pensées; **I'm not a t. reader, I can't read your thoughts,** je ne suis pas devin; (*b*) **the mere t. of it,** rien que d'y penser; **have you ever given it a single t.?** y avez-vous jamais pensé? **I didn't give it another t.,** je n'y ai pas repensé; (*c*) **thoughts,** esprit *m,* pensée; **to collect one's thoughts,** rassembler ses idées, ses esprits; **her thoughts were elsewhere,** son esprit était ailleurs; (*d*) **contemporary t.,** la pensée contemporaine. **3.** (*a*) réflexion *f,* considération *f*; **after much t.,** après mûre réflexion; **to give a great deal of t. to sth.,** réfléchir beaucoup à qch.; **on second thoughts,** (toute) réflexion faite; après réflexion; (*b*) pensées, rêverie *f,* méditation *f*; **to be deep, lost,** *Lit:* **wrapt, in t.,** être perdu, absorbé, dans ses pensées; être plongé dans ses réflexions. **4.** (*a*) intention *f,* dessein *m*; **I had no t. of offending you,** je n'avais pas l'intention de vous offenser; **you must give up all thought(s) of seeing him,** il faut renoncer à le voir; il ne faut plus penser à le voir; **his one t. is to get money,** il ne pense qu'à l'argent; (*b*) (*usu. neg.*) *O:* **I had no t. of meeting you here,** je ne m'attendais pas à vous rencontrer ici. **5.** *adv.phr. F: O:* **a t. too sweet,** un tout petit peu trop sucré.

thought² *see* THINK².

thoughtful ['θɔːtf(u)l] *a.* **1.** (*a*) pensif, méditatif; rêveur, -euse; (*b*) réfléchi, prudent. **2.** prévenant; plein d'égards (**of,** pour); **he was t. enough to warn me,** il a eu la prévenance, l'attention, de m'avertir. **3.** (*of book, writer*) profond. **-fully** *adv.* **1.** (*a*) pensivement; d'un air pensif, rêveur, méditatif; (*b*) d'une manière réfléchie, prudente. **2.** avec prévenance.

thoughtfulness ['θɔːtf(u)lnis] *n.* **1.** (*a*) méditation *f*, recueillement *m*; (*b*) réflexion *f*, prudence *f*. **2.** prévenance *f*; égards *mpl* (**of,** pour, envers).

thoughtless ['θɔːtlis] *a.* **1.** irréfléchi; étourdi; **t. action,** étourderie *f*; acte inconsidéré. **2. t. of others,** qui manque d'égards, de prévenance, pour les autres. **-ly** *adv.* **1.** étourdiment; sans réflexion. **2. to treat s.o. t.,** manquer d'égards envers qn.

thoughtlessness ['θɔːtlisnis] *n.* **1.** irréflexion *f*; étourderie *f*. **2.** manque d'égards, de prévenance (**of,** pour, envers).

thousand ['θauz(ə)nd] *num.a. & n.* mille (*m*) *inv*; *n.* millier *m*; **the year 4000 B.C.,** l'an quatre mille av. J.-C.; *Jur: Adm:* **the year one t. nine hundred and thirty,** l'an mil neuf cent trente; **a t. years,** mille ans; un millénaire; **about a t. men,** un millier d'hommes; quelque mille hommes; **three hundred t. men,** trois cent mille hommes; **thousands of people,** des milliers de gens; **in thousands, in hundreds of thousands,** par milliers, par centaines de mille; **he's one in a t.,** c'est un homme entre mille; **a t. and one,** mille un; *F:* **I've got a t. and one things to ask you,** j'ai mille et une choses à vous demander; **no, no, a t. times no!** non, non, et cent fois non!

thousandfold ['θauz(ə)n(d)fould] **1.** *a.* multiplié par mille. **2.** *adv.* mille fois autant.

thousandth ['θauz(ə)n(t)θ] *num.a. & n.* millième (*mf*).

thraldom ['θrɔːldəm] *n. Lit:* esclavage *m*, assujetissement *m*, servitude *f*.

thrall [θrɔːl] *n. Lit:* **1.** esclave *mf*, serf *m* (**of, to,** de). **2. kept in t.,** maintenu en esclavage *m*.

thrash [θræʃ] **1.** *v.tr.* (*a*) (i) battre (qn, une bête); rosser, tanner le cuir à (qn); **to t. s.o. soundly,** donner une bonne raclée à qn; (ii) battre (un adversaire) à plate(s) couture(s); (*b*) **to t. out,** (i) débattre, creuser (une question); discuter (une question) à fond; (ii) arriver à (une solution, la vérité, etc.); (*c*) battre (le blé); (*d*) **to t. the water,** battre l'eau; (*e*) **to t. one's arms and legs about,** se débattre des mains et des pieds. **2.** *v.i.* (*a*) (*of water*) battre, clapoter (**against,** contre); (*b*) (*of pers.*) **to t. about,** se débattre des mains et des pieds. **thrashing** *n.* (*a*) volée *f* (de coups), *F:* raclée *f*, rossée *f*; **to give s.o. a t.,** donner une raclée à qn; (*b*) *Sp: etc:* défaite *f*; **to give one's opponent a sound t.,** battre son adversaire à plate(s) couture(s); (*c*) battage *m* (du blé).

thread¹ [θred] *n.* **1.** (*a*) filament *m*, fil *m* (de soie, d'une plante, etc.); **his life hung by a t.,** sa vie ne tenait qu'à un fil; *Paperm:* **t. mark,** filigrane *m* (des billets de banque); (*b*) filet *m* (d'eau, de fumée, de lumière, etc.). **2.** (*a*) *Needlew:* fil (de coton, de nylon, etc.); **gold t.,** fil d'or; **button t.,** fil à boutons; gros fil; (*b*) *Tex:* fil (de trame, de chaîne); *Needlew:* **drawn t. work,** ouvrage *m*, travail *m*, à jour(s); **the t. of life,** la trame de la vie; **to lose the t. of the conversation,** perdre le fil de la conversation; **to gather up the threads of a story,** reprendre les fils d'une histoire; (*c*) **(length of) t.,** brin *m*, bout *m* (de coton, de soie, etc.). **3.** *Tchn:* filet (d'une vis, d'un boulon, etc.).

thread² *v.tr.* **1.** (*a*) enfiler (une aiguille); (*b*) enfiler (des perles) (**on,** sur); (*c*) enfiler (une ficelle, un élastique (**through sth.,** dans qch.); (*d*) **to t. one's way between the cars,** se faufiler, s'insinuer, entre les voitures. **2.** *Tchn:* (*a*) fileter (une vis, etc.); tarauder (un tuyau, un écrou, etc.); (*b*) (*of screw, etc.*) **to t. into sth.,** se visser dans qch. **threading** *n.* **1.** enfilement *m* (d'une aiguille, etc.). **2.** *Tchn:* filetage *m* (d'une vis, etc.); taraudage *m* (d'un tuyau, etc.).

threadbare ['θredbεər] *a.* (*a*) (*of clothes, etc.*) râpé, élimé, usé (jusqu'à la corde); (*b*) (*of subject, argument, joke, etc.*) usé (jusqu'à la corde), rebattu.

threadworm ['θredwəːm] *n. Ann:* nématode *m*; oxyure *m*.

threat [θret] *n.* menace *f*; **to utter a t.,** proférer une menace; **idle t.,** menace en l'air; **there is a t. of rain,** la pluie menace.

threaten ['θret(ə)n] *v.tr.* **1.** (*a*) menacer (qn); *Jur:* intimider (qn); **to t. s.o. with sth.,** menacer qn de qch.; **(to be) threatened with sth.,** (être) menacé de qch.; **race threatened with extinction,** race en voie de disparition; **the threatened strike didn't come off,** cette menace de grève n'a pas abouti; (*b*) **to t. to do sth.,** menacer de faire qch.; **this situation threatens to become dangerous,** cette situation menace de devenir dangereuse. **2.** *v.i.* **a storm is threatening,** l'orage menace, un orage s'annonce. **threatening** *a.* (ton, air) menaçant; (lettre) de menaces; **t. language,** menaces (verbales); *Jur:* intimidation *f*; **the weather looks t.,** le temps menace. **threateningly** *adv.* d'une manière menaçante.

three [θriː] *num.a & n.* trois (*m*); (*a*) **every t. months,** tous les trois mois; **twenty-t.,** vingt-trois; **t. and a half,** trois et demi; **to be t. (years old),** avoir trois ans; **he leaves at t. thirty, at half past t.,** il part à trois heures trente, à trois heures et demie; **to come in t. by t., in threes,** entrer par trois; *Cards:* **t. of diamonds,** trois de carreau; (*at dominoes, etc.*) **double t.,** double-trois *m*, *pl.* doubles-trois; **t. star hotel, brandy,** hôtel, cognac, trois-étoiles; *Th:* **t. act play,** pièce *f* en trois actes; *Pol:* **the Big T.,** les Trois (Grands); **t. sided, t. party, conversations,** conversations tripartites, triparties; (*b*) **t.-stranded rope,** corde à trois cordons; **t.-bladed propeller,** hélice tripale; **t.-pointed,** à trois pointes; **t. seater,** triplace *m*; *Av:* **t.-engine(d) aircraft,** trimoteur *m*; (*c*) *U.S:* **t.-ring circus,** (i) cirque *m* contenant trois arènes et montrant plusieurs numéros à la fois; (ii) situation *f* comique pleine d'activité désordonnée; cirque.

three-colour(ed) [θriː'kʌlər, -'kʌləd] *a. Phot:* trichrome; **t.-colour process,** trichromie *f*.

three-cornered [θriː'kɔːnəd] *a.* triangulaire; **t.-c. hat,** tricorne *m*; **t.-c. discussion,** débat *m* à trois.

three-course ['θriːkɔːs] *a.* (repas) à trois plats.

three-dimensional [θriːd(a)i'menʃənəl] *a.* tridimensionnel; à trois dimensions.

threefold ['θriːfould] **1.** *a.* triple. **2.** *adv.* trois fois autant; **to increase t.,** tripler.

three-handed [θriː'hændid] *a. Cards: etc:* **t.-h. game,** partie *f* à trois.

three-legged [θriː'legid] *a.* (tabouret, etc.) à trois pieds; *Games:* **t.-l. race,** course *f* à trois pieds.

threepence ['θrep(ə)ns] *n.* trois pence *mpl*.

threepenny ['θrep(ə)ni] *a.* coûtant trois pence, à, de, trois pence; *A:* **t. (bit),** pièce *f* de trois pence.

three-piece ['θriːpiːs] *a.* en trois pièces; *Cost:* **t.-p. suit,** trois-pièces *m inv*; *Furn:* **t.-p. suite,** canapé et deux fauteuils assortis.

three-ply ['θriːplai] *a.* (*of wool, etc.*) à trois fils; (*of rope*) en trois brins.

three-point ['θriːpɔint] *a. Av:* **t.-p. landing,** atterrissage *m* trois points; *Aut:* **t.-p. turn,** demi-tour *m* en trois manœuvres.

three-quarter [θri:ˈkwɔ:tər] **1.** *a.* **t.-q. length coat,** trois-quarts *m inv*; **t.-q. face portrait,** portrait *m* de trois quarts; *Rugby Fb:* **t.-q. (back),** trois-quarts. **2.** *adv.* **the room was t.-quarters full,** la salle était pleine aux trois quarts, aux trois quarts pleine.

threescore [ˈθri:skɔ:r] *a. A: & Lit:* soixante; **t. (years) and ten,** soixante-dix ans.

threesome [ˈθri:səm] *n.* (*a*) groupe *m* de trois personnes; (*b*) *Golf:* partie de trois; trois-balles *m inv.*

three-speed [ˈθri:spi:d] *a.* à trois vitesses.

three-storey(ed), *NAm:* **-story, -storied** [θri:ˈstɔ:ri(d)] *a.* (maison) à trois étages.

three-way [ˈθri:wei] *a.* (division, etc.) en trois; (discussion, etc.) à trois.

three-wheeler [θri:ˈ(h)wi:lər] *n.* (*a*) (petite) voiture à trois roues; trois-roues *m inv*; (*b*) tricycle *m.*

threnody [ˈθrenədi] *n.* chant *m* funèbre.

thresh [θreʃ] *v.tr.* **1.** battre (le blé). **2.** (*of ship's screw, of whale's tail, etc.*) **to t. the water,** battre l'eau. **threshing** *n.* battage *m* (du blé); **t. floor,** aire *f*; **t. machine,** batteuse *f.*

thresher [ˈθreʃər] *n.* (*a*) (*pers.*) batteur, -euse, en grange; (*b*) (*machine*) batteuse.

threshold [ˈθreʃould] *n.* **1.** seuil *m*, pas *m* (d'une porte, etc.); **on the t.,** sur le seuil; au seuil; **to cross the t.,** franchir le seuil; **to be on the t. of life,** être au seuil, au début, de la vie. **2.** (*a*) *Physiol:* **t. of audibility, of hearing,** seuil d'audibilité; **t. of pain,** seuil de douleur; (*b*) *Ph: etc:* seuil (de fission, de réaction).

thrice [θrais] *adv. A: & Lit:* trois fois.

thrift [θrift] *n.* économie *f*, épargne *f. Mil: etc:* **t. shop,** magasin spécialisé dans la vente des articles de seconde main.

thriftiness [ˈθriftinis] *n.* économie *f*, épargne *f.*

thriftless [ˈθriftlis] *a.* **1.** dépensier. **2.** imprévoyant.

thriftlessness [ˈθriftlisnis] *n.* **1.** gaspillage *m.* **2.** imprévoyance *f.*

thrifty [ˈθrifti] *a.* **1.** économe, épargnant. **2.** *NAm:* prospère; florissant. **-ily** *adv.* avec économie; (vivre) frugalement.

thrill¹ [θril] *n.* (*a*) frisson *m*, tressaillement *m*; **t. of pleasure,** frisson de plaisir; (*b*) (vive) émotion; **the crowd had the t. of their lives,** la foule était électrisée; **it gave me quite a t.,** ça m'a fait quelque chose.

thrill² **1.** *v.tr.* (*a*) faire frissonner, faire frémir (qn); *F:* **she's thrilled with her new car,** elle est ravie de sa nouvelle voiture; (*b*) faire vibrer le cœur de (qn); émouvoir (qn); émotionner (qn); électriser (son auditoire); **to be thrilled at the sight of sth.,** ressentir une vive émotion à la vue de qch. **2.** *v.i. esp. Lit:* tressaillir, frissonner (de joie). **thrilling** *a.* (spectacle, etc.) émouvant, saisissant, émotionnant; (voyage) mouvementé; (roman, etc.) sensationnel, à sensation; *Rac:* **t. finish,** arrivée palpitante.

thriller [ˈθrilər] *n.* pièce *f*, film *m*, à suspense.

thrive [θraiv] *v.i.* (*p.t. & p.p.* **thrived** [θraivd]; *A: & N.Am: p.t.* **throve** [θrouv]; *p.p.* **thriven** [ˈθrivn]) (*a*) (*of child, plant*) se (bien) développer; *F:* profiter; (*of adult*) se bien porter; (*of business, etc.*) bien marcher, bien aller; **children who t. on milk,** enfants à qui le lait profite bien; **plant that thrives in all soils,** plante qui s'accommode de tous les sols; (*b*) (*of pers.*) prospérer (**on sth.,** de qch.); **to t. on other people's misfortunes,** s'engraisser de la misère d'autrui. **thriving** *a.* (*of pers., plant, etc.*) vigoureux; bien portant; (*of pers., business*) prospère, florissant.

thro' [θru:] *prep. F:* = THROUGH.

throat [θrout] *n.* (*a*) *Anat:* gorge *f*; **to cut s.o.'s t.,** couper la gorge à qn; **he's cutting his own t.,** il travaille à sa propre ruine; **they were cutting each other's, one another's, throats,** ils se faisaient une concurrence désastreuse; **t. microphone,** laryngophone *m*; (*b*) (*gullet*) gorge, gosier *m*; **the back of the t.,** le fond de la gorge; l'arrière-gorge *f*, *pl.* arrière-gorges; **to have a sore t.,** avoir mal à la gorge; **to clear one's t.,** s'éclaircir la voix, la gorge; se racler la gorge; *Med:* **t. spray,** insufflateur *m*; *F:* **he's always ramming it down my t.,** il m'en rabat toujours les oreilles.

throatiness [ˈθroutinis] *n.* qualité gutturale (de la voix).

throaty [ˈθrouti] *a.* (*of voice*) d'arrière-gorge; guttural, -aux.

throb¹ [θrɔb] *n.* palpitation *f*, pulsation *f* (du pouls, du cœur, etc.); vrombissement *m* (d'une machine).

throb² *v.i.* **(throbbed)** (*a*) (*of heart, etc.*) battre fort, palpiter; (*of engine, etc.*) vrombir; **London is a city throbbing with activity,** Londres est une ville palpitante d'activité; (*b*) **my finger is throbbing,** mon doigt lancine. **throbbing** **1.** *a.* (*of heart, etc.*) palpitant; (*of engine*) vrombissant; **t. pain,** douleur lancinante; élancement *m.* **2.** *n.* (*a*) battement fort, palpitation *f*, pulsation *f* (du cœur, etc.); vrombissement *m* (d'une machine); (*b*) élancement *m* (d'un panaris).

throes [θrouz] *n.pl.* douleurs *fpl*, angoisse *f*, agonie *f*; **the t. of death,** les affres *fpl* de la mort; l'agonie; *F:* **we're in the t. of moving house,** nous sommes en plein déménagement.

thrombosis [θrɔmˈbousis] *n. Med:* thrombose *f*; **coronary t.,** infarctus *m* du myocarde.

throne [θroun] *n.* (*a*) trône; **to come to the t., to ascend,** *Lit:* **mount, the t.,** monter sur le trône; **the heir to the t.,** l'héritier du trône; **the power behind the t.,** l'Éminence grise; (*b*) *F:* (*lavatory*) trône.

throng¹ [θrɔŋ] *n.* (*a*) foule *f*, affluence *f*; (*b*) cohue *f.*

throng² **1.** *v.i.* s'assembler en foule; affluer (à, dans, un endroit); **to t. round s.o.,** se presser autour de qn; **they thronged into the square,** ils arrivèrent en foule sur la place. **2.** *v.tr.* encombrer, emplir; **the room was thronged with people,** la pièce était bondée. **thronging** *a.* **a t. mass,** une foule grouillante (de gens).

throttle¹ [ˈθrɔtl] *n.* **1.** gosier *m.* **2.** *Mec.E:* (*a*) *Mch:* régulateur *m*; prise *f* de vapeur; (*b*) *I.C.E:* étrangleur *m*; obturateur *m*; **t. control, lever,** manette *f* des gaz; **to open, to close, the t.,** ouvrir, fermer, les gaz.

throttle² **1.** *v.tr.* étrangler (qn); saisir, serrer (qn) à la gorge. **2.** (*a*) *v.tr. Mch: I.C.E:* étrangler (la vapeur, le moteur); (*b*) *v.i.* **to t. down,** mettre le moteur au ralenti; *I.C.E:* couper, fermer, les gaz; *Av:* **to t. back,** couper, fermer, les gaz. **throttling** *n.* **1.** étranglement *m*, *Jur:* strangulation *f* (de qn). **2.** *Mch: I.C.E:* étranglement; *Mch:* manœuvre *f* de registre.

through [θru:] **I.** *prep.* **1.** (*a*) à travers; par; d'un côté à l'autre de (qch.); d'un bout à l'autre de (qch.); **t. a hedge,** au travers d'une haie; **to come, go, t. sth.,** traverser qch.; passer par qch.; **the path goes, leads, t. the forest,** le sentier traverse, passe par, la forêt; **I'm on my way t. Paris,** je suis de passage à Paris; **to look t. the window, t. a telescope,** regarder par la fenêtre, dans un télescope; **he came in t. the window,** il est entré par la fenêtre; **to go t. s.o.'s pockets,** fouiller qn; *Aut:* **to go t. a red light,** brûler un feu (rouge); **he's been t. it, t. a lot,** il en a vu de dures; il a mangé de la vache enragée; **to speak t. one's nose,** parler du nez; **he got t. his exam,** il a été reçu à son examen; *F:* **to put s.o. t. it,** faire subir à qn un interrogatoire très serré; **I'm half way t. this book,** j'ai lu la moitié de ce livre; (*b*) (*time*) pendant, durant; **all t. his life,** durant, pendant, toute sa vie; **t. the ages,** à travers les âges; *esp. NAm:* **Monday t. Friday,** de lundi à vendredi; du lundi au vendredi. **2. t. s.o.,** par qn; par l'entremise, l'intermédiaire, de qn; **t. sth.,** par le moyen de qch.; **to send sth. t. the post,** envoyer qch. par la poste. **3.** (*a*) en conséquence de, par suite de, à cause de, par (qch.); **t. ignorance,** par ignorance; **absent t. illness,** absent par suite, pour cause, de maladie; **to act t. fear,** agir sous le coup de la peur; (*b*) par l'action de (qn, qch.); **it's (all) t. me that he missed his train,** c'est à cause de moi qu'il a manqué son train. **II.** *adv.* **1.** (*a*) à travers; **the water poured t.,** l'eau coulait à travers; **to let s.o. t.,** laisser passer qn; **his trousers are t. at the knees,** son pantalon est percé aux genoux; *F:* **England are t. to the semi-final,** l'Angleterre jouera dans la demi-finale; (*b*) **t. and t.,** de bout en bout; de part en part; (connaître un quartier, etc.) comme le fond de sa poche; *F:* **to be soaked t.,** être trempé jusqu'aux os; (*c*) d'un bout à l'autre; jusqu'au bout; jusqu'à la fin; **to read a book (right) t.,** lire un livre d'un bout à l'autre; **to see, carry, sth. t.,** mener qch. à bonne fin; **we must go t. with it,** il faut aller jusqu'au bout; **to be t. with sth.,** (i) avoir fini qch.; (ii) en avoir (eu) assez; **are you t. with your work?** avez-vous fini votre travail? **I'm t. with you, we're t.,** j'en ai fini avec toi; c'est fini entre nous; **to be t.,** (i) *esp. NAm:* avoir terminé, fini (de parler, etc.); (ii) *F:* être fichu. **2.** (*a*) directement; **to book t. to Paris,** prendre un billet direct pour Paris; (*b*) **to get t. to s.o.,** (i) *Tp:* obtenir la communication avec qn; (ii) *F:* faire comprendre qch. à qn; *Tp:* **I'll put you t. to the secretary,** je vous passe la, le, secrétaire; **you're t.,** vous avez la communication. **III.** *a.* **1.** *Tchn:* (*of bolt, etc.*) traversant; *Const:* **t. stone,** parpaing *m.* **2.** (*of train, road, ticket*) direct; *Rail:* **t. coach,** wagon de groupage; **t. carriage for Paris,** voiture directe pour Paris; **t. passenger to Paris,** voyageur, -euse, direct(e) pour Paris; **t. traffic,** transit *m*; *P.N:* **no t. road,** voie sans issue.

throughout [θru:'aut] **1.** *prep.* (*a*) **t. the country,** dans tout le pays; **t. the world,** à travers le monde; (*b*) (*time*) **t. the year,** pendant toute l'année; **t. his life,** durant, pendant, toute sa vie. **2.** *adv.* (*a*) partout; **the coat is lined with fur t.,** le manteau est entièrement doublé de fourrure; (*b*) (*time*) tout le temps.

throughput ['θru:put] *n.* (*a*) capacité *f*; consommation *f*; débit *m*; (*b*) *Cmptr:* (i) débit, rendement *m*; (ii) capacité de traitement.

throughway ['θru:wei] *n. NAm:* autoroute *f.*

throw[1] [θrou] *n.* **1.** (*a*) jet *m*, lancement *m* (de qch.); *Sp:* lancer *m* (du javelot, etc.); **t. of dice,** coup *m* de dés; (*b*) distance (à laquelle on lance un objet); **long t.,** jet de longue portée; (*c*) *Wr:* mise *f* à terre (de l'adversaire). **2.** (*a*) *Mch:* volée *f* (du piston); (*b*) maneton *m* (de vilebrequin). **3.** *NAm:* (*a*) couvre-lit *m*, *pl.* couvre-lits; (*b*) *Cost:* écharpe.

throw[2] *v.tr.* (*p.t.* **threw** [θru:]; *p.p.* **thrown** [θroun]) **1.** (*a*) jeter, lancer (une balle, etc.); *Sp:* lancer (le disque, etc.); *v.i* **he can t. a hundred metres,** il est capable de lancer à cent mètres; **to t. s.o. a kiss,** envoyer un baiser à qn; **to t. the dice,** jeter les dés; (*at dice*) **to t. a five, a six,** amener cinq, six; **to t. stones at s.o., at a dog,** lancer, jeter, des pierres sur, à, qn, à un chien; **to t. sth. in s.o.'s face,** jeter qch. à la figure de qn; **don't t. that in my face,** ne me faites pas de reproches à ce sujet; **to t. a glance at s.o.,** jeter un coup d'œil à, sur, qn; **to t. oneself forwards, backwards,** se jeter en avant; se rejeter en arrière; **to t. oneself into sth.,** (i) se jeter dans (la rivière, etc.); (ii) se lancer à corps perdu dans (une entreprise); **to t. oneself on s.o.'s mercy, generosity,** s'en remettre à la merci, la générosité, de qn; *F:* **she threw herself at him,** elle s'est jetée à sa tête; **to t. temptation in s.o.'s way,** exposer qn à la tentation; **to t. the blame on s.o.,** rejeter la faute sur qn; (*b*) **to t. a sheet over sth.,** couvrir qch. d'un drap; **to t. a shawl over one's shoulders,** jeter un châle sur ses épaules; **to t. s.o. into prison,** jeter, mettre, qn en prison; **to t. s.o. into confusion,** jeter qn dans l'embarras; **to t. a switch,** basculer un interrupteur; **to t. open the door,** ouvrir la porte toute grande; **to t. open one's house to s.o.,** ouvrir sa maison à qn; **to t. s.o. out of work,** mettre qn au chômage. **2.** (*a*) projeter (de l'eau, etc.); (*b*) projeter (une image, une ombre) (**on,** sur); **to t. light on the matter,** jeter de la lumière sur la question; éclairer la question. **3. to t. a fit,** (i) tomber en convulsions; (ii) *F:* piquer une crise de nerfs; *F:* **to t. a party,** organiser une soirée. **4.** (*a*) *Wr:* renverser (un adversaire); (*b*) (*of horse*) **to t. its rider,** désarçonner son cavalier; (*of rider*) **to be thrown,** vider les arçons; être désarçonné. **5.** (*of reptile*) **to t. its skin,** muer. **6.** (*of animals*) mettre bas. **7.** tourner, façonner (un pot). **8.** *F:* étonner, déconcerter (qn); **this question threw me for a moment,** pendant un moment je ne savais que répondre à sa question. **9.** *F:* perdre délibérément (un match). **throw about** *v.tr.* (*a*) jeter (des objets) çà et là; éparpiller, disséminer (des objets); **to t. one's money about,** gaspiller son argent; (*b*) (i) **to t. one's arms about,** faire de grands gestes; **to t. oneself about,** se démener; (ii) **to be thrown about,** être ballotté. **throw aside** *v.tr.* (*a*) jeter (qch.) de côté; écarter (qch.); (*b*) se dépouiller de (toute haine, etc.). **throw away** *v.tr.* (*a*) jeter (sa cigarette, etc.); rejeter (qch.); jeter, mettre (qch.) au rebut; (*b*) gaspiller; **to t. away a chance,** laisser passer une occasion; **to t. away one's life,** se sacrifier inutilement; (*c*) (*of actor*) **to t. away a line,** énoncer une phrase avec une indifférence calculée. **throw back** *v.tr.* (*a*) jeter (un poisson dans l'eau, etc.); renvoyer, relancer (une balle, etc.); (*of mirror*) refléter, réfléchir (l'image, etc.); réverbérer (la lumière, la chaleur); (*b*) repousser (les volets, etc.); **to t. one's head back,** rejeter la tête en arrière; (*c*) retarder (un travail, etc.); (*d*) **to be thrown back upon s.o., sth.,** être forcé de se rabattre sur qn, qch. **throw down** *v.tr.* (*a*) jeter (qch.) de haut en bas; (*b*) jeter (qch.) à terre, par terre; abattre (ses cartes, etc.); **to t. oneself down,** se jeter sur le sol; **to t. down one's arms,** (i) abandonner ses armes; (ii) se rendre. **throw in** *v.tr.* (*a*) jeter (qn, qch.) dedans; *Fb:* **to t. in the ball,** *v.i.* **to t. in,** remettre la balle en touche; (*b*) ajouter (qch.); donner (qch.) en plus; (*c*) intercaler, insérer (une observation, un mot); placer (un mot); (*d*) **to t. in one's lot with s.o.,** *v.i. U.S:* **to t. in with s.o.,** partager le sort de qn; (*e*) **to t. in one's hand, one's cards,** abandonner, quitter, la partie; s'avouer vaincu; **to t. in the towel,** (i) *Box:* jeter l'éponge; (ii) *Fig:* s'avouer vaincu. **throwing** *n.* **1.** jet *m*, lancement *m; Sp:* lancer *m* (du disque, etc.). **2.** projection *f* (d'une image). **3.** renversement *m* (d'un cavalier). **4.** tournage *m* (d'un pot). **throw off** *v.tr.* **1.** (*adv. use*) (*a*) jeter (de la vapeur, etc.); (*b*) enlever, ôter (ses vêtements); se débarrasser, se défaire, de (qn, qch.); lever (le masque); guérir (d'un rhume, etc.); (*c*) composer (un poème, etc.) au pied levé. **2.** (*prep. use*) (*a*) **to t. s.o. off his bicycle,** faire tomber qn de sa bicyclette; (*b*) **to t. the dogs, the police, off the scent,** dépister les chiens, la police. **throw on** *v.tr.* mettre, passer, (ses vêtements) à la hâte. **throw out** *v.tr.* (*a*) jeter (qn, qch.) dehors; jeter, mettre (qch.) au rebut; mettre (qn) à la porte; *Cr:* mettre (le batteur) hors jeu en lançant la balle sur le guichet; (*b*) jeter, émettre (des rayons, etc.); répandre (de la chaleur, etc.); **to t. out roots,** pousser des racines; (*c*) rejeter, repousser (un projet de loi, etc.); (*d*) **to t. out one's chest,** bomber la poitrine; (*e*) lancer (un défi, etc.); **to t. out a suggestion,** émettre une proposition (sans insister); (*f*) (i) troubler, déconcerter (un orateur, etc.); (ii) **to t. s.o. out in his calculations,** tromper les calculs de qn. **throw over** *v.tr.* (*a*) abandonner (un ami, etc.); lâcher, plaquer (un amant, etc.); (*b*) renverser (un levier). **throw together** *v.tr.* (*a*) assembler (qch.) à la hâte; (*b*) **chance had thrown us together,** le hasard nous avait réunis. **throw up** *v.tr. & i.* (*a*) jeter (qch.) en l'air; (*b*) *F:* vomir, rendre; **volcano that throws up lava,** volcan *m* qui vomit de la lave; (*c*) lever haut, mettre haut (les mains, etc.); (*d*) construire (une maison, etc.) à la hâte; (*e*) faire ressortir (une couleur, etc.); (*f*) renoncer à, abandonner (une affaire, etc.); **to t. up one's job,** donner sa démission; **to feel like throwing everything up,** avoir envie de tout plaquer.

throwaway[1] ['θrouəwei] *a.* **1.** (couche, etc.) à jeter, jetable. **2.** *F:* **a t. line, remark,** un aparté.

throwaway[2] *n. F:* prospectus *m.*

throwback ['θroubæk] *n.* **1.** *Biol:* régression *f*; atavisme *m.* **2.** retour *m* (en arrière); **it's a t. to the 16th century,** ça remonte au 16ème siècle.

thrower ['θrouər] *n.* **1.** lanceur, -euse (de javelot, etc.); **discus t.,** discobole *m.* **2.** *Cer:* potier *m.*

throw-in ['θrouin] *n. Fb:* (rentrée *f* en) touche *f*; remise *f* en jeu (du ballon).

throw-out ['θrouaut] *n. Com:* **throw-outs,** rebuts *mpl*; articles défectueux, pièces *fpl* de rebut.

thru [θru:] *prep. NAm: & F:* = THROUGH.

thrum [θrʌm] *v.tr. & i.* pincer (de la guitare); tapoter (le piano); tambouriner (sur la vitre).

thrush[1] [θrʌʃ] *n. Orn:* grive *f.*

thrush[2] *n. Med:* muguet *m.*

thrust[1] [θrʌst] *n.* **1.** (*a*) poussée *f*; (*b*) coup *m* de pointe; *Fenc:* coup d'estoc; *Fenc:* **t. and parry,** la botte et la parade; **the cut and t. of political debate,** le jeu d'attaques et de ripostes des débats politiques; **that was a t. at you,** c'était une attaque à votre adresse; (*c*) *Mil:* poussée (d'une armée). **2.** (*a*) *Mec: Mec.E:* poussée, butée *f*; *Arch:* poussée (d'une voûte); (*b*) *Av: Nau:* poussée (d'une hélice).

thrust[2] *v.* (*p.t. & p.p.* **thrust**) **1.** *v.tr.* (*a*) pousser (qn, qch.) (avec force); **to t. sth. into sth.,** enfoncer, fourrer, qch. dans qch.; **to t. one's hands into one's pockets,** fourrer, plonger, les mains dans ses poches; (*b*) **to t. sth. on s.o.,** forcer qn à accepter qch.; imposer (son opinion) à qn; **to t. oneself (up) on s.o.,** s'imposer à qn, chez qn; (*c*) **to t. oneself, one's way, through the crowd,** se frayer un chemin à travers la foule. **2.** *v.i.* **to t. at s.o.,** porter un coup de pointe à qn (avec sa canne, etc.); *Fenc:* porter un coup d'estoc à qn; **to cut and t.,** frapper d'estoc et de taille; *Fig:* **to t. and parry,** riposter du tac au tac. **thrust aside, away** *v.tr.* repousser, écarter (qn, qch., *Lit:* la tentation). **thrust forward** *v.tr.* (*a*) pousser (qn, qch.) en avant; avancer, tendre, brusquement (la main, etc.); (*b*) **to t. oneself forward,** (i) se faire valoir, se mettre en avant; (ii) s'ingérer dans une affaire. **thrusting** *a.* (*a*) entreprenant; dynamique; (*b*) arriviste.

thruster ['θrʌstər] *n. F:* (*pers.*) arriviste *mf.*

thruway ['θru:wei] *n. NAm:* autoroute *f.*

thud[1] [θʌd] *n.* bruit sourd.

thud[2] *v.i.* **(thudded)** tomber, frapper, avec un bruit sourd; **his feet went thudding along the corridor,** ses pas résonnaient sourdement dans le couloir.

thug [θʌg] *n.* **1.** *Hist:* étrangleur *m.* **2.** brute *f*, brutal *m.*

thumb[1] [θʌm] *n.* pouce *m*; *F:* **he's all thumbs,** il est maladroit de ses mains; **to be under s.o.'s t.,** être sous la domination de qn; **she's got him right under her t.,** elle le mène à la baguette; elle le fait marcher comme elle veut; **to stick out like a sore t.,** choquer la vue; *F:* **thumbs up!** bravo! *F:* **to give the thumbs up, down, to a proposal,** accepter, rejeter, une proposition; **t. index,** (i) onglets *mpl*; (ii) répertoire *m* à onglets; **t.-indexed edition,** édition à onglets.

thumb[2] *v.tr. & i.* **1. to t. (through) a book,** feuilleter, parcourir, un livre; **well thumbed book,** livre bien feuilleté. **2. to t. one's nose at s.o.,** faire un pied de nez à qn. **3. to t. a lift,** faire de l'auto-stop, du stop.

thumbmark ['θʌmmɑ:k] *n.* marque *f* de pouce.

thumbnail ['θʌmneil] *n.* ongle *m* du pouce; **t. sketch,** (i) *Art:* croquis *m* minuscule, hâtif; (ii) description concise.

thumbprint ['θʌmprint] *n.* empreinte *f* de pouce.

thumbscrew ['θʌmskru:] *n.* vis *f* à oreilles.

thumbstall ['θʌmstɔ:l] *n.* **1.** poucier *m* (de cordonnier, etc.). **2.** *Med:* doigtier *m* pour pouce.

thumbtack ['θʌmtæk] *n. NAm:* punaise *f.*

thump[1] [θʌmp] *n.* **1.** coup sourd; cognement *m* (d'un mécanisme, etc.); **to fall with a t.,** tomber lourdement, avec un bruit sourd. **2.** coup de poing.

thump[2] *v.tr. & i.* bourrer (qn) de coups; *F:* cogner (qn); cogner (sur la table); **they began to t. one another,** ils ont commencé à se cogner; **to t. out a tune,** taper un air (sur le piano); **my heart was thumping,** mon cœur battait à grands coups. **thumping** *a. F:* énorme; **a t. big lie,** un gros mensonge.

thunder[1] ['θʌndər] *n.* **1.** (*a*) tonnerre *m*; **clap, peal, of t.,** coup *m* de tonnerre; **roll of t.,** roulement *m*, grondement *m*, de tonnerre; **there's t. in the air,** (i) le temps est à l'orage; (ii) *Fig:* l'atmosphère est orageuse; (*b*) **t. of applause,** tonnerre d'applaudissements; **voice of, like, t.,** voix de tonnerre; voix tonnante. **2.** (*a*) *Lit:* foudre *m*; (*b*) **to steal s.o.'s t.,** anticiper qn; couper l'herbe sous le pied à qn.

thunder[2] *v.i. & tr.* **1.** tonner; **it's thundering,** il tonne; **the avalanche thundered down,** l'avalanche roula dans un bruit de tonnerre; **the train thundered past,** le train a passé avec un bruit de tonnerre. **2. to t. out an order,** donner un ordre d'une voix tonnante. **thundering 1.** *a.* (*a*) tonnant; fulminant; **t. applause,** tonnerre d'applaudissements; (*b*) (i) **to be in a t. rage,** être dans une rage à tout casser; (ii) *F: O:* **what a t. nuisance!** ce que c'est embêtant! **what a t. (great) lie!** quel gros mensonge! **2.** *n.* tonnerre *m*; (*b*) bruit retentissant; bruit de tonnerre.

thunderbolt ['θʌndəboult] *n.* **1.** (coup *m* de) foudre *f*; **the news came upon me like a t.,** cette nouvelle a été un coup de foudre pour moi. **2.** nouvelle foudroyante; coup de foudre.

thunderclap ['θʌndəklæp] *n.* **1.** coup *m* de tonnerre. **2.** *Fig:* coup de tonnerre, de foudre.

thundercloud ['θʌndəklaud] *n.* nuage orageux.

thunderous ['θʌnd(ə)rəs] *a.* **1.** *O:* (*of weather*) orageux. **2.** (*of voice, etc.*) tonnant; **t. applause,** tonnerre *m* d'applaudissements.

thundershower ['θʌndəʃauər] *n.* averse accompagnée de tonnerre.

thunderstorm ['θʌndəstɔ:m] *n.* orage *m.*

thunderstruck ['θʌndəstrʌk] *a.* abasourdi, foudroyé; **to be t.,** tomber des nues; être atterré; **I was t. by the news,** cette nouvelle m'a foudroyé.

thundery ['θʌndəri] *a.* (temps, ciel) orageux; (temps, pluie) d'orage; **t. shower,** averse accompagnée de tonnerre; **the weather's t.,** le temps est à l'orage.

thurible ['θju:(ə)ribl] *n. Ecc:* encensoir *m.*

Thursday ['θə:zdi] *n.* jeudi *m*; **Maundy T.,** jeudi saint; **he's coming on T.,** il viendra jeudi.

thus [ðʌs] *adv.* **1.** *Lit:* ainsi; de cette façon; de cette manière. **2.** ainsi, donc; **t., when he arrived,** donc, lorsqu'il est arrivé. **3. t. far,** jusqu'ici; jusque-là; **t. much,** autant que cela (et pas davantage).

thwack [θwæk] *n.* coup *m*; claque *f*, taloche *f.*

thwart[1] [θwɔ:t, *Nau:* θɔ:t] *n.* banc *m* de nage.

thwart[2] *v.tr.* contrarier (qn); déjouer (une intrigue, les projets de qn); **to be thwarted,** essuyer un échec.

thy [ðai] *poss.a.* (**thine,** *before a vowel*) *A: & Lit:* ton, *f.* ta, *pl.* tes; (*in the fem. before a vowel sound*) ton; **t. glory,** ta gloire; **thine own son,** ton propre fils.
thyme [taim] *n. Bot:* thym *m*; **wild t.,** serpolet *m.*
thyroid ['θaiərɔid] *a. & n.* thyroïde (*f*).
thyself [ðai'self] *pers.pron. A: & Lit:* toi(-même).
ti [tiː] *n. Mus:* si *m.*
tiara [ti'ɑːrə] *n.* **1.** *Ecc:* tiare *f.* **2.** diadème *m.*
Tiber (the) [ðə'taibər] *Pr.n. Geog:* le Tibre.
Tibet [ti'bet] *Pr.n. Geog:* Tibet *m.*
Tibetan [ti'bet(ə)n] **1.** *a. Geog:* tibétain. **2.** *n. Geog:* Tibétain, -aine.
tibia, *pl.* **-ae** ['tibiə, -iː] *n. Anat: etc:* tibia *m.*
tic [tik] *n. Med:* tic *m.*
tich [titʃ] *n. F:* (*of pers.*) **a (little) t.,** un (petit) bout de chou.
tichy ['titʃi] *a. F:* minuscule.
tick¹ [tik] *n.* **1.** (*a*) **t.(-tock),** tic-tac *m* (d'une pendule); *F:* **on the t.,** à l'heure tapante; *Turf: F:* **t.-tack man,** aide *m* de bookmaker (qui fait des signaux à bras); (*b*) *F:* moment *m*, instant *m*; **just a t.! half a t.!** un moment! une seconde! **2.** marque *f*, pointage *m*, coche *f*; **to put a t. against a name,** cocher un nom.
tick² **1.** *v.i.* (*a*) (*of clock*) **to t.,** *F:* **to t.-tock,** faire tic-tac; tictaquer; **the minutes are ticking by,** le temps passe; (*b*) *F:* **I'd like to know what makes him t.,** je voudrais bien savoir ce qui le pousse. **2.** *v.tr.* = TICK OFF (*a*). **ticking¹** *n.* **1.** tic-tac *m* (d'une pendule). **2.** **t. off,** (*a*) pointage *m*; (*b*) *F:* réprimande *f*, savon *m.* **tick off** *v.tr.* (*a*) pointer (un article sur une liste, etc.); cocher (un nom); (*b*) *F:* attraper (qn); **to get ticked off,** se faire rembarrer; (*c*) *U.S: F:* **to t. s.o. off,** embêter qn; **he's really ticked off,** il est drôlement en rogne. **tick over** *v.i.* (*a*) *I.C.E:* (*of engine*) tourner au grand ralenti; (*b*) **my business is just ticking over,** mes affaires vont doucement.
tick³ *n. Arach:* tique *f* (du bétail, etc.).
tick⁴ *n. F:* crédit *m*; **to buy, get, sth. on t.,** acheter qch. à crédit.
tick⁵ *n.* enveloppe *f*, toile *f* (à matelas).
ticker ['tikər] *n.* **1.** *F:* (*a*) montre *f*; pendule *f*; (*b*) *F:* cœur *m*, palpitant *m.* **2.** *Tg:* télégraphe imprimeur; **t. tape,** bande *f* (de téléimprimeur); ruban *m* (de téléscripteur).
ticket¹ ['tikit] *n.* **1.** (*a*) billet *m* (de chemin de fer, de théâtre, de loterie, etc.); ticket *m* (de métro, d'autobus, etc.); **complimentary t.,** billet de faveur; *Rail:* **single t.,** billet simple; (billet d')aller *m*; **return t.,** billet d'aller et retour; **left-luggage t., cloakroom t.,** bulletin *m*, ticket, de consigne; **platform t.,** ticket de quai; **season t.,** carte *f* d'abonnement; **season-t. holder,** abonné(e); **t. collector, inspector,** contrôleur, -euse (de billets); (*b*) *Aut: F:* **(parking) t.,** papillon *m*, P.V. *m*; **to get a t.,** attraper un P.V. **2.** *Com:* **(price) t.,** étiquette *f.* **3.** *Pol: U.S:* (*a*) liste *f* des candidats; (*b*) *F:* **the democratic t.,** le programme du parti démocrate. **4.** (*a*) *Mil:* **to get one's t.,** être libéré (du service); (*b*) *Nau: F:* **to get one's (master's) t.,** passer (son brevet de) capitaine. **5.** *P:* **that's the t.!** voilà qui fera l'affaire! à la bonne heure!
ticket² *v.tr.* **(ticketed)** étiqueter (des marchandises).
ticking² ['tikiŋ] *n.* toile *f*, coutil *m*, à matelas.
tickle¹ ['tikl] *n.* chatouillement *m*; **he gave her a t.,** il lui a fait des chatouilles *f*; **to have a t. in one's throat,** avoir un chatouillement dans le gosier.
tickle² **1.** *v.tr.* (*a*) chatouiller (qn); (*of food, wine*) **to t. the palate,** chatouiller le palais; **to t. s.o.'s fancy,** amuser qn; (*b*) *F:* amuser (qn); **to be tickled to death, tickled pink, at, by, sth.,** (i) s'amuser beaucoup de qch.; (ii) être enchanté, ravi, de qch.; (*c*) *Fish:* pêcher (la truite, etc.) à la main. **2.** *v.i.* **my hand tickles,** la main me démange. **tickling** **1.** *a.* qui chatouille; **t. cough,** toux d'irritation. **2.** *n.* (*a*) chatouillement *m*; (*b*) *Fish:* pêche *f* à la main (de la truite).
tickler ['tiklər] *n. F:* (*a*) vrai problème; colle *f*; (*b*) sujet délicat.
ticklish ['tikliʃ] *a.* **1.** chatouilleux, -euse; **to be t.,** être chatouilleux. **2.** (*a*) (*of pers.*) susceptible; (*b*) (*of subject, task, etc.*) délicat; (*of undertaking*) scabreux; (*of question*) chatouilleux; **to be in a t. situation,** se trouver dans une situation délicate.
tidal ['taid(ə)l] *a.* **1.** (*of energy, etc.*) marémoteur; **t. power station,** usine marémotrice; **t. wave,** (i) raz *m* de marée; (*on river*) barre *f* de flot; (ii) flot *m* de la marée; (iii) vague *f* (d'enthousiasme, etc.). **2.** (*of river, etc.*) à marée; **t. basin,** bassin *m* à flot.
tidbit ['tidbit] *n.* = TITBIT.
tiddler ['tidlər] *n. F:* (*a*) *Ich:* petit poisson; *esp.* épinoche *f*; (*b*) petit enfant; mioche *mf.*
tiddl(e)y¹ ['tidli] *a. F:* ivre, pompette.
tiddl(e)y² *a. F:* minuscule.
tiddlywinks ['tidliwiŋks] *n.* jeu *m* de (la) puce.
tide¹ [taid] *n.* **1.** *A:* temps *m*, saison *f*; *Ecc:* **Ascension t.,** temps, semaine *f*, de l'Ascension. **2.** marée *f*; **rising t., flood t.,** marée montante; flux *m*; **ebb t.,** marée descendante, jusant *m*; **high t.,** marée haute; **low t.,** marée basse; **neap t.,** marée de morte-eau; **spring t.,** grande marée; marée de vive eau; **t. race,** raz *m* de marée; **t. gate,** porte *f* à flot; écluse *f* (de bassin); **t. gauge,** maré(o)métre *m*, maré(o)graphe *m*; échelle *f* de marée; **rise, fall, of the t.,** montée *f*, baisse *f*, de l'eau; **against the t.,** à contre-marée; *Fig:* à contre-courant; *Fig:* **the rising t. of discontent,** le mécontentement qui croît de jour en jour; *Nau:* **to go out with the t.,** partir à la marée.
tide² *v.i.* (*a*) *Nau:* faire marée; (*b*) **to t. in, out,** entrer avec le flot, sortir avec le jusant. **tide over** *v.tr.* aider (qn) à surmonter une difficulté; dépanner (qn).
tidemark ['taidmɑːk] *n.* **1.** (*a*) ligne *f* de marée haute, des hautes eaux; (*b*) laisse *f* de haute mer. **2.** *F:* ligne de crasse (dans une baignoire, etc.).
tidewater ['taidwɑːtər] *n.* eau *f* de marée.
tideway ['taidwei] *n.* lit *m* de la marée.
tidiness ['taidinis] *n.* bon ordre; le goût de l'ordre.
tidings ['taidiŋz] *n.pl. Lit:* nouvelle(s) *f(pl).*
tidy¹ ['taidi] *a.* **1.** (*a*) (*of desk, room*) bien rangé, en (bon) ordre; **a clean and t. room,** une pièce propre et nette; (*b*) ordonné, qui a de l'ordre; **he's very t.,** il a beaucoup d'ordre. **2.** *F:* assez bon; **to cost a t. penny,** coûter chaud; **a t. sum,** une somme rondelette. **-ily** *adv.* avec ordre; (habillé) avec soin.
tidy² *n.* vide-poches *m inv*; **sink t.,** coin *m* d'évier.
tidy³ *v.tr.* ranger; mettre de l'ordre dans (une chambre); **to t. one's hair,** s'arranger les cheveux; **to t. oneself (up),** faire un bout de toilette; **to t. away the books,** ranger les livres; **to t. (things) up,** ranger.
tie¹ [tai] *n.* **1.** lien *m*; attache *f*; **family ties,** liens de famille; **ties of friendship,** liens de l'amitié. **2.** (*a*) lien (de corde, de paille, d'osier, etc.); (*b*) *Nau:* itague *f*; (*c*) lacet *m*, cordon *m* (de soulier); (*d*) *Cost:* cravate *f*; **bow t.,** nœud *m* papillon; (*on invitation*) **black t.** = smoking *m*; **old school t.,** (i) cravate portée par les anciens élèves d'une école; (ii) franc-maçonnerie des anciens d'une école. **3.** *Const: etc:* crampon *m*; *Rail: NAm:* traverse *f*; *Const:* **t. beam,** longrine *f.* **4.** *Mus:* liaison *f.* **5.** (*a*) *Sp:* match *m*, course *f*, à égalité; **t. breaker,** match de barrage; (*b*) **(cup) t.,** = match de championnat; (*c*) **the election ended in a t.,** les candidats obtinrent un nombre égal de suffrages.
tie² **(tied; tying)** **1.** *v.tr.* (*a*) (i) attacher (un chien à sa niche, etc.); lier (qn à un poteau); **to t. two things together,** lier deux choses ensemble; *Fig:* **to t. s.o.'s hands,** lier les mains à qn; **to be tied hand and foot,** (i) être ligoté; (ii) *Fig:* avoir les mains liées; **to be tied to one's bed,** être cloué au lit (par la maladie,

etc.); (*b*) lier, nouer (un lacet, une ficelle, etc.); faire (un nœud, sa cravate); attacher, nouer (les brides de son capuchon); (*c*) *Mus:* lier (deux notes). **2.** *v.i. Sp: etc:* être, arriver, à égalité (**with,** avec); (*of candidates*) obtenir un nombre égal de suffrages; *Sch:* **to t. for first place,** être premier ex æquo (**with,** avec). **tied** *a.* **1.** assujetti (à son service, etc.). **2. t. cottage, house** = logement *m* de fonction; **t. house,** débit de boissons astreint par bail à vendre la bière d'une certaine brasserie. **3.** *Mus:* **t. notes,** notes liées. **tie down** *v.tr.* (*a*) immobiliser (qn) en l'attachant contre terre; assujettir (un objet qui pourrait se déplacer); (*b*) assujettir (qn) à certaines conditions; **to t. s.o. down to facts,** obliger qn à ne pas s'écarter des faits; (*c*) **tied down to one's job,** assujetti à ses fonctions. **tie in** *v.i.* (*a*) se rattacher (à qch.); (*b*) avoir un rapport (avec qch.). **tie on** *v.tr.* attacher (une étiquette, etc.) avec une ficelle. **tie up 1.** *v.tr.* (*a*) attacher, ficeler (un paquet, etc.); se nouer (les cheveux); lier, ficeler (le haut d'un sac); bander, panser (un bras blessé, etc.); (*b*) attacher (un animal); ligoter (qn); *v.tr. & i.* amarrer (un bateau); (*c*) immobiliser (ses capitaux); (*d*) *F:* **to be tied up,** être très occupé; avoir beaucoup à faire; *NAm:* **the traffic was all tied up,** il y avait un embouteillage. **2.** *v.i.* avoir des rapports (avec qch.); **our firm is tied up with theirs,** notre maison a des accords avec la leur; **that ties up with what I was just saying,** cela rejoint ce que je viens de dire. **tying** *n.* **1.** nouage *m* (d'un nœud, etc.). **2. t. up,** (*a*) ficelage *m* (d'un paquet, etc.); (*b*) mise *f* à l'attache (d'un cheval, etc.); ligotage *m* (de qn); (*c*) immobilisation *f* (de ses capitaux).

tie-in ['taiin] *n. NAm:* rapport *m*; association *f*.

tie-on ['taiɔn] *a.* **t.-on label,** étiquette *f* à œillets.

tiepin ['taipin] *n.* épingle *f* de cravate.

tier [tiər] *n.* rangée *f* (de sièges, de barriques, etc.); étage *m*; **tiers of an amphitheatre,** gradins *m* d'un amphithéâtre; **two-t. postal service system,** courrier *m* à deux vitesses; **to arrange in tiers,** disposer par étages; étager; **to rise in tiers,** s'étager.

tiered ['tiəd] *a.* (*a*) à gradins, à étages; (*b*) **three-t. cake,** pièce montée à trois étages; **three-t. stand,** étagère *f* à trois tablettes.

Tierra del Fuego [ti'ɛərədel'fweigou] *Pr.n. Geog:* la Terre de Feu.

tie-up ['taiʌp] *n.* **1.** (*a*) amarrage *m* (pour un canot); (*b*) *NAm:* (i) *Aut:* embouteillage *m*; (ii) suspension forcée (du travail). **2.** rapport *m* (entre deux choses).

tiff [tif] *n.* petite querelle; *F:* bisbille *f*.

tiffin ['tifin] *n.* (*Anglo-Indian*) déjeuner *m*.

tig [tig] *n.* (jeu *m* de) chat *m*.

tiger ['taigər] *n.* **1.** (*a*) *Z:* tigre *m*; (*b*) homme (i) féroce, (ii) sanguinaire. **2.** (*a*) *Ent:* **t. moth,** écaille *f*; *Bot:* **t. lily,** lis tigré; (*b*) *Lap:* **tiger's eye,** œil *m* de tigre.

tight [tait] **I.** *a.* **1.** (*of partition, etc.*) imperméable (à l'eau, à l'air, etc.); (*of ship, container*) étanche; (*of joint*) hermétique. **2.** (*a*) (*of cord, etc.*) raide, tendu; **to draw a cord t.,** serrer un cordon; **to keep a t. hand, hold, over s.o.,** tenir qn serré; tenir qn de court; (*b*) (*of clothes*) **(skin) t.,** collant; **too t.,** étriqué; trop juste; **t. shoes,** chaussures trop petites, (trop) étroites; *F:* **to be in a t. corner, a t. spot,** être en mauvaise passe; être dans le pétrin; (*c*) (*of furniture, mortise, etc.*) bien ajusté; (*of knot, screw*) serré; (*d*) **t. schedule,** horaire minuté; **I work to a very t. schedule,** mon temps est très minuté. **3.** (*a*) (*of money, credit*) resserré, rare; *F:* **money's a bit t. with me,** je suis à court d'argent; (*b*) *Sp:* (*of race*) serré, chaudement disputé. **4.** *F:* **to be t.,** être ivre, soûl; **to get t.,** prendre une cuite. **II.** *adv.* **1.** hermétiquement; **shut t., t. shut,** (porte) hermétiquement close; (yeux) bien fermés. **2.** (*a*) fortement; **to hold sth. t.,** tenir qch. serré; **hold t.!** tenez bon! tenez ferme! **to screw a nut up t.,** serrer un écrou à bloc; (*b*) étroitement; **to squeeze sth. t.,** serrer qch. étroitement. **tightly** *adv.* **1.** (fermer) hermétiquement; **eyes t. shut,** yeux bien fermés. **2.** (*a*) fortement, fermement; **to hold on t. to sth.,** se cramponner à qch.; (*b*) étroitement; **to fit t.,** être bien ajusté; **to fit too t.,** être (trop) serré, trop juste; **we were t. packed,** nous étions serrés comme des sardines.

tighten ['tait(ə)n] **1.** *v.tr.* (*a*) serrer, resserrer (une vis, un nœud, etc.); bloquer (un écrou); bander, tendre (un ressort); tendre, raidir (un cordage, etc.); **to t. one's belt,** (i) serrer sa ceinture; (ii) *Fig:* se serrer la ceinture; (*b*) **to t. (up),** renforcer (un blocus, des restrictions). **2.** *v.i.* (*a*) se (res)serrer; **his lips tightened,** ses lèvres se sont serrées; (*b*) (*of spring*) se bander; (*of cable, etc.*) devenir tendu; se tendre; raidir. **tightening** *n.* **1.** serrage *m*, (res)serrement *m* (d'une vis, etc.). **2.** raidissement *m* (d'un cordage); bandage *m* (d'un ressort). **3.** (*a*) renforcement *m* (d'un blocus, etc.); (*b*) *Fin:* resserrement (du crédit, etc.).

tightfisted [tait'fistid] *a. F:* **to be t.,** être très près de ses sous.

tight-fitting [tait'fitiŋ] *a.* **1.** (vêtement) collant. **2.** (*of joint, etc.*) bien ajusté; (*of door*) qui ferme hermétiquement.

tightlaced [tait'leist] *a.* **1.** *O:* (*of figure*) serré dans son corset. **2.** *F:* collet monté *inv*; guindé; prude.

tight-lipped ['taitlipt] *a.* les lèvres serrées; **to be t.-l.,** ne rien dire (**about sth.,** au sujet de qch.).

tightness ['taitnis] *n.* **1.** étanchéité *f*; herméticité *f*. **2.** (*a*) raideur *f* (d'un cordage); (*b*) *Med:* oppression *f* (de la poitrine); (*c*) étroitesse *f* (d'un lien); force *f* (d'une étreinte); (*d*) étroitesse (d'un vêtement).

tightrope ['taitroup] *n.* corde raide; **t. walker,** funambule *mf*; *Fig:* **t. walking,** acrobatie *f* politique.

tights [taits] *n.pl. Cost:* collant *m*; *Th:* maillot *m*.

tightwad ['taitwɔd] *n. F:* avare *m*; radin, -ine.

tigress ['taigris] *n.f. Z:* tigresse.

Tigris (the) [ðə'taigris] *Pr.n. Geog:* le Tigre.

tike [taik] *n.* = TYKE.

tilde ['tildə] *n. Gram:* tilde *m*.

tile¹ [tail] *n.* (*a*) tuile *f* (de toiture, etc.); **crest, ridge, t.,** tuile faîtière; *F:* **to spend a night on the tiles,** traîner dehors toute la nuit; **to have a t. loose,** être toqué, timbré; (*b*) carreau *m*; **floor(ing) t.,** carreau de pavage, de revêtement de sol; **wall t.,** carreau de revêtement; (*c*) **t. works,** tuilerie *f*; **t. kiln,** tuilerie.

tile² *v.tr.* (*a*) couvrir de tuiles, en tuiles; (*b*) carreler (un plancher). **tiled** *a.* (*a*) (toit) de, en, tuiles; (*b*) (pavage) carrelé, en carreaux; (paroi) à carreaux vernissés, revêtue de carrelage. **tiling** *n.* **1.** (*a*) pose *f* des tuiles; (*b*) carrelage *m*; pose des carreaux. **2.** *coll.* (*a*) couverture *f* en tuiles; (*b*) carrelage, carreaux.

tiler ['tailər] *n.* (*a*) couvreur *m* (en tuiles); (*b*) tuilier *m*; (*c*) carreleur *m*.

till¹ [til] *v.tr.* labourer, cultiver (un champ, etc.). **tilling** *n.* labour *m*, culture *f*.

till² *n. Com:* tiroir-caisse *m*, *pl.* tiroirs-caisses; **t. money,** encaisse *f*; *F:* **to be caught with one's hand in the t.,** être surpris la main dans le sac.

till³ 1. *prep.* (*a*) jusqu'à; **t. tomorrow,** jusqu'à demain; **t. now, t. then,** jusqu'ici, jusque-là; **from morning t. night,** du matin au soir; **(goodbye) t. Thursday!** à jeudi! **wait t. after the holidays,** attendez jusqu'après les vacances; (*b*) **not t. Monday,** pas avant lundi; **he won't come t. after dinner,** il ne viendra qu'après le dîner; **I'd never heard of it t. now,** c'est la première fois que j'en entends parler. **2.** *conj.* (*a*) jusqu'à ce que + *sub.*; **t. all the doors are shut,** jusqu'à ce que toutes les portes soient fermées; **to laugh t. one cries,** rire aux larmes; (*b*) **I'm not going t. I get my money,** je ne sortirai d'ici que lorsque j'aurai mon argent.

tillage ['tilidʒ] *n.* **1.** labour *m*, labourage *m*, culture *f.* **2.** terres *fpl* en labour; labours.

tiller¹ ['tilər] *n. Nau:* barre franche (de direction).

tiller² *n.* laboureur *m*, cultivateur *m*.

tilt¹ [tilt] *n.* **1.** inclinaison *f*, pente *f.* **2.** (*a*) *A:* joute *f*; (*b*) *A:* coup *m* de lance; *Fig:* **to have a t. at s.o.,** jouter avec qn; (*c*) **(at) full t.,** à toute vitesse; à fond de train; **to run full t. into sth.,** donner en plein contre qch.

tilt² **1.** *v.i.* (*a*) **to t. (up),** s'incliner; pencher; **to t. backwards, forwards,** incliner vers l'arrière, vers l'avant; **to t. over,** (i) se pencher, s'incliner; (ii) (*of table, etc.*) se renverser; (*b*) (*of bench, etc.*) **to t. up,** basculer. **2.** *v.i. A:* jouter (**with s.o.,** avec qn); *Fig:* **to t. at s.o.,** donner un coup de patte à qn (dans un débat, etc.). **3.** *v.tr.* (*a*) pencher, incliner (un tonneau, sa chaise, etc.); **to t. one's hat over one's eyes,** rabattre son chapeau sur ses yeux; **to t. one's chair back,** se balancer, se renverser, sur sa chaise; (*b*) culbuter, (faire) basculer. **tilted** *a.* incliné, penché. **tilting** **1.** *a.* (*a*) incliné, penché; (*b*) inclinable; (*c*) basculant. **2.** *n.* (*a*) inclinaison *f*, pente *f*; (*b*) basculage *m*, culbutage *m*; (*c*) *A:* joute *f.*

tilt³ *n* (*a*) *Veh:* bâche *f*, banne *f*; (*b*) *Nau:* tendelet *m*.

tilth [tilθ] *n. Agr:* **1.** labour *m*, culture *f.* **2.** (*a*) couche *f* arable; (*b*) cultures.

timber¹ ['timbər] *n.* **1.** (*a*) bois *m* d'œuvre; **building t.,** bois de construction, de charpente; **the t. trade,** le commerce du bois; **t. merchant,** marchand *m* de bois; **t. yard,** chantier *m* (de bois de charpente); (*b*) **standing t.,** bois sur pied; arbres de haute futaie; **to fell t.,** abattre, couper, le bois; **to put an area under t.,** boiser une région. **2.** (*a*) **(piece of) t.,** poutre *f*, madrier *m*; (*b*) *N.Arch:* membre *m*; (*c*) *Nau:* **t. hitch,** nœud *m* de bois, d'anguille. **3.** *U.S:* trempe *f* (de qn).

timber² *v.tr. O:* boiser, blinder (un puits de mine, etc.). **timbered** *a.* (*a*) (maison, etc.) en bois; **half t.,** à, en, colombage; (*b*) (*of land*) boisé. **timbering** *n.* **1.** boisage *m*, boisement *m* (d'une région). **2.** (*a*) boisage; (i) blindage *m* (d'un puits de mine); (ii) armature *f* (de bois); (*b*) **half t.,** colombage *m*.

timberline ['timbəlain] *n. For:* limite *f* des arbres.

timberwork ['timbəwəːk] *n.* **1.** construction *f* en bois. **2.** charpente *f.*

timbre [tɛ̃ː(m)br, 'tæmbər] *n.* timbre *m* (de la voix).

Timbuktu [timbʌk'tuː] *Pr.n. Geog:* Tombouctou *m*.

time¹ [taim] *n.* **1.** temps *m*; **t. will show,** qui vivra verra; *Prov:* **t. is money,** le temps c'est de l'argent; **in (the course of) t.,** avec le temps; à la longue; **a race against t.,** une course contre la montre. **2.** (*a*) **in a short t.,** en peu de temps; sous peu; **in three weeks' t.,** en trois semaines; **in a month's t.,** dans un mois; **in no t. (at all), in next to no t.,** en un rien de temps, en moins de rien; **within the required t.,** dans le délai prescrit; **to take a long t. over sth.,** mettre longtemps à faire qch.; **we haven't seen him for a long t.,** voilà longtemps que nous ne l'avons vu; **for some t. past,** depuis quelque temps; **for some t. (to come),** pendant quelque temps; **a short t. after, after a short t.,** peu (de temps) après; **after a t.,** après quelque temps; au bout d'un certain temps; **after a long t.,** longtemps après; après un long intervalle; **what a (long) t. he is taking!** il n'en finit pas! il prend son temps! **all this t.,** pendant tout ce temps; **he does it all the t.,** il le fait toujours, tout le temps; *Sp:* **to keep the t.,** chronométrer; *Cin:* **running t.,** durée *f* de projection (d'un film); *Gram:* **t. clause,** proposition temporelle; (*b*) *Fin:* **t. bill,** échéance *f* à terme; *El:* **t. switch,** minuterie *f* (d'escalier); *Artil:* **t. bomb,** bombe *f* à retardement; *Phot:* **t. exposure,** pose *f.* **3.** (*a*) **my t. is my own,** je suis libre de mon temps; **when I have the t.,** quand j'aurai le temps; **to have t. on one's hands,** avoir du temps à perdre; **to have no t. to do sth.,** ne pas avoir le temps de faire qch.; *F:* **I've no t. for him,** il m'embête; **to gain t.,** gagner du temps; **to play for t.,** chercher à gagner du temps; **you've plenty,** *F:* **heaps, of t.,** vous avez tout le temps qu'il vous faut; **there's no t. to be lost, to lose,** il n'y a pas de temps à perdre; **to make up for lost t.,** rattraper le temps perdu; **to lose no t. doing sth.,** s'empresser, se hâter, à faire qch.; **to waste t.,** perdre du temps; **to make t. to do sth.,** trouver le temps de faire qch.; **it takes t.,** cela prend du temps; **to take one's t. over sth.,** mettre le temps à faire qch.; **take your t.,** prenez votre temps; **time's up!** l'heure a sonné! c'est l'heure! *Box:* **t.!** allez! (*in public house*) **t., gentlemen, please!** on ferme! *Fb: etc:* **to play extra t.,** jouer les prolongations *fpl*; (*b*) **convict nearing the end of his t.,** forçat qui a bientôt fait, fini, son temps; *F:* **to do t.,** faire de la prison, de la taule; **if I had my t. over again,** si j'avais à recommencer ma vie. **4.** époque *f*; (*a*) **sign of the times,** un signe de l'époque; **in times past, in former times,** autrefois, jadis; dans le temps (passé); **the good old times,** le bon vieux temps; **in happier times,** en un temps plus heureux; **in times to come,** à l'avenir; dans l'avenir; **in our times, these times,** de nos jours; (*b*) **to be ahead of, in advance of, one's t.,** avoir des idées avancées; **to move with the times,** *F:* être à la page; **to be behind the times,** retarder, être en retard, sur son siècle; *F:* ne pas être à la page; **times are bad,** les temps sont difficiles, durs. **5.** moment *m*; (*a*) **at the t. of delivery,** au moment de la livraison; **I didn't know it at the t.,** je n'en savais rien (i) à ce moment-là, (ii) à cette époque; **at that t.,** en ce temps-là; **at the present t.,** à l'heure qu'il est; actuellement; à présent; **at a given t.,** à un moment donné, déterminé; **at the t. fixed,** à l'heure convenue, dite; **at one t. it was different,** autrefois, dans le temps, il n'en était pas ainsi; **at no t.,** (i) jamais; (ii) à aucun moment; **at times,** parfois, quelquefois; par moments; **at all times,** (i) en tout temps; toujours; (ii) à n'importe quel moment; **between times,** entre temps; **(at) any t. (you like),** n'importe quand; quand vous voudrez; **if at any time . . .,** si à l'occasion . . .; **some t. or other,** un jour ou l'autre; **some time next month,** dans le courant du mois prochain; **this t. next year,** l'an prochain à pareille époque, à la même date; **this t. tomorrow,** demain à la même heure; **by the t. that I got there,** lorsque je suis arrivé; **from t. to t.,** de temps en temps; de temps à autre; **from that t. (onwards),** dès lors; à partir de ce moment-là; **at the proper t.,** en temps utile; **we shall see when the t. comes,** nous verrons (cela) quand le moment sera venu; **now is the t., our t., your t., to . . .,** c'est le (bon) moment pour . . .; **to choose one's t.,** choisir son heure, le moment; **this is no t., this is not the t., to . . .,** ce n'est pas le moment de . . ., (*b*) **in due t. and place,** en temps et lieu; **all in good t.,** chaque chose en son temps; **in his own good t.,** à son heure. **6.** heure *f*; (*a*) **Greenwich mean t.,** l'heure de Greenwich; **standard t.,** heure du fuseau; **(standard) t. belt, t. zone,** fuseau *m* horaire; **summer t.,** *NAm:* **daylight saving t.,** heure d'été, *Fr.C:* heure avancée; (*b*) (*o'clock*) **what's the t.?** quelle heure est-il? **what t. do you make it?** quelle heure avez-vous? *W. Tel: etc:* **t. signal,** signal *m* horaire; **to look at the t.,** regarder (à) sa montre; regarder quelle heure il est; **watch that keeps (good) t., that loses t.,** montre qui est toujours à l'heure, qui retarde; **t. of day,** heure du jour; **at any t. of the day or night,** à n'importe quelle heure du jour ou de la nuit; (*c*) **dinner t.,** l'heure du dîner; **(dead) on t.,** à l'heure (exacte); **to be ahead of, behind,**

t., être en avance, en retard; **I was just in t. to see it,** je suis arrivé juste à temps pour le voir; **to start in good t.**, (i) s'y prendre (bien) à temps; (ii) se mettre en route de bonne heure; **it is t. we left,** il est temps de songer à partir; *F:* **it's high t.! and about t. too!** ce n'est pas, c'est pas, trop tôt! (*d*) **t. of the year,** époque de l'année; saison *f*; **it was holiday t.**, c'était l'époque des vacances; (*e*) **before one's, its, t.**, prématurément; **his t. had not yet come,** son heure n'était pas encore venue; (*of pregnant woman*) **to be nearing her t.**, approcher de son terme. **7.** *Ind: etc:* (*a*) **to be paid by t.**, être payé à l'heure; **to put in t.**, faire des heures; **to work, to be on, short t.**, être en chômage partiel; (*b*) (*in factory, etc.*) **t. clock,** pendule *f* de pointage; **t. card,** fiche *f* de pointage; **t. sheet,** feuille *f* de présence; semainier *m*; (*c*) **t. and motion study,** étude des temps et mouvements; **t. and motion expert,** spécialiste *mf* des temps et méthodes. **8.** *F:* **to have a good t. (of it),** (i) bien s'amuser; (ii) mener une vie agréable; **to have a high old t.**, faire la noce; **to have a bad, rough, t. (of it),** (i) manger de la vache enragée; en voir de dures; (ii) passer un mauvais quart d'heure; **to give s.o. a rough t.**, en faire voir de dures à qn. **9.** fois *f*; **five times,** cinq fois; **this is the third t.**, c'est la troisième fois; **next t.**, la prochaine fois; **another t.**, une autre fois; **the first t. I saw him,** la première fois que je l'ai vu; **to do sth. several times over,** faire qch. à plusieurs reprises, plusieurs fois; **four times running,** quatre fois de suite, à quatre reprises; **t. and t. again, t. after t.**, à maintes reprises; maintes et maintes fois; **he succeeds every t.**, il réussit à chaque coup; **every t. that . . .**, chaque fois que . . .; **to do two things at a t.**, faire deux choses à la fois; **to run upstairs four at a t.**, monter l'escalier quatre à quatre; **for weeks at a t.**, des semaines durant, d'affilée; **it costs me £6 a t. to have my hair done,** ça me coûte six livres chaque fois que je me fais coiffer; **four times two is eight,** quatre fois deux font huit; **three times as big as the other,** trois fois plus grand que l'autre; **six times as much,** six fois autant. **10.** (*a*) **at the same t.**, en même temps; (faire deux choses) à la fois; *Prov:* **you can't be in two places at the same t.**, on ne peut être à la fois au four et au moulin; (*b*) **at the same t., you mustn't forget that . . .**, d'autre part, tout de même, néanmoins, il ne faut pas oublier que . . .. **11.** (*a*) *Mus:* **t. value,** valeur *f* (d'une note); (*b*) *Mus:* mesure *f*; **duple, triple, t.**, mesure à deux, trois, temps; **t. signature,** fraction *f* indiquant la mesure; **to beat t.**, battre la mesure; (*c*) **in strict t.**, en mesure; **to keep t., be in t.**, chanter, etc. en mesure; **to get out of t.**, perdre la mesure; (*d*) *Mus:* tempo *m*; **to quicken, slow, the t.**, presser, ralentir, le tempo, le mouvement; *Gym: etc:* **in quick t.**, au pas accéléré. **12.** *F:* **the big t.**, le haut de l'échelle; **to be in the big t., to have made the big t.**, être en haut de l'échelle; **big-t. operator,** gros trafiquant; **small-t. crook,** petit escroc.

time² *v.tr.* **1.** (*a*) fixer l'heure de (qch.); **to t. one's arrival to coincide with one's friend's,** s'arranger pour arriver en même temps que son ami; (*b*) **to t. a blow, a remark,** choisir le moment de porter un coup, de placer un mot; (*of remark, etc.*) **well timed,** opportun, à propos; **ill timed,** inopportun, mal à propos; (*c*) régler (une horloge); (*d*) *I.C.E:* régler, ajuster (l'allumage, les soupapes); caler (le distributeur, *Mch:* une soupape); mettre (le moteur) au point. **2.** calculer la durée de (qch.); *Phot:* calculer (le temps de pose). **3.** (*a*) **to t. how long it takes s.o. to do sth.**, mesurer le temps que qn met à faire qch.; (*b*) *Sp: etc:* chronométrer (qn, une course); prendre le temps (d'un coureur); **timed race,** course *f* contre la montre; (*c*) *Mil: etc:* minuter (une opération, etc.). **timing** *n.* **1.** (*a*) *I.C.E:* réglage *m* (de l'allumage); *Mch:* calage *m* (d'une soupape); (*b*) *I.C.E:* distribution *f*. **2.** *Phot:* calcul *m* (du temps de pose). **3.** (*a*) *Sp: etc:* chronométrage *m*; (*b*) *Mil: etc:* minutage *m* (d'une opération). **4.** (*a*) **error of t.**, mauvais calcul; erreur *f* de jugement; **good, bad, t.**, à-propos *m*, manque *m* d'à-propos (d'une observation); opportunité *f*, inopportunité *f* (d'une démarche); (*b*) *Sp: etc:* rythme *m* (d'un mouvement).

time-consuming ['taimkənsju:miŋ] *a.* (travail, etc.) qui prend beaucoup de temps.

time-honoured ['taimɔnəd] *a.* (*of custom, etc.*) consacré (par l'usage); vénérable, séculaire.

timekeeper ['taimki:pər] *n.* **1.** (*a*) *Ind:* contrôleur *m* (de présence); (*b*) *Sp:* chronométreur. **2.** (*of pers., watch*) **to be a good t.**, être toujours à l'heure.

timekeeping ['taimki:piŋ] *n.* **1.** *Ind:* contrôle *m*, pointage *m*, de présence. **2.** *Sp: etc:* chronométrage *m*; minutage *m*. **3. good t.**, ponctualité *f* (de qn); exactitude *f* (d'une montre).

timeless ['taimlis] *a.* (*a*) éternel; (*b*) intemporel.

timeliness ['taimlinis] *a.* opportunité *f*; à-propos *m* (d'une intervention, etc.).

timely ['taimli] *a.* opportun, à propos; **I made a t. escape,** je me suis échappé juste à temps.

timepiece ['taimpi:s] *n.* pendule *f*; chronomètre *m*; montre *f*.

timer ['taimər] *n.* **1.** (*pers.*) chronométreur *m*. **2.** (*device*) (*a*) *I.C.E: etc:* commutateur *m* d'allumage; (*b*) minuterie *f*; *Dom.Ec:* compte-minutes *m inv*; **egg t.**, sablier *m*.

time(-)saving ['taimseiviŋ] **1.** *a.* qui économise du temps; qui permet de gagner du temps. **2.** *n.* économie *f* de temps.

timeserver ['taimsə:vər] *n.* opportuniste *mf*.

timeserving ['taimsə:viŋ] *n.* opportunisme *m*.

timetable ['taimteibl] *n.* **1.** horaire *m*; *Rail:* indicateur *m* (des chemins de fer). **2.** (*a*) *Sch:* emploi *m* du temps; (*b*) *Ind:* plan *m* de mise en exécution.

timework ['taimwə:k] *n.* travail *m* à l'heure; **to be on t.**, travailler à, être payé à, l'heure.

timeworker ['taimwə:kər] *n.* ouvrier, -ière, qui travaille à l'heure.

timeworn ['taimwɔ:n] *a.* *O:* **1.** usé par le temps. **2.** séculaire, vénérable.

timid ['timid] *a.* timide, peureux. **-ly** *adv.* timidement.

timidity [ti'miditi] *n.* timidité *f*.

timorous ['timərəs] *a.* timoré, timide. **-ly** *adv.* timidement.

Timothy ['timəθi] *Pr.n.m.* Timothée.

timpani ['timpəni] *n.pl.* *Mus:* timbales *fpl*.

timpanist ['timpənist] *n.* *Mus:* timbalier *m*.

tin¹ [tin] *n.* **1.** *Metall:* étain *m*; **t. mine,** mine *f* d'étain; **t.-bearing,** stannifère. **2.** (*a*) **t. (plate),** fer-blanc *m*; **t. mug,** timbale *f*; *Mil: etc:* *F:* **t. hat,** casque *m*; *F:* **t. pan alley,** les compositeurs et éditeurs, le monde, de la musique populaire; (*b*) tôle *f*; **t. roof,** toit *m* en tôle ondulée; (*c*) *Dom.Ec:* (*for cake*) moule *m*; (*for tart*) tourtière *f*; *Bak:* **t. loaf,** pain cuit au moule; pain anglais; (*d*) boîte *f* (en fer-blanc); boîte de conserves; **t. of sardines,** boîte de sardines; **t. opener,** ouvre-boîtes *m inv*.

tin² *v.tr.* **(tinned) 1.** *Metalw:* étamer. **2.** mettre (des sardines, etc.) en boîtes. **tinned** *a.* **1.** *Metalw:* (fer, etc.) étamé. **2.** (*of meat, etc.*) en boîte; **t. foods,** conserves *fpl*. **tinning** *n.* **1.** *Metalw:* étamage *m*. **2.** mise *f* en boîte(s) (de conserves).

tincture¹ ['tiŋ(k)tjər] *n.* **1.** teinture *f* (d'iode, etc.). **2.** teinte *f*; nuance *f*. **3.** *Her:* émail *m*, -aux; teinture.

tincture² *v.tr.* teindre, colorer.

tinder ['tindər] *n.* mèche *f* de briquet; **(German) t.**, amadou *m*; **t. box,** briquet *m* (à silex); *NAm:* chose *f* inflammable; *Fig:* situation explosive.

tine [tain] *n.* **1.** dent *f*, fourchon *m* (de fourche); dent, pointe *f* (de herse, etc.). **2.** *Ven:* andouiller *m*.
tinfoil ['tin'fɔil] *n.* **1.** feuille *f* d'étain; étain battu en feuilles. **2.** papier *m* (d')étain, papier (d')aluminium.
ting[1] [tiŋ] *n.* tintement *m* (d'une cloche).
ting[2] *v.i. & tr.* (faire) tinter.
ting-a-ling ['tiŋəliŋ] *n. & adv.* drelin drelin (*m*).
tinge[1] [tin(d)ʒ] *n.* teinte *f*, nuance *f*; soupçon *m*; **a t. of irony,** une teinte, une pointe, d'ironie.
tinge[2] *v.tr.* teinter, colorer; **sky tinged with pink,** ciel teinté de rose; **words tinged with malice,** paroles teintées de malice; **memories tinged with sadness,** souvenirs empreints de tristesse.
tingle[1] ['tiŋgl] *n.* **1. t. in the ears,** tintement *m* d'oreilles. **2.** picotement *m*, fourmillement *m* (de la peau); **to have a t. in one's legs,** avoir des fourmis dans les jambes.
tingle[2] **1.** *v.i.* (*a*) (*of ears*) tinter; (*b*) picoter; **my hand tingles,** j'ai des picotements dans la main; **to t. with impatience,** vibrer d'impatience; **breeze that makes the blood t.,** brise qui fouette le sang. **2.** *v.tr.* (*a*) faire tinter (les oreilles); (*b*) faire picoter (la peau). **tingling 1.** *a.* (*a*) (oreilles) qui tintent; (*b*) **t. sensation,** picotement *m*. **2.** *n.* = TINGLE[1].
tingly ['tiŋgli] *a.* **t. sensation,** picotement *m*.
tininess ['taininis] *n.* petitesse *f* (extrême).
tinker[1] ['tiŋkər] *n.* (*a*) chaudronnier ambulant; étameur ambulant; (*b*) *Dial:* bohémien *m*; (*c*) *F:* bousilleur *m*; gâcheur *m* (d'ouvrage).
tinker[2] **1.** *v.tr.* **to t. (sth.) up,** retaper, rafistoler (une machine, etc.). **2.** *v.i.* bricoler; **to t. with the radio,** passer du temps à rafistoler le poste de radio. **tinkering** *n.* bricolage *m*; rafistolage *m*.
tinkle[1] ['tiŋkl] *n.* tintin *m*, tintement *m* (de clochettes, de verres); *F:* **I'll give you a t.,** je vous passerai un coup de fil.
tinkle[2] **1.** *v.i.* tinter; **tinkling bells,** cloches argentines; **to t. on the piano,** tapoter sur le piano. **2.** *v.tr.* faire tinter (une sonnette, des grelots). **tinkling** *n.* tintement *m* (de clochettes, de verres).
tinny ['tini] *a.* **1. food with a t. taste,** aliment *m* qui a un goût d'étain, de boîte de conserve. **2.** (son) grêle, fêlé; **to sound t.,** rendre un son métallique, fêlé.
tinplate ['tinpleit] *n.* fer-blanc *m*.
tinpot ['tinpɔt] *a. F:* mesquin, misérable; **a t. dictator,** un dictateur au petit pied.
tinsel ['tins(ə)l] **1.** *n.* clinquant *m*; (*Christmas decorations*) cheveux *mpl* d'ange. **2.** *a.* (*a*) (fil, etc.) de clinquant; (*b*) *Fig:* d'un faux brillant; clinquant.
tinsmith ['tinsmiθ] *n.* étameur *m*; ferblantier *m*.
tint[1] [tint] *n.* **1.** teinte *f*, nuance *f*; **red with a blue t.,** teinte rouge bleuâtre; **warm tints,** tons chauds; **half t.,** demi-teinte *f*, *pl.* demi-teintes. **2.** *Engr:* (*in line engraving*) grisé *m*. **3.** *Hairdr:* colorant *m*.
tint[2] *v.tr.* **1.** teinter, colorer; *Opt:* **tinted glasses,** verres teintés; *Hairdr:* **to have one's hair tinted,** se faire faire une coloration. **2.** *Engr:* ombrer, hachurer (une gravure). **tinting** *n.* coloration *f*.
tintack ['tintæk] *n.* broquette *f*; clou *m* de tapisserie.
tintinnabulation [tintinæbju'leiʃ(ə)n] *n.* tintinnabulement *m*.
tinware ['tinwɛər] *n. coll.* ferblanterie *f*.
tiny ['taini] *a.* minuscule; **a t. little house,** une toute petite maison; **a t. bit,** un tout petit peu.
tip[1] [tip] *n.* **1.** bout *m*, extrémité *f*, pointe *f*; **on the tips of the toes,** sur la pointe des pieds; **to have sth. on the t. of one's tongue,** avoir qch. sur le bout de la langue; **from t. to toe,** de la tête aux pieds; *Cu:* **asparagus tips,** pointes d'asperge. **2.** (*a*) bout ferré, embout *m* (d'une canne, etc.); **steel t.,** fer *m* (de bout de chaussure); (*b*) *Bill:* procédé *m* (de queue).
tip[2] *v.tr.* **(tipped) 1.** mettre un bout à (un soulier); embouter (une canne, etc.); **arrow tipped with poison,** flèche à bout empoisonné. **2.** couper le bout à (qch.). **tipped** *a.* **gold-t., silver-t.,** à bout doré, d'argent; **(filter) t. cigarettes,** cigarettes à bout filtre.
tip[3] *n.* **1** pente *f*, inclinaison *f*. **2.** coup léger; tape *f*. **3.** pourboire *m*. **4.** *Turf: St. Exch: etc:* tuyau *m*; **if you take my t. . .,** si vous m'en croyez . . .; **to give s.o. a t.,** tuyauter, renseigner, qn. **5.** *Civ.E: etc:* (*a*) chantier *m* de versage; *Min:* terri(l) *m*; **rubbish t.,** dépotoir *m*; (*b*) tas *m*, monceau *m* (d'ordures, etc.); (*c*) **t. car, truck,** wagon, wagonnet, basculant, à bascule; **t. cart,** tombereau *m* (à bascule).
tip[4] *v.* **(tipped) 1.** *v.tr.* (*a*) (i) **to t. (sth.) over,** renverser (qch.); chavirer (un canot, etc.); (ii) **to t. up,** soulever (un strapontin); faire basculer (une charrette); *Min:* verser (un wagon); (*b*) **to t. out,** déverser, décharger (le contenu de qch.); **to t. sth. into sth.,** verser qch. dans qch.; **to t. sth. (out) on the ground,** déverser qch. par terre; **to t. rubbish,** verser, déposer, des immondices; (*c*) faire pencher, faire incliner; **to t. one's hat over one's eyes,** rabattre son chapeau sur ses yeux; *O:* **to t. one's hat to s.o.,** tirer son chapeau à qn; (*d*) toucher légèrement, effleurer (qch.); (*e*) donner un pourboire à (qn); **to t. s.o. ten pence,** donner dix pence de pourboire à qn; (*f*) *Turf: St.Exch: etc:* tuyauter (qn); donner un tuyau à (qn); **to t. a certain horse to win,** pronostiquer qu'un certain cheval sera le gagnant; *F:* **he's widely tipped for the job,** on lui donne toutes les chances pour le poste; **to t. s.o. off,** (i) donner un tuyau à qn; (ii) avertir qn. **2.** *v.i.* **to t. over,** se renverser, basculer; (*of boat, etc.*) chavirer; **to t. up,** (*of plank, etc.*) se soulever; basculer. **tipping 1.** *a.* (wagon, etc.) basculant, à bascule. **2.** *n.* (*a*) inclinaison *f*; **t. over,** renversement *m* (de qch.); chavirement *m* (d'un canot); (*b*) basculage *m*; **t. apparatus,** culbuteur *m* (pour wagons, etc.); (*c*) **t. (out),** versage *m*, déversement *m* (du contenu d'un wagon, etc.); *P.N:* **no t.,** décharge interdite; (*d*) **tippings,** déblai *m* (d'une mine, etc.); (*e*) (système *m* des) pourboires *mpl*; distribution *f* de pourboires; (*f*) *Turf:* tuyautage *m*.
tip-off ['tipɔf] *n.* avertissement *m*; tuyau *m*; **to give s.o. a t.-o.,** tuyauter, renseigner, qn.
tipper ['tipər] *n.* **1. (waggon) t.,** (i) basculeur *m*, culbuteur *m*; verseur *m*; (ii) élévateur *m* à bascule. **2.** wagon, wagonnet, basculant, à bascule. **3. to be a good t.,** donner des pourboires généreux.
tippet ['tipit] *n.* pèlerine *f*, collet *m* (de fourrure).
tipple[1] ['tipl] *n. F:* boisson *f* alcoolique; **what's your t.?** qu'est-ce que vous allez prendre?
tipple[2] *v.i. F:* se livrer à la boisson; *P:* picoler.
tipple[3] *n. NAm: Min:* (*a*) basculeur *m* de wagons; (*b*) chantier *m* de versage.
tippler ['tiplər] *n.f.* buveur, -euse.
tipsiness ['tipsinis] *n.* (légère) ivresse.
tipstaff, *pl.* **-staffs, -staves** ['tipstɑːf, *n. Jur:* huissier *m*.
tipster ['tipstər] *n. Turf: etc:* pronostiqueur *m*.
tipsy ['tipsi] *a.* (*a*) gris, ivre; *F:* pompette; **slightly t.,** un peu éméché; **to get t.,** se griser, s'enivrer; (*b*) (titubation, rire, etc.) d'ivrogne; (*c*) *Cu:* **t. cake** = diplomate *m*. **-ily** *adv.* (d'une voix) qui accuse l'ivresse.
tiptoe[1] ['tiptou] *n. & adv.* **(on) t.,** sur la pointe des pieds.
tiptoe[2] *v.i.* marcher sur la pointe des pieds; **to t. into, out of, the room,** entrer, sortir, sur la pointe des pieds.
tiptop ['tiptɔp] *a.* excellent; (hôtel, etc.) de premier ordre; **I feel t.,** je me sens à merveille.
tip-up ['tipʌp] *a.* (charrette, cuvette, etc.) à bascule; **t.-up seat,** strapontin *m*.
tirade [tai'reid] *n.* tirade *f*; diatribe *f* **(against,** contre); **t. of invective,** tirade, bordée *f*, d'injures.

tire¹ ['taiər] **1.** *v.tr.* fatiguer, lasser; **to t. oneself (out) doing sth.,** se fatiguer, se lasser, à faire qch.; **to t. s.o. out,** (i) épuiser, briser, qn de fatigue; (ii) excéder, assommer, qn; lasser la patience de qn. **2.** *v.i.* se fatiguer, se lasser (**of s.o., sth.,** de qn, de qch.); **he never tires of telling me,** il ne se lasse pas de me le dire. **tired** *a.* (*a*) fatigué; las, *f.* lasse; **to get t.,** devenir las; se fatiguer; **she was t. out,** elle n'en pouvait plus de fatigue; *F:* **you make me t.,** tu m'ennuies, m'embêtes; *F:* **t. carpet,** tapis usé; (*b*) **to be t. of sth.,** être las de qch.; **to grow, get, t. of doing sth.,** se lasser de faire qch.; *F:* **I'm t. of you,** j'en ai assez de vous; **t. of arguing, he consented,** de guerre lasse, il a donné son consentement. **tiredly** *adv.* avec lassitude. **tiring** *a.* (*a*) fatigant, lassant; (*b*) ennuyeux.

tire² *n.* **1.** *Veh:* bandage *m*, cercle *m*, de fer (d'une roue de charrette, etc.). **2.** *NAm: Aut: Cy:* = TYRE.

tiredness ['taiədnis] *n.* lassitude *f*, fatigue *f*.

tireless ['taiəlis] *a.* inlassable, infatigable. **-ly** *adv.* infatigablement, inlassablement.

tiresome ['taiəsəm] *a.* **1.** fatigant; (discours) fastidieux, ennuyeux. **2.** exaspérant; (*of child*) assommant; **how t.!** que c'est ennuyeux, assommant!

tiro, *pl.* **-o(e)s** ['tairou, -ouz] *n.* novice *mf*; débutant, -ante.

'tis [tiz] = **it is,** *see* BE.

tissue ['tisju:] *n.* **1.** tissu *m* (de soie, coton, etc.); *Fig:* **t. of lies, nonsense,** tissu de mensonges, d'absurdités. **2.** *Biol:* tissu (nerveux, musculaire, etc.). **3.** (*a*) **t. (paper),** papier *m* de soie; (*b*) mouchoir *m* en papier.

tit¹ [tit] *n. Orn:* mésange *f*; **blue t.,** mésange bleue; **coal t.,** mésange noire; **great t.,** (mésange) charbonnière *f*.

tit² *n.* **t. for tat,** un prêté pour un rendu; donnant donnant; **to give s.o. t. for tat,** (i) rendre à qn la pareille; (ii) (*verbally*) riposter du tac au tac.

tit³ *n. P:* (*a*) bout *m* de sein; (*b*) sein *m*, néné *m*.

Titan ['tait(ə)n] **1.** *Pr.n.m.* Titan. **2.** *n.m.* titan.

titanic [tai'tænik] *a.* titanesque; géant, colossal.

titanium [tai'teiniəm] *n. Ch:* titane *m*.

titbit ['titbit] *n.* morceau friand; friandise *f*; *F:* bonne bouche.

titfer ['titfər] *n. P:* chapeau *m*.

tithe [taið] *n. Hist:* dîme *f*; **t. barn,** grange *f* de la dîme, aux dîmes.

Titian ['tiʃiən] *Pr.n.m. Hist: of Art:* le Titien.

titillate ['titileit] *v.tr.* chatouiller (le palais); émoustiller (les sens). **titillating** *a.* titillant, chatouillant; émoustillant.

titillation [titi'leiʃ(ə)n] *n.* titillation *f*, chatouillement *m*.

titivate ['titiveit] **1.** *v.tr.* faire (qn) beau; pomponner (qn). **2.** *v.i.* se faire beau.

title¹ ['taitl] *n.* titre *m*. **1.** (*a*) **to give s.o. a t.,** donner un titre à, titrer, qn; (*b*) **t. of nobility,** titre de noblesse; **to have a t.,** avoir un titre de noblesse, être titré; (*c*) *Sp:* **to hold the t.,** (dé)tenir le titre (de champion); **t. holder,** tenant, -ante, du titre; *Box:* **t. fight, non t. fight,** combat *m* comptant, ne comptant pas, pour le titre. **2.** (*a*) titre (d'un livre, d'un chapitre); intitulé *m* (d'un journal, d'un acte); *Publ:* **t. piece,** conte *m*, morceau *m*, qui donne le titre au recueil; *Th:* **t. rôle,** rôle *m* qui donne le titre à la pièce; *Typ:* **t. page,** (page *f* de) titre; (*with embellishments*) frontispice *m*; (*b*) **to publish fifty titles a year,** publier cinquante livres *mpl*, ouvrages *mpl*, par an. **3.** (*a*) **t. to property,** titre de propriété; (*b*) **t. (deed),** titre (constitutif) de propriété; acte *m*.

title² *v.tr.* intituler (un livre, etc.). **titled** *a.* (*of pers.*) titré; **to be t.,** avoir un titre (de noblesse).

titmouse ['titmaus] *n. Orn:* mésange *f*.

titrate ['taitreit] *v.tr. Ch: Ind:* titrer (une solution).

titter¹ ['titər] *n.* **1.** rire étouffé. **2.** petit rire nerveux.

titter² *v.i.* **1.** avoir un petit rire étouffé. **2.** rire nerveusement, bêtement. **tittering** *n.* petits rires.

tittle ['titl] *n.* **not one t.,** pas un iota.

tittle-tattle¹ ['titltætl] *n.* commérages *mpl*.

tittle-tattle² *v.i.* bavarder; potiner, cancaner.

titty ['titi] *n. P:* = TIT³.

titular ['titjulər] **1.** *a.* (*a*) titulaire; (*b*) (*of function, office, etc.*) nominal; (*c*) **t. possessions,** terres attachées à un titre. **2.** *n. Jur:* titulaire *mf* (d'un droit, etc.).

tizzy ['tizi] *n. F:* **to be in a t.,** ne (pas) savoir où donner de la tête.

to [tu:; *unstressed before consonant* tə; *unstressed before vowel* tu] **I.** *prep.* à. **1.** (*a*) **to go to church, to school,** aller à l'église, à l'école; **what school do you go to?** à quelle école allez-vous? **I'm off to Paris,** je pars pour Paris; **he went to France, to Japan,** il est allé en France, au Japon; **she returned home to her family,** elle est rentrée auprès de sa famille; **I am going to the grocer's,** je vais chez l'épicier; **from town to town,** de ville en ville; **flights to the Continent,** vols à destination du Continent; (*b*) **the road to London,** la route de Londres; **journey to Paris,** voyage à Paris; **the shortest way to the station,** le plus court chemin pour aller à la gare; **to bed!** (i) je vais me coucher; (ii) allez vous coucher! **2.** (*a*) vers, à; **to the east,** vers l'est; *P.N:* **to the trains,** accès aux quais; **to the station,** direction de la gare; **to the right, left,** à droite, à gauche; (*b*) **the rooms to the back,** les chambres de derrière. **3. elbow to elbow,** coude à coude; **I told him so to his face,** je le lui ai dit en face; **to clasp s.o. to one's heart,** serrer qn sur son cœur; **to fall to the ground,** tomber à, par, terre. **4.** (*of time*) (*a*) **from morning tonight,** du matin au soir; **from day to day,** de jour en jour; d'un jour à l'autre; (*b*) **ten minutes to six,** six heures moins dix. **5.** (*a*) jusqu'à; **to this day,** jusqu'à ce jour; **to count up to ten,** compter jusqu'à dix; **moved to tears,** ému jusqu'aux larmes; **fight to the death,** bataille à mort; (*b*) **to a high degree,** à un haut degré; **generous to a fault,** généreux à l'excès; **accurate to a millimetre,** exact à un millimètre près; **a year to the day,** un an jour pour jour; (*c*) **to cut sth. down to a minimum,** réduire qch. au minimum. **6.** (*a*) **to this end,** à cet effet, dans ce but; **to sit down to dinner,** se mettre à table (pour dîner); (*b*) **to my despair,** à mon grand désespoir; **to everyone's surprise,** à la surprise de tous. **7.** en; **to run to seed,** monter en graine; **to put to flight,** mettre en fuite; **to pull to pieces,** mettre en pièces. **8. what tune is it sung to?** sur quel air cela se chante-t-il? **9. heir to s.o., to an estate,** héritier de qn, d'une propriété; **ambassador to the King of Sweden,** ambassadeur auprès du roi de Suède; **apprentice to a joiner,** apprenti chez un menuisier; **the key to the door,** la clef de la porte. **10.** (*a*) (*effecting a comparison*) **superior to,** supérieur à; **compared to this,** comparé à, en comparaison de, celui-ci; **that's nothing to what I have seen,** cela n'est rien à côté de ce que j'ai vu; (*b*) (*expressing a proportion*) **three is to six as six is to twelve,** trois est à six ce que six est à douze; **six votes to four,** six voix contre quatre; **three goals to nil,** trois buts à zéro; **to bet ten to one,** parier dix contre un; **it's a thousand to one (that) it won't happen,** il y a mille à parier contre un que cela n'arrivera pas. **11. to all appearances,** selon les apparences; **not to my taste,** pas à mon goût; **to the best of my recollection,** autant que je m'en souvienne. **12. to drink to s.o.,** boire à la santé de qn. **13.** (*concerning*) **what did he say to my suggestion?** qu'est-ce qu'il a dit de ma proposition? **is that all there is to it?** c'est tout? **there's nothing to it,** (i) ça ne vaut pas la peine; (ii) c'est simple comme bonjour. **14.** (*used to form the dative*) (*a*) **to give sth. to s.o.,** donner qch. à qn;

who did you give it to? à qui l'avez-vous donné? **to speak to s.o.,** parler à qn; **to whom?** à qui? **what's that to you?** qu'est-ce que cela vous fait? **to keep sth. to oneself,** garder qch. pour soi; **to allude to sth.,** faire allusion à qch.; (*b*) envers, pour; **he has been a father to me,** il a été comme un père pour moi; (*c*) **known to the ancients,** connu des anciens; **used to doing sth.,** accoutumé à faire qch. **II.** (*with the infinitive*) **1.** (*a*) (*purpose, result*) pour; **he came to help me,** il est venu (pour) m'aider; **we must eat (in order) to live,** il faut manger pour vivre; **so to speak,** pour ainsi dire; **born to rule,** né pour régner; (*b*) (i) de, à, pour; **happy to do it,** heureux de le faire; **ready to listen,** prêt à écouter; **old enough to go to school,** d'âge à aller à l'école; (ii) (*inf. with pass. force*) à, pour; **too hot to drink,** trop chaud pour qu'on puisse le boire; (*c*) (*parenthetic*) (i) **to hear him talk you would imagine that he's somebody,** à l'entendre parler on s'imaginerait qu'il est important; (ii) (*expressing subsequent fact*) **he left the house never to return to it again,** il quitta la maison pour n'y plus revenir. **2.** (*a*) **to have a letter to write,** avoir une lettre à écrire; **to have a lot to do,** avoir beaucoup à faire; **there was not a sound to be heard,** on n'entendait pas le moindre bruit; **he is not a man to forget his friends,** il n'est pas homme à oublier ses amis; (*b*) à, de; **tendency to do sth.,** tendance à faire qch.; **desire to do sth.,** désir de faire qch. **3.** (*inf. with substantival function*) **to be or not to be,** être ou ne pas être; **to lie is shameful, it is shameful to lie,** il est honteux de mentir; **it is better to do nothing,** il vaut mieux ne rien faire; **to learn to do sth.,** apprendre à faire qch.; **to refuse to do sth.,** refuser de faire qch. **4.** (*inf. in finite clause*) (*a*) **it seemed to grow,** il semblait croître; (*b*) **I wish him to do it,** je veux qu'il le fasse. **5.** (*in headline*) **a hundred employees to go,** cent employés vont recevoir leur congé. **6.** (*with ellipsis of verb*); **take it; it would be absurd *not* to,** prenez-le; ce serait absurde de ne pas le faire, de manquer l'occasion; **we shall have to,** il le faudra bien; **you ought to,** vous devriez le faire; **I want to,** je voudrais bien; j'ai envie de le faire. **III.** *adv.* (*stressed*) **1.** (*a*) **ship moored head to** (= *to the wind*), navire amarré vent debout; **to put the horses to** (= *to the carriage*), atteler les chevaux; (*b*) **to turn to, set to, with a will,** se mettre résolument à l'ouvrage; **to come to** (= *to one's senses*), reprendre connaissance; (*c*) **to pull the door to,** fermer la porte. **2. to go to and fro,** aller et venir; faire la navette; *Mec.E:* **to-and-fro movement,** mouvement *m* de va-et-vient.

toad [toud] *n.* **1.** (*a*) *Amph:* crapaud *m*; (*b*) *P:* type répugnant, sale type. **2.** *Cu:* **t. in the hole,** saucisses cuites au four dans de la pâte à crêpes.

toadstool ['toudstu:l] *n. F:* champignon, *esp.* champignon vénéneux.

toady[1] ['toudi] *n.* lécheur *m* (de bottes).

toady[2] *v.i.* **to t. to s.o.,** lécher les bottes à qn, flagorner qn.

toast[1] [toust] *n.* **1.** pain grillé, toast *m*; **piece, round, of t.,** rôtie *f*, toast; **t. rack,** porte-rôties *m inv*, porte-toasts *m inv.* **2.** (*a*) personne à qui, chose à laquelle, on porte un toast; (*b*) toast; **to give, propose, a t.,** porter un toast; **t. master,** annonceur *m* des toasts.

toast[2] **1.** *v.tr.* (*a*) rôtir, griller (du pain); *F:* **to t. one's feet (in front of the fire),** se chauffer les pieds; (*b*) **to t. s.o.,** porter un toast à (la santé de) qn; boire à la santé de qn. **2.** *v.i.* rôtir, griller. **toasting** *n.* rôtissage *m*, grillage *m*; **t. fork,** fourchette *f* à rôties.

toaster ['toustər] *n.* grille-pain *m inv*; toaster *m.*

tobacco, *pl.* **-os** [tə'bækou, -ouz] *n.* **1.** *Bot:* **t. (plant),** tabac *m.* **2.** tabac (à fumer); **chewing t.,** tabac à chiquer, mâcher; **t.-coloured,** tabac *inv.*

tobacconist [tə'bækənist] *n.* débitant, -ante (de tabac); **tobacconist's (shop),** débit *m* de tabac.

toboggan[1] [tə'bɔgən] *n.* toboggan *m*; **(Swiss) t.,** luge *f*; *Sp:* **t. run,** piste *f* de toboggan.

toboggan[2] *v.i.* faire du toboggan; **to t. down a slope,** descendre une côte en toboggan. **tobogganing** *n.* (sport *m* du) toboggan.

Toby ['toubi] **1.** *Pr.n.m.* Tobie. **2.** *n.* **t. (jug),** pot *m* à bière (en forme de gros bonhomme à tricorne).

tocsin ['tɔksin] *n.* tocsin *m.*

tod [tɔd] *n. P:* **on my, his, t.,** tout seul.

today [tə'dei] *adv. & n.* aujourd'hui (*m*); (*a*) **a week ago t.,** il y a aujourd'hui huit hours; **t. week,** (d')aujourd'hui en huit; **today's paper,** le journal d'aujourd'hui, du jour; *F:* **he's here t. and gone tomorrow,** il est comme l'oiseau sur la branche; *Com:* **today's date, price,** la date, le prix, du jour; (*b*) **the young people of t.,** les jeunes d'aujourd'hui, de nos jours.

toddle[1] ['tɔdl] *n.* **1.** pas chancelants (d'un jeune enfant). **2.** *F: O:* petite promenade; balade *f.*

toddle[2] *v.i.* **1.** (*of young child*) marcher à petits pas chancelants. **2.** *F: O:* (*of adult*) trottiner; **to t. along,** aller, faire, son petit bonhomme de chemin.

toddler ['tɔdlər] *n.* enfant qui commence à marcher.

toddy ['tɔdi] *n.* grog chaud.

to-do [tə'du] *n. F:* bruit *m*, remue-ménage *m*; **what a to-do!** quelle affaire! **there was a great to-do about it,** l'affaire a fait grand bruit.

toe[1] [tou] *n.* **1.** orteil *m*; doigt *m* de pied; **big, little, t.,** gros, petit, orteil; *P:* **to turn up one's toes,** mourir; casser sa pipe; **on the tips of one's toes,** sur la pointe des pieds; *Fig:* **to be on one's toes,** être alerte. **2.** (*a*) bout *m*, pointe (de soulier, etc.); **t. cap,** bout rapporté; (*b*) *Golf:* pointe (de la crosse).

toe[2] *v.tr.* **1.** (i) tricoter, (ii) refaire, la pointe d'(une chaussette); mettre, remettre, un bout à (un soulier). **2.** *Sp:* **to t. the line, the mark,** s'aligner; *Fig:* **to t. the (party) line,** (i) s'aligner avec son parti; (ii) obéir; s'exécuter. **3.** (*a*) *Fb:* botter (le ballon) avec la pointe du pied; (*b*) *Golf:* frapper (la balle) avec la pointe de la crosse. **toed** *a.* **1.** (*with adj. or num. prefixed*) **two-t., three-t.,** à deux, trois, orteils; **square-t., pointed-t.,** (souliers) à bouts carrés, pointus. **2.** (chaussettes) dont les doigts sont marqués.

toehold ['touhold] *n.* **1.** *Mount: etc:* prise *f* de pied. **2.** *Fig:* prise précaire.

toenail ['touneil] *n.* ongle *m* d'orteil.

toff [tɔf] *n. F: O:* aristo *m*; **the toffs,** le gratin.

toffee, toffy ['tɔfi] *n.* (*a*) caramel *m* au beurre; **t. apple,** pomme enrobée de sucre et montée en sucette; *F:* **he can't sing for t.,** il ne sait pas chanter du tout; *F:* **t. nosed,** dédaigneux; (*b*) (bonbon *m* au) caramel.

tog [tɔg] *v.tr. & i.* **(togged)** *F:* **to t. s.o. up, out,** attifer qn; **to t. (oneself) up,** s'attifer; se mettre sur son trente et un; **to be (all) togged up,** en grand tralala.

toga ['tougə] *n. Rom.Ant:* toge *f.*

together [tə'geðər] *adv.* ensemble; (*a*) **to go, belong, t.,** aller ensemble; **we stand or fall t.,** nous sommes tous solidaires; **t. with,** (i) avec (qn, qch.); ainsi que (qn, qch.); (ii) en même temps que (qn, qch.); (*b*) **to gather, collect, t.,** (i) réunir, rassembler; (ii) se réunir, se rassembler; **to add t.,** additionner (ensemble); **to bring t.,** rassembler, réunir; (*c*) **to act t.,** agir de concert; **all t.,** tout le monde ensemble; tous à la fois; **now all t.!** tous en chœur! (*d*) **for hours t.,** des heures durant; pendant des heures et des heures.

togetherness [tə'geðənis] *n. F:* **1.** unité *f*, harmonie *f.* **2.** solidarité *f.*

toggle ['tɔgl] *n.* **1.** (*a*) *Nau:* **t. (pin),** cabillot *m* (d'amarrage); (*b*) *Cost:* olive *f* (de duffel-coat); (*c*) barrette *f* (de chaîne de montre). **2.** *El:* **t. switch,** interrupteur *m* à bascule; basculeur *m.*

Togo ['tougou] *Pr.n. Geog:* Togo *m.*

Togolese [tougou'li:z] *Geog:* **1.** *a.* togolais. **2.** *n.* Togolais, -aise.
togs [tɔgz] *n.pl. F:* fringues *fpl*, frusques *fpl*.
toil¹ [tɔil] *n.* travail dur, pénible; labeur *m*, peine *f*; **t. and trouble,** peine et ennuis *mpl*.
toil² *v.i.* travailler, peiner **(at,** à); **to t. and moil,** peiner, travailler dur; **to t. up a hill,** gravir péniblement une colline; **to t. on,** continuer péniblement (i) son travail, (ii) sa route.
toiler ['tɔilər] *n.* travailleur, -euse.
toilet ['tɔilit] *n.* **1.** toilette *f*; **to make one's t.,** faire sa toilette; **t. case,** nécessaire *m*, trousse *f*, de toilette; **t. soap, water,** savon *m*, eau *f*, de toilette; **t. table,** (table *f* de) toilette; coiffeuse *f*. **2.** (*a*) (*lavatory*) cabinets *mpl*; *P.N:* **toilets,** toilettes; **t. paper,** papier *m* hygiénique; **t. roll,** rouleau *m* de papier hygiénique; **to go to the t.,** aller aux cabinets; (*b*) *U.S:* cabinet *m* de toilette.
toiletries ['tɔilitriz] *n.pl.* articles *mpl* de toilette.
toilsome ['tɔilsəm] *a. Lit:* pénible, laborieux.
toing ['tuiŋ] *n.* **t. and froing,** va-et-vient *m*.
token ['touk(ə)n] *n.* **1.** indication *f*, marque *f*, témoignage *m* (d'identité, de respect, etc.); **in t., as a t., of sincerity,** en signe, en témoignage de bonne foi; **by this, by the same, t.,** (i) donc; d'ailleurs; (ii) pareillement; **t. money,** monnaie *f* fiduciaire; **t. payment, strike,** paiement *m*, grève *f*, symbolique, d'avertissement. **2.** (*a*) *O:* signe; **love t.,** gage *m* d'amour; (*b*) jeton *m* (de présence); (*c*) jeton (pour distributeur automatique, etc.); (*d*) **gift t.,** bon *m* d'achat; **book t.,** chèque-livre *m*, *pl.* chèques-livres.
Toledo [tɔ'leidou] *Pr.n. Geog:* Tolède.
tolerable ['tɔlərəbl] *a.* (*a*) (*of pain, etc.*) tolérable, supportable; (*b*) passable; assez bon; **we're in t. health,** nous nous portons assez bien. **-ably** *adv.* passablement; **I'm t. well,** je me porte assez bien.
tolerance ['tɔlərəns] *n.* **1.** tolérance *f* (d'une drogue); **increasing t.,** accoutumance *f* (à une drogue). **2.** (*a*) tolérance (religieuse, etc.); (*b*) **to show great t.,** faire preuve de beaucoup de tolérance, d'une grande indulgence. **3.** (*a*) (*minting*) tolérance; (*b*) *Mec.E: etc:* tolérance, écart *m* admissible.
tolerant ['tɔlərənt] *a.* (*a*) *Med:* **t. of a drug,** (malade) tolérant vis-à-vis d'une drogue; (*b*) (*of parent, etc.*) tolérant, indulgent. **-ly** *adv.* avec tolérance.
tolerate ['tɔləreit] *v.tr.* (*a*) *Med:* tolérer (une drogue); (*b*) tolérer, supporter (la douleur, la contradiction, etc.); **I will not t. this behaviour,** je ne supporterai pas une telle conduite; *F:* **I can't t. him,** je ne peux pas le souffrir, le sentir.
toleration [tɔlə'reiʃ(ə)n] *n* tolérance *f*.
toll¹ [toul] *n.* **1.** (*a*) droit *m* de passage; péage *m*; **t. gate, bar,** barrière *f* (de péage); **t. bridge,** pont *m* à péage, pont payant; **t. house,** (bureau *m* de) péage; **t. road,** route *f* à péage; (*b*) droit de place (au marché). **2.** (*of disease, etc.*) **to take its t.,** (i) faire beaucoup de victimes; (ii) laisser ses traces **(of s.o.,** sur qn); **accident that takes a heavy t. of human life,** accident qui occasionne beaucoup de morts; **the t. of the road,** les accidents de la route. **3.** *NAm: Tp:* **t. call,** communication interurbaine; **to call t. free,** faire un libre-appel.
toll² *n.* tintement *m*, son *m* (de cloche); (*for death*) glas *m*.
toll³ **1.** *v.tr.* (*a*) tinter, sonner (une cloche); *v.i.* **to t. for the dead,** sonner pour les morts; (*b*) (*of bell, clock*) sonner (l'heure); **to t. s.o.'s death,** sonner le glas pour la mort de qn. **2.** *v.i.* (*of bell*) tinter, sonner; (*for death*) sonner le glas. **tolling** *n.* tintement *m* (de cloche); (*for death*) glas *m*.
tollway ['toulwei] *n. NAm:* autoroute *f* à péage.
Tom [tɔm] *Pr.n.m.* (*dim. of Thomas*) Thomas, Tom. **1.** *F:* **any T., Dick or Harry,** n'importe qui, le premier venu. **2. t. (cat),** matou *m*; *NAm:* **t. (turkey),** dindon *m*. **3. T. Thumb,** le petit Poucet, Tom Pouce.
tomahawk ['tɔməhɔ:k] *n.* hache *f* de guerre (des Peaux-Rouges); tomahawk *m*.
tomato, *pl.* **-oes** [tə'mɑ:tou, -ouz; *NAm:* tə'meitou] *n.* tomate *f*; *Cu:* **t. sauce,** sauce *f* tomate.
tomb [tu:m] *n.* tombe *f*; tombeau *m*.
tombac ['tɔmbæk] *n. Metall:* tombac *m*.
tombola ['tɔmbələ] *n.* tombola *f*.
tomboy ['tɔmbɔi] *n.f.* **she's a real t.,** c'est un garçon manqué. **tomboyish** ['tɔmbɔiiʃ] *a.* (manières, etc.) de garçon manqué.
tombstone ['tu:mstoun] *n.* pierre tombale.
tome [toum] *n.* (*a*) tome *m*; (*b*) gros volume.
tomfool [tɔm'fu:l] *F:* **1.** *n.* idiot *m*, niais *m*. **2.** *a.* idiot; **t. scheme,** projet insensé.
tomfoolery [tɔm'fuləri] *n. F:* bêtise(s) *f(pl)*, niaiserie(s) *f(pl)*.
Tommy ['tɔmi] **1.** *Pr.n.m.* (*dim. of* **Thomas**) Thomas, Tom. **2.** *n.* **a t.,** un simple soldat; *F:* un troufion.
tommygun ['tɔmigʌn] *n. Mil:* mitraillette *f*.
tommyrot ['tɔmirɔt] *n. F:* bêtises *fpl*, inepties *fpl*; **that's all t.,** tout ça c'est de la blague.
tomorrow [tə'mɔrou] *adv. & n.* demain (*m*); **t. morning,** demain matin; **t. week,** (de) demain en huit; **the day after t.,** après-demain; *Prov:* **never put off till t. what you can do today,** ne remettez pas au lendemain ce que vous pouvez faire le jour même; **who knows what t. holds?** qui sait ce que demain nous réserve?
tomtit ['tɔmtit] *n. Orn:* mésange bleue.
tomtom ['tɔmtɔm] *n.* tam-tam *m*, *pl.* tam-tams.
ton [tʌn] *n. Meas:* **1.** tonne *f*; **metric t.,** tonne (métrique) (= 1000 kg); *F:* **there's tons of it,** il y en a des tas; **this suitcase weighs a t.,** cette valise est rudement lourde. **2.** *Nau:* **gross, register, t.,** tonneau *m* de jauge; **t. of displacement,** tonne de déplacement. **3.** *F:* vitesse de 100 milles à l'heure.
tonal ['toun(ə)l] *a.* tonal, -aux.
tonality [tou'næliti] *n.* tonalité *f*.
tone¹ [toun] *n.* **1.** son *m*; sonorité *f*; **t. (colour),** timbre *m* (de la voix, d'un instrument de musique); **this radio has a good t.,** ce poste a une bonne sonorité; **t. quality,** timbre (d'un intrument, etc.); *Rec:* **t. control,** touche *f* de tonalité; **t. arm,** bras *m* de lecture (d'un tourne-disque); *Tp:* **ringing t.,** tonalité d'appel. **2.** (*a*) ton *m*, voix *f*; intonation *f*; **t. of voice,** accent *m*; **in an impatient t.,** d'un ton d'impatience; **in a low t.,** sur un ton bas; d'une voix basse; (*b*) **to give a serious t. to a discussion,** donner un ton sérieux à une discussion; *Fin: etc:* **the t. of the market,** l'allure *f*, l'atmosphère *f*, du marché; (*c*) *Med:* tonicité *f*, tonus *m* (des muscles, etc.). **3.** *Mus: Ac:* ton; **whole t.,** ton entier; **quarter t.,** quart *m* de ton; *Mus:* **t. poem,** poème *m* symphonique. **4.** ton, nuance *f* (d'une couleur); *Phot:* ton (d'une épreuve); **warm tones,** tons chauds; *Art:* **half t.,** similigravure *f*, *F:* simili *f*. **5.** *Ling:* (*a*) ton; accent tonique; (*b*) accent de hauteur.
tone² **1.** *v.tr.* (*a*) adoucir les tons (d'un tableau); **toned paper,** papier (i) teinté, (ii) crémé; (*b*) **to t. down,** adoucir, atténuer (une couleur, etc.); (*on painting*) estomper (des details trop crus); **the editor had to t. down the article,** le rédacteur a dû atténuer les termes de l'article; (*c*) **to t. up,** tonifier (qn, les muscles, etc.); (*d*) *Phot:* virer (une épreuve). **2.** *v.i.* (*a*) **to t. (in) with sth.,** s'harmoniser avec qch.; (*b*) (*of voice, etc.*) **to t. down,** s'adoucir; (*c*) (*of pers., muscles, etc.*) **to t. up,** se tonifier. **toning** *n.* (*a*) *Phot:* virage *m* (des épreuves); (*b*) **t. down,** atténuation *f*, adoucissement *m*; (*c*) **t. up,** tonification *f*.
tone-deaf [toun'def] *a.* atteint d'amusie.
tone-deafness [toun'defnis] *n.* amusie *f*.
toneless ['tounlis] *a.* **1.** (couleur) sans éclat. **2.** (voix)

blanche, atone. **-ly** *adv.* d'une voix blanche, atone.

tongs [tɔŋz] *n.pl.* **(pair of) t.,** pince(s) *f(pl)*, tenailles *fpl*; *Glassm:* morailles *fpl*; **fire t.,** pincettes *fpl*; *Dom.Ec:* **sugar t.,** pince à sucre.

tongue¹ [tʌŋ] *n.* **1.** langue *f*; (*a*) *Med:* **coated t.,** langue pâteuse; **to put out, stick out, one's t.,** tirer la langue **(at s.o.,** à qn); *Fig:* **to have one's t. hanging out,** (i) tirer la langue; avoir soif; (ii) s'attendre à qch.; (*b*) **to have a ready, glib, t.,** avoir la langue déliée, bien pendue; **to find one's t.,** retrouver la parole; **with one's t. in one's cheek,** avec une ironie masquée; **t. twister,** mot *m*, phrase *f*, difficile à prononcer; phrase à décrocher la mâchoire; **to give s.o. a t. lashing,** tancer qn vertement; *Ven:* (*of hounds*) **to give t.,** donner de la voix; aboyer. **2.** langue, idiome *m* (d'un peuple); **the German t.,** la langue allemande; *esp. B:* **the gift of tongues,** le don des langues. **3.** langue (de terre, de feu); patte *f*, languette *f* (de chaussure); battant *m* (de cloche); aiguille *f* (d'une balance); *Mus:* anche *f* (de hautbois).

tongue² *v.tr. Mus:* (*on wind instrument*) **to t. a passage,** détacher les notes d'un passage. **tonguing** *n. Mus:* (*on wind instrument*) coup *m* de langue.

tongue-tied ['tʌŋtaid] *a.* muet, -ette (de timidité, etc.); interdit.

tonic ['tɔnik] **1.** *a.* (*a*) *Med: etc:* tonique, remontant, fortifiant; *Toil:* **t. lotion,** (lotion *f*) tonique *m*; (*b*) (*drink*) **t. water,** *n.* **t.,** eau tonique; **gin and t. (water),** gin-tonic *m*; (*c*) *Gram:* (accent) tonique; (*d*) *Mus:* (note) tonique. **2.** *n.* (*a*) *Med:* tonique, remontant *m*, fortifiant *m*; (*of news, etc.*) **to act as a t. on s.o.,** réconforter, remonter, qn; *Toil:* **skin t.,** (lotion) tonique; (*b*) *Mus:* tonique *f*.

tonicity [tou'nisiti] *n.* tonicité *f* (des muscles, etc.).

tonight [tə'nait] *adv. & n.* (*a*) ce soir; (*b*) cette nuit.

tonnage ['tʌnidʒ] *n.* **1.** *Nau:* tonnage *m*, jauge *f*; **register(ed) t.,** tonnage net; tonnage de jauge. **2.** tonnage (d'un port, d'un pays).

tonne [tʌn] *n. Meas:* tonne *f* (métrique).

tonsil ['tɔnsl] *n. Anat:* amygdale *f*.

tonsillectomy [tɔnsi'lektəmi] *n.* amygdalectomie *f*.

tonsillitis [tɔnsi'laitis] *n.* angine *f*; amygdalite *f*.

tonsure¹ ['tɔnʃər] *n.* tonsure *f*.

tonsure² *v.tr.* tonsurer (un ecclésiastique).

tontine [tɔn'ti:n] *n. Ins:* tontine *f*.

ton-up ['tʌnʌp] *a. F:* **t.-up boys,** motards *mpl* bolides (qui font du cent milles à l'heure).

tonus ['tounəs] *n. Med:* tonicité *f*, tonus *m*.

Tony ['touni] *Pr.n.m.* (*dim. of Antony*) Toine.

too [tu:] *adv.* **1.** trop, par trop; **it's t. difficult,** c'est trop difficile; **t. difficult a job,** un travail (par) trop difficile; **t. many people,** trop de gens; **t. far,** trop loin; **to work t. much, t. hard,** travailler trop, trop travailler; **50p t. much,** 50p de trop; **this job's t. much for me,** ce travail est au-dessus de mes forces; **I've listened to him t. long,** je l'ai trop écouté; **I know him all t. well,** je ne le connais que trop; **you're t. kind,** vous êtes très, trop, gentil; **he's not t. well today,** il ne va pas très bien aujourd'hui. **2.** (*also*) aussi; également; **you're coming t.,** vous venez aussi; **he t. is a painter,** lui aussi est peintre. **3.** (*moreover*) d'ailleurs; de plus; en outre; **30° in the shade and in September t.,** 30° à l'ombre et en septembre en plus.

toodle-oo ['tu:dl'u:] *int. F: O:* au revoir! salut!

tool¹ [tul] *n.* **1.** outil *m*; instrument *m*; ustensile *m*; **(set of) tools,** outillage *m*; **garden, gardening, tools,** outils de jardinage; **power t.,** outil à moteur; **t. holder,** (i) porte-outil *m*; (ii) manche spécial pour divers outils; **t. set,** jeu *m* d'outils; **t. rack,** râtelier à outils. **2.** (*a*) instrument, créature *f*; **to make a t. of s.o.,** se servir de qn (dans un but intéressé); **he was a mere t. in their hands,** il était devenu leur créature; (*b*) **you have to learn the tools of your trade,** on ne peut pratiquer un métier sans apprentissage.

tool² *v.tr.* **1.** (*a*) ciseler (le cuir, une reliure); **tooled leather,** cuir repoussé; (*b*) *Mec.E:* usiner, travailler (une pièce de fonte). **2. t. (up),** outiller (une usine, etc.); *v.i.* s'outiller. **tooling** *n.* **1.** (*a*) *Leath:* ciselage *m*; (*b*) *Mec.E:* usinage *m*. **2.** outillage *m*.

toolbag ['tulbæg] *n.* sac *m* à outils; (*of bicycle, etc.*) sacoche *f*.

toolbox ['tulbɔks] *n.* boîte *f*, coffre *m*, à outils.

toolkit ['tulkit] *n.* outillage *m*; jeu *m* d'outils.

toolmaker ['tu:lmeikər] *n.* fabricant *m* d'outils; outilleur *m*; taillandier *m*.

toolshed ['tu:lʃed] *n.* resserre *f*, remise *f*.

toot¹ [tu:t] *n.* son *m*, appel *m*, de clairon, etc; *Nau:* coup *m* de sirène; *Aut:* coup, appel, de klaxon.

toot² **1.** *v.tr.* **to t. a horn, a trumpet,** sonner du cor, de la trompette; *Aut:* **to t. the horn,** klaxonner. **2.** *v.i.* (*of pers.*) sonner du cor; (*of instrument*) sonner; *Aut:* klaxonner. **tooting** *n.* sonnerie *f* (de la trompette, etc.); *Aut:* coups *mpl* de klaxon.

tooth¹, *pl.* **teeth** [tu:θ, ti:θ] *n.* **1.** dent *f*; **(set of) teeth,** denture *f*, dentition *f*; **first, milk, teeth,** dents de lait; **buck teeth,** dents proéminentes; **(set of) false teeth,** dentier *m*; *F:* râtelier *m*; **t. glass, mug,** verre *m* à dents; **t. powder,** poudre *f* dentifrice; dentifrice *m*; **to have a fine set of teeth,** avoir de belles dents; **to cut one's teeth,** faire, percer, ses dents; **to have a t. out,** se faire arracher une dent; **to kick s.o. in the teeth,** traiter qn avec mépris; **to cast, fling, sth. in s.o.'s teeth,** reprocher qch. à qn; **in the teeth of all opposition,** malgré, en dépit de, toute opposition; **to show, bare, one's teeth,** montrer les dents; **armed to the teeth,** armé jusqu'aux dents; **to fight t. and nail,** se battre avec acharnement; *F:* **to get one's teeth into sth.,** se mettre pour de bon à faire qch.; s'acharner à faire qch.; **to set one's teeth,** serrer les dents; *F:* **she's a bit long in the t.,** elle n'est plus dans sa première jeunesse. **2.** dent (de scie, de peigne); dent (de roue d'engrenage); **teeth of a wheel,** denture; *Mec.E:* **gear teeth,** dents d'engrenage.

tooth² **1** *v.tr.* denter (une roue). **2.** *v.i.* (*of cogwheels*) s'engrener. **toothed** *a.* **1.** (*of animal*) denté; (*of leaf, etc.*) dentelé. **2.** *Mec.E: etc:* **t. wheel,** roue dentée. **toothing** *n.* **1.** taille *f* des dents (d'une scie, d'une roue). **2.** dents *fpl*, denture *f* (d'une roue).

toothache ['tu:θeik] *n.* mal *m*, rage *f*, de dents; **to have t.,** avoir mal aux dents.

toothbrush ['tu:θbrʌʃ] *n.* brosse *f* à dents.

toothcomb ['tu:θkoum] *n.* peigne fin; **to go through (a document) with a fine t.,** passer (un document) au peigne fin, au crible.

toothless ['tu:θlis] *a.* sans dents; édenté.

toothpaste ['tu:θpeist] *n.* pâte *f* dentifrice; dentifrice *m*.

toothpick ['tu:θpik] *n.* cure-dent(s) *m*.

toothsome ['tu:θsəm] *a.* savoureux.

toothy ['tu:θi] *a.* à dents saillantes; (*childish speech*) **t. pegs,** dents.

tootle¹ ['tu:tl] *v.i.* corner, klaxonner (de façon continue).

tootle² *v.i. F: A:* **to t. along,** aller, suivre, son petit bonhomme de chemin.

top¹ [tɔp] **I.** *n.* **1.** haut *m*, sommet *m*, cime *f*, faîte *m* (d'un arbre, d'une montagne); sommet (d'une tour, de la tête); **at the t. of the stairs,** en haut de l'escalier; **at the t. of the tree,** (i) en haut de l'arbre; (ii) *Fig:* au premier rang de sa profession; **from t. to bottom,** de haut en bas; de fond en comble; **from t. to toe,** de la tête aux pieds; de pied en cap; **to put sth. on (the) t. of sth.,** mettre qch. sur qch., (tout) en haut de qch.; **to be, to come out, on t.,** avoir (pris) le dessus; avoir l'avantage; **it's just one thing on t. of another,** ça n'arrête jamais; **on t. of it all,** et pour comble (de malheur), et en plus de tout cela; **to be, to feel, on t. of the world,** être, se sentir, en pleine forme. **2.** surface *f*, dessus *m* (d'une table, etc.); impériale *f* (d'un autobus); **t. of the milk,** crème (séparée du lait). **3.** (*a*) dessus (d'une chaussure); revers *m* (d'une botte à revers, d'un bas); couvercle *m* (d'une boîte, d'une casserole, etc.); bouchon *m*, capsule *f* (d'une bouteille, etc.); capuchon *m* (de stylo, etc.); **t. boots,** bottes *fpl* à revers; *F:* **to blow one's t.,** s'emporter; sortir de ses gonds; (*b*) *Cost:* (i) haut, corsage *m* (d'une robe); (ii) (*separate garment*) haut. **4.** tête (de page, de carte, etc.); haut (d'une page, etc.). **5.** haut bout (de la table); **at the t. of the street,** au bout de la rue; *Sch:* **to be (at) the t. of the form,** être le premier, la première, de la classe; (*of actor, etc.*) **to be (at) the t. of the bill,** faire tête d'affiche; *F:* **he's (the) tops!** c'est le dessus du panier! **6. to shout, sing, at the t. of one's voice,** crier, chanter, à tue-tête, à pleine gorge; **to be on t. of one's form,** être, se sentir, en pleine forme; *F:* **(the) t. of the morning (to you),** bien le bonjour! **7.** *Hort:* **turnip tops, carrot tops,** fanes *f* de navets, de carottes. **8.** *Nau:* hune *f*; **main t.,** grand-hune *f*. **II.** *a.* **1.** supérieur; du dessus, du haut, d'en haut; **the t. floor, storey,** le dernier étage; **t. stair, step,** dernière marche (en montant); **t. hat,** chapeau *m* haut de forme; **car with a t. speed of 150 km.p.h.,** voiture avec un plafond de 150 km/h; **t. people,** personnalités *fpl*; *F:* **the t. brass,** (i) *Mil:* les officiers supérieurs; (ii) les gros bonnets; *F:* **to be t. dog,** avoir le dessus; *Adm:* **t. secret,** ultra-secret; top secret; **to be, to feel, on t. form,** être, se sentir, en pleine forme; *Aut:* **t. gear,** prise (directe). **2.** premier; principal, -aux; **t. pupil,** premier, -ère, de la classe; **he got the t. mark,** *F:* **came t., in history,** il a eu la meilleure note en histoire; **one of the world's t. ten players,** un des dix meilleurs joueurs du monde; *Com:* **t. ten, twenty** = palmarès *m* (de la chanson).

top² *v.tr.* (**topped** [tɔpt]) **1.** écimer (un arbre, une plante); étêter (un arbre); **to t. and tail gooseberries,** éplucher des groseilles à maquereau. **2.** (*a*) surmonter, couronner, coiffer (**with,** de); *Cu:* garnir (un dessert, etc.) (**with,** de); **to t. up a drink, a glass,** remplir un verre (à ras bords); *F:* **let me t. you up,** encore un peu? *Aut:* **to t. up,** *NAm:* **t. off (the battery, the oil, the tank, etc.),** ajouter de l'eau, de l'huile, de l'essence; faire un appoint; **to t. out,** *NAm:* **t. off, a building,** célébrer l'achêvement de la construction d'un immeuble; (*b*) **and to t. it all,** et pour comble (de malheur), et en plus de tout cela. **3.** excéder, surpasser; **the takings have topped a thousand pounds,** les recettes dépassent mille livres; **to t. s.o. by a head,** dépasser qn de la tête. **4.** atteindre le sommet (d'une colline, etc.). **5. to t. a list, a class,** être à la tête d'une liste, de la classe. **6.** *Golf:* calotter (la balle). **topped** *a. esp. Lit:* **cloud-t. peaks,** sommets couronnés de nuages; **ivory-t. walking stick,** canne à pomme d'ivoire. **topping 1.** *a. F: O:* excellent, formidable. **2.** *n.* (*a*) (i) écimage *m*, étêtement *m* (d'un arbre); (ii) **t. out,** *NAm:* **t. off,** cérémonie *f* qui marque l'achèvement de la construction d'un immeuble; (*b*) *Cu: F:* garniture *f* (pour un dessert, etc.).

top³ *n.* **(spinning, peg) t.,** toupie *f*; **humming t.,** toupie d'Allemagne.

topaz ['toupæz] *n. Lap:* topaze *f*.

top-bracket ['tɔpbrækit] *a.* de première catégorie.

top(-)coat ['tɔpkout] *n.* **1.** *Cost:* pardessus *m*, manteau *m*. **2.** *Paint:* couche *f* de finition.

top(-)dress ['tɔpdres] *v.tr. Agr:* fumer en surface.

tope [toup] *v.i. F: O:* boire (avec excès); picoler.

topee ['toupi] *n.* casque colonial.

topflight ['tɔpflait] *a.* de premier ordre; excellent.

topheavy [tɔp'hevi] *a.* (*a*) trop lourd du haut; peu stable; (*b*) *Nau:* (*of ship*) trop chargé dans les hauts.

tophole ['tɔphoul] *a. A:* épatant; excellent; au poil.

topi ['toupi] *n.* casque colonial.

topic ['tɔpik] *n.* matière *f* (d'un écrit, d'une discussion); sujet *m*, thème *m* (de conversation).

topical ['tɔpik(ə)l] *a.* **t. question,** question d'actualité.

topicality [tɔpi'kæliti] *n.* actualité *f*.

topknot ['tɔpnɔt] *n.* (*a*) huppe *f* (d'un oiseau); (*b*) petit chignon.

topless ['tɔplis] *a.* (danseuse) aux seins nus; (*of swimsuit*) monokini; **to go t.,** aller torse nu.

topmast ['tɔpməst] *n. Nau:* mât *m* de hune.

topmost ['tɔpmoust] *a.* le plus haut; le plus élevé.

topnotch ['tɔpnɔtʃ] *a. O:* de premier ordre, rang.

topographer [tə'pɔgrəfər] *n.* topographe *m*.

topographic(al) [tɔpə'græfik(l)] *a.* topographique. **-ally** *adv.* topographiquement.

topography [tə'pɔgrəfi] *n.* **1.** topographie *f*. **2.** anatomie *f* topographique.

topologic(al) [tɔpə'lɔdʒik(l)] *a.* topologique.

topology [tə'pɔlədʒi] *n.* topologie *f*.

topper ['tɔpər] *n. F:* chapeau *m* haut de forme.

topple ['tɔpl] **1.** *v.i.* **to t. (down, over),** tomber, s'écrouler, culbuter, dégringoler; **to bring the government toppling,** faire tomber, renverser, le gouvernement. **2.** *v.tr.* (*a*) **to t. sth. down, over,** faire tomber, faire dégringoler, qch; (*b*) faire écrouler (un édifice, etc.); (*c*) renverser (un gouvernement, etc.).

top-rank(ing) ['tɔpræŋk(iŋ)] *a.* de premier rang; **t.-r. civil servant,** haut fonctionnaire.

topsail ['tɔpsl] *n. Nau:* hunier *m*; (*of cutter*) flèche *f*.

topside ['tɔpsaid] *n.* **1.** *Cu:* tende *f* de tranche (de bœuf). **2.** *Nau:* **topsides,** accastillage *m* (d'un navire).

topsoil ['tɔpsɔil] *n.* terre végétale; couche *f* arable.

topsy-turvy [tɔpsi'tə:vi] *adv. & a.* sens (*m*) dessus dessous; **the whole world's (turned) t.-t.,** c'est le monde renversé; c'est le monde à l'envers; **everything's t.-t.,** tout est en désarroi.

top-up ['tɔpʌp] *n. F:* (*a*) *Aut:* (remplissage *m* d')appoint *m*; (*b*) (*when serving drinks*) **let me give you a t.-up,** encore un peu?

toque [touk] *n. Cost:* toque *f*.

tor [tɔ:r] *n.* pic *m*, butte rocheuse.

torch [tɔ:tʃ] *n.* **1.** torche *f*, flambeau *m*; **to carry a, the, t. for a cause,** embrasser, épouser, une cause. **2. (electric) t.,** lampe *f* (électrique) (de poche).

torchbearer ['tɔ:tʃbɛərər] *n.* porte-flambeau *m inv*.

torchlight ['tɔ:tʃlait] *n.* lumière *f* de torche(s), de flambeau(x); **t. procession,** retraite *f* aux flambeaux.

toreador ['tɔriədɔ:r] *n.* toréador *m*, torero *m*.

torment¹ ['tɔ:ment] *n. esp. Lit:* tourment *m*, torture *f*, supplice *m*; **the torments of jealousy,** les tourments de la jalousie; **he suffered torments,** il souffrait le martyre; **to be in t.,** être au supplice.

torment² [tɔ:'ment] *v.tr.* (*a*) *esp. Lit:* tourmenter, torturer (qn); **tormented with remorse,** tourmenté par les remords; en proie aux remords; (*b*) taquiner (qn, un chat, etc.); harceler (qn, un animal, etc.).

tormentor [tɔ:'mentər] *n.* bourreau *m*.

tornado, *pl.* **-oes** [tɔ:'neidou, -ouz] *n.* tornade *f*.

torpedo¹, *pl.* **-oes** [tɔ:'pi:dou, -ouz] *n.* **1.** *Ich:* **t. (fish),** torpille *f*. **2.** *Navy: etc:* torpille; **t. boat,** vedette lance-torpilles; **t. tube,** (tube *m*) lance-torpille(s) *m inv*.

torpedo² *v.tr.* torpiller (un navire, *Fig:* la paix).

torpid ['tɔ:pid] *a.* engourdi, torpide; **t. state,** engourdissement *m* (d'un animal).

torpidity [tɔ:'piditi], **torpor** ['tɔ:pər] *n.* torpeur *f*, engourdissement *m*.

torque [tɔ:k] *n. Mec: Ph: etc:* moment *m* de torsion, de rotation; **starting t.,** couple de, au, démarrage.

torrent ['tɔrənt] *n.* torrent *m*; **it's raining in torrents,**

il pleut à torrents, à verse; **t. of abuse, of tears,** torrent, déluge *m*, d'injures, de larmes.
torrential [tɔ'renʃ(ə)l] *a.* torrentiel; **t. rain,** une pluie diluvienne, torrentielle.
torrid ['tɔrid] *a.* (chaleur, zone, terre) torride.
torsion ['tɔ:ʃ(ə)n] *n. Mec: etc:* torsion *f*; *Mch: Aut:* **t. bar,** barre *f* de torsion.
torso, *pl.* **-os** ['tɔ:sou, -ouz] *n.* torse *m.*
tort [tɔ:t] *n. Jur:* acte *m* dommageable; préjudice *m*; délit civil.
tortoise ['tɔ:təs] *n. Rept:* tortue *f.*
tortoiseshell ['tɔ:təʃel] *n.* (*a*) écaille *f* (de tortue); **t. comb,** peigne en écaille; (*b*) **t. cat,** chat écaille de tortue.
tortuous ['tɔ:tjuəs] *a.* (sentier, moyen) tortueux; **to have a t. mind,** avoir l'esprit tortu. **-ly** *adv.* tortueusement.
tortuousness ['tɔ:tjuəsnis] *n.* tortuosité *f* (d'un sentier, de la pensée, etc.).
torture¹ ['tɔ:tʃər] *n.* **1.** torture *f*; **to put s.o. to (the) t.,** mettre qn à la torture, au supplice; **instrument of t.,** instrument *m* de torture; **t. chamber,** chambre *f* de torture. **2.** torture, tourment *m*, supplice.
torture² *v.tr.* **1.** torturer (qn); mettre (qn) à la torture, au supplice; **tortured by remorse,** tenaillé par le remords. **2.** torturer (un texte). **torturing 1.** *a. Lit:* (remords, etc.) torturant. **2.** *n.* (mise *f* à la) torture.
torturer ['tɔ:tʃərər] *n.* (*a*) tortionnaire *m*; (*b*) *Hist:* bourreau *m.*
Tory ['tɔ:ri] *a.* & *n. Pol:* tory (*m*).
Toryism ['tɔ:riizm] *n. Pol:* torysme *m.*
tosh [tɔʃ] *n. F: O:* bêtises *fpl*, blague(s) *f(pl)*.
toss¹ [tɔs] *n.* **1.** (*a*) lancée *f*, lancement *m* (d'une balle, etc.); (*b*) **t. (of a coin),** coup *m* de pile ou face; **to win, lose, the t.,** gagner, perdre, à pile ou face. **2. t. of the head,** brusque mouvement de tête. **3. to take a t.,** faire une chute (de cheval, etc.).
toss² **(tossed** [tɔst]) **1.** *v.tr.* (*a*) lancer, jeter (une balle, etc.) en l'air; (*of bull*) lancer (qn) en l'air; **to t. sth. to s.o.,** jeter qch. à qn; **to t. s.o. in a blanket,** faire sauter qn en l'air sur une couverture; **to t. the salad,** mélanger, *F:* fatiguer, la salade; (*b*) **to t. a coin,** jouer à pile ou face; *v.i.* **to t. for sth.,** jouer qch. à pile ou face; **who's going to pay?—I'll t. you for it,** qui va payer?—décidons-le à pile ou face; (*c*) **to t. one's head,** relever la tête (d'un air dédaigneux); (*d*) agiter, secouer, ballotter; **to be tossed about,** être ballotté, cahoté. **2.** *v.i.* (*a*) **to t. and turn, to t. (about) in bed,** se tourner et se retourner dans son lit; (*b*) **to t. on the waves,** être ballotté par les flots; (*of ship*) **to pitch and t.,** tanguer; (*c*) (*of waves*) s'agiter. **tossing** *n.* **1.** (*a*) lancement *m* en l'air (d'une balle, etc.); (*b*) **t. (up) of a coin,** jeu *m* de pile ou face. **2.** agitation *f*, ballottement *m.* **toss off** *v.tr.* avaler d'un trait (un verre de vin); expédier (une tâche).
toss-up ['tɔsʌp] *n.* (*a*) (*of coin*) coup *m* de pile ou face; (*b*) affaire *f* à issue douteuse; **it's a t.-up,** les chances sont égales.
tot¹ [tɔt] *n.* **1. (tiny) t.,** tout(e) petit(e) enfant; **books for tiny tots,** livres *mpl* pour les tout petits. **2.** *F:* goutte *f*, petit verre (de whisky, etc.).
tot² **(totted) 1.** *v.tr.* **to t. up,** additionner; faire le total; **he has totted up 2,500 hours flying time,** il totalise 2,500 heures de vol. **2.** *v.i.* (*of expenses, etc.*) **to t. up,** s'élever (**to,** à).
total¹ ['tout(ə)l] **1.** *a.* (*a*) total, -aux; global, -aux; **the t. population,** la population totale; **t. amount,** somme totale, globale; **t. war,** guerre totale; (*b*) **they were in t. ignorance of it,** ils l'ignoraient complètement; **t. failure,** échec complet; **t. eclipse,** éclipse totale. **2.** *n.* total *m*; montant *m*; tout *m*; **grand t.,** total global; **sum t.,** somme totale; **the t. amounts to £100,** la somme s'élève à £100. **-ally** *adv.* totalement.
total² *v.tr.* & *i.* **(totalled,** *NAm:* **totaled) 1.** additionner, totaliser (les dépenses). **2. to t., to t. up to, £100,** s'élever à, se monter à, totaliser, £100.
total³ *v.tr. F:* démolir (qch.) complètement.
totalitarian [toutæli'tɛəriən] *a. Pol:* totalitaire.
totalitarianism [toutæli'tɛəriənizm] *n. Pol:* totalitarisme *m.*
totality [tou'tæliti] *n.* totalité *f.*
totalization [tout(ə)lai'zeiʃ(ə)n] *n.* totalisation *f.*
totalizator ['tout(ə)laizeitər] *n. Turf:* totalisateur *m*, totaliseur *m* (des paris).
totalize ['tout(ə)laiz] *v.tr.* additionner, totaliser.
tote¹ [tout] *n. Turf: F:* = TOTALIZATOR.
tote² *v.tr. esp. NAm:* transporter (des marchandises, etc.); porter (un sac, un revolver, etc.).
totem ['toutəm] *n.* totem *m*; **t. pole,** mât *m* totémique; mât-totem *m.*
t'other, tother ['tʌðər] *a.* & *pron. Dial:* & *F:* = **the other.**
totter¹ ['tɔtər] *n.* chancellement *m.*
totter² *v.i.* **1.** (*of pers.*) chanceler, tituber; **to t. in, out,** entrer, sortir, d'un pas mal assuré, chancelant. **2.** (*of building, government*) menacer ruine; chanceler, branler. **tottering** *a.* chancelant; titubant; **t. steps,** pas chancelants, mal assurés.
totter³ *n. F:* chiffonnier *m.*
tottery ['tɔtəri] *a.* chancelant, titubant.
toucan ['tu:kæn] *n. Orn:* toucan *m.*
touch¹ [tʌtʃ] *n.* **1.** toucher *m*, contact *m*; **I felt a t. on my arm,** j'ai senti qu'on me touchait le bras; **the engine starts at the first t. of the starter,** le moteur démarre du premier coup. **2.** (le sens du) toucher; tact *m*; **hard, soft, to the t.,** dur, mou, au toucher. **3.** (*feel*) toucher; **the cold t. of marble,** le contact froid du marbre. **4.** (*a*) léger coup; **t. of, with, a stick,** léger coup de baguette; **to give one's horse a t. of the spurs,** toucher son cheval de l'éperon; (*b*) touche *f* (de pinceau); coup (de crayon); **to add a few touches to a picture,** faire quelques retouches à un tableau; **to put the finishing touch(es), to add the final t., to sth.,** mettre la dernière main, la dernière touche, à qch. **5.** (*a*) **sculptor with a bold, light, t.,** sculpteur *m* au ciseau hardi, délicat; **delicate t. (with, of, the brush),** coup de pinceau délicat; **he's lost his t.,** il a perdu la main; **this room needs a woman's t.,** toute influence féminine fait défaut dans cette pièce; (*b*) *Mus:* toucher; **to have a light t. (on the piano),** avoir un toucher délicat. **6.** (*a*) pointe *f*, grain *m*, nuance *f*, soupçon *m*; **t. of garlic,** pointe d'ail; **a t. of bitterness,** une nuance d'amertume; **there's a t. of colour in her cheeks,** ses joues ont pris un peu de couleur; **the first touches of autumn,** les premières atteintes de l'automne; **a t. of originality,** une note d'originalité; (*b*) **t. of flu,** petite grippe. **7.** contact; **to be in t. with s.o.,** être, se tenir, en contact avec qn; être en rapport avec qn; **to get in t. with s.o.,** joindre, contacter, qn; prendre, se mettre en, contact avec qn; se mettre en communication avec (la police); **I'll be in t.,** je vous ferai signe; **to put s.o. in t. with s.o.,** mettre qn en relations, en rapport, avec qn; **to keep in t. with s.o.,** rester en contact avec qn; **to keep s.o. in t. with sth.,** tenir qn au courant de qch.; **to be out of t. with foreign affairs,** ne plus être au courant des affaires étrangères; **to be out of t., to have lost t., with s.o.,** ne plus être en communication avec qn. **8.** *Fb:* touche; **kick into t.,** envoi *m* de touche. **9.** (*a*) **it was t. and go whether we would catch the train,** nous courions grand risque de manquer le train; **it was t. and go with him,** il revient de loin; il a frôlé la mort; (*b*) **a t.-and-go affair,** une affaire très risquée; une affaire hasardeuse. **10.** *F:* **to make a t., to put the t. on s.o.,** emprunter de l'argent à qn, taper qn; **easy, soft, t.,** per-

sonne *f* à qui on emprunte de l'argent facilement.

touch² *v.* **I.** *v.tr.* **1.** (*a*) toucher; **to t. sth. with one's finger,** toucher qch. du doigt; **to t. s.o. on the shoulder, on the arm,** toucher qn à l'épaule; toucher le bras à qn; **he touched his hat to me,** il m'a salué; **t. wood!** touche du bois! **don't t.!** n'y touchez pas! **I wouldn't t. it with a bargepole,** *U.S:* **a ten foot pole,** je ne voudrais pas y toucher avec des pincettes; (*of ship*) **to t. the bottom,** *v.i.* **to t.,** toucher le fond; toucher; (*b*) (*be in contact with*) toucher (à) (qch.); **his garden touches mine,** son jardin touche au mien, le mien; (*c*) toucher, effleurer (les cordes de la harpe); faire jouer (un ressort); **he touched the bell,** il a appuyé sur le bouton de la sonnette; *Equit:* **to t. one's horse with the spur,** piquer son cheval de l'éperon; (*d*) *v.ind.tr.* **to t. on a subject,** aborder, effleurer, un sujet; (*e*) toucher, atteindre; *Fenc:* toucher, boutonner (son adversaire); **the law can't t. him,** la loi ne peut rien contre lui; **the curtains t. the floor,** les rideaux descendent jusqu'au plancher; **no one can t. him in comedy,** il n'y a personne pour l'égaler dans la comédie; (*f*) **I never t. wine,** je ne bois jamais de vin. **2.** produire de l'effet sur (qch.); *F:* (*of remedy, etc.*) **to t. the spot,** aller à la racine du mal; **to t. s.o. on a raw, tender, spot,** toucher qn à l'endroit sensible. **3.** toucher, émouvoir, attendrir (qn); **to be touched by s.o.'s kindness,** être touché de, par, la bonté de qn; **to t. s.o. to the quick,** toucher qn au vif. **4.** *O:* toucher, regarder (qn); **the question touches you closely,** la question vous touche de près. **5. flowers touched by the frost,** fleurs atteintes par la gelée. **6.** *F:* **to t. s.o. for a fiver,** taper, faire casquer, qn de cinq livres. **II.** *v.i.* (*a*) (*of pers., thgs*) se toucher; (i) être en contact; (ii) venir en contact; **the two ships touched,** les deux navires ont touché; (*b*) *Nau:* **to t. at a port,** faire escale à un port. **touch down 1.** *v.tr. & i. Rugby Fb:* toucher dans les buts. **2.** *v.i. Av:* atterrir; faire escale. **touched** *a F:* **t. (in the head),** toqué, timbré. **touching 1.** *a.* touchant, émouvant, attendrissant. **2.** *n.* (*a*) touche *f*; contact *m*; (*b*) **t. up,** (i) retouches *fpl*; (ii) avivage *m* (d'une couleur). **touchingly** *adv.* d'une manière touchante, émouvante. **touch off** *v.tr.* décharger (un canon, etc.); faire partir, faire exploser (une mine). **touch up** *v.tr.* (*a*) faire des retouches à (un tableau); (*of paintwork*) faire des raccords (de peinture); aviver, rafraîchir (les couleurs de qch.); enjoliver (un récit); retaper, fignoler (un ouvrage); (*b*) toucher (un cheval) du fouet.

touchdown ['tʌtʃdaun] *n.* **1.** *Rugby Fb:* touché-en-but *m.* **2.** *Av:* atterrissage *m.*

touché ['tu:ʃei] *int.* touché!

touchiness ['tʌtʃinis] *n.* susceptibilité *f*, irascibilité *f.*

touchline ['tʌtʃlain] *n. Fb: etc:* ligne *f* de touche.

touchstone ['tʌtʃstoun] *n.* pierre *f* de touche.

touch-type ['tʌtʃtaip] *v.i.* taper au toucher. **touch-typing** *n.* dactylographie *f* au toucher.

touchwood ['tʌtʃwud] *n.* amadou *m.*

touchy ['tʌtʃi] *a.* susceptible, irascible; **to be t.,** se froisser, s'offusquer, facilement; **he's very t. on that point,** il n'entend pas raillerie là-dessus.

tough [tʌf] *a.* **1.** dur, tenace; (bois, etc.) résistant; (viande) coriace. **2.** (*of pers., etc.*) fort, solide; **to become t. (through training),** s'endurcir; *F:* **a t. guy,** un dur. **3.** (*of pers.*) raide, inflexible; opiniâtre; *F:* **he's a t. customer,** il n'est pas commode; c'est un dur à cuire; **to be, get, t. with s.o.,** être, se montrer, dur envers qn. **4.** *F:* (*a*) (*of task, etc.*) rude, difficile; **it was a t. job,** ç'a été une rude besogne; (*b*) **t. luck!** pas de chance! **that's t.!** c'est dur pour vous! **5.** *NAm: F:* (*a*) (homme) brutal, violent; (*b*) *n.* brute *f*; voyou *m.* **-ly** *adv.* **1.** durement; avec ténacité. **2.** vigoureusement. **3.** avec opiniâtreté.

toughen ['tʌf(ə)n] **1.** *v.tr.* (*a*) durcir; **toughened glass,** verre trempé; (*b*) endurcir (qn). **2.** *v.i.* (*a*) durcir; (*b*) (*of pers.*) s'endurcir.

toughness ['tʌfnis] *n.* **1.** dureté *f*; ténacité *f*; résistance *f*; (*of meat*) coriacité *f.* **2.** (*a*) force *f*, solidité *f*; (*b*) résistance à la fatigue. **3.** (*a*) inflexibilité *f*, opiniâtreté *f*; (*b*) *F:* caractère *m* peu commode (de qn). **4.** difficulté *f* (d'un travail).

toupee, toupet ['tu:pei] *n. Hairdr:* (mèche) postiche (*m*).

tour¹ [tuər] *n.* **1.** voyage *m* (circulaire); excursion *f*; **conducted, guided, t.,** (i) voyage organisé; (ii) (*in museum, etc.*) visite guidée; **package t.,** *U.S:* **all-expense t.,** voyage à forfait, à prix forfaitaire; **walking t.,** excursion, randonnée *f*, à pied. **2.** tournée *f*; (*a*) **t. of inspection,** tournée d'inspection; **t. of duty,** (i) tour *m* d'équipe, de service; (ii) journée *f* (de travail); (*b*) *Th:* tournée *f.*

tour² *v.tr. & i.* (*a*) **to t. (in) a country,** faire le tour d'un pays; voyager dans un pays; (*b*) *Th:* **to t. the provinces,** (*of company*) faire une tournée en province; (*of play*) passer en province. **touring** *a.* **t. car,** voiture *f* de tourisme; *Th:* **t. company,** troupe *f* en tournée.

tourer ['tuərər] *n.* voiture *f* de tourisme.

tourism ['tuərizm] *n.* tourisme *m.*

tourist ['tuərist] *n.* touriste *mf*; **t. agency,** agence *f*, bureau *m*, de tourisme; **t. centre,** centre *m*, ville *f*, touristique; **t. information,** renseignements *mpl* touristiques; **the t. trade,** le tourisme; *Av: etc:* **t. class,** classe *f* touriste; *F:* **t. trap,** attrape-touristes *m inv.*

touristy ['tuəristi] *a. Pej:* (trop) touristique.

tournament ['tuənəmənt] *n.* **1.** *Hist:* (*a*) tournoi *m*; (*b*) carrousel *m.* **2.** tournoi (de tennis, de bridge).

tourniquet ['tuənikei] *n. Med:* tourniquet *m*, garrot *m.*

tousle ['tauzl] *v.tr.* ébouriffer, écheveler (les cheveux de qn); **tousled hair,** cheveux ébouriffés.

tout¹ [taut] *n.* **1.** (*for hotels*) rabatteur, -euse; (*for insurance companies*) démarcheur, -euse; (*for shops, shows, etc.*) racoleur *m*; **ticket t.,** revendeur, -euse, de billets au marché noir. **2. (racing) t.,** (i) individu qui suit secrètement l'entraînement des chevaux, à l'affût de tuyaux; (ii) donneur, -euse, de tuyaux.

tout² **1.** *v.i. Turf:* suivre secrètement les chevaux de course à l'entraînement; espionner dans les écuries. **2.** (*a*) *v.i.* **to t. for custom,** racoler des clients; (*b*) *v.tr.* (i) **to t. s.o. for his custom,** importuner qn avec des offres de service; (ii) **to t. a product (around),** faire l'article d'un produit. **touting** *n.* **1.** racolage *m*, démarchage *m.* **2.** *Turf:* espionnage *m.*

tow¹ [tou] *n.* **1.** (câble *m* de) remorque *f.* **2. to take a car in t.,** prendre une voiture en, à la, remorque; **to be taken in t.,** se mettre à la remorque; **to be on, in, t.,** être à la remorque; (*of boat*) être à la traîne; *F:* **he always has his family in t.,** il trimbale toujours toute sa famille avec lui; *Aut:* **on t.,** en remorque; **t. hook,** croc *m* de remorque; **t. bar,** (i) timon *m* de remorque; (ii) barre *f* de remorquage (d'un planeur); *U.S:* **t. car, truck,** dépanneuse *f.*

tow² *v.tr.* remorquer (un navire, une voiture); prendre (un navire, une voiture) en, à la, remorque; touer (un chaland); (*from towpath*) haler (une péniche, un chaland); **my car's been towed away by the police,** la police a saisi ma voiture. **towing** *n.* remorque *f*, remorquage *m*; touage *m*; (*from towpath*) halage *m.*

tow³ *n.* étoupe (blanche); filasse *f*; (*of pers.*) **t.-headed,** aux cheveux (blond) filasse.

towage ['touidʒ] *n.* (*a*) remorquage *m*, touage *m*; (*on canal*) halage *m*; (*b*) (frais de) remorquage.

toward [tə'wɔ:d, twɔ:d] *prep. Lit:* = TOWARDS.

towards [tə'wɔ:dz, twɔ:dz] *prep.* **1.** vers; du côté de; **t. the town,** vers la ville, du côté de la ville; **he came**

t. me, il est venu vers moi. **2.** envers, à l'égard de (qn); **his feelings t. me,** ses sentiments *mpl* envers, pour, moi; ses sentiments à mon égard. **3.** pour; **to save t. the children's education,** économiser pour, en vue de, l'éducation des enfants; **would you like to give something t. it?** voudriez-vous y contribuer quelque chose? **4.** (*of time*) vers; sur; **t. evening,** vers le soir; **t. the end of his life,** sur la fin de sa vie.

towel[1] ['tauəl] *n.* **1.** serviette *f* (de toilette); essuie-main(s) *m inv*; **roller t.,** essuie-main(s), serviette, sans fin (pour rouleau); **tea t.,** *NAm:* **dish t.,** torchon *m* (à vaisselle); **t. rail,** porte-serviettes *m inv*. **2. sanitary t.,** serviette hygiénique, périodique.

towel[2] *v.tr.* **(towelled,** *NAm:* **toweled)** essuyer, frotter (qn) avec une serviette; **to t. oneself (dry),** s'essuyer (après le bain, etc.). **towelling,** *NAm:* **toweling** *n.* **1.** friction *f* avec une serviette. **2.** tissu-éponge *m*; **t. robe,** peignoir *m* en tissu-éponge.

tower[1] ['tauər] *n.* **1.** (*a*) *Arch: Const:* tour *f*; **the T. of Babel,** la tour de Babel; **the T. of London,** la Tour de Londres; **church t.,** clocher *m*; **clock t.,** tour de l'horloge (de Westminster, etc.); *Hyd.E:* **water t.,** château *m* d'eau; *Av:* **control t.,** tour de contrôle; **t. block,** tour, immeuble-tour *m*, *pl.* immeubles-tours; **he is a t. of strength,** c'est un puissant appui, un puissant secours; (*b*) *Ind: Ch:* **fractionating t.,** tour de fractionnement. **2.** (*a*) *Civ.E: etc:* pylône *m*; (*b*) *Rail: U.S:* **signal t.,** cabine *f* de signaux.

tower[2] *v.i.* **1. to t. above, over, sth.,** dominer qch. **2.** (*of bird*) planer; monter très haut (en l'air). **towering** *a.* **1.** (*a*) très haut, très élevé; (*b*) *Lit:* (ambitions) sans bornes. **2.** (*of rage*) violent; **in a t. rage,** au paroxysme de la colère.

towline ['toulain] *n.* (câble *m* de) remorque *f*.

town [taun] *n.* **1.** (*a*) ville *f*; **fortified t.,** place forte; **to go out on the t.,** faire la bombe, la noce; **t. life,** vie urbaine; **t. clerk** = secrétaire *mf* de mairie; secrétaire de municipalité; **t. council,** conseil municipal; **t. hall,** hôtel *m* de ville; mairie *f*; **t. house,** (i) maison *f* de ville; hôtel particulier; (ii) résidence urbaine; **t. centre,** centre *m* de la ville; centre(-)ville; (*b*) *U.S:* (*in New England*) commune *f*; (*c*) (*inhabitants*) **the whole t. is talking about it,** toute la ville en parle. **2.** (*without article*) (*a*) **to live in T.,** habiter Londres; (*b*) **to go into t.,** aller, se rendre, à la, en, ville; **she's in t. shopping,** elle fait ses courses en ville; **he's out of t.,** il est à la campagne, en voyage; **man, woman, about t.,** mondain, -aine; *F:* **to go to t.,** (i) bien s'amuser; (ii) dépenser à pleines mains; *Sch:* **t. and gown,** les habitants de la ville et les étudiants.

townee ['tauni(:)] *n. Pej:* habitant, -ante, de la ville.

townsfolk ['taunzfouk] *n.pl.* habitants *m* de la ville; citadins *m*.

township ['taunʃip] *n.* **1.** commune *f*; bourg *m*. **2.** (*a*) *NAm:* municipalité *f*, *Fr.C:* canton *m*; (*b*) *U.S:* (*in New England*) commune. **3.** (*in S. Africa*) banlieue noire.

townsman, *pl.* **-men** ['taunzmən] *n.m.* habitant de la ville; citadin.

townspeople ['taunzpi:pl] *n.pl.* habitants *m* de la ville; citadins *m*.

townswoman, *pl.* **-women** ['taunzwumən, -wimin] *n.f.* habitante de la ville; citadine.

towpath ['toupɑ:θ] *n.* chemin *m* de halage.

towrope ['touroup] *n.* (câble *m* de) remorque *f*.

toxaemia, *NAm:* **toxemia** [tɔk'si:miə] *n. Med:* toxémie *f*.

toxic ['tɔksik] *a.* toxique.

toxicologic(al) [tɔksikə'lɔdʒik(l)] *a. Med:* toxicologique.

toxicologist [tɔksi'kɔlədʒist] *n.* toxicologue *mf*.

toxicology [tɔksi'kɔlədʒi] *n. Med:* toxicologie *f*.

toxin ['tɔksin] *n. Bio-Ch:* toxine *f*.

toy[1] [tɔi] *n.* (*a*) jouet *m*; (*child's word*) joujou *m*, *pl.* joujoux; **t. shop,** magasin *m* de jouets; **t. trumpet,** trompette *f* d'enfant; **t. soldier,** soldat *m* de plastique, de plomb; (*b*) **t. dog,** chien *m* de manchon; bichon *m*; **t. poodle,** caniche nain.

toy[2] *v.i.* **1. to t. with sth.,** jouer avec, manier, qch.; **to t. with one's food,** manger du bout des lèvres, des dents; **to t. with an idea,** caresser une idée. **2. to t. with s.o.,** badiner, flirter, avec qn.

trace[1] [treis] *n.* **1.** *usu.pl.* trace(s) *f(pl)* (de qn, d'un animal); empreinte *f* (d'un animal). **2.** (*a*) trace, vestige *m*; **they could find no t. of him,** on n'a pas pu retrouver sa trace; **there's not a t. of it,** (i) il n'en reste pas trace; (ii) cela ne se voit plus; (*b*) trace, quantité *f* minime; soupçon *m*.

trace[2] *v.tr.* **1. to t. (out),** tracer (un plan, une ligne de conduite, etc.). **2.** (*a*) faire le tracé d'(un plan, un diagramme); (*b*) calquer (un dessin). **3.** suivre la trace, la piste (de qn, d'une bête); recouvrer (des objets perdus); **they traced him as far as Paris,** on a suivi sa piste jusqu'à Paris; **to t. the evil to its source,** remonter à la source du mal. **4.** retrouver les vestiges, relever les traces (d'un ancien édifice, etc.); retracer, retrouver (une influence, etc.). **trace back** *v.tr.* **to t. sth. back to its source,** remonter jusqu'à l'origine de qch.; **to t. one's family back to the Conqueror,** faire remonter sa famille à Guillaume le Conquérant. **tracing** *n.* **1.** tracement *m*; calquage *m*; **t. paper,** papier *m* calque, à calquer; *Dressm: etc:* **t. wheel,** roulette *f* (à patron). **2.** calque *m*.

trace[3] *n. Harn:* trait *m*; **in the traces,** attelé; *F:* (*of pers.*) **to kick over the traces,** (i) s'insurger; ruer dans les brancards; (ii) s'émanciper; faire des frasques.

tracer ['treisər] *n.* **1.** (*pers.*) traceur, -euse (d'un plan, etc.); calqueur, -euse. **2.** *Mil: etc:* **t. shell,** traçant *m*; **t. bullet,** (balle) traçante *f*. **3.** (*a*) *Ch:* **t. (substance),** substance révélatrice; (*b*) traceur (radioactif).

tracery ['treisəri] *n.* **1.** *Arch:* réseau *m*, remplage *m* (d'une rosace). **2.** nervures *fpl* (d'une feuille, etc.).

trachea, *pl.* **-eae** [trə'ki:ə, -ii:] *n.* (*a*) *Anat:* trachée-artère *f*, trachée *f*; (*b*) *Nat.Hist:* trachée.

tracheal [trə'ki:əl] *a. Anat: Ent:* trachéal, -aux.

tracheotomy [træki'ɔtəmi] *n. Surg:* trachéotomie *f*.

trachoma [træ'koumə] *n. Med:* trachome *m*.

track[1] [træk] *n.* **1.** (*a*) *Ven:* voie *f*, foulées *fpl*, trace(s) *f(pl)*, piste *f* (d'un animal); **to follow the t.,** suivre la piste; (*b*) trace(s), piste (de qn); sillage *m* (d'un navire); sillon *m* (d'une roue); **to follow in s.o.'s tracks,** suivre la voie tracée par qn; **to be on s.o.'s t.,** suivre la piste de qn; **to throw s.o. off the t.,** dépister qn; *F:* **to be off the t.,** divaguer; **to be on the right t.,** être dans la bonne voie, sur la voie; **to be on the wrong t.,** avoir perdu la piste; être égaré; **to keep t. of s.o., of sth.,** suivre les progrès de qn, d'une affaire; **I've lost t. of him,** je l'ai perdu de vue; *F:* **to make tracks,** partir, filer; **to stop in one's tracks,** s'arrêter net; (*c*) *Veh:* écartement *m* des roues, voie. **2.** (*a*) piste, chemin *m*, sentier *m*; **cart t.,** chemin de terre; **mule t.,** sentier muletier; **cycle t.,** piste cyclable; (*b*) *Sp:* **(running, racing) t.,** piste; **t. racing,** courses *fpl* de, sur, piste; **t. and field events,** épreuves *fpl* d'athlétisme; **racing t.,** piste de vitesse; (*of racehorse, car, F: of pers.*) **t. record,** carrière *f*, dossier *m*, antécédents *mpl*; (*c*) *Rail:* voie (ferrée); **single-t., double-t., line,** ligne *f* à une voie, à deux voies; **the train left the t.,** le train a déraillé; (*d*) *Mec.E: etc:* chemin de roulement, de glissement; (*e*) *Rec: etc:* piste (de disque); voie, piste (de bande magnétique); **sound t.,** piste sonore. **3.** route *f*, chemin; cours *m* (d'une comète). **4.** *Veh:* chenille *f*; **t., half-t., vehicle,** véhicule chenillé, semi-chenillé.

track[2] **1.** *v.tr.* (*a*) suivre (une bête, un voleur, etc.) à la piste; traquer (un malfaiteur); suivre (un missile) à la trace; (*b*) tracer (une voie, etc.). **2.** *v.i.* (*a*) (*of gear wheels, etc.*) être en alignement; (*b*) *Rec:* (*of stylus*) suivre la piste. **track down** *v.tr.* dépister (le gibier, un criminel, etc.); découvrir (qch.). **tracked** *a.* (vehicule) chenillé; **half-t.,** semi-chenillé. **tracking** *n.* **1.** poursuite *f* (d'un animal, de qn) à la piste; **t. (down),** dépistage *m* (du gibier, d'un criminel, d'une erreur, etc.). **2.** (*a*) *Elcs: Space:* poursuite; **t. systems,** systèmes *mpl* de repérage et de poursuite; **t. station,** station *f* de dépistage; (*b*) *Cin:* **t. shot,** travelling *m* en poursuite.

tracker ['trækər] *n.* traqueur *m* (de gibier); **t. dog,** chien policier.

tracklayer ['trækleiər] *n. esp. U.S: Rail:* (*pers.*) poseur *m* de voie.

tracklaying ['trækleiiŋ] *n.* **1.** *Rail:* pose *f* de voie. **2.** *esp. U.S:* **t. vehicle,** véhicule *m* à chenilles.

trackless ['trækIis] *a.* **1.** sans chemins, sans sentiers; (forêt) vierge. **2.** *NAm:* **t. trolley,** trolleybus *m.*

tracksuit ['træks(j)u:t] *n. Sp:* survêtement *m.*

tract¹ [trækt] *n.* **1.** étendue *f* (de pays, de sable, d'eau); nappe *f* (d'eau); région (montagneuse, etc.). **2.** *Anat:* appareil *m* (respiratoire, digestif).

tract², *n.* petit traité; brochure *f*, tract *m.*

tractable ['træktəbl] *a.* **1.** (*of pers., character*) docile; traitable; menable. **2.** (*of material*) facile à ouvrer; ouvrable.

traction ['trækʃ(ə)n] *n.* traction *f*, tirage *m*; (*a*) **steam t.,** traction à vapeur; **t. wheels,** roues motrices (d'une locomotive, etc.); **t. cable,** câble tracteur; **t. engine,** tracteur *m*; (*b*) *Med:* traction.

tractive ['træktiv] *a.* tractif; (force) de traction.

tractor ['træktər] *n.* tracteur *m*; **t.-drawn,** tracté.

trad [træd] *F:* **1.** *a.* traditionnel. **2.** *n.* jazz *m* (de la Nouvelle Orléans (et ses dérivés).

trade¹ [treid] *n.* **1.** (*a*) métier *m*; commerce *m*; **to follow, carry on, a t.,** exercer un métier; **he's a plumber by t.,** il est plombier de son métier; **everyone to his t.,** chacun son métier; (*b*) (corps de) métier; **the building t.,** le bâtiment; **the publishing t.,** l'édition *f*; **the printing t.,** l'imprimerie *f*; **to be in the t.,** être du métier; **t. name,** (i) (*product*) appellation commerciale; (ii) (*firm*) raison commerciale; **t. secret,** secret *m* de fabrique; **t. journal,** journal professionnel; **t. discount,** remise *f*, escompte *m*; (*c*) **t. association,** syndicat professionnel; **t., trades, union,** syndicat (ouvrier); (*of workers*) **to form a t. union,** se syndiquer; **t., trades, unionism,** syndicalisme (ouvrier); **t., trades, unionist,** syndicaliste *mf*; (ouvrier, - ière) syndiqué(e). **2.** (*a*) commerce; négoce *m*, affaires *fpl*; **to be in t.,** être dans le commerce; être commerçant, -ante; **wholesale, retail, t.,** commerce de gros, de détail; **balance of t.,** balance commerciale; **the tea t.,** le commerce du thé; **it's good for t.,** cela fait marcher le commerce; **he's doing a roaring t.,** il fait des affaires d'or; (*b*) *NAm:* (i) transaction (commerciale); (ii) clientèle *f* (d'une maison); (*c*) **t. winds, trades,** (vents) alizés *mpl*; (*d*) **(illicit) t.,** trafic *m.*

trade² **1.** *v.i.* (*a*) faire le commerce, le négoce (**in sth.,** de, en, qch.; **with s.o.,** avec qn); faire des affaires, entretenir des relations commerciales (**with s.o.,** avec qn); (*b*) **to t. on s.o.'s ignorance,** exploiter, tirer profit de, l'ignorance de qn; (*c*) *NAm:* (i) se ravitailler (**at, with,** chez); (ii) **to t. with s.o.,** faire un troc avec qn. **2.** *v.tr.* **to t. sth. for sth.,** échanger, troquer, qch. contre qch; *NAm:* **to t. places with s.o.,** changer de place avec qn. **trade in** *v.tr.* donner (une voiture, etc.) en reprise. **trade off** *v.tr.* échanger (qch. contre qch.). **trading** *n.* (*a*) commerce *m*, négoce *m*; **t. year,** année *f* d'exploitation; exercice *m*; **t. company,** société commerciale; **t. stamp,** timbre-prime *m*, *pl.* timbres-prime(s); (*b*) **(illicit) t.,** trafic *m.*

trade-in ['treidin] *n.* objet donné en reprise.

trademark ['treidmɑ:k] *n.* marque *f* de fabrique, de commerce; **registered t.,** marque déposée.

trade-off ['treidɔf] *n. esp. U.S:* échange *m.*

trader ['treidər] *n.* **1.** négociant, -ante; commerçant, -ante; marchand, -ande. **2.** *Nau:* navire marchand.

tradesman, *pl.* **-men** ['treidzmən] *n.m.* marchand, fournisseur; **tradesmen's entrance,** entrée *f* des fournisseurs.

tradition [trə'diʃ(ə)n] *n.* tradition *f*; **t. has it that ...,** selon la tradition ....

traditional [trə'diʃ(ə)nəl] *a.* traditionel. **-ally** *adv.* traditionnellement.

traditionalism [trə'diʃ(ə)nəlizm] *n.* traditionalisme *m.*

traditionalist [trə'diʃ(ə)nəlist] *n.* traditionaliste *mf.*

traduce [trə'dju:s] *v.tr. O:* calomnier, diffamer (qn).

traffic¹ ['træfik] *n.* **1.** (*a*) *A:* commerce *m*, négoce *m* (**in,** de); (*b*) *Pej:* trafic *m*; **the drug t.,** le trafic des stupéfiants. **2.** (*a*) mouvement *m*, circulation *f*; **road t.,** circulation routière; **t. jam,** embouteillage *m*; bouchon *m*; **heavy t.,** circulation intense; **through t.,** circulation directe; **t. regulations,** règlements *mpl* sur la circulation; **t. island,** refuge *m*; **t. lights, signals,** feux *mpl* de circulation, de signalisation routière; **t. control,** régulation *f* de la circulation; (*b*) **ocean t.,** navigation *f* au long cours; (*c*) **rail(way) t.,** trafic ferroviaire; **goods, passenger, t.,** trafic marchandises, voyageurs; **t. manager, superintendent,** chef *m* du mouvement.

traffic² *v.tr. & i.* (**trafficked** ['træfikt]) *Pej:* trafiquer (**in drugs,** en stupéfiants).

trafficker ['træfikər] *n. Pej:* trafiquant, -ante, trafiqueur, -euse (**in,** de, en).

trafficator ['træfikeitər] *n. Aut: O:* flèche *f* de direction.

tragedian [trə'dʒi:diən] *n.* (*a*) auteur *m* tragique; (*b*) *Th:* (*f.* **tragedienne** [trədʒi:di'en]) tragédien, -ienne.

tragedy ['trædʒidi] *n.* (*a*) *Th:* tragédie *f*; le tragique; (*b*) tragédie; **to make a t. out of sth.,** prendre qch. au tragique; **the t. of his death,** sa mort tragique.

tragic ['trædʒik] *a.* tragique; (*a*) **t. actor, actress,** tragédien, -ienne; *F:* **to put on a t. act,** jouer la tragédie; (*b*) **t. event,** événement *m* tragique; **the t. side of the story is that ...,** le tragique de l'histoire c'est que .... **-ally** *adv.* tragiquement.

tragicomedy [trædʒi'kɔmidi] *n.* tragi-comédie *f*, *pl.* tragi-comédies.

tragicomic(al) [trædʒi'kɔmik(l)] *a.* tragicomique.

trail¹ [treil] *n.* **1.** (*a*) traînée *f* (de sang, de fumée, etc.); panache *m* (de fumée); queue *f* (d'un météore); (*b*) *Artil:* flèche *f*, crosse *f* (d'affût); (*c*) *Fish:* **t. net,** (i) traîneau *m*, traîne *f*; (ii) chalut *m.* **2.** (*a*) piste *f*, trace (d'une bête, de qn); trace (d'un colimaçon); *Ven:* voie *f* (d'une bête); (*of hounds*) **to pick up the t.,** retrouver la trace; **false t.,** fausse piste; **to be on the t. of s.o.,** être sur la piste de qn; **to leave ruin in one's t.,** laisser la ruine sur son passage; (*b*) sentier (battu); piste (dans une forêt, etc.).

trail² **1.** *v.tr.* (*a*) **to t. sth. (along),** traîner qch. après soi; (*of car, etc.*) remorquer (une caravane, etc.); **to let one's dress t. in the dust,** traîner sa robe dans la poussière; *Fig:* **to t. one's coat,** inviter les attaques; chercher noise à tout le monde; (*b*) traquer, suivre à la piste (une bête, un criminel); (*of crook*) suivre, filer (une victime). **2.** *v.i.* (*a*) traîner; **your skirt is trailing (on the ground),** votre jupe traîne (par terre); **with a boat trailing behind,** avec un bateau à la traîne; (*b*) (*of pers.*) **to t. along,** se traîner; **to t. behind,** traîner derrière (les autres); *Fig:* (*of team, etc.*) être en retard sur les autres; **her voice trailed away, off, in the distance,** sa voix se perdit dans le lointain; (*c*) (*of plant*) grimper, ramper. **trailing**

1. *a.* (*a*) (*of skirt, etc.*) traînant; (*b*) (*of plant*) grimpant, rampant; (*c*) *Av:* **t. edge,** bord *m* de fuite (de l'aile). **2.** *n.* (*a*) traîne *f*, traînement *m*; (*b*) poursuite *f* (de qn) à la piste.

trailblazer ['treilbleizər] *n.* pionnier *m.*

trailer ['treilər] *n.* **1.** (*pers.*) traqueur *m.* **2.** *Aut: etc:* (*a*) remorque *f*; (*b*) *NAm:* caravane *f* (de camping). **3.** *Cin:* film *m* annonce.

train¹ [trein] *n.* **1.** traîne *f*, queue *f* (d'une robe); queue (d'un paon, d'une comète); **t. bearer,** porte-queue *m inv*; caudataire *m* (d'un cardinal, etc.). **2.** (*a*) suite *f*, cortège *m*, équipage *m* (d'un prince, etc.); (*b*) *Mil:* équipage, train *m*; (*c*) **the evils that follow in the t. of war,** les maux que la guerre traîne à sa suite. **3.** (*a*) train, convoi *m* (de wagons, de péniches); succession *f*, série *f*, enchaînement *m* (d'événements, de circonstances); **t. of thought,** chaîne *f* d'idées; (*b*) *Min:* traînée *f* (de poudre); (*c*) *O:* **to set sth. in t.,** mettre qch. en train. **4.** *Tchn:* système *m* d'engrenages; rouage(s) *m(pl)* (d'une montre, d'une horloge); **wheel t.,** train de roues. **5.** (*a*) *Rail:* train; **passenger, goods, t.,** train de voyageurs, de marchandises; **fast t.,** (train) rapide *m*; **express t.,** train express; **slow, stopping, t.,** train omnibus; **relief t.,** train supplémentaire; **excursion t.,** train d'excursion, à prix réduit; **by t.,** (voyager) par, en, chemin de fer; **t. journey,** voyage *m* en, par, chemin de fer; *P.N:* **to the trains,** accès aux quais; (*b*) rame *f* (du métro); (*c*) **t. ferry,** ferry(-boat) *m*; (*d*) *F:* **the gravy t.,** le bon filon; **to ride the gravy t.,** taper dans l'assiette au beurre; se la couler douce.

train² **1.** *v.tr.* (*a*) former, instruire (qn); dresser (un animal); former (le caractère, l'esprit); exercer (l'oreille); **he was trained at . . .,** il sort de (telle ou telle école); **to t. s.o. for sth., to do sth.,** exercer qn à qch., à faire qch.; **to t. s.o. in the use of a weapon,** instruire qn à se servir d'une arme; (*b*) *Sp:* entraîner (un coureur, un cheval de course, etc.); (*c*) *Hort:* palisser, mettre en espalier (un arbre fruitier, une vigne); (*d*) pointer (un canon); braquer, diriger (une lunette, un projecteur, etc.) (**on,** sur); *Navy:* orienter (un canon). **2.** *v.i.* (*a*) s'exercer; *Mil:* faire l'exercice; (*b*) *Sp:* s'entraîner; (*c*) **to t. for sth.,** s'exercer, se préparer, à qch.; **to t. as a typist,** suivre un cours de dactylographie. **trained** *a.* (*a*) (soldat, etc.) instruit; (chien, etc.) dressé; (œil) exercé; **t. nurse,** infirmière diplômée; (*b*) *Sp:* entraîné.

trainee [trei'ni:] *n.* stagiaire *mf*; élève *mf.*

trainer ['treinər] *n.* **1.** (*pers.*) (*a*) dresseur *m* (d'animaux); (*b*) *Sp: Turf:* entraîneur *m* (d'athlètes, de chevaux de course); (*c*) *Artil: U.S:* pointeur *m.* **2.** *Av:* **t. (aircraft),** avion-école *f*, *pl.* avions-écoles.

training ['treiniŋ] *n.* **1.** (*a*) éducation *f*, instruction *f*, formation *f*; **physical t.,** éducation physique; **vocational t.,** éducation professionnelle; **I'm a historian by t.,** je suis historien de formation; **he had received a good t.,** il avait fait un bon apprentissage; **t. centre,** centre *m* de formation; (*b*) *Mil:* **military t.,** dressage *m* militaire; *Navy:* **t. ship,** navire-école *m*; **t. base,** base *f* école; (*c*) *Sp:* entraînement *m*; **to go into t.,** s'entraîner; **to be in t.,** (i) être à l'entraînement; (ii) être bien entraîné; être en forme; **to be out of t.,** ne plus être en forme; (*d*) dressage (d'un animal). **2.** *Hort:* palissage *m* (d'une plante, d'un arbre fruitier). **3.** *Artil:* orientation *f* (d'une pièce).

trainload ['treinloud] *n.* **t. of coal,** train chargé de houille; **t. of tourists,** plein train de touristes.

traipse [treips] *v.i.* **to t. around,** traîner çà et là; se balader; **to t. through the streets,** battre le pavé.

trait [treit] *n.* trait *m* (de caractère, etc.).

traitor ['treitər] *n.* traître *m* (**to,** à); **to turn t.,** passer à l'ennemi; se vendre.

traitorous ['treit(ə)rəs] *a.* traître, *f* traîtresse; perfide. **-ly** *adv.* traîtreusement, en traître.

traitress ['treitris] *n.f.* traîtresse.

trajectory [trə'dʒekt(ə)ri] *n.* trajectoire *f.*

tram¹ [træm] *n.* *Tex:* **t. (silk),** trame *f.*

tram² *n.* **1.** tramway *m*; **t. driver,** conducteur *m* de tramway; wattman *m.* **2.** *Min:* benne *f*, berline *f.*

tramcar ['træmkɑ:r] *n.* *O:* tramway *m.*

tramline ['træmlain] *n.* **1.** ligne de tramways. **2.** **tramlines,** (*a*) voie *f* de tramway; (*b*) *Ten:* le couloir.

trammel¹ ['træm(ə)l] *n.* **the trammels of superstition,** les entraves *fpl* de la superstition.

trammel² *v.tr.* **(trammelled,** *NAm:* **trameled)** entraver, empêtrer (**with,** de); **trammelled by prejudices,** entravé par les préjugés.

tramp¹ [træmp] *n.* **1.** bruit *m* de pas marqués; **I heard the (heavy) t. of the guard,** j'ai entendu le pas lourd de la garde. **2.** promenade *f* à pied. **3.** (*pers.*) chemineau *m*, vagabond, -onde, clochard, -arde. **4.** *Nau:* **(ocean) t., t. steamer,** tramp *m.*

tramp² *v.i. & tr.* **1.** marcher à pas marqués; marcher lourdement. **2.** **to t. on sth.,** piétiner, écraser, qch. **3.** (*a*) se promener, voyager, à pied; **to t. the country,** parcourir le pays à pied; **to t. wearily along,** suivre péniblement son chemin; (*b*) vagabonder; **to t. the streets,** battre le pavé.

trample ['træmpl] **1.** *v.i.* **to t. on sth., s.o.,** piétiner, écraser, qch., qn; **to t. on s.o.'s feelings,** fouler aux pieds les susceptibilités de qn. **2.** *v.tr.* (*a*) **to t. s.o., sth., under foot,** fouler qn, qch., aux pieds; **to t. down the grass,** fouler l'herbe; **child trampled to death,** enfant écrasé (sous les pieds de la foule); (*b*) piétiner (le sol).

trampoline [træmpə'li:n] *n.* *Gym: etc:* tremplin *m.*

tramway ['træmwei] *n.* (voie *f* de) tramway *m.*

trance [trɑ:ns] *n.* (*a*) *Med:* (i) extase *f*; (ii) catalepsie *f*; (*b*) **(hypnotic) t.,** transe *f*, hypnose *f*; **to send s.o. into a t.,** hypnotiser qn.

tranny ['træni] *n.* *F:* transistor *m.*

tranquil ['træŋkwil] *a.* tranquille, serein; calme.

tranquillity, *NAm: also* **tranquility** [træŋ'kwiliti] *n.* tranquillité *f*, calme *m*, sérénité *f.*

tranquillization, *NAm:* **tranquilization** [træŋkwilai'zeiʃ(ə)n] *n.* tranquillisation *f.*

tranquillize, *NAm:* **tranquilize** ['træŋkwilaiz] *v.tr.* tranquilliser, calmer, apaiser (qn, l'esprit, etc.).

tranquillizer, *NAm:* **tranquilizer** ['træŋkwilaizər] *n.* *Med: etc:* tranquillisant *m*, calmant *m.*

transact [træn'zækt] *v.tr.* **to t. business with s.o.,** faire des affaires avec qn; **the business was successfully transacted,** la transaction, l'affaire, a été conclue à notre satisfaction.

transaction [træn'zækʃ(ə)n] *n.* **1.** conduite *f* (d'une affaire); **business transactions,** les affaires; le commerce. **2.** opération (commerciale); affaire (faite); **cash t.,** opération, marché *m*, au comptant. **3.** **transactions,** mémoires *mpl*, procès-verbaux *mpl*, comptes rendus des séances (d'une société savante).

transalpine [trænz'ælpain] *a.* transalpin.

transatlantic [trænzət'lænti:k] *a.* transatlantique.

transceiver [træn'si:vər] *n.* *W.Tel:* émetteur-récepteur *m*, *pl.* émetteurs-récepteurs.

transcend [træn'send] *v.tr.* **1.** transcender; dépasser les bornes de (la raison, etc.); aller au delà de (ce que l'on peut concevoir). **2.** surpasser (qn).

transcendence, transcendency [træn'sendəns(i)] *n.* transcendance *f.*

transcendent [træn'sendənt] *a.* transcendant.

transcendental [trænsen'dent(ə)l] *a.* *Phil:* transcendantal, -aux.

transcendentalism [trænsen'dentəlizm] *n.* *Phil:* transcendantalisme *m.*

transcontinental [trænzkɔnti'nent(ə)l] *a.* transcontinental, -aux.
transcribe [træns'kraib] *v.tr.* **1.** copier, transcrire; traduire (des notes sténographiques). **2.** *Mus:* transcrire (un morceau pour un autre intrument).
transcript ['trænskript] *n.* (*a*) transcription *f*, copie *f*; (*b*) traduction *f* (de notes sténographiques).
transcription [træns'kripʃ(ə)n] *n.* **1.** = TRANSCRIPT. **2.** *Mus:* transcription *f*.
transect [træn'sekt] *v.tr.* couper transversalement.
transept ['trænsept] *n. Ecc.Arch:* (*a*) transept *m*; (*b*) **(arm of the) t.,** croisillon *m*.
transfer¹ ['trænsfə(:)r] *n.* **1.** (*a*) transfert *m*; transport *m* (de qch. à un autre endroit); déplacement *m*, mutation *f* (d'un fonctionnaire, etc.); *Av:* **t. passengers,** voyageurs *mpl* en transit; *Fb: etc:* **t. fee,** prix *m* de transfert (d'un joueur); (*b*) *Jur:* transfert, transmission *f* (d'un droit, etc.); translation *f*, mutation (de biens); *Fin:* transfert (d'actions); **(capital) t. tax,** (i) droits de succession; (ii) droit de mutation (entre vifs); (*c*) *Bank: etc:* transport *m* (d'une somme d'un compte à un autre); *Bank:* **t. of funds,** virement *m* de fonds. **2.** (*a*) *Jur:* **(deed of) t.,** acte *m* de cession; (*b*) *St.Exch:* (feuille *f* de) transfert. **3.** (*a*) *Lith:* report *m*; transport (sur la pierre); (*b*) *Cer: Needlew: etc:* décalque *m*; (*c*) **t. (picture),** décalcomanie *f*.
transfer² [træns'fə:r] *v.tr.* **(transferred) 1.** (*a*) transférer (qch., qn, d'un endroit à un autre); déplacer (un fonctionnaire, etc.); muter (un militaire, etc.); *Tp:* **transfer(red) charge call,** communication *f* en PCV; (*b*) *Jur:* transmettre (des droits, etc.); céder (un privilège, etc.); (*c*) *Bank: etc:* virer (une somme). **2.** (*a*) *Lith: Phot:* reporter (un plan, etc.); (*b*) *Needlew: etc:* calquer, décalquer (un dessin).
transferable [træns'fə:rəbl] *a.* transmissible; *Jur:* (droit, bien) cessible; (droit) communicable, transférable; (*on ticket, etc.*) **not t.,** non cessible.
transference ['trænsfərəns] *n. Psy:* transfer *m*; **thought t.,** transmission *f* de pensée.
transfiguration [trænsfigjə'reiʃ(ə)n] *n.* transfiguration *f*.
transfigure [træns'figər] *v.tr.* transfigurer; **to become transfigured,** se transfigurer.
transfix [træns'fiks] *v.tr.* **1.** transpercer (qn avec une lance, etc.). **2.** rendre (qn) immobile; **transfixed with fear,** pétrifié, cloué au sol, par la peur.
transform [træns'fɔ:m] *v.tr.* **1.** transformer; métamorphoser. **2.** (*a*) *Ch: Mec:* transformer, changer, convertir (**into,** en); (*b*) *El:* transformer (le courant).
transformation [trænsfə'meiʃ(ə)n] *n.* (*a*) transformation *f*; métamorphose *f*; (*b*) *Ch: Mec: etc:* conversion *f*; (*c*) *El:* transformation (du courant).
transformer [træns'fɔ:mər] *n. El:* transformateur *m*; **t. station,** station transformatrice.
transfuse [træns'fju:z] *v.tr. Med:* (*a*) transfuser (du sang); (*b*) faire une transfusion de sang (à qn).
transfusion [træns'fju:ʒ(ə)n] *n. Med:* **blood t.,** transfusion *f* de sang, transfusion sanguine.
transgress [træns'gres] *v.tr. & i.* transgresser, violer, enfreindre (la loi, etc.); pécher.
transgression [træns'greʃ(ə)n] *n.* (*a*) transgression *f*, violation *f* (d'une loi); infraction *f* (à la loi); (*b*) péché *m*.
transgressor [træns'gresər] *n.* transgresseur *m*; pécheur, *f.* pécheresse.
tranship [træn'ʃip] **1.** *v.tr.* transborder (des voyageurs, des marchandises). **2.** *v.i.* changer de bateau.
transhipment [træn'ʃipmənt] *n.* transbordement *m*.
transience ['trænziəns] *n.* nature passagère, transitoire (d'un phénomène, etc.).
transient ['trænziənt] *a.* transitoire; (bonheur, etc.) passager; (beauté, etc.) éphémère; *NAm:* **t. visitor,** *n.* **transient,** client, -ente, de passage.
transistor [træn'zistər] *n. Elcs:* transistor *m*; **t. (set, radio),** poste *m* à transistors, *F:* transistor.
transistorize [træn'zistəraiz] *v.tr.* transistoriser.
transit ['trænsit] *n.* **1.** (*a*) passage *m*, voyage *m* (à travers un pays, etc.); (*b*) passage (d'une planète sur le disque du soleil, d'un astre au méridien); **t. circle,** cercle méridien. **2.** transport *m* (de marchandises, etc.); **goods lost in t.,** marchandises perdues en cours de route. **3.** *Cust:* transit *m*; **goods in t.,** marchandises en transit; **t. duty,** droit *m* de transit.
transition [træn'siʒ(ə)n] *n.* transition *f*; passage *m* (du jour à la nuit, de la crainte à l'espoir); **t. period,** période *f* de transition; période transitoire.
transitional [træn'siʒən(ə)l] *a.* transitionnel; de transition; *Arch: Art:* **t. style,** style *m* de transition.
transitive ['trænzitiv] *a. & n.* **t. (verb),** (verbe) transitif (*m*). **-ly** *adv.* transitivement.
transitory ['trænsit(ə)ri] *a.* transitoire, passager; (bonheur, etc.) fugitif; (désir, etc.) momentané; (gloire, etc.) de courte durée.
translatable [træns'leitəbl] *a.* traduisible.
translate [træns'leit] *v.tr.* **1.** traduire (un livre, etc.) (**from,** de; **into,** en). **2.** (*a*) transférer (un évêque) (**to,** à); (*b*) *B:* **Enoch was translated (to heaven),** Énoch fut enlevé au ciel.
translation [træns'leiʃ(ə)n] *n.* **1.** (*a*) traduction *f* (d'un livre, etc.); **simultaneous t.,** traduction simultanée; (*b*) traduction; ouvrage traduit; *Sch:* version (latine, etc.). **2.** (*a*) translation *f* (d'un évêque); (*b*) *Mec: etc:* **movement of t.,** mouvement *m* de translation; (*c*) *B:* enlèvement *m* (au ciel).
translator [træns'leitər] *n.* traducteur, -trice.
transliterate [trænz'litəreit] *v.tr.* translit(t)érer; transcrire (en caractères différents, phonétiques).
transliteration [trænzlitə'reiʃ(ə)n] *n.* translit(t)ération *f*; transcription *f*.
translucence [trænz'lu:səns] *n.* translucidité *f*.
translucent [trænz'lu:sənt] *a.* translucide.
transmigrate [trænsmai'greit] *v.i.* (*of people*) migrer; (*of souls*) transmigrer.
transmigration [trænsmai'greiʃ(ə)n] *n.* migration *f*; (*of souls*) transmigration *f*.
transmissible [trænz'misəbl] *a.* transmissible.
transmission [træns'miʃ(ə)n] *n.* **1.** (*a*) transmission *f* (d'un message, d'un colis, etc.); (*b*) *Ph: etc:* transmission (de la chaleur, du son, etc.); (*c*) *W.Tel: T.V: etc:* transmission. **2.** *Aut:* **the t. (gear, system),** la transmission; **t. shaft,** arbre *m* de transmission. **3.** programme télévisé, radiodiffusé.
transmit [trænz'mit] *v.tr.* **(transmitted)** (*a*) transmettre (un colis, un ordre, une maladie, etc.); (*b*) *Ph: etc:* transmettre (la lumière, etc.); *Mec.E:* **to t. a motion to sth.,** imprimer, communiquer, un mouvement à qch.; (*c*) *W.Tel:* transmettre (un message).
transmitter [trænz'mitər] *n.* (*a*) *Tg: etc:* transmetteur *m*; émetteur *m*; *Tg: W.Tel:* **t. receiver,** emetteur-récepteur *m*; (*b*) *W.Tel: T.V:* (poste) émetteur; poste d'émission.
transmogrify [trænz'mɔgrifai] *v.tr. Hum:* transformer, métamorphoser (qch. en qch.).
transmutation [trænzmju:'teiʃ(ə)n] *n.* transmutation *f* (**into,** en).
transmute [trænz'mju:t] *v.tr.* (*a*) transformer, changer, convertir (**into,** en); (*b*) *Alch:* transmuer.
transom ['trænsəm] *n.* **1.** *Arch: Const:* traverse *f*, linteau *m* (de fenêtre, de porte). **2.** **t. window,** (i) fenêtre *f* à meneau horizontal; (ii) *NAm:* imposte *f*.
transparence [træns'pær(ə)ns, -'pɛər-] *n.* transparence *f*; clarté *f* (du verre, etc.).
transparency [træns'pærənsi, -'pɛər-] *n.* **1.** (*a*) transparence *f*; (*b*) limpidité *f* (de l'eau, etc.). **2.** (*a*) (*picture*) transparent *m*; (*b*) *Phot:* diapositive *f*; **colour t.,** diapositive en couleur.

transparent [træns'pærənt, -'pɛər-] *a.* **1.** (verre, etc.) transparent; (eau, quartz, etc.) limpide. **2.** évident, clair, qui saute aux yeux.

transpiration [trænspi'reiʃ(ə)n] *n.* transpiration *f.*

transpire [træns'paiər] **1.** *v.tr.* (*of body, plant, etc.*) exsuder (un fluide); exhaler (une odeur). **2.** *v.i.* (*a*) *Physiol: Bot:* transpirer; (*b*) (*of news, secret*) transpirer, se répandre; **it transpired that . . .,** on a appris que . . .; (*c*) arriver, se passer.

transplant¹ ['trænsplɑːnt, 'trɑː-] *n.* **1.** *Hort:* plant repiqué. **2.** *Surg:* (*a*) transplantation *f*, greffe *f*; **heart t.,** greffe du cœur; (*b*) transplant *m*, greffon *m.*

transplant² [træns'plɑːnt, trɑː-] *v.tr.* (*a*) *Hort:* transplanter (des arbres, etc.); repiquer (des plants); (*b*) transplanter, transporter (une population, etc.); (*c*) *Surg:* transplanter, greffer (un organe).

transplantation [trænsplɑː'nteiʃ(ə)n] *n.* transplantation *f.*

transport¹ ['trænspɔːt] *n.* **1.** transport *m* (de marchandises, de voyageurs, de troupes, etc.); **public t.,** les transports en commun; **road, rail, t.,** transport routier, ferroviaire; **t. charges,** frais *mpl* de transport. **2.** moyen *m* de transport; *Navy:* (bâtiment *m* de) transport; *Av:* **t. aircraft, plane,** (avion *m* de) transport; avion cargo; *F:* **have you got t.?** est-ce que vous avez une, votre, voiture? **3.** transport (de joie).

transport² [træns'pɔːt] *v.tr.* **1.** (*a*) transporter (des voyageurs, des marchandises); (*b*) *Cmptr:* acheminer (une carte); faire défiler (une bande). **2.** (*usu. passive*) **to be transported with joy,** être transporté de joie.

transportable [træns'pɔːtəbl] *a.* transportable.

transportation [trænspɔː'teiʃ(ə)n] *n.* **1.** (*a*) *esp. NAm:* (i) transport *m*; (ii) moyen *m* de transport; (*b*) *NAm: Rail: etc:* billet *m.* **2.** *Jur: A:* transportation *f.*

transporter [træns'pɔːtər] *n.* **1.** (*pers.*) entrepreneur *m* de transports. **2.** (*a*) transporteur *m*, transporteuse *f*; **car t.,** camion *m*, wagon *m*, transporteur de voitures; (*b*) **t. bridge,** (pont) transbordeur *m.*

transpose [træns'pouz] *v.tr.* **1.** transposer (des mots, les termes d'une équation, etc.). **2.** *Mus:* transposer. **transposing** *Mus:* **1.** *a.* (instrument) transpositeur. **2.** *n.* transposition *f.*

transposition [trænspə'ziʃ(ə)n] *n.* (*a*) *Mus:* transposition *f*; (*b*) transposition, inversion *f* (de lettres, etc.); (*c*) *Tp:* croisement *m* (technique) des fils.

trans-sexual [træn(z)'seksjuəl] *a.* & *n.* *Psy:* transsexuel, -elle.

trans-ship [træn(z)'ʃip] = TRANSHIP.

trans-Siberian [træn(z)sai'biəriən] *a.* transsibérien.

transsubstantiate [trænsəb'stænʃieit] *v.tr.* *Theol:* transsubstantier.

transsubstantiation [trænsəbstænʃi'eiʃ(ə)n] *n.* *Theol:* transsubstantiation *f.*

Transvaal ['trɑːnzvɑːl] **1.** *Pr.n.* **the T.,** le Transvaal. **2.** *a.* transvaalien.

transversal [trænz'vəːs(ə)l] **1.** *a.* transversal, -aux. **2.** *n.* *Mth:* transversale *f.* **-ally** *adv.* transversalement.

transverse ['trænzvəːs] *a.* transversal, -aux; transverse; *Mth:* **t. line,** transversale *f*; *Const:* **t. beam,** traverse *f.* **-ly** *adv.* transversalement, en travers.

transvestism [trænz'vestizm] *n.* travestisme *m.*

transvestite [trænz'vestait] *n.* travesti, -ie.

trap¹ [træp] *n.* **1.** (*a*) *Ven: etc:* piège *m*; (*for big game*) trappe *f*; (*for hares, etc.*) panneau *m*; **to set a t.,** dresser, tendre, un piège (**for,** à); **to catch an animal in a t.,** prendre une bête au piège; *Mil:* **tank t.,** (obstacle *m*) antichar (*m*); (*b*) *Atom.Ph:* piège (à particules); (*c*) piège, ruse *f*, attrape *f*; **police t.,** (i) souricière *f*; (ii) *Aut:* zone *f* de contrôle de vitesse; **he's fallen into his own t.,** il est pris à son propre piège; **he fell into the t.,** il s'y laissa prendre; **to walk, fall, straight into the t.,** donner, tomber, en plein dans le piège, dans le lacs. **2.** (*a*) **t. (door),** (i) trappe; abattant *m*; (ii) *Min:* porte *f* d'aérage; (*b*) *Th:* trappe; trappillon *m*; (*c*) trappe (de colombier); (*d*) *P:* bouche *f*, gueule *f*; **shut your t.!** ta gueule! la ferme! **3.** (*a*) *Sp:* (projecteur *m*) ball-trap *m*, *pl.* ball-traps (pour pigeons artificiels); boîte *f* de lancement (pour pigeons vivants); (*b*) (*in dog racing*) box *m* (de départ). **4.** *Tchn:* collecteur *m* (d'eau, d'huile, etc.); *Civ.E: Plumb:* siphon *m*; **sink t.,** puisard *m.* **5.** *Veh:* charrette anglaise; cabriolet *m.* **6.** *esp. NAm: Mus:* **traps,** instruments *mpl* à percussion.

trap² *v.tr.* **(trapped) 1.** (*a*) prendre (une bête, qn) au piège; piéger (une bête); **to t. one's finger in the door,** se coincer le doigt dans la porte; **trapped by the flames,** cerné par les flammes; (*b*) tendre des pièges; (*c*) *v.i.* *Can:* trapper. **2.** *Tchn:* arrêter (un gaz, etc.) au moyen d'un siphon. **trapping** *n.* *Ven:* (i) piégeage *m*; (ii) métier de trappeur.

trapeze [trə'piːz] *n.* *Gym: etc:* trapèze *m*; **to perform on the flying t.,** faire du trapèze volant, de la voltige; **t. artist,** trapéziste *mf*; voltigeur, -euse.

trapezist [trə'piːzist] *n.* *Gym: etc:* trapéziste *mf.*

trapezium [trə'piːziəm] *n.* *Mth:* trapèze *m.*

trapezoid ['træpizɔid] *n.* *Mth:* trapézoïde *m.*

trapper ['træpər] *n.* *Ven:* piégeur *m*; *NAm:* trappeur *m.*

trappings ['træpiŋz] *n.pl.* **1.** harnachement *m*, caparaçon *m.* **2.** atours *mpl*; apparat *m*; **the t. of authority,** l'apparat de l'autorité.

Trappist ['træpist] *a.* & *n.* *Ecc:* trappiste (*m*).

traps [træps] *n.pl.* *F:* effets (personnels); **to pack (up) one's t.,** faire ses valises; plier bagage.

trapshooting ['træpʃuːtiŋ] *n.* *Sp:* ball-trap *m.*

trash [træʃ] *n.* (*a*) chose(s) *f*(*pl*) sans valeur; camelote *f*; *NAm:* détritus *mpl*, déchets *mpl*, ordures *fpl*; **t. can,** poubelle *f*; boîte *f* à ordures; (*b*) littérature *f* de camelote; (*c*) **to talk a lot of t.,** dire des sottises; (*d*) *coll.* (*of pers.*) vauriens *mpl*, propres à rien *mpl.*

trashy ['træʃi] *a.* (marchandises, etc.) sans valeur, de rebut, de pacotille; (littérature) de camelote.

trauma, *pl.* **-as, -ata** ['trɔːmə, -əz, -ətə] *n.* *Med: Psy:* trauma *m.*

traumatic [trɔː'mætik] *a.* *Med:* traumatique.

traumatism ['trɔːmətizm] *n.* *Med:* traumatisme *m.*

travail¹ ['træveil] *n.* *A.* & *Lit:* douleurs *fpl* de l'enfantement; travail *m*; **woman in t.,** femme en travail.

travail² *v.i.* *A.* & *Lit:* (*of woman*) être en travail (d'enfantement).

travel¹ ['træv(ə)l] *n.* **1.** (*a*) voyages *mpl*; **t. agency, agent,** agence *f*, agent *m*, de voyages; **t. goods,** articles *mpl* de voyage; (*b*) **I met him on, in the course of, my travels,** j'ai fait sa connaissance en voyage. **2.** *Mec: Mch:* course *f* (du piston, du chariot); déplacement *m* (d'une pièce mécanique); *Ball:* course, trajet *m* (d'un mobile, d'un projectile).

travel² *v.i.* **(travelled,** *NAm:* **traveled) 1.** (*a*) voyager; faire des voyages; **he has travelled a great deal, widely,** il a beaucoup voyagé; **to t. round the world,** faire le tour du monde; **to t. all over the world,** courir le monde; **to t. through a country,** parcourir, traverser, un pays; (*b*) aller, marcher; faire route; (*of news*) circuler, se répandre; **light travels faster than sound,** la lumière va, se propage, plus vite que le son; **the train was travelling at 150 km an hour,** le train marchait à 150 km à l'heure; **this wine won't t.,** ce vin ne voyage pas. **2. to t. (for a firm),** voyager (pour une maison); représenter une maison; **to t. in wine,** voyager pour les vins. **3.** *Mec.E:* (*of part*) se mouvoir, se déplacer. **travelled,** *NAm:* **traveled** *a.* (*of pers.*) **much, well, t.,** qui a beaucoup voyagé. **travelling,** *NAm:* **traveling 1.** *a.* (*a*) (cirque) ambulant; (prédicateur) itinérant; **t. salesman,** voyageur *m* de commerce; (*b*) *Mec.E:* (trottoir, etc.)

roulant; (grue) mobile. **2.** *n.* (*a*) voyages *mpl*; **t. expenses,** frais *mpl* de voyage, de route; *Com: etc:* frais de déplacement; indemnité *f* de voyage; **t. scholarship,** bourse *f* de voyage; **t. companion,** compagnon *m* de voyage; **t. clock,** réveil *m* de voyage; (*b*) *Cin:* **t. platform,** travelling *m*; **t. shot,** prise *f* de vues en travelling.

travelator ['trævəleitər] *n.* trottoir, tapis, roulant.

travelogue, *NAm: also* **travelog** ['trævəlɔg] *n.* documentaire *m* de voyage.

travelstained ['trævəlsteind] *a.* sali par le voyage.

traverse¹ ['trævəs] *n.* **1.** *Mount:* (i) traverse *f* (sur la face d'un escarpement); vire *f*; (ii) traversée *f*. **2.** (*a*) *Mth:* (ligne) transversale *f*; (*b*) *Surv:* cheminement *m*. **3.** *Mec.E: Const: etc:* traverse, entretoise *f* (de châssis, de cadre, etc.).

traverse² **1.** *v.tr.* (*a*) *Lit:* traverser, passer à travers (une région, le corps); passer (un pont, la mer); (*b*) *Mec.E:* charioter (une pièce); (*c*) *Surv:* faire un cheminement (d'une région). **2.** *v.i.* (*a*) *Mount:* prendre une traverse; (*b*) (*of horse*) se traverser. **traversing** *n.* **1.** *Mount:* prise *f* d'une traverse. **2.** *Surv:* (levé *m* par) cheminement *m*.

travesty¹ ['trævəsti] *n.* travestissement *m* (d'une pièce de théâtre, etc.); **a t. of the truth,** un travestissement de la vérité.

travesty² *v.tr. Lit:* parodier, travestir (une histoire, un personnage, etc.).

trawl¹ [trɔ:l] *n. Fish:* (*a*) **t. (net),** chalut *m*, traille *f*; (*b*) **t. (line),** palangre *f*.

trawl² *Fish:* **1.** *v.i.* pêcher à la traille, au chalut; chaluter. **2.** *v.tr.* (*a*) traîner (un chalut); (*b*) prendre (le poisson) à la traille, au chalut. **trawling** *n.* pêche *f* au chalut; chalutage *m*.

trawler ['trɔ:lər] *n.* **1.** (*pers.*) (*also* **trawlerman**) pêcheur *m* au chalut; chalutier *m*. **2.** (*ship*) chalutier.

tray [trei] *n.* **1.** (*a*) plateau *m*, *Fr. C:* cabaret *m*; **tea t.,** plateau à thé; **hawker's t.,** éventaire *m*; *Surg: etc:* **instrument t.,** plateau à instruments; (*b*) **a t. of sandwiches,** un plateau de sandwiches; (*c*) casier *m*, châssis *m* (d'une malle, etc.); (*d*) (*in office, etc.*) corbeille *f* (à correspondance); **in t.,** corbeille à correspondance reçue; **out t.,** corbeille à courrier à expédier, à documents à classer. **2.** *Phot: etc:* cuvette *f*.

traycloth ['treiklɔθ] *n.* napperon *m* (de plateau).

treacherous ['tretʃərəs] *a.* (homme, caractère) traître, déloyal, -aux; (*of action*) déloyal; perfide; **t. ice,** glace traîtresse. **-ly** *adv.* (agir) en traître, traîtreusement, perfidement.

treachery ['tretʃəri] *n.* trahison *f*; perfidie *f*; **act of t.,** perfidie.

treacle [tri:kl] *n.* mélasse *f*; **t. tart,** tarte *f* à la mélasse.

treacly ['tri:kli] *a.* (*a*) sirupeux; (*b*) *Fig:* doucereux, mielleux.

tread¹ [tred] *n.* **1.** (*a*) pas *m*; **heavy t.,** pas lourd; **to walk with measured t.,** marcher à pas mesurés; (*b*) bruit *m* de pas. **2.** (*a*) giron *m* (de marche d'escalier); (*b*) semelle *f* (d'une chaussure); (*c*) fourchon *m*, étrier (d'échasse); (*d*) échelon *m* (d'échelle, etc.); (*e*) *Rail:* surface *f*, table *f*, de roulement (d'un rail); (*f*) *Aut:* (i) bande *f* de roulement, chape *f*, (ii) sculpture *f* (d'un pneu); **non-skid t.,** roulement antidérapant.

tread² *v.* (*p.t.* **trod** [trɔd]; *p.p.* **trodden** ['trɔd(ə)n]) **1.** *v.i.* marcher; poser les pieds; **to t. on sth.,** marcher sur qch.; **to t. on s.o.'s toes,** (i) marcher sur les pieds de qn; (ii) offenser, froisser, qn; **we shall have to t. carefully, lightly, warily,** nous marchons sur des œufs. **2.** *v.tr.* (*a*) marcher sur (le sol); **to t. down,** piétiner (le sol, etc.); **to t. sth. under foot,** écraser qch. du pied; fouler qch. aux pieds; **well trodden path,** (i) chemin battu; (ii) chemin (très) fréquenté; (*b*) *O:* **to t. a path,** suivre un chemin; (*c*) **to t. grapes,** fouler la vendange; *Swim:* **to t. water,** nager debout; (*d*) (*of male bird*) couvrir, côcher (la femelle). **treading** *n* (*a*) piétinement *m*; foulage *m* (des raisins); (*b*) *Swim:* **t. water,** nage *f* debout.

treadle ['tredl] *n.* pédale *f* (de machine à coudre, etc.); **t. machine,** machine *f* à pédale.

treadmill ['tredmil] *n.* (*a*) *A:* (*in prisons*) moulin *m* de discipline; (*b*) besogne ingrate (quotidienne).

treason ['tri:z(ə)n] *n. Jur:* trahison *f*; **high t.,** haute trahison; lèse-majesté *f*.

treasonable ['tri:z(ə)nəbl] *a.* séditieux; traître; (acte) de trahison.

treasure¹ ['treʒər] *n.* trésor *m*; **art treasures,** trésors, richesses *fpl*, artistiques; **t. hunt,** chasse *f* au(x) trésor(s); *F:* **my help's a real t.,** ma femme de ménage est une perle.

treasure² *v.tr.* **1.** priser, estimer, faire beaucoup de cas de (qch.). **2. to t. sth. (up),** garder qch. soigneusement; **to t. sth. in one's memory,** garder précieusement le souvenir de qch.

treasure(-)house ['treʒəhaus] *n. O:* trésor *m*.

treasurer ['treʒərər] *n.* trésorier, -ière; économe *mf*.

treasury ['treʒəri] *n.* **1.** (*a*) trésor (public); trésorerie *f*; (*in Eng.*) **the T.** = le Ministère des finances; *Fin:* **t. bonds, bills,** bons *mpl* du Trésor; (*b*) trésor (d'une cathédrale, etc.). **2.** anthologie *f* (de poésie).

treat¹ [tri:t] *n.* **1.** (*a*) régal, -als *m*; festin *m*; (*b*) *P:* **to stand t.,** payer la tournée; **it's my t.,** c'est ma tournée; c'est moi qui paie. **2.** plaisir *m*; délice *m*; **it would be a great t. to go to the theatre,** ce serait une véritable fête d'aller au théâtre; **to give oneself a t.,** faire un petit extra; **a t. in store,** un plaisir à venir. **3.** *P: adv. phr.* **a (fair) t.,** à merveille; **that whisky went down a t.!** ce whisky m'a fait du bien.

treat² *v.i. & tr.* **1.** *v.i.* (*a*) **to t. with s.o.,** traiter, négocier, avec qn; pactiser avec (l'ennemi); (*b*) (*of book, etc.*) **to t. of a subject,** traiter d'un sujet. **2.** *v.tr.* traiter (qn, qch.); **to t. s.o. well,** bien traiter qn; **to t. s.o., an animal, roughly,** malmener, maltraiter, qn, un animal; **my father still treats me like a child,** mon père me traite toujours en enfant; **to t. sth. as a joke,** considérer qch. comme une plaisanterie. **3.** *v.tr.* (*a*) **to t. s.o. to the theatre,** inviter qn au théâtre; **to t. oneself to oysters,** s'offrir des huîtres; (*b*) *F:* arroser (des électeurs). **4.** *v.tr.* (*a*) *Med:* traiter (un malade, une maladie); **to t. s.o. for rheumatism,** soigner qn pour le rhumatisme; **he was treated in hospital,** il a reçu des soins à l'hôpital; (*b*) traiter (un métal); **to t. wood with creosote,** imprégner le bois de créosote. **5.** *v.tr. Lit: Mus: etc:* traiter (un sujet, un thème).

treatise ['tri:tiz] *n.* traité *m* (**on,** de).

treatment ['tri:tmənt] *n.* **1.** (*a*) traitement *m* (de qn); (*b*) traitement (d'une matière, d'un sujet). **2.** traitement (médical).

treaty ['tri:ti] *n.* **1.** traité *m* (de paix, de commerce); convention *f*. **2.** accord *m*; contrat *m*; **to sell sth. by private t.,** vendre qch. de gré à gré, à l'amiable.

treble¹ ['trebl] **I.** *a.* **1.** triple. **2.** *Mus:* **t. voice,** (voix *f* de) soprano *m*; **t. clef,** clef *f* de sol. **II.** *adv.* trois fois autant. **III.** *n.* **1.** triple *m*. **2.** (*crochet*) **plain t.,** brides *fpl* simples. **3.** (*a*) *Mus:* dessus *m*; (*b*) (*pers., voice*) soprano *m*; (*c*) *Elcs:* **t. control,** touche *f* de tonalité aiguë. **trebly** *adv.* trois fois autant.

treble² **1.** *v.tr.* tripler (la valeur, le nombre). **2.** *v.i.* (se) tripler.

tree [tri:] *n.* **1.** (*a*) arbre *m*; **fruit t.,** arbre fruitier; **timber t.,** arbre de haute futaie; *Geog:* **the t. line, limit,** la limite des arbres; *Fig:* **to be at the top of the t.,** être au sommet, au haut, de l'échelle; **to get to the top of the t.,** arriver; *F:* **to be up a (gum) t.,** être dans une impasse, dans le pétrin; (*b*) **the t. of life,** l'arbre de la vie; (*c*) *Bot:* **t. fern,** fougère arborescente; (*d*) *Amph:* **t. frog,** rainette verte; (*e*) *Orn:* **t. creeper,**

grimpereau *m* des bois; **t. pipit,** pipit *m* des arbres. **2. family t.,** arbre généalogique. **3.** *A:* **gallows t.,** gibet *m,* potence *f.* **4.** (*a*) *O: Const:* poutre *f;* (*b*) **(shoe) t.,** embauchoir *m* (pour chaussures).

treeless ['tri:lis] *a.* sans arbres.

treetop ['tri:tɔp] *n.* cime *f* d'un arbre; *Av:* **to skim the treetops,** voler en rase-mottes.

trefoil ['tri:fɔil, 'tref-] *n.* **1.** *Bot:* trèfle *m;* **bird's foot t.,** lotier *m.* **2.** *Arch: Her:* trèfle; *Arch:* trilobe *m.*

trek¹ [trek] *n.* **1.** (*in S. Africa*) (*a*) voyage *m* en chariot (à bœufs); (*b*) étape *f* (d'un voyage); (*c*) *Hist:* migration *f.* **2. a long t.,** un trajet long et pénible (surtout à pied).

trek² *v.i.* **(trekked) 1.** (*in S. Africa*) voyager en chariot (à bœufs). **2.** faire un trajet long et pénible (surtout à pied).

trellis¹ ['trelis] *n.* treillis *m,* treillage *m;* **t. window,** fenêtre treillissée.

trellis² *v.tr.* **1.** treillisser, treillager (une fenêtre, etc.). **2.** échalasser (une vigne).

trelliswork ['treliswə:k] *n.* treillis *m,* treillage *m.*

tremble¹ ['trembl] *n.* tremblement *m;* (*in voice*) tremblotement *m;* **to be all of a t.,** être tout tremblant; trembloter.

tremble² *v.i.* **1.** trembler, vibrer. **2.** trembler, frissonner; frémir; **to t. like a leaf,** trembler comme une feuille; **to t. with fear,** trembler de peur. **trembling 1.** *a.* tremblant, tremblotant. **2.** *n.* tremblement *m;* tremblotement *m* (d'une feuille, de la voix); **in fear and t.,** tout tremblant.

trembler ['tremblər] *n.* **1.** (*pers.*) trembleur, -euse. **2.** *El:* trembleur.

tremendous [tri'mendəs] *a.* **1.** terrible, épouvantable. **2.** *F:* immense, énorme; formidable; **a. t. lot of sth.,** une quantité énorme de qch.; **there was a t. crowd,** il y avait un monde fou; **a t. difference,** une énorme différence. **-ly** *adv.* **1.** terriblement. **2.** énormément; **it was t. successful,** c'était un succès fou.

tremolo ['treməlou] *n. Mus:* tremolo *m.*

tremor ['tremər] *n.* **1.** (*a*) tremblement *m,* frémissement *m;* frisson *m* (de peur); (*b*) *Med:* tremblement; trémulation *f.* **2.** trépidation *f* (des vitres, etc.); **earth t.,** tremblement de terre; secousse *f* sismique.

tremulous ['tremjuləs] *a.* tremblotant, frémissant; (sourire) timide, craintif; **t. voice,** voix tremblante, chevrotante. **-ly** *adv.* en tremblant, en tremblotant; timidement.

trench¹ [tren(t)ʃ] *n.* **1.** *Agr: Hort:* tranchée *f,* fossé *m;* (*for draining*) rigole *f;* **water, irrigation, t.,** fossé d'irrigation; **t. plough,** rigoleuse *f.* **2.** *Mil:* tranchée; **communication t.,** boyau, -aux *m;* **t. warfare,** guerre *f* de tranchées; **t. coat,** trench-coat *m.*

trench² *v.tr.* creuser un fossé, une tranchée, dans (le sol); *v.i.* creuser des fossés.

trenchant ['tren(t)ʃənt] *a.* **1.** *Lit:* (*of sword, etc.*) tranchant. **2.** (*a*) (style, ton) tranchant, net, incisif; (*b*) (*of reply, epigram*) mordant, caustique.

trencher ['tren(t)ʃər] *n. A:* tranchoir *m,* tailloir *m.*

trencherman, *pl.* **-men** ['tren(t)ʃəmən] *n.* **good, stout, t.,** grand, gros, beau, mangeur.

trend¹ [trend] *n.* direction *f* (d'un cours d'eau, etc.); tendance *f,* marche *f* (de l'opinion publique, etc.); **current trends,** tendances actuelles.

trend² *v.i.* se diriger, s'orienter **(to, towards,** vers).

trendsetter ['trendsetər] *n.* lanceur, -euse, de modes, de nouvelles coutumes, etc.

trendy ['trendi] *a. F:* à la page; dans le vent.

trepan¹ [tri'pæn] *n. Surg: Min:* trépan *m.*

trepan² *v.tr.* **(trepanned)** *Surg: Min:* trépaner.

trepidation [trepi'deiʃ(ə)n] *n.* trépidation *f;* agitation violente; émoi *m.*

trespass¹ ['trespəs] *n.* **1.** (*a*) contravention *f* de la loi; (*b*) *Theol:* offense *f,* péché *m;* **forgive us our trespasses,** pardonne-nous nos offenses. **2.** *Jur:* (*a*) violation *f* des droits de qn; (*b*) **t. to land,** violation *f* de propriété (sur un bien foncier).

trespass² *v.i.* **1.** *A: & Lit:* transgresser la loi; pêcher **(against,** contre); **as we forgive them that t. against us,** comme nous pardonnons à ceux qui nous ont offensés. **2.** *Jur:* (*a*) **to t. (up)on s.o.'s rights,** violer, enfreindre, les droits de qn; (*b*) **to t. (on s.o.'s property),** entrer, passer sans autorisation, sur la propriété de qn; (*c*) *O:* **I don't wish to t. on your time,** je ne veux pas abuser de vos moments. **trespassing** *n.* violation *f* des droits d'autrui; **t. on s.o.'s land,** violation *f* de propriété (foncière).

trespasser ['trespəsər] *n.* **1.** *Theol:* pécheur, *f.* pécheresse. **2.** *Jur:* (*a*) violateur *m* des droits d'autrui; (*b*) auteur *m* d'une violation de propriété (foncière); intrus *m;* *P.N:* **trespassers will be prosecuted,** défense d'entrer sous peine d'amende.

tress [tres] *n.* (*a*) tresse *f,* boucle *f* (de cheveux); (*b*) *Lit:* **tresses,** chevelure *f,* cheveux *mpl* (d'une femme).

trestle ['tresl] *n.* tréteau *m,* chevalet *m;* **t. bridge,** pont *m* de, sur, chevalets; **t. table,** table *f* à tréteaux; **t. bed,** lit *m* de sangle.

trews [tru:z] *n.pl. Cost:* (*a*) pantalon *m* en tartan (porté par les soldats écossais); (*b*) *F:* pantalon.

triad ['traiæd] *n.* triade *f;* groupe *m* de trois. **2.** *Ch:* élément trivalent. **3.** *Mus:* accord *m* parfait.

trial ['traiəl] *n.* **1.** *Jur:* (*a*) jugement *m* (d'un litige, d'un accusé); **to bring s.o. to t.,** faire passer qn en jugement; **they were sent for t.,** ils furent renvoyés en jugement; **t. by jury,** jugement par jury; (*b*) procès *m;* **criminal t.,** procès criminel; **famous trials,** causes célèbres; *U.S:* **t. judge** = juge *m* d'instance; (*c*) *Hist:* **t. by combat,** combat *m* judiciaire. **2.** (*a*) essai *m;* épreuve *f;* **t. of strength,** épreuve de force; *Sp:* **t. (game),** match *m* de sélection; (*b*) **to give sth. a t.,** faire l'essai de qch.; **on t.,** à l'essai; **to proceed by t. and error,** procéder par tâtonnements, par approximations successives; *Com:* **t. order,** commande *f* d'essai; *Book-k:* **t. balance,** balance *f* de vérification; (*c*) essai (technique) (d'un appareil, d'un véhicule, etc.); *Veh:* **speed t.,** essai de vitesse; **t. run,** essai sur route; *Av:* **t. flight,** vol *m* d'essai; (*d*) *usu. pl.* concours *m* (de chiens de berger). **3.** épreuve douloureuse; peine *f,* adversité *f;* **that child is a great t. to his parents,** cet enfant fait le martyre de ses parents.

triangle ['traiæŋgl] *n.* **1.** *Mth: etc:* triangle *m;* *Mec:* **t. of forces,** triangle des forces; *F:* **the eternal t.,** l'éternel triangle; le ménage à trois. **2.** (*a*) *Draw: U.S:* équerre *f* (en triangle); triangle; (*b*) *Mus:* triangle.

triangular [trai'æŋgjulər] *a.* triangulaire; en triangle.

triangulate [trai'æŋgjuleit] *v.tr. Surv:* trianguler.

triangulation [traiæŋgju'leiʃ(ə)n] *n.* triangulation *f.*

tribal ['traib(ə)l] *a.* **1.** qui vit en tribus. **2.** tribal; de tribu; **t. system,** système tribal; tribalisme *m.*

tribalism ['traibəlizm] *n.* tribalisme *m;* système tribal.

tribe [traib] *n.* **1.** tribu *f;* **the twelve tribes of Israel,** les douze tribus d'Israël; *F:* une smala (d'enfants). **2.** *Nat.Hist:* tribu.

tribesman, *pl.* **-men** ['traibzmən] *n.m.* membre (i) d'une tribu, (ii) de la tribu.

tribulation [tribju'leiʃ(ə)n] *n.* tribulation *f,* affliction *f.*

tribunal [tr(a)i'bju:nəl] *n.* tribunal *m,* -aux.

tribune¹ ['tribju:n] *n. Rom.Hist: etc:* tribun *m.*

tribune² *n.* tribune *f* (d'orateur).

tributary ['tribjut(ə)ri] **1.** *a.* tributaire. **2.** *n.* (*a*) tributaire *m;* (*b*) *Geog:* affluent *m* (d'un fleuve).

tribute ['tribju:t] *n.* **1.** *Hist:* **t. (money),** tribut *m;* **to pay t.,** payer tribut **(to,** à). **2.** tribut, hommage *m;* **to pay a t. to s.o.,** rendre hommage à qn; **to pay a last t. to s.o.,** rendre à qn les derniers devoirs; **floral**

tributes, gerbes *fpl* et couronnes *fpl* (de fleurs).

trice¹ [trais] *n.* **in a t.,** (faire qch.) en un clin d'œil, en moins de rien.

trice² *v.tr. Nau:* **to t. (up),** hisser (une voile).

tricentenary, *esp. U.S:* **tricentennial** [trai-sen'ti:nəri, -'teniəl] *a. & n.* tricentenaire (*m*).

triceps ['traiseps] *n. Anat:* **t. (muscle),** triceps *m.*

trick¹ [trik] *n.* **1.** (*a*) tour *m*, ruse *f*, finesse *f*; supercherie *f*; **by a t.,** (obtenir qch.) par ruse; (*b*) farce *f*, tour; **to play a t. on s.o.,** faire une farce, une blague, à qn; **my eyes must have been playing tricks on me, playing me tricks,** j'ai dû avoir la berlue; **that was a nasty, mean, dirty, t.!** ça c'était un vilain tour! **you've been up to your tricks again,** vous avez encore fait des vôtres; (*c*) truc *m*; **the tricks of the trade,** les trucs, les tours, les astuces *fpl*, du métier; **that should do the t.,** ça fera l'affaire; *Phot: Cin:* **t. photography,** truquage *m*, trucage *m*; (*d*) tour d'adresse; **to teach a dog tricks,** apprendre des tours à un chien; **card t.,** tour de cartes; **conjuring t.,** tour de prestidigitation, de passe-passe; *F:* **the whole bag of tricks,** tout le bataclan; tout le tremblement; **t. riding,** voltige *f* (à cheval); **t. cyclist,** (i) cycliste acrobate; (ii) *F:* psychiatre *mf*; **he doesn't miss a t.,** rien ne lui échappe; *F:* **how's tricks?** (i) comment vas-tu? (ii) quoi de neuf? **2.** manie *f*; habitude *f*; tic *m*; **he has a t. of repeating himself,** il se répète toujours. **3.** *Cards:* levée *f*; **to take a t.,** faire une levée, un pli.

trick² *v.tr.* **1.** attraper, duper (qn); mystifier (qn); **I've been tricked,** on m'a refait, on m'a eu; **to t. s.o. into doing sth.,** amener qn par ruse à faire qch.; **to t. s.o. out of sth.,** (i) frustrer qn de qch.; (ii) escroquer qch. à qn. **2.** *F: O:* **to t. s.o. out,** parer, attifer, qn.

trickery ['trikəri] *n.* tricherie *f*; duperie *f*; **piece of t.,** fraude *f*; supercherie *f*; **by t.,** (obtenir qch.) par ruse.

trickiness ['trikinis] *n.* **1.** fourberie *f.* **2.** complication *f*, délicatesse *f* (d'un mécanisme, d'une situation, etc.).

trickle¹ ['trikl] *n.* (*a*) filet *m* (d'eau, etc.); **sales were down to a t.,** il n'y avait presque plus de ventes; (*b*) *El:* **t. charger,** chargeur *m* à régime lent.

trickle² **1.** *v.i.* (*a*) couler (goutte à goutte); suinter; **water was trickling down the wall,** l'eau dégoulinait le long du mur; **tears were trickling down her cheeks,** les larmes coulaient le long de ses joues; **news is beginning to t. through, out, from the devasted area,** on commence à recevoir peu à peu des nouvelles de la région sinistrée; (*b*) **the ball just trickled into the hole,** la balle a roulé tout doucement dans le trou. **2.** *v.tr.* laisser dégoutter (un liquide); laisser tomber (un liquide) goutte à goutte. **trickling** *n.* dégouttement *m*; écoulement *m* goutte à goutte.

trickster ['trikstər] *n.* escroc *m*; **confidence t.,** voleur, -euse, à l'américaine.

tricky ['triki] *a.* **1.** rusé; astucieux; *F:* **he's a t. customer,** c'est un rusé, un malin. **2.** compliqué, délicat; **t. job,** tâche délicate, difficile.

tricolo(u)r ['trikələr] *n.* drapeau tricolore (français).

tricorn(e) ['traikɔ:n] *a. & n.* (chapeau) tricorne (*m*).

tricuspid [trai'kʌspid] *a.* tricuspide.

tricycle ['traisikl] *n.* tricycle *m.*

trident ['traidənt] *n.* trident *m* (de Neptune, etc.).

triennial [trai'eniəl] *a.* triennal, -aux. **1.** qui a lieu tous les trois ans. **2.** qui dure trois ans; *Hort:* (plante) trisannuelle. **-ally** *adv.* tous les trois ans.

trier ['traiər] *n. F:* **to be a t.,** ne pas se laisser décourager; **he's a t.,** il fait toujours de son mieux.

trifle¹ ['traifl] *n.* **1.** (*a*) chose *f* sans importance; bagatelle *f*, vétille *f*; **to quarrel over a mere t.,** se quereller pour un oui, pour un non; se quereller sur un rien; **it's not exactly a t.,** ce n'est pas une petite affaire; (*b*) petite somme d'argent; **it was sold for a mere t.,** on l'a vendu pour un rien; (*c*) *adv.phr.* **a t.,** un tout petit peu, (un) tant soit peu; quelque peu; **a t. too wide, too short,** trop large, trop court, d'un doigt. **2.** *Cu:* = diplomate *m.*

trifle² **1.** *v.i.* (*a*) jouer, badiner (**with,** avec); **he's not a man to be trifled with,** on ne joue pas, plaisante pas, avec lui; (*b*) **to t. with sth.,** manier nonchalamment (sa canne, etc.); jouer avec (son lorgnon, etc.); **to t. with one's food,** manger du bout des dents; (*c*) s'amuser, s'occuper, à des futilités, à des riens. **2.** *v.tr.* **to t. away,** gaspiller; **to t. one's time away,** gaspiller son temps. **trifling** **1.** *a.* insignifiant, peu important, sans importance; négligeable; **t. incidents,** menus incidents; **that's a t. matter,** c'est peu de chose; ce n'est qu'une bagatelle; *Iron:* **the t. sum of 10,000 francs,** la bagatelle de 10,000 francs. **2.** *n.* (*a*) badinage *m* (**with,** avec); (*b*) gaspillage *m* du temps (en futilités).

triforium, *pl.* **-ia** [trai'fɔ:riəm, -iə] *n.* triforium *m.*

trigger¹ ['trigər] *n.* (*a*) *Mec.E: etc:* déclencheur *m*; poussoir *m* (à ressort); **t. action,** déclenchement *m*; **t. mechanism,** mécanisme *m* de déclenchement; (*b*) *Sm.a:* détente *f*, *F:* gâchette *f*; **t. finger,** index *m* (avec lequel on presse sur la détente); **to be quick on the t.,** *F:* **to be t. happy,** ne pas hésiter à tirer; *F:* avoir la gâchette facile.

trigger² *v.tr.* (*a*) déclencher (le départ du coup d'une arme à feu); (*b*) **to t. (off),** déclencher, provoquer (une explosion, une révolution, etc.).

trigonometric(al) [trigənə'metrik(l)] *a.* trigonométrique. **-ally** *adv.* trigonométriquement.

trigonometry [trigə'nɔmitri] *n.* trigonométrie *f.*

trilateral [trai'læt(ə)rəl] *a.* trilatéral, -aux.

trilby ['trilbi] *n.* **t. (hat),** chapeau mou.

trilingual [trai'liŋgw(ə)l] *a.* trilingue.

trill¹ [tril] *n.* **1.** *Mus:* trille *m.* **2.** chant perlé, trille (des oiseaux). **3.** *Ling:* consonne roulée.

trill² **1.** *v.i. Mus: etc:* faire des trilles; **trilling laugh,** rire perlé. **2.** *v.tr.* (*a*) *Mus: etc:* triller (une note); (*b*) *Ling:* **trilled consonant,** consonne roulée.

trillion ['triliən] *n.* **1.** trillion *m* (10^{18}). **2.** *U.S:* billion *m* (10^{12}).

trilogy ['trilədʒi] *n.* trilogie *f.*

trim¹ [trim] *n.* **1.** **in good t.,** (i) en bon ordre; (ii) (*of pers.*) en bonne santé; en (bonne) forme; **in fighting t.,** prêt pour le combat. **2.** (*a*) *Nau: Av:* assiette *f*; *Av:* équilibrage *m*; **in t., out of t.,** équilibré, non équilibré; (*b*) *Nau:* orientation *f* (des voiles); **sailing t.,** allure *f.* **3.** *Hairdr:* coupe *f*; **just a t.,** simplement rafraîchir.

trim² *a.* (*a*) soigné; coquet; (*of pers.*) **to have a t. figure,** avoir une tournure élégante; **a t. little garden,** un petit jardin coquet, bien tenu; (*b*) *Nau:* (navire) bien voilé.

trim³ *v.tr.* **(trimmed)** **1.** (*a*) arranger, mettre en état (qch.); (*b*) tailler (une haie, un arbre); ébarber, rogner (les tranches d'un livre); égaliser, rafraîchir (la barbe, etc.); *Hairdr:* couper, rafraîchir (les cheveux de qn); **to t. (the wick of) a lamp,** moucher une lampe; *Cu:* **to t. meat,** habiller, parer, la viande; **to t. off the fat,** enlever le gras. **2.** (*a*) équilibrer (un navire, un avion); arrimer (le chargement); (*b*) *Nau:* orienter, appareiller (les voiles). **3.** (*a*) *Dressm: etc:* orner, garnir, agrémenter (une robe, etc.) (**with,** de); garnir (un chapeau); *esp. NAm:* décorer (l'arbre de Noël); **trimmed with lace,** garni de dentelles. **trimming** *n.* **1.** (*a*) arrangement *m*, mise *f* en état (de qch.); (*b*) taille *f* (des haies, des arbres); ébarbage *m* (des tranches d'un livre, des pièces coulées); **t. machine,** (i) *Metall: etc:* ébarbeuse *f*; (ii) *Bookb:* rogneuse *f*; **trimmings,** rognures *fpl*, ébarbures *fpl* (de fer, de bois, de papier, etc.). **2.** (*a*) *Nau: Av:* équilibrage *m* (d'un navire, d'un avion); arrimage *m* (du chargement); (*b*) *Nau:* orientation *f* (des voiles). **3.** (*a*) garnissage *m* (de chapeaux, de linge, etc.); *Cu:* apprêt *m* (d'un mets); (*b*) garniture *f*, ornement *m* (de vêtements, de rideaux, etc.); (*often pl.*) passementerie *f* (pour vêtements, etc.); *Cu: F:* **the (usual) trimmings,** accompagnements *mpl*, garniture (d'un plat).

trimaran ['traimǝræn] *n. Nau:* trimaran *m*.

trimester [trai'mestǝr] *n.* trimestre *m*.

trimmer ['trimǝr] *n.* **1.** (*pers.*) (*a*) *Ind:* appareilleur *m*; pareur, -euse; (*b*) garnisseur, -euse (de chapeaux, etc.); (*d*) *Nau:* arrimeur *m*. **2.** (*a*) machine *f* à trancher (le bois, etc.); *Paperm: Bookb: etc:* massicot *m*; (*b*) *Av:* (dispositif) compensateur *m*; *Av: Nau:* équilibreur *m*.

trimness ['trimnis] *n.* air soigné (de qn, de qch.); apparence bien tenue (d'un jardin, etc.).

Trinidad ['trinidæd] *Pr.n. Geog:* (île de) Trinidad, (île de) la Trinité.

Trinity ['triniti] *n.* **1.** (*a*) *Theol:* **the (Holy) T.,** la (sainte) Trinité; **T. Sunday,** (fête *f* de) la Trinité; (*b*) *F:* **t.,** groupe *m* de trois. **2.** *Sch:* **T. term,** troisième trimestre (universitaire).

trinket ['triŋkit] *n.* (*a*) petit objet de parure; petit bijou; breloque *f*; (*b*) bibelot *m*.

trinomial [trai'noumiǝl] *a. & n. Mth:* trinôme (*m*).

trio, *pl.* **-os** ['tri:ou(z)] *n. Mus: etc:* trio *m*.

trip¹ [trip] *n.* **1.** (*a*) excursion *f*; voyage *m* d'agrément; tour *m*; **honeymoon t.,** voyage de noces; **the t. takes two hours,** on fait le trajet en deux heures; *Nau:* **maiden t.,** premier voyage; **round t.,** (i) voyage circulaire; *Nau:* croisière *f*; (ii) voyage d'aller et retour; (*b*) **(drug) t.,** voyage. **2.** pas léger. **3.** (*a*) faux pas; trébuchement *m*; (*b*) faute *f*; faux pas; (*c*) croc-en-jambe *m*, *pl.* crocs-en-jambe; croche-pied *m*, *pl.* croche-pieds; (*d*) **t. wire,** fil tendu (en guise de traquenard ou d'avertisseur). **4.** *Mec.E:* **t. gear,** (i) déclic *m*; (ii) culbuteur *m* (de bennes); **t. hammer,** marteau *m* à bascule, à soulèvement.

trip² (**tripped** [tript]) **1.** *v.i.* (*a*) **to t. (along),** aller d'un pas léger; (*b*) trébucher; faire un faux pas; (*of horse*) broncher; **to t. over sth.,** trébucher sur, buter contre, qch.; (*c*) **to t. (up),** se tromper; **to t. (up) over a word,** trébucher sur un mot; (*d*) *Mec.E:* (i) (*of catch, etc.*) se déclencher; (ii) (*of part of mechanism*) basculer, culbuter; (*e*) *P:* (*drugs*) faire un voyage; être en voyage. **2.** *v.tr.* (*a*) **to t. s.o. (up),** (i) faire, donner, un croc-en-jambe, un croche-pied, à qn; (*of obstacle*) faire trébucher, faire tomber, qn; (ii) prendre qn en défaut, en erreur; (*b*) *Mec.E:* déclencher (une pièce de machine); culbuter (un levier, etc.).

tripartite [trai'pɑ:tait] *a.* tripartite; divisé en trois.

tripe [traip] *n.* (*a*) *Cu:* tripe(s) *f*(*pl*); (*b*) bêtises *fpl*; **that's all, a lot of, t.,** tout ça c'est des sottises.

triphase ['traifeiz] *a. El:* (courant) triphasé.

triple¹ ['tripl] *a.* triple; *Mus:* **t. time,** mesure *f* ternaire, à trois temps; *Hist:* **the T. Alliance,** la Triplice, la triple Alliance. **-ply** *adv.* triplement.

triple² **1.** *v.tr.* tripler. **2.** *v.i.* (se) tripler.

triplet ['triplit] *n.* (*a*) *Mus:* triolet *m*; (*b*) *Pros:* tercet *m*; (*c*) (*of pers.*) triplé(e).

triplex ['tripleks] *a.* (planche) en trois épaisseurs; (machine) à trois cylindres.

triplicate¹ ['triplikǝt] **1.** *a.* triplé; triple. **2.** *n.* triple *m*; triplicata *m*; **invoice in t.,** facture *f* en triplicata, en trois exemplaires.

triplicate² ['triplikeit] *v.tr.* **1.** tripler. **2.** rédiger (un document) en trois exemplaires.

tripod ['traipɔd] *n.* trépied *m*.

tripos ['traipɔs] *n. Sch:* = licence *f* ès lettres, ès sciences (à Cambridge).

tripper ['tripǝr] *n.* (*pers.*) excursionniste *mf*; **they're (just) day trippers,** ils sont venus passer la journée.

triptych ['triptik] *n. Art:* triptyque *m*.

trisect [trai'sekt] *v.tr. Mth: etc:* diviser, couper (une ligne, un angle) en trois.

trisyllabic [traisi'læbik] *a. Pros:* tris(s)yllabe, tris(s)yllabique.

trisyllable [trai'silǝbl] *n. Pros:* tris(s)yllabe *m*.

trite [trait] *a.* banal, -als; rebattu; **t. remarks,** lieux communs; banalités *fpl*. **-ly** *adv.* banalement.

triteness ['traitnis] *n.* banalité *f*.

tritium ['tritiǝm] *n. Ch:* tritium *m*.

triton ['trait(ǝ)n] *n. Myth: Moll: Amph:* triton *m*.

triturate ['tritjǝreit] *v.tr.* triturer; broyer.

trituration [tritjǝ'reiʃ(ǝ)n] *n.* trituration *f*.

triumph¹ ['traiǝmf] *n.* **1.** *Rom.Ant:* triomphe *m*. **2.** (*a*) triomphe, succès *m*; **to achieve great triumphs,** remporter de grands succès; (*b*) air *m* de triomphe; jubilation *f*; **he came home in t.,** il est rentré chez lui en triomphe.

triumph² *v.i.* **1.** *Rom.Ant:* triompher. **2.** triompher; **to t. over one's enemies,** triompher de ses ennemis; l'emporter sur ses ennemis; **now it was my turn to t.,** c'était alors à moi de chanter, crier, victoire.

triumphal [trai'ʌmf(ǝ)l] *a.* triomphal, -aux.

triumphant [trai'ʌmfǝnt] *a.* triomphant; triomphateur, -trice; **the Church T.,** l'Église triomphante; **a t. expression,** un air de triomphe. **-ly** *adv.* en triomphe; d'un air de triomphe.

triumvirate [trai'ʌmvirit] *n.* (*a*) *Rom.Hist:* triumvirat *m*; (*b*) trio *m* (de personnes).

triune ['traiju:n] *a.* d'une unité triple; trin.

trivet ['trivit] *n. Dom.Ec:* trépied *m*, chevrette *f*.

trivia ['triviǝ] *n.pl.* des vétilles *fpl*, des riens *mpl*; **to get bogged down in t.,** s'embarrasser de questions *fpl* sans importance.

trivial ['triviǝl] *a.* **1.** (*a*) insignifiant; sans importance; **t. offence,** peccadille *f*; **t. matter,** bagatelle *f*; (*b*) (*of pers.*) superficiel; frivole. **2.** banal, -als.

triviality [trivi'æliti] *n.* **1.** (*a*) insignifiance *f* (d'une perte, d'une offense, etc.); (*b*) banalité *f* (d'une observation, etc.). **2. to talk polite trivialities,** dire des futilités; parler pour ne rien dire.

trivialize ['triviǝlaiz] *v.tr.* banaliser (qch. d'important).

trochaic [trou'keiik] *a. & n. Pros:* trochaïque (*m*).

trochee ['trouki:] *n. Pros:* trochée *m*, chorée *m*.

trod, trodden *see* TREAD².

troglodyte ['trɔglǝdait] *n.* troglodyte *m*.

Trojan ['troudʒǝn] **1.** *a. A. Hist:* troyen; de Troie; **the T. War,** la guerre de Troie; **the T. Horse,** le cheval de Troie. **2.** *n.* (*a*) *A. Hist:* Troyen, -enne; (*b*) **like a T.,** (se battre) vaillamment, avec courage; (travailler) sans relâche.

troll¹ [troul] *n. Fish:* (*a*) cuiller *f*; (*b*) moulinet *m* (de canne à pêche).

troll² **1.** *v.tr.* chantonner (un air, une chanson). **2.** *v.i. Fish:* **to t. for pike,** pêcher le brochet à la cuiller.
trolling *n.* pêche *f* à la cuiller.

troll³ *n. Myth:* troll *m*.

trolley ['trɔli] *n.* **1.** (*a*) chariot *m*; (*two wheeled*) diable *m*; **luggage t.,** chariot à bagages; (*b*) **shopping t.,** (i) (*in supermarket, etc.*) chariot, *F:* caddie *m*; (ii) (*belonging to customer*) poussette *f*; **dinner, tea, t.,** table roulante. **2.** *Ind:* **overhead t.,** chariot (de pont roulant, etc.). **3. t. (wheel),** (poulie *f* de) trolley *m*; *NAm:* **t. car,** tramway *m* à trolley.

trolleybus ['trɔlibʌs] *n.* trolleybus *m*.

trollop ['trɔlǝp] *n.f. A:* **1.** souillon. **2.** putain *f*.

trombone [trɔm'boun] *n. Mus:* trombone *m*.

trombonist [trɔm'bounist] *n.* tromboniste *mf*.

troop¹ [tru:p] *n.* **1.** troupe *f*, bande *f* (de personnes). **2.** *Mil:* (*a*) **troops,** troupes *fpl*; **to raise troops,** lever des troupes; **shock troops,** troupes de choc; **t. train,** train *m* militaire; **t. carrier,** (i) véhicule blindé de transport de personnel; (ii) avion *m* de transport de troupes; (*b*) (*unit*) peloton *m* (de cavalerie, de l'arme blindée). **3.** *Scout:* troupe.

troop² **1.** *v.i.* **to come trooping up,** s'attrouper, s'assembler; **to t. off, in,** partir, entrer, en groupe, en bande. **2.** *v.tr. Mil:* **to t. the colour,** faire la parade du drapeau; présenter le drapeau. **trooping** *n. Mil:* **t. (of) the colour,** parade *f* du drapeau; présentation *f* du drapeau.

trooper ['tru:pər] *n.* **1.** (*a*) *Mil:* cavalier *m*; soldat *m* de la cavalerie; *F:* **to swear like a t.,** jurer comme un charretier; (*b*) cheval *m* de cavalerie; (*c*) *U.S: Austr:* membre *m* de la police montée. **2.** = TROOPSHIP.

troopship ['tru:pʃip] *n.* (navire *m* de) transport *m* de troupes.

trophy ['troufi] *n.* **1.** trophée *m* (de guerre, de chasse, etc.). **2.** *Sp:* trophée.

tropic ['trɔpik] *n.* (*a*) *Astr: Geog:* tropique *m*; (*b*) **the tropics,** les tropiques.

tropical ['trɔpik(ə)l] *a.* (*a*) (climat, etc.) tropical, -aux; (maladie, etc.) des tropiques; **t. heat,** chaleur tropicale.

tropism ['trɔpizm] *n. Biol:* tropisme *m*.

troposphere ['trɔpəsfiər] *n. Meteor:* troposphère *f*.

trot¹ [trɔt] *n.* **1.** *Equit: etc:* trot *m*; **at a brisk t.,** au grand trot; **to set off at a t.,** partir au trot; *Sp: F:* **they've had 22 wins on the t.,** ils ont gagné la partie vingt-deux fois à la file, de suite; *F:* **to keep s.o. on the t.,** ne laisser aucun repos à qn. **2.** *P:* **to have the trots,** avoir la diarrhée, la courante.

trot² **(trotted)** **1.** *v.i.* (*a*) *Equit:* trotter; aller le trot, au trot; (*b*) (*of pers.*) trotter; (*of child, etc.*) trottiner; (*c*) *F: O:* **I must be trotting (along),** il faut que je file. **2.** *v.tr.* (*a*) trotter (un cheval); (*b*) **to t. s.o. round,** faire voir la ville à qn. **trot out** *v.tr.* (*a*) faire trotter, faire parader (un cheval) (devant un client); (*b*) faire étalage de (ses connaissances, etc.); désenterrer (de vieux griefs); *F:* **he can always t. out excuses,** il est toujours prêt à débiter des excuses. **trotting** *n.* trot *m*; **t. race,** course *f* de trot (attelé).

troth [trouθ] *n. A: & Lit:* **1.** foi *f*; **by my t.!** sur ma foi! **2. in t.,** en vérité.

trotter ['trɔtər] *n.* **1.** cheval *m* de trot; trotteur, -euse. **2.** (*a*) *Cu:* **sheep's, pigs', trotters,** pieds *mpl* de mouton, de porc; (*b*) *F:* **trotters,** pieds.

troubadour ['tru:bəduər] *n. Lit:* troubadour *m*.

trouble¹ ['trʌbl] *n.* **1.** (*a*) peine *f*; chagrin *m*; affliction *f*; malheur *m*; **he told me his troubles,** il m'a raconté ses malheurs; **his troubles are over,** il est au bout de ses malheurs; (*b*) ennui *m*; difficulté *f*; **money troubles,** soucis *mpl* d'argent; **what's the t.?** qu'est-ce qu'il y a? **we must get to the root of the t.,** il faut chercher la source du mal; **the t. is that . . .,** l'ennui, la difficulté, c'est que . . .; **you'll have t. with him,** il va vous causer des difficultés, des ennuis; (*c*) **to be in t.,** avoir des ennuis, des difficultés; **to get into t.,** (i) s'attirer des ennuis, des désagréments; (ii) *F:* (*of unmarried woman*) devenir enceinte; **to get into t. with the police,** avoir affaire à la police; **to get s.o. into t., to make t. for s.o.,** créer, susciter, des ennuis à qn; *F:* **to get a girl into t.,** rendre une femme enceinte; **to get s.o. out of t.,** tirer qn d'affaire; **to keep out of t.,** éviter des ennuis; **to be looking, asking, for t.,** se préparer des ennuis; (*d*) **to make t.,** semer la discorde; **to make t. for oneself,** s'attirer des ennuis; **there will be t.,** il y aura du vilain, *F:* de la casse; (*e*) **there was t. in the streets,** il y a eu des désordres dans la rue; **t. spot,** point *m* névralgique; **labour troubles,** conflits ouvriers; (*f*) *Med:* trouble(s); **eye t.,** (i) troubles de vision; (ii) affection *f* de l'œil; **stomach t.,** troubles digestifs; **to have heart t.,** être malade du cœur; (*g*) *Mec.E: etc:* panne *f*; **to locate, trace, the t.,** trouver la source de la panne; *Aut: etc:* **engine t.,** panne de moteur; **we had a t.-free journey,** nous avons eu un trajet sans incidents. **2.** dérangement *m*; peine; mal; **to take the t. to do sth., to go to the t. of doing sth.,** prendre, se donner, la peine de faire qch.; **to go to, put oneself to, to take, a great deal of t.,** se donner beaucoup de mal, de peine; **it's not worth the t.,** cela n'en vaut pas la peine; ce n'est pas la peine; **nothing's too much t. for him,** rien ne lui coûte; **to have had all one's t. for nothing,** en être pour sa peine.

trouble² **1.** *v.tr.* (*a*) affliger, chagriner (qn); inquiéter, préoccuper (qn); **I'm troubled about his future,** son avenir me préoccupe, m'inquiète; **don't let it t. you!** que cela ne vous inquiète pas! ne vous tourmentez pas à ce sujet! (*b*) affliger, faire souffrir (qn); **how long has this cough been troubling you?** depuis combien de temps souffrez-vous de cette toux? (*c*) déranger, incommoder (qn); donner de la peine à (qn); **I'm so sorry to t. you,** excusez-moi de vous déranger; *usu. Iron:* **may I t. you to shut the door?** cela vous dérangerait-il de fermer la porte? **2.** *v.i.* (*a*) s'inquiéter, se tracasser (**about,** au sujet de, à propos de); (*b*) se déranger; se mettre en peine; **don't t. to write,** ne vous donnez pas la peine d'écrire; **don't t.! you needn't t.!** ne vous dérangez pas! **troubled** *a.* **1.** (*of liquid*) trouble; **to fish in t. waters,** pêcher en eau trouble. **2.** (*a*) inquiet; agité; **a t. soul,** une âme agitée, troublée; **t. sleep,** sommeil agité; (*b*) *Pol: Hist:* **t. period,** époque *f* de troubles. **troubling** *a.* inquiétant.

troublemaker ['trʌb(ə)lmeikər] *n.* fomentateur, -trice, de troubles; agitateur, -trice.

troubleshooter ['trʌb(ə)lʃu:tər] *n.* **1.** *Mec.E: etc:* dépanneur *m*; déceleur *m*, détecteur *m*, de pannes. **2.** *Pol: Ind: etc:* médiateur, -trice; conciliateur, -trice.

troublesome ['trʌb(ə)lsəm] *a.* ennuyeux; (enfant) énervant; (rival) gênant; (toux) pénible.

troublous ['trʌbləs] *a. A:* troublé, agité.

trough [trɔf] *n.* **1.** (*a*) *Husb: etc:* **(feeding) t.,** auge *f*; mangeoire *f*; **drinking t.,** abreuvoir *m*; (*b*) *Tchn:* auge (de meule); *Ch: Ph:* cuve *f*, cuvette *f* (à mercure, à eau); *El:* **accumulator t.,** bac *m* d'accumulateur; (*c*) **book t.,** bac à livres; (*d*) **kneading t.,** pétrin *m* (de boulanger). **2.** *Geol:* auge. **3.** (*a*) **t. of the sea,** creux *m* de la lame; (*b*) *Ph: Mth:* creux (d'une onde, d'un graphique); (*c*) *Meteor:* dépression *f* (barométrique); zone dépressionnaire.

trounce [trauns] *v.tr.* (*a*) *O:* rosser (qn); (*b*) *Sp:* écraser; battre à plate(s) couture(s). **trouncing** *n.* (*a*) *O:* raclée *f*; (*b*) *Sp:* défaite écrasante.

troupe [tru:p] *n.* troupe *f* (de comédiens, etc.).

trouper ['tru:pər] *n. Th:* membre *m* d'une troupe.

trouser ['trauzər] *n.* **(pair of) trousers,** pantalon *m*; **t. suit,** tailleur-pantalon *m*; **t. press,** presse-pantalon *m*; *F:* **she's the one who wears the trousers,** c'est elle qui porte la culotte; *F:* **to be caught with one's trousers down,** être pris au dépourvu.

trousseau ['tru:sou] *n.* trousseau *m*.

trout [traut] *n.* **1.** *Ich:* (*inv. in pl.*) truite *f*; **rainbow t.,** truite arc-en-ciel; **salmon t.,** truite saumonée; **t. fishing,** pêche *f* à la truite. **2.** *P:* (*woman*) **old t.,** vieille bique.

trove [trouv] *n.* **treasure t.,** trésor (découvert par le pur effet du hasard).

trowel ['trauəl] *n.* **1.** *Const:* truelle *f*, gâche *f*. **2.** *Hort:* déplantoir *m*, houlette *f*.

troy¹ [trɔi] *n. Meas:* **t. (weight),** poids *m* troy (pour l'or et l'argent); **t. ounce,** once *f* troy (31g, 1).

Troy² *Pr.n. A.Geog:* Troie *f*.

truancy ['tru:ənsi] *n. Sch:* absentéisme *m* scolaire.

truant ['tru:ənt] *n. Sch:* élève absent (de l'école) sans permission; **to play t.,** faire l'école buissonnière.

truce [tru:s] *n.* trêve *f*; **let's call it a t.!** faisons la paix!

truck¹ [trʌk] *n.* **1.** troc *m*, échange *m*. **2.** *Hist:* **t. (system),** paiement *m* des ouvriers en nature. **3.** *F: O:* rapports *mpl*, relations *fpl* (avec qn); **I've no t. with him,** (i) je n'ai pas affaire à lui; (ii) je n'ai rien à faire avec lui. **4.** *NAm:* produits maraîchers; **t. gardener, farmer,** maraîcher *m*.

truck² *n.* **1.** (*a*) (*four-wheeled*) chariot *m*, fardier *m*; **fork-lift t.,** chariot élévateur à fourche; (*b*) *Min:* berline *f*, benne *f*, bac *m*; (*c*) *esp. NAm: Aut:* camion *m*; **heavy t.,** gros routier; *U.S:* **wrecking t.,** camion de dépannage, dépanneuse *f*. **2.** *Rail:* wagon *m* (à marchandises); **cattle t.,** fourgon *m* à bestiaux.

truck³ *v.tr.* camionner (des marchandises). **trucking** *n. esp. NAm:* camionnage *m*.

truckdriver ['trʌkdraivər], **trucker** ['trʌkər] *n. NAm:* camionneur *m*; routier *m*.

truckle¹ ['trʌkl] *n.* **t. bed,** lit gigogne.

truckle² *v.i.* ramper, s'abaisser (**to,** devant).

truculence ['trʌkjuləns] *n.* agressivité *f*; férocité *f*.

truculent ['trʌkjulənt] *a.* agressif; féroce. **-ly** *adv.* agressivement; férocement.

trudge¹ [trʌdʒ] *n.* marche *f* pénible; **a long t.,** un trajet long et pénible.

trudge² *v.i.* marcher lourdement, péniblement; **to t. along,** cheminer, avancer, péniblement.

true I. *a.* **1.** vrai; exact; **t. adventures,** aventures vécues; **it's only too t.,** ce n'est que trop vrai; **it is t. that . . .,** il est vrai que . . .; **if it were t. that . . .,** s'il était vrai que . . . +*sub.*; (*of wish, etc.*) **to come t.,** se réaliser; **this also holds t. for . . .,** il en est de même pour . . .. **2.** véritable; vrai, réel; (*a*) **t. repentance,** repentir *m* sincère, véritable; **his t. nature,** son véritable caractère; **to get a t. idea of the situation,** se faire une idée juste de la situation; (*b*) *Tchn:* **t. time,** temps vrai, heure vraie; **t. horizon,** horizon réel. **3.** (*a*) *Mec.E: Carp:* juste, droit, rectiligne; **to make a piece t.,** ajuster une pièce; (*b*) (terrain) égal, uni; **the table isn't t.,** la table n'est pas d'aplomb. **4.** (*a*) fidèle; loyal; **t. friend,** ami loyal; **to be t. to oneself,** ne pas se démentir; **to be t. to one's promise,** rester fidèle à une promesse; *O:* **he's a t. blue,** c'est un homme loyal, fidèle; (*b*) *A:* (*of pers.*) honnête; *Jur:* **a jury of twelve good men and t.,** un jury de douze citoyens de bonne renommée. **5.** (*of voice, instrument*) juste. **II.** *adv.* **1.** *F: O:* vraiment; (pour de) vrai. **2.** (chanter, viser) juste; (*of wheel*) **to run t.,** tourner rond, sans balourd; **the wheel is not running t.,** la roue est désaxée, faussée. **III.** *n. Mec.E: etc:* **out of t.,** (i) (*of vertical post, member, etc.*) hors d'aplomb; (ii) (*of horizontal member, etc.*) dénivelé; (iii) (*of metal plate, etc.*) gauchi, gondolé; (*of wheel rim*) voilé; (*of axle, etc.*) faussé, dévoyé; (*of timber*) déjeté; (iv) (*of wheel*) décentré, excentré, désaxé; **to run out of t.,** (i) se décentrer; (ii) être décentré; tourner à faux; ne pas tourner rond. **truly** ['tru:li] *adv.* **1.** (*a*) vraiment, véritablement; **a t. difficult situation,** une situation vraiment difficile; **I am t. grateful to him,** je lui suis sincèrement reconnaissant; **I t. believe that . . .,** je crois vraiment, sincèrement, que . . .; (*b*) *Corr:* **yours t.** = je vous prie d'agréer, de croire à, mes sentiments distingués; (*c*) *P:* **yours t.,** votre serviteur; moi-même. **2.** en vérité; à vrai dire; *F:* **(really and) t.?** vrai de vrai? **3.** (servir qn) fidèlement, loyalement. **4.** vraiment, justement; **it may t. be called tragic,** on peut bien le qualifier de tragique.

trueborn ['tru:bɔ:n] *a. O:* vrai, véritable; **a t. Englishman,** un vrai Anglais d'Angleterre.

truehearted [tru:'hɑ:tid] *a. O:* fidèle; loyal, -aux.

true(-)love ['tru:lʌv] *n.* bien-aimé(e); **t. knot** (*also* **true lover's knot**), lacs *m* d'amour (en 8 couché).

truffle ['trʌfl] *n.* truffe *f*; **t. hound,** chien truffier.

truism ['tru:izm] *n.* truisme *m*; vérité *f* de La Palisse.

trump¹ [trʌmp] *n. A: & Lit:* trompette *f*; **the last t.,** la trompette du jugement dernier.

trump² *n. Cards:* **t. (card),** atout *m*; **spades are trumps,** c'est pique atout; **to play trumps,** jouer l'atout; **to call no trumps,** appeler, demander, sans-atout; *Fig:* **to play one's t. card,** jouer son atout; *F:* **he always turns up trumps,** (i) la chance le favorise; (ii) on peut toujours compter sur lui.

trump³ *v.tr. & i.* **1.** *Cards:* couper (une carte); jouer atout. **2. to t. up,** inventer, forger (une excuse); **to t. up a charge against s.o.,** forger, fabriquer, une accusation contre qn; **trumped-up story,** histoire inventée.

trumpery ['trʌmpəri] **1.** *n.* friperie *f*, camelote *f*. **2.** *a.* (*a*) (marchandises) de camelote; (*b*) (argument, etc.) spécieux.

trumpet¹ ['trʌmpit] *n.* **1.** *Mus:* trompette *f*; **t. call,** coup *m* de trompette; sonnerie *f* de trompette; *Mil:* **t. major,** trompette-major *m*, *pl.* trompettes-majors. **2.** (*a*) **(ear) t.,** cornet *m* acoustique; (*b*) *O:* pavillon *m* (de phonographe, de cornet avertisseur, etc.).

trumpet², *v.* **(trumpeted) 1.** *v.i.* (*a*) trompeter; sonner de la trompette; (*b*) (*of elephant*) barrir. **2.** *v.tr.* publier (qch.) à cor et à cri; célébrer (un succès) à grand bruit. **trumpeting** *n.* **1.** sonnerie *f* de trompette. **2.** (*of elephant*) barrit *m*, barrissement *m*.

trumpeter ['trʌmpitər] *n.* (*a*) *Mil: etc:* trompette *m*; (*b*) (*by profession*) trompettiste *m*.

truncate [trʌŋ'keit] *v.tr.* tronquer (un corps, un texte, etc.). **truncated** *a. Cryst: etc:* tronqué; *Mth:* **t. cone,** tronc *m* de cône; cône tronqué.

truncheon ['trʌn(t)ʃ(ə)n] *n.* bâton *m* (d'agent de police); matraque *f*, casse-tête *m inv*; **rubber t.,** matraque en caoutchouc.

trundle¹ ['trʌndl] *n.* **t. bed,** lit gigogne.

trundle² **1.** *v.tr.* (*a*) faire rouler, faire courir (un cerceau, etc.); (*b*) pousser (une brouette, une voiture à bras). **2.** *v.i.* (*of hoop, etc.*) rouler.

trunk [trʌŋk] *n.* **1.** (*a*) tronc *m* (d'arbre); (*b*) tronc (du corps); *Art:* torse *m*; (*c*) *Anat:* tronc (d'artère, etc.); **t. roads,** grandes routes; **t. line,** (i) *Rail:* ligne principale; grande ligne; (ii) *Tp:* l'inter; **t. call,** appel interurbain; (*d*) *Arch:* fût *m* (d'une colonne). **2.** (*a*) malle *f*; (*b*) *NAm: Aut:* coffre. **3.** trompe *f* (d'éléphant). **4.** *Cost:* **trunks,** (i) short-slip *m*; (ii) short *m*; maillot *m* (de bain) (pour hommes).

trunnion ['trʌnjən] *n. Artil: Mch:* tourillon *m*.

truss¹ [trʌs] *n.* **1.** (*a*) botte *f* (de foin, de paille); (*b*) *Hort:* touffe *f* (de fleurs). **2.** (*a*) *Const:* (i) armature *f* (de poutre, etc.); (ii) ferme *f* (de comble, de pont); (iii) cintre *m* (de voûte); **t. girder,** poutre armée; ferme *f*; (*b*) *Civ.E:* treillis *m* (métallique). **3.** *Med:* bandage *m* herniaire.

truss² *v.tr.* **1.** *Const: Tchn:* armer, renforcer (une poutre, etc.); **trussed beam, girder,** poutre armée, renforcée. **2.** (*a*) *Cu:* trousser, brider (une volaille); *F:* **to t. s.o. up like a fowl,** ligoter qn.

trust¹ [trʌst] *n.* **1.** confiance *f* (**in,** en); **to put one's t. in s.o., sth.,** mettre sa confiance en qn; se reposer sur qn, qch.; **on t.,** (i) (accepter, acheter, qch.) de confiance; (ii) *Com:* (fournir des marchandises) à crédit. **2.** espérance *f*, espoir *m*; **it is my firm t. that . . .,** j'espère avec confiance que . . .; j'ai le ferme espoir que . . .. **3.** (*a*) responsabilité *f*, charge *f*; **to be in a position of t.,** occuper un poste de confiance; (*b*) garde *f*; dépôt *m*; **he committed it to my t.,** il l'a confié à mes soins, à ma garde; **a sacred t.,** un dépôt sacré. **4.** (*a*) *Jur:* fidéicommis *m*, fiducie *f*; **to hold sth. in t.,** tenir qch. par fidéicommis; administrer (un bien, etc.) par fidéicommis; (*b*) **National T.,** société *f* pour la conservation des sites et monuments. **5.** (*a*) *Ind: etc:* trust *m*, syndicat *m*, cartel *m*; *St.Exch:* **investment t.,** trust de placement; coopérative *f* de placement; **unit t.,** société d'investissement à capital variable; (*b*) **brains t.,** brain-trust *m*, *pl.* brain-trusts. **6.** *Pol:* **t. territories,** territoires *mpl* sous tutelle.

trust² **1.** *v.tr.* (*a*) se fier à (qn, qch.); se confier à, en (qn, qch.); mettre sa confiance en (qn, qch.); **he's not to be trusted,** on ne peut pas se fier à lui; **to t. s.o. with sth.,** confier qch. à qn; **to t. s.o. to do sth.,** se fier à qn du soin de faire qch.; *F:* **t. him to say that!** c'est bien de lui! **I couldn't t. myself to speak,** j'étais trop ému pour me risquer à rien dire; *F:* **she won't t. him out of her sight,** elle le surveille tout le temps; (*b*) **to t. sth. to, with, s.o.,** confier qch. à qn, aux soins de qn, à la garde de qn; (*c*) *Com:* *F:* faire crédit à (un client); (*d*) espérer (que + *ind.*); exprimer le vœu (que + *sub.*); **I t. he is not ill,** j'espère bien qu'il n'est pas malade. **2.** *v.i.* (*a*) se confier (**in,** en); se fier (**in,** à); mettre sa confiance (**in,** en); **I want someone I can t. in,** il me faut une personne de confiance; (*b*) mettre ses espérances, son espoir (en qch.); **to t. to luck,** se confier au hasard; **to t. in God,** s'abandonner à Dieu. **trusted** *a.* (personne) de confiance; **tried and t.,** (ami, remède) éprouvé; (ami) à toute épreuve. **trusting** *a.* plein de confiance; confiant. **trustingly** *adv.* avec confiance.

trustee [trʌs'tiː] *n.* **1.** *Jur:* (*a*) fidéicommissaire *m*, fiduciaire *m*; curateur, -trice; **the Public T.,** le curateur de l'État aux successions; (*b*) dépositaire *m*, consignataire *m*; (*c*) (*with powers of attorney*) mandataire *m*. **2.** administrateur, curateur (d'un musée, etc.); **board of trustees,** conseil *m* d'administration.

trusteeship [trʌs'tiːʃip] *n.* **1.** fidéicommis *m*. **2.** administration *f*, curatelle *f*. **3.** *Pol:* tutelle *f*.

trustful ['trʌstf(u)l] *a.* plein de confiance; confiant. **-fully** *adv.* avec confiance.

trustfulness ['trʌstf(u)lnis] *n.* confiance *f*.

trustiness ['trʌstinis] *n.* fidélité *f*, loyauté *f*.

trustworthiness ['trʌstwəːðinis] *n.* **1.** (*of pers.*) loyauté *f*, honnêteté *f*. **2.** crédibilité *f*, véracité *f* (d'un témoignage, etc.).

trustworthy ['trʌstwəːði] *a.* **1.** (*of pers.*) digne de confiance, de foi; loyal; honnête; irrécusable; **a t. person,** une personne de confiance. **2.** (renseignement) digne de foi; (témoignage) irrécusable.

trusty ['trʌsti] *a.* *A:* & *Lit:* sûr, fidèle; loyal, -aux.

truth [truːθ, *pl.* truːðz] *n.* (*a*) vérité *f*; véracité *f*; **to speak, tell, the t.,** dire la vérité; *Jur:* **the t., the whole t., and nothing but the t.,** la vérité, toute la vérité, rien que la vérité; **the real, plain, unvarnished, honest, t.,** la pure vérité; la vérité pure et simple; **the t. (of the matter) is, to tell the t., I forgot it,** pour dire la vérité, à dire vrai, je l'ai oublié; **there's some t. in what you say,** il y a du vrai dans ce que vous dites; *Prov:* **t. will out,** la vérité finit toujours par se découvrir; (*b*) chose vraie; **I told him some, a few, home truths,** je lui ai dit son fait, ses quatre vérités.

truthful ['truːθf(u)l] *a.* **1.** (*of pers.*) véridique. **2.** (témoignage, etc.) vrai; (portrait, etc.) fidèle. **-fully** *adv.* **1.** véridiquement; sans mentir. **2.** fidèlement.

truthfulness ['truːθf(u)lnis] *n.* **1.** (*of pers.*) véracité *f*. **2.** vérité *f*; véracité (d'une assertion, etc.); fidélité *f* (d'un portrait, etc.).

try¹ [trai] *n.* **1.** essai *m*, tentative *f*; **to have a t. at (doing) sth.,** essayer de faire qch.; s'essayer à qch.; **to have another t.,** ressayer (qch.); **let's have a t.!** essayons toujours! **at the first t.,** du premier coup. **2.** *Rugby Fb:* **to score a t.,** marquer un essai; **to convert a t.,** transformer un essai (en but).

try² (*p.t.* & *p.p.* **tried** [traid]) **I.** *v.tr.* **1.** (*a*) éprouver (qn); mettre (qn, qch.) à l'épreuve; faire l'épreuve de (qch.); **to t. s.o.'s courage,** mettre à l'épreuve le courage de qn; (*b*) *Lit:* éprouver; affliger; **a people sorely tried,** une nation fort, durement, éprouvée; (*c*) **to t. one's eyes (reading),** se fatiguer les yeux (à lire). **2.** essayer; faire l'essai de (qch.); **to t. a dish,** goûter (à) un mets. **3.** vérifier (un mécanisme); ajuster (des poids); essayer (un cordage, une voiture). **4.** *Jur:* (*a*) juger (une cause, un accusé); **to be tried for theft,** passer en correctionnelle pour vol; (*b*) *U.S:* (*of advocate*) plaider (une cause). **5.** essayer, tenter; **to t. an experiment,** tenter une expérience; **to t. one's strength against s.o.,** se mesurer avec qn; **to t. the door, the window,** essayer (d'ouvrir) la porte, la fenêtre. **6. to t. to do,** *F:* **and do, sth.,** tâcher, essayer, de faire qch.; **she tried to smile,** elle a essayé de sourire; **she was trying hard to keep back her tears,** elle faisait de grands efforts pour retenir ses larmes; **it's worth trying,** cela vaut la peine d'essayer. **II.** *v.i.* **1.** faire un effort, des efforts; **to t. again,** faire un nouvel effort; essayer de nouveau; **you must t. harder,** il faut faire de plus grands efforts. **2. to t. for (sth.),** tâcher d'obtenir (qch.); poser sa candidature à (un emploi). **tried** *a.* **well t.,** (remède) éprouvé; **t. and trusted,** (ami) à toute épreuve. **trying** **1.** *a.* (*a*) difficile, pénible; dur; (*b*) vexant, contrariant, *F:* agaçant; (*c*) **t. light,** lumière fatigante (pour les yeux). **2.** *n.* (*a*) *Jur:* jugement *m* (d'une cause, d'un accusé); (*b*) **t. on,** essayage *m* (de vêtements). **try on** *v.tr.* (*a*) essayer (un vêtement); (*b*) *F:* **to t. it on (with s.o.),** bluffer; chercher à donner le change (à qn); **you're (just) trying it on!** ça ne marche pas, ne prend pas! **try out** *v.tr.* faire l'essai de (qch.); essayer, expérimenter (un nouveau procédé).

try-on ['traiɔn] *n.* *F:* (*a*) bluff *m*; (*b*) ballon *m* d'essai.

tryout ['traiaut] *n.* **1.** premier essai, essai préliminaire (d'une machine, etc.). **2.** *NAm:* *Th:* audition *f*; *Sp:* épreuve *f* de sélection.

tryst [trist] *n.* *Lit:* rendez-vous *m* amoureux.

tsar [tsɑːr] *n.* tsar *m*, czar *m*.

tsarevitch ['tsɑːrəvitʃ] *n.* tsarévitch *m*, czarévitch *m*.

tsarina [tsɑː'riːnə] *n.f.* tsarine, czarine.

tsarist ['tsɑːrist] **1.** *a.* tsariste. **2.** *n.* tsariste *mf*.

tsetse ['t(s)etsi] *n.* *Ent:* **t. (fly),** (mouche *f*) tsé-tsé *f*.

tub [tʌb] *n.* **1.** (*a*) baquet *m*, bac *m*; *Hort:* bac, caisse *f* (à fleurs, à arbustes); *Paperm:* bac, cuve *f*; *F:* **t. thumper,** harangueur *m*; orateur *m* de carrefour; (*b*) baquet (à lessive); (*in washing machine*) cuve; (*c*) *Com:* carton *m* (à glaces, à crème etc.); (*d*) *Furn:* **t. chair,** crapaud *m*. **2.** (*a*) *F:* baignoire *f*; (*b*) **a hot t.,** un bain chaud. **3.** (*a*) *Nau:* *F:* **old t.,** vieux sabot; (*b*) *Row:* canot *m* d'entraînement.

tuba ['tjuːbə] *n.* *Mus:* tuba *m*.

tubby ['tʌbi] *a.* *F:* (*of pers.*) dodu, -ue, boulot, -otte.

tube [tjuːb] *n.* **1.** (*a*) tube *m*; tuyau *m*; **angle, bent, t.,** tube coudé; **seamless t.,** tube sans soudure; (*b*) tube (de couleur, de dentifrice); *Austr:* *F:* boîte *f* (de bière); (*c*) *Mch:* *etc:* **boiler t.,** tube de chaudière; *Aut:* *etc:* **inner t.,** chambre *f* à air (d'un pneu); (*d*) *Ch:* *Ph:* *etc:* **test t.,** éprouvette *f*; (*e*) *Rail:* *F:* (*in London*) **the t.** = le métro; **t. station** = station *f* de métro; (*f*) *Med:* *etc:* (i) drain *m* (pour plaie profonde); (ii) tube, canule *f*, sonde *f* (pour tubage); **stomach t.,** sonde pour tubage gastrique. **2.** *Anat:* tube; canal, -aux *m*; **Fallopian tubes,** trompes *fpl* de Fallope; **bronchial tubes,** les bronches *fpl*. **3.** *El:* *Elcs:* *T.V:* *etc:* (*a*) tube (électronique, thermionique); lampe *f*; **cathode-ray t.,** tube cathodique, à rayons cathodiques; **picture, television, t.,** tube cathodique pour télévision; (*b*) *U.S:* *F:* **the t.,** la télé.

tubeless ['tjuːblis] *a.* (pneu) sans chambre (à air).

tuber ['tjuːbər] *n.* (i) racine tubéreuse; (ii) tubercule *m*.

tubercle ['tjuːbəːkl] *n.* *Anat:* *Med:* tubercule *m*.

tubercular [tjuː'bəːkjulər] *a.* *Med:* *Bot:* tuberculeux.

tuberculin [tju'bəːkjulin] *n.* *Med:* tuberculine *f*; **t. test,** épreuve *f* de la tuberculinisation; tuberculinodiagnostic *m*; **t.-tested milk,** lait garanti exempt de tuberculose; = lait cru certifié.

tuberculosis [tjubəːkju'lousis] *n. Med:* tuberculose *f*; **t. of the lungs,** tuberculose pulmonaire.
tuberculous [tju'bəːkjuləs] *a. Med:* tuberculeux.
tubful ['tʌbful] *n.* cuvée *f*, plein baquet (**of,** de).
tubing ['tjuːbiŋ] *n. coll.* tubes *mpl*; tuyauterie *f*; **rubber t.,** tuyau(x) *m(pl)* en caoutchouc.
tubular ['tjuːbjulər] *a.* (*a*) tubulaire; (*b*) *Mus:* **t. bells,** carillon *m* (d'orchestre).
tuck¹ [tʌk] *n.* **1.** *Dressm:* (petit) pli; rempli *m*, plissé *m.* **2.** *Sch: F:* gâteaux *mpl*, friandises *fpl*, sucreries *fpl*; **t. box,** boîte *f* à provisions.
tuck² *v.tr.* **1.** *Dressm:* faire des plis à (un vêtement). **2.** replier; serrer, mettre; **to t. one's legs under one,** replier les jambes sous soi; **she tucked her arm in(to) mine,** elle a passé son bras sous le mien; **to t. a rug round s.o.,** envelopper qn d'une couverture; **the bird tucked its head under its wing,** l'oiseau a replié, caché, sa tête sous son aile; **to t. sth. into, away in, a drawer,** serrer qch. dans un tiroir; **village tucked away in the valley,** village blotti au fond de la vallée. **tuck in 1.** *v.tr.* serrer, rentrer (qch.); replier (le bord d'un vêtement, etc.); **to t. in the bedclothes,** border le lit; **to t. s.o. in,** border qn (dans son lit). **2.** *v.i. F:* manger à belles dents; **t. in!** allez-y! mangez! **tuck into** *v.i. F:* **to t. into a meal,** attaquer un repas. **tuck up** *v.tr.* (*a*) relever, retrousser (sa jupe, ses manches); (*b*) border (qn) (dans son lit).
tucker¹ ['tʌkər] *n.* **1.** *A.Cost:* fichu *m*, guimpe *f*; *F:* **in one's best bib and t.,** endimanché. **2.** *Austr: F:* nourriture *f*, mangeaille *f*.
tucker² *v.tr. F:* fatiguer (qn); **tuckered (out),** épuisé, éreinté.
tuck-in ['tʌkin] *n. F:* (*a*) (*of bed*) **there isn't enough t.-in,** les couvertures *fpl* ne sont pas assez larges; (*b*) **to have a good t.-in,** s'envoyer un bon repas.
tuckshop ['tʌkʃɔp] *n. Sch: F:* annexe *f* de la cantine où se vendent les friandises.
Tudor ['tjuːdər] *Pr.n.* **the Tudors,** la maison des Tudors; *Arch:* **T. style,** style Tudor, élisabéthain.
Tuesday ['tjuːzdi] *n.* mardi *m*; **he comes on Tuesdays,** il vient le mardi; **every T.,** tous les mardis.
tufa ['t(j)uːfə] *n. Geol:* tuf *m* calcaire, volcanique.
tuft [tʌft] *n.* **1.** (*a*) touffe *f* (d'herbe); (*b*) touffe (de plumes, de cheveux); huppe *f*, aigrette *f* (d'un oiseau); (*in brush*) **t. of bristles,** loquet *m* de soies. **2.** (*a*) barbiche *f*; mouche *f*; (*b*) toupet *m* (de cheveux).
tufted ['tʌftid] *a. Orn:* huppé; **t. heron,** héron *m* à aigrette; aigrette; **t. duck,** morillon *m.*
tug¹ [tʌg] *n.* **1.** (*a*) traction (subite); saccade *f*; **to give a good t.,** tirer fort; **he gave a t. at the bell,** il a tiré (sur) la sonnette; **I felt a t. at my sleeve,** je me sentis tiré par la manche; **t. of war,** (i) *Sp:* lutte *f* de traction à la corde; lutte à la jarretière; (ii) lutte acharnée et prolongée; (*b*) **to feel a t. at one's heartstrings,** avoir un serrement de cœur. **2.** *Nau:* remorqueur *m.*
tug² (**tugged** [tʌgd]) **1.** *v.tr. & i.* tirer (qch.) avec effort; **to t. at sth.,** tirer (sur) qch.; **to t. (at) one's moustache,** tirer (sur), torturer, tourmenter, sa moustache. **2.** *v.tr. Nau:* remorquer (un navire).
tugboat ['tʌgbout] *n. Nau:* remorqueur *m.*
tuition [tju(ː)'iʃ(ə)n] *n.* instruction *f*, enseignement *m*; **private t.,** leçons particulières.
tulip ['tjuːlip] *n. Bot:* **1.** tulipe *f.* **2. t. tree,** tulipier *m.*
tulle [tjuːl] *n. Tex:* tulle *m.*
tumble¹ ['tʌmbl] *n.* **1.** (*a*) culbute *f*, chute *f*; **he had a nasty t.,** il a fait une rude, mauvaise, chute; (*b*) *Dom.Ec:* **t. drier,** séchoir rotatif (à air chaud); *Fr.C:* sécheuse *f.* **2.** *Gym:* culbute (d'acrobate). **3.** désordre *m*; **everything was in a t.,** tout était en désordre.
tumble² **1.** *v.i.* (*a*) **to t. (down, over),** tomber (par terre); faire une chute; culbuter, faire la culbute; **building that is tumbling down,** édifice qui s'écroule, qui tombe en ruine; (*b*) **to t. about,** s'agiter; (*c*) se jeter (précipitamment) (**into,** dans); **to t. into bed,** se jeter dans son lit; **to t. into one's clothes,** enfiler ses vêtements à la hâte; **to t. out of the window,** tomber par la fenêtre; **they were tumbling over one another,** ils se bousculaient; (*d*) (*of acrobat, pigeon*) faire des culbutes; (*e*) *F:* **to t. to an idea, to a fact,** comprendre, saisir, une idée; se rendre compte d'un fait. **2.** *v.tr.* (*a*) **to t. sth., s.o., down, over,** culbuter, renverser, faire tomber, qch., qn; (*b*) bouleverser, déranger; mettre en désordre (un lit).
tumbledown ['tʌmb(ə)ldaun] *a.* croulant, délabré; (mur) à moitié écroulé; (maison) qui tombe en ruine(s).
tumbler ['tʌmblər] *n.* **1.** *Orn:* **t. (pigeon),** (pigeon) culbutant *m.* **2.** (*toy*) poussa(h) *m.* **3.** verre *m* (à boire) sans pied; gobelet *m.* **4.** (*a*) *El:* culbuteur *m* (d'interrupteur, etc.); (*b*) gorge *f* (de serrure); **t. lock,** serrure *f* à gorge(s).
tumblerful ['tʌmbləful] *n.* plein verre (**of,** de).
tumbrel ['tʌmbrəl], **tumbril** ['tʌmbril] *n. Hist:* charrette *f* (des condamnés).
tumefaction [tjuːmi'fækʃ(ə)n] *n.* tuméfaction *f.*
tumefy ['tjuːmifai] **1.** *v.tr.* tuméfier. **2.** *v.i.* se tuméfier.
tumescent [tjuː'mesənt] *a.* tumescent.
tumid ['tjuːmid] *a.* **1.** *Med:* enflé, gonflé. **2.** *O:* (style, etc.) enflé.
tummy ['tʌmi] *n. F:* ventre *m*; **t. ache,** mal *m* de ventre; **to have t. trouble,** avoir l'estomac dérangé.
tumour, *NAm:* **tumor** ['tjuːmər] *n. Med:* tumeur *f.*
tumult ['tjuːmʌlt] *n.* **1.** tumulte *m*; fracas *m.* **2.** tumulte, agitation *f*, trouble *m*, émoi *m* (des passions).
tumultuous [tju'mʌltjuəs] *a.* tumultueux; **t. meeting,** réunion orageuse; **t. session,** séance mouvementée. **-ly** *adv.* tumultueusement.
tumulus, *pl.* **-i** ['tjuːmjuləs, -ai] *n.* tumulus *m.*
tun [tʌn] *n.* **1.** tonneau *m*, fût *m.* **2.** *Brew:* cuve *f.*
tuna ['t(j)uːnə] *n. Ich:* thon *m.*
tundra ['tʌndrə] *n. Geog:* toundra *f.*
tune¹ [tjuːn] *n.* **1.** air *m* (de musique); *F:* **give us a t.!** faites-nous un peu de musique! jouez-nous un air! *Fig:* **to call the t.,** donner la note; **to change one's t.,** changer de ton, de gamme, de note; **to be fined to the t. of £50,** avoir une amende de £50. **2.** (*a*) *Mus:* accord *m*; **the piano is in, out of, t.,** le piano est d'accord, désaccordé; **to get out of t.,** se désaccorder; (*of singer, player*) **to be out of t.,** détonner; **to sing in, out of, t.,** chanter juste, faux; (*b*) *I.C.E:* **in perfect t.,** (moteur) au point. **3.** accord, harmonie *f*; **to be in t. with s.o., with one's surroundings,** être en bon accord avec qn, avec son milieu.
tune² *v.tr. & i.* **1.** *Mus:* accorder, mettre d'accord (un instrument); (*of orchestra*) **to t. up,** s'accorder. **2.** *El: W.Tel: etc:* **to t. one circuit to another,** accorder un circuit sur un autre; *W.Tel: etc:* **to t. in to Paris,** capter, prendre, Paris. **3.** *I.C.E: Mch: etc:* **to t. (up),** caler, régler, (re)mettre au point (un moteur); (*of engine*) **to be tuned (up),** être au point. **tuning** *n.* **1.** *Mus:* accord *m* (d'un piano, d'un orgue, etc.); **fine t.,** accord précis; **t. fork,** diapason *m.* **2.** *I.C.E: Mch:* **t. (up),** calage *m*, réglage *m*; (re)mise *f* au point. **3.** *W.Tel: etc:* réglage de la tonalité, des tonalités; **t. in to a station,** accrochage *m* d'un poste; **t. dial,** cadran *m* d'accord.
tuneful ['tjuːnful] *a.* mélodieux, harmonieux. **-fully** *adv.* mélodieusement.
tunefulness ['tjuːnfulnis] *n.* qualité mélodieuse (d'un air, etc.).
tuneless ['tjuːnlis] *a.* discordant; sans mélodie.
tuner ['tjuːnər] *n.* **1.** (*pers.*) (*a*) *Mus:* accordeur *m* (de pianos, etc.); (*b*) *I.C.E: etc:* metteur *m* au point. **2.** (*device*) *W.Tel: etc:* syntonisateur *m*; tuner *m.*
tungsten ['tʌŋstən] *n. Ch:* tungstène *m.*

tunic ['tju:nik] *n.* tunique *f.*
Tunisia [tju:'niziə] *Pr.n. Geog:* Tunisie *f.*
Tunisian [tju:'niziən] **1.** *a.* tunisien. **2.** *n.* Tunisien, -ienne.
tunnel¹ ['tʌn(ə)l] *n.* **1.** (*a*) tunnel *m*; **to drive a t. through a mountain,** percer un tunnel à travers, sous, une montagne; *Mec: etc:* **wind t.,** tunnel aérodynamique; soufflerie *f*; (*b*) *Nat.Hist:* galerie (creusée par une taupe, etc.); (*c*) **t. vision,** rétrécissement *m* du champ visuel. **2.** *Fish:* **t. net,** verveux *m.*
tunnel² *v.tr. & i.* (**tunnelled,** *NAm:* **tunneled** ['tʌnld]) **to t. through, into, a hill,** percer un tunnel à travers, dans, sous, une colline; **rats had tunnelled under the foundations,** les rats avaient creusé des galeries sous les fondements. **tunnelling,** *NAm:* **tunneling** *n.* percement *m* d'un tunnel, de tunnels.
tunny ['tʌni] *n. Ich:* **t. (fish),** thon *m.*
tuppence ['tʌp(ə)ns] *n. F: O:* = TWOPENCE.
tuppenny ['tʌp(ə)ni] *a. F: O:* = TWOPENNY; **t. halfpenny** = TWOPENNY-HALFPENNY.
turban ['tə:bən] *n. Cost:* turban *m.*
turbid ['tə:bid] *a.* **1.** (liquide) trouble, bourbeux. **2.** (esprit) trouble, brouillon.
turbidity [tə:'biditi] *n.* turbidité *f.*
turbine ['tə:bain] *n.* turbine *f*; **gas, steam, t.,** turbine à gaz, à vapeur; **t. engine,** turbomoteur *m.*
turbo-electric [tə:boui'lektrik] *a.* turbo-électrique.
turbofan ['tə:boufæn] *n. Av:* turboréacteur *m* à double flux.
turbogenerator [tə:bou'dʒenəreitər] *n. El:* turbogénérateur *m*, turbogénératrice *f.*
turbojet ['tə:boudʒet] *a. & n. Av:* **t. (engine),** turboréacteur *m* (à simple flux); **t. (aircraft),** avion *m* à turboréacteur.
turboprop ['tə:bouprɔp] *a. & n. Av:* **t. (engine),** turbopropulseur *m*; **t. (aircraft),** avion *m* à turbopropulseur.
turbot ['tə:bət] *n. Ich:* turbot *m.*
turbulence ['tə:bjuləns] *n.* **1.** (*a*) turbulence *f*, agitation *f*; (*b*) indiscipline *f.* **2.** *Meteor: Av:* turbulence.
turbulent ['tə:bjulənt] *a.* **1.** turbulent, tumultueux; (*b*) insubordonné. **2.** *Meteor: Av:* turbulent, agité. **-ly** *adv.* d'une manière turbulente.
turd [tə:d] *n. P:* **1.** merde *f*, crotte *f.* **2.** (*pers.*) couillon, -onne.
tureen [tjuə'ri:n] *n.* **(soup) t.,** soupière *f.*
turf¹, *pl.* **turves, turfs** [tə:f, tə:vz, tə:fs] *n.* (*a*) (i) gazon *m*; (ii) motte *f* de gazon; (*b*) (*in Ireland*) tourbe *f*; **t. cutting,** extraction *f* de la tourbe; (*c*) *Rac:* **the t.,** le turf, les courses *fpl* de chevaux; **t. accountant,** bookmaker *m.*
turf² *v.tr.* **1.** gazonner (un terrain). **2.** *F:* **to t. s.o. out,** flanquer qn à la porte.
turgid ['tə:dʒid] *a.* **1.** turgide, enflé, gonflé. **2.** (style, etc.) boursouflé, ampoulé. **-ly** *adv.* avec emphase.
Turk [tə:k] *n.* (*a*) Turc, *f.* Turque; (*b*) *F:* tyran *m*; **he's a young T.,** c'est un petit démon.
Turkey¹ ['tə:ki] *Pr.n. Geog:* Turquie *f.*
turkey² *n.* (*a*) *Orn:* **t. (cock),** dindon *m*; **hen t.,** dinde *f*; (*b*) *Orn:* **t. buzzard,** vautour *m* aura; (*c*) *Cu:* dinde, dindonneau *m*; *F:* **to talk t.,** parler franchement; en venir aux faits, *P:* **cold t.,** manque *m* de drogues.
Turkish ['tə:kiʃ] **1.** *a.* turc, *f.* turque; (bain) turc; *Hist:* **the T. Empire,** l'Empire *m* ottoman, du Croissant; **T. delight,** rahat-lo(u)koum *m*; **T. towel,** serviette *f* éponge. **2.** *n. Ling:* turc *m.*
turmeric ['tə:mərik] *n. Bot: Dy: etc:* curcuma *m.*
turmoil ['tə:mɔil] *n.* (*a*) trouble *m*, tumulte *m*, agitation *f*; **the whole town is in a t.,** toute la ville est agitée, est en ébullition; (*b*) remous *m* (des eaux); tourbillon *m.*
turn¹ [tə:n] *n.* **1.** tour *m*, révolution *f* (d'une roue); **with a t. of the wrist,** avec un tour de poignet; *Fig:* **to give another t. to the screw,** serrer la vis (à qn); **the meat is done to a t.,** la viande est cuite à point. **2.** (*a*) changement *m* de direction; virage *m*; *Aut:* **sharp t.,** virage à la corde; **no right, left, t.,** défense de tourner à droite, à gauche; **U turn,** demi-tour *m*; **three-point t.,** demi-tour *m* en trois manœuvres; *Ski:* **kick t.,** virage en plaine; conversion *f*; **at every t.,** à tout bout de champ; (*b*) tournure *f* (des affaires); **to take a tragic t.,** tourner au tragique; **the patient has taken a t. for the better, the worse,** l'état du malade s'est amélioré, a empiré; (*c*) **t. of the tide,** étale *m*; changement, renversement *m*, de la marée; **the milk is on the t.,** le lait est en train de tourner; **at the t. of the century,** au tournant du siècle; (*d*) *Fin:* **jobbers' t.,** écart *m* entre le prix d'achat et celui de vente; (*e*) *F:* choc *m*, coup *m*; **it gave me quite a t.,** ça m'a donné un (vrai) coup; **you gave me such a t.!** vous m'avez donné une belle peur! (*f*) *F:* **she had one of her turns,** elle a eu une de ses crises, de ses attaques. **3.** tour, petite promenade; **to take a t. in the garden,** faire un tour, vingt pas, dans le jardin. **4.** (*a*) tour (de rôle); **it's your t.,** c'est votre tour; c'est à vous (de jouer); **each in (his) t., t. and t. about,** chacun (à) son tour; **in t.,** tour à tour; à tour de rôle; **to speak out of (one's) t.,** parler mal à propos; **to take turns with s.o.,** relayer qn; **they take it in turns to drive,** ils se relaient au volant; (*b*) *Th:* numéro *m* (de music-hall, etc.). **5.** (*a*) **to do s.o. a good t.,** rendre (un) service à qn; **to do s.o. a bad t.,** jouer un mauvais tour à qn; *Prov:* **one good t. deserves another,** à beau jeu beau retour; un service en vaut un autre; (*b*) intention *f*, but *m*; **it will serve my t.,** cela fera mon affaire (pour le moment). **6.** (*a*) disposition *f*; **humorous t. of mind,** esprit *m* humoristique; (*b*) forme *f*; **t. of phrase,** tournure de phrase; (*c*) **to have a good t. of speed,** (i) (*of car*) être rapide; (ii) (*of horse*) être capable de fournir un effort à grande allure. **7.** (*a*) tournant *m*, coude *m* (d'un chemin, etc.); **(sharp) t.,** virage; **twists and turns,** tours et détours *mpl*; (*b*) tour (d'une corde); tour, spire *f* (d'une spirale).
turn² **I.** *v.tr.* **1.** (faire) tourner (une roue, une manivelle); (faire) tourner, faire jouer (une clef dans la serrure); (*with passive force*) **it won't t.,** ça ne marche pas, ne tourne pas; **to t. the knife in the wound,** retourner le fer dans la plaie; **to t. the gas low,** mettre le gaz en veilleuse. **2.** tourner (une page, etc.); retourner (un matelas, le foin, etc.); **to t. a garment inside out,** retourner un vêtement; **to t. everything upside down,** mettre tout sens dessus-dessous; **he turned the body over,** il a retourné le corps; *F:* **he didn't t. a hair,** il n'a pas bronché, sourcillé; **onions t. my stomach,** les oignons m'écœurent, me soulèvent le cœur. **3. he turned his steps towards home,** il a dirigé ses pas vers la maison; **he never turned anyone from his door,** il n'a jamais renvoyé personne (de sa porte); **to t. aside a blow,** détourner, faire dévier, un coup; **to t. the conversation,** donner un autre tour à la conversation; **to t. one's thoughts to God,** tourner ses pensées vers Dieu. **4.** tourner, retourner (la tête); tourner, diriger (les yeux) (vers qch.); **t. your face this way,** tournez-vous de ce côté; regardez de ce côté. **5. they turned the laughter, his argument, against him,** ils ont retourné les rires, son argument, contre lui; **he turns everyone against him,** il se met tout le monde à dos. **6.** (*a*) **to t. the corner,** (i) tourner le coin; *Fig:* passer le moment critique; (*b*) **he's turned forty,** il a quarante ans passés; il a passé la quarantaine; **it's turned seven,** il est sept heures passées. **7.** (*a*) changer, convertir, transformer **(into,** en); **to t. the water into wine,** changer l'eau en vin; **his love turned to hate,** son amour s'est changé, s'est

transformé, en haine; **to t. a theatre into a cinema,** convertir un théâtre en cinéma; (*b*) faire devenir; rendre; **the heat has turned the milk sour,** la chaleur a fait tourner le lait; **autumn turns the leaves yellow,** l'automne *m* fait jaunir les feuilles; (*c*) **success has turned his head,** le succès lui a tourné la tête. **8.** (*a*) tourner, façonner au tour (un pied de table, etc.); **well turned sentence,** phrase bien tournée; (*b*) *Knit:* **to t. a heel,** faire le talon. **II.** *v.i.* **1.** (*a*) tourner; **the wheel turns,** la roue tourne; **to t. a complete circle,** virer un cercle complet; **my head's turning,** la tête me tourne; (*b*) **everything turns on your answer,** tout dépend de votre réponse. **2.** (*a*) **to toss and t.,** se tourner et se retourner (dans son lit); (*b*) (*of edge of tool*) **to t. (up, over),** se rebrousser; (*c*) **to t. upside down,** se retourner. **3.** se tourner, se retourner; **he turned to look at the landscape,** il s'est retourné pour regarder le paysage; *Mil:* **right t.! left t.!** à droite! à gauche! **4.** (*a*) tourner, se diriger; **the path turns to the left,** le chemin tourne à gauche; **he turned to the left,** il a tourné à gauche; **he turned towards home,** il s'est dirigé vers la maison; **the wind is turning,** le vent change; (*b*) se diriger (vers qch.); s'adresser (à qn); **my thoughts often t. to this subject,** mes réflexions se portent souvent sur ce sujet; **to t. to another subject,** passer à une autre question; **to t. to the dictionary,** consulter le dictionnaire; **I don't know where, which way, to t.,** je ne sais pas de quel côté (me) tourner, où donner de la tête; **I didn't know to whom to t.,** je ne savais pas à qui m'adresser. **5.** (*a*) **the tide is turning,** la marée change; **his luck has turned,** sa chance a tourné; (*b*) **to t. against s.o.,** se retourner contre qn. **6.** (*a*) se changer, se convertir, se transformer (**into,** en); **caterpillars t. into butterflies,** la chenille se transforme en papillon; **it is turning to rain,** le temps se met à la pluie; **everything he touches turns to gold,** tout ce qu'il touche se change en or; (*b*) **to t. acid,** tourner au vinaigre; (*of milk*) **to t. (sour),** tourner; **it's turning cold,** le temps tourne au froid, il commence à faire froid; **the leaves are beginning to t.,** les feuilles *fpl* commencent à jaunir; **he turned red,** il a rougi; *Ch:* **to t. red, blue,** virer au rouge, au bleu; (*c*) **to t. sulky,** devenir maussade; **to t. socialist,** devenir socialiste. **turn around** *v.tr. & i. esp. NAm:* = TURN ROUND. **turn away 1.** *v.tr.* (*a*) détourner (la tête, les yeux, etc.); (*b*) détourner, écarter; (*c*) renvoyer (qn); *Th: etc:* **to t. people away,** refuser du monde. **2.** *v.i.* se détourner; **to t. away from s.o.,** (i) tourner le dos à qn; (ii) délaisser, abandonner, qn. **turn back 1.** *v.tr.* (*a*) faire faire demi-tour à (qn); faire revenir (qn) sur ses pas; (*b*) rabattre (son col, etc.). **2.** *v.i.* rebrousser chemin; se retourner; faire demi-tour. **turn down** *v.tr.* (*a*) rabattre (un col); plier, corner (la page d'un livre); **to t. down the bed,** faire la couverture; ouvrir le lit; (*b*) *Cards:* renverser (une carte) (face à la table); (*c*) baisser (le gaz, la radio, etc.); (*d*) repousser (une offre); refuser (un candidat, etc.); écarter (une réclamation); *F:* **she turned me down flat,** elle m'a refusé catégoriquement. **turned** *a.* **1. (lathe, machine) t.,** façonné, fait, au tour; **t. work,** tournage *m.* **2.** (*a*) retourné; *Typ:* **t. letter,** caractère retourné; blocage *m*; (*b*) (*of collar, etc.*) **t. down,** rabattu; (*c*) **t. in,** rentré; (*d*) **t. up,** (col, etc.) relevé; (nez) retroussé. **turn in 1.** *v.tr.* (*a*) **to t. in one's toes,** tourner les pieds en dedans; (*b*) *F:* rendre, rapporter (qch.); (*c*) *F:* quitter, abandonner (son emploi); (*d*) *F: esp. U.S:* livrer, vendre (qn) à la police; (*e*) *Sp: Th: etc:* **to t. in a good score, performance, etc.,** bien réussir. **2.** *v.i.* (*a*) **his toes t. in,** il a les pieds tournés en dedans; (*b*) **he turned in at the gate,** arrivé à la porte, il est entré; (*c*) *F:* se coucher, se pieuter. **turning** *n.* **1.** (*a*) mouvement *m* giratoire, rotatoire; rotation *f*, giration *f*; *Aut: etc:* **t. circle,** rayon *m* de braquage; (*b*) changement *m* de direction; virage *m*; *Fig:* **t. point,** point décisif; moment *m* critique; **at the t. point of his career,** au tournant de sa carrière; (*c*) retournage *m* (de la terre, d'un vêtement, etc.). **2.** (*a*) tournage *m*; travail *m* au tour; (*b*) **turnings,** tournures *fpl*, copeaux *mpl* de tour. **3.** (*a*) tournant *m* (d'une route); coude *m*; virage; (*b*) **the first t. to the right,** la première route, rue, à droite. **turn off 1.** *v.tr.* (*a*) fermer, couper (l'eau, le gaz); éteindre (le gaz, l'électricité); fermer (un robinet, la radio, etc.); (*b*) *P:* **he turns me off,** il me dégoûte. **2.** *v.i.* (*a*) changer de route; tourner (à droite, à gauche); **I turned off to the left,** j'ai pris (la route) à gauche; j'ai tourné à gauche; (*b*) **we turned off the main road,** nous avons quitté la grande route; **a small street turning off the High Street,** une petite rue qui fait coin, fait angle, avec la Grande Rue. **turn on 1.** *v.tr.* (*a*) ouvrir, faire couler (l'eau); ouvrir (le robinet, la radio, etc.); allumer, ouvrir (le gaz); allumer (l'électricité); **shall I t. on the light?** voulez-vous que j'allume? (*b*) **to t. s.o. on,** (i) *F:* éveiller l'intérêt, la curiosité, de qn; (ii) *P:* exciter qn (sexuellement). **2.** *v.i.* **to t. on s.o.,** attaquer qn; se retourner contre qn; s'en prendre à qn. **turn out 1.** *v.tr.* (*a*) mettre, *F:* flanquer (qn) à la porte; déloger, évincer (un locataire); (*b*) mettre (le bétail) au vert; (*c*) *Nau:* réveiller (les hommes); *Mil:* alerter (les troupes); (*d*) vider, retourner (ses poches, etc.); **to t. out a drawer,** (i) vider, (ii) mettre de l'ordre dans un tiroir; **to t. out a room,** nettoyer une pièce à fond; (*e*) *Cu:* démouler (une crème, etc.); (*f*) couper, éteindre (le gaz, l'électricité); (*g*) produire, fabriquer (des marchandises); **turned out by the dozen,** confectionnés à la douzaine; (*h*) (*of pers.*) **well turned out,** élégant, soigné; (*i*) **to t. one's toes out,** tourner les pieds en dehors. **2.** *v.i.* (*a*) sortir; **the whole town turned out to see it,** toute la ville est sortie pour le voir, le regarder; (*b*) *F:* se lever, sortir du lit; (*c*) **his toes t. out,** il a les pieds tournés en dehors; (*d*) **to t. out well, badly,** bien, mal, tourner; réussir, mal réussir; **it will t. out all right,** cela s'arrangera; **I don't know how it will t. out,** je ne sais pas comment cela finira; **as it turned out,** comme il est arrivé; en l'occurrence; **she's turned out (to be) beautiful,** elle est devenue belle; (*e*) **he turned out to be the son of an old friend of mine,** il s'est trouvé qu'il était le fils d'un de mes anciens amis; **it turns out that . . .,** il se trouve que . . .. **turn over 1.** *v.tr.* (*a*) retourner (qch.); tourner (une page); **to t. over the pages of a book,** feuilleter un livre; **please t. over,** tournez s'il vous plaît; *Agr:* **to t. over the soil,** retourner le sol; **to t. (sth.) over in one's mind,** ruminer (une idée); délibérer (une question); retourner (un projet) dans sa tête; (*b*) **to t. sth. over to s.o.,** remettre qch. entre les mains de qn; **the thief was turned over to the police,** on a remis le voleur entre les mains de la police. **2.** *v.i.* se tourner, se retourner; (*of car, etc.*) **to t. right over,** capoter; faire panache. **turn round 1.** *v.tr.* retourner (qch., qn). **2.** *v.i.* (*a*) tourner; (*of crane, etc.*) virer, pivoter; (*b*) tourner, se retourner; faire volte-face; (*in one's opinions, etc.*) tourner casaque, virer de bord; **t. round and let me see your face,** tournez-vous (un peu) que je voie votre visage; (*c*) **to t. round on s.o.,** se retourner contre qn; s'en prendre à qn. **turn up 1.** *v.tr.* (*a*) relever (le col de son pardessus); retrousser (ses manches); *F:* **to t. up one's nose at sth.,** renifler sur qch.; (*b*) retourner (le sol, une carte); déterrer (qch.); (*c*) trouver, se reporter à (une citation, etc.); (*d*) *F:* **it turns me up!** ça m'écœure! *P:* **t. it up!** arrête! j'en ai marre! (*e*) remonter (une mèche, une lampe); monter (le gaz); **to t. up the radio,** mettre la radio plus fort. **2.** *v.i.* (*a*) se relever, se replier; (*of edge of tool*) se rebrousser; **his**

nose turns up, il a le nez retroussé; (*b*) **the ten of diamonds turned up,** le dix de carreau est sorti; (*c*) arriver, se présenter (à l'improviste); **he turned up ten minutes late,** il est arrivé, s'est amené, dix minutes en retard; **he'll t. up one of these days,** il reparaîtra un de ces jours; **something is sure to t. up,** il se présentera sûrement une occasion; **until something better turns up,** en attendant mieux.
turnabout ['tə:nəbaut] *n.* retournement *m*; revirement *m*; volte-face *f inv.*
turnaround ['tə:nəraund] *n. esp. NAm:* (*a*) retournement *m*; revirement *m*; (*b*) *Trans:* rotation *f* (d'un navire, d'un avion, etc.).
turncoat ['tə:nkout] *n. Pol: etc:* renégat *m.*
turndown ['tə:ndaun] *a.* (col, etc.) rabattu.
turner ['tə:nər] *n. Ind:* tourneur *m.*
turnery ['tə:nəri] *n.* atelier *m* de tourneur.
turnip ['tə:nip] *n. Hort:* navet *m.*
turnkey ['tə:nki(:)] *n.* geôlier, -ière.
turnoff ['tə:nɔf] *n.* sortie *f* (d'autoroute, etc.).
turn-off *n. F:* **it's a right t.-o.!** c'est vraiment dégoûtant!
turnout ['tə:naut] *n.* **1.** concours *m*, assemblée *f* (de gens); **there was a large t. at his funeral,** il y avait foule à son enterrement. **2.** nettoyage *m* à fond (d'une pièce, etc.). **3.** *Ind:* production *f*, rendement *m.*
turnover ['tə:nouvər] *n.* **1.** *Com:* (*a*) chiffre *m* d'affaires; (*b*) écoulement *m*, rotation *f* (des marchandises); **t. of staff,** changement *m* de personnel. **2.** *Cu:* **apple t.,** chausson *m* aux pommes.
turnpike ['tə:npaik] *n.* (*a*) *Hist:* barrière *f* de péage; (*b*) *U.S:* autoroute *f* (à péage).
turnstile ['tə:nstail] *n.* tourniquet(-compteur) *m* (pour entrées); moulinet *m.*
turntable ['tə:nteibl] *n.* **1.** (*a*) *Rail:* plaque tournante; (*b*) *Artil:* plate-forme tournante. **2.** *Rec:* platine *f* (de tourne-disques).
turn(-)up ['tə:nʌp] *n.* (*a*) revers *m* (de pantalon); (*b*) *Cards:* retourne *f*; *F:* **what a t. (for the book)!** ça c'est une sacrée surprise!
turpentine ['tə:p(ə)ntain] *n.* (*a*) térébenthine *f*; (*b*) *Tchn:* **(oil of) t.,** essence *f* de térébenthine.
turpitude ['tə:pitju:d] *n.* turpitude *f.*
turps [tə:ps] *n. F:* essence *f* de térébenthine; **t. substitute,** white-spirit *m.*
turquoise ['tə:kwɔiz, -kwɑ:z] *n.* **1.** *Lap:* turquoise *f.* **2.** *a. & n.* **t. (blue),** turquoise (*m*) *inv.*
turret ['tʌrit] *n.* **1.** *Arch:* tourelle *f.* **2.** *Mil: Navy:* **(gun) t.,** tourelle (de pièce d'artillerie, de mitrailleuse). **3.** *Mec.E:* tourelle.
turreted ['tʌritid] *a. Arch:* (château) à tourelles.
turtle ['tə:tl] *n.* **1.** (*a*) tortue *f* de mer; **t. soup,** consommé *m* à la tortue; *F:* **to turn t.,** *Nau:* chavirer; (*of motor car, etc.*) capoter; faire panache; (*b*) *Cost:* **t. neck,** col (i) montant, (ii) *NAm:* roulé; **t.-necked sweater,** chandail *m* à col (i) montant, (ii) *NAm:* roulé. **2.** *Orn:* **t. dove,** tourterelle *f* des bois; *F:* **a pair of t. doves,** un couple d'amoureux, de tourtereaux.
Tuscan ['tʌskən]. **1.** *a. Geog: Arch:* toscan. **2.** *n.* (*a*) *Geog:* Toscan, -ane; (*b*) *Ling:* toscan *m.*
Tuscany ['tʌskəni] *Pr.n. Geog:* Toscane *f.*
tush [tʌʃ] *int. O:* bah! taratata!
tusk [tʌsk] *n.* défense *f* (de sanglier, d'éléphant, etc.).
tussle¹ ['tʌsl] *n.* lutte *f*, mêlée *f*, corps-à-corps *m*; **to have a t.,** en venir aux mains (**with s.o.,** avec qn).
tussle² *v.i.* **to t. with s.o.,** lutter avec qn; **to t. over sth.,** se disputer qch.
tussock ['tʌsək] *n.* touffe *f* d'herbe.
tut¹ [tʌt] *int.* **t. (tut)!** allons donc!
tut² *v.i.* **to t. (tut) at sth.,** faire un bruit désapprobateur, une exclamation désapprobatrice.
tutelage ['tju:tilidʒ] *n.* (*a*) tutelle *f*; **child in t.,** enfant en tutelle; (*b*) (période *f* de) tutelle.
tutelar, tutelary ['tju:tilər, -ləri] *a.* tutélaire.
tutor¹ ['tju:tər] *n.* **1.** *Sch:* (*a*) directeur, -trice, des études (d'un groupe d'étudiants); (*b*) **private t.,** précepteur *m.* **2.** *Jur:* tuteur, -trice (d'un mineur, etc.).
tutor² *v.tr.* instruire (qn); **to t. a boy in Latin,** donner à un élève des leçons particulières de latin.
tutorial [tju(:)'tɔ:riəl] *a.* **1.** (*a*) (cours, etc.) d'instructions; (*b*) (fonctions, etc.) de répétiteur, de préparateur. **2.** *n. Sch:* cours (individuel) fait par le directeur d'études.
tutti-frutti ['tuti'fruti] *n. Comest:* plombières *f.*
tutu ['tu:tu:] *n. Cost:* tutu *m.*
tu-whit, tu-whoo [tu'wittu'wu:] *int.* hou hou!
tux [tʌks] *n. NAm: F:* = TUXEDO.
tuxedo [tʌk'si:dou] *n. NAm: Cost:* smoking *m.*
twaddle¹ ['twɔdl] *n. F:* fadaises *fpl*; futilités *fpl*; **to talk t.,** dire, débiter, des balivernes, des sottises.
twaddle² *v.i. F:* dire, conter, des balivernes.
twain [twein] *a. & n. Lit:* deux; **in t.,** en deux.
twang¹ [twæŋ] *n.* **1.** bruit sec (de la corde d'un arc); son aigu (d'une guitare). **2. nasal t.,** ton nasillard; nasillement *m*; **to speak with a t.,** nasiller; parler d'une voix nasillarde.
twang² **1.** *v.tr.* (*a*) lâcher (la corde de l'arc tendu); (*b*) faire résonner (les cordes d'une harpe); **to t. a guitar,** *v.i.* **to t. on a guitar,** pincer de la guitare. **2.** *v.i.* (*a*) (*of string, etc.*) résonner; (*b*) (*of pers.*) nasiller.
tweak¹ [twi:k] *n.* pinçon *m*; **he gave her nose a t.,** il lui a doucement tordu le nez.
tweak² *v.tr.* pincer; serrer entre les doigts (en tordant); **to t. a boy's ear,** tirer l'oreille à un gamin.
twee [twi:] *a. F: Pej:* gentillet, mignard.
tweed [twi:d] *n.* **1.** *Tex:* tweed *m*; cheviote écossaise. **2. tweeds,** complet *m*, costume *m*, de tweed.
tweedy ['twi:di] *a. F:* **1.** (tissu) qui tient du tweed. **2.** *Pej:* (*of pers.*) qui affecte la tenue d'un propriétaire rural.
'tween [twi:n] **1.** *adv. & prep. A: & Lit:* entre. **2.** *Nau:* **'t.-decks,** (i) *n.* le faux-pont, l'entrepont *m*; (ii) *adv.* dans l'entrepont.
tweet¹ [twi:t] *n.* pépiement *m*, gazouillement *m* (d'un oiseau).
tweet² *v.i.* (*of bird*) pépier, gazouiller.
tweeter ['twi:tər] *n. W.Tel:* haut-parleur aigu; tweeter *m.*
tweezers ['twi:zəz] *n.pl.* brucelles *fpl*; (*for hairs*) pince *f* à épiler; épiloir *m.*
twelfth [twelfθ] **1.** *num.a. & n.* douzième (*mf*); **Louis the T.,** Louis Douze; **T. Night,** le jour des Rois. **2.** *n.* (*fractional*) douzième *m.*
twelve [twelv] *num.a. & n.* douze (*m*); **t. o'clock,** (i) (*midday*) midi *m*; (ii) (*midnight*) minuit *m.*
twelvemonth ['twelvmʌnθ] *n. O:* année *f*; **this day t.,** (i) d'aujourd'hui en un an; (ii) il y a un an aujourd'hui.
twelve-tone ['twelvtoun] *a. Mus:* dodécaphonique; **t.-tone system,** dodécaphonisme *m.*
twentieth ['twentiiθ] **1.** *num.a. & n.* vingtième (*mf*); **(on) the t. of June,** le vingt juin. **2.** *n.* (*fractional*) vingtième *m.*
twenty ['twenti] *num.a. & n.* vingt (*m*); **t.-one,** vingt et un; **t.-two,** vingt-deux; **about t. people,** quelque vingt personnes; une vingtaine de personnes; **the twenties,** les années vingt (1920–1929).
twerp [twə:p] *n. P:* andouille *f*; pauvre type *m.*
twice [twais] *adv.* deux fois; **t. as big as sth.,** deux fois plus grand que qch.; **t. as slow,** deux fois plus lent; **t. over,** à deux reprises; **to think t. before doing sth.,** y regarder à deux fois avant de faire qch.; **he didn't have to think t. before accepting,** il a accepté sans hésiter; **he did not have to be asked t.,** il ne se fit pas prier.

twiddle¹ ['twidl] *n.* **to give sth. a t.,** tourner, faire tournoyer, qch.
twiddle² *v.tr. & i.* **to t. (with) sth.,** jouer avec, tripoter, qch.; **to t. one's thumbs,** se tourner les pouces.
twig¹ [twig] *n.* **1.** brindille *f* (de branche); ramille *f.* **2. (dowser's hazel) t.,** baguette *f* (divinatoire).
twig² *v.tr.* **(twigged)** *O:* comprendre, saisir; piger; **I soon twigged his little game,** j'ai bien vu dans son jeu.
twilight ['twailait] *n.* **1.** crépuscule *m*, demi-jour *m*; **in the (evening) t.,** au crépuscule, entre chien et loup, à la brune; **in the t. of life,** dans le crépuscule de la vie. **2.** *attrib.* crépusculaire.
twill [twil] *n. Tex:* (tissu) croisé (*m*), sergé (*m*).
twin¹ [twin] *a. & n.* **1.** jumeau, -elle; **t. brother, t. sister,** frère jumeau, sœur jumelle; *Astr:* **the Twins,** les Gémeaux *mpl.* **2.** *a.* (*a*) *Med:* **t. birth,** accouchement *m* de jumeaux; (*b*) jumeau, jumelé; **t. beds,** lits jumeaux; **t. columns,** colonnes géminées; **t. towns,** villes jumelées; **t.-engine(d) aircraft,** avion bimoteur; (*c*) *Cost:* **t. set,** twin-set *m.*
twin² *v.* **(twinned) 1.** *v.tr.* jumeler (des villes). **2.** *v.i.* **to t. with sth.,** s'apparier à qch. **twinning** *n.* jumelage *m* (de deux villes, etc.).
twine¹ [twain] *n.* **1.** ficelle *f*, fil retors. **2.** entrelacement *m*, enchevêtrement *m.*
twine² **1.** *v.tr.* tordre, tortiller (des fils); entrelacer (une guirlande, les doigts, etc.); **to t. sth. about, round, sth.,** (en)rouler qch. autour de qch.; **she twined her arms round me,** elle m'a entouré de ses bras. **2.** *v.i.* (*a*) se tordre, se tortiller; **to t. round sth.,** s'enrouler, s'enlacer, autour de qch.; (*b*) (*of road, etc.*) serpenter. **twining** *a.* (*a*) *Bot:* (plante, tige) volubile; (*b*) (sentier, etc.) sinueux.
twinge [twin(d)ʒ] *n.* (*a*) élancement *m* (de douleur); légère atteinte (de goutte, etc.); (*b*) **t. of conscience,** remords *m* (de conscience).
twinkle¹ ['twiŋkl] *n.* **1.** scintillement *m*, clignotement *m* (des étoiles, de feux lointains). **2.** clignement *m* (des paupières); pétillement *m* (du regard); **a mischievous t. in the eye,** un éclair de malice dans les yeux; **in a t.,** en un clin d'œil.
twinkle² **1.** *v.i.* (*a*) (*of light, star*) scintiller, étinceler, clignoter; (*of object in motion*) papillonner; (*b*) **his eyes twinkled (with amusement, mischief),** ses yeux pétillaient (d'envie de rire, de malice). **2.** *v.tr.* **to t. one's eyes,** clignoter des yeux. **twinkling 1.** *a.* (*of star, etc.*) scintillant, étincelant, clignotant; **t. eyes,** yeux pétillants d'envie de rire, de malice. **2.** *n.* scintillement *m*, étincellement *m*, clignotement *m*; **in the t. of an eye,** en un clin d'œil.
twirl¹ [twəːl] *n.* **1.** tournoiement *m*; (*of dancer, etc.*) pirouette *f.* **2.** volute *f* (de fumée, etc.); *Arch:* enroulement *m*, volute; *Conch:* spire *f*; (*in writing*) enjolivure *f* en spirale; fioriture *f.*
twirl² **1.** *v.tr.* (*a*) faire tournoyer; faire des moulinets avec (une canne, etc.); (*b*) tortiller (sa moustache); **to t. one's thumbs,** se tourner les pouces. **2.** *v.i.* tournoyer; (*of dancer*) pirouetter.
twist¹ [twist] *n.* **1.** (*a*) fil retors; retors *m*, cordon *m*, cordonnet *m*; (*b*) torsade *f*, tortillon *m* (de cheveux); écheveau *m* (de laine); tortillon, cornet *m* (de papier); **sweet in a t. of paper,** bonbon *m* dans une papillote; (*c*) **t. (tobacco),** tabac mis en corde; **t. of tobacco,** rouleau *m*, boudin *m*, de tabac. **2.** (*a*) (effort *m* de) torsion *f*; **to give one's ankle a t.,** se fouler la cheville, se donner une entorse; (*b*) tors *m*, torsion (des brins d'un cordage); (*c*) *Sp:* effet (donné à une balle); **with a t. of the wrist,** avec un tour de poignet; (*d*) contorsion *f* (des traits, du visage); (*e*) *Danc:* twist *m.* **3.** (*a*) spire *f*; **t. of rope round a post,** tour de corde autour d'un poteau; (*b*) tournant *m*, coude *m* (d'une rue, etc.); **road full of twists and turns,** chemin plein de tours et de détours; **final t. in a story,** tour inattendu à la fin d'un récit; (*c*) *F:* **to be round the t.,** être fou, cinglé. **4.** (*a*) gauchissement *m* (d'une pièce de bois); déformation *f*; (*b*) perversion *f* (du sens d'un texte); (*c*) perversion (d'esprit); **to have a t. in one's character,** avoir l'esprit faussé.
twist² **1.** *v.tr.* (*a*) tordre, tortiller (ses cheveux, un cordage, etc.); tirebouchonner (son mouchoir); *Tex: etc:* retordre (le fil); **to t. together,** torsader; câbler (des fils métalliques); **to t. sth. round sth.,** rouler, entortiller, qch. autour de qch.; *F:* **she can t. him round her little finger,** elle le mène par le bout du nez; (*b*) se tordre (le bras, etc.); se déboîter (le genou); **to t. one's ankle,** se donner une entorse; se fouler la cheville; **to t. s.o.'s arm,** (i) tordre, retourner, le bras à qn; (ii) *Fig:* exercer une pression sur qn; (*c*) dénaturer (les paroles de qn, le sens d'un texte); altérer (la vérité, le sens de qch.); (*d*) donner de l'effet à (une balle). **2.** *v.i.* (*a*) (*of worm, etc.*) se tordre; se tortiller; (*b*) former une spirale; (*of smoke*) former des volutes; (*c*) **to get all twisted (up),** s'entortiller; (*d*) (*of road, etc.*) tourner; faire des détours; **to t. and turn,** serpenter; (*e*) **to t. round in one's seat,** se tourner sur son siège; (*f*) *Danc:* twister. **twisted** *a.* **1.** tordu, tors; (fil, etc.) retors; *Arch:* **t. pillar,** colonne torse. **2.** (*distorted*) tordu; (*of tree*) tortueux; (*of limb*) contourné; **face t. with pain,** traits contractés, tordus, par la douleur. **3.** (*of meaning, etc.*) perverti, dénaturé, altéré; **t. mind,** esprit tordu, faussé. **twisting** *a.* (sentier) tortueux.
twister ['twistər] *n.* **1.** *F:* escroc *m.* **2.** *F: O:* question déconcertante; **that's a t. for you!** voilà qui vous donnera du fil à retordre! **3.** *NAm: F:* tornade *f.*
twisty ['twisti] *a.* **1.** tortueux. **2.** *F:* malhonnête.
twit¹ [twit] *n. P:* andouille *f*, imbécile *m.*
twit² *v.tr.* **(twitted)** narguer, taquiner (qn); **to t. s.o. with sth.,** railler qn de qch.
twitch¹ [twitʃ] *n.* **1.** saccade *f*; petit coup sec. **2.** élancement *m* (de douleur); **t. of conscience,** remords *m* de conscience. **3.** (*a*) contraction soudaine (du visage); crispation nerveuse (des mains); mouvement convulsif (d'un membre); (*b*) **facial t.,** tic (nerveux).
twitch² **1.** *v.tr.* (*a*) tirer vivement, donner une saccade à (qch.); (*b*) contracter (ses traits); crisper (les mains, le visage); (*of cat*) **to t. its tail,** faire de petits mouvements de la queue. **2.** *v.i.* (*of face*) se contracter nerveusement; (*of eyelids*) clignoter; (*of hands*) se crisper nerveusement.
twitter¹ ['twitər] *n.* **1.** gazouillement *m*, gazouillis *m.* **2.** *F:* (*of pers.*) **to be in a t.,** être tout en émoi, dans tous ses états.
twitter² *v.i.* (*of bird*) gazouiller. **twittering** *n.* gazouillement *m.*
'twixt [twikst] *prep. A: & Poet:* entre.
two [tuː] *num.a. & n.* deux (*m*); (*a*) **twenty-two,** vingt-deux; *Gym: etc:* **one t.! one t.!** une deux! une deux! **no t. men are alike,** il n'y a pas deux hommes qui se ressemblent; **to break, fold, sth. in t.,** casser, plier, qch. en deux; **to walk in twos, t. by t., t. and t.,** marcher deux à deux, (deux) par deux; *Fig:* **to put t. and t. together,** tirer ses conclusions (après avoir rapproché les faits); *F:* **that makes t. of us,** c'est aussi mon cas; et moi aussi; **t. fours, four twos, are eight,** deux fois quatre, quatre fois deux, font huit; **at t. (o'clock),** à deux heures; **a mother of t.,** la mère de deux enfants; *Cards:* **t. of spades,** deux de pique; *Mus:* **t.-four time,** mesure *f* à deux quatre; (*b*) **t.-yearly,** biennal; **t.-horse carriage,** voiture *f* à deux chevaux; *Mus:* **t. part song,** chanson *f* à deux voix; **t.-headed,** bicéphale; *Her:* (aigle) double, à deux têtes; *Aut:* **t.-door,** (voiture) à deux portes; **t.-wheeler,** deux-roues *m inv*; **t.-seater,** voiture, avion *m*, à deux places; biplace *m*; **t.-engine(d),** bimoteur; *El:* **t.-phase,** (courant) biphasé.

two-bit ['tu:bit] *a. NAm: F:* insignifiant.
two-colour ['tu:kʌlər] *a.* de deux couleurs; *Typewr:* (ruban) bicolore; *Typ:* **t.-c. process,** bichromie *f.*
two-edged ['tu:edʒd] *a.* (épée, argument) à deux tranchants, à double tranchant; ambigu.
two-faced ['tu:feist] *a.* (*of pers.*) hypocrite.
twofer ['tu:fər] *n. U.S:* deux billets, etc. vendus pour le prix d'un.
twofold ['tu:fould] **1.** *a.* double; (cordage) à deux brins. **2.** *adv.* doublement; **kindness returned t.,** bontés rendues au double.
two-handed [tu:'hændid] *a.* **1. t.-h. sword,** épée *f* à deux mains, espadon *m.* **2.** *Z: etc:* bimane. **3.** *Cards: etc:* (jeu) qui se joue à deux.
two-legged [tu:'legd, -'legid] *a.* bipède.
twopence ['tʌpəns] *n.* deux pence *m*; *F:* **it isn't worth t.,** ça ne vaut pas chipette, pas un sou.
twopenny ['tʌp(ə)ni] *a.* à, de, deux pence.
twopenny-halfpenny ['tʌp(ə)ni'heipni] *a. O:* **1. a t.-h. stamp,** un timbre de deux pence et demi. **2.** *F:* insignifiant; **all that fuss over a t.-h. ring!** tout ça pour une méchante bague de quatre sous!
two-piece ['tu:pi:s] *a. & n.* **t.-p. (suit, swimsuit),** complet *m*, tailleur *m*, maillot *m* de bain, en deux pièces; deux-pièces *m.*
two-ply ['tu:plai] *a.* (cordage) à deux brins; (laine) deux fils.
two-sided [tu:'saidid] *a.* **1.** (*of contract, etc.*) bilatéral. **2.** (*of question, argument, etc.*) qui comporte deux points de vue.
twosome ['tu:səm] *n.* jeu, partie, à deux joueurs; danse par couples; paire *f*, couple *m* (d'amis, etc.).
two-step ['tu:step] *n. Danc: Mus:* pas *m* de deux.
two-stroke ['tu:strouk] *a.* (moteur, cycle) à deux temps; **t.-s. mixture,** (mélange *m*) deux-temps *m.*
two-time ['tu:taim] *v.tr. NAm: F:* tromper (qn).
two-tone ['tu:toun] *a.* (*a*) (peinture, voiture) deux tons; (*b*) (klaxon, etc.) à deux notes.
two-way ['tu:wei] *a.* **1.** (rue) à double sens; (miroir) sans tain; *El:* (commutateur) à deux directions. **2.** *Telecom:* bilatérale; **t.-w. radio,** poste émetteur-récepteur; **t.-w. trade,** commerce *m* dans les deux sens.
tycoon [tai'ku:n] *n. F:* magnat *m*, grand manitou.
tyke [taik] *n. F:* **1.** vilain chien. **2. (dirty) t.,** salaud *m.* **3.** *NAm:* enfant *m*; môme *m.*
tympanum, *pl.* **-a, -ums** ['timpənəm, -ə, -əmz] *n. Anat: Arch: Hyd.E:* tympan *m.*
type¹ [taip] *n.* **1.** type *m*; (*a*) **people, books, of this t.,** des personnes, des livres, de ce genre; **people of every t.,** des gens de toutes sortes; *F:* **she's not my t.,** elle n'est pas mon genre; *Nat.Hist:* **t. genus,** genre type; (*b*) *F:* **the t. with the red beard,** le type, l'individu, à barbe rousse. **2.** *Typ:* (i) caractère *m*, type; (ii) *coll.* caractères; **to print in large t.,** imprimer en gros caractères; **in t.,** composé; **to distribute the t.,** distribuer le plomb; **t. face,** œil *m* (de caractère); (iii) (*with pl.* **types**) sorte *f* de caractère.
type² *v.tr.* **1.** être le type de, typer (qn, qch.). **2.** *Med:* déterminer le groupe (sanguin, etc.).
type³ *v.tr.* écrire à la machine; dactylographier; *F:* taper (une lettre, etc.) (à la machine); *v.i.* **he types well,** il tape bien. **typing** *n.* dactylographie *f*, *F:* dactylo *f*; **t. error,** faute *f* de frappe; **t. paper,** papier *m* machine; **t. pool,** pool *m* de dactylos.
typecast ['taipkɑ:st] *v.tr. Th: Cin:* (i) faire jouer à (un acteur) le rôle d'un personnage qui lui ressemble; (ii) donner toujours les mêmes rôles à (un acteur).
typescript ['taipskript] *n.* texte dactylographié.
typesetter ['taipsetər] *n.* (*pers.*) compositeur *m.*
typesetting ['taipsetiŋ] *n. Typ:* composition *f*; **t. machine,** machine *f* à composer.
typewriter ['taipraitər] *n.* machine *f* à écrire.
typewriting ['taipraitiŋ] *n.* dactylographie *f.*
typewritten ['taiprit(ə)n] *a.* (document, etc.) écrit, tapé, à la machine, dactylographié.
typhoid ['taifɔid] *a. Med:* typhoïde; (bacille) typhoïdique; **t. fever,** *n.* **t.,** (fièvre *f*) typhoïde *f.*
typhoon [tai'fu:n] *n. Meteor:* typhon *m.*
typhus ['taifəs] *n. Med:* typhus *m.*
typical ['tipik(ə)l] *a.* typique; **the t. Frenchman,** le Français typique; *F:* **isn't that t. (of him, her)!** c'est bien de lui, d'elle! **-ally** *adv.* typiquement; **he's t. French,** c'est le vrai type français.
typify ['tipifai] *v.tr.* **1.** (*of symbol, etc.*) représenter (qch.); symboliser (qch.). **2.** (*of specimen, etc.*) être caractéristique de (sa classe, etc.); (*of pers.*) être le type de, personnifier (l'officier, etc.).
typist ['taipist] *n.* **(copy) t.,** dactylographe *mf*, *F:* dactylo *mf*; **audio t.,** dactylo audio-magnéto; **typist's error,** faute *f* de frappe.
typographer [tai'pɔgrəfər] *n.* typographe *m.*
typographic(al) [taipə'græfik(l)] *a.* typographique. **-ally** *adv.* typographiquement.
typography [tai'pɔgrəfi] *n.* typographie *f.*
tyrannical [ti'rænik(ə)l] *a.* tyrannique. **-ally** *adv.* tyranniquement.
tyrannize ['tirənaiz] *v.i. & tr.* faire le tyran; **to t. (over) s.o.,** tyranniser qn.
tyranny ['tirəni] *n.* tyrannie *f.*
tyrant ['tairənt] *n.* tyran *m.*
tyre ['taiər] *n.* (*a*) (*usu.* **tire**) bandage *m*, cercle *m* (d'une roue de charrette, etc.); (*b*) (*NAm:* **tire**) *Aut: etc:* pneu *m*, *pl.* pneus; pneumatique *m*; **cross ply, radial ply, t.,** pneu à carcasse croisée, radiale; **t. lever,** démonte-pneu *m*, *pl.* démonte-pneus.
tyro ['tairou] *n.* novice *mf*; débutant, -ante.
Tyrol (the) [ðəti'roul] *Pr.n. Geog:* le Tyrol.
Tyrolean [tirə'li:ən] *a. Geog:* tyrolien; *Cost:* **T. hat,** chapeau tyrolien.
tzar [tsɑ:r] *n., etc.* = TSAR, *etc.*

U

U, u [juː] *n.* (la lettre) U, u *m*; *Geog:* **U-shaped valley,** vallée (à profil) en U; *F:* **U and non U,** ce qui est bien, comme il faut, et ce qui ne l'est pas; *Mec.E:* **U-bolt,** étrier *m*; *Aut:* **U turn,** demi-tour *m, pl.* demi-tours; *P.N:* **no U turns,** demi-tour interdit; *Cin:* **U film,** film *m* pour tout le monde; **U boat,** sous-marin allemand.
ubiquitous [juː'bikwitəs] *a.* doué d'ubiquité; qui se trouve, que l'on rencontre, partout; omniprésent.
ubiquity [juː'bikwiti] *n.* ubiquité *f*; omniprésence *f*.
udder ['ʌdər] *n.* mamelle *f*, pis *m* (de vache, etc.).
ufologist [juː'fɔlədʒist] *n.* ufologue *mf*.
Uganda [ju(ː)'gændə] *Pr.n. Geog:* Ouganda *m*.
Ugandan [ju(ː)'gændən] *Geog:* **1.** *a.* ougandais. **2.** *n.* Ougandais, -aise.
ugh [ʌχ, uː] *int.* pouah! beuh!
ugli *pl.* **ugli(e)s** ['ʌgli,-iz] *n.* tangelo *m*.
uglify ['ʌglifai] *v.tr.* enlaidir.
ugliness ['ʌglinis] *n.* laideur *f*.
ugly ['ʌgli] *a.* (*a*) (*of pers.*) laid; **she's as u. as sin,** elle est laide comme les sept péchés capitaux; **u. person,** laideron *m*; **to grow u.,** (s')enlaidir; **u. duckling,** vilain petit canard; *F:* **an u. customer,** un sale type; **to turn, cut up, u.,** se mettre en colère, en rogne; (*b*) (*of thg*) vilain; (incident, scène) regrettable; **u. piece of furniture,** vilain meuble; **u. wound,** vilaine blessure; **u. rumour,** bruit sinistre.
uh [əː] *int.* euh!
Ukraine [juː'krein] *Pr.n. Geog:* Ukraine *f*.
Ukrainian [juː'kreiniən] *Geog:* **1.** *a.* ukrainien. **2.** *n.* (*a*) Ukrainien, -ienne; (*b*) *Ling:* ukrainien *m*.
ukulele [juːkə'leili] *n. Mus:* guitare hawaïenne.
ulcer ['ʌlsər] *n.* ulcère *m*; **peptic u.,** ulcère simple de l'estomac, du duodénum.
ulcerate ['ʌlsəreit]. *Med:* **1.** *v.tr.* ulcérer; **ulcerated wound,** blessure ulcérée, ulcéreuse. **2.** *v.i.* s'ulcérer.
ulceration [ʌlsə'reiʃ(ə)n] *n.* ulcération *f*.
ulcerative ['ʌls(ə)rətiv] *a. Med:* ulcératif.
ulcerous ['ʌls(ə)rəs] *a. Med:* ulcéreux.
ullage ['ʌlidʒ] *n. Winem: etc:* creux *m* du tonneau.
ulna ['ʌlnə] *n. Anat:* cubitus *m*.
Ulster ['ʌlstər]. **1.** *Pr.n. Geog:* (i) Ulster *m*; (ii) Irlande *f* du Nord. **2.** *n. Cost:* **u.,** ulster *m*.
Ulsterman, *pl.* **-men** ['ʌlstəmən] *n.m.* Ulstérien.
Ulsterwoman, *pl.* **-women** ['ʌlstəwumən, -wimin] *n.f.* Ulstérienne.
ulterior [ʌl'tiəriər] *a.* **1.** ultérieur. **2.** secret; **u. designs,** desseins secrets; **u. motive,** motif secret, caché; **without u. motive,** sans arrière-pensée.
ultimate ['ʌltimət] **1.** *a.* (*a*) final, -als; **u. goal, end, purpose,** but final; **u. decision,** décision définitive; (*b*) **u. truth,** vérité fondamentale; (*c*) *Ling:* (*of syllable*) ultime, dernier. **2.** *n.* (*a*) **the u.,** l'absolu; (*b*) le fin du fin; **the u. in luxury,** le summum du luxe; **it's the u. in vulgarity,** c'est du dernier vulgaire. **-ly** *adv.* (*a*) à la fin; en fin de compte; finalement; (*b*) fondamentalement.
ultimatum, *pl.* **-tums, -ta** [ʌlti'meitəm, -təmz, -tə] *n.* ultimatum *m*; **to deliver an u. to s.o., to present s.o. with an u.,** adresser un ultimatum à qn.
ultimo ['ʌltimou] *adv. Com:* du mois dernier; **on the tenth u.,** le dix du mois dernier.
ultra ['ʌltrə] **1.** *a.* extrême. **2.** *n Pol:* ultra *mf*.
ultrahigh [ʌltrə'hai] *a. Ph:* **u. frequency,** très haute fréquence.
ultramarine [ʌltrəmə'riːn] *a. & n.* **u. (blue),** (bleu d')outremer (*m*).
ultramodern [ʌltrə'mɔd(ə)n] *a.* ultramoderne.
ultramontane [ʌltrə'mɔntein] *a. & n.* ultramontain, -aine.
ultrasensitive [ʌltrə'sensitiv] *a.* ultrasensible.
ultrashort [ʌltrə'ʃɔːt] *a. Ph:* ultra-court.
ultrasonic [ʌltrə'sɔnik] **1.** *a.* ultrasonique. **2.** *n.pl.* (*usu. with sg. const.*) **ultrasonics,** science *f* des ultrasons.
ultraviolet [ʌltrə'vaiələt] *a. Ph:* ultra(-)violet; **u. rays,** rayons ultra(-)violets; *Med:* **u. treatment,** traitement aux rayons ultra(-)violets.
ultra vires [ʌltrə'vaiəriːz, ultrə'viːreiz] *Lt.adj. & adv.phr. Jur:* au delà des pouvoirs.
ululate ['juːljuleit] *v.i.* (*of owl, etc.*) ululer, huer, (*of jackal, etc.*) hurler.
ululation [juːlju'leiʃ(ə)n] *n.* ululation *f*, ululement *m* (du hibou, etc.); hurlement *m* (du chacal, etc.).
Ulysses ['juːlisiːz, ju(ː)'lisiːz] *Pr.n.m.* Ulysse.
umber ['ʌmbər] **1.** *n. Art:* terre *f* d'ombre, de Sienne; ombre *f*; **burnt u.,** terre d'ombre brûlée. **2.** *a.* couleur *inv* d'ombre.
umbilical [ʌm'bilik(ə)l] *a. Anat:* ombilical, -aux; **u. cord,** cordon ombilical.
umbilicus [ʌm'bilikəs] *n.* ombilic *m*, nombril *m*.
umbrage ['ʌmbridʒ] *n.* (*a*) *A:* ombrage *m*, ressentiment *m*; (*b*) **to take u. at sth.,** prendre ombrage, se froisser, de qch.
umbrella [ʌm'brelə] *n.* **1.** (*a*) parapluie *m*; **to put up one's u.,** ouvrir son parapluie; **to put down, to fold (up), one's u.,** fermer, replier, son parapluie; **telescopic u.,** parapluie télescopique; **beach u.,** parasol *m*; **u. stand,** porte-parapluies *m inv*; **u.-shaped,** en forme de parasol; (*b*) parasol (de chef de tribu, etc.); (*c*) **under the u. of the United Nations,** sous la protection des Nations Unies; (*d*) *Mil.Av:* **air, aerial, u.,** parapluie aérien, ombrelle *f* de protection aérienne. **2.** ombrelle (de méduse, etc.).
umlaut ['umlaut] *n. Ling:* (*a*) inflexion *f* vocalique, métaphonie *f*; (*b*) (*sign*) tréma *m*.
umph [hm] *int.* hum! hmm!
umpire¹ ['ʌmpaiər] *n. Sp: etc:* arbitre *m*, juge *m*; **to be an u. at a match,** arbitrer un match.
umpire² *v.tr. Sp: etc:* arbitrer (un match, etc.).
umpteen [ʌmp'tiːn] *a. F:* je ne sais combien; **she's got u. books on Africa,** elle a des tas de livres sur l'Afrique; **to have u. reasons for doing sth.,** avoir trente-six raisons de faire qch.
umpteenth [ʌmp'tiːnθ] *a. F:* **that's the u. time I've told you,** c'est la n^ième^ fois que je te le dis.
'un [ən] *pron. P:* (= *one*) **a little 'un,** un petit, une petite; **he's a bad 'un,** c'est un sale type.
un- [ʌn] *pref.* (*expressing negation*) **1.** in-. **2.** non. **3.** dé-. **4.** peu, mal. **5.** (ne) pas. **6.** a-. **7.** anti-. **8.** sans. **9.** manque *m* de, absence *f* de (qch.). **10.** indigne de (qn, qch.); dénué de (qch.); exempt de (qch.).
unabashed [ʌnə'bæʃt] *a.* **1.** sans perdre contenance; sans se déconcerter, sans se décontenancer. **2.** aucunement ébranlé.
unabated [ʌnə'beitid] *a.* qui n'a pas diminué; non diminué; **for three days the storm continued u.,** pen-

dant trois jours l'orage a continué sans répit.
unabbreviated [ʌnə'bri:vieitid] *a.* non abrégé.
unable [ʌn'eibl] *a.* incapable; **to be u. to do sth.,** ne pas pouvoir faire qch.; être dans l'impossibilité de faire qch.; **he seems u. to understand you,** il semble être incapable de vous comprendre; **we are u. to help you,** nous ne sommes pas en mesure de vous aider; **I was u. to persuade him,** je n'ai pas pu le persuader.
unabridged [ʌnə'bridʒd] *a.* non abrégé; intégral, -aux; **u. edition,** édition intégrale.
unaccented, unaccentuated [ʌnək'sentid, -'sentjueitid] *a.* inaccentué; *Ling:* (*of syllable, etc.*) non accentué; atone; *Mus:* **u. beat,** temps faible.
unacceptable [ʌnək'septəbl] *a.* inacceptable; (théorie) irrecevable; (conduite) inadmissible; **conditions u. to us,** conditions que nous ne pouvons pas agréer.
unaccommodating [ʌnə'kɔmədeitiŋ] *a.* (*of pers.*) peu accommodant; désobligeant.
unaccompanied [ʌnə'kʌmp(ə)nid] *a.* **1.** non accompagné; seul. **2.** *Mus:* sans accompagnement; **passage for u. violin,** passage pour violon seul.
unaccomplished [ʌnə'kʌmpliʃt, -'kɔm-] *a.* **1.** (projet) inaccompli, non réalisé; (travail) inachevé. **2.** (*of pers.*) médiocre.
unaccountable [ʌnə'kauntəbl] *a.* (*a*) (phénomène) inexplicable; (*b*) (conduite) bizarre, étrange. **-ably** *adv.* inexpliquablement.
unaccounted [ʌnə'kauntid] *a.* **these £10 are u. for in the balance sheet,** ces £10 ne figurent pas au bilan; **five of the passengers are still u. for,** on reste sans nouvelles de cinq passagers; **two books are still u. for,** il manque toujours deux livres.
unaccustomed [ʌnə'kʌstəmd] *a.* **1.** inaccoutumé, inhabituel. **2.** (*of pers.*) **u. to sth., to doing sth.,** peu habitué à qch., à faire qch.; **u. as I am to public speaking,** n'ayant pas l'habitude de faire des discours.
unacknowledged [ʌnək'nɔlidʒd] *a.* **1.** (*a*) *esp. Jur:* (enfant) non reconnu; (*b*) (citation) sans nom d'auteur. **2.** (lettre) restée sans réponse.
unacquainted [ʌnə'kweintid] *a.* **1. to be u. with s.o.,** ne pas connaître qn; **I am u. with him,** (i) il m'est étranger; (ii) je n'ai pas fait sa connaissance. **2. to be u. with sth.,** ignorer qch.; ne pas être au courant de qch.
unadaptable [ʌnə'dæptəbl] *a.* (*of pers.*) qui ne s'adapte pas aux circonstances.
unadapted [ʌnə'dæptid] *a.* mal adapté, peu adapté (**to sth.,** à qch.).
unaddressed [ʌnə'drest] *a.* (colis, etc.) sans adresse, qui ne porte pas d'adresse.
unadopted [ʌnə'dɔptid] *a.* **1.** non adopté; (*of measure*) **to remain u.,** rester en souffrance. **2. u. road,** rue non prise en charge par la municipalité.
unadorned [ʌnə'dɔ:nd] *a. Lit:* sans ornement, sans parure; **beauty u.,** la beauté sans parure, sans fard; **the u. truth,** la vérité pure, toute nue.
unadulterated [ʌnə'dʌltəreitid] *a.* pur; sans mélange; (vin) non frelaté; **u. joy,** joie *f* sans mélange; **the u. truth,** la vérité pure et simple.
unadventurous [ʌnəd'ventʃərəs] *a.* peu aventureux.
unadvertised [ʌn'ædvətaizd] *a.* (*of product, meeting, etc.*) sans publicité; (*of action, etc.*) discret, -ète.
unadvisable [ʌnəd'vaizəbl] *a.* (*a*) (*of action*) peu sage, imprudent; (*b*) **alcohol is u. for people suffering from heart complaints,** l'alcool est à déconseiller aux cardiaques.
unadvised [ʌnəd'vaizd] *a. esp. Lit:* imprudent.
unaesthetic [ʌni:s'θetik] *a.* inesthétique.
unaffected [ʌnə'fektid] *a.* **1.** (*a*) sans affectation; sincère; **u. joy,** joie qui n'a rien de simulé; (*b*) naturel, simple; (style) sans recherche, sans apprêt; (*c*) (*pers.*) sans affectation, sans pose; naturel; **u. modesty,** modestie simple. **2.** (*of pers.*) impassible, insensible (**by sth.,** à qch.); **to be u. by s.o.'s influence,** être réfractaire aux influences de qn. **3. u. by air or water,** inaltérable à l'air ou à l'eau. **-ly** *adv.* sans affectation; (*a*) sincèrement; (*b*) naturellement, simplement.
unaffiliated [ʌnə'filieitid] *a.* non affilié (**to,** à).
unafraid [ʌnə'freid] *a. esp. Lit:* sans peur.
unaided [ʌn'eidid] *a.* sans aide, sans assistance; **he did it u.,** il l'a fait tout seul, à lui seul.
unaired [ʌn'ɛəd] *a.* non aéré.
unalike [ʌnə'laik] *a.* dissemblable, différent; **they are not u.,** ils se ressemblent un peu.
unalleviated [ʌnə'li:vieitid] *a.* sans soulagement; **u. boredom,** ennui mortel.
unalloyed [ʌnə'lɔid] *a. Lit:* (bonheur) parfait.
unalterable [ʌn'ɔ:lt(ə)rəbl] *a.* immuable, invariable. **-ably** *adv.* immuablement, invariablement.
unaltered [ʌn'ɔ:ltəd] *a.* inchangé; toujours le même; sans changement.
unambiguous [ʌnæm'bigjuəs] *a.* non équivoque; (réponse) sans ambiguïté; **u. terms,** termes clairs. **-ly** *adv.* clairement; sans ambiguïté.
unambitious [ʌnæm'biʃəs] *a.* **1.** (*of pers.*) sans ambition; peu ambitieux. **2.** (projet) modeste.
un-American [ʌnə'merik(ə)n] *a.* antiaméricain; contraire à l'esprit américain.
unamiable [ʌn'eimiəbl] *a.* peu aimable; (caractère) désagréable, rébarbatif, bourru.
unanimity [ju:nə'nimiti] *n.* unanimité *f*, accord *m*.
unanimous [ju(:)'næniməs] *a.* unanime; **they were u. in accusing him,** ils étaient unanimes à l'accuser; **to reach a u. decision,** se prononcer à l'unanimité; **u. vote,** résolution adoptée à l'unanimité. **-ly** *adv.* à l'unanimité; **u. elected,** élu à l'unanimité.
unannounced [ʌnə'naunst] *a.* sans être annoncé; **he marched in u.,** il est entré sans se faire annoncer.
unanswerable [ʌn'ɑ:ns(ə)rəbl] *a.* (argument) incontestable, irréfutable; **u. question,** question à laquelle on ne peut pas répondre.
unanswered [ʌn'ɑ:nsəd] *a.* **1.** sans réponse; **u. letter,** lettre sans réponse; **our letter has remained u.,** notre lettre est restée sans réponse. **2.** (argument) irréfuté.
unappealing [ʌnə'pi:liŋ] *a.* peu attrayant.
unappeased [ʌnə'pi:zd] *a.* (*of hunger*) inassouvi.
unappetizing [ʌn'æpitaiziŋ] *a.* peu appétissant.
unappreciated [ʌnə'pri:ʃieitid] *a.* peu apprécié, peu estimé; dont on ne fait pas grand cas.
unappreciative [ʌnə'pri:ʃiətiv] *a.* (public) insensible; (compte rendu, etc.) peu favorable.
unapproachable [ʌnə'proutʃəbl] *a.* **1.** inabordable, inaccessible; **an u. sort of person,** une personne d'un abord difficile. **2.** incomparable, sans pareil.
unarmed [ʌn'ɑ:md] *a.* (*of pers.*) non armé; **u. combat,** combat sans armes.
unashamed [ʌnə'ʃeimd] *a.* sans honte; sans pudeur; **to be u. about doing sth.,** ne pas avoir honte de faire qch. **-ly** [ʌnə'ʃeimidli] *adv.* sans honte; sans pudeur.
unasked [ʌn'ɑ:skt] *a.* **1.** (faire qch.) spontanément; **she came to help us quite u.,** elle est venue nous aider sans qu'on le lui demandât. **2. u. (for),** (cadeau, etc.) qu'on n'a pas demandé.
unassailable [ʌnə'seiləbl] *a.* (forteresse, position) inattaquable; (conclusion) irréfutable; **his reputation is u.,** sa réputation est hors d'atteinte.
unassimilated [ʌnə'simileitid] *a.* inassimilé; **u. knowledge,** connaissances mal assimilées.
unassisted [ʌnə'sistid] *a.* sans aide, sans assistance; **he did it u.,** il l'a fait tout seul.

unassuming [ʌnə'sjuːmiŋ] *a.* sans prétention(s); modeste. **-ly** *adv.* modestement, sans prétention(s).
unattached [ʌnə'tætʃt] *a.* **1.** qui n'est pas attaché (**to,** à); indépendant (**to,** de). **2.** (journaliste, etc.) libre; *Mil:* (officier) disponible, en disponibilité; (*of pers.*) **to be u.,** être libre, sans attaches.
unattainable [ʌnə'teinəbl] *a.* inaccessible (**by,** à); hors de (la) portée (**by,** de).
unattended [ʌnə'tendid] *a.* **1.** (*a*) (*of pers.*) seul; sans escorte; (*b*) **to leave one's car u.,** laisser sa voiture sans surveillance; *P.N:* **do not leave your luggage u.,** surveillez toujours vos bagages. **2. u. to,** négligé.
unattractive [ʌnə'træktiv] *a.* peu attrayant, sans attrait, peu séduisant; (personne) peu sympathique; **she is not u.,** elle ne manque pas de charme.
unauthenticated [ʌnɔː'θentikeitid] *a.* (*a*) dont l'authenticité n'est pas établie; (*b*) *Jur:* (*of document*) non légalisé.
unauthorized [ʌn'ɔːθəraizd] *a.* **1.** non autorisé; sans autorisation; *P.N:* **no entry to u. persons, no u. access,** accès interdit à toute personne étrangère au service.
unavailability [ʌnəveilə'biliti] *n.* indisponibilité *f.*
unavailable [ʌnə'veiləbl] *a.* **1.** (*a*) indisponible; (*b*) qu'on ne peut se procurer; (article) épuisé; (*c*) (*of pers.*) pas libre; non disponible. **2. ticket u. for certain trains,** billet non valable pour certains trains.
unavailing [ʌnə'veiliŋ] *a.* inutile; (*of tears*) vain, inefficace; (*of efforts*) infructueux. **-ly** *adv.* inutilement; en vain.
unavoidable [ʌnə'vɔidəbl] *a.* (*a*) inévitable; (sort) auquel on ne peut échapper; (*b*) (événement) qu'on ne peut prévenir; **my absence was u.,** mon absence a été due à un cas de force majeure. **-ably** *adv.* (*a*) inévitablement; (*b*) **u. detained,** retenu pour raison majeure.
unaware [ʌnə'wɛər] *a.* ignorant, non informé, pas au courant (**of sth.,** de qch.); **to be u. of sth.,** ignorer, ne pas se douter de, qch.; **I was u. that . . .,** j'ignorais que . . . + *ind. or sub.*; **I'm not u. that . . .,** je n'ignore pas que . . . + *ind.*
unawares [ʌnə'wɛəz] *adv.* **1.** inconsciemment; sans s'en rendre compte. **2. to take, catch, s.o. u.,** prendre qn au dépourvu.
unbalance¹ [ʌn'bæləns] *n.* déséquilibre *m.*
unbalance² *v.tr.* **1.** déséquilibrer (un volant). **2.** déranger, déséquilibrer (l'esprit de qn). **unbalanced** *a.* **1.** (*a*) (volant) mal équilibré (*b*) (esprit, etc.) déséquilibré, dérangé. **2.** (*of account*) non soldé.
unbandage [ʌn'bændidʒ] *v.tr.* débander (une plaie).
unbaptized [ʌnbæp'taizd] *a.* non baptisé.
unbar [ʌn'bɑːr] *v.tr.* débarrer (une porte).
unbearable [ʌn'bɛərəbl] *a.* insupportable, intolérable; **in this heat, the office is u.,** par cette chaleur le bureau n'est pas tenable. **-ably** *adv.* insupportablement; **it's u. hot,** il fait une chaleur étouffante.
unbeatable [ʌn'biːtəbl] *a.* imbattable.
unbeaten [ʌn'biːt(ə)n] *a.* invaincu; (champion, record) qui n'a pas encore été battu.
unbecoming [ʌnbi'kʌmiŋ] *a.* **1.** peu convenable; malséant (**to,** à); **it's u. of him to act in this manner,** il lui sied mal d'agir de la sorte. **2.** (*of garment*) peu seyant.
unbeknown [ʌnbi'noun] **1.** *a. Lit:* inconnu (**to,** de). **2.** *adv.* (*also F:* **unbeknownst) to do sth. u. to anyone,** faire qch. à l'insu de tous.
unbelief [ʌnbi'liːf] *n.* incrédulité *f.*
unbelievable [ʌnbi'liːvəbl] *a.* incroyable; **it's u. that . . .,** il est incroyable que + *sub.* **-ably** *adv.* incroyablement; **u. stupid,** d'une sottise incroyable.
unbeliever [ʌnbi'liːvər] *n.* incrédule *mf.*
unbelieving [ʌnbi'liːviŋ] *a.* incrédule.
unbend [ʌn'bend] *v.* (*p.t. & p.p.* **unbent** [ʌn'bent]) **1.** *v.tr.* (*a*) détendre (un arc); (*b*) redresser (une tige d'acier, etc.); déplier (la jambe). **2.** *v.i.* (*a*) s'abandonner, se laisser aller (un peu); se détendre; (*b*) se redresser; (*of limb*) se déplier. **unbending** *a.* (*a*) inflexible, ferme; (*b*) (caractère) inflexible, rigide; **u. attitude,** attitude intransigeante.
unbias(s)ed [ʌn'baiəst] *a.* impartial, -aux; neutre; sans parti pris; non prévenu (**against s.o.,** contre qn); (conseil) désintéressé.
unbidden [ʌn'bid(ə)n] *a. O:* **to do sth. u.,** faire qch. spontanément, sans y avoir été invité.
unbind [ʌn'baind] *v.tr.* (*p.t. & p.p.* **unbound** [ʌn'baund]) (*a*) délier (un prisonnier, les mains); (*b*) débander (une plaie). **unbound** *a.* **1.** délié. **2.** (*of book*) non relié; broché.
unbleached [ʌn'bliːtʃt] *a.* (*a*) écru; **u. linen,** toile bise, écrue; (*b*) (cheveux) non oxygénés.
unblemished [ʌn'blemiʃt] *a.* sans défaut.
unblinking [ʌn'bliŋkiŋ] *a.* (*of pers.*) impassible; (regard) fixe; **with u. eyes,** sans ciller (des yeux).
unblock [ʌn'blɔk] *v.tr.* dégager, désencombrer (un passage); déboucher (un tuyau, etc.).
unblushing [ʌn'blʌʃiŋ] *a.* **1.** sans rougir. **2.** sans vergogne; impudent; éhonté. **-ly** *adv.* **1.** sans rougir. **2.** sans vergogne, sans honte.
unbolt [ʌn'boult] *v.tr.* **1.** déverrouiller (une porte). **2.** déboulonner (un rail, etc.).
unborn ['ʌnbɔːn] *a.* qui n'est pas (encore) né; **u. child,** enfant à naître; **generations yet u.** [ʌn'bɔːn], générations à venir; générations futures.
unbosom [ʌn'buzəm] *v.tr. A: & Lit:* **to u. oneself to s.o.,** ouvrir son cœur à qn.
unbounded [ʌn'baundid] *a.* sans bornes; illimité; (*of conceit, ambition, etc.*) démesuré.
unbowed [ʌn'baud] *a.* invaincu, insoumis.
unbreakable [ʌn'breikəbl] *a.* incassable; (*of promise*) sacré, inviolable.
unbreathable [ʌn'briːðəbl] *a.* irrespirable.
unbribable [ʌn'braibəbl] *a.* incorruptible.
unbridled [ʌn'braid(ə)ld] *a.* **1.** (cheval) (i) débridé, (ii) sans bride. **2.** (*of passion*) débridé, effréné.
unbroken [ʌn'brouk(ə)n] *a.* **1.** (*a*) non brisé, non cassé; (*b*) intact; **u. spirit,** courage inentamé; (*c*) (*of rule*) toujours observé, respecté; (*of promise*) inviolé; **the peace remained u. for ten years,** la paix n'a pas été troublée pendant dix ans; *Sp:* **record still u.,** record qui n'a pas été battu; (*d*) (*of silence*) ininterrompu, continu; (*of ground*) non accidenté; **u. sheet of ice,** nappe de glace continue. **2.** (*a*) (cheval) non rompu, non dressé; (*b*) **u. spirit,** esprit insoumis. **3.** *Agr:* **u. ground,** terre vierge.
unbuckle [ʌn'bʌkl] *v.tr.* déboucler (une ceinture).
unbuilt [ʌn'bilt, 'ʌnbilt] *a.* **u. plot, plot of u. ground,** terrain vague, non construit.
unburden [ʌn'bəːd(ə)n] *v.tr.* **1.** (*a*) décharger, débarrasser; (*b*) **to u. the mind,** soulager, alléger, l'esprit; **to u. oneself, one's heart,** s'épancher; **to u. oneself to s.o.,** se confier à qn; **to u. oneself of a secret,** se soulager du poids d'un secret. **2. to u. one's sorrows to s.o.,** épancher ses chagrins dans le sein de qn.
unburied [ʌn'berid] *a.* non enseveli, non enterré.
unbusinesslike [ʌn'biznislaik] *a.* **1.** (*of pers.*) peu commerçant; qui n'a pas le sens des affaires. **2.** (procédé) irrégulier, incorrect, contraire à toutes les règles du commerce; **to conduct one's affairs in an u. way,** mal conduire ses affaires.
unbutton [ʌn'bʌt(ə)n] *v.tr.* déboutonner (son manteau). **unbuttoned** *a.* déboutonné; (*of garment*) **to come u.,** se déboutonner.
uncalled [ʌn'kɔːld] *a.* **u. for,** (i) (*of remark*) déplacé; (ii) (*of rebuke*) immérité, injustifié; (*of insult*) gratuit.

uncanny [ʌn'kæni] *a.* d'une étrangeté inquiétante; mystérieux; **u. noise,** bruit qui vous donne la chair de poule. **-ily** *adv.* d'une manière étrange.
uncared-for [ʌn'kɛədfɔːr] *a.* négligé; **to leave a garden u.-for,** laisser un jardin à l'abandon.
uncaring [ʌn'kɛəriŋ] *a.* qui ne se soucie pas (des autres); indifférent.
uncarpeted [ʌn'kɑːpitid] *a.* sans tapis, sans moquette.
uncatalogued [ʌn'kætəlɔgd] *a.* qui n'est pas catalogué; qui ne figure pas dans le catalogue.
unceasing [ʌn'siːsiŋ] *a.* (*a*) incessant, continu, continuel; (*b*) (travail) assidu; (effort) soutenu. **-ly** *adv.* sans cesse; sans arrêt.
uncensored [ʌn'sensəd] *a.* (article, etc.) qui n'a pas été soumis à la censure.
unceremonious [ʌnseri'mouniəs] *a.* sans cérémonie; (*of pers.*) sans façons. **-ly** *adv.* sans cérémonie; brusquement.
uncertain [ʌn'səːt(ə)n] *a.* incertain. **1.** (*a*) (*of amount*) indéterminé; (*b*) (résultat) douteux; **it's u. who will win,** on ne sait pas au juste qui gagnera. **2.** (*a*) mal assuré; (avenir) incertain, douteux; **u. steps,** pas chancelants; **u. temper,** humeur inégale; **he told him in no u. terms,** il lui a dit sans mâcher ses mots; (*b*) **his memory is u.,** sa mémoire vacille; **to be u. of the future,** être incertain de l'avenir; **to be u. what to do,** hésiter sur le parti à prendre. **-ly** *adv.* d'une façon incertaine.
uncertainty [ʌn'səːt(ə)nti] *n.* **1.** incertitude *f* (d'un résultat); **there is some u. about . . .,** l'incertitude règne au sujet de . . .; **u. about, as to, the future,** incertitude quant à l'avenir; **to be in a state of u.,** être dans l'incertitude; **to remove any u.,** pour dissiper toute équivoque. **2.** incertitude; **to prefer a certainty to an u.,** préférer le certain à l'incertain.
unchain [ʌn'tʃein] *v.tr.* désenchaîner.
unchallengeable [ʌn'tʃælindʒəbl] *a.* (affirmation) indiscutable; (argument) irréfutable; (droit) incontestable; (témoignage, preuve) irrécusable.
unchallenged [ʌn'tʃælin(d)ʒd] *a.* **1.** (*a*) (interlocuteur) que personne ne vient contredire; **to continue u.,** continuer sans être contredit; (*b*) (droit) indisputé, incontesté; **to let (sth.) go, pass, u.,** ne pas relever (une affirmation); ne pas contester (un droit); ne pas récuser (un témoignage). **2.** *Mil:* **to let s.o. pass u.,** laisser passer qn sans interpellation.
unchangeable [ʌn'tʃeindʒəbl] *a.* inchangeable; immuable.
unchanged [ʌn'tʃein(d)ʒd] *a.* inchangé; intact; *Med:* **his condition remains u.,** son état est stationnaire. **unchanging** *a.* invariable, immuable.
uncharitable [ʌn'tʃæritəbl] *a.* peu charitable.
uncharted [ʌn'tʃɑːtid] *a.* non porté sur la carte; inexploré.
unchaste [ʌn'tʃeist] *a. A: & Lit:* impudique; impur.
unchastened [ʌn'tʃeis(ə)nd] *a.* (*of pers.*) aucunement ravalé; **he was u. by his experience,** son expérience n'a rien rabattu de ses prétentions.
unchecked [ʌn'tʃekt] *a.* **1.** (avance) sans (la moindre) opposition; (passion) sans frein; (colère) non contenue; **the enemy advanced u.,** l'ennemi s'est avancé sans qu'on lui oppose de résistance. **2.** (compte rendu, bilan) non vérifié.
unchivalrous [ʌn'ʃivəlrəs] *a. Lit:* peu courtois.
unchristian [ʌn'kristjən] *a.* **1.** (désir) peu chrétien. **2.** *F:* peu convenable; **at this u. hour,** à cette heure indue.
uncial ['ʌnsiəl] **1.** *a.* (*of letters, MS*) oncial, -aux. **2.** *n.* (écriture) onciale (*f*).
uncircumcised [ʌn'səːkəmsaizd] *a.* incirconcis.
uncivil [ʌn'siv(i)l] *a.* incivil, impoli.
uncivilized [ʌn'sivilaizd] *a.* non civilisé, incivilisé; barbare; *F:* **at this u. hour,** à cette heure indue.
unclaimed [ʌn'kleimd] *a.* non réclamé; (droit) non revendiqué.
unclasp [ʌn'klɑːsp] **1.** *v.tr.* (*a*) défaire (un bracelet); (*b*) desserrer (le poing). **2.** *v.i.* (*of hands*) se desserrer.
unclassifiable [ʌn'klæsifaiəbl] *a.* inclassable.
unclassified [un'klæsifaid] *a.* non (classé) secret.
uncle ['ʌŋkl] *n.* **1.** oncle *m*; *Fig:* **rich u.,** oncle d'Amérique; *U.S: F:* **U. Tom,** noir *m* qui s'insinue dans les bonnes grâces des blancs. **2.** *F: O:* **my watch is at my uncle's,** ma montre est chez ma tante.
unclean [ʌn'kliːn] *a.* **1.** impur, immonde; *B:* **u. spirit,** esprit immonde. **2.** *Lit:* malpropre, sale.
unclear [ʌn'kliər] *a.* (*of statement*) peu clair; obscur, incertain, vague.
uncleared [ʌn'kliəd] *a.* **1.** **u. ground,** terrain indéfriché. **2.** (*a*) (*of debt*) non liquidé; (*b*) **u. goods,** marchandises non dédouanées; (*c*) (chèque) non compensé.
unclench [ʌn'klen(t)ʃ] *v.tr.* desserrer (le poing).
uncloak [ʌn'klouk] *v.tr. Lit:* découvrir (des projets); démasquer, dévoiler (une imposture).
unclog [ʌn'klɔg] *v.tr.* **(unclogged)** débloquer (une machine); déboucher, décrasser (une conduite).
unclothed [ʌn'klouðd] *a.* nu; sans vêtements.
unclouded [ʌn'klaudid] *a.* **1.** (*of sky, future*) sans nuage(s); (*of vision*) clair. **2.** (*of liquid*) clair.
uncluttered [ʌn'klʌtəd] *a.* (*a*) (pièce) qui n'est pas encombrée (de meubles); (*b*) (style) dépouillé.
unco ['ʌŋkou] *adv. Scot: A: & Lit:* très.
uncoil [ʌn'kɔil] **1.** *v.tr.* dérouler. **2.** *v.i. & pr.* (*of snake, rope*) **to u. (itself),** se dérouler.
uncollected [ʌnkə'lektid] *a.* (*of luggage*) non réclamé; **u. taxes,** impôts non perçus.
uncoloured [ʌn'kʌləd] *a.* (*a*) non coloré; **u. account of sth.,** rapport impartial de qch.; (*b*) incolore.
uncombed [ʌn'koumd] *a.* (*of hair, wool*) non peigné; (*of hair*) mal peigné.
uncomely [ʌn'kʌmli] *a.* peu joli; peu gracieux.
uncomfortable [ʌn'kʌmf(ə)təbl] *a.* **1.** inconfortable; incommode; (fauteuil) peu confortable; (vêtement) gênant; **this is a very u. armchair,** on est très mal (assis) dans ce fauteuil. **2.** **to make things u. for s.o.,** attirer, créer, des ennuis à qn. **3.** **to feel, be, u.,** (i) être mal à l'aise; (ii) se sentir gêné; **to be, feel, u. about sth.,** être inquiet au sujet de qch.; **to make s.o. feel u.,** mettre qn mal à son aise; troubler qn. **-ably** *adv.* **1.** peu confortablement. **2.** **the enemy were u. near,** la proximité de l'ennemi était inquiétante.
uncommitted [ʌnkə'mitid] *a.* (*a*) (*of pers.*) non engagé; libre; indépendant; **to be u. to any course of action,** n'être engagé à aucune ligne de conduite; (*b*) *Pol:* neutraliste, non aligné.
uncommon [ʌn'kɔmən] **1.** *a.* (*a*) peu commun; **u. word,** mot peu usité; **not u.,** assez fréquent; (*b*) peu ordinaire; (événement) qui sort de l'ordinaire. **2.** *adv. F: A:* singulièrement. **-ly** *adv.* **1.** **not u.,** assez souvent. **2.** singulièrement; **u. good,** excellent.
uncommunicative [ʌnkə'mjuːnikətiv] *a.* peu communicatif; renfermé, taciturne.
uncomplaining [ʌnkəm'pleiniŋ] *a.* qui ne se plaint pas; patient, résigné; **-ly** *adv.* sans se plaindre.
uncomplicated [ʌn'kɔmplikeitid] *a.* peu compliqué, simple, facile.
uncomplimentary [ʌnkɔmpli'ment(ə)ri] *a.* peu flatteur, -euse.
uncomprehending [ʌnkɔmpri'hendiŋ] *a.* incompréhensif.
uncompromising [ʌn'kɔmprəmaiziŋ] *a.* intransigeant. **-ly** *adv.* **u. honest,** d'une honnêteté intransigeante.
unconcealed [ʌnkən'siːld] *a.* non dissimulé; **u. dis-**

like, aversion que l'on ne cherche pas à dissimuler.

unconcern [ʌnkən'sə:n] *n.* insouciance *f*; indifférence *f*; **to show u. in the face of danger,** se montrer indifférent en face du danger.

unconcerned [ʌnkən'sə:nd] *a.* (*a*) insouciant, indifférent; **u., he went on speaking,** sans se (laisser) troubler, il a continué de parler; (*b*) **he seems entirely u. about his results,** il ne semble pas du tout s'inquiéter au sujet de ses résultats. **-ly** [ʌnkən'sə:nidli] *adv.* d'un air indifférent; sans se (laisser) troubler.

unconditional [ʌnkən'diʃənəl] *a.* inconditionnel; sans réserve; **u. surrender,** soumission sans condition. **-ally** *adv.* inconditionnellement; (accepter) sans réserve; **to surrender u.,** se rendre sans condition.

unconfirmed [ʌnkən'fə:md] *a.* non confirmé.

uncongenial [ʌnkən'dʒi:niəl] *a.* **1.** (*of pers.*) peu sympathique, antipathique. **2.** (*a*) (climat) peu favorable (**to,** à); (*b*) (travail, ambiance) peu agréable.

unconnected [ʌnkə'nektid] *a.* (*a*) sans rapport, (**with,** avec); **the two events are totally u.,** les deux événements n'ont aucun rapport entre eux; (*b*) (style) décousu.

unconquerable [ʌn'kɔŋkərəbl] *a.* (ennemi) invincible; (courage) indomptable; (curiosité) irrésistible; (désir) irrépressible; (difficulté) insurmontable.

unconquered [ʌn'kɔŋkəd] *a.* (*a*) (passion) indomptée; (difficulté) insurmontable; (*b*) (peuple, pays) inconquis.

unconscionable [ʌn'kɔnʃənəbl] *a.* déraisonnable, excessif; **to take an u. time doing sth.,** mettre un temps invraisemblable à faire qch.

unconscious [ʌn'kɔnʃəs] *a.* **1.** inconscient; **to be u. of doing sth.,** ne pas avoir conscience de faire qch.; **to be u. of sth.,** ne pas avoir conscience, ne pas s'apercevoir, de qch. **2.** sans connaissance; **to become u.,** perdre connaissance; s'évanouir; **to knock s.o. u.,** assommer qn raide. **3.** *n. Psy:* **the u.,** l'inconscient *m.* **-ly** *adv.* inconsciemment; sans s'en rendre compte.

unconsciousness [ʌn'kɔnʃəsnis] *n.* **1.** inconscience *f* (**of,** de). **2.** évanouissement *m.*

unconsecrated [ʌn'kɔnsikreitid] *a.* non consacré.

unconsidered [ʌnkən'sidəd] *a.* **1.** (*of remark, opinion*) inconsidéré. **2.** *Lit:* **u. trifle,** vétille *f.*

unconstitutional [ʌnkɔnsti'tju:ʃənəl] *a.* inconstitutionnel, anticonstitutionnel. **-ally** *adv.* inconstitutionnellement, anticonstitutionnellement.

unconstrained [ʌnkən'streind] *a.* non contraint; sans contrainte; libre; (acte) spontané; **u. laughter,** hilarité débordante.

unconsummated [ʌn'kɔnsəmeitid] *a.* **u. marriage,** mariage inconsommé.

uncontested [ʌnkən'testid] *a.* (droit) incontesté; *Pol:* **u. seat,** siège (à la Chambre) qui n'est pas disputé.

uncontrollable [ʌnkən'trouləbl] *a.* (enfant, peuple) ingouvernable; (mouvement) irréprimable; (désir) irrésistible, irrépressible; **u. laughter,** fou rire; **fits of u. temper,** violents accès de colère. **-ably** *adv.* irrésistiblement; **she sobbed u.,** elle ne pouvait s'arrêter de sangloter.

uncontrolled [ʌnkən'trould] *a.* sans frein; **u. passions,** passions effrénées; **u. inflation,** inflation rampante.

uncontroversial [ʌnkɔntrə'və:ʃ(ə)l] *a.* (sujet) qui ne soulève, ne provoque, pas de controverses.

unconventional [ʌnkən'venʃənəl] *a.* peu conventionnel; non-conformiste. **-ally** *adv.* de manière peu conventionnelle.

unconvinced [ʌnkən'vinst] *a.* sceptique (**of,** au sujet de); **I am still u.,** je ne suis toujours pas convaincu. **unconvincing** *a.* (témoignage, etc.) peu convaincant; (excuse) peu vraisemblable. **unconvincingly** *adv.* d'une manière peu convaincante.

uncooked [ʌn'kukt] *a.* (aliment) non cuit, cru.

uncooperative [ʌnkou'ɔp(ə)rətiv] *a.* peu coopératif.

uncoordinated [ʌnkou'ɔ:dineitid] *a.* non coordonné; (manœuvre) qui manque de coordination.

uncork [ʌn'kɔ:k] *v.tr.* déboucher (une bouteille).

uncorrected [ʌnkə'rektid] *a.* **1.** (*of exercise, proof*) non corrigé. **2.** (*of error*) non rectifié; *Ph:* **result u. for temperature, for pressure,** résultat brut.

uncorroborated [ʌnkə'rɔbəreitid] *a.* non corroboré, non confirmé.

uncorrupted [ʌnkə'rʌptid] *a.* incorrompu; intègre.

uncouple [ʌn'kʌpl] *v.tr.* dételer, découpler (des wagons, une locomotive).

uncouth [ʌn'ku:θ] *a.* (*of pers., behaviour*) grossier; **u. manner,** manières gauches, frustes.

uncover [ʌn'kʌvər] *v.tr.* (*a*) dévoiler, révéler, découvrir (*b*) *Chess:* découvrir, dégarnir (une pièce).

uncovered [ʌn'kʌvəd] *a.* **1.** mis à nu, à découvert; découvert; (*of pers.*) **to remain u.,** rester la tête découverte. **2.** *Bank:* (achat, vente) à découvert.

uncreasable [ʌn'kri:səbl] *a.* (tissu) infroissable.

uncritical [ʌn'kritik(ə)l] *a.* dépourvu de sens critique; sans discernement; (auditoire) peu exigeant.

uncross [ʌn'krɔs] *v.tr.* décroiser (les jambes). **uncrossed** *a.* **1.** non croisé. **2.** (chèque) non barré.

uncrowned [ʌn'kraund] *a.* **1.** sans couronne. **2.** non couronné.

uncrushable [ʌn'krʌʃəbl] *a.* (tissu) infroissable.

unction ['ʌŋkʃ(ə)n] *n.* onction *f.*

unctuous ['ʌŋktjuəs] *a. A:* & *Lit:* onctueux. **-ly** *adv.* onctueusement; d'un air, d'un ton, onctueux.

unctuousness ['ʌŋktjuəsnis] *n. Lit:* onctuosité *f.*

uncultivated [ʌn'kʌltiveitid] *a.* (terrain) inculte, incultivé; (personne) inculte, sans culture.

uncultured [ʌn'kʌltʃəd] *a.* (esprit) inculte; (*of pers.*) peu lettré; sans culture, inculte; (accent) peu raffiné.

uncurbed [ʌn'kə:bd] *a.* (*a*) (autorité) sans restriction; (*b*) (*of passion*) déchaîné.

uncurl [ʌn'kə:l] **1.** *v.tr.* défriser, déboucler (les cheveux); déplier (ses jambes). **2.** *v.i.* & *pr.* (*of cat*) s'étirer; (*of snake*) se dérouler.

uncut [ʌn'kʌt] *a.* **1.** sans coupure, sans entaille. **2.** (*a*) (*of hedge*) non coupé, non taillé; (diamant) brut, non taillé; (*b*) (*of play, edition*) sans coupures, intégral.

undamaged [ʌn'dæmidʒd] *a.* non endommagé; indemne; en bon état; (réputation) intacte.

undamped [ʌn'dæmpt] *a.* (courage) non affaibli.

undated [ʌn'deitid] *a.* non daté; sans date.

undaunted [ʌn'dɔ:ntid] *a.* (*a*) intrépide; (*b*) aucunement intimidé; aucunement ébranlé (**by,** de, par).

undeceive [ʌndi'si:v] *v.tr. esp. Lit:* désabuser (**of,** de); détromper, désillusionner (qn).

undecided [ʌndi'saidid] *a.* (*a*) (problème) indécis, non résolu; (procès) pendant; (*b*) (*of pers.*) indécis, irrésolu; (*c*) **he was u. whether he would go or not,** il se demandait s'il irait ou non; **to be u. how to act,** ne pas savoir quel parti prendre.

undeclared [ʌndi'klɛəd] *a.* (*of war*) non déclaré; *Cust:* **u. goods,** marchandises non déclarées.

undefeated [ʌndi'fi:tid] *a.* invaincu; (champion) qui n'a pas (encore) été battu.

undefended [ʌndi'fendid] *a.* **1.** sans défense. **2.** *Jur:* (*a*) (accusé) qui n'est pas représenté par un avocat; (*b*) **u. case, trial,** débats non contentieux; **u. suit,** cause où le défendeur s'abstient de plaider.

undefiled [ʌndi'faild] *a.* sans souillure; immaculé.

undefinable [ʌndi'fainəbl] *a.* indéfinissable.

undefined [ʌndi'faind] *a.* **1.** non défini. **2.** indéterminé; vague.

undelivered [ʌndi'livəd] *a.* non livré, non remis; *Post:* (colis) en souffrance; **if u. return to sender,** en cas de non-livraison prière de retourner à l'expéditeur.

undemanding [ʌndi'mɑːndiŋ] *a.* peu exigeant.

undemocratic [ʌndemə'krætik] *a.* antidémocratique.

undemonstrative [ʌŋdi'mɔnstrətiv] *a.* (*of pers.*) peu expansif, peu démonstratif; réservé.

undeniable [ʌndi'naiəbl] *a.* indéniable, incontestable; (témoignage) irrécusable; **of u. worth,** dont la valeur s'impose. **-ably** *adv.* incontestablement.

undenominational [ʌndinɔmi'neiʃənəl] *a.* non confessionnel.

under ['ʌndər] **I.** *prep.* **1.** sous; au-dessous de; (*a*) **the dog is u. the table,** le chien est sous la table; **u. water,** sous l'eau; **here's a table, get u. it,** voici une table, mettez-vous dessous; **put it u. that,** mettez-le là-dessous; **to wear a waistcoat u. one's jacket,** porter un gilet sous son veston; **he pulled a stool out from u. the table,** il a tiré un tabouret de sous la table; **to look for, to file, sth. u.** *miscellaneous,* chercher, classer, qch. sous la rubrique *divers;* (*b*) (*less than*) **all their books were u. £5,** tous leurs livres coûtaient moins de £5; **salaries u. £5000,** salaires inférieurs à, au-dessous de, £5000; **he's u. thirty,** il a moins de trente ans; **people u. thirty, the u. thirties,** les moins de trente ans; **children u. ten,** les enfants au-dessous de dix ans; **in u. ten minutes,** en moins de dix minutes; **to speak u. one's breath,** parler à mi-voix. **2.** (*a*) **u. lock and key,** sous clef; **visible u. the microscope,** visible au microscope; **to be u. sentence of death,** être condamné à mort; **to be u. orders to do sth.,** avoir reçu l'ordre de faire qch.; **u. these conditions,** dans ces conditions; **u. the circumstances,** dans les circonstances; **u. the terms of the agreement,** aux termes de la convention; **u. his father's will,** d'après le testament de son père; **she wrote it u. a pseudonym,** elle l'a écrit sous un pseudonyme; (*b*) **he had a hundred men u. him,** il avait cent hommes sous ses ordres; **to be u. s.o.,** être sous les ordres de qn; **to be, to come, u. the authority of the Home Office,** relever du Ministère de l'Intérieur; **u. government control,** soumis au contrôle de l'État; **to be u. the influence of alcohol,** *F:* **to be u. the influence,** être sous l'empire de la boisson; **u. Louis XIV,** sous Louis XIV; *F:* **to be u. the doctor,** être sous les ordres du médecin. **3.** en; (*a*) **u. repair,** en (voie de) réparation; **u. construction,** en construction; **patient u. observation,** malade en observation; **the question is u. examination,** la question a été prise en considération; (*b*) **field u. wheat,** champ mis en blé. **II.** *adv.* **1.** (au-)dessous; **to stay u. for two minutes,** rester deux minutes sous l'eau; *F:* **to get out from u.,** se tirer d'affaire; *Com: etc:* **as u.,** comme ci-dessous; **children seven years old and u.,** des enfants (âgés) de sept ans et au-dessous. **2.** en soumission; **to keep a rebellion u.,** mater une rébellion.

under-age [ʌndər'eidʒ] *a.* mineur; **u.-a. sex, drinking,** indulgence sexuelle, consommation *f* d'alcool, par les mineurs.

underarm 1. *adv.* [ʌndər'ɑːm, 'ʌndərɑːm] *Cr: Ten:* **to bowl, to serve, u.,** lancer, servir, la balle par en-dessous. **2.** *a.* ['ʌndərɑːm] (*a*) *Cr: Ten:* (lancement, coup, etc.) par en-dessous; (*b*) **u. deodorant,** désodorisant *m* pour les aisselles.

underbelly ['undəbeli] *n.* (*a*) bas-ventre *m*, *pl.* bas-ventres (d'un animal); poitrine *f* (de porc); (*b*) point *m* vulnérable; point faible.

underbid [ʌndə'bid] *v.tr. & i.* (*p.t.* **underbid;** *p.p.* **underbid(den)** [-'bidn]) **1.** faire des soumissions, offrir des conditions, plus avantageuses que celles de (qn d'autre). **2.** *Cards:* **to u. (one's hand),** demander au-dessous de son jeu.

underblanket ['ʌndəblæŋkit] *n.* protège-matelas *m.*

underbody ['ʌndəbɔdi] *n. Aut:* dessous *m* de caisse.

underbrush ['ʌndəbrʌʃ] *n.* sous-bois *m.*

undercapitalization [ʌndəkæpitəlai'zeiʃ(ə)n] *n. Pol.Ec:* sous-capitalisation *f.*

undercapitalized [ʌndə'kæpitəlaizd] *a.* (*of industry*) sous-capitalisé.

undercarriage ['ʌndəkæridʒ] *n. Av:* train *m* d'atterrissage.

undercharge [ʌndə'tʃɑːdʒ] **1.** *v.tr.* **they undercharged him,** on ne lui a pas, on ne l'a pas, fait assez payer; **they undercharged her, she was undercharged, by 50p,** on aurait dû lui, la, faire payer 50 pence de plus. **2.** *v.i.* demander trop peu (**for sth.,** pour qch.).

underclothes ['ʌndəklouðz] *n.pl.*, **underclothing** ['ʌndəklouðiŋ] *n.* sous-vêtements *mpl*; vêtements *mpl* de dessous; (*women's*) lingerie *f*, dessous *mpl.*

undercoat ['ʌndəkout] *n.* **1.** duvet *m* (d'un chien). **2.** (*a*) *Paint:* couche *f* de fond, première couche; (*b*) *NAm: Aut:* couche, revêtement *m*, antirouille.

undercoating ['ʌndəkoutiŋ] *n.* = UNDERCOAT 2.

undercook [ʌndə'kuk] *v.tr.* ne pas assez cuire.

undercover ['ʌndəkʌvər] *a.* secret, -ète, clandestin; **u. agent,** agent secret.

undercurrent ['ʌndəkʌrənt] *n.* **1.** courant *m* de fond; (*in sea*) courant sous-marin. **2.** *Fig:* **u. of discontent,** vague *f* de fond de mécontentement.

undercut[1] ['ʌndəkʌt] *n.* **1.** *Cu:* filet *m* (de bœuf). **2.** coup tranchant (coupé en dessous).

undercut[2] *v.tr.* (*p.t. & p.p.* **undercut;** *pr.p.* **undercutting**) **1.** couper, lifter (la balle). **2.** *Com:* (*a*) faire des soumissions plus avantageuses que celles de (qn); (*b*) vendre moins cher que (qn).

underdeveloped [ʌndədi'veləpt] *a.* **1.** (cliché) insuffisamment développé. **2.** (enfant) retardé; (muscle) pas assez développé. **3. u. countries,** pays sous-développés; **u. area,** région sous-exploitée.

underdog ['ʌndədɔg] *n.* (*a*) perdant, -ante; (*b*) opprimé, -ée, défavorisé, -ée; **to plead for, to side with, the underdog(s),** plaider la cause des opprimés.

underdone [ʌndə'dʌn] *a. Cu:* (*a*) pas assez cuit; (*b*) pas trop cuit; (bœuf, etc.) saignant; (bifteck) bleu.

underdrawers ['ʌndədrɔːəz] *n. pl. U.S: Cost:* caleçon *m* (d'homme).

underemployed [ʌndərem'plɔid] *a.* sous-employé; (*of resources*) sous-exploité.

underemployment [ʌndərem'plɔimənt] *n.* sous-emploi *m* (de qn); sous-exploitation *f* (de ressources).

underestimate[1], **underestimation** [ʌndə(r)-'estimeit, -esti'meiʃ(ə)n] *n.* sous-estimation *f*, sous-évaluation *f.*

underestimate[2] *v.tr.* sous-estimer, sous-évaluer (les dépenses, un adversaire); méconnaître, mésestimer (les difficultés, un concurrent).

underexpose [ʌndəreks'pouz] *v.tr. Phot:* sous-exposer (un film).

underexposure [ʌndəreks'pouʒər] *n. Phot:* sous-exposition *f* (d'un film).

underfed [ʌndə'fed] *a.* sous-alimenté; mal nourri. **underfeeding** *n.* sous-alimentation *f.*

underfelt ['ʌndəfelt] *n.* thibaude *f* (pour moquette).

underfloor ['ʌndəflɔːr] *a.* **u. heating,** chauffage *m* par le sol.

underfoot [ʌndə'fut] *adv.* sous les pieds; **it's wet u.,** il fait mouillé à marcher; **the snow crunched u.,** la neige craquait sous les pieds; **to trample, tread, sth. u.,** fouler qch. aux pieds.

under(-)gardener ['ʌndəgɑːdnər] *n.* aide-jardinier *m*, *pl.* aides-jardiniers.

undergarment [ˈʌndəgɑːmənt] *n.* sous-vêtement *m*; vêtement *m* de dessous.

undergo [ʌndəˈgou] *v.tr.* (*p.t.* **underwent** [-ˈwent]; *p.p.* **undergone** [-ˈgɔn]) **1.** (*a*) passer par, subir (un changement); **to u. a complete change,** subir une métamorphose complète; **undergoing repairs,** en (voie de) réparation; (*b*) subir (une épreuve, un examen); **to u. an operation,** subir une opération *Med:* **to u. treatment,** suivre un traitement. **2.** éprouver (une déception); **she has undergone much suffering,** elle a subi, passé par, de dures épreuves.

undergrad [ʌndəˈgræd] *n. F:* = UNDERGRADUATE.

undergraduate [ʌndəˈgrædjuət] *n.* étudiant, -ante (qui prépare la licence); **in my u. days,** lorsque j'étais étudiant; **u. life,** la vie d'étudiant.

underground 1. *adv.* [ʌndəˈgraund] (*a*) sous (la) terre; **to work u.,** travailler sous (la) terre; (*b*) clandestinement, secrètement; **to go u.,** passer dans la clandestinité. **2.** *a.* [ˈʌndəgraund] (*a*) (travail) sous (la) terre; (tuyau) sous le sol; (lac, câble) souterrain; **u. railway,** chemin de fer souterrain; **u. gallery, passage,** souterrain *m*; **u. workings,** chantier souterrain, travaux souterrains; (*b*) (*of organization, press*) clandestin, secret, -ète; **u. movement,** mouvement clandestin; (*in occupied country*) résistance *f*. **3.** *n.* [ˈʌndəgraund] (*a*) chemin de fer souterrain; **the u.** = le métro; (*b*) (*in occupied country, etc.*) **the u.,** la résistance.

undergrowth [ˈʌndəgrouθ] *n.* broussailles *fpl*; sous-bois *m*.

underhand [ˈʌndəhænd] **1.** *adv. A: & Lit:* (agir) en sous-main, en cachette. **2.** *a.* secret, -ète; clandestin; (*of pers.*) sournois; **to behave in an u. way,** agir en sous-main; **u. dealings,** agissements clandestins.

underhanded [ʌndəˈhændid] **1.** *a.* = UNDERHAND 2. **2.** *a. esp. U.S:* à court de personnel, de main-d'œuvre. **-ly** *adv.* en sous-main, en cachette.

underinsured [ʌndərinˈsjuːəd] *a.* sous-assuré.

underlay¹ [ˈʌndəlei] *n.* thibaude *f* (pour moquette); assise *f* (pour carrelage).

underlay² [ʌndəˈlei] *v.tr.* (*p.t. & p.p.* **underlaid** [-ˈleid]) **to u. sth. with sth.,** mettre qch. sous qch.; **carpet underlaid with felt,** moquette sur thibaude.

underlie [ʌndəˈlai] *v.tr.* (*p.t.* **underlay** [-ˈlei]; *p.p.* **underlain** [-ˈlein] *pr.p.* **underlying** [-ˈlaiiŋ]) **1.** être sous (qch.), en dessous de (qch.). **2.** être à la base, à l'origine, de (qch.); servir de base à (qch.). **underlying** *a.* **1.** au-dessous; (*of rock*) sous-jacent. **2.** (i) (principe) fondamental, -aux; (qui sert) de base; (ii) caché, secret, -ète; **u. causes of an event,** raisons profondes d'un événement.

underline [ʌndəˈlain] *v.tr.* **1.** souligner (un mot). **2.** souligner, appuyer sur, insister sur (un fait). **underlining** *n.* soulignement *m*, soulignage *m*.

underling [ˈʌndəliŋ] *n. Pej:* subalterne *mf*, subordonné, -ée; inférieur, -e.

undermanager [ˈʌndəmænidʒər] *n.* sous-chef *m*.

undermanned [ʌndəˈmænd] *a.* à court de personnel, de main-d'œuvre; **to be u.,** manquer de personnel.

undermentioned [ˈʌndəmenʃ(ə)nd] *a.* (cité, mentionné) ci-dessous; **the u. persons,** les personnes dont les noms suivent.

undermine [ʌndəˈmain] *v.tr.* (*a*) miner, saper (la côte, une muraille); (*of sea, river*) affouiller (les falaises, les berges); **foundations undermined by water,** fondements minés par l'eau; (*b*) saper (un principe, l'autorité de qn); miner (la santé de qn); ébranler (la confiance de qn); **to u. the foundations of society,** attaquer les bases de la société.

undermost [ˈʌndəmoust] *a.* le plus bas, *f.* la plus basse; inférieur.

underneath [ʌndəˈniːθ] **1.** *prep.* au-dessous de; sous; **he pushed the letter u. the door,** il a glissé la lettre sous la porte; **he pulled it (out) from u. the blanket,** il l'a tiré de dessous la couverture. **2.** *adv.* au-dessous; dessous; **he picked up the book and found the ticket u.,** il a soulevé le livre et a trouvé le billet en dessous. **3.** *n.* dessous *m*; **the u. of the box is black,** la boîte est noire en dessous. **4.** *a.* d'en dessous.

undernourished [ʌndəˈnʌriʃt] *a.* sous-alimenté.

undernourishment [ʌndəˈnʌriʃmənt] *n.* sous-alimentation *f*.

underpants [ˈʌndəpænts] *n.pl.* (*for men*) slip *m*; (*with legs*) caleçon *m*.

underpart [ˈʌndəpɑːt] *n.* partie inférieure.

underpass [ˈʌndəpɑːs] *n.* (*a*) passage *m* en dessous, inférieur; (*b*) (passage) souterrain (*m*).

underpay [ʌndəˈpei] *v.tr.* (*p.t. & p.p.* **underpaid** [-ˈeid]) sous-payer, sous-rémunérer (un ouvrier, etc.). **underpaid** *a.* (travail, ouvrier) sous-payé; (colis, etc.) insuffisamment affranchi.

underpin [ʌndəˈpin] *v.tr.* **(underpinned)** (*a*) étayer (un mur); (*b*) étayer (une société).

underplay [ʌndəˈplei] *v.tr.* **1.** *Fig:* **to u. one's hand,** cacher son jeu. **2.** minimiser l'importance de qch.); **to u. a part,** ne pas faire assez ressortir un rôle.

underpopulated [undəˈpɔpjuleitid] *a.* sous-peuplé.

underprice [ʌndəˈprais] *v.tr.* mettre un prix trop bas à (un article).

underprivileged [ʌndəˈprivilidʒd] *a.* déshérité, défavorisé; économiquement faible; *n.pl.* **the u.,** les défavorisés (sociaux); les économiquement faibles.

underproduction [ʌndəprəˈdʌkʃ(ə)n] *n. Ind:* sous-production *f*.

underproductive [ʌndəprəˈdʌktiv] *a. Ind:* sous-productif.

underrate [ʌndəˈreit] *v.tr.* sous-estimer (un adversaire, les difficultés, l'importance de qch., etc.).

underscore [ˈʌndəskɔːr] *v.tr.* [*a*) souligner (un titre, etc.); (*b*) faire ressortir, mettre en évidence (un fait).

underseal¹ [ˈʌndəsiːl] *n. Aut:* couche *f* antirouille (pour dessous de châssis).

underseal² *v.tr.* **to u. (the chassis of) a car,** traiter contre la rouille le châssis d'une voiture.

undersecretary [ʌndəˈsekrit(ə)ri] *n.* sous-secrétaire *mf*; **permanent u.,** directeur général (d'un ministère).

undersell [ʌndəˈsel] *v.tr.* (*p.t. & p.p.* **undersold** [-ˈsould]) **1.** vendre moins cher que (qn). **2.** vendre (qch.) au-dessous de sa valeur.

undersexed [ʌndəˈsekst] *a.* de, à, faible libido.

undershirt [ˈʌndeʃəːt] *a. NAm:* (*for men*) maillot *m*.

undershoot [ʌndəˈʃuːt] *v.tr. & i.* (*p.t. & p.p.* **undershot** [-ˈʃɔt]) *Av:* **to u. (the runway),** se présenter, atterrir, trop court (sur la piste).

underside [ˈʌndəsaid] *n.* dessous *m*.

undersigned [ʌndəˈsaind] *a. & n.* **I, the u.,** je soussigné(e); **the u. declare that . . .,** les soussignés déclarent que . . . .

undersize(d) [ʌndəˈsaiz(d)] *a.* de (trop) petite taille, trop petit; (*of pers.*) rabougri.

underskirt [ˈʌndəskəːt] *n.* jupon *m*.

underslung [ʌndəˈslʌŋ] *a.* (ressort) sous l'essieu; *Aut:* (châssis) surbaissé; (voiture) à carrosserie surbaissée.

understaffed [ʌndəˈstɑːft] *a.* à court de personnel; **the office is u.,** le bureau manque de personnel.

understand [ʌndəˈstænd] *v.* (*p.t. & p.p.* **understood** [-ˈstud]) **1.** *v.tr.* (*a*) comprendre, entendre; **I don't u. French,** je ne comprends pas le français; **he can't make himself understood in German,** il ne peut pas se faire comprendre en allemand; **he understands business matters,** il s'y connaît en affaires; **this sentence can be understood in several ways,** cette phrase peut s'interpréter de plusieurs façons; **no one understands me,** (i) personne ne me comprend; (ii) je suis un incompris, une incomprise; **to u. each other, one another,** se comprendre, s'entendre; **I quite u. that he must be tired,** je comprends très bien qu'il soit fatigué; **I don't u. why he did it,** je ne comprends pas pourquoi il l'a fait; **do you u. what he's talking about?** comprenez-vous quelque chose à ce qu'il raconte? **what I can't u. is that . . .,** ce que je ne comprends pas, c'est que + *sub.*; **I can u. your being angry,** je comprends que vous soyez fâché; **I can't u. it,** je ne (le) comprends pas; **I'm at a loss to u. it, I can't u. a word of it, I don't u. the first thing about it,** je n'y comprends (absolument) rien; **(is that) understood?** (vous avez, c'est bien) compris? (c'est) entendu? **that's easily understood,** cela se comprend facilement; (*b*) **I understood that I was to be paid for my work,** j'ai cru comprendre que je devais être payé pour mon travail; **I u. (that) you're coming to work here,** si j'ai bien compris vous venez travailler ici; **am I to u. that . . .?** ai-je bien compris que . . .? **he is understood to be, it is understood that he is, abroad,** il paraît, on croit, qu'il est à l'étranger; **it must be understood, you must u., that . . .,** il doit être (bien) entendu, il faut (bien) comprendre, que . . .; **to give s.o. to u. that . . .,** laisser entendre à qn que . . .; **I have made it understood, I have let it be understood, that . . .,** j'ai laissé entendre que . . .; (*c*) *Gram:* sous-entendre (un mot); présumer, supposer (une condition); **in this sentence the verb is understood,** dans cette phrase le verbe est sous-entendu; **that's understood,** cela va sans dire; cela va de soi. **2.** *v.i.* comprendre; **now I u.!** je comprends, j'y suis, maintenant! **you don't u.,** vous n'y êtes pas; **do you u.?** vous comprenez? **he left yesterday, I u.,** il est parti hier, si j'ai bien compris, si je ne me trompe (pas); **to u. about sth.,** comprendre qch. **understanding 1.** *a.* compréhensif, bienveillant (**about sth.,** au sujet de qch.); **u. parents,** parents compréhensifs, qui comprennent; **u. smile,** sourire (i) d'intelligence, (ii) entendu; **he behaved in a very u. way,** il a agi avec beaucoup de discernement. **2.** *n.* (*a*) compréhension *f*, entendement *m*, intelligence *f*; **the age of u.,** l'âge de discernement *m*; **lacking in u.,** incompréhensif, inintelligent; **according to my u. of it,** si je l'ai bien compris; (*b*) entente *f*, accord *m*; **spirit of u.,** esprit d'entente; (*c*) accord, arrangement *m*; **they had an u., there was an u. between them,** ils étaient d'intelligence; **to come to, to reach, an u. with s.o.,** s'entendre, s'arranger, avec qn; (*d*) condition *f*; **on the u. that he gives it me back,** à (la) condition qu'il me le rende, qu'il me le rend; **on the firm u. that . . .,** à la condition expresse que . . .. **understandingly** *adv.* avec compréhension.

understandable [ʌndə'stændəbl] *a.* compréhensible; intelligible; **that's u.,** cela se comprend (facilement); c'est bien normal. **-ably** *adv.* naturellement; à juste titre.

understate [ʌndə'steit] *v.tr.* minimiser, amoindrir.

understatement [ʌndə'steitmənt] *n.* **1.** amoindrissement *m* (des faits); *Ling:* litote *f*. **2. to say it's expensive is an u.,** dire que c'est cher est bien audessous de la vérité; *F:* **that's the u. of the year!** si tu crois que c'est assez dire!

understudy[1] ['ʌndəstʌdi] *n. Th:* doublure *f*.

understudy[2] *v.tr. Th:* doubler (un rôle, un acteur).

undertake [ʌndə'teik] *v.tr.* (*p.t.* **undertook** [-'tuk]; *p.p.* **undertaken** [-'teik(ə)n]) **1.** entreprendre (un voyage, etc.). **2.** (*a*) se charger de, entreprendre (une tâche); assumer (une responsabilité); **to u. to do sth.,** se charger de, s'engager à, faire qch.; (*b*) **to u. that . . .,** garantir, assurer, que . . .. **undertaking** [ʌndə'teikiŋ] *n.* **1.** (*a*) action *f* d'entreprendre (qch.); entreprise *f* (de qch.); (*b*) ['ʌndəteikiŋ] métier *m* d'entrepreneur des pompes funèbres. **2.** entreprise (commerciale, industrielle); **it's quite an u.,** c'est toute une affaire; c'est une grande entreprise. **3.** engagement *m*, promesse *f*; *Jur:* soumission *f*; **he gave an u. to do it, that he would do it,** il s'est engagé à, il a promis de, le faire.

undertaker ['undəteikər] *n.* entrepreneur *m* des pompes funèbres; *F:* croque-mort.

undertone ['ʌndətoun] *n.* **1. in an u.,** (parler) à mi-voix, à voix basse; (parler) bas. **2.** (*a*) **u. of discontent,** courant sourd de mécontentement; (*b*) **grey with blue undertones,** gris nuancé de bleu.

undervalue [ʌndə'vælju:] *v.tr.* **1.** sous-évaluer (des marchandises). **2.** mésestimer (qn, qch.).

undervest ['ʌndəvest] *n. esp. NAm:* (*for men*) maillot *m*, tricot *m*, de corps; (*for women*) chemise américaine, *Fr.C:* camisole *f*.

underwater 1. ['ʌndəwɔ:tər] *a.* sous-marin; **u. camera, photography,** caméra, photographie, sous-marine; **u. fishing,** pêche sous-marine, subaquatique. **2.** [ʌndə'wɔ:tər] *adv.* sous l'eau; sous la mer.

underwear ['ʌndəwεər] *n.* sous-vêtements *mpl*; vêtements *mpl* de dessous (*for women*) lingerie *f*, dessous *mpl*.

underweight [ʌndə'weit] *a.* (article) d'un poids insuffisant; (*of pers.*) **to be u.,** ne pas peser assez.

underworld ['ʌndəwə:ld] *n.* **1.** *esp. Myth:* **the u.,** les enfers *mpl*. **2.** pègre *f*, milieu *m*.

underwrite ['ʌndərait] *v.tr.* (*p.t.* **underwrote** [-rout]; *p.p.* **underwritten** [-ritn]) **1.** *Fin:* garantir, souscrire (une émission); soumissionner (un emprunt, une nouvelle émission). **2.** *Ins:* souscrire (une police, un risque); **policy underwritten at Lloyd's, in London,** police souscrite chez Lloyd, à Londres. **underwriting** *n.* **1.** *Fin:* garantie *f* (d'émission); souscription *f* (d'un risque). **2.** (*a*) souscription (d'une police, d'un risque); (*b*) assurance *f* maritime.

underwriter ['ʌndəraitər] *n.* **1.** *Fin:* syndicataire *m*; soumissionnaire *mf*; **the underwriters,** le syndicat de garantie. **2.** *Ins:* **marine u.,** assureur *m* maritime; **Lloyd's underwriters,** assureurs du Lloyd.

undeserved [ʌndi'zə:vd] a. (*of praise, reproach*) immérité. **-ly** [ʌndi'zə:vidli] *adv.* **1.** à tort; injustement. **2.** (être décoré) sans le mériter, sans l'avoir mérité. **undeserving** *a.* (*of pers.*) sans mérite; (*of thg*) peu méritoire; **u. of attention,** qui ne mérite pas l'attention; indigne d'attention.

undesirable [ʌndi'zaiərəbl] *a.* & *n.* indésirable (*mf*); **an u. character,** un personnage peu désirable.

undetected [ʌndi'tektid] *a.* non détecté, non décelé; (*of mistake*) **to go u.,** passer inaperçu.

undetermined [ʌndi'tə:mind] *a.* **1.** (*of quality, date*) indéterminé, incertain. **2.** (*of question*) indécis; *esp. Lit:* (*of pers.*) irrésolu, indécis.

undeterred [ʌndi'tə:d] *a.* sans se laisser décourager (**by,** par); **u. by the weather, he went out for a walk,** en dépit du mauvais temps, il est sorti se promener.

undeveloped [ʌndi'veləpt] *a.* (*a*) non développé; (*of land, resources*) inexploité, non exploité; (*of mind*) non formé; (*b*) (*of film*) non développé.

undeviating [ʌn'di:vieitiŋ] *a.* **1.** (cours, chemin) droit, direct. **2.** constant; (fidélité) qui ne se dément pas.

undies ['ʌndiz] *n.pl. F:* (*esp. for women*) lingerie *f*.

undigested [ʌnd(a)i'dʒestid] *a.* (*of food*) non digéré, mal digéré; (*of facts*) mal assimilé.

undignified [ʌn'dignifaid] *a.* peu digne; qui manque de dignité, de tenue; **to be u.,** manquer de dignité.

undiluted [ʌndai'lju:tid] *a.* non dilué, non délayé; (vin) pur; (acide) concentré; (joie) sans mélange.

undiminished [ʌndi'miniʃt] *a.* non diminué; sans

diminution; **my respect for him remains u.,** mon respect pour lui n'a point diminué.

undiplomatic [ʌndiplə'mætik] *a.* peu diplomatique; peu adroit; (*of pers.*) peu diplomate.

undipped [ʌn'dipt] *a. Aut:* **to drive with u. headlights,** conduire avec les phares allumés; ne pas se mettre en code.

undiscernible [ʌndi'sə:nəbl] *a.* indiscernable.

undiscerning [ʌndi'sə:niŋ] *a.* (esprit) sans discernement, peu pénétrant.

undischarged [ʌndis'tʃɑ:dʒd] *a.* **1.** non déchargé. **2.** (débiteur) non libéré (d'une obligation); *Jur:* **u. bankrupt,** failli non réhabilité; **u. debt,** dette non liquidée. **3.** (devoir) inaccompli.

undisciplined [ʌn'disiplind] *a.* indiscipliné.

undisclosed [ʌndis'klouzd] *a.* non révélé.

undiscovered [ʌndis'kʌvəd] *a.* non découvert; caché; **u. country,** terre inconnue.

undiscriminating [ʌndis'krimineitiŋ] *a.* sans discernement, qui manque de discernement. **-ly** *adv.* **to praise u.,** prodiguer des éloges sans discernement.

undisguised [ʌndis'gaizd] *a.* non déguisé; (*of feelings*) non dissimulé; franc, *f.* franche; sincère; **to show u. satisfaction,** manifester une satisfaction sincère. **-ly** [ʌndis'gaizidli] *adv.* ouvertement; franchement.

undismayed [ʌndis'meid] *a.* non découragé; **he was quite u. by the incident,** l'incident ne l'a nullement consterné.

undisputed [ʌndis'pju:tid] *a.* incontesté, indisputé.

undistinguished [ʌndis'tiŋgwiʃt] *a.* médiocre; banal, -als; quelconque; (*of appearance*) peu distingué.

undisturbed [ʌndis'tə:bd] *a.* **1.** (*a*) *esp. Lit:* (*of pers.*) tranquille; (*b*) (*of sleep*) paisible, calme. **2.** (*of peace*) que rien ne vient troubler; (*of papers*) non dérangé, non déplacé.

undivided [ʌndi'vaidid] *a.* **1.** indivisé; entier. **2.** non partagé; **he gave her his u. attention,** il lui a donné toute son attention. **3. u. opinion,** opinion unanime.

undo [ʌn'du:] *v.tr.* (*p.t.* **undid** [-'did] *p.p.* **undone** [-'dʌn]) **1.** détruire, annuler (une œuvre); réparer (une faute); **you can't u. the past,** ce qui est fait est fait. **2.** défaire (un nœud, un bouton, un tricot); décrocher (une agrafe); ouvrir (un fermoir); desserrer (une vis); défaire, déficeler (un paquet); délacer (ses chaussures); dégrafer, déboutonner (sa robe). **undoing** *n. esp. Lit:* ruine *f*, perte *f*; **drink was his u.,** l'alcool a causé sa perte. **undone** *a.* **1.** (*a*) défait; **to come u.,** (*of knot, button*) se défaire; (*of hair*) se dénouer; (*of screw*) se desserrer; (*of shoe*) se délacer; (*of dress*) se dégrafer; (*of seam*) se découdre, se défaire; (*of parcel*) se déficeler; (*b*) *Hum: A:* **I am u.!** je suis perdu! **2.** inaccompli; **we have left u. those things which we ought to have done,** nous n'avons pas fait les choses que nous aurions dû faire.

undomesticated [ʌndə'mestikeitid] *a.* **he's completely u.,** il ne sait rien faire dans la maison.

undoubted [ʌn'dautid] *a.* (fait) incontestable. **-ly** *adv.* indubitablement, incontestablement.

undramatic [ʌndrə'mætik] *a.* (ouvrage, style) peu dramatique, qui manque de sens dramatique.

undrawn [ʌn'drɔ:n] *a.* **the curtains were still u.,** les rideaux n'étaient toujours pas tirés.

undreamed, undreamt [ʌn'dri:md, ʌn'dremt] *a.* **u. of,** (i) insoupçonné; (ii) inimaginable.

undress¹ [ʌn'dres] (**undressed** [ʌn'drest]) **1.** *v.i.* & *pr.* se déshabiller. **2.** *v.tr.* (*a*) déshabiller; (*b*) ôter les pansements (d'une plaie). **undressed** *a.* **1.** (*a*) déshabillé; (*b*) en déshabillé. **2.** (*a*) (tissu) inapprêté; (bois) en grume; **u. stone,** pierre non taillée; (*b*) *Cu:* (*of meat*) non accommodé; (*of lobster*) nature *inv*; (*of salad*) non assaisonné; (*d*) **u. wound,** blessure non pansée.

undress² *n. A: & Lit:* (*for women*) déshabillé *m*, négligé *m*; *Mil:* **u.** ['ʌndres] **uniform,** petite tenue; *F:* **in a state of u.,** peu vêtu; en petite tenue.

undrinkable [ʌn'driŋkəbl] *a.* imbuvable; non potable.

undue [ʌn'dju:] *a.* **1.** (paiement) inexigible, indu. **2.** (*a*) (*of exaction*) injuste, injustifiable; (*of reward*) immérité; **u. influence,** abus d'influence; (*b*) (*of haste*) exagéré, indu; **u. optimism,** optimisme peu justifié. **unduly** *adv.* **1.** (*a*) (réclamer, payer) indûment. **2.** (*a*) injustement; (*b*) à l'excès, trop; **u. high price,** prix excessif; **to be u. optimistic,** faire preuve d'un optimisme peu justifié; **he worries u., he's u. worried, about his health,** sa santé le préoccupe trop.

undulate ['ʌndjuleit] **1.** *v.tr.* onduler. **2.** *v.i.* onduler, ondoyer. **undulating** *a.* ondulé, onduleux; (blé) ondoyant; **u. country,** pays vallonné.

undulation [ʌndju'leiʃ(ə)n] *n.* **1.** ondulation *f.* **2.** accident *m* (de terrain); mouvement *m* (de terrain).

undying [ʌn'daiiŋ] *a.* immortel; (*of love*) éternel.

unearned [ʌn'ə:nd] *a.* **1.** (*of reward, punishment*) immérité. **2.** (*of money*) non gagné (par le travail); **u. income,** rentes *fpl.*

unearth [ʌn'ə:θ] *v.tr.* **1.** (*a*) déterrer, exhumer; (*b*) découvrir, dénicher (qch.); **wherever did you u. that?** où diable as-tu déniché ça? **2.** faire sortir (un animal) de son trou, de son terrier.

unearthly [ʌn'ə:θli] *a.* **1.** céleste, sublime. **2.** (*a*) surnaturel; mystérieux; (*b*) *Lit:* **u. pallor,** pâleur mortelle; **u. light,** lueur sinistre; (*c*) *F:* **at an u. hour,** à une heure impossible; **u. din,** vacarme de tous les diables; **for some u. reason,** pour une raison absurde.

unease [ʌn'i:z] *n. esp. Lit:* malaise *m*; gêne *f.*

uneasy [ʌn'i:zi] *a.* (*a*) mal à l'aise; gêné; (*b*) inquiet, -ète; (sommeil) agité; (calme) troublé; **there was an u. silence,** il y a eu un silence gêné; **to be u.,** être inquiet, anxieux (**about,** au sujet de); **to be u. in one's mind about sth.,** ne pas avoir l'esprit tranquille au sujet de qch. **-ily** *adv.* (*a*) d'un air gêné; (*b*) avec inquiétude; (dormir) d'un sommeil agité.

uneatable [ʌn'i:təbl] *a.* immangeable; pas mangeable.

uneaten [ʌn'i:t(ə)n] *a.* non mangé; **u. food,** restes *mpl.*

uneconomic [ʌni:kə'nɔmik] *a.* **1.** non économique. **2.** (travail) pas rentable.

uneconomical [ʌni:kə'nɔmik(ə)l] *a.* (*of method, car*) peu économique.

unedifying [ʌn'edifaiiŋ] *a.* peu édifiant.

unedited [ʌn'editid] *a.* (texte) non édité; (film) non monté.

uneducated [ʌn'edjukeitid] *a.* **1.** (*of pers.*) sans éducation. **2.** (*of speech, accent*) populaire.

unemotional [ʌni'mouʃən(ə)l] *a.* **1.** (*of pers.*) peu émotif; peu émotionnable; (*of reaction*) peu émotionnel; (*of style*) neutre, dépourvu de passion. **2.** (*of pers.*) impassible; qui ne montre aucune émotion. **-ally** *adv.* sans émotion; avec impassibilité.

unemployable [ʌnim'plɔiəbl] *a.* (*of pers.*) inapte à travailler.

unemployed [ʌnim'plɔid] *a.* **1.** (*of pers.*) (*a*) désœuvré, inoccupé; (*b*) *Ind:* en chômage; sans travail; *n.pl.* **the u.,** les chômeurs *mpl.* **2.** (*of time*) inemployé; (*of machine*) inutilisé; **u. capital,** fonds inactifs.

unemployment [ʌnim'plɔimənt] *n. Ind:* chômage *m*; manque *m* de travail; **u. benefit,** *NAm:* **u. compensation,** allocation *f*, indemnité *f*, de chômage; **u. figures,** statistiques du chômage.

unencumbered [ʌnin'kʌmbəd] *a.* non encombré (**by, with,** de); *Jur:* **u. estate,** propriété franche d'hypothèques.

unending [ʌn'endiŋ] *a.* **1.** interminable, qui n'en finit plus; sans fin. **2.** éternel.

unendurable [ʌnin'djuərəbl] *a.* insupportable.
unenforceable [ʌnin'fɔːsəbl] *a.* non exécutoire.
unengaged [ʌnin'geidʒd] *a.* libre.
un-English [ʌn'iŋgliʃ] *a.* peu anglais; (i) indigne d'un Anglais; (ii) contraire à l'esprit anglais.
unenlightened [ʌnin'lait(ə)nd] *a.* (peuple, siècle) peu éclairé; ignorant. **unenlightening** *a.* (remarque) qui jette peu de lumière (sur une question).
unenterprising [ʌn'entəpraiziŋ] *a.* (*of pers.*) peu entreprenant, qui manque d'initiative; (*of plan*) qui manque d'audace.
unenthusiastic [ʌninθjuːzi'æstik] *a.* peu enthousiaste; **he seems rather u. about it,** ça n'a pas l'air de l'enthousiasmer. **-ally** *adv.* sans enthousiasme.
unenviable [ʌn'enviəbl] *a.* peu enviable.
unequal [ʌn'iːkwəl] *a.* (*a*) (*of size, amount*) inégal, -aux; (*b*) **he was u. to the job,** il n'était pas à la hauteur de la tâche; **to be u. to doing sth.,** ne pas être de force à faire qch. **-ally** *adv.* inégalement.
unequalled [ʌn'iːkwəld] *a.* inégalé; sans égal.
unequivocal [ʌni'kwivək(ə)l] *a.* clair, net; sans équivoque; (réponse) sans ambiguïté; (refus) catégorique. **-ally** *adv.* sans équivoque; nettement.
unerring [ʌn'əːriŋ] *a.* infaillible, sûr; **with u. aim, he hit the target,** visant avec precision, il a touché la cible. **-ly** *adv.* infailliblement, sûrement.
unescorted [ʌni'skɔːtid] *a.* non accompagné.
unessential [ʌni'senʃ(ə)l] **1.** *a.* non essentiel. **2.** *n.pl.* **unessentials,** le superflu, l'accessoire *m*.
unethical [ʌn'eθik(ə)l] *a.* (conduite) qui manque de probité.
uneven [ʌn'iːv(ə)n] *a.* **1.** inégal, -aux; (*a*) rugueux; (chemin) raboteux; (*b*) (terrain) accidenté; **the floorboards are u.,** les planches ne sont pas de niveau; (*c*) **u. breathing,** respiration irrégulière; **u. temper,** humeur inégale. **2.** (nombre) impair. **-ly** *adv.* **1.** inégalement; **the opponents were u. matched,** les adversaires étaient de force inégale; **u. distributed load,** charge répartie inégalement. **2.** irrégulièrement.
unevenness [ʌn'iːv(ə)nnis] *n.* inégalité *f*; (*a*) rugosité *f*; (*b*) dénivellement *m*; anfractuosité *f* (d'un terrain); (*c*) irrégularité *f* (de la respiration).
uneventful [ʌni'ventf(u)l] *a.* (voyage) sans incidents; **u. life,** vie calme, peu mouvementée. **-fully** *adv.* **to pass u.,** se passer sans incidents.
unexceptionable [ʌnik'sepʃənəbl] *a.* (conduite) irréprochable; (personne) tout à fait convenable.
unexceptional [ʌnik'sepʃən(ə)l] *a.* ordinaire; banal, -als; (incident) qui n'a rien d'exceptionnel.
unexciting [ʌnik'saitiŋ] *a.* plat; (conte) insipide, peu passionnant; (vie) monotone; **u. day,** journée calme; **this restaurant serves very u. food,** on sert des repas très ordinaires dans ce restaurant.
unexpected [ʌniks'pektid] **1.** *a.* (visiteur, résultat) inattendu; (événement) imprévu; (départ) inopiné; (secours, bonheur) inespéré; **u. meeting,** rencontre inopinée; **it was completely u.,** on ne s'y attendait pas du tout. **2.** *n.* **you must allow for the u.,** il faut parer à l'imprévu. **-ly** *adv.* de manière inattendue; **to arrive u.,** arriver à l'improviste.
unexpired [ʌniks'paiəd] *a.* (bail) non expiré; (passeport, billet) non périmé, encore valable.
unexplained [ʌniks'pleind] *a.* inexpliqué.
unexploded [ʌniks'ploudid] *a.* (obus) non explosé, non éclaté.
unexploited [ʌniks'plɔitid] *a.* inexploité.
unexplored [ʌniks'plɔːd] *a.* (pays, etc.) inexploré.
unexposed [ʌniks'pouzd] *a.* **1.** *Phot:* (film) vierge. **2.** non découvert; (criminel) non démasqué.
unexpressed [ʌniks'prest] *a.* inexprimé.
unexpurgated [ʌn'ekspə(ː)geitid] *a.* (livre, texte) non expurgé; **u. edition,** édition intégrale.

unfading [ʌn'feidiŋ] *a.* qui ne se fane, ne se flétrit, pas; (souvenir) ineffaçable, impérissable.
unfailing [ʌn'feiliŋ] *a.* **1.** qui ne se dément pas; (moyen, remède) infaillible, certain, sûr; (courage) inlassable; (zèle) infatigable; (mémoire) sans défaillance; (bonté) inaltérable; (espoir) inébranlable; **to be u. in one's duty,** ne jamais faillir à son devoir. **2.** (source, réserve) intarissable, inépuisable. **-ly** *adv.* infailliblement, immanquablement.
unfair [ʌn'fɛər] *a.* **1.** injuste (**to s.o.,** envers qn); peu équitable; **to be u. to s.o.,** défavoriser qn; **it's u.!** ce n'est pas juste! **to have an u. advantage over everybody else,** être avantagé au détriment de tous les autres; **he has been put at an u. disadvantage,** il a été défavorisé, désavantagé. **2.** (*a*) inéquitable; (prix) exorbitant; (*b*) **u. competition,** concurrence déloyale. **-ly** *adv.* **1.** injustement; peu équitablement; **he has been u. treated,** il est (la) victime d'une injustice. **2.** (jouer) déloyalement; **to act u.,** agir avec mauvaise foi.
unfairness [ʌn'fɛənis] *n.* **1.** injustice *f*; partialité *f*. **2.** déloyauté *f*; mauvaise foi.
unfaithful [ʌn'feiθf(u)l] **1.** *a.* (*a*) **to be u. to (s.o.),** tromper, être infidèle à (sa femme, son mari); (*b*) (compte rendu) inexact, infidèle. **2.** *n.pl. Ecc:* **the u.,** les infidèles *mpl*. **-fully** *adv.* infidèlement.
unfaithfulness [ʌn'feiθf(u)lnis] *n.* infidélité *f*.
unfaltering [ʌn'fɔːltəriŋ] *a.* sans défaillance; **u. voice,** voix ferme; **u. steps,** pas assurés. **-ly** *adv.* (parler) d'une voix ferme; (marcher) d'un pas bien assuré.
unfamiliar [ʌnfə'miliər] *a.* **1.** peu familier, peu connu; **u. face,** visage étranger, inconnu; **u. phrase,** expression peu habituelle. **2.** (*of pers.*) **to be u. with sth.,** ne pas connaître, mal connaître, qch.; ne pas être au fait de qch.; **I'm totally u. with this town,** je ne connais pas du tout cette ville; **he is quite u. with this subject,** il ne sait absolument rien de ce sujet.
unfamiliarity [ʌnfəmili'æriti] *n.* **1.** caractère étranger (d'un lieu). **2.** ignorance *f* (**with,** de); **u. with legal procedure,** inexpérience *f* de la procédure.
unfashionable [ʌn'fæʃ(ə)nəbl] *a.* démodé, passé de mode; qui n'est pas, qui n'est plus, à la mode. **-ably** *adv.* sans se préoccuper de la mode.
unfasten [ʌn'fɑːs(ə)n] *v.tr.* **1. to u. sth. from sth.,** détacher, délier, qch. de qch. **2.** défaire, dégrafer (un vêtement, un bracelet); desserrer (une ceinture); défaire (une cravate, un nœud); ouvrir, déverrouiller (une porte); **to come unfastened,** (*of garment*) se dégrafer; se déboutonner; (*of knot*) se défaire, se dénouer; (*of belt*) se desserrer.
unfathomable [ʌn'fæðəməbl] *a.* (abîme, mystère) insondable; (visage) impénétrable, inscrutable.
unfathomed [ʌn'fæðəmd] *a.* (gouffre, mystère) insondé; **u. depths,** profondeurs inexplorées.
unfavourable, *NAm:* **unfavorable** [ʌn'feiv(ə)rəbl] *a.* défavorable, peu favorable (**to,** à); (moment) peu propice, inopportun; (vent) contraire; (critique) adverse; **u. weather, report,** temps, compte rendu, défavorable; **to appear in an u. light,** se montrer sous un jour désavantageux. **-ably** *adv.* défavorablement; **to be u. disposed towards sth., s.o.,** être hostile, opposé, à qch., à qn; **his work compares u. with his brother's,** ses œuvres supportent mal la comparaison avec celles de son frère.
unfeeling [ʌn'fiːliŋ] *a.* (*of pers.*) insensible, impitoyable; dur; **u. heart,** cœur froid, indifférent. **-ly** *adv.* (agir) sans pitié, impitoyablement; (répondre) froidement, durement.
unfeigned [ʌn'feind] *a.* non simulé; sincère. **-ly** [ʌn'feinidli] *adv.* sincèrement.
unfeminine [ʌn'feminin] *a.* peu féminin.
unfenced [ʌn'fenst] *a.* (terrain, etc.) sans clôture.

unfermented [ʌnfə'mentid] *a.* non fermenté.
unfertilized [ʌn'fəːtilaizd] *a.* (œuf) non fécondé.
unfettered [ʌn'fetəd] *a. Lit:* sans entrave(s).
unfilial [ʌn'filiəl] *a.* peu filial, -aux.
unfinished [ʌn'finiʃt] *a.* **1.** inachevé, incomplet, -ète; **u. game,** partie interrompue; **to have some u. business,** avoir (i) quelques affaires pendantes, (ii) une affaire à régler. **2.** *Ind:* non façonné; non usiné.
unfit [ʌn'fit] *a.* **1.** (*a*) impropre, peu propre (**for,** à); **u. for (human) consumption, u. to eat,** impropre à la consommation, non comestible; **u. to drink,** imbuvable; non potable; **u. for publication,** impubliable; **this house is u. for habitation,** cette maison est inhabitable; **road u. for heavy traffic,** chemin impraticable aux poids lourds; (*b*) (*of pers.*) **u. for military service,** inapte au service militaire; **to be u. for one's job,** ne pas convenir à son poste; **u. to rule,** indigne de régner. **2.** (*physically*) (*a*) **to be u.,** être en mauvaise santé; ne pas être en forme; **he's u. to travel,** il n'est pas en état de voyager; **u. for duty,** incapable de faire son service; (*b*) *Mil:* **to be discharged as u.,** être réformé; **to be declared u.,** être déclaré inapte.
unfitness [ʌn'fitnis] *n.* **1. u. for sth., to do sth.,** inaptitude *f* à qch., à faire qch. **2.** mauvaise santé.
unfitted [ʌn'fitid] *a.* **to be u. for sth., to do sth.,** (i) (*of equipment*) être impropre à qch., à faire qch.; (ii) (*of pers.*) ne pas convenir à (un poste); être (iii) être indigne de faire qch. **unfitting** *a.* peu convenable; (*of remark*) mal à propos, déplacé.
unfix [ʌn'fiks] *v.tr.* détacher, défaire; *Mil:* **to u. bayonets,** remettre la baïonnette.
unflagging [ʌn'flægiŋ] *a.* (intérêt) soutenu; (courage, vigueur) inlassable; (optimisme) inébranlable. **-ly** *adv.* inlassablement, infatigablement.
unflappable [ʌn'flæpəbl] *a. F:* imperturbable; **he is completely u.,** il garde toujours son calme.
unflattering [ʌn'flætəriŋ] *a.* peu flatteur (**to,** pour); **her hat was most u.,** son chapeau ne la mettait point en valeur. **-ly** *adv.* d'une manière peu flatteuse.
unfledged [ʌn'fledʒd] *a.* **1.** (oiseau) sans plumes. **2.** *Lit:* (*of pers.*) sans expérience (de la vie).
unflinching [ʌn'flinʃiŋ] *a.* qui ne bronche pas; résolu; stoïque, impassible; **with u. eyes,** d'un regard franc. **-ly** *adv.* sans broncher; résolument.
unfold [ʌn'fould] **1.** *v.tr.* (*a*) déplier, ouvrir (un journal, une serviette); déployer (une carte); **to u. one's arms,** décroiser les bras; (*b*) révéler; exposer (ses intentions, un projet); dévoiler, découvrir (ses plans, un secret). **2.** *v.i. & pr.* se déployer, se dérouler; (*of flower*) s'ouvrir, s'épanouir; (*of story, action*) se dérouler.
unforced [ʌn'fɔːst] *a.* **1.** qui n'est pas forcé. **2.** spontané; **u. laugh,** rire franc.
unforeseeable [ʌnfɔː'siːəbl] *a.* imprévisible.
unforeseen [ʌnfɔː'siːn] *a.* imprévu, inattendu; **unless something u. happens,** sauf imprévu; **u. circumstances,** (i) circonstances imprévues; (ii) *Jur:* force majeure.
unforgettable [ʌnfə'getəbl] *a.* inoubliable.
unforgivable [ʌnfə'givəbl] *a.* impardonnable; inexcusable. **-ably** *adv.* **he was u. rude,** on ne pouvait pas lui pardonner son impolitesse.
unforgiven [ʌnfə'giv(ə)n] *a.* impardonné.
unforgiving *a.* implacable, impitoyable.
unforgotten [ʌnfə'gɔt(ə)n] *a.* inoublié.
unformed [ʌn'fɔːmd] *a.* **1.** (os) qui n'est pas (encore) formé. **2.** (masse) informe. **3.** (esprit) inculte.
unformulated [ʌn'fɔːmjuleitid] *a.* informulé.
unforthcoming [ʌnfɔːθ'kʌmiŋ] *a.* réservé; **to be u. about sth.,** être, se montrer, réticent au sujet de qch.
unfortified [ʌn'fɔːtifaid] *a.* non fortifié; sans fortifications; **u. town,** ville ouverte.
unfortunate [ʌn'fɔːtjənət] **1.** *a.* (*a*) malheureux, malchanceux; **he's been most u.,** il n'a pas eu beaucoup de chance; (*b*) (accident, événement) malheureux, malencontreux; (erreur) regrettable; **u. state of affairs,** situation regrettable, fâcheuse; **u. consequences,** suites malheureuses; **u. choice of words,** choix de mots peu heureux; **in u. circumstances,** dans de tristes circonstances; **it's u. that she has to leave today,** il est dommage qu'elle soit obligée de partir aujourd'hui; **how (very) u.!** quel malheur! quel dommage! **2.** *n.* malheureux, -euse; *coll. Lit:* **the u.,** les infortunés *mpl.* **-ly** *adv.* malheureusement; par malheur; **an u. worded statement,** déclaration formulée d'une façon regrettable; **u. for him,** malheureusement pour lui.
unfounded [ʌn'faundid] *a.* sans fondement; **u. rumour,** bruit dénué de tout fondement; **u. criticism,** critique injustifiée.
unframed [ʌn'freimd] *a.* sans cadre.
unfreeze [ʌn'friːz] *v.* (*p.t.* **unfroze** [ʌn'frouz]; *p.p.* **unfrozen** [ʌn'frouz(ə)n]) **1.** *v.tr.* (*a*) (faire) dégeler; décongeler; (*b*) dégeler, débloquer (des crédits). **2.** *v.i.* (se) dégeler. **unfrozen** *a.* (*a*) (terrain) (i) dégelé, (ii) non gelé; (produit alimentaire) (i) décongelé, (ii) non congelé; (*b*) (crédit) dégelé, débloqué.
unfrequented [ʌnfri'kwentid] *a.* peu fréquenté; **u. spot,** endroit écarté.
unfriendliness [ʌn'frendlinis] *n.* manque *m* d'amitié (**towards,** pour); froideur *f* (**towards,** envers, à l'égard de); hostilité *f* (**towards,** envers, contre).
unfriendly [ʌn'frendli] *a.* **1.** (ton, sentiment) peu amical, -aux; inamical, -aux; **u. action,** action inamicale, hostile; **to be u. to(wards) s.o.,** être mal disposé envers qn; traiter qn avec froideur. **2.** (*of circumstances*) défavorable; **u. reception,** accueil froid.
unfrock [ʌn'frɔk] *v.tr.* défroquer (un prêtre, etc.).
unfruitful [ʌn'fruːtf(u)l] *a.* stérile, infertile; **u. research,** recherche infructueuse, improductive.
unfulfilled [ʌnful'fild] *a.* (*a*) (prophétie) inaccomplie; (*b*) (désir) non satisfait, inassouvi; (*of prayer*) inexaucé; (*of pers.*) **to feel u.,** éprouver un sentiment d'insatisfaction; (*c*) (devoir) inaccompli; (promesse) non tenue.
unfunny [ʌn'fʌni] *a.* qui n'est pas drôle.
unfurl [ʌn'fəːl] **1.** *v.tr.* (*a*) déferler (une voile, un drapeau); (*b*) dérouler (un parapluie). **2.** *v.i.* se déployer.
unfurnished [ʌn'fəːniʃt] *a.* non meublé.
ungainliness [ʌn'geinlinis] *n.* air *m* gauche.
ungainly [ʌn'geinli] *a.* gauche, disgracieux.
ungallant [ʌn'gælənt] *a.* peu galant; discourtois.
ungenerous [ʌn'dʒen(ə)rəs] *a.* peu généreux.
ungentlemanly [ʌn'dʒentlmənli] *a.* peu galant, discourtois; **u. behaviour,** manque *m* de savoir-vivre.
ungetatable [ʌnget'ætəbl] *a. F:* inaccessible.
unglazed [ʌn'gleizd] *a.* **1.** (*of window*) non vitré; sans vitres. **2.** (*a*) (papier) non glacé; *Phot:* **u. print,** épreuve mate; (*b*) *Cer:* non verni, non émaillé; (*of brick*) non vitrifié; **u. porcelain,** biscuit *m*; (*c*) (gâteau) non glacé.
ungodliness [ʌn'gɔdlinis] *n.* impiété *f.*
ungodly [ʌn'gɔdli] *a.* (*a*) impie, irréligieux; (*b*) *F:* **an u. row,** un bruit de tous les diables; **he got up at an u. hour,** il s'est levé à une heure impossible, indue.
ungovernable [ʌn'gʌv(ə)nəbl] *a.* **1.** (peuple, pays) ingouvernable. **2.** (désir, passion) irrésistible; **he has fits of u. temper,** il a des emportements *m* de colère.
ungraceful [ʌn'greisf(u)l] *a.* disgracieux; gauche. **-fully** *adv.* sans grâce; gauchement.
ungracious [ʌn'greiʃəs] *a.* peu gracieux; peu aimable; **it would be u. of me to refuse,** j'aurais mauvaise grâce de refuser. **-ly** *adv.* avec mauvaise grâce.

ungraciousness [ʌn'greiʃəsnis] *n.* mauvaise grâce.
ungrammatical [ʌngrə'mætik(ə)l] a. non grammatical, -aux; incorrect. **-ally** *adv.* incorrectement.
ungrateful [ʌn'greitf(u)l] *a.* **to be u. to s.o.,** être peu reconnaissant envers qn **(for sth.,** de qch.); se montrer ingrat envers qn; (*b*) (sol) ingrat; **u. task,** tâche ingrate. **-fully** *adv.* avec ingratitude.
ungratefulness [ʌn'greitf(u)lnis] *n.* ingratitude *f.*
ungratified [ʌn'grætifaid] *a.* (désir) inassouvi.
ungrudging [ʌn'grʌdʒiŋ] *a.* donné de bon cœur; (*of admiration*) (très) sincère. **-ly** *adv.* de bon cœur; généreusement.
unguarded [ʌn'gɑːdid] *a.* **1.** (*a*) non gardé; sans surveillance; (ville) sans défense; **to leave the goal u.,** dégarnir le but; (*b*) *Cards:* (roi) sec; *Chess:* (pièce) non gardée. **2.** (*of remark*) inconsidéré, irréfléchi; **in an u. moment,** dans un moment d'inattention. **3.** (précipice) sans garde-fou; (mécanisme) sans dispositif protecteur. **-ly** *adv.* inconsidérément; par inadvertance.
unguent ['ʌŋgwənt] *n.* onguent *m.*
ungulate ['ʌŋgjuleit] *a. & n. Z:* ongulé (*m*).
unhallowed [ʌn'hæloud] *a.* non béni, non consacré.
unhampered [ʌn'hæmpəd] *a.* non entravé **(by,** par); libre (de ses mouvements); **u. by rules,** sans être gêné par des règles.
unhand [ʌn'hænd] *v.tr. A: & Lit:* lâcher (qn).
unhandy [ʌn'hændi] *a. esp. Lit:* maladroit, gauche.
unhappiness [ʌn'hæpinis] *n.* chagrin *m,* tristesse *f.*
unhappy [ʌn'hæpi] *a.* **1.** (*a*) malheureux, triste; **to make s.o. u.,** causer du chagrin à qn; rendre qn malheureux; **to be u. at leaving s.o.,** avoir du chagrin de quitter qn; **to be u. with s.o., sth.,** être mécontent de qn, qch.; (*b*) inquiet; **I'm u. about leaving the house empty,** je n'aime pas laisser, ça m'inquiète de laisser, la maison vide. **2.** (*of remark*) malheureux, malencontreux; **an u. state of affairs,** une situation regrettable. **-ily** *adv.* (*a*) malheureusement; par malheur; (*b*) tristement; d'un air triste; (*c*) **they're u. married,** c'est un ménage malheureux.
unharmed [ʌn'hɑːmd] *a.* (*of pers.*) sain et sauf; indemne; (*of thg*) intact; non endommagé.
unharness [ʌn'hɑːnis] *v.tr.* (*a*) déharnacher (un cheval); (*b*) dételer (un cheval).
unhealthiness [ʌn'helθinis] *n.* **1.** insalubrité *f* (de l'air, d'un endroit). **2.** mauvaise santé; état maladif.
unhealthy [ʌn'helθi] *a.* **1.** (air, endroit) malsain, insalubre. **2.** (*a*) (*of pers.*) maladif; (*b*) (*of state of mind, influence*) malsain; **u. curiosity,** curiosité morbide.
unheard [ʌn'həːd] *a.* **1.** non entendu; **to condemn s.o. u.,** condamner qn sans l'avoir entendu. **2. u. of,** (i) inouï; (ii) (auteur) inconnu; (iii) sans précédent; **that's u. of!** c'est vraiment incroyable!
unheated [ʌn'hiːtid] *a.* non chauffé.
unheeded [ʌn'hiːdid] *a.* négligé, ignoré; **his warning went u.,** on n'a pas tenu compte de son avertissement. **unheeding** *a.* inattentif **(of,** à); insouciant **(of,** de).
unhelpful [ʌn'helpf(u)l] *a.* (*a*) (critique) peu utile; (conseil) vain, futile; (*b*) (*of pers.*) peu secourable, peu obligeant; **don't be so u.!** tâche donc un peu de nous aider! **-fully** *adv.* inutilement.
unheralded [ʌn'herəldid] *a. esp. Lit:* **1.** qui n'est pas annoncé. **2.** imprévu, inattendu.
unhesitating [ʌn'heziteitiŋ] *a.* qui n'hésite pas; **u. reply,** réponse faite sans hésitation; réponse prompte. **-ly** *adv.* sans hésiter; sans hésitation.
unhindered [ʌn'hindəd] *a.* sans obstacle; sans être dérangé **(by,** par); **to go u.,** passer librement.
unhinge [ʌn'hindʒ] *v.tr.* déranger, détraquer (l'esprit de qn). **unhinged** *a.* (esprit) détraqué.
unhitch [ʌn'hitʃ] *v.tr.* **1.** détacher, décrocher (qch.). **2.** dételer (un cheval).
unholy [ʌn'houli] *a. F:* **u. muddle,** désordre affreux; **there was an u. row,** il y a eu un charivari de tous les diables.
unhook [ʌn'huk] **1.** *v.tr.* (*a*) décrocher (un tableau); (*b*) dégrafer (un vêtement); (*of dress*) **to come unhooked,** se dégrafer. **2.** *v.i.* (*a*) se décrocher; (*b*) se dégrafer.
unhoped [ʌn'houpt] *a.* **u. for,** inespéré; inattendu.
unhorse [ʌn'hɔːs] *v.tr. esp. Lit:* désarçonner.
unhurried [ʌn'hʌrid] *a.* lent; **in an u. way,** sans se presser.
unhurt [ʌn'həːt] *a.* (*of pers.*) sans mal, sans blessure; sain et sauf; **to escape u.,** sortir indemne.
unhygienic [ʌnhai'dʒiːnik] *a.* non hygiénique.
unicellular [juːni'seljulər] *a. Biol:* unicellulaire.
unicorn ['juːnikɔːn] *n. Myth: Her:* licorne *f.*
unidentified [ʌnai'dentifaid] *a.* non identifié; **u. flying object,** objet volant non identifié.
unidirectional [juːnid(a)i'rekʃən(ə)l] *a. Ph: etc:* unidirectionnel.
unification [juːnifi'keiʃ(ə)n] *n.* unification *f.*
uniform ['juːnifɔːm] **1.** *a.* (*of colour, style*) uniforme; (*of temperature*) constant; **these boxes are all of u. size,** ces boîtes sont toutes de la même grandeur; **to make u.,** uniformiser. **2.** *n. Mil: Sch:* uniforme *m*; **in u.,** en tenue, en uniforme; **out of u.,** en civil. **-ly** *adv.* uniformément.
uniformed ['juːnifɔːmd] *a.* en uniforme, en tenue.
uniformity [juːni'fɔːmiti] *n.* (*a*) uniformité *f*, unité *f* (de style); (*b*) constance *f* (d'un courant).
unify ['juːnifai] **1.** *v.tr.* unifier un parti politique. **2.** *v.i.* s'unifier. **unifying** *a.* unificateur, -trice.
unilateral [juːni'lætərəl] *a.* unilatéral, -aux; **u. disarmament,** désarmement unilatéral. **-ally** *adv.* unilatéralement.
unilingual [juːni'liŋgwəl] *a.* unilingue.
unimaginable [ʌni'mædʒinəbl] *a.* inimaginable, inconcevable.
unimaginative [ʌni'mædʒinətiv] *a.* dénué, qui manque, d'imagination; peu imaginatif. **-ly** *adv.* sans imagination; d'une manière peu imaginative.
unimaginativeness [ʌni'mædʒinətivnis] *n.* manque *m* d'imagination.
unimpaired [ʌnim'pɛəd] *a.* (*of health, hearing*) non altéré; intact; (*of force, quality*) non diminué; **his mind is u.,** il conserve toute sa vigueur d'esprit.
unimpeachable [ʌnim'piːtʃəbl] *a.* (*a*) inattaquable; (droit) incontestable; **I have it from an u. source,** je le tiens de source sûre; (*b*) (témoignage, témoin) irrécusable; (conduite) irréprochable, impeccable.
unimpeded [ʌnim'piːdid] *a.* non entravé.
unimportant [ʌnim'pɔːtənt] *a.* sans importance; peu important; **it's quite u.,** cela n'a pas la moindre importance.
unimposing [ʌnim'pouziŋ] *a.* (air, aspect) peu imposant, peu impressionnant.
unimpressed [ʌnim'prest] *a.* qui n'est pas impressionné, peu impressionné **(by,** par); **I was u. by his speech,** son discours ne m'a fait aucune impression.
unimpressive [ʌnim'presiv] *a.* peu impressionnant; (discours) peu convaincant; (paysage) peu frappant.
uninflammable [ʌnin'flæməbl] *a.* ininflammable.
uninfluential [ʌninflu'enʃ(ə)l] *a.* sans influence.
uninformed [ʌnin'fɔːmd] *a.* **1.** mal informé, mal renseigné **(about,** sur). **2.** (*of pers.*) ignorant; (*of mind*) inculte.
uninhabitable [ʌnin'hæbitəbl] *a.* inhabitable.
uninhabited [ʌnin'hæbitid] *a.* inhabité, désert; sans habitants.
uninhibited [ʌnin'hibitid] *a.* sans inhibitions, qui n'a pas d'inhibitions; (*of emotion, etc.*) non refréné.

uninitiated [ʌni'niʃieitid] *a.* non initié (**in,** à); *n. pl.* **the u.,** les profanes *m,* les non-initiés *m.*

uninjured [ʌn'indʒəd] *a.* sans blessure, sans mal; sain et sauf; indemne.

uninspired [ʌnin'spaiəd] *a.* qui manque d'inspiration; (*of style*) banal, -als. **uninspiring** *a.* qui n'est pas inspirant; (plutôt) médiocre.

uninsured [ʌnin'ʃuəd] *a.* non assuré (**against,** contre).

unintelligent [ʌnin'telidʒənt] *a.* inintelligent.

unintelligible [ʌnin'telidʒibl] *a.* inintelligible. **-ibly** *adv.* inintelligiblement.

unintended [ʌnin'tendid] *a.* (*a*) (résultat) non voulu; (*b*) involontaire, non intentionnel.

unintentional [ʌnin'tenʃən(ə)l] *a.* involontaire; non intentionnel; fait sans intention; **it was quite u.,** ce n'était pas fait exprès. **-ally** *adv.* involontairement; sans intention; (froisser qn) sans le vouloir; **he did it quite u.,** il ne l'a pas fait exprès.

uninterested [ʌn'int(ə)restid] *a.* non intéressé (**in,** par); indifférent (**in,** à). **uninteresting** *a.* inintéressant; non intéressant; sans intérêt.

uninterrupted [ʌnintə'rʌptid] *a.* **1.** ininterrompu; sans interruption. **2.** continu; **u. correspondence,** correspondance suivie. **-ly** *adv.* sans interruption.

uninvited [ʌnin'vaitid] *a.* **u. guest,** (i) visiteur, -euse, inattendu(e), (ii) intrus, -use; **to come u.,** venir sans invitation; **to do sth. u.,** faire qch. sans y avoir été invité. **uninviting** *a.* peu attirant, peu attrayant; (*of food*) peu appétissant.

union ['ju:niən] *n.* **1.** (*a*) union *f* (**with,** avec); (*b*) mariage *m*; (*c*) concorde *f*; **in perfect u.,** (vivre ensemble) en parfaite harmonie. **2.** (*a*) **the (American) U.,** les États-Unis, l'Union (américaine); **customs u.,** union douanière; (*b*) syndicat (ouvrier); **to form, join, a u.,** se syndiquer; **u. member,** syndiqué(e); membre *m* du, d'un, syndicat; **u. regulations,** règles syndicales; **non-u. workers,** ouvriers, -ières, non syndiqué(e)s; *NAm:* **u. shop,** atelier *m* d'ouvriers syndiqués. **3.** *Mec.E:* **u. (joint),** raccord *m.* **4. U. Flag, Jack,** pavillon *m* britannique. **5.** *U.S: Cost:* **u. suit,** combinaison *f.*

unionism ['ju:niənizm] *n.* **1.** *Ind:* syndicalisme (ouvrier). **2.** *Pol:* unionisme *m.*

unionist ['ju:niənist] *n.* **1.** *Ind:* syndicaliste *mf*; syndiqué(e). **2.** *Pol:* unioniste *mf*; *Hist:* **the u. party,** le parti unioniste.

unionize ['ju:niənaiz] **1.** *v.tr.* syndiquer (des ouvriers). **2.** *v.i.* se syndiquer.

uniparous [ju:'nipərəs] *a. Biol:* unipare.

unique [ju:'ni:k] *a.* unique; seul en son genre; **a u. opportunity,** une occasion exceptionnelle; **his position is u.,** son cas est tout à fait particulier. **-ly** *adv.* d'une manière unique; exceptionnellement.

uniqueness [ju:'ni:knis] *n.* caractère *m* unique, exceptionnel; nature *f* unique, extraordinaire.

unisex ['ju:niseks] *a.* (boutique) unisexe.

unison ['ju:nis(ə)n, -z(ə)n] *n.* **1.** *Mus:* unisson *m*; **in u.,** à l'unisson (**with,** de); **they all replied in u.,** ils ont tous répondu en même temps. **2. to be in u. with s.o.** être en accord avec qn.

unit ['ju:nit] *n.* **1.** unité *f*; *Mth:* **units and tens,** unités et dizaines; *Com: Ind:* **each box contains a hundred units,** chaque boîte contient cent unités; **u. price,** prix unitaire, de l'unité. **2.** unité (de longueur, de poids, etc.); **standard u.,** module *m*; *Ph:* **u. of mass,** unité de masse; **thermal u.,** unité thermique; *Mec:* **u. of energy, of work,** unité d'énergie, de travail; **u. of velocity,** unité de vitesse; *Tp:* **u. charge,** taxe *f* unitaire; *Fin:* **monetary u.,** unité monétaire; **u. trust,** société d'investissement à capital variable. **3.** (*a*) **in England the county is the largest administrative u. for local government,** en Angleterre le comté est la plus grande division administrative; **information u.,** service *m* d'informations; *Med:* **intensive care u.,** centre *m* de soins intensifs; **X-ray u.,** service de radiologie; *Mil:* **administrative u.,** unité administrative; **auxiliary units,** formations *f* auxiliaires; **fighting u.,** *U.S:* **combat u.,** unité combattante; **air force u.,** unité, groupe *m,* de l'armée de l'air; (*b*) *Mec.E:* unité, élément *m*; **control u.,** élément de contrôle, de réglage; **construction u.,** élément de construction; **standardized units,** éléments normalisés; *Aut:* **motor u.,** bloc-moteur *m*; **the engine forms a u. with the transmission,** le moteur fait bloc avec la transmission; *Cmptr:* **central processing u.,** unité centrale; **input/output u.,** élément, dispositif *m* (d')entrée-sortie; **(visual) display u.,** console *f* de visualisation; visuel *m*; (*c*) *Const:* **u. construction,** préfabrication *f*; **u. furniture,** mobilier par éléments; **kitchen u.,** élément de cuisine; **hob u.,** table *f* de cuisson.

Unitarian [ju:ni'tɛəriən] *a. & n. Rel:* unitarien, -ienne; unitaire (*mf*).

Unitarianism [ju:ni'tɛəriənizm] *n. Rel:* unitarisme *m.*

unitary ['ju:nit(ə)ri] *a.* (système, etc.) unitaire.

unite [ju:'nait] **1.** *v.tr.* (*a*) unir; **to u. one country to, with, another,** réunir un pays à un autre; **to u. idealism with common sense,** allier l'idéalisme au bon sens; (*b*) mettre (les gens) d'accord; unifier (un parti); **common interests that u. two countries,** intérêts communs qui allient deux pays; (*c*) unir (en mariage). **2.** *v.i.* (*a*) s'unir, s'unifier (**with,** à); (*b*) (*of two or more pers. or thgs*) s'unir; se réunir; (*of party*) s'unifier; (*of states*) se confédérer; *Ch:* (*of atoms*) s'unir, se combiner; **to u. against s.o., sth.,** s'unir contre qn, qch.; *Pol:* faire bloc contre (un parti); **to u. in doing sth.,** se mettre d'accord pour faire qch. **united** *a.* uni; unifié; **u. efforts,** efforts conjugués; **u. we stand, divided we fall,** l'union fait la force; **to present a u. front,** présenter un front uni; *Geog:* **the U. Kingdom (of Great Britain and Northern Ireland),** le Royaume-Uni (de Grande-Bretagne et de l'Irlande du Nord); **the U. States (of America),** les États-Unis (d'Amérique); **the U. Arab Republic,** la République Arabe Unie.

unity ['ju:niti] *n.* (*a*) unité *f*; accord *m*; **national, political, u.,** unité nationale, politique; *Prov:* **u. is strength,** l'union fait la force; (*b*) **there is no u. in his work,** ses œuvres manquent d'harmonie; **u. of time, place, action,** unité de temps, de lieu, d'action.

univalent [ju:ni'veilənt] *a. Ch:* univalent.

universal [ju:ni'və:s(ə)l] *a.* (*a*) universel; **u. suffrage,** suffrage universel; **he's a u. favourite,** tout le monde l'aime; (*b*) *Mec.E:* **u. joint,** joint universel. **-ally** *adv.* universellement; par tout le monde.

universality [ju:nivə:'sæliti] *n.* universalité *f.*

universalize [ju:ni'və:səlaiz] *v.tr.* universaliser.

universe ['ju:nivə:s] *n.* univers *m*; **the wonders of the u.,** les merveilles de la création.

university [ju:ni'və:siti] *n.* université *f*; **he's been to u., he's had a u. education,** il a fait des études supérieures; **when I was at u.,** quand j'étais à la faculté; **London U.,** l'université de Londres; **u. professor,** professeur de faculté; **u. student,** étudiant, -ante, à l'université; **u. town,** ville universitaire; **the Open U.** = le centre de Télé-enseignement universitaire.

unjust [ʌn'dʒʌst] *a.* injuste (**to,** envers, avec); **my suspicions were u.,** mes soupçons étaient mal fondés. **-ly** *adv.* injustement.

unjustifiable [ʌndʒʌsti'faiəbl] *a.* injustifiable. **-ably** *adv.* sans justification.

unjustified [ʌn'dʒʌstifaid] *a.* injustifié; non justifié; **he was absolutely u. in doing that,** il était absolument dans son tort en faisant cela.

unkempt [ʌn'kem(p)t] *a.* **1.** (*of hair*) mal peigné; (*of appearance*) négligé, débraillé; (*of pers.*) dépeigné; débraillé. **2.** (*of garden*) mal tenu.

unkind [ʌn'kaind] *a.* (i) dur; méchant; (ii) peu aimable; pas gentil; *esp. Lit:* (*of weather*) peu favorable; **u. fate,** sort impitoyable, cruel; **that's very u. of him,** ce n'est pas gentil de sa part; **to say u. things to s.o.,** dire des méchancetés *f* à qn; **to be u. to s.o.,** être méchant avec qn. **-ly 1.** *adv.* (i) méchamment, durement; (ii) peu aimablement; **to take u. to sth.,** mal accepter qch.; **don't take it u. if I say it frankly,** ne le prenez pas en mauvaise part, si je vous le dis franchement. **2.** *a.* peu aimable, peu gentil; (*of remark*) méchant.

unkindness [ʌn'kaindnis] *n.* manque *m* de gentillesse; méchanceté *f*; rigueur *f* (du climat).

unknot [ʌn'nɔt] *v.tr.* **(unknotted)** dénouer; défaire les nœuds (d'une ficelle, etc.).

unknowing [ʌn'nouiŋ] *a.* ignorant; inconscient (**of,** de). **-ly** *adv.* inconsciemment; sans le savoir.

unknown [ʌn'noun] **1.** *a.* (*a*) inconnu (**to,** à, de); ignoré (**to,** de); (écrivain) inconnu; **u. person,** inconnu, -ue; **the U. Soldier,** le Soldat inconnu; *Jur:* **verdict against person or persons u.,** verdict contre inconnu; **this is a process u. to us, this process is u. to us,** c'est un procédé qui nous est inconnu; *adv.* **he did it u. to me,** il l'a fait à mon insu; (*b*) *Mth: etc:* **u. quantity,** (quantité) inconnue (*f*); **he's an u. quantity,** on ne sait pas comment il va réagir. **2.** *n.* (*a*) (*pers.*) inconnu; (*b*) *Mth:* inconnue; (*c*) **the u.,** l'inconnu.

unlace [ʌn'leis] *v.tr.* délacer, défaire (ses chaussures).

unladen [ʌn'leid(ə)n] *a. Nau:* sans charge; *Av: Veh:* **u. weight,** poids à vide.

unladylike [ʌn'leidilaik] *a.* indigne d'une femme bien élevée; mal élevée; (*of manners*) peu distingué.

unlaid [ʌn'leid] *a.* (*a*) (*of carpet*) **still u.,** pas encore posé; **the table was still u.,** la table n'était pas encore mise.

unlamented [ʌnlə'mentid] *a.* non regretté.

unlatch [ʌn'lætʃ] *v.tr.* ouvrir (une porte).

unlawful [ʌn'lɔːf(u)l] *a.* (*a*) illégal, -aux; contraire à la loi; (*b*) (moyen) illicite; (acte) irrégulier, illégitime. **-fully** *adv.* (*a*) illégalement; contrairement à la loi; (*b*) illicitement; irrégulièrement.

unlearn [ʌn'lɔːn] *v.tr.* (*p.t. & p.p.* **unlearnt** [-'lɔːnt] *occ.* **unlearned** ['lɔːnd]) désapprendre (qch.). **unlearned** [ʌn'lɔːnid] *a.* ignorant; inculte.

unleash [ʌn'liːʃ] *v.tr.* (*a*) lâcher (des chiens); (*b*) **to u. a nuclear war,** déclencher une guerre nucléaire.

unleavened [ʌn'levənd] *a.* (pain) sans levain, azyme.

unless [ʌn'les] *conj.* à moins que + *sub*; **he will do nothing u. you ask him to,** il ne fera rien à moins que vous ne le lui demandiez; **u. I'm mistaken,** à moins que je (ne) me trompe; **u. I hear to the contrary,** sauf avis contraire.

unlettered [ʌn'letəd] *a.* peu lettré; inculte.

unlicensed [ʌn'laisənst] *a.* (*a*) non autorisé; illicite; (*b*) non breveté; **u. premises,** établissement où la vente des boissons alcooliques n'est pas autorisée; **u. taxi,** taxi marron; (*c*) (*of car*) = sans vignette.

unlike [ʌn'laik] *a. & prep.* (*a*) différent, dissemblable; **u. s.o., sth.,** différent de qn, qch.; **they're completely u.** ils ne se ressemblent pas du tout; **he's not u. his sister,** il ressemble assez à la sœur; **he, u. his father,** lui, contrairement à son père; (*b*) **it's u. him to do such a thing,** cela ne lui ressemble pas de faire une chose pareille; **that was very u. him!** on ne s'attendait pas à ça de sa part!

unlikeable [ʌn'laikəbl] *a.* (*of pers.*) antipathique; peu sympathique; (*of thg*) peu agréable.

unlikelihood, unlikeliness [ʌn'laiklihud, -'laiklinis] *n.* improbabilité *f.*

unlikely [ʌn'laikli] *a.* **1.** (*a*) improbable, peu probable; (*of explanation*) invraisemblable; **that's most, very, u.,** c'est fort improbable; **it's not (at all) u.,** c'est très probable; cela se pourrait bien; **it's u. to happen,** cela ne risque pas d'arriver; (*b*) **he's u. to do it,** il est peu probable qu'il le fasse. **2. he's an u. man for the job,** il ne semble pas être destiné à ce travail; **we found the ring in a most u. place,** nous avons retrouvé la bague dans un endroit auquel nous n'aurions jamais pensé; *F:* **she wears the most u. clothes,** elle s'habille d'une façon invraisemblable.

unlimited [ʌn'limitid] *a.* (*of time*) illimité; sans limites; (*of patience*) sans borne(s); (*of hired car*) **u. mileage** = kilométrage illimité; **there were u. supplies of beer,** la bière était à discrétion.

unlined[1] [ʌn'laind] *a.* sans doublure.

unlined[2] *a.* (visage) sans rides; (papier) non réglé.

unlisted [ʌn'listid] *a.* qui ne figure pas sur une liste; *St.Exch:* non inscrit à la cote (officielle).

unlit [ʌn'lit] *a.* non éclairé.

unload [ʌn'loud] *v.tr. & i.* **1.** (*a*) décharger (un bateau, une voiture, des marchandises); (*b*) *Fig:* se débarrasser, se défaire, de (qch.); *St.Exch:* **to u. stock on the market,** se décharger d'un paquet d'actions. **2.** décharger (un fusil, un appareil). **unloaded** *a.* **1.** déchargé. **2.** (*a*) non chargé; sans chargement; (*b*) (fusil) non armé, non chargé. **unloading** *n.* déchargement *m*; débarquement *m.*

unlock [ʌn'lɔk] *v.tr.* **1.** ouvrir (une porte). **2.** révéler, découvrir (un secret). **3.** (*a*) débloquer (une roue, un écrou); (*b*) *Aut:* **to u. the steering gear,** déverrouiller le mécanisme de direction. **unlocked** *a.* (*of door*) qui n'est pas fermé à clef.

unlooked [ʌn'lukt] *a.* **u. for,** inattendu, imprévu.

unloose(n) [ʌn'luːs(n)] *v.tr.* délier, détacher; **to unloosen one's grip,** lâcher prise; **to u. s.o.'s tongue,** délier la langue à qn.

unlovable [ʌn'lʌvəbl] *a.* peu attachant.

unloved [ʌn'lʌvd] *a.* qui n'est pas aimé. **unloving** *a.* peu affectueux, peu aimant; froid.

unlovely [ʌn'lʌvli] *a.* (*of pers.*) sans charme.

unlucky [ʌn'lʌki] *a.* **1.** (*a*) (*of pers.*) malheureux, malchanceux; **to be u.,** ne pas avoir de chance; *F:* avoir de la déveine; **it was u. for him that she arrived just at that moment,** malheureusement pour lui, elle est arrivée à cet instant précis; (*b*) (*of thg*) malheureux, malencontreux; **u. day,** jour de malheur; **that's u.,** ce n'est pas de chance. **2.** qui porte malheur; **u. star,** étoile maléfique; **don't walk under a ladder, it's u.,** ne passez pas sous une échelle, ça porte malheur. **-ily** *adv.* malheureusement, par malheur.

unmake [ʌn'meik] *v.tr.* (*p.t. & p.p.* **unmade** [-'meid]) défaire; détruire. **unmade** *a.* qui n'est pas fait; (lit) défait; (chemin) non goudronné.

unman [ʌn'mæn] *v.tr.* **(unmanned)** *A: & Lit:* (*a*) émasculer (une nation); (*b*) décourager, démoraliser (qn). **unmanned** *a.* (*of vehicle*) sans équipage; (*of counter*) non occupé; *Rail:* (*of level crossing*) non géré; *Space:* **u. flight,** vol inhabité, non habité; **the reception desk must never be left u.,** il doit toujours y avoir quelqu'un au bureau de réception.

unmanageable [ʌn'mænidʒəbl] *a.* **1.** (*of pers.*) intraitable; (*of child, horse*) indocile; (*of vehicle, ship*) difficile à manœuvrer. **2.** (*of large book*) difficile à manier, peu maniable; **u. hair,** cheveux difficiles à coiffer.

unmanly [ʌn'mænli] *a.* (*a*) efféminé; (*b*) lâche.

unmannerliness [ʌn'mænəlinis] *n. Lit:* manque *m* de savoir-vivre; impolitesse *f.*

unmannerly [ʌn'mænəli] *a. Lit:* qui manque de savoir-vivre; impoli; mal élevé.

unmarked [ʌn'mɑːkt] *a.* (*a*) sans marque(s), sans

tache(s); **u. (police) car,** voiture (de police) banalisée; (*b*) *Games:* (joueur) démarqué; (*c*) **my essay was still u.,** ma dissertation n'était toujours pas corrigée.
unmarketable [ʌn'mɑːkitəbl] *a.* invendable.
unmarriageable [ʌn'mæridʒəbl] *a.* immariable.
unmarried [ʌn'mærid] *a.* célibataire; qui n'est pas marié; **he remained u.,** il est resté célibataire; **u. mother,** mère célibataire; **u. state,** célibat *m.*
unmask [ʌn'mɑːsk] **1.** *v.tr.* démasquer (qn); *Lit:* dévoiler (un complot). **2.** *v.i. & pr.* se démasquer. **unmasked** *a.* démasqué; sans masque.
unmatched [ʌn'mætʃt] *a.* sans égal, sans pareil; incomparable (**for courage,** pour son courage; **as a boxer,** comme boxeur).
unmentionable [ʌn'menʃənəbl] **1.** *a.* (événement, chose) dont il ne faut pas parler. **2.** *n.pl. A: Hum:* **unmentionables,** sous-vêtements *m.*
unmerciful [ʌn'məːsif(u)l] *a.* impitoyable; sans pitié. **-fully** *adv.* impitoyablement; sans pitié.
unmerited [ʌn'meritid] *a.* immérité.
unmethodical [ʌnmi'θɔdik(ə)l] *a.* **1.** peu méthodique. **2.** (*of pers.*) qui manque de méthode.
unmindful [ʌn'maindf(u)l] *a. Lit:* **to be u. of sth.,** être peu soucieux de qch.; **u. of one's own interests,** sans penser à ses propres intérêts.
unmistakable [ʌnmis'teikəbl] *a.* (*a*) (preuve) indubitable; (sentiment) clair; **u. difference,** différence marquée, manifeste; (*b*) facilement reconnaissable. **-ably** *adv.* sans aucun doute; clairement, nettement.
unmitigated [ʌn'mitigeitid] *a.* **1.** (mal) non mitigé, que rien ne vient adoucir. **2.** (*intensive*) véritable; **u. lie,** pur mensonge; **an u. disaster,** un échec total.
unmixed [ʌn'mikst] *a.* sans mélange; pur.
unmolested [ʌnmə'lestid] *a.* sans être molesté; (vivre) en paix.
unmortgaged [ʌn'mɔːgidʒd] *a.* non hypothéqué.
unmotivated [ʌn'moutiveitid] *a.* (*a*) sans motif(s), non motivé; (*b*) (*of pers.*) dépourvu d'ambition.
unmounted [ʌn'mauntid] *a.* **1.** (*a*) (*of gem*) non serti; (*b*) (*of photo*) non encadré. **2.** (soldat) à pied.
unmourned [ʌn'mɔːnd] *a.* non pleuré; **he died u.,** personne n'a pleuré sa mort.
unmoved [ʌn'muːvd] *a.* impassible; **u. by sth.,** aucunement ému de, par, qch.; **he remained u. by all our arguments, all our arguments left him quite u.,** tous nos arguments le laissaient indifférent.
unmusical [ʌn'mjuːzik(ə)l] *a.* **1.** peu mélodieux. **2.** (*of pers.*) peu musicien, -ienne.
unnameable [ʌn'neiməbl] *a.* innommable.
unnamed [ʌn'neimd] *a.* (*of pers.*) au nom inconnu; anonyme; (*of thg*) innom(m)é.
unnatural [ʌn'nætjərəl] *a.* qui n'est pas naturel; (*a*) anormal, -aux; (*b*) (*of vice*) contre nature; (*c*) (*of style*) peu naturel; artificiel; affecté; **u. laugh,** rire forcé. **-ally** *adv.* **1.** (i) de manière peu naturelle; (ii) de manière anormale; **he hoped not u. that she would come,** naturellement il espérait qu'elle viendrait. **2.** perversement. **3.** artificiellement.
unnavigable [ʌn'nævigəbl] *a.* innavigable.
unnecessary [ʌn'nesis(ə)ri] *a.* peu nécessaire; inutile, superflu; **it is u. to say that,** (il est) inutile de dire que. **-ily** *adv.* **1.** inutilement, pour rien. **2. to travel with u. bulky luggage,** voyager avec trop de bagages.
unneeded [ʌn'niːdid] *a.* inutile; dont on n'a pas besoin.
unneighbourly, *NAm:* **unneighborly** [ʌn'neibəli] *a.* peu obligeant; **to behave in an u. manner,** se conduire en mauvais voisin.
unnerve [ʌn'nəːv] *v.tr.* faire perdre son courage, son sang-froid, à (qn); **it unnerved him,** cela l'a déconcerté. **unnerving** *a.* déconcertant, déroutant.
unnoticed [ʌn'noutist] *a.* **1.** inaperçu, inobservé; qui échappe à l'attention; **to pass u.,** passer inaperçu. **2. to let an insult pass u.,** ne pas relever une injure.
unnumbered [ʌn'nʌmbəd] *a.* **1.** *esp. Lit:* innombrable. **2.** (*of page*) non numéroté; sans numéro.
unobjectionable [ʌnəb'dʒekʃ(ə)nəbl] *a.* (personne) à qui on ne peut rien reprocher; (chose) à laquelle on ne peut trouver à redire.
unobservant [ʌnəb'zəːvənt] *a.* peu perspicace; peu observateur, -trice.
unobserved [ʌnəb'zəːvd] *a.* inaperçu, inobservé; **he went out u.,** il est sorti sans être vu.
unobstructed [ʌnəb'strʌktid] *a.* **1.** non bouché, non obstrué; (chemin) non encombré; **u. view,** vue dégagée, libre. **2.** sans rencontrer d'obstacle(s).
unobtainable [ʌnəb'teinəbl] *a.* impossible à obtenir; impossible à se procurer; *Tp:* **the number is u.,** il est impossible d'avoir le numéro.
unobtrusive [ʌnəb'truːsiv] *a.* discret, -ète; **he always tried to remain u.,** il cherchait toujours à s'effacer. **-ly** *adv.* discrètement; d'une manière effacée.
unoccupied [ʌn'ɔkjupaid] *a.* **1.** (*of pers.*) inoccupé, désœuvré; sans occupation. **2.** (*a*) (*of house*) inoccupé, inhabité; (*b*) *Mil:* **u. zone,** zone libre; **the town was still u.,** la ville n'était toujours pas occupée. **3.** (*of table, seat*) libre, disponible.
unofficial [ʌnə'fiʃ(ə)l] *a.* (*of meeting*) non officiel; (renseignement) officieux; **u. strike,** grève sauvage; **in an u. capacity,** à titre non officiel; **from an u. source,** de source officieuse; **it's still u.,** on ne l'a pas encore confirmé. **-ally** *adv.* non officiellement; officieusement, à titre officieux.
unopened [ʌn'oupənd] *a.* non ouvert, qui n'a pas été ouvert; (*of letter*) non décacheté.
unopposed [ʌnə'pouzd] *a.* sans opposition; (avancer) sans rencontrer d'opposition, de résistance; *Pol:* **u. candidate,** candidat unique; *Parl:* **the bill was given an u. second reading,** le projet de loi a été accepté sans opposition à la deuxième lecture.
unorganized [ʌn'ɔːgənaizd] *a.* (*a*) mal organisé; (*b*) *Pol:* **u. labour,** main-d'œuvre inorganisée.
unoriginal [ʌnə'ridʒin(ə)l] *a.* sans originalité; peu original, -aux, qui manque d'originalité.
unorthodox [ʌn'ɔːθədɔks] *a.* peu orthodoxe.
unostentatious [ʌnɔsten'teiʃəs] *a.* peu fastueux, sans ostentation; simple; sobre; (*of behaviour*) peu ostentatoire; (*of ceremony*) sans faste. **-ly** *adv.* (agir) sans ostentation; (vêtu) simplement, sobrement.
unostentatiousness [ʌnɔsten'teiʃəsnis] *n.* manque *m* d'ostentation; simplicité *f.*
unpack [ʌn'pæk] **1.** *v.tr.* déballer, dépaqueter (des objets); défaire (une valise). **2.** *v.i.* défaire sa valise. **unpacking** *n.* déballage *m*; **the u. didn't take long,** nous n'avons pas été longtemps à défaire nos bagages.
unpaid [ʌn'peid] *a.* non payé. **1.** (*of pers.*) qui ne reçoit pas de salaire; non salarié; (*of post*) non rétribué, non rémunéré; **u. services,** services à titre gracieux. **2.** (*a*) (*of bill*) impayé; (*of debt*) non acquitté; (*of letter*) non affranchi; **to leave an account u.,** laisser arrérager un compte; (*b*) (*of money*) non versé.
unpalatable [ʌn'pælətəbl] *a.* (*a*) d'un goût désagréable; (*b*) (*of truth*) désagréable.
unparalleled [ʌn'pærəleld] *a.* (*of beauty*) incomparable, sans égal; (*of action, event*) sans précédent.
unpardonable [ʌn'pɑːd(ə)nəbl] *a.* impardonnable; inexcusable. **-ably** *adv.* inexcusablement.
unparliamentary [ʌnpɑːlə'ment(ə)ri] *a.* (langage, action) peu parlementaire.
unpatented [ʌn'peitəntid, -'pæ-] *a.* non breveté.
unpatriotic [ʌnpeitri'ɔtik, -pæ-] *a.* (*of pers.*) peu patriote; (*of action*) peu patriotique; **to be u.,** être

mauvais patriote. **-ally** *adv.* (agir) en mauvais patriote.
unpaved [ʌn'peivd] *a.* non pavé, sans pavés.
unperceived [ʌnpə'si:vd] *a.* inaperçu.
unperforated [ʌn'pə:fəreitid] *a.* sans perforations.
unperturbed [ʌnpə'tə:bd] *a.* **1.** impassible. **2.** non déconcerté, non découragé (**by,** par).
unpick [ʌn'pik] *v.tr.* défaire (une couture).
unpin [ʌn'pin] *v.tr.* (**unpinned**) détacher (qch.) (**from,** de).
unplaced [ʌn'pleist] *a.* (cheval, etc.) non placé; (candidat) non classé.
unplanned [ʌn'plænd] *a.* (événement) imprévu; (enfant) non prévu.
unplayable [ʌn'pleiəbl] *a.* injouable.
unpleasant [ʌn'plezənt] *a.* désagréable, déplaisant; **u. weather,** mauvais temps; **he made some u. remarks,** il a dit des choses désobligeantes; **she was very u. with me,** elle a été très désagréable avec moi. **-ly** *adv.* désagréablement.
unpleasantness [ʌn'plezəntnis] *n.* **1.** caractère *m* désagréable (de qch.); aspect déplaisant (d'un endroit). **2.** ennui *m*; **there was some u.,** il y a eu une dispute.
unpleasing [ʌn'pli:ziŋ] *a.* peu agréable; déplaisant.
unplug [ʌn'plʌg] *v.tr.* (**unplugged**) **1.** déboucher (une ouverture, un tuyau). **2.** débrancher (une télévision).
unplumbed [ʌn'plʌmd] *a. Lit:* **u. depths,** profondeurs insondées.
unpoetic(al) [ʌnpou'etik(l)] *a.* peu poétique.
unpolished [ʌn'pɔliʃt] *a.* **1.** (*a*) non poli; mat; (*of stone*) brut; (*b*) (*of floor, furniture*) non ciré, non astiqué; (*of shoes*) non ciré. **2.** (*a*) (*of pers.*) fruste, rude; (*b*) (style) fruste, non poli.
unpolluted [ʌnpə'lu:tid] *a.* impollué, non pollué.
unpopular [ʌn'pɔpjulər] *a.* impopulaire; **he makes himself u. with everybody,** il se fait mal voir de tout le monde; **he's u. with his employees,** ses employés ne l'aiment pas (beaucoup); **this decision was very u.,** cette décision a été très mal accueillie.
unpopularity [ʌnpɔpju'læriti] *n.* impopularité *f.*
unpopulated [ʌn'pɔpjuleitid] *a.* non peuplé.
unpractical [ʌn'præktik(ə)l] *a.* **1.** (*of pers.*) peu pratique. **2.** (*of plan*) impracticable, irréalisable.
unpractised [ʌn'præktist] *a.* inexercé, inexpérimenté; **u. in business,** sans expérience des affaires.
unprecedented [ʌn'presidentid] *a.* sans précédent.
unpredictable [ʌnpri'diktəbl] *a.* imprévisible; (*of weather*) incertain; **she's u.,** on ne sait jamais ce qu'elle va faire, comment elle va réagir.
unprejudiced [ʌn'predʒudist] *a.* impartial, -aux; sans parti pris; sans préjugés, sans prévention(s).
unpremeditated [ʌnpri'mediteitid] *a. Jur:* (délit) non prémédité.
unprepared [ʌnpri'pɛəd] *a.* **1.** (*a*) non préparé; (discours) improvisé, impromptu; (*b*) **to find everything u.,** trouver que rien n'a été préparé, que rien n'est prêt. **2. to be u. for sth.,** ne pas s'attendre à qch. **3.** sans préparation, sans préparatifs; **to go u. into an undertaking,** se lancer à tête perdue dans une entreprise; **I took the exam quite u.,** j'ai passé l'examen sans l'avoir suffisamment préparé.
unpreparedness [ʌnpri'pɛədnis, -'pɛəridnis] *n.* impréparation *f* (**for,** à).
unprepossessing [ʌnpri:pə'zesiŋ] *a.* (*of pers.*) peu engageant; peu avenant; **a man of u. appearance,** un homme qui fait mauvaise impression.
unpresentable [ʌnpri'zentəbl] *a.* peu présentable.
unpretentious [ʌnpri'tenʃəs] *a.* sans prétention(s); modeste; simple **-ly** *adv.* modestement; simplement.
unpriced [ʌn'praist] *a.* (article) dont le prix n'est pas marqué.
unprincipled [ʌn'prinsip(ə)ld] *a.* (*of pers.*) sans principes; (conduite) peu scrupuleuse, sans scrupules.
unprintable [ʌn'printəbl] *a.* (*of comment, reply*) qu'on n'oserait pas, qu'on ne peut, répéter.
unproductive [ʌnprə'dʌktiv] *a.* improductif; (terre) ingrate, stérile.
unprofessional [ʌnprə'feʃ(ə)n(ə)l] *a.* (*a*) **u. conduct,** conduite contraire au code professionnel; (*b*) **for an architect he's very u.,** comme architecte il est plutôt amateur. **-ally** *adv.* (*a*) contrairement au code professionnel; (*b*) en amateur.
unprofitable [ʌn'prɔfitəbl] *a.* peu profitable; sans profit; **-ably** *adv.* sans profit.
unpromising [ʌn'prɔmisiŋ] *a.* peu prometteur, -euse; **the weather looks u.,** le temps s'annonce mal.
unprompted [ʌn'prɔmptid] *a.* spontané.
unpronounceable [ʌnprə'naunsəbl] *a.* imprononçable.
unprotected [ʌnprə'tektid] *a.* **1.** sans protection, sans défense. **2.** *Tchn:* (*of moving part*) sans gardefou.
unproved, unproven [ʌn'pru:vd; -'pru:v(ə)n] *a.* improuvé; non prouvé.
unprovoked [ʌnprə'voukt] *a.* non provoqué; fait sans provocation.
unpublicized [ʌn'pʌblisaizd] *a.* non publié.
unpublished [ʌn'pʌbliʃt] *a.* inédit, non publié; **the u. facts,** les faits qui n'ont pas été révélés au public.
unpunctual [ʌn'pʌŋktjuəl] *a.* inexact, peu ponctuel.
unpunished [ʌn'pʌniʃt] *a.* impuni; **to go u.,** rester impuni.
unqualified [ʌn'kwɔlifaid] *a.* **1.** (*a*) non qualifié; **to be u. for sth.,** ne pas avoir les qualités requises pour qch.; **to be u. to do sth.,** être incompétent à faire qch.; (*b*) (médecin, professeur) sans diplôme(s), non diplômé; **she's u. for the job,** elle n'est pas qualifiée pour occuper le poste; **I'm quite u. to talk about it,** je ne suis nullement qualifié pour en parler. **2.** (*a*) (*of accusation*) sans réserve; **u. denial,** dénégation catégorique; **u. praise,** éloges sans réserve; **it was an u. success,** c'était un succès formidable; (*b*) (adjectif) non modifié.
unquenchable [ʌn'kwenʃəbl] *a.* (soif, feu) inextinguible; (soif, curiosité) insatiable.
unquenched [ʌn'kwenʃt] *a.* (feu) non éteint; (désir), inassouvi; **u. thirst,** soif non étanchée.
unquestionable [ʌn'kwestjənəbl] *a.* indiscutable; (droit) incontestable; **u. fact,** fait indiscutable. **-ably** *adv.* incontestablement; sans aucun doute; **she is u. guilty,** elle est indiscutablement coupable.
unquestioned [ʌn'kwestjənd] *a.* **1.** indiscuté, incontesté. **2. to let a statement pass u.,** laisser passer une affirmation sans la relever. **unquestioning** *a.* (obéissance) aveugle; **u. trust,** confiance absolue. **unquestioningly** *adv.* aveuglément; sans question.
unquiet [ʌn'kwaiət] *a. A: & Lit:* inquiet, -ète; agité; **u. times,** époque troublée.
unquote ['ʌnkwout] *v.i.* (*used only in imp.*) (*in dictation*) fermez les guillemets; (*in report*) fin de citation. **unquoted** *a.* **u. securities,** valeurs non cotées.
unratified [ʌn'rætifaid] *a.* qui n'a pas été ratifié.
unravel [ʌn'ræv(ə)l] *v.* (**unravelled,** *NAm:* **unraveled**) **1.** *v.tr.* (*a*) effiler, effilocher (un tissu); défaire (du tricot); (*b*) débrouiller, démêler (de la ficelle); dénouer, démêler (une intrigue); débrouiller (un mystère). **2.** *v.i. & pr.* (*a*) **to u. (itself), to come unravelled,** (*of cloth*) s'effiler, s'effilocher; (*of knitting*) se défaire; (*of rope*) se détordre; (*b*) (*of facts*) s'éclaircir.

unread [ʌn'red] *a.* qui n'a pas été lu; **to leave sth. u.,** ne pas lire qch.; **he left the magazine on the table u.,** il a laissé la revue sur la table sans la lire.
unreadable [ʌn'riːdəbl] *a.* (livre, écriture) illisible.
unreadiness [ʌn'redinis] *n.* impréparation *f*; manque *m* de préparation.
unready [ʌn'redi] *a.* **to be u. for sth.,** ne pas être prêt à qch.; être mal préparé pour qch.
unreal [ʌn'riəl] *a.* irréel; sans réalité; **everything seemed u. to him,** il avait l'impression de rêver.
unrealistic [ʌnriə'listik] *a.* irréaliste.
unreality [ʌnri'æliti] *n.* irréalité *f.*
unrealizable [ʌnriə'laizəbl] *a.* irréalisable.
unrealized [ʌn'riəlaizd] *a.* (*a*) (espoir, désir) irréalisé; (*b*) *Fin:* (capital) non réalisé.
unreasonable [ʌn'riːz(ə)nəbl] *a.* **1.** (*of pers.*) déraisonnable; **don't be u.,** soyez raisonnable; **you are being most u.,** vous n'êtes pas raisonnable. **2.** (*a*) (supposition) déraisonnable; (demande) immodérée; (prix) excessif; (*b*) **at this u. hour,** à cette heure indue. **-ably** *adv.* d'une manière peu raisonnable.
unreasoning [ʌn'riːz(ə)niŋ] *a.* (*of pers.*) qui ne raisonne pas; **u. hatred,** haine irraisonnée, aveugle.
unrecognizable [ʌnrekəg'naizəbl] *a.* méconnaissable; impossible, difficile, à reconnaître.
unrecognized [ʌn'rekəgnaizd] *a.* **1.** méconnu. **2.** (*of government*) non reconnu. **3. he mingled u. with the crowd,** il s'est mêlé à la foule sans être reconnu.
unrecorded [ʌnri'kɔːdid] *a.* **1.** (*of fact, comment*) non enregistré, non mentionné. **2.** (*a*) (*of music, tape*) non enregistré; (*b*) (*of tape*) vierge.
unredeemed [ʌnri'diːmd] *a.* **1.** (pécheur) non racheté; (mauvais caractère) non compensé (**by,** par). **2.** (*a*) (promesse) non remplie, non tenue; (*b*) (objet) non dégagé (du crédit municipal); (*c*) *Fin:* (emprunt) non amorti, non remboursé; (traite) non honorée; (hypothèque) non purgée.
unreel [ʌn'riːl] **1.** *v.tr.* dérouler (un film, un câble). **2.** *v.i. & pr.* se dérouler.
unrefined [ʌnri'faind] *a.* **1.** brut; non raffiné. **2.** (homme, goût) peu raffiné, grossier; **u. manners,** manières frustes.
unreformed [ʌnri'fɔːmd] *a.* (*of pers.*) qui ne s'est pas corrigé; (*of law*) non amendé.
unrefreshed [ʌnri'freʃt] *a.* encore fatigué.
unregistered [ʌn'redʒistəd] *a.* (*of pers.*) non inscrit; (*of luggage*) non enregistré; (*of parcel*) non recommandé; (voiture) non immatriculée; **u. birth,** naissance non déclarée.
unregretted [ʌnri'gretid] *a.* que l'on ne regrette pas; **she died u.,** personne n'a pleuré sa mort.
unrehearsed [ʌnri'həːst] *a.* (*of play*) (joué) sans répétition(s); (*of speech*) improvisé.
unrelated [ʌnri'leitid] *a.* (*a*) (*of events*) sans rapport (**to each other,** l'un avec l'autre); **these facts are totally u.,** il n'y a aucun rapport entre ces faits; (*b*) (*of pers.*) **they are u.,** il n'y a aucun lien de parenté entre eux.
unrelenting [ʌnri'lentiŋ] *a.* (*a*) (*of pers.*) implacable, inexorable (**towards,** à, pour, à l'égard de); **he was u.,** il restait inflexible; (*b*) (*of struggle*) acharné; sans rémission.
unreliability [ʌnrilaiə'biliti] *n.* **1.** manque *m* de sérieux (d'une entreprise, de qn). **2.** (*a*) inexactitude *f* (d'un résultat); (*b*) manque de fiabilité (d'une machine).
unreliable [ʌnri'laiəbl] *a.* **1.** (homme) auquel, à qui, on ne peut pas se fier, sur lequel, sur qui, on ne peut pas compter; (caractère) instable. **2.** (*a*) (renseignement) sujet à caution; (résultat) incertain; **an u. source,** une source douteuse; (*b*) (machine) non fiable; (horloge) à laquelle on ne peut se fier; **u. map,** carte peu fiable.
unrelieved [ʌnri'liːvd] *a.* **1.** (*of pain*) non soulagé; sans soulagement. **2.** qui manque de relief, de variété; **she was dressed in u. black,** elle était vêtue tout de noir; **the u. monotony of the concrete walls,** la monotonie absolue des murs de béton; **news of u. gloom,** nouvelles uniformément désolantes; **u. boredom,** ennui mortel.
unremarkable [ʌnri'mɑːkəbl] *a.* médiocre, (qui ne sort pas de l')ordinaire; quelconque.
unremitting [ʌnri'mitiŋ] *a.* **1.** (travail) ininterrompu; sans relâche; infatigable; **u. efforts,** efforts soutenus. **2.** (*of pers.*) **he was u. in his attentions,** son assiduité ne s'est pas démentie un instant. **-ly** *adv.* sans cesse, sans relâche; (travailler) inlassablement.
unremunerative [ʌnri'mjuːnərətiv] *a.* peu rémunérateur, -trice; mal payé.
unrepealed [ʌnri'piːld] *a.* (*of law, etc.*) non abrogé.
unrepeatable [ʌnri'piːtəbl] *a.* (*a*) (remarque) qu'on ne peut, qu'on n'oserait pas, répéter; (*b*) *Com:* (prix) exceptionnel; (offre) unique.
unrepentant [ʌnri'pentənt] *a.* impénitent; **to die u.,** mourir dans le péché; **she was u. about what she had done,** elle ne s'est pas repentie de ce qu'elle avait fait.
unreported [ʌnri'pɔːtid] *a.* (*of accident*) non signalé.
unrepresentative [ʌnrepri'zentətiv] *a.* peu représentatif; peu typique.
unrepresented [ʌnrepri'zentid] *a.* non représenté; (nation) sans représentant, sans délégué.
unrequited [ʌnri'kwaitid] *a.* **u. love,** amour non payé de retour, non partagé.
unreserved [ʌnri'zəːvd] *a.* **1.** sans réserve; (*a*) franc, *f.* franche; (*b*) (*of approval*) entier; **u. praise,** éloges sans réserve. **2. u. seats,** places non réservées. **-ly** [ʌnri'zəːvidli] *adv.* sans réserve; (*a*) franchement; (*b*) **to trust s.o. u.,** avoir pleine confiance en qn.
unresisting [ʌnri'zistiŋ] *a.* soumis, docile.
unresolved [ʌnri'zɔlvd] *a.* **1.** (*of pers.*) irrésolu, indécis. **2.** (problème, etc.) non résolu, irrésolu.
unresponsive [ʌnri'spɔnsiv] *a.* difficile à émouvoir.
unrest [ʌn'rest] *n.* troubles *mpl*; **social u.,** malaise social; **labour, industrial, u.,** agitation ouvrière; **there was u. among the workers,** les ouvriers s'agitaient.
unrestrained [ʌnri'streind] *a.* non réprimé, effréné; **u. laughter,** rires immodérés. **-ly** [ʌnri'streinidli] *adv.* librement; sans contrainte.
unrestricted [ʌnri'striktid] *a.* sans restriction; illimité; (pouvoir) absolu; (accès) libre.
unrevealed [ʌnri'viːld] *a.* non révélé; non divulgué.
unrevenged [ʌnri'vendʒd] *a.* invengé.
unrewarded [ʌnri'wɔːdid] *a.* non récompensé; sans récompense. **unrewarding** *a.* (*a*) peu rémunérateur, -trice; (*b*) (travail, sujet, etc.) ingrat.
unrig [ʌn'rig] *v.tr.* (**unrigged**) *Nau:* dégréer (un navire); désappareiller (une grue).
unrighteous [ʌn'raitʃəs] *a.* (*of pers., action*) **1.** mauvais, malveillant, méchant. **2.** inique, injuste.
unripe [ʌn'raip] *a.* vert; qui n'est pas mûr; (*of wheat*) en herbe.
unrivalled, *NAm: also* **unrivaled** [ʌn'raiv(ə)ld] *a.* sans rival; incomparable; hors de pair; **our goods are u.,** nos articles sont sans concurrence.
unroadworthy [ʌn'roudwəːði] *a.* (*of vehicle*) qui n'est pas en état de rouler, en état de marche.
unroll [ʌn'roul] **1.** *v.tr.* dérouler (une carte, du tissu); déferler (une bannière). **2.** *v.i. & pr.* se dérouler.
unromantic [ʌnrə'mæntik] *a.* peu romantique; terre à terre.

unruffled [ʌn'rʌf(ə)ld] *a.* **1.** (*of pers.*) calme, serein; **u., he continued to speak,** sans se troubler, il a continué de parler. **2.** (*of sea*) calme, uni; (*of hair, feathers*) lisse.
unruled [ʌn'ru:ld] *a.* (*of paper*) uni; non réglé.
unruliness [ʌn'ru:linis] *n.* indiscipline *f*, turbulence *f* (d'un enfant); caractère fougueux (d'un cheval).
unruly [ʌn'ru:li] *a.* (enfant) indiscipliné, insoumis, turbulent; (cheval) fougueux.
unsaddle [ʌn'sædl] *v.tr.* **1.** desseller (un cheval); débâter (un âne). **2.** désarçonner (un cavalier).
unsafe [ʌn'seif] *a.* **1.** dangereux; peu sûr; (*of undertaking*) hasardeux; (*of chair*) peu solide; (*of rope*) mal assujetti. **2.** exposé au danger; **to feel u.,** éprouver un manque de sécurité.
unsaid [ʌn'sed] *a.* non prononcé; **to leave sth. u.,** passer qch. sous silence; **it's better left u.,** mieux vaut ne rien dire.
unsalaried [ʌn'sælərid] *a.* non rémunéré.
unsaleable [ʌn'seiləbl] *a.* (*of goods*) invendable.
unsalted [ʌn'sɔ:ltid] *a.* (*of meat, fish*) non salé; **u. butter,** beurre frais.
unsatisfactory [ʌnsætis'fækt(ə)ri] *a.* peu satisfaisant; qui laisse à désirer; (*of explanation*) peu convaincant; (*of system*) défectueux; **it's most u.,** cela laisse beaucoup à désirer. **-ily** *adv.* d'une manière peu satisfaisante.
unsatisfied [ʌn'sætisfaid] *a.* **1.** peu satisfait (**with,** de). **2. to be u. about sth.,** avoir des doutes sur qch.; **I'm still u. about it,** je n'en suis pas encore convaincu. **3.** (*of appetite*) non rassasié. **unsatisfying** *a.* **1.** peu satisfaisant. **2.** peu convaincant. **3.** (*of meal, etc.*) insuffisant.
unsavoury, *NAm:* **unsavory** [ʌn'seiv(ə)ri] *a.* **1.** (*a*) (goût) désagréable; (plat) d'un goût désagréable; (*b*) **u. smell,** mauvaise odeur; odeur désagréable. **2.** (scandale) répugnant; (réputation) équivoque.
unscathed [ʌn'skeiðd] *a.* indemne; sain et sauf.
unscented [ʌn'sentid] *a.* (savon, etc.) sans parfum.
unscheduled [ʌn'ʃedju:ld] *a.* (départ) imprévu; qui n'est pas indiqué dans l'horaire.
unscholarly [ʌn'skɔləli] *a.* peu savant.
unschooled [ʌn'sku:ld] *a.* (*a*) *O:* (*of pers.*) sans instruction; (*b*) (cheval) non dressé.
unscientific [ʌnsaiən'tifik] *a.* non scientifique; peu scientifique. **-ally** *adv.* peu scientifiquement.
unscramble [ʌn'skræmbl] *v.tr.* déchiffrer.
unscrew [ʌn'skru:] **1.** *v.tr.* dévisser (un boulon, etc.). **2.** *v.i.* se dévisser.
unscripted [ʌn'skriptid] *a.* sans préparation.
unscrupulous [ʌn'skru:pjuləs] *a.* peu scrupuleux; sans scrupules. **-ly** *adv.* peu scrupuleusement.
unscrupulousness [ʌn'skru:pjuləsnis] *n.* indélicatesse *f*; manque *m* de scrupules.
unsealed [ʌn'si:ld] *a.* descellé; (*of letter*) décacheté.
unseasonable [ʌn'si:z(ə)nəbl] *a.* (*of fish, fruit*) hors de saison; **this weather's very u.,** ce temps n'est pas normal pour la saison.
unseasoned [ʌn'si:z(ə)nd] *a.* **1.** (*of food*) non assaisonné. **2.** (*of timber*) vert, non conditionné.
unseat [ʌn'si:t] *v.tr.* **1.** désarçonner (un cavalier). **2.** *Parl:* faire perdre son siège à (un député).
unseaworthy [ʌn'si:wə:ði] *n.* (navire) innavigable; en mauvais état de navigabilité.
unsecured [ʌnsi'kjuəd] *a.* (*of loan*) non garanti, à découvert; (*of debt*) sans garantie.
unseeded [ʌn'si:did] *a.* *Ten:* (*of player*) non classé.
unseeing [ʌn'si:iŋ] *a.* qui ne voit pas; aveugle; **to look at s.o., sth., with u. eyes,** regarder qn, qch., sans (le) voir. **unseen 1.** *a.* (*a*) inaperçu, invisible; **to do sth. u.,** faire qch. sans être vu; (*b*) **to buy sth. (sight) u.,** acheter qch. sans l'avoir vu; *Sch:* **u. translation,** *n.* **u.,** version *f*. **2.** *n.* **the u.,** le surnaturel.
unseemliness [ʌn'si:mlinis] *n.* *O:* inconvenance *f*.
unseemly [ʌn'si:mli] *a.* *O:* inconvenant.
unselfconscious [ʌnself'kɔnʃəs] *a.* naturel; sans contrainte. **-ly** *adv.* sans contrainte.
unselfish [ʌn'selfiʃ] *a.* généreux; sans égoïsme; (motif) désintéressé. **-ly** *adv.* généreusement.
unselfishness [ʌn'selfiʃnis] *n.* désintéressement *m*.
unsentimental [ʌnsenti'ment(ə)l] *a.* (*a*) peu sentimental, -aux; (*b*) (*of pers.*) prosaïque; terre à terre.
unserviceable [ʌn'sə:visəbl] *a.* (*a*) inutilisable; (*b*) (*of machine*) hors d'usage.
unsettle [ʌn'setl] *v.tr.* ébranler (les idées de qn); troubler le repos de (qn). **unsettled** *a.* **1.** (pays) troublé, instable; (temps) variable, changeant; (esprit) inquiet, troublé; **the u. state of the weather,** l'incertitude *f* du temps. **2.** (esprit, caractère) indécis, irrésolu; **I'm still u. in my mind about it,** je ne suis pas encore décidé là-dessus. **3.** (*a*) (*of question, dispute*) indécis; (*b*) (*of bill*) impayé, non réglé. **unsettling** *a.* troublant.
unsex [ʌn'seks] *v.tr.* émasculer (un mâle); déféminiser (une femelle).
unshackle [ʌn'ʃækl] *v.tr.* désentraver (un cheval); ôter les fers à (un prisonnier). **unshackled** *a.* sans entraves; libre.
unshakeable [ʌn'ʃeikəbl] *a.* inébranlable.
unshaken [ʌn'ʃeik(ə)n] *a.* inébranlé, ferme.
unshaved, unshaven [ʌn'ʃeivd, -'ʃeiv(ə)n] *a.* non rasé.
unsheathe [ʌn'ʃi:ð] *v.tr.* dégainer (une épée, etc.).
unsheltered [ʌn'ʃeltəd] *a.* sans abri, non abrité, sans protection (**from,** contre).
unship [ʌn'ʃip] *v.tr.* (**unshipped**) *Nau:* décharger, débarquer.
unshod [ʌn'ʃɔd] *a.* **1.** (*a*) (*of pers.*) déchaussé; (*b*) (*of horse*) déferré. **2.** (*of pers.*) les pieds nus.
unshrinkable [ʌn'ʃriŋkəbl] *a.* *Tex:* irrétrécissable.
unsighted [ʌn'saitid] *a.* invisible, qui n'est pas en vue.
unsightliness [ʌn'saitlinis] *n.* laideur *f*.
unsightly [ʌn'saitli] *a.* laid; désagréable à voir; **landscape marred by u. advertisements,** paysage déparé par des panneaux qui offusquent la vue.
unsigned [ʌn'saind] *a.* non signé, sans signature.
unsinkable [ʌn'siŋkəbl] *a.* insubmersible.
unskilful, *NAm:* **unskillful** [ʌn'skilf(u)l] *a.* malhabile, inhabile, maladroit (**in, at,** à).
unskilled [ʌn'skild] *a.* (*of pers.*) inexpérimenté (**in,** à); inexpert (**in,** dans, en); **u. in, at, doing sth.,** inexpérimenté à faire qch.; *Ind:* **u. worker,** ouvrier non qualifié; **u. labour,** main-d'œuvre non spécialisée.
unslept [ʌn'slept] *a.* **u. in,** (lit) non défait.
unsling [ʌn'sliŋ] *v.tr.* (*pt. & p.p.* **unslung** [-'slʌŋ]) dégréer, décrocher (un hamac, etc.).
unsmiling [ʌn'smailiŋ] *a.* sérieux; qui ne sourit pas.
unsmoked [ʌn'smoukt] *a.* non fumé.
unsociability [ʌnsouʃə'biliti], **unsociableness** [ʌn'souʃəblnis] *n.* insociabilité *f*.
unsociable [ʌn'souʃəbl] *a.* sauvage; peu sociable.
unsocial [ʌn'souʃ(ə)l] *a.* **1.** insocial, -aux; **to work u. hours,** travailler à des heures indues, quand la plupart des gens sont libres. **2.** = UNSOCIABLE.
unsold [ʌn'sould] *a.* invendu.
unsoldierly [ʌn'souldʒəli] *a.* peu militaire.
unsolicited [ʌnsə'lisitid] *a.* non sollicité; volontaire; **to do sth. u.,** faire qch. spontanément.
unsolvable [ʌn'sɔlvəbl] *a.* insoluble.
unsolved [ʌn'sɔlvd] *a.* (problème) non résolu.
unsophisticated [ʌnsə'fistikeitid] *a.* (*a*) (*of pers.*) ingénu, simple; (*of wine*) sans prétention; (*b*) *Tchn:* peu évolué; primitif.
unsound [ʌn'saund] *a.* (*a*) (*of pers.*) malsain, mala-

dif; (*of health*) précaire, chancelant; **to be of u. mind,** ne pas avoir toute sa raison; **to commit suicide while of u. mind,** se suicider en état de démence temporaire; (*b*) (*of timber*) avarié; (*of fruit*) gâté; (*c*) (*of foundations, bridge*) peu solide; en mauvais état; dangereux; (*d*) (*of theory, argument*) mal fondé; (*of doctrine, opinion*) faux; discutable; (*of decision*) peu judicieux; (*of investment*) peu sûr, hasardeux; (*of politician*) incompétent; **it is financially u.,** c'est de la mauvaise finance.

unsparing [ʌn'spɛəriŋ] *a.* prodigue; **to be u. in one's efforts,** être infatigable; ne pas ménager ses efforts. **-ly** *adv.* sans ménager ses efforts.

unspeakable [ʌn'spiːkəbl] *a.* **1.** (douleur) indicible; (joie) ineffable. **2.** *F:* détestable, exécrable; **it's u.!** ça n'a pas de nom! **he's really u.!** il est au-dessous de tout! **-ably** *adv.* **1.** indiciblement. **2.** *F:* **u. bad,** exécrable.

unspecified [ʌn'spesifaid] *a.* non spécifié; **certain u. persons,** certaines personnes, dont on taira les noms.

unspent [ʌn'spent] *a.* **1.** (*of money*) non dépensé. **2.** (*of cartridge*) qui n'a pas servi.

unspoilt [ʌn'spɔilt], *occ.* **unspoiled** [ʌn'spɔild] *a.* (*a*) intact; (*b*) (enfant) qui n'a pas été gâté; **he has remained u. despite his success,** son succès ne lui a pas tourné la tête; (*c*) (paysage) qui n'a pas été défiguré.

unspoken [ʌn'spouk(ə)n] *a.* non prononcé; tacite.

unsporting [ʌn'spɔːtiŋ], **unsportsmanlike** [ʌn'spɔːtsmənlaik] *a.* peu loyal, -aux; déloyal.

unstable [ʌn'steibl] *a.* instable.

unstained [ʌn'steind] *a.* **1.** (*a*) sans tache; (*b*) *Lit:* (*of reputation*) sans souillure. **2.** (*of wood*) non teint.

unstamped [ʌn'stæmpt] *a.* **1.** (*of silver, gold*) non poinçonné. **2.** (*a*) (*of letter*) sans timbre, non affranchi; (*b*) *Adm: Jur:* (*of document*) non estampillé.

unstatesmanlike [ʌn'steitsmənlaik] *a.* peu digne d'un homme d'État; peu diplomatique.

unsteadiness [ʌn'stedinis] *a.* (*a*) manque *m* d'aplomb; manque de sûreté (de la main); (*b*) démarche chancelante (d'un ivrogne).

unsteady [ʌn'stedi] *a.* (*a*) (*of table*) instable, peu stable; branlant; (*of legs, footsteps*) chancelant; (*of hand, voice*) mal assuré; (*of position, foothold*) mal assuré; incertain; **to be u. on one's legs, feet,** marcher d'un pas chancelant; tituber; (*b*) (*of flame*) tremblant, vacillant. **-ily** *adv.* (marcher) d'un pas chancelant, en titubant; (tenir qch.) d'une main tremblante; (écrire) d'une main tremblante.

unsterilized [ʌn'sterilaizd] *a.* non stérilisé.

unstick [ʌn'stik] *v.tr.* (*p.t. & p.p.* **unstuck** [-'stʌk]) décoller (qch.); **to come unstuck,** (i) se décoller; (ii) *F:* (*of plan*) s'effondrer.

unstinted [ʌn'stintid] *a.* (*a*) (*of supplies*) abondant; sans restriction; (*b*) = UNSTINTING (*b*).

unstinting [ʌn'stintiŋ] *a.* (*a*) généreux, prodigue; (*b*) sans réserve; (admiration) sans bornes; **u. efforts,** efforts illimités; **to give u. praise,** ne pas ménager ses louanges. **-ly** *adv.* (*a*) abondamment; (*b*) généreusement; (louer qn) sans réserve.

unstitch [ʌn'stitʃ] *v.tr.* dépiquer, découdre (une couture); **to come unstitched,** se découdre.

unstop [ʌn'stɔp] *v.tr.* **(unstopped)** déboucher.

unstoppable [ʌn'stɔpəbl] *a.* (*of shot*) imparable; **he's u. now,** on a l'impression que (désormais) tout va lui réussir.

unstressed [ʌn'strest] *a.* inaccentué; atone.

unstring [ʌn'striŋ] *v.tr.* (*p.t. & p.p.* **unstrung** [-'strʌŋ]) **1.** débander (un arc); **to u. a violin,** (i) ôter, (ii) détendre les cordes d'un violon. **2.** défiler, désenfiler (des perles, etc.). **3.** (*of pers.*) **to be unstrung,** avoir les nerfs à fleur de peau.

unstudied [ʌn'stʌdid] *a.* spontané; naturel.

unsubdued [ʌnsəb'djuːd] *a.* indompté.

unsubmissive [ʌnsəb'misiv] *a.* insoumis; rebelle.

unsubsidized [ʌn'sʌbsidaizd] *a.* non subventionné.

unsubstantial [ʌnsəb'stænʃ(ə)l] *a.* insubstantiel; (repas) léger, peu nourrissant.

unsubstantiated [ʌnsəb'stænʃieitid] *a.* (*of accusation*) non prouvé; (*of rumour*) non corroboré.

unsubtle [ʌn'sʌtl] *a.* peu subtil.

unsuccessful [ʌnsək'sesf(u)l] *a.* **1.** (*of effort*) vain, infructueux; (*of application*) refusé; (*of outcome, marriage*) malheureux; **u. attempt,** tentative qui n'a abouti à rien; **u. outcome,** insuccès *m*; échec *m*; **it was completely u.,** cela a été un échec complet. **2.** (*of pers.*) **to be u.,** ne pas réussir; échouer; **u. candidate,** candidat refusé; (*at election*) non élu. **-fully** *adv.* sans succès; en vain.

unsuitability [ʌns(j)uːtə'biliti] *n.* **1.** inaptitude *f* (de qn à qch.). **2.** caractère *m* impropre (de qch. à qch.).

unsuitable [ʌn's(j)uːtəbl] *a.* **1.** (*pers.*) peu fait (pour qch.); **he's quite u. for the job,** ce n'est pas l'homme qu'il faut pour ce poste. **2.** (*of thg*) impropre, mal adapté (à qch.); (*of time*) inopportun; (*of marriage*) mal assorti; **u. for, to, the occasion,** qui ne convient pas à la circonstance; **you have chosen a most u. time to . . .,** vous avez mal choisi le moment de . . .; **film u. for children,** film à déconseiller aux enfants; **the climate is u. for wheat,** le climat ne convient pas au blé. **-ably** *adv.* **u. dressed,** habillé d'une façon qui ne convient pas à l'occasion.

unsuited [ʌn's(j)uːtid] *a.* (*of pers.*) inapte (à qch.); **they are u. to each other,** ils s'accordent mal.

unsullied [ʌn'sʌlid] *a.* sans souillure, sans tache.

unsung [ʌn'sʌŋ] *a.* *Lit:* (*of deed*) non célébré; (*of hero*) méconnu.

unsupported [ʌnsə'pɔːtid] *a.* (*a*) (*of statement*) sans preuves; (*b*) (*of pers.*) non appuyé; non soutenu.

unsure [ʌn'ʃuər] *a.* **1.** (*of position*) peu sûr; précaire. **2.** (*of pers.*) peu sûr, incertain (**about,** de); **to be u. of oneself,** manquer de confiance en soi-même.

unsurmountable [ʌnsə(ː)'mauntəbl] *a.* insurmontable; **our difficulties are not u.,** il nous sera possible de surmonter nos difficultés.

unsurpassable [ʌnsə(ː)'pɑːsəbl] *a.* insurpassable.

unsurpassed [ʌnsə(ː)'pɑːst] *a.* sans égal, -aux.

unsuspected [ʌnsəs'pektid] *a.* insoupçonné (**by,** de); dont on ne soupçonnait pas l'existence. **unsuspecting** *a.* qui ne se doute de rien; **u. by nature,** peu soupçonneux.

unsuspicious [ʌnsəs'piʃəs] *a.* peu soupçonneux.

unsweetened [ʌn'swiːtnd] *a.* non sucré.

unswerving [ʌn'swəːviŋ] *a.* (*of loyalty*) constant, ferme. **-ly** *adv.* sans s'écarter du but; **u. loyal,** d'une loyauté inébranlable.

unsympathetic [ʌnsimpə'θetik] *a.* (*a*) peu compatissant; indifférent; (*b*) antipathique; **I find the characters of this novel u.,** les personnages de ce roman me sont peu sympathiques. **-ally** *adv.* froidement; d'un ton, d'un air, indifférent.

unsystematic [ʌnsistə'mætik] *a.* non systématique; sans méthode. **-ally** *adv.* sans méthode.

untainted [ʌn'teintid] *a.* non corrompu; (*of food*) non gâté; (*of reputation*) sans tache, sans souillure.

untalented [ʌn'tæləntid] *a.* peu doué.

untam(e)able [ʌn'teiməbl] *a.* (*of animal*) inapprivoisable, indomptable; (*of spirit*) indomptable.

untamed [ʌn'teimd] *a.* (*of animal*) inapprivoisé, indompté; (*of spirit*) indompté.

untangle [ʌn'tæŋgl] *v.tr.* démêler (de la laine, une ficelle); éclaircir (un mystère); débrouiller (une affaire compliquée).

untapped [ʌn'tæpt] *a.* (ressources) inexploitées.

untarnished [ʌn'tɑːniʃt] *a.* non terni, sans tache.

untasted [ʌn'teistid] *a.* auquel on n'a pas goûté; **to send a dish away u.,** renvoyer un plat sans y goûter.

untaught [ʌn'tɔːt] *a.* (*a*) (*of pers.*) sans instruction; ignorant; (*b*) (*of skill*) naturel, spontané.

untaxable [ʌn'tæksəbl] *a.* non imposable.

untaxed [ʌn'tækst] *a.* (*a*) exempt, exempté, d'impôts; (produit) non imposé; (*b*) (*of car*) = sans vignette.

unteachable [ʌn'tiːtʃəbl] *a.* **1.** (*of pers.*) à qui l'on ne peut rien apprendre; incapable d'apprendre. **2.** (*of subject, art*) impossible à enseigner.

untenable [ʌn'tenəbl] *a.* (position) intenable; (théorie) insoutenable.

untenanted [ʌn'tenəntid] *a.* sans locataire(s).

untended [ʌn'tendid] *a.* (malade) non soigné, sans soins; (jardin) non entretenu.

untested [ʌn'testid] *a.* inéprouvé, qui n'a pas (encore) été mis à l'épreuve; (*of invention, drug*) non essayé; (*of water, etc.*) non analysé.

unthinkable [ʌn'θiŋkəbl] *a.* inconcevable, impensable; **it's u. that . . .,** il est inconcevable que + *sub.*

unthinking [ʌn'θiŋkiŋ] *a.* (*of pers.*) étourdi. **-ly** *adv.* (faire qch.) sans réfléchir, étourdiment.

unthought [ʌn'θɔːt] *a.* **u. of,** à quoi on n'a pas pensé.

unthread [ʌn'θred] *v.tr.* désenfiler, défiler.

untidiness [ʌn'taidinis] *n.* désordre *m*; manque *m* d'ordre, de soin.

untidy [ʌn'taidi] *a.* (*a*) (*of room*) en désordre; mal rangé; (*of hair*) ébouriffé; (*of writing*) brouillon; **u. appearance,** tenue débraillée; *Mus:* **his playing is u.,** son jeu manque de netteté; (*b*) (*of pers.*) désordonné; qui manque d'ordre. **-ily** *adv.* sans ordre; **she's always u. dressed,** elle a toujours l'air débraillé.

untie [ʌn'tai] *v.* **(untied; untying) 1.** *v.tr.* dénouer (sa ceinture); défaire, délier (un nœud, un paquet); déficeler (un paquet); détacher (un chien). **2.** *v.i. & pr.* (*of knot*) **to u. itself, to come untied,** se défaire, se dénouer.

until [ʌn'til] **1.** *prep.* (*a*) jusqu'à; **u. tomorrow,** jusqu'à demain; **u. now,** jusqu'ici, jusque-là; **she didn't arrive u. yesterday,** elle n'est arrivée qu'hier; (*b*) **not u. (after) eight o'clock,** pas avant huit heures (passées); **it wasn't u. I met her that . . .,** ce n'est qu'après notre rencontre que . . .; **I've never seen it u. now,** c'est la première fois que je le vois. **2.** *conj.* (*a*) jusqu'à ce que + *sub.*; **u. all the windows are open,** jusqu'à ce que toutes les fenêtres soient ouvertes; (*b*) **he won't come u. he's invited,** il ne viendra pas avant d'être invité; **I won't leave him u. he's completely recovered,** je ne le quitterai pas tant qu'il n'est pas tout à fait guéri.

untilled [ʌn'tild] *a.* non cultivé, non labouré.

untimely [ʌn'taimli] **I.** *a.* **1.** (*of death*) prématuré; **to come to an u. end,** mourir avant l'âge. **2.** (*of snow*) hors de saison. **3.** (*of question, action*) inopportun, intempestif; mal à propos. **II.** *adv.* **1.** prématurément; avant l'heure. **2.** inopportunément; mal à propos.

untiring [ʌn'taiəriŋ] *a.* infatigable, inlassable. **-ly** *adv.* infatigablement, inlassablement.

unto ['ʌntu(ː), 'ʌntə] *prep. A: & Lit:* **1. to liken sth. u. sth.,** comparer qch. à, avec, qch.; *B:* **suffer little children to come u. me,** laissez venir à moi les petits enfants; **u. us a child is born,** un enfant nous est né; **and I say u. you . . .,** et je vous dis . . .. **2.** vers; **to turn u. s.o.,** se tourner vers qn.

untold [ʌn'tould] *a.* (richesse) immense, énorme; **u. suffering,** souffrances inouïes; **u. joy,** joie indicible.

untouchable [ʌn'tʌtʃəbl] **1.** *a.* intouchable; intangible. **2.** *n.* (*in India*) intouchable *mf*, paria *m.*

untouched [ʌn'tʌtʃt] *a.* **1.** (*a*) non touché; **food product u. by (human) hand,** produit alimentaire non manié; (*b*) **he'd left the meal u.,** il n'avait pas touché à son repas. **2.** (*of pers.*) indemne, sain et sauf; (*of thg*) intact. **3.** (*of pers.*) indifférent, insensible (**by,** à).

untoward [ʌntə'wɔːd; *NAm:* ʌn'tɔːd] *a.* fâcheux, malencontreux, malheureux; **I hope nothing u. has happened,** j'espère qu'il n'est pas arrivé un malheur.

untraceable [ʌn'treisəbl] *a.* introuvable.

untrained [ʌn'treind] *a.* qui n'a pas reçu de formation professionelle; (cheval) non dressé; **u. ear,** oreille inexercée.

untrammelled [ʌn'træməld] *a.* non entravé (**by,** par); libre (**by,** de).

untransferable [ʌntræns'fəːrəbl] *a.* non transmissible; *Jur:* (droit, propriété) incessible.

untranslatable [ʌntræns'leitəbl] *a.* intraduisible.

untravelled [ʌn'trævəld] *a.* **1.** (*of pers.*) qui n'a jamais voyagé. **2.** (pays) inexploré, peu fréquenté.

untried [ʌn'traid] *a.* **1.** qui n'a pas été essayé; non essayé. **2.** (moteur, système) qui n'a pas été mis à l'épreuve; **u. troops,** troupes qui n'ont pas encore vu le feu. **3.** (détenu, cas) qui n'a pas encore été jugé.

untrodden [ʌn'trɔd(ə)n] *a. Lit:* (chemin) peu fréquenté; **u. snow,** neige immaculée, vierge.

untroubled [ʌn'trʌbəld] *a.* calme, tranquille; **he seemed u. by the news,** la nouvelle ne semblait nullement le troubler.

untrue [ʌn'truː] *a.* **1.** faux, *f.* fausse; erroné; **it's absolutely u.,** c'est complètement faux. **2.** *Mec.E:* faux; qui n'est pas juste. **3.** (*of pers.*) infidèle (**to,** à); déloyal, -aux (**to,** envers).

untrustworthiness [ʌn'trʌstwəːðinis] *n.* **1.** (*of pers.*) manque *m* d'honnêteté. **2.** caractère douteux; exactitude.

untrustworthy [ʌn'trʌstwəːði] *a.* **1.** (*of pers.*) indigne de confiance; à qui on ne peut pas se fier. **2.** (renseignement) douteux, sujet à caution; (témoignage) récusable.

untruth [ʌn'truːθ, *pl.* -'truːðz] *n.* mensonge *m*; **to tell an u.,** dire, commettre, un mensonge.

untruthful [ʌn'truːθf(u)l] *a.* **1.** (*of pers.*) menteur; **he's an u. boy,** c'est un garçon qui ne dit jamais la vérité. **2.** (*of story*) mensonger; faux, *f.* fausse. **-fully** *adv.* mensongèrement; en mentant.

untruthfulness [ʌn'truːθf(u)lnis] *n.* **1.** (*of pers.*) caractère menteur. **2.** fausseté *f* (d'un témoignage).

untuned [ʌn'tjuːnd] *a.* (instrument) mal accordé; (moteur) qui n'est pas réglé.

untuneful [ʌn'tjuːnf(u)l] *a.* peu mélodieux.

unturned [ʌn'təːnd] *a.* (*of card*) non (re)tourné; **to leave no stone u.,** mettre tout en œuvre, remuer ciel et terre (**to do sth.,** pour accomplir qch.).

untutored [ʌn'tjuːtəd] *a. esp. Lit:* (*of pers.*) peu instruit; (esprit, goût) non formé.

untwine [ʌn'twain] *v.tr.* détordre, détortiller.

untwist [ʌn'twist] **1.** *v.tr.* détordre, détortiller (des fils); dévisser (le couvercle d'un bocal, etc.). **2.** *v.i. & pr.* **to u. (itself), to come untwisted,** se détordre.

unusable [ʌn'juːzəbl] *a.* inutilisable.

unused *a.* **1.** [ʌn'juːzd] (*a*) dont on ne se sert pas; inutilisé; non employé; (bâtiment) désaffecté; (*b*) qui n'a pas encore servi; (*of clothes*) neuf. **2.** [ʌn'juːst] (*of pers.*) peu habitué (**to sth.,** à qch.); **to be u. to doing sth.,** ne pas avoir l'habitude de faire qch.

unusual [ʌn'juːʒuəl] *a.* peu commun; peu ordinaire; insolite; **it's u.,** (i) cela se fait peu; (ii) cela se voit rarement; **it's u. to see him at the theatre,** il est rare qu'on le voie au théâtre; **nothing u.,** rien d'anormal; **of u. interest,** d'un intérêt exceptionnel. **-ally** *adv.* exceptionnellement; rarement; **u. tall,** d'une taille exceptionnelle; **he was u. attentive,** il s'est montré plus attentif que d'habitude.

unutterable [ʌn'ʌt(ə)rəbl] *a.* inexprimable, indicible; *F:* **u. fool,** parfait idiot. **-ably** *adv.* d'une façon inexprimable; **u. lazy,** d'une paresse inimaginable.
unvaried [ʌn'vɛərid] *a.* invariable; non varié; (nourriture) qui manque de variété.
unvarnished [ʌn'vɑːniʃt] *a.* **1.** (*of surface*) non verni; (*of pottery*) non vernissé. **2. the plain u. truth,** la vérité pure et simple.
unvarying [ʌ'vɛəriiŋ] *a.* invariable; constant.
unveil [ʌn'veil] **1.** *v.tr.* dévoiler (un secret); inaugurer (une statue). **2.** *v.i.* se dévoiler. **unveiled** *a.* sans voile. **unveiling** *n.* inauguration *f* (d'une statue).
unverified [ʌn'verifaid] *a.* non contrôlé, non vérifié.
unversed [ʌn'vəːst] *a. Lit:* peu versé **(in,** dans).
unvoiced [ʌn'vɔist] *a.* **1.** (*of vowel, consonant*) sourd, muet; non voisé. **2.** (*of opinion*) non exprimé.
unwanted [ʌn'wɔntid] *a.* **1.** non voulu; **u. child,** enfant non désiré. **2.** superflu; *Toil:* **u. hair,** poils superflus; **to give away all one's u. books,** se débarrasser de tous les livres dont on n'a plus besoin.
unwarranted [ʌn'wɔrəntid] *a.* injustifié; **u. insult,** injure gratuite; **u. familiarity,** familiarité indue.
unwary [ʌn'wɛəri] *a.* imprudent, inprévoyant.
unwashed [ʌn'wɔʃt] *a.* non lavé; *n. F: O:* **the great u.,** les prolétaires, les prolos.
unwavering [ʌn'weivəriŋ] *a.* constant, ferme; inébranlable. **-ly** *adv.* résolument; sans hésiter.
unweaned [ʌn'wiːnd] *a.* (enfant, chaton) non sevré.
unwearable [ʌn'wɛərəbl] *a.* (vêtement) immettable.
unwearying [ʌn'wiəriiŋ] *a.* inlassable, infatigable.
unweighted [ʌn'weitid] *a. Pol.Ec:* (*of index*) non pondéré; **u. figures,** chiffres bruts.
unwelcome [ʌn'welkəm] *a.* (*a*) (visiteur) importun; **u. visits,** visites importunes; **a not u. visit,** une visite opportune; (*b*) (*of news*) fâcheux.
unwell [ʌn'wel] *a.* indisposé; souffrant.
unwholesome [ʌn'houlsəm] *a.* malsain.
unwieldy [ʌn'wiːldi] *a.* **1.** (*of pers.*) lourd et gauche. **2.** peu maniable; difficile à manier.
unwilling [ʌn'wiliŋ] *a.* (consentement) donné à contrecœur; (complice) malgré lui; **to be u. to do sth.,** ne pas vouloir faire qch.; **I was u. that my wife should know, for my wife to know,** je ne voulais pas que ma femme le sache. **-ly** *adv.* à contrecœur; de mauvaise grâce.
unwillingness [ʌn'wiliŋnis] *n.* **1.** mauvaise grâce. **2.** manque *m* d'enthousiasme **(to do sth.,** à faire qch.).
unwind [ʌn'waind] *v.* (*p.t. & p.p.* **unwound** [-'waund]) **1.** *v.tr.* dérouler; dépelotonner (une pelote de laine). **2.** *v.i.* (*a*) se dérouler; (*of ball of wool*) se dépelotonner; (*b*) *F:* se détendre, se relaxer.
unwise [ʌn'waiz] *a.* (*of pers.*) imprudent; peu prudent, peu sage; (*of action*) peu judicieux; **that was very u. of you,** c'était très imprudent de votre part. **-ly** *adv.* imprudemment.
unwitting [ʌn'witiŋ] *a.* accidentel, non intentionnel. **-ly** *adv.* sans le savoir; sans le vouloir.
unwomanly [ʌn'wumənli] *a.* peu féminin.
unwonted [ʌn'wountid] *a. Lit:* inaccoutumé.
unworkable [ʌn'wəːkəbl] *a.* **1.** (projet) impracticable; (organisation) difficile à gouverner. **2.** (gisement) inexploitable.
unworldliness [ʌn'wəːldlinis] *n.* (*a*) détachement *m* de ce monde; (*b*) simplicité *f*, candeur *f*.
unwordly [ʌn'wəːldli] *a.* **1.** (*a*) détaché de ce monde; (*b*) simple, candide. **2.** qui n'est pas de ce monde.
unworthiness [ʌn'wəːðinis] *n.* indignité *f* (d'une action **(of sth., s.o.,** etc.).
unworthy [ʌn'wəːði] *a.* indigne **(of sth., s.o.,** de qch., de qn); **u. of notice,** qui ne mérite pas qu'on y fasse attention.
unwounded [ʌn'wuːndid] *a.* non blessé; indemne.
unwrap [ʌn'ræp] *v.tr.* **(unwrapped)** défaire (un paquet); détortiller (un bonbon); **to come unwrapped,** (*of parcel*) se défaire, (*of contents*) sortir de l'enveloppe.
unwritten [ʌn'rit(ə)n] *a.* non écrit (*of tradition*) oral, -aux; (*of agreement*) verbal, -aux; **an u. law,** une convention toujours respectée; **according to the u. law,** selon la tradition (établie); **this is an u. rule of the game,** c'est une des conventions du jeu.
unyielding [ʌn'jiːldiŋ] *a.* qui ne cède pas; raide, ferme; (*of pers., determination*) inébranlable, ferme; **u. grip,** prise de fer.
unyoke [ʌn'jouk] *v.tr.* dételer, découpler.
unzip [ʌnzip] *v.* **(unzipped) 1.** *v.tr.* ouvrir la fermeture éclair (*R.t.m.*). **2.** *v.i. F:* (*of garment*) **it unzips at the side,** ça s'ouvre sur le côté.
up[1] [ʌp] **I.** *adv.* **1.** (*a*) en montant; vers le haut; **all the way up, the whole way up, right up (to the top),** jusqu'au haut (de la colline); jusqu'en haut (de l'escalier); **half way up,** jusqu'à mi-hauteur; **to live three flights up,** habiter au troisième, *NAm:* au quatrième (étage); **to throw sth. up in the air,** jeter qch. en l'air; **to put one's hand up,** lever la main; **hands up!** haut les mains! **to put up the results,** afficher les résultats; (*b*) **to walk up and down,** se promener de long en large; **to go up north,** aller dans le nord; **to go up to London for the day,** aller passer la journée à Londres; **he's going up to Oxford,** il va faire ses études à l'université d'Oxford; **to come up before the bench,** être cité devant les magistrats; (*c*) **from £10 up,** à partir de £10. **2.** (*a*) haut, en haut; **what are you doing up there?** qu'est-ce que vous faites là-haut? **up above,** en haut; **up above sth.,** au-dessus de qch.; **before the sun was up,** avant le lever du soleil; **the new building is up,** le nouveau bâtiment est terminé; (*in car*) **would you like the window up a bit?** voulez-vous que je remonte un peu la glace? *Turf:* **Comet with Thomas up,** Comet monté par Thomas; **the cat's back was up,** le chat faisait le gros dos; **the river's up,** la rivière est en crue; **this road's always up,** cette route est toujours en réparation; (*b*) en dessus; **to lay sth. face up,** placer qch. face en dessus; (*on packing case*) **this side up,** haut; dessus; **put it the other way up,** retournez-le; (*c*) **up in London,** à Londres; **up in Yorkshire,** au nord dans le Yorkshire; **up at Oxford,** à l'université d'Oxford. **3.** (*a*) **prices are 10% up on last year's,** les prix ont augmenté de dix pour cent depuis l'année dernière; **bread is up again,** le pain a encore augmenté; **the temperature is going up,** la température monte; **business is looking up,** les affaires sont à la hausse; *F:* **he's something quite high up in the civil service,** il est haut placé dans l'administration; *Sp:* **to be one goal up,** *Golf:* **one hole up,** mener par un but; avoir un trou d'avance; **to be one up on s.o.,** (i) avoir un point d'avance sur un adversaire; (ii) avoir l'avantage sur qn; (*b*) *Mch:* **steam is up,** nous sommes sous pression; **his blood was up,** le sang lui bouillait; (*c*) **to be well up in a subject,** connaître un sujet à fond; (*d*) **speak up!** parlez plus fort! **4.** (*close proximity*) (*a*) **lean it up against the wall,** appuyez-le contre le mur; **they were standing close up to each other,** ils se tenaient tout près l'un de l'autre; (*b*) **to be up against difficulties,** se heurter à des difficultés; **to be up against it,** être dans le pétrin. **5.** (*a*) debout; levé; **to be up late,** veiller tard; **to be up all night,** ne pas se coucher de la nuit; **I was up late this morning,** je me suis levé tard ce matin; **he's always up and about by seven,** à sept heures il est toujours levé et au travail; (*after illness*) **to be up and about again,** être de nouveau sur pied; **to be up and coming,** (i) (*of pers.*) être plein d'avenir; promettre bien; (ii) (*of thg*) être progressif; (*b*) **up with X!** vive X! **6.** (*a*) **to be up**

in arms, être en révolte; (*b*) *F:* **what's up?** qu'est-ce qui se passe? qu'y a-t-il? **what's up with you?** qu'est-ce qui vous prend? **something's up,** il y a quelque chose (i) qui ne va pas, (ii) qui se mijote. **7. time is up,** il est l'heure (de fermer, de finir); **his leave is up,** sa permission est expirée; (*of prisoner*) **his time is up,** son temps est fini; *F:* **the game's up, it's all up,** tout est perdu; c'est fichu; **I thought it was all up with me,** j'ai cru que ma dernière heure était venue; **it's all up with him,** c'en est fait de lui; il a son compte. **8.** (*a*) **to go up to s.o.,** s'approcher de qn; **covered in mud up to the ears,** couvert de boue jusqu'aux oreilles; **where, what page, are you up to?** où en êtes-vous (du livre que vous lisez)? (*b*) **up to now, up to here,** jusqu'ici; **up to then,** jusqu'alors, jusque-là; **to be up to date,** être moderne, à la mode, *F:* à la page; **an up-to-date house,** une maison moderne; **up to £100 a week,** jusqu'à £100 par semaine; **up to what age?** jusqu'à quel âge? (*c*) **to be up to one's job,** être à la hauteur de sa tâche; **he's not up to it,** il n'est pas capable de le faire; **he's not up to the journey,** il n'est pas à même de faire le voyage; **I don't feel up to it,** je ne m'en sens pas le courage; **I don't feel up to much,** je ne me sens pas bien; **it's not up to much,** ça ne vaut pas grand-chose; (*d*) **he's up to something,** il a quelque chose en tête; il mijote quelque chose; **what are the children up to?** qu'est-ce que font les enfants? (*e*) **it's up to him to do it,** c'est à lui de le faire; **it's up to you to accept,** il ne tient qu'à vous d'accepter. **II.** *prep.* **1.** au haut de; dans le haut de; **to go up the stairs,** monter l'escalier; **the cat is up a tree,** le chat est en haut d'un arbre. **2. up the river,** en amont; vers la source de la rivière; **it's u. river from here,** c'est en amont d'ici; **to go up the street,** remonter la rue; **further up the street,** plus loin dans la rue; **to walk up and down the platform,** arpenter le quai. **III.** *a.* ascendant, montant; *Rail:* **up line,** voie en direction de Londres (ou d'un terminus important); **up train,** train montant. **IV.** *n.* (*a*) **ups and downs,** (i) ondulations *fpl* (du terrain); (ii) les hauts et les bas, les vicissitudes *fpl* (de la vie); (iii) avatars *mpl* (de la politique); (iv) *Com:* oscillations *fpl* (du marché); **life is full of ups and downs,** la vie est faite de hauts et de bas; *attrib.* **up-and-down movement,** (i) mouvement *m* de montée et de descente; (ii) jeu vertical (d'une pièce); (*b*) *F:* **to be on the up and up,** être en train de monter, de faire son chemin.

NOTE. *When* **up** *is an integral part of a verb, e.g.* **come up, go up, get up, take up,** *the user should consult the verb in question.*

up² *v.* **(upped) 1.** *v.tr.* (*a*) **to up the swans,** recenser les cygnes; (*b*) *F:* hausser (les prix); (*c*) *F:* lever (son bâton); **to up sticks,** déménager. **2.** *v.i. P:* se lever d'un bond; **they upped and went,** sans plus attendre ils sont partis. **upping** *n.* **swan u.,** recensement *m* des cygnes.

up-and-coming ['ʌpænd'kʌmiŋ] *a.* (*of pers.*) qui est plein d'avenir, qui promet; entreprenant; prometteur; (*of town*) progressif.

up-and-over ['ʌpænd'ouvər] *a.* **u.-a.-o. door,** porte basculante (d'un garage, etc.).

upbeat ['ʌpbi:t] *n. Mus:* levé *m*; temps *m* faible.

upbraid [ʌp'breid] *v.tr.* reprocher, faire des reproches à (qn); réprimander (qn).

upbringing ['ʌpbriŋiŋ] *n.* éducation *f*; **what sort of (an) u. has she had?** comment a-t-elle été élevée?

upchuck ['ʌptʃʌk] *v.i. U.S: F:* vomir, rendre.

upcoming ['ʌpkʌmiŋ] *a.* prochain.

upcountry [ʌp'kʌntri] *esp. NAm: Austr:* (*a*) *n.* l'intérieur *m* (du pays); (*b*) *a.* de l'intérieur (du pays); (*c*) *adv.* **to go u.,** aller vers l'intérieur.

update [ʌp'deit] *v.tr.* (*a*) mettre (qch.) à jour; (*b*) moderniser (qch.).

upend [ʌp'end] *v.tr.* mettre (qch.) debout.

upgrade¹ ['ʌpgreid] *n.* pente ascendante; montée *f* (d'une ligne de chemin de fer); **to be on the u.,** (i) (*of prices*) monter; (ii) (*of business*) reprendre, se relever; (iii) (*of invalid*) être en voie de guérison.

upgrade² [ʌp'greid] *v.tr.* **1.** améliorer (un produit). **2.** monter en grade (un fonctionnaire); nommer (qn), élever (qch.), à un niveau supérieur. **upgrading** *n.* **1.** amélioration *f.* **2.** montée *f* en grade; avancement *m.*

upheaval [ʌp'hi:v(ə)l] *n.* bouleversement, agitation *f*; **political u.,** commotion politique.

uphill 1. *a.* ['ʌphil] (*a*) (*of road*) montant; (*b*) (*of struggle*) pénible, difficile. **2.** *adv.* [ʌp'hil] **to go u.,** monter.

uphold [ʌp'hould] *v.tr.* (*p.t. & p.p.* **upheld** [-'held]) soutenir (une opinion); prêter son appui à (qn); confirmer (une décision); **to u. the law,** faire observer la loi.

upholder [ʌp'houldər] *n.* défenseur *m* (d'une cause).

upholster [ʌp'houlstər] *v.tr.* (i) capitonner, rembourrer, (ii) tapisser, couvrir (un canapé) (**with, in,** de). **upholstered** *a.* (i) capitonné, rembourré, (ii) tapissé, couvert; **u. in velvet,** garni de velours; *F:* **she's well u.,** elle est bien rembourrée.

upholsterer [ʌp'houlstərər] *n.* tapissier *m* (garnisseur, décorateur); tapissier en ameublement.

upholstery [ʌp'houlstəri] *n.* **1.** capitonnage *m,* rembourrage *m* (d'un fauteuil). **2.** (i) tapisserie *f* d'ameublement; (ii) garniture intérieure (d'une voiture); **leather u.,** garniture en cuir. **3.** (*trade*) tapisserie.

upkeep ['ʌpki:p] *n.* (frais *mpl* d')entretien *m.*

upland ['ʌplənd] **1.** *n. usu. pl.* **the uplands,** le haut pays; les hautes terres. **2.** *a.* (village) des montagnes.

uplift¹ ['ʌplift] *n.* **1.** (*a*) élévation *f* (du terrain); (*b*) **u. bra,** soutien-gorge au maintien parfait. **2. moral u.,** inspiration (morale).

uplift² [ʌp'lift] *v.tr.* **1.** soulever, élever (qch.). **2.** élever (l'âme, le cœur). **uplifted** *a.* (*a*) (*of hand*) levé; (*b*) exalté, inspiré.

up-market ['ʌpmɑ:kit] *a.* haut de gamme; de qualité supérieure.

upmost ['ʌpmoust] *a.* = UPPERMOST 1.

upon [ə'pɔn] *prep.* (= ON) sur; **on** *and* **upon** *are interchangeable in meaning; in modern English* **upon** *is used more formally; in certain phrases, however,* **upon** *is preferable:* **u. my word!** ma foi! mon Dieu! **the enemy was u. us,** l'ennemi nous attaquait; **I came u. it by accident,** je l'ai trouvé par hasard; **you brought it u. yourself,** ne t'en prends qu'à toi-même!

upper ['ʌpər] **I.** *a.* **1.** (*a*) supérieur; (plus) haut; (plus) élevé; de dessus; d'au-dessus; **the u. air,** les couches supérieures de l'atmosphère; **u. jaw, lip,** mâchoire, lèvre, supérieure; **the u. branches,** les hautes branches; **u. storey,** étage supérieur; *Nau:* **u. deck,** pont supérieur; *Th:* **u. circle,** deuxième balcon *m*; **temperature in the u. twenties,** température qui dépasse 25°; (*b*) **u. reaches,** amont *m* (d'une rivière); **the u. Rhine,** le haut Rhin; **U. Canada,** le haut Canada; **U. Egypt,** la Haute-Égypte. **2.** supérieur; **u. end of the table,** haut bout de la table; *Parl:* **the U. House,** la Chambre haute; **the u. classes,** la haute société; **u.-class milieu,** milieu aristocratique; **the u. middle classes,** la haute bourgeoisie; *Sch:* **the u. school,** les grandes classes; **to gain the u. hand,** prendre le dessus; **to let s.o. get the u. hand,** se laisser subjuguer par qn. **3.** *Mus:* (*a*) (clavier) du côté droit; (*b*) (registre) aigu. **II.** *n.* empeigne *f*; *F:* **to be down on one's uppers,** être dans la gêne.

uppermost ['ʌpəmoust] **1.** *a.* (*a*) le plus haut; le plus élevé; (*b*) de la plus grande importance; **to be**

u., tenir le premier rang; **the problem (which is) u. in our minds,** le problème qui nous préoccupe le plus. **2.** *adv.* (le plus) en dessus; **face u.,** face en dessus.

uppish ['ʌpiʃ], **uppity** ['ʌpiti] *a. F:* présomptueux, arrogant; **he's getting very u.,** il se croit quelqu'un.

upright ['ʌprait] **I.** *a.* **1.** (*of line*) vertical, -aux; perpendiculaire; (*of wall, writing*) droit; **u. piano,** piano droit; **u. freezer,** congélateur armoire. **2.** (*of pers., dealings*) droit, juste, honnête. **II.** *adv.* debout; (*of pers.*) **to stand u.,** se tenir droit; **sitting u. on his chair,** assis raide sur sa chaise; **to put, stand, sth. u.,** mettre qch. debout, d'aplomb. **III.** *n.* **1. out of u.,** hors d'aplomb. **2.** *Carp: etc:* montant *m*; **uprights of a ladder,** montants d'une échelle; *Fb:* **the uprights,** les montants de but. **3.** piano droit.

uprightness ['ʌpraitnis] *n.* droiture *f*, honnêteté *f*.

uprising [ʌp'raiziŋ] *n.* soulèvement *m* (du peuple); insurrection *f*.

uproar ['ʌprɔːr] *n.* tumulte *m*, vacarme *m*, tapage *m*; brouhaha *m*, chahut *m*; **the town was in an u.,** la ville était en effervescence.

uproarious [ʌp'rɔːriəs] *a.* tumultueux; **u. laughter,** grands éclats de rire. **-ly** *adv.* tumultueusement; (rire) à grands éclats; **u. funny,** désopilant.

uproot [ʌp'ruːt] *v.tr.* déraciner, extirper (une plante, un mal); **to u. s.o. from his home,** arracher qn de son foyer; **to feel uprooted,** se sentir déraciné.

upsadaisy ['ʌpsədeizi] *int. F:* houp là!

upset[1] ['ʌpset] *n.* **1.** renversement *m* (d'un bateau). **2.** (*a*) désorganisation *f*; désordre *m*; remue-ménage *m inv*; (*b*) ennui *m*; **that's going to cause a bit of an u.,** cela va causer des difficultés; (*c*) bouleversement (d'esprit); (*d*) indisposition *f*; dérangement *m* (d'estomac).

upset[2] [ʌp'set] *v.* (*p.t. & p.p.* **upset;** *pr.p.* **upsetting**) **1.** *v.tr.* (*a*) renverser; (faire) chavirer (un bateau); (*b*) désorganiser, bouleverser, déranger (les projets de qn); (*c*) troubler, émouvoir, bouleverser (qn); **the least thing upsets him,** il s'impressionne pour un rien; **don't u. yourself,** ne vous en faites pas; ne vous frappez pas; (*d*) indisposer (qn); déranger (l'estomac); troubler (la digestion); **beer upsets me,** la bière me rend malade. **2.** *v.i.* (*of cup, contents*) se renverser; (*of boat*) chavirer. **upsetting 1.** *a.* bouleversant, inquiétant. **2.** *n.* renversement *m*; désorganisation *f*; dérangement *m* (de projets).

upset[3] [*before noun* 'ʌpset, *otherwise* ʌp'set] *a.* **1.** (*a*) renversé; (*of boat*) chaviré; (*b*) (*of pers.*) bouleversé; ému; **don't get, be, u.,** ne vous en faites pas; (*c*) (estomac) dérangé. **2.** (*at auctions*) **u. price,** mise *f* à prix.

upshot ['ʌpʃɔt] *n.* résultat *m*; **what will be the u. of it?** cela finira comment? **the u. of it all was that he resigned,** en fin de compte il a donné sa démission.

upside ['ʌpsaid] **1.** *adv.phr:* **upside down,** (*a*) sens dessus dessous; la tête en bas; **to hold sth. u. down,** tenir qch. à l'envers; (*b*) en désordre; **to turn everything u. down,** tout bouleverser; tout mettre sens dessus dessous. **2.** *a. F:* **upside-down,** renversé; **pineapple u.-down cake,** gâteau renversé à l'ananas.

upstage[1] [ʌp'steidʒ] **1.** *n. Th:* arrière-scène *f*. **2.** *a.* (*a*) *Th:* de l'arrière-scene; (*b*) *F:* arrogant, hautain. **3.** *adv.* à l'arrière-scène.

upstage[2] *v.tr.* reléguer (qn) au second plan; souffler la vedette à (qn).

upstairs 1. *adv.* [ʌp'stɛəz] (i) en haut (de l'escalier); (ii) à l'étage; aux étages supérieurs; **to come, go, u.,** monter (l'escalier); *F:* **to kick s.o. u.,** donner de l'avancement à qn (pour s'en débarrasser); *F:* **he hasn't got much u.,** il n'est pas très intelligent. **2.** (*a*) *a.* ['ʌpstɛəz] (*of room*) d'en haut, du haut; à l'étage (supérieur); **we have an u. sitting room,** nous avons un salon au premier; (*b*) *n. F:* **(the) u.** [ʌp'stɛəz] l'étage; les pièces d'en haut; **the house has no u.,** la maison n'a pas d'étage.

upstanding [ʌp'stændiŋ] *a.* (*of pers.*) (*a*) droit, qui se tient bien; **a fine u. man,** un gars solide; (*b*) honnête.

upstart ['ʌpstɑːt] *n.* parvenu, -ue; nouveau riche.

upstate *U.S:* **1.** *a.* ['ʌpsteit] de l'intérieur (d'un État). **2.** *adv.* [ʌp'steit] (aller) vers l'intérieur (d'un État).

upstream 1. *adv.* [ʌp'striːm] (*a*) en amont **(from,** de); (*b*) en remontant le courant; à contre-fil de l'eau. **2.** *a.* ['ʌpstriːm] d'amont.

upstroke ['ʌpstrouk] *n.* **1.** (*in writing*) délié *m*. **2.** course montante, ascendante (du piston).

upsurge ['ʌpsəːdʒ] *n.* poussée *f*; vague *f* (d'enthousiasme); regain *m* (d'activité).

upswept ['ʌpswept] *a. Aut: Av:* surélevé; profilé; **u. hair(style),** coiffure relevée.

upswing ['ʌpswiŋ] *n.* **1.** mouvement ascendant. **2.** amélioration *f* sensible; **business is on the u.,** les affaires sont en progression constante.

uptake ['ʌpteik] *n. F:* entendement *m*; **to be quick on the u.,** avoir la compréhension facile; avoir l'esprit vif; **he's a bit slow on the u.,** il est lent à comprendre.

uptight ['ʌptait] *a. F:* (i) tendu; agité; crispé; (ii) fâché; **to get u.,** s'énerver.

up-to-date [ʌptə'deit] *a.* très récent; (*of method*) moderne; (*of pers.*) qui est dans le vent.

uptown *esp. U.S:* **1.** *adv.* [ʌp'taun] dans, vers, les quartiers résidentiels de la ville. **2.** *n.* ['ʌptaun] les quartiers résidentiels; **u. society,** les milieux bourgeois.

upturn[1] ['ʌptəːn] *n.* amélioration *f*; progression *f* (dans les affaires); avancement *m*.

upturn[2] [ʌp'təːn] *v.tr.* retourner; mettre à l'envers; renverser. **upturned** *a.* (*a*) retourné; renversé; (*b*) (nez) retroussé; (yeux) tournés vers le ciel.

upward ['ʌpwəd] **1.** *a.* montant, ascendant; **u. movement,** mouvement ascensionnel; **u. slope,** pente ascendante; **u. tendency, movement,** tendance *f* à la hausse, mouvement de hausse. **2.** *adv.* = UPWARDS.

upwards ['ʌpwədz] *adv.* **1.** de bas en haut; vers le haut; en montant; **to look u.,** regarder en haut. **2.** en dessus; **to put sth. face u. on the table,** mettre qch. à l'endroit sur la table; (*of pers.*) **lying face u.,** couché sur le dos. **3.** au-dessus; **£100 and u.,** £100 et au-dessus; **u. of 500 pupils,** plus de 500 élèves; **children from ten (years) u.,** des enfants à partir de dix ans.

upwind 1. *adv.* [ʌp'wind] (aller) contre le vent. **2.** *a.* ['ʌpwind] (être) contre le vent.

Ural ['jurəl] *Pr.n.* **the U. (river),** l'Oural *m*; **the U. mountains, the Urals,** les monts Ourals, l'Oural.

uranium [ju'reiniəm] *n. Ch:* uranium *m*.

Uranus [ju'reinəs] *Pr.n.m. Myth: Astr:* Uranus.

urban ['əːbən] *a.* urbain; **u. areas,** agglomérations urbaines; **u. sprawl,** urbanisation incontrôlée, sauvage.

urbane [əː'bein] *a.* courtois; d'une politesse raffinée. **-ly** *adv.* courtoisement; avec urbanité.

urbanism ['əːbənizm] *n.* urbanisme *m*.

urbanity [əː'bæniti] *n.* urbanité *f*; courtoisie *f*.

urbanization [əːbənai'zeiʃ(ə)n] *n.* urbanisation *f*.

urbanize ['əːbənaiz] *v.tr.* urbaniser.

urchin ['əːtʃin] *n.* **1.** *F:* (*a*) **(street) u.,** galopin *m*; (*b*) gosse *mf*. **2. sea u.,** oursin *m*.

Urdu ['uəduː] *n. Ling:* ourdou *m*.

urea [ju'riːə] *n. Ch:* urée *f*.

ureter [ju'riːtər] *n. Anat:* uretère *m*.

urethra [ju'riːθrə] *n. Anat:* urètre *m*.

urge[1] [əːdʒ] *n.* impulsion *f*; poussée *f*; **to feel an u. to do sth.,** se sentir le besoin de faire qch.

urge[2] *v.tr.* **1.** (*a*) **to u. s.o. (on),** encourager, exciter, qn; **to u. a horse forward,** pousser, presser, un cheval; **to u. s.o. to do sth.,** pousser qn à faire qch.; (*b*) hâter, pousser (qch.); **to u. on a piece of work,** hâter un travail. **2.** insister sur (un point); **I urged that . . .,** j'ai fait valoir que . . .. **3.** conseiller fortement, recommander (une démarche); **to u. the necessity of doing sth.,** insister sur la nécessité de faire qch.

urgency ['ə:dʒənsi] *n.* **1.** urgence *f*; **it's a matter of u.,** il y a urgence; c'est urgent. **2.** nécessité urgente.

urgent ['ə:dʒənt] *a.* urgent, pressant; **u. need,** besoin pressant; **u. case,** case urgent, pressant; **the matter is u.,** l'affaire presse; c'est urgent; **the doctor had an u. call,** on a appelé le médecin d'urgence; **at their u. request,** sur leurs instances pressantes. **-ly** *adv.* d'urgence; avec instance; **a doctor is u. required,** on demande d'urgence un médecin; **to press u. for sth.,** réclamer qch. de façon urgente.

uric ['ju:rik] *a.* (acide) urique.

urinal ['ju:rin(ə)l, ju:'rain(ə)l] *n.* **1. (bed) u.,** urinal *m*, -aux. **2.** urinoir *m*; *F:* pissotière *f*.

urinary ['ju:rinəri] *a. Anat:* urinaire.

urinate ['ju:rineit] *v.i.* uriner.

urine ['ju:rin] *n.* urine *f*.

urn [ə:n] *n.* **1.** urne *f*. **2. tea u.,** fontaine *f* à thé.

urogenital [ju(:)rou'dʒenit(ə)l] *a. Anat:* urogénital, -aux.

urological [jurou'lɔdʒik(ə)l] *a.* urologique.

urologist [ju'rɔlədʒist] *n.* urologue *mf*.

urology [ju'rɔlədʒi] *n. Med:* urologie *f*.

Ursa ['ə:sə] *n. Astr:* **U. Major, U. Minor,** la Grande, la Petite, Ourse.

urticaria [ə:ti'kɛəriə] *n. Med:* urticaire *f*.

Uruguay ['urugwai] *Pr.n. Geog:* Uruguay *m*.

Uruguayan [uru'gwaiən] *Geog:* **1.** *a.* uruguayen. **2.** *n.* Uruguayen, -enne.

us *pers. pron., objective case.* **1.** (*unstressed*) [əs] nous; **he sees us,** il nous voit; **in front of, behind, us,** devant, derrière, nous; **he gave it to us,** il nous l'a donné; **tell us,** dites-nous; **he wrote us a letter,** il nous a écrit une lettre; **he stayed with us a month,** il est resté un mois chez nous; **there are three of us,** nous sommes trois. **2.** (*stressed*) [ʌs] (*a*) nous; **that concerns *us* alone,** cela ne regarde que nous; **between them and us,** entre eux et nous; **as for us Englishmen,** quant à nous autres Anglais; (*b*) (*after the verb* **to be**) **he couldn't believe that it was us,** il ne pouvait pas croire que c'était nous. **3.** (= **me**) (*a*) nous; **it appears to us that . . .,** nous sommes persuadé que . . .; (*b*) *F:* **let's have a look,** laissez-moi regarder; **give us a bit of it,** donnez-m'en un peu.

usable ['ju:zəbl] *a.* utilisable, employable.

usage ['ju:sidʒ] *n.* **1.** traitement *m*; **this book has had rough u.,** ce livre a été maltraité. **2.** usage *m*; **an old u.,** une vieille coutume; **sanctified by u.,** consacré par l'usage. **3.** (*a*) emploi *m*, usage (d'un mot); (*b*) utilisation *f*.

use¹ [ju:s] *n.* **1.** (*a*) emploi *m*, usage *m*; utilisation *f*; **the u. of steel in building,** l'emploi de l'acier dans la construction; **to make u. of sth.,** se servir de qch.; utiliser qch.; employer qch.; **to make good u. of sth., to put sth. to good u.,** bien employer qch; tirer profit de qch.; **everything has a, its, u.,** il y a un emploi pour tout; **I'll find a u. for it,** je trouverai un moyen de m'en servir; **word in everyday u.,** mot d'usage courant; **not in u., out of u.,** hors d'usage; (mot) desuet, tombé en désuétude; (*on door of lift*) hors de service; **for u. in case of fire,** à employer en cas d'incendie; **for u. in schools,** à l'usage des écoles; **directions, instructions, for u.,** mode d'emploi; *Pharm:* **for external u.,** pour usage externe; (*b*) usage; **to improve with u.,** s'améliorer à l'usage. **2.** jouissance *f*, usage; (*a*) **to have full u. of one's faculties,** jouir de toutes ses facultés; **to lose the u. of a leg,** perdre l'usage d'une jambe; (*b*) **to have the u. of the bathroom,** avoir le droit de se servir de la salle de bains; **you can have the u. of my car while I'm in London,** tu peux te servir de ma voiture pendant que je suis à Londres; (*c*) *Jur:* usufruit *m*; **full right and u. (of sth.),** plein usufruit, pleine jouissance (de qch.). **3.** utilité *f*; **to be of u.,** être utile (**for sth.,** à qch.); **can I be of any u. (to you)?** puis-je vous être utile à quelque chose? **it's of no u. to me,** je n'en ai pas besoin; **it's not much u.,** cela ne sert pas à grand-chose; *F:* **a fat lot of u. that'll be to you!** si tu crois que ça va t'avancer! *F: Iron: **you're*** **a lot of u.!** je vous retiens! *F:* **he's no u.,** il est incapable; **to have no u. for sth.,** ne savoir que faire de qch.; **I've no further u. for it,** je n'en ai plus besoin; *F:* **I haven't much u. for him,** il ne me dit rien; **it was no u.,** c'était inutile; **it's no u. discussing the question,** inutile de discuter la question; **it's no u. crying,** ce n'est pas la peine de pleurer; **it's no u. my talking,** je perds ma peine à parler; **it's no u.(, I can't do it)!** c'est peine perdue(; je ne peux pas le faire); **is it any u. writing to him?** est-ce que ça servirait de lui écrire? **what's the u. of doing it, of going there?** à quoi bon le faire, y aller? **4.** *A:* usage, coutume *f*.

use² [ju:z] *v.tr.* **1.** (*a*) employer, se servir de (qch.); **are you using this knife?** est-ce que vous vous servez de ce couteau? **u. your head!** ne sois pas si bête! **u. your eyes!** ouvrez les yeux! (*of thg*) **to be used for sth.,** servir à qch.; **I used the money to rebuild my garage,** j'ai utilisé l'argent à reconstruire mon garage; **this word is no longer used,** ce mot est désuet; **word used figuratively,** mot employé au (sens) figuré; (*b*) **to u. force,** avoir recours à la force; **to u. discretion,** agir avec discrétion; **to u. one's influence,** user de son influence; **to u. every means (at one's disposal),** employer tous les moyens (à sa disposition); (*c*) *esp. U.S: F:* **I could u. some coffee,** je prendrais volontiers du café. **2.** (*a*) (bien, mal) agir envers qn; **this tool has been roughly used,** cet outil a été maltraité; **it will last a long time if you u. it carefully,** cela vous servira longtemps si vous le traitez avec soin; *F:* **how's the world been using you?** comment ça va? (*b*) **I feel I've been used,** j'ai l'impression qu'on s'est tout bonnement servi de moi. **3.** (*a*) **to u. sth. (up),** épuiser, consommer, qch.; **we've used (up) all the milk,** il ne reste plus de lait; (*b*) **to u. up scraps, leftovers,** utiliser, *Cu:* accommoder, les restes. **4.** (*as aux. p.t.*) [ju:st] **when we were children we used to play together,** quand nous étions enfants nous jouions ensemble; **my father used to tell me that . . .,** mon père m'a souvent raconté que . . .; **it used to be a pleasant town to live in,** c'était autrefois une ville agréable à habiter; **things aren't what they used to be,** ce n'est plus comme autrefois; **she used not, usen't, to like oysters,** autrefois elle n'aimait pas les huîtres; **I used not to like him,** *F:* **didn't use to** ['ju:stə] **like him,** autrefois je ne l'aimais pas. **used** *a.* **1.** [ju:zd] usé, usagé; (timbre-poste) oblitéré; (nappe) sale, qui a déjà servi; **u. car,** voiture d'occasion; **hardly u.,** presque neuf. **2.** [ju:st] **u. to (doing) sth.,** habitué, accoutumé, à (faire) qch.; **I'm not u. to it,** je n'en ai pas l'habitude; **to get u. to sth.,** s'habituer à qch.; **you'll get u. to it in time,** vous vous y ferez à la longue.

useful ['ju:sf(u)l] *a.* **1.** utile; pratique; **this book was very u. to me,** ce livre m'a été très utile, m'a rendu grand service; **it's u. to know,** c'est utile à savoir; **it will come in very u.,** cela rendra bien service; **a u. man to know,** un homme utile à connaître; **to make oneself u.,** se rendre utile; **this machine has a u. life of ten years,** cette machine donnera dix ans de service; **he played a u. game,** il s'est acquitté honorablement; **to be u. with a gun,** savoir manier un fusil. **-fully** *adv.* utilement; **one might u. write a book on . . .,** on pourrait utilement écrire un livre sur . . ..

usefulness ['ju:sf(u)lnis] *n.* utilité *f*; **it has outlived its u.,** cela ne sert plus à rien.
useless ['ju:slis] *a.* inutile; bon à rien; vain, infructueux; (remède) inefficace; **a map without a key is u.,** une carte sans légende est inutilisable; **it would be u. to make further requests,** d'autres demandes seraient inutiles; **a u. person,** un(e) incompétent(e); *F:* **to be worse than u.,** être au-dessous de tout. **-ly** *adv.* inutilement; en vain.
uselessness ['ju:slisnis] *n.* inutilité *f*; (*of pers.*) incompétence *f.*
user ['ju:zər] *n.* usager, -ère (de la route, d'un moyen de transport); utilisateur, -trice (d'un appareil); abonné, -ée (du téléphone).
usher¹ ['ʌʃər] *n.* (*a*) *Jur:* **court u.,** (huissier) audiencier *m*; (*b*) *Th: Cin:* placeur *m*; (*at wedding*) **the ushers,** les garçons *mpl* d'honneur.
usher² *v.tr.* **1.** précéder (un roi) comme huissier. **2. to u. s.o. in,** introduire, faire entrer, qn; **to u. s.o. into the presence of s.o.,** introduire qn en présence de qn; **to u. in a new epoch,** inaugurer une époque. **3.** *v.i. F:* (*at wedding*) servir de garçon(s) d'honneur.
usherette [ʌʃə'ret] *n.f. Th: Cin:* ouvreuse.
usual ['ju:ʒuəl] *a.* usuel, habituel, ordinaire; **at the u. time,** à l'heure habituelle; **the u. terms,** les conditions d'usage; **it's u. to pay in advance,** il est d'usage de payer d'avance; **it's the u. practice,** c'est la pratique courante; **earlier, later, than u.,** plus tôt, plus tard, que d'habitude; **more than u.,** plus que d'habitude; **as u.,** comme d'ordinaire, d'habitude; **business as u.,** les affaires continuent, la vente continue (pendant les réparations); *n. F:* (*in bar*) **(are you having) your u.?** votre demi, votre whisky, etc., comme d'habitude? **-ally** ['ju:ʒu(ə)li] *adv.* ordinairement, habituellement; d'ordinaire, d'habitude, de coutume; **I u. get up at seven,** j'ai l'habitude de me lever à sept heures; **he was more than u. polite,** il s'est montré encore plus poli que d'habitude.
usufruct ['ju:zjufrʌkt] *n. Jur:* usufruit *m* **(of,** de).
usufructuary [ju:zju'frʌktjəri] *a. & n. Jur:* usufruitier, -ière; **u. right,** droit *m* usufructuaire.
usurer ['ju:ʒərər] *n.* usurier, -ière.
usurious [ju:'zju:riəs] *a.* (intérêt *m*, etc.) usuraire.
usurp [ju:'zə:p, -'sə:p] **1.** *v.tr.* usurper (un trône, un titre) **(from,** sur). **2.** *v.i.* **to u. (up)on s.o.'s rights,** empiéter, usurper, sur les droits de qn.
usurpation [ju:zə'peiʃ(ə)n, -sə:-] *n.* usurpation *f.*
usurper [ju'zə:pər, -sə:-] *n.* usurpateur, -trice.
usury ['ju:ʒuri] *n.* usure *f.*
utensil [ju(:)'tens(ə)l] *n.* ustensile *m*; **(set of) kitchen utensils,** batterie *f* de cuisine.
uterine ['ju:tərain] *a.* utérin.
uterus ['ju:tərəs] *n. Anat:* utérus *m.*
utilitarian [ju:tili'tɛəriən] *a. & n.* utilitaire (*mf*).
utilitarianism [ju:tili'tɛəriənizm] *n.* utilitarisme *m.*
utility [ju'tiliti] *n.* (*a*) utilité *f*; **u. vehicle, car,** véhicule, voiture, utilitaire, tous usages; *Com:* **u. goods,** articles *m* utilitaires, de consommation courante; **u. room,** pièce réservée à la lessive, au repassage; (*b*) **public utilities, public u. services,** *NAm:* **utilities,** services publics; (*c*) *NAm:* entreprise *f* de service public.
utilizable [ju:ti'laizəbl] *a.* utilisable.
utilization (ju:tilai'zeiʃ(ə)n] *n.* utilisation *f*; mise *f* en valeur; *Bank:* réalisation *f;* **better u. of resources,** mobilisation *f* des resources.
utilize ['ju:tilaiz] *v.tr.* utiliser, se servir de (qn, qch.); tirer profit de, mettre en valeur (qch.).
utmost ['ʌtmoust] **1.** *a.* extrême; dernier; **the u. ends of the earth,** les (derniers) confins, les extrémités *fpl* de la terre; **the u. poverty,** la misère la plus profonde; **with the u. contempt,** avec le plus grand mépris; **it is of the u. importance that he should be present,** il est de la dernière importance qu'il soit présent; **with the u. ease,** avec la plus grande facilité. **2.** *n.* **to the u.,** le plus possible; au suprême degré; **I'll help you to the u. of my ability,** je vous aiderai autant qu'il est en mon pouvoir; **to do one's u. to achieve sth.,** faire tout son possible pour arriver à un but.
utopia (ju:'toupiə] *n.* utopie *f.*
utopian [ju:'toupiən] **1.** *a.* utopique; d'utopie. **2.** *n.* utopiste *mf.*
utter¹ ['ʌtər] *a.* complet, -ète; absolu; **he's an u. stranger to me,** il m'est complètement étranger; **we were in u. darkness,** il faisait noir comme dans un four; **u. rubbish,** (i) de la pure camelote; (ii) des absurdités; **he's an u. fool,** il est complètement idiot; **u. poverty,** la misère la plus profonde; **to my u. horror,** à ma grande horreur. **-ly** *adv.* complètement, absolument; **u. stupid,** d'une bêtise extrême.
utter² **1.** *v.tr.* (*a*) jeter, pousser (un cri); proférer (un mot); lancer (un juron); **never u. his name in her presence,** il ne faut jamais prononcer son nom devant elle; **I didn't u. a word,** je n'ai pas desserré les dents; (*b*) dire; débiter (des mensonges). **2.** *v.tr.* émettre, mettre en circulation (de la fausse monnaie). **3.** *v.i. F:* **he didn't u.,** il n'a pas desserré les dents; **he looked at me without uttering,** il m'a regardé sans mot dire.
utterance ['ʌtərəns] *n.* **1.** expression *f* (des sentiments); émission *f* (d'un son); **to give u. to one's feelings,** exprimer ses sentiments. **2.** articulation *f.* **3. utterances,** propos *mpl*, mots *mpl* (de qn).
uttermost ['ʌtəmoust] *a. & n.* = UTMOST; **the u. ends of the earth,** les derniers confins, les extrémités *fpl* de la terre.
uvula, *pl.* **-as, -ae** ['ju:vjulə, -əs, -i:] *n. Anat:* uvule *f*, luette *f.*
uvular ['ju:vjulər] *a.* uvulaire.
uxorious [ʌk'sɔ:riəs] *a.* (mari) (i) trop dévoué à sa femme, (ii) dominé par sa femme.
uxoriousness [ʌk'sɔ:riəsnis] *n.* attachement exagéré (d'un mari) pour sa femme.

V

V, v [viː] *n.* (la lettre) V, v *m.* **V-shaped,** en (forme de) V; **V-necked dress,** robe à encollure, en pointe, en V; **V sign,** (i) *Hist:* (1939–45) le V de la victoire; (ii) geste *m* obscène, de dérision.

vac [væk] *n. Sch: F:* vacances *fpl.*

vacancy [ˈveikənsi] *n.* vide *m.* **1.** vacuité *f.* **2.** absence *f* d'idées. **3.** espace *m* vide, lacune *f.* **4.** (*a*) place vacante, poste vacant; (*for dignitary, professional*) vacance *f*; **to fill a v.,** pourvoir un poste vacant, un vide; (*b*) (*at hotel*) chambre *f* libre; (*at camp site*) place libre; *P.N:* **no vacancies,** complet.

vacant [ˈveikənt] *a.* **1.** vacant, vide, libre; **v. space,** place vide; **v. site,** *NAm:* **v. lot,** terrain *m* vague; **v. room, seat,** chambre, place, libre, inoccupée; (*of official post*) **to be v.,** vaquer; **v. possession,** libre possession (d'un immeuble). **2.** (esprit) inoccupé; (regard) distrait, vague, sans expression; **with a v. stare,** le regard perdu. **-ly** *adv.* d'un air distrait; d'un regard perdu.

vacate [vəˈkeit] *v.tr.* (*a*) quitter (un emploi); (*b*) quitter (un siège); évacuer (un appartement); quitter (une chambre d'hôtel); déménager (d'une maison); *Jur:* **to v. the premises,** vider les lieux. **vacating** *n.* (*a*) **v. of office,** démission *f*; (*b*) évacuation *f* (d'une maison).

vacation¹ [vəˈkeiʃ(ə)n] *n.* **1.** (*a*) **the v.,** les vacances *fpl*; **the long v.,** *Jur:* les vacances judiciaires, les vacations *fpl*; *Sch:* (*at university*) les grandes vacances; (*b*) *NAm:* **to take a v.,** prendre des vacances; **to be on v.,** être en vacances. **2.** (*a*) **v. of office,** démission *f*; (*b*) évacuation *f* (d'une maison).

vacation² *v.i. NAm:* prendre, passer, ses vacances.

vacationist, vacationer [vəˈkeiʃ(ə)nist, -ər] *n. NAm:* vacancier, -ière; (*in summer*) estivant, -ante.

vaccinate [ˈvæksineit] *Med:* **1.** *v.tr.* vacciner (*esp.* contre la variole); **to get vaccinated,** se faire vacciner. **2.** *v.i.* faire une vaccination, des vaccinations.

vaccination [væksiˈneiʃ(ə)n] *n. Med:* vaccination *f*; **smallpox v.,** vaccination contre la variole.

vaccine [ˈvæksiːn] *n. Med:* vaccin *m*; **(smallpox) v.,** vaccin antivariolique.

vaccinee [væksiˈniː] *n. U.S:* personne vaccinée.

vacillate [ˈvæsileit] *v.i.* vaciller; (i) chanceler (en marchant); (ii) hésiter (entre deux opinions). **vacillating 1.** *a.* vacillant, irrésolu. **2.** *n.* vacillation *f.*

vacillation [væsiˈleiʃ(ə)n] *n.* vacillation *f.*

vacuity [væˈkju(ː)iti] *n.* **1.** vacuité *f*, vide *m* (de qch.). **2. vacuities,** bêtises *fpl*, niaiseries *fpl.*

vacuous [ˈvækjuəs] *a.* vide d'expression; (observation, rire) bête; **he's completely v.,** c'est un parfait idiot; **v. look,** air hébété, regard vide d'expression. **-ly** *adv.* avec des yeux vides d'expression; (rire) bêtement.

vacuum, *pl.* **-ua, -uums** [ˈvækjuəm, -juə, -juəmz] *n.* **1.** *Ph:* vide *m*, vacuum *m*; **to produce, create, a v. in a vessel,** faire le vide dans un récipient; **v. flask,** *NAm:* **bottle,** bouteille isolante; *El:* **v. lamp,** lampe *f* à vide; *Elcs:* **v. tube,** tube *m* (à vide) électronique; **v. pump,** pompe *f* à vide; *Ind: Com:* **v. packing,** emballage *m* sous vide. **2. v. cleaner,** aspirateur *m.*

vacuum(-clean) [ˈvækjuəm(kliːn)] *v.tr.* passer (une pièce) à l'aspirateur.

vacuum-packed [vækjuəmˈpækt] *a.* emballé, serti, sous vide.

vade mecum [veidiˈmiːkəm, vɑːdiˈmeikəm] *n.* vade-mecum *m inv*, aide-mémoire *m inv.*

vagabond [ˈvægəbɔnd] **1.** *a.* vagabond, errant. **2.** *n.* (*a*) vagabond, -onde; chemineau *m*; (*b*) vaurien *m.*

vagary [ˈveigəri] *n.* caprice *m*; **the vagaries of fashion,** les caprices de la mode.

vagina [vəˈdʒainə] *n. Anat:* vagin *m.*

vaginal [vəˈdʒain(ə)l] *a. Anat:* vaginal; *Med:* **v. douche,** douche vaginale.

vagrancy [ˈveigrənsi] *n.* **1.** *Jur:* vagabondage *m.* **2.** *NAm:* caprice *m.*

vagrant [ˈveigrənt] **1.** *a.* errant. **2.** *n.* (*a*) *Jur:* vagabond, -onde; (*b*) mendiant, -ante; chemineau *m.*

vague [veig] *a.* (*of pers., look*) vague; (*of impression, memory*) imprécis; (*of colour*) indéterminé, indécis; (*of shape, outline*) estompé, flou; **I haven't the vaguest idea,** je n'en ai pas la moindre idée; **I had a v. idea that he was dead,** j'avais vaguement l'idée qu'il était mort; **he was rather v. about the date,** (i) il n'a pas précisé la date; (ii) il n'était pas sûr de la date. **-ly** *adv.* vaguement.

vagueness [ˈveignis] *n.* vague *m*, imprécision *f.*

vain [vein] *a.* **1.** (*of pleasure, hope*) vain, mensonger, creux; **v. promises,** vaines promesses; promesses vaines. **2.** (*unavailing*) vain, inutile, stérile, **v. efforts,** efforts vains, futiles. **3.** (*conceited*) vaniteux, orgueilleux; **she was v. about her beauty,** elle était fière de sa beauté; **as v. as a peacock,** fier comme Artaban. **4.** *adv.phr.* **in v.,** en vain; (*a*) vainement; **we protested in v.,** nous avons eu beau protester; **to labour in v.,** travailler inutilement; perdre sa peine; **it was all in v.,** c'était peine perdue; (*b*) **to take God's name in v.,** prendre le nom de Dieu en vain; *F:* **who's taking my name in v.?** qui est-ce qui parle de moi? **-ly** *adv.* **1.** vainement, en vain, inutilement. **2.** vaniteusement, avec vanité.

vainglorious [veinˈglɔːriəs] *a.* vaniteux, orgueilleux. **-ly** *adv.* vaniteusement.

vainglory [veinˈglɔːri] *n.* vaine glorie; gloriole *f.*

valance [ˈvæləns] *n.* (*a*) frange *f* de lit; (*b*) lambrequin *m* (d'un ciel de lit, d'une fenêtre).

vale [veil] *n. A: & Lit:* vallon *m*; vallée *f*; **this v. of tears,** cette vallée de larmes.

valediction [væliˈdikʃ(ə)n] *n.* **1.** adieux(x) *m*(*pl*). **2.** *NAm:* = VALEDICTORY 2.

valedictorian [vælidikˈtɔːriən] *n. NAm: Sch:* membre *m* d'une promotion qui prononce le discours d'adieu.

valedictory [væliˈdiktəri] **1.** *a.* (allocution, dîner) d'adieu. **2.** *n. NAm: Sch:* discours *m* d'adieu (à la sortie d'une promotion, etc.).

valence [ˈveiləns] *n. Ch: Atom.Ph:* valence *f.*

valency [ˈveilənsi] *n.* = VALENCE.

Valentine [ˈvæləntain] **1.** *Pr.n.* Valentin *m*, Valentine *f*; **Saint Valentine's Day,** la Saint-Valentin (le 14 février). **2.** *n.* (*a*) carte envoyée le jour de la Saint-Valentin; (*b*) celui, celle, qui reçoit cette carte; **Robert is my v.,** c'est Robert que j'aime.

valerian [vəˈliəriən] *n. Bot: Pharm:* valériane *f.*

valet¹ [ˈvælei, ˈvælit] *n.* (*a*) valet *m* de chambre; (*b*) (*in hotel*) employé qui s'occupe de l'entretien des vêtements des clients; **v. service,** buanderie *f* et nettoyage *m.*

valet² *v.tr.* (**valeted** ['vælitid]) servir (qn) comme valet de chambre.
valetudinarian [vælitju:di'nɛəriən] *a. & n.* valétudinaire (*mf*).
Valhalla [væl'hælə] *n. Myth:* Walhalla *m.*
valiant ['væliənt] *a.* vaillant, valeureux, brave. **-ly** *adv.* vaillamment, valeureusement.
valid ['vælid] *a.* (contrat) valide, valable; (passeport) en règle; **v. argument,** argument valable, solide; **ticket v. for three months, no longer v.,** billet bon pour trois mois, périmé. **-ly** *adv.* validement.
validate ['vælideit] *v.tr.* valider, rendre valable (un acte); *U.S:* **to v. an election,** valider une élection.
validation [væli'deiʃ(ə)n] *n.* validation *f.*
validity [və'liditi] *n.* validité *f*; justesse *f*; force *f* (d'un argument).
valise [və'li:s, -i:z] *n.* **1.** *NAm:* valise *f*; sac *m* de voyage. **2.** *Mil:* sac de voyage (d'officier).
Valkyrie ['vælkiri] *n.f. Myth:* Walkyrie, Valkyrie.
valley ['væli] *n.* **1.** vallée *f*; (*small*) vallon *m*; **the Rhone V.,** la vallée du Rhône; **up, down, v.,** en montant, en descendant, la vallée; en amont, en aval. **2.** *Const:* noue (cornière), cornière *f* (de toit).
valor ['vælər] *n. NAm:* = VALOUR.
valorization [vælərai'zeiʃ(ə)n] *n.* valorisation *f.*
valorize ['væləraiz] *vtr. Com: Fin:* valoriser.
valorous ['vælərəs] *a. Lit:* valeureux, vaillant.
valour, *NAm:* **valor** ['vælər] *n. Lit:* valeur *f*, vaillance *f*, bravoure *f.*
valuable ['væljuəbl] **1.** *a.* (*a*) (*of object, help, time*) précieux; (object) de valeur, de prix; **v. gift,** cadeau de valeur; *Jur:* **for v. consideration,** à titre onéreux; (*b*) évaluable. **2.** *n.pl.* **valuables,** objets *m* de valeur, de prix.
valuation [vælju'eiʃ(ə)n] *n.* **1.** (*a*) évaluation *f*, estimation *f*, appréciation *f*; *Jur:* prisée *f* et estimation; expertise *f*; **to get a v. of sth.,** faire expertiser qch.; **to make a v. of the goods,** faire l'expertise des marchandises; (*b*) inventaire *m* (d'une succession). **2.** valeur estimée; (*a*) **to set too high, too low, a v. on goods,** surestimer, sous-estimer, des marchandises; (*b*) **to take, accept, s.o. at his own v.,** estimer qn selon l'opinion qu'il a de lui-même.
valuator ['væljueitər] *n.* estimateur *m*, commissaire-priseur *m, pl.* commissaires-priseurs.
value¹ ['vælju(:)] *n.* **1.** valeur *f*, prix *m*; **to be of v.,** avoir de la valeur; **of great v.,** de grande, de haute, valeur; **of little v.,** de peu de valeur; **to be of little v.,** valoir peu de chose; **of no v.,** sans valeur; **it is nothing of any v.,** ce n'est rien qui vaille; **to lose, to fall, in v.,** s'avilir; *Fin:* se dévaloriser; **loss of v., fall in v.,** dévalorisation *f*; **to have a certain v.,** valoir son prix; **to set a high, low, v. on sth.,** attacher un grand prix, peu de prix, à qch.; faire grand cas, peu de cas, de qch.; **to set a v. upon sth.,** (i) priser qch.; (ii) évaluer qch.; *Com:* attribuer une cote de valeur à qch.; **to set too high a v. on sth.,** attacher trop de valeur, trop de prix, à qch.; surestimer qch.; **v. judgment,** jugement *m* de valeur; **commercial, market, v.,** valeur vénale, marchande, négociable; cours *m*; *St.Exch: Adm:* **v. added tax,** taxe *f* à la valeur ajoutée; *Ins:* **replacement v.,** valeur de remplacement. **2. to pay s.o. the v. of a lost article,** rembourser à qn le prix d'un article perdu; *Com:* **for v. received,** valeur reçue; **to get (good) v. for one's money,** en avoir pour son argent; **he gives you v. for money,** il vous en donne pour votre argent; **it's v. for money,** cela vaut son prix, n'est pas cher. **3.** (*a*) *Mth:* **positive, negative, v.,** valeur positive, négative; (*b*) *Th:* **to give full v. to each word,** détailler les mots, la phrase; (*c*) **sense of values,** sentiment *m* des valeurs.
value² *v.tr.* **1.** *Com:* évaluer, estimer, apprécier, priser (des marchandises); faire l'expertise (d'un mobilier); **to get sth. valued,** faire expertiser qch. **2.** estimer, tenir à, faire grand cas de (qn, qch.); **if you v. your life,** si vous tenez à la vie. **valued** *a.* estimé, précieux; **my v. friend Mr Martin,** M. Martin dont l'amitié m'est si précieuse. **valuing** *n.* évaluation *f*, estimation *f*, appréciation *f.*
valueless ['væljulis] *a.* sans valeur.
valuer ['væljuər] *n.* estimateur *m*; **official v.,** commissaire-priseur *m, pl* commissaires-priseurs; expert *m.*
valve [vælv] *n.* **1.** (*a*) soupape *f*; **(clack, flap) v.,** (soupape à) clapet *m*; valve *f*; (*b*) *I.C.E:* **inlet, outlet, v.,** soupape d'admission, d'échappement; (*c*) (*tap, cock*) robinet *m*; **valves and fittings,** robinetterie *f*; (*d*) *Aut: Cy:* valve (de chambre à air); **v. cap,** capuchon *m*, chapeau *m*; (*e*) vanne *f*; **gas, water, v.,** vanne à gaz, d'eau; *Hyd.E:* **(sluice) v.,** vanne de communication; (*f*) *Mus:* piston *m* (d'un instrument en cuivre). **2.** *Anat:* valvule *f* (du cœur). **3.** *Elcs: W.Tel:* lampe *f* (de radio); valve.
valved [vælvd] *a.* à valve(s), à soupape(s); *Mus:* (instrument) à pistons; *Moll:* **two-v.,** (coquille) bivalve.
valvular ['vælvjulər] *a. Med: etc:* valvulaire.
vamoose [və'mu:s] *v.i. F:* décamper, filer.
vamp¹ [væmp] *n. Mus: F:* accompagnement tapoté, improvisé.
vamp² *v.tr.* **1.** *v.tr. & i. Mus: F:* tapoter au piano (un accompagnement improvisé); improviser (un accompagnement). **2. to v. up,** (*a*) rafistoler (qch.); (*b*) fagoter (un article).
vamp³ *n.f. F: O:* femme fatale; vamp.
vamp⁴ *F: O:* **1.** *v.tr.* (*of woman*) vamper (un homme). **2.** *v.i.* jouer la femme fatale.
vampire ['væmpaiər] *n.* **1.** *Myth & Fig:* vampire *m.* **2.** *Z:* **v. (bat),** vampire.
van¹ [væn] *n. Mil: etc:* (i) avant-garde *f*; (ii) front *m* (de bataille); *Fig:* **to be in the v.,** être à l'avant-garde.
van² *n. Veh:* **1.** (*a*) fourgon *m*; **furniture, removal, v.,** voiture *f* de déménagement; **delivery v.,** camion *m*, camionnette *f*, de livraison; *W.Tel:* **outside broadcasting v.,** car *m* de radio-reportage; (*b*) **gipsy v.,** roulotte *f.* **2.** *Rail:* wagon *m*, fourgon; **goods, luggage, v.,** fourgon à marchandises, à bagages; **guard's v.,** fourgon du chef de train; fourgon de queue.
van³ *n. Ten:* avantage *m*; **v. in,** avantage au servant, dedans; **v. out,** avantage au relanceur, dehors.
vanadium [və'neidiəm] *n. Ch:* vanadium *m.*
vandal ['vænd(ə)l] *n.* vandale *mf.*
vandalism ['vændəlizm] *n.* vandalisme *m*; **piece of v.,** acte *m* de vandalisme.
vandalize ['vændəlaiz] *v.tr.* saccager (un bâtiment, etc.); **several pictures have been vandalized,** plusieurs tableaux ont été mutilés par des vandales.
vane [vein] *n.* **1.** (*a*) **(wind, weather) v.,** girouette *f*; (*b*) moulinet *m* (d'un anémomètre); turbine *f* (d'un compteur à eau). **2.** (*a*) bras *m* (de moulin à vent); (*b*) pale *f* (d'hélice de ventilateur); aube *f*, ailette, palette *f* (de turbine); aube (de tunnel aérodynamique); **the vanes,** l'aubage *m* (d'une turbine, d'un tunnel aérodynamique); (*c*) *Ball:* ailette *f* (d'une bombe, torpille); **the vanes,** l'empennage *m.* **3.** *Surv:* **(sight) v.,** pinnule *f* (d'une alidade); viseur *m* (de compas); **slide v.,** voyant *m* (d'une mire de nivellement). **4.** *Orn:* lame *f* (d'une plume).
vanguard ['vængɑ:d] *n. Mil:* tête *f* d'avant-garde; *Fig:* **to be in the v. of a movement,** être un des pionniers d'un mouvement.
vanilla [və'nilə] *n.* **1.** *Bot:* **v. (plant),** vanille *f*, vanillier *m*; (*b*) **v. (pod),** gousse *f* de vanille. **2.** *Cu:* **v. (flavouring),** vanille; **flavoured with v., v. flavoured,**

vanillé, parfumé à la vanille; **v. ice,** glace à la vanille; **v. sugar,** sucre vanillé.
vanillin [və'nilin] *n. Ch:* vanilline *f.*
vanish ['væniʃ] *v.i.* disparaître; (*of visions, suspicions*) se dissiper, s'évanouir; (*of difficulties*) s'aplanir; **to make sth. v.,** faire disparaître qch.; (*of magician*) escamoter qch.; **to v. from sight,** disparaître aux yeux de qn; **to v. into thin air,** se volatiliser; **he's vanished,** il a disparu; il s'est éclipsé; **she saw her last hope v.,** elle a vu s'évanouir son dernier espoir. **vanishing 1.** *a.* qui disparaît; *Toil: O:* **v. cream,** crème *f* de jour. **2.** *n.* disparition *f*; *Art:* **v. point,** point *m* de fuite; *Fig:* **profits have dwindled to v. point,** les bénéfices se sont réduits à néant; **to do a v. trick,** (i) faire un tour d'escamotage, de passe-passe; (ii) *F:* disparaître; s'éclipser.
vanity ['væniti] *n.* **1.** vanité *f*, vide *m* (des grandeurs humaines); futilité *f* (d'une tentative). **2.** vanité; orgueil *m*; **to do sth. out of v.,** faire qch. par vanité, pour la gloriole. **3.** (*a*) **v. bag,** (petit) sac de dame (pour soirée); **v. case,** (i) nécessaire *m* de maquillage; (ii) mallette *f*, trousse *f*, de toilette; (*b*) *NAm: Furn:* coiffeuse *f*. **4.** *U.S:* **v. press,** maison *f* d'édition qui publie les livres aux frais des auteurs.
vanquish ['væŋkwiʃ] *Lit:* **1.** *v.tr.* vaincre; triompher de (qn, ses passions). **2.** *v.i.* être vainqueur; vaincre.
vanquisher ['væŋkwiʃər] *n.* vainqueur *m.*
vantage ['vɑːntidʒ] *n.* **1. (point of) v., v. point,** terrain avantageux, position avantageuse; avantage *m* du terrain. **2.** *Ten:* avantage; **v. in, out,** avantage dedans, dehors.
vapid ['væpid] *a.* insipide, plat; **v. style,** style fade.
vapidity [və'piditi] *n.* évent *m* (d'une boisson); fadeur *f*, insipidité *f* (d'une boisson, de la conversation.).
vapor ['veipər] *n. NAm:* = VAPOUR.
vaporization [veipərai'zeiʃ(ə)n] *n.* **1.** vaporisation *f*. **2.** pulvérisation *f* (d'un liquide); *I.C.E:* carburation *f* (du combustible).
vaporize ['veipəraiz] **1.** *v.tr.* (*a*) vaporiser, gazéifier; (*b*) pulvériser, vaporiser (un liquide); *I.C.E:* carburiser (le combustible). **2.** *v.i.* (*a*) se vaporiser, se gazéifier; (*b*) (*of liquid*) se pulvériser.
vaporizer ['veipəraizər] *n.* (*a*) (*evaporator*) vaporisateur *m*; *I.C.E: etc:* réchauffeur *m*; (*b*) atomiseur *m*, vaporisateur.
vaporous ['veipərəs] *a. Lit:* (ciel, style) vaporeux.
vapour, *NAm:* **vapor** ['veipər] *n.* **1.** (*a*) vapeur *f*; buée *f* (sur les vitres); **v. laden,** (atmosphère) humide; (*b*) *Ph:* vapeur (d'eau, d'alcool); **v. bath,** (i) *Med:* bain *m* de vapeur; (ii) étuve *f* humide (de hammam); *Av:* **v. trail,** traînée *f* de condensation. **2.** *Med: A:* **to have the vapours,** avoir des vapeurs.
variability [vɛəriə'biliti] *n.* variabilité *f* (du temps, etc.); *Nat.Hist:* inconstance *f* (de type).
variable ['vɛəriəbl] **1.** *a.* (*a*) variable, changeant, inconstant; *Astr:* **v. star,** étoile variable; *Mec:* **v. motion,** mouvement varié; *Mth:* **v. quantity,** quantité variable; (*b*) *Mec.E:* **v. (at will),** réglable. **2.** *n. Mth:* variable *f*; *Pol.Ec:* **random v.,** variable aléatoire. **-ably** *adv.* variablement.
variance ['vɛəriəns] *n.* **1.** désaccord *m*; discorde *f*; **to be at v. with s.o.,** être en désaccord, en contradiction, avec qn; avoir un différend avec qn; **historians are at v. on this point,** les historiens diffèrent entre eux, ne sont pas d'accord, sur ce point; **theory at v. with the facts,** théorie incompatible, en contradiction, avec les faits. **2.** (*a*) variation *f* (de température, volume, etc.); (*b*) *Stat: Ch:* variance *f*.
variant ['vɛəriənt] **1.** *a.* différent **(from,** de); *Lit:* **v. reading,** variante *f*. **2.** *n. Lit:* variante.
variation [vɛəri'eiʃ(ə)n] *n.* **1.** variation *f*, changement *m*; **magnetic v.,** déclinaison magnétique (locale). **2.** différence *f*; écart *m*; **v. between two readings,** écart entre deux lectures (d'un appareil scientifique). **3.** *Mus:* variations **(on,** sur).
varicoloured, *NAm:* **-colored** ['vɛərikʌləd] *a.* aux couleurs variées; versicolore.
varicose ['værikous] *a. Med:* **1.** variqueux; **v. vein,** varice *f*. **2. v. stockings,** bas *m* à varices.
varied *a. see* VARY.
variegated ['vɛərigeitid] *a.* **1.** varié, divers. **2.** bigarré, bariolé; diapré; versicolore; *Nat.Hist:* panaché; (*of flower, leaf*) **to become v.,** se panacher.
variegation [vɛəri'geiʃ(ə)n] *n.* diversité *f* de couleurs; bigarrure *f*; *Bot:* panachure *f*, diaprure *f*.
variety [və'raiəti] *n.* **1.** (*a*) variété *f*, diversité *f*; **hillocks that give v. to the landscape,** petites collines qui accidentent le paysage; *Prov:* **v. is the spice of life,** le changement donne du piquant à la vie; (*b*) **a v. of patterns,** un assortiment d'échantillons; **a large, wide, v. of materials,** un grand choix de tissus; **for a v. of reasons,** pour des raisons diverses; **in a v. of ways,** de diverses manières, diversement; *NAm:* **v. store,** grand magasin. **2.** *Nat.Hist:* variété *f* (de fleur, etc.). **3.** *Th:* **v. show, theatre,** spectacle *m*, théâtre *m*, de variétés; **v. turns,** numéros *mpl* de music-hall. **4.** *NAm:* **v. meat,** abats *mpl.*
variola [və'raiələ] *n. Med:* variole *f*; petite vérole.
various ['vɛəriəs] *a.* **1.** varié, divers; **of v. kinds,** de diverses sortes; **to talk about v. things,** parler de chose(s) et d'autre(s). **2.** (*a*) différent, dissemblable; divers; **known under v. names,** connu sous des noms divers; (*b*) plusieurs; plus d'un; **for v. reasons,** pour plusieurs raisons; **at v. times,** à différentes reprises; en diverses occasions; **in v. ways,** de diverses, plusieurs, manières; diversement. **-ly** *adv.* diversement; de diverses, plusieurs, manières.
varlet ['vɑːlit] *n.m. A:* coquin, vaurien.
varmint ['vɑːmint] *n. Dial:* **1.** vermine *f*. **2.** *F: A:* **young v.,** petit polisson.
varnish[1] ['vɑːniʃ] *n.* **1.** vernis *m*; **spirit v.,** vernis à l'alcool; **transparent, clear, v.,** vernis blanc; *Toil:* **nail v.,** vernis à ongles; **v. remover,** (i) *Ind: etc:* décapant *m* pour vernis; (ii) *Toil:* dissolvant *m*. **2. (coat of) v.,** (enduit *m* de) vernis; vernissage *m*, vernissure *f*.
varnish[2] *v.tr.* **1.** vernir (du bois, un tableau); vernir, vernisser (de la poterie). **2.** *Fig: O:* **to v. (over),** farder (les faits), glisser sur, vernir (les défauts de qn); maquiller (la vérité). **varnishing** *n.* vernissage *m*, vernissure *f*; peinture *f* au vernis; **v. day,** vernissage *m* (au Salon de peinture).
varnisher ['vɑːniʃər] *n.* vernisseur *m.*
varsity ['vɑːsiti] *n. F:* **1.** université *f*; fac *f*; **the V. match,** match *m* entre Oxford et Cambridge. **2.** *U.S:* équipe *f* universitaire.
vary ['vɛəri] **1.** *v.tr.* varier, diversifier; accidenter (son style); donner de la variété à (un programme); **to v. one's methods,** varier de méthode. **2.** *v.i.* (*a*) varier, changer; être variable; **to v. in quality,** varier en qualité; (*b*) **to v. from sth.,** dévier, s'écarter, de, différer de, qch.; (*c*) *Biol:* s'écarter du type; présenter une variation; (*d*) **as to the date, authors v.,** quant à la date, les auteurs ne sont pas d'accord, varient là-dessus. **varied** *a.* **1.** varié, divers. **2.** *Nat.Hist:* multicolore, diversicolore. **varying 1.** *a.* qui varie; variable, changeant; varié, divers; **with v. results,** avec des résultats divers. **2.** *n.* variation *f*, changement *m*.
vascular ['væskjulər] *a. Nat.Hist:* vasculaire.
vase [vɑːz] *n.* vase *m*; **flower v.,** vase à fleurs.
vasectomy [və'sektəmi] *n. Surg:* vasectomie *f*.
Vaseline ['væsəliːn] *n. R.t.m:* Vaseline *f*.
vasoconstrictor [veizoukən'striktər] *a. & n. Anat:* vasoconstricteur (*m*), -trice.

vasomotor ['veizoumoutər] *a. & n. Anat:* vasomoteur (*m*), -trice.

vassal ['væs(ə)l] *a. & n.* **1.** *Hist:* vassal (*m*), -aux; feudataire (*m*) (**to,** de). **2.** subordonné, vassal.

vassalage ['væsəlidʒ] *n.* **1.** *Hist:* vassalité *f*, vasselage *m.* **2.** *Fig:* sujétion *f.*

vast [vɑːst] *a.* vaste, immense; **a v. number of people,** un nombre incalculable de gens; **his v. knowledge,** l'étendue *f* de ses connaissances; **to spend a v. amount, v. sums, (of money),** dépenser énormément d'argent; **there's a v. difference between them,** il y a une différence énorme entre eux. **-ly** *adv.* vastement, immensément; **they're not v. different,** il y a peu de différence entre eux.

vastness ['vɑːstnis] *n.* immensité *f*; vaste étendue *f*; amplitude *f* (de l'espace, etc.).

vat [væt] *n.* (*a*) cuve *f*; bac *m*; *Dy:* **v. dyes,** colorants *mpl* de cuve; *Vit:* **v. for carrying grapes,** bouge *m*; (*b*) (*contents*) cuvée *f.*

vatful ['vætful] *n.* cuvée *f.*

Vatican ['vætikən] *n.* **the V.,** le Vatican; **the V. library,** la bibliothèque vaticane, la Vaticane; **V. City,** la cité du Vatican; *Hist:* **the V. State,** les États pontificaux; **the V. Council,** le concile du Vatican.

vaudeville ['vɔːdəvil] *n. Th:* **1.** vaudeville *m.* **2.** spectacle varié; spectacle de music-hall.

vault¹ [vɔːlt, vɔlt] *n.* **1.** (*a*) *Arch:* voûte *f*; **barrel, tunnel, v.,** voûte en berceau, cylindrique; **fan v.,** voûte en éventail; **ribbed v.,** voûte d'ogives, à nervures; *Lit:* **the v. of heaven,** la voûte céleste; (*b*) *Const:* chapelle *f* (de four de boulangerie); voûte (d'un fourneau); (*c*) *Anat:* voûte (du crâne). **2.** (*a*) souterrain *m*; **bank v.,** chambre forte; (*b*) (i) **(wine) v.,** cave *f*, cellier *m*; (ii) *pl.* **vaults,** débit *m* de boissons; (*c*) **family v.,** caveau *m* de famille.

vault² **1.** *v.tr.* **to v. (over),** voûter (une cave). **2.** *v.i.* (*of roof*) se voûter. **vaulted** *a.* voûté; en (forme de) voûte. **vaulting** *n.* voûte(s) *f* (*pl*); **barrel v.,** voûte en berceau.

vault³ *n. Gym:* saut *m* (de barrière, en s'aidant de la main); saut au cheval; **pole v.,** saut *m* à la perche.

vault⁴ **1.** *v.i.* (*a*) **to v. over a gate,** sauter (une barrière), franchir (une barrière) d'un saut (en s'aidant de la main, des mains); (*b*) **to v. into the saddle,** sauter en selle. **2.** *v.tr.* sauter (une barrière), franchir (une barrière) d'un saut (en s'aidant de la main, des mains). **vaulting** *n. Gym:* exercise *m* du saut; voltige *f* (sur le cheval); **v. horse,** cheval(-sautoir) *m*; **pole v.,** saut à la perche.

vaulter ['vɔːltər, 'vɔl-] *n,* sauteur, -euse; (*acrobatic*) voltigeur, -euse; **pole v.,** sauteur *m* à la perche.

vaunt [vɔːnt] *Lit:* **1.** *v.i. A:* se vanter; fanfaronner. **2.** *v.tr.* (*a*) vanter (qch.); **our much vaunted justice,** notre justice tant vantée, si célèbre; (*b*) se vanter de (qch.), se faire gloire de (qch.). **vaunting** *n.* vanterie *f*, jactance *f.*

veal [viːl] *n. Cu:* veau *m*; **v. cutlet,** côtelette *f* de veau; **v. olive,** alouette *f* sans tête.

vector ['vektər] *n. Mth: Ph:* vecteur *m*; **v. function,** fonction vectorielle.

vectorial [vek'tɔːriəl] *a. Mth:* vectoriel.

vee [viː] *n.* V (dans certains termes techniques).

veep [viːp] *n.m. U.S: F:* vice-président *m.*

veer¹ ['viər] *n.* **1.** changement *m* de direction, saute *f* (de vent, *esp.* à droite). **2.** (*of ship*) virage *m* vent arrière. **3.** revirement *m* (d'opinion).

veer² **1.** *v.i.* (*a*) (*of wind*) tourner, sauter (*esp.* à droite); (*b*) (*of ship*) virer (vent arrière); changer de bord; **to v. at anchor,** rôder sur son ancre; **to v. off course,** dévier du cap fixé; dévier de sa route; (*c*) *Fig:* **the conversation veered to politics,** la conversation a tourné à la politique; (*d*) (*of pers.*) **to v. round,** changer d'opinion; **to v. round to an opinion,** se ranger à une opinion. **2.** *v.tr.* (faire) virer (un navire) vent arrière.

veer³ *v.tr. Nau:* **to v. (away, out),** filer (du câble); *v.i.* **to v. and haul,** (i) filer et haler (un cordage) alternativement; (ii) *Fig:* manœuvrer avec adresse.

veg [vedʒ] *n. F:* légume(s) *m*(*pl*).

vegan ['viːgen] *n.* végétalien, -ienne.

veganism ['viːgənizm] *n.* végétalisme *m.*

vegetable ['vedʒ(i)təbl] **1.** *a.* (*a*) végétal, -aux; **the v. kingdom,** le règne végétal; **v. life,** la vie végétale; **v. oils,** huiles végétales; (*b*) *Fig:* **to lead a v. existence,** mener une existence végétative. **2.** *n.* (*a*) *Bot:* végétal *m*; (*b*) *Hort: Cu:* légume *m*; **green vegetables,** légumes verts; **early vegetables,** primeurs *fpl*; **v. dish,** légumier *m*; **v. garden,** (jardin) potager (*m*); **v. slicer,** coupe-légumes *m inv*; (*c*) **to live like a v.,** végéter; mener une vie végétative.

vegetal ['vedʒit(ə)l] *a. & n. Bot:* végétal (*m*), -aux.

vegetarian [vedʒi'tɛriən] *a. & n.* végétarien, -ienne.

vegetarianism [vedʒi'tɛəriənizm] *n.* végétarisme *m.*

vegetate ['vedʒiteit] *v.i.* végéter; **to v. in an office,** végéter, moisir, dans un bureau.

vegetation [vedʒi'teiʃ(ə)n] *n.* végétation *f.*

vegetative ['vedʒitətiv, -teitiv] *a.* végétatif; *Fig:* **v. existence,** existence végétative.

vehemence ['viːəməns] *n.* véhémence *f* (du vent, d'un orateur); impétuosité *f*, ardeur *f* (de la jeunesse).

vehement ['viːəmənt] *a.* (vent, orateur) véhément; (vent) impétueux; (amour) passionné; (effort) violent. **-ly** *adv.* avec véhémence; impétueusement.

vehicle ['viːikl] *n.* **1.** (*a*) véhicule *m*, voiture *f*; *Adm:* **commercial v.,** véhicule industriel; (véhicule) utilitaire (*m*); **(extra) long v.,** convoi *m* grande longueur; convoi exceptionnel; (*at ferry*) **v. check-in,** contrôle *m* des véhicules; (*b*) *Space:* **space v.,** véhicule spatial; **launching v.,** véhicule de lancement, lanceur *m.* **2.** véhicule (de la pensée); **the newspaper as a v. for advertising,** le journal comme moyen de publicité; (*b*) *Med:* (agent) vecteur (*m*) (d'un maladie). **3.** *Paint: Pharm:* véhicule; *Pharm:* excipient *m.*

vehicular [vi'hikjulər] *a.* des véhicules, des voitures; **v. traffic,** circulation *f* des voitures.

veil¹ [veil] *n.* **1.** *Cost:* (*a*) voile *m* (de religieuse, de deuil); **bridal v.,** voile de mariée; *Ecc:* **to take the v.,** prendre le voile; (*b*) voilette *f* (de chapeau). **2.** (*a*) *Jew.Ant:* **the v. of the temple,** le voile du temple; (*b*) *Lit:* **beyond the v.,** au delà de la tombe. **3.** *F:* voile, déguisement *m*; **under the v. of anonymity, of secrecy,** sous le voile de l'anonyme, du secret; **to draw, throw, a v. over sth.,** jeter un voile sur qch.

veil² *v.tr.* **1.** voiler (son visage, un tableau); **to v. oneself,** se voiler; **to v. one's face,** se voiler la face. **2.** *O:* voiler, cacher, dissimuler (ses sentiments, desseins). **veiled** *a.* **1.** voilé, couvert d'un voile. **2.** voilé, caché, dissimulé; **in v. terms,** (s'exprimer) en termes voilés; **v. hostility,** hostilité sourde; **scarcely v. hostility,** hostilité à peine déguisée. **veiling** *n.* **1.** action *f*, fait *m*, de voiler (la face), de dissimuler (la vérité, etc.). **2.** *coll.* voile(s) *m*(*pl*).

vein¹ [vein] *n.* **1.** *Anat:* veine *f*; **he has foreign blood in his veins,** du sang étranger coule dans ses veines. **2.** *Bot: Ent:* nervure *f* (de feuille, d'aile); veine (de feuille). **3.** *Geol: Min:* veine, filon *m.* **4.** (*in wood, marble*) veine. **5.** veine, disposition *f*, humeur *f*; **the poetic v.,** la veine poétique; **other remarks in the same v.,** d'autres observations faites dans le même esprit.

vein² *v.tr. Paint:* veiner, marbrer (une porte). **veined** *a.* **1.** veiné, à veines. **2.** *Bot: Ent:* nervuré. **veining** *n.* **1.** *Paint:* (*action*) veinage *m*; **v. brush,** veinette *f.* **2.** *coll.* (*a*) veinure *f*, marbrure *f*; (*b*) veines *fpl*; *Bot: Ent:* nervures *fpl.*

velar ['viːlər] *a. & n. Ling:* vélaire (*f*).

veld(t) [velt] *n.* veld(t) *m.*

vellum ['veləm] *n.* vélin *m*; **v. paper,** papier vélin.
velocipede [vi'lɔsipi:d] *n.* **1.** *A:* vélocipède *m.* **2.** *NAm:* tricycle *m* d'enfant.
velocity [vi'lɔsiti] *n.* vitesse *f*, *occ.* vélocité *f.*
velour(s) [və'luər] *n. Com:* **1.** *Tex:* velouté *m*; velours *m* de laine. **2.** feutre taupé; **v. (hat),** chapeau (en feutre) taupé.
velum, *pl.* **-la** ['vi:ləm, -ə] *n. Anat:* voile *m* du palais.
velvet ['velvit] *n.* **1.** *Tex:* velours *m;* **brocaded, figured, v.,** velours broché, façonné; **ribbed, corduroy, v.,** velours à côtes, côtelé; **as soft as v.,** velouté; *F:* **to be on v.,** (i) jouer sur le, du, velours; (ii) mener une vie de château. **2.** *Nat.Hist:* velouté *m.* **3.** *P:* **black v.,** mélange *m* de champagne et de stout. **4. v. coat, collar,** habit *m*, col *m*, de velours; *Fig:* **with v. tread,** à pas feutrés; **an iron hand in a v. glove,** une main de fer sous un gant de velours.
velveteen [velvi'ti:n] *n Tex:* velours *m* de coton; velvet *m.*
velvety ['velviti] *a.* velouté, velouteux; doux comme du velours; (vin) velouté, qui a du velouté.
venal ['vi:n(ə)l] *a.* vénal, aux.
venality [vi'næliti] *n.* vénalité *f.*
vend [vend] *v.tr.* (*a*) *Jur:* vendre; (*b*) faire le commerce de (choses de peu de valeur); vendre (des journaux). **vending** *n.* vente *f*; **v. machine,** distributeur *m* automatique.
vendetta [ven'detə] *n.* vendetta *f.*
vendor ['vendɔ:r] *n.* **1.** *Com: Jur:* vendeur, -euse. **2.** *also* ['vendər] (*a*) vendeur, -euse; **street v.,** marchand, -ande, des quatre saisons; marchand ambulant; (*b*) (*machine*) distributeur *m* automatique.
veneer¹ [və'niər] *n.* **1.** (*a*) placage *m*, revêtement *m* (de bois mince); (*b*) bois *m* de placage, bois à plaquer. **2.** *Fig:* masque *m*, apparence extérieure (de connaissances); **a v. of politeness,** un vernis de politesse.
veneer² *v.tr.* plaquer (le bois).
venerable ['ven(ə)rəbl] *a.* (vieillard, etc.) vénérable.
venerate ['venəreit] *v.tr.* vénérer; avoir de la vénération pour (qn).
veneration [venə'reiʃ(ə)n] *n.* vénération *f* **(for,** pour); **to hold s.o. in v.,** avoir de la vénération pour qn.
venereal [vi'niəriəl] *a. Med:* vénérien.
venereology [viniəri'ɔlədʒi] *n. Med:* vénéréologie *f.*
venery ['venəri] *n. A:* vénérie *f*; la chasse.
Venetian [vi'ni:ʃ(ə)n] *Geog:* **1.** *a.* vénitien; de Venise; **V. glass,** verre *m* de Venise; *Needlew:* **V. lace,** point *m* de Venise; *Furn:* **V. blinds,** jalousies *fpl* (à lames mobiles). **2.** *n.* Vénitien, -ienne.
Venezuela [vene'zweilə] *Pr.n.* le Vénézuéla.
Venezuelan [vene'zweil(ə)n] *Geog:* **1.** *a.* vénézuélien. **2.** *n.* Vénézuélien, -ienne.
vengeance ['ven(d)ʒəns] *n.* vengeance *f*; **to take v. on s.o.,** tirer vengeance de qn; se venger de qn; **to take v. for sth.,** tirer vengeance de qch.; venger qch.; *F:* **with a v.,** furieusement; à outrance; pour de bon; (travailler) d'arrache-pied.
vengeful ['ven(d)ʒf(u)l] *a.* (*of pers.*) vindicatif.
vengefulness ['ven(d)ʒf(u)lnis] *n.* caractère vindicatif, esprit *m* de vengeance.
venial ['vi:niəl] *a.* (*a*) *Theol:* (péché) véniel; (*b*) (*of fault*) léger, pardonnable, excusable, véniel.
veniality [vi:ni'æliti] *n.* (*a*) *Theol:* caractère véniel (d'un péché); (*b*) caractère léger, véniel (d'une faute).
Venice ['venis] *Pr.n. Geog:* Venise *f.*
venison ['ven(i)z(ə)n] *n. Cu:* venaison *f*; **haunch of v.,** quartier *m* de chevreuil.
venom ['venəm] *n.* venin *m.*
venomous ['venəməs] *a.* **1.** (*of animal*) venimeux; (*of plant*) vénéneux. **2.** (*of criticism*) venimeux, envenimé; **v. tongue,** langue de vipère. **-ly** *adv.* d'une manière venimeuse, avec venin.
venous ['vi:nəs] *a.* (système, sang) veineux.
vent¹ [vent] *n.* **1.** (*a*) trou *m*, orifice *m* (pour laisser entrer l'air, sortir un gaz); évent *m*; **v. hole,** évent; prise *f* d'air (d'un réservoir à essence); aspirail *m*, -aux (d'un fourneau); soupirail *m*, -aux (d'un puits d'aérage); *Metall:* trou d'air, d'évent (d'un moule); *El:* trou d'aération (d'un élément de pile); (*b*) *Ball:* évent (d'une fusée spatiale); (*c*) *Mus:* **vents of a flute,** trous d'une flûte; (*d*) tuyau de cheminée; *Geol:* cheminée *f* (de volcan); *Aer:* cheminée (de parachute). **2.** libre cours; **to give v. to one's grief, one's anger,** donner libre cours à sa douleur, à sa colère; **to give v. to one's indignation,** manifester son indignation; *Lit:* **to give v. to one's spleen,** décharger sa bile.
vent² *v.tr.* (*a*) décharger, vider (une canalisation) des gaz; (*b*) évacuer (les gaz d'une canalisation, la vapeur d'une chaudière); (*c*) munir (un réservoir) d'un évent, d'une prise d'air; (*d*) décharger, laisser éclater, exhaler, jeter (sa colère); **to v. one's spleen, one's anger, on s.o.,** décharger sa bile, épancher sa colère, sur qn.
vent³ *n. Cost:* fente *f* (dans la basque d'un veston).
ventilate ['ventileit] *v.tr.* **1.** aérer (une chambre); ventiler (un tunnel); éventer (une houillère). **2.** agiter (une question) (au grand jour); mettre (une question) en discussion.
ventilation [venti'leiʃ(ə)n] *n.* **1.** ventilation *f*, aération *f*, aérage *m*; *Min:* **v. shaft,** puits *m* de ventilation, d'aération, d'aérage. **2.** mise *f* en discussion publique (d'une question).
ventilator ['ventileitər] *n.* **1.** ventilateur *m*, aérateur *m*; *Nau:* manche *f* à air. **2.** (*in window, over door*) vasistas *m.* **3.** *Aut:* volet *m* d'aération; persienne *f* (de capot); (*window*) déflecteur *m.* **4.** *Med:* appareil *m* à respiration artificielle; poumon artificiel.
ventral ['ventr(ə)l] *a. Anat: Nat.Hist:* ventral, -aux; *Ich:* **v. fins,** *npl.* **ventrals,** (nageoires) ventrales.
ventricle ['ventrik(ə)l] *n. Anat:* ventricule *m.*
ventriloquism [ven'triləkwizm] *n.* ventriloquie *f.*
ventriloquist [ven'triləkwist] *n.* ventriloque *mf.*
venture¹ ['ventʃər] *n.* **1.** risque *m;* entreprise hasardeuse, risquée; **desperate v.,** tentative désespérée; *Scout:* **V. Scout,** routier *m.* **2.** *Com:* entreprise, spéculation *f*; **joint v.,** entreprise à risques partagés. **3. at a v.,** au hasard; (tirer) au jugé.
venture² **1.** *v.tr.* (*a*) **to v. to do sth.,** oser faire qch.; se risquer à faire qch.; **I v. to affirm he knew nothing about it,** j'ose affirmer qu'il n'en savait rien; **I ventured to go in,** je me hasardai à entrer; (*b*) **to v. an opinion,** se hasarder, se risquer, à donner une opinion; (*c*) hasarder, aventurer, risquer (sa vie, son argent); *Prov:* **nothing v. nothing gain,** qui n'ose rien ne gagne rien. **2.** *v.i.* (*a*) se risquer (**on sth.,** à faire qch.), prendre le risque (de faire qch.); (*b*) **to v. into unknown country,** s'aventurer en pays inconnu; **to v. out (of doors),** se risquer à sortir; **to v. too far,** être trop osé; aller trop loin.
venturer ['ventʃurər] *n.* aventurier *m.*
venturesome ['ventʃəsəm] *a.* **1.** (*of pers.*) aventureux, entreprenant. **2.** (*of action*) risqué, hasardeux.
venue ['venju:] *n.* **1.** *Jur:* lieu *m* du jugement; **to change the v. of a trial,** renvoyer une affaire devant une autre cour. **2.** lieu de réunion; rendez-vous *m*; **v. of the meet,** rendez-vous de chasse.
Venus ['vi:nəs] *Pr.n.f.* Vénus; *Anat:* **mount of V.,** mont *m* de Vénus; *Bot:* **Venus's flytrap,** dionée *f*, attrape-mouches *m inv.*; **Venus's slipper,** sabot *m* de Vénus.

veracious [və'reiʃəs] *a.* (*of pers., account*) véridique. **-ly** *adv.* véridiquement, avec véracité.
veracity [və'ræsiti], **veraciousness** [və'reiʃəsnis] *n.* véracité *f*, véridicité *f* (de qn, d'un rapport).
veranda(h) [və'rændə] *n. Arch:* véranda *f.*
verb [vəːb] *n. Gram:* verbe *m.*
verbal ['vəːb(ə)l] *a.* **1.** (*a*) (*of agreement, promise*) verbal, -aux, oral, -aux; *Dipl:* **v. note,** note verbale; (*b*) **v. dispute,** dispute de mots; *F:* **v. diarrhoea,** verbomanie *f*; (*c*) (*of translation*) mot à mot, mot pour mot; littéral, -aux. **2.** *Gram:* **v. noun,** *n.* **v.,** nom verbal. **-ally** *adv.* **1.** verbalement, oralement; de vive voix. **2.** littéralement; (traduire) mot à mot.
verbalize ['vəːbəlaiz] *v.tr.* (*a*) *Gram:* employer (un nom) comme verbe; (*b*) rendre (une idée) par des mots; *Psy:* verbaliser (une expérience).
verbatim [vəː'beitim] **1.** *adv.* mot à mot; textuellement. **2.** *a.* (*of reprint*) reproduit exactement, exact, mot à mot; **v. report,** compte rendu sténographique (des débats).
verbena [və(ː)'biːnə] *n. Bot:* verveine *f*; **lemon(-scented) v.,** citronnelle *f.*
verbiage ['vəːbiidʒ] *n.* verbiage *m.*
verbose [vəː'bous] *a.* (écrivain, style) verbeux, diffus. **-ly** *adv.* avec verbosité, verbeusement.
verbosity [vəː'bɔsiti] *n.* verbosité *f*, prolixité *f.*
verdant ['vəːdənt] *a. Lit:* vert, verdoyant.
verdict ['vəːdikt] *n.* **1.** *Jur:* (*a*) verdict *m*; **to bring in a v. of guilty, not guilty,** rendre un verdict de culpabilité, de non-culpabilité; **to return a v.,** prononcer, rendre, un verdict; **to reach a v.,** conclure, décider; (*b*) (*in coroner's court*) **the jury returned a v., of suicide,** le jury a conclu au suicide; **open v.,** jugement *m* (i) qui ne formule aucune conclusion sur les circonstances dans lesquelles la mort a eu lieu, (ii) qui conclut au crime sans désigner le coupable. **2.** jugement, décision *f*, avis *m*, opinion *f*; **to give one's v.,** se prononcer.
verdigris ['vəːdigris] *n.* vert-de-gris *m.*
verdure ['vəːdʒər] *n.* (*a*) verdure *f*; (i) couleur verte; (ii) herbage *m*, feuillage *m*; (*b*) *Lit:* verdeur *f*, jeunesse *f*, vigueur *f.*
verge[1] [vəːdʒ] *n.* **1.** (*a*) bord *m* (d'un fleuve); orée *f* (d'une forêt); *Civ.E:* accotement *m* (d'une route); **sitting on the grass v. of the road,** assis sur l'herbe du bord de la route; (*b*) bordure *f* (d'une plate-bande); (*c*) **on the v. of manhood,** au seuil de l'âge viril; **he is on the v. of ruin,** il est à deux doigts de la ruine; **on the v. of tears,** au bord des larmes. **2.** *Ecc:* verge (portée devant l'évêque).
verge[2] *v.i.* (*a*) **to v. on sth.,** toucher à, être contigu, -uë, à, être voisin de, côtoyer, qch.; (*b*) **courage verging on foolhardiness,** courage qui confine à la témérité; **colour verging on red,** couleur qui tire sur le rouge; **he was verging on sixty,** il frisait la soixantaine.
verger ['vəːdʒər] *n.* (*a*) *Ecc:* bedeau *m*; (*b*) huissier *m* à verge.
Vergil ['vəːdʒil] *Pr.n.m. Lt.Lit:* Virgile.
verifiable [veri'faiəbl] *a.* vérifiable.
verification [verifi'keiʃ(ə)n] *n.* vérification *f*, contrôle *m.*
verify ['verifai] *v.tr.* **1.** confirmer (une affirmation, un fait); **this verifies my suspicions, my fears,** cela confirme mes soupçons, mes craintes. **2.** vérifier, contrôler (des renseignements, des comptes).
verily ['verili] *adv. A: & B:* en vérité, vraiment.
verisimilitude [verisi'militjuːd] *n.* vraisemblance *f*; **beyond the bounds of v.,** au-delà du vraisemblable.
veritable ['veritəbl] *a.* véritable. **-ably** *adv.* véritablement.
verity ['veriti] *n. Lit:* vérité *f.*
vermicelli [vəːmi'tʃeli] *n. Cu:* vermicelle *m.*
vermicide ['vəːmisaid] *n. Pharm:* vermicide *m.*
vermiform ['vəːmifɔːm] *a.* vermiforme.
vermifugal ['vəːmifjuːg(ə)l] *a.* vermifuge.
vermifuge ['vəːmifjuːdʒ] *n.* vermifuge *m.*
vermilion [və'miljən] **1.** *n.* vermillon *m.* **2.** *a.* (de) vermillon *inv*, vermeil.
vermin ['vəːmin] *n.* (*a*) (*body parasites; Pej: people*) vermine *f*; (*b*) *Z:* les animaux *mpl* nuisibles.
verminous ['vəːminəs] *a.* couvert de vermine.
vermouth ['vəːməθ] *n.* vermout(h) *m.*
vernacular [və'nækjulər] *n.* **1.** *a. Ling:* vernaculaire; du pays. **2.** *n.* (*a*) langue *f* vernaculaire du pays; (*b*) la langue vulgaire; (*c*) langage *m*; jargon *m.*
vernal ['vəːn(ə)l] *a.* printanier; du printemps; *Astr: Bot:* vernal, -aux.
veronal ['verən(ə)l] *n. Pharm:* véronal *m.*
Veronica [və'rɔnikə] **1.** *Pr.n.f.* Véronique. **2.** *n.* (*a*) *Bot:* véronique *f*; (*b*) *Ecc:* véronique, suaire *m.*
verruca, *pl.* **-ae** [ve'ruːkə, -siː] *n.* verrue *f.*
versant ['vəːsənt] *n.* versant *m* (d'une montagne).
versatile ['vəːsətail] *a.* **1.** (*a*) (*of pers.*) (i) aux talents variés; (ii) capable d'entreprendre n'importe quoi, qui se plie à tout; **v. mind,** esprit souple; (*b*) (*of tool, machine, etc.*) polyvalent, d'une grande souplesse d'emploi; universel. **2.** *Nat.Hist:* versatile.
versatility [vəːsə'tiliti] *n.* **1.** (*a*) souplesse *f*, universalité *f* (d'esprit), (faculté *f* d')adaptation *f*; (*b*) polyvalence *f*, grande souplesse d'emploi (d'un outil, d'une machine). **2.** *Nat.Hist:* versatilité *f* (d'un organe).
verse [vəːs] *n.* **1.** vers *m.* **2.** (*of song*) couplet *m*; (*of poem, hymn*) strophe *f*, stance *f*. **3.** *coll.* vers *mpl*; **free v.,** vers libres; **light v.,** poésie légère. **4.** *Ecc:* verset *m* (de la Bible).
versed [vəːst] *a.* versé (**in,** en, dans); **v. in the arts,** versé dans les arts; **to be well v. in mathematics,** être fort instruit dans les mathématiques.
versification [vəːsifi'keiʃ(ə)n] *n.* **1.** versification *f.* **2.** facture *f* (du vers); métrique *f* (d'un auteur).
versifier ['vəːsifaiər] *n.* versificateur, -trice.
versify ['vəːsifai] *v.tr. & i.* versifier; mettre (un récit, etc.) en vers.
version ['vəːʃ(ə)n] *n.* **1.** (*a*) version *f*, traduction *f*; **the English v. of the Bible,** la version anglaise de la Bible; **the T.V. version of a novel,** l'adaptation *f* d'un roman à la télévision; (*b*) *Sch: Scot:* thème latin. **2.** version (des faits); interprétation *f* (d'un fait); **he gave us a very different v. of the affair,** il nous a donné de cette affaire un récit très différent; **according to his v.,** d'après lui. **3. the military v. of this aircraft,** la version militaire de cet avion.
verso ['vəːsou] *n.* **1.** verso *m* (d'une page). **2.** *Num:* revers *m* (d'une médaille).
versus ['vəːsəs] *prep. Jur: Sp:* contre; **Martin v. Thomas,** Martin contre Thomas.
vertebra, *pl.* **-ae** ['vəːtibrə, -iː] *n.* vertèbre *f.*
vertebral ['vəːtibrəl] *a. Anat:* vertébral, -aux.
vertebrate ['vəːtibreit] **1.** *a.* (*a*) (animal) vertébré; (*b*) des vertébrés. **2.** *n.* vertébré *m.*
vertex, *pl.* **-ices** ['vəːteks, -tisiːz] *n.* **1.** sommet *m* (d'un angle, d'une courbe). **2.** *Anat:* vertex *m.*
vertical ['vəːtik(ə)l] **1.** *a.* (*a*) vertical, -aux; **v. line,** (ligne) verticale (*f*); **v. elevation,** altitude *f*; (*b*) *Artil: Ball:* (écart, etc.) en hauteur; (*c*) **v. cliff,** falaise *f* à pic, à la verticale; *Av:* **v. take-off, landing,** décollage, atterrissage, vertical. **2.** *n.* (*a*) *Mth:* verticale *f*; (*b*) *Astr:* (cercle) vertical (*m*). **-ally** *adv.* verticalement, à la verticale; *Av:* **to take off, land v.,** décoller, atterrir, à la verticale.
verticality [vəːti'kæliti] *n.* verticalité *f.*
vertiginous [vəː'tidʒinəs] *a.* vertigineux.
vertigo ['vəːtigou] *n. Med:* vertige *m.*

verve [vəːv] *n.* verve *f*; **to play, act, with v.,** jouer avec verve.

very[1] ['veri] **I.** *a.* **1.** *Lit:* (*real, true*) vrai, véritable; parfait. **2.** (*emphatic use*) (*a*) (*identical*) même; **he lives in this v. house,** il habite ici même; **sitting in this v. room,** assis dans cette pièce même; **you are the v. man I wanted to see,** vous êtes justement l'homme que je voulais voir; **come here this v. minute!** venez ici à l'instant! **this v. day,** aujourd'hui même; **it was a year ago to the v. day,** c'était il y a un an jour pour jour; **these are his v. words,** ce sont là ses propres paroles; (*b*) **at the v. beginning,** tout au commencement; **he knows our v. thoughts,** il connaît jusqu'à nos pensées; (*c*) **the v. idea frightens me,** la seule pensée m'effraie; **I shudder at the v. thought of it,** je frémis rien que d'y penser. **II.** *adv.* **1.** très; (*in affective uses*) fort, bien; **v. good,** (i) très bon, fort bon; (ii) très bien, fort bien; **he is v. well known in Paris,** il est très connu à Paris; **that's v. kind of you,** c'est bien gentil à vous; **you are v. kind,** vous êtes bien bon; **so v. little,** si peu; **I took only a v. little,** j'en ai pris très peu; **it isn't so v. difficult,** ce n'est pas tellement difficile; ce n'est pas si difficile que ça; **v. (v.) few,** très (très) peu; **are you hungry?—yes, v.,** avez-vous faim?—oui, très; **he wore a v. pleased expression,** il avait l'air tout à fait satisfait; (*with past part.*) **I was v. (much) surprised,** j'en ai été très surpris; (*with comparatives*) **I feel v. much better,** je me sens beaucoup mieux; **it is v. much better to wait,** il vaut bien mieux attendre. **2.** (*emphatic use*) **the v. first,** le tout premier; **we were the v. first to arrive,** nous sommes arrivés les tout premiers; **the v. last,** le tout dernier; **the v. best,** tout ce qu'il y a de mieux, de meilleur; **it was the v. last thing I expected,** c'était (absolument) la dernière chose à laquelle je m'attendais; **the v. next day,** dès de lendemain; **at the v. most, least,** tout au plus, au moins; **at the v. latest,** au plus tard; **the v. same,** absolument le même; précisément le même; **it's my v. own,** c'est à moi tout seul.

Very[2] ['viəri] *Pr.n. Mil:* **V. light,** fusée éclairante; **V. (light) pistol,** pistolet *m* lance-fusée(s).

vesical ['vesik(ə)l] *a. Anat: Med:* vésical, -aux.

vesicle ['vesikl] *n. Anat: Nat.Hist: Med:* vésicule *f.*

Vesper ['vespər] *n. Ecc:* **vespers,** vêpres *fpl*; **the v. bell,** la cloche des vêpres, du soir.

vessel ['ves(ə)l] *n.* **1.** (*receptacle*) récipient *m.* **2.** *Nau:* navire *m*; bateau *m*; bâtiment *m*; **merchant v.,** navire marchand; **passenger v.,** navire à passagers, à voyageurs; paquebot *m*; **fishing v.,** navire de pêche; pêcheur *m.* **3.** *Anat: Bot:* vaisseau *m.*

vest[1] [vest] *n.* **1.** *NAm:* (*waistcoat*) gilet *m.* **2.** (*a*) (*for men*) maillot *m* de corps; (*knitted*) tricot *m* de corps; **string v.,** gilet en point noué, en filet maille (aérée); *Sp:* **running, boxing, rowing, v.,** maillot; (*b*) (*for women*) chemise américaine; *Fr.C:* camisole *f*; (*c*) (*for baby*) brassière *f.*

vest[2] **1.** *v.tr.* (*a*) **to v. s.o. with authority,** investir, revêtir, qn de l'autorité; (*b*) **to v. property in s.o.,** assigner des biens à qn; **right vested in the Crown,** droit dévolu à la Couronne; **authority vested in the people,** autorité exercée par le peuple; (*c*) *Lit: Ecc:* vêtir, revêtir (un dignitaire, le prêtre). **2.** *v.i.* (*a*) (*of priest*) revêtir ses vêtements sacerdotaux; se revêtir; (*b*) (*of property*) **to v. in s.o.,** être dévolu à qn. **vested** *a. Jur:* **v. interests,** droits acquis; **to have a v. interest in (sth.),** avoir des capitaux, être intéressé, dans (une entreprise); avoir un intérêt matériel à (qch.).

vestal ['vest(ə)l] *a. Rom.Ant:* **v. virgin,** vestale *f.*

vestibule ['vestibjuːl] *n.* **1.** (*a*) vestibule *m*, antichambre *f*; (*b*) (*of public building*) salle *f* des pas perdus; (*c*) *NAm: Rail:* soufflet *m*; **v. train,** train *m* à soufflets. **2.** *Anat:* vestibule (de l'oreille).

vestige ['vestidʒ] *n.* (*a*) vestige *m*, trace *f* (de civilisation); **not a v. of common sense,** pas la moindre trace, pas un grain, de bon sens; **without a v. of clothing,** complètement nu; (*b*) *Biol:* organe *m* qui persiste à l'état rudimentaire.

vestigial [ves'tidʒiəl] *a.* (*a*) résiduel; (*b*) *Biol:* (organe) qui persiste à l'état rudimentaire.

vestment ['vestmənt] *n.* vêtement *m* (de cérémonie); *Ecc: esp.* chasuble *f*; **(church) vestments,** vêtements sacerdotaux.

vestry ['vestri] *n. Ecc:* **1.** sacristie *f.* **2.** conseil paroissial.

vesture ['vestjər] *n. Lit:* vêtement(s) *m(pl).*

Vesuvius [vi'suːviəs] *Pr.n. Geog:* le Vésuve.

vet[1] [vet] *n.* vétérinaire *mf*; véto *m.*

vet[2] *v.tr.* **(vetted)** *F:* **1.** (*a*) examiner, traiter (un animal); (*b*) examiner (qn) médicalement. **2.** (*a*) revoir, mettre au point (l'œuvre littéraire de qn); (*b*) *Adm:* effectuer un contrôle de sécurité sur (un candidat). **vetting** *n.* examen *m* (médical); contrôle *m* de sécurité (sur un candidat).

vetch [vetʃ] *n. Bot:* vesce *f.*

veteran ['vet(ə)r(ə)n] **1.** *n.* vétéran *m*; *F:* vieux *m* de la vieille; **(war) v.,** ancien combattant. **2.** *a.* (*a*) de vétéran, des vétérans; vieux, *f.* vieille, ancien; **v. soldier,** vieux soldat; **v. army,** armée *f* de vétérans; (*b*) *Aut:* **v. car,** (i) (*in Eng.*) ancêtre *m* (vieille voiture d'avant 1905), (ii) (*international categories*) vétéran *m* (1905–1918).

veterinarian [vet(ə)ri'nɛəriən] *n.* vétérinaire *mf.*

veterinary ['vet(ə)rin(ə)ri] *a.* vétérinaire; **v. surgeon,** vétérinaire *mf.*

veto[1], *pl.* **-oes** ['viːtou, -ouz] *n.* veto *m*; **right of v.,** droit *m* de veto; **to have the right, power, of v.,** avoir le veto.

veto[2] *v.tr.* mettre son veto à (qch.); interdire (qch.).

vex [veks] *v.tr.* vexer, fâcher, ennuyer, chagriner (qn). **vexed** *a.* **1.** vexé, dépité. **2. v. question,** question controversée, très débattue, non résolue. **vexing** *a.* vexant, ennuyeux, chagrinant.

vexation [vek'seiʃ(ə)n] *n.* **1.** (*a*) action *f* de vexer; (*b*) action de se tourmenter. **2.** (*a*) contrariété *f*, ennui *m*; (*b*) chagrin *m*, dépit *m.*

vexatious [vek'seiʃəs] *a.* **1.** (*of pers., thg*) fâcheux, irritant, ennuyeux; tracassier. **2.** *Jur:* vexatoire. **-ly** *adv.* **1.** d'une manière vexante, fâcheuse. **2.** à seule fin de contrarier.

via ['vaiə] *prep.* via, par la voie de; par (une route).

viability [vaiə'biliti] *n.* viabilité *f.*

viable ['vaiəbl] *a.* viable.

viaduct ['vaiədʌkt] *n.* viaduc *m.*

vial ['vaiəl] *n.* fiole *f*; ampoule *f.*

viands ['vaiəndz] *n.pl. A: & Lit:* aliments *m*; **choice v.,** mets délicats.

viaticum [vai'ætikəm] *n. Ecc:* viatique *m.*

vibes [vaibz] *n.pl. F:* **1.** *Mus:* vibraphone *m.* **2.** vibrations *f*; **the v. are good,** ça marche, ça gaze.

vibrancy ['vaibrənsi] *n.* vibrance *f*, qualité vibrante.

vibrant ['vaibrənt] *a.* vibrant; **city v. with activity,** ville palpitante d'activité; **v. personality,** nature émotive.

vibraphone ['vaibrəfoun] *n. Mus:* vibraphone *m.*

vibrate [vai'breit] **1.** *v.i.* (*a*) vibrer; **voice vibrating with emotion,** voix vibrante d'émotion; (*b*) *Ph:* vibrer, osciller. **2.** *v.tr.* faire vibrer; faire osciller. **vibrating 1.** *a.* vibrant; (mouvement) vibratoire, oscillant. **2.** *n. Tchn:* vibrage *m.*

vibration [vai'breiʃ(ə)n] *n.* vibration *f*; *Ph: etc:* oscillation *f*, pulsation *f.*

vibrator [vai'breitər] *n.* **1.** (*a*) *El:* vibrateur *m*, vibreur *m*; (*b*) *Mus:* anche *f* (d'harmonium, etc.). **2.** *Med:* (*for massage*) **(electric) v.,** vibromasseur *m.*

vibratory [vai'breitəri] *a. Ph: etc:* vibratoire.

viburnum [vaiˈbəːnəm] *n. Bot:* viorne *f.*

vicar [ˈvikər] *n.* **1.** *Ch. of Eng:* pasteur *m*; = curé *m.* **2.** *R.C.Ch:* **v. apostolic,** vicaire apostolique. **3. the V. of Christ,** le vicaire de Jésus-Christ.

vicarage [ˈvikəridʒ] *n. Ch. of Eng:* presbytère *m* (d'un *vicar*); cure *f.*

vicar-general [ˈvikəˈdʒenərəl] *n. Ch. of Eng: R.C.Ch:* vicaire général, grand vicaire.

vicarious [vaiˈkɛəriəs] *a.* **1.** (*of power, authority*) délégué. **2.** (*a*) (châtiment) souffert (i) par un autre, (ii) pour un autre; **v. pleasure,** plaisir donné par le plaisir d'un autre; (*b*) (méthode) de substitution. **-ly** *adv.* (*a*) par délégation; par substitution, par procuration; (*b*) à la place d'un autre.

vice[1] [vais] *n.* **1.** vice *m*; (*a*) **to sink into v.,** tomber dans le vice, la débauche; **the V. Squad,** la brigade des mœurs, *F:* les Mœurs; (*b*) **avarice is a v.,** l'avarice est un vice. **2.** défaut *m*, défectuosité. **3.** (i) vice, (ii) nature vicieuse (d'un cheval); **stable v.,** tic *m.*

vice[2], *NAm:* **vise** *n. Tls:* étau *m*; **bench v.,** étau, servante *f*, d'établi; **v. clamp, jaw,** mâchoire *f.*

vice[3] *n. F:* = VICE-CHAIRMAN, -PRESIDENT; *Sch:* = VICE-CHANCELLOR.

vice[4] [ˈvaisi] *prep.* en remplacement de (qn).

vice-admiral [vaisˈædmərəl] *n.* vice-amiral *m.*

vice-chairman, *pl.* **-men** [vaisˈtʃɛəmən] *n.* vice-président, -ente, *pl.* vice-président(e)s.

vice-chairmanship [vaisˈtʃɛəmənʃip] *n.* vice-présidence *f*, *pl.* vice-présidences.

vice-chancellor [vaisˈtʃɑːnsələr] *n.* **1.** vice-chancelier *m*, *pl.* vice-chanceliers. **2.** *Sch:* recteur *m* (d'une université).

vice-chancellorship [vaisˈtʃɑːnsələʃip] *n.* **1.** fonction *f*, dignité *f*, de vice-chancelier. **2.** *Sch:* rectorat *m* (d'université).

vice-consul [vaisˈkɔns(ə)l] *n.* vice-consul *m*, *pl.* vice-consuls.

vice-consulate [vaisˈkɔnsjulət] *n.* (*post or premises*) vice-consulat *m*, *pl.* vice-consulats.

vicelike [ˈvaislaik] *a.* **held in a v. grip,** serré dans une poigne de fer, comme dans un étau.

vice-marshal [vaisˈmɑːʃ(ə)l] *n. Mil.Av:* **air v.-m.,** général *m* de division aérienne.

vice-presidency [vaisˈprezidənsi] *n.* vice-présidence *f.*

vice-president [vaisˈprezidənt] *n.* vice-président *m*, *pl.* vice-présidents.

viceroy [ˈvaisrɔi] *n.m.* vice-roi, *pl.* vice-rois.

vice versa [vais(i)ˈvəːsə] *Lt. adv.phr.* vice versa.

vicinity [viˈsiniti] *n.* **1.** voisinage *m*, proximité *f* (**to, with,** de). **2.** alentours *mpl*, environs *mpl*; **in the v. of Dover,** à proximité de, dans les environs de, Douvres; **in the immediate v. of the factory,** aux abords de l'usine.

vicious [ˈviʃəs] *a.* **1.** vicieux, dépravé. **2.** (*of horse*) vicieux, méchant. **3.** (*a*) méchant, haineux; **v. gossip,** commérages méchants; **she has a v. tongue,** c'est une mauvaise langue; (*b*) rageur; violent; (combat) acharné. **-ly** *adv.* **1.** vicieusement. **2.** incorrectement. **3.** (*a*) méchamment, haineusement; (*b*) rageusement; violemment.

viciousness [ˈviʃəsnis] *n.* **1.** nature vicieuse. **2.** méchanceté *f* (d'une critique).

vicissitude [viˈsisitjuːd] *n.* vicissitude *f.*

victim [ˈviktim] *n.* **1.** victime (offerte en sacrifice). **2. to be the v. of s.o.,** être la victime de qn; **v. of s.o.'s trickery,** dupe *f* de la fourberie de qn; **v. of an accident,** accidenté, -ée; (*of fire*) incendié, -ée; (*of flood*) inondé, -ée; (*of fire, flood, shipwreck, etc.*) sinistré, -ée; **to die a v. to smallpox,** mourir victime de la petite vérole; **to fall a v. to s.o.'s charm,** succomber au charme de qn.

victimization [viktimaiˈzeiʃ(ə)n] *n.* (*in strike settlement*) représailles *fpl* (contre des individus).

victimize [ˈviktimaiz] *v.tr.* (*a*) prendre (qn) comme victime; (*b*) exercer des représailles contre (les meneurs d'une grève, etc.); **he felt that he was being victimized,** il se croyait brimé.

victor [ˈviktər] *n.* vainqueur *m*, triomphateur, -trice.

Victoria [vikˈtɔːriə] **1.** *Pr.n.f.* Victoria; *Hist:* **Queen V.,** la reine Victoria; *Mil:* **V. Cross,** Croix *f* de Victoria; *Can:* **V. Day,** fête nationale célébrée le lundi qui précède le 24 mai. **2.** *n. Hort:* **v. (plum),** (variété *f* de) grosse prune rouge; (*c*) *A.Veh:* victoria *f.*

Victorian [vikˈtɔːriən] **1.** *a.* victorien, du règne de la reine Victoria. **2.** *n.* Victorien, -ienne.

Victoriana [viktɔːriˈɑːnə] *n.* bric-à-brac *m*, antiquités *fpl*, de l'ère victorienne.

victorious [vikˈtɔːriəs] *a.* **1.** victorieux, vainqueur *m*; **to be v. over s.o.,** être victorieux de qn; vaincre, battre, qn. **2.** (journée, etc.) de victoire. **-ly** *adv.* victorieusement, en vainqueur.

victory [ˈviktəri] *n.* **1.** victoire *f*; **to gain a, the, v.,** remporter la victoire (**over,** sur); être victorieux. **2.** *Art:* **(statue of) v.,** victoire; **the Winged V. of Samothrace,** la Victoire ailée de Samothrace.

victual [ˈvit(ə)l] *v.* (**victualled,** *NAm:* **victualed** [ˈvitld]) **1.** *v.tr.* approvisionner; ravitailler (un navire, une garnison). **2.** *v.i.* s'approvisionner, se ravitailler. **victualling,** *NAm:* **victualing** *n.* approvisionnement *m*, ravitaillement *m.*

victuals [ˈvit(ə)lz] *n.pl.* (i) vivres *mpl*, provisions *fpl*; (ii) victuailles *fpl.*

victualler, *NAm: also* **victualer** [ˈvitlər] *n.* (*a*) approvisionneur *m*; pourvoyeur *m*; fournisseur *m* de vivres; (*b*) **licensed v.,** débitant *m* de boissons.

video [ˈvidiou] *n. T.V:* vidéo *m*; **v. tape,** bande *f* vidéo; **v. (cassette) recorder,** magnétoscope *m*; **v. recording,** enregistrement *m* sur magnétoscope; **v. cassette,** vidéocassette *f.*

videophone [ˈvidioufoun] *n.* vidéophone *m.*

vie [vai] *v.* (**vied** [vaid], **vying** [ˈvaiiŋ]) **1.** *v.i.* le disputer (**with s.o.,** à qn); rivaliser (**with s.o.,** avec qn); **to v. with each other in doing sth.,** (*of two pers.*) faire qch. à l'envi l'un de l'autre, les uns des autres; faire qch. à qui mieux mieux. **2.** *v.tr. U.S:* mettre (de l'argent) en jeu; jouer (une somme). **vying** *n.* rivalité *f.*

Vienna [viˈenə] *Pr.n. Geog:* Vienne *f.*

Viennese [viəˈniːz] *Geog:* **1.** *a.* viennois; *Cu:* **V. bread,** viennoiserie *f.* **2.** *n.* Viennois, -oise.

Vietnam [vietˈnɑːm, -ˈnæm] *Pr.n.* le Vietnam.

Vietnamese [vietnəˈmiːz] *Geog:* **1.** *a.* vietnamien. **2.** *n.* Vietnamien, -ienne.

view[1] [vjuː] *n.* vue *f.* **1.** (*a*) regard *m*, coup *m* d'œil; (*of collection*) **on v. (to the public),** ouvert au public; **private v.,** entrée *f* sur invitation personnelle; avant-première *f*, *pl.* avant-premières (d'une exposition, etc.); vernissage *m* (d'une exposition de peinture); (*b*) *Jur:* descente *f* sur les lieux. **2.** (*a*) **exposed to, hidden from, v.,** exposé, caché, aux regards; **in v.,** en vue; **in full v. of the crowd,** sous les regards de la foule; **at last a hotel came into v.,** enfin nous avons aperçu un hôtel; **we were in v. of land,** nous étions en vue de la terre; (*b*) (*of telescope*) **field of v.,** champ *m*; **angle of v.,** angle *m* de champ. **3.** (*scene, prospect*) (*a*) vue, perspective *f*; **front v.,** vue de face; **from here you have a good v. of the castle,** d'ici on a une très belle vue du château; **you will get a better v. from here,** vous verrez mieux d'ici; **views of Paris,** vues de Paris; (*b*) *Arch: Draw:* **front, back, v.,** élévation *f* du devant, du derrière; **sectional v.,** vue en coupe; profil *m*; (*c*) **to keep sth. in v.,** ne pas perdre qch. de vue. **4.** (*mental survey*) aperçu *m*, exposé *m.* **5.** manière *f* de voir; opinion *f*, idée *f*, avis *m*; **point of v.,** point *m* de vue; **to express a v.,** exprimer une opinion, un avis; **to have very decided views on sth.,** avoir des idées arrêtées au sujet de qch.; **in my v.,** à mon avis; **to share s.o.'s views,** partager les sentiments de qn. **6. in v. of what has happened,** en considération de, en raison de, ce qui est arrivé; **in v. of these facts,** prenant ces faits en considération; **in v. of the great heat,** vu la grande chaleur. **7.** (*intention*) vue, intention *f*, but *m*, dessein *m*; **to fall in with, meet, s.o.'s views,** se mettre d'accord avec qn; **to have sth. in v.,** avoir qch. en vue; **with this in v.,** à cette fin; **with a v. to doing sth.,** en vue de, dans le but de, faire qch.; avec l'idée de faire qch.

view² *v.tr.* **1.** (*a*) regarder, porter sa vue sur (qn, qch.); visionner (des diapositives); *T.V:* regarder (une émission); (*b*) inspecter, examiner (qch.); visiter (une maison à vendre). **2.** envisager, regarder (qch.); **the prosposal was viewed unfavourably by the authorities,** la proposition était regardée d'un œil peu favorable par les autorités. **3.** voir, apercevoir (qn, qch.). **4.** *v.i. T.V:* regarder la télévision. **viewing** *n.* **1.** examen *m*, inspection *f*. **2.** *Opt: Elcs:* vision *f*, visualisation *f*; *Phot:* visée *f*; **v. window,** fenêtre *f* d'observation; *T.V:* **v. time,** temps *m* d'antenne.

viewer ['vjuər] *n.* **1.** (*pers.*) (*a*) spectateur, -trice; *T.V:* téléspectateur, -trice; (*b*) inspecteur, -trice. **2.** (*device*) visionneuse *f*.

viewfinder ['vju:faindər] *n. Phot:* viseur *m*.

viewpoint ['vju:pɔint] *n.* point *m* de vue; **from the international v.,** du point de vue international.

vigil ['vidʒil] *n.* **1.** veille *f*; **to keep v.,** veiller. **2.** *Ecc:* vigile *f*.

vigilance ['vidʒiləns] *n.* vigilance *f*.

vigilant ['vidʒilənt] *a.* vigilant, éveillé, alerte. **-ly** *adv.* vigilamment, avec vigilance.

vigilante [vidʒi'lænti] *n.* membre *m* d'un comité de surveillance.

vignette¹ [vi'njet] *n.* **1.** vignette *f*. **2.** *Phot:* buste *m* sur un fond dégradé.

vignette² *v.tr.* peindre (qn) en buste sur un fond dégradé; *Phot:* dégrader (un portrait).

vigor ['vigər] *n. NAm:* = VIGOUR.

vigorous ['vigərəs] *a.* **1.** vigoureux, robuste; (coup) solide; **v. in body and mind,** robuste de corps et d'esprit; *Hort:* **v. plant,** plante vigoureuse. **2.** (*a*) (*of style, opposition*) vigoureux; (*b*) (*of colour*) corsé. **-ly** *adv.* vigoureusement.

vigour, *NAm:* **vigor** ['vigər] *n.* **1.** vigueur *f*, énergie *f*; vitalité *f*; **the v. of youth,** la sève de la jeunesse; **man of v.,** homme énergique. **2. v. of style,** vigueur (de style). **3.** *NAm:* **laws in v.,** lois en vigueur.

Viking ['vaikiŋ] *Hist:* **1.** *n.* Viking *m*. **2.** *a.* viking; **V. ship,** drakkar *m*.

vile [vail] *a.* **1.** *A: & Lit:* vil; (i) sans valeur; (ii) abject. **2.** vil; bas, infâme, ignoble; **a v. calumny,** une calomnie infâme; **the vilest of men,** le dernier des hommes. **3.** *F:* abominable, exécrable; **he lived in a v. hovel,** il vivait dans un taudis infect; **v. weather,** un sale temps; **he's in a v. temper,** il est d'une humeur exécrable. **-ly** *adv.* **1.** *A: & Lit:* abjectement. **2.** vilement, bassement. **3.** d'une manière abominable, exécrable.

vileness ['vailnis] *n.* **1.** bassesse *f*, caractère *m* ignoble (de qn, d'un sentiment). **2.** *F:* caractère exécrable; **the v. of the weather,** le temps abominable.

vilification [vilifi'keiʃ(ə)n] *n.* dénigrement *m*.

vilify ['vilifai] *v.tr.* diffamer, dénigrer (qn); calomnier (qn).

villa ['vilə] *n.* (*a*) villa *f*; (*b*) pavillon *m* de banlieue.

village ['vilidʒ] *n.* **1.** village *m*; bourgade *f*; bourg *m*; **the whole v. was talking about it,** tout le village en parlait; **the v. grocer,** l'épicier du village; **v. inn,** auberge *f* de campagne. **2.** *U.S:* petite municipalité.

villager ['vilidʒər] *n.* villageois, -oise.

villain ['vilən] *n.* (*a*) scélérat *m*; *F:* **you little v.!** petit garnement! petite coquine! (*b*) *Th:* **the v. (of the piece),** le traître; **so you are the v. of the piece!** alors c'est vous qui êtes responsable de tout ça!

villainous ['vilənəs] *a.* **1.** vil, infâme; **v. deed,** infamie *f*. **2.** *F:* abominable, exécrable. **-ly** *adv.* **1.** d'une manière infâme. **2.** *F:* abominablement.

villainy ['viləni] *n.* **1.** infamie *f* (d'une action). **2.** action infâme.

villein ['vilin] *n. Hist:* vilain *m*; serf *m*.

vim [vim] *n. F:* vigueur *f*, énergie *f*; **full of v.,** plein d'entrain.

vinaigrette [vin(e)i'gret] *n. Cu:* vinaigrette *f*.

vindicate ['vindikeit] *v.tr.* **1.** défendre, soutenir (qn); justifier, faire l'apologie de (qn, sa conduite); prouver, maintenir (son dire); **to v. one's character,** se justifier. **2. to v. one's rights,** revendiquer ses droits; faire valoir son bon droit.

vindication [vindi'keiʃ(ə)n] *n.* défense *f*; justification *f*; **in v. of his conduct,** pour justifier, en justification de, sa conduite.

vindicator ['vindikeitər] *n.* défenseur *m*.

vindictive [vin'diktiv] *a.* **1.** vindicatif; (acte) de vengeance; **v. damages,** dommages-intérêts infligés à titre de pénalité. **2.** vindicatif, rancunier. **-ly** *adv.* par rancune, par esprit de vengeance.

vindictiveness [vin'diktivnis] *n.* caractère vindicatif; esprit *m* de vengeance; esprit rancunier.

vine [vain] *n.* **1.** vigne *f*; **v. growing,** viticulture *f*; **v. grower,** viticulteur *m*; vigneron, -onne; **v.-growing country, region,** pays, région, viticole, vinicole; **v. harvest,** vendange *f*. **2.** *NAm:* plante grimpante. **3.** sarment *m*, tige *f* (de houblon, etc.).

vinegar ['vinigər] *n.* **1.** vinaigre *m*; **wine, cider, v.,** vinaigre de vin, de cidre; **tarragon v.,** vinaigre à l'estragon; *Cu:* **oil and v. dressing,** vinaigrette *f*. **2.** *NAm: F:* vigueur *f*, allant *m*.

vinegary ['vinigəri] *a.* **1.** (goût, etc.) de vinaigre. **2.** *F:* (ton) acerbe, aigre.

vineleaf ['vainli:f] *n.* feuille *f* de vigne.

vineyard ['vinjəd] *n.* clos *m*, champ *m* de vigne; vignoble *m*; **the best vineyards,** les meilleurs crus.

vino ['vi:nou] *n. F:* vin *m*; gros rouge, pinard *m*.

vintage ['vintidʒ] *n.* **1.** (*a*) récolte *f* du raisin; vendanges *fpl*; (*b*) (*crop*) vendange; **the 1964 v.,** le cru de 1964; (*c*) temps *m* de vendange, les vendanges. **2.** (*a*) année *f* (de belle récolte); **of the 1964 v.,** de l'année 1964; **v. year,** année de bon vin; grande année; **v. wine,** vin de grand cru; grand vin; **v. champagne,** champagne *m* d'origine; **guaranteed v.,** appellation contrôlée; **bicycle of 1920 v.,** bicyclette du modèle de 1920; (*b*) *Aut:* **v. car,** vintage *m*, voiture construite entre 1916 et 1930.

vintner ['vintnər] *n.* négociant *m* en vins.

vinyl ['vainil] *n. Ch:* vinyle *m*.

viol ['vaiəl] *n. Mus:* voile *f*; **bass v.,** (i) basse *f* de viole; (ii) *U.S:* contrebasse *f*.

viola¹ [vi'oulə] *n. Mus:* **1.** alto *m* (à cordes); **v. player,** altiste *mf*. **2.** viole *f*; **v. da gamba,** viole de gambe; **v. d'amore,** viole d'amour.

viola² [vi'oulə] *n.* **1.** *Bot:* violacée *f*. **2.** *Hort:* pensée *f* (unicolore); violette *f* (de jardin).

violate ['vaiəleit] *v.tr.* **1.** violer (un secret); profaner (un sanctuaire); manquer à (une règle); violer, enfreindre (la loi); **to v. s.o.'s privacy,** faire intrusion auprès de qn. **2.** violer, outrager (une femme).

violation [vaiə'leiʃ(ə)n] *n.* **1.** violation *f* (d'un serment, d'une loi); viol *m*, profanation *f* (d'un sanctuaire); manquement *m*, infraction *f* (à une règle); infraction (à un ordre); **v. of s.o.'s privacy,** intrusion *f* auprès de qn. **2.** viol (d'une femme).

violator ['vaiəleitər] *n.* **1.** violateur, -trice (des lois). **2.** violateur, violeur *m* (d'une femme).

violence ['vaiələns] *n.* **1.** (*a*) violence *f*, intensité *f*; (*b*) **to use v.,** user de violence. **2.** *Jur:* **to commit acts of v., to resort to v.,** se livrer, se porter, à des voies de fait; **robbery with v.,** vol avec aggression, avec coups et blessures.

violent ['vaiələnt] *a.* **1.** violent; *Aut:* (freinage) brutal; **v. storm,** orage violent; tempête *f*; **to die a v. death,** mourir de mort violente; **to be in a v. temper,** être furieux, monté; (*of pers.*) **to become v.,** se livrer à des actes de violence; s'emporter. **2.** (*a*) violent, vif, aigu, -uë, fort; **v. pain,** douleur aiguë, violente; **v. dislike,** vive aversion; **v. fever,** fièvre violente; (*b*) **v. colours,** couleurs criardes, crues; **hair of a v. red,** cheveux d'un roux éclatant. **-ly** *adv.* **1.** violemment, avec violence; **his heart was beating v.,** son cœur battait à se rompre. **2.** vivement; extrêmement; **after supper I became v. ill,** après le souper j'ai été terriblement malade; **to fall v. in love with s.o.,** tomber follement amoureux de qn.

violet ['vaiələt] **1.** *n.* (*a*) *Bot:* violette *f*; **Parma v.,** violette de Parme; **shrinking v.,** personne *f* timide; (*b*) (*colour*) violet *m.* **2.** *a.* **v. (coloured),** violet, de couleur violette.

violin [vaiə'lin] *n.* violon *m*; **first v.,** premier violon, violon principal; **second v.,** second violon; **v. case,** boîte *f* à violon.

violinist ['vaiəlinist] *n.* violoniste *mf.*

violoncellist [vaiələn'tʃelist] *n.* violoncelliste *mf.*

violoncello [vaiələn'tʃelou] *n.* violoncelle *m.*

viper ['vaipər] *n.* (*a*) *Rept:* vipère *f*; (*b*) (*pers.*) vipère; **to cherish a v. in one's bosom,** réchauffer un serpent dans son sein.

viperish ['vaipəriʃ] *a.* vipérin, de vipère; *Fig:* **v. tongue,** langue venimeuse, de vipère.

virago [vi'rɑːgou] *n.f.* virago, mégère.

viral ['vairəl] *a. Med:* viral.

Virgil ['vəːdʒil] *Pr.n.m. Lt.Lit:* Virgile.

virgin ['vəːdʒin] **1.** *n.* (*a*) vierge *f*; **the (Blessed) V.,** la Sainte Vierge; *Hist:* **the V. Queen,** la Reine Vierge (Elizabeth I); *Geog:* **the V. Islands,** les îles *fpl* Vierges; (*b*) *Astr:* **the V.,** la Vierge. **2.** *a.* (*a*) de vierge; virginal, -aux; *Theol:* **v. birth,** (la) maternité divine; (*b*) **v. forest,** forêt *f* vierge; **v. snow,** neige virginale; **v. (vegetable) oil,** huile vierge, naturelle.

virginal ['vəːdʒin(ə)l] **1.** *a.* virginal, -aux; de vierge. **2.** *n. A.Mus:* **virginal(s), pair of virginals,** virginal *m.*

Virginia [və(ː)'dʒiniə] **1.** *Pr.n.*(*a*) Virginie; (*b*) *Geog:* la Virginie; *Bot:* **V. creeper,** vigne *f* vierge. **2.** *n.* **V. (tobacco),** tabac *m* de Virginie; virginie *f.*

virginity [və(ː)'dʒiniti] *n.* virginité *f.*

Virgo ['vəːgou] *Pr.n. Astr:* la Vierge.

virile ['virail] *a.* viril, mâle; *Anat:* **the v. member,** le membre viril.

virility [vi'riliti] *n.* virilité *f.*

virologist [vaiə'rɔlədʒist] *n.* virologiste *m*, virologue *m.*

virology [vaiə'rɔlədʒi] *n.* virologie *f.*

virtual ['vəːtjuəl] *a.* de fait, en fait; **he's the v. head of the business,** c'est lui le vrai chef de la maison; **this was a v. admission of guilt,** de fait c'était un aveu. **-ally** *adv.* virtuellement; de fait; **I'm v. certain of it,** j'en suis pratiquement certain.

virtue ['vəːtjuː] *n.* **1.** vertu *f*; **Christian virtues,** vertus chrétiennes; **the four cardinal virtues,** les trois vertus cardinales; *O:* **woman of easy v.,** femme de petite vertu, de mœurs faciles; **to make a v. of necessity,** faire de nécessité vertu. **2.** qualité *f*; avantage *m*; **the hotel has the v. of being cheap,** l'hôtel se recommande par son bon marché. **3.** efficacité *f* (de certaines drogues, de certaines eaux); **plants that have healing virtues,** plantes qui ont des propriétés curatives. **4.** *prep.phr.* **by v. of,** en vertu de; en raison de; à titre de; **by v. of one's office,** à titre d'office.

virtuosity [vəːtju'ɔsiti] *n. Mus: etc:* virtuosité *f.*

virtuoso, *pl.* **-sos, -si** [vəːtju'ouzou, -zouz, ziː] *n. Mus: etc:* virtuose *mf*; **he gave a v. performance,** il a fait montre d'une grande virtuosité.

virtuous ['vəːtjuəs] *a.* vertueux. **-ly** *adv.* vertueusement.

virulence ['vir(j)uləns] *n.* virulence *f.*

virulent ['vir(j)ulənt] *a.* virulent; **v. satire,** satire venimeuse. **-ly** *adv.* avec virulence.

virus, *pl.* **-uses** ['vairəs, -əsiz] *n. Med:* virus *m*; **v. disease,** maladie virale, à virus.

visa[1] ['viːzə] *n.* (*on passport, document*) visa *m*; **transit v.,** visa de transit.

visa[2] *v.tr.* (**visaed** ['viːzəd]) viser, apposer un visa à (un passeport).

visage ['vizidʒ] *n.* **1.** *Lit:* visage *m*, figure *f.* **2.** *NAm:* aspect *m*, visage (de qch.).

vis-à-vis ['viːzɑːviː] **1.** *n.* vis-à-vis *m.* **2.** *adv.* vis-à-vis (**to, with, s.o.,** de qn). **3.** *prep.* **to sit vis-à-vis s.o.,** être assis vis-à-vis de qn; **v.-à-v. the economic situation,** par rapport à la situation économique.

viscera ['visərə] *n.pl. Anat:* viscères *mpl.*

visceral ['visər(ə)l] *a. Anat:* viscéral, -aux.

viscid ['visid] *a.* visqueux, gluant.

viscidity ['vi'siditi] *n.* viscosité *f.*

viscose ['viskous] *n. Ch: Ind:* viscose *f.*

viscosity [vis'kɔsiti] *n.* viscosité *f.*

viscount ['vaikaunt] *n.m.* vicomte.

viscountcy ['vaikauntsi] *n.* vicomté *f.*

viscountess ['vaikauntis] *n.f.* vicomtesse.

viscounty ['vaikaunti] *n.* viscomté *f.*

viscous ['viskəs] *a.* visquex.

vise [vais] *n. NAm:* = VICE[2].

visé ['viːzei] *n. & v.tr.* (**viséd**) = VISA[1,2].

visibility [vizi'biliti] *n.* (*a*) visibilité *f*; **good, bad, v.,** bonne, mauvaise, visibilité; **v. was down to a few yards,** la visibilité était réduite à quelques mètres; (*b*) *Aut: Av:* vue *f*; champ visuel, de visibilité; **car with good front and rear v.,** voiture avec une bonne visibilité avant et arrière.

visible ['vizibl] *a.* visible; (*a*) **to become v.,** apparaître; **with v. satisfaction,** avec une satisfaction évidente; **v. horizon,** horizon visuel; (*b*) *F:* **I'm not v.!** je ne puis voir personne! **-ibly** *adv.* visiblement, manifestement; (grandir, etc.) à vue d'œil.

Visigoth ['vizigɔθ] *n. Hist:* Wisigoth, -e.

vision ['viʒ(ə)n] *n.* **1.** (*a*) vision *f*, vue *f*; **within the range of v.,** à portée de vue; **beyond our v.,** au delà de notre vue; **the accident had impaired his v.,** cet accident avait affaibli sa vue; *Med:* **double v.,** double vision, diplopie *f*; **field, angle, of v.,** champ, angle, visuel; (*b*) **man of v.,** homme d'une grande perspicacité, qui voit loin dans l'avenir. **2.** (*a*) imagination *f*, vision; **visions of wealth,** visions de richesses; (*b*) vision, apparition *f*; **he has, sees, visions,** il a des visions. **3.** *T.V:* image *f.*

visionary ['viʒ(ə)nəri] **1.** *a.* (*of pers.*) visionnaire, rêveur. **2.** *n.* visionnaire *mf.*

visit[1] ['vizit] *n.* **1.** (*a*) **(social) v.,** visite *f;* **courtesy v.,** visite de politesse; **to pay s.o. a v.,** faire (une) visite à qn, rendre visite à qn; **to return s.o.'s v.,** rendre sa visite à qn; *F:* **to pay a v.,** aller faire pipi; (*b*) visite (d'un médecin, d'un représentant); (*c*) *NAm:* causerie *f*, causette *f* (**with s.o.,** avec qn). **2.** visite, séjour *m*; **to be on a v. to,** *NAm:* **with, friends,** être en visite chez des amis. **3.** tournée d'inspection, visite d'inspection; *Jur:* **v. to the scene of a crime,** descente *f* sur les lieux; **domiciliary v.,** visite domiciliaire; *Nau:* **right of v. (and search),** droit *m* de visite (en mer).

visit[2] *v.tr.* **1.** (*a*) rendre visite, faire (une) visite, à (qn); aller voir (qn); (*b*) (*of doctor*) visiter (un malade); (*of representative*) passer chez (un client); (*c*) visiter, aller voir (un endroit); **we visited the mus-**

eums, nous avons visité les musées; (*d*) *v.i. NAm:* **to v. with s.o.,** (i) être en visite chez qn; (ii) bavarder avec qn. **2.** (*of official*) visiter, inspecter; *Jur:* **to v. the scene of a crime,** faire une descente sur les lieux. **3.** *B:* punir (qn, un péché); **to v. the sins of the fathers upon the children,** punir les enfants pour les péchés des pères. **visiting 1.** *a.* (*a*) en visite; *Sp:* **the v. team,** les visiteurs; (*b*) **v. lecturer,** conférencier, -ière, de l'extérieur; **v. professor,** professeur (de faculté) invité; *U.S:* **v. nurse,** infirmière visiteuse. **2.** *n.* (*a*) visites *fpl*; **to go v.,** aller en visites; **v. card,** carte *f* de visites; **v. hours,** heures *f* de visite (dans un hôpital); (*b*) (*of museum*) **worth v.,** qui vaut la visite.

visitation [vizi'teiʃ(ə)n] *n.* **1.** (*a*) visite *f* (d'inspection; (*of bishop*) visite pastorale; (*b*) tournée *f* (d'inspection); (*c*) *F:* visite fâcheuse, trop prolongée. **2.** *Ecc:* **(Feast of) the V.,** (fête *f* de) la Visitation. **3. v. (of God),** épreuve *f*; châtiment *m.*

visitor ['vizitər] *n.* (*a*) visiteur, -euse; **to have visitors,** avoir du monde; recevoir des visites; (*b*) visiteur (d'un musée); client, -ente (d'un hôtel); **visitor's book,** livre des voyageurs (à un hôtel); (*for distinguished visitors*) livre d'or (d'un hôtel de ville); **visitors' tax,** taxe *f* de séjour; **a v. from Mars,** un voyageur venu de Mars; (*c*) **health v.,** infirmière visiteuse.

visor ['vaizər] *n.* **1.** (*a*) *Arm:* visière *f* (de casque); (*b*) *esp. NAm:* visière (de casquette). **2.** *Aut:* **sun v.,** (*a*) pare-soleil *m inv*; (*over windscreen*) parasol *m.*

vista ['vistə] *n.* **1.** échappée *f* de vue; (*in forest*) percée *f*, éclaircie *f.* **2.** perspective *f*; *Rail:* **v. dome,** vistadôme *m*; *Fig:* **to open up new vistas,** ouvrir de nouvelles perspectives, de nouveaux horizons.

visual ['vizjuəl, 'viʒ-] *a.* **1.** visuel; *Mil: Nau:* **v. signal, signalling,** signal *m*, signalisation *f*, optique; *Sch:* **v. methods (of teaching),** enseignement *m* par l'image. **2.** perceptible à l'œil. **3.** *Anat:* **v. nerve,** nerf *m* optique. **-ally** *adv.* visuellement.

visualization [vizjuəlai'zeiʃ(ə)n] *n.* visualisation *f.*

visualize ['vizjuəlaiz, 'viʒ-] *v.tr.* (*a*) rendre (qch.) visible; (*b*) se représenter (qch.); évoquer l'image de (qch.).

vital ['vait(ə)l] **I.** *a.* **1.** vital, -aux; essentiel à la vie; **v. organ,** partie vitale; **v. force,** force vitale. **2.** essentiel; capital, -aux; vital; **question of v. importance,** question d'une importance vitale, de toute première importance; **it is v. that . . .,** il est indispensable, essentiel, que . . . + *sub.* **3.** mortel; fatal, -als; **v. error,** erreur fatale, irrémédiable. **4.** (*of pers.*) vif, plein d'entrain. **II.** *n.pl.* **vitals. 1.** *Anat: etc:* organes vitaux. **2.** parties essentielles, vitales (de qch.). **vitally** *adv.* d'une manière vitale; **v. important question,** question d'une importance vitale, de toute première importance; **it is v. important that . . .,** il est essentiel que . . .; il faut absolument que . . . + *sub.*

vitality [vai'tæliti] *n.* **1.** vitalité *f* (d'un organisme); vitalité, vigueur *f* (d'une institution). **2.** vie *f*, vigueur (de qn, de style); **I wish I had her v.,** j'aimerais bien avoir son énergie *f.*

vitalize ['vaitəlaiz] *v.tr.* vitaliser, vivifier. **vitalizing** *a.* (*of power, influence, etc.*) vivifiant.

vitamin ['v(a)itəmin] *n. Bio-Ch:* vitamine *f*; *Med:* **v. deficiency,** carence *f* vitaminique, en vitamines; (*disease*) avitaminose *f*; **with added vitamins,** vitaminé.

vitiate ['viʃieit] *v.tr.* **1.** vicier (le sang, l'air). **2.** *Jur:* vicier (un contrat). **vitiated** *a.* (air, etc.) vicié.

vitiation [viʃi'eiʃ(ə)n] *n.* viciation *f.*

viticulture ['vitikʌltjər] *n.* viticulture *f.*

vitreous ['vitriəs] *a.* **1.** *Ch: Geol:* vitreux. **2.** *Anat:* **v. body,** corps vitré (de l'œil).

vitrification [vitrifi'keiʃ(ə)n] *n.* vitrification *f.*

vitrify ['vitrifai] **1.** *v.tr.* vitrifier. **2.** *v.i.* se vitrifier. **vitrified** *a.* vitrifié.

vitriol ['vitriəl] *n.* **(oil of) v.,** (huile *f* de) vitriol *m*; acide *m* sulfurique; **to throw v. at s.o.,** lancer du vitriol sur qn, vitrioler qn.

vitriolic [vitri'ɔlik] *a.* (acide) vitriolique; *Fig:* **v. criticism,** critique mordante.

vitriolize ['vitriəlaiz] *v.tr.* vitrioler.

vituperate [vi'tju:pəreit] **1.** *v.tr.* injurier, *Lit:* vitupérer (qn); vilipender (qn). **2.** *v.i.* déblatérer, vitupérer (**against s.o., sth.,** contre qn, qch.).

vituperation [vitju:pə'reiʃ(ə)n] *n.* injures *fpl*, insultes *fpl*, invectives *fpl*; vitupération *f.*

vituperative [vi'tju:pərətiv] *a.* injurieux, vitupérateur, -trice.

Vitus ['vaitəs] *Pr.n.m. Ecc:* (Saint) Guy: *Med:* **Saint Vitus's dance,** chorée *f*; danse *f* de Saint-Guy.

viva¹ ['vi:və] *int. & n.* vivat (*m*).

viva² ['vaivə] *n. Sch: F:* = VIVA VOCE 3.

vivacious [vi'veiʃəs] *a.* (*of pers.*) vif, animé, enjoué; **to be v.,** (i) avoir de la vivacité; (ii) se montrer plein d'entrain, de verve. **-ly** *adv.* avec enjouement, avec verve, avec entrain, d'un air enjoué.

vivacity [vi'væsiti] *n.* vivacité *f*; verve *f*, entrain *m.*

vivarium, *pl.* **-iums, -ia** [vai'vɛəriəm, -iəmz, -iə] *n.* (*for animals, plants*) vivarium *m*; (*fish*) vivier *m.*

vivat ['vaivæt] *int. & n.* vivat (*m*).

viva voce ['vaivə'vousi, -'voutʃi] **1.** *adv.* de vive voix, oralement. **2.** *a.* oral, -aux. **3.** *n. Sch:* (*often shortened to* **viva**) examen oral, *F:* (l')oral *m.*

vivid ['vivid] *a.* **1.** (*of light, colour*) vif, éclatant, brillant; **v. flash of lightning,** éclair aveuglant. **2.** (*a*) (*of pers.*) vif, vigoureux; (*b*) **v. imagination,** imagination vive; **I have a v. recollection of the scene,** j'ai un souvenir très vif, très net, de la scène; **v. description of sth.,** description vivante de qch. **-ly** *adv.* **1.** vivement, avec éclat. **2. to describe sth. v.,** décrire qch. d'une manière vivante, sous de vives couleurs.

vividness ['vividnis] *n.* **1.** vivacité *f*, éclat *m* (de la lumière, des couleurs). **2. the v. of his style,** la vigueur, le pittoresque, de son style.

vivify ['vivifai] *v.tr.* vivifier, (r)animer.

viviparous [vi'vipərəs] *a. Bot: Z:* vivipare.

vivisect [vivi'sekt, 'vivisekt] *v.tr.* pratiquer des vivisections sur (des animaux).

vivisection [vivi'sekʃ(ə)n] *n.* vivisection *f.*

vivisectionist [vivi'sekʃənist] *n.* **1.** vivisecteur *m.* **2.** partisan *m* de la vivisection.

vixen ['viks(ə)n] *n.f.* **1.** *Z:* renarde. **2.** *F:* mégère.

viz [viz] (*when reading aloud usu.* **namely** ['neimli]) *adv.* (*abbr. for* VIDELICET) à savoir; c'est-à-dire.

vizier [vi'ziər] *n. Hist:* vizir *m*; **grand v.,** grand vizir.

vizor ['vaizər] *n.* = VISOR.

vocab ['voukæb] *n. Sch: F:* vocabulaire *m.*

vocable ['voukəbl] *n.* vocable *m.*

vocabulary [və'kæbjuləri] *n.* **1.** vocabulaire *m*, lexique *m*; glossaire *m.* **2.** vocabulaire (d'une langue, d'un auteur); lexique (d'une langue); **to enlarge one's v.,** enrichir son vocabulaire.

vocal ['vouk(ə)l] **1.** *a.* (*a*) (*of sound, music*) vocal, -aux; (*of communication*) verbal, oral; **v. score,** partition *f* de chant; *Anat:* **v. cords,** cordes vocales; (*b*) *Ling:* (*of vowel*) voisé; (*of consonant*) sonore; (*c*) *F:* **the most v. member of the audience,** le membre de l'auditoire qui s'est fait le plus entendre. **2.** *n.* (*a*) *Ling:* son vocal; (*b*) *Mus:* **vocals,** musique vocale; vocaux *m*, chant *m.* **-ally** *adv.* **1.** (*a*) vocalement, oralement; (*b*) (protester) à haute voix. **2.** par des chants.

vocalic [və'kælik] *a. Ling:* vocalique.

vocalist ['voukəlist] *n.* chanteur *m*, cantatrice *f.*

vocalization [voukəlai'zeiʃ(ə)n] *n.* **1.** prononciation *f*, articulation *f.* **2.** *Mus: Ling:* vocalisation *f.*

vocalize ['voukəlaiz] **1.** *v.tr.* (*a*) prononcer, articuler (un mot); chanter (un air); (*b*) *Ling:* (i) vocaliser (une consonne); (ii) sonoriser, voiser (une consonne); (*c*) *Mus:* vocaliser (un air). **2.** *v.i.* (*a*) *Mus:* faire des vocalises, vocaliser; (*b*) *F:* (i) chanter, chantonner; (ii) se faire entendre.

vocation [vou'keiʃ(ə)n] *n.* **1.** vocation *f* **(for teaching,** d'enseignant). **2.** vocation, profession *f*, métier *m*; **to miss one's v.,** manquer sa vocation.

vocational [vou'keiʃ(ə)n(ə)l] *a.* (enseignement, cours) professionnel; **v. guidance,** orientation professionnelle; **v. adviser,** *NAm:* **v. guidance counselor,** orienteur professionnel.

vocative ['vɔkətiv] *a.* & *n. Gram:* **v. (case),** (cas) vocatif *m*; **in the v.,** au vocatif.

vociferate [və'sifəreit] *v.i.* & *tr.* (*a*) vociférer, crier **(against,** contre); (*b*) crier à pleins poumons.

vociferation [vəsifə'reiʃ(ə)ŋ] *n.* **1.** cri *m*, clameur *f*. **2.** vocifération *fpl*, cris, clameurs.

vociferous [və'sifərəs] *a.* vociférant, bruyant. **-ly** *adv.* bruyamment; (protester) à haute voix.

vodka ['vɔdkə] *n.* vodka *f*.

vogue [voug] *n.* vogue *f*, mode *f*; **to be in v.,** être en vogue, à la mode; **to bring sth. into v.,** mettre qch. en vogue, à la mode; **v. word,** mot à la mode.

voice[1] [vɔis] *n.* **1.** voix *f*; (*a*) **to raise, lower, one's v.,** hausser, baisser, la voix; **in a low v.,** à voix basse, à mi-voix; **to speak in a loud v.,** parler à haute voix, à voix haute; **he likes to hear his own v.,** il aime à s'entendre parler; (*of singer*) **she's not in (good) v.,** elle n'est pas en voix; **loss of v.,** extinction de voix; **v. test,** audition *f*; **v. box,** larynx *m*; **v. production,** (i) élocution *f*, diction *f*; (ii) *Mus:* mise *f* de voix; *TV:* **v. over,** voix hors champ; (*b*) **the v. of conscience,** la voix de la conscience. **2.** (*a*) voix, suffrage *m*; **I count on your v.,** je compte sur votre voix; (*b*) **to give v. to (sth.),** exprimer (son indignation, etc.); **we have no v. in the matter,** nous n'avons pas voix au chapitre; **with one v.,** tout d'une voix, à l'unanimité. **3.** *Gram:* voix (du verbe); **in the active, passive, v.,** à la voix active, passive; à l'actif, au passif. **4.** *Ling:* son voisé.

voice[2] *v.tr.* **1.** exprimer, énoncer (une opinion); **to v. the general feeling,** exprimer, interpréter, le sentiment général, l'opinion générale. **2.** *Mus:* harmoniser (un tuyau d'orgue). **3.** *Ling:* voiser, sonoriser (une consonne).

voiced [vɔist] *a.* **1.** *with adj. prefixed* **low(-)v., loud(-)v.,** à la voix basse, forte. **2.** *Ling:* (consonne) sonore, voisée.

voiceless ['vɔislis] *a.* **1.** sans voix; muet; *Med:* aphone; **the v. minorities,** les minorités qui ne savent pas se faire entendre. **2.** *Ling:* sourd, non voisé.

void[1] [vɔid] **I.** *a.* **1.** (*a*) *Lit:* vide; (*b*) *Cards:* **v. suit,** couleur *f* dont on n'a pas de cartes dans son jeu. **2.** (*of office*) vacant, inoccupé; **to fall v.,** devenir inoccupé, vaquer. **3.** *Jur:* (*of deed, contract*) **(null and) v.,** nul, *f.* nulle; **to make v.,** annuler, frapper de nullité; **v. (voting) paper,** bulletin nul. **4.** *Poet:* vain, inutile. **5.** dépourvu, dénué **(of,** de); **proposal v. of reason,** proposition dénuée, dépourvue, de raison. **II.** *n.* vide *m*; **to fill the v.,** combler le vide; **the aching v. in his heart,** la perte douloureuse qui lui tenait au cœur; *F:* **to have an aching v.,** avoir l'estomac creux.

void[2] *v.tr.* **1.** *Jur:* résoudre, annuler (un contrat, etc.). **2.** évacuer (des matières fécales, etc.).

voile [vɔil] *n. Tex:* voile *m*.

volatile ['vɔlətail] **1.** *a.* (*a*) *Ch: etc:* volatil, gazéfiable; **v. oil,** huile volatile; (*b*) (i) gai, vif, folâtre; (ii) volage, inconstant. **2.** *n.* substance volatile.

volatility [vɔlə'tiliti] *n.* **1.** *Ch:* volatilité *f*. **2.** caractère (i) gai, vif, (ii) volage; inconstance *f*.

volatilize [vɔ'lætilaiz] *v. Ch:* **1.** *v.tr.* volatiliser (un liquide). **2.** *v.i.* se volatiliser.

volcanic [vɔl'kænik] *a.* volcanique; *Fig:* **v. temperament,** tempérament *m* volcanique.

volcano, *pl.* **-oes** [vɔl'keinou, -ouz] *n.* volcan *m*.

vole[1] [voul] *Cards:* **1.** *n.* vole *f*. **2.** *v.i.* faire la vole.

vole[2] *n. Z:* campagnol *m*; **water v.,** rat *m* d'eau.

volition [vɔ'liʃ(ə)n] *n.* volition *f*, volonté *f*; **to do sth. of one's own v.,** faire qch. de son propre gré.

volley[1] ['vɔli] *n.* **1.** volée *f*, salve *f* (d'armes à feu, de canon); volée, grêle *f* (de coups de bâton); grêle (de pierres); **to fire, discharge, a v.,** tirer une volée, une salve. **2.** volée, bordée *f* (d'injures, d'invectives). **3.** *Sp:* (balle prise de) volée; **half v.,** demi-volée *f*.

volley[2] **1.** *v.tr.* (*a*) *Mil:* tirer une volée, une salve, de (projectiles); (*b*) *Sp:* **to v. the ball, a return,** *v.i.* **to v.,** relancer la balle à la volée; **to half v. (the ball),** prendre la balle à la demi-volée. **2.** *v.i.* (*of guns*) partir ensemble.

volleyball ['vɔlibɔ:l] *n. Sp:* volley-ball *m*; **v. player,** volleyeur, -euse.

volt[1] [voult] *n. Equit: Fenc:* volte *f*.

volt[2] *n. El. Meas:* volt *m*.

voltage ['voultidʒ] *n. El:* tension *f*; **high, low, v.,** haute, basse, tension.

voltaic [vɔl'teiik] *a. El:* voltaïque.

volte-face[1] ['vɔltfɑ:s] *n.* volte-face *f inv*; **to make a v.-f.,** faire volte-face.

volte-face[2] *v.i.* faire volte-face.

voltmeter ['voultmi:tər] *n. El:* voltmètre *m*.

volubility [vɔlju'biliti] *n.* volubilité *f*.

voluble ['vɔljubl] *a.* (*of speech*) facile, aisé; (*of pers.*) volubile; (*of tongue*) délié, bien pendu; **to be a v. talker,** parler avec beaucoup de volubilité. **-bly** *adv.* avec volubilité.

volume ['vɔlju(:)m] *n.* **1.** volume *m*, livre *m*; tome *m*; **work in six volumes, six-v. work,** ouvrage en six volumes; **v. one,** volume premier, premier volume, tome premier; **it speaks volumes for him,** cela en dit long en sa faveur. **2. volumes of smoke,** nuages *mpl*, tourbillons *mpl*, de fumée; **volumes of water,** flots *mpl* torrents *mpl*, d'eau. **4.** *Ch: Ph:* volume; cubage *m*; **unit of v.,** unité *f* de volume; *I.C.E:* **v. of charge,** cylindrée *f*. **5. v. of business, exports,** volume des affaires, des exportations. **6.** *Mus: W.Tel:* volume (de la voix, du son); *W.Tel:* **to turn the v. up, down,** augmenter, diminuer, le volume; **v. control,** (i) réglage *m* de volume; (ii) bouton *m* de (réglage de) volume.

volumetric [vɔlju'metrik] *a. Ch: Ph:* volumétrique.

voluminous [və'lju:minəs] *a.* **1.** (auteur) volumineux, prolifique. **3.** (paquet) volumineux; (vêtement) ample. **-ly** *adv.* abondamment.

voluntary ['vɔlənt(ə)ri] **1.** *a.* (*a*) volontaire; (*of offer*) spontané; **v. service,** service volontaire; **v. confession of guilt,** confession volontaire; aveu spontané; (*b*) *Adm: Pol.Ec:* non-gouvernement, -aux; **v. organization,** organisation bénévole; (*c*) *Physiol:* (nerf, muscle) volontaire. **2.** *n. Ecc.Mus:* morceau d'orgue. **-ily** *adv.* (*a*) volontairement; de son plein gré; (*b*) bénévolement.

volunteer[1] [vɔlən'tiər] *n.* (*a*) *Mil:* volontaire *m*; **as a v.,** en volontaire; **v. service,** service volontaire; **v. army,** armée de volontaires; (*b*) **to call for volunteers,** demander des volontaires.

volunteer[2] **1.** *v.tr.* offrir volontairement, spontanément (ses services); donner spontanément (des renseignements); **to v. to do sth.,** se proposer (volontairement) pour faire qch.; s'offrir (pour une tâche); (*b*) *Mil:* s'engager comme volontaire.

voluptuous [və'lʌptjuəs] *a.* voluptueux, sensuel. **-ly** *adv.* voluptueusement.

voluptuousness [və'lʌptjuəsnis] *n.* sensualité *f*.

volute [və'lju:t] *n. Arch:* volute *f*.

voluted [və'lju:tid] *a.* voluté.

vomit[1] ['vɔmit] *n.* vomissure *f*, vomi *m*.

vomit² *v.tr. & i.* (*a*) vomir, rendre; **to v. blood,** vomir du sang; **he vomits up everything he eats,** il rejette, il rend, tout ce qu'il mange; (*b*) (*of chimney*) **to v. smoke,** vomir de la fumée. **vomiting** *n.* vomissement *m.*

vomitory ['vɔmitəri] *a. & n. Med:* vomitif (*m*).

voodoo¹ ['vu:du:] *n.* **1.** vaudou *m.* **2. v. (doctor, priest),** vaudou, *pl.* -ous, -oux; sorcier *m* (nègre).

voodoo² *v.tr.* (*of voodoo doctor*) ensorceler.

voodooism, voodouism ['vu:duizm] *n.* vaudou *m.*

voracious [vɔ'reiʃəs, vɔr-] *a.* vorace, dévorant; (appétit) dévorant, de loup; **v. reader,** lecteur vorace, grand dévoreur de livres. **-ly** *adv.* (manger) voracement, avec voracité; (lire) avidement.

voracity [vɔ'ræsiti] *n.* voracité *f.*

vortex, *pl.* **-ices, -exes** ['vɔ:teks, -isi:z, -eksiz] *n.* tourbillon *m* (de fumée, poussière); (*whirlpool*) gouffre *m*; *Fig:* **the v. of politics,** le tourbillon de la politique.

votary ['voutəri] *n.* fervent, -ente (**of,** de); dévot, -ote (**of,** à).

vote¹ [vout] *n.* **1.** (*a*) vote *m*, scrutin *m*; **secret v.,** scrutin secret; **popular v.,** consultation *f* populaire; **v. of an assembly,** délibération *f* d'une assemblée; **to put a question to the v.,** mettre une question aux voix; **to take the v.,** procéder au scrutin; (*b*) **(individual) v.,** voix *f*, suffrage *m*; **postal v.,** vote postal; **to give one's v. to s.o.,** donner son vote, sa voix, à qn; **to count, tell, the votes,** compter les votes; dépouiller le scrutin; **to record one's v.,** voter; **votes for women!** le droit de vote aux femmes! *coll.* **to lose the trade union v.,** perdre les suffrages des syndicalistes; (*c*) droit *m* de voter; **to have the v.,** avoir le droit de voter. **2.** motion *f*, résolution *f*; **v. of censure,** motion de censure; **v. of confidence,** vote de confiance; **to carry a v.,** adopter une résolution.

vote² **1.** *v.i.* voter (**for, against,** pour, contre); donner sa voix, son vote (**for sth.,** pour qch.); prendre part au vote; **to v. by (a) show of hands,** voter à mains levées; **to v. Communist,** voter communiste; **v. for Thomas!** votez Thomas! **2.** *v.tr.* (*a*) voter (une somme, *Parl:* un crédit); **to v. £50,000 for the victims of the disaster,** voter 50,000 livres pour les sinistrés; (*b*) *F:* **I v. (that) we go,** je propose que nous y allions. **3.** (*a*) **to v. down,** repousser (une motion); (*b*) **to v. s.o. in,** élire qn. **voting 1.** *a.* (*of assembly, member*) votant; (*of elector*) voteur, -euse. **2.** *n.* (participation *f* au) vote; scrutin *m*; **result of the v.,** vote; **v. paper,** bulletin *m* de vote.

voter ['voutər] *n.* (*a*) votant, -ante; (*b*) électeur, -trice; **registered v.,** inscrit *m.*

votive ['voutiv] *a.* votif; **v. offering,** ex-voto *m inv.*

vouch [vautʃ] **1.** *v.tr.* (*a*) affirmer, garantir (qch.); **I can v. that he wasn't there,** je peux garantir qu'il n'y était pas; (*b*) prouver, confirmer (une affirmation). **2.** *v.i.* (*a*) **to v. for the truth of sth.,** témoigner de, répondre de, attester, la vérité de qch.; **I can v. for it,** je m'en porte garant; (*b*) **to v. for s.o.,** répondre de qn; se rendre garant de qn; **I can v. for his honesty,** je le garantis honnête.

voucher ['vautʃər] *n.* (*a*) justification produite à l'appui de dépenses; pièce justificative; *Book-k:* pièce comptable; (*b*) *Com:* fiche *f*, bon *m*; (*for receipt*) recépissé *m*, quittance *f*; *Mil:* **issue v.,** bon de distribution, de sortie; (*c*) **cash v.,** bon de caisse; **gift v.,** (i) bon d'achat; (ii) coupon-prime *m*, *pl.* coupons-prime; **luncheon, v.,** chèque-repas *m*, *pl.* chèques-repas; chèque-restaurant *m*, *pl.* chèques-restaurant; *Mil:* **travel v.,** feuille *f* de route.

vouchsafe [vauʃ'seif] *v.tr. Lit:* (*a*) **to v. s.o. sth.,** accorder, octroyer, qch. à qn; (*b*) **to v. to do sth.,** daigner faire qch.

vow¹ [vau] *n.* vœu *m*, serment *m*; **to take the vows,** prononcer, faire, ses vœux; **to make a v.,** faire un vœu; **to take a v. of poverty,** faire vœu de pauvreté; **to break a v.,** violer un vœu.

vow² *v.tr.* vouer, jurer; **to v. obedience,** jurer obéissance; **to v. vengeance against s.o.,** faire vœu de se venger sur qn; **to v. to do sth.,** faire vœu, jurer, de faire qch.; *v.i.* **to v. and protest,** jurer ses grands dieux.

vow³ *v.tr. A:* affirmer, déclarer (**that,** que); **she vowed that she was delighted,** elle se déclara enchantée.

vowel ['vauəl] *n. Ling:* voyelle *f*; **v. sound,** son vocalique.

voyage¹ ['vɔiidʒ] *n.* **(sea) v.,** voyage *m* sur mer; (grande) traversée; **v. by air,** voyage aérien; **v. in space,** voyage spatial.

voyage² *v.i. Lit:* voyager, *esp.* sur, par, mer.

voyager ['vɔiidʒər] *n.* voyageur, -euse, par mer, par avion, dans l'espace; passager, -ère.

voyeur [vwɑ:'jə:r] *n.* voyeur, -euse.

voyeurism [vwɑ:'jə:rizm] *n.* voyeurisme *m.*

vulcanite ['vʌlkənait] *n.* vulcanite *f*, ébonite *f.*

vulcanization [vʌlkənai'zeiʃ(ə)n] *n. Ind:* vulcanisation *f.*

vulcanize ['vʌlkənaiz] *v.tr.* vulcaniser (le caoutchouc).

vulgar ['vʌlgər] *a.* **1.** vulgaire, commun; de mauvais goût; **v. expressions,** expressions vulgaires; **to make v. remarks,** dire des vulgarités *fpl*; **to be v. in one's speech,** s'exprimer vulgairement; *A:* **the v. herd,** le vulgaire; le commun des hommes. **2.** (*a*) vulgaire; commun; **v. errors,** erreurs très répandues, vulgaires; (*b*) **the v. tongue,** la langue commune; la langue vulgaire; (*c*) *Mth:* **v. fraction,** fraction *f* ordinaire. **-ly** *adv.* **1.** vulgairement, trivialement. **2.** *A:* vulgairement, communément.

vulgarian [vʌl'gɛəriən] *n.* (*a*) personne vulgaire; (*b*) parvenu(e) mal décrassé(e).

vulgarism ['vʌlgərizm] *n.* expression *f* vulgaire.

vulgarity [vʌl'gæriti] *n.* vulgarité *f*, grossièreté *f.*

vulgarization [vʌlgərai'zeiʃ(ə)n] *n.* vulgarisation *f.*

vulgarize ['vʌlgəraiz] *v.tr.* **1.** vulgariser (une science, etc.). **2.** vulgariser, trivialiser (son style, etc.).

vulgate ['vʌlgit, -eit] *n.* **the V.,** la Vulgate.

vulnerability [vʌln(ə)rə'biliti] *n.* vulnérabilité *f.*

vulnerable ['vʌln(ə)rəbl] *a.* (*a*) vulnérable; **v. to criticism,** sensible à la critique; **that's his v. spot,** c'est son point faible, son talon d'Achille; (*b*) *Cards:* (*at bridge*) vulnérable.

vulture ['vʌltʃər] *n. Orn:* vautour *m.*

vulva ['vʌlvə] *n. Anat:* vulve *f.*

vying *see* VIE.

W

W, w ['dʌblju:] *n.* (la lettre) W, w, *m.*
wacky ['wæki] *a. esp. NAm: F:* cinglé; loufoque.
wad¹ [wɔd] *n.* **1.** (*a*) tampon *m*, bouchon *m* (d'ouate); (*b*) liasse *f* (de billets de banque); (*c*) *F:* sandwich *m.* **2.** *Sm.a:* bourre *f* (de cartouche).
wad² *v.tr.* **(wadded) 1.** bourrer (une arme à feu). **2.** *Dressm: Needlew:* ouater, capitonner. **wadding** *n.* **1.** ouatage *m*, capitonnage *m*; rembourrage *m.* **2.** ouate *f* (pour vêtements); bourre *f* (pour armes à feu).
waddle¹ ['wɔdl] *n.* dandinement *m.*
waddle² *v.i.* (*a*) (*of duck*) marcher cahin-caha; (*b*) (*of pers.*) se dandiner (comme un canard); marcher en canard; **to w. along,** avancer en se dandinant.
wade [weid] **1.** *v.i.* marcher dans l'eau, dans la vase; **to w. across a stream,** passer à gué un cours d'eau; **to w. through a book,** venir péniblement à bout d'un livre; **to w. in,** (i) entrer dans l'eau; (ii) *F:* intervenir; prendre part (à qch.); (iii) *F:* s'attaquer à son adversaire; *F:* **to w. into s.o.,** s'attaquer à qn. **2.** *v.tr.* passer à gué (un cours d'eau). **wading 1.** *a. Orn:* **w. bird,** échassier *m.* **2.** *n.* partaugeage *m* dans l'eau; *U.S:* **w. pool,** grenouillère *f* (pour enfants).
wader ['weidər] *n.* **1.** *Orn:* échassier *m.* **2. waders,** bottes cuissardes imperméables.
wadi ['wɔdi] *n. Geog:* oued *m.*
wafer¹ ['weifər] *n.* **1.** *Cu:* gaufrette *f*; **to cut sth. w. thin,** couper qch. en tranches fines, ténues. **2.** *Ecc:* hostie *f.* **3.** *Jur:* cachet *m* de papier rouge.
waffle¹ [wɔfl] *n. Cu:* gaufre *f*; **w. iron,** gaufrier *m.*
waffle² *n. F:* verbosité *f*; verbiage *m.*
waffle³ *v.i. F:* parler pour ne rien dire; (*in writing*) faire du remplissage; **he just waffles on,** (il n'a rien à dire mais) il ne sait pas s'arrêter.
waft¹ [wɑ:ft] *n. Lit:* bouffée *f* (de vent, de parfum).
waft² *Lit:* **1.** *v.tr.* (*of wind*) **to w. a sound, a scent, through the air,** porter, transporter, un son, un parfum, dans les airs; **music wafted on the breeze,** musique *f* qui flotte, qui arrive, sur la brise. **2.** *v.i.* (*of sound, scent*) **to w. along,** être transporté par le vent; flotter sur la brise.
wag¹ [wæg] *n.* agitation *f*; hochement *m* (de la tête); (*of dog*) **with a w. of his tail,** en remuant la queue.
wag² *v.* **(wagged) 1.** *v.tr.* agiter, remuer (le bras); **to w. its tail,** (*of dog*) remuer, agiter, la queue; (*of bird*) hocher la queue; **to w. one's finger at s.o.,** menacer qn du doigt; **to w. one's head,** hocher la tête. **2.** *v.i.* s'agiter, se remuer; (*of dog*) **his tail was wagging,** sa queue frétillait; **to set (people's) tongues wagging,** faire aller les langues. **wagging** *n.* agitation *f* (de la queue); hochement *m* (de la tête); **there was a lot of tongue w.,** on jasait beaucoup.
wag³ *n. F:* plaisantin *m*, farceur, -euse.
wage¹ [weidʒ] *n.* (*a*) salaire *m*; paie *f*; gages *mpl* (de domestique); **basic w.,** salaire de base; **living w.,** minimum vital; **to get one's weekly w.,** recevoir son salaire de la semaine; *F:* toucher sa semaine; **to earn good wages,** être bien payé; **w. earner,** (i) salarié, -iée; (ii) soutien *m* de famille;**w. packet,** (i) enveloppe *f* de paie; (ii) paie *f*, salaire; (*b*) *Lit:* salaire, récompense *f*; **the wages of sin is death,** la mort est le salaire du péché.
wage² *v.tr.* **to w. war,** faire la guerre (**with, on, against,** à).
wager¹ ['weidʒər] *n.* **1.** pari *m*; gageure *f*; **to lay, make, a w.,** faire un pari, une gageure; parier, gager.
wager² *v.tr.* parier, gager (cent livres, etc.); **to w. that . . .,** parier que . . ..
waggish ['wægiʃ] *a. F:* plaisant, badin.
waggle ['wæg(ə)l] *v.tr. & i. F:* = WAG².
wag(g)on ['wægən] *n.* (*the spelling* **waggon** *is now rare except for* **1.** (*a*)) **1.** (*a*) (*usu. horse drawn*) charrette *f* (à quatre roues), chariot *m*; **covered w.,** chariot bâché; (*b*) *F:* **to be on the w.,** s'abstenir de boissons alcooliques; (*c*) = WAG(G)ONLOAD. **2.** *Aut:* (*a*) **station w.,** break *m*; *NAm:* **patrol w.,** *F:* **paddy w.,** voiture *f* cellulaire, *F:* panier *m* à salade; (*b*) *Mil: esp. U.S:* voiture *f*, fourgon *m.* **3.** (*a*) *Rail:* wagon (découvert); **goods w.,** wagon à marchandises; **covered goods w.,** fourgon; (*b*) *Rail: Min:* wagonnet *m*; *Min:* berline *f.*
wag(g)oner ['wægənər] *n.* roulier *m*, charretier *m.*
wag(g)onette [wægə'net] *n. Veh:* break *m.*
wag(g)onload ['wægənloud] *n.* charretée *f* (de foin, etc.); *Rail:* (charge *f* de) wagon *m.*
Wagnerian [vɑ:g'niəriən] *a. & n. Mus:* wagnérien, -ienne; wagnériste (*mf*).
wagtail ['wægteil] *n. Orn:* bergeronnette *f*, hochequeue *m*, lavandière *f.*
waif [weif] *n.* enfant abandonné; **waifs and strays,** enfants abandonnés.
wail¹ [weil] *n.* cri plaintif; plainte *f*; vagissement *m* (de nouveau-né); hurlement *m* (de sirène, etc.).
wail² *v.i.* (*a*) gémir; (*of new-born child*) vagir; (*of siren*) hurler; (*b*) **to w. over sth.,** se lamenter, pleurer, sur qch. **wailing 1.** *a.* (cri, chant) plaintif. **2.** *n.* plainte(s) *f*(*pl*), lamentation(s) *f*(*pl*); (*at Jerusalem*) **the W. Wall,** le mur des Lamentations.
wain [wein] *n.* **1.** *A:* charrette *f*; **hay w.,** charrette à foins. **2.** *Astr:* **Charles's W.,** la Grande Ourse.
wainscot¹ ['weinskɔt] *n.* lambris *m*; boiseries *fpl.*
wainscot² *v.tr.* **(wainscot(t)ed)** lambrisser, boiser. **wainscot(t)ing** ['weinskɔtiŋ] *n.* **1.** lambrissage *m*, boisage *m.* **2.** lambris *m*, boiseries *fpl.*
waist [weist] *n.* (*a*) (*of pers., dress*) taille *f*, ceinture *f*; mi-corps *m*; **down, up, to the w.,** jusqu'à la ceinture; jusqu'à mi-corps; **w. measurement,** tour *m* de taille; **to put one's arm round s.o.'s w.,** prendre qn par la taille; *Wr:* **w. lock,** ceinture; (*b*) étranglement *m* (d'un sablier, d'un violon); rétrécissement *m* (d'un tuyau); (*c*) *Nau:* embelle *f*, passavant *m* (d'un navire); (*d*) *NAm: Cost:* corsage *m.*
waistband ['weistbænd] *n.* ceinture *f.*
waistcoat ['weis(t)kout] *n. Tail:* gilet *m*; **single-, double-, breasted, w.,** gilet droit, croisé.
waisted ['weistid] *a.* **long, short, w.,** long, court, de taille.
waistline ['weistlain] *n. Dressm:* taille *f*; **to watch, to think of, one's w.,** surveiller sa ligne.
wait¹ [weit] *n.* **1.** (*a*) attente *f*; **we had a long w.,** nous avons dû attendre longtemps; (*b*) **to lie in w.,** se tenir en embuscade; être à l'affût; **to lie in w. for s.o.,** tendre un guet-apens à qn; attendre qn au passage. **2. waits,** chanteurs *mpl* de noëls (qui vont de porte en porte à l'approche de Noël).

wait² 1. *v.i.* (*a*) attendre; **w. a moment, a minute, a bit,** attendez un moment, un instant, un peu; *P.N:* **w.!** (piétons) attendez! **to keep s.o. waiting,** faire attendre qn; **to wait for s.o., sth.,** attendre qn, qch.; **what are you waiting for?** qu'attendez-vous? **I'll be late so don't w. up for me,** comme je rentrerai tard tu n'as qu'à te coucher; **we're waiting to be served,** nous attendons qu'on nous serve; **w. until tomorrow,** attendez jusqu'à demain; **I shall w. until he's ready,** j'attendrai qu'il soit prêt; *Com:* **repairs while you w.,** réparations *fpl* à la minute; *Prov:* **everything comes to him who waits,** tout vient à point à qui sait attendre; **(we must) w. and see,** il faudra voir; **w.-and-see policy,** politique *f* attentiste; attentisme *m*; (*b*) **to w. at,** *NAm:* **on, table,** servir (à table); faire le service; *v.ind.tr.* **to w. on s.o.,** (i) servir qn; (ii) *A:* présenter ses respects à qn; **to w. on s.o. hand and foot,** être aux petits soins auprès de qn. **2.** *v.tr.* (*a*) attendre, guetter (une occasion, un signal); (*b*) **don't w. dinner for me,** ne m'attendez pas pour vous mettre à table. **waiting** *n.* **1.** attente *f*; *P.N: Aut:* **no w.,** stationnement interdit; **w. room,** salle *f* d'attente, salle des pas perdus (de gare); antichambre *f* (chez un médecin); **to be on the w. list,** être sur la liste d'attente; **to play a w. game,** jouer un jeu d'attente. **2.** (*a*) **w. (at table),** service *m* (à table); (*b*) **gentleman-in-w.,** gentilhomme servant, de service (**to,** auprès de); **lady-in-w.,** dame *f* d'honneur.

waiter ['weitər] *n.* **1.** garçon *m* (de restaurant); **head w.,** maître *m* d'hôtel; **wine w.,** sommelier *m*; **w.!** garçon! **2. dumb w.,** servante *f*; monte-plats *m inv.*

waitress ['weitris] *n.f.* serveuse; **w.!** mademoiselle!

waive [weiv] *v.tr.* renoncer à, abandonner (ses prétentions, ses droits); déroger à (un principe); ne pas insister sur (une condition).

waiver ['weivər] *n. Jur:* **w. of a right,** renonciation *f* à un droit; **w. of a claim,** désistement *m* (de revendication).

wake¹ [weik] *n.* (*a*) *Nau:* sillage *m*; (*b*) **in the w. of the storm,** à la suite de la tempête; **to follow in s.o.'s w.,** marcher sur les traces de qn.

wake² *n.* **1.** (*in Ireland*) veillée *f* de corps. **2.** (*N. of Eng.*) **wakes week,** semaine *f* de congé annuel.

wake³ *v.* (*p.t.* **woke** [wouk] **waked** [weikt]; *p.p.* **woke, waked, woken** ['wouk(ə)n]) **1.** *v.i.* (*a*) veiller; être éveillé; rester éveillé; (*b*) **to w. (up),** se réveiller; **come on, w. up!** allons, (i) réveillez-vous! (ii) remuez-vous! secouez-vous! **to w. (up) with a start,** se réveiller en sursaut; **he is waking up to the truth,** la vérité se fait jour dans son esprit. **2.** *v.tr.* (*a*) **to w. s.o. (up),** (*from sleep*) réveiller qn; (*from inaction*) tirer qn de sa torpeur; **to be hard to w.,** avoir le sommeil dur; **w. me at six,** réveillez-moi à six heures; (*b*) **to w. the dead,** réveiller, ranimer, les morts; (*c*) éveiller, exciter (une émotion, un souvenir); (*d*) (*in Ireland*) veiller (un mort). **waking 1.** *a.* éveillé; **w. hours,** heures *fpl* de veille. **2.** *n.* **1.** veille *f*; **between sleeping and w.,** entre la veille et le sommeil. **2. w. (up),** réveil *m*. **3.** (*in Ireland*) veillée *f* (d'un mort).

wakeful ['weikf(u)l] *n.* **1.** (*a*) éveillé; peu disposé à dormir; (*b*) sans sommeil; **w. night,** nuit blanche. **2.** vigilant.

wakefulness ['weikf(u)lnis] *n.* **1.** insomnie *f*. **2.** vigilance *f*.

waken ['weik(ə)n] **1.** *v.tr.* (*a*) éveiller, réveiller (qn); **noise fit to w. the dead,** bruit *m* à réveiller les morts; (*b*) éveiller, exciter (une émotion). **2.** *v.i.* se réveiller, s'éveiller. **wakening** *n* réveil *m*.

wakey ['weiki] *int. F:* **w. (w.!)** debout! réveillez-vous!

wale [weil] *n.* marque *f*, trace *f* (d'un coup de fouet).

Wales [weilz] *Pr.n. Geog:* le pays de Galles; **New South W.,** la Nouvelle Galles du Sud; **the Prince of W.,** le Prince de Galles.

walk¹ [wɔːk] *n.* **1.** marche *f*; **it's half an hour's w. from here,** c'est à une demi-heure de marche à pied d'ici; **it's only a short w. (from here),** ce n'est qu'une petite promenade. **2.** promenade (à pied); tour *m*; **to go for a w.,** (aller) se promener; faire un tour, une promenade; **charity w., sponsored w.,** promenade en groupe entreprise au profit d'une œuvre de bienfaisance; **to take s.o. for a w.,** emmener qn en promenade; **to take the dog for a w.,** sortir, promener, le chien. **3.** (*a*) manière *f* de marcher; démarche *f*; marche, allure *f*; **I know him by his w.,** je le reconnais à sa démarche; (*b*) **to go, move, at a w.,** aller, avancer, marcher, au pas; (*of horse*) **to drop into a w.,** se mettre au pas. **4.** (*a*) allée *f* (de jardin); avenue *f*, promenade; (*b*) trottoir *m*; (*c*) **covered w.,** allée couverte; promenoir *m*; *Arch:* péristyle *m*, ambulatoire *m*; (*d*) *NAm:* trottoir *m*; **cross w.,** passage clouté (pour piétons). **5. w. of life,** (i) milieu *m*; position sociale; (ii) métier *m*, carrière *f*.

walk² I. *v.i.* **1.** marcher; cheminer; **to w. on, in, the road,** marcher sur la chaussée; **to w. two paces forward,** faire deux pas en avant; **to w. on all fours,** marcher à quatre pattes; **to w. in one's sleep,** être somnambule; **I'll w. a little way with you,** je vais vous accompagner un bout de chemin; **to w. with a limp,** boiter (en marchant); *NAm: P.N:* **w.! don't w.!** (piétons) passez! attendez! **2.** (*a*) (*as opposed to ride, drive, etc.*) aller à pied; **to w. home, back,** rentrer, retourner, à pied; **I had to w.,** j'ai dû faire le trajet à pied; (*b*) (*with preps.*) **to w. up, down, the street, the stairs,** monter, descendre, la rue, l'escalier; **to w. up and down,** (i) monter et descendre à pied; (ii) se promener de long en large; faire les cent pas; **to w. up to s.o.,** s'approcher de qn; **to w. across, over, to speak to s.o.,** traverser (la rue, etc.) pour parler à qn; **to w. into, out of, a room,** entrer dans une, sortir d'une, pièce; **please w. in,** entrez sans frapper; **to w. into s.o., sth.,** se heurter à, contre, qn, qch.; **to w. through the town, the crowd,** traverser la ville, la foule (à pied); (*c*) (*for exercise, pleasure*) se promener (à pied); **I like walking** j'aime bien me promener. **3.** (*of horse, rider*) aller au pas. **4.** (*of ghost*) revenir. **II.** *v.tr.* **1. to w. the streets,** (i) courir les rues; battre le pavé; (ii) (*of prostitute*) faire le trottoir; (*of sentry*) **to w. one's beat, one's round,** faire sa faction; *Th:* **to w. the boards,** être acteur, actrice. **2.** (*a*) faire marcher, faire promener (un stupéfié); (*b*) **to w. s.o. off his feet,** exténuer, éreinter, qn à force de le faire marcher; (*c*) **to w. a horse,** (i) conduire, promener, un cheval (au pas); (ii) mettre un cheval au pas; (*d*) **to w. the dog,** promener le chien. **walk away** *v.i.* s'en aller; partir; *Sp:* **to w. away from a competitor,** distancer facilement, semer, un concurrent; *F:* **to w. away with sth.,** (i) emporter, (ii) voler, faucher, qch. **walking 1.** *a.* (voyageur, spectre) ambulant; *Mil:* **w. cases, w. wounded,** blessés *mpl* qui marchent, qui peuvent marcher; **he's a w. dictionary,** c'est un dictionnaire ambulant, vivant. **2.** *n.* marche *f*; promenades *fpl* à pied; **two hour's w.,** deux heures de marche, de promenade; **it's within ten minutes' w. distance,** c'est à moins de dix minutes de marche; **it's within w. distance,** on peut aisément s'y rendre à pied; *Th:* **w.-on part,** rôle *m* de figurant(e); **at a w. pace,** au pas; *Sp:* **w. race,** concours *m* de marche; **w. shoes,** chaussures *fpl* de marche; **w. stick,** canne *f*; *F:* **to give s.o. his w. orders, papers,** congédier qn; donner son congé à qn. **walk off 1.** *v.i.* s'en aller; partir; *F:* **to w. off with sth.,** (i) emporter, (ii) voler, faucher, qch. **2.** *v.tr.* **to w. off one's lunch,** faire une promenade de digestion. **walk on** *v.i.* (*a*) continuer à marcher; (*b*) *Th:* figurer (sur la scène); faire, remplir, un rôle de figurant(e). **walk out** *v.i.* (*a*) sortir (**in a rage,** en colère); *Ind:* débrayer, se mettre en grève; (*b*) *F:* **to**

w. out on s.o., (i) abandonner, plaquer, qn; (ii) quitter qn en colère. **walk over** *v.i. Sp:* **to w. over the course,** inspecter le terrain (avant l'épreuve). **walk round** *v.i.* faire le tour.

walkabout ['wɔ:kəbaut] *n.* (*a*) *Austr:* (*of aborigines*) voyage *m* dans le désert; (*b*) bain *m* de foule; **to go w.,** prendre un bain de foule.

walkaway ['wɔ:kəwei] *n. Sp:* victoire *f* facile.

walker ['wɔ:kər] *n.* **1.** marcheur, -euse; promeneur, -euse; **he's a fast, slow, w.,** il marche vite, lentement. **2. baby w.,** trotteuse *f.* **3.** *Th:* **w. on,** figurant, -ante.

walkie-talkie [wɔ:ki'tɔ:ki] *n. W.Tel:* talkie-walkie *m, pl.* talkies-walkies.

walk-on ['wɔ:kɔn] *n. Th:* **w.-on (part),** rôle *m* de figurant(e).

walkout ['wɔ:kaut] *n.* (*a*) (*at meeting, etc.*) **to cause a w.,** provoquer le départ d'un groupe, d'une faction; (*b*) *Ind: etc:* débrayage *m,* mise *f* en grève.

walkover ['wɔ:kouvər] *n. Sp:* victoire *f* facile; **it was a w.!** c'était facile, *F:* fastoche!

walk-up ['wɔ:kʌp] *a. & n. NAm:* (immeuble *m*) sans ascenseur.

walkway ['wɔ:kwei] *n.* allée (couverte); passage (couvert); **moving w.,** tapis roulant.

wall¹ [wɔ:l] *n.* (*a*) mur *m;* **partition w.,** paroi *f;* **party w.,** mur mitoyen; **cavity w.,** mur double; **bearing w.,** mur d'appui, de support; **to leave only the four walls standing,** ne laisser que les quatre murs; **between these four walls,** entre ces quatre murs; **w. bracket,** console murale; **w. lamp,** (lampe *f* d')applique *f;* **w. paintings,** peintures murales; **w. clock,** pendule murale; **w. map,** carte murale; **w. to w. carpet(ing),** moquette *f; esp. U.S: F:* **w. to w. grin,** sourire énorme; (*b*) **surrounding w.,** mur d'enceinte; **dry(-stone) w.,** mur de pierres sèches; **sea w.,** digue *f,* endiguement *m;* **the town walls,** les murs, les murailles *fpl,* de la ville; **Hadrian's W.,** le mur d'Adrien; **the Great W. of China,** la grande muraille de Chine; **the Berlin W.,** le mur de Berlin; **W. Street,** la Bourse, le centre financier, de New-York; (*c*) muraille, paroi (de rochers); (*d*) paroi (d'une chaudière, d'une cellule); flanc *m* (d'un pneu); **white w. tyre,** pneu à flancs blancs; (*e*) *Fig:* **to come up against a blank w.,** se heurter à un mur; **to have one's back to the w.,** en être réduit à la dernière extrémité; **to go to the w.,** (i) être mis à l'écart; (ii) être ruiné, acculé; faire faillite; **the weakest always goes to the wall,** le plus faible est toujours battu; **to bang, beat, one's head against a (brick) w.,** donner de la tête, se battre la tête, contre un mur; *F:* **you might as well talk to a brick w.,** autant vaut parler à un sourd; **you're driving me up the w.,** vous allez me rendre fou.

wall² *v.tr.* **1. to w. (in),** murer, entourer de murs; **to w. up,** murer, maçonner (une fenêtre, une porte); *A:* emmurer (un prisonnier). **walled** *a.* **1.** (*of garden, town*) muré; clos de murs, d'une enceinte. **2.** (*with adj. or noun prefixed*) **double-w.,** à double paroi; **brick-w. house,** maison *f* en brique. **walling** *n.* **1. w. (in),** murage *m* (d'une ville, d'un jardin); **w. up,** (i) *A:* emmurement *m* (de qn); (ii) murage *m,* maçonnage *m* (d'une fenêtre). **2.** murs *mpl,* maçonnerie *f.*

wallaby ['wɔləbi] *n. Z:* wallaby *m.*

wallah ['wɔlə] *n.* (*a*) (*in India*) employé *m,* garçon *m;* **punkah-w.,** tireur *m* de panka; (*b*) *F:* type *m.*

wallcovering ['wɔ:lkʌvəriŋ] *n. Com:* tapisserie *f.*

wallet ['wɔlit] *n.* portefeuille *m.*

wall-eyed ['wɔ:laid] *a.* **1.** (*of horse, pers.*) vairon. **2.** (*of pers.*) à strabisme divergent.

wallflower ['wɔ:lflauər] *n.* **1.** *Bot:* giroflée *f* jaune. **2.** *F:* (*at a dance*) **to be a w.,** faire tapisserie.

Walloon [wɔ'lu:n] **1.** *a. Geog:* wallon. **2.** *n.* (*a*) Wallon, -onne; (*b*) *Ling:* wallon *m.*

wallop¹ ['wɔləp] *n. F:* **1.** gros coup; fessée *f.* **2. to fall with a w., to go (down) w.,** tomber lourdement, avec fracas. **3.** *F:* bière (brune).

wallop² *v.tr. F:* rosser (qn); tanner le cuir à (qn); *Sp:* battre (qn) à plate(s) couture(s). **walloping** *F:* **1.** *a. O:* énorme; **a w. great lie,** un gros mensonge. **2.** *n.* rossée *f;* **to give s.o. a w.,** (i) rosser qn; (ii) *Sp:* battre qn à plate(s) couture(s).

wallow¹ ['wɔlou] *n.* trou bourbeux, mare bourbeuse.

wallow² *v.i.* (*of animals*) se vautrer; (*of ship*) être ballotté (par les flots); (*of pers.*) **to w. in blood,** se baigner, se plonger, dans le sang; **to be wallowing in luxury,** être à la paille jusqu'au ventre.

wallpaper ['wɔ:lpeipər] *n.* papier peint.

walnut ['wɔ:lnʌt] *n.* **1.** noix *f;* **pickled walnuts,** cerneaux confits au vinaigre; **w. oil,** huile *f* de noix; **w. stain,** brou *m* de noix. **2.** *Bot:* **w. (tree),** noyer *m.* **3.** (bois *m* de) noyer.

walrus ['wɔ:lrəs] *n. Z:* morse *m; F:* **w. moustache,** moustache à la gauloise.

waltz¹ [wɔ:ls] *n. Danc: Mus:* valse *f.*

waltz² *v.i. & tr.* **1.** valser; **to w. with s.o.,** faire valser qn. **2.** *F:* danser (de joie, etc.); **to w. off,** partir, s'en aller. **waltzing** *n.* valse *f.*

wan [wɔn] *a.* pâlot, -otte; blême; **to grow w.,** pâlir, blêmir; **w. light,** lumière blafarde; **w. smile,** sourire triste. **-ly** *adv.* (briller) faiblement; (sourire) tristement.

wand [wɔnd] *n.* **1.** baguette *f* (de fée, de magicien). **2.** bâton *m* (de commandement); verge *f* (d'huissier).

wander¹ ['wɔndər] *n.* balade *f;* **to go for a w. in the woods,** aller se promener dans les bois.

wander² **1.** *v.i.* (*a*) errer (sans but); se promener au hasard; **to w. about,** aller à l'aventure; se balader; **to w. (about) aimlessly,** errer à l'abandon; **to w. about the world,** rouler sa bosse (un peu partout); **his eyes wandered over the scene,** ses regards se promenaient sur cette scène; **to let one's thoughts w.,** laisser vaguer ses pensées; (*b*) **to w. from the subject,** sortir du sujet; digresser; **my thoughts were wandering,** je n'étais pas à la conversation; **his mind wanders at times, is apt to w.,** il a des absences; (*c*) **to w. (in one's mind),** divaguer; radoter. **2.** *v.tr. A: & Lit:* **to w. the world,** errer de par le monde. **wandering 1** *a.* (*a*) errant, vagabond; (*of tribe*) nomade; **w. minstrels,** ménestrels ambulants; (*b*) (esprit) distrait; **w. attention,** attention vagabonde; (*c*) *Med:* qui a le délire; qui divague; (*d*) (discours, récit) incohérent. **2.** *n.* (*a*) vagabondage *m;* errance *f;* **wanderings,** pérégrinations *fpl;* (*b*) rêverie *f;* inattention *f;* (*c*) *Med:* égarement *m* (de l'esprit); délire *m;* **in his wanderings,** dans ses divagations.

wanderer ['wɔndərər] *n.* vagabond, -onde.

wanderlust ['wɔndəlʌst] *n.* manie *f,* passion *f,* des voyages.

wane¹ [wein] *n.* **to be on the w.,** (*of moon*) décroître; (*of pers., civilization*) être à, sur, son déclin; (*of beauty*) être sur le retour; **his star is on the w.,** son étoile pâlit.

wane² *v.i.* décroître, décliner; (*of beauty*) être sur le retour; (*of enthusiasm*) s'affaiblir, s'attiédir; **his star, his glory, is waning,** son étoile pâlit; sa gloire diminue. **waning 1.** *a.* décroissant, déclinant; (*of light*) défaillant, faiblissant; **w. moon,** lune décroissante; lune à son déclin. **2.** *n.* décroissance *f,* décroissement *m* (de la lune); déclin *m* (de la beauté); décadence *f* (d'un empire); attiédissement *m* (de l'enthousiasme).

wangle¹ ['wæŋgl] *n. F:* moyen détourné; truc *m.*

wangle² *v.tr. & i.* **1.** obtenir (qch.) par subterfuge; carotter, fricoter (qch); resquiller; **I'll w. it somehow,** je me débrouillerai, démerderai. **2.** cuisiner (des comptes). **wangling** *n.* resquillage *m,* carottage *m.*

wangler [ˈwæŋglər] *n. F:* resquilleur, -euse.
wanness [ˈwɔnnis] *n.* pâleur *f.*
want¹ [wɔnt] *n.* **1.** (*a*) *O:* manque *m*, défaut *m*; **w. of imagination,** manque d'imagination; **w. of respect,** manque de respect; **for w. of sth.,** faute de qch.; à défaut de qch.; par manque de (prévoyance); **for w. of money,** faute d'argent; **for w. of something better to do,** faute de mieux; *Prov:* **for w. of a nail the shoe was lost, for w. of a shoe the horse was lost,** faute d'un point Martin perdit son âne; (*b*) *O:* (*now usu.* **need**) **to be in w. of sth.,** avoir besoin de qch.; *esp. NAm: Journ:* **w. ad,** offre *f* d'emploi; demande *f* (**for,** de). **2.** indigence *f*, misère *f*, besoin *m*; **to be in w.,** être dans le besoin, dans la gêne; **war on w.,** lutte *f* contre la misère. **3.** besoin *m*; **to minister, to attend, to s.o.'s wants,** pourvoir aux besoins de qn.
want² **1.** *v.i.* (*a*) manquer (de); *O:* **to w. for bread,** manquer de pain; **to w. for nothing,** ne manquer de rien; (*b*) **her family will see to it that she doesn't w.,** sa famille veillera à ce qu'elle ne se trouve pas dans la gêne, le besoin; (*c*) *esp. U.S: F:* **if you w. in there's nothing stopping you,** si tu le veux rien ne t'empêche (i) d'entrer, (ii) d'y prendre part; **I w. out** (i) moi je me sauve; (ii) je ne veux plus rien avoir avec cette affaire. **2.** *v.tr.* (*a*) *O:* (*be without*) manquer de, ne pas avoir (qch.); **I w. one card,** il me manque une carte; *impers. NAm:* **it still wanted an hour to dinner-time,** il y avait encore une heure à passer avant le dîner; (*b*) (*need*) (*of pers.*) avoir besoin de (qch.); (*of thg*) exiger, réclamer, demander (qch.); **to w. rest,** avoir besoin de repos; **he wants a new hat,** il lui faut un nouveau chapeau; **situation that wants tactful handling,** situation qui demande à être maniée avec tact; **I shall w. you,** j'aurai besoin de vous; **have you everything you w.?** avez-vous tout ce qu'il vous faut? **we've more than we w.,** nous en avons plus qu'il n'en faut; **you shall have as much as you w.,** vous en aurez autant que vous voudrez; **I've had all I want(ed),** j'en ai assez; **the goods can be supplied as (and when) they are wanted,** on peut fournir les articles au fur et à mesure des besoins; **that's the very thing I w., that's just what I w.,** c'est juste ce qu'il me faut; cela fait tout juste mon affaire; **I have the very thing you w.,** j'ai juste votre affaire; **the very man we w.,** l'homme de la circonstance; **wanted, a good cook,** on demande, on recherche, une bonne cuisinière; *Journ:* **wanted ad,** offre *f* d'emploi; demande *f* (**for,** de); **he's wanted by the police,** il est recherché par la police; (*c*) **you w. to be on your guard,** il faut vous méfier; **your hair wants cutting,** vous avez besoin de vous faire couper les cheveux; **it wants some doing,** ce n'est pas (si) facile à faire; (*d*) (*desire*) désirer, vouloir; **he knows what he wants,** il sait ce qu'il veut; *Prov:* **the more you get the more you w.,** l'appétit vient en mangeant; **do you w. any?** en voulez-vous? **is that all you w.?** est-ce tout ce que vous voulez? **what more do you w.?** que voudriez-vous de plus? **what, how much, do you w. for this armchair?—I w. fifty pounds,** combien vendez-vous ce fauteuil?—j'en demande cinquante livres; *Iron:* **you don't w. much!** tu n'es pas dégoûté! **you're wanted,** on vous demande; **we're not wanted here,** nous sommes de trop ici; **they don't w. to have me,** ils ne veulent pas de moi; **what does he w. with me?** que me veut-il? **to w. sth. from s.o.,** désirer, vouloir, qch. de qn; **what do you w. of him?** que lui voulez-vous? **I w. to tell you that . . .,** je voudrais vous dire que . . .; **to w. to see, to speak to, s.o.,** demander qn; **he could have done it if he had wanted to,** il l'aurait bien fait s'il avait voulu; **don't come unless you w. to, if you don't w. to,** ne venez pas à moins que le cœur ne vous en dise; **I don't w. it known,** je ne veux pas que cela se sache; **what do you w. done?** que désirez-vous qu'on fasse? **I don't w. you turning everything upside down,** je ne veux pas que vous mettiez tout sens dessus dessous. **wanted** *a.* **1.** désiré, voulu; demandé. **2.** (criminel) recherché par la police. **wanting 1.** *a.* (*a*) manquant, qui manque; **to be w.,** faire défaut; **there is something w.,** le compte n'y est pas; (*b*) (*of pers.*) **to be w. in sth.,** manquer de qch.; **w. in intelligence,** dépourvu d'intelligence; *Lit:* **to be found w.,** se trouver en défaut; **he was tried and found w.,** il n'a pas supporté l'épreuve. **2.** *prep.* sans; sauf; **he arrived w. both money and luggage,** il est arrivé sans argent ni bagages.
wanton¹ [ˈwɔntən] **1.** *a.* (*a*) *O:* (*of woman*) licencieuse, impudique; **w. thoughts,** pensées *fpl* impudiques; (*b*) gratuit; sans motif; **w. cruelty,** cruauté gratuite; **w. destruction,** destruction pour le simple plaisir de détruire. **2.** *n.f. O:* femme impudique. **-ly** *adv.* (*a*) *O:* impudiquement; (*b*) (blesser, insulter) sans motif.
wantonness [ˈwɔntənnis] *n.* **1.** *O:* libertinage *m.* **2.** gratuité *f* (d'une insulte, etc.).
wapiti [ˈwɔpiti] *n. Z:* wapiti *m.*
war¹ [wɔːr] *n.* guerre *f*; (*a*) **atomic, nuclear, w.,** guerre atomique, nucléaire; **global w.,** guerre planétaire, universelle; **holy w.,** guerre sainte; **cold w.,** guerre froide; **civil w.,** guerre civile; **w. of nerves,** guerre des nerfs; **state of w.,** état *m* de guerre; **in time of w.,** en temps de guerre; **w. establishment, strength,** effectif(s) *m(pl)* de guerre; **to set a unit on a w. footing,** mettre une unité sur pied de guerre; **preparations for w.,** préparatifs *mpl* de guerre; **w. zone,** zone *f* de guerre; *Lit:* **to let loose the dogs of w.,** déchaîner les fureurs de la guerre; **to start a w.,** déclencher une guerre; **to be at w. with a country,** être en état de guerre avec un pays; **to make, wage, w. on, against, a country,** faire la guerre à, contre, un pays; **to go to the war(s),** partir à la guerre; **w. game,** kriegspiel *m*; exercise *m* sur la carte; jeu de stratégie militaire; **w. correspondent,** correspondant, -ante, de guerre; **I did my w. work in a hospital,** pendant la guerre j'ai travaillé dans un hôpital; **w. widow,** veuve *f* de guerre; **w. grave,** sépulture *f* militaire; **w. cemetery,** cimetière *m* militaire; **w. memorial,** monument *m* aux morts; **w. crimes,** crimes *mpl* de guerre; **w. criminal,** criminel, -elle, de guerre; **w. dance,** danse guerrière; (*b*) *Hist:* **the Trojan W.,** la guerre de Troie; **the Wars of the Roses,** la guerre des Deux Roses; **the American Civil W.,** *U.S:* **the w. between the States,** la guerre de Secession; **the Great W.** (1914–1918), la Grande Guerre; **the first, second, World W., World W. I, II,** la première, deuxième, guerre mondiale; (*c*) guerre, lutte *f*, conflit *m*; **class w.,** lutte des classes; *Pol.Ec:* **price w.,** guerre des prix; **w. of words,** dispute *f*, altercation *f*; **to wage w. on, against s.o., sth.,** faire la guerre à, contre, qn, à qch.; lutter, militer, contre qch.
war² *v.i.* **(warred) to w. against s.o., sth.,** mener une campagne contre qn, qch.; lutter contre qn, qch.; **to w. against abuses,** faire la guerre aux abus. **warring** *a.* **w. nations,** nations *fpl* en guerre.
warble¹ [ˈwɔːbl] *n.* gazouillement *m*, gazouillis *m.*
warble² **1.** *v.i.* (*a*) gazouiller; (*of lark*) grisoller; (*b*) *F:* (*of pers.*) chanter. **2.** *v.tr.* chanter (qch.) en gazouillant; *F:* (*of pers.*) roucouler (une chanson). **warbling 1.** *a.* (oiseau) gazouillant; (son) mélodieux. **2.** *n.* = WARBLE¹.
warbler [ˈwɔːblər] *n. Orn:* fauvette *f.*
warcry [ˈwɔːkrai] *n.* cri *m* de guerre.
ward¹ [wɔːd] *n.* **1.** (*pers.*) pupille *mf*; *Jur:* **w. in Chancery, w. of court,** pupille sous tutelle judiciaire. **2.** (*a*) **hospital w.,** salle *f* d'hôpital; (*of medical student*) **to walk the wards,** assister aux leçons cliniques; (*b*)

quartier *m* (d'une prison). **3.** *Adm:* **electoral w.,** circonscription électorale.

ward² *v.tr.* **to w. off,** parer, écarter (un coup); détourner, écarter (un danger); prévenir (une maladie).

warden ['wɔ:d(ə)n] *n.* **1.** (*a*) directeur *m* (d'une institution, d'une prison); **w. of a hostel,** (i) directeur, -trice, d'un foyer; (ii) (*of youth hostel*) père *m* aubergiste, mère *f* aubergiste; (*b*) (*freemasonry*) surveillant *m*; (*c*) gardien *m*; conservateur *m* (d'un parc national); (*d*) gouverneur *m* (d'une ville); **Lord W. of the Cinque Ports,** gouverneur des Cinq Ports. **2. traffic w.,** contractuel, -elle; *NAm:* **game w.,** garde-chasse *m, pl.* gardes-chasse.

warder ['wɔ:dər] *n.* gardien, -ienne (de prison, de musée).

wardress ['wɔ:dris] *n.f.* gardienne (de prison, de musée).

wardrobe ['wɔ:droub] *n.* **1.** *Furn:* armoire *f*, garde-robe *f, pl.* garde-robes; **hanging w.,** penderie *f.* **2.** (ensemble *m* de) vêtements *mpl*; garde-robe; **to have a large w.,** avoir beaucoup de vêtements; *Th:* **w. keeper,** *f.* **w. mistress,** costumier, -ière.

wardroom ['wɔ:dru(:)m] *n.* *Navy:* carré *m* des officiers.

wardship ['wɔ:dʃip] *n.* tutelle *f.*

ware [wɛər] *n.* **1.** *coll.* (*a*) articles fabriqués; **aluminium w.,** ustensiles *mpl* en aluminium; **cast-iron w.,** poterie *f* en fonte; (*b*) *Cer:* faïence *f.* **2. wares,** marchandise(s) *f(pl)*; **to cry one's wares,** crier sa marchandise.

warehouse¹ ['wɛəhaus] *n.* **1.** entrepôt *m*; magasin *m*; *Cust:* **bonded w.,** entrepôt de la douane; *Com:* **ex w.,** à prendre en entrepôt. **2.** (*for furniture*) garde-meuble *m, pl.* garde-meubles.

warehouse² ['wɛəhauz] *v.tr.* (*a*) (em)magasiner; (*b*) *Cust:* entreposer (des marchandises). **warehousing** *n.* (*a*) (em)magasinage *m*; (*b*) *Cust:* entreposage *m* (de marchandises).

warehouseman, *pl.* **-men** ['wɛəhausmən] *n.m.* garde-magasin, *pl.* gardes-magasin; magasinier.

warfare ['wɔ:fɛər] *n.* la guerre; **conventional w.,** guerre classique, conventionnelle; **guerilla w.,** guérilla *f*; **trench w.,** guerre de tranchées; **naval w.,** guerre navale, guerre sur mer; **bacteriological, germ, w.,** guerre bactériologique; **chemical w.,** guerre chimique; **class w.,** la lutte des classes.

warhead ['wɔ:hed] *n.* (*a*) cône *m* de charge (d'une torpille); (*b*) ogive *f*; tête *f* (de fusée); **atomic, nuclear, w.,** ogive atomique, nucléaire; tête nucléaire.

warhorse ['wɔ:hɔ:s] *n.* **1.** *A:* destrier *m*; cheval *m* de bataille. **2.** *F:* **an old w.,** (i) un vieux soldat; (ii) un vétéran de la politique.

wariness ['wɛərinis] *n.* circonspection *f*; prudence *f.*

warlike ['wɔ:laik] *a.* (exploit, maintien) guerrier; (peuple) belliqueux; (air) martial.

warlock ['wɔ:lɔk] *n.m.* *A:* sorcier, magicien.

warlord ['wɔ:lɔ:d] *n.* seigneur *m* de la guerre.

warm¹ [wɔ:m] **I.** *a.* **1.** (*a*) chaud; **to be w.,** (i) (*of water*) être chaud; (ii) (*of pers.*) avoir chaud; **the water's only just w.,** l'eau n'est que tiède; **to get w.,** se réchauffer; *Games:* **you're getting warmer,** tu brûles; **to keep w.,** se tenir chaud; **to keep a dish w.,** garder un plat au chaud; *F:* **to keep a place w. for s.o.,** garder un emploi pour qn; (*b*) (vêtement) chaud; (*c*) *Meteor:* **w. front,** front chaud; (*of weather*) **it's getting warmer,** il commence à faire plus chaud. **2.** (*a*) (accueil) chaleureux; **to meet with a w. reception,** être accueilli (i) chaleureusement, (ii) *Iron:* par des huées; (*b*) **w. heart,** cœur généreux, chaud; **w. smile,** sourire accueillant; (*c*) **it was w. work,** c'était une rude besogne; *F:* **to make things, it, w. for s.o.,** en faire voir de dures à qn; (*d*) (*of colour*) chaud; **w. tints,** tons chauds; **w. red,** rouge chaud, à tons chauds. **3.** *esp. N. of Eng: F:* (*of pers.*) riche, cossu. **II.** *n.* **1. to have a w.,** se réchauffer. **2. British w.,** pardessus *m* beige de coupe militaire. **-ly** *adv.* **1.** (vêtu) chaudement. **2.** (*a*) (applaudir) chaudement; (accueillir qn, remercier qn) chaleureusement; (*b*) (répondre) avec chaleur.

warm² **1.** *v.tr.* (*a*) **to w. sth. (up),** (faire) chauffer qch.; **to w. up the soup,** (faire) réchauffer le potage; **to w. oneself by the fire, in the sun,** se chauffer près de feu, au soleil; *Aut:* **to w. up the engine,** chauffer le moteur; (*b*) **wine, news, that warms the heart,** vin, nouvelle, qui réchauffe le cœur; **that will w. the cockles of your heart,** voilà qui vous réchauffera. **2.** *v.i.* (*a*) (se) chauffer; s'échauffer, se réchauffer; **to w. to s.o.,** concevoir de la sympathie pour qn; se sentir attiré vers qn; (*b*) **to w. (up),** (i) s'animer; (ii) devenir plus cordial, plus animé; *F:* se dégeler; (iii) *Sp:* se mettre en train. **warming 1.** *a.* chauffant; qui réchauffe. **2.** *n.* (*a*) chauffage *m*; **w. pan,** bassinoire *f*; (*b*) **w. up,** (i) réchauffage *m*; (ii) *Sp:* mise *f* en train.

warm-blooded [wɔ:m'blʌdid] *a.* **1.** (animal) à sang chaud. **2.** (*of pers.*) passionné, au sang chaud.

warmer ['wɔ:mər] *n.* **dish w.,** chauffe-plats *m inv*; **foot w.,** chaufferette *f.*

warmhearted [wɔ:m'hɑ:tid] *a.* au cœur chaud, généreux; (accueil) chaleureux. **-ly** *adv.* chaleureusement, avec chaleur.

warmonger ['wɔ:mʌŋgər] *n.* belliciste *mf.*

warmongering ['wɔ:mʌŋg(ə)riŋ] *n.* bellicisme *m*; propagande *f* de guerre.

warmth [wɔ:mθ] *n.* **1.** chaleur *f* (du soleil, du feu). **2.** (*a*) ardeur *f*; chaleur; (*b*) cordialité *f*, chaleur (d'un accueil); (*c*) emportement *m*, vivacité *f.*

warm-up ['wɔ:mʌp] *n.* réchauffement *m*; **come and have a w.-up by the fire,** viens te réchauffer auprès du feu; (*b*) *Sp:* mise *f* en train; **w.-up match,** match *m* préparatoire, d'entraînement; *esp. U.S:* **w.-up suit,** survêtement *m.*

warn [wɔ:n] *v.tr.* **1.** (*a*) avertir; prévenir; **to w. s.o. of a danger,** avertir qn d'un danger; **to w. s.o. against sth.,** mettre qn en garde, sur ses gardes, contre qch.; **he warned her against going, he warned her not to go,** il lui a conseillé (fortement) de ne pas y aller; **you have been warned!** vous voilà averti, prévenu! (*b*) **I shan't w. you again,** tenez-vous-le pour dit. **2.** informer, donner l'éveil à (qn); **to w. the police,** alerter la police. **3. to w. s.o. off,** (i) déconseiller qch. à qn; (ii) *Turf:* exclure qn des champs de course. **warning** *n.* (*a*) avertissement *m*; avis *m*, préavis *m*; **to sound a note of w.,** (i) donner l'alarme; (ii) recommander la prudence; **gale w.,** avis, signal *m*, de tempête; **air-raid w.,** alerte *f*; **strike w.,** préavis de grève; **w. strike,** grève *f* d'avertissement; **without w.,** sans préavis; sans déclaration préalable; **w. signal,** signal avertisseur, signal d'alarme; **w. device,** (appareil, dispositif) avertisseur; **w. bell,** sonnette *f*, sonnerie *f*, avertisseuse; **w. light,** (i) avertisseur lumineux; voyant (lumineux); (ii) *Nau:* feu *m* d'avertissement; *Aut:* **hazard w. lights,** feux *mpl* de détresse; *Navy:* **w. shot,** coup *m* de semonce; **w. sign,** (i) signe avertisseur, signe précurseur; (ii) pancarte *f*, plaque *f*, d'avertissement; **w. system,** système *m*, dispositif *m*, d'avertissement; *Mil:* **early w. system,** système de surveillance avancée; (*b*) **he was let off with a w.,** il en a été quitte pour une réprimande; **I'm giving you faire w.,** vous voilà averti! (*c*) **let this be a w. to you,** que cela vous serve de leçon, d'exemple, d'avertissement; (*d*) *Turf:* **w. off,** exécution *f* (d'un jockey).

warp¹ [wɔ:p] *n.* **1.** *Tex:* chaîne *f*; (*for tapestry*) lisse *f*, lice *f.* **2.** voilure *f*, courbure *f* (d'une planche); gauchissement *m.*

warp² **I.** *v.tr.* **1.** (*a*) déjeter, (faire) fausser, gauchir (le bois, une tôle); faire travailler (le bois); (*b*) fausser, pervertir (l'esprit, le caractère). **2.** ourdir (un tissu). **II.** *v.i.* se déformer; (*of timber*) se déjeter, gauchir; (*of sheet metal*) se fausser, (se) gondoler. **warped** *a.* (*a*) (bois) gauchi, gondolé; (*b*) (esprit) perverti, faussé; **w. nature,** caractère mal fait. **warping** *n.* **1.** (*a*) gauchissement *m* (d'une planche); gondolement *m* (d'une tôle); voilure *f*, voilement *m* (d'une roue); (*b*) perversion *f* (de l'esprit, du caractère). **2.** *Tex:* ourdissage *m.*

warpaint ['wɔːpeint] *n.* peinture *f* de guerre.

warpath ['wɔːpɑːθ] *n.* **to be on the w.,** (i) être parti en campagne; (ii) en vouloir à tout le monde; **the boss is on the w.,** le patron est d'une humeur massacrante.

warrant¹ ['wɔrənt] *n.* **1.** garantie *f*; **a w. for s.o.'s good behaviour,** une garantie pour la bonne conduite de qn. **2.** autorisation *f*; justification *f*. **3.** (*a*) mandat *m*, ordre *m*; *Jur:* **w. of arrest,** mandat d'arrêt, d'arrestation; mandat d'amener; **there's a w. out against him, for his arrest,** il est sous le coup d'un mandat d'amener; **search w.,** mandat de perquisition; (*b*) autorisation écrite; autorité *f*; pouvoir *m*; (*c*) certificat *m*; **warehouse w.,** certificat d'entrepôt; warrant *m*; (*d*) *Adm:* mandat; chèque *m*; **w. for payment,** ordonnance *f* de paiement; **travel w.,** feuille *f* de route; **royal w.,** brevet *m* de fournisseur du souverain. **4.** *Mil:* **w. officer,** adjudant *m.*

warrant² *v.tr.* **1.** garantir, certifier (qch.); répondre de (qch.); **it won't happen again, I w. you!** cela n'arrivera pas deux fois, je vous en réponds! **2.** justifier; **nothing can w. such conduct,** rien ne justifie une pareille conduite; rien ne peut excuser une telle conduite.

warrantable ['wɔrəntəbl] *a.* (*a*) justifiable; (*b*) que l'on peut garantir.

warrantee [wɔrən'tiː] *n.* receveur, -euse, d'une garantie.

warrantor ['wɔrəntɔːr] *n. Jur:* garant, -ante.

warranty ['wɔrənti] *n.* **1.** autorisation *f*; justification *f* (**for doing sth.,** pour faire qch., pour avoir fait qch.). **2.** *Com:* garantie *f*; **breach of w.,** rupture *f* de garantie.

warren ['wɔrən] *n.* **(rabbit) w.,** (i) garenne *f*, clapier *m*; (ii) enchevêtrement *m* de petites rues.

warrior ['wɔriər] *n.* guerrier *m*; **the Unknown W.,** le Soldat inconnu; **w. tribes,** tribus guerrières.

Warsaw ['wɔːsɔ] *Pr.n. Geog:* Varsovie *f.*

warship ['wɔːʃip] *n.* navire *m*, vaisseau *m*, de guerre.

wart [wɔːt] *n.* verrue *f*; *F:* **to paint s.o. warts and all,** peindre un portrait très exact de qn (sans le flatter).

warthog ['wɔːthɔg] *n. Z:* phacochère *m.*

wartime ['wɔːtaim] *n.* temps *m* de guerre; **in w.,** en temps de guerre.

warty ['wɔːti] *a.* verruqueux.

wary ['wɛəri] *a.* (*a*) avisé, prudent, circonspect; précautionneux; **to keep a w. eye on s.o.,** guetter qn; surveiller qn attentivement; (*b*) **to be w. of sth.,** se méfier de qch.; **be w. of strangers,** méfiez-vous des étrangers. **-ily** *adv.* avec circonspection; prudemment.

was *see* BE.

wash¹ [wɔʃ] *n.* **1.** (*a*) lavage *m*; savonnage *m*; **to give sth. a w.,** laver qch.; (*b*) (*of pers.*) **to have a w.,** se laver; **to have a w. and brush up,** faire un brin, un bout, de toilette; (*c*) lessive *f*, blanchissage *m*; **to send clothes to the w.,** donner du linge à laver, à blanchir; *F:* **it will all come out in the w.,** (i) les faits se révèleront un jour ou l'autre; (ii) ça se tassera; *Aut:* **car w.,** (i) lavage de voitures; (ii) lave-auto *m.* **2.** (*a*) *Med: Vet:* lotion *f* (pour plaies); **mouth w.,** collutoire *m*; (*b*) *Hort:* lessive (insecticide); *Vit:* (*against mildew*) bouillie *f.* **3.** (*a*) (*for walls*) **colour w.,** badigeon *m*; (*b*) couche légère (de couleur sur une surface); (*c*) *Art:* lavis *m* (d'aquarelle, d'encre de Chine); **w. drawing,** dessin *m* au lavis. **4.** (*a*) remous *m* (des vagues); (*b*) *Nau:* remous (d'un navire).

wash² **I.** *v.tr.* **1.** (*a*) laver; **to w. sth. in cold w.,** laver qch. à l'eau froide; **to w. one's face, one's hands,** se laver le visage, les mains; *F:* **to w. one's hands of sth., s.o.,** se laver les mains de qch., de qn; **I w. my hands of the affair,** je ne suis plus pour rien dans l'affaire; **to be washed of one's sins,** expier ses péchés; (*b*) *v.pr.* & *i.* **to w. (oneself),** se laver; (*c*) *Med:* lotionner, déterger (une plaie). **2.** (*a*) blanchir, lessiver, laver (le linge); **w. in cool, hot, water,** à laver à l'eau tiède, chaude; **hand w. only,** laver à la main seulement; (*b*) (*with passive force*) (*of fabric*) supporter le lavage; **material that washes well,** tissu *m* qui lave bien; *F:* **that won't w.!** ça ne prend pas! **3.** *Ind:* débourber (le minerai, le charbon); épurer (le gaz). **4.** (*a*) **to w. the walls,** badigeonner les murs (**with,** de); (*b*) *Art:* laver (un dessin). **5.** (*of sea*) baigner (une côte); **to w. s.o., sth., ashore,** rejeter qn, qch., sur le rivage; **sailor washed overboard,** matelot enlevé par une lame. **II.** *v.i.* **the waves washed over the deck,** les vagues *fpl* balayaient le pont; **waves washing against the cliff,** vagues qui baignent la falaise. **wash away** *v.tr.* (*a*) enlever (une tache) par le lavage; **to w. one's sins away,** se laver de ses péchés; (*b*) (*of running water*) **to w. away the gravel from a river bed,** enlever le gravier du lit d'une rivière; **the flood washed away part of the river bank,** l'inondation a dégradé la berge; (*c*) emporter, entraîner; **washed away by the tide,** emporté, enlevé, par la mer. **wash down** *v.tr.* (*a*) laver (les murs) à grande eau; (*b*) (*of the rain*) emporter, entraîner (le sol, le gravier); *F:* **to w. down one's dinner with a glass of beer,** arroser son dîner d'un verre de bière. **washing** *n.* **1.** (*a*) lavage *m*; ablutions *fpl*; (*b*) *Ecc:* lavement *m* (des pieds, des mains); ablution *f* (du calice). **2.** (*a*) blanchissage *m*, lessive *f* (du linge); **to do the w.,** faire la lessive; **w. machine,** machine *f* à laver; **w. powder,** lessive (en poudre), détergent *m*; (*b*) linge (i) à laver, (ii) lavé; la lessive; *F:* **to take in one another's w.,** se rendre mutuellement service; (*c*) **to do the w. up,** faire la vaisselle, (*in restaurant*) la plonge; **w.-up bowl,** cuvette *f*, bassine *f*; **w.-up water,** eau *f* de vaisselle; **w.-up machine,** machine à laver la vaisselle, lave-vaisselle *m inv*; *Fr.C:* laveuse *f* à vaisselle. **3.** *Ind:* débourbage *m* (du charbon, du minerai); épurage *m* (du gaz). **4.** (*a*) badigeonnage *m* (d'une surface); (*b*) *Art:* lavis *m* (d'un dessin). **wash off** *v.tr.* enlever, effacer (qch.) par le lavage; (*with passive force*) **it will w. off,** (i) cela s'effacera à l'eau; (ii) cela s'en ira à la lessive. **wash out** *v.tr.* (*a*) enlever (une tache); (*b*) **to w. out a few clothes, things,** faire une petite lessive; *F:* **to be completely washed out,** être complètement lessivé, vanné, à plat; (*c*) laver, rincer, nettoyer (une tasse, une bouteille); (*d*) *Art:* dégrader (une couleur); (*of colour, material*) **washed out,** délavé, déteint; (*e*) *Min:* **to w. out the gold,** extraire l'or (en lavant le sable, etc.); (*f*) *Sp:* (*of match*) **to be washed out,** être décommandé à cause de la pluie; (*g*) (*with passive force*) (*of stain, colour*) partir au lavage; **it will w. out,** cela s'en ira à la lessive. **wash up** **1.** *v.tr.* & *i.* (*a*) **to w. up (the dishes),** laver, faire, la vaisselle; (*b*) (*of sea*) rejeter (qn, qch.) sur le rivage; **wreckage washed up by the sea,** débris rejetés par la mer; (*c*) *F:* **to be (all) washed up,** (i) être fini, *F:* fichu; (ii) (*of plan*) être tombé à l'eau; **he's all washed up,** c'est un homme fini, liquidé. **2.** *v.i.* (*a*) **the water washed up on the bank,** l'eau refluait sur la berge; (*b*) *U.S:* se laver (les mains et la figure).

washable ['wɔʃəbl] *a.* lavable.

wash-and-wear [wɔʃənd'wɛər] *a.* lavé-repassé.
washbasin ['wɔʃbeis(ə)n] *n.* (cuvette *f* de) lavabo *m.*
washboard ['wɔʃbɔːd] *n.* planche *f* à laver.
washbowl ['wɔʃboul] *n.* cuvette *f*; (*large*) bassine *f*.
washcloth ['wɔʃklɔθ] *n. U.S:* = gant *m* de toilette.
washday ['wɔʃdei] *n.* jour *m* de la lessive.
washer¹ ['wɔʃər] *n.* **1.** (*pers.*) laveur, -euse; (*b*) **w. up,** *F:* **w. upper,** laveur, -euse, de vaisselle; (*in restaurant*) plongeur, -euse. **2.** (*device*) (*a*) *F:* (i) machine *f* à laver; (ii) lave-vaisselle *m inv*; (*b*) *Aut:* **windscreen w.,** lave-glace *m, pl.* lave-glaces.
washer² *n.* rondelle *f*; bague *f* (d'appui); **rubber w.,** rondelle de caoutchouc; **tap w.,** rondelle de robinet.
washerwoman, *pl.* **-women** ['wɔʃəwumən, -wimin] *n.f.* blanchisseuse.
wash(-)hand ['wɔʃhænd] *a.* **w. basin,** (cuvette *f* de) lavabo *m.*
wash-house ['wɔʃhaus] *n.* (*a*) buanderie *f*, lavanderie *f*; (*b*) lavoir (public); (*c*) *U.S:* blanchisserie *f*.
washleather ['wɔʃleðər] *n.* **1.** peau *f* de chamois; chamois *m* lavable; **w. gloves,** gants *mpl* chamois. **2.** peau de chamois (pour nettoyage de vitres).
washout ['wɔʃaut] *n.* **1.** lavage *m*, rinçage *m*. **2.** (*a*) fiasco *m*; **the whole thing's a w.,** c'est une perte sèche! (*b*) (*pers.*) raté *m*; zéro *m.*
washrag ['wɔʃræg] *n. U.S:* = gant *m* de toilette.
washroom ['wɔʃru(ː)m] *n.* (*a*) *esp. NAm:* (*in hotel, etc.*) toilette *f*; (*b*) salle *f* d'eau; cabinet *m* de toilette.
washstand ['wɔʃstænd] *n.* **1.** *Furn:* (*a*) table *f* de toilette; (*b*) *NAm:* lavabo *m*. **2.** *U.S: Aut:* installation *f*, aire *f*, de lavage.
washtub ['wɔʃtʌb] *n. Dom.Ec:* baquet *m* (à lessive).
washup ['wɔʃʌp] *n.* (*a*) lavage *m* (de vaisselle); (*b*) *F:* stérilisation *f* des mains (avant une opération); (*c*) *NAm:* **to have a w.,** se laver (les mains et la figure).
washy ['wɔʃi] *a. F:* (*a*) fade, fadasse; **w. tea, coffee,** lavasse *f*; (*b*) (*of colour*) délavé.
wasn't = **was not,** *see* BE.
wasp¹ [wɔsp] *n. Ent:* guêpe *f*; **wasps' nest,** guêpier *m*; (*of pers.*) **w. waist,** taille *f* de guêpe.
Wasp² *n. NAm:* Américain blanc protestant d'origine anglo-saxonne.
waspish ['wɔspiʃ] *a. F: O:* méchant; acerbe; (ton) aigre. **-ly** *adv.* d'une manière acerbe; d'un ton aigre.
wastage ['weistidʒ] *n.* **1.** (*a*) déperdition *f*, perte *f* (de chaleur); (*b*) gaspillage *m*. **2.** *coll.* déchets *mpl*, rebuts *mpl.*
waste¹ [weist] *a.* **1.** (*a*) **w. land, ground,** (i) terre *f* inculte, en friche; (ii) terre indéfrichable; (iii) (*in town*) terrains *mpl* vagues; (*of ground*) **to lie w.,** rester en friche; (*b*) **to lay w.,** dévaster, ravager, piller (un pays). **2.** (*a*) **w. products,** déchets *mpl*; **w. paper,** papier *m* de rebut; **waste-paper basket,** corbeille *f* à papier; **w. water,** (i) eaux ménagères; (ii) *Ind:* eaux résiduaires, usées; (*b*) *Ind:* (produit) non utilisé, perdu.
waste² *n.* **1.** région *f* inculte; désert *m*. **2.** gaspillage *m* (d'argent, d'efforts); **w. of time,** perte *f* de temps; **to run, go, to w.,** (i) (*of liquid*) se perdre, se gaspiller; (ii) (*of land, garden*) s'affricher; être envahi par de mauvaises herbes. **3.** (*a*) déperdition *f* (de force, d'énergie); (*b*) détérioration *f*, dépérissement *m* (de tissus); (*c*) *Ind:* freinte *f*. **4.** (*a*) déchets *mpl*; débris *mpl*; résidu(s) *m(pl)*; rebut *m*; *Min:* déblais *mpl*; *Atom.Ph:* **radioactive w.,** déchets, résidus, radioactifs; **w. disposal,** élimination *f*, destruction *f*, des déchets, des résidus; *Dom.Ec:* **w. disposal unit,** broyeur *m* à ordures; (*b*) *Hyd.E:* trop-plein *m*; **w. pipe,** tuyau *m* d'écoulement (du trop-plein); écoulement *m* (d'une baignoire).
waste³ **1.** *v.tr.* consumer, épuiser, faire dépérir (qn, le corps); **patient wasted by a disease,** malade miné par une maladie. **2.** *v.tr.* (*a*) gaspiller (les provisions, son argent); gâcher (du papier); dissiper, dilapider (une fortune); perdre, gaspiller (du temps); **nothing is wasted,** rien ne se perd; **I haven't any time to w. on him,** je n'ai pas de temps à perdre pour lui; **that would be wasted on me,** ce serait trop beau pour moi; **to w. one's life,** gâcher sa vie; **he's wasted in that job,** cet emploi est bien au-dessous de ses capacités; **to w. one's words,** (i) parler en pure perte; (ii) prêcher dans le désert; **you're wasting your energy,** vous vous dépensez inutilement; **the joke was wasted on him,** il n'a pas compris la plaisanterie; *Prov:* **w. not, want not,** qui épargne gagne; (*b*) perdre (une occasion). **3.** *v.i.* (*a*) se perdre; s'user, se consumer; s'épuiser; (*b*) (*of living being*) **to w. (away),** dépérir; s'affaiblir; maigrir; (*of limb*) s'atrophier. **wasted** *a.* **1.** (pays) dévasté, ravagé. **2.** (*a*) (malade, corps) affaibli, amaigri; (membre) atrophié. **3.** (argent) gaspillé; **w. life,** vie manquée; **w. time,** (i) temps perdu; (ii) (*in mechanical movement*) temps mort. **wasting** *n.* **1.** gaspillage *m* (de ses ressources, de son temps); dissipation *f*, dilapidation *f* (de sa fortune). **2.** **w. (away),** dépérissement *m*, amaigrissement *m* (du corps); atrophie *f* (d'un membre).
wastebin ['weistbin], *NAm:* **wastebasket** ['weistbɑːskit] *n.* corbeille *f* à papier.
wasteful ['weistful] *a.* gaspilleur, -euse; (dépense) en pure perte; **don't be so w. with the hot water!** ne gaspillez pas l'eau chaude! **-fully** *adv.* prodigalement, avec prodigalité; (dépenser) en pure perte.
wastefulness ['weistfulnis] *n.* prodigalité *f*; gaspillage *m.*
waster ['weistər] *n.* (*a*) gaspilleur, -euse; **time w.,** (i) personne qui perd son temps; (ii) travail, chose, qui vous fait perdre votre temps; (*b*) propre *m* à rien.
wastrel ['weistrəl] *n.* vaurien *m*; propre *m* à rien.
watch¹ [wɔtʃ] *n.* **1.** *A:* veille *f*; (*still so used in*) **in the watches of the night,** pendant les heures de veille. **2.** garde *f*; surveillance *f*; **to be on the w. for s.o.,** épier, guetter, qn; **to keep w.,** monter la garde; **to keep (a) good, close, w.,** faire bonne garde; **to keep a close w. on, over, s.o.,** surveiller qn de près; **to keep a w., on one's tongue,** (i) surveiller son langage; (ii) savoir se taire; **to set a w. on s.o.,** faire surveiller qn; **w. tower,** tour *f* d'observation, de guet; (*in prison camp*) mirador *m*. **3.** (*a*) *coll. Hist:* **the w.,** la garde, le guet; (*b*) *Adm:* **w. committee,** comité *m* qui veille au maintien de l'ordre de la commune. **4.** *Nau:* (*a*) quart *m*; **to be on w.,** être de quart; **to keep, come on, w.,** faire, prendre, le quart; **the officer of the w.,** l'officier *m* du quart; (*b*) (*men*) bordée *f*; **the port, starboard, w.,** la bordée de bâbord, de tribord. **5.** montre *f*; **it's six o'clock by my w.,** il est six heures à ma montre; **w. chain,** chaîne *f* de montre, de gilet; **w. spring,** ressort *m* de montre.
watch² **1.** *v.i.* (*a*) veiller; **I watched all night,** j'ai veillé jusqu'au jour; (*b*) garder (un troupeau); **to w. by a sick person,** veiller auprès d'un malade; (*c*) **to w. (out),** être aux aguets; être sur ses gardes; **w. out!** attention! prenez garde! **w. out for X!** gare à X! (*d*) **to w. (out) for s.o., sth.,** attendre qn, qch.; guetter qn, qch. **2.** *v.tr.* (*a*) veiller (un mort); garder, veiller sur (qn, qch.); (*b*) observer; regarder attentivement; *Prov:* **a watched pot never boils,** plus on désire une chose plus elle se fait attendre; **to w. s.o. closely,** surveiller qn de près; ne pas quitter qn des yeux; **to have s.o. watched,** faire surveiller qn; **we are being watched,** on nous observe; **to w. birds,** observer les oiseaux; (*c*) avoir l'œil sur (qch.); **we shall have to w. the expenses,** il nous faudra avoir l'œil sur la dépense; **w. the step!** attention à la marche! **w. your**

step! (i) prenez garde de tomber; (ii) allez-y discrètement; *F:* **w. it!** attention! (*d*) regarder (qn, qch.); **I watched her working,** je la regardais travailler; **to w. a football match,** assister à un match de football; **to w. the course of events, s.o.'s career,** suivre le cours des événements, la carrière de qn; *Jur:* **to w. a case,** veiller (en justice) aux intérêts de qn; (*e*) **to w. one's opportunity, one's time,** guetter l'occasion, le moment propice. **watching** *n.* **1.** veille *f*; veillée *f.* **2. bird w.,** observation *f* des oiseaux.

watchband ['wɔtʃbænd] *n.* bracelet *m* de montre.

watchdog ['wɔtʃdɔg] *n.* chien *m* de garde; *F:* **w. committee,** comité *m* qui veille à la dépense.

watcher ['wɔtʃər] *n.* **1.** veilleur, -euse (d'un mort, d'un malade). **2.** (*a*) observateur, -trice; **bird w.,** ornithologue *mf* amateur; (*b*) **to be a weight w.,** surveiller son poids.

watchful ['wɔtʃful] *a.* vigilant; alerte; attentif; **to be w.,** être ses gardes; **to keep a w. eye on, over, s.o.,** surveiller qn de près; **to be w. of s.o.,** observer, épier, qn d'un œil méfiant, d'un œil jaloux. **-fully** *adv.* avec vigilance; d'un œil attentif.

watchmaker ['wɔtʃmeikər] *n.* horloger *m.*

watchmaking ['wɔtʃmeikiŋ] *n.* horlogerie *f.*

watchman, *pl.* **-men** ['wɔtʃmən] *n.m.* gardien; *Nau:* homme de garde; **night w.,** gardien de nuit.

watchstrap ['wɔtʃstræp] *n.* bracelet *m* de montre.

watchword ['wɔtʃwəːd] *n.* mot *m* d'ordre.

water¹ ['wɔːtər] *n.* eau *f.* **1.** (*a*) **spring w.,** eau de source; **hard, soft, w.,** eau calcaire, douce; **sea w., salt w.,** eau de mer, eau salée; **fresh w.,** (i) (*newly drawn*) eau fraîche; (ii) (*not salt*) eau douce; **drinking w.,** eau potable; **w. carrier,** (i) porteur, -euse, d'eau; (ii) *Astr:* le Verseau; *F:* **to get into hot w.,** se mettre dans de mauvais draps; **to drink a glass of cold w.,** boire un verre d'eau fraîche; **to pour cold w. on a scheme,** jeter une douche froide sur un projet; **to put w. in one's wine,** couper son vin d'eau; *Prov:* **you can lead a horse to w. but you cannot make him drink,** on ne saurait faire boire un âne qui n'a pas soif; **my shoes let in w.,** mes chaussures prennent l'eau; **to take in w.,** (i) (*of ship*) embarquer son eau; faire de l'eau; (ii) (*of locomotive*) faire de l'eau; **w. repellent, resisting,** hydrofuge; imperméable; *Ch:* **w. soluble,** hydrosoluble; *Myth:* **w. sprite,** ondin, -ine; (*b*) **w. supply,** (i) arrivée *f* d'eau; (ii) service *m* des eaux; **w. pipe,** tuyau *m* d'eau; **w. main,** conduite *f* d'eau; **main(s) w.** = eau de la ville; **running w.,** eau courante; **w. heater,** chauffe-eau *m inv*; **w. closet,** water-closet *m*; toilettes *fpl*; **w. bed,** matelas *m* à eau; *Adm:* **w. rate,** taxe *f* d'abonnement à l'eau; **w. jug,** pot *m*, cruche *f*, broc *m* à eau; **w. bottle,** gourde *f*, bidon *m* (à eau); **hot w. bottle,** bouillotte *f*; *Cu:* **w. ice,** sorbet *m*; **w. biscuit,** *NAm:* **cracker,** petit biscuit croustillant; *Hyd.E:* **w. tower,** château *m* d'eau; (*c*) **w. mill,** moulin *m* à eau; *I.C.E:* **w.-cooled engine,** moteur *m* à refroidissement d'eau; (*e*) *Art:* **to paint in w. colours,** faire de l'aquarelle; (*painting*) **w. colour,** aquarelle *f*; (*paint*) **water colours,** couleurs *fpl* à eau; (*f*) *Sp:* **w. polo,** polo *m* nautique; water-polo *m*; **w. skiing,** ski *m* nautique; **to w. ski,** faire du ski nautique; *Rac:* **w. jump,** douve *f*, brook *m*. **2.** (*a*) **w. level,** niveau *m* piézométrique; **w. table,** niveau hydrostatique; (*b*) (*mineral springs*) **to take, drink, the waters,** prendre les eaux; faire une cure; (*c*) **the waters of the Danube,** les eaux du Danube; **on land and w.,** sur terre et sur mer; **on the other side of the w.,** de l'autre côté de l'Atlantique; **by water,** par eau; en bateau; (transporter des marchandises) par voie d'eau; **under w.,** (i) (*of land, roots*) submergé; inondé; (ii) (*of submarine*) en plongée; (iii) (nager) entre deux eaux; **above w.,** à flot; surnageant; **to keep (oneself), to keep one's head, above w.,** (i) se maintenir à la surface, sur l'eau; (ii) arriver à se subvenir; faire face à ses engagements; **deep w.,** eau profonde; (*of pers.*) **to get into deep water,** avoir de gros ennuis; (*d*) **high w.,** marée haute; hautes eaux; **low w.,** marée basse; eaux basses; (*e*) *Bot:* **w. lily,** nénuphar *m*; (*f*) *Orn:* **w. hen,** poule *f* d'eau; *Z:* **w. buffalo,** kérabau *m*; **w. rat,** rat *m* d'eau; campagnol nageur; *Ent:* **w. boatman,** notonecte *m or f*; *Moll:* **w. snail,** hélice *f* aquatique. **3.** (*a*) **toilet, lavender, w.,** eau de toilette, de lavande; (*b*) *Med:* **w. on the brain,** hydrocéphalie *f*; **w. on the knee,** hydarthrose *f* du genou; *Obst:* **breaking of the waters,** perte *f* des eaux; (*c*) (*saliva*) **it brings w. to one's mouth,** cela fait venir l'eau à la bouche; (*d*) **to pass w.,** uriner. **5.** transparence *f*, eau (d'un diamant); **diamond of the first w.,** diamant de première eau; *F: O:* **a liar of the first w.,** un menteur de premier ordre.

water² **1.** *v.tr.* (*a*) arroser (une plante, un jardin); (*b*) diluer, délayer (un liquide); **to w. one's wine,** couper son vin; (*c*) faire boire, donner à boire à, abreuver (des bêtes); (*d*) *Tex:* **watered silk,** soie moirée. **2.** *v.i.* (*a*) (*of eyes*) pleurer, larmoyer; **it makes one's mouth w.,** cela fait venir l'eau à la bouche; (*b*) (*of ship*) faire de l'eau; faire provision d'eau; (*c*) (*of animals*) aller à l'abreuvoir; s'abreuver. **water down** *v.tr.* diluer, délayer (un liquide); atténuer (une expression, une affirmation); **to w. down one's claims,** en rabattre; **a watered-down version of sth.,** une version édulcorée de qch. **watering** *n.* **1.** (*a*) arrosage *m* (d'une plante); **w. can,** arrosoir *m*; (*long spouted*) chantepleure *f*; (*b*) irrigation *f* (des champs). **2.** dilution *f* (d'un liquide). **3.** abreuvage *m* (des bêtes); **w. place,** (i) (*for cattle*) abreuvoir *m*; (ii) (*for ships*) aiguade *f*; (iii) ville *f* d'eau, station thermale; (iv) station balnéaire, plage *f*. **4.** *Tex:* moirage *m* (de la soie). **5.** (*of eyes*) larmoiement *m.*

waterborne ['wɔːtəbɔːn] *a.* (*a*) (*of vessel*) à flot, flottant; (*b*) (*of goods*) transporté par voie d'eau; (*c*) (*of disease*) d'origine hydrique.

waterbutt ['wɔːtəbʌt] *n.* tonneau *m* pour recueillir l'eau de pluie.

watercourse ['wɔːtəkɔːs] *n.* cours *m* d'eau.

watercress ['wɔːtəkres] *n.* *Bot:* cresson *m* de fontaine.

waterfall ['wɔːtəfɔːl] *n.* chute *f* d'eau; cascade *f.*

waterfowl ['wɔːtəfaul] *n.* (*a*) oiseau *m* aquatique; (*b*) *coll.* gibier *m* d'eau; sauvagine *f.*

waterfront ['wɔːtəfrʌnt] *n.* bord *m* de mer; bord de l'eau; les quais *mpl.*

waterglass ['wɔːtəglɑːs] *n.* *Com:* silicate *m* (i) de potasse, (ii) de soude; *F:* verre *m* soluble.

wateriness ['wɔːt(ə)rinis] *n.* insipidité *f*, fadeur *f* (d'un potage, de qch. cuit à l'eau).

waterline ['wɔːtəlain] *n.* (ligne *f* de) flottaison *f.*

waterlogged ['wɔːtəlɔgd] *a.* **1.** (*a*) (navire) plein d'eau, entre deux eaux; (*b*) (bois) alourdi par absorption d'eau. **2.** (terrain) détrempé, envahi par les eaux, imbibé d'eau; (sous-sol) aqueux.

Waterloo [wɔːtə'luː] *Pr.n.* **the Battle of W.,** la bataille de Waterloo; **to meet one's W.,** arriver au désastre.

watermark¹ ['wɔːtəmɑːk] *n.* **1.** *Nau:* laisse *f* (de haute, de basse, mer). **2.** *Paperm:* filigrane *m.*

watermark² *v.tr.* *Paperm:* filigraner.

waterpower ['wɔːtəpauər] *n.* énergie *f* hydraulique.

waterproof¹ ['wɔːtəpruːf] **1.** *a.* imperméable; (montre) étanche; **w. sheet,** bâche *f*. **2.** *n.* *Cost:* imperméable *m.*

waterproof² *v.tr.* imperméabiliser. **waterproofing** *n.* imperméabilisation *f.*

watershed ['wɔːtəʃed] *n.* **1.** *Geog:* (*a*) ligne *f* de partage des eaux; (*b*) *NAm:* bassin *m* hydrographique. **2.** *Fig:* point décisif; tournant *m*.

waterside ['wɔːtəsaid] *n.* bord *m* de l'eau; les quais *mpl*; **on the w.,** au bord de l'eau; sur la rive; **w. flowers,** fleurs du bord de l'eau; *U.S:* **w. workers,** dockers *mpl*.

waterspout ['wɔːtəspaut] *n.* **1.** tuyau *m*, descente *f* (d'eau). **2.** *Meteor:* trombe *f*.

watertight ['wɔːtətait] *a.* **1.** étanche (à l'eau); imperméable (à l'eau); (*of vessel*) **to be w.,** retenir l'eau; *Nau:* **w. bulkhead,** cloison étanche. **2.** (*of argument*) irréfutable; (*of regulation*) qui a prévu tous les cas.

waterway ['wɔːtəwei] *n.* voie navigable.

waterwheel ['wɔːtə(h)wiːl] *n.* roue *f* hydraulique.

waterworks ['wɔːtəwəːks] *n.pl.* (*a*) usine *f* de distribution d'eau; usine hydraulique; (*b*) *Med: F:* voies *fpl* urinaires; (*c*) *F:* **to turn on the w.,** se mettre à pleurer; ouvrir la fontaine.

watery ['wɔːtəri] *a.* (*a*) (terrain) humide; (*b*) aqueux; qui contient de l'eau; (*c*) noyé d'eau; **w. eyes,** yeux (i) larmoyants, (ii) mouillés de larmes; **w. soup,** potage trop clair; (*d*) (*of colour*) déteint; délavé; (*e*) (temps) pluvieux; (ciel) chargé de pluie; **w. moon,** lune entourée d'un halo; (*f*) *Lit:* **to find a w. grave,** être enseveli par les eaux.

watt [wɔt] *n. El.Meas.* watt *m*.

wattage ['wɔtidʒ] *n. El:* puissance *f*, consommation *f*, en watts.

wattle[1] ['wɔtl] *n.* **1.** clayonnage *m*; **w.-and-daub wall,** mur en clayonnage revêtu de boue, d'argile. **2.** *Austr: Bot:* (*a*) acacia *m*; (*b*) mimosa *m*.

wattle[2] *n.* caroncule *f* (d'un oiseau); barbillon *m* (d'un poisson).

wave[1] [weiv] *n.* **1.** (*a*) *Nau:* vague *f*, lame *f*; **crest, hollow, of a w.,** crête *f*, creux *m*, d'une vague; **bow w.,** lame d'étrave; (*b*) *Art:* **new w.,** nouvelle vague; (*c*) **w. of enthusiasm,** vague d'enthousiasme; **w. of anger,** bouffée *f* de colère; **a w. of bitterness swept over him,** un flot d'amertume l'envahit. **2.** (*a*) *Ph:* onde *f* (électrique, magnétique); **light w.,** onde lumineuse; *Av:* **shock w.,** onde de choc; (*b*) *W.Tel: Elcs:* **hertzian w.,** onde hertzienne; **long waves,** grandes ondes; **medium, short, waves,** ondes moyennes, courtes; **w. band,** gamme *f* d'ondes, plage *f* (d'ondes). **3.** (*a*) ondulation *f* (des cheveux); **to have a natural w. (in one's hair),** avoir les cheveux ondulés naturellement; (*b*) *Hairdr:* ondulation; **blow w.,** brushing *m*. **4.** (*a*) balancement *m*, ondoiement *m*; (*b*) geste *m*, signe *m* (de la main, du chapeau); **with a w. of his** hand, d'un geste, d'un signe, de la main.

wave[2] **1.** *v.i.* (*a*) s'agiter; (*of flag*) flotter (au vent); (*of corn, grass, plume*) ondoyer, onduler; (*b*) **to w. to s.o.,** (i) faire signe à qn (en agitant le bras, un mouchoir); (ii) saluer qn de la main; **I waved to him to stop,** je lui ai fait signe d'arrêter; (*c*) **my hair waves naturally,** mes cheveux ondulent naturellement. **2.** *v.tr.* (*a*) agiter (le bras, un mouchoir); brandir (un parapluie, une canne); **to w. one's hand,** faire signe de la main; **to w. one's arms about,** agiter les bras; (*b*) **to w. goodbye to s.o.,** agiter la main, son mouchoir, en signe d'adieu; **to w. s.o. aside, away,** écarter qn d'un geste; faire signe à qn de s'écarter; **he waved us on,** de la main il nous a fait signe de continuer; **he waved me back,** de la main il m'a fait signe de (i) revenir, (ii) reculer; **to w. aside an objection,** écarter une objection; (*c*) *Hairdr:* onduler (les cheveux); **to have one's hair waved,** se faire faire une mise en plis. **waving** *n.* **1.** (*a*) agitation *f* (d'un mouchoir); **w. of the hand,** geste *m*, mouvement *m*, de la main; (*b*) ondoiement *m*, ondulation *f* (du blé). **2.** *Hairdr:* ondulation (des cheveux).

wavelength ['weivleŋθ] *n. Ph:* longueur *f* d'onde; *F:* **we weren't on the same w.,** nous n'étions pas sur la même longueur d'onde.

waver ['weivər] *v.i.* vaciller. **1.** (*of flame*) trembloter. **2.** (*a*) hésiter, être indécis (entre deux opinions); (*of the voice*) se troubler; (*of courage*) défaillir; **to w. in one's resolution,** chanceler dans sa résolution; (*b*) *Mil:* (*of troops*) fléchir. **wavering** **1.** *a.* (*a*) (*of flame*) vacillant, tremblotant; (*b*) (homme, esprit) irrésolu, indécis, vacillant; (voix) défaillante; (courage) défaillant. **2.** *n.* (*a*) tremblement *m*, vacillement *m* (d'une flamme); (*b*) vacillation *f*, irrésolution *f* (de l'esprit); trouble *m* (de la voix); défaillance *f* (du courage).

waverer ['weivərər] *n.* indécis, -ise; irrésolu, -ue.

waviness ['weivinis] *n.* caractère onduleux, ondulé (d'une surface); ondulations naturelles (des cheveux).

wavy ['weivi] *a.* onduleux; ondulé; **w. line,** ligne tremblée; **w. hair,** chevelure ondoyante.

wax[1] [wæks] *n.* **1.** (*a*) cire *f*; **to mould s.o. like w.,** façonner, former (le caractère de) qn comme de la cire; *Ecc:* **w. taper,** cierge *m*; **w. doll,** poupée *f* de cire; (*b*) *Petr:* **(paraffin) w.,** cire (minérale), paraffine *f*; **w. paper,** papier paraffiné. **2.** (*a*) *Physiol:* **(ear) w.,** cérumen *m* (des oreilles); (*b*) **fossil, mineral, w.,** cire fossile; (*c*) *Ski:* fart *m*.

wax[2] *v.tr.* (*a*) cirer, encaustiquer (un plancher, un meuble); astiquer (un meuble); *Ski:* farter; (*b*) *Bootm:* empoisser (le fil). **waxed** *a.* (*a*) ciré; (parquet) frotté à la cire; (cuir) en cire; **w. moustache,** moustache cosmétiquée; (*b*) *Bootm:* (fil) poissé. **waxing** *n.* (*a*) cirage *m*; encaustiquage *m*; (*b*) empoissage *m* (du fil); (*c*) *Ski:* fartage *m*.

wax[3] *v.i.* **1.** (*of the moon*) croître; **to w. and wane,** croître et décroître. **2.** *esp. Lit:* devenir, se faire; **to w. eloquent in support of sth.,** déployer toute son éloquence en faveur de qch.; **he waxed indignant,** il s'indigna. **waxing** *n.* croissance *f* (de la lune).

waxen ['wæks(ə)n] *a.* (*a*) de cire, en cire; (*b*) cireux; (teint) de cire; **w. pallor,** pâleur cireuse.

waxwing ['wækswiŋ] *n. Orn:* jaseur *m*.

waxwork ['wækswəːk] *n.* (*a*) figure *f* de cire; (*b*) **waxworks,** (musée *m* de) figures de cire.

waxy ['wæksi] *a.* cireux; (teint) de cire.

way[1] [wei] *n.* **1.** chemin *m*, route *f*, voie *f*; **over, across, the w.,** de l'autre côté de la route, du chemin, de la rue; **the house, the people, over, across, the w.,** la maison, les gens, d'en face; *Rail:* **permanent w.,** voie ferrée; *U.S:* **w. train,** (train *m*) omnibus *m*; **w. station,** halte *f*. **2.** (*a*) (*route*) **the w. to the station,** le chemin qui mène, qui conduit, à la gare; le chemin de la gare; **to show s.o. the w.,** montrer la route à qn; **to ask one's w.,** demander son chemin; **to lose one's w.,** s'égarer, se perdre; **that's the w. to ruin,** c'est là le chemin de la ruine; **the right w.,** le bon chemin; la bonne route; **to go the wrong w.,** se tromper de chemin; faire fausse route; **to go the nearest, shortest, w.,** prendre par le plus court; **to know one's w. about (a house),** connaître les âtres; *F:* **he knows his w. about, around,** il sait se débrouiller; il est débrouillard; **to prepare the w.,** préparer les voies; **to start on one's w.,** se mettre en route; **on the w.,** chemin faisant; en chemin; en cours de route; **to stop on the w.,** s'arrêter en chemin; **to be on one's, the, w. to Paris,** être en route pour, sur la route de, Paris; **on my, the, w. home,** en revenant chez moi; en rentrant; **he's well on the w. to doing it,** il est en bonne voie de le faire; *F:* **there's a baby on the w.,** elle attend un bébé; **to go the w. of all things, of all flesh,** aller où va toute chose; mourir; **to go one's w.,** passer son chemin; **to go one's own w.,** (i) faire à sa guise; (ii) se désolidariser d'avec ses collègues; faire bande à part; **to go out of one's w.,** s'écarter de son chemin; dévier de sa route; faire un détour; **to go out of one's w. to oblige s.o.,** se déranger, se donner de la peine, pour être agréable à qn; **the village is rather out of the w.,** le village est un peu écarté; **that's nothing out of the w.,** rien d'extraordinaire à cela; *Ecc:* **the W. of the Cross,** le chemin de la Croix; (*b*) **w. in,** entrée *f*; **w. out,** sortie *f*; **w. through,** passage *m*; **to find a w. out, in,** trouver moyen de sortir, d'entrer; **to find a w. out of a deadlock,** trouver une issue à une impasse; **to leave s.o. a w. out,** laisser à qn le moyen de s'échapper, de sortir (d'une difficulté); **easy w. out,** solution *f* de facilité; (*c*) **to find one's w. to a place,** parvenir à un endroit; **can you find your w. out?** vous savez le chemin pour sortir? **however did it find its w. into print?** comment en est-on venu à l'imprimer? **to make one's w. towards a place, towards s.o.,** se diriger vers, se rendre dans, un endroit; **to make, work, push, one's w. through the crowd,** se frayer un chemin, s'ouvrir un chemin, à travers la foule; **he made his w. into the house,** il a pénétré dans la maison; **to make one's w. back,** retourner, revenir; **how to make one's w. (in the world),** le moyen de parvenir; **to work one's w. up,** (i) s'élever; (ii) s'élever à force de travail; **to pay one's w.,** se suffire; **firm that pays its w.,** entreprise qui fait, qui couvre, ses frais; **to see one's w. to doing sth.,** se croire à même de faire qch.; **couldn't you see your w. to doing it?** ne trouveriez-vous pas moyen de le faire? (*d*) **to stand in s.o.'s w.,** être dans le chemin de qn; barrer le passage à qn; **I don't wish to stand in the w. of your happiness,** je ne voudrais pas faire obstacle à votre bonheur; **to stand in the w. of a scheme,** s'opposer à un projet; **the obstacles that stand in our w.,** les obstacles qui se dressent sur notre chemin; **to put difficulties in s.o.'s w., in the w. of sth.,** opposer, créer, des difficultés à qn; apporter des difficultés à qch.; **to get in one another's w.,** se gêner (les uns les autres); **to be in s.o.'s w.,** gêner, embarrasser, qn; **this table is in the w.,** cette table nous gêne, est encombrante; **to get out of s.o.'s w.,** faire place à qn; céder le pas à qn; **to get out of the w.,** se ranger, s'effacer; s'ôter du chemin; s'écarter (pour laisser passer qn); **(get) out of the w.!** rangez-vous! ôtez-vous de là, de mon chemin! **to get s.o., sth., out of the w.,** se débarrasser de qn; écarter, éloigner, qn, qch.; **to keep out of the w.,** se tenir à l'écart; **to keep out of s.o.'s w.,** éviter qn; **to make w. for s.o.,** laisser passer qn; faire place à qn; (*e*) *Jur:* **right of w.,** servitude *f* de passage. **3.** (*distance*) **to go a little w., part of the w., with s.o.,** faire un bout de chemin avec qn; **all the w.,** tout le long du chemin; jusqu'au bout; **I flew most of the w.,** j'ai fait la plupart du voyage en avion; **I've come a long w.,** j'ai fait une longue traite; *F:* **he's come a long w.,** il a bien réussi (dans la vie); **it's a long w. to London, London's a long w. from here,** Londres est bien loin; **it's a long w. from Paris to Rome,** il y a loin de Paris à Rome; **to have a long w. to go,** avoir beaucoup de chemin à faire; **a little, short, w. off,** à peu de distance; pas trop loin; **it's only a short w. (off),** c'est assez proche; *Fig:* **he'll go a long w.,** il ira loin; **a little sympathy goes a long w.,** un peu de sympathie fait grand bien; **a little of it goes a long w.,** on en use très peu, il en faut très peu; **to make one's money go a long w.,** savoir ménager ses sous; **by a long w.,** de beaucoup; **not by a long w.,** il s'en faut de beaucoup; **you're a long w. out, out by a long w.,** vous êtes loin de compte; vous vous trompez de beaucoup. **4.** (*direction*) (*a*) côté *m*, direction *f*; **which w. is the wind blowing?** d'où vient, souffle, le vent? *F:* **so that's the w. the wind's blowing!** ça se passe donc comme ça! **this w., that w.,** de ce côté-ci, par ici; de ce côté-là, par là; **(step) this w.!** (venez, passez) par ici! **is this the way?** c'est par ici? **which w. did you come?** par où êtes-vous venu? **which w. did he go?** par où est-il passé? **which w. do we go?** de quel côté, par où, allons-nous? **this w. and that,** de-ci de-là; de tous (les) côtés; **he didn't know which w. to look,** il était tout décontenancé; **to look the other w.,** détourner les yeux; **I've nothing to say one w. or the other,** je n'ai rien à dire pour ou contre; **they set off, each going his own w.,** ils sont partis chacun de son côté; **I'm going your w.,** je vais de votre côté; **the next time you're that w.,** la prochaine fois que vous passerez par là; *F:* **down our w.,** chez nous; **he lives Hampstead w.,** il habite du côté de Hampstead; **if the chance comes your w.,** si vous en trouvez l'occasion; (*b*) sens *m*; **both ways,** dans les deux sens; **the wrong w.,** à contre-sens; **to brush sth. the wrong w.,** brosser qch. à rebours, à rebrousse-poil; **the wrong w., up,** sens dessus dessous; à l'envers; **to hold sth. (the) right w. up,** tenir qch. dans le bon sens; (*c*) voie (d'un robinet); **two-w. cock,** robinet à deux voies; (*d*) **to split a sum of money three ways,** partager une somme entre trois personnes. **5.** (*means*) moyen *m*; **to find a w. of doing sth.,** trouver (le) moyen de faire qch.; *Adm:* **ways and means,** voies et moyens; *Parl:* **Committee of Ways and Means** = Commission *f* du Budget. **6.** (*a*) façon *f*, manière *f*; **in this w.,** de cette façon; **in a friendly w.,** en ami; amicalement; **speaking in a general w.,** (parlant) d'une manière générale; **in such a w. as to . . .,** de façon à . . .; **in no w.,** en aucune facon; en rien; nullement; *esp. U.S: F:* **no w.!** jamais de la vie! **without in any w. wishing to criticize,** sans aucunement vouloir critiquer; **that's the w.!** ça y est! voilà! à la bonne heure! **in such and such a way,** de telle et telle façon; **to go, set, about it the right w.,** s'y prendre de la bonne manière, comme il faut; **you're going the right w. to make him angry,** ça c'est la meilleure manière de le mettre en colère; **the best w. is to say nothing,** le mieux est de ne rien dire; **in one w. or another,** de façon ou d'autre; d'une façon ou d'une autre; **there are no two ways about it,** il n'y a pas à discuter; **to go on in the same old w.,** aller toujours son train; **I don't like the w. things are going,** l'allure des affaires est assez inquiétante; **they'll never finish it the w. things are going,** ils n'en finiront jamais, au train où vont les choses; **w. of doing sth.,** manière, façon, de faire qch.; **w. of speaking, writing,** façon de parler, d'écrire; **our w. of living,** notre train *m*, genre *m*, de vie; **his w. of looking at things,** sa manière de voir; **it isn't what he says, it's the w. he says it,** ce n'est pas ce qu'il dit mais le ton dont il le dit; **to my w. of thinking,** selon moi; à mon sens; **that's not my w. (of doing things),** ce n'est pas ma manière de faire; **that's his w.,** c'est sa manière de faire; **that's always the w. with him,** il est toujours comme ça; **to do things in one's own w.,** faire les choses à sa guise, à sa façon, à sa manière; **to have a w. of one's own, one's own w., of doing sth.,** avoir une façon à soi de faire qch.; avoir sa méthode; **he's a genius in his w.,** c'est un génie dans son genre; **he does what he can for them in his small w.,** il les aide dans la mesure de ses moyens; **you'll soon get into our ways,** vous vous ferez bientôt à nos habitudes; **to get, fall, into the w. of doing sth.,** (i) prendre l'habitude de faire qch.; s'habituer à faire qch.; (ii) apprendre à faire qch.; **you'll get into the w. of it,** vous vous y ferez; **that's one w. of looking at it!** c'est une manière de voir; (*b*) **engaging ways,** petites façons engageantes; gentillesses *fpl*; **I know his little ways,** je connais ses petites manies; **he has a w. with children,** il sait prendre les enfants; (*c*) **to have one's (own) w.,** faire à sa tête; **to get one's (own) w.,** (en) faire à sa volonté; arriver à ses fins; **he wants his own w.,** il veut n'en faire qu'à sa tête; **if I had my w.,** si on me laissait faire; **have it your own w.,** (i) faites à votre guise; faites ce que vous voulez; (ii) soit; **he had it all his own w.,** il n'a pas rencontré de résistance; **you can't have it both ways,** on ne peut pas être et avoir été. **7.** (*respect*) **in many ways,** à bien des égards; **in some ways,** à certains points de vue; **in every w.,** sous tous les rapports, en tous points; **in one w.,** d'un certain point de vue; **you're right in a w.,** en un certain sens vous avez raison. **8.** cours *m*, course *f*; **I met him in the ordinary w. of business,** je l'ai rencontré dans le courant de mes affaires. **9.** (*a*) **the flood is making w.,** l'inondation fait des progrès; (*b*) *Nau:* erre *f*; **ship under w.,** navire en marche, en route; **to get under w.,** (i) *Nau:* appareiller; (ii) se mettre en route; (iii) (*of meeting*) commencer; **an important experiment is under w.,** une expérience importante est en cours. **10.** (*state, condition*) (*a*) (*of mind, body, estate*) **to be in a good, bad, w.,** être bien, mal, en point; **things seem in a bad w.,** les choses ont l'air d'aller mal; **his business is in a bad w.,** ses affaires vont mal, périclitent; **to be in a good w. of business,** faire de bonnes affaires; (*b*) **to be in a fair w. to . . .,** être en voie de, en (bonne) passe de (faire fortune, etc.); **to put s.o. in the w. of earning a few pounds,** mettre qn à même de gagner quelques livres. **11. to be in a small w. of business,** avoir un petit commerce; **to be in a large, big, way of business,** faire de grosses affaires; **to be doing quite well in a small w.,** aller (toujours) son chemin. **12.** (*a*) **by the way,** (i) chemin faisant; en route; (ii) incidemment; en passant; **(let it be said) by the w.,** soit dit en passant; **all this is by the w.,** tout ceci est par parenthèse; (iii) à (ce) propos; **by the w., did you see him yesterday?** à propos, l'avez-vous vu hier? **by the w.!** ah, j'y pense! (*b*) **by w. of,** (i) (*via*) par la voie de, par (un endroit); (ii) en guise de, a titre de; **by w. of introduction, of warning,** à titre d'introduction, d'avertissement; (iii) **what have you by w. of, in the w. of, fruit?** qu'est-ce que vous avez comme fruits? (iv) (*followed by gerund*) **he's by w. of being a socialist,** il se dit, il fait profession d'être, socialiste; (v) **he asked after her dog by w. of changing the conversation,** il a demandé des nouvelles de son chien, histoire de changer de sujet. **13.** *N.Arch:* **ways,** couettes *fpl*.

way² *adv. F:* **it was w. back in the twenties,** cela remonte aux années vingt; **w. down south,** là-bas dans le sud; **to be w. out,** (i) être original, excentrique, (ii) faire une grosse erreur; se tromper sérieusement.

waybill ['weibil] *n. Com:* feuille *f* de route; bulletin *m*, bordereau *m*, d'expédition.

wayfarer ['weifɛərər] *n.* voyageur, -euse (à pied).

wayfaring ['weifɛəriŋ] *n.* voyages *mpl* (à pied); **w. man,** voyageur *m* (à pied).

waylay [wei'lei] *v.tr.* (*p.t. & p.p.* **waylaid** [wei'leid]) **1.** attirer (qn) dans une embuscade; tendre un guet-apens à (qn); **to be waylaid,** tomber dans un guet-apens. **2.** arrêter (qn) au passage (pour lui parler).

wayside ['weisaid] *n.* bord *m* de la route; **to fall by the w.,** rester en chemin; **w. chapel, inn,** chapelle *f*, auberge *f*, au bord de la route; **w. flowers,** fleurs qui poussent en bordure de route.

wayward ['weiwəd] *a.* (*of pers.*) (*a*) volontaire, rebelle; entêté; (*b*) capricieux; **to be w.,** avoir des caprices.

waywardness ['weiwədnis] *n.* (*a*) entêtement *m*, caractère *m* volontaire; (*b*) caractère capricieux.

we [wi(:)] *pers. pron. nom. pl.* **1.** (*a*) (*unstressed*) nous; **we were playing,** nous jouions; **here we are!** nous voilà! **we both thank you,** nous vous remercions tous (les) deux; (*b*) (*stressed*) nous; **we are English, they are French,** nous, nous sommes anglais, eux sont français; **you don't think that we did it!** vous ne pensez pas que c'est nous qui l'avons fait? **we English,** nous autres Anglais; (*c*) (*indefinite*) on; nous; **as we say in England,** comme on dit en Angleterre; **we all make mistakes sometimes,** tout le monde se trompe parfois. **2.** (*plural of majesty, editorial* **we**) nous; **we are convinced that . . .,** nous sommes convaincu que . . ..

weak [wi:k] *a.* **1.** (*a*) faible; (*of health*) débile; (*of body*) infirme; **w. in body,** faible de corps; **to have a w. heart,** être cardiaque; **to have w. (eye-)sight,** avoir la vue faible; *F:* **I feel all w. at the knees,** j'ai les jambes en coton; **to grow w.,** s'affaiblir; **w. with hunger,** affaibli par la faim; **to feel as w. as a kitten,** se sentir mou, molle, comme une chiffe; *F:* **to be w. in the head,** être faible d'esprit; **the weaker sex,** le sexe faible; (*b*) (mémoire) faible. **2.** (*a*) (style) sans vigueur; (décision) qui dénote de la faiblesse; **in a w. moment,** dans un moment de faiblesse; (*b*) (*of pers.*) faible; inefficace; (*of argument*) faible, peu solide; **his w. side, spot,** son côté, son point, faible; (*c*) **the weaker pupils,** les élèves moins doués; **to be w. in French,** être faible en français; (*d*) *Mus:* **w. beat,** temps *m* faible. **3.** (*a*) (*of solution*) dilué, étendu; **w. tea,** thé (i) trop faible, (ii) léger; (*b*) *I.C.E:* **w. mixture,** mélange *m* pauvre. **4.** (*a*) *Gram:* (conjugaison) faible; (*b*) (syllable) non accentuée. **-ly** *adv.* (*a*) faiblement; sans force; (*b*) sans énergie.

weaken ['wi:k(ə)n] **1.** *v.tr.* affaiblir; amollir (l'esprit, le courage); appauvrir (la constitution de qn); **the floods have weakened the foundations of the house,** les inondations ont miné les fondations de la maison; *I.C.E:* **to w. the mixture,** appauvrir le mélange. **2.** *v.i.* s'affaiblir, faiblir, s'amollir; (*of sound*) fléchir; *I.C.E:* (*of mixture*) s'appauvrir; **his courage weakened,** son courage a fléchi, faibli; **the dollar has weakened,** le dollar a baissé. **weakening 1.** *a.* affaiblissant; faiblissant. **2.** *n.* affaiblissement *m*, amollissement *m*; fléchissement *m*; défaillance *f* (du courant, *Fin:* du dollar); *I.C.E:* appauvrissement *m* (du mélange).

weakhearted [wi:k'hɑ:tid] *a.* sans courage; mou, *f.* molle.

weak-kneed [wi:k'ni:d] *a.* (*a*) faible des genoux; (*b*) sans caractère; mou, *f.* molle.

weakling ['wi:kliŋ] *n.* (*a*) être *m* faible, débile; enfant chétif; (*b*) **he's a w.,** c'est un faible, un mou.

weakly ['wi:kli] *a.* (*of pers.*) débile, chétif.

weakminded [wi:k'maindid] *a.* (*a*) faible d'esprit; (*b*) irrésolu, indécis, qui manque de résolution.

weakness ['wi:knis] *n.* (*a*) faiblesse *f* (de corps, de caractère, d'un lien); débilité *f* (de corps); *I.C.E:* pauvreté *f* (du mélange); **the w. of his argument,** la faiblesse de son argument; (*b*) faible *m*; **to have a w. for sth., s.o.,** avoir un faible pour qch., qn.

weal¹ [wi:l] *n. A: & Lit:* bien *m*, bien-être *m*, bonheur *m*; **the common w.,** le bien commun.

weal² *n.* marque *f*, trace *f* (d'un coup de fouet).

wealth [welθ] *n.* **1.** richesse(s) *f(pl)*; opulence *f*; **he was a man of great w.,** il était très riche. **2.** abondance *f*, profusion *f* (de détails, etc.).

wealthy ['welθi] **1.** *a.* riche; opulent; **w. heiress,** grosse héritière. **2.** *n.* **the w.,** les riches *mpl*.

wean [wi:n] *v.tr.* (*a*) sevrer (un nourrisson); (*b*) **to w. s.o. (away) from a bad habit,** détacher, détourner, qn d'une mauvaise habitude. **weaning** *n.* sevrage *m*.

weapon ['wepən] *n.* arme *f*; **atomic, nuclear, weapons,** armes atomiques, nucléaires; **the carrying of weapons is illegal,** le port d'armes est prohibé.

weaponry ['wepənri] *n. coll.* armes *fpl*; armements *mpl*.

wear¹ [wɛər] *n.* **1.** (*a*) **men's, children's, w.,** vêtements *mpl* pour enfants; (*in department store*) **men's w. department,** rayon *m* hommes; **evening w.,** toilettes *fpl* de soirée; **for country w.,** pour la campagne; (*b*) (*of material*) **to stand hard w.,** être d'un bon usage; **these shoes still have some w. in them,** ces chaussures sont toujours portables. **2.** usure *f*; détérioration *f* (par usure); fatigue *f* (d'une machine); dégradation *f* (d'une route); **w. and tear,** usure; dépréciation *f*, détérioration; dégradation (d'un immeuble); **the cost of w. and tear,** les frais *mpl* d'entretien; *Jur:* **fair w. and tear,** usure naturelle, normale (du mobilier loué, etc.); **to be the worse for w.,** (*of garment*) être usé, défraîchi; (*of machine*) être abîmé, fatigué; *F:* (*of pers.*) (i) être épuisé; (ii) être amoché (après une bagarre; (iii) avoir la gueule de bois.

wear² *v.* (*p.t.* **wore** [wɔːr]; *p.p.* **worn** [wɔːn]) **1.** *v.tr.* porter (un vêtement); **she was wearing a blue dress,** elle portait une robe bleue; **blue is being worn,** le bleu se porte (beaucoup) actuellement; **to wear black,** porter du noir; **I've nothing (fit) to w.,** je n'ai rien à me mettre sur le dos, rien de mettable; **he was wearing his slippers,** il était en pantoufles; **to w. one's hair long,** porter les cheveux longs; **she wears her age well,** elle porte bien son âge; *F:* **I won't w. it,** je ne marche pas. **2.** *v.tr.* user; **to w. holes in sth.,** faire des trous à qch. (à force d'usage); **to w. oneself out,** s'éreinter (à force de travail); **worn with anxiety,** usé par les soucis; **to w. a surface flat,** araser une surface. **3.** (*with passive force*) (*a*) s'user; (*of garment*) **to w. into holes,** se trouer; (*of stone*) **to w. smooth,** se lisser par le frottement; (*of pers.*) **to be worn to a shadow,** ne plus être que l'ombre de soi-même; (*b*) **to w. well,** (i) (*of material*) être de bon usage; faire bon usage; (ii) (*of pers.*) bien porter son âge; **this coat has worn well,** ce manteau m'a bien servi; **it will w. for ever,** c'est inusable. **wear away 1.** *v.tr.* user, ronger; effacer. **2.** *v.i.* (*a*) s'user; s'effacer; (*b*) se consumer (de chagrin, d'inquiétude, etc.). **wear down 1.** *v.tr.* user; **to w. one's heels down,** user ses talons; **to w. down the enemy's resistance,** user à la longue, épuiser peu à peu, la résistance de l'ennemi; **to w. s.o. down,** briser la résistance à qn. **2.** *v.i.* s'user. **wearing 1.** *a.* fatigant, lassant; épuisant; **a very w. day,** une journée très fatigante. **2.** *n.* (*a*) **w. apparel,** vêtements *mpl*, habits *mpl*; (*b*) usure *f*; **w. surface,** surface *f* de frottement, d'usure; **w. quality,** résistance *f* à l'usure; durabilité *f*. **wear off** *v.i.* s'effacer; disparaître; (*of pain*) se calmer; **the novelty soon wore off,** la nouveauté a vite passé. **wear on** *v.i.* (*of time*) s'écouler (lentement); s'avancer; **as the evening wore on,** à mesure que la soirée s'avançait. **wear out 1.** *v.tr.* (*a*) user (ses vêtements, etc.); **to w. oneself out,** s'user; s'épuiser; se consumer; **to w. oneself out with work,** se tuer au travail, à travailler; (*b*) épuiser (la patience de qn); (*c*) *Lit:* **to w. out one's days in captivity,** passer le reste de ses jours dans la captivité. **2.** *v.i.* s'user; **this material will never w. out,** ce tissu ne s'use pas, est inusable. **worn** *a.* **1.** (*a*) **w. (out),** (vêtement) usé, fatigué, râpé; (*b*) (rocher) rongé par les intempéries; (*c*) usé, fatigué; (visage) marqué par les soucis; **travel-w.,** fatigué par le voyage; **w. features,** traits usés (par le chagrin, par l'âge, etc.); **I'm absolutely w. out!** je suis épuisé, éreinté! **2.** (*of idea, etc.*) **w. out,** rebattu, usé.

wearable ['wɛərəbl] *a.* (*of garment*) mettable.

wearer ['wɛərər] *n.* **clothes too heavy for the w.,** vêtements trop lourds pour celui, celle, qui les porte.

weariness ['wiərinis] *n.* **1.** fatigue *f*, lassitude *f*. **2.** dégoût *m*, ennui *m*.

wearisome ['wiəris(ə)m] *a.* fatigant, ennuyeux.

weary¹ ['wiəri] *a.* fatigué; las *f*, lasse; *F:* **a w. Willie,** un fainéant, un traîne-la-patte. **2.** las, dégoûté (**of,** de); **to be w. of life,** être dégoûté de la vie; **to grow w. of waiting,** se lasser d'attendre. **3.** fatigant, ennuyeux; **a w. day,** une journée fatigante; **it was a w. climb,** la montée était pénible. **-ily** *adv.* **1.** (répondre, regarder qn) d'un ton, d'un air, las, fatigué. **2.** (marcher, etc.) péniblement.

weary² *v.* (**wearied**) **1.** *v.i.* (*a*) se lasser, se fatiguer; *esp. Lit:* **to w. of (doing) sth.,** se lasser de (faire) qch.; **to w. of s.o.,** se fatiguer de la compagnie de qn; (*b*) trouver le temps long. **2.** *v.tr.* (*a*) lasser, fatiguer (qn); (*b*) **he wearies me with all his complaints,** je suis las de ses plaintes éternelles. **wearied** *a.* lassé; fatigué. **wearying** *a.* fatigant, ennuyeux; **I find it very w.,** cela me fatigue beaucoup.

weasel ['wiːz(ə)l] *n.* (*a*) *Z:* belette *f*; (*b*) *F:* fouine *f*.

weather¹ ['weðər] *n.* (*a*) temps *m* (qu'il fait); **in all weathers,** par tous les temps; **fine w.,** beau temps; **the w. is settled, we're in for a spell of fine w.,** le temps est au beau; **what's the w. like?** quel temps fait-il? **in spite of bad w.,** en dépit du mauvais temps; **in this, in such, w.,** par un temps pareil; **w. permitting,** si le temps le permet; (*b*) *Nau:* **heavy w.,** gros temps; (*of ship*) **to make heavy w.,** bourlinguer; (*of pers.*) **to make heavy w. (of sth.),** faire un tas d'histoires (pour faire qch.); avoir toutes les peines du monde (à faire qch.); (*c*) *F:* (*of pers.*) **to be under the w.,** être (i) indisposé, souffrant, (ii) déprimé; (*d*) **w. (situation), state of the w.,** état *m* du temps; **w. report, bulletin,** bulletin *m* météorologique; **w. forecast,** prévisions *fpl* météorologiques; **w. map, chart,** carte *f* météorologique; **w. station,** station *f* météorologique; **w. ship,** navire-météo *m*; (*e*) **w. side,** (i) côté exposé au vent; (ii) *Nau:* bord *m* du vent; *Fig:* **to keep one's w. eye open,** veiller au grain.

weather² **1.** *v.tr.* (*a*) (*usu. passive*) *Geol:* **weathered rocks,** roches désagrégées; (*b*) *Nau:* **to w. (out) a storm,** étaler, remonter, une tempête; *Fig:* **to w. the, a, storm,** se tirer d'affaire; *Pol:* se maintenir contre des attaques. **2.** *v.i.* (*a*) (*of rock*) se désagréger, s'altérer; (*b*) (*of copper, building*) prendre la patine; se patiner. **weathering** *n.* (*a*) désagrégation *f*, altération *f* (des roches); (*b*) patine *f*.

weatherbeaten ['weðəbiːtən] *a.* **1.** battu des vents; battu par la tempête. **2.** (*a*) (*of pers., face*) hâlé, basané; (*b*) (*of thg*) dégradé par le temps.

weatherboarding ['weðəbɔːdiŋ] *n.* *Const:* planches *fpl* à recouvrement.

weatherbound ['weðəbaund] *a.* retenu, arrêté, par le mauvais temps.

weathercock ['weðəkɔk] *n.* (*a*) girouette *f*; (*b*) *F:* (*pers.*) girouette; **to be a w.,** tourner, virer, à tous les vents.

weatherman, *pl.* **-men** ['weðəmæn, -men] *n.* *F:* météorologue *m*, météo *m*.

weatherproof¹ ['weðəpruːf] *a.* (*a*) à l'épreuve du gros temps; étanche; (*b*) qui résiste aux intempéries.

weatherproof² *v.tr.* protéger contre les intempéries.

weatherstrip ['weðəstrip] *n.* (*for door, window*) bourrelet *m* étanche; calfeutrage *m*.

weave¹ [wiːv] *n.* *Tex:* **1.** armure *f*; **plain w.,** armure toile. **2.** tissage *m*; texture *f*.

weave² *v.* (*p.t.* **wove** [wouv]; *p.p.* **woven** ['wouv(ə)n]) **1.** *v.tr.* (*a*) *Tex:* tisser; (*b*) *Lit:* **skilfully woven plot,** intrigue bien imaginée; **to w. a spell,** composer un charme; (*c*) tresser (une guirlande, un panier); entrelacer (des fils, des rameaux). **2.** *v.i.* (*a*) *Tex:* être tisserand, -ande (de métier); (*b*) **to w. through the traffic,** se frayer un chemin parmi les voitures; (*c*) *F:* **to get weaving,** s'y mettre; **get weaving!** vas-y! **weaving** *n* (*a*) *Tex:* (i) tissage *m*; (ii) (*trade*) tissanderie *f*; (*b*) entrelacement *m* (de rameaux, etc.).

weaver ['wiːvər] *n.* **1.** *Tex:* tisserand, -ande; tisseur, -euse. **2.** *Orn:* **w. (bird),** tisserin *m*.

web [web] *n.* **1.** tissu *m*; **w. of lies,** tissu de mensonges. **2. spider's w.,** toile *f* d'araignée. **3.** *Nat.Hist:* palmure *f* (d'un palmipède); **w.-footed, w.-toed,** palmipède; aux pieds palmés. **4.** *Paperm:* rouleau *m* (de papier).

webbed [webd] *a.* palmé; **w. foot,** pied palmé.

webbing ['webiŋ] *n.* **1.** sangles *fpl* (de chaise, de lit, etc.). **2.** toile *f* à sangles; ruban *m* à sangles.

wed [wed] *v.* (*p.t. & p.p.* **wedded,** *occ.* **wed;** *pr.p.* **wedding**) **1.** *v.tr.* (*a*) épouser (qn); se marier avec (qn); (*b*) (*of priest*) marier (un couple); (*of parent*) marier (sa fille); (*c*) unir (des qualités, etc.). **2.** *v.i.* se marier. **wedded** *a.* marié; **my (lawful) w. wife, husband,** mon épouse, époux, légitime; **w. life,** vie conjugale.

wedding ['wediŋ] *n.* mariage *m;* noce(s) *f(pl);* **church w.,** mariage religieux, à l'église; **w. day,** jour *m* de mariage; **silver, golden, diamond, w.,** noces d'argent, d'or, de diamants; **w. ring,** alliance *f;* **w. dress,** robe *f* de mariée; **the w. guests,** les invités (au mariage); **w. breakfast,** repas *m* de noces; **w. cake,** gâteau *m* de noces (en pièce montée); **w. present,** cadeau *m* de mariage, de noces; **w. card** = faire-part *m inv* de mariage; **w. night,** nuit *f* de noces; *Mus:* **w. march,** marche nuptiale.

we'd = (i) **we had,** *see* HAVE[2]; (ii) **we would,** *see* WILL[3].

wedge[1] [wedʒ] *n.* **1.** *Tchn:* (*a*) coin *m* (de serrage); cale *f* (de fixation); *Mec.E:* clavette *f,* clef; *Bootm:* **w. heeled shoes,** chaussures *fpl* à semelles compensées; (*b*) **splitting w.,** coin à fendre; **to drive in a w.,** enfoncer un coin; *Fig:* **it's the thin end of the w.,** c'est un premier empiétement; c'est un pied de pris. **2. w. of cake,** morceau *m* (triangulaire) de gâteau.

wedge[2] *v.tr.* **1.** *Tchn:* coincer; caler (des rails). **2. to w. (up),** caler (un meuble); **to w. a door open,** maintenir une porte ouverte avec une cale. **3. to w. sth. in sth.,** insérer, enfoncer, serrer, qch. dans qch.; **I was wedged in between two large women,** je me suis trouvé coincé entre deux grosses femmes. **4. to w. sth. apart, open,** fendre, forcer, qch. avec un coin.

wedge-shaped ['wedʒʃeipt] *a.* en (forme de) coin.

wedlock ['wedlɔk] *n.* (*a*) *Jur:* mariage *m;* **to be born out of w.,** être illégitime; (*b*) *Lit:* la vie conjugale.

Wednesday ['wenzdi] *n.* mercredi *m;* **on Wednesdays,** le mercredi; **every W.,** tous les mercredis; **Ash W.,** le mercredi des Cendres.

wee[1] [wi:] *a. F:* tout petit; minuscule; **a w. bit,** un tout petit peu; **a w. drop of whisky,** un doigt, une larme, de whisky.

wee[2] *n. & v.i. F:* = WEE(-)WEE[1,2].

weed[1] [wi:d] *n.* **1.** mauvaise herbe; **garden running to, overgrown with, weeds,** jardin envahi par les mauvaises herbes. **2.** *F:* (*a*) *O:* **the w.,** le tabac; (*b*) marijuana *f,* herbe *f.* **3.** *F:* personne étique, chétive.

weed[2] **1.** *v.tr.* (*a*) désherber (un jardin); arracher les mauvaises herbes de (l'allée); (*b*) **to w. out,** éliminer (les candidats faibles); **to w. out the bad (from the good),** éliminer, rejeter, ce qui est de mauvaise qualité. **2.** *v.i.* arracher, enlever, les mauvaises herbes. **weeding** *n.* désherbage *m;* sarclage *m.*

weedkiller ['wi:dkilər] *n.* herbicide *m;* désherbant *m.*

weeds [wi:dz] *n.pl. O:* **(widow's) weeds,** vêtements *mpl* de deuil (d'une veuve); deuil *m* de veuve.

weedy ['wi:di] *a.* **1.** couvert de mauvaises herbes. **2.** *F:* (*of pers.*) étique, chétif; à l'air malingre.

week [wi:k] *n.* **1.** (*a*) semaine *f;* **what day of the w. is it?** quel jour de la semaine sommes-nous? **next, last, w.,** la semaine prochaine, dernière; **w. in w. out,** toutes les semaines que Dieu nous envoie; **I haven't seen him for,** *esp. NAm:* **in, weeks,** je ne l'ai pas vu depuis des semaines; *Ecc:* **Holy W.,** la semaine sainte; (*b*) semaine, huit jours; **once, twice, a w.,** une fois, deux fois, par semaine; **every w.,** tous le huit jours; **within a w.,** sous huitaine; **a w. from now, today w., in a week's time,** (d')aujourd'hui en huit; dans une huitaine; **tomorrow w., Tuesday w.,** demain, mardi, en huit; **yesterday w.,** il y a eu hier huit jours; **in a w. or so,** dans une huitaine; **in six weeks' time,** dans six semaines; **a w. ago today,** il y a (aujourd'hui) huit jours; **I'm taking a week's holiday, a w. off,** je vais prendre huit jours de congé; *Ind: etc:* **forty hour w.,** semaine de quarante heures; **a week's wages,** le salaire hebdomadaire, de la semaine; *F:* la semaine; **to be paid by the w.,** être payé à la semaine. **2.** (*opposed to Sunday*) la semaine; **what I can't get done in the w. I do on Sundays,** ce que je n'arrive pas à faire en semaine je le fais le dimanche.

weekday ['wi:kdei] *n.* jour *m* ouvrable; jour de semaine; **on weekdays,** en semaine; **weekdays only,** (i) la semaine seulement; (ii) sauf samedi et dimanche.

weekend[1] [wi:k'end] *n.* fin *f* de semaine; week-end *m;* **to have one's weekends free,** être libre le week-end; **w. cottage,** résidence *f* secondaire (où on passe le week-end); *Rail:* **w. return,** aller (et) retour *m* valable du vendredi soir jusqu'au lundi.

weekend[2] *v.i.* passer le week-end, la fin de semaine.

weekender [wi:k'endər] *n.* **they're weekenders,** ils viennent, vont, y passer le week-end.

weekly ['wi:kli] **1.** *a.* (*a*) (salaire) de la semaine; (revue, visite, paiement) hebdomadaire; (*b*) (locataire) à la semaine; *Sch:* **w. boarder** = demi-pensionnaire *mf.* **2.** *n.* (journal *m,* revue *f*) hebdomadaire (*m*). **3.** *adv.* par semaine; tous les huit jours; **twice w.,** deux fois par semaine; **to be paid w.,** être payé à la semaine.

weeny ['wi:ni] *a. F:* minuscule.

weep[1] [wi:p] *n.* **to have a good w.,** pleurer à chaudes larmes; pleurer tout son content, son soûl; **to have a little w.,** verser quelques larmes.

weep[2] (*p.t. & p.p.* **wept** [wept]) **1.** *v.i.* (*a*) pleurer; **to w. bitterly,** pleurer amèrement; pleurer à chaudes larmes; **to w. for joy,** pleurer de joie; **to w. for s.o.,** (i) pleurer (la mort de) qn; (ii) pleurer sur les malheurs de qn; **to w. for one's lost youth,** pleurer sa jeunesse perdue; **it's enough to make you w.,** c'est à faire pleurer; **I could have wept to see it,** je gémissais de le voir; (*b*) (*of wall, rock*) suinter, suer; (*of tree*) pleurer; (*of sore*) couler, exsuder; **the smoke was making my eyes w.,** la fumée m'a fait venir les larmes aux yeux. **2.** *v.tr.* **to w. tears of joy,** pleurer de joie; **to w. one's heart, one's eyes, out,** pleurer à chaudes larmes. **weeping** **1.** *a.* (*a*) (enfant) qui pleure; (*b*) (*of rock*) suintant, humide; *Med:* (eczéma) humide; (*c*) *Bot:* **w. willow,** saule pleureur. **2.** *n.* (*a*) pleurs *mpl,* larmes *fpl;* **a fit of w.,** une crise de larmes; (*b*) suintement *m* (d'un mur); exsudation *f.*

weepy ['wi:pi] *a. F:* (*a*) larmoyant; (yeux) mouillés de larmes; (*b*) **to feel w.,** se sentir une envie de pleurer.

weever ['wi:vər] *n. Ich:* vive *f.*

weevil ['wi:v(i)l] *n. Ent:* charançon *m.*

wee(-)wee[1] ['wi:wi:] *n. F:* (*child's word*) pipi *m.*

wee(-)wee[2] *v.i. F:* faire pipi.

weft [weft] *n. Tex:* (*a*) trame *f;* (*b*) **w. (yarn),** fil *m* de trame.

weigh [wei] **1.** *v.tr.* (*a*) peser (un paquet); faire la pesée de (qch.); **to w. sth. in one's hand,** soupeser qch.; **to w. oneself,** se peser; (*b*) peser, mesurer, ménager (ses paroles); **to w. sth. in one's mind,** considérer qch.; **to w. the consequences (of sth.),** calculer les conséquences (de qch.); **to w. the pros and (the) cons,** peser le pour et le contre; **to w. one thing against another,** mettre deux choses en balance; (*c*) *Nau:* **to w. anchor,** lever l'ancre; appareiller. **2.** *v.i.* (*a*) peser, avoir du poids; **to w. heavy, light,** peser lourd, peu; **it weighs two kilos,** ça pèse deux kilos; (*b*) **it's weighing on my mind,** cela me trouble, me tracasse; (*c*) **that doesn't w. with me,** je ne fais pas grand cas de cela. **weigh down** *v.tr.* (*a*) faire pencher (la balance); (*b*) surcharger; appesantir; **branch weighed down with fruit,** branche surchargée de fruits; **weighed down by heavy responsibilities,** accablé de grosses responsabilités. **weigh in** *v.i.* (*a*) (*of jockey, boxer*) se faire peser avant la course, le match; (*b*) *F:* (*of pers.*) arriver, s'amener; **to w. in (with an argument),** intervenir avec un argument. **weighing** *n.* **1.** (*a*) pesée *f* (de qch.); **w. machine,** machine *f* à peser; (*b*) **w. in,** pesage *m* (d'un jockey, d'un boxeur); **w.-in room,** le pesage. **2.** *Nau:* levage *m* (de l'ancre); appareillage *m.* **weigh out.** **1.** *v.tr.* peser en petites quantités. **2.** *v.i.* (*of jockey*) se faire peser avant la course. **weigh up** *v.tr.* **to w. up the situation,** peser la situation; **to w. s.o. up,** estimer (i) la valeur, (ii) les intentions, de qn.

weighbridge ['weibridʒ] *n.* pont-bascule *m, pl.* ponts-bascules; poids public.

weigh-in ['weiin] *n. Box: Turf:* pesée *f.*

weight¹ [weit] *n.* **1.** (*a*) poids *m*; **to try, feel, the w. of sth.,** soupeser qch.; **to sell by w.,** vendre au poids; **to give good w., short w.,** faire bon poids, faux poids; **it's ten pounds in w.,** cela pèse dix livres; **it's worth its w. in gold,** cela vaut son pesant d'or; **what a w.!** que ça pèse lourd! que c'est lourd! (*of pers.*) **to lose w.,** perdre du poids; **to gain, put on, w.,** prendre du poids; **to watch one's w.,** surveiller son poids; **to have a w. problem,** peser trop; *Fig:* **to pull one's w.,** y mettre du sien; *Turf:* **to carry w.,** être handicapé; (*b*) *Tchn:* poids; pesanteur *f; Ph: Ch:* **atomic, molecular, w.,** poids atomique, moléculaire; **dead w.,** poids utile (d'un véhicule). **2.** (*a*) poids (en cuivre); **set of weights,** série *f* de poids; **weights and measures,** poids et mesures *fpl*; (*b*) (*corps lourd*) poids (d'une horloge); olive *f* (de plomb); gueuse *f* (d'athlétisme); *Fish:* lest *m* (d'un filet); **weights and dumb bells,** poids et haltères *mpl*; **w. lifting,** haltérophilie *f*; **w. lifter,** haltérophile *mf*; **to do w. training,** faire des haltères. **3.** charge *f*; **this pillar bears the w. of the whole building,** cette colonne soutient tout le bâtiment; **to give way under the w. of sth.,** fléchir sous le poids de qch.; **he feels the w. of his responsibilities,** sa responsabilité lui pèse; **that takes a w. off my mind,** cela me soulage; *F:* **I'm going to take the w. off my feet for a bit,** je vais m'asseoir, me reposer, un peu. **4.** force *f* (d'un coup); **blow with no w. behind it,** coup sans force. **5.** importance *f*; **to give w. to an argument,** donner du poids à un argument; **what he says carries w.,** sa parole a du poids, de l'autorité; **he doesn't carry much w. with the committee,** il n'a pas beaucoup d'influence auprès du comité; **the w. of the evidence was against him,** les témoignages pesaient contre lui; *F:* **to throw one's w. about,** faire l'important.

weight² *v.tr.* **1** (*a*) attacher un poids à (qch.); lester, plomber (un filet, un corde); plomber (une canne); (*b*) **to w. sth. down,** retenir, maintenir, qch. avec un poids; (*c*) *Fig:* **the circumstances are weighted in his favour,** les circonstances lui sont favorables. **weighted** *a.* (*a*) chargé d'un poids; lesté; (*of walking stick*) plombé; (*b*) *Stat:* (*of average, index*) pondéré. **weighting** *n.* (*a*) lestage *m*, plombage *m* (d'un filet); plombage (d'une canne); (*b*) *Stat:* pondération *f*; *Adm:* **London w.,** indemnité *f* de résidence pour Londres.

weightless ['weitlis] *a.* (*a*) qui pèse presque rien; (*b*) *Space:* **w. conditions,** état *m* d'apesanteur.

weightlessness ['weitlisnis] *n.* (*a*) absence *f* de poids; (*b*) *Space:* apesanteur *f.*

weighty ['weiti] *a.* **1.** pesant, (très) lourd. **2.** (*a*) (motif) grave, important, sérieux; (raisonnement) puissant, d'un grand poids; (*b*) (*occ. of pers.*) qui exerce une grande influence. **-ily** *adv.* **1.** pesamment. **2.** (raisonner) puissamment, avec force.

weir [wiər] *n.* **1.** barrage *m* (dans un cours d'eau); **w. keeper,** barragiste *m.* **2.** déversoir *m* (d'un étang).

weird ['wiəd] *a.* (*a*) mystérieux; d'une étrangeté inquiétante; (*b*) étrange, bizarre. **-ly** *adv.* (*a*) mystérieusement, étrangement inquiétante; (*b*) étrangement.

weirdie ['wiədi] *n. F:* excentrique *mf*; drôle d'oiseau.

weirdness ['wiədnis] *n.* (*a*) étrangeté inquiétante, mystérieuse (d'un spectacle, etc.); (*b*) caractère *m* étrange, bizarre (de qn, des vêtements).

weirdo, weirdy ['wiədou, -di] *n. F:* = WEIRDIE.

welcome¹ ['welkəm] *a.* **1.** (*a*) bienvenu; **to make s.o. w.,** faire bon accueil à qn; **you're always w.,** vous êtes toujours le bienvenu; (*b*) *as int.* **w.!** soyez le bienvenu, la bienvenue, (chez nous)! **w. to England!** soyez le(s) bienvenu(s) en Angleterre! **2.** (*of thg*) bienvenu; agréable; **this is w. news,** nous nous réjouissons de cette nouvelle; **this cheque is most w.,** ce chèque est très acceptable, tombe à merveille. **3.** **you're w. to borrow any of my books,** ma bibliothèque est à votre disposition; **you're w. to it,** (i) c'est à votre service, à votre disposition; (ii) *Iron:* je ne vous l'envie pas; grand bien vous fasse! **you're w. to try,** libre à vous d'essayer; *esp. NAm:* (*on being thanked*) **you're w.!** je vous en prie!

welcome² *n.* (*a*) bienvenue *f*; **to outstay, overstay, one's w.,** lasser l'amabilité de ses hôtes; s'incruster; (*b*) accueil *m*; **to give s.o. a hearty w.,** faire bon accueil à qn; **he gave us a very poor, cold, w.,** il nous a reçus froidement; *NAm:* **w. mat,** paillasson *m;* **to put out the w. mat for s.o.,** accueillir qn à bras ouverts.

welcome³ *v.tr.* **1.** (*a*) souhaiter la bienvenue à (qn); faire bon accueil à (qn); bien accueillir (qn); (*b*) accueillir, recevoir, avec plaisir; **to w. the, an, opportunity to do sth.,** se réjouir de, saluer, l'occasion de faire qch.; **his efforts weren't welcomed,** ses efforts ont reçu peu d'encouragement. **2.** accueillir; **to w. s.o. warmly,** faire un accueil chaleureux à qn. **welcoming** *a.* (sourire, etc.) accueillant.

weld¹ [weld] *n.* soudure *f*; ligne *f* de soudure.

weld² *Metalw:* **1.** *v.tr.* (*a*) souder (deux pièces); unir (deux pièces) à chaud; (*b*) *Fig:* **to w. (together),** unir, joindre, étroitement. **2.** *v.i.* (*of metals*) se souder. **welding** *n. Metalw:* **1.** (*process*) soudure *f*, soudage *m*; **arc w.,** soudure à l'arc; **w. torch,** chalumeau soudeur. **2.** (ligne *f* de) soudure.

welder ['weldər] *n.* **1.** (*pers.*) soudeur *m.* **2.** soudeuse *f*; machine *f* à souder.

welfare ['welfɛər] *n.* bien-être *m*; bonheur *m*; **to have s.o.'s w. at heart,** avoir à cœur le bonheur, le bien-être, de qn; **public w.,** bien-être et santé publics; **social w.,** sécurité sociale; **child w.,** protection *f* de l'enfance; puériculture sociale; **w. work,** = assistance sociale; **w. centre** = centre d'assistance sociale; **w. worker** = assistant(e) social(e); **the W. State,** l'État *m* providence.

well¹ [wel] *n.* **1.** (*a*) *A: & Lit:* source *f*, fontaine *f*; (*b*) **hot w.,** source chaude (d'eau minérale). **2.** puits *m*; **artesian w.,** puits artésien; **w. water,** eau *f* de puits; *Petr:* **oil w.,** puits de pétrole; **to drive, sink, a w.,** forer, creuser, un puits. **3.** (*a*) (*shaft*) puits, cage *f* (d'un ascenseur); cage, jour *m* (d'un escalier); (*b*) *Mec.E: etc:* fond *m* de carter, etc. (formant réservoir d'huile); vivier *m*, réservoir *m* (d'un bateau de pêche); *Av:* **landing gear w.,** compartiment *m* de logement de train; *Cu:* **make a w. in the flour,** faire un fontaine dans la farine.

well² *v.i.* (*of water, spring*) **to w. up, out,** jaillir; *Lit:*

sourdre; **tears were welling from her eyes,** des larmes jaillissaient de ses yeux.

well[3] **I.** *adv.* (*comp.* **better,** *sup.* **best,** *q.v.*) **1.** (*a*) **to work w.,** bien travailler; **to do as w. as one can,** faire de son mieux; **this boy will do w.,** ce garçon ira loin; **w. done!** bravo! très bien! **w. played!** bien joué! *F:* **to do oneself w.,** bien se soigner; bien manger (et bien boire); **it wouldn't look w. if we refused,** si on refusait cela ferait mauvaise impression; **you would do w. to be quiet (about it),** vous feriez bien, le mieux serait, de vous taire; **I know him w.,** je le connais bien; **I know only too w. what patience it needs,** je ne sais que trop quelle patience cela exige; **I can't very w. do it,** il ne m'est guère possible de le faire; **he accepted, as w. he might,** il a accepté et rien d'étonnant; **one might as w. say that black is white,** autant dire que blanc est noir; **you might (just) as w. stay,** (i) autant vaut rester; (ii) vous n'êtes pas de trop; **very w.!** (très) bien! entendu! (*b*) **everyone speaks w. of him,** tout le monde parle bien, dit du bien, de lui; **to do w. by s.o.,** se montrer généreux envers qn; **she deserves w. of you,** elle mérite bien votre reconnaissance; **he meant it w.,** il l'a fait, l'a dit, à bonne intention; (*c*) **you're w. out of it,** soyez heureux d'en être quitte; **the fete went off w.,** la fête s'est bien passée; *O:* **w. met!** heureuse rencontre! vous arrivez bien à propos! **2.** (*intensive*) **it's w. worth trying,** cela vaut bien la peine d'essayer, *F:* ça vaut le coup; **it's w. after six!** il est six heures bien sonnées; **he's w. over fifty,** il a largement dépassé la cinquantaine; **to be w. up in a subject,** connaître un sujet à fond; bien posséder un sujet. **3. pretty w. all,** presque tout; **it's pretty w. finished,** c'est presque, pratiquement, terminé; *F:* **it serves him damn w., jolly w., right!** il l'a bien cherché, mérité! **4.** (*a*) **as w.,** aussi; **take me as w.,** emmenez-moi aussi; **I need some as w.,** il m'en faut également; (*b*) **as w. as,** de même que; comme; ainsi que; **by day as w. as by night,** de jour comme de nuit; le jour comme la nuit. **5.** (*a*) (*introducing remark*) **w., as I was telling you,** eh bien, donc, comme je vous disais; **w., who was it?** eh bien, qui était-ce? **w., here we are (at last)!** enfin nous voilà! **you told him?—w., I'm afraid I didn't,** vous le lui avez dit?—eh bien, non! (*b*) (*exclamatory*) ça alors! pas possible! **(oh) w.! (ah) w.!** (i) eh bien! (ii) (*expressing resignation*) tant pis! **w., w.!** (i) (eh bien,) que voulez-vous! (ii) (*expressing incredulity*) vrai de vrai? **w., that's life!** enfin, quoi! c'est la vie! (*c*) **w. then,** eh bien, alors; **w. then, why worry about it?** eh bien alors, pourquoi se faire du mauvais sang? **6.** (*used as comb. fm. with participles to give a virtual adj.; a hyphen is incorrect if the adj. is predicative, and permissible but not obligatory if it precedes the noun*) **w. advised,** sage, prudent, judicieux; **w. balanced,** bien équilibré; (*of pers.*) posé; **w. behaved,** (i) (*of child*) bien élevé, sage; (ii) (*of animal*) bien dressé; **w. built,** bien construit; bien bâti; solide; **w. chosen,** bien choisi; **w. disposed,** (i) (*of pers.*) bien disposé (envers); (ii) (*of thgs*) bien arrangé, bien disposé; **w. educated,** instruit; cultivé; **w. fed,** bien nourri; **w. informed,** bien renseigné; instruit; (*of pers., mind*) averti; **to be w. informed on a subject,** bien connaître un sujet; connaître un sujet à fond; **w. intentioned,** bien intentionné; **w. kept,** (*of garden*) bien (entre)tenu; soigné; (*of hands*) soigné; (*of secret*) bien gardé; **w. known,** (bien) connu; célèbre; (*of expert*) réputé; **it is w. known that . . .,** tout le monde sait que . . .; **w. made,** bien fait, bien fini; de fabrication soignée; (*of garment*) de coupe soignée; **w. mannered,** poli, bien élevé; qui a du savoir-vivre; **w. matched,** bien assorti; (*of teams*) de force égale; **w. meaning,** bien intentionné; **w. meant,** fait avec une bonne intention, avec les meilleures intentions; **w. off,** *F:* **w. lined,** *esp. NAm: F:* **w. fixed, w. heeled,** *Austr: F:* **w. in,** riche; prospère; **to be very w. off,** avoir de la fortune, *F:* avoir de quoi; **you don't know when you're well off,** vous ne connaissez pas votre bonheur; **w. oiled,** (i) (*of machinery*) bien graissé; (ii) *F:* (*of pers.*) ivre; **w. paid,** bien payé, bien rétribué; **w. preserved,** bien conservé; (*pers.*) **w. read,** instruit, qui a de la culture; **w. spent,** (*of money, time*) bien utilisé; bien employé; (*of money*) dépensé avantageusement; **w. spoken,** qui parle bien, qui a un accent cultivé; **w. stocked,** bien approvisionné; (*of shop*) bien achalandé; **w. timed,** opportun, bien calculé; **w. worn,** (i) (*of garment*) usé; fortement usagé; (*of book*) qui a beaucoup servi; (*of argument*) rebattu; usé jusqu'à la corde. **II.** *a.* **(better; best) 1.** (*in good health*) **to be w.,** être bien portant, en bonne santé; se porter, aller, bien; **how are you?—very w., thank you,** comment allez-vous?—très bien, merci; **I don't feel w.,** je ne me sens pas bien; **he's not very w.,** il est indisposé, souffrant; **to get w.,** guérir; se rétablir; se remettre; *esp. U.S:* **he's not a w. man,** il ne se porte pas bien; il n'a pas de santé. **2.** (*a*) (*advisable*) **it is w. to . . .,** il est opportun de . . .; **it would be w. to . . .,** il serait bon, utile, recommandable, de . . .; **it would be just as w. if you were present,** il y aurait avantage à ce que vous soyez présent; **it might be as w. to . . .,** peut-être conviendrait-il de . . .; il serait peut-être bon de . . .; (*b*) (*lucky*) **it was w. for him that nobody saw him,** heureusement pour lui personne ne l'a vu; (*c*) (*satisfactory*) **all's w. that ends w.,** tout est bien qui finit bien; **all's w.!** tout va bien! (*d*) **that's all very w., but . . .,** tout cela est bel et bon, c'est bon à dire, mais . . .; **it is all very w. for you to say that . . .,** libre à vous, permis à vous, de dire que . . .; **w. and good!** soit! bon! **that's all very w. and good, but . . .,** tout ça c'est très bien, mais . . . . **III.** *n.* **1.** *pl.* **the w. and the sick,** les bien portants et les malades. **2. to wish s.o. w.,** vouloir du bien à qn; être bien disposé envers qn.

we'll = (i) **we shall,** *see* SHALL; (ii) **we will,** *see* WILL[3].

wellbeing ['welbiiŋ] *n.* bien-être *m;* **physical and moral w.,** santé physique et morale.

wellbred [wel'bred] *a.* (*of pers.*) (i) bien élevé; (ii) de bonne famille.

welldigger ['weldigər] *n.* puisatier *m.*

wellies ['weliz] *n.pl. F:* bottes *fpl* en caoutchouc.

wellington ['weliŋtən] *n.* **wellingtons, w. boots,** bottes *fpl* en caoutchouc.

wellnigh ['welnai] *adv. Lit:* presque.

well-to-do [weltə'du:] *a.* aisé, riche; cossu; *n.pl.* **the w.-to-do,** les riches, les fortunés.

wellwisher ['welwiʃər] *n.* partisan, -ane (d'une cause, etc.); **surrounded by wellwishers,** entouré d'admirateurs.

Welsh[1] [welʃ] **1.** *a.* gallois; du pays de Galles; *Furn:* **W. dresser,** vaisselier *m.* **2.** *n.* (*a*) *pl.* **the W.,** les Gallois *mpl*; (*b*) *Ling:* gallois *m.*

welsh[2] *v.tr. & i.* filer, décamper, sans payer; lever le pied; **to w. on s.o.,** manquer à une obligation à qn.

Welshman, -woman, *pl.* **-men, -women** ['welʃmən, -wumən, -mən, -wimin] *n.* Gallois, -oise.

welt [welt] *n.* **1.** *Bootm:* trépointe *f* (de semelle). **2.** marque *f*, trace *f* (d'un coup); vergeture *f.*

welter[1] ['weltər] *n.* (*a*) confusion *f*, désordre *m*; (*b*) masse confuse, fouillis *m* (de choses disparates).

welter[2] *v.i. esp. Lit:* se vautrer, se rouler (dans la boue); nager, baigner dans (le sang.)

welterweight ['weltəweit] *n. Box:* (*pers.*) poids mi-moyen; welter *m.*

wen [wen] *n. Med:* kyste sébacé; *F:* loupe *f.*

wench[1] [wen(t)ʃ] *n.f.* (*a*) *F: & Hum:* (jeune) fille, jeune femme; **great strapping w.,** grande gaillarde;

(*b*) *A:* **(serving) w.,** serveuse (dans une auberge); **kitchen w.,** fille de cuisine.
wench² *v.i. F:* **to go wenching,** courir le jupon.
wend [wend] *v.tr. Lit:* **to w. one's way,** porter, diriger, ses pas se diriger, s'acheminer (**to,** vers); **to w. one's way homeward,** s'acheminer vers sa maison.
went *see* GO².
wept *see* WEEP²
were *see* BE.
we're = **we are,** *see* BE.
weren't = **were not,** *see* BE.
werewolf, *pl.* **-wolves** ['wiəwulf, -wulvz; 'wəː-] *n. Myth:* loup-garou *m, pl.* loups-garous.
Wesleyan ['wesliən] *a. & n.* wesleyen, -enne.
west [west] **1.** *n.* (*a*) ouest *m*, occident *m*; **house facing (the) w.,** maison exposée à l'ouest; **on the w., to the w.,** à l'ouest (**of,** de); (*b*) **the W.,** l'Occident; (*c*) *U.S:* **the W.,** les États occidentaux (des États-Unis); **the Far W.,** le Far-West; **the Mid(dle) W.,** les États de la Prairie. **2.** *adv.* (*a*) à l'ouest, à l'occident; **to travel w.,** voyager vers l'ouest; (*b*) **to go w.,** (i) partir pour l'ouest; (ii) *F:* mourir; casser sa pipe; *Mill:* passer l'arme à gauche; **there's another plate gone w.!** encore une assiette de cassée! **3.** *a.* (*a*) ouest *inv.*; (vent) d'ouest; (mur) qui fait face, qui est exposé, à l'ouest; **the W. Country,** le sud-ouest de l'Angleterre; **the W. End,** le quartier du centre-ouest de Londres; *U.S:* **the W. Side,** les quartiers ouest de New York; (*b*) (*in Pr.n. Geog:*) **W. Africa,** l'Afrique occidentale; **W. Berlin,** Berlin Ouest; **W. Germany,** l'Allemagne de l'Ouest; **W. German,** *a. & n. F:* ouest-allemand, -ande; **the W. Indies,** les Antilles *fpl*; **W. Indian,** (i) *a.* des Antilles; antillais; (ii) *n.* Antillais, -aise.
westbound ['wes(t)baund] *a.* allant vers l'ouest; (*on underground*) en direction de la banlieue ouest.
westerly ['westəli] **1.** *a.* (vent) d'ouest, qui vient de l'ouest; (courant) qui se dirige vers l'ouest; **w. point,** point situé à, vers, l'ouest. **2.** *adv.* vers l'ouest. **3.** *n.pl.* **westerlies,** vents *mpl* d'ouest.
western ['westən] **1.** *a.* (*a*) ouest, de l'ouest; occidental, -aux; **W. Europe,** l'Europe occidentale; *Pol:* **the W. powers,** les puissances occidentales; (*b*) **W. Australia,** l'Australie occidentale. **2.** *n.* (*a*) occidental (*pl.* -aux), -ale; (*b*) *Cin:* western *m.*
westerner ['westənər] *n.* (*a*) occidental (*pl.* -aux), -ale; (*b*) *U.S:* habitant, -ante, des États occidentaux.
westernization [westənai'zeiʃ(ə)n] *n.* occidentalisation *f.*
westernize ['westənaiz] *v.tr.* occidentaliser (un peuple); **to become westernized,** s'occidentaliser.
westward ['westwəd] **1.** *a.* (*a*) à l'ouest; (*b*) (du côté) de l'ouest. **2.** *adv.* = WESTWARDS.
westwards ['westwədz] *adv.* vers l'ouest; à l'ouest.
wet¹ [wet] *a.* **(wetter; wettest) 1.** (*a*) mouillé, humide; **to get w.,** se mouiller; **to get one's feet w.,** se mouiller les pieds; **to be w. through, w. to the skin, dripping w.,** être trempé, mouillé, jusqu'aux os; **sopping, soaking, w.,** (*of clothes*) mouillé à tordre; (*of pers.*) trempé jusqu'aux os; **cheeks w. with tears,** joues baignées de larmes; **ink still w.,** encre encore fraîche; *F:* (*pers.*) **w. blanket,** rabat-joie *m inv*; trouble-fête *m inv*; (*b*) **w. weather,** temps humide, pluvieux; temps de pluie; **three w. days,** trois jours de pluie; **when it's w.,** quand il pleut; **the w. season,** la saison des pluies; (*c*) *El:* **w. cell,** pile *f* à élément humide; (*d*) **w. nurse,** nourrice *f*; (*e*) *F:* (i) bête, idiot; (ii) *Pol:* modéré; **he's w. behind the ears,** on lui pincerait le nez qu'il en sortira encore du lait. **2.** *F:* (*of country, state*) qui permet la vente des boissons alcooliques.
wet² *n.* **1.** humidité *f.* **2.** pluie *f*; **to go out in the w.,** sortir sous la pluie. **3.** *F:* (*pers.*) (i) poule mouillée; (ii) *Pol:* modéré(e).
wet³ *v.tr.* **(wetted)** mouiller, humecter; imbiber (une éponge); arroser (de la pâte); (*of child*) **to w. the bed,** mouiller le lit; **to w. one's pants,** *F:* **oneself,** mouiller sa culotte. **wetting** *n.* mouillage *m*, mouillement *m*; arrosage *m* (de la pâte); **to get a w.,** se faire tremper; **bed w.,** incontinence *f* nocturne.
wether ['weðər] *n. Husb:* bélier châtré; mouton *m.*
wetness ['wetnis] *n.* (*a*) humidité *f*; (*b*) *F:* bêtise *f.*
we've = **we have,** *see* HAVE².
whack¹ [(h)wæk] *F:* **1.** *n.* (*a*) coup (de bâton) retentissant, bien appliqué; claque *f*, taloche *f*; (*b*) **to have a w. at sth.,** essayer de faire qch.; tenter le coup; (*c*) part *f*, portion *f*, (grand) morceau; **he didn't get his w.,** il n'a pas eu sa part; **he did, paid, more than his w.,** il a fait, a payé, plus que sa part. **2.** *int.* v'lan!
whack² *v.tr. F:* (*a*) battre (qn) (à coups retentissants); rosser (qn); (*b*) *Sp:* battre (ses adversaires) à plate(s) couture(s). **whacked** *a. F:* épuisé, éreinté. **whacking** *F:* **1.** *a. & adv.* énorme; **a w. great cabbage,** un fameux chou; **a w. great lie,** un mensonge de taille. **2.** *n.* (*a*) rossée *f*, raclée *f*; (*b*) *Sp:* **we gave them a w.,** on les a bien battus.
whacker ['(h)wækər] *n. F:* **1.** quelque chose de colossal; **what a w.! isn't it a w.!** il est pépère, celui-là! **2.** *O:* gros mensonge; **what a w.!** en voilà une forte!
whacko [(h)wæ'kou] *int. P: O:* magnifique!
whacky ['(h)wæki] *a.* = WACKY.
whale¹ [(h)weil] *n.* (*a*) *Z:* baleine *f*; cétacé *m*; **blue w.,** baleine bleue; **sperm w.,** cachalot *m*; **white w.,** bél(o)uga *m*; **w. calf,** baleineau *m*; **w. oil,** huile *f* de baleine; **w. hunter** = WHALER; (*b*) *F:* **we had a w. of a time,** on s'est drôlement bien amusés.
whale² *v.i.* faire la pêche à la baleine. **whaling** *n.* pêche *f*, chasse *f*, à la baleine; **w. ship,** baleinier *m.*
whalebone ['(h)weilboun] *n.* (*a*) (fanon *m* de) baleine *f*; (*b*) busc *m*, baleine (d'un corset).
whaler ['(h)weilər] *n.* (*pers., vessel*) baleinier *m.*
wham ['(h)wæm] *int. F:* vlan!
wharf, *pl.* **-s, wharves** [(h)wɔːf, -s, (h)wɔːvz] *n.* appontement *m*; quai *m*; *Com:* **ex w.,** à prendre sur quai.
wharfage ['(h)wɔːfidʒ] *n.* quayage *m*; droits *mpl* de quai, de bassin.
what [(h)wɔt] **I.** *a.* **1.** (*relative*) (ce, la chose, etc.) que, qui; **he took w. little I had left,** il m'a pris le peu qui me restait. **2.** (*interrogative, direct or indirect*) quel, *f.* quelle, *pl.* quels, quelles; **w. time is it?** quelle heure est-il? **tell me w. books you want,** dites-moi quels livres vous désirez; **w. right has he to give orders?** de quel droit donne-t-il des ordres? **w. good, w. use, is this?** à quoi cela sert-il? **what's the date (today)?** quelle est la date (aujourd'hui)? **w. sort of (a) book is it?** quelle sorte, quelle espèce, de livre est-ce? **w. colour, w. size, is it?** c'est de quelle couleur, de quelle taille? **3.** (*exclamatory*) **w. an idea!** quelle idée! **w. a fool he is!** qu'il est bête! comme il est bête! **w. a fuss about nothing!** voilà bien du bruit pour rien! **w. a question!** quelle question! **w. a man!** quel homme! **w. a pity!** quel dommage! **w. a (long) time you are getting dressed!** comme vous êtes longtemps à vous habiller! **w. a lot of people!** que de gens! que de monde! **II.** *pron.* **1.** (*rel.*) ce qui, ce que; **w. is done cannot be undone,** ce qui est fait est fait; **I don't know w. has happened,** je ne sais pas ce qui est arrivé; **w. I like is a detective story,** ce que j'aime c'est un roman policier; **w. is most remarkable is that . . .,** ce qu'il y a de plus remarquable c'est que . . .; **this is w. it's all about,** voici ce dont il s'agit; **but that's not w. I said,** mais je n'ai pas dit cela; **come w. may,** advienne que pourra; **he never speaks of w. he has gone through,** il ne parle jamais de ce qu'il a enduré; **w. with golf and tennis I have no time to write,** entre le golf et le tennis il ne me reste pas une minute pour écrire; *P:* **to give s.o. w. for,** (i) laver la tête à qn; (ii) flan-

quer une bonne raclée à qn. **2.** (*interrogative*) (*a*) (*direct*) qu'est-ce qui? qu'est-ce que? que? quoi? **w. has happened?** qu'est-ce qui est arrivé? **what's happening?** que se passe-t-il? **w. on earth are you doing here?** qu'est-ce que vous pouvez bien faire ici? **w. is it?** (i) qu'est-ce? qu'est-ce que c'est? (ii) qu'est-ce qu'il y a? **what's that?** qu'est-ce que cela? qu'est-ce que c'est que ça? **what's that you're telling me?** qu'est-ce que vous me dites? **w. will become of him?** que deviendra-t-il? **what's the matter?** qu'y a-t-il? qu'est-ce qu'il y a? **what's her address?** quelle est son adresse? **what's his name?** quel est son nom? comment s'appelle-t-il? **what's that to you?** qu'est-ce que cela vous fait? est-ce que ça vous regarde? **w. is there to see in this town?** qu'y a-t-il à voir dans cette ville? **what's the good, the use?** à quoi bon? **w. do you want?** qu'est-ce que vous voulez? **what's to be done?** que faire? **w. did I tell you?** quand je vous le disais! je vous l'avais bien dit! **w. will people say?** que dira-t-on? **what's the French for *dog*?** comment dit-on *dog* en français? **w. else could bring me here?** quoi d'autre pourrait m'amener ici? **w. could be more beautiful?** quoi de plus beau? **w. do seven and eight make?** combien font sept et huit? **w. is the rent?** de combien est le loyer? **w. do I owe you?** combien vous dois-je? (*in shop*) c'est combien? ça fait combien? **w. is he like?** comment est-il? **w. do you take me for?** pour qui me prenez-vous? **what's it made of?** en quoi est-ce? c'est en quoi? **w. are you thinking of?** à quoi pensez-vous? **w. about the £10 I lent you?** et les £10 que je vous ai prêtées? **w. about a game of bridge?** si on faisait une partie de bridge? **w. about you?** et vous donc? **w. about that coffee?** et ce café? **what's that for?** à quoi cela sert-il? à quoi ça sert? **w. did he do that for?** pourquoi a-t-il fait cela? **w. (on earth) for?** mais pourquoi donc? **and w. if she hears about, of, it?** et si elle l'apprend? **w. then?** et après? *F:* **so w.?** et (puis) après? et alors? *F:* **d'you think I'm mad or w.?** dis, tu me crois donc fou? **paper, pens, pencils, and w. not, and w. have you,** du papier, des stylos, des crayons et d'autres choses encore, et que sais-je encore; **w. did you say?** vous disiez? pardon? **w. of it?** qu'est-ce que cela fait? eh bien, et puis après? (*b*) (*indirect*) ce qui, ce que; **tell me what's happened,** dites-moi ce qui s'est passé; **I don't know w. you want,** je ne sais pas ce que vous désirez; **he didn't know w. to say, do,** il ne savait que dire, faire; **there were books and I don't know w.,** il y avait des livres et que sais-je encore; **tell me w. you're crying for,** dites-moi pourquoi vous pleurez; **I'll tell you w.,** je vais vous dire; écoutez; **he knows what's w.,** il s'y connaît; **I'll show you what's w.!** on verra de quel bois je me chauffe! **3.** (*exclamatory*) (*a*) **w. he has suffered!** ce qu'il a souffert! **w. next!** par exemple! (*b*) **w.! you can't come!** comment! vous ne pouvez pas venir! *F:* **w.! no eggs!** quoi! pas d'œufs! *O:* **nice girl, w.!** joli brin de fille, hein!

what-d'ye-call-'em, -her, -him, -it ['(h)wɔtjəkɔːləm, -ər, -im, -it] *n. F:* machin *m*, truc *m*; (*of pers.*) chose *mf*; **Miss What-d'ye-call-her,** mademoiselle Chose.

whate'er [(h)wɔt'ɛər] *pron. Poet:* = WHATEVER.

whatever [(h)wɔt'evər] **1.** *pron.* (*a*) (*relative*) tout ce qui, tout ce que; **w. you like,** tout ce qui vous plaira; tout ce que vous voudrez; (*b*) quoi qui, quoi que + *sub.*; **w. it is, may be,** quoi que ce soit; **w. happens, keep calm,** quoi qui survienne, restez calme; **he shall have w. he wants,** quoi qu'il désire, il l'aura; **w. she says, may say,** en dépit de ce qu'elle dit; (*c*) *F:* **pens, pencils, paper and w.,** des stylos, des crayons, du papier et tout ce que vous voulez; . . . **or w.,** (i) ou quelque chose de ce genre; (ii) ou tout ce que vous voulez. **2.** *a.* (*a*) **w. price they are asking,** quel que soit le prix qu'on demande; **w. mistakes I (may) have made,** quelles que soient les erreurs que j'ai faites; (*b*) (*emphatic*) **under any pretext w.,** sous quelque prétexte que ce soit; **no hope w.,** pas le moindre espoir; **is there any hope w.?** y a t-il un espoir quelconque? **none w.,** pas un seul; **nothing w.,** absolument rien.

what-ho [(h)wɔt'(h)ou] *int. F:* (*a*) *O:* eh bien! tiens! (*b*) bonjour! salut!

whatnot ['(h)wɔtnɔt] *n.* **1.** *Furn:* étagère *f.* **2.** *F:* machin *m*, truc *m*.

what's-her-, -his-, -its-, name ['(h)wɔtsə, -iz, -its, neim] *n. F:* = WHAT-D'YE-CALL-HER, *etc.*

whatsit ['(h)wɔtsit] *n. F:* machin *m*, truc *m*.

whatsoever [(h)wɔtsou'evər] **1.** *pron. Lit:* **w. it may be,** quoi que ce soit. **2.** *a.* (*emphatic*) = WHATEVER 2 (*b*).

wheat [(h)wiːt] *n.* blé *m*, froment *m*; **to plant land with w.,** mettre une terre en blé; **to divide the w. from the chaff,** séparer le bon grain de l'ivraie.

wheatear ['(h)wiːtiər] *n. Orn:* traquet *m* (motteux), cul-blanc *m*.

wheaten ['(h)wiːt(ə)n] *a.* (pain) de froment, de blé.

wheatgerm ['(h)wiːtdʒəːm] *n.* germes *mpl* de blé.

wheatmeal ['(h)wiːtmiːl] *n.* farine grossière, grosse farine, de froment.

wheatsheaf ['(h)wiːtʃiːf] *n.* gerbe *f* de blé.

wheedle ['(h)wiːdl] *v.tr.* enjôler, cajoler, câliner, embobeliner (qn); **to w. s.o. into doing sth.,** amener qn à faire qch. à force de cajoleries; **to w. money from, out of, s.o.,** soutirer de l'argent à qn. **wheedling 1.** *a.* (*of manner, etc.*) enjôleur, cajoleur, câlin; **w. voice,** voix pateline. **2.** *n.* enjôlement *m*, cajolerie *f*, câlinerie *f*.

wheel[1] [(h)wiːl] *n.* **1.** roue *f*; (*small*) roulette *f*; (*a*) **on wheels,** sur roues, sur roulettes; **to run on wheels,** marcher sur des roues, sur des roulettes; **meals on wheels,** repas livrés à domicile (aux personnes âgées, etc.); *F:* **my wheels,** ma bagnole; *Aut:* **spare w.,** roue de secours; **w. disc,** enjoliveur *m*; **w. alignment,** (i) parallélisme *m* des roues; (ii) réglage *m* du train avant; *Adm:* **w. clamp,** sabot *m* de Denver; **to put one's shoulder to the w.,** pousser à la roue; se mettre à l'œuvre; **the fifth w.,** la cinquième roue du carrosse; *Av:* **landing wheels,** roues (du train) d'atterrissage; **nose w.,** roue (d'atterrisseur) avant; (*b*) *Hyd.E:* **hydraulic w.,** roue hydraulique; **bucket w.,** roue (hydraulique) à augets, à godets; (*c*) *Mec.E:* roue (de transmission, d'engrenage, de turbine, etc.); **toothed w., gear w.,** roue dentée, à dents, roue d'engrenage; **the wheels,** les rouages *mpl* (d'un mécanisme, d'une montre); **the wheels of government,** les rouages de l'administration; **there are wheels within wheels,** c'est une affaire très compliquée, dont il faut connaître les dessous; c'est plus compliqué que cela n'en a l'air; (*d*) **(steering) w.,** (i) *Aut:* volant (de direction); (ii) *Nau:* roue du gouvernail; la barre; **to be at the w.,** (i) *Aut:* être au volant; (ii) *Nau:* tenir la barre, le gouvernail; (iii) *Fig:* tenir la barre, être à la tête de l'entreprise, des affaires; **the man at the w.,** (i) *Aut:* le conducteur; l'homme au volant; (ii) *Nau:* l'homme de barre, le timonier; (iii) *Fig:* l'homme à la tête des affaires, *F:* le grand patron; (*e*) **(grinding) w.,** meule *f*; (*f*) **potter's w.,** tour *m* de potier; **spinning w.,** rouet *m*; (*g*) **cutting w.,** molette *f* (à couper le verre, etc.); **pastry w.,** roulette (à couper la pâte); *Needlew:* **tracing w.,** roulette (à piquer, à pointiller); (*h*) *Hist:* **to condemn a criminal to the w.,** condamner un criminel à la roue; **to break s.o. on the w.,** rouer qn; (*h*) **big w.,** (i) (*at fair*) grande roue; (ii) *NAm: F:* gros bonnet, grosse légume; **the w. of fortune,** la roue de la fortune. **2.** *Mil: etc:* (mouvement de) conversion *f*; **left, right, w.,** conversion à gauche, à droite.

wheel² **1.** *v.tr.* (*a*) **to w. sth. about, (a)round,** tourner qch.; faire pivoter (qch.); *Mil:* **to w. a line of men,** faire faire une conversion à une ligne d'hommes; (*b*) rouler (une brouette, etc.); pousser, conduire (une bicyclette) à la main; **to w. sth. in a barrow,** transporter qch. en brouette; **to w. a child in a pram,** promener un enfant dans son landau. **2.** *v.i.* (*a*) tourner en rond, en cercle; tournoyer; (*b*) *Mil:* opérer, effectuer, une conversion; **to w. about,** faire la roue; **left w.!** par file à gauche, gauche! (*c*) (*of pers.*) **to w. about, round,** faire demi-tour; se retourner (brusquement); faire volte-face; (*d*) *F:* **to w. and deal,** brasser des affaires (plus ou moins louches). **wheeled** *a.* **1.** roulant; à roues; sur roues. **2.** (*with adj. prefixed*) **two-w., three-w.,** à deux, à trois, roues. **wheeling** *n.* **1.** tournoiement *m* (des oiseaux, etc.). **2.** *Mil:* conversion *f.* **3.** *F:* **w. and dealing,** brassage *m* d'affaires (plus ou moins louches).

wheelbarrow ['(h)wi:lbærou] *n.* brouette *f.*

wheelbase ['(h)wi:lbeis] *n. Veh:* empattement *m.*

wheelchair ['(h)wi:ltʃɛər] *n.* fauteuil roulant.

wheeler ['(h)wi:lər] *n.* **1.** (*pers.*) *F:* **w. dealer,** brasseur *m* d'affaires (plus ou moins louches). **2.** *Veh:* (*with number prefixed*) **two-w., three-w.,** voiture *f* à deux, à trois, roues.

wheelhouse ['(h)wi:lhaus] *n. Nau:* abri *m* de navigation; la timonerie.

wheelwright ['(h)wi:lrait] *n.* charron *m.*

wheeze¹ [(h)wi:z] *n.* **1.** respiration asthmatique, sifflante. **2.** *F: O:* ruse *f*, truc *m*; **a good w.,** une bonne astuce.

wheeze² **1.** *v.i.* (*a*) respirer péniblement, en asthmatique; (*b*) (*of horse*) corner. **2.** *v.tr.* **to w. out sth.,** dire qch. d'une voix asthmatique. **wheezing** *n.* (*a*) respiration *f* asthmatique; sifflement gras (d'asthmatique); (*b*) (*of horse*) cornage *m.*

wheezy ['(h)wi:zi] *a.* (*a*) (*of pers.*) asthmatique; *F:* poussif; (*b*) (*of horse*) cornard; poussif; (*c*) **a w. old barrel organ,** un vieil orgue de Barbarie asthmatique.

whelk [(h)welk] *n. Moll:* buccin *m.*

whelp¹ [(h)welp] *n.* (*a*) jeune chien *m*, chiot *m*; (*b*) petit *m* (d'un fauve); (*c*) *F:* (i) mauvais garnement; (ii) petit morveux.

whelp² *v.i. & tr.* (*of animals*) mettre bas (des petits).

when [(h)wen] **I.** *adv.* **1.** (*interr.*) quand? **w. will you come?** quand viendrez-vous? **w. will the wedding be?** à quand le mariage? **w. ever, w. on earth, will he come?** quand donc, quand diable, viendra-t-il? *F:* (*when pouring drinks*) **say w.!** arrêtez-moi! comme ça? **2. the day w. I first met her,** le jour où je l'ai rencontrée pour la première fois; **one day w. I was on duty,** un jour que j'étais de service; **at the very time w . . .,** au moment même où . . .; alors même que . . . **II.** *conj.* **1.** quand, lorsque; **w. I came into the room,** lorsque je suis entré dans la pièce; **w. I was young,** quand j'étais jeune; **w. I think of what he must have suffered!** quand je pense à ce qu'il a dû souffrir! (*elliptical*) **w. writing I get very tired,** en écrivant je me fatigue beaucoup; *Cu:* **w. cool, turn out onto a dish,** après refroidissement, démouler sur un plat. **2. the prince will arrive on the 10th., w. he will open the new university,** le prince arrivera le dix et inaugurera la nouvelle université. **3. he walked there w. he could have taken the car,** il y est allé à pied, alors qu'il aurait pu faire le trajet en voiture; **what's the good of telling you w. you won't listen to me?** à quoi bon vous le dire du moment que vous ne voulez pas m'écouter? **III.** *pron.* **1.** (*interr.*) **until w. can you stay?** jusqu'à quand pouvez-vous rester? **since w. have you been living in Paris?** depuis quand habitez-vous Paris? **2.** (*rel.*) **since w. I have always bought a car of that make,** depuis quand j'achète toujours cette marque de voiture; **until w. I shall stay here,** jusqu'à quand je resterai ici. **IV.** *n.* **the w. and the how of it,** quand et comment cela est arrivé.

whence [(h)wens] *adv. A: & Lit:* d'où; **no one knows w. he comes,** personne ne sait d'où il vient; **w. I conclude that . . .,** d'où je conclus que . . . .

whenever, *Poet:* **whene'er** [(h)wen'evər, -'ɛər] *conj. & adv.* (*a*) toutes les fois, chaque fois, que; **w. I see it I think of you,** chaque fois que je le vois je pense à vous; **I go w. I can,** j'y vais aussi souvent que possible; (*b*) à n'importe quel moment (que); **come w. you like,** venez quand vous voudrez, à n'importe quel moment; **Sunday, Monday, or w.,** dimanche, lundi, ou n'importe quel jour.

where [(h)wɛər] **I.** *interr. adv.* (*a*) où; **w. am I?** où suis-je? **tell me w. he is,** dites-moi où il est; **w. did you put it?** où l'avez-vous mis? (*in work*) **w. have you got to? w. are you?** (i) où êtes-vous? (ii) (*in book, etc.*) où en êtes-vous? **w. should I be if I had followed your advice?** qu'est-ce que je serais devenu si j'avais suivi vos conseils? (*b*) par où; **w. is the exit?** par où sort-on? (*c*) **w. is the use, the good, of it?** à quoi bon (faire) cela? **w. can be the harm in doing it?** qu'y a-t-il de mal à faire cela? **II.** *rel. conj. & adv.* (*a*) (là) où; **I'll stay w. I am,** je resterai (là) où je suis; **go w. you like,** allez où vous voudrez; (*b*) **that's w. we've got to,** voilà où nous en sommes; **that is w. you are mistaken,** voilà, c'est là, que vous vous trompez; (*c*) **he came to (the place) w. I was fishing,** il est venu à l'endroit où je pêchais; **I can see it from w. we are,** je le vois d'où nous sommes; (*on form*) **delete w. inapplicable,** rayer les mentions inutiles; (*d*) où, dans lequel; **the house w. I was born,** la maison où, dans laquelle, je suis né; **they went to Paris w. they stayed a week,** ils sont allés à Paris et y sont restés huit jours. **III.** *pron.* **w. are you going to?** où allez-vous? **w. does he come from?** d'où vient-il? **IV.** *n.* **the w. and the when,** le lieu et la date; le lieu et l'heure.

whereabouts ['(h)wɛərəbauts] **1.** *adv. & conj.* où; de quel côté; **do you know w. the town hall is?** savez-vous de quel côté se trouve l'hôtel de ville? **2.** *n.* lieu *m* où se trouve qn, qch.; **nobody knows his w.,** personne ne sait où il est.

whereafter [(h)wɛə'rɑ:ftər] *rel. adv. A: & Lit:* après quoi; à la suite de quoi.

whereas [(h)wɛə'ræz] *conj.* **1.** *Jur: etc:* (*introducing preamble*) attendu que, vu que, puisque. **2.** alors que, tandis que + *ind.*

whereat [(h)wɛə'ræt] *adv. & conj. A: & Lit:* à quoi, sur quoi, etc.; **w. he replied that . . .,** à quoi il a répondu que . . . .

whereby [(h)wɛə'bai] *adv.* **1.** *A: & Lit:* (*interr.*) par quoi? par quel moyen? **2.** *Lit: Jur:* (*rel.*) par lequel.

wherefore ['(h)wɛəfɔ:r] **1.** *adv. A: & Lit:* (*a*) (*interr.*) pourquoi? pour quelle raison? (*b*) (*rel.*) donc; pour cette raison. **2.** *n.* **the whys and the wherefores,** les pourquoi et les comment.

wherein [(h)wɛə'rin] *adv. & conj. A: & Lit:* **1.** (*interr.*) en quoi? **w. have we offended you?** en quoi vous avons-nous offensé? **2.** (*rel.*) dans lequel; (là) où; **w. the difficulty lies,** là où se trouve la difficulté.

whereof [(h)wɛə'rɔv] *adv. & conj. A: & Lit:* **1.** (*interr.*) en quoi? de quoi? **2.** (*rel.*) (*a*) de quoi, dont; (*b*) duquel, dont.

whereon [(h)wɛə'rɔn] *adv. & conj. Lit:* (*rel.*) (*a*) *A:* sur quoi; **the day w. . . .,** le jour où . . .; (*b*) sur quoi; après quoi; **w. he left us,** sur quoi il nous a quitté.

wheresoever, *Poet:* **wheresoe'er** [(h)wɛəsou'evər, -'ɛər] *adv. & conj. esp. Lit:* = WHEREVER.

whereupon [(h)wɛərə'pɔn] *adv. & conj. Lit:* (*rel*) (*a*) *A:* sur quoi, sur lequel; (*b*) sur quoi; après quoi; **w. he left us,** sur quoi il nous a quitté.

wherever [(h)wɛə'revər] *conj. & adv.* **1.** partout où;

n'importe où; **I shall remember it w. I go,** où que j'aille, je m'en souviendrai; **I'll go w. you want (me to),** j'irai où vous voudrez (que j'aille); **w. possible,** partout où cela est possible; *F:* **at home, in the office, or w.,** chez moi, au bureau ou n'importe où. **2. w. they come from,** d'où qu'ils viennent; **he comes from Glossop, w. that may be,** il est originaire d'un endroit qui s'appellerait Glossop.

wherewith [(h)wɛə'wiθ] *adv. & conj. A: & Lit:* (*rel.*) (*a*) avec lequel; avec quoi; (*b*) = WHEREUPON (*b*).

wherewithal ['(h)wɛərwiðɔːl] *n. F:* **the w.,** l'argent *m*, le nécessaire, les moyens *mpl*; **I haven't the w. to buy it,** je n'ai pas de quoi l'acheter.

whet [(h)wet] *v.tr.* **(whetted) 1.** aiguiser, affûter, repasser (un outil, un couteau, etc.). **2.** stimuler, aiguiser (l'appétit, les désirs, etc.).

whether ['(h)weðər] *conj.* **1.** (*indirect question*) si; **I don't know w. it's true,** je ne sais pas si c'est vrai; **it's doubtful, uncertain, w . . .,** il est douteux, peu certain, si . . ., **I want to know w. . . . or w. . . .,** je voudrais savoir si . . . ou si . . .; **it depends on w. you're in a hurry or not,** cela dépend (de) si vous êtes pressé ou non. **2.** (*conditional*) **w. it rains or (w. it) snows, he always goes out,** soit qu'il pleuve, soit qu'il neige, il sort toujours; **w. he comes or not, or no, we shall leave,** qu'il vienne ou non, qu'il vienne ou qu'il ne vienne pas, nous allons partir; **w. or not . . .,** qu'il en soit ainsi ou non . . .

whetstone ['(h)wetstoun] *n.* pierre *f* à aiguiser, à repasser.

whew [hjuː] *int.* **1.** (*of relief, fatigue*) ouf! **2.** (*astonishment*) mon Dieu!

whey [(h)wei] *n.* petit lait.

which [(h)witʃ] **I.** *a.* **1.** (*interr.*) quel, *f.* quelle; *pl.* quels, *f.* quelles? **w. colour do you like best?** quelle couleur aimez-vous le mieux? **w. way do we go?** par où allons-nous? **w. way is the wind blowing?** d'où vient le vent? **w. one?** lequel? laquelle? **w. ones?** lesquels? lesquelles? **I know w. one you want,** je sais celui que vous désirez. **2.** (*rel.*) lequel, *f.* laquelle; *pl.* lesquels, *f.* lesquelles; **he stayed here two weeks during w. time he never left the house,** il est resté ici deux semaines, pendant lesquelles il n'a pas quitté la maison; **he came at noon, at w. time I'm usually in the garden,** il est venu à midi, heure à laquelle je suis ordinairement au jardin. **II.** *pron.* **1.** (*inter.*) lequel, *f.* laquelle; *pl.* lesquels, *f.* lesquelles? **w. have you chosen?** lequel, laquelle, avez-vous choisi(e)? **w. of you?** lequel d'entre vous? **w. of the two (girls) is the prettier?** laquelle des deux est la plus jolie? **w. would you rather have?** lequel préférez-vous? **I can never tell w. is w.,** je ne sais jamais les distinguer; **I don't know w. to choose,** je ne sais (pas) lequel choisir; **I don't mind w.,** n'importe (lequel). **2.** (*rel.*) (*a*) qui; que; lequel; **the house w. is for sale,** la maison qui est à vendre; **the book w. I bought yesterday,** le livre que j'ai acheté hier; (*b*) ce qui, ce que; **he looked like a retired colonel, which in fact he was,** il avait l'air d'un colonel en retraite, ce qu'il était en effet; **he was back in London, w. I didn't know,** il était de retour à Londres, fait que j'ignorais. **3.** (*a*) **to w., at w.,** auquel, *f.* à laquelle; *pl.* auxquels, *f.* auxquelles; **of w., from w.,** duquel, *f.* de laquelle; *pl.* desquels, *f.* desquelles; dont; **the house of w. I am speaking,** la maison dont je parle; **the countries to w. we are going, w. we're going to,** les pays où nous irons; **the pen w. I'm writing with,** le stylo avec lequel j'écris; **the town in w. we live,** la ville où nous demeurons, que nous habitons; (*b*) **he insists that actors should have talent, in w. he is right,** il exige que les acteurs aient du talent, (ce) en quoi il a raison; **there are no trains on Sunday, w. I hadn't thought of,** il n'y a pas de trains le dimanche, ce à quoi je n'avais pas pensé; **after w. he went out,** après quoi il est sorti.

whichever [(h)witʃ'evər] *pron. & a.* **1.** *pron.* (*a*) celui qui; celui que; n'importe lequel, laquelle; **take w. you like best,** prenez celui que vous préférez; **w. of you comes in first,** celui (d'entre vous) qui arrive le premier; (*b*) n'importe lequel; **w. you choose, you will have a good bargain,** n'importe lequel vous choisirez, vous aurez fait une bonne affaire. **2.** *a.* (*a*) le . . . que; n'importe quel; **take w. book you prefer,** prenez le livre que vous préférez; (*b*) n'importe quel; quelque . . . que; **w. way he turned he saw nothing but sand,** de quelque côté qu'il se soit tourné, de n'importe quel côté il se tournait, il ne voyait (rien) que du sable.

whiff [(h)wif] *n.* bouffée *f* (de vent, de fumée, d'air, etc.); odeur *f* (de vin, etc.); **to go out for a w. of fresh air,** sortir pour respirer un peu, pour prendre l'air; **what a w.!** qu'est-ce que sa pue!

whiffy ['(h)wifi] *a. F:* puant, qui pue.

Whig [(h)wig] *n. Pol.Hist:* whig *m.*

while¹ [(h)wail] *n.* **1.** (*a*) (espace *m* de) temps *m*; **after a w.,** au bout de quelque temps; quelque temps après; **after a little w., a little w. later,** peu de temps après; **for a (short) w.,** pendant quelque temps; pendant un moment; **in a short, little, w.,** sous peu; avant peu; **a short, little, w. ago,** il n'y a pas bien longtemps; **a long w.,** longtemps; **a long w. ago,** il y a longtemps; **a good w.,** pas mal de temps; **it will be a good w. before you see him again,** vous ne le reverrez pas de si tôt; **it will take me quite a w.,** cela me prendra un certain temps, pas mal de temps; **stay a little w. longer,** restez encore un peu; **all the w.,** tout le temps; **once in a w.,** de temps en temps; de temps à autre; (*b*) *adv.phr. A:* **the w.,** en attendant; pendant ce temps. **2. to be worth (one's) w.,** valoir la peine; *F:* valoir le coup; **it's not worth our w. waiting,** cela ne vaut pas, ce n'est pas, la peine d'attendre; **it is perhaps worth w. pointing out that . . .,** il vaut peut-être la peine de faire remarquer que . . .; **I'll make it worth your w.,** vous serez bien payé de votre peine.

while² *v.tr.* **to w. away,** faire passer (le temps); tuer (une heure, le temps); **I played patience to w. away the time,** j'ai fait des réussites pour me désennuyer.

while³ *conj.* **1.** (*a*) (*during the time that*) pendant que, tandis que; **w. (he was) here,** pendant qu'il était ici; **w. in Paris,** pendant son séjour à Paris; **w. reading I fell asleep,** tout en lisant, je me suis endormi; **w. this was going on,** sur ces entrefaites; (*b*) (*as long as*) tant que; **w. there's life there's hope,** tant qu'il y a de la vie il y a de l'espoir. **2.** (*concessive*) quoique, bien que; **w. I admit, w. admitting, it's difficult, I don't think it's impossible,** quoique j'admette, tout en reconnaissant, que c'est difficile, je ne le crois pas impossible. **3.** (*whereas*) tandis que; **one of the sisters was (dressed) in white w. the other was all in black,** une des sœurs était vêtue de blanc, tandis que l'autre était tout en noir.

whilst [(h)wailst] *conj.* = WHILE³.

whim [(h)wim] *n.* caprice *m*; fantaisie *f*, lubie *f*; **passing w.,** toquade *f*; **a sudden w. of his,** un caprice qui lui a pris.

whimper¹ ['(h)wimpər] *n.* **1.** (i) pleurnicherie *f*, pleurnichement *m*; (ii) geignement *m*, plainte *f*. **2.** (*of dog*) petit cri plaintif; plainte.

whimper² **1.** *v.i.* (*a*) pleurnicher, geindre; (*b*) (*of dog*) pousser de petits cris plaintifs. **2.** *v.tr.* dire (qch.) en pleurnichant. **whimpering 1.** *a.* pleurnicheur; geignard; (chien) qui pousse de petits cris plaintifs. **2.** *n.* (*a*) pleurnichement *m*, pleurnicheries *fpl*; (*b*) plaintes *fpl*; (*c*) petits cris plaintifs (d'un chien).

whimsical ['(h)wimzik(ə)l] *a.* **1.** (*of pers., mind*) capricieux, fantasque. **2.** (*of thg*) bizarre, baroque. **-ally** *adv.* **1.** capricieusement. **2.** bizarrement.

whimsicality [(h)wimzi'kæliti] *n.* **1.** caractère capricieux, fantasque. **2.** bizarrerie *f* (de caractère).

whimsy ['(h)wimzi] *n.* (*occ.* **whimsey)** fantaisie *f.*

whin [(h)win] *n. Bot:* ajonc *m*; genêt épineux.

whine¹ [(h)wain] *n.* **1.** plainte *f*; pleurnicherie *f*, geignement *m* (d'un enfant); gémissement *m*, geignement (d'un chien). **2.** jérémiade *f.*

whine² *v.i. & tr.* (*of pers.*) se plaindre; (*of child*) pleurnicher; (*of dog*) gémir, geindre; **you've nothing to w. about,** il n'y a pas de quoi vous plaindre; **stop whining!** assez de jérémiades! **whining 1.** *a.* (*a*) geignant; (enfant) pleurnicheur; (ton) plaintif, pleurard; **w. voice,** voix dolente; (*b*) geignard. **2.** *n.* (*a*) gémissement *m*, geignement *m*; (*b*) jérémiades *fpl*; plaintes *fpl*; **stop your w.!** assez de jérémiades!

whinge [(h)windʒ] *v.* = WHINE².

whinny¹ ['(h)wini] *n.* hennissement *m* (de cheval).

whinny² *v.i.* (*of horse*) hennir.

whip¹ [(h)wip] *n.* **1.** fouet *m*; **riding w.,** stick *m*; cravache *f*; *F:* **to get a fair crack of the w.,** avoir sa (bonne) part; en tirer un bon parti. **2.** *Parl:* (*a*) (membre désigné par un parti comme) chef *m* de file; whip *m*; (*b*) appel *m* aux membres d'un groupe; **three-line w.,** appel urgent. **4.** fouettement *m*, coup *m* de fouet (d'un câble, etc.). **5.** *Cu:* **strawberry w.** = mousse *f* aux fraises.

whip² *v.* (**whipped** [(h)wipt]) **I.** *v.tr.* **1.** (*a*) fouetter (un cheval); donner le fouet à (un enfant); **to w. a top,** fouetter, faire aller, un sabot; **the rain was whipping the window panes,** la pluie fouettait, cinglait, les vitres; (*b*) *Cu:* battre (des œufs); fouetter (de la crème); **whipped cream,** crème fouettée; (*c*) *F:* vaincre (qn); battre (qn) à plate(s) couture(s). **2.** (*a*) *Nau:* surlier, garnir (un cordage); (*b*) ligaturer (un brancard, une canne à pêche); (*c*) *Needlew:* **to w. a seam,** surjeter une couture; faire un surjet. **3. to w. sth. off,** ôter, enlever, qch. d'un geste rapide; **he whipped a revolver out of his pocket, he whipped out a revolver,** il a sorti vivement, brusquement, un revolver (de sa poche); **he whipped it away, out of sight,** il l'a caché d'un mouvement rapide. **II.** *v.i.* **1.** fouetter; **the rain was whipping against the panes,** la pluie fouettait, cinglait (contre) les vitres. **2. to w. in, out, off,** entrer, sortir, partir, brusquement; **to w. round,** se retourner vivement; **to w. round the corner,** tourner vivement le coin. **3.** (*of cable*) **to w. back,** fouetter. **whipping** *n.* **1.** (*a*) fouettage *m* (d'un cheval, d'un sabot, de la crème, etc.); *Com:* **w. cream,** crème à fouetter; *Toys:* **w. top,** sabot *m*; (*b*) **to get a w.,** (i) recevoir le fouet; être fouetté; (ii) *Sp:* être battu à plate(s) couture(s); **w. boy,** (i) *Hist:* jeune garçon élevé avec un prince et qui reçoit le fouet au lieu de celui-ci; (ii) *F:* bouc *m* émissaire. **2.** fouettement *m* (de la pluie, etc.). **3.** (*a*) *Nau:* surliure *f* (d'un cordage); (*b*) ligature(s) *f(pl)* (d'une canne à pêche, etc.). **whip up** *v.tr.* (*a*) activer, stimuler (un cheval); toucher (un cheval) (du fouet); (*b*) *Parl:* faire passer un appel urgent à (des membres d'un parti); **to w. up one's friends,** rallier ses amis; (*c*) battre (des œufs, etc.); *F:* **I'll w. you up something to eat,** je vais te préparer rapidement quelque chose à manger.

whipcord ['(h)wipkɔːd] *n.* **1.** (*a*) mèche *f* de fouet; (*b*) corde *f* à fouet. **2.** *Tex:* whipcord *m.*

whiphand ['(h)wiphænd] *n.* main *f* du fouet; *Fig:* **to have, hold, the w.,** avoir l'avantage; avoir le dessus; **to have the w. over, of, s.o.,** avoir barre(s) sur qn; avoir la haute main sur qn.

whiplash ['(h)wiplæʃ] *n.* coup *m* de fouet; *F:* **tongue like a w.,** langue *f* qui cingle.

whipper-in [(h)wipər'in] *n. Ven:* piqueur *m.*

whippersnapper ['(h)wipəsnæpər] *n. F:* jeune homme suffisant, qui fait l'important.

whippet ['(h)wipit] *n.* (*dog*) whippet *m.*

whipround ['(h)wipraund] *n. F:* quête *f*; **to have a w. for s.o.,** organiser une souscription en faveur de qn.

whir¹,² [(h)wəːr] *n. & v.i.* = WHIRR¹,².

whirl¹ [(h)wəːl] *n.* **1.** (*a*) mouvement *m* giratoire, giration *f* (d'une roue, etc.); (*b*) tourbillon *m*, tourbillonnement *m*, tournoiement *m*; **a w. of pleasure,** un tourbillon de plaisirs; **my head's in a w.,** la tête me tourne.

whirl² 1. *v.i.* (*a*) **to w. (round),** (i) tourbillonner, tournoyer; (ii) se retourner vivement; (*of dancer*) pirouetter; **whirling dervish,** derviche tourneur; **my head's whirling,** la tête me tourne; j'ai le vertige; (*b*) **to w. along,** filer à toute vitesse, à toute allure; **the thoughts that were whirling through my head,** les pensées qui tourbillonnaient dans mon cerveau. **2.** *v.tr.* (*a*) faire tournoyer, faire tourbillonner (les feuilles mortes, etc.); (*b*) entraîner (à toute vitesse, à fond de train); **the train whirled us along,** le train nous emportait à toute vitesse.

whirligig ['(h)wəːligig] *n.* **1.** (*a*) *Toys:* tourniquet *m*; (*b*) manège *m* de chevaux de bois. **2.** tournoiement *m.*

whirlpool ['(h)wəːlpuːl] *n.* tourbillon *m* (d'eau); remous *m* d'eau; gouffre *m*, maelström *m.*

whirlwind ['(h)wəːlwind] *n.* tourbillon *m* (de vent); trombe *f* (de vent); **to come in like a w.,** entrer en trombe, en coup de vent.

whirr¹ [(h)wəːr] *n.* bruissement *m* (d'ailes); ronflement *m*, ronronnement *m* (de machines); vrombissement *m* (d'une hélice d'avion, etc.).

whirr² *v.i.* (*of machinery, etc.*) ronfler, ronronner; (*of propeller*) vrombir.

whisk¹ [(h)wisk] *n.* **1.** (*rapid movement*) **a w. of the tail, of a duster,** un coup de queue, de torchon. **2.** (*a*) (*for dusting*) époussette *f*; plumeau *m*; (*for beating eggs*) fouet *m*, batteur *m*; (*b*) **fly w.,** chasse-mouches *m inv.*

whisk² 1. *v.i.* **to w. away, off,** partir comme un trait, comme une flèche; **to w. past,** passer comme le vent. **2.** *v.tr.* (*a*) (*of cow, etc.*) **to w. its tail,** agiter sa queue; (*b*) **to w. sth. away, off,** enlever qch. d'un geste rapide; **to w. away a fly,** chasser une mouche (d'un revers de main); **to w. s.o. away,** entraîner, emporter, qn à toute vitesse; (*c*) *Cu:* battre (des œufs); fouetter (de la crème).

whisker ['(h)wiskər] *n.* **whiskers,** favoris *mpl* (d'homme); moustache(s) *f(pl)* (de chat, de souris, etc.); *F:* **he thinks he's the cat's whiskers,** il se croit quelqu'un; *Sp: F:* **to win by a w.,** gagner dans un mouchoir.

whiskered ['(h)wiskəd] *a.* (homme) qui a des favoris, des moustaches.

whisky ['(h)wiski] *n.* (*Irish or U.S:* **whiskey)** whisky *m*; **a w. and soda,** un whisky soda; **w. on the rocks,** whisky frappé.

whisper¹ ['(h)wispər] *n.* **1.** (*a*) chuchotement *m*; **to speak in a w., in whispers,** parler bas; **to say sth. in a w.,** chuchoter qch.; dire qch. tout bas; (*b*) *Lit:* bruissement *m* (des feuilles); murmure *m* (de l'eau). **2.** rumeur *f*, bruit *m.*

whisper² 1. *v.i.* chuchoter; parler bas; *Lit:* (*of leaves*) susurrer; (*of water*) murmurer; **to w. to s.o.,** chuchoter à l'oreille de qn; dire, souffler, qch. à l'oreille de qn. **2.** *v.tr.* (*a*) **to w. sth. to s.o.,** dire, chuchoter, un mot à l'oreille de qn; souffler qch. à l'oreille de qn; **whispered conversation,** conversation *f* à voix basse; (*b*) *O:* faire circuler secrètement (une nouvelle); **it is whispered that . . .,** le bruit court que . . .. **whispering** *n.* **1.** (*a*) chuchotement *m*; (*b*) *Pej:* chuchoterie(s) *f(pl)*; **w. campaign,** campagne sournoise, de chuchoteries; (*c*) *Arch:* **w. gallery,** voûte *f* acoustique; galerie *f* à écho. **2.** *Lit:* bruissement *m* (de feuilles); murmure *m* (d'eaux).

whist [(h)wist] *n. Cards:* whist *m*; **dummy w.,** whist à trois (avec un mort); **w. player,** joueur, -euse, de whist; **w. drive,** tournoi *m* de whist.

whistle¹ ['(h)wisl] *n.* **1.** sifflement *m*; coup *m* de sifflet; *Sp:* **final w.,** coup de sifflet final. **2.** (*a*) sifflet *m*; **to blow a w.,** donner un coup de sifflet; *F:* **to blow the w. on sth.,** (i) révéler, dévoiler, qch.; (ii) mettre le holà à qch.; **to blow the w. on s.o.,** dénoncer qn; *Sp:* **to blow the w. for a foul, for half time,** siffler une faute, la mi-temps; (*b*) **tin w.,** *A:* **penny w.,** flageolet *m*. **3.** *P:* **to wet, whet, one's w.,** s'arroser la gorge; se rincer la dalle.

whistle² **1.** *v.i.* (*a*) (*of pers., bird, wind, etc.*) siffler; **to w. for one's dog, for a taxi,** siffler son chien, un taxi; *F:* **he can w. for his money,** il peut courir après son argent; **you can w. for it!** tu peux toujours courir! **the bullet whistled past his ear,** la balle a passé en sifflant tout près de son oreille; (*b*) donner un coup de sifflet. **2.** *v.tr.* (*a*) siffler, siffloter (un air); (*b*) *F:* **to w. s.o., sth., down the wind,** laisser aller qn, qch.; ne plus se soucier de qn, de qch.; (*c*) *F:* **I'll w. up a few friends to help us,** je vais trouver quelques amis pour nous aider; **can you w. up some more sandwiches?** peux-tu préparer encore quelques sandwichs? **whistling** **1.** *a.* (oiseau, etc.) siffleur; **w. sound,** sifflement *m*; *Nau:* **w. buoy,** bouée *f* à sifflet. **2.** *n.* sifflement *m*; sifflerie *f*.

whistler ['(h)wislər] *n.* **1.** siffleur, -euse. **2.** oiseau siffleur. **3.** *Z:* siffleur, marmotte canadienne, *Fr.C:* siffleux *m*.

whistle-stop¹ ['(h)wis(ə)lstɔp] *n. esp. U.S:* (*a*) *Rail:* halte *f* (à arrêt facultatif); **w.-s. tour,** (i) tournée électorale rapide (faite par train spécial); (ii) tour rapide; (*b*) *F:* patelin *m*, bled *m*.

whistle-stop² *v.i. U.S:* faire une tournée électorale par train spécial.

whit¹ [(h)wit] *n.* (*usu. in neg.*) brin *m*; **he's not a w. the better for it,** il ne s'en porte nullement mieux.

Whit² *a. & n.* **W. Sunday,** (le dimanche de) la Pentecôte; **W. Monday,** le lundi de la Pentecôte.

white [(h)wait] **I.** *a.* **1.** (*a*) blanc, *f.* blanche; **as w. as snow,** blanc comme la neige; **we had a w. Christmas,** il a neigé à Noël; **w. hair,** cheveux blancs; **he's going w.,** il commence à blanchir; **w. wedding,** mariage *m* en blanc; *Cu:* **w. sauce,** sauce blanche; **w. meat,** chair blanche, blanc *m* (de poulet); *Com:* **w. goods,** (i) articles *mpl* de blanc; (ii) appareils ménagers (réfrigérateurs, machines à laver, etc.); *U.S:* **the W. House,** la Maison Blanche; *Geog:* **W. Russia,** Russie Blanche; (*b*) **the w. races,** les races blanches; **a w. man,** (i) un blanc; (ii) *esp. U.S:* un homme loyal; (*c*) **w. with fear,** blanc de peur; **to turn, go, w.,** devenir blanc, pâle, blême; blanchir, blêmir; **as w. as a ghost, as a sheet,** pâle comme la mort, comme un linge; (*d*) **w. wine,** vin blanc; **w. bread,** pain blanc; **w. coffee,** café *m* au lait; (*e*) **w. metal, alloy,** (i) métal blanc; (ii) antifriction *f*; **w. iron,** (i) fer blanc; (ii) fonte blanche; **w. spirit,** white-spirit *m*. **2.** *Lit:* (*of pers.*) pur, innocent; (*of reputation*) sans tache. **II.** *n.* **1.** blanc *m*. **2. zinc w.,** blanc de zinc. **3. dressed in w.,** habillé en blanc, de blanc; **whites,** (i) *Com:* linge blanc; (ii) *Sp:* pantalon blanc; *Com:* **w. sale,** vente *f* de blanc; **wash your whites with X,** lavez votre linge avec X. **4.** (*pers.*) blanc, *f.* blanche. **5.** (*a*) **the w. of an egg,** un blanc d'œuf; (*b*) **the w. of the eyes,** le blanc des yeux; *F:* **to turn up the whites of one's eyes,** (i) faire des yeux de carpe pâmée; (ii) tourner de l'œil.

whitebait ['(h)waitbeit] *n. Cu:* blanchaille *f*; **a dish of w.** = une friture.

white-collar ['(h)wait'kɔlər] *a.* **w.-c. worker,** employé *m* de bureau; col-blanc *m*, *pl.* cols-blancs.

white-faced ['(h)wait'feist] *a.* au visage pâle.

whitefish ['(h)waitfiʃ] *n. Ich:* **1.** corégone *m*. **2.** poisson *m* à chair blanche et non huileuse.

white-haired ['(h)wait'hɛəd] *a.* aux cheveux blancs.

Whitehall ['(h)waithɔ:l] *n.* l'Administration *f* britannique.

white-headed [(h)wait'hedid] *a.* (*a*) *Z:* à tête blanche; (*b*) (*pers.*) aux cheveux blancs; *Fig:* **the w.-h. boy,** le chouchou de la famille.

white-hot ['(h)wait'hɔt] *a.* chauffé, porté, à blanc.

white-livered ['(h)waitlivəd] *a. Fig:* (*of pers.*) poltron, pusillanime.

whiten ['(h)wait(ə)n] **1.** *v.tr.* (*a*) blanchir (les cheveux, le linge); (*b*) blanchir à la chaux, badigeonner en blanc. **2.** *v.i.* (*a*) blanchir; (*b*) (*of pers.*) pâlir, blêmir. **whitening** *n.* **1.** blanchiment *m* (d'un mur). **2.** blanchissement *m* (des cheveux).

whiteness ['(h)waitnis] *n.* (*a*) blancheur *f* (de la neige, de la peau); (*b*) pâleur *f* (du visage); (*c*) *A:* & *Lit:* innocence *f*, pureté *f*.

whiteout ['(h)waitaut] *n.* brouillard blanc aveuglant (particulier aux régions polaires).

whitethorn ['(h)waitθɔ:n] *n. Bot:* aubépine *f*.

whitethroat ['(h)waitθrout] *n. Orn:* fauvette grisette.

whitewall ['(h)waitwɔ:l] *n. U.S:* **w. (tire),** pneu *m* avec une bande blanche peinte sur le côté extérieur.

whitewash¹ ['(h)waitwɔʃ] *n.* **1.** blanc *m*, lait *m*, de chaux; badigeon *m* à la chaux; **to give a wall a coat of w.,** badigeonner un mur (en blanc). **2.** blanchiment *m* (d'une réputation). **3.** *Sp:* *F:* défaite *f* à zéro.

whitewash² *v.tr.* **1.** (*a*) peindre, blanchir, à la chaux; badigeonner en blanc; (*b*) blanchir, disculper (qn). **2.** *Sp:* *F:* battre (ses adversaires) sans qu'ils aient marqué un point. **whitewashing** *n.* **1.** peinture *f* à la chaux; badigeonnage *m*. **2.** blanchiment *m* (d'une réputation).

whitewood ['(h)waitwud] *n. Com:* bois blanc.

whitey ['(h)wəiti] *n. U.S:* *Pej:* (i) blanc, blanche; (ii) *coll.* les blancs.

whither ['(h)wiðər] *adv. & conj. A:* & *Lit:* **1.** (*interr.*) où? vers quel lieu? **2.** (*rel.*) (là) où; **I shall go w. fate leads me,** j'irai là où me mènera le destin.

whiting ['(h)waitiŋ] *n. Ich:* merlan *m*.

whitish ['(h)waitiʃ] *a.* blanchâtre.

whitlow ['(h)witlou] *n. Med:* panaris *m*.

Whitsun(tide) ['(h)witsən(taid)] *n.* (fête *f*, saison *f*, de) la Pentecôte.

whittle ['(h)witl] *v.tr.* **to w. (down),** amenuiser, parer (un bâton, une cheville); **to w. down, away, one's capital,** rogner son capital.

whiz(z) [(h)wiz] *n. F:* **w. kid,** jeune prodige *m*.

whizz¹ [(h)wiz] **1.** *int.* pan! **2.** *n.* (*a*) sifflement *m* (d'une balle); (*b*) *esp. U.S:* *F:* as *m*, crack *m* **(at,** en).

whizz² *v.i.* (*of bullet, etc.*) siffler; **cars were whizzing past, by,** des voitures passaient à toute vitesse.

who [hu:] *pers. pron. nom.* **1.** (*interr.*) qui? qui est-ce qui? *occ.* lequel, etc., quel, etc.; **w. is it?** qui est-ce? **w. is that woman?** qui, quelle, est cette femme? **w. on earth told you that?** qui diable vous a dit cela? **who's speaking?** qui est-ce qui parle? *Tp:* c'est de la part de qui? **w. did you say?** qui ça? **tell me who's w.,** dites-moi qui sont tous ces gens-là; **w. does he think he is?** pour qui se prend-il? **w. of us can still remember it?** qui, lesquels, d'entre nous se le rappelle(nt) encore? (*b*) *F:* (*grammatically incorrect, in formal speech always* **whom) w. do you want?** qui voulez-vous? **w. were you talking to?** à qui parliez-vous? **2.** (*a*) (*rel.*) qui; **the friends w. came yesterday,** les amis qui sont venus hier; (*b*) (*to avoid ambiguity*) lequel; **Louise's father, w. is very rich,** le père de Louise, lequel est très riche; (*c*) (*independent rel.*) (celui) qui; **deny it w. will,** le nie qui voudra.

whoa [wou] *int.* (*a*) (*to stop horse*) **w. (back)!** ho! holà! (*b*) *F:* (*to pers.*) doucement! attendez!

whodun(n)it [hu:'dʌnit] *n. F:* roman policier.

whoever [hu(:)'evər] *pers. pron. nom.* **1.** celui qui, etc.; quiconque; **w. finds it may keep it,** celui qui le trouvera pourra le garder. **2.** qui que + *sub.*; **w. you are, speak!** qui que vous soyez, parlez! **w. wrote that letter,** qui que ce soit qui ait écrit cette lettre; *F:* . . . **or w.,** ou qui que ce soit. **3.** *F:* (*replaces* **whomsoever** *in ordinary conversation*) **w. she marries,** celui qu'elle épousera; **w. you like,** qui vous voudrez.

whole [houl] **I.** *a.* **1.** (*a*) *A:* sain; en bonne santé; *B:* **his hand was made w.,** sa main fut guérie; (*b*) (*of pers.*) sain et sauf; (*of thg*) intact. **2.** (*a*) (*entire*) intégral, -aux; entier; complet, -ète; total, -aux; **ox roasted w.,** bœuf rôti entier; **he swallowed it w.,** (i) il l'a avalé sans le mâcher; (ii) *F:* il a pris ça pour de l'argent comptant; **a w. loaf,** un pain entier, *Mth:* **w. number,** nombre entier; **w. life insurance,** assurance *f* en cas de décès, pour la vie entière; (*b*) (*emphatic*) tout, entier, tout entier; **to tell the w. truth,** dire toute la vérité; **the w. world,** le monde entier; **to last a w. week,** durer toute une semaine; **I never saw him the w. evening,** je ne l'ai pas vu de (toute) la soirée; **w. families died of it,** des familles entières en sont mortes; *F:* **the w. lot of you,** vous tous. **II.** *n.* tout *m*, totalité *f*, ensemble *m*; **the w. of the school,** l'école entière; toute l'école; **nearly the w. of our resources,** la presque totalité de nos ressources; **he spent the w. of that year in London,** il a passé toute cette année-là à Londres; **the w. amounts to . . .,** le total se monte à . . .; **as a w.,** dans son ensemble; en totalité; **taken as a w.,** pris dans sa totalité; **on the w.,** à tout prendre; en somme; dans l'ensemble.

wholehearted [houl'hɑ:tid] *a.* (qui vient) du cœur; (rire) épanoui. **-ly** *adv.* de bon, de grand, cœur.

wholehogger [houl'hɔgər] *n. F:* jusqu'au-boutiste *mf.*

wholemeal ['houlmi:l] *n. Mill:* bisaille *f*; **w. bread,** pain complet.

wholeness ['houlnis] *n.* état complet; intégralité *f*; intégrité *f.*

wholesale ['houlseil] **1.** *n. & a.* (*a*) *n.* (vente *f* en) gros *m*; **w. and retail,** gros et détail; (*b*) **w. trade,** commerce *m* de gros, en gros; **w. dealer, merchant,** grossiste *mf*; commerçant, -ante, en gros; **w. price,** prix *m* de, en, gros; (*c*) *a.* **by w. borrowing,** en empruntant de tous côtés; **a w. slaughter,** un massacre, une tuerie en masse. **2.** *adv.* (*a*) **to sell, buy, w.,** vendre, acheter, en gros; (*b*) en masse; en bloc.

wholesaler ['houlseilər] *n.* grossiste *mf*; commerçant, -ante, en gros.

wholesome ['houlsəm] *a.* (aliment) sain; (air, climat) salubre; (remède) salutaire.

wholesomeness ['houlsəmnis] *n.* nature saine (de la nourriture); salubrité *f* (de l'air).

wholly ['houlli] *adv.* **1.** tout à fait; complètement, entièrement. **2.** intégralement, en totalité.

whom [hum] *pers. pron.* (*objective case*) **1.** (*interr.*) qui? qui est-ce que? **w. did you see?** qui avez-vous vu? qui est-ce que vous avez vu? **to w., of w., are you speaking?** à qui, de qui, parlez-vous? **I don't know to w. to turn,** je ne sais à qui m'adresser. **2.** (*rel.*) (*a*) (*direct object*) que; lequel, *f.* laquelle; *pl.* lesquels, *f.* lesquelles; **the man w. you saw,** l'homme que vous avez vu; (*b*) (*indirect object and after prep.*) qui; **he wanted to find somebody to w. he might talk,** il voulait trouver quelqu'un à qui parler; **the friend of w. I speak,** l'ami dont je parle; **these two men, both of w. were quite young,** ces deux hommes, qui tous deux étaient tout jeunes. **3.** (*independent rel.*) celui que, etc.; qui; **w. the gods love die young,** qui est aimé des dieux meurt jeune.

whomsoever [hu:msou'evər] *pers. pron esp. Lit:* **1.** celui (quel qu'il soit) que; **w. they choose,** celui qu'ils choisiront. **2.** qui que ce soit que.

whoop¹ [hu:p] **1.** *int.* houp! **2.** *n.* (*a*) *Ven:* huée *f*; (*b*) *Med:* quinte *f* (de la coqueluche); (*c*) cri *m* (de joie); (*d*) *NAm:* (h)ululement *m* (d'un hibou).

whoop² *v.i.* (*a*) *Ven:* huer; (*b*) *Med:* faire entendre la toux convulsive de la coqueluche; **whooping cough,** coqueluche; (*c*) crier, pousser des cris (de joie); (*d*) *NAm:* (*of owl*) (h)ululer; (*e*) *F:* **to w.** [wu:p] **it up,** (i) faire la noce; (ii) *NAm:* faire un bruit infernal.

whoopee [wu'pi:] *n. F: O:* **to make w.,** (i) faire la noce, la bombe; (ii) bien s'amuser.

whoops [(h)wu:ps] *int.* houp-là!

whop [(h)wɔp] *v.tr.* **(whopped)** *F:* (*a*) battre, rosser (qn); (*b*) battre, rouler (une équipe). **whopping** *F:* **1.** *a.* énorme; **w. great lie,** mensonge *m* de taille. **2.** *n.* rossée *f*, raclée *f.*

whopper ['(h)wɔpər] *n. F:* (*a*) quelque chose de colossal, d'énorme; (*b*) mensonge *m* de taille.

whore¹ [hɔ:r] *n.f.* prostituée; putain; *P:* **w. house,** bordel *m.*

whore² *v.i.* (*a*) (*of man*) **to w., to go whoring,** fréquenter les prostituées; courir la gueuse; (*b*) (*of woman*) se prostituer. **whoring** *n.* (*a*) prostitution *f*; (*b*) débauche *f.*

whorl [(h)wɔ:l] *n.* **1.** *Bot:* verticille *m.* **2.** tour *m* d'une spirale; spire *f*, volute *f*; vortex *m* (d'une coquille).

whorled [(h)wɔ:ld] *a.* (*of flowers*) verticillé; (*of shell*) convoluté, turbiné; *Arch:* voluté.

whortleberry ['(h)wɔ:t(ə)lberi] *n. Bot:* airelle *f* myrtille.

whose [hu:z] *poss.pron.* **1.** de qui? (*ownership*) à qui? **w. are these gloves?** à qui sont ces gants? **w. daughter are you?** de qui êtes-vous la fille? **w. fault is it?** à qui la faute? **w. book did you take?** à qui est le livre que vous avez pris? **2.** (*rel.*) (*a*) dont; **the pupil w. work I showed you,** l'élève dont je vous ai montré le travail; (*b*) (*after prep.*) de qui; duquel, *f.* de laquelle; *pl.* desquels, *f.* desquelles; **the man to w. wife I gave the money,** l'homme à la femme de qui, duquel, j'ai donné l'argent.

whosoever [hu:sou'evər] *pron. esp. Lit:* (*emphatic*) = -WHOEVER.

why [(h)wai] **1.** *adv. & conj.* (*a*) pourquoi? pour quelle raison? **w. didn't you say so?** pourquoi ne l'avez-vous pas dit? **w. not?** pourquoi pas? (*b*) (*rel.*) pourquoi; **that is (the reason) w. . . .,** voilà pourquoi . . .; **w. he should always be late I do not understand,** qu'il soit toujours en retard, je ne me l'explique pas; **I'll tell you w.,** je vais vous dire pourquoi. **2.** *n.* (*pl.* **whys)** pourquoi *m*, raison *f*; **I like to know the whys and wherefores of a thing,** j'aime à savoir le pourquoi et le comment d'une chose. **3.** *int.* (*a*) (*surprise*) **w., it's David!** tiens, mais c'est David! (*b*) (*protest*) **w., you're not afraid, are you?** voyons, vous n'avez pas peur? **w., what's the harm?** mais quel mal y a-t-il? (*c*) (*hesitation*) **w. I really don't know,** vraiment, franchement, je ne sais pas; (*d*) (*introducing apodosis*) **if this doesn't do, w. we must try something else,** si ceci ne réussit pas, alors, eh bien, il faudra essayer autre chose.

wick [wik] *n.* **1.** mèche *f* (d'une lampe, d'une bougie). **2.** *P:* **he gets on my w.,** il me tape sur les nerfs.

wicked ['wikid] *a.* **1.** (*evil*) mauvais, méchant; pervers; (crime) atroce, affreux; **a w. lie,** un mensonge (i) inique, (ii) mal intentionné; *n.pl.* **the w.,** les méchants. **2.** (*a*) (*of weather*) affreux, atroce; (*of pain*) cruel, atroce; **he's got a w. temper,** il a très mauvais caractère;

(*b*) **it's w. to waste so much food,** c'est un crime de gaspiller tant de nourriture; **it's a w. shame that . . .,** il est scandaleux que + *sub.*; (*c*) (*mischievous*) malicieux, espiègle; *F:* (*to child*) **you w. little thing!** petit vilain! petite vilaine! **3.** *F:* excellent; **a w. shot,** un coup de tonnerre. **-ly** *adv.* **1.** méchamment. **2.** (*a*) terriblement, affreusement; **w. expensive,** hors de prix; (*b*) malicieusement; **she was smiling w.,** elle avait un sourire malicieux.

wickedness ['wikidnis] *n.* méchanceté *f*; perversité *f*; atrocité *f* (d'un crime).

wicker ['wikər] *n.* (*a*) osier *m*; **w. chair,** chaise *f* en osier (tressé), en vannerie; (*b*) = WICKERWORK.

wickerwork ['wikəwə:k] *n.* vannerie *f*; osier (tressé).

wicket ['wikit] *n.* **1.** guichet (d'une porte, etc.). **2.** (*a*) **w. (door),** porte à piétons; (*b*) **w. (gate),** petite porte à claire-voie; portillon *m* (de passage à niveau). **3.** *NAm:* (*in bank*) guichet. **4.** *Cr:* (*a*) guichet; **w. keeper,** gardien *m* de guichet; (*b*) le terrain entre les guichets; **soft w.,** terrain mou; *Fig:* **to be on a good, a sticky, w.,** être dans une position avantageuse, difficile. **5.** *NAm:* (*at croquet*) arceau *m*.

wide [waid] **I.** *a.* **1.** large; **the roads gets wider after the village,** au-delà du village la route s'élargit; **to be five metres w.,** avoir cinq mètres de large, de largeur; **how w. is the room?** quelle est la largeur de la pièce? **to give a w. yawn,** bâiller en ouvrant largement la bouche; *Cin:* **w. screen,** grand écran; *Aut:* (*on vehicle*) **w. load** = convoi exceptionnel. **2.** (*of range, experience, knowledge*) étendu, vaste, ample; (*of influence*) répandu; **the w. world,** le vaste monde; **there is a w. difference between . . .,** il y a une grande différence entre . . .; **in a wider sense,** par extension; *Phot:* **w. angle of view,** grand angle de champ. **3.** (*a*) (vêtement) ample, large; (*b*) (vues, opinions) larges, libérales, sans étroitesse; **in the widest sense of the word,** dans l'acception la plus large du mot. **4.** (*a*) éloigné, loin; **to be w. of the mark,** être loin de compte; (*b*) *Cr:* **w. ball,** *n.* **w.,** balle écartée, qui passe hors de la portée du batteur. **5.** *F:* **a w. boy,** un malin, un débrouillard. **II.** *adv.* **1.** (*a*) loin; **far and w.,** de tous côtés; partout; (*b*) **w. apart,** espacé; **with one's legs w. apart,** les jambes très écartées. **2.** (ouvrir, etc.) largement, grandement; **to fling the door open w., w. open,** ouvrir la porte toute grande; **w.-open door,** porte toute grande ouverte; **to open one's eyes w.,** ouvrir les yeux tout grands; **to be w. awake,** être complètement, bien, éveillé; *Box:* **to leave oneself w. open,** se découvrir; *Fig:* **to leave oneself w. open to criticism,** prêter le flanc à, s'exposer à, la critique; *Aut:* **to take a bend w.,** prendre un virage large. **-ly** *adv.* **1.** largement; **w. read newspaper,** journal répandu, très lu, à grande circulation; **w. known,** très connu, connu partout; **to be w. read,** (i) (*of author*) avoir un public très étendu; (ii) (*of pers.*) avoir beaucoup lu; **he has travelled w.,** il a beaucoup voyagé. **2.** (planter) à de grands intervalles. **3.** extrèmement, très; **w. different versions of what happened,** versions très différentes de ce qui est arrivé.

wide-angle ['waidæŋgl] *a. Phot:* **w.-a. lens,** objectif *m* grand angulaire.

wide-eyed ['waidaid] *a.* les yeux grands ouverts, les yeux écarquillés; **he looked at me in w.-e. amazement,** il m'a regardé avec des yeux comme des soucoupes.

widen ['waid(ə)n] **1.** *v.tr.* (*a*) élargir; agrandir (qch.) en large; donner plus d'ampleur à (un vêtement); (*b*) évaser (un trou); (*c*) étendre (l'influence, les limites, de qch.). **2.** *v.i.* (*a*) **to w. (out),** s'élargir; s'agrandir (en large); s'évaser; (*b*) **the breach is widening,** la rupture s'accentue; (*c*) (*of influence*) s'étendre.

widening *n.* **1.** élargissement *m*; agrandissement *m* (en large). **2.** extension *f* (d'une influence).

widespread ['waidspred] **1.** (*of plain, wings*) étendu. **2.** répandu; universel; **w. opinion,** opinion largement répandue; **w. damage,** de grands dégâts.

widgeon ['widʒən] *n. Orn:* canard siffleur.

widow¹ ['widou] *n.* (*a*) veuve *f*; **she was left a w. at (the age of) thirty,** elle a été laissée veuve à l'âge de trente ans; **widow's pension,** pension *f* de veuve; (*b*) *Arach:* **black w.,** veuve noire.

widow² *v.tr.* **to be widowed,** devenir veuf, veuve; perdre son mari, sa femme. **widowed** *a.* (homme) veuf; (femme) veuve; **his w. mother,** sa mère qui est veuve; **w. life,** veuvage *m*.

widower ['widouər] *n.m.* veuf.

widowhood ['widouhud] *n.* veuvage *m*.

width [widθ] *n.* **1.** largeur *f* (d'une route, de la poitrine); ampleur *f* (d'un vêtement); grosseur *f* (d'un pneu); **to be three metres in w.,** avoir trois mètres de large. **2.** largeur (d'idées). **3.** *Tex:* lé *m*, laize *f*, largeur (d'un tissu); **double w.,** grande largeur.

widthwise ['widθwaiz] *adv.* dans la largeur.

wield [wi:ld] *v.tr. esp. Lit:* manier (l'épée, la plume); **to w. power,** exercer le pouvoir; avoir l'autorité.

wiener ['wi:nər] *n. NAm: Comest:* saucisse *f* de Frankfort; **w.** (*also* **weenie) roast,** barbecue *m* de saucisses de Frankfort.

wife, *pl.* **wives** [waif, waivz] *n.f.* **1.** femme (mariée); *esp. Adm: & Lit:* épouse; **Mr Martin and his w.,** M. Martin et sa femme; **she was his second w.,** il l'avait épousée en secondes noces; **the baker's, butcher's, grocer's, w.,** la boulangère, la bouchère, l'épicière; **his common law w.,** sa concubine; **battered wives,** femmes battues; *P:* **the w.,** la ménagère, la bourgeoise. **2.** (*a*) *A:* femme; commère; (*b*) **old wives' remedy, tale,** remède *m*, conte *m*, de bonne femme.

wifely ['waifli] *a.* conjugal, -aux; de bonne épouse.

wig [wig] *n.* (*a*) perruque *f*; **w. block, stand,** tête *f* à perruque; champignon *m*; (*b*) postiche *m*.

wigeon ['widʒən] *n. Orn:* canard siffleur.

wigged [wigd] *a.* (juge, etc.) à perruque.

wigging ['wigiŋ] *n. F: O:* verte semonce; savon *m*; **to give s.o. a good w.,** tancer vertement qn; **to get a good w.,** se faire laver la tête; recevoir un savon.

wiggle¹ ['wigl] *v. F:* (*a*) *v.tr.* agiter, remuer (qch); **to w. one's hips,** se tortiller les hanches; (*b*) *v.i.* se remuer, se tortiller; (*of fish*) frétiller; (*c*) *v.i. & tr.* **to w. (one's way) out of a difficulty,** se tirer, s'extraire, d'une position difficile; **to try to w. out of it,** chercher une échappatoire.

wiggle² *n. F:* tortillement *m* (du corps, etc.); **to give sth. a w.,** agiter, remuer, qch.

wiggly ['wigli] *a. F:* qui se remue, se tortille; **w. line,** trait ondulé.

wigmaker ['wigmeikər] *n.* perruquier, -ière.

wigwam ['wigwæm] *n.* wigwam *m*.

wilco ['wilkou] *int. esp. U.S: W.Tel:* (= **will comply**) j'exécute.

wild [waild] **I.** *a.* **1.** (*of animal, plant*) sauvage; **w. flowers,** fleurs *f* des champs, sauvages; **w. country,** pays inculte, sauvage. **2.** (*a*) (vent) furieux, violent; (torrent) impétueux; **w. sea,** mer agitée; **a w. (and stormy) night,** une nuit de tempête; (*b*) (animal) farouche, inapprivoisé; *F:* **w. horses wouldn't drag it out of me,** rien au monde ne me le ferait dire; (*c*) (*of pers.*) dissipé, dissolu; (*of adolescent*) indiscipliné; (*of behaviour*) déréglé; (*d*) *Cards:* (carte) libre. **3.** (*a*) **w. applause,** applaudissements *mpl* frénétiques; **w. enthusiasm,** enthousiasme délirant, débordant; **w. eyes,** yeux égarés; **w. with joy, with rage,** fou de joie, de colère; **it makes me w. to think that . . .,** j'enrage, cela me met en rage, quand je pense que . . .; **to drive s.o. w.,** mettre qn en fureur; **to be w. about s.o., sth.,**

être emballé pour qn, qch.; **I'm not w. about it,** ça ne m'emballe pas; (*b*) (idée) fantasque; (projet) insensé, extravagant; **w. talk,** propos *mpl* en l'air; **w. rumour,** bruit extravagant, sans fondation; **w. promises,** promesses extravagantes; **to make a w. guess (at the answer),** répondre à tout hasard, à l'aveuglette; **to make a w. rush at sth.,** se ruer sur qch. **II.** *adv.* (*a*) (*of plant*) **to grow w.,** retourner, pousser, à l'état sauvage; (*b*) **to run w.,** (i) (*of children*) mener une vie sans discipline; (ii) (*of hooligans*) se livrer à des actes de violence; (iii) (*of escaped bull, etc.*) s'emballer. **III.** *n.* (*of animal*) **in the w.,** à l'état sauvage; **the call of the w.,** l'appel *m* de la jungle; **in the wilds,** dans une région sauvage, déserte; dans la brousse; **he lives in the wilds of Africa,** il habite au fin fond de l'Afrique. **wildly** *adv.* **1.** (écrire, parler) d'une manière extravagante; **to talk w.,** dire des folies; **to rush about w.,** courir çà et là comme un fou; **w. happy,** follement heureux; **to be w. excited,** être dans les nues; *F:* **I'm not w. enthusiastic about it,** ça ne m'emballe pas. **2.** (vivre, se comporter) d'une manière déréglée. **3.** (répondre) au hasard, au petit bonheur; **to hit out w.,** lancer des coups au hasard.

wildcat[1] ['waildkæt] *n.* (*a*) chat *m* sauvage; (*b*) *F:* **w. scheme,** projet insensé, extravagant; spéculation risquée; **w. strike,** grève sauvage.

wildebeest ['wildibi:st, 'vil-] *n. Z:* gnou *m.*

wilderness ['wildənis] *n.* (*a*) désert *m*; lieu *m* sauvage; **a voice in the w.,** *B:* **the voice of one crying in the w.,** une voix qui prêche dans le désert; *F:* (*of politician, party*) **to be in the w.,** ne plus être au pouvoir; (*b*) partie inculte, laissée à l'état sauvage (d'un jardin).

wildfire ['waildfaiər] *n.* (*of report, etc.*) **to spread like w.,** se répandre comme une traînée de poudre.

wildfowl ['waildfaul] *n. coll.* (*a*) gibier *m* à plume; (*b*) gibier d'eau; sauvagine *f.* **wildfowling** *n.* chasse *f* au gibier d'eau, à la sauvagine.

wildfowler ['waildfaulər] *n.* chasseur *m* au, de, gibier d'eau, à la sauvagine.

wildlife ['waildlaif] *n.* faune *f* (et flore *f*).

wildness ['waildnis] *n.* **1.** état *m* sauvage (d'un pays, d'un animal); état inculte (d'une région). **2.** (*a*) fureur *f*, impétuosité *f* (du vent, des vagues); déchaînement *m* (de la tempête); (*b*) nature *f* farouche (du gibier); (*c*) dérèglement *m* (de mœurs); égarements *mpl* (de conduite). **3.** frénésie *f* (d'applaudissements); extravagance *f* (d'idées, de paroles).

wile [wail] *n. usu.pl.* ruse *f*, artifice *m*; **to fall a victim to s.o.'s wiles,** succomber aux séductions de qn.

wilful, *NAm:* **willful** ['wilf(u)l] *a.* **1.** (*of pers.*) obstiné, entêté, volontaire. **2.** (*of action*) fait avec intention; fait exprès, de propos délibéré, à dessein; *Jur:* **w. murder,** homicide volontaire, prémédité; **w. damage,** bris *m*; dommage délibéré. **-fully** *adv.* **1.** obstinément; avec entêtement. **2.** exprès, à dessein.

wilfulness, *NAm:* **willfulness** ['wilf(u)lnis] *n.* **1.** obstination *f*, entêtement *m.* **2.** préméditation *f.*

wiliness ['wailinis] *n.* astuce *f*; caractère rusé.

will[1] [wil] *n.* **1.** (*a*) volonté *f*; **to have a strong, weak, w.,** avoir la volonté forte, faible; **w. of iron, iron w.,** volonté de fer; **he has a w. of his own,** il sait ce qu'il veut; il est volontaire; **strength of w.,** force de volonté; **the w. to live,** la volonté de vivre; **where there's a w. there's a way,** vouloir c'est pouvoir; **with the best w. in the world,** avec la meilleure volonté du monde; **to do sth. of one's own free w.,** faire qch. de bonne volonté; *Phil:* **free w.,** libre arbitre *m*; (*b*) **to work with a w.,** travailler de bonne volonté, de bon cœur. **2.** (*a*) décision *f*; volonté; *B:* **Thy w. be done,** que ta volonté soit faite; **to impose one's w. on s.o.,** imposer sa volonté à qn; (*b*) bon plaisir; gré *m*; **at w.,** à volonté; à discrétion; **to do sth. of one's own free w.,** faire qch. de son plein gré; **to do sth. against one's w.,** faire qch. contre son gré, à contrecœur. **3. good, ill, w.,** bonne, mauvaise, volonté. **4.** *Jur:* testament *m*; acte *m* de dernière volonté; **the last w. and testament of . . .,** les dernières volontés de . . .; **to make one's w.,** faire son testament; **to mention s.o. in one's w.,** mettre, coucher, qn sur son testament.

will[2] *v.tr.* (*p.t. & p.p.* **willed**) **1.** (*a*) *A: & Lit:* **God so willed (it),** Dieu l'a voulu ainsi; (*b*) **to w. s.o. to do, into doing, sth.,** faire faire qch. à qn par un acte de volonté, en lui imposant sa volonté; (*by hypnotism*) suggestionner qn. **2.** léguer (qch.); disposer de (qch.) par testament.

will[3] *modal aux v. def.* (*I* **will,** *you, he, we, etc.,* **will**; *A: thou* **wilt**; *p.t. & condit.* **would** [wud]; *I will, he will, etc. are often contracted into* **I'll** [ail], **he'll** [hi:l] *etc.*; *I would, they would, etc., to* **I'd** [aid], **they'd** [ðeid] *etc.*; *will not and would not to* **won't** [wount], **wouldn't** ['wud(ə)nt]) **I.** vouloir. **1.** (*a*) *esp. Lit:* **do as you w.,** faites comme vous voudrez; **I would have stayed there for ever,** j'aurais voulu y rester toujours; **what would you have me do?** que voulez-vous que je fasse? **say what you w., you won't be believed,** quoi que vous disiez, on ne vous croira pas; (*b*) *esp. Lit:* (*optative*) **would (that) I were a bird!** je voudrais être un oiseau! **would to God it wasn't true!** plût à Dieu que cela ne fût pas vrai! **2.** (*consent*) **I w. not do it,** je refuse de le faire; **I w. not have that said of me,** je ne veux pas qu'on dise cela de moi; **I wouldn't do it for anything,** je ne le ferais pour rien au monde; **he could if he would,** il le pourrait s'il le voulait; *F:* **will do!** d'accord! je le ferai! **the wound wouldn't heal,** la blessure ne voulait pas se cicatriser; **the engine won't start,** le moteur ne veut pas démarrer; **just wait a moment, w. you?** voulez-vous bien attendre un instant? **would you pass the mustard please?** voudriez-vous bien me passer la moutarde? **he w., would, have none of it,** (i) il n'en veut, n'en voulait, à aucun prix; (ii) il refuse, refusait, d'en entendre parler; **I w.** *not* **have it!** je ne le veux pas! **won't you sit down?** asseyez-vous, je vous en prie; *will* **you be quiet!** voulez-vous bien vous taire? **3.** (*emphatic*) **accidents** *will* **happen,** on ne peut pas éviter les accidents; **he** *will* **go out in spite of his cold,** il persiste à sortir malgré son rhume; **he** *will* **get in my way,** il est toujours dans mon chemin; **the doctor** *will* **have his little joke,** il aime (à) plaisanter, le docteur; **I quite forgot!—you would!** j'ai oublié!—c'est bien de vous! *F:* **I wouldn't know,** je ne saurais dire. **4.** (*habit*) **this hen w. lay up to six eggs a week,** cette poule pond jusqu'à six œufs par semaine; **she would often return home exhausted,** elle rentrait souvent très fatiguée. **5.** (*conjecture*) **that would be your cousin?** ça c'est sans doute votre cousin? **you'll be tired,** vous devez être fatigué. **II.** (*used as aux. v. forming future tenses*) **1.** (*used in the 1st pers.; for the 2nd and 3rd pers. see* SHALL) **I won't be caught again,** on ne m'y reprendra plus. **2.** (*simple future; used in the 2nd and 3rd pers.; for the 1st pers. see* SHALL) (*a*) **w. he be there?—he w.,** y sera-t-il?—oui (, il y sera); **no, he won't,** non (, il n'y sera pas); **but I shall starve!—no, you won't,** mais je mourrai de faim!—mais non; **you won't forget, w. you?** vous n'oublierez pas, hein? **you'll write to me, won't you?** vous m'écrirez, n'est-ce pas? **he told me he would be there,** il m'a dit qu'il serait là; (*b*) (*immediate future*) **Mr Long w. explain the situation to you,** M. Long va vous expliquer la situation; (*c*) (*in injunctions*) **you'll be here at three,** soyez ici à trois heures; (*d*) (*in Scot. & N. of Engl.* **I will = I shall**) **we will be there,** nous serons là. **3.** (*conditional*) **he would come if you invited him,** il viendrait si vous l'invitiez; **had he, if he had, let go he would have fallen,** s'il avait lâché prise il serait tombé. **willing** *a.* **1.** (*a*) de bonne volonté; bien disposé; serviable; **w. men,** hommes de bonne volonté; **w. hands,** mains empressées; (*b*) consentant. **2. to be w. to do sth.,** vouloir bien faire qch.; être disposé à faire qch.; **w. to help,** prêt à rendre service; complaisant; **I am more than w. to come with you,** je ne demande pas mieux que de vous accompagner; **I am able and w. to help them,** je peux les aider et je le ferai très volontiers; **w. or not,** bon gré mal gré; **God w.,** s'il plaît à Dieu; *F:* **to show w.,** faire preuve de bonne volonté. **willingly** *adv.* **1.** volontairement; de plein gré. **2.** (*a*) de bonne volonté; de bon cœur; (*b*) volontiers; avec plaisir; de grand cœur.

William ['wiliəm] **1.** *Pr.n.m.* Guillaume: **W. the Conqueror,** Guillaume le Conquérant. **2.** *Hort:* **W. pear,** poire *f* Williams; *Bot:* **sweet w.,** œillet *m* de poète.

willies ['wiliz] *n.pl. F:* **to have the w.,** avoir le trac, la frousse; **it gives me the w.,** cela me met les nerfs en pelote, en boule.

willingness ['wiliŋnis] *n.* **1.** bonne volonté; **with the utmost w.,** de très bon cœur. **2.** consentement *m*; **to express one's w. to do sth.,** accepter de faire qch.; consentir à faire qch.

will-o'-the-wisp [wiləðə'wisp] *n.* feu follet.

willow ['wilou] *n.* **1.** (*a*) *Bot:* **w. (tree),** saule *m*; **weeping w.,** saule pleureur; (*b*) *Cer:* **w. pattern plate,** assiette *f* à décoration à la chinoise en teinte bleue, à motif de saule pleureur. **2.** *Cr: F:* **the w.,** la batte.

willowy ['wiloui] *a.* souple, svelte, élancé.

willpower ['wilpauər] *n.* volonté *f*; **lack of w.,** manque *m* de volonté.

willy-nilly ['wili'nili] *adv.* bon gré mal gré.

wilt¹ [wilt] **1.** *v.i.* (*a*) (*of plant*) se flétrir, se faner; (*b*) (*of pers.*) dépérir, languir; (*c*) *F:* perdre contenance (devant des reproches); se dégonfler. **2.** *v.tr.* (*of the heat*) flétrir (les fleurs).

wilt² *see* WILL³.

wily ['waili] *a.* rusé, astucieux; malin, -igne; roublard; **he's a w. old bird,** c'est un vieux roublard.

wimple ['wimpl] *n.* guimpe *f* (de religieuse).

win¹ [win] *n. Sp:* victoire *f*; **to have three wins in succession,** gagner trois fois de suite; **to back a horse for a w.,** jouer un cheval gagnant.

win² *v.tr. & i.* (*p.t. & p.p.* **won** [wʌn]; *pr.p.* **winning**) **1.** gagner (une bataille, une course, un pari); remporter, gagner (un prix); remporter la victoire; **to w. money from s.o.,** gagner de l'argent à qn; *Rac:* **to w. by a length,** gagner d'une longueur; **to back a horse to w.,** jouer un cheval gagnant; *F:* **you (just) can't w.,** j'aurai, on aura, toujours tort; **you can't win them all,** on ne peut pas plaire à tout le monde. **2.** acquérir (de la popularité, la bienveillance de qn); captiver (l'attention de qn); gagner (la confiance de qn); **to w. s.o.'s love,** se faire aimer de qn. **3. to w. all hearts,** gagner, conquérir, tous les cœurs; **to w. s.o. away from sth.,** détourner, détacher, qn de qch.; **see whether you can w. him over,** essayez de le persuader de se mettre avec nous; **I won him round to my point of view,** j'ai réussi à lui faire accepter mon point de vue. **4. he won his way to the top of his profession,** il a réussi à atteindre le sommet de sa profession; **to w. through,** y arriver, parvenir, réussir; venir à bout. **5.** *O:* extraire (le charbon, le minerai). **winning 1.** *a.* (*a*) gagnant; **w. number,** numéro gagnant; (*in a lottery*) numéro sortant; **the w. side,** les vainqueurs *mpl; Sp:* **w. streak, sequence,** suite *f* de victoires; (*b*) attrayant, séduisant, (sourire) engageant. **2.** *n.* (*a*) victoire *f*; acquisition *f* (de qch.); **the w. of a battle,** le gain d'une bataille; (*b*) *Min:* extraction *f* (du charbon); (*c*) **winnings,** gains (aux courses).

wince¹ [wins] *n.* crispation *f* (de douleur); tressaillement *m*.

wince² *v.i.* faire une grimace de douleur, tressaillir de douleur; **the remark made him w.,** à cette observation il s'est crispé.

winch¹ [win(t)ʃ] *n. Mec.E:* (*a*) manivelle *f*; (*b*) *Mec.E:* treuil *m* (de hissage).

winch² *v.tr. Mec.E: etc:* **to w. sth., s.o., up,** soulever hisser, monter, qch., qn, à l'aide d'un treuil; **to w. sth. in,** amener, rentrer, qch. à l'aide d'un treuil.

wind¹ [wind] *n.* **1.** vent *m*; (*a*) **north, south, w.,** vent du nord, du sud; **east, west, w.,** vent d'est, d'ouest; **house exposed to all the winds,** maison exposée à tous les vents; *Fig:* **to see, to find out, which way the w. blows,** regarder de quel côté vient le vent; *F:* **there's something in the w.,** il se prépare, se mijote, quelque chose; *F:* **to go like the w.,** aller comme le vent; **to sow the w. and reap the whirlwind,** semer le vent et récolter la tempête; *F:* **to have, get, the w. up,** avoir le trac, la frousse; avoir une peur bleue; **to put the w. up s.o.,** faire une peur bleue à qn; (*b*) **head w.,** vent debout; **following w.,** vent arrière; *Nau:* vent de poupe; **to sail against the w.,** avoir le vent droit debout; **to sail, run, before the w.,** courir vent arrière; **to sail with w. and tide,** avoir vent et marée; **in the teeth of the w.,** contre le vent; **to sail into the w.,** venir, aller, au lof; *F:* **to sail close to the w.,** friser (i) l'indécence, (ii) la malhonnêteté; *F:* **to take the w. out of s.o.'s sails,** déjouer les projets de qn; couper l'herbe sous le pied de qn; (*c*) *Av:* **w. indicator,** indicateur *m* de direction du vent; **w. sock, sleeve,** manche *f* à air; *F:* biroute *f*. **2.** *Ven:* vent; *F:* **to get w. of sth.,** avoir vent de qch.; éventer (un secret, etc.). **3.** *Med:* vent(s); flatuosité *f*; **to break w.,** lâcher des gaz; **to have w.,** (i) roter; (ii) péter. **4.** souffle *m*, respiration *f*; haleine *f*; **to get one's second w.,** reprendre haleine; **let me get my w.,** laissez-moi souffler. **5.** *Ind:* vent; air *m*, vent, de soufflerie; *Mus:* **w. chest,** laie *f*, sommier *m* (d'un orgue); **w. tunnel,** soufflerie; tunnel *m* aérodynamique. **6.** *Mus:* **w. instrument,** instrument *m* à vent; (*in orchestra*) **the w.,** les instruments à vent.

wind² *v.tr.* **1.** [waind] (*p.t. & p.p.* **winded** ['waindid] *or* **wound** [waund]) **to w. the horn,** sonner du cor de la trompe. **2.** [wind] **(winded)** (*a*) *Ven:* (*of hounds*) avoir vent (du gibier); (*b*) couper la respiration, le souffle, à (qn); essouffler (qn, un cheval); (*c*) laisser souffler (un cheval). **winded** [windid] *a.* hors d'haleine; essoufflé.

wind³ [waind] *v.* (*p.t. & p.p.* **wound** [waund]) **I.** *v.i.* **1.** tourner; faire des détours; serpenter; (*of path, river*) serpenter; (*of staircase*) monter en colimaçon; **river that winds across the plain,** rivière *f* qui serpente à travers la plaine; **the road winds up, down, the hill,** le chemin monte, descend, en serpentant. **2.** (*of thread*) **to w. round sth.,** s'enrouler autour de qch. **II.** *v.tr.* **1.** enrouler; *Tex:* dévider, envider (le fil); dévider (la soie); **to w. wool into a ball,** enrouler de la laine en peloton; **to w. cotton on a reel,** bobiner du coton; *Fish:* **to w. in the line,** ramener la ligne; **she wound her arms round the child,** elle a entouré l'enfant de ses bras. **2. to w. a bobbin,** enrouler le fil sur une bobine; *El:* **to w. a dynamo,** armer une dynamo. **3.** remonter (l'horloge). **4.** *Min:* **to w. up,** hisser, remonter (le minerai). **winding 1.** *a.* (chemin, cours d'eau) sinueux, qui serpente; (chemin) anfractueux; (route) en lacets; **w. streets,** rues tortueuses; **w. staircase,** escalier tournant, en vis, en colimaçon. **2.** *n.* (*a*) mouvement sinueux; cours sinueux; serpentement *m*; replis *mpl;* (*b*) (i) *Tex:* bobinage *m*, embobinage *m*; *El:* enroulement *m*, bobinage; (ii) *A:* **w. sheet,** linceul *m*, suaire *m*; (*c*)

Min: remonte *f*, remontée *f*; **w. gear,** (i) *Min:* appareils *mpl*, machine *f*, d'extraction; (ii) treuil *m* (d'un ascenseur); (*d*) **w. (up),** (i) remontage *m* (d'une horloge, d'une montre); (ii) bandage *m* (d'un ressort); (*e*) **windings,** méandres *mpl* (d'une rivière); zigzags *mpl* (d'une route); (*f*) enroulement (d'une bobine, etc.); *El:* **armature w.,** enroulement d'enduit; (*g*) **w. up,** fin *f*, conclusion *f* (de qch.); *Com:* liquidation *f*, dissolution *f* (d'une société); clôture *f* (d'un compte).

wind up 1. *v.tr.* (*a*) enrouler (un cordage, etc.); (*b*) bander (un ressort); remonter (une horloge); *F:* (*of pers.*) **to be all wound up,** être excité, énervé; (*c*) finir, terminer (qch.); *Com:* liquider (une société); régler, clôturer (un compte); **he wound up his speech by announcing that . . .,** il a terminé son discours en faisant savoir que . . .. **2.** *v.i. F:* finir; se terminer; **he'll w. up in prison,** il finira en prison.

windbag ['windbæg] *n. F:* orateur verbeux; moulin *m* à paroles; **what a w.!** quel bavard!

windblown ['windbloun] *a.* **1.** emporté par le vent. **2. w. hair,** cheveux ébouriffés par le vent.

windborne ['windbɔːn] *a.* porté par le vent.

windbreak ['windbreik] *n. Hort: etc:* abrivent *m*; brise-vent *m inv*; abat-vent *m inv.* **2.** *For:* volis *m.*

windcheater ['windtʃiːtər] *n. Cost:* blouson *m*; *Fr.C:* coupe-vent *m inv.*

winder ['waindər] *n.* **1.** (*pers.*) (*a*) *Tex:* bobineur, -euse; dévideur, -euse; (*b*) remonteur, -euse (d'horloges). **2.** (*device*) (*a*) *Tex:* bobinoir *m*; dévidoir *m*; (*b*) remontoir *m* (d'une horloge, d'une montre); (*c*) *Aut:* lève-glace(s) *m inv* (de portière).

windfall ['windfɔːl] *n.* **1.** fruit abattu par le vent; fruit tombé. **2.** (*a*) aubaine *f*; bonne fortune; (*b*) héritage inattendu.

windjammer ['win(d)dʒæmər] *n. Nau:* grand voilier.

windlass ['windləs] *n.* treuil *m*; *Nau:* guindeau *m.*

windmill ['windmil] *n.* moulin *m* à vent; **to tilt at windmills,** se battre contre des moulins à vent.

window ['windou] *n.* (*a*) fenêtre *f*; **casement w.,** fenêtre croisée, à battants; **sash w.,** fenêtre à coulisse, à guillotine; *Fr.C:* fenêtre anglaise; **bay, bow, w.,** fenêtre en saillie; *Ecc.Arch:* **stained-glass w.,** vitrail, -aux *m*; **rose w.,** rosace *f*; **w. frame,** (i) formant *m*, (ii) châssis *m*, de fenêtre; **w. cleaner,** laveur *m* de vitres, de carreaux; **to look in at, out of, the w.,** regarder par, à la, fenêtre; **to break a w.,** casser une vitre, un carreau; (*b*) **French w.,** porte-fenêtre *f*, *pl.* portes-fenêtres; (*c*) (*of ticket office*) guichet *m*; (*d*) **(shop) w.,** vitrine *f*, devanture *f*; **w. display,** étage *m*; **w. dressing,** (i) (l'art de) l'étalage; (ii) *F:* façade *f*, décor *m* de théâtre, camouflage *m*; **w. dresser,** étalagiste *mf*; *F:* **w. shopping,** lèche-vitrines *m*; **to go w. shopping,** faire du lèche-vitrines; (*e*) *Aut: Rail:* vitre *f*; glace *f*; *Aut:* **rear w.,** lunette *f* arrière; (*f*) fenêtre (d'une enveloppe); panneau transparent; (*g*) *Anat:* fenêtre (du tympan).

windowledge ['windouledʒ] *n.* rebord *m* de fenêtre.

windowless ['windoulis] *n.* sans fenêtres.

windowpane ['windoupein] *n.* vitre *f*, carreau *m.*

windowsill ['windousil] *n.* (i) rebord *m*, (ii) (*inside*) appui *m*, tablette *f*, de fenêtre.

windpipe ['windpaip] *n. Anat:* trachée *f.*

windpower ['windpauər] *n.* énergie éolienne.

windscreen ['windskriːn] *n.* **1.** abrivent *m*; abat-vent *m inv*; brise-vent *m inv.* **2.** *Aut:* parebrise *m inv*; **w. wiper,** essuie-glace *m*, *pl.* essuie-glaces; **w. washer,** lave-glace *m*, *pl.* lave-glaces.

windshield ['windʃiːld] *n. NAm:* = WINDSCREEN 2.

windstorm ['windstɔːm] *n.* tempête *f* de vent.

windsurfer ['windsəːfər] *n. Sp:* **1.** planche *f* à voile. **2.** (*pers.*) véliplanchiste *mf.*

windsurfing ['windsəːfiŋ] *n.* **to go w.,** faire de la planche à voile.

windswept ['windswept] *a.* balayé par le vent; **w. hair,** cheveux ébouriffés.

windward ['windwəd] **1.** *a.* au vent; *Geog:* **the W. Islands,** les îles *fpl* du Vent. **2.** *n.* côté *m* au vent; **lying to (the) w. of . . .,** situé au vent de . . ..

windy ['windi] *a.* **1.** venteux; (journée) de grand vent; **it's very w.,** il fait beaucoup de vent. **2.** (*of place*) balayé par le vent; exposé au vent, aux quatre vents. **3.** *F:* **to be w.,** avoir le trac, la frousse.

wine¹ [wain] *n.* (*a*) vin *m*; **white, red, rosé, w.,** vin blanc, rouge, rosé; **dry, sweet, w.,** vin sec, doux; **sparkling w.,** vin mousseux; **w. merchant,** négociant *m* en vins; marchand *m* de vins; **w. cellar,** cave *f* (à vin); **w. bottle,** bouteille *f* à vin; **w. cooler,** rafraîchissoir *m*, rafraîchisseur *m* (à vin); (*in restaurant*) **wine list,** carte *f* des vins; **w. waiter,** sommelier, -ière; **w. producing district,** pays *m* vignoble, de vignobles; **w. vinegar,** vinaigre *m* de vin; (*b*) **rhubarb, ginger, w.,** vin de rhubarbe, de gingembre.

wine² *v.tr.* **to w. and dine s.o.,** fêter qn.

wine-coloured ['wainkʌləd] *a.* couleur de vin; lie de vin *inv.*

wineglass ['wainglɑːs] *n.* verre *m* à vin.

winepress ['wainpres] *n.* pressoir *m.*

wing¹ [wiŋ] *n.* **1.** (*a*) aile *f* (d'oiseau, d'insecte); **w. span, spread,** envergure *f*; **to take s.o. under one's w.,** prendre qn sous son aile, sous sa protection; *Lit:* **fear lent him wings,** la peur lui donnait des ailes; (*b*) vol *m*, essor *m*; **to shoot a bird on the w.,** tirer un oiseau au vol, à la volée; (*of bird*) **to be on the w.,** voler; **to take w.,** s'envoler; prendre son vol, son essor; (*c*) *Mil.Av:* **wings,** insigne *m* de pilote. **2.** *Av:* aile (d'un avion); **delta w.,** aile (en) delta; **w. span,** envergure *f*; **w. flap,** volet *m* (d'aile). **3.** (*a*) battant *m* (d'une porte); (*b*) aile (d'un bâtiment); pavillon *m* (d'un hôpital); *Th:* **the wings,** la coulisse, les coulisses; **in the wings,** (i) dans la coulisse; (ii) à la cantonnade; (*c*) *Mil:* aile, flanc *m* (d'une armée); *Sp:* (i) aile; (ii) (*pers.*) ailier *m*; **the w. halves,** les demis *mpl* aile; *Pol:* **the left w. (of the party),** l'aile gauche (du parti); (*d*) aile (d'un moulin à vent, d'une selle); oreille *f*, ailette (d'une vis); **w. bolt, screw,** boulon *m*, vis, à oreilles; *Furn:* **w. chair,** fauteuil *m* à oreillettes. **4.** *Aut:* aile (d'une voiture); **w. mirror,** rétroviseur *m* de côté. **5.** *Mil.Av:* escadre aérienne; *U.S:* brigade aérienne; **w. commander,** lieutenant-colonel *m.*

wing² *v.tr. & i.* **1.** (*a*) empenner (une flèche); (*b*) *Lit:* **fear winged his steps, his flight,** la peur lui donnait des ailes; (*c*) (*of bird*) **to w. its way,** voler. **2.** frapper, blesser (un oiseau) à l'aile; **I've winged him,** je lui ai mis du plomb dans l'aile. **winged** [wiŋd, *Lit: often* 'wiŋid] *a.* (*a*) ailé; *Ven:* **w. game,** gibier *m* à plumes; (*b*) (*with adj. prefixed*) **white(-)w.,** aux ailes blanches.

wingding ['wiŋdiŋ] *n. U.S. F:* soirée *f*, fête *f*, surprise-partie *f.*

winger ['wiŋər] *n. Fb: etc:* ailier *m.*

wingless ['wiŋlis] *a.* sans ailes; aptère.

wink¹ [wiŋk] *n.* clignement *m* d'œil; clin *m* d'œil; **with a w.,** en clignant de l'œil; *F:* **to tip s.o. the w.,** prévenir, avertir, qn; **to have forty winks,** faire un petit somme, une petite sieste; **I didn't sleep a w., didn't get a w. of sleep, all night,** je n'ai pas dormi, fermé l'œil, de toute la nuit; **a nod's as good as a w. to him,** il entend à demi-mot.

wink² **1.** *v.i.* (*a*) cligner de l'œil, cligner les yeux; **to w. at s.o.,** cligner de l'œil, lancer un clignement d'œil, à qn; (*b*) **to w. at an abuse,** fermer les yeux sur un abus; (*c*) (*of star, light*) clignoter. **2.** *v.tr.* **she winked an eye,** elle a cligné de l'œil. **winking 1.** *a.* (*of* *light*) clignotant. **2.** *n.* clignement *m* de l'œil; clignotement *m*; **as easy as w.,** simple comme bonjour; *F:* **like w.,** en un clin d'œil; (*b*) clignotement (d'une lumière).

winker ['wiŋkər] *n. Aut: F:* clignotant *m.*

winkle¹ [wiŋkl] *n.* **1.** *Moll:* bigorneau *m.* **2.** *F:* **w. pickers,** chaussures *fpl* à bout pointu.

winkle² *v.tr. F:* **to w. out,** extraire (qch); déloger (qn).

winner ['winər] *n.* (*a*) vainqueur *m*; gagnant, -ante; *Turf:* (cheval) gagnant; (*in lottery*) **the w. of the big prize,** le gagnant du gros lot; **to back a w.,** (i) *Turf:* jouer un cheval gagnant; (ii) *F:* jouer gagnant, bien miser; (*at fair*) **every time a w.!** à tous les coups l'on gagne! (*b*) *F:* roman, pièce, à grand succès; **this book will be a w.,** ce livre a un succès assuré.

winnow ['winou] *v.tr.* (*a*) *Agr:* vanner (le grain); **to w. (away, out) the chaff from the grain,** séparer l'ivraie d'avec le grain; (*b*) **to w. the evidence,** passer les témoignages au crible. **winnowing** *n.* **1.** (*a*) vannage *m*; **w. basket,** van *m*; (*b*) examen minutieux. **2. winnowings,** vannure *f.*

winnower ['winouər] *n.* **1.** (*pers.*) vanneur, -euse. **2.** (*machine*) vanneuse *f*; tarare *m.*

winsome ['winsəm] *a.* captivant, séduisant. **-ly** *adv.* d'une manière captivante.

winsomeness ['winsəmnis] *n.* charme *m* attrait *m.*

winter¹ ['wintər] *n.* hiver *m*; **in w.,** en hiver; *Lit:* **he has seen sixty winters,** il compte soixante hivers; **winter clothing,** vêtements *mpl* d'hiver; **w. resort,** station hivernale; **w. visitors,** hivernants *mpl*; **w. sports,** sports *mpl* d'hiver; **w. quarters,** quartiers *mpl* d'hiver.

winter² **1.** *v.i.* hiverner, passer l'hiver (**at,** à). **2.** *v.tr.* hiverner (le bétail). **wintering** *n.* hivernage *m.*

winter-flowering [wintə'flauəriŋ] *a.* (*of planet*) hibernal, -aux; hiémal, -aux.

wintergreen ['wintəgri:n] *n. Bot:* gaulthérie *f*; *Pharm:* **oil of w.,** essence *f* de wintergreen.

winterize ['wintəraiz] *v.tr. esp. N Am:* mettre (une voiture, une maison, etc.) en condition pour passer l'hiver; *Fr.C:* hivériser.

wintertime, *Lit:* **wintertide** ['wintətaim, -taid] *n.* l'hiver *m.*

wint(e)ry ['wint(ə)ri] *a.* d'hiver; hivernal, -aux; **w. weather,** temps *m* d'hiver; **w. smile,** sourire glacial.

wipe¹ [waip] *n.* coup *m* de torchon, de mouchoir, d'éponge; **to give sth. a w. (over),** essuyer qch.; donner un coup de torchon à qch.

wipe² **1.** *v.tr.* essuyer (une table, une assiette); **to w. one's face, one's hands,** s'essuyer la figure, les mains; **to w. one's eyes,** s'essuyer les yeux. **2.** *v.i.* **the windscreen wiper isn't wiping,** l'essuie-glace ne marche pas; **I'll wash if you'll w.,** je vais laver si tu veux bien essuyer (la vaisselle). **wipe away** *v.tr.* essuyer (ses larmes); enlever, ôter (une tache). **wipe off** *v.tr.* enlever, essuyer (une éclaboussure,); régler, liquider (une dette); *F:* **that'll w. the smile off his face,** ça va lui enlever le sourire; (*of earthquake*) **to w. a town off the map,** rayer une ville de la carte. **wipe out** *v.tr.* (*a*) essuyer (une baignoire, etc.); (*b*) liquider, amortir (une dette); effacer (un souvenir, son passé); passer l'éponge sur (qch.); (*c*) exterminer (une armée); **the fire wiped out the whole district,** l'incendie a rasé tout le quartier. **wipe up** *v.tr. & i.* nettoyer, enlever (une saleté); essuyer (la vaisselle). **wiping** *n.* essuyage *m*; **w. out,** liquidation *f*, amortissement *m* (d'une dette); effacement *m* (d'un souvenir).

wiper ['waipər] *n.* **1.** (*pers.*) essuyeur, -euse. **2.** racleur *m*; *Aut:* **windscreen w.,** essuie-glace(s) *m.*

wire¹ ['waiər] *n.* **1.** fil *m* métallique, fil de fer; (*a*) **w. drawing,** tréfilage *m*, étirage *m*; **w. netting,** treillis *m*, treillage *m*, métallique, en fil de fer; *Mil:* **barbed w.,** (fil de fer) barbelé (*m*); **(barbed) w. entanglements,** des barbelés; **w. brush,** brosse *f* en fil de fer; **w. mattress,** sommier *m* métallique; (*b*) **telegraph, telephone, w.,** fil télégraphique, téléphonique; **w. tapping,** captage *m* de messages télégraphiques, téléphoniques; branchement *m* pour écoute clandestine; *F:* **to get one's wires crossed,** se tromper, s'embrouiller; *U.S: Tp:* **party w.,** ligne partagée; **live w.,** (i) fil sous tension, fil électrisé; (ii) *F:* homme, femme, dynamique; *Com:* **cheese w.,** fil à couper le beurre; (*in circus*) **the high w.,** la corde raide; *F:* **to pull the wires,** tirer les ficelles, faire jouer le piston; **w. pulling,** intrigues *fpl*; **w. puller,** intrigant, -ante. **2.** *O:* télégramme *m*, dépêche *f.*

wire² **1.** *v.tr.* (*a*) rattacher (qch.) avec du fil de fer; monter (des fleurs) sur fil de fer; grillager (une ouverture); (*b*) *El:* faire l'installation électrique (d'une maison); **to w. a hall for sound,** sonoriser une salle. **2.** *v.i. & tr.* télégraphier (à qn); **he wired that he would arrive at twelve,** il a télégraphié qu'il arriverait vers midi. **wiring** *n.* **1.** (*a*) montage *m* (de fleurs, etc.) sur fil de fer; (*b*) *El:* pose *f* (de fils électriques); (*c*) *Mil:* pose des barbelés. **2.** installation *f* électrique (d'une maison, etc.).

wirecutter ['waiəkʌtər] *n. Tls:* (*a*) coupe-fil *m inv*; (*b*) **(pair of) wirecutters,** pince(s) coupante(s).

wirehaired ['waiəhɛəd] *a.* (chien terrier) à poil dur.

wireless ['waiəlis] **1.** *a.* sans fil. **2.** *n. O:* télégraphie *f*, téléphonie *f*, sans fil; radio *f*; **w. (set),** poste *m* de T.S.F., radio.

wiry ['waiəri] *a.* (*a*) (*of hair*) raide, rude; (*b*) (*of pers.*) vigoureux, (sec et) nerveux.

wisdom ['wizdəm] *n.* sagesse *f*; **w. tooth,** dent *f* de sagesse.

wise¹ [waiz] *a.* **1.** sage; prudent; **a w. man,** un sage; **the Three W. Men,** les (Rois) Mages *mpl*; **to get, grow, wise(r),** (i) s'assagir; (ii) acquérir de l'expérience; **it wouldn't be w. to do it,** il ne serait pas sage, prudent, de le faire; **w. after the event,** sage après coup. **2.** (*a*) **to look w.,** prendre un (petit) air entendu; (*b*) **I'm no wiser than you,** je n'en sais pas plus long que vous; **he's none, not any, the wiser (for it),** il n'en sait pas plus long pour cela; **without anyone being the wiser,** (faire qch.) à l'insu de tout le monde; (*c*) *F:* **to get w. to a fact,** saisir un fait; se rendre compte d'un fait; **to put s.o. w. (to sth.),** avertir qn (de qch.); mettre qn au courant, à la page. **-ly** *adv.* (*a*) sagement, prudemment; (*b*) **to shake one's head w.,** secouer la tête d'un air entendu.

wise² *n. Lit:* manière *f*, façon *f*; guise *f*; **in no w.,** en aucune manière, façon; nullement, aucunement.

wise³ *v. F:* **to w. s.o. up,** mettre qn à la page; **w. me up about it,** mets-moi au courant.

-wise [waiz] *adv.* **1.** dans le sens de . . .; **lengthwise,** dans le sens de la longueur; longitudinalement. **2.** en ce qui concerne . . .; **healthwise, salarywise,** en ce qui concerne la santé, la paie.

wiseacre ['waizeikər] *n.* prétendu sage; pédant *m.*

wisecrack¹ ['waizkræk] *n.* bon mot.

wisecrack² *v.i.* dire des bons mots; faire de l'esprit.

wish¹ [wiʃ] *n.* (*a*) désir *m*; **I have no w. to go, to see it,** je n'ai pas envie d'y aller, de le voir; **the w. to please,** le désir de plaire; **by my father's w.,** sur le désir de mon père; **it was done against, contrary to, my wishes,** cela s'est fait à l'encontre de mon désir, contre mon gré; **you shall have your w.,** votre désir sera exaucé; (*b*) **to make a w.,** faire un vœu; **your w. will come true,** ton vœu se réalisera; (*c*) souhait *m*, vœu; **to send all good wishes to s.o.,** adresser tous ses vœux de bonheur à qn; présenter ses souhaits à qn; **New Year's wishes,** souhaits (et félicitations) à l'occasion du nouvel an; (*at end of letter*) **with best wishes,** (bien) amicalement.

wish² **1.** *v.ind.tr.* **to w. for sth.,** désirer, vouloir, souhaiter, qch.; **to w. for happiness, for peace,** désirer, souhaiter, le bonheur, la paix; **to have everything one can, could, w. for,** avoir tout à souhait; **I couldn't w. for anything better,** je ne pourrais désirer mieux; **what more can you, do you w. for?** que voudriez-vous de plus? **2.** *v.tr.* vouloir; (*a*) **to w. to do sth.,** désirer, vouloir, faire qch.; **I w. it to be done,** je désire, je veux bien, que cela se fasse; (*b*) **I w. I were a bird!** je voudrais être un oiseau! **I w. I were in your place,** je voudrais bien être à votre place; **I w. I had seen it!** j'aurais bien voulu voir cela! **I w. I hadn't left so early,** je regrette d'être parti si tôt; **I w. he would come!** que ne vient-il! **how I w. I could (do it)!** si seulement je pouvais (le faire)! (*c*) **it's to be wished that . . .,** il est à souhaiter que . . .; (*d*) **he wishes me well,** il est bien disposé envers moi; **he wishes nobody ill,** il ne veut du mal à personne; **to w. s.o. a pleasant journey,** souhaiter à qn bon voyage; **to w. s.o. good-night,** souhaiter bonne nuit à qn; dire bonsoir à qn; (*e*) **it was wished on me,** j'ai été obligé de l'accepter.

wishbone ['wiʃboun] *n.* fourchette *f*, bréchet *m*.

wishful ['wiʃf(u)l] *a.* (*a*) **w. to do sth., of doing sth.,** désireux de faire qch.; (*b*) *F:* **that's a bit of w. thinking** = c'est prendre ses désirs pour des réalités.

wishywashy ['wiʃiwɔʃi] *a. F:* fade, insipide.

wisp [wisp] *n.* (*a*) bouchon *m*, poignée *f* (de paille, d'herbe); (*b*) tortillon *m*, toron *m* (de paille); **w. of smoke,** traînée *f* de fumée; **w. of hair,** mèche folle; **little w. of a girl,** tout petit bout de fillette.

wistaria [wis'tiəriə] *n. Bot:* glycine *f*.

wistful ['wistf(u)l] *a.* plein d'un vague désir, d'un vague regret; (regard, air) désenchanté; mélancolique; **w. smile,** sourire (i) de regret, (ii) pensif. **-fully** *adv.* avec un regard plein d'un vague désir, d'un vague regret; d'un air songeur et triste.

wit¹ [wit] *n.* **1.** (*often pl.*) esprit *m*, entendement *m*; intelligence *f*; **he hasn't the w., the wits, to see it,** il n'est pas assez intelligent pour s'en apercevoir; **to have quick wits,** avoir l'esprit vif; **to have lost one's wits,** avoir perdu l'esprit, la raison; **to collect one's wits,** se ressaisir; **to have, keep, one's wits about one,** avoir, conserver, toute sa présence d'esprit; **he has all his wits about him,** c'est un malin; **to be at one's wit's end,** ne plus savoir que faire; **to have, to engage in, a battle of wits,** jouer au plus fin; **to live by one's wits,** vivre d'expédients; **to put one's wits to work on a problem,** s'attaquer à un problème. **2.** vivacité *f* d'esprit; **flash of w.,** trait *m* d'esprit; **sparkling with w.,** étincelant d'esprit.

wit² *n.* (*pers.*) bel esprit; homme, femme, d'esprit.

wit³ *v.tr. Jur:* **to w.,** à savoir . . .; c'est-à-dire . . .. **witting** *a.* (*of insult*) fait de propos délibéré. **wittingly** *adv.* sciemment; à dessein.

witch [witʃ] *n.* (*a*) sorcière *f*; **w. hunt,** chasse *f* aux sorcières; (*b*) *F:* **old w.,** vieille sorcière; (*c*) *Anthr:* **w. doctor,** sorcier guérisseur; (*d*) *Bot:* **w. hazel,** hamamélis *m*.

witchcraft ['witʃkrɑːft] *n.* **1.** sorcellerie *f*. **2.** *F:* magie; **as if by w., like w.,** comme par magie.

witchery ['witʃəri] *n.* (*a*) ensorcellement *m*, enchantment *m*; (*b*) fascination *f*; magie *f*.

witching ['witʃiŋ] *a.* **1.** enchanteur, -eresse. **2.** magique; *Lit: & Hum:* **the w. hour,** minuit *m*.

with [wið] *prep.* avec **1.** (*expressing accompaniment*) (*a*) **to travel, work, w. s.o.,** voyager, travailler, avec qn; **he is staying w. friends,** il est chez des amis; **to mingle w. the crowd,** se mêler à la foule; **the king (together) w. his courtiers,** le roi accompagné de ses courtisans; **I have nobody to go out w.,** je n'ai personne avec qui sortir; **there I am w. nobody to talk to,** me voilà sans personne à qui parler; **I'll be w. you in a moment,** je serai à vous dans un moment; **some cheese to eat w. it,** du fromage pour manger avec; **question that is always w. us,** question qui est toujours d'actualité; (*b*) (*having*) **knife w. a silver handle,** couteau à manche d'argent; **girl w. blue eyes,** jeune fille aux yeux bleus; **child w. a cold,** enfant enrhumé; **w. his hat on,** le chapeau sur la tête; **w. his (over)coat on,** en pardessus; **w. your intelligence you'll easily guess what followed,** intelligent comme vous l'êtes vous devinerez facilement la suite; (*c*) **w. child,** enceinte; (*of animal*) **w. young,** pleine; (*d*) **he came in w. a suitcase,** il est entré avec une valise; **have you a pencil w. you?** avez-vous un crayon sur vous? **to leave a child w. s.o.,** laisser un enfant à la garde de qn; **the decision rests, lies, w. you,** c'est à vous de décider; (*e*) (*in spite of*) **w. all his faults . . .,** malgré tous ses défauts . . .; (*f*) **what will happen to her w. both her parents dead?** que va-t-elle devenir maintenant que son père et sa mère sont morts? **2.** (*expressing association*) (*a*) **to correspond w. s.o.,** correspondre avec qn; **to have to do w. s.o.,** avoir affaire avec qn; **to have nothing to do w. s.o.,** n'avoir rien à faire avec qn; **the next move is w. him,** c'est à lui d'agir maintenant; **w. him all men are equal,** tous les hommes sont égaux à ses yeux; **to be patient w. s.o.,** être patient avec qn; **to be honest w. oneself,** être sincère envers soi-même; **it's a habit w. me,** c'est une habitude chez moi; **to use one's influence w. s.o.,** agir auprès de qn; **all is well w. him,** il va bien; (*b*) **I sympathize w. you,** je vous plains; **I don't agree w. you,** je ne suis pas de votre avis; **I'm w. you,** je vous suis; je comprends; **I'm not w. you,** je ne (vous) comprends pas; *F:* **to be w. it,** être à la page, dans le vent; (*c*) **to rise w. the lark,** se lever avec l'alouette; **w. these words he dismissed me,** là-dessus il m'a congédié; **he said this w. a smile,** il a accompagné ces mots d'un sourire; **w. a cry,** en poussant un cri; (*d*) (*against*) **to compete w. s.o.,** concourir avec qn; **to fight w. s.o.,** se battre contre qn. **3.** (*dissociation*) **to part w. sth.,** se dessaisir, se défaire, de qch. **4.** (*expressing instrument*) (*a*) **to cut sth. w. a knife,** couper qch. avec un couteau, au couteau; **to walk w. (the aid of) a stick,** marcher avec une canne; **to fight w. swords,** se battre à l'épée; **to take sth. w. both hands,** prendre qch. à deux mains; **to strike w. all one's might,** frapper de toutes ses forces; (*b*) **to tremble w. rage,** trembler de rage; **to be stiff w. cold,** être engourdi par le froid; **to be ill w. measles,** être malade de la rougeole; (*c*) **to fill a vase w. water,** remplir un vase d'eau; **lorry loaded w. timber,** camion chargé de bois; **it's pouring w. rain,** il pleut à verse. **5.** (*forming adv. phrs.*) **to work w. a will,** travailler avec courage; **to advance w. great strides,** (s')avancer à grands pas; **to receive s.o. w. open arms,** recevoir qn à bras ouverts; **w. all due respect,** avec tout le respect que je vous dois; **w. your permission,** si vous voulez bien me le permettre; **w. this object (in view),** dans ce but; **I say it w. regret,** je le dis à regret; **w. a few exceptions,** à part quelques exceptions. **6.** (*elliptical*) **away w. care!** bannissons les soucis! *F:* **down w. the police!** à bas les flics! **to hell w. him!** qu'il aille au diable!

withal [wi'ðɔːl] *adv. A: & Lit:* aussi; de plus.

withdraw [wið'drɔː] *v.* (*p.t.* **withdrew** [-'druː] *p.p.* **withdrawn** [-'drɔːn]) **1.** *v.tr.* (*a*) retirer (sa main); retirer, enlever (un étai); (*b*) ramener (des troupes) en arrière; faire replier (des troupes); lever (une sentinelle); (*c*) *Bank:* retirer (une somme d'argent); **to w. coins from circulation,** retirer des pièces de la circulation; (*d*) retirer (une offre, une promesse, sa candidature); revenir sur (une promesse); renoncer à (une réclamation); **to w. a charge,** se rétracter; **to w. an order,** (i) *Com:* annuler une commande; (ii) *Adm:* rapporter un décret; *Jur:* **to w. an action,**

abandonner un procès; retirer sa plainte. **2.** *v.i.* (*a*) se retirer (**from,** de); s'éloigner; *Mil:* (*of outpost*) se replier; (*of candidate*) **to w. in favour of s.o.,** se désister pour qn; (*b*) **to w. into oneself, into silence,** se renfermer en soi-même, dans le silence. **withdrawn** *a.* (*of pers.*) réservé.

withdrawal [wið'drɔːəl] *n.* **1.** (*a*) retrait *m* (de troupes, d'une somme d'argent); **w. of capital,** retrait de fonds; *Bank:* **w. notice,** avis *m* de retrait de fonds; *Med:* **w. symptoms,** (*from alcohol*) symptômes *mpl* d'abstinence; (*from drugs*) (état *m*, crise *f*, de) manque *m*; (*b*) rappel *m* (d'un décret, d'un ordre); rétractation *f* (d'une promesse, d'une accusation); retrait (d'une plainte). **2.** (*a*) retraite *f*; *Mil:* repli *m* repliement *m* (des troupes); (*b*) **w. of a candidate,** désistement *m* d'un candidat.

withe [wiθ] *n.* brin *m*, lien *m*, d'osier.

wither ['wiðər] **1.** *v.i.* (*of plant, etc.*) **to w. (up, away),** se dessécher, se flétrir, se faner; (*of flowers, beauty*) passer; (*of pers.*) dépérir. **2.** *v.tr.* (*a*) (*of wind, heat*) dessécher, flétrir, faner (une plante, etc.); (*b*) **to w. s.o. with a look,** foudroyer qn du regard, d'un regard. **withered** *a.* desséché, flétri, fané; **w. arm,** bras atrophié. **withering 1.** *a.* (*a*) qui dessèche, qui flétrit; (*b*) (regard) foudroyant, écrasant; (ton) de souverain mépris; **to give s.o. a w. look,** foudroyer qn du regard. **2.** *n.* dessèchement *m*; **w. away,** dépérissement *m*; amenuisement *m* (d'un parti politique, etc.). **witheringly** *adv.* d'un regard foudroyant, d'un ton de mépris.

withers ['wiðəz] *n.pl.* garrot *m* (du cheval, du bœuf).

withershins ['wiðəʃinz] *adv. esp. Scot:* à contresens.

withhold [wið'hould] *v.tr.* (*p.t. & p.p.* **withheld** [-'held]) **1.** (*a*) refuser (son consentement, son aide); (*b*) taire, supprimer (un fait, etc.); **to w. the truth from s.o.,** cacher la vérité à qn; (*c*) *Jur:* détenir (des biens).

within [wið'in] **1.** *adv.* (*a*) *A: & Lit:* à l'intérieur; chez soi; (*b*) *Th:* à la cantonade; (*c*) *adv.phr.* **from w.,** de l'intérieur; **seen from w.,** vu de l'intérieur, du dedans. **2.** *prep.* (*a*) *O: & Lit:* à l'intérieur de, en dedans de; **w. four walls,** entre quatre murs; **the enemy is w. our frontiers,** l'ennemi est dans nos frontières; **he thought w. himself that . . .,** il pensait dans son for intérieur que . . . .; **a voice w. me,** une voix intérieure; (*b*) (*not beyond*) **w. reason,** dans des limites raisonnables; **to keep w. the law,** rester dans (les bornes de) la légalité; **to keep, live, w. one's income,** vivre selon ses moyens; (*c*) **w. sight,** en vue; **w. call,** à (la) portée de la voix; **w. two miles of the town,** à moins de deux milles de la ville; **w. a radius of ten kilometres,** dans un rayon de dix kilomètres; **we were w. an inch of death,** nous étions à deux doigts de la mort; (*d*) (*in expressions of time*) **w. an hour,** avant une heure; en moins d'une heure; **w. the week,** avant la fin de la semaine; dans la semaine; **w. a year of his death,** moins d'un an (i) après, (ii) avant, sa mort; **w. the next week,** dans le courant de la semaine prochaine; **w. the next five years (from now),** d'ici cinq ans; **w. the required time,** dans le délai prescrit; **w. twenty-four hours,** dans les vingt-quatre heures; **w. a short time,** (i) à court délai; (ii) peu de temps après.

without [wið'aut] **1.** *adv. A: & Lit:* (*a*) à l'extérieur, au dehors; (*b*) *adv. phr.* **from w.,** de l'extérieur; **seen from w.,** vu de l'extérieur, du dehors. **2.** *prep.* (*a*) *A: & Lit:* en dehors de; (*b*) sans; **to be w. food,** manquer de nourriture; **he came back w. any money,** il est revenu sans argent; **w. any difficulty,** sans aucune difficulté; **rumour w. foundation,** bruit dénué de fondement; **not w. difficulty,** non sans difficulté; **w. end,** sans fin; **he passed by w. seeing me, w. being seen,** il est passé sans me voir, sans être vu; **it goes w. saying that . . .,** il va sans dire, va de soi, que . . .; **can you do it w. his knowing about it?** pouvez-vous le faire sans qu'il le sache? **they are w. any knowledge of French,** ils ignorent le français; **to do, go, w. sth.,** se passer de qch.

withstand [wið'stænd] *v.tr.* (*p.t. & p.p.* **withstood** [-'stud]) résister à (qn, la douleur, la pression, etc.); **to w. the heat,** supporter la chaleur; *Mil: etc:* **to w. an attack,** soutenir une attaque.

withy ['wiði] *n.* brin *m*, lien *m*, d'osier.

witless ['witlis] *a.* (*a*) sans intelligence; sot, *f.* sotte; (*b*) imbécile; faible d'esprit; (*c*) (*of action*) stupide.

witness¹ [witnis] *n.* **1.** témoignage *m*; **to bear w. to, of, sth.,** rendre, porter, témoignage de qch.; témoigner de qch.; attester qch.; **I call you to w.,** j'en appelle à votre témoignage. **2.** (*pers.*) (*a*) témoin *m* (d'un incident, d'un mariage); (*b*) *Jur:* **w. to a document, a deed,** témoin instrumentaire; témoin à un acte; (*c*) *Jur:* **to call s.o. as w.,** citer qn comme témoin; **w. for the defence, for the prosecution,** témoin à décharge, à charge; **w. box,** *U.S:* **stand,** barre *f* des témoins; **to go into the w. box,** paraître à la barre.

witness² 1. *v.tr.* (*a*) être spectateur, témoin (d'une scène); assister à (une entrevue, etc.); attester (un acte); certifier (une signature). **2.** *v.i.* **to w. to sth.,** témoigner de qch; **to w. against, for, s.o.,** témoigner contre qn, en faveur de qn.

witticism ['witisizm] *n.* trait *m* d'esprit; bon mot.

wittiness ['witinis] *n.* esprit *m*; sel *m* (d'une observation, etc.).

witty ['witi] *a.* (*of pers.*) spirituel; (*of remark*) spirituel; piquant; plein d'esprit. **-ily** *adv.* spirituellement; avec esprit.

wizard¹ ['wizəd] *n.* (*a*) sorcier *m*, magicien *m*; (*b*) *Fig:* génie *m*; crack *m*; **to be a financial w.,** avoir le génie de la finance, des affaires; **he's a w. on the violin,** c'est un violiniste génial, de génie.

wizard² *a. F: O:* épatant, excellent.

wizardry ['wizədri] *n.* (*a*) sorcellerie *f*, magie *f*; (*b*) *Fig:* génie *m*; **his financial w.,** son habileté géniale en matières financières.

wizened ['wizənd] *a.* ratatiné; (*of cheeks*) parcheminé; **to become w.,** se ratatiner; se parcheminer.

wo(a) [wou] *int.* (*to horse*) ho! holà!

woad [woud] *n.* guède *f*.

wobble¹ ['wɔbl] *n.* (*a*) vacillation *f*; branlement *m*, oscillation *f*; tremblement *m*; *Aut:* **front-wheel w.,** shimmy *m*; (*b*) chevrotement *m* (de la voix).

wobble² *v.i.* **1.** (*a*) vaciller; osciller; (*of table*) branler; (*of pers.*) chanceler; (*of wheel*) tourner à faux; (*b*) (*of voice, etc.*) chevroter. **2.** *F: O:* (*of pers.*) hésiter.

wobbly ['wɔbli] *a.* (*a*) branlant, vacillant; hors d'aplomb; **w. chair,** chaise boiteuse, branlante; **my legs feel w.,** j'ai les jambes en coton; (*b*) (*of voice, etc.*) chevrotant.

wodge [wɔdʒ] *n.* gros morceau (de pain, etc.)

woe [wou] *n. esp. Lit:* malheur *m*, chagrin *m*, peine *f*; **to tell a tale of w.,** faire le récit de ses malheurs; **w. is me!** pauvre de moi! malheureux que je suis!

woebegone ['woubigɔn] *a.* (air, visage) désolé, abattu; (*of pers.*) **to look w.,** avoir l'air désolé.

wo(e)ful ['wouf(u)l] *a. esp. Lit:* (air) affigé, malheureux; (nouvelle) attristante. **-fully** *adv.* tristement.

wog [wɔg] *n. Pej:* **1.** Arabe *m*, Levantin *m*, Égyptien *m*; = bicot *m*, bougnoule *m*. **2.** étranger, -ère (au teint basané).

wok [wɔk] *n.* poêle *f* à frire chinoise.

wold [would] *n. Geog:* (*used mainly in Pr.n.*) (petite) chaîne de collines crayeuses (ou calcaires).

wolf¹, *pl.* **wolves** [wulf, wulvz] *n.* (*a*) *Z:* loup *m*; **she w.,** louve *f*; **w. cub,** louveteau *m*; **to be as hungry as a w.,** avoir une faim de loup; **to cry w.,** crier au loup; **that will keep the w. from the door,** (i) voilà quelque chose pour écarter la faim; (ii) cela vous, nous, mettra à l'abri du besoin; **a w. in sheep's clothing,** un loup déguisé en brebis; (*b*) *F:* coureur *m* de jupons; *F:* **w. whistle,** sifflement admiratif (au passage d'une jolie fille); *F:* **lone w.,** (i) cavalier seul; (ii) célibataire endurci, vieux bouc.

wolf² *v.tr.* **to w. (down) one's food,** engloutir, dévorer, sa nourriture.

wolfhound ['wulfhaund] *n.* chien *m* de loup; **Irish w.,** lévrier *m* d'Irlande.

wolfish ['wulfiʃ] *a.* (*a*) de loup; (*b*) vorace; **w. appetite,** appétit énorme.

wolfram ['wulfrəm] *n. Miner:* wolfram *m.*

wolfsbane ['wulfsbein] *n. Bot:* aconit *m.*

wolverine ['wulvəri:n] *n. Z:* glouton *m.*

woman, *pl.* **women** ['wumən, 'wimin] *n.f.* femme; **single w.,** femme célibataire; **a young w.,** une jeune femme; **an old w.,** une vieille femme; une vieille; *F: O:* **the little w.,** ma femme; (*of man*) **to run after women,** courir le jupon; **woman's man,** galant *m*; **Women's Liberation Movement,** *F:* **Women's Lib.,** le Mouvement pour la Libération de la Femme (M.L.F.); **Women's libber,** (i) membre *m*, (ii) partisan, -ane, du M.L.F.; *Journ:* **women's page,** page *f* des lectrices; **women's magazines,** revues féminines; **w. doctor,** femme médecin; **w. artist,** femme peintre; **w. friend,** amie; **it was a w. driver,** il y avait une femme au volant.

womanhater ['wumənheitər] *n.* misogyne *m.*

womanhood ['wumənhud] *n.* **1. to grow to w.,** devenir femme; devenir adulte. **2.** *coll. O:* les femmes.

womanish ['wuməniʃ] *a.* (*of man*) efféminé.

womanize ['wumənaiz] *v.i. F:* courir les femmes, courir le jupon.

womanizer ['wumənaizər] *n.* coureur *m* de femmes.

womankind ['wumənkaind] *n. coll.* les femmes.

womanliness ['wumənlinis] *n.* féminité *f.*

womanly ['wumənli] *a.* féminin; de femme; **she has a very w. nature,** elle est très femme.

womb [wu:m] *n. Anat:* matrice *f*, utérus *m.*

wombat ['wɔmbæt] *n. Z:* wombat *m*, phascolome *m.*

womenfolk ['wiminfouk] *n.f.pl.* (*a*) *coll.* les femmes; (*b*) *F:* **his w.,** les femmes de sa famille.

wonder¹ ['wʌndər] *n.* **1.** merveille *f*, miracle *m*, prodige *m*; **to work, do, wonders,** faire, accomplir, opérer, des merveilles, des miracles; faire des prodiges; faire merveille; **the seven wonders of the world,** les sept merveilles du monde; **a nine-days' w.,** la merveille d'un jour; **it's a w. (that) he hasn't lost it,** c'est merveille, miracle, qu'il ne l'ait pas perdu; **no, little, small, w. that the scheme failed,** il n'est guère étonnant que le projet n'ait pas réussi; **he's ill and no, little, w.,** il est malade et ce n'est pas étonnant, et rien d'étonnant. **2.** (*a*) étonnement *m*, surprise *f*; (*b*) émerveillement *m*, admiration *f*; **to fill s.o. with w.,** émerveiller qn. **3.** *a. F:* **w. product,** produit miracle *a. inv.*

wonder² **1.** *v.i.* s'étonner, s'émerveiller (**at,** de); **I don't w. at it,** cela ne m'étonne pas, ne me surprend pas; **can you w. that he refused?** comment s'étonner qu'il ait refusé? **it's not to be wondered at that he left,** il n'est pas étonnant, rien d'étonnant, qu'il soit parti; **I shouldn't w.,** cela ne m'étonnerait pas, ne me surprendrait pas. **2.** *v.tr.* (*a*) **to w. that . . .,** s'étonner que . . .; (*b*) se demander, vouloir savoir; **one wonders!** sait-on jamais? **I w. whether he'll come,** je me demande, je voudrais savoir, s'il viendra; **one wonders whether . . .,** c'est à se demander . . .; **I w. who invented that,** je suis curieux de savoir qui a inventé cela; **I w. why!** je voudrais bien savoir pourquoi! **their son will help them—I w.!** leur fils leur viendra en aide—vous croyez? **are you going to London tonight?—why?—oh, I just wondered,** allez-vous à Londres ce soir?—pourquoi?—oh, pour rien! **wondering** *a.* étonné, émerveillé. **wonderingly** *adv.* d'un air étonné; avec étonnement.

wonderful ['wʌndəf(u)l] *a.* merveilleux, prodigieux, admirable; **she's a w. mother,** c'est une mère merveilleuse; **it was w.!** c'était merveilleux, magnifique! **we had a w. time,** nous nous sommes très bien amusés. **-fully** *adv.* merveilleusement; **w. well,** merveilleusement bien; à merveille.

wonderland ['wʌndəlænd] *n.* pays *m* des merveilles.

wonderment ['wʌndəmənt] *n. esp. Lit:* étonnement *m*; émerveillement *m.*

wondrous ['wʌndrəs] *a. A: & Lit:* étonnant; merveilleux. **-ly** *adv.* merveilleusement.

wonky ['wɔŋki] *a. F: O:* patraque; chancelant, branlant; (*of chair, table*) boiteux; **to feel w.,** se sentir patraque.

wont¹ [wount] *a. Lit:* **to be w. to do sth.,** avoir coutume, avoir l'habitude, de faire qch.

wont² *n. Lit:* coutume *f*, habitude *f*; **according to his w., as is, was, his w.,** selon sa coutume; à, selon, suivant, son habitude.

won't = **will not,** *see* WILL³.

wonted ['wountid] *a. Lit:* habituel, accoutumé.

woo [wu:] *v.tr. A: & Lit:* **1.** faire la cour à, courtiser (une femme). **2.** rechercher, courtiser (la fortune, la célébrité). **3. to w. s.o. to do sth.,** solliciter qn de faire qch.

wood [wud] *n.* **1.** (*a*) (*collection of trees*) bois *m*; *For:* peuplement *m*; **pine w.,** bois de pins; **you can't see the w. for the trees,** les arbres cachent la forêt; **we're not out of the w. yet,** nous ne sommes pas encore tirés d'affaire; (*b*) *attrib.* des bois; (fleur) sylvestre; (oiseau, bête) sylvicole; *Bot:* **w. anemone,** anémone *f* des bois; *Orn:* **w. pigeon,** (pigeon *m*) ramier *m*; *Myth:* **w. nymph,** dryade *f*. **2.** (*a*) (*material*) bois; **box made of w.,** boîte faite de bois; boîte en bois; *F:* **touch w.!** *U.S:* **knock on w.!** touchez du bois! (*b*) **w. ash,** cendre *f* de bois; **w. floor,** plancher *m* de bois; *Engr:* **w. block,** planche *f*, bois; **w. engraving,** gravure *f* sur bois debout; **w. carving,** sculpture *f* sur bois; **w. carver,** sculpteur *m* sur bois; **w. alcohol,** alcool *m* méthylique; *Paperm:* **w. pulp,** pâte *f* à papier. **3.** *Wine-m:* **the w.,** le tonneau, le fût; **wine in the w.,** vin logé; vin en fût; **beer (drawn) from the w.,** bière tirée au fût. **4.** *Bowls:* boule *f*. **5.** *Mus:* = WOODWIND.

woodbine ['wudbain] *n. Bot:* (*a*) chèvrefeuille *m* des bois; (*b*) *U.S:* vigne *f* vierge.

woodchuck ['wudtʃʌk] *n. Z:* marmotte *f* d'Amérique.

woodcock ['wudkɔk] *n.* (*usu. inv. in pl.*) *Orn:* bécasse *f* (des bois).

woodcraft ['wudkrɑ:ft] *n.* **1.** connaissance *f* de la forêt. **2.** (pratique *f* du) travail sur bois.

woodcut ['wudkʌt] *n.* gravure *f* sur bois.

woodcutter ['wudkʌtər] *n.* bûcheron *m.*

wooded ['wudid] *a.* boisé; **w. country,** pays boisé, couvert.

wooden ['wud(ə)n] *a.* **1.** de bois, en bois; **w. shoes,** sabots *mpl.* **2.** (*a*) (*of movement, manner*) raide, gauche; **w. face,** visage fermé; (*b*) *F* **w.(-headed),** stupide; à l'esprit obtus.

woodenness ['wudənnis] *n.* maintien compassé.

woodland ['wudlənd] *n.* pays boisé; bois *m*(*pl*); **w. scenery,** paysage boisé.

woodlark ['wudlɑ:k] *n. Orn:* alouette *f* des bois.

woodlouse, *pl.* **-lice** ['wudlaus, -lais] *n.* cloporte *m.*
woodman, *pl.* **-men** ['wudmən] *n.m.* **1.** bûcheron. **2.** garde forestier.
woodpecker ['wudpekər] *n. Orn:* pic *m*; **green w.,** pivert *m.*
woodpile ['wudpail] *n.* tas *m*, monceau *m*, de bois.
woodshed ['wudʃed] *n.* bûcher *m*; *F:* **there's something nasty in the w.,** il se passe du vilain.
woodsman, *pl.* **-men** ['wudzmən] *n.m. esp. U.S:* chasseur (en forêt); trappeur.
woodstack ['wudstæk] *n.* = WOODPILE.
woodwind ['wudwind] *n. Mus:* **the w.,** les bois *mpl*; **w. instrument,** instrument *m* à vent en bois.
woodwork ['wudwəːk] *n.* **1.** travail *m* du bois; (*a*) construction *f* en bois; charpenterie *f*; (*b*) menuiserie *f*, ébénisterie *f*. **2.** bois travaillé; (*a*) boiserie *f*, charpente *f*; (*b*) menuiserie, ébénisterie.
woodworm ['wudwəːm] *n. Ent:* ver *m* du bois; **this table's got w.,** cette table est vermoulue.
woody ['wudi] *a.* **1.** (pays) boisé. **2.** *Bot:* ligneux.
wooer ['wuːər] *n. A: & Lit:* prétendant *m.*
woof[1] [wuːf] *n. Tex:* trame *f.*
woof[2] [wuf] *n.* (*of dog*) aboi *m*, aboiement *m.*
woof[3] [wuf] *v.i.* (*of dog*) aboyer.
wool [wul] *n.* **1.** laine *f*; (*a*) **w. grower,** éleveur, -euse, de moutons; **dyed in the w.,** teint en laine; **a dyed in the w. reactionary,** un conservateur à tous crins; *F:* **to pull the w. over s.o.'s eyes,** jeter de la poudre aux yeux de qn; (*b*) **the w. industry,** l'industrie lainière; **the w. trade,** le commerce des laines; **combed w.,** laine peignée; **w. cloth,** tissu *m* de laine; **pure w. suit,** complet *m* pure laine; (*c*) **knitting, darning, w.,** laine à tricoter, à repriser; **a ball of w.,** une pelote de laine. **2.** (*a*) pelage *m* (d'animal); (*b*) *Bot:* laine, duvet *m*; (*c*) *F:* cheveux crépus, laine. **3. mineral w.,** laine minérale; **steel, wire, w.,** paille *f* de fer.
woolgathering ['wulgæð(ə)riŋ] *F:* (*a*) *n.* rêvasserie *f*; (*b*) (*used verbally*) **to be w.,** rêvasser; **he's always w.,** il a toujours l'esprit ailleurs.
woollen, *NAm:* **woolen** ['wulən] *a. & n.* **w. materials, woollens,** (i) *Tchn:* tissus *mpl* de laine cardée; (ii) (*in general parlance*) laines *fpl*, lainages *mpl*; **w. dress,** robe *f* de laine.
woolliness, *NAm: also* **wooliness** ['wulinis] *n.* **1.** nature laineuse (**of,** de). **2.** *F:* imprécision *f* (de raisonnement, du style); nébulosité *f* (d'idées); manque *m* de netteté; flou *m* (des contours).
woolly, *NAm: also* **wooly** ['wuli] **1.** *a.* (*a*) laineux; de laine; **w. clouds,** nuages ouatés; **w. hair,** cheveux crépus; *F:* **wild and w.,** rude; (*b*) (*of fruit*) cotonneux; pâteux; (*c*) *F:* peu net; imprécis; nébuleux; (*of painting, outline, etc.*) flou; **w. ideas,** idées vagues, nébuleuses; **w. minded,** aux idées imprécises, vagues; **w. style,** style qui manque de précision. **2.** *n. F:* tricot *m*, laine *f*; **put on your w.,** mets ton tricot; **winter woollies,** vêtements chauds d'hiver.
woolsack ['wulsæk] *n. Parl:* **the W.,** le siège du *Lord Chancellor* (à la Chambre des Lords).
wop [wɔp] *n. P: Pej:* Italien *m*, macaroni *m.*
word[1] [wəːd] *n.* **1.** (*a*) mot *m*; vocable *m*; **w. for w.,** (répéter qch.) mot pour mot; (traduire qch.) mot à mot, textuellement; **a play on words,** un jeu de mots; **in a, one, w.,** en un mot; bref; **in a few words,** en quelques mots; **in other words,** en d'autres mots; **I told him in so many words that . . .,** je lui ai dit en termes propres, en termes exprès, que . . .; **in the full sense of the w.,** dans toute la force, l'acception, du terme; **he doesn't know a w. of Latin,** il ne sait pas un mot de latin; **bad isn't the w. for it,** mauvais n'est pas assez dire; (*b*) **w. group,** groupe *m* de mots; locution *f*, membre *m* de phrase; **w. picture,** description imagée, pittoresque; portrait *m* en prose (de qn); *Med:* **w. blindness,** dyslexie *f*; (*of actor*) **to be w. perfect,** savoir son rôle sur le bout du doigt; (*c*) *Cmptr:* mot machine; **key w.,** mot-clef *m*; (*d*) **spoken words,** paroles *fpl*; **in the words of Voltaire,** selon (l'expression de) Voltaire; comme Voltaire a dit; **I can't put it into words,** je n'arrive pas à l'exprimer par des mots; **song without words,** romance *f* sans paroles; **to ask s.o. to say a few words,** demander à qn de prendre la parole, de dire quelques mots; **he's a man of few words,** c'est un homme qui parle peu, qui ne parle pas beaucoup; **I can't get a w. out of him,** je ne peux pas le faire parler; **I couldn't get a w. in (edgeways),** je n'ai pas pu placer un mot; **he didn't say a w.,** il n'a rien dit; il n'a pas soufflé mot; **not a w.!** pas un mot! bouche close! **without a w.,** sans mot dire; **with these words, he went,** ce disant, sur ces mots, là-dessus, il est parti; **you're putting words into my mouth,** vous me prêtez des paroles (que je n'avais aucune intention de dire); **you've taken the words out of my mouth,** c'est exactement ce que j'allais dire; **words fail me!** j'en perds la parole! **too stupid for words,** d'une bêtise sans nom; **too beautiful for words,** d'une beauté ineffable; **hard words,** paroles dures; **fine words,** belles paroles; (*e*) **may I have a w. with you, I'd like a w. with you,** puis-je vous parler un instant? **I'll have a w. with him about it,** je lui en toucherai deux mots; **to put in a good w. for s.o.,** dire, glisser, un mot en faveur de qn; **he never has a good w. for anyone,** il ne peut pas s'empêcher de dire du mal de son prochain; **a w. in, out of, season,** un conseil opportun, inopportun; (*f*) **to have words with s.o.,** se disputer, se quereller, avec qn; **words were running high,** la querelle s'échauffait. **2.** (*speech*) parole; **by w. of mouth,** de vive voix; verbalement; **battle of words,** guerre *f* oratoire. **3.** (*message*) avis *m*; nouvelle *f*; **to send s.o. w. of sth.,** faire part à qn de qch.; faire savoir qch. à qn; **we received w. that . . .,** on nous a apporté la nouvelle que . . . . **4. to give s.o. one's w.,** donner sa parole à qn; **to keep one's w.,** tenir (sa) parole; **to break one's w.,** manquer à sa parole; **I give you my w., (you can) take my w. for it,** je vous en donne ma parole; je vous en réponds; **I'll take your w. for it,** je vous crois sur parole; je m'en rapporte à vous; **he's a man of his w., he's as good as his w.,** c'est un homme de parole; **his w. is as good as his bond,** sa parole vaut sa signature; **my w.!** tiens! mon Dieu! **5.** (*a*) **w. of command,** ordre *m*; **to give the w. to do sth.,** donner (i) l'ordre, (ii) le signal, de faire qch.; (*b*) mot de passe. **6.** *Theol:* (*a*) **the w. of God, God's w.,** la parole de Dieu; (*b*) **the W. (of God, of the Father),** le Verbe.
word[2] *v.tr.* formuler, rédiger (un document, etc.); **it might have been differently worded,** on aurait pu l'exprimer autrement, en d'autres termes. **wording** *n.* **1.** rédaction *f* (d'un document); libellé *m* (d'une traite, d'une lettre de change); énoncé *m* (d'un acte, d'un problème). **2.** (*a*) mots *mpl*; langage *m*; (choix *m* de) termes *mpl* (d'un article, d'un acte, etc.); (*b*) phraséologie *f.*
wordbook ['wəːdbuk] *n.* vocabulaire *m*, lexique *m.*
wordiness ['wəːdinis] *n.* verbosité *f*; prolixité *f.*
wordless ['wəːdlis] *a.* sans paroles.
wordy ['wəːdi] *a.* verbeux, prolixe, diffus.
work[1] [wəːk] *n.* **1.** travail, -aux *m*; **to be at w.,** travailler; être au travail; **the forces at w.,** les forces *fpl* en jeu; **to be hard at w.,** être en plein travail; **he was hard at w. ploughing, gardening,** il était en plein labour, en plein jardinage; *Prov:* **all w. and no play makes Jack a dull boy,** on ne peut pas toujours travailler sans se délasser; **to start w., to set to w.,** se mettre au travail; **to stop, knock off, w.,** cesser le travail; suspendre le travail (pour la journée). **2.** (*a*)

travail, ouvrage *m*, besogne *f*, tâche *f*; **I've w. to do,** j'ai (du travail) à faire; **to have too much w. to do,** avoir trop à faire; **to get through a lot of w.,** abattre de la besogne; **to give s.o. a piece, a job, of w. to do,** donner une tâche à qn; **let's get down to w.!** au travail! **a fine piece of w.,** un beau travail; **the brandy had done its w.,** l'eau-de-vie avait fait son effet; **I'll have my w. cut out to finish in time,** j'aurai de quoi faire pour finir à l'heure; **you'll have your w. cut out with him,** il vous donnera du fil à retordre; **day's w.,** (travail d'une) journée; **it's all in a day's w.,** c'est l'ordinaire de mon existence; c'est comme ça tous les jours; **good w.!** bien fait! (*b*) **it was thirsty w.,** c'était un travail qui donnait soif. **3.** (*a*) **the works of God,** les œuvres *fpl* de Dieu; **good works,** bonnes œuvres; (*b*) ouvrage, œuvre; **the works of Shakespeare,** les œuvres *fpl,* l'œuvre *m,* de Shakespeare; **a w. of art, of genius,** une œuvre d'art, de génie. **4.** (*a*) travail, emploi *m*; **office w.,** travail de bureau; **to be off w.,** ne pas travailler (parce qu'on est malade); **to be out of w.,** être en chômage; chômer; (*b*) (lieu *m* de) travail; bureau *m*, usine *f*, etc.; **he's not at w. today,** il ne travaille pas, il n'est pas à son bureau aujourd'hui. **5.** *Mil:* **works,** ouvrages, travaux; **defensive works,** ouvrages défensifs; **field works,** travaux de campagne. **6.** *Civ.E:* **works,** travaux; **public works,** travaux publics; *P.N:* **road works ahead!** *U.S:* **w. zone!** travaux! chantier! **7. works,** rouages *mpl,* mécanisme *m* (d'une montre, etc.); *F:* **the whole works,** tout le bataclan, tout le tralala! *P:* **to give s.o. the works,** (i) passer qn à tabac; (ii) tuer, descendre, qn; (iii) recevoir qn avec la croix et la bannière; *esp. U.S:* **to shoot the works,** tenter le coup; aller jusqu'au bout. **8. works,** usine *f*; atelier *m*; **engineering works,** atelier de constructions mécaniques; **works council,** comité *m* d'entreprise. **9. chased, hammered, w.,** ouvrage ciselé, martelé; *Publ:* **art w.,** illustration *f* (d'un ouvrage). **10.** *Nau:* **upper works,** accastillage *m*, œuvres mortes.

work² *v.* (*p.t. & p.p.* **worked** [wə:kt] *A: and in a few expressions* **wrought** [rɔ:t]) **I.** *v.i.* **1.** (*a*) travailler; **to w. hard,** travailler dur; **to w. like a navvy, a slave, a horse,** *U.S:* **a beaver,** travailler comme un bœuf, un forçat, comme quatre; **to w. a 40-hour week,** faire une semaine de 40 heures; *Ind:* **to w. to rule,** faire la grève du zèle; **to w. in leather, in brass,** travailler dans le cuir, dans le cuivre; **to w. on a newspaper,** collaborer à un journal; **he's working on an edition of** *Hamlet*, il travaille, prépare, une édition de *Hamlet;* (*b*) **to w. for a good cause,** travailler pour une bonne cause; **to w. for an end,** travailler pour atteindre un but; **to w. against s.o.,** intriguer, travailler, contre qn; **working from the principle that . . .,** partant du principe que . . .. **2.** (*a*) (*of machine*) fonctionner, aller, marcher; **system that works well,** système qui fonctionne bien; **the pump isn't working,** la pompe ne marche, fonctionne, pas; **the lift isn't working,** l'ascenseur est hors de service, est en panne; **these tools w. by compressed air,** ces outils sont actionnés par l'air comprimé; (*b*) **drug that works,** médicament qui produit son effet; **his plan didn't w.,** son projet a échoué, n'a pas réussi; *F:* **that won't w. with me,** ça ne prend pas avec moi. **3.** (*of yeast*) fermenter. **4.** (*a*) *O:* (*of face, features*), se crisper, se contracter; **his mouth was working,** sa bouche se crispait; (*b*) (*of sailing ship*) **to w. to windward,** chasser dans le vent; louvoyer; (*of angler*) **to w. upstream,** remonter le courant. **5.** (*of nut, etc.*) **to w. loose,** se desserrer; se détacher. **II.** *v.tr.* **1.** faire travailler (qn, un cheval, etc.); **he works his staff too hard,** il exige trop de travail de son personnel; il surmène son personnel; **to w. oneself to death,** se tuer à force de travailler. **2.** faire travailler, faire fonctionner, faire marcher (une machine, etc.); *Nau: etc:* manœuvrer (un navire, les voiles, une pompe); **it's worked by steam, by electricity,** cela marche à la vapeur, à l'électricité. **3.** opérer (un miracle, une guérison); exercer (une influence); amener (un changement); produire (un effet); **to w. mischief,** semer la discorde; **the destruction wrought by the fire,** la dévastation causée par l'incendie; **I'll w. it, things, so that . . .,** je ferai de sorte que + *sub*. **4.** broder (un dessin, des initiales); **the flowers are worked in silk,** les fleurs sont brodées à la soie. **5.** (*a*) **to w. an incident into a book,** introduire un incident dans un livre; **his keys had worked a hole in his pocket,** ses clefs avaient fini par faire un trou dans sa poche; (*b*) **to w. one's hands free,** parvenir à dégager ses mains; (*c*) **to w. one's way down, up,** descendre, monter, petit à petit, avec précaution; **they worked their way through the crowd,** ils se sont frayé un chemin à travers la foule. **6.** (*a*) travailler, façonner (le bois, le fer); ouvrer (les métaux précieux); pétrir (l'argile); travailler (la pâte); (*b*) **to w. the iron into a horseshoe,** façonner, forger, le fer en fer à cheval; (*c*) **to w. oneself (up) into a rage,** laisser monter sa colère; (*d*) **to w. sth. over,** (i) *F:* examiner qch. minutieusement; (*b*) *NAm:* refaire qch.; *F:* **to w. s.o. over,** (i) fouiller qn; (ii) tabasser qn. **7.** (*a*) exploiter (une mine, une carrière); (*b*) *Com:* (*of representative*) **to w. the south-east,** faire, couvrir, le sud-est. **8.** *Nau:* **to w. one's passage,** payer son passage par son travail; (*of student*) **to w. one's way through university,** travailler pour payer ses études. **work in** *v.tr.* incorporer, mélanger (qch. à qch.); introduire (un incident dans un roman, etc.). **working 1.** *a.* (*a*) (i) qui travaille; **w. man, woman,** ouvrier, -ière; **w. wife,** femme mariée qui travaille; **the w. classes,** la classe ouvrière; **w.-class family,** famille ouvrière; **w.-class district,** quartier populaire; (ii) **he's very hard w.,** c'est un grand travailleur; (iii) **w. party,** *Pol: Ind:* groupe *m* de travail; *Mil:* atelier *m*, équipe *f*; (*b*) qui fonctionne; **w. parts of a machine,** mécanisme *m* d'une machine; organes *mpl* mobiles; (*c*) **w. agreement,** modus vivendi *m*; **w. majority,** majorité suffisante; **w. theory,** théorie *f* qui donne des résultats. **2.** *n.* (*a*) travail *m*; **w. clothes,** vêtements *mpl* de travail; **w. hours,** heures *fpl* de travail; **w. day,** (i) jour ouvrable; (ii) journée *f* (de travail); **w. lunch,** déjeuner *m* d'affaires; (*b*) (i) manœuvre *f* (d'une machine, etc.); (ii) mise *f* en œuvre (d'un procédé); exploitation *f* (d'une mine, d'une forêt); *Min:* **w. face,** front *m* de taille; **w. expenses,** frais généraux; frais d'exploitation; **w. capital,** capital *m* d'exploitation; fonds *m* de roulement; (iii) fonctionnement *m* (d'une loi); fonctionnement, pratique *f* (d'un système); application *f* (d'une règle); (*c*) marche *f*, fonctionnement, jeu *m* (d'un mécanisme); *Tg:* **multiple(x) w.,** communication *f* multiplex; *Mec.E:* **w. speed,** vitesse *f* de régime; **in w. order,** en état de fonctionnement, marche; **to be in good w. order,** bien fonctionner; (*d*) **the workings of the mind,** le travail de l'esprit; (*e*) fermentation *f* (du vin, de la bière); (*f*) contraction *f*, crispation *f* (des traits, de la bouche); (*g*) *Min:* **workings,** chantiers *mpl* d'exploitation; (*h*) *Mth:* **w. out,** résolution *f* (d'un problème). **work off 1.** *v.tr.* se débarrasser de (qch.); cuver (sa colère); **to w. off one's bad temper on s.o.,** passer sa mauvaise humeur sur qn; **I'm doing some gardening to try to w. off a bit of fat,** je fais du jardinage pour essayer de perdre du poids. **2.** *v.i.* (*of nut, etc.*) se détacher. **work on** *v.i.* (*a*) continuer à travailler; (*b*) **have you any data to w. on?** avez-vous des données sur lesquelles vous baser? (*c*) influencer (qn); agir sur (l'esprit de) (qn); travailler (qn). **work out 1.** *v.tr.* (*a*) exécuter (un projet); mener à bien (une entreprise); développer (une idée); **to w. out**

one's own salvation, faire son salut; **to w. out one's (own) destiny,** être l'artisan de sa propre destinée; (*b*) faire (un calcul); calculer (un prix); résoudre (un problème); (*c*) (*of mine, seam*) **to be worked out,** être épuisé. **2.** *v.i.* (*a*) sortir peu à peu; (*b*) **I wonder how it will all w. out,** je me demande comment cela finira, va finir; **it worked out very well for me,** je m'en suis bien trouvé; (*c*) **how much does it all w. out at?** le total s'élève à combien? **it works out at £10 a head,** cela fait £10 par personne; (*d*) *Sp:* s'entraîner. **work up 1.** *v.i.* (*a*) (of skirt) remonter; (*b*) avancer par degrés; **what are you working up to?** à quoi voulez-vous en venir? **2.** *v.tr.* (*a*) préparer (un discours); élaborer (un article); *Com:* **to w. up a connection,** se faire une clientèle; (*b*) **to get worked up,** s'échauffer, s'énerver.

workability [wə:kə'biliti] *n.* maniabilitié *f.*

workable ['wə:kəbl] *a.* (*a*) *Tchn:* (*of material*) maniable; (*b*) (mine) exploitable; (*c*) (projet) réalisable.

workaday ['wə:kədei] *a.* de tous les jours; **w. clothes,** habits *mpl* de tous les jours.

workaholic [wə:kə'hɔlik] *n. F:* bourreau *m* de travail.

workbag ['wə:kbæg] *n. Needlew:* sac *m* à ouvrage.

workbasket ['wə:kbɑ:skit] *n. Needlew:* corbeille *f* à ouvrage.

workbench ['wə:kben(t)ʃ] *n.* établi *m.*

workbox ['wə:kbɔks] *n. Needlew:* boîte *f* à ouvrage.

workday ['wə:kdei] *n.* jour *m* ouvrable.

worker ['wə:kər] *n.* (*a*) travailleur, -euse; **heavy w.,** travailleur de force; **hard w.,** travailleur assidu; **to be a hard w.,** travailler dur; (*b*) *Ind:* ouvrier, -ière; (*as opposed to management*) **the workers,** le personnel; (*c*) *Ent:* **w. (bee, ant),** ouvrière; (*d*) **w. of miracles,** faiseur, -euse, de miracles.

workforce ['wə:kfɔ:s] *n.* main-d'œuvre *f.*

workhouse ['wə:khaus] *n.* **1.** *A:* asile *m* des pauvres; hospice *m.* **2.** *U.S:* maison *f* de correction.

workless ['wə:klis] *a.* sans travail; *n.pl.* **the w.,** les chômeurs *mpl,* les sans-travail *mpl.*

workman, *pl.* **-men** ['wə:kmən] *n.m.* ouvrier.

workmanlike ['wə:kmənlaik] *a.* bien fait, bien travaillé; **to do sth. in a w. manner,** faire qch. en professionnel.

workmanship ['wə:kmənʃip] *n. Ind:* exécution *f*; travail *m,* façon *f*; **sound w.,** fabrication, exécution, soignée; **fine (piece of) w.,** beau travail.

work(-)out ['wə:kaut] *n. Sp:* séance *f* d'entraînement.

workpeople ['wə:kpi:pl] *n.pl.* ouvriers *mpl.*

workroom ['wə:kru:m] *n.* atelier *m*; salle *f* de travail.

workshop ['wə:kʃɔp] *n.* atelier *m.*

workshy ['wə:kʃai] *a.* fainéant; **to be w.,** bouder, renâcler, à la besogne.

worktable ['wə:kteibl] *n.* table *f* de travail; *Needlew:* table à ouvrage.

work-to-rule [wə:ktə'ru:l] *n. Ind:* grève *f* du zèle.

world [wə:ld] *n.* monde *m.* **1.** (*a*) **in this w.,** en ce monde; **the other, next, w., the w. to come,** l'autre monde; **he's not long for this w.,** il n'en a pas pour longtemps à vivre; **to bring a child into the w.,** mettre un enfant au monde; **he wants the best of both worlds,** il veut tout avoir; **the end of the w.,** la fin du monde; **w. without end,** jusqu'à la fin des siècles; éternellement; (*b*) **the whole w.,** le monde entier; **to be alone in the w.,** être seul au monde; **the happiest man in the w.,** l'homme le plus heureux du monde; **he lives in a w. of his own,** il vit dans un monde à part; **what in the w. is the matter with you?** que diable avez-vous? **I wouldn't do it for (anything in) the w.,** je ne le ferais pour rien au monde. **2.** (*earth*) **to go round the w.,** faire le tour du monde; **round-the-w. trip, tour,** voyage *m* autour du monde; **he has seen the w.,** il a vu du pays; **map of the w.,** carte universelle; (*in two hemispheres*) mappemonde *f*; **(all) the w. over, all over the w.,** dans le monde entier; **to the end of the w.,** jusqu'au bout du monde; **it's a small w.!** (que) le monde est petit! **the Old, New, W.,** l'ancien, le nouveau, monde; **the English-speaking w.,** le monde anglophone; *Pol:* **w. power,** puissance mondiale; **w. politics,** politique mondiale; **w. war,** guerre mondiale; **w. record,** record mondial; *Fb:* **the W. Cup,** la coupe du monde; **w. history,** histoire universelle. **3.** (*human affairs*) **it's the way of the w.,** ainsi va le monde; **what is the w. coming to?** où allons-nous? **man of the w.,** homme qui connaît la vie, qui a l'expérience du monde; **w.-weary,** las, *f.* lasse, de ce monde; *F:* **it's out of this w.,** c'est (qch. d')extraordinaire, (d')épatant; c'est mirifique; **he's gone up in the w.,** il a fait du chemin; **to come down in the w.,** déchoir; **all the w. knows,** c'est bien connu; **w. famous,** célèbre, connu, dans le monde entier; **all the w. and his dog,** tout le monde sans exception. **4.** (*a*) **the w. of literature, of letters, the literary w.,** le monde littéraire; **the theatrical w.,** le milieu du théâtre; (*b*) **the animal, vegetable, mineral, w.,** le monde animal, végétal, minéral. **5.** *F:* **that will do you a w. of good,** cela vous fera un bien infini; **there's a w. of difference between . . .,** il y a une difference énorme entre . . ., **their opinions are worlds apart,** leurs opinions sont totalement différentes; **she thinks the w. of him,** elle l'admire énormément.

worldliness ['wə:ldlinis] *n.* mondanité *f*; attachement *m* aux biens de ce monde.

worldly ['wə:ldli] *a.* (*a*) de ce monde; matériel; **he's a child in w. matters, he's not w. wise,** il n'a aucune expérience du monde; **w. wisdom,** la sagesse du monde, du siècle; **all his w. goods,** toute sa fortune; (*b*) mondain; **w.(-)minded,** attaché aux choses matérielles, aux biens de ce monde.

worldwide ['wə:ldwaid] **1.** *a.* universel; mondial, -aux; **the w. problem of . . .,** le problème planétaire de . . . **2.** *adv.* dans le monde entier.

worm[1] [wə:m] *n.* **1.** ver *m*; (*a*) *Fig:* **the w. has turned,** il en a assez de se laisser mener par le bout du nez; **he's a w.,** c'est un minable; **worm's-eye view,** perspective vue (i) d'en bas, (ii) d'une humble position; *U.S: F:* **that's opening another can of worms,** nous allons nous fourrer dans un véritable guêpier; (*b*) *Ent:* asticot *m*; **meal w.,** ver de farine; (*c*) *Med: Vet:* **to have worms,** avoir des vers; *Pharm:* **w. powder,** poudre *f* à vers; poudre vermifuge. **2.** (*a*) filet *m* (de vis); (*b*) **w. (screw),** vis *f* sans fin.

worm[2] *v.tr.* (*a*) **he wormed himself, his way, along the tunnel,** il a avancé dans le tunnel en rampant, en se tortillant; **to w. one's way out of, into, sth.,** se faufiler hors de, dans, qch.; **to w. oneself into s.o.'s favour, confidence,** s'insinuer dans les bonnes grâces de qn, dans la confiance de qn; (*b*) **to w. a secret out of s.o.,** tirer un secret de, arracher un secret à qn; **I'll w. it out of him,** je saurai lui tirer les vers du nez; (*c*) **to w. a dog,** débarrasser un chien de ses vers.

wormcast ['wə:mkɑ:st] *n.* déjection *f* de ver de terre.

wormeaten ['wə:mi:t(ə)n] *a.* (*a*) mangé aux vers; (*of wood*) vermoulu; (*of fruit*) véreux; (*b*) suranné, désuet.

wormhole ['wə:mhoul] *n.* (*in wood, in the ground*) trou *m* de ver; (*in cloth, wood*) piqûre *f* (de ver).

wormwood ['wə:mwud] *n. Bot:* armoise (amère); *Lit:* **life to him was gall and w.,** la vie pour lui n'était qu'amertume et dégoût.

wormy ['wə:mi] *a.* **1.** infesté, plein, de vers; véreux; piqué des vers. **2.** vermiforme, vermiculaire.

worrier ['wʌriər] *n.* personne qui se tracasse, qui se fait de la bile; **he's such a w.,** il se fait trop de soucis.
worrisome ['wʌrisəm] *a.* tracassant, inquiétant.
worry¹ ['wʌri] *n.* ennui *m*, souci *m*, tracas *m*; **financial worries,** soucis d'argent; **it's causing me a lot of w.,** cela m'inquiète beaucoup; **that's the least of my worries,** c'est le moindre, le dernier, de mes soucis; *F:* **what's your w.?** qu'est-ce qui ne va pas?
worry² **1.** *v.tr.* (*a*) (*of dog, wolf*) attaquer, harceler (les moutons); (*b*) tourmenter, tracasser, harceler, importuner (qn); inquiéter (qn); **don't w. him,** laissez-le tranquille; **something is worrying him,** il y a quelque chose qui le préoccupe, qui le travaille; **it worries me,** cela m'inquiète. **2.** *v.i.* se tourmenter, se tracasser, s'inquiéter; se faire du souci, de la bile, du mauvais sang; **he keeps worrying about that business,** cette affaire lui travaille l'esprit; **don't (you) w.!** *F:* **not to w.!** ne vous tracassez, inquiétez, pas! ne vous en faites pas! **don't (you) w. about me,** ne vous inquiétez pas pour moi; **it's nothing to w. about,** ce n'est rien d'inquiétant; **what's the use of worrying?** à quoi bon se tourmenter? *F:* **I should w.!** ce n'est pas mon affaire! **worried** *a.* tourmenté, tracassé, soucieux; **I'm w. about this,** cela m'inquiète, me tracasse; **he's w. about the car,** il est inquiet au sujet de la voiture; **he looks w.,** il a l'air préoccupé, soucieux. **worriedly** *adv.* anxieusement, soucieusement; avec inquiétude. **worrying** **1.** *a.* tracassant, inquiétant. **2.** *n.* tracasserie *f*, tracas *m*, tourment *m*; inquiétude *f*.
worryguts ['wʌrigʌts] *n. P:* personne qui se fait de la bile, qui se tracasse.
worse [wə:s] **1.** *a. & n.* pire, plus mauvais; **I'm a w. player than he (is),** je joue plus mal que lui; **in w. condition,** dans un plus mauvais état; **this is (getting) w. and w.,** c'est, ça va, de mal en pis; **you're only making things w.,** vous ne faites qu'empirer les choses; **to make matters w. . . .,** par, pour, surcroît de malheur . . .; **that only made matters w.,** cela n'a pas arrangé les choses; **it might have been w.,** il n'y a que demi-mal; **he escaped with nothing w. than a fright,** il en fut quitte pour la peur; **what is w. . . .,** qui pis est . . .; **to go from bad to w.,** aller de mal en pis; **to get w.,** devenir pire; s'altérer; (*of illness*) s'aggraver, empirer; **I am none the w. for it,** je ne m'en trouve pas plus mal; **I think none the w. of him because he accepted,** je n'ai pas moins bonne opinion de lui parce qu'il a accepté. **2.** *n.* (*a*) **there was w. to follow, to come,** ce qui a suivi était encore pire; **I have seen w., been through w., than that,** j'en ai vu bien d'autres; (*b*) **to change for the w.,** s'altérer; **change for the w.,** changement *m* en mal; altération *f*; **he has taken a sudden turn for the w.,** son état s'est subitement aggravé. **3.** *adv.* (*a*) plus mal; *Lit:* pis; **he has been taken w.,** il va plus mal; son état a empiré; **w. still,** ce qui est pire; **you might do w. than to accept,** vous pourriez faire pire que d'accepter; **to think w. of s.o. for doing sth.,** estimer qn moins pour avoir fait qch.; **he is w. off than before,** sa situation a empiré; (*b*) **the noise went on w. than ever,** le vacarme a recommencé de plus belle.
worsen ['wə:s(ə)n] **1.** *v.tr.* empirer, aggraver (un mal); rendre pire. **2.** *v.i.* empirer, devenir pire; (*of health*) s'aggraver; **the situation has since worsened,** la situation a empiré depuis. **worsening** *n.* aggravation *f*.
worship¹ ['wə:ʃip] *n.* **1.** culte *m*; **divine w.,** le culte divin; **freedom of w.,** liberté *f* du culte; **forms of w.,** formes *fpl* de culte; **hours of w.,** heures *fpl* des offices; **place of w.,** lieu consacré au culte; église *f*, temple *m*; **to be an object of w.,** être un objet d'adoration. **2.** (*title*) **His W. the Mayor,** monsieur le maire; **yes, your W.,** oui, monsieur le maire, monsieur le juge.
worship² **(worshipped)** **1.** *v.tr.* (*a*) rendre un culte à, adorer (un dieu, une idole); vénérer (un saint, une relique); **to w. the golden calf,** adorer le veau d'or; (*b*) adorer (qn); avoir un véritable culte pour (qn); **to w. money,** faire son idole de l'argent; **he worships the ground she treads on,** il vénère jusqu'au sol qu'elle foule. **2.** *v.i.* **the church where his family had worshipped for years,** l'église où sa famille a fait ses dévotions pendant des années; **where does he w.?** à quelle église, à quel temple, va-t-il?
worshipful ['wə:ʃipf(u)l] *a.* honorable (titre des membres des Corporations de Londres, des juges de paix).
worshipper ['wə:ʃipər] *n.* adorateur, -trice; (*in church*) **the worshippers,** les fidèles *mpl*.
worst¹ [wə:st] **1.** *a.* (le) pire, (le) plus mauvais; **that was his w. mistake,** c'était sa plus grave erreur; **his w. enemy,** son pire ennemi. **2.** *n.* **the w. that could happen,** le pire, la pire chose, qui puisse arriver; **the w. of the storm is over,** le plus fort de l'orage est passé; **the w. of it is that . . .,** le pire c'est que + *ind.*; **that's the w. of cheap shoes,** c'est l'inconvénient des chaussures bon marché; **when things are at their, the, w.,** quand les choses vont au plus mal; (*in a fight*) **to get the w. of it,** avoir le dessous; **he's prepared for the w.,** il s'attend au pire; **at the w., if it comes to the w., if the w. comes to the w.,** *U.S:* **if the worse comes to the w.,** en mettant les choses au pire; au pis aller; **the w. is yet to come,** on n'a pas encore vu le pire; **do your w.!** allez-y! essayez toujours! **the w. is over,** le plus mauvais moment est passé; **the w. has happened!** c'est la catastrophe! **and that's not the w. of it!** et ce n'est pas le pire! et il y a pire encore! **3.** *adv.* (le) plus mal; *Lit:* (le) pis; **that frightened me w. of all,** c'est cela qui m'a effrayé le plus.
worst² *v.tr.* battre, vaincre, défaire (qn); **to be worsted,** succomber; avoir le dessous.
worsted ['wustid] *n. Tex:* laine peignée; peigné *m*.
worth [wə:θ] **1.** *a.* valant; (*a*) **to be w. so much, nothing,** valoir tant; ne rien valoir; **what is the franc w.?** combien vaut le franc? **two cars w. £3000 each,** deux voitures valant £3000 chacune; **it's not w. much,** cela ne vaut pas grand-chose; **whatever it may be w.,** vaille que vaille; **I tell you this for what it's w.,** je vous passe ce renseignement sans y attribuer grande valeur; **it would be as much as my life is w.,** ce serait risquer ma vie; (*b*) **it's not w. the trouble,** cela ne, n'en, vaut pas la peine; **is it w. while? is it w. it?** cela (en) vaut-il la peine? **it isn't w. it,** ça ne vaut pas le coup; **it's not w. anything,** cela ne vaut pas quatre sous; **this novel is not w. reading,** ce roman ne vaut pas la peine, ne mérite pas, d'être lu; **something w. having,** une chose précieuse; **life wouldn't be w. living,** la vie serait intolérable; **it's w. thinking about,** cela mérite réflexion; **it's worth knowing,** c'est bon à savoir; **the castle is w. a visit,** le château vaut la visite; (*c*) **he's w. millions,** il est riche à millions; **that is all I am w.,** voilà toute ma fortune; **he was pulling for all he was w.,** il tirait de toutes ses forces. **2.** *n.* valeur *f*, mérite *m*; **of great, little, no, w.,** de grande, de peu de, d'aucune, valeur; **give me £4 w. of petrol,** donnez-moi pour £4 d'essence; **to have, to want, one's money's w.,** en avoir, en vouloir, pour son argent.
worthiness ['wə:ðinis] *n.* mérite *m*.
worthless ['wə:θlis] *a.* sans valeur; qui ne vaut rien; **he's completely w.,** c'est un vaurien.
worthlessness ['wə:θlisnis] *n.* peu *m* de valeur; nature *f* méprisable (de qn).
worthwhile [wə:θ'(h)wail] *a.* qui en vaut le peine, *F:* le coup; **at last I've found a w. job,** j'ai enfin trouvé un poste qui me donne satisfaction.
worthy ['wə:ði] **1.** *a.* digne; (*a*) **a w. man,** un digne homme; un homme estimable; **a w. life,** une vie

honorable, vertueuse; (*b*) **to be w. of s.o., of sth.,** être digne de qn, de qch.; **to be w. to do sth.,** être digne de faire qch.; **w. of respect,** digne de respect; **it is w. of note that . . .,** il est à noter que . . .; (*c*) **the town has no museum w. of the name,** la ville n'a aucun musée digne du nom. **2.** *n. F:* personnage *m* (de l'endroit); **the village worthies,** les notables *mpl* du village. **-ily** *adv.* **1.** dignement. **2.** à juste titre.

wotcher ['wɔtʃər] *int. P:* **w. mate!** salut, mon vieux!

would *see* WILL.

would-be ['wudbi:] *a.* prétendu, soi-disant; **w.-be assassin,** prétendu assassin.

wound[1] [wu:nd] *n.* (*a*) blessure *f*; **w. in the arm,** blessure au bras; **bullet w.,** blessure par balle; (*b*) plaie *f*; **to reopen a w.,** rouvrir une plaie; *Fig:* **to rub salt in the w.,** retourner le fer dans la plaie.

wound[2] [wu:nd] *v.tr.* blesser; faire une blessure à (qn); **wounded in the shoulder,** blessé, atteint, à l'épaule; **to w. s.o.'s pride,** blesser qn dans son amour-propre; **to w. s.o.'s feelings,** blesser les susceptibilités de qn; froisser qn. **wounded** *a.* blessé; **the w. man,** le blessé; *n.pl.* **the w.,** les blessés; **w. pride,** orgueil froissé. **wounding** *a.* blessant; **he found it w. to his pride,** cela a blessé son amour-propre.

wound[3] [waund] *see* WIND[2, 3].

wow[1] [wau] *F:* **1.** *int.* oh là là! **2.** *n.* succès fou; **it's a w.,** c'est sensationnel.

wow[2] *v.tr. F:* emballer (qn).

wrack[1] [ræk] *n.* varec(h) *m*, goémon *m*.

wrack[2] *n.* **to go to w. and ruin,** aller à la ruine; (s'en) aller à vau-l'eau; (*of house, etc.*) se délabrer.

Wraf [ræf] *n.f. F:* membre *m* de la *Women's Royal Air Force.*

wraith [reiθ] *n.* apparition *f*.

wrangle[1] ['ræŋgl] *n.* dispute *f*, querelle *f*.

wrangle[2] *v.i.* se disputer, se quereller; se chamailler. **wrangling** *n.* disputes *fpl*, querelles *fpl*.

wrangler ['ræŋglər] *n.* **1.** querelleur, -euse. **2.** *NAm:* cowboy *m*.

wrap[1] [ræp] *n.* (*a*) *usu. pl.* **wraps,** (i) couvertures *fpl* (de voyage); (ii) châles *mpl*; (*b*) pèlerine *f*, manteau *m*; **evening w.,** manteau du soir, sortie *f* de bal; (*c*) *F:* **to keep sth. under wraps,** garder qch. secret.

wrap[2] **(wrapped** [ræpt]) **1.** *v.tr.* (*a*) envelopper; emballer; **to w. sth. (up) in paper,** envelopper, empaqueter, qch. dans du papier; **to w. up a parcel,** faire un paquet; *P:* **w. up!** la ferme! (*b*) **to w. oneself up,** *v.i.* **to w. up,** s'envelopper; s'emmitoufler; **w. up warmly!** couvrez-vous bien! **to w. a baby (up) in a shawl,** emmitoufler un bébé dans un châle; **mountain wrapped in mist,** montagne enveloppée de brouillard; *Fig:* **wrapped in mystery,** enveloppé, entouré, de mystère. **2.** *v.tr.* **to w. sth. round sth.,** enrouler, entortiller, qch. autour de qch.; **the cable wrapped (itself) round the capstan,** le câble s'enroula sur le cabestan; *F:* **he wrapped his car round a tree,** il a encadré un arbre. **3.** *v.tr. F:* **to w. up a deal,** boucler une affaire; **it's all wrapped up,** tout est arrangé. **4.** *v.i.* (*of garment*) **to w. over,** croiser. **5.** *v.tr.* bandeler (un pneu); *El:* **to w. a cable (in cotton),** guiper un câble (de coton). **wrapped** *a.* **1.** (*a*) **w. bread,** pain préemballé; **w. sweets,** bonbons *mpl* en papillotes *fpl*; (*b*) (*of pers.*) **w. up,** bien enveloppé; emmitouflé. **2.** (*a*) **w. in thought,** plongé, perdu, dans ses pensées; absorbé dans ses réflexions; (*b*) **to be w. up in sth.,** être uniquement préoccupé de qch.; **he is w. up in his work,** il est entièrement absorbé par son travail. **wrapping** *n.* **1.** (*a*) enveloppement *m*; mise *f* en paquet; **w. paper,** papier *m* d'emballage; *Com:* **gift w.,** emballage-cadeau *m*; (*b*) entortillage *m*, enroulement *m*. **2.** (*a*) enveloppe *f*, couverture *f*; (*b*) (i) papier *m*, (ii) toile *f*, d'emballage; (*c*) **wrappings,** bandelettes *fpl* (de momies).

wraparound ['ræpəraund] *n. Cost:* **w. (skirt),** jupe *f* portefeuille.

wrapover ['ræpouvər] *n. Cost:* **w. (skirt),** jupe *f* portefeuille.

wrapper ['ræpər] *n.* **1.** toile *f* d'emballage; feuille *f* de papier d'emballage; papillote *f* (de bonbon). **2.** (*a*) chemise *f* (d'un dossier); (*b*) **book w.,** (i) couverture *f* (d'un livre); couvre-livre *m*, *pl.* couvre-livres; (ii) liseuse *f*. **3.** bande *f* (de journal). **4.** *Cost:* saut-de-lit *m*, *pl.* sauts-de-lit.

wrap(-)round ['ræpraund] *a. Aut:* **w.(-)r. rear window,** lunette arrière panoramique.

wrath [rɔθ, rɔ:θ] *n. Lit:* courroux *m*.

wrathful ['rɔ(:)θf(u)l] *a. Lit:* courroucé, en colère.

wreak [ri:k] *v.tr.* assouvir (sa colère, haine); **to w. one's rage on, upon, s.o.,** décharger, passer, sa colère sur qn; **to w. (one's) vengeance upon s.o.,** exercer, assouvir, sa vengeance sur qn; se venger de qn.

wreath [ri:θ, *pl.* ri:ðz, ri:θs] *n.* **1.** couronne *f*, guirlande *f* (de fleurs); **funeral w.,** couronne mortuaire. **2.** volute *f*, panache *m* (de fumée).

wreathe [ri:ð] **1.** *v.tr.* (*a*) enguirlander; couronner (la tête de qn); **mountain wreathed with mist,** montagne entourée de brouillard; **face wreathed in smiles,** visage rayonnant; (*b*) tresser (des fleurs); (*c*) **to w. sth. round sth.,** enrouler, entortiller, qch. autour de qch. **2.** *v.i.* (*of smoke*) tourbillonner.

wreck[1] [rek] *n.* **1.** (*a*) *Jur:* **w. of the sea,** épaves *fpl* de mer; (*b*) navire naufragé, épave; *Ins:* **total w.,** navire entièrement perdu; (*c*) **my car's a total w.,** ma voiture est bonne pour la casse; **human wrecks,** épaves humaines; **to be a physical, nervous, w.,** avoir la santé détraquée, les nerfs détraqués. **2.** naufrage *m* (d'un navire); **to suffer w.,** faire naufrage; **to be saved from the w.,** échapper au naufrage.

wreck[2] *v.tr.* (*a*) faire faire naufrage à (un navire), causer le naufrage (d'un navire); (*of pers., ship*) **to be wrecked,** faire naufrage; (*b*) faire dérailler (un train); démolir (une voiture); démolir, détruire, ruiner (un bâtiment); **to w. one's health,** ruiner sa santé; (*c*) faire échouer, saboter (une entreprise); détruire, ruiner, briser (les espérances de qn); **to w. s.o.'s plans,** faire échouer les projets de qn. **wrecked** *a.* (*a*) (navire, marin) naufragé; (*b*) (édifice) ruiné, écroulé; (village) dévasté; (train) déraillé; **w. life,** existence brisée; **w. health,** santé ruinée. **wrecking** *n.* **1.** (*a*) destruction *f* (d'un navire); *Const:* démolition *f* (d'un bâtiment); (*b*) ruine *f* (d'une fortune, des espérances de qn); sabotage *m* (d'une entreprise). **2.** *NAm:* (*a*) *Nau:* sauvetage *m* (d'un navire); (*b*) *Aut:* dépannage *m*; **w. crew,** équipe *f*, de secours; **w. car,** camion *m* de dépannage; dépanneuse *f*.

wreckage ['rekidʒ] *n.* **1.** naufrage *m* (d'un navire, de la fortune de qn) **2.** *coll.* épaves éparses; débris *mpl*; ce qui reste (d'un sinistre); **piece of w.,** épave.

wrecker ['rekər] *n.* **1.** naufrageur *m*, pilleur *m* d'épaves. **2.** destructeur, -trice (d'une ville, d'une civilisation); *Const:* démolisseur *m* (de bâtiments). **3.** *NAm:* (*a*) *Nau:* (i) sauveteur *m*, (ii) exploiteur *m*, d'épaves; (*b*) *Aut:* (i) membre *m* d'une équipe de secours; (ii) camion *m* de dépannage; dépanneuse *f*; (iii) marchand *m* de voitures délabrées.

wren[1] [ren] *n. Orn:* troglodyte *m*.

Wren[2] *n.f.* membre *m* du *Women's Royal Naval Service.*

wrench[1] [ren(t)ʃ] *n.* **1.** (*a*) mouvement violent de torsion; effort violent; **to give sth. a w.,** tordre qch. violemment; **he gave his ankle a w.,** il s'est donné une entorse; il s'est foulé la cheville; (*b*) **the separation was a terrible w.,** la séparation fut un déchirement (de cœur) affreux; **it will be a w. to leave them,** il m'en coûtera de les quitter. **2.** *Tls:* clef *f*; **adjustable w.,** clef à ouverture variable, clef universelle; **pipe w.,** clef à tubes.

wrench² *v.tr.* **1.** (*a*) tordre; tourner violemment; **to w. the lid open,** forcer le couvercle; **to w. off, out,** arracher, enlever (avec un violent effort de torsion); (*b*) **to w. sth. from s.o.,** arracher qch. à qn; **she wrenched herself free,** d'une secousse elle se dégagea; (*c*) **to w. one's ankle,** se fouler la cheville; **to w. one's shoulder,** se fouler, se forcer, l'épaule. **2.** forcer, fausser (le sens d'un mot).

wrest [rest] *v.tr.* **1.** arracher (**from,** à); **to w. a confession from s.o.,** arracher un aveu à qn. **2.** forcer, fausser (le sens d'un passage).

wrestle¹ ['resl] *n.* (*a*) lutte *f* (corps à corps); (*b*) *Fig:* lutte (**with,** contre).

wrestle² **1.** *v.i.* (*a*) **to w. with s.o.,** lutter avec, contre, qn; **to w. (together),** lutter, se prendre corps à corps; *F:* **to w. with one's umbrella,** lutter avec son parapluie; (*b*) *Fig:* **to w. with sth.,** lutter contre (les difficultés); résister à (la tentation); être aux prises avec (l'adversité); s'attaquer à (un problème). **2.** *v.tr.* lutter avec, contre (qn); **to w. down one's opponent,** terrasser son adversaire (à la lutte). **wrestling** *n.* **1.** sport *m* de la lutte; lutte corps à corps; **freestyle w.,** lutte libre; **tag w.,** catch *m* à quatre. **2. w. with difficulties, temptation,** lutte contre les difficultés, la tentation.

wrestler ['reslər] *n.* lutteur *m.*

wretch [retʃ] *n.* **1.** malheureux, -euse; infortuné, -ée; **poor w.,** pauvre diable *m.* **2.** (*a*) misérable *mf*; **you w.!** misérable! (*b*) **you little w.!** petit fripon!

wretched ['retʃid] *a.* **1.** (*of pers.*) misérable, malheureux, infortuné; **to feel w.,** être mal en train; avoir le cafard; **to be in w. poverty,** être dans une misère affreuse. **2.** (*a*) pitoyable, lamentable; triste, pauvre (repas); **this coffee is w.,** ce café est une abomination; **what w. weather!** quel temps abominable! quel temps de chien! (*b*) **w. hovel,** taudis *m*; **w. lodgings,** appartement minable; (*c*) (*vague intensive*) **I can't find that w. umbrella,** je ne retrouve pas ce diable de parapluie; **what's that w. boy doing?** qu'est-ce qu'il fait, ce sacré garçon? **-ly** *adv.* **1.** misérablement. **2.** (s'acquitter) de façon pitoyable, lamentable. **3. to be w. poor,** être dans une misère affreuse; **to be w. ill,** être malade à faire pitié.

wretchedness ['retʃidnis] *n.* **1.** (*a*) misère *f*, malheur *m*; (*b*) tristesse *f.* **2.** mauvaise qualité.

wrick¹ [rik] *n.* **to give oneself a w.,** se donner un effort; **w. in the neck,** torticolis *m.*

wrick² *v.tr.* **to w. oneself, a muscle,** se donner, attraper, un effort; **to w. one's ankle,** se fouler la cheville; se donner une entorse.

wriggle¹ ['rigl] *n.* **1.** tortillement *m* du corps. **2.** détour *m*, sinuosité *f.*

wriggle² **1.** *v.i.* (*a*) (*of worm*) se tortiller; (*of fish*) frétiller; (*of pers.*) se tortiller, s'agiter; **to w. through a hedge,** se faufiler à travers une haie (en se tortillant); (*b*) **to w. out of a difficulty,** se tirer, s'extraire, d'une position difficile par des moyens évasifs; **to try to w. out of it,** chercher une échappatoire; (*c*) *Fig:* tortiller; tergiverser. **2.** *v.tr.* (*a*) tortiller (les doigts); agiter (les jambes); (*b*) **to w. one's way into sth.,** se faufiler, s'insinuer, dans qch. **wriggling.** **1.** *a.* = WRIGGLY. **2.** (*a*) tortillement *m*; (*b*) *Fig:* tergiversaion *f.*

wriggler ['riglər] *n.* **1.** (*a*) larve *f* de moustique; (*b*) enfant qui ne sait pas se tenir tranquille sur sa chaise. **2.** *Fig:* tergiversateur, -trice.

wriggly ['rigli] *a.* qui se tortille, se remue; frétillant.

wring¹ [riŋ] *n.* (mouvement *m* de) torsion *f*, action *f* de tordre; **to give the clothes a w.,** tordre le linge, passer le linge à l'essoreuse; **he gave my hand a w.,** il m'a donné une vigoureuse poignée de main.

wring² *v.tr.* (*p.t.* & *p.p.* **wrung** [rʌŋ]) **1.** tordre (qch); **to w. (out),** tordre, essorer (le linge); **to w. s.o.'s hand,** étreindre la main de qn; **to w. one's hands in despair,** se tordre les mains, les bras, de désespoir; **to w. a bird's neck,** tordre le cou à une volaille; *F:* **I'd like to w. his neck,** il m'exaspère à la fin! **2. to w. sth. out of, from, sth., s.o.,** exprimer, faire sortir (l'eau d'un vêtement mouillé); arracher (un secret à qn); arracher, extorquer (de l'argent à qn); **to w. tears from s.o.,** faire pleurer qn; arracher des larmes à qn. **wringing** **1.** *a.* **w. (wet),** (*of clothes*) mouillé à tordre; (*of pers.*) trempé jusqu'aux os. **2.** *n.* tordage *m*, essorage *m.*

wringer ['riŋər] *n.* *Laund:* essoreuse *f* (à rouleaux).

wrinkle¹ ['riŋkl] *n.* **1.** (*a*) (*on face*) ride *f*; (*b*) rugosité *f*; (*on water*) ondulation *f*, ride; (*c*) (*in garment*) faux pli. **2.** *F:* (*a*) renseignement *m* utile, tuyau *m*; (*b*) truc *m.*

wrinkle² **1.** *v.tr.* rider, plisser; (*a*) **to w. one's forehead,** froncer le(s) sourcil(s); (*b*) plisser, froisser, chiffonner (une robe); **her stockings were wrinkled,** ses bas faisaient des plis. **2.** *v.i.* **to w. (up),** se rider; se plisser; faire des plis. **wrinkled** *a.* (*of forehead*) ridé, plissé; (*of dress*) froncé, chiffonné; (*of skin*) ratatiné.

wrist [rist] *n.* (*a*) *Anat:* poignet *m*; (*b*) *Cost:* poignet *m* (d'une manche).

wristband ['ristbænd] *n.* **1.** poignet *m*, manchette *f* (de chemise). **2.** *Gym:* bracelet *m* de force (en cuir).

wristbone ['ristboun] *n.* *Anat:* os *m* du carpe; carpe.

wristlet ['ristlit] *n.* (*a*) bracelet *m*; (*b*) **woollen w.,** miton *m*; (*c*) *F:* **wristlets,** menottes *fpl.*

wristwatch ['ristwɔtʃ] *n.* montre-bracelet *f*, *pl.* montres-bracelets.

writ [rit] *n.* **1. Holy, Sacred, W.,** les saintes Écritures, l'Écriture sainte. **2.** *Jur:* acte *m* judiciaire, mandat *m*, ordonnance *f*; assignation *f*; **w. of attachment,** ordre *m* de saisie; **w. of possession,** envoi *m* en possession; **to serve a w. on s.o., issue a w. against s.o.,** assigner qn (en justice); signifier, faire donner, une assignation à qn; **a w. is out for his arrest,** il est sous le coup d'un mandat d'arrêt.

write [rait] *v.tr.* & *i.* (*p.t.* **wrote** [rout] *p.p.* **written** ['rit(ə)n] *A:* **writ** [rit]) **1.** *v.tr.* écrire; (*a*) **to w. one's name,** écrire son nom; **that was not written by me,** cela n'est pas écrit de ma main; **how is it written?** comment cela s'écrit-il? **the paper is written all over,** le papier est couvert d'écriture; **his guilt was written on his face,** on lisait sur son visage qu'il était coupable; **there's policeman written all over him,** il sent son policier d'une lieue; **writ large,** écrit en gros, en grosses lettres; (*b*) écrire (un roman, une lettre); rédiger (un article); faire, remplir, libeller (un chèque). **2.** *v.i.* écrire; (*a*) **to w. legibly,** écrire lisiblement; *with cogn. acc.* **he writes a good hand,** il a une belle écriture; **this pen won't w.,** ce stylo ne marche, ne va, pas; (*b*) **he writes,** il est écrivain; **to w. for a paper,** écrire dans, collaborer à, un journal; **he writes on, about, gardening,** il écrit des articles sur l'horticulture; (*c*) **he writes home every Sunday,** il écrit chez lui tous les dimanches; *F:* **that's nothing to w. home about,** il n'y a pas là de quoi s'émerveiller; ce n'est pas bien extraordinaire; **he wrote to me,** *F:* **he wrote me, yesterday,** il m'a écrit hier; **I have written to (ask) him to come,** je lui ai écrit de venir; **w. for our catalogue,** demandez notre catalogue. **write back** *v.i.* répondre (à une lettre). **write down** *v.tr.* (*a*) coucher, consigner (qch.) par écrit; inscire (son nom); marquer, noter (ses dépenses); (*b*) décrier, vilipender (qn), *F:* éreinter (qn, une pièce, un roman); (*c*) *Fin:* réduire (le capital). **write in** *v.tr.* (*a*) insérer (une correction, un mot); (*b*) **to w. in for**

sth., demander (un catalogue, etc.); *NAm:* **to w. in a complaint,** envoyer une plainte à la direction. **write off** *v.tr.* (*a*) écrire (un article) d'un trait; (*b*) **to w. off for sth.,** demander, commander, faire venir (un catalogue); (*c*) *Fin:* **to w. off capital,** réduire le capital; **to w. so much off for wear and tear,** déduire tant pour l'usure; (*d*) *Com:* **to w. off a bad debt,** défalquer une mauvaise créance; *F:* **my car can be written off,** ma voiture est bonne pour la casse. **write out** *v.tr.* (*a*) transcrire (qch.); mettre (une copie) au net; (*b*) **to w. sth. out in full,** écrire qch. en toutes lettres; (*c*) faire remplir, libeller (un chèque); *Med:* formuler, rédiger (une ordonnance). **write up** *v.tr.* (*a*) *Journ:* écrire, rédiger (un fait-divers, un compte rendu); (*b*) faire l'éloge de, *F:* prôner (qn, qch.); (*c*) mettre (son agenda, sa comptabilité) au courant, à jour; (*d*) *Sch:* **w. up your notes,** recopiez vos notes; (*e*) *Fin:* augmenter (la valeur des stocks). **writing** *n.* **1.** écriture *f*; (*a*) **the art of w.,** l'art d'écrire; **I'm very bad about letter w.,** je suis très mauvais correspondant; **at the time of w.,** au moment où j'écris; **w. case,** nécessaire *m* (contenant ce qu'il faut pour écrire); **w. desk, table,** pupitre *m*, bureau *m*, secrétaire *m*; **w. pad,** (i) sous-main *m*, *pl.* sous-mains; (ii) bloc-correspondance *m*, *pl.* blocs-correspondance; **w. paper,** papier *m* à lettres; (*b*) **his w. is bad,** il a une mauvaise écriture; **the w. on the wall,** un avertissement (d'une catastrophe imminente); **in w.,** (coucher qch, répondre) par écrit; **agreement in w.,** convention *f* par écrit; **to commit the facts to w.,** consigner les faits par écrit. **2.** (*a*) *Lit:* l'art d'écrire; **a fine piece of w.,** (i) un beau morceau; (ii) une œuvre bien écrite; (*b*) ouvrage *m* littéraire; **the writings of an author,** les ouvrages littéraires, l'œuvre *m*, d'un auteur. **3.** (*a*) **w. down,** inscription *f* (de son nom); (*b*) **w. in,** insertion *f* (d'un mot); (*c*) *Fin: Com:* **w. off,** déduction *f* (pour l'usure); défalcation *f* (d'une mauvaise créance); amortissement *m* (du capital); (*e*) **w. out,** mise *f* (d'une copie) au net; transcription *f* (de ses notes); (*f*) **w. up,** (i) *Journ:* rédaction *f* (d'un fait-divers); (ii) mise au courant, à jour (de son agenda). **written** *a.* écrit; par écrit; **the w. word,** le mot écrit; **w. consent,** consentement *m* par écrit; **w. law,** loi écrite.

write(-)down ['rait'daun] *n. Fin:* dépréciation *f*.

write-off ['raitɔf] *n.* **1.** *Book-k:* annulation *f* par écrit. **2.** *F:* **my car was a complete w.-o.,** ma voiture a été complètement démolie.

writer ['raitər] *n.* (*a*) scripteur *m* (d'un document, manuscrit); (*b*) **to be a good, bad, w.,** avoir une belle, mauvaise, écriture; (*c*) **the present w., the w. (of this letter),** celui qui écrit, l'auteur de cette lettre; (*d*) auteur *m* (d'un roman, du scénario); (*e*) écrivain; **woman w.,** femme écrivain; **writer's cramp,** crampe *f* des écrivains; (*f*) *Scot: Jur:* notaire *m*; **w. to the signet,** avoué *m*.

write-up ['raitʌp] *n.* **1.** *Journ:* article *m*; **a good w.-up,** un article élogieux. **2.** *Book-k:* augmentation *f* de la valeur comptable (du stock).

writhe [raið] *v.i.* (*a*) se tordre (de douleur); se contorsionner; **to w. in agony,** se tordre dans des souffrances atroces; (*b*) **he writhed under the insult,** il ressentit vivement cette injure. **writhing** *n.* contorsions *fpl.*

wrong¹ [rɔŋ] **I.** *a.* **1.** (*morally bad*) mauvais; **it is wrong to steal, stealing is w.,** c'est mal de voler; **that was very w. of you!** c'était très mal de votre part! **2.** (*a*) incorrect, inexact; erroné; faux, *f.* fausse; **my watch is w.,** ma montre n'est pas à l'heure; **w. use of a word,** emploi abusif d'un mot; **a w. expression,** une expression impropre; **his ideas are all w.,** il a des idées toutes de travers; (*b*) (*of pers.*) **to be w.,** avoir tort; se tromper; être dans l'erreur; **that's just where you are w.,** c'est justement ce qui vous trompe; **you were w. to contradict him,** vous avez eu tort de le contredire. **3.** (*a*) **to be in the w. place,** être mal placé; ne pas être à sa place; **to drive on the w. side of the road,** conduire du mauvais côté de la route; *F:* **to get out of bed on the w. side,** se lever du pied gauche; **the w. side of the material,** l'envers *m*, le revers, de l'étoffe; **your sock is w. side out,** votre chaussette est à l'envers; **to be w. side up,** être sens dessus dessous; **to be on the w. side of forty,** avoir (dé)passé la quarantaine; **to stroke a cat the w. way,** caresser un chat à rebrousse-poil; **you are setting about it in the w. way,** vous vous y prenez mal, de travers; **to take sth. the w. way,** prendre une observation à contre-pied; (*of food*) **it went down the w. way,** je l'ai avalé de travers; (*b*) (*mistaken*) **to take the w. train,** se tromper de train; **to back the w. horse,** miser sur le mauvais cheval; **to take the w. road,** se tromper de chemin, de direction; **I was sent the w. way,** on m'a mal dirigé; **to put s.o. on the w. track,** mettre qn sur une fausse piste; **to be on the w. scent, track,** suivre une mauvaise piste; faire fausse piste; **to come at the w. time,** venir dans un mauvais moment, mal à propos; **to do, say, the w. thing,** commettre un impair; faire une gaffe; mettre les pieds dans le plat; *Tp:* **w. number,** erreur *f* de numéro; **to dial the w. number,** composer un faux numéro; *Mus:* **w. note,** fausse note; *Typ:* **w. fount,** lettre *f* d'un autre œil, d'un œil étranger. **4.** (*amiss*) **what's w. with you?** qu'avez-vous? qu'est-ce qu'il y a qui ne va pas? **there's something w. with me,** j'ai quelque chose, il y a quelque chose, qui ne va pas; **there was something w. with our car,** nous avons eu des ennuis avec la voiture; **there's something w. somewhere,** il y a quelque chose qui cloche; **I hope there's nothing w.,** j'espère qu'il n'est rien arrivé (de malheureux); *F:* **what's w. with that?** qu'avez-vous à redire à cela? **II.** *n.* **1.** mal *m*; **to know right from w.,** distinguer le bien et le mal; **two wrongs do not make a right,** deux noirs ne font pas un blanc; **the king can do no w.,** le roi ne peut pas mal faire. **2.** (*a*) (*unjust action*) tort *m*, injustice *f*; **to acknowledge one's wrongs,** avouer ses torts; **to do s.o. w., to do w. to s.o.,** faire tort à qn; (*b*) *Jur:* (*tort*) dommage *m*, préjudice *m*. **3. to be in the w.,** être dans son tort; avoir tort; **to put s.o. in the w.,** mettre qn dans son tort. **III.** *adv.* mal. **1.** (*a*) inexactement, incorrectement; **to guess w.,** mal deviner; **you have spelt my name w.,** vous avez mal orthographié mon nom; (*b*) à tort; à faux; **you did w.,** vous avez mal agi; *F:* **you've got me w.,** vous m'avez mal compris; *Dial: & NAm:* **to get in w. with s.o.,** se faire mal voir de qn. **2. to go w.,** (*a*) (*of pers.*) (i) se tromper de chemin; se fourvoyer; faire fausse route; (ii) se tromper; commettre une erreur; (iii) se dévoyer; mal tourner; (*b*) (*of mechanism*) se déranger, se dérégler, se détraquer; (*of business*) aller mal; aller de travers; **something went w. with the electric light,** nous avons eu une panne d'électricité; **all our plans went w.,** tous nos projets ont avorté; **things have gone w.,** les choses ont mal tourné. **wrongly** *adv.* **1.** à tort, à faux; **I've been w. accused,** on m'a accusé injustement, à tort, à faux; **rightly or w.,** à tort ou à raison. **2.** mal; **to choose w.,** mal choisir.

wrong² *v.tr.* (*a*) faire (du) tort à (qn); faire injure à (qn), léser (qn); (*b*) être injuste pour, envers (qn).

wrongdoer ['rɔŋdu(:)ər] *n.* (*a*) auteur *m* d'une injustice; (*b*) *Jur:* malfaiteur *m*; délinquant, -ante.

wrongdoing ['rɔŋdu(:)iŋ] *n.* (*a*) mal *m*; injustice *f*; (*b*) **wrongdoings,** méfaits *mpl*; (*c*) infraction *f* à la loi.

wrong-foot ['rɔŋ'fut] *v.tr. Sp:* prendre (son adversaire) à contre-pied: *Fig:* prendre (qn) à l'improviste, au dépourvu, au pied levé.

wrongful ['rɔŋf(u)l] *a.* **1.** (*a*) injuste; *Jur:* **w. dismissal,** renvoi injustifié (d'un employé); (*b*) *Jur:* illégal, -aux; préjudiciable; dommageable. **2.** faux (héritier, roi). **-fully** *adv.* injustement, à tort.

wrongheaded [rɔŋ'hedid] *a.* qui a l'esprit pervers, de travers.

wrongness ['rɔŋnis] *n.* **1.** erreur *f*, inexactitude *f*. **2.** injustice *f* (d'une accusation, etc.).

wrought [rɔːt] **1.** *see* WORK[2]. **2.** *a.* (*a*) travaillé, ouvré, ouvragé, façonné; (*b*) (*of metals*) ouvré, forgé, battu; **w. iron,** (i) fer forgé; (ii) fer ouvré.

wry [rai] *a.* **(wrier, wryer)** tordu, tors; de travers; (sourire) forcé, pincé; **to pull a w. face,** faire la grimace; **he gave a w. smile,** il a grimacé un sourire. **-ly** *adv.* avec un sourire forcé; en grimaçant.

wuzzy ['wʌzi] *a.* *NAm:* *F:* **I feel w.,** la tête me tourne.

wych-elm ['witʃelm] *n.* *Bot:* orme blanc, de(s) montagne(s).

wynd [waind] *n.* *Scot:* venelle *f*.

X

X, x [eks] *n.* (la lettre) X, x *m*; **for x number of years,** pendant x années; *Ph:* **X rays,** rayons *mpl* X; *Cin:* **X (certificate) film,** film interdit aux moins de 18 ans.
xenon ['zenɔn] *n. Ch:* xénon *m.*
xenophobe ['zenoufoub] *a. & n.* xénophobe (*mf*).
xenophobia [zenou'foubiə] *n.* xénophobie *f.*
xenophobic [zenou'foubik] *a.* xénophobe.
xerocopy ['ziəroukɔpi] *n.* copie *f* xérographique.
xerography [ziə'rɔgrəfi] *n.* xérographie *f.*
Xerox[1] ['ziərɔks] *n. R.t.m.* machine *f* Xerox.
Xerox[2] *v.tr.* photocopier (qch.).
Xmas ['krisməs, 'eksməs] *n. F:* (= *Christmas*) Noël *m.*
X(-)ray[1] ['eksrei] *n.* **1. X rays,** rayons *mpl* X; **X-r. examination,** examen *m* radiographique, radioscopique, radioscopie *f*; **X-r. diagnosis,** radiodiagnostic *m*; **X-r. photograph,** radio(graphie) *f*; **X-r. photography,** radio(graphie); **X-r. treatment,** radiothérapie *f.* **2.** radio; radiographie, radioscopie *f.*
X-ray[2] *v.tr. Med:* radiographier (qn); **to be X-rayed,** se faire radiographier, *F:* passer à la radio.
xylograph ['zailougræf] *n.* xylographie *f.*
xylographic [zailou'græfik] *a.* xylographique.
xylography [zai'lɔgrəfi] *n.* xylographie *f.*
xylophone ['zailəfoun] *n. Mus:* xylophone *m.*
xylophonist [zai'lɔfənist] *n. Mus:* joueur, -euse, de xylophone.

Y

Y, y, *pl.* **y's, ys** [wai, waiz] *n.* (la lettre) Y, y, *m*; i grec; y-grec *m*; *Biol:* **Y chromosome,** chromosome *m* Y; **Y-shaped,** fourchu; à fourche; en Y.
yacht¹ [jɔt] *n.* yacht *m*; **sailing, motor, y.,** yacht à voiles, à moteur; **racing y.,** yacht de course; **y. club,** yacht-club *m*, *pl.* yacht-clubs.
yacht² *v.i.* faire du yachting. **yachting** *n.* yachting *m*; **to go y.,** faire du yachting; **y. cap,** casquette *f* de yachtman.
yachtsman, *pl.* **-men** [ˈjɔtsmən] *n.m.* yachtman, *pl.* yachtmen.
yack(ety-yack)¹ [ˈjæk(əti'jæk)] *n. P:* jacasserie *f*.
yack(ety-yack)² *v.i. P:* jacasser.
yah [jɑː] *int.* **1.** (*disgust*) pouah! **2.** (*derision*) oh, là là!
yahoo [jəˈhuː] *n. F:* brute *f*.
yak¹ [jæk] *n. Z:* ya(c)k *m*; vache *f* de Tartarie.
yak² *n. P:* jacasserie *f*.
yak³ *v.i. P:* jacasser.
yam [jæm] *n. Bot:* igname *f*.
yank¹ [jæŋk] *n. F:* secousse *f*, saccade *f*.
yank² *v.tr. F:* tirer (d'un coup sec); **to y. out a tooth,** arracher une dent d'un seul coup; **to y. s.o. off,** emmener qn de force.
Yank³, Yankee [ˈjæŋki] *n. F:* (*a*) Américain, -aine (des États-Unis); Yankee *mf*; (*b*) *U.S: usu. Pej:* habitant, -ante, des États du Nord.
yap¹ [jæp] *n.* jappement *m* (d'un chien).
yap² *v.i.* **(yapped)** (*a*) (*of dog*) japper; (*b*) *F:* (*of pers.*) jacasser. **yapping 1.** *a.* jappeur. **2.** *n.* (*a*) jappement *m* (d'un chien); (*b*) *F:* jacasserie *f*.
yappy [ˈjæpi] *a. F:* jappeur.
yarborough [ˈjɑːb(ə)rə] *n. Cards:* main *f* qui ne contient aucune carte au-dessus du neuf.
yard¹ [jɑːd] *n.* **1.** *Meas:* yard *m* (0,914m); (*in Canada*) verge *f*; **square y.,** yard carré (0,765 m²); **face a y. long,** figure longue d'une aune; **yards of statistics, statistics by the y.,** des statistiques à n'en plus finir. **2.** *Nau:* vergue *f*; **main y.,** grand-vergue *f*.
yard² *n.* **1.** (*a*) (i) cour *f* (de maison, de ferme, d'écurie, etc.); *Sch:* cour, préau *m*; (ii) *NAm:* jardin *m* (autour d'une maison); (iii) *Austr: pl. usu. with sg. const.* parc *m* à bétail, à bestiaux; (*b*) **New Scotland Y.,** *F:* **the Y.** = la Sûreté. **2.** (*a*) chantier *m*; **timber, lumber, y.,** chantier de bois; **builder's y.,** chantier (de construction); *N.Arch:* **repair y.,** chantier de radoub; **ship-building y.,** chantier de construction(s) navale(s); **naval (dock)y.,** *U.S:* **navy y.,** chantier de l'État; arsenal *m* maritime; (*b*) dépôt *m*; **coal y.,** dépôt de charbon; *Rail:* **goods y.,** dépôt de marchandises.
yardage [ˈjɑːdidʒ] *n.* métrage *m*.
yardarm [ˈjɑːdɑːm] *n. Nau:* bout *m* de vergue.
yardstick [ˈjɑːdstik] *n.* (i) yard *m* (en bois, en métal); (ii) *Fig:* (*as standard of comparison*) aune *f*, étalon *m*, jauge *f*; **to measure others by one's own y.,** mesurer les autres à son aune.
yarn¹ [jɑːn] *n.* **1.** (*a*) *Tex:* fil *m*; filé *m* (de coton); **woollen y.,** fil de laine; (*b*) *Nau:* **(rope) y.,** fil de caret; **spun y.,** bitord *m*. **2.** *F:* (i) histoire *f* de matelot; (ii) histoire merveilleuse; longue histoire; **to spin a y.,** raconter, débiter, une histoire.
yarn² *v.i. F:* débiter des histoires, bavarder.
yarrow [ˈjærou] *n. Bot:* achillée *f*, mille-feuille *f*.
yashmak [ˈjæʃmæk] *n. Cost:* litham *m*.
yaw¹ [jɔː] *n.* (*a*) *Nau:* embardée *f*; (*b*) *Av: etc:* (mouvement *m* de) lacet *m*.
yaw² *v.i.* (*a*) *Nau:* faire une embardée; (*b*) *Av: etc:* faire un mouvement de lacet.
yawl [jɔːl] *n. Nau:* **1.** yole *f*. **2.** sloop *m*, yawl *m*.
yawn¹ [jɔːn] *n.* bâillement *m*; **to give a y.,** bâiller; *F:* **the book is one long y.,** le livre est ennuyeux à mourir.
yawn² 1. *v.i.* (*a*) bâiller (de sommeil, etc.); (*b*) (*of chasm, etc.*) être béant; bâiller; **the gulf yawned at his feet,** le gouffre s'ouvrait, s'entrouvrait, à ses pieds. **2.** *v.tr. F:* **to y. one's head off,** bâiller à se décrocher la mâchoire. **yawning 1.** *a.* (*a*) qui bâille d'ennui; (*b*) (gouffre) béant, ouvert. **2.** *n.* bâillement *m*.
yaws [jɔːz] *n.pl. Med:* pian *m*.
ye¹ [jiː] *def. art. A:* (*& pseudo archaic*) le, la, les; **Ye Olde Shoppe,** la Vieille Boutique.
ye² *pers. pron.* (*a*) *pl. A: & Lit:* vous; **seek and ye shall find,** cherchez et vous trouverez; *F:* **ye gods!** grand Dieu! (*b*) *sg. F: & Dial:* tu, vous; **how d'ye do?** comment vas-tu? comment allez-vous?
yea [jei] **1.** *adv. B: & Lit:* (*a*) oui; (*b*) en vérité; voire. **2.** *n.* oui *m*; *U.S:* (*in voting*) **yeas and nays,** voix *fpl* pour et contre.
yeah [jɛə] *adv. P:* oui; *Iron:* **oh y.?** vraiment?
year [jiər] *n.* an *m*, année *f*; (*a*) *usu.* an; **in the y. (of our Lord, of grace) 1850,** en l'an, en l'année (du Seigneur, de grâce) 1850; **I have known him for ten years,** je le connais depuis dix ans; **the Thirty Years' War,** la Guerre de Trente Ans; **sentenced to ten years' imprisonment,** condamné à dix ans de prison; **a y. last, next, September,** il y a eu, il y aura, un an en septembre; **last y.,** l'an dernier; l'année dernière; **next y.,** l'an prochain; l'année prochaine; **this day next y.,** dans un an jour pour jour; **every y.,** tous les ans; chaque année; annuellement; **twice a y.,** deux fois par an; **to earn, to have, £10,000 a y.,** gagner £10,000 par an, avoir £10,000 de rente; **a y.-old child, a one-y.-old (child),** un enfant (âgé) d'un an; **to be ten years old,** avoir dix ans; **new y.,** nouvel an; **New Y.'s Day,** le jour de l'an; **Happy New Y.!** bonne année! **to see the old y. out, the new y. in,** faire la veillée, le réveillon, de la Saint-Sylvestre; réveillonner; (*b*) *usu.* année; **leap y.,** année bissextile; **calendar, civil, y.,** année civile; **financial, fiscal, tax, y.,** année budgétaire; exercice (financier); **school y.,** année scolaire; **half y.,** semestre *m*; **third y. student,** étudiant(e) de troisième année; **he was in my y.,** il est de ma promotion; **document valid for one y.,** document *m* valable pour un an; **for many long years,** pendant de longues années; **all the y. round,** (pendant) toute l'année; **y. in (and) y. out,** une année après l'autre; **y. by y.,** d'année en année; **years ago,** il y a bien des années; *F:* **it's years since I saw him, I haven't seen him for, in, years,** il y a des éternités que je ne l'ai vu; **the best years of our life,** les plus belles années de notre vie; **from his earliest years,** dès son plus jeune âge; **old for his years,** plus vieux que son âge; (enfant) précoce; **to be getting on in years, to advance in years,** prendre de l'âge; **advanced in years,** âgé; (*c*) *Vit:* millésime; **a good y. for claret,** une bonne année pour le bordeaux rouge.

yearbook ['jiəbuk] *n.* annuaire *m*, almanach *m*; recueil annuel (de jurisprudence etc.).
yearling ['jiəliŋ] *a.* & *n.* (animal *m*) d'un an; **y. (colt),** poulain *m* d'un an; yearling *m*.
yearlong ['jiəlɔŋ] *a.* qui dure un an, toute l'année.
yearly ['jiəli] **1.** *a.* annuel; (*a*) qui se fait, qui revient, chaque année; (*b*) qui dure un an. **2.** *adv.* annuellement; (i) une fois par an; (ii) tous les ans.
yearn [jəːn] *v.i.* **to y. for, after, sth.,** languir pour, après, qch.; soupirer pour, après, qch.; **to y. to do sth.,** avoir bien envie de faire qch.; brûler de faire qch. **yearning 1.** *a.* (désir) vif, ardent; (regard) plein d'envie, de désir. **2.** *n.* désir ardent; envie *f* (**for,** de). **yearningly** *adv.* avec envie.
yeast [jiːst] *n.* levure *f*; **brewer's y.,** levure de bière.
yell¹ [jel] *n.* **1.** (*a*) hurlement *m*; cri aigu; **to give a y.,** pousser un cri, un hurlement; (*b*) *NAm:* cri de guerre, de bataille (des étudiants, etc.). **2.** *F: O:* personne *f*, chose *f*, extrêmement drôle; **it was a y.,** c'était tordant.
yell² 1. *v.i.* hurler; crier à tue-tête; **to y. with pain,** hurler de douleur. **2.** *v.tr.* **to y. (out),** hurler, beugler (une chanson); hurler, *F:* gueuler (un ordre). **yelling** *n.* hurlements *mpl*; grands cris.
yellow¹ ['jelou] **1.** *a.* (*a*) jaune; **to turn, go, y.,** jaunir; **y. metal,** cuivre *m* jaune; laiton *m*; **the y. races,** les races *fpl* jaunes; **the y. peril,** le péril jaune; **the y. pages,** les pages *fpl* jaunes (de l'annuaire téléphonique); *Anat:* **y. body,** corps *m* jaune; (*b*) *F:* trouillard, lâche; **to turn y.,** caner. **2.** *n.* jaune *m*; **lemon y.,** jaune citron; **chrome y.,** jaune de chrome.
yellow² 1. *v.tr.* jaunir (qch.); **papers yellowed with age,** papiers jaunis par le temps. **2.** *v.i.* jaunir.
yellowbelly ['jeloubeli] *n. P:* froussard *m*; trouillard *m*.
yellowhammer ['jelouhæmər] *n. Orn:* bruant *m* jaune.
yellowish ['jelouiʃ] *a.* jaunâtre; jaunet.
yellowness ['jelounis] *n.* ton *m* jaune, teinte *f* jaune (de qch.); teint *m* jaune (de qn).
yelp¹ [jelp] *n.* jappement *m*, glapissement *m*.
yelp² *v.i.* japper, glapir. **yelping 1.** *a.* jappant, glapissant. **2.** *n.* jappement *m*, glapissement *m*; *Ven:* clabaudage *m* (des chiens).
Yemen (the) [ðə'jemən] *Pr.n. Geog:* le Yémen.
Yemeni(te) ['jeməni, -ait] **1.** *a.* yéménique, yéménite. **2.** *n.* Yéménite *mf*.
yen¹ [jen] *n. Num:* yen *m*.
yen² *n. F:* envie *f*; **to have a y. for sth.,** avoir envie de qch.
yen³ *v.i. F:* = YEARN.
yeoman, *pl.* **-men** ['joumən] *n.m.* **1.** *O:* petit propriétaire; *Hist:* franc-tenancier, *pl.* francs-tenanciers; *Fig:* **to do y. service,** rendre des services inestimables. **2.** (*a*) soldat du *yeomanry, q.v.*; (*b*) **Y. of the Guard,** hallebardier à la Tour de Londres.
yeomanry ['joumənri] *n. coll.* **1.** petits propriétaires; *Hist:* francs-tenanciers. **2.** *Hist:* corps de cavalerie composé de volontaires.
yep [jep] *adv. U.S: P:* oui.
yes [jes] **1.** *adv.* (*a*) oui; (*contradicting negation*) si; **to answer y. or no,** répondre par oui ou non; **to say y.,** dire oui; dire que oui; **y., certainly! oh y.!** mais oui! **are you hungry?—y. (, I am),** avez-vous faim?—oui; **you didn't hear me?—y., I did,** vous ne m'avez pas entendu?—(mais) si; (*b*) (*interrogatively*) **y.?** (i) vraiment? (ii) et puis après? (iii) vous désirez? (*in answer to summons*) **waiter!—y. sir,** garçon!—voilà, monsieur. **2.** *n.* (*pl.* **yeses** ['jesiz]) oui *m inv.*; **an emphatic y.,** un oui énergique.
yes-man, *pl.* **-men** ['jesmæn, -men] *n. F:* béni-oui-oui *m inv.*
yesterday ['jestədei] *adv.* & *n.* hier (*m*); **the day before y.,** avant-hier (*m*); **y. week,** il y a eu hier huit jours; **a week (from) y.,** d'hier en huit; **yesterday's paper,** le journal d'hier; **y. morning, evening,** hier (au) matin, (au) soir; *Lit:* **our yesterdays,** les jours *mpl* d'autrefois, d'antan.
yesteryear [jestə'jiər] *n. Poet:* **the snows of y.,** les neiges *fpl* d'antan.
yet [jet] **I.** *adv.* **1.** *esp. Lit:* (*a*) encore; **we have ten minutes yet,** nous avons encore dix minutes; **jobs y. to be done,** tâches *fpl* encore à faire; (*b*) **y. more,** encore plus; **y. again,** encore une fois; **y. one more,** encore un autre. **2.** déjà; jusqu'à présent; jusqu'ici; **not y.,** pas encore; **do not go y.,** ne partez pas encore; **it will not happen just y.,** cela n'arrivera pas tout de suite; **as y. nothing has been done,** jusqu'à maintenant, jusqu'à présent, jusqu'ici, on n'a rien fait. **3.** malgré tout; **I shall catch him y.!** je finirai bien par l'attraper! **I'll do it y.!** j'y arriverai! **4. not finished nor y. started,** pas achevé, pas même commencé, ni même commencé; **not me nor y. you,** ni moi ni vous non plus. **II.** *conj.* néanmoins, cependant; tout de même; **and y. I like him,** et cependant, et malgré tout, néanmoins, il me plaît.
yeti ['jeti] *n.* yeti *m*.
yew [juː] *n.* (*a*) *Bot:* **y. (tree),** if *m*; (*b*) (*wood*) (bois *m* d')if.
Yid [jid] *n. P: Pej:* Juif, Juive; youpin, -ine.
Yiddish ['jidiʃ] *a.* & *n. Ling:* yiddish (*m*).
yield¹ [jiːld] *n.* **1.** production *f*, produit *m*, débit *m* (d'une mine); rapport *m* (d'un arbre fruitier, d'une mise de fonds, etc.); rendement (d'un champ, d'une machine); **the y. on these shares is large,** ces actions *fpl* rapportent beaucoup; **net y.,** revenu net. **2.** affaissement *m* (des fondements, etc.); fléchissement *m* (d'une poutre, etc.); **y. point,** limite *f* de la résistance (élastique).
yield² 1. *v.tr.* (*a*) rendre, donner; offrir, présenter (une vue); émettre, exhaler (une odeur); (*b*) rapporter, produire, donner; **ground that yields well,** terre *f* qui donne un bon rendement, qui rend bien; **shares that y. high interest,** actions *fpl* à gros rendement; **to y. a 10% dividend,** produire, rapporter, rendre, un dividende de 10%; (*c*) céder (une forteresse à l'ennemi, un droit, etc.); **to y. ground,** céder le terrain; **to y. a point to s.o.,** céder à qn sur un point; concéder un point; *Lit:* **to y. (up) the ghost, one's soul,** rendre l'âme. **2.** *v.i.* (*a*) se rendre, se soumettre; céder (**to,** à); capituler (**to,** devant); **to y. to force, to reason,** céder devant la force; se rendre à la raison; **to y. to temptation,** succomber à la tentation; se laisser tenter; **to y. to s.o.'s wishes,** condescendre aux désirs de qn; (*b*) (*of rope, etc.*) céder; (*of beam, etc.*) s'affaisser, fléchir; **the plank yielded under our weight,** la planche a manqué, cédé, sous notre poids. **yielding 1.** *a.* (*a*) (*of pers.*) facile, complaisant; **in a y. moment,** dans un moment de faiblesse; (*b*) mou, *f.* molle; peu résistant; (*c*) souple, élastique, flexible. **2.** *n.* (*a*) rendement; (*b*) (i) soumission *f*; (ii) reddition *f* (d'une forteresse); cession *f* (d'un droit); (*c*) affaissement *m* (de fondements, etc.); fléchissement *m* (d'une poutre, etc.).
yin [jin] *n. Phil:* yin *m*.
yippee [ji'piː] *int. F:* hourra! bravo!
yob [jɔb], **yobbo** ['jɔbou] *n.m. P:* voyou, loubar(d).
yodel¹ ['joud(ə)l] *n. Mus:* (chant *m* à la) tyrolienne.
yodel² *v.i.* **(yodel(l)ing)** *Mus:* jodler, iodler; faire des tyroliennes.
yod(el)ler ['joud(ə)lər] *n.* jodleur, -euse, iodleur, -euse.
yoga ['jougə] *n.* yoga *m*.
yog(h)urt ['jɔgət] *n.* yaourt *m*, yog(h)urt *m*.
yogi ['jougi] *n.* yogi *m*.
yoke¹ [jouk] *n.* **1.** joug *m*; **y. of oxen,** attelage *m* de

bœufs; *Fig:* **the y. of convention,** le joug des conventions; **to throw off, cast off, the y.,** secouer le joug; s'affranchir du joug. **2.** (*for carrying two pails*) palanche *f*. **3.** *Dressm:* empiècement *m*. **4.** *El:* carcasse *f*, bâti *m* (de dynamo).

yoke² *v.tr.* **1.** accoupler (des bœufs); atteler (des bœufs) (**to the plough,** à la charrue); *Fig:* **to y. together,** unir (deux personnes en mariage). **2.** accoupler (les pièces d'un appareil).

yokel ['jouk(ə)l] *n.* rustre *m*; campagnard *m*.

yolk [jouk] *n.* (*a*) jaune *m* (d'œuf); *Cu:* **take the y. of an egg, one egg y.,** prenez un jaune d'œuf; (*b*) *Biol:* vitellus *m*; **y. bag, sac,** membrane vitelline.

yon [jɔn] *a. & adv. A: & Dial:* = YONDER.

yonder ['jɔndər] *Lit:* **1.** *adv.* **down, over, y.,** là-bas. **2.** *a.* ce . . .-là, *f.* cette . . .-là, *pl.* ces . . .-là; **y. elms,** ces ormes *mpl* là-bas; ces ormes-là.

yoohoo ['ju:hu:] *int.* ohé!

yore [jɔ:r] *n. A: & Lit:* **of y.,** (d')autrefois; **in days of y.,** au temps jadis; autrefois.

Yorkshire ['jɔ:kʃiər] *Pr.n. Geog:* le comté d'York; *Cu:* **Y. pudding,** pâte cuite servie avec du rosbif.

you [ju(:)] *pers. pron.* (i) *sg. & pl.* vous; (ii) *sg.* (*when addressing relatives, intimate friends, children, animals, deities, often*) tu, te, toi. **1.** (*unstressed*) (*a*) (*nom.*) vous; tu; **y. are very kind,** vous êtes bien aimable(s); tu es bien aimable; **how are y.?** comment allez-vous? comment vas-tu? **there y. are,** vous voilà, te voilà; **y. all,** vous tous; (*b*) (*as object of verb*) vous; te; **I hope to see y. tomorrow,** j'espère vous voir, te voir, demain; **I'll give y. some,** je vous en donnerai; je t'en donnerai; **I told y. so!** je vous, te, l'avais bien dit! (*c*) (*as object of preposition*) vous, toi; **between y. and me,** (i) entre vous et moi, entre toi et moi; (ii) entre nous soit dit; **away with y.!** allez-vous-en! va-t'en! **all of y.,** vous tous. **2.** (*stressed*) (*a*) vous; toi; **y. and I will go by train,** vous et moi, toi et moi, nous irons par le train; **I am older than y.,** je suis plus âgé que vous, que toi; **it's y.,** c'est vous, toi; **if I were y.,** (si j'étais) à votre place, à ta place; **hey! y. there!** eh! dites donc, là-bas! (*b*) (*in the imperative*) **don't y. be afraid!** n'ayez pas peur! **y. sit down and eat your lunch!** toi, assieds-toi et prends ton déjeuner! (*c*) (*in apposition*) **y. lawyers, y. Englishmen,** vous autres avocats, vous autres Anglais; **y. idiot (, y.)!** idiot que vous êtes, que tu es! espèce d'idiot! **y. darling!** tu es un amour! **3.** (*indefinite*) on; **y. never can tell,** on ne sait jamais; **the joy y. feel when y. meet a friend,** la joie qu'on ressent quand on recontre un ami.

you'd = (i) **you had,** *see* HAVE²; (ii) **you would,** *see* WILL³.

You-Know-Who [ju:nou'hu:] (*in lieu of*) *Pr.n.* qui-vous-savez *mf*.

you'll = (i) **you will;** (ii) **you shall.**

young [jʌŋ] **1.** *a.* (*a*) jeune; (*of animal*) petit; **younger,** plus jeune; **younger son, daughter,** fils cadet, fille cadette; **my younger brother,** mon frère cadet; **youngest,** le, la, plus jeune; le cadet, la cadette; **he is younger than I,** il est plus jeune, moins âgé, que moi; il est mon cadet; **she is two years younger than I,** elle est plus jeune que moi, elle est ma cadette, de deux ans; **when I was twenty years younger,** quand j'avais vingt ans de moins; **I am not so y. as I was,** je n'ai plus mes jambes de vingt ans; **a not-so-y. woman,** une femme plus très jeune; **y. man,** jeune homme; **y. woman, lady,** (i) jeune fille; (ii) jeune femme; **y. people,** jeunes gens; les jeunes; **Pliny the Younger,** Pline le Jeune; **the younger generation,** la jeune génération; **in his younger days,** dans son jeune temps; dans sa jeunesse; (*b*) **y. for his years,** jeune pour son âge; **y. in mind,** jeune d'esprit; **to grow, get, y. again, to grow younger,** rajeunir; (*c*) **y. wine,** vin vert; **the night is still y.,** la nuit n'est que peu avancée. **2.** *n.pl. inv.* (*a*) **the y.,** les jeunes gens; la jeunesse; **books for the y.,** livres *mpl* pour la jeunesse; **old and y.,** les grands et les petits; **y. and old,** tout le monde; (*b*) **animal and its y.,** animal et ses petits; **mare with y.,** jument pleine.

youngish ['jʌŋiʃ] *a.* assez jeune; *F:* jeunet, -ette.

youngster ['jʌŋstər] *n.* (*a*) jeune personne *f*, *esp.* garçon *m*; (*b*) petit, -ite; *F:* gosse *mf*.

your [jɔ:r] *poss.a.* **1.** (i) *sg & pl.* votre, *pl.* vos; (ii) *sg.* (*when addressing relatives, intimate friends, children, deities, often*) ton, *f.* ta, *pl.* tes; **y. house,** votre maison, ta maison; **y. friends,** vos ami(e)s, tes ami(e)s; **y. father and mother,** votre père et votre mère; (*in official style*) vos père et mère; ton père et ta mère; **the most recent of y. books, y. most recent book,** votre livre le plus récent; **have you hurt y. hand?** vous vous êtes fait mal à la main? **turn y. head(s),** tournez la tête; *Games: etc:* **y. turn!** à vous! **Y. Majesty,** votre Majesté. **2.** (*indefinite; cf.* YOU 3) son, *f.* sa, *pl.* ses; **you cannot alter y. nature,** on ne peut pas changer son caractère; **on y. right,** à (votre) droite. **3.** (*ethic*) **y. typical Frenchman,** le Français typique.

you're = **you are,** *see* BE.

yours [jɔ:z] *poss.pron.* (i) *sg. & pl.* le vôtre, la vôtre, les vôtres; (ii) *n.* (*when addressing relatives, inimate friends, children, often*) le tien, la tienne; les tiens, les tiennes; (*a*) **this is y.,** ceci est à vous, à toi; *F:* **the bathroom's all y.,** la salle de bains est libre maintenant; *Corr:* **y. (sincerely),** (i) bien amicalement; (ii) *Com:* veuillez agréer l'expression de mes sentiments distingués, respectueux; **y. is a nation of travellers,** vous êtes une nation de voyageurs; **he is a friend of y.,** c'est un de vos amis; c'est un ami à vous; **that's no business of y.,** cela ne vous regarde pas; ce n'est pas votre affaire; **that dog of y.,** votre chien; ton chien; *Com:* **y. of the 16th inst.,** votre estimée, votre honorée, du seize de ce mois; (*b*) (*your kindred*) **you and y.,** vous et les vôtres; toi et les tiens.

yourself [jɔ:'self], *pl.* **yourselves** [jɔ:'selvz] *pers. pron.* (*a*) (*emphatic*) (i) *sg. & pl.* vous, vous-même(s); (ii) (*when addressing relatives, intimate friends, children, deities, often*) toi(-même); *F:* **you don't look quite y.,** vous avez, tu as, l'air mal en train; (*b*) (*refl.*) (i) vous; (ii) te; **are you enjoying y., yourselves?** tu t'amuses bien? vous amusez-vous bien? **have you hurt y.?** vous êtes-vous fait mal? tu t'es fait mal? *F:* **have y. a good time,** amuse-toi bien; (*c*) (*after preposition*) **see for y., yourselves,** voyez vous-même(s); **speak for y.!** parle pour toi! **keep it for y.,** garde-le pour toi(-même), gardez-le pour vous(-même); **do you live by y.?** vous vivez, tu vis, (tout) seul? (*reciprocal*) **among yourselves,** entre vous; (*d*) (*used impersonally*) soi-(-même); (*refl.*) se; **you have to do it y.,** il faut le faire soi-même; **you can't take y. too seriously,** il ne faut pas se prendre trop au sérieux.

youth [ju:θ, *pl.* ju:ðz] *n.* **1.** jeunesse *f*, adolescence *f*, jeune âge *m*; **in his early y.,** dans sa première jeunesse; **she is not in the first blush of y., past her first y.,** elle n'est pas de la première jeunesse; *Myth:* **the fountain of Y.,** la Fontaine de Jouvence; *Prov:* **y. will have its way, its fling,** il faut que jeunesse se passe. **2.** jeune homme, adolescent *m*. **3.** *coll.* jeunes gens *mpl*, jeunesse (du village, etc.).

youthful ['ju:θf(u)l] *a.* **1.** (*of pers., face, fashion, etc.*) jeune; **to look y.,** avoir l'air jeune. **2.** (erreur, enthousiasme) de jeunesse. **-fully** *adv* en jeune homme; en jeune fille.

youthfulness ['ju:θf(u)lnis] *n.* jeunesse *f*; air *m* de jeunesse; air jeune.

you've = **you have.**

yowl¹ [jaul] *n.* hurlement *m* (de chien); miaulement *m* (de chat).

yowl² *v.i.* (*of dog*) hurler; (*of cat*) miauler.
yo-yo ['joujou] *n. Toys: R.t.m.* yo-yo *m.*
yucca ['jʌkə] *n. Bot:* yucca *m.*
yuck [jʌk] *int. F:* pouah!
yucky ['jʌki] *a. F:* dégueulasse.
Yugoslav ['ju:gouslɑ:v] *Geog:* **1.** *a.* yougoslave. **2.** *n.* Yougoslave *mf.*
Yugoslavia [ju:gou'slɑ:viə] *Pr.n. Geog:* Yougoslavie *f.*
Yugoslavian [ju:gou'slɑ:viən] *a.* yougoslave.
yule [ju:l] *n.* (*a*) *A:* Noël *m*; (*b*) **y. log,** bûche *f* de Noël.
yuletide ['ju:ltaid] *n. A:* l'époque *f* de Noël; les fêtes *fpl* de Noël.
yummy ['jʌmi] *a. F:* délicieux.
yum-yum [jʌm'jʌm] *int. F:* miam-miam!
yup [jup] *adv. U.S: P:* oui.

Z

Z, z, *pl.* **zs, z's** [zed, *U.S:* ziː, *pl.* zedz, ziːz] *n.* (la lettre) Z, z *m.*
Zaire [zɑː'iər] *Pr.n. Geog:* Zaïre *m.*
Zambezi (the) [ðəzæm'biːzi] *Pr.n. Geog:* le Zambèze.
Zambia ['zæmbiə] *Pr.n. Geog:* Zambie *f.*
Zambian ['zæmbiən] **1.** *a.* zambien. **2.** *n.* Zambien, -ienne.
zaniness ['zeininis] *n. F:* loufoquerie *f.*
zany ['zeini] *a. F:* loufoque.
zap[1] [zæp] *NAm:* **1.** *int F:* paf! **2.** *n.* bruit *m* de coup sec, d'explosion, etc.
zap[2] *v.tr. NAm:* (*a*) détruire; tuer (qn); (*b*) donner un coup à, cogner (qch.); battre (un adversaire).
zeal [ziːl] *n.* zèle *m*, ardeur *f*; **religious z.,** zèle, ferveur *f*; **to make a show of z.,** faire du zèle.
Zealand ['ziːlənd] *Pr.n. Geog:* **1.** (l'île *f* de) Seeland. **2. New Z.,** Nouvelle-Zélande *f.*
zealot ['zelət] *n.* **1.** *B. Hist:* zélote *m.* **2.** fanatique *mf*, zélateur (**for,** de).
zealotry ['zelətri] *n.* **1.** *Hist:* zélotisme *m.* **2.** fanatisme *n*, ferveur *f.*
zealous ['zeləs] *a.* zélé; zélateur, -trice; ardent; empressé; **z. for sth.,** plein de zèle pour qch. **-ly** *adv.* avec zèle.
zebra ['ziːbrə, 'zebrə] *n.* **1.** *Z:* zèbre *m*; **z. markings, stripes,** zébrures *fpl.* **2. z. crossing,** passage *m* pour piétons.
zebu ['ziːb(j)uː] *n.* zébu *m*; bœuf *m* à bosse.
zed [zed] *n.* (la lettre) z *m.*
zee [ziː] *n. NAm:* (la lettre) z *m.*
Zen [zen] *n. Rel:* **Z. (Buddhism),** (bouddhisme) zen *m.*
zenith ['zeniθ] *n. Astr:* zénith *m*; **at the z. of his fame,** à l'apogée *m*, au sommet, au zénith, de sa gloire.
zephyr ['zefər] *n. Lit:* zéphyr *m.*
zeppelin ['zepəlin] *n. Aer:* zeppelin *m.*
zero[1] ['ziərou] *n.* **1.** *Mth:* zéro *m*; **z. point two (0.2),** zéro virgule deux (0,2); **z. hour,** l'heure H; *F:* (*pers.*) **a z.,** un zéro, une nullité. **2.** (*a*) **z. (point),** (point *m*) origine *f*, zéro (d'une échelle graduée, etc.); **the thermometer is at z., below z.,** le thermomètre est à zéro, au-dessous de zéro; *Adm:* **z. rating,** imposition nulle; **exports are down to z.,** les exportations sont tombées à zéro, à néant; (*b*) *Surv:* **z. altitude,** altitude zéro.
zero[2] *v.tr.* (re)mettre (un instrument, etc.) à zéro. **zero in 1.** *v.tr. U.S: Artil:* régler le tir (d'une pièce) (**on a target,** sur un objectif). **2.** *v.i.* (*a*) *Artil:* **to z. in on sth.,** régler le tir sur qch.; (*b*) *Fig:* se diriger (**on sth.,** vers qch.).
zest [zest] *n.* **1.** (*a*) enthousiasme *m*, entrain *m*; verve *f*; **with z.,** (combattre, etc.) avec élan, avec entrain; (manger) avec appétit, de bon appétit; (*b*) saveur *f*, goût *m*; **to add z. to the adventure,** donner du piquant à l'aventure. **2.** zeste *m* (d'orange, de citron).
zestful ['zestf(ul)] *a.* plain d'enthousiasme, de verve.
zigzag[1] [zigzæg] **1.** *n.* zigzag *m*; **in zigzags,** en zigzag; **z. path,** sentier *m* en zigzag; **z. pattern,** dessin *m* à zigzags. **2.** *adv.* **the road runs z.,** le chemin fait des zigzags.
zigzag[2] *v.* **(zigzagged) 1.** *v.i.* zigzaguer; faire des zigzags. **2.** *v.tr.* (*a*) disposer (des obstacles, etc.) en zigzag; (*b*) traverser (une plaine, etc.) en zigzag. **zigzagging** *n.* zigzags *mpl*; marche *f* en zigzag.
zilch [ziltʃ] *n. esp. NAm: F:* zéro *m*; rien de rien.
zillion ['ziliən] *n. U.S: F:* des millions *mpl* (et des millions).
Zimbabwe [zim'babwei] *Pr.n. Geog:* Zimbabwe *m.*
zinc [ziŋk] *n.* **1.** zinc *m*; **z.(-)bearing,** zincifère; **z. oxide,** *Paint:* **z. white,** oxyde *m* de zinc, blanc *m* de zinc; *Pharm:* **z. ointment,** pommade *f* à l'oxyde de zinc; **z. works, trade,** zinguerie *f.* **2.** *Phot: Engr:* **z. engraving, etching,** zincogravure *f.*
zincblende ['ziŋkblend] *n. Miner:* blende *f.*
zing [ziŋ] *n. F:* vitalité *f*, entrain *m.*
zinnia ['ziniə] *n. Bot:* zinnia *m.*
Zion ['zaiən] *Pr.n.m.* Sion.
Zionism ['zaiənizm] *n. Pol:* sionisme *m.*
Zionist ['zaiənist] *a.* & *n. Pol:* sioniste (*mf*).
zip[1] [zip] *n.* **1.** sifflement *m* (d'une balle). **2.** *F:* énergie *f*, vitesse *f*; **put some z. into it!** mets-y du nerf! **3. z. (fastener, fastening),** fermeture *f* éclair *inv* (*R.t.m.*); *Belg:* tirette *f.*
zip[2] *v.* **(zipped) 1.** *v.i.* siffler (comme une balle); (*of car, etc.*) **to z. past,** passer comme un éclair. **2.** *v.tr.* **to z. in a lining,** attacher une doublure au moyen d'une fermeture éclair (*R.t.m.*); *F:* **z. me up,** agrafe ma robe.
zip[3] *n. U.S:* **z. code,** code postal.
zipper ['zipər] *n. F:* fermeture *f* éclair *inv* (*R.t.m.*); **z. bag,** (sac *m*) fourre-tout *m inv* à fermeture éclair.
zippy ['zipi] *a. F:* plein d'énergie; plein d'entrain, **look z.!** grouille-toi!
zircon ['zəːkɔn] *n. Miner:* zircon *m.*
zither ['ziðər] *n. Mus:* cithare *f.*
zodiac ['zoudiæk] *n. Astr:* zodiaque *m*; **the signs of the z.,** les signes *mpl* du zodiaque.
zodiacal [zou'daiək(ə)l] *a.* zodiacal, -aux.
zombi(e) ['zɔmbi] *n.* **1.** *Rel:* zombi *m.* **2.** *F:* abruti, -ie; **he walks about like a z.,** il a tout le temps un air hébété.
zonal ['zoun(ə)l] *a.* zonal, -aux.
zone[1] [zoun] *n.* zone *f*; *Geog:* **time z.,** fuseau *m* horaire; *Adm:* **no parking z.,** zone d'interdiction de stationner; **parking meter z.,** = zone bleue; *Mil:* **battle z.,** zone de l'avant; **danger z.,** zone dangereuse.
zone[2] *v.tr.* répartir (une ville, etc.) en zones. **zoned** *a.* **1.** *Town P:* réparti, découpé, en zones. **2.** *Bot: Z: Miner:* zoné. **zoning** *n.* répartition *f* en zones; *Town P:* zonage *m*, zoning *m.*
zoo [zuː] *n.* jardin *m* zoologique, *F:* zoo *m.*
zoological [zouə'lɔdʒik(ə)l, zuːə'lɔdʒik(ə)l] *a.* zoologique; **z. garden(s),** jardin *m* zoologique. **-ally** *adv.* zoologiquement.
zoologist [zou'ɔlədʒist, zuː-] *n.* zoologiste *m.*
zoology [zou'ɔlədʒi, zuː-] *n.* zoologie *f.*
zoom[1] [zuːm] *n.* **1.** bourdonnement *m*; vrombissement *m.* **2.** *Av:* (montée *f* en) chancelle *f.* **3.** *Cin:* zoom *m*; changement *m* rapide de plan; **z. lens,** zoom.
zoom[2] *v.i.* **1.** bourdonner; vrombir; **the cars are zooming along the road,** les voitures passent en trombe sur la route. **2.** *Av: F:* monter en chandelle. **3.** *Cin:* **to z. in,** changer de plan; faire un zoom.
zoophyte ['zouəfait] *n. Biol:* zoophyte *m.*
Zoroaster [zɔrou'æstər] *Pr.n.m. Rel.H:* Zoroastre.
zounds [zaundz] *int. A:* morbleu! ventrebleu! sacrebleu!
zucchini [zu'kiːni] *n.* courgette *f.*

Zulu ['zu:lu:] **1.** *a. Ethn:* zoulou *inv. in f, pl.* zoulous, **2.** *n.* (*a*) *Ethn:* Zoulou *mf*; (*b*) *Ling:* zoulou *m.*

Zululand ['zu:lu:lænd] *Pr.n. Geog:* le Zoulouland.

zwieback ['zwi:bæk] *n. Comest:* (genre *m* de) biscotte *f.*

zygote ['zaigout] *n. Biol:* zygote *m.*

Common abbreviations
Abréviations courantes

A., 1. *angström*, angström. 2. *answer*, réponse.
A.A., 1. *anti-aircraft* = défense contre avions, D.C.A. 2. *Automobile Association.* 3. *Alcoholics Anonymous*, Alcooliques Anonymes, AA.
A.A.A., 1. *Amateur Athletics Association.* 2. *American Automobile Association.*
A.A.U., 1. *Association of American Universities.* 2. *U.S: Amateur Athletic Union.*
A.B., 1. *Nau: able(-bodied) seaman*, matelot de deuxième classe. 2. *U.S: Artium Baccalaureus, Bachelor of Arts.*
A.B.A., 1. *Amateur Boxing Association.* 2. *American Bar Association.*
A.B.C., 1. *American Broadcasting Company.* 2. *Australian Broadcasting Corporation.*
A.B.M., *antiballistic missile*, engin antimissile.
Abp., *Archbishop*, archevêque.
abr., *abridged*, réduit.
abs., **absol.**, *absolute(ly)*, absolu(ment).
abs., *abstract*, abstrait.
A.B.T.A. ['æbtə] *Association of British Travel Agents.*
A.C., *El: alternating current*, courant alternatif, c.a.
A/C, a/c., *Com: account*, compte, c.
acad., (*a*) *academic*, académique; (*b*) *academy*, académie.
acct., (*a*) *account* compte, c(pte).; (*b*) *accountant*, comptable.
AC/DC, 1. *El: alternating current or direct current*, courant alternatif ou courant continu. 2. *F: bisexual*, bisexuel.
act., *Gram: active*, actif.
A.D., *anno Domini*, A.D., après Jésus-Christ, ap(r). J.-C.
ad., *advertisement*, annonce; affiche.
A.D.C., *aide-de-camp*, officier d'ordonnance.
adj., *adjective, adjectival*, adjectif.
Adjt, *adjutant*, adjudant.
ad lib., *ad libitum*, à volonté.
Adm., *Admiral*, amiral.
admin., *administration*, administration.
adv., 1. *adverb*, adverbe. 2. *advisory*, consultatif.
ad val., *Com: ad valorem*, selon la valeur.
A.E.C., *U.S: Atomic Energy Commission* = Commissariat à l'énergie atomique.
A.E.F., *American Expeditionary Forces.*
A.E.U., *Amalgamated Engineering Union.*
afft, *Jur: affidavit*, déclaration sous serment.
AFL-CIO, *American Federation of Labor and Congress of Industrial Organizations.*
A.F.M., *Air Force Medal.*
A.F.N., *American Forces Network.*
agitprop, *agitation and propaganda*, agitation et propagande.
A.G.M., *Annual General Meeting*, assemblée générale annuelle.
agri(c)., *agriculture*, agriculture, agr.
Agt, *agent*, commissionnaire, caire.
A.I., 1. *Amnesty International.* 2. *artificial insemination*, insémination artificielle.
A.I.D., 1. *U.S: Agency for International Development.* 2. *artificial insemination by donor*, insémination artificielle par donneur.
Ala., *Geog: Alabama.*
Alas., *Geog: Alaska.*
Ald(m)., *alderman*, conseiller municipal.
alt., 1. *altitude*, altitude. 2. *alternate*, alternatif, alterné. 3. *Mus: alto*, alto.
Alta, *Geog: Alberta.*
A.M., *U.S: Artium Magister*, Master of Arts.
a.m., *ante meridiem, before noon*, avant midi, a.m.
A.M.A., *American Medical Association.*
Am(er)., *America, American*, Amérique, Américain.
amp., *ampere*, ampère, amp.
A.M.P.A.S., *Academy of Motion Picture Arts and Sciences.*
anon., *anonymous*, anonyme.
AOB, *any other business.*
A.P.C., *Mil: armoured personnel carrier*, véhicule blindé de transport de troupe, de personnel.
A.P.O., *U.S: Army Post Office.*
app., *appendix*, appendice.
approx., *approximately*, à peu près.
apt., *U.S: apartment*, appartement.
A.P.T., *Rail: advanced passenger train.*
A.R.A., *Associate of the Royal Academy of Arts.*
A.R.A.M., *Associate of the Royal Academy of Music.*
A.R.C.M, *Associate of the Royal College of Music.*
Ariz., *Geog: Arizona.*
Ark., *Geog: Arkansas.*
arr., *arrives*, arrive.
A.S., *Anglo-Saxon*, Anglo-Saxon.
A.S.A., 1. *Advertising Standards Authority.* 2. *American Standards Association.*
A.S.C.A.P., *American Society of Composers, Authors and Publishers.*
A.S.C.E., *American Society of Civil Engineers.*
ASH [æʃ] *Action on Smoking and Health* = Ligue contre la Fumée du Tabac en Public, L.C.F.T.P.
ASLEF ['æzlef] *Associated Society of Locomotive Engineers and Firemen.*
A.S.P.C.A., *American Society for the Prevention of Cruelty to Animals.*
Ass(n)., *association*, association, A.
ass(t)., *assistant*, adjoint, aide, auxiliaire.
A.S.T., *U.S: Atlantic Standard Time.*
A.S.T.M.S., *Association of Scientific, Technical and Managerial Staffs.*
A.T.C., 1. *Air Training Corps* = préparation militaire supérieure (pour l'aviation), P.M.S. 2. *Air Traffic Control*, réglementation du trafic aérien.
Atty, *Jur: Attorney;* **Atty Gen.**, *Attorney General.*
A.T.V., *Associated Television.*
A.U.E.W., *Amalgamated Union of Engineering Workers.*
A.V., *Authorized Version*, la traduction anglaise de la Bible de 1611.
av., 1. *Meas: avoirdupois*, avoirdupoids, avdp. 2. *average*, (i) avaries, (ii) moyen(ne).
Av(e)., *Avenue*, avenue, av.
aw., atomic weight, poids atomique, p.at.
A.W.O.L. ['eiwɔl] *Mil: absent without leave*, en absence illégale.
A.Y.H.A., *American Youth Hostels Association.*

B., 1. *Mus: bass*, basse. 2. *black* (*pencil lead*).

b., 1. *born*, né. 2. *Cr: bowled.*
B.A., 1. *Bachelor of Arts* = licencié ès lettres. 2. *British Airways.*
B.A.C., *British Aircraft Corporation.*
b. & b., *bed and breakfast*, chambre et petit déjeuner.
B.A.O.R., *British Army of the Rhine.*
Bart, *baronet*, baronnet.
B.B., *double black (pencil).*
B.B.B., *U.S: Better Business Bureau.*
B.B.C., *British Broadcasting Corporation*, la Corporation britannique de radiodiffusion.
BC., 1. *before Christ*, avant Jésus-Christ, av. J.-C. 2. *British Columbia.* 3. *British Council.*
B.C.G., *Med: bacillus Calmette-Guérin*, bacille Calmette-Guérin.
B.D., *Bachelor of Divinity*, Bachelier en Théologie.
Bd, *Boulevard*, boulevard.
Bde, *Brigade*, brigade, bde.
B.Ed., *Bachelor of Education.*
Beds, *Geog: Bedfordshire.*
B.E.F., *British Expeditionary Force.*
B.E.M., *British Empire Medal.*
Berks., *Geog: Berkshire.*
B.F., *P: bloody fool.*
b/f, *Book-k: brought forward*, à reporter.
BFI, *British Film Institute.*
B.F.P.O., *British Forces Post Office.*
biog., *biographical, biography, biographer*, biographique, biographie, biographe.
bk, 1. *book*, livre. 2. *bank*, banque, banq., bque.
B. L., *Bachelor of Law*, licencié en droit.
bl., 1. *Com: bale*, balle, B.; ballot, bot. 2. *black*, noir. 3. *blue*, bleu. 4. *block*, bloc.
B/L, b/l, *Com: bill of lading*, connaissement, connt.
bldg, *building*, construction.
B.Litt., *Bachelor of Letters*, Bachelier ès Lettres, B. ès L.
blvd, *boulevard*, boulevard, boul., bd.
B.M., 1. *British Museum.* 2. *Bachelor of Medicine.*
B.M.A., *British Medical Association.*
B.Mus., *Bachelor of Music*, licencié en musique.
B.O., *body odour*, odeur corporelle.
B. of E., *Bank of England.*
Bor., Boro', *borough.*
B.P., *British Petroleum.*
Bp, *bishop*, évêque.
Br, *Ecc: brother*, frère, F(r).
B.R., *British Rail.*
B.R.C.S., *British Red Cross Society.*
Brig., *Mil:* (*a*) *brigade*, brigade, bde, brig.; (*b*) *brigadier.*
Brit., *Britain, British*, Grande-Bretagne, britannique.
bro(s)., *brother(s)*, frère(s).
B.R.S., *British Road Services.*
B/S, b.s., 1. *Com: balance sheet*, bilan. 2. *bill of sale*, acte de vente.
B.Sc., *Bachelor of Science*, licencié ès sciences.
B.S.C., *British Steel Corporation.*
B.S.I., *British Standards Institution*, institut britannique de normalisation.
B.S.T., (*a*) *British Summer Time*, heure d'été britannique; (*b*) *British Standard Time*, heure légale britannique.
B.T.U., *British thermal unit.*
Bucks., *Geog: Buckinghamshire.*
BUPA ['bu:pə] *British United Provident Association.*
B.V.M., *Blessed Virgin Mary*, la Sainte Vierge.

C., 1. *centum*, cent, c. 2. *Ph:* (*a*) *centigrade*, centigrade, c.; (*b*) *Celsius*, Celsius, C. 3. *Geog: Cape*, cap.
c., 1. *circa, circiter*, environ, env. 2. *Num:* (*a*) *cent*, cent, c.; (*b*) *centime*, centime, c. 3. *cube, cubic*, cube, cubique, cub. 4. *century*, siècle.
C.A., 1. (*a*) *chartered accountant*, expert comptable; (*b*) *chief accountant*, chef comptable. 2. *Fin: current account*, compte courant, C.C., c/c.
ca., *circa*, environ, env.
C.A.B., *Citizens' Advice Bureau.*
Caer., *Geog: Hist: Caernarvonshire.*
Cal., 1. *Ph: large, great, calorie*, grande calorie, C(al). 2. *Geog: California*, Californie.
Cam., Camb., *Geog: Cambridge.*
Cambs., *Geog: Cambridgeshire.*
Can., *Geog: Canada.*
Cantab., *Cantabrigiensis*, de l'Université de Cambridge.
C.A.P., *Common Agricultural Policy.*
cap., 1. *capitulum*, chapitre, ch(ap). 2. *Typ: capital*, majuscule. 3. *Geog: capital*, capitale, cap.
Capt., *captain*, capitaine, Cap., commandant, comm.
carr., *carriage*, port.
Cath., *Catholic*, catholique.
C.B., 1. *Companion of the Order of the Bath.* 2. *Mil: confinement to barracks*, consigne au quartier. 3. *W.Tel: citizens' band.*
C.B.C., *Canadian Broadcasting Corporation.*
C.B.E., (i) *Commander*, (ii) *Companion, of the Order of the British Empire.*
C.B.I., *Confederation of British Industries.*
C.B.S., *Columbia Broadcasting System.*
C.C., *county council.*
c.c., *Meas: cubic centimetres(s)*, centimètre(s) cube(s), cm^3, cc.
cc., *copies*, copies.
C.D., 1. *civil defence* = défense passive, D.P. 2. *Corps Diplomatique.*
Cdr, *Mil: commander*, commandant.
C.E.G.B., *Central Electricity Generating Board.*
C.Eng., *chartered engineer.*
CENTO ['sentou] *Central Treaty Organization*, Cento.
cert., *certificate*, certificat.
C.E.T., *Central European Time*, heure de l'Europe centrale.
cf., *Lt: confer*, comparez; voir.
C.G.S., *Mil: Chief of the General Staff*, chef de l'état-major.
C.H., 1. *Companion of Honour.* 2. *Fin: clearing house*, chambre de compensation, clearing. 3. *customs house*, (bureau de) douane. 4. *central heating*, chauffage central.
ch., 1. *chapter*, chapitre, ch(ap). 2. *church*, église.
Ch.B., *Bachelor of Surgery*, licencié en chirurgie.
Ches., *Geog:* Cheshire.
chq., *cheque*, chèque.
C.I., *Geog: Channel Islands*, îles Anglo-normandes.
c/i, *Com: certificate of insurance*, certificat d'assurance.
C.I.A., *U.S: Central Intelligence Agency*, service de renseignements.
C.I.D., *Criminal Investigation Department* = police judiciaire, P.J.
C.I.F., c.i.f., *Com: cost, insurance and freight*, coût, assurance, fret, C.A.F.
C.I.G.S., *Mil: Chief of the Imperial General Staff.*
C.-in-C., *Mil: commander-in-chief*, commandant en chef.
C.I.P., *F: Commercially Important Person.*
civ., (*a*) *civilian*, civil; (*b*) *civil*, civil.
cl., *Meas: centilitre*, centilitre, cl.
C.M., *Common Market*, Marché commun.
cm., *Meas: centimetre(s)*, centimètre(s), cm.
Cmdr., 1. *commodore.* 2. *commander.*
C.M.S., *Church Missionary Society.*

C.N.D., *Campaign for Nuclear Disarmament.*
Co., **1.** *Com: company*, compagnie, société, Cie, Co., Sté. **2.** *Adm: county.*
C.O., **1.** *Mil: commanding officer*, officier commandant. **2.** *conscientious objector*, objecteur de conscience.
c/o, *Post: care of*, aux bons soins (de), a.b.s.
C.O.D., **1.** *Com: cash on delivery, U.S: collect on delivery*, (livraison) contre remboursement. **2.** *Concise Oxford Dictionary.*
C. of E., *Church of England*, l'Église anglicane.
C.O.I., *Central Office of Information.*
Col., **1.** *Mil: colonel*, colonel, Col. **2.** *Geog:* (*a*) *Colombia*; (*b*) *Colorado.*
col., **1.** *column*, colonne. **2.** *colour*, couleur.
coll., *college*, collège.
Colo., *Geog: Colorado*, Colorado.
Com., *communist*, communiste.
COMECON ['kɔmikɔn] *Council for Mutual Economic Aid*, Conseil pour l'aide économique mutuelle, COMECON.
Cominform ['kɔminfɔːm] *Communist Information Bureau*, Kominform.
Comintern ['kɔmintəːn] *Communist International*, Komintern.
comp., (*a*) *comparative*, comparatif, compar.; (*b*) *compare*, comparer, compar.
comps, *compliments*, compliments.
Con., **1.** *consul*, consul. **2.** *Pol: Conservative*, conservateur.
conf., *conference*, conférence.
conj., *conjunction*, conjonction.
Conn., *Geog: Connecticut.*
Cons., *Pol: conservative*, conservateur.
cont., **1.** *contents*, contenu. **2.** *continued*, suite.
contd, *continued*, suite.
co-op., *cooperative society*, société coopérative.
Corn., *Geog: Cornwall.*
corp., **Corp.**, **1.** *corporation*, compagnie, Cie. **2.** *Mil: corporal*, caporal.
Coy, *esp. Mil: company*, compagnie.
cp., *compare*, comparer.
C.P., **1.** *Com: carriage paid*, port payé, p.p., franco, fco, fro. **2.** *Communist Party*, Parti communiste.
C.P.A., *U.S: Certified Public Accountant.*
C.P.I., *Consumer Price Index.*
Cpl, *corporal*, caporal.
C.P.O., *Navy: Chief Petty Officer.*
cr., *Book-k:* (*a*) *credit*, crédit, cr, avoir, Av.; (*b*) *creditor*, créancier.
Cres., *Crescent*, (nom de) rue.
crit., *criticism, critical*, critique.
C.R.O., *Criminal Records Office* = l'Identité judiciaire.
C.S., *Civil Service*, Administration civile.
C.S.C., *Civil Service Commission.*
C.S.E., *Sch: Certificate of Secondary Education*, certificat de fin d'études secondaires.
C.S.T., *U.S: Central Standard Time.*
C.T., *U.S: Central Time.*
C.U., *Cambridge University*, Université de Cambridge.
cu.ft., *cubic foot, feet*, pied(s) cube(s).
Cumb., *Geog:* Cumberland.
c.w.o., *Com: cash with order*, payable à la commande.
cwt(s), *Meas: hundredweight(s).*

D., **1.** *dimension(al)*, dimension(nel). **2.** *Pol: U.S: democrat*, démocrate.
d., **1.** *died, deceased*, mort, m. **2.** *Num: Lt: denarius, -ii*, penny, pence. **3.** *Com: debit*, doit, débit, D. **4.** *daughter*, fille. **5.** *date*, date. **6.** *departs*, part.
D.A., *U.S: District Attorney* = procureur de la République.
D/A, *Bank: deposit account*, compte de dépôts.
dag., *Meas: decagramme*, décagramme, dag.
Dak., *Geog: Dakota.*
dal., *Meas: decalitre*, décalitre, dal.
dam., *Meas: decametre*, décamètre, dam.
D. & C., *Med: dilation and curettage*, dilatation et curetage.
D.B.E., *Dame Commander of the Order of the British Empire.*
D.C., **1.** *District Commissioner*, commissaire régional. **2.** *El: direct current*, courant continu, c.c. **3.** *Geog: District of Columbia.* **4.** *Mus: da capo*, D.C.
D.C.L., *Doctor of Civil Law*, docteur en droit civil.
D.C.M., *Distinguished Conduct Medal.*
D.D., *Doctor of Divinity*, docteur en théologie.
D.D.T., *dichloro-diphenyl-trichloroethane*, D.D.T.
dec., *deceased*, décédé, déc.
Del., *Geog: Delaware.*
Dem., *Pol: U.S: Democrat*, démocrate.
dep., **1.** *departs*, part. **2.** *deputy*, suppléant.
dept, *department*, service; rayon.
D.E.S., *Department of Education and Science.*
D.F.C., *Distinguished Flying Cross.*
D.F.M., *Distinguished Flying Medal.*
D.G., **1.** *Dei gratia*, par la grâce de Dieu, D.G. **2.** *Director-General.*
dg., *Meas: decigramme*, décigramme, dg.
D.H.S.S., *Department of Health and Social Security.*
diam., *diameter*, diamètre.
dict., **1.** *dictionary*, dictionnaire. **2.** *dictation*, dictée.
Dip.Ed., *Diploma in Education* = Certificat d'aptitude au professorat de l'enseignement secondaire, C.A.P.E.S.
Dir., *director*, administrateur, directeur.
dist., **1.** *Adm: district*, arrondissement, arr., quartier, qer. **2.** *distance*, distance.
distr., *distribution*, distribution.
div., *Fin: dividend*, dividende, div.
D.I.Y., *do-it-yourself*, bricolage.
D.J., **1.** *dinner jacket*, smoking. **2.** *disc jockey*, présentateur de disques.
dl., *Meas: decilitre*, décilitre, d(éci)l.
D.Lit(t)., *Doctor of Letters*, docteur ès lettres.
D.M., *Deutsche Mark.*
dm., *Meas: decimetre(s)*, décimètre(s), dm.
D.Mus., *Doctor of Music*, docteur en musique.
D.N.A., *desoxyribonucleic acid*, acide désoxyribonucléique, A.D.N.
D.N.B., *Dictionary of National Biography.*
do, *ditto*, dito, do.
D.O.A., *dead on arrival.*
D.O.E., *Department of the Environment.*
dol., *dollar*, dollar, dol(l).
doz., *dozen*, douzaine, d(ou)z.
D.P., *displaced person*, personne déplacée, D.P.
D.Phil., *Doctor of Philosophy*, docteur en philosophie.
D.P.P., *Director of Public Prosecutions* = Procureur de la République.
dpt, *department*, service; rayon.
Dr, **1.** *doctor*, docteur, Dr. **2.** *Com: debtor*, débiteur. **3.** *Drive*, avenue, av.
D.S.C., *Navy: Distinguished Service Cross.*
D.Sc., *Doctor of Science*, docteur ès sciences.
D.S.M., *Navy: Distinguished Service Medal.*
D.S.O., *Distinguished Service Order.*
D.S.T., *U.S: Daylight Saving Time*, heure d'été.
D.T.(s) ['diː'tiː(z)] *Med: F: delirium tremens.*
D.T.I., *Department of Trade and Industry.*
D.V., *Deo volente*, si Dieu le veut.

E., *east*, est, E.
ea., *each*, chacun.
E. & O.E., *Com: errors and omissions excepted*, sauf erreur ou omission, s.e. & o.
E.C.G., *electrocardiogram*, électrocardiogramme.
ecol., *ecological, ecology*, écologique, écologie.
econ., *economic(s)*, économique.
ed., (*a*) *edition*, édition, éd(it).; (*b*) *editor*; (*c*) *edited.*
E.D.P., *electronic data processing*, informatique.
E.D.T., *U.S: Eastern Daylight Time.*
E.E.C., *European Economic Community*, Communauté économique européenne, C.E.E.
E.E.G., *Med: electroencephalogram*, électroencéphalogramme, E.E.G.
E.F.T.A. ['eftə] *European Free Trade Association*, Association européenne de libre-échange, A.E.L.E.
e.g., *exempli gratia*, par exemple, p.ex.
el., *U.S: elevated railroad*, chemin de fer, *F:* métro, aérien.
e.m.f., *El: electromotive force*, force électromotrice, f.é.m.
E.M.S., *European Monetary System*, Système Monétaire Européen, SME.
enc(l)., *enclosures(s)*, document(s) ci-inclus.
eng., **1.** (*a*) *engineer*, ingénieur, ing(én).; (*b*) *engineering*, génie. **2.** *engraving*, gravure.
E.N.S.A. ['ensə] *Entertainments National Service Association.*
E.N.T., *Med: ear, nose and throat*, oto-rhino-laryngologie, O.R.L.
E.P., *Rec: extended play*, super 45 tours.
E.R., *Elizabeth Regina*, la reine Elizabeth.
ERNIE ['ə:ni] *Cmptr: Electronic Random Number Indicator Equipment.*
E.S.N., *educationally subnormal*, arriéré.
esp., *especially*, surtout.
E.S.P., *extrasensory perception*, perception extrasensorielle.
Esq., *Esquire.*
est., **1.** *established.* **2.** *estimated*, estimatif.
E.S.T., **1.** *U.S:* (*a*) *Eastern Standard Time*; (*b*) *Eastern Summer Time.* **2.** *Med: electro-shock treatment*, électrochoc.
E.T.A., *estimated time of arrival.*
et al., *et alia, et alii*, et d'autres.
etc., *etcetera*, et cætera, etc.
et seq., *et sequentia*, et la suite.
E.T.U., *Electrical Trades Union.*
Eur., (*a*) *Europe*, Europe; (*b*) *European*, européen.
Euratom [ju:'rætɔm] *European Atomic Energy Community*, Euratom.
eve., **evg**, *evening*, soir.
ex., *example*, exemple, ex.
excl., *exclusive, excluding*, exclusif, à l'exclusion de.
exec., **1.** *Jur: executor*, exécuteur testamentaire. **2.** *executive.*
exp., **1.** *export*, exportation. **2.** *expenses*, frais. **3.** *expired*, périmé.
ext., **1.** *Tp: etc: extension.* **2.** *external*, externe.

F., **1.** *Ph: Fahrenheit*, Fahrenheit, F. **2.** *fine* (*pencil lead*).
f., **1.** *Meas:* (*a*) *foot, feet*, pied(s); (*b*) *fathom*, brasse. **2.** *Ph:* (*a*) *force*, force, F.; (*b*) *frequency*, fréquence, f.
F.A., **1.** *Football Association.* **2.** *P:* **sweet F.A.**, *sweet Fanny Adams*, rien du tout.
fac., *facsimile*, fac-similé.
fam., **1.** *family*, famille. **2.** *familiar*, familier, fam.
F.B.I., *U.S: Federal Bureau of Investigation.*
F.C., *Football Club.*
F.D.A., *U.S: Food and Drug Administration.*
Fed., *Federal*, fédéral.
fem., *feminine*, féminin, f.
ff., **1.** *following pages*, pages suivantes. **2.** *folios*, folios.
f'hold, *freehold*, tenu en propriété perpétuelle et libre.
F.I.F.A., ['fi:fə] *Federation of International Football Associations.*
fig., **1.** *figure*, figure, fig. **2.** *figurative*, figuré, fig.
Fla., *Geog: Florida*, Floride.
fl.oz., *Meas: fluid ounce(s).*
F/Lt, Flt Lt, *flight lieutenant*, capitaine d'aviation.
fm, *fathom*, brasse.
F.M., *W.Tel: Frequency Modulation*, modulation de fréquence, F.M.
fo., *folio*, folio, f°; in-folio, inf(0), in-fo.
F.O., *Foreign Office*, ministère des affaires étrangères.
f.o.b., *Com: free on board*, franco à bord, f. à b.
foll., *following*, suivant, suiv.
F.P., *freezing point*, point de congélation.
F.P.A., *Family Planning Association.*
Fr., **1.** *Geog:* (*a*) *France*, France, Fr.; (*b*) *French*, français. **2.** *Ecc: Father*, Père, P. **3.** *Ecc: friar*, frère, Fr. **4.** *Frau*, madame.
fr., **1.** *Num: franc(s)*, franc(s), fr. **2.** *from*, de.
F.R.A.M., *Fellow of the Royal Academy of Music.*
F.R.C.S., *Fellow of the Royal College of Surgeons.*
F.R.I.B.A., *Fellow of the Royal Institute of British Architects.*
F.R.I.C.S., *Fellow of the Royal Institution of Chartered Surveyors.*
F.R.S.., *Fellow of the Royal Society.*
ft, *Meas: foot, feet*, pied(s), p., pd.
F.T.C., *U.S: Federal Trade Commission.*
fur., *Meas: furlong.*
furn., *furnished*, meublé.
fwd, *forward.*

g., *Meas: gramme*, gramme, gr.
Ga, *Geog: Georgia*, Géorgie.
gal(l)., *Meas: gallon(s).*
G.A.T.T., *General Agreement on Tariffs and Trade*, accord général sur les tarifs douaniers et le commerce.
G.A.W., *U.S: guaranteed annual wage.*
G.B., *Geog: Great Britain*, Grande-Bretagne, G.B.
G.C.E., *General Certificate of Education.*
Gdns, *Gardens*, rue.
G.D.R., *German Democratic Republic*, République démocratique allemande, R.D.A.
Gen., *Mil: General*, général, gal.
gent., *gentleman*, monsieur.
G.G., **1.** *Governor General.* **2.** *Girl Guides.*
G.H.Q., *Mil: General Headquarters*, grand quartier général, C.Q.G.
G.I., *U.S: Mil:* (*a*) *Government issue, general issue*, matériel réglementaire de l'armée; (*b*) *F:* soldat (américain).
Glam., *Geog: Glamorganshire.*
G.L.C., *Adm: Greater London Council.*
Glos., *Geog: Gloucestershire.*
G-man, (*Government man*), agent de la police fédérale.
G.M.T., *Hor: Greenwich mean time*, temps moyen de Greenwich, temps universel, T.U.
G.M.W.U., *General and Municipal Workers' Union.*
G.N.P., *gross national product*, produit national brut, P.N.B.
G.O.C., *Mil: general officer commanding*, officier général commandant.
G.O.M., *Grand Old Man.*
G.O.P., *U.S: Grand Old Party*, le Parti républicain.
Gov., (*a*) *government*, gouvernement; (*b*) *governor*, gouverneur.

Govt, *government*, gouvernement.
G.P., *Med: General Practitioner*, médecin de médecine générale, M.G.
G.P.O., 1. *A: General Post Office* = Postes et Télécommunications, P.E.T. **2.** *U.S: Government Printing Office.*
gr., 1. *Com: gross*, (i) grosse(s), (ii) brut. **2.** *Meas: gramme(s)*, gramme(s), g.
G.R., *Georgius Rex*, le roi George.
grad., 1. *graduate*, diplômé. **2.** *gradient.*
G.R.T., *Com: gross registered tonnage*, jauge brute.
G.S.A., *Girl Scouts of America.*
gt, *great*, grand.
guar., *guaranteed*, avec garantie.

H., 1. *Ph: henry*, henry, H. **2.** *hydrant*, bouche d'eau. **3.** (*of pencil lead*) *hard*, dur.
h., 1. *hour(s)*, heure(s), h. **2.** *hecto-*, hecto-. **3.** *horse*, cheval. **4.** *hot*, chaud. **5.** *husband*, mari.
ha., *Meas: hectare*, hectare, ha.
h. & c., *hot and cold* (*water*), eau courante chaude et froide.
Hants., *Geog: Hampshire.*
HB, (*of pencil lead*) *hard black.*
H.C., *House of Commons*, Chambre des Communes.
H.C.F., *Mth: highest common factor*, plus grand commun diviseur, p.g.c.d.
H.E., 1. (*a*) *His Eminence*, son Éminence, S.E(m).; (*b*) *His, Her, Excellency*, son Excellence, S.E(xc). **2.** *high explosive*, haut explosif.
Herts., *Geog: Hertfordshire.*
HEW, *U.S: Department of Health, Education and Welfare.*
hf., *half*, moitié.
HF., *El: high frequency*, haute fréquence.
hg., *Meas: hectogramme*, hectogramme, hg.
H.G.V., *heavy goods vehicle*, poids lourd.
H.H., 1. *His, Her, Highness*, Son Altesse, S.A. **2.** *His Holiness*, Sa Sainteté, S.S.
H.I.M., *His, Her, Imperial Majesty*, sa Majesté Impériale, S.M.I.
hl., *Meas: hectolitre*, hectolitre, hl.
hm., *Meas: hectometre*, hectomètre, hectom., hm.
H.M., *His, Her, Majesty*, sa Majesté, S.M.
H.M.I., *His, Her, Majesty's Inspector* (*of schools*) = Inspecteur d'Académie.
H.M.S., *His, Her, Majesty's Ship.*
H.M.S.O., *His, Her, Majesty's Stationery Office*, service des fournitures et des publications de l'Administration.
ho., *house*, maison.
Hon., 1. *Honourable.* **2.** *Honorary*, honoraire.
Hons, *Sch: Honours.*
H.P., *hire purchase.*
h.p., 1. *high pressure*, haute pression, h.p. **2.** *Mec: horsepower*, cheval-vapeur, c.v., ch.v(ap).; chevaux, chx.
H.Q., *headquarters*, (i) poste de commandement, P.C.; (ii) quartier général, Q.G.; (iii) état-major, E.M.
H.R., *Pol:* **1.** *Hist: Home Rule*, autonomie. **2.** *U.S: House of Representatives*, Chambre des Représentants.
H.R.H., *His, Her, Royal Highness*, son Altesse Royale, S.A.R.
hr(s), *hour(s)*, heure(s).
ht., 1. *heat*, chaleur. **2.** *height*, hauteur.
H.T., *El: high tension*, haute tension, H.T.
H.W.M., *Nau: high water mark*, niveau de haute mer.
Hz., *El: hertz*, hertz, hz.

I., *Island, Isle*, île.
Ia, *Geog: Iowa.*
IAAF, *International Amateur Athletic Federation.*
I.B.A., *Independent Broadcasting Authority.*
ibid., *ibidem*, ibid.
I.B.M., *International Business Machines.*
i/c, *in charge* (*of*).
I.C.A., 1. *Institute of Contemporary Arts.* **2.** *Institute of Chartered Accountants.*
ICBM, *intercontinental ballistic missile*, missile balistique intercontinental.
I.C.E., *Institute of Civil Engineers.*
I.C.I., *Imperial Chemical Industries.*
ID, *identification*, identification.
id., *idem*, id.
Ida., *Geog: Idaho.*
i.e., *id est, that is*, c'est-à-dire, c.-à-d.
I.L.E.A., *Inner London Education Authority.*
Ill., *Geog: Illinois.*
ill(us)., (*a*) *illustrated*, illustré; (*b*) *illustration*, illustration.
I.L.O., *International Labour Organization*, Organisation internationale du travail, O.I.T.
I.L.P., *Pol: Independent Labour Party*, Parti travailliste indépendant.
I.M.F., *International Monetary Fund*, Fonds monétaire international, F.M.I.
in., *Meas: inch*, pouce, p(o).
Inc., *Incorporated.*
inc., 1. *increase*, augmentation. **2.** *income*, revenu.
incl., (*a*) *inclusive*, inclusivement; (*b*) *including*, y compris.
Ind., 1. *Independent*, indépendant. **2.** *Geog: Indiana.*
I.N.R.I., *Ecc: Iesus Nazarenus Rex Iudaeorum*, Jésus de Nazareth, Roi des Juifs.
ins., 1. *insurance*, assurance, asse. **2.** *Meas: inches*, pouces, ppo.
Inst., (*a*) *Institute*, institut; (*b*) *Institution*, institution.
inst., *Corr: instant*, courant, c., cour., ct.
I.O.M., *Geog: Isle of Man.*
I.O.W., *Geog: Isle of Wight.*
IPA, *International Phonetic Alphabet.*
I.Q., *intelligence quotient*, quotient intellectuel, Q.I.
I.R., *Inland Revenue*, le fisc.
I.R.A., *Irish Republican Army.*
I.R.S., *U.S: Internal Revenue Service.*
Is., *Isle, Island*, île.
I.S.B.N., *International Standard Book Number.*
I.T.A., *A: Independent Television Authority.*
I.T.N., *Independent Television News.*
ITV, *Independent Television.*
I.U.D., (*for birth control*) *intra-uterine device*, stérilet.
I.U.S., *International Union of Students*
I.V., *intravenous*, intraveineux.

J., 1. *El: joule*, joule, J., j. **2.** *Cards: jack*, valet. **3.** *Judge*, juge. **4.** *Justice*, justice.
J.C., *Jesus Christ*, Jésus-Christ, J.-C.
J.C.R., *Sch:* **1.** *Junior Common Room.* **2.** *Junior Combination Room.*
jn., *junction*, jonction.
Jnr, *Junior*, jeune, Je, Jne.
jour., *journal*, journal, jl.
J.P., *Justice of the Peace* = juge de paix.
Jr, *Junior*, jeune, Je, Jne.
Jun., *Junior*, jeune, Je, Jne.

K., 1. *Ph: Kelvin* (*scale*), (échelle de) Kelvin, K. **2.** *King('s)*, (du) roi. **3.** *Knight*, Chevalier, Ch(ev). **4.** *Mus: Köchel.*
k, *kilo*, kilo, k.
Kan(s)., *Geog: Kansas.*

K.B.E., *Knight Commander (of the Order) of the British Empire*, Chevalier de l'Ordre de l'Empire britannique.
kc., *El: kilocycle*, kilocycle, kc; kilohertz, kHz.
K.C.B., *Knight Commander (of the Order) of the Bath*, Chevalier Commandeur de l'Ordre du Bain.
K.E., *kinetic energy*, énergie cinétique.
Ken., *Geog: Kentucky.*
K.G., *Knight (of the Order) of the Garter*, Chevalier de l'Ordre de la Jarretière.
K.G.B., *secret police in the Soviet Union*, police secrète en Union soviétique, K.G.B.
kHz, *El: kilohertz*, kilohertz, kHz.
K.K.K., *U.S: Ku Klux Klan.*
km., *Meas: kilometre(s)*, kilomètre(s), km.
km.p.h., *kilometres per hour*, kilomètres (à l')heure, km/h.
K.O., *Box: knockout*, knock-out, k.o.
k.p.h., *Meas: kilometres per hour*, kilomètres (à l')heure, km/h.
Kt., *Knight*, Chevalier, Ch(ev).
kW, kw, *El: kilowatt*, kilowatt, kW.
kWhr, kwhr, *El: kilowatt-hour(s)*, kilowatt(s)-heure, kWh.
Ky, *Geog: Kentucky.*

L., **1.** *Lake*, lac. **2.** *Aut: learner (driver)*, apprenti conducteur. **3.** *Pol: Liberal*, libéral.
£, *Num: libra, librae, pound sterling*, livre(s) sterling, l(iv). s(t).
l., **1.** *Num: lira*, lire. **2.** *Meas: litre*, litre, l. **3.** *length*, longueur, long. **4.** *line*, ligne. **5.** *left*, gauche, g.
La., *Geog: Louisiana.*
L.A., **1.** *Library Association.* **2.** *Geog: Los Angeles.*
Lab., *Pol: Labour*, travailliste.
Lancs., *Geog: Lancashire.*
Lat., *Latin*, latin, lat.
lat., *Geog: latitude*, latitude, lat.
lb., *Meas: libra, pound*, livre, lb.
l.b.w., *Cr: leg before wicket.*
L.C.D., *Mth: lowest common denominator*, plus petit commun dénominateur, p.p.c.d.
L.C.M., *Mth: lowest common multiple*, plus petit commun multiple, p.p.c.m.
Ld, *Lord.*
Ldn, *Geog: London*, Londres.
L.E.A., *Adm: Local Education Authority.*
Leics., *Geog: Leicestershire.*
L.F., *El: low frequency*, basse fréquence.
l.h., *Mus: etc: left hand*, main gauche.
Lib., **1.** *Pol: Liberal*, libéral. **2.** *F: Liberation*, libération.
lib., *library*, bibliothèque, Bib.
Lieut., *Mil: Lieutenant*, lieutenant, Lieut, Lt.
Lieut.-Col., *Mil: Lieutenant-Colonel*, lieutenant-colonel, Lieut-Col.
Lincs., *Geog: Lincolnshire.*
Litt. D., *Litterarum Doctor, Doctor of Letters*, Docteur ès lettres.
ll., *lines*, lignes.
LL.B., *Legum Baccalaureus, Bachelor of Laws*, Bachelier en Droit.
LL.D., *Legum Doctor, Doctor of Laws*, Docteur en Droit.
loc. cit., *loco citato, in the passage already quoted*, l(oc), c(it).
long., *Geog: longitude*, longitude, long.
L.P., *long-playing (record)*, (disque) de longue durée, 33 tours.
L.P.G., *liquefied petroleum gas.*
L.R.A.M., *Licentiate of the Royal Academy of Music.*
LSD, *Pharm: lysergic acid diethylamide*, acide lysergique diéthylamide, LSD.
£.s.d., *A: librae, solidi, denarii, pounds, shillings, and pence.*
L.S.E., *London School of Economics.*
Lt., *Mil: Lieutenant*, lieutenant, Lieut., Lt.
L.T., **1.** *London Transport.* **2.** *El: low tension*, basse tension, B.T.
L.T.A., *Lawn Tennis Association.*
Ltd, *Com: Limited (company)*, à responsabilité limitée, *Fr.C:* Ltée; = Société Anonyme, S.A.
L.V., *luncheon voucher*, chèque-repas, ticket-repas.
L.W., *W.Tel: long waves*, grandes ondes, G.O.
L.W.M., *Nau: low water mark*, niveau de basse mer.

M., **1.** *Master*, Maître. **2.** Monsieur, M. **3.** *member*, membre. **4.** *motorway*, autoroute.
m., **1.** *metre(s)*, mètres, *m.* **2.** *mile(s)*, mille(s). **3.** (*a*) *male*, mâle; (*b*) *masculine*, masculin, m. **4.** *married*, marié. **5.** *mare*, jument. **6.** *milli-*, milli. **7.** *million(s)*, million(s). **8.** minute(*s*), minute(s), mn. **9.** *Num: mark*, mark. **10.** *month*, mois, m.
M.A., *Sch: Magister Artium, Master of Arts* = (i) maîtrise, (ii) maître (ès lettres).
mag., **1.** *F: magazine*, revue. **2.** *magneto*, magnéto.
Maj., *Mil: Major*, commandant, Cdt, Comm., Comt; Major, Maj.
Man(it)., *Geog: Manitoba.*
mar., **1.** *marine*, marin. **2.** *maritime*, maritime.
masc., *masculine*, masculin, m.
Mass., *Geog: Massachusetts.*
max., *maximum*, maximum, max.
M.B., *Medicinæ Baccalaureus, Bachelor of Medicine* = (i) licence, (ii) licencié, en médecine.
M.B.E., *Member of the Order of the British Empire*, membre de l'Ordre de l'Empire britannique.
M.C., **1.** *Master of Ceremonies*, maître des cérémonies. **2.** *U.S: Member of Congress*, député. **3.** *Military Cross* = Croix de guerre.
Md., *Geog: Maryland.*
M.D., **1.** *Medicinæ Doctor, Doctor of Medicine*, Docteur en médecine. **2.** *Managing Director* = Président-directeur général, P.-D.G. **3.** *mentally deficient*, débile.
Mddx., *Geog: Post: Middlesex.*
Me., *Geog: Maine.*
Med., *Geog: F: Mediterranean (Sea)*, (mer) Méditerranée.
med., **1.** *medieval*, médiéval. **2.** (*a*) *medical*, médical; (*b*) *medicine*, médecine. **3.** *medium*, moyen.
memo., *memorandum*, mémorandum, mém.
Messrs ['mesəz] Messieurs, MM.
Met., *Metropolitan*, métropolitain.
met(eor)., *meteorological*, météorologique.
mf., *Mus: mezzo forte*, mezz.f.
M.F., *W.Tel: medium frequency*, fréquence moyenne, intermédiaire.
mfd, *Com: manufactured*, fabriqué.
mfr(s), *Com: manufacturer(s)*, fabricant(s).
mg., *Meas: milligram(me)*, milligramme; mg.
Mgr, **1.** *manager*, directeur. **2.** *Ecc: Monsignor*, Monseigneur; Mgr.
M.I., MI, *Military Intelligence.*
Mich., *Geog: Michigan.*
MIDAS ['maidəs] *missile defence alarm system*, système d'alarme pour la défense contre les missiles.
Min., (*a*) *Minister*, Ministre, Min.; (*b*) *Ministry*, Ministère.
min., **1.** minimum, minimum, min. **2.** *minute(s)*, minute(s), mn. **3.** *Mus: minim*, blanche.
Minn., *Geog: Minnesota.*
misc., *miscellaneous*, divers.
Miss., *Geog: Mississippi.*

M.I.T., *Massachusetts Institute of Technology.*
mkt., *market*, marché.
M.L.A., *Modern Language Association* (*of America*).
M.L.R., *Fin: Minimum Lending Rate*, taux (officiel) d'escompte.
mm., *millimetre*(*s*), millimetre(s), mm.
Mo., *Geog: Missouri.*
M.O., **1.** *Medical Officer*, (i) (*in hospital*) chef de service; (ii) médecin militaire. **2.** *Post: money order*, mandat-poste.
mod., **1.** *modern*, moderne. **2.** *moderate*, modéré.
M.O.D., *Ministry of Defence.*
mod. cons., *F: modern conveniences*, confort moderne.
M.O.H., *Medical Officer of Health*, médecin de l'état civil.
mol., *Ch:* (*a*) *molecular*, moléculaire; (*b*) *molecule*, mol.
Mont., *Geog: Montana.*
M.O.T., *Ministry of Transport*; *F:* **M.O.T. test,** examen annuel obligatoire des véhicules âgés de trois ans ou plus.
M.P., **1.** (*a*) *Metropolitan Police*, police métropolitaine; (*b*) *Military Police*, police militaire. **2.** *Member of Parliament*, membre de la Chambre des Communes.
m.p.g., *miles per gallon* = litres au cent (kilomètres).
m.p.h., *miles per hour*, milles à l'heure.
M.P.S., *Member of the Pharmaceutical Society.*
Mr ['mistər] *Mister*, Monsieur, M.
M.R.C., *Medical Research Council.*
Mrs ['misiz] *Mistress*, Madame, Mme.
MS, *manuscript*, manuscit; **MSS**, *manuscripts*, manuscrits.
Ms [miz] madame ou mademoiselle.
M.S., **1.** *Mastery of Surgery.* **2.** *Master of Science.* **3.** *Med: multiple sclerosis*, sclérose en plaques.
M.Sc., *Master of Science.*
m.s.l., *mean sea level*, niveau moyen de la mer.
Mt., *Mount*, mont, montagne.
M.T.B., *motor torpedo boat*, vedette lance-torpilles.
Mus.D(oc)., *Musicae Doctor*, *Doctor of Music.*
M.W., *W.Tel: medium wave*, onde moyenne.
M.Y., *motor yacht*, yacht à moteur.

N., **1.** *North*, nord, N. **2.** *Ph: Newton*, Newton, N. **3.** (*chess*) *knight*, cavalier.
n., **1.** *noon*, midi, M. **2.** *name*, nom, N. **3.** *neuter*, neutre, n. **4.** *noun*, substantif.
N/A, *Adm: not applicable*, sans objet, S.O.
N.A.A.C.P., *U.S: National Association for the Advancement of Colored People.*
N.A.A.F.I. ['næfi] *Navy, Army, and Air Force Institutes* = coopérative militaire.
N.A.L.G.O. ['nælgou] *National and Local Government Officers' Association.*
NASA ['næsə] *U.S: National Aeronautics and Space Administration*, administration des questions aéronautiques et de l'espace.
nat., **1.** (*a*) *national*, national; (*b*) *nationalist*, nationaliste. **2.** *natural*, naturel.
N.A.T.O. ['neitou] *North Atlantic Treaty Organization*, Organisation du Traité de l'Atlantique Nord, OTAN.
NATSOPA [næt'soupə] *National Society of Operative Printers and Assistants.*
NATTKE ['nætki] *National Association of Theatrical, Television and Kine Employees.*
N.B., **1.** *nota bene*, N.B. **2.** *Geog: New Brunswick*, Nouveau-Brunswick.
NBC, *U.S: National Broadcasting Company.*
N.C., *Geog: North Carolina.*
N.C.B., *National Coal Board.*
N.C.O., *Mil: non-commissioned officer*, sous-officier, gradé.
N.D(ak)., *Geog: North Dakota.*
NE, N.E., *Geog: New England*, Nouvelle-Angleterre.
N.E.B., *New English Bible.*
Neb(r)., *Geog: Nebraska.*
NEDC (*also* **Neddy**), *National Economic Development Council.*
Nev., *Geog: Nevada.*
N.F., **1.** (*also* **Nfld**) *Geog: Newfoundland*, Terre-Neuve. **2.** *Pol: National Front.*
N.F.T., *National Film Theatre.*
NFU, *National Farmers' Union.*
N.G.A., *National Graphical Association.*
N.H., *Geog: New Hampshire.*
N.H.S., *National Health Service* = Sécurité Sociale, S.S.
N.J., *Geog: New Jersey.*
N.M., *Geog: New Mexico*, Nouveau Mexique.
No., **no.**, *number*, numéro, No, N°, n°.
N.O., *Geog: New Orleans*, Nouvelle-Orléans.
non seq., *non sequitur*, illogicité.
Northants., *Geog: Northamptonshire.*
Northumb., *Geog: Northumberland.*
Notts., *Geog: Nottinghamshire.*
NPA, *Newspaper Publishers' Association.*
nr, *near*, près.
N.S., *Geog: Nova Scotia*, Nouvelle-Écosse.
N.S.B., *National Savings Bank.*
N.S.P.C.C., *National Society for the Prevention of Cruelty to Children.*
N.S.W., *Geog: New South Wales.*
N.T., **1.** *B: New Testament*, Nouveau Testament, N.T. **2.** *Geog: Austr: Northern Territory*, Territoire du Nord. **3.** *National Theatre.*
NUJ, *National Union of Journalists.*
NUM, *National Union of Mineworkers.*
NUPE ['nju:pi] *National Union of Public Employees.*
NUR, *National Union of Railwaymen.*
NUS, *National Union of Students* = Union Nationale des Étudiants de France, UNEF.
NUT, *National Union of Teachers* = Fédération de l'éducation nationale, F.E.N.
N.Y., *Geog: New York.*
N.Y.C., *Geog: New York City.*
N.Z., *Geog: New Zeland*, Nouvelle-Zélande.

O., **1.** *Old*, vieux. **2.** *Geog: Ohio.* **3.** *El: ohm*, ohm. **4.** *Sch:* **O level,** *Ordinary level examination.*
O.A.P., (*a*) *Old Age Pension*, retraite de vieillesse; (*b*) *Old Age Pensioner*, retraité(e).
O.A.S., **1.** *on active service* (i) *Mil:* en service actif; (ii) *Post:* franchise militaire, F.M. **2.** *Organization of American States*, Organisation des États américains, O.E.A.
O.A.U., *Organization of African Unity*, Organisation de l'unité africaine, O.U.A.
ob., *obiit*, décédé.
O.B., **1.** *Old Boy.* **2.** *outside broadcast*, production extérieure.
O.B.E., (*Officer of the*) *Order of the British Empire.*
O.C., *Mil: Officer Commanding*, chef de corps.
O.E.C.D., *Organization for Economic Co-operation and Development*, Organisation de coopération et de développement économiques, O.C.D.E.
O.E.D., *Oxford English Dictionary.*
O.H.M.S., *On His, Her, Majesty's Service*, au service de Sa Majesté.
Okla., *Geog: Oklahoma.*
O.M., (*Member of the*) *Order of Merit.*
o.n.o., *or near*(*est*) *offer.*
Ont., *Geog: Ontario.*

o/p, *Publ: out of print*, tirage épuisé.
op. cit., *opere citato, in the work already quoted*, op. cit.
O.P.E.C. ['oupek] *Organization of Petroleum Exporting Countries*, Organisation des pays exportateurs de pétrole, O.P.E.P.
opp., **1.** *opposed*, opposé. **2.** *opposite*, en face.
ord., **1.** *ordinary*, ordinaire, ord. **2.** *order*, ordre.
Ore(g)., *Geog: Oregon.*
orig., (*a*) *original*, original; (*b*) *originally*, originairement.
O.S., **1.** *Chr: Old Style*, vieux style. **2.** *Nau: ordinary seaman*, matelot de pont. **3.** *Com: out of stock*, manque en magasin. **4.** *Ordnance Survey* = Institut Géographique National, I.G.N.
O.T., *B: Old Testament*, Ancien Testament, A.T.
O.U., *Sch: Oxford University.*
OXFAM ['ɔksfæm] *Oxford Committee for Famine Relief.*
Oxon., **1.** *Geog: Oxfordshire.* **2.** *Oxoniensis, of Oxford*, d'Oxford.
oz., *Meas: ounce(s)*, once(s)

P., (*chess*) *pawn*, pion.
p., **1.** *page*, page, p. **2.** *Mus: piano*, piano, p. **3.** *penny, pence.*
Pa., *Geog: Pennsylvania.*
P.A., **1.** *Press Association.* **2.** *personal assistant.* **3.** *public address* (*system*), sonorisation extérieure.
p.a., *per annum*, par an, p. an.
p. & p., *postage and packing*, port et emballage.
par(a)., *paragraph*, paragraphe.
pat., **1.** *patent*, brevet. **2.** *pattern*, modèle, mle.
P.A.Y.E., *pay-as-you-earn* = impôt retenu à la source, à la base.
pc., *piece*, morceau.
P.C., **1.** *Police Constable.* **2.** *Privy Councillor*, conseiller privé.
p.c., **1.** *postcard*, carte postale. **2.** *percent*, pour cent. p.c.
pd, *paid*, payé.
P.E., *physical education*, éducation physique.
P.E.I., *Geog: Prince Edward Island.*
P.E.N., (*also* **PEN Club**) *International Association of Poets, Playwrights, Editors, Essayists and Novelists.*
Penn(a)., *Geog: Pennsylvania.*
per pro., *per procurationem, by proxy*, par procuration, p.p., p. pon.
P.G., *paying guest*, pensionnaire.
Ph.D., *Doctor of Philosophy*, Docteur en Philosophie.
Phil., *Geog: Philadephia.*
Pl., *Place*, rue.
P.L.C., **p.l.c.**, *Public Limited Company.*
P.L.O., *Palestinian Liberation Organization*, Organization pour la Libération de la Palestine, O.L.P.
P.M., *Prime Minister*, premier ministre.
p.m., *post meridiem, after noon*, après midi, p.m., P.M.
P.M.G., **1.** *Postmaster General*, directeur général des Postes. **2.** *Paymaster General*, trésorier.
P.O., **1.** *Post Office* = Postes et Télécommunications, P.E.T.; **P.O. Box,** *post office box*, Boîte Postale, B.P. **2.** *postal order*, mandat-poste, M.-P. **3.** *Navy: Petty Officer*, officer marinier; *F:* chef.
pop., *population*, population.
poss., **1.** (*a*) *possible*, possible; (*b*) *possibly*, c'est possible.
P.O.W., *Prisoner of War*, prisonnier de guerre, P.G.
pp., *pages*, pages, pp.
p.p., *per procurationem*, par procuration, p.p., p. pon.
PPE, *Sch: philosophy, politics and economics*, philosophie, politique et économie.
P.P.S., **1.** *Adm: Parliamentary Private Secretary.* **2.** *post postsciptum, additional postscript.*
P.Q., *Geog: Province of Quebec*, Province de Québec.
Pr., *Prince*, Prince, Pr.
pr., **1.** *pair*, paire. **2.** *price*, prix.
P.R., **1.** *proportional representation*, représentation proportionnelle, R.P. **2.** *public relations* (*office*), service des relations publiques.
prep., (*a*) *preparation*, préparation; (*b*) *preparatory*, préparatoire.
Pres., *President*, président.
PRO., **1.** *public relations officer*, chef du service des relations publiques. **2.** *Public Record Office*, bureau des archives nationales.
prob., (*a*) *probable*, probable; (*b*) *probably*, probablement.
Prof., *Professor*, professeur.
prog., *programme*, programme.
prop., *proprietor*, propriétaire.
Prot., *Protestant*, protestant.
prox., *Com: proximo, of next month*, du mois prochain, prox.
P.S., (*also* **PS**) *postscript*, post-scriptum, P.S.
P.T., *physical training*, éducation physique.
P.T.A., *Parent-Teacher Association* = Association des Parents d'Élèves, A.P.E.
Pte, *Mil: Private*, simple soldat.
P.T.O., *please turn over*, tournez s'il vous plaît, T.S.V.P.
PVC, *polyvinyl chloride*, chlorure de polyvinyle.
Pvt., *Mil: Private*, simple soldat.

Q., **1.** *Queen('s)*, (de la) reine. **2.** *Geog: Quebec*, Québec.
q., *question*, question.
Q.C., *Jur: Queen's Counsel.*
q.e., *quod est, which is*, ce qui est.
Q.E.D., *quod erat demonstrandum, which was to be proved*, ce qu'il fallait démontrer, C.Q.F.D., Q.E.D.
Q.E.2., *F: Queen Elizabeth II*, (le paquebot) la reine Elizabeth II.
Q.M., *Mil: Quartermaster*, (i) *Nau:* maître de timonerie; (ii) *Mil:* officier chargé des vivres et des fournitures; **Q.M.G.**, *Quartermaster general* = Directeur de l'Intendance (militaire).
qr., **1.** *Meas: quarter*, quart. **2.** *quire* = (*approx.*) main de papier.
Quango ['kwæŋgou] *Quasi-autonomous non-governmental organisation.*
Que., *Geog: Quebec*, Québec.
q.v., *quod vide, which see*, voyez, voir, v., q.v.

R., **1.** (*a*) *Rex, king*, roi; (*b*) *Regina, queen*, reine. **2.** *Royal*, royal. **3.** *River*, rivière. **4.** *Ph: Réaumur*, Réaumur, R. **5.** (*chess*) *rook*, tour. **6.** *NAm: Republican*, républicain. **7.** *registered*, (i) déposé, (ii) *Post:* recommandé.
r., *right*, droit, d.
R.A., **1.** (*a*) *Royal Academy* = Académie des Beaux-Arts; (*b*) *Royal Academician* = membre de l'Académie des Beaux-Arts. **2.** *Mil: Royal Artillery.*
R.A.C., *Royal Automobile Club.*
R.A.D.A. ['rɑːdə] *Royal Academy of Dramatic Art.*
R.A.F., *Royal Air Force*, armée de l'air.
R. & D., *research and development*, recherche et développement.
R.C., *Roman Catholic*, catholique.
R.C.A., **1.** *Royal College of Art.* **2.** *Radio Corporation of America.*
R.C.M., *Royal College of Music.*
R.C.M.P., *Royal Canadian Mounted Police.*
R.C.P., *Royal College of Physicians.*

R.C.S., *Royal College of Surgeons.*
Rd, *road*, rue, r.
R.E., *Mil: Royal Engineers.*
recd., *received*, reçu, r.
ref., **1.** *Corr: reference*, référence, Réf. **2.** *referred*, rapporté. **3.** *referee*, arbitre.
reg., **1.** *regular*, régulier. **2.** *Post: registered*, recommandé, r. **3.** (*on gas oven*) *regulo.*
regd, *Post: registered*, recommandé, r.
Regt., *Regiment*, régiment, rég.
R.E.M., *Physiol: rapid eye movement*, mouvement oculaire rapide.
R.E.M.E., *Mil: Royal Electrical and Mechanical Engineers.*
Rep., **1.** (*a*) *Republic*, république; (*b*) *Republican*, républicain. **2.** *U.S: Representative.*
ret., **1.** *retired*, retraité. **2.** *returned*, renvoyé.
retd, **1.** *retired*, retraité. **2.** *returned*, renvoyé. **3.** *retained*, retenu.
Rev., *Ecc: Reverend*, révérend, Rd, Revd.
rev., *revolution*, tour, t(r).
R.G.S., *Royal Geographical Society.*
Rgt., *regiment*, régiment, rég.
Rh., *Med: rhesus*, rhésus, Rh.
r.h., *Mus: etc: right hand*, main droite.
R.H.S., **1.** *Royal Horticultural Society.* **2.** *Royal Humane Society.* **3.** *Royal Historical Society.*
R.I.B.A., *Royal Institute of British Architects.*
R.I.C.S., *Royal Institution of Chartered Surveyors.*
R.I.P., *requiescat in pace, may he, she, rest in peace*, qu'il, qu'elle, repose en paix, R.I.P.
R.L., *Rugby League.*
rly, *railway*, chemin de fer, c(h). de f.
rm, *room*, pièce, chambre.
R.M., **1.** *Post: Royal Mail.* **2.** *Navy: Royal Marines*, fusiliers marins.
R.M.A., *Royal Military Academy.*
R.N., **1.** *Royal Navy.* **2.** *NAm: Registered Nurse*, infirmière diplômée.
RNIB, *Royal National Institute for the Blind.*
RNID, *Royal National Institute for the Deaf.*
RNLI, *Royal National Lifeboat Institution.*
R.N.(V.)R., *Royal Naval* (*Volunteer*) *Reserve.*
rom., *Typ: roman type*, romain.
rpm, r.p.m., **1.** *reseale price maintenance.* **2.** *revolutions per minute*, tours (par) minute, t.m., t/mn.
R.R., *NAm: Railroad*, chemin de fer, c(h). de f.
R.S., *Royal Society.*
R.S.M., *Mil: Regimental Sergeant-major* = adjudant chef.
R.S.P.B., *Royal Society for the Protection of Birds.*
R.S.P.C.A., *Royal Society for the Prevention of Cruelty to Animals*, Société protectrice des animaux, S.P.A.
R.S.V.P., *please answer*, répondez s'il vous plaît, R.S.V.P.
Rt Hon., *Right Honourable*, très honorable.
Rt Rev., *Right Reverend*, très révérend.
R.U., *Rugby Union.*
R.U.C., *Royal Ulster Constabulary.*
R.V., (*of Bible*) *Revised Version.*
Ry, *Railway*, chemin de fer, c(h). de f.
R.Z.S., *Royal Zoological Society.*

S., **1.** *Saint*, Saint, S(t)., Ste. **2.** *South*, sud, S.
s., **1.** *Meas: second(s)*, second(s), s(ec). **2.** *A.Num: shilling(s).* **3.** *Gram:* (*a*) *singular*, singulier; (*b*) *substantive*, substantif. **4.** *son*, fils.
S.A., **1.** *Salvation Army*, Armée du Salut. **2.** *Geog: South Africa.* **3.** *Hist: Sturmabteilung, Storm troops*, section d'assaut, S.A.
s.a., *see also*, voir.
s.a.e., *stamped addressed envelope.*
SALT [sɔlt] *Strategic Arms Limitation Talks.*
Sask., *Geog: Saskatchewan.*
S.A.Y.E., *save-as-you-earn*, économie à la source.
S.C., **1.** *Geog: South Carolina*, Caroline du Sud. **2.** *Mil: Signal Corps*, service des transmissions.
Sc.D., *Doctor of Science*, Docteur ès Sciences.
S.C.E., *Scottish Certicate of Education.*
sch., *school*, école.
Scot., *Geog:* (*a*) *Scotland*, Écosse; (*b*) *Scottish*, écossais.
S.C.R., *Sch:* **1.** *Senior Common Room.* **2.** *Senior Combination Room.*
S.D(ak)., *Geog: South Dakota.*
S.D.P., *Pol: Social Democratic Party.*
S.E.A.T.O. ['siːtou] *South-East Asia Treaty Organization*, Organisation du Traité de l'Asie du Sud-Est, O.T.A.S.E.
sec., **1.** *secretary*, secrétaire. **2.** *second(s)*, seconde(s), s(ec).
Sen., **1.** (*a*) *Senate*, Sénat; (*b*) *Senator*, sénateur. **2.** *senior*, aîné; père.
S.E.N., *State Enrolled Nurse* = infirmière diplômée.
Sergt., *Mil: Sergeant*, sergent, sgt.
S.E.T., *Selective Employment Tax.*
S.F., *science fiction*, science-fiction.
Sgt., *Sergeant*, sergent, sgt.
SHAPE [ʃeip] *Supreme Headquarters Allied Powers Europe*, quartier général suprême des forces alliées en Europe.
S.J., *Societas Jesu, Society of Jesus*, Société de Jésus.
S.M., *Mil: Sergeant Major* = sergent major.
S.N.P., *Pol: Scottish National Party.*
So., *NAm:* (*a*) *south*, sud, S; (*b*) *southern*, austral, A.
S.O.B., *P: son of a bitch*, fils de pute.
Soc., **1.** *Society*, société, association. **2.** *Socialist*, socialiste.
SOGAT ['sougæt] *Society of Graphical and Allied Trades.*
Som., *Geog: Somerset.*
S.O.S., *W.Tg: save our souls*, signal de détresse, appel de détresse international, S.O.S.
sov., **1.** *sovereign*, souverain. **2.** *soviet*, soviet.
Sp., *Geog:* (*a*) *Spain*, Espagne; (*b*) *Spanish*, espagnol.
s.p., *Turf: starting price*, dernière cote avant le départ.
S.P.C.K., *Society for Promoting Christian Knowledge.*
sp. gr., *Ph: specific gravity*, gravité spécifique.
Sq., *Square*, place, square.
sq. ft., *Meas: square foot*, pied carré.
Sqn. Ldr, *Av: Squadron Leader.*
Sr., **1.** *senior*, aîné; père. **2.** *Señor.*
S.R.N., *State Registered Nurse.*
SS., *Saints*, Saints, SS.
S.S., **1.** *steamship*, steamer, ss. **2.** *German Hist: Schutzstaffel, Nazi special police force*, S.S.
St, **1.** *Street*, rue. **2.** *Saint*, Saint, S(t), Ste. **3.** *Strait*, détroit.
st., *Meas: stone.*
Sta., *Station*, gare.
Staffs., *Geog: Staffordshire.*
std., *standard*, ordinaire, standard.
STD, *Tp: subscriber trunk dialling* = (téléphone) automatique.
stg., *sterling.*
Sth., *South*, sud, S.
S.T.O.L. [stɔl] *Av: short takeoff and landing*, décollage et atterrissage courts.
sub., *subscription*, souscription.
subj., *subject*, sujet.
sup., *superior*, supérieur.
supp(l)., *supplement*, supplément.
Supt, *Superintendent.*

surg., (*a*) *surgeon*, chirurgien; (*b*) *surgical*, chirurgical; (*c*) *surgery*, chirurgie.
S.W.A.(L.)K. [swæk, swɔlk] *F:* (*on back of envelope*) *sealed with a* (*loving*) *kiss*.
S.W.A.P.O. ['swɑːpou] *South West African People's Organization.*
Sx., *Geog: Sussex.*
syn., (*a*) *synonym*, synonyme; (*b*) *synonymous*, synonyme.

t., *Meas: ton*(*s*), *tonne*(*s*), tonne(s), t.
T.A., *Mil: Territorial Army.*
T.A.B., *typhoid-paratyphoid A and B vaccine*, vaccin antityphoparatyphoïdique A et B, T.A.B.
T. & A.V.R., *Territorial and Army Volunteer Reserve.*
TASS [tæs] *Telegraphic news agency of the Soviet Union*, agence de presse de l'Union soviétique, TASS.
T.B., *Med:* (*a*) *tubercle bacillus*, bacille de Koch; (*b*) *F: tuberculosis*, tuberculose.
tbs(p)., *tablespoon(ful)*, cuiller à soupe.
T.C.P., *Ch: trichlorophenoxyacetic acid.*
tech(n)., **1.** *technical*, technique. **2.** *technology*, technologie.
tel., *telephone*, téléphone, tel.
temp., **1.** *temperature*, température, t. **2.** *temporary*, temporaire.
Tenn., *Geog: Tennessee.*
Tex., *Geog: Texas.*
TGWU, *Transport and General Workers Union.*
Th.D., *Doctor of Theology*, docteur en théologie.
T.N.T., *Exp: trinitrotoluene*, trinitrotoluène, T.N.T.
trans., (*a*) *translated*, traduit; (*b*) *translation*, traduction.
treas., (*a*) *treasurer*, trésorier; (*b*) *treasury*, trésor.
tsp., *teaspoonful*, cuiller à café.
TT., **1.** *teetotal*(*ler*), abstinent. **2.** *tuberculin tested*, garanti exempt de tuberculose. **3.** (*also* **T.T. race**) *Tourist Trophy.*
T.U., *Trade Union*, syndicat.
TUC, *Trades Union Congress.*
T.V. *television*, télévision, T.V.; **T.V. game**, jeu vidéo.

U., **1.** *Unionist.* **2.** *Cin: universal*, pour tout le monde. **3.** *university*, université.
U.A.E., *United Arab Emirates*, Émirats arabes unis. E.A.U.
U.A.R., *United Arab Republic*, République arabe unie, R.A.U.
U.C.C.A. ['ʌkə] *Universities Central Council on Admissions.*
U.D.A., *Ulster Defence Association.*
UDI, *Unilateral Declaration of Independence.*
U.D.R., *Ulster Defence Regiment.*
U.F.O. (*occ.* ['juːfou]) *unidentified flying object*, objet volant non identifié, O.V.N.I.
UHF, *W. Tel: ultra-high frequency*, fréquence ultra-haute.
UK., *Geog: United Kingdom*, Royaume-Uni.
ult., *Corr: ultimo*, dernier, der(r).
U.N., *United Nations*, Nations Unies.
UNA, *United Nations Association.*
UNESCO [ju'neskou] *United Nations Educational, Scientific and Cultural Organization*, Organisation des Nations Unies pour l'éducation, la science et la culture, UNESCO.
UNICEF ['juːnisef] *United Nations* (*International*) *Children's* (*Emergency*) *Fund*, Fonds international de secours à l'enfance, FISE.
univ., **1.** *universal*, universel. **2.** *university*, université.
UNO, U.N.O. ['juːnou] *United Nations Organization*, Organisation des Nations Unies, O.N.U.
U.S., *Geog: United States*, États-Unis, É.-U.
U.S.A., **1.** *Geog: United States of America*, États-Unis d'Amérique. **2.** *United States Army.*
U.S.A.F., *United States Air Force.*
U.S.M., **1.** *United States Mail.* **2.** *Mil: United States Marines.* **3.** *Fin: United States Mint.*
U.S.N., *United States Navy.*
U.S.N.R., *United States Naval Reserve.*
U.S.S., *United States Ship.*
U.S.S.R., *Union of Soviet Socialist Republics*, Union des républiques socialistes soviétiques, U.R.S.S.
Ut., *Geog: Utah.*
U.V., *ultra-violet*, ultraviolet, U.V.

V, *El: volt*, volt, v.
v., **1.** *vide, see*, voir, voyez, v. **2.** *Jur: etc: versus*, contre, c. **3.** *verse*, (i) *B:* verset, v.; (ii) *Lit:* strophe. **4.** *very*, très.
Va, *Geog: Virginia*, Virginie.
V.A., **1.** *Vice-Admiral.* **2.** *U.S: Veterans' Administration.*
V. & A., *Victoria & Albert Museum.*
V.A.T. (*also* [væt]) *value added tax*, taxe à la valeur ajoutée, T.V.A.
V.C., *Victoria Cross.*
V.D., *Med: Venereal Disease*, maladie vénérienne.
V.D.U., *visual display unit*, dispositif d'affichage.
V.E., *Victory in Europe*, victoire en Europe.
Ven., *Ecc: Venerable*, vénérable.
VG, *very good*, très bien.
VHF, *W. Tel: very high frequency*, très haute fréquence, THF.
V.I.P., *very important person*, personnage de marque.
Vis(c)., *Viscount*, vicomte, Vcte; *Viscountess*, Vicomtesse, Vctesse.
viz., *videlicet, namely*, c'est-à-dire, à savoir.
VOA, *W.Tel: Voice of America.*
vol., **1.** *Ph: volume*, volume, vol. **2.** *volume*, tome, t(om). **3.** *volunteer*, volontaire.
VP., *Vice-President*, vice-président.
V.R., *Victoria Regina, Queen Victoria*, la Reine Victoria.
vs., *versus*, contre, c.
V.S.O., *Voluntary Service Overseas.*
V.S.O.P., (*of brandy*) *Very Special Old Pale.*
Vt., *Geog: Vermont.*
VTOL, *Av: vertical take-off and landing* (*aircraft*), avion à décollage et atterrissage verticaux, ADAV.
vv., *verses*, (i) *B:* versets; (ii) *Lit:* strophes.

W., **1.** *El: watt*(*s*), watt(s), w. **2.** *west*, ouest, O.; *Nau:* W.
w., **1.** *Cr: wicket.* **2.** (*a*) *wide*, large; (*b*) *width*, largeur, larg. **3.** *with*, avec. **4.** *wife*, épouse.
W.A.A.C., *Hist:* (1914–18) *Women's Army Auxiliary Corps.*
W.A.A.F., *Hist:* (1939–45) *Women's Auxiliary Air Force.*
W.A.C., *U.S: Women's Army Corps.*
W.A.F., *U.S: Women in the Air Force.*
War., *Geog: Warwickshire.*
Wash., *Geog: Washington.*
W.A.S.P [wɔsp] *Pej: White Anglo-Saxon Protestant.*
WAVES, *U.S: Navy: Women's Appointed Volunteer Emergency Service.*
W.C., *water closet*, water-closet, W.C.
W.C.C., *World Council of Churches.*
W/Cdr, *Av: Wing Commander*, lieutenant-colonel.
W.D., *War Department*, Ministère de la guerre.
w/e., *week ending*, semaine se terminant . . .

W.E.A., *Workers' Educational Association.*
W.E.U., *Western European Union*, Union de l'Europe occidentale, U.E.O.
W.H.O., *World Health Organization*, Organisation mondiale de la santé, O.M.S.
W.I., 1. *Women's Institute.* **2.** *Geog: West Indies.*
Wilts., *Geog: Wiltshire.*
Wis., *Geog: Wisconsin.*
wk., *week*, semaine.
WL, *W.Tel: wavelength*, longueur d'onde.
Worcs., *Geog: Worcestershire.*
W.P., *weather permitting*, si le temps le permet.
W.P.B., *waste paper basket*, corbeille à papier(s).
W.P.C., *women police constable*, femme-agent.
w.p.m., *words per minute*, mots par minute.
W.R.A.C., *Women's Royal Army Corps* = Auxiliaire féminine de l'armée de terre, A.F.A.T.
W.R.A.F., *Women's Royal Air Force.*
W.R.N.S., *Women's Royal Naval Service*, Services féminins de la Flotte, S.F.F.
W.R.V.S., *Women's Royal Voluntary Service.*
wt., *weight*, poids, p.
W.Va., *Geog: West Virginia.*
WW, *World War*, Guerre mondiale.
W.W.F., *World Wildlife Fund.*
Wyo., *Geog: Wyoming.*

X., 1. *cross*, croix. **2.** *Cin: adults only* = interdit aux moins de 18 ans.
Xmas ['eksmas] *Christmas*, Noël.

Y., *U.S: F:* = Y.M.C.A., Y.W.C.A.
y., 1. *year*, an. **2.** *Meas: yard.*
Y.H.A., *Youth Hostels Association.*
Y.M.C.A., *Young Men's Christian Association.*
Yorks., *Geog: Yorkshire.*
yr., 1. *Corr: your*, votre, v. **2.** *year*, an.
yrs, 1. *Corr: yours*, votre, v. **2.** *years*, ans.
Y.W.C.A., *Young Women's Christian Association.*

Z., 1. *zero*, zéro. **2.** *zone*, zone.
Z.A.N.U. ['zɑːnuː] *Zimbabwe African National Union.*
Z.A.P.U. ['zɑːpuː] *Zimbabwe African People's Union.*

PART TWO

FRENCH–ENGLISH

Tableau des symboles phonétiques

Consonnes et semi-consonnes

[p]	pain [pɛ̃]; tape [tap]
[b]	beau [bo]; abbé [abe]; robe [rɔb]
[m]	mon [mɔ̃]; flamme [flam]; prisme [prism]
[f]	feu [fø]; bref [brɛf]; phrase [fraz]
[v]	voir [vwar]; vie [vi]; wagon [vagɔ̃]
[t]	table [tabl̥]; nette [nɛt]; théâtre [teɑtr̥]
[d]	donner [dɔne]; sud [syd]
[n]	né [ne]; canne [kan]; automne [otɔn]
[s]	sou [su]; rébus [rebys]; cire [sir]; scène [sɛn]; six [sis]
[z]	cousin [kuzɛ̃]; zéro [zero]; deuxième [døzjɛm]
[l]	lait [lɛ]; aile [ɛl]; facile [fasil]
[l̥]	table [tabl̥]; sensible [sɑ̃sibl̥]; noble [nɔbl̥]
[ʃ]	chose [ʃoz]; chercher [ʃɛrʃe]; schisme [ʃism]
[ʒ]	gilet [ʒilɛ]; manger [mɑ̃ʒe]; âge [ɑʒ]
[k]	camp [kɑ̃]; képi [kepi]; quatre [katr̥]; écho [eko]
[g]	garde [gard]; guerre [gɛr]; second [səgɔ̃]
[ɲ]	campagne [kɑ̃paɲ]; gnaule [ɲol]
[ŋ]	(*in words of foreign origin*) parking [parkiŋ]; smoking [smɔkiŋ]
[r]	rare [rar]; arbre [arbr̥]; rhume [rym]
[r̥]	être [ɛtr̥]; marbre [marbr̥]; neutre [nøtr̥]
[ks]	accident [aksidɑ̃]; action [aksjɔ̃]; xérose [kseroz]
[gz]	exister [egziste]; examen [egzamɛ̃]
[j]	yacht [jɔt, jat]; piano [pjano]; ration [rasjɔ̃]; voyage [vwajaʒ]; travailler [travaje]; cahier [kaje]
[w]	ouate [wat]; ouest [west]; noir [nwar]; (*also in words of foreign origin*) tramway [tramwɛ]; whist [wist]
[ɥ]	muet [mɥɛ]; huit [ɥit]; luire [lɥir]; aiguille [egɥij]

Voyelles

[i]	vite [vit]; signe [siɲ]; sortie [sɔrti]
[e]	été [ete]; donner, donné [dɔne]; légal [legal]
[ɛ]	elle [ɛl]; très [trɛ]; terre [tɛr]; rêve [rɛv]; père [pɛr]
[a]	chat [ʃa]; tache [taʃ]; toit [twa]; phare [far]
[ɑ]	âge [ɑʒ]; âgé [ɑʒe]; tâche [tɑʃ]
[ɔ]	donner [dɔne]; album [albɔm]; fort [fɔr]
[o]	dos [do]; impôt [ɛ̃po]; chaud [ʃo]
[u]	tout [tu]; goût [gu]; août [u]; cour [kur]
[y]	cru [kry]; ciguë [sigy]; mur [myr]
[ø]	feu [fø]; nœud [nø]; heureuse [ørøz]
[œ]	seul [sœl]; œuf [œf]; sœur [sœr]; cueillir [kœjir]
[ə]*	le [lə]; ce [sə]; entremets [ɑ̃trəmɛ]
[ɛ̃]	vin [vɛ̃]; plein [plɛ̃]; thym [tɛ̃]; prince [prɛ̃s]; plainte [plɛ̃t]
[ɑ̃]	enfant [ɑ̃fɑ̃]; temps [tɑ̃]; paon [pɑ̃]; centre [sɑ̃tr̥]; branche [brɑ̃ʃ]
[ɔ̃]	mon [mɔ̃]; plomb [plɔ̃]; longe [lɔ̃ʒ]; comte [kɔ̃t]
[œ̃]	un [œ̃]; lundi [lœ̃di]; humble [œ̃bl̥]

* The symbol (ə) (in brackets) indicates that the mute *e* is pronounced in careful speech but not in rapid speech.

A

A a [ɑ] *n.m.* (the letter) **A, a;** *F:* **il ne sait ni A ni B,** (i) he can't read, he doesn't know his ABC; (ii) he doesn't know A from B; **connaître un sujet depuis A jusqu'à Z,** to know a subject from A to Z, thoroughly, inside out.

à [a] prep. (*contracts with the article* **le** *into* **au,** *with the article* **les** *into* **aux**). **I.** (**à** *with a non-infinitive complement*). **1.** (*denoting direction*) (*a*) **courir à qn,** to run (up) to s.o.; **revenir à la surface,** to come (up) to the surface again; **aller à l'église, au cinéma,** to go to church, to the cinema; **monter à sa chambre,** to go up to one's room; **de Paris à Lyon,** from Paris to Lyons; **se rendre au Japon, aux Antilles, à la Guadeloupe, à Terre-Neuve,** to travel to Japan, to the West Indies, to Guadeloupe, to Newfoundland; (*elliptically*) **au feu!** fire! **au voleur!** stop thief! (*b*) **courir à sa perte,** to head for disaster; **(de) vingt à trente personnes,** between twenty and thirty people. **2.** (*denoting position*) (*a*) **au coin de la rue,** at the corner of the street, at the street corner; **à l'horizon,** on the horizon; **à la page deux,** on page two; **à l'ombre,** in the shade; **au grenier,** in the attic; **à la maison,** at home; **au théâtre,** at the theatre; **au Canada,** in Canada; **aux États-Unis,** in the United States; **à la Jamaïque,** in Jamaica; **à Cuba;** in Cuba; **à Paris,** in Paris; **à deux kilomètres d'ici,** two kilometres from here; **un livre à la main,** with a book in one's hand; (*b*) **au fond,** basically; fundamentally. **3.** (*denoting direction in time*) **du matin au soir,** from morning to night; **remettre une affaire à plus tard,** to put off, postpone, something; **à jamais,** for ever; **à demain!** see you tomorrow! **de lundi à vendredi,** from Monday to Friday, *NAm:* Monday thru Friday; **au revoir,** goodbye (for now). **4.** (*a*) **au premier mot,** at the first word; **à mon arrivée,** on my arrival; (*b*) **à deux heures,** at two o'clock; **au vingtième siècle,** in the twentieth century; **à l'avenir,** in (the) future; **à l'aube,** at dawn. **5. se battre homme à homme,** to fight man to man; *Ten:* **quinze à,** fifteen all; **monter l'escalier quatre à quatre,** to go upstairs four (steps) at a time; **peu à peu,** little by little, gradually. **6.** (*introducing the indirect object of many verbs*) (*a*) **attacher un cheval à un arbre,** to tie a horse to a tree; **attacher de l'importance à qch.,** to attach importance to sth.; **donner qch. à qn,** to give sth. to s.o., to give s.o. sth.; **parler à qn,** to speak to s.o.; **penser à qn, à qch.,** to think of s.o., sth.; **s'habituer à qch.,** to become used to sth.; **à quoi cela sert-il?** (i) what's that used for? (ii) what's the good of that? (*b*) **survivre à qn, à qch.,** to survive, outlive s.o., sth.; **prendre qn à témoin,** to call s.o. to witness; (*c*) **s'opposer à qch.,** to oppose sth.; **résister à qn, à qch.,** to resist s.o., sth.; (*d*) **cacher, voler, qch. à qn,** to hide, steal, sth. from s.o.; **boire à (même) la bouteille,** to drink (straight) from the bottle. **7. faire faire qch. à qn,** to get s.o. to do sth.; **faire savoir qch. à qn,** to tell s.o. about sth.; to inform s.o. of sth.; **laisser croire à qn que . . .,** to let s.o. think, believe, that . . .. **8.** (*possession, etc.*) **ce livre est à Paul,** this is Paul's book; this book belongs to Paul; **un ami à moi,** a friend of mine; **c'est à vous de décider,** it's for, up to, you to decide; **c'est à vous,** it's your turn; *W.Tel:* **à vous,** over (to you); **la parole est à X,** X will now speak. **9. tasse à thé,** teacup; **brosse à dents,** toothbrush; **moulin à vent,** windmill; **chambre à deux lits,** room with twin-beds; **voiture à toit ouvrant,** car with a sunshine roof; **homme à barbe noire,** man with a black beard; *Sp:* **rugby à quinze,** Rugby Union. **10.** (*a*) (*manner*) **à pied,** on foot; **à la main,** by hand; **fait à la main,** handmade; **arriver à l'improviste,** to arrive unexpectedly; **recevoir qn à bras ouverts,** to receive s.o. with open arms; **vendre des huîtres à la douzaine,** to sell oysters by the dozen; **à la française,** in the French manner, way; **un repas à l'anglaise,** a typical(ly) English meal; **manger à sa faim,** to eat one's fill; to eat as much as one can; **nous l'avons fait à trois,** there were three of us to do, doing it; (*b*) **à mon avis,** in my opinion; **à ce qu'il dit,** according to him, to what he says; **au reste,** moreover; besides; **à cette condition,** on this condition; (*c*) **à quel prix vendez-vous cela?** how much are you asking for that? **un timbre à deux francs,** a two-franc stamp. **11. indispensable à,** indispensable to (s.o.), for (sth.); **parallèle à,** parallel to; **hostile à,** hostile to; **c'est bien gentil à lui,** it's very kind of him. **II.** (*introducing verb in infinitive*) **1.** (*a*) **penser à faire qch.,** to think of doing sth.; **encourager qn à faire qch.,** to encourage s.o. to do sth.; (*b*) **j'ai à écrire une lettre,** I have to write a letter; **il ne me reste qu'à vous remercier,** it only remains for me to thank you; (*c*) **commencer à faire qch.,** to begin to do sth.; **apprendre à lire,** to learn to read. **2. une machine à coudre,** a sewing machine; **il est homme à se défendre,** he's the kind of man who will hit back; **il est à plaindre,** he is to be pitied; **j'ai une lettre à écrire,** I have a letter to write; **maison à vendre,** house for sale. **3. laid á faire peur,** frightfully ugly; **geler à pierre fendre,** to freeze hard; **un bruit à tout casser,** an ear-splitting noise. **4.** (*a*) **je suis prêt à vous écouter,** I'm ready to listen to you; **habile à coudre,** good at sewing; **facile à comprendre,** easy to understand; (*b*) **être le seul à faire qch.,** to be the only one to do sth.; **le troisième à arriver,** the third to arrive. **5. à partager les mêmes périls on apprend à se connaître,** by sharing the same dangers we learn to know each other; **à en juger par . . .;** judging by . . .; **à les en croire,** according to them; if we are to believe them.

abaissant [abɛsɑ̃] *a.* degrading; lowering.

abaisse [abɛs] *n.f. Cu:* thinly rolled pastry.

abaisse-langue [abɛslɑ̃g] *n.m.inv. Med:* tongue depressor.

abaissement [abɛsmɑ̃] *n.m.* **1.** lowering, pulling down (of blind, etc.); reduction (in prices). **2.** fall; subsidence, sinking; fall, drop (in temperature, prices). **3.** *Lit:* abasement, humiliation.

abaisser [abese] **I.** *v.tr.* **1.** to lower; to pull down (a blind); to let down (drawbridge). **2.** to lower (one's voice, prices); to reduce (prices, cost, pressure, etc.). **3.** *Lit:* to humble, abase. **4.** *Mth:* **a. une perpendiculaire à une ligne,** to drop a perpendicular to a line. **II. s'abaisser.** **1.** to fall away, dip, slope down, go down; **le terrain s'est abaissé,** the ground has subsided; **la température s'abaisse,** the temperature is falling. **2. s'a. devant Dieu,** to humble oneself before God. **3. s'a. à, jusqu'à faire qch.,** (i) to stoop so low as to do sth.; (ii) to condescend to do sth.

abandon [abɑ̃dɔ̃] *n.m.* **1.** (*a*) surrender, renunciation (of goods, rights, etc.); **faire l'a. de qch. à qn,** to make over, relinquish, surrender, sth. to s.o.; (*b*) *Sp:* retirement, withdrawal (from race). **2.** forsaking, desertion, abandonment (of children, duty). **3.** neglect; **à l'a.,** (completely) neglected; *Nau:* adrift, derelict; (*of children, garden*) running wild. **4.** lack of restraint; **parler avec un complet a.,** to speak freely, without reserve.

abandonné, -ée [abɑ̃dɔne] *a.* & *n.* **1.** (*of pers.*) abandoned, deserted; **les abandonnés,** waifs and strays; **navire a. en mer,** derelict; **maison abandonnée,** deserted house; *Com:* **modèle a.,** discontinued line. **2.** *O:* profligate, shameless, abandoned (person, conduct). **3.** untidy (appearance).

abandonner [abɑ̃dɔne] **I.** *v.tr.* **1.** (*a*) to forsake, desert, abandon; to leave; *Nau:* **a. un homme,** to maroon a man; **a. le bâtiment,** to abandon ship; *Av:* **a. le bord, un avion, en vol,** to bale out; *Mil:* **a. son poste,** to desert one's post; **mes forces m'abandonnent,** my strength is failing me; **abandonné par les médecins,** given up by the doctors; **a. la partie,** to throw in one's hand; (*b*) *v.i. Sp:* to give up, retire. **2.** to surrender, renounce, give up; **a. ses prétentions,** to renounce, surrender, one's claims. **II. s'abandonner.** **1.** (*a*) to neglect oneself; (*b*) to give way to despair. **2.** to be unconstrained; to let oneself go. **3. s'a. à (qch.),** to give oneself up to (sth.); to become addicted to (vice, etc.); to give way to (emotion). **4. s'a. à son sort,** to resign oneself to one's fate; **s'a. au sommeil,** to give way to sleep.

abaque [abak] *n.m.* (*a*) abacus, counting frame; (*b*) chart, graph, table, scale, diagram; nomography, plotter; (*c*) *Arch:* abacus.

abasourdir [abazurdir] *v.tr.* to astound, bewilder, stun; **nous sommes restés abasourdis de la nouvelle,** we were flabbergasted by the news.

abasourdissant [abazurdisɑ̃] *a.* stunning; astounding.

abasourdissement [abazurdismɑ̃] *n.m.* bewilderment, stupefaction.

abat [aba] *n.m.* **1.** *A:* slaughter. **2. pluie d'a.,** sudden shower. **3. abats,** (i) offal, *NAm:* variety meat; (ii) giblets.

abâtardi [abɑtardi] *a.* degenerate.

abâtardir [abɑtardir] *v.tr.* **1.** to cause to degenerate; to debase. **2. s'a.,** to degenerate, to deteriorate.

abâtardissement [abɑtardismɑ̃] *n.m.* degeneracy.

abat-jour [abaʒur] *n.m.inv.* (*a*) lampshade; (*b*) eyeshade; (*c*) sunblind, awning; (*d*) *slanting shutter;* **mettre la main en a.-j.,** to shade one's eyes with one's hand.

abattage [abataʒ *n.m.* **1.** (*a*) knocking down; pulling down (of buildings); (*b*) felling, cutting down, clearing (of trees, etc.); (*c*) *Min:* cutting, working; **face d'a.,** working face; (*d*) *Nau:* **a. en carène,** careening. **2.** leverage. **3.** slaughtering, killing; **grand a. de gibier,** heavy bag of game.

abattant [abatɑ̃] **1.** *a.* (*a*) depressing; **chaleur abattante,** heat that leaves one limp; (*b*) **siège a.,** tip-up seat. **2.** *n.m.* flap (of counter, table, envelope).

abattement [abatmɑ̃] *n.m.* **1.** (*a*) (physical) prostration; exhaustion; (*b*) despondency, dejection, depression, low spirits. **2.** *Fin:* abatement; allowance (against tax).

abatteur, -euse [abatœr, -øz] *n.* (*a*) **a. de besogne,** hard worker, *F:* slogger; (*b*) feller (of trees); (*c*) slaughterer.

abattis [abati] *n.m.* **1.** felling, clearing (of trees). **2.** heap of felled trees; **a. de maisons,** heap of fallen houses. **3.** *pl.* (*a*) *Cu:* giblets; (*b*) *P:* limbs; hands and feet.

abattoir [abatwar] *n.m.* slaughterhouse; abattoir.

abattr̥e [abatr̥] *v.* (*conj. like* BATTRE) **I.** *v.tr.* **1.** (*a*) to knock down, throw down, pull down; to overthrow; **a. une maison,** to pull down a house; **a. de la besogne,** to get through a lot of work; (*b*) to cover, do (miles, etc.); (*c*) to fell, cut down, clear (trees); (*d*) to strike off, lop off, cut off, *F:* chop off (head, limb). **2.** to slaughter, kill, destroy; *P:* to kill (s.o.), bump (s.o.) off; **a. un bœuf,** to slaughter an ox. **3.** (*a*) **a. un avion,** to bring down, shoot down, an aircraft; (*b*) **a. violemment le couvercle,** to bang down the lid. **4.** to lower; to damp (courage, enthusiasm); **a. les tentes,** to strike tents. **5.** to lay (dust, wind). **6.** (*of wind*) to blow down, beat down; **arbre, blé, abattu par le vent,** tree blown down by the wind, corn flattened by the wind; *Nau:* **a. navire en carène,** to careen a ship. **7.** to dishearten, depress; **ne vous laissez pas a.!** bear up! **8.** *Cards:* **a. ses cartes, son jeu,** to lay one's cards on the table, to lay down one's hand. **9.** *Nau:* to pay off; **a. à la côte,** to drift on-shore. **10.** *Tch:* (*a*) to blunt (an angle); to reduce (a surface); to chamfer (an edge); (*b*) to clinch (a rivet). **II. s'abattre** *v.pr.* **1.** to fall, to crash down, to collapse; **le mât s'abattit,** the mast came crashing down. **2. s'a. sur qch.,** to pounce on sth.; to swoop down, sweep down, on sth. **3.** (*of fever, heat, etc.*) to abate, to subside; **le vent s'abat,** the wind is falling. **4.** to become disheartened, depressed.

abattu [abaty] **1.** *a.* dejected, dispirited, low-spirited; **a. par la chaleur,** limp with the heat; **visage a.,** drawn face. **2.** *n.m.* **fusil à l'a.,** uncocked rifle.

abat-vent [abavɑ̃ *n.m.inv.* **1.** louvre boards. **2.** (chimney) cowl. **3.** *Hort:* windbreak.

abbatial, -aux [abasjal, -o] **1.** *a.* **terres abbatiales,** abbey lands; **église abbatiale,** abbey (church). **2.** *n.f.* **abbatiale,** abbey (church).

abbaye [abei] *n.f.* abbey.

abbé [abe] *n.m.* **1.** abbot. **2.** (*general designation of and mode of address for a* (*Roman Catholic*) *priest*) **J'en parlerai à monsieur l'a.,** I shall mention it to the priest; **(Monsieur) l'A. Constantin,** Father Constantin.

abbesse [abɛs] *n.f.* abbess.

abc [abese] *n.m.inv.* **1.** abc, alphabet. **2.** spelling book; primer. **3.** rudiments (of a science).

abcès [apsɛ] *n.m.* abscess, gathering; **a. au doigt,** gathered finger; **a. à la gencive,** gumboil.

abdication [abdikasjɔ̃] *n.f.* (*a*) abdication; (*b*) renunciation, surrender (of authority, rights).

abdiquer [abdike] **1.** *v.tr.* to abdicate (throne); to renounce, surrender (rights, etc.). **2.** *v.i.* to abdicate.

abdomen [abdɔmɛn] *n.m.* abdomen.

abdominal, -aux [abdɔminal, -o] *a.* abdominal.

abducteur [abdyktœr] *a.* & *n.m.* **(muscle) a.,** abductor (muscle).

abécédaire [abesedɛr] **1.** *a.* alphabetical. **2.** *n.m.* ABC, alphabet book.

abeille [abɛj] *n.f.* bee; **a. domestique,** hive bee, honey bee; **a neutre, a. ouvrière,** worker (bee); **a. mâle,** drone; **a. mère,** queen bee; **nid d'abeilles,** bees' nest, honeycomb; **serviette nid d'abeilles,** honeycomb towel; *Aut:* **radiateur nid d'abeilles,** honeycomb radiator.

abeiller, -ère [abɛje, -ɛr] *a.* relating to bees.

aberration [abɛrasjɔ̃] *n.f.* **1.** *Astr: Biol: Mth: Opt:* aberration; **a. de sphéricité,** spherical aberration. **2.** aberration (of mind, conduct).

abêtir [abɛtir] **1.** *v.tr.* stupefy; to make (s.o.) stupid. **2.** *v.i. & pr.* to grow, become, stupid.

abhorrer [abɔre] *v.tr.* to abhor, loathe.

abîme [abim] *n.m.* (*a*) abyss, chasm, depth(s); gulf; **les profonds abîmes de l'océan,** the ocean depths; **un a. de science,** a man of immense learning; a mine of information; (*b*) *Geol:* swallowhole.

abîmer [abime] *v.* **I.** *v.tr.* to spoil, damage, injure; **s'a. la santé,** to injure one's health; **livre abîmé par la pluie,** book spoilt by the rain. *F:* **se faire a.,** to get beaten up, knocked about. **II s'abîmer. 1.** (*a*) **s'a. dans les flots,** to sink, to be engulfed, swallowed up, by the sea; (*b*) **s'a. dans la douleur, dans ses pensées,** to be sunk in grief, lost in thought. **2.** to get spoiled; to spoil.

abject [abʒɛkt] *a.* abject (poverty); mean; contemptible, despicable (person, conduct).

abjectement [abʒɛktmɑ̃] *adv.* abjectly.

abjuration [abʒyrasjɔ̃] *n.f.* abjuration; renunciation (on oath); recantation.

abjurer [abʒyre] *v.tr.* to abjure, forswear; to renounce (on oath); to recant, retract.

ablatif, -ive [ablatif, -iv] *a. & n.m. Gram:* ablative (case); **à l'a.,** in the ablative; **a. absolu,** ablative absolute.

ablation [ablɑsjɔ̃] *n.f.* ablation.

ablution [ablysjɔ̃] *n.f.* ablution, washing; *F:* **faire ses ablutions,** to wash, to perform one's ablutions.

abnégation [abnegasjɔ̃] *n.f.* abnegation, self sacrifice.

aboi [abwa] *n.m. used in* **aux abois,** (i) (*of stag, enemy*) at bay; (ii) hard pressed, with his back against the wall; **ils sont aux abois,** they are in desperate straits.

aboiement [abwamɑ̃] *n.m.* bark, barking (of dog); bay, baying (of hound).

abolir [abɔlir] *v.tr.* to abolish, suppress; to cancel (a debt, etc.).

abolissement [abɔlismɑ̃] *n.m.*, **abolition** [abɔlisjɔ̃] *n.f.* **1.** abolition, suppression. **2.** repeal, annulment.

abolitionnisme [abɔlisjɔnism] *n.m. Hist:* abolitionism.

abolitionniste [abɔlisjɔnist] *a. & n. Hist:* abolitionist.

abominable [abɔminabl̩] *a.* abominable, foul; heinous (crime); **l'abominable homme des neiges,** the abominable snowman; *F:* **temps a.,** filthy weather.

abominablement [abɔminabləmɑ̃] *adv.* abominably.

abomination [abɔminasjɔ̃] *n.f.* **1.** abomination, abhorrence; **avoir qch., qn, en a.,** to loathe, sth., s.o. **2. ce café est une a.,** this coffee is abominable.

abominer [abɔmine] *v.tr.* to abominate, loathe.

abondamment [abɔ̃damɑ̃] *adv.* abundantly, plentifully, copiously; **peu a.,** scantily.

abondance [abɔ̃dɑ̃s] *n.f.* **1.** abundance, plenty; **une a. de fruits,** an abundance of fruit; **corne d'a.,** cornucopia. **2.** (*a*) wealth (of expression, details); **parler avec a.,** to have a great flow of words; **parler d'a.,** to speak off the cuff, extempore; (*b*) *Cards:* (*solo whist*) abundance.

abondant [abɔ̃dɑ̃] *a.* abundant, copious, plentiful; rich (style); luxuriant (foliage); copious, hearty (meal); profuse (excuses, bleeding); prolific (author); rich (vocabulary).

abonder [abɔ̃de] *v.i.* **1.** to abound (**en,** in); to be plentiful; **rivière qui abonde en poisson,** river with plenty of fish; **a. de biens,** to be blessed with riches. **2. a. dans le sens de qn,** to be entirely of s.o.'s opinion.

abonné, -ée [abɔne] *n.* **1.** subscriber (to paper, etc.). **2.** season-ticket holder. **3. abonnés du gaz, de l'électricité,** gas, electricity, consumers.

abonnement [abɔnmɑ̃] *n.m.* **1.** subscription (to paper, etc.); **prendre un a. au** *Figaro,* to subscribe to the *Figaro.* **2. (carte d') a.,** season ticket; **prendre un a.,** to take out a season ticket. **3.** *Adm:* (water, etc.) rate; (telephone) rental.

abonner [abɔne] **1.** *v.tr.* to enrol, to take out a subscription for (s.o.). **2.** (*a*) **s'a. à une revue,** to take out a subscription to a magazine; (*b*) *Rail: etc:* **s'a.,** to take a season ticket; (*c*) **s'a. au téléphone, etc.,** to have the telephone, etc., installed.

abord [abɔr] *n.m.* **1.** access, approach (to land); **île d'un a. difficile,** island difficult of access. **2.** *pl.* approaches (**d'un endroit,** to a place); surroundings, outskirts (**de,** of). **3.** (*of pers.*) **avoir l'a. facile, difficile,** to be approachable, not (very) approachable. **4.** *adv.phr.* **d'a., tout d'a.,** (i) straight away, at once; (ii) at first, to begin with; (iii) first, in the first place, first and foremost; **dès l'a.,** from the (very) first, from the outset; **à l'a., au premier a., de prime a.,** at first sight, to begin with.

abordable [abɔrdabl̩] *a.* **1.** easy to land on; easy of approach, easy of access; approachable, accessible; *F:* **vos prix ne sont pas abordables,** your prices are not reasonable, are beyond my means. **2.** (*of pers.*) easily approached; accessible, affable, kindly; **peu a.,** aloof, standoffish; grumpy.

abordage [abɔrdaʒ] *n.m. Nau:* **1.** boarding (as an act of war); grappling; **monter, sauter, à l'a. (d'un navire),** to board a ship. **2.** collision; **il y a eu un a. causé par le brouillard,** two ships collided in the fog. **3.** boarding (another boat); coming alongside.

aborder [abɔrde] **1.** *v.i.* to land; to make land; to berth; **a. à un port,** to reach a port. **2.** *v.tr.* (*a*) to accost (s.o.); (*b*) **a. une question, une difficulté,** to approach, tackle, a question; to meet, grapple with, a difficulty; (*c*) to board, grapple (ship in a fight); to come alongside (a ship); (*d*) to collide with, run foul of, run down (ship).

aborigène [abɔriʒɛn] **1.** *a.* aboriginal; native, indigenous (**de,** to). **2.** *n.m.* native (of a country).

abortif, -ive [abɔrtif, iv] *a.* **1.** abortive. **2.** *Jur:* **manœuvres abortives,** (procuring of) abortion.

Aboukir [abukir] *Pr.n.m. Geog:* Ab(o)ukir; *Hist:* **la bataille d'A.,** the battle of the Nile.

abouler [abule] *v.tr. P:* **1.** to bring; to hand over; **aboule ça ici!** bring it here! hand it over! **2. s'a.,** to arrive, turn up; **s'a. en retard,** to turn up late.

aboutir [abutir] *v.i.* **1. a. à, dans, en, qch.,** to end at, in, sth.; to lead to sth.; to converge on sth.; to result in sth.; **ce sentier aboutit à la grande route,** this path leads to the main road; **une pyramide aboutit en pointe,** a pyramid ends in a point; **n'a. à rien,** to lead, come, to nothing; *F:* to go up in smoke; **pour a. aux fins que nous poursuivons,** to attain the end (which) we have in view. **2.** (*a*) (*of plan, etc.*) to succeed; **ne pas a.,** to fail; to fall through; **faire a. qch.,** to bring sth. to a successful conclusion; (*b*) (*of abscess*) to come to a head, to burst.

aboyer [abwaje] *v.i.* **(j'aboie, j'aboierai)** (*of dog*) to bark; (*of hound*) to bay.

aboyeur, -euse [abwajœr, -øz] **1.** *a.* barking (dog). **2.** *n. F:* tout, *U.S:* barker in front of booth, etc.). **3.** *n.m. Orn:* sandpiper.

abracadabra [abrakadabra] *n.m.* abracadabra.

abracadabrant [abrakadabrɑ̃] *a. F:* stupendous, amazing; extraordinary; cock-and-bull (story).

abraser [abraze] *v.tr.* to abrade.

abrasif, -ive [abrazif, iv] *a. & n.m.* abrasive.

abrasion [abrazjɔ̃] *n.f.* abrasion.

abrégé [abreʒe] *n.m.* abridgment, précis, summary; abstract; **en a.,** in abridged, abbreviated, form; **a. d'histoire de France,** short history of France; **voici les faits en a.,** here are the facts in a few words.

abrégement [abrɛʒmɑ̃] *n.m.* **1.** (*a*) summarizing (of speech, etc.); (*b*) shortening (of syllable). **2.** abridgment); summary, précis; **a. (d'un ouvrage),** abridged edition (of a work).

abréger [abreʒe] *v.tr.* **(j'abrège, n. abrégeons; j'abrégerai) 1.** to shorten, to cut short (life, work, etc); **pour a.,** to be brief; to cut it short. **2.** to abridge, cut down (article); to abbreviate (word). **3.** (*of days, etc.*) **s'a.,** to grow shorter; to shorten.

abreuvage [abrœvaʒ] *n.m.*, **abreuvement** [abrœvmɑ̃] *n.m.* **1.** watering (of animals). **2.** (*a*) drenching (of meadow); (*b*) priming (of pump); (*c*) seasoning (of casks).

abreuver [abrœve] *v.tr.* **1.** to water (horses, cattle, etc.); to supply (animals) with drink. **2.** (*a*) to flood, irrigate (meadow, etc.); **l'Egypte est abreuvée par le Nil,** Egypt is watered by the Nile; (*b*) to prime (a pump); (*c*) to season (casks). **3. s'a.,** (i) (*of horse*) to drink; (ii) *F:* (*of pers.*) to drink copiously, to swill it down.

abreuvoir [abrœvwar] *n.m.* (*a*) watering place (in river, etc.); horse pond; **mener les chevaux à l'a.,** to water the horses; (*b*) drinking trough.

abréviation [abrevjasjɔ̃] *n.f.* **1.** shortening (of term of imprisonment). **2.** abbreviation (of word).

abri [abri] *n.m.* shelter, cover; screen; *Hort:* (tent) cloche; **a. public,** public shelter; **a. de sous-marins,** submarine pen; **a. bétonné,** bunker; *Prehist:* **a. sous roche,** rock shelter; **prendre a.,** to take cover; **famille sans a.,** homeless family; **à l'a.,** sheltered, under shelter, under cover; **mettre qch. à l'a.,** to shelter, screen, sth; **se mettre à l'a.,** to take shelter; **à l'a. de qch.,** sheltered, screened, from sth.; **se mettre à l'a. de la pluie,** to (take) shelter from the rain; **a. contre le vent,** windscreen; *Nau:* **à l'a. de la côte,** under the lee of the shore.

abribus [abribys] *n.m.* bus shelter.

abricot [abriko] **1.** *n.m.* apricot. **2.** *a.inv.* apricot-coloured.

abricoté [abrikɔte] **1.** *a.* apricot flavoured. **2.** *n.m.* slice of crystallized, candied, apricot.

abricotier [abrikɔtje] *n.m.* apricot tree.

abri-garage [abrigaraʒ] *n.m.* carport.

abriter [abrite] *v.tr.* **1.** to shelter, screen, shield, shade, protect; **a. des plantes contre le vent,** to screen plants from the wind. **2.** to house; **cet hôtel peut a. cent personnes,** this hotel can accommodate a hundred people. **3. s'a.,** to take cover, shelter (**contre,** from); **s'a. derrière qn,** to shelter behind s.o.

abrivent [abrivɑ̃] *n.m. Hort:* windbreak.

abrogation [abrɔgasjɔ̃] *n.f.* abrogation, rescinding, repeal (of law, etc.).

abroger [abrɔʒe] *v.tr.* **(j'abrogeai(s); n. abrogeons)** to abrogate, rescind, repeal (law, etc.).

abrupt [abrypt] *a.* **1.** sheer, steep (rock, descent). **2.** abrupt, blunt; **répondre d'un ton a.,** to give an abrupt, short, answer.

abruptemement [abryptmɑ̃] *adv.* **1.** sheerly, steeply. **2.** abruptly, sharply.

abruti, -ie [abryti] **1.** *a.* (*a*) stupefied, dazed; exhausted (by heat, work, etc.); **a. par l'alcool,** stupefied, sodden, with drink; (*b*) *F:* stupid, idiotic, moronic; **avoir un air a.,** to look stupid, moronic. **2.** *n. F:* idiot; **quel a.!** what a nit! **espèce d'a.!** you fool!

abrutir [abrytir] *v.* **1.** *v.tr.* (*a*) *O: & Lit:* to stupefy; (*b*) to exhaust (s.o.); ce travail m'abrutit, this work's exhausting me, wearing me out. **2. on s'abrutit à trop regarder la télévision,** too much television is mind destroying.

abrutissant [abrytisɑ̃] *a.* (*a*) *O: & Lit:* degrading; mind-destroying; (*b*) exhausting, wearing; **travail a.,** (i) exhausting, (ii) deadly dull, work.

abrutissement [abrytismɑ̃] *n.m.* **1.** *O:* degradation. **2. propagande qui cause l'a. des masses,** propaganda that stops people thinking for themselves.

absence [apsɑ̃s] *n.f.* **1.** absence; **en, pendant, mon a.,** in, during my absence; when I am, was, away; **en l'a. de ma secrétaire,** while, when, my secretary is away; **en l'a. d'une secrétaire,** as I have no secretary; **remarquer l'a. de qn,** to miss s.o.; **nous avons regretté votre a.,** we were sorry that you weren't with us; **briller par son a.,** to be conspicuous by one's absence; **a. de l'école,** non-attendance at, absence from, school; **faire des absences,** to play truant; *Mil: etc.* **a. illégale,** absence without leave. **2.** (*a*) **a. de goût,** (i) lack of taste; (ii) tastelessness; **a. d'imagination,** lack of imagination; (*b*) **a. d'esprit,** absence of mind; absentmindedness; **il a des absences,** he's apt to be absentminded; **dans un moment d'a.,** in an absentminded moment; without thinking. **3.** *Med:* **a. (épileptique),** epileptic vertigo.

absent, -ente [apsɑ̃, -ɑ̃t] **1.** *a.* (*a*) absent; away; **il est a. de Paris en ce moment,** he isn't in Paris at the moment; **quand ma femme est absente je suis obligé de faire la cuisine,** I have to do the cooking when my wife's away; **il est souvent a. à l'école,** he's often away from school; **a. sans permission,** absent without leave; (*b*) absent, missing; **chez cet animal les dents sont absentes,** this animal is edentate, has no teeth. **2.** *a.* (*pers.*) distrait; **son esprit est a.,** his mind is far away; *F:* he isn't with us. **3.** *n.* absentee; missing person; **les absents ont toujours tort,** the absent are always in the wrong.

absentéisme [apsɑ̃teism] *n.m.* absenteeism.

absenter (s') [sapsɑ̃te] *v.pr.* to go away (from home); to stay, stop, away (from school).

absidal, -aux [apsidal, -o] *a.* apsidal.

abside [apsid] *n.f. Ecc.Arch:* apse.

absidiole [apsidjɔl] *n.f. Ecc.Arch:* apsidal chapel

absinthe [apsɛ̃t] *n.f.* **1.** *Bot:* wormwood. **2.** (*drink*) absinthe.

absolu [apsɔly] **1.** *a.* absolute; (*a*) **zéro a.,** absolute zero; *Gram:* **ablatif a.,** ablative absolute; **poser une règle absolue,** to lay down a hard and fast rule; **refus a.,** flat refusal; **majorité absolue,** absolute majority; (*b*) **pouvoir a.,** absolute power; **caractère a.,** autocratic nature; (*c*) peremptory (tone, voice). **2.** *n.m. Phil:* **l'a.,** the absolute.

absolument [apsɔlymɑ̃] *adv.* (*a*) **régner a.,** to reign absolutely; **a. parlant,** speaking generally; (*b*) entirely (unnecessary); utterly (impossible); **j'ai a. oublié,** I completely forgot; **a. rien,** nothing whatever; (*c*) (to speak) peremptorily; **c'est a. défendu,** it is absolutely, strictly, forbidden; **je le veux a.,** I insist on it; **nier a. qch.,** to deny sth. flatly; (*d*) **vous devez a. y aller!** you simply *must* go (there)!

absolution [apsɔlysjɔ̃] *n.f.* **1.** *Theol:* absolution. **2.** *Jur:* discharge, acquittal.

absorbant [apsɔrbɑ̃] **1.** *a. & n.m.* absorbent (substance). **2.** absorbing, engrossing (book, task).

absorber [apsɔrbe] *v.tr.* **1.** (*of sponge, etc.*) to absorb, soak up (water, etc.); *Ch:* to occlude (a gas). **2.** to consume (food, etc.); to drink (beer, etc.); to take (medicine). **3.** to absorb, engross; to take up (time); **son travail l'absorbe,** he's completely wrapped up in his work. **4. s'a.,** to become absorbed, engrossed (**dans,** in); **être absorbé dans ses pensées,** to be lost in thought; **s'absorber dans la lecture d'un livre,** to be absorbed, lost, in a book.

absorption [apsɔrpsjɔ̃] *n.f.* absorption.

absoudre [apsudr] *v.tr.* (*pr.p.* **absolvant;** *p.p.* **absous,** *f.* **absoute;** *pr.ind.* **j'absous, il absout, n. absolvons, ils absolvent;** *pr.sub.* **j'absolve;** *p.h. & p.sub.* are lacking; *fu.* **j'absoudrai)** (*a*) **a. qn de qch.,** (i) to forgive s.o. sth.; (*b*) **a. qn de ses péchés,** to grant s.o. remission of his sins.

abstenir (s') [sapstənir] *v.pr.* (*conj. like* TENIR) to stand aside, aloof, *esp.* to abstain from voting; **s'a. de qch.,** to abstain from sth.; to forgo sth.; **s'a. de faire qch.,** to abstain, refrain, from doing sth; **dans le doute abstiens-toi,** when in doubt, don't.

abstention [apstɑ̃sjɔ̃] *n.f.* abstention (**de,** from).

abstentionnisme [apstɑ̃sjɔnism] *n.m. esp. Pol:* abstention (from voting, etc.).

abstentionniste [apstɑ̃sjɔnist] *a. & n. esp. Pol:* abstentionist.

abstinence [apstinɑ̃s] *n.f.* **1.** abstinence; abstemiousness; *Ecc:* **jour d'a.,** day of abstinence. **2.** abstention (**de,** from); *Med:* **symptômes d'a.,** withdrawal symptoms.

abstinent, -ente [apstinɑ̃, -ɑ̃t] **1.** *a.* abstemious. **2.** *n.* abstainer, teetotaller.

abstraction [apstraksjɔ̃] *n.f.* (*a*) abstraction; **faire a. de qch.,** to disregard sth.; **a. faite du style,** style apart; (*b*) **se perdre dans des abstractions,** to lose oneself in abstractions; (*c*) **dans un moment d'a.,** in an absentminded moment; **par a.,** absentmindedly.

abstraire [apstrɛr] *v.* (*conj. like* TRAIRE) **1.** *v.tr.* to abstract; to separate; to consider (sth.) apart (from sth.). **2. s'a. (dans, en, qch.),** to become engrossed (in sth.); to cut oneself off.

abstrait [apstrɛ] *a.* **1.** abstracted, absorbed. **2.** abstract (idea, etc.); abstruse, deep (question).

abstraitement [apstrɛtmɑ̃] *adv.* **1.** in the abstract. **2.** abstractedly; absentmindedly.

abstrus [apstry] *a.* abstruse, recondite.

absurde [apsyrd] **1.** *a.* absurd, preposterous, nonsensical. **2.** *n.m.* **l'a.,** absurdity; **réduire une théorie à l'a.,** to reduce a theory *ad absurdum.*

absurdement [apsyrdəmɑ̃] *adv.* absurdly, preposterously.

absurdité [apsyrdite] *n.f.* **1.** absurdity, preposterousness. **2. dire des absurdités,** to talk nonsense.

abus [aby] *n.m.* **1.** (*a*) abuse, misuse (**de,** of); **employer un terme par a.,** to misuse a term; (*b*) over-indulgence (**de,** in); **faire a. de qch.,** to indulge too freely in sth.; (*c*) violation (of rights); **a. de confiance,** breach of trust. **2.** abuse; corrupt practice; **réformer un a.,** to remedy an abuse. **3.** error, mistake; **c'est un a. (que) de croire que . . .,** it is a mistake to suppose that . . . . **4.** *F:* **il y a de l'a.!** that's going too far!

abuser [abyze] **1.** *v.i.* **a. de qch.,** (i) to misuse sth.; (ii) to take (an unfair) advantage of sth.; **vous abusez de vos forces,** you're overtaxing yourself; **a. du tabac,** to smoke too much; **a. de l'amabilité de qn,** to impose, on s.o., on s.o.'s kindness; **j'abuse de votre temps,** I am taking up too much of your time; **a. d'une femme,** to seduce a woman; **n'abusez point,** be moderate; **je ne voudrais pas a., j'ai peur d'a.,** I don't want to cause you any inconvenience; **vous abusez!** that's a bit much! **2.** *v.tr.* to deceive.

abusif, -ive [abyzif, -iv] *a.* **1.** incorrect (use of a word). **2.** excessive; **emploi a. de la force,** excessive, unwarranted, display of force; **mère abusive,** possessive mother.

abusivement [abyzivmɑ̃] *adv.* incorrectly, wrongly; **employer un mot a.,** to use a word incorrectly, in the wrong meaning.

abuter [abyte] **1.** *v.i. Carp:* to abut, to butt. **2.** *v.tr.* **a. un camion à un quai,** to back a lorry against a platform.

abyssal, -aux [abisal, -o] *a.* **1.** *Oc:* abyssal (fauna, etc.); **la région abyssale,** the ocean deeps. **2.** unfathomable.

Abyssinie [abisini] *Pr.n.f. Geog:* Abyssinia.

abyssinien, -ienne [abisinjɛ̃, -jɛn] *a. & n. Geog:* Abyssinian.

acabit [akabi] *n.m. F: often Pej:* nature (of person); (good, bad) quality (of fruit, etc.); **ils sont du même a.,** they're all tarred with the same brush.

acacia [akasja] *n.m. Bot:* **1. a. vrai,** acacia. **2. a. vulgaire, faux a.,** locust tree, false acacia.

académicien [akademisjɛ̃] *n.m.* academician, *esp.* member of the *Académie française.*

académie [akademi] *n.f.* **1.** (*a*) academy (of Plato, etc.); (*b*) educational district (of France). **2.** society (of letters, science, art); **l'A. française,** the French Academy (of letters). **3.** (*a*) riding school; (*b*) **a. de musique,** school of music; **a. de danse,** dancing school; **a. de dessin,** school of art, art school. **4.** (*a*) study from the nude; (*b*) *F:* body.

académique [akademik] *a.* **1.** academic(al); **les palmes académiques,** insignia of decoration granted by the French Ministry of Education; **séance a.,** sitting, meeting, of an Academy; **occuper un fauteuil a.,** to be a member of the French Academy; *Lit:* **style a.,** academic, *Pej:* pedantic, style; **débat a.,** academic discussion. **2.** *Art:* **figure a.,** nude; academy figure.

académisme [akademism] *n.m. Art:* academism.

acajou [akaʒu] *n.m.* **1.** mahogany. **2. noix d'a.,** cashew nut.

acanthe [akɑ̃t] *n.f. Bot: Arch:* acanthus.

acariâtre [akarjɑtr̥] *a.* (*esp. of women*) bad tempered, cantankerous, shrewish.

acariâtreté [akarjɑtrəte] *n.f.* cantankerousness.

accablant [akɑblɑ̃] *a.* **1.** overwhelming (misfortune, proof). **2.** overpowering, oppressive (heat).

accablé [akɑble] *a.* overwhelmed (with work, etc.); overcome, weighted down (with grief); tired out; **a. de fatigue,** worn out with fatigue; **a. par la chaleur,** prostrated by the heat.

accablement [akɑbləmɑ̃] *n.m.* dejection, despondency, depression; *Med:* prostration.

accabler [akɑble] *v.tr.* **1.** to overpower, overwhelm, crush; **a. qn d'injures,** to heap abuse on s.o. **2.** to overwhelm (*in a favourable sense*).

accalmie [akalmi] *n.f.* lull (in the storm, in war).

accaparant [akaparɑ̃] *a.* engrossing, absorbing.

accaparement [akaparmɑ̃] *n.m.* monopolizing; buying up (of stocks); cornering (of goods).

accaparer [akapare] *v.tr.* to corner, hoard (goods); to buy up (stocks); to seize upon (sth.); **a. la conversation,** to monopolize the conversation; **a. les meilleures places,** to secure, grab, corner, the best seats.

accapareur, -euse [akaparœr, -øz] *n.* (*a*) buyer-up (of food, etc.); monopolizer; monopolist; (*b*) *Pej:* grabber; (*c*) *a.* possessive (person).

accéder [aksede] *v.i.* **(j'accède, n. accédons; j'accéderai) 1.** to have access (à, to); **on accède à la porte par un escalier,** a flight of steps leads to the door. **2. a. à une requête,** to comply with a request; **a. à une condition,** to agree, assent, to a condition. **3. a. au trône,** to accede to the throne.

accélérateur, -trice [akseleratœr, -tris] **1.** *a.* accelerative, accelerating. **2.** *n.m.* accelerator; **a. de particules,** cyclotron; **a. d'électrons,** betatron; *Aut:* **appuyer sur l'a.,** to accelerate; to put on speed.

accélération [akselerasjɔ̃] *n.f.* (*a*) acceleration; **a. de la pesanteur,** gravitational acceleration; *Aut:* **pédale d'a.,** accelerator (pedal); (*b*) speeding up (of work).

accéléré [akselere] **1.** *a.* accelerated (motion). **2.** *a.* quick, fast, rapid. **3.** *n.m. Cin:* accelerated motion.

accélérer [akselere] *v.tr.* **(j'accélère, n. accélérons; j'accélérerai)** to accelerate; to speed up.

accent [aksɑ̃] *n.m.* **1.** accent; stress; **a. tonique,** tonic accent; **syllabe sans a.,** unstressed syllable. **2. a. grammatical,** grammatical accent; **a. aigu, grave,** acute, grave, accent. **3.** pronunciation; **parler le français avec un a. anglais,** to speak French with an

English accent. **4.** tone of voice; **son récit a l'a. de la vérité,** his account rings true. **5.** (*a*) **les accents du désespoir,** the accents of despair; (*b*) **les accents de la Marseillaise,** the strains of the Marseillaise.

accentuation [aksɑ̃tɥasjɔ̃] *n.f.* **1.** stressing (of syllables, etc.). **2.** accentuation; placing of the grammatical accents.

accentuer [aksɑ̃tɥe] *v.tr.* **1.** to stress (syllable, etc.); **syllabe non accentuée,** unstressed syllable. **2.** to mark (vowel) with an accent; to accentuate. **3.** to emphasize; **traits fortement accentués,** pronounced, strongly marked, features; **a. le chômage,** to increase, add to, unemployment. **4. s'a.,** to become accentuated, more pronounced.

acceptabilité [aksɛptabilite] *n.f.* acceptableness, acceptability.

acceptable [aksɛptabl̩] *a.* **1.** acceptable (**à,** to); **offre a.,** reasonable offer; **cadeau très a.,** very acceptable, welcome, gift. **2.** in fair condition; reasonably good; that will pass muster.

acceptablement [aksɛptabləmɑ̃] *adv.* acceptably, in an acceptable manner.

acceptant, -ante [aksɛptɑ̃, -ɑ̃t] *a. & n. Com:* acceptant.

acceptation [aksɛptasjɔ̃] *n.f.* acceptance.

accepter [aksɛpte] *v.tr.* to accept; to take up (a challenge); to take on (a bet); to honour, to accept (a bill); **a. de faire qch.,** (i) to agree to do sth.; (ii) to accept an invitation to do sth.; **a. qn comme, pour, arbitre,** to accept s.o. as an arbitrator.

accepteur [aksɛptœr] *n.m.* **1.** *Com:* acceptor, drawee (of bill). **2.** *Ch: Elcs:* acceptor.

acception [aksɛpsjɔ̃] *n.f.* acceptation, meaning, sense (of word, etc.).

accès [aksɛ] *n.m.* **1.** access, approach; **les a. de la gare,** the station approaches; **avoir a. à qch.,** to have access to sth.; **donner a. à qch.,** to give access, to lead, to sth.; **trouver a. auprès de qn,** to gain admission to s.o.; *Nau:* **carte d'a. à bord,** embarkation card; *P.N:* **a. aux quais,** to the trains. **2.** fit, attack, outburst; **a. de fièvre,** attack, bout, of fever; **a. de faiblesse,** fainting fit; **a. d'enthousiasme,** burst, fit, of enthusiasm; **a. de colère, de folie,** outburst of passion; fit of madness; **travailler par a.,** to work by fits and starts.

accessibilité [aksɛsibilite] *n.f.* accessibility.

accessible [aksɛsibl] *a.* **1.** accessible; **endroit a.,** accessible place; place that can be reached easily. **2.** (*of pers.*) (*a*) approachable; (*b*) **a. à la pitié,** open to pity; **a. à la flatterie,** susceptible to flattery.

accession [aksɛsjɔ̃] *n.f.* **1.** accession (to power, etc.); **a au trône,** accession to the throne. **2.** union (of Brittany with France, etc.). **3.** adherence, adhesion (to a contract, to a party).

accessit [aksɛsit] *n.m.* 'proxime accessit'; honourable mention; certificate of merit.

accessoire [aksɛswar] **1.** *a.* accessory; **jouer un rôle a.,** to play a subordinate part. **2.** *n.m.* accessory, appurtenance; *Th: etc:* **accessoires,** properties, *F:* props; **magasin des accessoires,** property room.

accessoiriste [aksɛswarist] *n. Th: etc:* props (man), property mistress.

accident [aksidɑ̃] *n.m.* **1.** accident; (*a*) **je l'ai retrouvé par accident,** I found it by accident, accidentally; (*b*) mishap; **a. de chemin de fer,** railway accident; **accidents du travail,** industrial injuries; **a. d'avion, d'aviation,** plane crash, air crash; **a. mortel,** fatality; **être victime d'un a.,** to meet with an accident; **nous sommes arrivés sans a.,** we arrived safely. **2.** *Mus:* accidental. **3. a. de terrain,** unevenness, irregularity, of the ground.

accidenté, -ée [aksidɑ̃te] **1.** *a.* (*a*) eventful (life); (*b*) uneven, broken (ground); (*c*) *F:* **voiture accidentée,** damaged car. **2.** *n.* victim of an accident; **les accidentés,** the injured, the casualties.

accidentel, -elle [aksidɑ̃tɛl] *a.* **1.** accidental, undesigned; **mort accidentelle,** death in, as a result of, an accident. **2.** *Mus:* **signes accidentels,** (i) accidentals; (ii) key signature.

accidentellement [aksidɑ̃tɛlmɛ̃] *adv.* accidentally; (to die) in, as the result of, an accident.

accidenter [aksidɑ̃te] *v.tr.* **1.** to give variety to (the landscape, etc.); to vary (one's style, etc.). **2.** *F:* to damage in an accident.

acclamatif, -ive [aklamatif, -iv] *a.* acclamatory.

acclamation [aklamasjɔ̃] *n.f.* acclamation, cheering; **discours salué d'acclamations,** speech greeted with cheers.

acclamer [aklame] *v.tr.* (*a*) to acclaim, applaud, cheer; to greet (s.o.) with cheers; (*b*) **a. qn empereur,** to acclaim s.o. emperor.

acclimatation [aklimatasjɔ̃] *n.f.* acclimatization; **jardin d'a.,** zoological gardens.

acclimatement [aklimatmɑ̃] *n.m.* acclimat(iz)ation.

acclimater [aklimate] *v.tr.* **1.** to acclimatize (**à,** to); to introduce (an idea). **2. s'a.,** to become, get, acclimatized.

accointance [akwɛ̃tɑ̃s] *n.f. usu. pl. Pej:* intimacy; dealings, relations (**avec,** with).

accointer (s') [sakwɛ̃te] *v.pr. Pej:* **s'a. avec qn,** to take up with s.o.

accolade [akɔlad] *n.f.* **1.** (formal) embrace. **2.** accolade; **recevoir l'a.,** to be knighted. **3.** *Mus: Typ:* brace, bracket. **4.** *Arch:* **arc en a.,** ogee arch.

accolader [akɔlade] *v.tr.* **1.** (*a*) to embrace (s.o.); (*b*) to confer the accolade upon (s.o.). **2.** to bracket.

accolement [akɔlmɑ̃] *n.m.* joining, bracketing.

accoler [akɔle] *v.* **I.** *v.tr.* (*a*) to join side by side; to couple; *Typ:* to brace, bracket; **accolé aux murs de la ville,** built on the town walls; (*b*) to tie up (vine, etc.). **II. s'accoler 1.** (*of plants*) to intertwine, to cling. **2.** *F:* **s'a. avec une femme,** to associate, to take up, *F:* to hook up, with a woman.

accolure [akɔlyr] *n.f.* **1.** twine (for tying up plant). **2.** *Bookb: pl.* bands. **3.** raft (of floated timber).

accommodant [akɔmɔdɑ̃] *a.* good-natured, easy-going, easy to deal with, accommodating; **peu a.,** not easy to deal with, (*of pers.*) difficult.

accommodation [akɔmɔdasjɔ̃] *n.f.* **1.** adapting; **a. d'une pièce aux usages d'un bureau,** adaptation, conversion, of a room for office use. **2.** *Physiol:* accommodation (of the eye).

accommodement [akɔmɔdmɑ̃] *n.m.* compromise, arrangement; **en venir à un a.,** to come to terms (**avec,** with); **politique d'a.,** give-and-take policy; *Com:* **a. avec ses créanciers,** composition with one's creditors.

accommoder [akɔmɔde] **I.** *v.tr.* **1.** (*a*) *A:* to make (s.o.) comfortable (in an armchair, etc.); (*b*) to suit (s.o.); to answer (s.o.'s) purpose; **difficile à a.,** difficult to please. **2.** to cook, prepare (food); **a. les restes,** to use up the scraps, the leftovers; **a. une salade,** to dress a salad. **3. a qch. à qch.,** to fit, adapt, sth. to sth. **II. s'accommoder 1.** (*a*) *A:* to make oneself comfortable, to settle down (in armchair, etc.); (*b*) **il s'accommode partout, à toutes les circonstances,** he makes himself at home everywhere; he's very adaptable. **2. s'a. de qch.,** to make the best of sth., to make shift, to put up, with sth.; **je m'accommode à tout,** anything will do for me. **3. s'a. à qch.,** to adapt to sth. **4. s'a. avec qn,** (i) to come to an agreement with s.o.; (ii) to compromise with s.o.; to compound with (creditor).

accompagnateur, -trice [akɔ̃paɲatœr, -tris] *n.* **1.** *Mus:* accompanist. **2.** courier (of tour).

accompagnement [akɔ̃paɲmɑ̃] *n.m.* **1.** *Mus:* accompaniment; **chanter sans a.,** to sing unaccompanied. **2.** *Mil: etc:* close support; **tir d'a.,** supporting fire; *Av:* **chasseur d'a.,** escort fighter. **3.** *pl. Cu:* garnish; vegetables (served with meat).

accompagner [akɔ̃paɲe] *v.tr.* **1.** (*a*) to go, come, with (s.o.); **est-ce que tu vas m'a.?** are you coming with me? **a. qn jusqu'à la gare,** to see s.o. off at the station; **a. qn un bout de chemin,** to go part of the way with s.o.; (*b*) to escort (s.o.); to act as courier to (a group of tourists); **accompagné de sa, son, secrétaire,** accompanied by his secretary; (*c*) **a. qn au piano,** to accompany s.o. on the piano; **elle s'accompagne elle-même,** she plays her own accompaniments. **2. il a accompagné ses mots d'un sourire,** he said it with a smile.

accompli [akɔ̃pli] *a.* accomplished (musician, linguist, etc.); **menteur a.,** out and out, thoroughgoing, liar, **fait accompli,** accomplished fact, *fait accompli.*

accomplir [akɔ̃plir] *v.tr.* **1.** to accomplish, achieve (purpose, etc.); to carry out, fulfil (order, promise, etc.); **que la volonté du Seigneur s'accomplisse,** the Lord's will be done. **2.** to complete, finish (apprenticeship, etc.); **il a quarante ans accomplis,** he's turned forty.

accomplissement [akɔ̃plismɑ̃] *n.m.* **1.** accomplishment, performance, carrying out (of work, duty); fulfilment (of wish). **2.** completion.

accord [akɔr] *n.m.* **1.** agreement, understanding; bargain; settlement; **un a. est intervenu d'après lequel . . .,** an agreement has been reached by which . . . . **2.** agreement (**sur,** on); harmony; **vivre en, de, bon a.,** to live in perfect harmony; **d'a.,** in agreement, in accordance (**avec,** with); **mettre d'a. deux points de vue,** to reconcile two points of view; **se mettre d'a., tomber d'a., avec qn,** to come to an agreement with s.o.; **être d'a. avec qn,** to agree with s.o.; **les témoins ne sont pas d'a.,** the witnesses disagree, differ; **mes comptes sont d'a.,** my accounts balance; **tout est d'a.,** everything is settled, arranged; **d'a.!** agreed! yes, I agree! *F:* O.K.! **d'un commun a.,** by common consent, by mutual agreement; **en a. avec,** in harmony, keeping, with. **3.** *Gram:* agreement, concordance (**avec,** with); **les règles d'a.,** the concords. **4.** *Mus:* chord; **a. parfait,** common chord; **faux a.,** discord; **a. arpégé, brisé, figuré,** broken chord; **a. de sensible,** dominant seventh (chord). **5.** (*a*) *Mus:* pitch, tune; **être d'a.,** to be in tune; **mettre des instruments d'a.,** to tune instruments; (*of piano, etc.*) **tenir l'a.,** to keep in tune; (*b*) *W.Tel:* **a. précis,** fine tuning; **a. silencieux,** aural null; *Elcs:* **a. d'antenne,** alignment input; (*c*) *Mec.E:* tuning.

accordage [akɔrdaʒ], **accordement** [akɔrdəmɑ̃] *n.m. Mus:* tuning.

accordéon [akɔrdeɔ̃] *n.m.* accordion; **a. hexagonal,** concertina; **a. à touches,** piano accordion; **en a.,** (i) (accordion-)pleated (skirt); (ii) *F:* crumpled (up) (mudguard, etc.); **voitures en a.,** pile-up; **ses bas sont en a.,** her stockings are coming down.

accordéoniste [akɔrdeɔnist] *n.* accordionist; accordion player, concertina player.

accorder [akɔrde] **I.** *v.tr.* **1.** (*a*) to reconcile (enemies, etc.); (*b*) *Gram:* **a. le verbe avec le sujet,** to make the verb agree with the subject. **2.** *Mus: W.Tel:* to tune (piano, radio, etc.); **a. les violons au ton du piano,** to tune the violins to the pitch of the piano. **3.** to grant (favour, etc.); **accorder des dommages-intérêts,** to award damages; **a. un escompte,** to allow a discount; **pouvez-vous m'a. quelques minutes?** can you spare me a few minutes? **a. à qn de faire qch.,** to give s.o. permission to do sth.; **on m'a accordé huit jours de congé,** I have been given a week's leave; **s'accorder dix minutes de repos,** to allow oneself ten minutes' rest. **II. s'accorder 1.** (*of pers.*) (*a*) to agree, come to an agreement (about sth.); to come to terms (**avec qn,** with s.o.); **s'a. sur le prix,** to agee on the price; **s'a. à, pour, faire qch.,** to agree to do sth.; (*b*) to get on (well, badly) (**avec qn,** with s.o.); **ils s'accordent mal ensemble,** they don't get on (at all) well; **ils s'accordent très bien,** they get on very well (together). **2.** (*of fact or thg*) to correspond, harmonize, tally, square, fit in (**avec,** with); **cette action ne s'accorde pas avec son caractère,** this action is not in keeping, in line, with his character; **cela ne s'accorde pas avec mes idées,** it doesn't fit in with my ideas; *Com:* **faire a. les livres,** to agree the books. **3. s.a. avec qch.,** (i) to fit in with, to be consistent with (theory, plan); (ii) (*of article of dress, etc.*) to go with, harmonize with (sth.). **4.** *Mus:* to tune (up).

accordeur [akɔrdœr] *n.m.* (piano) tuner.

accordoir [akɔrdwar] *n.m.* (piano) tuning key.

accostage [akɔstaʒ] *n.m.* **1.** accosting (s.o.). **2.** (*a*) *Nau:* drawing alongside (quay); (*b*) *Space:* docking.

accoster [akɔste] *v.tr.* **1.** to accost (s.o.); to go, come, up to (s.o.). **2.** (*a*) **a. un bateau le long du quai,** to moor, berth, a boat alongside (the quay); *v.i.* to berth, dock; *Space:* to dock; (*b*) *Nau:* to come on board (ship).

accotement [akɔtmɑ̃] *n.m.* (*a*) verge (of road); *P.N:* **a. non stabilisé,** soft verge; (*b*) *Rail:* shoulder.

accoter [akɔte] *v.tr.* to lean (sth. against sth.); to shore up (vessel, wall, etc.); **s'a. à, contre, un mur,** to lean against a wall; **accoté contre qch.,** leaning against sth.

accotoir [akɔtwar] *n.m.* armrest, elbow rest.

accouchée [akuʃe] *n.f.* mother (of newborn child); *Med:* **salle des accouchées,** maternity ward.

accouchement [akuʃmɑ̃] *n.m.* childbirth; labour; **a. prématuré, avant terme,** premature delivery.

accoucher [akuʃe] **1.** *v.i.* (*a*) **a. d'un garçon,** to give birth to a boy; **elle accouchera dans un mois,** her baby's due in a month's time; (*b*) *F:* **mais accouche(z) donc!** come on, out with it! **2.** *v.tr.* to deliver (a mother in childbirth).

accoucheur, -euse [akuʃœr, -øz] *n.* (*a*) obstetrician; accoucheur; (*b*) *n.f.* midwife.

accouder (s') [sakude] *v.pr.* to lean on one's elbow(s).

accoudoir [akudwar] *n.m.* **1.** armrest, elbow rest. **2.** *Arch:* balustrade.

accouple [akupl̩] *n.f.* leash.

accouplement [akupləmɑ̃] *n.m.* **1.** (*a*) coupling, join(ing), link(ing); yoking (of oxen); *Mec.E:* **a. à débrayage,** disengaging gear, clutch coupling; *Aut:* **a. direct,** direct drive; *Av:* **a. bendix,** bendix drive; **a. à glissement,** slip clutch; *Av: Min:* **a. à griffe(s),** dog clutch, coupling; *Mus:* (*organ*) **pédale d'a.,** coupler (pedal); (*b*) *El:* connecting. **2.** pairing, mating.

accoupler [akuple] *v.tr.* **1.** (*a*) to couple, to join pairs; to yoke (oxen); (*b*) *Husb:* to mate (animals); (*c*) to couple (up) (parts); (*d*) *El:* to connect, group (batteries, etc.). **2. s'a.,** (i) to pair off, to team up; (ii) to mate, pair; to copulate.

accourir [akurir] *v.i.* (*conj. like* COURIR; *aux.* **avoir** *or* **être)** to run (up); to flock, rush up; **ils ont accouru, sont accourus, à mon secours,** they ran, came running, to help me.

accoutrement [akutrəmɑ̃] *n.m. usu. Pej:* dress, garb; *F:* get-up.

accoutrer [akutre] *v.tr. usu. Pej:* to rig (s.o.) out (**de,** in); **accoutré d'une vieille capote,** rigged out in an old army greatcoat.

accoutumance [akutymɑ̃s] *n.f.* **1.** (*a*) familiarization (**à,** with); **l'a. diminue le plaisir,** even pleasure palls; (*b*) inurement (**à,** to); (*c*) *Med:* **a. (à une drogue),** tolerance (for a drug). **2.** habit, usage.

accoutumé, -ée [akutyme] *a.* (*a*) usual, habitual; **à l'heure accoutumée,** at the usual time; (*b*) **à l'accoutumée,** usually; **il est arrivé à huit heures comme à l'accoutumée,** he arrived at eight o'clock as usual.
accoutumer [akutyme] *v.tr.* **1.** (*a*) **a. qn à qch.,** to accustom s.o. to sth.; (*b*) **être accoutumé à qch.,** to be accustomed, used, to sth. **2. s'a. à la fatigue,** to become accustomed, hardened, to fatigue; **je ne puis pas m'a. à m'en passer,** I can't get used to doing without it.
accouvage [akuvaʒ] *n.m. Husb:* artificial incubation.
accréditation [akreditasjɔ̃] *n.f.* accreditation, accrediting (of an ambassador).
accrédité, -ée [akredite] **1.** *a.* of good standing; accredited; **notre représentant a.,** our authorized representative. **2.** *n.* agent; holder of a letter of credit.
accréditer [akredite] *v.tr.* **1.** (*a*) to accredit (an ambassador); (*b*) *Fin:* **a. un client,** to open an account for a client. **2.** (*a*) to credit, believe (sth.); (*b*) (*of rumour, etc.*) **s'a.,** to gain ground, to spread.
accréditif [akreditif] *n.m.* letter of credit.
accroc [akro] *n.m.* **1.** tear, rent (in clothes, etc.). **2.** hitch, difficulty, snag.
accrochage [akrɔʃaʒ] *n.m.* **1.** (*a*) hooking; *Aut:* catching, scraping (of vehicle); *Nau:* running foul; *Box:* clinch; (*b*) *Rail:* hitching on, coupling; (*c*) hanging (up) (of picture, etc.); (*d*) *El:* synchronization; synchronizing; *W.Tel:* picking up (of a station); (*e*) *Sp:* recovery (from a losing position). **2.** altercation, squabble; *Mil:* brush, skirmish.
accroche [akrɔʃ] *n.f.* eye-catching advertisement; striking (publicity) slogan.
accroche-casseroles [akrɔʃkasrɔl] *n.m.inv.* saucepan rack.
accrocher [akrɔʃe] **I. 1.** *v.tr.* (*a*) to hook, catch (sth.); **a. un poisson,** to hook a fish; **titre qui accroche le lecteur,** striking, eye-catching, title; **a. sa robe sur un clou,** to catch one's dress on a nail; *Aut:* **il a accroché mon pare-choc,** he caught, hit, my bumper; *F:* **a. qn,** to buttonhole s.o.; (*b*) *Rail:* to hitch on, couple (carriage, etc.); (*c*) to grapple (ship); (*d*) to hang (sth.) up; *Const:* to hang (door); **a. son manteau,** to hang up one's coat; *P:* **a. sa montre,** to pawn, pop, one's watch; (*e*) *W.Tel:* **a. une station,** to tune in to a station. **2.** *v.i.* **les négotiations ont accroché,** there has been a hitch in the negotiations. **II. s'accrocher 1. s'a. à qn, à qch.,** to fasten on to, cling to, grapple on to, s.o., sth. **2.** to get caught (**à,** on). **3.** (*a*) *Box:* to clinch; (*b*) *F:* to have a row.
accrocheur, -euse [akrɔʃœr, -øz] *a.* (*a*) tenacious, stubborn; (*b*) eye-catching (title).
accroire [akrwar] *v.tr.* (*used only in*) **faire a. à qn que . . .,** to make s.o. believe that . . .
accroissement [akrwasmɑ̃] *n.m.* **1.** (*a*) growth, growing (of plant, etc.); (*b*) increase, increasing; **taux d'a.,** rate of increase. **2.** (amount of) increase; *Mth:* **a. d'une fonction,** increment of a function.
accroître [akrwatr̥] **1.** *v.tr.* (*pr.p.* **accroissant;** *p.p.* **accru;** *pr.ind.* **j'accrois, il accroît, n. accroissons, ils accroissent;** *impf.* **j'accroissais;** *p.h.* **j'accrus;** *fu.* **j'accroîtrai**) to increase, enlarge, add to, augment; to enhance (reputation). **2. s'a.,** to increase, grow.
accroupir (s') [sakrupir] *v.pr.* to squat (down), to crouch (down); **accroupi,** squatting, crouching.
accru [akry] *n.m. Bot:* sucker.
accu [aky] *n.m. El: F:* accumulator, battery.
accueil [akœj] *n.m.* reception, welcome, greeting; **faire bon a. à qn,** to welcome s.o.; **a. hostile, défavorable,** hostile reception; *Com:* **faire (bon) a. à une traite,** to honour a bill; **centre d'a.,** rest centre.
accueillant [akœjɑ̃] hospitable, welcoming.
accueillir [akœjir] *v.tr.* (*conj. like* CUEILLIR) to receive, greet (s.o.); **bien a. qn,** to welcome s.o.; **mal a. qn,** to give s.o. a bad reception; *Com:* **a. une traite,** to meet, honour, a bill.
acculer [akyle] **1.** *v.tr.* to drive (s.o.) back (**contre,** against); to drive (s.o.) to the wall; to bring (animal) to bay, to a stand. **2.** *v.i. Nau:* (*a*) to pitch heavily astern; (*b*) to be down by the stern. **3. s'a. à, contre, qch.,** to set one's back against sth.; to stand at bay.
accumulateur [akymylatœr] *n.m.* accumulator; battery.
accumulation [akymylasjɔ̃] *n.f.* **1.** accumulating; storage (of energy); hoarding (of money); **chauffage par a.,** storage heating. **2.** accumulation, hoard; collection.
accumuler [akymyle] *v.tr.* to accumulate, amass; to gather (together); to hoard; to heap up, to pile up.
accusateur, -trice [akyzatœr, -tris] **1.** *a.* accusatory, accusing, incriminating. **2.** *n.* accuser, indicter, impeacher, arraigner; *Hist:* **a. public,** public prosecutor.
accusatif, -ive [akyzatif, -iv] *a. & n.m. Gram:* accusative, objective (case); **mot à l'a.,** word in the accusative.
accusation [akyzasjɔ̃] *n.f.* **1.** accusation, charge; **lancer, porter, une a. contre qn,** to bring an accusation against s.o. **2.** *Jur:* **mettre qn en a.,** to commit s.o. for trial. **3.** *Pol:* impeachment, arraignment.
accusé, -ée [akyze] **1.** *a.* prominent, pronounced, bold (feature, etc.); **rides très accusées,** strongly marked wrinkles. **2.** *n.* accused (of crime); (*in court*) defendant, prisoner at the bar. **3.** *n.m.* **a. de réception,** acknowledgement (of receipt) (of a letter).
accuser [akyze] *v.tr.* **1. a. qn de qch., de faire qch.,** to accuse s.o. of (doing) sth. **2. a. qch.,** to own to, profess, sth.; **elle accuse trente ans,** (i) she owns up to being thirty; (ii) she looks (at least) thirty. **3.** to define, show up, accentuate; **esquisse qui accuse tous les muscles,** sketch that brings out every muscle; **paroles qui accusent une grande ignorance,** words that betray, show, reveal, great ignorance. **4. a. réception de qch.,** to acknowledge (receipt of) sth.
acerbe [asɛrb] *a.* **1.** tart, sour; bitter. **2.** sharp, harsh; **réprimande a.,** sharp reproof; **discussion a.,** acrid discussion; **parler d'un ton a.,** to speak sharply.
acerbité [asɛrbite] *n.f.* acerbity. **1.** tartness, bitterness, sourness. **2.** sharpness, harshness; **répondre avec a.,** to answer, sharply.
acéré [asere] *a.* (*a*) sharp(-pointed); (*b*) sharp (blade, etc.); **langue acérée,** sharp, stinging, tongue.
acérer [adere] *v.tr.* (**j'acère; j'acérerai**) to sharpen, to give a keen edge to (sth.).
acétate [asetat] *n.m. Ch:* acetate; **a. de cuivre,** copper acetate; *Tex:* **a. de cellulose,** cellulose acetate.
acétique [asetik] *a. Ch:* acetic.
acétocellulose [asetɔselyloz] *n.f. Ch:* cellulose acetate.
acétone [asetɔn] *n.f. Ch:* acetone.
acétylène [asetilɛn] *n.m.* acetylene.
achalandage [aʃalɑ̃daʒ] *n.m. Com:* **1.** working up of a clientele. **2.** (*a*) custom, customers, clientele; (*b*) goodwill; (*c*) *F:* stock (of a shop).
achalandé [aʃalɑ̃de] *a.* **magasin bien a.,** (i) well patronized shop; (ii) *F:* well stocked shop.
achalander [aʃalɑ̃de] *v.tr. F:* to stock (shop).
acharné [aʃarne] *a.* **1. meute acharnée à la poursuite,** pack in hot, eager, pursuit; **hommes acharnés les uns contre les autres,** men fighting desperately against each other. **2. joueur a.,** inveterate gambler. **3. lutte acharnée,** desperate, bitter, struggle; **concurrence acharnée,** cut-throat competition.
acharnement [aʃarnəmɑ̃] *n.m.* relentlessness; **a. au**

travail, pour le travail, passion for work; **se battre avec a.,** to fight tooth and nail.

acharner [aʃarne] **I.** *v.tr. Ven:* **a. la meute après une bête,** to set the pack on (the track of) a quarry; **a. un chien,** to flesh, blood, a hound. **II. s'acharner 1. s'a. après, contre, sur, qn,** to be dead set against s.o.; to be always on to s.o.; to have one's knife into s.o.; **le malheur s'acharne après lui,** he is dogged by misfortune. **2. s'a. à, sur, qch.,** to work desperately hard at sth.; to slave (away) at sth.; **il s'acharne à vous nuire,** he is set on harming you.

achat [aʃs] *n.m.* **1.** purchase; buying; **faire l'a. de qch.,** to buy sth.; **aller faire ses achats,** to go shopping; **pouvoir d'a.,** purchasing power; **prix d'a.,** purchase price. **2.** purchase; **voilà mes achats,** look (at) what I've bought; this is what I've bought.

acheminement [aʃminmɑ̃] *n.m.* **1.** step, progress, (**à, vers,** towards). **2.** forwarding (of goods, parcels).

acheminer [aʃmine] *v.tr.* **1.** to set s.o. on his way (**sur, vers,** to(wards)). **2.** to dispatch, to convey (goods, etc.) (**sur, vers,** to). **3. s'a. vers la maison,** to set out for, make one's way, home.

acheter [aʃte] *v.tr.* **(j'achète, n. achetons; j'achèterai)** (*a*) **a. qch.,** to buy, purchase, sth.; **a. en gros, en détail,** to buy wholesale, retail; **j'ai acheté ce livre 50 francs,** I bought this book for 50 francs; **a. qch. (à) bon marché,** to buy sth. cheap; **vous l'achetez bien cher,** it's a high price to pay for it; **ces choses ne s'achètent pas,** such things are not for sale, cannot be bought; **a. chat en poche,** to buy a pig in a poke; (*b*) **a. qch. à qn,** to buy sth. from s.o.; (*c*) **a. qch. à, pour, qn,** to buy sth. for s.o.; **je vais lui a. un livre,** I'm going to buy him a book; (*d*) *F:* to bribe (s.o.), to buy (s.o.) off.

acheteur, -euse [aʃtœr, -øz] *n.* buyer, purchaser. *Jur:* vendee.

achevé [aʃve] **1.** *a.* (*a*) accomplished (horseman, etc.); perfect (piece of work); (*b*) *F:* **sot a.,** utter, absolute, fool; **menteur a.,** consummate, out and out, liar. **2.** *n.m.* finish, perfection (of work of art).

achèvement [aʃɛvmɑ̃] *n.m.* completion, finishing, (of work); **travail en a.,** work in process of completion; **date d'a.,** target date, completion date.

achever [aʃve] *v.* **(j'achève, n. achevons; j'achèverai) I.** *v.tr.* **1.** to end, conclude, finish (off), complete (piece of work, etc.); **avant d'a. ma lettre,** before closing, finishing, my letter; *F:* **achève!** out with it! **a. de faire qch.,** to finish doing sth.; **achève de boire ton café,** drink up your coffee. **2.** to dispatch (animal, etc.); to put (animal) out of pain; *F:* **cette grosse perte l'a achevé,** this heavy loss was the end of him. **II. s'achever 1.** to draw to a close; to end; **le jour s'acheva tristement,** the day closed, ended, sadly. **2.** (*of work*) to reach completion.

achigan [aʃigɑ̃] *n.m. Ich: Fr.C:* (black) bass.

Achille [aʃill] *Pr.n.m.* Achilles.

achoppement [aʃɔpmɑ̃] *n.m.* (*a*) *Lit:* obstacle; difficulty; (*b*) **pierre d'a.,** stumbling block.

achopper (s') [saʃɔpe] *v.pr.* to stumble (**à,** against); to come to grief.

achromatique [akrɔmatik] *a.* achromatic.

acide [asid] **1.** *a.* acid, sharp, tart, sour. **2.** *n.m.* acid.

acidifier (s') [sasidif,e] *v.pr.* to become acid, to turn sour.

acidité [asidite] *n.f.* acidity, sourness, tartness.

acidose [asidoz] *n.f. Med:* acidosis.

acidulé [asidyle] *a.* acidulous; **bonbons acidulés,** acid drops.

aciduler [asidyle] *v.tr.* **1.** to acidulate (drink, etc.). **2.** to make (stomach, etc.) acid. **3. s'a.,** to turn, become, acid.

acier [asje] *n.m.* steel; **lame d'a., en a.,** steel blade; **a. trempé,** hardened steel; **a. inoxydable,** stainless steel; **a. au chrome, au nickel,** chrome steel, nickel steel; **cœur d'a.,** heart of steel; **regard d'a.,** steely look.

aciérie [asjeri] *n.f.* steel works.

aciériste [asjerist] *n.m.* steel maker, manufacturer.

acné [akne] *n.f.* acne.

acolyte [akɔlit] *n.m.* **1.** *Ecc:* acolyte. **2.** (*a*) assistant, attendant, acolyte. (*b*) *Pej:* confederate, accomplice.

acompte [akɔ̃t] *n.m.* instalment, partial payment, payment on account; **payer par acomptes,** to pay by instalments; **recevoir un a.,** to receive something on account; **a. de, sur, dividende,** interim dividend.

aconit [akɔnit] *n.m. Bot:* aconite.

Açores (les) [lezasɔr] *Pr.n.f.pl. Geog:* the Azores.

à-côté [akote] *n.m.* **1.** aside (remark). **2.** *usu. pl.* (*a*) **à-côtés d'une question,** side issues of a question; **les à-côtés de l'histoire,** sidelights on history; (*b*) *F:* extras; **il a quelques à-côtés,** he makes a bit on the side.

à-coup [aku] *n.m.* jerk, jolt, jar, shock; **il travaille par à-coups,** he works by fits and starts; *El:* surge (of current); **sans à-coups,** smoothly.

acousticien, -ienne [akustisjɛ̃, -jɛn] *n.* acoustician.

acoustique [akustik] **1.** *a.* acoustical; acoustic (nerve, etc.); **cornet a.,** ear trumpet; **tuyau a.,** speaking tube; **voûte a.,** whispering gallery. **2.** *n.f.* (*a*) acoustics; (science of) sound; (*b*) **a. d'une salle,** acoustics of a hall.

acquéreur, [akerœr] *n.m.* acquirer, purchaser, buyer; *Jur:* vendee.

acquérir [akerir] *v.tr.* (*pr.p.* **acquérant;** *p.p.* **acquis;** *pr.ind.* **j'acquiers, il acquiert, n. acquérons, ils acquièrent;** *pr.sub.* **j'acquière, n. acquérions;** *impf.* **j'acquérais;** *p.h.* **j'acquis;** *fu.* **j'acquerrai**). **1.** (*a*) to acquire, obtain, get, win, gain; to get into (a habit); **l'expérience acquise au long d'une carrière,** the experience gained in the course of one's career; **a. de mauvaises habitudes,** to get into bad habits; *Prov:* **un bien en acquiert un autre,** money begets money; (*b*) (*of wine*) **a. en vieillissant,** to improve with age; (*c*) **s'a. une mauvaise réputation,** to get oneself a bad name. **2. a. une terre d'un voisin,** to purchase, buy, land from a neighbour.

acquêt [akɛ] *n.m.* acquisition; windfall.

acquiescement [akjɛsmɑ̃] *n.m.* acquiescence.

acquiescer [akjɛse] *v.i.* **(j'acquiesçai(s); n. acquiesçons) a. à qch.,** to acquiesce in sth.; to agree, assent, to sth.

acquis [aki] **1.** *a.* (*a*) acquired (knowledge, etc.); (*b*) **fait a.,** established, accepted, fact; **tenir pour a.,** to take for granted; **droits a.,** vested interests; **je vous suis tout a.,** I am entirely yours. **2.** *n.m.* acquired knowledge, attainments, experience.

acquisitif, -ive [akizitif, -iv] *a.* acquisitive.

acquisition [akizisjɔ̃] *n.f.* **1.** acquisition, acquiring; **faire l'a. de qch.,** to acquire, purchase, sth. **2.** (*a*) acquisition, purchase; (*b*) **acquisitions de l'esprit,** intellectual attainments.

acquit [aki] *n.m.* **1.** *Com:* (*a*) receipt, acquittance; **donner a. de qch.,** to give a receipt for sth.; **pour a.,** received (with thanks); paid; (*b*) *Cust:* clearance (of ship). **2.** discharge, release (from promise); **faire qch. par manière d'a.,** to do sth. as a matter of form. **3.** *Jur:* **sentence, ordonnance, d'a.,** order of acquittal.

acquit-à-caution [akiakosjɔ̃] *n.m. Cust:* permit; transire; excise bond. *pl. acquits-à-caution.*

acquittement [akitmɑ̃] *n.m.* **1.** discharge, payment (of debt, etc.). **2.** *Jur:* acquittal; **verdict d'a.,** verdict of not guilty.

acquitter [akite] **I.** *v.tr.* **1.** (*a*) **a. qn (d'une obligation, etc.),** to release s.o. (from an obligation, etc.); (*b*) **a. un accusé,** to acquit, discharge, an accused person. **2.** (*a*) **a. une obligation,** to fulfil an obligation; **a. une**

dette, to discharge a debt; (*b*) **a. une facture,** to receipt a bill. **II. s'acquitter 1. s'a. d'une obligation, d'un devoir,** to fulfil, carry out, discharge, an obligation, a duty; **s'a. de son devoir,** to do one's duty; **comment pourrai-je m'a. envers vous?** how can I repay you? **2. se bien, mal, a.,** to acquit oneself well, badly.

âcre [ɑkr̥] *a.* bitter, tart, pungent (taste, remark, etc.).

âcreté [akrəte] *n.f.* acidity, bitterness, pungency.

acrimonie [akrimɔni] *n.f.* acrimony, acrimoniousness; bitterness (of speech, quarrel).

acrimonieusement [akrimɔnjøzmɑ̃] *adv.* acrimoniously, bitterly.

acrimonieux, -euse [akrimɔnjø, -øz] *a.* acrimonious, bitter (quarrel, etc.).

acrobate [akrɔbat] **1.** *n.m. & f.* acrobat. **2.** *n.m. Z:* flying phalanger, flying squirrel.

acrobatie [akrɔbasi] *n.f.* (*a*) acrobatics; (*b*) acrobatic feat; (*c*) **a. aérienne,** stunt flying; aerobatics.

acrobatique [akrɔbatik] *a.* acrobatic.

acropole [akrɔpɔl] *n.f.* acropolis.

acrostiche [akrɔstiʃ] *a. & n.m.* acrostic.

acrylique [akrilik] *a. Ch:* acrylic.

acte [akt] *n.m.* **1.** (*a*) action, act, deed; **a. de courage,** brave action; **faire a. de bonne volonté,** to give proof of good will; **faire a. de souverain,** to exercise the royal prerogative; **a. de guerre,** act of war; (*b*) **a. de foi, de contrition,** act of faith, of contrition. **2.** *Jur:* (*a*) deed, title; any instrument embodying a transaction in real estate; **a. de vente,** bill of sale; **a. notarié, a. sur papier timbré,** deed executed and authenticated by a notary; (*b*) **a. judiciaire,** writ; **a. d'accusation,** bill of indictment; (*c*) record; **a. de naissance, de mariage, de décès,** birth, marriage, death, certificate; **a. de dernière volonté,** last will and testament; **prendre a. de qch.,** to record, note, take a note of, set down, sth.; **donner a. de qch.,** to grant, to admit sth.; (*d*) *pl.* records (of proceedings, etc.); transactions (of scientific body, etc.); *B:* **les Actes des Apôtres,** the Acts of the Apostles. **3.** *Th:* act.

acteur, -trice [aktœr, -tris] *n.* (*a*) actor, actress; **se faire a.,** to go on the stage; **a. à transformations,** quick-change artist; (*b*) participant (in an event).

actif, -ive [aktif, -iv] **1.** *a.* (*a*) active (supporter, drug, *Gram:* verb, voice); potent (drug, etc.); **a. à défendre ses amis,** active in the defence of one's friends; *Pol.Ec:* **population active,** gainfully employed, working, population; **armée active,** regular army; **service a.,** active service; (*b*) active, brisk, sprightly, agile, alert (person, etc.); **faire un commerce a.,** to do a brisk trade. **2.** *n.m.* (*a*) *Com:* assets; credit (account); **mettre qch. à l'a. de qn,** to credit s.o. with sth.; (*b*) *Gram:* **verbe à l'a.,** verb in the active voice.

action [aksjɔ̃] *n.f.* **1.** (*a*) action, act; **l'a. de marcher,** the action, act, of walking; **homme d'a.,** man of action; (*b*) action, deed, exploit; **a. d'éclat,** brilliant feat of arms. **2.** (*a*) (i) **a. sur qch.,** action, effect, on sth.; (ii) **a. sur qn,** influence over s.o.; **événements en dehors de notre a.,** events beyond our control; **sans a.,** ineffectual, ineffective; (*b*) **a. de l'eau, du feu, etc.,** agency, effect, of water, fire, etc.; (*c*) action, motion, working, functioning (of machine, etc.); (*of regulation, etc.*) **entrer en a.,** to come into force, into operation; **hors d'a.,** out of action, out of gear. **3.** (*a*) action, gesture (of orator, etc.); (*b*) *Th: Lit:* action; **scène qui retarde l'a.,** scene that delays the action; (*c*) plot (of play, novel). **4.** *Fin:* share; share certificate; **a. ordinaire,** ordinary share; **a. privilégiée,** preference share; **compagnie par actions,** joint-stock company; *Fig:* **ses actions montent, baissent,** his stock is going up, going down. **5.** *Jur:* action, lawsuit, trial; **intenter une a. à qn,** to bring an action against s.o.; to sue s.o.; **a. en divorce,** divorce suit. **6.** *Mil:* action, fight, engagement. **7.** *Sw.Fr:* **vente a.,** bargain offer.

actionnable [aksjɔnabl̥] *a. Jur:* actionable.

actionnaire [aksjɔnɛr] *n.m. & f.* shareholder.

actionnement [aksjɔnmɑ̃] *n.m.* activation.

actionner [aksjɔne] *v.tr.* **1.** (*a*) *Jur:* to sue (s.o.), to bring an action against (s.o.); **a. qn en dommages-intérêts,** to sue s.o. for damages; (*b*) *F:* **a. qn,** to rouse, stir, s.o. to action. **2.** *Mec.E:* to set (sth.) in action, in motion; to operate, drive, run (machine, etc.); **actionné à la main,** hand operated; **a. les freins,** to apply, put on, the brakes. **3.** *F:* **s'a.,** to buck up, get a move on.

activation [aktivasjɔ̃] *n.f.* activation.

activé [aktive] *a. Ch:* activated.

activement [aktivmɑ̃] *adv.* actively, briskly, busily.

activer [aktive] *v.tr.* **1.** (*a*) to stimulate; to rouse; to speed up; **a. un ouvrage,** to speed up, to press on with, a piece of work; *F:* **activez!** get a move on! (*b*) *Ch: etc:* to activate. **2. s'a.,** to be busy; to bustle about; **s'a. (à qch.),** to get on, press on (with sth.).

activiste [aktivist] *a. & n.* activist.

activité [aktivite] *n.f.* **1.** activity; potency (of drug, etc.); **maintenir l'a. de l'industrie,** to keep industry going. **2.** activity, quickness, briskness, dispatch. **3. en a.,** in activity, in action, in operation, in progress, at work; **en pleine a.,** in full operation; **un moment de grande a.,** a very busy time; **marché sans a.,** dull market; **l'usine est en a.,** the factory is working, is in production; **volcan en a.,** volcano in eruption; **être en a. (de service),** to be on active duty, on the active list; *Sch: etc:* **activités dirigées,** projects.

actrice *see* ACTEUR.

actuaire [aktɥɛr] *n.m. Ins:* actuary.

actualisation [aktɥalizasjɔ̃] *n.f.* **1.** *Phil:* actualization. **2.** *Pol.Ec:* updating; **taux d'a.,** rate of discount.

actualiser [aktɥalize] *v.tr.* **1.** to turn (sth.) into a reality; to actualize. **2.** to bring up to date. **3. s'a.,** to become a reality; to come into being.

actualité [aktɥalite] *n.f.* **1.** actuality, reality. **2.** question of the day, of the moment; **cette question est toujours d'a.,** this question is still, always, with us; **les actualités,** current events; *TV:* news.

actuel, -elle [aktɥɛl] *a.* of the present day; existing, current; **le gouvernement a.,** the present government; **l'état a. du pays,** the present state of the country, nation; **valeur actuelle,** present value; **à l'heure actuelle,** at the present time.

actuellement [aktɥɛlmɑ̃] *adv.* (just) now, at present, at the present time.

acuité [akɥite] *n.f.* acuteness, sharpness, keenness (of point, pain, etc.); **a. d'un son,** high pitch of a sound; **a. visuelle,** keenness of sight.

acuponcteur, acupuncteur [akypɔ̃ktœr] *n.m. Med:* acupuncturist.

acuponcture, acupuncture [akypɔ̃ktyr] *n.f. Med:* acupuncture.

acutangle [akytɑ̃gl̥] *a. Mth:* acute-angled.

adage [adaʒ] *n.m.* adage, (common) saying; proverb; **selon l'a.,** as the saying goes.

Adam [adɑ̃] *Pr.n.m.* Adam; *F:* **dans le costume d'A.,** in one's birthday suit.

adaptable [adaptabl̥] *a.* adaptable; flexible.

adaptateur, -trice [adaptatœr, -tris] **1.** *n.m. El: Mec.E: Phot:* adapter. **2.** *n.m. W.Tel:* convertor. **3.** *n.* adapter (of book for film, etc.).

adaptation [adaptasjɔ̃] *n.f.* adaptation, adjustment, accommodation (**à,** to); *W.Tel:* matching; **faculté d'a.,** adaptability.

adapter [adapte] **I.** *v.tr.* (*a*) **a. qch. à qch.,** (i) to fit, adjust, sth. to sth.; (ii) to adapt sth. to sth.; to make sth. suitable for sth.; **a. un tube à un autre,** to make one tube fit another; **a. un roman à la scène,** to adapt a novel for the stage; (*b*) *W.Tel:* to match. **II. s'adapter. s'a. aux conditions nouvelles,** to adapt, adjust, oneself to new conditions; **il sait s'a.,** he's very adaptable.

addenda [adɛ̃da] *n.m.inv.* addendum (**à,** to).

additif, -ive [aditif, -iv] **1.** *a.* additive. **2.** *n.m.* (*a*) supplement, addition; (*b*) *Ch: etc:* additive.

addition [adisjɔ̃] *n.f.* **1.** addition, adding (to); adding up; **faire l'a. des chiffres,** to add up, *F:* tot up, the figures; **l'a. du thym améliorera le ragoût,** the addition of some thyme will improve the stew. **2.** (*a*) addition, extension; **faire une a. à une maison,** to build an extension to a house; **en a. à,** in addition to; (*b*) *Mth:* addition; (*c*) (*in restaurant, etc.*) bill, *NAm:* check; (*d*) *Typ:* marginal note.

additionnel, -elle [adisjɔnɛl] *a.* additional, extra.

additionner [adisjɔne] *v.tr. & i.* to add (up), *F:* to tot up; **lait additionné d'eau,** watered down milk; **café additionné d'eau-de-vie,** coffee laced with spirits.

additionneuse [adisjɔnøz] *n.f.* adding machine, adder; *Cmptr:* **a. imprimante,** adding lister.

adducteur [adyktœr] **1.** *a.m. Anat: etc:* adducent. **2.** *n.m.* (*a*) *Anat:* adductor; (*b*) *Civ.E:* supply main.

adduction [adyksjɔ̃] *n.f.* **1.** adduction. **2.** (*a*) *Mch: I.C.E:* admission; intake; (*b*) **a. d'eau,** canalization; **adductions d'eau,** water supply.

adénoïde [adenɔid] *a. Med:* **végétations adénoïdes,** adenoids.

adent [adɑ̃] *n.m. Carp:* dovetail.

adepte [adɛpt] *n.m. & f.* (*a*) adept, initiate; (*b*) follower, adherent.

adéquat [adekwa] *a.* adequate; appropriate.

adhérence [aderɑ̃s] *n.f.* adhesion; adherence; **a. des roues (à la route),** grip of the wheels (on the road).

adhérent, -ente [aderɑ̃, -ɑ̃t] **1.** *a.* adherent (**à,** to); adhesive; **substance adhérente,** sticky substance. **2.** *n.* member; **a. d'un parti,** member, supporter, of a party.

adhérer [adere] *v.i.* **(j'adhère, n. adhérons; j'adhérerai) 1.** to adhere, stick, cling (**aux doigts, etc.,** to the fingers, etc.); (*of wheels*) **a. à la route,** to grip the road. **2.** to adhere, hold (to opinion, etc.). **3. a. (à un parti),** to join (a party).

adhésif, -ive [adezif, -iv] **1.** *a.* adhesive, sticky. **2.** *n.m.* adhesive.

adhésion [adezjɔ̃] *n.f.* **1.** adhesion, sticking; **force d'a.,** adhesiveness. **2.** (*a*) adhesion, adherence (**à,** to); membership (of a party); (*b*) agreement; approval; **donner son a. à un projet,** to support a plan.

ad hoc [adɔk] *Lt.adv.phr:* ad hoc, for the purpose.

adieu, *pl.* **-eux** [adjø] **1.** *int.* (*a*) goodbye! **dire a. à qn,** to say goodbye to s.o.; **dire a. à qch.,** to give up, renounce, sth.; (*b*) *Sw.Fr: S. of Fr:* hello! hi! **2.** *n.m.* farewell; **faire ses adieux à qn,** to say goodbye to s.o.; **baiser d'a.,** parting kiss.

adipeux, -euse [adipø, -øz] *a.* adipose, fatty (tissue, etc.).

adiposité [adipozite] *n.f.* adiposity.

adjacent [adʒasɑ̃] *a.* adjacent, contiguous (**à,** to); adjoining; bordering (**à,** on); *Mth:* **angles adjacents,** adjacent angles.

adjectif, -ive [adʒɛktif, -iv] **1.** *a.* adjectival (phrase, etc.). **2.** *n.m.* adjective; **a. attribut,** predicative adjective; **a. épithète,** attributive adjective.

adjectival, -aux [adʒɛktival, -o] *a.* adjectival.

adjoindre [adʒwɛ̃dr̥] *v.tr.* (*conj. like* JOINDRE) **1. a. qch. à qch.,** to unite, associate, sth. with sth. **2. a. qn à qn,** to give s.o. to s.o. as an assistant; **a. qn à un comité,** to add s.o. to a committee. **3. s'a. à d'autres,** to join (in) with others.

adjoint, -ointe [adʒwɛ̃, -wɛ̃t] **1.** *a.* assistant, deputy. **2.** *n.* assistant; **a. au maire,** deputy mayor.

adjonction [adʒɔ̃ksjɔ̃] *n.f.* **1.** adding, adjunction. **2.** addition (made to a text, etc.); annexe (of hospital).

adjudant [adʒydɑ̃] *n.m.* **1.** *Mil:* warrant officer class II; *U.S:* warrant officer (junior grade); **a.-chef,** warrant officer class I, U.S: chief warrant officer; **(capitaine) a.-major,** adjutant, *U.S:* executive officer. **2.** *Orn:* adjutant bird, crane.

adjudicataire [adʒydikatɛr] **1.** *a.* **partie a.,** (i) contracting party; (ii) purchasing party. **2.** *n.* (*a*) successful tenderer (for a contract); (*b*) highest bidder; purchaser (at auction).

adjudicateur, -trice [adʒydikatœr, -tris] *n.* adjudicator, awarder (of contract, etc.).

adjudication [adʒydikasjɔ̃] *n.f.* (*a*) adjudication, allocation, award; allocation (of contract); (*b*) **mettre qch. en a.,** (i) to invite tenders for sth.; (ii) to put sth. up for (sale by) auction; **a. forcée,** compulsory sale.

adjuger [adʒyʒe] *v.tr.* **(j'adjugeai(s); n. adjugeons) a. qch. à qn,** (i) to adjudge, award, allocate, sth. to s.o.; (ii) (*at auction*) to knock down sth. to s.o.; **une fois! deux fois! adjugé!** going! going! gone! **s'a. qch.,** to appropriate, take possession of, sth.

adjurer [adʒyre] *v.tr.* **a. qn de faire qch.,** to adjure, entreat, s.o. to do sth.

admettre [admɛtr̥] *v.tr.* (*conj. like* METTRE) **1.** to admit; to let (s.o.) in; **a. qn chez soi,** to admit, let, s.o. into one's house; **être admis à un examen,** to pass an examination. **2. a. qn à faire qch.,** to authorize, allow, permit, s.o. to do sth. **3.** (*a*) **a. qch.,** to admit, admit of, permit, allow, sth.; **l'usage admis,** the accepted custom; (*b*) **il admet que c'est vrai,** he admits, acknowledges, that it is true; **admettons que j'aie tort,** assuming, supposing, (that) I'm wrong.

administrateur, -trice [administratœr, -tris] *n.* **1.** (*a*) administrator, *f.* administratrix; (*b*) **a. foncier,** land agent, estate agent. **2.** director (of company, bank, etc.). **3.** trustee.

administratif, -ive [administratif, -iv] *a.* administrative.

administration [administrasjɔ̃] *n.f.* **1.** administering, dispensing (of justice, sacrament, etc.). **2.** (*a*) administration, direction, management (of business, etc.); **conseil d'a.,** board of directors; **mauvaise a.,** mismanagement, maladministration; (*b*) governing (of country). **3.** (*a*) governing body; board of directors; (*b*) government service; **entrer dans l'a.,** to become a civil servant; (*c*) authorities, officials.

administrer [administre] *v.tr.* **1.** to administer, manage, conduct (business, estate); to govern (country). **2.** to dispense (justice); to administer (sacraments). **3.** *Jur:* **a. des preuves,** to produce proofs.

admirable [admirabl̥] *a.* admirable, wonderful; **quel temps a.!** what glorious weather!

admirablement [admirabləmɑ̃] *adv.* admirably; wonderfully, perfectly.

admirateur, -trice [admiratœr, -tris] **1.** *a.* admiring. **2.** *n.* admirer; fan.

admiratif, -ive [admiratif, -iv] *a.* admiring (gesture, etc.).

admiration [admirasjɔ̃] *n.f.* admiration; **avoir de l'a. pour qn,** to admire, be full of admiration for, s.o.

admirer [admire] *v.tr.* to admire; **admiré de tous,** admired by all.

admissibilité [admisibilite] *n.f.* admissibility; *Sch:* **épreuves d'a. (à l'examen oral),** written examination.

admissible [admisibl̥] *a.* (*a*) admissible, allowable (excuse, proof, conduct); (*b*) **a. à un emploi,** eligible for a job; *Sch:* **(candidats) admissibles,** candidates who have qualified for the oral examination.

admission [admisjɔ̃] *n.f.* **1.** admission (**à, dans,** to);

a. à un club, admission to a club; **cotisation d'a.,** entrance fee. **2.** *Cust:* entry (of goods); **a. en franchise,** duty-free entry. **3.** *Mch: I.C.E:* intake; **période d'a.,** induction stroke; **soupape d'a.,** inlet valve. **4.** *St. Exch:* **a. à la cote,** admission to quotation.

admittance [admitɑ̃s] *n.f. El:* admisttance.

admixtion [admikstjɔ̃] *n.f.* admixture (**à,** with).

admonition [admɔnisjɔ̃] *n.f.* admonition.

adobe [adɔb] *n.m.* (*brick or house*) adobe.

adolescence [adɔlɛsɑ̃s] *n.f.* adolescence, youth.

adolescent, -ente [adɔlɛsɑ̃, -ɑ̃t] **1.** *a.* adolescent; *F:* teenage; **arbre a.,** young tree. **2.** *n.* adolescent; *F:* teenager; youth; *f.* girl (in her teens).

adon [adɔ̃] *n.m. Fr.C: F:* coincidence.

Adonis [adɔnis] **1.** *Pr.n.m. Myth:* Adonis. **2.** *n.m.* (*a*) adonis; (*b*) *Ent:* adonis.

adonner (s') [sadɔne] *v.pr.* (*a*) **s'a. à qch.,** to give oneself up to sth.; **s'a. à l'étude,** to devote oneself to study; **s'a. à une profession,** to take up a profession; (*b*) **s'a. à la boisson,** to take to drink.

adoptant, -ante [adɔptɑ̃, -ɑ̃t] *n.* adoptive parent.

adopté, -ée [adɔpte] *a. & n.* adopted, adoptive (child).

adopter [adɔpte] *v.tr.* **1. a. un enfant,** to adopt a child. **2.** (*a*) **a. un nom,** to adopt, take, assume, a name; **a. une cause,** to take up, embrace, a cause; (*b*) **a. un projet de loi, une résolution,** to pass, carry, a bill, a resolution; **adopté à l'unanimité,** carried unanimously.

adoptif, -ive [adɔptif, -iv] *a.* adopted, adoptive (child, parent, country).

adoption [adɔpsjɔ̃ *n.f.* adoption (of child, proposal, idea, fashion). *Parl:* passage, carrying (of bill); **mon pays d'a.,** my adopted country.

adorable [adɔrabl] *a.* adorable; charming, delightful; **vous êtes a. dans cette robe,** you look charming in that dress.

adorateur, -trice [adɔratœr, -tris] *n.* (*a*) adorer, worshipper; (*b*) ardent admirer; fan.

adoration [adɔrasjɔ̃] *n.f.* adoration. **1.** worship (of a god). **2.** profound admiration (**de,** for); **aimer qn à l'a.,** to adore, worship, s.o.

adorer [adɔre] *v.tr.* **1.** to adore, worship (a god). **2.** to adore, idolize, to be passionately fond of (s.o., sth.); **j'adore monter à cheval,** I adore, love, riding.

adossé [adose] *a.* **1.** back to back. **2. a. à qch.,** (i) with one's back against sth.; leaning against sth.; (ii) backed on to sth.

adosser [adose] *v.tr.* **1.** to place (two things) back to back. **2. a. qch. à, contre, qch.,** to place, lean, rest, sth. (with its back) against sth.; to back sth. against sth. **3. s'a. à, contre, qch.,** to lean (up) against sth.; **le village s'adosse à la colline,** the village is built against the hillside.

adouber [adube] *v.tr.* **1.** *A:* to dub (a knight). **2.** *Chess:* to adjust (a piece).

adoucir [adusir] *v.* **I.** *v.tr.* **1.** to soften (voice, water); to tone down (contrast, colour); to subdue (light, one's voice); to sweeten (drink). **2.** to alleviate, relieve, ease, mitigate, calm, allay (pain, sorrow, etc.). **3.** to pacify, mollify. **4.** to smooth (metal, wood, etc.); to smooth off (an angle); to (rough-)polish (glass). **5.** *Metall:* (*a*) to temper; (*b*) to soften (cast iron). **II. s'adoucir 1.** (*of voice*) to grow softer; to soften. **2.** (*of weather*) to grow milder. **3.** (*of pain*) to decrease. **4.** (*of character*) to mellow.

adoucissage [adusisaʒ] *n.m.* **1.** smoothing. **2.** *Metall:* tempering; softening.

adoucissement [adusismɑ̃] *n.m.* **1.** softening (of voice, temper, etc.). **2.** alleviation (of pain, etc.). **3.** smoothing (of surfaces, angles). **4.** (*a*) sweetening; (water) softening; (*b*) *Metall:* annealing.

adoucisseur [adusisœr] *n.m.* (water) softener.

adrénaline [adrenalin] *n.f. Med:* adrenalin(e).

adresse [adrɛs] *n.f.* **1.** (*a*) address; **carnet d'adresses,** address book; (*of restaurant, good shop, etc.*) **il m'a donné une bonne a.,** he told me where to go; (*b*) **une observation à votre a.,** a remark aimed at, meant for, you; (*c*) *Cmptr:* **a. absolue,** absolute, specific, address; **a. de mémoire,** memory location. **2.** (formal) address (to an assembly). **3.** (*a*) skill, dexterity; **tours d'a.,** tricks, sleight of hand; (*b*) tact, diplomacy; **dénué d'a.,** tactless, bungling.

adresser [adrɛse] *v.* **I.** *v.tr.* **1.** to address (letter, etc.); **lettre mal adressée,** letter incorrectly addressed. **2. on m'a adressé à vous,** I have been recommended to come and see you; I have been referred to you; **le médecin m'a adressé à un spécialiste,** the doctor sent me to a specialist. **3.** to address, aim (remarks, etc.); **cette remarque a été adressée à Martin,** this remark was aimed at, meant for, Martin; **a. un sourire à qn,** to smile at s.o. **II. s'adresser 1. s'a. à qn,** to apply to s.o.; **s'a. ici,** apply, enquire, here; **adressez-vous à l'agent,** ask the policeman. **2. s'a. à qn,** to speak to s.o.; **à qui pensez-vous vous a.?** to whom do you think you are speaking? **3. s'a. à l'imagination, au bon sens, de qn,** to appeal to s.o.'s imagination, s.o.'s common sense.

Adriatique [adriatik] *Geog:* **1.** *a.* Adriatic. **2.** *Pr. n.f.* **l'A.,** the Adriatic.

Adrien [adriɛ̃] *Pr.n.m. Rom. Hist:* Hadrian.

adroit [adrwa] *a.* **1.** (*a*) dexterous, deft, skilful, handy; **être a. de ses mains,** to be clever, good, with one's hands; (*b*) **phrase adroite,** neat sentence. **2.** shrewd, adroit (answer, diplomat).

adroitement [adrwatmɑ̃] *adv.* skilfully; cleverly; shrewdly; neatly.

adsorber [atsɔrbe] *v.tr. Ph:* to adsorb.

adsorption [atsɔrpsjɔ̃] *n.f. Ph:* adsorption.

adulation [adylasjɔ̃] *n.f. A:* adulation, flattery (**de,** of); sycophancy.

adulte [adylt] *a. & n.* adult, grown-up.

adultère¹ [adyltɛr] **1.** *a.* adulterous. **2.** *n.* adulterer, *f.* adulteress.

adultère² *n.m.* adultery; **commettre un a.,** to commit adultery.

adultérer [adyltere] *v.tr.* **(j'adultère, n. adultérons; j'adultérerai)** *A:* to adulterate (food, etc.); to falsify (document).

ad valorem [advalɔrɛm] *Lt.adj.phr.* **droits ad v.,** ad valorem duty.

advenir [advənir] *v.* (*conj. like* VENIR; *used only in the third pers.*) to occur, happen; to befall, chance; to come (about). **1.** *v.i.* **je ne sais ce qui en adviendra,** I don't know what will come of it; **quand le cas adviendra,** when the case arises. *Jur:* **le cas advenant que** + *sub.*, in the event of (something happening). **2.** *v.impers. Lit:* **or, il advint que . . .,** now it came to pass that . . .; **quoi qu'il advienne, advienne que pourra,** come what may.

adventice [advɑ̃tis] *a.* adventitious; casual.

adventif, -ive [advɑ̃tif, -iv] *a. Bot:* adventitious (root, etc.); *Geol:* parasitic (cone).

adverbe [advɛrb] *n.m.* adverb.

adverbial, -aux [advɛrbjal, -o] *a.* adverbial; **locution adverbiale,** adverbial phrase.

adversaire [advɛrsɛr] *n.m. & f.* adversary, opponent; enemy.

adverse [advɛrs] *a.* (*a*) *Jur:* **la partie a.,** the opposing party, the other side; (*b*) adverse, unfortunate, unfavourable; **fortune a.,** bad luck; **critique a.,** unfavourable criticism; (*c*) hostile.

adversité [advɛrsite] *n.f.* **1.** adversity; adverse circumstances. **2.** misfortune, trial.

aérage [aeraʒ *n.m.* **1.** ventilation (of room, etc.); airing (of room, clothes, etc.). **2.** aeration (of water).

aérateur [aeratœr] *n.m.* ventilator.

aération [aerasjɔ̃] *n.f.* = AÉRAGE.

aérer [aere] *v.tr.* **(j'aère, n. aérons; j'aérerai) 1.** (*a*) to ventilate (mine); to air (room); (*b*) to air (linen); to expose (water) to the air. **2.** to aerate (water).

aérien, -ienne [aerjɛ̃, -jɛn] *a.* **1.** aerial, atmospheric (phenomenon, etc.); aerial (plant); *Mil:* **les forces aériennes,** the air force; **défense aérienne,** air defence; **attaque aérienne,** air raid; *Av:* **ligne aérienne,** airline; **poste aérienne,** airmail. **2.** (light and) airy (footstep, texture, etc.). **3.** overhead (cable, etc.); elevated (railway).

aérium [aerjɔm] *n.m.* (open air) sanatorium.

aéro- [aerɔ] *pref.* aero-.

aérocâble [aerɔkabl̥] *n.m.* cableway.

aéro-club [aerɔklyb] *n.m.* flying club, aero club; *pl. aéro-clubs.*

aérodrome [aerɔdrom] *n.m.* aerodrome, airfield, *U.S:* airdrome.

aérodynamique [aerɔdinamik] **1.** *a.* aerodynamic. **2.** *n.f.* aerodynamics.

aérodyne [aerɔdin] *n.m.* aerodyne.

aérofrein [aerɔfrɛ̃] *n.m.* air brake.

aérogare [aerɔgar] *n.f.* air terminal.

aéroglisseur [aerɔglisœr] *n.m.* hovercraft.

aérogramme [aerɔgram] *n.m.* air letter (form).

aéromoteur [aerɔmɔtœr] *n.m.* wind engine.

aéronaute [aerɔnot] *n.m.* & *f.* aeronaut.

aéronautique [aerɔnotik] **1.** *a.* aeronautic(al). **2.** *n.f.* aeronautics; **ingénieur d'a.,** aircraft engineer.

aéronaval, -ale [aerɔnaval] **1.** *a.* air and sea (forces, etc.). **2.** *n.f.* **l'Aéronavale** = the Fleet Air Arm, *U.S:* the Naval Air Service.

aéronef [aerɔnɛf] *n.m.* aircraft; airship.

aérophare [aerɔfar] *n.m. Av:* air, aerial, beacon.

aérophotographie [aerɔfɔgrafi] *n.f.* aerial photography.

aéroport [aerɔpɔr] *n.m.* airport.

aéroporté [aerɔpɔrte] *a.* airborne.

aéroroute [aerɔrut] *n.f. Av:* air route, airway.

aérosol [aerɔsɔl] *n.m.* aerosol.

aérospatial, -aux [aerɔspasjal, -o] *a.* aerospace (equipment, etc.).

aérostat [aerɔsta] *n.m.* aerostat.

aérostatique [aerɔstatik] **1.** *a.* aerostatic. **2.** *n.f.* aerostatics.

Aérotrain [aerɔtrɛ̃] *n.m.* (*R.t.m.*) hovertrain.

aérotransporter [aerɔtrɑ̃spɔrte] *v.tr.* to transport, carry, by air; to fly (goods, passengers).

affabilité [afabilite] *n.f.* graciousness, affability (**avec, envers,** to, towards).

affable [afɑbl̥] *a.* gracious, affable (**à, envers, avec,** to towards, with).

affadir [afadir] *v.tr.* **1.** to make (food, etc.) insipid, tasteless. **2.** to make (sth.) dull, uninteresting. **3. s'a.,** to become insipid.

affaiblir [afɛblir] *v.tr.* **1.** (*a*) to weaken; to enfeeble, debilitate; **affaibli par la maladie,** weakened by illness; (*b*) to lessen, reduce; **a. le courage de qn,** to damp s.o.'s courage; *Phot:* **a. un cliché,** to reduce (the contrasts of) a negative. **2. s'a.,** to grow, become, weak(er), feeble(r); to lose one's strength; (*of sound*) to become, grow fainter; **ses forces s'affaiblissaient,** his strength was flagging; **la tempête s'affaiblit,** the storm is abating.

affaiblissement [afɛblismɑ̃] *n.m.* **1.** weakening; diminution (of strength, etc.). **2.** weakness, *Med:* debility.

affaire [afɛr] *n.f.* **1.** (*a*) business, concern; **ce n'est pas votre a.,** it's not, none of, your business; **occupez-vous de vos affaires,** mind your own business; **ça c'est mon a.,** (i) that's my business; (ii) (you can) leave that to me; **ce n'est pas l'a. de tout le monde,** it's not everybody's job; **c'est l'a. d'un médecin,** it's a case for a doctor; (*b*) **a. d'argent,** money matter; **a. de cœur,** love affair; **a. de conscience,** matter of conscience; **a. difficile,** difficult question, matter; **c'est (une) a. de goût,** it's a matter, question, of taste; **ce n'est que l'a. d'un instant,** it won't take a minute; **ça, c'est une autre a.,** that's another question, another matter; (*c*) (*thg, pers., required*) **ça fait, c'est, juste mon a.,** that's just what I need, what I was looking for; **cela ne fera pas l'a.,** that won't do; **il fera votre a.,** he's just the man for you; **faire son a. à qn,** (i) *F:* to give s.o. what he deserves, what he's asking for, what was coming to him; (ii) *P:* to do s.o. in, bump s.o. off; (*d*) (difficult, serious) business; **c'est une sale a.,** it's a nasty business, piece of work; **ce n'est pas une a.,** it's nothing serious; **ce n'est pas une petite a., c'est toute une a.,** it's quite a business, quite a proposition; **je n'en fais pas une a.,** I'm not making an issue of it; **en voilà une a.!** (i) here's a nice mess, a pretty kettle of fish! (ii) that's a lot of fuss about nothing! **la belle a.!** is *that* all? so what? **se tirer d'a.,** to get out of a difficulty; **se faire une a. de qch.,** to get all worked up about sth. **2.** (*a*) (business) transaction; deal; **une bonne a.,** a sound transaction, deal; a good stroke of business; **une mauvaise a.,** a bad bargain; **ils font des affaires d'or,** they're coining money, making money hand over fist; **faire des affaires avec qn,** to do business with s.o.; **chiffre d'affaires,** turnover; **homme d'affaires,** businessman; **femme d'affaires,** businesswoman; **voyage d'affaires,** business trip; **déjeuner d'affaires,** (i) business, (ii) working, lunch; (*b*) **les affaires,** business; **parler affaires,** to talk business; to talk shop; (*c*) firm, business; **une grosse affaire,** a large firm. **3.** (*a*) **affaires,** possessions, belongings, things; **ranger ses affaires,** to put one's things away; to tidy up; (*b*) **les affaires de l'État,** affairs of State; **ce n'est pas une a. d'État,** it's of no great importance; **le Ministère des Affaires étrangères** = the Foreign (and Commonwealth) Office, *U.S:* the State Department; *Fr.C:* **les Affaires Extérieures,** External Affairs. **4.** (*a*) *Jur:* case, lawsuit; **a. civile,** civil action; *Hist:* **l'a. Dreyfus,** the Dreyfus case; (*b*) **l'a. de la rue X,** the X Street crime, murder. **5. a. (d'honneur),** duel.

affairé [afere] *a.* busy; **faire l'a.,** to make a show of being busy; to bustle, fuss, around; **ils entraient et sortaient d'un air a.,** they were bustling in and out.

affairer (s') [safere] *v.pr.* to lead a busy life; **s'a. autour de qn,** to fuss round, around, s.o.; **s'a. à tout remettre en place,** to be busy tidying up.

affairiste [aferist] *n.m.* & *f.* speculator; *F:* get-rich-quick type; **ce n'est qu'un a.,** he thinks of nothing but (of) making money, getting rich.

affaissement [afɛsmɑ̃] *n.m.* **1.** subsidence; sinking; collapse (of floor, roof, tyre); setting (of foundation); sagging (of floor, beam). **2.** depression, dejection, despondency; *Med:* prostration, collapse.

affaisser (s') [safɛse] *v.pr.* (*a*) (*of thg*) to subside, give way, cave in, collapse, sink; (*of material*) to give, yield; (*of beam, etc.*) to sag; (*of earth*) to settle; (*b*) (*of pers.*) to sink down, back (in chair); to collapse; (*c*) **il s'affaisse de jour en jour,** he is gradually declining, sinking.

affaler [afale] *v.* **I.** *v.tr. Nau:* **1.** (*a*) to haul down (rope); (*b*) to pay down (rope). **2.** to lower (object); **affale!** lower away! **II. s'affaler** (*a*) to collapse; **s'a. par terre,** to sink to the ground; (*b*) **s'a. dans un fauteuil,** to sink, *F:* flop, into an armchair.

affamant [afamɑ̃] *a.* **régime a.,** starvation diet.

affamé [afame] *a.* hungry, starving, ravenous, famished; *n.* **les affamés,** the hungry, the starving; **regarder qch. d'un œil a.,** to look hungrily at sth.

affamer [afame] *v.tr.* to starve (s.o.).

affectation [afɛktasjɔ̃] *n.f.* **1.** (*a*) affectation, affectedness; **sans a.,** unaffectedly; (*b*) pretence, affectation; **avec une a. de générosité,** with a show of generosity. **2.** (*a*) assignment, allocation, allotment (of sth.); *Fin:* **a. de fonds,** appropriation of funds; **a. hypothécaire,** mortgage charge; (*b*) *Mil: etc:* assignment, posting; **avoir une, être en, a. spéciale** = to be in a reserved occupation.

affecté [afɛkte] *a.* affected (person, manner).

affecter [afɛkte *v.tr.* **1.** (*a*) **a. qch. à un certain usage,** to assign sth. to, to appropriate, earmark, allocate, sth. for, to set sth. apart for, a certain use; (*b*) *Mil:* to detail, post, draft (soldier, detachment, for a particular service); *Navy:* **être affecté à un navire,** to be posted to a ship. **2. a. la mort,** to pretend to be dead; **a. de faire qch.,** to pretend to do sth. **3.** to have a partiality for (sth.); to make great use of (sth.). **4.** to assume, take on (shape, colour, etc.). **5.** (*a*) to affect, move, touch (s.o.); **vivement affecté de la nouvelle,** greatly moved by the news; (*b*) to affect, to have an effect on (career, health, etc.); **la grève a affecté plusieurs usines,** the strike hit several factories.

affectif, -ive [afɛktif, -iv] *a.* affective, emotional, emotive (use of a word, etc.).

affection [afɛksjɔ̃] *n.f.* affection. **1.** fondness, attachment, liking (**pour,** for); **prendre qn en a.,** to become attached to, fond of, s.o.; **avec a.,** affectionately. **2.** *Med:* disease, complaint, ailment.

affectionné [afɛksjɔne] *a.* affectionate, loving; *Corr:* **votre cousin(e) affectionnée(e),** your affectionate cousin.

affectionner [afɛksjɔne] *v.tr.* **1. a. qn,** to love, be fond of, s.o.; to be attached to s.o.; **affectionné de tous,** loved by all. **2. s'a. qn,** to gain s.o.'s affection.

affectueusement [afɛktɥøzmɑ̃] *adv.* affectionately; *Corr:* **a. à tous,** love to all.

affectueux, -euse [afɛktɥø, -øz] *a.* affectionate, loving.

affermer [afɛrme] *v.tr.* **1.** to lease (farm, etc.). **2.** to rent; to take (land, etc.) on lease.

affermir [afɛrmir] *v.tr.* **1.** to strengthen, make firm (foundations, etc.). **2.** to strengthen, consolidate (power, health, belief). **3. s'a.,** to become stronger; to strengthen; to harden; to set.

affermissement [afɛrmismɑ̃] *n.m.* strengthening; consolidation, hardening; setting.

affichage [afiʃaʒ] *n.m.* (*a*) billsticking, billposting; **tableau d'a.,** (i) notice board; *NAm:* billboard; (ii) *Trans:* arrivals and departures (board); (iii) *Sp:* telegraph board; *NAm:* bulletin board; (*b*) flaunting (of opinions, etc.); (*c*) *Elcs:* display; (*d*) *Av:* visual indicator.

affiche [afiʃ] *n.f.* poster, bill; placard; advertisement; **a. à la main,** handbill; **panneau à affiches,** (advertisement) hoarding, *NAm:* billboard; **a. de théâtre,** playbill; **la pièce a tenu l'a., est restée à l'a., pendant deux ans,** the play ran for two years.

afficher [afiʃe] *v.tr.* **1.** to stick, post (up) (bills, notices); **a. une vente,** to advertise, *NAm:* post, a sale; *P.N:* **défense d'a.,** stick, *NAm:* post, no bills. **2.** (*a*) to parade, show off, flaunt, make a display of (sth.); **a. son savoir,** to air one's knowledge; **a. son ignorance,** to expose, betray, one's ignorance; **a. sa pauvreté** to plead poverty; (*b*) **s'a.,** to show off, to draw attention to oneself; **il s'affiche avec sa maîtresse,** he takes his mistress everywhere.

afficheur [afiʃœr] *n.m.* billsticker, billposter.

affichiste [afiʃist] *n.m. & f.* poster designer.

affidavit [afidavit] *n.m. Jur:* affidavit.

affilage [afilaʒ] *n.m.* sharpening, setting, whetting.

affilée (d') [dafile] *adv.phr.* **cinq heures d'a.,** five hours at a stretch, at a time, on end; **livre vingt chapitres d'a.,** to read twenty chapters straight off.

affiler [afile] *v.tr.* **1.** to sharpen, whet, put an edge on (blade, etc.). **2.** to (wire-) draw (gold, silver).

affiliation [afiljasjɔ̃] *n.f.* affiliation.

affilié, -ée [afilje] *a. & n.* affiliated (member).

affilier [afilje] **1.** *v.tr.* to affiliate (**à,** to, with). **2. s'a. à un parti,** to join a party.

affiloir [afilwar] *n.m.* (*a*) oilstone; (*b*) knife sharpener, steel.

affiloire [afilwar] *n.f.* oilstone.

affinage [afinaʒ] *n.m.* **1.** (*a*) *Metall:* refining; smelting; (*b*) maturing (of wine, cheese). **2.** pointing (of nails, needles). **3.** (*a*) (thinning, fining down (of plank, etc.); (*b*) *Tex:* (fine) shearing (of cloth). **4.** *Tex:* hackling (of hemp); dressing (of flax).

affinement [afinmɑ̃] *n.m.* refinement.

affiner [afine] *v.* **I.** *v.tr.* **1.** (*a*) to improve, refine, make better; (*b*) to refine (iorn, gold); (*c*) to ripen, mature (cheese, etc.). **2.** (*a*) to sharpen (the intelligence); (*b*) to point (nails). **3.** to thin, fine down (board, etc.). **4.** *Tex:* to hackle (hemp). **II. s'affiner 1.** (*of pers.*) to become more refined; (*of features*) to become finer, fine down. **2.** (*of cheese, etc.*) to ripen, mature.

affinerie [afinri] *n.f. Metall:* **1.** (*a*) metal refinery; (*b*) wire-drawing mill. **2.** refining.

affinité [afinite] *n.f.* (*a*) affinity (**entre,** between); resemblance; similarity of character; (*b*) attraction; *Ch:* **a. pour un corps,** affinity for a body.

affirmatif, -ive [afirmatif, -iv] **1.** *a.* (*a*) affirmative, positive; **réponse affirmative,** answer in the affirmative; **signe a.,** nod (of agreement); (*b*) assertive, positive (person). **2.** *n.f.* **l'affirmative,** the affirmative; **dans l'affirmative,** if so, if you can; **répondre par l'affirmative,** to say, answer, yes.

affirmation [afirmasjɔ̃] *n.f* affirmation, assurance; assertion, statement; **a. trop générale,** sweeping statement; *Jur:* **a. de créance,** proof of indebtedness; **a. sous serment,** affidavit; statement on oath.

affirmativement [afirmativmɑ̃] *adv.* in the affirmative.

affirmer [afirme] *v.* **I.** *v.tr.* **1.** to insist; to affirm; to state positively; **je n'affirmerais pas que . . .,** I won't swear to it that . . .; **a. qch. sous, sur, par, serment,** to state sth. on oath, on affidavit. **2. a. son autorité,** to make one's authority felt. **II. s'affirmer** (*a*) to assert oneself; to assert one's authority; (*b*) **beaucoup de ses observations se sont affirmées justes,** many of his observations have proved correct, have been confirmed.

affleurer [aflœre] **1.** *v.tr.* (*a*) to bring (timbers, etc.) to the same level; to make flush; (*b*) **a. qch.,** to be level, even, flush, with sth.**2.** *v.i.* (*a*) to be even, level, flush; (*b*) *Geol:* (*of lode*) to outcrop.

affliction [afliksjɔ̃] *n.f.* affliction, sorrow.

affligé [afliʒe] *a.* **1.** afflicted; troubled (**de,** with); **a. de rhumatisme,** suffering from rheumatism; *n.* **les affligés,** the afflicted. **2.** grieved, distressed.

affligeant [afliʒɑ̃] *a.* distressing, painful, sad (news).

affliger [afliʒe] **1.** *v.tr.* **(j'affligeai(s); n. affligeons)** to afflict (**de,** with); to pain, distress, grieve. **2. s'a.,** to be grieved, distressed (about sth.); **ne vous affligez pas ainsi,** don't take it so much to heart.

affluence [aflyɑ̃s] *n.f.* **1.** *A:* affluence. **2.** crowd, concourse (of people); **heures d'a.,** rush hours.

affluent [aflyɑ̃] *n.m.* tributary (of river).

affluer [aflye] *v.i.* (*of liquid*) to flow (**vers,** towards; **dans,** into); (*of blood*) to rush, flow (**à,** to); **a. à, dans, un endroit,** to crowd, flock, to a place.

afflux [afly] *n.m.* (*a*) *Med: etc:* rush (of blood); (*b*) *El:* surge (of current); (*c*) crowd (of visitors).

affolé [afɔle] *a.* **1.** crazy, distracted, demented, frantic, panic-stricken; **il était a.,** he was scared out of his wits; **épouvante affolée,** wild, crazed, terror. **2.** spinning, crazy (compass needle).

affolement [afɔlmɑ̃] *n.m.* **1.** panic, *F:* flap. **2.** perturbation, unsteadiness, spinning (of magnetic needle). **3.** *(a)* racing (of engine, propeller, etc.); *(b)* disconnecting (of pulley, etc.).

affoler [afɔle] **I.** *v.tr.* **1.** to madden, distract; to drive (s.o.) crazy, to throw (crowd) into a panic. **2.** to disturb, perturb (needle of compass). **3.** *Mch:* *(a)* to let (machine) race; *(b)* to disconnect (part of machine). **II. s'affoler 1.** *(a)* to panic; to get in a panic; *(b)* to lose one's head; *F:* to go off the deep end. **2.** *(a)* *(of compass needle)* to spin; *(b)* *(of machine)* to begin to race.

afforestation [afɔrɛstasjɔ̃] *n.f.* (re-)afforestation.

affouiller [afuje] *v.tr.* *(of water)* to undermine, erode, wash away, lay bare (bank, foundation, etc.).

affourager [afuraʒe] *v.tr.* **(j'affourageais; n. affourageons)** to fodder (cattle).

affranchir [afrɑ̃ʃir] *v.tr.* **1.** *(a)* to free; to set free; to liberate (slave, etc.); **a. qn, qch., de qch.,** to free, release, s.o., sth., from sth.; *(b)* **s'a. du joug,** to cast off the yoke; **s'a. d'une habitude,** to break oneself of a habit. **2.** to pay the postage on (sth.); to frank; to stamp (letter); **colis affranchi,** pre-paid parcel; **machine à a. (les lettres),** franking machine, franker, *U.S:* postal meter. **3.** *Cards:* to unblock (suit).

affranchissement [afrɑ̃ʃismɑ̃] *n.m.* **1.** *(a)* emancipation, manumission, affranchisement, enfranchisement, liberation, setting free (of slave, etc.); *(b)* release, deliverance, exemption (from taxes, charges, etc.). **2.** *(a)* prepayment, stamping, franking; *(b)* postage, carriage (of letter, parcel, etc.).

affranchisseur [afrɑ̃ʃisœr] *n.m.* emancipator, liberator.

affres [afr̥] *n.f.pl.* anguish, spasm; **les a. de la mort,** (i) the pangs of death; (ii) the death throes, struggle; **les a. de la faim,** the pangs of hunger.

affrètement [afrɛtmɑ̃] *n.m.* *(a)* freighting (= *hiring out*) (of ship); *(b)* chartering (of ship); **a. au voyage,** trip charter; **a. à temps,** time charter.

affréter [afrete] *v.tr.* **(j'affrète, n. affrétons; j'affréterai)** *Nau:* *(a)* to freight (= *hire out*) (ship); *(b)* to charter (ship); **a. un navire en travers,** to charter a ship by the bulk.

affréteur [afretœr] *n.m.* *Nau:* *(a)* freighter; *(b)* charterer, shipper.

affreusement [afrøzmɑ̃] *adv.* terribly, frightfully; horribly, shockingly.

affreux, -euse [afrø, -øz] *a.* **1.** frightful, hideous, ghastly, atrocious; *n. F:* **c'est un a.,** he's a nasty piece of work, a shocker. **2.** frightful, horrible, dreadful, shocking (news, poverty, crime, etc.); **mal de tête a.,** splitting headache; **temps a.,** filthy, shocking, weather.

affriolant [afrijɔlɑ̃] *a.* tempting, enticing.

affriquée [afrike] *n.f.* *Ling:* affricate (consonant).

affront [afrɔ̃] *n.m.* affront, indignity, insult, snub, slight, *F:* slap in the face; **faire, infliger, un a. à qn,** to slight s.o.; to snub s.o.; **doubler ses torts d'un a.,** to add insult to injury.

affrontement [afrɔ̃tmɑ̃] *n.m.* **1.** facing, confronting (of enemy, danger, etc.). **2.** joining edge to edge; *Surg:* bringing into apposition.

affronter [afrɔ̃te] *v.tr.* **1.** to face, confront, brave, tackle (s.o., sth.); to encounter (enemy); **a. une épreuve avec courage,** to meet an ordeal bravely; **a. la colère de qn,** to brave the wrath of s.o.; **deux thèses s'affrontent,** there are two conflicting theories. **2.** *(a)* to join face to face, edge to edge; to bring together (metal plates, etc.); *(b)* *Surg:* to bring into apposition.

affubler [afyble] *v.tr.* *Pej:* **a. qn de qch.,** to dress s.o. up in sth.; **il s'était affublé d'un antique uniforme,** he'd got himself up in an ancient uniform.

affût [afy] *n.m.* **1.** hiding place; hide (for ornithologist, etc.); **chasse au cerf à l'a.,** deer stalking; **être, se mettre, à l'a. de qn, de qch.,** to lie in wait, be on the watch, lookout, for s.o., sth., **il est toujours à l'a. du scandale,** he keeps his ears open for scandal. **2.** *(a)* *Artil:* carriage, mount(ing); *(b)* stand, frame, rest, mounting (of telescope, etc.).

affûtage [afytaʒ] *n.m.* **1.** sharpening, grinding (of tool); setting (of saw). **2.** set of bench tools.

affûter [afyte] *v.tr.* to grind, sharpen, whet (tool); to set (saw); *Turf:* **a. un cheval,** to bring a horse to the top of its form.

affûteur [afytœr] *n.m.* **1.** *Ven:* (deer)stalker. **2.** (tool)-grinder, sharpener; setter (of saws). **3.** *Tls:* saw file.

affûteuse [afytøz] *n.f.* *(a)* sharpening machine (for taps); *(b)* grinding machine (for tools).

afghan, -ane [afgɑ̃, -an] *a. & n.* *Geog:* Afghan.

Afghanistan [afganistɑ̃] *Pr.n.m.* *Geog:* *Afghanistan.*

afin [afɛ̃] *adv.* **1. a. de (faire qch.),** to, in order to, so as to (do sth.); **a. d'obtenir cette grâce,** in order to obtain this favour. **2. a. que** + *sub.*, that, so that, in order that; **a. que les autres puissent le voir,** so that the others may see it.

africain, -aine [afrikɛ̃, -ɛn] *a. & n.* *Geog:* African.

africanisation [afrikanizasjɔ̃] *n.f.* *Pol:* africanization.

africaniste [afrikanist] *n. & a.* (student) of African races and languages.

Afrikander [afrikɑ̃dɛr] *n.m.* *Geog:* Afrikaner.

afrika(a)ns [afrikɑ̃] *n.m.* *Ling:* Afrikaans.

Afrique [afrik] *Pr.n.f.* *Geog:* **l'A. du Nord,** North Africa.

afro-asiatique [afroazjatik] *a.* Afro-Asian.

agaçant [agasɑ̃] *a.* annoying, irritating, provoking, *F:* aggravating.

agacement [agasmɑ̃] *n.m.* irritation, annoyance; setting (of teeth, nerves) on edge.

agacer [agase] *v.tr.* **(j'agaçai(s), n. agaçons). 1.** to set (teeth, nerves) on edge; to grate on (nerves, ears). **2. a. qn,** to provoke, annoy, irritate, s.o.; to get on s.o.'s nerves, to aggravate s.o.; **a. un chien,** to tease a dog.

agape [agap] *n.f.* *(a)* *Ecc.Hist:* agape, love-feast; *(b)* *A:* reunion (dinner); *(c)* *pl.* *Hum:* feast, spread.

agar-agar [agaragar] *n.m.* agar-agar.

agaric [agarik] *n.m.* *Fung:* agaric.

agate [agat] *n.f.* **1.** *Miner:* agate; **a. noire, d'Islande,** obsidian; **a. onyx,** sardonyx. **2.** glass marble.

agave, agavé [agav, agave] *n.m.* *Bot:* agave; **a. d'Amérique,** American aloe, sisal hemp.

âge [ɑʒ] *n.m.* **1.** age; *(a)* **quel â. avez-vous?** how old are you? **quand j'avais votre â.,** when I was your age; **à l'â. de six ans,** when he, she, was six; at six years old; *P:* **je ne t'ai pas demandé don â.,** mind your own business; **quel â. lui donnez-vous?** how old do you think he is, would you say he was? **accuser son â.,** to look one's age; **dès son â. le plus tendre,** from his earliest years; **mourir à un grand â., à un â. avancé, à un bel â.,** to die at a good old age; **être d'â. légal,** to be of age; **il n'est pas encore d'â.,** he's still a minor; he's not of age yet; **être en â. de se marier,** to be of an age to marry; *(of horse)* **hors d'â.,** aged; *(b)* **le bas â.,** infancy; **enfant en bas â.,** infant; **avoir l'â. de raison,** to have reached the age of discretion; **l'â. d'homme,** manhood; **être d'â. mûr, entre deux âges, d'un certain â.,** to be middle aged; **il est bien pour son â.,** he's marvellous for his age; *(c)* old age; **un homme d'â.,** an old man; **le troisième a.,** the over sixties; **à l'â. que j'ai, à mon â.,** at my age, at my time of life; **mourir avant l'â.,** to die before one's time; (*d*) *Psy:* **l'â. mental,** mental age. **2.** generation; **d'â. en â.,** from generation to generation. **3.** age, period, epoch; *Archeol:* **l'a. de (la) pierre,** the stone age; **l'â. de pierre polie,** the neolithic age; **l'â. de, du, bronze,** the bronze age; **l'â. de, du, fer,** the iron age; *Hist:* **le moyen â.,** the middle ages; **costumes du moyen â.,** medi(a)eval costumes; *Myth:* **l'â. d'or,** the golden age; **l'â. d'airain,** the brazen age; **l'â. de fer,** the iron age.

âgé [ɑʒe] *a.* **1.** old, aged; **â. de dix ans,** ten years old, **je suis plus, moins, â. que vous,** I am older, younger, than you. **2.** old, *Lit:* aged ['eidʒid]; **assez â.,** elderly.

agence [aʒɑ̃s] *n.f.* (*a*) agency (office); bureau; **a. de renseignement(s),** information bureau; **a. de placement,** employment bureau; **a. de presse,** press agency; **a. de tourisme, de voyages,** travel agency; (*b*) branch office.

agencement [aʒɑ̃smɑ̃] *n.m.* **1.** arrangement; fitting (together) (of parts of machine, etc.); layout (of radio set, gearbox, etc.). **2.** *pl.* fixtures, fittings.

agencer [aʒɑ̃se] *v.tr.* **(j'agençai(s), n. agençons),** to arrange, dispose (house, etc.); to fit (together), adjust (parts of machine, etc.); **local bien agencé,** well designed, well equipped, premises; **phrases mal agencées,** badly constructed sentences.

agenda [aʒɛ̃da] *n.m.* agenda, notebook; engagement book; diary.

agenouiller (s') [saʒnuje] *v.pr.* to kneel (down).

agenouilloir [aʒnujwar] *n.m.* prie-Dieu; hassock (in church); bench (for kneeling in church).

agent [aʒɑ̃] *n.m.* **1.** agent, agency, medium; **a. chimique,** chemical agent; **a. monétaire,** circulating medium. **2.** agent; (*a*) **a. de location, de publicité,** estate, advertising, agent; **a. maritime,** shipping agent; **a. en douanes,** customs broker; **a. d'assurance(s),** insurance agent; **a. diplomatique,** diplomatic agent; **a. (de police),** policeman, police constable; (*b*) **a. de change,** (i) *Fin:* stockbroker, exchange broker; (ii) *Com:* mercantile broker; *Com:* **a. de liaison,** contact man; **a. de recouvrements,** debt collector. **3.** *Mil:* **a. de liaison,** liaison officer; **a. de transmission,** runner, dispatch rider, *U.S:* messenger; **a secret,** secret agent; **a. double,** double agent.

agglomérant [aglɔmerɑ̃] **1.** *a.* binding (material). **2.** *n.m.* binding material, binder.

agglomérat [aglɔmera] *n.m. Geol:* agglomerate.

agglomératif, -ive [aglɔmeratif, -iv] **1.** *a.* agglomerative; binding (material). **2.** *n.m. Civ.E:* binder.

agglomération [aglɔmerasjɔ̃] *n.f.* **1.** packing (of snow), etc.); caking, balling. **2.** agglomeration, built-up area; **les grandes agglomérations urbaines,** the great urban centres; **l'a. londonienne,** Greater London.

aggloméré [aglɔmere] **1.** *a.* conglomerate; **panneau de fibres agglomérées,** fibreboard. **2.** *n.m.* (*a*) *Geol: Const:* conglomerate; (*b*) compressed fuel, briquette; (*c*) fibreboard; **a. de liège,** agglomerated cork.

agglomérer [aglɔmere] **1.** *v.tr.* **(j'agglomère, n. agglomérons; j'agglomérerai),** to agglomerate. **2. s'a.,** to agglomerate; to cohere, to bind; (*of fuel, etc.*) to cake, to ball.

agglutinant [aglytinɑ̃] **1.** *a.* (*a*) agglutinant, adhesive; (*b*) agglutinative (languages). **2.** *n.m.* bond (of conglomerates).

agglutination [aglytinasjɔ̃] *n.f.* **1.** agglutination; binding; caking. **2.** agglutinated mass, cake; *Bac:* clump (of microbes).

agglutiner [aglytine] *v.tr.* to agglutinate; to bind.

aggravant [agravɑ̃] *a. Med: Jur: etc:* aggravating (symptom, circumstance).

aggravation [agravasjɔ̃] *n.f.* **1.** aggravation (of disease, etc.); worsening (of weather, etc.). **2.** augmentation (of penalty); increase (of taxation).

aggraver [agrave] *v.tr.* **1.** (*a*) to aggravate (disease, crime); to worsen; (*b*) **s'a.,** to worsen, become worse; **son état s'est aggravé,** he has taken a turn for the worse. **2.** to increase, augment (penalty); to increase (difficulties, taxation).

agile [aʒil] *a.* agile, nimble; active, lithe; light footed; **esprit a.,** quick, agile, mind; **elle est a. de ses doigts,** she's clever with her fingers; **il a la langue agile,** he's never at a loss for a word, for an answer.

agilité [aʒilite] *n.f.* agility.

agio [aʒjo] *n.m. Fin:* agio (of exchange); premium.

agiotage [aʒjɔtaʒ] *n.m. Pej: Fin: St. Exch:* stock jobbing, agiotage; rigging the market; gambling.

agioter [aʒjɔte] *v.i. St.Exch:* to speculate, gamble.

agioteur, -euse [aʒjɔtœr, -øz] *n. St.Exch.* speculator, gambler.

agir [aʒir] *v.* **I.** *v.i.* to act. **1. a. de soi-même,** to act on one's own initiative; **maintenant agissons,** now let's get going, get down to it; **faire a. qn,** to get s.o. to act, to take action; **faire a. qch.,** to set sth. going, working; to bring sth. into action, to put sth. in motion; **bien, mal, a. envers qn,** to act, behave, well, badly, towards s.o.; **est-ce ainsi que vous agissez envers moi?** is that how you treat me? **2.** to act, operate, take effect; **médecine qui agit vite,** medicine that acts, takes effect, quickly; **a. sur qch.,** to act on sth.; **a. sur qn,** to exercise an influence on s.o.; **a. sur les sentiments de qn,** to work on s.o.'s feelings; *St. Exch:* **a. sur le marché,** to rig the market. **3.** *Jur:* **a. contre qn,** to take action, proceedings, against s.o.; **a. au criminel, criminellement, contre qn,** to prosecute s.o.; **a. civilement contre qn,** to sue s.o. **II.** *v.impers.* **s'agir (de)** (*a*) to concern; to be the matter; **de quoi s'agit-il?** what's the matter? what's it all about? what's up? **l'affaire dont il s'agit,** the matter in hand; **il ne s'agit pas d'argent,** it's not a question of money; **il s'agit de lui,** it concerns him; **il ne s'agit pas de cela,** that is not the question, not the point; that's neither here nor there; (*b*) **il ne s'agit que de les rendre heureux,** it is only a question of making them happy; **il s'agirait de savoir si . . .,** the question is whether . . .; **il s'agirait de se dépêcher,** we've got to hurry, it's a case of now or never.

agissements [aʒismɑ̃] *n.m.pl. usu. Pej:* dealings, manoeuvres (of criminals, etc.); machinations.

agitant [aʒitɑ̃] *a.* **1.** agitating, disquieting (news). **2.** *Med:* **paralysie agitante,** Parkinson's disease.

agitateur, -trice [aʒitatœr, -tris] **1.** *n.* (political) agitator. **2.** *n.m.* (*a*) *Ch:* stirring rod, glass rod; (*b*) stirring machine, agitator, mixer.

agitation [aʒitasjɔ̃] *n.f.* **1.** (*a*) shaking, stirring; tossing (of sth.); waving (of handkerchief, flag); (*b*) roughness (of the sea). **2.** (*a*) agitation; restlessness; fidgetiness; (*b*) commotion, ferment, agitation; **l'a. ouvrière,** (labour) unrest; (*c*) (state of) perturbation; excitement; disturbance; **il l'a trouvé dans un état de grande a.,** he found him greatly excited.

agité [aʒite] *a.* **1.** choppy, rough (sea); wild (sky). **2.** (*a*) *Med:* feverish, restless (patient); (*b*) restless, sleepless (night); broken, fitful (sleep); (*c*) agitated, tumultuous (crowd). **3.** (*a*) restless, excited, fidgety (person); (*b*) perturbed, troubled (mind); (*c*) unsettled (times); (*d*) **vie agitée,** hectic life. **4.** *n.* **c'est un(e) agité(e),** he's, she's, restless, unsettled.

agiter [aʒite] *v.* **I.** *v.tr.* **1.** (*a*) to wave (a handkerchief, a flag); **le chien agite sa queue,** the dog is wagging his tail; **le cheval agite la queue,** the horse is whisking, flicking, its tail; **le vent agitait ses cheveux,** the wind was ruffling her hair; (*b*) to shake (tree, bottle, etc.); to wave (arms); to flutter (fan, wings); to sway (tree, branches); to rouse (sea); *P:* **les a.,** to beetle off, to scram; **a. avant de s'en servir,** shake before use; (*c*) to stir (mixture, air); to fan (air). **2.** (*a*) to agitate; to excite (patient); **malade agité par la fièvre,** patient restless with fever; (*b*) to perturb, to trouble; (*c*) to stir up; **a. le peuple, les masses,** to stir up the masses. **3.** to discuss, to debate (a question). **II. s'agiter 1.** to be agitated; to bustle around; **s'a. dans l'eau,** to splash about in the water; **s'a. dans son sommeil,** to toss (about), thrash around, in one's sleep. **2.** to become agitated, excited; to get upset, worked up; (*of sea*) to get rough.

agneau, -eaux [aɲo] *n.m.* **1.** lamb; **(peau d')a.,** lambskin; **laine d'a.,** lamb's wool; **doux comme un a.,** as gentle as a lamb. **2.** (*opposed to* AGNELLE) wether lamb. **3.** *Theol:* **l'A. sans tache,** the Lamb (of God). **4.** *Cu:* lamb.

agnelage [aɲlaʒ] *n.m.* (*a*) lambing; (*b*) lambin season.

agneler [aɲle] *v.i.* **(elle agnèle, elle agnèlera),** to lamb.

agnelet [aɲlɛ] *n.m.* lambkin, young lamb.

agnelle [aɲɛl] *n.f.* ewe lamb.

agnosticisme [agnɔstisism] *n.m.* agnosticism.

agnostique [agnɔstik] *a. & n.* agnostic.

agonie [agɔni] *n.f.* death agony, death struggle, pangs of death; **être à l'a.,** to be at one's last gasp; **lente a.,** lingering death.

agonisant, -ante [agɔnizɑ̃, -ɑ̃t] **1.** *a.* dying, in the throes of death; **de sa voix agonisante,** with his dying breath. **2.** *n.* dying person; **prières pour les agonisants,** prayers for the dying.

agoniser [agɔnize] *v.i.* (*a*) to be dying, at the point of death; (*b*) (*of business*) to be on its last legs.

agoraphobie [agɔrafɔbi] *n.f. Med:* agoraphobia.

agrafage [agrafaʒ] *n.m.* fastening; clipping together; clamping; dowelling.

agrafe [agraf] *n.f.* **1.** hook, fastener; clasp (of medal, of album; buckle (of strap); (paper) clip; staple (for stapler); *Surg: etc:* suture clip; **a. de diamants,** diamond clasp; **agrafes et portes (de couturière),** hooks and eyes. **2.** *Const: etc:* (*a*) clamp; cleat; cramp iron; (*b*) dowel; (*c*) joint; (*d*) hasp, catch (of window, etc.). **3.** *Arch:* keystone (of arch).

agrafer [agrafe] *v.tr.* **1.** to fasten, clip together; to hook up; to buckle (belt); *F:* **agrafe-moi, ma robe!** do me up! **2.** *Const: etc:* (*a*) to clamp, cramp; (*b*) to dowel.

agrafeuse [agraføz] *n.f.* stapler.

agraire [agrɛr] *a.* agrarian; **mesures agraires,** land measures; *Jur:* **loi a.** land act.

agrandir [agrɑ̃dir] *v.* **I.** *v.tr.* **1.** (*a*) to make (sth.) larger; to enlarge (photograph, etc.); to increase, extend, (sth.); **a. qch. en long, en large,** to lengthen, widen, sth.; (*b*) to make (sth.) appear larger; to magnify; **a. sa taille,** to make oneself look taller; (*c*) to exaggerate (story, etc.). **2.** to uplift (the mind, etc.). **II. s'agrandir 1.** to grow larger; to become greater; to increase; to expand; **nous allons nous a.,** we are going to enlarge our premises. **2.** to become richer, more powerful, more important.

agrandissement [agrɑ̃dismɑ̃] *n.m.* **1.** (*a*) enlarging, extending; **a. en long, en large,** lengthening, widening; (*b*) extension (of factory, etc.); increase (of holding, etc.); *Phot:* enlargement. **2.** advancement; increase in power, in importance.

agrandisseur [agrɑ̃disœr] *n.m. Phot:* enlarger.

agrarianisme [agrarjanism] *n.m. Pol:* agrarianism.

agrarien, -ienne [agrarjɛ̃, -jɛn] *a. & n.* agrarian.

agréable [agreabl̩] *a.* **1.** agreeable, pleasant, pleasing; prepossessing (manner, etc.); **se rendre a. à qn,** to make oneself agreeable to s.o.; **a. au goût,** pleasant to the taste; **peu agréable,** disagreeable; *n.* **faire l'a.,** to make oneself pleasant **(auprès de,** to); *n.m.* **joindre l'utile àl'a.,** to combine business with pleasure. **2. sacrifice a. à Dieu,** sacrifice acceptable to God.

agréablement [agreabləmɑ̃] *adv.* agreeably; pleasantly.

agréé [agree] **1.** *a.* (*a*) approved (sample, etc.); (*b*) *Fr.C:* **comptable a.,** chartered accountant. **2.** *n.m. Jur:* counsel (before a *tribunal de commerce*).

agréer [agree] **1.** *v.tr.* to accept, recognize, agree to (sth.); **a. un contrat,** to approve an agreement; *Corr:* **veuillez a. l'assurance de mes salutations distinguées,** yours truly; yours faithfully. **2.** *v.* to please; **si cela lui agrée,** if that suits him.

agreg [agrɛg] *n.f. Sch: F:* = AGRÉGATION 2 (*b*).

agrégat [agrega] *n.m.* aggregate.

agrégation [agregasjɔ̃] *n.f.* **1.** (*a*) aggregation, binding; **matière d'a.,** binding mateiral (of raod, etc.); (*b*) aggregate, agglomeration. **2.** *Sch:* **(concours d') a.,** competitive examination for posts on the teaching staff of *lycées* and universities.

agrégé, -ée [agreʒe] **1.** *n.* aggregate (matter). **2.** *a. & n. Sch:* (graduate) who has passed the *agrégation* examination.

agrément [agremɑ̃] *n.m.* **1.** (*a*) pleasure, amusement; **voyage d'a.,** pleasure trip; **livres d'a.,** light reading; (*b*) attractiveness, pleasantness, charm. **2.** *usu. pl.* (*a*) amenities (of place); charm (of person); (*b*) ornament(ation), *Cost:* trimmings; *Mus:* **notes d'a.,** grace notes. **3.** approval; consent.

agrémenter [agremɑ̃te] *v.tr.* to ornament; to trim (dress, etc.).

agresser [agrɛse] *v.tr.* to attack (without provocation).

agresseur [agrɛsœr] *n.m.* agressor; assailant.

agressif, -ive [agresif, -iv] *a.* aggressive.

agression [agrɛsjɔ̃] *n.f.* agression; unprovoked assault; **être victime d'une a.,** to be assaulted, attacked.

aggressivement [agresivmɑ̃] *adv.* aggressively.

agreste [agrɛst] *a. Lit:* **1.** rustic; rural (site). **2.** uncouth (person, manners.).

agricole [agrikɔl] *a.* agricultural (produce, etc.); **comice(s) agricole(s),** agricultural show; **grande, petite, exploitation a.,** large-scale, small-scale, farming; large, small, farm; smallholding.

agriculteur [agrikyltœr] **1.** *n.m.* agriculturist, farmer. **2.** *a.* agricultural (people).

agricultural, -aux [agrikyltyral, -o] *a.* agricultural.

agriculture [agrikyltyr] *n.f.* agriculture, farming.

agriflamme [agriflam] *n.m. Hort:* flame gun.

agripper [agripe] *v.tr.* (*a*), to clutch (at), grip (sth., s.o.); to seize (hold of) sth.; (*b*) **il s'agrippait au bord de la fenêtre,** he was clinging to the window sill.

agro [agrɔ] *n.m. F:* (*a*) = *Institut national agronomique*; (*b*) a student at this college.

agronome [agrɔnɔm] *n.m.* agronomist, agricultural economist.

agronomie [agrɔnɔmi] *n.f.* agronomy; agronomics.

agronomique [agrɔnɔmik] *a.* agronomic(al); **l'Institut national a.,** (university level) college for students of agronomics.

agrumes [agrym] *n.m.pl.* citrus fruits.

aguerrir [agɛrir] *v.* **1.** *v.tr.* to harden (s.o.) to war; to train (troops). **2. s'a. à, contre, qch.,** to become hardened to sth.; to learn to take sth. in one's stride.

aguets [agɛ] *n.m.pl.* **être, se tenir, aux a.,** to be on the watch, on the lookout; **avoir l'oreille aux a.,** to keep one's ears open.

aguichant [agiʃɑ̃] *a.* seductive; provocative.

aguicher [agiʃe] *v.tr.* to excite, arouse (s.o.); *F:* to lead (s.o.) on.

ah [ɑ] *int.* ah! oh! **ah, que c'est beau!** isn't it beautiful! **ah oui!** well yes, of course.

ahuri, -ie [ayri] *a.* (*a*) disconcerted; bewildered; flabbergasted; (*b*) confused, dazed, stupefied.

ahurir [ayrir] *v.tr.* to bewilder; to disconcert; to dumbfound, flabbergast; to confuse, stupefy.

ahurissant [ayrisɑ̃] *a.* (*a*) bewildering; disconcerting; flabbergasting; (*b*) *F:* **il a un culot a.,** he's got the hell of a cheek.

ahurissement [ayrismɑ̃] *n.m.* bewilderment, confusion; stupefaction; **il ne revient pas de son a.,** he can't get over it.

aï [ai] *n.m. Z:* three-toed sloth.

aide[1] [ɛd] *n.f.* (*a*) help, assistance, aid; **venir en a. à qn, venir à l'aide de qn, donner a. à qn,** to help s.o.; **recourir à l'a. d'un médecin,** to call in a doctor; **appeler à l'a.,** to call for help; **à l'a.!** help! **à l'a. de qch., avec l'a. de qn,** with the help, assistance, of sth., s.o.; **faire qch. sans a.,** to do sth. without help, on one's own; (*b*) **a. de l'État** = national assistance.

aide[2] *n.m. & f.* **1.** assistant, helper; *Nau:* mate; *Surv:* chainman; **a. de cuisine,** assistant cook; **a. de camp,** aide-de-camp; **a. familiale** = mother's help. **2.** *n.m.* **a. auditif,** hearing aid.

aide-comptable [ɛdkɔ̃tabl̥] *n.m.* assistant accountant; *pl. aides-comptables.*

aide-mécanicien [ɛdmekanisjɛ̃] *n.m.* garage hand; *pl. aides-mécaniciens.*

aide-mémoire [ɛdmemwar] *n.m.inv.,* (*a*) manual; (*b*) memorandum; (*c*) *Dipl:* aide-memoire.

aide-ouïe [ɛdwi] *n.m.inv.* hearing aid.

aider [ede] *v.* **I. 1.** *v.tr.* to help, assist, aid (s.o.); **je me suis fait a. par un ami,** I got a friend to help me, to give a hand; **à qui se lève matin Dieu aide et prête la main,** the early bird catches the worm; **a. qn à faire qch.,** to help s.o. to do sth.; to lend s.o. a hand; **a. qn à monter, à descendre, à entrer, à sortir,** to help s.o. up, down, in, out; **a. qn à mettre, à ôter, son pardessus,** to help s.o. on, off, with his overcoat; **Dieu aidant,** with God's help. **2.** *v.i.* **a. à qch.,** to contribute to(wards) sth. **II. s'aider 1.** *Prov:* **aide-toi et le ciel t'aidera,** God helps those who help themselves. **2.** (*a*) **s'a. de qch.,** to make use of sth.; **s'a. d'un dictionnaire,** to consult a dictionary; (*b*) **il faut s'aider les uns les autres,** we must help one another.

aïe [aj] *int.* (*indicating twinge of pain*) ow! ouch!

aïeul [ajœl] *n.m.* **1.** (*pl.* **aïeuls**) grandfather. **2.** (*pl.* **aïeux** [ajø]) ancestor.

aïeule [ajœl] *n.f.* **1.** grandmother. **2.** ancestress.

aigle [ɛgl̥] **1.** (*a*) *n.m. & f. Orn:* eagle; **a. impérial,** imperial eagle; **a. royal, fauve, doré,** golden eagle; **grand a. des mers,** erne, sea eagle; **un regard, des yeux, d'a.,** keen, penetrating, glance; **aux yeux d'a.,** eagle-eyed; (*b*) *n.m.* genius, mastermind; **ce n'est pas un a.,** he's no genius. **2.** *n.m.* (*a*) lectern; (*b*) **l'A.,** (the constellation) Aquila. **3.** *n.m. Ich:* **a. de mer,** eagle ray. **4.** (*a*) *n.f. Her:* eagle; **a. de sable éployée,** eagle displayed sable; **double a., a. à deux têtes,** double-headed eagle; (*b*) *n.m. or f. Mil:* eagle, standard; **les aigles romaines,** the Roman eagles; **l'a. noir de Prusse,** the black eagle of Prussia; **a. impérial,** imperial eagle; **l'a. impériale (des armées napoléoniennes),** the imperial eagle; (*c*) *n.m.* (*skating*) **grand a.,** spread-eagle.

aiglefin [ɛgləfɛ̃] *n.m. Ich:* haddock.

aiglette [ɛglɛt] *n.f. Her:* eaglet.

aiglon, -onne [ɛglɔ̃, ɔn] *n. Orn:* eaglet, young eagle; *Hist:* **L'A.,** Napoleon II.

aigre [ɛgr̥] *a.* (*a*) sour, sharp, acid, tart; *n.m.* **tourner à l'a.,** (i) (*of food, etc.*) to turn sour; (ii) (*of pers.*) to become acrimonious; (iii) (*of quarrel*) to turn nasty; **sentir l'a.,** to smell sour; (*b*) (*of pers.*) sour; bitter; (*c*) **son a.,** harsh, shrill, sound.

aigre-doux, -douce [ɛgrədu, -dus] *a.* sweet and sour (sauce); snide, *F:* catty (remark).

aigrefin[1] [əgrafɛ̃] *n.m. Ich:* haddock.

aigrefin[2] *n.m.* swindler; (financial) shark.

aigrement [ɛgrəmɑ̃] *adv.* acrimoniously; bitterly.

aigrette [ɛgrɛt] *n.f.* **1.** (*a*) aigrette (of heron, of egret); crest (of peacock, etc.); horn (of owl); tuft; (*b*) *Cost:* aigrette, plume; (*c*) *Bot:* egret; tassel (of maize); (*d*) *El:* aigrette, brush (discharge). **2.** *Orn:* egret; tufted heron.

aigreur [ɛgrœr] *n.f.* (*a*) sourness, tartness, acidity; (*b*) sourness (of temper); acerbity, bitterness; (*c*) *Metall:* brittleness; (*d*) *Med:* **aigreurs,** acidity.

aigri [ɛgri] *a.* embittered, soured.

aigrir [ɛgrir] *v.* **1.** *v.tr.* (*a*) to turn (sth.) sour; to sour (food, mil, etc.); (*b*) to embitter (person). **2.** *v.i.* to turn, grow, sour, to sour; (*of milk*) to turn. **3.** (*a*) **le vin s'aigrit,** the wine is turning acid; (*b*) **son caractère s'est aigri,** he has become embittered.

aigu, -uë [egy] *a.* **1.** sharp, pointed (instrument); *Mth:* **angle a.,** acute angle. **2.** acute, sharp (pain); intense (curiosity); keen, bitter (conflict, jealousy); penetrating (look); keen (mind). **3.** shrill, sharp, high-pitched (sound). **4.** *Gram:* **accent a.,** acute accent.

aigue-marine [ɛgmarin] *n.f. & a. inv.* aquamarine; *pl. aigues-marines.*

aiguillage [egɥijaʒ] *n.m. Rail:* **1.** switching, shifting of points; shunting (of train); **poste d'a.,** signal box. **2.** points, *U.S:* switches. **3.** orientation; **faire une erreur d'a.,** to take the wrong turning, course.

aiguille [egɥij] *n.f.* **1.** needle; **a. à coudre, à repriser, à tricoter,** sewing, darning, knitting, needle; **a. à passer, à lacet,** bodkin; **a. hypodermique,** hypodermic needle; **travail à l'a.,** needlework; **discuter sur la pointe d'une a.,** to split hairs; **chercher une a. dans une botte de foin,** to look for a needle in a haystack. **2.** (*a*) **a. de glace,** icicle; *Geol:* **a. (rocheuse),** needle; spine; **a. de pin,** pine needle; *Ich:* **a. de mer,** pipe fish, garfish; (*b*) **a. à tracer,** scriber; **a. de graveur,** etching needle; (*c*) *Rail:* tongue rail, point rail, blade; **a. de raccordement,** points, *U.S:* switches. **3.** (*a*) needle, point (of obelisk, peak, etc.); (church) spire. **4.** needle (of compass, speedometer, etc.); hand (of watch, clock); **petite a.,** hour hand; **grande a.,** minute hand; **a. trotteuse,** second hand.

aiguillé [egɥije] *a.* needle-shaped.

aiguiller [egɥije] *v.tr. Rail:* to shunt, *U.S:* switch, (a train); **a. la police sur une fausse piste,** to put the police on to a false track.

aiguilleur [egɥijœr] *n.m. Rail:* pointsman, *U.S:* switchman; *Av:* **a. du ciel,** air traffic controller.

aiguillon [egɥijɔ̃] *n.m.* **1.** (*a*) goad; (*b*) incentive. **2.** (*a*) *Bot:* prickle, thorn; (*b*) sting (of wasp).

aiguillonner [egɥijɔne] *v.tr.* **1.** to goad (oxen). **2.** to urge (s.o.) on; to inspire (s.o.); to rouse (s.o.), stir (s.o.) up.

aiguisé [eg(ɥ)ize] *a.* sharp (knife); keen (appetite).

aiguiser [eg(ɥ)ize] *v.tr.* **1.** (*a*) to whet (scythe); to sharpen, set, put, an edge on, grind (knife, etc.); to set (saw, razor); (*b*) to point; to sharpen (tool) to a point; **a. un crayon,** to sharpen a pencil. **2.** to make keen; to excite, stimulate, quicken (wits, appetite, etc.); to whet (appetite).

aiguiseur, -euse [eg(ɥ)izœr, øz] *n.* **1.** grinder, sharpener (of tools, etc.). **2.** *n.m. F:* (razor-) stropping machine.

aiguisoir [eg(ɥ)izwar] *n.m.* (*a*) (knife) sharpener; (*b*) whetstone.

ail [aj] *n.m.* **1.** *Bot:* allium. **2.** garlic; **gousse d'a.,** clove of garlic; *pl. ails, aulx* [o].

aile [ɛl] *n.f.* **1.** (*a*) wing; **sur l'a.,** on the wing; (*of bird*)

battre des ailes, to beat its wings; **battre de l'a.,** (i) (*of wounded bird*) to flutter; (ii) (*of pers.*) to be flustered, embarrassed; **avoir du plomb dans l'a., en avoir dans l'a.,** (i) (*of bird*) to be winded; (ii) (*of pers.*) to be hard hit; **la peur lui donnait des ailes,** fear lent him wings; **voler de ses propres ailes,** to stand on one's own feet; **vouloir voler avant d'avoir ses ailes,** to want to run before one can walk; (*b*) flipper (of penguin). **2.** (*a*) wing (of building, of the stage); wing, flank (of army); sail (of windmill); arm (of semaphore); blade (of propeller, of turbine); helix (of ear); wing, ala (of nose); flange (of girder); (*b*) *Aut:* wing, *NAm:* fender; *Av:* wing, aerofoil, *NAm:* airfoil; **a. courbe,** cambered wing; **a. en flèche,** swept-back wing; **a. à fente,** slotted wing; **a. en delta,** delta wing; **a. cantilever, a. en porte à faux,** cantilever wing; (*c*) *Fb:* wing; **les demi a.,** the wing halves; *Rugby Fb:* **jouer trois quarts a.,** to play wing three-quarters.

ailé [ɛle] *a.* **1.** winged, feathered; *Nat. Hist:* alate. **2. vis ailée,** butterfly screw; thumb screw.

aileron [ɛlrɔ̃] *n.m.* **1.** (*a*) pinion (of bird); (*b*) fin (of shark, etc.). **2.** (*a*) console, scroll (of portal, etc.); (*b*) *Av:* aileron, wing tip; **a. compensé,** balanced aileron; (*c*) paddle board (of water wheel); (*d*) fin keel (of submarine); (*e*) fin; *Av: etc:* **a. stabilisateur,** stabilizer fin; **stabilisateur à a.,** fin stabilizer; (*f*) *N.Arch:* **a. de passerelle,** bridge wing.

ailette [ɛlɛt] *n.f.* **1.** small wing (of building, etc.). **2.** (*a*) radiating plate, (cooling) flange, rib, fin, gill (of radiator); **tube à ailettes,** fanned, gilled, tube; (*b*) lug, tenon (of machine part; stud (of shell)); **vis à ailettes,** wing nut, thumbscrew; (*c*) vane (of torpedo, fan, ventilator, etc.); wing, fin (of bomb, missile); fin (of aircraft); blade (of turbine); **à ailettes,** (i) (*of wheel, etc.*) bladed; (ii) (*of bomb, missile*) winged; (*d*) rib (of aircraft); (*e*) leaf (of hinge). **3.** *Tex:* flyer (of spindle).

ailier [elje] *n.m. Fb:* wing (player); winger.

ailler [aje] *v.tr. Cu:* to flavour with garlic.

ailleurs [ajœr] *adv.* **1.** elsewhere, somewhere else; **partout a.,** everywhere else, anywhere else; **nulle part a.,** nowhere else. **2.** (*a*) **d'a.,** (i) besides, moreover; (ii) from another place; (iii) however; (iv) come to that; for that matter; (*b*) **par a.,** (i) by another way, route; (ii) in other respects; (iii) from another source; (iv) (= **d'a.**) moreover; (v) incidentally.

ailloli [ajɔli] *n.m.* garlic mayonnaise.

aimable [ɛmabl̥] *a.* **1.** amiable, agreeable, pleasant; kind; **vous êtes bien a., c'est très a. de votre part,** it's very kind of you, very good of you; **peu a.,** ungracious; disagreeable. **2.** lovable, attractive.

aimablement [ɛmabləmɑ̃] *adv.* amiably.

aimant [ɛmɑ̃] *n.m.* magnet.

aimantation [ɛmɑ̃tasjɔ̃] *n.f.* magnetization.

aimanter [ɛmɑ̃te] *v.tr.* to magnetize.

aimer [eme] *v.tr.* **1.** (*a*) to like, care for, to be fond of (s.o., sth.); **a. qn d'amitié,** to be food friends with s.o.; **je ne l'aime guère,** I don't like it, him, very much; I don't think much of it; **se faire a. de qn,** to win s.o.'s affection; **j'aime beaucoup la musique,** I'm very fond of music; **plante qui aime un sol calcaire,** plant that likes a chalky soil; **a. (à) faire qch.,** to like doing sth.; **j'aurais aimé le voir,** I would like to have seen him; *Prov:* **qui m'aime aime mon chien,** love me, love my dog; (*b*) **j'aime autant le cidre (que le vin),** I like cider just as much (as wine); **j'aime(rais) autant rester ici (que de . . .),** I would just as soon stay here (as . . .); **j'aime autant qu'il ne m'attende pas,** I would just as soon he didn't wait for me; (*c*) **a. mieux,** to prefer; **j'aime, j'aimerais, mieux rester ici,** I would rather, would sooner, stay here; *F:* **j'aime mieux pas,** I'd rather not. **2. a. qn (d'amour),** to love s.o., to be in love with s.o.; **ils s'aiment,** they are in love (with each other). **3.** (*a*) **s'a.,** to think a lot of oneself; to be pleased with oneself; (*b*) **je ne m'aime pas dans cette robe,** I don't like myself in this dress.

aine [ɛn] *n.f. Anat:* groin.

aîné [ene] *a.* (*a*) elder (of two); eldest (of more than two); **mon frère a.,** (i) my elder brother; (ii) my eldest brother; **la branche aînée de la famille,** the elder, senior, branch of the family; *n.* **nos aînés,** our elders; **il est mon a.,** he is older than I (am); (*b*) senior; **M. Thomas a.,** Mr Thomas senior; **a. de trois ans,** senior by three years.

aînesse [ɛnɛs] *n.f.* **1.** primogeniture; **droit d'a.,** (i) law of primogeniture; (ii) birthright. **2.** *A:* seniority.

ainsi [ɛ̃si] **1.** *adv.* (*a*) like this, like that; in this, that, way; **c'est ainsi qu'il est devenu soldat,** and that was how he became a soldier; **s'il en est a.,** if that is the case, if (it is) so; **puisqu'il en est a. je n'ai plus rien à dire,** under the circumstances I have nothing more to say; **les choses étant a.,** if that's the way things are; **et a. de suite,** and so on, and so forth; **pour a. dire,** so to speak, as it were; (*b*) **a. soit-il,** (i) so be it; (ii) *Ecc:* amen; (*c*) for example, for instance; **il m'arrive des aventures; a., l'autre jour . . .,** things happen to me; for instance, the other day . . .. **2.** *conj.* (*a*) so; **a. vous ne venez pas?** so you're not coming? (*b*) as also; **cette règle a. que la suivante me paraît, paraissent, inutile(s),** this rule, as well as the next one, seems to me to be unnecessary.

aïoli [ajɔli] *n.m.* = AILLOLI.

air [ɛr] *n.m.* **I. 1.** (*a*) air, atmosphere; **privé d'a., sans a.,** airless; **cela manque d'a. ici,** it's close, stuffy, here; **donner de l'a. à,** to ventilate, to air; **à a. conditionné,** air conditioned; *Typ:* **donner de l'a. à la composition,** to lead out, space out, the type; **prendre l'a.,** to enjoy the fresh air; **vivre de l'a. du temps,** to live on (next to) nothing, on air; **ne pas laisser à l'a.,** not to be exposed to the air; **au grand a., en plein a.,** in the fresh air, in the open air; **vie au grand a.,** open-air life; **vie de plein a.,** outdoor life; **concert en plein a.,** open-air concert; *Aut:* **poste d'a.,** air line; (*b*) **la conquête de l'a.,** the conquest of the air; (*of aircraft*) **prendre l'a.,** to take off; **tenir l'a.,** (i) to keep flying; (ii) to be airworthy; **Ministère de l'A.** = Ministry of Defence; **Armée de l'A.** = Royal Air Force, United States Air Force; **École de l'a.** = R.A.F. College, U.S.A.F. Academy; (*c*) **en l'a.,** in the air; **être en l'a.,** to be in a state of (i) confusion, (ii) excitement; **mettre tout en l'a.,** to throw everything into confusion; to turn everything upside down; **paroles en l'a.,** idle talk; **parler en l'a.,** to talk wildly, at random; **il y a quelque chose dans l'a.,** there's something in the wind, something brewing. **2.** wind; **il fait de l'a.,** it's breezy; **courant d'a.,** draught; **il ne fait pas d'a.,** there's not a breath of air; **coup d'a.,** rush of air; **attraper un coup d'a.,** to catch a chill. **II. 1.** (*a*) appearance, look; **avoir bon a., grand a.,** (i) (*of pers.*) to look distinguished; (ii) (*of dress, etc.*) to be smart, becoming; **a. de famille,** family likeness; **avoir un faux a. de . . .,** to have a vague, remote, resemblance to . . .; to look vaguely like . . .; **il a un drôle d'a.,** he looks odd, funny; **la ville a un a. de fête,** the town is looking festive; (*b*) **avoir l'a.,** to look, to seem; **avoir l'a. fatigué,** to look tired; **il a l'a. d'un étranger,** he looks like (i) a stranger (here), (ii) a foreigner; **ils ont l'a. d'avoir peur,** they look as if they were afraid; **cela en a tout l'a.,** it looks like it; **n'avoir l'a. de rien,** (i) (*of pers.*) to seem, appear, insignificant, of no importance; (ii) (*of house, etc.*) to be unpretentious, to look nothing much (from the outside); (iii) (*of job*) to look (deceptively) easy; **le temps a l'a. d'être à la pluie,** it looks like rain. **2.** manner, way; **se donner des airs,** to give oneself airs, to (try to) look important; (*b*) *Equit:* **les airs du manège,** the paces of a horse. **III.** tune, air, melody; **a. varié,** theme with variations; **je connais des paroles sur cet a.-là,** I've heard that one before.

airain [ɛrɛ̃] *n.m. A: or Lit:* bronze, brass; **avoir un cœur, une âme, d'a.,** to have a heart of stone; *Pol.Ec:* **la loi d'a.,** (Lassalle's) iron law of wages.

aire [ɛr] *n.f.* **1.** (*a*) (plane) surface, floor; **a. (d'une grange),** threshing floor; *Geol:* **a. continentale,** continental shield; (*b*) *Trans: etc:* roadway, floor (of a bridge); (*on motorway*) parking area, picnic area; **a. de services (principale),** service area, *P.N:* services; *Av:* **a. d'atterrissage,** landing area, ground; **a. de manœuvre,** apron; **a. de stationnement,** tarmac; **a. de lavage,** (i) *Aut:* washing bay, *U.S:* car wash; (ii) *Av:* washdown, *U.S:* wash rack; *Space:* **a. de lancement,** launching site. **2.** area (of field, triangle, building, etc.); *Geog:* **a. de drainage,** drainage area, basin. **3.** eyrie (of eagle). **4. les aires du vent,** the points of the compass; **prendre l'a. du vent,** to see which way the wind is blowing.

airelle [ɛrɛl] *n.f. Bot:* **a. myrtille, noire,** bilberry, whortleberry, whinberry, *Scot:* blaeberry; *NAm:* blueberry, huckleberry; **a. coussinette,** cranberry.

aisance [ɛzɑ̃s] *n.f.* **1.** ease; (*a*) freedom (of movement, etc.); **faire qch. avec a.,** to do sth. easily, with ease; **donner de l'a. à qch.,** to ease sth.; **a. des coudes,** elbow room; *Jur:* **a. de voirie,** easement; (*b*) **jouir de l'a., être dans l'a.,** to be well off, comfortably off; **ils ont une belle a.,** they are very well off. **2. fosse d'aisances,** cesspool; *O:* **lieu, cabinet, d'aisances,** public convenience, lavatory.

aise [ɛz] **1.** *n.f.* ease, comfort; **être à l'a., à son a.,** (i) to be comfortable, to have (elbow) room; (ii) to be well off; **on tient à l'a. à six dans cette voiture,** this car holds six comfortably; **ne pas être à son a., se sentir mal à l'a.,** (i) to feel awkward, to feel uncomfortable; (ii) to feel indisposed, off colour; **être (très) à l'a.,** to be relaxed; **mettez-vous à votre a.,** make yourself comfortable; **il en prend à son a.,** (i) he takes things, it, easy; (ii) he's a cool customer; **faire qch. à son a.,** to do sth. at one's own convenience; **aimer ses aises,** to like one's comforts. **2.** *a. A: Lit:* **je suis bien a. de vous voir,** I am so pleased to see you.

aisé [eze] *a.* **1.** (*a*) easy, free (position, manner); comfortable (clothes); **morale aisée,** lax morals; **parler d'un ton a.,** to speak in a natural way; (*b*) comfortably off, well-to-do. **2.** easy (task).

aisément [ezemɑ̃] *adv.* **1.** (*a*) comfortably, freely; (*b*) **vivre a.,** to be comfortably off. **2.** easily, readily.

aisselle [ɛsɛl] *n.f.* **1.** armpit; **porter qch. sous l'a.,** to carry sth. under one's arm. **2.** *Bot:* axil(la).

Aix-la-Chapelle [ɛkslaʃapɛl] *Pr.n.f. Geog:* Aachen, Aix-la-Chapelle.

ajisme [aʒism] *n.m.* (*a*) The Youth Hostel movement; (*b*) (youth) hostelling.

ajiste [aʒist] *n.m. & f.* (youth) hosteller.

ajointer [aʒwɛ̃te] *v.tr.* to join up; to fit (boards, pipes, etc.), end to end.

ajonc [aʒɔ̃] *n.m. Bot:* furze, gorse.

ajour [aʒur] *n.m.* **1.** opening, hole, orifice (which lets the light through). **2.** (*a*) (ornamental) perforation, openwork (in carving, etc.); (*b*) *Needlew:* **ajours,** hemstitching.

ajouré [aʒure] *a.* perforated; openwork (design); *Carp:* **travail a.,** fretwork; *Needlew:* **travail a.,** drawn-thread work.

ajourer [aʒure] *v.tr.* (*a*) to pierce an opening (to let in light); **a. une mansarde,** to make a window in an attic; (*b*) (*of ornamental work*) to perforate, to pierce; (*c*) to hemstitch.

ajournement [aʒurnəmɑ̃] *n.m.* **1.** (*a*) postponement, adjournment (of meeting); (*b*) *Sch:* referring (of examinee); *Mil:* deferment (of conscript). **2.** *Jur:* writ of summons (to appear); subpoena.

ajourner [aʒurne] *v.tr.* **1.** (*a*) to postpone, put off, adjourn, defer (meeting, decision, journey, etc.); to delay (plan); *Pol:* to table (bill); (*b*) *Sch:* to refer (candidate); *Mil:* to grant deferment to (conscript). **2.** *Jur:* to subpoena (s.o.).

ajout [aʒu] *n.m.* addition, extension; eking-out piece; *Av:* **a. profilé,** fairing.

ajouté [aʒute] *n.m.* addition (to MS, contract).

ajouter [aʒute] *v.tr.* to add. **1. a. qch. à qch.,** to add sth. to sth.; **sans a. que . . .,** without adding that . . ., let alone the fact that . . .; **a. aux embarras de qn,** to add to s.o.'s difficulties. **2. "venez aussi," ajouta-t-il,** "you come too," he added; **nous devons a. que . . .,** it should also be stated that . . . **3. a. foi à qch.,** to believe sth.

ajustable [aʒystabl̩] *a.* adjustable.

ajustage [aʒystaʒ] *n.m.* **1.** fitting, trying on (of dress, etc.). **2.** *Mec.E:* (*a*) assembly (of machine); **atelier d'a.,** fitting shop; (*b*) **a. mécanique,** machining; (*c*) *Num:* gauging. **3.** fit; *Mec.E:* **a. serré,** tight fit; **a. lâche, à jeu,** loose fit.

ajustement [aʒstəmɑ̃] *n.m.* **1.** (*a*) adjusting, adjustment (of apparatus, prices, etc.); (*b*) arrangement, settlement (of quarrel, etc.). **2.** *pl.* fittings.

ajuster [aʒyste] *v.tr.* **1.** (*a*) to adjust, set (apparatus, tool); *Num:* to gauge; **tapis ajusté,** fitted carpet; (*b*) to true (sth.) up, to finish; (*c*) to set up (machine); (*d*) **a. son fusil,** to aim one's gun; **feu bien ajusté,** well aimed fire; (*e*) **a. qch. à qch.,** to fit, adjust, adapt, sth. to sth.; **cette clef s'ajuste à chacune des serrures,** this key fits each of the locks; **a. un vêtement à qn,** to fit a garment on s.o.; **mi-ajusté,** semi-fitting. **2.** to put (sth.) right, straight; to settle (sth.); **a. une querelle,** to settle, patch up, a quarrel; **laissez-moi m'a.,** let me put myself straight, tidy myself up; *F:* **comme vous voilà ajusté!** what a sight you look!

ajusteur [aʒystœr] *n.m.* (*a*) *Mec.E:* **a. sur métaux, a. mécanicien,** (metal) fitter, filer, bench hand; **a. de tubes (de chaudières),** tube setter; (*b*) *Num:* gauger.

alacrité [alakrite] *n.f.* liveliness; alacrity.

Aladin [aladɛ̃] *Pr.n.m.* Aladdin.

Alain [alɛ̃] *Pr.n.m.* Allan, Alan.

alaire [alɛr] *a. Av:* **charge a.,** wing load(ing); **surface a.,** wing area.

alaise [alɛz] *n.f. Med:* drawsheet.

alambic [alɑ̃bik] *n.m. Ch: Ind:* still; **passer qch. par., à, l'a.,** to distil sth.

alangui [alɑ̃gi] *a.* languid.

alanguir [alɑ̃gir] *v.* **1.** *v.tr.* (*usu. used in passive*) to make languid, to enfeeble. **2. s'a.,** to grow languid; to languish, flag, droop.

alanguissement [alɑgismɑ̃] *n.m.* languor.

alarmant [alarmɑ̃] *a.* alarming; frightening.

alarme [alarm] *n.f.* (*a*) alarm; **donner, sonner, l'a.,** to give, sound, the alarm; *Rail:* **tirer la sonnette d'a.,** to pull the communication cord; **porter l'a. dans un camp,** to raise the alarm, a scare; **prendre l'a.,** to take fright; (*b*) *Av:* warning signal; **a. lumineuse,** warning light.

alarmer [alarme] *v.* **1.** *v.tr.* to alarm, frighten, startle (s.o.); **la nouvelle ne nous a pas alarmés,** we were not alarmed at, by, the news. **2. s'a.,** to take fright; **il s'alarme pour un rien,** the least thing frightens him.

alarmiste [alarmist] *a. & n.* alarmist; **la presse a.,** the sensational press.

Alaska [alaska] *Pr.n.m. Geog:* Alaska; **en A.,** in Alaska.

albanais, -aise [albanɛ, -ɛz] *a. & n. Geog: Ling:* Albanian.

Albanie [albani] *Pr.n.f. Geog:* Albania.

albâtre [albɑtr̥] *n.m.* alabaster.
albatros [albatrɔs] *n.m. Orn:* albatross.
albigeois, -oise [albiʒwa, -waz] *a. & n. Geog:* (inhabitant, native) of Albi; *Hist:* **les A.**, the Albigenses, Albigensians.
albinisme [albinism] *n.m.* albinism.
albinos [albinos] *n. & a.inv.* albino.
Albion [albjɔ̃] *Pr.n.f. A.Geog:* Albion, Britain; *Lit:* **la perfide A.**, perfidious Albion.
album [albɔm] *n.m.* album.
albumen [albymɛn] *n.m. Biol:* albumen.
albumine [albymin] *n.f. Ch:* albumin.
alcali [alkali] *n.m. Ch:* alkali.
alcalin [alkalɛ̃] *a.* alkaline.
alcaloïde [alkalɔid] *a. & n.m. Ch:* alkaloid.
alchimie [alʃimi] *n.f.* alchemy.
alchimiste [alʃimist] *n.m.* alchemist.
alcool [alkɔl] *n.m.* (*a*) alcohol; **a. absolu**, pure, absolute, alcohol; **a. éthylique**, ethyl alcohol; **a. à brûler, dénaturé**, methylated spirits; *Med:* **a. à 90°** = surgical spirit, *U.S:* rubbing alcohol; **lampe à a.**, spirit lamp, *U.S:* alcohol lamp; (*b*) alcohol; spirits, hard liquor, *F:* the hard stuff; **je ne bois jamais d'a.**, (i) I never drink spirits; (ii) I don't drink (anything alcoholic); **a. blanc**, clear spirits (*e.g.* kirsch); **a. de poire** = pear brandy.
alcoolique [alkɔlik] **1.** *a.* alcoholic. **2.** *n.* (*a*) drunkard; (*b*) alcoholic.
alcoolisage [alkɔlizaʒ] *n.m. Winem:* fortification.
alcoolisation [alkɔlizasjɔ̃] *n.f.* alcoholization.
alcoolisé [alkɔlize] *a.* alcoholic (drink).
alcooliser [alkɔlize] *v.* **1.** *v.tr.* to acoholize; to fortify (wine). **2.** *F:* **s'a.**, to drink too much.
alcoolisme [alkɔlism] *n.m. Med:* alcoholism.
alcoolomètre [alkɔlɔmɛtr̥] *n.m.*, **alcoomètre** [alkɔmɛtr̥] *n.m.* alcohol(o)meter.
alcootest [alkɔtɛst] *n.m.* breathalyser test.
alcôve [alkov] *n.f.* alcove; **a. de dortoir**, cubicles.
alcyon [alsjɔ̃] *n.m.* **1.** halcyon. **2.** kingfisher.
aldéhyde [aldeid] *n.m. Ch:* aldehyde; **a. formique**, formaldehyde.
aldin [aldɛ̃] *a. Typ:* Aldine (edition, type).
aléa [alea] *n.m.* risk, hazard, chance; **l'affaire présente trop d'aléas**, the business is too hazardous.
aléatoire [aleatwar] **1.** *a.* aleatory (contract, etc.); problematical, chancy, uncertain (result); random (sampling). **2.** *n.m.* **l'a. du marché**, the risks, the unsettled state, uncertainties, of the market.
alêne [alɛn] *n.f.* **1.** *Tls:* awl; **a. plate**, bradawl. **2.** *Ich:* sharp-nosed skate.
alentour [alɑ̃tur] **1.** *adv.* around, round about; **le pays d'a.**, the surrounding, neighbouring, country. **2.** *n.m.pl.* **aux alentours de la ville**, in the vicinity of the town.
aléoute [aleut] *a. & n.*, **aléoutien, -ienne** [aleusjɛ̃, -jɛn] *a. & n. Geog:* Aleutian; **les (îles) Aléoutiennes**, the Aleutian Islands.
alerte [alɛrt] **1.** *int.* to arms! look out! **2.** *n.f.* alarm, (air-raid) warning; **être en a.**, to be on the alert, on the qui-vive; *Mil:* **fin d'a.**, all clear; *Av:* **a. en piste**, scramble; **point d'a.**, danger point; **une chaude a.**, a narrow escape, close shave. **3.** *a.* (*a*) alert, brisk, quick; (*b*) *A:* vigilant, watchful.
alertement [alɛrtəmɑ̃] *adv.* briskly.
alerter [alɛrte] *v.tr.* to alert, to give the alarm to (troops); to alert, warn (the police, etc.).
alésage [alezaʒ] *n.m.* **1.** *Metalw:* (*a*) boring (out); (*b*) broaching, reaming. **2.** bore (of rifle barrel); *I.C.E:* bore; internal diameter (of cylinder, etc.).
alèse [alɛz] *n.f. Med:* drawsheet.
alester [alɛste], **alestir** [alɛstir] *v.tr. Nau:* (*a*) to lighten (ship); (*b*) to trim up, tidy up (rigging).
alevin [alvɛ̃] *n.m. Pisc:* alevin, fry, young fish.
Alexandre [alɛksɑ̃dr̥] *Pr.n.m.* Alexander.
Alexandrie [alɛksɑ̃dri] *Pr.n.f. Geog:* Alexandria.
alexandrin, -ine [alɛksɑdrɛ̃, -in] *a. & n.m.* alexandrine.
alexie [alɛksi] *n.f. Med:* word blindness.
alezan, -ane [alzɑ̃, -an] *a. & n.* chestnut (horse); **a. châtain**, chestnut sorrel; **a. roux**, red bay.
alèze [alɛz] *n.f. Med:* drawsheet.
alfa [alfa] *n.m. Bot:* alfa (grass), esparto (grass).
algèbre [alʒɛbr̥] *n.f.* algebra; **résoudre un problème par l'a.**, to solve a problem algebraically; **c'est de l'a. pour moi**, it's all Greek to me.
algébrique [alʒebrik] *a.* algebraic.
Alger [alʒe] *Pr.n.m. Geog:* **1.** Algiers. **2.** *n.m. Hist:* (the Department of) Alger.
Algérie [alʒeri] *Pr.n.f. Geog:* Algeria; **en A.**, in Algeria.
algérien, -ienne [alʒerjɛ̃, -jɛn] *a. & n.* Algerian.
algérois, -oise [alʒerwa, -waz] *a. & n.* (inhabitant, native) of Algiers.
algide [alʒid] *a. Med:* algid (cholera, fever, etc.).
algie [alʒi] *n.f.* ache, pain.
algonkien [algɔ̃kjɛ̃] *a. & n.m. Geol:* Algonkian.
Algonquin(s) [algɔ̃kɛ̃] *n.m.(pl.) Ethn:* **1.** Algonquin(s). **2.** Algonquian(s).
algue [alg] *n.f. Bot:* alga, *pl.* algae, seaweed.
alias [aljɑs] *adv.* alias; otherwise (known as . . .).
alibi [alibi] *n.m.* alibi.
aliénable [aljenabl̥] *a. Jur:* alienable, transferable.
aliénation [aljenasjɔ̃] *n.f.* **1.** *Jur:* alienation, transfer (of rights, property, etc.). **2.** alienation, estrangement. **3. a. mentale**, insanity.
aliéné, -ée [aljene] *a. & n.* lunatic, mad(man), insane (person); **hospice d'aliénés**, mental hospital; **a. interdit**, certified lunatic.
aliéner [aljene] *v.tr.* **(j'aliène, n. aliénerai) 1.** (*a*) *Jur:* to alienate, part with, transfer, (property, rights, etc.); (*b*) **a. sa liberté**, to give up one's freedom. **2.** to alienate, estrange (affections, etc.); **s'a. la sympathie de l'électorat**, to lose the goodwill of the electorate. **3.** to derange, unhinge (the mind).
aliéniste [aljenist] *n.m. & f. Med:* alienist.
alignée [aliɲe] *n.f.* line, row (of houses, trees, etc.).
alignement [aliɲmɑ̃] *n.m.* **1.** alignment; aligning; *Mil:* dressing (of a line); *Mil:* **à droite a.!** right dress! (*b*) making up, balancing (of accounts, etc.); **a. des monnaies**, alignment of currencies. **2.** alignment, line (of wall, etc.); *Const:* **déborder, dépasser, l'a.**, to project beyond the building line; **maison frappée d'a.**, house scheduled for realignment. **3.** *Rail:* straight stretch (of line).
aligner [aliɲe] *v.tr.* **1.** to align, lay out, draw up, line up; to put (thgs) in a line; *Mil:* to dress (a line); **a. un terrain**, to mark out a plot (of ground); *Typ:* **a. des caractères**, (i) to align, (ii) to range, type; *F:* **les a.**, to pay out, cough up. **2. a. un compte**, to balance an account. **3. s'a.**, to be in line with; to fall into line; *Mil:* to dress; *P:* **tu peux toujours t'a.!** just you try it on! *Pol:* **la Hongrie s'aligne sur l'URSS**, Hungary follows the Soviet line.
aliment [alimɑ̃] *n.m.* **1.** (*a*) food, nutriment, sustenance; *Physiol:* **a. complet**, complete food; (*b*) *pl. Jur:* alimony. **2.** *Ins:* interest, risk, value.
alimentaire [alimɑ̃tɛr] *a.* **1. régime a.**, diet; *Jur:* **pension, provision, a.**, alimony; maintenance; *Adm: Hist:* **carte a.**, ration card. **2.** nutritious (food, plant, etc.); **produits alimentaires**, food (products); **conserves alimentaires**, tinned, canned, foods. **3.** *Physiol:* **canal, tube, a.**, alimentary canal; *Mch: etc:* **pompe a.**, feed pump.
alimentation [alimɑ̃tasjɔ̃] *n.f.* **1.** (*a*) alimentation, feeding (of plants, animals, etc.); supply (of town, market, etc.); **article d'a.**, foodstuff, food product;

Com: **(magasin d')a.,** grocer's shop; **(rayon d')a.,** grocery department, food counter; (*b*) food, nourishment; nutrition; **a. défectueuse,** malnutrition. **2.** *Tchn: Mch: etc:* feed(ing) (of boiler, etc.); feed mechanism (of gun); **pompe d'a.,** feed pump; **a. par pesanteur, par gravité,** gravity feed; *El:* **bloc d'a.,** power supply; **câble, fil, d'a.,** feeder.

alimenter [alimɑ̃te] *v.tr.* **1.** to feed, nourish (s.o.), to supply (market) with food; **ruisseaux qui alimentent une rivière,** streams that feed a river; *El:* **a. une usine en courant,** to supply a factory with current. **2.** *Jur:* **a. son épouse,** to provide, (i) maintenance, (ii) alimony, for one's wife.

alinéa [alinea] *n.m. Typ:* **1.** first line of paragraph, indented line; **en a.,** indented. **2.** paragraph, *F:* par.

alité [alite] *a.* confined to (one's) bed; *F:* laid up.

alitement [alitmɑ̃] *n.m.* confinement to bed; **trois jours d'a.,** three days in bed.

aliter [alite] *v.tr.* **1.** to confine (s.o.) to bed, to keep (s.o.) in bed. **2. a. des harengs,** to barrel herrings.

alizé [alize] *a. & n.m.* **les (vents) alizés,** the trade winds.

allaitant [alɛtɑ̃] *a.* suckling, nursing; **mère allaitante,** nursing mother; **brebis allaitante,** milch ewe.

allaitement [alɛtmɑ̃] *n.m.* suckling, nursing; **a. au biberon,** bottle feeding; **a. naturel,** breast feeding.

allaiter [alete] *v.tr.* to suckle (child or young); to feed (child) at the breast; to nurse (child).

allant [alɑ̃] **1.** *a.* (*a*) active, busy, bustling, lively (person); (*b*) (*of old people*) active, able to move, walk about. **2.** *n.m.* initiative, drive; energy.

alléchant [aleʃɑ̃] *a.* attractive, alluring, enticing, tempting (offer, food); appetizing (smell, etc.).

allécher [aleʃe] *v.tr.* **(j'allèche, n. alléchons; j'allécherai)** to allure, attract, entice, tempt.

allée [ale] *n.f.* **1. allées et venues,** coming and going, running about. **2.** (*a*) walk (*esp.* lined with trees); lane, avenue; (carriage) drive; (*b*) path (in garden); (*c*) passage, entrance, alley; (*d*) *Prehist:* **a. couverte,** passage grave, gallery tomb.

allégation [alegasjɔ̃] *n.f.* allegation.

allège [alɛʒ] *n.f.* **1.** *Nau:* lighter, hopper, barge; *Com:* **frais d'a.,** lighterage; **franco a.,** free over side. **2.** *Const:* (*a*) breast wall, basement (of window); (*b*) balustrade, rail (of window, etc.).

allégeance[1] [aleʒɑ̃s] *n.f.* **serment d'a.,** oath of allegiance.

allégeance[2] *n.f. Sp:* handicapping (of yachts).

allégement [alɛʒmɑ̃] *n.m.* **1.** lightening (of vessel); **2.** alleviation, relief (of pain, grief); reduction (of taxation).

alléger [aleʒe] *v.tr.* **(j'allège, n. allégeons; j'allégeai(s); j'allégerai) 1.** (*a*) to lighten (ships, etc.); to reduce (taxes); (*b*) to unburden; to ease the strain on (timbers, etc.); (*c*) to alleviate, relieve, soothe (pain, grief). **2. a. qn de qch.,** to relieve s.o. of (the weight of) sth. **3.** *Tchn:* to reduce the volume of (sth.); to plane down, file down, fine down.

allégorie [alegɔri] *n.f.* allegory; **par a.,** allegorically.

allégorique [alegɔrik] *a.* allegorical.

allegoriquement [alegɔrikmɑ̃] *adv.* allegorically.

allègre [alɛgr] *a.* lively, gay, jolly, cheerful; **caractère a.,** cheerful disposition; **avoir le cœur a.,** to be light-hearted; **marcher d'un pas a.,** to walk briskly.

allégrement [alɛgrəmɑ̃] *adv.* briskly; cheerfully.

allégresse [alegrɛs] *n.f.* joy, cheerfulness, liveliness; **plein d'a.,** full of joy.

allegretto [alegrɛtto] *adv. & n.m. Mus:* allegretto.

allegro [alegro] *adv. & n.m. Mus:* allegro.

alléguer [alege] *v.tr.* **(j'allègue, n. alléguons; j'alléguerai) 1.** to allege, urge, plead; **a. l'ignorance,** to plead ignorance. **2.** to cite, quote (author, etc.)

alléluia [alelyja] *n.m. & int. Ecc.* alleluia.

Allemagne [almaɲ] *Pr.n.f. Geog:* Germany; **l'A. de l'ouest, de l'est,** West, East, Germany; **l'ambassadeur d'A.,** the German ambassador.

allemand, -ande [almɑ̃, -ɑ̃d] **1.** *a. & n.* German; **querelle d'A.,** quarrel about nothing; **la langue allemande,** *n.m.* **l'allemand,** the German language, German.

aller[1] [ale] *v.* **I.** *v.i.* (*pr.p.* **allant;** *p.p.* **allé;** *pr.ind.* **je vais** (*A: & Dial:* **je vas), tu vas, il va, n. allons, v. allez, ils vont;** *pr. sub.* **j'aille, n. allions, ils aillent;** *imp.* **va (vas-y), allons, allez;** *impf.* **j'allais;** *p.h.* **j'allai;** *fu.* **j'irai;** *the aux. is* **être.) 1.** (*a*) to go; **a. à Paris,** to go to Paris; **navire allant à Bordeaux,** ship bound for Bordeaux; **a. chez qn,** to call on s.o.; to go and see s.o.; **qui va là?** who goes there?; **ne faire qu'a. et venir,** to be always on the go, on the move; **je ne ferai qu'a. et revenir,** I shall come straight back; **a. où va toute chose,** to go the way of all things, of all flesh; **où allons-nous?** (i) where are we going? (ii) what are things coming to? **il va sur ses quarante ans,** he is getting on for forty, he is nearly forty (years old); **il ira loin,** he will go far, will distinguish himself; **vous n'irez pas loin avec 50 francs,** 50 francs won't get you very far; **soyez tranquille, cela n'ira pas plus loin,** don't worry, it won't go any further; **le pauvre vieux n'ira pas loin,** the poor old chap won't last long; **a. jusqu'au bout,** to see it through; **nous irons jusqu'au bout,** we shall carry on to the end; (*b*) **a. en course, à la chasse, à la pêche, à pied, à cheval, en voiture, au galop, au trot;** *see these words;* (*c*) *with adv. acc.* **a. bon train,** to go at a good pace; **a. grand train,** to race along; *with cogn. acc.* **a. son (petit bonhomme de) chemin,** to go one's way, to jog along; (*d*) **allez, je vous écoute,** go on, go ahead, I'm listening; (*e*) **chemin qui va à la gare,** road leading to the station; **tous les chemins vont à Rome,** all roads lead to Rome; (*f*) **plat qui va au feu, allant au feu, au four,** fireproof, ovenproof, dish. **2.** (*a*) to go, be going (well, badly); **les affaires vont, ne vont pas,** business is good, slack; **tout va bien,** everything is going well, things are all right; **ça ira!** we'll manage! **ça n'irait pas du tout,** that would never do; **il y a quelque chose qui ne va pas,** there's something wrong; **je vous en offre cent francs—va pour cent francs!** I'll give you 100 francs for it—right, (we'll say) 100 francs! **cela va sans dire, cela va de soi,** that goes without saying; (*b*) (*of machine, clock, etc.*) to go, act, work, run; **la pendule va bien, mal,** (i) the clock's right, wrong; (ii) the clock keeps good, bad, time; **faire a. un commerce,** to run a business; **tout va comme sur des roulettes,** everything is going like clockwork; (*c*) (*of clothes, etc.*) **ce veston ne va pas bien,** this jacket doesn't fit well; (*d*) **c'est trop grand pour a. dans le panier,** it's too big to go, get, into the basket; (*e*) **comment allez-vous?** how are you? **je vais bien,** *F:* **ça va,** I'm well, I'm all right; **cela va mieux,** I'm better; **cela ne va pas,** I'm not feeling up to the mark. **3. a. à qn,** (i) (*of colours, etc.*) to suit s.o.; (ii) (*of clothes*) to fit s.o.; (iii) (*of climate, food*) to agree with s.o.; (iv) (*of plan, etc.*) to please, suit, s.o.; to be to s.o.'s liking; **cela vous va comme un gant,** (i) it fits you like a glove; (ii) it suits you down to the ground; **ça me va!** agreed! done! **ça va!** O.K.! **ça va comme ça,** it's all right as it is. **4.** (*of colours, etc.*) **a. avec qch.,** to go well with sth., to match sth.; **a. (bien) ensemble,** to go well together, to match; **bas qui ne vont pas ensemble,** odd stockings. **5.** (*a*) **(aller +** *inf.*) **a. voir qn,** to go and, to. see s.o., to call on s.o.; **a. trouver qn,** to go and find s.o.; **a. se promener,** to go for a walk; *F:* **allez vous promener!** go (and) jump in the lake! **n'allez pas vous imaginer que . . .,** don't imagine that . . .; **allez donc savoir!** how is one to know? (*b*) (*aux. use*) to be going, to be about (to do sth.); **il va s'en occuper,** he is going to see about it; **il va venir,** he'll be coming; **elle allait tout avouer,** she was about to confess everything; **sa santé va (en) empirant,** his health is steadily growing worse. **6.** (*a*) **j'y vais! on y va!** coming! **nous irons demain,** we will go there tomorrow; (*b*) **est-ce comme ça que vous y allez?** is that how you set about it, how you go to work? **allez-y doucement!** easy, gently (does it)! **y a. de tout son cœur,** to put one's heart and soul into it; **y a. carrément, franchement,** to make no bones about it; **il n'y va pas par quatre chemins,** he doesn't mince matters, beat about the bush; **maintenant allons-y!** now (let's get down) to it! **allons-y!** well, here goes! **vas-y! allez-y!** go! get on with it! fire away! (*c*) *F:* **y a. de qch.,** to lay, stake, sth.; **y a. de son reste,** to stake one's all; **y a. de sa personne,** (i) to take a hand in it oneself; (ii) *F:* to do one's bit. **7.** *v.impers.* **il va de soi que . . .,** it stands to reason, it goes without saying, that . . .; **il en va de même pour lui, pour moi,** it's the same with him, with me; **il y va de vingt francs,** it's a matter of twenty francs; **il y allait de sa vie,** it was a matter of life and death (for him); his life was at stake. **8.** *int.* **alons, dépêchez-vous!** come on, hurry up! **allons donc!** (i) come along! get a move on! (ii) nonsense! get on, along, with you! **allons bon!** there now! bother! **mais va donc!** get on with it! **II. s'en aller** (*pr.ind.* **je m'en vais;** *imp.* **va-t'en, allons-nous-en, allez-vous-en, ne t'en va pas, ne nous en allons pas;** *perf.* **je m'en suis allé(e), nous nous en sommes allé(e)s) 1.** to go away; to leave; **les voisins s'en vont,** the neighbours are moving; **les taches ne veulent pas s'en a.,** the stains won't come off, out; **allez-vous-en!** go away! **allons-nous-en!** let's go! **il faut que je m'en aille,** I must be going; **ses forces s'en allaient,** his strength was failing; **le malade s'en va,** the patient is sinking; **votre lait s'en va,** your milk is boiling over; **s'en aller en fumée,** to end in smoke. **2.** (= ALLER I 5 (*b*)); **je m'en vais vous raconter ça,** I'll tell you all about it.

aller[2], *n.m.* **1.** going; outward journey; **à l'a.,** on the way there; **cargaison d'a.,** outward cargo; **a.-retour, voyage d'a. et retour,** journey there and back; *Nau:* voyage out and home; **billet a.-retour, d'a. et retour,** return ticket; *F:* **un a.,** a single ticket; *M.Ins:* **police à l'a. et au retour,** round policy; *Sp:* **match a.,** away match. **2. pis a.,** last resort; **au pis a.,** at the worst, if the worst comes to the worst. *Mec.E:* **a.-retour du piston,** up and down stroke.

allergène [alɛrʒɛn] *n.m. Med:* allergen.

allergie [alɛrʒi] *n.f. Med:* allergy.

allergique [alɛrʒik] *a. Med:* allergic (**à,** to).

aller-retour [alertur] *n.m. F:* return (ticket).

alliage [aljaʒ] *n.m. Ch: Metall: etc:* **1.** alloying, blending. **2.** alloy; **sans a.,** pure, unalloyed.

alliance [aljɑ̃] *n.f.* **1.** (*a*) alliance; marriage, union; **entrer par a. dans une famille,** to marry into a family; **parent par a.,** relation by marriage; (*b*) **traité d'a.,** treaty of alliance. **2.** wedding ring.

allié, -ée [alje] **1.** *a.* (*a*) allied (nation, etc.); (*b*) related by marriage; **être bien a.,** to be well connected. **2.** *n.* (*a*) ally; *Hist:* **les Alliés,** the Allies; (*b*) relation by marriage; connection.

allier [alje] *v.* **I.** *v.tr.* (*impf. & pr.sub.* **n. alliions, v. alliiez) 1.** to ally, unite; **intérêts communs qui allient deux pays,** common interests that unite two countries; **a. une famille à, avec, une autre,** to unite one family with another by marriage. **2.** (*a*) to alloy, mix (metals); (*b*) to harmonize, blend, match (colours); (*c*) to combine, unite (qualities, words, etc.) (**à,** with). **II. s'allier 1.** (*a*) to form an alliance, to becomes allies, to ally; (*b*) **s'a. à une famille,** to marry into a family. **2.** (*a*) (*of fluids*) to mix; (*of metals*) to alloy; (*b*) (*of colours*) to harmonize, blend.

alligator [aligatɔr] *n.m. Rept:* alligator.

allitératif, -ive [aliteratif, -iv] *a.* alliterative.

allô, allo [alo] *int. Tp:* hullo! hallo! hello!

allocation [alɔkasjɔ̃] *n.f.* **1.** (*a*) allocation, granting (of money, of land, supplies, etc.); (*b*) *Fin:* allotment (of shares, etc.); (*c*) *Jur:* allocation, allowance (of items in an account, etc.). **2.** allowance, grant; **allocations familiales,** family allowances, *U.S:* dependents' allowances; **a. de maternité,** maternity benefit; **a. (de) chômage,** unemployment benefit.

allocution [alɔkysjɔ̃] *n.f.* (*a*) short speech, address; (*b*) *Ecc: Jur:* charge (by bishop; by judge to jury).

allonge [alɔ̃ʒ] *n.f.* **1.** (*a*) extension leaf (of a table); **mettre une a. à qch.,** to lengthen sth.; (*b*) adaptor (of retort, pipe, etc.); lengthening tube; (*c*) *Mch:* coupling rod; **a. de tige,** extension rod; (*d*) **a. de boucher,** meathook. **2.** rider (to a document). **3.** *Box:* reach. **3. Equit:** lunging rein, longe, lunge.

allongé, -ée [alɔ̃ʒe] **1.** *a.* long; elongated; **avoir une figure allongée,** (i) to have a long(-shaped) face; (ii) to have a face as long as a fiddle; *Anat:* **la moelle allongée,** the medulla oblongata. **2.** *a. Sp:* **coup a.,** follow through. **4.** *n.m. & f. Med:* recumbent patient.

allongement [alɔ̃ʒmɑ̃] *n.m.* **1.** (*a*) lengthening, extension (of canal, etc.); lengthening (of dress); (*b*) elongation (of metals, etc.); strain; (*c*) *Artil:* lifting (of fire); (*d*) *N.Arch:* jumboization. **2.** protraction, extension (of time). **3.** *Av:* aspect ratio (of wing).

allonger [alɔ̃ʒe] *v.* **I.** *v.tr.* **(j'allongeai(s); n. allongeons) 1.** (*a*) to lengthen, elongate; to let down (garment); **cette robe vous allonge,** this dress makes you look taller; (*b*) to add a piece to (sth.); (*c*) *Artil:* to lift (fire); (*d*) *Sp:* **a. l'allure,** to increase the pace; (*e*) *N.Arch:* to jumboize. **2.** (*a*) to stretch out (one's arm); to crane (one's neck); to extend, draw out (rope, etc.); (*b*) *F:* **a. qn,** to knock s.o. down; **a. un coup à qn,** to aim a blow at s.o.; **a. l'argent,** to hand over, fork out, the money. **3.** to protract, prolong (conversation, etc.). **II. s'allonger. 1.** (*of days, etc.*) to grow longer, lengthen. **2.** to stretch oneself out, to lie down at full length; *F:* **s'a. (par terre),** to fall flat on the ground; to come a cropper. **3.** to extend; *Sp:* **le peloton des coureurs allongé derrière,** the field strung out behind.

allouer [alwe] *v.tr. Adm:* (*a*) to grant (salary, etc.); **a. une dépense, un budget,** to allow, pass, an item of expenditure, a budget; (*b*) to allocate, apportion (shares, rations, etc.); *Jur:* **a. à qn une somme à titre de dommages-intérêts,** to award s.o. damages.

allumage [alymaʒ] *n.m.* (*a*) lighting (of lamp, fire); switching on (of electric light); (*b*) firing (of mine); **a. défectueux,** misfiring; (*c*) *I.C.E:* ignition; **point d'a.,** spark gar; **a. prématuré,** pre-ignition.

allumé [alyme] *a.* **1.** (*a*) alight; burning; (*of blast furnace*) in blast; (*b*) *F:* drunk, high, lit up; (*c*) *P:* (sexually) excited, randy.

allume-cigare [alymsigar] *n.m.* cigar lighter; *pl. allume-cigares.*

allume-gaz [alymgaz] *n.m.inv.* gas lighter (for cooker).

allumer [alyme] *v.tr.* **1.** (*a*) to light (lamp, fire, pipe); **veux-tu a.?** will you switch on, put on, the lights, light up? **a. un projecteur,** to switch on a searchlight; (*b*) **a. une pompe,** to prime, fetch, a pump. **2.** to inflame, excite, stir up (passions, people); **a. l'imagination,** to fire the imagination. **3. s'a.,** to take, catch, fire; (*of eyes*) to light up; **ça ne s'allume pas,** the light's not working; *I.C.E:* **s'a. prématurément,** to backfire.

allumette [alymɛt] *n.f.* **1.** match; **a. de sûreté,** safety match; **pochette d'allumettes,** book of matches; **frotter une a.,** to strike a match; (*b*) *F:* (*long, thin legs*)

allumettes, matchsticks. **2.** *Cu:* **a. au fromage,** cheese straw; **pommes allumettes,** game chips; straw potatoes.

allumeur, -euse [alymœr -øz] *n.* **1.** (*pers.*) lighter; igniter. **2.** *n.f. P:* **allumeuse,** sexpot. **3.** *n.m.* (*a*) lighter, igniting device; (*b*) *I.C.E:* distributor.

allure [alyr] *n.f.* **1.** (*a*) walk, gait, bearing; **allures d'un cheval,** paces of a horse; **avoir de l'a.,** (i) (*of horse*) to be a good stepper; (ii) (*of pers.*) to have style; **reconnaître qn à son a.,** to know s.o. by his walk; (*b*) pace; **marcher à (une) vive a.,** to walk at a brisk pace; (*c*) speed; **à toute a.,** at full, top, speed; all out; *Rac:* at full stretch; **pleine a.,** maximum speed; **a. économique de croisière,** cruising speed; (*d*) *Mch: etc:* working (of furnace, engine, etc.); **a. régulière,** smooth running; **a. de marche,** rating; **a. normale,** normal speed. **2.** (*a*) manner; way(s) of doing things; behaviour, conduct (of pers.); (*b*) aspect, look (of person, things, events); **l'a. des affaires,** the way things are going; **prendre bonne allure,** to look promising, to look well.

allusif, -ive [alyzif, -iv] *a.* allusive.

allusion [alyzjɔ̃] *n.f.* allusion (**à,** to); hint, innuendo; **faire a. à qn, qch.,** to refer to, make an allusion to, s.o., sth.; **c'est à vous que s'adresse cette a.,** that's a dig at you, that's meant for you.

alluvial, -iaux [alyvjal, -jo] *a. Geol:* alluvial.

alluvion [alyvjɔ̃] *n.f. Geol: usu. pl.* alluvium.

almanach [almana] *n.m.* (*a*) almanac; (*b*) yearbook.

aloès [alɔɛs] *n.m. Bot:* aloe; *Pharm:* **amer d'a.,** bitter aloes.

aloi [alwa] *n.m.* **1.** (*a*) *A:* degree of fineness (of coin); **monnaie d'a.,** sterling money; (*b*) **pièce de mauvais a.,** base coin, light coin. **2.** standard, quality, kind (of thgs, people); **de bon a.,** genuine.

alopécie [alɔpesi] *n.f. Med:* alopecia.

alors [alɔr] *adv.* **1.** (*a*) then, at that time, at the time; **que faisiez-vous a.,** what were you doing then, at the time? **jusqu'a.,** until then; (*b*) **la vie d'a.,** life then, in those days; **le ministre d'a.,** the minister at the time. **2.** (*a*) then, well then, in that case, in such a case, in such a case; **a. vous viendrez?** well then, you're coming? **et (puis) a.? a. quoi?** (i) and what then? (ii) so what? (*b*) therefore, so; **il n'était pas là, a. je suis revenu,** he wasn't there, so I came back. **3.** *conj. phr.* **a. (même) que,** (at the very time) when, even when; even though; **vous économisez, a. qu'il faudrait dépenser,** you're saving, when you should be spending; **a. même que je le pourrais,** even though I could. **4.** then, next.

alouette [alwɛt] *n.f.* **1.** *Orn:* (*a*) lark; **a. des champs,** skylark; **a. des bois,** woodlark; (*b*) **a. de mer,** summer snipe, sea lark, dunlin. **2.** *Cu:* **a. sans tête,** veal olive.

alourdi [alurdi] *a.* heavy, dull; **a. de sommeil,** drowsy; **a. par le sommeil,** heavy with sleep; *Fin:* **le marché est alourdi,** the market is dull.

alourdir [alurdir] **1.** *v.tr.* (*a*) to make (sth.) heavy; (*b*) to weigh (s.o., sth.) down; (*c*) to dull (the senses). **2. s'a.,** to grow, become, (i) heavy, (ii) stupid.

alourdissant [alurdisɑ̃] *a.* oppressive (heat, weather, etc.).

alourdissement [alurdismɑ̃] *n.m.* (process of) growing heavy; growing heaviness (of limbs, etc.); dulling (of the senses); **sensation d'a.,** feeling of heaviness.

aloyau, -aux [alwajo] *n.m. Cu:* sirloin (of beef).

alpaga [alpaga] *n.m. Z: Tex:* alpaca.

alpage [alpaʒ] *n.m.* (*in the Alps*) (*a*) alp, mountain pasture; (*b*) right of pasture (on mountain slopes); (*c*) season spent by livestock in mountain pastures.

alpe [alp] *n.f.* **1.** alp, mountain pasture (*esp.* in the Alps). **2.** (*a*) **Les Alpes,** the Alps; **les Alpes suisses,** the Swiss Alps; **cor des Alpes,** alpenhorn; **pavot des Alpes,** Alpine poppy; (*b*) **les Alpes australiennes,** the Australian Alps; **les Alpes néo-zélandaises, méridionales,** the Southern Alps.

alpestre [alpɛstr̥] *a.* Alpine (scenery, climate, resort, plant, etc.) alpestrine (plant).

alpha [alfa] *n.m.* **1.** *Gr.Alph:* alpha; **l'a. et l'oméga,** Alpha and Omega, the beginning and the end. **2.** *Ph:* alpha (particle, rays, radiation).

alphabet [alfabɛ] *n.m.* **1.** alphabet; **apprendre son a. à un enfant,** to teach a child his alphabet. **2.** *Sch:* spelling book.

alphabétique [alfabetik] *a.* alphabetical; **par ordre a.,** in alphabetical order, alphabetically.

alphabétiser [alfabetize] *v.tr.* to teach (s.o.) to read and write.

alpin [alpɛ̃] *a.* alpine (club, plant, troops).

alpinisme [alpinism] *n.m.* mountaineering.

alpiniste [alpinist] *n.m. & f.* alpinist; mountaineer.

Alsace [alzas] *Pr.n.f. Geog:* Alsace.

alsacien, -ienne [alzasjɛ̃, -jɛn] *a. & n. Geog:* Alsatian.

altérant [alterɑ̃] *a.* thirst producing.

altération [alterasjɔ̃] *n.f.* **1.** change (for the worse); impairing (of health, etc.); deterioration (of food, etc.); **a. de la voix,** breaking of the voice (with emotion) (after puberty). **2.** debasing, debasement (of coinage); adulteration (of food); falsification (of document); garbling (of text); misrepresentation (of facts). **3.** great thirst.

altercation [altɛrkasjɔ̃] *n.f.* altercation, dispute.

altéré [altere] *a.* **1.** faded (colour); drawn, haggard (face). **2.** thirsty; **a. de sang,** thirsting for blood.

altérer [altere] *v.tr.* **(j'altère, n. altérons; j'altérerai) 1.** (*a*) to change (for the worse); to spoil, taint, corrupt (meat, wine, character); to impair (health); **voix altérée par l'émotion,** voice faltering, husky, with emotion; (*b*) **s'a.,** to deteriorate; (*of colours*) to fade. **2.** (*a*) to tamper with (sth.); to adulterate (food); to debase (coinage); to falsify (document); to garble (text, history); **a. la vérité,** to twist the truth; (*b*) *Mus:* **a. une note,** to inflect a note. **3.** to make (s.o.) thirsty.

alternance [altɛrnɑ̃s] *n.f.* alternance (of seasons, leaves, strata, etc.); *Hort:* alternate bearing; **en a.,** alternately. **2.** *El:* alternation; **redresseur à deux alternances,** full-wave rectifier.

alternateur [altɛrnatœr] *n.m. El:* alternating-current generator; alternator.

alternatif, -ive [altɛrnatif, -iv] **1.** *a.* (*a*) alternate (colours); (*b*) *El:* alternating (current); (*c*) *Mec.E:* reciprocating (engine, saw, motion). **2.** *a.* alternative (plan, meaning, etc.). **3.** *n.f.* (*a*) alternation, succession; (*b*) alternative, option; choice.

alternativement [altɛrnativmɑ̃] *adv.* alternately, in turn.

alterne [altɛrn] *a.* alternate (leaves, angles, etc.).

alterner [altɛrne] **1.** *v.i.* (*a*) to alternate; (*b*) to take turns (**pour,** in + *ger.*); to take it in turn (**pour,** to + *inf.*); **ils alternent pour veiller,** they take it in turns to sit up. **2.** *v.tr.* to rotate (crops).

altesse [altɛs] *n.f.* highness; **son A. impériale,** his, her, Imperial Highness.

altier -ière [altje, -jɛr] *a.* haughty, proud, arrogant (tone, bearing).

altimètre [altimɛtr̥] *n.m. Surv: Av:* altimeter; altitude indicator; *Av:* **a. à contact,** altitude switch.

altiport [altipɔr] *n.m.* high altitude airport.

altiste [altist] *n.m. Mus:* viola player.

altitraceur [altitrasœr] *n.m. Surv: Av:* altitude recorder.

altitude [altityd] *n.f.* altitude; **a cent mètres d'a.,** at an altitude of 100 metres; **en a.,** at a high altitude; *Av:* **prendre de l'a.,** to climb; **vol à haute a.,** altitude

flight; **a. limite,** ceiling; *Med:* **cure d'a.,** high-altitude treatment; **mal d'a.,** (i) mountain, (ii) altitude, sickness; **ivresse d'a.,** altitude narcosis.
alto [alto] *n.m. Mus:* **1.** alto, counter-tenor (voice). **2.** viola, tenor violin. **3.** tenor saxophone (in E flat).
altocumulus [altɔkymylys] *n.m.inv. Meteor:* altocumulus.
altostratus [altɔstratys] *n.m.inv. Meteor:* altostratus.
altruisme [altryism] *n.m.* altruism.
altruiste [altryist] **a.** *a.* altruistic. **2.** *n.* altruist.
alumine [alymin] *n.f.* alumina, aluminium oxide.
aluminium [alyminjɔm] *n.m.* aluminium, *U.S:* aluminum; **sulfate d'a.,** aluminium sulphate.
alun [alœ̃] *n.m.* alum; *Toil:* **pierre d'a.,** styptic pencil.
alunir [alynir] *v.i.* to land on the moon.
alunissage [alynisaʒ] *n.m.* moon landing.
alvéolaire [alveɔlɛr] *a.,* alveolate; cellular; honeycomb (pattern), alveolar (nerve, vein, consonant).
alvéole [alveɔl] *n.m.* **1.** (*a*) alveole, alveolus; cell (of honeycomb, etc.); **alvéoles pulmonaires,** alveoli of the lungs; (*b*) pigeonhole (of desk, etc.); (*c*) chamber (of revolver). **2.** socket (of tooth); socket, seat(ing) (of diamond). **3.** cavity, pit (in stone, etc.); *El:* **alvéoles d'un grillage,** interstices of an accumulator grid. **4.** *Artil:* gun pit.
alysse [alis] *n.f.,* **alysson** [alisɔ̃] *n.m. Bot:* alyssum.
amabilité [amabilite] *n.f.* **1.** amiableness, amiability; kindness; **auriez-vous l'a. de me dire . . .?** would you be good enough, kind enough, to tell me . . .? **2.** **faites toutes sortes d'amabilités de ma part à . . .,** give my kindest regards to . . .
amadouement [amadumɑ̃] *n.m.* (*a*) wheedling, coaxing; (*b*) softening.
amadouer [amadwe] *v.tr.* (*a*) to coax, wheedle, persuade; (*b*) to soften.
amagnétique [amaɲetik] *a.* non-magnetic.
amaigrir [amɛgrir, -e-] *v.tr.* **1.** (*a*) to emaciate; **s'a.,** to grow thin; to lose weight; **il s'est amaigri de dix kilos,** he has lost ten kilos; (*b*) to thin down, reduce (column, beam, etc.). **2.** *Agr:* to impoverish (soil).
amaigrissant [amɛgrisɑ̃, -e-] *a.* slimming (diet).
amaigrissement [amɛgrismɑ̃] *n.m.* **1.** (*a*) wasting away, growing thin, emaciation; (*b*) reducing, slimming; **cure d'a.,** slimming cure. **2.** reducing (in thickness), thinning down (of beam, etc.).
amalgamation [amalgamasjɔ̃] *n.f.* **1.** amalgamation. **2.** *Fin:* merger.
amalgame [amalgam] *n.m.* **1.** *Ch: Dent:* amalgam. **2.** medley, mixture.
amalgamer [amalgame] *v.tr.* **1.** to amalgamate (*Metall:* gold, silver; *El:* zinc plates). **2.** to amalgamate (banks, companies, etc.).
amande [amɑ̃d] *n.f.* **1.** almond; **amandes amères, douces,** bitter, sweet, almonds; **amandes pilées,** ground almonds. **2.** *Bot:* kernel (of a drupe).
amandier [amɑ̃dje] *n.m.* almond tree.
amanite [amanit] *n.f. Fung:* **a. phalloïde,** death cup; **a. tue-mouches,** fly agaric.
amant, -ante [amɑ̃, -ɑ̃t] *n.* **1.** (*a*) *A:* lover, sweetheart; (*b*) **un amant de la nature,** a lover of nature. **2.** *n.* lover, *f.* mistress; **a. de cœur,** fancy man.
amarante [amarɑ̃t] *n.f. Bot:* amarant(h); **a. commune, à fleurs en queue,** love lies bleeding.
amariner [amarine] *v.tr. Nau:* **1.** to man (prize). **2.** **s'a.,** to find, get, one's sea legs.
amarrage [amaraʒ] *n.m. Nau:* **1.** (*a*) mooring, fastening; stowing (equipment); **droits d'a.,** berthing dues; (*b*) berth, moorings. **2.** lashing; **faire un a. sur une corde,** to lash a rope. **3.** lanyard (of knife).
amarre [amar] *n.f.* (*a*) (mooring) rope; painter, warp; **navire sur ses amarres,** ship at her moorings; (*of ship*) **rompre ses amarees,** to break adrift; (*b*) cable, hawser; **a. de retenue,** guy.
amarrer [amare] *v.tr. Nau: etc:* **1.** (*a*) to make fast, to moor (ship, etc.); **navire amarré à quai,** boat berthed, lying, at the quay; (*b*) to belay; to make (rope) fast; (*c*) to secure (gun); (*d*) *Const:* to brace (wall, etc.). **2.** to seize, lash (hawsers, etc.).
amaryllis [amarilis] *n.f. Bot:* amaryllis; **a. belle-dame,** belladonna lily.
amas [ama] *n.m.* **1.** (*a*) heap, pile, accumulation; **des a. de glace,** packs of ice; (*b*) store, hoard (of money, provisions); (*c*) gathering, mass (of people); (*d*) *Astr:* cluster; constellation; (*e*) *Cryst:* colony. **2.** *Min:* lode.
amasser [amase] *v.tr.* **1.** to heap up, pile up. **2.** to hoard (up); **a. pour sa vieillesse,** to save up for one's old age. **3.** to collect; to gather (troops, etc.) together; **une foule s'amassait,** a crowd was gathering.
amateur [amatœr] *n.m.* **1.** (*a*) lover (of sth.); **a. d'art,** art lover; **a. d'oiseaux,** bird fancier; **édition d'a.,** collector's, booklover's, edition; **être a. de qch.,** to be fond of, have a taste for, sth.; (*b*) bidder (at sale); **est-ce qu'il y a des amateurs?** any takers? **2.** amateur; **elle joue bien pour un a.,** she plays well for an amateur; *Sp:* **championnat d'a.,** amateur championship; **faire qch. en a.,** to do sth. as a hobby; *Pej:* to dabble in sth.; **travail d'a.,** (i) amateur, (ii) amateurish, work.
amateurisme [amatœrism] *n.m.* amateurism.
amazone [amazon] *n.f.* **1.** (*a*) *Myth:* Amazon; *Geog:* **l'A.,** the (river) Amazon; (*b*) horsewoman; **monter en a.,** to ride side saddle. **2.** *Cost:* riding habit.
Amazonie [amazɔni] *Pr.n.f. Geog:* Amazonia.
ambages [ɑ̃baʒ] *n.f.pl. used only in* **parler sans a.,** to speak straight out; not to beat about the bush.
ambassade [ɑ̃basad] *n.f.* **1.** (*a*) *Dipl:* embassy, mission; **envoyer une a. extraordinaire,** to send a special mission; **obtenir une a.,** to be appointed ambassador; (*b*) mission, errand. **2.** (*a*) ambassador's staff, embassy; (*b*) (*building*) embassy.
ambassadeur [ɑ̃basadœr] *n.m.* ambassador; envoy; **l'a. d'Angleterre,** the British ambassador; **a. auprès du roi, de la reine, d'Angleterre,** Ambassador to, at, the Court of St James's.
ambassadorial, -iaux [ɑ̃basadɔrjal, -jo] *a.* ambassadorial.
ambassadrice [ɑ̃basadris] *n.f.* ambassadress; (*a*) woman ambassador; (*b*) ambassador's wife.
ambiance [ɑ̃bjɑ̃s] *n.f.* surroundings, environment, atmosphere, ambience; **régulateur d'a.,** thermostat; *Fin:* **l'a. générale,** the prevailing tone; *F:* **il y a de l'a. ici,** there's a cheerful atmosphere here.
ambiant [ɑ̃bjɑ̃] *a.* surrounding (atmosphere, etc.); **millieu a.,** environment; **température ambiante,** room temperature.
ambidextre [ɑ̃bidɛkstr̥] *a.* ambidextrous.
ambigu, -uë [ɑ̃bigy] *a.* ambiguous.
ambiguïté [ɑ̃bigɥite] *n.f.* ambiguity, ambiguousness.
ambigument [ɑ̃bigymɑ̃] *adv.* ambiguously.
ambitieusement [ɑ̃bisjøzmɑ̃] *adv.* **1.** ambitiously. **2.** pretentiously.
ambitieux, -ieuse [ɑ̃bisjø, -jøz] **1.** *a.* (*a*) ambitious; (*b*) **style a.,** pretentious style. **2.** *n.* ambitious person; careerist; *Pej:* go-getter.
ambition [ɑ̃bisjɔ̃] *n.f.* ambition (**de,** of, for); **sans a.,** unambitious(ly).
ambitionner [ɑ̃bisjɔne] *v.tr.* to set one's heart on (sth., doing sth.).
ambivalence [ɑ̃bivalɑ̃s] *n.f.* ambivalence.
ambivalent [ɑ̃bivalɑ̃] *a.* ambivalent.
amble [ɑ̃bl̥] *n.m.* amble, pace; *U.S:* single-foot; **a. rompu,** rack; *Equit:* **aller l'a.,** to amble.
ambler [ɑ̃ble] *v.i.* (*of horse, etc.*) to amble (along).
ambre [ɑ̃br̥] *n.m.* **1. a. gris,** ambergris; **pomme d'a.,** pomander. **2. a. jaune,** (yellow) amber.

ambré [ɑ̃bre] *a.* **1.** perfumed with amber(gris). **2.** amber-coloured; warm (complexion, tint).
ambroisie [ɑ̃brwazi] *n.f.* ambrosia.
ambulance [ɑ̃bylɑ̃s] *n.f.* ambulance.
ambulancier [ɑ̃bylɑ̃sje] *n.m.* ambulance man.
ambulant [ɑ̃bylɑ̃] **1.** *a.* strolling, itinerant, travelling, mobile; **épicier a.,** mobile grocer; **comédiens ambulants,** strolling players; **marchand ambulant,** itinerant dealer; hawker; **cirque a.,** travelling circus; *Post:* **courrier a.,** mobile sorter; *Med:* **érysipèle a.,** migrant erysipelas; *F:* **c'est un cadavre a.,** he's a walking corpse; he looks like death warmed up. **2.** *n.m.* (*a*) pedlar, hawker; (*b*) *Adm:* itinerant collector (of excise, taxes, etc.); (*c*) *Post:* travelling sorter.
ambulatoire [ɑ̃bylatwar] *a. Med:* **malade a.,** walking case; **(fièvre) typhoïde a.,** ambulant typhoid.
âme [ɑm] *n.f.* **1.** (*a*) soul; **une bonne â.,** a well-meaning person, a good soul; **se donner corps et â. à qn.,** to give oneself body and soul to s.o.; **rendre l'â.,** to give up the ghost; **Dieu ait son â.,** God rest his soul; (*b*) (departed) soul, spirit; **les âmes en peine,** the souls in Purgatory; **aller comme une â. en peine,** to wander around like a lost soul; (*c*) heart, feeling, soul, spirit; **â. sœur,** kindred soul, spirit; **en mon â. et conscience,** to the best of my knowledge and belief; **état d'â.,** state of mind; mood; (*d*) inspiration, soul, life; moving spirit (of an undertaking); (*e*) **ne pas rencontrer â. qui vive,** not to meet a (living) soul. **2.** (*a*) bore (of gun, pump); (*b*) core (of statue, cable); (*c*) web (of girder, beam); centre rib (of rail); *Av: web* (*of wing*); (*d*) *Mus:* sound post (of violin).
améliorant [ameljɔrɑ̃] *a. Agr:* **culture améliorante,** cover crop.
amélioration [ameljɔrasjɔ̃] *n.f.* **1.** amelioration, improvement, change for the better; **a. de santé,** improvement of, in, health; **il y a a. dans les affaires,** business is improving; **travaux d'a.,** improvements. **2.** appreciation (of property, etc.).
améliorer [ameljɔre] *v.* **1.** *v.tr.* to improve (a property, the soil, a translation, etc.); **a. son état,** to improve one's situation. **2. s'a.,** to get better, to improve; **sa santé, le temps, s'améliore,** his health, the weather, is improving.
amen [amɛn] *int. & n.m.inv.* amen.
aménagement [amenaʒmɑ̃] *n.m.* **1.** (*a*) equipping, arranging; fitting out (of ship); (*b*) harnessing (of power). **2.** (*a*) arrangement, disposition (of house, etc.); (*b*) *pl.* fittings; amenities; fixtures, installations; (*c*) *pl. Nau: Av:* accommodation, berthing; *Nau:* **les aménagements de l'équipage,** the mess decks; (*d*) **a. urbain et rural,** town and country planning.
aménager [amenaʒe] *v.tr.* **(j'aménageai(s); n. aménageons) 1.** to divide, distribute (supplies, etc.); to plan (town). **2.** (*a*) to fit out (house, ship, etc.); **étable aménagée,** converted cowshed; **route aménagée,** made-up road; (*b*) to harness (water power.)
amende [amɑ̃d] *n.f.* **1.** fine; penalty; **être condamné à l'a., à une a.,** to be fined; **défense d'entrer sous peine d'a.,** trespassers will be prosecuted. **2. faire a. honorable,** to make (i) amends, (ii) due apology.
amendement [amɑ̃dmɑ̃] *n.m.* **1.** improvement (of the soil, etc.). **2.** (soil) conditioner. **3.** *Pol:* amendment (to a bill, etc.).
amender [amɑ̃de] *v.tr.* **1.** (*a*) to make better; to improve (soil, etc.); (*b*) (*of pers.*) **s'a.,** to turn over a new leaf. **2.** *Pol: etc:* to amend (bill, etc.).
amenée [amne] *n.f.* **1. tuyau, conduite, d'a.,** (i) *Civ.E:* branch pipe; (*ii*) *Hyd.E:* supply pipe, *El:* lead. **2.** inlet, intake (for air).
amener [amne] *v.tr.* **(j'amène, n. amenons; j'amènerai) 1.** (*a*) to bring; to bring up (reserves, etc.); to lay on (water, gas, etc.); **amenez votre ami avec vous,** bring your friend (with you); **a. qn à son opinion,** to bring s.o. round to one's point of view; **a. un sujet,** to lead up to a subject; **a. la conversation sur un sujet,** to bring the conversation round to a subject; **a. qn à faire qch.,** to get, induce, s.o. to do sth.; (*b*) **a. une querelle,** to bring about, lead to, a quarrel; **a. une mode,** to bring in a fashion. **2.** *Nau:* to haul down (signal); to strike (colours); to lower (boat, flag, sail). **3.** *P:* **s'a.,** to turn up; **amène-toi ici!** come (along) here!
aménité [amenite] *n.f.* **1.** charm, graciousness (of manners, greeting, etc.); charm, grace (of style). **2.** *pl. Iron:* insults; uncomplimentary remarks.
amenuiser [amənɥize] *v.tr.* to reduce, to thin (down); to whittle down.
amer[1], -ère [amɛr] **1.** *a.* (*of pers., taste, etc.*) bitter **2.** *n.m.* (*drink*) bitters.
amer[2] *n.m. Nau:* seamark, landmark.
amèrement [amɛrmɑ̃] *adv.* bitterly.
américain, -aine [amerikɛ̃, -ɛn] **1.** *a. & n.* American; **idiotisme a.,** Americanism; *Cu:* **homard à l'américaine,** lobster américaine; **2.** *n.m. Ling:* American (English). **3.** *n.f. Sp: Cy:* track relay (race).
américanisation [amerikanizasjɔ̃] *n.f.* Americanization.
américaniser [amerikanize] *v.tr.* **1.** to Americanize. **2. un monde qui s'américanise,** a world which is coming more and more under American influence.
américanisme [amerikanism] *n.m.* **1.** *Ling:* Americanism. **2.** American studies.
américaniste [amerikanist] *n.m. & f.* specialist in American studies.
amérindien, -ienne [amerɛ̃djɛ̃, -jɛn] *a. & n. Ethn:* Amerind, Amerindian, American Indian.
Amérique [amerik] *Pr.n.f. Geog:* America; **l'A. du Nord, du Sud,** North, South, America; **l'A. latine,** Latin America.
Amerlo(t), Amerloque [amɛrlo, amɛrlɔk] *n. P:* American, Yank.
amerrir [amerir] *v.i.* (*a*) *Av:* to alight, land (on the sea); (*b*) (*of space capsule*) to splash down.
amerrissage [amerisaʒ] *n.m.* (*a*) *Av:* alighting, landing (on the sea); **a. forcé,** ditching; (*b*) splashdown (of space capsule).
amertume [amɛrtym] *n.f.* bitterness.
améthyste [ametist] *n.f.* amethyst.
ameublement [amœbləmɑ̃] *n.m.* **1.** furnishing (of house, office, etc.). **2.** (*a*) set, suite of furniture; (*b*) furniture; **tissu d'a.,** furnishing fabric.
ameublir [amœblir] *v.tr.* **1.** *Agr:* to loosen, break up, mellow (soil). **2.** *Jur:* (*a*) to convert (realty) into personality; (*b*) to bring (one's realty) into the communal estate.
ameublissement [amœblismɑ̃] *n.m.* **1.** *Agr:* loosening, breaking up (of soil). **2.** *Jur:* (*a*) conversion (of realty) into personalty; (*b*) inclusion (of realty) in the communal estate.
ameuter [amøte] *v.tr.* **1.** *Ven:* to form (hounds) into a pack; to pack (hounds). **2.** (*a*) to stir up (the mob); (*b*) **s'a.,** to form a mob.
ami, -e [ami] **1.** *n.* (*a*) friend; **un de mes meilleurs amis,** one of my best friends; **a. intime,** close friend; **a. d'enfance,** childhood friend; **un a. de la maison,** a friend of the family; **en a.,** as a friend; **mon a.,** (i) (*between friends*) my dear fellow; (ii) (*from wife to husband*) my dear; **mon amie,** my dear, my love; **être sans amis,** to be friendless, without friends; (*b*) **son a.,** (i) her man friend; (ii) her lover; **sa petite amie,** (i) his girl friend; (ii) his mistress; (*c*) **un a. des arts,** a patron of art; (*of words*) **faux amis,** deceptive cognates; (*d*) *Geog:* **les Îles des Amis,** the Friendly Islands, Tonga; (*e*) **société des amis,** Society of Friends, *F:* Quakers. **2.** *a.* (*a*) friendly **(de,** to); **peuple a.,** ally, friendly state; (*b*) favourable (wind, etc.).

amiable [amjabl̥] *a. Jur:* **1.** friendly, conciliatory, amicable; **a. compositeur,** arbitrator. **2. à l'a.,** amicably; **différons à l'a.,** let us agree to differ; *Jur:* **arranger une affaire à l'a.,** to settle a difference out of court; **arrangement à l'a.,** amicable arrangement; **vente à l'a.,** private sale; sale by private contract.

amiablement [amjabləmɑ̃] *adv. Jur:* amicably, in a friendly manner; privately.

amiante [amjɑ̃t] *n.m. Miner:* asbestos; **carton d'a.,** asbestos board, sheet.

amibe [amib] *n.f.* amoeba.

amibien, -ienne [amibjɛ̃, -jɛn] *a. Med:* amœbic.

amical, -aux [amikal, -o] *a.* friendly (advice, tone, etc.); amicable (relations); **être a. avec qn,** to be friendly towards s.o.; **peu a.,** unfriendly; *Sp:* **match a.,** *n.m.* **amical,** friendly match; **association amicale,** *n.f.* **amicale,** (professional) association.

amicalement [amikalmɑ̃] *adv.* in a friendly way; like a friend; *Corr:* **bien a. à vous,** yours (ever).

amide [amid] *n.m. Ch:* amide.

amidon [amidɔ̃] *n.m.* starch.

amidonnage [amidɔnaʒ] *n.m. Laund:* starching.

amidonner [amidɔne] *v.tr. Laund:* to starch.

amincir [amɛ̃sir] *(a) v.tr.* to make (sth.) thinner; to fine down, thin down (wood); to machine down (metal); **la brume s'amincit,** the mist is clearing; *(b) v.i. F:* (*of pers.*) to get slimmer.

amincissant [amɛ̃sisɑ̃] **1.** *a.* (*of dress*) slimming; *U.S:* slenderizing. **2.** *n.m.* (paint) thinner.

amincissement [amɛ̃sismɑ̃] *n.m.* *(a)* thinning down, machining down; *(b)* (*of pers.*) growing thinner, slimmer.

amine [amin] *n.f. Ch: Pharm:* **a. de réveil,** amphetamine.

aminé [amine] *a. Ch:* **acide a.,** amino acid.

amiral, -aux [amiral, -o] **1.** *n.m.* admiral, flag officer; **a. de la flotte,** admiral of the fleet. **2.** *a.* **(vaisseau) a.,** (i) (*at sea*) flagship; (ii) (*in port*) guardship. **3.** *n.m. Conch:* admiral shell.

amirale [amiral] *n.f.* admiral's wife.

amirauté [amirote] *n.f.* **1.** Admiralty; **conseil d'a.** = (i) Board of Admiralty; (ii) High Court of Admiralty. **2.** *Geog:* **îles de l'A.,** the Admiralty Islands; **île de l'A.,** Admiralty Island (British Columbia).

amitié [amitje] *n.f.* **1.** friendship; **étroite a.,** close friendship; **concevoir de l'a. pour qn, prendre qn en a.,** to take a liking to s.o., to take to s.o.; **se lier d'a. avec qn,** to make friends with s.o., to become friendly with s.o.; **par a.,** out of friendship. **2.** *(a)* kindness, favour; **faites-moi l'a. de le lui dire,** do me the favour of telling him so; *(b) Corr:* **mes amitiés à votre sœur,** (i) my love, (ii) my best regards, *F:* all the best, to your sister; **sincères amitiés de . . .,** best wishes from . . ..

ammoniac, -iaque [amɔnjak] *a. Ch:* **gaz a.,** *n.* **ammoniac,** ammonia; **sel a.,** sal ammoniac.

ammoniaque [amɔnjak] *n.f. Ch:* ammonia.

ammoniaqué [amɔnjake] *a.* ammoniated; (tincture of) quinine.

ammonite [amɔnit] *n.f. Paleont:* ammonite.

amnésie [amnezi] *n.f. Med:* amnesia.

amnésique [amnezik] *Med:* *(a) a.* amnesic; *(b) n.* amnesia case; amnesiac.

amnistie [amnisti] *n.f.* amnesty.

amnistier [amnistje] *v.tr.* (*pr.sub. & impf.* **n. amnistiions, v. amnistiiez)** to amnesty, pardon.

amocher [amɔʃe] *v.tr. P:* to knock, bash (s.o.) about; to beat (s.o.) up.

amoindrir [amwɛ̃drir] **1.** *v.tr.* to reduce, decrease, lessen, diminish; to weaken; to belittle (s.o.); to mitigate (an evil); **a. la puissance de qn,** to curtail s.o.'s power. **2.** *v.i. & pr.* to diminish, to grow less.

amoindrissement [amwɛ̃drismɑ̃] *n.m.* reduction, lessening, decrease, diminution.

amok [amɔk] **1.** *a.* (running) amok. **2.** *n.m.* amok (frenzy). **3.** *n.m.* person running amok.

amollir [amɔlir] *v.* **1.** *v.tr.* to soften (substance, s.o.'s heart, etc.). **2. s'a.,** to soften, become soft; (*of courage, etc.*) to flag, weaken.

amollissement [amɔlismɑ̃] *n.m.* softening; weakening, flagging (of courage, etc.).

amonceler [amɔ̃sle] *v.tr.* **(j'amoncelle, n. amoncelons; j'amoncellerai)** to pile up, heap up, bank up; to accumulate.

amoncellement [amɔ̃sɛlmɑ̃] *n.m.* **1.** heaping (up), piling (up), banking up, accumulation. **2.** heap, pile; **a. de neige,** snowdrift.

amont [amɔ̃] *n.m.* *(a)* upper waters (of river); **en a., vers l'a.,** upstream; up river; **la Seine en a. de Paris,** the Seine above Paris; *(b)* **vent d'a.,** off-shore wind.

amoral, -aux [amɔral, -o] *a.* amoral.

amoralité [amɔralite] *n.f.* amorality.

amorçage [amɔrsaʒ] *n.m.* **1.** beginning, setting going (of sth.); priming (of pump, motor, etc.); building up (of magnetic field); *Med:* induction (of sleep). **2.** baiting (of hook, line).

amorce [amɔrs] *n.f.* **1.** beginning; initial section (of road, etc. under construction); **a. de négociations,** preliminary talks. **2.** *(a) Exp:* (i) primer, fuse, detonator; *(b) Sm.a:* percussion cap, cartridge cap; *(c) El:* fuse; *(d) Hyd.E:* priming (of pump); *(e) Metalw:* scarf (of weld). **3.** *Fish:* bait. **4.** *Cin: Rec:* leader.

amorcer [amɔrse] *v.tr.* **(j'amorçai(s); n. amorçons) 1.** *(a)* to begin, start (building, road, attack, subject, etc.); **a. des négociations,** to initiate negotiations; *(b)* to prime, fetch (pump); to cap (shell); *El:* to start, excite (dynamo); to strike (arc); *Metalw:* to scarf (weld); to fuse (bomb). **2.** *(a)* to bait (line, trap, etc.); *(b)* to entice, decoy (animal, person). **3. s'a.,** to begin; **une baisse des cours s'amorce,** stocks, shares, are showing a downward trend.

amorçoir [amɔrswar] *n.m. Tls:* *(a)* auger, twist bit, boring bit; *(b)* centre punch.

amorphe [amɔrf] *a.* **1.** *Ch: Miner: Biol:* amorphous. **2.** flabby; without personality; *F:* spineless.

amorti [amɔrti] *a.* **1.** *(a) Ph:* damped (wave); *(b) Tls:* **marteau a.,** cushioned hammer. **2.** *Nau:* **navire a.,** neaped ship. **3.** *n.f. Ten: etc:* drop shot.

amortir [amɔrtir] *v.tr.* **1.** *(a)* to deaden, muffle (sound); to subdue (light); to dull (pain); to damp (ardour); to damp, cool (passion); to tone down, flatten (colour); to break (fall); to absorb, deaden (shock); to break the force of (blow); *(b) Ph:* to damp down, damp out (oscillations). **2.** *Const:* to slack, slake (lime). **3.** *(a) Fin:* to redeem, pay off, extinguish, amortize (debt); **cela s'amortira tout seul,** it will pay for itself; *(b)* to allow for depreciation of, to write off (plant).

amortissable [amɔrtisabl̥] *a. Fin:* redeemable.

amortissement [amɔrtismɑ̃] *n.m.* **1.** breaking (of fall); absorption (of shock); **a. du son,** sound-proofing (of wall, etc.). **2.** *Fin:* *(a)* redemption, amortization, paying off, liquidation (of debt); **fonds, caisse, d'a.,** sinking fund; *(b)* depreciation.

amortisseur [amɔrtisœr] *n.m.* **1.** *(a) Mec.E:* **a. à moulinet,** air brake; **a. pneumatique,** air cushion; *(b) Aut: etc:* shock absorber, *U.S:* snubber. **2.** *El:* damper.

amour [amur] *n.m.* (*occ. f. in poetry, often f. in pl. in* **1, 2.**) **1.** *(a)* love, affection, passion; **a. d'une mère,** a mother's love; **l'a. du prochain,** love of one's neighbour; **avec a.,** lovingly; with loving care; **chagrin d'a.,** unhappy love affair; **a. platonique,** platonic love; **a. intéressé,** cupboard love; **chanson d'a.,** love song; **enfant de l'a.,** love child; **se marier par a.,** to marry for love; **mariage d'a.,** love match; **faire l'a.,** to make love, to have sexual intercourse (**avec,** with); **il n'y a point de laides amours,** beauty is in the eye of the beholder; **froides mains, chaudes amours,** cold hands, warm heart; (*b*) *pl.* love affairs; **les premières amours,** first love, calf love; **2.** (*object of one's love*) **mon a.,** my love, my darling; **l'a. de sa famille,** the idol of the family; **une de mes anciennes amours,** an old flame of mine; **les voitures sont ses seul(e)s amours,** cars are his sole passion. **3.** Cupid, Eros, the god of Love; **beau comme l'A.,** handsome as a Greek god; **quel a. d'enfant!** what an adorable child! **tu es un a.!** you('re an) angel! **sois un a.!** be a dear, be an angel! **quel a. de bague!** what a lovely, heavenly, ring!

amouracher (s') [samuraʃe] *v.pr.* to fall head over heels in love, to become infatuated (with s.o.).

amourette [amurɛt] *n.f.* **1.** love affair, passing fancy. **2.** *Cu:* **amourettes,** spinal marrow.

amoureusement [amurøzmɑ̃] *adv.* (*a*) lovingly; (*b*) amorously.

amoureux, -euse [amurø, -øz] **1.** *a.* (*a*) loving (care, look, gesture); **vie amoureuse,** love life; **être a. de qn, de qch.,** to be in love with s.o.; to be a lover of sth.; (*b*) amorous (look, gesture). **2.** *n.* suitor, lover; man, woman, in love.

amour-propre [amurprɔpr̥] *n.m.* (*a*) self respect, amour propre, (legitimate) pride; **blesser l'a.-p. de qn,** to hurt, wound, s.o.'s pride; (*b*) amour-propre, vanity, conceit; **pétri d'a.-p.,** eaten up with conceit.

amovible [amɔvibl̥] *a.* **1.** (*a*) (*of office*) revocable at pleasure; (*b*) removable (official). **2.** (*of parts of machine*) detachable; interchangeable; **siège a.,** sliding seat.

ampérage [ɑ̃peraʒ] *n.m. El:* amperage.

ampère [ɑ̃pɛr] *n.m. El.Meas:* ampere.

ampèremètre [ɑ̃pɛrmɛtr̥] *n.m. El:* ammeter.

amphétamine [ɑ̃fetamin] *n.f.* amphetamine.

amphi [ɑ̃fi] *n.m. F:* (*a*) *Sch:* lecture room (*b*) *Sch:* lecture; (*c*) *Av: Mil:* briefing.

amphibie [ɑ̃fibi] **1.** *a.* (*a*) *Nat.Hist:* amphibious (plant, animal); (*b*) **appareil a., voiture a.,** amphibian; *Mil:* **opération a.,** combined operation. **2.** *n.m.* (*a*) *Nat.Hist:* amphibian; (*b*) *Veh:* amphibian.

amphibiens [ɑ̃fibjɛ̃] *n.m.pl. Z:* Amphibia.

amphithéâtre [ɑ̃fiteɑtr̥] *n.m.* **1.** amphitheatre; **en a.,** in tiers; tier upon tier. **2.** lecture room.

amphore [ɑ̃fɔr] *n.f.* (*a*) *Archeol:* amphora; (*b*) jar.

ample [ɑ̃pl̥] *a.* **1.** ample, full (dress, skirt, etc.). **2.** roomy, spacious (shop, theatre, etc.). **3.** full (account); plentiful, ample (supply); **jusqu'à plus a. informé,** until fuller information is available.

amplement [ɑ̃pləmɑ̃] *adv.* amply; fully; **nous avons a. le temps,** we have plenty of time.

ampleur [ɑ̃plœr] *n.f.* **1.** width, fullness (of garment); copiousness (of meal); volume (of voice); extent (of damages). **2. devant l'a. du désastre,** in view of the extent, the scope, of the disaster.

ampli [ɑ̃pli] *n.m. F:* amplifier.

amplificateur, -trice [ɑ̃plifikatœr, -tris] **1.** *a.* magnifying; amplifying. **2.** *n.m.* amplifier.

amplification [ɑ̃plifikasjɔ̃] *n.f.* **1.** (*a*) amplification, development (of a subject); (*b*) exaggeration. **2.** *Opt:* magnification; *W.Tel: etc.* amplification.

amplifier [ɑ̃plifje] *v.tr.* (*impf. & pr.sub.* **n. amplifiions, v. amplifiiez**) **1.** (*a*) to amplify, develop (subject, etc.); (*b*) to embroider (story); to exaggerate; to magnify (danger). **2.** *Opt:* to magnify.

amplitude [ɑ̃plityd] *n.f.* **1.** *Lit:* amplitude, vastness (of space, etc.). **2.** amplitude (of star, of oscillation); *W.Tel:* **modulation d'a.,** amplitude modulation. **3.** range; **a. thermique,** range of temperature.

ampoule [ɑ̃pul] *n.f.* **1.** phial. **2.** (*a*) bulb (of thermometer, electric light); (electronic) tube; (*b*) container (of vacuum flask); **a. de rechange,** refill. **3.** blister (on foot, metal, etc.).

ampoulé [ɑ̃pule] *a.* inflated, bombastic (speech).

amputation [ɑ̃pytasjɔ̃] *n.f.* **1.** (*a*) amputation (of limb, etc.); (*b*) curtailment, cutting down (of book, etc.); reduction (of claim). **2.** *F:* cut; **faire des amputations dans un article,** to make cuts in an article.

amputé, -ée [ɑ̃pyte] *n.* amputee.

amputer [ɑ̃pyte] *v.tr.* **1.** to amputate (a limb); **a. qn,** to amputate s.o.'s limb; **il fut amputé du bras gauche,** his left arm was amputated. **2.** to cut down, curtail (article, etc.); to cut, reduce (claim) (**de,** by).

amulette [amylɛt] *n.f.* amulet, charm.

amusant [amyzɑ̃] *a.* amusing, entertaining; funny.

amuse-gueule [amyzgœl] *n.m.* cocktail snack; *pl. amuse-gueules.*

amusement [amyzmɑ̃] *n.m.* (*a*) entertaining, amusing; **faire qch. pour son a.,** to do sth. for one's own amusement; (*b*) amusement, recreation, pastime.

amuser [amyze] *v.* **I.** *v.tr.* to amuse, entertain, divert; **en attendant il faut a. la salle,** in the meantime we must keep the audience amused; **si tu penses que ça m'amuse!** if you think I enjoy (doing) that! **II. s'amuser** (*a*) to enjoy oneself; to have a good time; **je ne me suis jamais aussi bien amusé,** I've had the time of my life; **les enfants s'amusent dans le jardin,** the children are playing in the garden; **amusez-vous bien!** enjoy yourselves! (*b*) **s'a. aux dépens de qn,** to amuse oneself at s.o.'s expense; to make fun of s.o.; **s'a. à faire qch.,** to enjoy doing sth.; to amuse oneself doing sth.; *F:* **ne t'amuse pas à recommencer,** don't you dare do that again; **si tu crois que je vais m'amuser à faire ça,** if you think I've nothing better to do than that; **si je dois m'amuser à y aller à pied,** if I'm expected to walk there.

amusette [amyzɛt] *n.f.* **1.** pastime; diversion. **2.** *Belg:* frivolous person.

amuseur, -euse [amyzœr, -øz] *n.* entertainer.

amygdale [ami(g)dal] *n.f.* tonsil; *Med:* **inflammation des amygdales,** tonsillitis.

amygdalectomie [ami(g)dalɛktɔmi] *n.f. Surg:* tonsillectomy.

amygdalite [ami(g)dalit] *n.f. Med:* tonsillitis.

an [ɑ̃] *n.m.* year; **l'an passé, dernier,** last year; **deux fois par an,** twice a year; **tous les ans,** every year; **avoir dix ans,** to be ten (years old); **ami de vingt ans,** friend of twenty years' standing; **bon an, mal an,** taking one year with another; **en l'an 1200,** in the year 1200; **le jour de l'an, le nouvel an,** New Year's day.

anacarde [anakard] *n.m. Bot:* cashew nut.

anacardier [anakardje] *n.m.* cashew tree.

anachorète [anakɔrɛt] *n.m.* anchorite; recluse.

anachronique [anakrɔnik] *a.* anachronistic.

anachronisme [anakrɔnism] *n.m.* anachronism.

anaconda [anakɔ̃da] *n.m. Rept:* anaconda.

anagrammatique [anagramatik] *a.* anagrammatic(al).

anagramme [anagram] *n.f.* anagram.

anal, -aux [anal, -o] *a. Anat:* anal.

analgésie [analʒezi] *n.f. Med:* analgesia.

analgésique [analʒezik] *a. & n.m.* analgesic.

analogie [analɔʒi] *n.f.* analogy.

analogique [analɔʒik] *a.* analogical; *Elcs:* **calculatrice a.,** analog(ue) computer.

analogue [analɔg] **1.** *a.* analogous (**à,** to, with); similar (**à,** to). **2.** *n.m.* analogue, parallel.

analphabète [analfabɛt] *a. & n.* illiterate.

analphabétisme [analfabetism] *n.m.* illiteracy.

analyse [analiz] *n.f.* analysis. **1.** (*a*) **a. grammaticale,** parsing; **a. logique,** analysis; **faire l'a. d'une phrase,** (i) to parse; (ii) to analyse, a sentence; **en dernière a.,** in the last analysis, when all is said and done, all things considered; (*b*) *Ch:* **a. quantitative,** quantitative analysis; **a. volumétrique,** volumetric analysis; **a. qualitative,** qualitative analysis; *Med:* **laboratoire d'analyses,** pathology laboratory; *Mth:* **a. infinitésimale,** (differential and integral) calculus. **2.** abstract, résumé, précis.

analyser [analize] *v.tr.* to analyse (facts, etc.); **a. une phrase,** (i) to parse, (ii) to analyse, a sentence.

analyseur [analizœr] *n.m.* analyser.

analyste [analist] *n.m. & f.* analyst.

analytique [analitik] **1.** *a.* analytic(al); **géométrie a.,** analytic geometry. **2.** *n.f.* analytics.

analytiquement [analitikmɑ̃] *adv.* analytically.

ananas [anana(s)] *n.m.* (*a*) pineapple; (*b*) pineapple plant; **serre à a.,** pinery.

anarchie [anarʃi] *n.f.* anarchy.

anarchique [anarʃik] *a.* anarchic(al); anarchistic.

anarchisant [anarʃizɑ̃] *a.* with anarchist tendencies, leanings.

anarchiser [anarʃize] *v.tr.* to anarchize.

anarchisme [anarʃism] *n.m.* anarchism.

anarchiste [anarʃist] *a. & n.* anarchist.

anastigmat [anastigma], **anastigmatique** [anastigmatik] *a.* anastigmatic (lens).

anathématiser [anatematize] *v.tr.* to anathematize, curse.

anathème [anatɛm] *n.m.* anathema.

anatife [anatif] *n.m. Crust:* barnacle.

anatomie [anatɔmi] *n.f.* **1.** anatomy; *Med:* **a. pathologique,** morbid anatomy; *F:* **une belle a.,** a lovely figure. **2. pièce d'a.,** anatomical figure.

anatomique [anatɔmik] *a.* anatomical.

anatomiquement [anatɔmikmɑ̃] *adv.* anatomically.

anatomiste [anatɔmist] *n.m. & f.* anatomist.

ancestral, -aux [ɑ̃sɛstral, -o] *a.* ancestral.

ancêtre [ɑ̃sɛtr̥] *n.m.* (*a*) ancestor; **la maison de ses ancêtres,** his (i) ancestral, (ii) family, home; (*b*) **la montgolfière est l'a. de l'avion,** Montgolfier's balloon is the ancestor of the aeroplane; (*c*) *F:* old man.

anche [ɑ̃ʃ] *n.f.* **1.** *Mus:* reed, tongue (of oboe, clarinet, etc.); **jeu d'anches,** reed-stop (of organ). **2.** spout (of hopper). **3.** *Const: etc:* leg, sheer (of gin, etc.).

anchois [ɑ̃ʃwa] *n.m.* anchovy; **a. de Norvège,** sprat; **beurre d'a., sauce aux a.,** anchovy paste, sauce; *F:* **serrés comme des a.,** packed like sardines.

ancien, -ienne [ɑ̃sjɛ̃, -jɛn] *a.* **1.** ancient, old, antique; **monument a.,** ancient monument; **meubles anciens,** antique furniture. **2.** ancient, old(en), early, bygone, past; **les peuples anciens,** people of antiquity; **le grec a.,** ancient, classical, Greek; **l'A. Testament,** the Old Testament. **3.** former, late, old, ex-(teacher, pupil, etc.); **a. président,** past president; **a. élève,** old pupil, old boy (of a school); *U.S:* alumnus; **anciens combattants,** ex-servicemen, *esp. U.S.* veterans. **4.** senior (captain, officer, etc.); **les élèves anciens, les anciens,** the senior pupils; **il est votre a.,** he is senior to you. **5.** *n.m.* (*a*) **les anciens,** the ancients; (*b*) *Ecc: Pol:* elder; (*c*) **les anciens du village,** the older inhabitants of the village; *F:* **l'a.,** the old man, father; (*d*) *Scout:* patrol leader; (*e*) **aimer l'a.,** to like (i) antique furniture, antiques, (ii) old buildings.

ancienneté [ɑ̃sjɛnte] *n.f.* **1.** age, antiquity (of monument, race, etc.); **de toute a.,** from time immemorial. **2.** seniority, length of service; **a. de grade,** seniority in rank; **avancer à l'a.,** to be promoted by seniority.

ancillaire [ɑ̃silɛr] *a.* ancillary.

ancolie [ɑ̃kɔli] *n.f. Bot:* aquilegia, columbine.

ancrage [ɑ̃kraʒ] *n.m.* **1.** *Nau:* (*a*) anchoring; (*b*) anchorage; **(droits d')a.,** anchorage dues. **2.** *Mec.E: Civ.E: etc:* (*a*) anchoring, anchorage, fixing; (*b*) bracing, staying; (*c*) wall tie; **plaque, tige, d'a.,** anchor plate, tie.

ancre [ɑ̃kr̥] *n.f.* **1.** anchor; **a. de veille,** sheet anchor; **lever l'a.,** to weigh anchor; *F:* to leave, to get moving; *Aer:* **a. de ballon,** balloon anchor, grapnel. **2.** *Const: etc:* anchor, cramp iron, tie (plate) (of wall, furnace, etc.); brace, stay (of boiler).

ancrer [ɑ̃kre] *v.tr.* **1.** to anchor (ship, balloon). **2.** *Const:* to brace, tie, stay, anchor (chimney, engine, boiler, etc.). **3. s'a.,** to settle in, get a firm footing.

andalou, -ouse [ɑ̃dalu, -uz] **1.** *a.& s. Geog:* Andalusian. **2.** *n.m. Ling:* Andalusian (dialect). **3.** *n.m.* Andalusian horse.

Andalousie [ɑ̃daluzi] *Pr.n.f. Geog:* Andalusia.

andante [ɑ̃dɑ̃t] *adv. & n.m. Mus:* andante.

andantino [ɑ̃dɑ̃tino] *adv. & n.m. Mus:* andantino.

Andes [ɑ̃d] *Pr.n.f.pl. Geog:* **les A.,** the Andes; **la Cordillère des A.,** the Andean, the Great, Cordillera.

andin [ɑ̃dɛ̃] *a. Geog:* Andean.

andorran, -ane [ɑ̃dɔrɑ̃, -an] *a. & n. Geog:* Andorran.

Andorre [ɑ̃dɔr] *Pr.n.Geog:* **le val, la principauté d'A.,** the Vale, Principality, of Andorra.

andouille [ɑ̃duj] *n.f.* **1.** *Cu:* chitterlings (made into sausages). **2. faire l'a.,** to play the fool.

andouiller [ɑ̃duje] *n.m. Ven:* tine (of antler).

andouillette [ɑ̃dujɛt] *n.f. Cu:* (small) sausage (for frying) made of chitterlings.

André [ɑ̃dre] *Pr.n.m.* Andrew.

androgène [ɑ̃drɔʒɛn] (*a*) *a.* androgenic; (*b*) *n.m.* androgen, male hormone.

androgyne [ɑ̃drɔʒin] **1.** *a.* (*a*) *Bot:* androgynous; (*b*) *Z:* hermaphroditic. **2.** *n.m.* (*a*) *Bot:* androgyne; (*b*) *Z:* hermaphrodite.

Andromaque [ɑ̃drɔmak] *Pr.n.f.* Andromache.

Andromède [ɑ̃drɔmɛd] *Pr.n.f.* Andromeda.

âne [ɑn] *n.m.* **1.** (*a*) donkey, ass; **â. mâle,** jack(-ass), jackass; **promenade à â., à dos d'â.,** donkey ride; *F:* **têtu comme un â.,** as stubborn as, mule; pig-headed; *Prov:* **on ne saurait faire boire un â. qui n'a pas soif,** you may lead a horse to water but you cannot make him drink; **faute d'un point Martin perdit son â.,** for want of a nail the shoe was lost; (*b*) **en dos d'â.,** ridged, razor-backed; **colline en dos d'â.,** hog's back; **pont en dos d'â.,** humpbacked bridge. **2.** *F:* fool, ass, dunce; **bonnet d'â.,** dunce's cap.

anéantir [aneɑ̃tir] *v.tr.* **1.** to reduce to nothing; to annihilate, destroy (empire, town, etc.); **a. les espérances de qn,** to dash, put an end to, s.o.'s hopes; **je suis anéanti,** I am exhausted, dead beat. **2. s'a.** (*a*) to come to nothing, to vanish; to melt into thin air; (*b*) to humble, abase, oneself (before God).

anéantissant [aneɑ̃tisɑ̃] *a.* exhausting (work); overwhelming (misfortune).

anéantissement [aneɑ̃tismɑ̃] *n.m.* **1.** destruction, annihilation (of hope, empire, etc.). **2.** (state of) prostration, exhaustion.

anecdote [anɛkdɔt] *n.f.* anecdote.

anémie [anemi] n.f. *Med:* an(a)emia; **a. pernicieuse,** pernicious anaemia.

anémier [anemje] *v.tr.* to make (s.o.) an(a)emic; **s'a.,** to become an(a)emic.

anémique [anemik] *a.* **1.** an(a)emic. **2.** feeble; weak.

anémomètre [anemɔmɛtr̥] *n.m.* anemometer, wind gauge, indicator; **a. badin,** airspeed indicator.

anémone [anemɔn] *n.f.* **1.** *Bot:* anemone; **a. sylvie,** wood anemone. **2.** *Coel:* **a. de mer,** sea anemone.

ânerie [ɑnri] *n.f. F:* **1.** stupidity; **il est d'une â.!** what an idiot! **2. faire des âneries,** to make an ass, a fool, of oneself; **dire des âneries,** to talk tripe.

anéroïde [anerɔid] *a. Meteor:* aneroid (barometer).

ânesse [ɑnɛs] *n.f.* she ass, jenny; **lait d'â.,** ass's milk.

anesthésiant [anɛstezjɑ̃] *a. & n.m. Med:* an(a)esthetic.

anesthésie [anɛstezi] *n.f. Med:* an(a)esthesia; **a. générale, a. locale,** general, local, an(a)esthetic.
anesthésier [anɛstezje] *v.tr. Med:* to an(a)esthetize.
anesthésique [anɛstezik] *a. & n.m. Med:* an(a)esthetic.
anesthésiste [anɛstezist] *n.m. & f. Med:* an(a)esthetist.
aneurine [anœrin] *n.f.* vitamin B.
anévrisme, -ysme [anevrism] *n.m. Med:* aneurism, aneurysm.
ange [ɑ̃ʒ] *n.m.* **1.** angel; **a. gardien,** guardian angel; **a. déchu,** fallen angel; *Art:* **a. joufflu,** chubby little cherub; **être aux anges,** to be in the seventh heaven (of delight), to walk on air; *F:* **faiseuse d'anges,** abortionist; *F:* **un a. passe,** an angel is passing; *F:* **sois un a.!** be an angel! *Swim:* **saut de l'a.,** swallow dive; *U.S:* swan dive; **2.** *Ich:* **a. (noir, de mer),** (black) angel fish; monk fish.
angelet [ɑ̃ʒlɛ] *n.m.* little angel, cherub.
angélique [ɑ̃ʒelik] **1.** *a.* angelic(al); **la salutation a.,** the Hail Mary. **2.** *n.f. Cu:* angelica.
angelot [ɑ̃ʒlo] *n.m.* **1.** = ANGELET. **2.** *Ich:* monk fish, angel fish, ray, shark.
angélus [ɑ̃ʒelys] *n.m. Ecc:* angelus (bell).
angevin, -ine [ɑ̃ʒvɛ̃, -in] *a. & n.* Angevin(e), (i) of Angers; (ii) *Hist:* of Anjou.
angine [ɑ̃ʒin] *n.f. Med:* **1.** quinsy; tonsillitis. **2. a. de poitrine,** angina (pectoris).
anglais, -aise [ɑ̃glɛ, -ɛz] **1.** *a.* English (language, etc.); British (army, goods, etc.); *F:* **filer à l'anglaise,** to take French leave, to slip away; *Cu:* **pommes (de terre) à l'anglaise,** boiled potatoes. **2.** *n.* Englishman, Englishwoman, Briton; **les A.,** the English; the British. **3.** *n.m.* English (language); **l'a. correct,** the King's, Queen's, English. **4. anglaises,** ringlets.
angle [ɑ̃gl] *n.m.* **1.** (*a*) angle; **a. aigu, obtus,** acute, obtuse, angle; **a. droit,** right angle; **à angles droits,** rectangular; (*of house*) **faire a. avec la rue,** to stand at an angle to the street; *Av:* **a. critique,** stalling angle; **a. de cap,** track course; **a. mort,** dead angle; *Join: etc:* **abattre les angles de qch.,** to chamfer sth.; **soudure d'a.,** fillet weld; *Mec.E:* **roue d'a.,** bevel wheel, mitre wheel; **engrenage d'a.,** bevel gear; **fer d'a.,** angle iron; (*b*) *Tls:* **a. oblique,** bevel rule, mitre square. **2.** edge (of a tool); **à angles vifs,** with sharp edges. **3.** (*a*) corner, angle (of wall, room, etc.); **armoire d'a.,** corner cupboard; **boutique d'a.,** corner shop; **l'a. de la rue,** the street corner; **à l'a. du chemin,** at the bend of the road; (*b*) *Arch:* quoin (of building). **4.** angle, point of view; **a. d'attaque,** approach (to a subject).
angledozer [ɑ̃glədozɛr] *n.m.* angledozer.
Angleterre [ɑ̃glətɛr] *Pr.n.f.* **1.** *Geog:* England; **la bataille d'A.,** the Battle of Britain (1940). **2.** *Lacem:* **point d'A.,** Brussels (bobbin) lace.
anglican, -ane [ɑ̃glikɑ̃, -an] *a. & n. Rel:* Anglican; **l'Église anglicane,** the Church of England, the Anglican Church.
anglicanisme [ɑ̃glikanism] *n.m. Rel:* Anglicanism.
anglicisant, -ante [ɑ̃glisizɑ̃, -ɑ̃t] *n.* student of English; English scholar; Anglicist.
angliciser [ɑ̃glisize] *v.tr.* to anglicize (word, etc.).
anglicisme [ɑ̃glisism] *n.m. Ling:* Anglicism.
angliciste [ɑ̃glisist] *n.m. & f.* Anglicist.
anglo- [ɑ̃glo] *pref.* Anglo-.
anglo-américain [ɑ̃gloamerikɛ̃] *a.* Anglo-American.
anglo-catholique [ɑ̃glokatɔlik] *a. & n.m. & f. Ecc:* Anglo-Catholic.
anglo-irlandais, -aise [ɑ̃gloirlɑ̃dɛ, ɛz] *a. & n. Hist:* Anglo-Irish(man, -woman).
anglomane [ɛ̃glɔman] *n.m. & f.* anglomaniac.
anglomanie [ɑ̃glɔmani] *n.f.* anglomania.
anglo-normand, -ande [ɑ̃glɔnɔrmɑ̃, -ɑ̃d] **1.** *Hist:* (*a*) *a. & n.* Anglo-Norman; (*b*) *n.m. Ling:* Anglo-Norman. **2.** *a. Geog:* **les îles Anglo-Normandes,** the Channel Islands.
anglophile [ɑ̃glɔfil] *a. & n.* anglophil(e), pro-English.
anglophilie [ɑ̃glɔfili] *n.f.* anglophilia.
anglophobe [aglɔfɔb] **1.** *a.* anglophobi(a)c. **2.** *n.* anglophobe.
anglophobie [ɑ̃glɔfɔbi] *n.f.* anglophobia.
anglophone [ɑ̃glɔfɔn] *a. & n.* English-speaking (person).
anglo-saxon, -onne [ɑ̃glɔsaksɔ̃, -ɔn] *a. & n.* Anglo-Saxon; **les pays anglo-saxons,** the English-speaking countries.
angoissant [ɑ̃gwasɑ̃] *a.* distressing (news); agonizing, heart-rending (sight); tense, anxious (moment).
angoisse [ɑ̃gwas] *n.f.* anguish; distress; agony; **les angoisses de la mort,** the pangs of death.
angoissé [ɑ̃gwase] *a.* distressed, anxious; **j'étais a.,** my heart was in my mouth.
Angola [ɑ̃gɔla] *Pr.n.m. Geog:* Angola.
angolais, -aise [ɑ̃gɔlɛ, -ɛz] *a. & n.,* **angolan,-ane** [ɑ̃gɔlɑ̃, -an] *a. & n. Geog:* Angolan.
Angora [ɑ̃gɔra] **1.** *a. usu. inv.* angora (wool); **poil de chèvre a.,** mohair. **2.** *n.m.* (*a*) angora rabbit; (*b*) Persian cat; (*c*) angora (goat).
angstrœm, angström [ɑ̃gstrœm] *n.m. Ph.Meas:* angström.
anguille [ɑ̃gij] *n.f.* (*a*) *Ich:* eel; **il y a a. sous roche,** (i) there's something in the wind; (ii) there's something fishy going on; (*b*) **a. de mer,** conger eel.
angulaire [ɑ̃gylɛr] **1.** *a.* angular; *Const:* **pierre a.,** cornerstone. **2.** *n.m. Phot:* **grand a.,** wide-angle lens.
anguleux, -euse [ɑ̃gylø, -øz] *a.* angular, bony (face, elbows, etc.); rough, rugged (outline, etc.); **caractère a.,** awkward disposition.
anicroche [anikrɔʃ] *n.f.* difficulty, hitch, snag; **se passer sans a.,** to go smoothly, without a hitch.
aniline [anilin] *n.f. Ch: Dy:* aniline.
animal¹ -aux [animal, -o] *n.m.* animal; **société protectrice des animaux,** society for the prevention of cruelty to animals; *F:* **quel a.!** what a brute! what a beast! **il en a de la chance, cet a.-là!** what a lucky brute! **espèce d'a.!** you bastard!
animal² -aux, *a.* **1.** animal (kingdom, matter, etc.); **chaleur animale,** animal warmth. **2.** animal, sensual, brute (instinct, etc.).
animalier [animalje] *a. & n.m.* painter, sculptor, of animals.
animant [animɑ̃] *a.* stimulating, exciting.
animateur, -trice [animatœr, -tris] **1.** *a.* life-giving (power, etc.); stimulating (person). **2.** *n.* (*a*) stimulating person; life and soul (of an enterprise); (*b*) *T.V: etc.* compère; M.C., emcee; quiz, question, master; (*c*) *Cin:* animator. **3.** *n.m. Mec:* prime mover.
animation [animasjɔ̃] *n.f.* **1.** animation, liveliness, vivacity; **l'a. des rues,** the bustle in the streets; **ville pleine d'a.,** town full of life; **a. du marché,** buoyancy of the market. **2.** *Cin:* animation.
animé [anime] *a.* **1.** animated, spirited, lively (person, discussion, etc.), busy (street); **cheval a.,** fresh, frisky, horse; **marché a.,** brisk, buoyant, market. **2.** *Cin:* **dessin a.,** cartoon.
animer [anime] *v.tr.* **1.** to animate; to give life to (s.o., sth.); **animé par un nouvel espoir,** buoyed up with new hope; **son visage s'anima,** his face lit up. **2.** (*a*) to move, propel; to drive (machine); (*b*) **animé d'un sentiment de jalousie,** prompted by feelings of jealousy. **3.** to enliven (conversation); to stir up (feelings); **la conversation s'animait,** the conversation was getting more lively, was warming up; **la rue s'anime le soir,** the street wakes up at night.

animosité [animozite] *n.f.* animosity, spite **(contre,** against); **avoir, garder, de l'a. contre qn,** to nurse a grudge against s.o.; **agir par a.,** to act out of spite.

anion [anjɔ̃] *n.m. Ph:* anion.

anis [ani(s)] *n.m.* (*a*) *Bot:* anise; (*b*) **(graine d')a.,** aniseed; **à l'a.,** aniseed-flavoured; (*c*) aniseed aperitif.

ankylose [ɑ̃kiloz] *n.f. Med:* ankylosis.

ankyloser [ɑ̃kiloze] *v.tr.* (*a*) *Med:* to ankylose; (*b*) **s'a.,** to become, get, stiff; **être ankylosé,** to be stiff.

annal, -aux [anal, -o] *a. Jur:* valid for one year; **location annale,** yearly letting.

annales [anal] *n.f.pl.* annals, (public) records; **les annales du crime,** the annals of crime.

annamite [anamit] **1.** *a. & n. Geog:* Annamese, Annamite. **2.** *n.m. Ling:* Annamese.

Anne [ɑn] *Pr.n.f.* Anna, Ann(e).

anneau, -eaux [ano] *n.m.* **1.** ring; *Bot:* annulus; **a. de rideau,** curtain ring; **a. nuptial, de mariage,** wedding ring; **a. épiscopal,** episcopal, bishop's, ring; *Gym:* **les anneaux,** the rings; **jeu des anneaux,** hoop-la. **2.** (*a*) link (of chain); *F:* **l'a. manquant,** the missing link; (*b*) ringlet, curl (of hair); (*c*) coil (of serpent); (*d*) bow (of key). **3.** (*a*) *Tchn:* ring, collar; hoop (of hub, etc.); **a. brisé,** key ring, split ring; **a. à fiche,** ring-bolt, eye-bolt; (*b*) *Mount:* sling (of rope).

année [ane] *n.f.* year; **a. solaire,** solar year; **a. civile,** calendar year; **bonne a!** happy new year! **a. budgétaire, d'exercice, fiscale,** financial, fiscal, year; **a. scolaire,** school, academic, year; **payer à l'a.,** to pay by the year; **d'a. en a.,** year by year; **une a. après l'autre,** year in year out.

année-lumière [anelymjɛr] *n.f.* light year; *pl. années-lumière.*

annelé [anle] *a.* ringed (column, worm, etc.).

annexe [anɛks] *n.f.* **1.** (*a*) annex(e); outbuilding; (*b*) *Ecc:* chapel of ease. **2.** dependency (of a state). **3.** (*a*) rider (to bill); schedule (to act); supplement, appendix (to book, report); (*b*) enclosure (with letter). **4.** *a.* **établissement a.,** annex(e); **lettre a.,** covering letter; **industries annexes,** subsidiary industries; **revenus annexes,** supplementary income.

annexer [anɛkse] *v.tr.* **1.** to annex (territory). **2.** to append, attach (document, etc.); **pièces annexées (à une lettre),** enclosures.

annexion [anɛksjɔ̃] *n.f.* annexation.

Annibal [anibal] *Pr.n.m. A.Hist:* Hannibal.

annihilant [aniilɑ̃] *a.* annihilating.

annihilation [aniilasjɔ̃] *n.f.* annihilation.

annihiler [aniile] *v.tr.* **1.** to annihilate, destroy (army, etc.). **2.** *Jur:* to annul, cancel.

anniversaire [anivɛrsɛr] **1.** *a.* anniversary (festival, ceremony). **2.** *n.m.* anniversary (of victory, birth, death, etc.); (wedding) anniversary; **l'a. de ma naissance, mon a.,** my birthday.

annonce [anɔ̃s] *n.f.* **1.** (*a*) announcement, notification, notice; *Ecc:* **faire l'a. d'un mariage,** to publish the banns; **les annonces de la semaine,** the weekly notices; (*b*) *Cards:* declaration; bid; (*c*) sign, indication. **2.** advertisement; **petites annonces,** classified advertisements, small ads.

annoncer [anɔ̃se] *v.tr.* **(j'annonçai(s); n. annonçons) 1.** to announce, give notice of, give out (sth.); **a. une mauvaise nouvelle à qn,** to break bad news to s.o.; **2.** to advertise (sale, etc.). **3.** (*a*) to promise, foretell, give promise of; **tout semble a. le succès,** everything points to success; **cela n'annonce rien de bon, s'annonce mal,** it looks unpromising; no, nothing, good will come of that; (*b*) to give proof of (sth.); to show (sth.); **cela annonce de l'intelligence,** that shows intelligence. **4.** to announce (s.o.), to show (s.o.) in.

annonceur [anɔ̃sœr] *n.m.* **1.** advertiser. **2.** *W.Tel: T.V:* announcer.

annonciateur, -trice [anɔ̃sjatœr, -tris] **1.** *n.m.* (*a*) *Tp: etc:* indicator board, annunciator (board); **a. à volets,** drop indicator, drop annunciator; **a. de fin,** ring-off signal; (*b*) *El:* **a. de couplage,** interlocking signal. **2.** *a.* **signes annonciateurs du printemps,** signs that spring is on the way.

annonciation [anɔ̃sjasjɔ̃] *n.f. Ecc:* annunciation; **fête de l'A.,** Feast of the Annunciation, Lady Day.

annoncier [anɔ̃sje] *n.m. Journ:* **1.** (*a*) publicity editor; (*b*) advertising agent. **2.** advertiser.

annotateur, -trice [anɔtatœr, -tris] *n.* annotator, commentator (of text, etc.).

annotation [anɔtasjɔ̃] *n.f.* **1.** annotating, making notes. **2.** annotation, note.

annoter [anɔte] *v.tr.* to annotate (text); to write notes (in book).

annuaire [anɥɛr] *n.m.* **1.** annual, yearbook. **2.** almanac, calendar; **a. des marées,** tide table. **3.** (yearly) list; **l'A. militaire,** the Army list; *U.S.:* the Army Register; **l'A. de la Marine,** the Navy List; **l'A. du téléphone, téléphonique,** telephone directory; *F:* the phone book; **a. de l'université,** university calendar.

annuel, -elle [anɥɛl] *a.* annual, yearly; **plante annuelle,** annual; **rente annuelle,** annuity.

annuellement [anɥɛlmɑ̃] *adv.* annually, yearly.

annuité [anɥite] *n.f.* **1.** annual instalment (in repayment of debt). **2.** annuity.

annulaire [anylɛr] *a.* **1.** annular, ring-shaped. **2.** *a. & n.m.* **(doigt) a.,** ring finger, third finger.

annulation [anylasjɔ̃] *n.f. Jur: etc:* annulment; quashing, setting aside, (of judgment); abatement (of writ); voidance (of contract); cancelling, cancellation (of contract); setting aside (of will).

annuler [anyle] *v.tr.* (*a*) *Jur:* to annul; to render void, repeal, rescind (law, judgment); to set aside (will); (*b*) to cancel (contract, etc.); to call off (a deal); **a. un ordre de grève,** to call off a strike; (*c*) to cancel (cheque, etc.); (*d*) **ce catalogue annule les précédents,** this catalogue cancels all previous issues; **ces deux forces s'annulent,** these two forces counterbalance, cancel, each other, cancel out; (*e*) *Fb:* to disallow (a goal).

anoblir [anɔblir] *v.tr.* to raise (s.o.) to the peerage.

anoblissement [anɔblismɑ̃] *n.m.* ennoblement **(de,** of); raising to the peerage.

anode [anɔd] *n.f. El:* anode, positive pole.

anodin [anɔdɛ̃] **1.** *a.* harmless; innocuous; slight (injury); mild (criticism). **2.** *n.m.* palliative, painkiller, analgesic.

anodique [anɔdik] *a. El:* anodic, anodal; anode (current).

anomalie [anɔmali] *n.f.* (*a*) anomaly; (*b*) *Biol:* anomaly; aberration; abnormality; deviation.

ânon [ɑnɔ̃] *n.m.* ass's foal, ass's colt.

ânonnement [ɑnɔnmɑ̃] *n.m.* stumbling, painful, delivery; stammering; humming and hawing.

ânonner [ɑnɔne] *v.tr.* to stumble, blunder, through (speech); to hum and haw.

anonymat [anɔnima] *n.m.* anonymity; **écrire sous l'a.,** to write anonymously; **garder l'a.,** to remain anonymous.

anonyme [anɔnim] *a.* (*a*) anonymous (writer, letter, etc.); (*b*) *Com:* **société a. (par actions),** joint-stock company, limited (-liability) company.

anonymement [anɔnimmɑ̃] *adv.* anonymously.

anorak [anɔrak] *n.m. Cost:* anorak.

anorexie [anɔrɛksi] *n.f. Med:* anorexia.

anormal, -aux [anɔrmal, -o] *a.* (*a*) abnormal; **évolution anormale d'une maladie,** unexpected evolution of an illness; **enfants anormaux,** educationally subnormal children; *n. F:* **c'est un a.,** he's round the

bend; (*b*) unjust; unfair; (*c*) extraordinary; **il fait une chaleur anormale,** it's exceptionally hot.
anormalement [anɔrmalmɑ̃] *adv.* abnormally.
anse [ɑ̃s] *n.f.* **1.** handle (of jug, basket); shackle (of padlock); *Arch:* **voûte en a. de panier,** basket-handle arch. **2.** (*a*) loop, bight (of rope, etc.); *Anat:* loop; (*b*) **a. à vis,** screw eye(bolt). **3.** *Geog:* bight, cove.
antagonique [ɑ̃tagɔnik] *a.* antagonistic.
antagonisme [ɑ̃tagɔnism] *n.m.* antagonism; **éveiller l'a. de qn,** to antagonize s.o.
antagoniste [ɑ̃tagɔnist] **1.** *a.* antagonistic, opposed; *Mec:* **force a.,** (i) antagonistic force; (ii) controlling force, counter-check; **couple a.,** opposing couple. **2.** *n.* antagonist, opponent.
antan [ɑ̃tɑ̃] *adv. A: & Lit:* yesteryear; **où sont les neiges d'a.?** where are the snows of yesteryear?
antarctique [ɑ̃tarktik] *Geog:* (*a*) *a.* Antarctic; **cercle a.,** Antarctic circle; (*b*) *Pr.n.m.* **l'A.,** Antarctica, the Antarctic.
anté- [ɑ̃te] *pref.* ante-; pre-.
antécédent [ɑ̃tesedɑ̃] **1.** *a.* antecedent, previous, anterior (**à,** to). **2.** *n.m.* (*a*) antecedent; (*b*) *pl.* previous history, past record; antecedents.
antéchrist [ɑ̃tekrist] *n.m.* antichrist.
antédiluvien, -ienne [ɑ̃tedilyvjɛ̃, -jɛn] *a.* antediluvian.
antenne [ɑ̃tɛn] *n.f.* **1.** *W.Tel: etc:* (*a*) aerial, antenna; **a. de télévision,** television aerial; **a. fermée, en cadre,** loop aerial; *Av:* **a. pendante,** trailing aerial; (*b*) **passer sur les antennes,** to be broadcast, televised. **2.** (*a*) antenna, *F:* feeler (of insect); (*b*) branch (of pipeline); *Rail:* branch line (with sidings); (*c*) *Mil:* **a. chirurgicale,** advanced surgical unit.
anténuptial, -aux [ɑ̃tenypsjal, -o] *a.* antenuptial.
antépénultième [ɑ̃tepenyltjɛm] *a. & n.f.* antepenultimate.
antérieur, -eure [ɑterjœr] *a.* **1.** (*a*) anterior (**à,** to); former (period); earlier (date); previous (year) (**à,** to); prior (engagement) (**à,** to); antecedent (**à,** to); **a. au mariage,** pre-marital; (*b*) *Gram:* **futur a.,** future perfect; **passé a.,** past anterior. **2.** anterior (muscle); fore (limb, etc.); front (wall, vowel, etc.).
antérieurement [ɑ̃terjœrmɑ̃] *adv.* previously, earlier; **son livre a paru a. au vôtre,** his book appeared before yours.
anthère [ɑ̃tɛr] *n.f. Bot:* anther.
anthologie [ɑ̃tɔlɔʒi] *n.f.* anthology.
anthologique [ɑ̃tɔlɔʒik] *a.* anthological.
anthracite [ɑ̃trasit] **1.** *n.m. Miner:* anthracite. **2.** *a.inv.* charcoal grey.
anthrax [ɑ̃traks] *n.m.* **1.** *Med:* (*a*) carbuncle; (*b*) **a. malin,** anthrax. **2.** *Ent:* anthrax.
anthropoïde [ɑ̃trɔpɔid] *a. & n.m.* anthropoid (ape).
anthropologie [ɑ̃trɔpɔlɔʒi] *n.f.* anthropology.
anthropologique [ɑ̃trɔpɔlɔʒik] *a.* anthropological.
anthropologiste [ɑ̃trɔpɔlɔʒist] *n.m.,* **anthropologue** [ɑ̃trɔpɔlɔg] *n.m.* anthropologist.
anthropométrie [ɑ̃trɔpɔmetri] *n.f.* anthropometry.
anthropométrique [ɑ̃trɔpɔmetrik] *a.* anthropometric(al); *Adm:* **service a.,** criminal anthropometry department (= Criminal Records Office); **fiche a.** = (criminal's) dossier.
anthropomorphisme [ɑ̃trɔpɔmɔfism] *n.m.* anthropomorphism.
anthropophage [ɑ̃trɔpɔfaʒ] **1.** *a.* anthropophagous, cannibalistic, man-eating. **2.** *n.m. & f.* cannibal.
anti¹- [ɑ̃ti] *pref.* anti-.
anti²- *pref.* ante-.
antiaérien, -ienne [ɑ̃tiaerjɛ̃, -jɛn] *a.* anti-aircraft (gun, defence).
antialcoolique [ɑ̃tialkɔlik] **1.** *a.* (*a*) anti-alcohol (league, etc.); (*b*) teetotal. **2.** *n.* teetotaller.
antialcoolisme [ɑ̃tialkɔlism] *n.m.* antialcoholism; teetotalism.
antiatomique [ɑ̃tiatɔmik] *a.* antinuclear; **abri a.,** fall-out shelter; **manifestation a.,** ban-the-bomb demonstration.
antibiotique [ɑ̃tibjɔtik] *a. & n.m.* antibiotic.
antibrouillage [ɑ̃tibrujaʒ] *n.m. W.Tel: etc:* anti-jamming.
antibrouillard [ɑ̃tibrujar] *a. & n.m. Aut:* **(phare) a.,** fog lamp.
antibuée [ɑ̃tibɥe] *a. & n.m. Aut:* **(dispositif) a.,** demister.
anticalcaire [ɑ̃tikalkɛr] *n.m. Mch:* scale preventer, scale remover.
anticancéreux, -euse [ɑ̃tikɑ̃serø, -øz] *a.* **centre, sérum, a.,** cancer hospital, serum.
anticathode [ɑ̃tikatɔd] *n.f. X-rays:* anticathode.
antichambre [ɑ̃tiʃɑ̃br̥] *n.f.* waiting room, antechamber; **pilier d'a.,** hanger-on (of minister, etc.).
antichar [ɑ̃tiʃar] *Mil:* **1.** *a.* anti-tank. **2.** *n.m.* anti-tank device.
antichoc [ɑ̃tiʃɔk] *a.inv.* shock-proof; *Med:* **traitement a.,** anti-shock treatment.
anticipatif, -ive [ɑ̃tisipatif, -iv] *a.* anticipatory, anticipative; **paiement a.,** prepayment.
anticipation [ɑ̃tisipasjɔ̃] *n.f.* **1.** anticipation; **payer par a.,** to pay in advance; **littérature d'a.** = science fiction. **2.** encroachment (on s.o.'s rights, etc.).
anticiper [ɑ̃tisipe] **1.** *v.tr.* to anticipate (sth.), to forestall (s.o.'s action); **plaisir anticipé,** anticipated pleasure; **avec mes remerciements anticipés,** thanking you in anticipation; *Fin:* **dividende anticipé,** advanced dividend; **remboursement anticipé,** redemption before due date. **2.** *v.i.* (*a*) **a. sur les droits de qn,** to encroach on s.o.'s rights; (*b*) **a. sur les événements,** to anticipate events; **a. sur ses revenus,** to spend one's income in advance; (*c*) *Sp: etc.* to anticipate one's opponent's moves.
anticlérical, -ale, -aux [ɑ̃tiklerikal, -o] *a. & n.* anticlerical.
anticléricalisme [ɑ̃tiklerikalism] *n.m.* anticlericalism.
anticlimax [ɑ̃tiklimaks] *n.m.* anticlimax.
anticlinal, -aux [ɑ̃tiklinal, -o] *n.m. Geol:* anticline.
anticoagulant [ɑ̃tikɔagylɑ̃] *a. & n.m.* anticoagulant.
anticolonialisme [ɑ̃tikɔlɔnjalism] *n.m.* anticolonialism.
anticonceptionnel, -elle [ɑ̃tikɔ̃sɛpsjɔnɛl] *a.* (*a*) contraceptive; (*b*) birth-control (measures, etc.).
anticonstitutionnel, -elle [ɑ̃tikɔ̃stitysjɔnɛl] *a.* anticonstitutional.
anticorps [ɑ̃tikɔr] *n.m.* antibody.
anticyclique [ɑ̃tisiklik] *a.* anticyclic.
anticyclonal [ɑ̃tisiklɔnal] *a. Meteor:* anticyclonic; **aire anticyclonale,** high-pressure area.
anticyclone¹ [ɑ̃tisiklon] *n.m. Meteor:* anticyclone.
anticyclone², *a.* **abri a.,** cyclone cellar.
anticyclonique [ɑ̃tisiklɔnik] *a. Meteor:* anticyclonic.
antidate [ɑ̃tidat] *n.f.* antedate.
antidater [ɑ̃tidate] *v.tr.* to antedate (contract, etc.).
antidéflagrant [ɑ̃tideflagrɑ̃] *a.* explosion-proof; flameproof.
antidémocratique [ɑ̃tidemɔkratik] *a.* antidemocratic.
antidérapant [ɑ̃tiderapɑ̃] *a. & n.m.Aut: etc:* **(pneu) a.,** non-skid (tyre).
antidétonant [ɑ̃tidetɔnɑ̃] *a. & n. I.C.E:* anti-knock.
antidiphtérique [ɑ̃tidifterik] *a.* **vaccin a.,** diphtheria vaccine.

antidote [ɑ̃tidɔt] *n.m. Med:* antidote.
anti-éblouissant [ɑ̃tiebluisɑ̃] *a.* anti-dazzle.
antienne [ɑ̃tjɛn] *n.f. Ecc.Mus:* antiphon.
antifading [ɑ̃tifadiŋ] *a. & n.inv.* **(dispositif) a.,** automatic volume control.
antifasciste [ɑ̃tifasist, -ʃist] *a. & n.m. & f. Pol:* anti-fascist.
anti-g [ɑ̃tiʒe] *a.inv. Av:* **vêtement, combinaison, a.-g.,** (anti) G suit.
antigaz [ɑ̃tigaz] *a.* anti-gas.
antigel [ɑ̃tiʒɛl] *n.m. & a.inv.* antifreeze.
antigène [ɑ̃ntiʒɛn] *n.m. Med:* antigen.
antigivreur, -euse [ɑ̃tiʒivrœr, -øz] *(a) a. Av:* anti-icing; *Aut:* de-icing; *(b) n.m. Av:* anti-icer; *Aut:* de-icer.
antihéros [ɑ̃tiero] *n.m.* antihero.
antihistaminique [ɑ̃tiistaminik] *a. & n.m. Med:* antihistamine.
antihygiénique [ɑ̃tiiʒjenik] *a.* unhygienic, insanitary.
anti-incrustant [ɑ̃tiɛ̃krystɑ̃] *Mch:* **1.** *a.* scale-preventing. **2.** *n.m.* scale preventer.
antillais, -aise [ɑ̃tijɛ, -ɛz] *a. & n. Geog:* West-Indian.
Antilles [ɑ̃tij] *Pr.n.f.pl. Geog:* **les A.,** the West Indies; **la Mer des A.,** the Caribbean (Sea).
antilog [ɑ̃tilɔg] *n.m. Mth: F:* antilog.
antilogarithme [ɑ̃tilɔgaritm] *n.m. Mth:* antilogarithm.
antilope [ɑ̃tilɔp] *n.f. Z:* antelope.
antimagnétique [ɑ̃timaɲetik] *a.* antimagnetic.
antimatière [ɑ̃timatjɛr] *n.f.* antimatter.
antimilitarisme [ɑtimilitarism] *n.m.* antimilitarism.
antimilitariste [ɑ̃timilitarist] *n.* antimilitarist.
antimissile [ɑ̃timisil] *a.* anti-missile; **missile a.-m.,** anti-missile missile.
antimite(s) [ɑ̃timit] *(a) a.* mothproof; *(b) a.* moth destroying; *n.m.* mothkiller.
antimoine [ɑ̃timwan] *n.m. Ch:* antimony.
antimonarchique [ɑ̃timɔnarʃik] *a.* anti-monarchic(al).
antimonarchisme [ɑ̃timɔnarʃism] *n.m.* anti-monarchism.
antimonarchiste [ɑ̃timɔnarʃist] *n.m. & f.* anti-monarchist.
antinazi, -e [ɑ̃tinazi] *a. & n.* anti-nazi.
antinévralgique [ɑ̃tinevralʒik] *a & n.m. Pharm:* antineuralgic.
antipaludique [ɑ̃tipalydik] *a.* antimalaria(l).
antipape [ɑ̃tipap] *n.m. Rel.H:* antipope.
antiparasitage [ɑ̃tiparazitaʒ] *n.m. W.Tel: El:* suppression.
antiparasitaire [ɑ̃tiparazitɛr] **1.** *n.m.* pesticide. **2.** *a.* pest-destroying.
antiparasite [ɑ̃tiparazit] **1.** *(a) a.* pesticidal; *(b) n.m.* pesticide. **2.** *a. & n.m. W.Tel: Aut: etc:* **(dispositif) a.,** suppressor.
antiparlementaire [ɑ̃tiparləmɑ̃tɛr] *a. Pol: (a)* antiparliamentary; *(b)* unparliamentary (language).
antipathie [ɑ̃tipati] *n.f.* antipathy.
antipathique [ɑ̃tipatik] *a.* antipathetic; repugnant.
antipersonnel [ɑ̃tipɛrsɔnɛl] *a.inv.* antipersonnel.
antiphone [ɑ̃tifɔn] *n.m. Ecc:* antiphon.
antipodal, -aux [ɑ̃tipɔdal, -o] *a.* antipodean.
antipode [ɑ̃tipɔd] *n.m.* **les antipodes,** the antipodes; **aux antipodes,** (i) at the antipodes; (ii) diametrically opposed; poles apart.
antipoliomyélite [ɑ̃tipɔljɔmjelit] *a.* **vaccination a.,** polio vaccination.
antipolitique [ɑ̃tipɔlitik] *a.* impolitic, ill-advised.
antiprogressif, -ive [ɑ̃tiprɔgrɛsif, -iv] *a.* reactionary.
antiprotectionniste [ɑ̃tiprɔtɛksjɔnist] **1.** *a.* free-trade (policy). **2.** *n.* antiprotectionist; free trader.
antiquaire [ɑ̃tikɛr] *n.m.* antiquary, antiquarian; antique dealer.
antique [ɑ̃tik] **1.** *a. (a)* ancient; **la Grèce a.,** ancient, classical, Greece; *(b)* old, ancient; antique; *(c)* old-fashioned, antiquated. **2.** *(a) n.m. O:* work of art (of classical antiquity); *(b) n.m. coll.* the antique, classical antiquity. **3.** *n.m. Typ:* antique.
antiquité [ɑ̃tikite] *n.f.* **1.** antiquity, ancientness. **2.** ancient times, antiquity. **3. l'a. grecque,** ancient Greek civilization. **4.** *(a)* **les antiquités,** the works of classical antiquity; *(b)* antiques; **magasin d'antiquités,** antique shop.
antirabique [ɑ̃tirabik] *a. Med:* anti-rabic.
antiracisme [ɑ̃tirasism] *n.m.* antiracialism, antiracism.
antiradar [ɑ̃tiradar] *a. & n.m.* anti-radar (device).
antireligieux, -euse [ɑ̃tirəliʒjø, øz] *a.* antireligious.
antirépublicain, -aine [ɑ̃tirepyblikɛ̃, -ɛn] *a. & n.* antirepublican.
antirévolutionnaire [ɑ̃tirevɔlysjɔnɛr] *a. & n.* antirevolutionary.
anti-roman [ɑ̃tirɔmɑ̃] *n.m. Lit:* anti-novel; *pl. anti-romans.*
antirouille [ɑ̃tiruj] **1.** *n.m.* rust preventive. **2.** *a.inv.* rustproof, non-rusting; rust-preventing.
antiroulis [ɑ̃tiruli] *n.m. Nau: Av:* (gyro) stabilizer.
antiscorbutique [ɑ̃tiskɔrbytik] *a. & n.m. Pharm:* antiscorbutic.
antiségrégationniste [ɑ̃tisegregasjɔnist] *n.m. & f.* antisegregationist.
antisémite [ɑ̃tisemit] *n.m. & f.* antisemite.
antisémitique [ɑ̃tisemitik] *a.* antisemitic.
antisémitisme [ɑ̃tisemitism] *n.m.* antisemitism.
antisepsie [ɑ̃tisɛpsi] *n.f. Med:* antisepsis.
antiseptique [ɑ̃tisɛptik] *a. & n.m. Med:* antiseptic.
antisérum [ɑ̃tiserɔm] *n.m. Med:* antiserum.
antisocial, -aux [ɑ̃tisɔsjal, -o] *a.* antisocial.
anti-sous-marin [ɑ̃tisumarɛ̃] *a.* anti-submarine.
antisoviétique [ɑ̃tisɔvjetik] *a.* anti-Soviet.
antispasmodique [ɑ̃tispasmɔdik] *a. & n.m. Pharm:* antispasmodic.
antistrophe [ɑ̃tistrɔf] *n.f. Pros:* antistrophe.
antitétanique [ɑ̃titetanik] *a. & n.m. Med:* antitetanus (serum).
antithèse [ɑ̃titɛz] *n.f.* antithesis.
antitoxine [ɑ̃titɔksin] *n.f. Med:* antitoxin.
antitoxique [ɑ̃titɔksik] *a. & n.m. Med:* antitoxic.
antitrust [ɑ̃titrœst] *a.inv.* antitrust.
antituberculeux, -euse [ɑ̃titybɛrkylø, -øz] *a. Med:* antitubercular; **centre a.,** tuberculosis centre.
antivenimeux, -euse [ɑ̃tivənimø, -øz] *a.* antivenomous.
antivirus [ɑ̃tivirys] *n.m.* antivirus.
antivivisection(n)iste [ɑ̃tivivisɛksjɔnist] *n.m. & f.* antivivisectionist; **société a.,** antivivisection society.
antivol [ɑ̃tivɔl] *a.inv. & n.m.* anti-theft, thief-proof (lock, device).
Antoine [ɑ̃twan] *Pr.n.m.* Ant(h)ony.
antonyme [ɑ̃tɔnim] **1.** *a.* antonymous. **2.** *n.m.* antonym.
antre [ɑ̃tr̥] *n.m.* **1.** *(a)* cave, cavern; *(b)* den, lair, retreat (of animal, brigand, etc.). **2.** *Anat:* sinus.
anucléaire [anykleɛr] *a Atom. Ph:* anuclear.
anurèse [anyrɛz] *n.f.,* **anurie** [anyri] *n.f. Med:* anuresis; anuria.
anus [anys] *n.m.* anus.
Anvers [ɑ̃vɛr(s)] *Pr.n.m. Geog:* Antwerp.
anversois, -oise [ɑ̃vɛrswa, -waz] *a. & n.* (native, inhabitant) of Antwerp.

anxiété [ɑ̃ksjete] *n.f.* **1.** anxiety; **avec a.,** anxiously.
anxieusement [ɑ̃ksjøzmɑ̃] *adv.* anxiously.
anxieux, -ieuse [ɑ̃ksjø, -jøz] *a.* anxious, uneasy.
aorte [aɔrt] *n.f. Anat:* aorta.
aortique [aɔrtik] *a. Anat:* aortic, aortal.
août [u] *n.m.* August; **en a., au mois d'a.,** in (the month of) August; **le premier, le sept., a.,** (on) the first, the seventh, of August, (on) August (the) first, (the) seventh.
apaisant [apɛzɑ̃] *a.* appeasing, soothing (news, effect, etc.).
apaisement [apɛzmɑ̃] *n.m.* appeasement; appeasing; calming (down); alleviation (of suffering).
apaiser [apeze] *v.tr.* **1.** to appease, calm, pacify (s.o.); **la foule s'apaisait,** the crowd was calming down, becoming quieter. **2.** to soothe (pain); to appease, satisfy (hunger); to quench (thirst); to calm (fears); **le vent s'apaisait,** the wind was dropping.
apanage [apanaʒ] *n.m.* ap(p)anage.
aparté [aparte] *n.m.* **1.** *Th:* aside, stage whisper; **en a.,** aside, in a stage whisper. **2.** private conversation.
apartheid [aparteid] *n.m.* apartheid.
apathie [apati] *n.f.* apathy, listlessness; indifference.
apathique [apatik] *a.* apathetic, listless; lackadaisical.
apatride [apatrid] *a. & n.m. & f. Jur:* stateless (person).
apatridie [apatridi] *n.f.* statelessness.
Apennins [apɛnɛ̃] *n.m.pl. Geog:* Apennines.
apercevoir [apɛrsəvwar] *v.* (*pr.p.* **apercevant;** *p.p.* **aperçu;** *pr.ind.* **j'aperçois, n. apercevons, ils aperçoivent,** *pr.sub.* **j'aperçoive, n. apercevions,** *imperf.* **j'apercevais;** *p.h.* **j'aperçus,** *fu.* **j'apercevrai) I.** *v.tr.* to perceive, see; to catch sight of, catch a glimpse of (s.o., sth.); **je n'ai fait que l'a.,** I caught only a glimpse of him; **cela ne s'aperçoit pas,** it isn't visible, noticeable; evident; it doesn't show; **enfin nous avons aperçu un hôtel,** at last we saw a hotel. **II. s'apercevoir de qch.,** to realize, notice, sth.; to become aware, conscious, of sth.; **sans s'en a.,** without being aware of it, without noticing it.
aperçu [apɛrsy] *n.m.* **1.** glimpse; **a. sur la campagne,** glimpse of the country. **2.** general idea, outline, summary; **par a.,** at a rough estimate.
apériodique [aperjɔdik] *a. Mec: El:* aperiodic.
apéritif [aperitif] *n.m.* aperitif, drink; **viens prendre l'a. chez moi demain soir,** come round and have a drink tomorrow evening.
aperture [apɛrtyr] *n.f. Ling:* aperture.
apesanteur [apəzɑ̃tœr] *n.f.* weightlessness.
à-peu-près [apøprɛ] *n.m.inv.* approximation; rough estimate, guess; **calculer une somme par à-p.-p.,** to make a rough calculation.
apeuré [apœre, -øre] *a.* scared, frightened.
apeurer [apœre] *v.tr.* to frighten, scare.
apex [apɛks] *n.m.* apex.
aphasie [afazi] *n.f. Med:* aphasia.
aphis [afis] *n.m. Ent:* aphis, plant louse, green fly.
aphone [afɔn] *a. Med:* voiceless.
aphonie [afɔni] *n.f. Med:* loss of voice.
aphorisme [afɔrism] *n.m.* aphorism.
aphrodisiaque [afrɔdizjak] *a. & n.m. Pharm:* aphrodisiac.
aphteux, -euse [aftø, -øz] *a. Med: Vet:* **fièvre aphteuse,** foot-and-mouth disease.
à-pic [*apik*] *n.m.* cliff, bluff, steep; *pl. à-pics.*
apicole [apikɔl] *a.* apiarian; **exploitation a.,** bee keeping.
apiculteur [apikyltœr] *n.m.* apiarist, bee keeper.
apiculture [apikyltyr] *n.f.* apiculture, bee keeping.
apitoiement [apitwamɑ̃] *n.m.* commiseration, pity, compassion; **porté à l'a.,** compassionate.
apitoyant [apitwajɑ̃] *a.* piteous, pitiful.
apitoyer [apitwaje] *v.tr.* **(j'apitoie, n. apitoyons; j'apitoierai)** to move (to pity); to incite to pity; **s'a. sur qn,** to pity s.o., to feel pity for s.o.; **s'a. sur le sort de qn,** to commiserate with s.o.
apivore [apivɔr] *a. & n.* bee-eating (creature).
aplaner [aplane] *v.tr.* to plane, smooth (wood).
aplanir [aplanir] *v.tr.* to flatten, smooth (surface); to plane (wood); to planish (metal); to level (road, etc.); to smooth out (imperfections); to ease, smooth down, iron out (difficulties); to settle (dispute).
aplati [aplati] *a.* **1.** (*a*) flattened, flat; (*b*) deflated. **2.** oblate (spheroid, etc.).
aplatir [aplatir] *v.* **I.** *v.tr.* **1.** to make (sth.) flat, to bring (sth.) level; to flatten (surface, seam); to flat (metal); to blunt (angle); *Metalw:* to clench (rivet); to hammer down (rivet head); to squash; **a. qch. à coups de marteau,** to beat sth. flat. **2.** *F:* **a. qn,** (i) to knock s.o. flat, to send s.o. sprawling; (ii) to floor s.o.; (iii) to beat s.o. to a frazzle. **II. s'aplatir 1.** to become flat, flattened out; (*of balloon*) to collapse; (*of tyre*) to get flat. **2. s'a. par terre,** (i) to lie down flat on the ground; (ii) *F:* to fall down flat, to come a cropper.
aplatissage [aplatisaʒ] *n.m.* pressing; crushing (down); flattening; hammering down (of rivet).
aplatissement [aplatismɑ̃] *n.m.* **1.** flatness; oblateness (of ellipsoid); **l'a. de la terre aux pôles,** the flattening of the earth at the poles. **2.** *Fig:* humiliation.
aplomb [aplɔ̃] *n.m.* **1.** (*a*) perpendicularity, equilibrium, balance; **d'a.,** upright, vertical(ly), plumb; **bien d'a. sur ses pieds,** steady on one's feet; *F:* **je ne suis pas d'a. aujourd'hui,** I'm out of sorts, off colour, today; **voilà qui vous remettra d'a.,** that will revive you, buck you up; **il me faut dix mille francs pour me remettre d'a.,** I want ten thousand francs to get straight; **hors d'a.,** (i) out of plumb, out of true; (ii) *F:* wobbly, shaky; **à l'a. de qch.,** straight above, below sth.; *Tchn:* plumb with sth. **2.** (self-)assurance, coolness; **perdre son a.,** to lose one's assurance, one's nerve; **avoir l'a. de dire, de faire, qch.,** to have the cheek, nerve, to say, do, sth.
apocalypse [apɔkalips] *n.f.* apocalypse, revelation; *B:* **l'A.,** the Book of Revelation, the Apocalypse; **les quatre cavaliers de l'A.,** the four horsemen of the Apocalypse.
apocalyptique [apɔkaliptik] *a.* apocalyptic(al).
apocryphe [apɔkrif] **1.** *a.* (*a*) apocryphal; (*b*) of doubtful authenticity. **2.** *n.pl. B:* **les Apocryphes,** the apocryphal books.
apogée [apɔʒe] *n.m. Astr:* apogee; **la lune est à son a.,** the moon is at apogee; **à l'a. de sa gloire,** at the height, zenith, of one's fame.
apolitique [apɔlitik] *a.* apolitical.
apolitisme [apɔlitism] *n.m.* apolitical attitude.
Apollon [apɔlɔ̃] **1.** *Pr.n.m. Myth:* Apollo; *Art:* **A. du Belvédère,** Apollo Belvedere.
apologétique [apɔlɔʒetik] **1.** *a.* apologetic(al), vindicatory. **2.** *n.f. Theol:* apologetics.
apologie [apɔlɔʒi] *n.f.* apology, apologia (**de,** for); defence, vindication, (written) justification (**de,** of); **faire l'a. de qn, de qch.,** to vindicate, justify, defend, s.o., sth.; NOTE: *never* = EXCUSE, *q.v.*
apologique [apɔlɔʒik] *a.* apologetic, by way of justification, defence.
apologiste [apɔlɔʒist] *n.m. & f.* apologist.
apoplectique [apɔplɛktik] *a. & n.* apoplectic.
apoplexie [apɔplɛksi] *n.f. Med:* apoplexy; **attaque d'a.,** apoplectic seizure, *F:* stroke.
apostasie [apɔstazi] *n.f.* apostasy.
apostasier [apɔstazje] *v.i.* (*pr.sub. & impf.* **n. apostasiions, v. apostasiiez**), to apostatize, to become an apostate; to renounce one's party, one's principles.

apostat, -ate [apɔsta, -at] *a. & n.* apostate.
a posteriori [apɔsterjɔri] *Lt.adv.phr. Log:* a posteriori; **méthode a p.,** a posteriori method.
apostolique [apɔstɔlik] *a.* **1.** apostolic (times, Church, etc.). **2.** apostolic, papal; **vicaire a.,** vicar apostolic; **pères apostoliques,** apostolic fathers.
apostrophe[1] [apɔstrɔf] *n.f.* (*a*) *Rh:* apostrophe; (*b*) reproach, reprimand.
apostrophe[2] *n.f. Gram:* apostrophe.
apostropher [apɔstrɔfe] *v.tr.* to address (s.o.) rudely; to shout at (s.o.); to hurl abuse at (s.o.).
apothéose [apɔteoz] *n.f.* **1.** apotheosis; deification. **2.** *Th:* grand finale.
apothicaire [apɔtikɛr] *n.m. A:* apothecary.
apôtre [apotr̥] *n.m.* apostle.
Appalaches [apalaʃ] *Pr.n.m.pl. Geog:* **les (monts) Appalaches,** the Appalachian Mountains.
appalachien, -ienne [apalaʃjɛ̃, -jɛn] *a. Geog:* Appalachian; **relief a.,** Appalachian relief.
apparaître [aparɛtr̥] *v.i.* (*conj. like* PARAÎTRE; *the auxiliary is usu.* **être,** *occ.* **avoir**) **1.** to appear; to become visible, to come into sight; **a. à travers le brouillard,** to loom out of the fog; **un spectre lui était apparu,** a ghost had appeared to him. **2.** (*a*) to become evident, apparent; (*b*) **le projet lui apparaissait impossible,** the plan seemed impossible to him.
apparat [apara] *n.m.* state, pomp, show, display; **dîner d'a.,** banquet; **lettres d'a.,** illuminated letters.
apparaux [aparo] *n.m.pl.* **1.** *Nau:* tackle, gear; **les gros a.,** the purchase. **2.** *Gym:* apparatus.
appareil [aparɛj] *n.m.* **1.** (*a*) *Lit:* display, magnificence, pomp; (*b*) **mettre en jeu l'a. de la justice,** to put the machinery of the law in motion; (*c*) **dans le plus simple a.,** in the nude. **2.** (*a*) apparatus; equipment; *Ind:* (*sg. or pl.*) plant; **appareils de laboratoire,** laboratory apparatus; **a. auxiliaire, de secours,** stand-by equipment; **a. de pêche,** fishing tackle; *Min:* **a. de forage,** drilling rig; *Anat:* **a. digestif,** digestive system; (*b*) device, appliance, fixture, apparatus; gear, mechanism; **a. à gaz,** gas appliance; *Rail:* **a. de voie,** switch gear; (*c*) machine; (i) *Tp:* telephone; **qui est à l'a.?** who's speaking? **gardez l'a.!** hold the line! (ii) *Av:* aircraft, plane; **a. de chasse,** fighter; **a. d'école,** training aircraft, trainer; (iii) *Phot:* **a. (photographique),** camera; (iv) **a. de prothèse,** prosthesis, artificial limb, etc.; *Dent:* **a. (dentaire),** brace; (v) **a. à sous,** slot machine; fruit machine, one-armed bandit. **3.** *Med:* dressing; splint; plaster. **4.** *Const:* (*a*) height (of stones); **assise de grand a.,** course of large stones; (*b*) bond. **5.** *Lit:* **a. critique,** critical apparatus.
appareillage[1] [aparɛjaʒ] *n.m.* **1.** (*a*) installation, fitting (up), setting up of workshop, etc.); (*b*) *Const:* bonding (of stones, bricks); (*c*) *Nau:* getting under way; weighing; setting sail; (*d*) fitting with artificial limbs; *Adm:* **centre d'a.,** artificial limb supply centre. **2.** (*a*) fittings, equipment, accessories; **a. électrique,** electrical equipment; (*b*) *Ind:* plant.
appareillage[2] *n.m.,* **appareillement** [aparɛjmɑ̃] *n.m.* **1.** matching (of colours, etc.). **2.** pairing, mating (of animals for breeding); pairing (of oxen for the yoke).
appareiller [apareje] *v.tr.* **1.** to install, fit up (workshop, etc.). **2.** *Const:* to bond (stones, bricks). **3.** to spread (net). **4.** *Nau:* (*a*) **a. une voile,** to trim a sail; (*b*) *v.i.* to get under way.
appareilleur [aparɛjœr] *n.m.* (*a*) trimmer, fitter, dresser (of stone, etc.); (*b*) *Const:* (i) house carpenter; (ii) foreman mason; (*c*) **a. à gaz,** gas fitter.
apparemment [aparamɑ̃] *adv.* apparently.
apparence [aparɑ̃s] *n.f.* **1.** (*a*) appearance, look; **quelque a. de (la) vérité,** some semblance of truth; **selon toute a.,** to all appearances; (*b*) **sous de fausses apparences,** under false pretences; **en a.,** outwardly, on the surface; ostensibly; **plus difficile en a. qu'en réalité,** less difficult than it looks. **2. avoir de l'a.,** (i) (*of pers.*) to have a good presence; (ii) (*of thg*) to look well; **pour sauver les apparences,** for the sake of appearances; to save face.
apparent [aparɑ̃] *a.* **1.** (*a*) visible, apparent; **peu a.,** hardly noticeable; (*b*) obvious, evident. **2.** apparent, not real; **mouvement a. du soleil,** apparent movement of the sun; **piété apparente,** outward piety. **3.** *Jur:* **héritier a.,** heir apparent.
apparenté [aparɑ̃te] *a.* (*a*) related (by marriage); *Jur:* affinitive (**à, avec,** to); **bien a.,** well connected; (*b*) *Ch:* **éléments apparentés,** related, affinitive, elements; (*c*) closely connected.
apparenter (s') [saparɑ̃te] *v.pr.* **1.** to marry (into a family). **2.** to have sth. in common (**à,** with).
apparier [aparje] *v.tr.* (*impf. & pr.sub.* **n. appariions, v. appariiez**) **1.** to match, pair (socks, horses, etc.); to pair off (opponents). **2.** to couple, pair, mate (birds for breeding); (*of birds*) **s'a.,** to mate.
appariteur [aparitœr] *n.m.* mace bearer (of university court, of corporation).
apparition [aparisjɔ̃] *n.f.* **1.** appearance; coming out; publication (of book, etc.); emergence (of new state, etc.); **faire une courte a.,** to make a brief appearance. **2.** (*a*) apparition, ghost, spectre; (*b*) vision (of angels, etc.).
appartement [apartəmɑ̃] *n.m.* (*a*) flat, *NAm:* apartment; suite, set of rooms; **a. de passage,** pied-à-terre; **plantes d'a.,** indoor, house, plants; (*b*) (*in château, etc.*) **les grands appartements,** the state apartments; (*c*) *Fr.C:* room.
appartenance [apartənɑ̃s] *n.f.* **1. a. à un parti,** adherence to, membership of, a party. **2.** property **3.** *pl.* (*a*) appurtenances (of house, castle); (*b*) *Equit:* (saddle) accessories.
appartenir [apartənir] *v.i.* (*conj. like* TENIR) **1.** (*a*) to belong (**à,** to); to be owned (**à,** by); **cette maison lui appartient en propre,** this house is his own personal property; **cela n'appartient pas à mes fonctions,** this does not come within the scope of my duties; (*b*) **je ne m'appartiens pas,** I'm not my own master; I've no time to call my own. **2.** *v. impers.* **à tous ceux qu'il appartient,** to all whom it may concern; **il ne m'appartient pas de le critiquer,** it is not for me to criticize him; *Iron:* **il vous appartient bien de me critiquer,** you're a fine one to criticize me.
appât [apɑ] *n.m.* **1.** (*a*) bait; **a. de fond,** ground bait; **mettre l'a. à la ligne,** to bait the line; **mordre à l'a.,** to rise to the bait; (*b*) lure (of success). **2.** soft food (for poultry).
appâter [apɑte] *v.tr.* **1.** to lure (birds, fishes, etc.) with a bait; to entice (pers.). **2.** to feed (poultry) forcibly; to cram (geese). **3.** to bait (a hook, etc.).
appauvrir [apovrir] *v.* **1.** *v.tr.* to impoverish; **a. la constitution de qn,** to weaken s.o.'s constitution. **2. s'a.,** to grow poorer; (*of soil*) to lose its fertility.
appauvrissement [apovrismɑ̃] *n.m.* impoverishment (of country, of health, etc.); degeneration (of race); deterioration (of stock); thinning (of blood).
appel [apɛl] *n.m.* **1.** (*a*) appeal; calling in (of specialist, etc.); **faire a. à qn,** to appeal to s.o., to send for s.o., to call on s.o.'s services; **faire a. à tout son courage,** to summon up all one's courage; **le moteur part au premier a.,** the engine starts at the first touch of the switch; (*b*) *Jur:* appeal at law; **avis d'a.,** notice of appeal; **Cour d'a.,** Court of Appeal; **faire a. d'une décision,** to appeal against a decision; **juger en a. (d'une décision),** to hear an appeal (from a decision); **casser un jugement en a.,** to quash a sentence on appeal; **jugement sans a.,** final judgment. **2.** call; **l'a.**

du printemps, the call of spring; **l'a. de la mer,** sea fever; **l'a. de la conscience,** the voice of conscience; **cri d'a.,** call for help; **a. d'incendie,** fire alarm; *Fin:* **faire un a. de fonds,** to call up capital; *Com:* **faire un a. d'offres,** to invite bids, tenders; *Mil:* **l'a. aux armes,** the call to arms; **a. de mobilisation,** mobilization order; **a. d'une classe,** calling up, call-up, of a class; *Tg: Tp:* **touche d'a.,** call key; **signe d'a.,** ringing tone; **a. téléphonique,** (tele)phone call; **a. avec préavis,** personal call, *U.S:* person to person call; *Av:* **a. particulier,** selective calling. **3.** roll call, callover; **feuille d'a.,** roll; *Nau:* muster roll; *Mil:* **l'a. du soir,** tattoo; **manquant à l'a.,** missing. **4.** *Tchn:* **a. d'air,** intake of air; **vitesse d'a.,** inflow; **a. d'un aimant,** pull of a magnet. **5.** reference mark; *Typ:* **a. de note,** footnote reference, superior figure. **6.** *Sp:* take-off; **un bon coup d'a. sur le tremplin,** a good kick-off from the springboard.

appelant, -ante [aplɑ̃, -ɑ̃t] *Jur:* (*a*) *a.* appealing (party, etc.); (*b*) *n.* appellant (against a judgement); **se porter a.,** to appeal.

appeler [aple] *v.* **I.** *v.tr.* **(j'appelle, n. appelons, j'appellerai) 1.** (*a*) to call, call to (s.o.); **a. au secours,** to call for help; (*b*) to call, hail (taxi); **a. qn de la main, du geste,** to beckon (to) s.o.; (*c*) *Tp:* **a. qn (au téléphone),** to ring s.o. up, *NAm:* to call s.o.; **a. Paris à l'automatique,** to dial Paris; **a. un taxi, un médecin,** to phone for a taxi, a doctor; **a. l'ascenseur,** to ring for the lift, *NAm:* to call the elevator. **2.** (*a*) to call in, send for, summon (s.o.); *Jur:* to summon (s.o.) to attend; **faire a. un médecin,** to call in, send for, a doctor; *Mil:* **a. une classe,** to call up a class; *Jur:* **a. qn en justice,** to summon(s) s.o., to sue s.o.; **a. qn à témoin,** to call s.o. to witness; *Fin:* **capital appelé,** called up capital; (*b*) **être appelé à qch.,** to be destined for sth. **3.** to call (by name); to term, name; **nous l'avons appelé David,** we have called him David; **a. les choses par leur nom,** to call a spade a spade; **vous a. appelez cela danser?** do you call that dancing? **4.** (*a*) to appeal to, call on (s.o., sth.); **a. qn à faire qch.,** to call on, invite, s.o. to do sth.; (*b*) to call for (sth.); to invite (criticism); **ce problème appelle une solution immédiate,** the problem calls for an immediate solution. **5.** to provoke, arouse, attract; *Prov:* **un malheur en appelle un autre,** misfortunes never come singly. **6.** *v.i.* (*a*) *Jur:* **a. d'un jugement,** to appeal against a sentence; **j'en appelle de votre décision,** I challenge your decision; (*b*) **en appeler à qn,** to appeal to s.o.; **j'en appelle à votre témoignage,** I call you to witness. **II. s'appeler,** to be called, named; **comment vous appelez-vous?** what is your name? **je m'appelle David,** my name is David; *F:* **voilà qui s'appelle pleuvoir!** that's rain with a vengeance!

appellation [apɛlasjɔ̃] *n.f.* **1.** (*a*) appellation; name; **a. injurieuse,** abusive term; (*b*) nomenclature; designation; trade name; (*c*) *Vit:* **a. contrôlée,** guaranteed vintage; **vin sans a.,** non-vintage wine. **2.** *Jur:* appeal at law.

appendice [apɛ̃dis] *n.m.* **1.** appendix, supplement (of book). **2.** annex(e), appendage (of building). **3.** (*a*) *Anat: Bot:* (i) appendix; (ii) appendage. **4.** (*a*) neck (of balloon); (*b*) tail (of aircraft).

appendicectomie [apɛ̃disɛktɔmi] *n.f. Med:* append(ic)ectomy.

appendicite [apɛ̃disit] *n.f. Med:* appendicitis; **a. chronique,** grumbling appendix.

appentis [apɑ̃ti] *n.m.* **1.** *Const:* (*a*) lean-to (building, roof); (*b*) outhouse; shed.

appesantir [apəzɑ̃tir] *v.* **1.** *v.tr.* (*a*) to weigh (sth., s.o.) down; **yeux appesantis par le sommeil,** eyes heavy with sleep; (*b*) to bring (sth.) down heavily. **2. s'a. sur un sujet,** to go on and on about a subject.

appétissant [apetisɑ̃] *a.* (*a*) appetizing, tempting; (*b*) alluring.

appétit [apeti] *n.m.* **1.** appetite; **couper l'a. à qn,** to spoil, take away, s.o.'s appetite; **demeurer, rester, sur son a.,** (i) to eat sparingly, to curb one's appetite; (ii) to remain unsatisfied; **manger de bon a., avec a.,** to eat heartily, with relish; **avoir un a. de loup, de cheval,** to eat like a horse; **avoir un a. d'oiseau,** to have a small, poor, appetite; to peck at one's food; **avoir bon a.,** to have a hearty appetite; **je n'ai plus d'a.,** I'm off my food; *Prov:* **l'a. vient en mangeant,** (i) once you start eating you realize that you're hungry; (ii) the more you get the more you want. **2.** desire, craving (**de,** for); **a. sexuel,** sexual desire; **a. du gain,** craving for money.

applaudir [aplodir] **1.** *v.tr.* to applaud (s.o., sth.); **se faire a. à tout casser,** to get tremendous applause, to bring the house down. **2.** *v.i.* to applaud, clap. **3. s'a. (de qch.),** to congratulate oneself, pat oneself on the back (for having done sth.).

applaudissement [aplodismɑ̃] *n.m. usu. pl.* **1.** applause, clapping. **2.** *Lit:* approval.

applicable [aplikabl̩] *a.* (*a*) applicable; **cette règle est a. à tous les cas,** this rule applies to all cases; **a. à partir du premier janvier,** to take effect from the first of January; **mot a.,** appropriate, suitable, word; (*b*) chargeable (against sth.).

applicateur [aplikatœr] *n.m.* (*device*) applicator.

application [aplikasjɔ̃] *n.f.* **1.** (*a*) application, applying; **première a. de peinture,** first coat of paint; (*b*) *Needlew:* **broderie d'a.,** appliqué (work); (*c*) **bois d'a.,** veneer. **2.** application (of a rule); **a. de la loi,** enforcement of the law; **mettre une théorie en a.,** to put a theory into practice; **faire l'a. de qch. à qch.,** to apply sth. to sth.; **en a. de ce décret,** in pursuance of this decree; *Mil: etc:* **école d'a.,** school of instruction. **3.** application (to one's work); industriousness.

applique [aplik] *n.f.* **1.** application (against wall, etc.); **lampe d'a.,** bracket lamp. **2.** applied ornament; *Needlew:* appliquéd ornament; *Bookb:* (i) paste-on label; (ii) (leather) inlay. **3.** (*a*) (wall) bracket (for lamp, etc.); (*b*) sconce, bracket lamp.

appliqué [aplike] *a.* **1.** hard working, painstaking (person); careful (handwriting). **2.** applied (sciences). **3.** *Needlew:* appliquéd (trimming).

appliquer [aplike] *v.* **I.** *v.tr.* **1.** to apply (sth. to sth.); **a. une couche de peinture sur qch.,** to apply a coat of paint to sth.; **un coup bien appliqué,** a well planted blow. **2. a. une loi à un cas particulier,** to apply a law to a special case; **a. (les dispositions de) la loi,** to bring, put, the law into operation; *Jur:* **a. le maximum de la peine,** to impose the maximum penalty. **3. a. son esprit à ses études,** to apply one's mind to one's studies. **II. s'appliquer 1. s'a. à qch.,** to apply oneself to sth., to take pains over sth.; **il s'applique à apprendre le français,** he is making a serious effort to learn French. **2.** (*of law, etc.*) to apply (**à,** to); **à qui s'applique cette remarque?** to whom does this remark apply?

appoint [apwɛ̃] *n.m.* **1.** (*a*) *Com: Fin:* balance, odd money; **le public est tenu de faire l'a.,** no change given; (*b*) **ressources d'a.,** additional (sources of) income; *Aut:* **faire l'a.,** to top up (battery, engine oil, etc.); **chauffage, éclairage, d'a.,** auxiliary heating, lighting; **siège d'a.,** extra chair. **2.** contribution; **apporter son a. à qch.,** to contribute to sth., to take a part in sth.

appointements [apwɛ̃tmɑ̃] *n.m.pl.* salary; *Ecc:* stipend; **toucher ses a.,** to draw one's salary.

appointer [apwɛ̃te] *v.tr.* to sharpen (pencil, etc.).

appointir [apwɛ̃tir] *v.tr. Tchn:* to point (needles, stakes, etc.).

apponṭage [apɔ̃taʒ] *n.m.* landing on flight deck (of

aircraft carrier); **officier d'a.,** landing officer; **crosse, crochet, d'a.,** arrester hook.

appontement [apɔ̃tmɑ̃] *n.m. Nau:* (*usu.* wooden) wharf, jetty, pier, quay; landing stage.

apponter [apɔ̃te] *v.i.* to land (on deck of aircraft carrier).

apport [apɔr] *n.m.* **1.** (*action of bringing*) contribution, contributing; (*a*) *Fin:* **a. de capitaux,** contribution of capital; **capital d'a.,** initial capital; **actions d'a.,** founder's, promoter's, shares; (*b*) *Jur:* **a. de pièces,** deposit(ing) of documents (in a suit); (*c*) *Jur:* **biens d'a.,** estate brought in by husband or wife on marriage; (*d*) *Civ.E:* **terres d'a.,** earthworks; (*e*) *Pol.Ec:* inflow; influx; **a. d'argent frais,** injection of new money. **2.** (*thing brought*) (*a*) *Fin:* initial share (in undertaking); (*b*) *Jur:* **a. dotal,** dowry; marriage portion; (*c*) *Tchn:* coating, layer, deposit; (*d*) *Agr:* **un gros a. de fumier,** a heavy dressing of manure; (*e*) **a. de chaleur, a. calorifique,** heat supply, input.

apporter [apɔrte] *v.tr.* **1.** to bring **(qch. à qn,** sth. to s.o.). **2. a. du soin à faire qch.,** to do sth. carefully; **a. des difficultés (à qch.),** to put difficulties in the way (of sth.); to raise difficulties. **3.** *Fin:* **a. des capitaux,** to bring in capital. **4.** to cause, bring about (changes etc.); **ce que l'avenir apportera,** what the future has in store.

apposer [apoze] *v.tr.* (*a*) to affix, place, put; **a. une affiche sur un mur,** to stick a bill on a wall; *Jur:* **a. sa signature à un acte,** to append one's signature to a deed; (*b*) **a. une clause à un acte,** to insert a clause in, add a clause to, an act.

apposition [apozisjɔ̃] *n.f.* **1.** *Adm:* affixing, appending (of seal, signature, etc.). **2.** *Gram:* apposition; **mot en a.,** word in apposition.

appréciable [apresjabl̥] *a.* appreciable; **a. aux sens,** perceptible; **à une distance a.,** at an appreciable, a considerable, distance.

appréciateur, -trice [apresjatœr, -tris] **1.** *a.* appreciative. **2.** *n.* (*a*) appreciator **(de,** of); (*b*) *Com: etc:* appraiser, valuer.

appréciatif [apresjatif] *a.* **devis a.,** estimate.

appréciation [apresjasjɔ̃] *n.f.* **1.** valuation, estimating, estimation, estimate; judging (of distance); **faire l'a. des marchandises,** to value, to make a valuation of, goods; *Jur:* **l'a. du juge,** the judge's summing up. **2.** judgement; opinion; appreciation (of work of art, meal, etc.). **3.** appreciation, rise in value.

apprécier [apresje] *v.tr.* (*pr.sub. & impf.* **n. appréciions, v. appréciiez**). **1.** (*a*) to appraise, to estimate the value of (sth.); to value (sth.); (*b*) to determine, estimate (temperature, distance, sound); to judge (distance); to appreciate, judge (differences, distinctions). **2.** to appreciate (meal, good thing).

appréhender [apreɑ̃de] *v.tr.* **1.** *Jur:* **a. qn (au corps),** to seize, arrest, to apprehend, s.o. **2.** to dread, fear (sth.).

appréhensif, -ive [apreɑ̃sif, -iv] *a.* apprehensive.

appréhension [apreɑ̃sjɔ̃] *n.f.* apprehension **(de,** of).

apprendre [aprɑ̃dr̥] *v.tr.* (*conj. like* PRENDRE). **1.** (*a*) to learn (lesson, trade, etc.); **a. (de qn) à faire qch.,** to learn (from s.o.) (how) to do sth.; **a. facilement,** to find learning easy; *Prov:* **on apprend à tout âge,** it is never too late to learn; (*b*) to learn, hear (of), get to know of (piece of news, etc.); **je l'ai appris de bonne part,** I have it on good authority. **2.** (*a*) **a. qch. à qn,** to teach s.o. sth.; **a. à qn à faire qch.,** to teach, show, s.o. how to do sth.; *F:* **je vous apprendrai à me parler de la sorte!** I'll teach you to speak to me like that! **ça vous apprendra!** serve(s) you right! (*b*) to inform s.o. of sth.; to tell s.o. sth.; *F:* **vous ne m'apprenez rien!** you're telling me!

apprenti, -ie [aprɑ̃ti] *n.* apprentice; *Jur:* articled clerk; **a. menuisier,** carpenter's apprentice; **a. conducteur,** learner (driver); **je ne suis qu'un a.,** I'm only a beginner, a novice.

apprentissage [aprɑ̃tisaʒ] *n.m.* apprenticeship; (*in liberal professions*) articles; **être en a. chez qn,** to be apprenticed, articled, to s.o.; **faire l'a de la vie,** to learn by experience.

apprêt [aprɛ] *n.m.* **1.** dressing, finishing (of fabrics, hides, etc.). **2.** (*a*) affectation, affectedness; (*b*) finish (of fabrics, etc.); dress; (*c*) *Paint:* primer; size.

apprêtage [aprɛtaʒ] *n.m. Tchn:* **1.** dressing, finishing (of fabrics). **2.** *Paint:* priming, sizing.

apprêté [aprete] *a.* (*a*) affected, stiff (style, manner, etc.); (*b*) **papier a.,** glazed, glossy, paper.

apprêter [aprete] *v.* **I.** *v.tr.* **1.** to prepare (meal, etc.). **2.** to dress, finish, stiffen (fabrics, etc.); to finish (leather) . **3.** *Paint:* to prime (surface). **II. s'apprêter 1.** to get ready (to go out, etc.); to get dressed, to tidy oneself (up). **2.** (*of storm, trouble, etc.*) to be on the way, to be brewing.

apprivoisé [aprivwaze] *a.* tame (animal, etc.).

apprivoisement [aprivwazmɑ̃] *n.m.* taming, domestication.

apprivoiser [aprivwaze] *v.* **1.** *v.tr.* to tame (animal); to win over (s.o.). **2. s'a.,** (i) (*of animal*) to become domesticated; (ii) (*of pers.*) to become more sociable.

approbateur, -trice [aprɔbatœr, -tris] *a.* approving (gesture, speech, etc.).

approbatif, -ive [aprɔbatif, -iv] *a.* approving (gesture), (gesture, look, etc.) of approval.

approbation [aprɔbasjɔ̃] *n.f.* (*a*) approval **(de qch.,** of sth.); consent, authorization; (*b*) certifying (of accounts, of document); passing (of accounts); (*c*) **a. tacite,** tacit approval; *Com:* **pour a.,** for approval.

approchable [aprɔʃabl̥] *a.* approachable, accessible (place, person).

approchant [aprɔʃɑ̃] *a.* approximating, similar **(de,** to); **offre approchante,** near offer; **je n'ai jamais rien vu d'a.,** I never saw anything like it, anything approaching it; **voilà ce qu'il a dit, ou quelque chose d'a.,** that is what he said, or something like it.

approche [aprɔʃ] *n.m.* **1.** (*a*) approach; advance; **l'a. de l'hiver,** the approach of winter; **à son a.,** as he came up; **d'une a. difficile,** difficult of access; **un homme d'a. facile,** an easily approachable man; **une nouvelle a. du problème,** a new approach to the problem; (*b*) *Av:* **a. à vue,** visual approach; (*c*) *Ven:* **chasse à l'a.,** deerstalking; (*d*) *Z:* mating. **2. approches d'une ville,** approaches of a town.

approcher [aprɔʃe], *v.* **1.** *v.tr.* (*a*) **a. qch. de qn, de qch.,** to bring, draw, sth. near (to) s.o., sth.; **approchez votre chaise,** pull up your chair; (*b*) to approach, come near (s.o., sth.); to come close to (s.o., sth.); **ne m'approchez pas,** don't come near me; **on ne peut pas l'a.,** (i) you can never see him; (ii) he's unapproachable. **2.** *v.i.* (*a*) to approach, draw near, come nearer; **l'heure approche,** it will soon be time; **la nuit approchait,** night was falling; it was beginning to get dark; **faites-le a.,** ask him to come (here, in); bring him to me; (*b*) **a. de qn, de qch.,** to approach s.o., sth.; **nous approchons de Paris,** we are getting near Paris; **a. du but,** to be nearing one's goal; (*c*) **a. de qn, de qch.,** to resemble s.o., sth.; **il n'y a pas de pays qui en approche,** there is no country like it; **cela approche de la folie,** that borders on insanity; (*d*) *Golf:* to play an approach shot; (*e*) *Z:* to mate. **3. s'a. de qn, de qch.,** to come up to s.o., sth.; **le navire s'approchait de la terre,** the ship was nearing land; **s'a. de la perfection,** to be almost perfect.

approfondi [aprɔfɔ̃di] *a.* elaborate, careful, extensive (research); **enquête approfondie,** searching enquiry; **connaissance approfondie,** thorough knowledge.

approfondir [aprɔfɔ̃dir] *v.tr.* **1.** (*a*) to deepen, excavate (river bed, etc.); (*b*) **cela approfondit ma tristesse,** it increases my sadness. **2.** to go deeply, thoroughly, into (sth.); to study (sth.) thoroughly; **a. une affaire,** to get to the root of a matter.

approfondissement [aprɔfɔ̃dismɑ̃] *n.m.* **1.** deepening, excavating, excavation (of canal, etc.). **2.** investigation, analysis (of question).

appropriation [aprɔprijasjɔ̃] *n.f.* **1.** appropriation (of property, etc.); **a. de fonds,** embezzlement. **2.** *A: & Belg:* cleaning; tidying up.

approprié [aprɔprije] *a.* appropriate, adapted (**à,** to); proper, suitable (term, measure, etc.).

approprier [aprɔprije] *v.tr.* (*pr.sub. & impf.* **n. appropriions, v. appropriiez**) **1.** to arrange (sth.) to fit (sth.); to adapt (sth. to sth.). **2.** *A: & Belg:* to clean; to tidy (sth.). **3. s'a. qch.,** to appropriate sth.

approuver [apruve] *v.tr.* **1.** (*a*) **a. qch.,** to approve of, *U.S:* to approbate, sth.; **a. de la tête,** to nod approval; (*b*) **a. qn de faire, d'avoir fait, qch.,** to commend s.o. for doing sth. **2.** to consent to, agree to (sth.); **a. qch. officiellement,** to agree formally to sth.; *Com:* **a. une facture,** to pass an invoice; **a. un contrat,** to ratify a contract; *Adm:* **a. une nomination,** to confirm an appointment; **a. un appel,** to endorse an appeal; **lu et approuvé,** read and approved.

approvisionné [aprɔvizjɔne] *a.* stocked, supplied (**de, en,** with); **bien a.,** well stocked.

approvisionnement [aprɔvizjɔnmɑ̃] *n.m.* **1.** provisioning, supplying (of town, army); catering (for s.o.); stocking (of shop). **2.** supply, stock, provisions; **faire un a. de qch.,** to lay in a supply of sth.

approvisionner [aprɔvizjɔne] *v.* **1.** *v.tr.* to supply (**de,** with); to cater for (s.o.); to stock (shop). **2. s'a.,** to get a stock, a supply (**en, de,** of); to lay in provisions; **s'a. chez (qn),** to deal with, get one's supplies from (s.o.); to shop at (s.o.'s).

approximatif, -ive [aprɔksimatif, -iv] *a.* approximate; rough (calculation, estimate).

approximation [aprɔksimasjɔ̃] *n.f.* approximation; rough estimate.

approximativement [aprɔksimativmɑ̃] *adv.* approximately, roughly; **dans une heure a.,** in an hour or so.

appui [apɥi] *n.m.* **1.** (*a*) support, prop, stay, shore; **mettre un a. à un mur,** to shore up a wall; (*b*) rest; *Arch:* balustrade; **a. de fenêtre,** window ledge, window sill; **a. de porte,** door sill; **a. d'escalier,** banisters. **2.** support; (*a*) **mur d'a.,** supporting, retaining, wall; **barre d'a.,** handrail; **à hauteur d'a.,** elbow high; (*b*) **a. moral,** moral support; **prêter son a. à qn,** to support s.o., to back s.o up; **être sans appui(s),** to be friendless; (*c*) *Mil:* **a. direct,** close, *U.S:* direct, support; **tir d'a.,** covering fire.

appui-bras [apɥibra] *n.m.* armrest; *pl. appuis-bras.*

appuie- [apɥi] *compound nouns of which the first element is* **appui-** *have an alternative form* **appuie-**, *in which case they are invariable.*

appui-jambes [apɥiʒɑ̃b] *n.m.* leg rest; *pl. appuis-jambes.*

appui-queue [apɥikø] *n.m. Bill:* cue rest: *F:* jigger; *pl. appuis-queue.*

appui-tête [apɥitɛ] *n.m.* headrest; *pl. appuis-tête.*

appuyé [apɥije] *a.* laboured, heavy (joke, irony).

appuyer [apɥije] *v.* **(j'appuie, n. appuyons; j'appuierai) I.** *v.tr.* **1.** (*a*) to support; to prop (up) (joist, wall, etc.); (*b*) **a. une pétition,** to support a petition (**par,** by); **a. une proposition,** to second a proposal. **2.** (*a*) to lean, rest; **a. qch. contre qch.,** to lean sth., rest sth., against sth.; **a. son opinion sur qch.,** to base, rest, one's opinion on sth.; **théorie appuyée sur des faits,** theory supported by facts; (*b*) to press (sth. on sth.); *Mus:* **a. (sur) une note,** to dwell on a note. **II.** *v.i.* to bear (**sur,** on); (*a*) **poutre qui appuie sur deux montants,** beam resting, bearing, on two uprights; (*b*) **a. sur son stylo,** to press on one's pen; **a. sur le bouton,** to press the button; **a. sur une syllabe,** to stress a syllable; *Mil:* **appuyez à droite, à gauche!** (i) on the right, left, close! (ii) feel your right! feel your left! **appuyez à droite à la sortie du village,** bear right at the end of the village. **III. s'appuyer 1. s'a. sur, contre, à, qch.,** to lean, rest, on, against, sth.; **s'a. sur qn,** (i) to lean on s.o.; (ii) to rely, depend, on s.o. **2. s'a. d'une autorité,** to base oneself on an authority. **3.** *P:* **s'a. un bon dîner, un gentil petit voyage,** to stand oneself, treat oneself to, a good dinner, a nice little trip.

âpre [ɑpr̥] *a.* **1.** rough, harsh; **voix â.,** rasping voice; **goût â.,** tart taste; **vin â.,** rough wine. **2.** bitter, biting, sharp (frost, rebuke); scathing (irony); **temps â.,** raw weather. **3.** keen (competition, etc.); **homme â. (au gain),** grasping man.

âprement [ɑprəmɑ̃] *adv.* bitterly, harshly, roughly.

après [aprɛ] **I.** *prep.* **1.** (*order in time, space*) (*a*) after; **il est arrivé a. moi,** he arrived after me; **a. tout,** after all; **jour a. jour,** day after day; **a. vous, monsieur!** after you, sir! (*in shop*) **et a. cela, madame?** anything else, madam? **a. quoi,** after which; (*b*) **je suis, viens, a. lui,** I am, come, next to him. **2.** *F:* **courir a. qn,** to run after s.o.; **jurer, maugréer, a. qn,** to swear, grumble, at s.o.; **il est toujours a. moi,** he's always nagging at me, getting at me. **3.** *prep. phr.* **d'a.,** according to, after, from; **d'a. ce qu'il a dit,** by, according to, what he said; **d'a. l'horloge il est trois heures,** according to the clock it is three; **peint d'a. nature,** painted from nature; **paysage d'a. Turner,** landscape after Turner; **texte d'a. Cicéron,** text adapted from Cicero; **d'a. l'article 12,** under article 12; **d'a. vos instructions,** in accordance with your instructions. **4. après** + *perf.inf.* **a. avoir dîné,** after dinner. **II.** *adv.* **1.** (*a*) afterwards, later; **parlez d'abord, je parlerai a.,** you speak first, I shall speak afterwards; **six semaines a.,** six weeks later; **le jour (d')a.,** the next day, the day after; *F:* **eh bien, et puis a.?** well, what of it? what about it? so what? **et a.?** what then? (*b*) *conj.phr.* **a. que,** after, when; **a. que je fus parti,** after I had gone; **a. que j'aurai fini,** when I have finished. **2.** *F:* **tout le monde leur court a.,** everybody runs after them.

après-demain [aprɛdmɛ̃] *adv. & n.m.inv.* the day after tomorrow.

après-dîner [aprɛdine] *n.m.* evening; **discours d'a.-d.,** after-dinner speech; *pl. après-dîners.*

après-guerre [aprɛgɛr] *n.m.* post-war period, conditions; aftermath of war; *pl. après-guerres.*

après-midi [aprɛmidi] *n.m. or f.inv.* afternoon; **trois heures de l'a.-m.,** three in the afternoon, three p.m.

après-rasage [aprɛrazaʒ] *a.inv.* **lotion a.-r.,** aftershave lotion.

après-ski [aprɛski] *n.m.inv.* **tenue d'a.-s.,** après-ski outfit; **des a.-s.,** snowboots.

après-vente [aprɛvɑ̃t] *a.inv. Com:* **service a.-v.,** aftersales service.

âpreté [ɑprəte] *n.f.* **1.** roughness, harshness (of wine, voice, etc.); tartness (of fruit). **2.** asperity (of tone, etc.); sharpness, bitterness (of weather, reproach).

a priori [apriɔri] *Lt.adv.phr. & a.* a priori; **raisonnement a p.,** a priori reasoning.

à-propos [aprɔpo] *n.m.* **1.** aptness, appropriateness, relevance (of an expression, etc.); **le don de (saisir) l'à-p.,** the knack of saying, doing, the right thing; **votre observation manque d'à-p.,** your remark is not to the point, is irrelevant. **2.** opportuneness; **manque d'à-p.,** untimeliness.

apte [apt] *a.* **1. a. à faire qch., à qch.,** fit, fitted, suited, qualified, to do sth., for sth.; **peu a. (à faire qch.),** unsuitable, ill-equipped (to do sth.); **a. à naviguer,** seaworthy; **a. au service,** fit for military service; *Jur:* **a. à hériter,** entitled to inherit. **2.** apt, suitable (example, etc.); **peu a.,** unsuitable.

aptère [aptɛr] *a.* wingless; *Sculp:* **victoire aptère,** wingless victory.

aptéryx [apteriks] *n.m. Orn:* kiwi.

aptitude [aptityd] *n.f.* aptitude, fitness (**à, pour,** to); *Jur:* capacity; **avoir une a. à (faire qch.),** to have the capacity (for doing sth.); to have a gift (for sth.); **test d'a.,** aptitude test.

apurement [apyrmɑ̃] *n.m.* **1.** auditing, agreeing (of accounts). **2.** discharge (of liability).

apurer [apyre] *v.tr.* **1.** to audit, pass, agree (accounts). **2.** to discharge (liability).

aquaplane [akwaplan] *n.m.* (*a*) aquaplane; surfboard; (*b*) aquaplaning; surfriding.

aquaplaniste [akwaplanist] *n.m. & f.* surf rider.

aquarelle [akwarɛl] *n.f. Art:* aquarelle; watercolour; **peindre à l'a.,** to paint in water colours.

aquarelliste [akwarɛlist] *n.m. & f.* water colourist.

aquarium [akwarjɔm] *n.m.* aquarium; **a. d'eau de mer,** oceanarium.

aquatinte [akwatɛ̃t] *n.f. Engr:* aquatint.

aquatique [akwatik] *a.* **1.** aquatic (bird, plant, sport). **2.** marshy, watery (land).

aqueduc [ak(ə)dyk] *n.m.* **1.** *Civ.E.:* (*a*) aqueduct; (*b*) culvert, conduit. **2.** *Anat:* aqueduct, canal.

aqueux, -euse [akø, -øz] *a.* **1.** *Anat: Ch: etc:* aqueous, water; **humeur aqueuse,** aqueous humour. **2.** waterlogged (ground); watery, waxy (potato).

aquilegia [akɥileʒja] *n.f.,* **aquilégie** [akɥileʒi] *n.f. Bot:* aquilegia; *F:* columbine.

aquilin [akilɛ̃] *a.* aquiline (profile, etc.); **nez a.,** Roman nose.

Aquin [akɛ̃] *Pr.n.m.* **Saint Thomas d'A.,** St Thomas Aquinas.

aquitain, -aine [akitɛ̃, -ɛn] *a. & n.* Aquitanian.

Aquitaine [akitɛn] *Pr.n.f. Hist:* (province of) Aquitaine; *Geog:* **bassin d'A.,** Basin of Aquitaine.

ara [ara] *n.m. Orn:* macaw.

arabe [arab] **1.** *a. & n.* (*a*) Arab (person, horse); **République a. unie,** United Arab Republic; (*b*) *a.* Arabian (customs, etc.). **2.** *a. & n.m. Ling: etc:* Arabic (language, numerals, etc.).

arabesque [arabɛsk] **1.** *a.* arabesque, Arabian (architecture, etc.). **2.** *n.f. Danc:* arabesque.

Arabie [arabi] *Pr.n.f. Geog:* Arabia; **A. séoudite, saoudite,** Saudi Arabia.

arabique [*arabik*] *a. used esp. in* **le désert a.,** the Arabian desert; *Com:* **gomme a.,** gum arabic.

arabisant, -ante [arabizɑ̃, -ɑ̃t] *n.* Arabic scholar, Arabist.

arable [arabl̥] *a.* arable (land, etc.).

arachide [araʃid] *n.f.* groundnut, peanut; *F:* monkey nut; **huile d'a.,** groundnut oil; **beurre d'a.,** peanut butter.

arachnides [araknid] *n.m.pl. Z:* Arachnida.

arachnoïde [araknɔid] **1.** *a. Anat: Bot:* arachnoid. **2.** *n.f. Anat:* arachnoid (membrane). **3.** *n.m. Z:* (*a*) arachnid; (*b*) spider monkey.

araignée [areɲe] *n.f.* (*a*) spider; **a. d'eau,** water spider; **toile d'a.,** cobweb, spider's web; *F:* **avoir une a. au, dans le, plafond,** to have a screw loose, to have bats in the belfry; (*b*) *F:* **a. de mer,** (i) *Crust:* spider crab; (ii) *Ich:* weever (fish).

araméen, -enne [arameɛ̃, -ɛn] *a. & n.m. Ling:* Aramaic.

arase [arɑz] *n.f. Const:* **(pierres d')a., les arases,** levelling course (of masonry).

arasé [arɑze], *a.* flush; *Furn:* **armoire arasée,** built-in cupboard.

arasement [arɑzmɑ̃] *n.m.* **1.** *Const: etc:* levelling (wall); making (wall) even, level, flush. **2.** (*a*) *Carp:* shoulder (of tenon); (*b*) *Const:* levelling course (of bricks or stones).

araser [arɑze] *v.tr.* **1.** to level (down) (wall, etc.); to make (wall) level, even; to make (two stones, etc.) flush; to plane (plank) even. **2.** to saw off (end); to square (plank); to cut off, strike off (heads of piles); to cut (rails, etc.) to length.

aratoire [aratwar] *a.* agricultural (implement).

araucaria [arokarja] *n.m.,* **araucarie** [arokari] *n.f. Bot:* araucaria, *F:* monkey puzzle.

arbalète [arbalɛt] *n.f. A.Arms:* crossbow.

arbalétrier [arbaletrije] *n.m.* **1.** *A.Mil:* crossbowman. **2.** *Const:* principal rafter (of roof, etc.).

arbitrage [arbitraʒ] *n.m.* **1.** arbitration; *Sp:* umpiring; refereeing; **conseil d'a.,** conciliation, arbitration, board (in industrial dispute). **2.** *Bank: etc:* arbitrage; **a. de change,** arbitration of exchange; *St.Exch:* **a. en reports,** jobbing in contango(e)s.

arbitraire [arbitrɛr] *a.* **1.** arbitrary (name, choice, etc.); discretionary (punishment, etc.); *n.m.* **laisser qch. à l'a. de qn,** to leave sth. to s.o.'s discretion. **2.** arbitrary, despotic, high-handed (government, power, action, etc.). **3.** *n.m.* arbitrariness.

arbitrairement [arbitrɛrmɑ̃] *adv.* arbitrarily. **1.** at will. **2.** despotically, in an overbearing manner.

arbitral, -aux [arbitral, -o] *a. Jur:* arbitral; **tribunal a.,** court of arbitration; **solution arbitrale, règlement a.,** settlement by arbitration; **commission arbitrale,** board of referees.

arbitre[1] [arbitr̥] *n.m.* (*a*) *Jur:* arbitrator, referee, adjudicator; **a. rapporteur,** referee (in commercial suit); (*b*) *Games:* referee, umpire; **a. de lignes,** *Fb:* **a. de touche,** linesman; (*in rugby*) touch judge; (*c*) arbiter (of fashion, etc.).

arbitre[2] *n.m. Phil:* **libre, franc, a.,** free will.

arbitrer [arbitre] *v.tr.* **1.** *Jur:* to arbitrate. **2.** *Games:* to referee (at), umpire (at) (match).

arborer [arbɔre] *v.tr.* to raise, erect, set up; to hoist (flag); to step (mast); **a. l'étendard de la révolte,** to raise, the standard of revolt; **a. une cravate rouge,** to wear, to sport, a red tie.

arborescence [arbɔresɑ̃s] *n.f. Bot:* arborescence.

arborescent [arbɔresɑ̃] *a. Bot:* arborescent; **fougère arborescente,** tree fern.

arborétum [arbɔretɔm] *n.m.* arboretum.

arboricole [arbɔrikɔl] *a.* tree-dwelling, arboreal (animal).

arboriculteur [arbɔrikyltœr] *n.m.* nurseryman.

arboriculture [arbɔrikyltyr] *n.f.* arboriculture; **a. fruitière,** orcharding, fruit growing.

arborisation [arbɔrizasjɔ̃] *n.f.* dendritic marking (of crystals).

arborisé [arbɔrize] *a. Miner:* dendritic.

arbousier [arbuzje] *n.m. Bot:* arbutus; **a. commun,** strawberry tree.

arbre [arbr̥] *n.m.* **1.** (*a*) tree; **jeune a.,** sapling; **a. fruitier,** fruit tree; **a. de plein vent,** standard; **a. en espalier,** espalier (tree); **a. vert,** evergreen (tree); **a. à feuille(s) caduque(s),** deciduous tree; **faire l'a. fourchu,** to walk on one's hands; to do a handstand; *Prov:* **se trouver entre l'a. et l'écorce,** to be between the devil and the deep blue sea; **les arbres cachent la forêt,** you can't see the wood for the trees; (*b*) **a. généalogique,** genealogical tree, family tree; **a. de Jessé,** tree of Jesse; (*c*) **l'a. de la Croix,** the Rood; (*d*) **a. de Noël,** Christmas tree; (*e*) **a. de la liberté,** tree of liberty. **2.** (*a*) *Bot: F:* **a. de Judée,** Judas tree; **a. à la gale, a. à la puce, a. à poison,** poison ivy; **a. à grives,** rowan, mountain ash; **a. aux lis, aux tulipes,**

tulip tree; **a. à pain,** bread(fruit) tree; **a. de paradis, de vie,** thuya, tree of life, arbor vitae; **a. du voyageur,** traveller's tree; (*b*) *Anat:* **a. de vie,** arbor vitae; **a. respiratoire,** respiratory system. **3.** *Mec.E:* shaft, spindle, axle; *Clockm: etc:* arbor; *Mec.E.:* **a. moteur, de commande,** main shaft, driving shaft; **a. d'entraînement,** (i) drive shaft; (ii) quill shaft; **a. fou,** loose shaft; **a. d'accouplement,** coupling shaft; **a. creux,** hollow spindle; tubular shaft; **a. à excentrique(s), a. excentré, excentrique,** eccentric shaft; **a. coudé, a. manivelle, a. vilebrequin,** crankshaft; **a. de tour,** lathe spindle; mandrel; **a. à cardan, a. de cardan(s),** cardan shaft; **a. à cames,** camshaft; **a. de transmission,** line shaft; *Aut:* propeller shaft; *Aut:* **a. arrière,** back axle shaft; *I.C.E:* **a. de culbuteur,** rockershaft; *El:* **a. d'induit,** armature shaft; *N.Arch:* **a. de l'hélice, a. porte-hélice,** propeller shaft.

arbrisseau, -eaux [arbriso] *n.m.* shrub; **plantation d'arbrisseaux,** shrubbery.

arbuste [arbyst] *n.m.* bush, (arborescent) shrub; **plantation d'arbustes,** shrubbery.

arc [ark] *n.m.* **1.** (*a*) bow; **tir à l'a.,** archery; **à la portée de l'a.,** within bowshot; **corde de l'a.,** bowstring; **avoir plus d'une corde à son a.,** to have more than one string to one's bow; (*b*) *Mec.E:* **ressort à a.,** bow spring; *Tls:* **scie à a.,** bow saw. **2.** (*a*) *Arch:* arch; **a. en plein cintre, a. roman,** semicircular arch; **a. brisé, aigu,** gothic arch; **a. en fer à cheval,** horseshoe arch; **a. de triomphe,** triumphal arch; (*b*) **l'a. des sourcils, de l'aorte,** the arch of the eyebrows, of the aorta; **a. dentaire,** dental arch. **3.** (*a*) *Mth:* **a. de cercle,** arc of a circle; (*b*) *Mec.E:* **a. denté,** toothed arc, segmental rack; (*c*) *El:* **a. voltaïque,** voltaic arc; **a. électrique,** electric arc; **soudure en a.,** arc welding; **lampe à a.,** arc lamp.

arcade [arkad] *n.f.* **1.** (*a*) archway; (*b*) **arcades,** arcade. **2.** (*a*) arch (of saddle, etc.); *Anat:* **a. dentaire, orbitaire,** dental, orbital, arch; (*b*) bridge (of pair of spectacles); (*c*) **a. feinte,** blind arch.

arcadé [arkade] *a.* arcaded (court, walk, etc.).

arcature [arkatyr] *n.f.* *Arch:* arcature; blind arcade.

arc-boutant [arkbutɑ̃] *n.m.* **1.** *Arch:* (*a*) flying buttress; (*b*) *Civ.E:* abutment pier. **2.** *Const: etc:* strut, stay; **arcs-boutants d'un parapluie,** stretchers of an umbrella. **3.** *Row:* outrigger; *pl. arcs-boutants.*

arc-bouter [arkbute] *v.tr.* **1.** to buttress; to support (wall) with flying buttresses. **2.** to prop up, shore up (wall, etc.). **3. s'a.-b. contre un mur,** to brace oneself against a wall.

arc-doubleau [arkdublo] *n.m.* *Arch:* transverse rib; *pl. arcs-doubleaux.*

arceau, -eaux [arso] *n.m.* **1.** arch (of vault). **2.** ring bow (of padlock); (croquet) hoop. **3.** *Med:* (bed)-cradle.

arc-en-ciel [arkɑ̃sjɛl] *n.m.* rainbow; *pl. arcs-en-ciel.*

archaïque [arkaik] *a.* archaic (style, etc.); antiquated (appearance, etc.).

archaïsme [arkaism] *n.m.* archaism.

archange [arkɑ̃ʒ] *n.m.* archangel.

arche¹ [arʃ] *n.f.* **1.** ark; **l'a. de Noé,** Noah's ark; **l'a. d'alliance, l'a. sainte,** the Ark of the Covenant. **2.** *Husb:* **a. d'élevage,** coop.

arche² *n.f.* **1.** (*a*) arch (of bridge, etc.); (*b*) *Geol:* **a. naturelle,** natural arch. **2.** (croquet) hoop.

archéologie [arkeɔlɔʒi] *n.f.* arch(a)eology.

archéologique [arkeɔlɔʒik] *a.* arch(a)eological.

archéologiquement [arkeɔlɔʒikmɑ̃] *adv.* arch(a)eologically; from an arch(a)eological point of view.

archéologue [arkeɔlɔg] *n.m.* & *f.* arch(a)eologist.

archer [arʃe] *n.m.* archer, bowman.

archet [arʃɛ] *n.m.* (*a*) bow; **a. de violon,** violin bow; **scie à a.,** bow saw; (*b*) *Rail:* pantograph.

archétype [arketip] *n.m.* archetype, prototype.

archevêché [arʃəveʃe] *n.m.* **1.** archbishopric, archdiocese. **2.** archbishop's palace.

archevêque [arʃəvɛk] *n.m.* archbishop.

archiconnu [arʃikɔny] *a.* very well known; only too well known.

archicube [arʃikyb] *n.m.* *Sch: F:* graduate of the *École Normale Supérieure.*

archidémon [arʃidemɔ̃] *n.m.* arch-fiend.

archidiacre [arʃidjakr̥] *n.m.* *Ecc:* archdeacon.

archidiocèse [arʃidiɔsɛz] *n.m.* *Ecc:* archdiocese; archbishopric.

archiduc [arʃidyk] *n.m.* archduke.

archiépiscopal, -aux [arʃiepiskɔpal, -o] *a.* archiepiscopal.

archiépiscopat [arʃiepiskɔpa] *n.m.* **1.** archiepiscopacy. **2.** archiepiscopate.

Archimède [arʃimɛd] *Pr.n.m.* *Gr.Hist:* Archimedes; *Ph:* **le principe d'A.,** Archimedes' principle; **vis d'A.,** *Hyd:* Archimedean screw; *Ind:* spiral conveyor.

archimillionnaire [arʃimiljɔnɛr] *a.* & *n.* *F:* multimillionaire.

archipel [arʃipɛl] *n.m.* *Geog:* archipelago.

archisec, -sèche [arʃisɛk, -sɛʃ] *a.* *F:* bone-dry.

archisecret [arʃisɛkrɛ] *a.* *F:* top secret; hush-hush.

architecte [arʃitɛkt] *n.m.* architect; **a. paysagiste,** landscape gardener; **a. naval,** naval architect; **a. urbaniste,** town planner.

architectural, -aux [arʃitɛktyral, -o] *a.* architectural.

architecture [arʃitɛktyr] *n.f.* architecture; **a. navale,** naval architecture.

architrave [arʃitrav] *n.f.* *Arch:* architrave.

archives [arʃiv] *n.f.pl.* archives; records; *Publ:* **exemplaire des a.,** file copy; **les archives nationales** = the (Public) Record Office.

archiviste [arʃivist] *n.m.* & *f.* **1.** archivist; keeper of public records. **2.** *Com: etc:* clerk (in charge of records); filing clerk.

arçon [arsɔ̃] *n.m.* **1.** *Harn:* saddle bow; *Gym:* **cheval d'arçons,** (vaulting) horse. **2.** *Tls:* (*a*) *Tex:* (felter's) bow; (*b*) frame (of saw); (*c*) **foret, drille, à a.,** fiddle drill, bow drill.

arçonner [arsɔne] *v.tr.* *Tex:* to card, clean (cotton, wool, etc.) with a (felter's) bow.

arctique [arktik] (*a*) *a.* arctic; **cercle a.,** arctic circle; (*b*) *Pr.n.m.* *Geog:* **l'A.,** the Arctic.

ardemment [ardamɑ̃] *adv.* ardently, passionately, zealously; eagerly.

Ardennes (les) [lezardɛn] *Pr.n.f.pl.* *Geog:* the Ardennes; **la Bataille des Ardennes,** the Battle of the Bulge.

ardent [ardɑ̃] *a.* **1.** burning hot, scorching, blazing (fire, etc.); **soleil a.,** scorching sun; **cheveux d'un blond a.,** reddish blond hair; **rouge a.,** fiery red. **2.** ardent, passionate, eager; **socialiste a.,** red-hot Socialist; **a. sportif,** keen sportsman.

ardeur [ardœr] *n.f.* **1.** heat (of sun, fire, etc.). **2.** eagerness, ardour, fervour; **cheval plein d'a.,** high-spirited, high-mettled, horse.

ardoise [ardwaz] *n.f.* (*a*) slate; **(couleur) gris a.,** slate grey (colour); *Const:* **(feuille d')a.,** slate; **couvrir un toit en a.,** to slate a roof; (*b*) **a. (à écrire),** (writing) slate; **crayon d'a.,** slate pencil; (*c*) *F:* **inscrire les consommations à l'a.,** to chalk up the drinks.

ardoisé [ardwaze], *a.* slate-colour(ed), bluish-grey.

ardoiser [ardwaze] *v.tr.* to slate (roof).

ardoisier, -ière [ardwazje, -jɛr] **1.** *a.* slaty; **schiste a.,** slate clay, shale. **2.** *n.m.* (*a*) owner of a slate quarry; (*b*) slate worker, slate quarryman. **3.** *n.f.* **ardoisière,** slate quarry.

ardu [ardy] *a.* **1.** steep, abrupt, difficult (path, etc.). **2.** arduous, difficult, hard (task, etc.); **travail a.,** uphill work.

are [ar] *n.m.* *Meas:* are (= 100 square metres).

arec [arɛk] *n.m.*, **areca** [areka] *n.m.* **1.** *Bot:* areca palm (tree). **2. (noix d')a.,** areca nut, betel nut.

aréna [arena] *n.f. Fr.C:* arena; skating rink.

arène [arɛn] *n.f.* **1.** *A: & Poet:* sand. **2.** arena; bull-ring; **les arènes d'Arles,** the amphitheatre of Arles.

aréole [areɔl] *n.f. Anat: Bot: Med:* areola.

arête [arɛt] *n.f.* **1.** (*a*) (fish) bone; **poisson plein d'arêtes,** bony fish; **grande a.,** backbone (of fish); **dessin en a. de hareng,** *Arch:* **de poisson,** herringbone pattern; (*b*) ridge, rib (of sword blade, bayonet). **2.** (*a*) *Const: etc:* line; **a. d'un comble,** hip of a roof; **pierre d'a.,** quoin stone; **a. de voûte,** groin (of an arch); (*b*) bridge (of the nose); (*c*) *Av:* **a. dorsale,** dorsal fin (of fuselage); (*d*) *Geog:* arête, (serrate) ridge. **3.** beard (of ear of barley, etc.).

arêtière [arɛtjɛr] *n.f. Const:* arris tile, hip tile.

argent [arʒɑ̃] *n.m.* **1.** silver; **vaisselle d'a.,** (silver) plate; **a. en feuille,** silver foil, silver leaf; *Prov:* **la parole est d'a., le silence est d'or,** speech is silvern, silence is golden. **2.** money; **a. de poche,** pocket money; **a. liquide,** ready money, cash (in hand); **l'a. lui fond entre les mains,** money just slips through his fingers; **en avoir pour son a.,** (i) to have one's money's worth; to have good value for one's money; (ii) to have a run for one's money.

argenté [arʒɑ̃te] *a.* **1.** silver(ed), silvery; **gris a.,** silver-grey; **renard a.,** silver fox. **2.** silver-plated. **3.** *F:* rich, *U.S:* well-heeled; **touristes bien argentés,** tourists with well-lined pockets.

argenter [arʒɑ̃te] *v.tr.* to silver.

argenterie [arʒɑ̃tri] *n.f.* (silver) plate; silverware.

argenteur [arʒɑ̃tœr] **1.** *a.m.* silvering (salt). **2.** *n.m.* silverer, silver plater.

argentin[1] [arʒɑ̃tɛ̃] *a.* silvery (waves); silver-toned (voice); tinkling (bell).

argentin[2], -ine *a. & n. Geog:* Argentinian; **la République Argentine,** *n.f.* **l'Argentine,** Argentina, the Argentine (Republic).

argile [arʒil] *n.f.* (*a*) clay; **a. à blocaux,** boulder clay; **a. schisteuse,** shale; (*b*) **a. cuite,** terracotta, earthenware; (*c*) **une statue, un colosse, aux pieds d'a.,** an idol with feet of clay.

argileux, -euse [arʒilø, -øz] *a.* clayey.

argilifère [arʒilifɛr] *a.* clay-bearing.

argon [argɔ̃] *n.m. Ch:* argon.

argonaute [argɔnot] *n.m.* **1.** *Myth:* Argonaut. **2.** *Moll:* argonaut, paper nautilus.

argot [argo] *n.m.* slang; jargon; **a. des voleurs,** thieves' cant; **a. du milieu,** underworld slang; **a. scolaire,** schoolboy slang.

argotique [argɔtik] *a.* slangy (language); **expression a.,** (i) cant phrase; (ii) slang expression.

argotisme [argɔtism] *n.m.* slang expression.

arguer [argɥe] *v.* **(j'arguë** [ʒargy] **n. arguïons** [nuzargyjɔ̃]) **1.** *v.tr.* (*a*) *Lit:* to infer, assert, deduce; (*b*) *Jur:* **a. une pièce de faux,** to assert a deed to be forged. **2.** *v.i.* to argue.

argument [argymɑ̃] *n.m.* **1.** argument; **par manière d'a.,** for argument's sake; **tirer a. de qch.,** to argue from sth. **2.** outline, summary, plot, argument (of book, etc.); synopsis (of contents).

argumentaire [argymɑ̃tɛr] *a. & n.m. Com:* sales (talk, gambit); **rédiger un a.,** to draw up a list of selling points.

argumentateur, -trice [argymɑ̃tatœr, -tris], *Pej:* **1.** *a.* argumentative. **2.** *n.* arguer.

argumenter [argymɑ̃te] *v.i.* (*a*) to argue (**contre,** against); (*b*) *F:* to be argumentative.

argumenteur, -euse [argymɑ̃tœr, -øz] *n.* arguer.

Argus [argys] **1.** *Pr.n.m. Myth:* Argus. **2.** *n.m.* **l'A. (de l'Automobile)** = Glass's Guide; **l'A. de la Presse,** a press-cutting agency.

argutie [argysi] *n.f.* quibble; cavil(ling).

aria [arja] *n.f. Mus:* aria.

aride [arid] *a.* arid, dry, barren (country, subject).

aridité [aridite] *n.f.* aridity, aridness, barrenness.

aristocrate [aristɔkrat] *n.m. & f.* aristocrat.

aristocratie [aristɔkrasi] *n.f.* aristocracy.

aristocratique [aristɔkratik] *a.* aristocratic.

Aristote [aristɔt] *Pr.n.m. Gr.Phil:* Aristotle; **la logique d'A.,** Aristotelian logic.

arithméticien, -ienne [aritmetisjɛ̃, -jɛn] *n.* arithmetician.

arithmétique [aritmetik] **1.** *a.* arithmetical. **2.** *n.f.* (*a*) arithmetic; (*b*) **une a.,** an arithmetic book.

arlequin [arləkɛ̃] *n.m. Th:* Harlequin; **habillé en a.,** dressed in motley; **manteau d'a.,** proscenium arch.

arlequinade [arləkinad] *n.f.* (*a*) *Th:* harlequinade; (*b*) (piece of) buffoonery.

arlésien, -ienne [arlezjɛ̃, -jɛn] *a. & n. Geog:* Arlesian; of Arles.

armada [armada] *n.f. Hist:* armada; **l'Invincible A.,** the Invincible Armada.

armadille [armadij] *n.f. Crust:* wood louse.

armateur [armatœr] *n.m. Nau:* (*a*) fitter-out (of ship, expedition); (*b*) (ship)owner.

armature [armatyr] *n.f.* **1.** frame, brace, armature (of window, etc.); reinforcement (of concrete work); truss (of girder, etc.). **2.** armouring, sheathing, (of electric cable). **3.** *El:* (*a*) armature (of magnet, small dynamo, magneto); (*b*) plate (of condenser). **4.** *E:* **a. de soupape, de pompe,** valve gear, pump gear. **5.** *Mus:* key signature.

arme [arm] *n.f.* **1.** arm, weapon; **salle d'armes,** (i) armoury; (ii) fencing school; **armes à feu,** firearms; **armes portatives,** small arms; **armes classiques, traditionnelles, conventionnelles,** conventional weapons; **a. non classique, a. non conventionnelle,** non-conventional weapon; advanced weapon; **a. nucléaire,** nuclear weapon; **a. de dissuasion,** deterrent; **nation en, sous les, armes,** nation in arms; **prendre les armes,** (i) to take up arms, to rise up in arms (**contre,** against); (ii) *Mil:* to parade under arms; **porter les armes,** (i) to bear, carry, arms; (ii) to be a soldier; **aux armes!** to arms! *Mil:* guard turn out! **le métier, la carrière, des armes,** the military profession; **suspension d'armes,** cessation of hostilities; **frères d'armes,** brothers in arms; **place d'armes,** (i) parade ground; (ii) (*tactics*) assembly area; **portez armes!** shoulder arms! **passer qn par les armes,** to have s.o. (court-martialled and) shot; **sans armes,** unarmed; **à armes égales,** on equal terms; **avec armes et bagages,** (with) bag and baggage. **2.** arm (as a branch of the army); **douze mille hommes de toutes armes,** twelve thousand men of all arms, services. **3.** *pl. Her:* (coat of) arms.

armé [arme] *a.* (*a*) armed; **troupe armée,** body of troops; **agression à main armée,** hold-up; (*b*) fortified; strengthened; **poutre armée,** trussed beam; **béton a.,** reinforced concrete; **verre a.,** wired glass; (*c*) cocked; **pistolet à l'a., à demi a.,** pistol at full cock, at half cock.

armée [arme] *n.f.* **1.** *Mil:* (*a*) army, force(s); **a. de métier,** professional army; **a. permanente,** standing army; **a. active,** regular army; **l'a. de terre,** the army, the land forces; **l'a. de l'air,** the air force; **l'a. de mer,** the navy, the naval forces; (*b*) army; **a. de secours,** relieving army; **la 8ième a.,** the 8th army; **groupe d'a.,** army group; (*c*) *Hist:* **la Grande A.,** the Grande Armée. **2.** (*a*) **le Dieu des armées,** the Lord of Hosts; (*b*) **l'A. du Salut,** the Salvation Army; (*c*) **toute une a. de fonctionnaires,** a whole army of officials.

armement [arməmɑ̃] *n.m.* **1.** (*a*) arming, equipping (of army); (*b*) armament, equipment; **officier d'a.,** ordnance officer; (*c*) *pl.* armaments; weaponry; **course aux armements,** arms race. **2.** strengthening, bracing (of girder, etc.); sheathing (of cable, etc.). **3.** *Nau:* (*a*) (i) commissioning, fitting out; (ii) equipment, gear, stores; **mettre un navire en a.,** to put a ship in commission; **port d'a.,** port of registry; (*b*) (i) manning; (ii) crew (of boat, gun, etc.); (*c*) merchant shipping. **4.** (*a*) loading (of gun); arming (of fuse); (*b*) setting (of camera shutter, etc.); cocking (of loaded fire arm); (*c*) mounting, fitting up (of machine, etc.). **5.** mounting gear (of machine).

Arménie [armeni] *Pr.n.f. Geog:* Armenia.

arménien, -ienne [armenjɛ̃, -jɛn] *a. & n.* Armenian.

armer [arme] **I.** *v.tr.* **1.** to arm (**de,** with); **vol à main armée,** armed robbery; **l'éléphant est armé de défenses,** the elephant is armed with tusks. **2.** (*a*) to fortify (a town); (*b*) to strengthen, brace; to wind (a dynamo); to sheathe, armour (a cable). **3.** *Nau:* (*a*) to equip, fit out, commission (ship); (*b*) to man (boat, etc.); to rig (capstan); (*c*) **a. les avirons,** to ship the oars. **4.** (*a*) to arm (a fuse); (*b*) to set (an apparatus); to cock (firearm); (*c*) to mount (machine, battery of guns, etc.); to fit up (machine). **5. a. la clef,** to put the key signature (to a piece of music). **II.** *v.i.* **1.** *Mil:* to arm, prepare for war. **2.** *Nau:* (*a*) **le navire arme à Brest,** the ship is being commissioned at Brest; (*b*) **a. sur un navire,** to serve on a vessel. **III. s'armer. 1.** to arm oneself; to take up arms. **2. s'a. de courage, de patience,** to summon up (one's) courage, patience.

armistice [armistis] *n.m.* armistice; truce; **journée, anniversaire, de l'A.,** Armistice Day, Remembrance Day.

armoire [armwar] *n.f.* (*a*) cupboard, *esp. NAm:* closet; **a. à linge,** linen cupboard, press; **a. à provisions,** store cupboard; **a. de cuisine,** kitchen cupboard; (*b*) wardrobe.

armoiries [armwari] *n.f.pl. Her:* (coat of) arms, armorial bearings.

armorial, -aux [armɔrjal, -o] *a.* armorial.

armoricain, -aine [armɔrikɛ̃, ɛn] *a. & n. Geog:* Armorican; **massif a.,** Armorican massif.

Armorique [armɔrik] *Pr.n.f. Geog:* Armorica.

armoriste [armɔrist] *n.m.* heraldic artist.

armure [armyr] *n.f.* **1.** (*a*) armour; **a. complète,** suit of armour; (*b*) **a. d'un navire de guerre,** armour (plating) of a warship; (*c*) defence (of animals). **2.** *Tex:* (*a*) cording and healds (of loom); (*b*) draught (of warp); (*c*) weave, pattern, design. **3.** *El:* (*a*) pole piece (of dynamo); (*b*) armouring; sheathing (of cable). **4.** *Mus:* key signature.

armurier [armyrje] *n.m.* **1.** arms manufacturer; gunsmith. **2.** *Mil: etc:* armourer.

arnaque [arnak] *n.f. P:* swindle, trickery.

arnaquer [arnake] *v.tr. P:* to cheat, swindle.

arnaqueur, -euse [arnakœr, -øz] *n. P:* swindler.

arnica [arnika] *n.f. Bot: Pharm:* arnica.

aromate [arɔmat] *n.m.* aromatic; spice.

aromatique [arɔmatik] *a.* **1.** aromatic, spicy. **2.** *Ch:* **carbures aromatiques,** aromatics.

aromatisation [arɔmatizasjɔ̃] *n.f. Ch:* aromatization.

aromatiser [arɔmatize] *v.tr.* **1.** to give aroma to (sth.); *Cu:* to flavour. **2.** *Ch:* to aromatize.

arome, arôme [arom] *n.m.* aroma; flavour.

aronde [arɔ̃d] *n.f. Carp:* **queue d'a.,** dovetail; **assembler qch. à, en, queue d'a.,** to dovetail sth.

arpège [arpɛʒ] *n.m. Mus:* arpeggio.

arpentage [arpɑ̃taʒ] *n.m.* surveying, land measuring; **faire l'a. d'un terrain,** to measure a piece of ground.

arpenter [arpɑ̃te] *v.tr.* **1.** to survey, measure (land). **2. a. le terrain,** to stride over the ground; **il arpentait le quai,** he was tramping, pacing, up and down the platform.

arpenteur [arpɑ̃tœr] *n.m.* (land) surveyor.

arpion [arpjɔ̃] *n.m. P:* (*a*) foot; (*b*) toe.

arqué [arke] *a.* arched, curved; cambered (beam, etc.); high-bridged (nose); bandy-legged (horse); **jambes arquées,** bow legs.

arquer [arke] **1.** *v.tr.* to bend, arch, curve (wood, iron, etc.); to camber (surface); **a. le dos,** to bend, hump, the back; (*of cat*) to arch its back. **2.** *v.i.* to bend; to sag; to buckle. **3. s'a.,** to bend; to become bent, arched.

arrachage [araʃaʒ] *n.m.* pulling up, rooting up, (of plants, etc.); lifting (of potatoes); pulling out, wrenching out, drawing, extraction (of tooth, nail, etc.).

arraché [araʃe] **1.** *a. Her:* erased. **2.** *n.m. Sp:* (*weight-lifting*) snatch; **gagner à l'a.,** to snatch a win, to win with a terrific effort.

arrache-clou [araʃklu] *n.m. Tls:* nail drawer; *pl. arrache-clous.*

arrachement [araʃmɑ̃] *n.m.* **1.** rooting up (of tree, etc.). **2.** (*a*) parting; (*b*) wrench; **nous ne pouvons le quitter sans a.,** we can't leave it, him, without a wrench. **3.** *Const:* toothing. **4.** (*a*) *Mec:* tearing, wrenching, stripping; **effort d'a.,** wrenching force; (*b*) *Med: etc:* wrench. **5.** landslide.

arrache-pied (d') [daraʃpje] *adv.phr.* without interruption; **travailler d'a.-p.,** (i) to work steadily, (ii) to slave away; **parler deux heures d'a.-p.,** to talk for two hours at a stretch, without stopping.

arracher [araʃe] *v.tr.* to tear (out, up, away); to, pull (up, out, away); to draw (nail); to root up, uproot (tree); to lift (potatoes); to extract (money from s.o.); to extract, pull out (tooth); to tear down, pull down (poster); to extract (promise, secret); **a. qch. de qch.,** to pull sth. off, from, out of, sth.; **a. qch. à qn, des mains de qn,** to snatch sth. from s.o., s.o.'s hands; **a. qn de son foyer,** to drag, uproot, s.o. from his home; **a. les yeux à qn,** to tear s.o.'s eyes out; **s'a. les cheveux,** to tear one's hair; **a. qn à la mort,** to snatch, rescue, s.o. from the jaws of death; **a. qn au sommeil,** to rouse s.o. from his sleep; **la sonnerie du réveil m'a arraché du lit,** the alarm dragged me out of bed; **a. qn à son travail,** to tear s.o. away from his work; **cela m'arrache le cœur,** it breaks my heart.

arracheur, -euse [araʃœr, -øz] *n.* **1.** (*pers.*) tearer (down); (potato, etc.) lifter. **2.** (*device*) **arracheuse,** (i) grubbing plough, grubber, (ii) (potato) lifter; (beet) puller.

arrachoir [araʃwar] *n.m.* (*device*) (potato) lifter; (beet) puller.

arraisonnement [arɛzɔnmɑ̃] *n.m. Nau:* **1.** boarding (of ship). **2. a. de la patente (d'un navire),** examination of the bill of health, sanitary report.

arraisonner [arɛzɔne] *Nau:* **1.** *v.tr.* **a. un navire,** (i) to hail, speak, a vessel; (ii) to stop and examine a ship. **2.** *v.i.* **a. avec les autorités du port,** to report to the port authorities.

arraisonneur [arɛzɔnœr] *a.* **navire a.,** examination vessel.

arrangeant [arɑ̃ʒɑ̃] *a.* accommodating, helpful.

arrangement [arɑ̃ʒmɑ̃] *n.m.* **1.** (*a*) arranging, putting in order; **mal prendre ses arrangements,** to arrange, plan, things badly; (*b*) arrangement (of furniture, etc.); (*c*) *Mus:* **a. pour violon,** arrangement for violin. **2.** agreement; settlement; understanding; **sauf a. contraire,** unless otherwise agreed.

arranger [arɑ̃ʒe] *v.* (**j'arrangeais n. arrangeons**). **I.** *v.tr.* **1.** (*a*) to arrange (furniture, etc.); to put (books, room) in order; to tidy (up) (room); to straighten (one's tie, etc.); (*b*) *F:* **le voilà bien arrangé!** he does look a mess! **a. qn de la belle manière,** to tell s.o. off (in no uncertain terms); *P:* **on vous a arrangé,** you've been had, taken for a ride; (*c*) *Mus:* to arrange (song for violin, etc.). **2.** to repair, overhaul (car, watch, etc.); to mend (watch). **3.** to organize (concert, etc.);

a. qch. d'avance, to arrange, plan, sth. in advance. **4.** to settle (quarrel, etc.); **je vais essayer d'a. les choses,** I'll try to put things right; **cela n'arrangera rien,** that won't (be much) help. **5. faire qch. pour a. qn,** to do sth. to help s.o.; **on ne peut a. tout le monde,** you can't please everybody. **II. s'arranger 1.** (*a*) to manage; **si vous pouvez vous a. pour le voir,** if you can manage, make the time, to see him; **arrangez-vous pour être là,** you must make sure to be there; **il s'arrange de tout,** he's very adaptable; (*b*) to tidy oneself up; to get dressed. **2.** (*a*) **s'a. avec qn,** to come to an agreement, to terms, with s.o.; **arrangez-vous,** settle it among yourselves; (*b*) **cela s'arrangera,** things will turn out all right; **cela s'arrangera tout seul,** that will sort itself out.

arrangeur, -euse [arɑ̃ʒœr, -øz] *n. esp. Mus:* arranger.

arrérages [areraʒ] *n.m.pl.* **1.** arrears (of wages, rent, etc.); **2.** back interest; **coupon d'a.,** interest, dividend, warrant; **toucher ses a.,** to draw one's pension, dividends.

arrestation [arɛstasjɔ̃] *n.f.* arrest; **mettre qn en a.,** to take s.o. into custody; **en état d'a.,** under arrest.

arrêt [arɛ] *n.m.* **1.** (*a*) stop, stoppage; stopping; **a. d'urgence,** emergency stop; **point d'a.,** (i) stopping place, point; (ii) *Mus:* pause (over a rest); **faire un a. au cours de son voyage,** to break one's journey, *NAm:* to stop over; **a. en cours de route,** break of journey, *NAm:* stopover; **trajet sans a.,** non-stop journey; **dix minutes d'a.,** ten minutes' stop, halt; ten minutes' break; **temps d'a.,** pause, halt; **marquer un temps d'a.,** to pause, halt, mark time; **mettre a. à un chèque,** to stop a cheque; *Med:* **a. (de cœur),** heart failure; *Mch: etc:* **a. (inopiné),** breakdown; *W.Tel: T.V:* **a. d'émission,** break in transmission; **robinet d'a.,** stopcock; *Rail:* **signal d'a.,** stop signal; (*b*) (bus, etc.) stop; **a. facultatif,** request stop; **ne pas descendre avant l'a.,** do not get off before the bus, train, etc., stops; (*c*) stop, catch (of door, etc.); tumbler (of a lock); **cran d'a.,** safety catch; *Cy:* **a. de pied,** toeclip. **2.** (*a*) decree, general order; **les arrêts de la Providence,** the decrees of Providence; (*b*) *Jur:* judgement, adjudication (delivered by **Cour d'assises, Cour d'appel,** or **Cour de cassation**); **prononcer, rendre, un a.,** to pronounce, deliver, judgement; **a. par défaut,** judgement by default; **a. de défense,** stay of execution; **a. de mort,** death sentence. **3.** (*a*) seizure, impounding, attachment; **faire a. sur des marchandises,** to impound, seize, goods; (*b*) *Nau:* detention (of ship). **4.** arrest; **ordre, mandat d'a.,** warrant for the arrest (of s.o.); **mettre un officier aux arrêts,** to put an officer under arrest; **arrêts à la chambre, arrêts domestiques,** house arrest. **5.** *Fb:* tackle; *Rugby Fb:* **a. de volée,** fair catch. **6.** *Ven:* set; **chien d'a.,** setter, pointer; *Fig:* **rester, tomber, en a. devant qn, qch.,** to stop and stare at s.o., sth.

arrêté [arete] **1.** *a.* (*a*) (*of ideas, etc.*) fixed, decided; **homme aux opinions arrêtées,** dogmatic person, man with set ideas, with decided views; **dessein a.,** settled design; (*b*) *Sp:* **départ a.,** standing start. **2.** *n.m.* (*a*) decision, order, decree; **a. ministériel,** departmental order (signed by a minister); **a. municipal,** by(e)-law; **a. d'exécution,** decree providing for the enforcement of a law; (*b*) *Com:* **a. de compte(s),** settlement (of an account).

arrêter [arete] *v.* **I.** *v.tr.* **1.** to stop (s.o., sth.); to check (attack); to bring (vehicle) to a standstill; to hold up; to detain, delay, keep back; to stem (flood, torrent, etc.); **a. un cheval,** pull up a horse; **rien ne l'arrêtera,** nothing will stop him, he will stick at nothing; **quel obstacle vous arrête?** what's stopping you? **a. le vent,** to break (the force of) the wind; *Aut:* **a. le moteur,** to switch off the engine; **a. le paiement d'un chèque,** to stop (payment of) a cheque; **a. la croissance,** to arrest growth; **le brouillard, la neige, a complètement arrêté toute circulation,** fog, snow, has brought traffic to a standstill; *Fb:* **a. un but,** to stop, save, a goal; *Ven:* (*of dog*) **a. le gibier,** to point game. **2.** to fix, fasten, secure (shutter, plank, etc.); **a. l'attention,** to arrest attention; *Needlew:* **a. un point,** to fasten off a stitch; *Knit:* **a. les mailles,** to cast off. **3.** to arrest, seize (criminal); to seize (contraband, books, etc.); **l'assassin n'est pas encore arrêté,** the murderer is still at large. **4.** to decide sth.; **a. un jour,** to fix, appoint, settle, a day; **a. un programme,** to draw up a programme. **5.** *Com:* to make up, close, settle (account). **II.** *v.i.* to stop, halt; **dites au chauffeur d'arrêter devant l'hotel de ville,** tell the driver to stop at, in front of, the town hall; **elle n'arrête jamais de parler,** she never stops talking; *int.* **arrête! arrêtez!** stop (it)! that's enough! **III. s'arrêter 1.** to stop, to come to a stop, to a standstill; *Mec:* (*of moving body*) to come to rest; **s'a. court,** to stop short; **la voiture s'est arrêtée,** the car stopped, drew up; **s'a. en route,** to break one's journey; **s'a. de faire qch.,** to stop doing sth; **s'a. de fumer,** to give up smoking; **s'a. chez qn,** to call at s.o.'s; **passer sans s'a.,** to pass without stopping. **2.** to fix one's attention (on sth.); to dwell, insist (on sth.); **il ne faut pas s'a. aux apparences,** one should not pay too much attention to (outward) appearances.

arrhes [ar] *n.f.pl.* (*a*) deposit; **verser des a.,** to pay a deposit; (*b*) fine; **stipulation d'a.,** right to annul a sale by paying a fine.

arriération [arjerasjɔ̃] *n.f. Psy:* retardation; backwardness (of child, etc.).

arrière [arjɛr] **1.** *adv.* **(en) a.** (*a*) behind; **rester en a.,** to remain, stay behind; to lag behind; **avoir le vent en a.,** to have the wind astern; **en a. de qn, de qch.,** behind s.o., sth.; **il est resté en a. de sa classe,** he stayed at the bottom of the class; **en a. de son siècle, de son temps,** behind the times; (*b*) **locataire en a. pour ses loyers,** tenant in arrears with his rent; (*c*) **en a.,** backwards; *int.* **arrière!** (stand) back! **revenir en a.,** to come back; **retourner en a.,** to go, turn, back; **regarder en a.,** to look back; *Nau:* **en a. (à) toute (vitesse)!** full speed astern! **faire marche (en) a.,** to back; *Nau:* to go astern; *Aut:* to reverse; *Fig:* to back down, retract. **2.** *a.inv.* back; **essieu a.,** back axle, rear axle; *Aut:* **feu a.,** rear light; **à moteur a.,** rear-engined; **siège, banquette, a.,** back seat (of car); **siège a. (de motocyclette),** pillion seat; *Needlew:* **point a.,** backstitch. **3.** *n.m.* (*a*) back, back part, rear (of house, etc.); *Mil:* **l'a.,** the rear; *Aut:* **un modèle tout à l'a.,** a rear-engined model; (*b*) *Nau:* stern (of ship); **vers l'a.,** aft, abaft; **sur l'a.,** astern; **aller à l'a.,** to go aft. **4.** *n.m. Fb:* (full) back; *Rugby Fb:* full back; *Fb:* **a. gauche,** left back.

arriéré [arjere] **1.** *a.* (*a*) late, behind(hand), in arrears; **paiement a.,** overdue, outstanding, payment; (*b*) **enfant a.,** backward child; (*of pers.*) **être a.,** to be behind the times; **idées arriérées,** oldfashioned ideas; *Pol.Ec:* **pays arriérés,** under-developed countries. **2.** *n.m.* arrears (of account, correspondence, etc.); backlog; **a. du loyer,** arrears of rent; *Mil:* **a. de solde,** back pay; **a. de permissions,** accumulated leave.

arrière-bassin [arjɛrbasɛ̃] *n.m.* inner dock; *pl. arrière-bassins.*

arrière-bouche [arjɛrbuʃ] *n.f.* back of the mouth; fauces; *pl. arrière-bouches.*

arrière-boutique [arjɛrbutik] *n.f.* back premises (of a shop); back shop, *U.S:* back store; *pl. arrière-boutiques.*

arrière-bras [arjɛrbra] *n.m.inv. Anat:* upper arm.

arrière-cour [arjɛrkur] *n.f.* backyard; *pl. arrière-cours.*

arrière-cuisine [arjɛrkɥizin] *n.f.* scullery, back kitchen; *pl. arrière-cuisines.*

arrière-défense [arjɛrdefɑ̃s] *n.f. Fb:* (the) back-line defence, the backs; *pl. arrière-défenses.*

arrière-fond [arjɛrfɔ̃], *n.m.* innermost depth; *pl. arrière-fonds.*

arrière-garde [arjɛrgard) *n.f.* **1.** *Mil:* rearguard. **2.** *Navy:* rear squadron; *pl. arrière-gardes.*

arrière-gorge [arjɛrgɔrʒ] *n.f.* back of the throat; **voix d'a.-g.,** throaty voice; *pl. arrière-gorges.*

arrière-goût [arjɛrgu] *n.m.* aftertaste, faint taste **(de,** of); *pl. arrière-goûts.*

arrière-grand-mère [arjɛrgrɑ̃mɛr] *n.f.* great-grandmother; *pl. arrière-grand-mères.*

arrière-grand-père [arjɛrgrɑ̃pɛr] *n.m.* great-grandfather; *pl. arrière-grands-pères.*

arrière-grands-parents [arjɛrgrɑ̃parɑ̃] *n.m.-pl.inv.* great-grandparents.

arrière-main [arjɛrmɛ̃] *n.m. or f.* **1.** *Ten: etc:* **(coup d')a.-m.,** backhand (stroke). **2.** (hind)quarters (of horse); *pl. arrière-mains.*

arrière-neveu, -nièce [arjɛrnəvø, -njɛs] *n.* grand-nephew, -niece.

arrière-pays [arjɛrpei] *n.m.inv.* hinterland.

arrière-pensée [arjɛrpɑ̃se] *n.f.* (*a*) mental reservation; (*b*) ulterior motive; *pl. arrière-pensées.*

arrière-petit-fils, -petite-fille [arjɛpətifis, -pətitfij] *n.* great-grandson, -grand-daughter; *pl. arrière-petits-fils, -petites-filles.*

arrière-petit-neveu, -petite-nièce [arjɛrpətinvø, -pətitnjɛs] great-grand-nephew, -niece; *pl. arrière-petits-neveux, -petites-nièces.*

arrière-petits-enfants [arjɛrpətizɑ̃fɑ̃] *s.m.pl.* great-grandchildren.

arrière-plan [arjɛrplɑ̃] *n.m.* background; **à l'a.-p.,** in the background; at the back; *Th:* upstage; **ce projet est passé à l'a.-p.,** this plan has been shelved; **se trouver relégué à l'a.-p.,** to be pushed into the background; to be upstaged; *pl. arrière-plans.*

arrière-pont [arjɛrpɔ̃] *n.m. Nau:* after deck; *pl. arrière-ponts.*

arrière-port [arjɛrpɔr] *n.m.* inner harbour; *pl. arrière-ports.*

arriérer [arjere], *v.* **1.** *v.tr.* **(j'arrière, n. arriérons, j'arriérerai)** to postpone, delay, defer (payment, etc.). **2. s'a.,** to fall into arrears.

arrière-saison [arjɛrsɛzɔ̃] *n.f.* (*a*) late season, late autumn, *NAm:* fall; (*b*) **les pommes de terre sont chères dans l'a.-s.,** potatoes are expensive at the end of the season; *pl. arrière-saisons.*

arrière-scène [arjɛrsɛn] *n.f. Th:* **1.** back of the stage; **à l'a.-s.,** backstage. **2.** back curtain; backcloth; backdrop; *pl. arrière-scènes.*

arrière-train [arjɛrtrɛ̃] *n.m.* (hind)quarters (of animal); *F:* (*of pers.*) rump, rear; *pl. arrière-trains.*

arrimage [arimaʒ] *n.m. Nau: etc:* (*a*) stowing, trimming (of ship's cargo, etc.); **bois d'a.,** dunnage; (*b*) stowage; (*c*) trim (of ship); (*d*) docking (of spacecraft).

arrimer [arime] *v.tr.* **1.** *Nau: etc:* (*a*) to stow (cargo, etc.); (*b*) to trim (ship). **2.** (*a*) to secure (gun for travelling, etc.); (*b*) *Space:* to dock.

arrimeur [arimœr] *n.m. Nau:* (*a*) stower, trimmer; (*b*) stevedore.

arrivage [arivaʒ] *n.m.* arrival; consignment (of goods); *Fin:* **a. de fonds de l'étranger,** accession of funds from abroad.

arrivant, -e [arivɑ̃, -ɑ̃t] *n.* (*pers.*) arrival; **le dernier a.,** the last comer; **les nouveaux arrivants,** the new arrivals, the newcomers.

arrivé, -ée [arive] **I.** *n* (*pers.*) arrival; **un nouvel a.,** a newcomer; a new arrival. **II.** *n.f.* **1.** arrival, coming, advent; **on attend son arrivée pour la semaine prochaine,** he is expected to arrive next week; **à mon arrivée,** when I arrived; *Trans:* **arrivées,** arrivals; *Post:* **heures d'arrivée,** times of delivery. **2.** *Mch:* inlet (for steam, etc.); intake, admission; *Tchn:* **arrivée (d'huile),** (oil) feed. **3.** *Sp:* (winning) post; finish; **ligne d'arrivée,** finishing line.

arriver [arive] *v.i.* (*aux.* **être**). **1.** (*a*) to arrive, come; **a. en voiture,** to come by car; **il est arrivé en courant,** he came running up; **il arrive de voyage,** he is just back from a journey; **a. chez soi,** to arrive, get back home; **a. à temps,** to be on, in, time; **a. en retard,** to be late; **l'avion devait a. à midi,** the plane was due at midday; **arrivez (vite)!** hurry up! (*b*) **a. à un endroit,** to reach, get to, arrive at, a place; **a. à bon port,** to arrive safely; **le paquet m'est arrivé trop tard,** the parcel reached me too late; **ma fille m'arrive déjà à l'épaule,** my daughter comes up to my shoulder already; **a. à la vérité,** to arrive at, get at, the truth; **a. au fait,** to come to the point; (*c*) **j'en étais arrivé là lorsque . . .,** I had got to that point when . . .; **en a. aux coups,** to come to blows. **2.** (*a*) to succeed; **c'est un homme qui arrivera,** he is a man who will succeed, get on, do well; **avec du courage on arrive à tout,** with courage one can get anywhere, one can achieve anything; (*b*) **a. à faire qch.,** to succeed in doing sth.; **je n'arrive pas à y croire,** I just can't believe it; **comment y a.?** how can it be done? *F:* **tu y arrives?** can you do, manage, get, make, it? **3.** to happen, occur; **cela arrive tous les jours,** it happens every day; *Prov:* **un malheur n'arrive jamais seul,** misfortunes never come singly; **cela ne nous arrivera jamais,** it will never happen to us; **cela n'arrive qu'à nous!** just our luck! *impers.* **il lui est arrivé un accident,** he had an accident; **quoi qu'il arrive,** whatever happens, whatever may happen; **il m'arrive souvent d'oublier,** I often forget, I'm apt to forget.

arrivisme [arivism] *n.m.* unscrupulous ambition.

arriviste [arivist] *n.m. & f.* climber, pusher; careerist; go-getter.

arrogance [arɔgɑ̃s] *n.f.* arrogance.

árrogant, -ante [arɔgɑ̃, -ɑ̃t] (*a*) *a.* arrogant, overbearing; (*b*) *n.* arrogant person.

arroger (s') [sarɔʒe] *v.tr.pr.* **(je m'arrogeai(s); n.n. arrogeons); s'a. un droit, un privilège,** to assume, claim, a right, a privilege; **s'a. la meilleure chambre,** to take the best room as a matter of course.

arrondi [arɔ̃di] **1.** *a.* (*a*) rounded, round; **(visage a.,** round face; **chiffre a.,** rounded number; (*b*) well rounded (sentence, etc.). **2.** *n.m.* (*a*) round, rounded form; round-off (of edge, etc.); *Av:* fillet, fillet radius; (*b*) *Av:* flare out; **atterrissage avec a.,** flared landing; (*c*) hemline (of skirt.)

arrondir [arɔ̃dir] *v.* **I.** *v.tr.* **1.** (*a*) to round (sth.) (off); to make (sth.) round; **a. sa fortune,** to get together a considerable capital; **a. son champ,** to add to, to round off, one's land; **les yeux arrondis par l'étonnement,** in wide-eyed astonishment; (*b*) **a. les angles,** to round off the angles; to smooth things over; *Ling:* **a. une voyelle,** to round a vowel; (*c*) *Mth:* **a. un résultat,** to correct a result (to the nearest whole number, to so many places of decimals). **2.** *Nau:* **a. un cap,** to round, double, a cape. **3.** *Av:* to flare out (before touchdown). **II. s'a.,** to become rounded; to round out, fill out.

arrondissement[arɔ̃dismɑ̃]*n.m.***1.**(*a*)rounding(off) (of sentence, territory, etc.); (*b*) roundness. **2.** *Adm:* arrondissement; (i) major subdivision of *département;* (ii) (*in Paris, large city*) = (London) borough; (postal) district.

arrosage [arozaʒ] *n.m.* **1.** (*a*) watering; sprinkling, spraying (of lawn, etc.); wetting, moistening (of dough, etc.); *F:* **un bon a.,** a good soaking; *Mil:* heavy bombing, shelling; **a. des rues,** watering of the streets; **voiture d'a.,** water cart; (*b*) irrigation (of a meadow); (*c*) watering, diluting (of wine, etc.); (*d*) celebrating (with drinks).

arroser [aroze] *v.tr.* (*a*) to water (streets, plants); to sprinkle, spray (lawn); *Cu:* **a. un rôti,** to baste a joint; *Mil:* **a. une ville,** to bomb, shell, a town; **yeux arrosés de larmes,** eyes bathed in tears; **j'ai été bien arrosé,** I got a (thorough) soaking; *F:* **s'a. la gorge,** to wet one's whistle; **bifteck arrosé d'une bouteille de bordeaux,** steak served with a bottle of claret; **café arrosé,** laced coffee; **ça s'arrose!** we must drink to that! (*b*) **a. une prairie,** to irrigate a meadow; **rivière qui arrose une région,** river that waters a district; **la Seine arrose Paris,** the Seine flows through Paris; (*c*) to water, dilute (wine, milk).

arroseur *n.m.,* **arroseuse** *n.f.* [arozœr, -øz] *Hort: etc:* (*device*) sprinkler.

arrosoir [arozwar] *n.m.* watering can.

arsenal, -aux [arsənal, -o] *n.m.* **1.** (*a*) arsenal; (*b*) **a. maritime, de la marine,** naval dockyard; (*c*) **a. d'artillerie,** gun factory. **2. il emporta son a. de drogues,** he took his whole stock of drugs with him.

arsenic [arsənik] *n.m. Ch:* arsenic.

art [ar] *n.m.* **1.** (*a*) art, craft; **l'a. militaire, de la guerre,** the art of war; **l'a. culinaire,** the art of (good) cooking; (*b*) art; **l'a. pour l'a.,** art for art's sake; **a. égyptien, italien,** Egyptian, Italian art; **beaux-arts,** fine arts; **œuvre d'a.,** work of art; **ville d'a.,** city of artistic interest; **histoire de l'a.,** history of art; (*c*) **arts plastiques, graphiques,** plastic, graphic, arts; **le septième, le huitième, a.,** cinema, television; (*d*) *Sch: Fr.C:* **maître-ès-arts,** master of arts. **2.** *Civ.E:* **travaux, ouvrages, d'a.,** (generic term for) bridges, tunnels, viaducts, etc.; constructive works.

artefact [artefakt] *n.m. Biol:* artefact, artifact.

artère [artɛr] *n.f.* **1.** *Anat:* artery; **on a l'âge de ses artères,** a man is as old as he feels. **2.** *Trans:* main highway; thoroughfare.

artériel, -ielle [arterjɛl] *a. Physiol:* arterial; **tension artérielle,** blood pressure.

artériosclérose [arterjɔskleroz] *n.f. Med:* arteriosclerosis.

artésien, -ienne [artezjɛ̃, -jɛn] *a.* Artesian (well).

arthrite [artrit] *n.f. Med:* arthritis; **a. sèche, déformante,** rheumatoid arthritis.

arthritique [artritik] *a. & n. Med:* arthritic (patient).

arthro- [artrɔ] *pref.* arthro-.

arthropode [artrɔpɔd] *n.m.* arthropod.

arthrose [artroz] *n.f. Med:* osteoarthritis.

artichaut [artiʃo] *n.m. Bot:* globe artichoke; *Cu:* **fonds d'artichauts,** artichoke hearts.

article [artikl̥] *n.m.* **1.** (*a*) *Bot: Ent:* joint; (*b*) critical point; **être à l'a. de la mort,** to be at the point of death. **2.** (*a*) article, clause (of treaty, etc.); **a. de foi,** article of faith; (*b*) item (of bill, etc.); **articles divers,** sundries; (*c*) article (in newspaper, etc.); **a. de tête, de fond,** editorial, leader; leading article. **3.** *Com:* article, commodity, *pl.* goods, wares; **a. (en) réclame,** special offer; **articles de voyage,** travel goods; **articles de ménage,** household requisites; **articles de toilette,** toilet requisites, toiletries. **4.** *Gram:* **a. défini, indéfini,** definite, indefinite, article.

articulaire [artikylɛr] *a. Anat:* articular, articulatory; *Med:* **rhumatisme a.,** rheumatoid arthritis.

articulation [artikylasjɔ̃] *n.f.* **1.** (*a*) *Anat: etc:* articulation, joint; *Bot:* node; **a. du doigt,** knuckle; (*b*) connection, joint; **accouplement à a.,** jointed coupling; **a. à. rotule,** ball-and-socket joint. **2.** articulation, (manner of) speech. **3.** *Jur:* numeration (of facts).

articulé [artikyle] *a.* (*a*) articulate(d); jointed (limb, coupling, etc.); hinged; *Mec.E:* **courroie articulée,** chain belt, link belt; (*b*) articulate (speech).

articuler [artikyle] *v.tr.* **1.** to articulate, hinge, link, joint. **2.** to articulate; pronounce distinctly; **mal a.,** to mumble. **3.** *Jur:* (*a*) to enumerate, to set forth (facts); (*b*) to state (fact) clearly, definitely.

artifice [artifis] *n.m.* **1.** artifice; contrivance; stratagem; **user de tous les artifices pour . . .,** to resort to every trick in order to. . .. **2.** (*a*) **feu d'a.,** fireworks, firework display; **pièce d'a.,** set piece.

artificialité [artifisjalite] *n.f.* artificiality.

artificiel, -ielle [artifsjɛl], *a.* artificial; imitation (pearl, etc.); false (teeth, etc.); **lumière, glace, fleur, artificielle,** artificial light, ice, flowers; **jambe artificielle,** artificial leg; **classification artificielle,** arbitrary classification; **rire a.,** forced laugh.

artificiellement [artifisjɛlmɑ̃] *adv.* artificially.

artillerie [artijri] *n.f.* **1.** artillery, ordnance; **a. de campagne,** field artillery; **a. légère, lourde,** light, heavy, artillery; **a. navale,** naval artillery; **a. antichars,** *Belg:* **anti-blindés,** anti-tank artillery; **a. antiaérienne,** anti-aircraft artillery; **a. d'assaut,** assault artillery, guns; *Aut:* **roue type a.,** artillery-type wheel. **2.** gunnery.

artilleur [artijœr] *n.m.* artilleryman, gunner.

artimon [artimɔ̃] *n.m. Nau:* **(mât d')a.,** mizzenmast; **voile d'a.,** mizzen (sail); **a. de cape,** storm mizzen.

artisan, -ane [artizɑ̃, -ɑŋ] *n.* artisan, craftsman.

artisanal, -aux [artizanal, -o] *a.* artisanal; **métier a.,** craft; **production artisanale,** small-scale production (by craftsmen).

artisanat [artizana] *n.m.* **1.** craftsmen (as a class); **l'a. indigène,** the native craftsmen. **2.** (*a*) cottage industry; (*b*) **a. d'expression,** arts and crafts, handicrafts; **produits d'a. régional,** local handicrafts.

artiste [artist] **1.** *n.* (*a*) artist (including musician, etc.); **a. peintre,** painter; (*b*) *Th: Mus:* performer; (*c*) *Th:* actor, actress; singer; dancer; entertainer; artiste (of variety stage); **entrée des artistes,** stage entrance. **2.** *a.* artistic (temperament, style).

artistique [artistik] *a.* artistic.

artistiquement [artistikmɑ̃] *adv.* artistically.

arum [arɔm] *n.m. Bot:* arum.

aryen, -enne [arjɛ̃, -ɛn] *a. & n.* Aryan.

as [ɑs] *n.m.* **1.** (*a*) *Cards: etc:* ace; **amener deux as,** to throw two aces; **as de pique,** (i) ace of spades; (ii) *F:* rump (of fowl); parson's nose; *P:* **être aux as, plein aux as,** to be rolling (in it); (*b*) (*dominoes*) one; **l'as blanc,** one blank; (*c*) *F:* **l'as,** (table) No. 1 (in restaurants, etc.). **2.** (*a*) *Av:* ace; (*b*) *F:* first-rater; *Games:* crack player, star; **au tennis c'est un as,** he's an ace at tennis; *Aut:* **as du volant,** crack (racing) driver. **3.** *Row:* single-sculler (skiff).

asbeste [azbɛst] *n.m. Miner:* asbestos.

asbestose [azbɛstoz] *n.f. Med:* asbestosis.

ascendance [asɑ̃dɑ̃s] *n.f.* **1.** *Astr:* ascent. **2.** lineage; **l'une et l'autre famille avait une a. canadienne,** both families were of Canadian ancestry.

ascendant [asɑ̃dɑ̃] **1.** *a.* ascending (movement, *Meteor:* current, *Mus:* scale, *Mth:* series); upward (motion, etc.); *Av:* **vol a.,** climbing flight; *Mch:* **course ascendante,** up stroke (of piston); *Mch: etc:* **tuyau a.,** standpipe. **2.** *n.m.* (*a*) *Astr: etc:* ascendant; **astre qui est à l'a.,** star in the ascendant; (*b*) ascendancy, influence; (*c*) **ascendants,** ancestry.

ascenseur [asɑ̃sœr] *n.m.* lift, *NAm:* elevator; **a. de marchandises,** goods hoist; **a. à tous les étages,** lift to all floors. *Hyd.E:* **a. à sas,** canal lift.

ascension [asɑ̃sjɔ̃] *n.f.* (*a*) ascent, ascension; rising (of sap, etc.); *Av:* climb; **faire l'a. d'une montagne,** to climb a mountain; **a. d'un astre,** ascension of a star; *Av:* **angle d'a.,** climbing; angle; **a. verticale,** (i) *Av:* vertical climb; (ii) *Astr:* right ascension; *Ecc:* **fête, jeudi, de l'A.,** Ascension Day; *Geog:* **l'île de l'A.,**

Ascension Island; (*b*) progress, ascent; rise; **l'a. de Bonaparte,** the rise of Bonaparte.

ascensionnel, -elle [asɑ̃sjɔnɛl] *a.* ascensional; upward (motion); *Aer:* **force ascensionnelle,** lifting power, lift; **vitesse ascensionnelle,** rate of climb, climbing speed; *Mch:* **mouvement a.,** up-stroke.

ascensionner [asɑ̃sjɔne] *v.i. Mount:* to climb.

ascensionniste [asɑ̃sjɔnist] *n.m. & f.* climber, mountaineer.

ascète [asɛt] *n.m. & f.* ascetic.

ascétique [asetik] *a. & n.* ascetic; **vie a.,** ascetic life.

ascétisme [asetism] *n.m.* asceticism.

ascorbique [askɔrbik] *a.* ascorbic (acid).

asdic [asdik] *n.m. Nav:* asdic (*Allied Submarine Detection Investigation Committee*).

asepsie, aseptie [asɛpsi] *n.f. Med:* asepsis.

aseptique [asɛptik] *a. Med:* aseptic.

asexué [asɛksɥe] *a.* **asexuel, -elle** [asɛksɥɛl] *a. Biol:* asexual.

asiatique [azjatik] *a. & n. Geog:* Asiatic, Asian; **grippe a.,** Asian flu.

Asie [azi] *Pr.n.f. Geog:* Asia; **l'A. Mineure,** Asia Minor.

asile [azil] *n.m.* **1.** (*a*) *Jur:* sanctuary; **droit d'a.,** right of sanctuary; (*b*) **a. politique, diplomatique,** political, diplomatic, asylum. **2.** shelter, refuge, retreat; **lieu d'a.,** (place of) refuge; **sans a.,** homeless; without refuge; *A:* **a. des pauvres** = workhouse; **a. de nuit,** night shelter, *F:* dosshouse; **a. d'aliénés,** mental hospital, *O:* lunatic asylum; **a. des marins,** sailors' home; *Lit:* **a. de paix,** haven of peace; **le dernier a.,** the grave.

asinien, -ienne [azinjɛ̃, -jɛn] *a. Z:* asinine.

asocial, -ale, -aux [asɔsjal, -o] *a. & n.* asocial, maladjusted (person).

asparagus [asparagys] *n.m.* **1.** *Bot:* asparagus. **2.** asparagus-fern.

aspect [aspɛ] *n.m.* **1.** sight, aspect; **au premier a.,** at first sight, at a first glance. **2.** (*a*) aspect, appearance, look; **avoir un a. imposant** [aspɛk ɛ̃pozɑ̃], to look imposing; **considérer une affaire sous tous ses aspects,** to look at a problem from every angle, from all points of view; **je n'aime pas l'a. de l'affaire,** I don't like the look of the thing; (*b*) get-up (of book, etc.). **3.** *Astrol:* aspect, relative positions (of stars).

asperge [aspɛrʒ] *n.f.* (*a*) asparagus; **a. plumeuse,** asparagus fern; **plant d'asperges,** asparagus bed; (*b*) *F:* tall, thin person, beanpole.

asperger [aspɛrʒe] *v.tr.* **(j'aspergeai(s) n. aspergeons)** to sprinkle (linen, etc.) with water; **a. qn d'eau bénite,** to sprinkle s.o. with holy water; **une voiture nous a aspergés d'eau sale,** a (passing) car sprayed us with dirty water.

aspergès [aspɛrʒɛs] *n.m. Ecc:* **1.** aspergillum, holy-water sprinkler. **2.** asperges.

aspérité [asperite] *n.f.* **1.** unevenness, ruggedness, roughness (of surface, etc.). **2.** asperity, harshness, sharpness (of character, voice).

asperme [aspɛrm] *a. Bot:* seedless.

aspersion [aspɛrsjɔ̃] *n.f.* aspersion, sprinkling; spraying (of wound, etc.); *Agr:* drench.

aspersoir [aspɛrswar] *n.m.* **1.** *Ecc:* aspergillum. **2.** rose (of watering can).

asphaltage [asfaltaʒ] *n.m. Civ.E: etc:* asphalting.

asphalte [asfalt] *n.m.* (*a*) asphalt; **a. minéral,** pitch, bitumen; (*b*) *F:* **arpenter l'a.,** to pace up and down the streets.

asphalter [asfalte] *v.tr.* to asphalt (road, etc.).

asphérique [asferik] *a. Opt:* aspheric(al).

asphodèle [asfɔdɛl] *n.m. Bot:* asphodel; **a. rameux,** branched lily, king's rod; **a. blanc,** king's spear.

asphyxiant [asfiksjɑ̃] (*a*) asphyxiating, suffocating; **gaz a.,** poison gas; (*b*) stifling, suffocating (atmosphere, etc.).

asphyxie [asfiksi] *n.f.* asphyxia, asphyxiation, suffocation; *Min: etc:* gassing; **a. économique,** economic strangulation.

asphyxié, -ée [asfiksje] *a. & n.* asphyxiated, suffocated (person); *Min: etc:* gassed.

asphyxier [asfiksje] *v.tr.* (*pr.sub. & impf.* **n. asphyxiions, v. asphyxiiez)** **1.** to asphyxiate, suffocate; *Min: etc:* to gas; **il s'est asphyxié,** he suffocated, gassed, himself. **2.** to stifle.

aspic[1] [aspik] *n.m. Rept:* asp.

aspic[2] *n.m. Cu:* aspic.

aspidistra [aspidistra] *n.m. Bot:* aspidistra.

aspirant, -ante [aspirɑ̃, -ɑ̃t] **1.** *a.* sucking; **pompe aspirante,** suction pump; **ventilateur a.,** suction fan; *I.C.E:* **course aspirante,** induction stroke, admission stroke. **2.** *n.* (*a*) candidate; (*b*) *n.m. Navy:* midshipman; *Nau:* **a. pilote,** apprentice pilot; (*c*) *Mil* = officer cadet. **3.** *n.m.* strainer (of pump).

aspirateur, -trice [aspiratœr, -tris] **1.** *a.* aspiratory; suction (device). **2.** *n.m. Ch: Ind: Med:* (gas, air) exhauster; aspirator; *Dom.Ec:* vacuum cleaner; **a. à céréales,** grain elevator; *Mec.E: etc:* (i) exhaust fan, suction fan; (ii) suction conveyor; **a. de buées,** extractor fan; **passer une pièce à l'a.,** to vacuum-clean a room.

aspiration [aspirasjɔ̃] *n.f.* **1.** aspiration, yearning (**à, vers,** for, after); **aspirations à la scène,** hankering after the stage. **2.** *Ling:* aspiration. **3.** (*a*) inspiration, inhaling (of air into the lungs, etc.); (*b*) suction, sucking up (of water into pump, etc.); exhaustion; **ventilateur à a.,** exhaust fan; (*c*) *I.C.E:* admission, induction; **clapet d'a.,** intake valve.

aspiré [aspire] *a. Ling:* aspirate(d).

aspirée [aspire] *n.f. Ling:* aspirate.

aspirer [aspire] **1.** *v.i.* to aspire (**à,** to, after), to aim at; to long for; to yearn for; **a. à faire qch.,** to long to do sth. **2.** *v.tr.* (*a*) to inhale, breathe (in) (air, scent, etc.); to sniff up (powder, etc.); (*b*) to suck up, suck in, draw (up) (water, etc.); (*c*) *Ling:* to aspirate, breathe (a sound); **l'h est aspirée en allemand,** the h is aspirated in German.

aspirine [aspirin] *n.f. Pharm:* aspirin.

assagir [asaʒir] *v.tr.* to make (s.o.) wiser; to sober (s.o.) (down); **le mariage l'a assagi,** marriage has made him settle down; **voilà qui l'assagira,** that will knock some sense into him.

assaillant [asajɑ̃] **1.** *a.* attacking, assaulting. **2.** *n.m.* assailant, attacker, assaulter; aggressor, besieger.

assaillir [asajir] *v.tr.* (*pr.p.* **assaillant,** *p.p.* **assailli,** *pr. ind.* **j'assaille, n. assaillons, ils assaillent,** *impf.* **j'assaillais,** *p.h.* **j'assaillis,** *fu.* **j'assaillirai)** to assault, attack; **à mon retour j'ai été assailli de questions,** when I came back I was bombarded with questions.

assainir [asɛnir] *v.tr.* to make (sth.) healthier; to cleanse, purify (atmosphere, etc.); to sweeten (soil, stable, etc.); to drain (marshes); to improve the sanitation of (town); to stabilize (currency, etc.); **a. les finances, l'administration,** to reorganize finance, administration, *F:* to set one's house in order.

assainissant [asɛnisɑ̃] *a.* cleansing, purifying.

assainissement [asɛnismɑ̃] *n.m.* cleansing, purifying, purification; drainage (of ground); disinfecting (of goods); sweetening (of soil, etc.); improving of the sanitation (of town); *Fin:* stabilization.

assaisonnement [asɛzɔnmɑ̃] *n.m.* **1.** seasoning, flavouring (dish); dressing (of salad). **2.** condiment, seasoning, flavouring. **3.** spice, zest, piquancy.

assaisonner [asɛzɔne] *v.tr.* to season, flavour (**de,** with); to dress (salad).

assassin, -ine [asasɛ̃, -in] **1.** *n.* assassin, murderer, *f.* murderess; **à l'a!** murder! **2.** *a.* (*a*) murderous (horde, etc.); (*b*) provocative, bewitching (smile).

assassinat [asasina] *n.m.* assassination, murder; *Jur:* premeditated murder, *U.S:* murder in the first degree.

assassiner [asasine] *v.tr.* **1.** to assassinate, murder. **2.** *F:* (*a*) to murder (song, etc.); (*b*) to worry, pester, bore (s.o.) to death (**de,** with).

assaut [aso] *n.m.* **1.** (*a*) assault, attack, onslaught; charge; **canon d'a.,** assault gun; **troupes d'a.,** storm troops; storming party; **a. à la baïonnette,** bayonet charge; (*b*) **les assauts répétés d'une maladie,** the repeated attacks, onslaughts, of a disease. **2.** match, bout; **a. de lutte,** wrestling bout; **a. de boxe,** sparring match.

assauvagir [asovaʒir] *v.i. & pr.* to grow wild.

asséchage [aseʃaʒ] *n.m.,* **assèchement** [asɛʃmɑ̃] *n.m.* drying, draining, drainage (of land, road, pond, etc.); pumping dry (of a mine).

assécher [aseʃe] *v.* **(j'assèche, n. asséchons; j'assècherai) 1.** *v.tr.* to dry, drain (marsh, etc.); to pump (mine, etc.) dry; to pump out (mine). **2.** *v.i. & pr.* (*of land, stream, etc.*) to become dry, to dry up.

assemblage [asɑ̃blaʒ] *n.m.* **1.** assemblage, gathering, collection, combination; blending (of wines, etc.); **a. de circonstances,** combination of circumstances. **2.** assembling, assembly (of parts of machine, etc.); *Bookb:* gathering, collating, assembling (of sheets). **3.** (*a*) framework, support, structure; (*b*) *Carp: Metalw: etc:* joint, jointing, joining, coupling, connection; **a. à queue d'aronde,** dovetail joint; **a. à tenon et mortaise,** mortise-and-tenon joint; (*c*) *El:* connection; **a. en quantité,** parallel connection. **4.** *Metalw:* bond.

assemblée [asɑ̃ble] *n.f.* (*a*) assembly; meeting; **a. générale d'actionnaires,** general meeting of shareholders; **l'a. des fidèles,** the congregation; (*b*) *Pol:* **A. nationale** = House of Commons, *U.S:* House of Representatives.

assembler [asɑ̃ble] *v.* **I.** *v.tr.* **1.** to assemble; to call (people) together; to convene (committee, etc.); to collect, gather; to blend (wines, etc.); *Nau:* **a. l'équipage,** to muster the crew. **2.** to assemble, fit together (machine, etc.); to collate (documents); *Bookb:* to collate, gather (sheets); *Cmptr:* to assemble (program(me); to link (modules); *El:* to connect, join up (cells); *Carp: Mec.E: etc:* to join (up); to joint; to couple; **a. deux morceaux à plat,** to butt-joint two pieces. **II. s'a.,** to assemble, meet, gather; *Prov:* **qui se ressemble s'assemble,** birds of a feather flock together.

assembleur, -euse [asɑ̃blœr, -øz] *n.* **1.** assembler; fitter (of machines, etc.). **2.** collector, gatherer; *Bookb:* collator (of sheets). **3.** *n.f.* (*machine*) *Bookb:* gatherer; *Cmptr:* collator, collating machine. **4.** *n.m.* *Comptr:* assembly program(me), routine.

assener, asséner [asene] *v.tr.* **(j'assène, n. assenons, n. assénons, j'assènerai, j'assénerai)** to strike (blow); **coup bien asséné,** telling, well-planted, blow.

assentiment [asɑ̃timɑ̃] *n.m.* assent, consent, agreement; **avoir l'a. de tous,** to be supported unanimously; **sourire d'a.,** smile of consent.

asseoir [aswar] *v.* **I.** *v.tr.* (*pr.p.* **asseyant;** *p.p.* **assis;** *pr.ind.* **j'assieds** [asje] **il assied, n. asseyons, ils asseyant,** or **j'assois, il assoit, ils assoient;** *pr.sub.* **j'asseye, n. asseyions,** or **j'assoie;** *imp.* **assieds, asseyons, asseyez;** *impf.* **j'asseyais** or **j'assoyais;** *p.h.* **j'assis;** *p.sub.* **j'assisse;** *fu.* **j'assiérai, j'assoirai) 1.** to set, seat; **asseyez-le sur le gazon,** sit him down on the grass. **2.** to place, lay, establish (foundations, etc.); **a. une pierre,** to bed a stone; **a. une statue sur un piédestal,** to stand a statue on a pedestal; **a. une tente, un camp,** to pitch a tent, a camp; *Av:* **a. l'appareil,** to pancake; **a. l'impôt sur le revenu,** to base taxation on income. **3.** (*a*) **a. une pension sur qn,** to settle a pension on s.o.; (*b*) **a. un impôt sur les tabacs,** to impose, to lay, to levy, a tax on tobacco. **II. s'asseoir 1.** to sit down; **faire a. qn,** to ask s.o. to sit down; **s'a. (sur son séant),** to sit up; *F:* **s'a. sur qn,** to sit on s.o.; *F:* **les ordres du patron, moi, je m'assois dessus,** I don't care a damn about the boss's orders! **2.** (*of house, gun, etc.*) to settle.

assermenté [asɛrmɑ̃te] *a.* (*a*) sworn (in); **fonctionnaire a.,** sworn official; *Hist:* **(prêtre) non a.,** non-juring (priest); (*b*) (witness, etc.) on oath.

assermenter [asɛrmɑ̃te] *v.tr.* to swear (s.o.) in; to administer the oath to (s.o.).

assertion [asɛrsjɔ̃] *n.f.* assertion.

asservi [asɛrvi] *a.* *Mec.E:* servo (appliance); **moteur a.,** servomotor.

asservir [asɛrvir] *v.tr.* **1.** to enslave, subjugate, subdue; to reduce (nation) to slavery. **2.** (*of actuating device, etc.*) to bring (part) under control. **3. s'a.,** to submit.

asservissant [asɛrvisɑ̃] *a.* enslaving; servile (yoke); **avoir un emploi a.,** to be tied down to one's job.

asservissement [asɛrvismɑ̃] *n.m.* **1.** (*a*) reduction to slavery; (*b*) subjection (**à,** to), enslavement; subservience. **2.** control (of mechanism); servo control.

assesseur [asɛsœr] *n.m.* (*a*) *Jur:* **(juge) a.,** assessor (to magistrate, etc.); (*b*) **être secondé par ses assesseurs,** to be supported by one's assistants.

assez [ase] *adv.* **1.** (*a*) enough; **vous travaillez bien a.,** you work quite enough; **elle parle a. bien l'anglais,** she speaks English quite, fairly, well; **c'est a. parlé!** enough said! that's enough talking! (*b*) **assez de** + *n.:* **il y a a. de temps que je l'attends,** I've been waiting for her long enough; **avez-vous a. d'argent?** have you enough money? **j'en ai assez!** I've had enough of it, I'm sick, tired, of it! I'm fed up! **en voilà a. sur ce sujet!** that's enough about that! **c'en est a.!** that's enough of that! **a. de larmes!** stop crying! (*c*) **c'est assez** + *inf:* **c'est a. parler,** I, you, have said enough; that's enough talking; (*d*) **être a. près pour voir,** to be near enough to see; **il n'avait pas a. pour vivre,** he hadn't enough to live on; (*e*) *int.* **assez!** that's enough! stop! **2.** rather, fairly, tolerably; **elle est a. jolie,** she's quite pretty; **je suis a. de votre avis,** I'm rather inclined to agree with you; **arriver a. tard,** to arrive somewhat late; **avoir a. de bon sens,** to have a fair amount, plenty, of (common) sense; **il parle a. peu,** he doesn't talk much.

assidu [asidy] *a.* (*a*) assiduous; industrious, hard-working, persevering (pupil, etc.); **efforts assidus,** untiring efforts; **travailleur a.,** hard worker; (*b*) persistent, unremitting, unceasing, constant (care, work, attention, etc.); (*c*) regular, constant (visitor).

assiduité [asidɥite] *n.f.* **1.** (*a*) assiduity; steadiness; perseverance; **a. à (faire) qch.,** assiduity, steadiness, in (doing) sth.; **a. au travail,** devotion to work; (*b*) *Sch: etc:* regular attendance. **2.** constant attention(s), constant care; **fréquenter qn avec a.,** to be a frequent visitor at s.o.'s house.

assidûment [asidymɑ̃] *adv.* assiduously, unremittingly. **il y travaille a.,** he is hard at work on it.

assiégé, -ée [asjeʒe] *a. & n.* besieged; **les assiégés,** the besieged.

assiégeant [asjeʒɑ̃] **1.** *a.* besieging (army, etc.). **2.** *n.m.* besieger.

assiéger [asjeʒe] *v.tr.* **(assiégeant, j'assiège, n. assiégeons, j'assiégerai) 1.** (*a*) to besiege; to lay siege to (s.o., sth.); (*b*) **a. qn de demandes,** to pester s.o. with requests. **2.** to surround, crowd round.

assiette [asjɛt] *n.f.* **1.** (*a*) laying (down) (of foundations); bedding (of stone); pitching (of camp);

laying out (of railway line); (*b*) establishment (of tax, of rates); funding (of annuity). **2.** (*a*) seat (on horse); trim (of boat); *Av: Nau:* **angle d'a.,** trim angle; **avoir une bonne a.,** (i) *Equit:* to have a good seat; (ii) (*of ship*) to be in good trim; *F:* **ne pas être dans son a.,** to be out of sorts, off colour, not to be up to the mark; (*b*) position; situation, site (of building, etc.); disposition (of camp); lie (of land); *For:* **a. des coupes,** felling plan; (*e*) set (of stone, beam, etc.); (*of foundation, gun, etc.*) **prendre son a.,** to set, to settle, to bed down. **3.** foundation, bottom, bed (of a road); basis (of a tax). **4.** (*a*) plate; **a. plate,** dinner plate; **a. creuse, à soupe,** soup plate; **a. à dessert,** dessert plate; **manger dans une a.,** to eat from, off, a plate; *F:* **a. au beurre,** cushy job; (*b*) **a. anglaise,** assorted cold meat, *U.S:* cold cuts; **a. de charcuterie,** plate of assorted delicatessen.

assiettée [asjete] *n.f.* plate(ful).

assignataire [asiɲatɛr] *a.* **banque a.,** warrant bank.

assignation [asiɲasjɔ̃] *n.f.* **1.** *Fin:* assignment, transfer (of shares, of funds) (**à,** to). **2.** *Jur:* (*a*) serving of a writ, summons, process; (*b*) writ of summons; subpoena; **signifier, faire, donner, envoyer, une a. à qn,** to serve a writ on s.o.; to issue a summons to s.o.; to subpoena (witness); (*c*) **a. à résidence,** placing under forced residence.

assigner [asiɲe] *v.tr.* **1.** (*a*) to assign; to fix, appoint (time, meeting, etc.); **a. une tâche à qn,** to assign, allot, a job to s.o.; (*b*) **a. une somme à un paiement,** to assign, earmark, a sum for payment, to allocate a sum to a payment; (*c*) **a. une dépense sur le trésor public,** to charge an expense to public funds. **2.** *Jur:* (*a*) to summon, subpoena, cite (witness, etc.); (*b*) (i) to issue a writ against (s.o.); (ii) to have a writ issued against (s.o.); (iii) to serve a writ on (s.o.).

assimilation [asimilasjɔ̃] *n.f.* **1.** (*a*) assimilation (of food, knowledge, etc.); (*b*) assimilation (of racial groups, etc.); **politique d'a.,** policy of assimilation. **2.** *Mil: Navy:* correlation (of ranks).

assimilé [asimile] **1.** *a.* (*a*) *Mil: Navy:* **être a. à . . .,** to rank as, with; ranked as; **a. au grade de capitaine,** ranking, ranked, as a captain; (*b*) assimilated (immigrants, etc.). **2.** *n.m.* (*a*) **officiers et assimilés,** officers and equivalent; **cadres et assimilés,** executives and acting executives.

assimiler [asimile] *v.tr.* **1.** (*a*) to assimilate (food, knowledge, etc.); **ces minéraux s'assimilent facilement,** these minerals are easily assimilated; (*b*) to assimilate (immigrants, etc.). **2.** (*a*) to assimilate; to compare (**à,** to, with); (*b*) **a. à,** to class as, to put in the same category as.

assis [asi] *a.* (*a*) seated; **nous étions a. auprès du feu,** we were sitting, seated, round the fire; *F:* **en rester a.,** to be flabbergasted; *Her:* **lion a.,** lion sejant; (*b*) *Rail: Th: etc:* **places assises,** seats; **il n'y a plus de places assises,** standing room only; **bien a. sur l'eau,** well trimmed (ship).

assise[1] [asiz] *n.f.* **1.** seating, laying (of foundation). **2.** (*a*) seating, foundation; bed(plate) (of engine, etc.); **ajuster l'a. d'une soupape,** to seat a valve; (*b*) *Geol:* bed, stratum. **3.** *Const:* course (of masonry); layer (of cement). **4.** (*a*) *Jur:* **les assises,** the assizes; **cour d'assises,** Assize Court; **être renvoyé devant la cour d'assises,** to be committed for trial; **avocat d'assises,** criminal lawyer; (*b*) **assises d'un congrès, etc.,** sittings of a congress, etc.; (*c*) *Hist:* **les Assises de Jérusalem,** the Assizes of Jerusalem.

Assise[2] *Pr.n.f. Geog:* Assisi.

assistance [asistɑ̃s] *n.f.* **1.** presence, attendance (*esp.* of magistrate or priest). **2.** (*a*) audience; *Ecc:* congregation; (*b*) spectators, onlookers. **3.** (*a*) assistance, help, aid; **faire qch. sans assistance,** to do sth. unaided; **a. sociale,** welfare work; *Com:* **a. maritime,** salvage; (*b*) *A:* **L'A. publique** = (i) National Assistance Board; (ii) Child Welfare; *Jur:* **a. judiciaire,** legal aid.

assistant, -ante [asistɑ̃, -ɑ̃t] **1.** *n. usu. pl.* (*a*) bystander, onlooker, spectator; (*b*) member of the audience; **quelques-uns d'entre vous, messieurs, les assistants,** some of you gentlemen here. **2.** *n.* (*a*) assistant; **l'a. du chirurgien,** the surgeon's assistant; (*b*) foreign assistant (in school); (*c*) *Sch:* demonstrator (of practical work); laboratory assistant; (*d*) **assistante sociale,** welfare worker, officer; (*in hospital*) medical social worker.

assisté, -ée [asiste] *a. & n. Adm:* (person) in receipt of (national) assistance; **enfants assistés,** children in care.

assister [asiste] **1.** *v.i.* **a. à qch.,** to attend sth., to be (present) at sth., to take part in sth.; **a. à une partie de football,** to attend a football match. **2.** *v.tr.* (*a*) to help, assist (s.o.); **a. qn de ses conseils,** to give s.o. advice; (*b*) **prêtre assisté de deux enfants de chœur,** priest attended by two altar boys.

association [asɔsjasjɔ̃] *n.f.* **1.** (*a*) association (of words, ideas); (*b*) *El:* connecting, grouping, coupling (of cells); (*c*) *Jur:* **a. de malfaiteurs,** conspiracy. **2.** (*a*) society, company; association, fellowship; **a. syndicale,** trade union; **a. de secours,** friendly society; **a. de bienfaisance,** charity, charitable institution; (*b*) *Com:* partnership.

associé, -ée [asɔsje] **1.** *a.* associated; joint; **porteurs, souscripteurs, associés,** joint holders (of stock); *Adm:* **territoires associés,** associated territories. **2.** *n.* (*a*) *Com:* partner; **a. principal,** senior partner; **a. commandité,** acting partner; **a. commanditaire,** sleeping partner; (*b*) associate, honorary member (of learned body, etc.).

associer [asɔsje] *v.* (*pr. sub. & impf.* **n. associions, v. associiez**) **I.** *v.tr.* **1.** (*a*) to associate, unite, join; **a. qn à qch.,** to make s.o. a party to sth., to associate s.o. with sth.; **a. des idées,** to associate ideas; (*b*) *El:* to connect, join up (cells, etc.). **2. s'a. qn, a. qn à sa maison, à ses travaux,** to take s.o. into partnership. **II. s'associer 1. s'a. à qch.,** to share in, participate in, join in, sth; **s'a. à un crime,** to be a party to a crime. **2. s'a. à, avec, qn,** (i) to join forces with s.o.; (ii) to enter into partnership with s.o.

assoiffé, -ée [aswɑfe] thirsty; **a. de sang,** bloodthirsty.

assolement [asɔlmɑ̃] *n.m. Agr:* rotation (of crops); **a. triennal,** three course system.

assombrir [asɔ̃brir] *v.* **1.** *v.tr.* (*a*) to darken, obscure; **ciel assombri,** cloudy, overcast, sky; (*b*) to cast a gloom over (s.o., sth.); **visage assombri,** gloomy face. **2. s'a.,** to become dark; to cloud over.

assommant [asɔmɑ̃] *a.* **1.** *O:* overwhelming (heat, argument, etc.). **2.** *F:* boring, tedious, deadly dull; **il est a., cet enfant-là!** that child is a plague!

assommer [asɔme] *v.tr.* **1.** (*a*) **a. un bœuf,** to fell an ox; **a. qn,** to brain s.o.; to club s.o. to death; (*b*) to knock (s.o.) senseless; to stun, to cosh (s.o.). **2.** *F:* to bore (s.o.) (to death); to pester (s.o.).

assommeur, -euse [asɔmœr, -øz] **1.** *n.m.* (*a*) slaughterer, slaughterman; (*b*) ruffian (armed with club), tough. **2.** *n.m. & f. F:* (*pers.*) bore.

assommoir [asɔmwar] *n.m. O:* (*a*) pole-axe; (*b*) club, bludgeon, cosh; *U.S:* blackjack; *F:* **porter un coup d'a. à qn,** to deal s.o. a knock-out blow.

assomption [asɔ̃psjɔ̃] *n.f.* **1.** *Ecc:* **(fête de) l'A. (de la Sainte Vierge),** (feast of) the Assumption (of the Blessed Virgin). **2.** *Geog:* **Assomption,** Asuncion.

assonance [asɔnɑ̃s] *n.f. Ling: Pros:* assonance.

assorti [asɔrti] *a.* **1.** matched, matching, paired; **bien a.,** well matched; **couple mal a.,** ill assorted couple;

couleurs assorties, colours that match; **pull avec jupe assortie,** jumper with matching skirt. **2.** assorted, mixed (sweets, nails, etc.). **3.** **bien assorti,** well stocked (shop, etc.); **fromages assortis,** choice of cheeses; (*in restaurant*) cheese board, platter.

assortiment [asɔrtimɑ̃] *n.m.* **1.** matching; **a. parfait de couleurs,** perfect match(ing) of colours. **2.** (*a*) assortment, variety, collection (of goods, etc.); **ample a. d'échantillons,** wide range of patterns; **a. de charcuterie,** assorted delicatessen; (*b*) set (of tools).

assortir [asɔrtir] *v.* **(j'assortis, n. assortissons) 1.** *v.tr.* match (colours, etc.); **a. son style à la matière,** to suit one's style to the subject. **2.** **s'a.,** to match, blend, harmonize; to go well together.

assoupi [asupi] *a.* **1.** dozing; somnolent. **2.** dormant (volcano, etc.).

assoupir [asupir] *v.* **1.** (*a*) to make (s.o.) drowsy, sleepy, heavy; to send (s.o.) to sleep; (*b*) to calm, deaden, lull (pain, the senses). **2.** **s'a.,** to drop off to sleep; to doze off; to grow sleepy, drowsy; (*of pain, grief*) to die down; (*of sound*) to die away.

assoupissant [asupisɑ̃] *a.* soporific.

assoupissement [asupismɑ̃] *n.m.* **1.** calming, lulling (of pain, etc.). **2.** drowsiness, somnolence.

assouplir [asuplir] *v.* **1.** *v.tr.* (*a*) to (make) supple; to soften; **a. du cuir,** to supple, soften, leather; (*b*) to ease, relax (regulations). **2.** **s'a.,** to become supple; to soften; **s'a. les muscles,** to limber up.

assouplissement [asuplismɑ̃] *n.m.* suppling (of leather); softening; easing (of regulations); **exercices d'a., assouplissements,** limbering-up exercises.

assourdir [asurdir] *v.tr.* **1.** to make (s.o.) deaf; to deafen. **2.** (*a*) to deaden, damp, muffle (sound); to muffle (drum, bell, oars); to mute (violin); *Const:* to soundproof; *Ling:* to unvoice (consonant); (*b*) to soften, subdue, tone down (light, colour).

assourdissant [asurdisɑ̃] *a.* deafening (noise, etc.).

assourdissement [asurdismɑ̃] *n.m.* **1.** (*a*) deafening! (*b*) deadening (of sound); muffling (of drum, oars); *Ling:* unvoicing (of consonant); (*c*) softening, subduing (of light). **2.** temporary deafness.

assouvir [asuvir] *v.* **1.** *v.tr.* to satiate, state, appease, satisfy (hunger, passions); **a. sa soif,** to slake, quench, one's thirst. **2.** **s'a.,** to become appeased.

assouvissement [asuvismɑ̃] *n.m.* satisfying, satisfaction (of hunger, etc.); quenching (of thirst).

assuétude [asyetyd] *n.f. Med:* addiction.

assujettir [asyʒetir] *v.tr.* **1.** (*a*) to subdue, subjugate (province, etc.), to bring (province, etc.) into subjection; (*b*) **a. qn à faire qch.,** to compel, oblige, s.o. to do sth. **2.** to fix, fasten (**à,** to); make (sth.) secure. **3.** to subject, to make liable (**à,** to).

assujettissant [asyʒetisɑ̃] *a.* exacting, demanding (work).

assujettissement [asyʒetismɑ̃] *n.m.* **1.** (*action*) subjection, subjugation. **2.** (*a*) (*state*) subjection, subservience (to s.o., sth.); (*b*) tie; **la grandeur a ses assujettissements,** greatness has its obligations.

assumer [asyme] *v.tr.* to assume; to take upon oneself (right, responsibility, etc.); **a. les frais,** to take charge of the expenditure; **a. son service,** to take up one's duties.

assurable [asyrabl̥] *a. Ins:* assurable, insurable.

assurance [asyrɑ̃s] *n.f.* **1.** (*a*) assurance; (self) confidence; **parler avec a.,** to speak with confidence; **perdre son a.,** to lose one's self assurance; (*b*) *Corr:* **agréez l'a. de mes sentiments distingués,** yours faithfully; (*c*) **vous pouvez l'acheter en toute a.,** you can buy it with complete confidence. **2.** security, pledge; **demander, recevoir, des assurances,** to ask for, receive, assurances. **3.** (*a*) making sure, safe; *Mount:* **(point d')a.,** belay; (*b*) *Com:* insurance, assurance; **police d'a.,** insurance policy; **prime d'a.,** insurance premium; **compagnie, société, d'assurances,** insurance company; **a. sur la vie, a.-vie,** life insurance; **a. contre les accidents, a.-accident,** accident insurance; **a. contre l'incendie, a.-incendie,** fire insurance; **a. contre les accidents du travail,** employers' liability insurance; **a. maritime,** marine insurance; **a. vis-à-vis des tiers, aux tiers,** third-party insurance; **a. collective,** group insurance; *Aut:* **a. tous risques,** *Sw. Fr:* **a. casco,** comprehensive insurance; **agent d'assurance(s),** insurance agent; **courtier d'assurance(s),** insurance broker; (*c*) *Adm:* **assurances sociales,** social, national, State, insurance; **a. chômage** = unemployment insurance, benefits; **a. invalidité** = disability pension; **a. vieillesse** = retirement pension; **a. maternité** = maternity benefits; **a. maladie** = sickness benefits.

assuré, -ée [asyre] **1.** *a.* firm, sure (step, voice, etc.); assured, confident (air, person); certain (cure); secure, safe (retreat); **voix mal assurée,** unsteady, quavering, voice; **d'une main assurée,** with a sure hand; **il n'y a encore rien d'a.,** there is nothing fixed yet. **2.** *n. Ins:* policy holder; the insured.

assurément [asyremɑ̃] *adv.* assuredly, surely, undoubtedly, certainly; **a. non!** certainly not! **oui, a.!** yes, of course!

assurer [asyre] *v.* **I.** *v.tr.* **1.** (*a*) to make (sth.) firm, steady; to fix, secure, fasten, strengthen, steady (sth.); to prop up (wall); to make fast (rope); *Mount:* to belay; to secure; **a. qn sec,** to give s.o. a tight rope; (*b*) to ensure (result); **a. un pays,** to make a country secure; **a. sa fortune,** to consolidate one's fortune; **a. une rente à qn,** to settle an annuity on s.o.; **ma retraite m'assure de quoi vivre,** my pension gives me enough to live on; **a. ses arrières,** (i) *Mil:* to protect one's rear; (ii) to protect oneself against any eventuality; **le courrier littéraire sera assuré par M. X,** the literary column will be in the hands of Mr X; **un service régulier est assuré entre Paris et Londres,** there is a regular service between Paris and London; **s'a. qch.,** to secure, make certain of, sth.; (*c*) **a. une créance,** to stand security for a debt. **2.** **a qch. à qn, a. qn de qch.,** to assure s.o. of sth.; **il m'a assuré qu'il voulait bien le faire,** he assured me that he was willing to do it; **c'est bien vrai, je te l'assure, je t'assure,** it's quite true, I (can) assure you. **3.** *Ins:* **a. qn,** to insure s.o.; **se faire a. sur la vie,** to take out a life insurance (policy); **a. un immeuble contre l'incendie,** to insure a building against fire. **II.** **s'assurer 1.** to settle oneself firmly; **s'a. sur ses pieds,** to steady oneself on one's feet. **2.** **s'a. de qch.,** to make sure, certain, of sth.; **je vais m'en a.,** I'll go and see. **3.** to take out an insurance, to insure oneself (**contre,** against).

assureur [asyrœr] *n.m. Ins:* (*a*) insurer; (*b*) underwriter.

Assyrie [asiri] *Pr.n.f. A.Geog:* Assyria.

assyrien, -ienne [asirjɛ̃, -jɛn] *a.* & *n.* Assyrian.

aster [astɛr] *n.m.* **1.** *Biol:* aster. **2.** *Bot:* aster; **a. de Chine,** China aster; **a. œil-du-Christ,** Michaelmas daisy, *U.S:* aster.

astériser [asterize] *v.tr.* to asterisk, to put an asterisk against (word, etc.).

astérisque [asterisk] *n.m. Typ:* asterisk.

astéroïde [asterɔid] *n.m. Astr:* **1.** asteroid. **2.** planetoid, minor planet.

asthmatique [asmatik] *a.* & *n.m.* & *f. Med:* asthmatic.

asthme [asm] *n.m. Med:* asthma; **a. d'été, des foins,** hay-fever; **être atteint d'a., avoir de l'a.,** to suffer from, to have, asthma; **crise d'a.,** attack of asthma.

asticot [astiko] *n.m.* maggot; *Fish:* gentle.

asticoter [astikɔte] *v.tr. F:* (*a*) to tease, worry; to plague; (*b*) **j'ai qch. qui m'asticote sous le pied,** I've got an itching under the foot.

astigmate, astigmatique [astigmat, astigmatik] *a. Med:* astigmatic(al).

astigmatisme [astigmatism] *n.m.,* **astigmie** [astigmi] *n.f. Med: Opt:* astigmastism.

astiquage [astikaʒ] *n.m.* polishing; tidying up.

astiquer [astike] *v.tr.* to polish; *F:* **s'a.,** to tidy oneself up.

astragale [astragal] *n.m.* **1.** *Anat:* ankle bone. **2.** *Arch:* astragal (of column, etc.).

astrakan [astrakɑ̃] *n.m. Com:* astrakhan (fur).

astral, -aux [astral, -o] *a.* astral (influence, body, etc.); **esprits astraux,** astral spirits.

astre [astr̥] *n.m.* heavenly body; star; **louer qn jusqu'aux astres,** to praise s.o. to the skies; **contempler les astres,** (i) to look at the stars; (ii) (*of dreamer*) to stargaze; **consulter les astres,** to consult the stars.

astreignant [astrɛɲɑ̃] *a.* exacting, demanding.

astreindre [astrɛ̃dr̥] *v.tr.* (*pr.p* **astreignant,** *p.p.* **astreint,** *pr.ind.* **j'astreins, il astreint, n. astreignons,** *impf.* **j'astreignais,** *p.h.* **j'astreignis,** *fu.* **j'astreindrai**) to compel, oblige; to tie down (**à un devoir,** to a duty); **être astreint à faire qch.,** to be compelled to do sth.; **astreint au service militaire,** liable to military service; **s'a. à un régime sévère,** to keep to a strict diet.

astreinte [astrɛ̃t] *n.f.* obligation; **les astreintes de la vie moderne,** the pressures of modern life.

astringence [astrɛ̃ʒɑ̃s] *n.f.* astringency.

astringent [astrɛ̃ʒɑ̃] *a. & n.m. Med:* astringent.

astro- [astrɔ] *pref.* astro-.

astrologie [astrɔlɔʒi] *n.f.* astrology.

astrologique [astrɔlɔʒik] *a.* astrologic(al).

astrologue [astrɔlɔg] *n.m.* astrologer.

astronaute [astrɔnot] *n.m. & f.* astronaut, space traveller, spaceman, -woman.

astronauticien, -ienne [astrɔnotisjɛ̃, -jɛn] *n.* research worker in astronautics.

astronautique [astrɔnotik] *n.f.* astronautics.

astronome [astrɔnɔm] *n.m.* astronomer.

astronomie [astrɔnɔmi] *n.f.* astronomy.

astronomique [astrɔnɔmik] *a.* astronomic(al); **heure a.,** sidereal time; *F:* **la vente atteint aux chiffres astronomiques,** the sales have been astronomical.

astronomiquement [astrɔnɔmikmɑ̃] *adv.* astronomically.

astrophysicien, -ienne [astrɔfizisjɛ̃, -jɛn] *n.* astrophysicist.

astrophysique [astrɔfizik] **1.** *a.* astrophysical. **2.** *n.f.* astrophysics.

astuce [astys] *n.f.* **1.** astuteness, artfulness, wiliness, craftiness; **politicien plein d'a.,** tricky politician. **2.** wile; **les astuces du métier,** the tricks of the trade. **3.** witticism; pun; **je ne saisis pas l'a.,** I don't see it, get it. **4.** *F:* gadget; gimmick.

astucieusement [astysjøzmɑ̃] *adv.* astutely.

astucieux, -ieuse [astysjø, -jøz] *a.* astute, artful, wily, crafty, cunning, tricky (person, behaviour); **réponse astucieuse,** crafty, clever, answer.

asymétrie [asimetri] *n.f.* asymmetry.

asymétrique [asimetrik] *a.* asymmetrical.

atavique [atavik] *a.* atavistic; *Biol:* **retour a.,** throwback.

atavisme [atavism] *n.m.* atavism.

atchoum [atʃum] *int.* (*sneeze*) atishoo.

atelier [atəlje] *n.m.* **1.** (*a*) (work)shop, workroom, atelier; loft; **a. de réparations,** repair shop; *Mec.E:* **a. de montage, d'assemblage,** assembly shop; **a. d'ajustage,** fitting shop; **a. de constructions mécaniques,** machine shop; **a. de tissage,** weaving shed; **a. de constructions navales,** shipyard; **il est monté contremaître après cinq ans d'a.,** he became a foreman after five years on the factory floor; **camion a.,** repair van; (*b*) lodge (of freemasons); (*c*) studio (of artist, etc.). **2.** (*a*) staff (of workshop, etc.); (printer's) chapel; working party.

atermoiement [atɛrmwamɑ̃] *n.m.* **1.** *Com: Jur:* arrangement with creditors for extension of time for payment; **a. d'une lettre de change,** renewal of a bill. **2.** *pl. F:* delays, excuses; shillyshally(ing).

athée [ate] **1.** *a.* atheistic(al) (person, argument). **2.** *n.* atheist.

athéisme [ateism] *n.m.* atheism.

athéistique [ateistik] *a.* atheistic(al) (philosophy).

athénée [atene] *n.m.* **1.** athenaeum. **2.** *Belg: Sw.Fr:* public secondary school.

Athènes [atɛn] *Pr.n.f. Geog:* Athens.

athénien, -ienne [atenjɛ̃, -jɛn] *a. & n.* Athenian.

athlète [atlɛt] *n.m. & f.* athlete; athletic man; *Med:* **pied de l'a.,** athlete's foot.

athlétique [atletik] **1.** *a.* athletic; (*of pers.*) strong, vigorous. **2.** *n.f.* athletics.

athlétiquement [atletikmɑ̃] *adv.* athletically.

athlétisme [atletism] *n.m.* athletics, **épreuves d'a.,** athletic events, track and field events.

Atlantide [atlɑ̃tid] *Pr. n.f.* Atlantis.

atlantique [atlɑ̃tik] *a.* **l'océan A.,** *n.m.* **l'A.,** the Atlantic (Ocean); *Pol:* **la Charte de l'A.,** the Atlantic Charter; **Organisation du Traité de l'A. Nord,** North Atlantic Treaty Organisation.

Atlas [atlas] **1.** *Pr.n.m. Myth: Geog:* Atlas. **2.** *n.m.* (*a*) *Anat:* atlas; (*b*) (*book of maps*) atlas.

atmosphère [atmɔsfɛr] *n.f.* **1.** atmosphere; **humidité de l'a.,** atmospheric humidity; **une a. de vacances,** a holiday atmosphere, feeling. **2.** *Ph:* (*pressure of* 760 *mm. of mercury*) atmosphere.

atmosphérique [atmɔsferik] *a.* atmospheric; *W.Tel:* **parasites atmosphériques, les atmosphériques,** *n.f.pl.,* atmospherics; **perturbations atmosphériques,** atmospheric disturbances.

atoca [atɔka] *n.m. Fr.C: Bot:* cranberry.

atoll [atɔl] *n.m. Geog:* atoll.

atome [atom] *n.m.* (*a*) *Ph:* atom; (*b*) particle; bit; *F:* (*of pers.*) scrap; mite; **atomes de poussière,** specks of dust; **pas un a. de vérité,** not an atom of truth.

atome-gramme [atomgram] *n.m. Ph:* atomgramme, gram(me)-atom; *pl. atomes-grammes.*

atomicité [atɔmisite] *n.f. Ch:* atomicity.

atomique [atɔmik] *a.* atomic (theory, weight, etc.); **masse a.,** atomic mass; **nombre, numéro a.,** atomic number; **sciences atomiques,** atomics; **bombe a.,** atom(ic) bomb; **guerre a.,** atomic warfare; **énergie a.,** atomic energy, nuclear power; **sous-marin à propulseur, propulsion, a.,** nuclear(-powered, -propelled), submarine; **pile a.,** atomic reactor; **centre a.,** atomic research station; **usine a.,** atomic energy plant; **Commissariat à l'énergie a.** = Atomic Energy Authority, *U.S:* Atomic Energy Commission.

atomisation [atɔmizasjɔ̃] *n.f.* atomization.

atomisé, -ée [atɔmize] *n.* person subjected to an atom bomb attack; **les atomisés de Hiroshima qui survécurent à l'explosion de la bombe,** the people who survived the atom bomb attack on Hiroshima.

atomiser [atɔmize] *v.tr.* (*a*) to atomize; (*b*) *F:* to A-bomb; to smash to smithereens.

atomiseur [atɔmizœr] *n.m.* atomizer, spray.

atomisme [atɔmism] *n.m.* the atomic theory.

atomiste [atɔmist] *n.m.* nuclear, atomic, physicist.

atomistique [atɔmistik] (*a*) *n.f.* nucleonics, nuclear engineering; atomics; (*b*) *a.* atomic.

atone [atɔn] *a.* **1.** dull, vacant, lack-lustre (look). **2.** atonic; *Ling:* unstressed, unaccented.

atout [atu] *n.m. Cards:* trump; **a. maître,** master trump; **jouer a.,** to play a trump, to play trumps; **avoir tous les atouts dans son jeu,** to hold all the winning cards, to have every chance of winning.

atoxique [atɔksik] *a. Biol:* non-poisonous.

âtre [ɑtr̥] *n.m.* **1.** fireplace, hearth; **coin de l'â.,** chimney corner. **2.** *Ind:* (*a*) hearth (of forge, etc.); (*b*) (blacksmith's) forge.

atroce [atrɔs] *a.* (*a*) atrocious, heinous, abominable (crime, etc.); (*b*) **douleur a.,** excruciating, agonizing, pain; **j'avais une peur a. de le rencontrer,** I was in dread of meeting him; (*c*) awful, ghastly; **d'une laideur a.,** hideously ugly; **rhume a.,** shocking cold.

atrocement [atrɔsmɑ̃] *adv.* **1.** atrociously, shockingly. **2.** dreadfully; awfully, horribly, terribly.

atrocité [atrɔsite] *n.f.* **1.** atrociousness (of sth.) **2.** (*a*) atrocious act, atrocity; (*b*) *F:* **on m'a raconté des atrocités sur votre compte,** I have been hearing dreadful things about you; (*c*) *F:* **ce tableau est une a.,** this picture is a real horror, a shocker.

atrophie [atrɔfi] *n.f. Med:* (*a*) atrophy (of limb, liver); degeneration; (*b*) wasting (away), emaciation.

atrophié [atrɔfje] *a.* atrophied (liver, intelligence); wasted, withered (arm); emaciated; degenerated.

atrophier [atrɔfje], *v.tr.* to atrophy (limb, intelligence); **s'a.,** to atrophy; to waste (away).

atropine [atrɔpin] *n.f. Ch:* atropin(e).

attabler (s') [satable] *v.pr.* to sit down to table.

attachant [ataʃɑ̃] *a.* **1.** interesting (book); fascinating (spectacle). **2.** engaging, attractive (personality).

attache [ataʃ] *n.f.* **1.** fastening; tying up; sewing on; **chien d'a.,** guard dog; *Civ.E: etc:* **point d'a.,** connection; **pièce d'a.,** fastening; **rivets d'a.,** jointing rivets; *Nau:* **droit d'a.,** mooring right; **droits d'a.,** mooring dues, moorage; **port d'a.,** home port; port of registry; **borne d'a.,** *Nau:* bollard; *El:* terminal. **2.** tie, fastener, fastening, attachment; (*a*) head rope (of horse); lead, leash, chain (of dog); cord, guy (rope); tether; **mettre un chien à l'a.,** to put a dog on the lead, on the chain; **tenir qn comme un chien d'a., comme un chien à l'a.,** to keep s.o. on a string; **nos attaches dans ce pays,** our close ties, links, with this country; **sans attaches,** unattached, unconnected; (*b*) rivet (for mending china); *El:* (wire) clamp; *Cost:* loop, tab; **a. de diamants,** diamond clasp; *Rail:* **a. de rail,** rail fastening; (*c*) *Anat:* origin, attachment (of muscle); **a. de la main, du pied,** wrist joint, ankle joint; (*d*) *Civ.E: etc:* connection, bond, brace; binder (of reinforced concrete beam); (*e*) *Bot:* tendril.

attaché, -ée [ataʃe] **1.** *a.* (*a*) fastened, tied up; chained (dog); **yeux attachés au sol,** eyes fixed on the ground; (*b*) **être a. à qn, à qch.,** to be attached, devoted, to s.o., to sth.; **a. à une opinion,** wedded to an opinion; **rester a. à une opinion,** to cling to an opinion; (*c*) **mon bonheur est a. au vôtre,** my happiness is bound up with yours; (*d*) **des mains finement attachées,** delicately jointed hands; (*e*) attached; dependent on; (*f*) *St.Exch:* **coupon a.,** cum dividend. **2.** *n. Dipl: etc:* attaché; **a. militaire, commercial,** military, commercial, attaché; **a. de presse,** press attaché; **a. d'administration,** junior civil servant.

attachement [ataʃmɑ̃] *n.m.* (*a*) **a. pour qn,** attachment, affection, for s.o.; **a. à l'étude,** fondness for study; (*b*) **rompre un a.,** to break off a liaison.

attacher [ataʃe] *v.* **I. 1.** *v.tr.* to attach; (*a*) to fasten, bind; to tie (up), to do up; **a. un cheval,** to tie up, tether, a horse; **a. avec une boucle,** to buckle; **a. avec des clous,** to nail (on, together); **a. avec une corde,** to rope (together); to tie on, together, with string; **a. avec des épingles,** to pin (on, together); **a. avec des rivets, avec des vis,** to rivet, screw (on, together); (*b*) **a. de l'importance à qch.,** to attach importance to sth.; (*c*) **a. un nouveau secrétaire à une ambassade,** to attach a new secretary to an embassy; **tout ce qui nous attache à la vie,** all that makes us cling to life. **2.** *v.i. Cu: F:* **les pommes de terre ont attaché,** the potatoes have caught; **casserole qui n'attache pas,** non-stick saucepan. **II. s'attacher 1.** (*a*) to attach oneself, to cling, stick (**à,** to); to fasten (**à,** on); to be attached, stuck (**à,** to); to be fastened, tied (**à,** on, to); **le lierre s'attache aux arbres,** ivy clings to trees; **collier qui s'attache avec une agrafe,** necklace that fastens with a clip; **une certaine importance s'y attache,** some importance is attached to it; **s'a. aux faits,** to stick to the facts; (*b*) **s'a. à qn,** to become, grow, fond of, attached to, devoted to, s.o. **2. s'a. à une tâche,** to apply oneself to a job; **s'a. (surtout) à qch., à faire qch.,** to pay particular attention to sth.

attaquable [atakabl̥] *a.* **1.** attackable; open to attack, assailable (town, etc.). **2.** contestable (fact, opinion, etc.); (codicil, etc.) open to attack.

attaquant, -ante [atakɑ̃, -ɑ̃t] **1.** *a.* assailing, attacking. **2.** *n.* assailant, attacker.

attaque [atak] *n.f.* **1.** (*a*) *Mil: etc:* attack, assault, onslaught; **a. concertée,** concerted attack; **reprise d'a.,** renewed attack; **corps d'a.,** attacking party; **passer à l'a.,** to take the offensive; **repasser à l'a.,** to return to the attack; **monter une a.,** to stage an attack; (*b*) *Av:* **a. aérienne,** air raid, attack; *Av: Nau:* **bord d'a.,** leading edge (of wing, propeller); **angle d'a.,** leading angle; **son angle d'a. vis-à-vis d'un problème,** his approach to a problem; (*c*) attack, assault (**de,** on); hold-up (**de,** of) (of a car, train, etc.); **a. de front,** direct, frontal, attack; **subir une a.,** to be attacked; **diriger de violentes attaques contre qn,** to attack s.o. violently; (*d*) *Sp:* attack; *Cards:* lead; (*e*) *Row:* beginning of a stroke; catch (as in the blade grips the water); **d'attaque,** vigorously; **il y va d'a.,** he goes at it tooth and nail, hammer and tongs; **être d'a.,** (i) to have plenty of pluck; (ii) to be on top form; (iii) *Mil:* (*of troops*) to be fit; **il est toujours d'a.,** he is still going strong; (*d*) *Med:* attack (of gout); bout (of fever, influenza); **a. d'épilepsie,** epileptic fit; **a. d'apoplexie,** (apoplectic) stroke; **a. de nerfs,** fit of hysterics. **2.** *Mec.E:* **a. directe,** direct drive (of motor); **pignon d'a.,** driving pinion. **3.** *Mus:* (*a*) short fugue theme; (*b*) entry (of instrument); attack (of note); **chef d'a.,** first violin, leader (of the orchestra).

attaquer [atake] *v.tr.* **1.** (*a*) to attack (enemy, stronghold, etc.); to set upon, assault (s.o., enemy); *Mil:* **a. de front,** to make, to launch a front(al) attack; **attaquez!** engage! (*b*) to attack, criticize, (s.o., s.o.'s opinions); (*of acid*) to attack, eat into, corrode (metal); **a. les abus, les préjugés,** to attack abuses, préjudices; **a. qn sur un sujet,** to tackle s.o. on a subject; *Jur:* **a. (la validité d')un testament,** to contest a will; **a. qn en justice,** to prosecute, sue, bring an action against, s.o.; **le poumon droit est attaqué,** the right lung is affected; (*c*) *v.i.* to attack; to take the offensive. **2.** (*a*) to tackle, get to work on (meal, subject, piece of work, etc.); (*b*) *Mus:* to attack, *F:* to strike up; **bien a. la note,** to hit the note well; **a. faux,** to hit the wrong note; (*c*) *Cards:* **a. trèfle, de la reine,** to lead clubs, the queen; (*d*) *Ling:* to attack; (*e*) *Nau:* **a. un cap,** to sail towards a headland; (*f*) (*of acids, etc.*) to corrode; to etch. **3.** (*of piece of mechanism*) to drive, operate, engage with (another piece). **4. s'attaquer à qn, à qch.,** to attack, make an attack on, tackle, s.o., sth.; **s'a. à une difficulté, à un problème,** to grapple with a difficulty, a problem.

attardé [atarde] *a.* **1.** belated (traveller, etc.); late; behindhand; *n.* **les attardés,** the laggards. **2.** behind the times; *n.* **les attardés,** old fogies, back numbers. **3.** *a. & n. Sch:* backward (child).

attarder [atarde] *v.* **I.** *v.tr.* to keep (s.o.) late; to delay (s.o.); **une crevaison nous a attardés,** we were delayed by a puncture. **II. s'attarder 1.** (*a*) to be delayed; (*b*) to stay (too) late; to stay up late; **s'a. à faire qch.,** to stay (up) late doing sth.; (*c*) to linger, loiter; to lag behind, dawdle; **s'a. en route,** to dawdle on the way. **2. s'a. à qch.,** to waste one's time on, to linger over, sth. **3.** to be behind the times.

atteindre [atɛ̃dr̥] *v.* (*pr.p.* **atteignant;** *p.p.* **atteint;** *pr.ind.* **j'atteins, il atteint, n. atteignons;** *impf.* **j'atteignais;** *p.h.* **j'atteignis;** *fu.* **j'atteindrai) 1.** *v.tr.* to reach; to overtake; to attain; (*a*) **a. la ville,** to reach, to get to, the town; **a. qn,** to catch s.o. up, to overtake s.o.; **a. l'ennemi,** to catch up with, to come up to, the enemy; **comment puis-je vous a.?** (i) how can I reach, get to, you? (ii) how can I get in touch with you?; **a. son but,** to attain, achieve, one's end; **a. l'âge de soixante ans,** to reach the age of sixty; (*b*) **je ne puis pas l'a.,** I can't reach it; **très peu de montagnes atteignent 8000 mètres,** very few mountains reach a height of 8000 metres; **a. un prix élevé,** to reach, fetch, a high price; (*c*) **a. le but,** to hit the target, the mark; **ne pas a. le but,** to fall short of the mark; **a. une couche pétrolifère,** to strike oil; **être atteint (d'un coup de feu) à la jambe,** to be wounded, shot, in the leg; **être atteint d'une maladie,** to be struck down by a disease; (*of trees, etc.*) to be attacked by a disease; **le poumon est atteint,** the lung is affected; **gravement atteint par une faillite,** heavily hit by a bankruptcy. **2.** *v.i.* **a. à qch.,** to reach, attain (to), sth. (with difficulty); **a. à son but,** to achieve one's aim.

atteinte [atɛ̃t] *n.f.* **1.** reach; **se mettre hors de l'a. de qn,** to get, beyond, out of s.o.'s reach; **hors d'a.,** beyond reach, out of reach; **se dérober, se soustraire, à l'a. de la loi,** (i) to circumvent, get round, *F:* dodge, the law; (ii) to get out of the clutches of the law. **2.** blow, stroke, attack; **légère a. au bras,** slight blow on the arm; **a. au crédit de qn,** blow to s.o.'s credit; **légère a. de goutte,** twinge, touch, of gout; **porter a. à l'autorité de qn,** to undermine s.o.'s authority; **a. portée aux privilèges,** breach of privilege; **porter a. aux intérêts de qn,** to interfere with s.o.'s interests, to affect s.o.'s interests.

attelage [atlaʒ] *n.m.* **1.** harnessing; yoking (of oxen). **2.** (*a*) team; pair (of horses); yoke (of oxen); (*b*) *Veh:* carriage (and horses). **3.** *Civ.E: etc:* attachment; (*a*) tying, fastening; hooking on; *Rail;* coupling; (*b*) tie; hook, fastening.

atteler [atle] *v.tr.* **(j'attelle, n. attelons; j'attellerai) 1.** (*a*) to harness, put to (horses, etc.); to yoke (oxen); (*b*) **s'a. à une tâche,** to settle down to a job; **toujours attelé à son travail,** always hard at work, at it. **2. a. une voiture,** to put horses to a carriage; **voiture attelée de quatre chevaux,** carriage drawn by four horses; *Rac:* **course attelée,** trotting race. **3.** *Rail:* **a. des wagons,** to couple (up) wagons.

attelle [atɛl] *n.f. Med:* splint.

attellement [atɛlmɑ̃] *n.m.* harnessing; yoking (of oxen); putting (the) horses to.

attenant [atnɑ̃] *a.* contiguous (**à,** to); adjoining; bordering; **jardin a. au mien,** garden next to mine.

attendre [atɑ̃dr̥] *v.* **I.** *v.tr.* **1.** (*a*) to wait for (s.o., sth.), to await (s.o., sth.); **qu'attendez-vous?** what are you waiting for? **a. qn au passage,** to lie in wait for s.o.; **le déjeuner nous attend,** lunch is ready; **le train n'attend pas,** the train won't wait; **l'avenir nous attend,** the future lies before us; **aller a. qn à la gare,** to go to meet, to go and meet, s.o. at the station; **faire a. qch. à qn,** to keep s.o. waiting for sth., to make s.o. wait for sth.; **il se fait a.,** he's keeping us waiting; **tu t'es fait a.!** and about time too! **a. de faire qch.,** to wait (until it is time) to do sth.; **attendez voir,** (i) just wait; wait and see; (ii) let me see; **a. d'avoir soixante ans,** to wait until one is sixty; **a. que qn fasse qch.,** to wait for s.o. to do sth.; **j'attendrai (jusqu'à ce) qu'il soit prêt,** I shall wait until he's ready; (*b*) *v.i.* **perdre son temps à a.,** to waste one's time waiting; **attendons jusqu'à demain,** let's wait until tomorrow; **attendez (donc)!** wait a bit! just a moment, a minute! **sans plus a.,** without waiting any longer; *Prov:* **tout vient à point à qui sait a.,** everything comes to him who waits; **il ne perdra rien pour a.,** he's got it coming to him; **un plat qui n'attend pas,** a dish that won't stand keeping; (*c*) **en attendant,** meanwhile, in the meantime; **en attendant son arrivée,** until he arrives; while waiting for him to arrive; **en attendant de vous voir,** until I see you; (*d*) *v.i. F:* **a. après qn, qch.,** to wait for, to want, s.o., sth.; **portez-lui ce livre, il attend après,** take that book to him, he is waiting for it. **2.** to expect; **on l'attend la semaine prochaine,** he is expected next week; **femme qui attend un bébé,** expectant mother. **II. s'attendre. s'a. à qch.,** to expect sth.; **il faut s'a. à tout,** one must be prepared, ready, for anything; **je m'y attendais,** I expected as much.

attendri [atɑ̃dri] *a.* **regard a.,** fond, compassionate, look; **yeux attendris,** eyes brimming with tears.

attendrir [atɑ̃drir] *v.tr.* **1.** to make (meat) tender, to tenderize. **2.** to soften (s.o.'s heart), to move (s.o.); to touch (s.o.); **cela attendrirait un cœur de pierre,** it would melt a heart of stone. **3. s'a. sur qch.,** to be moved (to tears), touched, by sth.; **elle s'attendrissait sur leur bébé,** she gushed over their baby; **il s'attendrit facilement,** he is very emotional.

attendrissant [atɑ̃drisɑ̃] *a.* moving, touching, affecting.

attendrissement [atɑ̃drismɑ̃] *n.m.* **1.** (*of meat, etc.*) tenderizing. **2.** pity, emotion; **a. sur soi-même** self pity; **larmes d'a.,** tears of emotion.

attendu [atɑ̃dy] (*a*) *prep.* considering (the circumstances); owing to (the events); in consideration of (his services); (*b*) *conj.phr.* **a. que** + *ind.*, considering that; seeing that; *Jur:* whereas.

attentat [atɑ̃ta] *n.m.* (criminal) attempt; outrage; **a. contre la vie de qn,** attempted murder; **victime d'un a.,** victim of a crime, of an attack; *Jur:* **a. aux mœurs,** indecent behaviour, immoral offence; **a. à la sûreté de l'État,** high treason.

attentatoire [atɑ̃tatwar] *a. Jur:* **action a. à l'autorité,** action that is a challenge to, in contempt of, authority; **mesure a. à la liberté,** measure that constitutes an attempt upon liberty.

attente [atɑ̃t] *n.f.* **1.** (*a*) wait(ing); **être dans l'a. de qch.,** to be waiting for sth; **salle d'a.,** waiting room; **rester en a.,** to be held over; **liste d'a.,** waiting list; *Mil:* **combat d'a.,** delaying action; (*b*) *Surg:* **ligature d'a.,** temporary ligature; (*c*) **circuit d'a.,** (i) *Av:* holding pattern, orbiting; (ii) *Th:* holding circuit. **2.** expectation(s), anticipation; **contre toute a.,** contrary to all expectations; **remplir l'a. de qn, répondre à l'a. de qn,** to come up to s.o.'s expectations; **être dans l'a. de qch.,** to be waiting for sth.; *Corr:* **dans l'a. de votre réponse,** awaiting your reply.

attenter [atɑ̃te] *v.i.* to make an attempt (**à,** on against); **a. à la vie de qn, a. sur qn,** to make an attempt on s.o.'s life; **a. à ses jours,** to attempt suicide; **a. à la liberté de qn,** to interfere with s.o.'s liberty.

attentif, -ive [atɑ̃tif, -iv] *a.* **1.** (*a*) attentive (**à,** to); careful; **il n'est pas a.,** he doesn't pay attention; **il**

écoutait d'un air a., he was listening attentively; (*b*) **être a. à qch.,** to look after sth., to see to sth.; **être a. à sa santé,** to look after oneself, one's health. **2. examen a.,** careful examination.

attention [atɑ̃sjɔ̃] *n.f.* (*a*) attention, care; **appliquer toute son a. à qch.,** to give one's whole mind to sth.; to devote one's whole attention to sth.; **faute d'a.,** through not paying attention; **écouter avec a.,** to listen attentively; *Com: etc:* **à l'a. de M. X,** (for the) attention of Mr X; **indigne de son a.,** beneath his notice; **porter, tourner, diriger, son a. vers, sur, qch.,** to turn one's attention to sth.; to bring one's mind to bear on sth.; (*of object or fact*) **attirer l'a.,** to catch the eye; to be conspicuous; **faire a. à sa santé,** to take care of one's health; **ne faire aucune a., ne pas prêter la moindre a., à qch.,** to take no, not the least, notice of sth.; **(faites) a.!** (i) take care! look out! watch it! (ii) *Sch:* pay attention! **a. à la peinture,** mind the paint, wet paint; **a. au départ!** (i) *Rail:* = stand clear of the doors! mind the doors! (ii) (*on bus*): = hold tight! *P.N:* **a. aux portes,** stand clear of the gates! **a. au train,** beware of (the) trains; **a., descente rapide,** caution, steep hill; **a. aux travaux,** road works ahead; **faites a. à, de, ne pas vous perdre,** be careful not to get lost; **faites a. (à ce) que personne ne sorte,** take care, be sure, that no one leaves the house; **faites a. qu'il n'a que dix ans,** remember, don't forget, that he is only ten (years old); (*b*) **être plein d'attention(s) pour qn,** to be full of attention, consideration, for s.o.; (*c*) **il a eu l'a. de m'avertir,** he was considerate enough to warn me.

attentionné [atɑ̃sjɔne] *a.* attentive; **être a. pour qn,** to be full of attention, consideration, for s.o.

attentisme [atɑ̃tism] *n.m.* wait-and-see policy.

attentivement [atɑ̃tivmɑ̃] *adv.* attentively, carefully; closely.

atténuant [atenɥɑ̃] *a. Jur:* mitigating, extenuating, (circumstances).

atténuation [atenɥasjɔ̃] *n.f.* **1.** (*a*) attenuation, lessening, abatement, diminishing, reducing; dimming, subduing (of light); toning down (of colour); breaking (of fall); mitigation, reduction (of punishment, sentence); (*b*) emaciation, wasting (of body); (*c*) *Phot:* reduction (of negative), softening (of contrasts). **2.** extenuation (of crime).

atténué [atenɥe] *a.* attenuated, diminished; *Jur:* **responsabilité atténuée,** diminished responsibility.

atténuer [atenɥe] *v.tr.* **1.** (*a*) to attenuate, lessen, diminish, reduce; to tone down (colour); to dim, subdue (light); to mitigate (punishment, consequences); **a. une chute,** to break a fall; (*b*) to emaciate, waste; to make (s.o.) thin; (*c*) *Phot:* to reduce (negative, etc.), to soften, tone down (contrasts). **2.** to extenuate, palliate (offence); to render (crime, etc.) less grave; **circonstances qui atténuent son action,** circumstances in extenuation of his action. **3. s'a.,** to lessen, to diminish; to fade.

atterrant [atɛrɑ̃] *a. Lit:* overwhelming; shattering, crushing, staggering (news); startling, astounding.

atterré [atere] *a.* (*a*) overwhelmed, crushed (by news); **ils se contemplèrent atterrés,** they looked at each other in consternation; (*b*) horrorstricken, horrorstruck.

atterrement [atɛrmɑ̃] *n.m.* (*a*) stupefaction, consternation; (*b*) state of prostration.

atterrer [atere] *v.tr.* **1.** to throw (to the ground); to strike down, to fell; to bring down (opponent). **2.** to overwhelm, astound, stupefy, shatter.

atterrir [aterir] **1.** *v.i.* (*a*) *Nau:* to make, sight, land; to make a landfall; (*b*) (*of boat*) to ground, to run ashore; (*c*) *Av:* to alight, to land; **a. trop court,** to undershoot; **a. trop long,** to overshoot; **a. brutalement,** to crash (land); *F:* **a. finalement dans un bar,** to land up in a bar. **2.** *v.tr.* to ground (boat), to run (boat) ashore.

atterrissage [aterisaʒ] *n.m.* **1.** *Nau:* (*a*) making (the) land; landfall; (*b*) grounding (of ship); running ashore. **2.** *Av:* landing; touchdown; **a. trop long,** overshoot; **a. trop court,** undershoot; **a. à vue,** visual landing; **a. aux instruments,** instrument landing; **a. sans visibilité,** blind landing; **a. brutal,** crash landing; **pont d'a.,** landing deck (of aircraft carrier); *Space:* **a. en douceur,** soft landing. **3.** *Tg:* (*a*) landing (of marine cable); (*b*) point of emergence of cable (from the sea).

atterrisseur [aterisœr] *n.m. Av:* undercarriage; landing gear.

attestation [atɛstasjɔ̃] *n.f.* attestation; (*a*) **a. du médecin,** doctor's certificate; *Jur:* **a. du titre,** warranty of title; **a. sous serment, sur l'honneur,** affidavit; (*b*) testimonial, certificate.

attester [atɛste] *v.tr.* **1. a. qch.,** to attest, certify, sth.; to bear testimony, bear witness, testify, to sth.; to vouch for, sth.; **a. que qch. est vrai,** to attest, certify that sth. is true. **2. a. qn (de qch),** to call s.o. to witness (to sth.); **j'en atteste les cieux,** as heaven is my witness; **a. l'autorité de qn en faveur d'une affirmation,** to advance a statement on the authority of s.o.

attiédir [atjedir] *v.tr.* to make tepid, lukewarm; (i) to cool (hot water, etc., s.o.'s ardour); (ii) to warm, to take the chill off (cold water).

attifer [atife] *v.tr. F: usu. Pej:* to dress (s.o.) up, to get (s.o.) up, to deck (s.o.) out (**de,** in); **je ne m'attiferais pas comme ça!** I wouldn't get myself up like that! **comme la voilà attifée!** what a sight, fright, she looks! **attifée de pierreries,** smothered in jewels.

attiger [atiʒe] *v.i.* **(j'attigeais, n. attigeons)** *P:* to exaggerate; to shoot a line; **tu attiges!** come off it!

attique [atik] **1.** *a. Ant:* Attic; Athenian. **2.** *n.m. Arch:* attic (storey).

attirail [atiraj] *n.m.* **1.** apparatus, gear; outfit; set (of tools, etc.); appliances, utensils; implements; **a. de pêche,** fishing tackle. **2.** *F:* paraphernalia.

attirance [atirɑ̃s] *n.f.* attraction (**vers,** to); lure, fascination (of pleasure, place, etc.).

attirant [atirɑ̃] *a.* attractive; drawing (force, etc.); alluring, engaging (manners, smile).

attirer [atire] *v.tr.* **1.** (*a*) (*of magnet, sun, etc.*) to attract, draw; **sa pièce attire un grand public,** his play is a great draw; (*b*) **a. qch. à, sur. qn,** to bring sth. on s.o.; **a. la colère de qn sur qn,** to bring down s.o.'s wrath on s.o.; **a. à soi, s'a., l'attention publique,** to attract public attention; **s'a. des critiques, des éloges,** to come in for criticism, praise; **vous vous l'êtes attiré vous-même,** you have brought it (up)on yourself. **2.** to entice, lure; **a. qn dans un piège,** to lure s.o. into a trap; **a. qn par des promesses,** to entice s.o. with promises; *Jur:* **a. une mineure,** to decoy a girl under age; **affiche qui attire les regards,** poster that attracts attention; **a. l'imagination,** to appeal to the imagination.

attisée [atize] *n.f.* armful of firewood; *Fr. C:* good fire, good blaze.

attiser [atize] *v.tr.* **1.** to stir (up), poke (up) (fire); *Mch: etc:* to stoke (fire); **a. les haines,** to stir up hatred. **2.** to fan (fire, discontent).

attitré [atitre] *a.* regular, appointed, recognized; **fournisseurs attitrés de sa Majesté,** purveyors by appointment to his, her, Majesty; **mon marchand de légumes a.,** my usual, regular, greengrocer.

attitrer [atitre] *v.tr.* to appoint (ambassador).

attitude [atityd] *n.f.* **1.** attitude, posture; **être toujours en a.,** to be always striking attitudes, posing; **a. hostile, intransigeante,** hostile, uncompromising, attitude (**envers, à l'égard de, pour, en face de,** towards). **2.** behaviour.

attractif, -ive [atraktif, -iv] *a.* attractive, drawing (power, force of magnet); gravitational (force).

attraction [atraksjɔ̃] *n.f.* **1.** (*a*) attraction, pull (of magnet, etc.); *Ph:* **a. universelle,** gravitation; **a. moléculaire,** molecular attraction; (*b*) attraction, attractiveness (of place, person, etc.); **exercer une a. sur qn,** to attract s.o.; (*c*) number (in cabaret). **2. attractions,** attractions; sideshows; *Th:* variety show; cabaret show.

attrait [atrɛ] *n.m.* **1.** (*a*) attraction, lure; attractiveness; charm (of youth, etc.); **l'a. de la mer,** the call of the sea; **les attraits d'une carrière dans le commerce,** the attraction of a business career; **dépourvu d'a.,** unattractive; (*b*) inclination; **se sentir de l'a. pour qn,** to feel drawn towards s.o., to feel a liking, a sympathy, for s.o.; (*c*) **attraits,** charms (of woman). **2.** *Fish:* bait.

attrapade [atrapad] *n.f.,* **attrapage** [atrapaʒ] *n.m. F:* **1.** quarrel, set-to. **2.** ticking off.

attrape [atrap] *n.f.* (*a*) *A:* trap, gin, snare (for birds, etc.); (*b*) trick, hoax; **faire une a. à qn,** to play a trick, a practical joke, on s.o.; to take s.o. in; **c'est une a.,** there's a catch in it.

attrape-mouche(s) [atrapmuʃ] *n.m.inv.* **1.** flytrap, flypaper. **2.** *Bot:* Venus' flytrap.

attrape-nigaud [atrapnigo] *n.m.* trick; booby trap; *pl. attrape-nigaud(s).*

attrape-poussières [atrappusjɛr] *n.m. inv.* **1.** air strainer, dust trap. **2.** *F:* white elephant.

attraper [atrape], *v.tr.* to catch. **1.** (*a*) to (en)trap, (en)snare (animal); (*b*) **a. qn,** to trick, cheat, s.o., to take s.o. in. **2.** (*a*) to seize (ball, thief, idea, etc.); **a. un autobus,** to catch a bus; **vous avez bien attrapé la ressemblance,** you have caught the likeness; **en a. pour dix ans,** to get ten years' (imprisonment); (*b*) to hit; **une pierre l'a attrapé au front,** a stone hit him, caught him, on the forehead; (*c*) **a. froid,** to catch a chill; **a. un rhume,** to catch cold; (*d*) **a. qn sur le fait,** to catch s.o. in the act, red-handed; (*e*) *F:* **a. qn,** to scold s.o., to give s.o. a good talking to; **on va vous a.,** you'll catch it, get it in the neck; *Aut: etc:* **a. une contravention,** to get a ticket; **se faire a.,** (i) to get hauled over the coals, to catch it; (ii) to let oneself be cheated, taken in.

attrape-touristes [atrapturist] *n.m.inv. F:* tourist trap.

attrayant [atrɛjɑ̃] *a.* attractive, engaging, alluring, enticing; **peu a.,** unattractive.

attribuable [atribɥabl̥] *a.* attributable, ascribable, (**à,** to); **erreur a. à . . .,** error due to . . . .

attribuer [atribɥe] *v.tr.* **1.** to assign, allot (**à,** to); to confer (**à,** (up)on); to award; **a. des rôles, des fonctions,** to allocate duties (**à,** to); *Th:* **a. un rôle à qn,** to cast s.o. for a part. **2.** to attribute, ascribe (fact, book, etc.) (**à,** to); to impute (crime, mistake) (**à,** to); to attach (importance to sth.); **a. un projet à qn,** to give s.o. the credit for a plan; **tableau attribué à Hogarth,** painting believed to be by Hogarth. **3. s'a. qch.,** to claim, lay claim to, sth.; to take (a duty) upon oneself.

attribut [atriby] *n.m.* attribute.

attribution [atribysjɔ̃] *n.m.* **1.** (*a*) assigning, attribution, attributing (**à,** to); allocation, allocating (of duties); awarding (of scholarships, etc.); *Th:* casting (of parts); *Gram:* **complément d'a.,** indirect object; *St.Exch:* **actions d'a.,** bonus shares; **avis d'a.,** letter of allotment; (*b*) **a. (d'essence, de sucre),** (i) quota, (ii) ration (of petrol, sugar). **2.** *usu. pl.* (*a*) prerogative, competence, powers; **cela entre dans ses attributions,** this comes within his competence, his province; (*b*) duties, functions, responsibilities.

attristant [atristɑ̃] *a.* saddening, depressing (news, etc.); **temps a.,** gloomy, depressing, weather.

attristé [atriste] *a.* sad (face); sorrowful (look); **contempler qch. d'un œil a.,** to gaze sadly at sth.

attrister [atriste] *v.tr.* (*a*) to sadden, grieve; **cela m'attriste d'entendre . . .,** it makes me sad to hear . . .; (*b*) **s'a. de qch.,** to be sad, grieve, about sth.

attroupement [atrupmɑ̃] *n.m.* crowd (of demonstrators, etc.); *Jur:* unlawful, riotous, assembly; **la loi contre les attroupements** = the Riot Act.

attrouper [atrupe] *v.tr.* to gather (mob, etc.) together; **les manifestants s'attroupaient,** the demonstrators were gathering.

atypique [atipik] *a. Med: etc:* atypic(al).

aubaine [obɛn] *n.f.* (*a*) windfall, godsend; (*b*) *Fr.C:* bargain, good buy.

aube[1] [ob] *n.f.* **1.** dawn; **à l'a. (du jour),** at dawn, at break of day, at daybreak, at first light; **l'a. de la civilisation,** the dawn of civilization. **2.** *Ecc:* alb.

aube[2] *n.f.* (*a*) *Nau: Hyd.E:* paddle, blade, float(board) (of wheel); **roue à aubes,** paddle (wheel); **vapeur à roue à aubes,** paddleboat; (*b*) *Mch: etc:* blade, vane (of turbine); vane (of fan).

aubépine [obepin] *n.f. Bot:* hawthorn, may (tree); **fleurs d'a.,** may (blossom).

aubère [obɛr] *a. & n.m.* red roan (horse).

auberge [obɛrʒ] *n.f.* inn; **tenir a.,** (i) to keep an inn; (ii) *F:* to keep open house; **auberges de jeunesse,** youth hostels; **il prend notre maison pour une a.,** he treats our house like a hotel.

aubergine [obɛrʒin] **1.** *n.f. Bot:* aubergine, eggplant. **2.** *a.inv.* aubergine-coloured.

aubergiste [obɛrʒist] *n.m. & f.* innkeeper.

aubette [obɛt] *n.f. esp. Belg:* newspaper kiosk.

aubriétie [obriesi] *n.f. Bot:* aubrietia.

auburn [obœrn] *a.inv.* auburn.

aucun, -une [okœ̃, -yn] **1.** *pron.* (*a*) anyone, any; **il travaille plus qu'a.,** he works more than anyone (else); (*b*) (*with implied negation*) **de tous vos soi-disant amis, a. interviendra-t-il?** will any of your so-called friends intervene? (*c*) (*with negation expressed or understood, accompanied by* **ne** *or* **sans**) (i) no one, nobody; (ii) none, not any; **je ne me fie à a. d'entre eux,** I don't trust any of them; **a. (des deux) ne viendra,** neither (of them) will come; (iii) not one; **de tous ces élèves a. n'a répondu,** not one of these pupils answered; (*d*) *pl. Lit:* some, some people; **d'aucuns prétendent qu'il est encore en vie,** there are some who maintain that he is still alive. **2.** *a.* (*a*) any; **un des plus beaux livres qui aient été écrits sur a. sujet,** one of the finest books that have been written on any subject; (*b*) (*with implied negation*) **avez-vous aucune intention de le faire?** have you any intention of doing it? (*c*) **vendre qch. sans a. bénéfice,** to sell sth. without any profit; **sans aucune exception,** without any exception; **le fait n'a aucune importance,** the fact is of no importance; **sans mentionner a. nom,** without mentioning any names; **il n'a jamais fait a. mal à personne,** he never did anyone any harm.

aucunement [okynmɑ̃] *adv.* (*with negation expressed or understood*) in no way, not at all, by no means, not in the slightest, not in the least; **je n'en suis a. étonné,** I am not at all, in no way, astonished; **je ne le connais a.,** I don't know him at all, *F:* from Adam; **je ne m'attendais a. à ce qu'il vînt,** I never expected him to come; **il ne s'en porte a. mieux,** he is not any better for it.

audace [odas] *n.f.* **1.** audacity, audaciousness; boldness, daring. **2.** audacity, impudence; **vous avez l'a. de me dire cela!** you have the audacity, impudence, cheek, nerve, to tell me that!

audacieusement [odasjøzmɑ̃] *adv.* **1.** audaciously, boldly, daringly. **2.** impudently.

audacieux, -euse [odasjø, -øz], *a.* **1.** audacious, bold, daring. **2.** impudent; brazen (lie, etc).

au-deçà [odsa] *A:* (*a*) *adv.* on this side; (*b*) *prep.phr.* **a.-d. de,** on this side of; without going as far as.

au-dedans [odədɑ̃] (*a*) *adv.* inside; (*b*) *prep.phr.* **a.-d. de,** inside; within.

au-dehors [odəɔr] (*a*) *adv.* outside; (*b*) *prep.phr.* **a.-d. de,** outside, beyond.

au-delà [odla] (*a*) *adv.* beyond; (*b*) *n.m.* **l'a.-d.,** the next world, the hereafter; (*c*) *prep.phr.* **a.-d. de,** beyond, on the other side of; **n'allez pas a.-d. de cent francs,** don't go above, beyond, a hundred francs.

au-dessous [odsu] *adv.* **1.** (*a*) below, under (it); **sur la table et a.-d.,** on the table and under it; **le château est en haut de la colline, le village est a.-d.,** the castle is at the top of the hill, with the village down below; (*b*) below, underneath; **les locataires a.-d.,** the tenants below, downstairs; (*c*) **les enfants âgés de sept ans et a.-d.,** children of seven years and under; (*d*) **musique transposée deux tons a.-d.,** music transposed two tones lower, two tones down. **2.** *prep.phr.* **a.-d. de:** (*a*) below, under; **le village est a.-d. du château,** the village lies at the foot of the castle; **cinquante kilomètres au-d. de Paris,** fifty kilometres below, down river from, Paris; **a.-d. du genou,** below the knee; (*b*) **les locataires a.-d. de nous,** the tenants (on the floor) below us; **quinze degrés a.-d. de zéro,** fifteen degrees below zero; **a.-d. de la moyenne, du pair,** below the average, below par; **il est a.-d. de lui de se plaindre,** it is beneath him to complain; (*c*) **épouser qn a.-d. de soi,** to marry beneath one; (*d*) **a.-d. de cinq ans,** under five (years of age); **quantités a.-d. de 30 kilos,** quantities of less than 30 kilos; **acheter qch. au-d. de sa valeur,** to buy sth. for less than it is worth; (*e*) **son travail était a.-d. de mon attente,** his work fell short of what I expected; **je suis a.-d. de la tâche,** I'm not up to the job; **être a.-d. de tout,** to be worse than useless.

au-dessus [odsy] *adv.* **1.** (*a*) above (it); **le village est en bas de la colline, le château a.-d.,** the village is at the foot of the hill, with the castle (up) above (it); (*b*) **une terrasse avec une marquise a.-d.,** a terrace with an awning over it, above; **la salle de bains est a.-d.,** the bathroom is upstairs; (*c*) **mille francs et a.-d.,** a thousand francs and upwards; *Post:* **a.-d., par 50 gr.,** for each additional 50 gr.; (*d*) **musique transposée un ton a.-d.,** music transposed a tone higher. **2.** *prep.phr.* **au-dessus de:** (*a*) above; **le château est situé a.-d. du village,** the castle stands above the village; (*b*) **il a son nom a.-d. de la porte,** his name is above, over, the door; **les avions volaient a.-d. de nos têtes,** the planes were flying overhead; **l'eau leur montait jusqu'a.-d des genoux,** the water came up above their knees; **deux degrés a.-d. de zéro,** two degrees above zero; **a.-d. de cinquante francs,** more than fifty francs; **cinquante kilomètres a.-d. de Paris,** fifty kilometres above, up river from, Paris; **a.-d. de la moyenne,** above average; **le colonel est a.-d. du commandant,** a colonel is higher than a major; (*c*) **a.-d. de cinq ans,** over five (years of age); **elle a une sagesse a.-d. de son âge,** she is wise beyond her years; (*d*) **la tâche est a.-d. de leurs forces,** the job is too much for them, beyond them; **vivre a.-d. de ses moyens,** to live beyond one's means.

au-devant [odvɑ̃] *used only in such phrases as* **aller, courir, se jeter, se précipiter, a.-d. 1.** *adv.* (*a*) **quand il y a du danger, je vais a.-d.,** when there is danger ahead, I go to meet it; (*b*) **quand je prévois une objection je vais a.-d.,** when I anticipate an objection, I take steps in advance. **2.** *prep.phr.* **a.-d. de:** (*a*) **aller, courir, a.-d. de. qn,** to go, run, to meet s.o.; **aller a.-d. des désirs de qn,** to anticipate s.o.'s wishes; (*b*) **aller a.-d. d'un danger,** to anticipate a danger; **aller a.-d. d'un complot,** to forestall a plot; (*c*) **aller a.-d. du danger, d'une défaite,** to court danger, failure.

audibilité [odibilite] *n.f.* audibility.

audible [odibl̥] *a.* audible.

audience [odjɑ̃s] *n.f.* (*a*) audience, hearing; **recevoir qn sur lettre d'a.,** to interview s.o. by appointment; (*b*) (*of king*) **tenir une a.,** to hold an audience; (*c*) *Jur:* hearing (by the court); sitting, session, court; **plaider en pleine a., en a. publique,** to plead in open court; **a. à huis clos,** hearing in camera; **tenir a.,** to hold a court, a sitting; **l'a. est reprise,** the case is resumed.

audiencier [odjɑ̃sje] *a.* & *n.m. Jur:* **(huissier) a.,** court crier; usher.

audiofréquence [odjofrekɑ̃s] *n.f.* audiofrequency.

audio(-)visuel, -elle [odjɔvizɥɛl] *a.* audiovisual.

auditeur, -trice [oditœr, -tris] *n.* **1.** hearer, listener; **les auditeurs,** the audience; *W.Tel: T.V:* **programme des auditeurs,** request programme. **2.** *Adm:* **a. à la Cour des comptes** = Commissioner of Audit.

auditif, -ive [oditif, -iv] *a.* auditory (nerve, meatus); auditive; **prothèse auditive, aide a.,** hearing aid; **mémoire auditive,** aural memory.

audition [odisjɔ̃] *n.f.* **1.** (*a*) hearing (of sounds); audition; (*b*) **juger d'un opéra à la première a.,** to judge an opera at the first hearing. **2.** (*a*) **a. de piano,** (private) piano recital; (*b*) audition (of singer, etc.); (*c*) *Jur:* **a. des témoins,** hearing, examination, of the witnesses; **nouvelle a.,** rehearing.

auditionner [odisjɔne] **1.** *v.tr.* to audition (s.o.). **2.** *v.i.* to have an audition, to audition (for a part).

auditoire [oditwar], *n.m.* **1.** (*a*) auditorium; (*b*) *Jur:* court. **2.** audience; *Ecc:* congregation.

auditorium [oditɔrjɔm] *n.m.* (*a*) auditorium; (*b*) (broadcasting, television) studio.

auge [oʒ] *n.f.* **1.** (feeding, water) trough; **a. d'écurie,** manger. **2.** *Hyd.E:* (*a*) = AUGET 2; (*b*) flume, channel (for leading water to mill).

auget [oʒɛ] *n.m.* **1.** (small) trough; seed trough, water trough (of a bird cage). **2.** *Hyd.E:* bucket (of water wheel); **roue à augets,** bucket, overshot, wheel.

augmentation [ɔgmɑ̃tasjɔ̃] *n.f.* **1.** increase, augmentation; *Adm:* increment; **a. de salaire,** rise, increase, in wages, *U.S:* raise; **a. de prix,** increase in prices; **être en a.,** to be rising, on the increase. **2.** *Mus:* augmentation. **3.** *Knit:* **faire une a.,** to make a stitch, to make one.

augmenter [ɔgmɑ̃te] **1.** *v.tr.* to increase, augment, enlarge; **a. ses terres,** to extend, add to, one's estate; **édition augmentée,** enlarged edition; **a. une douleur,** to aggravate a pain; **a. le prix de qch.,** to raise, put up, the price of sth.; **a. qn,** to raise, increase, s.o.'s (i) salary, wages, (ii) rent; *Mus:* **en augmentant,** crescendo. **2.** *v.i.* to increase (*a*) **le crime augmente beaucoup,** crime is on the increase; **empêcher les frais d'a.,** to keep expenses down; **la valeur a augmenté de 10% par rapport à l'année dernière,** the value is 10% up on last year; (*b*) *Nau:* **a. de toile,** to crowd on sail; (*c*) *Knit:* to make a stitch, to make one; **a. de deux points au commencement du rang suivant,** increase two at the beginning of the next row.

augure[1] [ɔgyr] *n.m. Rom.Ant:* augur; **le Collège des augures,** the College of Augurs.

augure[2] *n.m.* augury, omen; **prendre les augures,** to take the auguries; **prendre qch. à bon a.,** to take sth. as a good omen; **de bon a.,** auspicious; **de mauvais a.,** ominous; **oiseau de mauvais a.,** bird of ill omen.

augurer [ɔgyre] *v.tr.* to augur, forecast; **a. l'avenir,** to forecast, foresee, the future; **a. bien de qch.,** to augur well of sth., to feel optimistic about sth.; **a. mal de qch.,** to augur ill of sth., to feel pessimisitic about sth.

Auguste[1] [ɔgyst] **1.** *Pr.n.m.* Augustus; **le siècle d'A.,** the Augustan Age. **2.** *n.m.* **l'a.,** the "funny man" (at circus).

auguste[2] *a.* august, majestic.

Augustin [ɔgystɛ̃] **1.** *Pr.n.m.* Augustine. **2.** *a. & n.m. Ecc:* **(religieux) a.,** Augustinian (friar); **les Augustins,** the Austin friars.

aujourd'hui [oʒurdɥi] today; (*a*) *adv.* **il arrive a.,** he is coming today; **c'est quel jour a.?** what day is it today? **c'est a. le cinq, c'est a. dimanche,** today is the fifth, is Sunday; **les jeunes gens d'a.,** (the) young people (of) today; **le journal d'a.,** today's paper; **(d')a. en huit, en quinze,** today week, today fortnight; **il y a a. huit jours,** a week ago today; **je ne l'ai pas vue d'a.,** I have not seen her, set eyes on her, today; **ce n'est pas d'a. que je la connais,** I have known her for a long time; **c'est pour a. ou pour demain?** hurry up! are you coming today or next week? (*b*) *n.* **a. passé, on ne pourra plus y aller,** after today we shall no longer be able to go there.

aulne [on] *n.m. Bot:* alder.

aulx [o] *see* AIL 2.

aumône [ɔmon] *n.f.* alms; **faire l'a. à qn,** to give alms to s.o.; **donner qch. en a. à qn,** to give s.o. sth. out of charity; **réduit à l'a.,** reduced to begging.

aumônier [ɔmonje] *n.m.* **1.** almoner. **2.** chaplain; **aumônier militaire,** army chaplain.

aune¹ [on] *n.m. Bot:* alder.

aune² *n.f. A.Meas:* ell ($1^{m}\cdot188$); *Fig:* **figure longue d'une a.,** face as long as a fiddle.

auparavant [oparavɑ̃] *adv.* before(hand), previously; **a. il faut s'assurer de . . .,** first we must make sure of . . .; **l'année d'a.,** the preceding year, the year before; **comme a.,** as before.

auprès [oprɛ] *adv.* **1.** (*a*) close to, near to; **voilà l'église, la maison est tout a.,** there is the church; the house is close to it; (*b*) **il n'y a rien à mettre a.,** there is nothing to be compared with it. **2.** *prep.phr.* **a. de:** (*a*) close to, by, close by, beside, near; **tout a. de qn, de qch.,** close beside s.o., sth.; **il a toujours une garde-malade a. de lui,** he always has a nurse with him, at hand, in his service; **ambassadeur a. du roi de Suède,** ambassador to the King of Sweden; **avocat a. du tribunal,** advocate attached to the tribunal; (*b*) (*indicating a moral relation*) **agir a. de qn,** to use one's influence with s.o.; **être bien a. de qn,** to be in favour with s.o., to be in s.o.'s good books; **trouver grâce a. de qn,** to find favour in s.o.'s sight; (*c*) compared with, in comparison with.

aura [ɔra] *n.f. Med: etc:* aura; **a. épileptique,** epileptic aura.

auréole [ɔreɔl] *n.f.* **1.** (*a*) halo (of saint); *Com:* **détachant qui ne laisse pas d'a.,** stain remover which leaves no ring; (*b*) halo (of moon); corona (of sun); (*c*) *Min:* blue cap (of safety lamp). **2.** *Phot:* halation.

auréoler [ɔreɔle] *v.tr.* (*a*) to surround with a halo; (*b*) to exalt, glorify.

auréomycine [ɔreɔmisin] *n.f. Med:* aureomycin.

auriculaire [ɔrikylɛr] *a.* auricular (confession, etc.); **témoin a.,** auricular witness; **le doigt a.,** *n.m.* **l'a.,** the little finger; *Artil: etc:* **protecteur a.,** ear protector.

auricule [ɔrikyl] *n.f.* **1.** *Anat: Bot:* auricle (of the heart, of a petal); **a. de l'oreille,** lower lobe of the ear. **2.** *Bot:* auricula. **3.** *Echin:* auricula, auricle. **4.** *Moll:* auricula.

auriculiste [ɔrikylist] *n.m. Med:* ear specialist; aural surgeon.

aurifère [ɔrifɛr] *a.* gold-bearing; **champ a.,** goldfield.

Aurigny [ɔriɲi] *Pr.n.m. Geog:* Alderney; **vache d'A.,** Alderney cow.

auriol [ɔriɔl] *n.m. Orn:* oriole.

auriste [ɔrist] *n.m. Med:* ear specialist; aural surgeon.

aurochs [ɔrɔks] *n.m. Z:* aurochs, urus, wild ox.

aurore [ɔrɔr] **1.** *n.f.* (*a*) dawn, daybreak; break of day; **l'a. commence à paraître, à poindre,** dawn is breaking; **l'a. de la civilisation,** the dawn of civilization; (*b*) **a. australe,** aurora australis; **a. boréale,** aurora borealis, northern lights; **a. polaire,** aurora polaris, polar light. **2.** (*a*) *a. inv.* (saffron, golden) yellow; (*b*) *n.f. Ent:* orange tip (butterfly). **3.** *Pr.n.f.* Aurora.

auscultation [ɔskyltasjɔ̃] *n.f. Med:* auscultation.

ausculter [ɔskylte] *v.tr. Med:* to sound (patient, etc.).

auspice [ɔspis] *n.m. usu. pl.* (*a*) *Rom.Ant:* auspice; **prendre les auspices,** to take the auspices; (*b*) auspice, omen; **mauvais a.,** ill omen; **l'année commence sous d'heureux, de fâcheux, auspices,** the year begins auspiciously, inauspiciously.

aussi [osi] **1.** *adv.* (*a*) (*in comparative sentences*) as **pas a.,** not so, not as; **il est a. grand que son frère,** he is as tall as his brother; **ce tableau est deux fois a. grand que celui-là,** this painting is twice as large as that one; **tout a. au sud, à l'est, que Paris,** as far south, east, as Paris; **ma méthode est tout a. bonne que la vôtre,** my method is quite as good as yours; **je le connais a. peu que son frère,** I don't know him any better than I know his brother; (*b*) so; **après avoir attendu a. longtemps,** after waiting so long, for such a long time; **un homme a. travailleur que vous,** a man as hardworking as you; **avez-vous jamais entendu une symphonie a. bizarre?** have you ever heard such a peculiar symphony? (*c*) (i) also, too; **vous venez a.,** you are coming too; **gardez a. ceux-là,** keep those too, as well; (ii) so; **moi a.,** so am I, so can I, so do I, so shall I, so did I, so was I, *etc.*; **et moi a. je suis peintre,** and I too am a painter; **"j'ai froid"—"moi a.",** "I'm cold"—"so am I"; (*d*) *conj.phr.* **a. bien que,** as well as, (both) . . . and . . .; **le vieillard, a. bien que sa femme se frottaient les mains,** (both) the old man and his wife rubbed their hands; (*e*) **a. bizarre qu'il soit, semble** however odd, peculiar, it may be, seem. **2.** *conj.* (*a*) therefore, consequently, so; **la vie est chère ici, a. nous devons, devons-nous, économiser,** the cost of living is high here, so we have to economize; (*b*) *F:* **a., c'est ta faute,** after all, it's your fault; (*c*) **a. bien,** moreover, for that matter, in any case, besides, and as a matter of fact, though; **il faut patienter un peu, a. bien n'avez-vous que vingt ans,** you must have patience; after all, you are only twenty.

aussitôt [osito] (*a*) *adv.* immediately, directly, at once; **a. dit, a. fait,** no sooner said than done; **a. après,** immediately after; **a. après son retour je suis parti,** as soon as, the minute, he returned I left; (*b*) *conj.phr.* **a. que** + *ind.*, as soon as; **il se repentit de ses paroles a. qu'il les eut prononcées,** he repented (of) his words as soon as he had said them; (*c*) **a.** + *p.p.* **a. l'argent reçu je vous paierai,** as soon as I get the money I will pay you.

austère [ɔstɛr] *a.* austere (life); strict (fast); severe (style); stern (countenance).

austèrement [ɔstɛrmɑ̃] *adv.* austerely.

austérité [ɔsterite] *n.f.* austerity. **1.** austereness, strictness, sternness; **la période d'a.,** the days of austerity; **mesures d'a.,** austerity measures. **2.** *usu. pl.* asceticism, mortification of the flesh.

austral, -als, -aux [ɔstral, -o] *a.* southern (hemisphere, etc.); **aurore australe,** southern lights.

Australasie [ɔstralazi] *Pr.n.f.* Australasia.

australasien, -ienne [ɔstralazjɛ̃, -jɛn] *a. & n.* Australasian.

Australie [ɔstrali] *Pr.n.f* Australia; **l'A. méridionale,** South Australia; **l'A. occidentale,** Western Australia.

australien, -ienne [ɔstraljɛ̃, -jɛn] *a. & n.* Australian.

austro-hongrois, -oise [ɔstroɔ̃grwa, -waz] *a. & n. Hist:* Austro-Hungarian.

autant [otɑ̃] *adv.* **1.** (*a*) as much, so much; as many;

so many; **je ne le savais pas a. respecté,** I did not know he was so much respected; (*of promises, etc.*) **a. en emporte le vent,** it's all idle talk, it's all gone with the wind; **on ne peut pas en dire a. de tout le monde,** one cannot say as much for everybody; **je consens, mais à charge d'a.,** I consent, but on condition that I do the same for you; **a. vous l'aimez, a. il vous hait,** he hates you as much as you love him; **tout a.,** quite as much, quite as many; **encore a., une fois a.,** twice as much, as much again, as many again; **deux fois a.,** twice as much; **rendre à qn six fois a.,** to repay s.o. sixfold; *F:* **cela vaut a.,** it's just as well; **j'aimerais a. aller au cinéma,** I would just as soon go to the cinema; (*b*) (i) **le travail est fini ou a. vaut,** the work is as good as finished; **a. vaut rester ici,** we may as well stay here; **a. vaudrait dire que . . .,** one might as well say that . . .; (ii) **ils ont a. dire accepté,** they have practically accepted; **cela vous coûtera neuf cent quatre-vingt-dix-sept francs, a. dire mille,** that will cost you nine hundred and ninety-seven francs, (let us) say a thousand; **la bataille était a. dire perdue,** the battle was as good as lost; **a. le faire tout de suite,** better do it right away; **a. ne rien faire du tout,** we might as well do nothing at all. **2. a. que:** (*a*) as much as, as many as; **a. que possible,** as much as possible; **a. que de besoin,** as much as is necessary; **faites a. que vous pourrez,** do as much as you can; **j'en sais a. que toi,** your guess is as good as mine; **c'est a. ta faute que la mienne,** it is as much your fault as mine; **il est a. à craindre qu'elle,** he is as much to be feared as she is; *F:* **a. ça qu'autre chose,** it's all the same to me; (*b*) as far as, as near as; **a. qu'il est possible,** as far as it is possible; **a. que j'en puis(se) juger,** as far as I can judge; **pour a. qu'il est en mon pouvoir,** within the limits of my power, my authority; to the best of my ability; (*c*) **a. que nous désirions vous aider,** much as we would like to help you. **3. a. de,** as much, as many, so much, so many; (*a*) **ils ont a. de terrain, a. d'amis, que vous,** they have as much land, as many friends, as you; **ce sont a. de (voleurs, etc.**), they are nothing better than (a pack of thieves, etc.); **les garçons grimpent comme a. de singes,** the boys climb like so many monkeys; (*b*) **ce sera a. de moins à payer,** it will be so much the less to pay; **c'est a. de gagné,** that's so much gained, so much to the good. **4. d'autant,** accordingly; **d'a. plus,** especially, particularly; **d'a. plus, moins (que),** all the more, less (because); **j'en suis surpris, d'a. plus qu'au fond il est honnête,** I am all the more surprised because basically he is honest; **cela vous sera d'a. plus facile que vous êtes jeune,** it will be all the easier for you as you are young. **5. pour a.,** for all that; **elle ne s'en fait pas pour a.,** she doesn't worry for all that.

autarchie [otarʃi] *n.f. Pol:* autarchy.

autarcie [otarsi] *n.f.* autarky.

autel [ɔtɛl] *n.m.* **1.** altar; **maître a.,** high altar; **a. latéral,** side altar; **nappe d'a.,** altar cloth; **pierre d'a.,** altar stone, altar table; **tableau d'a.,** altarpiece; **conduire qn à l'a.,** (i) to give s.o. away (in marriage); (ii) to marry s.o.

auteur [otœr] *n.m.* **1.** (*a*) author, maker, originator; founder (of race); perpetrator (of crime); promoter, sponsor (of scheme); **a. d'un accident,** party at fault in an accident; **être l'a. de la ruine de qn,** to be the cause of s.o.'s downfall; (*b*) *Jur:* principal. **2.** (*a*) author, writer (of book); composer (of song); painter (of picture); **femme a.,** woman writer; **droit d'a.,** copyright; **droits d'a.,** royalties; **un droit d'a. de 10%,** a royalty of 10%; (*b*) **citer ses auteurs,** to quote one's authorities.

authenticité [ɔtɑ̃tisite] *n.f.* authenticity, genuineness.

authentification [ɔtɑ̃tifikasjɔ̃] *n.f.* authentication; **cachet d'a.,** approved stamp.

authentique [ɔtɑ̃tik] *a.* authentic, genuine; **c'est un fait a.,** it's a positive fact; **bourgogne a.,** genuine burgundy; *Jur:* **acte a.,** instrument drawn up by a solicitor; **copie a.,** certified copy; *Fin:* **cours a.,** official quotation.

authentiquement [ɔtɑ̃tikmɑ̃] *adv.* authentically, genuinely.

authentiquer [ɔtɑ̃tike] *v.tr.* to authenticate, certify, legalize (document, etc.).

autisme [ɔtism] *n.m. Psy:* autism.

autiste [ɔtist], **autistique** [ɔtistik] *a. Psy:* autistic.

auto [ɔto] *n.f. F: O:* (motor) car.

auto- [ɔtɔ] *pref.* **1.** auto-. **2.** self-. **3.** motor.

auto-allumage [ɔtɔalymaʒ] *n.m. I.C.E:* **1.** self, spontaneous, ignition. **2.** pre-ignition.

auto-amorçage [ɔtɔamɔrsaʒ] *n.m.* automatic priming (of pump engine, etc.).

autobiographe [ɔtɔbjɔgraf] *n.m. & f.* autobiographer.

autobiographie [ɔtɔbjɔgrafi] *n.f.* autobiography.

autobiographique [ɔtɔobjɔgrafik] *a.* autobiographic(al).

autobus [ɔtɔbys] *n.m. Aut:* bus.

autocar [ɔtɔkar] *n.m.* (*a*) (motor) coach; **a. de luxe,** luxury coach; (*b*) (country) bus.

autochenille [ɔtɔʃnij] *n.f.* caterpillar tractor (*R.t.m.*); half-track vehicle.

autochtone [ɔtɔktɔn] **1.** *a.* aboriginal. **2.** *n.* autochthon.

autoclave [ɔtɔklav] **1.** *a.* hermetically-sealed, pressure-sealed. **2.** *n.m.* (*a*) *Ch: Ind:* **(marmite) a.,** autoclave, digester; (*b*) *Med:* sterilizer; (*c*) *Cu: O:* pressure cooker.

autocollant [ɔtɔkɔlɑ̃] *a.* self-adhesive.

autoconsommation [ɔtɔkɔ̃sɔmasjɔ̃] *n.f.* subsistence farming.

autocopie [ɔtɔkɔpi] *n.f.* **1.** duplicating (of documents). **2.** photocopy.

autocopier [ɔtɔkɔpje] *v.tr.* (*pr.sub. & impf.* **n. autocopiions, v. autocopiiez**) to duplicate.

autocrate [ɔtɔkrat] **1.** *n.* autocrat. **2.** *a.* autocratic.

autocratie [ɔtɔkrasi] *n.f.* autocracy.

autocratique [ɔtɔkratik] *a.* autocratic.

autocratiquement [ɔtɔkratikmɑ̃] *adv.* autocratically.

autocritique [ɔtɔkritik] *n.f.* self criticism.

autocuiseur [ɔtɔkɥizœr] *n.m.* pressure cooker.

autodafé [ɔtɔdafe] *n.m. Hist:* auto-da-fé.

autodébrayage [ɔtɔdebrɛjaʒ] *n.m. Aut:* automatic clutch.

autodéfense [ɔtɔdefɑ̃s] *n.f.* self-defence.

auto-démarrage [ɔtɔdemaraʒ] *n.m. Mch: I.C.E: etc:* self starting.

autodétermination [ɔtɔdetɛrminasjɔ̃] *n.f. Pol:* self determination.

autodidacte [ɔtɔdidakt] **1.** *a.* self-taught, self-educated. **2.** *n.* autodidact.

autodrome [ɔtɔdrom] *n.m.* motor-racing track; car-testing track.

auto-école [ɔtɔekɔl] *n.f.* school of motoring, driving school; *pl. auto-écoles.*

autofinancement [ɔtɔfinɑ̃smɑ̃] *n.m. Fin:* ploughing back of profits.

autogare [ɔtɔgar] *n.f.* coach, bus, station.

autogenèse [ɔtɔʒənɛz] *n.f. Biol:* autogenesis.

autograissage [ɔtɔgrɛsaʒ] *n.m. Mec.E:* self lubrication.

autograisseur, -euse [ɔtɔgrɛsœr, -øz] *a. Mec.E:* self-lubricating (bearing, etc.).

autographe [ɔtɔgraf] **1.** *a.* autograph; handwritten (letter, etc.). **2.** *n.m.* autograph.

autographier [ɔtɔgrafje] *v.tr.* (*pr.sub. & impf.* **n. autographiions, v. autographiiez**) to autograph.
autographique [ɔtɔgrafik] *a.* autographic.
autogreffe [ɔtɔgrɛf] *n.f. Surg:* autograft.
autoguidage [ɔtɔgidaʒ] *n.m.* **(retour par) a.,** homing; **cellule d'a.,** homing eye.
autoguidé [ɔtɔgide] *a.* self-directional, homing (missile).
autogyre [ɔtɔʒir] *n.m. Av:* autogyro.
autolubrifiant [ɔtɔlybrifjɑ̃] *a.* self-lubricating.
autolubrication [ɔtɔlybrifikasjɔ̃] *n.f. Mec.E:* self lubrication.
auto-marché [ɔtɔmarʃe] *n.m.* car mart; *pl. auto-marchés.*
automate [ɔtɔmat] *n.m.* automaton, robot.
automation [ɔtɔmasjɔ̃] *n.f.* automation.
automatique [ɔtɔmatik] **1.** *a.* automatic (action); self-acting (apparatus); **à mise en marche a.,** self-starting; **2.** *n.m.* (*a*) automatic (telephone); (*b*) automatic (pistol). **3.** *n.f. Tchn:* (*a*) automatics; (*b*) automation.
automatiquement [ɔtɔmatikmɑ̃] *adv.* automatically.
automatisation [ɔtɔmatizasjɔ̃] *n.f.* automation.
automatisme [ɔtɔmatism] *n.m.* **1.** *Physiol: Med:* automatism. **2.** *Tchn:* (*a*) automatic working; (*b*) automatic device.
automitrailleuse [ɔtɔmitrajøz] *n.f.* armoured car.
automnal, -aux [ɔtɔ(m)nal, -o] *a.* autumnal.
automne [ɔtɔn] *n.m. occ. f.* autumn, *NAm:* fall; **l'équinoxe d'a.,** the autumnal equinox; **en a., à l'à.,** in autumn; **une soirée d'a.,** an autumn evening.
automobile [ɔtɔmɔbil] **1.** *a.* (*a*) self-propelling; **voiture a.,** motor vehicle; **canot a.,** motor boat; (*b*) **club a.,** automobile club; **assurance a.,** car, motor, insurance; **accessoires automobiles,** car accessories. **2.** *n.f* (motor) car, *NAm:* automobile; *Mil:* **a. blindée,** armoured car; **salon de l'a.,** motor show.
automobilisme [ɔtɔmɔbilism] *n.m.* motoring.
automobiliste [ɔtɔmɔbilist] *n.m. & f.* motorist.
automoteur, -trice [ɔtɔmɔtœr, -tris] **1.** *a.* self-propelling (vehicle); self-acting (valve, etc.); **train a.,** multiple unit (Diesel) train. **2.** *n.f.* railcar. **3.** *n.m. Nau:* self-propelled barge.
autoneige [ɔtɔnɛʒ] *n.f. Fr.C:* snowmobile.
autonome [ɔtɔnɔm] *a.* autonomous, self-governing; independent (state, etc.); self-contained (apparatus).
autonomie [ɔtɔnɔmi] *n.f.* (*a*) autonomy; self-government; independence; (*b*) self-sufficiency; (*c*) *Tchn:* cruising radius, range; (*d*) *Av:* endurance.
autonomiste [ɔtɔnɔmist] *n.* autonomist.
autoportrait [ɔtɔpɔrtrɛ] *n.m.* self portrait.
autopropulsé [ɔtɔprɔpylse] *a.* self-propelled.
autopsie [ɔtɔpsi] *n.f.* autopsy; **a. (cadavérique),** post mortem (examination).
autopsier [ɔtɔpsie] *v.tr.* to perform a post mortem (examination) on; *U.S:* to autopsy.
autoradio [ɔtɔradjɔ] *n.m.* car radio.
autorail [ɔtɔraj] *n.m.* railcar.
auto-régénérateur, -trice [ɔtɔregeneratœr, -tris] *a. Atom.Ph:* breeder (reactor, etc.).
autorégulateur, -trice [ɔtɔregylatœr, -tris] *Mec.E:* **1.** *a.* self-regulating. **2.** *n.m.* self-acting regulator.
auto-relieur [ɔtɔrəljœr] *n.m.* spring-back binder; *pl. auto-relieurs.*
autorisation [ɔtɔrizasjɔ̃] *n.f.* **1.** (*a*) authorization, authority; permission; permit; **donner à qn une a. pour faire qch.,** to authorize s.o. to do sth.; **a. d'exporter,** export permit; (*b*) *Av:* **a. de vol,** flight clearance. **2.** licence; *NAm:* license.
autorisé [ɔtɔrize] *a.* **1.** authorized, authoritative; **tenir qch. d'une source autorisée,** to have sth. from an authoritative source. **2.** (*a*) permitted, permissible, allowed; (*b*) *Breed:* approved (stallion).
autoriser [ɔtɔrize] *v.tr.* **1. a. qn à faire qch.,** to authorize, empower, s.o. to do sth., to give s.o. authority to do sth. **2.** to justify, authorize, sanction (an action); **ces découvertes autorisent à penser que . . .,** these discoveries entitle us to believe that . . . **3.** to allow, permit, give permission (to do sth.). **4. s'a. de qn, de qch.,** to act on the authority of s.o., of sth., to quote s.o. as a reason for doing sth.
autoritaire [ɔtɔritɛr] **1.** *a.* authoritative, dictatorial, overbearing, *F:* bossy. **2.** *n.* authoritarian.
autoritairement [ɔtɔritɛrmɑ̃] *adv.* authoritatively; in an overbearing manner.
autoritarisme [ɔtɔritarism] *n.m.* **1.** authoritarianism. **2.** *F:* bossiness.
autorité [ɔtɔrite] *n.f.* **1.** (*a*) authority; **exercer son a. sur qn,** to exercise authority over s.o.; **a. paternelle,** parental authority; **ce professeur n'a pas d'a. sur ses élèves,** this teacher can't keep order; **il veut tout emporter d'a.,** he wants his own way in everything, *F:* he wants to run the whole show; **agir de pleine a.,** to act with full powers; **faire qch. d'a.,** to do sth. on one's own (responsibility), off one's own bat, to take it upon oneself to do sth.; **territoire soumis à l'a. de . . .,** area within the jurisdiction of; (*b*) **avoir de l'a. sur qn,** to have influence, authority, over s.o.; **faire a. en qch.,** to be an authority on sth.; *Jur:* **cas d'espèce qui font a.,** leading cases; **parler avec a.,** to speak authoritatively, with authority; **sa parole a de l'a.,** his word carries weight. **2.** (*a*) **l'a. fiscale,** the (income) tax people; **les autorités,** the authorities, the powers that be; (*b*) **citer une a.,** to quote an authority; to quote chapter and verse.
autoroute [ɔtɔrut] *n.f.* motorway, *U.S:* freeway, thruway, superhighway; **a. à péage,** toll motorway, *U.S:* turnpike (road).
autoroutier, -ière [ɔtɔrutje, -jɛ] *a.* **système a.,** motorway system, network.
auto-stop [ɔtɔstɔp] *n.m.* hitch hiking; **faire de l'a.,** to hitch-hike, *F:* to thumb a lift.
auto-stoppeur, -euse [ɔtɔstɔpœr, -øz] *n.* hitch hiker; *pl. auto-stoppeurs, auto-stoppeuses.*
autosuggestion [ɔtɔsygʒɛtjɔ̃] *n.f.* auto-suggestion.
autour[1] [otur] **1.** *adv.* round, around (it, them); **une vieille ville avec des murs tout a.,** an old walled town. **2.** *prep. phr.* **a. de,** round, about; **nous nous sommes assis a. de la table,** we sat down round the table; **ce qui se passe a. de nous,** what is going on around us; *F:* **il a a. de cinquante ans,** he is (somewhere) about fifty; **tourner a. de la qestion, a. du pot,** to beat about the bush.
autour[2] *n.m. Orn:* **a. (des palombes),** goshawk.
autovaccin [ɔtɔvaksɛ̃] *n.m. Med:* autovaccine.
autre [otr̥] *a. & pron.* **1.** (*a*) other, further; **tous les autres verbes que ceux en -er,** all verbs other than those in *-er*; **je ne pourrai pas y aller; entre autres raisons je suis à court d'argent,** I can't go; for one thing I'm short of money; **une a. semaine, un a. jour,** another week, another day; **une a. fois,** later; another time; **un jour ou l'a.,** one day, some time, or other; **les défauts des autres,** the failings of others; **d'autres vous diront que . . .,** others, other people, will tell you that . . .; **tous les autres sont là,** all the others are there; **encore un a.,** one more; another (one); **encore bien d'autres,** many more besides; **en voici un a. exemple,** here is another example; **il se croit un a. Napoléon,** he thinks he is a second, another, Napoleon; **toute a. femme aurait agi de la même façon,** any other woman would have acted in the same way; **les choux et autres légumes,** cabbages and (all) other vegetables; **les choux et d'autres légumes,** cabbages

and some other vegetables; **de l'a. côté du champ,** on the other side of the field; **l'a. monde,** the next world; **sans faire d'a. observation,** without making any further observation; **sans a. perte de temps,** without further loss of time; **la science est une chose, l'art en est une a.,** science is one thing, art is another; **il parle d'une façon et agit d'une a.,** he says one thing and does something else, another; **parler d'une chose et d'une a., de chose(s) et d'autre(s),** to talk about one thing and another, about this, that and the other; **c'était un touriste comme un a.,** he was just an ordinary tourist; **c'est une raison comme une a.,** it's as good a reason as any; **c'est un homme pas comme les autres,** he is an exceptional man; *F:* **l'a. lundi,** Monday week; *F:* **comme dit l'a.,** as the saying goes, as they say; (*b*) (*stressing the pers. pron*) **vous autres hommes vous êtes seuls coupables,** it is you men who are alone to blame; **nous autres Anglais,** we English (people); **vous autres,** you others, all of you; (*c*) **cela peut arriver d'un jour à l'a.,** it may happen any day; **je l'attends d'un moment à l'a.,** I expect him any moment; **je le vois de temps à a.,** I see him now and again, now and then; (*d*) **l'un et l'a.,** both; **les uns et les autres,** (i) all (and sundry), one and all; (ii) both parties; **il a parlé aux uns et aux autres,** he spoke to them all; **l'un et l'a. a été puni, ont été punis,** both were punished; (*e*) **l'un ou l'a.,** either; **ni l'un ni l'a.,** neither; **ni l'un ni l'a. ne sont venus,** neither of them came; **je ne les connais ni l'un ni l'a.,** I don't know either of them; **je n'ai vu ni les uns ni les autres,** I didn't see any of them; (*f*) **l'un . . ., l'a. . . .,** one . . ., the other . . .; **l'un dit ceci, l'a. dit cela,** one says this and the other says that; **les uns . . ., les autres . . .,** some . . ., others . . .; some . . ., some . . .; **ils s'en allèrent les uns par ci les autres par là,** they went off, some one way, some another; **sans prendre parti ni pour les uns ni pour les autres,** without taking either side; **l'un ne va pas sans l'a.,** you can't have one without the other; **qui voit l'un voit l'a.,** there's no difference between them, you can't tell the two apart; **l'un vaut l'a.,** there's no difference between them, the one's just as good, as bad, as the other; (*g*) **l'un l'a.,** each other, one another; **elles se moquent les unes des autres,** they make fun of each other; **l'un auprès de l'a., auprès l'un de l'a.,** near each other, near one another; (*h*) **l'un dans l'a., l'un portant l'a., on se fait mille francs,** one thing with another, on an average, we earn a thousand francs; **une année dans l'a.,** taking one year with another. **2.** (*a*) other, different; **j'ai maintenant une a. maison,** I've a new house, a different house, now; *Prov:* **autres temps autres mœurs,** other days other ways; **il est a. que je ne le pensais,** he is different from what I thought; **cela a fait de lui un a. homme,** it made a new man of him; **une tout a. femme,** quite a different woman; **j'ai des idées autres,** I have different ideas, my ideas are different; **elle a de bien autres idées,** she has very different ideas; **être d'une a. opinion,** to think otherwise; **c'est tout (l')un ou tout (l')a.,** there is no happy medium, it's either one thing or the other; *F:* **en voilà bien d'une a.!** here we go again! **j'en sais d'autres,** I can do better than that; **j'en ai vu bien d'autres,** that's nothing, I've been through worse than that; (*b*) someone, something, else; **adressez-vous à un a., à quelqu'un d'a.,** ask someone else, somebody else; **je l'ai pris pour un a.,** I mistook him for someone else; **il n'est pas plus bête qu'un a.,** he is no more stupid than anyone else; **nul a., personne (d')a., ne l'a vu,** no one else, nobody else, saw him; **je ne demande rien d'a.,** I don't ask for anything more, I ask for nothing more; **que pouvait-il faire d'a.?** what else could he do? **que pouvaient-ils faire d'a. que de l'inviter**? what could they do but invite him? **qui d'a. que lui aurait pu le faire?** who else could have done it? **(dites cela) à d'autres!** nonsense! don't tell me! tell that to the marines! (*c*) *indef. pron. m.* (i) **a. chose,** something else; something different; **j'ai a. chose d'important à vous dire,** I have something else of importance to tell you; **avez-vous a. chose à faire?** have you anything else to do? **c'est a. chose que je n'avais d'abord pensé,** it is different from what I had first thought; (ii) **a. chose, ma mère est partie hier,** not only that, but my mother left yesterday; **c'est tout a. chose!** that's quite a different thing! **a. chose est de parler, a. chose d'agir,** it's one thing to talk, it's another to act.

autrefois [otrəfwa] *adv.* formerly, in the past; once; **il y avait a. un roi,** once upon a time there was a king; **c'était l'usage a.,** it was the custom in former times, in olden days; **d'a.,** of long ago; **sa vie d'a.,** his past life; **les hommes d'a.,** men of old, of olden times; **des chants d'a.,** old-time songs.

autrement [otrəmɑ̃] *adv.* otherwise. **1.** (*a*) differently; **il parle a. que vous,** he speaks differently from you; **faisons a.,** let us set about it in another way; **il ne put faire a. que d'obéir,** he had no alternative but to obey; (*b*) **c'est bien a. sérieux,** that is far more serious. **2.** or (else); **venez demain, a. il sera trop tard,** come tomorrow, otherwise it will be too late.

Autriche [otriʃ] *Pr.n.f. Geog:* Austria.

autrichien, -ienne [otriʃjɛ̃, -jɛn] *a. & n. Geog:* Austrian.

autruche [otryʃ] *n.f. Orn:* ostrich; *F:* **avoir un estomac d'a.,** to have a cast-iron stomach; **pratiquer une politique d'a.,** to bury one's head in the sand.

autrui [otrɥi] *pron.indef.* others, other people; **convoiter le bien d'a.,** to covet one's neighbour's property; *Com:* **pour le compte d'a.,** for account of a third party; **ne fais pas à a. ce que tu ne voudrais pas qu'on te fît,** do as you would be done by.

auvent [ovɑ̃] *n.m.* **1.** (*a*) open shed; (*b*) porch roof; window roof; (*c*) canopy (of tent). **2.** *Ind:* hood (over hearth, etc.). **3.** *Hort:* screen, matting. **4.** *Const:* weatherboard. **5.** *Aut:* **auvents de capot,** bonnet louvres. **6.** visor (of helmet).

auxiliaire [ɔksiljɛr, o-] **1.** *a.* auxiliary (verb, troops, etc.); **machine a.,** auxiliary engine; **bureau a.,** sub-office; **services auxiliaires de l'armée,** non-combatant services. **2.** *n.* auxiliary; (*a*) helper, assistant; *Adm:* temporary civil servant; **c'est un a. précieux,** he's a valuable helper; **a. familiale** = mother's help; (*b*) *n.m.pl. Mil:* auxiliaries; (*c*) *n.m. Nau:* auxiliary cruiser; (*d*) *Av: Nau:* **les auxiliaires,** the auxiliary engines.

avachi [avaʃi] *a.* (*a*) (*of boots, etc.*) out of shape (through much use); (*b*) flabby, sloppy (figure); (*c*) **c'est un homme a.,** he has gone to seed.

avachir [avaʃir] *v.tr.* **1.** to soften (leather, etc.). **2.** to enervate, to make flabby. **3. s'a.,** (i) to become flabby, sloppy; (ii) to let oneself go, to go to seed.

aval[1] [aval] *n.m. Fin:* endorsement (on bill); **donner son a. à un billet,** to endorse, back, a bill; **donneur d'a.,** guarantor, backer (of bill).

aval[2] *n.m.* **1.** downstream side; **les villages d'a.,** the villages downstream; **canal d'a.,** tail race (of lock); **porte d'a.,** tail gate, aft gate; **en a.,** downstream; *Rail:* down the line. **2.** *Tg:* down side.

avalaison [avalɛzɔ̃] *n.f.* **1.** (*a*) spate, freshet; (*b*) heap of stones (deposited by a torrent). **2.** downstream migration (of fish).

avalanche [avalɑ̃ʃ] *n.f.* avalanche; **a. de pierres,** avalanche of stones; **a. boueuse,** mud avalanche; **a. électronique, ionique,** avalanche of electrons, ions; **a. d'injures,** shower of insults; **ce fut une a. de lettres,** letters came pouring in, arrived in shoals.

avalé [avale] *a.* drooping (shoulders, etc.); flabby

(cheeks); **lapin à oreilles avalées,** lop-eared rabbit; **chien à oreilles avalées,** dog with floppy, hanging, ears.

avaler [avale] *v.tr.* **1.** (*a*) *A:* to lower (cask into cellar, etc); (*b*) **a. une branche,** to lop off a bough; (*c*) *Min:* **a. un puits,** to sink a shaft. **2.** to swallow (down); **cela s'avale facilement,** it goes down easily; **a. son repas,** to bolt one's meal; **a. son vin à grandes gorgées,** to gulp down one's wine; **a. la fumée,** to inhale; *F:* **a. qn, qch., des yeux,** to devour s.o. with one's eyes, to eye sth. greedily; **a. un roman,** to race through a novel; **a. une couleuvre, une insulte,** to pocket an insult; **celle-là est dure à a.,** that's a tall story, I can hardly swallow that; **j'ai avalé de travers,** it went down the wrong way; **a. ses mots,** to swallow one's words; **a. le morceau, la pilule, la médecine, le calice,** to take one's medicine, one's punishment; **tu auras du mal à leur faire a. ça,** you'll have a job to make them believe that; **a. les kilomètres,** to eat up the miles; *F:* **tu as avalé ta langue?** have you lost your tongue?

avale-tout [avaltu] *n.m.inv. P:* glutton.

avaliser [avalise] *v.tr. Com:* to endorse, back (bill).

avaliste [avalist] *n.m. Com:* surety, backer.

à-valoir [avalwar] *n.m.inv.* advance (payment).

avance [avɑ̃s] *n.f.* **1.** advance, lead; **mouvement d'a. et de recul,** backward and forward movement; **l'a. rapide de l'indice du coût de la vie,** the rapid rise, climb, of the cost of living index; **a. et recul,** move and counter-move; **avoir de l'a. sur qn,** to be ahead, in advance, of s.o., to have the start of s.o.; **garder son a. sur qn,** to maintain one's lead over s.o.; **prendre de l'a. sur un concurrent,** to draw away from a competitor; to steal a march on a competitor; to overtake a competitor; **ma montre prend de l'a.,** my watch gains; **ma montre a dix minutes d'a.,** my watch is ten minutes fast; **(prendre un train) avec cinq minutes d'a.,** (to catch a train) with five minutes in hand, to spare; *F:* **la belle a.!** much good that will do you! *Sp:* **donner de l'a. à qn,** to give s.o. a (head) start; *Golf:* **tant de trous d'a.,** so many holes up; *El:* **a. d'une magnéto,** magneto lead; *I.C.E:* **mettre de l'a. à l'allumage,** to advance the ignition; **réduire l'a.,** to retard the ignition; **levier d'a.,** ignition lever; *Mch:* **a. à l'échappement,** exhaust lead. **2.** *Mec.E:* feed movement, travel (of tool); **mécanisme d'a.,** feed mechanism, feeding gear. **3.** projection; **l'a. d'un toit,** the projecting part, eaves, of a roof; **balcon qui forme a.,** balcony that juts out. **4.** (*a*) **a. (de fonds),** advance, loan; *Fin:* **par a., à titre d'a.,** by way of advance, as an advance; **faire une a. de mille francs à qn,** to advance s.o. a thousand francs; **faire les avances d'une entreprise,** to advance funds for an enterprise; (*b*) **faire des avances à qn,** to make approaches, advances, overtures, to s.o.; **faire la moitié des avances,** to meet s.o. half way; **faire les premières avances,** to make the first move. **5.** *adv.phr.* (*a*) **d'a., à l'a., par a.,** in advance, beforehand; **jouir d'a. de qch.,** to look forward to sth.; **savourer un plaisir d'a.,** to anticipate a pleasure; **payer qn d'a., à l'a.,** to pay s.o. in advance; **payé d'a.,** prepaid; **payable à l'a.,** payable in advance; *Corr:* **je vous remercie d'a.,** thanking you in anticipation; **retenir, louer, une place huit jours à l'a.,** to book a seat a week in advance; **chose décidée à l'a.,** foregone conclusion; (*b*) **l'horloge est en a.,** the clock is fast; **partir en a.,** to go off in advance (of the party); **arriver en a.,** to arrive in advance, before the others; **je suis en a. d'une demi-heure,** I am half an hour early; *Sch:* **il est en a. sur sa classe,** he is ahead of his class; **être en a. sur son temps,** to be ahead, in advance, of one's time; **la moisson est en a. cette année,** the harvest is early this year.

avancé [avɑ̃se] *a.* advanced; (*a*) **position avancée,** advanced, forward, position; *Rail:* **signal a.,** distant signal; (*b*) **opinions avancées,** advanced, progressive, left-wing, ideas; **c'est un esprit a.,** he's a progressive; (*c*) **élève a.,** pupil ahead of his class; **les pommiers sont bien avancés cette année,** the apple trees are in advance this year; (*d*) **à une heure avancée de la nuit,** late in the night, well on in the night; **à une heure peu avancée,** quite early on; *Fr.C:* **heure avancée,** summer time; daylight saving time; **l'été est bien a.,** summer is nearly over; (*e*) **a. en âge,** elderly, getting on (in years); **à un âge a.,** late in life, at an advanced age; (*f*) (*of fruit*) overripe; **viande avancée,** high meat; (*g*) *F:* **vous voilà bien a.!** a lot of good that's done you! **vous n'en êtes pas plus a.,** you're no further forward.

avancée [avɑ̃se] *n.f.* **1.** prominence, bulge, projection, protuberance; *Const:* **a. du toit,** eaves. **2.** advance (of sea, ice, etc.).

avancement [avɑ̃smɑ̃] *n.m.* **1.** (*a*) advancing, putting forward; *Mec.E:* **a. automatique,** automatic feed; (*b*) putting forward (of dinner hour, event, etc.); (*c*) furtherance (of plan); (*d*) promotion; **a. à l'ancienneté,** promotion by seniority. **2.** advance(ment), progress; going ahead; **l'a. des sciences,** the progress of science.

avancer [avɑ̃se] *v.* **(j'avançai(s); n. avançons) I.** *v.tr.* **1.** (*a*) to advance, put forward; to stretch out, hold out (one's hand, etc.); **a. des chaises,** to pull forward chairs; *Chess:* **a. un pion,** to advance a pawn; *Min:* **a. une galerie,** to drive a gallery; (*b*) **a. une proposition,** to put forward, advance, a proposal; **a. ses raisons,** to produce, set out, give, one's reasons. **2.** to make (sth.) earlier; to hurry (sth.) on; **la réunion a été avancée du 14 au 7,** the meeting has been brought forward from the 14th to the 7th; **a. l'heure du dîner,** to put dinner forward; **a. une montre,** to put a watch on; **a. son travail,** to push on with, get ahead with, one's work; *Hort:* **a. une plante,** to bring on, force, a plant. **3. a. de l'argent à qn,** to advance money to s.o., to lend s.o. money. **4.** to promote, forward, further, advance (science, s.o.'s interests, etc.); **a. qn,** to promote s.o.; **à quoi cela vous avancera-t-il?** what good will that do you? how much better (off) will you be for it? *F:* **cela ne va pas nous a. beaucoup,** it won't get us much further forward. **II.** *v.i.* **1.** to advance; (*a*) to move, go, step, forward; (*of ship*) to make headway; (*of watch*) (i) to be fast; (ii) to gain; **a. à grands pas,** to stride along; **a. à pas de loup, à tâtons,** to creep along, feel, grope, one's way; **a. d'un pas,** to take one step forward; **chaque année la mer avance un peu plus sur notre terrain,** each year the sea encroaches a little further on our land; **faire a. qn,** to bring s.o. forward; **faire a. les troupes,** to advance the troops, to move the troops forward; **faire a. des renforts,** to bring up reinforcements; **faire a. sa voiture jusqu'à la porte,** to drive one's car up to the door; **a. en âge,** to be getting on, to get on, in years; **montre qui avance d'une minute par jour,** watch that gains a minute a day; **la nuit avance,** the night is getting on; **l'été avance,** summer is almost over; (*b*) to progress, to get on, to make headway; **le travail avance,** the work is going forward; **les choses n'avancent plus,** things are at a standstill; **la lune avance,** the moon is waxing; *Prov:* **plus on se hâte moins on avance,** more haste less speed; (*c*) to advance, be promoted (in a service). **2.** (*a*) to be ahead of time; **l'horloge avance,** the clock is fast; **vous avancez de dix minutes,** your watch is ten minutes fast; **a. sur son époque,** to be ahead, in advance, of one's time; (*b*) (*of promontory, roof, etc.*) to jut out, to project, to protrude. **III. s'avancer 1.** to move forward, to advance; **s'a. vers qch.,** to make one's way, to head, towards sth.; **s'a. d'un pas,** to take a, one, step forward; **s'a. péniblement,** to drag oneself along. **2.** to progress; **la nuit s'avance,** the night is getting on, is far advanced; **il s'est trop avancé pour reculer,** he has gone too far to withdraw. **3.** (*of promontory, etc.*) to jut out; **une langue de terre s'avance dans la mer,** a strip of land runs out into the sea.

avant [avɑ̃] **I. 1.** *prep.* before; **a. le temps,** too soon, prematurely; **venez a. midi,** come before twelve o'clock; **a. J.-C.,** B.C.; **il sera ici a. une heure,** he will be here, (i) by one o'clock; (ii) within an hour; **je le verrai a. quinze jours (d'ici),** I shall see him within, in less than, a fortnight; **pas a. lundi,** not before Monday; **pas a. de nombreuses années,** not for many years to come; **l'article se place a. le nom,** the article is placed before the noun; **les dames a. les messieurs,** ladies first; **(surtout et) a. tout,** first of all, above all; **a. toute chose,** in the first place. **2.** (*a*) *prep.phr.* **a. de,** + *inf.* **je vous reverrai a. de partir,** I shall see you before I leave; (*b*) *conj.phr.* **a. que** + *sub.* **je vous reverrai a. que vous (ne) partiez,** I shall see you again before you leave; **a. que vous ayez fini je serai parti,** by the time (that) you have finished I shall be gone; (*c*) **pas a. de, que,** not before, not until; **ne partez pas a. d'en recevoir l'ordre, a. qu'on vous le dise,** don't go until you are told; (*d*) *n.m.inv. Jur:* **a. faire droit, dire droit,** injunction, interim order. **3.** *adv.* (*a*) (= AUPARAVANT) **il était arrivé quelques mois a.,** he had arrived some months before; (*b*) **réfléchis a., tu parleras après,** think first, speak later; (*c*) **n'allez pas jusqu'à l'église, sa maison est a.,** do not go as far as the church, his house is before (you come to) it; **les dames passent a.,** ladies take precedence; **il l'a mentionné a. dans la préface,** he mentioned it before, earlier, in the preface. **4.** *adv.* (*a*) far, deep; **pénétrer très a. dans les terres,** to penetrate far inland; **le harpon pénétra très a. dans les chairs,** the harpoon sank deep into the flesh; (*b*) far, late; **très a. dans la journée,** very late in the day. **5.** *adv.phr.* **en a.,** in front, before, forward, ahead; **en a.!** forward! *Mil:* **en a., (marche)!** quick march! **envoyer qn en a.,** to send s.o. ahead, on (in front); **aller en a.,** to push ahead, press on; **regarder en a.,** to look ahead; **faire deux pas en a.,** to move forward two steps; **mettre en a. un candidat,** to put a candidate forward; **mettre en a. une question,** to bring up a question; *Nau:* **en a. (à) toute (vitesse),** full (steam) ahead; *prep.phr.* **il est bien en a. de son siècle,** he is well ahead, in advance, of his time; **il est à quelques mètres en a. de nous,** he is a few metres in front of us. **6.** (*in adj. relation to n.*) (*a*) fore, forward, front; **la partie a. du navire,** the fore part of the ship; **roue a.,** front wheel; *Aut:* **à traction a.,** with front-wheel drive; (*b*) **d'a.,** previous; **la nuit d'a.,** the night before; (*c*) *Ling:* **voyelle d'a.,** front vowel; *Nau:* **cabine d'a.,** fore cabin. **II.** *n.m.* **1.** (*a*) *Nau:* (i) bow, head; (ii) eyes (of a ship); (iii) the steerage; **présenter l'a. à la lame,** to be head to sea; **le logement de l'équipage est à l'a.,** the crew's quarters are forward; **par tribord a.,** on the starboard bow; **aborder un navire par l'a.,** to collide with a ship head on; **sur, à, l'a. du mât,** before the mast; **aller de l'a., pousser de l'a., marcher de l'a.,** to go, forge, ahead; *Row:* **a. partout!** give way! **retourner sur l'a.,** to come forward; *Aut:* **un modèle tout à l'a.,** a front-wheel drive model; (*b*) front; nose (of plane); *Mch:* crank end (of piston); head end (of locomotive piston). **2.** *Fb: etc.* forward. **3.** *Mil:* **l'a.,** the front; the forward area(s).

avantage [avɑ̃taʒ] *n.m.* **1.** (*a*) advantage; **a. pécuniaire,** monetary gain; **faire à qn tous les avantages possibles,** to give s.o. every (possible) advantage; **a. en nature,** perquisite; **il ne m'en revient aucun a.,** I'm not getting any advantage, benefit, from it; **être à l'a. de qn,** to turn out to s.o.'s advantage; **sa connaissance du français lui est un a. précieux,** his knowledge of French is a great asset to him; **tirer a. de qch.,** to turn sth. to advantage; **prendre a. de qch.,** to take advantage of sth.; **s'habiller à son a.,** to dress to the best advantage; **il est à son a. en uniforme,** he looks his best in uniform; **il a changé à son a.,** he has changed for the better; **parler à l'a. de qn,** to speak in s.o.'s favour; **je n'ai pas l'a. de le connaître,** I have not the pleasure, privilege, of knowing him; (*b*) *Jur:* gift, donation; **à titre d'a.,** as a gift. **2.** (*a*) *Sp:* **donner l'a. à qn,** to give s.o. odds; **accorder, concéder, donner un a. à qn,** to give s.o. points; **il a l'a.,** the odds are in his favour; (*b*) *Ten:* (ad)vantage; (*c*) **avoir l'a. sur qn,** to have the advantage of, over, s.o.; **remporter l'a. sur qn,** to get the better, best, of s.o.; **trouver de l'a. à faire qch.,** to find it an advantage, advantageous, to do sth.; **il y a a. à** + *inf.*, it is best to, it comes cheaper to, + *inf.*; **il y aura a. à ce que vous soyez présent,** it will be a good thing, just as well, if you are present.

avantagé [avɑ̃taʒe] *a.* **1. être fort a. par rapport aux autres,** to enjoy many advantages over others; **a. par la nature,** well endowed; **2.** *Sp:* **joueur a.,** player who has been given a start, been given odds.

avantager [avɑ̃taʒe] *v.tr.* **(j'avantageai(s); n. avantageons)** (*a*) to favour (s.o.); to give (s.o.) an advantage; (*b*) **l'uniforme l'avantage,** he looks his best in uniform.

avantageur [avɑ̃taʒœr] *n.m. Sp:* scratch player.

avantageusement [avɑ̃taʒøzmɑ̃] *adv.* advantageously, to advantage.

avantageux, -euse [avɑ̃taʒø, -øz] *a.* **1.** (*a*) advantageous, favourable; *Com:* **prix a.,** reasonable price; **cet article est très a.,** this article is very good value; (*b*) **robe avantageuse,** becoming dress; (*c*) **poitrine avantageuse,** well-developed bust. **2.** conceited, vain; **prendre un ton a.,** to adopt a superior tone.

avant-bassin [avɑ̃basɛ̃] *n.m. Nau:* outer basin, dock; *pl. avant-bassins.*

avant-bras [avɑ̃bra] *n.m.inv. Anat:* forearm.

avant-cale [avɑ̃kal] *n.f. Nau:* fore hold; *pl. avant-cales.*

avant-centre [avɑ̃sɑ̃tr̥] *n.m. Fb:* centre forward; *pl. avant-centres.*

avant-corps [avɑ̃kɔr] *n.m.inv. Arch: etc:* projecting part (of building).

avant-cour [avɑ̃kur] *n.f. Arch:* forecourt; *pl. avant-cours.*

avant-coureur [avɑ̃kurœr] **1.** *n.m.* forerunner; *Mil:* scout; *pl. avant-coureurs.* **2.** *a.m.* premonitory (symptom); **choc a.-c. (de séisme),** preliminary tremor.

avant-courrier, -ière [avɑ̃kurje, -jɛr] *n.* **1.** forerunner, precursor, herald. **2.** *n.m.* (*b*) advance publicity manager (of circus); *pl. avant-courriers, -ières.*

avant-dernier, -ière [avɑ̃dɛrnje, -jɛr] *a. & n.* last but one, penultimate; **l'avant-dernière fois,** the time before last; *pl. avant-derniers, -ières.*

avant-garde [avɑ̃gard] *n.f.* (*a*) *Mil:* advance(d) guard; **détachement d'a.-g.,** advance(d) party; (*b*) **hommes d'a.-g.,** men in the van (of reform, etc.); pioneers; *Pol:* **les éléments d'a.-g.,** the avant-garde; (*c*) **livre d'a.-g.,** avant-garde book; **technique d'a.-g.,** technique ahead of its time; *pl. avant-gardes.*

avant-goût [avɑ̃gu] *n.m.* foretaste; anticipation; first impression; *pl. avant-goûts.*

avant-guerre [avɑ̃gɛr] *n.m. or f.* pre-war period; **prix d'a.-g.,** pre-war prices; *pl. avant-guerres.*

avant-hier [avɑ̃tjɛr] *adv.* the day before yesterday; **la nuit d'a.-h.,** the night before last; **a.-h au soir,** the night, evening, before last.

avant-main [avɑ̃mɛ̃] *n.m.* **1.** *Anat:* flat of the hand. **2.** *Z:* forequarters, forehand (of horse). **3.** *Ten:* **coup d'a.-m.,** forehand stroke; *pl. avant-mains.*

avant-plan [avɑ̃plɑ̃] *n.m. Art: Phot: etc:* foreground; *pl. avant-plans.*
avant-pont [avɑ̃pɔ̃] *n.m. Nau:* foredeck; *pl. avant-ponts.*
avant-port [avɑ̃pɔr] *n.m. Nau:* outer harbour; outport; *pl. avant-ports.*
avant-poste [avɑ̃pɔst] *n.m. Mil:* outpost; **réseau d'a.-p.,** outpost screen, system; *pl. avant-postes.*
avant-première [avɑ̃prəmjɛr] *n.f.* (*a*) private view, preview (of art exhibition, etc.); *Th:* dress rehearsal; (*b*) *Journ:* pre-performance write-up; *pl. avant-premières.*
avant-propos [avɑ̃prɔpo] *n.m.inv.* **1.** preface, foreword, avant-propos (to book). **2. après quelques a.-p.,** after a few preliminary remarks.
avant-scène [avɑ̃sɛn] *n.f. Th:* (*a*) proscenium, apron, forestage; (*b*) **(loge d')a.-s.,** stage box; *pl. avant-scènes.*
avant-titre [avɑ̃titr̥] *n.m.* half-title (of book); *pl. avant-titres.*
avant-toit [avɑ̃twa] *n.m.* eaves (of roof); **comble avec a.-t.,** umbrella roof; *pl. avant-toits.*
avant-train [avɑ̃trɛ̃] *n.m.* (*a*) *Aut:* front-axle unit; (*b*) wheels (of plough); (*c*) *Artil:* limber; *pl. avant-trains.*
avant-veille [avɑ̃vɛj] *n.f.* two days before; **l'a.-v. de Noël,** two days before Christmas; *pl. avant-veilles.*
avare [avar] **1.** *a.* (*a*) miserly; avaricious; (*b*) **il n'est pas a. de son argent,** he's not mean with his money. **2.** *n.m. & f.* miser.
avarice [avaris] *n.f.* avarice; miserliness.
avaricieux, -ieuse [avarisjø, -jøz] *a.* avaricious, miserly, grasping; *n.* **un vieil a.,** an old miser.
avarie [avari] *n.f.* **1.** damage (to ship, engine, etc.); **subir une a.,** to be damaged; to break down; **faire subir une a. à qch.,** to damage sth.; **2.** *M.Ins:* (*a*) **déclaration d'avaries,** (ship's) protest; **avaries matérielles de mer,** damage done by sea water; (*b*) **avaries-frais,** average; **règlement d'avaries,** adjustment of average; **répartiteur d'avaries,** average adjuster.
avarié [avarje] *a.* damaged, spoiled (goods, etc).
avarier [avarje] *v.tr.* (*pr.sub. & impf.* **n. avariions, v. avariiez**) to damage (goods, etc.); **ces denrées se sont avariées,** these goods have (i) been damaged, (ii) deteriorated, perished, gone bad.
avatar [avatar] *n.m.* (*a*) *Hindu Rel:* avatar; (*b*) transformation, change; phase; *pl.* ups and downs (of political life, etc.); (*c*) mishap, misadventure.
Ave [ɑve] *n.m.,* **avé** [ɑve] *n.m.* **1. Ave,** Ave; **L'Ave Maria,** the Hail Mary. **2. avé,** Ave Maria (bead).
avec [avɛk] **I.** *prep.* with. **1.** (*a*) (*accompaniment, collaboration*) **je vous ai vu a. lui,** I saw you with him; **déjeuner a. qn,** to lunch with s.o.; **je crois a. vous que . . .,** like you, I believe that . . .; **le public est a. nous,** the public is behind us; (*b*) (*indicating an adjunct or special feature*) **il est sorti a. son parapluie,** he has gone out with his umbrella; **elle ressemble à sa sœur, a. des traits plus réguliers,** she is like her sister, but with more regular features; *Com:* **et a. cela, madame?** anything else, madam? (*c*) (*contemporaneity*) **il se lève a. le soleil,** he gets up at sunrise; **il est arrivé a. la nuit,** he arrived when it was getting dark; **le paysage change a. les saisons,** the countryside changes with the seasons. **2.** (*a*) (*suggesting cause*) **on n'y arrive plus, a. cette vie chère,** it is becoming impossible to manage with the cost of living as high as it is; (*b*) (*equivalent to* **malgré**) **a. tous ses défauts, je l'aime,** with, in spite of, all his faults, I love him; **a. tout le respect que je vous dois,** with all due respect. **3.** (*manner*) **combattre a. courage,** to fight with courage; **ce mot s'écrit a. un seul "t,"** this word is written with (only) one "t." **4.** (*means, instrument*) **cela viendra a. le temps,** that will come in time; **a. l'aide de qn,** with s.o.'s help; **ouvrir une porte a. une clef,** to open a door with a key. **5. un métal qui se combine a. un acide,** a metal which combines with an acid; **se marier a. qn,** to marry s.o., to get married to s.o.; **lier conversation a. qn,** to get into conversation with s.o. **6.** (*conformity*) **être d'accord a. qn,** to agree with s.o.; **s'harmoniser a. qch.,** to harmonize, be in keeping, with sth.; **mot qui rime a. un autre,** word that rhymes with another. **7.** (*comparison*) **soutenir la comparaison a. qch.,** to stand, bear, comparison with sth. **8.** (*opposition: equivalent to* **contre**) **lutter a. qch.,** to struggle with sth; **se battre a. qn,** to fight s.o. **9.** (*in expressing personal relationship*) **être bien, mal, a. qn,** to be on good, bad, terms with s.o.; **être sévère a. qn,** to be hard on s.o.; **être franc a. qn,** to be frank with s.o. **10.** (*equivalent to* **en ce qui concerne**) **a. elle on ne sait jamais,** with her you never can tell; **c'est une idée qui ne me viendrait jamais a. vous,** it is an idea which would never occur to me as far as you are concerned. **11.** *F:* **elle est grande et a. ça mince,** she is tall, and, what's more, slim; **a. ça qu'il n'a pas triché!** don't say he didn't cheat! **II.** *prep.phr.* **d'avec** from; **distinguer, séparer, le bon d'a. le mauvais,** to distinguish (the) good from (the) bad; **divorcer d'a. sa femme,** to divorce one's wife. **III.** *adv.* with it, with them; *F:* **il a pris mon chapeau et s'est sauvé a.,** he took my hat and ran off with it.
aveline [avlin] *n.f. Bot:* filbert, hazel nut, cob (nut).
avelinier [avlinje] *n.m. Bot:* hazel tree.
aven [avɛn] *n.m. Geol:* swallowhole.
avenant [avnɑ̃] *a.* **1.** pleasing, prepossessing (person, manners, etc.); **mal a.,** uncouth (manner, etc.). **2. à l'a.,** in keeping, in conformity, correspondingly; **ils se sont conduits à l'a.,** they acted accordingly; **le bâtiment est beau et le jardin est à l'a.,** the building is beautiful and the garden is in keeping with it. **3.** *n.m.* (*a*) codicil (to treaty); (*b*) additional clause (to insurance policy); (*c*) rider (to verdict).
avènement [avɛnmɑ̃] *n.m.* (*a*) advent (of Christ, etc.); coming (of Messiah); **depuis l'a. de l'automobile,** since the invention of the (motor) car; (*b*) **a. au trône,** accession to the throne.
avenir [avnir] *n.m.* future; **qu'est-ce que l'a. nous réserve?** what has the future in store for us? **prédire l'a.,** to predict the future; **jeune homme d'un grand a., de beaucoup d'a.,** young man of great promise; **c'est un homme d'a.,** he's a coming man, a man with a future; *Sp:* **un joueur d'a.,** a coming player; **situation sans a.,** job with no future, dead-end occupation; **assurer l'a. de qn,** to make provision for s.o.; **dans l'a.,** at some future date; **dans un a. très prochain,** in the very near future; **à l'a. je serai plus circonspect,** in future I shall be more cautious.
à-venir [avnir] *n.m.inv. Jur:* writ of summons (to opposing counsel); **signifier un à-v. à la partie adverse,** to serve a writ on the other party.
Avent [avɑ̃] *n.m. Ecc:* Advent.
aventure [avɑ̃tyr] *n.f.* **1.** (*a*) adventure; **homme d'aventures,** adventurous man, adventurer; **vie d'a.,** life of adventure; **a. effrayante,** terrifying experience; (*b*) intrigue, (love) affair. **2.** (*a*) chance, luck, venture; **tenter l'a.,** to try one's luck; **l'a. est au coin de la rue,** the unexpected is always round the corner; **avoir part en une a.,** to have a share in a venture; **à l'a.,** at random; **aller, errer, à l'a.,** to wander about aimlessly; **vivre à l'a.,** to live in a happy-go-lucky fashion; **mettre tout à l'a.,** to leave everything to chance; **par a., d'a.,** by chance; (*b*) *Com:* **prêt à l'a., à la grosse a.,** bottomry. **3. dire, tirer, la bonne a. (à qn),** to tell (s.o.'s) fortune; **diseuse de bonne a.,** fortune teller.
aventuré [avɑ̃tyre] *a.* risky, chancy.
aventurer [avɑ̃tyre] *v.tr.* to risk (life, etc.). **2. s'a. en**

pays inconnu, to venture into an unknown country; (*b*) to expose oneself (to risks); to take risks.

aventureusement [avɑ̃tyrøzmɑ̃] *adv.* adventurously, venturesomely; in an adventurous manner.

aventureux, -euse [avɑ̃tyrø, -øz] *a.* adventurous, venturesome; **homme a. au jeu,** reckless gambler; **projet a.,** hazardous, risky, plan; *n.* **jeune a.,** a rash, venturesome, young man.

aventurier, -ière [avɑ̃tyrje, -jɛr] *n.* adventurer; **c'est un a.,** he lives by his wits.

avenue [avny] *n.f.* (*in town*) avenue; (*leading to house*) (carriage) drive; **les avenues du pouvoir,** the paths to power.

avéré [avere] *a.* authenticated, established (fact, etc.); (fact) beyond doubt; **prendre qch. pour a.,** to take sth. for granted; **crime a.,** patent and established crime; **ennemi a.,** avowed enemy; **voleur a.,** known thief; **marxistes avérés,** professed Marxists.

avérer [avere] *v.* **(j'avère, n. avérons; j'avérerai) 1.** *v.tr. Jur:* to aver (fact). **2. s'a.,** to be proved correct; to be confirmed; **s'a. faux,** to be proved false.

avers [avɛr] *n.m. Num:* obverse (of coin).

averse [avɛrs] *n.f.* sudden shower, downpour; **essuyer une a.,** to be caught in a shower; **une a. de félicitations,** a flood, stream, of congratulations.

aversion [avɛrsjɔ̃] *n.f.* aversion (**pour,** to, for); dislike (**pour,** to, for, of); **avoir une a., de l'a., pour qch., pour, contre, qn,** to have an aversion to, for, sth., s.o., a distaste for sth., a dislike for s.o.; **prendre qn en a.,** to take a dislike to s.o.

averti [avɛrti] *a.* (*a*) experienced (observer, etc.); **un homme a.,** an experienced man, an expert; (*b*) **a. de qch.,** aware, warned, of sth.; **se tenir pour a.,** to be on one's guard; to take the hint; **vous voilà a.!** I give you fair warning!

avertin [avɛrtɛ̃] *n.m. Vet:* staggers.

avertir [avɛrtir] *v.tr.* **1. a. qn de qch.,** to warn, notify, advise, inform, s.o. of sth., to give s.o. notice, warning, of sth.; **je l'en avais averti,** I had warned him of it, against it; **je vous en avertis!** I give you fair warning! **2.** *Aut:* to signal (intention to turn).

avertissement [avɛrtismɑ̃] *n.m.* **1.** (*a*) warning; **renvoyer qn sans a. préalable,** to discharge s.o. at a moment's notice; (*b*) reprimand; *Sp:* warning (by the referee); **lettre envoyée à titre d'a.,** (i) letter sent as a reminder; (ii) warning letter; (*c*) danger signal, sign; warning signal; **a. de tempête,** gale warning; (*d*) **a. (au lecteur),** prefactory note, foreword (to book); (*e*) *Jur:* **billet d'a.,** summons to appear before a magistrate. **2.** *Adm:* demand note.

avertisseur [avɛrtisœr] *n.m.* **1.** warner; *Th:* callboy. **2.** (*a*) warning signal, alarm; *Tp:* annunciator; *Aut:* horn; *Ind:* hooter; *Rail:* signal; **a. d'incendie,** fire alarm; *P.N.:* **avertisseurs sonores interdits,** no hooting; (*b*) *a.* **signal a.,** warning signal.

aveu, -eux [avø] *n.m.* **1.** *Hist:* recognition between a vassal and his overlord; **homme sans a.,** vagabond, vagrant. **2.** *Jur:* consent, authorization; **obtenir l'a. de qn pour faire qch.,** to obtain s.o.'s consent to do sth. **3.** avowal, confession; *Jur:* admission; **faire l'a. d'une erreur,** to own up to a mistake; **faire des aveux complets,** to make a full confession; **de l'a. de tout le monde,** by common consent; **il est certain, de l'a. de tout le monde, que . . .,** everyone agrees that . . .

aveuglant [avœglɑ̃], *a.* blinding; dazzling.

aveugle [avœgl̥] **1.** (*a*) *a.* blind, sightless; **devenir a.,** to go blind; **a. d'un œil,** blind in one eye; *Opt:* **point a.,** blind spot; *F:* **a. comme une taupe,** as blind as a bat; (*b*) *n.* **un, une, a.,** a blind man, woman; **les aveugles,** the blind; **aveugles de guerre,** blinded ex-servicemen. **2.** *Arch:* **fenêtre a., arcade a.,** blind window, arch; **mur a.,** blind wall; *Tchn:* **écrou a.,** blind nut; **trou a.,** dead hole; **bout a. (d'un tuyau),** blind end. **3.** blind, unreasoning (hatred); implicit (confidence, etc.); **avoir une confiance a. en qn,** to trust s.o. implicitly, unreservedly; **obéissance a.,** blind, unquestioning, obedience; **être a. aux défauts, pour, devant, les défauts, de qn,** to be blind to s.o.'s faults; **suivre qn en a.,** to follow s.o. blindly, unreasoningly; **aller à l'a.,** to grope one's way; to go blindly on; **sujet auquel les savants travaillent encore à l'a.,** subject at which scientists are still working in the dark.

aveuglement [avœgləmɑ̃] *n.m.* **1.** *A:* blinding; **depuis son a.,** since his blindness. **2.** (moral, mental) blindness; **l'a. de la passion,** the blindness of passion.

aveuglément [avœglemɑ̃] *adv.* blindly, blindfold; **obéir a.,** to obey blindly, without question.

aveugle-né, -née [avœglәne] *a. & n.* (man, woman) blind from birth; *pl. aveugles-né(e)s.*

aveugler [avœgle] *v.tr.* **1.** (*a*) to blind (s.o.); (*b*) (*of light, etc.*) to dazzle, blind; (*c*) **aveuglé par la colère,** blind with rage; **s'a. sur les défauts de qn,** to shut one's eyes, turn a blind eye, to s.o.'s faults. **2.** *Nau:* (*a*) **a. une voie d'eau,** to stop a leak; (*b*) **a. une fenêtre,** to wall up, block, a window.

aveuglette (à l') [alavœglɛt] *adv.phr.* blindly; **aller à l'a.,** to go blindly on; **avancer à l'a. vers qch.,** to feel, grope, one's way to sth.; **choisir qch. à l'a.,** to choose sth. at random; **lancer des coups à l'a.,** to hit out blindly; *Av:* **voler à l'a.,** to fly blind.

aveulir [avølir] *v.tr.* to enervate; to sap (s.o.'s) energy; to deaden (feelings, etc.); **il s'aveulit,** he's going to pieces.

aviaire [avjɛr] *a.* **peste a.,** fowl plague, fowl pest.

aviateur, -trice [avjatœr, -tris] *n.* aviator; airman, -woman; **mal des aviateurs,** altitude sickness.

aviation [avjasjɔ̃] *n.f.* aviation; **a. civile, commerciale, militaire,** civil, commercial, military aviation; **compagnie d'a.,** airline; **champ, terrain, d'a.,** airfield; flying ground; **base d'a.,** air base; **usine d'a.,** aircraft factory.

avicole [avikɔl] *a.* **élevage a.,** (i) poultry farming; (ii) poultry farm.

aviculteur [avikyltœr] *n.m.* **1.** bird fancier. **2.** poultry farmer, *U.S:* poultryman.

aviculture [avikyltyr] *n.f.* aviculture. **1.** bird fancying. **2.** poultry farming.

avide [avid] *a.* **1.** greedy; **a. de qch.,** (i) greedy for sth.; (ii) eager for sth.; **espérances avides,** eager hopes; **a. de sang,** bloodthirsty; **a. de tout savoir,** eager for knowledge. **2.** covetous (**de,** of); grasping (hands, nature).

avidement [avidmɑ̃] *adv.* greedily, hungrily; covetously; **écouter a.,** to listen eagerly.

avidité [avidite] *n.f.* avidity, greed(iness); voracity (for food); **manger avec a.,** to eat greedily; **écouter avec a.,** to listen eagerly.

avilir [avilir] *v.tr.* **1.** to degrade, debase, lower. **2.** *Com:* to depreciate, lower, bring down (currency, prices, etc.). **3. s'a.,** (i) to lower, demean, oneself; (ii) (*of goods*) to depreciate; to come down (in value).

avilissant [avilisɑ̃] *a.* debasing, degrading.

avilissement [avilismɑ̃] *n.m.* **1.** debasement, degradation. **2.** depreciation; fall (in price).

avion [avjɔ̃] *n.m.* aircraft, aeroplane, *F:* plane, *U.S:* airplane; **j'ai fait une partie du trajet en a.,** I flew part of the way; **par a.,** (by) air mail; **a. commercial,** commercial aircraft; **a. de ligne,** airliner; **a. de transport,** transport aircraft; **a. transbordeur,** air ferry; **a. de tourisme,** private aircraft; **a. bimoteur,** twin-engine aircraft; **a. de bombardement,** bomber; **a. de chasse,** fighter; **a. de pénétration,** intruder; **a. de reconnaissance,** reconnaissance aircraft: **a. ravitailleur,** tanker; **a. d'attaque au sol,** ground attack aircraft; **a.**

à réaction, jet aircraft; **a. à géométrie variable,** swing-wing aircraft; **a. à décollage et atterrissage court,** short take-off and landing aircraft.

avion-citerne [avjɔ̃sitɛrn] *n.m. Av:* tanker (aircraft); *pl. avions-citernes.*

avion-école [avjɔ̃ekɔl] *n.m.* trainer, training aircraft; *pl. avions-écoles.*

avionique [avjɔnik] *n.f. Av:* avionics.

avionneur [avjɔnœr] *n.m.* (*a*) airframe designer; (*b*) airframe manufacturer.

avion-taxi [avjɔ̃taksi] *n.m.* charter aircraft; air taxi; *pl. avions-taxis.*

aviron [avirɔ̃] *n.m.* **1.** oar; *Fr.C:* (canoe) paddle; **a. de couple,** scull; **avirons de couple, accouplés,** double-banked oars; **avirons de, en, pointe,** single-banked oars; **a. de galère,** sweep; **les avirons dans l'eau!** hold water! **engager son a.,** to catch a crab; **coup d'a.,** stroke. **2. l'a.,** rowing; **cercles d'a.,** rowing clubs.

avironner [avirɔne], *v.i. Fr.C:* to paddle (a canoe).

avis [avi] *n.m.* **1.** (*a*) opinion, judgment, decision; **a. d'expert,** expert advice, opinion; **exprimer, émettre, un a.,** to express a view, an opinion; **ne pas être du même a. que qn,** to disagree with s.o.; **sauf meilleur a. je crois que . . .,** with all due deference I think that . . .; *Prov:* **deux a. valent mieux qu'un,** two heads are better than one; **à, selon, mon a.** in my opinion; I consider (that); **de l'a. de tous,** in the opinion, judgment, of all; **être du même a. que qn,** to be of the same opinion as s.o.; **je suis tout à fait de votre a.,** I agree with you; *F:* I'm with you; **j'ai changé d'a.,** I have changed my mind; **êtes-vous d'a. de rester ici?** do you agree with staying here? (*b*) advice, counsel; **a. paternel,** fatherly advice; **donner des a. à qn sur qch.,** to advise s.o. on sth.; **prendre, demander, l'a. de qn,** to ask s.o.'s advice. **2.** notice, notification, announcement; **a. (au public),** notice (to the public); **donner a. de qch.,** to give notice of sth.; **donner a. à qn de qch.,** to advise s.o. of sth.; **a. par écrit,** notice in writing; **a. peu voilé,** broad hint; **jusqu'à nouvel a.,** until further notice, until further orders; until you hear further; **à moins d'a. contraire,** unless I (you) hear to the contrary; *Com:* **note, lettre, d'a.,** advice note, notification of dispatch; **a. de livraison,** delivery note; **suivant a.,** as per advice; *St.Exch:* **a. d'exécution,** contract note.

avisé [avize] *a.* prudent, circumspect; far-seeing; intelligent, shrewd; **être trop a. pour faire qch.,** to be too cautious, wary, to do sth.; **il est trop a. pour . . .,** he knows better than to . . .; **acheteur a.,** discriminating purchaser; **bien a.,** well advised; **mesures mal avisées,** ill advised, thoughtless, measures; *n.* **c'est un mal a.,** he is thoughtless.

aviser [avize] *v.* **I. 1.** *v.tr. A: & Lit:* (*a*) to perceive, to catch a glimpse of (sth., s.o.); (*b*) **a. qn de qch.,** to inform, warn, *Com:* advise, s.o. of sth.; **a. qn de faire qch.,** to give s.o. notice to do sth.; **a. qn que** + *ind.,* to warn s.o. that . . . **2.** *v.i.* **a. à qch.,** to decide what to do about (situation, etc.), to see about sth.; **vous ferez bien d'y a.,** you had better look into it; **a. à faire qch.,** to see about doing sth.; **a. à ce que qch. se fasse,** to take steps to have sth. done; **il est temps d'a.,** it is time to decide, to make up one's mind. **II. s'aviser 1. s'a. de qch.,** to think of sth.; **il ne s'avise de rien,** he never thinks of anything; **s'a. de faire qch.,** (i) to take it into one's head to do sth.; (ii) to take it upon oneself to do sth.; **ne vous en avisez pas!** don't dare to do such a thing! you'd better not! **2. s'aviser que,** to notice, to realize.

aviso [avizo] *n.m.* sloop; **a.-torpilleur,** torpedo gunboat; **a. d'escorte,** corvette; **canonnière-aviso,** gunboat; *U.S: Navy:* **a. de croisière,** cruising cutter.

avitaminose [avitaminoz] *n.f.* vitamin deficiency.

aviver [avive] *v.tr.* **1.** (*a*) to revive, brighten (colours, etc.); to touch up (colour, picture); to irritate (wound, sore); to excite, stir up (passion); to fan, revive, stir up (fire); to sharpen (appetite); **a. d'anciennes rancunes,** to revive ancient grudges; (*b*) to burnish (metalwork); to polish (marble); (*c*) *Metalw:* to clean up (surfaces for soldering). **2.** to put a keen edge on (tool, etc.).

avocat¹, -ate [avɔka, -at] *n.* **1.** *Jur:* barrister(-at-law), counsel; *Scot:* advocate; **a. consultant, a. conseil,** counsel in chambers, consulting barrister; **a. général,** assistant public prosecutor (in a court of appeal); **plaider par a.,** to be represented by counsel; **être reçu a.,** to be called to the bar. **2.** pleader, advocate; *Ecc:* **a. du diable,** devil's advocate.

avocat² *n.m. Bot:* avocado (pear).

avocat-avoué [avɔkaavwe] *n.m.* = attorney; *pl. avocats-avoués.*

avocatier [avɔkatje] *n.m. Bot:* avocado (tree).

avocette [avɔsɛt] *n.f. Orn:* avocet.

avoine [avwan] *n.f.* oat(s); **a. commune,** common oat; **farine d'a.,** oatmeal; **flocons d'a.,** porridge oats; **bouillie d'a.,** (oatmeal) porridge; **galette d'a.,** oatcake; *F: A:* **semer sa folle a.,** to sow one's wild oats.

avoir¹ [avwar] *v.tr.* (*pr.p.* **ayant;** *p.p.* **eu;** *pr.ind.* **j'ai, tu as, il a, n. avons, v. avez, ils ont.;** *pr.sub:* **j'aie, tu aies, il ait, n. ayons, v. ayez, ils aient;** *imp.* **aie, ayons, ayez;** *impf.* **j'avais;** *p.h.* **j'eus, tu eus, il eut, n. eûmes, v. eûtes, ils eurent;** *p.sub.* **j'eusse;** *fu.* **j'aurai; avoir** *is the auxiliary of all transitive and of many intransitive verbs*). **1.** (*a*) to have, possess; **a. beaucoup d'amis,** to have many friends; **il a deux voitures,** he runs two cars; **il a des poulets,** he keeps chickens; **il a encore son père,** his father is still alive; **a. une opinion,** to hold an opinion; (*b*) **qu'est-ce que vous avez là?** what have you (got) there? **a. des amis à dîner,** to have friends to dinner; **en juin nous avons eu du beau temps,** in June we had fine weather; **Dieu ait son âme,** God rest his, her, soul; (*c*) **a. les yeux bleus,** to have blue eyes; **a. les mains pleines, les poches vides, les yeux ouverts,** to have one's hands full, one's pockets empty, one's eyes open; *Fig:* **il a le bras long,** he is very influential; **a. qn, qch., en horreur,** to have a horror of s.o., sth.; (*d*) **a. dix ans,** to be ten (years old); **mur qui a trois mètres de haut,** wall that is three metres high; (*e*) *for the verbal phrases* **avoir affaire, faim, froid, pitié, raison,** *etc., see under these words.* **2.** (*a*) to get, obtain (sth.); **j'ai eu ce cheval (à) bon marché,** I got, bought, this horse cheap; **j'ai bien eu mon train ce matin,** I caught my train all right this morning; **la propriété qu'il a eue de son père,** the property which he inherited from his father; **j'ai eu sa réponse ce matin,** I had, got, his answer this morning; *P:* **a. une femme,** to have, go to bed with, a woman; (*b*) **a. un enfant,** to have, give birth to, a child. **3.** *F:* to get the better of (s.o.), to pull a fast one on (s.o.); **on l'a eu!** he's been had! he's been taken for a ride! **4.** *Lit:* = FAIRE, *etc., chiefly in p.h.;* **il eut un mouvement brusque,** he made a sudden movement. **5.** to be ill; **qu'avez-vous? qu'est-ce que vous avez?** what's the matter with you? **a. la rougeole,** to have measles. **6. en avoir:** (*a*) **nous en avons pour deux heures,** it will take us two hours; we'll be two hours; **j'en ai assez,** I've had enough (of it), I'm tired, sick, of it; I'm through (with it); **j'en ai eu pour 100 francs,** (i) it cost me 100 francs; (ii) I had 100 francs' worth; (*b*) **en a. à, contre, qn,** to have a grudge against s.o.; **est-ce à moi que vous en avez?** are you getting at me? **7.** (*a*) **a. qch. à faire,** to have sth. to do; **je n'ai rien à faire,** I have nothing to do; **j'ai à travailler,** I've work to do; **vous n'avez pas à vous inquiéter,** you have no need to worry; (*b*) **je n'ai que faire de cela,** I don't need that. **8.** *impers.* **y avoir:** (*a*) **qu'est-ce qu'il peut y a. dans ce tiroir?** I wonder what's in this drawer? **combien y a-t-il de blessés?** how many wounded are there? **il n'y en a qu'un,** there is only one; **un homme comme il y en a peu,** man in a thousand; **il y en a qui disent que . . .,** there are people who, some people, say that . . .; **il y en a un qui va être surpris,** someone is in for a surprise; **il n'y a pas de quoi,** please . . .! don't mention it; *U.S:* you're welcome! **qu'est-ce qu'il y a à voir!** what is there to see? (*b*) **il doit y a. quelque chose,** there must be something wrong; **qu'est-ce qu'il y a?** what's the matter? *F:* what's up? **qu'y a-t-il à présent?** what now? (*c*) **il y a deux ans,** two years ago; **il y avait six mois que j'attendais,** I had been waiting for six months; (*d*) **combien y a-t-il d'ici (à) Londres?** how far is it (from here) to London? **9.** (*aux. use*) **j'ai fini,** I've finished; **attendez que nous ayons fini,** wait until we've finished; **je l'ai déjà vu, je les ai déjà vus,** I have already seen him, I have seen them, before; **je l'ai vu, vue, hier,** I saw him, her, yesterday; **j'ai eu vingt ans hier,** I was twenty yesterday; **j'ai eu bientôt fini de m'habiller,** I (had) soon finished dressing, **quand il eut fini de parler, quand il a eu fini de parler,** when he had finished speaking; **j'aurai bientôt fini,** I shall soon have finished.

avoir² *n.m.* property; possessions; **tout mon a.,** all I possess, have; *Com:* **doit et a.,** debit and credit.

avoirdupois [avwardypwa] *n.m. Meas:* avoirdupois.

avoisinant [avwazinɑ̃] *a.* neighbouring; nearby.

avoisiner [avwazine] *v.tr.* **a. qch.,** to be near sth., close, adjacent, to sth., to border on sth.

avortement [avɔrtəmɑ̃] *n.m.* **1.** (*a*) **a. spontané,** miscarriage; (*b*) **a. provoqué,** (procured) abortion; (*c*) (*of animal*) casting (of young). **2.** failure, miscarriage, falling through (of plan, etc.).

avorter [avɔrte] *v.i.* **1.** to miscarry, to abort; **faire a. (qn),** to procure abortion; to bring on a miscarriage. **2.** (*of animals*) to cast (young). **3.** *Bot:* to develop imperfectly; to fail to ripen; to abort; **arbres avortés,** stunted trees. **4. projet qui a avorté,** plan that (has) miscarried, proved abortive, has gone wrong, come to nothing, fallen through.

avorteur, -euse [avɔrtœr, -øz] *n.* abortionist.

avorton [avɔrtɔ̃] *n.m.* abortion; stunted plant, animal; puny, undersized, child; *Pej:* **(petit) a.,** little shrimp, squirt.

avouable [avwabl̥] *a.* avowable (fact, motive); **c'est un métier plus a.,** it's a more respectable trade.

avoué¹ [avwe] *n.m. Jur:* = solicitor, *U.S:* attorney.

avoué² *a.* **1.** (*a*) acknowledged, admitted (fact); (*b*) confessed (author of . . .). **2.** ostensible (purpose).

avouer [avwe] *v.tr.* **1.** (*a*) to acknowledge, recognize (s.o., debt, etc.); (*b*) **a. qn pour frère,** to acknowledge, own, s.o. as one's brother; **s'a. coupable,** to admit one's guilt; **s'a. vaincu,** to acknowledge oneself beaten, to acknowledge defeat. **2.** to confess, admit, own up to (fault, etc.); **elle avoue trente ans,** she admits to being thirty; **ceci me surprend, je l'avoue,** this surprises me, I confess, I must say; **a. avoir fait qch.,** to confess, own (up), to having done sth.

avril [avril] *n.m.* April; **en a.,** in April; **au mois d'a.,** in the month of April; **pluie d'a.,** April showers; **le sept a.,** (on) the seventh of April, (on) April (the) seventh; **le premier a.,** (i) the first of April; (ii) April Fools' Day; **poisson d'a.!** April fool!

avunculaire [avɔ̃kylɛr] *a.* avuncular.

axe [aks] *n.m.* **1.** axis (*pl.* axes) (of plant, the earth, ellipse, etc.); **grand a., petit a.,** major, minor, axis; *Civ.E:* **a. d'une route, d'un pont,** centre line of a road, of a bridge; **a. de circulation,** major route; **conduire sur l'a. de la chaussée,** to drive on the crown of the road; *Mth:* **a. des *x*, des *y*,** *x*-axis, *y*-axis; **axes de coordonnées,** co-ordinate axes; *Mec:* **axes principaux d'un corps,** principal axes of a body; **cristal à deux axes,** biaxial crystal. **2.** *Mch: Mec.E: etc:* axle, spindle, pin; **a. de pompe,** pump spindle; **a. d'une grue,** pin of a crane; *I.C.E.: etc:* **a. du piston,** gudgeon pin. **3.** *Hist:* axis; **les Puissances de l'A.,** the Axis powers. **4.** (*a*) *Mil:* **a. de progression,** main direction of advance; **a. (principal) de ravitaillement,** main line of supply; main supply route; (*b*) *Av:* **a. de sustentation,** lift axis; **a. de descente,** glide path, line of descent; **a. balisé,** radio range course; **a. balisé d'atterrissage,** radio landing beam; **a. de référence,** datum line.

axer [akse] *v.tr. Mch:* to centre; **être axé sur, autour de,** to follow (a tendency, etc.), to centre on.

axial, -aux [aksjal, -o] *a.* axial (line, plane); *Mec:* **effort de compression axiale,** collapsible load; **éclairage a.,** central overhead lighting (of streets).

axillaire [aksilɛr] *a. Anat: Bot:* axillary.

axiomatique [aksjɔmatik] *a.* axiomatic(al).

axiome [aksjom] *n.m.* axiom.

axis [aksis] *n.m. Anat:* axis (second vertebra).

ayant [ɛjɑ̃]. **1.** *See* AVOIR. **2.** *n.m. Jur:* **a. cause,** assign, trustee, executor; *pl. ayants cause;* **a. droit,** rightful claimant or owner; interested party; beneficiary; *pl. ayants droit.*

azalée [azale] *n.f. Bot:* azalea.

azimut [azimyt] *n.m. Astr: etc:* azimuth; *Nau: Surv: etc:* **prendre un a.,** to take a bearing; *F:* **dans tous les azimuts,** everywhere, all over the place; **direction tous azimuts,** facing all ways, all directions.

azimutal, -aux [azimytal, -o] *a.* azimuth(al); **cercle a.,** azimuth circle; **compas a.,** azimuth compass.

azimuté [azimyte] *a. F:* crazy, round the bend.

Azincourt [azɛkur] *Pr.n.m. Geog: Hist:* Agincourt.

azotate [azɔtat] *n.m. Ch:* nitrate; **a. de potasse,** nitre, saltpetre.

azote [azɔt] *n.m. Ch:* nitrogen.

azoté [azɔte] *a.* nitrogenous; **engrais azotés,** nitrate fertilizers, nitrates.

azoter [azɔte] *v.tr.* to nitrogenize.

azotique [azɔtik] *a. Ch:* nitric.

azotite [azɔtit] *n.m. Ch:* nitrite.

aztèque [aztɛk] *a. & n. Ethn: Hist:* Aztec.

azur [azyr] *n.m.* **1.** azure, blue; *Geog:* **la Côte d'Azur,** the French Riviera; *Her:* **champ d'a.,** field azure; **pierre d'a.,** lapis lazuli. **2.** *Com:* blue (for laundry).

azuré [azyre] *a.* **1.** (sky-)blue, azure. **2.** tinged with blue.

azurer [azyre] *v.tr.* **1.** *Dom.Ec: Ind:* to blue (linen, etc.). **2.** to tinge with blue.

azyme [azim] **1.** *a.* **pain a.,** unleavened bread, wafer. **2.** *n.m. Jew.Rel:* **fête des azymes,** feast of unleavened bread.

B

B, b [be] *n.m.* (the letter) B, b.
baba¹ [baba] *n.m. Cu:* (rum) baba.
baba² *a.inv. F:* dumbfounded, flabbergasted; **j'en suis resté b.,** I was absolutely amazed.
Babel [babɛl] *Pr.n.f.* Babel; **la tour de B.,** the Tower of Babel; **c'est une vraie tour de B.,** it's a perfect Babel, it's pandemonium.
babeurre¹ [babœr] *n.m.* buttermilk.
babeurre² *n.m.* dasher (of churn).
babil [babi(l)] *n.m.* **1.** prattling (of child); twittering (of birds); babbling (of a brook). **2.** prattle (of children).
babillage [babijaʒ] *n.m.* = BABIL.
babillard, -arde [babijar, -ard] **1.** *a.* garrulous, talkative; **cours d'eau b.,** babbling brook. **2.** *n.* chatterbox.
babillement [babijmɑ̃] *n.m.* = BABIL.
babiller [babije] *v.i.* to prattle; to chatter; (*of brook*) to babble.
babines [babin] *n.f.pl. Z:* pendulous lips (of monkey, etc.) chops (of ruminants); *F:* lips (of pers.); **s'essuyer les b.,** to wipe one's lips; **vous vous en lécherez les b.,** it will make you lick your lips.
babiole [babjɔl] *n.f.* curio, knick-knack, trinket.
bâbord [babɔr] *n.m. Nau:* port (side); **la barre toute à b., b. toute! b. la barre!** hard a-port! **la terre par b.!** land on the port side! *Row:* **aviron de b.,** stroke-side oar.
bâbordais [babɔrdɛ] *n.m. Nau:* man of the port watch; **les b.,** the port watch.
babouche [babuʃ] *n.f.* Turkish slipper; mule.
babouin [babwɛ̃] *n.m.* baboon.
Babylone [babilɔn] *Pr.n.f. A.Geog:* Babylon.
Babylonie [babilɔni] *Pr.n.f. A.Geog:* Babylonia.
babylonien, -ienne [babilɔnjɛ̃, -jɛn] *a.* & *n.* Babylonian.
baby-sitting [bɛbisitiŋ] *n.m. F:* **faire du b.-s.,** to baby-sit.
bac¹ [bak] *n.m.* **1.** (*a*) ferry (boat); pontoon; **b. à piétons,** passenger ferry; **b. à voitures,** car ferry; **b. transbordeur,** train ferry; **passer qn dans un b.,** to ferry s.o. across; **passer le b.,** to cross the ferry; (*b*) *Jur:* **droit de b.,** ferry (right). **2.** tank, vat; pot (of electric cell); jar, box, container (of accumulator); box, container (for food, etc.); (miner's) truck, tub; **b. à laver,** wash tub; **b. à glace,** ice tray (in fridge); *Belg:* **b. à ordures,** dustbin.
bac² *n.m. F:* = BACCALAURÉAT.
baccalauréat [bakalɔrea] *n.m.* **1. b. (de l'enseignement secondaire)** = General Certificate of Education (A Level); *Scot:* Scottish Higher Certificate of Education; (*in Eire*) School Leaving Certificate. **2. b. en droit,** degree granted when a student has passed his first two examinations for the *Licence en Droit*.
baccara(t)¹ [bakara] *n.m. Cards:* baccarat.
baccarat² *n.m. Glassm:* crystal (made at Baccarat).
bacchanale [bakanal] *n.f.* **1.** *Rom.Ant:* **les bacchanales,** the bacchanalia. **2.** *F: O:* (*a*) noisy, uproarious, dance; (*b*) orgy; drunken revel.
bacchante [bakɑ̃t] *n.f.* **1.** *Ant:* bacchante. **2.** *pl. F:* moustache.
bâche [bɑʃ] *n.f.* **1.** tank, cistern; **b. d'alimentation,** feed tank. **2.** *Hort:* forcing frame. **3.** (coarse canvas) cover (for hayricks, etc.); awning; **b. goudronnée,** tarpaulin; **b. de campement,** ground sheet. **4.** *P:* cap.
bachelier, -ière [baʃəlje, -jɛr] *n. Sch:* student who has passed the *baccalauréat, q.v.*
bâcher [bɑʃe] *v.tr.* to sheet (sth.) over; to cover (sth.) with a tarpaulin.
bachique [baʃik] *a.* bacchic; **scène b.,** bacchanalian scene; **chanson b.,** drinking song.
bachot¹ [baʃo] *n.m.* wherry, punt.
bachot² *n.m. F:* = BACCALAURÉAT; **boite à b.,** crammer.
bachotage [baʃɔtaʒ] *n.m. Sch: F:* cramming.
bachoter [baʃɔte] *Sch: F: v.tr.* & *i.* to cram.
bachoteur¹ [baʃɔtœr] *n.m.* wherryman.
bachoteur², -euse [baʃɔtœr, -øz] *n. F:* student cramming, swotting up, for an exam.
bacillaire [basilɛr] **1.** *a.* bacillary. **2.** *n.m.* & *f.* tubercular patient.
bacille [basil] *n.m.* **1.** *Biol:* bacillus. **2.** *Ent:* stick insect.
bacillose [basiloz] *n.f. Med:* bacillosis; bacillus infection; *esp.* pulmonary tuberculosis.
bâclage [bɑklaʒ] *n.m.* **1.** *Nau:* closing, blocking (of a harbour, port). **2.** *F:* doing (sth.) perfunctorily; scamping, botching (up) (of work).
bâcle [bɑkl̥] *n.f.* bar (of door).
bâclé [bɑkle] *a.* **1.** blocked (harbour, etc.). **2.** slapdash (work, etc.); **un travail b.,** a botched (up) job.
bâcler [bɑkle] *v.tr.* **1.** *A:* to bar, bolt (door, etc.). **2.** *Nau:* (*a*) to block up, close (port, harbour). **3.** *F:* to do (sth.) perfunctorily; to botch (up) (work).
bactéricide [bakterisid] **1.** *a.* bactericidal. **2.** *n.m.* bactericide.
bactérie [bakteri] *n.f.* bacterium, *pl.* -ia.
bactérien, -ienne [bakterjɛ̃, -jɛn] *a.* bacterial.
bactériologie [bakterjɔlɔʒi] *n.f.* bacteriology.
bactériologique [bakterjɔlɔʒik] *a.* bacteriological; **guerre b.,** bacteriological, germ, warfare.
bactériologiste [bakterjɔlɔʒist] **bactériologue** [bakterjɔlɔg] *n.m. or f.* bacteriologist.
bactériophage [bakterjɔfaʒ] *n.m.* bacteriophage.
badaud, -aude [bado, -od] *a.* & *n.* idler; rubberneck.
badaudage [badodaʒ] *n.m.* rubbernecking.
badauder [badode] *v.i.* to stroll about (idly); to rubberneck.
baderne [badɛrn] *n.f. F: Pej:* **une (vieille) b.,** an old fogey, an old fossil, an old stick-in-the-mud.
badigeon [badiʒɔ̃] *n.m.* (colour)wash, distemper (for walls, etc.); **b. à la chaux,** whitewash.
badigeonnage [badiʒɔnaʒ] *n.m.* (*a*) whitewashing; (*b*) colourwashing, distempering; (*c*) *Med:* painting (with iodine, etc.).
badigeonner [badiʒɔne] *v.tr.* (*a*) **b. une surface de qch.,** to brush over a surface with sth.; **b. un mur en blanc, en couleur,** to whitewash, to colourwash, distemper a wall; (*b*) *Med:* to paint **(d'iode, à l'iode,** with iodine).
badigeonneur [badiʒɔnœr] *n.m.* (*a*) whitewasher; (*b*) *F: Pej:* poor painter, dauber.
badin [badɛ̃] *n.m. Av:* airspeed indicator.
badinage [badinaʒ] *n.m.* joking; banter.

badine[2] [badin] *n.f.* cane, switch.

badiner [badine] *v.i.* to jest, joke; **b. de tout,** to turn everything into a joke; **on ne badine pas avec l'amour,** one should never laugh at love.

badinerie [badinri] *n.f.* joking; banter.

badminton [badmintɔn] *n.m.* badminton.

bâdrant [bɑdrɑ̃] *a. Fr.C:* bothersome.

baffe [baf] *n.f. P:* slap, clip on the ear.

Baffin [bafɑ̃] *Pr.n.m. Geog:* **la terre de B.,** Baffin Island.

bafouer [bafwe] *v.tr.* to ridicule, jeer at (s.o.); to flout (regulations).

bafouillage [bafujaʒ] *n.m. F:* (*a*) stammering, spluttering; (*b*) nonsense; (*c*) *I.C.E:* missing, misfiring.

bafouille [bafuj] *n.f. P:* letter.

bafouiller [bafuje] *v.tr. & i. F:* (*a*) to splutter, stammer; (*b*) to talk nonsense, through one's hat; (*c*) (*of engine*) to miss, to misfire.

bâfrer [bɑfre] *P:* **1.** *v.i.* to stuff oneself, to guzzle. **2.** *v.tr.* to wolf one's food.

bâfreur, -euse [bɑfrœr, -øz] *n. P:* glutton, greedy-guts.

bagage [bagaʒ] *n.m.* **1. plier b.,** (i) to pack up one's bags, *Mil:* one's kit; (ii) *F:* to do a bunk, to clear out. **2.** *esp. pl.* luggage, *esp. U.S:* baggage; **bagages non accompagnés,** luggage in advance; **bagages à main,** hand luggage; **fourgon à bagages,** luggage van, *U.S:* baggage car; **voyager avec peu de b.,** to travel light.

bagagiste [bagaʒist] *n.m.* porter; luggage, baggage, handler.

bagarre [bagar] *n.f.* scuffle; brawl; free-for-all.

bagarrer [bagare] *v.i. F:* **1.** to fight, to battle (**pour,** for). **2. se b.,** to fight, to quarrel, to brawl.

bagarreur, -euse [bagarœr, -øz] *a. & n. F:* quarrelsome, violent (persons, character); *n.* brawler.

bagatelle [bagatɛl] *n.f.* trifle, bagatelle; **se fâcher pour une b.,** to take offence at a (mere) trifle; **acheter qch. pour une b.,** to buy sth. for a song.

bagnard [baɲar] *n.m.* convict.

bagne [baɲ] *n.m.* (*a*) *A:* convict prison; **b. flottant,** hulks; (*b*) **condamné à cinq ans de b.,** sentenced to five years' penal servitude; *F:* **quel b.!** what a hole!

bagnole [baɲɔl] *n.f. Aut: F:* **(vieille) b.,** banger, jalopy; **c'est une belle b.,** she's a nice job.

bagou(t) [bagu] *n.m. F:* glibness (of tongue); **avoir du b.,** to have the gift of the gab.

baguage [bagaʒ] *n.m.* ringing (of birds, trees).

bague [bag] *n.f.* **1.** (*a*) (jewelled) ring; (*b*) **b. (d'un cigare),** band (round a cigar). **2.** *Mec.E:* **b. d'assemblage,** collar, sleeve; thimble coupling, joint; **b. de serrage,** set collar, ring; clamping collar, ring; jubilee clip; **b. d'espacement,** sleeve; **b. à bride,** adapter; **b. de roulement,** ball race; bearing race. **3.** *Mch:* (*a*) **b. (de garniture) de piston,** piston ring, packing ring; (*b*) **b. d'appui,** washer.

baguenauder [bagnode] *v.i. & pr. F:* to mooch about, loaf around.

baguer[1] [bage] *v.tr.* **1.** to ring (bird); **cigare bagué d'or,** cigar with a gold band. **2.** to ring (tree).

baguer[2] *v.tr. Needlew:* to tack, baste (pleats. etc.).

baguette [bagɛt] *n.f.* **1.** rod, wand, stick; long thin loaf of French bread; **baguettes,** chopsticks; **b. magique,** magic wand; **baguettes de tambour,** drumsticks; **b. (de chef d'orchestre),** baton; *F:* **commander, mener, faire marcher, qn à la b.,** to rule s.o. with a rod of iron; **passer par les baguettes,** to run the gauntlet. **2.** *Join: etc.* moulding, beading, fillet, reed.

baguier [bagje] *n.m.* ring case, ring stand.

bah [bɑ] *int.* bah! pooh!

Bahamas [baama] *Pr.n.f.pl. Geog:* **les (îles) B., l'archipel des B.,** the Bahamas.

Bahrain [barɛ̃], **Bahreïn** [bareɛ̃] *Pr.n.m. Geog:* **les îles B.,** Bahrain, Bahrein.

bahut [bay] *n.m.* (*a*) *A. Furn:* (round-topped) chest; (*b*) sideboard; (*c*) *P:* school; (*d*) *P:* taxi.

bai [bɛ] *a.* bay (horse); **b. châtain,** chestnut bay.

baie[1] [bɛ] *n.f. Geog:* bay; **la grande B. de l'Australie, la grande B. australienne,** the Great Australian Bight.

baie[2] *n.f. Arch:* bay, opening; **fenêtre en b.,** bay window.

baie[3] *n.f. Bot:* berry.

baignade [bɛɲad] *n.f.* **1.** bathe, swim. **2.** bathing place.

baigner [beɲe] **1.** *v.tr.* (*a*) to bathe, to steep; **baigné de soleil,** bathed in sunlight; **il était baigné de sueur,** he was dripping with sweat; (*b*) (*of sea*) to wash (coast, etc.); (*of river*) to water (a district); (*c*) to bath, give a bath to (dog, baby, etc.). **2.** *v.i.* to soak, steep (in sth.); **il baignait dans son sang,** he was weltering in his own blood. **3. se b.** (*a*) to have, take a bath; *U.S:* to bathe; (*b*) to bathe, to have a swim.

baigneur, -euse [bɛɲœr, -øz] *n.* (*a*) bather; (*b*) small (naked) (china, plastic) doll.

baignoire [bɛɲwar] *n.f.* **1.** bath; (bath)tub. **2.** *Th:* ground-floor box. **3.** *Nau:* upper part of submarine's conning tower.

bail, baux [baj, bo] *n.m.* lease (by landlord to tenant); **b. à ferme,** farming lease; **prendre une maison à b.,** to take a lease on a house; **donner une maison à b.,** to lease a house; *F:* **ça fait un b. que je l'ai vu,** I haven't seen him for ages.

baille [bɑj] *n.f. Nau:* (*a*) tub, bucket, pail; (*b*) *P:* **la (grande) b.,** the sea, the drink.

bâillement [bɑjmɑ̃] *n.m.* **1.** yawn, yawning; **étouffer un b.,** to stifle a yawn. **2.** gaping (of seam, etc.); **b. des rideaux,** gap between the curtains.

bâiller [bɑje] *v.i.* **1.** to yawn; *F:* **b. à se décrocher la mâchoire,** to yawn one's head off. **2.** (*of seams, etc.*) to gape; to fit badly; (*of door*) to be, to stand, ajar.

bailleur, -eresse [bajœr, bajrɛs] *n.* **1.** *Jur:* lessor. **2. b. de fonds,** (i) *Com:* sleeping partner; (ii) financial backer.

bailli [baji] *n.m. A:* bailiff, magistrate, judge.

bailliage [bajaʒ] *n.m. A:* **1.** bailiwick; (*in Fr. or Switz.*) bailliage. **2.** bailiff's court.

bâillon [bɑjɔ̃] *n.m.* gag; **mettre un b. à qn,** to gag s.o.

bâillonner [bɑjɔne] *v.tr.* to gag; **b. la presse,** to muzzle the press.

bain [bɛ̃] *n.m.* **1.** (*a*) bath; **prendre un b.,** to have, to take, a bath; *U.S:* to bath(e); **donner un b. à qn,** to bath s.o.; **b. de mousse,** bubble bath; **bains de soleil,** sunbathing; **prendre un b. de soleil, des bains de soleil,** to sunbathe; **(corsage, haut) b.-de-soleil,** halter top, sun top; **b. de bouche,** mouth wash; **salle de bain(s),** bathroom; *Cost:* **peignoir, sortie, de b.,** bath(ing) wrap, bathrobe; *F:* **être dans le b.,** (i) to be implicated in sth.; (ii) to be in the know; **ils sont dans le même b.,** they're in the same boat; (*b*) bath(tub); (*c*) **bains publics,** public baths, *U.S:* bath house; (*d*) *pl.* baths, watering place, spa; (*e*) swim, bathe (in sea, etc.); bathing; **bains de mer,** (i) sea bathing; (ii) seaside resort; *Cost:* **costume, maillot, de b.,** swimming costume, swimsuit, *U.S:* bathing suit; **slip de b.,** bathing slip. **2.** (*a*) *Husb:* (sheep) dip; *Phot:* **b. révélateur, de développement,** developing bath; **b. de fixage, fixateur,** fixing bath.

bain-marie [bɛ̃mari] *n.m. Dom.Ec:* bain-marie, double saucepan, boiler; *pl. bains-marie.*

baïonnette [bajɔnɛt] *n.f.* bayonet; **mettre, remettre, la b.,** to fix, unfix, bayonets; **charge à la b.,** bayonet charge; *Mec.E: etc:* **joint en b.,** bayonet joint; *El:* **douille à b.,** bayonet socket.

baisemain [bɛzmɛ̃] *n.m.* hand kissing, kissing of hands.
baiser[1] [beze] *v.tr.* (*a*) to kiss (s.o.); (*b*) *P:* to have sex with (s.o.); (*c*) *P:* **se faire b.,** to be had.
baiser[2] *n.m.* kiss; **b. de paix,** kiss of peace; **b. d'adieu,** parting kiss.
baissant [besɑ̃] *a.* declining, diminishing; setting (sun); failing (sight).
baisse [bɛs] *n.f.* **1.** fall, falling, subsidence (of water, of ground, etc.); ebb (of tide); **température en b.,** falling temperature. **2. b. (de prix),** fall, drop (in prices); *St.Exch:* **spéculations à la b.,** bear speculations; **actions en b.,** falling shares.
baisser [bese] **1.** *v.tr.* to lower (a curtain, a blind); to pull down (blind, etc.); to open (car window); *Aut:* to dip (headlights); **le store est baissé,** the blind is down; **b. la tête, le front,** (i) to bend down one's head; (ii) to hang one's head; **b. brusquement la tête,** to duck; **donner tête baissée dans un piège,** to fall headlong into a trap; **b. les yeux,** to look down; **yeux baissés,** downcast eyes; **b. le nez,** to hang one's head in shame; **b. la voix,** to lower one's voice; **b. la radio,** to turn down the radio; **b. le ton,** to climb down (a little); **b. le prix de qch.,** to lower, reduce, cut, bring down, the price of sth.. **2.** *v.i.* (*a*) to go, come, down; to be on the decline; (*of tide*) to ebb; (*of fire*) to burn low, burn down; *Th:* **les lumières baissent,** the lights are going down; **le baromètre baisse,** the barometer is going down; **la température baisse,** it's getting colder; **le jour baisse,** night is falling; it's getting dark; **sa vue, sa mémoire, baisse,** his sight, memory, is failing; **le malade baisse,** the patient is sinking; **il a baissé dans mon estime,** he's gone down in my estimation; (*b*) (*of prices*) to fall; to come, to go, down; **la valeur de ces maisons a baissé,** these houses have gone down in value. **3. se b.,** to stoop; to bend down.
baissier [besje] *n.m. St.Exch:* bear.
bajoues [baʒu] *n.f.pl.* (*of pig, etc.*) cheeks, chaps, chops; *Pej:* (*of pers.*) flabby, pendulous, cheeks.
bakchich [bakʃiʃ] *n.m.* baksheesh; tip.
bal, *pl.* **bals** [bal] *n.m.* **1.** ball; dance; **b. travesti,** fancy dress ball; **b. public,** public dance; **robe de b.,** dance dress, evening dress. **2.** ballroom; dance hall.
balade [balad] *n.f. F:* **faire une b.,** (i) to go for a walk, stroll; (ii) to go for a run in the car.
balader [balade] *F:* **1.** *v.tr.* (*a*) to take (s.o.) out for a walk; (*b*) to drag (sth.). **2. se b.,** to go for a walk.
baladeur,-euse [baladœr, -øz] **1.** *a.* wandering, roving (instinct); **train b.,** sliding gear. **2.** *n.f.* **baladeuse,** (*a*) trailer (of car, etc.); (*b*) (*in market, etc.*) barrow; (*c*) portable lamp, inspection lamp.
balafre [balafr̥] *n.f.* **1.** cut, slash, gash (*esp.* in face); sabre cut. **2.** scar.
balafrer [balafre] *v.tr.* **1.** to cut, gash, slash (*esp.* the face). **2. visage balafré,** scarred face.
balai [balɛ] *n.m.* **1.** (*a*) broom; (long-handled) brush; **b. mécanique,** carpet sweeper; **manche à b.,** (i) broomstick, brush handle; (ii) *Av:* joystick; (iii) *F:* thin, lanky person, beanpole; **donner un coup de b.,** (i) to sweep (a room); *Fig:* (ii) to make a clean sweep; (*b*) *F:* last bus, underground train, etc. (at night). **2.** *El:* brush (of commutator). **3.** *Aut:* blade (of windscreen wiper).
balance [balɑ̃s] *n.f.* **1.** (*a*) balance, (pair of) scales; weighing machine; **b. à bascule,** weighbridge; **b. à levier, b. romaine,** Roman balance, steelyard; **faire pencher la b., incliner la b., emporter la b.,** to turn, to tip, the scales, the balance; (*b*) *Astr:* **la B.,** Libra, the Scales. **2.** indecision; **être en b.,** to be undecided; **la victoire était, restait, en b.,** victory hung in the balance. **3.** (*a*) *Com:* **b. d'un compte,** balance, balancing, of an account; **faire la b.,** to make up the balance (sheet); **compte en b.,** account that balances; **b. du commerce, b. commerciale,** balance of trade; **b. des paiements,** balance of payments; (*b*) **b. des forces au pouvoir,** balance of power. **4.** *Fish:* shrimp net.
balancé [balɑ̃se] *a.* well balanced (sentence, etc.); *F:* **elle est bien balancée,** she's got a wonderful figure.
balancement [balɑ̃smɑ̃] *n.m.* **1.** swing(ing), sway(ing), rocking (of boat, trees, etc.). **2.** balance (of figures in picture, etc.)
balancer [balɑ̃se] *v.* **(je balançai(s); n. balançons) I.** *v.tr.* **1.** to balance (weights, etc.); *Com:* **b. un compte,** to balance an account; **b. le pour et le contre,** to weigh up the pros and cons. **2.** to swing (one's arms, etc.); to rock (s.o. in a hammock, etc.); to sway (one's hips); **b. un enfant sur ses genoux,** to rock a child on one's knees. **3.** *F:* (*a*) to throw, chuck (stones, etc.); (*b*) to fire (employee); to give (s.o.) the sack, the push; to throw (s.o., sth.) out; **il a tout balancé,** (i) he's thrown everything away; (ii) he's given it all up. **II.** *v.i. Lit:* to waver, hesitate. **III. se balancer:** (*a*) to swing; to sway, to rock; (*of ship*) **se b. sur ses ancres,** to ride at anchor; **se b. sur sa chaise,** to rock backwards and forwards on one's chair; (*b*) to see-saw; to play on a swing; (*c*) *P:* **je m'en balance!** I don't care, give, a damn!
balancier[1] [balɑ̃sje] *n.m.* scale manufacturer.
balancier[2] *n.m.* **1.** balancing pole (of tightrope walker). **2.** (*a*) *Clockm: etc:* (i) pendulum (bob); (ii) balance wheel (of watch); (*b*) handle (of pump, etc.); (*c*) *Mch:* beam (of beam engine).
balançoire [balɑ̃swar] *n.f.* (*a*) seesaw; (*b*) (child's) swing; (*c*) (*at fair*) swing-boat.
balayage [balɛjaʒ] *n.m.* **1.** sweeping (of room, etc.); sweeping up (of dirt, etc.). **2.** *Rad: Elcs: T.V:* scan(ning), sweep; **fréquence de b.,** sweep frequency.
balayer [baleje] *v.tr.* **(je balaie, je balaye; je balaierai, je balayerai) 1.** to sweep (out) (room, etc.); to sweep up (dirt, etc.); **le vent a balayé les nuages,** the wind has swept away the clouds; **b. l'ennemi,** to drive away the enemy. **2.** *Rad: Elcs: T.V:* to scan, to explore, to sweep.
balayette [balɛjɛt] *n.f.* (hearth, hand) brush.
balayeur, -euse [balɛjœr, -øz] **1.** *n.* (*pers.*) (road) sweeper. **2.** *n.f.* (*machine*) **balayeuse,** road sweeper.
balayures [balɛjyr] *n.f.pl.* sweepings.
balbutiant [balbysjɑ̃] *a.* stuttering, stammering.
balbutiement [balbysimɑ̃], *n.m.* (*a*) stuttering, stammering; mumbling; (*b*) **l'informatique n'était alors qu'à ses premiers balbutiements,** data processing was then only in its infancy.
balbutier [balbysje] *v.* (*pr.sub. & impf.* **n. balbutiions, v. balbutiiez**) *v.i. & tr.* to stutter; to stammer; to mumble (sth.).
balcon [balkɔ̃] *n.m.* **1.** *Arch:* balcony. **2.** *Th:* dress circle.
balconnet [balkɔnɛ] *n.m.* half-cup brassière.
baldaquin [baldakɛ̃] *n.m.* baldachin, canopy (of bed, etc.).
Bâle [bɑl] *Pr.n.f. Geog:* Basle, Basel.
baléare [balear] *a. & n.* **les (îles) Baléares,** the Balearic Islands.
baleine [balɛn] *n.f.* **1.** whale; **b. à bosse,** humpbacked whale; **blanc de b.,** spermaceti. **2.** (whale)bone (of a corset, etc.); *pl.* ribs (of an umbrella).
baleiné [balene] *a.* boned (brassière); stiffened (collar).
baleineau, -eaux [balɛno] *n.m.* whale calf.
baleinier, -ière [balenje, -jɛr] **1.** *a.* whaling (vessel, industry). **2.** *n.f.* **baleinière,** whaleboat; **b. de sauvetage,** lifeboat.
balénoptère [balenɔptɛr] *n.m. Z:* rorqual; **b. à bec,** piked whale.

balisage [balizaʒ] *n.m.* (*a*) *Nau:* buoys; *Av: etc:* beacons, markings, signs; **projecteur de b.,** direction beacon; (*b*) *Nau:* beaconing, buoying; *Av:* (aerodrome) lights, lighting; signalling, marking out (with beacons).
balise [baliz] *n.f.* (*a*) *Nau:* beacon; seamark; **b. flottante,** buoy; (*b*) *Av:* (approach) light, marker; (radio) beacon; (*c*) *Rad:* **b. radar,** radar beacon.
baliser [balize] *v.tr.* (*a*) *Nau:* to beacon, buoy, mark out (channel); (*b*) *Av:* to equip (airport) with (approach) lights; to mark out (route) with beacons.
baliseur [balizœr] *n.m.* (*a*) **(bateau) b.** = Trinity House boat; (*b*) (*pers.*) = Trinity (House) buoy keeper.
balistique [balistik] **1.** *a.* ballistic; **engin b.,** ballistic missile. **2.** *n.f.* ballistics.
baliverne [balivɛrn] *n.f.* futile remark; **débiter des balivernes,** to talk twaddle, nonsense.
balkanique [balkanik] *a. Geog:* Balkan (state, etc.).
ballade [balad] *n.f. Lit: Mus:* (*a*) ballade; **les ballades de Villon,** Villon's ballades; (*b*) ballad.
ballant [balɑ̃] **1.** *a.* swinging, dangling (arms, etc.); **assis les pieds ballants,** sitting with one's feet dangling. **2.** *n.m.* (*a*) swing, rocking motion; roll, sway (of vehicle, etc.); (*b*) *Nau:* slack (in rope).
ballast [balast] *n.m.* **1.** *Civ.E: etc:* ballast, bottom (of road, railway track). **2.** *Nau:* ballast tank (of submarine, etc.)
ballastage [balastaʒ] *n.m.* **1.** *Civ.E: etc:* ballasting (of railway track, etc.). **2.** *Nau:* (i) ballasting; (ii) unballasting.
ballaster [balaste] *v.tr.* **1.** *Civ.E: etc:* to ballast (railway track, etc.). **2.** *Nau:* (i) to ballast; (ii) to unballast.
balle¹ [bal] *n.f.* **1.** ball; (*a*) **b. de golf, de tennis,** golf ball, tennis ball; **jouer à la b.,** to play ball; *F:* **vous avez la b. belle,** now's your chance; **b. au mur** = fives; *Ten:* **faire des, quelques, balles,** to have a knock-up; **b. de filet,** net (ball); **b. de match, de set,** match point, set point. **2.** bullet; shot; **b. de fusil,** rifle bullet; **b. morte,** spent bullet; **b. perdue,** stray bullet; **à l'épreuve des balles,** bullet-proof.
balle² *n.f.* (*a*) *Com:* bale (of cotton, etc.); (*b*) *P:* **quelle b.!** what an ugly mug!
balle³ *n.f.* husk, chaff (of wheat); *Bot:* glume (of flower); *P:* **peau de b.,** nothing at all, damn all.
baller [bale] *v.i.* to hang (down); to be slack; **laisser b. ses bras,** to let one's arms dangle.
ballerine [balrin] *n.f.* **1.** *Th:* ballerina, ballet dancer. **2.** *Bootm:* ballerina shoe.
ballet [balɛ] *n.m. Th:* ballet; **maître de b.,** ballet master.
ballon [balɔ̃] *n.m.* **1.** (*a*) balloon; **b. dirigeable,** airship, dirigible; **b. d'observation,** observation balloon; **b. de protection, de barrage,** barrage balloon; **envoyer, lancer, un b. d'essai,** (i) to send up a pilot balloon; (ii) to put out a feeler; **monter en b.,** to go up in a balloon; **b. d'enfant,** toy balloon; (*b*) *Med:* **b. d'oxygène,** oxygen bottle. **2.** (*a*) ball; **b. de football, de rugby,** football, rugby ball; (*b*) **b. d'entraînement (pour boxeurs, à boxer**), punchball. **3.** (*a*) *Ch:* balloon flask; *Ind:* carboy; (*b*) **(verre) b.,** brandy glass, balloon glass. **4.** *Nau:* ball signal.
ballonné [balɔne] *a.* distended, swollen; blown out.
ballonnement [balɔnmɑ̃] *n.m.* distending (of stomach, etc.); ballooning (of skirt, etc.).
ballonner [balɔne] **1.** *v.tr.* to distend (the stomach). **2.** *v.i. & pr.* (*a*) to swell, to bulge (out), to become distended; (*of skirt, etc.*) to balloon (out).
ballon-panier [balɔ̃panje] *n.m.inv. Fr.C: Sp:* basketball.
ballon-sonde [balɔ̃sɔ̃d] *n.m. Meteor:* sounding balloon; *pl. ballons-sondes.*
ballot [balo] *n.m.* **1.** bundle, package. **2.** *F:* nit(wit), clot; *a.* **t'es pas b.?** are you mad?
ballottage [balɔtaʒ] *n.m. Pol: etc:* failure to gain absolute majority; **scrutin de b.,** second ballot, *U.S:* run-off election.
ballotter [balɔte] **1.** *v.tr.* to toss, to shake (about); **ballotter qn (de l'un à l'autre),** to drive, chase, s.o. from pillar to post. **2.** *v.i.* (*of door, etc.*) to rattle, shake; to swing to and fro; (*of ship*) to toss (on the water).
ballottine [balɔtin] *n.f. Cu:* meat roll, galantine.
ball-trap [baltrap] *n.m.* (clay pigeon) shooting; *NAm:* skeet shooting; *pl. ball-traps.*
bal(l)uchon [balyʃɔ̃] *n.m. F:* bundle (*esp.* of clothes); **faire son b.,** to pack up.
balnéaire [balneɛr] *a.* **station b.,** (i) seaside resort; (ii) spa.
balourd, -ourde [balur, -urd] **1.** *a. & n.* awkward, clumsy, stupid (person); lout; **un grand b.,** a great hulking fellow. **2.** *n.m. Mec.E:* unbalance.
balourdise [balurdiz] *n.f.* **1.** awkwardness, clumsiness; stupidity. **2.** stupid blunder; *F:* clanger.
balsa [balza] *n.m. Bot:* balsa (wood).
balsamier [balzamje] *n.m. Bot:* balsam (tree).
balsamine [balzamin] *n.f. Bot:* balsam; busy Lizzie.
balte [balt] *a.* **les pays baltes,** the Baltic States.
baltique [baltik] *a. & Pr.n.f. Geog:* **la (mer) B.,** the Baltic (Sea).
balustrade [balystrad] *n.f.* **1.** balustrade. **2.** (hand-) rail; railing.
balustre [balystr̥] *n.m.* (*a*) baluster; (*b*) *pl.* banisters (of stairs); (*c*) splat (of chair).
balzan [balzɑ̃] *a.* **cheval b.,** horse with white stockings.
balzane [balzan] *n.f.* white stocking (of horse).
bambin, -ine [bɑ̃bɛ̃, -in] *n. F:* little child; tiny tot.
bamboche [bɑ̃bɔʃ] *n.f. F:* spree, lark; **faire (une) b.,** to live it up.
bambocher [bɑ̃bɔʃe] *v.i. F:* to live it up.
bambocheur, -euse [bɑ̃bɔʃœr, -øz] *n. F:* reveller; **c'est un b.,** he likes living it up.
bambou [bɑ̃bu] *n.m. Bot:* bamboo (cane); *Cu:* **pousses de b.,** bamboo shoots; *Pol:* **rideau de b.,** bamboo curtain; *F:* (*in tropics*) **coup de b.,** sunstroke; *P:* **il a le coup de b.,** (i) he's mad, crackers, nuts; (ii) he's tired out, whacked.
ban [bɑ̃] *n.m.* **1.** (*a*) *A:* (public) proclamation (of event); (*b*) roll of drum (before proclamation); (*c*) round of (rhythmical) applause; **un b. pour Monsieur le maire!** = three cheers for the mayor! (*d*) *pl.* banns (of marriage). **2.** *Hist:* (proclamation of) banishment; **mettre qn au b.,** (i) to banish s.o.; (ii) to send s.o. to Coventry; **être au b. de la société,** to be outlawed by society. **3. le b. et l'arrière-ban,** (i) *Hist:* the ban and the arrière-ban; (ii) the whole lot.
banal [banal] *a.* **1.** (*m.pl.* **banaux**) *Hist:* communal (mill, bakehouse). **2.** (*m.pl.* **banals**) commonplace, banal, ordinary, trite; **parler de choses banales,** to engage in small talk; **ça, c'est peu b.!** that's unusual, a bit out of the ordinary!
banalement [banalmɑ̃] *adv.* in a banal, commonplace, manner; tritely.
banalisation [banalizasjɔ̃] *n.f.* **1.** standardization (of sth.). **2.** *Rail:* (*a*) signalling (of track) for two-way working; (*b*) use of engine by several crews.
banaliser [banalize] *v.tr.* **1.** to make (sth.) commonplace, ordinary; **voiture banalisée,** unmarked police car. **2.** *Rail:* to signal (track) for two-way working; **b. une locomotive,** to have an engine manned by several crews.
banalité [banalite] *n.f.* **1.** banality, triteness. **2.** *pl.* small talk; clichés, platitudes.

banane [banan] *n.f.* **1.** *Bot:* banana. **2.** *F:* (*a*) medal, gong; (*b*) *Aut:* overrider; (*c*) helicopter, chopper.
bananier [bananje] *n.m.* **1.** *Bot:* banana tree. **2.** *Nau:* banana boat.
banc [bɑ̃] *n.m.* **1.** bench, seat, form; **b. d'église,** pew; **b. d'œuvre,** churchwardens' pew; *Row:* **b. à coulisses,** sliding seat; *Pol:* **le b. des ministres** = the Treasury bench, the government front bench; *Jur:* **b. des magistrats,** magistrates' bench; *Jur:* (*in Eng.*) **cour du b. de la reine, du roi,** Queen's, King's, Bench Division (of the High Court of Justice); **b. des prévenus, des accusés,** dock; **b. des témoins,** witness box. **2.** (*a*) (work)bench; *Mec.E:* bed (of lathe); table (of drilling machine); **b. d'essai,** testing bench, test bed (for engines); testing ground (for sth. new). **3.** (*a*) layer, bed (of rock, etc.); *Min:* seam (of coal); (*b*) **b. de sable,** sandbank; **b. de vase,** mudbank; **b. de glace,** ice floe, ice field; *Fr.C:* **b. de neige,** snowbank; **b. de roches,** reef; **b. d'huîtres,** oyster bed; *Geog:* **b. continental,** continental shelf; **le Banc de Terre-Neuve,** the Banks (of Newfoundland); *Nau:* **toucher au b.,** to run aground. **4.** shoal, school (of fish).
bancable [bɑ̃kabl̩] *a. Fin:* bankable, negotiable.
bancaire [bɑ̃kɛr] *a.* pertaining to banking; **opérations bancaires,** bank(ing) transactions; **chèque b.,** banker's draft, bank cheque.
bancal, -als [bɑ̃kal] *a.* (*a*) (person) who limps; (*b*) wobbly, rickety (furniture, etc.).
banco [bɑ̃ko] *n.m. Cards:* banco; **faire b.,** to go banco.
bandage [bɑ̃daʒ] *n.m.* **1.** (*a*) bandaging, binding up (of wound); (*b*) bandage; **b. herniaire,** truss. **2.** (steel, rubber) tyre; hoop, band (of wheel). **3.** tightening, winding (up) (of spring); stringing, bending (of bow).
bandagiste [bɑ̃daʒist] *n.m. & f. Med:* truss manufacturer, supplier.
bande¹ [bɑ̃d] *n.f.* **1.** (*a*) band, strip (of cloth, paper, metal, etc.); stretch, belt (of land); stripe (on cloth, cup, etc.); **mettre un journal sous b.,** to put a wrapper round a newspaper; **b. de téléimprimeur,** ticker tape; **b. dessinée, illustrée,** strip cartoon, comic strip; *Agr:* **culture en bandes de niveau,** strip contour farming; *Aut:* **b. de stationnement,** layby; *Av:* **b. d'envol,** airstrip, landing strip; (*on road*) **b. médiane,** white line; (*b*) (surgical) bandage; **b. adhésive,** adhesive tape; (*c*) (reel of) (cine) film; **bandes vierges,** (film) stock; **tourner une b. d'essai,** to have a film test; **b. sonore,** sound track; **b. magnétique,** magnetic tape; **b. vidéo,** video tape; (*d*) (steel) tyre (of wheel); **b. de roulement,** tread (of tyre); (*e*) *Bill:* cushion; **par la b.,** in a round-about way, indirectly; (*f*) *Opt:* band (of the spectrum); *W.Tel:* **b. de fréquences,** frequency band; (*g*) (feeding) belt, strip (of machine gun). **2.** *Her:* bend. **3.** *Nau:* (*a*) side (of ship); (*b*) keel, list(ing); **donner de la b.,** to keel (over), to careen, to have a list.
bande² *n.f.* **1.** band, party, troop; **b. de voleurs,** gang of thieves; **il fait b. à part,** he goes his own way, he keeps himself to himself; **être de la b. de qn,** to belong to s.o.'s group; **toute la b.,** the whole gang, the whole lot of them; **b. d'imbéciles!** you idiots! you stupid lot! **b. noire,** terrorist gang. **2.** flight, flock (of birds); pack (of wolves); herd (of buffaloes); school, shoal (of porpoises); pride (of lions).
bandé [bɑ̃de] *a.* (*a*) *Her:* bendy; (*b*) **les yeux bandés,** blindfold(ed); **main bandée,** bandaged hand.
bandeau, -eaux [bɑ̃do] *n.m.* **1.** (*a*) headband; (*b*) **cheveux en bandeaux,** hair parted in the middle; (*c*) **b. royal,** diadem. **2.** bandage (on head); **mettre un b. à qn,** to blindfold s.o. **3.** *Arch:* string course.
bandelette [bɑ̃dlɛt] *n.f.* (*a*) narrow band, strip (of cloth); (*b*) *pl.* bandages, wrappings (of mummies).
bander [bɑ̃de] **1.** *v.tr.* (*a*) to bandage, bind (up) (wound); to put a bandage on (s.o., sth.); **b. les yeux à, de, qn,** to blindfold s.o.; (*b*) to tighten, stretch, wind up (spring, etc.); **b. un arc,** (i) to bend, (ii) to string, a bow. **2.** *v.i.* (*a*) to be stretched tight; (*b*) *V:* to have an erection.
banderille [bɑ̃drij] *n.f.* (*bullfighting*) banderilla.
banderole [bɑ̃drɔl] *n.f.* banderole, streamer.
bandit [bɑ̃di] *n.m.* (*a*) *O:* bandit, brigand, highwayman; (*b*) crook, swindler, rogue.
bandoulière [bɑ̃duljɛr] *n.f.* **1.** shoulder strap (of bag, etc.); **porter, mettre, qch. en b.,** to carry, sling, sth. over, across, one's shoulder. **2.** *Mil:* bandolier.
bang [bɑ̃g] *n.m. inv. Av:* (super)sonic boom.
banian [banjɑ̃] *n.m. Bot:* banyan (tree).
banjo [bɑ̃ʒo] *n.m. Mus:* banjo.
banlieue [bɑ̃ljø] (*a*) *n.f.* suburbs; commuter belt; *Rail:* **ligne, gare, de b.,** suburban line, station; (*b*) *n.m. Belg:* stopping train.
banlieusard, -arde [bɑ̃ljøzar, -ard] *n. F:* commuter; **c'est un b.,** (i) he lives in the suburbs; (ii) he's very suburban.
banne [ban] *n.f.* **1.** cart (for coal, etc.). **2.** hamper, large basket. **3.** awning, blind (of shop, etc.).
banneret [banrɛ] *n.m. Hist:* banneret; **chevalier b.,** knight banneret.
banneton [bantɔ̃] *n.m.* **1.** basket (without handles). **2.** *Fish:* corf.
banni, -e [bani] **1.** *a.* banished, outlawed. **2.** *n.* exile, outlaw.
bannière [banjɛr] *n.f.* banner; **il s'est rangé sous la b. des écologistes,** he's joined the ranks of the ecologists; **la b. étoilée,** the star-spangled banner (of the U.S.A.).
bannir [banir] *v.tr.* to banish, to exile, to outlaw; **il a banni complètement le café,** he has completely given up drinking coffee.
bannissement [banismɑ̃] *n.m.* banishment.
banquable [bɑ̃kabl̩] *a. Fin:* bankable, negotiable.
banque [bɑ̃k] *n.f.* **1.** (*a*) banking; (*b*) bank; **b. d'émission,** bank of issue, issuing house; **billet de b.,** banknote; **carnet, livret, de b.,** bank book; **avoir un compte en b. chez . . .,** to bank with . . .; **employé de b.,** bank clerk; (*c*) *Med:* **b. de, du sang,** blood bank; **b. des yeux,** eye bank; (*d*) *Cmptr:* **b. de données,** data bank. **2.** *Cards:* bank; **faire sauter la b.,** to break the bank.
banqueroute [bɑ̃krut] *n.f. Jur:* bankruptcy; **faire b.,** to go bankrupt.
banqueroutier, -ière [bɑ̃krutje, -jɛr] *n.* bankrupt (*usu.* fraudulent).
banquet [bɑ̃kɛ] *n.m.* banquet, feast; **salle de b.,** banqueting hall.
banquette [bɑ̃kɛt] *n.f.* **1.** bench, seat, form; **b. de piano,** piano stool; *Th:* **jouer devant les banquettes,** to play to an empty house. **2.** (*a*) *Civ.E: etc:* bank (of earth, etc.); verge; (*b*) (foot)path (of bridge, tunnel); (*c*) **b. de fenêtre,** windowledge, window seat.
banquier [bɑ̃kje] *n.m. Fin: Cards:* banker.
banquise [bɑ̃kiz] *n.f.* ice floe, ice pack.
bantam [bɑ̃tam] *n.m. Husb:* bantam.
Bantou, -e [bɑ̃tu] *a. & n. Ethn:* Bantu.
baobab [baɔbab] *n.m. Bot:* baobab (tree).
baptême [batɛm] *n.m.* **1.** baptism, christening; **donner le b. à qn,** to baptize, to christen, s.o.; **recevoir le b.,** to be baptised; **nom de b.,** Christian name, baptismal name. **2.** blessing (of a bell); naming (of a ship); **b. de l'air,** first flight; *Nau:* **b. de la ligne,** (ducking on) crossing the line.
baptiser [batize] *v.tr.* (*a*) to baptize (s.o.), to christen (s.o., ship, etc.); to bless (bell, etc.); (*b*) to christen, to nickname; **on l'avait baptisé "le Balafré,"** they had nicknamed him "Scarface"; (*c*) *F:* **b. son vin,** to water down one's wine.

baptismal, -aux [batismal, -o] *a.* baptismal.
baptistaire [batistɛr] *a.* **registre b.,** register of baptisms; **extrait b.,** certificate of baptism.
baptiste [batist] *a. & n. Ecc:* Baptist.
baptistère [batistɛr] *n.m. Ecc:* baptist(e)ry.
baquet [bakɛ] *n.m.* **1.** tub, bucket. **2.** *Aut:* **(siège en) b.,** bucket seat.
bar¹ [bar] *n.m. Ich:* bass; **b. commun,** sea perch.
bar² *n.m.* (*a*) (public) bar; **le b. du coin,** the bar, café, pub, on the corner; the local; **b.-tabac,** bar with tobacco licence. (*b*) (*counter*) bar; **prendre une consommation au b.,** to have a drink at the bar.
bar³ *n.m. Meteor. Meas:* bar.
barachois [baraʃwa] *n.m. Fr.C:* sandbar (in a river).
baragouin [baragwɛ̃] *n.m.* gibberish, jargon.
baragouinage [baragwinaʒ] *n.m.* jabbering.
baragouiner [baragwine] *v.tr. & i. F:* (*a*) to speak a language badly; **b. l'anglais,** to talk broken English; (*b*) to jabber.
baragouineur, -euse [baragwinœr, -øz] *n.* jabberer.
baraka [baraka] *n.f.* (good) luck; **avoir la b.,** to be lucky.
baraque [barak] *n.f.* (*a*) hut, shack, shed; (*b*) *F:* hovel, hole (of a place); **quelle b.!** what a dump! (*c*) stall (at fair, etc.).
baraquement [barakmɑ̃] *n.m. usu. pl.* shacks; *Mil:* hutted camp.
baraquer [barake] **1.** *v.tr. A:* to lodge (troops, etc.) in huts. **2.** *v.i.* (*of camel*) to kneel down.
baraterie [baratri] *n.f. Jur:* barratry.
baratin [baratɛ̃] *n.m. P:* (*a*) chatter; (sales) patter; **faire du b.,** to spin a yarn, to shoot a line; (*b*) smooth talk.
baratiner [baratine] *v.tr. & i. P:* (*a*) to talk a lot, to chatter; to have the gift of the gab; (*b*) to shoot a line; to spin a yarn; to make sales talk; (*c*) to chat up (a girl).
baratineur, -euse [baratinœr, -øz] *n. P:* (*a*) gasbag; (*b*) smooth talker.
baratte [barat] *n.f.* churn.
baratter [barate] *v.tr.* to churn (milk).
barbacane [barbakan] *n.f.* **1.** *Fort:* (*a*) barbican, outwork; (*b*) loop(hole). **2.** drainage channel (in wall).
Barbade [barbad] *Pr.n.f. Geog:* Barbados.
barbant [barbɑ̃] *a. F:* boring.
barbare [barbar] **1.** *a.* (*a*) barbaric; (*b*) barbarous. **2.** *n.m. & f.* barbarian.
barbaresque [barbarɛsk] **1.** *a.* Berber; **les États barbaresques,** the Barbary States. **2.** *n.m. & f.* Berber.
barbarie¹ [barbari] *n.f.* **1.** barbarism. **2.** barbarousness, barbarity, cruelty.
Barbarie² *Pr.n.f. Geog:* the Barbary States.
barbarisme [barbarism] *n.m. Gram:* barbarism.
barbe¹ [barb] *n.f.* **1.** (*a*) beard; **sans b.,** cleanshaven; **faire la b. à qn,** to shave s.o.; **il avait une b. de huit jours,** he had a week's beard, a week's growth; **brosse, savon, à b.,** shaving brush, soap; **parler dans sa b.,** to mutter, to mumble; **rire dans sa b.,** to laugh up one's sleeve; *Comest:* **b. à papa,** candy floss, *NAm:* cotton candy; (*b*) *F:* **quelle b.!** what a drag! what a bore! **la b.!** that'll do! shut up! (*c*) **vieille b.,** old fogey; (*d*) beard (of goat, bird, etc.); whiskers (of cat); barb(el), wattle (of fish); wattle (of bird); barb (of feather, fish hook); beard (of wheat). **2.** *Tchn:* (*a*) bur(r) (on casting, etc.); (*b*) *pl.* deckle edge (of paper).
barbe² *a. & n.m.* **(cheval) b.,** barb, Barbary horse.
barbeau¹, -eaux [barbo] *n.m.* **1.** *Ich:* **b. commun,** barbel; **b. de mer,** red mullet. **2.** *P:* pimp.
barbeau² **1.** *n.m. Bot:* cornflower. **2.** *a.inv.* **(bleu) b.,** cornflower blue, light blue.
Barbe-Bleue [barbəblø] *Pr.n.m.* Bluebeard.
barbecue [barbəkju] *n.m.* barbecue.
barbelé [barbəle] *a.* barbed (arrow, hook); **fil de fer b.,** *n.m.* **barbelé,** barbed wire; *Mil:* **des barbelés,** barbed wire entanglement.
barber [barbe] *F:* **1.** *v.tr.* to bore (s.o.) (to death). **2.** **se b.,** to be bored (stiff).
barbiche [barbiʃ] *n.f.* short (pointed) beard; goatee.
barbier [barbje] *n.m.* (*a*) (*pers. who shaves s.o.*) barber; (*b*) *Fr.C:* (men's) hairdresser, *esp. NAm:* barber; **salon de b.,** hairdresser's (shop), *NAm:* barbershop.
barbillon [barbijɔ̃] *n.m.* **1.** wattle (of cock, fish); barbel (of fish); *pl.* barbels (of horse, cattle). **2.** *Ich:* barbel; **b. de mer,** red mullet.
barbital [barbital] *n.m. Pharm:* barbitone, *esp. NAm:* barbital.
barbiturique [barbityrik] *Pharm:* (*a*) *a.* barbituric; (*b*) *n.m.* barbiturate.
barbiturisme [barbityrism] *n.m. Med:* barbiturism, addiction to barbiturates; barbiturate poisoning.
barbotage [barbɔtaʒ] *n.m.* (*a*) paddling, splashing (about) (in water); (*b*) bubbling (of gas through liquid).
barboter [barbɔte] **1.** *v.i.* (*a*) to paddle, splash (about) (in water); (*b*) (*of gas*) to bubble (through liquid). **2.** *v.tr. P:* to steal, pinch, nick (sth.).
barboteur, -euse [barbɔtœr, -øz] *n.* **1.** (*a*) paddler; (*b*) *P:* thief, scrounger. **2.** *n.m. Ch:* bubbler, blower. **3.** *n.f.* (child's) playsuit, rompers.
barbotière [barbɔtjɛr] *n.f.* duckpond.
barbotin [barbɔtɛ̃] *n.m. Mec.E:* sprocket wheel.
barbouillage [barbujaʒ] *n.m.* **1.** (*a*) daubing, smearing; (*b*) scrawling, scribbling. **2.** (*a*) bad picture, daub; (*b*) scrawl, scribble.
barbouiller [barbuje] *v.tr.* **1.** (*a*) to daub, to smear (with paint); (*b*) to smear, dirty (one's face); to blot (paper with ink); **visage barbouillé de larmes,** tear-stained face. **2.** to scribble, scrawl; **b. un article,** to scribble off an article. **3.** *F:* **ça me barbouille l'estomac, le cœur,** it makes me feel sick, turns my stomach.
barbouilleur, -euse [barbujœr, -øz] *n.* **1.** dauber; so-called artist. **2.** **b. (de papier),** scribbler, hack.
barbu [barby] **1.** *a. & n.* bearded (man). **2.** *n.f. Ich:* **barbue,** brill.
barcarolle [barkarɔl] *n.f. Mus:* barcarol(l)e.
Barcelone [barsəlɔn] *Pr.n.f. Geog:* Barcelona.
bard [bar] *n.m.* (wheelless) hand barrow.
barda [barda] *n.m. Mil: etc: P:* kit; luggage, gear.
bardage [bardaʒ] *n.m.* **1.** hand transport (of heavy materials). **2.** boarding (to protect a painting, etc.).
bardane [bardan] *n.f. Bot:* burdock.
barde¹ [bard] *n.f.* **1.** *Arm:* bard (protecting warhorse). **2.** *Cu:* bard, bacon (put over roast).
barde² *n.m.* bard, poet.
bardeau, -eaux [bardo] *n.m.* **1.** *Const:* shingle (board). **2.** *Z:* hinny.
barder¹ [barde] *v. impers. F:* **ça va b.!** things are really going to hot up! **c'est là que ça a commencé à b.!** and then the fun began!
barder² *v.tr.* **1.** *Hist:* to bard; **chevalier bardé de fer,** steel-clad knight; **malle bardée d'étiquettes,** trunk stuck all over with labels. **2.** *Cu:* to bard (fowl, etc.).
bardot [bardo] *n.m. Z:* hinny.
barème [barɛm] *n.m.* **1.** ready reckoner. **2.** (*a*) scale (of marks, of salaries); (*b*) (printed) table, schedule (of prices, etc.); (price) list.
barge [barʒ] *n.f.* **1.** barge, lighter. **2.** (rectangular) haystack.

baril [bari(l)] *n.m.* (*a*) barrel, keg, cask; (*b*) *Meas: Petr:* barrel (42 gallons).
barillet [barijɛ] *n.m.* **1.** small barrel, keg, cask. **2.** barrel piston chamber (of pump); cylinder (of revolver); *Clockm: etc:* **b. (de ressort),** spring box, spring drum.
barilleur [barijœr] *n.m.* cooper.
bariolage [barjɔlaʒ] *n.m.* (*a*) painting, daubing, with different colours; (*b*) medley, splashes (of colours); gaudy colour scheme; variegation; *Mil: etc:* (*camouflage*) disruptive painting.
bariolé [barjɔle] *a.* gaudy, multicoloured; splashed with colour; variegated.
barioler [barjɔle] *v.tr.* to variegate; to paint, to daub (sth.) in many colours, in gaudy colours.
bariolure [barjɔlyr] *n.f.* medley, splashes (of colours); gaudy colour scheme; variegation.
barmaid [barmɛd] *n.f.* barmaid.
barman [barman] *n.m.* barman; *pl. barmen, barmans.*
barn [barn] *n.m. Atom.Ph.Meas:* barn (10^{-24} cm^2).
barographe [barɔgraf] *n.m. Meteor:* barograph.
baromètre [barɔmɛtr̥] *n.m.* barometer; **b. anéroïde,** aneroid barometer; **b. enregistreur,** recording barometer.
barométrique [barɔmetrik] *a.* barometric.
baron [barɔ̃] *n.m.* **1.** baron; **les (hauts) barons de la finance, de l'industrie,** financial tycoons. **2.** *P:* protector (of prostitute).
baronnage [barɔnaʒ] *n.m.* **1.** baronage. **2.** barony.
baronne [barɔn] *n.f.* baroness; **bonjour madame la b.,** good morning, Lady X; (*said by servant*) good morning, your ladyship, my lady.
baronnet [barɔnɛ] *n.m.* baronet.
baronnie [barɔni] *n.f. A:* barony.
baroque [barɔk] *a.* odd, strange, bizarre (ideas, etc.); *Arch:* baroque (style).
baroud [barud] *n.m. Mil: F:* fighting; **b. d'honneur,** last-ditch battle, last stand.
baroudeur [barudœr] *n.m. Mil: F:* (keen) fighter.
barouf(le) [baruf(l̥)] *n.m. P:* noise, din, row, racket.
barque [bark] *n.f. Nau:* **1.** boat; **quelle b.!** what an old tub! **b. de pêcheur,** fishing boat, smack; **patron de b.,** skipper; **bien mener, bien conduire, sa b.,** to manage one's affairs well; to play one's cards well; **c'est lui qui mène la b.,** he's the boss. **2. trois-mâts b.,** barque.
barquette [barkɛt] *n.f.* (small) boat-shaped pastry.
barracuda [barakyda] *n.m. Ich:* barracuda.
barrage [baraʒ] *n.m.* **1.** barring, blocking (off) (of road, etc.); blocking (of harbour); damming (of valley); closing, closure (of street). **2.** (*a*) barrier, obstruction; (harbour) boom; **b. routier, de route,** roadblock; **b. de police,** police roadblock, cordon; (*b*) *Hyd.E:* **b. (de retenue),** barrage, dam; weir; (*c*) *Mil:* **b. aérien,** anti-aircraft barrage; **(tir de) barrage,** barrage (fire).
barre [bar] *n.f.* **1.** (*a*) bar, rod, rail (of metal, wood, etc.); (wooden) batten; bar (of chocolate); *F:* **c'est le coup de b.,** you've paid over the odds; it's a real rip-off, racket; (*b*) bar, barrier; *Danc:* barre; **b. d'appui,** handrail; *Gym:* **b. fixe,** horizontal bar; **barres parallèles,** parallel bars; *Aut:* **b. de connexion,** crossbar, tie rod (of steering gear); *Mch: Aut:* **b. de torsion,** torsion bar; (*c*) *Nau:* tiller (of boat); helm (of ship); **homme de b.,** man at the wheel, helmsman; **être à la b., prendre, tenir, la b.,** to be at the helm; (*d*) *Nau:* **barres de hune,** crosstrees; (*e*) *Jur:* **b. d'un tribunal,** bar of a lawcourt; **b. des témoins** = witness box, *NAm:* witness stand; **paraître à la b.,** to appear before the court, at the bar. **2.** (sand)bar (of river, harbour); (harbour) boom; **b. d'eau,** (tidal) bore; **b. de flot,** tidal wave; **b. de plage,** surf. **3.** *pl.* bars (of horse's mouth). **4.** (*a*) line, dash, stroke; **b. d'un t,** cross(bar) of a t; (*b*) *Mus:* **b. de mesure,** bar (line); **double b.,** double bar; (*c*) *Her:* bend sinister; (*d*) *Games:* **jeu de barres,** prisoners' base.
barré [bare] **1.** *a.* (*a*) obstructed; *P.N:* **route barrée,** road closed; (*b*) **chèque b.,** crossed cheque; (*c*) *Her:* bendy sinister; (*d*) *Dent:* **dent barrée,** impacted tooth; (*e*) *Row:* coxed; **un deux b.,** a coxed pair.
barreau, -eaux [baro] *n.m.* **1.** small bar, rail; rung (of ladder); stretcher (of chair); **fenêtre garnie de barreaux,** barred window; **être derrière les barreaux,** to be behind (prison) bars. **2.** *Jur:* bar; **être reçu, admis, au b.,** to be called to the bar; **rayer qn du b.,** to disbar s.o.
barrement [barmɑ̃] *n.m.* crossing (of cheque).
barrer [bare] *v.* **I.** *v.tr.* **1.** (*a*) to bar (door, etc.); *Fr.C:* to lock (window, etc.); (*b*) to bar, obstruct (the way); to dam (stream); to block, close (road); **b. le passage, la route, à qn,** (i) to block s.o.'s way; (ii) to thwart s.o. **2.** to cross (a *t*, an *A*); **b. un chèque,** to cross a cheque. **3.** to cross out, strike out (word, etc.). **4.** (*a*) *Nau:* to steer (a boat); (*b*) *Row:* to cox. **II.** *P:* **se b.,** to clear off, to beat it, to scram; **barre-toi!** get lost! push off!
barrette[1] [barɛt] *n.f. Ecc:* biretta; (cardinal's) cap.
barrette[2] *n.f.* **1.** (*a*) (small) bar, rod, stick; *Aut:* **b. (verticale),** overrider; (*b*) brooch, *NAm:* pin; **b. de médaille,** bar of medal; (*c*) (hair) slide; (shoe) strap. **2.** *Ind:* damper (of furnace).
barreur [barœr] *n.m.* **1.** *Nau:* man at the helm; helmsman. **2.** *Row:* cox; **un deux sans b.,** a coxless pair.
barricade [barikad] *n.f.* **b. (de rue),** (street) barricade; **de l'autre côté de la b.,** on the opposing side; on the other side of the fence.
barricader [barikade] *v.tr.* to barricade (street, door, etc.); **se b. dans une chambre,** (i) to barricade oneself in a room (**contre,** against); (ii) to shut, lock, oneself up in one's room (so as not to be disturbed).
barrière [barjɛr] *n.f.* **1.** barrier; fence (around a field); *Rail:* (ticket collectors') gate, barrier; gate (of level crossing); *Aut:* **b. de dégel,** barrier closing road to heavy traffic during a thaw; **b. à bascule,** drop-arm barrier; *Av:* **b. antisouffle,** blast wall; *Geog:* **b. naturelle,** natural frontier; **la Grande B.,** the Great Barrier Reef. **2.** *Hist:* gate (of town, castle, etc.); toll gate, turnpike. **3.** *Turf: etc:* starting gate. **4.** *Ph:* **b. de potentiel,** potential barrier.
barrique [barik] *n.f.* large barrel (*approx.* 200 litres); cask, butt, hogshead; *F:* **il est gros comme une b.,** he's as round as a barrel.
barrir [barir] *v.i.* (*of elephant*) to trumpet.
barrissement [barismɑ̃] *n.m.,* **barrit** [bari] *n.m.* trumpeting (of elephant).
bartavelle [bartavɛl] *n.f.* **(perdrix) b.,** rock partridge.
baryte [barit] *n.f. Ch: Miner:* baryta, barium oxide.
baryté [barite] *a. Med:* **bouillie barytée,** barium meal.
baryton [baritɔ̃] *a. & n.m. Mus:* baritone (voice).
baryum [barjɔm] *n.m. Ch: Miner:* barium.
barzoï [barzɔi] *n.m. Z:* borzoi.
bas, basse [bɑ, bɑs] **I.** *a.* **1.** low; **maison basse de toit, à toit b.,** house with a low roof; **b. sur pattes, b. sur, de, jambes,** short-legged; *Box: etc.* **coup b.,** blow below the belt; **enfant en b. âge,** infant; **avoir la vue basse,** to be short-sighted; **voix basse,** low, deep, voice; **parler à voix basse,** to whisper, to speak under one's breath; **maintenir les prix b.,** to keep prices down, low; **prix les plus b.,** rock-bottom prices; **le soleil est b.,** the sun is low; *Meteor:* **plafond b.,** low ceiling (of clouds); **mer basse,** low water, tide; **la tête basse,** with one's head down; with a hang-dog look; **le moral est très b.,** morale is very low. **2.** mean,

base, low; **motif b.,** base, mean, contemptible, motive; **terme, style, b.,** vulgar expression, style. **3.** low(er); **les basses classes,** (i) the lower classes (of society); (ii) *Sch:* the lower forms, *NAm:* grades; *Cu:* **b. morceaux,** cheap cuts (of meat); **le b. clergé,** the lower clergy; *Pol:* **la Chambre basse,** the Lower House; **la partie basse d'une ville, la basse ville,** the lower (part of a) town; **les bas quartiers,** the poor districts (of a town); **terres, régions, basses,** lowlands; **le b. Rhin,** the lower Rhine; **la basse Normandie,** Lower Normandy; *Ling:* **b. latin,** low Latin; dog Latin; **b. allemand,** low German; *Rom.Hist:* **le B.-Empire,** the Lower, Later, Byzantine, Empire; **en ce b. monde,** here below; **au b. mot,** at the lowest estimate, valuation. **II.** *adv.* **1.** low (down); **être assis trop b.,** to be sitting too low down; **quelques marches plus b.,** a few steps further down, lower down; **dix lignes plus b.,** ten lines (further) down; **les hirondelles volent b.,** the swallows are flying low; **voir plus b.,** see below; **mettre qn plus b. que terre,** to humiliate s.o.; *St.Exch:* **les cours sont tombés très b.,** shares are down; **le malade est bien b.,** the patient is very low. **2.** (*a*) **chapeaux b.!** hats off! **chapeau b.,** (i) hat in hand; (ii) I take my hat off to you; *F:* **b. les mains, les pattes!** hands off! keep your paws off! (*to dog*) **b. les pattes!** paws (down)! *Nau:* **mettre b. une voile,** to haul down a sail; **mettre pavillon b.,** (i) *Nau:* to lower, strike, the colours; (ii) *F:* to climb down; (*b*) (*of animals*) **mettre b.,** to give birth to, drop (young); (*of mare*) to foal; (*of sheep*) to lamb; (*of goat*) to kid; (*of bitch*) to pup, whelp; (*of sow*) to farrow; **mettre b. avant terme,** to cast, slip, its young; (*c*) **mettre b. les armes,** (i) *Mil:* to lay down one's arms; (ii) to give up (arguing); **mettre b. les outils,** to down tools. **3. vous chantez trop b.,** you are singing (i) in too low a key; (ii) too softly; **parler (tout) b.,** to (speak in a) whisper; **rire tout b.,** to chuckle to oneself; **entre haut et b.,** half aloud. **III.** *n.m.* **1.** lower part (of sth.); (*a*) **b. d'une échelle, d'une page,** foot, bottom, of a ladder, of a page, foot (of a hill); **l'étage du b.,** the lower storey; **b. du dos,** small of the back; **le, les, b. du navire,** the ship's bottom; *Tail:* **b. américains,** turn-ups (of trousers), *U.S:* cuffs; *Typ:* **b. de casse,** (i) lower case; (ii) small letters; **de haut en b.,** from top to bottom, from head to toe; **regarder qn de haut en b.,** to look s.o. up and down; (*b*) *adv.phr.* **en b.,** (down) below; **aller en b.,** to go down(stairs); *Nau:* **tout le monde en b.!** all hands below! **les gens d'en b.,** the people below, downstairs; **la tête en b.,** upside down; **tomber la tête en b.,** to fall head first; **ce vase s'élargit par en b.,** this vase is wider at the bottom; *prep.phr.* **en b. de, au b. de,** at the foot of, at the bottom of; **au b. de, en b. de, l'escalier,** downstairs; *adv.phr.* **à b.,** down; **mettre, jeter, à b.,** to demolish, pull down (house); to overthrow (s.o., government); **à b. X!** down with X! *prep.phr.* **tomber à b. de son cheval,** to fall off one's horse; **sauter à b. de son lit,** to jump out of bed. **2.** low state (of sth.); **b. de l'eau,** low water; **les hauts et les b.,** the ups and downs (of life, etc.). **3.** stocking; **b. à côtes,** ribbed stocking; **b. diminué, proportionné,** fully-fashioned stocking; **b. extensible,** stretch nylons; **b. filet,** fishnet, mesh, stocking; **b. fin,** sheer stocking; **b. indémaillable,** non-run stocking; *Med:* **b. à varices, b. élastique,** elastic, support, stocking. **IV. basse** *n.f.* **1.** *Mus:* (*a*) bass part; **basse chiffrée, continue, figurée,** figured bass, thorough bass, basso continuo; (*b*) bass (voice, singer); **basse chantante, basse-taille,** basso cantante, singing bass; **basse profonde, basse-contre, basse noble,** basso profundo; (*c*) (*instrument*) (i) 'cello; (ii) euphonium; *A:* **basse de hautbois,** bassoon; **basse de viole,** bass viol; (*d*) bass strings (of instrument). **2.** *Nau:* shoal, flat, sandbank.

basalte [bazalt] *n.m. Geol:* basalt.

basaltique [bazaltik] *a. Geol:* basaltic.

basané [bazane] *a.* sunburnt, (sun)tanned, weather-beaten, swarthy (complexion, etc.).

basaner [bazane] *v.tr.* to bronze, tan (face, etc.).

bas-bleu [bablø] *n.m.* bluestocking; *pl. bas-bleus.*

bas-côté [bakote] *n.m.* **1.** (side) aisle (of church). **2.** shoulder, side (of road, etc.); **défense de stationner sur les bas-côtés,** no parking on the verge.

basculant [baskylɑ̃] *a.* rocking, tilting; **wagon b.,** tip wagon; **pont b.,** drawbridge; **siège b.,** tip-up seat.

bascule [baskyl] *n.f.* **1.** rocker; bascule, scale; **mouvement de b.,** rocking motion; **(jeu de) b.,** seesaw(ing); **chaise, cheval, à b.,** rocking chair, horse; **(balance à) b.,** weighbridge, weighing machine; **b. romaine,** platform scales, (with steelyard); **wagon à b.,** tip wagon. **2.** *Elcs:* **(montage en) b.,** bistable trigger circuit, flip-flop circuit.

basculement [baskylmɑ̃] *n.m.* **1.** (*a*) rocking, swinging; seesaw(ing); (*b*) tipping (up), tilting (over). **2.** toppling, falling, over; overbalancing.

basculer [baskyle] *v.tr. & i.* **1.** (*a*) to rock, to swing; to seesaw; **levier basculé par une came,** lever rocked by a cam; (*b*) to tip (up), to tilt (over); **(faire) b. une charrette,** to tip a cart. **2.** to fall over, to overbalance; **tout a basculé,** the whole lot toppled over.

basculeur [baskylœr] *n.m.* **1.** tip(per), rocker. **2.** *El:* rocker switch.

base [bɑz] *n.f.* **1.** (*a*) lower part, foot, bottom, base (of mountain, etc.); foundation(s) (of building); **jeter, poser, les bases,** to lay the foundation; *Toil:* **b. de maquillage,** foundation cream, (makeup) base; (*b*) *Anat:* *Mth:* base (of heart, triangle, etc.); (*c*) *Surv:* base (line); (*d*) *Mec.E:* base plate (of machine). **2.** *Mil:* *etc:* base (of operations); **b. de ravitaillement,** supply base; **b. aérienne, navale,** air, naval, base; **b. de lancement (d'engins),** (missile) launching site. **3.** (*a*) basis, foundation; grounds (of suspicion, etc.); **être à la b. de qch.,** to be at the root, the source, of sth.; **argument qui pèche par la b.,** fundamentally unsound argument; **sans b.,** without foundation; **vocabulaire, l'anglais, de b.,** basic vocabulary, English; **traitement de b.,** basic salary; **produits à b. d'amidon,** starch products; **boisson à b. de gin,** = gin cocktail; *Cmptr:* **b. de temps,** time base; **documents, données, de b.,** source documents, data; (*b*) *Pol:* *etc:* **la b.,** the rank and file, the grassroots (of a trade union, etc.). **4.** *Mth:* base, radix (of system of notation); radix, root, basis (of logarithm). **5.** *Ch:* base. **6.** *Elcs:* base (electrode) (of transistor).

base-ball [bɛzbol] *n.m.* baseball.

baseballeur [bɛzbɔlœr] *n.m. Sp:* baseball player.

baser [bɑze] **1.** *v.tr.* to base, ground, found (opinion, etc.) **(sur,** on); **avions américains basés en Grande-Bretagne,** American aircraft based in Great Britain. **2. se b. sur qch.,** to base one's argument on sth.

bas-fond [bafɔ̃] *n.m.* **1.** low ground, hollow; swamp; flat; **les b.-fonds de la société,** the dregs of society; **les b.-fonds du journalisme,** the gutter press. **2.** shallow, shoal (in sea, river); *pl. bas-fonds.*

basilic[1] [bazilik] *n.m. Bot:* basil.

basilic[2] *n.m. Myth:* *Rept:* basilisk; **regarder qn d'un œil de b.,** to give s.o. a withering look.

basilical, -aux [bazilikal, -o] *a. Arch:* basilical.

basilique[1] [bazilik] *a. & n.f. Anat:* basilic (vein).

basilique[2] *n.f. Arch:* basilica.

basin [bazɛ̃] *n.m. Tex:* cotton damask.

basique [bɑzik] *a.* **1.** *Ch:* *Metall:* basic (salt, process, etc.); **scorie b.,** basic slag. **2.** basic (facts, etc.).

basket(-ball) [baskɛt(bɔl)] *n.m.* basketball.

basketteur, -euse [baskɛtœr, -øz] *n.* basketball player.

bas-mât [bɑmɑ] *n.m. Nau:* lower mast; *pl. bas-mâts.*

basquais, -aise [baskɛ, -ɛz] **1.** *a.* Basque; *Cu:* **poulet (à la) basquaise,** Basque chicken (cooked with onion, tomato, etc.). **2.** *n.f.* **Basquaise,** Basque (woman).

basque¹ [bask] **1.** *a. & n.* Basque; **le Pays b.,** the Basque country. **2.** *n.m. Ling:* Basque.

basque² *n.f.* (*a*) skirt, tail (of jacket, etc.); **être toujours pendu aux basques de qn.,** to be always at s.o.'s heels; (*b*) **soutien-gorge à b.,** long-line brassière.

bas-relief [bɑrəljɛf] *n.m. Arch: etc:* bas relief, low relief; *pl. bas-reliefs.*

basse. *see* BAS.

basse-cour [bɑskur] *n.f.* (*a*) farmyard; (*b*) poultry, fowl; *pl. basses-cours.*

basse-fosse [bɑsfos] *n.f.* dungeon; **cul de b.-f.,** deepest dungeon, oubliette; *pl. basses-fosses.*

bassesse [bɑsɛs] *n.f.* **1.** baseness, lowness (of birth, expression, action, etc.); degradation. **2.** low, mean, contemptible, action; **homme prêt à toutes les bassesses,** man who would stoop to anything.

basset¹ [bɑsɛ] *n.m.* basset (hound); **b. allemand,** dachshund.

basset² *n.m. Mus:* **cor de b.,** tenor clarinet in F, basset horn.

basse-taille [bɑstɑj] *n.f. Mus:* basso cantante; singing bass; *pl. basses-tailles.*

bassin [basɛ̃] *n.m.* **1.** basin, bowl, pan; pan (of scale); *Med:* **b. (de lit),** bedpan. **2.** (*a*) ornamental lake; pond, pool; basin (of a fountain); (*b*) *Hyd.E:* reservoir, tank; **b. filtrant,** filter bed. **3.** dock, basin (of port); **b. à flot,** wet dock; **b. à marée,** tidal dock, basin; **b. de radoub,** dry dock, graving dock; **entrer au b.,** to dock. **4.** (*a*) *Geol:* basin; *Oc:* depression; **le b. parisien,** the Paris basin; (*b*) (river) basin; **b. de réception,** catchment area.; **le b. de la Tamise,** the Thames basin; (*c*) **b. houiller,** coal basin. **5.** *Anat:* pelvis.

bassinant [basinɑ̃] *a. P:* boring.

bassine [basin] *n.f.* pan, vat; **b. à confitures,** preserving pan; **b. à vaisselle,** washing-up bowl, basin.

bassiner [basine] *v.tr.* **1.** to bathe (wound, etc.). **2.** *A:* **b. un lit,** to warm a bed (with a warming pan). **3.** *P:* to bore, annoy, plague (s.o.).

bassinet [basinɛ] *n.m.* **1.** *Arm:* basinet, basnet. **2.** *Anat:* pelvis (of the kidney).

bassinoire [basinwar] *n.f.* **1.** warming pan. **2.** *P:* (*pers.*) bore; pain (in the neck).

bassiste [bɑsist] *n.m. & f. Mus.* **1.** (double) bass player. **2.** tuba player.

basson [bɑsɔ̃] *n.m. Mus:* **1.** bassoon. **2.** bassoonist.

bassoniste [bɑsɔnist] *n.* bassoonist.

bastide [bastid] *n.f.* **1.** *Hist:* fortified town (in S. Fr.); fortification. **2.** *Dial:* (*S. of Fr.*) (small) country house, farm.

bastille [bastij] *n.f.* fortress; *Hist:* **la B.,** the Bastille.

bastingage [bastɛ̃gaʒ] *n.m. Nau:* **1.** *A:* hammock netting. **2.** (*a*) bulwark, topside; (*b*) (hand)rail; **accoudé aux bastingages,** leaning over the rails.

bastion [bastjɔ̃] *n.m.* (*a*) *Fort:* bastion; (*b*) bastion, bulwark, stronghold (of liberty, etc.).

bastonnade [bastɔnad] *n.f.* **1.** *A:* beating (with a stick). **2.** bastinado.

bastos [bastɔs] *n.m. P:* bullet, slug.

bastringue [bastrɛ̃g] *n.m. F:* **1.** (*a*) (cheap) dance hall; (*b*) (dance) band; (*c*) noise, din, racket. **2.** luggage; kit, gear; paraphernalia.

bas-ventre [bɑvɑ̃tr] *n.m.* lower abdomen; *pl. bas-ventres.*

bât [bɑ] *n.m.* pack(saddle); **cheval de b.,** packhorse; **c'est là que le b. (le) blesse,** that's his weak point.

bataclan [bataklɑ̃] *n.m. F:* belongings, kit, gear, paraphernalia; **et tout le b.,** and all the rest of it, and so on; **vendez tout le b.!** sell the whole lot.

bataille [batɑj] *n.f.* **1.** battle, fight; **b. terrestre, aérienne, navale,** land, air, naval, battle; **b. de vaincu,** losing battle; **le fort de la b.,** the thick, the brunt of the fight, battle; **champ de b.,** battlefield; **livrer b. à,** to give battle to, to join battle with; **la b. contre l'inflation,** the battle, the fight, against inflation; **en b.,** (i) in battle order, formation; (ii) *A:* in battle array. **2.** (*a*) **il portait son chapeau en b.,** his hat was all crooked, cockeyed; (*b*) **cheveux en b.,** dishevelled hair. **3.** *Cards:* beggar-my-neighbour.

batailler [bataje] *v.i.* to fight; to battle; **il est toujours prêt à b.,** he's always spoiling for a fight; *F:* **j'ai dû b. pendant une heure pour ouvrir la porte,** I had to battle for an hour to open the door.

batailleur, -euse [batajœr, -øz] **1.** *a.* quarrelsome, pugnacious, aggressive. **2.** *n.* fighter; battler.

bataillon [batajɔ̃] *n.m.* (*a*) *Mil:* battalion; **commandant de b.,** battalion commander; **b. d'Afrique,** French disciplinary battalion (formerly stationed in North Africa); (*b*) **elle a un b. d'enfants,** she has a whole swarm, army, of children.

bâtard, -arde [bɑtar, -ard] *a. & n.* (*a*) **(enfant) b., bâtarde,** bastard (child), illegitimate (child); (*b*) bastard, hybrid, counterfeit (product, etc.); **(chien) b.,** mongrel; **(écriture) bâtarde,** bastard hand(writing); *Typ:* **format b.,** bastard size.

batardeau, -eaux [batardo] *n.m.* **1.** *Fort: etc:* batardeau. **2.** *Hyd.E:* coffer(dam), caisson.

bâtardise [bɑtardiz] *n.f.* illegitimacy; bastardy.

bateau, -eaux [bato] *n.m.* (*a*) boat; (merchant) vessel, craft; **b. à voiles,** sailing boat; **b. à vapeur,** steamboat, steamer; **b. à moteur,** motor boat, motor launch; **b. à rames,** rowing boat; **b. de plaisance,** pleasure boat; **b. de pêche,** fishing boat, smack; **b. de sauvetage,** lifeboat; **b. de guerre,** warship, battleship; **faire du b. à voiles, à rames,** to go sailing, rowing; *Rail:* **le train du b.,** the boat train; **je suis venu en, par, b.,** I came by boat; *F:* **monter un b. à qn,** to have s.o. on, pull s.o.'s leg; (*b*) *Cost:* **encolure b.,** boat neck, scoop neck (of dress, etc.); (*c*) entrance (to garage, drive, etc., where pavement slopes down).

bateau-citerne [batositɛrn] *n.m.* tanker; *pl. bateaux-citernes.*

bateau-feu [batofø] *n.m. Nau:* lightship, light vessel; *pl. bateaux-feux.*

bateau-lavoir [batolavwar] *n.m. A:* (*boat*) wash-house (on the Seine); *pl. bateaux-lavoirs.*

bateau-mouche [batomuʃ] *n.m.* river boat (in Paris, etc.); water bus; *pl. bateaux-mouches.*

bateau-phare [batofar] *n.m.* lightship, light vessel; *pl. bateaux-phares.*

bateau-pompe [batopɔ̃p] *n.m.* fire boat; *pl. bateaux-pompes.*

batelage¹ [batlaʒ] *n.m. Nau:* **(frais de) b.,** lighterage, waterage (charges).

batelage² *n.m.* juggling, tumbling; acrobatics.

bateler [batle] *v.i.* **(je batelle, n. batelons, je batellerai)** to juggle, to tumble; to do trick, acrobatics.

bateleur, -euse [batlœr, -øz] *n.* (*a*) *A:* juggler, tumbler; acrobat; (*b*) *Pej:* **quel b.!** what a buffoon!

batelier, -ière [batəlje, -jɛr] *n.* boatman, boat woman; waterman; ferryman, -woman; **b. de chaland,** bargeman, bargee, lighterman.

batellerie [batɛlri] *n.f.* **1.** inland water transport. **2.** *coll:* small (river, canal) craft.

bat-flanc [baflɑ̃] *n.m.inv.* (*a*) swinging bail (of horse stall); (*b*) wooden partition (in a dormitory).

bath [bat] *a.inv. P:* super, fantastic, stupendous; **t'es b.,** you're really great.

bathyal, -aux [batjal, -o] *a. Oc:* bathyal.

bathymètre [batimɛtr̥] *n.m. Oc:* bathometer, bathymeter.
bathymétrie [batimetri] *n.f. Oc:* bathymetry.
bathyscaphe [batiskaf] *n.m.* bathyscaph(e).
bathysphère [batisfɛr] *n.f.* bathysphere.
bâti [bɑti] *n.m.* **1.** frame(work), structure, support, stand; **b. de fenêtre,** window frame; **b. moteur,** engine mounting. **2.** *Needlew:* tacking, basting.
batifolage [batifɔlaʒ] *n.m. F:* **1.** romping; larking, playing, about, around. **2.** flirting.
batifoler [batifɔle] *v.i. F:* to romp; to lark, play about, around.
batillage [batijaʒ] *n.m.* wake (of boat).
bâtiment [bɑtimɑ̃] *n.m.* **1. (l'industrie du) b.,** (the) building (trade); **il est du b.,** (i) he's in the same line of business; (ii) he's one of us. **2.** building; **bâtiments de ferme,** farm buildings; **usine en trois corps de b.,** factory in three main buildings. **3.** ship, vessel; **b. de guerre,** warship, battleship.
bâtiment-école [bɑtimɑ̃ekɔl] *n.m. Nau:* training ship; *pl. bâtiments-écoles.*
bâtir [bɑtir] *v.tr.* **1.** to build; to construct; **b. une maison,** to build a house; **(se) faire b. une maison,** to have a house built; **terrain à b.,** building land, site; **b. une fortune,** to build up a fortune; **b. sur le sable,** to build on sand; **b. une théorie,** to develop a theory; **homme bien bâti,** well built man; **homme bâti comme moi,** a man of my build. **2.** *Needlew:* to tack, baste; **coton à b.,** tacking thread.
bâtisse [bɑtis] *n.f.* (*a*) masonry, bricks and mortar; (*b*) large building; **ce n'est qu'une grande b.,** it's a great (ugly) barracks of a place.
bâtisseur, -euse [bɑtisœr, -øz] *n.* builder.
batiste [batist] *n.f. Tex:* batiste, lawn, cambric.
bâton [bɑtɔ̃] *n.m.* **1.** (*a*) stick, staff, rod; **b. ferré,** iron-shod pole, alpenstock; **b. (d'agent de police),** truncheon; **bâtons de ski,** ski sticks; *Toil:* **b. d'oranger,** orange stick; **b. d'une chaise,** rung, stretcher, of a chair; *F:* **vie de b. de chaise,** fast living; **b. de vieillesse,** support, prop, of old age; **donner des coups de b. à qn,** to beat s.o.; **mettre des bâtons dans les roues,** to put a spoke in s.o.'s wheel; to throw a spanner in the works; (*b*) *Arch:* **bâtons rompus,** zigzag moulding; **travailler à bâtons rompus,** to work by fits and starts; **conversation à bâtons rompus,** desultory, rambling, conversation; (*c*) staff, pole; **b. d'une croix,** staff of a cross; **b. de pavillon,** flagstaff, flagpole; (*d*) (*wand of office*) **b. pastoral,** pastoral staff, crozier; **b. de maréchal,** field-marshal's baton; **b. de chef d'orchestre,** conductor's baton; **b. de magicien,** conjurer's wand; **tour de b.,** (i) conjuring trick; (ii) illicit gains, pickings, perks. **2.** stick, roll; **b. de rouge (à lèvres),** lipstick. **3.** stroke (of the pen, etc.); **apprendre à un enfant à faire des bâtons,** to teach a child to write; *Typ:* **capitale b.,** block letter.
bâtonner [bɑtɔne] *v.tr.* to beat, cudgel, cane.
bâtonnet [bɑtɔnɛ] *n.m.* **1.** small stick; **b. de dynamite,** stick of dynamite; *Toil:* **b. (d'oranger),** orange stick. **2.** (*a*) *Biol:* rod bacterium; (*b*) *Anat:* (i) rodlike cell; (ii) *pl.* rods (of retina).
bâtonnier [bɑtɔnje] *n.m.* leader, president, of the barristers (attached to a French lawcourt).
batracien [batrasjɛ̃] *n.m. Z:* batrachian.
battage [bataʒ] *n.m.* **1.** (*a*) beating (of carpet, etc.); churning (of butter); threshing (of corn); **b. d'or,** gold beating; **b. des pieux,** pile driving; (*b*) field of fire (of gun). **2.** *F:* blatant publicity (campaign), promotion (of a product, a person); hard sell (technique).
battant [batɑ̃] **I.** *a.* (*a*) beating; **pluie battante,** driving, pelting, rain; downpour; **porte battante,** (i) banging door; (ii) swing door, self-closing door; **le cœur b.,** with a pounding heart; **tambour b.,** with drums beating; **mener qn tambour b.,** to treat s.o. high-handedly; **mener les choses tambour b.,** to hurry, to hustle things on; **(tout) b. neuf,** brand new; (*b*) striking; **à onze heures b., battantes,** on the stroke of eleven. **II.** *n.m.* **1.** (*a*) clapper, tongue (of bell); (*b*) lift (of latch); (*c*) *Nau:* fly (of flag); slab (of sail); (*d*) *Tex:* batten, lathe, lay (of loom). **2.** (*a*) leaf, flap (of table, counter, etc.); leaf (of door, shutter); **porte à deux battants,** double door, folding doors; **ouvrir les portes à deux battants,** to fling the gates wide open; (*b*) door (of cupboard, etc.). **3.** (*pers.*) *Sp: etc:* fighter, battler; trier, goer.
batte [bat] *n.f.* **1.** beating; **b. de l'or,** gold beating. **2.** (*a*) beater, mallet; rammer; (*b*) (cricket) bat.
battée [bate] *n.f.* jamb (of door, window).
battellement [batɛlmɑ̃] *n.m. Const:* eaves.
battement [batmɑ̃] *n.m.* **1.** (*a*) beat(ing) (of drum); stamp(ing), tap(ping) (of feet); clapping (of hands); flutter(ing) (of wings, of eyelids); flapping (of sails); banging (of door); rattling (of shutters); **b. de paupières,** blink(ing); **regarder qn avec un b. de paupières,** to blink at s.o.; (*b*) beat(ing), throb(bing), pulsation; **chaque b. de cœur,** every heartbeat; **avoir des battements de cœur,** (i) to suffer from palpitations; (ii) to be in a flutter; (*c*) swing(ing) (of pendulum); tick-tock (of clock); *Danc:* high kick; (*d*) *Cards:* shuffling; (*e*) *Ph:* (i) beating, pulsation (of oscillations); (ii) (interference) beat. **2.** interval (between two events, etc.); **deux heures de b.,** two clear hours (before starting); **b. de vingt minutes entre les deux trains,** twenty minutes' wait between the two trains. **3.** shutter catch (on window).
batterie [batri] *n.f.* **1.** *Mus:* (*a*) beat (of drum); roll (on side-drum); (*b*) quick succession of notes; broken chords; (*c*) percussion instruments, drums; drum kit; **il joue de la b.,** he plays the drums. **2.** *Artil:* (*a*) (*number of guns*) battery; **b. antiaérienne,** anti-aircraft battery; **pièces en b.,** guns in firing position, in action; **en b.!** action! (*b*) (*unit*) troop; *NAm:* battery; **b. d'instruction,** training battery. **3.** (*a*) set, collection; **b. de chaudières, de fours à coke,** battery, range, bank, of boilers, of coke ovens; **b. de projecteurs,** bank of spotlights; **b. de cuisine,** (i) (set of) kitchen utensils; (ii) *P:* one's whole set of medals, all one's gongs; (*b*) *Husb:* battery (for raising chicks); **poulet de b.,** battery hen; (*c*) **b. électrique,** electric battery; **b. de rechange,** refill (for torch, etc.).
batteur, -euse [batœr, -øz] *n.* **1.** *n.m.* (*pers.*) (*a*) **b. d'or,** gold beater; **b. en grange,** thresher; (*b*) *Ven:* beater; (*c*) *F:* **b. de pavé,** loafer, idler; (*d*) *Cr:* batsman; (*baseball*) batter, striker; (*e*) *Mus:* drummer (in pop group, etc.). **2.** *n.m.* (*device*) (*a*) *Dom.Ec:* **b. à œufs,** egg beater, whisk; (*b*) *Agr:* beater drum (of threshing machine); (*c*) **b. de coton,** cotton breaker, shaker. **3.** *n.f.* (*a*) *Agr:* threshing machine, thresher; (*b*) *Metalw:* beater.
battoir [batwar] *n.m.* (*a*) (carpet) beater; (*b*) washerwoman's beetle; (*c*) *F:* (large) hand.
battre [batr̥] *v.* (*pr.p.* **battant,** *p.p.* **battu,** *pr.ind.* **je bats** [ba], **tu bats, il bat, n. battons, ils battent;** *p.h.* **je battis,** *fu.* **je battrai**) to beat. **1.** *v.tr.* (*a*) to beat, thrash, flog, s.o.; **b. qn à coups de poings, avec une canne,** to punch, to cane, s.o.; **b. qn comme plâtre,** to beat the living daylights out of s.o.; **b. un tapis,** to beat a carpet; **b. le tambour,** to beat the drum; **b. du blé,** to thresh wheat; **b. le beurre,** to churn butter; **battez-moi ces œufs,** beat these eggs (up) for me; (*b*) **b. le fer (avec un marteau),** to hammer iron; **b. le fer à froid,** to cold-hammer iron; *Prov:* **b. le fer pendant qu'il est chaud,** to strike while the iron is hot; *Mil:* **b. une position,** to fire on a position; (*c*) to beat, defeat (s.o.); **battre qn à plate(s) couture(s),** to beat, lick, s.o. hollow; (*d*) **b. la campagne,** (i) to scour, comb,

the countryside; (ii) to be delirious; *Ven:* **b. un bois, les buissons,** to beat a wood, the bushes; (*e*) *Nau:* **b. un pavillon,** to fly a flag; (*f*) **b. les cartes,** (i) *Cards:* to shuffle, (ii) *Cmptr:* to joggle, the cards. **2.** *v.tr. & i.* (*a*) **b. la mesure,** to beat time; **la montre bat,** the watch is ticking; (*b*) **b. le réveil,** to beat, sound, the reveille; **le cœur lui battait,** his heart was beating; **la nouvelle nous fit b. le cœur,** we were thrilled at the news; (*c*) **la pluie bat (contre) les carreaux,** the rain beats, lashes, against the windowpanes; **la mer bat les rochers,** the sea breaks against the rocks; **île battue par les flots,** island washed by the waves; **battu par les vagues,** buffeted by the waves; **porte qui bat,** banging door; **voile qui bat dans le vent,** sail flapping in the wind; **le vent faisait b. les volets,** the shutters were banging, rattling, in the wind; (*d*) **b. des mains,** to clap one's hands, to applaud; **b. du pied,** (i) to stamp one's foot; (ii) to tap (with) one's foot; **b. des paupières,** to blink; (*e*) *Rel:* **b. sa coulpe,** to beat one's breast (in penitence). **3. se b.,** to fight; **se b. avec, contre, qn,** to fight, to argue, (with, against) s.o.; **se b. en duel,** fight a duel; **il se bat avec ses devoirs,** he's struggling with his prep, homework.

battu [baty] *a.* **1.** (*a*) beaten; **enfant b., femme battue,** battered baby, wife; **avoir l'air d'un chien b.,** to look cowed; to have a hangdog look; **avoir les yeux battus,** to have rings, circles, round one's eyes; (*b*) **armée battue,** defeated army. **2.** *Metalw:* **fer b.,** wrought iron; **or b.,** beaten gold. **3. chemin b.,** trodden path; **suivre les sentiers battus, le chemin b.,** to follow the beaten track.

battue [baty] *n.f. Ven:* battue, beat.

batture [batyr] *n.f. Fr.C:* sandbank.

bau, -aux [bo] *n.m. N.Arch:* beam; **maître b.,** midship beam.

baud [bo] *n.m. Telecom. Meas:* baud.

baudet [bodɛ] *n.m.* **1.** (i) (he-)ass, donkey; (ii) stallion (ass). **2.** *Carp:* (sawyer's) trestle, sawpit horse.

baudrier [bodrije] *n.m.* crossbelt, shoulder belt; *Astr:* **le B. d'Orion,** Orion's belt.

bauge [boʒ] *n.f.* **1.** (*a*) lair, wallow (of wild boar); (*b*) *F:* **c'est une vraie b.,** it's a real pigsty. **2.** *Const:* clay and straw mortar.

baume [bom] *n.m.* **1.** (*a*) balm, balsam; **b. de, du, Canada,** Canada balsam; *Pharm:* **b. de benjoin,** friar's balsam; (*b*) *Lit:* balm, consolation; **mettre du b. dans le cœur de qn,** to console s.o. **2.** *Bot:* **b. sauvage, des champs,** wild mint; **b. vert,** garden mint, spearmint.

baumier [bomje] *n.m. Bot:* balsam (tree).

baux[1,2] *see* BAIL, BAU.

bauxite [boksit] *n.f. Miner:* bauxite.

bavard, -arde [bavar, -ard] **1.** *a.* (*a*) talkative; garrulous; *NAm:* gabby; **il est b. comme une pie,** he'd talk the hind leg off a donkey; (*b*) indiscreet, gossiping. **2.** *n.* (*a*) chatterbox; (*b*) gossip, *F:* blabbermouth.

bavardage [bavardaʒ] *n.m.* (*a*) chattering, nattering; gossiping; (*b*) chatter, natter; gossip; tittle-tattle.

bavarder [bavarde] *v.i.* (*a*) to chatter, natter; (*b*) to gossip; to blab, to tell tales.

bavarois, -oise [bavarwa, -waz] *a. & n. Geog:* Bavarian.

bave [bav] *n.f.* (*a*) slaver, dribble; slobber (of dog); slime (of snail); froth, foam (of horse, of mad dog); spittle (of toad); (*b*) spiteful talk, mudslinging.

baver [bave] *v.i.* (*a*) to dribble; to slobber; to foam at the mouth; (*b*) *P:* **en b.,** (i) to be taken aback, struck all of a heap; (ii) to have a rough time of it; (*c*) (*of pen*) to run; (*of ink*) to smudge.

bavette [bavɛt] *n.f.* **1.** (*a*) (baby's) bib, feeder; (*b*) bib (of overalls, etc.). **2.** *Cu:* **b. d'aloyau,** undercut of the sirloin.

baveux, -euse [bavø, -øz] *a.* dribbling, slobbery (mouth); **omelette baveuse,** moist, runny, omelette; **plaie baveuse,** weeping wound; *Typ:* **lettres baveuses,** blurred, smeared letters.

Bavière [bavjɛr] *Pr.n.f. Geog:* Bavaria.

bavocher [bavɔʃe] *v.i. Typ: etc:* to blur; to smear; to mackle.

bavochure [bavɔʃyr] *n.f.* blur, smear; *Typ:* mackle.

bavoir [bavwar] *n.m.* (baby's) bib.

bavure [bavyr] *n.f.* **1.** *Metall:* burr, wire edge (of casting, etc.); barb (of metal); **2.** (*a*) smudge, smear; *Typ:* mackle; **sans bavure(s),** (i) faultlessly, faultless; (ii) impeccably, impeccable; (*b*) slip-up, mistake.

bayer [baje] *v.i.* **(je baye, baie, n. bayons; je bayerai, baierai) b. aux corneilles,** to stand stargazing.

bazar [bazar] *n.m.* **1.** (oriental) bazaar. **2.** (*a*) general shop, store; **de b.,** (of) poor quality; shoddy; (*b*) *F:* untidy room, etc.; **quel b.!** what a shambles! (*c*) *F:* **tout son b.,** all one's things, gear; **et tout le b.,** and all the rest of it; and the whole caboodle.

bazarder [bazarde] *v.tr. F:* to get rid of (sth.); to chuck (sth.) out; to flog, to sell off (sth.).

bazooka [bazuka] *n.m. Artil:* bazooka.

bé [be] *n.m.* (the letter) b.

bê [bɛ] *onomat:* baa.

beagle [bigl̩] *n.m.* beagle.

béant [beɑ̃] *a.* (wide) open; gaping (wound); yawning (chasm); **regarder qch. bouche béante,** to stare open-mouthed at sth.; **les yeux béants,** wide-eyed.

béat, -ate [bea, -at] *a.* (*a*) *Ecc:* blessed; (*b*) self-satisfied, smug; **sourire b.,** self-satisfied smile.

béatification [beatifikasjɔ̃] *n.f.* beatification (of martyr, etc.).

béatifier [beatifje] *v.tr.* (*pr.sub. & impf.*) **n. béatifiions, v. béatifiiez)** *Ecc:* to beatify (s.o.).

béatifique [beatifik] *a.* beatific (vision).

béatitude [beatityd] *n.f.* **1.** *Ecc:* (*a*) beatitude; (*b*) **les (huit) béatitudes,** the Beatitudes. **2.** bliss.

beatnik [bitnik] *n.m. & f.* beatnik.

beau [bo] **bel** [bɛl] *f.* **belle** [bɛl] *pl.* **beaux** [bo] **belles.** (*The form* **bel** *is used* (i) *before m.sg. n. beginning with a vowel or a mute* **h;** (ii) *in the expression* **bel et bien;** (iii) *in* **Charles le Bel** *and* **Philippe le Bel;** (iv) *occ. as in* **un bel et charmant enfant.) I.** *a.* **1.** beautiful, handsome, good-looking; lovely; **un bel homme,** a handsome, good-looking, man; **une belle femme,** a beautiful woman; **le b. sexe,** the fair sex; **de beaux arbres,** beautiful, fine, trees; **la mer est belle,** the sea is (i) beautiful, (ii) calm; *Hist:* **Philippe le Bel,** Philip the Fair. **2.** fine; (*a*) **de beaux sentiments,** fine, noble, feelings; **belle action,** fine deed; **une belle vie,** a full life; **trouver une belle mort,** to die a glorious death; **cela n'est pas b. de votre part,** that was unworthy of you; *F:* **ce n'est pas b. de parler la bouche pleine,** it's not polite to speak with your mouth full; (*b*) **b. danseur,** excellent dancer; *Prov:* **les beaux esprits se recontrent,** great minds think alike; **c'est un b. parleur,** (i) he's a good speaker, (ii) he's got a smooth tongue; (iii) he's got the gift of the gab; **un b. talent,** a promising, talented, gifted, artist, writer, etc.; **un bel âge,** a ripe old age; **belle santé,** good health; **belle occasion,** good, fine, opportunity; **il a une belle situation,** he has an excellent job; **belle fortune,** large, handsome, tidy, comfortable, fortune; **b. poulet,** good-sized, sizeable, chicken; **c'est trop b. pour être vrai,** it's too good to be true; **ce serait trop b.!** that would be too much (to hope for)! *Cards:* **avoir (un) b. jeu,** to have a good hand, good cards; **il est b. joueur,** he's a good loser; **voir tout du b. côté,** to see the bright, sunny, side of everything; (*c*) smart, spruce; **un b. monsieur,** a smartly, dressed man; **le b. monde,** society, the fashionable set; **se faire b.,** to smarten oneself up, **vous voilà b.!** you *do* look smart! (*d*) **b. temps,** fine, beautiful, weather; **ami des beaux jours,** fairweather friend; **un (de ces) beau(x), jour(s),** one (of these) fine day(s); (*e*) *Iron:* **le bel avantage, ma foi!** well, that's a great advantage! **tout cela est fort b. mais . . .,** that's all very fine, well, but . . .; **vous avez fait du b. travail!** you *have* done well! *F:* **il en dit de belles,** he really comes out with them!; **j'en ai entendu de belles sur votre compte,** I've heard some nice things about you! **vous en avez fait une belle!** you *have* put your foot in it! (*f*) (*intensive*) **j'ai eu une belle peur,** I had an awful fright! **au b. milieu de la rue,** right in the middle of the road; **il y a beau temps qu'il est parti,** it's a long time, ages, since he went away; **une belle congestion pulmonaire,** a bad attack of pneumonia; **belle correction,** good thrashing; **b. tapage,** terrific din, racket; **un b. gâchis,** a fine mess; **son bras n'est pas b. à voir, est dans un bel état,** his arm is in an awful state; *P:* **un b. salaud,** a real, regular, bastard. **3.** *adv.phrs.* **bel et bien,** entirely, well and truly; **il est bel et bien venu,** he really did come; **vous voilà bel et bien grand-père!** so you've actually become a grandfather! *O:* **tout b.!** steady (on)! gently! **de plus belle,** all the more; (even) more, worse, than ever; **il recommença de plus belle,** he began again harder, worse, than ever. **4.** *v.phrs.* (*a*) **l'échapper belle,** to have a narrow escape, a close shave; (*b*) **il ferait b. voir cela,** that would be a fine thing to see; (*c*) **avoir b. faire qch.,** to do sth. in vain; **j'avais b. chercher, je ne trouvais rien,** however hard I looked, I found nothing; **vous avez b. parler,** you can talk until you're blue in the face. **II. beau, belle,** *n.* **1.** (*a*) **une belle,** a beauty, a beautiful woman; **la Belle et la Bête,** Beauty and the Beast; **la Belle au bois dormant,** the Sleeping Beauty; (*b*) *A:* **un b.,** a dandy, a beau, *NAm:* a buck; **un vieux b.,** an old roué; (*of dog*) **faire le b.,** to sit up and beg. **2.** *n.m.* (*a*) **le b.,** the beautiful; **l'amour du b.,** love of beauty; (*b*) **le b. de l'histoire c'est que . . .,** the best part of the story is that . . .; *F:* **c'est du b.!** that was very clever, wasn't it? (*c*) fine weather; **le temps est au b. (fixe),** the weather is fine, is set fair; (*d*) **n'acheter que du b.,** to buy the best only. **3.** *n.f.* (*a*) **jouer, faire, la belle,** to play (i) the deciding game, (ii) *Cards:* the rubber game; (*b*) *Nau:* waist (of ship); **en belle,** abeam; (*c*) **se faire la belle,** to escape; to break out (of prison).

beaucoup [boku] **1.** *n.m.inv.* (*a*) much, a great deal, a lot; **il reste encore b. à faire,** there's still a lot to do; **c'est déjà b. s'il veut bien, qu'il veuille bien, vous parler,** it's (quite) something that he condescended to speak to you; (*b*) (a great) many, a lot; **b. pensent que . . .,** many people think that . . .; **b. de,** much; (a great) many; a great deal of, a lot of; **avoir b. d'argent,** to have plenty, a lot, of money; **avec b. de soin,** very carefully; **il y est pour b.,** he has had a great deal to do with it; **b. d'entre nous, d'entre vous,** many of us, of you; (*c*) *adv.phr.* **de b.,** much, by far, by a great deal; **c'est de b. le meilleur,** it's far and away the best; it's the best by a long chalk; **il s'en faut de b. que je sois riche,** I'm far from being rich. **2.** *adv.* much; **il vous aime b.,** he is very fond of you; **elle parle b.,** she talks a lot; **elle parle b. trop,** she talks far too much; **il est b. plus âgé que sa femme,** he is much older than his wife; **il a b. voyagé,** he has travelled a great deal.

beau-fils [bofis] *n.m.* **1.** son-in-law. **2.** stepson; *pl. beaux-fils.*

beau-frère [bofrɛr] *n.m.* brother-in-law; *pl. beaux-frères.*

beau-père [bopɛr] *n.m.* **1.** father-in-law. **2.** stepfather; *pl. beaux-pères.*

beaupré [bopre] *n.m. Nau:* bowsprit.

beauté [bote] *n.f.* **1.** beauty; **être dans toute sa b.,** to be in the flower of one's beauty; **être en b.,** to be looking one's best; *F:* **finir en b.,** to end with a flourish, in a blaze of glory; **grain de b.,** beauty spot, mole; **des bijoux de toute b.,** magnificent jewels; **institut de b.,** beauty parlour; **produits de b.,** beauty preparations, cosmetics; *F:* **se (re)faire une b.,** to put one's makeup on. **2.** beauty, beautiful woman. **3. les beautés artistiques de l'Italie,** the art treasures of Italy; **les beautés touristiques,** the sights.

beaux-arts [bozar] *n.m.pl.* fine arts; **école des b.-a.,** *F:* **les B.-A.,** art school (of university standing).

beaux-parents [boparɑ̃] *n.m.pl.* parents-in-law, *F:* in-laws.

bébé [bebe] *n.m.* **1.** baby; **faire le b.,** to behave childishly, like a baby. **2.** *Com:* (baby) doll. **3.** *attrib.* **b. gazelle, lapin,** baby gazelle, rabbit.

bébé-éprouvette [bebeepruvɛt] *n.m.* test-tube baby; *pl. bébés-éprouvette.*

bébête [bebɛt] *a. F:* silly, babyish; **rire b.,** giggle.

bec [bɛk] *n.m.* **1.** (*a*) beak, bill (of bird); **au b. long, court, jaune,** long-, short-, yellow-billed; **coup de b.,** peck; **donner un coup de b. à qn,** (i) to peck s.o.; (ii) *F:* to have a dig at s.o.; **l'oiseau se fait le bec,** the bird is sharpening its beak; (*b*) snout, beak (of certain fishes, etc.) **2.** *F:* mouth; **claquer du b.,** to be hungry, starving; **fin b.,** gourmet; **être, rester, le b. dans l'eau,** to be, stranded, left in the lurch, high and dry; **ferme ton b.!** shut up! **clouer, clore, le b. à qn,** to shut s.o. up; **avoir bon b.,** to have the gift of the gab; **prise de b.,** quarrel, slanging match. **3.** (*a*) nose (of tool); nozzle (of tube); lip (of jug); spout (of coffee pot); peak (of bicycle saddle); mouthpiece (of clarinet); *Av:* **b. d'attaque,** leading edge (of wing); (*b*) **b. de plume,** pen nib; (*c*) **b. à gaz,** gas jet, burner; **b. Bunsen,** Bunsen burner; *P:* **tomber sur un b. (de gaz),** to come a cropper; (*d*) *Geog:* (*in place names*) bill; **le B. de Portland,** Portland Bill.

bécane [bekan] *n.f. F:* bicycle, bike.

bécarre [bekar] *a. & n.m. Mus:* natural (sign); **mi b.,** E natural.

bécasse [bekas] *n.f.* (*a*) *Orn:* **b. (des bois),** woodcock; **b. de mer,** oystercatcher; (*b*) *F:* **c'est une petite b.,** she's a little idiot.

bécasseau, -eaux [bekaso] *n.m. Orn:* (*a*) sandpiper; (*b*) young woodcock.

bécassine [bekasin] *n.f.* (*a*) *Orn:* snipe; (*b*) *F:* naïve girl.

bec-croisé [bɛkkrwaze] *n.m. Orn:* crossbill.

bec-de-cane [bɛkdəkan] *n.m.* (*a*) catch (in a lock); (*b*) (door) handle; *pl. becs-de-cane.*

bec-de-lièvre [bɛkdəljɛvr̥] *n.m.* harelip; *pl. becs-de-lièvre.*

becfigue [bɛkfig] *n.m. Orn:* (i) (garden) warbler; (ii) blackcap; (iii) waxwing; (iv) pipit.

bêchage [bɛʃaʒ] *n.m.* digging, turning over (of earth).

béchamel [beʃamɛl] *a. & n.f. Cu:* **(sauce) b.,** béchamel sauce, white sauce.

bêche [bɛʃ] *n.f. Hort: etc:* spade.

bêcher [beʃe] *v.tr.* **1.** to dig, to turn over (earth). **2.** *F:* to run (s.o.) down, to pull (s.o.) to pieces.

bécot [beko] *n.m. F:* kiss, peck.

bécoter [bekɔte] *v.tr. F:* to give (s.o.) a kiss, a peck.

becquée [beke] *n.f.* beakful, billfull; *F:* (*to a child*) **encore une b.!** another little mouthful, bite!

becquerel [bɛk(ə)rɛl] *n.m. Rad.-A. Meas:* becquerel, curie.

becquetance [bɛktɑ̃s] *n.f. P:* food, grub.

becqueter [bɛkte] *v.tr.* **(je becquète, n. becquetons; je becquèterai)** (*a*) (*of bird*) to peck at (sth.); (*b*) *P:* (*of pers.*) to eat; **il n'y a rien à b.,** there's no grub.

bectance [bɛktɑ̃s] *n.f. P:* food, grub.

becter [bɛkte] *v.tr.* = BECQUETER.

bedaine [bədɛn] *n.f. F:* stomach, (pot)belly; paunch, corporation.
bédane [bedan] *n.m. Tls:* mortise, (cold) chisel.
bedeau, -eaux [bədo] *n.m. Ecc:* verger.
bedon [bədɔ̃] *n.m. F:* (pot)belly, paunch, corporation.
bedonnant [bədɔnɑ̃] *a. F:* corpulent, pot-bellied.
bedonner [bədɔne], *v.i. F:* to get stout; to get a paunch, a corporation.
bédouin, -ouine [bedwɛ̃, -win] *a. & n.* bedouin.
bée [be] **1.** *a.f.* **bouche b.,** agape; **rester bouche b. devant qch.,** to stand gaping, open-mouthed, in front of sth.; **regarder qch. bouche b.,** to gape at sth. **2.** *n.f. Hyd.E:* mill leat, *esp. NAm:* flume.
béer [bee] *v.i. Lit:* (*of pers.*) (i) to stand open-mouthed (in astonishment, etc.); (ii) to daydream.
beffroi [befrwa] *n.m.* **1.** belfry. **2.** (alarm) bell (hung in belfry).
bégaiement [begɛmɑ̃] *n.m.* **1.** stammering, stuttering. **2.** lispings (of baby). **3.** early attempts, tentative beginnings.
bégayant [begɛjɑ̃] *a.* (*a*) stuttering, stammering; (*b*) *Lit:* hesitant, faltering.
bégayer [begeje] *v.* (**je bégaye, bégaie, n. bégayons; je bégayerai, bégaierai**) **1.** *v.i.* (*a*) to stutter, to stammer; **homme qui bégaie,** man with a stammer; (*b*) (*of babies*) to lisp. **2.** *v.tr.* **b. une excuse,** to stammer out an excuse.
bégayeur, -euse [begɛjœr, -øz] *a.* stuttering, stammering.
bégonia [begɔnja] *n.m. Bot:* begonia.
bègue [bɛg] **1.** *a.* stuttering, stammering. **2.** *n.* stutterer, stammerer.
bégueule [begœl] **1.** *n.f.* prude. **2.** *a.* prudish.
béguin [begɛ̃] *n.m.* **1.** (*a*) hood (of beguine nun); (*b*) bonnet (for baby, etc.). **2.** (*a*) *F:* **avoir le b. pour qn,** to have a crush on s.o.; (*b*) *P:* **c'est mon b.,** I've got a thing on him, her.
béguinage [beginaʒ] *n.m.* beguine convent.
béguine [begin] *n.f. Ecc:* beguine.
bégum [begɔm] *n.f.* begum.
beige [bɛʒ] *a. & n.m.* beige.
beigne[1] [bɛɲ] *n.f. P:* blow, slap, clout; **donner, flanquer, une b. à qn,** to give s.o. a clip on the ear.
beigne[2] *n.m. Fr.C:* doughnut, *NAm:* donut.
beignet [bɛɲɛ] *n.m. Comest:* (*a*) fritter; **b. de, aux, pommes,** apple fritter; (*b*) doughnut.
bel[1] [bɛl] *n.m. Ph.Meas:* bel.
bel[2]. *See* BEAU.
bélandre [belɑ̃dr̥] *n.f.* canal barge.
bêlement [bɛlmɑ̃] *n.m.* bleating.
bélemnite [belɛmnit] *n.f. Paleont:* belemnite.
bêler [bele] *v.i.,* to bleat; **qu'est-ce que vous avez à b. comme ça?** what on earth are you bellyaching, bleating, about?
belette [bəlɛt] *n.f. Z:* weasel.
belge [bɛlʒ] *a. & n. Geog:* Belgian.
belgicisme [bɛlʒisism] *n.m.* Belgian word, expression.
Belgique [bɛlʒik] *Pr.n.f.* Belgium.
bélier [belje] *n.m.* **1.** *Z:* ram. **2.** (*a*) *A. Mil:* battering ram; (*b*) *Civ.E:* **b. (à pilotage),** pile driver, ram(mer); **b. mécanique,** bulldozer; (*c*) *Hyd.E:* **b. hydraulique,** hydraulic ram. **3.** *Astr:* **le B.,** the Ram, Aries.
bélière [beljɛr] *n.f.* **1.** clapper ring (of bell); ring (of watch, etc.). **2.** sheep bell (of the bell-wether).
belladone [beladɔn] *n.f. Bot:* belladonna, deadly nightshade.
belle. *See* BEAU.
belle-dame [bɛldam] *n.f.* **1.** *Bot:* deadly nightshade. **2.** *Ent:* painted lady (butterfly); *pl. belles-dames.*
belle-de-jour [bɛldəʒur] *n.f. Bot:* convolvulus, bindweed; *pl. belles-de-jour.*
belle-de-nuit [bɛldənɥi] *n.f.* **1.** *Bot:* marvel of Peru, four o'clock. **2.** *F:* prostitute, lady of the night; *pl. belles-de-nuit.*
belle-famille [bɛlfamij] *n.f.* wife's family, husband's family; *F:* in-laws; *pl. belles-familles.*
belle-fille [bɛlfij] *n.f.* **1.** daughter-in-law. **2.** stepdaughter; *pl. belles-filles.*
bellement [bɛlmɑ̃] *adv.* well and truly; **il est b. en prison,** he's well and truly in prison.
belle-mère [bɛlmɛr] *n.f.* **1.** mother-in-law. **2.** stepmother; *pl. belles-mères.*
belle-sœur [bɛlsœr] *n.f.* sister-in-law; *pl. belles-sœurs.*
bellicisme [belisism] *n.m.* bellicosity, warmongering.
belligérance [beliʒerɑ̃s] *n.f.* belligerence.
belligérant [beliʒerɑ̃] *a. & n.* belligerent.
belliqueux, -euse [belikø, -øz] *a.* warlike, bellicose (nation, etc.); aggressive, quarrelsome (person, etc.)
belote [bəlɔt] *n.f. Cards:* belote; = pinocle.
belouga [beluga] *n.m.,* **béluga** [belyga] *n.m. Z:* beluga, white whale.
belvédère [bɛlvedɛr] *n.m.* **1.** belvedere, gazebo. **2.** (*at beauty spot*) viewpoint.
Belzébuth [bɛlzebyt] *Pr.n.m. B.Hist:* Beelzebub.
bémol [bemɔl] *n.m. Mus:* flat; **clarinette en si b.,** B-flat clarinet.
bémoliser [bemɔlize] *v.tr. Mus:* to flatten; to mark (note) with a flat; *NAm:* to flat (note).
ben [bɛ̃] *adv. P:* = BIEN; **b. oui!** why, yes!
bénarde [benard] *n.f.* pin key lock, double-sided lock.
bénédicité [benedisite] *n.m.* grace (before meal).
bénédictin, -ine [benediktɛ̃, -in] *a. & n.* Benedictine (monk, nun); **un vrai b.,** a scholar; **un travail de b.,** a work of painstaking scholarship.
bénédiction [benediksjɔ̃] *n.f.* blessing, benediction; consecration (of church, colours); (*of priest*) **donner la b.,** to give, pronounce, the blessing; **il a donné sa b. au projet,** he gave the plan his blessing; **quelle b.!** what a blessing! what a godsend!
bénef [benɛf] *n.m. P:* profit; **petits bénefs,** perks.
bénéfice [benefis] *n.m.* **1.** profit, gain; **réaliser de gros bénéfices,** to make large, handsome, profits; **vendre qch. à b.,** to sell sth. at a profit; **participation aux bénéfices,** profit sharing; **petits bénéfices,** perquisites, *F:* perks. **2.** benefit; *Th: Sp:* **représentation, match, à b.,** benefit performance, match; *Jur:* **b. du doute,** benefit of the doubt. **3.** *Ecc:* living, benefice.
bénéficiaire [benefisjɛr] **1.** *a. Com:* **solde b.,** profit balance; **compte b.,** account showing a credit balance; **marge b.,** profit margin. **2.** *n.* (*a*) recipient, payee (of cheque, etc.); (*b*) *Ecc: Jur: etc:* beneficiary.
bénéficier [benefisje] *v.ind.tr.* (*impf. & pr.sub.* **n. bénéficiions, v. bénéficiiez**) to profit (**de,** by); to have the advantage (**de,** of); to gain (**de,** by, from); **faire b. qn d'une expérience,** to give s.o. the benefit of one's experience; *Jur:* **il a bénéficié d'une ordonnance de non-lieu,** he was discharged; **bénéficiant d'une remise de dix pour cent,** subject to a discount of ten per cent.
bénéfique [benefik] *a.* (*a*) *Astrol:* benefic, beneficent (planet); (*b*) favourable, beneficial (**à,** to).
Bénélux [benelyks] *Pr.n.m.* Benelux.
benêt [bənɛ] **1.** *a.m.* silly, stupid. **2.** *n.m.* simpleton.
bénévolat [benevɔla] *n.m.* voluntary service, work.
bénévole [benevɔl] *a.* **1.** *Lit:* benevolent, kindly, indulgent (person). **2.** unpaid (service, work); **organisation b.,** voluntary organization; **infirmière b.,** voluntary nurse.
bénévolement [benevɔlmɑ̃] *adv.* **1.** *Lit:* benevolently, kindly, out of kindness. **2.** gratuitously, voluntarily; **il travaille b.,** he does voluntary work.
Bengale [bɛ̃gal] *Pr.n.m.* **1.** *Geog:* Bengal. **2.** *Pyr:* **feu de B.,** (i) Bengal light; (ii) light signal; flare.

Bengali [bɛ̃gali] **1.** *a. & n. Geog:* Bengali, Bengalese. **2.** *n.m. Ling:* Bengali.
bénignité [beniɲite] *n.f.* (*a*) *Lit:* benignity, kindness; (*b*) mildness (of climate, of a disease).
bénin, -igne [benɛ̃, -iɲ] *Lit: a.* (*a*) benign, kindly, indulgent (person, criticism, etc.); (*b*) slight, minor (accident, etc.); **tumeur bénigne,** benign, non-malignant, tumor; **forme bénigne de (la) rougeole,** mild form of measles.
béni-oui-oui [beniwiwi] *n.m.inv. F:* yes-man.
bénir [benir] *v.tr.* **1.** (*a*) to bless, to grant blessings to (s.o.); **(que) Dieu vous bénisse!** (may) (God) bless you! (*b*) to bless, to ask God's blessing on (s.o.); to bless (a marriage); (*c*) to glorify, to render thanks to (God); **le ciel en soit béni!** thank heaven(s)! **2.** to consecrate (church, bread, etc.).
bénit [beni] *a.* consecrated, blessed; **pain b.,** consecrated bread, holy bread; **eau bénite,** holy water.
bénitier [benitje] *n.m.* **1.** *Ecc:* holy water basin; stoop, stoup; font. **2.** *Conch:* giant clam.
Benjamin [bɛ̃ʒamɛ̃] **1.** *Pr.n.m.* Benjamin. **2.** *n.m. & f.* **benjamin, -ine,** benjamin, youngest child.
benjoin [bɛ̃ʒwɛ̃] *n.m. Com:* (gum) benzoin; benjamin.
benne [bɛn] *n.f.* (*a*) *Min: etc:* skip, tub, bucket, truck; (*b*) scoop (of crane); bucket (of dredger); (*c*) **(camion à) b. (basculante),** dumper (lorry, truck); tip(per) wagon; (*d*) (cable) car.
Benoist, Benoît [bənwa] *Pr.n.m.* Benedict.
benthique [bɛ̃tik] *a. Oc:* benthic (fauna, etc.).
benthos [bɛ̃tɔs] *n.m. Oc:* (*a*) benthos; (*b*) benthic flora and fauna.
benzène [bɛ̃zɛn] *n.m. Ch:* benzene.
benzine [bɛ̃zin] *n.f.* benzine.
benzol [bɛ̃zɔl] *n.m. Ch:* benzol(e).
béquille [bekij] *n.f.* **1.** crutch. **2.** *Veh: etc:* prop; stand (of motor cycle); *Av:* tail skid; *Nau:* (i) leg, shore, prop; (ii) tiller (of rudder). **3.** (*a*) catch (in a lock); (*b*) (door) handle.
béquiller [bekije] **1.** *v.i. F:* to walk on crutches. **2.** *v.tr. Nau:* to shore up, prop up (ship).
ber(s) [bɛr] *n.m.* **1.** *N.Arch:* (launching) cradle. **2.** *Fr.C:* (baby's) cradle, crib.
berbère [bɛrbɛr] **1.** *a. & n. Ethn:* Berber. **2.** *n.m. Ling:* Berber.
bercail [bɛrkaj] *n.m. not used in the pl.* fold (of the Church, etc.); **ramener au b. la brebis égarée,** to bring the lost sheep back to the fold.
berçant [bɛrsɑ̃] *a. & n.f. Fr.C:* **(chaise) berçante,** rocking chair.
berce [bɛrs] *n.f.* **1.** *Bot:* **b. commune,** hogweed. **2.** *Belg: Sw.Fr:* cradle.
berceau, -eaux [bɛrso] *n.m.* **1.** cradle, cot, *esp. NAm:* crib; **dès le b.,** from the cradle, from birth, from infancy; **le b. d'un mouvement populaire,** the birthplace of a popular movement; *F:* **il les prend au b.,** he's a baby snatcher. **2.** (*a*) *Aut: N.Arch: Typ: etc:* cradle, bed, support; *Artil:* cradle (of gun); *Aut: Av:* **b. (du) moteur,** engine mounting; (*b*) *Arch:* **voûte en b.,** barrel vault; (*c*) *Hort:* arbo(u)r, bower.
bercelonnette [bɛrsəlɔnɛt] *n.f.* bassinet, (rocking) cradle, cot.
bercement [bɛrsəmɑ̃] *n.m.* **1.** rocking, lulling. **2.** swaying.
bercer [bɛrse] *v.tr.* **(je berçai(s); n. berçons) 1.** to rock (a baby); **j'ai été bercé là-dedans,** I was brought up to it from my cradle. **2.** (*a*) to soothe (grief, s.o.); (*b*) **b. qn de promesses,** to delude s.o. with promises. **3.** **se b. d'une illusion, d'un espoir,** to cherish, indulge in, an illusion, a hope; to delude oneself.
berceur, -euse [bɛrsœr, -øz] **1.** *a.* soothing, lulling. **2.** *n.f.* (*a*) rocking chair; (*b*) *Mus:* (i) lullaby, cradle song; (ii) berceuse.
béret [berɛ] *n.m.* beret.
berge¹ [bɛrʒ] *n.f.* (steep) bank (of river, railway track, road); slope, side (of valley).
berge² *n.f. P:* (*usu. pl.*) year; **un gosse de six berges,** a six-year old kid.
berger, -ère [bɛrʒe, -ɛr] *n.* **1.** (*a*) shepherd, shepherdess; **chien de b.,** sheepdog; **b. allemand,** Alsatian (dog); **l'étoile du b.,** the evening star; (*b*) *Ecc:* shepherd, pastor. **2.** *n.f. Furn:* wing chair.
bergerette [bɛrʒərɛt] *n.f. Orn:* wagtail.
bergerie [bɛrʒəri] *n.f.* **1.** *Husb:* sheepfold; sheep pen. **2.** *Art: Lit:* pastoral (poem, painting, etc.).
bergeronnette [bɛrʒərɔnɛt] *n.f. Orn:* wagtail.
béribéri [beriberi] *n.m. Med:* beriberi.
berkélium [bɛrkeljɔm] *n.m. Ch:* berkelium.
berlander [bɛrlɑ̃de] *v.i. Fr.C:* to dawdle, to waste time, words.
Berlin [bɛrlɛ̃] *Pr.n. Geog:* Berlin; **B.-Ouest, B.-Est,** West Berlin, East Berlin.
berline [bɛrlin] *n.f.* (*a*) *A:* berlin(e); (*b*) *Aut:* (four-door) saloon, *NAm* sedan; (*c*) *Min:* truck, tram.
berlingot [bɛrlɛ̃go] *n.m.* **1.** *Comest:* (boiled) sweet; humbug. **2.** (pyramid-shaped) carton (of milk).
berlinois, -oise [bɛrlinwa, -waz] *Geog:* **1.** *a.* of, from, Berlin. **2.** *n.* Berliner.
berlue [bɛrly] *n.f.* **avoir la b.,** to be seeing things; to delude, to deceive, oneself.
berme [bɛrm] *n.f.* **1.** *Fort:* berm. **2.** (foot)path, verge (by canal, ditch, etc.).
bermuda(s) [bɛrmyda] *n.m. Cost:* Bermuda shorts.
Bermudes [bɛrmyd] *Pr.n.f.pl. Geog:* **les (îles) B.,** Bermuda.
bernache [bɛrnaʃ] *n.f.,* **bernacle** [bɛrnakl̩] *n.f.* **1.** *Crust:* barnacle. **2.** *Orn:* barnacle goose, brent goose.
bernardin, -ine [bɛrnardɛ̃, -in] *n.* Bernardine, Cistercian (monk, nun).
bernard-l'(h)ermite [bɛrnarlɛrmit] *n.m. Crust:* hermit crab, soldier crab.
berne¹ [bɛrn] *n.f. A:* tossing in a blanket.
berne² *n.f.* **1.** *Nau:* **pavillon en b.,** flag at half mast. **2.** *Mil:* **drapeau en b.,** flag furled and craped.
Berne³ *Pr.n. Geog:* Bern(e).
berner [bɛrne] *v.tr.* **1.** *A:* to toss (s.o.) in a blanket. **2.** (*a*) to ridicule (s.o.); (*b*) to fool, to hoax (s.o.).
bernicle [bɛrnikl̩] *n.f.,* **bernique¹** [bɛrnik] *n.f. Moll:* limpet.
bernique² *int. F:* no go! nothing doing!
bernois, -oise [bɛrnwa, -waz] *a. & n. Geog:* Bernese.
bertillonnage [bɛrtijɔnaʒ] *n.m.* Bertillon system (of anthropometry).
béryl [beril] *n.m. Miner:* beryl.
béryllium [beriljɔm] *n.m. Ch:* beryllium.
besace [bəzas] *n.f. A:* (beggar's) bag; (pilgrim's) scrip.
besaiguë [bəzegy] *n.f. Tls:* **1.** *Carp:* mortising axe. **2.** glazier's hammer.
besant [bəzɑ̃] *n.m. Num: Arch: Her:* bezant.
bésef [bezɛf] *adv. P:* = BÉZEF.
besicles [bəzikl̩] *n.f.pl. A:* spectacles; *F:* specs.
bésigue [bezig] *n.m. Cards:* bezique.
besogne [bəzɔɲ] *n.f.* (piece of) work; task, job; **se mettre à la b.,** to set to work; **rude b.,** hard job; **aller vite en b.,** (i) to work, to act, quickly; (ii) *F:* to cut corners; **abattre de la b.,** to get through a lot of work; **voilà de la belle b.!** here's a pretty kettle of fish, a fine mess!
besogner [bəzɔɲe] *v.i.* to work hard, to slave.
besogneux, -euse [bəzɔɲø, -øz] *a. & n.* poor, impecunious, hard-up (person).
besoin [bəzwɛ̃] *n.m.* **1.** (*a*) need, want, necessity, requirement; **pourvoir, subvenir, aux besoins de qn,** to

provide for s.o.'s needs; **si le b. s'en faisait sentir,** if the necessity arose; **pour le b. de la cause,** for the sake of the cause; *F:* **faire ses (petits) besoins,** to relieve oneself, to spend a penny; to go to the loo; **au b.,** if necessary, if need(s) be; *F:* at a pinch; **en cas de b.,** in case of necessity, emergency; (*b*) **avoir b. de qch., qn,** to need, require, want, sth., s.o.; **j'ai grand b. de son aide,** I'm badly in need of, I really need, his help; **il n'a pas b. de venir lundi,** he needn't come, there is no need for him to come, on Monday; **(il n'y a, je n'ai) pas b. de dire qu'elle était là,** needless to say, it goes without saying that, she was there; **vous aviez bien b. d'aller lui parler de cela!** you *would* go and tell him about that! (*c*) *impers. Lit:* **il n'est b. d'insister,** no need to insist; **s'il (en) est b., si b. (en) est,** if necessary, if need(s) be. **2.** poverty, indigence; **être dans le b.,** to be in need, in straitened circumstances; **vieillards dans le b.,** needy, impoverished, old people.

bessemer [bɛsmɛr] *n.m. Metall:* **(convertisseur) b.,** Bessemer converter.

bestiaire [bɛstjɛr] *n.m. Lit:* bestiary.

bestial, -aux[1] [bɛstjal, -o] *a.* bestial, beastly, brutish.

bestialité [bɛstjalite] *n.f.* bestiality; brutishness.

bestiaux[2] [bɛstjo] *n.m.pl.* livestock, cattle; **cinquante b.,** fifty head of cattle.

bestiole [bɛstjɔl] *n.f.* (*a*) small, tiny, animal, creature; (*b*) insect, *esp. U.S:* bug.

best-seller [bɛstsɛlœr] *n.m.* best-seller; *pl. best-sellers.*

bêta[1]**-asse** [bɛta, -ɑs] *F:* (*a*) *a.* silly, stupid; (*b*) *n.* idiot, nit(wit).

bêta[2] [bɛta] *n.m.* **1.** *Gr.Alph:* beta. **2.** *Atom.Ph:* **particules, rayons, b.,** beta particles, rays.

bétail [betaj] *n.m. coll.* livestock, cattle, grazing stock; **gros b.,** cattle (including horses, asses, mules); **menu, petit, b.,** smaller livestock.

bêtatron [bɛtatrɔ̃] *n.m. Atom.Ph:* betatron.

bête [bɛt] *n.f.* **1.** *n.* (*a*) beast; animal; **b. à quatre pieds,** four-footed beast; **b. à cornes,** horned beast; **b. de trait,** draught animal; (*on farm*) **les bêtes,** the livestock; **donner aux bêtes,** to feed the animals; *F:* **reprendre du poil de la b.,** (i) to take a hair of the dog (that bit you); (ii) to perk up, pick up; (*b*) **petites bêtes,** (i) insects; (ii) vermin; **b. à bon Dieu,** ladybird; **il y a une b. dans ma pomme,** there's a maggot, an inhabitant, in my apple; **chercher la petite b.,** to be over-critical, *F:* always picking holes, nitpicking. **2.** (*a*) *n.* fool, idiot, nit(wit); **faire la b.,** (i) to pretend to be stupid; (ii) to act foolishly, stupidly; (*b*) *a.* stupid, silly, foolish; **que je suis b.!** how silly, stupid, of me! **pas si b.!** I'm not such a fool (as all that)! not likely! **il n'est pas si b. qu'il en a l'air,** he's not as stupid, as daft, as he looks; **il est b. comme un âne, comme ses pieds,** he's a real idiot, fool; (*c*) *a.* **c'est b. comme chou,** it's as easy as pie, as anything.

bétel [betɛl] *n.m. Bot:* betel.

bêtement [bɛtmɑ̃] *adv.* stupidly, foolishly, idiotically; **tout b.,** purely and simply.

Bethléem [bɛtleɛm] *Pr.n.m. B.Hist:* Bethlehem.

bêtifier [betifje] **1.** *v.tr.* (*pr.sub. & impf.* **n. bêtifiions, v. bêtifiiez**) to stupefy, dull; to make (s.o.) stupid. **2.** *v.i.* (*a*) to talk nonsense; (*b*) to play the fool.

bêtise [betiz] *n.f.* **1.** stupidity, folly, silliness; **être d'une b. extrême,** to be exceedingly stupid. **2.** nonsense, absurdity; **dire des bêtises,** to talk nonsense, rubbish; **quelle b.!** what nonsense! how ridiculous! **faire des bêtises,** to play the fool. **3.** blunder, silly, stupid, mistake; **faire une grande b.,** to do something extremely stupid, silly. **4.** trifle; **dépenser tout son argent en bêtises,** to fritter away one's money. **5. bêtises de Cambrai** = mint humbugs.

béton [betɔ̃] *n.m.* **1.** *Const:* concrete; **b. armé,** reinforced concrete. **2.** *Fb:* **faire le b.,** to pack the defence.

bétonnage [betɔnaʒ] *n.m.* **1.** *Const:* concreting. **2.** *Fb:* packing the defence.

bétonner [betɔne] *v.tr.* **1.** to concrete; to build with concrete. **2.** *Fb:* to pack the defence.

bétonneuse [betɔnøz] *n.f.* **bétonnière** [betɔnjɛr] *n.f.* concrete mixer, cement mixer.

bette [bɛt] *n.f. Bot:* (spinach) beet; **b. à carde (blanche), b. à côtes,** seakale beet, Swiss chard.

betterave [bɛtrav] *n.f. Bot:* beet(root); **b. sucrière,** sugar beet; **b. fourragère,** mangel-wurzel, fodder beet.

betteravier, -ière [bɛtravje, -jɛr] **1.** *a.* **l'industrie betteravière,** the beet industry. **2.** *n.m.* sugar beet grower.

beuglement [bøgləmɑ̃] *n.m.* lowing (of cattle); bellow(ing) (of bull); *F:* (*of pers.*) bawling; (*of radio, etc.*) blaring.

beugler [bøgle] *v.i.* (*of cattle*) to low; (*of bull*) to bellow; *F:* (*of pers.*) to bawl; (*of radio, etc.*) to blare; *v.tr.* **b. une chanson,** to bawl, bellow, out a song.

beurre [bœr] *n.m.* **1.** butter; **b. salé, demi-sel,** salted, slightly salted, butter; **b. fondu,** melted butter; *Cu:* **au b.,** with melted butter, cooked in butter; **b. d'anchois,** anchovy butter; **au b. noir,** with black butter; *F:* **avoir un œil au b. noir,** to have a black eye; **nous sommes entrés comme dans du b.,** we got in very easily; *P:* **c'est du b.,** it's dead easy, a cinch; **cela compte pour du b.,** that doesn't count; *F:* **il a fait son b.,** he's made his packet; **ça mettra du b. dans les épinards,** that will improve matters, ease the situation. **2. b. de cacao,** cocoa butter; **b. de cacahouètes,** peanut butter.

beurrer [bœre] *v.tr.* to butter (bread, a dish, etc.).

beurrerie [bœreri] *n.f.* **1.** dairy. **2.** the butter industry.

beurrier, -ière [bœrje, -jɛr] **1.** *a.* **l'industrie beurrière,** the butter industry; **région beurrière,** butter-producing district. **2.** *n.m.* butter dish.

beuverie [bøvri] *n.f.* drinking session; booze-up.

bévatron [bevatrɔ̃] *n.m. Atom.Ph:* bevatron.

bévue [bevy] *n.f.* blunder, mistake, slip.

bey [bɛ] *n.m.* bey.

Beyrouth [berut] *Pr.n. Geog:* Beirut.

bézef [bezɛf] *adv. P:* **il n'y en a pas b.,** there's not much, a lot (of it); there's not many, a lot (of them).

biacide [biasid] *a. & n.m. Ch:* diacid.

biais, -aise [bjɛ, -ɛz] **1.** *a. Arch:* oblique, sloping, slanting, bevelled; **voûte biaise,** skew(ed) arch. **2.** *n.m.* (*a*) skew (of tool, of arch); slant (of wall); **en b.,** on the slant, slantwise, at an angle; aslant, askew; **tailler un tissu dans le b.,** to cut material on the bias; **regarder qn de b.,** to look sideways, askance, at s.o.; (*b*) (indirect) manner, means (of doing sth.); expedient; **aborder de b. une personne, une question,** to approach a person, a question, in a roundabout way, indirectly; **il faut considérer ce problème par deux b.,** we must look at this question from two angles. **3.** *n.m. Dressm:* bias binding.

biaiser [bjeze] *v.i.* **1.** to be on the slant; to edge off, to turn off, away (towards sth.). **2.** to beat about the bush; to dodge the issue.

biaural, -aux [biɔral *a.* binaural.

bibasique [bibazik] *a. Ch:* dibasic.

bibelot [biblo] *n.m.* **1.** curio, knick-knack, trinket. **2.** *pl.* odds and ends.

biberon [bibrɔ̃] *n.m.* (baby's feeding) bottle; **nourrir, élever, un enfant au b.,** to bottle-feed a child.

biberonner [bibrɔne] *v.i. F:* to booze, to tipple.

bibi [bibi] *n.m.* **1.** *P:* I, me, myself, yours truly;

number one. **2.** *F:* (woman's) hat.
bibine [bibin] *n.f. P:* tasteless drink, *esp.* beer; slops.
bibite [bibit] *n.f. Fr.C: P:* bug, insect.
bible [bibl] *n.f.* bible; **la B.,** the Bible.
bibliobus [bibliɔbys] *n.m.* mobile library, *NAm:* bookmobile.
bibliographe [bibliɔgraf] *n.m. & f.* bibliographer.
bibliographie [bibliɔgrafi] *n.f.* bibliography.
bibliographique [bibliɔgrafik] *a.* bibliographic(al).
bibliomane [bibliɔman] *n.m. & f.* bibliomaniac; book lover, collector.
bibliomanie [bibliɔmani] *n.f.* bibliomania, book collecting.
bibliophile [bibliɔfil] *n.m. & f.* bibliophile.
bibliophile [bibliɔfili] *n.f.* love of books, bibliophily.
bibliothécaire [bibliɔtekɛr] *n.m. & f.* librarian.
bibliothéconomie [bibliɔtekɔnɔmi] *n.f.* library science.
bibliothèque [bibliɔtɛk] *n.f.* **1.** (*a*) (*building, room*) library; **b. de prêt,** lending library; (*b*) *Rail:* bookstall, *NAm:* news stand. **2.** bookcase. **3.** library; collection, series, of books; *F:* **c'est une b. ambulante, vivante,** he's a walking encyclopaedia.
biblique [biblik] *a.* biblical.
bicaméral, -aux [bikameral, -o] *a. Pol:* bicameral, double-chamber (system, etc.).
bicaméralisme [bikameralism] **bicamérisme** [bikamerism] *n.m. Pol:* bicameral system.
bicarbonate [bikarbɔnat] *n.m. Ch:* bicarbonate.
bicentenaire [bisɑ̃tnɛr] *n.m.* bicentenary; *esp. NAm:* bicentennial.
bicéphale [bisefal] *a. & n.m.* bicephalous, two-headed (animal).
biceps [bisɛps] *a. & n.m. Anat:* biceps (muscle); *F:* **avoir du, des, b.,** to be muscular.
biche [biʃ] *n.f.* **1.** *Z:* hind, doe; **ventre de b.,** reddish-white; **table à pieds de b.,** table with cabriole legs; **aux yeux de b.,** doe-eyed. **2.** *F:* **ma b.,** my darling.
bicher [biʃe] *v.i.* **1.** *F:* **ça biche?** how's things? **ça biche, les affaires?** how's business? **2.** *P:* to be delighted, pleased as punch.
bichette [biʃɛt] *n.f.* **1.** *Z:* young, small, hind. **2.** *F:* **ma b.,** my darling, dear.
bichlorure [biklɔryr] *n.m. Ch:* bichloride, dichloride.
bichon, -onne [biʃɔ̃, ɔn] *n.* **1.** lap-dog, toy dog. **2.** *F:* **mon b.,** my darling, love, dear.
bichonner [biʃɔne] *v.tr.* **1.** (*a*) to make (s.o.) spruce, smart; (*b*) to mollycoddle (s.o.). **2. se b.,** to spruce oneself up.
bichromate [bikrɔmat] *n.m. Ch:* bichromate, dichromate.
bicolore [bikɔlɔr] *a.* bicolour(ed), two-tone.
biconcave [bikɔ̃kav] *a.* biconcave.
biconvexe [bikɔ̃vɛks] *a.* biconvex.
bicoque [bikɔk] *n.f.* poky little house; shack.
bicorne [bikɔrn] **1.** *a. Nat.Hist: Anat:* bicornuate. **2.** *n.m.* cocked hat, bicorne.
bicot [biko] *n.m.* **1.** *Z:* kid. **2.** *F: Pej.* Arab, wog.
biculturalisme [bikyltyralism] *n.m.* biculturalism.
biculturel, -elle [bikyltyrel] *a.* bicultural.
bicuspide [bikyspid] *a.* bicuspid, bicuspidate.
bicyclette [bisiklɛt] *n.f.* bicycle; **b. à moteur,** motorized bicycle; moped; **aller à, en, b.,** to ride a bicycle, to cycle; **faire de la b.,** to go cycling, to cycle.
bidasse [bidas] *n.m. Mil: P:* squaddie; *U.S:* G.I.
bide [bid] *n.m.* **1.** *P:* (*a*) belly; (*b*) **c'est du b.,** it's a load of rubbish, codswallop. **2.** *F: esp. Th:* **la pièce a fait un b.,** the play's a flop.
bidet [bidɛ] *n.m.* **1.** pony, nag. **2.** *Hyg:* bidet.
bidoche [bidɔʃ] *n.f. P:* meat (*esp.* poor quality).
bidon [bidɔ̃] **1.** *n.m.* (*a*) can, tin, drum (for oil, etc.); **b. à lait,** milk churn; (*b*) *Mil. etc:* water bottle; (*c*) *P:* belly; **se remplir le b.,** to stuff oneself; (*d*) *P:* **c'est du b.,** it's a load of rubbish, codswallop; *P:* **c'est pas du b.,** it's the honest truth. **2.** *a. P:* fake, phoney.
bidonnant [bidɔnɑ̃] *a. P:* hilarious, screamingly funny; **c'est b.,** it's a scream.
bidonner (se) [səbidɔne] *v.pr. P:* to laugh one's head off.
bidonville [bidɔ̃vil] *n.m.* shantytown.
bidule [bidyl] *n.m. P:* thing, thingummy, whatsit.
bief [bjɛf] *n.m. Hyd.E:* **1.** (canal) reach, level; **b. d'amont,** head bay; **b. d'aval, de fuite,** tail bay, aft bay. **2.** millcourse, millrace.
bielle [bjɛl] *n.f.* (*a*) (tie) rod; (*in compression*) push rod; crank arm; *Aut:* **b. d'accouplement,** track link; (*b*) **tête de b.,** *Mch:* crank head; *I.C.E:* big end; **pied de b.,** *Mch:* crosshead; *I.C.E:* little end.
biellette [bjɛlɛt] *n.f. Mec.E:* (*a*) small rod; (*b*) link.
bien [bjɛ̃] **1.** *adv.* **1.** well; **livre b. écrit,** well written book; **il parle b.,** he is a good speaker, he speaks well; **écoutez b. ceci,** now, listen carefully to this; **se conduire b.,** to behave; **il faut b. les soigner, les soigner b.,** they must be well looked after; **vous avez b. fait,** you did the right thing; **c'est b. fait (pour lui),** it serves him right; **aller, se porter, b.,** to be well, in good health; **tout va b.,** all's well, everything's O.K., fine; *Iron:* **voilà qui commence b.,** that's a fine start! **vous arrivez joliment b.,** you've come just in the nick of time; **b.!** (i) good! (ii) that's enough! that will do! (iii) all right! **très b.! fort b.!** very good! well done! (*agreeing with speaker*) hear, hear! **2.** (*a*) right, proper; **c'est b.!** good! all right! **comme c'est b. à vous d'être venu!** how good of you to come! **ce n'est pas b. de vous moquer de lui,** it's not kind of you to make fun of him; (*b*) comfortable; **êtes-vous b. dans ce fauteuil?** are you comfortable in that armchair? **vous ne savez pas quand vous êtes b.,** you don't know when you're well off; (*c*) **je ne me sens pas très b.,** I don't feel very well; **il est moins b.,** he's not as well (as he was); (*d*) **être b. avec qn,** to be on good terms with s.o.; (*e*) of good appearance, position, quality, etc.; **il est b. de sa personne,** he's a fine figure of a man; **tu es très b. dans cette robe,** that dress suits you perfectly. **3.** (*emphatic*) (*a*) indeed, really, quite; **c'est b. cela,** that's right; **il y a b. deux ans que je ne l'ai vue,** it's at least, it must be, two years since I (last) saw her; **je l'ai regardé b. en face,** I looked him full in the face; **être b. d'accord,** to be entirely in agreement; (in letter) **b. à vous,** yours; **je veux b. le croire,** I can quite believe it, him; **qu'est-ce que ça peut b. être?** what ever, what on earth, can it be? **c'est b. lui,** it really *is* him; **c'est b. de lui,** it's just like him; that's typical of him; *F:* **c'est b. à moi, ça?** you're sure that's mine? **est-ce b. le train pour Paris?** is this the right train for Paris? **je l'avais b. dit!** didn't I say so? **voulez-vous b. vous taire!** *do* shut up! **il est b. entendu que . . .,** it is quite understood that . . .; **b. entendu,** of course; **je m'en doutais b.,** I thought as much; **il est b. venu, mais j'étais occupé,** he did come, but I was busy; **je ne veux pas que tu fasses cela.—mais vous le faites b., vous!** I don't want you to do that.—but, *you* do it, don't you? *Iron:* **c'est b. le moment de parler come ça!** a fine time, what a time, to talk like that! (*b*) very; **b. malheureux,** very unhappy; **vous venez b. tard,** you're very late; **b. loin de, que,** far from; **c'est b. simple,** it's quite, very, simple; (*c*) much, many, a great deal, a great many, a lot; **b. plus, b. moins,** much more, much less; a lot more, a lot less; **il a b. souffert,** he's suffered, been through, a great deal; (*d*) **j'ai eu b. de la peine, b. du mal, à la convaincre,** I had a great, a good, deal of

trouble in convincing her; **je l'ai vu b. des fois,** I have seen him many times; **b. d'autres,** many others; *F:* lots more; (*e*) **j'irais b. avec vous mais . . .,** I'd love to go with you but . . .; **j'y suis b. obligé,** I just, really, have to. **4.** *adv. phr.* (*a*) **aussi b.,** in any case, after all, anyway; just as well, just as easily; (*b*) **tant b. que mal,** somehow (or other), after a fashion; **je m'en suis acquitté tant b. que mal,** I got through. **5.** *conj.phr.* (*a*) **b. que** +*sub.*, though, although; **je le respecte, b. qu'il ne me soit pas sympathique,** I respect him (even) though I don't like him; (*b*) **si b. que** +*ind.*, so that, and so, with the result that; **il ne reparut plus, si b. qu'on le crut mort,** he failed to come back, and so he was thought dead; (*c*) **ou b.,** or else, otherwise. **6.** *int.* **eh b.!** (oh) well! **eh b. donc!** well then! **eh b. ça alors!** well, I'm damned! well, fancy that! **II.** *n.m.* **1.** (*a*) good; **le b. et le mal,** good and evil; right and wrong; **faire le b.,** to do good; **homme de b.,** good, upright, man; (*b*) **le b. public,** the public good; **c'est pour votre b.,** it's for your own good, for your benefit; **cela m'a fait beaucoup de b.,** it did me a lot of good; **grand b. vous fasse!** much good may it do you! **vouloir du b. à qn, vouloir le b. de qn,** to wish s.o. well; **une personne qui vous veut du b.,** a well-wisher; **tout le monde dit du b., parle en b., de lui,** everyone speaks well of him. **2.** (*a*) possession, property, assets, wealth, goods (and chattels); fortune; **il a du b. (au soleil),** he's well-to-do, wealthy, a landowner, a man of property; (*b*) *Jur:* **biens meubles, mobiliers,** personal property, personal estate; **biens immobiliers,** real estate; **biens fonciers,** landed property; **biens dotaux,** dowry; **biens successoraux,** hereditaments; **biens vacants,** ownerless property; derelict; (*c*) *Pol.Ec:* **biens de consommation,** consumer goods; **biens de production,** capital goods. **3.** (*a*) **je trouve qu'il a changé en b.,** I think there's a change for the better; (*b*) **mener une affaire à b.,** to bring a matter to a satisfactory conclusion; (*c*) *F:* **en tout b. (et) tout honneur,** with the best of intentions.

bien-aimé, -ée [bjɛ̃nɛme] *a. & n.* beloved, darling; *Hist:* **(Louis) le B.-A.,** Louis XV; *pl. bien-aimé(e)s.*

bien-être [bjɛ̃nɛtr̥] *n.m. no pl.* (*a*) well-being; **sentiment de b.-ê.,** feeling of well-being; (*b*) (material) well-being; comfort; welfare (of population, etc.).

bienfaisance [bjɛ̃fəzɑ̃s] *n.f.* (*a*) benevolence; (*b*) charity; **bureau de b.,** charitable organization.

bienfaisant [bjɛ̃fəzɑ̃] *a.* **1.** (*of pers*) charitable, kindly. **2.** beneficial, salutary (remedy, etc.).

bienfait [bjɛ̃fɛ] *n.m.* **1.** benefit, kindness, service. **2.** gift, blessing, boon; **un b. du ciel,** a godsend.

bienfaiteur, -trice [bjɛ̃fɛtœr, -tris] *n.* benefactor, benefactress; **b. du peuple,** people's friend.

bien-fondé [bjɛ̃fɔ̃de] *n.m. no pl.* validity, merits, reasonableness (of opinion, argument); *Jur:* cogency (of claim, etc.).

bien-fonds [bjɛ̃fɔ̃] *n.m.* real estate, landed property; *pl. biens-fonds.*

bienheureux, -euse [bjɛ̃nœrø, -øz] *a. & n.* **1.** blissful, happy. **2.** *Ecc:* blessed; **les b.,** the blessed, the blest.

bien-jugé [bjɛ̃ʒyʒe] *n.m. no pl.*; *Jur:* just and lawful decision, sentence, verdict.

biennal, -aux [bjenal, -o] **1.** *a.* biennial, two-yearly. **2.** *n.f.* **biennale,** biennial festival, etc.

bien-pensant, -e [bjɛ̃pɑ̃sɑ̃(t)] *a. & n.* (*a*) right-minded (person); (*b*) *Pej:* self-righteous (person).

bienséance [bjɛ̃seɑ̃s] *n.f.* propriety, decorum; **observer les bienséances,** to observe the rules of etiquette.

bienséant [bjɛ̃seɑ̃] *a.* decorous, proper; **il est b. aux jeunes gens de respecter la vieillesse,** it is right and proper for young people to respect old age.

bientôt [bjɛ̃to] *adv.* (very) soon, before long; **à b.!** see you soon! goodbye for now! **c'est b. dit!** easier said than done! **b. après,** soon after(wards), shortly (afterwards), not long after(wards).

bienveillance [bjɛ̃vɛjɑ̃s] *n.f.* benevolence, kindness (**envers, pour,** to); goodwill; **par b.,** out of kindness.

bienveillant [bjɛ̃vɛjɑ̃] *a.* kind, kindly, benevolent (**envers, pour,** to); **examinateur b.,** lenient examiner.

bienvenu, -e [bjɛ̃vny] **1.** *a.* well-timed, opportune (remark, etc.). **2.** *n.* **soyez le b., la b.!** welcome! **vous êtes toujours le b.,** you're always welcome; we're always pleased to see you.

bienvenue [bjɛ̃vny] *n.f.* welcome; **souhaiter la b. à qn,** to welcome s.o.

bière[1] [bjɛr] *n.f.* beer; **b. blonde,** lager; light ale, pale ale; **b. brune,** brown ale.

bière[2] *n.f.* coffin.

biffe [bif] *n.f. P:* infantry.

biffer [bife] *v.tr.* to cross out, strike out, put a line through (word, etc.).

biffin [bifɛ̃] *n.m.* **1.** *P:* ragman, rag-and-bone man. **2.** *F:* infantryman.

biffure [bifyr] *n.f.* (*a*) crossing out, striking out (of word); (*b*) line (through a word).

bifocal, -aux [bifɔkal, -o] *a.* bifocal (lens, etc.).

bifteck [biftɛk] *n.m.* (beef)steak; **b. de cheval,** horse-(meat) steak; *P:* **gagner son b.,** to earn a living.

bifurcation [bifyrkasjɔ̃] *n.f.* bifurcation, fork, branching (of road, tree trunk, etc.); change of direction, branching out (in career, etc.).

bifurquer [bifyrke] *v.i.* to fork, bifurcate, divide; to branch off; **la route bifurque à Noyon,** the road forks at Noyon; **nous avons bifurqué vers, sur, la ville,** we turned off towards the town; **b. vers la politique,** to go, to branch out, into politics.

bigame [bigam] **1.** *a.* bigamous. **2.** *n.* bigamist.

bigamie [bigami] *n.f.* bigamy.

bigarade [bigarad] *n.f.* bitter, Seville, orange.

bigarré [bigare] *a.* (*a*) variegated, multicoloured (shirt, etc.); (*b*) motley, mixed (crowd, group, etc.).

bigarreau, -eaux [bigaro] *n.m.* whiteheart (cherry).

bigarrer [bigare] *v.tr.* to variegate, mottle; to make a medley of (sth.); to give variety to (sth.).

bigarrure [bigaryr] *n.f.* (*a*) medley, mixture, variegation (of colours); (*b*) medley, variety, disparity (of group, etc.).

bigle [bigl̥] *a. & n. O: & Hum:* cross-eyed (person).

bigler [bigle] *F:* **1.** *v.i.* to squint, to have a squint, to be cross-eyed. **2.** *v.tr.* to squint, to have a squint (at sth.).

bigleux, -euse [biglø, -øz] *a. & n.* **1.** *F:* cross-eyed (person). **2.** *P:* short-sighted (person); **t'es b.?** are you blind?

bigophone [bigɔfɔn] *n.m. F:* telephone; blower; **coup de b.,** ring, tinkle.

bigorne [bigɔrn] *n.f.* **1.** two-beaked anvil, two-horned anvil. **2.** beak, horn (of anvil).

bigorneau, -eaux [bigɔrno] *n.m. Moll:* winkle.

bigorner [bigɔrne] *v.tr.* (*a*) *Metalw:* to work (sth.) on an anvil; (*b*) *P:* to bash, to smash (up). **2. se b.,** *P:* to have a punch-up.

bigot, -ote [bigo, -ɔt] **1.** *a.* (over-)devout, bigoted. **2.** *n.* (religious) bigot.

bigoterie [bigɔtri] *n.f.* (religious) bigotry.

bigoudi [bigudi] *n.m.* (hair) curler, roller.

bigre [bigr̥] *int. F:* gosh! my God!

bigrement [bigrəmɑ̃] *adv. F:* **vous avez b. raison!** you're dead right! **il fait b. froid,** it's awfully cold.

bigue [big] *n.f.* **1.** (*a*) hoisting gin, sheers; (*b*) *pl.* sheerlegs. **2.** *Nau:* mast crane, jumbo derrick.

bihebdomadaire [biɛbdɔmadɛr] *a.* twice-weekly (magazine, etc.).

bijou, -oux [biʒu] *n.m.* jewel, gem; *pl.* jewellery; *F:* **mon b.!** my precious! my pet!
bijouterie [biʒutri] *n.f.* **1.** (*a*) jeweller's trade, business; (*b*) jeweller's (shop). **2.** jewellery, jewels.
bijoutier, -ière [biʒutje, -jɛr] *n.* jeweller.
bikini [bikini] *n.m. Cost:* bikini.
bilabiale [bilabjal] *a. & n.f. Ling:* bilabial.
bilan [bilɑ̃] *n.m.* **1.** *Fin:* (*a*) balance sheet; statement of account; **faire, dresser, un b.,** to draw up a balance sheet; (*b*) schedule (of assets and liabilities); **déposer son b.,** to file one's petition (in bankruptcy). **2.** (*a*) evaluation, results, consequences (of a situation); assessment (of facts); **faire le b. de la situation,** to take stock of the situation; (*b*) **faire le b. de santé de qn,** to give s.o. a complete (medical) check-up.
bilatéral, -aux [bilateral, -o] *a.* bilateral, two-sided (paralysis, contract, etc.).
bilboquet [bilbɔkɛ] *n.m.* **1.** *Toys:* (*a*) cup-and-ball; (*b*) (weighted figure) tumbler. **2.** *Typ:* (piece of) job work.
bile [bil] *n.f.* **1.** *Physiol:* bile. **2.** (*a*) bad temper; **échauffer la b. de, à, qn,** to rouse s.o.'s anger; (*b*) **il se fait de la b.,** he's fretting, worried sick.
biler (se) [səbile] *v.pr. F:* to get worked up, all hot and bothered; to be worried sick.
bileux, -euse [bilø, -øz] *a. F:* easily upset; **il n'est pas b.,** he doesn't let things worry him, get on top of him.
biliaire [biljɛr] *a. Anat:* biliary (vessels, etc); *Med:* **calcul b.,** biliary calculus, gallstone; **cirrhose b.,** cirrhosis (of the liver).
bilieux, -ieuse [biljø, -jøz] *a. & n.* **1.** bilious (temperament, complexion). **2.** irritable, irascible (person).
bilingue [bilɛ̃g] *a.* bilingual.
billard [bijar] *n.m.* **1.** (game of) billiards; **b. russe,** bar billiards; **b. électrique, japonais,** pinball, pin table. **2.** billiard table; *F:* **monter, passer, sur le b.,** to have an operation. **3.** billiard (i) room, (ii) saloon.
bille¹ [bij] *n.f.* **1.** (*a*) billiard ball; (*b*) *P:* face, mug; **il a une bonne b.,** he looks pleasant enough; **il a une b. de billard,** he's as bald as a coot. **2.** *Toys:* marble, alley; **jouer aux billes,** to play marbles. **3.** *Mec.E: etc:* ball; **roulement à billes,** ball bearing(s); **stylo (à) b.,** ballpoint (pen); *Toil:* **flacon (à) b.,** roll-on (bottle).
bille² *n.f.* (saw)log, billet (of timber).
billet [bijɛ] *n.m.* **1.** *esp.Lit:* note, short letter; **b. doux,** love letter. **2.** notice, invitation; **b. de faire part,** card announcing a family event (birth, marriage, death). **3.** ticket; **b. simple, b. d'aller,** single, *NAm:* one-way, ticket; **b. de retour, d'aller (et) retour,** return, *NAm:* round trip, ticket; **b. d'avion,** air, plane, ticket; **b. de quai,** platform ticket; **b. circulaire,** round trip ticket; **b. de cinéma,** cinema ticket; *Th: etc:* **b. de faveur,** complimentary ticket. **4.** *Com: Fin:* (*a*) note, promissory note, bill; **b. au porteur,** bill payable to bearer; (*b*) **b. (de banque),** (bank)note; *NAm:* bill; (*c*) *F: O:* ten-franc note. **5. b. de santé,** certificate, bill, of health. **6.** permit, permission; *Sch: etc:* **b. de sortie,** pass, exeat. **7.** *Mil:* **b. de logement,** billet.
billette [bijɛt] *n.f.* **1.** billet (of firewood, of metal). **2.** *Arch:* billet (moulding).
billetterie [bijɛtri] *n.f.* (*a*) ticketing; (*b*) ticket office.
billevesée [bijvəze] *n.f.* stupid idea, nonsense.
billion [biljɔ̃] *n.m.* **1.** billion (10^{12}); *U.S:* trillion. **2.** *A:* milliard (10^9); *U.S:* billion.
billon [bijɔ̃] *n.m.* **1.** *Agr:* ridge of earth (formed by two plough furrows); **labourer en billons,** to rafter (field). **2. (monnaie de) b.,** copper, nickel, coinage.
billonnage [bijɔnaʒ] *n.m. Agr:* ridging (of field).
billot [bijo] *n.m.* (*a*) block (of wood); chopping block; (butcher's) block, (*b*) executioner's block; *F:* **j'en mettrais ma tête sur le b.,** I'd stake my life on it; (*c*) **b. d'enclume,** anvil block, stock.
bilobé [bilɔbe] *a. Arch: Biol:* bilobate, bilobed.
bimane [biman] *Z: a. & n.* bimanous, bimanal (animal).
bimbeloterie [bɛ̃blɔtri] *n.f.* **1.** toy, fancy goods, business, trade. **2.** toys, fancy goods, knick-knacks, odds and ends.
bimbelotier [bɛ̃blɔtje] *n.m.* maker of, dealer in, toys, fancy goods.
bimensuel, -elle [bimɑ̃sɥɛl] *a.* fortnightly, bimonthly, *esp. NAm:* semimonthly.
bimensuellement [bimɑ̃sɥɛlmɑ̃] *adv.* twice a month, every fortnight, *esp. NAm:* semimonthly.
bimestriel, -elle [bimɛstriɛl] *a.* bimonthly, occurring every other month, every two months.
bimétallique [bimetalik] *a.* bimetallic.
bimoteur [bimɔtœr] *a. & n.m.* twin-engine(d) (aircraft).
binage [binaʒ] *n.m. Agr:* second dressing, harrowing, hoeing.
binaire [binɛr] *a. Mth: etc:* binary.
binard, binart [binar] *n.m.* (low) dray, lorry (for carting stone).
biner [bine] **1.** *v.tr.* (*a*) *Agr:* to dig, harrow, dress, (ground) for a second time; (*b*) to hoe. **2.** *v.i. Ecc:* to celebrate mass twice in one day.
binette¹ [binɛt] *n.f. Agr. Hort:* hoe.
binette² *n.f. P:* face, mug.
bineur [binœr] *n.m.*, **bineuse** [binøz] *n.f. Agr:* cultivator, light plough.
binocle [binɔkl̩] *n.m.* eyeglasses, pince-nez.
binoculaire [binɔkylɛr] *a.* binocular (vision, etc.).
binôme [binom] *n.m. Mth:* binomial; **le b. de Newton,** the binomial theorem.
binômial, -aux [binomjal, -o] *a. Mth:* binomial.
binon [binɔ̃] *n.m. Cmptr:* bit.
binot [bino] *n.m. Agr:* = BINEUR.
biochimie [bjɔʃimi] *n.f.* biochemistry.
biochimique [bjɔʃimik] *a.* biochemical.
biodégradable [bjɔdegradabl̩] *a.* biodegradable.
biogenèse [bjɔʒənɛz] *n.f. Biol:* biogenesis.
biographe [bjɔgraf] *n.m. & f.* biographer.
biographie [bjɔgrafi] *n.f.* biography.
biographique [bjɔgrafik] *a.* biographic(al).
biologie [bjɔlɔʒi] *n.f.* biology.
biologique [bjɔlɔʒik] *a.* biologic(al).
biologiste [bjɔlɔʒist] *n.m. & f.* biologist.
bionique [bjɔnik] *n.f.* bionics.
biophysique [bjɔfizik] *n.f.* biophysics.
biopsie [biɔpsi] *n.f. Surg:* biopsy.
biosphère [bjɔsfɛr] *n.f.* biosphere.
biosynthèse [bjɔsɛ̃tɛz] *n.f.* biosynthesis.
bioxyde [biɔksid] *n.m. Ch:* dioxide.
biparti [biparti] *a.* **bipartite** [bipartit] *a.* bipartite.
bipède [bipɛd] **1.** *a.* two-footed, two-legged, biped(al). **2.** *n.m.* biped.
biphasé [bifɑze] *a. El:* two-phase, diphase (current).
biplace [biplas] *a. & n.m. Aut: Av:* two-seater.
biplan [biplɑ̃] *a. & n.m.* **(avion) b.,** biplane.
bipolaire [bipɔlɛr] *a. El: Ph: etc:* bipolar, two-pole.
bipolarité [bipɔlarite] *n.f.* bipolarity.
biquadratique [bikwadratik] *a. & n.f. Mth:* biquadratic (equation).
bique [bik] *n.f. F:* **1.** nanny goat; **peau de b.,** goatskin. **2.** (*of woman*) old bag, old hag, old cow.
biquet, -ette [bikɛ, -ɛt] *n.* **1.** *Z:* kid. **2.** *F:* **mon b.,** my pet, my love.
biquotidien, -ienne [bikɔtidjɛ̃, jɛn] *a.* occurring, published, twice a day, twice-daily.
birbe [birb] *n.m. F:* **vieux b.,** old man, old geezer.

biréacteur [bireaktœr] *n.m.* twin-jet (aircraft).
biréfringence [birefrɛ̃ʒɑ̃s] *n.f. Opt:* double refraction, birefringence.
biréfringent [birefrɛ̃ʒɑ̃] *a. Opt:* doubly-refractive, birefringent.
birman, -ane [birmɑ̃, -an] **1.** *a. & n.m. & f. Geog:* Burmese. **2.** *n.m. Ling:* Burmese.
Birmanie [birmani] *Pr.n.f. Geog:* Burma.
biroute [birut] *n.f. Mil.Av: F:* (wind) sock, sleeve.
bis¹, bise [bi, biz] *a.* greyish-brown, brownish-grey; **teint b.,** dark, swarthy, complexion; **toile bise,** unbleached linen; **pain b.,** brown bread.
bis² [bis] **1.** *adv. & n.m.* (*a*) *Th: etc:* encore; (*b*) *Mus:* repeat. **2.** *adv.* (*in an address*) **10 b.,** (i) 10A; (ii) 10B.
bisaïeul, -eule [bizajœl] *n. Lit:* great-grandfather, great-grandmother; *pl. bisaïeul(e)s.*
bisannuel, -elle [bizanɥɛl] *a.* biennial.
bisbille [bisbij] *n.f. F:* petty quarrel, tiff, bickering; **être en b. avec qn,** to be at loggerheads, with s.o.
Biscaye [biskaj] *Pr.n. Geog:* Biscay; **le golfe de B.,** the Bay of Biscay.
biscornu [biskɔrny] *a.* **1.** (*a*) mis-shapen, crooked; (*b*) irregular, badly proportioned (building), etc.). **2.** *F:* bizarre, queer (ideas); illogical (argument).
biscotte [biskɔt] *n.f.* rusk.
biscuit [biskɥi] *n.m.* **1.** biscuit; cracker; **b. à la cuiller,** sponge finger; **b. de savoie,** sponge cake; **b. de mer,** (i) ship's biscuit; (ii) *F:* cuttlebone; **b. de chien,** dog biscuit; *Husb:* **b. de fourrage,** cake (of oats, peas, etc.). **2.** *Cer:* unglazed porcelain, biscuitware, bisque.
biscuiterie [biskɥitri] *n.f.* (*a*) biscuit factory; (*b*) biscuit trade.
bise¹ [biz] *n.f.* north wind.
bise² *n.f. F:* kiss; **donner une b. à qn,** to kiss s.o.
biseau, -eaux [bizo] *n.m.* **1.** (*a*) chamfered, bevelled, edge; feather edge; chamfer, bevel; **taillé en b.,** bevel-edged, bevelled, chamfered; (*b*) *Clockm: etc:* bezel; *Mus:* lip (of a recorder, etc.). **2.** *Tls:* bevel.
biseautage [bizotaʒ] *n.m.* **1.** bevelling, chamfering. **2.** marking (of playing cards).
biseauter [bizote] *v.tr.* **1.** to bevel, chamfer. **2.** to mark (playing cards).
biser¹ [bize] *v.tr.* to re-dye (cloth).
biser² *v.i. Agr:* (*of grain*) to darken, deteriorate.
biser³ *v.tr. F:* to kiss.
biset [bizɛ] *n.m. Orn:* rock pigeon.
bisexué [bisɛkɥe] **bisexual, -elle** [bisɛksɥɛl] *a.* bisexual.
bismuth [bismyt] *n.m.* bismuth.
bison [bizɔ̃] *n.m. Z:* bison; *esp. U.S:* buffalo.
bisou [bizu] *n.m. F:* kiss, smacker.
bisque [bisk] *n.f. Cu:* bisque.
bissecteur, -trice [bisɛktœr, -tris] **1.** *a.* bisecting (line, etc.). **2.** *n.f.* **bissectrice,** bisector, bisecting line.
bissection [bisɛksjɔ̃] *n.f. Mth:* bisection.
bisser [bise] *v.tr.* (*a*) to give an encore of, to repeat (a song, etc.); (*b*) to encore (a song, performer, etc.).
bissextile [bisɛkstil] *a.f.* **année b.,** leap year.
bissexué [bisɛksɥe], **bissexuel, -elle** [bisɛksɥɛl] *a.* bisexual.
bistouri [bisturi] *n.m. Surg:* bistoury, lancet.
bistournage [bisturnaʒ] *n.m. Husb:* castration (by twisting of the cord).
bistourner [bisturne] *v.tr.* **1.** to wring, to wrench. **2.** *Husb:* to castrate (by twisting the cord).
bistre [bistr̥] *a. & n.m.* bistre, blackish-brown; **teint b.,** swarthy complexion.
bistré [bistre] *a.* brown, swarthy (skin).
bistrer [bistre] *v.tr.* to darken, to tan (complexion).
bistro(t) [bistro] *n.m. F:* = pub; **le b. du coin,** the local.
bisulfate [bisylfat] *n.m. Ch:* bisulphate.
bisulfite [bisylfit] *n.m. Ch:* bisulphite.
bisulfure [bisylfyr] *n.m. Ch:* disulphide, bisulphide.
bit [bit] *n.m. Cmptr:* bit.
bitos [bitɔs] *n.m. P:* hat, titfer.
bitte [bit] *n.f. Nau:* bitt; bollard (on ship).
bitter [bitɛr] *n.m.* bitters.
bitture [bityr] *n.f.* **1.** *Nau:* range of cable. **2.** *P:* **prendre une b.,** to get drunk, canned, stoned.
bitturer(se) [səbityre] *v.pr. P:* to get drunk, canned.
bitumage [bitymaʒ] *n.m. Civ.E:* **1.** asphalting. **2.** tarring.
bitume [bitym] *n.m. Miner:* **1.** bitumen, asphalt. **2.** (mineral) pitch, tar.
bitum(in)er [bitym(in)e] *v.tr.* **1.** to cover (road, etc.) with bitumen; to asphalt. **2.** to tar; **carton bitumé,** tarred felt.
bitum(in)eux, -euse [bitym(in)ø, -øz] *a. Miner:* **1.** bituminous, asphaltic. **2.** tarry.
biture [bityr] *n.f.* = SE BITTURE.
biturer(se) [səbityre] *v.pr. P:* = BITTURER.
bivalent [bivalɑ̃] *a. Ch:* bivalent, divalent.
bivalve [bivalv] *a. & n.m. Moll:* bivalve.
bivouac [bivwak] *n.m. Mil:* bivouac; **feu de b.,** watch fire.
bivouaquer [bivwake] *v.i. Mil:* to bivouac.
bizarre [bizar] *a.* peculiar, eccentric, odd, strange, queer, bizarre; *n.m.* **le b.,** the bizarre; **le b. de l'affaire, c'est que . . .,** the funny thing is, that . . .
bizarrement [bizarmɑ̃] *adv.* peculiarly, strangely.
bizarrerie [bizarri] *n.f.* **1.** peculiarity, strangeness, oddness. **2.** whimsicalness, eccentricity; **on lui pardonne ses bizarreries,** people forgive his oddities.
bizutage [bizytaʒ] *n.m. Sch:F:* initiation, ragging (of freshmen).
bizuter [bizyte] *v.tr. Sch: F:* to rag (a freshman).
bizut(h) [bizy] *n.m. Sch: F:* freshman, fresher.
blabla(bla) [blabla(bla)] *n.m. F:* claptrap, boloney; padding, waffle (in a speech, etc.).
blackboulage [blakbulaʒ] *n.m.* blackballing; *F:* failing (of an exam candidate).
blackbouler [blakbule] *v.tr.* to blackball; *F:* to fail (candidate).
black-out [blakaut] *n.m.* blackout; **faire le b.-o. sur un scandale,** to hush up, cover up, a scandal.
blafard, -arde [blafar, -ard] *a.* pallid, wan, pale (moon, light, etc.).
blague [blag] *n.f.* **1. b. (à tabac)** (tobacco) pouch. **2.** *F:* (*a*) tall story; bunkum; **tout ça c'est de la b.,** it's all bunkum, nonsense; **ne racontez pas de blagues,** you're having me on; **b. à part,** seriously, joking apart; **sans b.?** really? you're joking! no kidding? (*b*) (practical) joke; trick, hoax; **il m'a fait une sale b.,** he played a dirty trick on me. **3.** mistake, blunder.
blaguer [blage] *F:* **1.** *v.i.* to talk through one's hat; **tu blagues!** you're joking, kidding, having me on. **2.** *v.tr.* to tease, make fun of (s.o., sth.).
blagueur, -euse [blagœr -øz] *F:* **1.** *n.* joker, comedian. **2.** *a.* teasing, bantering, ironical (remark).
blair [blɛr] *n.m. P:* nose, conk, hooter.
blaireau, -eaux [blɛro] *n.m.* **1.** *Z:* badger. **2.** (*a*) shaving brush; (*b*) *Art:* (badger hair) brush; badger.
blairer [blere] *v.tr. P:* **je ne peux pas le b.,** I can't stick him, stand him at any price.
blâmable [blɑmabl] *a.* blameworthy, blamable.
blâme [blɑm] *n.m.* **1.** blame, disapproval; **rejeter le b. de qch. sur qn,** to lay all the blame for sth. on s.o. **2.** *Adm:* reprimand; **donner un b. à qn,** to reprimand s.o.; **recevoir un b.,** to incur a reprimand, censure.
blâmer [blɑme] *v.tr.* **1.** to blame (s.o., action); to find fault with (s.o.); to censure (government, etc.); **b. qn de faire, d'avoir fait, qch.,** to blame s.o. for

doing, having done, sth. **2.** *Adm:* to reprimand.

blanc, blanche [blɑ̃, blɑ̃ʃ] **I.** *a.* **1.** white; **b. comme (la) neige,** white as snow, snow-white; **vieillard à cheveux blancs,** white-haired old man. **2.** light-coloured, pale; **la race blanche,** the white race; **b. de peur,** white with fear; **b. de colère,** livid with anger; **b. comme un linge,** as white as a sheet; **verre b.,** colourless glass; **vin b.,** white wine. **3.** innocent, pure. **4.** blank (page, etc.); plain, unlined (paper); **nuit blanche,** sleepless night; **examen b.,** mock examination; **mariage b.,** unconsummated marriage; **voix blanche,** toneless voice; **vers blancs,** blank verse; *Ten:* **jeu b.,** love game. **II.** *n.m.* **1.** white; **robe d'un b. sale,** dingy white dress; **b. cassé,** off white; **être habillé de b., être en b.,** to be dressed in white; **mariage en b.,** white wedding; **je vous l'écris noir sur b.,** I'm putting it in black and white. **2.** (*white part*) (*a*) **le b. des yeux,** the whites of the eyes; **regarder qn dans le b. des yeux,** to look s.o. straight in the eye; **rougir jusqu'au b. des yeux,** to blush to the roots of one's hair; (*b*) **b. d'une cible,** bull's eye of a target; **donner, mettre, dans le b.,** to hit the bull's eye; (*c*) blank, gap, space; **laisser des blancs,** to leave blanks; **chèque en b.,** blank cheque; (*d*) (*in dominoes*) **double b.,** double blank. **3.** white (man). **4.** (*a*) **saigner qn à b.,** to bleed s.o. white; **chauffer un métal à b.,** to bring a metal to a white heat; **chauffé à b.,** white-hot; (*b*) **cartouche à b.,** blank cartridge; **tirer à b.,** to fire a blank, blanks. **5.** (*white substance*) (*a*) **b. de poulet,** breast of chicken, chicken breast; *esp. U.S:* white meat; **b. d'œuf,** white of egg, egg white; (*b*) **b. de billard,** billiard chalk; **b. de chaux,** whitewash; (*c*) *Paint:* **b. de zinc,** zinc white, oxide of zinc; **b. de céruse, d'argent, de plomb,** white lead; (*d*) **(articles de) b.,** linen, *NAm:* white goods; **magasin de b.,** linen shop; **vente de b.,** sale of linen, white sale; (*e*) white wine. **6.** *Hort:* **b. du rosier, de la vigne,** rose, vine, mildew. **III. blanche,** *n.f.* **1.** white (woman). **2.** *Bill:* white (ball). **3.** *Mus:* minim; *esp. NAm:* half note.

blanc-bec [blɑ̃bɛk] *n.m.* callow youth; greenhorn, tenderfoot; *pl. blancs-becs.*

blanchaille [blɑ̃ʃɑj] *n.f.* **1.** *Fish:* small fry, bait. **2.** *Cu:* whitebait.

blanchâtre [blɑ̃ʃɑtr̥] *a.* whitish, off-white.

Blanche-Neige [blɑ̃ʃnɛʒ] *Pr.n.f. Lit:* Snow White.

blanchet [blɑ̃ʃɛ] *n.m.* (*a*) white woollen cloth; (*b*) cloth filter; strainer; (*c*) *Typ:* (press) blanket.

blancheur [blɑ̃ʃœr] *n.f.* **1.** whiteness, paleness; **d'une b. de perle,** pearl-white. **2.** *Lit:* purity, innocence.

blanchiment [blɑ̃ʃimɑ̃] *n.m.* **1.** (*a*) whitening; (*b*) whitewashing (of wall, etc.) (*c*) *Cu: Agr:* blanching (of vegetables). **2.** *Tex:* bleaching.

blanchir [blɑ̃ʃir] **1.** *v.tr.* (*a*) to whiten, to make (sth.) white; *Typ:* **b. la composition,** to space out the matter; (*b*) *Tex:* to bleach; (*c*) to wash, launder; **donner du linge à b.,** to send clothes to the wash; **cette déclaration l'a blanchi complètement,** this statement has completely exonerated him; (*d*) **b. (à la chaux),** to whitewash (ceiling, wall, etc.); (*e*) *Cu: Agr:* to blanch (vegetables). **2.** *v.i.* (*a*) to whiten, to turn white; **il commence à b.,** he's turning, going, grey, white; (*b*) to blanch, to turn pale. **3. se b.,** to clear oneself, one's name.

blanchissage [blɑ̃ʃisaʒ] *n.m.* **1.** washing, laundering (of linen, etc.); **liste du b.,** laundry list. **2.** *Ind:* refining (of sugar).

blanchissant [blɑ̃ʃisɑ̃] *a.* (*a*) whitening, growing white; greying (hair); **l'aube blanchissante,** the brightening dawn; (*b*) paling (skin, etc.).

blanchissement [blɑ̃ʃismɑ̃] *n.m.* (*a*) whitening; turning, going, white; (*b*) blanching, turning pale.

blanchisserie [blɑ̃ʃisri] *n.f.* **1.** laundry. **2.** *Tex:* bleachery.

blanchisseur, -euse [blɑ̃ʃisœr, -øz] *n.* launderer, laundryman, *f.* laundress; washerwoman.

blanc-manger [blɑ̃mɑ̃ʒe] *n.m. Cu:* = blancmange; *pl. blancs-mangers.*

blanc-seing [blɑ̃sɛ̃] *n.m.* signature to a blank document; **donner b.-s. à qn,** to give s.o. a free hand, full power; *pl. blancs-seings.*

blanquette [blɑ̃kɛt] *n.f. Cu:* blanquette (of veal).

blasé, -ée [blɑze] *a. & n.* blasé, indifferent (person).

blaser [blɑze] **1.** *v. tr.* to blunt, cloy (the palate, etc.); to make (s.o.) blasé, indifferent. **2. se b.,** to become blasé, indifferent (**de, sur, qch.,** to sth.); **on se blase de ces plaisirs,** these pleasures pall.

blason [blazɔ̃] *n.m. Her:* (*a*) coat of arms, armorial bearings, blazon; (*b*) heraldry, armory.

blasonner [blazɔne] *v.tr. Her:* **b. un écu,** to blazon an escutcheon.

blasphémateur, -trice [blasfematœr, -tris] **1.** *n.* blasphemer. **2.** *a.* blaspheming, blasphemous.

blasphématoire [blasfematwar] *a.* blasphemous.

blasphème [blasfɛm] *n.m.* blasphemy.

blasphémer [blasfeme] *v.tr. & i.* **(je blasphème, n. blasphémons; je blasphémerai)** to blaspheme.

blastoderme [blastɔdɛrm] *n.m. Biol:* blastoderm.

blastomère [blastɔmɛr] *n.m. Biol:* blastomere.

blastomycose [blastɔmikoz] *n.f. Med:* blastomycosis.

blatérer [blatere] *v.i.* **(il blatère; il blatérera)** (*of camel*) to roar; (*of ram*) to bleat.

blatte [blat] *n.f. Ent:* cockroach, blackbeetle.

blazer [blazœr] *n.m. Cost:* blazer.

blé [ble] *n.m.* **1.** wheat, corn; **b. dur,** hard wheat, durum wheat; **b. tendre,** soft wheat; **champ de b.,** wheatfield; **grenier à b.,** granary; **halle aux blés,** corn exchange; **b. en herbe,** corn in the blade. **2. b. noir,** buckwheat; *Fr.C:* **b. d'Inde,** maize, (Indian) corn.

bled [blɛd] *n.m.* (*a*) (*in NAfrica*) inland country, interior; **dans le b.,** up country; (*b*) *F:* **en plein b.,** at the back of beyond, in the sticks; **un sale b.,** a godforsaken place; a dump.

blêmir [blemir] *v.i.* **1.** to turn pale, livid; to blanch; to turn ghastly pale. **2.** (*of light, etc.*) to grow dim, faint, wan.

blêmissement [blemismɑ̃] *n.m.* turning pale, paleness.

blennorragie [blɛnɔraʒi] *n.f. Med:* gonorrhoea.

blépharite [blefarit] *n.f. Med:* blepharitis.

blèsement [blɛzmɑ̃] *n.m.* lisping, lisp.

bléser [bleze] *v.i.* **(je blèse, n. blésons; je bléserai)** to lisp.

blésité [blezite] *n.f.* lisping.

blessant [blɛsɑ̃] *a.* hurtful, cutting (remark, etc.).

blessé, -ée [blese] **1.** *a.* (*a*) wounded, injured, hurt; **b. au bras,** wounded in the arm; **b. à mort,** fatally injured; (*b*) hurt, upset; **être b. de qch.,** to be hurt, offended, at, by, sth. **2.** *n.* wounded, injured, person; casualty; **les blessés,** the wounded, the injured, the casualties; **les grands blessés,** the severely wounded, injured; **un mort et trois blessés,** one dead and three injured.

blesser [blese] **1.** *v.tr.* (*a*) to wound, injure, hurt; **ces souliers me blessent,** these shoes hurt, pinch, me; (*b*) to offend, hurt, upset (s.o.); **b. la vue, les yeux, l'oreille,** to offend the eye, to shock, grate on, the ear; **b. qn dans son orgueil,** to hurt s.o.'s pride; **cette suspicion de ta part me blesse,** I resent your suspiciousness. **2. se b.:** (*a*) to injure, wound, hurt, damage, oneself (**avec,** with); **il s'est blessé (à) la tête,** he's hurt his head; (*b*) to take offence (**de,** at); **il se blesse pour un rien,** he's very quick to take offence.

blessure [blesyr] *n.f.* wound, injury; **faire une b. à qn,** to wound s.o.; **b. légère, dans les chairs,** flesh wound; *Jur:* **coups et blessures,** assault and battery.

blet, blette[1] [blɛ, blɛt] *a.* overripe, sleepy (fruit).
blette[2] [blɛt] *n.f.* = BETTE.
blettir [bletir] *v.i.* (*of fruit*) to become overripe; to go soft, sleepy.
bleu [blø] **1.** *a.* blue; **enfant aux yeux bleus,** blue-eyed child; **conte b.,** fairytale; tall story; **b. de froid,** blue with cold; **colère bleue,** towering rage; **j'en suis resté b.,** I was flabbergasted; **biftek b.,** very rare steak; *Med:* **enfant b.,** blue baby. **2.** *n.m.* (*a*) blue (colour); **b. clair, b.,** light blue; **b. foncé,** dark blue; **b. (de) ciel, horizon,** sky blue; **b. de Prusse,** Prussian blue; **b. marine,** navy (blue); **b. (de) roi,** royal blue; **b. d'outremer,** ultramarine (blue); **de l'encre bleu-noir,** blue-black ink; *Artil:* **tirer dans le b.,** to fire at random; (*b*) bruise; **j'ai le bras couvert de bleus,** my arm's covered with bruises, black and blue; (*c*) *F:* novice, greenhorn, *esp. NAm:* tenderfoot; *Mil:* raw recruit, rookie; (*d*) *Comest:* blue cheese; (*e*) *Cu:* **poisson au b.,** fish *au bleu*; (*f*) **bleu(s) (de chauffe, de travail),** overalls, dungarees, boiler suit; (*g*) *Tchn:* blueprint.
bleuâtre [bløɑtr̥] *a.* bluish.
bleuet [bløɛ] *n.m. Bot:* **1.** cornflower. **2.** *Fr.C:* (Canada) blueberry.
bleuir [bløir] *v.tr. & i.* to make (sth.) blue; to become, turn, go, blue.
bleuissement [bløismɑ̃] *n.m.* making (sth.) blue; becoming, turning, going, blue.
bleuté [bløte] *a.* bluish, blue-tinged (light, etc.); blue-tinted (spectacles, etc.).
bleuter [bløte] *v.tr.* to give a blue tinge to (glass, steel, etc.).
blindage [blɛ̃daʒ] *n.m.* **1.** *Civ.E: Min:* timbering, poling, sheeting (of trench, etc.). **2.** *Mil: etc:* armour, (armour) plate, (armour) plating; **plaque de b.,** armour plate. **3.** *El:* screen(ing) (of valve); shrouding (of transformer, etc.).
blindé [blɛ̃de] *a.* **1.** (*a*) *Mil: etc:* armoured, armour-plated; **abri b.,** bombproof shelter; **train b.,** armoured train; **division blindée,** armoured division; **non b.,** soft-skinned (vehicle); (*b*) *F:* **b. contre qch.,** proof against sth., hardened, immune, to sth.; (*c*) *P:* blind drunk. **3.** *Mil:* (*a*) *n.f.* **blindée,** armoured car; (*b*) *n.m.pl.* **les blindés,** the armour. **4.** *El:* screened (valve); shrouded (transformer).
blinder [blɛ̃de] *v.tr.* **1.** *Civ.E: Min:* to sheet, pole, timber (trench, mine shaft, etc.). **2.** *Mil:* to armour (plate); to plate (ship, etc.); to make bombproof. **3.** *El:* to screen, shroud. **4.** *F:* to harden (s.o.), make (s.o.) immune (**contre qch.,** to sth.).
blizzard [blizar] *n.m.* blizzard.
bloc [blɔk] *n.m.* **1.** (*a*) block, lump (of wood, stone, etc.); *Sp:* **b. de départ,** starting block; **tout d'un b.,** in one go; **coulé en b.,** cast in one piece; **acheter qch. en b.,** to buy sth. en bloc; **acquérir des droits (de traduction, etc.) en b.,** to buy rights outright; **visser, serrer, qch. à b.,** to screw sth. (up) as tightly as possible; **serrer les freins à b.,** to jam the brakes on hard; **hisser un signal à b.,** to hoist a signal close up; *F:* **gonflé à b.,** full of beans, raring to go; (*b*) block (of houses); **b. technique,** design department, technical services block (of factory, etc.). **2.** *Pol: etc:* group; coalition; bloc; **faire b.,** to join sides, unite, combine, form a bloc **(avec, contre,** with, against); **le b. occidental,** the Western bloc, the West. **3.** pad (of paper); **b. à dessin,** sketch pad. **4.** unit; *Cin:* **b. sonore,** sound unit; *Cmptr:* **b. logique,** package. **5.** *F:* prison, nick, clink.
blocage [blɔkaʒ] *n.m.* **1.** (*a*) *Const:* rubble (stone); (*b*) *Typ:* turning (of letters). **2.** (*a*) jamming, clamping, sticking (of piece of machinery, etc.); locking on, seizing (of brakes); **vis de b.,** locking screw; (*b*) jamming on (of brakes); (*c*) *Pol.Ec:* pegging; *Fin:* freezing; **b. des prix et des salaires,** prices and wage freeze; (*d*) *Sp:* blocking (of ball, etc.); *Bill:* jamming (of the balls).
blocaille [blɔkɑj] *n.f. Const:* rubble (stone).
bloc-cuisine [blɔkkɥizin] *n.m.* kitchen unit; *pl. blocs-cuisines.*
bloc-cylindres [blɔksilɛ̃dr̥] *n.m. Aut:* cylinder block, engine block; *pl. blocs-cylindres.*
bloc-diagramme [blɔkdjagram] *n.m. Geog:* (block) diagram; *pl. blocs-diagrammes.*
bloc-évier [blɔkevje] *n.m.* sink unit; *pl. blocs-éviers.*
blockhaus [blɔkos] *n.m.* **1.** *Fort:* blockhouse, pill-box. **2.** *Navy:* armoured tower; **b. de commandement,** conning tower.
bloc-moteur [blɔkmɔtœr] *n.m. Aut:* engine block; *pl. blocs-moteurs.*
bloc-notes [blɔknɔt] *n.m.* writing pad; (reporter's, shorthand) notebook; *pl. blocs-notes.*
bloc-système [blɔksistɛm] *n.m. Rail:* block system (signalling).
blocus [blɔkys] *n.m.* blockade; **faire le b. d'un port,** to blockade a port; **lever, forcer, le b.,** to raise, to run, the blockade.
blond, -onde [blɔ̃, -ɔ̃d] **1.** *a.* fair, blond (hair, person); fair-haired (person); **bière blonde,** lager; pale ale; **un demi de blonde** = a half of lager; **(cigarette) blonde,** Virginia cigarette. **2.** *n.* fair-(haired) man, woman; blond(e); *F:* **il va voir sa blonde,** he's off to see his sweetheart, his girl(friend). **3.** *n.m.* **cheveux (d'un) b. doré,** golden hair; **b. ardent,** auburn; **b. vénitien,** strawberry blond, Titian red; **b. platine,** platinum blond; **b. cendré,** ash blond.
blondasse [blɔ̃das] *a.* insipidly fair, washed out (hair).
blondeur [blɔ̃dœr] *n.f.* blondness, fairness.
blondin,[1] **-ine** [blɔ̃dɛ̃, -in] *n.* blond(e).
blondin[2], *n.m.* cableway.
blondinet, -ette [blɔ̃dinɛ, -ɛt] *n.* fair haired child.
blondir [blɔ̃dir] **1.** *v.i.* (*of hair, person*) to go blond, to get fairer, lighter. **2. elle s'est blondi les cheveux,** she's bleached her hair.
bloquer [blɔke] **1.** *v.tr.* (*a*) to combine; to put, group, mass, together; (*b*) *Const:* to block up, fill up (wall) with rubble; (*c*) *Typ:* **b. une lettre,** to turn a letter; (*d*) to blockade (port, etc.); (*e*) to jam, clamp (piece of machinery, etc.); **b. les roues,** to lock the wheels; **b. les freins,** to jam the brakes on; **b. une porte,** to jam, wedge, a door; **bloqué par la neige, le brouillard,** snowbound, fogbound; *F:* **me voilà bloqué à l'hôpital,** here I am stuck in hospital; (*f*) to stop (cheque); to block (bank account); to freeze (prices, wages); (*g*) to block, obstruct (road, etc.); **b. le chemin à qn,** to block, be in, stand in, s.o.'s way; (*h*) *Sp:* to block (ball, etc.); (*i*) *Belg: F:* to swot up, mug up (subject). **2. se b.,** to jam, stick, lock; to get jammed, stuck.
blottir (se) [səblɔtir] *v.pr.* to curl up, crouch; **village blotti au fond de la vallée,** village tucked away, nestling, in the valley; **se b. dans son lit,** to curl up, snuggle up, down, in bed; **blotti dans un coin,** huddled, huddling, in a corner.
blouse [bluz] *n.f.* (*a*) overall, smock; (surgeon's) gown; (*b*) (woman's) (over)blouse, smock.
blouser [bluze] **1.** *v.tr. F:* to cheat, trick, con (s.o.); to take (s.o.) in. **2.** *v.i.* (*of dress, etc.*) to blouse. **3.** *F:* **se b.,** to make a mistake, a blunder.
blouson [bluzɔ̃] *n.m.* (lumber)jacket; windcheater; *NAm:* windbreaker; *F: O:* **b. noir** = teddy boy.
blue-jean(s) [blu(d)ʒin(z)] *n.m. Cost:* jeans; *pl. blue-jeans.*
blues (bluz] *n.m. Mus:* blues.
bluff [blœf] *n.m.* bluff; **faire du b.,** to bluff; **c'est un**

coup de b., its all bluff; he's bluffing.
bluffer [blœfe] *v.tr. & i.* (*a*) *Cards:* to bluff (s.o.); (*b*) *F:* to trick (s.o.); to have (s.o.) on; **il ne fait que b.,** he's only bluffing; he's just trying it on.
bluffeur, -euse [blœfœr, -øz] *n.* bluffer.
boa [bɔa] *n.m.* **1.** *Rept:* boa; **b. constricteur,** boa constrictor. **2.** *Cost:* boa.
bob [bɔb] *n.m. F:* bob(sleigh).
bobard [bɔbar] *n.m. F:* tall story.
bobinage [bɔbinaʒ] *n.m.* **1.** winding, reeling. **2.** *El:* winding, coiling.
bobine [bɔin] *n.f.* **1.** (*a*) reel (of tape, etc.); bobbin (in sewing machine, etc.); spool (in typewriter, camera, etc.); roll (of film, paper, etc.); **b. de fil,** reel, spool, of cotton, of thread; (*b*) *El:* coil; **b. d'allumage,** ignition coil. **2.** *P:* face, mug.
bobiner [bɔbine] *v.tr.* to wind, reel (cotton, etc., on bobbin); to coil (wire, etc.).
bobineur, euse [bɔbinœr, -øz] *n. Tex: El:* **1.** (*pers.*) winder. **2.** *n.f.* **bobineuse,** winding machine, winder.
bobinier [bɔbinje] *n.m. El:* (*pers.*) coil winder.
bobinoir [bɔbinwar] *n.m. Tex: El:* winding machine, winder.
bobo [bobo] *n.m. F:* (*child's language*) (*a*) pain; sore; bump, bruise, cut; **avoir (du) b,** to have a sore, a pain; **ça fait bobo?** does it hurt? is it sore? (*b*) **avoir un b. au doigt,** to have a sore on one's finger.
bobonne [bɔbɔn] *n.f. P:* (*to wife*) **(ma) b.,** my dear, my love, my pet.
bobsleigh [bɔbslɛ(g)] *n.m.* bobsleigh.
bocage [bɔkaʒ] *n.m.* **1.** *Lit:* copse. **2.** *Geog:* bocage.
bocal, -aux [bɔkal, -o] *n.m.* (wide-mouthed, short-necked) bottle, jar; **mettre des fruits en b.,** to bottle fruit; **b. à poissons rouges,** goldfish bowl.
bocard [bɔkar] *n.m. Metall:* ore crusher, stamping mill.
bocardage [bɔkardaʒ] *n.m. Metall:* crushing, stamping (of ore).
bocarder [bɔkarde] *v.tr. Metall:* to crush, stamp (ore).
Boccace [bɔkas] *Pr.n.m.* Boccaccio.
boche [bɔʃ] *a. & n. F: Pej:* German, Boche, Kraut.
bock [bɔk] *n.m.* (*a*) beer glass; (*b*) glass of beer (*approx.* ¼ l./½ pt).
Boer [bur] *n. & a. inv. in f., var. in pl.* Boer.
boët(t)e [bwɛt] *n.f. Fish:* bait.
bœuf, *pl. bœufs* [bœf, bø] *n.m.* **1.** (*a*) ox, bullock; **jeune b.,** steer; **bœufs à l'engrais,** beeves, *NAm:* beefs; **b. gras** [bøgrɑ], fatted ox, prize ox; **bœufs de boucherie,** beef cattle; **fort comme un b.,** as strong as an ox; (*b*) **b. musqué,** musk ox; **b. à bosse,** zebu. **2.** beef; **b. (à la) mode,** stewed beef. **3.** *a.inv. F:* tremendous, amazing, great; **c'est b.,** it's fantastic.
bog(g)ie [bɔʒi] *n.m. Rail: etc:* bogie (truck), radial truck.
bogue [bɔg] *n.f. Bot:* chestnut bur, *NAm:* shuck.
Bohême [bɔem] *Pr.n.f.* Geog: Bohemia.
bohème 1. a. & n. bohemian; **mener une vie de b.,** to lead a bohemian, an unconventional, a free and easy, life. **2.** *n.f.* bohemia, the artistic world.
bohémien, -ienne [bɔemjɛ̃, -jɛn] *a. & n.* **1.** *Geog:* Bohemian. **2.** gipsy.
boire¹ [bwar] *v.tr.* (*pr.p.* **buvant;** *p.p.* **bu, bue;** *pr.ind.* **je bois** [bwa], **il boit, n. buvons, ils boivent;** *pr. sub.* **je boive, n. buvions;** *impf.* **je buvais;** *p.h.* **je bus, n. bûmes;** *fu.* **je boirai) 1.** to drink; **b. qch. à petits coups,** to sip sth., **b. qch. d'un (seul) trait, d'un seul coup,** to drink sth. at one gulp, straight off; to knock sth. back; **b. à la bouteille,** to drink from the bottle; **b. à sa soif,** to drink one's fill; **b. un verre jusqu'à la dernière goutte,** to drain a glass; *F:* **b. un coup,** to have a drink; **tu viens b. un verre?** are you coming for a drink? **ce vin se boit bien, se laisse b.,** this wine is very drinkable, goes down well; **faire b. qn,** to give s.o. a drink, something to drink; **faire b. les chevaux,** to water the horses; **b. les paroles de qn,** to drink in s.o.'s every word; *F:* **b. la, une, tasse,** to get a mouthful (when swimming); **ce n'est pas la mer à b.,** it's not all that hard (to do); **il y a à b. et à manger,** it's got its pros and cons. **2.** to drink (alcohol); **il boit trop,** he drinks too much; **il a (trop) bu, il a bu un coup (de trop),** he's had one too many; **il boit comme un trou,** he drinks like a fish; **il a commandé à boire,** he ordered a drink, the drinks. **3.** (*of plants, porous substances, etc.*) to soak up, absorb (moisture); (*of plant*) to drink.
boire² *n.m.* drink, drinking; **le b. et le manger,** food and drink, eating and drinking.
bois [bwa] *n.m.* **1.** wood, forest; **petit b.,** spinney, grove, thicket. **2.** timber (trees); *esp. Fr.C:* **b. debout,** standing timber; **abattre, couper, le b.,** to cut down, fell, timber; *F:* (*of aircraft*) **casser du b.,** to crash-land. **3.** wood, timber, lumber; **b. de chauffage, b. à brûler,** firewood; **petit b.,** kindling; **b. d'œuvre,** timber, lumber; **chantier de b.,** timber yard; **travail du b.,** woodwork; **train de b.,** float, raft, of timber; **jambe de b.,** wooden leg; **meubles en b.,** wooden furniture; *Fr.C:* **maison en b. rond,** log house; **b. dur,** *Fr.C:* **b. franc,** hardwood; **b. tendre,** softwood; **b. de sapin, b. blanc,** deal, whitewood; **b. de rose,** rosewood; **b. de mai,** hawthorn; **b. des îles,** West Indian hardwood; **il n'est pas de b.,** he's got *some* feelings; he's only human; **je leur ferai voir de quel b. je me chauffe,** I'll show them (what I'm made of); *F:* **touchez du bois!** touch, *U.S:* knock on, wood! **4.** (*a*) woodcut; (*b*) frame(work) (of chair, racket, etc.); **b. de lit,** bedstead; **b. de fusil,** rifle stock; **b. de drapeau,** flagstaff; (*c*) *Mus:* **les b.,** the woodwind. **5.** *pl.* antlers (of deer).
boisage [bwazaʒ] *n.m.* (*a*) timbering (of shaft, gallery, etc.); (*b*) scaffold(ing), timber(ing), framing; frame(work).
boisé [bwaze] *a.* wooded, well timbered (country); **pays b.,** woodland(s), wooded country.
boisement [bwazmɑ̃] *n.m.* afforestation (of region).
boiser [bwaze] *v.tr.* **1.** to timber, prop (mine). **2.** *For:* to afforest; to plant with timber.
boiserie [bwazri] *n.f. Const:* woodwork, wainscot (ing), panelling.
boisseau, -eaux [bwaso] *n.m.* **1.** (*a*) *Meas: A: & Fr.C:* bushel; (*b*) **mettre la lumière sous le b.,** to hide one's light under a bushel. **2.** (*a*) drain tile; chimney (flue) tile; (*b*) *Mch: I.C.E:* throttle chamber.
boisselier [bwasəlje] *n.m.* (dry) cooper.
boisson [bwasɔ̃] *n.f.* (*a*) drink, beverage; **boissons alcoolisées, non alcoolisées,** alcoholic, soft, drinks; **il s'est adonné à la boisson,** he's taken to drink; (*b*) *Fr.C:* hard liquor, spirits.
boîte [bwat], *n.* **1.** box; **b. en fer,** tin, can; canister; **b. à conserves,** tin, can; **conserves en b.,** tinned, canned, food; **b. à pain,** bread bin; **b. de secours,** first-aid box; *Aut:* **b. à gants,** glove box, compartment; **mettre en b.,** to box (goods); to tin, can (sardines); **b. aux lettres,** (i) letterbox, pillarbox, postbox, *NAm:* mailbox; (ii) (*at house, etc.*) letterbox, *NAm:* mailbox; **b. postale 260,** Post Office box 260; **b. d'allumettes,** box of matches; **b. à allumettes,** matchbox; **b. à outils,** toolbox; **b. à musique,** musical box, *NAm:* music box; **b. à violon,** violin case; **b. à malice, à surprise,** jack-in-the-box; *Anat:* **b. crânienne, du crâne,** brain-pan. **2.** *Tchn:* **b. d'une serrure,** case of a lock; *Mch:* **b. à feu,** firebox; **b. à vapeur,** steam chest; *Aut:* **b. de vitesses,** gearbox; **b. de l'embrayage,** clutch casing; *Rail:* **b. de l'essieu,** axle box; *El:* **b. à fusible,** fuse

box; *Av:* **b. noire,** flight recorder; black box. **3.** (*a*) *F:* one's office, shop, school, etc.; **sale b.,** rotten hole; **quelle b. affreuse!** what a hole! what a dump! (*b*) **b. (de nuit),** nightclub.

boiter [bwate] *v.i.* to limp, walk with a limp; **b. d'un pied,** to be lame in one foot; **b. bas,** to limp badly; **homme qui boite,** lame man, man with a limp.

boiterie [bwatri], *n.f.* lameness.

boiteux, -euse [bwatø, -øz] **1.** *a.* (*a*) lame, limping; **le facteur est b.,** the postman walks with a limp; **cheval b.,** lame horse; (*b*) wobbly, rickety, shaky (furniture, argument, etc.); **vers b.,** clumsy, faulty, lines; limping verses. **2.** *n.* **un b., une boiteuse,** a lame man, woman; a cripple; **le b.,** the man with the limp.

boîtier [bwatje] *n.m.* case, casing; **b. de montre,** watch case; **b. de chirurgien,** surgeon's instrument case.

boitiller [bwatije] *v.i.* to limp slightly, have a slight limp.

boitte [bwat] *n.f. Fish:* bait.

bol¹ [bɔl] *n.m.* (*a*) *Physiol:* **b. alimentaire,** (alimentary) bolus; (*b*) *Pharm: Vet:* bolus, pellet.

bol² *n.m.* **1.** (*a*) bowl, basin; (*b*) *P:* luck; **manque de b.,** bad luck. **2.** bowl(ful).

bolchevik, bolchevique [bɔlʃəvik] *a. & n.* Bolshevik, Bolshevist.

bolchevisme [bɔlʃəvism] *n.m.* Bolshevism.

bolcheviste [bɔlʃəvist] *a. & n.* Bolshevist.

bolduc [bɔldyk] *n.m.* (thin) coloured ribbon (for tying up boxes of chocolates, etc.).

bolée [bɔle] *n.f.* bowl(ful), basin(ful) (of soup, etc.).

boléro [bɔlero] *n.m. Danc: Mus: Cost:* bolero.

bolet [bɔlɛ] *n.m. Fung:* boletus.

bolide [bɔlid] *n.m.* (*a*) *Meteor:* bolide, fireball, meteor; (*b*) racing car; **lancé comme un b. sur la route,** hurtling along the road.

Bolivie [bɔlivi], *Pr.n.f. Geog:* Bolivia.

bolivien, -ienne [bɔlivjɛ̃, -jɛn] *a. & n. Geog:* Bolivian.

bollard [bɔlar] *n.m. Nau:* bitt, bollard.

Bologne [bɔlɔɲ] *Pr.n.f. Geog:* Bologna.

bolonais, -aise [bɔlɔnɛ, -ɛz] *a. & n. Geog:* Bolognese.

bombance [bɔ̃bɑ̃s] *n.f. F:* feast(ing); carousing; **faire b.,** to feast; to go on a spree, a binge.

bombardement [bɔ̃bardəmɑ̃] *n.m.* **1.** (*a*) *Artil:* bombardment, shelling, gunfire; (*b*) pelting, showering (with stones, etc.); bombarding (with questions, etc.). **2.** *Av:* bombing; **b. aérien,** air raid; **avion de b.,** bomber. **3.** *Ph:* bombardment.

bombarder [bɔ̃barde] *v.tr.* **1.** (*a*) to bombard, bomb, shell; **maison bombardée,** bombed, shelled, house; (*b*) *Ph:* to bombard (with neutrons, etc.); (*c*) **b. qn de pierres,** to pelt s.o. with stones; **b. qn de questions,** to fire questions at s.o.; **être bombardé de lettres,** to be inundated with letters. **2.** *F:* **on l'a bombardé ministre,** he's been made a minister out of the blue.

bombardier [bɔ̃bardje] *n.m. Mil:* **1.** *A:* bombardier. **2.** *Av:* (*a*) (*aircraft*) bomber; (*b*) (*pers*) bomb aimer; *NAm:* bombardier.

bombe [bɔ̃b] *n.f.* **1.** bomb; **b. à fragmentation,** fragmentation, scatter, bomb; **b. à retardement,** delayed-action bomb, time bomb; **b. incendiaire,** incendiary bomb; **b. lacrymogène,** tear gas bomb, grenade; **b. fumigène,** smoke bomb; **b. atomique, b. A.,** atom(ic) bomb, A bomb; **b. à hydrogène, b. H.,** hydrogen bomb, H bomb; **b. volante,** flying bomb; *F:* doodlebug; **attaque, attentat, à la b.,** bomb attack; **lâcher, larguer, une b.,** to release, drop, a bomb; *F:* **entrer en, comme une, b.,** to come bursting in; **cela a fait l'effet d'une b.,** it was a real bombshell. **2.** (*a*) *Med:* **b. au cobalt,** cobalt bomb; (*b*) *Cu:* **b. glacée,** *bombe glacée;* (*c*) *Geol:* **b. volcanique,** volcanic bomb; (*d*) *Com:* aerosol; **b. à peinture,** paint spray. **3.** riding hat, cap. **4.** *F:* party, do; booze-up; **faire la b.,** to go on a binge.

bombé [bɔ̃be] *a.* convex, curved, rounded, bulging; **avoir le dos b.,** to be round-shouldered; **chaussée bombée,** cambered road; **une cuiller bombée (de sucre),** a heaped spoonful (of sugar).

bombement [bɔ̃bmɑ̃] *n.m.* bulge, bulging, convexity; camber (of road).

bomber [bɔ̃be] **1.** *v.tr.* (*a*) to cause (sth.) to bulge, belly; **b. la poitrine,** to throw out one's chest; **b. le torse,** to swagger; (*b*) to bend, curve, arch (one's back, etc.); (*c*) to camber (road). **2.** *v.i.* (*of wall, etc.*) to bulge (out).

bombonne [bɔ̃bɔn] *n.f.* = BONBONNE.

bombyx [bɔ̃biks] *n.m. Ent:* bombyx.

bon¹, bonne¹ [bɔ̃, bɔn] **I.** *a.* **1.** good, upright, honest (person, etc.); **le b. M. Seguin,** good old M. Seguin; **mon b. monsieur,** my dear sir; **bonne action,** good deed. **2.** good (book, smell, etc.); **bonne histoire,** good story; **bonne soirée,** pleasant evening; **j'aime un b. fauteuil,** I like a nice, comfortable, armchair; **j'ai trouvé le rôti b.,** I enjoyed the roast; **la bonne société,** polite society; *F:* **cela est b. à dire,** it's easier said than done. **3.** (*of pers.*) clever, capable; good (at one's work, etc.); **b. en anglais,** good at English. **4.** good, right, correct, proper, sound; **si j'ai bonne mémoire,** if my memory serves me well; **en b. état,** in good, working, order; **la bonne voie, route,** the right path, track; *Ten:* **la balle est bonne,** the ball is in. **5.** good, kind(-hearted) **(pour, envers,** to); **c'est un b. garçon,** *F:* **un b. type, un b. gars,** he's a good sort, he's all right; **il se montre b. pour sa mère,** he's very kind to his mother; **vous êtes bien b. de m'inviter,** it's very good, kind, of you to invite me. **6.** good, profitable, advantageous (investment, etc.); **acheter qch. à b. marché,** to buy sth. cheap(ly); **c'est b. à savoir, à se rappeler,** it's worth knowing, remembering; **c'est toujours b. à avoir,** it's always worth having; no point in not having it; **à quoi b.?** what's the good of it? **à quoi b. se plaindre?** what's the use, the good, the point, of complaining? **puis-je vous être b. à quelque chose?** can I do anything for you, be of any help to you? **cet exercice est b. pour le dos,** this exercise is good for the back. **7.** good; fit, suitable; **b. à manger,** (i) good to eat; (ii) fit, safe, to eat; *Mil:* **b. pour le service,** fit for duty; **il n'est b. qu'à cela,** that's all he's fit for; **elle n'est bonne à rien,** she's no good at anything; she's useless; **si b. vous semble,** if you think it advisable; **il est b. que vous sachiez,** it's just as well that you should know; **trouver b. de faire qch.,** to think fit, think it advisable, to do sth. **8.** good, favourable (omen, etc.); **souhaiter une, la, bonne année à qn,** to wish s.o. a happy New Year; **b. week-end, dimanche!** have a good weekend, Sunday! **bonne chasse!** good hunting! **9.** good, sound, safe (security, credit, etc.); **il est b. pour 25,000 frs.,** he is good for 25,000 frs.; **billet b. pour trois mois,** ticket available, valid, for three months; **son affaire est bonne, son compte est b.!** he's in for it! **10.** good, full, considerable; **un b. rhume,** a bad cold; **j'ai attendu deux bonnes heures,** I waited a full, a good, two hours, (for) two solid hours; **arriver b. premier,** to come in an easy first; **prendre une bonne moitié de qch.,** to take a good half of sth.; **donner bonne mesure,** to give full measure. **11. pour de b.,** *Lit:* **tout de b.,** seriously, in earnest, really, truly; **est-ce pour de b.?** are you serious? **il pleut pour de b.,** it's raining in real earnest; **c'est b.!** good! enough said! **12.** *int.* **b.!** right! good! fine! **b., je viendrai,** all right, I'll come. **II.** *adv.* **tenir b.,** to stand fast, to hold one's own; **tenez b.!** hold tight! hold on (tight)! **sentir b.,** to smell good; **il fait b. vivre,** it's good to be alive; **il ne fait pas b. se promener dans ce quartier,** it's not safe to walk in this district. **III.** *s.* (*a*) **les bons,** the good, the righteous; *F:* the goodies; (*b*) **cela a du b.,** it has its good points; it has some advantages; there's some good in it; **il y a du b. dans ce livre,** this book has some good parts; **le b. de l'histoire,** the best part of the story; (*c*) **en voilà une (bien) bonne!** that's a good one!

bon² *n.m.* **1.** order, voucher, ticket; coupon, form; **b. de caisse,** cash voucher; *Com:* **b. de livraison,** delivery note; **b. d'achat,** gift voucher; **b. d'essence,** petrol coupon. **2.** *Fin:* (*a*) bond, bill, draft; **b. au porteur,** bearer bond; **b. du Trésor,** treasury bond, exchequer bill; (*b*) I.O.U., note of hand.

bonace [bɔnas] *n.f.* lull, calm (before or after a storm).

bonasse [bɔnas] *a.* weak(-willed), (too) easy-going.

bonbon [bɔ̃bɔ̃] *n.m.* (*a*) sweet, *NAm:* candy; **bonbons anglais,** fruit drops, (boiled) fruit sweets; **bonbons acidulés,** acid drops; (*b*) *Belg:* biscuit.

bonbonne (bɔ̃bɔn] *n.f.* (*a*) *Ind:* carboy; (*b*) demijohn.

bonbonnière [bɔ̃bɔnjɛr] *n.f.* **1.** sweet box, bonbonnière, *NAm:* candy box. **2.** daintily furnished, neat, little flat; bijou flat, *NAm:* apartment.

bond [bɔ̃] *n.m.* **1.** bound, leap, jump, spring; **faire un b.,** to leap, spring; **les loyers ont fait un b.,** rents have shot up; **franchir qch. d'un b.,** to clear sth. at one bound; **se lever d'un b.,** to spring, leap, to one's feet; **progresser par bonds,** to advance by leaps and bounds; **b. en avant,** breakthrough (in technology, etc.). **2.** (*of ball, etc.*) bounce, rebound; **prendre la balle au b.,** (i) to catch the ball on the bounce, the rebound; (ii) to seize, jump at, the opportunity; **faire faux b. à qn,** to leave s.o. in the lurch, let s.o. down, stand s.o. up.

bonde [bɔ̃d] *n.f.* **1.** (*a*) bung (of cask); (*b*) plug (of sink, bath); **lâcher, lever, la b.,** to pull the plug out; (*c*) *Hyd.E:* sluice gate (of pond); **lâcher la b. à sa colère,** to let loose one's anger. **2.** (*a*) bunghole (of cask) (*b*) plughole (of bath, etc.); (*c*) drainage hole, outlet (of pond, etc.).

bondé [bɔ̃de] *a.* chock-full, crammed (bus, etc.); **des trains bondés de vacanciers,** trains chock-a-block, crammed, with holiday makers; *Th:* **salle bondée,** packed house.

bondieuserie [bɔ̃djøzri] *n.f.* **1.** religiosity, bigotry. **2.** *Pej:* devotional objects, religious knick-knacks.

bondir [bɔ̃dir] *v.i.* **1.** (*a*) to leap, bound; to spring, jump, up; **b. sur qch.,** to spring at, pounce on, sth.; **il a bondi de colère,** he flew into a rage; **cela me fait b.,** it infuriates me, it makes me wild to hear it; (*b*) to rush, dash, off; (*c*) to gambol; to leap, skip about. **2.** (*of ball, etc.*) to bounce.

bondissement [bɔ̃dismɑ̃] *n.m.* (*a*) bound(ing), leaping; (*b*) gambolling, frisking (of lambs, etc.).

bondon [bɔ̃dɔ̃] *n.m.* **1.** (*a*) bung; (*b*) bunghole. **2.** (cylindrical) cheese.

bonheur [bɔnœr] *n.m.* **1.** good fortune, good luck, success; **j'ai eu le b. de le connaître,** I had the good fortune to know him; **porter b. à qn,** to bring s.o. (good) luck; **quel b.!** what a blessing! **par b.,** luckily, fortunately, as luck would have it; **au petit b.,** haphazardly; **au petit b. la chance,** trusting to luck. **2.** happiness; **faire le b. de qn,** to make s.o. happy; **quel b. de voyager en avion,** what a pleasure, delight, it is to travel by air.

bonhomie [bɔnɔmi] *n.f.* simple good-heartedness; good nature; bonhomie; **avec b.,** goodnaturedly.

bonhomme [bɔnɔm] *n.m.* **1.** *A:* simple goodnatured man. **2.** *F:* fellow, chap, bloke, *esp. NAm:* guy; **un vilain b.,** a nasty piece of work; **pourquoi pleures-tu, mon b.?** what are you crying for, sonny, my little chap? **il va son petit b. de chemin,** he's jogging quietly along; (*in car*) he's bumbling along; **dessiner des bonshommes,** to draw funny people, figures; **b. de, en, pain d'épice,** gingerbread man, **b. de neige,** snowman; *pl. bonshommes* [bɔ̃zɔm].

boni [bɔni] *n.m.* **1.** *Fin:* surplus, balance in hand. **2.** bonus, profit.

boniche [bɔniʃ] *n.f. Pej:* young maid (servant).

bonification [bɔnifikasjɔ̃] *n.f.* **1.** improvement (of land, etc.). **2.** (*a*) *Com:* allowance, bonus; *Ins:* **b. pour non sinistre,** no claims bonus; (*b*) *Sp:* advantage.

bonifier [bɔnifje] (*pr.sub. & impf.* **n. bonifiions, v. bonifiiez) 1.** *v.tr.* (*a*) to improve, ameliorate (field, one's character, etc.); (*b*) *Com:* to make up, make good (shortage, etc.); (*c*) to give (s.o.) a bonus. **2.** (*of wine, etc.*) **se b.,** to improve.

boniment [bɔnimɑ̃] *n.m.* (*a*) sales talk; **faire du b. à qn,** to try to coax s.o.; (*b*) *F:* tall story; **tout ça c'est du b.,** that's all eyewash, claptrap.

bonimenter [bɔnimɑ̃te] *v.i. F:* to hand out the sales talk.

bonjour [bɔ̃ʒur] *n.m.* good day, good morning, good afternoon; hello; how d'you do? *NAm: F:* hi! **(dis) b. à ta mère (de ma part),** (give) my regards, remember me, to your mother.

bonne² [bɔn] *n.f.* maid(servant); **b. à tout faire,** maid of all work; **b. d'enfants,** nursery nurse, nanny.

Bonne-Espérance [bɔnɛsperɑ̃s] *Pr.n. Geog:* **Cap de B.-E.,** Cape of Good Hope.

bonne-maman [bɔnmamɑ̃] *n.f. F:* grandma(ma), gran(ny), nan: *pl. bonnes-mamans.*

bonnement [bɔnmɑ̃] *adv.* **tout b.,** simply, plainly, frankly; **je lui ai dit tout b. que . . .,** I just, simply, told him that. . . .

bonnet [bɔnɛ] *n.m.* **1.** (*a*) (brimless) cap, hat; (woman's, child's) bonnet; **prendre qch. sous son b.,** to do sth. off one's own bat; to take it upon oneself to do sth.; **opiner du b.,** to fall in with the majority; **c'est b. blanc et blanc b.,** it's six of one and half a dozen of the other; **b. de nuit,** nightcap; **être triste comme un b. de nuit,** to be as cheerful as the grave; **b. de bain,** bathing cap, swimming cap; **b. de douche,** shower cap; *Mil:* **b. de police,** forage cap; **b. à poil,** bearskin, busby; **b. d'évêque,** (i) bishop's mitre; (ii) *Cu: F:* parson's nose (of fowl); (*b*) **gros b.,** big shot, big noise, bigwig. **2.** (*a*) *Cost:* cup (of brassière); (*b*) second stomach, honeycomb stomach, reticulum (of ruminant).

bonneterie [bɔntri] *n.f.* **1.** hosiery. **2.** hosiery trade; hosier's (shop).

bonnetier, -ière [bɔntje, -jɛr] *n.* hosier.

bonniche [bɔniʃ] *n.f. Pej:* young maid(servant).

bon-papa [bɔ̃papa] *n.m. F:* grandpa(pa), grandad; *pl. bons-papas.*

bonsoir [bɔ̃swar] *n.m.* good evening, goodnight; **dire b., souhaiter le b., à qn,** to say good evening, goodnight, to s.o.; *F:* **tout est dit, b.!** there's nothing more to be said; there's an end of it! and that's that!

bonté [bɔ̃te] *n.f.* **1.** (*a*) goodness, kindness; kindliness; **sourire plein de b.,** kindly, benevolent, smile; **ayez la b. de me dire . . .,** please tell me . . .; **b. divine, du ciel!** good heavens! (*b*) *pl.* kindnesses, kind actions; **je ne m'attendais pas à tant de bontés,** I didn't expect such kindness. **2.** goodness, good quality, excellence (of things).

bonze [bɔ̃z] *n.m.* **1.** bonze, Buddhist priest, monk. **2.** *F:* big shot. **3.** *F:* **vieux b.,** old fogey, dodderer.

bonzerie [bɔ̃zri], *n.f.* bonze, Buddhist, monastery.

bonzesse [bɔ̃zɛs] *n.f.* bonze, Buddhist nun.

bookmaker, *F:* **book** [buk(mɛkœr)], *n.m.* bookmaker, *F:* bookie.

boom [bum] *n.m.* **1.** *Com: Fin:* boom. **2.** *F:* (young people's) party.

boomerang [bumrɑ̃g] *n.m.* boomerang; *F:* **son projet a fait b.,** his plan boomeranged, backfired.

borate [bɔrat] *n.m. Ch:* borate.

borax [bɔraks] *n.m. Ch:* borax.

borborygme [bɔrbɔrigm] *n.m. usu pl.* rumbling(s), gurgling(s) (in the stomach).

bord [bɔr] *n.m.* **1.** *Nau:* side (of ship); **jeter qch., tomber, par-dessus b.,** to throw sth., to fall, overboard; **moteur hors bord,** outboard (motor); **b. du vent, sous le vent,** weather side, lee side; **faux b.,** list; **le long du b.,** alongside; **être b. à quai,** to be alongside the quay; (*b*) tack, leg; **courir, tirer, un b.,** to make a tack; (*c*) **les hommes du b.,** the ship's company, the crew; **être du même b.,** to be on the same side, of the same opinion; **journal de b.,** ship's log; logbook (of ship, aircraft, etc.); **à b. d'un navire, d'un avion,** on board, aboard, a ship, an aircraft; **à b.,** on board (ship); aboard; **avoir qn à son b.,** to have s.o. aboard. **2.** (*a*) edge (of table, etc.); border, hem (of garment); edge, verge (of cliff, etc.); rim, brim (of vase, etc.); lip (of cup, wound, etc.); **b. du trottoir,** kerb, *NAm:* curb; **au b. du tombeau,** at death's door; **au b. des larmes,** on the verge of tears; **remplir un verre jusqu'au b.,** to fill a glass to the brim; **au b. de la route,** at, on, the roadside; at, on, the side of the road; **auberge au b., sur le b., de la route,** wayside, roadside, inn; **hôtel au b. du lac,** lakeside hotel; **je l'ai trouvé au b. de la rivière,** I found it on the river bank; **aller au b. de la mer,** to go to the seaside; **maison au b. de la mer,** seaside house; **maison sur le b. de la mer,** house on the sea front, the (sea) shore; **b. à b.,** edge to edge; *Av:* **b. d'attaque, b. de fuite,** leading edge, trailing edge (of wing); (*b*) brim (of hat); **chapeau à larges bords,** broad-brimmed, wide-brimmed, hat.

bordage [bɔrdɑʒ] *n.m.* **1.** *Nau:* plank(ing), sheathing, plating (of ship). **2.** edging (of dress, etc.); **b. de pierres,** stone kerb, *NAm:* curb; **3.** *Fr.C:* inshore ice.

bordé [bɔrde] **1.** *a.* edged, fringed, bordered (**de,** with); **mouchoir b. de dentelle,** lace-edged handkerchief; **boulevard b. d'arbres,** tree-lined boulevard; **2.** *n.m.* (*a*) edging, border, (of garment, etc.); (*b*) *Nau:* planking, planks, plating (of ship).

bordeaux [bɔrdo] *n.m.* Bordeaux (wine); **b. rouge,** claret; *a.inv.* claret(-coloured), maroon.

bordée [bɔrde] *n.f. Nau:* **1.** broadside (guns, fire); **lâcher une b.,** to let fly a broadside; **b. de jurons,** torrent of abuse; *Fr.C:* **b. (de neige),** heavy snowfall. **2.** tack; **courir une b.,** to make a tack; **tirer des bordées,** to tack; *F:* **tirer, courir, une b.,** to go on a binge, a pub crawl. **3.** watch; **b. de tribord, de bâbord,** starboard watch, port watch.

bordel [bɔrdɛl] *n.m.* brothel; *P:* **quel b.!** what a mess! what a shambles! **tout le b.,** the whole damn lot.

bordelais, -aise [bɔrdəlɛ, -ɛz] **1.** *a. & n.* (native, inhabitant) of Bordeaux. **2.** *n.m.* **le B.,** the Bordeaux region. **3.** *n.f.* **bordelaise:** (*a*) Bordeaux cask of about 225 litres; (*b*) Bordeaux bottle of about ¾ litre.

border [bɔrde] *v.tr.* **1.** to border; to edge, fringe (sth. with sth.); **les peupliers qui bordent le chemin,** the poplars lining the road; *Nau:* **navire qui borde la côte,** ship skirting the coast; **b. un lit,** to tuck in the bedclothes; **b. qn (dans son lit),** to tuck s.o. in, up. **2.** *Nau:* to plank, plate (a ship). **3.** to ship (oars). **4.** *Nau:* **b. une voile,** to haul the sheets taut.

bordereau, -eaux [bɔrdəro] *n.m.* statement; invoice, account (of goods, cash, etc.); note, abstract, schedule; **b. de(s) prix,** price list; **b. d'expédition,** dispatch note; **b. de livraison,** delivery note; **b. d'achat,** contract note, purchase note; **b. de crédit,** credit note; **b. de versement,** paying-in slip; **b. de paie, de salaire,** wage(s) slip; salary advice (note).

bordure [bɔrdyr] *n.f.* **1.** (*a*) border, rim; fringe, edging, edge (of garment, etc.); kerb, *NAm:* curb (of pavement, etc.); **papier à b. noire,** black-edged paper; (*b*) binding (of hat, etc.); welt (of glove, etc.). **2.** frame, surround (of mirror, etc.).

bore [bɔr] *n.m. Ch:* boron.

boréal, -aux [bɔreal, -o] *a.* boreal, north(ern).

borgne [bɔrɲ] *a.* **1.** (*a*) one-eyed, blind in one eye; *n.* **un(e) b.,** one-eyed man, woman; (*b*) *Mec.E:* **trou b.,** recessed hole. **2.** disreputable, shady house, street, etc.); **café b.,** low dive.

borique [bɔrik] *a. Ch:* boric, boracic (acid).

boriqué [bɔrike] *a. Pharm:* **pommade boriquée,** boracic ointment; **compresse en coton b.,** boracic lint compress.

bornage [bɔrnaʒ] *n.m. Surv:* demarcation, marking out (of land boundaries); **pierre de b,** boundary stone.

borne [bɔrn] *n.f.* **1.** (*a*) boundary mark, stone, post; (*b*) **b. kilométrique** = milestone; *Nau:* **b. d'amarrage,** bollard (on wharf); **il était planté là comme une b.,** he stood there like a post; (*c*) *F:* kilometre; (*d*) *pl.* boundaries, limits, bounds, confines (of kingdom, knowledge, etc.); **dépasser toutes les bornes,** to go too far; **sans bornes,** boundless, limitless, unlimited. **2.** *El:* terminal; **b. de mise à la terre, b. de masse,** earth, *NAm:* ground, terminal.

borné [bɔrne] *a.* limited, restricted (intelligence, etc.); narrow (mind); narrow-minded (person).

borne-fontaine [bɔrn(ə)fɔ̃tɛn] *n.f.* (*a*) public drinking fountain; (*b*) *Fr.C:* fire hydrant; *pl. bornes-fontaines.*

borner [bɔrne] **1.** *v.tr.* (*a*) to mark out, to mark the boundary of (field, etc.); **b. une route,** to set up milestones along a road; (*b*) to form the boundary of (country, etc.); **le chemin qui borne la forêt,** the path bordering the forest; (*c*) to limit, restrict (view, power, etc.); to set limits, bounds, to (ambition, desires). **2. se b.** (*a*) to restrict, limit, oneself; to exercise self restraint; **je me borne au strict nécessaire,** I confine myself to the absolute essentials; **se b. à faire qch.,** to limit oneself to doing sth.; (*b*) (*of things*) to be confined, limited, restricted (**à qch.,** to sth.); **toute leur science se borne à cela,** this is the (full) extent of their knowledge; **voici à quoi se borne son raisonnement,** this is what his argument comes down to.

bosnien, -ienne [bɔznjɛ̃, - jɛn] *a. & n. Hist:* Bosnian.

Bosnie [bɔzni] *Pr.n.f. Hist:* Bosnia.

Bosphore (le) [ləbɔsfɔr] *Pr.n.m. Geog:* the Bosphorus.

bosquet [bɔskɛ] *n.m.* grove, thicket, copse.

bossage [bɔsaʒ] *n.m. Arch:* boss.

bosse [bɔs] *n.f.* **1.** hump (of hunchback, camel, etc.); *F:* **il a roulé sa b. partout,** he's knocked about, been about, a bit; he's a rolling stone. **2.** (*a*) bump, lump, swelling (on the head, etc.); (*b*) unevenness, bump (in the ground); **avoir la b. du commerce,** to have a good head for business. **3.** *Nau:* painter (of boat).

bosselage [bɔslaʒ] *n.m.* embossing.

bosseler [bɔsle] *v.tr.* **(je bosselle, n. bosselons; je bossellerai) 1.** to emboss (plate, etc.). **2.** to dent, bash (things); **casserole toute bosselée,** battered saucepan.

bosselure [bɔslyr] *n.f.* **1.** (*on silverware*) relief **2.** inequality, unevenness, bumpiness (of surface).

bosser [bɔse] *v.i. P:* to work hard; to slave, slog.

bosseur, -euse [bɔsœr, -øz] *n. P:* hard worker, slogger.

bossoir [bɔswar] *n.m. Nau:* **1.** (*a*) cathead; (*b*) bow (of ship). **2.** davit; **les bras de b.,** the davit guys.

bossu, -ue [bɔsy] **1.** *a.* hunchbacked (person); humped (animal); **tu deviens b.,** you're getting a stoop. **2.** *n* hunchback.

bossué [bɔsɥe] *a.* battered (kettle, etc.).

bossuer [bɔsɥe] *v.tr.* = BOSSELER 2.

boston [bɔstɔ̃] *n.m.* **1.** *Cards:* boston. **2.** *Danc:* boston; hesitation waltz.

bostonien, -ienne [bɔstɔnjɛ̃, jɛn] *a. & n. Geog:* (native, inhabitant) of Boston (U.S.A.).

bostonnais, -aise [bɔstɔnɛ, -ɛz] *n. Fr.C:* American; Bostonian.

bot [bo] *a.* **pied b.,** (i) clubfoot; (ii) clubfooted person; **main bote,** club hand.

botanique [bɔtanik] **1.** *a.* botanical. **2.** *n.f.* botany.

botaniste [bɔtanist] *n.m. & f.* botanist.

botte¹ [bɔt] *n.f.* bunch, bundle (of carrots, etc.); truss, bundle, sheaf (of hay); bale (of hemp, etc.).

botte² *n.f.* (high) boot; **bottes à l'écuyère,** riding boots; **bottes de mer,** seaboots, jackboots; **bottes d'égoutier, bottes cuissardes,** waders; **bottes de, en, caoutchouc,** wellingtons, rubber boots, gumboots; **sous la b. de l'envahisseur,** under the heel of the invader; **la b. de l'Italie,** the boot of Italy; *F:* **à propos de bottes,** apropos of nothing at all, without rhyme or reason; *F:* **en avoir plein les bottes,** to be fed up with sth.

botte³ *n.f. Fenc:* pass, thrust, lunge, hit.

botte⁴ *n.f. Sch: F:* students who leave the *École Polytechnique* with the highest marks.

bottelage [bɔtlaʒ] *n.m.* trussing, tying up (of hay).

botteler [bɔtle] *v.tr.* **(je bottelle, n. bottelons; je bottellerai)** to bundle, tie up, truss (hay, etc.).

botter [bɔte] **1.** *v.tr.* (*a*) to put (s.o.'s) boots, shoes, on; to supply (s.o.) with boots; **être bien botté,** to be well shod; **le Chat botté,** Puss in Boots; (*b*) *F:* to boot, kick (a ball, etc.); **il lui a botté les fesses,** he booted him, gave him a kick in the backside. **2.** *v.i. Fb: F:* to kick the ball. **3. se b.,** to put one's boots on.

bottier [bɔtje] *n.m.* bootmaker, shoemaker.

bottillon [bɔtijɔ̃] *n.m.* ankle boot; bootee.

Bottin [bɔtɛ̃] *Pr.n.m. R.t.m.* French telephone and street directory.

bottine [bɔtin] *n.f.* ankle boot; (baby's) bootee.

bouc [buk] *n.m.* (*a*) (billy) goat; **b. émissaire,** scapegoat; *F:* **puer comme un b., puer le b.,** to stink, pong; (*b*) **(barbe de) b.,** goatee (beard).

boucan [bukɑ̃] *n.m. P:* hullabaloo, row, din, uproar; **un b. de tous les diables,** the devil of a row.

boucane [bukan] *n.f. Fr.C:* smoke.

boucané [bukane] *a.* tanned, weatherbeaten, swarthy (complexion).

boucaner [bukane] *v.tr.* (*a*) to smoke, cure (meat, fish, etc.); (*b*) to tan (s.o.'s skin).

boucanier [bukanje] *n.m.* buccaneer, pirate.

bouchage [buʃaʒ] *n.m.* (*a*) filling up, in, plugging, stopping (up) (of gas, etc.); blocking (up), clogging (of pipe, etc.); corking (of bottle); (*b*) blocking up, walling up (of passage, etc.).

bouche [buʃ] *n.f.* **1.** (*of pers.*) mouth; (*a*) **avoir, parler, la b. pleine,** to have, to talk with, one's mouth full; **une pipe à la bouche,** with a pipe in his mouth; **avoir bonne, mauvaise, b.,** to have a pleasant, a nasty, taste in one's mouth; **garder qch. pour la bonne b.,** to save something until last, as a titbit; **cela fait venir l'eau à la b.,** it makes your mouth water; **faire la petite b.,** to turn one's nose up; **embrasser qn à pleine b.,** to kiss s.o. full on the lips, passionately; **manger à pleine b.,** to eat greedily, to gobble one's food; **provisions de b.,** food; **dépense de b.,** housekeeping expenses; **avoir une douzaine de bouches à nourrir,** to have a dozen mouths to feed; **c'est une fine b.,** he's a gourmet; **les bouches inutiles,** unproductive people; *Med:* **à prendre par la b.,** to be taken internally; (*b*) **elle n'osait pas ouvrir la b.,** she dared not open her mouth; **je l'ai appris de sa propre b.,** I had it from his, her, own lips; **son nom est dans toutes les bouches,** everyone's talking about him; **demeurer b. close,** to remain silent, to hold one's tongue; **b. cousue!** not a word! mum's the word! don't breathe a word (of it); *P:* **ta b.!** shut up! dry up! *F:* **il en avait la b. pleine, plein la b.,** he was full of it, he couldn't talk of anything else; **de b. à oreille,** (i) by word of mouth; (ii) off the record, unofficially. **2.** mouth (of horse, fish, etc.); **cheval sans b., fort en b.,** hard-mouthed horse; **cheval à la b. chatouilleuse,** tender-mouthed horse. **3.** mouth (of river, etc.); opening, aperture (of crater, well, etc.); muzzle (of gun); slot (of money box, etc.); nozzle; **b. de métro,** underground entrance, *NAm:* subway entrance; *Civ.E: etc:* **b. d'accès,** manhole (of sewer); **b. d'eau,** hydrant; **b. d'incendie,** fire hydrant, *NAm:* fireplug; **b. de chaleur,** hot air vent; **b. d'aération,** air vent; **b. d'égout,** gully hole.

bouché [buʃe] *a.* **1.** blocked, choked (pipe, etc.); **nez b.,** blocked, stuffed-up, nose; **avoir l'esprit b., être b.,** to be dull-witted, dense, thick; **être b. à l'émeri,** to be a complete moron; **temps b.,** cloudy, overcast, weather. **2. cidre b.,** bottled cider.

bouche-à-bouche [buʃabuʃ] *n.m. inv.* mouth-to-mouth resuscitation; kiss of life.

bouchée [buʃe] *n.f.* **1.** mouthful; **mettre les bouchées doubles,** to do a job in double quick time; **ne faire qu'une b. d'un mets,** to eat a dish quickly, greedily; **ne faire qu'une b. de qn, de qch.,** to make short work of s.o., sth. **2.** *Cu:* small patty, pasty; **b. aux huîtres,** oyster patty; **b. à la reine,** chicken vol-au-vent.

boucher¹ [buʃe] **1.** *v.tr.* to fill up, in (gap, etc.); to block (up), choke (up), clog (pipe, etc.); to block (the view, etc.); **b. un trou,** to plug, block up, stop (up), a hole; **cela servira à b. un trou,** that will do as a stopgap; that will tide us over; **b. une bouteille,** to cork a bottle; **b. une fenêtre,** to block up, wall up, a window; **b. le passage à qn,** to block, stand in, s.o.'s way. **2. se b.,** (*of pipe, etc.*) to get blocked (up), choked (up), clogged; **se b. le nez,** to hold one's nose; **se b. les oreilles,** to put one's fingers in one's ears; to refuse to listen.

boucher² *n.m.* butcher.

bouchère [buʃɛr] *n.f.* (*a*) butcher's wife; (*b*) (woman) butcher.

boucherie [buʃri] *n.f.* **1.** (*a*) butcher's (shop); (*b*) (*trade*) butchery. **2.** butchery, slaughter.

bouche-trou [buʃtru] *n.m.* substitute, stopgap, stand-in; *pl. bouche-trous.*

bouchon [buʃɔ̃] *n.m.* **1.** *A:* bush, sign (of tavern). **2.** wisp, handful (of straw). **3.** (*a*) stopper, plug, bung (of cask); cap, top (of bottle); **b. (de liège),** cork; **vin qui sent le b.,** corked wine; **b. de verre,** glass stopper; **b. à l'émeri,** ground (glass) stopper; *I.C.E:* **b. de radiateur,** radiator cap; *Mec.E:* **b. de vidange, de trop-plein,** drain(ing) plug, tap; (*b*) (traffic) hold-up, jam; (*c*) **b. d'air,** airlock (in pipe). **4.** *Fish:* float, bob (of line).

bouchonner [buʃɔne] *v.tr.* (*a*) to rub down, wisp down (horse); (*b*) to (molly)coddle, cosset (child).

bouchot [buʃo] *n.m.* mussel bank, bed, farm.

bouclage [buklaʒ] *n.m.* (*a*) *F:* imprisonment, locking up; (*b*) surrounding, sealing off, cordoning off (of area).

boucle [bukl] *n.f.* **1.** buckle (on belt, shoe, etc.). **2.** (*a*) loop, bow (of ribbon, string, etc.); **b. à nœud coulant,** running loop; (*b*) *Nau:* bight, eye (of rope); (*c*) loop, sweep (of river); bend (of river, road); (*of river*) **décrire de nombreuses boucles,** to meander; (*d*)

Av: loop; (*e*) *Cmptr: etc:* loop. **3.** ring; **b. de rideau,** curtain ring; **boucles d'oreilles,** earrings. **4.** curl, ringlet, lock (of hair). **5.** *Sp:* lap.

bouclé [bukle] *a.* curly (hair).

boucler [bukle] **1.** *v.tr.* (*a*) to buckle, fasten (belt, etc.); *P:* **boucle-la! la boucle!** belt up! shut up! *F:* **b. une affaire,** to settle, clinch, a matter; **b. les comptes,** to close the books; *F:* **il n'y a plus qu'à b.,** we'll have to close down, shut up shop; **b. sa valise,** (i) to shut one's suitcase; (ii) to get ready to leave; (*b*) to loop, tie up, knot (ribbon, cord, etc.); **b. la boucle,** (i) *Av:* to loop the loop; (ii) to come full circle; (*c*) *F:* to lock up, imprison (s.o.); to put (s.o.) inside; (*d*) to surround, seal off, to cordon off, (an area); (*e*) *Sp:* to lap (competitor). **2.** *v.i.* (*of hair*) to curl, to be curly.

bouclette [buklɛt] *n.f.* **1.** small buckle. **2.** small ring. **3.** small curl (of hair). **4.** *Tex:* **laine b.,** knop wool, bouclé wool.

bouclier [buklije] *n.m.* (*a*) buckler, shield; (*b*) *Civ.E:* shield; (*c*) *Space:* **b. thermique,** heat shield; (*d*) *Crust:* carapace; *Geol:* **b. canadien,** Laurentian shield.

Bouddha [buda] *Pr.n.m.* Buddha.

bouddhique [budik] *a.* Buddhist.

bouddhisme [budism] *n.m.* Buddhism.

bouddhiste [budist] *a. & n.m. & f.* Buddhist.

bouder [bude] **1.** *v.i.* to sulk. **2.** *v.tr.* (*a*) **b. qn,** to refuse to have anything to do with s.o.; **il boude la peinture moderne,** he can't bear modern paintings.

bouderie [budri] *n.f.* sulkiness; (fit of the) sulks.

boudeur, -euse [budœr, -øz] **1.** *a. & n.* sulky, sullen (person). **2.** *n.f.* **boudeuse,** double back-to-back settee.

boudin [budɛ̃] *n.m.* **1.** (*a*) *Cu:* **b. (noir),** black pudding, *NAm:* blood sausage; **b. blanc,** white pudding; *F:* (*of undertaking*) **s'en aller en eau de b.,** to go to pot, down the drain; to fizzle out; (*b*) *F:* **boudins,** fat, podgy, fingers; (*c*) *Belg:* bolster. **2.** (*a*) corkscrew curl; ringlet; roll, twist (of tobacco, etc.); (*b*) *Min: etc:* sausage (of explosive); (*c*) *Mec.E: etc:* flange (on wheel, etc.).

boudiné, -ée [budine], *a.* (*a*) **boudinée dans une robe trop étroite,** bursting, bulging, out of a tight dress; (*b*) podgy (fingers, etc.).

boudiner [budine]. **1.** *v.tr.* (*a*) *Tex:* to rove, slub; (*b*) *Tchn:* to coil (wire). (*c*) *F:* **cette robe me boudine,** this dress makes me bulge. **2. se b. dans ses vêtements,** to squeeze into, bulge out of, one's clothes.

boudoir [budwar] *n.m.* (*a*) boudoir; (*b*) *Comest:* (trifle) sponge, *NAm:* ladyfinger.

boue [bu] *n.f.* **1.** mud, slush; filth, dirt; **il me considère comme la b. de ses souliers,** he treats me like dirt; **couvrir qn de b.,** to throw, sling, mud at s.o. **2.** (building) clay. **3.** sediment, mud, sludge; (*in river, etc.*) silt; *Oc:* ooze; **boues minérales,** mud baths; **bain de b.,** mud bath; **boues activées,** *Med:* radioactive mud; *Hyg:* activated sludge.

bouée [bwe], *n.f. Nau:* **1.** buoy; **b. sonore,** sonobuoy; **b. à sifflet,** whistling buoy; **b. à cloche,** bell buoy; **b. d'amarrage, de corps-mort,** mooring buoy; **b. lumineuse,** light buoy, floating light. **2. b. de sauvetage,** lifebuoy; **b. culotte,** breeches buoy.

boueur [buœr] *n.m.* dustman, refuse collector, *NAm:* garbage man, garbage collector.

boueux, -euse [buø, -øz] **1.** *a.* (*a*) muddy (road, boots, etc.); (*b*) smudged, smudgy, thick, blurred (writing, print, etc.). **2.** *n.m.* = BOUEUR.

bouffant [bufɑ̃] **1.** *a.* puffed (sleeve, etc.); full (skirt); baggy (trousers); **cheveux bouffants,** bouffant hair-do. **2.** *n.m.* puff (of sleeve).

bouffarde [bufard] *n.f. F:* (tobacco) pipe.

bouffe¹ [buf] *a.* **opéra b.,** opera bouffe, comic opera; musical comedy.

bouffe² *n.f. F:* **1.** food, grub, nosh. **2.** eating; **venez, c'est l'heure de la b.,** grub up!

bouffée [bufe] *n.f.* **1.** puff (of smoke); whiff (of scent); **tirer une b. de sa pipe,** to take a puff at one's pipe; **b. de chaleur,** blast of hot air; *Med:* hot flush. **2.** (out)burst, gust, fit (of eloquence, anger, etc.); **travailler par bouffées,** to work by fits and starts.

bouffer [bufe]. **1.** *v.i.* (*of dress, etc.*) to puff (out), swell out, balloon out, fill out; (*of bread*) to rise. **2.** *F:* (*a*) *v.i.* to eat greedily; to gobble, scoff, guzzle; (*b*) *v.tr. & i.* to eat (sth.); **j'ai bien bouffé,** that was a bloody good meal; **on n'a rien à b.,** there's no grub; (*of car*) **b. de l'essence,** to be heavy on petrol; **b. du kilomètre,** to eat up the miles; (*c*) to blow (money); **b. un million en six mois,** to run through a million in six months.

bouffetance [buftɑ̃s], *n.f. F:* food, grub, nosh.

bouffi [bufi] *a.* puffy, puffed (up), swollen (eyes, etc.); bloated (face, etc.); *Com:* **(hareng) b.,** bloater.

bouffir [bufir]. **1.** *v.tr.* to swell, puff up, out. **2.** *v.i.* to become swollen, bloated; to puff up, swell.

bouffissure [bufisyr] *s.f.* **1.** swelling, puffiness (of the face, etc.). **2.** turgidity (of style).

bouffon [bufɔ̃]. **1.** *n.m.* buffoon, clown, fool, jester. **2.** *a.* (*f.* **bouffonne** [bufɔn]) farcical, comical.

bouffonner [bufɔne] *v.i.* to play, act, the buffoon, the fool.

bouffonnerie [bufɔnri] *n.f.* buffoonery; clowning; antics; **faire des bouffonneries,** to play the fool.

bougainvillée [bugɛ̃vile] *n.f.* , **bougainvillier** [bugɛ̃vilje] *n.m. Bot:* bougainvillea.

bouge [buʒ] *n.m.* **1.** bulge (of wall, etc.); swell (of wheel nave). **2.** (*a*) hovel, dump; **sa cuisine est un b.,** her kitchen is a real pigsty; (*b*) low dive, sleazy bar.

bougeoir [buʒwar] *n.m.* (flat) candlestick.

bougeotte [buʒɔt] *n.f. F:* **avoir la b.,** to be fidgety, have the fidgets; to be always on the move, have itchy feet.

bouger [buʒe] *v.* **(je bougeai(s); n. bougeons) 1.** *v.i.* (*a*) to move, budge, stir; **rester sans b.,** to stand, remain, still; **ne bougez pas!** don't move! keep still! *Phot:* **ne bougeons plus!** hold it! (*b*) **les prix ne bougent pas,** prices are steady; (*c*) *Pol:* (*of workers, etc.*) to stir. **2.** *v.tr. F:* **il ne faut rien b.,** you mustn't move, shift, anything. **3.** *F:* **se b.,** to move; **il ne veut pas se b.,** he won't shift, budge.

bougie [buʒi] *n.f.* **1.** candle; **à la b., aux bougies,** by candlelight. **2.** (*a*) *Ph. Meas: A:* candlepower; (*b*) *Com:* **lampe de 100 bougies,** 100 watt bulb. **3.** *I.C.E:* **b. (d'allumage),** spark(ing) plug. **4.** *P:* face, mug.

bougon, -onne [bugɔ̃, -ɔn] *F:* **1.** *n.* grumbler, *esp. NAm:* grouch. **2.** *a.* grumpy, grouchy.

bougonnement [bugɔnmɑ̃] *n.m. F:* grumbling, grousing.

bougonner [bugɔne] *v.i. F:* to grumble, grouse.

bougran [bugrɑ̃] *n.m. Tex:* buckram.

bougre [bugr] *n.m. F:* **1.** chap, bloke; *esp. NAm:* guy; **c'est un bon b.,** he's not a bad sort; **le pauvre b.,** the poor devil; **mauvais b.,** ugly customer. **2.** (*a*) **b. de temps,** filthy weather; **b. d'imbécile,** damn(ed) fool, bloody idiot; (*b*) *int.* blast! damn it! **b. que ça fait mal!** that hurts like blazes.

bougrement [bugrəmɑ̃] *adv.* damn(ed); **il fait b. chaud,** it's damn hot.

bouillabaisse [bujabɛs] *n.f. Cu:* bouillabaisse, Provençal fish soup.

bouillant [bujɑ̃] *a.* **1.** boiling; **de l'eau bouillante,** boiling water. **2.** fiery, hot-headed, impetuous; **b. de colère,** seething with anger; **b. d'impatience,** bursting with impatience.

bouille [buj], *n.f.* **1.** *P:* face, mug, dial. **2.** (wooden) tub for collecting grapes.

bouilleur [bujœr] *n.m.* **1.** (brandy) distiller; **b. de cru,** home distiller. **2.** *Mch:* water space, room (of boiler).

bouilli [buji] *Cu:* **1.** *a.* boiled. **2.** *n.m.* boiled meat.
bouillie [buji] *n.f.* **1.** gruel; **mettre en b.,** to mash, pulp; **légumes en b.,** watery, mushy, vegetables; **les malheureux voyageurs ont été réduits en b.,** the unfortunate passengers were crushed to a pulp. **2.** *Paperm:* pulp.
bouillir [bujir] *v.* (*pr.p.* **bouillant;** *p.p.* **bouilli;** *pr.ind.* **je bous** [bu], **tu bous, il bout, n. bouillons, v. bouillez, ils bouillent;** *pr.sub.* **je bouille, n. bouillions;** *imp.* **bous, bouillons, bouillez;** *impf.* **je bouillais;** *p.h.* **je bouillis;** *p.sub.* **je bouillisse;** *fu.* **je bouillirai**) **1.** *v.i.* to boil; **commencer à b.,** to come to the boil; **cesser de b.,** to go off the boil; **faire b. qch.,** to boil sth.; *F:* **cela fera b. la marmite,** that will keep the pot boiling; **b. de colère,** to seethe with anger; **cela me fait b.,** that makes my blood boil. **2.** *v.tr. F:* to boil (milk, etc.).
bouilloire [bujwar] *n.f.* kettle.
bouillon [bujɔ̃] *n.m.* **1.** (*a*) bubble (given off by boiling liquid); **bouillir à gros bouillons,** to boil fast; **le sang sortait à gros bouillons,** the blood was gushing out, welling out; (*b*) bleb, air bubble (in glass); blowhole (in metal); (*c*) *Cost:* puff. **2.** (*a*) *Cu:* (meat, vegetable) stock; **b. gras,** clear (meat) soup; bouillon; beef tea; **b. de légumes,** vegetable soup; **b. cube,** stock cube; **boire un b.,** (i) to get a mouthful (when swimming); (ii) *F:* to come to grief, to suffer a heavy loss (in business); (*b*) **b. de culture,** (i) *Bac:* culture medium; (ii) breeding ground (for discontent, etc.). **3.** *pl. Com:* returns, remainders, unsold copies (of book, newspapers).
bouillonnant [bujɔnɑ̃] *a.* bubbling, seething, foaming, frothing; **b. de vie.,** bubbling over with life.
bouillonnement [bujɔnmɑ̃] *n.m.* bubbling, foaming, frothing; **b. de la jeunesse,** effervescence, impetuousness, of youth.
bouillonner [bujɔne] **1.** *v.i.* (*a*) to bubble, seethe, foam, froth up; **b. de colère,** to boil, seethe, with anger; (*b*) *Com:* (*of newspaper, magazine*) to remain unsold. **2.** *v.tr. Dressm:* to gather (material) into puffs.
bouillotte [bujɔt] *n.f.* hot water bottle.
bouillotter [bujɔte] *v.i.* to boil gently, to simmer.
boulaie [bulɛ] *n.f.* birch plantation.
boulange [bulɑ̃ʒ] *n.f. F:* bakery trade.
boulanger¹, -ère [bulɑ̃ʒe, -ɛr] *n.* baker; *f.* (i) baker's wife; (ii) (woman) baker.
boulanger² *v.tr.* **(je boulangeai(s); n. boulangeons)** *Bak:* to knead (the flour).
boulangerie [bulɑ̃ʒri] *n.f.* **1.** bakery trade. **2.** (*a*) bakery, bakehouse; (*b*) baker's (shop).
boule [bul] *n.f.* **1.** (*a*) ball, sphere, globe; **être rond comme une b.,** to be short and fat, podgy; **foudre en b.,** ball lighting; **arbre en b.,** bushy-topped tree; (*of hedgehog, etc.*) **se rouler, se mettre, en b.,** to curl (itself) up; *F:* **se mettre en b.,** to get angry; *F:* **il me met en b.,** he gets my back up; *F:* **j'ai les nerfs en b.,** my nerves are all on edge; **b. dans la gorge,** lump in one's throat; (*b*) *F:* head, nut; **perdre la b.,** to go off one's head, round the bend; (*c*) *Mch:* **boules du régulateur,** governor flyballs; *Nav:* **b. de signaux,** (red or black) ball; (*d*) **b. de scrutin,** ballot (ball), voting ball; (*e*) **b. d'amortissement, de balustre,** banister knob. **2.** (*a*) *Games:* (croquet, hockey) ball; bowl; **jouer aux boules,** to play bowls; **jeu de boules,** (game of) bowls; **lancer la b.,** to bowl; (*b*) *Gaming:* **la b.,** (i) the ball (thrown into the cup); (ii) (the game of) boule.
bouleau, -eaux [bulo] *n.m. Bot:* (silver) birch (tree); birchwood.
boule-de-neige [buldənɛʒ] *n.f. Bot:* guelder rose; snowball tree; *pl. boules-de-neige.*
bouledogue [buldɔg] *n.m.* bulldog.
bouler [bule] **1.** *v.i.* to roll, go rolling (along); *F:* **envoyer b. qn,** to send s.o. packing. **2.** *v.tr.* **b. les cornes d'un taureau,** to pad a bull's horns.
boulet [bulɛ] *n.m.* **1.** (*a*) *Artil:* **b. (de canon),** cannonball; **tirer sur qn à boulet(s) rouge(s),** to go for s.o. hammer and tongs; **passer comme un b. (de canon),** to hurtle past, by; (*b*) *A.Jur:* ball and chain; *Fig:* **c'est un b. qu'il traînera toute sa vie,** it, he, she, will be a millstone round his neck all his life. **2.** *Com:* (coal) nut. **3.** fetlock joint, pastern joint (of horse).
boulette [bulɛt] *n.f.* **1.** small ball, pellet (of paper, etc.). **2.** (*a*) *Cu:* forcemeat ball; meatball; **b. (de pâte),** dumpling; (*b*) *Vet: etc:* (poison) ball; bolus. **3.** *F:* **faire une b.,** to drop a brick, a clanger; to put one's foot in it.
boulevard [bulvar] *n.m.* boulevard; **théâtre de b.** = variety show; (*in Paris*) **les boulevards extérieurs,** the boulevards following the line of the old fortifications.
boulevardier, -ière [bulvardje, -jɛr] *a.* facile (humour).
bouleversant [bulvɛrsɑ̃] *a.* distressing; staggering.
bouleversé [bulvɛrse] *a.* distressed, upset; **avoir l'esprit b.,** to be completely shattered, bowled over.
bouleversement [bulvɛrsəmɑ̃] *n.m.* (*a*) overthrow, overturning, upsetting, upheaval (of system, etc.); (*b*) disorder, confusion, disruption; (*c*) distress, anxiety (of s.o.).
bouleverser [bulvɛrse] *v.tr.* (*a*) to upset, overturn, overthrow; to turn (sth.) upside down; to throw (sth.) into confusion; (*b*) to unsettle, upset, distress, overwhelm (s.o.); **la nouvelle l'a complètement bouleversé,** the news bowled him over.
boulier [bulje] *n.m.* (*a*) **b. (compteur),** abacus, counting frame; (*b*) billiard scoring board.
boulimie [bulimi] *n.f. Med:* bulimia, morbid hunger.
boulimique [bulimik] *a. & n.* bulimic (subject).
bouline [bulin] *n.f. Nau:* bowline; **naviguer à la b.,** to sail close-hauled, close to the wind; **nœud de b.,** bowline knot.
boulingrin [bulɛ̃grɛ̃] *n.m.* lawn; grass.
bouliste [bulist] *n.m. & f.* bowls player.
boulle [bul] *n. Furn:* boul(l)e, buhl; **cabinet de b.,** buhl, boul(l)e, cabinet.
boulodrome [bulɔdrom] *n.m.* bowling alley.
boulon [bulɔ̃] *n.m. Mec.E: etc:* bolt, pin; **b. à écrou,** screw bolt; **b. à œil,** eyebolt; **b. à oreilles,** wing bolt; **b. mécanique,** machine bolt; *Rail:* **b. d'attelage,** coupling pin.
boulonnage [bulɔnaʒ] *n.m. Mec.E: etc:* bolting (down).
boulonnais, -aise [bulɔnɛ, -ɛz] *a. & n. Geog:* (native, inhabitant) of Boulogne.
boulonner [bulɔne] **1.** *v.tr. Mec.E: etc:* to bolt (down). **2.** *v.i. F:* to work hard; to slog, slave (away).
boulonnerie [bulɔnri] *n.f.* **1.** nut-and-bolt (i) works, (ii) trade. **2.** *coll:* nuts and bolts.
boulot, -otte [bulo, -ɔt] **1.** *a. & n.* fat, dumpy, plump, tubby, chubby (person). **2.** *n.m. F:* work; **quel est son b.?** what's his job?
boulotter [bulɔte] *v.tr. & i. F:* to eat, tuck in; **il n'y a rien à b.,** there's no grub.
boum [bum] **1.** *int. & n.m.* bang! crash! boom! **2.** *n.m. Com: Fin:* boom; **en plein b.,** in full spate, full swing. **3.** *n.f.* young people's party.
boumer [bume] *v.i. P:* **ça boume!** it's going fine! **ça boume?** how's things?
bouquet¹ [bukɛ] *n.m.* **1.** (*a*) bunch of flowers, posy, bouquet; *Cu:* **b. garni,** (bunch of) mixed herbs, bouquet garni; (*b*) cluster, clump (of trees, etc.); plume, tuft (of feathers). **2.** bouquet (of wine). **3.** *Pyr:*

crowning piece, finishing piece (of firework display); *F:* **ça c'est le b.!** that takes the biscuit! that's the last straw!

bouquet² *n.m.* **1.** *Ven:* (*a*) hare; (*b*) buck rabbit. **2.** *Crust:* prawn.

bouquetière [buktjɛr] *n.f.* flower seller, girl, woman.

bouquetin [buktɛ̃] *n.m. Z:* ibex.

bouquin¹ [bukɛ̃] *n.m.* (*a*) old book; (*b*) *F:* book.

bouquin² *n.m.* (*a*) hare; (*b*) buck rabbit.

bouquiner [bukine] *v.i.* **1.** to hunt after, to collect, old books; to browse in bookshops. **2.** *F:* to read.

bouquiniste [bukinist] *n.m.* & *f.* second-hand bookseller (esp. in Paris).

bourbe [burb] *n.f.* mud (of pond, etc.); mire.

bourbeux, -euse [burbø, -øz] *a.* muddy, miry.

bourbier [burbje] *n.m.* slough, (quag)mire; **se tirer d'un b.,** to get out of a scrape, out of a mess.

bourbillon [burbijɔ̃] *n.m.* core (of boil, abscess, etc.).

bourdaine [burdɛn] *n.f. Bot:* black alder.

bourde [burd] *n.f. F:* **1.** lie; **raconter des bourdes à qn,** to lie to s.o.; to have s.o. on. **2.** blunder, bloomer; (schoolboy's) howler; **faire une b.,** to put one's foot in it; to drop a brick, a clanger.

bourdon¹ [burdɔ̃] *n.m.* pilgrim's staff.

bourdon² *n.m.* **1.** *Mus:* (*a*) drone (of bagpipes, etc.); (*b*) drone bass; (*c*) bourdon stop (of organ). **2.** great bell. **3.** (*a*) *Ent:* bumblebee, humble bee; **faux b.,** drone; (*b*) *P:* **avoir le b.,** to be down (in the dumps).

bourdon³ *n.m. Typ:* omission, out.

bourdonnement [burdɔnmɑ̃] *n.m.* buzz(ing), hum(ming) (of insects); hum(ming) (of engine); murmur(ing), drone, droning (of crowd, voices, etc.); *Med:* buzzing in the ears.

bourdonner [burdɔne] **1.** *v.i.* (*of insects*) to buzz, hum; (*of crowd, etc.*) to murmur; (*of voices*) to drone; (*of ears*) to buzz, ring. **2.** *v.tr.* to hum (tune, song).

bourdonneur, -euse [burdɔnœr, -øz] **1.** *a.* humming (insect, etc.). **2.** *n.m. Orn:* hummingbird. **3.** *n.f. Ap:* **bourdonneuse,** drone layer (of hive).

bourg [bur] *n.m.* **1.** small market town. **2.** *Eng. Hist:* borough; **b. pourri,** rotten borough.

bourgade [burgad] *n.f.* straggling village, township.

bourgeois, -oise [burʒwa, -waz] *a.* & *n.* **1.** *n. A:* (*a*) burgess, burgher; citizen; (*b*) commoner. **2.** *a.* & *n.* (*a*) middle-class (person); **les petits b.,** the lower middle class; **en b.,** in plain, civilian, clothes; **quartier b.,** residential area; **cuisine bourgeoise,** simple, family, home, cooking; (*b*) *Pej:* (*esp. in art circles*) philistine; *a.* bourgeois; **c'est du dernier b.!** it's horribly, hopelessly, middle class! (*c*) *P:* **la bourgeoise,** the wife, the missus.

bourgeoisement [burʒwazmɑ̃] *adv.* in a middle-class way, style; **vivre b.,** to live comfortably, in a middle-class way. *Adm:* **occuper b. un local,** to occupy premises for residential purposes.

bourgeoisie [burʒwazi] *n.f. coll.* **1.** *A:* burgesses, citizens, freemen (of a city); **droit de b.,** freedom of a city. **2.** the middle class(es); **la haute, la petite, b.,** the upper, lower, middle class.

bourgeon [burʒɔ̃] *n.m.* **1.** *Bot:* bud. **2.** *F: O:* spot, pimple. 3. *Anat:* **b. gustatif,** gustatory, taste, bud.

bourgeonnement [burʒɔnmɑ̃] *n.m.* **1.** *Bot:* (*a*) budding; (*b*) budding time. **2.** *Med:* granulation.

bourgeonner [burʒɔne] *v.i.* **1.** *Bot:* to bud, shoot; to come out (in bud). **2.** *F:* (*of the nose, etc.*) to come out in spots. **3.** *Med:* (*of wound*) to granulate.

bourgmestre [burgmɛstr̥] *n.m.* burgomaster.

Bourgogne [burgɔɲ] **1.** *Pr.n.f. Hist: Geog:* Burgundy. **2.** *n.m.* (*also* **vin de B.,**) burgundy (wine).

bourgot [burgo] *n.m. Fr.C:* moose caller.

bourguignon, -onne [burgiɲɔ̃, -ɔn] *a.* & *n.* **1.** Burgundian; *Cu:* **bœuf b.,** bœuf bourguignon. **2.** *n.m. P:* sun.

bourguignotte [burgiɲɔt] *n.f.* **1.** *A.Arms:* burgonet (helmet). **2.** *Mil: F:* steel helmet; tin hat.

bouriate [burjat] *n.m. Ethn:* Buriat, Buryat.

bourlinguer [burlɛ̃ge] *v.i.* **1.** (*a*) *Nau:* (*of ship*) to labour, toil, strain (in a seaway); to make heavy weather; (*b*) **il a bourlingué dans les mers de Chine,** he has sailed the China Seas; (*c*) *F:* **b. de par le monde,** to knock about the world.

bourlingueur, -euse [burlɛ̃gœr, -øz] *F:* **1.** *a.* adventurous. **2.** *n.* adventurer, rolling stone; **c'est un grand b.,** he's knocked about a bit.

bourrache [buraʃ] *n.f. Bot:* borage.

bourrade [burad] *n.f.* blow, push, shove; thump, slap (on the back, etc.); dig, poke, prod (in the ribs).

bourrage [buraʒ] *n.m.* **1.** stuffing (of chair, etc.); cramming, packing tight (of cupboard, bag, etc.); filling (of pipe with tobacco); tamping (of firearms, mines, etc.); packing (of stuffing-box); *Sch:* cramming; *F:* **b. de crâne,** eyewash; bluff; propaganda. **2.** (*material used*) stuffing, filling, packing.

bourrasque [burask] *n.f.* squall, gust of wind; (snow) flurry.

bourratif [buratif] *a. F:* stodgy, filling (food).

bourre¹ [bur] *n.f.* **1.** flock, padding, wadding (for stuffing chairs, etc.); waste, fluff, linters (of cotton, etc.); *Bot:* down, floss (of buds); *Tex: etc:* **b. de soie,** floss silk, silk waste. **2.** wad (of firearm). **3.** *P:* **de première b.,** first-class, first-rate.

bourre² *n.m. P:* policeman, cop.

bourré [bure] *a.* (*a*) stuffed, crammed (**de qch.,** with sth., full of sth.); full, packed tight, cram full; (*b*) *P:* drunk, stoned, sloshed.

bourreau, -eaux [buro] *n.m.* **1.** executioner; hangman. **2.** tormentor, torturer; **être le b. de qn,** to torment, torture, s.o.; **c'est un b. de travail,** he's a glutton for work; **b. des cœurs,** ladykiller.

bourrée [bure] *n.f.* faggot, bundle of firewood.

bourrèlement [burɛlmɑ̃] *n.m. Lit:* anguish, (tormenting) pain; pangs (of remorse, etc.).

bourreler [burle] *v.tr.* **(je bourrelle, n. bourrelons; je bourrellerai)** to torment, torture (s.o. mentally); **bourrelé de remords,** conscience stricken.

bourrelet [burlɛ] *n.m.* **1.** (*a*) pad, wad, cushion; (*b*) draught excluder, weather strip(ping). **2. b. de graisse,** roll, fold, of fat (round the neck, etc.); *F:* spare tyre (round the waist). **3.** (*a*) rim, flange (of pipe, wheel; fillet; (*b*) bead (of tyre).

bourrelier [burəlje] *n.m.* harness maker, saddler.

bourrellerie [burɛlri] *n.f.* harness maker's business, trade, shop; saddlery.

bourrer [bure] **1.** (*a*) *v.tr.* to stuff (cushion, etc.); to cram, pack tight (cupboard, bag, etc.); to fill (pipe with tobacco); *F:* **b. un élève de latin,** to cram, a pupil with Latin; *F:* **il est bourré de complexes,** he's one mass of complexes; *F:* **b. le crâne à qn,** to stuff, fill, s.o.'s head with nonsense; **aliment qui bourre,** stodgy, filling, food; **bourré à craquer,** full to bursting; **b. qn de coups,** to beat s.o. up; (*b*) *Mil: Min:* to ram (charge) home; to stem, tamp (blast hole, mine); *Mch:* to pack (piston, stuffing box). **2. se b.,** (i) to stuff oneself, fill oneself up (**de chocolat, etc.,** with chocolate, etc.); (ii) *F:* to get drunk, canned, stoned.

bourriche [buriʃ] *n.f.* basket, hamper (for oysters, game, etc.).

bourrichon [buriʃɔ̃] *n.m. F:* **se monter le b.,** to get excited, to work oneself up into a state.

bourricot [buriko] *n.m.* (small) donkey.

bourrin [burɛ̃] *n.m. P:* horse, nag.

bourrique [burik] *n.f.* **1.** (*a*) she ass; (*b*) *F:* dunce, duffer, ignoramus; **faire tourner qn en b.,** to drive s.o. crazy, round the bend. **2.** *P:* policeman, cop.

bourriquet [burikɛ] *n.m.* **1.** ass's colt. **2.** windlass, winch.

bourru [bury] *a.* rough, rude, surly, churlish, gruff.

bourse [burs] *n.f.* **1.** (*a*) purse, bag, pouch; **b. bien garnie,** well lined purse; **la b. ou la vie!** your money or your life! **tenir les cordons de la b.,** to hold the purse strings; **sans b. délier,** without spending a penny; **faire b. à part,** to keep separate accounts; **faire b. commune,** to share expenses, to pool resources; (*b*) *Anat: pl.* scrotum. **2.** *Sch:* **b. (d'études),** grant; scholarship, exhibition; **b. de voyage,** travelling scholarship. **3.** stock exchange, stock market; **en B.,** on the Stock Exchange; **jouer à la B.,** to speculate; **b. de commerce,** commodities exchange; **b. de l'emploi** = employment exchange, job centre.

boursicotage [bursikɔtaʒ] *n.m. St.Exch:* speculation (in a small way); dabbling.

boursicoter [bursikɔte] *v.i. St.Exch:* to speculate (in a small way), dabble.

boursicoteur, -euse [bursikɔtœr, -øz] *n.,* **boursicotier, -ière** [bursikɔtje, -jɛr] *n. St.Exch:* speculator in a small way.

boursier, -iere [bursje, -jɛr] **1.** *a.* **opérations boursières,** Stock Exchange transactions. **2.** *n.* (*a*) *Sch:* scholarship, grant, holder; (*b*) *St.Exch:* speculator.

boursouflage [bursuflaʒ] *n.m.,* **boursouflement** [bursufləmɑ̃] *n.m.* puffing up, puffiness (of flesh, etc.); blistering (of paint); turgidity (of style).

boursouflé [bursufle] *a.* swollen, puffy, bloated (face, etc.); blistered (paint); turgid (style).

boursoufler [bursufle] **1.** *v.tr.* to swell, puff up, (face); to blister (paint). **2.** (*of paint*) **se b.,** to blister.

boursouflure [bursuflyr] *n.f.* swelling, puffiness (of face, etc.); blister (on paint); turgidity (of style).

bouscueil [buskœj] *n.m. Fr.C:* break-up (of ice); débâcle.

bousculade [buskylad] *n.f.* scuffle; hustle; jostling; **une b. vers la porte,** a rush for the door.

bousculer [buskyle] *v.tr.* **1. b. des objets,** to knock things over, turn everything upside down. **2. b. qn,** to jostle s.o., barge, bump, knock, into s.o., knock against s.o. **3. b. qn,** to rush s.o.; **il est toujours bousculé,** he's always in a rush.

bouse [buz] *n.f.* cow dung; cowpat.

bousier [buzje] *n.m. Ent:* dung beetle.

bousillage [buzijaʒ] *n.m.* **1.** *Const:* cob, daub. **2.** *F:* (*a*) bungling, botching (of piece of work); wrecking, smashing (up) (of car); (*b*) bungle, botch(-up).

bousiller [buzije] *v.tr. F:* to bungle, botch (up) (a piece of work); to wreck, crash, smash up (a car); **b. qn,** to kill s.o., bump s.o. off, do s.o. in.

bousilleur, -euse [buzijœr, -øz] *n. F:* botcher, bungler.

boussole [busɔl] *n.f.* compass; **b. de marine,** mariner's compass; **b. de poche,** pocket compass; *F:* **perdre la b.,** (i) to be all at sea; (ii) to go haywire.

boustifaille [bustifɑj] *n.f. P:* food, grub, nosh.

bout [bu] *n.m.* **1.** end, extremity; **le haut b. de la table,** the head of the table; **le bas b. de la table,** the foot, bottom, of the table; **l'autre b.,** the other, the far, end (of the street, etc.); **assembler deux planches b. à b.,** to join two planks end to end, end on; to butt-joint two planks; **je n'en vois pas le b.,** I'm nowhere near the end of it; **je n'arrive pas à joindre les deux bouts,** I can't make both ends meet; **de b. en b.,** from beginning to end, from end to end; *Nau:* from stem to stern; **je connais Paris de b. en b.,** I know Paris inside out; **d'un b. à l'autre,** from one end to the other, from beginning to end; **lire un livre d'un b. à l'autre,** to read a book from cover to cover, from start to finish; **d'un b. de la semaine, de l'année, à l'autre,** week in week out, year in year out; **au b. du compte,** after all; when all's said and done; **au b. de la rue,** at the end, bottom, top, of the street; **aller au b. du monde,** to go to the ends of the earth; *F:* **c'est le b. du monde,** (i) it's a godforsaken hole, a dump; (ii) it's the outside limit; **au b. d'une heure, de quelques jours,** after, at the end of, an hour, a few days; **nous ne sommes pas encore au b.,** we're not yet through with it, out of the wood(s); **jusqu'au b.,** to the (very) end; **aller jusqu'au b.,** (i) to go the whole way; (ii) to go on to the bitter end, to see it through; **aller jusqu'au b. de ses idées,** to follow one's ideas to their logical conclusion; **être à b.,** to be exhausted, all in; **pousser, mettre, qn à b.,** to exasperate s.o., to drive s.o. round the bend; **à b. de patience,** at the end of one's patience, one's tether; **être au b. de son rouleau, à b. de ressources,** (i) to have run out of money, of resources; (ii) to be at the end of one's tether; **venir à b. de la résistance de qn,** to break down s.o.'s resistance; **venir à b. d'une épidémie,** to stamp out an epidemic; **venir à b. de (faire) qch.,** to succeed in doing sth.; *Ecc:* **(messe du) b. de l'an,** mass, memorial service (held on the anniversary of s.o.'s death). **2.** end, tip, end-piece; **b. du doigt, du nez, de la langue,** tip of the finger, nose, tongue; **avoir un mot sur le b. de la langue,** to have a word on the tip of one's tongue; **b. de sein,** nipple, teat; **b. de pied, b. renforcé,** toecap; **b. de pipe,** mouthpiece of a pipe; **b. de l'archet (d'un violon),** point of the bow; **b. ferré, b. de canne,** ferrule (of walking stick); **b. d'un fusil,** muzzle of a gun; **à b. portant,** (at) point blank (range); *Mil:* with open sights; **b. filtre,** filter tip (of cigarette); *El:* **b. mort,** dead end (of coil); *Nau:* **(bon) b.,** hauling end (of rope); **tenir le bon b.,** to have the best of it; **on ne sait jamais par quel b. le prendre,** one never knows how to approach, tackle, him; *P:* **mettre les bouts,** to run away, do a bunk. **3.** bit, fragment, end; **b. de papier,** scrap of paper; **b. de ficelle,** piece of string; **b. de cigarette,** cigarette end, butt, stub; **un b. de jardin,** a bit of a garden; **écrivez-moi un b. de lettre,** write me a note, a line or two; **un tout petit b. de femme,** a tiny little (slip of a) woman; **un b. de temps,** a little while; **un bon b. de temps,** quite a while; **nous avons fait un b. de chemin ensemble,** we went part of the way together; **nous avons fait un bon b. de chemin,** we've come, we went, a good way; **c'est un bon b. de chemin,** it's a good step; *Cin: T.V:* **b. d'essai,** screen test.

boutade [butad] *n.f.* **1.** whim, caprice; **travailler par b.,** to work by fits and starts. **2.** sudden outburst (of bad temper); tirade. **3.** sally, flash of wit.

bout-dehors [budəɔr] *n.m. Nau:* boom; **b.-d. de foc,** jib boom; *pl. bouts-dehors.*

boute-en-train [butɑ̃trɛ̃] *n.m.inv.* exhilarating companion; the life and soul of the party; **c'est un b.-en-t.,** he's a real live wire.

bouteille [butɛj] *n.f.* (*a*) bottle; **nous allons boire une b.,** we'll have a bottle (of wine) together; **b. d'eau,** bottle(ful) of water; **b. isolante,** vacuum flask; **mettre du vin en bouteilles,** to bottle wine; **mise en bouteilles,** bottling; *F:* **aimer la b.,** to like one's drink, to be fond of the bottle; *F:* **prendre de la b.,** to be, get, long in the tooth; (*b*) **b. à gaz,** gas cylinder; **b. d'oxygène,** oxygen cylinder; *El:* **b. de Leyde,** Leyden jar, electric jar.

bouteillon [butɛjɔ̃] *n.m. Mil:* dixie.

bouter [bute] *v.tr. A:* to push out; **b. l'ennemi hors de France,** to drive the enemy out of France.

bouteur [butœr] *n.m. Civ.E:* bulldozer.

boutique [butik] *n.f.* (*a*) shop; (small, general) store; **tenir b.,** to run a shop; **fermer b.,** to shut up shop, to close down; **parler b.,** to talk shop; *F:* **j'en ai assez de cette sale b.!** I'm sick of this rotten dump! (*b*) (fashion) boutique; (*c*) **b. (en plein vent),** (market) stall.

boutiquier, -ière [butikje, -jɛr] *n.* shopkeeper.

boutoir [butwar] *n.m.* snout (of a boar); *Fig:* **coup de b.,** (i) cutting, aggressive, remark; (ii) staggering blow.

bouton [butɔ̃] *n.m.* **1.** bud; **b. de rose,** rosebud; **en b.,** budding, in bud. **2.** button; **b. à queue,** shank button; **b. de plastron de chemise,** stud; **b. de col,** collar stud; **boutons de manchette (jumelés),** cuff links. **3.** knob (of door, radio, etc.); handle (of door, lid, etc.); (push) button (of machine, etc.); button (of foil); button, tail pin (of violin, etc.); **b. (électrique),** switch; **b. de réglage (du volume),** volume control (knob); **tourner le b.,** to switch, turn (the radio, etc.) on, off; **b. de sonnerie, de sonnette, d'appel,** bellpush. **4.** spot, pimple (on face, etc.); **couvert de boutons,** spotty, pimply.

bouton-d'or [butɔ̃dɔr] *n.m. Bot:* buttercup; *pl. boutons-d'or.*

boutonnage [butɔnaʒ] *n.m.* buttoning (up); **b. devant,** front fastening.

boutonner [butɔne] **1.** *v.i.* (*of dress, etc.*) **(se) b. par derrière,** to button at the back. **2.** *v.tr.* (*a*) to button (up) (coat, etc.); (*b*) *Fenc:* to touch (opponent).

boutonneux, -euse [butɔnø, -øz] *a.* spotty, pimply (face, etc.).

boutonnière [butɔnjɛr] *n.f.* **1.** buttonhole; **porter une fleur à la b.,** to wear a buttonhole, *NAm:* a boutonniere. **2.** *Surg:* incision; buttonhole; **faire une b. à qn,** to pink s.o. (with rapier).

bouton-pression [butɔ̃prɛsjɔ̃] *n.m.* press stud, snap fastener; *F:* popper; *pl. boutons-pression.*

bouturage [butyraʒ] *n.m.* propagation (of plants) by cuttings; piping (of carnations).

bouture [butyr] *n.f. Hort:* cutting, slip; **b. d'œillet,** piping.

bouturer [butyre] **1.** *v.i.* (*of plants*) to make suckers. **2.** *v.tr.* to propagate by cuttings; to pipe (carnations).

bouvet [buvɛ] *n.m. Tls:* grooving plane.

bouvier, -ière [buvje, -jɛr] *n.* (*a*) cowherd, cowhand; cowgirl; cowman; herdsman, -woman; (*b*) drover, cattleman.

bouvillon [buvijɔ̃] *n.m.* steer, young bullock.

bouvreuil [buvrœj] *n.m. Orn:* bullfinch.

bovidés [bɔvide] *n.m.pl. Z:* Bovidae.

bovin, -ine [bɔvɛ̃, -in] **1.** *a.* bovine (race, eyes, etc.). **2.** *n.m.pl.* bovines, cattle.

bovinés [bɔvine] *n.m.pl. Z:* bovines, cattle.

bowling [bɔliŋ] *n.m.* **1.** (tenpin) bowling. **2.** (tenpin) bowling alley.

box¹ [bɔks] *n.m.* **1.** horse box, loose box, stall (in stable). **2.** (*a*) cubicle (in dormitory); (*b*) *Jur:* **b. des accusés,** dock. **3.** *Aut:* lock-up (garage); *pl. boxes.*

box² *n.m.*, **box-calf** [bɔkskalf] *n.m.* box calf.

boxe [bɔks] *n.f.* boxing.

boxer¹ [bɔkse] *v.i. & tr.* to box, spar.

boxer² [bɔksɛr] *n.m.* boxer (dog).

boxeur [bɔksœr] *n.m.* boxer.

boy [bɔj] *n.m.* (*native servant*) boy.

boyau, -aux [bwajo] *n.m.* **1.** bowel, gut; **(corde de) b.,** (cat)gut. **2.** (*a*) hose(pipe); (*b*) *Cy:* tubular tyre. **3.** narrow alley(way); *Min:* narrow gallery; *Mil:* communication trench.

boycott(age) [bɔjkɔt(aʒ)] *n.m.* boycott(ing).

boycotter [bɔjkɔte] *v.tr.* to boycott.

boycotteur, -euse [bɔjkɔtœr, -øz] *n.* boycotter.

brabançon, -onne [brabɑ̃sɔ̃, -ɔn] *a. & n.* Brabantine; **la Brabançonne,** the Belgian national anthem.

Brabant [brabɑ̃] **1.** *Pr.n.m. Geog:* Brabant. **2.** *n.m. Agr:* all-metal wheel plough.

bracelet [braslɛ] *n.m.* **1.** bracelet, bangle; strap, bracelet, band (of wristwatch); **b. de force,** (leather) wrist-band, wristlet. **2.** metal band, ring.

bracelet-montre [braslɛmɔ̃tr̥] *n.m.* wristwatch; *pl. bracelets-montres.*

brachial, -iaux [brakjal, -jo] *a. Anat:* brachial (artery, etc.).

brachiopode [brakjɔpɔd] *n.m. Moll:* brachiopod.

brachycéphale [brakisefal] *a. & n.* brachycephalic (person).

braconnage [brakɔnaʒ] *n.m.* poaching.

braconner [brakɔne] *v.i.* to poach.

braconnier [brakɔnje] *n.m.* poacher.

bractée [brakte] *n.f. Bot:* bract.

brader [brade] *v.tr.* to sell off (goods); to sell (sth.) dirt cheap.

braderie [bradri] *n.f.* (*a*) (outdoor) jumble sale, rummage sale; (*b*) clearance sale.

braguette [bragɛt] *n.f.* flies, fly (of trousers).

brahmane [braman] *n.m.* Brahmin.

brahmanisme [bramanism] *n.m.* Brahminism.

brahmine [bramin] *n.f.* Brahmanee.

brai [brɛ] *n.m.* pitch, tar.

braillard, -arde [brɑjar, -ard] **1.** *a. F:* bawling, yelling, noisy (crowd, etc.); howling, squalling (child). **2.** *n.* bawler; loudmouth; **petit b.,** noisy brat.

braille [brɑj] *n.m.* braille.

braillement [brɑjmɑ̃] *n.m.* bawling, yelling, squalling; uproar.

brailler [brɑje] **1.** *v.i.* to bawl, shout, yell; (*of child*) to squall, howl. **2.** *v.tr.* to bawl (out) (a song); to chant (a slogan).

brailleur, -euse [brɑjœr, -øz] *a. & n. F:* = BRAILLARD.

braiment [brɛmɑ̃] *n.m.* bray(ing) (of donkey).

braire [brɛr] *v.i.* (*pr.ind.* **il brait, ils braient;** *fu.* **il braira, ils brairont;** *condit.* **il brairait, ils brairaient**) **1.** (*of donkey*) to bray. **2.** *F:* = BRAILLER.

braise [brɛz] *n.f.* (*a*) (glowing) embers; live charcoal; cinders of wood; **des yeux de b.,** glowing, burning, eyes; **être sur la b.,** to be on tenterhooks; (*b*) *P:* cash, bread, dough.

braiser [breze] *v.tr. Cu:* to braise.

braisière [brɛzjɛr] *n.f. Dom.Ec:* braising pan.

bramement [brammɑ̃] *n.m.* (*a*) troat(ing), bell(ing) (of stag); (*b*) howling, wailing.

bramer [brame] *v.i.* (*a*) (*of stag*) to troat, bell; (*b*) to howl, wail.

bran [brɑ̃] *n.m.* (*a*) bran; (*b*) **b. de scie,** sawdust.

brancard [brɑ̃kar] *n.m.* **1.** shaft, pole (of stretcher, cart, etc.); **ruer dans les brancards,** (i) (*of horse, etc.*) to kick when between the shafts; (ii) *Fig:* to jib; to kick over the traces. **2.** stretcher, *NAm:* litter.

brancardier [brɑ̃kardje] *n.m.* stretcher bearer.

branchage [brɑ̃ʃaʒ] *n.m.* (*a*) *coll.* branches, boughs (of trees); (*b*) *pl.* cut, lopped (off), branches.

branche [brɑ̃ʃ] *n.f.* **1.** (*a*) branch, limb, bough (of tree); **céleris en branches,** sticks of celery; *P:* **vieille b.,** old mate; **avoir de la b.,** to look distinguished; (*b*) **notre b. de la famille,** our branch of the family; **la b. maternelle,** the maternal line; the mother's side; (*c*) branch (of nerve, river, etc.); branch, division (of industry, etc.); **branches des bois d'un cerf,** tines of a stag's antlers. **2.** leg (of compasses, dividers); side (of spectacle frame); prong (of pitchfork); blade (of propeller); shank (of key); arm (of horseshoe); **b. à coulisse,** telescopic leg (of tripod).

branché [brɑ̃ʃe] *a. F:* **être b. sur qn, qch.,** to be in (close) touch, contact, with s.o., sth.; **tu es b.?** (i) do you get it? are you with me? (ii) have you been filled in?

branchement [brɑ̃ʃmɑ̃] *n.m.* (*a*) plugging in, connecting (up), connection (of electric appliance);

tap(ping) (of telephone line, gas main, etc.); branch (-ing), branch line, junction (of pipes, wires, etc.); **(tube de) b.**, branch pipe; (*b*) *Rail:* branch line; **b. de voie,** junction, points; (*c*) *Cmptr:* branch, jump, (control) transfer.

brancher [brɑ̃ʃe] **1.** *v.i. & v.pr.* (*of bird*) to perch, roost (on a branch). **2.** *v.tr.* to plug in, connect (up) (electric appliance); *Tp:* to put (s.o.) through; to tap (telephone line, gas main, etc.); **b. une sonnerie sur le circuit de lumière,** to run a bell off the light circuit.

branchette [brɑ̃ʃɛt] *n.f.* small branch; twig.

branchial, -iaux [brɑ̃ʃjal, -jo] *a. Z:* branchial.

branchies [brɑ̃ʃi] *n.f.pl. Z:* branchiae, gills (of fish).

branchu [brɑ̃ʃy] *a.* branchy, branching.

brandade [brɑ̃dad] *n.f. Cu:* **b. (de morue),** salt cod pounded with garlic, oil, and cream.

brande [brɑ̃d] *n.f.* **1.** heather. **2.** heath(land).

Brandebourg [brɑ̃dbur] **1.** *Pr.n.m. Geog:* Brandenburg. **2.** (*a*) *n.m. Cost:* frog (and loop); **à brandebourgs,** frogged.

brandir [brɑ̃dir] *v.tr.* to brandish, flourish (weapon, etc.); to wave (sth. to attract attention).

brandon [brɑ̃dɔ̃] *n.m.* (fire)brand; torch (of twisted straw); **c'est un b. de discorde,** he's a firebrand.

branlant [brɑ̃lɑ̃] *a.* shaky; loose (tooth, etc.); rickety (chair, staircase); ramshackle (building).

branle [brɑ̃l] *n.m.* (*a*) oscillation (of bell, etc.); **mettre une cloche en b.,** to set a bell swinging, ringing; (*b*) impulse, impetus; **donner le b. à qch.,** to give an impetus to sth., get the ball rolling; **mettre qch. en b.,** to set, get, sth. going; **se mettre en b.,** to get going.

branle-bas [brɑ̃lbɑ] *n.m.inv.* **1.** *Navy: etc:* **faire le b.-b. de combat,** to clear the decks for action; **b.-b.!** action stations! **2.** bustle, commotion, confusion; **toute la ville était en b.-b.,** the whole town was in turmoil; **il met toute la maison en b.-b.,** he's turning the whole house upside down.

branlement [brɑ̃lmɑ̃] *n.m.* shaking, nodding, wagging (of one's head).

branler [brɑ̃le] **1.** *v.tr.* to shake, nod, wag (one's head). **2.** *v.i.* to shake, move, rock; to be loose, shaky, rickety; **dent qui branle,** loose tooth; (*of tool*) **b. dans le manche,** to have a loose handle. **3.** *P:* (*a*) *v.tr. & pr.* **(se) b.,** to masturbate; (*b*) *v.i.* **je ne sais pas ce qu'elle b.,** I don't know what the (bloody) hell she's up to.

braquage [brakaʒ] *n.m.* **1.** turning (of car wheels, aircraft controls); **(angle de) b.,** (steering) lock (of car); **rayon, cercle, de b.,** turning circle; **b. (au) maximum,** full lock. **2.** *P:* hold-up.

braque [brak] **1.** *n.m. Ven:* pointer. **2.** *a. F:* hare-brained, crazy, nutty, daft.

braquer [brake] **1.** *v.tr.* (*a*) **b. un fusil sur qn, qch.,** to aim, point, level, a gun at s.o., sth.; **b. une lunette sur qn, qch.,** to fix, train, direct, a telescope on s.o., sth.; (*b*) **il a toujours l'œil braqué sur nous,** he's got his eye on us all the time; **b. son attention sur qch.,** to fix one's attention on sth.; (*c*) *Aut:* to manoeuvre, *U.S:* maneuver, turn (car, etc.); (*d*) to antagonize (s.o.); **b. qn contre qn, qch.,** to turn s.o. against s.o., sth.; **il est braqué contre le projet,** he's dead against the plan. **2.** *v.i. Aut:* to turn the (steering) wheel; **braquez à gauche!** left hand down! **b. au maximum,** to apply full lock; **voiture qui braque mal,** car with a poor lock.

braquet [brakɛ] *n.m. Cy:* gear ratio.

bras [bra] *n.m.* **1.** (*a*) arm; *Fig:* **avoir le b. long,** to have a lot of influence, *F:* clout; **allonger le b. vers qch.,** to reach for sth.; **offrir le b. à qn,** to offer s.o. one's arm; **avoir un panier au b.,** to have a basket on, over, one's arm; **b. dessus b. dessous,** arm in arm; **les b. m'en tombent,** I'm astounded; **cela m'a coupé b. et jambes,** it bowled me over, stunned me; **rester les b. croisés,** to twiddle one's thumbs; **vivre de ses b.,** to be a manual worker; **ouvrir les b. à qn,** to receive s.o. with open arms; **avoir qn, qch., sur les bras,** to have s.o., sth., on one's hands; **être le b. droit de qn,** to be s.o.'s right hand (man); **à bras (d'hommes),** by hand; **voiture à b.,** handcart; **tenir qch. à b. tendu(s), à bout de b.,** to hold sth. at arm's length; **en b. de chemise,** in one's shirtsleeves; (*b*) hand, worker, workman; **manquer de b.,** to be short-handed. **2.** arm(rest) (of chair); leg (of sheers); arm (of lever, anchor); jib (of crane); limb (of cross); handle (of pump, etc.); *Nau:* brace (of a yard); *Mch:* **b. de manivelle,** crank arm; *Rec:* **b. de lecture,** pickup arm; **b. de mer,** arm of the sea; **b. d'un fleuve,** arm of a river; **b. mort,** backwater.

brasage [brazaʒ] *n.m. Metalw:* brazing.

braser [brɑze] *v.tr. Metalw:* to braze.

brasero [brɑzero] *n.m.* brazier, charcoal pan.

brasier [brɑzje] *n.m.* glowing fire; blaze; hotbed (of violence, etc.); **la voiture n'était plus qu'un b.,** the car was reduced to a blazing mass.

brasiller [brazije] *v.i.* (*of sea*) to glitter, sparkle.

bras-le-corps (à) [abralәkɔr] *adv.phr.* **saisir qn à b.-le-c.,** to seize s.o. round the waist.

brassage [brasaʒ] *n.m.* **1.** brewing (of beer). **2.** mixing, stirring, churning (up); *I.C.E:* **b. des gaz,** mixture. **3.** *Nau:* bracing (of yard); *Av:* swinging (of propeller).

brassard [brasar] *n.m.* armband; **b. de deuil,** black armband.

brasse [bras] *n.f.* **1.** *Swim:* **b. (coulée),** breast stroke; **nager la b.,** to swim breast stroke; **b. papillon,** butterfly stroke. **2.** *Nau.Meas:* fathom.

brassée [brase] *n.f.* armful.

brasser [brase] *v.tr.* **1.** to brew (beer, etc.). **2.** to mix, stir, churn (up); *F:* **b. des affaires,** to be doing good business; **b. les cartes,** to shuffle the cards. **3.** (*a*) *Nau:* to brace (yard); (*b*) *Av:* to swing (propeller).

brasserie [brasri] *n.f.* **1.** brewery. **2.** brewing; beer-making (industry). **3.** restaurant (with bar).

brasseur, -euse [brasœr, -øz] *n.* **1.** brewer. **2. b. d'affaires,** big businessman; tycoon.

brassière [brasjɛr] *n.f.* **1.** (*a*) (child's sleeved) vest, *NAm:* undershirt; (*b*) **b. de sauvetage,** life jacket, *NAm:* life vest; (*c*) *Fr.C:* brassière, *F:* bra. **2.** *pl.* shoulder straps, slings (of bag, etc.).

brasure [brazyr] *n.f.* **1.** braze; (brazed) seam, joint. **2.** brazing, hard-soldering. **3.** hard solder.

bravache [bravaʃ] **1.** *n.m.* blusterer, bully. **2.** *a.* swaggering, blustering; **d'un air b.,** blusteringly.

bravade [bravad] *n.f.* bravado; **par b.,** out of bravado.

brave [brav] *a.* **1.** brave, courageous, bold; gallant (man, deed, etc.); **faire le b.,** to bluster, to brag. **2.** (*preceding the noun*) good, honest, worthy; **c'est un b. homme,** *F:* **un b. type,** he's a good sort.

bravement [bravmɑ̃] *adv.* bravely, courageously, boldly; gallantly.

braver [brave] *v.tr.* to brave. **1.** to face (sth.) bravely; **toujours prêt à b. le danger,** always ready to face danger. **2.** to defy, dare (s.o.).

bravo [bravo] **1.** *int.* bravo! good! well done! hear, hear! **2.** *n.m.pl.* **des bravos,** applause, cheers.

bravoure [bravur] *n.f.* **1.** bravery, gallantry. **2.** bravura (of performance, etc.); *Lit:* **morceau de b.,** purple passage.

break[1] [brɛk] *n.m. Aut:* estate (car), station wagon.

break[2] *n.m.* **1.** *Mus:* break. **2.** *Box:* **b.!** break!

brebis [brәbi] *n.f.* **1.** ewe. **2.** sheep; **b. égarée,** lost sheep; *Fig:* **b. galeuse,** black sheep.

brèche [brɛʃ] *n.f.* breach, opening, gap, break (in wall, hedge, etc.); hole (in ship's side); notch (in

blade); *Mil:* **monter sur la b.,** to stand in the breach; **être toujours sur la b.,** to be always on the go; **battre qn en b.,** to disparage s.o.; to run s.o. down.
bréchet [breʃɛ] *n.m. Anat:* breastbone, sternum.
bredouillage [brədujaʒ] *n.m.* **bredouillement** [brədujmɑ̃] *n.m.* mumbling, spluttering.
bredouille [brəduj] *a.inv.* **rentrer, revenir, b.,** to come back, home, empty handed.
bredouiller [brəduje] **1.** *v.i.* to mumble, splutter. **2.** *v.tr.* **b. une excuse,** to mumble an excuse.
bredouilleur, -euse [brədujœr, -øz] **1.** *a.* mumbling, spluttering. **2.** *n.* mumbler.
bref, brève [brɛf, brɛv) **1.** *a.* brief, short; **soyez b.!** be brief! make it short! **répondre d'un ton b.,** to give a curt answer; **raconter qch. en b.,** to relate sth. in a few words, briefly. **2.** *adv.* briefly, in a word, in short; **b., il accepte,** in short, to cut a long story short, he accepts. **3.** *n.m. Ecc:* (Papal) brief. **4.** *n.f.* (*a*) *Pros:* short syllable; (*b*) *Ling:* short vowel.
bréhaigne [breɛɲ] *a. O:* (*of mare, etc.*) barren.
brelan [brəlɑ̃] *n.m. Cards:* three of a kind, pair royal; **b. d'as,** three aces.
breloque [brəlɔk] *n.f.* **1.** charm (on bracelet, etc.). **2.** *Mil:* break-off; **battre la b.,** (i) to sound the dismiss; (ii) to sound the all clear (after air raid, etc.); (iii) to wander (in one's mind); (iv) (*of watch*) to go erratically; **mon cœur bat la b.,** my heart is (i) racing, (ii) giving out, (iii) playing me up; *F:* **la télé bat la b.,** the telly's on the blink.
brème [brɛm] *n.f. Ich:* bream.
Brême [brɛm] *Pr.n.f. Geog:* Bremen.
Brésil [brezil] *Pr.n.m.* Brazil.
brésilien, -ienne [breziljɛ̃, -jɛn] *a. & n.* Brazilian.
brésiller [brezije] *Tchn: & Lit:* **1.** *v.tr.* to break (sth.) into small pieces; to crumble, pulverize. **2.** *v.i. & pr.* **(se) b.,** to crumble.
Bretagne [brətaɲ] *Pr.n.f. Geog:* **1.** Brittany; **Basse-B.,** Lower, Western, Brittany. **2.** Britain (in GRANDE-BRETAGNE, *q.v.*).
bretèche [brətɛʃ] *n.f.* **1.** *Fort:* bartizan. **2.** bay, bow, window.
bretelle [brətɛl] *n.f.* **1.** strap; **b. de fusil,** rifle sling; **l'arme à la b.,** with one's rifle slung over one's shoulder. **2.** *Cost:* (*a*) shoulder strap; (*b*) **(paire de) bretelles,** (pair of) braces, *NAm:* suspenders. **3.** (*a*) *Rail:* scissors crossover; (*b*) access road; (motorway) spur; sliproad (to, from, motorway).
breton, -onne [brətɔ̃, -ɔn] **1.** *a. & n. Geog:* Breton. **2.** *n.m. Ling:* Breton.
bretonnant [brətɔnɑ̃] *a.* of Lower Brittany; **Breton b.,** Breton-speaking Breton.
brett(el)er [brɛtle, brete] *v.tr.* **(je brettelle** [brɛtɛl], **n. brettelons** [brɛtlɔ̃]; **je brettellerai)** to tool, tooth (stone, etc.); to hatch, chase (jewellery).
bretzel [brɛdzɛl] *n.m. Comest:* pretzel.
breuvage [brœvaʒ] *n.m.* **1.** beverage, drink. **2.** draught, potion.
brevet [brəvɛ] *n.m.* **1.** *Hist:* (letters) patent, (royal) warrant; (*b*) **b. (d'invention),** (letters) patent; **prendre un b.,** to take out a patent. **2.** (*a*) diploma, certificate; *Sch:* = (G.C.E.) O-level; *Mil:* **b. d'état-major** = staff college certificate; *Nau:* **passer son b. de capitaine,** to obtain one's master's certificate; *F:* to get one's ticket; *Av:* **b. de pilote,** pilot's licence, *Mil:* wings; (*b*) guarantee (of peace, character, etc.). **3.** *Jur:* (*a*) **b. d'apprentissage,** indentures, articles; (*b*) **(acte en) b.,** contract delivered by notary in original.
brevetable [brəvtabl̩] *a.* patentable.
breveté, -ée [brəvte] *a.* **1.** patented (invention); **inventeur b.,** inventor holding letters patent. **2.** certificated, qualified; **officier b. (d'état-major)** = officer who has passed staff college.
breveter [brəvte] *v.tr.* **(je brevète, n. brevetons; je brevèterai)** to patent (invention); **faire b. une invention,** to take out a patent for an invention.
bréviaire [brevjɛr] *n.m. Ecc:* breviary.
brévité [brevite] *n.f. Ling:* shortness (of vowel, etc.).
bribe [brib] *n.f. usu. pl.* **des bribes,** scraps, fragments, bits, odds and ends; **bribes de conversation,** snatches, scraps, of conversation; **apprendre qch. par bribes,** to learn sth. piecemeal, bit by bit.
bric [brik] *n.m. used in:* **de b. et de broc,** from one source and another, haphazardly; **de b. ou de broc,** some way or other.
bric-à-brac [brikabrak] *n.m.inv.* (*a*) odds and ends, bric-à-brac; jumble; **marchand de b.-à-b.,** secondhand dealer; (*b*) **(boutique de) b.-à-b.,** secondhand shop; *F:* junk shop.
brick [brik] *n.m. Nau:* brig.
bricolage [brikɔlaʒ] *n.m.* pottering about, doing odd jobs; **un mordu du b.,** a do-it-yourself enthusiast.
bricole [brikɔl] *n.f.* **1.** (*a*) breast strap (for barrow, etc.); (*b*) breast harness (of horse, etc.). **2.** *usu. pl.* odd jobs, trifles, odds and ends; **une petite b.,** a little something; **s'occuper à des bricoles,** to potter about the house, to do odd jobs.
bricoler [brikɔle] **1.** *v.tr.* **b. une affaire,** to arrange a piece of business (often shady); **il a bricolé une table,** he's knocked together, up, a table; **il a bricolé le moteur,** he's tinkered with the engine. **2.** *v.i.* to do odd jobs (about the house).
bricoleur, -euse [brikɔlœr, -øz] *n.* handyman; do-it-yourself enthusiast.
bride [brid] *n.f.* **1.** (*a*) bridle; **mettre la b. à un cheval,** to bridle, put the bridle on, a horse; (*b*) rein(s); **aller à b. abattue, à toute b.,** to ride at full speed, to ride full tilt; *F:* to ride hell for leather; **lâcher la b. à un cheval, à qn,** to give (free) rein to a horse, to s.o.; to give a horse, s.o., his head; **laisser à un cheval, à qn, la b. sur le cou,** (i) to give a horse his head; (ii) to give s.o. a free hand; **tenir un cheval en b.,** to curb, check, a horse; **tenir qn en b., tenir la b. haute à qn,** to keep a tight rein on s.o.; **fureur sans b.,** unbridled fury. **2.** (*a*) string (of bonnet, etc.); (*b*) *Needlew:* bar (of buttonhole, etc.); loop (for button, etc.). **3.** *Mec.E: etc:* (*a*) strap, tie; **b. de serrage,** clamp, cramp; (*b*) flange, collar (of cylinder, pipe, etc.); **tuyau à brides,** flanged pipe.
bridé [bride] *a.* tied up, constricted; **yeux bridés,** slant(ing) eyes.
brider [bride] *v.tr.* **1.** (*a*) to bridle (horse); (*b*) to keep (s.o., emotion, etc.) in check; **b. ses passions,** to check, restrain, curb, one's passions. **2.** (*a*) to tie up, fasten (up); *Cu:* to truss (fowl); **cette robe me b.,** this dress is too tight for me; (*b*) *Needlew:* to bind (buttonhole); (*c*) *Nau:* to lash, seize (cable, etc.); (*d*) to flange, clamp (pipes).
bridge [bridʒ] *n.m.* **1.** *Cards:* bridge; **b. aux enchères,** auction bridge; **b. contrat,** contract bridge; **faire un b.,** to have a game, hand, of bridge. **2.** *Dent:* bridge.
bridger [bridʒe] *v.i.* **(je bridgeai(s); n. bridgeons)** to play bridge.
bridgeur, -euse [bridʒœr, -øz] *n.* bridge player.
bridon [bridɔ̃] *n.m.* snaffle (bridle).
briefing [brifiŋ] *n.m.* briefing.
brièvement [briɛvmɑ̃] *adv.* briefly, in short.
brièveté [briɛvte] *n.f.* shortness, brevity, briefness.
brigade [brigad] *n.f.* **1.** *Mil:* brigade; *Av:* **b. aérienne,** group, *U.S:* wing. **2.** (*a*) squad, party, detachment (of policemen, etc.); (*b*) gang, party (of workmen, etc.); **chef de b.,** foreman.
brigadier [brigadje] *n.m.* **1.** (*a*) *Mil:* corporal; (*in artillery*) bombardier; (*b*) **b. (de police),** (police) sergeant; (*c*) foreman (of gang of workmen, etc.). **2.** *Nau:* bowman, bow oar(sman).

brigadier-chef [brigadjeʃɛf] *n.m. Mil:* lance sergeant; *pl. brigadiers-chefs.*
brigand [brigɑ̃] *n.m.* (*a*) brigand, bandit; (*b*) crook; **le petit b.,** the little ruffian, scoundrel, rascal.
brigandage [brigɑ̃daʒ] *n.m.* brigandage, robbery, banditry.
brigantin [brigɑ̃tɛ̃] *n.m. Nau:* brigantine.
brigantine [brigɑ̃tin] *n.f. Nau:* spanker (sail).
brigue [brig] *n.f. Lit:* intrigue; corrupt practices.
briguer [brige] *v.tr.* to solicit, canvass for (sth.); **b. des voix,** to canvass (for votes).
brillamment [brijamɑ̃] *adv.* brilliantly.
brillance [brijɑ̃s] *n.f.* brilliance; *Opt:* brilliancy, *T.V:* brightness (of image, etc.); *Mus:* brightness of tone.
brillant [brijɑ̃] **1.** *a.* brilliant; (*a*) sparkling, glittering, bright (light, gem, colour, etc.); shiny, glossy (hair, etc.); sparkling (conversation); (*b*) splendid, striking; **b. orateur,** brilliant speaker; **spectacle b.,** splendid sight; (*c*) **je ne suis pas b.,** I'm not too good, not feeling too well; **la situation n'est pas brillante,** the situation is far from brilliant. **2.** *n.m.* (*a*) brilliancy, brilliance, brightness, lustre, sparkle, glitter (of gem, metal, etc.); glossiness (of paper, material); (*b*) polish, shine (on shoes, etc.). **3.** *n.m.* brilliant (diamond).
brillanter [brijɑ̃te] *v.tr.* **1.** to make (sth.) shine, sparkle, glitter; to polish; *Tex:* to gloss, glaze (thread). **2.** to cut (diamond) into a brilliant.
brillantine [brijɑ̃tin] *n.f. Toil:* brilliantine.
briller [brije] *v.i.* to shine. **1.** (*of steel*) to glisten, glint, gleam; (*of candle, water*) to glimmer; (*of stars*) to glitter, sparkle, twinkle; (*of moon, satin*) to shimmer; (*of headlights*) to glare; (*of embers*) to glow; *Prov:* **tout ce qui brille n'est pas or,** all that glitters is not gold. **2.** to shine, do well, be successful; **b. dans la conversation,** to be a brilliant conversationalist; **b. par son absence,** to be conspicuous by one's absence.
brimade [brimad] *n.f.* **1.** rough joke (played on freshmen, recruits, new boys). **2.** *pl.* (*a*) ragging, *U.S:* hazing; (*b*) persecution, bullying, victimization.
brimbalement [brɛ̃balmɑ̃] *n.m.* (*a*) swinging (to and fro), dangling; (*b*) wobbling (of wheel).
brimbaler [brɛ̃bale] *F:* **1.** *v.i.* (*a*) to swing (to and fro), to dangle; (*b*) (*of wheel*) to wobble. **2.** *v.tr.* to carry, cart (sth.) about.
brimborion [brɛ̃bɔrjɔ̃] *n.m.* bauble, knick-knack.
brimer [brime] *v.tr.* (*a*) to rag, *U.S:* haze (recruit, etc.); (*b*) to persecute, bully, victimize; **il se croyait brimé,** he felt he was being picked on, got at.
brin [brɛ̃] *n.m.* **1.** (*a*) shoot (of tree); **un beau b. de fille,** a fine strapping girl; a handsome girl; (*b*) blade (of grass, etc.); sprig, twig (of myrtle, etc.); spray (of mimosa); wisp (of straw). **2.** *F:* bit, fragment; **pas un b. de pain,** not a scrap, not a crumb, of bread; **un b. d'air,** a breath of air; **avec un b. d'envie,** with a touch of envy; **un b. de toilette,** a lick and a promise; a quick wash (and brush up). **3.** staple (of wool, flax, etc.); ply (of wool); strand (of rope, wire, etc.). **4.** stick, rib (of fan, etc.); **gros b.,** butt (of rod); **brins d'une antenne,** wires of an aerial. **5.** *adv.* **il est un b. ennuyeux,** he's a bit of a bore.
brindille [brɛ̃dij] *n.f.* twig, sprig; *pl.* brushwood.
bringue[1] [brɛ̃g] *n.f. P:* **grande b.,** lanky, gangling, girl.
bringue[2] *n.f. P:* binge; **faire la b.,** to be, go, on the binge, on a booze-up.
bringuebaler [brɛ̃gbale] **brinquebaler** [brɛ̃kbale] *v. F:* = BRIMBALER.
brio [brijo] *n.m.* (*a*) *Mus:* **con b.,** con brio; (*b*) **parler avec b.,** to talk brilliantly, with spirit.
brioche [brijɔʃ] *n.f. Cu:* brioche; *F:* **prendre de la b.,** to develop a paunch.
brioché [brijɔʃe] *a. Bak:* **pain b.** = milk bread, loaf.
brique [brik] *n.f.* **1.** brick; **b. tubulaire, creuse,** hollow brick; **maison de, en, briques,** brick(-built) house; *P:* **bouffer des briques,** to live on air. **2.** bar, cake (of soap); block, slab (of concrete, etc.); *Nau:* **b. à pont,** holystone. **3.** *a.inv.* brick-red.
briquer [brike] *v.tr.* (*a*) *Nau:* to holystone (deck); (*b*) to scrub down.
briquet[1] [brikɛ] *n.m.* (*a*) *A:* tinder box; **battre le b.,** to strike a light; (*b*) (cigarette, cigar) lighter.
briquet[2] *n.m.* beagle.
briquetage [briktaʒ] *n.m.* (*a*) brickwork; (*b*) imitation brickwork.
briqueter [brikte] *v.tr.* **(je briquette, n. briquetons; je briquetterai)** (*a*) to brick (sth.); to face (sth.) with bricks; (*b*) to face (wall) in imitation brickwork.
briqueterie [briktri] *n.f.* brickfield, brick works.
briqueteur [briktœr] *n.m.* bricklayer.
briquetier [briktje] *n.m.* brick manufacturer.
briquette [brikɛt] *n.f.* briquette.
bris [bri] *n.m.* **1.** breaking (of seals, glass, etc.). **2.** *Jur:* (*a*) wilful damage (to property); (*b*) **b. de prison,** prison breaking; **b. de clôture,** breach of close.
brisant [brizɑ̃] **1.** *a.* **explosif b.,** high explosive; **obus b.,** high-explosive shell. **2.** *n.m.* (*a*) reef, shoal; (*b*) *pl.* breakers; (*c*) = BRISE-LAMES.
brise [briz] *n.f.* breeze; *Nau:* **forte b.,** stiff breeze.
brisé [brize] *a.* broken; **être tout b.,** to be sore, aching, all over; **b. de fatigue,** exhausted, tired out.
brisées [brize] *n.f.pl. Ven:* (*a*) broken boughs (to mark track of deer in wood); (*b*) track (of deer, etc.); **suivre les b. de qn,** to follow in s.o.'s footsteps, to follow s.o.'s lead, example; **aller, courir, sur les b. de qn,** to compete with s.o. on his home ground; **revenir sur ses b.,** to retrace one's steps.
brise-fer [brizfɛr] *n.m. or f. inv.* destructive child.
brise-glace [brizglas] *n.m.inv.* **1.** (*a*) ice fender (of a bridge pier); (*b*) ice beam (of ship). **2.** (*ship*) ice breaker.
brise-jet [brizʒɛ] *n.m.inv.* tap nozzle.
brise-lames [brizlam] *n.m.inv.* **1.** breakwater, mole. **2.** groyne (across beach).
brise-mottes [brizmɔt] *n.m.inv. Agr:* brake harrow.
briser [brize] **1.** *v.tr.* (*a*) to break, smash; **b. une porte,** to break, burst, open a door; **b. qch. en éclats,** to smash sth. to bits, to smithereens; (*b*) to break up (clods of earth, ship, etc.); to pound (up), crush (ore, etc.); (*c*) to break (treaty, etc.); to crush, break down (opposition, etc.); to exhaust (s.o.); to wear (s.o.) out; **brisé par la douleur,** crushed by grief; **cela me brise le cœur,** it breaks my heart; (*d*) to break off (conversation, etc.). **2.** *v.i. & pr.* (*a*) **b. avec qn,** to break with s.o.; (*b*) (*of waves*) **(se) briser,** to break; (*c*) (*of china, glass, etc.*) **se b.,** to break; to be smashed, shattered; **cela se brise comme du verre,** it's as brittle as glass; **espoirs qui se brisent,** shattered hopes.
brise-tout [briztu] *a. & n.m. or f. inv.* clumsy (person) (who breaks everything); destructive child; **c'est un b.-t.,** he's like a bull in a china shop.
briseur, -euse [brizœr, -øz] *n.* breaker; **b. de grève,** strike breaker.
brise-vent [brizvɑ̃] *n.m.inv. Hort: etc:* windbreak.
bristol [bristɔl] *n.m.* (*a*) Bristol board; (*b*) visiting card.
brisure [brizyr] *n.f.* **1.** break, crack. **2.** break (of hinge); folding joint (of shutter). **3.** *Her:* brisure.
britannique [britanik] (*a*) *a.* British; **les Iles Britanniques,** the British Isles; (*b*) *n.m. & f.* Briton, British subject, *U.S:* Britisher; *pl.* the British.
broc [bro] *n.m.* pitcher, (large) jug.
brocante [brɔkɑ̃t] *Com:* dealing in antiques, bric-à-

brac and secondhand goods; (*as shop sign*) Antiques.

brocanter [brɔkɑ̃te] *v.i. & tr.* to deal in, sell, antiques, bric-à-brac and secondhand goods.

brocanteur, -euse [brɔkɑ̃tœr, -øz] *n.m. & f.* dealer in antiques, bric-à-brac and secondhand goods.

brocarder [brɔkarde] *v.tr.* to gibe at (s.o.); to lampoon (s.o.); to launch squibs at (s.o.).

brocart [brɔkar] *n.m. Tex:* brocade.

brochage [brɔʃaʒ] *n.m.* **1.** *Bookb:* stitching, sewing. **2.** *Tex:* brocading, figuring (of material).

broche [brɔʃ] *n.f.* **1.** *Cu:* (*a*) spit; (*b*) **b. de boucher,** meat skewer. **2.** *Tchn:* peg, pin; **b. de charnière,** hinge pin; **b. d'une serrure,** gudgeon of a lock; *El:* **fiche à deux broches,** two-pin plug. **3.** *Tex:* spindle. **4.** *Cost:* brooch. **5.** *Dent:* broach; *Surg:* pin.

broché [brɔʃe] **1.** *a.* (*a*) *Tex:* brocaded; (*b*) **livre b.,** paperback (book), paper-bound book. **2.** *n.m. Tex:* (*a*) brocading (of material); (*b*) brocade.

brocher (brɔʃe] *v.tr.* **1.** *Bookb:* to stitch, sew (book). **2.** *Tex:* to brocade, figure (material); **tissu broché d'or,** gold brocade.

brochet [brɔʃɛ] *n.m. Ich:* pike.

brochette [brɔʃɛt] *n.f.* **1.** (*a*) skewer; (*b*) *Cu:* kebab. **2.** (*a*) **b. de décorations,** row of medals, decorations; (*b*) row (of people, etc.).

brocheur, -euse [brɔʃœr, øz], *n.* **1.** *n.m. & f.* (*a*) *Bookb:* stitcher, sewer; (*b*) *Tex:* brocade weaver. **2.** *n.f. Bookb:* (i) stitching machine; (ii) staple press; stapler. **3.** *n.m. Tex:* brocade loom.

brochure [brɔʃyr] *n.f.* **1.** *Bookb:* stitching, sewing (of books). **2.** brochure, booklet, pamphlet. **3.** *Tex:* brocaded pattern.

brocoli [brɔkɔli] *n.m. Hort:* broccoli.

brodequin [brɔdkɛ̃] *n.m.* **1.** laced boot. **2.** *A.Th:* **le b.,** the sock. **3.** *pl. Hist:* (the torture of) the boot.

broder [brɔde] *v.tr.* to embroider; **b. une histoire,** to embroider, embellish, elaborate (on), a story.

broderie [brɔdri] *n.f.* (*a*) (piece of) embroidery; (*b*) embroidering; **b. anglaise,** broderie anglaise.

brodeur, -euse [brɔdœr, øz] *n.* **1.** (*a*) embroiderer; *f.* embroideress. **2. brodeuse,** embroidering machine.

broiement [brwamɑ̃] *n.m.* = BROYAGE.

bromate [brɔmat] *n.m. Ch:* bromate.

brome [brom] *n.m. Ch:* bromine.

bromure [brɔmyr] *n.m. Ch:* bromide.

bronche [brɔ̃ʃ] *n.f. Anat:* bronchus, *pl.* bronchi.

broncher [brɔ̃ʃe] *v.i.* **1.** (*of horse*) (*a*) to stumble; (*b*) to shy. **2.** (*a*) to falter, waver, flinch; **sans b.,** without turning a hair; (*b*) *F:* to budge, move.

bronchiole [brɔ̃ʃjɔl] *n.f. Anat:* bronchiole.

bronchique [brɔ̃ʃik] *a. Anat:* bronchial.

bronchite [brɔ̃ʃit] *n.f. Med:* bronchitis.

bronchitique [brɔ̃ʃitik] *a. & n. Med:* bronchitic.

broncho-pneumonie [brɔ̃kɔpnømɔni] *n.f. Med:* broncho-pneumonia; *pl. broncho-pneumonies.*

bronchoscopie [brɔ̃kɔskɔpi] *n.f. Med:* bronchoscopy.

brontosaure [brɔ̃tɔzɔr] *n.m. Paleont:* brontosaurus.

bronzage [brɔ̃zaʒ] *n.m.* **1.** (*a*) bronzing; (*b*) browning, blueing (of gun barrels, etc.). **2.** (sun)tan.

bronze [brɔ̃z] *n.m.* **1.** (*a*) bronze; (*b*) **un beau b.,** a fine bronze (statue). **2. b. à canon,** gunmetal.

bronzé [brɔ̃ze] *a.* (*a*) bronze(d) (statue, etc.); (*b*) (sun)-tanned, sunburnt, brown, bronze(d) (face, etc.).

bronzer [brɔ̃ze] **1.** *v.tr.* (*a*) to bronze (statue, etc.); (*b*) to brown, blue (gun barrels, etc.); (*c*) to tan (skin, etc.). **2.** *v.i. & pr.* **(se) b.,** to (get a) tan, go brown; **il se bronze au balcon,** he's sunbathing on the balcony.

bronzier [brɔ̃zje] *n.m.* maker of bronzes.

brook [bruk] *n.m. Rac:* water jump.

broquette [brɔkɛt] *n.f.* (tin)tack.

brossage [brɔsaʒ] *n.m.* brushing.

brosse [brɔs] *n.f.* **1.** brush; (*a*) **b. à cheveux, à habits,** hairbrush, clothes brush; **b. à dents,** toothbrush; **b. métallique,** wire brush; *Mch:* **b. à tubes,** scaling brush; **donner un coup de b. à qch., à qn,** to give sth. a brush, to give s.o. a brush (down); **enlever la boue d'un coup de b.,** to brush off the mud; *Hairdr:* **cheveux en b.,** crew cut; (*b*) (paint) brush; **passer la b. sur qch.,** to paint sth. out. **2.** *Ven:* brush (of fox).

brosser [brɔse] *v.tr.* **1.** to brush (carpet, coat, etc.).; to scrub (floor); to brush down (a horse); **se b.,** to brush oneself down, to brush one's clothes; **se b. les dents,** to brush, clean, one's teeth; *F:* **tu peux te b.!** you can whistle for it; *Belg:* **b. un cours,** to cut a lecture. **2.** to paint (boldly); **b. les décors d'une pièce,** to paint the scenery for a play. **3.** *Sp:* to cut (ball).

brosserie [brɔsri] *n.f.* (*a*) brush factory; (*b*) brush trade; (*c*) brushware.

brosseur [brɔsœr] *n.m.* **1.** *Tchn:* brusher, cleaner, polisher. **2. b. de décors,** scene painter.

brossier [brɔsje] *n.m.* brushmaker; dealer in brushes.

brou [bru] *n.m.* **1.** husk, hull, *U.S:* shuck (of walnut, almond, etc.). **2. b. de noix,** walnut stain.

broue [bru] *n.f. Fr.C: P:* froth; **faire de la b.,** to talk big, to show off.

brouet [bruɛ] *n.m.* (thin) gruel, broth; *F:* skilly.

brouette [bruɛt] *n.f.* **1.** *A:* sedan chair (on two wheels). **2.** wheelbarrow.

brouettée [bruete] *n.f.* barrowful, barrowload.

brouetter [bruete] *v.tr.* to carry, push (sth.) in a wheelbarrow; to barrow.

brouhaha [bruaa] *n.m.* hubbub, uproar, commotion; hullabaloo; hum (of conversation).

brouillage [brujaʒ] *n.m.* (*a*) *W.Tel: Elcs:* jamming, interference; *Rad:* **zone de b.,** interference area, mush area; (*b*) *Elcs: Tp:* scramble, scrambling.

brouillard [brujar] *n.m.* **1.** fog, mist, haze; **il fait du b.,** it's foggy; **arrêté par le b., pris dans le b.,** fog-bound; **je suis dans le b.,** I can't make head or tail of it; *T.V:* **b. de fond,** background mush. **2.** *Com:* day book; counter cash book.

brouillasse [brujas] *n.f.* = BRUINE.

brouillasser [brujase] *v.impers.* = BRUINER.

brouille [bruj] *n.f.* quarrel; disagreement; **être en b. avec qn,** to be on bad terms with s.o.

brouillé [bruje] *a.* **1.** jumbled, mixed, confused; blurred (photograph, etc.); **œufs brouillés,** scrambled eggs; **teint b.,** blotchy complexion. **2. être b. avec qn,** to be on bad terms with s.o.

brouiller [bruje] *v.* **I.** *v.tr.* **1.** to mix up, jumble; to throw (sth.) into confusion; muddle (s.o.); **b. des œufs,** to scramble eggs; **b. les cartes,** (i) to shuffle the cards; (ii) to spread confusion, sow discord; **la pluie brouille les fenêtres,** the rain is blurring, misting (up), the windows. **2.** to cause a misunderstanding between (people). **3.** (*a*) *W.Tel: Elcs:* to jam (a transmission); (*b*) *Tp: Elcs:* to scramble. **II. se brouiller 1.** (*a*) to become mixed, confused; **le temps se brouille,** (i) the weather is breaking up; (ii) things are looking black; (*b*) (*of eyes*) to grow dim; **yeux brouillés de larmes,** eyes blurred with tears. **2.** to quarrel, fall out.

brouilleur [brujœr] **1.** *a. W.Tel: Elcs:* (*a*) jamming; **émetteur b.,** jamming station; (*b*) scrambling. **2.** *n.m.* (*a*) *W.Tel: Elcs:* jammer, jamming transmitter; (*b*) *W.Tel: Elcs: Tp:* **(circuit) b.,** scrambler.

brouillon, -onne [brujɔ̃, -ɔn]. **1.** *a.* disorganized; unmethodical; muddleheaded. **2.** *n.* muddler. **3.** *n.m.* (*a*) (rough) draft, rough copy; *Sch:* rough work; **(papier) b.,** scrap, *U.S:* scratch, paper; **(cahier de) b.,** rough (note)book; (*b*) = BROUILLARD 2.

broussaille [brusɑj] *n.f. usu. pl.* brushwood, undergrowth, scrub, bush(es); **cheveux en b.,** (i) thick, shaggy, (ii) tousled, unkempt, hair; **sourcils en b.,** shaggy eyebrows.

broussailleux, -euse [brusɑjø, -øz] *a.* bushy (country, hair, eyebrows); covered with bushes, with scrub; **terrain b.,** scrubland.

broussard [brusar] *n.m.* bushman.

brousse[1] [brus] *n.f.* (i) **la b.,** *Geog:* the bush; (ii) *Austr:* the outback; *F:* the back of beyond.

broutage [brutaʒ] *n.m.* **broutement** [brutmɑ̃] *n.m.* **1.** browsing, grazing. **2.** *Mec.E:* jumping, judder(ing) (of brake, tool); grab(bing) (of brake).

brouter [brute] **1.** *v.tr. & i.* **b. (l'herbe),** to browse, graze (on the grass). **2.** *v.i.* (*of brake, tool*) to chatter, jump, judder; (*of brake*) to grab.

broutille [brutij] *n.f.* trifle; thing of no importance.

broyage [brwajaʒ] *n.m.* pounding; pulverizing (of coal, etc.); crushing, grinding (of stone, etc.); *Tex:* braking (of hemp).

broyer [brwaje] *v.tr.* **(je broie, n. broyons; je broierai)** to pound, pulverize, crush, grind; *Tex:* to brake (hemp, etc.); **b. des couleurs,** to grind, colours; *Fig:* **b. du noir,** to be down in the dumps, have the blues.

broyeur, -euse [brwajœr, -øz] **1.** *a.* crushing, grinding (mill, etc.). **2.** *n.m. & f.* (*pers*) crusher, grinder; *Tex:* hemp braker, dresser. **3.** *n.m.* crusher, grinder; (coal) pulverizer; grinding mill; *Dom.Ec:* **b. d'ordures,** waste, *NAm:* garbage, disposal unit.

brrr [brrr] *int.* brr . . .!

bru [bry] *n.f.* daughter-in-law.

bruant [bryɑ̃] *n.m. Orn:* bunting; **b. jaune,** yellowhammer.

brucelles [brysɛl] *n.f.pl.* tweezers.

bruche [bryʃ] *n.m. Ent:* **b. des pois,** pea beetle, weevil.

brugnon [bryɲɔ̃] *n.m. Hort:* nectarine.

brugnonier [bryɲɔnje] *n.m. Hort:* nectarine (tree).

bruine [brɥin] *n.f.* fine rain; drizzle; Scotch mist.

bruiner [brɥine] *v.impers.* to drizzle.

bruire [brɥir] *v.i.* (*pr.p* **bruissant;** *pr.ind.* **il bruit, ils bruissent;** *impf.* **il bruissait**); to rustle, rumble; (*of machinery*) to hum; (*of water*) to murmur, plash; (*of bees*) to buzz.

bruissement [brɥismɑ̃] *n.m.* rustling; hum(ming) (of machinery); murmur(ing), (of brook); buzzing (of bees).

bruit [brɥi] *n.m.* **1.** (*a*) noise; sound; **lutte contre le b.,** noise abatement campaign; **b. de vaisselle,** clatter of dishes; **b. métallique,** clang; **b. de marteaux,** (sound of) hammering; **b. de pas,** (sound of) footsteps; **b. sourd,** thud, thump; **faire du b.,** to make a noise, be noisy; **quel b.!** what a row, din, racket! **ne faites pas de b.!** don't make a noise! *Elcs: etc:* **b. parasite,** parasitic noise; **b. de fond,** background noise; (*b*) noise, fuss; **beaucoup de b. pour rien,** much ado about nothing; **faire grand b. de qch.,** to make a great to-do, a great fuss, about sth.; **sans b.,** noiselessly, silently, without any fuss, quietly; (*c*) *Med:* (cardiac, respiratory) murmur. **2.** rumour, report; **le b. court que . . .,** rumour has it that . . . .

bruitage [brɥitaʒ] *n.m. Th: Cin: T.V:* sound effects.

bruiter [brɥite] *v.tr. Th: Cin: T.V:* to produce sound effects.

bruiteur [brɥitœr] *n.m. Th: Cin: T.V:* sound effects man.

brûlage [brylaʒ] *n.m.* **1.** (*a*) burning (of weeds, grass, etc.); burning off (of paint); (*b*) singeing (of hair). **2.** scorching (of clothes, etc.); roasting (of coffee).

brûlant [brylɑ̃] *a.* (*a*) burning, on fire; **café b.,** boiling (hot), scalding (hot), coffee; **il a les mains brûlantes,** his hands are burning hot; **soleil b.,** scorching, blazing, sun; **question brûlante,** burning question; (*b*) fiery, passionate (words, etc.).

brûlé [bryle] **1.** *a.* burnt; *Cu:* **crème brûlée,** caramel custard; **vin b.,** mulled wine; *F:* **cerveau b., tête brûlée,** daredevil. **2.** *n.m.* (*a*) **odeur, goût, de b.,** smell, taste, of burning; burnt smell, burnt taste; **sentir le b.,** (*of opinions*) to smack of heresy; (*of business, etc.*) (i) to look fishy; (ii) to look bad; (*b*) *Fr.C:* burnt-out woodland area, *NAm:* brûlé(e); (*c*) **crier comme un b.,** to scream like a madman.

brûle-parfum(s) [brylparfœ̃] *n.m.inv.* perfume burner.

brûle-pourpoint (à) [abrylpurpwɛ̃] *adv.phr.* point-blank; *A:* **tirer sur qn à b.-p.,** to fire at s.o. at close range; **dire qch. à qn à b.-p.,** (i) to tell s.o. sth. point-blank, to his face; (ii) to spring sth. on s.o.

brûler [bryle] **I.** *v.tr.* to burn. **1.** (*a*) to burn (down) (house, etc.); to burn (up) (rubbish, etc.); to burn away (metal); to burn out (s.o.'s eyes, electrical resistor, etc.); to cauterize (a wound); to burn off (paint); **elle fut brûlée vive,** (i) she was burnt to death; (ii) she was burnt at the stake; **se b. les doigts,** to burn one's fingers; **b. la cervelle à qn,** to blow s.o.'s brains out; (*b*) *Agr:* **b. le terrain, la brousse,** to burn the ground; (*c*) to use, consume, burn (fuel, electricity); (*d*) **prendre une ville sans b. une cartouche,** to take a town without firing a shot; (*e*) (*of acid*) to corrode. **2.** (*a*) to scorch; to burn (toast); to roast (coffee); to singe (hair); **le lait est brûlé,** the milk has caught; **se b. la langue,** to burn, scald, one's tongue; **l'argent lui brûle la poche,** money burns a hole in his pocket; **terre brûlée par le soleil,** sun-scorched earth; *F:* **b. la route, le pavé,** to scorch, tear, along the road; (*b*) *Rail:* **b. une gare,** to run through a station without stopping; **b. un signal,** to overrun a signal; *Aut:* **b. les feux, un feu rouge,** to jump the lights, to go through a red light; *Rac:* **b. un concurrent,** to race past a competitor; to leave a competitor standing; (*c*) **la gelée a brûlé les bourgeons,** the frost has nipped the buds; **la fumée me brûlait les yeux,** the smoke made my eyes smart. **3.** *F:* **b. un espion,** to uncover a spy; **il est brûlé,** his cover's blown. **II.** *v.i.* **1.** to burn, to be on fire, to be alight; *Med:* to be feverish; (*of wound*) to smart; **b. lentement, sans flamme,** to smoulder; **b. sec,** to burn like tinder; **laisser b. la lumière,** to leave the light on; *F:* **on brûle ici,** it's baking, unbearably hot, here; *Games:* **tu brûles,** you're getting hot. **2. b. de curiosité,** to be consumed with curiosity; **b. d'indignation,** to seethe with indignation; **b. (du désir) de faire qch.,** to be burning, dying, to do sth.; **les mains lui brûlent,** (i) his hands are hot; (ii) *F:* he is dying to be up and doing; *F:* **les pieds lui brûlent,** he is itching to be off. **3.** (*of meat*) to burn; (*of milk*) to catch.

brûleur [brylœr] *n.m.* **1. b. de café,** coffee roaster. **2.** burner (of gas cooker, etc.); **b. à mazout,** oil-fired furnace.

brûloir [brylwar] *n.m.* (*machine*) (coffee) burner, roaster.

brûlot [brylo] *n.m.* **1.** (*a*) *A.Nau:* fire ship; (*b*) *Fig:* firebrand. **2.** *Cu:* burnt brandy (cooked with sugar). **3.** *Fr.C:* gnat, midge.

brûlure [brylyr] *n.f.* **1.** (*a*) burn, scald; (*b*) **(sensation de) b.,** burning, stinging, smarting (sensation); **b. d'estomac,** heartburn. **2.** *Agr: Hort:* frost nip; scorching (by sun); blight (on corn).

brume [brym] *n.f.* haze, mist, fog (*esp.* at sea); **b. de chaleur,** heat haze.

brumeux, -euse [brymø, -øz] *a.* (*a*) foggy; misty, hazy; (*b*) obscure, vague, hazy (ideas, etc.).

brumisateur [brymizatœr] *n.m. Toil:* atomizer, spray.

brun, brune [brœ̃, bryn] **1.** *a.* brown (cloth, hair, etc.); dark, dusky, swarthy (skin, person); sunburnt, (sun)tanned (complexion); **un (homme) b., une (femme) brune,** a dark(-haired, -skinned) man, woman; **une belle brune,** a lovely brunette; **(bière) brune,** brown ale. **2.** *n.m.* brown (colour); **b. foncé,** dark brown. **3.** *n.f.* **à la brune,** at dusk, at twilight.

brunante [brynɑ̃t] *n.f. Fr.C:* dusk; twilight.

brunâtre [brynɑ̃tr] *a.* brownish.

brunette [brynɛt] *n.f.* brunette.

brunir [brynir] **1.** *v.i.* to become dark, (sun)tanned; to (go) brown. **2.** *v.tr.* (*a*) to darken, tan; (*b*) to burnish (gold, etc.); (*c*) to polish, planish (metal).

brunissage [brynisaʒ] *n.m.* (*a*) burnishing; (*b*) polishing, planishing.

brunissement [brynismɑ̃] *n.m.* tanning (of skin); (sun)tan.

brunisseur, -euse [brynisœr, -øz] *n.* burnisher.

brunissoir [bryniswar] *n.m. Tls:* burnisher, polisher, polishing tool.

brunissure [brynisyr] *n.f.* **1.** burnish, polish (of metals). **2.** *Agr:* (potato) blight, rot.

brushing [brœʃiŋ] *n.m. Hairdr:* blow-dry; **se faire un b.,** to blow-dry one's hair.

brusque [brysk] *a.* **1.** abrupt, off-hand, curt, brusque (person, manner). **2.** sudden, abrupt (stop, etc.); *Aut:* **tournant b.,** sudden turning, sharp bend.

brusquement [bryskəmɑ̃] *adv.* **1.** abruptly, brusquely, curtly. **2.** suddenly, abruptly; **la route plonge b.,** the road dips sharply.

brusquer [bryske] *v.tr.* **1.** to be brusque, curt with (s.o.); to treat (s.o.) harshly. **2. b. les choses,** to rush things; **attaque brusquée,** surprise attack.

brusquerie [bryskəri] *n.f.* abruptness, brusqueness.

brut [bryt] *a.* **1.** unpolished (marble, etc.); undressed (timber, skin); unrefined (sugar); crude (oil, etc.); rough, uncut (diamond); extra-dry (champagne); **produit b.,** primary product; **matières brutes,** raw materials; **fonte brute,** pig iron; **or b.,** gold in nuggets; *Metall:* **b. de fonte, de coulée,** rough cast; **à l'état b.,** in the rough; **faits bruts,** bald, hard, facts. **2.** *Com:* gross (profit, value, weight, etc.); *adv.* **affaire qui produit un million b.,** business which produces a million gross. **3.** *n.m.* crude (oil).

brutal, -aux [brytal, -o] *a.* (*a*) brutal, savage; (*b*) coarse, rough; **force brutale,** brute force; **coup b.,** brutal, savage, blow; **les faits brutaux,** the hard facts; **vérité brutale,** plain, unvarnished, truth; **être b. avec qn,** to treat s.o. roughly, harshly; **arrêt b.,** sudden stop, abrupt stop; *Veh: etc:* **frein, embrayage, b.,** fierce brake, clutch.

brutalement [brytalmɑ̃] *adv.* (*a*) brutally, savagely, harshly, roughly; (*b*) bluntly, plainly; (*c*) abruptly, suddenly.

brutaliser [brytalize] *v.tr.* to ill-treat, maltreat; to treat (s.o.) brutally, roughly, harshly; to bully (s.o.).

brutalité [brytalite] *n.f.* **1.** (*a*) brutality, brutishness; (*b*) brutality, savagery, savage cruelty; (*c*) coarseness, roughness; (*d*) suddenness, abruptness. **2.** brutal act.

brute [bryt] *n.f.* (*a*) *Lit:* brute beast; (*b*) (*pers.*) brute; beast; boor; **sale b.!** filthy beast! **frapper comme une b.,** to hit out brutally, violently.

Bruxelles [brysɛl] *Pr.n.f. Geog:* Brussels.

bruyamment [brɥijamɑ̃] *adv.* noisily, loudly; **rire b.,** to laugh boisterously.

bruyant [brɥijɑ̃] *a.* **1.** noisy; resounding (success). **2.** loud (applause); boisterous (laughter).

bruyère [bryɛr] *n.f.* **1.** (*a*) heather, heath; (*b*) heath (land); moor(land); **terre de b.,** heath mould. **2.** briar; **racine de b.,** briar root; **pipe en b., de b.,** briar pipe.

bryone [brijɔn] *n.f. Bot:* bryony.

buanderie [bɥɑ̃dri] *n.f.* wash house, laundry.

buandier, -ière [bɥɑ̃dje, -jɛr] *n.* laundryman, laundress; washerwoman.

bubon [bybɔ̃] *n.m. Med:* bubo.

bubonique [bybɔnik] *a. Med:* bubonic (plague).

Bucarest [bykarɛst] *Pr.n.f. Geog:* Bucharest.

buccal, -aux [bykal, -o] *a. Anat:* buccal (cavity, etc.); *Med:* **vaccin b.,** oral vaccine.

bûche [byʃ] *n.f.* (*a*) log; **b. de Noël,** yule log; *F:* **ramasser une b.,** to come a cropper; (*b*) *F:* duffer, blockhead, drip.

bûcher[1] [byʃe] *n.m.* **1.** woodshed. **2.** (*a*) stake; **monter, mourir, sur le b.,** to be burnt at the stake; (*b*) (funeral) pyre.

bûcher[2] *v.tr. & i. F:* to work hard, slog away (at sth.); to swot (sth. up); to swot, *NAm:* grind, for an exam.

bûcheron [byʃrɔ̃] *n.m.* (*a*) woodcutter, woodman; logger; (*b*) lumberman, lumberer, lumberjack.

bûchette [byʃɛt] *n.f.* stick, twig (of dry wood).

bûcheur, -euse [byʃœr, -øz] *F:* **1.** *n.* hard worker, swot, slogger, *NAm:* grind. **2.** *a.* hard-working (student, etc.).

bucolique [bykɔlik] *a. & n.f.* bucolic, pastoral (poem).

budget [bydʒɛ] *n.m.* budget; **b. de la marine, de la guerre,** navy, army, estimates; **inscrire, porter, qch. au b.,** to budget for sth.; **boucler le b.,** to balance the budget, make both ends meet.

budgétaire [bydʒetɛr] *a.* budgetary; fiscal (year); financial (period).

budgétisation [bydʒetizasjɔ̃] *n.f.* inclusion (of item) in budget; budgeting.

budgétiser [bydʒetize] *v.tr.* to include (sth.) in the budget; to budget for (sth.).

buée [bɥe] *n.f.* steam, vapour, condensation (on window panes, etc.); blur (of breath on mirror); mist, moisture (on mirror).

buffet [byfɛ] *n.m.* **1.** (*a*) sideboard; **b. de cuisine,** (kitchen) dresser; (*b*) **b. (d'orgue),** organ chest. **2.** buffet (meal); **b. de gare,** station buffet, refreshment room.

buffetier, -ière [byftje, -jɛr] *n.* manager(ess) (of station buffet, refreshment room.

buffle [byfl] *n.m. Z:* buffalo; **cuir (de) b.,** buffalo hide.

bufflesse [byflɛs] *n.f.*, **bufflonne** [byflɔn] *n.f. Z:* cow buffalo.

bugle[1] [bygl] *n.m. Mus:* (key) bugle; flugelhorn.

bugle[2] *n.f. Bot:* bugle.

building [bildiŋ] *n.m.* large modern block (of flats, offices).

buire [bɥir] *n.f.* ewer, flagon.

buis [bɥi] *n.m. Bot:* (*a*) box(tree); (*b*) box(wood).

buisson [bɥisɔ̃] *n.m.* **1.** bush; *B:* **b. ardent,** burning bush. **2.** thicket, spinney; *Ven: & Fig:* **trouver, faire, b. creux,** to draw a blank; to find the bird flown.

buissonneux, -euse [bɥisɔnø, -øz] *a.* bushy (country, etc.).

buissonnier, -ière [bɥisɔnje, -jɛr] *a.* (*a*) *A:* (animal, etc.) that lives in bushes; (*b*) **faire l'école buissonnière,** to play truant, *U.S:* to play hook(e)y.

bulbe [bylb] *n.m.* **1.** *Bot:* bulb, corm. **2.** *Anat:* bulb; **b. (rachidien),** medulla oblongata. **3.** *Arch:* rounded dome, cupola.

bulbeux, -euse [bylbø, -øz] *a.* bulbous.

bulgare [bylgar] **1.** *a. & n. Geog:* Bulgarian. **2.** *n.m. Ling:* Bulgarian.

Bulgarie [bylgari] *Pr.n.f. Geog:* Bulgaria.

bulldozer [buldozœr] *n.m.* bulldozer.

bulle [byl] *n.f.* **1.** *Ecc.Hist:* (papal) bull. **2.** (*a*) bubble (of air, water, etc.); **b. de savon,** soap bubble; **faire des bulles,** to blow bubbles; (*b*) *Med:* blister, bleb; (*c*) balloon (in comic strips, etc.). **3. (papier) b.,** *n.m.* **du b.,** manila (paper).

bulletin [byltɛ̃] *n.m.* **1.** bulletin; report, summary (of news, etc.); **b. météorologique,** weather report; **b. d'actualités,** news bulletin; *Sch:* **b. trimestriel,** end-of-term report. **2.** ticket, receipt, certificate; form; **b. de paie,** pay (advice) slip; *Com:* **b. de commande,** order form; **b. (d'enregistrement) de bagages,** luggage ticket, luggage check; **b. de consigne,** cloakroom ticket, left-luggage ticket; **b. de vote,** ballot, voting, paper; **b. blanc,** blank voting paper, blank vote.

bulleux, -euse [bylø, -øz] *a.* covered with bubbles, blisters; bubbly; *Geol: Med:* vesicular (rock, fever).

bungalow [bœ̃galo] *n.m.* bungalow.

buraliste [byralist] *n.m.* & *f.* (*a*) clerk (in post office, etc.); (*b*) receiver of taxes; (*c*) tobacconist.

bure [byr] *n.f.* (*a*) *Tex:* frieze; rough homespun; (*b*) frock (of monk).

bureau, -eaux [byro] *n.m.* **1.** desk; bureau; **b. à cylindre,** roll-top desk; **b. ministre,** kneehole desk; *Pol:* **déposer un projet de loi sur le b.,** to table a bill. **2.** (*a*) office; study; **ceci fera d'excellents bureaux,** this will be very good office space; **b. d'études,** design, planning, department, office; **b. de poste,** post office; **b. central,** (i) main post office; (ii) *Tp:* exchange; **b. de police,** police station; **b. de douane,** custom(s) house; **b. de location,** box office; **b. de placement,** employment agency, bureau; **b. de tabac,** tobacconist's (shop); (*b*) (office) staff. **3.** board, committee, executive. **4.** department, division, bureau (of the civil service, etc.); **Deuxième B.,** Intelligence Branch, Service; *U.S:* G2 (Division).

bureaucrate [byrokrat] *n.m.* & *f.* bureaucrat.

bureaucratie [byrokrasi] *n.f.* bureaucracy, officialdom; *F:* red tape.

bureaucratique [byrokratik] *a.* bureaucratic; **style b.,** formal, official, style.

bureaucratisation [byrokratizasjɔ̃] *n.f.* bureaucratization.

bureaucratiser [byrokratize] *v.tr.* to bureaucratize, bring under official control.

burette [byrɛt] *n.f.* **1.** *Dom.Ec: Ecc:* cruet. **2.** *Ch:* burette. **3.** oilcan, oiler.

burin [byrɛ̃] *n.m.* **1.** (*a*) graver, etcher's needle, burin; (*b*) engraving, print. **2.** *Tls:* (cold) chisel.

burinage [byrinaʒ] *n.m.* **1.** graving. **2.** *Tchn:* chiselling, chipping.

buriner [byrine] *v.tr.* **1.** to engrave (copperplate, etc.); **visage buriné,** seamed face; chiselled, craggy, features. **2.** *Tchn:* to chisel, chip.

burineur [byrinœr] *n.m.* (*pers.*) chipper, trimmer, chiseller.

burlesque [byrlɛsk] *a.* **1.** burlesque (poem, etc.). **2.** comical, ludicrous, ridiculous (appearance, etc.).

burlesquement [byrlɛskəmɑ̃] *adv.* in a burlesque manner, comically, ludicrously, ridiculously.

burnous [byrnu(s)] *n.m.* burnous(e), cloak.

bus [bys] *n.m.* *F:* bus.

busard [byzar] *n.m.* *Orn:* harrier.

busc [bysk] *n.m.* **1.** *Cost:* (corset) steel; whalebone. **2.** *Hyd.E:* locksill. **3.** *Sm.a:* shoulder (of rifle butt).

buse[1] [byz] *n.f.* **1.** *Orn:* buzzard. **2.** *F:* fool.

buse[2] *n.f.* **1.** channel, tube, pipe; nozzle (of bellows, etc.); *Metall:* blast pipe; **b. d'injection,** injector (spray tip); *I.C.E:* **b. de carburateur,** carburettor choke tube. **2.** *Min:* **b. d'aérage,** air channel, pipe, shaft.

business [biznɛs] *n.m.* *F:* (*a*) complicated, fishy, business; (*b*) thingummy, what's it.

busqué [byske] *a.* hook(ed), aquiline, Roman (nose).

buste [byst] *n.m.* (*a*) chest (of pers.); bust (of woman); **peindre (qn) en b.,** to paint a half-length portrait (of s.o.); (*b*) (marble, etc.) bust.

bustier [bystje] *n.m.* long-line (strapless) brassière.

but [by(t)] *n.m.* **1.** mark (to aim at); target; objective; **un coup au b.,** a direct hit. **2.** *Fb: etc:* goal; **ligne de b.,** goal line; **entrée du b.,** goal mouth; **marquer un b.,** to score a goal. **3.** object, end, aim, goal, purpose; **mesure ayant pour b. d'assurer . . .,** measure intended to ensure . . .; **dans le b. de . . .,** with the object, aim, intention, of . . .; **dans le b. de frauder,** with intent to defraud; **dans ce b.,** with this aim in view; **cette loi vise un double b.,** this law has two objects, two aims; **aller droit au b.,** to go straight to the point; **errer sans b.,** to wander about aimlessly. **4.** *adv.phr.* (*a*) **b. à b.,** even, without any advantage to either party; (*b*) **tirer de b. en blanc,** to fire direct, point-blank; **faire une offre de b. en blanc,** to make an offer on the spur of the moment.

butane [bytan] *n.m.* *Ch:* butane.

butanier [bytanje] *n.m.* *Nau:* (butane) tanker.

buté [byte] *a.* stubborn, obstinate; **visage b.,** fixed, set, determined, expression.

butée [byte] *n.f.* **1.** *Mec.E: etc:* thrust; **palier de b.,** thrust block, bearing; **b. (d'arrêt),** stop. **2.** abutment, buttress.

buter [byte] **1.** *v.i.* (*a*) **b. contre qch.,** to strike, knock against sth.; to bump, bang, into, against, sth.; to stumble over sth.; **b. contre, sur, un problème,** to come up against a problem; (*b*) (*of beams, etc.*) to abut, rest **(contre,** against). **2.** *v.tr.* (*a*) to prop up, buttress, shore up (a wall); (*b*) to antagonize (s.o.); (*c*) *P:* to kill, bump (s.o.) off. **3.** (*a*) **se b. à qn,** to come across, bump into, s.o.; **se b. à un obstacle,** to come up against an obstacle; (*b*) **se b. à faire qch.,** to be set on doing sth.

buteur [bytœr] *n.m.* *Sp:* (goal) scorer.

butin [bytɛ̃] *n.m.* booty, spoils, plunder; loot.

butiner [bytine] **1.** *v.i.* (*of bees*) to gather pollen. **2.** *v.tr.* to gather, collect (information, etc.).

butoir [bytwar] *n.m.* stop, check; *Rail: etc:* buffer; **b. d'une porte,** door stop(per).

butor [bytɔr] *n.m.* **1.** *Orn:* bittern. **2.** lout, clod, oaf.

buttage [bytaʒ] *n.m.* *Hort:* earthing up (of plants).

butte [byt] *n.f.* **1.** knoll, hillock, mound; *Geol:* **b. témoin,** (flat-topped) outlier. **2. b. (de tir),** butts; **être en b. à qch.,** to be a butt for sth.

butter [byte] *v.tr.* (*a*) *Agr:* to ridge (ground); (*b*) *Hort:* to earth up (plants); (*c*) *P:* to bump (s.o.) off.

buvable [byvabl̥] *a.* (*a*) drinkable, fit to drink; (*b*) *Med:* to be taken orally.

buvard [byvar] **1.** *a.* & *n.m.* **(papier) b.,** blotting paper. **2.** *n.m.* blotter, blotting pad.

buvetier, -ière [byvtje, -jɛr] *n.* barkeeper; barman, barmaid.

buvette [byvɛt] *n.f.* **1.** refreshment bar (at railway station, etc.). **2.** pump room (in spa).

buveur, -euse [byvœr, -øz] *n.* drinker.

byronien, -ienne [birɔnjɛ̃, -jɛn] *a.* *Lit:* Byronic.

Byzance [bizɑ̃s] *Pr.n.* *A.Geog:* Byzantium.

byzantin, -ine [bizɑ̃tɛ̃, -in] **1.** *a.* & *n.* Byzantine. **2.** *a.* ill-timed, futile, pointless (discussions).

byzantiniste [bizɑ̃tinist] *n.m.* & *f.* Byzantinist.

C

C c [se] *n.m.* (the letter) C, c.
c' *See* CE[1].
ça [sa] *dem.pron.neut.* **1.** *F:* = CELA. **2.** *Psy:* **le ça,** the id.
çà [sa] **1.** *adv.* **çà et là,** this way and that; hither and thither; here and there. **2.** *int.* **ah çà!** now then! **ça alors!** you don't say!
cabale [kabal] *n.f.* **1.** *Jew.Rel.H:* cab(b)ala. **2.** cabal; (*a*) intrigue, scheme, plot; (*b*) faction, junta, clique.
cabaliste [kabalist] *n.m. Jew.Rel.H:* cab(b)alist.
cabalistique [kabalistik] *a.* cab(b)alistic.
caban [kabɑ̃] *n.m. Nau:* (sailor's) peajacket, reefing jacket, reefer, pilot coat.
cabane [kaban] *n.f.* (*a*) hut, shanty; *Pej:* shack; (log) cabin; shed (for tools, etc.); (rabbit)hutch; *Fr.C:* **c. à sucre,** saphouse; (*b*) *P:* jail, clink, nick.
cabanon [kabanɔ̃] *n.m.* **1.** (*a*) hut, shed; (*b*) (*in Provence*) (country) cottage; (*c*) (beach) hut, cabin, chalet. **2.** padded cell; *F:* **il est bon pour le c.,** he ought to be locked up.
cabaret [kabarɛ] *n.m.* **1.** (*a*) *A:* tavern, inn, public house; (*b*) night club, cabaret. **2.** liqueur stand.
cabaretier, -ière [kabartje, -jɛr] *n. A:* tavern keeper, innkeeper.
cabas [kabɑ] *n.m.* (*a*) frail, basket; (*b*) shopping basket, bag.
cabestan [kabɛstɑ̃] *n.m. Nau: etc:* capstan; *Petr:* cathead; **c. horizontal,** windlass; **c. à bras,** hand capstan; **grand c.,** main capstan; **virez au c.!** heave!
cabillau(d) [kabijo] *n.m.* codfish, fresh cod.
cabillot [kabijo] *n.m. Nau:* **c. d'amarrage,** toggle (pin); **c. de tournage,** belaying pin.
cabine [kabin] *n.f.* (*a*) cabin (in ship, aircraft, spacecraft, etc.); *Nau:* **la c.,** the saloon; **c. de luxe,** stateroom; *Av:* **c. de pilotage,** cockpit; flight deck; (*b*) hut; **c. de bains,** (bathing, beach) hut; **c. de douche,** shower cubicle; **c. téléphonique,** (tele)phone box; call box; *Rail:* **c. d'aiguillage,** signal box; (*c*) cab, house (of crane); cab (of locomotive, lorry); cage, car (of lift).
cabinet [kabinɛ] *n.m.* **1.** closet, small room; **c. de toilette** = dressing room (with washbasin (and bidet)); *F:* **les cabinets,** the lavatory, the loo, *NAm:* the john; **c. de travail,** study; (*in restaurant*) **c. particulier,** private dining room. **2.** (*a*) office; chambers (of barrister, etc.); (doctor's) consulting room, surgery, *NAm:* office; (*b*) practice (of lawyer, doctor, etc.); **c. d'experts-conseils,** business consultancy firm. **3.** collection (of works of art, etc.); **c. d'estampes,** print room (in museum); **c. de lecture,** reading room. **4.** *Pol:* (*a*) cabinet; **question de c.,** ministerial question; (*b*) **c. (d'un ministre),** (minister's) departmental staff; **chef de c.** = principal private secretary. **5.** *Furn:* cabinet.
câblage [kɑblaʒ] *n.m.* **1.** *Tex: El:* twisting, cabling (of yarn, wires, etc.). **2.** *El:* connecting up, wiring. **3.** cabling (of message).
câble [kɑbl] *n.m.* **1.** (*a*) cable, rope; *Nau:* **c. d'amarrage,** mooring cable; **c. de remorque,** towing line, tow(rope); (*b*) **c. métallique,** (i) wire rope, cable; (ii) stranded wire; *Mec.E:* **c. de frein,** brake cable. **2.** (*a*) *El:* cable, lead, flex, cord; **poser un c.,** to lay a cable; (*b*) *Telecom:* cable; (*c*) *Elcs:* **c. hertzien,** radio link.
câbler [kɑble] *v.tr.* **1.** to twist, lay (strands into cable). **2.** to cable (message).
câblodistribution [kablɔdistribysjɔ̃] *n.f.* cable television, *NAm:* community antenna television.
câblogramme [kɑblɔgram] *n.m.* cablegram, cable.
cabochard, -arde [kabɔʃar, -ard] *a. & n.* stubborn (person).
caboche [kabɔʃ] *n.f.* **1.** *F:* head, nut, noddle; **avoir la c. dure,** (i) to be thick-headed; (ii) to be obstinate, pigheaded. **2.** heavy-headed nail; *Bootm:* hobnail; *Furn:* stud (nail).
cabochon [kabɔʃɔ̃] *n.m.* **1.** (*a*) *Lap:* cabochon; (*b*) (glass) stopper (of decanter, etc.). **2.** *Furn:* stud (nail).
cabosser [kabɔse] *v.tr.* to dent (metal), bash in (hat); **vieux chapeau cabossé,** battered old hat.
cabot [kabo] *F:* **1.** *a. & n.m.* = CABOTIN. **2.** *n.m.* (*a*) dog; pooch, *Pej:* mutt; (*b*) *Mil:* corporal, corp.
cabotage [kabɔtaʒ] *n.m. Nau:* coasting; coastal trade; **grand c., petit c.,** offshore, inshore, coastal traffic.
caboter [kabɔte] *v.i. Nau:* to coast.
caboteur [kabɔtœr] *Nau:* **1.** *n.m.* coaster, coasting vessel. **2.** *a.* coastal (trade).
cabotin, -ine [kabɔtɛ̃, -in] *a. & n. F:* (*a*) third-rate actor, actress; ham (actor); (*b*) histrionic (person); **c'est un c., il est c.,** he's a show-off.
cabotinage [kabɔtinaʒ] *n.m.* **1.** third-rate, ham, acting. **2.** histrionics (in politics, etc.); showing off.
cabotiner [kabɔtine] *v.i. F:* to play to the gallery, show off.
caboulot [kabulo] *n.m. P:* seedy pub, dive.
cabrage [kɑbraʒ] *n.m.* rearing (up); *Av:* pulling up (of nose).
cabré [kɑbre] *a.* **1.** (*of horse*) rearing. **2.** rebellious, aggressive, (character, etc.).
cabrer [kɑbre] **1.** (*a*) *v.tr.* to rear up (horse); **c. qn contre qn,** to turn, set, s.o. against s.o.; (*b*) *v.tr. & i.* **c. (un avion),** to pull (the nose) up. **2. se c.,** (*of horse, etc.*) to rear (up); (*of pers.*) **se c. contre qch.,** to jib at sth., to rise in protest against sth.; to rebel against sth.
cabri [kabri] *n.m. Z:* kid.
cabriole [kabrijɔl] *n.f.* (*a*) leap, caper; **faire des cabrioles,** to caper about, cavort, cut capers; (*b*) *Danc:* cabriole; (*c*) *Equit:* capriole, goat's leap; (*d*) tumble, somersault; (*e*) subterfuge, way out.
cabrioler [kabrijɔle] *v.i.* to caper, cavort (about), to cut capers.
cabriolet [kabrijɔlɛ] *n.m. Veh:* (*a*) *A:* cab(riolet), gig; (*b*) *Aut:* cabriolet, convertible.
caca [kaka] *n.m. F:* excrement; big job; (*to child*) **as-tu fait c.?** have you done your job? **jette ça, c'est du c.,** throw that away, it's nasty, dirty; **c. d'oie,** yellowish green.
cacah(o)uète *n.f.*, **cacahouette** *n.f.* [kakawɛt] *n.f.* peanut, monkeynut.
cacao [kakao] *n.m. Bot:* cacao, cocoa bean; *Com:* cocoa.
cacaoté [kakaɔte] *a.* cocoa-flavoured.
cacaotier [kakaɔtje] *n.m.* **cacaoyer** [kakaɔje] *n.m. Bot:* cacao (tree).

cacaoui [kakawi] *n.m. Fr.C: Orn:* long-tailed duck, old squaw.
cacatoès [kakatɔɛs] *n.m. Orn:* cockatoo.
cacatois [kakatwa] *n.m. Nau:* royal (sail); **(mât de) c.,** royal mast; **c. de perruche,** mizzen royal.
cachalot [kaʃalo] *n.m. Z:* cachalot, sperm whale.
cache [kaʃ] **1.** *n.f. A:* hiding place, cache. **2.** *n.m.* (*a*) *Phot:* mask (for printing); (*b*) cover, guard.
cache-cache [kaʃkaʃ] *n.m.inv.* hide-and-seek.
cache-col [kaʃkɔl] *n.m.inv. Cost:* scarf, muffler.
Cachemire [kaʃmir] **1.** *Pr.n.m. Geog:* Kashmir. **2.** *n.m. Tex:* (*a*) cashmere; (*b*) Paisley pattern.
cache-nez [kaʃne] *n.m.inv.* scarf, muffler.
cache-pot [kaʃpo] *n.m.inv.* flowerpot holder.
cacher [kaʃe] **1.** *v.tr.* (*a*) to hide, conceal, secrete (s.o., sth.); (*b*) to conceal; to hide (one's face, etc.) from view; to cover up (picture, etc.); to mask, hide, (one's feelings, etc.); **douleur cachée,** secret grief; **c. qch, à qn,** to hide, conceal, keep back, sth. from s.o.; **il n'y a rien de caché dans cette affaire,** all is open and aboveboard in this transaction; **il ne cache pas que . . .,** he makes no secret of the fact that . . .. **2. se c.,** to hide, be hiding, be hidden, lie in hiding; to skulk; **se c. de qn,** to hide from, avoid, s.o.; to keep out of s.o.'s sight, way; **je ne m'en cache pas,** I make no secret of it; **en se cachant,** secretly, on the sly; **sans se c.,** openly.
cache-radiateur [kaʃradjatœr] *n.m.inv.* radiator cover.
cache-sexe [kaʃsɛks] *n.m.inv.* G-string.
cachet [kaʃɛ] *n.m.* **1.** (*a*) seal, stamp (on document); *Hist:* **lettre de c.,** order under the King's private seal; (*b*) mark, stamp, impress; **c. d'oblitération, de la poste,** postmark; **c. d'un fabricant,** maker's trademark; **le c. du génie,** the stamp, hallmark, of genius; **il a beaucoup de c.,** he has style, a certain cachet; **manteau qui a du c.,** stylish coat. **2.** (*for sealing documents*) stamp, seal. **3.** (*a*) **courir le c.,** to give private lessons (in pupils' homes); (*b*) fee (of artiste, counsel, consultant, etc.). **4.** *Pharm:* (*a*) *A:* cachet; (*b*) tablet, pill.
cachetage [kaʃtaʒ] *n.m.* sealing (of letters, etc.).
cache-tampon [kaʃtɑ̃pɔ̃] *n.m.inv.* (game of) hunt-the-thimble, hunt-the-slipper.
cacheter [kaʃte] *v.tr.* **(je cachette, n. cachetons; je cachetterai)** to seal (up) (letter, bottle, etc.); **cire à c.,** sealing wax; **vin cacheté,** vintage wine.
cachette [kaʃɛt] *n.f.* hiding place, hideout, hideaway; **en c.,** secretly, on the sly, on the quiet, in an underhand manner; **vendre en c.,** to sell under the counter.
cachexie [kaʃɛksi] *n.f.* cachexy, general debility; *Vet:* rot.
cachot [kaʃo] *n.m.* **1.** dungeon. **2.** (*a*) prison, gaol, jail; (*b*) solitary confinement.
cachotterie [kaʃɔtri] *n.f.* (affectation of) mystery; **faire des cachotteries,** to keep things secret.
cachottier, -ière [kaʃɔtje, -jɛr] *a. & n.* secretive, reticent, close (person).
cachou [kaʃu] *n.m.* (*a*) *Dy:* catechu; (*b*) cachou.
cacique [kasik] *n.m.* (*a*) cacique; (*b*) *Sch: F:* **c'est lui le c.,** he's come top, first; (*c*) *F:* boss, big shot, big noise.
cacophonie [kakɔfɔni] *n.f.* cacophony.
cacophonique [kakɔfɔnik] *a.* cacophonous.
cactus [kaktys] *n.m.* cactus.
cadastral, -aux [kadastral, -o] *a.* cadastral (register, survey).
cadastre [kadastr̥] *n.m. Adm:* **1.** cadastral survey; plan (of commune); land register; cadastre. **2.** survey (staff, operations).
cadastrer [kadastre] *v.tr. Adm:* **1.** to survey and value (parish). **2.** to register (property) in the land register.
cadavéreux, -euse [kadaverø, -øz] *a.* cadaverous; deathly; deadly pale.
cadavérique [kadaverik] *a.* cadaveric; deathly; deadly pale; **rigidité c.,** rigor mortis.
cadavre [kadɑvr̥] *n.m.* (*a*) corpse, (dead) body, *U.S:* cadaver; carcass (of dead animal); **c'est un c. ambulant,** he's a walking corpse; (*b*) *P:* empty (bottle); dead man.
caddie [kadi] *n.m. Golf:* caddie.
cadeau, -eaux [kado] *n.m.* present, gift; **en c.,** as a present; **faire un c. à qn,** to give s.o. a present; **j'aimerais mieux en faire c.,** I'd rather give it away; *F:* **il ne lui a pas fait de c.,** (i) he didn't spare him; (ii) he didn't help him much, was a fat lot of use to him.
cadenas [kadna] *n.m.* padlock; **fermer la porte au c.,** to padlock the door.
cadenasser [kadnase] *v.tr.* to padlock (door, etc.).
cadence [kadɑ̃s] *n.f.* **1.** cadence, rhythm (of verse, motion); **en c.,** rhythmically, in time; **forcer la c.,** to force the pace; **à la c. de . . .,** at the rate of . . .; *Artil: etc:* **c. du tir,** rate of fire. **2.** *Mus:* (*a*) cadence; (*b*) cadenza (in concerto).
cadencé [kadɑ̃se] *a.* rhythmic(al); measured (step, etc.); **pas c., marche!** quick march! **marcher au pas c.,** to march, walk, in step, in quick time.
cadencer [kadɑ̃se] *v.tr.* **(je cadençai(s); n. cadençons)** to give rhythm to (one's style, etc.); **c. son pas,** to get into, keep in, step.
cadet, -ette [kadɛ, -ɛt] **1.** *a. & n.* (*a*) **la (sœur) cadette,** the younger sister; the youngest sister; **il est mon c. de deux ans,** he's two years younger than I am; he's two years my junior; **avoir trois frères cadets,** to have three younger brothers; **c'est le c. de mes soucis,** that's the least of my worries; *Sp:* **épreuve des cadets,** junior event; (*b*) junior (in position, rank). **2.** *n.m. Hist:* cadet. **3.** *n.m. Golf:* caddie.
Cadix [kadis] *Pr.n.f. Geog:* Cadiz.
cadmium [kadmjɔm] *n.m. Ch:* cadmium.
cadogan [kadɔgɑ̃] *n.m.* = CATOGAN.
cadrage [kɑdraʒ] *n.m. Cin: Phot: etc:* centring (of image).
cadran [kadrɑ̃] *n.m.* **1.** (*of clock, barometer, etc.*) face, dial; (*of instrument, telephone, etc.*) dial; **c. solaire,** sundial; **faire le tour du c.,** (i) (*of hands of clock*) to go right round the clock; (ii) (*of pers.*) to sleep (right) round the clock. **2.** *Nau:* **c. de transmission d'ordres,** engine-room telegraph.
cadre [kɑdr̥] *n.m.* **1.** (*a*) frame (of picture, door, etc.), casing (of ship's screw, etc.); (*b*) (*on form, etc.*) space, box; (*c*) border (of map, etc.); (*d*) setting (of scene); surroundings; (*e*) compass, limits, bounds, framework; **sortir du c. de ses fonctions,** to go beyond (the limits of) one's duties; **dans le c. de ce programme,** as part of this programme; **ces produits n'entrent pas dans le c. de notre fabrication,** we do not manufacture these articles; (*f*) **c. d'emballage,** packing case; **c. de déménagement,** container; (*g*) *W.Tel:* frame aerial, loop aerial. **2.** (*a*) frame(work) (of bicycle, etc.); (*b*) *Lit:* outline, skeleton, plan (of book, etc.). **3.** (*a*) *Mil: etc:* **les cadres,** (i) commissioned and non-commissioned officers; (ii) cadre, staff (of skeleton unit, etc.); (*b*) *Ind: etc:* salaried staff; managerial staff; management; **c. supérieur,** senior executive, manager; (*c*) books (of company, etc.); *Mil: etc:* **c. de réserve,** reserve list; **hors c.,** not on the strength; specially employed; **être mis hors c.,** to be seconded, detached; **rayé des cadres,** dismissed. **4.** *Nau:* (*a*) cot; (*b*) berth.
cadrer [kadre] **1.** *v.i.* to agree, tally, conform, square, fit in (**avec,** with). **2.** *v.tr.* to centre (a photograph).
caduc, -uque [kadyk] *a.* **1.** (*a*) *A:* decaying, crumbling (building); (*b*) (*of pers.*) decrepit; (*c*) out of

date; oldfashioned. **2.** deciduous (leaf, etc.). **3.** *Jur:* null and void (legacy); lapsed (agreement); statute-barred (debt).

caecum [sekɔm] *n.m. Anat:* caecum.

cafard, -arde [kafar, -ard] **1.** *n.* (*a*) *A:* hypocrite; *a.* **air c.,** hypocritical, sanctimonious, air; (*b*) sneak, creep, talebearer. **2.** *n.m. F:* (*a*) *Ent:* cockroach; (*b*) **avoir le c.,** to be depressed, fed up, down in the dumps.

cafardage [kafardaʒ] *n.m.* talebearing, sneaking.

cafarder [kafarde] *v.i.* to tell tales; to sneak; to split on somebody.

cafardeur, -euse [kafardœr, -øz] *n.* = CAFARD 1 (*b*).

cafardeux, -euse [kafardø, -øz] *a.* depressed, fed up, browned off, down in the dumps.

café [kafe] *n.m.* **1.** coffee; (*a*) **c. vert, torrifié,** unroasted, roasted, coffee; **grain de c.,** coffee bean; **c. en grains,** whole coffee; coffee beans; **c. moulu,** ground coffee; **c. en poudre,** instant coffee; (*b*) **c. noir,** *esp. Sw.Fr:* **c. nature,** black coffee; **c. au lait, c. crème,** white coffee; **c. complet,** continental breakfast; **glace au c.,** coffee ice (cream); (*c*) *a. inv.* **c. (au lait),** coffee coloured. **2.** (*a*) *A:* coffee-house; (*b*) café; bar; pub; **c. tabac,** café with licence to sell tobacco; **garçon de c.,** waiter; barman.

caféier [kafeje] *n.m.* coffee tree.

caféine [kafein] *n.f.* caffeine.

cafetan [kaftɑ̃] *n.m. Cost:* kaftan, caftan.

caféteria [kæfeterja] *n.f.* cafeteria.

cafetier, -ière [kaftje, -jɛr] **1.** *n.* café owner. **2.** *n.f.* (*a*) coffee pot; (*b*) coffee machine, maker; **c. automatique, à pression,** percolator.

cafouillage [kafujaʒ] *n.m. F:* mess, muddle; missing, misfiring (of car engine).

cafouiller [kafuje] *v.i. F:* to get into a mess, a muddle; (*of car engine*) to miss, misfire; (*of T.V. set, etc.*) to be on the blink.

cafouilleur, -euse [kafujœr, -øz] *a. & n.* ham-fisted, muddle-headed (person); *n.* muddler.

cage [kaʒ] *n.f.* **1.** (*a*) (bird, lion, etc.) cage; (hen) coop; (rabbit) hutch; **mettre un oiseau en c.,** to cage a bird; *F:* **habiter une vraie c. à lapins,** to live in a poky little place; (*b*) cage (of mine shaft); (*c*) shell, carcass (of house); (*d*) *esp. Fb:* goal. **2.** (protective) cover; case, casing. **3.** (stair) well; (lift) shaft. **4.** *Mec.E:* **c. à billes,** ball race. **5.** *El:* **c. de Faraday,** Faraday cage, electrostatic screen.

cageot [kaʒo] *n.m.* (*a*) hamper; (*b*) crate.

cagibi [kaʒibi] *n.m. F:* **1.** hut; shed. **2.** poky little room; boxroom; lumber room.

cagne [kaɲ] *n.f. Sch: F:* second-year arts class preparing to compete for entrance to the *École normale supérieure.*

cagneux, -euse [kaɲø, -øz] **1.** *a. & n.* (*a*) knock-kneed (person); (*b*) crooked (legs); knock (knees). **2.** *n. Sch: F:* student in the *cagne.*

cagnotte [kaɲɔt] *n.f.* (*a*) *Games:* pool, kitty, *esp. NAm:* pot; (*b*) *F:* savings, nest egg.

cagot, -ote [kago, -ɔt] **1.** *n.* (canting) hypocrite. **2.** *a.* hypocritical, sanctimonious.

cagoule [kagul] *n.f.* (*a*) (monk's) cowl; (*b*) hood (of penitent, robber); (*c*) balaclava (helmet).

cahier [kaje] *n.m.* (*a*) notebook; exercise book; (*b*) **c. de papier à lettres,** six sheets, quarter of a quire, of notepaper; (*c*) *Typ:* signature; (*d*) periodical, review, journal.

cahin-caha [kaɛ̃kaa] *adv. F:* **aller c.-c.,** (i) (*of pers., health*) to be so-so; (ii) (*of pers.*) to struggle, limp, along; **les affaires vont c.-c.,** business is slow, slack.

cahot [kao] *n.m.* (*a*) jolt, bump (of vehicle); (*b*) vicissitudes, ups and downs (of life).

cahotage [kaɔtaʒ] *n.m.* = CAHOTEMENT.

cahotant [kaɔtɑ̃] *a.* **1.** jolting, jolty (car). **2.** rough, bumpy (road).

cahotement [kaɔtmɑ̃] *n.m.* (*a*) jolting, shaking, bumping; (*b*) jolt, bump.

cahoter [kaɔte] *v.tr. & i.* to jolt, shake, bump along (in cart, etc.); **vie cahotée,** life full of ups and downs.

cahoteux, -euse [kaɔtø, -øz] *a.* rough, bumpy (road).

cahute [kayt] *n.f.* hut, shanty, shack.

caïd [kaid] *n.m.* (*a*) (*in N.Africa*) kaid; (*b*) *P:* gang leader; (*c*) *P:* boss, big noise (in company, etc.); (*d*) *F:* **c'est le gros c. en maths,** he's our great maths expert.

caillage [kɑjaʒ] *n.m.* = CAILLEMENT.

caillasse [kajas] *n.f.* **1.** *Geol:* (gravelly) marl. **2.** road metal, loose stones, chippings.

caille [kɑj] *n.f. Orn:* quail; **gros comme une c.,** as plump as a partridge.

caillé [kɑje] *n.m.* curdled milk, curds.

caillebotis [kɑjbɔti] *n.m.* **1.** *Nau: etc:* grating. **2.** duckboard(s).

caillebotte [kɑjbɔt] *n.f.* curds.

caillebotter [kɑjbɔte] *v.tr.* to curdle, clot (milk).

caillement [kɑjmɑ̃] *n.m.* clotting, curdling (of milk, blood); coagulating, coagulation (of blood, etc.).

cailler [kɑje] *v.tr., i., & pr.* **1.** (*of milk, blood, etc.*) to clot, curdle; (*of blood, etc.*) to coagulate, congeal; **faire c. du lait,** to curdle milk. **2.** *P:* **ça caille, on se (les) caille,** it's bloody cold, bloody freezing.

caillette [kajɛt] *n.f.* fourth stomach, reed, rennet stomach, abomasum (of ruminants).

caillot [kajo] *n.m.* clot (of blood, etc.).

caillou, -oux [kaju] *n.m.* **1.** (*a*) pebble, stone; **cailloux d'empierrement,** (loose) chippings, road metal; **avoir le cœur dur comme un c.,** to have a heart of stone; (*b*) boulder, rock; (*c*) *Lap:* stone, rock. **2.** *P:* head, nut.

cailloutage [kajutaʒ] *n.m.* road metal(ling); *esp. Rail:* ballast(ing) (of track).

caillouter [kajute] *v.tr.* to metal (road); *esp. Rail:* to ballast (track).

caillouteux, -euse [kajutø, -øz] *a.* stony, flinty (road, etc.); pebbly, shingly (beach).

cailloutis [kajuti] *n.m.* broken stones, chippings, gravel; road metal.

caïman [kaimɑ̃] *n.m. Rept:* cayman, caiman.

Caïn [kaɛ̃] *Pr.n.m.* Cain.

Caire (le) [(lə)kɛr] *Pr.n.m. Geog:* Cairo.

cairn [kɛrn] *n.m.* cairn.

caisse [kɛs] *n.f.* **1.** (*a*) (packing) case; crate; **c. à savon,** soapbox; **mettre des marchandises en c.,** to case goods; (*b*) box (for tools, etc.); chest (for tea, etc.); tub (for plants); tank, cistern (for oil, water); *Nau:* **c. à eau douce,** freshwater tank; *Aut:* **c. de l'embrayage,** clutch casing; (*c*) *P:* chest; **il s'en va de la c.,** he's got a very bad chest. **2.** (*a*) case (of piano, clock); body(work) (of vehicle); (*b*) shell (of pulley). **3.** *Com: Fin:* (*a*) cash box; till; **c. (enregistreuse),** cash register; **les caisses de l'État,** the coffers of the State; (*b*) (i) pay desk, cash desk; (*in supermarket, etc.*) check-out; **payez à la c.,** pay at the (cash) desk, at the till; (ii) counting house; cashier's office; pay office; **tenir la c.,** to be in charge of the cash; to be cashier; **passer à la c.,** (i) to go to the cash desk; (ii) to pay; (iii) to be paid; (iv) to be paid off; (*c*) (i) cash (in hand); (ii) takings; **livre de c.,** cashbook; **faire la, sa, c.,** to balance (up) one's cash, *F:* do the till, cash up; **avoir tant d'argent en c.,** to have so much money in hand; (*d*) fund; **c. de défense,** fighting fund (of an association, etc.); *Pol:* **c. noire,** bribery fund, slush fund, *NAm:* boodle, graft; (*e*) **c. d'épargne,** savings bank. **4.** (*a*) *Mus:* drum; **c. claire,** (high-pitched) side drum, snare drum; **grosse c.,** bass drum; *F:* big drum; **battre la grosse c.,** run a big publicity campaign; (*b*) *Anat:* **c. du tympan,** middle ear.

caissette [kεsεt] *n.f.* small case, box.

caissier, -ière [kεsje, -jεr] *n.* (*a*) cashier (in shop, etc.); (*b*) *Bank:* cashier, teller.

caisson [kεsɔ̃] *n.m.* **1.** (*a*) box, case, chest; (*b*) *Mil:* wagon, caisson (for ammunition, etc.); *P:* **se faire sauter le c.,** to blow one's brains out. **2.** *Nau:* locker, bin. **3.** *Arch:* **plafond à caissons,** panelled, coffered, ceiling. **4.** caisson (for underwater work); *Med:* **mal(adie) des caissons,** caisson disease, decompression sickness; *F:* the bends.

cajoler [kaʒɔle] *v.tr.* **1.** *O:* to cajole, coax, wheedle. **2.** to pet, make a fuss of (child, etc.).

cajolerie [kaʒɔlri] *n.f.* cajoling, coaxing, wheedling.

cajoleur, -euse [kaʒɔlœr, -øz] **1.** *a.* cajoling, wheedling, coaxing. **2.** *n.* cajoler, wheedler, coaxer.

cajou [kaʒu] *n.m.* cashew (nut).

cake [kεk] *n.m.* fruit cake.

cal [kal] *n.m. Bot: Med:* callus, callosity; *pl. cals.*

calage [kalaʒ] *n.m.* **1.** (*a*) wedging, steadying (of chair leg, etc.); chocking (up) (of wheel, etc.); (*b*) propping (up). **2.** *Mec.E: etc:* (*a*) wedging, keying (of crank to shaft, etc.); fixing (of wheel on axle, etc.); jamming, locking (of valve, etc.); (*b*) stalling (of engine). **3.** adjustment; setting; *Mch:* timing, tuning (of valve, engine).

calamar [kalamar] *n.m.* = CALMAR.

calamine [kalamin] *n.f.* **1.** *Miner:* calamine. **2.** *I.C.E:* carbon (deposit).

calamité [kalamite] *n.f.* (*a*) calamity, disaster; (*b*) great misfortune.

calamiteux, -euse [kalamitø, -øz] *a.* calamitous, disastrous.

calandrage [kalɑ̃draʒ] *n.m. Tex: Paperm: etc:* calendering, hot-pressing, surfacing.

calandre [kalɑ̃dr̥] *n.f.* **1.** *Tex: Paperm: etc:* calender, roller. **2.** *Aut:* radiator grille.

calandrer [kalɑ̃dre] *v.tr. Tex: Paperm: etc:* to calender, roll, press; to surface.

calandreur, -euse [kalɑ̃drœr, -øz] *n. Tex: Paperm: etc:* calenderer.

calanque [kalɑ̃k] *n.f.* (*in the Mediterranean*) deep, narrow, creek.

calcaire [kalkεr] **1.** *a.* calcareous (rock, etc.); chalky (soil, etc.); **terrain c.,** limestone region; **eau c.,** hard water. **2.** *n.m.* (*a*) limestone; (*b*) *F:* fur (in kettle).

calcanéum [kalkaneɔm] *n.m. Anat:* calcaneum; heel bone.

calcédoine [kalsedwan] *n.f. Miner:* chalcedony.

calcification [kalsifikasjɔ̃] *n.f.* calcification.

calcination [kalsinasjɔ̃] *n.f.* calcination.

calciner [kalsine] **1.** *v.tr.* (*a*) to char; **rôti calciné,** joint burnt to a cinder; **désert calciné par le soleil,** sun-baked desert; (*b*) *Ch: Ind:* to calcine. **2. se c.,** to burn, be burnt, to a cinder.

calcium [kalsjɔm] *n.m. Ch:* calcium.

calcul¹ [kalkyl] *n.m.* (*a*) calculation, reckoning, computation; **faux c., erreur de c.,** miscalculation, mistake in reckoning, in adding up; **règle à calcul,** slide rule; **faire son c.,** to lay one's plans; **agir par c.,** to act from selfish, from ulterior, motives; **tout c. fait,** taking everything into account; (*b*) arithmetic; **faible en c.,** bad at sums; (*c*) *Mth:* **c. différentiel et intégral,** differential and integral calculus; **c. des probabilités,** theory of probability.

calcul² *n.m. Med:* calculus, stone (in the bladder).

calculable [kalkylabl̥] *a.* calculable, computable.

calculateur, -trice [kalkylatœr, -tris] **1.** (*a*) *n.* (*pers.*) reckoner, calculator; **c'est un bon c.,** he's good at figures; (*b*) *a.* calculating, shrewd (person, policy). **2.** *n.m.* (*a*) **c. (électronique),** (electronic) computer; (*b*) (pocket) calculator. **3.** *n.f.* (*a*) adding machine; (*b*) (large desk) calculator.

calculé [kalkyle] *a.* premeditated (malice); deliberate (insolence); calculated (insult).

calculer [kalkyle] *v.tr.* (*a*) to calculate, compute, reckon; **c. de tête,** to work sth. out sth., in one's head; **c. un prix,** to work out a price; **tout bien calculé,** taking everything into account; **c. vite et bien,** to be quick and accurate at figures; **machine à c.,** adding machine, desk calculator; (*b*) to plan, calculate (behaviour, etc.); to weigh (up) (consequences); to measure (efforts).

cale¹ [kal] *n.f. Nau:* **1.** (*a*) hold (of ship); **eau de c.,** bilge water; **fond de c.,** bilge; **à fond de c.,** down in the hold; **être à fond de c.,** to be down on one's uppers, down and out; (*b*) **c. à eau,** water tank. **2.** (*a*) **c. de construction, de lancement,** slip(way), (shipbuilding) stocks; **mettre un navire sur c.,** to lay down a ship; (*b*) **c. sèche,** dry dock; **c. de radoub,** graving dock.

cale² *n.f.* **1.** wedge, chock, block (to steady furniture, stop wheel, etc.); **mettre une voiture sur cales,** to put a car on blocks; *Av: etc:* **enlevez les cales!** chocks away! **2.** (*a*) prop, strut; (*b*) packing piece; (*c*) *Mec.E:* key (of shaft, etc.).

calé [kale] *a.* **1.** *Mch:* **piston c.,** (i) jammed piston; (ii) piston at one of the dead points; *Av:* **hélice calée,** dead airscrew. **2.** *F:* (*a*) **être c. en qch.,** to be well up in, know all about, sth.; (*b*) difficult, complicated (problem, etc.); (*c*) **ça c'est c.!** that's cunning, clever!

calebasse [kalbɑs] *n.f.* calabash, gourd; water bottle.

calèche [kalεʃ] *n.f. A.Veh:* barouche.

caleçon [kalsɔ̃] *n.m.* underpants, *NAm:* shorts; **c. long,** long underpants, *F:* long johns; **c. de bain,** swimming trunks, bathing trunks.

calédonien, -ienne [kaledɔnjɛ̃, -jεn] *a. & n. Geog:* Caledonian.

calembour [kalɑ̃bur] *n.m.* pun, play on words.

calendes [kalɑ̃d] *n.f.pl. Rom.Ant:* calends, kalends; **renvoyer qn, qch., aux c. grecques,** to put s.o., sth., off indefinitely.

calendrier [kalɑ̃drije] *n.m.* **1.** calendar; **bloc c., c. à effeuiller,** block calendar, tear-off calendar; **c. perpétuel,** perpetual calendar. **2.** timetable, programme (of journey, work, etc.).

cale-pied [kalpje] *n.m.inv. Cy:* toe clip.

calepin [kalpɛ̃] *n.m.* notebook.

caler¹ [kale] **1.** *v.tr.* (*a*) to wedge, steady (chair leg, etc.); to chock (up) (wheel, etc.); (*b*) to prop up; **c. un malade sur des coussins,** to prop up a patient on cushions; (*c*) *Mec.E: etc:* to wedge, key (crank to shaft, etc.); to fix (wheel on axle, etc.); to jam, lock (valve, etc.); (*d*) *Aut:* to stall (engine); *v.i.* (*of engine*) to stall; (*e*) to adjust; to time, tune (valve, engine, etc.). **2. se c.** (*a*) to settle (oneself) comfortably (in an armchair, etc.); (*b*) *F:* **se c. les joues, se les c.,** to stuff oneself, have a good feed.

caler² *v.i. Nau:* **navire qui cale vingt pieds,** ship that draws, whose draught is, twenty feet (of water); **navire qui cale trop,** ship that is too deep in the water.

caler³ **1.** *v.tr. Nau:* to house (mast); to strike (sail). **2.** *v.i. F:* to give in, give up.

caleter (se) [(sε)kalte] *v.i. & pr. P:* = (SE) CALTER.

calfat [kalfa] *n.m. Nau:* ca(u)lker.

calfatage [kalfataʒ] *n.m. Nau:* ca(u)lking.

calfater [kalfate] *v.tr. Nau:* to ca(u)lk.

calfeutrage [kalføtraʒ] *n.m.,* **calfeutrement** [kalføtrəmɑ̃] *n.m.* blocking up, stopping up, filling in (of gaps); draught-proofing (of room, etc.).

calfeutrer [kalføtre] **1.** *v.tr.* to block up, stop (up), fill (in) (gaps); **c. une pièce,** to make a room draughtproof. **2. se c. dans sa chambre,** (i) to make oneself snug, (ii) shut, lock, oneself up, in one's room.

calibrage [kalibraʒ] *n.m.* **1.** (*a*) gauging, measuring; (*b*) calibration (of thermometer, etc.); (*c*) *Com:* grading (of eggs, etc.). **2.** *Phot:* trimming (of print). **3.** *Typ:* casting off (of copy).

calibre [kalibr̥] *n.m.* **1.** (*a*) calibre, bore (of fire-arm, pipe, etc.); **fusil de c. 8 mm,** (i) *Mil:* 8-mm. calibre rifle; (ii) *Sp:* 8-mm gauge gun; **canon de gros c.,** heavy gun, large-bore gun; (*b*) size, diameter, calibre (of bullet, etc.); grade (of eggs, etc.); **il n'est pas de ce c.-là,** he's not a man of that calibre. **2.** (*a*) *Tls:* gauge, *NAm:* gage; measuring tool; **c. d'épaisseur (à lames),** feeler gauge, set of feelers; **c. de profondeur,** depth gauge; (*b*) (*for reproduction*) template, pattern, mould; profile; (*c*) *Mch.Tls:* jig, former. **3.** *P:* gun, shooter, *esp. NAm:* rod, piece.

calibrer [kalibre] *v.tr.* **1.** (*a*) to gauge, measure; (*b*) to calibrate (thermometer, etc.); (*c*) *Com:* to grade (eggs, etc.). **2.** *Phot:* to trim (print). **3.** *Typ:* to cast off (copy).

calice¹ [kalis] *n.m.* chalice; **boire, avaler, le c. d'amertume,** to drain the cup (of bitterness); **boire le c. jusqu'à la lie,** to drain the cup to its dregs.

calice² *n.m.* **1.** *Bot:* calyx. **2.** *Anat:* calix.

calicot [kaliko] *n.m.* **1.** (*a*) *Tex:* calico, *NAm:* unbleached muslin; (*b*) streamer, banner (bearing advertisement, etc.). **2.** *O:* draper's assistant.

califat [kalifa] *n.m.* caliphate.

calife [kalif] *n.m.* caliph.

Californie [kalifɔrni] *Pr.n.f. Geog:* California.

californien, -ienne [kalifɔrnjɛ̃, -jɛn] *a. & n.* Californian.

californium [kalifɔrnjɔm] *n.m. Ch:* californium.

califourchon [kalifurʃɔ̃] **1.** *adv.phr.* **à c.,** astride; **se mettre à c. sur qch.,** to sit astride (on), to straddle, sth. **2.** *n.m. Fr.C:* bottom, backside, behind.

câlin [kɑlɛ̃] **1.** *a.* coaxing, winning (child, ways, etc.); fond, affectionate (look, tone, etc.). **2.** *n.m. & f.* wheedler, coaxer.

câliner [kɑline] *v.tr.* to caress, fondle, cuddle, make a fuss of (child, etc.).

câlinerie [kɑlinri] *n.f.* **1.** fondness, tenderness. **2.** caress, fondle, cuddle.

calleux, -euse [kalø, -øz] *a.* callous, horny (hand, etc.).

calligraphe [kaligraf] *n.m. & f.* calligrapher, calligraphist.

calligraphie [kaligrafi] *n.f.* calligraphy, penmanship.

calligraphier [kaligrafje] *v.tr.* (*pr. sub. & impf.* **n. calligraphiions, v. calligraphiiez**) to write (letter, etc.) beautifully (and ornamentally), to calligraph.

calligraphique [kaligrafik] *a.* calligraphic.

callosité [kalozite] *n.f.* callosity, callus.

calmant [kalmɑ̃] **1.** *a.* calming, soothing (words, etc.); *Med:* tranquillizing, painkilling, sedative (drug). **2.** *n.m. Med:* tranquillizer, painkiller, sedative.

calmar [kalmar] *n.m.* calamary, squid.

calme¹ [kalm] *n.m.* calm, calmness; stillness (of air, night, etc.); peace (of mind, etc.); peace and quiet; quiet(ness), peacefulness; coolness, composure (of s.o.); **dans le c. de la nuit,** in the still of the night; **moment de c.,** lull; **du c.!** keep cool, calm! **retrouver son c.,** to recover one's equanimity, to calm down; *Nau:* **c. plat,** dead calm; **calmes équatoriaux,** doldrums.

calme² *a.* calm; still, quiet (air, night, etc.); unruffled, cool, composed (person, manner); smooth, serene (sea); *Com:* **marché c.,** flat, quiet, dull, market.

calmement [kalməmɑ̃] *adv.* calmly, quietly, coolly.

calmer [kalme] **1.** *v.tr.* to calm (down); to quieten (down), *esp. NAm:* to quiet down; to still, allay (fears, etc.); to soothe, ease (pain, conscience, etc.); to quench (thirst); to damp, cool (ardour, etc.); to pacify (child, mob, etc.); to abate (fever, etc.); to appease (hunger, etc.). **2. se c.,** to become calm; to calm down, cool down; to quieten down, *esp. NAm:* to quiet down; (*of storm, etc.*) to abate, die down, blow over; (*of wind, etc.*) to drop, subside.

calomel [kalɔmɛl] *n.m. Pharm:* calomel.

calomniateur, -trice [kalɔmnjatœr, -tris] **1.** *n.* slanderer, libeller, calumniator. **2.** *a.* slanderous, libellous.

calomnie [kalɔmni] *n.f.* calumny, slander, libel; **répandre des calomnies sur qn,** to cast aspersions on s.o.

calomnier [kalɔmnje] *v.tr.* to slander, libel (s.o.); to calumniate, malign.

calomnieusement [kalɔmnjøzmɑ̃] *adv.* slanderously, libellously.

calomnieux, -ieuse [kalɔmnjø, -jøz] *a.* slanderous, libellous.

calorie [kalɔri] *n.f. Ph.Meas:* calorie; **grande c.,** (large, great) calorie; **petite c.,** small calorie.

calorifère [kalɔrifɛr] **1.** *a.* heat-conveying. **2.** *n.m.* (*a*) (central) heating installation; (*b*) slow-combustion stove.

calorifique [kalɔrifik] *a. Ph:* calorific, thermal; **capacité c.,** heat capacity.

calorifuge [kalɔrifyʒ] **1.** *a.* (*a*) non-conducting; (heat-)insulating; (*b*) heat-proof (varnish, etc.). **2.** *n.m.* heat insulator, insulation; lagging.

calorifugeage [kalɔrifyʒaʒ] *n.m.* heat insulation, lagging.

calorifuger [kalɔrifyʒe] *v.tr.* (**je calorifugeai(s); n. calorifugeons**) to insulate, lag (pipe, etc.).

calorimètre [kalɔrimɛtr̥] *n.m. Ph:* calorimeter.

calorimétrie [kalɔrimetri] *n.f. Ph:* calorimetry.

calorimétrique [kalɔrimetrik] *a. Ph:* calorimetric(al) (unit, etc.).

calorique [kalɔrik] **1.** *n.m. Ph: A:* heat, caloric. **2.** *a. Physiol: etc:* calorific (value, etc.).

calorisation [kalɔrizasjɔ̃] *n.f. Metalw:* calorizing, calorization, aluminium plating.

calot¹ [kalo] *n.m.* **1.** *Games:* (large) marble; ally. **2.** *P:* eye.

calot² *n.m. Mil:* forage cap, *U.S:* garrison cap.

calotin [kalɔtɛ̃] *n.m. F: Pej:* **1.** priest. **2.** churchgoer.

calotte [kalɔt] *n.f.* **1.** (*a*) skullcap; (*b*) *Ecc:* calotte, zucchetto; *P: Pej:* **la c.,** (i) the priests, the clergy, the cloth; (ii) *Pol:* the clerical party; (*c*) crown (of hat). **2.** (*a*) *Arch:* calotte; *Mth:* **c. sphérique,** portion of a sphere; *Geol:* **c. glaciaire,** ice cap, ice sheet; *Anat:* **c. crânienne, du crâne,** top part of skull, skullcap; *Lit:* **la c. des cieux,** the vault, canopy, of heaven; (*b*) (watch)case, dome. **3.** *F:* cuff, clout (on the head); **flanquer une c. à qn,** to give s.o. a box on the ear.

calotter [kalɔte] *v.tr. F:* to cuff, clout (s.o.); to give s.o. a box on the ear.

calquage [kalkaʒ] *n.m.* tracing.

calque [kalk] *n.m.* (*a*) tracing, traced design; **prendre un c. de qch.,** to make, take, a tracing of sth., to trace sth.; (*b*) exact copy (of painting, poem, etc.); (*c*) **(papier-)c.,** tracing paper; (*d*) **elle est le c. de sa mère,** she's the dead spit, the spitting image, of her mother; (*e*) *Ling:* calque.

calquer [kalke] *v.tr.* **1.** to trace; make, take, a tracing of (sth.); **dessin calqué,** tracing. **2.** to copy closely, exactly; to imitate; **expression calquée sur l'anglais,** expression copied from, modelled on, the English.

calquoir [kalkwar] *n.m.* tracing point; tracer.

calter (se) [səkalte] *v.i. & pr. P:* to run away, make off, hop it.

calumet [kalymɛ] *n.m.* calumet; (Red Indian's) pipe;

fumer le c. de la paix avec qn, to smoke the pipe of peace with s.o.

calvados, *F:* **calva** [kalvados, kalva] *n.m.* apple brandy, calvados.

calvaire [kalvɛr] *n.m.* (*a*) **Le C.,** (Mount) Calvary; (*b*) agony; **sa vie fut un long c.,** his life was one long calvary; (*c*) wayside cross.

calvinisme [kalvinism] *n.m.* Calvinism.

calviniste [kalvinist] **1.** *a.* Calvinistic(al), Calvinist. **2.** *n.* Calvinist.

calvitie [kalvisi] *n.f.* baldness; **c. naissante,** incipient baldness.

calypso [kalipso] *n.m. Mus: Danc:* calypso.

camaïeu, -eux [kamajø] *n.m.* camaieu, monochrome (painting); *Engr:* tint drawing.

camail [kamaj] *n.m.* **1.** *R.C.Ch:* cape (worn over the surplice). **2.** *Orn:* neck feathers, hackles (of fowl).

camarade [kamarad] *n.m.* & *f.* comrade; friend; mate; (*as term of address*) comrade; **c. d'école, de collège,** school friend; **c. de classe, de promotion,** classmate; **faire c.,** to put one's hands up, to surrender.

camaraderie [kamaradri] *n.f.* (*a*) comradeship, companionship, goodfellowship; (*b*) (spirit of) mutual co-operation, camaraderie.

camarguais, -aise [kamargɛ, -ɛz] *a.* & *n. Geog:* (native, inhabitant) of the Camargue.

cambiste [kɑ̃bist] **1.** *n.m. Fin:* exchange broker, money changer. **2.** *a.* **marché c.,** exchange market.

Cambodge [kɑ̃bɔdʒ] *Pr.n.m. Hist: Geog:* Cambodia.

cambodgien, -ienne [kɑ̃bɔdʒjɛ̃, -jɛn] *a.* & *n. Geog:* Cambodian.

cambouis [kɑ̃bwi] *n.m.* dirty oil, grease.

cambrage [kɑ̃braʒ] *n.m.* bending; arching (of foot, back, etc.); cambering, curving (of wood, etc.).

cambré [kɑ̃bre] *a.* **1.** cambered, arched (beam, etc.); **pied très c.,** foot with a high instep. **2.** bent; **taille cambrée,** arched, curved, back; **jambes cambrées,** bow legs.

cambrement [kɑ̃brəmɑ̃] *n.m.* = CAMBRAGE.

cambrer [kɑ̃bre] **1.** *v.tr.* (*a*) to bend; to arch (one's foot, etc.); **c. la taille, les reins,** to throw out one's chest; to arch, straighten, one's back; to draw oneself up; (*b*) to camber, curve (wood, etc.). **2. se c.,** to throw out one's chest; to arch, straighten, one's back; to draw oneself up.

cambrien, -ienne [kɑ̃mbrijɛ̃, -jɛn] *a.* & *n.m. Geol:* Cambrian.

cambriolage [kɑ̃brijɔlaʒ] *n.m.* housebreaking, burglary; burgling.

cambrioler [kɑ̃brijɔle] *v.tr.* to break into (house); to burgle, *NAm:* burglarize.

cambrioleur, -euse [kɑ̃brijɔlœr, -øz] *n.* housebreaker; burglar.

cambrique [kɑ̃brik] *n.m. Ling:* Welsh, Cymric.

cambrous(s)e (kɑ̃bruz, -us] *n.f. F:* country; **maison en pleine c.,** house in the middle of nowhere, (out) in the sticks, at the back of beyond.

cambrure [kɑ̃bryr] *n.f.* camber, curve (of wood, etc.); arch (of foot, back); instep.

cambuse [kɑ̃byz] *n.f.* **1.** *Nau:* steward's room, storeroom. **2.** canteen (in shipyard). **3.** *P:* hovel, dump.

cambusier [kɑ̃byzje] *n.m. Nau:* **1.** steward, purser. **2.** (*a*) canteen keeper (in shipyard, etc.); (*b*) storekeeper.

came[1] [kam] *n.f. Mec.E:* cam, lifter, wiper; **arbre à cames,** camshaft; **moteur avec arbre à cames en tête,** overhead camshaft engine.

came[2] *n.f. P:* dope, junk; snow.

camé, -ée[1] [kame] *n. P:* drug addict, junkie.

camée[2] [kame] *n.m.* cameo.

caméléon [kameleɔ̃] *n.m.* (*a*) *Rept: Miner:* chameleon; (*b*) (*pers.*) chameleon, turncoat.

camél(l)ia [kamelja] *n.m. Bot:* camellia.

camelot [kamlo] *n.m.* **1.** *F:* cheapjack, street hawker. **2.** *A:* newsvendor; *Hist:* **les camelots du roi,** royalist group.

camelote [kamlɔt] *n.f.* (*a*) *F:* cheap goods, trash, junk, rubbish; **maison de c.,** jerry-built house; (*b*) *P:* goods; **fais voir ta c.!** let's have a look at your stuff.

caméra [kamera] *n.f.* film, *NAm:* movie, camera; cinecamera; *T.V:* camera.

cameraman [kameraman] *n.m. Cin:* cameraman; *pl. cameramen.*

camérier [kamerje] *n.m.* chamberlain (to Pope, cardinal).

camériste [kamerist] *n.f. A:* maid of honour, lady-in-waiting.

Cameroun (le) [ləkamrun] *Pr.n.m.* **1.** *Hist:* the Cameroons. **2.** *Geog:* the Cameroon (Republic).

camerounais, -aise [kamrunɛ, -ɛz] *a.* & *n.* Cameroonian.

camion [kamjɔ̃] *n.m.* **1.** (*a*) dray, wag(g)on; (*b*) *Aut:* lorry, *esp. NAm:* truck; **c. de déménagement,** removal van, pantechnicon. **2.** (painter's) kettle.

camion-benne [kamjɔ̃bɛn] *n.m.* dumper (truck), *U.S:* dump truck; *pl. camions-bennes.*

camion-citerne (kamjɔ̃sitɛrn] *n.m.* tanker (lorry), *NAm:* tank truck, tank trailer; *pl. camions-citernes.*

camionnage [kamjɔnaʒ] *n.m.* cartage, haulage; *NAm:* truckage, trucking.

camionner [kamjɔne] *v.tr.* to cart, carry, haul, *NAm:* truck (goods).

camionnette [kamjɔnɛt] *n.f.* van, *NAm:* delivery truck.

camionneur [kamjɔnœr] *n.m.* **1.** lorry driver, van driver, *NAm:* truck driver, trucker, teamster. **2.** haulier, haulage contractor, *NAm:* trucker.

camisole [kamizɔl] *n.f.* **1.** *Cost:* (*a*) *A:* nightshirt; (*b*) *A:* camisole, sleeved vest, spencer; (*c*) *Fr.C:* vest, *NAm:* undershirt. **2. c. de force,** strait-jacket.

camomille [kamɔmij] *n.f. Bot:* camomile; **tisane de c.,** camomile tea.

camouflage [kamuflaʒ] *n.m.* camouflage; disguising, hiding (truth, etc.); faking.

camoufler [kamufle] *v.tr.* to camouflage; to disguise, hide (truth, etc.); to fake.

camouflet [kamuflɛ] *n.m.* **1.** affront, insult, snub. **2.** *Mil.Min:* camouflet, stifler.

camp [kɑ̃] *n.m.* **1.** camp; **établir un c.,** to pitch (a) camp; **lever le c.,** to strike camp; *Mil:* **c. volant,** temporary camp; *Fig:* **être en c. volant,** to be somewhere only temporarily; **lit de c.,** camp bed; **c. de vacances,** holiday camp; **c. de concentration, d'internement,** concentration, internment, camp; *F:* **ficher le c.,** to clear off, scram. **2.** (*a*) party, faction, camp; **changer de c.,** to change sides; (*b*) *Games:* side; **tirer les camps,** to pick sides.

campagnard, -arde [kɑ̃paɲar, -ard] **1.** *a.* country (gentleman, accent, etc.); rustic (simplicity, etc.). **2.** *n.* countryman, countrywoman; rustic.

campagne [kɑ̃paɲ] *n.f.* **1.** (*a*) plain; open country; **en pleine c.,** in the open country; (*b*) country(side) (as opposed to town); **à la c.,** in the country; **vie de c.,** country life; (*c*) **(maison de) c.,** small estate, little place in the country. **2.** *Mil:* (the) field; **en c.,** in the field; on active service; **artillerie de c.,** field artillery; **tenue de c.,** field dress, combat kit; **entrer, se mettre, en c.,** (i) to begin operations, take the field; (ii) to set to work. **3.** (*a*) *Mil: Pol: etc:* campaign; *Mil:* **faire c.,** to campaign, fight a campaign; **faire c., se mettre en c., pour qn, contre qch.,** to campaign on s.o.'s behalf against sth.; **c. publicitaire, de publicité,** advertising campaign; publicity drive; **c. de calomnies,** smear campaign; (*b*) *Navy:* (i) cruise, (ii) (naval) campaign.

campagnol [kɑ̃paɲɔl] *n.m. Z:* (field) vole.
campanile [kɑ̃panil] *n.m. Arch:* campanile; bell tower.
campanule [kɑ̃panyl] *n.f. Bot:* campanula.
campé [kɑ̃pe] *a.* (*of pers.*) **bien c.,** well built, well made; **portrait bien c.,** well sketched portrait; **récit bien c.,** well constructed, well told story; **bien c. sur ses jambes,** standing firmly on his feet, firmly planted.
campêche [kɑ̃pɛʃ] *n.m.* **(bois de) c.,** Campeachy wood, logwood.
campement [kɑ̃pmɑ̃] *n.m.* **1.** camping. **2.** (*a*) encampment, camp; **établir un c.,** to camp, pitch camp; **replier le c.,** to strike camp; **matériel de c.,** camping equipment; (*b*) camping ground, place.
camper [kɑ̃pe] **1.** *v.i.* (*a*) to (en)camp, to pitch camp; to camp out; to go camping; (*b*) to install oneself provisionally, camp out (in a hotel, etc.). **2.** *v.tr.* (*a*) to encamp (troops); to put (troops) under canvas; (*b*) to place, fix, put; **il a campé son chapeau sur la tête,** he stuck his hat on his head; **c. là qn,** to leave s.o. in the lurch; (*c*) to construct (story, etc.); **écrivain qui campe bien ses personnages,** writer who is good at portraying characters; *Th:* **c. un personnage,** to play a part effectively. **3. se c.,** to stand, plant one's feet, firmly; **se c. devant qn,** to plant oneself in front of s.o.
campeur, -euse [kɑ̃pœr, -øz] *n.* camper.
camphre [kɑ̃fr̥] *n.m.* camphor; **essence de c.,** camphor oil.
camphré [kɑ̃fre] *a.* camphorated (oil, etc.).
camphrier [kɑ̃frije] *n.m. Bot:* camphor tree.
camping [kɑ̃piŋ] *n.m.* **1.** camping; **faire du c.,** to go camping. **2.** camp(ing) site.
campos [kɑ̃po] *n.m. F: O:* holiday, rest; **donner c. à qn,** to give s.o. a day off, an afternoon off.
campus [kɑ̃pys] *n.m.* campus.
camus [kamy] *a.* **1.** flat-, snub-nosed (person); pug-nosed (dog, etc.). **2.** flat, snub, pug (nose).
Canada [kanada] *Pr.n.m. Geog:* Canada; **au C.,** in Canada.
canadianisme [kanadjanism] *n.m. Ling:* Canadianism.
canadien, -ienne [kanadjɛ̃, -jɛn] **1.** *a. & n. Geog:* Canadian; **canadien français,** French Canadian. **2.** *n.f.* **canadienne** (*a*) sheepskin jacket, fur-lined lumber jacket; (*b*) Canadian canoe; (*c*) *Aut:* shooting brake, station wagon.
canaille [kanɑj] **1.** *n.f.* (*a*) *coll.* rabble, riff-raff; (*b*) scoundrel, rogue, bad lot; (*to child*) **petite c.!** you little devil, rascal! **2.** *a.* low, crooked (action, etc.); vulgar, coarse (song, etc.).
canaillerie [kanɑjri] *n.f.* **1.** low(-down) trick. **2.** (*a*) lowness, crookedness (of action, etc.); (*b*) vulgarity, coarseness (of song, etc.).
canal, -aux [kanal, -o] *n.m.* **1.** (*a*) channel (of river); **par le c. de la poste,** through (the medium of), via, the post; (*b*) **le C. de Mozambique,** the Mozambique Channel; (*c*) *Hyd.E:* (i) culvert; (ii) (mill) race. **2.** *Civ.E:* canal; **c. maritime, de navigation,** ship canal; **le C. de Suez,** the Suez Canal; **la Zone du C. (de Panama),** the Canal Zone; **c. d'irrigation,** irrigation canal. **3.** (*a*) pipe, spout, conduit, tube; **c. à air, d'aérage,** air passage, duct, flue; **c. de fuite,** waste pipe; (*b*) *Anat: Bot:* canal, duct, meatus; **c. alimentaire,** alimentary canal; **c. biliaire,** bile duct; **c. déférent,** vas deferens; (*c*) groove; **c. de graissage,** oil groove; (*d*) *T.V:* channel, *NAm:* airway.
canalisation [kanalizasjɔ̃] *n.f.* **1.** canalization (of river, etc.). **2.** (*a*) (system of) pipes, piping; conduit, mains ducting; (electric) conduit, cable, wiring; (*b*) pipeline (for mineral oils, etc.).
canaliser [kanalize] *v.tr.* **1.** to canalize (region, river, etc.). **2.** to channel, concentrate (resources, etc.); to direct (traffic, crowd, etc.).
cananéen, -enne [kananeɛ̃, -ɛn] *a. & n. B.Hist:* Canaanite.
canapé [kanape] *n.m.* **1.** *Furn:* sofa, couch, settee. **2.** *Cu:* (*a*) slice of bread fried in butter; (*b*) (cocktail) canapé.
canapé-lit [kanapeli] *n.m.* bed settee, studio couch; day bed; *pl. canapés-lits.*
canard [kanar] *n.m.* **1.** duck; (*male bird*) drake; **c. de Barbarie,** Muscovy duck; **c. sauvage,** wild duck, mallard; **c. siffleur,** wi(d)geon; **chasse aux canards,** duck shooting; *F:* **mon petit c.,** darling, ducky; *F:* **marcher comme un c.,** to waddle. **2.** *F:* (*a*) false report, hoax, canard; (*b*) newspaper, rag. **3.** lump of sugar dipped in coffee, brandy, etc. **4.** *Mus:* false note (on reed instrument, etc.).
canardeau, -eaux [kanardo] *n.m.* duckling.
canarder [kanarde] **1.** *v.i.* (*a*) (*of ship*) to pitch; (*b*) *Mus: F:* to play, sing, a false note. **2.** *v.tr. F:* to fire at (s.o.) from behind cover; to snipe at, take pot shots at (s.o.).
canardière [kanardjɛr] *n.f.* **1.** duck pond. **2.** screen (for duck shooting). **3.** duck gun, punt gun.
canari [kanari] *n.m. Orn:* canary; *a.inv.* **(jaune) c.,** canary (yellow).
Canaries [kanari] *Pr.n.f.pl. Geog:* **les (îles) C.,** the Canary Islands, the Canaries.
canasson [kanasɔ̃] *n.m. P:* horse, nag.
canasta [kanasta] *n.f. Cards:* canasta.
cancale [kɑ̃kal] *n.f.* Cancale oyster.
cancan [kɑ̃kɑ̃] *n.m. F:* **1.** (*a*) (piece of) ill natured gossip; (*b*) *pl.* tittle-tattle, gossip; **dire, faire, des cancans,** to gossip, talk (**sur,** about). **2.** cancan (dance).
cancaner [kɑ̃kane] *v.i.* **1.** *F:* to tittle-tattle, gossip, talk scandal. **2.** (*of duck*) to quack.
cancanier, -ière [kɑ̃kanje, -jɛr] *F:* **1.** *a.* fond of tittle-tattle, gossipy. **2.** *n.* gossip, scandalmonger, tattler.
cancer [kɑ̃sɛr] *n.m.* **1.** *Astr:* **le C.,** Cancer, the Crab; *Geog:* **le Tropique du C.,** the Tropic of Cancer. **2.** *Med:* cancer; **c. de la peau,** skin cancer.
cancéreux, -euse [kɑ̃serø, -øz] **1.** *a.* cancerous (tumour, etc.). **2.** *n.* cancer patient.
cancériforme [kɑ̃serifɔrm] *a. Med:* cancriform, cancroid.
cancérigène [kɑ̃seriʒɛn], **cancérogène** [kɑ̃serɔʒɛn] *a.* carcinogenic.
cancérologie [kɑ̃serɔlɔʒi] *n.f.* cancerology.
cancérologue [kɑ̃serɔlɔg] *n.m. & f.* cancer specialist, cancerologist.
cancre [kɑ̃kr̥] *n.m.* **1.** *Crust:* crab. **2.** *F:* dunce, duffer, dud.
cancrelat [kɑ̃krəla] *n.m.* cockroach.
cancroïde [kɑ̃krɔid] *n.m. Med:* cancroid (ulcer).
candélabre [kɑ̃delabr̥] *n.m.* (*a*) candelabrum, *pl.* candelabra; branched candlestick; (*b*) street lamp post (with branched lamps).
candeur [kɑ̃dœr] *n.f.* ingenuousness, artlessness.
candi [kɑ̃di] *a.m.* candied; **fruits candis,** crystallized fruit; **sucre c.,** sugar candy.
candidat, -ate [kɑ̃dida, -at] *n.* candidate; applicant (**à une place,** for a place); examinee; **se porter c. à la députation,** to stand for Parliament.
candidature [kɑ̃didatyr] *n.f.* candidature, *NAm:* candidacy; **poser sa c. à un poste,** to apply for a post.
candide [kɑ̃did] *a.* ingenuous, guileless, artless.
candidement [kɑ̃didmɑ̃] *adv.* ingenuously, guilelessly, artlessly.
candir (se) [səkɑ̃dir] *v.pr.* (*of sugar*) to candy, crystallize.

cane [kan] *n.f.* duck (as opposed to drake).
caner [kane] *v.i. P:* (*a*) to have the jitters; (*b*) to chicken out, to funk; (*c*) to die; to kick the bucket.
caneton [kantɔ̃] *n.m. Orn:* (male) duckling.
canette¹ [kanɛt] *n.f. Orn:* (female) duckling.
canette² *n.f.* = CANNETTE 2, 3.
canevas [kanvɑ] *n.m.* **1.** *Tex:* canvas. **2.** (*a*) *Art: Lit: Mus:* groundwork, sketch, outline (of drawing, novel, etc.); (*b*) *Surv:* (i) skeleton map; (ii) skeleton triangulation.
caniche [kaniʃ] *n.m. Z:* poodle.
caniculaire [kanikylɛr] *a.* **1.** canicular; **les jours caniculaires,** the dog days. **2.** sultry, scorching (heat, day, etc.).
canicule [kanikyl] *n.f.* heatwave; **la c.,** the dog days.
canif [kanif] *n.m.* penknife.
canin [kanɛ̃] **1.** *a.* canine; **exposition canine,** dog show. **2.** *n.f.* **(dent) canine,** canine (tooth), eyetooth.
caniveau, -eaux [kanivo] *n.m.* **1.** *Civ.E:* (*a*) gutter stone; (*b*) gutter, gully. **2.** trough, conduit (for cables).
cannage [kanaʒ] *n.m.* **1.** caning (of chairs, etc.). **2.** cane bottom, canework (of chair, etc.).
canne [kan] *n.f.* **1.** cane, reed; **c. à sucre,** sugar cane; **sucre de c.,** cane sugar. **2.** walking stick, cane; **c. (à) épée,** swordstick; **(escrime à) la c.,** singlestick (play); **c. blanche,** (i) blind man's stick, white stick; (ii) blind man, woman. **3. c. à pêche,** fishing rod. **4.** *Glassm:* blowing iron, blowpipe. **5.** *Fr.C:* can, tin (of tomatoes, etc.).
canné [kane] *a.* **chaise cannée,** cane(-seated) chair.
canneberge [kanbɛrʒ] *n.f. Bot:* cranberry.
cannelé [kanle] *a.* (*a*) fluted, channelled, grooved; (*b*) corrugated.
canneler [kanle] *v.tr.* (**je cannelle, n. cannelons; je cannellerai**) (*a*) to flute, channel, groove; (*b*) to corrugate.
cannelier [kanəlje] *n.m. Bot:* cinnamon tree.
cannelle¹ [kanɛl] *n.f.* cinnamon (bark).
cannelle² *n.f.* spigot, faucet, tap.
cannelure [kanlyr] *n.f.* **1.** (*a*) groove, channel, slot; *Arch:* flute, fluting (of column); (*b*) corrugation. **2.** *pl. Bot: etc:* striae. **3.** *Geol:* fault fissure.
canner [kane] *v.tr.* to cane (chair).
cannette [kanɛt] *n.f.* **1.** = CANNELLE². **2.** (beer) bottle. **3.** (*a*) *Tex:* cop, spool; (*b*) spool (of sewing machine).
cannibale [kanibal] **1.** *n.* cannibal. **2.** *a.* cannibal (tribe, etc.); cannibalistic (propensities, etc.).
cannibalisme [kanibalism] *n.m.* cannibalism.
canoë [kanɔe] *n.m.* canoe; **faire du c.,** to canoe, go canoeing.
canoéisme [kanɔeism] *n.m.* canoeing.
canoéiste [kanɔeist] *n.* canoeist.
canon¹ [kanɔ̃] *n.m.* **1.** (*a*) *Mil: etc:* gun, cannon; **c. à âme lisse,** smooth-bore gun; **c. rayé,** rifled gun; **c. de 105 mm, de 280 mm,** 105 mm, 280 mm gun; **c. antiaérien,** anti-aircraft gun; **c. antichar,** anti-tank gun; **c. de char,** tank gun; **c. de marine, de bord,** naval gun; **c. de chasse,** bow chaser; **c. de retraite,** sternchaser; **poudre à c.,** gunpowder; *F:* **chair à c.,** cannon fodder; (*b*) *coll.* artillery, the guns; **le gros c.,** the heavy guns. **2.** (*a*) barrel (of rifle, watch, pen, etc.); **fusil à deux canons,** double-barrelled gun; (*b*) barrel, pipe (of key, of lock); (*c*) spout (of watering can); (*d*) body (of syringe, etc.). **3.** (*a*) *A:* wine measure (= 0.058 l.); (*b*) *P:* **boire un c.,** to drink a glass of wine. **4.** *Vet:* cannon (bone), shin, shank (of horse). **5.** *pl. A.Cost:* can(n)ions, canons. **6.** *T.V: X rays:* **c. à électrons,** electron gun.
canon² *n.m.* **1.** *Ecc:* canon, rule (of an order, of the Mass, etc.); *a.* **droit c.,** canon law. **2.** (general) formula, rule, canon. **3.** *Mus:* canon, round, catch.
cañon [kaɲɔ̃] *n.m. Geog:* canyon, cañon.
canonial, -iaux [kanɔnjal, -jo] *a. Ecc:* **1.** canonic(al) (hours, etc.). **2.** pertaining to a canon (*chanoine*).
canonique [kanɔnik] *a.* canonical (book, etc.); **âge c.,** (i) canonical age (for priest's housekeeper); (ii) *F:* respectable age.
canonisation [kanɔnizasjɔ̃] *n.f. Ecc:* canonization.
canoniser [kanɔnize] *v.tr. Ecc:* to canonize.
canon-mitrailleuse [kanɔ̃mitrajøz] *n.m.* pompom; *pl. canons-mitrailleuses.*
canonnade [kanɔnad] *n.f.* cannonade, gunfire.
canonner [kanɔne] *v.tr.* to cannonade, to shell (enemy); to batter (fort).
canonnier [kanɔnje] *n.m.* gunner.
canonnière [kanɔnjɛr] *n.f.* **1.** *Navy:* gunboat. **2.** *Fort:* loophole (for gun). **3.** *Toys: A:* popgun.
canot [kano] *n.m.* (*a*) (open) boat; rowing boat, *NAm:* rowboat; dinghy; **grand c.,** longboat, pinnace; *Navy:* **c. major,** officers' boat; **petit c.,** jollyboat, gig; **c. automobile,** motorboat, motor launch; (*b*) *Fr.C:* canoe.
canotage [kanɔtaʒ] *n.m.* (*a*) boating; rowing; (dinghy) sailing; (*b*) *Fr.C:* canoeing; **faire du c.,** to canoe.
canoter [kanɔte] *v.i.* (*a*) to go (in for) boating, rowing, (dinghy) sailing; to row, to sail; (*b*) *Fr.C:* to go (in for) canoeing; to canoe.
canoteur [kanɔtœr] *n.m.* (*a*) rower, boater; (*b*) *Fr.C:* canoeist.
canotier [kanɔtje] *n.m.* **1.** rower, oarsman. **2.** straw hat, boater.
cantaloup [kɑ̃talu] *n.m.* cantaloup (melon).
cantate [kɑ̃tat] *n.f. Mus:* cantata.
cantatrice [kɑ̃tatris] *n.f.* (professional) singer.
cantharide [kɑ̃tarid] *n.f. Ent:* cantharis, Spanish fly.
cantilène [kɑ̃tilɛn] *n.f. Mus:* cantilena.
cantilever [kɑ̃tilevœr] *a. & n.m. Civ.E:* cantilever; **(pont) c.,** cantilever bridge.
cantine [kɑ̃tin] *n.f.* **1.** (*a*) *Mil: etc:* canteen; *Sch:* dining room, refectory; *Sch:* **déjeuner à la c.,** to have school lunch, dinner; (*b*) soup kitchen. **2.** *Mil:* (officer's) uniform case, tin trunk; **c. médicale,** field medical chest.
cantinier, -ière [kɑ̃tinje, -jɛr] *n. Mil: A:* canteen keeper, attendant.
cantique [kɑ̃tik] *n.m. Ecc:* (*a*) canticle; **le C. des cantiques,** the Song of Songs; (*b*) hymn.
canton [kɑ̃tɔ̃] *n.m.* **1.** (*a*) (*in Fr.*) canton (administrative district); (*b*) (*in Switz.*) canton; (*c*) *Fr.C:* **les cantons de l'Est,** the Eastern Townships. **2.** (*a*) *A:* district, region; (*b*) *Civ.E:* section (of road, railway, etc.); (*c*) *Rail:* block (in block system).
cantonade [kɑ̃tɔnad] *n.f. Th:* (the) wings; **parler à la c.,** (i) *Th:* to speak off; (ii) to speak to nobody in particular, to the company at large.
cantonais, aise [kɑ̃tɔnɛ, -ɛz] **1.** *a. & n. Geog:* Cantonese. **2.** *n.m. Ling:* Cantonese.
cantonal, -aux [kɑ̃tɔnal, -o] *a.* cantonal, district (committee, etc.).
cantonnement [kɑ̃tɔnmɑ̃] *n.m.* **1.** *Mil:* quartering, billeting (of troops). **2.** (*a*) section (of forest, etc.); forest range; stretch of river (with fishing rights); (*b*) *Mil:* quarters, billets, cantonment.
cantonner [kɑ̃tɔne] **1.** *v.tr.* to confine, limit (**dans qch.,** to sth.); to isolate (sick animals, etc.); *Mil:* to quarter, billet (troops). **2.** *v.i.* (*of troops*) to be billeted, quartered. **3. se c.** (*a*) to lock oneself away (in a room, etc.); (*b*) to confine, limit oneself (**dans qch.,** to sth.).
cantonnier [kɑ̃tɔnje] *n.m.* (*a*) roadman, roadmender; (*b*) *Rail:* line(s)man.

cantonnière [kɑ̃tɔnjɛr] *n.f. Furn:* (*a*) valence; (*b*) window drapery.

Cantorbéry [kɑ̃tɔrberi] *Pr.n. Geog:* Canterbury.

canular(d) [kanylar] *n.m. Sch: F:* (*a*) tall story; (*b*) hoax, practical joke, leg-pull; rag.

canule [kanyl] *n.f. Med:* nozzle (of syringe, etc.); cannula.

canulé [kanyle] *a.* nozzle-shaped.

canuler [kanyle] *v.tr.* (*a*) *P:* to bore, be a nuisance to (s.o.); (*b*) *Sch: F:* to play a practical joke on (s.o.).

caoutchouc [kautʃu] *n.m.* **1.** rubber; **c. synthétique,** synthetic rubber; **c. mousse** (*R.t.m.*), foam rubber, sponge rubber; *St.Exch:* **caoutchoucs,** rubber shares, rubbers. **2.** (*a*) waterproof (coat), mackintosh; (*b*) *pl.* galoshes, rubber overshoes, *NAm:* rubbers; (*c*) rubber band, elastic band.

caoutchoutage [kautʃutaʒ] *n.m.* treating with rubber, rubberizing.

caoutchouter [kautʃute] *v.tr.* to treat (sth.) with rubber, to rubberize.

caoutchouteux, -euse [kautʃutø, -øz] *a.* rubbery.

cap [kap] *n.m.* **1.** *Geog:* cape, headland, foreland; **le c. Horn,** Cape Horn; **le C.,** Capetown; *Hist:* **la Colonie du c.,** Cape Colony; **franchir, doubler, un c.,** (i) to weather a cape; (ii) to round a cape; (iii) to weather, overcome, a difficulty; **quand on a franchi le c. de la quarantaine,** when one has, you've, turned forty. **2.** *Nau: Av:* course, heading, direction; **mettre le c. sur . . .,** to head for, to steer for . . ., **mettre le c. au large,** to stand out to sea; **c. au vent, au large,** head (on) to the wind, to sea; **changement de c.,** change of course; **c. de collision,** collision course; *Av:* **conservateur de c.,** directional gyro.

capable [kapab̥l] *a.* **1.** (*a*) capable; **c. de qch.,** capable of sth.; **être c. de faire qch.,** to be capable of doing sth.; to be fit, able to do sth.; to be equal to doing sth.; **il est c. de tout,** he's liable to do anything; he'll stop at nothing; **cette maladie est c. de le tuer,** this illness might well, may be enough to, kill him; (*b*) *Jur:* entitled, qualified, competent (to do sth.). **2.** capable, able, competent (person).

capacité [kapasite] *n.f.* **1.** capacity (of vase, accumulator, etc.); *El:* **c. (électrostatique),** capacitance; *Med:* **c. vitale,** vital capacity. **2.** (*a*) capacity, ability; capability; talent; **homme de grande, de haute, c.,** very capable man; **avoir les capacités pour faire qch.,** to be qualified to do sth.; **c. pour les affaires,** business ability; *Jur:* **certificat de c., en droit,** certificate entitling holder to practise in some branches of the legal profession; (*b*) *Jur:* capacity; **avoir c. pour faire qch.,** to be (legally) entitled, qualified, to do sth.; **c. légale,** legal capacity.

caparaçon [kaparasɔ̃] *n.m. Harn:* caparison, trappings.

caparaçonner [kaparasɔne] *v.tr.* to caparison (horse).

cape [kap] *n.f.* **1.** cape, cloak; **roman de c. et d'épée,** historical romance; cloak-and-dagger story; **sous c.,** secretly, on the sly, on the quiet; **rire sous c.,** to laugh up one's sleeve. **2.** *Nau:* **être, se tenir, à la c.,** to lie to, to be hove to; **(se) mettre à la c.,** to heave to.

capelage [kaplaʒ] *n.m. Nau:* **1.** rigging (of mast). **2.** masthead (under rigging).

capeler [kaple] *v.tr.* (**je capelle, n. capelons; je capellerai**) *Nau:* **1.** to rig (mast, spar, etc.). **2. canot capelé par une lame,** boat swamped by a sea.

capeline [kaplin] *n.f. Cost:* (*a*) *A:* riding hood; (*b*) sunbonnet, sun hat, floppy hat.

capésien, -ienne [kapesjɛ̃, -jɛn] *n. Sch: F:* student reading for the C.A.P.E.S. (*Certificat d'Aptitude pédagogique à l'Enseignement secondaire*).

capétien, -ienne [kapesjɛ̃, -jɛn] *a. & n. Hist:* Capetian.

Capharnaüm [kafarnaɔm] **1.** *Pr.n.m. B.Hist:* Capernaum. **2.** *n.m.* junk room; glory hole.

capillaire [kapilɛr] **1.** *a.* (*a*) capillary (tube, attraction); *Anat:* **les vaisseaux capillaires,** *n.* **les capillaires,** the capillary blood vessels, the capillaries; (*b*) **lotion c.,** hair lotion, hair tonic; **artiste c.,** hair stylist. **2.** *n.m. Bot:* maidenhair (fern).

capillarité [kapilarite] *n.f. Ph:* capillarity, capillary attraction.

capilliculture [kapilikyltyr] *n.f.* hair care, treatment.

capilotade [kapilɔtad] *n.f. F:* **mettre qn en c.,** to beat s.o. to a pulp, black and blue; to make mincemeat of s.o.; **mettre qch. en c.,** to smash sth. to pieces, to smithereens.

capitaine [kapitɛn] *n.m.* **1.** *Mil: Nau:* captain; *Nau:* skipper; *Mil.Av:* **c. (d'aviation)** = flight lieutenant; *U.S:* (air) captain; *Navy:* **c. de corvette,** lieutenant commander; **c. de frégate,** commander; **c. de vaisseau,** captain; *Nau:* **c. de la marine marchande,** captain, master (in the merchant navy); **c. de port,** harbour master; **c. au long cours,** master mariner. **2.** chief, head, leader (of band, gang, etc.); captain (of football team, etc.); *Mil:* **un grand c.,** a great (military) leader; **les capitaines d'industrie,** the captains of industry.

capital, -aux [kapital, -o] **1.** *a.* (*a*) *Jur:* capital (crime, etc.); **la peine capitale,** capital punishment; the death penalty; (*b*) fundamental, essential, chief, principal; **le point c.,** the essential, the main, point; **une décision capitale,** a major decision; **son défaut c.,** his greatest fault; **d'une importance capitale,** of capital, paramount, cardinal, importance; **les sept péchés capitaux,** the seven deadly sins; (*c*) *Typ:* **lettre capitale,** *n.f.* **capitale,** capital (letter); **(écrire en) capitales d'imprimerie,** (write in) block capitals. **2.** *n.m.* (*a*) *Fin:* capital, assets; **c. et intérêt,** principal and interest; **c. social,** registered capital; (*b*) *Pol.Ec:* **c. réel,** capital assets; **association c.-travail,** profit-sharing scheme. **3.** *n.f.* **capitale,** capital (city).

capitalisable [kapitalizab̥l] *a.* capitalizable (interest, etc.).

capitalisation [kapitalizasjɔ̃] *n.f.* capitalization (of interest, etc.).

capitaliser [kapitalize] **1.** *v.tr.* to capitalize (interest, etc.). **2.** *v.i.* to save; to put money by.

capitalisme [kapitalism] *n.m.* capitalism.

capitaliste [kapitalist] **1.** *a.* capitalist, capitalistic. **2.** *n.* capitalist.

capitation [kapitasjɔ̃] *n.f. A.Adm:* capitation, poll tax, head money.

capiteux, -euse [kapitø, -øz] *a.* (*a*) (*of wine, etc.*) heady; (*b*) sensuous (charm, etc.); exciting, alluring (woman).

Capitole (le) [ləkapitɔl] *n.m.* the Capitol (of ancient Rome, Toulouse, Washington).

capiton [kapitɔ̃] *n.m.* **1.** *Com:* silk waste. **2.** *Furn:* (*a*) cap, boss (between buttons); (*b*) (upholstery) stuffing, padding.

capitonnage [kapitɔnaʒ] *n.m.* (*a*) upholstering, stuffing, padding; (*b*) (upholstery) stuffing, padding.

capitonner [kapitɔne] *v.tr.* to upholster, stuff, pad (furniture).

capitulaire [kapitylɛr] *a.* capitular (act, letter); **salle c.,** chapter house.

capitulation [kapitylasjɔ̃] *n.f.* capitulation, surrender; **c. sans conditions,** unconditional surrender.

capituler [kapityle] *v.i.* to capitulate, surrender; **forcer qn à c.,** to bring s.o. to terms, make s.o. give in.

capon, -onne [kapɔ̃, -ɔn] *F:* **1.** *a.* cowardly; yellow. **2.** *n.* coward, funk.
caporal, -aux [kapɔral, -o] *n.m.* **1.** *Mil: etc:* corporal; **c. d'ordinaire,** mess corporal; *Hist: F:* **le Petit C.,** Napoleon. **2.** caporal (tobacco).
caporal-chef [kapɔralʃɛf] *n.m. Mil:* lance-sergeant; senior corporal; *pl. caporaux-chefs.*
caporaliser [kapɔralize] *v.tr.* to militarize, Prussianize.
caporalisme [kapɔralism] *n.m.* (*a*) militarism; (*b*) authoritarianism.
capot[1] [kapo] *n.m.* **1.** (*a*) cover, hood, casing (of arc lamp, etc.); *Aut:* bonnet, *NAm:* hood (of car); *Av:* cowl(ing) (of aircraft engine); (*b*) *Nau:* tarpaulin. **2.** *Nau:* companion (hatch).
capot[2] *Cards:* **1.** *n.m. A:* capot. **2.** *a.inv.* **être c.,** not to take a single trick.
capotage [kapɔtaʒ] *n.m.* **1.** capsizing (of boat). **2.** *Aut: Av:* overturning.
capote [kapɔt] *n.f.* **1.** *Cost:* (*a*) *Mil:* greatcoat, overcoat; (*b*) (lady's) bonnet. **2.** *Aut:* adjustable hood, top (of convertible). **3.** *P:* **c. anglaise,** contraceptive sheath; French letter; rubber.
capoter[1] [kapɔte] *v.tr.* to put a hood on, close the hood on (vehicle).
capoter[2] *v.i.* **1.** *Nau:* to capsize, turn turtle. **2.** *Aut: Av:* to overturn.
câpre [kɑpr̥] *n.f. Bot: Cu:* caper.
caprice [kapris] *n.m.* caprice, whim, freak; **avoir, faire, des caprices,** to be capricious, fickle, moody, temperamental; **faire qch. par c.,** to do sth. on a sudden impulse; **les caprices de la mode,** the vagaries of fashion; **avoir un c. pour qn,** to take a passing fancy to s.o.
capricieusement [kaprisjøzmɑ̃] *adv.* capriciously, whimsically.
capricieux, -ieuse [kaprisjø, -jøz] *a. & n.* capricious, freakish, whimsical; temperamental (person); **temps c.,** changeable weather.
capricorne [kaprikɔrn] *n.m.* **1.** *Astr:* Capricorn, the Goat; *Geog:* **le Tropique du C.,** the Tropic of Capricorn. **2.** *Ent:* capricorn beetle.
câprier [kɑprije] *n.m. Bot:* caper bush, plant.
caprin, -ine [kaprɛ̃, -in] *a. Z:* caprine, goat-like.
capsulage [kapsylaʒ] *n.m.* capsuling, capping (of bottles, etc.).
capsule [kapsyl] *n.f.* **1.** *Anat: Bot: Pharm:* capsule. **2.** *Ch:* **c. d'évaporation,** evaporating dish. **3.** *Sm.a: Min:* (firing) cap, primer; **c. (fulminante),** cap (in toy gun). **4.** (*a*) (metallic) capsule, cap, crown cork (of bottle); (*b*) seal (of bottle). **5. c. (spatiale),** (space) capsule.
capsuler [kapsyle] *v.tr.* to seal, cap, put a capsule on (bottle).
captage [kaptaʒ] *n.m.* **1.** collecting, impounding (of waters); *El:* picking up (of current). **2.** water catchment.
captateur, -trice [kaptatœr, -tris] *n. Jur:* inveigler; **c. de succession d'héritage,** legacy hunter.
captation [kaptasjɔ̃] *n.f. Jur:* inveigling of an inheritance.
captatoire [kaptatwar] *a. Jur:* inveigling, insidious (means of obtaining an inheritance).
capter [kapte] *v.tr.* **1.** to captivate, capture (s.o.); to win (s.o.) over, gain; to rivet (s.o.'s attention). **2.** to collect, pick up (electric current, etc.); to catch, impound (waters). **3.** *W.Tel: Tp:* to intercept, pick up (messages); to tap (a line).
captieusement [kapsjøzmɑ̃] *adv.* speciously.
captieux, -ieuse [kapsjø, -jøz] *a.* fallacious, specious (argument, etc.).
captif, -ive [kaptif, -iv] *a. & n.* **1.** captive, *n.* prisoner; **être c. du plaisir,** to be a slave to pleasure. **2. ballon c.,** captive balloon.
captivant [kaptivɑ̃] *a.* captivating (person, etc.); enthralling, gripping (book, film, etc.).
captiver [kaptive] *v.tr.* to captivate, enthral, charm (s.o.); to capture (s.o.'s attention).
captivité [kaptivite] *n.f.* captivity.
capture [kaptyr] *n.f.* **1.** capture, seizure (of ship, etc.); catching (of thief, etc.). **2.** capture, prize.
capturer [kaptyre] *v.tr.* to capture, seize (ship, etc.); to catch (whale, etc.).
capuche [kapyʃ] *n.f.* hood.
capuchon [kapyʃɔ̃] *n.m.* **1.** (*a*) hood (on coat, etc.); (monk's) cowl; (*b*) hooded cloak, cape; (*c*) *Nat.Hist:* **à c.,** hooded (seal, etc.). **2.** cap (of pen, tyre valve); cap, top, lid (of tube of toothpaste, etc.); (chimney) cowl.
capucin [kapysɛ̃] *n.m.* **1.** Capuchin (friar). **2.** (*a*) *Z:* capuchin (monkey); (*b*) *Ven: F:* hare.
capucine [kapysin] *n.f.* **1.** Capuchin (nun). **2.** *Bot:* nasturtium.
caque [kak] *n.f.* herring barrel; *Prov:* **la c. sent toujours le hareng,** what's bred in the bone will come out in the flesh.
caquelon [kaklɔ̃] *n.m. Dom.Ec:* fondue dish.
caquet [kakɛ] *n.m.* **1.** cackle, cackling (of hens). **2.** (noisy) chatter, cackle, gossip, tittle-tattle; **elle lui a rabattu, rabaissé, le c.,** she shut him up.
caquetage [kaktaʒ] *n.m.* **1.** cackle, cackling (of hens). **2.** (noisy) chatter(ing), cackle, cackling, gossip(ing).
caqueter [kakte] *v.i.* (**je caquette, n. caquetons; je caquetterai**) **1.** (*of hen*) to cackle. **2.** to gossip, chatter, cackle.
caqueteur, -euse [kaktœr, -øz] *n. F:* chatterer, tattler, gossip.
car[1] [kar] *conj.* for, because; *n.m.inv.* **les si et les c.,** the whys and wherefores.
car[2] *n.m.* (*a*) bus; coach; (*b*) **c. de police,** police van; **c. de radio-reportage,** outside broadcasting van, mobile broadcasting unit.
carabe [karab] *n.m. Ent:* ground beetle.
carabin [karabɛ̃] *n.m. F:* medical student, medic.
carabine [karabin] *n.f.* (cavalry) carbine; rifle; **c. à air comprimé,** air rifle, air gun.
carabiné [karabine] *a. Nau:* **vent c.,** strong, stiff, gale; *F:* **rhume c.,** heavy cold; **fièvre carabinée,** violent, raging, fever.
carabinier [karabinje] *n.m.* **1.** *A:* carabineer. **2.** (*in Italy*) police officer; (*in Spain*) frontier guard.
Carabosse [karabɔs] *Pr.n.f.* **la fée C.,** the wicked fairy (Carabossa).
caracole [karakɔl] *n.f. Equit:* caracole, half turn.
caracoler [karakɔle] *v.i.* (*a*) *Equit:* to caracole, prance about; (*b*) to gambol, caper.
caractère [karaktɛr] *n.m.* **1.** character, letter; graphic sign; *Mth: etc:* symbol; *Typ:* (metal) type; **écrire en petits caractères,** to write in a small hand; **écrivez en caractères d'imprimerie,** write in block letters, in (block) capitals; please print; *Typ:* **en petits, gros, caractères,** in small, large, type, print. **2.** characteristic, feature; **l'affaire a pris un c. grave,** the matter has taken a serious turn; **publication de c. officiel,** publication of an official nature; *Biol:* **c. héréditaire, acquis,** hereditary, acquired, character. **3.** (*a*) character, nature, disposition; **avoir (un) mauvais c.,** to be bad-tempered, ill natured; **avoir (un) bon c.,** to be good-tempered, good-natured; (*b*) personality, character; **avoir du c.,** to have character; **manquer de c.,** to lack strength of character; to have no backbone, no spirit; to be spineless; **cette maison a beaucoup de c.,** this house has plenty of character.
caractériel, -ielle [karakterjɛl] **1.** *a.* of, pertaining

to, character; *Psy:* **trouble c.,** psychopathic disorder. **2.** *a. & n.* **(enfant) c., caractérielle,** psychoneurotic (child); problem (child).

caractérisation [karakterizasjɔ̃] *n.f.* characterization.

caractérisé [karakterize] *a.* typical, unquestionable, indisputable; **une rougeole caractérisée,** a clear, typical, unmistakable, case of measles.

caractériser [karakterize] **1.** *v.tr.* to characterize, be characteristic of, distinguish (sth.); **symptômes qui caractérisent une maladie,** characteristic symptoms of an illness. **2. se c.,** to be characterized, distinguished (**par,** by).

caractéristique [karakteristik] **1.** *a.* characteristic, distinctive, typical. **2.** *n.f.* (*a*) characteristic; feature; (*b*) *pl.* specifications (of car, aircraft, etc.).

caractérologie [karakterɔlɔʒi] *n.f.* characterology.

carafe [karaf] *n.f.* **1.** (glass) decanter, carafe. **2.** *F:* **rester en c.,** (i) to be left in the lurch; (ii) to be left out of it, out in the cold.

carafon [karafɔ̃] *n.m.* small decanter; small carafe.

caraïbe [karaib] **1.** *Ethn:* (*a*) *a.* Caribbean; (*b*) *n.* Carib. **2.** *n.m. A.Ling:* Carib. **3.** *Geog:* **la mer des Caraïbes,** the Caribbean (Sea).

carambolage [karɑ̃bɔlaʒ] *n.m.* (*a*) *Bill:* cannon, *NAm:* carom; (*b*) *F:* (multiple) pile-up (of cars).

caramboler [karɑ̃bɔle] **1.** *v.i. Bill:* to cannon, *NAm:* to carom. **2.** *v.tr. F:* **c. une voiture,** to run into a car; **dix voitures se sont carambolées sur l'autoroute,** there has been a pile-up of ten cars on the motorway.

carambouillage [karɑ̃bujaʒ] *n.m.,* **carambouille** [karɑ̃buj] *n.f. F:* fraudulent conversion.

caramel [karamɛl] *n.m. Cu:* caramel, burnt sugar; **bonbons au c., des caramels,** caramels; **c. (dur) au beurre,** butterscotch, toffee.

caramélisation [karamelizasjɔ̃] *n.f. Cu:* caramelization.

caraméliser [karamelize] **1.** *v.tr.* (*a*) to caramelize (sugar); (*b*) to mix caramel with (sth.); (*c*) to coat (mould) with caramel. **2. se c.,** (*of roast*) to brown (well); (*of sugar*) to caramelize.

carapace [karapas] *n.f.* carapace, shell (of lobster, etc.).

carapater (se) [səkarapate] *v.pr. P:* to hop it, scarper, scram.

carat [kara] *n.m.* **1.** (*a*) carat; **or à dix-huit carats,** eighteen-carat gold; *Lap:* carat (weight) (0·2 gr.).

Caravage (le) [ləkaravaʒ] *Pr.n.m.* Caravaggio.

caravane [karavan] *n.f.* **1.** (*a*) caravan, desert convoy; (*b*) conducted party, procession (of tourists, schoolchildren, etc.). **2.** *Veh:* caravan, *NAm:* (house) trailer, camper.

caravanier [karavanje] **1.** (*in desert*) (*a*) *n.m.* caravaneer; (*b*) *a.* **chemin c.,** caravan route, track. **2.** *n.m. Aut:* caravan(n)er.

caravan(n)ing [karavaniŋ] *n.m.* **faire du c.,** to go caravan(n)ing.

caravansérail [karavɑ̃seraj] *n.m.* caravanserai.

caravelle [karavɛl] *n.f.* **1.** *A.Nau:* car(a)vel. **2.** *Av: R.t.m:* Caravelle (air liner).

carbonate [karbɔnat] *n.m. Ch:* carbonate; **c. de soude,** carbonate of soda, sodium carbonate; *Com:* washing soda.

carbone [karbɔn] *n.m. Ch:* carbon; *Com:* **(papier) c.,** carbon (paper).

carbonifère [karbɔnifɛr] *a. & n.m.* carboniferous.

carbonique [karbɔnik] *a. Ch:* carbonic; **anhydride c., gaz c.,** carbon dioxide; **acide c.,** carbonic acid.

carbonisation [karbɔ̃nizasjɔ̃] *n.f.* carbonization.

carboniser [karbɔnize] *v.tr.* to carbonize (bones, etc.); to char (wood); to burn (meat, etc.) to a cinder; **être carbonisé,** to be burnt to death.

carbon(n)ade [karbɔnad] *n.f. Cu:* **bifteck à la c.,** charcoal-grilled steak.

carbonyle [karbɔnil] *n.m.* carbonyl.

carborundum [karbɔrɔ̃dɔm] *n.m.* carborundum.

carburant [karbyrɑ̃] **1.** *n.m.* (motor) fuel. **2.** *a.* containing hydrocarbon; *I.C.E:* **mélange c.,** mixture (of petrol and air).

carburateur [karbyratœr] *n.m. I.C.E:* carburettor, *NAm:* carburetor.

carburation [karbyrasjɔ̃] *n.f.* **1.** *Metall:* carburization. **2.** *I.C.E:* carburation.

carbure [karbyr] *n.m. Ch:* carbide.

carburé [karbyre] *a.* **1.** *Metall:* carburized. **2.** *I.C.E:* carburetted (air).

carburer [karbyre] **1.** *v.tr. Metall:* to carburize. **2.** *v.i.* (*a*) *I.C.E:* to vaporize (fuel); **le moteur carbure mal,** the mixture is wrong; (*b*) *F:* to work, to go well; **ça carbure,** it's going fine, like a bomb.

carcajou [karkaʒu] *n.m. Z:* carcajou, wolverine.

carcan [karkɑ̃] *n.m.* (*a*) *Hist:* iron collar; (*b*) yoke, restraint.

carcasse [karkas] *n.f.* **1.** carcass, carcase; *F:* body (of living person). **2.** frame(work) (of umbrella, etc.); shell, skeleton (of house, ship, etc.); carcass (of ship, electric motor); shape (of hat, etc.); casing (of tyre).

carcéral, -aux [karseral, -o] *a.* prison (life).

carcinome [karsinɔm] *n.m. Med:* carcinoma.

cardage [kardaʒ] *n.m. Tex:* **1.** carding, combing (of wool, etc.). **2.** teaseling (of cloth).

Cardan [kardɑ̃] *Pr.n.m. & n.m. Mec.E:* **c., joint de C.,** universal joint, Cardan joint.

carde [kard] *n.f.* **1.** *Cu:* chard. **2.** *Tex:* card, carding brush; teasel (frame).

carder [karde] *v.tr. Tex:* **1.** to card (wool, etc.). **2.** to teasel (cloth).

cardeur, -euse [kardœr, -øz] *n. Tex:* **1.** carder, teaseler. **2.** *n.f.* **cardeuse,** carding machine, carder.

cardiaque [kardjak] **1.** *a.* cardiac (nerves, murmur, etc.); **crise c.,** heart attack; **être c.,** to have heart trouble, a weak heart. **2.** *n.* cardiac; heart case.

cardigan [kardigɑ̃] *n.m. Cost:* cardigan.

cardinal, -aux [kardinal, -o] **1.** *a.* cardinal (point, number, virtue); chief (altar, etc.). **2.** *n.m. R.C.Ch:* cardinal. **3.** *n.m. Orn:* cardinal (bird).

cardinalat [kardinala] *n.m.* cardinalate, cardinalship.

cardinalice [kardinalis] *a. Ecc:* of a cardinal; **revêtir la pourpre c.,** to don the scarlet; **élever qn à la dignité c.,** to make s.o. a cardinal.

cardiogramme [kardjɔgram] *n.m. Med:* cardiogram.

cardiographe [kardjɔgraf] *n.m. Med:* cardiograph.

cardiographie [kardjɔgrafi] *n.f. Med:* cardiography.

cardiologie [kardjɔlɔʒi] *n.f.* cardiology.

cardiologue [kardjɔlɔg] *n.* cardiologist.

cardio-vasculaire [kardjɔvaskylɛr] *a. Anat: Med:* cardiovascular.

cardite [kardit] *n.f. Med.* carditis.

cardon [kardɔ̃] *n.m. Bot:* cardoon.

carême [karɛm] *n.m.* **1.** Lent. **2.** (Lenten) fast(ing); **faire (son) c.,** to keep Lent, to fast; **face de c.,** dismal face. **3.** (course of) Lenten sermons.

carême-prenant [karɛmprənɑ̃] *n.m. A:* Shrovetide; *pl. carêmes-prenants.*

carénage [karenaʒ] *n.m.* **1.** *Nau:* (*a*) careening, careenage (of ship); (*b*) careening beach; careenage. **2.** *Av: Aut:* streamlining; fairing (of the lines).

carence [karɑ̃s] *n.f.* **1.** *Jur:* insolvency. **2.** default(-ing), reneging; shirking of one's obligations; inefficiency. **3.** *Med:* deficiency (**de,** in, of); **maladie de, par, c.,** deficiency disease.

carène [karɛn] *n.f.* **1.** *N.Arch:* bottom, (underwater)

hull (of ship); **abattre un navire en c.,** to careen a ship. **2.** *Bot:* carina, keel.
caréner [karene] *v.tr.* (**je carène; je carénerai**) **1.** *Nau:* to careen (ship). **2.** *Av: Aut:* to streamline.
caressant [karɛsɑ̃] *a.* affectionate (child, etc.); tender (look, etc.); soft, gentle (wind).
caresse [karɛs] *n.f.* (*a*) caress; **faire des caresses à,** to caress (s.o.); to pat, stroke, make a fuss (of dog); (*b*) *O:* flattery.
caresser [karese] *v.tr.* **1.** (*a*) to caress, fondle, stroke; to pat, make a fuss of (animal); **c. qn du regard,** to look affectionately at s.o.; (*b*) *O:* to flatter (s.o.). **2.** to cherish (hope, etc.); to toy with (idea).
cargaison [kargɛzɔ̃] *n.f.* (*a*) cargo, freight; (*b*) *F:* load (of passengers, etc.).
cargo [kargo] *n.m. Nau:* cargo boat, freighter; tramp (steamer); **c. mixte,** cargo and passenger vessel.
cargue [karg] *n.f. Nau:* brail (of sail).
carguer [karge] *v.tr. Nau:* to take in, clew (up), brail (up) (sail).
cariatide [karjatid] *n.f. Arch:* caryatid.
caribou [karibu] *n.m. Z:* caribou.
caricatural, -aux [karikatyral, -o] *a.* caricatural.
caricature [karikatyr] *n.f.* (*a*) caricature; cartoon; (*b*) *F:* **quelle c. que cette femme!** what a fright that woman is!
caricaturer [karikatyre] *v.tr.* to caricature (s.o.).
caricaturiste [karikatyrist] *n.* caricaturist; cartoonist.
carie [kari] *n.f.* (*a*) *Med:* caries, decay (of bone); **c. dentaire,** dental caries, tooth decay; (*b*) blight (of trees); smut, bunt (of cereals).
carié [karje] *a.* decayed, carious, bad (tooth).
carier (se) [səkarje] *v.tr. & pr.* to rot, decay.
carillon [karijɔ̃] *n.m.* (*a*) chime(s), carillon; **(horloge à) c.,** chiming clock; (*b*) peal of bells; (*c*) (door) chime(s); (*d*) *Mus:* tubular bells, chimes.
carillonnement [karijɔnmɑ̃] *n.m.* (*a*) chiming, ringing (of bells); (*b*) jingling (of doorbell).
carillonner [karijɔne] **1.** *v.i.* (*a*) to chime the bells; to ring a peal; (*b*) (*of bells*) to chime; (*c*) **c. à la porte,** to ring the (door) bell loudly. **2.** *v.tr.* to chime (air); to announce (church festival) with a full peal; **fête carillonnée,** high festival.
carillonneur [karijɔnœr] *n.m.* bellringer.
carlin [karlɛ̃] *n.m.* pugdog.
carlingue [karlɛ̃g] *n.f.* **1.** *Nau:* ke(e)lson. **2.** *Av:* cabin.
carliste [karlist] *n.m. & f. Hist:* Carlist.
carmagnole [karmaɲɔl] *n.f. Hist:* (*a*) jacket (worn by Revolutionaries in 1793); (*b*) *Mus: Danc:* carmagnole.
carme [karm] *n.m. Ecc:* Carmelite (friar), White friar.
Carmel [karmɛl] *Pr.n.m.* (*a*) *Ecc:* **le C.,** the Carmelite order; (*b*) Carmelite monastery, convent.
carmélite [karmelit] *n.f. Ecc:* Carmelite (nun).
carmin [karmɛ̃] *a.inv. & n.m.* carmine.
carminé [karmine] *a.* carmine-coloured, ruby.
carnage [karnaʒ] *n.m.* carnage, slaughter.
carnassier, -ière [karnasje, -jɛr] **1.** *a.* carnivorous, flesh-eating (animal); *Z:* carnassial (tooth). **2.** *n.m.* carnivore; *pl.* **les carnassiers,** the Carnivora. **3.** *n.f.* **carnassière,** (*a*) *Z:* carnassial (tooth); (*b*) game bag.
carnation [karnasjɔ̃] *n.f.* (*a*) *Art:* flesh tint, carnation; (*b*) **c. de blonde,** fair skin, complexion.
carnaval, -als [karnaval] *n.m.* **1.** carnival. **2. Sa Majesté C.,** King Carnival; *F:* **c'est un vrai c.,** he looks a real clown.
carnavalesque [karnavalɛsk] *a.* carnivalesque.
carne [karn] *n.f.* **1.** *F:* (*a*) tough meat; (*b*) old horse; screw. **2.** *P:* **quelle c.!** what a pig, brute! (*of woman*) what a bitch, slut!
carné [karne] *a.* **1.** flesh-coloured. **2. régime c.,** meat diet.
carneau, -eaux [karno] *n.m.* (boiler) flue.
carnet [karnɛ] *n.m.* **1.** (*a*) notebook; memo book; **c. d'adresses,** address book; *Com:* **c. de commandes,** order book; *Sch:* **c. (de notes)** = (school) report; (*b*) *O:* **c. de bal,** dance card; (*c*) **c. à souche(s),** counterfoil book; **c. de chèques,** cheque book; **c. de timbres,** book of stamps; **c. (de tickets d'autobus, etc.),** book of tickets; (*d*) *Aut: etc:* **c. de route, de bord,** logbook.
carnier [karnje] *n.m.* game bag.
carnivore [karnivɔr] *Z:* **1.** *a.* carnivorous, flesh-eating (animal). **2.** *n.m.* carnivore, *pl.* Carnivora.
carolingien, -ienne [karɔlɛ̃ʒjɛ̃, -jɛn] *a. & n. Hist:* Carolingian, Carlovingian.
Caron [karɔ̃] *Pr.n.m. Myth:* Charon.
caroncule [karɔ̃kyl] *n.f. Anat: Bot: Z:* caruncle; *usu. pl.* wattles (of turkey).
carotide [karɔtid] *a. & n.f. Anat:* carotid (artery).
carottage [karɔtaʒ] *n.m. F:* (*a*) stealing, pinching; (*b*) swindling, diddling.
carotte [karɔt] *n.f.* **1.** *Bot: Hort:* carrot; *F:* **Poil de c.,** Ginger; *a.inv.* **cheveux (rouge) c.,** carroty, ginger, red hair; *F:* **ses carottes sont cuites,** he's cooked his goose, he's done for. **2.** (*a*) plug (of tobacco); *F:* tobacconist's sign; (*b*) *Min:* core (sample). **3.** *F:* (*a*) **tirer une c. à qn,** to swindle, diddle, s.o.; (*b*) *Ten:* drop shot.
carotter [karɔte] *v.tr. F:* (*a*) to steal, pinch; (*b*) to do (s.o.); to swindle, diddle (s.o.); (*c*) *Mil:* **c. une permission,** to wangle leave.
carotteur, -euse [karɔtœr, -øz] *n.*, **carottier, -ière** [karɔtje, -jɛr] *n. F:* thief; swindler; diddler; trickster.
caroube [karub] *n.f. Bot:* carob (bean).
caroubier [karubje] *n.m. Bot:* carob tree.
Carpates [karpat] *Pr.n.f.pl. Geog:* **les C.,** Carpathian Mountains, Carpathians.
carpe[1] [karp] *n.m. Anat:* carpus, wrist.
carpe[2] *n.f. Ich:* carp; *Swim:* **saut de c.,** jack-knife (dive); **faire des sauts de carpe,** to bounce around; **faire des yeux de c.,** make sheep's eyes; **bâiller comme une c.,** to yawn one's head off.
carpeau, -eaux [karpo] *n.m. Ich:* young carp.
carpette [karpɛt] *n.f.* rug; *F:* **s'aplatir comme une c.,** to behave like a doormat.
carpien, -ienne [karpjɛ̃, -jɛn] *a. Anat:* carpal (bone, etc.).
carquois [karkwa] *n.m.* quiver; *Lit:* **il a vidé son c.,** he has shot his bolt.
Carrare [karar] **1.** *Pr.n. Geog:* Carrara. **2.** *n.m.* Carrara marble.
carre [kɑr] *n.f.* (*a*) cross section (of board, etc.); (*b*) corner (of book, etc.); (*c*) edge (of skate, ski); **lâcher les carres,** to flatten, take the edge off, the skis.
carré, -ée [kare] **1.** *a.* (*a*) square (figure, garden, etc.); square, broad (shoulders); *Mth:* **nombre c.,** square number; **dix mètres carrés,** ten-square metres; **partie carrée,** foursome, date; *F:* **tête carrée,** (i) level-headed, (ii) stubborn, man; (*b*) plain, straightforward, blunt (answer, person); outspoken (person); **être c. en affaires,** to be honest in business. **2.** *n.m.* (*a*) *Mth:* square (of a number); **élever au c.,** to square; **le c. de 6, six au c.,** 6 squared; (*b*) **c. de papier,** slip of paper; **c. de soie,** silk square; **c. (d'un escalier),** landing; **c. de choux,** cabbage patch; *Nau:* **c. (des officiers),** wardroom; (*c*) *Cu:* loin (of lamb, etc.); (*d*) *Cards:* **c. de valets,** four jacks; (*e*) *Fr.C:* (public) square. **3.** *n.f.* **carrée** (*a*) *Mus: A:* breve; (*b*) *F:* room, digs.
carreau, -eaux [karo] *n.m.* **1.** small square; **tissu à carreaux,** check(ed) material; *Art:* **mettre un croquis**

au c., to square up a sketch. **2.** (*a*) (floor, wall) tile; flag(stone); (*b*) (window) pane; **regarder aux carreaux,** to look out of, in at, the window; (*c*) *F:* monocle; *pl.* glasses, specs. **3.** (*a*) floor (of room); **coucher qn sur le c.,** to lay s.o. out; **rester sur le c.,** (i) to be killed on the spot; (ii) to be out of the running; (*b*) (*in Paris*) **le c. des Halles,** the (floor of the) market; (*c*) *Min:* **c. de mine,** pit head. **4.** *Cards:* diamond; **se garder, se tenir, à c.,** to take every precaution; to keep one's weather eye open. **5.** *Lacem:* pillow. **6.** (tailor's) goose. **7.** *A:* bolt, quarrel.

carrefour [karfur] *n.m.* (*a*) crossroads; (*in town*) square, circus; **tête de c.,** T-junction; *Fig:* **être au c.,** to be at the parting of the ways; (*b*) symposium.

carrelage [karlaʒ] *n.m.* **1.** tiling. **2.** tiling, tiles; tile(d) floor, wall; flagstone pavement, floor(ing).

carreler [karle] *v.tr.* (**je carrelle, n. carrelons; je carrellerai**) **1.** to tile (floor, walls); to lay (floor) with flags; to pave (yard). **2.** to draw squares on, to square (sheet of paper, etc.).

carrelet [karlɛ] *n.m.* **1.** square ruler. **2.** large needle; *Bootm:* sewing awl. **3.** *Fish:* square dipping net. **4.** *Ich:* plaice.

carreleur [karlœr] *n.m.* tile layer, tiler; paver.

carrément [karemɑ̃] *adv.* (*a*) square(ly); **pièce coupée c.,** square-cut piece; (*b*) **il y est allé c.,** he made no bones about it; he didn't beat about the bush; **je lui ai dit c. ce que je pensais,** I told him straight, in no uncertain terms, what I thought.

carrer [kare] **1.** *v.tr.* to square (plank, number, etc.). **2. se c.,** to settle (down) (**dans un fauteuil,** in an armchair).

carrier [karje] *n.m.* **1.** quarryman, quarrier. **2.** **(maître) c.,** quarry-owner.

carrière[1] [karjɛr] *n.f.* **1.** (*a*) *A:* racecourse, arena; (*b*) course (of life); **être au bout de sa c.,** to be at the end of one's life; **la c. du succès,** the road to success. **2. donner c. à un cheval,** to give free rein to a horse; **donner (libre) c. à son imagination,** to give free rein, free play, full scope, to one's imagination; **donner c. à ses sentiments, à ses opinions, se donner c.,** to let oneself go. **3.** career; **c. politique, des armes,** political, military, career; **militaire de c.,** regular (soldier); **diplomate de c.,** professional, career, diplomat; **il est de la c.,** he is in the diplomatic service.

carrière[2] *n.f.* (stone) quarry.

carriériste [karjerist] *n.* careerist.

carriole [karjɔl] *n.f.* *Veh:* **1.** light cart, carriole. **2.** *Fr.C:* (horsedrawn) sled, sleigh; *NAm:* car(r)iole, carryall.

carrossable [karɔsabl̩] *a.* **route c.,** road suitable for motor vehicles.

carrosse [karɔs] *n.m.* (*a*) (horse-drawn) coach; **c. d'apparat,** state coach; *F:* **rouler c.,** to live in great style; (*b*) *Fr.C:* **c. de bébé,** pram, *NAm:* baby carriage.

carrosser [karɔse] *v.tr.* *Aut:* to fit the body to (chassis); *P:* **elle est bien carrossée,** she comes out in the right places.

carrosserie [karɔsri] *n.f.* *Aut:* **1.** coachbuilding. **2.** body, coachwork (of car, etc.).

carrossier [karɔsje] *n.m.* *Aut:* coachbuilder.

carrousel [karuzɛl] *n.m.* **1.** *Hist:* (*a*) tournament; (*b*) tiltyard. **2.** *Equit:* carousel. **3.** *Fig:* merry-go-round, roundabout (of cars, aircraft, etc.).

carrure [karyr] *n.f.* **1.** breadth (of pers., of coat) across the shoulders; **homme d'une belle c.,** well-built, burly, man. **2.** broadness, squareness (of jaw, etc.).

carry [kari] *n.m.* = CURRY.

cartable [kartabl̩] *n.m.* (school) satchel.

carte [kart] *n.f.* **1.** map; chart; **c. d'état-major** = Ordnance Survey map; **c. météorologique,** meteorological, weather, map, chart; **c. routière,** road map; **c. du ciel,** astronomical map, chart; **dresser la c. d'une région,** to map (out) an area. **2.** (piece of) card(board); (*a*) **c. (à jouer),** (playing) card; **jouer aux cartes,** to play cards; **donner, faire, les cartes,** to deal (the cards); **jouer cartes sur table,** to put one's cards on the table; to show one's hand; **c'était la c. forcée,** it was Hobson's choice; **voir le dessous des cartes,** to be in the know; **brouiller les cartes,** to complicate matters, to confuse the issue; (*b*) **c. (de visite),** (visiting, *NAm:* calling) card; (*c*) **c. (postale),** (post)card; **c. de correspondance,** (plain) postcard; **c. de vœux,** greetings card; **c. d'anniversaire,** birthday, anniversary, card; (*d*) **c. d'entrée,** admission card; **c. d'abonnement,** season ticket; **c. de circulation,** (rail, bus, etc.) pass; **c. d'identité,** identity card; **c. de lecteur,** library, reader's, ticket; *Aut:* **c. grise** = (vehicle) registration document; *Adm:* **c. de commerce,** trading licence; *War Adm:* **c. d'alimentation,** ration book; **femme en c.,** registered prostitute; (*e*) **donner carte blanche à qn,** to give s.o. carte blanche, a free hand; (*f*) *Cmptr: etc:* **c. perforée, mécanographique,** punch card; (*g*) **c. (de restaurant),** menu; **carte du jour,** menu for the day; **c. des vins,** wine list; **manger à la c.,** to eat à la carte; (*h*) *Com:* card (of buttons, etc.); **c. d'échantillons,** sample card.

cartel[1] [kartɛl] *n.m.* **1.** *A:* cartel, challenge. **2.** (*a*) dial case (of clock); (*b*) (hanging) wall clock.

cartel[2] *n.m.* **1.** cartel, trust; combine. **2.** *Pol:* coalition, cartel.

carte-lettre [kart(ə)lɛtr̥] *n.f.* lettercard; *pl. cartes-lettres.*

cartellisation [kartɛlizasjɔ̃] *n.f.* cartellization.

carter [kartɛr] *n.m.* *Mch:* case, casing, housing (of gear, etc.); cover (of small machines, etc.); *Aut:* crankcase; **fond de c.,** sump.

cartésianisme [kartezjanism] *n.m.* *Phil:* Cartesianism.

cartésien, -ienne [kartezjɛ̃, -jɛn] *a. & n.* *Phil: Mth:* Cartesian.

carthaginois, -oise [kartaʒinwa, -waz] *a. & n.* *Hist: Geog:* Carthaginian.

cartilage [kartilaʒ] *n.m.* *Anat:* cartilage; (*in meat*) gristle.

cartilagineux, -euse [kartilaʒinø, -øz] *a.* *Anat:* cartilaginous; *Cu:* gristly.

cartographe [kartɔgraf] *n.* cartographer.

cartographie [kartɔgrafi] *n.f.* cartography.

cartographique [kartɔgrafik] *a.* cartographic(al).

cartomancie [kartɔmɑ̃si] *n.f.* cartomancy, fortune telling (by cards).

cartomancien, -ienne [kartɔmɑ̃sjɛ̃, -jɛn] *n.* fortune teller (by cards).

carton [kartɔ̃] *n.m.* **1.** cardboard; pasteboard; **c. ondulé,** corrugated paper, cardboard; **c. gris,** chipboard; **c. épais,** millboard; **poupée de c.,** papier mâche doll; *F:* **maison de c.,** jerry-built house. **2.** (*a*) (cardboard) box; carton; **c. à chapeau(x),** hatbox; **c. à dessins,** portfolio; (*b*) (cardboard) file. **3.** (*a*) *Art:* cartoon, sketch (for canvas, tapestry); (*b*) *Geog:* inset (map). **4.** (*at shooting range*) **faire un c.,** to fill a target; **faire un bon c.,** to make a good score.

cartonnage [kartɔnaʒ] *n.m.* **1.** (*a*) making of cardboard articles; cardboard trade; (*b*) *coll.* (cardboard) boxes, cases, packing. **2.** *Bookb:* (binding in) paper boards; boarding, casing; **c. pleine toile,** (binding in) cloth boards; **c. souple,** limp boards.

cartonner [kartɔne] *v.tr.* to bind (book) in boards, to case (book); **livre cartonné,** hardback (book).

cartonnerie [kartɔnri] *n.f.* **1.** cardboard factory. **2.** cardboard trade.

cartonnier, -ière [kartɔnje, -jɛr] *n.* **1.** cardboard manufacturer, seller. **2.** *n.m.* filing cabinet.

carton-paille [kartɔ̃pɑj] *n.m.* strawboard; *pl. cartons-pailles.*
carton-pâte [kartɔ̃pɑt] *n.m.* papier mâché; pasteboard; *pl. cartons-pâtes.*
cartouche [kartuʃ] **1.** *n.m. Arch: etc:* cartouche, scroll (round title, etc.). **2.** *n.f.* (*a*) cartridge; **cent cartouches,** a hundred rounds (of ammunition); **c. à balle, à blanc,** ball cartridge, blank cartridge; **c. de chasse,** sporting cartridge; (*b*) *Phot: Elcs: etc:* cartridge; **c. de stylo,** refill cartridge; (*c*) *Com:* carton (of cigarettes).
cartoucherie [kartuʃri] *n.f.* cartridge factory, store.
cartouchière [kartuʃjɛr] *n.f.* (*a*) cartridge pouch; (*b*) cartridge belt.
carvi [karvi] *n.m. Bot:* **(graines de) c.,** caraway (seeds).
caryatide [karjatid] *n.f. Arch:* caryatid.
cas [kɑ] *n.m.* **1.** (*a*) case, instance, circumstance; **c. limite,** borderline case; **c. imprévu,** unforeseen event; emergency; *Ins:* act of God; **dans le premier c.,** in the first instance; **c'est bien le c. de le dire,** there's no mistake about it; *F:* you can say that again; **c'est le c. ou jamais de . . .,** now if ever, now or never, is the time . . .; it's (a case of) now or never; (*b*) (legal) case, cause; **c. d'espèce,** concrete case, case in point; **c'est un c. d'espèce,** it depends upon the particular circumstances; **c. de divorce,** grounds for divorce; (*c*) (medical) case; **c. de rougeole,** case of measles. **2.** case, matter, affair, business; **ce n'est pas le c.,** this is not the case; **c. de conscience,** matter of conscience. **3. faire (grand) c. de qn, de qch.,** to value s.o., sth., (highly); to have a high opinion of s.o.; to set great store by sth.; **faire peu de c. de qch.,** to have a poor opinion of sth.; **je ne fais pas grand c. de votre ami,** I don't think much of your friend; **ne faire aucun c. de qch.,** to leave sth. out of account; to take no notice of sth. **4.** *Gram:* case; **au c. nominatif,** in the nominative case. **5. en, dans, ce c.,** in that case, if that is the case, if so, under those circumstances; **en aucun c.,** under no circumstances, on no account, not on any account; **en tout c., dans tous les c.,** in any case, in all events; **dans tous les c. il est trop tard,** its too late now, anyway, anyhow; **le c. échéant,** should the occasion arise; **selon le c.,** as the case may be; **en c. de nécessité,** if need be, if necessary; **au c. où, dans le c. où, il viendrait,** if he comes; **au c. où il serait exact,** should it prove correct.
casanier, -ière [kazanje, -jɛr] *a. & n.* stay-at-home; *n.* homebird, *U.S:* homebody.
casaque [kazak] *n.f.* **1.** (*a*) *A. Cost:* (musketeer's) surtout; (*b*) **tourner c.,** (i) to flee, turn tail; (ii) to desert one's party, change sides, *F:* to rat. **2.** (*a*) blouse, jacket (of jockey); (*b*) *O:* (woman's) overblouse.
casbah [kazba] *n.f.* casbah, kasbah.
cascade [kaskad] *n.f.* cascade, waterfall, falls; **c. d'un glacier,** ice fall; **cascades de rires,** peals of laughter; *El:* **montage en c.,** connection in series.
cascader [kaskade] *v.i.* **1.** *Lit:* to cascade. **2.** *F: O:* to live a wild life.
cascadeur, -euse [kaskadœr, -øz] **1.** *a. F: O:* wild, loose, fast (life, etc.). **2.** *n.* (*a*) *F: O:* reveller; (*b*) *Cin:* stuntman, stuntgirl; (*c*) trapeze artist, acrobat.
case [kɑz] *n.f.* **1.** (native) hut, cabin. **2.** (*a*) compartment, division (of drawer, etc.); locker; pigeonhole; **c. postale,** Post Office, P.O., box; (*b*) division, space (on printed form); (*c*) square (of chessboard); *F:* **il lui manque une c., il a une c. vide, une c. en moins,** he's got a screw loose.
caséeux, -euse [kazeø, -øz] *a.* caseous, cheesy.
caséine [kazein] *n.f. Ch:* casein.
casemate [kazmat] *n.f. Fort:* casemate.
caser [kɑze] **1.** *v.tr.* to put, stow, (sth.) away; **c. des papiers,** to file, pigeonhole, papers; *F:* **c. qn,** to find a job, for s.o.; **il est bien casé,** he's got a good home, a good job; **elle a trois filles à c.,** she has three daughters to marry. **2. se c.,** to (get married and) settle down; to find a job, somewhere to live.
caserne [kazɛrn] *n.f.* (*a*) *Mil:* barracks; *Pej: F:* barrack of a place; **quand j'étais à la c.,** when I was in the army; **plaisanteries de c.,** coarse jokes, barrack-room jokes; (*b*) **c. de pompiers,** fire station.
casernement [kazɛrnəmɑ̃] *n.m.* **1.** barracking, quartering (of troops). **2.** barrack block.
caserner [kazɛrne] *v.tr.* to quarter (troops) in barracks, to barrack (troops).
casernier, -ière [kazɛrnje, -jɛr] *n.m.* barrack warden.
cash [kaʃ] *adv. F:* **payer c.,** to pay cash (down).
casier [kɑzje] *n.m.* **1.** (*a*) (set of) pigeonholes; (*b*) pigeonhole, locker; (*c*) **c. judiciaire,** police record; **son c. judiciaire est vierge,** he has a clean record. **2.** (*a*) (wine)bin, rack; **c. à bouteilles,** bottle, wine, rack; **c. d'une malle,** tray of a trunk; (*b*) **c. à musique,** music cabinet; (*c*) *Fish:* **c. (à homards),** lobsterpot.
casino [kazino] *n.m.* casino.
casoar [kazɔar] *n.m.* **1.** *Orn:* cassowary. **2.** plume (worn by cadets of Saint-Cyr).
caspien, -ienne [kaspjɛ̃, -jɛn] *a. Geog:* **la (mer) Caspienne,** the Caspian (Sea).
casque [kask] *n.m.* **1.** (*a*) helmet (of soldier, fireman, etc.); crash helmet (of motorcyclist); **c. colonial,** tropical helmet, sun helmet; topee; **Casques bleus,** United Nations troops; (*b*) *W.Tel: Tp:* **c. (téléphonique),** headphones, headset. **2.** *Nat.Hist:* galea, hood, casque; *Bot:* helmet. **3.** *Hairdr:* (hair) drier.
casqué [kaske] *a.* helmeted; **c. d'un bonnet de coton,** wearing a cotton nightcap.
casquer [kaske] *v.i. P:* to pay (up), fork out, shell out; to foot the bill.
casquette [kaskɛt] *n.f.* (peaked) cap (of schoolboy, jockey, etc.); *Mil: etc:* (officer's) hat.
cassable [kasabl̥] *a.* breakable.
cassage [kasaʒ] *n.m.* breaking.
Cassandre [kasɑ̃dr̥] **1.** *Pr.n.f. Gr.Lit:* Cassandra. **2.** *n.m. & f.* defeatist, Cassandra.
cassant [kasɑ̃] *a.* **1.** (*a*) brittle (china, etc.); (*b*) crisp, crunchy (fruit, etc.); (*c*) *Metall:* short (steel, etc.). **2.** curt, abrupt, imperious (tone of voice); **être c. avec qn,** to be short with s.o. **3.** *P:* **c'est pas trop c.,** it won't (exactly) break your back.
cassate [kasat] *n.f. Comest:* cassata.
cassation [kasasjɔ̃] *n.f.* **1.** *Jur:* cassation, annulment, quashing, setting aside (of sentence, will, etc.); **Cour de c.,** supreme court of appeal. **2.** *Mil:* reduction (of N.C.O. to the ranks).
casse[1] [cas] *n.f. Typ:* case; **bas, haut, de c.,** lower case, upper case.
casse[2] *n.f. Bot:* cassia.
casse[3] *n.f.* **1.** (*a*) breaking; breakage, damage; **il y aura de la c.,** (i) something will get broken; (ii) *F:* there'll be trouble, a row; (*b*) things broken, breakages; **payer la c.,** to pay for the breakages, the damage; (*c*) *Com:* **vendre à la c.,** to sell for scrap; **envoyer une voiture à la c.,** to send a car to the scrapyard.
casse[4] *n.m. P:* burglary, break-in.
cassé [kase] *a.* broken; worn out, broken down (person, etc.); cracked (voice).
casse-cou [kasku] *n.m.inv.* **1.** deathtrap; **crier c.-c. à qn,** to warn s.o. (of a danger). **2.** daredevil, reckless individual.
casse-croûte [kaskrut] *n.m.inv.* **1.** snack (meal). **2.** snack bar.
casse-gueule [kasgœl] **1.** *P: n.m.inv.* dangerous

spot, deathtrap. **2.** *a. & n.* dangerous, tricky, daredevil, reckless (undertaking).

cassement [kasmɑ̃] *n.m.* **1. c. de tête,** (i) worry, anxiety; (ii) splitting headache. **2.** *P:* burglary, break-in.

casse-noisette(s) [kasnwazɛt] *n.m.inv.* (pair of) nutcrackers; *NAm:* nutcracker; **menton en c.-n.,** nutcracker chin.

casse-noix [kasnwɑ] *n.m.inv.* **1.** (pair of) nutcrackers; *NAm:* nutcracker. **2.** *Orn:* nutcracker.

casse-pieds [kaspje] *a. & n.m.inv. F:* **ce qu'il est c.-p., quel c.-p.,** what a bore, pain in the neck.

casse-pierre(s) [kaspjɛr] *n.m.inv.* **1.** (*a*) stonebreaker's hammer; (*b*) *Civ.E:* (*machine*) stonebreaker, stone crusher. **2.** *Bot:* pellitory.

casse-pipes [kaspip] *n.m.inv.* (*a*) shooting gallery; (*b*) *P:* war; front (line).

casser [kase] **1.** *v.tr.* (*a*) to break (plate, etc.); to snap (twigs); to crack (nuts, etc.); to crack, ruin (voice); to crush (stones); **c. du bois,** (i) to chop wood; (ii) *Av:* to crash on landing; *F:* **c. la tête, les oreilles, à qn,** to deafen s.o.; *F:* **c. les pieds (à qn),** to be a bore, a pain in the neck (to s.o.); *F:* **c. le cou, la figure,** *P:* **la gueule, à qn,** to smash, kick, s.o.'s face in; *F:* **c. sa pipe,** to die, kick the bucket; *P:* **c. le morceau,** (i) to confess, come clean; (ii) to denounce, grass on, s.o.; *F:* **ça ne casse rien, ça ne casse pas trois pattes à un canard,** it's not up to much, it's nothing to write home about, there's nothing extraordinary about that, it's no great shakes; **un spectacle à tout c.,** a marvellous, fantastic, super, show; **se faire applaudir à tout c.,** to bring the house down; **cela vaut 1,000 francs à tout c.,** it's worth 1,000 francs at the very most, at the outside; (*b*) to cashier, break (officer); to reduce an N.C.O. (to the ranks); to demote , dismiss (employee); (*c*) *Jur:* to annul, quash, set aside (verdict, etc.). **2.** *v.i.* to break, snap, give way; **l'assiette a cassé en tombant,** the plate fell and broke; **cela casse comme du verre,** it breaks like glass. **3. se c.,** to break, snap, give way; **elle s'est cassé la jambe,** she's broken her leg; *F:* **se c. la figure,** (i) to fall flat on one's face, come a cropper; (ii) to kill oneself; (iii) to fail, come a cropper; **se c. la tête,** to rack one's brains; *P: Iron:* **ne te casse pas la tête!** don't strain yourself! don't overdo it! **se c. le nez à la porte de qn,** to find nobody in, at home; **il s'est cassé le nez,** he's failed, come a cropper.

casserole [kasrɔl] *n.f.* **1.** (*a*) (sauce)pan; **veau à la, en c.,** braised veal; (*b*) *P:* **passer à la c.,** (i) to get bumped off; (ii) to go through a tough time; (iii) to be raped. **2.** *P:* (*a*) tinny piano; (*b*) (film) projector.

casse-tête [kastɛt] *n.m.inv.* **1.** (*a*) (war) club (*b*) truncheon, baton. **2.** puzzle, *F:* headache; **c.-t. chinois,** Chinese puzzle. **3.** din, racket.

cassette [kasɛt] *n.f.* (*a*) casket case; (*b*) moneybox; *A:* **c. du roi,** King's privy purse; (*c*) *Rec:* cassette.

casseur, -euse [kasœr, -øz] **1.** *n.* (*a*) breaker; person who damages things; **c. de pierres,** stonebreaker; (*b*) *F:* **c'est une grande casseuse,** she's always breaking things; (*c*) **c. (d'assiettes),** rowdy, aggressive, person, troublemaker; (*d*) scrap (metal) merchant; **dépôt de c.,** breaker's yard; **c. de voitures,** (car) breaker; (*e*) *P:* burglar. **2.** *a.* aggressive (look, etc.).

Cassin [kasɛ̃] *Pr.n.m. Geog:* **le mont C.,** Monte Cassino.

cassine [kasin], *n.f.* (*a*) *A:* (country) cottage; (*b*) *F:* hovel, shack.

cassis[1] [kasis] *n.m.* **1.** blackcurrant. **2.** blackcurrant bush. **3.** blackcurrant liqueur.

cassis[2] [kɑsi] *n.m. Civ.E:* cross-drain, open gutter (across road).

cassis[3] [kasis] *n.m. P:* head, nut, block.

cassolette [kasɔlɛt] *n.f.* (*a*) incense burner; (*b*) *Cu:* ramekin.

cassonade [kasɔnad] *n.f.* brown sugar.

cassoulet [kasulɛ] *n.m. Cu:* (*a*) earthenware dish; (*b*) cassoulet; stew of beans, pork, goose, etc. (made in Languedoc).

cassure [kasyr] *n.f.* (*a*) break, fracture, crack; (*b*) *Geol:* fault; (*c*) fold mark (in linen), crease.

castagnette [kastaɲɛt] *n.f.* castanet.

caste [kast] *n.f.* caste; **esprit de c.,** class consciousness; **être hors c.,** to be an outcaste.

castel [kastɛl] *n.m.* manor house.

castillan, -ane [kastijɑ̃, -an] **1.** *a. &. n. Geog:* Castilian. **2.** *n.m. Ling:* Castilian.

Castille [kastij] *Pr.n.f. Geog:* Castile.

castor [kastɔr] *n.m.* **1.** (*a*) *Z:* beaver; (*b*) *Com:* beaver fur; (*c*) **c. du Chili,** *Z:* coypu; *Com:* nutria; (*d*) **c. du Canada,** musquash (fur). **2. mouvement des castors,** group of people building their own houses.

castrat [kastra] *n.m.* eunuch; *Mus:* castrato.

castration [kastrasjɔ̃] *n.f.* castration; gelding (of stallion); neutering; spaying (of bitch, etc.).

castrer [kastre] *v.tr.* to castrate; to geld (stallion); to neuter; to spay (bitch, etc.).

castrisme [kastrism] *n.m. Pol:* Castroism.

casuel, -elle [kazɥɛl] **1.** *a.* (*a*) *A: & Lit:* fortuitous, accidental; (*b*) *Gram:* **flexions casuelles,** case endings. **2.** *n.m.* perquisites, fees (in addition to fixed salary); *Ecc:* surplice fees.

casuiste [kazɥist] *n.m. Theol:* casuist.

casuistique [kazɥistik] *n.f. Theol:* casuistry.

catabolisme [katabɔlism] *n.m. Biol:* catabolism.

catachrèse [katakrɛz] *n.f. Rh:* catachresis.

cataclysme [kataklism] *n.m.* cataclysm, disaster.

cataclysmique [kataklismik] *a.* cataclysmic, cataclysmal.

catacombes [katakɔ̃b] *n.f.pl.* catacombs.

catadioptre [katadiɔptr̥] *n.m.* reflector; (*on road surface*) cat's eye.

catafalque [katafalk] *n.m.* catafalque.

cataire [katɛr] *n.f. Bot:* catmint, *NAm:* catnip.

catalan, -ane [katalɑ̃, -an] **1.** *a. & n. Geog:* Catalan, Catalonian. **2.** *n.m. Ling:* Catalan.

catalepsie [katalɛpsi] *n.f. Med:* catalepsy.

cataleptique [katalɛptik] *a. & n. Med:* cataleptic (patient, etc.).

Catalogne [katalɔɲ] **1.** *Pr.n.f. Geog:* Catalonia. **2.** *n.f. Fr.C: Tex:* **couvertures de, en, c.,** rugs of rough multicoloured wool.

catalogue [katalɔg] *n.m.* catalogue; list; **c. méthodique,** subject catalogue; **faire le c. de . . .,** to catalogue, list (objects).

cataloguer [katalɔge] *v.tr.* (*a*) to catalogue, list; (*b*) *F:* to size (s.o.) up, label (s.o.).

catalyse [kataliz] *n.f. Ch:* catalysis.

catalyser [katalize] *v.tr.* to catalyse.

catalyseur [katalizœr] **1.** *a.* catalytic. **2.** *n.m.* catalyst.

catalytique [katalitik] *a. Ch:* catalytic.

catamaran [katamarɑ̃] *n.m. Nau:* catamaran; *Av:* floats (of seaplane).

cataphote [katafɔt] *n.m. R.t.m:* = CATADIOPTRE.

cataplasme [kataplasm] *n.m. Med:* poultice; **c. sinapisé,** mustard poultice, plaster; *F:* **c'est un bon c. pour l'estomac,** it's a good lining for the stomach.

catapultage [katapyltaʒ] *n.m.* catapulting; *Av:* catapult launch(ing); **crochet de c.,** catapulting hook.

catapulte [katapylt] *n.f.* catapult.

catapulter [katapylte] *v.tr.* to catapult.

cataracte [katarakt] *n.f.* **1.** cataract, falls; *Lit:* **les cataractes du ciel,** the sluice gates of heaven; torrents of rain. **2.** *Med:* cataract; **se faire opérer de la c.,** to have a cataract operation.

catarrhal, -aux [kataral, -o] *a. Med:* catarrhal.
catarrhe [katar] *n.m. Med:* catarrah.
catarrheux, -euse [katarø, -øz] *a. & n.* catarrhal (person).
catastrophe [katastrɔf] *n.f.* catastrophe, disaster; **c. financière,** crash; **c'est la c.!** the worst has happened; *Av:* **atterrir en c.,** to make a forced landing.
catastrophé [katastrɔfe] *a. F:* overwhelmed, dumbfounded; **mine catastrophée,** amazed, dismayed, expression.
catastropher [katastrɔfe] *v.tr. F:* to overwhelm, dumbfound; to bowl (s.o.) over.
catastrophique [katastrɔfik] *a.* catastrophic, disastrous.
catch [katʃ] *n.m.* (all-in) wrestling.
catcheur, -euse [katʃœr, -øz] *n.* (all-in) wrestler.
catéchèse [kateʃɛz] *n.f. Ecc:* (*a*) *A:* catechesis; (*b*) catechism.
catéchisation [kateʃizasjɔ̃] *n.f.* catechization.
catéchiser [kateʃize] *v.tr.* (*a*) *Ecc:* to catechize; (*b*) to tell (s.o.) what to say, indoctrinate (s.o.); to preach at, lecture (s.o.).
catéchisme [kateʃism] *n.m.* catechism; **aller au c.,** to go to catechism class.
catéchiste [kateʃist] *n.* catechist.
catéchumène [katekymɛn] *n.m. & f.* (*a*) *Ecc:* catechumen; (*b*) new member, novice.
catégorie [kategɔri] *n.f.* category; type, grade (of goods, person, etc.); **de la même c.,** of the same quality; **légumes, de première c.,** first-class, class one, prime, vegetables; **de dernière c.,** of poor quality.
catégorique [kategɔrik] *a.* (*a*) *Phil:* categorical (proposition, etc.); (*b*) categorical, explicit, clear (answer, etc.); **refus c.,** flat refusal.
catégoriquement [kategɔrikmɑ̃] *adv.* categorically; explicitly, clearly; (to refuse) flatly.
catégorisation [kategɔrizasjɔ̃] *n.f.* categorization, classification.
caténaire [katenɛr] **1.** *a. & n.f.* **(suspension) c.,** catenary (suspension); overhead wires (of electric railway). **2.** *a.* **réaction c.,** chain reaction.
catgut [katgyt] *n.m. Surg:* catgut.
catharsis [katarsis] *n.f. Gr.Lit: Psy:* catharsis.
cathédrale [katedral] *n.f.* cathedral.
Catherine [katrin] *Pr.n.f.* Catherine, Katherine; (*of woman*) **coiffer sainte C.,** to be still unmarried on one's twenty-fifth birthday.
catherinette [katrinɛt] *n.f.* unmarried girl of 25 and over.
cathéter [katetɛr] *n.m. Surg:* catheter.
cathode [katɔd] *n.f. El:* cathode.
cathodique [katɔdik] *a. El:* cathodic; **rayons cathodiques,** cathode rays; **tube à rayons cathodiques, tube c.,** cathode ray tube.
catholicisme [katɔlisism] *n.m.* (Roman) Catholicism.
catholicité [katɔlisite] *n.f.* **1.** catholicity; orthodoxy. **2.** the (Roman) Catholic Church.
catholique [katɔlik] *a.* **1.** (*a*) *Ecc:* catholic, universal; orthodox; (*b*) *F:* **ce n'est pas (très) c.,** I don't like the look, the sound, of it; it looks, sounds, fishy, doubtful, dubious. **2.** *a. & n.* (Roman) Catholic.
cati [kati] *n.m. Tex:* gloss, lustre.
catilinaire [katilinɛr] *n.f.* (*a*) Catilinarian oration (of Cicero); (*b*) *Lit:* diatribe, outburst.
catimini (en) [ɑ̃katimini] *adv.phr. F:* stealthily, on the sly; **entrer, sortir, en c.,** to steal, sneak, in, out.
catin [katɛ̃] *n.f. P: O:* prostitute, whore.
cation [katjɔ̃] *n.m. El:* cation.
catir [katir] *v.tr. Tex:* to press, gloss (material).
catissage [katisaʒ] *n.m. Tex:* pressing, glossing.
catisseur, -euse [katisœr, -øz] *n. Tex:* (piece) presser, glosser.
catogan [katɔgɑ̃] *n.m.* ribbon for tying back hair.
Caton [katɔ̃] *Pr.n.m. Rom.Hist:* Cato.
catoptrique [katɔptrik] *Ph:* **1.** *a.* catoptric(al), reflecting. **2.** *n.f.* catoptrics.
Caucase (le) [ləkokaz] *Pr.n. Geog:* the Caucasus.
caucasien, -ienne [kokazjɛ̃, -jɛn] *a. & n. Geog:* Caucasian.
cauchemar [koʃmar] *n.m.* nightmare; **avoir le c.,** to have a nightmare; *F:* **il me donne le c.,** he's a bugbear, my pet aversion.
caudal, -aux [kodal, -o] *a. Z:* caudal.
cauri(s) [kori] *n.m.* cowrie (shell).
causal [kozal] *a.* no *m.pl. Gram: Phil:* causal.
causalité [kozalite] *n.f. Phil:* causality.
causant [kozɑ̃] *a. F:* chatty, talkative (person).
cause [koz] *n.f.* **1.** cause; **c. de défiance,** cause, reason, for distrust; **c. première, seconde,** prime, secondary, cause; **être (la) c. de qch.,** to be the cause of sth.; **c'est elle qui en est c.,** it's her fault; **pour quelle c.?** for what reason? on what grounds? **et pour c.,** and for a very good reason; **absent pour c. de santé,** absent for health reasons, on medical grounds; **à c. de,** because of, on account of; owing to; for the sake of; **c'est à c. de moi qu'il a manqué le train,** it was my fault he missed the train; **c'est à c. de toi!** it's all because of you! **2.** (*a*) *Jur:* cause, (law) suit; action; **c. célèbre,** famous trial, cause célèbre; **avocat sans c.,** briefless barrister; **confier une c. à un avocat,** to brief a barrister; **affaire en c.,** case before the court; **entendre une c.,** to hear a case; **la c. est entendue,** there's nothing more to add; **être en c.,** (i) to be party to a suit; (ii) to be concerned, involved, in sth.; **mettre qn en c.,** (i) to summon, sue, s.o.; (ii) to implicate s.o.; **mettre en c. la probité de qn,** to question s.o.'s honesty; **cela est hors de c.,** that's beside the point, irrelevant; **mettre qn, qch., hors de c.,** (i) to rule (plaintiff, argument) out of court; (ii) to exonerate s.o.; **en tout état de c.,** at all events, in any case; **en connaissance de c.,** with full knowledge of the case, the facts; (*b*) **souffrir pour une c.,** to suffer in a cause; **faire c. commune avec qn,** to make common cause with s.o.; to side with s.o.
causer[1] [koze] *v.tr.* to cause, be the cause of (sth.); **c. un changement,** to bring about a change.
causer[2] *v.i. F:* (*a*) to talk, chat (**de,** about); **c. avec, à, qn,** to have a chat, a talk, with s.o.; **causez toujours,** you can talk as much as you like (I'm not listening); (*b*) to blab, squeal, give the game away; **faire c. qn,** to pump s.o., make s.o. talk.
causerie [kozri] *n.f.* (*a*) talk, chat; (*b*) causerie, informal talk, lecture.
causette [kozɛt] *n.f. F:* little chat; **faire la c., un brin de c.,** to have a little chat, a natter.
causeur, -euse [kozœr, -øz] **1.** *n.* chatterer. **2.** *n.f. Furn:* **causeuse,** sociable, causeuse, love seat.
causse [kos] *n.m. Geog:* causse.
causticité [kostisite] *n.f.* (*a*) *Ch:* causticity; (*b*) causticity, caustic humour; biting, stinging, nature (of remark, etc.).
caustique [kostik] **1.** *a.* (*a*) *Ch:* caustic; (*b*) biting, caustic, cutting (remark, etc.). **2.** *n.m Ch: Pharm:* caustic. **3.** *n.f. Opt:* caustic (curve).
caustiquement [kostikmɑ̃] *adv.* caustically, bitingly.
cautère [kotɛr] *n.m. Med:* cautery; *F:* **c'est un c. sur une jambe de bois,** it won't do any good whatever.
cautérisation [koterizasjɔ̃] *n.f.* cauterization.
cautériser [koterize] *v.tr.* to cauterize (wound, etc.).
caution [kosjɔ̃] *n.f.* **1.** security, guarantee, bail (bond); **donner, fournir, c. pour qn, se porter c. pour qn,** to go, stand, bail for s.o., to bail s.o. out; **mettre**

qn en liberté sous c., to release s.o. on bail; *Com:* **verser une c.,** to pay a deposit; **sujet à caution,** unreliable, unconfirmed (news, etc.). **2.** surety, security, guaranty, bail (bondsman); **se porter c. pour qn,** (i) to go bail for s.o.; (ii) *Com:* to stand surety, security, for s.o.

cautionnement [kosjɔnmɑ̃] *n.m. Com:* (*a*) surety bond, guarantee; (*b*) security, guarantee, guaranty; **c. judiciaire,** bail.

cautionner [kosjɔne] *v.tr.* (*a*) to stand surety, as guarantor, for (s.o.); *Jur:* to go, stand, bail for (s.o.); to bail (s.o.) out; (*b*) to answer for, guarantee (sth.).

cavalcade [kavalkad] *n.f.* **1.** cavalcade, procession; pageant. **2.** swarm, unruly gang (of children, etc.).

cavalcader [kavalkade] *v.i.* **1.** *A:* to cavalcade; to ride (in a cavalcade). **2.** (*of gangs of people, etc.*) to swarm (about).

cavale [kaval] *n.f.* **1.** *Lit:* mare. **2.** *P:* escape, break-out (from prison); **être en c.,** to be on the run.

cavaler [kavale] *P:* **1.** *v.i. & pr.* **(se) c.,** to run (at full speed); to run away, scarper, make tracks, do a bunk. **2.** *v.tr.* **c. qn,** to get on s.o.'s nerves, plague, pester, s.o.

cavalerie [kavalri] *n.f.* **1.** *Mil:* cavalry; **c. légère,** light cavalry, light horse; **c. motorisée,** motorized cavalry. **2.** stable (of circus horses, etc.).

cavaleur [kavalœr] *n.m. P:* skirt chaser, womaniser.

cavalier, -ière [kavalje, -jɛr] **1.** (*a*) *n.* rider; horseman, horsewoman; **habit de c.,** riding costume; *B:* **les (Quatre) cavaliers de l'Apocalypse,** the (four) Horsemen of the Apocalypse; (*b*) *a.* **piste cavalière,** (i) riding track, (ii) bridle path; (*in forest, etc.*) **allée cavalière,** ride. **2.** (*a*) *n.m. Mil:* trooper, cavalryman; (*b*) *n.m. Chess:* knight; (*c*) *n.m. A:* gentleman, gallant; *Hist:* **Cavaliers et Têtes rondes,** Cavaliers and Roundheads; (*d*) *n.m.* escort (to a lady); (*e*) *n.m & f.* partner (at dance); **faire c. seul,** to act alone, go it alone. **3.** *n.m. Tchn:* (*a*) staple; (*b*) rider (of balance). **4.** *a.* cavalier, free and easy; offhand (manner, etc.); **à la cavalière,** in a cavalier, offhand, manner.

cavalièrement [kavaljɛrmɑ̃] *adv.* in a cavalier manner; off-handedly.

cave¹ [kav] *a.* **1.** hollow, sunken (cheeks, eyes). **2.** *Anat:* **veine c.,** vena cava.

cave² *n.f.* **1.** (*a*) cellar, vault; **avoir une bonne c.,** to keep a good cellar (of wine); **de la c. au grenier,** from top to bottom; thoroughly; (*b*) cellar nightclub. **2. c. à liqueurs,** cellaret, liqueur cabinet.

cave³ *n.f. Cards:* money put up by each player (at beginning of game); stake.

cave⁴ *n.m. P:* **1.** outsider (as opposed to a member of the underworld). **2.** clot, dupe; sucker; *a.* **ce qu'elle est c.!** what a sucker!

caveau, -eaux [kavo] *n.m.* **1.** (*a*) small (wine) cellar, vault; (*b*) nightclub. **2.** burial vault.

caver¹ [kave] *v.tr. A: & Lit:* to hollow (out), dig (out), excavate, undermine. **2. se c.,** (*of eyes, etc.*) to become hollow, sunken.

caver² *Cards:* **1.** *v.tr. A:* to put up (a sum of money as a stake). **2.** *v.i.* to put up a stake; *A:* to bet, bank (on sth.); **c. au plus fort,** to put up an amount equal to the highest on the table. **3. se c. de deux cents francs,** to put up two hundred francs (as a stake).

caverne [kavɛrn] *n.f.* (*a*) cave, cavern; *Prehist:* **homme des cavernes,** caveman; (*b*) den (of thieves); (*c*) *Anat:* cavity (in lungs, etc.).

caverneux, -euse [kavɛrnø, -øz] *a.* **1.** (*a*) cavernous, caverned (mountain, rock); (*b*) *Anat:* cavern(ul)ous; spongy (tissue). **2.** cavernous, hollow, sepulchral (voice).

cavernicole [kavɛrnikɔl] *Nat.Hist:* (*a*) *a.* cavernicolous (animal, etc.); (*b*) *n.m. & f.* cavernicole.

cavet [kavɛ] *n.m. Arch:* cavetto, hollowed moulding.

caviar [kavjar] *n.m.* **1.** caviar; **c. rouge,** salmon caviar. **2. passer au c.,** to censor (newspaper article, etc.).

caviarder [kavjarde] *v.tr.* to censor (newspaper article, etc.).

caviste [kavist] *n.m.* cellarman.

cavité [kavite] *n.f.* cavity, hollow; pit (in metal); *Anat:* **c. articulaire,** socket (of bone).

Cayenne [kajɛn] *Pr.n.f. Geog:* Cayenne (Island); **poivre de C.,** cayenne pepper.

ce¹ [s(ə)] *dem. pron. neut.* (**c'** *before parts of* **être** *beginning with a vowel*) it, that. **1.** (*as neut. subject of* **être, devoir être, pouvoir être**) (*a*) (*with adj. or adv. complement*) **c'est faux!** it's not true! it's untrue! **ce doit être faux,** it's probably untrue; **le voilà, ce n'est pas trop tôt!** there he is, and about time too! **est-ce** [ɛs] **assez?** is that enough? (*b*) (*with noun or pron. as complement*; *with a 3rd pers. pl. complement the verb should be in the plural, but colloquial usage allows the singular*) **c'est moi, c'est nous, ce sont eux,** *F:* **c'est eux,** it is I, we, they; *F:* it's me, us, them; **est-ce vous, Jean?** is that you, John? **c'est un bon soldat,** he's a good soldier; **ce ne sont pas mes chaussures** they, these, are not my shoes; *inv.phr.* **si ce n'est,** escept, unless; **personne si ce n'est vos parents,** no one except (possibly) your parents; (*c*) **ce . . . ici** = CECI; **ce n'est pas ici un hôtel!** this is not a(n) hotel! (*d*) **ce . . . là** = CELA; **ce n'est pas là mon parapluie,** that is not my unbrella; **est-ce que ce sont là vos enfants?** are these, those, your children? (*e*) (*representing a subject which has been isolated in order to stress it*) **Paris, c'est bien loin! c'est bien loin, Paris!** it's a long way to Paris! Paris is a long way off; **le temps, c'est de l'argent,** time is money; (*f*) (*anticipating the subject*) **c'est demain dimanche,** tomorrow is Sunday; (*g*) (i) *F:* (*as temporary subject when an adj. is followed by a noun clause or an inf. subject; careful speech requires* **il**) **c'était inutile de sonner,** you need not have rung; (ii) **c'est assez qu'il veuille bien pardonner,** it is enough that he is willing to forgive; **c'est à vous de vous en occuper,** it's up to you to see to it; (*h*) **c'est . . . qui, c'est . . . que** (*used to bring a word into prominence*); **c'est un bon petit garçon que Jean!** what a fine little chap John is! **ce serait imprudence que d'y aller,** it would be unwise to go (there); **c'est moi qui lui ai écrit,** it was I, *F:* me, who wrote to him; **est-ce à moi que vous parlez?** are you speaking to me? (*i*) (i) **c'est que** (*introducing a statement*) **c'est que maman est malade,** you see, the point is, mother's ill; **c'est qu'il fait froid!** it's cold and no mistake! **s'il chante, c'est qu'il est de bonne humeur,** when, if, he sings it means, it's because, he's in a good mood; (ii) **ce n'est pas qu'il n'y tienne pas,** it's not that he isn't keen on it; it isn't that he's not keen on it; (iii) **est-ce que** [ɛskə] (*introducing a question*) **est-ce que je peux entrer?** may I come in? **est-ce qu'il est là?** is he there? **2.** *literary use, always* [sə] (*a*) (*used as subject to* **devenir, laisser, sembler, venir**) **voilà, ce me semble, un avis excellent,** that, to my mind, is excellent advice; (*b*) (*used as object to* **faire, dire, etc.**) **pour ce faire,** in order to do this, with this intention; **ce faisant,** in so doing; **ce disant,** saying which, this; so saying, with these words. **3.** (*used as neut. antecedent to a rel. pron.*) (*a*) **ce qui, ce que, etc.** = what; **je sais ce qui est arrivé,** I know what's happened; **voilà ce que j'ai répondu,** this is what I answered; **je sais ce que c'est que la pauvreté,** I know what poverty is; **si vous saviez ce que c'est que de vivre seul!** if you knew what it means, what it's like, to live alone; **voilà ce que c'est que mentir,** that's what comes of telling lies; **c'est ce qu'il a dit,** that's what he said; so he said; **voici ce dont il s'agit,** this is the point; this is what it's all about;

ce qu'il y a de plus remarquable, c'est que . . ., what is most remarkable is that . . .; **à ce qu'on dit,** by, according to, from, what they say; **voici ce à quoi** [səakwa] **j'avais pensé,** this is what I had thought of; (*b*) **ce qui, ce que, etc.** = which; **il est déjà parti, ce que je ne savais pas,** he's already gone, and I didn't know, (a fact) which I didn't know; (*c*) **tout ce qui, que,** everything, all (that); **voici tout ce que j'ai d'argent,** here's all the money I've got; **faites tout ce que vous voudrez,** do whatever you like; (*d*) *F:* **ce que . . .!** how . . .! **(qu'est-)ce qu'elle a changé!** how she has changed! **ce que tu es grandi!** well, you *have* grown! **4.** (= CELA) **on l'a attaqué et ce** [sə] **en plein jour,** he was attacked, and in broad daylight; **sur ce . . .,** thereupon . . .; *A:* **depuis ce . . .,** since then. **5.** *conj.phr.* **tenez-vous beaucoup à ce qu'il vienne?** are you very anxious for him to come? **6.** *prep.phr.* **pour ce qui est de la qualité et du prix,** with regard to, as regards, quality and price; **pour ce qui est de cela,** for that matter.

ce² (cet), cette, ces [sə (sɛt), sɛt, se or sɛ] *dem.a.* (*The form* **cet** *is used before a n. or adj. beginning with a vowel or* **h** *mute.*) this, that, *pl.* these, those. **1. un de ces jours,** one of these days; **il fera de l'orage cette nuit,** there will be a storm tonight; **j'ai mal dormi cette nuit,** I slept badly last night; **je l'ai vu, je le verrai, ce matin, cet été,** I saw him, I'll see him, this morning, this summer, during the summer. **2.** (*a*) that, these; **mon père, ce héros au sourire si doux,** my father, that hero with the gentle smile; **c'est une de ces personnes dont on ne peut pas se débarrasser,** he's, she's, one of those people, the sort of person, you can't get rid of; (*b*) the; **il a eu cette sensation que . . .,** he experienced the feeling that . . .; **rien de ce genre,** nothing of the kind. **3.** (*a*) **ce dernier,** the latter; (*b*) *F:* **mais laissez-la donc, cette enfant!** do leave the child alone! **4.** *pl.* **que prendront ces messieurs?** what will you take, gentlemen? **ces dames sont au salon,** the ladies are in the drawing room. **5. ce . . . -ci,** this; **ce . . . -là,** that; **prenez cette tasse-ci,** take this cup; **je n'oublierai jamais ce jour-là,** I shall never forget that day; **je le verrai ces jours-ci,** I'll see him in a day or two. **6.** *F:* (*a*) **eh bien, et cette jambe?** well, how's that leg of yours? **cette question!** what an absurd question! (*b*) **je lui ai écrit une de ces lettres!** I wrote him such a letter! **j'ai une de ces faims!** I'm ravenous!

céans [seɑ̃] *adv.* (*a*) *A:* (here) within, in this house; (*b*) **le maître de c.,** the master of the house.

ceci [səsi] *dem. pron. neut. inv.* this (thing, fact, etc.); **écoutez bien c.,** (now) listen to this; **le cas offre c. de particulier, que . . .,** the case is peculiar in (this) that . . ..

cécité [sesite] *n.f.* blindness; **c. verbale,** word blindness.

cédant, -ante [sedɑ̃, -ɑ̃t] *Com: Jur:* **1.** *a.* granting, assigning (party). **2.** *n.* grantor, assignor.

céder [sede] *v.* **(je cède; je céderai) 1.** *v.tr.* (*a*) to give up, part with, yield (**à,** to); to surrender (right); **c. sa place à qn,** to give up one's seat to s.o.; **c. le pas à qn,** to let s.o. go first, give way to s.o.; (*b*) *Jur:* to transfer, make over, assign (**à,** to); to dispose of, sell (lease); **maison à c.,** business for sale; **je vous le céderai pour cent francs,** I will let you have it for a hundred francs; (*c*) **ne le c. en rien à qn,** to be s.o.'s equal, to be in no way inferior to s.o.; **le c. à qn en qch.,** to yield to s.o. in sth., to be inferior to s.o. in sth.; **pour l'intelligence elle ne (le) cède à personne,** in intelligence she's second to none. **2.** *v.i.* to yield, give way (under pressure); (*a*) **c. sous le pied,** to give beneath the foot; **le câble a cédé sous l'effort,** the rope gave way, parted, under the strain; **c. au sommeil,** to succumb to sleep; **forcer qn à c.,** to bring s.o. to terms; (*b*) to give in, submit (**à,** to); *F:* to knuckle under; **il a cédé à nos désirs,** he gave in to us.

cédille [sedij] *n.f. Gram:* cedilla.

cédrat [sedra] *n.m. Bot:* (*a*) citron (tree); (*b*) citron.

cédratier [sedratje] *n.m. Bot:* citron (tree).

cèdre [sɛdr̥] *n.m. Bot:* (*a*) cedar (tree, wood); (*b*) *Fr.C:* thuja, arbor vitae, cedar.

cédulaire [sedylɛr] *a.* pertaining to income tax schedules; **impôts cédulaires,** scheduled taxes.

cédule [sedyl] *n.f.* schedule (of taxes); **c. d'impôts,** tax bracket.

cégétiste [seʒetist] **1.** *n.m. & f.* member of the C.G.T. (*Confédération générale du travail*). **2.** *a.* **délégué c.,** C.G.T. delegate.

ceindre [sɛ̃dr̥] *v.tr.* (*pr.p.* **ceignant;** *p.p.* **ceint;** *pr. ind.* **je ceins, il ceint, n. ceignons;** *p.d.* **je ceignais;** *p.h.* **je ceignis;** *fu.* **je ceindrai**) *Lit:* **1.** to gird; (*a*) **c. une épée,** to gird on, buckle on, a sword; **c. l'écharpe municipale,** to put on, assume, one's sash of office; **c. la couronne,** to put on, assume, the crown; (*b*) **c. qn de qch.,** to gird, encircle, s.o. with sth.; **se c. les reins, c. ses reins,** to gird up one's loins. **2.** (*of a wreath, etc.*) to encircle (s.o.'s head, etc.); **tête ceinte d'une couronne de lauriers,** head wreathed with laurels. **3. c. une ville de murailles,** to encircle, surround, a town with walls.

ceinture [sɛ̃tyr] *n.f.* **1.** (*a*) belt; girdle, sash; waistband (of skirt, trousers); **c. de grossesse,** maternity corset; *Med:* **c. orthopédique,** surgical corset, belt; *A:* **c. de chasteté,** chastity belt; **c. de sauvetage,** lifebelt; **c. de parachute,** parachute harness; *Aut: Av:* **c. de sécurité,** seat belt, safety belt; (*judo*) **c. marron, noire,** brown, black, belt; *F:* **se serrer, se mettre, la c., faire c.,** to tighten one's belt; to go without (sth.); (*b*) waist, middle (of the body); **coup au-dessous de la c.,** blow below the belt; (*c*) *Wr:* hold round the waist, waist lock; (*d*) *Anat:* **c. pelvienne,** pelvic girdle; **c. scapulaire,** pectoral, scapular, arch, girdle. **2.** enclosure; circle (of walls); belt (of hills); **c. de verdure, verte,** green belt. **3.** *Rail:* **chemin de fer de c.,** circle line (round a town); **la grande, la petite, C.,** the outer, inner, circle railway. **4.** *Arch:* cincture (of column).

ceinturer [sɛ̃tyre] *v.tr.* **1.** to girdle, surround; **ville ceinturée de murs,** walled town. **2.** *Wr:* to grip round the waist; *Rugby Fb:* to tackle (a player).

ceinturon [sɛ̃tyrɔ̃] *n.m. Mil:* belt, swordbelt.

cela [səla, sla] *F:* **ça** [sa] *dem. pron. neut.* (*a*) that (thing, fact, etc.); **qu'est-ce que c'est que c.,** *F:* **que ça?** what's that? **il y a deux ans de c.,** that was two years ago; **c'est pour c. que je viens,** that's what I've come for, why I've come; **sans c. je ne serais pas venu,** but for that, otherwise, I wouldn't have come; **à c. près, à part c., nous sommes d'accord,** we are agreed, with that one exception, except on that point; **s'il n'y a que c. de nouveau,** if that's all that's new; (*b*) that, it (**cela** *is the pron. used as neut. subject to all verbs other than* **être,** *and may be used with* **être** *as more emphatic than* **ce**) **c. ne vous regarde pas,** that's, it's, no business of yours; **la voir si malheureuse, c. m'est pénible,** to see her, seeing her, so unhappy is very painful to me; **ça y est!** that's that! that's it! (*c*) *F:* (*disparagingly of people and things*) **c'est ça les hommes!** that's what men are like! that's men for you! **ça arrive en retard et ça veut qu'on l'attende,** he, she, etc., comes late, and then expects me, us, to wait for him, her, etc. (*d*) *F:* **ceci . . . cela; il m'a dit ceci et c.,** he told me this, that and the other; **comment allez-vous?—comme (ci comme) ça,** how are you?—so-so, middling; (*e*) (*idiomatic uses*) **ça alors!** you don't say! *F:* well I'm damned! **c'est ça!** that's it! that's right!; **ce n'est plus c.,** it's no longer what it was, it's not the same any more; **il n'y a que c. pour me tenir éveillé,** that's the only thing that will keep me awake; **ah, pour cela, oui!** yes, indeed! yes, of course! (*in shop*) **et avec c., madame?** anything else, madam? **une petite femme haute comme ça,** a little woman no taller than that, only so high; **je suis comme ça,** I'm like that; *F:* **comme ça, vous déménagez?** so you're moving, are you? **allons, pas de ça!** hey! none of that! **ce n'est pas si facile que ça,** it isn't as easy as all that; **où ça?** where('s that)? **comment ça?** how come? **ça oui!** yes indeed! definitely! **ça non!** never! not on your life!

céladon [seladɔ̃] *n.m. & a.inv.* willow-green, celadon.

célébrant [selebrɑ̃] *a. & n.m. Ecc:* celebrant.

célébration [selebrasjɔ̃] *n.f.* celebration.

célèbre [selɛbr̥] *a.* celebrated, famous (**par,** for); **le cas si tristement c. de . . .,** the notorious case of . . ..

célébrer [selebre] *v.tr.* **(je célèbre; je célébrerai) 1.** to celebrate (mass, etc.); (i) to solemnize (rite); (ii) to observe, keep (feast); **c. des funérailles,** to hold a funeral. **2.** to celebrate, extol (s.o.); **c. les louanges de qn,** to sing s.o.'s praises.

célébrité [selebrite] *n.f.* (*a*) celebrity; fame; (*b*) (*pers.*) celebrity.

celer [səle] *v.tr.* **(je cèle je cèlerai)** *A: & Lit:* to conceal, keep secret (**à,** from).

céleri [sɛlri] *n.m* celery; **pied de c.,** head of celery; **morceau, branche, de c.,** stick of celery.

céleri-rave [sɛlrirav] *n.m.* celeriac; *pl. céleris-raves.*

célérité [selerite] *n.f.* speed, rapidity; **avec une étonnante c.,** with astonishing speed, at an astonishing rate.

célesta [selɛsta] *n.m. Mus:* celesta, celeste.

céleste [selɛst] *a.* **1.** celestial, heavenly; *Lit:* **la voûte c.,** the vault of heaven; **bleu c.,** sky blue, celeste. **2.** *A:* **le C. Empire,** the Celestial Empire.

célibat [seliba] *n.m.* celibacy, single life.

célibataire [selibatɛr] *a. & n.* unmarried, single, celibate (man, woman); *n.m.* bachelor; *n.f.* spinster.

celle, celle-ci, celle-là *pron. See* CELUI.

cellérier, -ière [selerje, -jɛr] *n. Ecc:* cellarer; *f.* cellaress.

cellier [selje] *n.m.* storeroom (for wine, etc.); still-room.

cellulaire [selylɛr] *a.* **1.** cellular (tissue, girder, etc.). **2. voiture c.,** police van, *F:* Black Maria; **prison c.,** solitary confinement.

cellule [selyl], *n.f.* **1.** cell (of prison, honeycomb, etc.); *Mil:* **dix jours de c.,** ten days in the cells; *F:* ten days' cells. **2.** *Biol:* cell. **3.** *Av:* airframe. **4. c. photoélectrique,** photoelectric cell, photocell; *T.V:* electric eye. **5.** *Rec:* cartridge.

cellulite [selylit] *n.f. Med:* cellulitis.

celluloïd [selylɔid] *n.m.* celluloid.

cellulose [selyloz] *n.f. Ch: Com:* cellulose.

cellulosique [selylozik] *a.* cellulose (varnish, etc.).

celte [sɛlt] **1.** *a.* Celtic. **2.** *n.m. & f.* Celt.

celtique [sɛltik] *a.* Celtic.

celui, celle, *pl.* **ceux, celles** [səlɥi, sɛl, sø, sɛl] *dem.pron.* **1.** (*completed by an adj. clause*) (*a*) the one, *pl.* those; **c. qui était parti le dernier,** the one who started last; (*b*) he, she, *pl.* those; **c. qui mange peu dort bien,** he who eats little sleeps well; **celui dont je t'ai parlé,** the one, the man, I told you about; **celle à qui j'ai écrit,** the one, the woman, I wrote to, to whom I wrote. **2.** (*followed by* **de**) **mes livres et ceux de Jean,** my books and John's; **les hommes d'aujourd'hui et ceux d'autrefois,** the men of today and those of former times. **3. tous ceux ayant la même idée,** all those with the same idea; **toutes les maisons sont en bois sauf celles voisines de l'église,** all the houses are built of wood except those near the church. **4. celui-ci, ceux-ci,** this (one), these; the latter; **celui-là, ceux-là,** that (one), those; the former; **ceux-ci coûtent plus cher que ceux-là,** these cost more than those do; **ah, celui-là! quel idiot!** oh him! that idiot! **autre exemple, plus technique c.-la,** another example, a more technical one this time.

cément [semɑ̃] *n.m.* **1.** *Anat:* cement (of tooth). **2.** *Metall:* cement, cementation powder.

cémentation [semɑ̃tasjɔ̃] *n.f. Metall:* cementation, case hardening.

cémenter [semɑ̃te] *v.tr. Metall:* to case-harden, face-harden (steel); to cement (armour-plate).

cénacle [senakl̥] *n.m.* **1.** *Ant:* cenacle; *esp. B:* upper room (of the Last Supper). **2.** (literary) club, group, coterie.

cendre [sɑ̃dr̥] *n.f.* (*a*) ash(es), cinders; **laisser tomber de la c. (de cigarette) sur son pantalon,** to drop (cigarette) ash on one's trousers; **mettre, réduire, une ville en cendres,** to reduce a town to ashes; **le mercredi des Cendres,** Ash Wednesday; **visage couleur de c.,** ashen face; (*b*) *pl.* (mortal) remains, ashes; (*c*) **cendres volcaniques,** volcanic ash.

cendré [sɑ̃dre] *a.* ash-grey, ashen, ashy.

cendrée [sɑ̃dre] *n.f.* **1.** *Sp: etc:* (*a*) cinders (for track, etc.); (*b*) cinder track, dirt track. **2.** *Ven:* dust shot.

cendrer [sɑ̃dre] *v.tr.* **1.** to colour (wall, etc.) ash-grey. **2.** to cinder (path, track).

cendreux, -euse [sɑ̃drø, -øz] *a.* **1.** ashy, ashen, ash-grey. **2.** full of ashes; ashy, gritty.

cendrier [sɑ̃drije] *n.m.* (*a*) ashpan (of stove); ash pit, ash hole (of furnace); ash box (of locomotive); (*b*) ashtray.

Cendrillon [sɑ̃drijɔ̃] **1.** *Pr.n.f.* Cinderella. **2.** *n.f.* (household) drudge, slavey.

cène [sɛn] *n.f.* (*a*) **La (Sainte) C.,** the Last Supper; (*b*) *Ecc:* (*in Protestant Church*) Holy Communion, Lord's Supper.

cenelle [sənɛl] *n.f. Bot:* haw (of hawthorn).

cenellier [sənɛlje] *n.m. Bot: Fr.C:* hawthorn.

cénobite [senɔbit] *n.m.* c(o)enobite (monk).

cénotaphe [senɔtaf] *n.m.* cenotaph.

cens [sɑ̃s] *n.m.* **1.** *Rom.Ant:* census. **2.** (*a*) *Hist:* (*in feudal system*) (quit) rent; (*b*) *Adm:* quota (of taxes payable); rating; **c. électoral,** property qualification (for the franchise).

censé [sɑ̃se] *a.* **être c. savoir faire qch.,** to be considered competent to do sth.; to be supposed to be able to do sth.; **je ne suis pas c. le savoir,** I'm not required to know that; **nul n'est c. ignorer la loi,** ignorance of the law is no excuse.

censément [sɑ̃semɑ̃] *adv.* (i) supposedly; (ii) practically; **il est c. le maître,** (i) he's supposed to be the master; (ii) to all intents and purposes he is the master.

censeur [sɑ̃sœr] *n.m.* **1.** *Rom.Ant:* censor. **2.** critic, faultfinder. **3.** censor (of the press, etc.). **4.** *Sch:* vice-principal, deputy headmaster, headmistress (of *lycée*).

censitaire [sɑ̃sitɛr] *a. & n.m. Hist:* **(électeur) c.,** elector qualified by property, by his assessment.

censurable [sɑ̃syrabl̥] *a.* censurable, open to censure.

censure [sɑ̃syr] *n.f.* **1.** (*a*) *Rom.Ant:* censorship; (*b*) censorship (of the press, etc.); (*c*) *Cin: etc:* (board of) censors; (*d*) *Psy:* (the) censor. **2.** (*a*) *O:* censure, blame; **les censures de l'Église,** the censure of the Church; (*b*) **motion de c.,** vote of censure.

censurer [sɑ̃syre] *v.tr.* (*a*) to censure, find fault with (s.o., sth.); (*b*) to censor (film, etc.).

cent¹ [sɑ̃] **1.** (*a*) *num.a.* (*takes a plural* **s** *when multiplied by a preceding numeral but not when followed by another numeral; does not vary when used as an* *ordinal*) (a, one) hundred; **c. élèves,** a hundred pupils; **deux cents hommes,** two hundred men; **deux cent cinquante hommes,** two hundred and fifty men; **page deux cent,** page two hundred; **l'an trois cent,** the year three hundred; **cent un** [sɑ̃ œ̃], one hundred and one; **je te l'ai dit c. fois,** (if I've told you once) I've told you a hundred times; **vous avez c. fois raison,** you're absolutely right; **c. fois mieux,** a hundred times better; *F:* **je ne vais pas t'attendre (pendant) c. sept ans,** I'm not going to wait for you for ever; **faire les c. pas,** to pace up and down; *F:* **faire les quatre cents coups,** (i) to kick up a hell of a racket; (ii) to paint the town red; (iii) to be up to all sorts of tricks; *F:* **être aux c. coups,** to be desperate; *F:* **je vous le donne en c.,** I'll give you a hundred guesses; guess! (*b*) *n.m.inv.* a hundred; **sept pour c.,** seven per cent; *F:* **il y a c. à parier contre un que . . .,** it's a hundred to one that . . .; *Ch:* **solution à trente pour c.,** thirty per cent solution; **c. pour c.,** a hundred per cent. **2.** *n.m.var. Com:* **un c. d'œufs,** a hundred eggs; *F:* **il gagne des mille et des cents,** he earns a packet; *Sp:* **le c. mètres,** the hundred metres.

cent² [sɛn(t)] *n.m. esp. Fr.C:* (*coin*) cent.

centaine [sɑ̃tɛn] *n.f.* (approximate) hundred; **une c. de francs,** about a hundred francs, a hundred francs or so; **des centaines de livres,** hundreds of books; **quelques centaines de francs,** a few hundred francs; **atteindre la c.,** to live to be a hundred; **les gens mourent par centaines, par centaines de mille,** people died in hundreds, in thousands.

centaure [sɑ̃tɔr] *n.m. Myth:* centaur.

centauré [sɑ̃tɔre] *n.f. Bot:* centaury.

centenaire [sɑ̃tnɛr]. **1.** *a.* age-old; **plusieurs fois c.,** hundreds of years old; **chêne c.,** ancient oak. **2.** *n.m. & f.* centenarian. **3.** *n.m.* centenary (anniversary).

centenier [sɑ̃tənje] *n.m. Rom.Hist:* centurion.

centennal, -aux [sɑ̃tɛnal, -o] *a.* centennial.

centésimal, -aux [sɑ̃tezimal, -o] *a.* centesimal (fraction, scale, etc.).

centiare [sɑ̃tjar] *n.m. Meas:* centiare (one sq metre, or about 1⅕ square yards).

centième [sɑ̃tjɛm] **1.** *num. a. & n.* hundredth. **2.** *n.m.* hundredth (part). **3.** *n.f. Th:* hundredth performance.

centigrade [sɑ̃tigrad] *a.* centigrade.

centigramme [sɑ̃tigram] *n.m.* centigram(me).

centilitre [sɑ̃tilitr̥] *n.m.* centilitre.

centime [sɑ̃tim] *n.m.* (*a*) centime; **ne pas avoir un c.,** to be hard up; (*b*) *Adm:* **centimes additionnels,** special surtax.

centimètre [sɑ̃timɛtr̥] *n.m.* **1.** centimetre, *NAm:* centimeter. **2.** tape measure.

centrage [sɑ̃traʒ] *n.m.* centring, centering; adjusting (or work in lathe, etc.).

central, -aux [sɑ̃tral, -o] **1.** *a.* central; (*a*) middle (point, etc.); **quartier c. de la ville,** town centre; **Amérique centrale,** Central America; (*b*) principal, main, head (office, etc.); **(prison) centrale** = county gaol; **École centrale,** (university level) State school of engineering; **chauffage c.,** central heating. **2.** n.m. **c. téléphonique,** telephone exchange. **3.** *n.f.* (*a*) **centrale (électrique),** power station; **centrale thermique, nucléaire,** thermal, nuclear, power station; (*b*) **centrale (syndicale),** group of affiliated trade unions.

centralement [sɑ̃tralmɑ̃] *adv.* centrally; in the centre.

centralisateur, -trice [sɑ̃tralizatœr, -tris] *a.* centralizing (force, etc.).

centralisation [sɑ̃tralizasjɔ̃] *n.f.* centralization, centralizing.

centraliser [sɑ̃tralize] *v.tr.* to centralize.

centre [sɑ̃tr̥] *n.m.* **1.** (*a*) centre, *NAm:* center; central point; middle, midst; **c. commercial,** shopping precinct, shopping centre; **c. d'intérêt,** centre of interest; **il se croit le c. de l'univers,** he thinks that the world revolves round him; *Rail:* **c. de triage,** shunting, marshalling, yard; (*b*) *Pol:* centre; **le c. droit, gauche,** the centre right, left; (*c*) *Fb: etc:* (i) centre (player); (ii) centre (pass). **2.** *Mec: etc:* **c. d'un levier,** fulcrum of a lever; **c. de gravité,** centre of gravity; *Ph:* **c. d'attraction, de gravitation,** centre of attraction; *Meteor:* **c. de dépression,** storm centre.

centrer [sɑ̃tre] *v.tr.* (*a*) to centre (**sur,** on); to adjust (wheel, tool, lens, etc.); **c. l'attention du lecteur sur qch.,** to focus the reader's attention on sth.; (*b*) *Fb: etc:* to centre the ball.

centreur [sɑ̃trœr] *n.m. Tls:* centring tool.

centrifugation [sɑ̃trifygasjɔ̃] *n.f.* centrifugation, centrifuging.

centrifuge [sɑ̃trifyʒ] *a.* centrifugal (force, etc.).

centrifuger [sɑ̃trifyʒe] *v.tr.* to centrifuge (liquid); to separate (cream).

centrifugeur [sɑ̃trifyʒœr] *n.m.*, **centrifugeuse** [sɑ̃trifyʒøz] *n.f.* centrifuge; centrifugal machine; (cream) separator.

centripète [sɑ̃tripɛt] *a.* centripetal (force, etc.).

centriste [sɑ̃trist] *Pol:* **1.** *a.* (of the) centre. **2.** *n.m. & f.* centrist; **les centristes,** the centre.

centuple [sɑ̃typl̥] *a. & n.m.* centuple, hundredfold; **mille est (le) c. de dix,** a thousand is a hundred times as much as ten.

centupler [sɑ̃typle] *v.tr. & i.* to centuple; to increase a hundred times, a hundredfold.

centurie [sɑ̃tyri] *n.f. Rom.Ant:* century.

centurion [sɑ̃tyrjɔ̃] *n.m. Rom.Ant:* centurion.

cep [sɛp] *n.m.* **1.** *Hort:* **c. de vigne** [sɛdviɲ, sɛpdəviɲ] vinestock, vine plant. **2.** *Agr:* sole (of plough).

cépage [sepaʒ] *n.m.* (variety of) vine.

cèpe [sɛp] *n.m. Fung:* boletus, cepe.

cependant [s(ə)pɑ̃dɑ̃] **1.** *conj.* yet, still, nevertheless, however, though. **2.** *adv. A:* meanwhile, in the meantime; **c. que,** while, whilst.

céphalique [sefalik] *a.* cephalic.

céphalopode [sefalɔpɔd] *n.m. Moll:* cephalopod; *pl.* cephalopoda.

céphalo-rachidien, -ienne [sefalɔraʃidjɛ̃, -jɛn] *a.* cephalo-rachidian.

céramique [seramik] **1.** *a.* ceramic (arts, etc.); **industries céramiques,** pottery industry. **2.** *n.f.* (*a*) ceramics, (art of) pottery; (*b*) ceramic, pottery; **dalles en c.,** ceramic tiles; (*c*) ceramic, piece of pottery; pot.

céramiste [seramist] *n.m. & f.* ceramist.

Cerbère [sɛrbɛr] **1.** *Pr.n.m. Myth:* Cerberus. **2.** *n.m.* ill-tempered hall porter, janitor, etc.

cerceau, -eaux [sɛrso] *n.m.* **1.** hoop; **c. de baril,** barrel hoop; **faire courir un c.,** to bowl, trundle, a hoop. **2.** (*a*) half hoop, round frame, bail (of cart tilt); (*b*) cradle (over bed).

cerclage [sɛrklaʒ] *n.m.* hooping (of barrels, etc.); tyring (of wheel).

cercle [sɛrkl̥] *n.m.* **1.** (*a*) circle; **faire c.,** to lie, stand, in a circle, in a ring; to make a circle; **les avions décrivaient des cercles au-dessus de nos têtes,** the planes were circling overhead; **c. d'activités,** circle, sphere, range, of activities; **c. vicieux,** vicious circle; *Geog:* **c. (polaire) arctique,** Arctic Circle; **(arc de) grand c.,** great circle; (*b*) circle, set (of friends, etc.); **c. littéraire,** literary circle, society; (*c*) club; **c. militaire, des officiers,** officers' club. **2.** (binding) hoop, ring; **vin en cercles,** wine in the wood; **c. d'une roue,** tyre of a wheel. 3. (*a*) dial, circle; *Artil:* **c. de pointage,** dial (of dial sight); (*b*) **quart de c.,** quadrant.

cercler [sɛrkle] *v.tr.* **1.** to encircle, to ring; **lunettes cerclées d'or,** gold-rimmed spectacles; **yeux cerclés de bistre,** eyes with dark rings round them. **2.** to hoop (barrel); to tyre (wheel); **cerclé de fer,** iron-bound.

cercueil [sɛrkœj] *n.m.* coffin, *esp. U.S:* casket; **c. de plomb,** leaden shell.

céréale [sereal] *n.f.* cereal; **commerce des céréales,** corn, grain, trade.

céréalier, -ière [serealje, -jɛr] **1.** *a.* cereal (production, etc.). **2.** *n.* cereal grower.

cérébelleux, -euse [serebɛllø, -øz] *a. Anat:* cerebellar (artery, etc.).

cérébral, -ale, -aux [serebral, -o] **1.** *a.* (*a*) cerebral (artery, etc.); (*b*) **travail c.,** intellectual work; **surmenage c.,** mental exhaustion. **2.** *n.* intellectual, thinker.

cérébro-cardiaque [serebrɔkardjak] *a. Med:* cerebro-cardiac (neuropathy, etc.); *pl. cerebro-cardiaques.*

cérébro-spinal [serebrɔspinal] *a. Anat: Med:* cerebro-spinal; *pl. cérébro-spinaux.*

cérémonial, -als [seremɔnjal] **1.** *a. A:* ceremonial. **2.** *n.m.* ceremonial; **c. de la cour,** court etiquette.

cérémonie [seremɔni] *n.f.* ceremony; **faire une visite de c.,** to pay a ceremonial, formal, call (**à,** on); **tenue, habit, de c.,** dress suit; *Mil:* **uniforme de c.,** (full) dress uniform; **sans c.,** without ceremony; **faire des cérémonies,** to stand on ceremony, make a fuss; **sans plus de c.,** without (any) more ado; **maître de c.,** master of ceremonies.

cérémonieusement [seremɔnjøzmɑ̃] *adv.* ceremoniously; formally.

cérémonieux, -ieuse [seremɔnjø, -jøz] *a.* ceremonious, formal.

Cérès [serɛs] *Pr.n.f. Myth:* Ceres.

cerf [sɛr] *n.m.* (*a*) *Z:* stag, hart; **c. commun,** (red) deer; (*b*) *Cu:* venison.

cerfeuil [sɛrfœj] *n.m. Bot:* chervil.

cerf-volant [sɛrvɔlɑ̃] *n.m.* **1.** *Ent:* stag beetle. **2.** kite; *pl. cerfs-volants.*

cerisaie [s(ə)rizɛ] *n.f.* cherry orchard.

cerise [s(ə)riz] **1.** *n.f.* cherry. **2.** *n.m.* &. *a.inv.* cherry-red; cerise.

cerisier [s(ə)rizje] *n.m.* (*a*) cherry tree; (*b*) cherry-wood.

cérium [serjɔm] *n.m. Ch:* cerium.

cerne [sɛrn] *n.m.* **1.** ring, circle (round moon, etc.); ring, (dark) shadow (round eyes). **2.** age ring (of tree).

cerneau, -eaux [sɛrno] *n.m.* green walnut.

cernement [sɛrnəmɑ̃] *n.m.* **1.** surrounding, encircling (of army); investing (of town, etc.). **2.** *For:* girdling, ringing (of tree).

cerner [sɛrne] *v.tr.* **1.** (*a*) to encircle, surround (army, etc.); to invest (town); **avoir les yeux cernés,** to have rings, (dark) shadows, round one's eyes; (*b*) to grasp, determine (argument, etc.). **2.** to shell, husk (walnuts). **3.** *For:* (*a*) to dig round (tree); (*b*) to girdle, ring (tree).

céroplastique [serɔplastik] *n.f.* ceroplastics, wax modelling.

certain, -aine [sɛrtɛ̃, -ɛn] **1.** *a.* (*a*) certain, sure, unquestionable (proof, news, etc.); **il est c. qu'il viendra,** it's certain, definite, that he'll come; he'll definitely come; **tenir qch. pour c., pour chose certaine,** to look on sth. as a certainty; *F:* **c'est sûr et c.,** it's absolutely certain; (*b*) **il est c. de réussir,** he's sure, certain, to succeed; **j'en suis c.,** I'm sure, certain, of it; **moi, je n'en suis pas bien c.,** I'm not so sure myself; I'm not entirely convinced; (*c*) fixed, stated (date, price, etc.). **2.** *indef. a. & pron.* (*a*) some, certain; **certains, (de) certaines gens, affirment que . . .,** some (people) maintain that . . .; **après un c. temps,** after a certain time; **jusqu'à un c. point,** up to a point; **d'un c. âge,** middle-aged; elderly; **dans un c. sens,** in a sense, in a way; (*b*) *often Pej:* **un c. M. Martin,** a certain Mr Martin.

certainement [sɛrtɛnmɑ̃] *adv.* certainly, undoubtedly; **il réussira c.,** he is sure to succeed; **vous l'avez c. lu,** I'm sure you've read it; **c.!** of course! by all means!

certes [sɛrt] *adv* (*a*) *O:* most certainly; **oui c.!** yes indeed! (*b*) (*indicating a concession*) **c. je n'irais pas jusqu'à dire que . . .,** I really wouldn't go as far as to say that . . ..

certificat [sɛrtifika] *n.m.* certificate; **c. de bonne vie et mœurs,** certificate of good character; **montrer ses certificats,** to show one's testimonials, references; **c. de chargement,** certificate of receipt; **c. de navigabilité,** certificate of (i) seaworthiness, (ii) airworthiness; **c. d'origine,** (i) *Com:* certificate of origin; (ii) pedigree (of dog, etc.); *Fin:* **c. provisoire,** share certificate, (provisional) scrip; *Cust:* **c. d'entrepôt,** warrant; *Sch: A:* **c. de licence, d'études supérieures,** (i) each of the four examinations for the *licence*; (ii) certificate so obtained; **c. d'aptitude professionnelle,** certificate of education for those who have received vocational training; **c. d'aptitude pédagogique à l'enseignement secondaire** (C.A.P.E.S.) = (postgraduate) diploma of education; *A:* **c. d'études (primaires),** certificate given after an examination at the end of an elementary course of studies.

certificateur [sɛrtifikatœr] *n.m.* certifier, guarantor.

certification [sɛrtifikasjɔ̃] *n.f. Jur: Com:* certification, authentication; **c. d'une signature,** witnessing of a signature.

certifié, -ée [sɛrtifje] *a. & n. Sch:* **(professeur) c.** = qualified (graduate) teacher.

certifier [sɛrtifje] *v.tr.* (*pr. sub. & p.d.* **n. certifiions, v. certifiiez)** to certify, attest, assure; **c. qch. à qn,** to assure s.o. of sth.; **c. une signature,** to witness, authenticate, a signature; *Jur:* **copie certifiée,** attested, certified, copy; **c. une caution,** to guarantee a surety.

certitude [sɛrtityd] *n.f.* certainty, certitude; **j'en ai la c.,** I'm sure of it; **dire qch. avec c.,** to speak with assurance.

cérumen [serymɛn] *n.m. Physiol:* cerumen, earwax.

céruse [seryz] *n.f.* (*a*) white lead; (*b*) *Th: etc:* ceruse (for making up).

cerveau, -eaux [sɛrvo] *n.m.* (*a*) brain; *Anat:* **c. antérieur** = forebrain; **c. moyen** = midbrain; **c. postérieur** = hindbrain; **rhume de c.,** cold in the head, head cold; **vin qui monte au c.,** heady wine; (*b*) mind, intellect, brains; **homme à c. étroit, vide,** shallow-brained, emptyheaded, man; *F:* **avoir le c. dérangé, fêlé,** to be mad, cracked, nuts; (*c*) intellectual; brain; mastermind (of a plan, etc.); **c. brûlé,** hothead; (*d*) **c. électronique,** electronic brain.

cervelas [sɛrvəla] *n.m. Comest:* saveloy.

cervelet [sɛrvəlɛ] *n.m. Anat:* cerebellum.

cervelle [sɛrvɛl] *n.f.* (*a*) *Anat:* brain (as matter); **brûler, faire sauter, la c. à qn,** to blow s.o.'s brains out; *Cu:* **c. de veau,** calves' brains; (*b*) mind, intellect, brains; **se creuser la c.,** to rack one's brains; **vous me rompez la c.,** you're giving me a headache, getting on my nerves (with that noise); *F:* **idée qui me trotte dans la c.,** idea running through my head; (*of pers.*) **sans c.,** brainless, dimwitted; **elle a une c. de moineau,** she's completely feather-brained, scatter-brained, empty-headed.

cervical, -aux [sɛrvikal, -o] *a. Anat:* cervical.

cervidés [sɛrvide] *n.m.pl. Z:* Cervidae, deer family.

cervin [sɛrvɛ̃] *Pr.n.m. Geog:* **le Mont C.,** the Matterhorn.

cervoise [sɛrvwaz] *n.f. A:* barley beer.

ces *see* CE².

César [sezar] *Pr.n.m.* Caesar; **Jules C.,** Julius Caesar.

césarien, -enne [sezarjɛ̃, -jɛn] **1.** *a. Hist:* Caesarean, Caesarian. **2.** *a.f. & n.f. Obst:* **(opération) césarienne,** Caesarean (section).
césium [sezjɔm] *n.m. Ch:* caesium.
cessant [sɛsɑ̃] *a.* **toute(s) affaire(s) cessante(s),** immediately.
cessation [sɛsasjɔ̃] *n.f.* cessation, ceasing, discontinuance, termination, stoppage; **c. des hostilités, de paiements,** suspension of hostilities, of payments.
cesse [sɛs] *n.f.* **sans c.,** unceasingly; constantly, incessantly, continually; without stopping; **elle parle sans c.,** she never stops talking; **il n'aura (pas) de c. qu'il n'ait réussi,** he won't stop, rest, until he's succeeded.
cesser [sese] *v.* to cease, leave off, stop. **1.** *v.i.* **faire c. qch.,** to put a stop to sth.; **c. de faire qch.,** to stop, doing sth; **c. de fumer,** to give up smoking; **il n'a pas cessé de nous observer,** he's been watching us all this time. **2.** *v.tr.* **c. le travail,** to stop, leave off, work; **c. les affaires,** to give up business; **c. toutes relations avec qn,** to break off all relations with s.o.; **c. les paiements,** to stop, suspend, discontinue, payment(s); *Mil:* **cessez le feu!** cease fire!
cessez-le-feu [seselfø] *n.m.inv.* ceasefire.
cessible [sesibl̥] *a. Jur:* transferable, assignable; (*of pension, etc.*) negotiable.
cession [sɛsjɔ̃] *n.f. Jur:* transfer, assignment; **faire c. de qch. à qn,** to transfer, assign, surrender, sth. to s.o.
cessionnaire [sɛsjɔnɛr] *n.m.* (*a*) *Com:* transferee, assignee; holder (of bill); *Jur:* assignee, cessionary; (*b*) endorser (of cheque).
c'est-à-dire [sɛtadir] *conj.phr.* **1.** that is (to say); i.e., in other words. **2. c.-à-d. que** + *ind.*, the fact, the thing, is that . . .; indeed . . .; **vous l'avez prévenu?—c.-à-d. que non,** you let him know?—well, no, well, actually, I'm afraid I didn't.
césure [sezyr] *n.f. Pros:* caesura.
cet *see* CE².
cétacé [setase] *Z: a. & n.m.* cetacean.
cette *see* CE².
ceux *see* CELUI.
cévenol, -ole [sevnɔl] *a. & n. Geog:* (nature, inhabitant) of the Cévennes (region).
Ceylan [selɑ̃] *Pr.n.m. Geog:* Ceylon.
chabot [ʃabo] *n.m. Ich:* (*a*) bullhead, lasher; (*b*) chub, miller's thumb.
chacal [ʃakal] *n.m. Z:* jackal; *pl. chacals.*
chacon(n)e [ʃakɔn] *n.f. Mus:* chaconne.
chacun, -une [ʃakœ̃, -yn] *indef.pron.* **1.** each (one), every one; **chacune d'elles a refusé,** each (one), every one, of them refused; **trois francs c.,** three francs each; **ils ont pris c. son, leur, chapeau,** each of them took his hat; **nous avons pris c. notre chapeau,** each of us took his hat; **ils sont partis c. de son côté, c. de leur côté,** they (all) went their separate ways. **2.** everybody, everyone; **c. pour soi,** every man for himself; **c. son goût,** every man to his taste; **c. son tour,** each in turn; *F:* **tout un c.,** all and sundry; every Tom, Dick and Harry.
chafouin, -ine [ʃafwɛ̃, -in] *a.* foxy-looking, sly-looking (person).
chagrin¹ [ʃagrɛ̃] **1.** *a.* (*a*) *A:* sad, downcast; troubled, distressed; (*b*) *Lit:* morose, peevish. **2.** *n.m.* (*a*) grief, sorrow, affliction, trouble; **avoir du c.,** to be sorrowful, grieved; **faire du c. à qn,** to grieve, distress, s.o.; **usé par le c.,** careworn; **mourir de c.,** to die of a broken heart; (*b*) *A:* vexation, chagrin, peevishness.
chagrin² *n.m.* shagreen, grain (leather).
chagrinant [ʃagrinɑ̃] *a.* distressing, sad; annoying, vexing.
chagriner¹ [ʃagrine] *v.tr.* **1.** to grieve, distress, afflict; **cela me chagrine lorsque je vois que . . .,** I feel aggrieved when I see that . . ., (*b*) *A:* to vex, annoy. **2. se c.,** to grieve; to fret.
chagriner² *v.tr.* to shagreen, grain (leather); **papier chagriné,** pebbled, granulated, paper.
chah [ʃa] *n.m.* shah.
chahut [ʃay] *n.m. F:* noise, din; **faire du c.,** to make, kick up, a din, a racket, a rumpus; to create an uproar.
chahuter [ʃayte] *F:* **1.** *v.i.* to make, kick up, a din, a racket, a rumpus; to create an uproar. **2.** *v.tr.* (*a*) to knock (things) about, send (things) flying; (*b*) to rag (schoolmaster, etc.); (*c*) to boo (play, speaker, etc.); to heckle, barrack (speaker).
chahuteur, -euse [ʃaytœr, -øz] *F:* (*a*) *a.* rowdy, disorderly (student, etc.); (*b*) *n.* rowdy, ragger, heckler.
chai [ʃɛ] *n.m.* wine and spirits store(house).
chaînage [ʃɛnaʒ], *n.m.* **1.** *Surv:* chaining, chain measuring. **2.** *Const:* (*a*) tying, clamping (of walls); (*b*) tie irons, (series of) clamps, ties.
chaîne [ʃɛn] *n.f.* **1** (*a*) chain (of iron, gold, etc.); **c. de montre,** watch chain; **c. de sûreté,** door chain, safety chain; **c. de bicyclette,** bicyle chain; *Aut:* **chaînes à neige,** snow chains; (*b*) chains, shackles, fetters, bonds; **mettre un chien à la c.,** to chain up a dog; **briser sa c., ses chaînes,** to burst one's fetters, one's chains; to escape from bondage; (*c*) *Surv:* **c. d'arpenteur,** surveying chain, surveyor's chain; (*d*) *Nau:* cable; **tour de c.,** foul cable; **les chaînes,** the hawse; **le navire a cassé sa chaîne,** the ship has parted her cable; **c. de port,** harbour (chain) boom; (*e*) (*of pers.*) **faire la c.,** to form a chain (in order to pass buckets, etc.) **c. de montage,** assembly line; **c. de fabrication,** production line; **travail à la c.,** assembly line, production line, work. **2.** chain, succession, sequence, series; (*a*) **c. de montagnes,** range, chain, of mountains; **c. de chalands,** string of barges; **c. d'idées,** train of thought; **c. du commandement,** chain of command; **c. de combat,** firing line; (*b*) chain (of hotels, etc.); (*c*) chain letter. **3.** *Const:* **c. de liaison,** stone pier (in brickwork); brick pier (in rubble work). **4.** *Ch: Elcs: etc:* chain; (hi-fi) system; *W.Tel: T.V:* network; station; *T.V:* channel. **5.** *Tex:* warp.
chaîner [ʃɛne] *v.tr.* **1.** *Surv:* to chain, to measure (land) with a chain. **2.** *Const:* to chain, tie (walls, etc.).
chaînette [ʃɛnɛt] *n.f.* **1.** small chain; *Cy: etc:* **c. antivol,** chain lock. **2.** *Mth:* **(arc en) c.,** catenary (curve). **3.** *Needlew:* **point de c.,** chainstitch.
chaînon [ʃɛnɔ̃] *n.m.* (*a*) link (of chain); (*b*) *Geog:* secondary chain (of mountains).
chair [ʃɛr] *n.f.* flesh. **1. c. vive,** raw flesh; **en c. et en os,** in the flesh, in person; **être (bien) en c.,** (i) (*of chicken*) to be nice and plump; (ii) (*of pers.*) to be plump, *F:* tubby; **c. à canon,** cannon fodder. **2.** (*a*) *A:* meat (as opposed to fish); **n'être ni c. ni poisson,** to be neither fish nor fowl (nor good red herring); (*b*) **c. (à saucisse),** sausagemeat; (*c*) flesh, pulp (of peach, melon, etc.). **3.** (*a*) skin, outer surface of flesh; **avoir la c. fraîche,** to have a rosy complexion; **c. de poule,** gooseflesh, goose pimples; *U.S:* goose bumps; **cela vous donne, on en a, la c. de poule,** it makes your flesh creep; it makes you shudder; *F:* it gives you the creeps; *a.inv.* **(couleur) c.,** flesh-coloured; (*b*) *pl. Art:* flesh parts; *Paint:* flesh tints. **4.** body; **la résurrection de la c.,** the resurrection of the body; *B:* **le Verbe s'est fait c.,** the Word was made flesh; **c. de sa c.,** his, her, own flesh and blood.
chaire [ʃɛr] *n.f.* **1.** chair, throne; **la c. de saint Pierre, la c. pontificale,** the Chair of St. Peter, the Holy See; **c. d'un évêque,** bishop's throne. **2.** pulpit; **monter en**

c., to go into the pulpit. **3.** (*a*) chair, desk, rostrum (of lecturer); (*b*) *Sch:* chair, professorship; **il a été nommé à la c. d'anglais,** he has been appointed to the chair of English.

chaise [ʃɛz] *n.f.* **1.** (*a*) chair, seat; **c. de paille, c. cannée,** straw-, came-bottomed chair; **c. haute, c. d'enfant,** (baby's) high chair; **c. longue,** (i) chaise longue, couch; (ii) deckchair; **faire de la c. longue,** to have a rest, put one's feet up; **c. à bascule,** *Fr.C:* **c. berçante,** rocking chair; **être assis entre deux chaises,** to be in an awkward position; to fall between two stools; **porter qn en c., faire la c. à qn,** to make a chair (with one's arms); to give s.o. a chair; (*b*) **c. roulante,** wheelchair, bath chair; **c. percée,** (night) commode; (*c*) *Jur: U.S:* **c. électrique,** electric chair. **2.** *A:* **c. à porteurs,** sedan chair; **c. de poste.,** post chaise. **3.** *Const:* frame, timberwork (of windmill, etc.). **4.** support, bracket; **c. de coussinet,** plummer block; *Rail:* **c. de rail,** (rail) chair; *N.Arch:* **c. d'hélice,** "A" bracket. **5.** *Nau: etc:* rope sling; **nœud de c.,** bowline hitch.

chaisier, -ière [ʃɛzje, -jɛr] **1.** *n.* chairmaker. **2.** chair attendant (in park, etc.).

chaland[1] [ʃalɑ̃] *n.m.* barge, lighter; **transport par chalands,** lighterage.

chaland[2], -ande [ʃalɑ̃, -ɑ̃d] *n. A:* customer.

chalcédoine [kalsedwan] *n.f. Miner:* chalcedony.

chaldaïque [kaldaik] *a. & n.* = CHALDÉEN.

Chaldée [kalde] *Pr.n.f. A.Geog:* Chaldea.

chaldéen, -enne [kaldeɛ̃, -ɛn] *a. & n.* Chaldean.

châle [ʃɑl] *n.m.* shawl.

chalet [ʃalɛ] *n.m.* **1.** (*a*) (Swiss, etc.) chalet; (*b*) country cottage. **2.** *A:* **c. de nécessité,** public convenience.

chaleur [ʃalœr] *n.f.* **1.** (*a*) heat, warmth; **il fait une grande c.,** it's very hot; **vague de c.,** heatwave; **c. étouffante,** sultry weather; (*on label*) **craint la c.,** store in a cool place; *Ph:* **c. spécifique, c. latente,** specific, latent, heat; *Med:* **éprouver des chaleurs,** to flush, have hot flushes; **sensation de c.,** (i) glow (after cold bath, etc.); (ii) burning sensation; *Med:* **coup de c.,** heatstroke; (*b*) **les chaleurs,** the hot weather; **dans les grandes chaleurs,** during the hot season; (*c*) *Art:* **c. de coloris,** warmth of colour; (*d*) ardour, zeal; **dans la c. du combat,** in the heat of the battle; **parler avec c.,** to speak warmly, enthusiastically. **2.** heat, rut (of animals); **en c.,** on heat, *esp. NAm:* in heat.

chaleureusement [ʃalørøzmɑ̃] *adv.* warmly.

chaleureux, -euse [ʃalørø, -øz] *a.* warm (thanks, etc.); cordial, hearty (welcome, etc.); glowing (colour, terms); enthusiastic (applause, etc.); **remercier qn en termes c.,** to thank s.o. warmly.

châlit [ʃɑli] *n.m.* bedstead.

challenge [ʃalɑ̃ʒ] *n.m. Sp:* challenge match, tournament.

challenger [ʃalɑ̃ʒɛr] *n.m. Sp: etc:* challenger.

chaloir [ʃalwar] *v.impers. A: & Lit: used only in* **peu me chaut, peu m'en chaut,** I don't care (a rap); I care not.

chaloupe [ʃalup] *n.f. Nau:* launch, longboat; *Fr.C:* rowing boat, *NAm:* rowboat; **c. à moteur,** motor launch.

chaloupé [ʃalupe] *a.* swaying, swinging, rocking (dance, walk).

chalumeau, -eaux [ʃalymo] *n.m.* **1.** (drinking) straw; **c. de roseau,** reed. **2.** *Mus:* pipe. **3.** blowlamp, blowtorch; **c. oxyacétylénique,** oxyacetylene torch. **4.** *Fr.C:* spout (for collecting sap of maple tree).

chalut [ʃaly] *n.m. Fish:* trawl; **pêcher au c.,** to trawl.

chalutage [ʃalytaʒ] *n.m. Fish:* trawling.

chalutier [ʃalytje] (*a*) (*boat*) trawler; (*b*) trawler(man).

chamade [ʃamad] *n.f.* **battre la c.,** to be in a panic; **mon cœur battait la c.,** my heart was thumping, beating wildly.

chamaille [ʃamɑj] *n.f. F:* squabble, row, quarrel.

chamailler (se) [səʃamaje] *v.pr. F:* to bicker, squabble, quarrel.

chamaillerie [ʃamɑjəri] *n.f. F:* **1.** bickering, quarrelling, squabbling. **2.** squabble, row, quarrel.

chamailleur, -euse [ʃamɑjœr, -øz] *a. & n.* quarrelsome (person).

chamarrer [ʃamare] *v.tr. Lit:* to bedizen, bedeck, adorn.

chambard [ʃɑ̃bar] *n.m. F:* (*a*) disorder, shambles; upset, upheaval; (*b*) din, racket; **faire du c.,** to make, kick up, a row, a shindy.

chambardement [ʃɑ̃bardəmɑ̃] *n.m. F:* upset, upheaval; general reshuffle.

chambarder [ʃɑ̃barde] *v.tr. F:* (*a*) to upset, ransack (room, etc.); **tout c.,** to turn everything upside down; **c. les plans de qn,** to upset s.o.'s applecart; (*b*) to rearrange, reorganize.

chambellan [ʃɑ̃belɑ̃] *n.m.* chamberlain.

chambouler [ʃɑ̃bule] *v.tr. F:* to ruin, mess up (plans, etc.); **tout c.,** to turn everything topsy-turvey, upside down.

chambranle [ʃɑ̃brɑ̃l] *n.m.* frame casing (of door, window); (standing) window frame; mantelpiece.

chambre [ʃɑ̃br̥] *n.f.* **1.** (*a*) bedroom; **c. à coucher,** (i) bedroom; (ii) bedroom suite; **c. à grand lit, à deux (personnes),** double room; **c. à deux lits,** room with twin beds; twin-bedded room; **c. à un lit,** single room; **c. d'amis,** spare (bed)room, guest room; **c. d'enfants,** nursery; **c. meublée,** furnished room, bed-sitting-room, *F:* bed-sit(ter); **faire c. à part,** to sleep in separate rooms; **faire sa c.,** to clean (out), tidy (up), one's room; **c. forte,** safety vault, strong room; **c. froide, frigorifique,** cold (storage) room, cold store; **travailler en c.,** to work at home; **ouvrier en c.,** homeworker; **stratège en c.,** armchair strategist; **musique de c.,** chamber music; (*b*) *Nau:* **c. des cartes,** charthouse, chart room; (*c*) *Navy:* cabin; (*d*) **c. des machines,** engine room; **c. de chauffe,** boiler room, *Nau:* stokehold; (*e*) **c. à gaz,** gas chamber. **2.** *Adm: Jur:* chamber, house; division of a court of justice; **c. de commerce,** chamber of commerce; **c. des députés,** Chamber of Deputies; **C. basse,** Lower House, Lower Chamber; **C. haute,** Upper House, Upper Chamber; *Fin:* **c. de compensation,** clearing house. **3.** *Tchn:* chamber (of gun, lock, etc.); cavity, space; *Physiol:* chamber (of the eye); *Aut: Cy:* **c. à air,** inner tube (of tyre); **pneu sans c.,** tubeless tyre; *I.C.E: Mec.E:* **c. de combustion, d'explosion,** combustion chamber; **c. à bulles,** bubble chamber; *Phot:* **c. noire,** (i) camera obscura; (ii) camera (body); (iii) darkroom.

chambrée [ʃɑ̃bre] *n.f.* **1.** room(ful) (of people sharing a room). **2.** *Mil:* barrackroom.

chambrer [ʃɑ̃bre] *v.tr.* (*a*) to confine, lock up (s.o.); to keep (s.o.) locked up; (*b*) to bring (wine) to room temperature.

chambrette [ʃɑ̃brɛt] *n.f.* little (bed)room.

chambrière [ʃɑ̃brijɛr] *n.f.* **1.** *A:* chambermaid. **2.** long whip, lunging whip. **3.** (cart)prop.

chameau, -eaux [ʃamo] *n.m.* **1.** (*a*) camel; (*b*) *F: a. & n.* **quel c.! ce qu'il, ce qu'elle, est c.!** (*of man*) what a beast, brute! (*of woman*) what a cow, bitch! **2.** *Nau:* camel (for raising ships).

chamelier [ʃaməlje], *n.m.* camel-driver, cameleer.

chamelle [ʃamɛl] *n.f.* she-camel.

chamois [ʃamwa]. **1.** *n.m. Z:* chamois; **(peau de) c.,** washleather, chamois leather, shammy (leather). **2.** *a. inv.* buff(-coloured).

champ [ʃɑ̃] *n.m.* field. **1.** (*a*) **c. de blé,** field of corn, of wheat, cornfield; **fleur des champs,** wild flower;

courir les champs, to wander about the country; **aux champs,** in the fields; **aller aux champs,** to go into the country; **prendre, couper, à travers champs,** to go, cut, across country; **donner la clef des champs à qn,** to give s.o. his liberty; **prendre la clef des champs,** to decamp, run off; **en plein(s) champ(s),** in the open (fields); **à tout bout de c.,** repeatedly; at every, any, moment; (*b*) **c. de foire,** fairground; **c. d'aviation,** airfield; **c. de courses,** racecourse, *NAm:* racetrack; **parier contre le c.,** to lay against the field; **c. de neige,** snowfield; **c. de glace,** icefield; (*c*) *Mil:* **c. de bataille,** battlefield; **c. d'honneur,** battlefield; field of honour; **mort au c. d'honneur,** killed in action; **c. de manœuvres,** drill, exercise, parade, ground; **c. de tir,** (i) firing, shooting, rifle, range; *Artil:* practice ground; (ii) field of fire (of gun); **c. de mines,** minefield; (*d*) *A:* **c. clos,** lists; *Fig:* battlefield. **2.** (*a*) field of action; sphere, range, scope; **prendre du c. (pour sauter, etc.),** to give oneself (plenty of) room (to jump, etc.); **donnez-moi du c.,** give me (some) elbow room; **laisser le c. libre à qn,** to leave s.o. a clear field; *F:* **le c. est libre,** the coast's clear; **ses lectures embrassent un c. très étendu,** his reading covers a very wide range of subjects; **élargir le c. de son activité,** to extend the scope of one's activities; (*b*) *Cin: etc:* shot, picture; *Opt:* field (of telescope, etc.); **c. optique, c. visuel, c. de vision,** field of view, of vision; *Phot:* **profondeur de c.,** depth of focus; **hors c.,** off camera. **3.** *El: Elcs: Rad:* field; **c. magnétique,** magnetic field. **4.** (*a*) *Her:* field (of coat of arms); (*b*) *Art:* field, ground (of picture); (*c*) *Surg:* **c. opératoire,** operative field.

Champagne [ʃɑ̃paɲ] **1.** *Pr.n.f. Geog:* Champagne; **C. humide,** wet Champagne; **c. pouilleuse,** dry Champagne. **2.** *n.m.* (*also* **vin de C.**) champagne. **3.** *n.f.* **fine c.,** liqueur brandy.

champagnisation [ʃɑ̃paɲizasjɔ̃] *n.f. Wine-m:* champagnization.

champagniser [ʃɑ̃paɲize] *v.tr.* to champagnize (wine).

champenois, -oise [ʃɑ̃pənwa, -waz] **1.** *a. & n.* (native, inhabitant) of Champagne. **2.** *a. Wine-m:* **méthode champenoise,** (natural) champagnization method; champagne method.

champêtre [ʃɑ̃pɛtr̥] *a.* rustic, rural; **vie c.,** country life; **garde c.,** country, village, policeman.

champignon [ʃɑ̃piɲɔ̃] *n.m.* **1.** (*a*) **c. (comestible),** mushroom; edible fungus; **c. vénéneux,** poisonous fungus; **c. de couche, de Paris,** cultivated mushroom, button mushroom; **blanc de c.,** mushroom spawn; **pousser comme un c.,** to (spring up like a) mushroom; **ville c.,** mushroom town, boom town; **c. atomique,** mushroom cloud; (*b*) *Med:* fungoid growth. **2.** (*a*) **c. de modiste,** milliner's hatstand; (*b*) cowl (of chimney); (*c*) *Rail:* head (of rail); (*d*) *Aut: F:* accelerator (pedal); **appuyer sur le c.,** to put one's foot down, step on the gas.

champignonnière [ʃɑ̃piɲɔnjɛr] *n.f.* mushroom bed.

champignonniste [ʃɑ̃piɲɔnist] *n.m.* mushroom grower.

champion, -ionne [ʃɑ̃pjɔ̃, -jɔn]. **1.** *n.* (*a*) *Sp: etc:* champion; (*b*) champion, defender (of a cause, etc.). **2.** *a. F:* great, champion; **c'est c.!** it's first-rate!

championnat [ʃɑ̃pjɔna] *n.m.* championship.

chançard, -arde [ʃɑ̃sar, -ard] *a. & n. F:* lucky (man, woman); **quel c.!** he's a lucky devil!

chance [ʃɑ̃s] *n.f.* **1.** chance, likelihood; **vous avez toutes les chances d'être accusé, il y a toutes les chances (pour) que vous soyez accusé,** there is every chance, every likelihood, that you will be accused; **donner une c. à qn,** to give s.o. a chance; **il a peu de chances de réussir, de succès,** he has little chance of succeeding; he's very unlikely to succeed; **il a des chances égales d'être nommé,** he has an even, a fifty-fifty, chance of being appointed; **il a des chances d'être choisi,** he stands a good chance of being chosen; **il y a une c.,** it's just possible; **il y a une c. sur cent (pour) qu'elle le voie,** it's a hundred to one against her seeing him. **2.** (good) luck, fortune; **la c. lui sourit,** fortune smiles on him; **tenter la c.,** to try one's luck, to chance it; **souhaiter bonne c. à qn,** to wish s.o. luck; **bonne c.!** good luck! **quelle c.!** what a bit, stroke, of luck! what a blessing! **avoir de la c.,** to be lucky, fortunate; **il n'a pas eu de c.,** he was unlucky; **porter c. à qn,** to bring s.o. luck; **c'est bien ma c.!** just my luck! **pas de c.!** hard luck! **par c.,** luckily, fortunately, by a stroke of luck.

chancelant [ʃɑ̃slɑ̃] *a.* staggering, wavering, unsteady; **pas chancelants,** staggering, tottering, unsteady, footsteps; **santé chancelante,** (i) delicate, poor, health; (ii) delicate constitution.

chanceler [ʃɑ̃sle] *v.i.* **(je chancelle, n. chancelons; je chancellerai)** to stagger, totter, wobble; to be unsteady (on one's legs); **avancer, reculer, entrer, sortir, en chancelant,** to stagger, totter, forward, back, in, out; **trône qui chancelle,** tottering throne; **c. dans sa résolution,** to waver, falter, in one's resolution.

chancelier [ʃɑ̃səlje] *n.m.* chancellor; (*in Britain*) **Grand C.,** Lord Chancellor; **C. de l'Échiquier,** Chancellor of the Exchequer.

chancelière [ʃɑ̃səljɛr] *n.f.* **1.** chancellor's wife. **2.** footmuff.

chancellerie [ʃɑ̃sɛlri] *n.f.* **1.** chancellery. **2.** chancery (of an embassy).

chanceux, -euse [ʃɑ̃sø, -øz] *a.* **1.** *A:* hazardous, chancy. **2.** lucky, fortunate; **vous voilà bien c.!** you're lucky! you're in luck!

chancir [ʃɑ̃sir] *v.i. & pr.* to go mouldy.

chancre [ʃɑ̃kr̥] *n.m. Bot: Med: Vet:* canker; *Med:* **c. syphilitique, mou,** soft chancre; *P:* **manger comme un c.,** to eat like a horse, to make a pig of oneself.

chandail [ʃɑ̃daj] *n.m. Cost:* jumper, sweater, pullover.

Chandeleur (la) [laʃɑ̃dlœr] *n.f. Ecc:* Candlemas.

chandelier, -ière [ʃɑ̃dəlje, -jɛr] *n.* **1.** tallow chandler; candlemaker. **2.** *n.m.* candlestick; candelabra.

chandelle [ʃɑ̃dɛl] *n.f.* **1.** (*a*) (tallow) candle; **économies de bouts de c.,** cheeseparing economy; **travailler à la c.,** to work by candlelight; **brûler la c. par les deux bouts,** to be extravagant (with money); to burn the candle at both ends; **le jeu n'en vaut pas la c.,** the game is not worth the candle; **tenir la c.,** to act as go-between in a love affair; **en voir trente-six chandelles,** to see stars; (*b*) (church) candle, taper; **je vous dois une fière c.,** I owe you more than I can repay. **2.** (*a*) icicle; (*b*) *P:* dewdrop, snot (at the end of the nose). **3.** (*a*) **c. romaine,** Roman candle; (*of aircraft*) **monter en c.,** to climb vertically, to rocket; *Av:* **(montée en) c.,** vertical climb, chandelle; (*b*) *Ten: Cr: etc:* lob; *Fb:* high kick; (*c*) *Gym:* shoulder stand. **4.** *Const: etc:* stay, prop, shore, pillar, upright.

chanfrein¹ [ʃɑ̃frɛ̃] *n.m.* nose, forehead (of horse).

chanfrein² *n.m.* chamfered edge, chamfer, bevelled edge.

change [ʃɑ̃ʒ] *n.m.* **1.** *A:* change. **2.** *Fin:* exchange; **gagner, ne pas perdre, au c.,** to gain on, by, the exchange; to lose nothing on the deal; **lettre de c.,** bill of exchange; **lettre de c. sur l'intérieur, sur l'extérieur,** inland, foreign, bill; **bureau de c.,** foreign exchange office; **opérations de c.,** (foreign) exchange transactions; **cours du c.,** exchange rate, rate of exchange; **au c. du jour,** at the current rate of exchange; **contrôle des changes,** exchange control. **3.** *Ven:* **donner le c. aux chiens,** to put hounds on the wrong scent;

donner le c. à qn, to put s.o. on a false scent, trail; to sidetrack s.o.

changeable [ʃɑ̃ʒabl̩] *a.* changeable, alterable.

changeant [ʃɑ̃ʒɑ̃] *a.* changing, altering; changeable, variable; **caractère changeant,** changeable, fickle, disposition; **d'humeur changeante,** fitful; **temps c.,** unsettled weather; **taffetas c.,** shot silk.

changement [ʃɑ̃ʒmɑ̃] *n.m.* change (of air, of residence, of condition, etc.); changing; alteration; *Sch:* **c. (de section, de classe),** transfer; **il vous faudrait un c. d'air, d'occupation,** you need a change; *P.N:* **c. de propriétaire,** under new management; **c. de marée,** turn of the tide; **c. de vent,** shift of wind; **c. en mal, en mieux,** change for the worse, for the better; **c. de vitesse,** (i) change of gear; gear change; (ii) change (-speed) gear; gear change; *Rail:* **c. de voie,** points, turn-off; *Th:* **c. à vue,** transformation scene.

changer [ʃɑ̃ʒe] *v.* **(je changeai(s); n. changeons) 1.** *v.tr.* to change; to exchange; **c. un billet de banque,** to change a (bank)note; **c. des dollars contre des francs,** to change dollars into francs; **c. des meubles contre des tableaux,** to exchange furniture for pictures; **c. les draps,** to change the sheets; *Th:* **c. le décor,** to shift, change, the scenery; **c. un bébé,** to change a baby's nappy, *NAm:* diaper; to change a baby. **2.** *v.tr.* (*a*) to change, alter; **c. sa manière de vivre,** to change one's way of life; **cette robe vous change,** that dress makes you look different; **voilà qui change les choses du tout au tout,** that makes all the difference; (*b*) **la campagne me changera,** the country will be a (good) change for me; it will be a change for me to stay in the country; **une promenade me changera les idées,** a walk will take my mind off things. **3.** *v.i.* (*a*) to (undergo a) change; to alter; **le temps va c.,** the weather's going to change; **il a changé en mal, en mieux,** he's changed for the worse, for the better; **c. de couleur,** to change colour; **c. de visage,** to change, alter, one's expression; *Iron:* **pour c.,** (just) for a change; (*b*) **c. de train,** to change (trains); **c. de main,** to change hands, use the other hand; **c. de mains,** to change hands, ownership; **c. de place avec qn,** to change seats with s.o.; **c. de places,** to changes places; **c. de maison,** to move (house); **la rue a changé de nom,** the name of the street has been changed; **le magasin a changé de propriétaire,** the shop is under new management; **c. de vêtements, se c.,** to change (one's clothes); to get changed; (*of snake*) **c. de peau,** to change, shed, slough, its skin; **c. d'avis,** to change one's mind, one's opinion; **c. de sujet,** to change the subject; **c. de route,** (i) to take another road; (ii) *Nau:* to alter course; **c. de vitesse,** to change gear; **la rivière a changé de cours,** the river has shifted its course; **c. de ton,** to change one's tune.

changeur, -euse [ʃɑ̃ʒœr, -øz] **1.** *n.* (*pers.*) money changer. **2.** *n.m. W.Tel:* **c. de fréquence,** frequency changer. **3.** *n.m. Rec:* **c. de disques,** record changer.

Changhai [ʃɑ̃gaj] *Pr.n.m. Geog:* Shanghai.

chanoine [ʃanwan] *n.m. Ecc:* canon; *F:* **vie de c.** easy life.

chanson [ʃɑ̃sɔ̃] *n.f.* **1.** song; **c. à boire,** drinking song; **c. de route,** marching song; **c. de marins,** sea shanty; **c. réaliste,** cabaret song, music hall song; *F:* **c'est toujours la même c.!** it's always the same old story; **voilà bien une autre c.!** that's quite another story! *A:* **chansons (que tout cela)!** nonsense! **2.** song, lay, verse chronicle; **la c. de Roland,** the Song of Roland.

chansonner [ʃɑ̃sɔne] *v.tr.* to write satirical songs about (s.o.); to lampoon (s.o.).

chansonnette [ʃɑ̃sɔnɛt] *n.f.* little song, ditty; comic song.

chansonnier [ʃɑ̃sɔnje] *n.m.* **1.** chansonnier (who sings in cabaret, in clubs). **2.** song book.

chant¹ [ʃɑ̃] *n.m.* **1.** singing, song; **leçon, maître, de c.,** singing lesson, master; **le c. des oiseaux,** the song of the birds; **c'était son c. du cygne,** it was his swan song; **c. du grillon,** chirping of the cricket; **c. du coq,** crowing of the cock; **au c. du coq,** at cockcrow. **2.** (*a*) song; **c. de victoire,** song of victory; **c. de guerre,** battle song, war song; **c. de Noël,** Christmas carol; (*b*) melody, air; (*c*) *Ecc:* **c. grégorien,** Gregorian chant; **c. funèbre,** dirge; (*d*) *Mus:* canto (in harmony). **3.** *Lit:* (*a*) song, lyric; (*b*) canto (of long poem).

chant² *n.m.* edge, side; **pierres (posées) de c., sur c.,** stones set on edge, edgewise.

chantage [ʃɑ̃taʒ] *n.m.* blackmail; extortion; **c. sentimental,** emotional blackmail; **faire du c.,** to blackmail.

chantant [ʃɑ̃tɑ̃] *a.* (*a*) musical (verse, etc.); **accent c.,** sing-song, lilting, accent; (*b*) melodious, tuneful; **air c.,** catchy tune; (*c*) **soirée chantante,** musical evening.

chanteau, -eaux [ʃɑ̃to] *n.m.* **1.** hunk (of bread). **2.** cutting (of cloth); *Tail:* gore.

chantepleure [ʃɑ̃tplœr] *n.f.* **1.** (*a*) wine funnel; *Ind:* colander; (*b*) long-spouted watering can, sprayer; (*c*) tap (of cask). **2.** (*a*) weephole (in wall); (*b*) spout (of gutter).

chanter [ʃɑ̃te] *v.* to sing **1.** *v.tr.* to sing (song, etc.); **c. qch. sur l'air de . . .,** to sing sth. to the tune of . . .; **c. victoire,** to exult; to crow; *Ecc:* **c. la messe,** to sing mass; **pain à c.,** (unconsecrated) host, wafer; **c. toujours la même chanson, la même antienne,** to be always harping on (the same string); *F:* **qu'est-ce que vous me chantez là?** what's this fairy tale you're telling me? *what* are you talking about? **2.** *v.i.* (*a*) (*of bird, pers., kettle*) to sing; (*of cock*) to crow; (*of cricket*) to chirp; (*of butter*) to sizzle; **il chante en parlant,** he's got a sing-song accent; *F:* **c'est comme si je chantais,** I'm wasting my breath; **faire c. qn,** to blackmail s.o.; **faire c. qn sur un autre ton,** to make s.o. sing another tune; (*b*) *F:* **est-ce que cela vous chante?** do you like the idea (of it)? does it appeal to you?

chanterelle¹ [ʃɑ̃trɛl] *n.f.* **1.** decoy (bird). **2.** *Mus:* first, highest, string (of violin, etc.); chanterelle; *F:* **appuyer sur la c.,** to hammer a point home, to rub it in.

chanterelle² *n.f. Fung:* chanterelle.

chanteur, -euse [ʃɑ̃tœr, -øz] (*a*) *n.* singer, vocalist; **c. des rues,** street singer; busker; **c. de charme,** crooner; **maître chanteur,** (i) *Mus.Hist:* mastersinger, meistersinger; (ii) blackmailer; (*b*) *a.* **oiseau c.,** songbird.

chantier [ʃɑ̃tje] *n.m.* **1.** gantry, stand (for barrels). **2.** (*a*) yard, depot, site; **c. (de construction),** (i) building site; (ii) builder's yard; (iii) road works; **c. de bois,** timberyard, lumberyard; **travailler au c., sur le c.,** to work on (the) site; **avoir une œuvre en c., sur le c.,** to have a piece of work in hand; **quel c.!** what a mess! what a shambles! *P.N:* **c.,** men at work, road works, road up; **fin de c.,** road clear; **c. interdit au public,** no admittance except on business; (*b*) *Min:* **c. d'exploitation,** working(s); (*c*) *Fr.C:* lumber camp; shanty. **3.** *Nau:* **c. naval, c. de construction navale,** shipyard; **c. de l'État,** naval (dock)yard; **vaisseau sur le c.,** vessel on the slips. **4.** *Rail:* **c. de voies de garage et de triage,** shunting yard.

chantonnement [ʃɑ̃tɔnmɑ̃] *n.m.* humming, singing softly; crooning.

chantonner [ʃɑ̃tɔne] *v.tr. & i.* to hum; to sing softly; to croon.

chantoung [ʃɑ̃tuɲ] *n.m. Tex:* shantung.

chantourner [ʃɑ̃turne] *v.tr.* to cut, saw (sth.) round a curved outline; to jigsaw; **scie à c.,** (i) (*hand*) bow saw, whipsaw, fretsaw; (ii) (*machine*) jigsaw, scroll saw.

chantre [ʃɑ̃tr̥] *n.m.* **1.** *Ecc:* cantor; chorister; **grand c.,** precentor. **2.** *Lit:* (*a*) poet; (*b*) songster; **les chantres des bois,** the woodland chorus.

chanvre [ʃɑ̃vr̥] *n.m.* hemp; **c. du Bengale,** Bengal hemp; **c. indien,** Indian hemp, hashish; **c. de Manille,** Manila hemp; **c. de la Nouvelle-Zélande,** New Zealand flax, flax lily; **cordage de, en, c.,** hemp(en) rope; **cravate de c.,** hangman's noose.

chanvrier, -ière [ʃɑ̃vrije, -jɛr] **1.** *a.* hemp (industry, etc.). **2.** *n.* hemp grower, worker.

chaos [kao] *n.m.* chaos; **tout est dans le c.,** everything is in a state of confusion, is chaotic.

chaotique [kaɔtik] *a.* chaotic, confused.

chapardage [ʃapardaʒ] *n.m. F:* theft, thieving, pinching, pilfering.

chaparder [ʃaparde] *v.tr. F:* to steal, pinch, pilfer.

chapardeur, -euse [ʃapardœr, -øz] *F:* **1.** *a.* thieving, pinching, pilfering. **2.** *n.* thief, pilferer.

chape [ʃap] *n.f.* **1.** *Ecc:* cope. **2.** covering; (*a*) *Aut: etc:* tread (of tyre); (*b*) coping (of bridge); (*c*) *Mec.E:* fork joint, yoke, clevis; **c. de cardan,** cardan fork; **chapes d'un moufle,** straps of a pulley block; (*d*) shell (of pulley).

chapeau, -eaux [ʃapo] *n.m.* **1.** hat; (*a*) **c. mou,** (soft) felt hat, trilby, *NAm:* fedora; **c. gibus, c. claque,** opera hat, crush hat; **c. de paille,** straw hat; **c. de soleil,** sunhat; **c. à cornes, de gendarme,** cocked hat; **c. de cardinal, le c. rouge,** cardinal's hat, the red hat; **ruban de c.,** hatband; **saluer qn d'un coup de c., donner un coup de c. à qn,** to raise one's hat to s.o.; **tirer son c. à qn,** to take off one's hat to s.o.; **c.!** bravo! well done! I take my hat off to you; **chapeaux bas!** hats off! **c. bas,** hat in hand; **faire passer le c.,** to pass the hat round; *P:* **il travaille du c.,** he's crazy, nutty; (*b*) *Bot:* pileus, cap (of mushroom); (*c*) *Orn:* cap (of bird); (*d*) *Mus:* **c. chinois,** jingling Johnnie. **2.** cover; (*a*) *Cu:* piecrust; lid, top (of vol-au-vent, etc.); (*b*) cap (of fountain pen, etc.); *Aut:* **c. de roue,** hub cap; *F:* **prendre un virage sur les chapeaux de roues,** to screech round a corner. **3.** *Typ: Journ:* introductory paragraph.

chapeauter [ʃapote] *v.tr.* (*a*) **elle était bien chapeautée,** she was wearing a lovely hat; (*b*) to be in charge (of); **il chapeaute les trois services,** he's in charge of the three departments.

chapelain [ʃaplɛ̃] *n.m. Ecc:* chaplain (attached to private chapel).

chapelet [ʃaplɛ] *n.m.* **1.** rosary; chaplet; **dire son c.,** tell one's beads; *F:* **défiler son c.,** to have one's say, speak one's mind; **c. d'invectives,** string of abuse; **c. de bombes,** stick of bombs; **c. de péniches, d'îles,** string of barges, of islands; **c. d'oignons,** string, rope, of onions; **réservoirs en c.,** reservoirs arranged in series. **2. pompe à c., c. hydraulique,** chain pump.

chapelier, -ière [ʃapəlje, -jɛr] **1.** *a.* hat(-making) (trade, etc.). **2.** *n.* hatter.

chapelle [ʃapɛl] *n.f.* **1.** (*a*) chapel (in private house, etc.); (side) chapel (of church); chapel of ease (of parish); **c. de la (Sainte) Vierge,** Lady Chapel; **c. ardente,** chapelle ardente; mortuary chapel; (*b*) *esp. Ecc:* choir and/or orchestra; **maître de c.,** choir master; (*c*) *Ecc:* ornaments and plate (for the celebration of mass); (*d*) *Lit: Art:* clique, coterie. **2.** *Const:* vault (of baking oven). **3.** *Mch:* **c. de pompe,** pump case; *I.C.E:* **soupapes en c.,** side valves.

chapellerie [ʃapɛlri] *n.f.* **1.** hat trade, hat industry. **2.** hatshop.

chapelure [ʃaplyr] *n.f. Cu:* breadcrumbs.

chaperon [ʃaprɔ̃] *n.m.* **1.** (*a*) *A:* hood; *Lit:* **le Petit C. rouge,** Little Red Riding Hood; (*b*) *Sch:* = (graduate's) hood. **2.** chaperon. **3.** (*a*) *Const:* coping (of wall); (*b*) protecting lid or cover.

chaperonner [ʃaprɔne] *v.tr.* **1.** to hood (falcon, etc.). **2.** to chaperon (young woman). **3.** *Const:* to cope (wall).

chapiteau, -eaux [ʃapito] *n.m.* **1.** (*a*) *Arch:* capital (of column); (*b*) cornice (of wardrobe, etc.). **2.** head (of still, rocket). **3.** big top (of circus).

chapitre [ʃapitr̥] *n.m.* **1.** *Ecc:* chapter (of canons); **salle du c.,** chapter house; **avoir voix au c.,** to have a say in the matter. **2.** (*a*) chapter (of book); (*b*) head(ing), item (of expenditure, etc.); **nous traiterons demain ce c.,** we will deal with this subject, matter, tomorrow; **elle est sévère sur le c. de la discipline,** she is strict as regards, in the matter of, discipline.

chapitrer [ʃapitre] *v.tr.* (*a*) *Ecc:* to rebuke in chapter; (*b*) *F:* to tell (s.o.) off, to tear (s.o.) off a strip.

chapon [ʃapɔ̃] *n.m. Cu:* capon.

chaque [ʃak] **1.** *a.* each, every; **c. chose à sa place,** everything in its place; **c. fois qu'il vient,** whenever, every time, he comes; *F:* **c. deux jours,** every other day. **2.** *pron. F:* (= CHACUN) **ces livres coûtent 100 francs c.,** these books cost 100 francs each.

char [ʃar] *n.m.* **1.** (*a*) chariot; (*b*) waggon; **c. à bœufs,** ox cart, bullock cart; **c. funèbre,** hearse; *A:* **c. à bancs,** (horse) charabanc; (*c*) **c. (de carnaval),** float; (*d*) *Lit:* **le c. de l'État,** the Ship of State; (*e*) *Fr.C:* car, *NAm:* automobile. **2.** *Mil:* **c. (de combat),** *O:* **c. d'assaut,** tank; **les chars,** the armour; **régiment de chars,** armoured, tank, regiment; *U.S:* tank battalion.

charabia [ʃarabja] *n.m. F:* jargon, gibberish, gobbledegook.

charade [ʃarad] *n.f.* charade.

charançon [ʃarɑ̃sɔ̃] *n.m. Ent:* weevil.

charançonné [ʃarɑ̃sɔne] *a.* weevil(l)ed, weevil(l)y.

charbon [ʃarbɔ̃] *n.m.* **1.** (*a*) **c. (de terre),** coal; **c. sans fumée,** smokeless fuel; (*b*) coal dust; **avoir un c. dans l'œil,** to have a bit of grit in one's eye; (*c*) **c. (de bois),** charcoal; **c. animal,** animal charcoal; **c. actif, activé,** active, activated, charcoal; **être sur des charbons ardents,** to be on tenterhooks; (*d*)*Draw:* charcoal (pencil, drawing); (*e*) *Ch:* carbon; **c. de cornue,** gas carbon; *El:* **balai de c.,** carbon brush. **2.** (*a*) *Agr:* smut, black rust (of cereal, etc.); (*b*) *Med: Vet:* anthrax.

charbonnage [ʃarbɔnaʒ] *n.m.* **1.** coal mining. **2.** *usu. pl.* collieries, coalfield; **les charbonnages de France,** the (French) National Coal Board.

charbonner [ʃarbɔne] **1.** *v.tr.* (*a*) to blacken (sth.) with charcoal; to scrawl (words, etc.) in charcoal; **se c. le visage,** to black(en) one's face; (*b*) to make a charcoal sketch of (sth.). **2.** *v.i.* (*a*) to char, carbonize; (*b*) *Nau:* to coal ship; to bunker.

charbonneux, -euse [ʃarbɔnø, -øz] *a.* **1.** coaly, carbonaceous; **dépot c.,** sooty deposit, carbon deposit. **2.** *Med:* anthracic, anthracoid, carbuncular; **mouches charbonneuses,** anthrax-carrying flies; **bactéridie charbonneuse,** anthrax bacillus.

charbonnier, -ière [ʃarbɔnje, -jɛr] **1.** *a.* (*a*) charcoal (trade, etc.); (*b*) coal (mining) (industry, etc.); **(navire) c.,** collier, coaler. **2.** *n.* (*a*) (*pers.*) charcoal burner; *Prov:* **c. est maître dans sa maison, chez soi,** a man's house is his castle; **la foi du c.,** simple faith; (*b*) coal merchant; coalman. **3.** *n.f.* **charbonnière,** charcoal kiln.

charcuter [ʃarkyte] *v.tr. F:* to hack up (piece of meat); to hack (s.o.) to pieces, butcher (s.o.); **c. son menton en se rasant,** to gash one's chin shaving.

charcuterie [ʃarkytri] *n.f.* **1.** pork butchery; delicatessen trade. **2.** pork butcher's business, shop; = delicatessen (shop). **3. assiette de c.,** plate of assorted delicatessen.

charcutier, -ière [ʃarkytje, -jɛr] *n.* **1.** pork butcher. **2.** *F:* surgeon, sawbones; butcher.

chardon [ʃardɔ̃] *n.m.* **1.** thistle. **2.** *pl.* (clustered) spikes (on iron railing. etc.).

chardonneret [ʃardɔnrɛ] *n.m. Orn:* goldfinch.

charentais, -aise [ʃarɑ̃tɛ, -ɛz] *a. & n.* (native, inhabitant) of Charente.

charge [ʃarʒ] *n.f.* **1.** (*a*) load, burden; (*on ship, etc.*) cargo; **bête de c.,** beast of burden; **cheval, mulet, de c.,** packhorse, pack mule; (*of vehicle*) **c. utile,** (i) carrying capacity; (ii) live weight, load; (iii) payload; **c. maximum (de rupture),** ultimate, breaking, load; *Nau:* **ligne de c.,** loadline; (*of taxi*) **prendre (un client) en c.,** to pick up (a fare); **prise en c.,** minimum fare; **être à c. à qn,** to be a burden to s.o.; (*b*) (*action*) loading (ship, etc.); **navire en c.,** ship loading. **2.** *Tchn:* (*a*) load; stress; **c. de sécurité, admissible,** safe load; **c. à vide,** weight empty; **facteur de c.,** load factor; (*b*) (*of furnace, gun, etc.*) **c. d'explosif,** explosive charge; **c. creuse,** hollow(-shaped) charge; (*c*) *Hyd.E: etc:* **c. d'eau,** head of water; (*d*) *El:* charge (of battery, etc.); load (of circuit, etc.); **conducteur en c.,** live conductor; **mettre une batterie en c.,** to put a battery on charge. **3.** (*a*) charge, responsibility, trust; **prendre qn, qch., en c.,** to take charge of s.o., sth., assume, take, responsibility for s.o., sth.; take over sth.; *Ecc:* **avoir c. d'âmes,** to have a cure of souls; **cela est à votre c.,** that's part of your duty; **enfants confiés à ma c.,** children entrusted to me, in my charge, in my care; **femme de c.,** housekeeper; (*b*) office; **charges publiques,** public offices; **c. d'avoué,** solicitor's practice. **4.** charge, expense; **les réparations sont à la c. du locataire,** the tenant is responsible for repairs; **charges sociales,** national insurance contributions (paid by employer); **être à la c. de qn,** to be dependent on s.o., to be supported by s.o.; **charges de famille,** dependents; **deux enfants à c.,** two dependent children; **loyer plus les charges,** rent plus service charge (and maintenance costs); **cahier des charges,** (i) specifications; (ii) articles and conditions (of sale, etc.); **j'accepte, mais à c. de revanche,** I accept, but only on condition that you let me do the same for you some time; **à c. pour vous de payer,** on condition, provided, that you pay. **5.** exaggeration (of story); *Th:* overacting (of part); *Art: Lit:* caricature (of character, portrait). **6.** *Mil:* charge; **sonner la c.,** to sound the charge; **revenir à la c.,** to return to the charge; to have another try. **7.** *Jur:* charge, indictment; **témoin à c.,** witness for the prosecution.

chargé [ʃarʒe] **1.** *a.* loaded, laden; charged; **bateau fortement c.,** heavily laden ship; **train très c.,** crowded train; **avoir la conscience chargée,** to have a guilty conscience; **jour c.,** full, busy, day; **regard c. de reconnaissance,** look full of gratitude; *Lit:* **mourir c. d'ans,** to die at a ripe old age; **temps c.,** heavy, overcast, weather; **dès chargés,** loaded dice; *Artil:* **obus c.,** live shell. **2. lettre chargée** = registered letter (value declared). **3.** (*a*) *n.m. Dipl:* **c. d'affaires,** chargé d'affaires; (*b*) *n. Sch:* **chargé(e) de cours** = (university) lecturer.

chargement [ʃarʒəmɑ̃] *n.m.* **1.** (*a*) loading (of lorry, etc.); lading (of ship); shipping (of cargo); loading (of camera); **navire en c.,** ship loading; *Rail:* **voie de c.,** goods siding; (*b*) *Artil: Sm.a:* loading (of gun, rifle, pistol, etc.); filling (of cartridge, shell, bomb, etc.); (*c*) *El:* charging (of battery); (*d*) registration (of letter). **2.** (*a*) load, cargo, freight; (*b*) registered letter, parcel.

charger [ʃarʒe] *v.tr.* **(je chargeai(s); n. chargeons)** (*a*) to load (lorry, truck, ship, etc.); **c. des marchandises,** to load, *Nau:* to ship, goods; **navire chargé de blé,** ship laden with wheat; *F:* (*of taxi driver*) **c. un client,** to pick up a fare; (*b*) to weigh (down); **toiture qui charge trop les murs,** roof that overloads the walls; **chargé de paquets,** weighed down with parcels; **table chargée de mets,** table laden with food; **le temps se charge,** it's becoming overcast; it's clouding over; **mets qui chargent l'estomac,** food that lies heavy on the stomach; (*c*) **c. sa mémoire de dates inutiles,** to clutter up one's mind with useless dates; **c. qn de reproches,** to heap reproaches on s.o.; **l'air est chargé du parfum des fleurs,** the air is heavy with the scent of flowers; (*d*) to load (gun, camera, etc.); to fill (pipe); to put a refill into (a pen); (*e*) *El:* to charge (battery). **2.** (*a*) to entrust (s.o. with (doing) sth.); to instruct (s.o. to do sth.); **être chargé de l'entretien,** to be in charge of, responsible for, the maintenance; (*b*) **se c. de (faire) qch.,** to undertake (to do) sth.; **je m'en chargerai,** I'll see to it, take care of it. **3.** to turn (a portrait) into a caricature; to caricature (s.o.); to exaggerate, embroider (a story); *Th:* to overact (a part). **4.** (*of troops, bull, etc.*) to charge; **chargez!** charge! at them! **5.** *Jur:* to charge, accuse, indict (s.o.); **c. qn d'un crime,** to charge s.o. with a crime. **6.** *Her:* to charge.

chargeur [ʃarʒœr] *n.m.* **1.** (*pers.*) loader; *Nau:* shipper. **2.** (*a*) *Sm.a:* magazine; (cartridge, loading) clip; **c. automatique,** self loader; (*b*) *Phot:* cassette; (*c*) *El:* (battery) charger.

chariot [ʃarjo] *n.m.* **1.** (*a*) (four-wheeled) wag(g)on, cart; *Astr:* **le Grand C.,** the Great Bear, Charles's Wain; *NAm:* the (Big) Dipper; **le petit C.,** the Little Bear; the Little Dipper; (*b*) *NAm:* baby walker; (*c*) truck, trolley; *Cin:* dolly; **c. élévateur à fourche,** fork-lift truck; **c. à bagages,** luggage trolley. **2.** (*a*) carriage (of typewriter); (*b*) *Av:* **c. d'atterrissage,** landing gear, undercarriage.

charitable [ʃaritabl̥] *a.* charitable, benevolent (**envers,** to, towards); **œuvre, fondation, c.,** charity.

charitablement [ʃaritabləmɑ̃] *adv.* charitably, benevolently.

charité [ʃarite] *n.f.* **1.** charity, love; **faire qch. par c.,** to do sth. out of, for, charity; *A:* **dame de c.,** district visitor; *Ecc:* **les Filles, les Sœurs, de la C.,** the Sisters of Charity; *Prov:* **c. bien ordonnée commence par soi-même,** charity begins at home. **2.** act of charity; giving to charity; **faire la c. à qn,** to give money, a donation, to s.o.; **vivre de charités,** to live on charity.

charivari [ʃarivari] *n.m.* din, row, racket.

charlatan, -ane [ʃarlatɑ̃, -an] *n.* charlatan, quack, mountebank; **remède de c.,** quack remedy.

charlatanerie [ʃarlatanri] *n.f.* charlatanry, quackery; *F:* **tout ça c'est de la c.,** that's all eyewash.

charlatanesque [ʃarlatanɛsk] *a.* quack (remedy, etc); quackish.

charlatanisme [ʃarlatanism] *n.m.* charlatanism, quackery; deception, trickery.

Charles [ʃarl] *Pr.n.m.* Charles; *Hist:* **C. le Téméraire,** Charles the Bold (of Burgundy).

charleston [ʃarlɛstɔn] *n.m. Danc:* charleston.

Charlot [ʃarlo] *Pr.n.m. F:* Charley, Charlie; *Cin:* Charlie Chaplin.

Charlotte [ʃarlɔt] **1.** *Pr.n.f.* Charlotte. **2.** *n.f. Cu:* (*a*) apple charlotte; (*b*) **c. russe,** charlotte russe. **3.** *A.Cost:* mob cap.

charmant [ʃarmɑ̃] *a.* charming, delightful (person, thing); **prince c.,** prince charming.

charme¹ [ʃarm] *n.m.* **1.** charm, spell; **être sous le c.,** to be under the spell; **tenir ses auditeurs sous le c.,** to hold one's audience spellbound; **rompre le c.,** to break the spell; **se porter comme un c.,** to be in the best of health, to be as fit as a fiddle. **2.** (*a*) charm, attraction; **elle a beaucoup de c.,** she's absolutely charming; **cela donne du c. au paysage,** it lends a charm, a beauty, to the landscape; **c'est ce qui en fait le c.,** that's what makes it so attractive; **faire du**

c., to turn on the charm; (*b*) *pl.* (physical) attractions, charms (of a woman).

charme² *n.m. Bot:* hornbeam.

charmer [ʃarme] *v.tr.* **1.** to charm, bewitch (snake, etc.); *A:* to charm away (cares, etc.). **2.** to charm, delight, enchant; **tableau qui charme les yeux,** picture that delights, charms, the eye; **être charmé de faire qch.,** to be delighted to do sth.; **elle est charmée du cadeau,** she's delighted, enchanted, with the gift.

charmeur, -euse [ʃarmœr, -øz] **1.** *a.* charming, appealing (look, etc.). **2.** *n.* (*a*) **c. de serpents,** snake charmer; (*b*) charming, delightful, person.

charmille [ʃarmij] *n.f.* (*a*) hedge(row); (*b*) bower, arbour.

charnel, -elle [ʃarnɛl] *a.* (*a*) carnal, fleshly (desires, etc.); (*b*) worldly (goods, etc.).

charnellement [ʃarnɛlmɑ̃] *adv.* carnally.

charnier [ʃarnje] *n.m.* (*a*) *A: & Lit:* charnel (house); (*b*) (open) grave.

charnière [ʃarnjɛr] *n.f.* (*a*) stamp hinge; hinge, butt hinge joint; *F:* **nom à c.,** double-barrelled name; (*b*) *Mil:* (point of) junction (of two armies, etc.); bridge; **l'une des grandes charnières de l'histoire,** one of the great turning points of history.

charnu [ʃarny] *a.* fleshy, plump; pulpy (fruit).

charognard [ʃarɔɲar] *n.m.* **1.** *Orn:* vulture. **2.** *P:* (*pers.*) shark, vulture.

charogne [ʃarɔɲ] *n.f.* **1.** carrion, decaying carcass. **2.** *P:* (*pers.*) (dirty) swine; (*woman*) bitch.

charpente [ʃarpɑ̃t] *n.f.* (*a*) frame(work), framing, skeleton (of building, etc.); **bois de c.,** timber; (*b*) frame (of body); (*of pers.*) **avoir la c. solide,** to be solidly built; (*c*) framework, skeleton, structure (of novel, etc.).

charpenté [ʃarpɑ̃te] *a.* built, constructed; **homme solidement c.,** well built man; **pièce de théâtre bien charpentée,** well constructed play.

charpenter [ʃarpɑ̃te] *v.tr.* **1.** to cut (timber) into shape. **2.** (*a*) to frame (up) (roof, etc.); (*b*) to construct (novel, etc.).

charpenterie [ʃarpɑ̃tri] *n.f.* **1.** carpentry. **2.** (*a*) carpenter's (work)shop; (*b*) timberyard.

charpentier [ʃarpɑ̃tje] *n.m.* carpenter; **matelot c.,** ship's carpenter; **c. du bord,** shipwright.

charpie [ʃarpi] *n.f.* (*a*) *A:* lint; shredded linen; (*b*) **mettre qch. en c.,** to tear sth. to pieces, to shreds; *F:* **il vous mettra en c.,** he'll make mincemeat of you; **viande en c.,** meat cooked to shreds.

charretée [ʃarte] *n.f.* cartload, cartful.

charretier, -ière [ʃartje, -jɛr] **1.** *n.m.* carter, carrier; **langage de c.,** coarse language. **2.** *a.* **porte charretière,** carriage gate(way); **chemin c., voie charretière,** cart track.

charrette [ʃarɛt] *n.f.* cart; **c. anglaise,** dogcart, trap; **c. à bras,** handcart, barrow; *Hist:* **c. (des condamnés),** tumbrel.

charriable [ʃarjabl̩] *a.* cartable, transportable.

charriage [ʃarjaʒ] *n.m.* (*a*) cartage, haulage, carriage; (*b*) *Geol:* thrusting; overthrust.

charrier [ʃarje] *v.* (*impf. & pr.sub.* **n. charriions, v. charriiez) 1.** *v.tr.* (*a*) to cart, carry, transport; (*b*) to carry along, wash down, drift; **rivière qui charrie du sable,** river that carries, brings down, sand; **nuages charriés par le vent,** wind-driven clouds; (*c*) *P:* to poke fun at, to kid (s.o.); **sans c.,** joking aside. **2.** *v.i. P:* to exaggerate; to shoot a line, pile it on; **il charrie vraiment!** he's really having you on.

charroi [ʃarwa] *n.m.* cartage, haulage, carriage.

charron [ʃarɔ̃] *n.m.* cartwright (and ploughwright); wheelwright.

charroyer [ʃarwaje] *v.tr.* **(je charroie; je charroierai)** to transport (sth.) in a cart, to cart (sth.).

charroyeur [ʃarwajœr] *n.m.* carter, carrier.

charrue [ʃary] *n.f.* (*a*) plough, *NAm:* plow; **mener, pousser, la c.,** to drive the plough; *F:* **mettre la c. devant les bœufs,** to put the cart before the horse; (*b*) *Fr.C:* snowplough, *NAm:* snowplow.

charte [ʃart] *n.f.* **1.** charter; **compagnie à c.,** chartered society; *Eng.Hist:* **la Grande C.,** Magna Carta; *Pol: Hist:* **la C. de l'Atlantique,** the Atlantic Charter. **2.** (ancient) deed; title; **l'École des chartes,** the School of Palaeography and Librarianship (in Paris).

charte-partie [ʃartəparti] *n.f. Nau:* charter party; *pl. chartes-parties.*

charter [tʃartœr] *n.m.* **(avion) c.,** charter, chartered aircraft; **vol c.,** charter flight.

chartisme [ʃartism] *n.m. Eng.Hist:* chartism.

chartiste [ʃartist] *a. & n.* **1.** (student) of the *École des chartes.* **2.** *Eng.Hist:* chartist.

chartreux, -euse [ʃartrø, -øz] **1.** *n. Ecc:* Carthusian (monk, nun). **2.** *n.f.* Carthusian monastery; charterhouse.

chartrier [ʃartrije] *n.m.* **1.** custodian of charters. **2.** (*a*) collection of charters; (*b*) charter room.

Charybde [karibd] *Pr.n.m. Gr.Myth:* Charybdis; **tomber de C. en Scylla,** to fall out of the frying pan into the fire.

chas [ʃa] *n.m.* eye (of needle).

chasse [ʃas] *n.f.* **1.** (*a*) hunting; (game) shooting; hunt, shoot; **c. à courre,** (stag, fox)hunt(ing); **c. à tir,** (i) (game) shooting; (ii) shoot; **c. au furet,** ferreting; **c. au lévrier,** coursing; **c. au renard,** foxhunt(ing); **c. aux perdrix,** partridge shoot(ing); **c. aux oiseaux,** fowling; **c. au lapin,** rabbiting, rabbit shooting; **c. au daim (à l'affût),** deerstalking; **c. aux souris,** mousing; **c. à l'homme,** manhunt; *F:* **c. au mari,** husband hunting; **c. aux soldes,** bargain hunting; **c. aux appartements,** flat hunting; **c. sous-marine,** underwater fishing; **aller à la c.,** to go hunting, shooting; **la c. est ouverte, fermée,** the shooting season has begun, ended; **c. fermée,** close season; **la c. vient de passer,** the hunt has just gone by; **fusil de c.,** (i) sporting gun; (ii) fowling piece; **couteau, habit, de c.,** hunting knife, coat; **faire bonne c.,** to have good sport, make a good bag; (*b*) **c. gardée,** private game preserve; *Fig:* **ah non, c. gardée!** no poaching! hands off! **louer une c.,** to rent a shoot; (*c*) chase; **donner la c. à qch., à qn, prendre qch., qn, en c.,** to chase, pursue, give chase to, sth., s.o.; **faire la c. à qch.,** to hunt sth., down, out; (*d*) *Mil.Av:* **la c.,** the fighter aircraft; the fighters; **pilote de c.,** fighter pilot. **2.** (*a*) **c. (d'eau),** flushing system, flush; **tirer la c. (d'eau),** to flush the lavatory, pull the chain; (*b*) *Mec.E:* play (of wheels, etc.); *Aut:* trail (of front wheels); (*c*) *Typ:* overrun (of page).

châsse [ʃɑs] *n.f.* **1.** *Ecc:* reliquary, shrine. **2.** mounting; frame (of spectacles).

chassé [ʃase] *n.m. Danc:* chassé.

chasse-clou(s) [ʃasklu] *n.m. Tls:* nail punch, nail set; *pl. chasse-clous.*

chassé-croisé [ʃasekrwaze] *n.m.* (*a*) *Danc:* set to partners; (*b*) rearrangement, reshuffling (of staff, etc.); chassé-croisé; *pl. chassés-croisés.*

chasse-marée [ʃasmare] *n.m.inv.* **1.** fish cart. **2.** coasting lugger.

chasse-mouches [ʃasmuʃ] *n.m.inv.* fly whisk, fly swat(ter).

chasse-neige [ʃasnɛʒ] *n.m.inv.* **1.** snowplough. **2.** *Ski:* stem; snowplough; **virage (en) c.-n.,** snowplough turn, stem turn.

chasse-pierres [ʃaspjɛr] *n.m.inv. Rail:* cowcatcher.

chassepot [ʃaspo] *n.m. A:* chassepot (rifle).

chasser [ʃase] **1.** *v.tr.* (*a*) to chase, hunt; **c. le renard, la perdrix,** to go foxhunting, partridge shooting; **c. à courre,** to ride to hounds; to hunt, go hunting; **c. au fusil,** to shoot, go shooting; **c. au furet,** to ferret; (*b*) to drive, chase (s.o.) out, away; to turn (s.o.) out; to expel (s.o.); to dismiss (employee); *B:* to cast out (devils); to dispel (fog, etc.); to drive (nail) in; **c. qn du pays,** to drive, expel s.o. from the country; **c. qn de son esprit,** to dismiss s.o. from one's mind, from one's thoughts; **c. une mouche (du revers de la main),** to brush away a fly; **le vent chassait la pluie contre les vitres,** the wind was driving the rain against the windowpanes; **c. une mauvaise odeur,** to get rid of a nasty smell. **2.** *v.i.* (*a*) to hunt, go hunting, go shooting; **c. au lion,** to hunt lions; *Fig:* **c. sur les terres de qn,** to poach on s.o.'s preserves; (*b*) to drive; **nuages qui chassent du nord,** clouds driving from the north; **navire qui chasse sur ses ancres,** ship dragging her anchors; (*c*) *Aut:* to skid; *Nau:* (*of anchor*) to drag; (*d*) *Typ:* (i) (*of type*) to drive out; (ii) (*of matter*) to overrun.

chasseresse [ʃasrɛs] *n.f. Lit:* huntress; **Diane c.,** Diana the Huntress.

chasseur, -euse [ʃasœr, -øz] **1.** *n.* (*a*) hunter, *f.* huntress; huntsman; **il est bon c.,** he's a good shot; **c. de têtes,** headhunter; **c. d'images,** keen photographer; news cameraman; **c. d'autographes,** autograph hunter; (*b*) (sportsman with) gun. **2.** *n.m.* (*in hotel, etc.*) commissionaire; porter; messenger (boy); page(boy); *NAm:* bellhop, bellboy. **3.** *n.m.* (*a*) *A.Mil:* rifleman, light infantryman, chasseur; **les chasseurs (à pied),** the light infantry; **chasseurs à cheval,** light cavalry; **c. à cheval,** light cavalryman; (*b*) **les chasseurs alpins,** the mountain light infantry. **4.** *n.m.* (*a*) *Mil:* **c. de chars,** tank destroyer; (*b*) *Mil.Av:* fighter; **c. tout temps,** all-weather fighter; (*c*) *Navy:* **c. de sous-marins,** submarine chaser.

chasseur-bombardier [ʃasœrbɔ̃bardje] *n.m.* fighter-bomber; *pl. chasseurs-bombardiers.*

chassie [ʃasi] *n.f.* matter, gum, rheum (in the eyes).

chassieux, -euse [ʃasjø, -øz] *a.* gummy, rheumy (eyes); rheumy-eyed, bleary-eyed (person).

châssis [ʃɑsi] *n.m.* (*a*) frame; stretcher of a canvas; **c. de porte, de fenêtre,** door frame, window frame; **c. mobile,** sash; **c. dormant,** sash (frame); **c. à guillotine,** sash window; (*b*) *Hort:* (cold, forcing) frame; **culture sous c.,** forcing; (*c*) *Aut:* chassis; *Rail:* underframe (of carriage); *Aut:* **faux c.,** sub-frame; (*d*) *Typ:* chase.

chaste [ʃast] *a.* chaste, pure.

chastement [ʃastəmɑ̃] *adv.* chastely, purely.

chasteté [ʃastəte] *n.f.* chastity; purity.

chasuble [ʃazybl̥] *n.f. Cost:* (*a*) *Ecc:* chasuble; (*b*) **robe c.,** pinafore dress, *NAm:* jumper.

chat, chatte [ʃa, ʃat] *n.* **1.** (*a*) cat; *m.* tom(cat); *f.* queen, she cat; **le C. botté,** Puss in Boots; **petit c.,** kitten; *F:* **mon petit c., ma petite chatte,** my dear, my pet, my darling; *Pej: A:* **c. fourré,** judge; **il n'y avait pas un c. dans la rue,** there wasn't a soul in the street; **appeler un c. un c.,** to call a spade a spade; **acheter c. en poche,** to buy a pig in a poke; **avoir un c. dans la gorge,** to have a frog in one's throat; *Prov:* **ne réveillez pas le c. qui dort,** let sleeping dogs lie; **à bon c. bon rat,** tit for tat; **c. échaudé craint l'eau froide,** once bitten twice shy; **le c. parti, les souris dansent,** when the cat's away the mice will play; (*b*) *a. F:* caressing, feline (manner, etc.). **2. c. à neuf queues,** cat(-o'-nine-tails). **3.** *Games:* (*a*) tag, tig, he; **jouer au c.,** to play tag, tig, he; **c. perché,** off-ground tag, tig, he; (*b*) (*pers.*) it, he.

châtaigne [ʃɑtɛɲ] *n.f.* (*a*) *Bot:* (sweet) chestnut; **c. d'eau,** water caltrop, water chestnut; (*b*) *P:* blow, biff, clout.

châtaigneraie [ʃɑtɛɲrɛ] *n.f.* chestnut grove, plantation.

châtaignier [ʃɑtɛɲe] *n.m.* chestnut (tree, wood).

châtain [ʃɑtɛ̃] (*a*) *a.* (*usu. inv. in fem., occ.* **-aine**) (chestnut-)brown; **une femme châtain(e),** a brown-haired woman; **cheveux c. clair,** light brown hair; (*b*) *n.m.* chestnut brown.

château, -eaux [ʃɑto] *n.m.* **1.** castle; stronghold; (*a*) **c. fort,** (fortified) castle; **bâtir des châteaux en Espagne,** to build castles in the air; **c. de cartes,** house of cards; (*b*) *Vit:* château; **vin mis en bouteille au c.,** château-bottled wine; *P:* **c.-la-pompe,** (drinking) water, Adam's ale. **2.** (*a*) country seat; mansion; manor; hall; (*b*) (royal) palace; **le c. de Versailles,** the palace of Versailles. **3. c. d'eau,** water tower; *Rail:* tank. **4.** *N.Arch:* superstructure; *A:* **c. d'avant,** forecastle, fo'c'sle.

chateaubriand, châteaubriant [ʃɑtobrijɑ̃] *n.m. Cu:* chateaubriand, porterhouse steak.

châtelain [ʃɑtlɛ̃] *n.m.* **1.** *Hist:* lord (of the manor). **2.** owner, tenant, of a château.

châtelaine [ʃɑtlɛn] *n.f.* **1.** *Hist:* chatelaine, lady (of the manor). **2.** (*a*) (woman) owner, tenant, of a château; (*b*) wife of owner, tenant, of a château. **3.** *Cost:* chatelaine (for keys, etc.).

châtelet [ʃɑtlɛ] *n.m.* small castle.

chat-huant [ʃaɥɑ̃] *n.m. Orn:* tawny owl, brown owl, wood owl; *pl. chats-huants.*

châtié [ʃɑtje] *a.* polished (style, verse).

châtier [ʃɑtje] *v.tr.* (*p.d. & pr.sub.* **n. châtiions, v. châtiiez)** *Lit:* to punish, chastise, castigate (child, etc.); to chasten (one's passions, etc.); to polish (style); **c. son corps,** to mortify the flesh; **c. l'impudence de qn,** to punish s.o. for his impudence; *Prov:* **qui aime bien châtie bien,** spare the rod and spoil the child.

chatière [ʃatjɛr] *n.f.* **1.** (*a*) cat door, flap; (*b*) ventilation hole (in roof); (*c*) narrow underground passage. **2.** cat trap.

châtiment [ʃɑtimɑ̃] *n.m. Lit:* punishment, chastisement, castigation; **c. corporel,** corporal punishment.

chatoiement [ʃatwamɑ̃] *n.m.* shimmer(ing), iridescence, sheen.

chaton¹ [ʃatɔ̃] *n.m.* **1.** kitten. **2.** *Bot:* catkin.

chaton² *n.m. Lap:* **1.** bezel, setting (of stone). **2.** stone (in its setting).

chatonner [ʃatɔne] *v.i.* **1.** to kitten, to have kittens. **2.** (*of tree*) to grow catkins.

chatouille [ʃatuj] *n.f. F:* **faire des chatouilles à qn,** to tickle s.o.; **craindre les chatouilles,** to be ticklish.

chatouillement [ʃatujmɑ̃] *n.m.* tickling; **éprouver un c. dans la gorge,** to have a tickle in one's throat.

chatouiller [ʃatuje] *v.tr.* to tickle; *F:* **c. les côtes à qn,** to give s.o. a thrashing; **vin qui chatouille le palais,** wine that pleases, excites, the palate; **c. la curiosité,** to excite, arouse, curiosity; **c. l'amour-propre de qn,** to flatter s.o.'s vanity.

chatouilleux, -euse [ʃatujø, -øz] *a.* (*a*) ticklish; (*b*) sensitive, touchy; **c. sur le point d'honneur,** touchy where honour is concerned, touchy on a point of honour.

chatoyant [ʃatwajɑ̃] *a.* shimmering, glistening, iridescent; sparkling (stone, imagination, etc.); **soie chatoyante,** shot silk.

chatoyer [ʃatwaje] *v.i.* **(il chatoie; il chatoiera)** to shimmer, glisten, sparkle; **style qui chatoie,** sparkling, colourful style.

châtré [ʃɑtre] *a. & n.m.* castrated (man); eunuch; *F:* **voix de c.,** high-pitched, falsetto, voice.

châtrer [ʃɑtre] *v.tr.* (*a*) to castrate, emasculate; to geld (stallion); to neuter (cat); to spay (bitch, etc.); (*b*) to bowdlerize, expurgate, mutilate (literary work).

chatterie [ʃatri] *n.f.* **1.** *usu. pl.* wheedling ways, coaxing. **2.** *pl.* delicacies, dainties.

chatterton [ʃatɛrtɔn] *n.m. El:* (adhesive) insulating tape.

chat-tigre [ʃatigr̥] *n.m. Z:* tiger cat; *pl. chats-tigres.*

chaud, chaude [ʃo, ʃod] **1.** *a.* (*a*) warm; hot; **soupe toute chaude,** steaming hot, piping hot, soup; **avoir la tête chaude,** to be hot-headed; **affaire chaude,** sharp tussle, brisk engagement; **guerre chaude,** shooting war; **chaude dispute,** heated discussion; **animal à sang c.,** warm-blooded animal; **pleurer à chaudes larmes,** to weep bitterly; **il n'est pas c. pour le projet,** he's not keen on, not over-enthusiastic about, the project; **j'aime à manger c.,** I like my food hot; **nouvelle toute chaude,** (piece of) really hot news; **tout c. de . . .,** straight from . . ., hotfoot from . . .; **voix chaude,** sultry voice; *Art:* **tons chauds,** warm tints; *Prov:* **il faut battre le fer pendant qu'il est c.,** strike while the iron is hot, make hay while the sun shines; *F:* **ça a dû coûter c.,** it must have cost a pretty penny; *F:* **il fera c. quand elle commencera à travailler!** that'll be the day when she starts working! (*b*) warm, warming; **couverture chaude,** warm blanket; (*c*) *P:* **être c.,** to be highly sexed; to feel sexy, randy; **c'est un c. lapin,** he's a sexy devil. **2.** *n.m.* heat, warmth; hot, warm, state; **tenir qch. au c.,** to keep sth. hot; (*on label*) **tenir au c.,** to be kept in a warm place; **cela ne me fait ni c. ni froid,** it makes no difference, it's all the same, to me; **souffler le c. et le froid,** to blow hot and cold; to lay down the law; **prendre un c. et froid,** to catch a chill; **marqué à c.,** branded; (*of pers.*) **avoir c.,** to be, feel, warm, hot; *F:* **il a eu c.,** he was scared stiff; he had a narrow escape. **3.** *n.f.* **chaude,** *Metall:* heat.

chaudement [ʃodmɑ̃] *adv.* warmly; **être vêtu c.,** to be warmly dressed; **protester c.,** to protest hotly.

chaude-pisse [ʃodpis] *n.f.inv. Med: P:* V.D., clap.

chaud-froid [ʃofrwa] *n.m. Cu:* chaudfroid; **c.-f. de poulet,** cold jellied chicken; *pl. chauds-froids.*

chaudière [ʃodjɛr] *n.f.* **1.** *A:* copper (for washing, etc.). **2.** (central heating) boiler; **c. à vapeur,** steam boiler, steam generator.

chaudron [ʃodrɔ̃] *n.m.* cauldron, *esp. NAm:* caldron.

chaudronnerie [ʃodrɔnri] *n.f.* **1.** (*a*) boiler-making; hollow-ware manufacture; (*b*) boiler trade; hollow-ware trade; (*c*) sheet metal work(ing). **2. grosse c.,** boilers and industrial hollow-ware; **petite c.,** domestic hollow-ware. **3.** (*a*) boiler works; coppersmith's, tinsmith's works; hollow-ware factory; (*b*) = ironmonger's, hardware shop.

chaudronnier, -ière [ʃodrɔnje, -jɛr] **1.** *n.* (*a*) boiler maker; brazier; coppersmith; tinsmith; hollow-ware maker; (*b*) = ironmonger; (*c*) sheet metal worker. **2.** *a.* **industrie chaudronnière,** boiler-making, hollow-ware industry.

chauffage [ʃofaʒ] *n.m.* (*a*) heating, warming (of room, etc.); (*b*) heating system, apparatus; *Aut:* (car) heater; **c. central,** central heating; **c. urbain,** district heating; **c. à l'électricité, au gaz, au mazout,** electric, gas, oil, heating; **bois de c.,** firewood; **le c. est détraqué,** the boiler, the heating, is out of order; (*c*) stoking, firing (of boiler).

chauffant [ʃofɑ̃] *a.* heating, warming; **couverture chauffante,** electric blanket; **plaque chauffante,** hot plate.

chauffard [ʃofar] *n.m. F:* (*a*) roadhog; (*b*) hit-and-run driver.

chauffe [ʃof] *n.f.* **1.** heating. **2.** *Mch:* firing, stoking; **surface de c.,** heating surface; **chef de c.,** head stoker; *Nau:* leading stoker; *Nau:* **chambre de c.,** stokehold. **3.** *Metall:* fire chamber (of furnace).

chauffe-assiette(s) [ʃofasjɛt] *n.m.* plate warmer, hot plate; *pl. chauffe-assiettes.*

chauffe-bain [ʃofbɛ̃] *n.m.* water heater; *pl. chauffe-bains.*

chauffe-eau [ʃofo] *n.m.inv.* water heater; immersion heater.

chauffe-pieds [ʃofpje] *n.m.inv.* footwarmer.

chauffe-plats [ʃofpla] *n.m. inv.* chafing dish; hot plate; plate warmer.

chauffer [ʃofe] **1.** *v.tr.* (*a*) to heat (up), warm (up); **c. une maison au gaz,** to heat a house with gas, to have gas heating; (*b*) **c. le fer à blanc, au rouge,** to make iron white-hot, red-hot; **chauffé à blanc, au rouge,** white-hot, red-hot; **c. une chaudière, une locomotive,** to fire, stoke (up), a boiler, an engine; to get up, raise, steam; (*c*) *F:* to cram, coach (s.o.) for an examination; **il faut c. l'affaire,** we must strike while the iron is hot; **c. qn (à blanc),** to incite s.o., get s.o. going; (*d*) *P:* to steal, pinch, nick. **2.** *v.i.* (*a*) to get, become, hot, warm; **l'eau chauffe,** the water is heating (up), warming (up); (*b*) *F:* **ça chauffe, ça va c.,** things are getting hot, are beginning to hum; (*c*) (*of bearing, etc.*) to overheat, run hot. **3. se c.,** to warm oneself (**au soleil,** in the sun); **se c. (les muscles),** to limber up; **se c. au mazout,** to have oil-fired (central) heating.

chaufferette [ʃofrɛt] *n.f.* footwarmer.

chaufferie [ʃofri] *n.f.* boiler room; *Nau:* stokehold.

chauffeur, -euse [ʃofœr, -øz] *n.* **1.** stoker, fireman (of steam engine, etc.). **2.** *Aut:* (*a*) *O:* driver; (*b*) *n.m.* chauffeur, *f.* chauffeuse; **c. de camion,** lorry driver; **elle est c. de taxi,** she's a taxi driver; **les chauffeurs du dimanche,** weekend drivers. **3.** *n.f.* low fireside chair.

chaufour [ʃofur] *n.m.* limekiln.

chaulage [ʃolaʒ] *n.m.* liming (of ground, etc.); whitewashing (of walls, etc.).

chauler [ʃole] *v.tr.* to lime (hides, etc.); to treat (ground, etc.) with lime; to limewash (fruit trees, etc.); to whitewash (walls, etc.).

chaumage [ʃomaʒ] *n.m. Agr:* cutting (of stubble).

chaume [ʃom] *n.m.* **1.** (*a*) straw, haulm; (*b*) thatch; **couvrir un toit de, en, c.,** to thatch a roof; **toit de c.,** thatched roof; (*c*) (i) stubble; (ii) stubble field. **2.** *Bot:* culm, haulm (of grasses).

chaumer [ʃome] *v.tr. Agr:* to clear (field) of stubble.

chaumière [ʃomjɛr] *n.f.* thatched cottage.

chaussant [ʃosɑ̃] *a.* (shoe) that fits well; comfortable (shoe).

chausse [ʃos] *n.f.* **1.** *pl. A. Cost:* **des chausses, une paire de chausses,** hose, breeches; **tirer ses chausses,** to take to one's heels. **2.** straining bag (for wine, etc.).

chaussée [ʃose] *n.f.* **1.** (*a*) dyke, embankment; (*b*) causeway (across marsh, etc.); **la C. des Géants,** the Giant's Causeway. **2.** roadway, carriageway, *NAm:* pavement; **c. bombée,** cambered road; **c. déformée,** road in poor condition; *P.N:* temporary road surface. **3.** reef, line of rocks.

chausse-pied [ʃospje] *n.m.* shoehorn; *pl. chausse-pieds.*

chausser [ʃose] *v.tr.* **1.** to put on one's (shoes, boots, etc.); **chaussé de pantoufles,** wearing (his) slippers; **c. les étriers,** to put one's feet into the stirrups; **c. ses lunettes,** to put one's spectacles on. **2.** (*a*) to put shoes on (s.o.); **se c.,** to put one's shoes, boots, on; **c. une idée,** to get sth. into one's head; (*b*) to supply, fit, (s.o.) with footwear, to make footwear for (s.o.); **se faire c. chez B.,** to buy, get, one's shoes at B.'s; **souliers qui chaussent bien,** shoes that fit well; **ce soulier chausse étroit,** this shoe comes in a narrow fitting; **combien chaussez-vous?** what size do you take (in shoes)? **3.** *Aut:* to put tyres on (car). **4.** *Hort:* to earth up (tree).

chaussette [ʃosɛt] *n.f.* sock; *pl. Com:* half-hose; **en chaussettes,** in one's socks, in one's stockinged feet; *Mil: etc:* **c. russe,** footcloth; *P:* **chaussettes à clous,** hobnailed boots.

chausseur [ʃosœr] *n.m.* footwear specialist.

chausson [ʃosɔ̃] *n.m.* **1.** (*a*) slipper; (*b*) ballet shoe; (*c*) (baby's) bootee; **2.** *Sp:* French boxing, foot boxing, savate. **3.** *Cu:* **c. aux pommes,** apple turnover.

chaussure [ʃosyr] *n.f.* **1.** (*a*) footwear; (*b*) (boot and) shoe industry, trade. **2.** shoe; **un paire de chaussures,** a pair of shoes; **chaussures de marche,** walking shoes; **chaussures de ski,** ski boots; *F:* **trouver c. à son pied,** to find exactly what one wants.

chauve [ʃov] **1.** *a.* (*a*) bald; **à tête c.,** bald-headed; *F:* **c. comme un genou, comme un œuf, comme une bille,** as bald as a coot; (*b*) bare, denuded (mountain, etc.). **2.** *n.m.* bald(-headed) person.

chauve-souris [ʃovsuri] *n.f. Z:* bat; *pl. chauves-souris.*

chauvin, -ine [ʃovɛ̃, -in] **1.** *n.* chauvinist. **2.** *a.* chauvinist(ic); jingoist(ic).

chauvinisme [ʃovinism] *n.m.* chauvinism; jingoism.

chauviniste [ʃovinist] *a. & n.* = CHAUVIN.

chaux [ʃo] *n.f.* lime; **c. vive,** quicklime; **c. éteinte,** slaked lime; **pierre à c.,** limestone; **lait, blanc, de c.,** whitewash; **blanchir un mur à la c.,** to whitewash a wall; **bâtir à c. et à sable, à c. et à ciment,** to build firmly, solidly; (*of pers.*) **être bâti à c. et à sable,** to have an iron constitution.

chavirer [ʃavire] **1.** *v.i.* (*a*) (*of boat, etc.*) to capsize, turn turtle, overturn; (*b*) **les nations les plus grandes chavirent,** (even) the greatest nations collapse, fall; (*c*) to sway, reel, spin (round); **ses yeux chaviraient,** he was showing the whites of his eyes. **2.** *v.tr.* (*a*) to upset, capsize, overturn (boat); to cant (boat for repairs); (*b*) to turn (sth.) upside down, to overturn (sth.); to knock (sth.) over; (*c*) *F:* **j'en suis tout chaviré,** it's completely upset me.

chéchia [ʃeʃja], *n.f. Cost:* chechia.

check-list [tʃeklist] *n.f. Av: etc: F:* checklist; *pl. check-lists.*

chef [ʃɛf] *n.m.* **1.** (*a*) *A: & Hum:* head; (*b*) *Lit:* **il pense de son c.,** he thinks for himself; **faire qch. de son (propre) c.,** to do sth. on one's own authority, off one's own bat; *Jur:* **du c. de sa femme,** in one's wife's right; (*c*) *Her:* chief (of shield). **2.** head (of family, etc.); chief, chieftain (of tribe, etc.); leader (of political party, etc.); principal, head (of business); foreman (of jury); conductor (of orchestra); founder (of school of thought, etc.); **c. de famille,** head of family; householder; **c. d'état,** head of state; **c. de bande,** ringleader; **c. (cuisinier, de cuisine),** chef; **c. de musique,** bandmaster; *Row:* **c. de nage,** stroke (oar); **c. d'équipe,** (i) *Sp:* captain; (ii) *Ind:* foreman; charge hand; *Adm:* **c. de bureau,** chief clerk; **c. de service,** head of department, departmental manager; **c. du personnel,** personnel, staff, manager; **c. de cabinet** = (minister's) principal private secretary; *Ind:* **c. d'atelier** (shop) foreman; **ingénieur en c.,** chief engineer; (*in shop*) **c. de rayon,** head of department, department(al) manager; **les chefs d'industrie,** the captains of industry; *Rail:* **c. de gare,** station manager; **c. de train,** guard, *NAm:* conductor; *Nau:* **c. de quart,** officer of the watch; *Mil:* **commandant en c.,** commander-in-chief; **c. de bataillon,** major; **c. de patrouille,** patrol leader. **3.** *Jur:* **c. d'accusation,** count of an indictment, charge.

chef-d'œuvre [ʃɛdœvr̥] *n.m.* masterpiece, chef-d'œuvre; *pl. chefs-d'œuvre.*

chef-lieu [ʃɛfljø] *n.m.* chief town (of department); = county town, *NAm:* county seat; *pl. chefs-lieux.*

cheftaine [ʃɛftɛn] *n.f. Scout:* (i) captain; (ii) Brown owl; (iii) cubmaster.

cheik(h) [ʃɛk] *n.m.* sheik(h).

chelem [ʃlɛm] *n.m. Cards:* slam; **grand c.,** grand slam; **petit c.,** little slam.

chemin [ʃ(ə)mɛ̃] *n.m.* **1.** (*a*) way, road; **la ligne droite est le plus court c. d'un point à un autre,** a straight line is the shortest distance between two points; *F:* **c. des écoliers,** roundabout way, longest way round; **demander son c.,** to ask one's way; **c'est sur mon c.,** it's on my way; **nous avons beaucoup de c. à faire,** we've a long way to go; **il y a dix minutes de c.,** it's ten minutes away, from here; **faire la moitié du c.,** to meet s.o. half way; **il fera son c.,** he'll get on, he'll make his way, in the world; **cette idée fait du c.,** this idea is gaining ground; **aller (toujours) son c.,** to jog along; **c. faisant,** on the way; **faire un bout de c. avec qn,** to go part of the way with s.o.; **montrer le c.,** to lead, show, the way; **être en bon c.,** to be getting on well; **nous sommes dans le bon c.,** we're on the right road, track; **à moitié c.,** half way; **se mettre en c. pour, prendre le c. de, la France,** to set out for France; **être dans, sur, le c. de qn,** to be, stand, in s.o.'s way; **le c. de la gare,** the way to the station; **ne pas y aller par quatre chemins, par trente-six chemins,** to go straight to the point; **s'arrêter en c.,** to stop on the way; (*b*) *Nau:* **faire du c.,** to make headway; **c. est,** easting; (*c*) road, path, track; route; **c. piéton,** footpath; *A:* **grand c.,** highway, high road; **voleur de grand c.,** highwayman; **c. de traverse,** side road; short cut; **c. vicinal,** by-road, minor road; **c. de terre,** dirt track; **c. creux,** sunken road, lane; **c. de halage,** towpath; *F:* **être toujours sur les chemins,** to be always on the go; *Mec.E:* **c. de roulement pour billes,** ball race. **2. c. de fer,** railway, *NAm:* railroad; **aller, voyager, en, par, c. de fer,** to go, travel, by rail, by train. **3. c. de table,** (table) runner.

chemineau, -eaux [ʃ(ə)mino] *n.m.* tramp, vagrant.

cheminée [ʃ(ə)mine] *n.f.* **1.** (*a*) fireplace; **un feu dans la c.,** a fire in the grate; **pierre de la c.,** hearthstone; (*b*) **c. prussienne,** stove; (*c*) **(manteau de) c.,** mantelpiece, chimneypiece. **2.** (*a*) chimney (stack); **(conduit de) c.,** flue; **c. d'usine,** factory chimney; **feu de c.,** chimney (on) fire; (*b*) funnel, smokestack (of locomotive, steamer); (*c*) chimney (of lamp). **3. c. d'aération,** air shaft, ventilating shaft. **4.** (*a*) **c. volcanique,** vent (of a volcano); (*b*) *Mount:* chimney.

cheminement [ʃ(ə)minmɑ̃] *n.m.* **1.** tramping; walking; trudging (along); **le c. des eaux,** the advance of the water. **2.** *Mil:* advancing (to position, *esp.* under cover). **3. c. de la pensée,** (i) advance, progress, march, of thought; (ii) processes of thought. **4.** *Surv:* plane table traversing.

cheminer [ʃ(ə)mine] *v.i.* **1.** to continue on one's way; **c. sous la pluie,** to trudge, plod, along in the rain. **2.** *Mil:* to advance (to position, *esp.* under cover). **3.** *Surv:* to traverse.

cheminot [ʃ(ə)mino] *n.m.* railway employee, railwayman, *NAm:* railroader.

chemisage [ʃ(ə)mizaʒ] *n.m.* (*a*) jacketing, casing (of boiler, cylinder, etc.); (*b*) lining (of gun, cylinder, etc.).

chemise [ʃ(ə)miz] *n.f.* **1.** shirt; **c. empesée,** starched shirt; **en bras, en manches, de c.,** in one's shirtsleeves; **c. de nuit,** nightshirt; (woman's) nightdress; **c. américaine,** (woman's) vest, *NAm:* undershirt; **se moquer de qch. comme de sa première c.,** not to care a damn, two hoots about sth.; *Hist:* **Chemises rouges,** Red Shirts; **Chemises noires,** Blackshirts; **Chemises brunes,** Brownshirts; *Arm:* **c. de mailles,** shirt of mail. **2.** (*a*) folder, portfolio (for papers); (*b*) jacket(ing), casing, sheathing (of boiler, cylinder, etc.); **c. de vapeur,** steam jacket; **c. d'eau,** water jacket; (*c*) lining (of cylinder, furnace, etc.); (*d*) *I.C.E:* **c. (de cylindre),** (cylinder) liner, sleeve (of sleevevalve engine); (*e*) facing (of wall).

choisir [ʃwazir] *v.tr.* to choose, select, pick; **c. entre, parmi, plusieurs choses,** to choose from, between, several things; **c. si l'on part, c. de partir,** to choose whether one will leave, to choose to leave.

choix [ʃwa] *n.m.* choice, choosing, selection; **l'embarras du c.,** the difficulty of choosing; **faites votre c.,** take your pick; **je vous laisse le c.,** choose for yourself; **nous n'avons pas d'autre c. que de . . .,** we have no option, choice, but to . . .; (*on a menu*) **viande ou poisson au c.,** choice of meat or fish; **de premier c.,** (of the) best quality, first-class; class one, grade one; **morceaux de viande de c.,** prime cuts; *Adm:* **avancer au c.,** to be promoted by selection, on merit.

choléra [kɔlera] *n.m. Med:* cholera.

cholérine [kɔlerin] *n.f. Med:* cholerine.

cholérique [kɔlerik] *Med:* **1.** *a.* choleraic. **2.** *n.* cholera patient.

cholestérol [kɔlɛsterɔl] *n.m. Med:* cholesterol.

chômage [ʃomaʒ] *n.m.* **1.** *A:* abstention from work (on feast days, etc.). **2.** unemployment; **être en c.,** to be unemployed, out of work, *F:* jobless; **allocation, indemnité, de c.,** unemployment benefit; *F:* dole; **s'inscrire au c.,** to sign on (the dole); **c. saisonnier,** seasonal unemployment; **c. partiel,** short-time working; **c. d'une usine,** shutting down of a works.

chômer [ʃome] **1.** *v.tr. & i. A:* to take a holiday (on feast days, etc.); to keep (feast day); **fête chômée,** public holiday. **2.** to be, lie, idle; to be unemployed, out of work; (*of field*) to lie fallow; **les usines chôment,** the works are at a standstill, are standing idle; **laisser c. son argent,** to let one's money lie idle.

chômeur, -euse [ʃomœr, -øz] *n.* unemployed worker; **les chômeurs,** the unemployed.

chope [ʃɔp] *n.f.* (*a*) beer mug, pint pot, tankard; (*b*) mugful.

choper [ʃɔpe] *v.tr. P:* **1.** to steal, pinch. **2.** to arrest; **se faire c.,** to get nabbed. **3.** to catch (cold).

chopine [ʃɔpin] *n.f.* (*a*) *F:* half-litre, *NAm:* half-liter, bottle; **tu viens boire une c.?** are you coming for a drink? (*b*) *Fr.C.Meas:* pint (0.568 l.).

choquant [ʃɔkɑ̃] *a.* shocking, displeasing, disagreeable, offensive; **un abus c.,** a gross, glaring, abuse.

choquer [ʃɔke] **1.** *v.tr.* (*a*) to strike, knock, bump (sth. against sth.); **nous avons choqué nos verres,** we clinked, chinked, glasses; (*b*) to shock, displease, offend; **être choqué de qch.,** to be scandalized, shocked, at, by, sth.; **sons qui choquent l'oreille,** sounds that grate on the ear; **mot qui choque,** offensive, rude, word; (*c*) to distress; **j'ai été choqué de le voir tellement changé,** I was shocked, it gave me a shock, to see such a change in him. **2. se c.,** to be shocked, scandalized; to take offence (**de,** at).

choral, -als [kɔral]. **1.** *a.* choral; **société chorale,** choral society. **2.** *n.m.* choral(e). **3.** *n.f.* **chorale,** choral society; choir.

chorée [kɔre] *n.f. Med:* chorea; *F:* Saint Vitus's dance.

chorégraphe [kɔregraf] *n.m. & f.* choreographer.

chorégraphie [kɔregrafi] *n.f.* choreography.

chorégraphique [kɔregrafik] *a.* choreographic.

choriste [kɔrist] *n.m.* chorister (in church); choir member; chorus singer (in opera).

chorus [kɔrys] *n.m.* **faire c.,** to chorus s.o.'s words; to express approval, repeat a request in chorus.

chose [ʃoz] **1.** *n.f.* thing; (*a*) **un tas de choses,** a pile, heap, of things; **j'ai un tas de choses à faire,** I've loads, masses, of things to do; **c'est de deux choses l'une,** you have the choice of two things; **dites bien des choses de ma part à . . .,** remember me, give my regards, to . . .; **j'ai bien des choses à vous raconter,** I've a lot (of things) to tell you; **la c. en question,** the case in point; **je vais vous expliquer la c.,** I'll explain it, the matter, to you; **cela n'est plus la même c.,** that alters the case; **je vois la c.,** I see how things stand, I understand; **c. curieuse, personne n'en savait rien,** curiously enough nobody knew anything about it; **avant toute c.,** first of all, above all; **dans l'état actuel des choses,** as things are, stand, at the moment; **ce n'est pas c. aisée de . . .,** it's no easy matter to . . .; **il fait bien les choses,** he does things in style; **ne pas faire les choses à demi,** not to do things by halves; *Jur:* **c. jugée,** res judicata; (*b*) property, goods; chattel. **2.** (*a*) *n.m. & f. F:* **Monsieur C, Madame C,** Mr, Mrs, What-d'ye-call-him, -her; **le petit Chose,** little What's-his-name; (*b*) what's it, thingummy; **passe-moi le c.,** pass me the what's-its-name. **3.** *a.inv. F:* **être, se sentir, tout c.,** to feel funny, queer; **vous avez l'air tout c.,** you look upset, out of sorts.

chott [ʃɔt] *n.m. Geog:* saline lake, chott.

chou, -oux [ʃu] *n.m.* **1.** cabbage; **c. pommé,** garden cabbage; **c. frisé,** kale; **c. de Bruxelles,** Brussels sprout; **c. de Milan,** Savoy (cabbage); **c. rouge,** red cabbage; **c. marin,** seakale; *F:* **aller planter ses choux,** to go and live in, to retire to, the country; **faire ses choux gras de qch.,** to thrive on, feather one's nest with, sth.; **faire c. blanc,** to draw a blank; **mon petit c.,** darling, dear; **être dans les choux,** (i) to be in a fix, a mess; (ii) come in last, be nowhere, lose; **rentrer dans le c. à qn,** to attack, go for, s.o.; **feuille de c.,** poor quality newspaper, rag. **2.** bow, rosette, chou (of ribbon). **3.** *Cu:* **c. à la crème,** cream bun; **pâte à choux,** choux pastry. **4.** *a. inv. F:* pretty, lovely.

choucas [ʃuka] *n.m.* jackdaw.

chouchou, -oute [ʃuʃu, -ut] *n. F:* pet, darling; blue-eyed boy; **le c. du prof,** teacher's pet.

chouchouter [ʃuʃute] *v.tr. F:* to pet, coddle (child).

choucroute [ʃukrut] *n.f. Cu:* sauerkraut.

chouette[1] [ʃwɛt] *n.f. Orn:* **c. des clochers, c. effraie,** screech owl, barn owl; **c. des bois,** wood owl, brown owl; **c. hulotte,** tawny owl.

chouette[2] *a. & int. F:* terrific, marvellous, great; **c. (alors)!** great! fantastic! splendid!

chou-fleur [ʃuflœr] *n.m.* cauliflower; **oreille en c.-f.,** cauliflower ear; *pl. choux-fleurs.*

chou-navet [ʃunavɛ] *n.m.* swede; *pl. choux-navets.*

chou-palmiste [ʃupalmist] *n.m. Bot:* palm cabbage; *pl. choux-palmistes.*

chou-rave [ʃurav] *n.m.* kohlrabi; *pl. choux-raves.*

chow-chow [ʃuʃu] *n.m.* chow (dog); *pl. chows-chows.*

choyer [ʃwaje] *v.tr.* **(je choie; je choierai)** to pet, coddle; **c. un espoir,** to cherish a hope.

chrême [krɛm] *n.m. Ecc:* chrism, holy oil.

chrestomathie [krɛstɔmati] *n.f.* chrestomathy, anthology.

chrétien, -ienne [kretjɛ̃, -jɛn] *a. & n.* Christian.

chrétiennement [kretjɛnmɑ̃] *adv.* in a Christian manner, like a Christian.

chrétienté [kretjɛ̃te] *n.f.* Christendom.

Christ [krist] *n.m.* **1. le C.** [ləkrist], Christ; **Jésus-C.** [ʒezykri], Jesus Christ. **2.** crucifix.

christiania [kristjanja] *n.m. Ski:* christiania, christie (turn).

christianisation [kristjanizasjɔ̃] *n.f.* christianization.

christianiser [kristjanize] *v.tr.* to christianize.

christianisme [kristjanism] *n.m.* Christianity.

Christophe [kristɔf] *Pr.n.m.* Christopher.

chromage [kromaʒ] *n.m.* chromium plating.

chromate [krɔmat] *n.m. Ch:* chromate.

chromatique [krɔmatik] *a.* (*a*) *Mus: Opt: etc:* chromatic; (*b*) *Biol:* chromosomal.

chromatiquement [krɔmatikmɑ̃] *adv. Mus:* chromatically.
chromatisme [krɔmatism] *n.m. Art: Mus:* chromatism, chromatic aberration.
chrome [krom] *n.m.* **1.** (*a*) *Ch:* chromium; (*b*) chromium fitting; *F:* **faire (briller) les chromes,** to polish the chrome (of cars, bicycles, etc.). **2.** *Com:* chrome; **jaune de c.,** chrome yellow.
chromé [krome] *a.* **1. cuir c.,** chrome(-tanned) leather; **veau c.,** box calf; **acier c.,** chrome steel. **2.** chromium-plated (metal).
chromer [krome] *v.tr.* to chromium-plate (metal); to chrome (leather, steel).
chromique [krɔmik] *a. Ch:* chromic (acid).
chromo [krɔmo] *n.m. F:* chromo(lithograph); colour print.
chromosome [krɔmozom] *n.m. Biol:* chromosome.
chromosomique [krɔmozomik] *a. Biol:* chromosomal.
chronicité [krɔnisite] *n.f.* chronicity (of disease, etc.).
chronique[1] [krɔnik] *a.* chronic (disease, etc.).
chronique[2] *n.f.* **1.** chronicle. **2.** *Journ:* (financial, etc.) news, report, column.
chroniquement [krɔnikmɑ̃] *adv.* chronically.
chroniqueur, -euse [krɔnikœr, -øz] *n.* **1.** chronicler. **2.** *Journ:* columnist; reporter.
chrono [krɔnɔ] *n.m. F:* stopwatch; **du 220 (km/h) (au) c.,** recorded speed of 220 (km/h).
chronologie [krɔnɔlɔʒi] *n.f.* chronology.
chronologique [krɔnɔlɔʒik] *a.* chronological.
chronologiquement [krɔnɔlɔʒikmɑ̃] *adv.* chronologically.
chronométrage [krɔnɔmetraʒ] *n.m.* time-keeping; timing.
chronomètre [krɔnɔmɛtr̥] *n.m.* **1.** chronometer. **2.** stopwatch.
chronométrer [krɔnɔmetre] *v.tr.* **(je chronomètre; je chronométrerai)** *Sp:* to keep the time; to time (race, etc.).
chronométreur [krɔnɔmetrœr] *n.m.* **1.** *Sp:* timekeeper. **2.** *Ind:* time (and motion) study expert.
chronométrique [krɔnɔmetrik] *a.* chronometric(al).
chrysalide [krizalid] *n.f. Ent:* chrysalis, pupa; *Fig:* **sortir de sa c.,** to come out of one's shell.
chrysanthème [krizɑ̃tɛm] *n.m. Bot:* chrysanthemum.
chrysocal(e) [krizɔkal] *n.m. Metall:* pinchbeck.
chrysolithe [krizɔlit] *n.f. Miner:* chrysolite, olivine.
chuchotement [ʃyʃɔtmɑ̃] *n.m.* whisper(ing).
chuchoter [ʃyʃɔte] **1.** *v.i.* to whisper; **parler en chuchotant,** to speak in a whisper. **2.** *v.tr.* **c. qch. à l'oreille de qn,** to whisper sth. in s.o.'s ear.
chuchoterie [ʃyʃɔtri] *n.f.* whisper(ing); whispered conversation.
chuchoteur, -euse [ʃyʃɔtœr, -øz] **1.** *a.* whispering. **2.** *n.* whisperer.
chuintant [ʃɥɛ̃tɑ̃] *a. & n.f. Ling:* **(consonne) chuintante,** tongue-and-after-gum consonant; **sons chuintants,** hushing sounds (*e.g.* ʃ, ʒ).
chuintement [ʃɥɛ̃tmɑ̃] *n.m.* (*a*) *Ling:* pronunciation of *s* as *sh*; lisping; (*b*) hissing.
chuinter [ʃɥɛ̃te] *v.i.* **1.** (*of owl*) to hoot. **2.** (*a*) *Ling:* to pronounce *s* as *sh;* to lisp; (*b*) (*of gas*) to hiss.
chut [ʃyt,] *int.* hush! sh!
chute [ʃyt] *n.f.* **1.** (*a*) fall; **faire une c. (de cheval, de bicyclette),** to have a fall, a tumble, a spill; *F:* to come a cropper; to fall off one's horse, bicycle; **c. libre,** free fall; *P.N:* **c. de pierres,** danger! falling stones; *Th:* **c. du rideau,** fall of the curtain; **c. de pluie, de neige,** rainfall, snowfall; **c. du jour,** nightfall; **c. des feuilles,** autumn, *NAm:* fall; **c. des cheveux,** hair loss; **c. des prix,** fall, drop, in prices; (*b*) (down)-fall, collapse (of ministry, etc.); **la c. de l'homme,** the fall; **c. d'eau,** waterfall; **les Chutes Victoria,** the Victoria Falls; **hauteur de c.,** (i) fall, head (of water); (ii) drop (of pile ram); **il m'a entraîné dans sa c.,** he has dragged me down with him; *Th:* **c. d'une pièce,** failure, *F:* flop, of a play; *Cards:* **avoir deux levées de c.,** to be two tricks down; (*c*) drop, fall (in pressure, temperature, etc.); *El:* **c. de potentiel,** voltage drop. **2.** pitch (of roof); hang (of dress); cadence (of voice, etc.); **c. des reins,** small of the back. **3.** (*a*) off-cut (of wood); (*b*) snippets, trimmings (of cloth, etc.); (*c*) scrap (of metal). **4.** *Ind: Min:* shoot.
chuter [ʃyte] *v.i.* (*a*) *F:* to fall, tumble, down; to come a cropper; (*b*) *Th:* (*of play*) to be a failure, to flop; (*c*) *Cards:* **c. de deux levées,** to be two tricks down.
Chypre [ʃipr̥] *Pr.n.f. Geog:* **(l'île de) C.,** Cyprus.
chypriote [ʃiprijɔt] *a. & n. Geog:* Cypriot.
ci[1] [si] *adv.* **de ci, de là,** here and there, on all sides; **ci-gît . . ., ci-gisent . . .,** here lies . . ., here lie . . ..
ci[2] *dem. pron. neut. inv. F:* **faire ci et ça,** to do this, that, and the other; **comme ci, comme ça,** so so.
ci-après [siaprɛ] *adv.* here(in)after; later, further on, below (in the book, etc.).
cibiche [sibiʃ] *n.f. F:* cigarette, fag, ciggie.
cibiste [sibist] *n.* user of citizen band radio; C.B. user.
cible [sibl̥] *n.f.* target, mark; **servir de c. aux railleries de qn,** to be a butt, the target, for s.o.'s jokes.
ciboire [sibwar] *n.m. Ecc:* pyx, ciborium.
ciboule [sibul] *n.f. Bot: Cu:* spring onion.
ciboulette [sibulɛt] *n.f. Bot: Cu:* chive(s).
ciboulot [sibulo] *n.m. P:* head, noddle, nut.
cicatrice [sikatris] *n.f.* scar.
cicatriciel, -ielle [sikatrisjɛl] *a.* cicatricial (mark, etc.); **tissu c.,** scar tissue.
cicatrisant [sikatrizɑ̃] *a. & n.m.* healing, cicatrizing (lotion, etc.).
cicatrisation [sikatrizasjɔ̃] *n.f.* cicatrization, healing, closing (up) (of wound, etc.).
cicatriser [sikatrize] **1.** *v.tr.* to heal (wound, etc). **2.** *v.i. & pr.* (*of wound, etc.*) to heal (up), scar over.
cicéro [sisero] *n.m. Typ:* pica, twelve-point type.
Cicéron [siserɔ̃] *Pr.n.m. Lit:* Cicero.
cicérone [siserɔn] *n.m.* guide, cicerone.
cicéronien, -ienne [siserɔnjɛ̃, -jɛn] *a. Lit:* Ciceronian.
ci-contre [sikɔ̃tr̥] *adv.* (*a*) opposite, in the margin; *Book-k:* **porté ci-c.,** as per contra; (*b*) annexed (circular, etc.).
ci-dessous [sidsu] *adv.* hereunder, below, undermentioned.
ci-dessus [sidsy] *adv.* above(-mentioned).
ci-devant [sidvɑ̃] **1.** *adv.* previously, formerly. **2.** *n.m. & f. inv. Fr. Hist:* ci-devant, aristocrat.
cidre [sidr̥] *n.m.* cider; **c. bouché,** champagne cider.
cidrerie [sidrəri] *n.f.* **1.** cider house. **2.** cidermaking.
ciel, *pl.* **ciels, cieux** [sjɛl, sjø] *n.m.* **1.** (*a*) sky, firmament, heaven; **à c. ouvert,** in the open air, out of doors; **(couleur) bleu (de) c.,** sky-blue; **élever qn aux cieux, jusqu'au c.,** to laud s.o. to the skies; **être suspendu entre c. et terre,** to hang in mid-air; (*b*) (*pl. often* **ciels**) climate; **les ciels de l'Italie,** the skies of Italy; *Art:* **les ciels de Turner,** Turner's skies. **2.** heaven; **notre Père qui es aux cieux,** our Father which art in Heaven; **le royaume des cieux,** the Kingdom of Heaven; *F:* **tomber du c.,** to come out of the blue; **(juste) c.!** (good) heavens! heavens above! **3.** (*pl.* **ciels**) (*a*) *Ecc:* baldachin, canopy; (*b*) *Furn:* (bed) tester; (*c*) *Min:* roof (of quarry, etc.); **carrière à c. ouvert,** open(cast) quarry.
cierge [sjɛrʒ] *n.m.* **1.** *Ecc:* candle; **brûler un c. à un saint,** to burn a candle to a saint. **2.** *Bot:* cereus.

cigale [sigal] *n.f. Ent:* cicada.
cigare [sigar] *n.m.* **1.** cigar. **2.** *P:* head, nut.
cigarette [sigarɛt] *n.f.* cigarette.
cigarillo [sigarijo] *n.m.* cigarillo.
cigogne [sigɔɲ] *n.f.* **1.** *Orn:* stork. **2.** *Mch: etc:* crank lever.
ciguë [sigy] *n.f. Bot: Med:* hemlock.
ci-inclus [siɛ̃kly] *a. & adv.* (*inv. when it precedes the noun*) **la copie ci-incluse,** the enclosed copy; **ci-i. copie de votre lettre,** enclosed, herewith, a copy of your letter.
ci-joint [siʒwɛ̃] *a. & adv.* (*inv. when it precedes the noun*) attached, herewith, hereto (annexed); **les pièces ci-jointes,** the enclosed, attached documents; **vous trouverez ci-j. quittance,** please find receipt attached.
cil [sil] *n.m.* **1.** (eye)lash. **2.** *Nat.Hist:* cilium, hair; filament.
ciliare [siljɛr] *a.* ciliary.
cilice [silis] *n.m.* hair shirt.
cillement [sijmɑ̃] *n.m.* blinking.
ciller [sije] *v.i.* to blink; **personne n'ose c. devant lui,** no one dares move, bat, an eyelid in his presence.
cimaise [simɛz] *n.f. Arch:* cyma, picture rail, ogee moulding, dado.
cime [sim] *n.f.* **1.** summit (of hill, etc.); top (of tree, mast, etc.); peak (of mountain). **2.** *Bot:* cyme.
ciment [simɑ̃] *n.m.* cement; **c. armé,** reinforced concrete.
cimentation [simɑ̃tasjɔ̃] *n.f.* cementing.
cimenter [simɑ̃te] *v.tr.* to cement; to render (with cement); **c. une alliance,** to cement, consolidate, an alliance.
cimenterie [simɑ̃tri] *n.f.* cement works.
cimeterre [simtɛr] *n.m.* scimitar.
cimetière [simtjɛr] *n.m.* cemetery, graveyard, burial ground; churchyard.
cimier¹ [simje] *n.m.* crest (of helmet).
cimier² *n.m.* haunch (of venison); rump, buttock (of beef).
cinabre [sinabr̥] *n.m.* (*a*) cinnaber; (*b*) *Art:* vermilion.
ciné [sine] *n.m. P:* flicks, pictures, *NAm:* movies.
cinéaste [sineast] *n.m. & f.* film producer, director, maker.
ciné-club [sineklœb] *n.m.* film club, cine-club; *pl. ciné-clubs.*
cinéma [sinema] *n.m.* **1.** cinema, *NAm:* motion pictures, movies; **faire du c.,** to be a film actor, movie actor; **acteur de c.,** film actor, *NAm:* movie actor; **c. muet,** silent films; **industrie du c.,** film industry; *NAm:* motion picture, movie, industry; *F:* **c'est du c.,** it's all an act, all put on. **2.** (*theatre*) cinema, pictures, film theatre, *NAm:* movie theater.
cinémascope [sinemaskɔp] *n.m. R.t.m:* cinemascope.
cinémathèque [sinematɛk] *n.f.* film library.
cinématique [sinematik] *Mec:* **1.** *a.* kinematic(al). **2.** *n.f.* kinematics.
cinématographe [sinematɔgraf] *n.m.* cinematograph.
cinématographie [sinematɔgrafi] *n.f.* cinematography.
cinématographier [sinematɔgrafje] *v.tr.* to film.
cinématographique [sinematɔgrafik] *a.* cinematographic; film (production, etc.).
cinéphile [sinefil] *n.* film enthusiast.
cinéraire [sinerɛr] **1.** *a.* cinerary (urn, etc.). **2.** *n.f. Bot:* cineraria.
cinérama [sinerama] *n.m. R.t.m:* cinerama.
ciné-roman [sinerɔmɑ̃] *n.m.* film story; *pl. ciné-romans.*
cinétique [sinetik] **1.** *a.* kinetic, motive (energy, etc.). **2.** *n.f.* kinetics.
cing(h)alais, -aise [sɛ̃galɛ, -ɛz] **1.** *a. & n. Geog:* Sin(g)halese. **2.** *n.m. Ling:* Sin(g)halese.
cinglant [sɛ̃glɑ̃] *a.* lashing (rain, etc.); cutting, biting (wind, etc.); bitter (cold); stinging, cutting, scathing (remark).
cinglé [sɛ̃gle] *a. P:* cracked, potty; **il est complètement c.,** he's nuts, crackers.
cingler¹ [sɛ̃gle] *v.i. Nau: O:* (*a*) to sail (before the wind), to scud along; (*b*) to steer a given course.
cingler² *v.tr.* **1.** to lash, cut (horse, etc.) with a whip; to lash out at (s.o.); **la grêle lui cinglait le visage,** the hail stung his face. **2.** *Metall:* to shingle, forge (bloom).
cinoche [sinɔʃ] *n.m. P:* cinema, flick house.
cinoque [sinɔk] *a. P:* mad, crazy.
cinq [sɛ̃k] *num.a.inv. & n.m.inv.* (*as card. a. before a noun or adj. beginning with a consonant sound* [sɛ̃] five; **c. (petits) garçons** [sɛ̃(pti)garsɔ̃], five (little) boys; **c. hommes** [sɛ̃kɔm], five men; **j'en ai c.** [sɛ̃k], I've got five; **Henri C.,** Henry the Fifth; **le c. mars** [sɛ̃(k)-mars], March the fifth; **il était moins c.,** it was a near thing, a close shave; **je lui ai répondu en c. lettres,** I told him to go to blazes, to go to hell.
cinquantaine [sɛ̃kɑ̃tɛn] *n.f.* (approximate) fifty; **une c. de personnes,** about, some, fifty people; fifty or so people; **avoir passé la c.,** to be in one's fifties.
cinquante [sɛ̃kɑ̃t] *num.a.inv. & n.m. inv.* fifty; **billet de c. francs,** fifty-franc note; **page c.,** page fifty; **demeurer au numéro c.,** to live at number fifty; **les années c.,** the fifties (1950–1959).
cinquantenaire [sɛ̃kɑ̃tnɛr] **1.** *n.m.* fiftieth anniversary, jubilee. **2.** *a.* fifty year(s) old.
cinquantième [sɛ̃kɑ̃tjɛm] **1.** *num.a. & n.* fiftieth. **2.** *n.m.* fiftieth (part).
cinquième [sɛ̃kjɛm] **1.** *num. a. & n.m. & f.* fifth; **loger au c. (étage),** to live on the fifth floor, *NAm:* the sixth floor. **2.** *n.m.* fifth (part). **3.** *n.m. Sch:* **(classe de) c.,** = second form, year (of secondary school).
cinquièmement [sɛ̃kjɛmmɑ̃] *adv.* fifthly, in (the) fifth place.
cintrage [sɛ̃traʒ] *n.m.* bend(ing) (of pipes, etc.).
cintre [sɛ̃tr̥] *n.m.* **1.** concave surface; curve, bend. **2.** *Arch:* (*a*) arch (of tunnel, etc.); (*b*) soffit (of arch); **arc en plein c.,** semicircular arch. **3.** coathanger. **4.** *Th:* **les cintres,** the flies.
cintré [sɛ̃tre] *a.* (*a*) arched (window, etc.); (*b*) bent, curved (timber, etc.); (*c*) fitted (jacket, etc.); **taille cintrée,** nipped-in waist; (*d*) *F:* **il est complètement c.,** he's nuts, crackers.
cintrer [sɛ̃tre] *v.tr.* (*a*) to bend, curve (pipe, rail, etc.); (*b*) to arch (window); (*c*) to take in (jacket, etc.) at the waist.
cipaye [sipaj] *n.m.* sepoy; **la révolte des cipayes,** the Indian Mutiny.
cirage [siraʒ] *n.m.* **1.** waxing, polishing (of floors, etc.). **2.** (wax, shoe) polish; *F:* **être dans le c.,** (i) *Av:* to be flying blind; (ii) not to understand, to be all at sea.
circoncire [sirkɔ̃sir] *v.tr.* (*pr.p* **circoncisant;** *p.p.* **circoncis;** *pr.ind.* **je circoncis;** *pr.sub.* **je circoncise;** *p.h.* **je circoncis;** *fu.* **je circoncirai)** to circumcise.
circoncision [sirkɔ̃sizjɔ̃] *n.f.* circumcision.
circonférence [sirkɔ̃ferɑ̃s] *n.f.* **1.** (*a*) circumference; (*b*) girth (of tree). **2.** perimeter, boundaries (of town, etc.).
circonflexe [sirkɔ̃flɛks] *a.* circumflex (accent).
circonlocution [sirkɔ̃lɔkysjɔ̃] *n.f.* circumlocution; **parler par circonlocutions,** to speak in a roundabout way; *F:* to beat about the bush.
circonscription [sirkɔ̃skripsjɔ̃] *n.f.* **1.** circumscription, circumscribing. **2.** *Adm: etc:* division, district,

area; **c. électorale,** electoral district, ward; constituency; **c. de remise gratuite,** radius of free delivery, free delivery area (of telegrams, etc.).

circonscrire [sirkɔ̃skrir] (*conj. like* ÉCRIRE) **1.** *v.tr.* to circumscribe; (*a*) to draw a line round (sth.); (*b*) to surround, encircle (**par,** with, by); (*c*) to limit, bound; **c. son sujet,** to define the scope of one's subject; **c. un incendie,** to bring a fire under control. **2. se c.,** to be bounded, limited; **tout le débat se circonscrit autour d'une seule idée,** the whole debate centres on, is centred around, one idea.

circonspect [sirkɔ̃spɛ (kt)] *a.* circumspect, prudent, cautious, wary, guarded.

circonspection [sirkɔ̃spɛksjɔ̃] *n.f.* circumspection, caution, wariness; **avec c.,** circumspectly, warily, cautiously.

circonstance [sirkɔ̃stɑ̃s] *n.f.* **1.** circumstance, incident, event, case, occasion; **dans la c.,** in this instance; **en pareille c.,** under such circumstances, in such a case; **à la hauteur des circonstances,** equal to the occasion; **eu égard aux, étant donné les, circonstances,** all things considered, in the circumstances; **profiter de la c.,** to make the most of the opportunity; **vers de c.,** occasional verse; **paroles de c.,** words suited to the occasion; appropriate, suitable, words. **2.** *Jur:* **circonstances et dépendances,** appurtenances; **circonstances aggravantes, atténuantes,** aggravating, extenuating circumstances.

circonstancié [sirkɔ̃stɑ̃sje] *a.* circumstantial, detailed (account).

circonstanciel, -ielle [sirkɔ̃stɑ̃sjɛl] *a.* (*a*) circumstantial; **des mesures rigoureusement circonstantielles,** measures strictly due to the emergency, to exceptional circumstances; (*b*) *Gram:* **complément c.,** adverbial complement.

circonvenir [sirkɔ̃vnir] *v.tr.* (*conj. like* VENIR) to circumvent, thwart; to outwit (s.o.).

circonvolution [sirkɔ̃vɔlysjɔ̃] *n.f. Anat: Arch:* convolution; *Arch:* circumvolution (of volute, etc.).

circuit [sirkɥi] *n.m.* **1.** (*a*) circumference, compass (of town, etc.); (*b*) *Sp:* round, lap; circuit (for motor racing, etc.); (*c*) **c. (touristique),** (organized) trip, tour; (*d*) **circuits commerciaux,** commercial trading, channels; channels of circulation. **2.** deviation, circuitous route; detour. **3.** *El:* circuit; **mettre en c.,** to connect, switch on; **couper le c.,** to switch off; **rétablir le c.,** to switch on (again); **mettre une lampe hors c.,** to disconnect a lamp; **c. ouvert, fermé,** open, closed, circuit; **télévision à c. fermé,** closed-circuit television; *Elcs:* **c. imprimé,** printed circuit; **c. intégré,** integrated circuit.

circulaire [sirkylɛr] **1.** *a.* circular; **billet c.,** excursion ticket; **scie c.,** circular saw; *Mec.E:* **mouvement c.,** rotary motion. **2.** *n.f.* circular.

circulairement [sirkylɛrmɑ̃] *adv.* in a circle.

circulant [sirkylɑ̃] *a.* circulating; *Fin:* **billets circulants,** notes in circulation.

circulation [sirkylasjɔ̃] *n.f.* **1.** circulation (of air, blood, news, etc.); **mettre un livre en c.,** to put a book into circulation; **mettre un bruit en c.,** to spread, circulate, a rumour. **2.** traffic; **c. aérienne,** air traffic; **c. à sens unique, à deux sens,** one-way, two-way, traffic; *P.N:* **c. interdite,** no thoroughfare; **arrêt de c.,** traffic block; **accident de la c.,** road accident; *Rail:* **c. des trains,** running of trains. **3.** *Fin:* currency, circulation (of banknotes, etc.). **4. libre c. des travailleurs,** free movement of workers.

circulatoire [sirkylatwar] *a. Anat:* circulatory.

circuler [sirkyle] *v.i.* **1.** (*of blood, air, etc.*) to circulate, flow; **faire c. l'air,** to circulate the air; **faire c. la bouteille,** to pass, hand, the bottle round. **2.** to circulate, move about; *P.N:* **défense de c. sur l'herbe!** please keep off the grass! **circulez!** move along! **les autobus circulent jour et nuit,** the buses run day and night; **des bruits circulent,** rumours are going about, round; **faire c. une nouvelle,** to spread a piece of news.

circumnavigation [sirkɔmnavigasjɔ̃] *n.f.* circumnavigation.

cire [sir] *n.f.* **1.** (*a*) wax; **c. d'abeilles,** beeswax; **c. à cacheter,** sealing wax; (*b*) (wax) polish. **2.** *Orn:* cere (of beak).

ciré [sire] **1.** *a.* waxed, polished; **toile cirée,** oilcloth, American cloth. **2.** *n.m. Cost:* (suit of) oilskins.

cirer [sire] *v.tr.* to wax (thread, etc.); to polish (floors, etc.); **c. des chaussures,** to polish shoes; *F:* **c. les bottes à qn,** to lick s.o.'s boots.

cireur, -euse[1] [sirœr, -øz] **1.** *n.* (*pers.*) (*a*) shoeblack; (*b*) (floor) polisher. **2.** *n.f.* (*machine*) (electric) (floor) polisher.

cireux, -euse[2] [sirø, -øz] *a.* waxy, wax-like, waxen.

cirier, -ière [sirje, -jɛr] **1.** *a.* wax-producing, wax (tree, bee, etc.). **2.** *n.m.* (*a*) wax chandler, wax-taper maker; worker in wax; (*b*) *Bot:* wax myrtle. **3.** *n.f.* **cirière,** wax-making bee.

ciron [sirɔ̃] *n.m. Arach:* (cheese, itch) mite.

cirque [sirk] *n.m.* **1.** (*a*) circus; (*b*) amphitheatre. **2.** *Geol:* cirque, corrie, cwm.

cirr(h)e [sir] *n.m.* **1.** *Bot:* cirrus, tendril. **2.** *Ich:* barbel. **3.** *Z:* tentacle.

cirrhose [siroz] *n.f. Med:* cirrhosis.

cirro-cumulus [sirɔkymylys] *n.m.inv. Meteor:* cirrocumulus.

cirro-stratus [sirɔstratys] *n.m.inv. Meteor:* cirrostratus.

cirrus [sirys] *n.m.inv. Meteor:* cirrus; *F:* mare's tail.

cisaille [sizɑj] *n.f.* **1.** parings, cuttings (of metal). **2.** (*a*) *Bookb: etc:* guillotine; cutting press; (*b*) *sg. or pl.* shears; wirecutters; *Hort:* **c. à haies,** hedge clipper(s); **c. à bordures,** edging shears.

cisaillement [sizɑjmɑ̃] *n.m.* **1.** (*a*) cutting, shearing (of metal); (*b*) clipping (of coins); (*c*) pruning (of branches); (*d*) shearing (off) (of rivet). **2.** *Mec:* shearing (stress), shear.

cisailler [sizɑje] **1.** *v.tr.* (*a*) to cut, shear (metal); to clip (coins); to prune (branches). **2. se c.,** (*of metal*) to shear (off).

cisalpin [sizalpɛ̃] *a. A.Hist: A.Geog:* on the Roman side of the Alps; Cisalpine; *Hist:* **République cisalpine,** Cisalpine Republic.

ciseau, -eaux [sizo] *n.m.* **1.** chisel; **c. à froid,** cold chisel. **2.** *pl.* (*a*) scissors; *Hort: etc:* shears, clippers; **coup de ciseaux,** snip (of the scissors); *Dressm:* **ciseaux à denteler,** pinking shears; (*b*) *Wr: etc:* scissors.

ciselage [sizlaʒ] *n.m.* = CISELLEMENT.

ciseler [sizle] *v.tr.* **(je cisèle; je ciselerai)** (*a*) to chase, engrave (gold, silver); to chisel, carve (wood); to tool, emboss (leather); to cut, shear (velvet); **visage délicatement ciselé,** finely chiselled features; (*b*) to polish up, work on (poem, etc.).

ciseleur [sizlœr] *n.m.* engraver; carver.

cisellement [sizɛlmɑ̃] *n.m.* chiselling (of wood); chasing, engraving (of gold, silver); tooling, embossing (of leather); cutting, shearing (of velvet).

ciselure [sizlyr] *n.f.* chasing, engraving (of gold, silver); chiselling, carving (of wood); tooling, embossing (of leather).

cistercien, -ienne [sistɛrsjɛ̃, -jɛn] *a. & n.* **1.** *Geog:* (native, inhabitant) of Cîteaux. **2.** *Ecc:* Cistercian.

citadelle [sitadɛl] *n.f.* citadel; stronghold.

citadin, -ine [sitadɛ̃, -in] **1.** *n.* townsman, townswoman. **2.** *a.* (belonging to a) town, city.

citation [sitasjɔ̃] *n.f.* **1.** quotation, citation. **2.** *Jur:* citation, (writ of) summons; **c. des témoins,** subpoena of witnesses; **notifier une c. à qn,** (i) to serve a summons on s.o.; (ii) to subpoena s.o. **3.** *Mil:* **c. (à l'ordre du jour)** = mention in dispatches.

cité [site] *n.f.* (*a*) city; (large) town; **droit de c.,** freedom of the city; **gagner droit de c.,** to be accepted; (*b*) **c. (ouvrière),** housing estate; **c. universitaire** = students' hall(s) of residence.

Cîteaux [sito] *Pr.n.m. Geog:* Cîteaux; *Ecc:* **L'ordre de C.,** the Cistercian Order.

cité-dortoir [sitedɔrtwar] *n.f.* dormitory town; *pl. cités-dortoirs.*

cité-jardin [siteʒardɛ̃] *n.f.* garden city; *pl. cités-jardins.*

citer [site] *v.tr.* **1.** to quote, cite; **c. qn en exemple,** to quote s.o., hold s.o. up, as an example. **2.** *Jur:* to summon (s.o. before the court), to subpoena (witness). **3.** *Mil:* **c. qn (à l'ordre du jour)** = to mention s.o. in dispatches.

citerne [sitɛrn] *n.f.* tank, cistern, reservoir.

cithare [sitar] *n.f. Mus:* **1.** *Gr.Ant:* cithara. **2.** zither.

citoyen, -enne [sitwajɛ̃, -ɛn] *n.* citizen; **droits de c.,** civic rights, citizenship; **c. d'honneur** = freeman of a city; *F:* **c'est un drôle de c.!** he's a queer customer!

citoyenneté [sitwajɛnte] *n.f.* citizenship; **c. d'honneur d'une ville** = freedom of a city.

citrate [sitrat] *n.m. Ch:* citrate.

citrique [sitrik] *a. Ch:* citric (acid).

citron [sitrɔ̃] *n.m.* **1.** *Bot:* (*generic term including*) lemon, lime, citron; **bois de c.,** citrus wood. **2.** (*a*) lemon; **c. pressé,** fresh lemon juice; **essence de c.,** lemon oil; **écorce de c.,** lemon peel; (*b*) *a.inv.* lemon-yellow, lemon(-coloured); (*c*) *P:* head, nut.

citronnade [sitrɔnad] *n.f.* still lemonade, lemon squash.

citronné [sitrɔne] *a.* (*a*) lemon-scented; (*b*) lemon-flavoured.

citronnelle [sitrɔnɛl] *n.f.* **1.** *Bot:* citronella.

citronnier [sitrɔnje] *n.m. Bot:* lemon tree; citrus (tree).

citrouille [sitruj] *n.f.* **1.** *Bot:* pumpkin, gourd. **2.** *P:* (*a*) head, nut; (*b*) idiot, fathead.

cive [siv] *n.f. Bot: Cu:* chive(s).

civet [sivɛ] *n.m. Cu:* stew (of venison, etc.); **c. de lièvre** = jugged hare.

civette[1] [sivɛt] *n.f.* **1.** *Z:* civet (cat). **2.** *Com:* civet (perfume).

civette[2] *n.f. Bot: Cu:* chive(s).

civière [sivjɛr] *n.f.* **1.** stretcher. **2.** bier (for coffin).

civil [sivil] *a.* civil. **1.** (*a*) civil (rights, etc.); **guerre civile,** civil war; (*b*) *Jur:* **droit c.,** civil law; (*c*) **liste civile,** civil list; (*d*) lay, secular (as opposed to ecclesiastical); civilian (as opposed to military); **mariage c.,** civil marriage; *n.m.* **un c.,** (i) a layman; (ii) a civilian; **dans la vie c., dans le c.,** in private, civilian, life; **en c.,** (i) (*of police*) in plain clothes; (ii) *Mil:* in civilian clothes, in mufti; *F:* in civvies. **2.** *A:* polite, courteous.

civilement [sivilmɑ̃] *adv.* civilly. **1.** *Jur:* (*a*) **se marier c.,** to contract a civil marriage, to be married at a registry office; **enterré c.,** buried without religious ceremony; (*b*) **poursuivre qn c.,** to bring a civil action against s.o.; **c. responsable,** liable for damages. **2.** *A:* politely, courteously.

civilisable [sivilizabl̩] *a.* civilizable.

civilisateur, -trice [sivilizatœr, -tris] **1.** *a.* civilizing. **2.** *n.* civilizer.

civilisation [sivilizasjɔ̃] *n.f.* civilization.

civiliser [sivilize] **1.** *v.tr.* to civilize. **2. se c.,** to become civilized, *F:* more civilized.

civilité [sivilite] *n.f.* **1.** civility, politeness, courtesy. **2. présenter ses civilités à qn,** to present one's compliments to s.o.

civique [sivik] *a.* civic (duties, etc.); civil (rights); *Sch:* **instruction c.,** civics; *esp. Fr.C:* **bibliothèque c.,** municipal, public, library.

civisme [sivism] *n.m.* good citizenship.

clabaudage [klabodaʒ] *n.m.* **1.** yelping, baying. **2.** ill-natured talk, (spiteful) gossip, backbiting.

clabauder [klabode] *v.i.* **1.** (*of dog*) to yelp, bark a lot; *Ven:* to give tongue falsely. **2. c. sur, contre, qn,** to say ill-natured things about s.o.

clabauderie [klabodri] *n.f.* = CLABAUDAGE **2.**

clabaudeur, -euse [klabodœr, -øz] **1.** *a. & n.* yelping, *Ven:* baying (hound). **2.** (*a*) *a.* gossiping; (*b*) *n.* gossip, scandalmonger.

clac [klak] *int.* crack! slam! snap!

clafoutis [klafuti] *n.m. Cu:* **c. aux pommes, c. limousin,** apples, (black) cherries, baked in batter.

claie [klɛ] *n.f.* **1.** (*a*) wattle, hurdle; *A:* **traîner qn sur la c.,** to drag s.o. to execution; (*b*) **c. à fruits,** (wicker) fruit tray. **2.** (*a*) screen, riddle; (*b*) *Hyd.E:* grid. **3.** fence (round field, etc.).

clair [klɛr] **1.** *a.* clear; (*a*) unclouded, limpid (water, etc.); **vitres claires,** transparent window panes; **teint c.,** clear complexion; **ciel c.,** cloudless sky; **voix claire,** clear voice; (*b*) obvious, manifest, plain (meaning, etc.); **explication claire,** lucid explanation; **il est c. qu'elle a tort,** she is obviously wrong; **voilà qui est c.!** that's clear (enough)! **c. comme le jour,** crystal clear, as clear as daylight, as crystal; **sa conduite n'est pas claire,** his behaviour is suspicious, *F:* fishy; **il passe le plus c. de son temps à . . .,** he spends most, the best, better, part, of his time in . . .; (*c*) bright, light (room, dress, etc.); **il fait c.,** (i) it's day(light); (ii) there's plenty of light; **il ne fait pas c.,** there isn't much light here; (*d*) light, pale (colour); **robe bleu c.,** pale blue dress; (*e*) thin (soup); light, thin (fabric). **2.** *adv.* plainly, clearly; **parler c.,** to speak clearly; **je commence à (y) voir c.,** I'm beginning to see, to understand. **3.** *n.m.* (*a*) light; **c. de lune,** moonlight; **au c. de (la) lune,** in the moonlight; **les clairs d'une peinture,** the (high) lights in a painting; (*b*) thin place (in stocking, etc.); (*c*) **en c.,** in plain language; **message en c.,** message in clear (*i.e.* not in code); (*d*) **tirer du vin au c.,** to decant wine; **tirer une affaire au c.,** to clear a matter up; **sabre au c.,** with drawn sword.

claire [klɛr] *n.f.* fattening pond (for oysters).

clairement [klɛrmɑ̃] *adv.* clearly, plainly.

clairet, -ette [klɛrɛ, -ɛt] **1.** *a.* **(vin) c.,** light-red wine; **voix clairette,** thin, high-pitched, voice. **2.** *n.f.* **clairette,** light sparkling wine.

claire-voie [klɛrvwa] *n.f.* **1.** open-work, lattice (-work); **porte à c.-v.,** (wicket) gate; **clôture à c.-v.,** fence, paling; **cloison à c.-v.,** grating; **caisse à c.-v.,** crate. **2.** (*a*) *Nau:* skylight, deadlight; (*b*) *Arch:* clerestory.

clairière [klɛrjɛr] *n.f.* **1.** clearing, glade. **2.** *Tex:* thin place.

clair-obscur [klɛrɔpskyr] *n.m. Art:* chiaroscuro, light and shade; *pl. clairs-obscurs.*

clairon [klɛrɔ̃] *n.m.* **1.** (*a*) bugle; (*b*) bugler. **2.** (*a*) clarion stop (of organ); (*b*) upper register (of clarinet).

claironnant [klɛrɔnɑ̃] *a.* loud, brassy (sound); **voix claironnante,** loud and piercing voice.

claironner [klɛrɔne] **1.** *v.i.* (*a*) to sound the bugle; (*b*) to shout loudly. **2.** *v.tr.* **c. une nouvelle,** to trumpet a piece of news.

clairsemé [klɛrsəme] *a.* scattered, sparse, (population, etc.); thinly sown (corn); thin (hair).

clairvoyance [klɛrvwajɑ̃s] *n.f.* perspicacity, clear-sightedness, shrewdness, acumen.

clairvoyant, -ante [klɛrvwajɑ̃, -ɑ̃t] *a.* perceptive, perspicacious, clear-sighted, shrewd.

clam [klam] *n.m. Moll:* clam.

clamecer [klamse] *v.i. P:* to die, snuff it.

clamer [klame] *v.tr.* **c. son innocence,** to protest one's innocence.

clameur [klamœr] *n.f.* (*a*) clamour; outcry; **c. publique,** hue and cry; (*b*) howling, roaring, (of wind, etc.).

clam(p)ser [klamse, klɑ̃pse] *v.i. P:* to die, kick it.

clan [klɑ̃] *n.m.* **1.** clan; **chef de c.,** head of the clan. **2.** set, clique.

clandestin, -ine [klɑ̃dɛstɛ̃, -in] *a.* clandestine, secret; underground; illicit (betting, etc.); **armée clandestine,** underground forces; **passager c.,** stowaway.

clandestinement [klɑ̃dɛstinmɑ̃] *adv.* clandestinely; secretly, illicitly.

clandestinité [klɑ̃dɛstinite] *n.f.* clandestineness; **dans la c.,** in secret; **passer dans la c.,** to go under ground.

clapet [klapɛ] *n.m.* **1.** *Tchn:* (*a*) valve; **c. d'admission,** inlet valve; **c. d'échappement,** exhaust valve; **boîte à c.,** (i) clack box; (ii) valve chest; **c. à charnière,** clack valve; (*b*) *I.C.E:* poppet valve, mushroom valve. **2.** *El:* rectifier. **3.** *P:* **elle a un de ces clapets!** she never stops (talking)!

clapier [klapje] *n.m.* **1.** rabbit burrow. **2.** rabbit hutch; **(lapin de) c.,** tame rabbit. **3.** *Geol:* (*in the Alps*) scree.

clapir [klapir] **1.** *v.i.* (*of rabbit*) to squeal. **2. se c.,** (*of rabbit*) to hide, squat, cower (in the burrow).

clapotage [klapɔtaʒ] *n.m.*, **clapotement** [klapɔtmɑ̃] *n.m.* lapping (of waves).

clapoter [klapɔte] *v.i.* (*of waves*) to lap; **mer qui clapote,** choppy sea.

clapoteux, -euse [klapɔtø, -øz] *a.* choppy (sea).

clapotis [klapɔti] *n.m.* lap(ping) (of waves).

clappement [klapmɑ̃] *n.m.* click(ing) (of the tongue).

clapper [klape] *v.i.* **c. de la langue,** to click (with) one's tongue.

claquage [klakaʒ] *n.m.* strain, pulling (of a muscle).

claquant [klakɑ̃] *a. P:* exhausting.

claque[1] [klak] *n.f.* **1.** slap, smack (on face, etc.); *F:* **tête à claques,** unpleasant, nasty, face. **2.** *Th:* hired clappers; claque. **3.** *P:* **il en a sa c.,** (i) he's on his last legs; (ii) he's fed up with it, he's had enough of it. **4.** *Fr.C:* galoshes, *NAm:* rubbers.

claque[2] *a. & n.m.* **(chapeau) c.,** opera hat, crush hat.

claqué [klake] *a. F:* fagged out, dog-tired.

claquement [klakmɑ̃] *n.m.* slam(ming), bang(ing) (of a door); chattering (of teeth); crack(ing) (of whip); clatter(ing) (of clogs, etc.); flap(ping) (of flag); snap(ping) (of fingers); click(ing) (of heels, tongue); *I.C.E:* slapping of pistons.

claquemurer [klakmyre] *v.tr. & pr.* **(se) c.,** to shut, coop (s.o., oneself) up.

claquer [klake] **1.** *v.i.* (*a*) (*of door*) to slam, bang; (*of clogs, etc.*) to clatter; (*of flag*) to flap; (*of piston, etc.*) to slap; **c. des mains,** to clap; applaud; **il claque des dents,** his teeth are chattering; *F:* **c. du bec,** to be hungry, starving; (*b*) *P:* (*of pers.*) to die, kick the bucket; (*of business*) to go to pieces, go bust; (*of machinery*), to give up, go phut; (*of light bulb*) to go; **le moteur m'a claqué dans les mains,** the engine died on me. **2.** *v.tr. & i.* **(faire) c.,** to slam, bang (door); to crack (whip); to snap (one's fingers); to click (one's heels). **3.** *v.tr.* (*a*) to slap, smack (child, etc.); (*b*) *F:* to tire, wear, (s.o.) out; (*c*) *F:* to squander, blue (money). **4. se c.** (*a*) *F:* to tire, wear, oneself out; (*b*) **se c. un muscle, un ligament,** to pull a muscle, tear a ligament.

claquet [klakɛ] *n.m.* clapper (of mill hopper).

claquette [klakɛt] *n.f.* **1.** *Ecc:* clapper; *Cin:* clapperboard. **2. (danse à) claquettes,** tap dancing, dance.

claquoir [klakwar] *n.m.* clapper; *Cin:* clapperboard.

clarification [klarifikasjɔ̃] *n.f.* **1.** clarifying (of liquid). **2.** clarification, enlightenment.

clarifier [klarifje] **1.** *v.tr.* (*a*) to clarify (wine, etc.); (*b*) to clarify, enlighten (the mind). **2. se c.,** to (become) clear.

clarine [klarin] *n.f.* cattle bell, cowbell.

clarinette [klarinɛt] *n.f.* (*a*) clarinet; (*b*) clarinettist.

clarinettiste [klarinɛtist] *n.* clarinettist.

clarisse [klaris] *n.f. Ecc:* **(sœur) c.,** nun of the order of St Clare.

clarté [klarte] *n.f.* **1.** clearness, clarity; (*a*) limpidity (of water, etc.); transparency (of glass, etc.); (*b*) lucidity, perspicuity (of style, etc.); **avoir de la c. d'esprit,** to be clear-minded; (*c*) *Lit:* **avoir des clartés sur un sujet,** to have some knowledge of a subject. **2.** light, brightness (of sun, etc.); **à la c. de la lune,** by the light of the moon, by moonlight; **les premières clartés du soleil,** the first gleams of the sun.

classe [klas] *n.f.* **1.** class, division, category; *Adm: etc:* rank; grade; **c. d'âge,** age group; **les hautes classes,** the upper classes; **la c. moyenne,** the middle class(es); **la c. ouvrière,** the working class(es); **produits de première c.,** top quality goods; *Av: etc:* **c. touriste,** tourist class; **billet de première, deuxième c.,** first-, second-class ticket; *F:* **avoir de la c.,** to have class, style. **2.** *Sch:* (*a*) class; form; *NAm:* grade; **hautes classes, classes supérieures,** upper forms; senior school; **la petite classe,** the junior school, the juniors; **c. de français,** French class; (*b*) **aller en c.,** to go to school; **être en c.,** to be in, at, school; **faire la c.,** to teach; **livre de c.,** schoolbook; **(salle de) c.,** classroom, schoolroom; **en sortant de c.,** on coming out of school. **3.** *Mil:* (*a*) annual contingent (of recruits); **la c. 1965,** the 1965 class, the 1965 levy; **faire ses classes,** to undergo basic training; (*b*) (*rank*) **(soldat de) deuxième c.,** private; *Mil.Av:* aircraftman, *U.S:* airman (basic); **(soldat de) première c.,** lance-corporal, *U.S:* private first class; *Mil.Av:* leading, senior, aircraftman, *U.S:* airman first class.

classement [klasmɑ̃] *n.m.* **1.** classification, classing (of plants, etc.); position, place (in class, race, etc.); *Sch:* **c. trimestriel,** end of term list; **donner le c.,** to give the results (of a competition). **2.** (*a*) sorting out, arranging (of articles); grading (of ore, etc.); *Rail:* marshalling (of trucks); (*b*) filing (of documents).

classer [klase] **1.** *v.tr.* (*a*) to classify (animal, etc.); to class; **monument classé,** scheduled, listed, monument; **classés par pays,** classified according to country; *Turf:* **non classés,** also ran; (*b*) to sort out, arrange (articles); to grade (ore, etc.); *Rail:* to marshal (trucks); (*c*) to file (documents); **c. une affaire,** to consider a matter closed. **2. ces faits se classent dans une autre catégorie,** these facts fall into another category; *Sp: etc:* **se c. troisième,** to be placed, come in, third.

classeur [klasœr] *n.m.* **1.** (*a*) rack (for letters, etc.); (index) file; (looseleaf) binder; (*b*) filing cabinet. **2.** (*pers.*) sorter (of letters, coal, etc.).

classicisme [klasisism] *n.m.* classicism.

classificateur, -trice [klasifikatœr, -tris] **1.** *n.* classifier. **2.** *a.* classifying.

classification [klasifikasjɔ̃] *n.f.* classification.

classifier [klasifje] *v.tr.* (*impf. & pr.sub.* **n. classifiions, v. classifiiez**) to classify.

classique [klasik] **1.** *a.* (*a*) *Sch:* academic, for school use; **livres classiques,** school books; (*b*) classical (period, music, etc.); classic (beauty, etc.); **études classiques,** classical studies; (*c*) standard (work, etc.); classic (example, joke, etc.); **guerre c.,** conventional warfare; *F:* **c'est le coup c.,** it's the same old story. **2.** *n.m.* **les classiques grecs, français,** the Greek, French, classics.

claudication [klodikasjɔ̃] *n.f. Lit:* limp(ing).
claudiquer [klodike] *v.i. Lit:* to limp.
clause [kloz] *n.f. Jur: etc:* clause; **c. additionnelle,** additional clause; rider; **c. pénale,** penalty clause; **c. de style,** formal clause.
claustral, -aux [klostral, -o] *a.* monastic.
claustration [klostrasjɔ̃] *n.f.* **1.** cloistering (in monastery, etc.). **2.** (close) confinement.
claustrer [klostre] **1.** *v.tr.* (*a*) to cloister; (*b*) to confine, shut up. **2. se c.,** to shut oneself up.
claustrophobie [klostrɔfɔbi] *n.f. Med:* claustrophobia.
claveau, -eaux [klavo] *n.m. Const: Arch:* archstone, voussoir; **c. droit,** keystone.
clavecin [klavsɛ̃] *n.m. Mus:* harpsichord.
claveciniste [klavsinist] *n.m. & f. Mus:* harpsichord player, harpsichordist.
clavetage [klavtaʒ] *n.m. Mec.E:* keying, wedging, cottering (of machine parts, etc.).
claveter [klavte] *v.tr.* **(je clavette; je clavetterai)** *Mec.E:* to key, wedge, cotter.
clavette [klavɛt] *n.f. Mec.E:* key (bolt), pin, cotter (pin).
clavicorde [klavikɔrd] *n.m. Mus:* clavichord.
clavicule [klavikyl] *n.f. Anat:* clavicle, collarbone.
clavier [klavje] *n.m.* **1.** keyboard (of piano, typewriter, etc.). **2.** range, compass (of clarinet, etc.).
claviste [klavist] *n.m. & f. Typ:* machine compositor.
clayette [klɛjɛt] *n.f.* (*a*) wire tray, rack; (wire) shelf (in fridge); (*b*) crate (for fruit, etc.).
clayon [klɛjɔ̃] *n.m.* **1.** (*a*) wicker tray (for draining cheeses, etc.); (*b*) *Dom.Ec:* cake rack. **2.** wattle enclosure.
clé [kle] *n.f.* = CLEF.
clébard [klebar], **clebs** [klɛps] *n.m. P:* dog, pooch, tyke.
clef [kle] *n.f.* **1.** key; (*a*) **c. de maison,** house key; latchkey; **fausse c.,** skeleton key; **fermer une porte à c.,** to lock a door; **donner un tour de c. à la porte,** to lock the door; **tenir qch. sous c.,** to keep sth. under lock and key; **la c. est sur la porte,** the key is in the lock; **louer une maison clefs en main,** to rent a house with immediate, vacant, possession; **mettre la c. sous la porte,** to do a moonlight flit; (*b*) **Orléans, c. de la vallée de la Loire,** Orléans, gateway to the Loire Valley; **position c.,** key position; **industrie c.,** key industry; (*c*) key (to a code, a mystery); clue (to a puzzle); **roman à c.,** novel introducing real characters under fictitious names. **2.** *Mus:* (*a*) clef; **c. de sol,** treble clef; (*b*) key signature; **jouer avec des dièses à la c.,** to play in sharp keys. **3. c. de voûte,** keystone, crown (of arch). **4.** (*a*) *Tls:* wrench, spanner; **c. anglaise,** adjustable spanner, monkey wrench; **c. à douille, en, à, tube,** box spanner; **c. fermée,** ring spanner; **c. plate,** (open) end wrench; (*b*) *Plumb:* handle (of tap); plug (of cock); (*c*) *Civ.E:* **c. (de tuyau de poêle),** damper; (*d*) *Mus:* peg (of stringed instrument). **5.** *El:* switch (key); *Tp:* **c. d'appel,** call(ing) key; call button; *Tg:* **c. Morse,** Morse key. **6.** *Wr:* lock.
clématite [klematit] *n.f. Bot:* clematis.
clémence [klemɑ̃s] *n.f.* **1.** clemency, mercy, leniency (**pour, envers,** to(wards)). **2.** mildness (of the weather).
clément [klemɑ̃] *a.* **1.** clement, merciful, lenient (**pour, envers,** to, towards). **2.** mild (weather, etc.).
clémentine [klemɑ̃tin] *n.f. Hort:* clementine.
clenche [klɑ̃ʃ] *n.f.*, **clenchette** [klɑ̃ʃɛt] *n.f.* latch (of door lock).
Cléopâtre [kleɔpɑtr̥] *Pr.n.f. A.Hist:* Cleopatra.
cleptomane [klɛptoman] *n.* kleptomaniac.
cleptomanie [klɛptomani] *n.f.* kleptomania.
clerc [klɛr] *n.m.* **1.** (*a*) *Ecc:* cleric; clerk; (*b*) *A:* learned man, scholar; (*c*) **il n'est pas besoin d'être grand c. pour . . .,** one doesn't have to be a genius in order to . . . **2.** clerk (in office); **petit c.,** junior clerk.
clergé [klɛrʒe] *n.m.* clergy.
clérical, -aux [klerikal, -o] *a. & n. Ecc:* clerical.
cléricalisme [klerikalism] *n.m. Ecc:* clericalism.
clic [klik] *n.m. & int.* click, clicking.
clic-clac [kliklak] *n.m.* crack(ing) (of whip, etc.); clatter (of sabots, etc.); clanking (of machinery); click-clack.
clichage [kliʃaʒ] *n.m. Typ:* (*a*) stereotyping; (*b*) electrotyping.
cliché [kliʃe] *n.m.* **1.** *Typ:* plate (of type); block (of illustration); stereotype. **2.** *Phot:* negative. **3.** cliché.
clicher [kliʃe] *v.tr. Typ:* (*a*) to stereotype; (*b*) to take electros of (pages of book, etc.).
clicheur [kliʃœr] *n.m. Typ:* stereotyper, electrotyper, blockmaker.
client, -ente [klijɑ̃, -ɑ̃t] *n.* **1.** *Rom.Ant:* client, dependent. **2.** client; customer; (doctor's) patient; (portrait painter's) sitter; (taxi driver's) fare; (hotel) guest, patron; *F:* **c'est un drôle de c.,** he's a queer customer.
clientèle [klijɑ̃tɛl] *n.f.* **1.** *Rom.Ant:* clients, dependents. **2.** (*a*) practice (of barrister, doctor); customers, clientele (of shop); (*b*) custom; **accorder sa c. à . . .,** to patronize.
clignement [kliɲmɑ̃] *n.m.* blink(ing), wink(ing); flicker of the eyelids; **regarder qn avec un c. d'yeux,** to blink at s.o.; **faire un c. d'œil,** to wink.
cligner [kliɲe] *v.tr. & i.* **c. les yeux, des yeux,** to screw up one's eyes; to blink; **c. de l'œil à qn,** to wink at s.o.
clignotant [kliɲɔtɑ̃]. **1.** *a.* blinking (eyes); twitching (eyelid); twinkling (star); flashing, winking (light); **signal c.,** (i) *Nau:* intermittent signal; (ii) *Aut:* flashing light. **2.** *n.m. Aut:* indicator, *U.S:* flasher.
clignotement [kliɲɔtmɑ̃] *n.m.* blinking (of eyes); twitching (of eyelid); twinkling (of star); flickering, flashing, winking (of light).
clignoter [kliɲɔte] *v.i.* (*a*) **c. des yeux,** to blink; (*b*) (*of eyelid*) to twitch; (*of star*) to twinkle; (*of light*) to flicker, flash.
climat [klima] *n.m.* **1.** climate. **2.** *Fig:* atmosphere.
climatérique [klimaterik] *a. A.Med: etc:* climacteric.
climatique [klimatik] *a.* climatic (conditions, etc.); **station c.,** health resort.
climatisation [klimatizasjɔ̃] *n.f.* air conditioning.
climatiser [klimatize] *v.tr.* to air-condition.
climatiseur [klimatizœr] *n.m.* air conditioner.
climatologie [klimatɔlɔʒi] *n.f.* climatology.
climatologique [klimatɔlɔʒik] *a.* climatological.
clin[1] [klɛ̃] *n.m. Mec.E:* **joint à c.,** lap joint; *N.Arch:* **bordé à clin(s),** clinker built.
clin[2] **d'œil** [klɛ̃dœj] *n.m.* wink; **en un c. d'œ.,** in the twinkling of an eye.
clinicien [klinisjɛ̃] *a. & n.m.* **(médecin) c.,** clinician.
clinique [klinik] **1.** *a.* clinical (lecture, etc.). **2.** *n.f.* (*a*) clinical lecture; (*b*) clinic; nursing home.
clinomètre [klinɔmɛtr̥] *n.m. Surv: Av:* clinometer.
clinquant [klɛ̃kɑ̃] *n.m.* **1.** tinsel; **(bijoux de) c.,** imitation, costume, jewellery; **c. du style,** showiness of style. **2.** *El: etc:* foil. **3.** *a.* flashy, tawdry.
clip [klip] *n.m.* clip.
clipper [klipœr] *n.m.* **1.** *A.Nau:* clipper. **2.** *Av:* transport aircraft.
clique [klik] *n.f.* **1.** clique, gang, set. **2.** *Mil:* (drum and bugle) band.
cliques [klik] *n.f.pl.* (*a*) *A:* wooden shoes, pattens; (*b*) *F:* **prendre ses c. et ses claques,** to pack up and leave; to scram.

cliquet [klikɛ] *n.m. Mec.E: etc:* catch, pawl; ratchet.
cliqueter [klikte] *v.i.* **(il cliquette, il cliquettera)** (*of chains, etc.*) to rattle, clank; (*of swords, etc.*) to click; (*of glasses, etc.*) to clink, chink; (*of keys, etc.*) to jingle, jangle; *Aut:* to pink.
cliquetis [klikti] *n.m.* rattling, rattle, clank(ing) (of chains, etc.); click(ing), clash (of swords, etc.); clink(ing), chinking (of glasses, etc.); jingling, jingle, jangling, jangle (of keys, etc.); *Aut:* pinking.
clisse [klis] *n.f.* (*a*) wicker covering (of bottle); (*b*) wicker tray (for draining cheeses).
clitoris [klitɔris] *n.m. Anat:* clitoris.
clivage [klivaʒ] *n.m.* **1.** cleaving (of diamonds, etc.). **2.** cleavage (of rocks, etc.). **3.** gulf, rift (in society).
cliver [klive] **1.** *v.tr.* to cleave, split (diamonds, etc.). **2. se c.,** (*of rock, etc.*) to cleave, split.
cloaque [klɔak] **1.** *n.f. Rom.Ant:* **la grande C.,** the Cloaca Maxima. **2.** *n.m.* (*a*) cesspool; **c. de vices,** sink of iniquity; (*b*) *Anat: Z:* cloaca.
clochard, -arde [klɔʃar, -ard] *n. F:* tramp, *NAm:* hobo.
cloche [klɔʃ] *n.f.* **1.** bell; **fleurs en c.,** bell-shaped flowers; *F:* **déménager à la c. de bois,** to do a moonlight flit; **voilà un autre son de c.,** that's quite a different version; *Nau:* **c. flottante,** bellbuoy. **2.** (*a*) bell (of gasometer); *Ch:* belljar; *Hort:* cloche; *Dom.Ec:* dish cover; **c. à plongeur,** diving bell; **(chapeau) c.,** cloche (hat); (*b*) *P:* **se taper la c.,** to have a good nosh, stuff oneself. **3.** *P:* imbecile, idiot; **avoir l'air c.,** to look stupid.
cloche-pied (à) [aklɔʃpje] *adv.phr.* **sauter à c.-p.,** to hop (on one foot); **s'éloigner à c.-p.,** to hop away.
clocher[1] [klɔʃe] *n.m.* belfry, bell tower; steeple; **disputes de c.,** petty local quarrels; **esprit de c.,** parochialism; **course au c.,** point-to-point (race).
clocher[2] *v.i.* (*a*) *A:* to limp, hobble; (*b*) *F:* **il y a quelque chose qui cloche,** there's something wrong, a hitch, somewhere.
clocheton [klɔʃtɔ̃] *n.m. Arch:* pinnacle (turret).
clochette [klɔʃɛt] *n.f.* **1.** small bell, handbell. **2.** *Bot:* (any) small bellflower.
cloison [klwazɔ̃] *n.f.* **1.** partition, division; **mur de c.,** dividing wall. **2.** *Nat.Hist:* septum. **3.** (*a*) *Aut:* baffle plate (of silencer); (*b*) *Nau: Av:* bulkhead; **c. étanche,** (i) *Nau:* watertight bulkhead; (ii) *Av:* pressure bulkhead; (iii) *Fig:* watertight compartment.
cloisonnage [klwazɔnaʒ] *n.m.* partitioning.
cloisonné [klwazɔne] *a.* **1.** partitioned off (room). **2.** *Nat.Hist:* septate(d). **3.** *Art:* cloisonné (enamel).
cloisonnement [klwazɔnmɑ̃] *n.m.* **1.** partitioning (off) (of room, etc.). **2.** *Nat.Hist:* septation.
cloisonner [klwazɔne] *v.tr.* to partition (off) (room, etc.).
cloître [klwatr̥] *n.m.* **1.** cloister(s) (of monastery, etc.). **2.** monastery, convent; **vie de c.,** cloistered life.
cloîtrer [klwatre] **1.** *v.tr.* (*a*) to cloister (s.o.); **nonne cloîtrée,** enclosed nun; (*b*) to shut (s.o.) up, away; to cloister (s.o.). **2. se c.,** (*a*) to enter a convent, a monastery; (*b*) to shut oneself up, away; to live the life of a recluse.
clone [klɔn] *n.m. Biol:* clone.
clope [klɔp] *n.m. P:* fag, cig.
clopin-clopant [klɔpɛ̃klɔpɑ̃] *adv. F:* **aller c.-c.,** to limp along, hobble about; **commerce qui va c.-c.,** business that has its ups and downs.
clopiner [klɔpine] *v.i.* to hobble, limp.
cloporte [klɔpɔrt] *n.m. Crust:* woodlouse, *NAm:* sowbug.
cloque [klɔk] *n.f.* **1.** (*a*) lump, swelling (from insect bite, etc.); (*b*) blister (on hand, paint, etc.). **2.** *Agr:* rust (of wheat); *Arb:* blight; curl (of peach tree, etc.).
cloqué [klɔke] *a. Agr:* rusty (wheat); *Arb:* blighted, curled (leaf).
cloquer [klɔke] *v.i.* (*of paint, skin, etc.*) to blister.
clore [klɔr] **1.** *v.tr.def.* (= FERMER, *which has taken its place in most uses*) (*p.p.* **clos;** *pr.ind.* **je clos, il clôt, ils closent;** *fu.* **je clorai**) (*a*) *A: & Lit:* to close shut (up); (*b*) *A:* to enclose (park, etc.); (*c*) to end (discussion, etc.); to conclude (bargain); to close (account); **c. les débats,** to close the meeting; to adjourn. **2.** (*of meeting, etc.*) **se c.,** to (come to an) end.
clos [klo] **1.** *a.* (*a*) closed, shut; **à la nuit close,** after dark; *Jur:* **à huis c.,** in camera; (*b*) finished, concluded. **2.** *n.m.* enclosure; **c. (de vigne),** vineyard.
clôture [klotyr] *n.f.* **1.** enclosure, fence, fencing; paling(s); **c. de fer,** iron railing; **c. métallique,** wire fence; **mur de c.,** enclosing wall; *Jur:* **bris de c.,** breach of close. **2.** (*a*) closing, closure (of offices, etc.); *Ven:* **c. de la chasse,** close of season; (*b*) conclusion, end (of sitting, etc.); **prononcer la c. des débats,** to declare the discussion closed; *St.Exch:* **cours en c.,** closing price. **3.** *Com:* closing, winding up (of account).
clôturer [klotyre] *v.tr.* **1.** to enclose, shut in (field, etc.). **2.** to close, terminate, end, conclude (session); *Pol:* **c. les débats,** to closure the debate. **3.** *Com:* to close, wind up (accounts, etc.).
clou [klu] *n.m.* **1.** (*a*) nail; **c. à tête perdue, c. étêté,** brad; **c. doré,** brass-headed nail; stud; **souliers à gros clous,** hobnailed boots; **attacher qch. avec un c.,** to nail sth. up, down; *F:* **ça ne vaut pas un c.,** it's not worth anything; *F:* **des clous!** nothing doing! no fear! *F:* **mettre qch. au c.,** to pawn sth., put sth. up the spout; (*b*) stud (of pedestrian crossing); **traverser dans les clous,** to cross at a pedestrian crossing; (*c*) **c. cavalier,** staple; **c. à crochet,** hook; (*d*) *F:* star turn, chief attraction (of show, etc.); (*e*) *Mil: P:* cells; **au c.,** in clink. **2.** *Med:* boil, carbuncle. **3.** *Cu:* **c. de girofle,** clove. **4. (vieux) c.,** (i) ancient car, old crock; (ii) old bike, boneshaker.
clouage [kluaʒ] *n.m.* nailing.
clouer [klue] *v.tr.* **1.** to nail, tack (sth.); *F:* **c. le bec à qn,** to shut s.o. up. **2.** (*a*) to pin (sth., s.o.) down; to rivet; **c. au sol,** to pin down; **rester cloué sur place,** to stand stock still, to be rooted to the spot; **être cloué à son lit,** to be bedridden; (*b*) *Chess:* to pin (a piece).
cloutage [klutaʒ] *n.m.* studding (of shoe, etc.).
clouté [klute] *a.* studded (shoes, etc.); **passage c.,** pedestrian crossing.
clouter [klute] *v.tr.* to stud (shoe, etc.).
clouterie [klutri] *n.f.* (*a*) nail trade; (*b*) nail, factory.
cloutier [klutje] *n.m.* (*a*) nailer, nailsmith; (*b*) nail dealer.
clovisse [klɔvis] *n.f. Moll:* clam.
clown [klun] *n.m.* clown; buffoon.
clownesque [klunɛsk] *a.* clownish.
club [klœb] *n.m.* **1.** (political, sporting) club; **(fauteuil) c.,** large leather armchair. **2.** golf club, *F:* stick.
clystère [klistɛr] *n.m. A.Med:* clyster, enema.
coaccusé, -ée [kɔakyze] *n. Jur:* co-defendant.
coacquéreur [kɔakerœr] *n.m.* joint purchaser.
coadjuteur [kɔadʒytœr] *n.m. Ecc:* coadjutor.
coadministrateur [kɔadministratœr] *n.m.* co-director; *Jur:* co-trustee.
coagulable [kɔagylabl̥] *a.* coagulable.
coagulant [kɔagylɑ̃] *a. & n.m.* coagulant.
coagulateur, -trice [kɔagylatœr, -tris] *a.* coagulative.
coagulation [kɔagylasjɔ̃] *n.f.* coagulation, coagulating.
coaguler [kɔagyle] **1.** *v.tr.* to coagulate, congeal; to curdle (milk). **2.** *v.i. & pr.* **(se) c.,** (*of blood, etc.*) to coagulate, congeal, clot; (*of milk*) to curdle.
coalisé, -ée [kɔalize] *a.* (*a*) allied; (*b*) *n.* **les coalisés,** the allies.

coaliser [kɔalize] **1.** *v.tr.* to unite, combine (powers, etc.) in a coalition. **2. se c.,** to form a coalition, to unite.
coalition [kɔalisjɔ̃] *n.f.* **1.** coalition, union, league; **ministère de c.,** coalition ministry. **2.** (hostile) combination, conspiracy.
coaltar [koltar] *n.m.* coal tar; gas tar.
coassement [kɔasmɑ̃] *n.m.* croak(ing) (of frog).
coasser [kɔase] *v.i.* (*of frog*) to croak.
coassocié, -ée [kɔasɔsje] *n.* copartner, joint partner.
coassurance [kɔasyrɑ̃s] *n.f.* mutual assurance.
coauteur [kɔotœr] *n.m.* **1.** joint author, co-author. **2.** accomplice (in crime).
cobalt [kɔbalt] *n.m.* cobalt.
cobaye [kɔbaj] *n.m.* *Z:* guinea pig; cavy; **servir de c.,** to act as a guinea pig.
cobelligérant [cɔbeliʒerɑ̃] *a. & n.m.* cobelligerent.
Coblence [kɔblɑ̃s] *Pr.n.f. Geog:* Koblenz.
cobra [kɔbra] *n.m. Rept:* cobra.
coca [kɔka] **1.** *n.m. or f. Bot:* coca. **2.** *n.f. Pharm:* coca.
cocagne [kɔkaɲ] *n.f.* **mât de c.,** greasy pole; **pays de c.,** land of milk and honey; land of plenty.
cocaïne [kɔkain] *n.f. Pharm:* cocaine.
cocaïnomane [kɔkainɔman] *n.m. & f.* cocaine addict.
cocarde [kɔkard] *n.f.* cockade; rosette; *Av:* roundel; fuselage marking; company crest (on aircraft).
cocardier, -ière [kɔkardje, -jɛr] (*a*) *a.* fond of uniform(s), of all things military; chauvinistic, jingoistic; (*b*) *n.* chauvinist, jingoist.
cocasse [kɔkas] *a. F:* comical, laughable.
cocasserie [kɔkasri] *n.f. F:* **1.** comical nature, oddity. **2.** *pl.* antics (of clown, etc.).
coccinelle [kɔksinɛl] *n.f. Ent:* coccinella; ladybird.
coccyx [kɔksis] *n.m. Anat:* coccyx.
coche¹ [kɔʃ] *n.m.* **1.** (*a*) *A:* stagecoach; (*b*) **faire la mouche du c.,** to buzz around, be a busybody; *F:* **manquer le c.,** to miss the bus, let an opportunity slip by. **2.** *A:* **c. (d'eau),** passenger barge.
coche² *n.f.* notch, nick; score (on tally stick); nock (of arrow).
cochenille [kɔʃnij] *n.f.* cochineal.
cocher¹ [kɔʃe] *n.m.* coachman, driver (of horse-drawn vehicle); **c. de fiacre,** cabman, *F:* cabby.
cocher² *v.tr.* (*a*) to nick, notch; to mark off; to score (tally); (*b*) to tick (off) (names, etc.).
cochère [kɔʃɛr] *a.f.* **porte c.,** carriage gateway, main entrance.
cochet [kɔʃɛ] *n.m.* cockerel.
Cochinchine [kɔʃɛ̃ʃin] *Pr.n.f. Geog:* Cochin-China.
cochon, -onne [kɔʃɔ̃n, -ɔn] **I.** *n.m.* **1.** (*a*) pig, hog, porker; **c. de lait,** suck(l)ing pig; **gardeur de cochons,** swineherd; **étable à cochons,** pigsty; **amis comme cochons,** as thick as thieves; *F:* **un c. n'y retrouverait pas ses petits,** what a pigsty! (*b*) *occ.* pork. **2.** *Z:* **c. d'Inde,** guinea pig. **II.** *a. & n. P:* **1.** *a.* indecent, dirty, smutty, foul (story, etc.); swinish (person, trick, etc.); **dix mille francs, c'est pas c.!** ten thousand francs, that's pretty good! **c. qui s'en dédit,** it's a deal. **2.** *n.* dirty pig; swine; **jouer un tour de c. à qn,** to play a dirty, rotten, trick on s.o.
cochonnaille [kɔʃɔnaj] *n.f. F:* (i) pork; (ii) cooked meats.
cochonner [kɔʃɔne] *v.tr. F:* to bungle, botch, muck up (piece of work, etc.).
cochonnerie [kɔʃɔnri] *n.f. P:* **1.** (*a*) filthiness; (*b*) **dire des cochonneries,** to talk smut. **2.** (*a*) trash, rubbish; (*b*) revolting food, pigwash. **3.** dirty, lousy, trick.
cochonnet [kɔʃɔnɛ] *n.m.* **1.** piglet. **2.** *Games:* (*a*) (*at bowls*) jack; (*b*) die with twelve faces; teetotum.
cockpit [kɔkpit] *n.m. Av: etc:* cockpit.
cocktail [kɔktɛl] *n.m.* (*a*) cocktail; (*b*) cocktail party; (*c*) *F:* mixture.
coco¹ [koko] *n.m.* **1.** (*a*) **noix de c.,** coconut; **huile, beurre, de c.,** coconut oil, butter; (*b*) *P:* head, nut; (*c*) *P:* stomach, belly. **2.** liquorice water.
coco² *n.m.* **1.** (*child's word*) egg. **2.** *F:* (*a*) fellow, bloke; **drôle de c.,** queer stick; (*b*) **mon petit c.,** my darling, my pet.
coco³ *n.f. P:* cocaine, snow, coke.
coco⁴ *a. & n. F:* communist, commie, red.
cocon [kɔkɔ̃] *n.m.* cocoon (of silkworm, etc.); **s'enfermer dans son c.,** to retire into one's shell.
cocorico [kɔkɔriko] *onomat. & n.m.* cock-a-doodle-doo!
cocoter [kɔkɔte] *v.i. P:* to stink.
cocotier [kɔkɔtje] *n.m.* coconut palm.
cocotte [kɔkɔt] *n.f.* **1.** (*a*) (*child's word*) hen, chicken; (*b*) bird made out of folded paper. **2.** *F:* (*a*) **ma c.,** darling; (*b*) prostitute, tart. **3.** *Cu:* (large) stewpan; casserole (dish). **4.** *F:* **hue, c.!** gee up!
cocotte-minute [kɔkɔtminyt] *n.f. R.t.m:* pressure cooker; *pl. cocottes-minute.*
cocu, -e [kɔky] *P:* **1.** *n.m.* deceived husband; cuckold; **avoir une chance de c.,** to have the devil's own luck. **2.** *a.* deceived.
cocuage [kɔkɥaʒ] *n.m. P:* cuckoldry.
cocufier [kɔkyfje] *v.tr. P:* to be unfaithful to, to cuckold.
coda [kɔda] *n.f. Mus:* coda.
codage [kɔdaʒ] *n.m.* coding.
code [kɔd] *n.m.* **1.** *Jur:* statute book; **c. civil** = Common Law; **c. pénal,** penal code; **c. de justice militaire,** military law; **c. de commerce,** commercial law; **c. maritime,** navigation laws; **se tenir dans les marges du c.,** to keep just within the law; **c. de la morale,** moral code; *Aut:* **C. de la route,** Highway Code; *Aut:* **se mettre en c.,** to dip one's headlights; **phares c.,** dipped headlights. **2.** code, cypher; **c. télégraphique,** telegraphic code.
codébiteur, -trice [kɔdebitœr, -tris] *n. Jur:* joint debtor.
codéine [kɔdein] *n.f. Ch:* codeine.
coder [kɔde] *v.tr.* to code (message).
codétenu, -ue [kɔdetny] *n.* fellow prisoner.
codex [kɔdɛks] *n.m.* codex; pharmacopoeia.
codicillaire [kɔdisilɛr] *a. Jur:* codicillary.
codicille [kɔdisil] *n.m. Jur:* codicil.
codification [kɔdifikasjɔ̃] *n.f.* codification, classification (of laws, etc.).
codifier [kɔdifje] *v.tr.* to codify (laws, etc.).
codirecteur, -trice [kɔdirɛktœr -tris] *n.* co-director; joint manager, manageress.
coefficient [kɔefisjɑ̃] *n.m.* coefficient, factor; **c. de dilatation,** coefficient of expansion; *Mec:* **c. d'écrasement, c. d'élasticité,** modulus of compression, of elasticity; **c. de sécurité,** safety factor.
coéquation [kɔekwasjɔ̃] *n.f. Adm:* proportional assessment.
coéquipier, -ière [kɔekipje, -jɛr] *n. Sp:* team mate.
coercible [kɔɛrsibl̩] *a. Ph:* coercible (gas, etc.).
coercitif, -ive [kɔɛrsitif, -iv] *a.* coercive.
coercition [kɔɛrsisjɔ̃] *n.f.* coercion.
cœur [kœr] *n.m.* heart. **1.** (*a*) **maladie de c.,** heart disease; **greffe du c.,** heart transplant; **opération à c. ouvert,** open-heart surgery; **tué d'une balle au c.,** killed by a bullet in the heart; **en c.,** heart-shaped; **faire la bouche en c.,** to simper; **joli comme un c.,** as pretty as a picture; *F:* **faire le joli c.,** to put on airs (and graces); (*b*) **avoir mal au c.,** to feel sick; **cela soulève le c.,** it's nauseating, sickening; *F:* **avoir le c. bien accroché,** to have a strong stomach. **2.** soul, feelings, mind; (*a*) **avoir qch. sur le c.,** to have sth.

on one's mind; **en avoir le c. net,** to get to the bottom of it, clear the matter up; **avoir la rage au c.,** to be raging, seething, with anger; **au fond du c.,** in one's heart of hearts; **parler à c. ouvert,** to speak freely, have a heart to heart talk; **remercier qn de tout (son) c., du fond de son c.,** to thank s.o. wholeheartedly, from the bottom of one's heart; **il me portait dans son c.,** he was very fond of me; **partir le c. léger,** to set off with a light heart; **de gaieté de c.,** with a light heart; **avoir le c. gros, serré,** to be heavy-hearted, sad at heart; **avoir la mort dans le c.,** to be sick at heart; **la chose qui lui tient au c.,** (i) the thing he has set his heart on, (ii) the thing that hurts him most; **avoir le c. sur la main,** to be generous; **homme de c.,** good-hearted man; **je serai de c. avec vous,** I'll be with you in spirit; **si le c. vous en dit,** if you feel like it; **vous n'aurez pas le c. de faire cela,** you wouldn't have the heart to do that; **des gens selon mon c.,** people after my own heart; **prendre, avoir, qch. à c.,** to take sth. to heart; **prendre, avoir, à c. de faire qch.,** to set one's heart on doing sth; (*b*) **apprendre, savoir, qch. par c.,** to learn, know, sth. by heart. **3.** courage, spirit, pluck; **donner du c. à qn,** to give s.o. courage; *F:* **avoir du c. au ventre,** to have plenty of guts; **faire contre mauvaise fortune bon c.,** to make the best of a bad job. **4.** (*a*) **avoir du, le, c. à l'ouvrage,** to have one's heart in one's work; **faire qch. de bon c., de grand c.,** to do sth. willingly, gladly; **faire qch. de mauvais c.,** to do sth. reluctantly, unwillingly; **rire de bon c.,** to laugh heartily; **y aller de bon c.,** to get down to it; **le c. n'y est pas,** his, my, heart isn't in it; (*b*) **donner son c. à qn,** to lose one's heart to s.o.; **aimer qn de tout son c.,** to love s.o. with all one's heart; *Prov:* **loin des yeux loin du c.,** out of sight, out of mind; (*c*) **c'est un bon c., il a bon c.,** he's kind-hearted; **ne pas avoir de c.,** to be heartless. **5.** middle, midst; core; **au c. de la ville,** in the centre of the town; **c. de palmier,** heart of palm; **c. d'un chou, d'un artichaut,** heart of a cabbage, of an artichoke; *F:* **avoir un c. d'artichaut,** to fall in love with every pretty girl, handsome boy, one meets; **fromage fait à c.,** ripe cheese; **au c. de l'hiver, de l'été,** in the depth of winter, the height of summer. **6.** *Cards:* heart(s); **avez-vous du c.?** have you any hearts?

coexistence [kɔɛgzistɑ̃s] *n.f.* coexistence (**avec,** with); *Pol:* **c. pacifique,** peaceful coexistence.

coexister [kɔɛgziste] *v.i.* to coexist (**avec,** with).

coffrage [kɔfraʒ] *n.m.* **1.** *Min: etc:* coffering, lining (of shaft, etc.). **2.** framing, shuttering, formwork, casing (for concrete work).

coffre [kɔfr̥] *n.m.* **1.** (*a*) chest, bin; cabinet; **c. à outils,** tool chest, toolbox; **c. à linge,** linen chest; (*b*) *Anat: F:* chest; **avoir le c. bon,** to be sound in wind and limb; (*c*) safe (deposit box); **les coffres de l'État,** the coffers of State, the Treasury; (*d*) boot, *NAm:* trunk (of car). **2.** case (of lock, piano, etc.). **3.** *Nau:* (*a*) **c. d'amarrage,** mooring buoy; (*b*) moorings. **4.** *Nau:* well deck.

coffre-fort [kɔfrəfɔr] *n.m.* safe; strongbox; *pl. coffres-forts.*

coffrer [kɔfre] *v.tr.* **1.** *F:* to put (s.o.) in prison, away. **2.** *Min: etc:* to coffer, line (shaft, etc.).

coffret [kɔfrɛ] *n.m.* small box; casket; **c. à bijoux,** jewel case; **c. à documents,** deed box.

cogérant, -ante [kɔʒerɑ̃, -ɑ̃t] *n.* joint manager, joint manageress.

cogestion [kɔʒɛstjɔ̃] *n.f.* joint management.

cogitation [kɔʒitasjɔ̃] *n.f.* cogitation, reflection.

cogiter [kɔʒite] *v.i.* to cogitate, think.

cognac [kɔɲak] *n.m.* cognac.

cognassier [kɔɲasje] *n.m. Bot:* quince (tree).

cogne [kɔɲ] *n.m. P:* policeman, cop.

cognée [kɔɲe] *n.f.* axe; hatchet.

cognement [kɔɲmɑ̃] *n.m.* knocking (of engine, etc.); thump(ing), banging.

cogner [kɔɲe] **1.** *v.tr.* (*a*) to drive in, hammer in (nail, etc.); (*b*) to knock, beat, thump, bump; **c. qn en passant,** to bump into s.o. (in passing); (*c*) *P:* to knock (s.o.) about; **il cogne dur,** he's a hard hitter. **2.** *v.i.* (*a*) to knock, thump (**sur,** on); to bump, bang (**contre,** against); **c. du poing sur la table,** to bang (one's fist) on the table; (*b*) (*of engine, etc.*) to knock. **3. se c. à, contre, qch.,** to knock against sth.; **se c. la tête contre les murs,** to bang one's head against a brick wall.

cogneur [kɔɲœr] *n.m. Box: etc:* hard hitter, bruiser.

cognitif, -ive [kɔgnitif, -iv] *a. Phil:* cognitive.

cognition [kɔgnisjɔ̃] *n.f. Phil:* cognition.

cohabitation [kɔabitasjɔ̃] *n.f.* cohabitation.

cohabiter [kɔabite] *v.i.* to cohabit (**avec,** with).

cohérence [kɔerɑ̃s] *n.f.* coherence; consistency.

cohérent [kɔerɑ̃] *a.* coherent; consistent.

cohéritier, -ière [kɔeritje, -jɛr] *n.* coheir(ess); joint heir(ess).

cohésif, -ive [kɔezif, -iv] *a.* cohesive.

cohésion [kɔezjɔ̃] *n.f.* cohesion, cohesiveness.

cohorte [kɔɔrt] *n.f.* **1.** *Rom.Mil:* cohort. **2.** *F:* mob, band (of people).

cohue [kɔy] *n.f.* crowd, mob, throng.

coi, coite [kwa, kwat] *a.* **se tenir c.,** to keep quiet, lie low; **en rester c.,** to be flabbergasted.

coiffe [kwaf] *n.f.* **1.** head dress, cap (*esp.* of regional costume. **2.** lining (of hat). **3.** cover; (*a*) *Nau: etc:* **c. blanche,** white cap cover; (*b*) *Artil:* breech cover; **c. de fusée,** fuse cap. **4.** caul (of newborn child).

coiffé [kwafe] *a.* **1. être c. d'un chapeau,** to be wearing a hat; **il est né c.,** he was born (i) with a caul, (ii) *F:* with a silver spoon in his mouth. **2. elle est bien coiffée ce soir,** her hair looks beautiful this evening; **je ne suis pas encore coiffée,** I haven't done my hair yet.**3. être c. de qn,** to be infatuated with s.o.

coiffer [kwafe] **1.** *v.tr.* (*a*) to cover (the head); to cap (bottle, etc.); **ce chapeau vous coiffe bien,** that hat suits you; **montagne coiffée de neige,** snow-capped mountain; (*b*) **c. un chapeau,** to put on a hat; (*c*) **c. qn,** to do s.o.'s hair; **il coiffe bien,** he's a good hairdresser; **se faire c.,** to have one's hair done; (*d*) *Sp: F:* to overtake; **se faire c. (au poteau),** to be beaten at the post; (*e*) *F:* to control, direct (an organization, etc.). **2.** (*a*) **se c. d'une casquette,** to put on, wear, a cap; (*b*) **se c.,** to do one's hair; (*c*) *F:* **se c. de qn,** to become infatuated with s.o.

coiffeur, -euse [kwafœr, -øz] **1.** *n.* hairdresser; hair stylist; *U.S:* (*for men*) barber. **2.** *n.f.* dressing table.

coiffure [kwafyr] *n.f.* **1.** headdress; headgear. **2.** hairstyle. **3.** hairdressing; **salon de c.,** hairdresser's; hairdressing salon; *U.S:* (*for men*) barbershop.

coin [kwɛ̃] *n.m.* **1.** (*a*) corner (of street, room, mouth, etc.); **maison du c., qui fait le c.,** corner house; **l'épicier du c.,** (i) the grocer on the corner; (ii) the local grocer; **place de c.,** corner seat; **mettre un enfant au c.,** to put a child in the corner (in disgrace); **c. repas,** dining area, recess; **regard en c.,** side glance; **regarder qn du c. de l'œil,** to look at s.o. out of the corner of one's eye; **il a visité les quatre coins du monde,** he has travelled all over the world; **reliure avec coins,** binding with leather corners; (*b*) (retired) spot, nook; **un petit c. pas cher,** a cheap, inexpensive, little place; *F:* **le petit c.,** the smallest room (in the house), the loo; **coins et recoins,** nooks and crannies; **chercher qch. dans tous les coins,** to look, everywhere, high and low for sth.; (*c*) **c. d'évier,** sink tidy; (*d*) **c. du feu,** inglenook; **au c. du feu,** by the fireside; (*e*) patch (of land, etc.); **c. des légumes,** vegetable plot; **c. de ciel bleu,** patch of blue sky. **2.** wedge, key, quoin, chock;

en c., wedge-shaped; **tranchant du c.,** thin end of the wedge. **3.** (*a*) stamp, die (for striking coins, medals); hallmark; **marqué au c. du génie,** bearing the stamp, the hallmark, of genius.
coinçage [kwɛ̃saʒ] *n.m.*, **coincement** [kwɛ̃smɑ̃] *n.m.* wedging, jamming.
coincer [kwɛ̃se] *v.* **(je coinçai(s); n. coinçons) 1.** *v.tr.* (*a*) to wedge (up), chock (up) (rails, etc.); (*b*) to jam (drawer, etc.); **voiture coincée entre deux camions,** car jammed, stuck, caught, between two lorries; (*c*) *F:* to corner (s.o.); **vous êtes coincé,** you're stymied; (*d*) *F:* to arrest (s.o.), run (s.o.) in. **2. se c.,** to jam, stick; to bind.
coïncidence [kɔɛ̃sidɑ̃s] *n.f.* coincidence.
coïncident [kɔɛ̃sidɑ̃] *a.* coincident, coinciding.
coïncider [kɔɛ̃side] *v.i.* to coincide (**avec,** with).
coin-coin [kwɛ̃kwɛ̃] *n.m.* (*of ducks*) quack(ing); *int.* quack! quack!
coing [kwɛ̃] *n.m. Bot:* quince.
coït [kɔit] *n.m.* coitus, coition.
coke [kɔk] *n.m.* coke.
cokéfaction [kɔkefaksjɔ̃] *n.f.* coking.
cokéfier [kɔkefje] *v.tr.* to coke.
cokerie [kɔkri] *n.f.* coking plant.
col [kɔl] *n.m.* **1.** (*a*) *A: & Lit:* neck (of pers.); (*b*) **homme au c. court,** short-necked man; (*c*) neck (of bottle, etc.); *Anat:* cervix (of uterus, etc.). **2.** collar (of dress, shirt, etc.); **faux c.,** (i) detachable collar; (ii) head (of froth on glass of beer); **c. raide, mou,** stiff, soft, collar; **c. cassé,** wing collar; **c. de fourrure, de dentelle,** fur, lace, collar. **3. c. blanc,** white-collar worker. **4.** *Geog:* col.
cola [kɔla] *n.m. Bot:* cola, kola.
col-bleu [kɔlblø] *n.m. F:* (*a*) sailor, bluejacket; (*b*) blue-collar worker; *pl. cols-bleus.*
colchique [kɔlʃik] *n.m. Bot:* colchicum; meadow saffron; autumn crocus.
cold-cream [kɔldkrim] *n.m.* cold cream.
col-de-cygne [kɔldəsiɲ] *n.m. Plumb: etc:* swan neck; *pl. cols-de-cygne.*
colégataire [kɔlegatɛr] *n.m. & f. Jur:* co-legatee, joint legatee.
coléoptère [kɔleɔptɛr] *n.m. Ent:* beetle; **les coléoptères,** the Coleoptera.
colère [kɔlɛr] **1.** *n.f.* (*a*) anger; *Lit:* wrath; **c. bleue, noire,** towering rage; **être en c.,** to be angry; **se mettre en c.,** to get angry **(contre qn,** with, *NAm:* at, s.o.); to lose one's temper; **avec c.,** angrily; (*b*) **il avait des colères terribles,** he was subject to terrible fits of anger. **2.** *a. Lit:* irate, angry (voice); irascible (person).
coléreux, -euse [kɔlerø, -øz] *a.*, **colérique** [kɔlerik] *a.* quick-tempered (person); irritable (disposition).
colibacille [kɔlibasil] *n.m.* colon bacillus.
colibri [kɔlibri] *n.m. Orn:* colibri; humming bird.
colifichet [kɔlifiʃɛ] *n.m.* (*a*) trinket; knick-knack; (*b*) *pl.* rubbish, trash.
colimaçon [kɔlimasɔ̃] *n.m.* snail; **escalier en c.,** spiral staircase.
colin [kɔlɛ̃] *n.m. Ich:* (*a*) hake; (*b*) coalfish.
colin-maillard [kɔlɛ̃majar] *n.m. Games:* **1.** blindman's buff. **2.** blind man (in blindman's buff).
colique [kɔlik] **1.** *a. Anat:* colic (artery, etc.). **2.** *n.f.* colic; severe stomach pains; **avoir la c.,** (i) to have stomach ache; (ii) to have diarrhoea; (iii) *F:* have the wind up; *F:* **quelle c.!** what a bore! what a bind!
colis [kɔli] *n.m.* parcel, packet, package; **par c. postal,** by parcel post.
Colisée (le) [ləkɔlize] *n.m. Rom.Ant:* the Coliseum.
colistier [kɔlistje] *n.m. Pol: etc:* fellow candidate.
colite [kɔlit] *n.f. Med:* colitis.
collaborateur, -trice [kɔlabɔratœr, -tris] *n.* (*a*) collaborator; fellow worker; associate; **collaborateurs d'une revue,** contributors to a magazine; (*b*) *Pol:* collaborator, collaborationist.
collaboration [kɔlabɔrasjɔ̃] *n.f.* collaboration (**avec,** with); joint authorship.
collaborer [kɔlabɔre] *v.i.* to collaborate (**avec,** with); **c. à un journal,** to contribute to a newspaper.
collage [kɔlaʒ] *n.m.* **1.** (*a*) gluing, sticking (of wood, etc.); pasting (of paper, etc.); *Art:* collage; **c. du papier (peint),** paper hanging; (*b*) *F:* (*of unmarried couple*) living together. **2.** *Paperm:* sizing. **3.** fining, clarifying (of wine).
collant [kɔlɑ̃] **1.** *a.* (*a*) sticky, tacky; **papier c.,** gummed paper; (*b*) tight-, close-, fitting; skintight (garment). **2.** *n.m.* (pair of) tights.
collante [kɔlɑ̃t] *n.f. Sch: F:* letter giving notice of the date and place of an examination.
collapsus [kɔlapsys] *n.m. Med:* collapse (of patient).
collatéral, -aux [kɔlateral, -o] *a.* collateral; *Arch:* **nef collatérale,** *n.m.* **c.,** (side) aisle; *Jur:* **(parents) collatéraux,** collaterals; relatives.
collation [kɔlasjɔ̃] *n.f.* **1.** (*a*) granting, conferment (of degree, etc.); (*b*) *Ecc:* advowson. **2.** collation (of documents, etc.); checking. **3.** light meal; snack.
collationnement [kɔlasjɔnmɑ̃] *n.m.* collating, collation (of documents, etc.); checking.
collationner [kɔlasjɔne] **1.** *v.tr.* (*a*) to collate, compare (two written documents); (*b*) to check (documents). **2.** *v.i.* to have a snack.
colle [kɔl] *n.f.* **1.** adhesive; paste; glue; size; **c. forte,** glue; **c. à bois,** wood glue; **c. de poisson,** fish glue, isinglass; **c. au caoutchouc,** rubber solution; **papier sans c.,** unsized paper. **2.** *Sch: etc: F:* (*a*) difficult, sticky, question; poser; (*b*) oral exam; (*c*) detention. **3.** *P:* **vivre à la c.,** to be living together, to shack up.
collecte [kɔlɛkt] *n.f.* (*a*) collection (for the poor, etc.); (*b*) *Ecc:* collect.
collecter [kɔlɛkte] *v.tr.* to collect.
collecteur, -trice [kɔlɛktœr, -tris] **1.** *n.* collector. **2.** *a. & n.m.* **(égout, grand) c.,** main sewer; *El:* **c., bague collectrice,** collector (ring), commutator (of dynamo, etc.); *W.Tel:* **c. d'ondes,** aerial; *I.C.E:* **c. d'échappement,** exhaust manifold.
collectif, -ive [kɔlɛktif, -iv] **1.** *a.* collective, joint (action, report, etc.); **ferme collective,** collective farm; **voyages collectifs,** group travel; **radiographie collective,** mass radiography. **2.** *n.m.* (*a*) *Gram:* collective noun; (*b*) *Adm:* block of flats; (*c*) *Fin:* **c. budgétaire,** bill of supply.
collection [kɔlɛksjɔ̃] *n.f.* **1.** collecting; gathering. **2.** (*a*) collection (of butterflies, etc.); file (of newspapers); *Com:* line (of samples); **présentation de c.,** fashion show; (*b*) *Publ:* series (of books).
collectionner [kɔlɛksjɔne] *v.tr.* to collect (stamps, etc.).
collectionneur, -euse [kɔlɛksjɔnœr, -øz] *n.* collector (of stamps, etc.).
collectivement [kɔlɛktivmɑ̃] *adv.* collectively.
collectivisation [kɔlɛktivizasjɔ̃] *n.f.* collectivization.
collectiviser [kɔlɛktivize] *v.tr.* to collectivize.
collectivisme [kɔlɛktivism] *n.m.* collectivism.
collectiviste [kɔlɛktivist] *n.* collectivist.
collectivité [kɔlɛktivite] *n.f.* collectivity. **1.** community; **collectivités nationales,** national organizations. **2.** common ownership.
collège [kɔlɛʒ] *n.m.* **1.** college; **le Sacré C.,** the College of Cardinals; **c. électoral,** electoral body, constituency; *esp. U.S:* electoral college. **2.** school; **c. d'enseignement secondaire** = secondary (modern) school, *NAm:* high school; **c. d'enseignement technique,** technical college; **c. libre,** private school.

collégial, -iaux [kɔleʒjal, -jo] **1.** *a.* collegial, collegiate. **2.** *n.f.* **collégiale,** collegiate church.
collégialité [kɔleʒjalite] *n.f.* collegial structure (of a society, etc.).
collégien, -ienne [kɔleʒjɛ̃, -jɛn] *n.* schoolboy, schoolgirl.
collègue [kɔlɛg] *n.* colleague; fellow worker, officer.
coller [kɔle] **1.** *v.tr.* (*a*) to paste, stick, glue (**à, sur,** to, on); **c. du papier peint sur un mur,** to paper a wall; **le sang avait collé ses cheveux,** her hair was matted with blood; **c. son visage à, contre, la vitre,** to glue one's face to the window; *F:* **c. une gifle à qn,** to slap s.o. in the face; (*b*) *F:* to put; **collez ça dans un coin,** stick it in a corner; **c. un élève,** (i) to keep a pupil in; (ii) to catch out a pupil (with a difficult question); **c. un candidat,** to fail a candidate; **il me colle!** he sticks to me like glue! (*c*) to size (paper); (*d*) to clarify, fine (wine). **2.** *v.i.* to stick, adhere, cling (**à,** to); **robe qui colle au corps,** clinging dress; *F:* **ça ne colle pas entre eux,** they don't hit it off; *F:* **ça colle?** how are things? O.K.? *F:* **ça ne colle pas,** there's something wrong; **ça colle,** that makes sense, *U.S:* that figures. **3.** (*a*) **se c.,** to stick, adhere closely; **elle s'est collée contre lui,** she clung to him; (*b*) *P:* **se c. avec qn,** to live with s.o., to shack up with s.o.
collerette [kɔlrɛt] *n.f.* **1.** collarette, ruff. **2.** *Bot:* annulus (of mushroom). **3.** *Mec.E: etc:* flange (of pipe, joint, etc.).
collet [kɔlɛ] *n.m.* **1.** (*a*) collar (of coat, dress, etc.); **saisir qn au c.,** to collar s.o., to seize s.o. by the scruff of the neck; **la police lui mit la main au c.,** the police arrested him; **un c. monté,** a stiff-necked, strait-laced, person; *a.inv.* **elle est très c. monté,** she is very prim (and proper), very formal; (*b*) short cape (of fur, etc.). **2.** neck (of tooth, screw, violin, etc.); shoulder (of racquet, etc.); *Bot:* neck, collar (of mushroom, etc.); *Cu:* **c. de mouton,** neck, scrag, of mutton. **3.** *Mch: Mec.E: etc:* flange, collar, fillet (of pipe, etc.). **4.** snare, springe, noose (for trapping small animals); **prendre, des lapins au c.,** to snare rabbits.
colleter [kɔlte] *v.tr.* **(je collette, n. colletons; je colletterai)** (*a*) to collar (s.o.); to seize (s.o.) by the collar; (*b*) **se c. avec qn,** to tussle, grapple, with s.o.; to come to grips with s.o.; **se c. avec les difficultés,** to struggle with problems.
colleur, -euse [kɔlœr, -øz] *n.* **1.** (*a*) gluer, paster; **c. d'affiches,** billsticker; (*b*) sizer (of paper, etc.). **2.** *F: Sch:* examiner (who asks sticky questions). **3.** *n.f. Cin:* **colleuse,** film splicer, splicing unit.
collier [kɔlje] *n.m.* **1.** necklace, necklet. **2.** (*a*) collar chain (of order, etc.); (*b*) **c. de chien,** dog collar; **cheval de c.,** draught horse; **donner un coup de c.,** to put one's back into it, to make a special effort; (*c*) **c. de barbe,** narrow beard (following line of jaw). **3.** (*a*) *Mec.E:* collar, ring; **c. de serrage,** clamping ring, clamp; **c. de fixation,** bracket, clip; **c. de frein,** brake band; **c. de palier,** bearing collar; (*b*) *Tchn:* clip. **4.** *Z:* collar, ring (on birds, etc.); **pigeon à c., au c.,** ringed, ring-necked, pigeon. **5.** *Cu:* neck (of beef, mutton).
collimateur [kɔlimatœr] *n.m.* *Astr: Surv:* collimator, laying prism; *Opt:* collimating lens.
colline [kɔlin] *n.f.* hill; **petite c.,** hillock.
collision [kɔlizjɔ̃] *n.f.* collision; impact; **entrer en c. avec qch.,** to collide with sth.; to run into (ship, car, etc.); **c. des intérêts,** clash of interests; **c. nucléaire,** nuclear collision.
collocation [kɔlɔkasjɔ̃] *n.f.* *Jur:* (establishing the) order of priority of creditors (in bankruptcy).
collodion [kɔlɔdjɔ̃] *n.m.* *Ch: etc:* collodion.
colloïdal, -aux [kɔlɔidal, -o] *a.* *Ch: etc:* colloidal.
colloïde [kɔlɔid] *a. & n.m.* *Ch: etc:* colloid, gel.
colloque [kɔlɔk] *n.m.* (*a*) discussion; conference, symposium; (*b*) conversation.
collusion [kɔlyzjɔ̃] *n.f.* *Jur: etc:* collusion.
collusoire [kɔlyzwar] *a.* *Jur:* collusive.
collutoire [kɔlytwar] *n.m.* *Pharm:* mouth wash.
collyre [kɔlir] *n.m.* *Pharm:* eyewash; eye lotion.
colmatage [kɔlmataʒ] *n.m.* **1.** *Agr:* warping (of land). **2.** (*a*) filling in (of potholes in road, etc.); (*b*) plugging (up) (of hole, etc.); (*c*) *Mil:* consolidation (of position).
colmater [kɔlmate] *v.tr.* **1.** *Agr:* to warp (land). **2.** (*a*) to fill in (potholes in road, etc.); (*b*) to plug (up) (hole, etc.); (*c*) *Mil:* to consolidate (position). **3. se c.,** to clog up; to become choked, to choke up.
colocataire [kɔlɔkatɛr] *n.m. & f.* joint tenant, cotenant.
Colomb [kɔlɔ̃] *Pr.n.m.* **Christophe C.,** Christopher Columbus.
colombage [kɔlɔ̃baʒ] *n.m.* *Const:* half timbering; **maison en c.,** half-timbered house.
colombe [kɔlɔ̃b] *n.f.* *Orn:* dove; **c. biset,** rock pigeon.
Colombie [kɔlɔ̃bi] *Pr.n.f.* *Geog:* **1.** Colombia. **2. la C. britannique,** British Columbia.
colombien, -ienne [kɔlɔ̃bjɛ̃, -jɛn] *a. & n.* *Geog:* Colombian.
colombier [kɔlɔ̃bje] *n.m.* dovecot(e), pigeon loft.
colombophilie [kɔlɔ̃bɔfili] *n.f.* pigeon fancying, breeding.
colon[1] [kɔlɔ̃] *n.m.* **1.** farmer, smallholder. **2.** colonist, settler. **3.** child at a holiday camp.
colon[2] *n.m.* *Mil: P:* colonel; **ben, mon c.!** well, I'm damned!
côlon [kolɔ̃, kɔ-] *n.m.* *Anat:* colon.
colonel [kɔlɔnɛl] *n.m.* *Mil:* colonel; *Mil.Av:* group captain.
colonelle [kɔlɔnɛl] *n.f.* colonel's wife; group captain's wife.
colonial, -iaux [kɔlɔnjal, -jo] **1.** *a.* colonial. **2.** *n.m.* (*a*) soldier of the colonial troops; (*b*) colonial.
colonialisme [kɔlɔnjalism] *n.m.* *Pol:* colonialism.
colonialiste [kɔlɔnjalist] *a. & n.* *Pol:* colonialist.
colonie [kɔlɔni] *n.f.* **1.** (*a*) colony; settlement; **vivre aux colonies,** to live in the colonies; (*b*) **c. de vacances,** children's holiday camp, *NAm:* vacation camp; (*c*) **la c. anglaise de Paris,** the English colony in Paris. **2.** colony (of animals).
colonisateur, -trice [kɔlɔnizatœr, -tris] **1.** *a.* colonizing (nation, etc.). **2.** *n.* colonizer.
colonisation [kɔlɔnizasjɔ̃] *n.f.* colonization, settlement.
coloniser [kɔlɔnize] *v.tr.* to colonize, settle (region).
colonnade [kɔlɔnad] *n.f.* *Arch:* colonnade.
colonne [kɔlɔn] *n.f.* **1.** (*a*) *Arch:* column, pillar; **c. de l'Église,** pillar of the Church; (*b*) **lit à colonnes,** four-poster bed; *Anat:* **c. vertébrale,** spinal column; (*c*) **c. de mercure,** column of mercury; **c. d'eau,** waterspout; (*d*) *Nau:* **c. d'habitacle,** binnacle. **2. c. montante,** (i) *Plumb: Ind:* rising main, riser (pipe); (ii) *El.E:* **c. montante,** service cable, service conductor, riser. **3.** *Mil:* column; (*a*) **c. par deux, par trois, par quatre,** column of twos, of threes, of fours; (*b*) **c. de secours,** relief (column); **c. de véhicules en marche,** column of moving vehicles; (*c*) *Navy:* **en c.,** line ahead; (*d*) *Pol:* **cinquième c.,** fifth column.
colophane [kɔlɔfan] *n.f.* rosin, colophony.
coloquinte [kɔlɔkɛ̃t] *n.f.* **1.** *Bot:* colocynth, bitter apple. **2.** *P:* head, nut.
colorant [kɔlɔrɑ̃] **1.** *a.* colouring, *NAm:* coloring (matter, etc.). **2.** *n.m.* colouring; dye.
coloration [kɔlɔrasjɔ̃] *n.f.* **1.** colouring, *NAm:* coloring, colo(u)ration; staining; **se faire faire une**

c., to have one's hair tinted. **2.** colour(ing) (of skin).

coloré [kɔlɔre] *a.* coloured, *NAm:* colored; **teint c.,** florid, ruddy, complexion; **style c.,** colourful, *NAm:* colorful, style.

colorer [kɔlɔre] **1.** *v.tr.* to colour, *NAm:* color, stain, tinge, tint; **c. qch. en vert,** to colour sth. green; **c. un récit,** to lend colour to a tale; **c. ses préjugés,** to disguise one's prejudices. **2. se c.,** (*of fruit, etc.*) to colour; (*of face*) to become flushed.

coloriage [kɔlɔrjaʒ] *n.m.* (*a*) colouring; (*b*) coloured drawing.

colorier [kɔlɔrje] *v.tr.* (*impf. & pr.sub.* **n. coloriions, v. coloriiez**) to colour, *NAm:* color (map, drawing).

coloris [kɔlɔri] *n.m.* colour(ing), *NAm:* color(ing) (of painting, fruit, etc.); shade; **c. du style,** brilliance, richness, of style; *Com:* **carte de c.,** shade card.

coloriste [kɔlɔrist] *n.m. & f.* **1.** *Art:* colourist, *NAm:* colorist. **2.** colourer, painter (of postcards, toys, etc.). **3.** hairdresser specializing in tinting.

colossal, -aux [kɔlɔsal, -o] *a.* colossal, gigantic, huge; enormous; tremendous.

colossalement [kɔlɔsalmɑ̃] *adv.* colossally.

colosse [kɔlɔs] *n.m.* colossus; giant.

colostomie [kɔlɔstɔmi] *n.f. Surg:* colostomy.

colportage [kɔlpɔrtaʒ] *n.m.* (*a*) hawking, peddling (of goods); (*b*) **c. de fausses nouvelles,** rumour mongering.

colporter [kɔlpɔrte] *v.tr.* (*a*) to hawk, peddle (goods); (*b*) to retail, spread (news).

colporteur, -euse [kɔlpɔrtœr, -øz] *n.* (*a*) door-to-door salesman; hawker, pedlar; (*b*) **c. de nouvelles,** newsmonger.

coltinage [kɔltinaʒ] *n.m.* porterage, carrying (of heavy loads on one's back).

coltiner [kɔltine] **1.** *v.tr.* to carry (heavy loads) on one's back. **2.** *F:* **je ne vais pas me c. ça tout seul,** I'm not going to do it alone.

coltineur [kɔltinœr] *n.m.* porter (who carries heavy loads); **c. de charbon,** coal heaver.

columbarium [kɔlɔ̃barjɔm] *n.m.* columbarium.

col(-)vert [kɔlvɛr] *n.m. Orn:* mallard; *pl. cols-verts.*

colza [kɔlza] *n.m. Bot:* rape, colza, coleseed; **huile de c.,** colza oil.

coma [kɔma] *n.m. Med:* coma.

comateux, -euse [kɔmatø, -øz] *a. Med:* comatose; *n.* **un c.,** a patient in a coma.

combat [kɔ̃ba] *n.m.* **1.** *Mil:* combat, fight, battle, engagement, action; (*a*) **c. corps à corps,** hand-to-hand fight(ing); **c. aérien,** aerial combat; **c. naval,** naval engagement, action; **c. terrestre,** land operation; **c. de rue,** street fight(ing); **engager le c.,** to go into action (**avec,** with); **mettre hors de c.,** to disable, to put out of action, to cripple; **hors de c.,** (i) (*of pers.*) hors de combat; disabled; (ii) (*of equipment*) out of action; (*b*) fight(ing); quarrel(ling); (*c*) **c. de boxe,** boxing match; (*d*) **c. de coqs,** cockfight. **2.** conflict, struggle; contest (of wits, etc.); **c. d'intérêts,** clash of interests.

combatif, -ive [kɔ̃batif, -iv] *a.* combative, pugnacious; **esprit c.,** fighting spirit; **il n'a rien de c.,** he's no fighter.

combativité [kɔ̃bativite] *n.f.* combativeness, pugnacity.

combattant, -ante [kɔ̃batɑ̃, -ɑ̃t] **1.** *a. Mil:* **unité combattante,** combatant, fighting, unit. **2.** *n.m.* (*a*) combatant, fighter; *Mil:* soldier, (i) on active service; (ii) in a fighting unit; **anciens combattants,** ex-servicemen, *U.S:* veterans; (*b*) fighter, brawler. **3.** *n.m.* (*a*) game cock, fowl; (*b*) *Orn:* ruff.

combattre [kɔ̃batr̥] *v.* (*conj. like* BATTRE) **1.** *v.tr.* to combat, to fight (against), to contend, battle, with (enemy, disease, temptation, opinion, etc.). **2.** *v.i.* to fight, strive, struggle; **c. pour, contre, qn, qch.,** to fight for, against, s.o., sth.

combe [kɔ̃b] *n.f. Geog:* (*in the Jura*) anticlinal valley.

combien [kɔ̃bjɛ̃] *adv.* (*& conj. when introducing a clause*) **1.** (*exclamative*) (*a*) how (much)! **si vous saviez c. je l'aime!** if you knew how much I love him! (*b*) how (many)! **c. de gens!** what a lot of people! **2.** (*interrogative*) (*a*) how much? **c. vous dois-je?** how much do I owe you? **(c'est) c.?** *F:* **ça fait c.?** how much is it? **depuis c. de temps est-il ici?** how long has he been here? **c. y a-t-il d'ici à Londres?** how far is it (from here) to London? **à c. sommes-nous de Paris?** how far are we from Paris? **c. vous a-t-il fallu pour venir?** how long did it take you to come? **c'est arrivé il y a je ne sais c. de temps,** it happened such a long time ago; (*b*) how many? **c. de fois?** how many times? how often? (*c*) *n.m.inv. F:* **le c. sommes-nous?** what's the date? **il y a un car tous les c.?** how often does the bus run?

combientième [kɔ̃bjɛ̃tjɛm] *a. & n. F:* **tu as été reçu (le) c. à l'examen?** where did you come in the exam?

combinaison [kɔ̃binɛzɔ̃] *n.f.* **1.** (*a*) combination, arrangement, grouping (of letters, ideas, etc.); (colour) scheme; *Mth:* combination; **c. financière,** combine; (*b*) plan, contrivance, scheme; **trouvez une c. pour en sortir!** find a way of getting out of this! (*c*) *Ch:* combination; compound. **2.** (*a*) (mechanic's) overalls, dungarees, boiler suit; *Av:* one-piece flying suit; (*b*) *Cost:* slip. **3.** combination lock (of safe).

combinard, -arde [kɔ̃binar, -ard] *a. & n. F:* schemer; **il est, c'est un, c.,** he knows all the tricks.

combinateur [kɔ̃binatœr] *n.m. El:* controller; multiple-contact, selector, switch; *Rail:* switchgroup.

combinatoire [kɔ̃binatwar] *a.* combinative; *Mth:* combinational.

combine [kɔ̃bin] *n.f. F:* scheme, trick; fiddle; **il a une c. pour entrer sans payer,** he knows a way of getting in without paying.

combiné [kɔ̃bine] **1.** *a.* combined, joint (action, etc.). **2.** *n.m.* (*a*) *Ch:* compound; (*b*) (telephone) receiver; (*c*) radiogram; (*d*) *Ski:* combined downhill and slalom competition; (*e*) *Cost:* corselette.

combiner [kɔ̃bine] *v.tr.* **1.** (*a*) to combine, unite (forces, etc.); to arrange, group (numbers, ideas, etc.); (*b*) *Ch:* to combine. **2.** to contrive, devise, think out, concoct (plan, etc.); **qu'est-ce que tu as combiné?** what have you dreamed up? **3. se c.,** to combine, unite (**à, avec,** with).

comble [kɔ̃bl̥] *n.m.* **1. pour c. de malheur,** to cap, crown, it all; **ça c'est le c., un c.!** that's the limit, the last straw! **2.** (*a*) roof (timbers); roofing; **c. à deux pans,** span roof; **c. brisé,** curb roof; **loger sous les combles,** to live in an attic; **de fond en c.,** from top to bottom; (*b*) highest point; height (of happiness, insolence); depth (of despair); summit (of fame, etc.); **elle était au c. de la joie,** she was overjoyed, wild with joy. **2.** *a.* (*a*) (*of measure, etc.*) heaped up, piled up; full to bursting, to overflowing; (*b*) (*of hall, etc.*) packed; **salle c.,** house filled to capacity.

comblé [kɔ̃ble] *a.* (*of pers.*) happy, contented, satisfied; **il est c.,** he has everything he could wish for.

combler [kɔ̃ble] *v.tr.* **1.** to fill (up), fill in (well, ditch, etc.); to make up, make good (a loss); **c. une lacune,** to fill a gap. **2.** to overload, overwhelm (s.o., sth.); **c. les vœux de qn,** to fulfil s.o.'s desires; **vous me comblez,** you are too kind.

comburant [kɔ̃byrɑ̃] **1.** *a. Ch: etc:* combustive. **2.** *n.m.* combustive agent; oxidant.

combustibilité [kɔbystibilite] *n.f.* combustibility.

combustible [kɔ̃bystibl̥] **1.** *a.* combustible. **2.** *n.m.* fuel; (*rockets*) propellant; **refaire sa provision de c., se réapprovisionner en c.,** to refuel.

combustion [kɔ̃bystjɔ̃] *n.f.* combustion, burning; **poêle à c. lente,** slow combustion stove; **moteur à c. interne,** internal combustion engine.

Côme [kom] *Pr.n.f. Geog:* Como; **le lac de C.,** lake Como.

comédie [kɔmedi] *n.f.* **1.** (*a*) comedy; **c. de mœurs,** comedy of manners; **c. musicale,** musical (comedy); (*b*) **jouer la c.,** (i) to act in a play; (ii) to put on an act; (*to children*) **allons! pas de c.!** come along! behave yourselves! **c'est toujours la même c.,** it's always the same; the same thing happens every time. **2.** *A:* play.

comédien, -ienne [kɔmedjɛ̃, -jɛn] *n.* (*a*) comedian, actor, *f.* actress; player; **comédiens ambulants,** strolling players; **c'est un(e) comédien(ne),** he, she, is always putting on an act; (*b*) (*child*) show-off.

comestible [kɔmɛstibl] **1.** *a.* edible, eatable; **denrées comestibles,** comestibles, food. **2.** *n.m.pl.* food.

comète [kɔmɛt] *n.f.* **1.** *Astr:* comet; *Pyr:* sky rocket; *Vit:* **l'année de la C.,** the Comet year (1811); **du vin de la c.,** excellent wine. **2.** *Bookb:* headband.

comice [kɔmis] *n.m.* **1.** *pl.* (*a*) *Rom.Ant:* comitia; (*b*) *Fr.Hist:* electoral meeting. **2. c. agricole,** agricultural association; **comices agricoles,** agricultural show.

comique [kɔmik] **1.** *Th: Lit:* (*a*) *a.* comic (actor, author, part, etc.); **le genre c.,** comedy; (*b*) *n.m.* (i) comedy; (ii) comic actor; (iii) comic; comedian. **2.** (*a*) *a.* comic(al), funny, ludicrous (story, face, etc.); (*b*) *n.m.* **le c. de l'histoire c'est que . . .,** the funny part, the joke, is that . . ..

comiquement [kɔmikmɑ̃] *adv.* comically.

comité [kɔmite] *n.m.* (*a*) committee, board; **c. consultatif,** advisory board, commission; **c. d'enquête,** board of enquiry; *Ind:* **c. d'entreprise,** joint production committee; *Th:* **c. de lecture,** reading, selection, committee; **c. secret,** secret session; (*b*) **être en petit c.,** to be a select party, an informal gathering; **dîner en petit c.,** a small (intimate) dinner party.

commandant [kɔmɑ̃dɑ̃] **1.** *a.* (*a*) commanding, in command of; (*b*) *F:* authoritarian; bossy. **2.** *n.m.* (*a*) (*function*) commander, commanding officer (of unit, etc.); commandant (of camp, base, etc.); *Nau:* captain (of ship) (whatever his rank); **c. en chef,** commander-in-chief; *Navy:* executive officer; first lieutenant; *Av:* **c. de bord,** captain; (*b*) (*rank*) *Mil:* major; *Mil. Av:* squadron leader; **c. en chef des forces aériennes** = Marshal of the Royal Air Force. **3.** *n.f.* wife of a *commandant.*

commande [kɔmɑ̃d] *n.f.* **1.** (*a*) *Com:* order; **faire, passer, une c.,** to place, put in, an order; **fait sur c.,** made to order; **ouvrage écrit sur la c. de l'éditeur,** work commissioned by the publisher; **payable à la c.,** cash with order; (*b*) (*goods ordered*) **livrer une c.,** to deliver an order; (*c*) **sourire de c.,** forced smile. **2.** *Mec.E:* (*a*) control, operation; **bouton de c.,** control knob; **c. à distance,** remote control; **levier de c.,** (i) control, operating, lever; (ii) *Av:* control column; (*b*) lever; **prendre les commandes,** (i) to take (over) the controls; (ii) to take control; **avion à double c.,** dual-control plane; (*c*) drive, driving (gear); **machine à c. électrique,** electrically driven machine.

commandement [kɔmɑ̃dmɑ̃] *n.m.* **1.** command, order; (*a*) *Rel:* **les Dix Commandements,** the Ten Commandments; (*b*) *Jur:* summons to pay before execution. **2.** authority; command; **avoir, prendre, le c.,** to be in, to take, command; **avoir le c. sur . . .,** to have authority over . . .. **3.** *Mil: Navy:* (*a*) order, (word of) command; (*b*) (*authority*) **c. en chef,** command-in-chief; **c. suprême, haut c.,** (i) higher command (of British forces); (ii) high command (of French, German, etc. forces).

commander [kɔmɑ̃de] **I.** *v.tr.* **1.** (*a*) to command; **il n'aime pas qu'on le commande,** he doesn't like being ordered about; (*b*) to order (sth.); **c. qch. à qn,** to give s.o. an order for sth., to order sth. from s.o.; **c. des marchandises, un dîner,** to order goods, a dinner; **c. une peinture,** to commission a painting; **ces choses-là ne se commandent pas,** these things are beyond our control; **il faut apprendre à vous c.,** you must learn to control yourself; (*c*) **c. le respect,** to command respect. **2.** *Mil: etc:* to command, to order; to be in charge, in command (of); **c. en chef,** to be commander-in-chief (of). **3.** (*a*) to command, dominate; **le fort commande la vallée,** the fort commands, dominates, the valley; (*b*) to give access to; **les pièces de cet appartement se commandent,** the rooms of this flat communicate with each other. **4.** *Mec.E:* (*a*) to control, operate (motion, valve, etc.); (*b*) to drive (machine, shaft, etc.). **II.** *v.i.* **1. c. à qn, à qch.,** to command, govern, control, s.o., sth.; **je lui ai commandé de se taire,** I told him to be quiet; **c. à son impatience,** to control, curb, one's impatience. **2. qui est-ce qui commande ici?** who's in charge here? who's giving the orders here?

commandeur [kɔmɑ̃dœr] *n.m.* commander (of the *Légion d'Honneur*).

commanditaire [kɔmɑ̃ditɛr] *a. & n.m. Com:* **(associé) c.** = sleeping partner.

commandite [kɔmɑ̃dit] *n.f. Com:* (*a*) **(société en) c.,** mixed liability company; limited partnership; (*b*) interest of, capital invested by, sleeping partner(s).

commandité [kɔmɑ̃dite] *a. & n.m. Com:* **(associé) c.,** active partner.

commanditer [kɔmɑ̃dite] *v.tr. Com:* to subscribe capital (to firm, etc.) as sleeping partner; to finance (enterprise, etc.).

commando [kɔmɑ̃do] *n.m. Mil:* commando (unit).

comme¹ [kɔm] *adv.* **1.** (*a*) as; **faites c. moi,** do as I do; **il a été vendu c. esclave,** he was sold as a slave; (*b*) like; **se conduire c. un fou,** to behave like a madman; **tout c. un autre,** (just) like anyone else; **sortir tous les jours, été c. hiver,** to go out every day, summer and winter alike; *F:* **j'ai c. une idée que . . .,** I have a sort of idea that . . .; *F:* **c. ci c. ça,** so so; **(alors) c. ça vous venez de Paris?** (and) so you come from Paris? (*c*) (as) . . . as . . .; **doux c. un agneau,** (as) gentle as a lamb; **blanc c. neige,** snow-white; *F:* **drôle c. tout,** awfully, terribly, funny; (*d*) **c. (si)** (**si** *is expressed only before a finite verb*), as if, as though; **il travaille c. s'il avait vingt ans,** he works as if he were twenty; **ils faisaient c. si rien ne s'était passé,** they pretended that nothing had happened; **il leva la main c. pour me frapper,** he lifted his hand as if to strike me; *F:* **c'est tout c.,** it amounts to the same thing; (*e*) *F:* **elle est partie, c. quoi tu n'as pas pu la rencontrer,** she's left, therefore, so, you couldn't have met her; (*f*) such as; **les bois durs c. le chêne et le noyer,** hard woods such as oak and walnut. **2.** (*immediately before finite verbs*) as; (*a*) **faites c. il vous plaira,** do as you please; **c'est arrivé à peu près c. je l'avais prédit,** it happened more or less as I predicted; (*b*) *adj. & adv. phr.* **c. il faut,** proper(ly); *F:* (*of pers.*) **il est très c. il faut,** (i) he's well-bred; (ii) he's prim and proper; **tiens-toi c. il faut,** (i) don't slouch; (ii) sit up, properly. **3.** as, in the way of; **qu'est-ce que vous avez c. légumes?** what have you (got) in the way of vegetables? **ce n'est pas mal c. film,** it's not bad as films go. **4.** *excl.* how! **c. vous avez grandi!** how you've grown! **c. je suis content de vous voir!** how glad I am to see you! *NAm:* am I glad to see you! **5.** *F:* (= COMMENT); how; **il y est arrivé Dieu sait c.,** he managed it, God knows how; **voilà c. il est,** that's just like him; that's his way.

comme² *conj.* **1.** as, seeing that; **c. vous êtes mon ami je vous dirai tout,** since you're my friend I will tell you everything. **2.** (just) as; **c. il allait frapper on l'arrêta,** (just) as he was about to strike he was arrested.

commémoratif, -ive [kɔmemɔratif, -iv] *a.* commemorative (**de,** of); memorial (service, etc.); **monument c.,** memorial.

commémoration [kɔmemɔrasjɔ̃] *n.f.* commemoration.

commémorer [kɔmemɔre] *v.tr.* to commemorate.

commençant, -ante [kɔmɑ̃sɑ̃, -ɑ̃t] **1.** *a.* beginning, early. **2.** *n.* beginner.

commencement [kɔmɑ̃smɑ̃] *n.m.* (*a*) beginning, start; **au c.,** at the beginning, the outset; **du c. jusqu'à la fin,** from beginning to end, from start to finish; (*b*) *pl.* beginnings; initial stage(s).

commencer [kɔmɑ̃se] *v.* **(je commencai(s); n. commençons)** to begin, start. **1.** (*a*) *v.tr.* **c. la leçon,** to begin the lesson; **c. un voyage,** to start on a journey; **c. un élève,** to ground a pupil; *v.i.* **pour c., je dois vous dire . . .,** to begin with, first of all, I must tell you . . .; (*b*) *v.i.* **c. à, de, faire qch.,** to begin to do sth., to begin doing sth.; **il commence à pleuvoir,** it's beginning, starting, to rain; **c. par faire qch.,** to begin by doing sth.; **nous allions c. sans vous,** we were going to start (eating, etc.) without you; **commencez!** fire away! *F:* **je commence à en avoir assez!** I've had just about enough! **2.** *v.i.* to begin; **la pluie vient de c.,** it's just started raining; **l'année commence le 1er janvier,** the year begins on January 1st.

commensal, -ale, -aux [kɔmɑ̃sal, -o] *n.* **1.** *Lit:* commensal, table companion. **2.** *Biol:* commensal.

commensurable [kɔmɑ̃syrabl̥] *a.* commensurable (**avec,** with, to).

comment [kɔmɑ̃] *adv.* **1.** *interr.* how; **c. allez-vous?** how are you? **c. (dites-vous)?** what (did you say)? **c. faire?** what can, should, I, we, etc., do? **c. s'appelle-t-il?** what is his name? **c. est-il, ce garçon?** what sort of young man is he? **faire qch. n'importe c.,** to do sth. in a slapdash manner, *F:* all anyhow. **2.** *excl.* what! why! **c.! vous n'êtes pas encore parti!** what, haven't you gone yet! **mais c. donc!** why of course, by all means! *F:* **ça vous a plu?—et c.!** did you like it?—we certainly did! and how! **3.** *n.m.inv.* **les pourquoi et les c.,** the whys and wherefores.

commentaire [kɔmɑ̃tɛr] *n.m.* **1.** commentary (**sur,** on); annotations (**sur,** on). **2.** comment; remark; *F:* **cela se passe de c.,** it speaks for itself; it's obvious; *F:* **sans c.!** no comment! *F:* **pas de c.!** that's final! I don't want any comments (from you)!

commentateur, -trice [kɔmɑ̃tatœr, -tris] **1.** *n.m. Lit:* commentator, annotator. **2.** *n. W.Tel: T.V:* (news) commentator.

commenter [kɔmɑ̃te] *v.tr.* **1.** to comment on; to annotate (text, etc.). **2.** to comment on, criticize (s.o., sth.).

commérage [kɔmeraʒ] *n.m. F:* (*a*) piece of gossip; (*b*) *pl.* gossip(ing); tittle-tattle.

commerçant, -ante [kɔmɛrsɑ̃, -ɑ̃t] **1.** *a.* commercial; business (district); **rue très commerçante,** busy shopping street; **peu c.,** bad at business. **2.** *n.* dealer; tradesman; shopkeeper; **c. en gros, en détail,** wholesaler, retailer; **les commerçants,** tradespeople.

commerce [kɔmɛrs] *n.m.* **1.** commerce, trade; (transaction of) business; **c. en, de, gros, en, de, détail,** wholesale, retail, trade; **c. intérieur, extérieur,** home, foreign, trade; **maison de c.,** business house; firm; **le c.,** (i) trade; (ii) the commercial world; **le petit c.,** (i) small traders; (ii) shopkeeping; **cela fait marcher le c.,** it's good for trade; **hors c.,** not for (general) sale; **c. des chevaux,** horse dealing; **(fonds de) c.,** business. **2.** *A: & Lit:* intercourse, dealings; **avoir, être en, c. avec qn,** to be in touch, in relationship, with s.o.; **être d'un c. agréable,** to be easy to get on with, pleasant to deal with.

commercer [kɔmɛrse] *v.i.* **(je commerçai(s); n. commerçons)** to trade, deal (**avec,** with).

commercial, -iale, -iaux [kɔmɛrsjal, -jo] **1.** *a.* commercial, trading, business (relations). **2.** *n.f. Aut:* (i) estate car, *NAm:* station wagon; (ii) small van.

commercialement [kɔmɛrsjalmɑ̃] *adv.* commercially.

commercialisation [kɔmɛrsjalizasjɔ̃] *n.f.* marketing.

commercialiser [kɔmɛrsjalize] *v.tr.* to commercialize (art, etc.); to market (product).

commère [kɔmɛr] *n.f.* gossip, busybody.

commettant [kɔmɛtɑ̃] *n.m.* **1.** *Com: Jur:* principal (to a deal). **2.** *pl. Pol:* constituents.

commettre [kɔmɛtr̥] *v.tr.* (*conj. like* METTRE) **1.** *Ropem:* to lay, twist (rope). **2.** (*a*) *A:* (= COMPROMETTRE) to expose; **c. sa réputation,** to risk one's reputation; **il eut soin de ne pas se c.,** he was careful not to commit himself; (*b*) *A:* **c. qch. à qn,** to commit, entrust, sth. to s.o., to s.o.'s keeping; to entrust s.o. with sth.; (*c*) *Jur:* **c. qn à qch.,** to appoint s.o. to sth.; to put s.o. in charge of sth. **3.** to commit (crime, sin, injustice); **c. une erreur,** to make a mistake.

comminatoire [kɔminatwar] *a.* (*a*) *Jur:* comminatory (decree, etc.); (*b*) threatening (letter).

commis [kɔmi] *n.m.* **1.** *O:* clerk; **c. aux écritures,** book-keeper; **les grands c.,** the higher civil servants. **2.** (*a*) *O:* shop assistant; (*b*) *A:* **c. voyageur,** commercial traveller.

commisération [kɔmizerasjɔ̃] *n.f.* commiseration.

commissaire [kɔmisɛr] *n.m.* (*a*) member of a commission, commissioner; commissary; **c. du gouvernement,** government representative; (*b*) **c. (de police)** = (police) superintendent; **c. principal** = chief superintendent; (*c*) *Navy:* **c. de la Marine,** supply and secretariat officer; *U.S:* supply officer; *Nau:* **c. du bord,** purser; (*d*) *Fin:* **c. aux comptes,** auditor; (*e*) *Fr.C:* **c. d'école,** school commissioner; (*f*) *Sp: etc:* steward; *Rac:* **c. des courses,** race steward.

commissaire-priseur [kɔmisɛrprizœr] *n.m.* (*a*) appraiser, valuer; (*b*) auctioneer; *pl. commissaires-priseurs.*

commissariat [kɔmisarja] *n.m.* **1.** (*a*) commissionership, commissaryship; **c. des comptes,** auditorship; (*b*) *Nau:* pursership. **2. c. (de police),** police station. **3. c. de la marine,** supply and secretariat branch; **c. de l'air** = air department (of Ministry of Defence).

commission [kɔmisjɔ̃] *n.f.* commission. **1.** (*a*) *Jur: etc:* charge, warrant; **avoir la c. de faire qch.,** to be commissioned, empowered, to do sth.; (*b*) *Com:* **maison de c.,** firm of commission agents, commission agency; **vente à c.,** sale on commission. **2.** (*a*) *Com:* commission, allowance; **c. de deux pour cent,** commission of two per cent; **3% de c.,** 3% commission; (*b*) *Fin:* brokerage. **3.** (*a*) message, errand; **faire des commissions,** to run errands; **j'ai fait toutes mes commisssions,** I've done all my shopping; (*b*) (*child's language*) **la petite, la grosse, c.,** number one, two. **4.** committee, board; **c. d'enquête,** board, committee, of inquiry.

commissionnaire [kɔmisjɔnɛr] *n.m.* **1.** *Com:* commission agent; broker; **c. exportateur, importateur,** export, import, agent; **c. de transport, de roulage,** forwarding agent, carrier. **2.** messenger; (*in hotels, theatres*) commissionaire.

commissionner [kɔmisjɔne] *v.tr.* to commission; to appoint (s.o.) as buyer on commission.

commissure [kɔmisyr] *n.f. Anat: Bot: etc:* commissure; corner (of the lips, etc.).

commode [kɔmɔd] **1.** *a.* (*a*) convenient, suitable, opportune (moment, etc.); handy (tool, etc.); convenient, comfortable (house, etc.); (*b*) **ce que vous me demandez là n'est pas c.,** what you are asking me isn't very easy; *F:* **c'est trop c.,** that's too easy; (*c*) *O:* accommodating, easy, adaptable (disposition, etc.); **c. à vivre,** easy to live with; *F:* **il n'est pas c., il est peu c.,** he's a tough, an awkward, customer. **2.** *n.f. Furn:* chest of drawers.

commodément [kɔmɔdemɑ̃] *adv.* comfortably.

commodité [kɔmɔdite] *n.f.* (*a*) convenience; **les commodités de la vie,** the comforts of life; **pour plus de c.,** for convenience sake; (*b*) commodiousness.

commotion [kɔmosjɔ̃] *n.f.* **1.** commotion, disturbance; **c. politique,** political upheaval; *Med:* **c. cérébrale,** concussion. **2.** shock, violent emotion.

commotionner [kɔmosjɔne] *v.tr.* (*a*) *Med:* to cause a state of shock; **il a été fortement commotionné,** he was severely concussed, he had severe concussion; (*b*) **cette nouvelle m'a commotionné,** this news has given me a terrible shock.

commuable [kɔmɥabl̩] *a. Jur:* commutable (sentence, etc.).

commuer [kɔmɥe] *v.tr. Jur:* to commute (penalty) (**en,** to).

commun [kɔmœ̃] **1.** *a.* (*a*) common (**à,** to); **jardin c. à deux maisons,** garden shared by two houses; **salle commune,** (i) common room; (ii) (*in hospital*) ward; **maison commune,** town hall, municipal buildings; **avoir des intérêts communs,** to have interests in common, to have common interests; **amis communs,** mutual friends; **vie commune,** community life; **d'un c. accord,** with one accord; *Mth:* **dénominateur c.,** common denominator; **en commun,** in common; **vivre en c.,** to live communally; (*b*) common; universal, general (custom, opinion, etc.); usual, ordinary, everyday (occurrence, etc.); **le sens c.,** common sense; *Gram:* **nom c.,** common noun; **lieu c.,** commonplace; **il est d'une force peu commune,** he's unusually strong; (*c*) vulgar; **terme c.,** vulgar, common, expression. **2.** *n.m.* (*a*) common run, generality (of persons, etc.); **le c. des mortels,** the ordinary, average, man; **hors du c.,** out of the ordinary; (*b*) *pl.* **les communs,** outhouses, outbuildings.

communal, -aux [kɔmynal, -o] *a.* **1.** common (land, property); *n.m.pl.* **les communaux,** common land. **2.** communal; council (property, etc.); **école communale,** *n.f.* **communale** = primary school.

communautaire [kɔmynotɛr] *a.* communal; **centre c.,** community centre.

communauté [kɔmynote] *n.f.* **1.** (*a*) community (of interests, ideas, etc.); (*b*) *Jur:* joint estate (of husband and wife). **2.** (*a*) community, corporation, society; (*b*) (religious) community, order; (*c*) *Pol:* community.

commune [kɔmyn] *n.f.* **1.** (*a*) *Fr.Hist:* free town; (*b*) (*in Engl.*) **la Chambre des Communes, les Communes,** the (House of) Commons. **2.** *Fr.Adm:* (*smallest territorial division*) commune, approx. = (i) parish, (ii) municipality. **3.** *Fr.Hist:* (*in 1789 and 1871*) **la C.,** the Commune.

communément [kɔmynemɑ̃] *adv.* commonly.

communiant, -ante [kɔmynjɑ̃, -ɑ̃t] *n. Ecc:* communicant; **premier c., première communiante,** person taking his, her, first communion.

communicable [kɔmynikabl̩] *a.* communicable (disease, etc.); *Jur:* transferable (right); (file, etc.) that can be made available.

communicant [kɔmynikɑ̃] *a.* communicating (rooms, etc.).

communicateur, -trice [kɔmynikatœr, -tris] *a.* connecting (wire, etc.).

communicatif, -ive [kɔmynikatif, -iv] *a.* **1.** communicative, talkative; **peu c.,** uncommunicative. **2.** infectious (laughter, etc.).

communication [kɔmynikasjɔ̃] *n.f.* **1.** communication; communicating; (*a*) **faire une c. (à une société savante),** to read a paper (to a learned society); *Jur:* **donner c. des pièces,** to give discovery of documents; (*b*) **c. d'idées,** interchange of ideas; **entrer, se mettre, en c. avec qn,** to get into communication with s.o.; to communicate with s.o.; **mettre deux personnes en c.,** to put two people in touch with each other; **communications de masse,** mass media; **portes de c.,** communicating doors; (*c*) *Tp:* **c. téléphonique,** (telephone) call; **c. en P.C.V.,** reverse, transferred, charge call, *NAm:* collect call; **mettez-moi en c. avec M. Martin,** put me through to Mr Martin; **vous avez la c.,** you're through; **la c. est mauvaise,** the line is bad. **2.** communication; message; **transmettre une c. à qn,** to pass on a message to s.o..

communier [kɔmynje] *v.* (*impf. & pr.sub.* **n. communiions, v. communiiez**) *v.i. Ecc:* to receive Holy Communion.

communion [kɔmynjɔ̃] *n.f.* **1.** communion; **appartenir à la même c.,** to belong to the same persuasion, faith. **2.** *Ecc:* (Holy) Communion.

communiqué [kɔmynike] *n.m.* communiqué; official statement; press release.

communiquer [kɔmynike] *v.* to communicate. **1.** *v.tr.* (*a*) to impart, convey (information, etc.); **c. qch. à qn,** to bring sth. to s.o.'s notice; **c. qch. par écrit à qn,** to report in writing to s.o. about sth.; **c. une maladie à qn,** to pass on an illness to s.o.; (*b*) (*in library*) to issue (a book). **2.** *v.i.* to be in communication; **porte qui communique au, avec le, jardin,** door that leads into the garden; **canal qui fait c. deux rivières,** canal that connects two rivers. **3. se c.** (*a*) *O:* to be communicative; (*b*) **l'incendie s'est communiqué aux maisons voisines,** the fire has spread to the neighbouring houses.

communisant, -ante [kɔmynizɑ̃, -ɑ̃t] *a.* communist (newspaper, etc.); *n.* **c'est un c.,** he's a Communist sympathizer.

communisme [kɔmynism] *n.m.* Communism.

communiste [kɔmynist] (*a*) *n.* Communist; (*b*) *a.* Communist; **la Chine c.,** Communist China.

commutateur [kɔmytatœr] *n.m. El:* **1.** commutator (of dynamo, etc.). **2.** switch; changeover, throw over, switch; **c. sélecteur,** selector switch.

commutatif, -ive [kɔmytatif, -iv] *a. Jur: Mth:* commutative.

commutation [kɔmytasjɔ̃] *n.f.* **1.** (*a*) *Jur:* commutation (of penalty); (*b*) *Gram:* replacement, substitution. **2.** *El:* changeover.

commutatrice [kɔmytatris] *n.f. El:* rotary converter, transformer.

commuter [kɔmyte] *v.tr.* **1.** *Jur:* to commute (penalty). **2.** *El:* to commutate, to switch over, change over (current).

Comores [kɔmɔr] *Pr.n. Geog:* **les îles C.,** the Comoro Islands.

compacité [kɔ̃pasite] *n.f.* compactness (of soil, etc.); density (of metal); denseness (of crowd).

compact [kɔ̃pakt] *a.* (*a*) compact, close, dense (mass, formation, etc.); **majorité compacte,** large, solid, majority; (*b*) **voiture compacte,** small (compact) car, *NAm:* compact.

compagne [kɔ̃paɲ] *n.f.* **1.** (female) companion; **c'était ma c. d'école,** I was at school with her. **2.** *Lit:* partner (in life); wife; (*of animals*) mate.

compagnie [kɔ̃paɲi] *n.f.* **1.** company, companionship; **tenir c. à qn,** to keep s.o. company; **fausser c. à qn,** to give s.o. the slip; **dame de c.,** (lady's) companion; **aller de c. avec . . .,** to go (hand in hand) with . . .; **ils ont voyagé de c.,** they travelled together. **2.** company, party, society; **toute la c.,** everybody; all of them, of us; **fréquenter la bonne, la mauvaise, c.,** to keep good, bad, company. **3.** (*a*) *Com: Th: etc:* company; **c. de navigation,** shipping company; **compagnies républicaines de sécurité,** state security police (in France); **c. aérienne,** airline; (*b*) *Com:* **la maison Thomas et Compagnie** (*usu.* **et Cie**), the firm of Thomas and Company (*usu.* and Co.); (*c*) *Ecc:* **la C. de Jésus,** the Society of Jesus. **4.** (*a*) *Mil:* company; (*b*) party; **c. de débarquement,** landing party. **5.** covey (of partridges).

compagnon [kɔ̃paɲɔ̃] *n.m.* **1.** (*a*) companion; comrade; **c. d'études,** fellow student; **c. de voyage,** travelling companion; **c'était mon c. de jeu,** I used to play with him; **c. d'infortune,** fellow sufferer; (*b*) *Ind:* (workman's) mate. **2.** journeyman. **3.** *Bot:* *F:* **c. blanc, rouge,** white, red, campion.

comparable [kɔ̃parabl̩] *a.* comparable (**à, avec, qch., qn,** to, with, sth., s.o.); **ce n'est pas c.,** there's no comparison.

comparablement [kɔ̃parabləmɑ̃] *adv.* comparably; in comparison (**à,** with).

comparaison [kɔ̃parɛzɔ̃] *n.f.* **1.** comparison; **hors de toute c.,** beyond compare; **il est sans c. le plus grand,** he is by far the tallest; **c. n'est pas raison,** comparisons are odious. **2.** simile.

comparaître [kɔ̃parɛtr̥] *v.i.* (*conj. like* PARAÎTRE) *Jur:* **c. (en justice),** to appear before a court of justice; **c. par avoué,** to be represented by counsel; **être appelé à c.,** to be summoned to appear.

comparant, -ante [kɔ̃parɑ̃, -ɑ̃t] *a.* & *n. Jur:* (person) appearing (before the court, etc.); *n.* appearer.

comparatif, -ive [kɔ̃paratif, -iv] **1.** *a.* comparative. **2.** *n.m. Gram:* **adjectif au c.,** comparative adjective.

comparativement [kɔ̃parativmɑ̃] *adv.* comparatively.

comparé [kɔ̃pare] *a.* comparative (anatomy, history, etc.).

comparer [kɔ̃pare] *v.tr.* to compare (**à, avec,** to, with).

comparse [kɔ̃pars] *n.* (*a*) *Th:* supernumerary; *F:* super; *Cin:* extra; **rôle de c.,** walk-on part; (*b*) associate, stooge; (*c*) person playing a minor role in an undertaking.

compartiment [kɔ̃partimɑ̃] *n.m.* compartment (of railway carriage, etc.); partition (of box, drawer, etc.); division; square (of chessboard, etc.).

compartimentage [kɔ̃partimɑ̃taʒ] *n.m.* partitioning; compartmentalization.

compartimenter [kɔ̃partimɑ̃te] *v.tr.* (*a*) to partition, to divide into compartments; (*b*) to compartmentalize.

comparution [kɔ̃parysjɔ̃] *n.f. Jur:* appearance (before the court); **non-c.,** non-appearance; default.

compas [kɔ̃pa] *n.m.* **1.** (*a*) (pair of) compasses; **c. à pointes sèches,** dividers; **c. quart de cercle,** wing compasses; **c. de réduction,** reduction compasses; *F:* **tout faire au c.,** to do everything with precision; **allonger le, son, c.,** to quicken one's pace; **avoir le c. dans l'œil,** to have an accurate eye; (*b*) *Mec.E:* *etc:* **c. d'épaisseur,** callipers. **2.** *Nau:* *etc:* **c. (de mer),** (mariner's) compass; **c. de route,** steering compass; **c. gyroscopique,** gyrocompass.

compassé [kɔ̃pase] *a.* stiff, formal (manner).

compasser [kɔ̃pase] *v.tr.* **1.** to measure (distances on map, etc.) with compasses; *Nau:* to prick (chart). **2.** *Lit:* to regulate, control (one's actions, etc.).

compassion [kɔ̃pasjɔ̃] *n.f.* compassion, pity; **avec c.,** compassionately.

compatibilité [kɔ̃patibilite] *n.f.* compatibility.

compatible [kɔ̃patibl̩] *a.* compatible (**avec,** with).

compatir [kɔ̃patir] *v.i.* **c. au chagrin de qn,** to sympathize with, feel for, s.o. in his grief.

compatissant [kɔ̃patisɑ̃] *a.* compassionate, sympathetic (**pour,** to, towards).

compatriote [kɔ̃patriɔ̃t] *n.m.* & *f.* compatriot, fellow countryman, countrywoman.

compensateur, -trice [kɔ̃pɑ̃satœr, -tris] **1.** *a.* compensating (spring, magnet, etc.); *El:* equalizing (current); balancing (dynamo); **pendule c.,** compensation pendulum. **2.** *n.m.* (*a*) compensator, balancer (of compass, etc.); (pressure) equalizer; *Av:* trimming tab, trimmer; (*b*) compensation pendulum.

compensation [kɔ̃pɑ̃sasjɔ̃] *n.f.* (*a*) compensation (of loss); set-off; **en c. de mes pertes,** as an offset to my losses; **il y a c.,** that makes up for it; (*b*) *Jur:* **c. des dépens,** sharing of the costs; *Fin:* **chambre de c.,** clearing house; (*c*) *Mec:* *El:* *etc:* equalization, balancing (of forces, etc.); compensation; (*d*) *Nau:* adjustment (of compass).

compensatoire [kɔ̃pɑ̃satwar] *a.* compensatory.

compensé [kɔ̃pɑ̃se] *a.* compensated; equalized; *Nau:* **gouvernail c.,** balanced rudder; *Bootm:* **semelle compensée,** wedge heel.

compenser [kɔ̃pɑ̃se] *v.tr.* (*a*) to compensate, make up for (sth.); to offset (fault, etc.); **c. une perte,** to make good a loss; (*b*) *Jur:* *etc:* to compensate, balance, set off (debts); **c. les dépens,** to divide out the costs; (*c*) *Nau:* to adjust (compass).

compère [kɔ̃pɛr] *n.m.* **1.** accomplice, associate (of conjuror, etc.). **2.** *F:* *O:* comrade, crony; **un bon c.,** a pleasant companion.

compère-loriot [kɔ̃pɛrlɔrjo] *n.m.* **1.** *Orn:* golden oriole. **2.** sty(e) (on the eyelid); *pl. compères-loriots.*

compétence [kɔ̃petɑ̃s] *n.f.* **1.** *Jur:* competence, competency, jurisdiction, powers (of court of justice, etc.); **cela ne rentre pas dans sa c., cela n'est pas de sa c.,** that does not come within his province, that is outside his scope; **sortir de sa c.,** to exceed one's powers. **2.** competence, ability, proficiency, skill (**pour faire qch.,** to do sth.).

compétent [kɔ̃petɑ̃] *a. Jur:* *etc:* competent (tribunal, authority, etc.); **c. en matière de finance,** conversant with finance; **il est d'un âge c. pour signer,** he is of a suitable, proper, age to sign; **je ne suis pas c. en la matière,** I am not competent to speak on the subject; *Com:* **adressez-vous au service c.,** apply to the department concerned.

compétiteur, -trice [kɔ̃petitœr, -tris] *n.* competitor.

compétitif, -ive [kɔ̃petitif, -iv] *a. Com:* competitive (prices, etc.).

compétition [kɔ̃petisjɔ̃] *n.f.* (*a*) competition, rivalry; **c. entre partis politiques,** political rivalry; (*b*) *Sp:* contest, match; **c. sportive,** sporting event.

compilateur, -trice [kɔ̃pilatœr, -tris] *n.* (*a*) compiler; (*b*) *Pej:* plagiarist.

compilation [kɔ̃pilasjɔ̃] *n.f.* **1.** compiling, compilation. **2.** *Pej:* plagiarism.

compiler [kɔ̃pile] *v.tr.* **1.** to compile. **2.** *Pej:* to plagiarize.

complainte [kɔ̃plɛ̃t] *n.f.* (*a*) *A:* plaint, lamentation; (*b*) *Lit:* *Mus:* (plaintive) ballad, lay.

complaire [kɔ̃plɛr] (*a*) *v.i.* (*conj. like* PLAIRE) *Lit:* **c. à qn,** to please, humour, gratify, s.o.; (*b*) **se c. dans, qch., à faire qch.,** to take pleasure, to delight, in sth., in doing sth.

complaisamment [kɔ̃plɛzamɑ̃] *adv.* **1.** obligingly, willingly. **2.** complacently, with satisfaction.

complaisance [kɔ̃plɛzɑ̃s] *n.f.* **1.** complaisance, obligingness; **faire qch. par c.,** to do sth. out of kindness; **faire qch. par c. pour qn,** to do sth. to oblige s.o.; **auriez-vous la c. de** + *inf.*, would you be so good, so kind, as to + *inf.*; *Com:* **billet, effet, de c.,** accommodation bill. **2.** complacence, complacency, (self-)satisfaction.

complaisant, -ante [kɔ̃plɛzɑ̃, -ɑ̃t] *a.* (*a*) obliging, accommodating (**envers, pour,** towards); willing (person, character, etc.); **prêter une oreille complaisante à qn,** to lend a sympathetic, willing, ear to s.o.; (*b*) **mari c.,** complaisant, indulgent, husband; (*c*) complacent, self-satisfied (smile, etc.).

complément [kɔ̃plemɑ̃] *n.m.* (*a*) complement; rest, remainder; **faire le c. de qch.,** to complement sth.; (*b*) *Gram:* complement; extension (of the subject, of the predicate); **c. (d'objet),** object (of verb); (*c*) *Bio-Ch:* complement; (*d*) *Mth:* complement (of angle).

complémentaire [kɔ̃plemɑ̃tɛr] *a.* complementary (angle, colour, etc.); **pour tout renseignement c., s'adresser à . . .,** for further information apply to . . ..

complet, -ète [kɔ̃plɛ, -ɛt] **1.** *a.* (*a*) complete, entire, whole (outfit, works, etc.); **rapport très c.,** very full, comprehensive, report; **examen c.,** full, thorough, examination; **c'est loin d'être c.,** it's a long way, far, from being complete; **athlète c.,** all-round athlete; **échec c.,** total, utter, failure; *F:* **c'est c.!** that's the last straw, the limit! **pain c.,** wholemeal bread; **café c., thé c.,** continental breakfast; (*b*) full (bus, *Th:* house, etc.); *P.N:* **c.,** full (up); (*outside boarding house*) no vacancies. **2.** *n.m.* (*a*) **c. (-veston),** suit; (*b*) **au c.,** complete, full; **nous étions présents au grand c.,** we turned out in full force.

complètement [kɔ̃plɛtmɑ̃] *adv.* completely, wholly, totally, fully; utterly (ruined); stark (naked).

compléter [kɔ̃plete] (*a*) *v.tr.* **(je complète, n. complétons; je compléterai)** to complete; to make (sth.) complete; **c. une somme,** to make up a sum (of money); (*b*) **les deux volumes se complètent,** the two volumes complement one another.

complétif, -ive [kɔ̃pletif, -iv] *a. & n. Gram:* **(proposition) complétive,** noun clause.

complexe [kɔ̃plɛks] **1.** *a.* complex (character, etc.); complicated (question); intricate (problem); *Gram:* **sujet c.,** compound subject; *Mth:* **nombre c.,** compound number. **2.** *n.m.* complex; **le c. industriel de la vallée du Rhône,** the Rhone valley industrial complex; *Psy:* **c. d'infériorité,** inferiority complex; *F:* **avoir des complexes,** to be inhibited, to be hung up.

complexé [kɔ̃plɛkse] *a. F:* inhibited, full of complexes; *F:* mixed up, hung up.

complexer [kɔ̃plɛkse] *v.tr. F:* to give (s.o.) a complex.

complexion [kɔ̃plɛksjɔ̃] *n.f. A:* constitution, disposition, temperament.

complexité [kɔ̃plɛksite] *n.f.* complexity.

complication [kɔ̃plikasjɔ̃] *n.f.* **1.** complication. **2.** complexity, intricacy. **3.** *Med:* complication(s).

complice [kɔ̃plis] *a. & n.* accessory (**de,** to); accomplice, abettor (**de,** of); **être c. d'une crime,** to be party to a crime; **c. en adultère,** co-respondent.

complicité [kɔ̃plisite] *n.f.* complicity; *Jur:* aiding and abetting; **agir de c. avec qn,** to act in collusion, in complicity, with s.o.

complies [kɔ̃pli] *n.f.pl. Ecc:* compline.

compliment [kɔ̃plimɑ̃] *n.m.* **1.** compliment; **faire des compliments à qn,** to pay s.o. compliments. **2.** *pl.* compliments, greetings; **faites-lui mes compliments,** (please) give him, her, my regards. **3.** congratulation; **(je vous fais) mes compliments,** I congratulate you; *Iron:* **mes compliments!** a nice mess you've made of it! **4.** speech of congratulation.

complimenter [kɔ̃plimɑ̃te] *v.tr.* to compliment (**de, sur,** on); to congratulate (**de, sur,** on).

complimenteur, -euse [kɔ̃plimɑ̃tœr, -øz] *a. & n.* obsequious (person); *n.* flatterer; **discours c.,** flattering speech.

compliqué [kɔ̃plike] *a.* complicated, elaborate, intricate (mechanism, etc.); involved (style, etc.); **je n'arrive pas, c'est trop c.,** I can't do it, it's too difficult; **personne compliquée,** *F:* **un c.,** difficult person.

compliquer [kɔ̃plike] **1.** *v.tr.* to complicate. **2. se c.,** to become complicated (**de,** with); to become involved; (*of plot*) to thicken; **il se complique l'existence,** he's making life difficult for himself.

complot [kɔ̃plo] *n.m.* plot, conspiracy; **tramer un c.,** to weave a plot; **chef de c.,** ringleader; **mettre qn dans le c.,** to let s.o. into the secret, into the plot.

comploter [kɔ̃plɔte] *v.tr. & i.* to plot, conspire (**contre,** against); **c. de faire qch.,** to plot to do sth.; *F:* **qu'est-ce que vous complotez là?** what are you up to now?

comploteur [kɔ̃plɔtœr] *n.m.* plotter.

compo [kɔ̃po] *n.f. Sch: F:* test; exam.

componction [kɔ̃pɔ̃ksjɔ̃] *n.f.* **1.** compunction. **2.** *Iron:* **avec. c.,** gravely, solemnly.

comportement [kɔ̃pɔrtəmɑ̃] *n.m.* behaviour, *NAm:* behavior; **psychologie du c.,** behaviourism.

comporter [kɔ̃pɔrte] *v.tr.* **1.** to allow, allow of; to admit of (sth.); **règle qui comporte des exceptions,** rule not without exceptions. **2.** to call for, require (sth.); **les précautions que comporte la situation,** the care which the situation demands. **3.** to comprise, include (sth.); **objectif qui comporte quatre éléments,** lens that comprises, is made up of, four elements; **les inconvénients que cela comporterait,** the difficulties which this would involve, entail. **4. se c.,** to behave, act (**vis-à-vis de, envers,** towards); **se c. mal,** to misbehave; **se c. en lâche, comme un lâche,** to act, behave, like a coward; **comment s'est-elle comportée devant la nouvelle?** how did she react to the news?

composant, -ante [kɔ̃pozɑ̃, -ɑ̃t] **1.** *a. & n.m.* component, constituent (part). **2.** *n.f.* **composante,** component (of voltage, force, velocity, etc.).

composé [kɔ̃poze] **1.** *a.* (*a*) compound (pendulum, interest, word, time, etc.); *Ch:* **corps c.,** compound; *Mec: etc:* **résistance composée,** combined strength; **temps c.,** compound tense; (*b*) *Bot:* composite (flower); *n.f.pl.* **composées,** Compositae; (*c*) composed (attitude, etc.). **2.** *n.m. Ch: Gram: etc:* compound.

composer [kɔ̃poze] **1.** *v.tr.* (*a*) to compose (poem, symphony, etc.); *Pharm:* to make up (prescription); *v.i. Mus:* to compose; *v.i. Sch:* to sit an examination; (*b*) *Typ:* to set (type); *Tp:* **c. un numéro,** to dial a number; (*c*) **les personnes qui composent notre famille,** the people who make up our family; all the members of our family; (*d*) **c. son visage,** to compose one's features; **se c. un visage de circonstance,** to put on a suitable expression. **2.** *v.i.* to compromise, come to terms (**avec,** with). **3. se c. (de),** to be made up (of), to consist (of).

compositeur, -trice [kɔ̃pozitœr, -tris] *n.* **1.** *Mus:* composer. **2.** *Typ:* compositor, typesetter.

composition [kɔ̃pozisjɔ̃] *n.f.* **1.** (*a*) composing, composition (of sonata, poem, etc.); construction (of novel, etc.); composition (of water, etc.); making up (of prescription, etc.); (*b*) *Typ:* typesetting, composition. **2.** (*a*) composition, compound, mixture; (*b*) *Lit: Mus: etc:* composition; *Sch:* (i) essay; (ii) test; paper. **3.** arrangement, compromise; **entrer en c. avec qn,** to come to terms with s.o.

compost [kɔ̃pɔst] *n.m. Agr:* compost.

compostage [kɔ̃pɔstaʒ] *n.m.* (date) stamping, punching (of ticket, etc.).

composter¹ [kɔ̃pɔste] *v.tr. Agr:* to compost (land).

composter² *v.tr.* to (date) stamp, punch (ticket, etc.).

composteur [kɔ̃pɔstœr] *n.m.* **1.** date stamp; punch; (automatic) ticket puncher. **2.** *Typ:* composing stick.

compote¹ [kɔ̃pɔt] *n.f.* (*a*) *Cu:* compote, stewed fruit; (*b*) *F:* **j'ai les jambes en c.,** my legs feel like jelly.

compote² *n.f. Sch: F:* test; exam.

compotier [kɔ̃pɔtje] *n.m.* fruit dish.

compréhensibilité [kɔ̃preɑ̃sibilite] *n.f.* comprehensibility.
compréhensible [kɔ̃preɑ̃sibl̥] *a.* comprehensible, understandable.
compréhensif, -ive [kɔ̃preɑ̃sif, -iv] *a.* **1.** comprehensive. **2.** (*pers.*) understanding.
compréhension [kɔ̃preɑ̃sjɔ̃] *n.f.* **1.** comprehension, understanding. **2.** understanding; **il est plein de c.,** he is full of sympathy.
comprendre [kɔ̃prɑ̃dr̥] *v.tr.* (*conj. like* PRENDRE) **1.** to comprise, include; **service non compris,** service not included; **jusqu'à et y compris le 31 décembre,** up to and including December 31st. **2.** to understand; **je ne comprends pas ce que vous voulez dire,** I don't understand what you mean; *F:* I don't get you; **je n'arrive pas à c. cette phrase,** I can't make sense of this sentence; **ai-je bien compris que...?** am I to understand, do you mean to say, that...? **vous m'avez mal compris,** you've misunderstood me; **il ne comprend rien de rien,** he hasn't a clue about anything; **je n'y comprends rien,** I can't make head or tail of it; **c'est à n'y rien comprendre,** it's incomprehensible; **ah! je comprends!** oh! I see! **je lui ai fait c. que** + *ind.* (i) I gave him to understand that...; (ii) I made it clear to him that...; **se faire c.,** to make oneself understood; **cela se comprend,** of course, that's understandable; **je comprends bien!** I can well imagine it!
comprenette [kɔ̃prənɛt] *n.f. F:* **il a la c. un peu dure,** he's a bit slow on the uptake.
compresse [kɔ̃prɛs] *n.f.* compress.
compresseur [kɔ̃prɛsœr] **1.** *n.m.* (*a*) *Mec.E:* compressor (of air, gas, fluid); (*b*) *I.C.E:* supercharger. **2.** *a.* compressing; *Civ.E:* **rouleau c.,** road roller.
compressible [kɔ̃prɛsibl̥] *a.* (*a*) compressible; (*b*) reducible (expenses, etc.).
compressif, -ive [kɔ̃prɛsif, -iv] *a.* compressive (bandage, etc.).
compression [kɔ̃mprɛsjɔ̃] *n.f.* **1.** *Mec:* compression (of gas, steam, etc.); *I.C.E:* **temps de c.,** compression stroke. **2.** (*strength of materials*) compression, crushing. **3.** restriction, cutback; **c. des dépenses,** spending cuts; **c. de crédit,** credit squeeze; **c. du personnel,** reduction of staff.
comprimable [kɔ̃primabl̥] *a.* compressible.
comprimé [kɔ̃prime] **1.** *a.* compressed; **air c.,** compressed air; **outil à air c.,** pneumatic tool. **2.** *n.m. Pharm:* tablet.
comprimer [kɔ̃prime] *v.tr.* **1.** to compress (gas, artery, etc.); **c. la taille,** to squeeze the waist in. **2.** to curb, repress, restrain (one's feelings, etc.); to repress, hold back (tears).
compris [kɔ̃pri) *a.* **bien c.,** (thoroughly) understood; **mal c.,** misunderstood; misinterpreted; *s.a.* COMPRENDRE.
compromettant [kɔ̃prɔmɛtɑ̃] *a.* compromising (situation, etc.).
compromettre [kɔ̃prɔmɛtr̥] (*conj. like* METTRE) **1.** *v.tr.* (*a*) to compromise (s.o., s.o.'s reputation, etc.); **être compromis dans un crime,** to be implicated in a crime; (*b*) to endanger, jeopardize (life, safety, etc.). **2.** *v.i.* to accept arbitration, to compromise. **3. se c.,** (i) to compromise oneself; (ii) to commit oneself.
compromis [kɔ̃prɔmi] *n.m.* (*a*) compromise, arrangement; (*b*) *Jur:* **mettre une affaire en c.,** to submit an affair for arbitration.
compromission [kɔ̃prɔmisjɔ̃] *n.f. usu. Pej:* **1.** compromising (with one's conscience); surrender (of principle). **2.** compromise.
comptabiliser [kɔ̃tabilize] *v.tr.* to account for (sth.), to enter (sth.) in the accounts.
comptabilité [kɔ̃tabilite] *n.f.* **1.** book-keeping, accountancy; **c. en partie simple, double,** single-, double-, entry book-keeping; **livre de c.,** account book; **tenir la c. d'une maison,** to keep the books, the accounts, of a firm; *Ind:* **c. de temps (du personnel),** time keeping. **2.** accounts department.
comptable [kɔ̃tabl̥] **1.** *Com: etc:* (*a*) *a.* book-keeping (work, etc.); **pièce c.,** voucher; **machine c.,** accounting machine; (*b*) *n.m.* accountant, bookkeeper; **expert c.,** (i) auditor; (ii) = chartered accountant. **2.** *a.* accountable, responsible; **être c. à qn de qch.,** to be accountable to s.o. for sth.
comptant [kɔ̃tɑ̃] **1.** *a.* **argent c.,** ready money, cash; *F:* **prendre qch. pour argent c.,** to take sth. for gospel truth. **2.** *adv.* **payer c.,** to pay (in) cash. **3.** *n.m.* cash; **payer au c.,** to pay (in) cash.
compte [kɔ̃t] *n.m.* account; (*a*) reckoning, calculation; **faire le c. des dépenses,** to add up expenses; **cela fait mon c.,** it's just the thing for me, that suits me; **il y trouve son c.,** he gets sth. out of it, there's sth. in it for him; **le c. y est,** it's the right amount, number; **vous êtes loin du c.,** you're wide of the mark; **ça ne fait pas le c.,** it doesn't come to the right amount; **c. rond,** round sum; **au bout du c.,** after all, when all is said and done; **en fin de c., tout c. fait,** all things considered; after all, taking everything into account; **à ce c.-là,** in that case; **tenir c. de qch.,** to take sth. into account, into consideration; **ne tenir aucun c. de qn, de qch.,** to ignore, disregard, s.o., sth.; **acheter qch. à bon c.,** to buy sth. cheap; **s'en tirer à bon c.,** to get off lightly; *F:* **il a son c., il en a pour son c.,** (i) he's done for, it's all up with him; (ii) he's drunk, he's had as much as he can carry; *F:* **son c. est bon,** he's for it, he'll get what's coming to him; (*b*) count; *Box:* **rester sur le plancher pour le c.,** to be counted out; (*c*) **tenir les comptes d'une maison,** to keep the accounts of a firm; **régler son c.,** to settle one's account; *F:* **régler son c. à qn,** to settle s.o.'s hash; **avoir un (petit) c. à régler avec qn,** to have a bone to pick with s.o.; **règlement de c.,** (i) settling of accounts; (ii) *F:* settling of scores; **donner, régler, son c. à un employé,** (i) to settle up with, (ii) to dismiss, an employee; **avoir un c. chez qn,** to have an account with s.o.; **c. en banque, bancaire,** banking account; **c. courant,** current account; **c. courant postal, c. chèque postal** = (National) Girobank account; **c. permanent** = credit account, *NAm:* charge account; **livre de comptes,** account book; **la Cour des Comptes** = the Audit Office; **faire ses comptes,** to make up one's accounts; **cela n'entre pas en ligne de c.,** that has nothing to do with the matter; **versement à c.,** payment on account; **mettre un malheur sur le c. de qn,** to ascribe, attribute, a misfortune to s.o., to blame s.o. for a misfortune; **apprendre qch. sur le c. de qn,** learn sth. about s.o.; **prendre qch. à son c.,** to accept responsibility for sth.; **être, se mettre, s'installer, à son c.,** to be, to set up, in business on one's own account; **faire qch. pour le c. de qn,** to do sth. on s.o.'s behalf; **pour mon c., j'aimerais mieux rester ici,** as far as I am concerned I'd prefer to stay here; **c. (con)joint,** joint account; (*d*) **demander des comptes à qn,** to call s.o. to account; **il ne doit de comptes à personne,** he is answerable to nobody; **rendre c. de qch.,** to account for sth.; **c. rendu,** (i) report; (ii) (book) review; **se rendre c. de qch.,** to realize, understand, sth.; *F:* **tu te rends c.!** would you believe it!
compte-gouttes [kɔ̃tgut] *n.m.inv. Pharm: etc:* dropper, pipette; **mesurer qch. au c.-g.,** to dole sth. out in driblets, sparingly.
compter [kɔ̃te] **1.** *v.tr.* (*a*) to count (up), reckon (up), compute (numbers, etc.); **c. jusqu'à dix,** to count up to ten; **dix-neuf tous comptés,** nineteen in all, all told; **marcher à pas comptés,** to walk with measured tread; **ses jours sont comptés,** his days are numbered; **il y a de cela vingt ans bien comptés,** a good twenty years

have passed since then; **sans c. que . . .**, not to mention that . . ., besides the fact that . . .; **mal c.**, to miscount; **il faut c. une heure pour faire cela,** we must allow, it will take an hour, to do this; **à c. de . . .**, (reckoning) from . . .; *Adm:* **à c. du 1er janvier,** to take effect on, with effect from, January 1st; (*b*) **c. cent francs à qn,** to pay s.o. a hundred francs; (*c*) *Com:* to charge; **nous ne comptons pas l'emballage,** there is no charge for packing; (*d*) to value; **c. sa vie pour rien,** to hold one's life of no account; (*e*) **c. faire qch.**, to expect, intend, to do sth.; to reckon on doing sth. **2.** *v.i* (*a*) **compter sur qn, sur qch.**, to depend, rely, on s.o., sth.; **comptez sur moi,** (you can) depend on me; **j'y compte bien,** I hope so; (*b*) **c. avec qn, qch.**, to reckon with s.o., sth.; (*c*) **ce tableau compte parmi les trésors du musée,** this painting is numbered among the treasures of the gallery; **c. parmi les meilleurs,** to rank among the best; (*d*) to count, to be of consequence; **cela ne compte pas,** that doesn't count; **ce qui compte c'est de réussir,** the main thing is to succeed.

compte-tours [kɔ̃ttur] *n.m.inv.* revolution, *F:* rev, counter; tachometer.

compteur [kɔ̃tœr, -øz] *n.m.* (*a*) meter; **c. d'électricité, à gaz, à eau,** electricity, gas, water, meter; *Aut:* **c. de vitesse,** speedometer; **c. kilométrique** = milometer; odometer; (*b*) *Atom.Ph:* **c. (de) Geiger,** Geiger counter.

comptine [kɔ̃tin] *n.f.* counting rhyme.

comptoir [kɔ̃twar] *n.m.* **1.** *Com:* counter; bar; **garçon de c.**, bartender. **2.** trading post. **3.** (marketing) syndicate. **4.** *Fin:* (*a*) bank; **c. d'escompte,** discount house; (*b*) branch (of bank).

compulser [kɔ̃pylse] *v.tr.* to examine, inspect, go through (documents, books, etc.).

compulsif, -ive [kɔ̃pylsif, -iv] *a.* compulsive (drinker, etc.).

compulsion [kɔ̃pylsjɔ̃] *n.f.* compulsion.

comput [kɔ̃pyt] *n.m.* computation (of calendar).

computation [kɔ̃pytasjɔ̃] *n.f.* computation.

computer [kɔ̃pyte] *v.tr.* to compute.

comte [kɔ̃t] *n.m.* count; (*in Engl.*) earl.

comté [kɔ̃te] *n.m.* (*a*) *Hist:* earldom; (*b*) county; (*c*) *Fr.C: Pol:* electoral circumscription.

comtesse [kɔ̃tɛs] *n.f.* countess.

con, conne [kɔ̃, kɔn] *P:* **1.** *a* (*no f. form*) bloody stupid, idiotic. **2.** *n.* bloody idiot, fool; cretin; **faire le c.**, to fool about.

concassage [kɔ̃kasaʒ] *n.m.* crushing, pounding, grinding.

concasser [kɔ̃kase] *v.tr.* to break, crush (stone, etc.); to grind (pepper, etc.); to pound.

concasseur [kɔ̃kasœr] *n.m.* crusher, crushing mill; *a.* **rouleau c.**, crushing roller.

concave [kɔ̃kav] *a.* concave.

concavité [kɔ̃kavite] *n.f.* (*a*) concavity; (*b*) concave side (of lens, etc.); (*c*) hollow, cavity.

concéder [kɔ̃sede] *v.tr.* **(je concède, n. concédons; je concéderai) 1.** to concede, grant, allow (privilege, etc.); grant (land, concession). **2. c. qu'on a tort,** to admit that one is wrong.

concentration [kɔ̃sɑ̃trasjɔ̃] *n.f.* **1.** (*a*) *Ph: Ch:* concentration, concentrating (of heat, etc.); (*b*) *Atom.Ph:* concentration, focusing; (*c*) **camp de c.**, concentration camp; (*d*) **les grandes concentrations urbaines,** large urban agglomerations; (*e*) integration, merging (of businesses). **2.** concentration (of the mind).

concentrationnaire [kɔ̃sɑ̃trasjɔnɛr] **1.** *a.* of a concentration camp. **2.** *n.m.f.* prisoner in a concentration camp.

concentré [kɔ̃sɑ̃tre] *a.* **1.** concentrated; condensed (milk). **2.** concentrating (mind); **caractère c.**, reserved character. **3.** *n.m.* extract, concentrate; **c. de tomates,** tomato concentrate, purée.

concentrer [kɔ̃sɑ̃tre] **1.** *v.tr.* to concentrate (heat, troops, etc.); to focus (sun's rays, etc.); to centre. **2. se c. (sur),** to concentrate (on); **taisez-vous, je me concentre,** be quiet, I'm trying to concentrate.

concentrique [kɔ̃sɑ̃trik] *a. Mth: etc:* concentric.

concept [kɔ̃sɛpt] *n.m.* concept.

conception [kɔ̃sɛpsjɔ̃] *n.f.* **1.** conception, conceiving (i) of offspring; (ii) of idea; *Ecc:* **Immaculée C.**, the Immaculate Conception. **2.** (*a*) conception, idea; (*b*) creation.

concernant [kɔ̃sɛrnɑ̃] **1.** *pr.p.* concerning, touching, relating to; **les frais me c.**, the expenses for which I am liable. **2.** (*with prepositional force*) concerning, about, with regard to, regarding.

concerner [kɔ̃sɛrne] *v.tr.* (*used in third pers. only*) to concern, affect; **pour, en, ce qui concerne cette affaire,** with regard to this matter; **en ce qui me concerne,** as far as I am concerned; **est-ce que cela vous concerne?** is it any business of yours?

concert [kɔ̃sɛr] *n.m.* concert. **1.** (*a*) entente (between powers, etc.); **agir de c. avec qn,** to act in cooperation with s.o.; to take concerted action with s.o. **2.** (*a*) *Mus:* concert; **salle de c.**, concert hall; (*b*) **ce fut un c. d'approbations,** there was a chorus of approval.

concertant, -ante [kɔ̃sɛrtɑ̃, -ɑ̃t] *a. Mus:* concerted (composition); concertante (part).

concertation [kɔ̃sɛrtasjɔ̃] *n.f. Pol:* dialogue.

concerté [kɔ̃sɛrte] *a.* concerted, united (action).

concerter [kɔ̃sɛrte] **1.** *v.tr.* to concert, arrange, devise (plan, etc.); to plan (scheme). **2. se c. (avec qn),** to act in concert (with s.o.); **ils se concertèrent,** they put their heads together, they worked together; **ils se concertèrent sur le moyen d'agir,** they took counsel together as to how to act.

concertiste [kɔ̃sɛrtist] *n.* concert performer; soloist (in a concerto).

concerto [kɔ̃sɛrto] *n.m. Mus:* concerto.

concessif, -ive [kɔ̃sɛsif, -iv] *a.* concessive.

concession [kɔ̃sɛsjɔ̃] *n.f.* concession. **1.** granting (of land, etc.); yielding (of point in dispute, etc.); **faire des concessions,** to make concessions. **2.** grant, concession; plot (in cemetery).

concessionnaire [kɔ̃sɛsjɔnɛr] **1.** *a.* concessionary (company, etc.). **2.** *n.* concessionnaire, licence holder; *Com:* agent, dealer.

concevable [kɔ̃svabl̩] *a.* conceivable.

concevoir [kɔ̃s(ə)vwar] *v.tr.* (*pr.p.* **concevant;** *p.p.* **conçu;** *pr.ind.* **je conçois n. concevons, ils conçoivent;** *impf.* **je concevais;** *p.h.* **je conçus;** *fu.* **je concevrai) 1.** to conceive (child); to become pregnant. **2.** (*a*) to conceive, imagine, form, devise, (idea, plan, etc.); **c. de l'amitié pour qn,** to take a liking to s.o.; **la maison est très bien conçue,** the house is very well designed; (*b*) **je ne conçois pas de ne jamais le revoir,** I don't imagine that I'll ever see him again; (*c*) to conceive, understand; **cela se conçoit facilement,** that is easily understood; (*d*) **télégramme ainsi conçu,** telegram worded as follows, that reads as follows.

concierge [kɔ̃sjɛrʒ] *n.* (house) porter; doorkeeper; caretaker (of flats, etc.), *NAm:* janitor; lodgekeeper (of country estate); *F:* **c'est une vraie c.**, he's, she's, a terrible gossip.

conciergerie [kɔ̃sjɛrʒəri] *n.f.* **1.** caretaker's lodge. **2.** *Hist:* **la Conciergerie,** the Conciergerie (prison). **3.** *Fr. C:* block of flats.

concile [kɔ̃sil] *n.m. Ecc:* council, synod.

conciliable [kɔ̃siljabl̩] *a.* reconcilable (qualities).

conciliabule [kɔ̃siljabyl] *n.m.* (*a*) *A:* secret meeting, secret assembly; (*b*) *F:* confabulation, confab.

conciliaire [kɔ̃siljɛr] *a.* conciliar.

conciliant [kɔ̃siljɑ̃] *a.* conciliating, conciliatory (reply, etc.).
conciliateur, -trice [kɔ̃siljatœr, -tris] **1.** *a.* conciliating. **2.** *n.* conciliator.
conciliation [kɔ̃siljasjɔ̃] *n.f.* conciliation, reconciliation; **comité de c.,** arbitration committee.
conciliatoire [kɔ̃siljatwar] *a.* conciliatory (measure, etc.)
concilier [kɔ̃silje] *v.tr.* (*impf. & pr.sub.* **n. conciliions, v. conciliiez**) **1.** to conciliate, reconcile (two parties, etc.). **2.** (*a*) to win, gain (hearts, esteem, etc.); (*b*) **se c.,** to agree (**avec,** with); **se c. qn, la faveur de qn,** to gain s.o.'s goodwill.
concis [kɔ̃si] *a.* concise, terse.
concision [kɔ̃sizjɔ̃] *n.f.* concision, conciseness, terseness; **avec c.,** concisely.
concitoyen, -enne [kɔ̃sitwajɛ̃, -ɛn] *n.* fellow citizen.
conclave [kɔ̃klav] *n.m. Ecc:* conclave.
concluant [kɔ̃klyɑ̃] *a.* conclusive, decisive (experiment, etc.); **peu c.,** inconclusive.
conclure [kɔ̃klyr] *v.* (*pr.p.* **concluant;** *p.p.* **conclu;** *pr.ind.* **je conclus, n. concluons, ils concluent;** *impf.* **je concluais;** *p.h.* **je conclus;** *fu.* **je conclurai**) to conclude. **1.** (*a*) *v.tr.* to end, finish; to bring (speech, etc.) to an end, to a conclusion; (*b*) *v.tr.* to arrive at (an understanding); **c. un traité,** to conclude a treaty; **c. un marché,** to drive, strike, clinch, a bargain; **c'est une affaire conclue,** (i) that's settled; (ii) it's a bargain, it's a deal; *F:* done! (*c*) *v.i.* to come to a conclusion. **2.** (*a*) *v.tr.* to decide; **nous avons conclu que . . .,** we came to the conclusion that . . .; (*b*) *v.i.* **c. à qch.,** to come to a conclusion about sth.; **c. à une opération immédiate,** to decide that an immediate operation is necessary; **le jury a conclu au suicide,** the jury returned a verdict of suicide.
conclusion [kɔ̃klyzjɔ̃] *n.f.* conclusion. **1.** close, end (of speech, meeting, etc.). **2.** concluding, settlement (of treaty, agreement, etc.). **3.** (*a*) inference; **en c.,** in short; to sum up; (*b*) *Jur:* finding, decision; (*c*) *pl. Jur:* pleas, submissions.
concombre [kɔ̃kɔ̃bɽ] *n.m.* cucumber.
concomitant [kɔ̃kɔmitɑ̃] *a.* concomitant, accompanying (circumstance, symptoms, etc.).
concordance [kɔ̃kɔrdɑ̃s] *n.f.* **1.** concordance, agreement (of evidence, etc.). **2.** *Gram:* sequence (of tenses). **3.** (*index*) concordance.
concordant [kɔ̃kɔrdɑ̃] *a.* concordant, agreeing, in agreement.
concordat [kɔ̃kɔrda] *n.m.* **1.** *Ecc:* concordat (between pope and sovereign). **2.** *Com:* (bankrupt's) certificate; composition.
concorde [kɔ̃kɔrd] *n.f.* concord, harmony.
concorder [kɔ̃kɔrde] *v.i.* (*of dates, evidence*) to agree, to tally (**avec,** with).
concourant [kɔ̃kurɑ̃] *a.* concurrent, converging (lines, etc.).
concourir [kɔ̃kurir] *v.i.* (*conj. like* COURIR) **1.** (*of lines, etc.*) to converge, to concur. **2.** to combine, unite; **c. à (faire) qch.,** to work towards (doing) sth.; **les témoignages concourent à prouver que . . .,** all evidence goes to prove that . . .. **3.** to compete; **c. (avec qn) pour un prix,** to compete (with s.o.) for a prize.
concours [kɔ̃kur] *n.m.* **1.** (*a*) *A: & Lit:* concourse, gathering (of people); (*b*) coincidence (of events); **par un c. de circonstances,** by a combination of circumstances. **2.** co-operation, assistance, help; **prêter son c. à qn,** to help, assist, s.o.; **c. financier,** financial aid; *Th: etc:* **avec le c. de . . .,** with the following cast . . .; those taking part were . . .; **avec l'aimable c. de X,** assisted by X. **3.** (*a*) competition; competitive examination; *Sp:* field events; *Sch:* **c. général,** competition between all the *lycées* at *baccalauréat* level; **c. d'entrée,** entrance examination; (*b*) (competitive) show; **c. agricole, hippique,** agricultural, horse, show; **c. de beauté,** beauty contest.
concret, -ète [kɔ̃krɛ, -ɛt] *a.* **1.** concrete, solid. **2.** concrete (term, etc.); **cas c.,** actual case, concrete example. **3.** *n.m.* (the) concrete (as opposed to the abstract).
concrétion [kɔ̃kresjɔ̃] *n.f.* **1.** coagulation. **2.** concrete mass, concretion; *Med:* **concrétions calcaires,** chalk stones.
concrétiser [kɔ̃kretize] *v.tr.* to put (idea, question) in concrete form; **nos projets commencent à se c.,** our plans are beginning to take shape.
concubin, -ine [kɔ̃kybɛ̃, -in] cohabitant; (*of woman*) (i) concubine; (ii) mistress.
concubinage [kɔ̃kybinaʒ] *n.m.* concubinage, cohabitation; **vivre en c.,** to live together (as man and wife).
concupiscence [kɔ̃kypisɑ̃s] *n.f.* concupiscence; sexual desire.
concurremment [kɔ̃kyramɑ̃] *adv.* **1.** concurrently, jointly; **agir c. avec qn,** to act jointly, in conjunction, with s.o. **2.** competitively, in competition (**avec,** with).
concurrence [kɔ̃kyrɑ̃s] *n.f.* **1.** (*a*) *A:* concurrence, coincidence (of events); (*b*) *Com: etc:* **jusqu'à c. de . . .,** to the amount of . . ., not exceeding . . ., up to . . .. **2.** competition, rivalry; *Com:* **faire c. à qn, à qch.,** to compete with s.o., with sth.; **prix défiant toute c.,** unbeatable price.
concurrencer [kɔ̃kyrɑ̃se] *v.tr.* (**je concurrençai(s); n. concurrençons**) to compete with (s.o., sth.) (in trade, etc.).
concurrent, -ente [kɔ̃kyrɑ̃, -ɑ̃t] **1.** *a.* (*a*) (*of forces, actions, etc.*) cooperative; (*b*) competitive, rival (industries, etc.). **2.** *n.* competitor (for prize, etc.); candidate (for post, etc.).
concurrentiel, -ielle [kɔ̃kyrɑ̃sjɛl] *a.* rival, competitive (companies, prices, etc.).
concussion [kɔ̃kysjɔ̃] *n.f.* misappropriation (of public funds).
condamnable [kɔ̃danabl̩] *a.* reprehensible, blameworthy.
condamnation [kɔ̃danasjɔ̃] *n.f.* condemnation. **1.** *Jur:* conviction, judgment, sentence; **c. à la prison,** prison sentence; **c. à mort,** death sentence; **passer c. sur qch.,** to admit that one is in the wrong (about sth.). **2.** reproof, blame, censure.
condamné, -ée [kɔ̃dane] *n.* convict; sentenced, condemned, person.
condamner [kɔ̃dane] *v.tr.* to condemn. **1.** (*a*) *Jur:* to convict, sentence, pass judgment on (criminal, etc.); **c. qn. à trois mois de prison,** to sentence s.o. to three months' imprisonment; **c. qn à 10,000 francs d'amende,** to fine s.o. 10,000 francs; **tentative condamnée à l'insuccès,** attempt doomed to failure; **le médecin l'a condamné,** the doctor has given him up; (*b*) to forbid; **la loi condamne la bigamie,** bigamy is forbidden by law; (*c*) **c. une porte,** to block up, fill in, a door; (*d*) **c. sa porte,** to bar one's door to visitors. **2.** to blame, censure, reprove (s.o.).
condensateur [kɔ̃dɑ̃satœr] *n.m. El: etc:* condenser; capacitor; *Opt:* condenser.
condensation [kɔ̃dɑ̃sasjɔ̃] *n.f.* condensation.
condensé [kɔ̃dɑ̃se] **1.** *a.* condensed; **lait c.,** condensed milk. **2.** *n.m.* résumé (of a literary work); digest.
condenser [kɔ̃dɑ̃se] (*a*) *v.tr.* to condense (gas, lecture, etc.) (**en,** into); **c. un article,** to cut down an article; (*b*) **se c.,** to condense.
condenseur [kɔ̃dɑ̃sœr] *n.m. Ph: Opt:* condenser.
condescendance [kɔ̃dɛsɑ̃dɑ̃s] *n.f.* condescension.
condescendant [kɔ̃dɛsɑ̃dɑ̃] *a.* condescending.
condescendre [kɔ̃dɛsɑ̃dɽ] *v.i.* to condescend (**à faire qch.,** to do sth.).

condiment [kɔ̃dimɑ̃] *n.m. Cu:* condiment, seasoning.
condisciple [kɔ̃disipl̩] *n.m.* fellow student, schoolmate.
condition [kɔ̃disjɔ̃] *n.f.* condition. **1.** (*a*) state; **en bonne c.,** in good condition; **être en c. de faire qch.,** to be in a position, in a fit state, to do sth.; (*b*) *pl.* conditions, circumstances; **voyager dans les meilleures conditions,** to travel under the most favourable conditions; **dans ces conditions . . .,** in these circumstances . . .; in that case . . .; (*c*) rank, station, status, position; *A:* **personne de c.,** person of rank. **2.** condition, stipulation; *pl.* terms; **conditions d'une vente,** clauses governing a sale; **conditions de faveur,** preferential terms; **faire ses conditions,** to name one's (own) terms; **imposer une c.,** to lay down a condition, stipulation; **offre sans c.,** unconditional offer; **se rendre sans c.,** to surrender unconditionally; **sous c.,** conditionally; **acheter qch. sous c.,** to buy sth. on approval; **tu peux partir quand tu veux, à c. de me prévenir,** you can leave when you like provided (that) you let me know. **3.** *A:* **être de, en, c. chez qn,** to be in service with s.o.
conditionné [kɔ̃disjɔne] *a.* **1.** (*a*) (*of work, goods*) in (good, bad) condition; **à air c.,** air-conditioned; (*b*) *Com:* **viande conditionnée,** prepackaged meat. **2.** *Log: Med: Psy:* conditioned (proposition, reflex).
conditionnel, -elle [kɔ̃disjɔnɛl] **1.** *a.* conditional. **2.** *n.m. Gram:* conditional (mood).
conditionnellement [kɔ̃disjɔnɛlmɑ̃] *adv.* conditionally.
conditionnement [kɔ̃disjɔnmɑ̃] *n.m.* **1.** (*a*) conditioning (of air, textiles, etc.); (*b*) *Com:* (i) packaging; (ii) package. **2.** *Psy:* conditioning.
conditionner [kɔ̃disjɔne] *v.tr.* **1.** to condition (air, textiles, etc.). **2.** to govern; **son arrivée conditionne notre départ,** our departure depends on his arrival. **3.** *Com:* to package. **4.** *Psy:* to condition (s.o.).
conditionneur, -euse [kɔ̃disjɔnœr, -øz] *n.* (*a*) *n.m.* **c. d'air,** air conditioner; (*b*) *n.m. & f. Com:* packager, packer.
condoléances [kɔ̃dɔleɑ̃s] *n.f.pl.* condolences; **offrir, présenter, ses c.,** to offer one's sympathy; **toutes mes c.,** (please accept) my sincere sympathy.
condor [kɔ̃dɔr] *n.m. Orn:* condor.
conductance [kɔ̃dyktɑ̃s] *n.f. El:* conductance.
conducteur, -trice [kɔ̃dyktœr, -tris] **1.** *n.* (*a*) leader, guide (of men, etc.); (*b*) **c. de bestiaux,** drover; (*c*) *Aut:* driver; (*d*) **c. d'une machine,** machine operator; **c. de travaux,** clerk of the works, (works) foreman. **2.** *a. Ph: El:* conducting, conductive. **3.** *n.m.* (*a*) *El: Ph:* conductor (of heat, electricity, etc.); (*b*) *El:* lead (wire), main.
conductibilité [kɔ̃dyktibilite] *n.f. El: Ph:* conductivity.
conductible [kɔ̃dyktibl̩] *a. El: Ph:* conductive.
conduction [kɔ̃dyksjɔ̃] *n.f. Ph: etc.:* conduction.
conductivité [kɔ̃dyktivite] *n.f. El:* conductivity.
conduire [kɔ̃dɥir] *v.tr.* (*pr.p.* **conduisant;** *p.p.* **conduit;** *pr.ind.* **je conduis, n. conduisons, ils conduisent;** *impf.* **je conduisais;** *p.h.* **je conduisis;** *fu.* **je conduirai**) **1.** (*a*) to conduct, escort (party, etc.); to lead (horse, blind man, etc.); to guide (child's first steps, etc.); **c. qn à la gare,** to take, drive, s.o. to the station; **on le conduisit à sa chambre,** he was shown to his room; *v.i.* **quel est le chemin qui conduit à la gare?** which is the way to the station? (*b*) **c. qn à faire qch.,** to induce, prevail on, s.o. to do sth. **2.** (*a*) to drive (horse, car, etc.); *v.i.* **il conduit bien,** he is a good driver; (*b*) to steer, row (boat). **3.** to convey, conduct (water, etc.); **corps qui conduit bien l'électricité,** good conductor of electricity. **4.** to direct, manage, supervise, run (sth.); **c. un orchestre,** to conduct an orchestra; **c. une affaire,** to manage a business. **5. se c.** (*a*) **être d'âge à se c.,** to be old enough to take care of oneself; (*b*) to behave; **se c. bien, mal, avec qn,** to behave well, badly.
conduit [kɔ̃dɥi] *n.m.* (*a*) *Techn:* conduit, duct, pipe, passage, channel; *Civ.E: Mec.E:* **c. d'aération,** air duct; **c. de ventilation,** ventilation shaft; *Nau:* **c. de chaîne,** hawse hole, pipe; **c. de cordage,** fairlead; (*b*) *Physiol:* **c. auditif,** auditory meatus; **c. lacrymal,** tear duct.
conduite [kɔ̃dɥit] *n.f.* **1.** (*a*) conducting, leading, escorting (of s.o.); *F:* **faire un bout de c. à qn,** to go part of the way with s.o.; (*b*) driving (of cart, car, etc.); navigation (of boat, balloon); **c. intérieure,** saloon (car), *NAm:* sedan; **c. à gauche,** left-hand drive; **leçons de c.,** driving lessons. **2.** direction, management, control (of affairs, etc.); command (of army, fleet, etc.); **être sous la c. de qn,** to be (i) under s.o.'s leadership; (ii) in s.o.'s care; **c. des travaux,** superintendence of works. **3.** conduct, behaviour; **c'est ma seule ligne de c.,** it's the only course open to me; **mauvaise c.,** misbehaviour; *Sch:* **zéro de c.,** no marks for conduct. **4.** pipe, conduit, duct; piping, tubing; **c. à air, d'air,** air duct; **c. d'eau,** water pipe, main(s); **c. de gaz,** gas pipe, main(s); **c. souple,** hose, flexible pipe; **tuyau de c.,** conduit pipe; *Hyd.E: etc:* **c. forcée,** (pressure) pipeline; **c. montante,** flow pipe, rising main.
cône [kon] *n.m.* **1.** cone; **c. de pin,** pine cone; *Geol:* **c. de déjection,** alluvial cone; *Astr:* **c. d'ombre,** umbra (of a planet, etc.); *Nau:* **c. de tempête,** storm cone; **c. de signalisation,** signal cone. **2.** (*shape*) taper; **en forme de c.,** cone-shaped, tapering.
confection [kɔ̃fɛksjɔ̃] *n.f.* **1.** putting together, making (up) (of garment, etc.); preparing, preparation (of meal); **elle nous a offert des gâteaux de sa c.,** she offered us some of her home made cakes. **2.** (*a*) (ready-to-wear) clothing industry; (*b*) **robe de c.,** ready-made dress; **vêtements de c.,** off-the-peg clothes.
confectionner [kɔ̃fɛksjɔne] *v.tr.* to make (up) (dress); to prepare (dish, etc.).
confédération [kɔ̃federasjɔ̃] *n.f.* confederation, confederacy.
confédéré [kɔ̃federe] **1.** *a.* confederate (nations); *Ind: Pol:* **syndicat non c.,** non-affiliated union. **2.** *n. Hist:* **les Confédérés,** the Confederates.
confédérer [kɔ̃federe] *v.tr.* (**je confédère, n. confédérons; je confédérai**) to confederate, unite.
conférence [kɔ̃ferɑ̃s] *n.f.* **1.** conference, discussion; **tenir c.,** to hold a conference; **c. au sommet,** summit (conference); **c. de presse,** press conference. **2.** lecture; **maître de conférences,** lecturer; **salle de conférences,** lecture room.
conférencier, -ière [kɔ̃ferɑ̃sje, -jɛr] *n.* lecturer.
conférer [kɔ̃fere] *v.* (**je confère, n. conférons; je conférerai**) **1.** *v.tr.* (*a*) to compare, collate (texts); (*b*) to confer, bestow, grant, award (privileges, etc.); **c. le grade de docteur à qn,** to confer a doctor's degree on s.o. **2.** *v.i.* to confer (**avec,** with); **nous avons conféré de votre affaire,** we talked your business over.
confesse [kɔ̃fɛs] *n.f.* **aller, être, à c.,** to go to, be at confession.
confesser [kɔ̃fɛse] *v.tr.* **1.** to confess, own; to plead guilty to (sth.), to own (up) to (sth.). **2.** *Ecc:* (*a*) to confess (one's sins); (*b*) to declare one's belief in (God, etc.); to confess (one's faith). **3.** (*of priest*) to confess (penitent); *v.i.* **ce prêtre ne confesse pas,** this priest doesn't hear confessions. **4. se c.,** to confess (one's sins); **se c. toutes les semaines,** to go to confession every week.
confesseur [kɔ̃fɛsœr] *n.m. Ecc:* **1.** (father) confessor. **2.** *Hist:* confessor (of one's religion, faith).

confession [kɔ̃fɛsjɔ̃] *n.f.* **1.** confession, avowal, admission (of crime, etc.); **faire la c. de qch.,** to confess, own up to, sth. **2.** *Ecc:* (*a*) confession (of sins); (*b*) **c. de foi,** confession of faith; (*c*) religious persuasion. **3.** *Ecc:* hearing of confession.

confessional, -aux [kɔ̃fɛsjɔnal, -o] *n.m. Ecc:* confessional.

confessionnel, -elle [kɔ̃fɛsjɔnɛl] *a.* denominational (matters, disputes).

confetti [kɔ̃feti] *n.m.pl.* confetti.

confiance [kɔ̃fjɑ̃s] *n.f.* **1.** confidence, faith, trust; **avoir c. en qn, qch., faire c. à qn, qch.,** to put trust in s.o., sth., to rely on s.o., sth., to trust s.o., sth.; **il n'a pas c. dans les médecins,** he doesn't believe in doctors; **acheter qch. de c.,** to buy sth. on trust; **il me faut un homme de c.,** I want a man whom I can trust, I can rely on; **abuser de la c. de qn,** to break faith with s.o.; **digne de c.,** trustworthy, reliable; **maison de c.,** reliable firm; **avec c.,** (i) confidently; (ii) trustingly, trustfully; **je vous parle en toute c.,** I know I can trust you (with what I have to say); *F:* **faites-moi c.,** (please) believe me; *Pol:* **vote de c.,** vote of confidence. **2.** confidence, sense of security; **manquer de c. en soi,** to lack self assurance.

confiant [kɔ̃fjɑ̃] *a.* **1.** confiding, trusting, trustful (**dans,** in). **2.** confident, sanguine (disposition, etc.). **3.** self-confident, assured (manner, etc.).

confidence [kɔ̃fidɑ̃s] *n.f.* confidence (imparted as a secret); **faire une c. à qn,** to tell s.o. a secret; **faire c. de qch. à qn,** to confide sth. to s.o.; **mettre qn dans la c.,** to let s.o. into the secret; **dire qch. en c.,** to say sth. in confidence, confidentially.

confident, -ente [kɔ̃fidɑ̃, -ɑ̃t] *n.* confidant, *f.* confidante.

confidentiel, -ielle [kɔ̃fidɑ̃sjɛl] *a.* confidential; **à titre c.,** confidentially, in confidence, privately.

confidentiellement [kɔ̃fidɑ̃sjɛlmɑ̃] *adv.* confidentially, in confidence.

confier [kɔ̃fje] *v.tr.* (*impf. & pr.sub.* **n. confiions, v. confiiez**) **1.** to trust, entrust, commit; **c. qch. à qn, à la garde de qn,** to entrust s.o. with sth. **2.** to confide, impart, disclose; **c. qch. à qn,** to tell s.o. sth. in confidence. **3.** (*a*) **se c. à qn, à qch.,** to put one's trust in s.o., in sth.; (*b*) **se c. à qn,** to confide in s.o.

configuration [kɔ̃figyrasjɔ̃] *n.f.* **1.** configuration, outline; form, shape; lie (of the land, etc.).

confiné [kɔ̃fine] *a.* (*a*) enclosed (atmosphere, etc.); stale (air); (*b*) **vivre c. chez soi,** to live a retired life.

confinement [kɔ̃finmɑ̃] *n.m.* confinement, confining.

confiner [kɔ̃fine] **1.** *v.i.* (*of country, etc.*) **c. à, avec, un pays,** to border on, adjoin, a country; **courage qui confine à la témérité,** courage verging on foolhardiness. **2.** (*a*) *v.tr.* to confine (s.o.); to shut (s.o.) up; (*b*) **se c. chez soi,** to live a retired life.

confins [kɔ̃fɛ̃] *n.m.pl.* confines, borders (of country); **aux c. de la science,** within the limits of science.

confire [kɔ̃fir] *v.tr.* (*pr.p.* **confisant;** *p.p.* **confit;** *pr.ind.* **je confis, n. confisons, ils confisent;** *impf.* **je confisais;** *p.h.* **je confis;** *fu.* **je confirai**) to preserve (fruit, etc.); to candy (peel, etc.); **c. au sel, au vinaigre,** to pickle.

confirmatif, -ive [kɔ̃firmatif, -iv] *a.* confirmative (judgment); corroborative (statement).

confirmation [kɔ̃firmasjɔ̃] *n.f.* **1.** confirmation, corroboration (of piece of news, etc.); **c. d'un jugement,** confirmation of a sentence; **il m'en a donné c.,** he gave me confirmation of it. **2.** *Ecc:* (sacrament of) confirmation; **donner la c. à qn,** to confirm s.o.

confirmer [kɔ̃firme] *v.tr.* **1.** to confirm (news, judgment, etc.); **c. un traité,** to ratify a treaty; **l'exception confirme la règle,** the exception proves the rule; **le bruit ne s'est pas confirmé,** the news proved false. **2.** *Ecc:* to confirm (s.o.).

confiscation [kɔ̃fiskasjɔ̃] *n.f.* confiscation; forfeiture, seizure (of property, etc.).

confiserie [kɔ̃fizri] *n.f.* (*a*) preserving (of fruit, etc.) in sugar; (*b*) confectioner's shop, sweetshop; *NAm:* candy store; (*c*) confectionery, sweets, *NAm:* candy.

confiseur, -euse [kɔ̃fizœr, -øz] *n.* = confectioner.

confisquer [kɔ̃fiske] *v.tr.* to confiscate, seize (goods, property, etc.).

confit [kɔ̃fi] **1.** *a.* **fruits confits,** crystallized fruit; **être c. en dévotion,** to be steeped in piety. **2.** *n.m. Cu:* conserve (of goose, etc.).

confiture [kɔ̃fityr] *n.f. often pl. Cu:* jam; **c. d'oranges,** (orange) marmalade.

confiturerie [kɔ̃fityrri] *n.f.* **1.** jam manufacture. **2.** jam factory.

conflagration [kɔ̃flagrasjɔ̃] *n.f.* cataclysm; (political) crisis.

conflit [kɔ̃fli] *n.m.* (*a*) conflict, struggle; clash (of interests); **c. (armé),** armed conflict; war; **être en c.,** (i) to be at variance; *F:* at loggerheads (**avec,** with); (ii) (*of interests, etc.*) to clash (**avec,** with); (*b*) *Jur:* conflict (of authority, scope).

confluence [kɔ̃flyɑ̃s] *n.f.* confluence.

confluent [kɔ̃flyɑ̃] *n.m.* confluence (of rivers, veins, etc.).

confluer [kɔ̃flye] *v.i.* to meet, join, unite; **l'Oise conflue avec la Seine,** the Oise flows into the Seine.

confondre [kɔ̃fɔ̃dr̥] *v.* **I.** *v.tr.* **1.** (*a*) to merge, mingle, intermingle; (*b*) to mistake, confuse; **je les confonds toujours,** I always mistake one for the other; **c. des noms,** to confuse names. **2.** (*a*) to astound, stagger (s.o.); **son insolence me confond,** I'm astounded by his insolence; (*b*) to confound (criminal, etc.); **c. un menteur,** to show up a liar. **II. se confondre. 1.** (*a*) (*of colours, etc.*) to blend (**en,** into); to merge (into one another); (*b*) (*of streams, etc.*) to intermingle, flow together; (*c*) (*of interests, etc.*) to be identical. **2. se c. en excuses,** to apologize profusely.

confondu [kɔ̃fɔ̃dy] *a.* **1.** disconcerted, abashed; **je suis tout c. de votre bonté,** I am overwhelmed by your kindness. **2.** dumbfounded, astounded (**de,** at).

conformation [kɔ̃fɔrmasjɔ̃] *n.f.* conformation, structure (of hills, parts of body, etc.).

conforme [kɔ̃fɔrm] *a.* conformable, true, according (**à,** to); consistent (**à,** with); **copie c. à l'original,** exact copy; *Adm:* **pour copie c.,** certified true copy; **il mène une vie c. à ses moyens,** he lives according to his means.

conformé [kɔ̃fɔrme] *a.* **bien c.,** well-formed (child, etc.); **mal c.,** mis-shapen (limb, etc.).

conformément [kɔ̃fɔrmemɑ̃] *adv.* according (**à,** to); in conformity, in accordance, in compliance (**à,** with); **c. à la loi,** according to the law; **c. à vos ordres,** in accordance with your orders; **c. au plan prévu,** according to the proposed plan.

conformer [kɔ̃fɔrme] *v.* **1.** *v.tr.* to model (**à,** on); **c. sa vie à certains principes,** to shape one's life according to certain principles. **2. se c. à qch.,** to conform to sth.; to comply with, abide by, sth.; *Com:* **se c. au modèle,** to keep (to) the pattern.

conformisme [kɔ̃fɔrmism] *n.m.* (*a*) conformism, *NAm:* conformity; (*b*) *Ecc:* conformity.

conformiste [kɔ̃fɔrmist] *n.m. & f.* (*a*) *Ecc:* conformist (of Ch. of Eng.); (*b*) conventionalist, conformist.

conformité [kɔ̃fɔrmite] *n.f.* conformity, similarity; *Ecc:* conformity; **être en c. de goûts avec qn,** to have similar tastes to s.o.; **en c. avec,** in accordance with, according to.

confort [kɔ̃fɔr] *n.m.* comfort(s); **hôtel avec tout le c. moderne,** hotel with every modern convenience, *F:* with all mod cons.

confortable [kɔ̃fɔrtabl̥] *a.* (*a*) comfortable, snug, cosy; (*b*) well off, comfortably off; **des appointements confortables,** a good salary.
confortablement [kɔ̃fɔrtabləmɑ̃] *adv.* comfortably.
confraternel, -elle [kɔ̃fratɛrnɛl] *a.* fraternal, brotherly.
confraternité [kɔ̃fratɛrnite] *n.f.* brotherliness.
confrère [kɔ̃frɛr] *n.m.* colleague, confrère, fellow member (of profession, society).
confrérie [kɔ̃freri] *n.f.* (religious) brotherhood, sisterhood; confraternity.
confrontation [kɔ̃frɔ̃tasjɔ̃] *n.f.* **1.** *Jur:* confrontation, confronting (of accused person with witness). **2.** comparison (**à, avec,** with); collation (of MSS.).
confronter [kɔ̃frɔ̃te] *v.tr.* **1.** *Jur: etc:* to confront; to bring (prisoner) face to face (**avec, à,** with). **2.** to collate (MSS.); to compare (materials, etc.) (**avec, à,** with).
confucianisme [kɔ̃fysjanism] *n.m. Rel.H:* Confucianism.
confus [kɔ̃fy] *a.* **1.** confused, mixed, chaotic, jumbled (heap, etc.); indistinct (noise); dim, blurred (vision); obscure, ambiguous (style, etc.); **mélange c.,** jumble (**de,** of). **2.** embarrassed, abashed, ashamed; **je suis c.,** I don't know where to put myself; **je suis c. de vous déranger,** I'm so sorry to disturb you.
confusément [kɔ̃fyzemɑ̃] *adv.* confusedly, vaguely, indistinctly.
confusion [kɔ̃fyzjɔ̃] *n.f.* confusion. **1.** (*a*) disorder, jumble, medley; **tout était en c.,** everything was in a mess, in disorder; **mettre la c. dans l'assemblée,** to throw the audience into confusion; *Med:* **c. mentale,** mental aberration; (*b*) mistake, error, misunderstanding; **c. de dates, de noms,** confusion of, mistake in, dates, names. **2.** confusion, embarrassment, shame; **être rouge de c.,** to blush with shame. **3.** *Jur:* **avec c. des peines,** the sentences to run concurrently.
congé [kɔ̃ʒe] *n.m.* **1.** (*a*) **prendre c. de qn,** to take (one's) leave of s.o.; **donner c. à qn,** to dismiss s.o.; (*b*) leave (of absence); **en c.,** on leave; **c. de maladie,** sick leave; (*c*) holiday; *esp. NAm:* vacation; **un après-midi de c.,** an afternoon off; *Ind:* **c. payé,** (i) paid holiday; (ii) *F: Pej:* holiday maker. **2.** (*a*) (notice of) discharge, dismissal; **donner son c. à qn,** to give s.o. his notice; **demander son c.,** to hand in one's resignation, to give notice; (*b*) **donner c. à un locataire,** to give a tenant notice to quit. **3.** authorization, permit; release (of wine from bond); *Nau:* **c. de navigation,** clearance certificate.
congédiable [kɔ̃ʒedjabl̥] *a.* liable to be discharged; due for discharge.
congédier [kɔ̃ʒedje] *v.tr.* (*impf. & pr.sub.* **n. congédiions, v. congédiiez**) **1.** to dismiss (servant, etc.). **2.** (*a*) to dismiss (caller); (*b*) *Mil: Navy:* to discharge (men); *Nau:* to pay off (crew).
congélateur [kɔ̃ʒelatœr] *n.m.* deep freeze, freezer (compartment).
congélation [kɔ̃ʒelasjɔ̃] *n.f.* (*a*) freezing (of water, etc.); congealing (of oil); **point de c. de l'eau,** freezing point of water; (*b*) deep freezing.
congeler [kɔ̃ʒle] *v.* (**il congèle; il congèlera**) **1.** *v.tr.* to freeze (water, etc.); to deep-freeze (food); **viande congelée,** frozen meat. **2. se c.,** to freeze.
congénère [kɔ̃ʒenɛr] **1.** *a. Biol:* congeneric; *Anat:* congenerous (muscle). **2.** *n.m. Biol:* congener; **lui et ses congénères,** he and his like.
congénital, -aux [kɔ̃ʒenital, -o] *a.* congenital.
congère [kɔ̃ʒɛr] *n.f.* snowdrift.
congestif, -ive [kɔ̃ʒɛstif, -iv] *a. Med:* congestive (disposition, etc.)
congestion [kɔ̃ʒɛstjɔ̃] *n.f. Med:* congestion; **c. cérébrale,** stroke; **c. pulmonaire,** pneumonia.
congestionné [kɔ̃ʒɛstjɔne] *a.* flushed, red (face).
congestionner [kɔ̃ʒɛstjɔne] *v.tr.* **1.** *Med:* to congest; to flush (face). **2. les voitures congestionnent la rue,** the cars are blocking the street. **3. se c.,** to become congested.
conglomérat [kɔ̃glɔmera] *n.m.* **1.** *Geol:* conglomerate. **2.** *Pol.Ec:* conglomerate.
conglomération [kɔ̃glɔmerasjɔ̃] *n.f.* conglomeration.
conglomérer [kɔ̃glɔmere] *v.tr.* (**je conglomère, n. conglomérons; je conglomérerai**) (*a*) to conglomerate; (*b*) **se c.,** to conglomerate, to unite, cluster together.
congolais, -aise [kɔ̃gɔlɛ, -ɛz] (*a*) *a. & n.* (native, inhabitant) of the Congo; Congolese; (*b*) *n.m. Cu:* coconut cake.
congratulation [kɔ̃gratylasjɔ̃] *n.f. Iron: F:* congratulation.
congratuler [kɔ̃gratyle] *v.tr. Iron: F:* to congratulate.
congre [kɔ̃gr̥] *n.m.* conger (eel).
congrégation [kɔ̃gregasjɔ̃] *n.f. Ecc:* **1.** (*a*) community (= group of monasteries); (*b*) congregation (of Cardinals). **2.** assembly.
congrès [kɔ̃grɛ] *n.m.* congress; **C. des États-Unis,** United States Congress; **membre du C.,** congressman.
congressiste [kɔ̃grɛsist] *n.m. & f.* participant at a congress.
congru [kɔ̃gry] *a.* **1.** (*a*) *A:* sufficient, adequate; (*b*) **portion congrue,** (i) *Ecc:* adequate emolument (of priest); (ii) (income providing a) bare living; **réduire qn à la portion congrue,** to put s.o. on short allowance. **2.** *Mth:* congruent.
congruence [kɔ̃gryɑ̃s] *n.f. Mth:* congruence.
conifère [kɔnifɛr] *n.m. Bot:* conifer.
conique [kɔnik, ko-] *a.* **1.** cone-shaped, conical. **2.** *Mth:* **section c.,** conic section. **3.** *Mec.E: etc:* coned, taper(ing) (shank, pin, etc.); **engrenage c.,** bevel gearing.
conjectural, -aux [kɔ̃ʒɛktyral, -o] *a.* conjectural.
conjecture [kɔ̃ʒɛktyr] *n.f.* conjecture, surmise, guess.
conjecturer [kɔ̃ʒɛktyre] *v.tr. & i.* to conjecture, surmise, guess; **il conjecture sur ce qu'il ignore,** he makes guesses about things he knows nothing about.
conjoint [kɔ̃ʒwɛ̃] *a.* **1.** conjoined, united, joint; *Fin:* **compte c.,** joint account; *Jur:* **legs c.,** joint legacy; **légataires conjoints,** co-legatees. **2.** *Jur:* married; *n.m.* **les conjoints,** husband and wife.
conjointement [kɔ̃ʒwɛ̃tmɑ̃] *adv.* (con)jointly.
conjoncteur [kɔ̃ʒɔ̃ktœr] *n.m. El:* circuit closer; cut-in; **c.-disjoncteur,** make-and-break (switch).
conjonctif, -ive [kɔ̃ʒɔ̃ktif, -iv] *a.* conjunctive, connective (tissue, etc.); *Gram:* **locution conjonctive,** conjunctive phrase.
conjonction [kɔ̃ʒɔ̃ksjɔ̃] *n.f.* **1.** conjunction, union, connection. **2.** *Gram:* conjunction.
conjonctive [kɔ̃ʒɔ̃ktiv] *n.f.* conjunctiva (of the eye).
conjonctivite [kɔ̃ʒɔ̃ktivit] *n.f. Med:* conjunctivitis.
conjoncture [kɔ̃ʒɔ̃ktyr] *n.f.* conjuncture; (combination of) circumstances; **dans la c. actuelle,** at this (present) juncture, under the present circumstances; *Pol: Ec:* **c. économique,** overall economic situation; **étude de c.,** study of the state of the economy.
conjugable [kɔ̃ʒygabl̥] *a. Gram:* conjugable.
conjugaison [kɔ̃ʒygɛzɔ̃] *n.f. Gram: Biol: etc:* conjugation (of verb, of cells, etc.); **grâce à la c. de leurs efforts,** thanks to their joint efforts.
conjugal, -aux [kɔ̃ʒygal, -o] *a.* conjugal; **vie conjugale,** married life; **le domicile c.,** home (of married couple).

conjugalement [kɔ̃ʒygalmɑ̃] *adv.* conjugally.
conjugué [kɔ̃ʒyge] *a.* (*a*) *Mth: Opt:* conjugate; *Bot:* **feuilles conjuguées,** conjugate leaves; (*b*) joint, combined (efforts, etc.); (*c*) *Mec.E:* paired, twin, interconnected; **machines conjuguées,** paired engines.
conjuguer [kɔ̃ʒyge] *v.tr.* **1.** *Gram:* to conjugate. **2. ils conjuguèrent leurs efforts,** they combined, united, their efforts.
conjuration [kɔ̃ʒyrasjɔ̃] *n.f.* **1.** conspiracy, plot. **2.** exorcism, conjuration.
conjuré, -ée [kɔ̃ʒyre] *n.* conspirator.
conjurer [kɔ̃ʒyre] *v.tr.* **1.** *A:* to plot, conspire. **2.** (*a*) to exorcise (demon); (*b*) to avert, ward off (danger, etc.). **3. c. qn de faire qch.,** to entreat, beg, beseech s.o. to do sth. **3. se c.,** to conspire (together) (**contre,** against).
connaissable [kɔnɛsabl̥] *a.* cognizable, knowable.
connaissance [kɔnɛsɑ̃s] *n.f.* **1.** (*a*) acquaintance, knowledge; **prendre c. de qch.,** to make oneself acquainted with, to study, examine, to enquire into, sth.; **avoir c. de qch.,** to be aware of sth.; **donner qch. à la c. de qn,** to inform s.o. of sth., to make sth. known to s.o., **il n'a jamais, à ma c., été malade,** he has never, to my knowledge, as far as I know, had a day's illness; **en c. de cause,** with full knowledge of the facts, on good grounds; (*b*) **une personne de ma c.,** someone I know, an acquaintance; **faire c. avec qn, faire la c. de qn,** to make s.o.'s acquaintance, to meet s.o.; **quand je fis sa c.,** when I first knew him; **lier c. avec qn,** to strike up an acquaintance with s.o.; **une figure de c.,** a familiar face; **en pays de c.,** (i) among familiar faces; (ii) on familiar ground; (*c*) **c'est une de mes connaissances,** he is an acquaintance of mine; *F:* **c'est une vieille c.,** I've known him, her, for ages; (*d*) *F:* **je l'ai rencontré avec sa c.,** I met him with his girl-friend. **2.** (*a*) knowledge, understanding; **avoir la c. de plusieurs langues,** to know several languages; **sa c. du droit,** his knowledge of the law; (*b*) *Jur:* cognizance; (*c*) *Phil:* cognition; (*d*) *pl.* learning, attainments, acquirements; **avoir de profondes connaissances en mathématiques,** to be very well versed in mathematics. **3.** consciousness; **perdre c.,** to lose consciousness, to faint; **reprendre c.,** to regain consciousness, *F:* to come round; **sans c.,** unconscious; **il a toute sa c.,** he's quite, fully, conscious.
connaissement [kɔnɛsmɑ̃] *n.m. Nau: Com:* bill of lading.
connaisseur, -euse [kɔnɛsœr, -øz] **1.** *n.* expert, connoisseur; **être bon c. en qch.,** to be a good judge of, an authority on, sth. **2.** *a.* **regarder qch. d'un œil c.,** to look at sth. with a critical eye.
connaître [kɔnɛtr̥] *v.tr.* (*pr.p.* **connaissant;** *p.p.* **connu;** *pr.ind.* **je connais, il connaît, n. connaissons;** *impf.* **je connaissais;** *p.h.* **je connus;** *fu.* **je connaîtrai**) to know. **1.** to be acquainted with (sth.); **c. les chemins,** to be familiar with the roads; **je connais tous les détails,** I am aware of all the circumstances; **il ne connaît pas l'amour,** he does not know what love is, has no experience of love; **je lui connaissais du talent,** I knew he had talent; **faire c. qch.,** to bring sth. to light, to make sth. known; **cette région connaît actuellement une famine,** that region is now experiencing a famine; **connaissez-vous la nouvelle?** have you heard the news? **si tu te tais, ni vu ni connu,** if you keep quiet, no one will be any the wiser; **il en connaît bien d'autres,** he has plenty more tricks up his sleeve. **2.** (*a*) to be acquainted with (s.o.); **c. qn de nom, de vue,** to know s.o. by name, by sight; **c. son monde,** to know the people one has to deal with; **il est connu ici,** he's well known around here; *F:* **je le connais par cœur, comme ma poche,** I know him through and through; I can read him like a book; **c'est connu!** I've heard that one before! *F:* **ça me connaît, le foot,** I know all there is to know about football; **je connais la musique,** it's always the same old story; (*b*) to make the acquaintance of (s.o.), to come to know (s.o.); **ils se sont connus en 1970,** they met in 1970; **se faire c.,** (i) to introduce oneself (by name); (ii) to become (well-)known; **je vous le ferai c.,** I'll introduce him to you. **3.** (*a*) to be versed in (science, art, language, etc.); **c. qch. à fond,** to be thoroughly conversant with sth., to have a thorough knowledge of sth.; to have a thorough command of (a language); **il n'y connaît rien,** he doesn't know anything about it; (*b*) to distinguish; **c. le bien du mal,** to know good from evil. **4.** *B:* to know (woman). **5.** *v.i. Jur:* **c. de qch.,** to take cognizance of sth. **6.** (*a*) **se c. en qch.,** to know all about, be a good judge of, sth.; *F:* **il s'y connaît,** he's an expert; (*b*) **il ne se connaît plus,** he has lost control of himself; **il ne se connaît plus de joie,** he's beside himself with joy; he's walking on air.
connecter [kɔnɛkte] *v.tr. El: Elcs:* to connect.
connerie [kɔnri] *n.f. P:* (piece of) damned stupidity.
connétable [kɔnetabl̥] *n.m. Hist:* High Constable.
connexe [kɔnɛks] *a. Jur: Bot: etc:* connected; allied; related.
connexion [kɔnɛksjɔ̃] *n.f.* **1.** connection (of parts, ideas, etc.); **à c. directe,** direct-acting. **2.** connecting organ, part; *El:* lead; connection.
connivence [kɔnivɑ̃s] *n.f.* connivance, complicity; **agir, être, de c. avec qn,** to act in complicity, in collusion, with s.o.
connotation [kɔnɔtasjɔ̃] *n.f.* connotation.
connu [kɔny] **1.** *a.* well known; famous; **un écrivain c.,** a well known writer; **elle est bien connue, celle-là!** everybody knows that joke, that's an old one! **2.** *n.m.* **passer, aller, du c. à l'inconnu,** to go from the known to the unknown.
conque [kɔ̃k] *n.f.* **1.** conch, marine shell. **2.** *Anat:* external ear.
conquérant [kɔ̃kerɑ̃] *a.* conquering (nation, etc.); *n.* **Guillaume le C.,** William the Conqueror; *F:* **air c.,** swaggering air, swagger.
conquérir [kɔ̃kerir] *v.tr.* (*pr.p.* **conquérant;** *p.p.* **conquis;** *pr.ind.* **je conquiers, n. conquérons, ils conquièrent;** *impf.* **je conquérais;** *p.h.* **je conquis;** *fu.* **je conquerrai**) (*a*) to conquer, subdue (country, people); (*b*) to gain, win (over), make a conquest of (s.o., sth.); **c. l'estime de qn,** to win, gain, s.o.'s esteem.
conquête [kɔ̃kɛt] *n.f.* **1.** (act of) conquest; (*a*) **faire la c. d'un pays,** to conquer a country; (*b*) **faire la c. de qn,** to gain s.o.'s sympathy, respect; to make a conquest of s.o.; **vous avez fait sa c.,** you have won his, her, heart. **2.** conquered territory; acquisition, possession.
consacré [kɔ̃sakre] *a.* **1.** consecrated, sacred (vessel, etc.); hallowed (ground). **2.** sanctioned, established (custom, etc.).
consacrer [kɔ̃sakre] *v.tr.* **1.** (*a*) to consecrate (altar, bread and wine, etc.); **c. un évêque, un prêtre,** to consecrate a bishop, ordain a priest; (*b*) to dedicate (one's life to God, etc.); to devote (one's time, energy, to sth.); **combien de temps pouvez-vous me c.?** how much time can you spare me? **2.** to sanctify, hallow (memory, place, etc.). **3.** to establish, sanction.
consanguin [kɔ̃sɑ̃gɛ̃] *a.* **1. frère c., sœur consanguine,** half brother, half sister (on father's side). **2.** inbred (horse, etc.).
consanguinité [kɔ̃sɑ̃gɥinite] *n.f.* **1.** consanguinity (through the father). **2.** inbreeding.
consciemment [kɔ̃sjamɑ̃] *adv.* consciously, knowingly.

conscience [kɔ̃sjɑ̃s] *n.f.* **1.** consciousness; *Phil:* self-consciousness; **perdre c.**, to lose consciousness ((i) to faint; (ii) to fall asleep); **avoir c. de qch., d'avoir fait qch.**, to be conscious, aware of sth., of having done sth.; **c. de soi,** self awareness; **prise de c.**, sudden awareness; **c'est la première fois que j'en ai pris c.**, it's the first time that it has come home to me. **2.** (*a*) conscience; **mauvaise c.**, guilty conscience; **c. large,** accommodating conscience; *F:* **il a la c. élastique,** he is not over-scrupulous; **(se) faire c. de faire qch.**, to scruple to do sth.; **avoir qch. sur la c.**, to have sth. on one's conscience; **faire qch. par acquit de c.**, to do sth. for conscience' sake; **dire qch. en c.**, to say sth. in good faith; **manque de c.**, unscrupulousness; **j'ai bonne c.**, my conscience is clear; (*b*) conscientiousness; **c. professionelle,** conscientious approach to one's work; professional integrity; **faire qch. avec c.**, to do sth. conscientiously; (*c*) **liberté de c.**, freedom of conscience.

consciencieusement [kɔ̃sjɑ̃sjøzmɑ̃] *adv.* conscientiously.

consciencieux, -ieuse [kɔ̃sjɑ̃sjø, -jøz] *a.* conscientious (person, work).

conscient [kɔ̃sjɑ̃] *a.* **1.** conscious, (fully) aware (**de,** of; **que,** that); *Phil:* self-conscious. **2. être c.**, sentient being.

conscription [kɔ̃skripsjɔ̃] *n.f. Mil:* conscription, *U.S:* draft.

conscrit [kɔ̃skri] *n.m.* (*a*) *Mil:* (i) one liable to conscription; (ii) conscript, recruit; *U.S:* draftee; (*b*) novice, greenhorn; *F:* sucker.

consécration [kɔ̃sekrasjɔ̃] *n.f.* **1.** (*a*) consecration (of church, bishop, etc.); ordination (of priest); (*b*) consecration (of bread and wine). **2.** ratification; establishing (of custom, reputation).

consécutif, -ive [kɔ̃sekytif, -iv] *a.* **1.** consecutive; **pendant trois jours consécutifs,** for three days running; *a. & n. Gram:* **(proposition) consécutive,** consecutive clause. **2. c. à,** following on; **fatigue consécutive à une longue marche,** fatigue resulting from a long walk.

consécutivement [kɔ̃sekytivmɑ̃] *adv.* consecutively, in succession.

conseil [kɔ̃sɛj] *n.m.* **1.** (*a*) *A: & Lit:* (firm) resolution; **ne savoir quel c. prendre,** not to know what decision to make; (*b*) counsel, (piece of) advice; **c'est un homme de bon c.**, he gives sound advice; **donner c. à qn,** to advise s.o.; **demander c. à qn,** to consult s.o., seek s.o.'s advice; **pouvez-vous me donner quelques conseils?** can you give me some hints, tips? *Prov:* **la nuit porte c.**, sleep on it. **2.** (*a*) *A:* (*of pers.*) counsellor, counsel; (*b*) **avocat-c.**, legal consultant; **ingénieur-c.**, consulting engineer. **3.** council, committee, board; **tenir c.**, to hold (a) council; **le c. des ministres,** the Cabinet; **c. d'État,** Council of State; **c. municipal** = borough, etc., council; **c. général** = county council, regional council; *Com:* **c. d'administration,** board of directors; *Mil:* **c. de guerre,** (i) war council; (ii) court-martial; **passer en c. de guerre,** to be court-martialled; *Sch: etc:* **c. de discipline,** disciplinary committee; *Jur:* **c. de famille,** family council; **c. de sécurité,** Security Council.

conseiller¹ [kɔ̃seje] *v.tr.* to advise, counsel; **c. qn,** to advise, give advice to, s.o.; **c. qch. à qn,** to recommend sth. to s.o.; **je ne vous le conseille pas,** I shouldn't if I were you; **c. à qn de faire qch.**, to advise, recommend, s.o. to do sth.

conseiller², -ère [kɔ̃sɛje, -jɛr] *n.* **1.** counsellor, adviser; **c. juridique, technique,** legal, technical, adviser; **c. fiscal** = tax consultant. **2. c. municipal,** town, borough, councillor; **c. général** = county councillor. **3.** *Jur:* **c. à la cour (d'appel),** judge of appeal.

conseilleur, -euse [kɔ̃sɛjœr, -øz] *n. Pej:* giver, dispenser, of (unwanted) advice.

consensus [kɔ̃sɛ̃sys] *n.m.* consensus (of opinion).

consentant [kɔ̃sɑ̃tɑ̃] *a. Jur:* consenting (party, etc.); in agreement, agreeing; **elle est consentante,** she's willing.

consentement [kɔ̃sɑ̃tmɑ̃] *n.m.* consent, assent; **c. universel,** universal, common, assent; **donner son c. à qch.**, to assent, consent, to sth.

consentir [kɔ̃sɑ̃tir] *v.* (*conj. like* SENTIR) **1.** *v.i.* to consent, agree; **c. à (faire) qch.**, to consent to (do) sth.; **je consens (à ce) qu'il vienne,** I consent, agree, to his coming; **il a fini par c.**, he finally agreed; *F:* he came round in the end. **2.** *v.tr.* (*a*) **c. un prêt,** to grant a loan; **c. une remise à qn,** to allow s.o. a discount; (*b*) to accept, admit (sth.).

conséquemment [kɔ̃sekamɑ̃] *adv.* (*a*) *A: & Lit:* consequentially; (*b*) consequently, in consequence.

conséquence [kɔ̃sekɑ̃s] *n.f.* consequence; (*a*) outcome, sequel, result; **il faut en subir les conséquences,** we, you, must take the consequences; **qu'est-ce que cela aura pour c.?** what will be the effect, the result, of it? **cela ne tire pas à c.**, it's of no consequence; *adv.phr.* **en c.**, in consequence, consequently; **agir en c.**, to take appropriate action; *prep.phr.* **en c. de . . .**, (i) in consequence of . . .; (ii) according to . . .; (*b*) inference; **tirer une c. de qch.**, to draw an inference, a conclusion, from sth.; (*c*) importance; **personne sans c.**, person of no importance, consequence.

conséquent [kɔ̃sekɑ̃] **1.** *a.* (*a*) consistent, rational (mind, speech, etc.); **il n'est pas c. dans ses actions,** he's not consistent in his actions; (*b*) *Mus:* **partie conséquente,** *n.f.* **conséquente, d'une fugue,** countersubject of a fugue; (*c*) consequent (river, valley); (*d*) *F:* **homme c., affaire conséquente,** important man, business; (*e*) **par c.**, consequently, accordingly, therefore. **2.** *n.m. Gram: Log: Mth:* consequent.

conservateur, -trice [kɔ̃sɛrvatœr, -tris] **1.** *n.* (*a*) keeper, warden; **c. de bibliothèque,** librarian; **c. d'un musée,** curator, keeper, of a museum; **c. des hypothèques,** registrar of mortgages; (*b*) *Pol:* conservative; *a.* **parti c.**, conservative party. **2.** *a.* preserving, preservative (process, etc.).

conservation [kɔ̃sɛrvasjɔ̃] *n.f.* **1.** (*a*) conserving, conservation; preserving, preservation (of fruit, meat, etc.); (*b*) preservation, care (of buildings, archives, health, etc.); **instinct de conservation,** instinct of self preservation; (*c*) retaining, keeping (of rights, situation, etc.); (*d*) registration (of mortgages); **c. des Eaux et forêts** = Forestry Commission. **2.** (state of) preservation; **meubles d'une belle c.**, well preserved, well kept, furniture.

conservatisme [kɔ̃sɛrvatism] *n.m. Pol: etc:* conservatism.

conservatoire [kɔ̃sɛrvatwar] **1.** *a. Jur:* conservatory (act, etc.); **mesures conservatoires,** measures of conservation. **2.** *n.m.* (*a*) repository, museum; **C. des arts et métiers,** museum and college of Arts and Crafts; (*b*) school, academy (of music, of dramatic art), *NAm:* conservatory; **le C. (de Paris),** the Paris conservatoire.

conserve [kɔ̃sɛrv] *n.f.* **1.** preserve; preserved, tinned, canned, food; **boîte de c.**, tin, can; **conserves au vinaigre,** pickles; **bœuf de c.**, tinned beef, corned beef, *NAm:* canned beef; **petits pois en c.**, tinned peas; **mettre en c.**, to tin, can; *F:* **je vais mettre cet argent en c.**, I'm going to hang on to this money. **2.** *Nau:* consort; **naviguer de c.**, to sail in company, together (**avec,** with).

conservé [kɔ̃sɛrve] *a.* **femme bien conservée,** well preserved woman.

conserver [kɔ̃sɛrve] *v.tr.* **1.** (*a*) to preserve, conserve (fruit, meat, etc.); **aliments conservés,** tinned, canned, bottled, foods; (*b*) to preserve, take care of (building, furniture, clothes, etc.). **2.** to keep, retain, maintain (rights, situation, etc.); **c. son sang-froid, sa tête,** to remain cool, to keep one's head; **c. l'allure,** to keep up, maintain, the speed; *Mil:* **c. une position,** to hold a position. **3. se c.,** (*of goods, etc.*) to keep; **articles qui ne se conservent pas,** perishable goods.

conserverie [kɔ̃sɛrvəri] *n.f.* **1.** canning industry. **2.** cannery, canning factory.

considérable [kɔ̃siderabl̩] *a.* considerable. **1.** *O:* notable, eminent; well-to-do (person). **2.** large, extensive (property, population, etc.); significant (change, etc.); **j'ai fait des dépenses considérables,** I have been, have gone, to considerable expense.

considérablement [kɔ̃siderabləmɑ̃] *adv.* considerably, significantly.

considérant [kɔ̃siderɑ̃] *n.m. Jur:* preamble.

considération [kɔ̃siderasjɔ̃] *n.f.* consideration. **1.** (*a*) attention, thought; **agir avec, sans, c.,** to act considerately, inconsiderately; **prendre qch. en c.,** to take sth. into consideration, into account; to consider (offer, etc.); **en c. de,** in consideration of, on account of; (*b*) *pl.* **considérations sur l'histoire,** reflexions on history. **2.** reason, motive; **je ne peux pas entrer dans ces considérations,** I can't go into these considerations. **3.** regard, esteem, respect; **n'avoir de c. pour personne,** to have no consideration for anyone, to be most inconsiderate; **jouir d'une grande c.,** to be highly respected; *Corr:* **veuillez agréer, Monsieur, l'assurance de ma parfaite, de ma haute, c.,** yours very truly; **par c. pour,** out of consideration, regard, for.

considéré *a.* [kɔ̃sidere] highly regarded, respected (person).

considérer [kɔ̃sidere] *v.tr.* **(je considère, n. considérons; je considérerai) 1.** to consider; to weigh up (matter); **tout bien considéré,** taking all things into consideration, all things considered, on the whole; **c'est à c.,** it must be borne in mind; **considérant que . . .,** considering that . . . . **2.** to contemplate, gaze on, look at (sth.). **3.** to regard, deem; **je considère votre lettre comme frivole,** I think your letter is flippant; **se c. comme responsable,** to consider, hold, oneself responsible; **on le considère beaucoup,** he is highly thought of.

consignataire [kɔ̃siɲatɛr] *n.m. & f.* **1.** *Jur:* depositary; trustee. **2.** *Com: Nau:* consignee.

consignation [kɔ̃siɲasjɔ̃] *n.f.* **1.** deposit (of money); **caisse des dépôts et consignations,** Deposit and Consignment Office. **2.** *Com:* (*a*) consignment (of goods); **marchandises en c.,** goods on consignment; (*b*) charging a deposit (on container).

consigne [kɔ̃siɲ] *n.f.* **1.** order(s), instructions (to sentry, etc.); **il a pour c. de ne laisser passer personne,** his orders are to let nobody pass; **observer la c.,** to obey orders; **c'est la c.,** those are the orders. **2.** (*a*) *Mil:* confinement (to barracks, etc.); (*b*) *Sch:* detention. **3.** *Rail:* left-luggage office; *NAm:* checkroom; **c. automatique,** left-luggage lockers. **4.** deposit (on bottle, etc.).

consigner [kɔ̃siɲe] *v.tr.* **1.** (*a*) to deposit (money, etc.); **bouteille consignée,** returnable bottle; **emballage non consigné,** non-returnable packing; (*b*) *Com:* to consign (goods, etc.) (**à,** to). **2. c. qch.,** to register, write down, enter, record, put on record (fact, etc.). **3.** (*a*) to confine (soldier) to barracks; to keep in (pupil); (*b*) to refuse admittance to (s.o.); **la salle est consignée,** the hall is closed; **c. sa porte à qn,** to bar one's door to s.o. **4.** *Rail:* **c. ses bagages,** to put, deposit, one's luggage in the left-luggage office, *NAm:* checkroom.

consistance [kɔ̃sistɑ̃s] *n.f.* **1.** (*a*) consistence, consistency (of syrup, cream, etc.); **prendre c.,** to thicken; (*b*) stability, firmness (of mind, character); **sans c.,** spineless. **2.** credit; **bruit sans c.,** unfounded, groundless, rumour.

consistant [kɔ̃sistɑ̃] *a.* firm, solid, stable (substance); thick (paint, etc.); **repas c.,** substantial meal; **information consistante,** reliable information.

consister [kɔ̃siste], *v.i.* to consist; **c. en qch.,** to consist, to be composed, of sth.; **c. dans qch.,** to consist in sth.; **le bonheur consiste à rendre heureux les autres,** happiness consists, lies, in making others happy.

consistoire [kɔsistwar] *n.m. Ecc:* consistory.

consœur [kɔ̃sœr] *n.f. esp. Iron:* fellow member, sister member, colleague.

consolable [kɔ̃sɔlabl̩] *a.* consolable.

consolant [kɔ̃sɔlɑ̃] *a.* consoling, comforting.

consolateur, -trice [kɔ̃sɔlatœr, -tris] **1.** *n.* consoler, comforter. **2.** *a.* consoling, consolatory.

consolation [kɔ̃sɔlasjɔ̃] *n.f.* consolation, solace, comfort; **apporter la c. à qn,** to bring comfort to s.o., to comfort s.o.; **paroles de c.,** words of comfort, comforting, consoling, words.

console [kɔ̃sɔl] *n.f.* **1.** *Arch:* console, corbel, bracket; *Const:* **grue à console,** wall crane. **2.** *Furn:* console (table), pier table. **3.** *Mus:* console (of organ); neck (of harp). **4.** *Cmptr:* console.

consoler [kɔ̃sɔle] (*a*) *v.tr.* to console, solace, comfort; **c. qn de sa peine,** to comfort, console, s.o. in his grief; **le temps console,** time is a healer; **si ça peut te c.,** if that's any comfort to you; (*b*) **se c. d'une perte,** to get over a loss; **elle s'est vite consolée,** she soon got over it.

consolidation [kɔ̃sɔlidasjɔ̃] *n.f.* **1.** consolidation, strengthening, reinforcing (of foundation, position, power, etc.). **2.** *Med:* healing (of wound); knitting (of fracture). **3.** *Fin:* funding (of floating debt).

consolidé [kɔ̃sɔlide] *a. Fin:* **dette consolidée,** funded debt; **fonds consolidés,** *n.* **consolidés,** consolidated fund; consols.

consolider [kɔ̃sɔlide] *v.tr.* **1.** to consolidate, strengthen, reinforce (foundations, position, etc.). **2.** *Med:* to heal (wound); to knit (fracture). **3.** to fund (debt); to consolidate (rates). **4. se c.** (*a*) to consolidate, strengthen; (*b*) *Med:* to heal, knit.

consommable [kɔ̃sɔmabl̩] *a.* consumable; edible, drinkable.

consommateur, -trice [kɔ̃sɔmatœr, -tris] *n.* (*a*) consumer (of products); (*b*) customer (in restaurant, café).

consommation [kɔ̃sɔmasjɔ̃] *n.f.* **1.** consummation, accomplishment (of work, etc.); perpetration (of crime); consummation (of marriage); **jusqu'à la c. des siècles,** until the end of time. **2.** consumption (of electricity, petrol); use; *Mil: Nau:* expenditure (of stores, equipment, etc.); **faire une grande c. de papier,** to go through, use (up), a lot of paper; **société de c.,** (i) co-operative stores; (ii) consumer society. **3.** drink (in café).

consommé [kɔ̃sɔme] **1.** *a.* consummate (skill, etc.); accomplished (writer, etc.). **2.** *n.m. Cu:* clear soup, consommé.

consommer [kɔ̃sɔme] *v.tr.* **1.** to consummate, accomplish, achieve (work, etc.); to perpetrate (crime); to consummate (marriage). **2.** to consume (electricity, etc.); to eat (food). **3.** (*a*) **cette voiture consomme trop (d'essence),** this car is heavy on petrol; (*b*) *v.i.* **c. au bar,** to have a drink (i) in, (ii) at, the bar. **4. ce plat se consomme froid,** this dish is eaten cold.

consomption [kɔ̃sɔ̃psjɔ̃] *n.f.* **1.** *A: & Lit:* (*a*) consumption; (*b*) consuming (by fire). **2.** *Med:* wasting, decline; *A:* consumption.

consonance [kɔ̃sɔnɑ̃s] *n.f. Mus: Ling:* consonance; **mots aux consonances harmonieuses, bizarres,** harmonious, queer sounding, words.

consonant [kɔ̃sɔnɑ̃] *a. Mus: Ling:* consonant.
consonne [kɔ̃sɔn] *n.f. Ling:* consonant.
consort, -orte [kɔ̃sɔr, -ɔrt] **1.** *a.* **prince c.,** prince consort. **2.** *n.m. pl.* (*a*) *Jur:* jointly interested parties; (*b*) *Pej:* **et consorts,** and company.
consortium [kɔ̃sɔrsjɔm] *n.m. Com: Fin:* consortium, syndicate.
conspirateur, -trice [kɔ̃spiratœr, -tris] **1.** *n.* conspirator, conspirer. **2.** *a.* conspiring, conspiratorial.
conspiration [kɔ̃spirasjɔ̃] *n.f.* conspiracy, plot.
conspirer [kɔ̃spire] *v.i.* **1.** to conspire, plot (**contre,** against). **2.** to conspire, tend, concur; **tout conspire à me mettre en retard,** everything's conspiring to make me late.
conspuer [kɔ̃spɥe] *v.tr.* to boo, shout down (play, speaker, etc.).
constamment [kɔ̃stamɑ̃] *adv.* constantly, continually, continuously.
constance [kɔ̃stɑ̃s] *n.f.* **1.** constancy; **travailler avec c.,** to work steadily. **2.** persistence, perseverance. **3.** constancy, invariability (of temperature, etc.).
constant, -ante [kɔ̃stɑ̃, -ɑ̃t] *a.* **1.** (*a*) constant (heart, friendship, etc.); (*b*) firm, unshaken (perseverance, etc.). **2.** established, patent (fact, etc.). **3.** (*a*) constant (temperature); continuous, uninterrupted (traffic, etc.); (*b*) *n.f. Mth: Ph: etc:* constant.
constat [kɔ̃sta] *n.m.* **1.** *Jur:* certified, official, statement, report; **c. à l'amiable,** unofficial account (of an incident); **c. d'huissier,** affidavit made by a process server. **2.** established fact.
constatation [kɔ̃statasjɔ̃] *n.f.* **1.** verification, establishment (of fact, etc.); noting, taking note; **procéder aux constatations d'usage,** to make routine investigations. **2. constatations d'une enquête,** findings of an enquiry.
constater [kɔ̃state] *v.tr.* **1.** to establish, verify, ascertain, note (fact, etc.); **c. une erreur,** to discover, find, a mistake; **vous pouvez c. vous-même qu'il est parti,** you can see for yourself that he's gone. **2.** to state, record (sth.); **c. un décès,** to certify a death.
constellation [kɔ̃stɛlasjɔ̃] *n.f.* constellation.
consteller [kɔ̃stɛle] *v.tr.* to constellate; **ciel constellé d'étoiles,** star-spangled sky; **robe constellée de pierreries,** dress studded, starred, with jewels.
consternant [kɔ̃stɛrnɑ̃] *a.* alarming, dismaying, (news).
consternation [kɔ̃stɛrnasjɔ̃] *n.f.* consternation, dismay.
consterner [kɔ̃stɛrne] *v.tr.* to dismay, stagger; to strike (s.o.) with consternation, with dismay.
constipation [kɔ̃stipasjɔ̃] *n.f. Med:* constipation.
constipé [kɔ̃stipe] *a.* (*a*) constipated; (*b*) *F:* (*of manner, etc.*) embarrassed, ill at ease, stiff.
constiper [kɔ̃stipe] *v.tr. Med:* to constipate; *abs.* **nourriture qui constipe,** constipating food.
constituant, -ante [kɔ̃stitɥɑ̃, -ɑ̃t] *a. & n.* **1.** *a.* component, constituent (part, element); *n.m.* constituent part. **2.** *a. Pol:* **l'Assemblée constituante,** *n.f.* **la Constituante,** the Constituent Assembly (of 1789); *n.m.* **les constituants,** members of Constituent Assembly. **3.** *n.f. Fr.C:* **constituante,** branch of Quebec university.
constitué [kɔ̃stitɥe] *a.* **1.** constituted, organized (authority, etc.); **les corps constitués,** official bodies. **2. enfant bien c.,** fine healthy child.
constituer [kɔ̃stitɥe] *v.tr.* to constitute. **1.** (*a*) to form, frame, make (up); **parties qui constituent le tout,** parts that constitute, (go to) make up, the whole; **appartement constitué de six pièces,** six-roomed flat, *NAm:* appartment; (*b*) to set up, institute (committee, etc.); to incorporate (an order, a society); to form (ministry, etc.); **ils se constituèrent en commission,** they resolved themselves into a committee. **2.** *Jur: etc:* (*a*) to constitute, appoint; **c. qn son héritier,** to make s.o. one's heir; **se c. prisonnier,** to give oneself up (to the police, etc.); (*b*) **c. une rente à qn,** to settle an annuity on s.o.
constitutif, -ve [kɔ̃stitytif, -iv] *a.* **1.** *Jur:* constitutive; conferring a right; **titre c. (d'une propriété),** title deed. **2.** constituent, component; **les éléments constitutifs de l'air,** the constituent elements of air.
constitution [kɔ̃stitysjɔ̃] *n.f.* **1.** constituting, appointing, establishing; **c. d'un comité,** forming of a committee; **c. de dot,** settlement of a dowry; *Jur:* **c. de partie civile,** institution of civil action; **c. d'avoué,** briefing, instructions, of lawyer. **2.** (*a*) **avoir une bonne c.,** to have a sound constitution, to be fit; (*b*) *Pol:* constitution. **3.** composition (of air, water).
constitutionnel, -elle [kɔ̃stitysjɔnɛl] *a.* constitutional.
constitutionnellement [kɔ̃stitysjɔnɛlmɑ̃] *adv.* constitutionally.
constricteur [kɔ̃striktœr] *n.m. & a.* **1. (muscle) c.,** constrictor (muscle). **2.** *Rept:* **boa c.,** boa constrictor.
constriction [kɔ̃striksjɔ̃] *n.f.* constriction (of muscle, chest, etc.).
constrictor [kɔ̃striktɔr] *a. & n.m. Rept:* **(boa) c.,** boa constrictor.
constructeur, -trice [kɔ̃stryktœr, -tris] **1.** *n.m.* constructor; maker, (structural) engineer; builder; **c. mécanicien,** mechanical engineer; **c. (d')automobile(s),** car manufacturer. **2.** *a.* constructive (idea).
constructif, -ive [kɔ̃stryktif, -iv] *a.* constructive.
construction [kɔ̃stryksjɔ̃] *n.f.* construction. **1.** (*a*) constructing, erecting, erection, building; **matériaux de c.,** building materials; **c. navale,** shipbuilding; **maison en c.,** house under construction; **c. mécanique,** (mechanical) engineering; **jeu de c.,** (i) box of bricks; (ii) construction set; (*b*) construction (of novel, etc.); structure (of sentence). **2.** structure, building.
construire [kɔ̃strɥir] *v.tr.* (*pr.p.* **construisant;** *p.p.* **construit;** *pr.ind.* **je construis, il construit, n. construisons;** *impf.* **je construisais;** *p.h.* **je construisis;** *fu.* **je construirai**) to construct. **1.** to build; to make, lay out (road, etc.); **pendant qu'on construit la maison,** while the house is being built. **2.** to assemble, put together (machine, etc.); *Gram:* **c. une phrase,** (i) to construct, (ii) to construe, a sentence; **c. une théorie,** to build up a theory.
consubstantiation [kɔ̃sypstɑ̃sjasjɔ̃] *n.f. Theol:* consubstantiation, real presence.
consubstantiel, -ielle [kɔ̃sypstɑ̃sjɛl] *a. Theol:* consubstantial; of one substance (**à, avec,** with).
consul [kɔ̃syl] *n.m.* consul; **le c. de France,** the French consul.
consulaire [kɔ̃sylɛr] *a.* consular.
consulat [kɔ̃syla] *n.m.* (i) consulate; (ii) consulship; *Fr.Hist:* **le Consulat,** the Consulate (1799–1804).
consultable [kɔ̃syltabl̩] *a.* (*of book, etc.*) available for consultation.
consultant, -ante [kɔ̃syltɑ̃, -ɑ̃t] *a.* consulting; **médecin c.,** *n.m.* **consultant,** consulting physician, consultant.
consultatif, -ive [kɔ̃syltatif, -iv] *a.* consultative, advisory; **à titre c.,** in an advisory capacity.
consultation [kɔ̃syltasjɔ̃] *n.f.* (*a*) consultation, conference; **entrer en c. avec qn,** to consult, confer, with s.o.; (*b*) (medical) advice, (legal) opinion; (*c*) *Med:* visit to a doctor; **cabinet de c.,** consulting room, surgery; *NAm:* (doctor's) office; **heures de c.,** surgery hours; **consultation externe,** out-patients department; *Jur:* **cabinet de c.,** chambers.
consulter [kɔ̃sylte] **1.** *v.tr.* (*a*) to consult, to ask the advice of, the opinion of, to refer to (s.o., sth.); **c. un médecin, un avocat,** to take medical, legal, advice;

ils se sont consultés, they put their heads together; **c. un dictionnaire,** to consult a dictionary; **ouvrage à c.,** work of reference; (*b*) **c. ses intérêts,** to look after one's own interests. **2.** *v.i. Med:* (i) to take surgery; (ii) to hold a consultation (with a colleague).

consumer [kɔ̃syme] *v.tr.* to consume. **1.** to wear away; to destroy; **consumé par le feu,** consumed by fire, burnt up; **consumé par l'ambition,** eaten up with ambition. **2.** *Lit:* to waste, spend (fortune, time, energy). **3. se c.,** to waste away; to pine; **se c. en efforts inutiles,** to wear oneself out in useless efforts.

contact [kɔ̃takt] *n.m.* **1.** contact, touch; **être, entrer, en c. avec qn, qch.,** to be in contact, come into contact, with s.o., sth.; **prendre c., se mettre en c., avec qn,** to get in touch with s.o., to contact s.o.; **prise de c.,** preliminary contacts; first meeting; **garder, perdre, le c.,** to keep, lose, touch; **lentille, verre, de c.,** contact lens. **2.** *El:* (*a*) connection, contact; **c. avec la terre,** contact to earth; **point de c.,** contact point; *Aut:* **clef de c.,** ignition key; **établir, mettre, le c.,** to make contact; to switch on; **couper le c.,** to break contact; to switch off; (*b*) switch, contact; **fiche, cheville, de c.,** contact plug.

contacter [kɔ̃takte] *v.tr.* to contact, get in touch with (s.o.).

contacteur [kɔ̃taktœr] *n.m. El:* contactor.

contagieux, -ieuse [kɔ̃taʒjø, -jøz] *a.* contagious, infectious, catching (disease, etc.); *n.* **un c.,** a contagious patient, case; **rire c.,** infectious laugh.

contagion [kɔ̃taʒjɔ̃] *n.f.* **1.** *Med: etc:* (*a*) contagion; (*b*) infectious, contagious, disease. **2. la c. du rire,** the infectiousness of laughter.

contagionner [kɔ̃taʒjɔne] *v.tr. Med:* to infect.

container [kɔ̃tɛnɛr] *n.m. Trans:* container.

contamination [kɔ̃taminasjɔ̃] *n.f.* (*a*) contamination; pollution; (*b*) *Med:* infection.

contaminer [kɔ̃tamine] *v.tr.* to contaminate; (*a*) to pollute (water, etc.); (*b*) *Med:* to infect.

conte [kɔ̃t] *n.m.* **1.** story, tale; **c. de fées,** fairytale; **contes de bonnes femmes,** old wives' tale. **2.** *A: & Lit:* (tall) story, yarn; **c. à dormir debout,** cock-and-bull story.

contemplateur, -trice [kɔ̃tɑ̃platœr, -tris] *n.* contemplator.

contemplatif, -ive [kɔ̃tɑ̃platif, -iv] **1.** *a.* contemplative. **2.** *n.* meditator; *Ecc:* contemplative.

contemplation [kɔ̃tɑ̃plasjɔ̃] *n.f.* **1.** contemplation (of picture, etc.). **2. plongé dans la c.,** lost in contemplation, in meditation. **3.** *Ecc:* contemplation.

contempler [kɔ̃tɑ̃ple] *v.tr.* to contemplate, to gaze at (nature, picture, etc.).

contemporain -aine [kɔ̃tɑ̃pɔrɛ̃, -ɛn] **1.** *a.* (*a*) contemporary; present-day (opinions, etc.); (*b*) contemporaneous (**de,** with). **2.** *n.* contemporary.

contenance [kɔ̃tnɑ̃s] *n.f.* **1.** capacity, content (of bottle, etc.); **c. d'un navire,** burden of a vessel; **d'une c. de dix litres,** capable of holding ten litres. **2.** countenance, bearing; **faire bonne c.,** to show a bold front; **perdre c.,** to lose one's composure; **faire qch. pour se donner une c.,** to do sth. to avoid losing face.

contenant [kɔ̃tnɑ̃] *n.m.,* **conteneur** [kɔ̃tnœr] *n.m.* container.

contenir [kɔ̃tnir] *v.tr.* (*conj. like* TENIR) to contain. **1.** to hold, have capacity for (certain quantity, number); **le théâtre contient mille places,** the theatre seats a thousand; **lettre contenant chèque,** letter enclosing cheque. **2.** to restrain; to keep, hold (crowd, feelings, etc.) in check; to suppress (anger); to hold back (tears); **c. l'ennemi,** to hold, contain, the enemy, to keep the enemy in check. **3. se c.,** to contain oneself, control one's emotions.

content [kɔ̃tɑ̃] **1.** *a.* (*a*) content; **être c. de son sort,** to be content, satisfied, with one's lot; (*b*) satisfied, pleased (**de,** with); **il est très c. ici,** he's very happy here; (*c*) pleased; **je suis très c. de vous voir,** I am very pleased to see you; **votre père ne sera pas c.,** your father won't like it; (*d*) glad; **je suis fort c. que vous soyez venu,** I'm so glad you've come. **2.** *n.m.* **manger tout son c.,** to eat one's fill; **s'amuser tout son c.,** to enjoy oneself to one's heart's content.

contentement [kɔ̃tɑ̃tmɑ̃] *n.m.* (*a*) content(ment); (*b*) satisfaction (**de,** at, with).

contenter [kɔ̃tɑ̃te] *v.* **1.** *v.tr.* to content, satisfy (s.o.); to gratify (curiosity, whim, etc.). **2. se c. de (faire) qch.,** to be content, satisfied, with (doing) sth.; **je me contenterai de faire remarquer que . . .,** I will merely point out that . . .; **il se contente d'un repas par jour,** he has only one meal a day.

contentieux, -ieuse [kɔ̃tɑ̃sjø, -jøz] **1.** *a.* contentious (matter). **2.** (*a*) *n.m. Adm:* contentious business, matters in dispute; litigation; (*b*) legal department (of bank, administration, etc.); **chef du c.,** (company's, etc.) solicitor.

contention[1] [kɔ̃tɑ̃sjɔ̃] *n.f.* **1.** application, exertion (of faculties); **c. d'esprit,** intentness of mind. **2.** *A:* contention, dispute.

contention[2] *n.f. Med:* retention (of fracture, etc.) in place.

contenu [kɔ̃tny] **1.** *a.* restrained, suppressed (passion, style, etc.). **2.** *n.m.* contents (of parcel, etc.); **le c. de sa lettre,** the content, tenor, of his letter.

conter [kɔ̃te] *v.tr.* to tell, relate (story, etc.); *F:* **allez c. ça ailleurs!** go and tell that to the marines! **elle ne s'en laisse pas c.,** you can't fool her.

contestable [kɔ̃tɛstabl̩] *a.* contestable, debatable, questionable.

contestataire [kɔ̃tɛstatɛr] **1.** *a.* contesting; anti-establishment. **2.** *n.* contestant, protester.

contestation [kɔ̃tɛstasjɔ̃] *n.f.* **1.** contesting; dispute; **être en c. avec qn,** to be at variance, at issue, with s.o.; **sans c. possible,** beyond all question, beyond dispute. **2.** *Pol:* protest.

conteste [kɔ̃tɛst] *adv.phr.* **sans c.,** indisputably, unquestionably, beyond question.

contester [kɔ̃tɛste] **1.** *v.tr.* to contest, dispute, challenge (point, right, etc.); **point contesté,** controversial point; **je lui conteste le droit,** I question his right. **2.** *v.i.* to take issue (**sur,** over); *Pol:* to protest.

conteur, -euse [kɔtœr, -øz] *n.* **1.** narrator, storyteller. **2.** storywriter.

contexte [kɔ̃tɛkst] *n.m.* (*a*) context; (*b*) **c. historique,** historical background (of an event).

contexture [kɔ̃tɛkstyr] *n.f.* **1.** (con)texture (of bones, muscles, etc.). **2.** structure, framework (of story, poem).

contigu, -uë [kɔ̃tigy] *a.* contiguous, adjoining, adjacent; **c. à, avec, qch.,** contiguous to, next to, adjacent to, sth.; **idées contiguës,** analogous, related, ideas.

contiguïté [kɔ̃tigɥite] *n.f.* contiguity, adjacency, proximity (of house, etc.).

continence [kɔ̃tinɑs] *n.f.* continence.

continent[1] [kɔtinɑ̃] *a.* continent.

continent[2] *n.m. Geog:* **1.** continent; **l'ancien, le nouveau, c.,** the old, the new, world. **2.** mainland.

continental, -aux [kɔ̃tinɑ̃tal, -o] *a.* continental.

contingence [kɔ̃tɛ̃ʒɑ̃s] *n.f. Phil:* contingency; **les contingences de la vie quotidienne,** everyday happenings.

contingent [kɔ̃tɛ̃ʒɑ̃] **1.** *a. Phil:* contingent. **2.** *n.m.* (*a*) *Mil:* contingent; **le c. annuel d'une classe est de 250.000 hommes,** the annual intake, call-up, *NAm:* draft, totals 250,000 men; (*b*) quota (*e.g.* immigration quota); (*c*) share, contribution.

contingentement [kɔ̃tɛ̃ʒɑ̃tmɑ̃] *n.m. Adm:* quota system of distribution; apportioning of quotas.

contingenter [kɔ̃tɛ̃ʒɑ̃te] *v.tr. Adm:* **1.** to establish, fix, quotas for (imports, etc.). **2.** to distribute (films, etc.) according to a quota.

continu [kɔ̃tiny] **1.** *a.* continuous, unbroken; unceasing, incessant; sustained (effort, etc.); endless (suffering); *El:* **courant c.,** direct current. **2.** *n.m. Phil: Ph: Mth:* continuum.

continuation [kɔ̃tinɥasjɔ̃] *n.f.* **1.** continuation (of work, etc.); *F:* **bonne c.!** keep up the good work! keep it up! **2.** duration; long spell, run (of bad weather, etc.).

continuel, -elle [kɔ̃tinɥɛl] *a.* continual, unceasing, ceaseless.

continuellement [kɔ̃tinɥɛlmɑ̃] *adv.* continually.

continuer [kɔ̃tinɥe] *v.tr. & i.* to continue; (*a*) to carry on, go on with, keep on with (studies, efforts, etc.); **c. sa route,** to continue on one's way; **c. à, de, faire qch.,** to continue to do sth., to go on doing sth.; **continuez!** go on! go ahead! keep it up! carry on! **la guerre continue,** the war is still going on; (*b*) to extend; **jardin qui continue jusqu'à la rivière,** garden that extends to the river.

continuité [kɔ̃tinɥite] *n.f.* continuity; continuation.

continûment [kɔ̃tinymɑ̃] *adv.* continuously.

continuum [kɔ̃tinyɔm] *n.m. Mth: Ph: etc:* continuum; **c. espace-temps,** space-time continuum.

contorsion [kɔ̃tɔrsjɔ̃] *n.f.* contortion; twisting (of face, etc.).

contorsionner (se) [səkɔ̃tɔrsjɔne] *v.pr.* to contort one's body; to writhe (about).

contorsionniste [kɔ̃tɔrsjɔnist] *n.m. & f.* contortionist.

contour [kɔ̃tur] *n.m.* **1.** outline, line, contour. **2.** *Surv:* contour (line). **3.** (*a*) edge, limit (of town, forest, etc.); (*b*) bend, turn (of road, etc.).

contourné [kɔ̃turne] *a.* (*a*) twisted, contorted, crooked (limb, tree, etc.); **style c.,** tortuous style; (*b*) (over) elaborate (furniture, etc.).

contournement [kɔ̃turnəmɑ̃] *n.m.* skirting (of mountain, etc.); *Rail:* **(voie de) c.,** loop line.

contourner [kɔ̃turne] *v.tr.* **1.** to shape, to trace the outline of (design, vase, etc.). **2.** to pass round, skirt (round), bypass (hill, wood, etc.); **c. la loi, une difficulté,** to get round, evade, circumvent, the law, a difficulty. **3.** to twist, warp, contort, distort.

contraceptif, -ive [kɔ̃trasɛptif, -iv] *a. & n.m.* contraceptive.

contraception [kɔ̃trasɛpsjɔ̃] *n.f.* contraception.

contractant [kɔ̃traktɑ̃] *Jur:* **1.** *a.* contracting (party). **2.** *n.m.* contracting party.

contracté [kɔ̃trakte] *a.* (*a*) *Gram:* contracted; (*b*) tense (muscles, etc.).

contracter¹ [kɔ̃trakte] *v.tr.* **1.** (*a*) to contract, enter into (alliance, marriage); (*b*) to incur, contract (debt); (*c*) **c. une assurance,** to take out an insurance policy. **2.** to acquire (habit); to contract, catch (disease).

contracter² **1.** *v.tr.* to contract, draw together; to tense (muscles); **visage contracté par la douleur,** face drawn with pain. **2. se c.,** (*of heart, etc.*) to contract; (*of muscle*) to tense up, to contract; *Ling:* (*of word, article*) to contract, be contracted (into).

contractile [kɔ̃traktil] *a. Physiol:* contractile, contractible (muscle, etc.).

contraction [kɔ̃traksjɔ̃] *n.f.* (*a*) contraction (of body, etc.); (*b*) *Ling:* contraction; (*c*) contraction, tensing (of muscle).

contractuel, -elle [kɔ̃traktɥɛl] **1.** *a.* contractual (obligation, etc.); **agent c.** = contractor working for the (local) council. **2.** *n.* = traffic warden.

contradicteur [kɔ̃tradiktœr] *n.m.* contradictor.

contradiction [kɔ̃tradiksjɔ̃] *n.f.* **1.** contradiction; *Jur:* opposition; **être en c. avec qn, avec les faits,** to be at variance with s.o., with the facts; **esprit de c.,** contrariness. **2.** contradiction, inconsistency; **en c. avec qch.,** inconsistent, incompatible, with sth.

contradictoire [kɔ̃tradiktwar] *a.* (*a*) contradictory (**à,** to); inconsistent (**à,** with); conflicting (accounts, etc.); (*b*) *Jur:* **jugement c.,** judgment after trial; (*c*) **débat c.,** debate.

contradictoirement [kɔ̃tradiktwarmɑ̃] *adv.* **1.** contradictorily. **2.** *Jur:* after hearing of both parties.

contraignant [kɔ̃trɛɲɑ̃] *a.* restricting, constraining.

contraindre [kɔ̃trɛ̃dr̥] *v.tr.* (*p.p.* **contraint;** *pr.ind.* **je contrains, n. contraignons, ils contraignent;** *impf.* **je contraignais;** *p.h.* **je contraignis;** *fu* **je contraindrai)** to constrain. **1.** to restrain (s.o., one's feelings). **2.** to compel, force; **c. qn à,** *occ.* **de, faire qch.,** to constrain, force, s.o. to do sth.; **je fus contraint de me taire,** I was obliged, compelled, to keep quiet; *Jur:* **c. qn par voie de justice,** to bring an action against s.o. **3. se c.** (*a*) to restrain oneself; (*b*) **se c. à faire qch.,** to force oneself to, to make oneself, do sth.

contraint [kɔ̃trɛ̃] *a.* constrained, cramped (posture, style, etc.); forced (smile); stiff, starched (manner); **c. et forcé,** under duress.

contrainte [kɔ̃trɛ̃t] *n.f.* constraint. **1.** restraint; **parler sans c.,** to speak freely. **2.** compulsion, coercion; **faire qch. par c.,** to be forced to do sth.; **agir sous la c.,** to act under pressure, under duress; *Jur:* **c. par corps,** imprisonment for debt.

contraire [kɔ̃trɛr] *a. & n.m.* **1.** *a.* contrary, opposite (direction, etc.); opposed, conflicting (interest, etc.); **en sens c.,** in the opposite direction; **sauf avis c.,** unless I, you, hear to the contrary; **c. à la règle, aux règlements,** against the rules. **2.** *a.* (*a*) adverse, opposed; **le sort lui est c.,** fate is against him; **vent c.,** adverse, contrary, wind; (*b*) **le climat lui est c.,** the climate does not agree with him. **3.** *n.m.* opposite; contrary; **c'est le c.,** it's the other way round; **il ne vous dit pas le c.,** he's not denying it; **au c., bien au c.,** on the contrary; **au c. de ses frères,** unlike his brothers.

contrairement [kɔ̃trɛrmɑ̃] *adv.* **c. à,** contrary to, in opposition to; unlike; **c. à son habitude, il sortit sans manteau,** contrary to his habit, he went out without a coat.

contralto [kɔtralto] *n.m. Mus:* contralto; *pl. contraltos.*

contrariant [kɔ̃trarjɑ̃] *a.* (*a*) perverse, contrary (person, spirit); (*b*) tiresome, irritating; **comme c'est c.!** how annoying!

contrarié [kɔ̃trarje], *a.* **1.** (**a**) thwarted; (*b*) annoyed, vexed.

contrarier [kɔ̃trarje] *v.tr.* (*impf. & pr.sub.* **n. contrariions, v. contrariiez) 1.** to thwart, oppose, cross, frustrate; **c. les desseins de qn,** to interfere with s.o.'s plans. **2.** to annoy, bother; **il cherche à le c.,** he's trying to annoy him.

contrariété [kɔ̃trarjete] *n.f.* **1.** (*a*) clash(ing) (of interests, tastes, colours, etc.); (*b*) **esprit de c.,** contrariness; perversity. **2.** vexation, annoyance; **éprouver une vive c.,** to be very much annoyed.

contrastant [kɔ̃trastɑ̃] *a.* contrasting (colours, etc.).

contraste [kɔ̃trast] *n.m.* contrast; **mettre une chose en c. avec une autre,** to contrast one thing with another; **être en c., faire c., avec,** to contrast with; **en c. avec le rouge,** in contrast to the red.

contrasté [kɔ̃traste] *a.* contrasted, contrasting (colours, etc.).

contraster [kɔ̃traste] *v.* to contrast. **1.** *v.i.* **c. avec qch.,** to contrast, stand in contrast, with sth.; **couleurs qui contrastent,** colours that set one another off. **2.** *v.tr.* to put (colours, etc.) in contrast.

contrat [kɔ̃tra] *n.m.* contract, agreement, deed; **rupture de c.,** breach of contract; **passer un c. avec qn,**

to enter into, conclude, an agreement with s.o.; **c. de mariage,** marriage settlement; *U.S:* premarital agreement; **c. d'assurance,** contract of insurance; **c. de vente,** bill of sale; *Cards:* **réaliser son c.,** to make one's contract; **c. de travail,** contract of employment; *U.S:* labor contract; **c. collectif,** collective agreement.

contravention [kɔ̃travɑ̃sjɔ̃] *n.f.* (*a*) *Jur:* contravention, infringement (of law, etc.); **être en c.,** to be contravening the law; (*b*) breach of police regulations, police offence; (*c*) (parking) ticket; (parking) fine; **donner,** *F:* **flanquer, une c. à qn,** to give s.o. a ticket, to book s.o.

contre [kɔ̃tr̥] **1.** *prep.* against; (*a*) **nager c. le courant,** to swim against the stream; **se battre c. qn,** to fight against, with, s.o.; **se fâcher c. qn,** to get angry with s.o.; **c. toute attente,** contrary to all expectation; **c. son habitude,** contrary to his usual practice; **l'Angleterre c. l'Irelande,** England versus Ireland; **je n'ai rien c.,** I have nothing against it, him, etc.; (*b*) from; **s'abriter c. la pluie,** to shelter from the rain; **sirop c. la toux,** cough mixture; (*c*) (in exchange) for; **échanger une chose c. une autre,** to exchange one thing for another; **livraison c. remboursement,** cash on delivery; (*d*) to; **parier à cinq c. un,** to bet five to one; (*e*) (close) to, by; **s'appuyer c. le mur,** to lean against the wall; **sa maison est tout c. la mienne,** his house adjoins mine. **2.** *adv.* against; **parler, voter, pour et c.,** to speak, vote, for and against; **la maison est tout c.,** the house is close by; **laisse la porte c.,** leave the door to. **3.** *n.m.* (*a*) **disputer le pour et le c.,** to argue the pros and cons; *adv.phr:* **par c.,** on the other hand; (*b*) *Box: Fenc:* counter; (*c*) *Bill:* kiss; (*d*) *Cards:* double.

contre-accusation [kɔ̃trakyzasjɔ̃] *n.f.* countercharge; *pl. contre-accusations.*

contre-alizé [kɔ̃tralize] *a.* & *n. Meteor:* countertrade; anti-trade (wind); *pl. contre-alizés.*

contre-allée [kɔ̃trale] *n.f.* side path, lane; service road; *pl. contre-allées.*

contre-amiral [kɔ̃tramiral] *n.m.* rear-admiral; *pl. contre-amiraux.*

contre-appel [kɔ̃trapɛl] *n.m. Mil:* check roll call, second call; *pl. contre-appels.*

contre-assurance [kɔ̃trasyrɑ̃s] *n.f.* reinsurance; *pl. contre-assurances.*

contre-attaque [kɔ̃tratak] *n.f. Mil:* counter attack; *pl. contre-attaques.*

contre-attaquer [kɔ̃tratake] *v.tr.* & *i.* to counter-attack.

contrebalancer [kɔ̃trəbalɑ̃se] *v.tr.* **(je contrebalançai(s); n. contrebalançons) 1.** to counterbalance, counterpoise, offset. **2.** *F:* **s'en c.,** not to give a damn; **il s'en contrebalance,** he couldn't care less.

contrebande [kɔ̃trəbɑ̃d] *n.f.* **1.** contraband, smuggling; **faire la c.** to be a smuggler; **faire entrer des marchandises en c.,** to smuggle in goods. **2.** contraband goods, smuggled goods.

contrebandier, -ière [kɔ̃trəbɑ̃dje, -jɛr] *n.* smuggler.

contrebas (en) [ɑ̃kɔ̃trəbɑ] *adv.phr.* (lower) down, on a lower level, below; **le café est en c. de la rue,** the café is below street level.

contrebasse [kɔ̃trəbas] *n.f. Mus:* (*a*) (double) bass; (*b*) (double) bass player.

contrebassiste [kɔ̃trəbasist] *n.m. Mus:* (double) bass player.

contrebasson [kɔ̃trəbasɔ̃] *n.m. Mus:* double bassoon, contrabassoon.

contrebatterie [kɔ̃trəbatri] *n.f. Mil:* counterbattery.

contre-biais [kɔ̃trəbjɛ] *n.m.inv.* diagonal cut against the twist (of cloth).

contre-bord (à) [akɔ̃trəbɔr] *adv.phr. Nau:* **courir à c.-b.,** to sail (i) on opposite tacks, (ii) on parallel and opposite courses.

contreboutant [kɔ̃trəbutɑ̃] *n.m.* **1.** *Arch: etc:* buttress. **2.** *Const: Civ.E:* shore.

contrebouter [kɔ̃trəbute] **contrebuter** [kɔ̃trəbyte] *v.tr. Civ.E: etc:* to buttress; to shore up.

contrecarrer [kɔ̃trəkɑre] *v.tr.* to cross, thwart, oppose (s.o., plans).

contrechamp [kɔ̃trəʃɑ̃] *n.m. Cin:* reverse shot.

contre-chant [kɔ̃trəʃɑ̃] *n.m. Mus:* counterpoint; *pl. contre-chants.*

contrechâssis [kɔ̃trəʃɑsi] *n.m.inv.* double (window) frame.

contrecœur[1] [kɔ̃trəkœr] *adv.phr.* **à c.,** unwillingly, reluctantly, grudgingly.

contrecœur[2] *n.m.* (*a*) *Const:* backplate (of fireplace); fireback; (*b*) *Rail:* guardrail, wingrail (at centre of crossover).

contrecoup [kɔ̃trəku] *n.m.* (*a*) rebound (of bullet, etc.); recoil; (*b*) jar (of blow, etc.); (*c*) after effects, consequence (of action, disaster); **les contrecoups de la guerre,** the repercussions of war.

contre-courant [kɔ̃trəkurɑ̃] *n.m.* **1.** (*a*) *Hyd:* countercurrent; **nager à c.-c.,** to swim against the current, the stream; *pl. contre-courants.*

contredanse [kɔ̃trədɑ̃s] *n.f.* **1.** quadrille (dance air). **2.** *F:* (parking) ticket, fine.

contredire [kɔ̃trədir] *v.tr.* (*pr.ind.* **je contredis, n. contredisons, v. contredisez;** *other tenses like* DIRE) to contradict; (*a*) to deny, refute; (*b*) to be inconsistent with, contrary to (sth.), to belie (expectations); **les événements contredisent ses espérances,** the events are at variance with his hopes; (*c*) **se c.,** to contradict oneself; **ces deux textes se contredisent,** these two texts do not agree.

contredit [kɔ̃trədi] *adv.phr.* **sans c.,** indisputably, unquestionably.

contrée [kɔ̃tre] *n.f.* (geographical) region.

contre-écrou [kɔ̃trekru] *n.m. Mec.E:* lock nut; *pl. contre-écrous.*

contre-effet [kɔ̃trefɛ] *n.m.* contrary effect; *pl. contre-effets.*

contre-enquête [kɔ̃trɑ̃kɛt] *n.f. Jur:* counter enquiry; *pl. contre-enquêtes.*

contre-épreuve [kɔ̃treprœv] *n.f.* **1.** *Engr:* (*a*) counterproof. **2.** *Tchn:* check test; *pl. contre-épreuves.*

contre-espionnage [kɔ̃trɛspjɔnaʒ] *n.m.* counter-espionage.

contre-essai [kɔ̃tresɛ] *n.m.* control experiment, check test; *pl. contre-essais.*

contre-expertise [kɔ̃trɛkspɛrtiz] *n.f.* counter-valuation; *pl. contre-expertises.*

contrefaçon [kɔtrəfasɔ̃] *n.f.* **1.** counterfeiting; fraudulently copying, imitating (trade-mark, etc.). **2.** counterfeit, forgery, fraudulent imitation; pirated edition.

contrefacteur [kɔ̃trəfaktœr] *n.m.* counterfeiter, forger (of document).

contrefaction [kɔ̃trəfaksjɔ̃] *n.f.* counterfeiting (of coins, etc.); forgery (of banknotes, etc.).

contrefaire [kɔ̃trəfɛr] *v.tr.* (*conj. like* FAIRE) **1.** (*a*) to imitate, mimic; (*b*) *O:* to feign; (*c*) to disguise (one's voice, writing, etc.). **2.** (*a*) to counterfeit (coin, etc.); to forge (signature, currency, etc.); (*b*) to pirate (book, etc.). **3.** to distort, deform (shape etc.).

contrefait [kɔ̃trəfɛ] *a.* **1.** counterfeit, forged (money, etc.). **2.** deformed (person).

contre-feu [kɔ̃trəfø] *n.m.* **1.** fireback. **2.** *For:* counter-fire; *U.S:* backfire; *pl. contre-feux.*

contre-fiche [kɔ̃trəfiʃ] *n.f. Const:* brace, strut; *pl. contre-fiches.*

contreficher (se) [səkɔ̃trəfiʃe] *v.pr. P:* **je m'en fiche et m'en contrefiche,** I don't give a damn, I couldn't care less.

contre(-)fil [kɔ̃trəfil] *n.m.* opposite direction (of watercourse, etc.); **travailler le bois à c.f.,** to work wood against the grain; *pl. contre-fils.*

contre-filet [kɔ̃trəfilɛ] *n.m. Cu:* sirloin; *pl. contre-filets.*

contrefort [kɔ̃trəfɔr] *n.m.* **1.** *Arch:* (close) buttress. **2.** *Geog:* counterfort, spur (of mountain); *pl.* foothills. **3.** stiffening (of shoe).

contre-haut (en) [ɑ̃kɔ̃trəo] *adv.phr.* higher up, on a higher level; above.

contre-indication [kɔ̃trɛ̃dikasjɔ̃] *n.f. Med:* contra-indication; *pl. contre-indications.*

contre-indiquer [kɔ̃trɛ̃dike] *v.tr. Med:* to contra-indicate; **c'est contre-indiqué,** it's inadvisable, unwise.

contre-interrogatoire [kɔ̃trɛ̃tɛrɔgatwar] *n.m. Jur:* cross-examination; *pl. contre-interrogatoires.*

contre-jour [kɔ̃trəʒur] *n.m.* **1.** (unfavourable) light from behind (for picture, etc.); **tableau pendu à c.-j.,** picture hung against the light; **photo prise à c.-j.,** photograph taken against the light; **assis à c.-j.,** sitting with one's back to the light. **2.** *Art: Cin: Phot:* backlighting; *pl. contre-jours.*

contremaître, -tresse [kɔ̃trəmɛtr̥ -trɛs] *n.* foreman, forewoman.

contremander [kɔ̃trəmɑ̃de] *v.tr.* to countermand, cancel, revoke (order, invitation, etc.).

contre-manifestant, -ante [kɔ̃trəmanifɛstɑ̃, -ɑ̃t] *n.* counterdemonstrator; *pl. contre-manifestant(e)s.*

contre-manifestation [kɔ̃trəmanifɛstasjɔ̃] *n.f.* counterdemonstration; *pl. contre-manifestations.*

contre-manifester [kɔ̃trəmanifɛste] *v.i. Pol:* to counterdemonstrate, to hold a counterdemonstration.

contremarche [kɔ̃trəmarʃ] *n.f.* **1.** *Mil:* countermarch. **2.** *Const:* riser (of stair).

contremarque [kɔ̃trəmark] *n.f.* **1.** countermark (on coin, gold plate, etc.). **2.** *Th:* passout ticket.

contre-mesure [kɔ̃trəmzyr] *n.f.* **1.** counter measure. **2.** *Mus:* **jouer à c.-m.,** to play against the beat; *pl. contre-mesures.*

contre-offensive [kɔ̃trɔfɑ̃siv] *n.f. Mil:* counter offensive; *pl. contre-offensives.*

contre-ordre [kɔ̃trɔrdr̥] *n.m.* = CONTRORDRE.

contrepartie [kɔ̃trəparti] *n.f.* **1.** (*a*) opposite, opposing, view (in debate, etc.); (*b*) *Com: Fin:* other party, other side (in transaction); *St. Exch:* **faire la c.,** to operate against one's client. **2.** compensation; **en c.,** in return; to make up for it. **3.** *Book-k:* (*a*) contra; **en c.,** per contra; (*b*) counterpart (of entry); duplicate (of register). **4.** *Mus:* counterpart.

contre-pas [kɔ̃trəpɑ] *n.m.inv. Mil:* half-pace.

contre-passer [kɔ̃trəpase] *v.tr.* **1.** *Com: Fin:* to return, to endorse back (bill to drawer). **2.** *Book-k:* to reverse, contra (item, entry).

contre(-)pente [kɔ̃trəpɑ̃t] *n.f.* reverse gradient; counterslope; *pl. contre-pentes.*

contre-performance [kɔ̃trəpɛrfɔrmɑ̃s] *n.f. Sp:* below standard performance; *pl. contre-performances.*

contrepèterie [kɔ̃trəpetri] *n.f.* spoonerism.

contre-pied [kɔ̃trəpje] *n.m.* **1.** *Ven:* back scent. **2. prendre le c.-p.,** to take the opposite course, view **(de,** to); **il prend toujours le c.-p. de ce qu'on lui dit,** he always does the opposite of what he's told; **à contre-pied de,** contrary to. **3.** *Sp:* **prendre son adversaire à c.-p.,** to wrong-foot one's opponent; **prendre la balle à c.-p.,** to take the ball on the wrong foot; *pl. contre-pieds.*

contre(-)placage [kɔ̃trəplakaʒ] *n.m.* plywood construction.

contre(-)plaqué [kɔ̃trəplake] *n.m.* plywood; *pl. contre-plaqués.*

contre-plongée [kɔ̃trəplɔ̃ʒe] *n.f. Cin:* low angle shot; *pl. contre-plongées.*

contrepoids [kɔ̃trəpwɑ] *n.m.* (*a*) *Mec.E: Mch:* balance weight (of clock, lift, etc.); counterweight, counter-balance; **faire c. à qch.,** to (counter)balance sth.; (*b*) balancing pole (of rope dancer).

contre-poil (à) [akɔ̃trəpwal] *adv.phr.* the wrong way (of the nap, of the hair); *F:* **prendre qn à c.-p.,** to rub s.o. up the wrong way; **prendre une affaire à c.-p.,** to start at the wrong end.

contrepoint [kɔ̃trəpwɛ̃] *n.m. Mus:* counterpoint.

contrepoison [kɔ̃trəpwazɔ̃] *n.m.* antidote, counter-poison.

contre-porte [kɔ̃trəpɔrt] *n.f. NAm:* screen door, inner door, stormdoor; *pl. contre-portes.*

contre-préparation [kɔ̃trəpreparasjɔ̃] *n.f. Mil:* counterpreparation; *pl. contre-préparations.*

contre(-)projet [kɔ̃trəprɔʒɛ] *n.m.* counterplan; *pl. contre-projets.*

contre-proposition [kɔ̃trəprɔpozisjɔ̃] *n.f.* counterproposal, counterproposition; *pl. contre-propositions.*

contrer [kɔ̃tre] **1.** *v.tr. Box:* to counter (blow). **2.** *v.tr. & i. Cards:* to double. **3.** *v.tr. F:* to thwart.

contre-rail [kɔ̃trəraj] *n.m. Rail:* guard rail, check rail; *pl. contre-rails.*

contre-réforme [kɔ̃trərefɔrm] *n.f. Rel.H.:* Counter Reformation.

contre-révolution [kɔ̃trərevɔlysjɔ̃] *n.f.* counter-revolution; *pl. contre-révolutions.*

contre-révolutionnaire [kɔ̃trərevɔlysjɔnɛr] *a. & n.* counter-revolutionary; *pl. contre-révolutionnaires.*

contreseing [kɔ̃trəsɛ̃] *n.m.* countersignature.

contresens [kɔ̃trəsɑ̃s] *n.m.* **1.** misinterpretation (of words, etc.); mistranslation (of passage, etc.); **prendre les paroles de qn à c., prendre le c. des paroles de qn,** to misunderstand what s.o. said. **2.** wrong way (of material). **3. à c.,** in the wrong way, direction; **voitures qui défilent à c.,** cars passing in opposite directions; **à c. de,** in the opposite direction to.

contresigner [kɔ̃trəsiɲe] *v.tr.* to countersign.

contretemps [kɔ̃trətɑ̃] *n.m.* **1.** (*a*) mishap, hitch; contretemps; (*b*) delay, inconvenience. **2.** note played against the beat, on the unaccented portion of the beat. **3.** (*a*) **arriver à c.,** to arrive at the wrong moment; (*b*) *Mus:* **jouer à c.,** to play out of time.

contre-terrorisme [kɔ̃trətɛrɔrism] *n.m.* counter-terrorism.

contre-terroriste [kɔ̃trətɛrɔrist] *a. & n.* counter-terrorist; *pl. contre-terroristes.*

contre-torpilleur [kɔ̃trətɔrpijœr] *n.m. A: Navy:* (*a*) destroyer; (*b*) light cruiser; *pl. contre-torpilleurs.*

contre-ut [kɔ̃tryt] *n.m. Mus:* top C.

contre-valeur [kɔ̃trəvalœr] *n.f. Fin:* exchange value; *pl. contre-valeurs.*

contrevenant, -ante [kɔ̃trəvnɑ̃, -ɑ̃t] **1.** *a.* contravening, offending (party, etc.). **2.** *n.* contravener, infringer (of regulations); offender.

contrevenir [kɔ̃trəvnir] *v.ind.tr.* (*conj. like* VENIR) to contravene, infringe.

contrevent [kɔ̃trəvɑ̃] *n.m.* **1.** (outside) shutter (of window). **2.** *Const:* brace, strut.

contre(-)vérité [kɔ̃trəverite] *n.f.* **1.** untruth, falsehood. **2.** ironical statement (intended to convey the contrary); *pl. contre-vérités.*

contre-visite [kɔ̃trəvizit] *n.f.* (*a*) *Adm: etc:* check survey; second inspection, check inspection; (*b*) *Med:* check visit; *pl. contre-visites.*

contre-voie (à) [akɔ̃trəvwa] *adv.phr. Rail:* **1. cir-**

culer à c.-v., to travel on the wrong track. **2. descendre à c.-v.,** to get out on the wrong side of the train.

contribuable [kɔ̃tribɥabl̩] *n.* taxpayer; **c. à l'impôt foncier** = ratepayer.

contribuer [kɔ̃tribɥe] *v.i.* **1.** to contribute; **nous y avons contribué pour une bonne part,** we made a handsome contribution to it. **2.** to contribute, conduce; **cela contribue pour beaucoup à la rendre heureuse,** that goes a long way towards making her happy; **il a beaucoup contribué à . . .,** he has played a great part in . . .; he has been instrumental in . . ..

contributif, -ive [kɔ̃tribytif, -iv] *a.* contributive, contributory.

contribution [kɔ̃tribysjɔ̃] *n.f.* **1.** *Adm:* tax; rate; **contributions indirectes,** indirect taxation; **c. foncière,** land tax; **(bureau des) contributions,** tax office; = Inland Revenue, *U.S:* Internal Revenue; **lever, percevoir, une c.,** to collect, levy, a tax. **2.** (*a*) contribution, share; **mettre qn à c.,** to call on s.o.'s services; **mettre qch à c.,** to make use of sth.; (*b*) contribution (to learning).

contrister [kɔ̃triste] *v.tr. A:* to sadden, grieve.

contrit [kɔ̃tri] *a.* contrite, penitent.

contrition [kɔ̃trisjɔ̃] *n.f.* contrition, penitence.

contrôlable [kɔ̃trolabl̩] *a.* that may be checked, verified, verifiable; controllable.

contrôle [kɔ̃trol] *n.m.* **1.** *Mil: etc:* roll, list, register; **c. de service,** duty roster; **rayer qn des contrôles de l'armée,** to remove s.o. from the army list. **2.** (*a*) hallmark; **poinçon de c.,** hall-mark stamp; (*b*) assay office. **3.** (*a*) checking, verification (of information, statements, etc.); (*b*) *Adm:* inspection, supervision (of services); *Com:* auditing, checking (of accounts, etc.); *Fin:* **c. des changes,** exchange control; *Th: etc:* **c. des billets,** checking of tickets; **(bureau de) c.,** ticket office; booking office, *NAm:* reservation office; (*c*) *Sp: Aut:* (i) check, checkpoint; (ii) control (point) (in reliability run, etc.); (*d*) *Sch:* **c. continu,** continuous assessment. **4.** (*a*) authority; **exercer un c. sévère sur qn,** to keep s.o. under strict supervision, to maintain strict control over s.o.; (*b*) **c. de soi-même,** self control; (*c*) **c. des naissances,** birth control. **5.** *Tchn:* control, monitoring, testing, regulation (of machine, craft, etc.); *Av:* **tour de c.,** control tower.

contrôler [kɔ̃trole] *v.tr.* **1.** to hallmark, stamp (gold, silver). **2.** to inspect, supervise (work, etc.); to check, audit (accounts); to check (tickets); to examine, inspect (passports); to verify, check (up) (information, a fact, etc.). **3.** (*a*) to control, supervise (operations, etc.); (*b*) to control (s.o.); **se c.,** to control oneself.

contrôleur, -euse [kɔ̃trolœr, -øz] *n.* **1.** (*a*) controller (of government department); auditor (of company accounts, etc.); **c. aux liquidations,** controller in bankruptcy; **c. des contributions,** assessor, inspector, of taxes; (*b*) inspector, examiner, supervisor (of work, etc.); *Rail:* ticket inspector; (*c*) *Av:* **c. de la circulation aérienne,** air traffic controller. **2.** *n.m.* checking machine, apparatus; regulator; *Rail:* master controller; **c. d'atelier,** time recorder.

contrordre [kɔ̃trɔrdr̩] *n.m.* counterorder, countermand; **il y a c.,** the orders have been changed; **sauf c.,** unless otherwise directed.

controuvé [kɔ̃truve] *a.* false, fabricated.

controversable [kɔ̃trɔvɛrsabl̩] *a.* controversial; debatable.

controverse [kɔ̃trɔvɛrs] *n.f.* controversy; debate; **hors de c.,** beyond dispute, indisputable.

controverser [kɔ̃trɔvɛrse] *v.tr.* to discuss, debate (question, etc.); **question controversée,** controversial, much debated, question.

contumace[1] [kɔ̃tymas] *n.f. Jur:* non-appearance (in court); **condamné par c.,** sentenced in absentia, sentenced in his absence.

contumace,[2] **contumax** [kɔ̃tymaks] *a. Jur:* contumacious, defaulting.

contus [kɔ̃ty] *a.* contused, bruised.

contusion [kɔ̃tyzjɔ̃] *n.f.* contusion, bruise.

contusionner [kɔ̃tyzjɔne] *v.tr.* to contuse, bruise.

conurbation [kɔ̃nyrbasjɔ] *n.f.* conurbation.

convaincant [kɔ̃vɛ̃kɑ̃] *a.* convincing.

convaincre [kɔ̃vɛ̃kr̩] *v.tr.* (*conj. like* VAINCRE) **1.** to convince (**de,** of, **que,** that); **j'en suis convaincu,** I'm sure of it; **se laisser c.,** to let oneself be persuaded; **je l'ai finalement convaincu,** I finally convinced him. **2.** to convict (s.o.), to prove (s.o.) guilty (**de,** of).

convaincu [kɔ̃vɛ̃ky] *a.* convinced; **parler d'un ton c.,** to speak with conviction.

convalescence [kɔ̃valɛsɑ̃s] *n.f.* (*a*) convalescence; **elle est en c.,** she's convalescing; **maison de c.,** (i) convalescent home; (ii) nursing home (for rest cure); (*b*) *Mil: etc:* sick leave.

convalescent, -ente [kɔ̃valɛsɑ̃, -ɑ̃t] *a. & n.* convalescent.

convection [kɔ̃vɛksjɔ̃] *n.f. Ph:* convection.

convenable [kɔ̃vnabl̩] *a.* **1.** suitable, fitting, appropriate, proper; **juger c. de faire qch.,** to think it proper, advisable, to do sth. **2.** decent, respectable; acceptable (behaviour); **peu c.,** unacceptable. **3.** *F:* adequate (salary, etc.).

convenablement [kɔ̃vnabləmɑ̃] *adv.* **1.** suitably, fittingly, appropriately. **2.** correctly, properly, decently. **3.** *F:* **on peut manger très c. à la cantine,** you can eat quite well in the canteen.

convenance [kɔ̃vnɑ̃s] *n.f.* **1.** conformity, agreement (of tastes, etc.). **2.** suitability, fitness, convenience, appropriateness, advisability; **pour des raisons de c. personnelle,** for personal reasons; **mariage de c.,** marriage of convenience; **trouver qch. à sa c.,** to find sth. suitable; **il le fera à sa c.,** he'll do it at his own convenience. **3. les convenances,** propriety, the proprieties; etiquette.

convenir [kɔ̃vnir] *v.i.* (*conj. like* VENIR) **1.** (*conj. with* **avoir**) (*a*) to suit, fit; **robe qui convient à la circonstance,** dress suitable for the occasion; **si cela vous convient,** if that suits you; **c'est exactement ce qui me convient,** it's just what I need; (*b*) *impers.* **il convient de . . .,** it is fitting, advisable, to . . .; **ce qu'il convient de faire,** (i) the right thing to do; (ii) the proper measures to take; **il convient que vous y alliez,** you should, ought to, go. **2.** (*conj. with* **avoir,** *and with* **être** *to denote a state of agreement*) (*a*) to agree; to come to an agreement; **c. de qch.,** to agree on, about, sth.; **ils sont convenus,** they are agreed; *impers.* **il fut convenu qu'ils le feraient venir,** it was agreed, arranged, that they would send for him; **comme convenu,** as agreed; (*b*) **c. de qch.,** to acknowledge, admit, sth.; **il convient qu'il a eu tort,** he admits that he was wrong; **j'ai eu tort, j'en conviens,** I was wrong, I admit.

convention [kɔ̃vɑ̃sjɔ̃] *n.f.* convention. **1.** (*a*) covenant, agreement, compact; **c. collective** = collective bargaining; collective (wage) agreement; *Pol:* **c. internationale,** international convention; (*b*) *Jur:* article, clause (of deed, etc.); **cela n'est pas dans les conventions,** this doesn't enter into the agreement. **2. les conventions (sociales),** the social conventions; **de c.,** conventional. **3.** *Pol:* (*a*) (extraordinary) assembly; *Fr.Hist:* **La C. (nationale),** the (National) Convention (1792–95); (*b*) *U.S:* Convention.

conventionné [kɔ̃vɑ̃sjɔne] *a.* **médecin c.** = National Health Service doctor.

conventionnel, -elle [kɔ̃vɑ̃sjɔnɛl] **1.** *a.* (*a*) conventional (value, symbol, *Mil:* weapons); (*b*) contractual (clause, etc.). **2.** *n.m. Fr.Hist:* member of the National Convention.

conventionnellement [kɔ̃vɑ̃sjɔnɛlmɑ̃] *adv.* **1.** *Jur:* by agreement. **2.** conventionally.

conventuel, -elle [kɔ̃vɑ̃tɥɛl] *a.* conventual (house, rule, etc.); monastic (life); **bâtiment c.,** (i) monastery, (ii) convent.
convenu [kɔ̃vny] *a.* **1.** agreed; stipulated (price, etc.); appointed (time). **2.** *Pej:* conventional (language, etc.).
convergence [kɔ̃vɛrʒɑ̃s] *n.f.* convergence.
convergent [kɔ̃vɛrʒɑ̃] *a.* convergent, converging (lines, etc.).
converger [kɔ̃vɛrʒe] *v.i.* **(convergeant; ils convergeaient)** (*of roads, lines, etc.*) to converge.
convers, -erse [kɔ̃vɛr, -ɛrs] *a.* **1.** *Ecc:* lay (brother, sister). **2.** *a. & n.f. Log:* **(proposition) converse,** converse (proposition).
conversation [kɔ̃vɛrsasjɔ̃] *n.f.* conversation, talk; **lier c., entrer en c., engager une c., avec qn,** to enter, get, into conversation with s.o.; **faire la c. à qn,** to chat with s.o., to entertain s.o.; **il a fait les frais de la c.,** he was the main subject of conversation; **langage, expressions, de la c.,** colloquial language, expressions; **c. téléphonique,** telephone call, conversation; **avoir de la c.,** to be a good conversationalist.
converser [kɔ̃vɛrse] *v.i.* to converse, talk (**avec,** with).
conversion [kɔ̃vɛrsjɔ̃] *n.f.* **1.** conversion (to a faith). **2.** conversion, change (**en,** into); *Mth:* **c. des fractions,** conversion of fractions. **3.** (*a*) *Mil: etc:* wheel(ing); (*b*) *Ski:* kick turn.
converti, -e [kɔ̃vɛrti] **1.** *a.* converted (sinner, etc.). **2.** *n.* convert.
convertibilité [kɔ̃vɛrtibilite] *n.f. Fin:* convertibility.
convertible [kɔ̃vɛrtibl̥] **1.** *a.* convertible (**en,** into). **2.** *n.m. Av:* convertiplane.
convertir [kɔ̃vɛrtir] *v.tr.* **1.** to convert (s.o. to a faith, to a point of view, etc.). **2.** to convert (sth. into sth.); *Com: Fin:* **c. des rentes,** to convert stock. **3. se c.** (*a*) to become converted (to a faith, etc.); (*b*) **la neige s'était convertie en boue,** the snow had turned (in)to slush.
convertissement [kɔ̃vɛrtismɑ̃] *n.m. St.Exch: Fin:* conversion (of securities into money).
convertisseur [kɔ̃vɛrtisœr] *n.m.* **1.** *Metall:* converter. **2.** *El: Elcs:* converter; **c. à vapeur de mercure,** mercury-vapour rectifier.
convexe [kɔ̃vɛks] *a.* convex.
convexité [kɔ̃vɛksite] *n.f.* convexity.
conviction [kɔ̃viksjɔ̃] *n.f.* **1.** conviction; **avoir la c. que . . .,** to be convinced that . . .; **sans grande c.,** without much conviction. **2.** *Jur:* **pièce à c.,** object, etc., produced in evidence; exhibit (in criminal case).
convier [kɔ̃vje] *v.tr.* (*impf. & pr.sub.* **n. conviions, v. conviiez**) **1.** to invite; **c. qn à un mariage,** to invite s.o. to a wedding. **2. c. qn à faire qch.,** to urge s.o. to do sth.
convive [kɔ̃viv] *n.* guest (at table).
convocation [kɔ̃vɔkasjɔ̃] *n.f.* convocation; inviting; calling together, convening (of assembly, etc.); *Jur:* summons; **recevoir une c.,** (i) to receive notice of a meeting; (ii) *Adm: etc:* to be asked to come for an interview; to receive a letter fixing an appointment.
convoi [kɔ̃vwa] *n.m.* **1.** convoy; (*a*) **c. administratif,** supply column; (*b*) *Nau:* (i) escorting vessel; (ii) merchant fleet under escort. **2. c. (funèbre),** funeral procession, funeral cortège. **3.** train, convoy; **c. automobile,** motorcade; *Rail:* **c. de marchandises,** goods freight, train.
convoiement [kɔ̃vwamɑ̃] *n.m.* convoying, escorting.
convoiter [kɔ̃vwate] *v.tr.* to covet, desire; to lust after, hanker after (s.o., sth.).
convoitise [kɔ̃vwatiz] *n.f.* covetousness; covetous desire, lust; **regarder qch., qn, avec c.,** to cast covetous glances on sth., to cast lustful eyes on s.o.
convoler [kɔ̃vɔle] *v.i.* (*of widow, widower*) to remarry, to marry again; *F:* **c. en justes noces,** to marry.
convoluté [kɔ̃vɔlyte] *a. Nat.Hist:* convolute(d), whorled.
convoquer [kɔ̃vɔke] *v.tr.* **1.** to summon, call together, convoke (assembly); to convene (meeting). **2.** *Adm: etc:* to invite (s.o.) to an interview; **le patron m'a convoqué dans son bureau,** the boss called me to his office.
convoyage [kɔ̃vwajaʒ] *n.m.* = CONVOIEMENT.
convoyer [kɔ̃vwaje] *v.tr.* **(je convoie, n. convoyons, ils convoient; je convoierai)** to convoy, escort (train, fleet, etc.).
convoyeur [kɔ̃vwajœr] *n.m.* **1.** (*a*) *Mil:* officer in charge of convoy; (*b*) *Nav:* (i) convoying officer; (ii) convoy (ship), escort (ship). **2.** *Mec.E: Ind:* conveyor.
convulser [kɔ̃vylse] *v.tr.* to convulse; **visage convulsé par la terreur,** face convulsed by, with, terror.
convulsif, -ive [kɔ̃vylsif, -iv] *a.* convulsive; **rire c.,** uncontrollable laughter.
convulsion [kɔ̃vylsjɔ̃] *n.f.* convulsion; **convulsions cloniques,** clonic spasms; **c. politique,** political upheaval.
convulsionner [kɔ̃vylsjɔne] *v.tr.* to convulse.
convulsivement [kɔ̃vylsivmɑ̃] *adv.* convulsively.
cooblig é, -ée [koɔbliʒe] *n. Jur:* co-obligant, co-obligor.
cooccupant, -ante [koɔkypɑ̃, -ɑ̃t] *n.* co-occupier.
coopérateur, -trice [koɔperatœr, -tris] **1.** *n.* (*a*) cooperator; fellow-worker; (*b*) member of cooperative. **2.** *a.* **agent c.,** cooperating agent.
coopératif, -ive [koɔperatif, -iv] **1.** *a.* cooperative (society, etc.). **2.** *n.f.* **coopérative,** (i) cooperative; (ii) cooperative stores; *F:* coop.
coopération [koɔperasjɔ̃] *n.f.* (*a*) cooperation; (*b*) = Voluntary Service Overseas.
coopératisme [koɔperatism] *n.m. Pol.Ec:* cooperation, the cooperative system.
coopérer [koɔpere] *v.i.* **(je coopère, n. coopérons; je coopérerai)** to cooperate; to work together; **c. au succès de qch.,** to contribute to the success of sth.
cooptation [koɔptasjɔ̃] *n.f.* co-optation, co-option.
coopter [koɔpte] *v.tr.* to co-opt.
coordinateur, -trice [koɔrdinatœr, -tris] *a. & n.* = COORDONNATEUR.
coordination [koɔrdinasjɔ̃] *n.f.* coordination.
coordonnateur, -trice [koɔrdɔnatœr, -tris] **1.** *a.* coordinating. **2.** *n.* (*pers.*) coordinator.
coordonné, -ée [koɔrdɔne] **1.** *a.* (*a*) coordinated (movement, etc.); (*b*) *Gram: etc:* coordinate (clause, etc.); (*c*) matching (sheets and towels, etc.). **2.** *n.f.pl.* (*a*) *Mth: Geog: Astr:* coordinates; *F:* **donnez-moi vos coordonnées,** give me your address and 'phone number; (*b*) *Cost: Com:* coordinates.
coordonner [koɔrdɔne] *v.tr.* to coordinate (**à, avec,** with), to arrange.
copain [kɔpɛ̃] *n.m. F:* pal, mate; *NAm:* buddy; **ils sont très copains,** they're great pals.
copartageant, -ante [kɔpartaʒɑ̃, -ɑ̃t] *n.* coparcener, coheir, coheiress.
coparticipant [kɔpartisipɑ̃] *n.m. Jur:* copartner.
coparticipation [kɔpartisipasjɔ̃] *n.f. Jur:* copartnership; **c. aux bénéfices,** profit sharing.
copeau, -eaux [kɔpo] *n.m.* shaving (of wood); chip, cutting (of wood, metal); **c. de tour,** turnings.
Copenhague [kɔpɛnag] *Pr.n.f. Geog:* Copenhagen.
copiage [kɔpjaʒ] *n.m. Sch:* cribbing, copying.
copie [kɔpi] *n.f.* **1.** copy, transcript; (*a*) *Adm: Jur:*

pour c. conforme, certified true copy; (*b*) *Journ: Typ:* (i) manuscript; (ii) copy; *F:* **être en mal de c.,** to lack subject material; (*c*) *Sch:* (i) fair copy (of exercise, etc.); (ii) (candidate's) paper; (iii) double sheet (of paper). **2.** copy, reproduction (of picture, statue, etc.); imitation (of novel, style, etc.). **3.** *Cin:* (print) copy; print.

copier [kɔpje] *v.tr.* (*impf. & pr.sub.* **n. copiions, v. copiiez) 1.** to copy, transcribe (manuscript, music, etc.); **c. qch. au propre, au net,** to make a fair copy of sth., to copy out sth. (neatly). **2.** to copy, reproduce (statue, picture); to imitate (s.o., style, etc.); *Sch:* to copy, crib.

copieur, -ieuse [kɔpjœr, -øz] *a. & n.* (*a*) *Sch: etc:* copier, cribber; (*b*) *n.m.* copying machine, photocopier.

copieusement [kɔpjøzmɑ̃] *adv.* copiously; **boire c.,** to drink deep.

copieux, -ieuse [kɔpjø, -jøz] *a.* copious; hearty, square (meal); generous (portion).

copilote [kɔpilɔt] *n.m. Av:* copilot.

copine [kɔpin] *n.f. F:* friend; *cf.* COPAIN.

copiste [kɔpist] *n.m. & f.* **1.** copyist, transcriber. **2.** copier, imitator.

coposséder [kɔpɔsede] *v.tr.* (*conj. like* POSSÉDER) *Jur:* to own jointly, to have joint ownership of (sth.).

copra(h) [kɔpra] *n.m.* copra; **huile de c.,** coconut oil.

coproduction [kɔprɔdyksjɔ̃] *n.f.* coproduction, joint production.

copropriétaire [kɔprɔprijetɛr] *n. Jur:* co-owner, joint owner.

copropriété [kɔprɔprijete] *n.f. Jur:* co-ownership, joint ownership.

copte [kɔpt] *a. & n.m.* **1.** *n.m.* (*a*) Copt; (*b*) *Ling:* Coptic. **2.** *a.* Coptic.

copulation [kɔpylasjɔ̃] *n.f. Physiol:* copulation.

copyright [kɔpirajt] *n.m.* copyright.

coq[1] [kɔk] *n.m.* **1.** (*a*) cock, *NAm:* rooster; **jeune c.,** cockerel; **le c. gaulois,** the French cockerel; **au chant du c.,** at cockcrow; **combat de coqs,** cockfight(ing); **c. de combat,** fighting cock; *F:* **rouge comme un c.,** red as a turkey cock; **jambes de c.,** wiry, spindly, legs; **vivre comme un c. en pâte,** to live in clover; **le c. du village,** the cock of the walk; *Box:* **poids c.,** bantam weight; *Cu:* **c. au vin,** coq au vin; (*b*) cock, male, of various birds; **c. faisan,** cock pheasant; **c. de bruyère,** capercaillie; wood grouse; **c. de roche,** cock of the rock. **2.** weathercock, vane.

coq[2] *n.m. Nau:* **(maître-)c.,** (ship's) cook.

coq-à-l'âne [kɔkalɑn] *n.m.inv.* sudden change of subject; **faire des coq-à-l'âne,** to skip from one subject to another.

coque [kɔk] *n.f.* **1.** (*a*) shell (of egg); **œuf à la c.,** (soft-)boiled egg; (*b*) shell, husk (of nut, fruit); (*c*) *Ent:* (= COCON) cocoon; **se renfermer dans sa c.,** to retire into one's shell; (*d*) *Moll:* cockle. **2.** (*a*) *N.Arch:* hull, bottom (of ship); **double c.,** double bottom; (*b*) *Av:* hull (of aircraft, *esp.* flying boat); fuselage; (*c*) *Veh: Mch:* body, shell (of car). **3.** loop (of ribbon, hair, etc.).

coquelet [kɔklɛ] *n.m. Cu:* cockerel.

coquelicot [kɔkliko] *n.m. Bot:* red poppy.

coquelourde [kɔklurd] *n.f. Bot:* pasque flower, dane flower, pulsatilla.

coqueluche [kɔklyʃ] *n.f.* **1.** *Med:* whooping cough. **2.** *Fig:* **être la c. de toutes les femmes,** to be the ladies' darling, idol.

coquerico [kɔkriko] *Onomat. & n.m.* cock-a-doodle-doo.

coquet, -ette [kɔkɛ, -ɛt] **1.** *a.* (*a*) coquettish, flirtatious (woman, smile, etc.); **elle est coquette,** (i) she likes pretty clothes; (ii) she likes to look attractive; **il est trop c.,** he's too conscious of his appearance; (*b*) charming (town); smart, stylish (clothes, etc.); *F:* **fortune assez coquette,** tidy fortune. **2.** *n.f.* **coquette,** flirt, coquette.

coquetier, -ière [kɔktje, -jɛr] **1.** *n. A:* wholesale egg merchant; poulterer. **2.** *n.m.* (*a*) egg cup; (*b*) *F:* **gagner le c.,** to hit the jackpot. **3.** *n.f.* egg boiler.

coquettement [kɔkɛtmɑ̃] *adv.* smartly, stylishly (dressed, etc.).

coquetterie [kɔkɛtri] *n.f.* **1.** (*a*) coquetry, flirtatiousness; **faire des coquetteries à qn,** to make advances to s.o., to lead s.o. on; (*b*) affectation; (*c*) fastidiousness (in dress); **avoir de la c. pour sa tenue,** to be fastidious, particular, about one's appearance. **2.** smartness, stylishness (of dress, etc.). **3.** *F:* **avoir une c. dans l'œil,** to have a cast in one's eye.

coquillage [kɔkijaʒ] *n.m.* **1.** shellfish. **2.** (empty) shell (of shellfish).

coquille [kɔkij] *n.f.* **1.** shell (of snail, oyster, etc.); **il ne sort jamais de sa c.,** he never goes out, he always stays at home; **rentrer dans sa c.,** to retire into one's shell. **2.** (*a*) *Moll:* **c. Saint-Jacques,** (i) scallop; (ii) scallop shell; (*b*) (i) (scallop-shaped) dish; (ii) *Cu:* dish (of fish, meat) served up in scallop shells. **3.** (*a*) shell (of egg, nut, etc.); (*of boat*) **c. de noix,** cockleshell; **peinture c. d'œuf,** off white paint; (*b*) **c. de beurre,** flake, shell, of butter; **c. d'épée,** hand guard, shell, of sword. **4.** (*a*) *Const:* soffit, underpart (of spiral stair); (*b*) *Metall:* chill, chill mould. **5.** (*a*) *Sp:* box, shield; (*b*) spinal plaster. **6.** *Typ:* misprint, *F:* literal.

coquillettes [kɔkijɛt] *n.f.pl. Cu:* pasta shells.

coquin, -ine [kɔkɛ̃, -in] **1.** *n. A:* rogue, rascal; *f.* loose woman, hussy; (*in Provence*) **c. de sort!** hang it! damn it! **petit c.! petite coquine!** you little rascal! **2.** *a.* mischievous, rascally.

cor [kɔr] *n.m.* **1.** *Ven:* tine (of antler); **un cerf (de) dix cors,** a five pronger. **2.** (*a*) *Ven:* **cor (de chasse),** (hunting) horn; **sonner du c.,** to sound, wind, blow, the horn; **réclamer qch. à c. et à cri,** to clamour for sth.; (*b*) *Mus:* **c. d'harmonie,** French horn; **c. à piston,** valve horn; **c. anglais,** English horn, cor anglais. **3.** corn (on toe, foot).

corail, -aux [kɔraj, -o] *n.m.* coral; **récif de c.,** coral reef; **lèvres de c.,** coral lips.

corailleur, -euse [kɔrajœr, -øz] *n.* (*a*) coral fisher; (*b*) coral worker.

corallien, -ienne [kɔraljɛ̃, -jɛn] *a.* coralline; **récif c.,** coral reef.

Coran (le) [ləkɔrɑ̃] *n.m.* The Koran.

corbeau, -eaux [kɔrbo] *n.m.* **1.** *Orn:* crow; **(grand) c.,** raven; **c. freux,** rook; **noir comme un c.,** raven black. **2.** (*a*) *Arch:* corbel, bracket; (*b*) writer of poison-pen letters; (*d*) rapacious person, shark.

corbeille [kɔrbɛj] *n.f.* **1.** (open) basket (without bow handle); **c. à pain,** breadbasket; **c. à papier,** waste(paper) basket; **c. de mariage,** wedding presents. **2.** (*a*) *Arch:* corbel, bell, base (of Corinthian capital); (*b*) (round, oval) flower bed. **3.** (*a*) stockbroker's central enclosure (in Paris Bourse); (*b*) *Th:* dress circle. **4.** *Bot:* **c. d'or,** rock alyssum; **c. d'argent,** sweet alyssum.

corbillard [kɔrbijar] *n.m.* hearse.

cordage [kɔrdaʒ] *n.m.* **1.** stringing (of racket, etc.). **2.** (*a*) rope; **c. en chanvre,** hemp rope; (*b*) *pl.* cordage, ropes; *Nau:* gear, rigging; (*c*) *coll:* strings (of racket, etc.).

corde [kɔrd] *n.f.* **1.** (*a*) rope, cord; **c. à linge,** clothes line; **danseur de c.,** tightrope dancer; **marcher, danser, être, sur la c. raide,** to be (walking) on a tightrope; *Gym:* **c. lisse,** climbing rope; **c. à nœuds,** knotted climbing rope; **c. à sauter,** skipping rope; **sauter à la**

c., to skip; **trop tirer sur la c.,** to go too far; to push one's luck; *F:* **il pleut des cordes,** it's raining cats and dogs; (*b*) string; **c. de boyau,** catgut; **c. de violon,** violin string; **instrument à cordes,** stringed instrument; (*in orchestra*) **les cordes,** the strings; **double c.,** double stopping; **toucher la c. de qn,** to touch upon s.o.'s favourite subject; (*c*) halter, hangman's rope; gallows; *F:* **se mettre la c. au cou,** (i) to put a halter round one's own neck; (ii) *P:* to get married, tied up; **parler de c. dans la maison d'un pendu,** to make a tactless remark; (*d*) *Rac:* **la c.,** the rails; **tenir la c.,** (i) to hug the rails, to be on the inside (lane); (ii) to have the advantage; *Aut:* **prendre un virage à la c.,** to cut a corner close; *Box:* **les cordes,** the ropes; **être dans les cordes,** to be in an unfavourable position; (*e*) *Tex:* thread; **drap usé jusqu'à la c., qui laisse voir la c.,** threadbare cloth; **plaisanterie usée jusqu'à la c.,** old joke. **2.** *Mth:* chord (of segment, of arc). **3.** *Anat:* (*a*) **cordes vocales,** vocal cords; **ce n'est pas dans mes cordes,** it's not in my line; (*b*) **c. dorsale,** spinal cord; **c. cervicale,** cervical nerve.

cordé [kɔrde] *a. Bot: Conch:* cordate, heart-shaped.

cordeau, -eaux [kɔrdo] *n.m.* **1.** line, string; **tiré au c.,** laid out by the line; perfectly straight. **2.** *Min: Mil: Exp:* fuse, match; **c. Bickford,** Bickford fuse, safety fuse. **3.** *Fish:* paternoster (line).

cordée [kɔrde] *n.f.* **1.** *Com:* **c. de bois,** cord of wood. **2.** *Fish:* hook length. **3.** *Mount:* rope; roped party; **premier de c.,** leader, first on the rope.

cordelette [kɔrdəlɛt] *n.f.* small cord, string.

cordelier, -ière [kɔrdəlje, -jɛr] **1.** *n.* Franciscan friar, nun; *m.* cordelier. **2.** *n.f.* **cordelière,** (*a*) cord ((i) worn by Franciscan friar, (ii) of dressing gown, etc.); (*b*) *Arch:* cable moulding.

corder [kɔrde] *v.tr.* **1.** to twist (hemp, etc.) into rope. **2.** (*a*) to cord (trunk, bale, etc.); (*b*) to string (racquet, etc.). **3.** *Com:* to measure (wood) by the cord.

corderie [kɔrd(ə)ri] *n.f.* (*a*) rope manufacture; rope trade; (*b*) rope factory.

cordial, -iaux [kɔrdjal, -jo] *a.* **1.** *Pharm:* stimulating (medicine); *n.m.* cordial; tonic. **2.** cordial, hearty, warm (welcome, etc.).

cordialement [kɔrdjalmɑ̃] *adv.* cordially, heartily; warmly; *Corr:* **c. vôtre,** yours sincerely, yours ever.

cordialité [kɔrdjalite] *n.f.* cordiality, heartiness.

cordier [kɔrdje] *n.m.* (*a*) ropemaker; (*b*) tailpiece (of violin).

cordillère [kɔrdijɛr] *n.f. Geog:* cordillera.

cordite [kɔrdit] *n.f. Exp:* cordite.

cordon [kɔrdɔ̃] *n.m.* **1.** (*a*) strand, twist (of cable, rope); **corde à trois cordons,** three-stranded rope; (*b*) cord, string; **c. de soie,** silk cord; **c. de sonnette,** bellpull; *A:* **demander le c.,** to ask the *concierge* to open the door; **c. de soulier,** shoelace; (*c*) ribbon, decoration (of an order, etc.); **c.(-)bleu,** (i) of the order of the Holy Ghost; (ii) *F:* cordon bleu (cook); (*d*) *Obst:* **c. ombilical,** umbilical cord; *Anat:* **c. médullaire,** spinal cord; (*e*) *El: Elcs:* cord, flex. **2.** (*a*) row, line (of trees, etc.); cordon (of police, troops); **c. sanitaire,** sanitary cordon; (*b*) *Arch:* string course, cordon (in wall); (*c*) milled edge (of coin, etc.). **3.** *Geog:* **c. littoral,** offshore bar.

cordonner [kɔrdɔne] *v.tr.* to twist, twine, cord (silk, hemp, etc.).

cordonnerie [kɔrdɔnri] *n.f.* **1.** (*a*) boot and shoe manufacture, trade; shoemaking; (*b*) shoemending. **2.** (*a*) shoemaker's, cobbler's shop; (*b*) shoemender's shop.

cordonnet [kɔrdɔnɛ] *n.m.* braid, cord, twist.

cordonnier, -ière [kɔrdɔnje, -jɛr] *n.* shoemaker; shoemender, shoe repairer; cobbler.

Cordoue [kɔrdu] *Pr.n.f Geog:* Cordoba.

Corée [kɔre] *Pr.n.f. Geog:* Korea.

coréen, -enne [kɔreɛ̃, -ɛn] *a. & n. Geog:* Korean.

coreligionnaire [kɔrəliʒjɔnɛr] *n.* co-religionist.

Corfou [kɔrfu] *Pr.n.f. Geog:* Corfu.

coriace [kɔrjas] *a.* **1.** tough, leathery (meat, etc.). **2.** hard, tough, hard-headed (person).

coriandre [kɔrjɑ̃dr̥] *n.f. Bot:* coriander.

coricide [kɔrisid] *n.m. Pharm:* corn cure, corn remover.

corindon [kɔrɛ̃dɔ̃] *n.m. Miner:* corundum.

Corinthe [kɔrɛ̃t] *Pr.n.f. Geog:* Corinth; *Cu:* **raisins de C.,** currants.

corinthien, -ienne [kɔrɛ̃tjɛ̃, -jɛn] *a. & n.* Corinthian.

cormoran [kɔrmɔrɑ̃] *n.m. Orn:* cormorant.

cornac [kɔrnak] *n.m.* elephant keeper, mahout.

cornage [kɔrnaʒ] *n.m.* **1.** *Vet:* wheezing, roaring (of horse). **2.** *Med:* wheezing, wheeze.

cornaline [kɔrnalin] *n.f. Lap:* cornelian.

cornard [kɔrnar] *n.m. P:* cuckold.

corne [kɔrn] *n.f.* **1.** (*a*) horn; **bêtes à cornes,** horned animals; *F:* **montrer les cornes,** to show fight; **donner un coup de c. à qn,** (*of bull*) to horn s.o., to gore s.o.; (*of ram, goat*) to butt s.o.; **avoir, porter, des cornes,** to be a cuckold; **faire les cornes à qn,** to jeer, mock, at s.o.; **peigne de c.,** horn comb; **c. à chaussure,** shoehorn; (*b*) horn, feeler (of snail); horn, antenna (of insect). **2.** (*a*) (hunting, shepherd's) horn; *Nau:* **c. de brume,** foghorn; (*b*) *Nau:* gaff (of fore-and-aft sail); (*c*) tip (of crescent, etc.); horns, cusps (of the moon); **chapeau à cornes,** cocked hat; (*d*) dog-ear (of page); **faire une c. à une carte de visite,** to turn down the corner of a visiting card. **3.** horny matter; **cornes cutanées,** callosities. **4. c. d'abondance,** cornucopia; horn of plenty.

corné [kɔrne] *a.* corneous, horny.

cornée [kɔrne] *n.f. Anat:* cornea.

cornéen, -enne [kɔrneɛ̃, -ɛn] *a. Anat:* corneal.

corneille [kɔrnɛj] *n.f. Orn:* crow, rook; **c. noire,** carrion crow; **c. mantelée,** hooded crow.

cornélien, -ienne [kɔrneljɛ̃, -jɛn] *a. Fr.Lit.Hist:* Cornelian (tragedy).

cornemuse [kɔrnəmyz] *n.f. Mus:* bagpipe(s); **joueur de c.,** piper.

corner[1] [kɔrne] **1.** *v.tr.* (*a*) to blare out (sth.); *F:* **c. qch. aux oreilles de qn,** to shout sth. into s.o.'s ear; (*b*) to turn down the corner of (page, etc.); **page cornée,** dog-eared page. **2.** *v.i.* (*a*) to sound a horn; *Aut:* to hoot, honk; (*b*) *F:* to shout; **la radio nous cornait dans les oreilles,** the radio was blaring; (*c*) (*of ears*) to ring; **les oreilles lui cornent,** his ears (i) are ringing, (ii) are burning; (*d*) (*of goat, ram*) to butt.

corner[2] [kɔrnɛr] *n.m. Fb:* corner.

cornet [kɔrnɛ] *n.m.* **1.** (*a*) *A:* small horn; (*b*) *Mus:* (i) **c. à pistons,** cornet; (ii) cornet stop (of organ). **2.** (*a*) **c. acoustique,** ear trumpet; **c. à dés,** dice box; **c. de papier,** cornet; paper cone; **c. de glace,** ice-cream cone; (*b*) *P:* **se mettre quelque chose dans le c.,** to have something to eat; (*c*) *Anat:* scroll bone, turbinate bone.

cornette [kɔrnɛt] *n.f.* **1.** (nun's winged) coif, cornet. **2.** *Mil: A:* (i) pennant, standard (of cavalry); (ii) *n.m. A:* cornet, ensign (of cavalry).

cornettiste [kɔrnɛtist] *n.m. & f. Mus:* cornetist, cornet player.

corniaud [kɔrnjo] *n.m.* **1.** mongrel (dog). **2.** *F:* idiot, twit.

corniche [kɔrniʃ] *n.f.* **1.** (*a*) *Arch:* cornice. **2.** ledge (of rock); **(route en) c.,** corniche (road).

cornichon [kɔrniʃɔ̃] *n.m.* **1.** gherkin. **2.** *F:* idiot, nitwit.

cornier, -ière [kɔrnje, -jɛr] **1.** *a.* (at the) corner, angle; *Const:* **poteau c.,** corner, angle, post. **2.** *n.f.*

cornière; (*a*) *Const:* valley (joining roofs); (*b*) angle (iron, bar).

cornique [kɔrnik] (*a*) *a.* Cornish; (*b*) *n.m. Ling:* Cornish.

corniste [kɔrnist] *n.m. Mus:* horn player.

cornouaillais, -aise [kɔrnwɑjɛ, -ɛz] *Geog:* **1.** *a.* Cornish. **2.** (*a*) *a. & n.* (native, inhabitant) of Cornouaille; (*b*) *n.m.* Breton dialect (of Cornouaille).

Cornouaille [kɔrnwɑj] *Pr.n.f. Geog:* Cornouaille (in Brittany).

Cornouailles [kɔrnwɑj] *Pr.n.f. Geog:* Cornwall.

cornouille [kɔrnuj] *n.f. Bot:* cornel berry; dogberry.

cornouiller [kɔrnuje] *n.m.* **1.** *Bot:* corneltree. **2.** *Com:* dogwood.

cornu [kɔrny] *a.* horned (animal).

cornue [kɔrny] *n.f.* (*a*) *Ch: Gasm:* retort; **charbon de c.,** retort carbon; (*b*) *Metall:* steel converter.

corollaire [kɔrɔlɛr] *n.m.* (*a*) *Log: Mth:* corollary; (*b*) consequence.

corolle [kɔrɔl] *n.f. Bot:* corolla.

coron [kɔrɔ̃] *n.m.* (*a*) miner's cottage; (*b*) mining village.

coronaire [kɔrɔnɛr] *a. Anat:* coronary.

corporatif, -ive [kɔrpɔratif, -iv] *a.* corporate, corporative.

corporation [kɔrpɔrasjɔ̃] *n.f.* (*a*) corporate body; (*b*) *Com.Hist:* (trade)guild.

corporel, -elle [kɔrpɔrɛl] *a.* corporeal (being, etc.); corporal (punishment, etc.); bodily (needs, etc.); tangible (property).

corporellement [kɔrpɔrɛlmɑ̃] *adv.* corporeally, corporally, bodily.

corps [kɔr] *n.m.* body. **1. un c. robuste,** a strong, robust, frame; **passer sur le c. de, à, qn,** (i) to run over s.o.; (ii) *Fig:* to trample s.o. underfoot; **je me demande ce qu'il a dans le c.,** I wonder (i) what stuff he's made of, (ii) what makes him tick; *F:* **avoir le diable au c.,** (i) to be very excited; (ii) to be angry; (iii) to be tireless; **prendre du c.,** to put on weight; **prendre c.,** to take shape; **il n'a rien dans le c.,** (i) he hasn't eaten anything; (ii) he has no strength, no energy; **gardes du c.,** bodyguards, lifeguards; *F:* **c'est un drôle de c.,** he's a strange character; *Jur:* **séparation de c.,** (judicial) separation from bed and board; *adv.phr.* **saisir qn à bras-le-c.,** to seize s.o. round the waist; **lutter c. à c.,** to fight hand to hand; **affronter c. à c. la réalité,** to come to grips with reality; *n.m.* **un c.-à-c.,** a tussle; hand-to-hand fight(ing); *Box:* a clinch. **2.** corpse, body; *NAm:* cadaver; **la levée du c. aura lieu à onze heures,** the coffin will leave the house at eleven o'clock. **3.** (*a*) *Ch: Ph:* body, substance, material; **c. simple,** element; **c. composé,** compound (body); (*b*) *Atom.Ph:* **c. noir,** black body; (*c*) *Med: Ch:* **c. étranger,** foreign body; (*d*) *Astr:* **c. céleste,** celestial, heavenly, body. **4. étoffe qui a du c., qui n'a pas de c.,** strong, flimsy, material; **vin qui a du c.,** full-bodied wine. **5.** (*a*) main part (of sth.); body (of coach, hub, etc.); barrel (of cylinder, pump, etc.); shell (of boiler, etc.); **faire c. avec qch.,** to be an integral part of sth.; (*b*) body, bodice (of dress); (*c*) *Const:* **c. de bâtiment, de logis,** main (part of a) building; (*d*) *Nau:* **perdu c. et biens,** lost with all hands; (*e*) dolphin, moorings; **(bouée de) c. mort,** (anchor) buoy; (*f*) *Typ:* **force de c.,** size of type body; (*g*) *Jur:* **c. du délit,** *corpus delicti.* **6.** (*organized body of men*) (*a*) **le c. diplomatique,** the diplomatic corps; **le c. médical, enseignant,** the medical, teaching, profession; (*b*) *Mil:* **c. d'armée,** (army) corps; **c. de garde,** guardhouse, guardroom; **plaisanterie de c. de garde,** barrackroom joke. **7.** corpus, collection of writing; **c. de preuves,** body of evidence.

corpulence [kɔrpylɑ̃s] *n.f.* stoutness, corpulence.

corpulent [kɔrpylɑ̃] *a.* stout, corpulent.

corpus [kɔrpys] *n.m. Lit: Jur:* corpus.

corpusculaire [kɔrpyskylɛr] *a.* corpuscular.

corpuscule [kɔrpyskyl] *n.m.* corpuscle.

correct [kɔrɛkt] *a.* (*a*) correct (language, etc.); accurate (copy etc.); (*of pers.*) **(très) c.,** conventional; **les occupants étaient corrects,** the occupying forces behaved correctly; (*b*) *F:* adequate; acceptable.

correctement [kɔrɛktəmɑ̃] *adv.* correctly; properly; accurately.

correcteur, -trice [kɔrɛktœr, -tris] **1.** *n.* corrector; *Sch:* examiner; marker (of papers); *Typ:* proofreader. **2.** *n.m. Tchn:* corrector; **c. de tonalité,** tone control. **3.** *a.* correcting; corrective (lenses, etc.).

correctif, -ive [kɔrɛtif, -iv] **1.** *a.* corrective; *Med:* **gymnastique corrective,** remedial exercises. **2.** *n.m.* (*a*) qualifying statement, rider; (*b*) *Med:* corrective.

correction [kɔrɛksjɔ̃] *n.f.* **1.** (*a*) correction, correcting (of exercise, fault, etc.); proofreading; correction (of proofs); **je crois, sauf c., qu'il vient demain,** unless I'm mistaken, he's coming tomorrow; (*b*) *Av: Nau: etc:* **c. de compas,** adjustment of the compass. **2.** punishment, thrashing; **tu vas recevoir une bonne c.!** you'll get a good hiding! **3.** correctness (of dress, speech, etc.); propriety (of behaviour).

correctionnel, -elle [kɔrɛksjɔnɛl] *a. Jur:* **peine correctionnelle,** penalty of more than five days' (but less than five years') imprisonment; **tribunal de police correctionnelle,** *n.f. F:* **correctionnelle,** court of summary jurisdiction.

corrélatif, -ive [kɔrelatif, -iv] *a. & n.m.* correlative.

corrélation [kɔrelasjɔ̃] *n.f.* correlation; **être en c. étroite,** to be closely connected, related.

correspondance [kɔrɛspɔ̃dɑ̃s] *n.f.* **1.** correspondence, agreement (of tastes, between things, etc.); conformity (of ideas). **2.** connection (between trains); interchange service; *Av:* connecting flight; (*of train, boat, etc.*) **assurer la c. avec . . .,** to connect with . . .; **j'attend la c.,** I'm waiting for the connection. **3.** (*a*) (business, etc.) dealings; (*b*) correspondence (with s.o. by letter); **être en c., entretenir une c., avec qn,** to correspond, be in correspondence, with s.o.; **enseignement par c.,** correspondence course; *Journ:* **(petite) c.,** letters to the editor; personal column; (*c*) mail, post; **ouvrir la c.,** to open, go through, the mail.

correspondant, -ante [kɔrɛspɔ̃dɑ̃, -ɑ̃t] **1.** *a.* corresponding (**à,** to, with); corresponding (angle, etc.); *a. & n.* **(membre) c.,** corresponding member (of institute, etc.). **2.** *n.* (*a*) *Com: Journ:* correspondent; (*b*) *Sch:* friend acting *in loco parentis* (in boarding schools); (*c*) penfriend.

correspondre [kɔrɛspɔ̃dr̥] *v.i.* **1.** to tally, agree, square, fit (**à,** with); to correspond (**à,** to, with); **la théorie ne correspond pas aux faits,** the theory does not square with the facts; **ornements qui se correspondent,** ornaments that match. **2.** to communicate; **ces deux pièces (se) correspondent,** these two rooms communicate with one another. **3. c. avec qn,** to correspond with, write to, s.o.

corrida [kɔrida] *n.f.* **1.** corrida, bullfight. **2.** *F:* carry-on; hassle; **quelle c.!** all hell broke loose!

corridor [kɔridɔr] *n.m.* corridor, passage.

corrigé [kɔriʒe] *n.m. Sch:* fair copy, correct version (of exercise); key; *F:* crib.

corriger [kɔriʒe] *v.tr.* **(je corrigeai(s); n. corrigeons) 1.** to correct, mark (exercise, etc.); to proofread; to correct (proofs); to sub-edit (article); to rectify (mistake, etc.); *Nau:* to adjust (compass); **c. qn d'une mauvaise habitude,** to cure, break, s.o. of a bad habit. **2.** to give (s.o.) a thrashing, a hiding.

corrigible [kɔriʒibl̥] *a.* corrigible, rectifiable.

corroboration [kɔrɔbɔrasjɔ̃] *n.f.* corroboration.
corroborer [kɔrɔbɔre] *v.tr.* to corroborate.
corrodant [kɔrɔdɑ̃] *a. & n.m.* corrodent, corrosive.
corroder [kɔrɔde] *v.tr.* to corrode, erode, eat away, wear away (metal, stone, etc.).
corroierie [kɔrwari] *n.f. Leath:* (*a*) currying; (*b*) curriery.
corrompre [kɔrɔ̃pr̥] *v.tr.* **1.** (*a*) to corrupt (morals, etc.); to deprave, spoil (taste, etc.); to debase (language); (*b*) to bribe, corrupt (s.o.); (*c*) **c. la viande,** to taint meat. **2. se. c.** (*a*) to become corrupt(ed); (*b*) (*of meat, etc.*) to become tainted.
corrompu [kɔrɔ̃py] *a.* corrupt, depraved (person, morals); tainted, putrid (meat); corrupt (text).
corrosif, -ive [kɔrozif, -iv] *a. & n.m.* corrosive.
corrosion [kɔrozjɔ̃] *n.f.* (*a*) corrosion, corroding (of metal, etc.); (*b*) *Geol:* corrosion, erosion (of river banks, etc.).
corroyage [kɔrwajaʒ] *n.m.* currying (of leather); welding (of metal).
corroyer [kɔrwaje] *v.tr.* **(je corroie, n. corroyons; je corroierai)** to curry (leather); to trim, rough-plane (wood); to weld (metal).
corroyeur [kɔrwajœr] *n.m.* currier.
corrupteur, -trice [kɔryptœr, -tris] **1.** *n.* corrupter; suborner, briber (of witness, etc.). **2.** *a.* corrupt (ing) (influence, etc.).
corruptible [kɔryptibl̥] *a.* corruptible.
corruption [kɔrypsjɔ̃] *n.f.* corruption. **1.** bribery (of witness). **2.** decomposition (of food, etc.). **3.** (*a*) depravity (of morals, tastes); (*b*) corrupt practices.
corsage [kɔrsaʒ] *n.m.* (*a*) bodice, body (of dress); (*b*) blouse, *NAm:* waist.
corsaire [kɔrsɛr] *a. & n.m.* **1.** *Hist:* (*ship*) corsair, privateer. **2.** corsair, privateer(sman); *Cost:* **pantalon c.,** (knee) breeches.
corse[1] [kɔrs] **1.** *a. Geog:* Corsican. **2.** (*a*) *n.m. & f.* Corsican; (*b*) *n.m. Ling:* Corsican.
Corse[2] *Pr.n.f. Geog:* Corsica.
corsé [kɔrse] *a.* full-bodied (wine, etc.); spicy (sauce, etc.); **histoire corsée,** risqué story; **affaire corsée,** sensational business.
corselet [kɔrsəlɛ] *n.m. Ent: Mil: Cost:* corselet.
corser [kɔrse] *v.tr.* to give body, volume, flavour, to (sth.); to enliven (sth.); **c. du vin,** to strengthen wine (by adding spirits); **c. l'action d'un drame,** to intensify the action of a drama; **l'affaire se corse,** (i) the plot thickens; (ii) things are getting serious.
corset [kɔrsɛ] *n.m.* corset; **c. orthopédique, médical,** (surgical) corset.
corseter [kɔrsəte] *v.tr.* **(je corsète, n. corsetons; je corsèterai)** to corset; *Fig:* to restrict, constrain.
corsetier, -ière [kɔrsətje, -jɛr] *n.* corset maker.
corso [kɔrso] *n.m.* **c. (fleuri),** procession of floral floats; *pl. corsi.*
cortège [kɔrtɛʒ] *n.m.* **1.** train, retinue, suite (of sovereign, etc.); cortège. **2.** procession; (funeral) cortège; **c. (nuptial),** bridal procession.
cortex [kɔrtɛks] *n.m. Anat: Bot:* cortex.
cortisone [kɔrtizɔn] *n.f. Med:* cortisone.
corvée [kɔrve] *n.f.* **1.** *Hist:* forced, statute, labour; corvée. **2.** *Mil: etc:* (*a*) fatigue (duty); **c. de cuisine(s),** cookhouse fatigue; *U.S:* kitchen police; **être de c.,** to be on fatigue; (*b*) **(détachment de) c.,** fatigue party. **3.** chore, drudgery; **quelle c.!** what a drag!
corvette [kɔrvɛt] *n.f. Navy:* corvette.
coryphée [kɔrife] *n.m.* **1.** *Gr.Th:* coryphaeus, leader of the chorus. **2.** ballerina (in the *corps de ballet*). **3.** leader, chief (of a sect, party).
coryza [kɔriza] *n.m. Med:* coryza, cold in the head.
cosaque [kɔzak] *n.m.* cossack.
cosécante [kɔsekɑ̃t] *n.f. Mth:* cosecant.
cosignataire [kɔsiɲatɛr] *n.m.* co-signatory.
cosinus [kɔsinys] *n.m. Mth:* cosine.
cosmétique [kɔsmetik] **1.** *a.* cosmetic. **2.** *n.m.* hair oil, hair cream.
cosmétologue [kɔsmetɔlɔg] *n.* cosmetics expert; beautician.
cosmique [kɔsmik] *a.* cosmic (rays, etc.).
cosmographie [kɔsmɔgrafi] *n.f.* cosmography.
cosmologie [kɔsmɔlɔʒi] *n.f.* cosmology.
cosmonaute [kɔsmɔnot] *n.m. & f.* cosmonaut.
cosmopolite [kɔsmɔpɔlit] *a.* cosmopolitan.
cosmos [kɔsmɔs] *n.m.* (*a*) *Phil:* cosmos; (*b*) *Space:* outer space.
cossard [kɔsar] *P:* (*a*) *n.m.* lazybones; (*b*) *a.* lazy.
cosse [kɔs] *n.f.* **1.** pod, husk, hull (of peas, etc.). **2.** (*a*) *Nau:* thimble, eyelet (of rope); (*b*) *El:* cable terminal (of cable). **3.** *P:* **avoir la c.,** to feel lazy.
cossu [kɔsy] *a.* wealthy, well-to-do, well-off (person); opulent.
costal, -aux [kɔstal, -o] *a. Anat:* costal.
costard [kɔstar] *n.m. P:* (man's) suit.
costaud, *f.* **costaude** [kɔsto, -od] *a. & n. F:* strong, sturdy (person); solid, tough, strong.
costume [kɔstym] *n.m.* (*a*) costume, dress; **c. national,** national costume; **c. de cérémonie, d'apparat,** ceremonial, formal, dress; *F:* **c. d'Adam, d'Ève,** birthday suit; *Th:* **répéter en c.,** to have a dress rehearsal; (*b*) (man's) (three-piece) suit.
costumé [kɔstyme] *a.* **bal c.,** fancy-dress ball.
costumer [kɔstyme] *v.tr.* to dress (s.o.) (up); **se c. en Turc,** to dress up as a Turk.
costumier, -ière [kɔstymje, -jɛr] *n.* **1.** costum(i)er, dealer in (fancy) costumes. **2.** *Th:* wardrobe keeper; wardrobe mistress.
cotangente [kɔtɑ̃ʒɑ̃t] *n.f. Mth:* cotangent.
cotation [kɔtasjɔ̃] *n.f. Fin:* quotation, quoting.
cote [kɔt] *n.f.* **1.** (*a*) quota, share, proportion (of expense, taxes, etc.); **c. mal taillée,** rough and ready settlement; (*b*) *Adm:* assessment; **c. mobilière,** assessment on income. **2.** (*a*) (indication of) dimensions; **c. d'origine,** standard size; (*b*) *Surv:* altitude (of a point in figures); elevation (above sea level); height; **c. d'alerte,** (i) *Hyd.E:* critical level, flood level; (ii) danger point; *Mil:* **la c. 304,** hill 304. **3.** (*a*) *Com: Jur:* (classification) mark, letter, figure, number (of document, etc.); serial number; (library) shelf mark, pressmark; (*b*) *Nau:* character, classification (of ship). **4.** (*a*) *St.Exch: Com:* quotation; **c. des prix,** (i) sharelist; (ii) *Com:* list of prices; **c. d'une voiture d'occasion,** quoted value of a secondhand car; **actions inscrites à la c.,** listed shares; **marché hors c.,** unofficial, *NAm:* over-the-counter, market; **c. d'amour,** favouritism; *F:* **avoir la c.,** to be popular (**auprès de,** with, by); (*b*) *Turf:* **c. d'un cheval,** odds on (or against) a horse; (*c*) *Sch:* mark; (*d*) **c. morale d'un film,** film rating.
côte [kot] *n.f.* **1.** rib; (*a*) *Anat:* **côtes flottantes,** floating ribs; *F:* **se tenir les côtes,** to split one's sides laughing; **on lui compterait les côtes,** he is nothing but skin and bone; *F:* **avoir les côtes en long,** to be lazy; *Cu:* **c. de bœuf,** rib of beef; **c. de porc,** pork chop; **côtes découvertes,** spare ribs (of pork); **c. première,** loin chop; **c. à c.,** side by side; (*b*) rib (of melon); midrib (of leaf); **tissu à côtes,** ribbed, corded, material. **2.** (*a*) slope (of hill); hillside; *Civ.E:* gradient; **vitesse en c.,** speed uphill; *Aut:* **démarrage en c.,** hill start; (*b*) hill, rise; **à mi-côte,** halfway up, down, the hill. **3.** coast, coastline; **les côtes de (la) France,** the coast of France; **la c. (d'Azur),** the (French) Riviera; *Nau:* **faire c.,** to beach, run aground; **jeter à la c.,** to drive ashore, to strand; *F:* **être à la c.,** to be on one's beam ends, hard up.
côté [kote] *n.m.* **1.** side (of human body); **couché sur le c.,** lying on one's side; **assis à mes côtés,** sitting by

my side. **2.** (*a*) side (of mountain, road, table, etc.); **passer de l'autre c. de la rue,** to cross the street; **demeurer de l'autre c. de la rue,** to live on the other side of the street; **appartement c. jardin,** flat overlooking the garden; *Ten:* **service ou c.?** side or service? **la tour penche d'un c.,** the tower leans to one side, leans sideways; *Nau:* **présenter le c. à qch.,** to be broadside on to sth.; **navire sur le c.,** ship on her beam ends; (*b*) **le c. scientifique,** the scientific aspect; **le bon, le mauvais, c. d'une affaire,** the good, bad, side of a matter; **il a un c. méchant,** there's a mean streak in him; **le vent vient du bon c.,** the wind is in the right quarter; **prendre les choses par le bon c.,** to look on the bright side of things; **être né du c. gauche,** to be illegitimate; **d'un c. à l'autre,** from side to side; **d'un c. . . ., d'un autre c. . . .,** on the one hand . . ., on the other hand . . .; **de mon c.,** for my part; *F:* **de ce c. il n'y a rien a craindre,** there's nothing to worry about on that score; (*c*) side, direction, way; **de tous (les) côtés,** on all sides; from all quarters; **de c. et d'autre,** here and there; **se diriger du c. de Paris,** to go towards, in the direction of, Paris; **il habitait du c. de la rivière,** he lived near the river; **se ranger du c. des plus forts,** to take sides with the stronger, the strongest; **les parents du c. du père,** relations on the father's side; **venez de ce c.,** come (i) this way, (ii) on this side; **de ce c.-ci, -là,** on this side, on that side; **ils s'en allèrent chacun de son c.,** they went their own separate ways; **de quel c.?** in which direction? which way? (*d*) *F:* **c. vitesse, cette voiture est remarquable,** as far as speed is concerned, speedwise, this car is remarkable. **3.** *adv.phr.* (*a*) **de c.,** sideways; on one side; **faire un saut de c.,** to leap aside, to jump sideways; **regard de c.,** sidelong glance; **mettre qch. de c.,** to put sth. aside, on one side; **mettre de l'argent de c.,** to put money by, aside; to save money; **laisser qn de c.,** to neglect s.o.; (*b*) **à c.,** to one side, near; **la maison est tout à c.,** the house is quite near; **il habite à c.,** he lives next door; **tirer à c.,** to miss the mark; **le salon est à c. de la cuisine,** the drawing room is next to the kitchen; **il se tenait à c. de moi,** he stood at, by, my side; he stood beside me; **à c. l'un de l'autre,** side by side; **vous êtes à c. de la question,** you're off the point; **passer à c. d'une difficulté,** to avoid a difficulty; **mes ennuis sont petits à c. des vôtres,** my troubles are small compared with yours; **il n'est rien à c. de vous,** he's nothing compared to you.

coteau, -eaux [kɔto] *n.m.* (*a*) slope, hillside; (*b*) hillock; small hill.

côtelé [kotle] *a. Tex:* ribbed; corded (material); **velours c.,** corduroy.

côtelette [kotlɛt, kɔ-] *n.f. Cu:* cutlet; **c. d'agneau, de porc,** lamb, pork, chop.

coter [kɔte] *v.tr.* **1.** *Mec.E: Surv: etc:* to mark the dimensions on (drawing, etc.); to put references on (maps, etc.); *Surv:* **point coté,** (i) reference point, landmark, (ii) spot height (on map, etc.). **2.** (*a*) *Com: Jur:* to classify, number, letter (documents, etc.); (*b*) *Nau:* to class (ship). **3.** (*a*) *Com: St.Exch:* to quote (price, etc.); *F:* **ma voiture est si vieille, elle n'est même pas cotée,** my car is so old it's not even listed (in the car buyer's guide); (*b*) **très coté,** (i) *Turf:* well backed; (ii) highly considered. **4.** *Sch:* to mark (exercise, etc.).

coterie [kɔtri] *n.f. Lit: Pol:* set, clique, coterie.

cothurne [kɔtyrn] *n.m.* (*a*) *Ant:* cothurnus, buskin; (*b*) *Lit:* tragic genre; tragedy.

côtier, -ière [kotje, -jɛr] **1.** *a.* (*a*) coast(ing) (pilot, etc.); coastal (defence, etc.); coastwise (trade, etc.); inshore (fishery); **navigation côtière,** coasting; (*b*) **fleuve c.,** short coastal river. **2.** *n.m.* coaster, coasting vessel.

cotillon [kɔtijɔ̃] *n.m.* **1.** *A:* petticoat; *F:* **courir le c.,** to flirt with women. **2.** *Danc:* cotill(i)on; **accessoires de c., cotillons,** party novelties.

cotisant, -ante [kɔtizɑ̃, -ɑ̃t] *a. & n.* paying member; subscriber (**de,** to).

cotisation [kɔtizasjɔ̃] *n.f.* (*a*) quota, share; contribution (to common fund); **c. de Sécurité Sociale** = National Insurance contribution; (*b*) subscription (to club, etc.).

cotiser [kɔtize] *v.i.* **1.** (*a*) to contribute (**pour,** towards); (*b*) to subscribe, pay one's subscription. **2. se c.,** to club together (in order to raise sum).

côtoiement [kotwamɑ̃] *n.m.* coming into contact with, encounter(s) with (society, a situation, etc.).

coton [kɔtɔ̃] **1.** *n.m.* cotton; (*a*) **fil de c.,** sewing cotton; **c. retors,** cotton thread; **c. à broder,** embroidery thread; **c. à repriser,** darning thread, cotton; (*b*) *P:* trouble, difficulty; *F:* **filer un mauvais c.,** to be in a bad way (in health, business). **2.** *n.m.* (*a*) **c. (hydrophile),** cotton wool; *F:* **j'ai les jambes en c.,** my legs feel like cotton wool, like jelly; **il a du c. dans les oreilles,** (i) he's deaf; (ii) he doesn't want to hear; **élever un enfant dans du c.,** to (molly)coddle a child; (*b*) down (on plants); (*c*) **c. de verre,** glass wool. **3.** *a. F:* difficult; **ça, c'est plutôt c.!** that's rather difficult.

cotonnade [kɔtɔnad] *n.f.* cotton fabric.

cotonner [kɔtɔne] **1.** *v.tr.* to cover (sth.) with cotton, with down, with fibres. **2.** *v.i. & pr.* (*a*) (*of material*) to become fluffy; (*b*) **fruit qui se cotonne,** fruit that becomes woolly, sleepy.

cotonnerie [kɔtɔnri] *n.f.* (*a*) cotton plantation; (*b*) cotton mill.

cotonneux, -euse [kɔtɔnø, -øz] *a.* cottony; downy (leaf, fruit, etc.); woolly, fleecy (clouds); muffled (sound); thick (fog); **style c.,** woolly style; **jambes cotonneuses,** shaky legs.

cotonnier, -ière [kɔtɔnje, -jɛr] **1.** *a.* cotton (industry, products, etc.). **2.** *n.* cotton worker, spinner. **3.** *n.m.* cotton plant.

coton-poudre [kɔtɔ̃pudr̥] *n.m. Exp:* guncotton; *U.S:* nitrocotton; *pl. cotons-poudre.*

côtoyer [kotwaje] *v.tr.* (**je côtoie, n. côtoyons; je côtoierai**) **1.** to coast along, keep close to, hug (shore, etc.); to skirt (forest, etc.). **2.** to border on (river, etc.); **cela côtoie le ridicule,** it's verging on the ridiculous.

cotre [kɔtr̥] *n.m. Nau:* cutter.

cottage [kɔtaʒ] *n.m.* (country) cottage.

cotte [kɔt] *n.f. Cost:* (*a*) *Mil:* **c. d'armes,** (i) tunic (worn over armour); (ii) coat of banded mail; **c. de mailles,** coat of mail; (*b*) *A:* short skirt, petticoat; (*c*) (workmen's) overalls; dungarees.

cotutelle [kɔtytɛl] *n.f. Jur:* joint guardianship.

cotuteur, -trice [kɔtytœr, -tris] *n. Jur:* joint guardian.

cotylédon [kɔtiledɔ̃] *n.m.* **1.** *Anat: Bot:* cotyledon.

cou [ku] *n.m.* neck (of animal, bottle, etc.); **la peau du c.,** the scruff of the neck; **couper le c. à qn,** to behead s.o.; **tendre le c.,** to offer oneself as a ready victim; **se jeter au c. de qn,** to throw one's arms round s.o.'s neck; *F:* **endetté jusqu'au c.,** up to the eyes in debt; **prendre ses jambes à son c.,** to take to one's heels.

couac [kwak] *n.m. Mus:* squeak, goosenote (on clarinet, etc.); false note (of voice).

couard [kwar] **1.** *a. Lit: Dial:* cowardly. **2.** *n.m.* coward.

couardise [kwardiz] *n.f. O:* cowardice.

couchage [kuʃaʒ] *n.m.* (*a*) lying in bed; (*b*) **(matériel de) c.,** bedding, bedclothes; **sac de c.,** sleeping bag; (*d*) *P:* sexual intercourse.

couchant [kuʃɑ̃] **1.** *a.* (*a*) **soleil c.,** setting sun, sunset; (*b*) *Ven:* **chien c.,** setter; **faire le chien c. auprès de qn,** to fawn on s.o. **2.** *n.m.* (*a*) setting sun; (*b*) sunset; (*c*) west.

couche [kuʃ] *n.f.* **1.** (*a*) *Lit:* bed; (*b*) *usu. pl.* confinement, labour; **femme en couches,** woman in labour; **couches laborieuses, pénibles,** difficult (child)birth; **fausse c.,** miscarriage; (*c*) **c. (de bébé),** (baby's) nappy, *NAm:* diaper; **c.-culotte,** shaped nappy. **2.** (*a*) *Geol:* bed, layer, stratum; **c. de houille,** coal bed, seam; (*b*) *Hort:* **c. de fumier,** hotbed; **champignons de c.,** cultivated mushrooms; (*c*) **couches sociales,** social strata, levels of society; (*d*) coat, coating (of paint, etc.); **c. d'apprêt,** primer; **c. de fond,** undercoat; **c. de glace,** sheet of ice; (*e*) layer (of butter, dirt, etc.); (*f*) *P:* **il a, il en tient, une c.!** he's really thick! what an idiot! **3.** *Mec.E:* **arbre de c.,** engine shaft, main shaft, power shaft.

couché [kuʃe] *a.* (*a*) lying (down); in bed; (*b*) **écriture couchée,** slanting, sloping, writing; (*c*) **papier c.,** art paper; coated paper.

coucher¹ [kuʃe] **I.** *v.* **1.** *v.tr.* (*a*) to put (child, etc.) to bed; (*b*) **je ne peux pas vous c.,** I can't put you up; (*c*) to lay (s.o., sth.) down; **la pluie a couché les blés,** the rain has flattened the wheat; **c. un navire,** to throw a vessel on her beam ends; **c. un fusil en joue,** to aim a gun; **c. qn en joue,** to take aim at s.o.; (*d*) **c. qch. par écrit,** to set, put, sth. down in writing; **c. qn sur son testament,** to mention s.o. in one's will. **2.** *v.i.* (*a*) **c. à l'hôtel, chez des amis,** to sleep, spend the night, at the hotel, with friends; (*b*) *F:* **c. avec qn,** to sleep with s.o.; *F:* **elle ne couche pas,** she doesn't sleep around; (*c*) (*to dog*) **(allez) c.! couche!** (lie) down! (*d*) *F:* **avoir un nom à c. dehors,** to have an impossible name. **II. se coucher** (*a*) **(aller) se c.,** to go to bed; **il est l'heure d'aller se c.,** it's bedtime; **je ne veux pas vous faire c. tard,** I don't want to keep you up; *F:* **se c. comme les poules,** to go to bed early; *F:* **va te c.!** buzz off, clear off! leave me alone! *Prov:* **comme on fait son lit on se couche,** as we make our bed, so must we lie; (*b*) to lie down; **se c. à plat ventre,** to lie on one's stomach; (*c*) *Nau:* (*of ship*) **se c. sur le flanc,** to heel over; (*d*) (*of sun, stars*) to set, go down.

coucher² *n.m.* **1.** (*a*) **l'heure du c.,** bedtime; (*b*) accommodation; **le c. et la nourriture,** board and lodging. **2. au c. du soleil,** at sunset, sundown.

coucherie [kuʃri] *n.f. P:* sexual intercourse.

couchette [kuʃɛt] *n.f.* **1.** (child's) cot, bed. **2.** *Nau:* berth, bunk; *Rail:* couchette.

coucheur [kuʃœr] *n.m. F:* **c'est un mauvais c.,** he's an awkward customer.

couci-couça [kusikusa] *adv. F:* so so.

coucou [kuku] *n.m.* **1.** (*a*) *Orn:* cuckoo; **(pendule à) c.,** cuckoo clock; (*b*) *int.* **c.! (me voilà!)** peep-bo! peek-a-boo! **2.** *Bot:* cowslip. **3.** *Av:* *P:* old plane, old crate, ancient kite.

coude [kud] *n.m.* **1.** elbow; **coudes au corps,** elbows in; **c. à c.,** side by side, close together, shoulder to shoulder; **c. à c. fraternel,** friendly jostling; **coup de c.,** (i) poke with the elbow; (ii) nudge; **donner un coup de c. à qn,** to nudge, jog, s.o.; **se serrer les coudes,** to help one another, to stick together; **jouer des coudes,** (i) to elbow one's way (through a crowd); (ii) to manœuvre (to gain one's own ends); *F:* **lever le c.,** to lift, bend, one's elbow, to booze; **huile de c.,** elbow grease; *P:* **se fourrer le doigt dans l'œil jusqu'au c.,** to be completely wrong. **2.** (*a*) bend (in road, etc.); (*b*) *Mec.E:* bend, elbow (of bar, pipe, etc.); crank (of shaft); *Mch:* *I.C.E:* **arbre à deux coudes,** two-throw crankshaft.

coudé [kude] *a.* bent, kneed, cranked; at an angle.

coudée [kude] *n.f.* **1.** *A.Meas:* cubit. **2.** *pl.* **avoir ses coudées franches,** (i) to have elbow room; (ii) to have a free hand, to have free scope.

cou-de-pied [kudpje] *n.m.* instep; *pl. cous-de-pied.*

couder [kude] *v.tr.* to bend (pipe, etc.) at an angle; to crank (shaft).

coudoiement [kudwamɑ̃] *n.m.* contact, association.

coudoyer [kudwaje] *v.tr.* **(je coudoie, n. coudoyons; je coudoierai) 1.** (*a*) *A:* to elbow (s.o.); (*b*) to brush against (s.o.). **2.** to be in contact with (s.o.); to rub shoulders with (s.o.).

coudre [kudr̥] *v.tr.* (*pr.p.* **cousant;** *p.p.* **cousu;** *pr.ind.* **je couds, il coud, n. cousons, ils cousent;** *impf.* **je cousais;** *p.h.* **je cousis;** *fu.* **je coudrai**) to sew, stitch; **c. un bouton à une robe,** to sew, stitch, a button on a dress; **c. une jupe,** to make, sew up, a skirt; **machine à c.,** sewing machine; **c. une plaie,** to sew up a wound.

coudrier [kudrije] *n.m.* hazel (tree).

couenne [kwan] *n.f.* **1.** (*a*) rind (of bacon); (*b*) (thick) skin; *P:* **quelle c.!** what a twerp, an idiot! **2.** *Med:* (diphtheric) membrane.

couette¹ [kwɛt] *n.f.* **1.** (*a*) *Dial:* feather bed; (*b*) duvet; continental quilt. **2.** *Mec.E:* bearing. **3.** *pl.* *N.Arch:* **couettes courantes,** bilge ways.

couette² *n.f. F:* lock (of hair); **elle était coiffée avec des couettes,** she wore her hair in bunches.

couffe [kuf] *n.f.,* **couffin** [kufɛ̃] *n.m.* frail, basket; moses basket.

coug(o)uar [kug(w)ar] *n.m. Z:* cougar, puma.

couic [kwik] *int.* eek! cheep! squeak! *P:* **faire c.,** to give one's last gasp, to die.

couille [kuj] *n.f. V:* testicle, ball; **une c. molle,** a drip; **avoir des couilles au cul,** to have guts.

couillon [kujɔ̃] *a. & n.m. P:* idiot, fathead, cretin.

couillonner [kujɔne] *v.tr. P:* to swindle (s.o.); **je me suis fait c.,** I've been had, done.

couinement [kwinmɑ̃] *n.m.* sqeak, squeal (of animal).

couiner [kwine] *v.i.* (*a*) (*of animal*) to squeak; (*of rabbit*) to scream; (*b*) (*of child*) to whine.

coulage [kulaʒ] *n.m.* **1.** pouring, running; casting; pouring (of molten metal, glass, soap, etc.). **2.** *F:* waste, wastage.

coulant [kulɑ̃] **1.** *a.* running, flowing (liquid); runny (jam, etc.); smooth (wine); **nœud c.,** slip knot, running knot; noose; **style c.,** easy, flowing, style; *F:* **personne coulante,** easy-going person. **2.** *n.m.* (*a*) sliding ring, sliding runner; **c. d'une ceinture,** loop of a belt; (*b*) *Hort:* runner (of a plant).

coule¹ [kul] *n.f. P:* **être à la c.,** to know the tricks of the trade; to know the ropes.

coule² *n.f.* (monk's) cowl.

coulé [kule] **1.** *a.* smooth (movement). **2.** *n.m.* (*a*) *Mus:* (i) slide, coulé; (ii) slur; (*b*) *Danc:* glide.

coulée [kule] *n.f.* **1.** running, flow(ing) (of liquid); **c. de lave,** lava flow. **2.** *Metall:* casting, tapping (of molten metal); **trou de c.,** tap(ping) hole, draw hole; **d'une seule c.,** in one movement, at one go. **3.** *Swim:* glide; push-off.

coulemelle [kulmɛl] *n.f. Fung:* parasol mushroom.

couler [kule] *v.* **1.** *v.tr.* (*a*) to run, draw, pour (liquid); (*b*) to cast, pour, run (molten metal); to pour (wax); **c. une pièce, une statue,** to cast a piece, a statue; (*c*) *Mch:* *I.C.E:* **c. (une bielle, etc.),** to burn out (a connecting rod, etc.); (*d*) *Const:* *etc:* to grout (masonry); to pour (concrete); (*e*) to sink (a ship); **c. qn,** to discredit s.o.; to ruin s.o.; (*f*) to slip, glide; **c. un mot à l'oreille de qn,** to drop, whisper, a word in s.o.'s ear; *Mus:* **c. un passage,** to slur a passage; (*g*) to pass, spend (time smoothly, pleasantly); **c. une vie heureuse,** to lead, spend, a happy life; *F:* **se la c. douce,** to take life easily, to have a good time. **2.** *v.i.* (*a*) (*of liquids, cheese, river, etc.*) to flow, run; **faire c. l'eau,** to turn the water on; **faire c. un bain,** to run a bath; **la sueur coule sur son front,** sweat is trickling, running, down his forehead; **ça coule de source,** (i) it's obvious; (ii) it follows naturally; **les années coulent,** the years slip by; (*b*) (*of barrel, fountain pen,* *etc.*) to leak; (*of nose*) to run; (*of verse*) to flow; (*c*) (*of ship*) to sink; (*d*) to slide, slip; **une tuile coula du toit,** a tile fell off the roof. **3. se c.,** to glide, slip; **se c. entre les draps,** to slip into bed; **se c. dans la foule,** to slip, disappear, into the crowd; **se c. le long du mur,** to hug the wall.

couleur [kulœr] *n.f.* **1.** (*a*) colour, *NAm:* color; tint; **couleurs fondamentales,** primary colours; **couleurs primitives, spectrales,** colours of the spectrum; *Ethn:* **gens de c.,** coloured people, coloureds; *Laund:* **la c., les couleurs,** coloureds; **photographie, télévision, en couleurs,** colour photography, television; **la c. d'un journal,** the (political) colour, tone, of a paper; **c. locale,** local colour; **suivant la c. du temps,** according to the state of things; **sous c. de me rendre service,** under the pretext of helping me, of doing me a service; *F:* **il en a vu de toutes les couleurs,** he's been through the mill, through a lot; *Cu:* (*of joint*) **prendre c.,** to brown; (*b*) colour, complexion; **perdre, reprendre, ses couleurs,** to become pale, to lose one's colour; to get back one's colour; **sans c.,** colourless, pale; (*c*) *Mil: etc: pl.* colours, flag; **envoyer, hisser, les couleurs,** to hoist the colours, the flag; (*d*) *Sp: Turf:* colours (of club, stable); (*e*) *a.inv.* **c. paille, c. chair,** straw coloured, flesh coloured. **2.** colour, paint; **c. à l'eau, à l'huile,** water colour; oil paint; **boîte de couleurs,** box of paints; *Com:* **marchand de couleurs** = ironmonger. **3.** *Cards:* suit; **jouer dans la c.,** to follow suit; **annoncer la c.,** (i) to call (trumps); (ii) *F:* to have one's say; to state one's case.

couleuvre [kulœvr̥] *n.f.* **c. (à collier),** grass snake; **c. lisse,** European smooth snake; **paresseux comme une c.,** bone-lazy; bone-idle; **avaler des couleuvres,** (i) to swallow an insult; (ii) to believe, swallow, anything.

coulis¹ [kuli] *a.m.* **vent c.,** draught (through crevice, etc.).

coulis² *n.m.* **1.** *Const:* grout(ing). **2.** *Metall:* molten metal. **3.** *Cu:* (meat, vegetable) broth, *occ.* purée; **c. de tomates,** tomato sauce.

coulissant [kulisɑ̃] *a.* sliding (door, panel, etc.).

coulisse [kulis] *n.f.* **1.** (*a*) groove, slot, runner; **fenêtre, porte, à c.,** sliding window, door; **regard en c.,** sidelong glance; (*b*) sliding door, panel; slide; **trombone à c.,** slide trombone. **2.** *Needlew:* hem (through which to pass tape). **3.** *Th:* (*a*) runner, groove (of scenery flat); (*b*) **les coulisses,** the wings, the slips; backstage; **les coulisses de la politique,** behind the scenes in politics; the corridors of power; **rester dans les coulisses,** to pull the strings.

coulissé [kulise] *a.* grooved, slotted.

coulisseau, -eaux [kuliso] *n.m.* (*a*) slide (of piece of machinery); (*b*) sliding block; (*c*) runner (of drawer, etc.).

coulisser [kulise] *Mec.E: etc:* **1.** *v.i.* to slide. **2.** *v.tr.* (*a*) to provide (sth.) with slides, runners; (*b*) *Needlew:* to run up (hem).

couloir [kulwar] *n.m.* **1.** (*a*) corridor, passage; *Pol:* lobby; **propos de couloir,** confidential information; (*b*) *Sp:* (*athletics*) lane; *Ten:* tramlines. **2.** *Ind: etc:* shoot, chute; *Cin:* **c. du film,** film channel, track. **3.** *Geog:* channel, gully; gorge. **4.** (*a*) *Av:* **c. aérien,** air corridor; (*b*) *Hist:* **le c. de Dantzig,** the Polish Corridor.

coup [ku] *n.m.* **1.** (*a*) knock, blow; rap, tap (on door); *Th:* **les trois coups,** the three knocks (given just before the curtain rises); **donner de grands coups dans la porte,** to pound, bang, at the door; **se donner un c. contre qch.,** to knock against sth.; **c. de bec,** peck; **c. de bâton,** blow (with a stick); **c. sur les doigts,** rap over the knuckles; **il a reçu un c. de poing, de pied,** he was punched, kicked; **c. de couteau, de poignard,** stab (with knife, dagger); **coup d'épée,** thrust, lunge; **c. de hache,** blow, stroke (with an axe); **ça m'a donné un c.!** it gave me such a shock! *F:* **tenir le c.,** to hold out; to stick it; **il tiendra le c.,** he's going to make it, he'll make it; **rendre c. pour c.,** to return blow for blow; to hit back, strike back; *F:* **faire les quatre cents coups,** to lead a reckless life; **c. bas,** hit below the belt; *Jur:* **coups et blessures,** assault and battery; **corps couvert de coups,** body covered with bruises; **enfoncer un clou à coups de marteau,** to hammer a nail in; *F:* **faire une traduction à coups de dictionnaire,** to do a translation with a dictionary; (*b*) **c. de feu,** shot; **c. de fusil,** (i) (gun)shot; (ii) report (of a gun); **c. au but,** direct hit; **c. manqué,** miss; **fusil à deux coups,** double-barrelled gun; **il fut tué d'un c. de fusil,** he was shot (dead); **c. de grisou,** firedamp explosion; (*c*) **c. de vent,** (i) gust, blast, of wind; (ii) sudden gale; squall; **entrer dans une pièce en c. de vent,** to burst into a room; **c. de tabac,** (i) squall; (ii) dangerous situation; trouble; **c. de froid,** (i) *Meteor:* cold snap; (ii) *Med:* chill, cold. **2.** (*normal action of sth.*) (*a*) **c. d'aile,** stroke, flap, of the wing; **c. de dents,** bite; **c. de queue,** flick of the tail; *F:* **c. de gueule,** shout; **boire qch. à petits coups,** to sip sth.; *F:* **un c. de rouge,** a glass of red wine; **allons boire un c.,** let's go and have a drink; **c. de crayon,** pencil stroke; **saluer qn d'un c. de chapeau,** to raise one's hat to s.o.; **c. de cloche,** stroke of the bell; **l'horloge sonna trois coups,** the clock struck three; **sur le c. de midi,** on the stroke of twelve; **c. de filet,** (i) cast; (ii) haul (of a net), draught (of fishes); (*b*) *Games:* (i) stroke, hit, drive; *Ten:* **c. droit,** forehand (stroke); (ii) *Golf:* stroke; (iii) *Fb:* kick; **c. franc,** free kick; **c. d'envoi,** kickoff; **c. de tête,** header; (iv) *Box:* blow, punch; **c. bas,** one below the belt; (v) *Cards:* **finir le c.,** to finish the hand; (vi) *Chess: etc:* move; (*c*) **c. de chance,** *F:* **c. de veine,** stroke of luck; **c. d'État,** coup (d'état); **c. d'éclat,** distinguished action, glorious deed; (*d*) (*sound*) **c. de tonnerre,** clap, peal, of thunder; **c. de sifflet,** (i) blast of a whistle; (ii) whistle; **c. de sonnette,** ring of the bell; **c. de téléphone,** telephone call. **3.** influence, power; **agir sous le c. de la peur,** to act through fear, out of fear; **j'ai répondu sous le c. de la colère,** I answered in a fit of anger; **elle est sous le c. d'une forte émotion,** she's in a very emotional state; **tomber sous le c. de la loi,** to come within the provisions of the law; **être sous le c. d'une condamnation,** to have a current conviction. **4.** (*a*) attempt; **c. d'essai,** trial shot, stroke; **à tous les coups l'on gagne,** you win every time; **marquer le c.,** to mark, celebrate, the occasion; **accuser le c.,** to mark the occasion; *F:* **ça vaut le c.,** it's worth while, it's worth trying; **ça ne vaut pas le c.,** it isn't worth it; **réussir un bon c.,** to make a hit; **c. de tête,** impulsive act; **faire qch. sur un c. de tête,** to act impulsively; *Iron:* **il a fait là un beau c.!** he made a fine mess of it! **il prépare un mauvais c.,** he's up to no good; *F:* **ça, c'est un sale c.!** what a dirty trick! **c'est encore un c. de ton ami,** it's another of your friend's tricks; *F:* **il est dans le c.,** (i) he knows what's going on; (ii) he's in on it; (*b*) **avoir le c. de main pour faire qch.,** to have the knack of doing sth.; (*c*) *adv.phr.* **d'un seul c.,** at one go; **faire qch. du premier c.,** to do sth. at the first attempt, shot; **j'ai deviné du premier c.,** I guessed straight off; **du même c., du c.,** (i) at the same time; (ii) as a result; and so; **il fut tué sur le c.,** he was killed outright; **sur le c., je n'ai pas compris,** at the time, I didn't understand; **pour le c.,** (i) as a result; (ii) this time; **après c.,** after the event; **tout à c., tout d'un c.,** suddenly, all of a sudden; **boire trois verres c. sur c.,** to drink three glasses one after the other; **encore un c.,** once again; once more; **à c. sûr,** definitely.

coupable [kupabl̥] **1.** *a.* (*a*) guilty (person); **c. de vol,** guilty of theft; **s'avouer c.,** to admit one's responsibility (for sth.); **elle se sent c.,** she feels guilty (about it); *Jur:* **plaider c.,** to plead guilty; (*b*) **action c.,** culpable act; **faiblesse c.,** reprehensible weakness. **2.** *n.m. & f.* culprit; guilty party.

coupage [kupaʒ] *n.m.* (*a*) blending, mixing (of wines); (*b*) diluting (of wine, etc., with water).

coupant [kupɑ̃] *a.* cutting, sharp; **outils coupants,** edge tools; **ton c.,** sharp tone.

coup-de-poing [kudpwɛ̃] *n.m.* (*a*) **c.-de-p. (américain),** knuckle duster; (*b*) *Prehist:* chellean pick, hand axe, *coup-de-poing.*

coupe[1] [kup] *n.f.* (*a*) cup; (*contents*) cup(ful); **c. à champagne,** champagne glass; **c. à fruits,** fruit dish, bowl; **boire la c. jusqu'à la lie,** to drain the cup to the dregs; *Prov:* **il y a loin de la c. aux lèvres,** there's many a slip 'twixt the cup and the lip; (*b*) *Sp:* (gold, silver) cup.

coupe[2] *n.f.* **1.** (*a*) cutting (of wheat, etc.); cutting out (of material); felling (of trees); **c. de cheveux,** haircut; **mettre un bois en c. réglée,** to make periodical cuttings in a wood; *F:* **mettre qn en c. réglée,** to exploit s.o.; **c. sombre,** (i) slight thinning (of forest area); (ii) drastic cut (in personnel, spending); (*b*) length (of material); piece (of wood); (*c*) cut (of a garment); **complet de bonne c.,** well cut suit; (*d*) *Arch: Draw: etc:* section; **c. longitudinale,** longitudinal section; **c. transversale,** cross section, transverse section; **machine vue en c.,** section of a machine; (*e*) outline (of face, etc.). **2.** *Cards:* cut, cutting; (*a*) **être sous la c. de qn,** (i) to lead after one's opponent has cut; (ii) to be under s.o.'s thumb; **tenir qn sous sa c.,** to have s.o. in one's power; (*b*) (*cheating*) **faire sauter la c.,** to make the pass, to slip the cut.

coupé [kupe] **1.** *a.* (*a*) cut (up, out); **costume mal c.,** badly cut suit; (*b*) **vin c. d'eau,** wine and water; (*c*) *Ten:* **coup c.,** drive with a cut. **2.** *n.m.* (*a*) *Veh:* coupé; *NAm: Aut:* two-door sedan; (*b*) *Danc:* coupée.

coupe-cigare(s) [kupsigar] *n.m.* cigar cutter; *pl. coupe-cigares.*

coupe-circuit [kupsirkɥi] *n.m.inv. El:* cutout, circuit breaker.

coupe-coupe [kupkup] *n.m.inv.* machete.

coupée [kupe] *n.f. Nau:* (*opening or port*) gangway; **échelle de c.,** accommodation ladder.

coupe-feu [kupfø] *n.m.inv. For:* firebreak.

coupe-file [kupfil] *n.m.inv.* (police, etc.) pass.

coupe-frites [kupfrit] *n.m.inv. Dom.Ec:* chip cutter, slicer.

coupe-gorge [kupgɔrʒ] *n.m.inv.* death trap; dangerous alley.

coupe-jarret [kupʒarɛ] *n.m.* cut-throat, assassin; *pl. coupe-jarrets.*

coupe-légumes [kuplegym] *n.m.inv. Dom.Ec:* vegetable cutter, slicer.

coupelle [kupɛl] *n.f.* **1.** small dish. **2.** *Ch:* cupel.

coupe-ongles [kupɔ̃gl] *n.m.inv.* nail clippers.

coupe-papier [kuppapje] *n.m.inv.* paper knife.

couper [kupe] *v.tr. & i.* to cut. **1.** (*a*) **c. de la viande en morceaux,** to cut up meat; **c. un arbre,** to cut down, fell, a tree; **c. la tête à qn,** to cut off s.o.'s head; **c. bras et jambes à qn,** (i) to disarm s.o.; (ii) to stun s.o.; (iii) to discourage s.o.; **c. l'herbe sous les pieds de qn,** to cut the ground from under s.o.'s feet; **c. dans le vif,** (i) to cut to the quick; (ii) to take extreme measures (to settle sth.); **c. le mal dans sa racine,** to strike at the root of an evil; **c. les cheveux à qn,** to cut, trim, s.o.'s hair; **un accent à c. au couteau,** an accent you could cut with a knife; **c. un vêtement,** to cut out a garment; (*b*) *Cards:* (i) to cut (the cards); **c'est à vous de c.,** it's your turn to cut; (ii) to trump; (*c*) *Games:* **c. une balle,** to cut, slice, a ball. **2.** (*a*) to cut, cross, intersect; **sentier qui coupe la route,** path that cuts across the road; **c. à travers champs,** to cut across country; **c. par le plus court,** to take a short cut; (*b*) *Aut:* **c. la route à qn,** to cut in; *Nau:* **c. la route d'un navire,** to cut across the bows of a ship. **3.** to cut off, interrupt, stop; (*a*) **c. (le) chemin à qn,** to cut s.o. off, to bar s.o.'s way; **c. la retraite à qn,** to cut off, intercept, s.o.'s retreat; **c. les vivres,** to cut off supplies; **c. les vivres à qn,** to stop s.o.'s allowance; **c. l'appétit à qn,** to spoil s.o.'s appetite, to take s.o.'s appetite away; **c. la parole à qn,** to interrupt s.o.; *F:* **c. court à qn,** to cut s.o. short; **c. le souffle à qn,** (i) to wind s.o.; (ii) to take s.o.'s breath away; *P:* **ça te la coupe!** that shakes you! *P:* **c. le sifflet, la chique, à qn,** to shut s.o. up; *Tp:* **c. la communication,** to ring off; *abs.* **ne coupez pas!** hold the line! *Cin:* **coupez!** cut! (*b*) **c. l'eau,** to turn off the water; *El:* **c. le courant,** to switch off the current; *Aut:* **c. l'allumage, le contact,** to cut off, switch off, the ignition. **4. c. du vin,** (i) to blend, (ii) to water down, dilute, wine. **5.** *v.ind.tr.F:* to avoid, get out of, doing sth.; **c. à une corvée,** to dodge, shirk, an unpleasant job; **il n'y coupera pas,** he won't get out of it. **6. se c.** (*a*) to cut oneself; **il s'est coupé, le, au, doigt,** he cut his finger; **il se couperait en quatre pour elle,** he'd do anything for her; (*b*) (*of roads, etc.*) to intersect; (*c*) *F:* to give oneself away.

coupe-racines [kuprasin] *n.m.inv. Agr:* root slicer, cutter.

couperet [kuprɛ] *n.m.* **1.** (meat) chopper, cleaver. **2.** blade, knife (of the guillotine).

couperose [kuproz] *n.f.* **1. c. verte,** green vitriol, ferrous sulphate; **c. bleue,** blue vitriol, copper sulphate. **2.** *Med:* acne roseacea; blotchiness.

couperosé [kuproze] *a. Med:* affected with acne rosacea; blotchy (complexion).

coupeur, -euse [kupœr, -øz] *n.* (*a*) cutter (of material, leather, etc.); (*b*) *A:* **c. de bourses,** pickpocket; **c. de cheveux en quatre,** hair splitter.

coupe-vent [kupvɑ̃] *n.m.inv.* **1.** windbreak. **2.** *Cost: Fr.C:* windcheater, *NAm:* windbreaker.

couplage [kuplaʒ] *n.m. Mec.E:* coupling, connecting (of wheels, etc.); coupling (of railway engines); *El: Elcs:* coupling.

couple [kupl] **I.** *n.m.* **1.** pair, couple; married couple; **c. de pigeons,** pair of pigeons; **arrangés par couples,** arranged in pairs. **2.** (*a*) *Mec: Ph:* couple; **c. moteur,** *Mec. E:* **couple (de torsion),** torque; *Ph:* **c. thermoélectrique,** thermocouple. **3.** *N.Arch:* frame, timber. **II.** *n.f.* **1.** *Ven: etc:* leash (for hounds, etc.). **2.** *A:* **une bonne c. de soufflets,** a couple of good blows.

coupler [kuple] *v.tr.* **1.** to couple; to attach (things) together. **2.** to leash (hounds).

couplet [kuplɛ] *n.m.* verse (of song); *pl.* song; *F:* tirade, little piece.

coupoir [kupwar] *n.m.* cutter.

coupole [kupɔl] *n.f.* (*a*) *Arch:* cupola, dome; **être reçu sous la c.,** to be made a member of the *Académie Française*; (*b*) *Mil: etc:* (revolving) gun turret.

coupon [kupɔ̃] *n.m.* **1.** *Com:* remnant (of material). **2.** (*a*) coupon; *Fin:* **c. d'action,** coupon; **c. attaché, détaché,** cum, ex, dividend; (*b*) *Th:* **c. de loge,** box ticket; *Rail:* **c. d'aller, de retour,** outward half, return half (of ticket).

coupon-réponse [kupɔ̃repɔ̃s] *n.m. Post:* **c.-r. (international),** (international) reply coupon; *pl. coupons-réponse.*

coupure [kupyr] *n.f.* **1.** (*a*) cut, gash (on finger, etc.); (*b*) cut, drain, irrigation channel. **2.** (*a*) cutting, piece cut out; **c. de journal,** newspaper cutting, clipping; (*b*) cut (in play, book, film); (*c*) *El:* **c. (de courant),** (power) cut; **il y aura une c. de 5 heures à 7 heures,** the gas, water, electricity, will be cut off between 5 and 7 o'clock; (*d*) gap, gulf; **la c. entre son passé et**

son avenir, the gap, break, between his past and his future. **3.** *Fin:* (bank)note (of small denomination); **c. de 50 francs,** 50 franc note.

cour [kur] *n.f.* **1.** (*a*) court (of sovereign); **vivre à la c.,** to live at court; **gens de c.,** courtiers; **être bien, mal, en c.,** to be in favour, out of favour; (*b*) courting, courtship; **faire la c. à qn,** to curry favour with s.o.; **faire la c. à une jeune fille,** to court a girl. **2. c. de justice,** court of justice; **messieurs, la C.!** = all rise! **Haute C.,** High Court (for impeachment of president, ministers). **3.** court, yard, courtyard; **c. de ferme,** farmyard; **c. d'honneur,** main courtyard; **c. de récréation, d'école,** schoolyard; playground; *Mil:* **c. de quartier,** barrack square; *Th:* **côté c.,** O.P. (side) (opposite prompter).

courage [kuraʒ] *n.m.* courage; valour; **perdre, prendre, c.,** to lose, take, courage, heart; **se sentir le c. de faire qch.,** to feel up to doing sth.; **prendre son c. à deux mains,** to pluck up courage; **être plein de c.,** to be full of energy; **(du) c.!** (i) cheer up! buck up! (ii) keep it up! keep going! **avoir le c. de ses opinions,** to have the courage of one's convictions; **vous n'auriez pas le c. de les renvoyer!** you wouldn't have the heart to dismiss them! **se battre avec c.,** to fight bravely, courageously.

courageusement [kuraʒøzmɑ̃] *adv.* (*a*) courageously, bravely; (*b*) zealously, with energy.

courageux, -euse [kuraʒø, -øz] *a.* **1.** courageous, brave. **2.** energetic; **il n'est pas très c. pour l'étude,** he doesn't show much enthusiasm for his studies.

couramment [kuramɑ̃] *adv.* **1.** easily, readily; **parler c. une langue étrangère,** to speak a foreign language fluently. **2.** generally, usually; **ce mot s'emploie c.,** this word is in current use.

courant, -ante [kurɑ̃, -ɑ̃t] **1.** *a.* (*a*) running; **chien c.,** hound; *Typ:* **titre c.,** running head(line); (*b*) flowing, running (water, etc.); **chambre avec eau courante,** bedroom with running water; (*c*) current (account, etc.); **dette courante,** floating debt; **le mois c.,** the present, current, month; **le cinq c.,** the fifth inst.; **fin c.,** at the end of this month; **vie courante,** everyday life; **mot d'usage c.,** word in current, general, use; **monnaie courante,** legal currency; **c'est monnaie courante,** it's quite usual; you often meet it; **prix c.,** (i) current price; (ii) price list; *Com:* **marque courante,** standard make; **de taille courante,** of standard size. **2.** *n.m.* (*a*) current; stream; running water; **suivre, remonter, le c.,** to go with, to stem, the tide; **c. d'air,** (i) draught; (ii) air current; **c. sous-marin,** undercurrent; undertow; **c. de population,** population movement; **le c. de l'opinion publique,** the trend of public opinion; **écrire au c. de la plume,** to write spontaneously; (*b*) *El:* **c. (électrique),** electric current; power; **couper le c.,** to cut off the current, to break contact; **c. continu, alternatif,** direct, alternating, current; **c. de repos,** quiescent current; (*c*) course; **dans le c. de l'année,** in the course of the year; **dans le c. de la semaine,** within the next week, some day this week; **c. des affaires,** course of events; **c. du marché,** current market prices; **il est au c.,** he knows about it; **mettre qn au c. d'une décision,** to inform s.o. of a decision; **il m'a mis au c.,** he told me all about it; **je me suis mis très vite au c.,** I got the hang of things very quickly; **le professeur est très au c. des nouvelles méthodes,** the teacher is very conversant with new methods; **3.** *n.f.* **courante** (*a*) *Mus:* *Danc:* courante; (*b*) *P:* (*diarrhœa*) **la c.,** the runs, trots.

courbatu [kurbaty] *a.* (*of pers.*) tired out, stiff, aching (all over).

courbature [kurbatyr] *n.f.* stiffness, tiredness; **avoir une c., des courbatures,** to be aching, stiff, all over.

courbaturer [kurbatyre] *v.tr.* to tire (s.o.) out; **je me sens tout courbaturé,** I'm stiff, aching, all over.

courbe [kurb] **1.** *a.* curved; curving. **2.** *n.f.* curve; graph; **la route fait une c.,** the road curves (round); *Mth:* **c. plane,** plane curve; *Mapm:* **c. de niveau,** contour (line); *Med:* **c. de température,** temperature graph.

courber [kurbe] **1.** *v.tr.* to bend, curve; **taille courbée par l'âge,** figure bowed with age; **c. le front, la tête,** (i) to bow one's head; (ii) to submit; **c. l'échine,** to submit. **2.** *v.i.* to bend; **c. sous le poids,** to bend under the weight. **3. se c.,** to bow, bend, stoop; **se c. devant qn,** (i) to bow; (ii) to submit to s.o.; **se c. en deux,** to bend double.

courbette [kurbɛt] *n.f.* (*a*) *Equit:* curvet; (*b*) bow; **faire des courbettes à qn,** to bow and scrape to s.o.

courbure [kurbyr] *n.f.* (*a*) curvature (of line, surface, etc.); **c. double, en S,** S curve; (*b*) bend, curve (of piece of wood, etc.); curve (of the back); (*c*) camber (of road, etc.); (*d*) sagging (of beam, etc.).

courette [kurɛt] *n.f.* small (court)yard.

coureur, -euse [kurœr, -øz] *n.* **1.** *n.m.* (*a*) runner; *Sp:* runner, racer; **c. de fond, de demi-fond,** long-distance, middle distance, runner; **c. de vitesse,** sprinter; **c. cycliste,** racing cyclist; **c. automobile,** racing driver; (*b*) **les (oiseaux) coureurs,** Ratitae; ratite birds. **2.** *n.m.* (*a*) wanderer, rover; *Can: Hist:* **c. de(s) bois,** trapper; (*b*) gadabout; **c'est un c. de bals, de cafés,** he's always at dances, in cafés; **c. (de filles),** womanizer; **c. de dot,** fortune hunter. **3.** *n.f.* **coureuse,** loose woman; *a.* **elle est un peu coureuse,** she's a bit of a man hunter.

courge [kurʒ] *n.f.* **1.** *Bot:* gourd; marrow; *NAm:* squash. **2.** *P:* clot, berk.

courgette [kurʒɛt] *n.f.* *Hort:* (small) marrow, courgette.

courir [kurir] *v.* (*pr.p.* **courant;** *p.p.* **couru;** *pr.ind.* **je cours, il court, n. courons, ils courent;** *pr.sub.* **je coure;** *p.h.* **je courus;** *fu.* **je courrai;** *the aux. is* **avoir**) **1.** *v.i.* (*a*) to run; **c. après qn, qch.,** to run after s.o., sth.; **c. après les femmes,** to run after the women; **j'ai couru le prévenir,** I ran to warn him; **je cours l'appeler,** I'll run and get him; **j'y cours,** I'll go at once; **cet acteur fait c. tout Paris,** the whole of Paris is rushing to see this actor; **monter, descendre, la colline en courant,** to run up, down, the hill; **arriver en courant,** to come running up; **faire qch. en courant,** to do sth. in a hurry; **cours acheter du pain,** run out and get some bread; **c. à sa fin,** to draw to an end; *F:* **tu peux toujours c.!** you can whistle for it! *P:* **c. sur le haricot à qn,** to get on s.o.'s nerves, s.o.'s wick; *NAm:* to bug s.o.; (*b*) to race, to run (in a race); **faire c. des chevaux,** to race, run, horses; (*c*) (*of ship*) to sail; **c. au large,** to stand out to sea; **c. à terre,** to stand in for the land; **c. devant le vent,** to run, scud, before the wind; **c. de l'avant,** to forge ahead; (*d*) to be current; **le bruit court que . . .,** rumour has it that . . ., they say that . . .; **faire c. un bruit,** to spread a rumour; *impers.* **il court des bruits sur lui,** there are rumours going round about him; **la mode qui court,** the present fashion; (*e*) (*of blood, wine*) to flow; (*of clouds*) to float; (*of water*) to rush; (*f*) **le mois qui court,** the current month; **par les temps qui courent, par le temps qui court,** nowadays, as things go, are, at present; *Fin:* **les intérêts qui courent,** the accruing interest; *F:* **laisse c.,** forget it, drop it. **2.** *v.tr.* to run after (sth.); to pursue, to chase; **c. le cerf,** to hunt the stag; to go staghunting; **c. un risque,** to run a risk; **c. sa chance,** to try one's luck. **3.** *with cogn. acc.* (*a*) **c. une course,** to run a race; **la coupe se courra demain,** the cup will be competed for tomorrow; (*b*) **c. le monde,** to roam the world; **passer son après-midi à c. les magasins,** to spend one's afternoon shopping; **c. les théâtres,** to be an inveterate theatre goer; **c. les filles, le jupon,** to run after girls, skirts; (*c*) *Nau:* **c. un bord,** to make a tack.

courlieu [kurljø] *n.m.* **courlis** [kurli] *n.m. Orn:* **c. (cendré), (grand) c.,** curlew; **c. corlieu,** whimbrel.

couronne [kurɔn] *n.f.* **1.** wreath, crown (of flowers, laurel, etc.); **c. funéraire,** (funeral) wreath; **en c.,** in a ring, circle. **2.** (*a*) (king's) crown; (ducal) coronet; **la triple c.,** the (pope's) tiara; (*b*) (*sovereignty*) the Crown; **aspirer, prétendre, à la c.,** to lay claim to the throne. **3.** (*a*) *Num:* (*in Scandinavia*) crown; (*b*) *Paperm:* crown (size). **4.** (*a*) ring; *Bot:* corona; *Anat:* crown (of tooth); *Astr:* **c. solaire,** solar corona; (*b*) loaf of bread (in the shape of a ring); (*c*) *Arch:* corona. **5.** *Mec.E:* rim (of pulley, wheel); **c. dentée,** crown gear, crown wheel, ring gear (of differential, etc.); **c. d'embrayage,** clutch ring.

couronné [kurɔne] *a.* **1.** (*a*) wreathed (with flowers, etc.); **lauréat c.,** prizewinner; **roman c.,** prizewinning novel; (*b*) crowned (sovereign); **tête couronnée,** sovereign. **2.** *Bot:* coronate(d). **3.** *Vet:* **cheval c.,** broken-kneed horse.

couronnement [kurɔnmɑ̃] *n.m.* **1.** (*a*) crowning, coronation (of king); (*b*) capping (of arch pier); top, cap (of building, column, etc.); coping (of wall, etc.); ridge (of roof); (*c*) climax; crowning achievement. **2.** scar (on horse's knee), broken knees.

couronner [kurɔne] *v.tr.* **1.** (*a*) to crown (with a wreath); to award a prize to (author, pupil, etc.); *F:* **et pour c. le tout . . .,** to cap, crown, it all . . .; **mes efforts furent couronnés de succès,** my efforts were crowned with success; (*b*) to crown; **c. qn roi,** to crown s.o. king. **2.** *Dent:* **c. une dent,** to crown a tooth. **3. c. un cheval,** to let a horse down on its knees; **se c. le genou,** to graze, skin, one's knee.

courre [kur] *v.tr. & i. A:* (= COURIR) *Ven: still used in* **chasse à c.,** hunt(ing).

courrier [kurje] *n.m.* **1.** courier; messenger. **2.** (*a*) mail, post, letters; **par retour du c.,** by return of post; **dépouiller son c.,** to open one's mail; **faire son c.,** to write one's letters; (*b*) (i) *A:* mail coach; (ii) mail boat; (iii) aircraft (flying a regular transport service); *Mil.Av:* courier, liaison aircraft. **3.** *Journ:* (*a*) (*title*) = Mail; (*b*) column; **c. des lecteurs,** letters to the Editor; **c. du cœur,** (women's) advice column; problem page; *F:* agony column.

courriériste [kurjerist] *n.m. Journ:* columnist.

courroie [kurwɑ] *n.f.* **1.** strap. **2.** *Mec.E:* belt; **c. de transmission,** driving belt; **c. de ventilateur,** fanbelt.

courroucé [kuruse] *a. esp. Lit:* angry, incensed (person).

courroucer [kuruse] *v.tr. Lit:* **(je courrouçai(s), n. courrouçons)** to anger, incense (s.o.); **se c.,** to become incensed.

courroux [kuru] *n.m. Lit:* anger, wrath, ire.

cours [kur] *n.m.* **1.** (*a*) course (of river); course, path (of sun, moon, etc.); **descendre le c. de la Tamise,** to go down the Thames; **c. d'eau,** river, watercourse, waterway, stream; **le c. des siècles,** the course of years; **suivre le c. de ses idées,** to follow the train of one's thoughts; **donner libre c. à son imagination,** to give free rein to one's imagination; **la maladie suit son c.,** the illness is running its course; **affaires en c.,** outstanding business; **travaux en c.,** work in progress, on hand; **année en c.,** current, present, year; **en c. de route,** during the journey; on the way; **en c. de production,** in production; **au c. de la conversation,** in the course of the conversation; (*b*) *Nau:* **long c.,** foreign trade; **voyage au long c.,** ocean voyage; **capitaine au long c.,** captain of an ocean-going vessel. **2.** circulation, currency (of money); **c. légal,** legal tender; **c. forcé,** forced currency; **avoir c.,** (i) to be legal tender; (ii) to be current, in current use; **donner c. à un bruit,** to spread a rumour. **3.** *St.Exch: etc:* quotation, price; **c. du marché,** market prices, rates; **c. du change,** rate of exchange; **au c. (du jour),** at the current daily price; **quel est le c. du sucre?** what is the quotation for sugar? **4.** (*a*) course (of lectures, etc.); lecture; lesson; **faire un c. d'histoire,** (i) to give a history lesson; (ii) to lecture on history; **c. par correspondance,** correspondence course; (*b*) text book, course; **c. élémentaire, moyen,** primary, intermediate, course. **5.** walk; avenue.

course [kurs] *n.f.* **1.** run, running; **au pas de c.,** at a run; *Mil:* at, *U.S.:* on, the double; **prendre sa c.,** to set off (running); **arrêté en pleine c.,** checked in full career. **2.** race, racing; **c. de chevaux,** horse race; **les courses,** the races; **c. de plat,** flat race; **c. d'obstacles,** (i) steeplechase; (ii) hurdle race; obstacle race; **c. de fond,** long-distance (i) running, (ii) race; **c. de vitesse,** sprint; **champ, terrain, de courses,** racecourse; **voiture de c.,** racing car; **c. sur piste, sur route,** track, road, racing; **c. de taureaux,** bullfight; *F:* **être dans la c.,** to be with it; to be in the know. **3.** (*a*) excursion, outing, trip; *Mount:* climb; (*b*) journey (*esp.* in taxi, etc.); **payer (le prix de) la c.,** to pay the fare; (*c*) (business) errand; **faire une c.,** to run an errand; **garçon de courses,** errand boy; **faire des courses,** (i) to go shopping; (ii) to run errands, messages. **4.** *Nau: A:* privateering. **5.** (*a*) path, way, course (of person, ship, planet, etc.); course, flight (of projectile); **je poursuivis ma c.,** I went on my way; *F:* (*of pers.*) **être à bout de c.,** to be worn out, exhausted; to be done in; (*b*) *Mec.E: etc:* movement, travel (of tool, etc.); stroke (of piston); **à bout de c.,** at full stroke; **à mi-c.,** at half stroke.

coursier, -ière [kursje, -jɛr] **1.** *n.m. Lit:* (i) charger; (ii) steed. **2.** *n.* messenger.

coursive [kursiv] *n.f. Nau:* alleyway, gangway.

court[1] [kur] **1.** *a.* (*a*) (*in space*) short; **avoir les jambes courtes, être c. de jambes,** to be short in the leg, to have short legs; **avoir la vue courte,** (i) to be short-sighted; (ii) to lack forethought; **avoir l'intelligence c.,** to be of limited intelligence; **avoir la respiration, le souffle, c.,** to be short-winded; to be short of breath; *Nau:* **vague, mer, courte,** choppy sea, short sea; **(le chemin) le plus c.,** the quickest way; a short cut; *F:* **il m'a donné 100 francs; c'est un peu c.,** he gave me 100 francs; it's a bit mean; (*b*) (*in time*) **c. intervalle,** short, brief, interval; **de courte durée,** short-lived; **avoir la mémoire courte,** to have a short memory; to be forgetful; **pour faire c.,** to cut a long story short; (*c*) *Cu:* **sauce courte,** thick sauce. **2.** *adv.* short; **s'arrêter c.,** to stop short, suddenly; **demeurer, rester, c.,** to be at a loss (for ideas, etc.); **tourner c.,** to turn sharply; **cheveux coupés c.,** short hair; **couper c. à qn, à qch.,** to cut s.o., sth., short. **3.** (*a*) *adv.phr.* **tout c.,** simply, only, merely; (*b*) **prendre qn de c.,** (i) to give s.o. short notice; (ii) to catch s.o. unawares; (*c*) *prep.phr.* **à c. (de),** short of; **à c. d'argent,** short of money, hard up; **il n'est jamais à c. d'arguments,** he's never at a loss for an argument, for an answer; **être à c.,** to be at a loss for words, for sth. to do.

court[2] [kur] *n.m.* **c. (de tennis),** (tennis) court.

courtage [kurtaʒ] *n.m. Com:* (*a*) broking, brokerage; (*b*) commission, brokerage.

courtaud, -aude [kurto, -od] *a. & n.* **1.** dock-tailed, crop-eared (animal). **2.** dumpy, squat, stocky (person).

court-bouillon [kurbujɔ̃] *n.m. Cu:* court-bouillon; *pl. courts-bouillons.*

court-circuit [kursirkɥi] *n.m. El:* short circuit; *pl. courts-circuits.*

court-circuitage [kursikɥitaʒ] *n.m. El:* short-circuiting.

court-circuiter [kursirkɥite] *v.tr.* (*a*) *El:* to short-circuit (resistance, etc.); (*b*) *F:* to short-circuit, bypass (sth.).

courtepointe [kurtəpwɛ̃t] *n.f.* quilt; (quilted) bedspread.

courtier, -ière [kurtje, -jɛr] *n. Com: Fin:* broker; agent; **c. d'assurances,** insurance broker; **c. maritime,** ship broker; **c. en vins,** wine broker.

courtisan [kurtizɑ̃] *n.m.* (*a*) courtier; (*b*) sycophant; *a.* **manières courtisanes,** flattering, obsequious, manners.

courtisane [kurtizan] *n.f. Hist: Lit:* courtezan, courtesan.

courtiser [kurtize] *v.tr.* (*a*) to pay court to, fawn on (s.o.); (*b*) to court, woo, to pay court to (woman).

court-jus [kurjy] *n.m. P:* short circuit.

courtois [kurtwa] *a.* courteous (**envers, avec, pour,** to); polite, urbane.

courtoisement [kurtwazmɑ̃] *adv.* courteously, politely; urbanely.

courtoisie [kurtwazi] *n.f.* **1.** courtesy, courteousness (**envers,** to, towards). **2.** (act of) courtesy.

couru [kury] *a.* **1.** sought after; **opéra très c.,** popular opera. **2.** *F:* **c'est c. (d'avance),** it's a cinch, a cert; **c'etait c.,** it was bound to happen.

couscous [kuskus] *n.m. Cu:* couscous.

couseuse [kuzøz] *n.f.* **1.** (*a*) sewer, seamstress; (*b*) *Bookb:* stitcher. **2.** stitching machine.

cousin¹ -ine [kuzɛ̃, -in] *n.* cousin; **c. germain,** first cousin; **cousins au second degré, cousins issus de germains,** second cousins; *F:* **cousin à la mode de Bretagne,** distant relation, sort of relation.

cousin² *n.m. Ent:* gnat, midge; *occ.* daddy-longlegs.

cousinage [kuzinaʒ] *n.m. O:* **1.** cousinship, cousinhood. **2. tout le c.,** all the cousins; *esp.* all the poor relations.

coussin [kusɛ̃] *n.m.* (*a*) cushion; *Belg:* pillow; **c. d'air,** air cushion; (*b*) pad(ding) (of horse's collar, etc.).

coussinet [kusinɛ] *n.m.* **1.** small cushion; pad. **2.** *Mec.E: etc:* (*a*) bearing; **c. de tête de bielle,** big end bearing; (*b*) *Rail:* **c. de rail,** rail chair; (*c*) *Arch: Civ.E:* coussinet, cushion (of Ionic column, etc.).

cousu [kuzy] *a.* sewn; **c. à la main,** *F:* **c. main,** hand sewn; *P:* **c'est du c. main,** it's first rate; **garder bouche cousue,** to keep one's mouth shut; to keep a secret; **bouche cousue!** not a word! **c. de fil blanc,** obvious; blatant; **être (tout) c. d'or,** to be rolling in money.

coût [ku] *n.m.* cost; **le c. de la vie,** the cost of living; **le c. d'une imprudence,** the price, the consequences, of a rash action.

coûtant [kutɑ̃] *a.m.* **à prix c.,** at cost price.

couteau, -eaux [kuto] *n.m.* **1.** (*a*) knife; **c. de cuisine,** kitchen knife; **c. à pain,** breadknife; **c. à découper,** carving knife, carver; **c. à légumes,** vegetable knife; **c. de poche, pliant,** pocket knife; **c. à cran d'arrêt,** flick knife; *NAm:* switch-blade (knife); **c. à palette,** palette knife; **c. de chasse,** hunting knife, *NAm:* bowie knife; **ils sont à couteaux tirés,** they're at daggers drawn; **mettre le c. sous, sur, la gorge à qn,** to force s.o. (to do sth.), to hold a pistol to s.o.'s head; (*b*) *Ph:* knife edge, fulcrum (of balance beam). **2.** *Moll:* **(manche de) c.,** razor shell, clam.

couteau-scie [kutosi] *n.m.* knife with serrated edge; *pl. couteaux-scies.*

coutelas [kutlɑ] *n.m.* (*a*) cutlass; (*b*) *Dom.Ec:* large (kitchen) knife.

coutelier, -ière [kutəlje, -jɛr] *n.* cutler.

coutellerie [kutɛlri] *n.f.* **1.** (*industry, wares*) cutlery. **2.** (*a*) cutlery shop; (*b*) cutlery works.

coûter [kute] *v.i.* **1.** to cost; **ça ne coûte rien,** it's free; **c. cher, peu,** to be expensive, inexpensive; **cela vous coûtera cher,** you shall pay dearly for this; **coûte que coûte,** at any cost, at any price, at all costs, whatever the cost; *F:* **ça coûtera ce que ça coutera!** hang the expense! *F:* **l'argent ne lui coûte guère,** money means nothing to him; **cela coûte les yeux de la tête,** it costs the earth; **cela lui a coûté la vie,** it cost him his life; *impers.* **j'ai voulu l'aider; il m'en coûta,** I tried to help him, to my cost. **2. rien ne lui coûte,** (i) nothing is an effort to him; (ii) he spares no effort; **ça ne coûte rien d'essayer,** there's no harm in trying; **il m'en coûte de le dire,** it pains me to have to say this.

coûteux, -euse [kutø, -øz] *a.* costly; expensive; dear; **peu c.,** inexpensive.

coutil [kuti] *n.m. Tex:* drill, twill; **c. pour matelas,** ticking.

coutre [kutr̥] *n.m.* coulter (of plough).

coutume [kutym] *n.f.* **1.** custom, habit; **avoir c. de faire qch.,** to be in the habit of doing sth.; to be accustomed to do sth.; **comme de c.,** as usual; **je me suis levé plus tard que c.,** I got up later than usual; **une fois n'est pas c.,** it doesn't matter for once; we're not making a habit of it. **2.** *Jur:* customary.

coutumier, -ière [kutymje, -jɛr] **1.** *a.* (*a*) *A:* in the habit of (doing sth.); *usu. Pej:* **il est c. du fait,** it's not the first time he's done that; (*b*) customary; usual; **droit c.,** (i) customary law; (ii) unwritten law, common law. **2.** *n.m. Jur:* customary.

couture [kutyr] *n.f.* **1.** sewing, needlework; **elle est dans la c.,** she does dressmaking; **haute c.,** haute couture; **maison de haute c.,** fashion house; *a.* **une veste c.,** a fashionable jacket. **2.** (*a*) seam (in dress, etc.); **sans c.,** seamless; **c. rabattue, plate,** run and fell seam; flat seam; **c. anglaise,** French seam; **faire une c. à grands points,** to tack, baste, a seam; **battre qn à plate(s) couture(s),** to beat s.o. hollow; **examiner qn, qch., sur, sous, toutes les coutures,** to examine s.o., sth., from every angle; (*b*) *Nau:* **c. à clin,** lapped seam.

couturé [kutyre] *a.* scarred (face).

couturier, -ière [kutyrje, -jɛr] *n.* (*a*) *n.m. & f.* dressmaker; couturier; (*b*) *n.f.* seamstress, needlewoman; (*c*) *n.f. Th:* rehearsal preceding the final dress rehearsal.

couvage [kuvaʒ] *n.m.* = COUVAISON (*b*).

couvain [kuvɛ̃] *n.m.* **1.** nest of insect eggs. **2.** *Ap:* brood comb.

couvaison [kuvɛzɔ̃] *n.f.* (*a*) brooding time, sitting time (of bird); (*b*) incubation, hatching (of eggs).

couvée [kuve] *n.f.* **1.** clutch (of eggs). **2.** brood (of chicks).

couvent [kuvɑ̃] *n.m.* (*a*) convent; **entrer au c.,** to go into a convent; (*b*) convent school; (*c*) monastery.

couventine [kuvɑ̃tin] *n.f.* (*a*) nun conventual; (*b*) convent schoolgirl.

couver [kuve] **1.** *v.tr.* (*a*) (*of hen, etc.*) to sit on (eggs); *v.i.* to brood, sit; **poule qui veut c.,** broody hen; (*b*) to incubate, to hatch (out) (eggs); (*c*) **c. des projets de vengeance,** to meditate schemes of vengeance; **c. un complot,** to hatch a plot; **c. une maladie,** to be sickening for an illness; **c. qn, qch., des yeux,** (i) to look longingly at sth.; (ii) to look fondly at s.o.; **il est couvé par sa mère,** his mother is overprotective. **2.** *v.i.* (*of fire, passion*) to smoulder; (*of riot, etc.*) to be brewing; **la conspiration couvait depuis longtemps,** the conspiracy had been hatching for a long time.

couvercle [kuvɛrkl̥] *n.m.* (*a*) lid, cover (of box, pot, saucepan, etc.); cap, top (of jar, etc.); **c. vissé,** screw cap; (*b*) *Mec.E:* cover (of piston).

couvert¹ [kuvɛr] *a.* covered. **1. allée couverte,** shady walk; **parler à mots couverts,** to speak in veiled terms; **ciel c.,** overcast sky. **2.** wearing a hat; **rester c.,** to keep one's hat on. **3.** dressed; **c. chaudement, bien c.,** warmly dressed, well wrapped up.

couvert² *n.m.* **1.** cover(ing), shelter; **le vivre et le c.,** board and lodging; **être à c.,** (i) to be under cover; (ii) *Com:* to be covered (for a credit); **se mettre à c.,**

to take cover; **se mettre à c. de la pluie,** to shelter from the rain; **mettre ses intérêts à c.,** to safeguard one's interests; **sous le c. de l'amitié,** under the cover, cloak, pretence, of friendship; **il a agi sous le c. de ses chefs,** he acted with the authority of his superiors. **2.** (*a*) (i) fork and spoon; (ii) cutlery; **c. à poisson,** fish knife and fork; (*b*) place setting (at table); **mettre le c.,** to lay, set, the table; **mettre trois couverts,** to set the table, to lay, for three; **vous trouverez toujours votre c. mis,** you can come and have a meal with us any time. (*c*) (*in restaurant*) cover charge.

couverte [kuvɛrt] *n.f. Cer:* glaze.

couverture [kuvɛrtyr] *n.f.* **1.** covering, cover; **c. de voyage,** (travelling) rug; **c. (de lit),** blanket; **c. chauffante,** electric blanket; **amener, tirer, la c. à soi,** to take the lion's share; **c. d'un livre,** (dust) cover of a book; **sous c. d'amitié,** under the cover, the cloak, of friendship; **servir de c. à qn,** to cover up for s.o.; *Mil:* **troupes de c.,** covering troops; *Av:* **c. aérienne,** air cover. **2.** *Const:* roofing; **c. en tuiles,** tiled roof. **3.** *Agr:* topping; **engrais en c.,** surface, top, dressing. **4.** (*a*) *Com:* cover; (*b*) *St.Exch:* margin, cover.

couveuse [kuvøz] *n.f.* **1.** sitting hen, brood hen, brooder; **c. artificielle,** incubator (for eggs). **2.** incubator (for infants).

couvrant [kuvrɑ̃] *a.* (*a*) covering, giving cover; (*b*) (paint, etc.) that covers well.

couvre-chef [kuvrəʃɛf] *n.m. F: & Hum:* headdress, headgear; *pl. couvre-chefs.*

couvre-feu [kuvrəfø] *n.m.inv.* curfew.

couvre-lit [kuvrəli] *n.m.* bedspread; **c.-l. piqué,** (eiderdown) quilt, *NAm:* comforter; *pl. couvre-lits.*

couvre-livre [kuvrəlivr̥] *n.m. Bookb:* (dust) jacket; book cover; *pl. couvre-livres.*

couvre-nuque [kuvrənyk] *n.m.* sun curtain (of cap); *pl. couvre-nuques.*

couvre-pied(s) [kuvrəpje] *n.m.* coverlet, bedspread; *pl. couvre-pieds.*

couvre-plat [kuvrəpla] *n.m.* dish cover; *pl. couvre-plats.*

couvreur [kuvrœr] *n.m.* roofer; **c. en tuiles, en ardoises,** tiler, slater; **c. en chaume,** thatcher.

couvrir [kuvrir] *v.tr.* (*pr.p.* **couvrant;** *p.p.* **couvert;** *pr.ind.* **je couvre, il couvre, n. couvrons;** *pr.sub.* **je couvre;** *impf.* **je couvrais;** *p.h.* **je couvris;** *fu.* **je couvrirai) I.** *v.tr.* **1.** to cover, to overlay, to screen (**de,** with); **être couvert de poussière,** to be covered with dust; **mur couvert de lierre,** wall overgrown with ivy; **c. qn de cadeaux,** to shower s.o. with gifts; **c. qn de son corps,** to shield s.o. with one's body; **c. qn,** to cover up for s.o.; **c. la retraite de l'armée,** to cover the army's retreat; *Ins:* **c. les risques,** to insure against risks; **le bruit de la cascade couvre les voix,** the noise of the waterfall drowns the sound of voices; **c. son jeu,** (i) *Cards:* to hide one's hand; (ii) to keep one's plans secret; *Cards:* **c. une carte,** to cover a card; **c. cinquante kilomètres en une heure,** to cover fifty kilometres in an hour; *Com:* **le prix de vente couvre à peine les frais,** the selling price barely covers the cost; **prière de nous c. par chèque,** kindly remit by cheque; **c. une enchère,** to make a higher bid; *Journ:* **c. un événement,** to cover an event. **2.** *Const:* **c. un toit d'ardoises, de tuiles, de chaume,** to slate, tile, thatch, a roof. **3.** (*of male animal*) to cover (female). **II. se couvrir. 1.** (*a*) to put on one's (outdoor) clothes; (*b*) to put on one's hat; (*c*) **se c. de gloire,** to cover oneself with glory. **2.** *Sp:* to cover, protect, oneself; *Fenc:* to guard one's body. **3.** (*of weather*) to become overcast. **4. les arbres se couvrent de feuilles,** the trees are coming into leaf.

cover-girl [kɔvœrgœrl] *n.f. F:* cover-girl; *pl. cover-girls.*

cow(-)boy [kaubɔj] *n.m.* cowboy; *pl. cow(-)boys.*

coxal, -aux [kɔksal, -o] *a. Anat:* coxal; **os c.,** hip bone.

coxalgie [kɔksalʒi] *n.f. Med:* coxalgia.

coyote [kɔjɔt] *n.m. Z:* coyote, prairie wolf.

crabe [krab] *n.m.* **1.** *Crust:* crab; **marcher en c.,** to walk sideways, crabwise; *F:* **c'est un panier de crabes,** they're always at each other's throats. **2.** caterpillar tracked vehicle.

crac [krak] *int. & n.m.* crack, snap; rip; *F:* **et crac! il est tombé par terre,** and bang! there he was on the floor.

crachat [kraʃa] *n.m.* **1.** spittle, spit; *Med:* sputum; **se noyer dans un c.,** to be defeated by the slightest problem. **2.** *F:* decoration, star; gong.

craché [kraʃe] *a. F:* **c'est son père tout c.,** he's the spitting image of his father; **c'est lui tout c.!** that's him all over, that's just like him!

crachement [kraʃmɑ̃] *n.m.* (*a*) spitting; **c. de sang,** spitting of blood; (*b*) crackling (of loudspeaker).

cracher [kraʃe] **1.** *v.i.* (*a*) to spit, expectorate; *F:* **il ne crache pas sur le champagne,** he doesn't turn up his nose at champagne; (*b*) (*of pen*) to splutter; (*c*) (*of loudspeaker*) to crackle. **2.** *v.tr.* (*a*) to spit (out) (saliva, blood, etc.); to expectorate; **c. du sang,** to spit blood; **c. des injures,** to hurl abuse; *F:* **j'ai dû c. mille francs,** I had to fork out, cough up, a thousand francs; (*b*) (*of chimney, volcano, etc.*) to belch out.

crachin [kraʃɛ̃] *n.m.* (fine) drizzle.

crachiner [kraʃine] *v.i.* to drizzle.

crachoir [kraʃwar] *n.m.* spitoon, *NAm:* cuspidor; *F:* **tenir le c.,** to monopolize the conversation; **tenir le c. à qn,** to listen to s.o. without getting a word in edgeways.

crachotement [kraʃɔtmɑ̃] *n.m.* sputtering, spluttering; *W.Tel:* crackling.

crachoter [kraʃɔte] *v.i.* to keep on spitting; to sputter, to splutter; *W.Tel:* to crackle.

crack [krak] *n.m.* (*a*) crack horse; (*b*) *F:* genius; ace; **c'est un c. en math,** he's a genius at maths.

cracking [krakiɲ] *n.m. Petr:* cracking (of crude oil).

Cracovie [krakɔvi] *Pr.n.f. Geog:* Cracow.

cracra [krakra], **crado, cradingue** [krado, -dɛ̃g] *a.inv. P:* filthy.

craie [krɛ] *n.f.* chalk; **c. de tailleur,** tailor's chalk, French chalk; **inscrire qch. à la c.,** to chalk sth. up.

craindre [krɛ̃dr̥] *v.tr.* (*pr.p.* **craignant;** *p.p.* **craint;** *pr.ind.* **je crains, il craint, n. craignons, ils craignent;** *pr.sub.* **je craigne;** *impf.* **je craignais;** *p.h.* **je craignis;** *fu.* **je craindrai**) (*a*) to fear, dread, be afraid of (s.o., sth.); **c. la mort,** to be afraid of death; **ne craignez rien!** don't be alarmed, frightened! **je crains de le laisser entrer,** I am afraid to let him in; **je crains qu'il (ne) soit mort,** I fear, I'm afraid, he's dead; **il est à c., il y a lieu de c., que . . . (ne) . . .,** it is to be feared that . . .; **il n'y a pas à c. qu'il revienne,** there is no fear of his coming back; **c. pour qn,** to have fears for s.o.'s safety, future; to be anxious about s.o.; (*b*) **ces plantes craignent le gel,** these plants can't stand the frost; **je crains le froid,** I can't stand the cold; *Com:* **craint l'humidité,** to be kept in a dry place.

crainte [krɛ̃t] *n.f.* fear, dread; **avoir une c. respectueuse de qn,** to stand in awe of s.o.; **dans la c. de tomber,** for fear of falling; **de c. que . . . (ne)** + *sub.*, lest; **il a parlé plus bas de c. qu'on ne l'entende,** he spoke more quietly for fear of being overheard; **sans c.,** (i) fearless; (ii) fearlessly; **soyez sans c., n'ayez c.,** have no fear; **avoir des craintes au sujet de qch.,** to entertain fears, to be under some apprehension, about sth.

craintif, -ive [krɛ̃tif, -iv] *a.* timid, timorous.

craintivement [krɛ̃tivmɑ̃] *adv.* timidly, timorously.
cramoisi [kramwazi] *a.* crimson; **devenir c.,** to flush crimson; to get purple in the face.
crampe [krɑ̃p] *n.f. Med:* cramp; **c. de l'écrivain,** writer's cramp; **c. du tennis,** tennis elbow; **c. d'estomac,** stomach cramp.
crampon [krɑ̃pɔ̃] *n.m.* **1.** *Const: etc:* cramp (iron), staple; clamp, holdfast. **2.** (*a*) climbing iron; (*b*) stud (for sole of boot); calk, cog (of horse's shoe); **c. à glace,** crampon. **3.** *Bot:* tendril; adventitious root. **4.** *a. & n.m. F:* **quel c.! qu'il est c.!** what a leech!
cramponnement [krɑ̃pɔnmɑ̃] *n.m.* clutching, clinging.
cramponner [krɑ̃pɔne] *v.tr.* **1.** (*a*) *Const:* to clamp, cramp, (stones, etc.) together; (*b*) *F:* to buttonhole, pester; to cling to (s.o.). **2. se c. à qn,** to hold on to, hang on to, cling (on) to, to clutch, sth., s.o.; **cramponne-toi!** hold on!
cran [krɑ̃] *n.m.* **1.** notch; (*a*) catch, tooth (of ratchet, etc.); cog (of wheel); *Sm.a:* **c. de l'armé,** full cock notch; **c. de sûreté,** safety catch; *F:* **être à c.,** to be on the point of losing one's temper; (*b*) hole (in belt, strap, etc.); **lâcher une courroie d'un cran,** to let a strap out a hole; *F:* **se serrer d'un c.,** to tighten one's belt; (*c*) *F:* **avoir du c.,** to have guts.
crâne [krɑn] **1.** *n.m.* skull, cranium; **fracture du c.,** fracture of the skull; **défoncer le c. à qn,** to brain s.o.; **avoir mal au c.,** to have a hangover; **avoir le c. étroit,** to be thickheaded; **bourrer le c. à qn,** to stuff s.o. with stories. **2.** *a. O:* swaggering, jaunty (air).
crâner [krɑne] *v.i. F:* (*a*) to swagger; to show off; (*b*) to brazen it out.
crâneur, -euse [krɑnœr, -øz] *n. F:* swaggerer, swanker; show-off.
crânien, -ienne [krɑnjɛ̃, -jɛn] *a. Anat:* cranial; **la boîte crânienne,** the skull.
craniologie [krɑnjɔlɔʒi] *n.f.* craniology.
cranter [krɑ̃te] *v.tr.* to notch (wheel, etc.).
crapaud [krapo] *n.m.* **1.** (*a*) toad; *P:* **c'est un vilain c.,** he's an ugly little squirt; (*b*) *F:* child, brat; (*c*) *Ich:* **c. de mer,** angler fish, sea devil; (*d*) *Lap:* blemish. **2.** (*a*) **(fauteuil) c.,** tub chair; (*b*) **(piano) c.,** baby grand (piano).
crapaudine [krapodin] *n.f.* **1.** *Miner:* toadstone. **2.** *Cu:* **poulet à la c.,** spatchcock (chicken). **3.** *Hyd.E:* grating, strainer (of inlet pipe of pond). **4.** *Mec.E:* (*a*) pivot bearing, box, hole; (*b*) socket, gudgeon (of door hinge, etc.).
crapette [krapɛt] *n.f. Cards:* crapette, Russian bank.
crapule [krapyl] *n.f.* **1.** *A:* debauchery, dissoluteness. **2.** *coll. A:* dissolute mob. **3.** scoundrel; crook, villain; *a.* dishonest, lowdown (pers., action).
crapuleusement [krapyløzmɑ̃] *adv.* dishonestly.
crapuleux, -euse [krapylø, -øz] *a.* (*a*) *A:* debauched, dissolute; (*b*) sordid, loathsome (crime).
craquage [krakaʒ] *n.m.* cracking (of heavy oil).
craquelé [krakle] **1.** *a.* crackled; *Cer:* craquelé. **2.** *n.m. Cer:* crackle (ware, china, glass).
craqueler [krakle] *v.tr.* **(je craquelle, n. craquelons; je craquellerai)** (*a*) to crack; *Cer:* to crackle; (*b*) **se c.,** to crack, to become cracked.
craquelure [kraklyr] *n.f.* crack; *Cer:* crackle; *Art:* craquelure.
craquement [krakmɑ̃] *n.m.* cracking (sound); crack, snap; crackling (of dried leaves, etc.); crunching (of snow); creaking (of shoes, etc.).
craquer [krake] *v.i.* **1.** (*a*) to crack; to make a cracking sound; (*of dried leaves, etc.*) to crackle; (*of hard snow*) to crunch; (*of shoes, etc.*) to creak, to squeak; **faire c. ses doigts,** to crack one's finger joints; (*b*) **les coutures ont craqué,** the seams have split; **plein à c.,** full to bursting; **son affaire craque,** his business is on the verge of collapse; (*c*) (*of pers.*) to crack up; (*d*) *v.tr.* **c. une allumette,** to strike a match. **2.** *v.tr. Petr:* to crack (oil).
craqueter [krakte] *v.i.* **(il craquette; il craquettera) 1.** to crackle. **2.** (*a*) (*of cricket*) to chirp; (*b*) (*of stork*) to clatter.
crash [kraʃ] *n.m. Av:* crash landing.
crasse [kras] **1.** *a.f.* gross, crass; *used esp. in* **ignorance c.,** crass ignorance. **2.** *n.f.* (*a*) (body) dirt, filth; **vivre dans la c.,** to live in squalor; (*b*) *Med:* **c. sénile,** senile keratosis; (*c*) *Metall:* dross, scum, slag; *Metalw:* hammer scale, forge scale; (*d*) *F:* **faire une c. à qn,** to play a dirty trick, to do the dirty, on s.o.
crasseux, -euse [krasø, -øz] *a.* (*a*) dirty, filthy, grimy (hands, linen, etc.); squalid (dwelling, etc.).
crassier [krasje] *n.m.* slag heap.
cratère [kratɛr] *n.m.* **1.** *Gr.Ant:* crater; (wine) bowl. **2.** *Geog:* crater (of volcano).
cravache [kravaʃ] *n.f.* riding whip, (hunting) crop; **à la c.,** brutally.
cravacher [kravaʃe] (*a*) *v.tr.* to flog (horse); to horsewhip (person); (*b*) *v.i. F:* to slog, to work like mad (to finish sth.).
cravate [kravat] *n.f.* (*a*) *Cost:* (i) tie; (ii) scarf; cravat; (*on invitation card*) **c. blanche,** white tie, tails; **c. noire,** black tie, dinner jacket, *U.S:* tuxedo; **épingle de c.,** tiepin; *Mil:* **c. d'un drapeau,** bow and tassels of colour stave; *F:* **c. de chanvre,** hangman's rope; *F:* **s'en jeter un derrière la c.,** to knock back a drink; (*b*) (*decoration*) insignia, ribbon; (*c*) *Wr:* headlock; (*d*) *Nau:* sling.
cravater [kravate] *v.tr.* **1.** to put a tie on (s.o.); **se c.,** to put on one's tie. **2.** to grab s.o. round, by, the neck; *Wr:* to put in a headlock. **3.** *P:* to dupe (s.o.); **je me suis fait c.,** I got taken for a ride.
crawl [krol] *n.m. Swim:* crawl.
crawler [krole] *v.i. Swim:* to crawl.
crayeux, -euse [krɛjø, -øz] *a.* chalky.
crayon [krɛjɔ̃] *n.m.* **1.** (*a*) pencil; **c. de plombagine,** *F:* **à mine de plomb,** lead pencil; **c. gras,** soft lead pencil; **écrit au c.,** written in pencil; pencilled; **c. de couleur,** coloured pencil, crayon; **c. feutre,** felt (tip) pen; **c. à bille,** ballpoint pen; **c. lithographique,** litho crayon; *U.S:* grease pencil; **dessin au c.,** pencil drawing; **coup de c.,** pencil stroke; (*b*) pencil drawing, sketch. **2.** stick; *Med:* pencil (of caustic, etc.); *Toil:* **c. de rouge à lèvres,** lipstick; **c. à sourcils,** eyebrow pencil; **c. noir,** (i) eyebrow, (ii) eye(liner), pencil.
crayonnage [krɛjɔnaʒ] *n.m.* **1.** pencilling; pencil marks. **2.** pencil sketch.
crayonner [krɛjɔne] *v.tr.* **1.** to draw (sth.) in pencil, to make a pencil sketch of (sth.). **2.** to pencil; to make a pencil note of (sth.). **3.** to draw (outline of sth.); to outline, describe (character, etc.).
créance [kreɑ̃s] *n.f.* **1.** belief, credence, credit; **hors de c.,** unbelievable, incredible; **trouver c.,** to be believed, credible; **ajouter c. à qch.,** to take sth. seriously. **2.** *A:* trust; *Dipl:* **lettres de c.,** letter of credence; credentials. **3.** debt; *Jur:* claim; **mauvaises créances,** bad debts; **c. exigible,** debt due; **créances gelées,** frozen credits; **c. hypothécaire,** debt secured by a mortgage.
créancier, -ière [kreɑ̃sje, -jɛr] *n.* creditor.
créateur, -trice [kreatœr, -tris] **1.** *a.* creative (power, genius). **2.** *n.* creator; (*a*) **le C.,** the Creator, God; (*b*) maker; inventor; (*c*) *Th:* creator (of a rôle).
créatif, -ive [kreatif, -iv] *a.* creative.
création [kreasjɔ̃] *n.f.* **1.** (*a*) creation, creating; **esprit de c.,** creativeness; **la c. (du monde),** the creation (of the world); (*b*) founding, establishment (of institution, etc.); creation (of work of art); *Com:* invention (of new product); *Th:* first production (of play); **c.**

d'un rôle, creation of a part. **2.** (*a*) **les merveilles de la c.,** the wonders of creation, of the universe; (*b*) *Com:* new product; **sa robe était une c. de chez Vénus et Cie,** her dress was a creation by Venus & Co.

créativité [kreativite] *n.f.* creativity.

créature [kreatyr] *n.f.* creature. **1.** created being; **c. humaine,** human being. **2.** (*a*) person, individual; *F:* **une belle c.,** a beautiful woman; (*b*) *Pej:* contemptible woman. **3.** creature, protégé (of minister, etc.).

crécelle [kresɛl] *n.f.* (hand) rattle; **quelle c.!** what a chatterbox! **voix de c.,** rasping voice.

crèche [krɛʃ] *n.f.* **1.** (*a*) *Husb:* manger, crib; (*b*) (Christ child's) crib. **2.** (*a*) day nursery, crèche; (*b*) *P:* pad.

crécher [kreʃe] *v.i.* *P:* to live; **où que tu crèches?** where do you hang out?

crédence [kredɑ̃s] *n.f.* **1.** credenza; sideboard. **2.** *Ecc:* credence (table).

credibilité [kredibilite] *n.f.* credibility.

crédit [kredi] *n.m.* **1.** *Lit:* credit, repute, influence; **être en c. auprès de qn,** to have credit, influence, with s.o. **2.** *Fin:* *Com:* credit; **c. bancaire,** bank credit; **c. en blanc, à découvert,** blank, open, credit; **c. d'impôt,** (i) tax rebate; (ii) tax credit; **lettre de c.,** letter of credit; **carte de c.,** credit card; **vendre, acheter, qch. à c.,** to sell, buy, sth. (i) on credit, *F:* on tick, (ii) on hire purchase; **faire c. à qn,** (i) to give s.o. credit; (ii) to trust s.o.; **ouvrir un c. chez qn,** to open a credit account, *F:* an account, with s.o.; **établissement, société, de c.,** loan society; credit establishment; bank; **c. foncier** = (government controlled) building society. **3.** credit(or) side (of ledger, balance sheet); **porter une somme au c. de qn,** to place a sum to s.o.'s credit, to credit s.o. with a sum. **4.** sum voted by Parliament for supply; **voter des crédits,** to vote supplies. **5.** *Sch:* *Can:* credit, mark.

crédit-bail [kredibaj] *n.m.* leasing.

créditer [kredite] *v.tr.* (*a*) **c. qn du montant d'une somme,** to credit s.o., s.o.'s account, with a sum; to place, carry, a sum to s.o.'s credit; **c. un compte,** to credit an account; (*b*) **c. qn de,** to give s.o. credit for; to credit s.o. with.

créditeur, -trice [kreditœr, -tris] **1.** *n.* creditor. **2.** *a.* having a credit; **compte c.,** account in credit; **solde c.,** credit balance.

credo [kredo] *n.m.inv.* creed, *esp.* the Apostles' Creed; credo; **c. politique,** political creed.

crédule [kredyl] *a.* credulous.

crédulité [kredylite] *n.f.* credulity, credulousness.

créer [kree] *v.tr.* **1.** to create. **2. c. une chaire,** to found a chair; **c. une armée,** to form an army; **créer qch. de toutes pièces,** to create sth. out of nothing; **c. une entreprise,** to set up a business; **se c. une clientèle,** to build up a clientele; **agence récemment créée,** recently established agency; **le pouvoir de c.,** the power of creation; **c. des difficultés à qn,** to create, cause, difficulties for s.o.; *Th:* **c. un rôle,** to create a part; **c. une pièce,** to produce a play (for the first time). **3.** *Com:* **chemises créées par Dumaine,** shirts styled by Dumaine.

crémaillère [kremajɛr] *n.f.* **1.** (*a*) pot hanger, hook; trammel (hook); *F:* **pendre la c.,** to give a house warming party. **2.** (*a*) *Mec.E:* *etc:* (toothed) rack; rack bar; **c. (et pignon),** rack and pinion; **engrenage à c.,** rack(-and-pinion) gearing; (*b*) *Rail:* rack rail; **chemin de fer à c.,** rack railway.

crémant [kremɑ̃] *a.* & *n.m.* slightly sparkling (Champagne).

crémation [kremasjɔ̃] *n.f.* cremation.

crématoire [krematwar] *a.* & *n.m.* crematory; **(four) crématoire,** crematorium.

crématorium [krematɔrjɔm] *n.m.* crematorium.

crème [krɛm] *n.f.* **1.** (*a*) cream; (*on boiled milk*) skin; **c. fouettée, Chantilly,** whipped cream; **fromage à la c.,** cream cheese; **fraises à la c.,** strawberries and cream; **café c.,** white coffee; *n.m.* *F:* **un grand c.,** a large cup of white coffee; (*b*) *F:* (*of pers.*) **la c.,** the cream; **c'est la c. des hommes,** he's the best of men, one of the best; (*c*) *Cu:* **c. anglaise,** (egg) custard; **c. pâtissière,** confectioner's custard; **c. brûlée,** crème brûlée; **c. au beurre,** butter cream; **c. (au) caramel,** caramel custard; cream caramel, crème caramel; **c. glacée,** *Fr.C:* **c. à la glace,** ice cream. **2.** (*a*) **c. pour chaussures,** shoe cream, polish; (*b*) *Toil:* **c. de beauté,** face, beauty, cream; **c. hydratante,** moisturizing cream; **c. à raser,** shaving cream; (*c*) *Ch:* **c. de tartre,** cream of tartar. **3. c. de menthe,** *crème de menthe,* peppermint liqueur. **4.** *a.inv.* cream(-coloured).

crémer[1] [kreme] *v.tr.* **(je crème, n. crémons; je crémerai)** to cremate.

crémer[2] *v.i.* (*of milk*) to cream.

crémerie [krɛmri] *n.f.* **1.** creamery, dairy. **2.** *O:* small restaurant (serving light meals); *F:* **changer de c.,** to move on; to go elsewhere.

crémeux, -euse [kremø, -øz] *a.* creamy.

crémier, -ière [kremje, -jɛr] *n.* dairyman, dairywoman.

Crémone [kremɔn] **1.** *Pr.n.f.* *Geog:* Cremona. **2.** *n.f.* espagnolette.

créneau, -eaux [kreno] *n.m.* **1.** (*a*) *Fort:* crenel, crenelle; (*b*) loophole; slit (in armoured turret, tank, etc.). **2.** (*a*) gap, space; *Aut:* **faire un c.,** to reverse into a parking space; (*b*) *Com:* market gap; opening; (*c*) available time; *W.Tel:* *T.V:* slot.

crénelage [krɛnlaʒ] *n.m.* **1.** *Fort:* (*a*) crenel(l)ation; (*b*) cutting of loopholes (in wall, etc.). **2.** toothing; milling (of coin).

crénelé [krɛnle] *a.* **1.** *Fort:* (*a*) crenel(l)ated (wall, etc.); (*b*) loopholed. **2.** *Bot:* crenate(d), crenelled (leaf, etc.). **3.** milled (coin).

créneler [krɛnle] *v.tr.* **(je crénelle, n. crénelons; je crénellerai) 1.** *Fort:* (*a*) to crenel(l)ate, crenel (wall, etc.); (*b*) to cut loopholes in, to loophole (wall, etc.). **2.** to notch, tooth (wheel, etc.); to mill (coin).

crénelure [krɛnlyr] *n.f.* crenel(l)ation, indentation; *Bot:* crenelling (of leaf).

créole [kreɔl] *a.* & *n.* *Ethn:* Creole.

créosote [kreɔzɔt] *n.f.* creosote.

créosoter [kreɔzɔte] *v.tr.* to creosote.

crêpage [krɛpaʒ] *n.m.* crimping, crisping (of hair, of crêpe); *F:* **c. de chignons,** fight (between women).

crêpe [krɛp] **1.** *n.f.* *Cu:* pancake; **faire sauter une crêpe,** to toss a pancake. **2.** *n.m.* (*a*) *Tex:* crêpe, crape; **c. de Chine,** crêpe de Chine; **c. satin,** satin crêpe; (*b*) black mourning crêpe; crape; **voile de c.,** mourning veil; (*c*) crêpe (rubber); **semelles (de) c.,** crêpe (-rubber) soles.

crêpelé [krɛple] *a.* (*of hair*) frizzy.

crêper [krepe] *v.tr.* (*a*) to backcomb (hair); to crimp (material); *F:* **se c (le chignon),** (*of women*) to fight, to tear each other's hair; (*b*) **se c.,** (*of hair*) to frizz.

crêperie [krɛpri] *n.f.* pancake bar.

crépi [krepi] *a.* & *n.m.* *Const:* roughcast.

crépine [krepin] *n.f.* **1.** fringe (on upholstered furniture). **2.** *Cu:* caul. **3.** strainer, rose (of pump, etc.).

crépir [krepir] *v.tr.* *Const:* to roughcast (wall, etc.).

crépissage [krepisaʒ] *n.m.* *Const:* roughcasting.

crépitation [krepitasjɔ̃] *n.f.* **1.** crackling (of fire, sparks, etc.). **2.** *Med:* **c. osseuse,** crepitation, crepitus; **c. pulmonaire,** crepitant rale.

crépitement [krepitmɑ̃] *n.m.* crackling; sputtering.

crépiter [krepite] *v.i.* (*of fire*) to crackle; (*of rain*) to patter; (*of candle flame, melted butter, etc.*) to sputter; **les applaudissements crépitèrent,** there was a ripple of applause.

crépon [krepɔ̃] *n.m.* *Tex:* crepon.

crépu [krepy] *a.* woolly, frizzy, fuzzy (hair).
crépusculaire [krepyskylɛr] *a.* (pertaining to the) twilight; crepuscular; **lumière c.,** twilight, half light.
crépuscule [krepyskyl] *n.m.* (*a*) twilight; **c. du soir,** evening twilight; dusk; (*b*) decline.
crescendo [kreʃɛndo, -ʃɛ̃do] *adv. & n.m.inv. Mus:* crescendo; **aller c.,** to grow louder and louder.
cresson [kresɔ̃] *n.m. Bot:* cress; **c. de fontaine,** watercress.
cressonnière [kresɔnjɛr] *n.f.* watercress bed, pond.
Crésus [krezys] *Pr.n.m. A.Hist:* Croesus; **c'est un C., il est riche comme C.,** he's as rich as Croesus.
crétacé [kretase] *a. & n.m. Geol:* cretaceous.
Crète [krɛt] *Pr.n.f. Geog:* Crete.
crête [krɛt] *n.f.* **1.** comb, crest (of bird); horn (of toad); **c. de coq,** cockscomb; *F:* **baisser la c.,** to look crestfallen. **2.** (*a*) crest, ridge (of mountain); crest (of wave); *Geog:* **(ligne de) c.,** watershed; (*b*) *Const:* crest, ridge (of roof); crest, top (of parapet, wall); (*c*) *Anat:* crest (of bone); (*d*) crest (of helmet). **3.** *El:* peak.
crête-de-coq [krɛtdəkɔk] *n.f. Bot:* cockscomb; *pl. crêtes-de-coq.*
crétin, -ine [kretɛ̃, -in] **1.** *n.* (*a*) *Med:* cretin; (*b*) *F:* idiot, cretin; **quel c.!** what a moron! **2.** *a. F:* idiotic, moronic; **vous êtes encore plus c. que lui,** you're even more of an idiot than he is.
crétinerie [kretinri] *n.f.* imbecility; stupidity.
crétinisme [kretinism] *n.m.* **1.** *Med:* cretinism. **2.** *F:* stupidity, idiocy.
crétois, -oise [kretwa, -waz] *a. & n. Geog:* Cretan.
cretonne [krətɔn] *n.f. Tex:* cretonne.
creusage [krøzaʒ] *n.m.,* **creusement** [krøzmɑ̃] *n.m.* digging (of hole, etc.); sinking (of well, etc.); cutting (of canal).
creuser [krøze] *v.tr.* **1.** (*a*) to hollow (out); to groove (wood, metal, etc.); to plough (a furrow); **c. ((dans) la terre),** to dig; **front creusé de rides,** brow furrowed with wrinkles, deeply lined forehead; **la maladie lui avait creusé les joues,** illness had hollowed his cheeks; **travail qui creuse l'estomac,** work that gives you an appetite, that whets the appetite; (*b*) to wear (sth.) hollow. **2.** (*a*) to excavate; to dig (out) (trench, etc.); to cut (canal); **c. un puits,** to bore, sink, a well; **c. un chemin sous terre,** to burrow one's way underground; **c. sa fosse, sa tombe,** to dig one's own grave; **cela a creusé un abîme entre eux,** it has created a gulf between them; (*b*) to examine (a problem, etc.); **c. une question,** to go thoroughly, deeply, into a question. **3. se c.,** to grow hollow; **ses joues se creusent,** his cheeks are falling in; **se c. la tête,** to rack one's brains.
creuset [krøzɛ] *n.m.* **1.** *Ch: Ind:* crucible, melting pot. **2.** *Metall:* crucible, well, hearth (of blast furnace).
creux, -euse [krø, -øz] **1.** *a.* hollow; **yeux c.,** sunken, deep-set, eyes; **joues creuses,** gaunt, hollow, cheeks; **voix creuse,** deep voice; **avoir l'estomac, le ventre, c.,** to be ravenous; **avoir la tête creuse,** to be empty-headed; *F:* **avoir le nez c.,** to be shrewd, far-seeing; **chemin c.,** sunken road; **heures creuses,** off-peak hours; **période creuse,** slack season; **assiette creuse,** soup plate; **paroles creuses,** empty, meaningless, words; *Dressm:* **pli c.,** inverted pleat; *Fin:* **marché c.,** sagging market; *Nau:* **mer creuse,** rough sea. **2.** *adv.* **sonner c.,** (i) to sound hollow; (ii) to sound empty, false; **songer, rêver, c.,** to dream futile dreams. **3.** *n.m.* (*a*) hollow (of the hand, shoulder, in the ground, etc.); hole (in tree, etc.); pit (of the stomach); trough (of wave, curve); belly (of sail); **sonner le c.,** to sound hollow; **c. d'un rocher,** cavity of a rock; **le c. des reins,** the small of the back; **c. de l'aisselle,** armpit; *Mec.E:* **c. d'une roue dentée,** clearance of a toothed wheel; *F:* **avoir un c. dans l'estomac,** to be ravenous; (*b*) **ce chanteur a du c., a un bon c.,** this singer has a fine bass voice.
crevaison [krəvɛzɔ̃] *n.f.* **1.** puncture (in tyre), *NAm:* flat. **2.** *P:* (*a*) death; (*b*) extreme fatigue; **quelle c.!** what a slog!
crevant [krəvɑ̃] *a. P:* **1.** killing, exhausting (work). **2.** hilarious, priceless, killing (story, etc.).
crevard, -arde [krəvar, -ard] *a. & n. P:* (*a*) dying (person); (*b*) hungry, starving (person).
crevasse [krəvas] *n.f.* crack (in skin, etc.); crack, fissure, crevice (in wall, etc.); fissure (in ground); crevasse (in glacier); **avoir des crevasses aux mains,** to have chapped hands.
crevasser [krəvase] *v.tr.* **1.** to crack; to make cracks, fissures, in (sth.); to chap (the hands). **2. se c.,** to crack; (*of hands*) to chap, get chapped.
crève [krɛv] *n.f. P:* (i) death; (ii) illness; **attraper la c.,** (i) to fall ill; (ii) to catch a cold; (iii) to catch one's death (of cold).
crevé [krəve] **1.** *a.* (*a*) burst; punctured (tyre); (*b*) *F:* dead; (*c*) *P:* worn out, fagged out. **2.** *n.m.* (*a*) *A.Cost:* slash; **manches à crevés,** slashed sleeves; (*b*) *P:* **petit c.,** little runt.
crève-cœur [krɛvkœr] *n.m.inv.* heartbreak; bitter disappointment.
crève-la-faim [krɛvlafɛ̃] *n.m.inv. F:* down-and-out.
crever [krəve] *v.* **(je crève, n. crevons; je crèverai) 1.** *v.i.* (*a*) to burst, split; **mon pneu a crevé,** *F:* **j'ai crevé,** I've got a puncture, *NAm:* a flat; **c. de jalousie, d'orgueil,** to be bursting with jealousy, with pride; **c. de rire,** to split one's sides laughing; (*b*) (*of animals*), *P:* (*of people*) to die; *F:* **c. de faim,** (i) to starve to death; (ii) to be starving, famished; **c. d'ennui,** to be bored to death; **il fait une chaleur à c.,** it's boiling; *F:* **je crève de froid, de chaleur,** I'm freezing (to death); I'm baking. **2.** *v.tr.* (*a*) to burst (balloon, bag, etc.); to puncture (tyre); **se c. les yeux à lire,** to ruin one's eyes reading (too much); **c. le cœur à qn.,** to break s.o.'s heart; **c. un œil à qn,** (i) to put out, gouge out, s.o.'s eye, (ii) (*accidentally*) to blind s.o. in one eye; *F:* **ça vous crève les yeux,** it's staring you in the face, it's under your very nose; it stands out, sticks out, a mile; (*b*) **c. un cheval,** to ride, work, a horse to death; (*c*) **se c. au travail,** to work oneself to death.
crevette [krəvɛt] *n.f.* **c. grise,** shrimp; **c. (rose),** prawn; **faire la pêche à la c.,** to shrimp, to go shrimping.
crevettier [krəvɛtje] *n.m.* (*a*) shrimping net; (*b*) shrimper, shrimp boat.
cri [kri] *n.m.* (*a*) cry (of persons, animals); squeal (of animal); chirp (of cricket, bird); squeak (of mouse); (*b*) shout, call; scream; **cri du cœur,** cri de cœur; **c. de guerre,** (i) war cry; (ii) *Pol: etc:* slogan; **c. d'angoisse, d'horreur,** shriek, scream, of anguish, horror; **pousser un c. aigu,** to scream, to shriek out; **jeter les hauts cris,** to make loud protests, to give vent to one's indignation; **appeler qn à grands cris,** to call loudly to, for, s.o.; (*c*) *F:* **le dernier c.,** the latest fashion, style; **c'est le dernier c.,** it's all the rage; it's the latest thing.
criailler [kri(j)ɑje] *v.i.* **1.** (*of pheasant, guinea fowl*) to cry; (*of goose*) to honk. **2.** to cry out, bawl, shout, squall. **3.** to whine, complain, *F:* grouse.
criaillerie [krijɑjri] *n.f. usu. pl.* whining, complaining.
criailleur, -euse [krijɑjœr, -øz] *F:* (*a*) *a.* whining, complaining; (*b*) *n.* whiner, complainer; *F:* grouser.
criant [kriɑ̃] *a.* glaring (mistake); striking (contrast, proof); **injustice criante,** flagrant, gross, injustice.
criard [kriar] **1.** *a.* (*a*) crying, squalling (child, etc.); *F:* **femme criarde,** scolding, nagging, woman; (*b*) **voix criarde,** shrill, high-pitched, piercing, voice;

dettes criardes, pressing debts; **couleur criarde,** loud, gaudy, colour. **2.** *n.* bawler, squaller; grumbler; nagger.

criblage [kriblaʒ] *n.m.* sifting, riddling (of grain, etc.); screening (of coal, gravel, etc.); grading (of fruit).

crible [kribl̩] *n.m.* sieve; riddle; *Min: Civ.E:* screen, jig, jigger; **c. à gravier, à sable,** gravel, sand, screen; **passer qch. au c.,** (i) to pass sth. through a sieve; to sift, sieve, screen, sth.; (ii) to go through sth. with a fine toothcomb.

criblé [krible] *a.* riddled (with holes, etc.); **être c. de dettes,** to be up to one's eyes in debt.

cribler [krible] *v.tr.* **1.** to sift, riddle, sieve; to pass (sth.) through a sieve; to screen (gravel, coal); to grade (fruit). **2.** to pierce (sth.) with holes; **c. qn, qch., de balles,** to riddle s.o., sth., with bullets; **c. qn de reproches,** to heap reproaches on s.o.; **c. qn de questions,** to bombard s.o. with questions.

cribleur, -euse [kriblœr, -øz] *n.* (*a*) sifter, riddler, screener; (*b*) *n.f.* **cribleuse,** sifter, sifting machine.

cric[1] [krik] *n.m.* (lifting) jack; **c. hydraulique,** hydraulic jack; **c. à vis,** screw jack; **soulever (qch.) au c., à l'aide d'un c.,** to jack (sth.) up.

cric[2] [krik] *int.* crack! snap!

cricket [krikɛt] *n.m. Sp:* cricket.

cricoïde [krikɔid] *a.* & *n.m. Anat:* cricoid (cartilage).

cri(-)cri [krikri] *n.m.inv.* **1.** chirping (of cricket). **2.** *Ent: F:* cricket.

criée [krije] *n.f.* **(vente à la) c.,** (sale by) auction.

crier [krije] *v.* (*pr.sub.* & *p.h.* **n. criions, v. criiez**) **1.** *v.i.* (*a*) to cry; to call out, to shout; to scream, shriek; to yell; **c. de douleur,** to cry out, scream, shriek, with pain; **c. comme un sourd,** to shout one's head off; **enfant qui crie,** squalling child; **c. contre, après, qn,** to rail, cry out, against s.o.; **ne criez pas!** don't shout! **c. au secours,** to shout for help; (*b*) (*of mouse, etc.*) to squeak; (*of cricket*) to chirp; (*of birds*) to call; (*c*) (*of door, axle, etc.*) to squeak, creak; (*d*) (*of colours*) to clash. **2.** *v.tr.* (*a*) **c. des légumes,** to cry, hawk, vegetables; *F:* **c. qch. sur les toits,** to cry sth. from the roof tops; (*b*) **c. une vente,** to put (goods) up for auction; (*c*) **c. un ordre,** to shout an order; **c. des injures à qn,** to shout abuse at s.o.; **c. famine, misère,** to cry famine; to complain of hardship, distress; **c. vengeance,** to call, cry out, for vengeance.

crieur, -euse [krijœr, -øz] *n.* (*a*) (street) hawker; **c. de journaux,** newspaper seller; *Hist:* **c. public,** town crier; (*b*) *Th:* call boy.

crime [krim] *n.m.* (*a*) crime, offence, *Jur:* felony; **c. capital,** capital offence, crime; **c. d'État,** treason; **c. d'incendie,** arson; (*b*) murder; **l'arme du c.,** the murder weapon; (*c*) **c'est un c. que d'avoir démoli cette maison,** it's a crime to have pulled down that house; **ce n'est pas un c.!** it's not a crime! it's not really serious!

Crimée [krime] *Pr.n.f. Geog:* Crimea.

criminaliser [kriminalize] *v.tr. Jur:* to refer (a case) to a criminal court.

criminaliste [kriminalist] *n.m.* criminal jurist.

criminalité [kriminalite] *n.f.* (*a*) criminality, criminal nature (of an act); (*b*) crime, delinquency; **c. juvénile,** juvenile delinquency.

criminel, -elle [kriminɛl] **1.** *a.* (*a*) guilty (of crime); *F:* **ce serait c. de la jeter,** it would be a crime to throw it away; (*b*) criminal (law, attempt, etc.). **2.** *n.* criminal; murderer; **voilà le c.,** that's the culprit. **3.** *n.m.* **avocat au c.,** criminal lawyer; **poursuivre qn au c.,** to take criminal proceedings against s.o.

criminellement [kriminɛlmɑ̃] *adv.* **1.** criminally (inclined, etc.). **2. poursuivre qn c.,** to take criminal proceedings against s.o.

criminologie [kriminɔlɔʒi] *n.f.* criminology.

criminologiste [kriminɔlɔʒist] *n.m.* & *f.* criminologist.

crin [krɛ̃] *n.m.* **1.** (*a*) hair (of animal), *esp.* horsehair; **le c.,** the mane and tail (of horse); **matelas de c.,** (horse)hair mattress; **à tous crins,** diehard, fanatical; **révolutionnaire à tous crins,** out and out revolutionary; *F:* **être comme un c., à c.,** to be bad-tempered, cantankerous; (*b*) **c. végétal,** vegetable horsehair.

crincrin [krɛ̃krɛ̃] *n.m. F:* **1.** squeaky violin, fiddle. **2.** squeaking, scraping (sound).

crinière [krinjɛr] *n.f.* **1.** mane (of horse, lion, etc.); **c. d'un casque,** (horsehair) plume. **2.** *F:* (*of pers.*) abundant crop of (untidy) hair; mop, mane.

crinoline [krinɔlin] *n.f. A. Cost:* crinoline.

crique [krik] *n.f.* creek, cove, bay.

criquet [krikɛ] *n.m. Ent:* locust; **c. pélerin, migrateur,** migratory locust.

crise [kriz] *n.f.* **1.** crisis; emergency; **c. ministérielle,** cabinet crisis; **c. économique,** economic crisis; slump; **c. du logement,** housing shortage. **2.** (*a*) *Med:* crisis (in an illness); (*b*) attack; **c. cardiaque,** heart attack; **c. d'épilepsie,** epileptic fit; **c. de foie,** bilious attack; **c. de nerfs,** attack of nerves; fit of hysterics; *F:* **piquer une c.,** (i) to have hysterics; (ii) to get in a rage; *F:* **faire prendre une c. (de nerfs) à qn,** to send s.o. up the wall.

crispant [krispɑ̃] *a. F:* irritating, annoying.

crispation [krispasjɔ̃] *n.f.* (*a*) crispation, shrivelling up (of leather); tensing (of the face); (*b*) nervous twitching, clenching (of the hands); wince (of pain); **donner des crispations à qn,** to get on s.o.'s nerves.

crispé [krispe] *a.* (*a*) nervous, strained (smile, etc.); (*b*) (*of pers.*) on edge; tense.

crisper [krispe] *v.tr.* (*a*) to shrivel up (leather, etc.); **le froid crispe la peau,** cold wrinkles the skin; (*b*) to contract (muscles, etc.); to clench (fists, etc.); **visage crispé par la souffrance,** face contorted, screwed up, with pain; *F:* **cela me crispe,** it irritates me, it gets on my nerves; (*c*) **se c.,** to contract; to become wrinkled; **ses mains se crispaient sur le volant,** his hands were clutching the wheel.

crispin [krispɛ̃] *n.m.* gauntlet (of glove); **gants à c.,** gauntlets.

criss [kris] *n.m.* kris, creese.

crissement [krismɑ̃] *n.m.* grating, grinding (of teeth); squeaking (of chalk on blackboard, etc.); squealing, screeching (of brakes); crunching (of gravel).

crisser [krise] *v.i.* to grate; to make a grating, grinding, rasping, sound; (*of brakes*) to squeal, screech; **c. des dents,** to grind one's teeth; **gravier qui crisse sous les pas,** gravel that crunches under one's feet.

cristal, -aux [kristal, -o] *n.m.* **1.** crystal; **c. de roche,** rock crystal. **2.** (*a*) crystal (glass); *pl.* crystal (ware); **boule de c.,** crystal ball; **voix de c.,** crystal-clear voice; (*b*) *Lit:* pure water, ice. **3.** *F:* **cristaux (de soude),** washing soda.

cristallerie [kristalri] *n.f.* (*a*) crystal (glass) manufacture; (*b*) (crystal) glassworks; (*c*) crystal (ware).

cristallier [kristalje] *n.m.* glass cutter and engraver.

cristallin, -ine [kristalɛ̃, -in] **1.** *a.* crystalline (rock, etc.); crystal-clear (water, etc.); (*of sound*) as clear as a bell. **2.** *n.m. Anat:* crystalline lens (of the eye).

cristallisation [kristalizasjɔ̃] *n.f.* crystallization, crystallizing.

cristallisé [kristalize] *a.* crystallized; **sucre c.,** granulated sugar.

cristalliser [kristalize] *v.tr.* & *i.* to crystallize.

cristallographie [kristalɔgrafi] *n.f.* crystallography.

critère [kritɛr] *n.m.* criterion; test; measure; **son seul c. c'est l'avis de son père,** his father's opinion is his only criterion.
critérium [kriterjɔm] *n.m.* **1.** *A:* criterion; test. **2.** *Sp:* (*a*) *Turf:* **c. des deux ans,** races to select the best two-year-old; (*b*) (eliminating) heat.
critiquable [kritikabl] *a.* criticizable, open to criticism.
critique¹ [kritik] *a.* (*a*) *Med:* **phase c.,** critical phase (of an illness); **l'âge c.,** the menopause; (*b*) critical; decisive; crucial; **dans une situation c.,** in a critical situation, in a tight spot; in an emergency.
critique² *a. & n.* **1.** *a.* (*a*) (*passing judgement*) critical; **examiner qch. d'un œil c.,** to examine sth. critically, with a critical eye; **esprit c.,** critical mind; (*b*) censorious, criticizing (mind, etc.). **2.** *n.m.* critic; **c. d'art,** art critic; **c. sévère,** harsh critic. **3.** *n.f.* (*a*) (art of) criticism; **c. des textes,** textual criticism; **c. dramatique,** dramatic criticism; (*b*) critical article, paper; review; **faire la c. d'une pièce,** to review a play; (*c*) censure; **être l'objet des critiques du public,** to incur the censure of the public, to be a target for public criticism; (*d*) *coll:* **la c.,** the (body of) critics.
critiquer [kritike] *v.tr.* to criticize; (*a*) to assess (sth.); to examine (sth.) critically; (*b*) to censure; to find fault with (s.o., sth.).
critiqueur [kritikœr] *n.m.* captious critic; criticizer.
croassement [krɔasmɑ̃] *n.m.* caw(ing) (of crow, rook); croak(ing) (of raven).
croasser [krɔase] *v.i.* (*of crow, rook*) to caw; (*of raven*) to croak.
croate [krɔat] *Geog:* **1.** *a.* Croatian. **2.** *n.* Croat(ian). **3.** *n.m. Ling:* Croat(ian).
Croatie [krɔasi] *Pr.n.f. Geog:* Croatia.
croc [kro] *n.m.* **1.** hook; **c. de boucherie,** meat hook; **c. à pommes de terre,** potato hook, Canterbury hoe; **c. à fumier,** muck rake; **c. de marinier,** boathook. **2.** canine tooth; fang (of dog, wolf); **moustache en c.,** curled-up moustache; **montrer ses crocs,** to show one's teeth; *P:* **avoir les crocs,** to be famished, ravenous.
croc-en-jambe [krɔkɑ̃ʒɑ̃b] *n.m.* trip (to bring down opponent); **faire un c.-en-j. à qn,** (i) to trip s.o. up; (ii) to pull a fast one on s.o.; *pl. crocs-en-jambe.*
croche [krɔʃ] *n.f. Mus:* quaver; *NAm:* eighth note; **double c.,** semiquaver; *NAm:* sixteenth note; **triple, quadruple, c.,** demisemiquaver, hemidemisemiquaver; *NAm:* thirty-second, sixty-fourth, note.
croche-pied [krɔʃpje] *n.m.* = CROC-EN-JAMBE. *pl. croche-pieds.*
crocher [krɔʃe] *v.tr. & i.* (*a*) *Nau:* to hook (on to) (sth.), to seize (sth.) with a hook; **l'ancre croche,** the anchor grips, bites, holds; (*b*) to grab hold of (sth.).
crochet [krɔʃɛ] *n.m.* **1.** (*a*) hook; **clou à c.,** hook nail; **c. à vis,** screw hook; **c. d'attelage,** *Rail:* coupling hook; **c. de boucherie,** meat hook; **c. à boutons,** buttonhook; **c. de bureau,** spike file; **vivre aux crochets de qn,** to live off, sponge on, s.o.; (*b*) crochet hook; **(travail au) c.,** crochet work; **faire du c.,** to crochet; **faire qch. au c.,** to crochet sth. **2.** (*a*) *Mec.E:* **c. d'arrêt,** pawl, catch; (*b*) **c. de serrurier,** picklock. **3.** (poison) fang (of snake). **4.** *Typ:* square bracket. **5.** **faire un c.,** (i) to make a detour; (ii) (*of road*) to take a sudden turn; (iii) to swerve (to avoid sth.). **6.** *Box:* **c. du gauche, du droit,** left, right, hook. **7.** *Mus:* hook (of quaver). **8.** *Arch:* crocket. **9.** **c. radiophonique,** talent contest (on radio, T.V.).
crochetage [krɔʃtaʒ] *n.m.* picking (of a lock).
crocheter [krɔʃte] *v.tr.* (**je crochète, n. crochetons; je crochèterai**) **1.** to pick (lock). **2.** to hook, to pick up with a hook.
crocheteur [krɔʃtœr] *n.m.* picklock; housebreaker.
crochu [krɔʃy] *a.* hooked (wire, nose, etc.); claw-like (fingers, hands); *F:* **avoir les doigts crochus, les mains crochues,** to be mean, tight-fisted; *Gr.Phil:* **atomes crochus,** interlocking atoms; *F:* **nous nous sommes senti des atomes crochus,** we hit it off together.
croco [krɔko] *n.m. F:* crocodile (skin); *F:* croc.
crocodile [krɔkɔdil] *n.m.* **1.** (*a*) crocodile; **larmes de c.,** crocodile tears; (*b*) **sac à main en c.,** crocodile (skin) handbag. **2.** *Rail:* alarm contact; contact ramp.
crocus [krɔkys] *n.m. Bot:* crocus.
croire [krwar] *v.* (*pr.p.* **croyant;** *p.p.* **cru;** *pr.ind.* **je crois, il croit, n. croyons, ils croient;** *impf.* **je croyais;** *p.h.* **je crus;** *fu.* **je croirai**) **1.** *v.tr.* (*a*) **c. qch.,** to believe sth.; **ne pas croire qch.,** to disbelieve sth.; not to believe sth.; **vous ne sauriez c. combien je suis content,** you can't think, imagine, how glad I am; **j'aime à c. que** + *ind.,* I hope, trust, that . . .; **il est à c. que** + *ind.,* it is probable that . . .; **tout porte à c., il faut c., que . . .,** there is every indication that . . .; it would seem that . . .; *F:* **faut pas c.!** don't you believe it! **je ne crois pas que cela suffise,** I don't think that will be enough; **je crois que oui, que non,** I believe, think, so, not; **n'en croyez rien!** don't believe it! *F:* not a bit of it! **vous croyez?** do you really think so? **à ce que je crois . . .,** in my opinion . . .; **c. qn riche,** to believe s.o. to be rich; **on se serait cru en octobre,** it felt like October; **je vous croyais anglais,** I thought you were English; **on croirait qu'il dort,** you'd think he was asleep; **je ne suis pas celle que vous croyez,** I'm not that kind of girl; **j'ai cru nécessaire de . . .,** I thought it necessary to . . .; **j'ai cru bien faire,** I believed, thought, I was doing right, the right thing; **j'ai cru devoir le prévenir,** I thought I ought to warn him; **il ne croyait pas si bien dire,** he didn't know how right he was; **il se croit tout permis,** he thinks he can do, get away with, anything; *F:* **qu'est-ce qu'il se croit?** who does he think he is? *F:* **il se croit (beaucoup), il s'en croit,** he thinks a lot of himself, he thinks he's the bee's knees; **je n'aurais pas cru cela de lui,** I wouldn't, would never, have thought it of him; (*b*) **c. qn,** to believe s.o., take s.o.'s word for sth.; **me croira qui voudra, mais . . .,** believe me or not, but . . .; *F:* **je te, vous, crois!** (i) I should think so! (ii) of course! **en croire qn,** (i) to take s.o.'s word for it; (ii) to take s.o.'s advice; **vous pouvez m'en c.,** take my word for it, you can take it from me; **s'il faut l'en c., à l'en c., ce n'est pas difficile,** according to him it is not difficult; **je ne pouvais en c. mes yeux, mes oreilles,** I couldn't believe my eyes, my ears. **2.** *v.i.* (*a*) to believe (in the existence of sth.); **c. aux fantômes,** to believe in ghosts; **c. à l'innocence de qn,** to believe in s.o.'s innocence; **le médecin crut à une rougeole,** the doctor thought it was measles; **c'est à ne pas y c.,** it's beyond belief; it's unbelievable; *Corr:* **veuillez c., je vous prie de c., à l'expression de mes sentiments distingués** = yours sincerely; (*b*) to believe (in), trust (in), to have faith in; **je ne crois pas à ses promesses,** I have no faith in his promises; **c. en Dieu,** to believe in God; **il ne croit plus,** he has lost his faith (in God).
croisade [krwazad] *n.f.* (*a*) *Hist:* crusade; **partir en c.,** to go on a crusade; (*b*) campaign (for, against, sth.).
croisé [krwaze] **1.** *a.* (*a*) crossed; **feu c.,** crossfire; **mots croisés,** crossword; *Pros:* **rimes croisées,** alternate rhymes; *Husb:* **race croisée,** crossbreed; (*b*) double-breasted (coat, etc.); (*c*) *Tex:* twilled (material). **2.** *n.m.* (*a*) *Hist:* crusader; (*b*) *Tex:* twill.
croisée [krwaze] *n.f.* **1.** crossing; **c. de chemins,** crossroads; **être à la c. des chemins,** to stand at the crossroads, at the parting of the ways. **2.** (*a*) casement; (*b*) casement window. **3.** *Ecc. Arch:* **c. (du transept),** transept; **c. d'ogives,** intersecting ribs (of a vault).

croisement [krwazmɑ̃] *n.m.* **1.** crossing, passing, meeting (of traffic, etc.); crossing (of legs, arms). **2.** crossing, intersection (of lines, roads, etc.); **c. de routes, de rues,** crossroads; junction; **c. dangereux,** dangerous crossroads. **3.** (*a*) crossing, crossbreeding, interbreeding (of animals); **faire des croisements de races,** to cross breeds; (*b*) crossbreed; cross (**entre . . . et . . .,** between . . . and . . .).

croiser [krwaze] **1.** *v.tr.* (*a*) to cross; to cut across, to intersect; **c. le fer avec qn,** to cross swords with s.o.; **c. les jambes,** to cross one's legs; **(se) c. les bras,** (i) to fold one's arms; (ii) to refuse to work; **c. qn dans l'escalier,** to meet, pass, s.o. on the stairs; **nos lettres se sont croisées,** our letters have crossed in the post; (*b*) to cross(breed), interbreed (animals, plants). **2.** *v.i.* (*of garment*) to lap, fold over; **habit qui ne croise pas assez,** coat that has not sufficient overlap. **3.** *v.i. Nau:* to cruise. **4. se c.** (*a*) to (inter)-cross; to intersect; **ces deux chemins se croisent,** these two paths intersect; **se c. avec qn,** to meet and pass s.o.; **leurs regards se croisèrent,** their eyes met; (*b*) *Hist:* to take the cross; to go on a crusade; (*c*) **le cheval peut se c. avec l'âne,** the horse can be crossed with the donkey.

croiseur [krwazœr] *n.m. Navy:* cruiser; **c. de bataille,** battle cruiser.

croisière [krwazjɛr] *n.f. Nau: etc:* (*a*) cruising; **navire en c.,** ship cruising; **vitesse de c.,** cruising speed; (*b*) cruise; expedition; (*c*) cruising fleet; blockage fleet.

croisillon [krwazijɔ̃] *n.m.* crosspiece, crossbar (of cross, window); (cross)bar (of chair, etc.); brace; *Arch:* transept; **fenêtre à croisillons,** lattice window.

croissance [krwasɑ̃s] *n.f.* growth; **c. économique,** economic growth, development; **en pleine c.,** growing rapidly; **arrêté dans sa c.,** stunted.

croissant¹ [krwasɑ̃] *a.* growing (plant, tendency, etc.); increasing (wealth, anxiety, etc.); rising (heat, etc.).

croissant² *n.m.* **1.** (*a*) *O:* waxing (of moon); (*b*) crescent (of moon); **en c.,** crescent-shaped. **2.** (*a*) *Cu:* croissant; (*b*) **c. à élaguer,** billhook; pruning hook.

croître [krwɑtr̥] *v.i.* (*pr.p.* **croissant;** *p.p.* **crû,** *f.* **crue;** *pr.ind.* **je crois, il croît, n. croissons, ils croissent;** *p.h.* **je crûs;** *fu.* **je croîtrai;** *pr.sub.* **je croisse;** *p.sub.* **je crûsse**) to grow, increase (in size); (*a*) (*of moon*) to wax; (*of river*) to rise, swell; (*of wind*) to rise; **c. en volume, en nombre,** to increase in volume, in number; **les jours croissent,** the days are lengthening, getting longer; **c. en beauté,** to grow in beauty; **cela ne fait que c. et embellir,** (i) it's getting better and better; (ii) *Iron:* it's getting worse and worse; **la chaleur ne cesse de c.,** the heat is getting more and more intense; **c. dans l'estime de qn,** to rise in s.o.'s esteem; (*b*) (*of plants*) to grow; **les pays où croissent la vigne et l'olivier,** lands of the vine and the olive; *Prov:* **mauvaise herbe croît toujours,** ill weeds grow apace.

croix [krwa] *n.f.* cross. **1.** (*a*) **la sainte C.,** the Holy Cross; **mettre en c.,** to crucify; **le chemin de (la) C.,** (i) the Way of the Cross; (ii) the stations of the Cross; **le signe de (la) c.,** the sign of the cross; **faire le signe de c.,** to cross oneself; **chacun a sa c., porte sa c.,** everyone has his cross to bear; (*b*) **c'est la c. et la bannière,** it's the devil of a job; **la Croix-Rouge,** the Red Cross (organization); *Hist:* **prendre la c.,** to go on a crusade; **la c. (de la Légion d'honneur),** the Cross of the Legion of Honour; *Mil:* **la c. de guerre,** the Military Cross. **2.** (*a*) **en forme de c.,** cross-shaped; in the shape of a cross; **mettre des bâtons en c.,** to lay sticks crosswise; **mettre les bras en c.,** to stretch one's arms out sideways; **marquer qch. d'une c.,** to mark sth. with a cross (against it); *F:* **faire une c. sur qch.,** to give sth. up for good; **faire une c. à la cheminée,** to mark sth. in red letters; (*b*) **c. de Saint-André,** St. Andrew's cross; **c. latine,** Latin cross; **c. de Malte,** Maltese cross; **c. gammée,** swastika; (*c*) *Typ:* **c. (mortuaire),** dagger; (*d*) *Astr:* **la C. du Sud,** the Southern Cross.

croquant¹ [krɔkɑ̃] *a.* crisp, crunchy (biscuit, etc.).

croquant² *n.m. Pej:* country bumpkin, yokel.

croque au sel (à la) [alakrɔkosɛl] *adv.phr. Cu:* raw and unseasoned except for salt.

croque-madame [krɔkmadam] *n.m.inv. Cu:* toasted cheese and ham sandwich topped with fried egg.

croque(-)mitaine [krɔkmitɛn] *n.m.* bogeyman; *pl. croque(-)mitaines.*

croque-monsieur [krɔkməsjø] *n.m.inv. Cu:* toasted cheese and ham sandwich.

croque-mort [krɔkmɔr] *n.m. F:* undertaker; **avoir une figure de c.-m.,** to have a funereal look; *pl. croque-morts.*

croquer [krɔke] **1.** *v.i.* (*a*) (*of fruit, gravel, etc.*) to crunch (between the teeth, underfoot); **pomme qui croque,** crunchy apple; (*b*) **c. dans une pomme,** to bite into an apple. **2.** *v.tr.* (*a*) to crunch, munch; **chocolat à c.,** plain chocolate; **c. de l'argent,** to squander one's money; (*b*) to sketch; *F:* **elle est jolie, mignonne, à c.,** she's as pretty as a picture; *F:* she's a sweetie; (*c*) *F:* **c. le marmot,** to cool, kick, one's heels.

croquet¹ [krɔkɛ] *n.m. Cu:* crisp almond biscuit.

croquet² *n.m. Games:* croquet.

croquette [krɔkɛt] *n.f.* (*a*) *Cu:* (potato, etc.) croquette; rissole; (*b*) chocolate drop.

croqueur, -euse [krɔkœr, -øz] *n.* (*a*) (*of pers., animal*) devourer; (*b*) *F:* **une croqueuse de diamants,** an expensive mistress, a gold digger.

croquignole [krɔkiɲɔl] *n.f.* small crunchy biscuit.

croquignolet, -ette [krɔkiɲɔlɛ, -ɛt] *a. F:* sweet, pretty, *NAm:* cute.

croquis [krɔki] *n.m.* sketch; rough drawing; **faire un c. de qch.,** to make a (rough) sketch of sth., to sketch sth.; *Mth:* **c. coté,** dimensional sketch.

crosne [kron] *n.m. Hort:* Japanese, Chinese, artichoke.

cross [krɔs] *n.m. F:* = CROSS-COUNTRY.

cross-country [krɔskuntri] *n.m. Sp:* cross-country run, race; cross-country running, racing.

crosse [krɔs] *n.f.* **1.** (bishop's) crook, crozier. **2.** *Sp:* (*a*) (hockey) stick; (golf) club; *Fr.C:* (*lacrosse*) crosse; (*b*) *F:* **chercher des crosses à qn,** to pick a quarrel with s.o. **3.** (*a*) crook; *Anat:* **c. de l'aorte,** arch of the aorta; (*b*) *Cu:* **c. de bœuf,** knuckle of beef; (*c*) *Mch:* crosshead (of piston); (*d*) *Mil:* butt (of rifle); grip (of pistol); *F:* **lever, mettre, la c. en l'air,** (i) to mutiny; (ii) to surrender; (*e*) scroll (of violin, etc.); (*f*) *Bot:* crosier (of a fern).

crotale [krɔtal] *n.m. Rept:* rattlesnake, *NAm: F:* rattler.

crotte [krɔt] *n.f.* **1.** (*a*) dung, dropping (of horse, sheep, etc.); *F:* **c'est de la c. (de bique),** it isn't worth anything, it's a load of rubbish; (*b*) *P:* shit; (*c*) **une c. de chocolat,** a chocolate; *F:* **ma petite c.,** my dear, (my) darling; (*d*) *int. F:* **c.!** damn! **2.** *O:* mud, slush.

crotté [krɔte] *a. F:* dirty; muddy, covered in mud.

crotter [krɔte] (*a*) *v.tr.* to dirty, soil; to cover in mud; (*b*) *v.i. F:* (*of animal*) to make droppings; (*of dog*) to make a mess; (*c*) **se c.,** to get dirty; to get covered with mud.

crottin [krɔtɛ̃] *n.m.* (*a*) (horse) dung, manure; (sheep) droppings; (*b*) small goat's-milk cheese.

croulant [krulɑ̃] **1.** *a.* (*of building*) crumbling, tumbledown, ramshackle; **empire c.,** tottering empire. **2.** *n.m. P:* (*esp. of one's parents*) **les croulants,** the old folk.

crouler [krule] *v.i.* (*of building, etc.*) (*a*) to be on the point of collapse, to totter; (*b*) to collapse, crumble, fall in; **faire c. un projet,** to ruin a plan; *Th:* **faire c. la salle (sous les applaudissements),** to bring down the house.

croup [krup] *n.m. Med:* croup; **faux c.,** false croup.

croupe [krup] *n.f.* **1.** (*a*) croup, crupper, rump, hind-quarters (of horse); **monter en c.,** to ride pillion; (*b*) *F:* behind, backside. **2.** (*a*) brow, crest (of hill); (*b*) *Arch:* hip (of roof).

croupetons (à) [akruptɔ̃] *adv.phr.* squatting, crouching; **se tenir à c.,** to squat (down).

croupi [krupi] *a.* (*of water*) stagnant, foul.

croupier [krupje] *n.m.* croupier (in casino).

croupière [krupjɛr] *n.f. Harn:* crupper; **tailler des croupières à qn,** to put difficulties, obstacles, in s.o.'s way.

croupion [krupjɔ̃] *n.m.* **1.** (*a*) rump (of bird); (*b*) *F:* parson's nose, *U.S:* pope's nose (of cooked chicken, etc.). **2.** *F:* backside, behind.

croupir [krupir] *v.i.* **1.** (*of pers.*) to lie, be sunk wallow (in filth, vice, idleness, etc.). **2.** (*of water, etc.*) to stagnate, grow foul.

croupissant [krupisɑ̃] *a.* stagnating; **eaux croupissantes,** stagnant water.

croustade [krustad] *n.f. Cu:* croustade.

croustillant [krustijɑ̃] *a.* **1.** crisp (biscuit, pie, etc.); crusty (loaf). **2.** *F:* spicy (story).

croustiller [krustije] *v.i.* (*of food*) to crunch (under the teeth); **pain qui croustille,** crisp, crunchy, bread.

croûte [krut] *n.f.* **1.** (*a*) crust (of bread, pie, etc.); rind (of cheese); **la c. terrestre,** the earth's crust; *Cu:* **c. au fromage** = cheese on toast; *F:* **casser la c.,** to eat; **casser une c.,** to have a snack; *P:* **à la c.!** let's eat! grub's up! *F:* **gagner sa c.,** to earn one's daily bread, one's bread and butter. **2.** (*a*) scab (on wound, etc.); (*b*) **c. de rouille,** layer of rust. **3.** undressed leather; hide. **4.** *F:* (*a*) daub, badly painted picture; (*b*) **une vieille c.,** an old fossil.

croûter [krute] *v.i. P:* to eat, nosh.

croûteux, -euse [krutø, -øz] *a.* scabby, covered with scabs.

croûton [krutɔ̃] *n.m.* **1.** crust, crusty end (of loaf). **2.** *Cu:* croûton (for soup). **3.** *P:* **(vieux) c.,** old fossil, old stick-in-the-mud.

croyable [krwajabl̩] *a.* believable, credible; **ce n'est pas c.,** it's unbelievable, incredible.

croyance [krwajɑ̃s] *n.f.* (*a*) belief (**à,** in); **c. en Dieu,** belief in God; (*b*) belief, conviction; **croyances religieuses,** religious beliefs; **c. politique,** political opinion.

croyant, -ante [krwajɑ̃, -ɑ̃t] **1.** *a.* believing; **il n'est pas c.,** he's a non-believer. **2.** *n.* (*a*) believer; (*b*) *pl.* (*Islam*) the Faithful.

cru[1] [kry] *a.* **1.** (*a*) raw, uncooked (food); raw (silk, material, etc.); crude (ore); untreated, raw (leather); crude, garish (colour, light); **dans le jour c.,** in broad daylight; **réponse crue,** blunt answer; **cette plaisanterie est un peu crue,** that's a rather coarse, crude, joke; **je vous le dis tout c.,** I'm not mincing my words; (*b*) **eau crue,** hard water. **2.** *adv.phr.* **à c.** (*a*) **être chaussé à c.,** to wear one's shoes without any socks; **monter à c.,** to ride bareback; (*b*) **construction à c.,** building without foundations. **3.** *n.m.* **manger du c.,** to eat raw food.

cru[2] *n.m.* vineyard; **les meilleurs crus,** (i) the best vineyards; (ii) the best wines; **un grand c.,** a vintage wine; **vin du c.,** local wine; **bouilleur de c.,** home distiller; **une histoire de son (propre) c.,** a story of his own invention.

cruauté [kryote] *n.f.* **1.** cruelty (**envers,** to). **2.** (act of) cruelty.

cruche [kryʃ] *n.f.* **1.** (*a*) (earthenware) jug, pitcher; (*b*) jugful. **2.** *F:* idiot, ass, twit.

cruchon [kryʃɔ̃] *n.m.* (*a*) small jug; (*b*) small jugful.

crucial, -iaux [krysjal, -jo] *a.* **1.** crucial, cross-shaped (incision, etc.). **2.** crucial (question, point).

crucifère [krysifɛr] *a.* cruciferous.

crucifiement [krysifimɑ̃] *n.m.* (*a*) crucifying, crucifixion; (*b*) **c. de la chair,** mortifying of the flesh.

crucifier [krysifje] *v.tr.* (*pr.sub. & impf.* **n. crucifiions, v. crucifiiez**) to crucify; **c. la chair,** to crucify, mortify, the flesh.

crucifix [krysifi] *n.m.inv.* crucifix.

crucifixion [krysifiksjɔ̃] *n.f.* crucifixion.

cruciforme [krysifɔrm] *a.* cruciform.

cruciverbiste [krysivɛrbist] *n.m. & f.* crossword enthusiast.

crudité [krydite] *n.f.* **1. crudités,** raw vegetable hors d'œuvres. **2.** (*a*) crudity, crudeness (of colours, etc.); glare (of light); (*b*) coarseness (of expression, etc.).

crue [kry] *n.f.* (*a*) rising, swelling (of waters, river, etc.); (*b*) flood; **rivière en c.,** river in spate.

cruel, -elle [kryɛl] *a.* cruel (**envers, avec,** to); **expérience cruelle,** bitter experience.

cruellement [kryɛlmɑ̃] *adv.* cruelly, bitterly, grievously; **c. éprouvé,** sorely tried.

crûment [krymɑ̃] *adv.* (*a*) crudely, roughly; **dire qch. c.,** to say sth. bluntly; (*b*) **éclairé c.,** garishly lit.

crustacé [krystase] *n.m.* **crustacés,** Crustacea, crustaceans; shellfish; **la crevette est un c.,** the prawn is a shellfish; *Cu:* **assiette de crustacés,** seafood platter.

crypte [kript] *n.f. Arch: Anat:* crypt.

cryptogramme [kriptɔgram] *n.m.* cryptogram; cipher (message).

cryptographie [kriptɔgrafi] *n.m.* cryptography, writing in cipher.

cubage [kybaʒ] *n.m.* **1.** cubature; finding the cubic contents (of pile of wood, etc.). **2.** cubage; cubic content, capacity; volume (of reservoir, etc.); air space (of room, etc.).

cubain, -aine [kybɛ̃, -ɛn] *a. & n. Geog:* Cuban.

cube [kyb] **1.** *n.m.* (*a*) *Mth:* cube; **le c. de 2 est 8,** the cube of 2 is 8; **élever (un nombre) au c.,** to cube (a number); (*b*) *Toys:* **jeu de cubes,** building blocks, (wooden) bricks. **2.** *a.* cubic; **mètre c., centimètre c.,** cubic metre, centimetre, *NAm:* meter, centimeter.

cuber [kybe] **1.** *v.tr.* (*a*) *Mth:* to cube (number, etc.); (*b*) to find the cubical contents of (sth.). **2.** *v.i.* (*a*) **réservoir qui cube vingt litres,** tank with a cubic capacity of twenty litres, *NAm:* liters; (*b*) *F:* **ça cube, ça finit par c.,** it mounts up; it's getting expensive.

cubique [kybik] **1.** *a.* (*a*) cubic; (*b*) *Mth:* **racine c.,** cube root. **2.** *n.f.* cubic (curve).

cubisme [kybism] *n.m. Art:* cubism.

cubiste [kybist] *a. & n.m. & f. Art:* cubist.

cubital, -aux [kybital, -o] *a. Anat:* ulnar.

cubitus [kybitys] *n.m. Anat:* ulna.

cucu(l) [kyky] *a. F:* **c. (la praline),** stupid, idotic, goofy.

cueillette [kœjɛt] *n.f.* (*a*) gathering, picking (of fruit, flowers, etc.); **la c. des fraises,** strawberry picking; (*b*) crop, harvest (of fruit, etc.).

cueilleur, -euse [kœjœr, -øz] *n.* picker, gatherer (of fruit, etc.).

cueillir [kœjir] *v.tr.* (*pr.p.* **cueillant;** *p.p.* **cueilli;** *pr.ind.* **je cueille, il cueille, n. cueillons;** *impf.* **je cueillais;** *p.h.* **je cueillis;** *fu.* **je cueillerai**) to gather, pick, pluck (flowers, fruit, etc.); **c. un baiser,** to steal, snatch, a kiss; **c. des lauriers,** to win laurels; *F:* **c. qn,** (i) to meet, collect s.o., to pick s.o. up, (ii) to arrest, nab, s.o.

cueilloir [kœjwar] *n.m.* **1.** (*implement*) fruit picker. **2.** fruit basket.

cui-cui [kɥikɥi] *int. & n.m.* cheeping, chirping, chirruping (of birds).

cuiller, cuillère [kɥijɛr] *n.f.* **1.** (*a*) spoon; **c. à des-**

sert, à entremets, dessert spoon; **c. à soupe,** soup spoon; **c. à café, petite c.,** (i) coffee spoon; (ii) teaspoon; **c. à pot,** ladle; *F:* **il n'y va pas avec le dos de la c.,** he goes the whole hog; he doesn't go in for half measures; *F:* **en deux, trois, coups de c. à pot,** in less than no time, in two shakes (of a lamb's tail); *F:* **être à ramasser à la petite c.,** (i) to be badly hurt, smashed up; (ii) to be completely exhausted, all in; (*b*) spoonful; *Fish:* spoon (bait), trolling spoon; **pêcher à la c.,** to troll, to spin (for trout, etc.); (*c*) *Tls:* spoon drill; **mèche à c.,** spoon bit; (*d*) safety catch (of grenade). **2.** *Civ.E:* scoop, bucket (of dredger). **3.** *P:* hand, paw.

cuillerée [kɥij(e)re] *n.f.* spoonful; (*to child*) **une c. pour maman,** one (spoonful) for mummy!

cuilleron [kɥijrɔ̃] *n.m.* bowl (of spoon).

cuir [kɥir] *n.m.* **1.** (*a*) *O:* skin; *still so used in* **blessure entre c. et chair,** oblique flesh wound; *P:* **tanner le c. à qn,** to give s.o. a good hiding; *Anat:* **c. chevelu,** scalp; (*b*) hide (of elephant, etc.). **2.** (*a*) leather; **c. vert, brut,** rawhide; **c. en croûte,** undressed leather; **c. jaune,** tan leather; **c. verni,** patent leather; **c. bouilli,** cuir-bouilli; **chaussures en c.,** leather shoes; (*b*) **c. à rasoir,** razor strop; (*c*) leather jacket. **3.** *F:* incorrect liaison, *e.g.:* **j'étais avec lui** [ʒetɛtavɛk lɥi], **il a fait une erreur** [il a fɛz yn ɛrœr], **s'en va en guerre** [sɑ̃vatɑ̃gɛr].

cuirasse [kɥiras] *n.f.* **1.** cuirass, breastplate; *Z:* cuirass; **trouver le défaut dans la c. de qn,** to find s.o.'s weak, vulnerable, spot. **2.** armour (plating) (of warship, tank); **plaque de c.,** armour plate.

cuirassé [kɥirase] **1.** *a.* (*a*) armour-plated, armoured; (*b*) **être c. contre (les supplications, etc.),** to be proof, be hardened, against (entreaties, etc.). **2.** *n.m.* armoured ship; **c. (de ligne),** battleship.

cuirassement [kɥirasmɑ̃] *n.m.* **1.** armouring (of ship, etc.). **2.** armour, armour plating.

cuirasser [kɥirase] *v.tr.* **1.** to put a cuirass, a breastplate, on (soldier); **se c.,** to put on one's cuirass; **se c. contre qch.,** to steel, harden, oneself against sth. **2.** to armour(-plate) (ship); to enclose, protect (machine).

cuirassier [kɥirasje] *n.m. Mil:* cuirassier.

cuire [kɥir] *v.* (*pr.p.* **cuisant;** *p.p.* **cuit;** *pr.ind.* **je cuis, il cuit, n. cuisons, ils cuisent;** *impf.* **je cuisais;** *p.h.* **je cuisis;** *fu.* **je cuirai) 1.** *v.tr.* (*a*) to cook; **c. à l'eau,** to boil; **c. au four,** to bake, to roast; *F:* **être dur à c.,** to be stubborn; *F:* **un dur à c.,** a tough nut, a tough customer; (*b*) to burn, fire, bake, kiln (bricks, pottery, etc.). **2.** *v.i.* (*a*) (*of food*) to cook; **c. à petit feu, à feu doux,** to cook slowly; to simmer; **le poulet a cuit trop longtemps,** the chicken is overcooked; **chocolat à c.,** cooking chocolate; *F:* **c. (dans son jus),** to be terribly hot; *F:* **on cuit dans cette salle,** this room's like an oven; **se c. au soleil,** to roast in the sun; *P:* **va te faire c. un œuf,** to hell with you! (*b*) to burn, smart; **les yeux me cuisent,** my eyes are smarting; *impers.* **il vous en cuira,** you'll be sorry for it; you'll regret it.

cuisant [kɥizɑ̃] *a.* smarting, burning (pain, etc.); biting (cold); caustic, biting, bitter (remarks); **déception cuisante,** bitter disappointment.

cuiseur [kɥizœr] *n.m.* large cooking pot.

cuisine [kɥizin] *n.f.* **1.** kitchen; *Nau:* (cook's) galley; **articles, ustensiles, batterie, de c.,** cooking utensils; *Mil:* **c. roulante,** field kitchen; **latin de c.,** dog Latin. **2.** (*a*) (art of) cooking, cookery; cuisine; **faire la c.,** to do the cooking; **il fait de la bonne c.,** he's a good cook; **c. au beurre, à l'huile,** cooking with butter, oil; **c. bourgeoise,** plain, home, cooking; **livre de c.,** cookery book, *NAm:* cookbook; (*b*) *F:* (dirty) tricks; **la c. parlementaire,** parliamentary intrigue. **3.** (cooked) food; **hôtel où la c. est bonne,** hotel renowned for its cusine, good cooking.

cuisiner [kɥizine] **1.** *v.i.* to cook; **elle cuisine bien,** she's a good cook. **2.** *v.tr.* (*a*) to cook (meat, etc.); **plats cuisinés,** ready-cooked dishes; takeaway meals; (*b*) *F:* **c. qn,** to interrogate, grill, s.o.

cuisinier, -ière [kɥizinje, -jɛr] *n.* **1.** cook. **2.** *n.m.* cookery book, *NAm:* cookbook. **3.** *n.f.* cooker, *NAm:* cookstove; **c. électrique,** electric cooker.

cuissard [kɥisar] *n.m.* **1.** *A.Arm:* cuisse, thigh piece. **2.** *Cy:* racing shorts.

cuissardes [kɥisard] *n.f.pl. & a.* **(bottes) c.,** (i) thigh boots; (ii) waders.

cuisse [kɥis] *n.f.* thigh; *Cu:* **c. de poulet,** chicken leg; *F:* drumstick; **cuisses de grenouilles,** frogs' legs; *F:* **se croire sorti de la c. de Jupiter,** to think a lot, no small beer, of oneself.

cuisseau, -eaux [kɥiso] *n.m. Cu:* leg (of veal).

cuisson [kɥisɔ̃] *n.f.* **1.** (*a*) cooking; **temps de c.,** cooking time; **le porc demande une longue c.,** pork has to be cooked for a long time; (*b*) burning, firing (of bricks, porcelain, etc.). **2.** burning (sensation); smarting (pain).

cuissot [kɥiso] *n.m. Cu:* haunch (of venison).

cuistance [kɥistɑ̃s] *n.f. P:* cookery, cooking.

cuistot [kɥisto] *n.m. F:* cook.

cuistre [kɥistr̥] *n.m. F: Pej:* (conceited) pedant; prig.

cuit [kɥi] *a.* (*a*) cooked; **bien c.,** well done; **c. à point,** done to a turn; **trop c.,** overdone, overcooked; **pas assez c.,** underdone, undercooked; **terre cuite,** terra cotta; (*b*) *F:* (*of pers., thg*) done for; **je suis c.,** it's all up with me, I've had it; **c'est c.!** that's it! we've had it! (*c*) *F:* **c'est du tout c.,** it's a cinch, a walkover.

cuite [kɥit] *n.f.* **1.** baking, firing (of bricks, etc.). **2.** *F:* **prendre une (bonne) c.,** to get drunk, plastered.

cuiter (se) [səkɥite] *v.pr. P:* to get drunk, tight, plastered.

cuivrage [kɥivraʒ] *n.m.* coppering (of metals, etc.); copper plating.

cuivre [kɥivr̥] *n.m.* **1.** (*a*) **c. (rouge),** copper; **casserole en c.,** copper saucepan; **doublé en c.,** (i) copper plated; (ii) copper bottomed; (*b*) **c. jaune,** brass; **les cuivres,** (i) copper(ware); brasses; (ii) *Mus:* the brass; (*c*) *Miner:* **minerai de c.,** copper ore. **2.** *Engr:* copperplate.

cuivré [kɥivre] *a.* **1.** copper coloured; **peau cuivrée, teint c.,** bronzed skin, complexion; **cheveux aux reflets cuivrés,** auburn hair. **2.** resonant, ringing (voice); *Mus:* **sons cuivrés,** brassy tones.

cuivrer [kɥivre] *v.tr.* **1.** to copper; to coat, sheath, (sth.) with copper. **2.** to bronze (the skin, the complexion). **3. se c.,** to turn the colour of copper, coppery.

cuivreux, -euse [kɥivrø, -øz] *a. Ch:* cuprous (oxide).

cul [ky] *n.m.* **1.** (*a*) *P:* backside, bottom, bum (of person); *V:* **le trou du c.,** the anus, shithole, arsehole, *NAm:* asshole; **c.-terreux,** country bumpkin, yokel, *NAm:* rube; *P:* **renverser qn c. par-dessus tête,** to send s.o. flying; **il en est tombé, resté, sur le c.,** he was flabbergasted; **se taper le c. par terre,** to roar with laughter; **lécher le c. à qn,** to lick s.o.'s boots, s.o.'s arse; **avoir le feu au c.,** to go like greased lightning; **ça vaut mieux qu'un coup de pied au c.,** it's better than a kick in the pants; **avoir qn dans le c.,** to hate s.o.'s guts; **ils l'ont dans le c.,** they've had it; that's really screwed them up; *Mil: P:* **tirer au c.,** to swing the lead; to shirk; **c'est un tire-au-c.,** he's a shirker; *P:* **quel c.!** *a.* **ce qu'il est c.!** what a bloody fool! (*b*) haunches, rump (of animal); **tirer un oiseau au c. levé,** to shoot a bird on the rise. **2.** (*a*) bottom (of bag, bottle, barrel); base (of bottle); **c.-de-basse-fosse,** dungeon; **faire c. sec,** to down one's drink in one go; **c. sec!** bottoms up! (*b*) *Nau:* stern (of ship); **trop sur c.,** too much by the stern; (*c*) *P:* **faire la bouche en c.-de-poule,** to pull a face; to pout.

culasse [kylas] *n.f.* **1.** (*a*) *Artil: Sm.a:* breech (of gun, rifle); **c. mobil,** bolt (of rifle); **fusil se chargeant par la c.,** breech loader; **bloc de c.,** breech block; (*b*) *Lap:* culet (of precious stone). **2.** *I.C.E:* cylinder head; **joint de c.,** cylinder head gasket.

cul-blanc [kyblɑ̃] *n.m. Orn:* wheatear; *pl. culs-blancs.*

culbute [kylbyt] *n.f.* (*a*) somersault; **faire la c.,** to turn a somersault; (*b*) tumble; heavy fall; **faire une c.,** to fall head over heels; (*c*) *F:* **faire la c.,** (*of ministry*) to fall; (*in business*) to become bankrupt; to go bust.

culbuter [kylbyte] **1.** *v.i.* (*a*) to turn a somersault; **la voiture a culbuté dans le fossé,** the car overturned in the ditch; (*b*) to fall head over heels; (*c*) *F:* (*of business*) to go bankrupt, bust; (*of ministry*) to fall, to collapse; (*d*) to topple over. **2.** *v.tr.* (*a*) to knock down, knock over, upset (s.o., sth.); to overwhelm (enemy); to overthrow, bring down (ministry); (*b*) *P:* to lay (a woman).

culbuteur [kylbytœr] *n.m.* **1.** *Toys:* tumbler. **2.** *I.C.E:* rocker arm. **3.** *Mec.E:* (*a*) tripper device; (*b*) tipper (for trucks, etc.).

cul-de-jatte [kydʒat] *n.m.* legless cripple; *pl. culs-de-jatte.*

cul-de-lampe [kydlɑ̃p] *n.m.* **1.** *Arch:* (*a*) pendant, cul-de-lampe; (*b*) bracket, corbel. **2.** *Typ:* tailpiece, cul-de-lampe; *pl. culs-de-lampe.*

cul-de-sac [kydsak] *n.m.* blind alley, cul-de-sac; *Rail:* blind siding; **votre emploi est un c.-de-s.,** you've got a dead end job; *pl. culs-de-sac.*

culée [kyle] *n.f.* **1.** *Arch:* pier (of buttress); *Civ.E:* abutment (pier) (of bridge). **2.** *Nau:* sternway.

culer [kyle] *v.i.* **1.** *Nau:* to make, gather, sternway; to drop astern; **nagez à c.!** backwater! **brasser à c.,** to brace aback. **2.** (*of wind*) to veer astern.

culinaire [kylinɛr] *a.* culinary; **l'art c.,** the art of cooking.

culminant [kylminɑ̃] *a.* (*a*) *Astr:* culminant; (*b*) **point c.,** culminating, highest, point (of range of mountains, of one's fortunes, etc.); zenith (of power, etc.); height, climax, peak (of glory).

culminer [kylmine] *v.i.* to culminate, reach its highest point; to reach its peak.

culot [kylo] *n.m.* **1.** (*a*) bottom, base (of lamp, bottle, etc.); (*b*) *Artil: Sm.a:* base (of cartridge case, shell, etc.); head (of cartridge); (*c*) *El:* base (of bulb); (*d*) *I.C.E:* body of spark(ing) plug; (*e*) *F:* cheek, nerve, *NAm:* gall; **tu ne manques pas de c., tu as du c.,** you've got a nerve! **2.** (*a*) *Metall:* slag, residue (left in crucible); (*b*) dottle (in tobacco pipe).

culottage [kylɔtaʒ] *n.m.* colouring, seasoning (of pipe).

culotte [kylɔt] *n.f.* **1.** *Cu:* buttock, rump, aitch bone (of beef). **2.** (*a*) **une c.,** *occ.* **des culottes, une paire de culottes,** knee breeches; **c. courte, longue,** short, long, trousers; **c. de cheval,** jodhpurs; riding breeches; **c. de golf,** plus fours; knickerbockers; **c. de peau,** (i) *A.Mil.Cost:* buckskins; (ii) *Pej: Mil:* colonel Blimp; *F:* **c'est la femme qui porte la c.,** it's the wife who wears the trousers; *F:* **user ses fonds de c. sur les bancs de l'école,** to idle away one's time at school; *F:* **trembler,** *P:* **faire, dans sa c.,** to be scared stiff, to have the jitters; (*b*) (woman's) briefs, panties, (child's) pants. **3.** *F:* **prendre une c.,** to lose heavily (at cards, etc.).

culotté [kylɔte] **1.** (*a*) (*of pipe*) seasoned; (*b*) (*of leather*) mellowed. **2.** *F:* full of cheek, nerve; cheeky; **il est c. comme tout,** he's got a, the, hell of a nerve.

culotter [kylɔte] *v.tr.* **1.** to put (s.o.'s) trousers on; **se c.,** to put one's trousers on. **2.** to colour, season (a pipe).

culottier, -ière [kylɔtje, -jɛr] *n.* trousers maker; breeches maker.

culpabilité [kylpabilite] *n.f.* culpability, guilt; *Jur:* **nier sa c.,** to plead not guilty; **sentiment de c.,** guilt complex.

culte [kylt] *n.m.* **1.** worship; **avoir le c. de l'argent,** to worship money; **avoir un c. pour qn; rendre, vouer, un c. à qn,** to (hero) worship s.o. **2.** (*a*) form of worship, cult, creed; religion; **liberté du c.,** freedom, liberty, of worship; (*b*) (protestant) (church) service.

cultivable [kyltivabl̥] *a.* suitable for cultivation.

cultivateur, -trice [kyltivatœr, -tris] *n.* **1.** agriculturist; farmer; **petits cultivateurs,** small farmers; smallholders; *a.* **les peuples cultivateurs,** agricultural people, farming communities. **2.** *n.m.* cultivator.

cultivé [kyltive] *a.* **1.** cultivated (land, etc.). **2.** cultured (mind, etc.); well-read; **gens cultivés,** cultured, educated, people.

cultiver [kyltive] *v.tr.* **1.** to cultivate, farm, till (the soil, etc.). **2.** (*a*) to cultivate, raise, grow (cereals, etc.); **c. son esprit,** to improve one's mind; **c. un goût,** to develop a taste; (*b*) **c. l'amitié de qn,** to cultivate s.o.'s friendship. **3.** to take an interest in (sth.); **c. les sciences,** to take up, study, devote oneself to, science. **4. se c.,** to broaden, improve, one's mind.

cultuel, -elle [kyltɥɛl] *a.* of, pertaining to, worship; **édifice c.,** place of worship.

cultural, -aux [kyltyral, -o] *a.* farming (methods).

culture [kyltyr] *n.f.* **1.** (*a*) cultivation (of the soil); **la grande, la petite, c.,** large-scale, small-scale, farming; **c. sèche,** dry farming; **c. fruitière,** fruit farming; (*b*) *pl.* land under cultivation. **2.** cultivation, cultivating (of plants); culture, rearing, breeding (of fish, oysters, etc.). **3.** *Biol: Bac:* **c. (microbienne, de tissus),** culture (of bacteria, of tissue); **bouillon de c.,** culture medium. **4.** (*a*) culture; education; **c. scientifique,** scientific knowledge, background; **c. physique,** physical training; *F:* P.T.; *Adm:* **maison de la c.** = arts centre; (*b*) **la c. gréco-romaine,** Graeco-Roman culture, civilization.

culturel, -elle [kyltyrɛl] *a.* cultural; educational; *Dipl:* **attaché c.,** cultural attaché.

culturisme [kyltyrism] *n.m.* body building.

cumin [kymɛ̃] *n.m. Bot:* (*a*) cum(m)in; **c. des prés,** caraway; (*b*) *Cu:* caraway seeds.

cumul [kymyl] *n.m.* **c. de fonctions,** plurality of offices, pluralism; **c. des traitements,** concurrent drawing of salary; *Jur:* **c. des peines,** non-concurrence of sentences.

cumulard [kymylar] *n.m. F: Pej:* pluralist; holder of several (paid) jobs; *F:* moonlighter.

cumulatif, -ive [kymylatif, -iv] *a.* cumulative.

cumuler [kymyle] *v.tr. & i.* **c. des fonctions,** to hold a plurality of offices; **c. deux traitements,** to draw two (separate) salaries; **il cumule,** he has more than one job, *F:* he's a moonlighter.

cumulus [kymylus] *n.m.inv. Meteor:* cumulus.

cunéiforme [kyneifɔrm] *a.* (*a*) *Anat:* cuneiform (bone); (*b*) **écriture c.,** cuneiform writing.

cupide [kypid] *a.* greedy, grasping; moneygrubbing.

cupidité [kypidite] *n.f.* cupidity; greed.

Cupidon [kypidɔ̃] *Pr.n.m. Myth:* Cupid.

cuprifère [kyprifɛr] *a.* cupriferous, copper-bearing.

cuprique [kyprik] *a.* cupric.

cupule [kypyl] *n.f. Bot:* cupule, cupula; cup (of acorn).

curable [kyrabl̥] *a.* curable (disease, etc.).

curage [kyraʒ] *n.m.* clearing, cleaning out (of drain, harbour, etc.); flushing (of drain).

curare [kyrar] *n.m.* curare.

curatelle [kyratɛl] *n.f. Jur:* trusteeship, guardianship.

curateur, -trice [kyratœr, -tris] *n. Jur:* trustee (of succession, etc.); guardian (of minor, lunatic).

curatif, -ive [kyratif, -iv] *a. & n.m.* curative.

cure [kyr] *n.f.* **1.** care; *used only in* **n'avoir c. de qch.,** not to care about, not to take any notice of, sth. **2.** *R.C.Ch:* (*a*) office of a parish priest; **obtenir une c.,** to be appointed parish priest, to be appointed to a parish; (*b*) parish; (*c*) presbytery. **3.** *Med:* (course of) treatment; cure; **c. thermale,** hydropathy, hydrotherapy; **c. d'amaigrissement,** slimming cure, diet; **faire une c. de lait,** to go on a milk diet; **elle a fait une c. à Vichy,** she took the waters at Vichy.

curé [kyre] *n.m. R.C.Ch:* (i) parish priest; (ii) *F:* (any) priest; **il veut se faire c.,** he wants to become a priest; *F:* **bouffer du c.,** to be (violently) anti-clerical.

cure-dent(s) [kyrdɑ̃] *n.m.* toothpick; *pl. cure-dents.*

curée [kyre] *n.f.* (*a*) *Ven:* parts of the stag given to the hounds; (*b*) the rush for the spoils; the rat race.

cure-ongles [kyrɔ̃gl̩] *n.m.inv. Toil:* nail cleaner.

cure-pipe [kyrpip] *n.m.* pipe cleaner; *pl. cure-pipes.*

curer [kyre] *v.tr.* (*a*) to pick (one's teeth, etc.); **se c. les ongles,** to clean one's nails; (*b*) to clear, clean, out (drain, harbour, etc.); to dredge (river, pond, etc.); (*c*) to scrape (pipe, etc.) clean.

cureter [kyrte] *v.tr. Surg:* to curette.

curet(t)age [kyr(ɛ)taʒ] *n.m. Surg:* curetting, curettage.

curette [kyrɛt] *n.f.* scraper; *Surg:* curette.

curie[1] [kyri] *n.f. Rom.Ant: R.C.Ch:* curia.

curie[2] *n.m. Ph:* curie.

curieusement [kyrjøzmɑ̃] *adv.* curiously, strangely, oddly, peculiarly.

curieux, -ieuse [kyrjø, -jøz] *a.* **1.** *A: & Lit:* (*of pers.*) (*a*) careful (**de,** of); (*b*) inquiring (mind); interested (**de qch.,** in sth.). **2.** (*a*) curious, interested; **je serai c. de voir cela,** I shall be curious, interested, to see it; (*b*) curious, inquisitive; (*c*) *n.m. & f.* inquisitive person; *F:* a nos(e)y parker, busybody; **un attroupement de c.,** a crowd of onlookers, bystanders; **il était venu en c.,** he came just to have a look. **3.** (*a*) (*of thg*) curious; odd, peculiar; **c'est c.,** that's odd, funny; **par une curieuse coïncidence,** by a strange coincidence; **ne me regarde pas comme une bête curieuse,** don't look at me as if I were a strange animal; **chose assez curieuse,** curiously enough; (*b*) *n.m.* **le plus c. de l'affaire est que . . .** (+ *ind.*), the oddest part of the business, the strangest thing about it, is that . . ..

curiosité [kyrjozite] *n.f.* **1.** curiosity; (*a*) interestedness; interest (**de,** for); **c. d'esprit,** inquisitiveness of mind; (*b*) inquisitiveness; *F:* nosiness; **par c.,** out of curiosity. **2.** curio; interesting thing, sight; **curiosités d'une ville,** sights of a town.

curiste [kyrist] *n.m. & f.* patient taking the cure, the waters (at a spa).

curling [kœliŋ] *n.m. Sp:* curling.

curseur [kyrsœr] *n.m. Tchn:* cursor, slide, runner (of mathematical instrument, etc.).

cursif, -ive [kyrsif, -iv] *a.* (*a*) cursive, running (handwriting); (*b*) cursory.

curviligne [kyrviliɲ] *a.* curvilinear, rounded.

curvimètre [kyrvimɛtr̩] *n.m. Surv:* curvometer.

cuspide [kyspid] *n.f. Anat: Bot:* cusp.

custode [kystɔd] *n.f.* **1.** *Ecc:* custodial (for the host, etc.). **2.** rear side panel (of car).

cutané [kytane] *a.* cutaneous; **maladie cutanée,** skin disease.

cuti [kyti] *n.f. Med: F:* = CUTIRÉACTION.

cuticule [kytikyl] *n.f.* cuticle, epidermis.

cutiréaction [kytireaksjɔ̃] *n.f. Med:* cutireaction; skin test.

cuvage [kyvaʒ] *n.m.,* **cuvaison** [kyvɛzɔ̃] *n.f.* fermenting, fermentation (of wine, beer) in vats.

cuve [kyv] *n.f.* (*a*) vat, tun (for fermenting wine, etc.); (*b*) (storage) tank; cistern; tub (of washing machine); **c. à lessive,** copper; laundry vat; *Phot:* **c. à laver, à développement,** washing, developing, tank.

cuvée [kyve] *n.f.* (*a*) vatful, tunful; **vin de première c.,** wine of the first growth; (*b*) product of whole vineyard; vintage.

cuvelage [kyvlaʒ] *n.m.* lining, timbering, tubbing (of mineshaft, etc.); lining (of borehole); casing (of well).

cuveler [kyvle] *v.tr.* (**je cuvelle, n. cuvelons; je cuvellerai**) to line, timber, tub (mineshaft, etc.); to line (borehole); to case, consolidate (well).

cuver [kyve] **1.** *v.i.* (*of wine, beer*) to ferment, work (in the vats). **2.** *v.tr. F:* **c. son vin,** to sleep off the effects of wine, *F:* to sleep it off; **c. sa colère,** to work off one's anger, to simmer down.

cuvette [kyvɛt] *n.f.* **1.** (wash)basin, (wash)bowl; **c. (de lavabo),** washbasin. **2.** bowl; pan (of W.C.); cup, cistern (of barometer); bulb (of thermometer); cap (of watch); *Phot:* (developing) dish. **3.** *Geog:* basin, depression; punchbowl.

cyanose [sjanoz] *n.f. Med:* cyanosis.

cyanure [sjanyr] *n.m. Ch:* cyanide.

cybernétique [sibɛrnetik] *n.f.* cybernetics.

cyclable [siklabl̩] *a.* **piste c.,** cycle track.

cyclamen [siklamɛn] *n.m. Bot:* cyclamen.

cycle [sikl̩] *n.m.* **1.** cycle (of events, poems, etc.); series (of lectures, etc.); **c. solaire,** solar cycle; **c. menstruel,** menstrual cycle; *Sch:* **premier c., second c.,** first, second, stage (of secondary education). **2.** *Veh:* cycle; **magasin, fabricant, de cycles,** cycle shop, manufacturer.

cyclique [siklik] *a.* cyclic(al).

cyclisme [siklism] *n.m. Sp:* cycling.

cycliste [siklist] **1.** *n.* cyclist. **2.** *a.* cycle (race, etc.); **coureur c.,** racing cyclist.

cycloïdal, -aux [siklɔidal, -o] *a. Mth:* cycloidal (curve, etc.).

cycloïde [siklɔid] *n.f. Mth:* cycloid.

cyclomoteur [siklɔmɔtœr] *n.m.* moped.

cyclomotoriste [siklɔmɔtɔrist] *n.m. & f.* moped rider.

cyclonal, -aux [siklɔnal, -o] *a. Meteor:* cyclonic.

cyclone [siklon] *n.m. Meteor:* (*a*) cyclone; **œil de c.,** centre, eye, of cyclone; (*b*) hurricane, cyclone; **elle est entrée comme un c.,** she came in like a whirlwind.

cyclonique [siklɔnik] *a. Meteor:* cyclonic.

cyclope [siklɔp] *n.m.* (*a*) *Gr.Myth: Crust:* cyclops; (*b*) **travail de c.,** colossal undertaking.

cyclopéen, -enne [siklɔpeɛ̃, -ɛn] *a.* cyclopean, gigantic; colossal.

cyclotourisme [siklɔturism] *n.m.* touring on bicycles.

cyclotron [siklɔtrɔ̃] *n.m. Atom.Ph:* cyclotron.

cygne [siɲ] *n.m.* (*a*) swan; **jeune c.,** cygnet; **c. mâle,** cob; **c. femelle,** pen; **duvet de c.,** swansdown; (*b*) *Tchn:* **col de c.,** swan neck.

cylindrage [silɛ̃draʒ] *n.m.* **1.** rolling (of roads, steel, etc.); pressing. **2.** *Tex:* calendering, mangling (of cloth); *Mch.Tls:* cylindrical turning; *Metall:* **c. à froid,** cold rolling.

cylindre [silɛ̃dr̩] *n.m.* **1.** *Mth:* cylinder; **c. de révolution,** cylinder of revolution. **2.** (*a*) *Mch: I.C.E:* cylinder; **moteur à quatre cylindres,** four-cylinder engine; (*b*) *Typ:* **c. d'impression,** printing cylinder, drum; (*c*) roller, roll (of rolling mill, mangle, calender, etc.); **c. compresseur,** road roller; (*d*) *Furn:* **bureau à c.,** roll top desk.

cylindrée [silɛ̃dre] *n.f. Mch: I.C.E:* cubic capacity (of cylinder, engine).

cylindrer [silɛ̃dre] *v.tr.* **1.** to roll (road, lawn, metal, etc.); to roll down (surfacing of road, etc.). **2.** to roll

(up) (paper, etc.). **3.** *Tex:* to calender, mangle (cloth).
cylindrique [silɛ̃drik] *a.* cylindrical.
cymbale [sɛ̃bal] *n.f. Mus:* cymbal.
cymbalier [sɛ̃balje] *n.m.* cymbal player, cymbalist.
cyme [sim] *n.f. Bot:* cyme.
cynégétique [sineʒetik] **1.** *a.* cynegetic. **2.** *n.f.* cynegetics, hunting.
cynique [sinik] **1.** *a.* (*a*) Cynic (philosophy); (*b*) cynical (person, attitude). **2.** *n.m.* (*a*) Cynic; (*b*) cynic.
cyniquement [sinikmɑ̃] *adv.* cynically.
cynisme [sinism] *n.m.* **1.** *Phil:* Cynicism. **2.** cynicism.
cynocéphale [sinɔsefal] **1.** *a.* cynocephalous, dog-headed. **2.** *n.m. Z:* cynocephalus; dog-faced baboon.
cynodrome [sinɔdrom] *n.m.* greyhound (racing) track; dog track.
cynophile [sinɔfil] *n.m. & f.* dog lover.
cyprès [siprɛ] *n.m. Bot:* cypress (tree).
cypriote [siprijɔt] *a. & n. Geog:* Cypriot.
cyrillique [sirilik] *a.* Cyrillic (alphabet, etc.).
cystique [sistik] *a. Anat: Med:* cystic (duct, calculus, etc.).
cystite [sistit] *n.f. Med:* cystitis.
cytise [sitiz] *n.m. Bot:* laburnum.
cytologie [sitɔlɔʒi] *n.f. Biol:* cytology.
cytoplasme [sitɔplasm] *n.m. Biol:* cytoplasm.

D

D, d [de] *n.m.* (the letter) D, d; **le système D** (= **dé-brouillard**), resourcefulness; wangling.
d'abord [dabɔr] *adv.phr. see* ABORD[4].
dac, d'ac [dak] *int. F:* O.K.
dactyle [daktil] *n.m. Pros:* dactyl.
dactylo [daktilo] (*a*) *n.f.* (*may be applied to a man*) typist; (*b*) *n.f.* typing; **il est bon à la d.,** he's good at typing; (*c*) *n.m. Fr.C:* typewriter.
dactylo-facturière [daktilɔfaktyrjɛr] *n.f.* typist invoice clerk; *pl. dactylos-facturières.*
dactylographe [daktilɔgraf] *n.m. & f. A:* (*a*) typist; (*b*) *Fr.C:* typewriter.
dactylographie [daktilɔgrafi] *n.f.* typing.
dactylographier [daktilɔgrafje] *v.tr.* to type.
dactylographique [daktilɔgrafik] *a.* typing (material, etc.).
dactylologie [daktilɔlɔʒi] *n.f.* dactylology.
dactyloscopie [daktilɔskɔpi] *n.f.* dactyloscopy.
dactyloscopique [daktilɔskɔpik] *a.* dactyloscopic; **examen d.,** examination of fingerprints.
dada [dada] *n.m. F:* **1.** (*in nursery language*) gee-gee; **aller à d.,** to ride a-cock-horse. **2.** (*a*) *A:* hobby-horse; (*b*) *F:* pet subject; **enfourcher son d.,** to get on to one's pet subject.
dadais [dadɛ] *n.m. F:* silly, awkward, boy.
dadaïsme [dadaism] *n.m. Art: Lit:* Dadaism.
dadaïste [dadaist] *n.m. & f. Art: Lit:* Dadaist.
dague [dag] *n.f.* **1.** dagger; *Navy:* dirk. **2.** dag (of two-year-old deer).
daguerréotype [dagɛreɔtip] *n.m. A.Phot:* daguerreotype.
dahlia [dalja] *n.m. Bot:* dahlia.
daigner [dɛɲe] *v.tr.* to deign, condescend; **le roi a daigné lui parler,** the king condescended to speak to him; **elle n'a même pas daigné me voir,** she wouldn't even see me.
daim [dɛ̃] *n.m.* (fallow) deer; buck; **(peau de) d.,** (i) buckskin, doeskin; (ii) suede.
daine [dɛn] *nf* doe.
dais [dɛ] *n.m.* canopy; **recouvert d'un d.,** canopied.
dallage [dalaʒ] *n.m.* **1.** paving (with flags, etc.) **2.** pavement, flagging, flagstones; **d. en céramique,** tiled floor.
dalle [dal] *n.f.* **1.** (*a*) *Const:* flag(stone); flooring tile; paving stone; (*b*) slab (of marble, etc.); **d. funéraire,** ledger. **2.** *P:* **je n'y vois que d.,** I can't see a damn thing.
daller [dale] *v.tr.* to pave (with flagstones, etc.); to flag (pavement, etc.); to tile (floor).
dalleur [dalœr] *n.m.* flag layer, pavio(u)r.
dalmatique [dalmatik] *n.f. Ecc.Cost:* dalmatic.
dalot [dalo] *n.m. Nau:* scupper (hole).
daltonien, -ienne [daltɔnjɛ̃, -jɛn] *a. & n.* colour blind (person).
daltonisme [daltɔnism] *n.m.* colour blindness.
dam [dɑ̃] *n.m.* **1. au grand d. de qn,** to the great displeasure of s.o. **2.** *Theol:* **peine du d.,** eternal damnation.
damage [damaʒ] *n.m.* ramming, tamping (of earth).
damasquinage [damaskinaʒ] *n.m.* damascening.
damasquiner [damaskine] *v.tr.* to inlay, damascene (blade, etc.).
damassé [damase] (*a*) *a. & n.m. Tex:* damask; **nappe damassée,** damask tablecloth; (*b*) *a.* **acier d.,** damask steel.
damasser [damase] *v.tr. Tex: Metalw:* to damask.
dame¹ [dam] *n.f.* **1.** (*a*) *A:* (noble) lady; **les dames de France,** the royal princesses of France; *F:* **elle fait la grande d.,** she puts on airs, she's all lah-di-dah; (*b*) lady; *P.N:* (*on public convenience*) **dames,** ladies; **que prendront ces dames?** what will the ladies take? what will you take, ladies? (*c*) **d. nature,** mother nature; (*d*) married woman; *F:* **et pour vous, ma petite d.?** what can I get you, love? *Jur:* **la d. Simon,** Mrs Simon; (*e*) **d. d'honneur,** lady-in-waiting; maid of honour; **d. de compagnie,** lady's companion; (*f*) (gentleman's) partner (at dance). **2.** *Games:* (*a*) **jeu de dames** = (game of) draughts, *U.S:* checkers; (*b*) (*at draughts*) = king; *Chess: Cards:* queen; (*at backgammon*) piece; *Cards:* **d. troisième,** guarded queen; **aller à d.,** (i) (*at draughts*) to make a king; (ii) *Chess:* to queen (a pawn). **3. dames,** rowlocks. **4.** *Civ.E: etc:* (paving) beetle; (earth) rammer. **5.** *Bot:* **d. d'onze heures,** star of Bethlehem.
dame² *int.* **d. oui!** well, yes! why, yes! rather! **vous y allez? d.!** are you going? what else can I do?
dame³ *n.f. Civ.E:* dam (across section of canal under construction); *Metall:* dam (stone) (of furnace).
dame-jeanne [damʒan] *n.f.* demijohn; *pl. dames-jeannes.*
damer [dame] *v.tr.* **1.** (*at draughts*) to crown (a piece); *F:* **d. le pion à qn,** to go one better than s.o.; to outwit, outdo, s.o. **2.** *Civ.E:* to ram, tamp (earth).
damier [damje] *n.m.* draught board (in Fr. with 100 squares); *U.S:* checkerboard; **tissu en d.,** check, chequered, material.
damnable [danabl̩] *a.* **1.** *Theol:* deserving of damnation. **2.** detestable, heinous; abominable.
damnation [dɑnasjɔ̃] *n.f.* damnation.
damné, -ée [dɑne] *a. & n.* damned; **souffrir comme un d.,** to go through hell; **être l'âme damnée de qn,** to be a mere tool in s.o.'s hands.
damner [dɑne] *v.tr.* **1.** to damn; *F:* **faire d. qn,** to drive s.o. crazy, to drive s.o. to exasperation. **2. se d.,** to incur damnation.
Damoclès [damɔklɛs] *Pr.n.m.* **l'épée de D.,** the sword of Damocles.
Danaïdes [danaid] *n.f.pl. Myth:* the Danaides.
dancing [dɑ̃siŋ] *n.m.* dance hall.
dandinement [dɑ̃dinmɑ̃] *n.m.* rolling gait, waddle.
dandiner [dɑ̃dine] *v.tr.* to dandle (baby); **se d.,** to have a rolling gait; to waddle.
dandy [dɑ̃di] *n.m.* dandy; *pl. dandys.*
Danemark [danmark] *Pr.n.m. Geog:* Denmark.
danger [dɑ̃ʒe] *n.m.* danger, peril; hazard; **à l'abri du d.,** out of harm's way; **courir un d.,** to be in danger; **il n'y a pas de d.,** it's quite safe; **mettre en d. la vie de qn,** to endanger s.o.'s life; **en d. de mort,** in danger, peril, of death; *Med:* **hors de d.,** off the danger list; *F:* **pas de d.!** no fear! not likely! **il n'y a pas de d. qu'il revienne,** it's not likely he'll come back.
dangereusement [dɑ̃ʒrøzmɑ̃] *adv.* dangerously.
dangereux, -euse [dɑ̃ʒrø, -øz] *a.* dangerous (**pour,** to, for); *Mil:* **zone dangereuse,** danger zone.
danois, -oise [danwa, -waz] **1.** *a.* Danish. **2.** *n.* (*cap.*

D) Dane; *Z:* **Grand D.,** Great Dane. **3.** *n.m. Ling:* Danish.

dans [dɑ̃] *prep.* **1.** (*of position*) in; (*a*) **d. une boîte,** in(side) a box; **il est d. sa chambre,** he's in his room; **qu'est-ce que vous avez d. la main?** what have you (got) in your hand? **il habite d. Paris même,** he lives (right) in Paris; **lire qch. d. un journal,** to read sth. in the newspaper; (*b*) within; **d. un rayon de dix kilomètres,** within a radius of ten kilometres; (*c*) into; **mettre qch. d. une boîte,** to put sth. in(to) a box; **il est entré d. leur chambre,** he went into their room; **tomber d. l'oubli,** to sink into oblivion; (*d*) (*with motion from a point within sth.*) **prendre qch. d. qch.,** to take sth. out of sth.; **boire d. un verre,** to drink out of a glass; **copier qch. d. un livre,** to copy sth. out of, from, a book; **découper un article d. le journal,** to cut an article out of the paper; (*e*) *Cu:* **un morceau d. la poitrine,** a cut off the breast. **2.** (*of time*) (*a*) in, within, during; **d. l'après-midi,** in, during, the afternoon; **d. le temps,** long ago, formerly; **payer d. les dix jours,** to pay within ten days; **je serai prêt à partir d. cinq minutes,** I shall be ready to leave in five minutes; (*b*) **il a d. les quarante ans,** he's about forty; **cela coûte d. les dix francs,** it costs about ten francs. **3.** (*a*) **être d. le commerce,** to be in trade; (*b*) **d. les circonstances,** in, under, the circumstances; **d. ce but,** with this aim in view; **d. l'espoir de,** in the hope of.

dansant [dɑ̃sɑ̃] *a.* **1.** dancing; **pas d.,** springy step. **2.** **thé d.,** tea dance, thé dansant; **donner une soirée dansante,** to give a dance. **3.** lively (tune).

danse [dɑ̃s] *n.f.* (*a*) dance, dancing; **d. du ventre,** belly dance; **elle aime la d.,** she's fond of dancing; *Med:* **d. de Saint-Guy,** St Vitus's dance; **ouvrir la d.,** to open the ball; *F:* **entrer en d.,** to join in (sth.); (*b*) dance tune.

danser [dɑ̃se] *v.i.* **1.** (*a*) to dance; *with cogn. acc.* **d. une valse,** to dance a waltz; **faire d. qn,** (i) to dance with s.o.; (ii) *F:* to lead s.o. a dance; **c'est un disque qui se danse,** it's a record, disc, you can dance to; **faire d. les écus,** to make the money fly; **ne savoir sur quel pied d.,** to be all at sea; (*b*) **le bouchon danse sur l'eau,** the cork is bobbing up and down on the water. **2.** (*of horse*) to prance.

danseur, -euse [dɑ̃sœr, -øz] *n.* **1.** (*a*) dancer, *esp.* ballet dancer, *f.* ballerina; (*b*) **d. de corde,** tightrope dancer; *Cy:* **pédaler en danseuse,** to stand up on the pedals. **2.** partner (at dance).

Danube [danyb] *Pr.n.m. Geog:* (the river) Danube; **paysan du D.,** (i) plain speaker; (ii) boor.

danubien, -ienne [danybjɛ̃, -jɛn] *a.* Danubian.

dard [dar] *n.m.* **1.** (*a*) *A:* dart, javelin; (*b*) *Fish:* spear, harpoon. **2.** (*a*) sting (of insect); forked tongue (of snake); (*b*) tongue (of flame). **3.** *Hort:* fruit spur. **4.** *Arch:* dart.

darder [darde] *v.tr.* **1.** to hurl, dart (pointed object); **il a dardé sur moi un regard chargé de haine,** he shot, flashed, a glance of hatred at me. **2.** to spear, harpoon (fish). **3.** (*of thorn, etc.*) to point.

dardillon [dardijɔ̃] *n.m.* **1.** small dart. **2.** barb (of fish hook).

dare-dare [dardar] *adv. F:* double-quick; **accourir d.-d.,** to come charging up.

darne [darn] *n.f. Cu:* slice, steak (of fish).

darse [dars] *n.f.* harbour, wet dock (in Mediterranean).

dartre [dartr̥] *n.f. Med: O:* (slight) skin trouble; scurf, dartre, herpes.

dartreux, -euse [dartrø, -øz] *a.* scabby, dartrous.

datation [datasjɔ̃] *n.f.* dating.

date [dat] *n.f.* date; **mettre la d.,** to date (a document); **sans d.,** undated (letter, etc.); **erreur de d.,** mistake in the date; **la lettre porte la d. du 5 mai,** the letter is dated (the) 5th May; **prendre d. pour qch.,** to fix a date for sth.; (*of event*) **faire d.,** to be momentous; to mark an epoch; **être le premier en d.,** to come first; **amitié de fraîche d., de vieille, de longue, d.,** recent, long standing, friendship;; **je le connais de longue d.,** I have known him for a long time; **à cette d.,** by then, by that time; *Com:* **en d. du 15 courant,** dated (the) 15th inst.; **à trente jours de d.,** thirty days after date; **d. limite,** deadline; *Fin:* **emprunt à longue, à courte, d.,** long-dated, short-dated, loan.

dater [date] **1.** *v.tr.* to date (letter, etc.); **lettre datée de Paris,** letter dated from Paris; **non daté,** undated. **2.** *v.i.* to date (**de,** from); **à d. de ce jour,** from today; **à d. du 15,** on and after (the) 15th; **de quand date votre dernier repas?** when did you last eat? **événement qui date,** memorable event; **robe qui date,** oldfashioned dress.

dateur [datœr] *n.m.* date marker, date stamp.

datif [datif] *a. & n.m. Gram:* dative (case); **au d.,** in the dative.

datte [dat] *n.f. Bot:* date.

dattier [datje] *n.m. Bot:* date palm, date tree.

daube [dob] *n.f. Cu:* stew; casserole; **bœuf en d.,** stewed, braised, beef.

dauber [dobe] *v.tr.* **1.** *Cu:* to stew, braise (beef). **2.** *A: & Lit:* to make fun of (s.o.).

daubière [dobjɛr] *n.f. Cu:* braising pan; casserole.

dauphin [dofɛ̃] *n.m.* **1.** *Z:* dolphin. **2.** (*a*) *Hist:* Dauphin; (*b*) heir apparent (to important position). **3.** shoe (of drainpipe).

dauphine [dofin] *n.f. Fr.Hist:* Dauphiness.

daurade [dorad] *n.f. Ich:* gilthead (bream); sea bream.

davantage [davɑ̃taʒ] *adv.* more; (*a*) **il m'en faut d.,** I need still more; **je n'en dis pas d.,** I shall say no more; **je ne l'interrogerai pas d.,** I won't question him any further; **vous êtes riche, mais il l'est d.,** you're rich, but he's richer; **nous ne resterons pas d.,** we will not stay any longer; **se baisser d.,** to stoop lower; **chaque jour d.,** more and more every day; (*b*) **elle en a d. que lui,** she's got more than he (has).

davier [davje] *n.m.* **1.** *Tls:* (*a*) *Dent:* forceps; (*b*) *Carp:* cramp. **2.** *Nau:* bow sheave.

de [də] (*before vowels and h 'mute'* **d'**; **de** + *def. art.* **le, les,** *are contracted into* **du, des.**) **I.** *prep.* **1.** (*a*) from; **il vient de Paris,** he comes from Paris; **l'idée est de vous,** the idea is yours, comes from you; **je l'ai oublié? c'est bien de moi,** did I forget it? that's just like me; **du matin au soir,** from morning till night; **de vous à moi . . .,** between ourselves . . .; **de vingt à trente personnes,** between twenty and thirty people; **de jour en jour,** from day to day; (*b*) (*time vaguely indicated*) **il est parti de nuit,** he left by night; **du temps de nos pères,** in the days of our fathers; (*c*) (*agent, means, instrument*) **accompagné de ses amis,** accompanied by his friends; **la statue est de Rodin,** the statue is by Rodin; **j'ai fait cela de ma propre main,** it's all my own work; (*d*) (*manner*) **il m'a regardé d'un air amusé,** he looked at me with an amused expression; **répondre d'une voix douce,** to answer in a gentle voice; (*e*) (*cause, origin*) **sauter de joie,** to leap for joy; **je tombe de fatigue,** I'm so tired, I'm ready to drop; **faire qch. de soi-même,** to do sth. of one's own accord; (*f*) (*measure*) **âgé de seize ans,** sixteen years old; **ma montre retarde de dix minutes,** my watch is ten minutes slow; **il est plus grand que moi de la tête,** he's a head taller than I am; **la terrasse a vingt mètres de long, est longue de vingt mètres,** the terrace is twenty metres long; **un chèque de £10,** a cheque for £10; (*g*) (*introducing complement of adj.*) **digne d'éloges,** worthy of praise; **altéré de sang,** thirsting for blood. **2.** (*a*) **le livre de Pierre,** Peter's book; **le toit de la maison,** the roof of the house; **le meilleur élève de la classe,** the best pupil in the class; **les rues de Paris,** the streets of Paris; **la conférence de Berlin,** the Berlin conference; **la chambre du second,** the room on the second, *NAm:* third, floor; **un hôtel de la rive gauche,** a hotel on the left bank; **scène de rivière hollandaise,** scene on a Dutch river; (*b*) (*material*) **un pont de fer,** an iron bridge; **robe de soie,** silk dress; (*c*) (*distinguishing mark*) **le chien de berger,** the sheepdog; (*cp.* **le chien du berger,** the shepherd's dog); **le journal d'hier,** yesterday's paper; **à quatre heures de l'après-midi,** at four (o'clock) in the afternoon; **la route de Paris,** the Paris road; **le professeur de français,** the French teacher; (*d*) (*partitive*) **un verre de vin,** a glass of wine; **une livre de café,** a pound of coffee; **quelque chose de bon,** something good; **je n'ai pas de sœurs,** I haven't any sisters; **je ne l'ai pas vu de la soirée,** I haven't seen him all evening. **3.** (*forming compound prepositions*) **près de la maison,** near the house; **autour du jardin,** round the garden; **à partir de ce jour-là,** from that day onward. **4.** (*connecting verb and object*) **nous approchons de Paris,** we're getting near Paris; **j'ai changé d'avis,** I've changed my mind; **manquer de courage,** to lack courage; **convenir d'une erreur,** to admit an error. **II.** (*serving as a link word*) **1.** *introducing an inf.* (*a*) **il est honteux de mentir,** it is shameful to lie; **le mieux était de rire,** it was best to laugh; **je crains d'être en retard,** I'm afraid of being late; **j'aime mieux attendre que de me faire mouiller,** I would rather wait than get wet; (*b*) (*the so-called 'historical infinitive'*) **la musique commença et les enfants de danser,** the music began, and the children started to dance. **2.** (*introducing an apposition or a predicative complement*) **la ville de Paris,** the city of Paris; **on l'a traité de lâche,** he was called a coward; **un drôle de type,** a funny chap; **il y eut trois hommes de tués,** three men were killed; **c'est un grand pas de fait,** that's a great step forward; *F:* **la robe est d'un réussi!** the dress is such a success! **III.** *partitive article* (*used also as pl. of* **un, une**) **n'avez-vous pas des amis?** haven't you got any friends? **sans faire de fautes,** without making any mistakes; **je ne veux pas qu'on lui mette de collier,** I won't have a collar put on him; **de grands artistes se trouvaient là,** there were some distinguished artists there; **je bois de l'eau,** (i) I drink water; (ii) I am drinking water; **donnez-nous de vos nouvelles,** let's hear from you; **avez-vous du pain?** have you any bread? **donnez-moi de ce vin,** give me some of that wine; **donnez-moi du bon vin,** give me some good wine; **manger de tous les plats,** to partake of every dish; to have something of everything; (*intensive*) **mettre des heures à faire qch.,** to spend hours over sth.

dé[1] [de] *n.m.* **1.** (*a*) *Gaming:* die; **jeter les dés,** to throw, cast, the dice; **dé pipé,** loaded die; **coup de dé,** cast of the die; **les dés sont jetés,** the die is cast; (*b*) *Cu:* **couper en dés,** to dice (vegetables, etc.). **2.** *Arch:* dado, die (of pedestal, etc.). **3.** *Mec.E:* bearing (bush), brass.

dé[2] *n.m.* **dé (à coudre),** thimble.

déambulatoire [deɑ̃bylatwar] *n.m. Ecc.Arch:* ambulatory.

déambuler [deɑ̃byle] *v.i.* to stroll (about), to walk up and down, to saunter.

débâcle [debɑkl] *n.f.* **1.** break(ing) up (of drift ice). **2.** (*a*) downfall, collapse (of business, etc.); *Pol:* landslide; *Fin:* crash; **d. de la santé,** breakdown in health; (*b*) *Mil: etc:* débâcle, rout.

débâcler [debɑkle] *v.i.* (*of ice*) to break up.

déballage [debalaʒ] *n.m.* **1.** unpacking. **2. (vente au) d.,** (i) spread of hawker's wares; (ii) sale (in temporary premises). **3.** *F:* confession; outpouring.

déballer [debale] *v.tr.* (*a*) to unpack (goods, cases); (*b*) *F:* (i) to disclose (a secret, etc.); (ii) to confess to (the truth).

débandade [debɑ̃dad] *n.f.* rout (of army, etc.); stampede (of horses, etc.); **à la d.,** in confusion; helter-skelter; **tout va à la d.,** everything's in a mess.

débander[1] [debɑ̃de] *v.tr.* **1.** to relax (sth. under tension); to unbend (bow); to unbrace (drum); to let down (spring); **se d. l'esprit,** to relax one's mind. **2.** to remove a bandage from, to unbandage, to unbind (wound).

débander[2] *v.tr.* **1.** *A:* to disband (troops, crew). **2. se d.,** (i) (*of crowd, etc.*) to disperse; (ii) *Mil: etc:* to break into a rout.

débaptiser [debatize] *v.tr.* to change the name (of pers., street, etc.); to rename.

débarbouiller [debarbuje] *v.tr.* **1.** to wash (s.o.'s) face. **2. se d.:** (*a*) to wash one's face; (*b*) (*of weather*) to clear up.

débarbouillette [debarbujɛt] *n.f. Fr.C:* (face) flannel, face cloth, *NAm:* washrag.

débarcadère [debarkadɛr] *n.m. Nau:* landing stage, wharf.

débardage [debardaʒ] *n.m.* unloading, unlading (of timber).

débarder [debarde] *v.tr.* **1.** *Nau:* to unload, discharge (timber, etc.). **2.** to convey (lumber, quarried stone) to the railhead.

débardeur [debardœr] *n.m.* **1.** docker, stevedore. **2.** *Cost:* tank top.

débarquement [debarkəmɑ̃] *n.m.* **1.** unloading, discharge (of cargo); landing, disembarkation (of passengers); **carte de d.,** landing card; **quai de d.,** arrival platform. **2.** (*a*) *Mil:* detraining; *Nau:* disembarkation; (*b*) *Mil: Navy:* landing; **troupes de d.,** landing force; **d. sur plage,** beaching. **3.** *Nau:* paying off, discharge (of crew).

débarquer [debarke] **1.** *v.tr.* (*a*) to unship, unload, discharge (cargo); to disembark, land (passengers); to drop (pilot); (*of bus*) to set down (passengers); (*b*) to pay off, discharge (crew); *F:* **d. qn,** to dismiss s.o.; to give s.o. the sack. **2.** *v.i.* to land, disembark (from boat); to alight (from train); *Mil:* to detrain; *F:* **elle a débarqué hier soir,** she turned up last night; *n.m.* **au d.,** on arrival, on landing.

débarras [debarɑ] *n.m.* (*a*) riddance; **bon d.!** good riddance! (*b*) boxroom; *F:* glory hole.

débarrasser [debarase] *v.tr.* **1.** to disencumber; to clear (table, etc.); **d. qn de qch.,** to relieve s.o. of sth.; **d. qn de qn,** to rid s.o. of s.o.; *F:* **d. le plancher,** to clear out. **2. se d. de qch., de qn,** to get rid of sth., of s.o.; to extricate, disentangle, oneself from sth., from s.o.

débarrer [debare] *v.tr.* to unbar (door, etc.).

débat [deba] *n.m.* **1.** (oral) discussion; debate; *pl. Pol:* (parliamentary) debates, proceedings. **2.** dispute; **trancher un d.,** to settle a dispute; **être en d. sur une question,** to be at issue on a question.

débâtir [debatir] *v.tr.* to unbaste, untack (garment).

débattement [debatmɑ̃] *n.m. Aut: etc:* clearance.

débattre [debatr̥] *v.tr.* (*conj. like* BATTRE) **1.** to debate, discuss; **prix à d.,** price by arrangement; **je n'ai pas débattu le prix,** I didn't haggle about the price. **2. se d.,** to struggle; **se d. dans l'eau,** to flounder, splash (about) in the water; **se d. contre une difficulté,** to struggle with a problem.

débauchage [deboʃaʒ] *n.m.* laying off (workmen).

débauche [deboʃ] *n.f.* debauchery, dissolute living; *Jur:* **excitation des mineurs à la d.,** incitement of minors to vice.

débauché, -ée [deboʃe] **1.** *a.* debauched, profligate. **2.** *n.* debauchee, libertine, rake; *f.* debauched woman.

débaucher [deboʃe] *v.tr.* **1.** (*a*) to entice (s.o.) away, to lead (s.o.) astray; **d. un ouvrier,** to entice a workman away (from his work), to induce him to strike;

d. la jeunesse, to corrupt the young; (*b*) *Ind:* to lay off (hands); to make (s.o.) redundant; (*c*) *F:* **arrête de travailler et débauche-toi un peu,** stop working for a minute and enjoy yourself. **2. se d.,** to become corrupted.

débaucheur [deboʃœr] *n.m.* corrupter; seducer.

débecter [debɛkte] *v.tr. P:* to disgust (s.o.); **ça me débecte,** it's disgusting.

débet [debɛ] *n.m. Fin:* balance due.

débile [debil] **1.** *a.* weakly (child); weak, feeble (body); poor (health); **avoir une volonté d.,** to be weak-willed. **2.** *n.* **un(e) d. (mental(e)),** a mental defective.

débilitant [debilitɑ̃] *a.* debilitating, weakening; *Fig:* demoralizing; *a. & n.m.* **(remède) d.,** debilitant.

débilité [debilite] *n.f.* debility, weakness; **d. mentale,** mental deficiency.

débiliter [debilite] *v.tr.* to debilitate, weaken.

débinage [debinaʒ] *n.m. F:* disparagement, running down.

débine [debin] *n.f. F:* poverty; **être dans la d.,** to be (stony) broke.

débiner [debine] *v.tr. F:* **1.** to disparage; to speak slightingly of (s.o.); to run (s.o.) down. **2. se d.,** to scram, to clear off.

débit[1] [debi] *n.m.* **1.** (*a*) (retail) sale; **marchandises de bon d.,** marketable, saleable, goods; (*b*) (retail) shop; *esp.* **d. de tabac,** tobacconist's (shop); **d. de boissons,** bar; *F:* = pub. **2.** cutting up (of logs, meat, etc.). **3.** (*a*) discharge, delivery (of pump, etc.); flow (of river, tap, etc.); rate (of traffic flow); (*b*) *Ind:* output; *El:* power supplied. **4.** delivery (of orator); **avoir le d. facile,** to have the gift of the gab, a glib tongue.

débit[2] *n.m. Com:* debit; **porter 1.000 francs au d. de qn,** to debit s.o. with 1,000 francs.

débitant, -ante [debitɑ̃, -ɑ̃t] *n.* (*a*) *O:* retailer; (*b*) **d. de tabac,** tobacconist.

débiter[1] [debite] *v.tr.* to retail; to sell (goods) retail. **2.** to cut up, convert (timber); to cut up (meat). **3.** to discharge, yield (so many litres an hour, etc.); *Ind:* to produce; **cette usine débite 250 voitures par jour,** the output from this factory is 250 cars a day. **4.** (*a*) *Th:* to recite (one's part); (*b*) *F: usu. Pej:* **d. une longue harangue,** to make a long speech; **d. des sottises,** to talk rubbish.

débiter[2] *v.tr. Com:* to debit; **d. une somme à qn, d. qn d'une somme,** to debit s.o. with an amount.

débiteur[1]**, -euse** [debitœur, -øz] *n.* **1.** *Pej: O:* person who holds forth, talks rubbish; **d. de calomnies,** scandalmonger. **2.** *Mec.E:* feeding device. **3.** shop assistant (who takes customers to cash desk).

débiteur[2]**, -trice** [debitœr, -tris] **1.** *n.* debtor. **2.** *a.* **compte d.,** debit account. **3.** *a. Cin:* **bobine débitrice,** top spool, delivery spool.

déblai [deblɛ] *n.m. Civ.E: Rail: etc:* **1.** excavation, cut(ting); **route en d.,** sunk road. **2.** spoil earth.

déblaiement [deblɛmɑ̃] *n.m.* clearing (of ground, etc.).

déblatérer [deblatere] *v.* **(je déblatère; je déblatérerai) 1.** *v.tr.* **d. des sottises,** to talk nonsense; **d. des injures,** to fling abuse (**contre,** at). **2.** *v.i.* **d. contre qn,** to rail against s.o.; to run s.o. down.

déblayer [debleje] *v.tr.* **(je déblaye, je déblaie) 1.** to clear away, remove (spoil earth, etc.); **d. la neige,** to shovel away the snow. **2. d. un terrain,** (i) to clear a piece of ground; (ii) to clear the ground, the way (for negotiations, etc.).

déblocage [deblɔkaʒ] *n.m.* freeing, releasing; *Fin:* unfreezing (of prices, etc.).

débloquer [deblɔke] *v.tr.* **1.** *A.Mil:* to raise the blockade of (town). **2.** to unjam (machine). **3.** to free, to release; *Fin:* to unfreeze (prices, etc.).

débobiner [debɔbine] *v.tr. El:* to unwind (coil).

déboire [debwar] *n.m.* disappointment; **essuyer bien des déboires,** to suffer many disappointments, setbacks.

déboisement [debwazmɑ̃] *n.m.* deforestation.

déboiser [debwaze] *v.tr.* to deforest, untimber, clear (land).

déboîtement [debwatmɑ̃] *n.m.* dislocation (of limb, etc.).

déboîter [debwate] *v.tr.* **1.** to disconnect, uncouple (pipe, etc.). **2.** to dislocate (joint); **se d. l'épaule,** to put one's shoulder out; **se d. le genou,** to twist one's knee. **3.** to remove (watch, etc.) from its case; *Bookb:* to uncase (book). **4.** *v.i.* (*a*) *Mil:* to break out of column; (*b*) *Aut:* to filter. **5.** (*of shoulder, etc.*) **se d.,** to come out of joint.

débonder [debɔ̃de] **1.** *v.tr.* to unbung (cask); to open the sluice gates of (reservoir); **d. son cœur,** to pour out one's heart. **2.** *v.i.* (*of liquid*) to gush out, to spill out.

débonnaire [debɔnɛr] *a.* goodnatured, easy-going.

débordant [debɔrdɑ̃] *a.* **1.** overflowing, brimming over (**de,** with); **d. de santé,** bursting with health. **2.** projecting, protruding; overlapping.

débordé [debɔrde] *a.* **1.** overflowing (river, etc.). **2.** overwhelmed, unable to keep pace, snowed under (with work, etc.). **3. drap d.,** untucked sheet.

débordement [debɔrdəmɑ̃] *n.m.* **1.** (*a*) overflowing (of river, etc.); **d. d'injures,** outburst of abuse; (*b*) *pl.* excesses, dissipation; dissolute living. **2.** *Mil:* outflanking (of enemy).

déborder [debɔrde] **1.** *v.tr. & i.* to overflow, brim over, run over; **verre plein à d.,** glass full to overflowing, to the brim; **elle déborde de vie,** she is bubbling over with vitality; **c'est la goutte d'eau qui fait d. le vase,** it's the last straw. **2.** *v.tr.* (*a*) to project, jut out, stick out, protrude, extend, beyond (sth.); to overlap (sth.); **dents qui débordent les lèvres,** protruding teeth; (*b*) *Mil:* to outflank (the enemy); (*c*) **d. les avirons,** to unship the oars; **d. (les couvertures d')un lit,** to untuck a bed; *Nau:* **d. (une embarcation),** to shove off, sheer off; (*d*) to remove the edging from (sth.); **d. une tôle,** to trim the edges of an iron plate.

débotter [debɔte] **1.** *v.tr.* to take off (s.o.'s) boots. **2.** *v.i. & pr.* to take off one's boots; *n.m.* **au débotté,** immediately on arrival.

débouchage [debuʃaʒ] *n.m.* **1.** uncorking (of bottle); unblocking (of pipe). **2.** *Mil:* setting (of time fuse).

débouché [debuʃe] *n.m.* **1.** (*a*) outlet, opening, issue (of passage, etc.); exit (from building, etc.); (*b*) inlet (into pond). **2.** opening; opportunity; *Com:* outlet; **quels débouchés y a-t-il pour lui?** what (career) prospects has he (got)?

déboucher[1] [debuʃe] *v.tr.* **1.** to clear (choked pipe, etc.). **2.** to uncork (bottle); *F:* **d. qn,** to awaken, arouse s.o.'s mind. **3.** *Mil:* to set (time fuse).

déboucher[2] *v.i.* to emerge, come out; **cette rue débouche sur la place,** this street runs into the square.

débouchoir [debuʃwar] *n.m.* **1.** *Dom.Ec:* rubber plunger. **2.** *Lap:* clearing iron.

déboucler [debukle] *v.tr.* **1.** to unbuckle (belt, etc.). **2.** to take the curl out of, to uncurl (hair). **3.** (*of hair*) **se d.,** to come out of curl.

débouler [debule] *v.i.* **1.** to fall head over heels; **d. l'escalier,** to roll downstairs. **2.** (*of game*) to start, bolt (from cover); *n.m.* **tirer un lapin au d.,** to shoot a rabbit as it bolts from cover.

déboulonnage [debulɔnaʒ] *n.m.,* **déboulonnement** [debulɔnmɑ̃] *n.m.* **1.** unriveting, unbolting. **2.** *F:* debunking.

déboulonner [debulɔne] *v.tr.* **1.** to unrivet; to unbolt. **2.** *F:* to debunk (s.o.).

débourbage [deburbaʒ] *n.m.* clearing out (of mud).
débourber [deburbe] *v.tr.* **1.** to cleanse, to clear (of mud); to clean out (cistern); **d. le vin,** to draw off, decant, wine. **2.** to haul (car, etc.) out of the mud.
débourrage [deburaʒ] *n.m.* **1.** unhairing (of skins). **2.** removal of stuffing (from armchair, etc.).
débourrer [debure] *v.tr.* **1.** to unhair (skins); to strip, clean (carding machine). **2.** to remove wad from (firearm), stuffing from (armchair, etc.), tobacco from (pipe); to untamp (blast hole).
débours [debur] *n.m.* disbursement; expenses; **faire des d.,** to lay out money.
déboursement [debursəmɑ̃] *n.m.* paying out, disbursement.
débourser [deburse] *v.tr.* to disburse, spend, lay out (money); **sans rien d.,** without spending a penny; **je suis toujours à d.,** I'm always dipping my hand into my pocket.
debout [dəbu], *adv.* **1.** (*a*) (*of thg*) upright, on end; (*of pers.*) standing; **mettre, dresser, qch. d.,** to stand sth. up, on end; (*on packing case, etc.*) **tenir d.,** to be kept upright; **se tenir d.,** to stand; (*of dog*) to stand on its hind legs; **elle est d. toute la journée,** she's on her feet all day; **argument qui ne tient pas d.,** argument that won't hold water; **se (re)mettre d.,** to stand up; **rester d.,** to remain standing; **d. les gardes!** up guards! **places d. seulement,** standing room only; **conte à dormir d.,** silly, extravagant, story; *Sp:* **record encore d.,** unbeaten record; (*b*) (*of pers.*) **être d.,** to be up; **allons, d.!** come on, get up! **il va mieux, il est déjà d.,** he's better, he's already up; (*c*) *Cust:* **passer d.,** to have a permit for transire. **2.** *Nau:* **d. à la mer, à la lame, au vent,** head on to the sea, to the wind; **vent d.,** head wind.
débouté [debute], **déboutement** [debutmɑ̃] *n.m. Jur:* nonsuit.
débouter [debute] *v.tr. Jur:* **1.** to dismiss (suit). **2. d. qn (de sa demande),** to nonsuit s.o.
déboutonner [debutɔne] *v.tr.* **1.** to unbutton; **rire à ventre déboutonné,** to split one's sides laughing. **2. se d.** (*a*) to unbutton oneself; (*b*) to get sth. off one's chest.
débraillé [debrɑje] **1.** *a.* untidy, slovenly (person); **tenue débraillée,** untidy, sloppy, appearance; **manières débraillées,** crude, rude, manners. **2.** *n.m.* untidiness, slovenliness.
débrancher [debrɑ̃ʃe] *v.tr. El: etc:* to disconnect; to unplug (iron, etc.).
débrayage [debrɛjaʒ] *n.m.* **1.** *Aut: Mec.E:* declutching, throwing out of gear. **2.** *Aut:* clutch. **3.** *F:* going on strike.
débrayer [debrɛje] *v.* **(je débraye, je débraie) 1.** *v.tr. Mec.E:* to disengage (part) out of gear. **2.** *v.i. Aut:* to release the clutch. **3.** *v.i. F:* (*a*) to go on strike; (*b*) to knock off.
débridé [debride] *a.* unbridled (tongue, etc.).
débridement [debridmɑ̃] *n.m.* **1.** unbridling (of horse). **2.** *Surg:* slitting up (of adhesion, etc.).
débrider [debride] *v.tr.* **1.** to unbridle (horse, etc.); (*hence*) to halt; **travailler dix heures sans d.,** to work ten hours at a stretch. **2.** *Surg:* to incise, slit up (adhesion, etc.); *Fig:* **d. les yeux à qn,** to open s.o.'s eyes. **3.** to unsling (load). **4.** *Cu:* to untruss (fowl).
débris [debri] *n.m.pl.* remains, debris, fragments; **d. de métal,** scrap (metal).
débrocher [debrɔʃe] *v.tr.* **1.** to unstitch (book). **2.** *Cu:* to unspit.
débrouillard, -arde [debrujar, -ard] *F:* **1.** *a.* resourceful; smart. **2.** *s.* resourceful person.
débrouillement [debrujmɑ̃] *n.m.* unravelling, sorting out.
débrouiller [debruje] *v.tr.* **I.** to unravel, disentangle (thread, etc.); to sort out (papers, etc.); **d. une affaire,** to clear up, straighten out, matters; **d. une signature,** to make out, decipher, a signature. **II. se débrouiller 1.** (*of the sky, etc.*) to clear (up). **2.** to extricate oneself (from difficulties); to manage; *F:* **qu'il se débrouille!** he'll have to sort it out himself! **débrouillez-vous!** that's your lookout!
débroussailler [debrusaje] *v.tr.* **1.** to clear (ground) of undergrowth. **2. d. (une question),** to clarify (a matter).
débucher[1] [debyʃe] *v.i. Ven:* (*of big game*) to break cover; *v.tr.* **(faire) d. un cerf,** to unharbour, start, a stag.
débucher[2] *n.m.*, **débuché** *n.m. Ven:* (i) breaking cover; (ii) (*on the horn*) gone away; **au débuché,** at the start.
débusquer [debyske] **1.** *v.tr.* (*a*) *Mil:* to drive (enemy) out of ambush; (*b*) to drive (s.o.) out (of refuge); (*c*) *Ven:* = DÉBUCHER[1]. **2.** *v.i. Mil: etc:* to come out (of ambush); to come out of hiding.
début [deby] *n.m.* **1.** *Games:* first turn, first play; first throw, first cast. **2.** first appearance (of actor, etc.); **faire son d.,** to make one's first appearance, one's début; (*of girl*) **faire son d. (dans le monde),** to come out; **société à ses débuts,** association in its infancy. **3.** beginning, start, outset; **dès le d.,** from the outset (**de,** of); right at the start; **au d. des hostilités,** at the outbreak of hostilities; **appointements de d.,** starting salary; **discours de d.,** maiden speech.
débutant, -ante [debytɑ̃, -ɑ̃t] *n.* **1.** beginner, tyro; actor, etc., making his début. **2.** *n.f.* débutante, *F:* deb.
débuter [debyte] *v.i.* **1.** *Games:* to play first; (*dice*) to throw first. **2.** to make one's first appearance, one's début (on stage, etc.); **d. dans la vie,** to start a career; **faire d. une jeune fille dans le monde,** to bring out a girl. **3.** to begin, start, commence; **vous travaillerez ici pour d.,** you will work here to begin with.
deçà [dəsa] (*a*) *adv. A:* on this side; **d. et delà,** here and there, on all sides; **jambe d., jambe delà,** astride; (*b*) *prep.phr.* **en d. de qch.,** (on) this side of sth.; **rester en d. de la vérité,** to be short of the truth.
décachetage [dekaʃtaʒ] *n.m.* unsealing, opening.
décacheter [dekaʃte] *v.tr.* (*conj. like* CACHETER) to unseal, break open (letter, etc.).
décade [dekad] *n.f.* **1.** (*a*) period of ten days; (*b*) (*period of ten years*) decade. **2.** (*series of ten*) decade.
décadence [dekadɑ̃s] *n.f.* decadence, decline, decay; **être en d.,** to be decadent, on the downgrade.
décadent [dekadɑ̃] **1.** *a.* decadent, declining, in decay. **2.** *n.m. Lit: Art:* Decadent.
décaèdre [dekaɛdr̥] *Mth:* **1.** *a.* decahedral. **2.** *n.m.* decahedron.
décaféiner [dekafeine] *v.tr.* to decaffeinate; **un café décaféiné,** *n.* **un décaféiné,** a (cup of) decaffeinated coffee.
décagone [dekagɔn] *n.m. Mth:* decagon.
décaissage [dekɛsaʒ] *n.m.* **1.** unpacking (of goods, etc.). **2.** *Hort:* planting out (of plant, shrub).
décaissement [dekɛsmɑ̃] *n.m.* **1.** = DÉCAISSAGE. **2.** *Com:* paying out (of cash).
décaisser [dekese] *v.tr.* **1.** to unpack, uncase (goods, etc.). **2.** *Hort:* to plant out (plant, shrub). **3.** *Com:* to pay out (cash).
décalage [dekalaʒ] *n.m.* **1.** (*a*) unwedging, unkeying; (*b*) unscotching (of wheel). **2.** staggering (of rivets). **3.** (*a*) shifting the zero (of instrument); (*b*) **d. horaire,** time lag, difference; (*c*) (amount of) shift.
décalaminage [dekalaminaʒ] *n.m. I.C.E:* decarbonizing, *F:* decoking.
décalaminer [dekalamine] *v.tr. I.C.E:* to decarbonize, *F:* to decoke (engine).
décalcomanie [dekalkɔmani] *n.f. Cer: etc:* transfer (process, picture).

décaler [dekale] *v.tr.* **1.** (*a*) to unwedge, unkey; (*b*) to unscotch (wheel). **2.** to set off (part of machine, etc.); to stagger (rivets). **3.** to shift the zero of (instrument); *El:* to displace, shift (the brushes, etc.); **magnéto décalée,** magneto out of adjustment; **d. l'heure,** to alter the time, change the time, the clock; *Ph:* **ondes décalées,** waves out of phase.
décalitre [dekalitr̥] *n.m. Meas:* decalitre.
décalogue [dekalɔg] *n.m. Ecc:* (the) Decalogue.
décalquage [dekalkaʒ] *n.m.* (*a*) transferring; (*b*) tracing off.
décalque [dekalk] *n.m.* **1.** (*a*) transferring; (*b*) tracing off; **papier à d.,** (i) transfer paper, (ii) carbon paper, tracing paper. **2.** (*a*) transfer; (*b*) tracing.
décalquer [dekalke] *v.tr.* **1.** to transfer (design, coloured picture). **2.** to trace off (drawing).
décamètre [dekamɛtr̥] *n.m. Meas:* decametre, *NAm:* decameter.
décamper [dekɑ̃pe] *v.i. F:* to decamp, clear out, clear off; **décampez d'ici!** get lost!
décanat [dekana] *n.m.* deanship.
décaniller [dekanije] *v.i.* = DÉCAMPER.
décantation [dekɑ̃tasjɔ̃] *n.f.* decantation, decanting.
décanter [dekɑ̃te] *v.tr.* to decant, pour off.
décapage [dekapaʒ] *n.m.* = DÉCAPEMENT.
décapant [dekapɑ̃] *n.m.* scouring solution; **d. pour vernis,** varnish remover.
décapeler [dekaple] *v.tr.* **(je décapelle, n. décapelons; je décapellerai)** *Nau:* **1.** to unrig (yard). **2.** to cast off a cable.
décapement [dekapmɑ̃] *n.m.* scouring, cleaning (of metals).
décaper [dekape] *v.tr.* to scour, clean (metal, etc.); to pickle, dip (metal objects); to strip (paint).
décapeur [dekapœr] *n.m.* (*pers.*) pickler, dipper (of metals).
décapitation [dekapitasjɔ̃] *n.f.* decapitation, beheading.
décapiter [dekapite] *v.tr.* to decapitate, behead.
décapode [dekapɔd] *n.m. Crust:* decapod.
décapotable [dekapɔtabl̥] *a. & n.f. Aut:* convertible; drop-head (coupé).
décapsulation [dekapsylasjɔ̃] *n.f. Surg:* decapsulation.
décapsuler [dekapsyle] *v.tr.* to open, to take the top off (a bottle).
décapsuleur [dekapsylœr] *n.m.* crown cork, bottle, opener.
décarburant [decarbyrɑ̃] *Metall: etc:* **1.** *a.* decarbonizing. **2.** *n.m.* decarbonizer.
décarburer [dekarbyre] *v.tr. Metall:* to decarbonize, decarburize (steel, iron).
décarcasser (se) [sədekarkase] *v.pr. F:* to wear oneself out.
décasyllabe, décasyllabique [dekasilab(ik)] *a.* decasyllabic; *n.m.* **décasyllabe,** decasyllabic verse.
décathlon [dekatlɔ̃] *n.m. Sp:* decathlon.
décati [dekati] *a.* (*of face*) wrinkled; that has lost its freshness; **vieillard d.,** decrepit old man.
décatir [dekatir] *v.tr.* **1.** *Tex:* to sponge, steam; to take the gloss, the finish, off (cloth). **2. se d.,** to lose one's freshness, one's beauty; to age.
decauville [dəkovil] *n.m.* narrow-gauge railway.
décavé [dekave] *a. F:* (*a*) (*of pers.*) ruined; (stony) broke; (*b*) (*of face*) drawn, pinched.
décaver [dekave] *v.tr. Cards: etc:* **d. qn,** to win the whole of s.o.'s stakes.
décédé, -ée [desede] *a. & n.* deceased.
décéder [desede] *v.i.* (*conj. like* CÉDER *aux.* être) *Adm:* to die, decease.
déceler [desle] *v.tr.* **(je décèle; je décèlerai) 1.** to disclose (fraud, etc.); to divulge, betray (secret). **2.** *El:* **d. des fuites,** to test for faults.
décembre [desɑ̃br̥] *n.m.* December; **en d., au mois de d.,** in (the month of) December.
decemment [desamɑ̃] *adv.* decently.
décence [desɑ̃s] *n.f.* (*a*) decency; (*b*) propriety, decency, decorum.
décennal, -aux [desenal, -o] *a.* decennial.
décennie [deseni] *n.f.* decade.
décent [desɑ̃] *a.* (*a*) decent; modest (attire, etc.); (*b*) proper, seemly (behaviour, etc.); **peu d.,** indecent, unseemly.
décentralisateur, -trice [desɑ̃tralizatœr, -tris] **1.** *a.* decentralizing. **2.** *n. Pol:* advocate of decentralization.
décentralization [desɑ̃tralizasjɔ̃] *n.f.* decentralization.
décentraliser [desɑ̃tralize] *v.tr.* to decentralize.
décentration [desɑ̃trasjɔ̃] *n.f.,* **décentrement** [desɑ̃trəmɑ̃] *n.m. Opt: Phot:* decentring, throwing off centre.
décentré [desɑ̃tre] *a.* out of centre, out of true, off centre; eccentric.
décentrer [desɑ̃tre] *v.tr. Opt: Mec.E: etc:* to put (lenses, axes, etc.) out of, off, centre; to decentre.
déception [desɛpsjɔ̃] *n.f.* disappointment; *F:* letdown; **éprouver une d.,** to be disappointed; **d. sentimentale,** unhappy love affair.
décernement [desɛrnəmɑ̃] *n.m.* awarding (of prize, etc.).
décerner [desɛrne] *v.tr.* **1.** *Jur:* **d. un mandat d'arrêt contre qn,** to issue a warrant for the arrest of s.o. **2.** to award (a prize, etc.); **d. un honneur à qn,** to confer an honour on s.o.
décès [desɛ] *n.m. esp. Adm:* decease; (natural) death; *Jur:* demise; **acte de d.,** death certificate; **fermé pour cause de d.,** closed on account of death.
décevant [des(ə)vɑ̃] *a.* **1.** *A:* deceptive; delusive (appearance, etc.). **2.** disappointing (result, etc.).
décevoir [desəvwar] *v.tr.* (*conj. like* RECEVOIR) **1.** *A:* to deceive, delude. **2.** to disappoint.
déchaînement [deʃɛnmɑ̃] *n.m.* (*a*) breaking loose; **le d. de la tempête,** the breaking of the storm; **un d. de l'opinion,** a great wave of public opinion; (*b*) outburst (of passion); outburst of fury, fit of rage.
déchaîner [deʃene] *v.tr.* **1.** to unchain, to let loose (dog, etc.); *F:* **les diables sont déchaînés,** all hell has broken loose. **2.** to unleash (passions, anger, etc.); **d. l'hilarité,** to provoke laughter. **3.** (*a*) **se d.,** to break out; **la tempête s'est déchaînée,** the storm broke; (*b*) **se d. contre qn,** to fly into a rage against s.o.
déchanter [deʃɑ̃te] *v.i. F:* to lower one's tone, to sing a different tune, to come down a peg.
déchaper [deʃape] *v.tr. Tchn:* to remove the cope from a mould.
décharge [deʃarʒ] *n.f.* **1.** (*a*) unloading (of cart, etc.); unlading, discharging (of ship, cargo); (*b*) discharge, volley (of gunfire, etc.); (*c*) *El:* discharge; **d. disruptive,** spark discharge; **d. électrique,** electric shock; (*d*) output (of accumulator). **2.** (*a*) relief, relieving, easing; *Arch:* **arc d.,** relieving arch; (*b*) (tax) rebate; **porter une somme en d.,** to mark a sum as paid; **d. de 50 pour cent,** composition of 50p in the £; (*c*) *Jur:* **témoin à d.,** witness for the defence; (*d*) *Jur:* release, acquittal (of accused person); (*e*) *Bank:* letter of indemnity. **3.** (*a*) discharge, outlet; **tuyau de d.,** wastepipe; (*b*) *Dy:* running (of colour). **4. d. (publique),** rubbish dump, tip; *P.N:* **d. interdite,** tipping prohibited. **5.** *Type:* offset sheet.
déchargement [deʃarʒəmɑ̃] *n.m.* unloading (of cart, firearm); unlading (of ship); discharging, unloading (of cargo).
déchargeoir [deʃarʒwar] *n.m.* **1.** wastepipe, overflow (pipe). **2.** *Tex:* cloth beam (of loom).
décharger [deʃarʒe] *v.tr.* **(je déchargeai(s); n. dé-**

chargeons) 1. (*a*) to unload (cart, etc.); to unlade, discharge (ship); to unship, discharge (cargo); to tip, dump (gravel); (*b*) to unload (firearm); (*c*) **d. sa conscience,** to ease one's mind (**de,** of); *A:* **d. son cœur,** to unburden one's heart; (*d*) **d. son fusil sur, contre, qn,** to let off, fire (off), one's gun at s.o.; (*e*) to discharge (accumulator). **2.** (*a*) to relieve, lighten, ease (horse, ship, etc.) of part of its load; to take the strain off (beam); (*b*) *Com:* to receipt; (*c*) **d. qn d'une accusation,** to acquit s.o. of a charge; **d. qn d'une dette,** to remit a debt; **failli déchargé, non déchargé,** discharged, undischarged, bankrupt. **3.** (*a*) to discharge, empty (reservoir, etc.); (*b*) *v.i. Typ:* **encre qui décharge,** ink that rubs off. **4.** (*a*) **se d.,** (*of gun*) to go off; (*of battery*) to run down; to discharge; (*of anger*) vent itself (**sur,** on); (*b*) **se d. de qn, de qch.,** to get rid of s.o., of sth.; **se d. d'un fardeau,** to put down, lay down, a load; **se d. de qch. sur qn,** to shift the responsibility of sth. on to s.o.; (*c*) **le fleuve se décharge dans un lac,** the river flows into a lake.

déchargeur [deʃarʒœr] *n.m.* **1.** *A:* stevedore, docker; (market) porter; **d. de charbon,** coalheaver. **2.** *El:* (spark, lightning) arrester.

décharné [deʃarne] *a.* **1.** fleshless (bones, etc.). **2.** emaciated, scraggy, bony (limbs, etc.); lank, skinny (body); gaunt (face); bare (tree); bald (style).

décharnement [deʃarnəmɑ̃] *n.m.* emaciation.

décharner [deʃarne] *v.tr.* **1.** to strip the flesh off (bone). **2.** to emaciate (s.o.).

déchaumer [deʃome] *v.tr. Agr:* to plough the stubble.

déchaussé [deʃose] *a.* barefoot(ed).

déchaussement [deʃosmɑ̃] *n.m.* (*a*) taking off of one's shoes; (*b*) laying bare.

déchausser [deʃose] *v.tr.* **1.** to take off (s.o.'s) shoes. **2.** to lay bare the roots of (tree); to bare, expose (tooth, foundations). **3. se d.,** to take off one's shoes; **ses dents se déchaussent,** his teeth are getting loose.

dèche [dɛʃ] *n.f. F:* poverty, distress; **être dans la d.,** to be hard up, (stony) broke.

déchéance [deʃeɑ̃s] *n.f.* **1.** fall (from grace); downfall; decline. **2.** *Jur: Fin:* forfeiture (of rights, etc.); **action en d. de brevet,** action for forfeiture of patent; **d. de la puissance paternelle,** loss of parental authority; *Ins:* **d. d'une police,** expiration of a policy.

déchet [deʃɛ] *n.m.* **1.** loss, decrease, diminution (of weight, value). **2.** (*a*) *usu. pl.* waste, refuse; **déchets radioactifs,** radioactive waste; **d. de métal,** scrap (metal); **déchets de viande,** scraps; (*b*) (*of pers.*) failure; **un d. de la société,** a social outcast.

déchevelé [deʃəvle], *a.* dishevelled.

déchiffonner [deʃifɔne] *v.tr.* to smooth out, iron out, creases (in material, etc.).

déchiffrable [deʃifrabl̥] *a.* decipherable (inscription); legible (writing).

déchiffrement [deʃifrəmɑ̃] *n.m.* deciphering.

déchiffrer [deʃifre] *v.tr.* to decipher, make out (inscription, etc.); to decode (message); to read, interpret (signals); to read, play (music) at sight; to sightread (music).

déchiffreur, -euse [deʃifrœr, -øz] *n.* decipherer (of inscription); decoder (of message); **d. de radar,** radar scanner.

déchiquetage [deʃiktaʒ] *n.m.* shredding; slashing.

déchiqueté [deʃikte] *a.* **1.** jagged (edge); ragged (coastline); **papier à bords déchiquetés,** deckle-edge paper. **2.** (*object*) cut to bits, to shreds.

déchiqueter [deʃikte] *v.tr.* **(je déchiquette; je déchiquetterai)** to cut, slash, tear (stuff, flesh, etc.) into strips, into shreds; to hack (chicken); to pull (s.o.'s reputation) to pieces.

déchiqueture [deʃiktyr] *n.f.* slash, long tear (in cloth, etc.).

déchirant [deʃirɑ̃] *a.* heartrending, harrowing; agonizing (pain).

déchirement [deʃirmɑ̃] *n.m.* tearing, rending (of material, etc.); **d. d'un muscle,** tearing of a muscle; **d. de cœur,** heartbreak.

déchirer [deʃire] *v.tr.* **1.** to tear, rend (garment, etc.); to tear up (paper, etc.); to tear open (envelope); **d. qch. en morceaux,** to tear sth. to pieces, to bits; **sons qui déchirent l'oreille,** ear-splitting sounds; **cris qui déchiraient le cœur,** heartrending cries; **d. qn,** to vilify, slander, s.o.; **il s'est déchiré un muscle,** he's torn a muscle. **2.** (*of material*) **se d.,** to tear.

déchirure [deʃiryr] *n.f.* (*a*) tear, rent, slit, rip; (*b*) lacerated wound, laceration.

déchloruré [deklɔryre] *a. Med:* (*of diet*) salt-free.

déchoir [deʃwar] *v.i.* (*p.p.* **déchu;** *pr.ind.* **je déchois, n. déchoyons, ils déchoient;** *p.h.* **je déchus;** *fu.* **je déchoirai;** *aux.* **être** *or* **avoir**) to fall (from honour, etc.); **ce quartier a déchu,** the district has gone down; **sa popularité déchoit,** his popularity is declining; **la maison déchoit de son prestige,** the firm is going down (in public estimation); **ce serait d.,** (i) it would mean loss of prestige; (ii) it would mean losing one's standing; **il est déchu de ses droits,** he has forfeited his rights.

déchristianiser [dekristjanize] *v.tr.* **1.** to dechristianize; to turn (s.o.) from Christianity. **2. se d.,** to turn (away) from Christianity.

déchu [deʃy] *a.* fallen; **ange d.,** fallen angel; **roi d.,** dethroned king; *Ins:* **police déchue,** expired policy; **d. de la nationalité française,** deprived of French nationality.

décibel [desibɛl] *n.m. Ph:* decibel.

décidé [deside] *a.* **1.** settled (matter, etc.). **2.** resolute, confident (person, manner); determined (character); **d'un ton d.,** decisively, resolutely. **3. être d. à faire qch.,** to be determined, resolved, to do sth.; to be bent on doing sth. **4. avoir une supériorité décidée sur qn,** to have a decided superiority over s.o.

décidément [desidemɑ̃] *adv.* **1.** *A:* resolutely, firmly. **2.** decidedly, positively, definitely; **d. je n'ai pas de chance,** I really haven't any luck! **d., elle est folle!** she must be mad!

décider [deside] **I.** *v.tr.* **1.** (*a*) to decide, settle (question, dispute); **voilà qui décide tout!** that settles it! (*b*) **l'assemblée décida la guerre, la paix,** the assembly decided on war, on peace. **2. d. qn à faire qch.,** to persuade, induce, s.o. to do sth. **3.** *v.i.* (*a*) **il faut que je décide,** I must decide, make a decision; **d. en faveur de qn,** to decide, *Jur:* to give a ruling, in favour of s.o.; to find for (the plaintiff); (*b*) **d. de qch.,** to decide, determine, sth.; **événement qui a décidé de sa carrière,** event that determined his career. **4. d. de** + *inf.*, to decide (after deliberation) to (do sth.); **j'ai décidé de partir demain,** I've decided to leave tomorrow; **d. que** + *ind.*, to decide, settle, that . . .; *impers.* **il fut décidé qu'on attendrait sa réponse,** it was decided to wait for his reply. **II. se décider 1.** to make up one's mind; to come to a decision. **2. se d. à qch., à faire qch.,** to make up one's mind (reluctantly) to do sth.; **je ne puis pas me d. à le faire,** I cannot bring myself to do it; **allons décidez-vous,** come on, make up your mind. **3. se d. pour qn, pour qch.,** to decide in favour of s.o., of sth.

décigramme [desigram] *n.m. Meas:* decigramme.

décilitre [desilitr̥] *n.m. Meas:* decilitre.

décimal, -aux [desimal, -o] *a.* decimal.

décimale [desimal] *n.f.* decimal.

décimation [desimasjɔ̃] *n.f.* decimation.

décime[1] [desim] *n.m.* **1.** one tenth of a franc; ten centimes. **2.** 10% tax.

décime[2] *n.f. Ecc: Hist:* tithe.

décimer [desime] *v.tr.* to decimate.

décimètre [desimɛtr̥] *n.m. Meas:* decimetre, *NAm:* decimeter.

décimo [desimo] *adv.* tenthly.

décintrage, décintrement [desɛ̃traʒ, -əmɑ̃] *n.m. Const:* centring (of arch).

décintrer [desɛ̃tre] *v.tr. Const:* to strike, remove, the centering of (arch).

décisif, -ive [desizif, -iv] *a.* **1.** decisive (battle, etc.); conclusive (evidence); **au moment d.,** at the critical, crucial, moment. **2.** positive, peremptory (tone).

décision [desizjɔ̃] *n.f.* decision. **1.** (*a*) **prendre, arriver à, une d.,** to take, come to, reach, a decision; to make up one's mind (**quant à, au sujet de,** about); **forcer une d.,** to bring matters to a head; (*b*) *Jur:* ruling, award; (*c*) *Mil:* (regimental) orders. **2.** resolution, determination.

décisivement [desizivmɑ̃] *adv.* decisively.

déclamateur, -trice [deklamatœr, -tris] *n. Pej:* (*a*) orator; *F:* tub thumper; (*b*) bombastic writer.

déclamation [deklamasjɔ̃] *n.f.* **1.** (art of) declamation; oratory; **il a une mauvaise d.,** he is no orator. **2.** (*a*) ranting, spouting; (*b*) bombastic speech.

déclamatoire [deklamatwar] *a.* declamatory, highflown (style); ranting, bombastic (speech).

déclamer [deklame] *v.tr.* **1.** to declaim (speech). **2.** (*a*) *Pej:* to rant; (*b*) *Lit:* **d. contre qn,** to rail against s.o.

déclarable [deklarabl̥] *a. Cust:* liable to duty.

déclarant, -ante [deklarɑ̃, -ɑ̃t] *n. Jur: Adm:* declarant.

déclaration [deklarasjɔ̃] *n.f.* declaration; (*a*) proclamation, announcement; **d. de guerre,** declaration of war; (*b*) notification (of birth, death, etc.); (*c*) **émettre une d.,** to make a statement; **d. sous serment,** affidavit; (*d*) **d. d'amour,** declaration of love; (*e*) *Cust:* **d. en douane,** customs declaration.

déclaré [deklare] *a.* declared, avowed (enemy, intention, etc.).

déclarer [deklare] *v.tr.* **1.** (*a*) to declare, make known (one's intentions, wishes, one's love, etc.); (*b*) *Cards:* **d. trèfle,** to declare, call, clubs. **2.** to declare, proclaim, announce, make public; (*a*) **d. qn roi,** to declare s.o. king; **déclaré coupable,** found guilty; **déclaré coupable de vol,** convicted of theft; (*b*) to notify (birth, death, etc.); (*c*) **d. la guerre à qn,** to declare war on s.o.; (*d*) *Cust:* **avez-vous quelque chose à d.?** have you anything to declare? **3.** (*a*) **se d.** (i) to speak one's mind; (ii) to declare one's love; (iii) (*of fire, disease*) to break out; **se d. pour, contre, qch.,** to declare for, against, sth.; (*b*) **se d. l'auteur du méfait,** to own up to the deed.

déclassé [deklase] **1.** *a.* (*a*) (*of pers.*) déclassé; (*b*) *Sp:* relegated (to lower division, etc.); (*c*) (*of hotel*) downgraded. **2.** *n.* **un(e) déclassé(e),** person who has lost social position.

déclassement [deklasmɑ̃] *n.m.* change of class.

déclasser [deklase] *v.tr.* **1.** to transfer (passengers) from one class to another. **2.** to lower the social position (of s.o.). **3.** *Mil:* to declare (weapon) obsolete; *Navy:* to strike (warship) off the list. **4.** *Navy:* to disrate (seaman).

déclenchement [deklɑ̃ʃmɑ̃] *n.m.* **1.** *Mec.E:* (*a*) releasing, disengaging (of part); (*b*) trigger action; *Phot:* (shutter) release. **2.** starting; setting (of sth.) in motion.

déclencher [deklɑ̃ʃe] *v.tr.* **1.** *Mec.E:* to release, disconnect, disengage (part). **2.** to set off (mechanism); to start (apparatus), to set (apparatus) in motion; to trigger off; *Mil:* **d. une attaque,** to launch an attack.

déclencheur [deklɑ̃ʃœr] *n.m. Phot:* shutter release.

déclic [deklik] *n.m.* **1.** pawl, catch; trigger; **chronomètre à d.,** stopwatch. **2.** click(ing sound).

déclin [deklɛ̃] *n.m.* decline, close (of day); wane, waning (of moon); fall (of the year); falling off (of talent); **le soleil est à, sur, son d.,** the sun is sinking, setting; **au d. de sa vie,** in his declining years.

déclinable [deklinabl̥] *a. Gram:* declinable.

déclinaison [deklinɛzɔ̃] *n.f.* **1.** (*a*) *Astr:* declination (of star); (*b*) **d. magnétique,** magnetic variation. **2.** *Gram:* declension.

décliner [dekline] **I.** *v.i.* **1.** (*of compass*) to deviate (from the true line). **2.** to wane; (*of star*) to decline; (*of day*) to draw to a close. **II.** *v.tr.* **1.** to decline, refuse (offer, etc.); to decline (responsibility); **d. une juridiction,** to refuse to acknowledge a jurisdiction. **2.** (*a*) *Gram:* to decline (noun, etc.); (*b*) **d. ses noms et prénoms,** to state, give, one's name.

décliquer [deklike] *v.tr.* to release (pawl); *Civ.E:* **d. le mouton,** to release the monkey (of pile driver).

déclive [dekliv] **1.** *a.* declivitous, sloping, inclined. **2.** *n.f.* slope.

déclivité [deklivite] *n.f.* declivity, slope, incline, gradient; **angle de d.,** angle of gradient.

déclouer [deklue] *v.tr.* (*a*) to unnail, to draw the nails out of (packing case, etc.); (*b*) **d. un tableau,** to take down a picture (from its nail).

décocher [dekɔʃe] *v.tr.* to shoot, let fly (bolt from crossbow); **d. un coup à qn,** to hit out at s.o.; **d. une remarque,** to fire a comment; **d. une œillade à qn,** to flash a glance at s.o.

décoiffer [dekwafe] *v.tr.* **1.** to remove (s.o.'s) hat; to uncap (fuse). **2.** to disarrange, tousle (s.o.'s) hair. **3. se d.,** (i) to remove one's hat; (ii) to let one's hair down; (iii) to disarrange one's hair.

décoinçage, décoincement [dekwɛ̃saʒ, -mɑ̃] *n.m.* loosening; unwedging.

décoincer [dekwɛ̃se] *v.tr.* **(n. décoinçons; je décoinçai(s))** to loosen (jammed part, etc.); to unwedge.

décolérer [dekɔlere] *v.i.* **(je décolère; je décolérerai)** to calm down; (*used esp. in the neg.*) **il ne décolérait pas,** he was in a constant state of anger; he was still fuming.

décollage [dekɔlaʒ] *n.m.* **1.** unsticking, ungluing. **2.** *Av:* takeoff.

décollation [dekɔlasjɔ̃] *n.m.* decapitation, beheading.

décollé [dekɔle] *a.* (*of ears*) sticking out.

décollement [dekɔlmɑ̃] *n.m.* **1.** unsticking, ungluing. **2.** coming unstuck, unglued; unsticking, loosening; *Med:* **d. de la rétine,** detachment of the retina.

décoller [dekɔle] **1.** *v.tr.* (*a*) to unstick, unglue; (*b*) to loosen, disengage, release (part). **2.** *v.i.* (*a*) (*of aircraft*) to rise from the ground; to take off; (*b*) *F:* **il ne décolle pas d'ici,** he won't budge, he's staying put. **3. se d.,** to come unstuck, undone; to work loose.

décolletage [dekɔltaʒ] *n.m.* (*a*) lowering of neckline; (*b*) *Metalw:* screw cutting.

décolleté [dekɔlte] **1.** *a.* **femme décolletée,** woman in low-necked, low cut, (evening) dress; **robe décolletée,** low-necked dress; **robe décolletée dans le dos,** dress cut low at the back. **2.** *s.m.* neck opening, neckline; **d. carré,** square neck; **d. en pointe,** V neck; **en grand d.,** in a low-cut dress, in full evening dress.

décolleter [dekɔlte] *v.tr.* **(je décollète, je décollette** *are theoretical forms; the pronunciation is always* [dekɔlt]) **1.** to cut out the neck of (dress). **2.** *Metalw:* to cut (screw); **tour à d.,** screw-cutting lathe. **3. se d.,** to wear a low-necked dress.

décolonisation [dekɔlɔnizasjɔ̃] *n.f.* decolonization.

décolorant [dekɔlɔrɑ̃] **1.** *a.* bleaching. **2.** *n.m.* bleaching agent, bleach.

décoloration [dekɔlɔrasjɔ̃] *n.f.* (*a*) discolo(u)ration, fading; (*b*) *Hairdr:* bleaching; (*c*) colourlessness (of complexion, style).

décolorer [dekɔlɔre] *v.tr.* **1.** to discolour; to fade; to take the colour out of (sth.); to bleach (hair). **2. se d.,** to lose colour, to fade, to bleach; (*of pers.*) to lose one's colour, to grow pale.

décombres [dekɔ̃bʀ̥] *n.m.pl.* rubbish, debris (of building); ruins.

décommandement [dekɔmɑ̃dmɑ̃] *n.m.* countermanding; cancelling.

décommander [dekɔmɑ̃de] *v.tr.* to countermand (order); to cancel (meeting, dinner); to put off (guest); **d. une grève,** to call off a strike.

décomposé [dekɔ̃poze] *a.* **1.** *Bot:* decomposite (leaves, etc.). **2.** (*a*) *Mch: I.C.E:* **huile décomposée,** spent oil; (*b*) **visage d.,** drawn face; face distorted by grief, terror; (*c*) decomposed, rotten.

décomposer [dekɔ̃poze] *v.tr.* **1.** *Ph: Ch: etc:* to decompose; **d. la lumière,** to split light; **d. une fraction,** to split up a fraction. **2.** to decompose, rot, decay (organic matter). **3.** to contort, distort (features). **4. se d.** (*a*) to decompose, rot, decay; (*b*) (*of face, features*) to become distorted (with terror, etc.).

décomposition [dekɔ̃pɔzisjɔ̃] *n.f.* **1.** *Ph: Ch: etc:* decomposition. **2.** decomposition, decay, rotting. **3.** distortion (of features).

décompresseur [dekɔ̃prɛsœr] *n.m. I.C.E:* (*a*) compression tap; (*b*) exhaust (valve) lifter; (*c*) decompressor.

décompression [dekɔ̃prɛsjɔ̃] *n.f. Mch: etc:* decompression; **robinet de d.,** (i) *I.C.E:* compression tap; (ii) *Mch:* pet cock.

décomprimer [dekɔ̃prime] *v.tr.* to decompress.

décompte [dekɔ̃t] *n.m.* **1.** (*a*) deduction (from sum to be paid); *Fig:* **trouver du d.,** to be disappointed (**à,** in); (*b*) balance. **2.** *Adm: Com:* detailed account; breakdown.

décompter [dekɔ̃te] **1.** *v.tr.* to deduct (sum from account). **2.** *v.i.* (*of clock*) to miscount (on striking).

déconcertant [dekɔ̃sɛrtɑ̃] *a.* disconcerting.

déconcerté [dekɔ̃sɛrte] *a.* disconcerted; taken aback.

déconcerter [dekɔ̃sɛrte] *v.tr.* **1.** *Lit:* to upset, confound, frustrate (s.o.'s plans). **2.** to disconcert (s.o.); to put (s.o.) out (of countenance). **3. se d.,** to lose one's assurance; to lose countenance; **sans se d.,** unabashed.

déconfit [dekɔ̃fi] *a.* crestfallen, discomfited.

déconfiture [dekɔ̃fityr] *n.f.* collapse, failure, downfall, ruin; bankruptcy (of non-trader); **tomber en d.,** to fail to meet one's liabilities.

décongélation [dekɔ̃ʒelasjɔ̃] *n.f.* defrosting, thawing (of meat, etc.).

décongeler [dekɔ̃ʒle] *v.tr.* **(je décongèle; je décongèlerai)** to thaw, defrost, defreeze (frozen meat, etc.).

décongestionner [dekɔ̃ʒɛstjɔne] *v.tr.* (*a*) *Med:* to relieve congestion in (the lungs, etc.); (*b*) to clear (street of traffic).

déconnecter [dekɔnɛkte] *v.tr. El:* to disconnect (lead, etc.).

déconner [dekɔne] *v.i. P:* (*a*) to talk rubbish, drivel; **tu déconnes!** what on earth are you talking about? (*b*) to fool around.

déconseiller [dekɔ̃seje] *v.tr.* **d. qch. à qn,** to advise s.o. against sth.; **d. qn de faire qch.,** to advise s.o. against doing sth.; **un livre à d. pour les jeunes,** a book unsuitable for young people.

déconsidération [dekɔ̃siderasjɔ̃] *n.f.* disrepute, discredit; **tomber en d.,** to fall into disrepute.

déconsidérer [dekɔ̃sidere] *v.tr.* **(je déconsidère; je déconsidérerai) 1.** to bring (s.o., sth.) into disrepute. **2. se d.,** to fall into discredit; to belittle oneself.

déconsigner [dekɔ̃siɲe] *v.tr.* **1.** *Rail:* to take (suitcase) out of left-luggage office. **2.** to return deposit (on bottle, etc.).

décontenancé [dekɔ̃tnɑ̃se] *a.* confused; put out.

décontenancer [dekɔ̃tnɑ̃se] *v.tr.* **(je décontenançai(s); n. décontenançons) 1.** to put (s.o.) out of countenance, to embarrass, confuse (s.o.). **2. se d.,** to lose countenance.

décontracté [dekɔ̃trakte] *a.* relaxed.

décontracter [dekɔ̃trakte] *v.tr.* **1.** to relax (muscle, mind, etc.). **2. se d.,** to relax.

décontraction [dekɔ̃traksjɔ̃] *n.f.* relaxation.

déconvenue [dekɔ̃vny] *n.f.* disappointment, mortification.

décor [dekɔr] *n.m.* **1.** decoration (of house, etc.); **peintre en d.,** house painter. **2.** *Th: Cin: T.V:* setting (of stage); set; *pl.* scenery; **peintre de décors,** scene painter; **il lui faut un changement de d.,** he needs a change. **3.** *F: Aut:* **rentrer dans le d.,** to drive off the road (into tree, etc.).

décorateur [dekɔratœr] *n.m.* (*a*) (interior) decorator; (*b*) (i) stage designer; (ii) scene painter.

décoratif, -ive [dekɔratif, -iv] *a.* decorative, ornamental.

décoration [dekɔrasjɔ̃] *n.f.* **1.** (*a*) (interior) decoration (of house, etc.); (*b*) ornamentation, embellishment (of church, etc.). **2.** decoration; medal; ribbon, star (of an order); **remise de décorations,** investiture.

décorativement [dekɔrativmɑ̃] *adv.* decoratively.

décorer [dekɔre] *v.tr.* **1.** to decorate, ornament; to do up (house, etc.). **2.** to decorate (s.o.).

décorner [dekɔrne] *v.tr.* to dehorn; to poll (cattle, etc.); *F:* **un vent à d. les bœufs,** a howling gale.

décorticage [dekɔrtikaʒ] *n.m.* husking (of rice); shelling (of nuts).

décortication [dekɔrtikasjɔ̃] *n.f.* barking (of timber).

décortiquer [dekɔrtike] *v.tr.* to decorticate; to bark (timber); to husk (rice); to hull (barley); to shell (nuts).

décorum [dekɔrɔm] *n.m.* decorum, propriety; etiquette; **observer le d.,** to observe the proprieties.

découcher [dekuʃe] *v.i.* (*a*) to sleep away from home, to sleep out; (*b*) to stay out all night.

découdre [dekudʀ̥] *v.tr.* (*conj. like* COUDRE) **1.** (*a*) to unpick, unstitch (garment); to rip up (seam); (*b*) (*of horned animal*) to rip open, to gore (dog, etc.); **en d.,** to cross swords; to fight. **2. se d.,** to come unsewn, unstitched.

découler [dekule] *v.i.* **1.** *A: & Lit:* to trickle, drip, flow. **2.** to ensue, proceed, follow (from); **il en découle que . . .,** it follows that. . . .

découpage [dekupaʒ] *n.m.* **1.** cutting up (of paper, cake, etc.); carving (of chicken, etc.). **2.** (*a*) cutting out (of patterns, etc.); punching, stamping, cutting (of sheet metal); punching, pinking (of leather, etc.); **matrices pour d.,** cutting dies; (*b*) cutout; (*c*) *Typ:* (i) cutting of the overlays; (ii) overlay.

découpé [dekupe] *a.* (*a*) cut out; **bois d.,** fretwork; (*b*) *Bot:* denticulate (leaf, etc.).

découper [dekupe] *v.tr.* **1.** to cut up (paper, cake, etc.); to carve (chicken, etc.); **couteau à d.,** carving knife. **2.** to cut out (design); to stamp (out), to punch, cut (metals); to punch, pink (leather); **d. un article dans un journal,** to cut an article out of a newspaper; **scie à d.,** fretsaw. **3. se d.,** to stand out, show up, project (**sur,** on, against).

découpeur, -euse [dekupœr, -øz] *n.* **1.** (*a*) (*pers.*) carver; (*b*) **d. en cuir,** (i) leather cutter, (ii) pinker; (*c*) *Cin:* cutter. **2.** *n.f.* **découpeuse** *Tex: etc:* shearing, cutting, pinking, machine.

découplé [dekuple] *a.* **bien d.,** well built, muscular (person).

découpler [dekuple] *v.tr.* **1.** to slip, uncouple (hounds). **2.** to uncouple (horses, trucks).
découpoir [dekupwar] *n.m.* **1.** *Metalw: etc:* cutter; (i) shear, (ii) stamp. **2.** *Needlew:* **d. à figures,** pinking iron.
découpure [dekupyr] *n.f.* **1.** (*a*) cutting out; (*b*) punching, stamping (out); (*c*) pinking; (*d*) fretwork. **2.** (*a*) piece cut out (by punch, etc.); stamping; (*b*) (newspaper) cutting. **3.** (*a*) indentation (in coastline, etc.); (*b*) *Bot:* denticulation (in leaf).
découragé [dekuraʒe] *a.* discouraged, disheartened, despondent, downcast.
décourageant [dekuraʒɑ̃] *a.* discouraging, dispiriting, disheartening, depressing; **vous êtes d.,** you're hopeless.
découragement [dekuraʒmɑ̃] *n.m.* discouragement; **tomber dans le d.,** to become disheartened, despondent.
décourager [dekuraʒe] *v.tr.* **(je décourageai(s); n. décourageons) 1.** to discourage, dishearten; **d. qn de (faire) qch.,** to discourage, deter, s.o. from (doing) sth; to put s.o. off (doing) sth. **2. d. un projet,** to discourage a scheme. **3. se d.,** to become discouraged, disheartened; to lose heart; **ne vous découragez pas!** don't lose heart! *F:* cheer up!
découronner [dekurɔne] *v.tr.* **1.** (*a*) to dethrone, depose (king, etc.); (*b*) to debunk (hero, etc.). **2.** to pollard (tree).
décours [dekur] *n.m.* **1.** waning (of the moon); **lune à son d.,** moon on the wane. **2.** abatement (of fever); decline (of illness).
décousu [dekusy] **1.** *a.* (a) (*of seam, etc.*) unsewn, unstitched; (*b*) disconnected, disjointed, incoherent (words, ideas, etc.); rambling, desultory (remarks, conversation); unmethodical (work). **2.** *n.m.* disjointedness, desultoriness.
décousure [dekusyr] *n.f.* **1.** *A:* seam rent. **2.** gash, rip (caused by horns, tusks).
découvert [dekuvɛr] **1.** *a.* (*a*) uncovered; **la tête découverte,** bareheaded; **à visage d.,** openly, frankly; (*b*) open (country, etc.); **coin de ciel d.,** bit of blue sky; (*c*) exposed, unprotected (town, etc.); *Ten:* **région découverte,** part of the court left uncovered (by player); (*d*) **compte d.,** overdrawn account. **2.** *n.m.* uncovered balance; overdraft. **3.** *adv. phr.* **à d.,** uncovered, unprotected, open; **agir, parler, à d.,** to act, speak, openly; **mettre qch. à d.,** to expose sth. to view; **crédit à d.,** unsecured credit; *St. Exch:* **vendre à d.,** to go a bear, to sell short.
découverte [dekuvɛrt] *n.f.* **1.** discovery (of land, etc.); *Mil:* scouting, reconnoitring; **aller à la d.,** to explore; to go in search of (sth.). **2.** (*a*) discovery, exposure, detection (of plot, etc.); (*b*) (scientific) discovery.
découvreur, -euse [dekuvrœr, øz] *n.* discoverer.
découvrir [dekuvrir] *v.tr.* (*conj. like* COUVRIR) **I. 1.** (*a*) to uncover; **d. un pot,** to take the lid off a pot; **d. une maison,** to take the roof off a house; (*b*) to expose, lay bare; to unveil (statue); to disclose (secret); to reveal (plan); **se d. la tête,** to bare one's head; **d. ses dents,** to show one's teeth; **d. son cœur,** to open one's heart; *Chess:* **d. une pièce,** to uncover a piece. **2.** to perceive, discern; *Nau:* to sight (land). **3.** (*a*) to discover (plot, etc.); to detect (error, criminal); to bring (crime, etc.) to light; **il ne pouvait pas d. qui elle était,** he couldn't find out who she was; **le projecteur découvrit l'avion,** the searchlight picked out the aircraft; **craindre d'être découvert,** to fear detection; (*b*) to discover (a virus, etc.); to be the first to find (sth.). **4.** *v.i.* (*of reef*) to uncover (at low tide). **II. se découvrir 1.** (*a*) to bare one's head; to take off one's hat; (*b*) to take off some of one's clothing. **2.** *Fenc:* to expose oneself. **3.** (*of sky*) to clear. **4.** to become perceptible; to come into sight. **5.** to come to light; **la vérité se découvre toujours,** truth will out.
décrassage, décrassement [dekrasaʒ, -mɑ̃] *n.m.* cleaning, scouring.
décrasser [dekrase] *v.tr.* **1.** to clean, cleanse, scour; to remove the fouling from (gun barrel); **d. une chaudière,** to scale, fur, a boiler. **2. se d.** (*a*) to clean oneself up; (*b*) to rise in the world.
décrassoir [dekraswar] *n.m.* toothcomb.
décrépir [dekrepir] *v.tr.* to strip the plaster, the roughcast, off (wall, etc.).
décrépit [dekrepi] *a.* decrepit, senile; broken-down (horse); tumbledown, dilapidated (house).
décrépitude [dekrepityd] *n.f.* decrepitude.
décret [dekrɛ] *n.m.* decree, fiat, order; *Adm:* **d. présidentiel** = Order in Council.
décréter [dekrete] *v.tr.* **(je décrète; je décréterai)** to decree; to enact (law).
décret-loi [dekrɛlwa] *n.m.* = Order in Council; *pl. décrets-lois.*
décrier [dekrije] *v.tr.* to disparage, decry, discredit (s.o., sth.); to run (s.o., sth.) down.
décrire [dekrir] *v.tr.* (*conj. like* ÉCRIRE) **1.** to describe, depict (sth.). **2.** *Mth: etc:* to describe, draw (curve, circle); **la route décrit une courbe,** the road follows a curve.
décrochage, décrochement [dekrɔʃaʒ, -mɑ̃] *n.m.* unhooking; disconnecting.
décrocher [dekrɔʃe] **1.** *v.tr.* to unhook, take down (coat from peg, etc.); to unsling (hammock); *Tp:* to pick, lift (receiver); to uncouple, disconnect (railway carriages, etc.); to undo (clasp, etc.); **se d. la mâchoire,** to dislocate one's jaw; **phrase à d. la mâchoire,** tongue twister; *F:* **d. les palmes, la croix,** to receive a decoration; **d. le grand succès,** to make a big hit. **2.** *v.i. Av:* to stall; *Mil:* to beat a retreat, withdraw.
décroisement [dekrwazmɑ̃] *n.m.* uncrossing.
décroiser [dekrwaze] *v.tr.* to uncross (one's legs, etc.).
décroissance [dekrwasɑ̃s] *n.f.* decrease; diminution (of population); decline (of strength); abatement (of fever); **nos importations sont en d.,** our imports are decreasing.
décroissement [dekrwasmɑ̃] *n.m.* waning (of moon); shortening (of days).
décroît [dekrwa] *n.m.* last quarter (of moon); **la lune est sur son d.,** the moon is in its last quarter.
décroître [dekrwatr̥] *v.i.* (*pr. p.* **décroissant;** *p.p.* **décru;** *pr.ind.* **il décroît, ils décroissent;** *p.h.* **il décrut:** *fu.* **il décroîtra**) to decrease, decline, diminish; **les jours commencent à d.,** the days are beginning to draw in; **la lune décroît,** the moon is on the wane; **aller (en) décroissant,** to decrease; to grow gradually less.
décrottage [dekrɔtaʒ] *n.m.* cleaning (of boots, etc.).
décrotter [dekrɔte] *v.tr.* to clean, to remove mud from (boots, etc.); to scrape (one's boots); *F:* to polish up (s.o.'s manners).
décrottoir [dekrɔtwar] *n.m.* shoe scraper; door scraper; **tapis d.,** (wire) door mat.
décrue [dekry] *n.f.* **1.** fall, subsidence (of river, etc.). **2.** decrease, diminution, fall (in numbers, etc.).
décrypter [dekripte] *v.tr.* to decipher (cryptogram).
déculotter [dekylɔte] *v.tr.* **1.** to take the trousers off, *F:* debag (s.o.). **2. se d.,** to take off, to let down, one's trousers; *F:* to grovel.
décuple [dekypl̥] *a. & n.m.* decuple; tenfold (amount).
décuplement [dekypləmɑ̃] *n.m.* multiplication by ten.
décupler [dekyple] *v.tr. & i.* to decuple; to increase, multiply, tenfold.

décuver [dekyve] *v.tr.* to tun, rack off (wine).
dédaigner [dedɛɲe] *v.tr.* to scorn, disdain; to turn up one's nose at (offer, etc.); **cette offre n'est pas à d.,** this offer is not to be disdained, is not to be sneezed at.
dédaigneusement [dedɛɲøzmɑ̃] *adv.* disdainfully, scornfully.
dédaigneux, -euse [dedeɲø, -øz] *a.* disdainful, contemptuous, scornful (**de,** of).
dédain [dedɛ̃] *n.m.* disdain, scorn (**de,** of); disregard (**de qch.,** of sth., **pour qn,** for s.o.); **avec d.,** disdainfully, scornfully; **témoigner du d. à qn,** to show contempt for s.o., to despise s.o.; **avoir le d. de qch.,** to have a contempt for sth.; **considérer qn avec d.,** to look down on s.o.
Dédale [dedal] **1.** *Pr.n.m. Gr.Myth:* Daedalus. **2.** *n.m.* **d.,** labyrinth, maze (of streets, etc.).
dedans [dədɑ̃] **1.** *adv.* inside; within; in (it, them, etc.); *F:* **mettre qn d.,** to put s.o. inside, in jug; **donner d.,** to fall into the trap; **de d.,** from within; **en d.,** (on the) inside; within; **il n'était pas si calme en d.,** he was not so calm inwardly; **en d. de,** within. **2.** *n.m.* inside, interior (of house, box, etc.); innermost heart (of person); **agir du d.,** to act from within (a party, etc.); **au d.,** (on the) inside; within; **au d. et au dehors,** (i) inside and out; (ii) at home and abroad; **au d. de,** inside, within.
dédicace [dedikas] *n.f.* **1.** *Ecc:* dedication, consecration (of building, etc.). **2.** dedication (of book, etc.).
dédicacer [dedikase] *v.tr.* **(je dédicaçai(s); n. dédicaçons)** to dedicate (book, etc.); to autograph (a book); to write a dedication in (book, etc.).
dédicatoire [dedikatwar] *a.* dedicatory.
dédier [dedje] *v.tr.* **1.** *Ecc:* to dedicate, consecrate (building, etc.). **2.** to dedicate, inscribe (book, etc.).
dédire (se) [sədedir] *v.pr.* (*conj. like* DIRE, *except pr. ind.* **v.v. dédisez**) **1. se d. d'une affirmation,** to take back what one has said; to retract a statement. **2. se d. d'une promesse,** to go back on one's word.
dédit [dedi] *n.m.* **1.** retraction, withdrawal. **2.** breaking (of promise). **3.** forfeit, penalty (for breaking contract, etc.).
dédommagement [dedɔmaʒmɑ̃] *n.m.* **1.** indemnification, indemnifying (**de qn,** of s.o.). **2.** indemnity, compensation, damages; **recevoir une somme en d. de qch.,** to receive a sum as, in, compensation for sth.
dédommager [dedɔmaʒe] *v.tr.* **(je dédommageai(s); n. dédommageons) 1.** to indemnify, compensate (s.o.); to make amends to (s.o.); **d. qn de qch.,** to indemnify, compensate, s.o. for sth.; **d. qn d'une perte,** to make good a loss to s.o.; **se faire d. par qn,** to receive compensation from s.o. **2. se d. de ses pertes,** to recoup one's losses.
dédoré [dedɔre] *a.* tarnished; with the gilt rubbed off.
dédorer [dedɔre] *v.tr.* to remove the gilt from (sth.).
dédouanage [dedwanaʒ] *n.m.,* **dédouanement** [dedwanmɑ̃] *n.m. Cust:* clearance (of goods).
dédouaner [dedwane] *v.tr. Cust:* to clear (goods); to take (goods) out of bond; **d. ses bagages,** to clear one's luggage through customs.
dédoublage [dedublaʒ] *n.m.* **1.** diluting (of alcohol). **2.** removing lining (of coat, etc.); unsheathing (of ship).
dédoublement [dedubləmɑ̃] *n.m.* **1.** opening out (of folded cloth, etc.). **2.** (*a*) dividing, splitting, into two; **d. de la personnalité,** split personality; (*b*) *Ch:* double decomposition; (*c*) running (of train) in two portions.
dédoubler [deduble] *v.tr.* **1.** to open out (folded cloth, etc.); **d. les rangs,** to form single file. **2.** (*a*) to divide, cut, split (sth.) into two; (*b*) to run (train) in two portions. **3.** to remove the lining of (garment). **4. se d.** (*a*) to unfold; to divide, split (into two parts); (*b*) *Psy:* to suffer from split personality.
déductif, -ive [dedyktif, -iv] *a. Phil:* deductive (reasoning).
déduction [dedyksjɔ̃] *n.f.* **1.** deduction, inference. **2.** *Com: etc:* deduction, allowance, abatement; **faire d. des sommes payées d'avance,** to deduct, to allow for, sums paid in advance; **sous d. de 10%,** less 10%; **sans d.,** terms net cash.
déduire [dedɥir] *v.tr.* (*conj. like* CONDUIRE) **1.** to deduce, infer (result). **2.** to deduct; **d. 5%,** to take off, deduct, 5%; to allow a deduction of 5%.
déesse [deɛs] *n.f.* goddess.
défaillance [defajɑ̃s] *n.f.* (*a*) (moral, physical) lapse; failing; failure (to do sth.); **sans d.,** without flinching; **moment de d.,** weak moment; **d. de mémoire,** lapse of memory; **d. cardiaque,** heart failure; **d. mécanique,** mechanical failure; (*b*) fainting fit; **tomber en d., avoir une d.,** to faint; (*c*) *Jur:* default(ing).
défaillant, -ante [defajɑ̃, -ɑ̃t] *a.* **1.** (*a*) failing (strength); declining (health); weak (heart); (*b*) (*of pers.*) **d. de fatigue,** exhausted; (*c*) (*of pers.*) faint. **2.** *Jur:* (*a*) *a.* defaulting; (*b*) *n.* defaulter, absconder.
défaillir [defajir] *v.i.* (*pr.p.* **défaillant;** *p.p.* **défailli;** *pr.ind.* **il défaille, n. défaillons;** *impf.* **je défaillais;** *p.h.* **je défaillis;** *fu. occ.* **je défaillerai**) (*a*) to become feeble, to lose strength; **sa mémoire commence à d.,** his memory is beginning to fail; (*b*) to flinch; **j'accomplirai le travail sans d.,** I'll do the job without flinching; (*c*) to faint; **d. de faim,** to feel faint with hunger; **à cette nouvelle son cœur défaillit,** his heart sank at the news.
défaire [defɛr] *v.tr.* (*conj. like* FAIRE) **I. 1.** to demolish (wall, etc.); to pull (sth.) to pieces; to cancel, annul (treaty); to break off (alliance, marriage). **2.** (*a*) to undo; to untie (parcel, knot); to unwrap (parcel); to unpack (suitcase); to unpick (seam); to undo, unzip (one's dress, etc.); to strip (bed); **d. ses cheveux,** to let one's hair down; **d. la table,** to clear the table; (*b*) *A: & Lit:* **d. qn de qn, de qch.,** to rid s.o. of s.o., of sth. **3.** to defeat, overthrow (army, etc.); to get the better of (s.o.). **II. se défaire 1.** (*of clothes, knot*) to come undone; (*of hair*) to come down; (*of things joined together*) to come apart. **2.** (*a*) **se d. de qn,** to kill s.o., *F:* to bump s.o. off; (*b*) **se d. de qn, de qch.,** to get rid of s.o., of sth.; to rid oneself of s.o., of sth.; **se d. de ses marchandises,** to sell off one's goods; **je ne veux pas m'en d.,** I don't want to part with it; **se d. d'une mauvaise habitude,** to get out of, break oneself of, a bad habit.
défait [defɛ] *a.* (*a*) drawn, distorted, haggard (features, face); (*b*) dishevelled, disarranged (hair, appearance); (*c*) defeated, overthrown (army, etc.).
défaite [defɛt] *n.f.* defeat.
défaitisme [defɛtism] *n.m.* defeatism.
défaitiste [defɛtist] *a. & n.* defeatist.
défalcation [defalkasjɔ̃] *n.f.* (*a*) deduction, deducting; writing-off (of bad debt); (*b*) sum, weight, deducted.
défalquer [defalke] *v.tr.* to deduct (sum from total); **d. une mauvaise créance,** to write off a bad debt.
défausser[1] [defose] *v.tr.* to true, straighten (rod, blade, etc.).
défausser[2] (se) [sədefose] *v.pr. Cards:* to discard **se d. à trèfle,** to discard one's clubs.
défaut [defo] *n.m.* **1.** (*a*) default, absence, (total) lack (of sth.); **d. de paiement,** failure to pay; non-payment; **le temps me fait d.,** I can't spare the time; **les provisions font d.,** there is a shortage of supplies; **la mémoire lui fait d.,** (his) memory fails him; *Bank:* **d. de provision,** no funds; **à d. de qch.,** in default of, for

lack of, sth.; (*b*) break in continuity; **le d. de l'armure,** the joint in the harness; *Fig:* the vulnerable point; (*c*) *Jur:* default; **faire d.,** to fail to appear, to default; **jugement par d.,** judgment by default. **2.** (*a*) fault, shortcoming; **chacun a ses défauts,** everyone has his failings; **c'est là son moindre d.,** that's the last thing one can reproach him with; (*b*) defect, flaw; **il y a un d. de fonctionnement,** it isn't working properly; **sans d.,** faultless, flawless; (*c*) *Ven:* **mettre les chiens en d.,** to throw the hounds off the scent; **mettre qn en d.,** to put s.o. on the wrong track; to deceive s.o.; **prendre qn en d.,** to catch s.o. out.

défaveur [defavœr] *n.f.* disfavour, discredit; **tomber en d.,** to fall into disfavour (**auprès de,** with).

défavorable [defavɔrabl̥] *a.* unfavourable (**à,** to); **les conditions (nous) sont défavorables,** conditions are against us.

défavorablement [defavɔrabləmɑ̃] *adv.* unfavourably.

défavoriser [defavɔrize] *v.tr.* to be unfair to (s.o.); **candidat défavorisé,** candidate at an unfair disadvantage.

défécation [defekasjɔ̃] *n.f.* **1.** *Ch:* defecation, clarification. **2.** *Physiol:* defecation.

défectible [defɛktibl̥] *a.* fallible.

défectif, -ive [defɛktif, -iv] *a.* defective (verb, etc.).

défection [defɛksjɔ̃] *n.f.* defection from, desertion of, a cause, a party, etc.; **faire d.,** to desert, to defect; *F:* to rat.

défectueusement [defɛktɥøzmɑ̃] *adv.* defectively.

défectueux, -euse [defɛktɥø, -øz] *a.* defective, faulty, imperfect.

défectuosité [defɛktɥɔzite] *n.f.* **1.** defectiveness. **2.** defect, flaw.

défendable [defɑ̃dabl̥] *a.* defensible (position, etc.).

défendeur, -eresse [defɑ̃dœr, -(ə)rɛs] *n. Jur:* defendant.

défendre [defɑ̃dr̥] *v.tr.* **I. 1.** (*a*) to defend (cause, prisoner, etc.); to champion (opinion, cause); to maintain, uphold (opinion, right); to stand up for (one's friends, etc.) (**contre,** against); **il sait d. son opinion,** he can hold his own; **faire qch. à son corps défendant,** to do sth., reluctantly, grudgingly; (*b*) to protect, shield, guard (**contre,** against, from); **les rideaux défendent la chambre du soleil,** the curtains protect the room from the sun. **2.** to forbid, prohibit; **fruit défendu,** forbidden fruit; **d. qch. à qn,** to forbid s.o. sth.; **d. à qn de faire qch.,** to forbid s.o. to do sth.; **il est défendu de fumer,** smoking (is) prohibited; **il m'est défendu de fumer,** I'm not allowed to smoke; **il défendit qu'on passât par là,** he forbade anyone to go that way. **II. se défendre 1.** (*a*) to defend oneself; *F:* **je me défends,** I'm holding my own, I'm getting along; **il se défend bien en affaires,** he's a good businessman; (*b*) *Lit:* **se d. d'avoir fait qch.,** to deny having done sth. **2. se d. de, contre, qch.,** to protect, shield, oneself from, against, sth.; **se d. de la pluie,** to protect oneself from the rain. **3. se d. de faire qch.,** to refrain from doing sth.; (*esp. in neg.*) **on ne peut se d. de l'aimer,** one can't help liking him. **4.** (*the pron. is the indirect object*) **se d. tout plaisir,** to deny oneself all pleasure.

défense [defɑ̃s] *n.f.* **1.** (*a*) defence; **combattre pour la d. de son pays,** to fight in defence of one's country; **prendre la d. de qn,** to undertake s.o.'s defence; to champion s.o.'s cause; **d. nationale, passive,** national, civil, defence; **d. contre avions,** anti-aircraft defence; **sans d.,** unprotected, defenceless; **être hors de d.,** to be unable to defend oneself; *Jur:* **légitime d.,** self defence; (*b*) *Jur:* defence; **moyens de d.,** plea (of defendant). **2.** (*a*) **d. côtière, aérienne,** coastal, air, defense; (*b*) tusk (of elephant, wild boar, etc.). **3.** prohibition, interdiction; *P.N:* **d. d'entrer, de fumer,** no admittance, no smoking; **faire d. à qn de faire qch.,** to forbid s.o. to do sth.

défenseur [defɑ̃sœr] *n.m.* **1.** (*a*) protector, defender (of child, town, etc.); (*b*) supporter, upholder (of a cause). **2.** *Jur:* counsel for the defence.

défensif, -ive [defɑ̃sif, -iv] **1.** *a.* defensive. **2.** *n.f.* **être, se tenir, sur la défensive,** to be, stand, on the defensive.

défensivement [defɑ̃sivmɑ̃] *adv.* defensively.

déféquer [defeke] **(je défèque, n. déféquons; je déféquerai) 1.** *v.tr. Ch:* to clarify, clear, purify (sth.). **2.** *v.i. Physiol:* to defecate.

déférence [deferɑ̃s] *n.f.* deference, respect, regard (**pour,** for); **par d. pour . . .,** in, out of, deference to. . . .

déférent, -ente [deferɑ̃, -ɑ̃t] *a.* **1.** deferential (manner, etc.). **2.** *Anat:* deferent; **canal d.,** vas deferens. **3.** *n.m. Num:* mint mark.

déférer [defere] *v.* **(je défère; je déférerai) I.** *v.tr.* **1.** *Jur:* (*a*) to submit, refer (case to a court); (*b*) **d. qn à la justice,** to hand over, give up, s.o. to justice; (*c*) **d. le serment à qn,** to administer, tender, the oath, to s.o.; to swear (witness); to swear in (jury). **2.** *A:* to confer, bestow (honour) (**à,** on). **II.** *v.i.* **d. à qn,** to defer to s.o.; **d. aux ordres de qn,** to comply with s.o.'s orders; **d. à une demande,** to accede to a request.

déferlant [defɛrlɑ̃] *a. Nau:* (*of wave*) breaking; **vague déferlante,** beachcomber; breaker.

déferlement [defɛrləmɑ̃] *n.m.* breaking (of waves); unfurling (of sail, flag); **d. d'enthousiasme,** wave of enthusiasm.

déferler [defɛrle] **1.** *v.tr. Nau:* to unfurl, shake out (sail, flag); to break (flag, signal); to set (sail). **2.** *v.i.* (*of waves*) to break; to comb; **la foule déferle dans la rue,** the crowd is surging down the street.

déferrage, déferrement [defɛraʒ, -ɛrmɑ̃] *n.m.* removal of iron (from sth.); unshoeing (of horse).

déferrer [defɛre] *v.tr.* **1.** to remove the iron from (sth.). **2.** to unshoe (horse).

défet [defɛ] *n.m. Bookb:* waste, odd, spare, sheet.

défeuillaison [defœjɛzɔ̃, -ø-] *n.f.* defoliation, fall of the leaves.

défeuiller [defœje] *v.tr.* **1.** to strip the leaves off, to defoliate (tree). **2.** (*of tree*) **se d.,** to shed its leaves.

défi [defi] *n.m.* (*a*) challenge; **lancer, jeter, un d. à qn,** to challenge s.o.; **relever un d.,** to take up a challenge; (*b*) defiance; **mettre qn au d. de faire qch.,** to defy, dare, s.o. to do sth.; **d'un air de d.,** defiantly.

défiance [defjɑ̃s] *n.f.* **1.** mistrust, distrust, suspicion, wariness; **inspirer, éveiller, la d.,** to arouse suspicion; **motion de d.,** motion of no confidence. **2. d. de soi-même,** diffidence, lack of self confidence.

défiant [defjɑ̃] *a.* mistrustful, distrustful, cautious, wary.

déficeler [defisle] *v.tr.* (*conj. like* FICELER) **1.** to untie, undo (parcel, etc.). **2. se d.,** to come untied, undone.

déficience [defisjɑ̃s] *n.f.* deficiency; **d. mentale,** mental deficiency; **d. (alimentaire),** malnutrition.

déficient [defisjɑ̃] *a.* deficient; **enfant d.,** mentally deficient child.

déficit [defisit] *n.m.* deficit, shortage (in cash, etc.); **être en d.,** to show a deficit.

déficitaire [defisitɛr] *a.* (account) showing a debit balance; (budget, etc.) showing a deficit; **récolte d.,** short crop.

défier [defje] *v.tr.* **1.** (*a*) to challenge; **d. qn au combat, aux échecs,** to challenge s.o. to fight, to a game of chess; (*b*) to defy (s.o., sth.); **je vous défie de faire mieux,** I defy you to do better; **le spectacle défie toute description,** the sight defies, is beyond, description; (*c*) to brave, to face (danger, death). **2. se**

d. de qn, de qch., to mistrust, distrust, s.o., sth.; **se d. de soi-même,** to be diffident.
défiguration [defigyrasjɔ̃] *n.f.*, **défigurement** [defigyrmɑ̃] *n.m.* disfigurement, disfiguration; defacement (of statue); distortion (of the truth).
défigurer [defigyre] *v.tr.* to disfigure (s.o., sth.); to deface (statue); to distort (the truth).
défilé [defile] *n.m.* **1.** defile, gorge; (mountain) pass. **2.** procession; *Mil: etc:* march past; *Av:* **d. (aérien),** flypast; **d. de mode,** fashion parade; **d. ininterrompu de visiteurs,** endless stream of visitors.
défilement [defilmɑ̃] *n.m.* defilade, defilading.
défiler[1] [defile] *v.tr.* **1.** to unstring, unthread (beads, necklace). **2.** *Mil:* to defilade (fortress); to put (company, etc.) under cover. **3. se d.** (*a*) (*of beads, etc.*) to come unstrung; (*b*) *Mil:* **se d. du feu de l'adversaire,** to take cover from the enemy's fire; (*c*) *F:* to slip off on the quiet.
défiler[2] *v.i.* (*a*) *Mil:* to defile; to file off; **d. en colonne par deux,** to file off in twos; (*b*) *Mil:* to march past; (*c*) to walk in procession; (*d*) **des centaines de voitures défilent vers la côte,** hundreds of cars are streaming towards the coast.
défini [defini] *a.* (*a*) definite; clearly defined; (*b*) *Gram:* definite (article, etc.); **passé d.,** past definite, preterite, past historic.
définir [definir] *v.tr.* to define; **d. un mot,** to explain the meaning of a word.
définissable [definisabl̩] *a.* definable.
définitif, -ive [definitif, -iv] *a.* definitive, final (resolution, judgment, etc.); **nommé à titre d.,** permanently appointed; *adv.phr.* **en définitive,** finally, when all is said and done.
définition [definisjɔ̃] *n.f.* **1.** definition; **par d.,** by that very fact; logically. **2.** clue (of crossword puzzle).
définitivement [definitivmɑ̃] *adv.* definitely; **il est parti d.,** he's gone away for good.
déflagrateur [deflagratœr] *n.m.* deflagrator; *El:* spark gap.
déflagration [deflagrasjɔ̃] *n.f.* deflagration, combustion.
déflagrer [deflagre] *v.i.* to deflagrate.
déflation [deflasjɔ̃] *n.f.* **1.** deflation (of the currency). **2.** *Geog:* wind erosion.
défléchir [defleʃir] *v.tr.* & *i.* to deflect.
déflecteur [deflɛktœr] *n.m. Mch: Aut: etc:* deflector.
défleuraison [deflœrɛzɔ̃] *n.f.* falling of blossom.
défleurir [deflœrir] **1.** *v.i.* & *pr.* (*of tree, etc.*) to lose its blossom. **2.** *v.tr.* to take the flowers off (plant).
défloraison [deflɔrɛzɔ̃] *n.f.* = DÉFLEURAISON.
défloration [deflɔrasjɔ̃] *n.f.* deflowering (of virgin).
déflorer [deflɔre] *v.tr.* **1.** to take the freshness off, to spoil (piece of news, etc.). **2.** to deflower (virgin).
défoliant [defɔljɑ̃] *n.m. Agr:* defoliant.
défoliation [defɔljasjɔ̃] *n.f.* defoliation.
défonçage, défoncement [defɔ̃saʒ, -smɑ̃] *n.m.* smashing in (of box, etc.); knocking down (of wall).
défoncé [defɔ̃se] *a.* **1.** bashed in; battered. **2. chemin d.,** rough, bumpy, road.
défoncer [defɔ̃se] *v.tr.* **(je défonçai(s); n. défonçons) 1.** to stave in (cask, boat); to smash in, bash in (box, door, etc.); to knock down (wall, etc.). **2.** to break up, cut up (road). **3.** *F:* **se d.,** to get high (on drug).
défonceuse [defɔ̃søz] *n.f. Agr:* heavy plough, trenching plough.
déforestation [defɔrɛstasjɔ̃] *n.f.* deforestation.
déformant [defɔrmɑ̃] *a.* distorting.
déformation [defɔrmasjɔ̃] *n.f.* **1.** (*a*) deformation; **d. professionnelle,** professional idiosyncracy, vocational bias; (*b*) *Phot:* distortion (of image). **2.** (*a*) buckling, warping; (*b*) buckled, warped, condition.
déformer [defɔrme] *v.tr.* **1.** to deform; to put (sth.) out of shape; *Phot:* to distort (image); *P.N:* **chaussée déformée,** uneven road surface. **2.** to warp, buckle. **3. se d.,** to get out of shape, to warp, to buckle.
défouler [defule] *v.tr.* **1.** *Psy:* to liberate. **2. se d.,** to unwind, *F:* to let off steam.
défourner [defurne] *v.tr.* to draw (pottery) from the kiln, (bread) from the oven.
défraîchi [defrɛʃi] *a.* (shop)soiled (goods); faded (flowers).
défraîchir [defrɛʃir] *v.tr.* **1.** to take away the newness, freshness, of (sth.). **2. se d.,** to lose one's, its, freshness; to fade.
défrayer [defreje] *v.tr.* **(je défraie, je défraye; je défraierai, je défrayerai) 1. d. qn,** to defray, pay, s.o.'s expenses; **être défrayé de tout,** to have all expenses paid. **2. d. la conversation,** (i) to monopolize the conversation; (ii) to be the subject of conversation; **d. la chronique,** to be in the news.
défrichage [defriʃaʒ] *n.m.* clearing (of land).
défriche [defriʃ] *n.f.*, **défriché** [defriʃe] *n.m. Agr:* clearing, cleared patch (in forest, etc.).
défrichement [defriʃmɑ̃] *n.m.* (*a*) clearing (of land); (*b*) cleared land.
défricher [defriʃe] *v.tr.* to clear, grub, reclaim (land for cultivation); to bring (land) into cultivation; to break (new ground); **d. un sujet,** to do pioneer work in a subject.
défricheur, -euse [defriʃœr, -øz] *n.* (*a*) *Agr:* land clearer; settler; (*b*) pioneer (in a subject).
défriper [defripe] *v.tr.* to smooth out (crumpled garment).
défriser [defrize] *v.tr.* to uncurl, to straighten (hair); *F:* **ça vous défrise?** are you put out?
défroisser [defrwase] *v.tr.* to take the creases out of (dress, etc.).
défroque [defrɔk] *n.f.* **1.** effects (of dead monk). **2.** *usu. pl.* cast-off clothing, *F:* cast-offs.
défroqué [defrɔke] *a.* & *n.m.* unfrocked (pirest); expriest, ex-monk.
défroquer [defrɔke] *v.tr.* **1.** to unfrock (priest, monk). **2. se d.,** to leave the priesthood, to renounce one's order.
défunt, -unte [defœ̃, -œ̃t] *a.* & *n.* defunct, deceased; **le roi d.,** the late king; **prier pour les défunts,** to pray for the dead.
dégagé [degaʒe] *a.* (*a*) free, untrammelled (movements, etc.); **allure dégagée,** swinging stride; (*b*) free and easy (tone, manner); (*c*) (*of sky, road*) clear; **vue dégagée,** open view.
dégagement [degaʒmɑ̃] *n.m.* **1.** redemption (of pledge, mortgage); taking out of pawn. **2.** (*a*) disengagement, release (of brake, etc.); *Fenc:* disengaging (of one's point); disengagement; *Mec.E:* backing off (tool); (*b*) loosening, slackening (of bolt, etc.); (*c*) relieving of congestion; clearing (of road, of the lungs, etc.); **escalier de d.,** (i) private staircase; (ii) emergency stairs; **porte de d.,** (side) exit (of cinema, etc.); (*d*) private passage (in suite of rooms); (*e*) *Fb:* clearance; (*f*) *Pol: Mil:* disengagement. **3.** (*a*) escape, release (of steam, gas, etc.); **tuyau de d.,** waste pipe; (*b*) emission, liberation (of heat). **4.** (*a*) open space, clearing (in front of house, etc.); (*b*) clearance (of car above the ground).
dégager [degaʒe] *v.tr.* **(je dégageai(s); n. dégageons) I. 1.** to redeem (pledge, mortgage); to take (sth.) out of pawn; **d. des titres,** to release (pledged) securities; **d. sa parole,** (i) to make good one's promise; (ii) to take back one's word. **2.** (*a*) to disengage; **d. le frein,** to release the brake; **d. une ville,** to relieve a town; **d. les blessés des décombres,** to pull the wounded clear of the wreckage, the ruins; **d. qn d'une promesse,** to release, absolve, s.o. from a promise; **d. sa responsabilité d'une affaire,** to disclaim responsibility

in a matter; (*b*) to relieve the congestion in, to clear (road, deck, etc.); *F:* **dégagez, s'il vous plaît,** move along, clear the way, please; *Arch:* **d. les vues,** to open vistas; (*c*) **robe qui dégage les épaules,** dress that leaves the shoulders bare; (*d*) **d. l'idée principale d'un texte,** to draw, derive, the main idea from a text; (*e*) *Mec.E: etc:* to free (a part); to loosen, slacken (bolt); to back off (a tool); *Fenc:* to disengage (the blade); *Fb:* to kick (ball) over the touchline; to clear (ball). **3.** to emit, give off (vapour, smell); to emit, give out (heat). **II. se dégager 1.** to free oneself, to get free (**de,** by); to get clear (**de,** of); to break loose, break away (**de,** from); to disengage oneself (**de,** from); to extricate oneself (**de,** from); **d'un effort violent il s'est dégagé,** he wrenched himself free; **se d. d'une promesse,** to go back on a promise; **le ciel se dégage,** the sky is clearing. **2.** (*of gas, smell etc.*) to be given off (**de,** by); to escape, emanate (**de,** from); to arise, to come off; **il se dégage de l'oxygène,** oxygen is given off. **3.** to emerge, come out; **la silhouette du navire s'est dégagée du brouillard,** the ship loomed up out of the fog; **la vérité se dégage peu à peu,** the truth is gradually coming out; **cette nécessité se dégage de l'étude des faits,** this need becomes apparent after a study of the facts.

dégaine [degɛn] *n.f. F:* awkward gait; awkward, strange, appearance.

dégainer [degene] *v.tr.* to unsheathe, draw (sword).

déganter (se) [sədegɑ̃te] *v.pr.* to take off one's gloves.

dégarni [degarni] *a.* empty; depleted; stripped; **armoire dégarnie,** empty cupboard; **arbre d.,** tree bare of leaves; **région dégarnie (de cheveux),** bald patch.

dégarnir [degarnir] *v.tr.* **1.** to dismantle, clear (room, etc.); to take the trimmings off (a dress); to strip (bed, etc.); to withdraw troops from (town, etc.); to unrig (ship, capstan); to thin out (tree); to draw (heavily) on (bank account). **2. se d.** (*a*) (*of tree*) to lose its leaves; (*of head*) to get bald; (*of hall, etc.*) to empty; (*b*) *F:* to run short of ready money.

dégarnissement [degarnismɑ̃] *n.m.* (*a*) dismantling, clearing (of room); (*b*) unrigging (of capstan).

dégât [degɑ] *n.m. usu. pl.* damage; **les gelées ont fait des dégâts dans les vignobles,** the frosts have made havoc of the vineyards.

dégauchir [degoʃir] *v.tr.* to surface, to rough plane (board, etc.); to straighten, to true (piece of machinery, etc.).

dégauchissage, dégauchissement [degoʃisaʒ,-ismɑ̃] *n.m.* surfacing, rough planing; straightening, truing up; trimming (of stone).

dégauchisseuse [degoʃisøz] *n.f.* surfacing machine, surfacer.

dégel [deʒɛl] *n.m.* **1.** thaw; **le temps est, se met, au d.,** it's beginning to thaw. **2.** *Pol: etc:* thaw (in relations between two countries).

dégelée [deʒle] *n.f.* shower of blows; thrashing.

dégèlement [deʒɛlmɑ̃] *n.m.* thawing.

dégeler [deʒle] *v.tr. & i., v. impers.* **(il dégèle; il dégèlera) 1.** to thaw; *Fin:* to unfreeze (assets, etc.); **d. un auditoire,** to warm up an audience. **2.** (*of pers.*) **se d.,** to thaw (out).

dégénération [deʒenerasjɔ̃] *n.f.* degeneration, degeneracy.

dégénéré, -ée [deʒenere] *a. & n.* (*a*) degenerate; (*b*) (mentally) defective; mental defective.

dégénérer [deʒenere] *v.i.* **(je dégénère; je dégénérerai)** to degenerate (**de,** from; **en,** into); (*of quality*) to deteriorate; **son rhume a dégénéré en bronchite,** his cold developed into bronchitis.

dégénérescence [deʒenerɛsɑ̃s] *n.f. Med:* degeneration.

dégénérescent [deʒenerɛsɑ̃] *a. Med:* degenerating; degenerative.

dégermer [deʒɛrme] *v.tr. Brew: Agr:* to degerm.

dégingandé [deʒɛ̃gɑ̃de] *a. F:* (*of pers.*) gangling, lanky, ungainly.

dégivrage [deʒivraʒ] *n.m.* de-icing; defrosting.

dégivrer [deʒivre] *v.tr. Av: Aut:* to de-ice; *Dom.Ec:* to defrost.

dégivreur [deʒivrœr] *n.m. Av: Aut:* de-icer; *Dom.Ec:* defroster.

déglacer [deglase] *v.tr.* (*conj. like* GLACER) **1.** to thaw, to melt the ice on (pond, etc.); to defrost (refrigerator). **2.** to take the glaze off (paper). **3.** *Cu:* to make a sauce by adding liquid to residue left after cooking (roast, etc.).

déglinguer [deglɛ̃ge] *v.tr. F:* to smash up, bust up; **ma bicyclette est toute déglinguée,** my bicycle is falling to pieces.

déglutir [deglytir] *v.tr. Physiol:* to swallow.

dégobiller [degɔbije] *P:* **1.** *v.i.* to be sick, to puke, to throw up. **2.** *v.tr.* to bring up (one's food).

dégoiser [degwaze] *v.tr. F: & Pej:* **1.** *v.tr.* to spout (speech, etc.); **qu'est-ce qu'il dégoise?** what's he rattling on about? **2.** *v.i.* to rattle on, to go on (and on).

dégommage [degɔmaʒ] *n.m.* (*a*) ungumming; (*b*) *F:* sacking (of s.o.).

dégommer [degɔme] *v.tr.* **1.** to ungum, unstick (sth.). **2.** *F:* (*a*); to give (s.o.) the sack; (*b*) to push (s.o.) out, to oust (s.o.); (*c*) to beat, to lick (s.o.) (at a game).

dégonflé, -ée [degɔ̃fle] (*a*) *a.* (*of tyre, etc.*) flat, soft; (*b*) *n.m. & f. F:* coward, chicken, *U.S:* yellow-belly.

dégonflement [degɔ̃fləmɑ̃] *n.m.* deflating; deflation.

dégonfler [degɔ̃fle] *v.tr.* **1.** to deflate, let the air out of (balloon, etc.). **2.** to reduce, bring down (swelling). **3.** *F:* to debunk (hero). **4. se d.** (*a*) (*of tyre, balloon, etc.*) to collapse, to go flat; (*b*) (*of swelling*) to subside, go down; (*c*) *F:* to chicken out; to get cold feet.

dégorgement [degɔrʒəmɑ̃] *n.m.* disgorging, cleansing, purifying.

dégorger [degɔrʒe] *v.* **(je dégorgeai(s); n. dégorgeons) 1.** *v.tr.* (*a*) to disgorge; **l'égout dégorge de l'eau sale,** the drain is discharging dirty water; **la rue a dégorgé un flot de gens,** a crowd of people surged from the street; (*b*) to free, clear, unstop (passage, pipe); (*c*) to purify, scour (wool, leather). **2.** *v.i. & pr.* (*a*) (*of sewer, pond*) to flow out, to discharge (**dans,** into); (*of gutter, stream*) to overflow; (*b*) *Cu:* **faire d. des concombres, etc.,** to salt cucumber, etc. (to make it release water).

dégouliner [deguline] *v.i.* (*of water*) to trickle, drip; **la pluie me dégoulinait dans le cou,** the rain was trickling down my neck.

dégourdi [degurdi] **1.** *a.* (*of pers.*) bright, sharp, smart; **il n'est pas très d.,** he's not very bright, he's not really on the ball. **2.** *n.* **c'est un d., une dégourdie,** he's, she's, pretty bright, got what it takes.

dégourdir [degurdir] *v.tr.* **1.** (*a*) to remove stiffness, numbness, from (the limbs); to revive (by warmth, movement, etc.); **je vais me d. les jambes,** I'm going to stretch my legs a bit; **d. qn,** to sharpen s.o.'s wits; **Paris l'a dégourdi,** Paris has polished him up, *F:* has taught him a thing or two; (*b*) **d. de l'eau,** to take the chill off water. **2. se d.** (*a*) to restore the circulation; to lose one's numb, stiff, feeling; to stretch one's limbs; (*b*) (*of water*) to grow warm; (*c*) to grow smarter, more alert.

dégourdissement [degurdismɑ̃] *n.m.* removal of numbness.

dégoût [degu] *n.m.* **1.** disgust, distaste, loathing; **il a**

un véritable d. pour la viande, he can't stand meat. **2.** dislike; **avoir du d. pour qch.,** to feel a dislike for sth., an aversion from sth.; **prendre qch. en d.,** to take a dislike to sth.; **il a pris sa vie en d.,** he grew weary of the life he was leading.

dégoûtant [degutɑ̃] *a.* disgusting, revolting, loathsome, nauseating (sight, smell, etc.).

dégoûté [degute] *a.* **1.** disgusted (**de,** with); sick (of); *F:* fed up; **d. de la viande,** off meat. **2.** fastidious, squeamish; *Iron:* **vous n'êtes pas d.!** you're not fussy! *n.* **faire le, la, dégoûté(e),** to turn up one's nose (at sth.).

dégoûter [degute] *v.tr.* (*a*) to disgust; **d. qn de qch.,** to give s.o. a distaste for sth.; to put s.o. off sth.; **tout cela me dégoûte,** I'm sick of it all; (*b*) **se d. de qn, de qch.,** to take a dislike to s.o., sth.; **il s'est dégoûté de Paris,** he got tired of (living in) Paris.

dégouttement [degutmɑ̃] *n.m.* dripping (of water, etc.).

dégoutter [degute] *v.i.* **1.** to drip, trickle, to fall drop by drop (**de,** from); **la pluie dégoutte de son chapeau,** the rain is dripping from his hat. **2.** to be dripping (**de,** with); **parapluie dégouttant d'eau,** dripping wet umbrella.

dégradant [degradɑ̃] *a.* degrading, lowering.

dégradation¹ [degradasjɔ̃] *n.f.* **1.** degradation (from rank, etc.); **d. civique,** loss of civil rights. **2.** (moral) degradation; **tomber dans la d.,** to lose all self respect. **3.** (*a*) defacement (of monument, etc.); (*b*) *usu. pl.* damage; dilapidation; **cette maison est dans un état de d. pitoyable,** this house is in a shocking state of repair. **4.** *Ph:* dissipation (of energy).

dégradation² *n.f.* shading off, graduation (of colours, light).

dégradé [degrade] *n.m.* (*of colours*) gradation; *Phot:* graduated shading.

dégrader¹ [degrade] *v.tr.* **1.** to degrade (s.o.) (from rank, etc.). **2.** to degrade, to debase (s.o.). **3.** to deface, damage (monument, etc.). **4.** *Ph:* to degrade (energy). **5. se d.** (*a*) to lower, demean, oneself; (*b*) to fall into disrepair; (*c*) *Ph:* (*of energy*) to dissipate.

dégrader² *v.tr.* to shade off, graduate (colours, light); *Phot:* to vignette; **écran de ciel dégradé,** gradual sky filter.

dégrafer [degrafe] *v.tr.* **1.** to unhook, unfasten, undo (dress, etc.); to unclasp (bracelet). **2. se d.** (*a*) (*of garment*) to come undone; (*b*) (*of pers.*) to undo one's dress.

dégraissage [degrɛsaʒ] *n.m.* **1.** skimming. **2.** cleaning.

dégraisser [degrese] *v.tr.* **1.** to remove the fat from (carcass of animal); to skim the fat off (soup, etc.). **2.** to remove the grease marks from, to dry clean (clothes, etc.); to scour (wool). **3.** to bevel off, trim (piece of wood).

dégraisseur, -euse [degrɛsœr, -øz] *n.* **1.** dry cleaner (of clothes, etc.); scourer (of wool). **2.** *n.f.* **dégraisseuse** (*a*) *Tex:* scouring machine; (*b*) *Leath:* grease extractor.

degré [dəgre] *n.m.* **1.** (*a*) step (of stair, ladder); degree (of musical scale); (*b*) degree (of circle, heat); **dix degrés au-dessous de zéro,** ten degrees below zero; (*c*) proof (of alcoholic drink). **2.** degree (of relationship, comparison); **cousins au second d.,** cousins once removed; second cousins; **d. de parenté,** degree of kinship; *Med:* **brûlure du troisième d.,** third degree burn; **les degrés de l'échelle sociale,** the rungs of the social ladder; **il est généreux au plus haut d.,** he is generous in the extreme; **par degré(s),** by degrees, gradually; *Mth:* **équation du second, du troisième, d.,** quadratic, cubic, equation.

dégréage, dégréement [degreaʒ, degremɑ̃] *n.m.* *Nau:* unrigging (of mast, etc.).

dégréer [degree] *v.tr.* *Nau:* to unrig (mast, etc.); to dismantle, take down (crane); to unsling (hammock).

dégressif, -ive [degrɛsif, -iv] *a.* degressive, graded (tax, etc.); **impôt d.,** degressive taxation.

dégrèvement [degrɛvmɑ̃] *n.m.* reduction, abatement (of tax).

dégrever [degrəve] *v.tr.* **(je dégrève; je dégrèverai)** (*a*) to reduce, diminish (tax); (*b*) to grant (s.o.) tax relief; to derate (industry); to reduce the assessment on (building); (*c*) to disencumber (estate).

dégringolade [degrɛ̃gɔlad] *n.f.* *F:* **1.** tumble, tumbling (downstairs, downhill). **2.** downfall (of financier); collapse (of prices, etc.).

dégringoler [degrɛ̃gɔle] *v.tr.* & *i.* *F:* **1.** to tumble down, to come rushing down; **il a dégringolé l'escalier,** he came tearing down the stairs. **2. maison (de commerce) qui dégringole,** firm that is losing business rapidly.

dégrisement [degrizmɑ̃] *n.m.* sobering up; disillusionment.

dégriser [degrize] *v.tr.* **1.** (*a*) to sober (s.o.) up; (*b*) to disillusion, disenchant (s.o.). **2. se d.,** to sober up.

dégrossir [degrosir] *v.tr.* to give a rough, preliminary, dressing to (sth.); to rough down, trim (timber); to roughhew (stone); to rough out (design, etc.); *F:* **d. qn,** to polish s.o. up; to lick s.o. into shape; **recrues mal dégrossies,** raw recruits.

dégrossissage, dégrossissement [degrosisaʒ, -sismɑ̃] *n.m.* roughing; trimming.

dégrouiller (se) [sedegruje] *v.pr.* *F:* to get a move on, to buck up.

déguenillé [degənije] *a.* ragged, tattered, in rags, in tatters; *n.* **un petit d.,** a little ragamuffin.

déguerpir [degɛrpir] *v.i.* to clear out, off, to decamp; **d. au plus vite,** to bolt; **faire d. l'ennemi,** to scatter the enemy.

dégueulasse [degœlas] a. *P:* disgusting, repulsive; *n.* **c'est un d.,** he's a rotten swine.

dégueuler [degœle] *v.i.* *P:* to spew, puke.

déguisement [degizmɑ̃] *n.m.* **1.** (*a*) disguise, get-up; (*b*) fancy dress, costume. **2.** dissimulation; **sans d.,** plainly, openly.

déguiser [degize] *v.tr.* **1.** to disguise; **d. un enfant en clown,** to dress a child up as a clown. **2.** to disguise, conceal (truth, etc.); **parler sans rien d.,** to speak plainly, openly. **3. se d.** (*a*) to disguise oneself; (*b*) to dress up.

dégustateur, -trice [degystatœr, -tris] *n.* wine taster.

dégustation [degystasjɔ̃] *n.f.* tasting, sampling (of wine, food); **ici, d. d'huîtres,** oysters served here.

déguster [degyste] *v.tr.* **1.** to taste, sample (wine, etc.); **d. sa liqueur,** to sip one's liqueur. **2.** (*a*) to eat, drink, with relish; to enjoy one's food; (*b*) to appreciate, enjoy (book, etc.). **3.** *P:* **d. des coups,** to get a good hiding; **qu'est-ce qu'on a dégusté!** we didn't half catch it!

déhaler [deale] *v.tr.* *Nau:* to warp out, haul out, shift (a ship).

déhanché [deɑ̃ʃe] *a.* (*a*) (*of horse*) hipshot; (*b*) (*of pers.*) who walks swaying the hips.

déhancher (se) [sedeɑ̃ʃe] *v.pr.* (*a*) to sway one's hips (when walking); (*b*) to lean one's weight on one hip.

déharnachement [dearnaʃmɑ̃] *n.m.* unharnessing, unsaddling.

déharnacher [dearnaʃe] *v.tr.* to unharness, unsaddle (horse).

déhiscence [deis(s)ɑ̃s] *n.f.* *Bot:* dehiscence.

dehors [dəɔr] **1.** *adv.* (*a*) out, outside; **coucher, dîner, d.,** to sleep, dine (i) out of doors, in the open, (ii) away from home; **mettre qn d.,** (i) to put, turn, s.o.

out (of doors); (ii) to dismiss s.o.; *Nau:* **toutes voiles d.,** with every sail set; (*b*) *Sp: Cr:* out; *Box:* **compter qn d.,** to count s.o. out; (*c*) **de d.,** from outside; **en d.,** (on the) outside; outwards; **en d. de la maison,** outside the house; **c'est en d. de mes pouvoirs,** its not within my competence; it's more than I can manage; **en d. du sujet,** beside the question; **cela s'est fait en d. de moi,** it was done (i) without my knowledge, (ii) without my participation; (*d*) **au d.,** on the outside; *P.N:* **ne pas se pencher au d.!** do not lean out of the window! **mettre une embarcation au d.,** to get out a boat; **au d. de ce pays,** outside, beyond, this country. **2.** *n.m.* (*a*) outside, exterior (of house, etc.); **affaires du d.,** foreign affairs; **agir du d.,** to act from without (a party, etc.); (*b*) *usu. pl.* (outward) appearance; **maison aux d. imposants,** house with an imposing exterior; (*c*) (*skating*) outside edge. **3.** *prep. A:* **dedans et d. le royaume,** within and without the kingdom.

déicide [deisid] **1.** *n.m. & f.* (*a*) (*pers.*) deicide; (*b*) (*crime*) deicide. **2.** *a.* deicidal.

déifier [deifje] *v.tr.* to deify; to make a god of (s.o., sth.).

déité [deite] *n.f.* deity.

déjà [deʒa] *adv.* **1.** already; **il est d. quatres heures,** it's already four o'clock; **d. en 1900,** as early as 1900. **2.** before, previously; **je vous ai d. vu,** I've seen you before. **3.** yet; **faut-il que vous partiez d.?** need you go just yet? **vous avez d. trop de travail,** you have too much work as it is; **ce n'est d. pas si mal,** that's not bad at all; **qu'est-ce que vous faites d.?** what did you say your job was?

déjanter [deʒɑ̃te] *v.tr. Aut:* to remove (tyre) from rim.

déjection [deʒɛksjɔ̃] *n.f.* **1.** *Physiol:* evacuation (of bowels); *pl.* dejecta, faeces. **2.** *Geol:* ejecta (of volcano, etc.).

déjeter [deʒte] *v.tr.* **(il déjette; il déjettera)** (*a*) to make (sth.) lopsided; to warp (wood); to buckle (metal); **elle a la taille déjetée,** she has one shoulder higher than the other; (*b*) **se d.,** to grow lopsided; (*of wood*) to warp; (*of metal*) to buckle.

déjeuner [deʒœne] **I.** *v.i.* (*a*) to (have) breakfast; (*b*) to (have) lunch; **il est resté à d.,** he stayed for lunch. **II.** *n.m.* **1.** lunch(eon); **petit d.,** breakfast; **d. sur l'herbe,** picnic (lunch). **2.** breakfast cup and saucer.

déjouer [deʒwe] *v.tr.* to thwart, foil (s.o.); to frustrate (plot); **d. les plans de qn,** to spoil s.o.'s plans.

déjucher [deʒyʃe] *v.i.* (*of fowls*) to come off the roost; *F:* **d. qn, faire d. qn,** to make s.o. come down from his perch.

déjuger (se) [sədeʒyʒe] *v.pr.* (*conj. like* JUGER) to reverse one's judgment, decision, etc.

delà [dəla] beyond. **1.** *prep. A. & Lit:* **d. les monts,** beyond the mountains; *prep. phr.* **par d. les mers,** beyond the seas. **2.** *adv.* **deçà (et) d.,** here and there; **au(-)d.,** beyond; **en d.,** further away; *n.m.* **l'au-d.,** the next world, the hereafter; *prep. phr.* **au d. de,** beyond; **n'allez pas au d. de 300 francs,** don't go above 300 francs; **il est allé au d. de ses promesses,** he was better than his word.

délabré [delabre] *a.* dilapidated, beyond repair; broken down (furniture); ramshackle (house); impaired (health); **manteau d.,** shabby coat.

délabrement [delabrəmɑ̃] *n.m.* ruinous condition; disrepair, decay.

délabrer [delabre] *v.tr.* **1.** to wreck, ruin (house, fortune, health). **2. se d.,** (*of house, etc.*) to fall into decay; (*of health*) to become impaired.

délacer [delase] *v.tr.* **(je délaçai(s); n. délaçons)** (*a*) to unlace; to undo (shoes, etc.); (*b*) **se d.,** to come unlaced, undone.

délai [delɛ] *n.m.* **1.** delay; **sans d.,** without delay, immediately. **2.** respite, time allowed (for completion of a job, etc.); **à court d.,** at short notice; **dans le d. prescrit, fixé,** within the required, allotted, time; **dans le plus bref d.,** as soon as possible; *Mil: etc:* **d. de route,** travelling time; *Com:* **d. de paiement, de congé,** term of payment, of notice; **d. de livraison un mois,** delivery within a month; **livrable dans un d. de trois jours,** can be delivered at three days' notice; **d. de préavis** = DÉLAI-CONGÉ.

délai-congé [delɛkɔ̃ʒe] *n.m. Jur: Com:* term of notice (to employee or employer); *pl. délais-congés.*

délaissé [delese] *a.* forsaken; **épouse délaissée,** deserted wife; **enfant d.,** abandoned child.

délaissement [delɛsmɑ̃] *n.m.* **1.** (*a*) desertion, abandonment, neglect (of wife, children, etc.); (*b*) loneliness; **être dans un grand d.,** to be completely alone. **2.** relinquishment, renunciation (of right, etc.); abandonment (of ship to insurer).

délaisser [delese] *v.tr.* **1.** to forsake, desert, abandon (s.o.). **2.** *Jur:* to relinquish, forgo (right, succession); to abandon (ship to insurer).

délassant [delɑsɑ̃] *a.* refreshing, relaxing (bath, rest, etc.); light, entertaining (reading).

délassement [delɑsmɑ̃] *n.m.* rest, relaxation.

délasser [delɑse] *v.tr.* (*a*) to rest, refresh (s.o.); (*b*) **se d.,** to (take some) rest, to relax.

délateur, -trice [delatœr, -tris] *n.* informer, spy.

délation [delasjɔ̃] *n.f.* denouncement.

délavage [delavaʒ] *n.m.* washing out (of colours, etc.).

délavé [delave] *a.* (*a*) washed out (colour, etc.); (*b*) **terre délavée,** sodden earth.

délaver [delave] *v.tr.* (*a*) to make faint in colour; to dilute, to weaken; (*b*) to soak (with water).

délayage [delɛjaʒ] *n.m.* thinning out (of paint, etc.).

délayé [deleje] *a.* (*a*) thin, watery; (*b*) wordy (style); *n.* **c'est du d.,** it's mere verbosity.

délayer [deleje] *v.tr.* **(je délaie, délaye; je délaierai, délayerai)** (*a*) to add water to (powder, etc.); to thin (paint, etc.) (**dans,** with); to water (liquid); **d. de la farine dans du lait,** to mix flour with milk; (*b*) **d. un discours,** to spin out, pad out, a speech.

Delco [dɛlko] *n.m. Aut: R.t.m.* distributor (*made by the Dayton Engineering Laboratories Company*).

déléatur [deleatyr] *n.m.inv. Typ:* delete (mark); dele.

délectable [delɛktabl̥] *a.* delectable; delicious, delightful.

délectablement [delɛktabləmɑ̃] *adv.* delectably, deliciously.

délecter [delɛkte] *v.tr.* **1.** to delight. **2. se d. à qch., à faire qch.,** to take delight in sth., in doing sth.

délégant, -ante [delegɑ̃, -ɑ̃t] *n. Jur:* delegant.

délégataire [delegatɛr] *n. Jur:* delegatee.

délégateur, -trice [delegatœr, -tris] *n. Jur:* delegator.

délégation [delegasjɔ̃] *n.f.* **1.** (*a*) delegation (of authority); **agir en vertu d'une, par, d.,** to act on the authority of s.o.; (*b*) delegation, deputing (of representatives); (*c*) assignment, transfer (of debt). **2.** *coll.* delegation, body of delegates.

délégatoire [delegatwar] *a.* delegatory (power, authority).

délégué, -ée [delege] *a. & n.* (*a*) delegate (at meeting, etc.); representative; (*b*) deputy (professor, etc.); (*c*) **d. du personnel,** shop steward; **d. syndical,** union representative.

déléguer [delege] *v.tr.* **(je délègue; je déléguerai) 1. d. qn pour faire qch.,** to delegate, depute, s.o. to do sth. **2. d. son pouvoir,** to delegate, hand over, one's powers; **d. une créance,** to assign a debt.

délestage [delɛstaʒ] *n.m.* (*a*) unballasting (of ship, etc.); (*b*) *El:* power cut.

délester [delɛste] *v.tr.* (*a*) to unballast (ship); (*b*) **d.**

qn d'un fardeau, to relieve s.o. of a load; **se d. le cœur,** to unburden oneself; *F:* **d. qn de son argent,** to steal s.o.'s money; (*c*) *El:* to cut off the power.

délétère [deletɛr] *a.* deleterious; noxious, poisonous (gas); pernicious (influence, etc.).

délibérant [deliberɑ̃] *a.* deliberative (assembly).

délibératif, -ive [deliberatif, -iv] *a.* deliberative (function); **avoir voix délibérative,** to be entitled to speak and vote.

délibération [deliberasjɔ̃] *n.f.* **1.** deliberation, debate, discussion; **la question est en d.,** the matter is under consideration. **2.** reflection, cogitation; **après mûre d.,** after careful consideration. **3.** resolution, decision, vote (of an assembly).

délibéré [delibere] **1.** *a.* deliberate; (*a*) determined, resolute (tone, manner); (*b*) intentional; **agir de propos d.,** to act deliberately, intentionally. **2.** *n.m. Jur:* consultation, private sitting (of judges).

délibérément [deliberemɑ̃] *adv.* deliberately.

délibérer [delibere] *v.* **1.** *v.i.* to deliberate, confer; **d. (avec qn) sur qch.,** to discuss a matter (with s.o.); **le jury s'est retiré pour d.,** the jury retired to consider its verdict. **2.** *v.i.* **d. de qch.,** to deliberate sth.; **elle délibérait de partir,** she was wondering whether to leave.

délicat [delika] *a.* **1.** delicate; dainty (dish, etc.). **2.** delicate, gentle (touch); fine, refined, discerning, sensitive (taste, person); tactful (behaviour). **3.** delicate; sensitive, tender (skin, flower, etc.); delicate, frail, weak (health). **4.** difficult, critical, ticklish (problem, etc.); tricky (job); delicate (situation). **5.** scrupulous, particular, tender (conscience); **d. sur la nourriture,** fussy about food; **peu d.,** not very scrupulous.

délicatement [delikatmɑ̃] *adv.* delicately; tastefully; tactfully.

délicatesse [delikatɛs] *n.f.* **1.** delicacy; fineness, softness (of texture, colouring, etc.). **2.** (*a*) gentleness (of touch); (*b*) refinement (of taste); scrupulousness (of conduct); tactfulness, thoughtfulness (of behaviour); **agir avec d.,** to behave tactfully. **3.** frailty, fragility (of object, etc.); tenderness (of skin, etc.). **4.** delicacy, difficulty, awkwardness (of situation, etc.). **5.** consideration (for s.o.); **elle avait des délicatesses pour moi,** she treated me very considerately.

délice [delis] *n.m.* delight; extreme pleasure.

délices [delis] *n.f.pl.* delight(s), pleasure(s); **faire les d. de qn,** to be the delight of s.o.; **faire ses d. de qch.,** to delight in sth.; **c'est un lieu de d.,** this place is heavenly.

délicieusement [delisjøzmɑ̃] *adv.* deliciously; delightfully.

délicieux, -euse [delisjø, -øz] *a.* delicious (food); delightful, charming (person, dress, etc.).

délictueux, -euse [deliktɥø, -ty-, -øz] *a. Jur:* **1.** punishable; **acte d.,** misdemeanour, offence. **2.** felonious; malicious (intent).

délié [delje] **1.** *a.* (*a*) slender, fine; **taille déliée,** slim figure; (*b*) nimble, agile (fingers); **avoir la langue déliée,** to be talkative, *F:* to have the gift of the gab; (*c*) **un esprit d.,** a sharp, subtle, astute, mind. **2.** *n.m. Typ: etc:* thin stroke.

délier [delje] *v.tr.* **1.** to untie, undo, unbind; to loose (fetters, prisoner); **d. les mains à qn,** to untie, unbind, s.o.'s hands; **le vin lui a délié la langue,** the wine loosened his tongue. **2. d. qn d'une promesse,** to release s.o. from a promise. **3.** (*a*) **se d.,** to come undone, untied; to come loose; **sa langue se déliait,** his tongue was beginning to wag; (*b*) **se d. d'un serment,** to free oneself from an oath.

délimitation [delimitasjɔ̃] *n.f.* delimitation, demarcation; **poteau de d.,** boundary post.

délimiter [delimite] *v.tr.* to delimit, demarcate (territory); to define, determine (responsibility, etc.).

délinéament [delineamɑ̃] *n.m.* outline, shape, contour.

délinéer [delinee] *v.tr.* to delineate, outline.

délinquance [delɛ̃kɑ̃s] *n.f.* delinquency; **d. juvénile,** juvenile delinquency.

délinquant, -ante [delɛ̃kɑ̃, -ɑ̃t] *a. & n. Jur:* delinquent; **jeunesse délinquante,** juvenile delinquents; **d. primaire,** first offender.

déliquescence [delikɛsɑ̃s] *n.f.* deliquescence; **tomber en d.,** to fall into decay.

déliquescent [delikɛsɑ̃] *a.* deliquescent.

délirant [delirɑ̃] *a.* delirious, raving, lightheaded; **joie d.,** frenzied joy.

délire [delir] *n.m.* **1.** delirium; **avoir le d., être en d.,** to be delirious; to wander (in one's mind). **2.** frenzy; **foule en d.,** ecstatic crowd.

délirer [delire] *v.i.* to be delirious, lightheaded; to wander (in one's mind); to rave; **d. de joie,** to be mad with joy.

délit [deli] *n.m. Jur:* misdemeanour, offence; **d. civil,** tort; **d. de presse,** violation of the press laws.

délivrance [delivrɑ̃s] *n.f.* **1.** deliverance, rescue, release. **2.** delivery, handing over (of property, certificate); issue (of tickets). **3.** *Obst:* (*a*) delivery of the afterbirth; (*b*) childbirth, confinement.

délivre [delivr̥] *n.m. Obst:* afterbirth.

délivrer [delivre] *v.tr.* **1.** to deliver; to rescue (captive, etc.); to release, set free (prisoner); **d. qn de ses liens,** to free s.o. from his bonds. **2.** to deliver, hand over (goods, etc.); to deliver, issue (certificate, ticket). **3.** *Obst:* **d. une femme,** to deliver a woman (i) of the afterbirth, (ii) of a child. **4. se d. de qn, de qch.,** to rid oneself, to get rid, of s.o., of sth.

délogement [delɔʒmɑ̃] *n.m.* eviction (of tenant).

déloger [delɔʒe] *v.* (*conj. like* LOGER) **1.** *v.i.* to go off; to leave (home); **délogez de là!** get out of here! **2.** *v.tr.* to drive (s.o.) out; to evict (tenant); to dislodge (the enemy).

déloyal, -aux [delwajal, -o] *a.* disloyal, unfaithful, false (friend, etc.); dishonest, unfair (practice); *Sp:* **jeu d.,** foul play; **coup d.,** foul.

déloyalement [delwajalmɑ̃] *adv.* disloyally, dishonestly.

déloyauté [delwajote] *n.f.* (*a*) disloyalty, treachery; unfairness; (*b*) disloyal act.

Delphes [dɛlf] *Pr.n.f.pl. Geog:* Delphi.

delphien, -ienne [dɛlfjɛ̃, -jɛn] *a.* Delphic (oracle).

delta [dɛlta] *n.m. Gr.Alph: Geog:* delta; *Av:* **aile (en) d.,** delta wing.

deltaplane [dɛltaplan] *n.m. Sp:* hang glider; **faire du d.,** to go hang gliding.

deltoïde [dɛltɔid] *a. & n.m.* deltoid (muscle).

déluge [delyʒ] *n.m.* (*a*) deluge, flood; torrent (of abuse); **après moi le d.!** when I'm gone I don't care what happens! **cela remonte au d.,** it's as old as the hills; (*b*) downpour (of rain).

déluré [delyre] *a.* sharp, knowing, smart.

délustrer [delystre] *v.tr. Tex:* to remove the sheen, lustre (from cloth); to sponge, steam (cloth).

démagnétisation [demaɲetizasjɔ̃] *n.f.* **1.** *Ph:* demagnetization. **2.** *Nau:* degaussing.

démagnétiser [demaɲetize], *v.tr.* **1.** *Ph:* to demagnetize. **2.** *Nau:* to degauss.

démagogie [demagɔʒi] *n.f.* demagogy.

démagogique [demagɔʒik] *a.* demagogic.

démagogue [demagɔg] *n.m.* demagogue.

démailler [demaje] *v.tr.* **1.** to unshackle (chain). **2.** to undo the meshes of (net). **3.** (*of stocking*) **se d.,** to ladder.

demain [dəmɛ̃] *adv & n.m.* tomorrow; **d. (au) soir,** tomorrow evening; **d. en huit,** tomorrow week; **à d.!** see you tomorrow! **le journal de d.,** tomorrow's paper; **ce n'est pas pour d.,** *F:* **c'est pas d. la veille,**

you won't see that in a hurry; it's not for a long time yet; **d. il fera jour,** tomorrow is another day.

démanché [demɑ̃ʃe] **1.** *a.* (*a*) (*of tool, etc.*) without a handle; (*b*) rickety (furniture, etc.); dislocated (shoulder, etc.); ungainly, awkward (pers.). **2.** *n.m. Mus:* shift.

démanchement [demɑ̃ʃmɑ̃] *n.m.* **1.** removal of handle (of tool, etc.). **2.** dislocation (of shoulder, etc.).

démancher [demɑ̃ʃe] **1.** *v.tr.* (*a*) to remove the handle of (tool, etc.); (*b*) **se d. le bras,** to put one's arm out (of joint). **2.** *v.i. Mus:* to shift (in playing the violin). **3. se d.** (*a*) (*of tool, etc.*) to lose its handle; (*b*) *F:* to fall to pieces, to collapse; (*c*) to put one's arm out (of joint); *F:* **se d. pour obtenir qch.,** to move heaven and earth to get sth.

demande [dəmɑ̃d] *n.f.* **1.** (*a*) request, petition, application (**de,** for); **faire la d. de qch.,** to ask for sth.; **d. (en mariage),** offer, proposal, of marriage; **faire qch. sur la d. de qn,** to act at s.o.'s request; *Adm:* **d. de remboursement de voyage,** fare, travel, claim; **il faut faire une d.**, you must fill in an application form; **faire une d. d'emploi,** to apply for a job; (*b*) *Com:* demand; **l'offre et la d.,** supply and demand; (*c*) **d. en divorce,** divorce petition. **2.** question, enquiry; **demandes et réponses,** questions and answers.

demander [dəmɑ̃de] *v.tr.* **1.** (*a*) to ask (for); to claim (damages, etc.); **d. du pain,** to ask for bread; **on nous a demandé nos passeports,** we were asked for our passports; **d. la permission,** to ask (for) permission; **je vous demande pardon,** I beg your pardon; **d. la main de (qn), d. (qn) en mariage,** to ask for s.o.'s hand (in marriage); **on vous demande,** you're wanted, somebody wants to see you; **combien demandez-vous de l'heure?** how much do you charge an hour? **d. qch. à qn,** to ask s.o. for sth.; **il demande qu'on,** *F:* **à ce qu'on, lui rende justice,** he asks for justice; (*b*) **d. à,** *occ.* **de, faire qch.,** to ask (permission) to do sth.; **je demande à parler,** may I, please let me, speak; **d. à manger,** to ask for something to eat; **je ne demande qu'à rester ici,** I ask for nothing better than to stay here; **d. à qn de faire qch.,** to ask s.o. to do sth. **2.** to desire, want, need, require; **on demande maçon,** builder wanted; **article très demandé,** article in great demand; **cela demande le plus grand soin,** it requires the greatest care; **la situation demande à être maniée avec tact,** the situation needs, calls for, tactful handling; **le voyage demande trois heures,** the journey takes three hours. **3.** to demand; **d. à qn plus qu'il n'en peut faire,** to demand, expect, from s.o. more than he can do; **c'est trop me d.,** it's too much to ask of me; **il ne faut pas lui en demander trop,** you mustn't expect too much from him. **4.** to ask, enquire; **d. quelle heure il est, d. l'heure,** to ask the time; **d. son chemin à qn,** to ask s.o. the way; *F:* **je ne t'ai rien demandé!** I didn't ask for your advice, opinion! **je ne t'ai pas demandé l'heure qu'il est,** mind your own business! **je vous (le) demande, je vous demande un peu!** I ask you! **5. se d.,** to ask oneself, to wonder; **c'est ce que je me demande,** that's what I'd like to know; **c'est à se demander, on se demande, s'il ne l'a pas fait exprès,** one wonders whether he didn't do it on purpose; **je me demande bien pourquoi, ce que, où,** I really can't think why, what, where.

demandeur, -euse [dəmɑ̃dœr, -øz] *n.* **1.** *A:* petitioner, constant applicant for favours. **2.** *Jur:* (*f.* **demanderesse** [dəmɑ̃drɛs]) plaintiff; **d. en divorce,** petitioner; **d. en appel,** appellant. **3.** *Com:* buyer. **4.** *Tp:* **d. (de la communication),** caller.

démangeaison [demɑ̃ʒɛzɔ̃] *n.f.* itching; **j'ai une d.,** I've got an itch; I'm itching; *F:* **une d. de faire qch.,** a longing, an itching, to do sth.

démanger [demɑ̃ʒe] *v.i.* (**il démangea(it);** *usu. with dative of person*) to itch; **l'épaule me démange,** my shoulder's itching; *Fig:* **la main lui démangeait,** he was itching, dying, for a fight.

démantèlement [demɑ̃tɛlmɑ̃] *n.m.* demolition, demolishing; breaking up; bringing down.

démanteler [demɑ̃tle] *v.tr.* (**je démantèle; je démantèlerai**) to demolish, destroy (fortifications, etc.); to break up (organization, etc.); to bring down (empire, etc.).

démantibuler [demɑ̃tibyle] *v.tr. F:* (*a*) to break up, smash up (object); **d. une machine,** to take, smash, a machine to pieces; (*b*) **se d.,** to come to pieces, to break up.

démaquillage [demakijaʒ] *n.m. Toil:* removal of makeup; **crème pour le d.,** cleansing cream, makeup remover.

démaquillant [demakijɑ̃] *n.m. Toil:* cleansing cream, makeup remover.

démaquiller [demakije] *v.tr.* (*a*) to remove makeup; (*b*) **se d.,** to remove one's makeup.

démarcage [demarkaʒ] *n.m.* = DÉMARQUAGE.

démarcatif, -ive [demarkatif, -iv] *a.* demarcating (line, etc.).

démarcation [demarkasjɔ̃] *n.f.* demarcation; **ligne de d.,** dividing line, boundary line; demarcation line.

démarchage [demarʃaʒ] *n.m. Com:* (*a*) door-to-door selling; (*b*) canvassing.

démarche [demarʃ] *n.f.* **1.** gait, step, walk; **d. majestueuse,** majestic bearing; **il avait une d. digne,** he moved with dignity. **2.** step; **faire une d. auprès de qn,** to approach s.o.; **faire les premières démarches,** to take the first steps; *Dipl:* **d. collective,** joint representations. **3.** process; **d. de la pensée,** thought process.

démarcheur, -euse [demarʃœr, -øz] *n. Com:* (*a*) door-to-door salesman, saleswoman; (*b*) canvasser.

démarquage [demarkaʒ] *n.m.* **1.** removal of the mark (from linen, plate, etc.). **2.** plagiarism. **3.** *Sp:* breaking free from one's opponent.

démarque [demark] *n.f. Com:* marking down (of goods at sales).

démarqué [demarke] *a. Sp:* unmarked.

démarquer [demarke] *v.tr.* **1.** (*a*) to remove the identification marks from (linen, plate, etc.); (*b*) *Com:* to mark down (goods). **2.** to plagiarize (book). **3.** *Sp:* to leave one's opponent unmarked. **4.** *Sp:* **se d.,** to break free from one's opponent.

démarrage [demaraʒ] *n.m.* **1.** unmooring (of ship). **2.** (*a*) start, starting (of engine, etc.); moving off (of car, etc.); **d. en côte,** hill start; **d. d'une affaire,** start of a business; (*b*) *Sp:* (sudden) spurt.

démarrer [demare] **1.** *v.tr.* (*a*) to unmoor, cast off (ship); (*b*) to start (car, etc.). **2.** *v.i.* (*a*) (*of ship*) to cast off; (*b*) (*of train, car, etc.*) to start, move off, get away; (*of driver*) to drive, away, off; **faire d.,** to start (car, etc.); (*c*) *Sp:* to put on a spurt; (*d*) **son affaire commence à d.,** his business is beginning to get going.

démarreur [demarœr] *n.m. Aut: Mch: etc:* starter (motor).

démasquer [demaske] *v.tr.* (*a*) to unmask; to expose, to show up (impostor); *Fig:* **d. ses batteries,** to show one's hand; (*b*) **se d.,** (i) to take off one's mask; (ii) *Fig:* to drop the mask.

démâtage [demɑtaʒ] *n.m.* dismasting.

démâter [demɑte] *v.tr.* to dismast (ship).

démêlage [demɛlaʒ] *n.m.* disentangling.

démêlé [demele] *n.m. usu. pl.* contention; (unpleasant) dealings; **il a eu des démêlés avec la police,** he's been in trouble with the police.

démêler [demele] *v.tr.* (*a*) to disentangle, unravel (string, silk, etc.) to untangle, comb out (hair); to tease (out) (wool); **d. un problème, un malentendu,** to sort out a problem, clear up a misunderstanding; **avoir qch. à d. avec qn,** to have sth. to discuss with s.o.; (*b*) *O:* **se d.,** to extricate oneself (from difficulty).

démêloir [demɛlwar] *n.m.* large-toothed comb.

démêlures [demɛlyr] *n.f.pl.* combings.

démembrement [demɑ̃brəmɑ̃] *n.m.* dismemberment, disruption (of empire, etc.); breaking up (of ship).

démembrer [demɑ̃bre] *v.tr.* to dismember; to cut up, joint (chicken, etc.); to divide up (kingdom).

déménagement [demenaʒmɑ̃] *n.m.* moving (house); **camion de d.,** furniture, removal, van; *F:* **votre d. est arrivé,** your furniture has arrived.

déménager [demenaʒe] *v.tr. & i.* **(je déménageai(s); n. déménageons) d. (ses meubles),** to move (house); *F:* **d. à la cloche de bois,** to do a moonlight flit; *F:* **il déménage!** he's off his head! he's round the bend! *F:* **allez! déménagez!** scram! buzz off!

déménageur [demenaʒœr] *n.m.* removal man, furniture remover; *U.S:* mover.

démence [demɑ̃s] *n.f.* (*a*) insanity, madness; *Jur:* lunacy; (*b*) *Med:* dementia; **d. précoce,** dementia praecox; (*c*) **c'est de la pure d.!** it's insane!

démener (se) [sədemne] *v.pr.* (*conj. like* MENER) **1.** to thrash about, throw oneself about; to struggle; **se d. comme un beau diable,** to thrash about like a cat on hot bricks. **2.** to exert oneself; to make a great effort.

dément, -ente [demɑ̃, -ɑ̃t] *a. & n.* mad, insane (person); *Jur:* lunatic; *Med:* demented person; **quel monde! c'est d.!** what a crowd! it's unbelievable!

démenti [demɑ̃ti] *n.m.* **1.** (flat) denial, contradiction; **donner, opposer, un d. formel à une accusation,** to deny an accusation; **ses actions donnent un d. à ses paroles,** his actions belie his words. **2.** failure (of efforts); disappointment (of expectations).

démentiel, -elle [demɑ̃sjɛl] *a.* mad, insane; **accès d.,** fit of madness.

démentir [demɑ̃tir] *v.tr.* (*conj. like* MENTIR) **1.** to give the lie to, to contradict (s.o., sth.); to deny, refute (fact). **2.** to belie; **il a démenti nos espérances,** he has not come up to our expectations; he has disappointed us. **3. se d.,** to contradict oneself; to go back on one's word; **politesse qui ne se dément jamais,** unfailing courtesy.

démerder (se) [sədemɛrde] *v.pr. P:* (*a*) to get a move on; (*b*) to get out of a mess.

démérite [demerit] *n.m.* demerit, fault; **faire à qn un d. de qch.,** to reproach s.o. for sth.

démériter [demerite] *v.i.* **1.** to act in a reprehensible manner. **2. d. auprès de qn,** to forfeit s.o.'s esteem; to come down in s.o.'s regard.

démesure [deməzyr] *n.f.* disproportion, excessiveness.

démesuré [deməzyre] *a.* beyond measure, huge, enormous; inordinate (pride); excessive (thirst); unbounded (ambition).

démesurément [deməzyremɑ̃], *adv.* enormously; inordinately.

démettre[1] [demɛtr̥] *v.tr.* (*conj. like* METTRE) to dislocate (joint); **se d. l'épaule,** to put one's shoulder out (of joint).

démettre[2] *v.tr.* **1. d. qn de ses fonctions,** to deprive s.o. of his office. **2. se d.,** to resign, retire; **se d. de ses fonctions,** to resign office, resign from one's job.

démeubler [demœble] *v.tr.* to remove the furniture from (house, etc.); to strip (house, etc.) of its furniture, fittings.

demeurant [dəmœrɑ̃] *n.m. now used only in adv. phr.* **au d.,** after all, all the same, for all that.

demeure [dəmœr] *n.f.* **1.** (*a*) *A:* tarrying, delay; *still so used in such phrases as* **sans plus longue d.,** without further delay; **il y a péril en la d.,** there is danger in delay; (*b*) **mettre qn en d. de payer,** to give s.o. notice to pay; **mise en d.,** formal notice, summons; (*c*) stay; **à d.,** fixed, permanent(ly); **meuble à d.,** fixture; **il est ici à d.,** he's here permanently, for good. **2.** (place of) residence; **dernière d.,** last resting place.

demeuré, -ée [dəmœre] **1.** *a.* halfwitted, mentally retarded. **2.** *n.* halfwit.

demeurer [dəmœre] *v.i.* **1.** (*conj. with* **être**) to remain; to stay, stop (in a place); **je demeure convaincu que . . .,** I remain convinced that . . .; **l'affaire n'en demeurera pas là,** the matter will not rest there; **demeurons-en là,** let's leave it at that; **ne pouvoir d. en place,** to be unable to keep still; **elle demeurait assise à nous écouter,** she sat listening to us; **d. en reste avec qn,** to remain under an obligation to s.o. **2.** (*conj. with* **avoir**) to live, reside; **d. à la campagne,** to live in the country; **il demeure rue de Rivoli,** he lives in the rue de Rivoli.

demi [dəmi] **1.** *a.* (*a*) half; **deux heures et demie,** (i) two and a half hours; (ii) half past two; **un d.-congé,** a half holiday; **une d.-heure,** half an hour; (*b*) semi-; **d.-cercle,** semicircle; (*c*) demi-; **d.-dieu,** demigod; (*d*) **d.-cuit,** half cooked. **2.** *n.m.* (*a*) **deux plus un d.,** two plus a half; (*beer*) **un d.** = half a pint; a half; (*b*) *Fb:* **les demis,** the halfbacks; *Rugby:* **d. de mêlée,** scrum half; **d. d'ouverture,** stand-off half; (*c*) **à d.,** (i) half; **à d. mort,** half dead; **faire les choses à d.,** to do things by halves; (ii) semi-; **à d. transparent,** semi-transparent. **3.** *n.f.* **demie,** half hour; **il est la demie,** it's half past.

NOTE. *in all the following compounds* DEMI *is inv.; the second component takes the plural.*

demi-arbre [dəmiarbr̥] *n.m. Aut:* halfshaft.

demiard [dəmjar] *n.m. Fr.C: Meas:* half pint.

demi-arrière [dəmiarjɛr] *n.m. Fb:* halfback.

demi-bas [dəmiba] *n.m. Cost:* kneesock.

demi-botte [dəmibɔt] *n.f.* half boot.

demi-bouteille [dəmibutɛj] *n.f.* half bottle.

demi-cercle [dəmisɛrkl̥] *n.m.* semicircle, half circle; **en d.-c.,** semicircular.

demi-circulaire [dəmisirkylɛr] *a.* semicircular.

demi-clef [dəmikle] *n.f. Nau:* half hitch.

demi-deuil [dəmidœj] *n.m.* half mourning.

demi-dieu [dəmidjø] *n.m.* demigod.

demi-douzaine [dəmiduzɛn] *n.f.* half dozen.

démieller [demjɛle] *v.tr.* to remove the honey from (honeycomb).

demi-fin, -fine [dəmifɛ̃, -fin] *a.* (*a*) (*of size*) medium; (*b*) (*of gold*) twelve carat; *n.* **bracelet en d.-f.,** twelve carat bracelet.

demi-finale [dəmifinal] *n.f. Sp:* semifinal.

demi-finaliste [dəmifinalist] *n.m. & f. Sp:* semifinalist.

demi-fond [dəmifɔ̃] *n.m.inv. Sp:* **(course de) d.-f.,** middle distance race.

demi-frère [dəmifrɛr] *n.m.* half brother.

demi-gros [dəmigro] *n.m.* **commerce de d.-g.,** wholesale dealing in small quantities; cash and carry.

demi-heure [dəmiœr] *n.f.* **une d.-h.,** half an hour; **deux d.-heures,** two half hours; **de d.-h. en d.-h., toutes les d.-heures,** every half hour.

demi-jour [dəmiʒur] *n.m.* (*a*) half light (of dawn); (*b*) twilight, dusk.

demi-journée [dəmiʒurne] *n.f.* half a day; **faire des d.-journées,** to work half days, to work half the day.

démilitarisation [demilitarizasjɔ̃] *n.m.* demilitarization.

démilitariser [demilitarize] *v.tr.* to demilitarize.

demi-litre [dəmilitr̥] *n.m.* half litre, *NAm:* liter.

demi-longueur [dəmilɔ̃gœr] *n.f. Sp:* half a length; a half length.

demi-lune [dəmilyn] **1.** *n.f.* (*a*) half moon; (*b*) *Fort:* demi-lune. **2.** *a.* semicircular.
demi-mal [dəmimal] *n.m.* small harm; **il n'y a que d.-m.,** it might have been worse.
demi-mesure [dəmiməzyr] *n.f.* half measure; **avec lui il n'y a jamais de d.-m.,** there's no halfway with him.
demi-mondain, -aine [dəmimɔ̃dɛ̃, -ɛn] **1.** *a.* belonging to the demi-monde. **2.** *n.f.* **demi-mondaine,** demi-mondaine.
demi-monde [dəmimɔ̃d] *n.m.* demi-monde; outskirts of society.
demi-mort [dəmimɔr] *a.* half dead.
demi-mot (à) [ad(ə)mimo] *adv.phr.* **entendre (qn) à d.-m.,** to (know how to) take a hint; **il a compris à d.-m.,** he caught on at once (to what I meant).
déminage [deminaʒ] *n.m.* mine clearance; bomb disposal.
déminer [demine] *v.tr.* to clear (a field) of mines.
démineur [deminœr] *n.m.* bomb disposal expert.
demi-pause [dəmipoz] *n.f. Mus:* minim rest.
demi-pension [dəmipɑ̃sjɔ̃] *n.f.* half board.
demi-pensionnaire [dəmipɑ̃sjɔnɛr] *n.m. & f.* half boarder; *Sch:* day boarder.
demi-place [dəmiplas] *n.f.* half fare (when travelling); half price (at theatre, etc.).
demi-portion [dəmipɔrsjɔ̃] *n.f. F: Pej:* small insignificant person; weed.
demi-quart [dəmikar] *n.m.* **1.** *Nau:* half point (of the compass). **2.** *Meas:* = 2 ounces.
demi-queue [dəmikø] *n.m.inv.* baby grand (piano).
demi-reliure [dəmirəljyr] *n.f. Bookb:* quarter binding; **d.-r. à (petits) coins,** half binding.
demi-saison [dəmisɛzɔ̃] *n.f.* between season, mid season; **vêtements de d.-s.,** spring, autumn, clothes.
demi-sang [dəmisɑ̃] *n.m.inv.* halfbred (horse).
demi-sel [dəmisɛl] **1.** *a. inv.* slightly salted (butter, etc.). **2.** *n.m.* (*a*) (slightly salted) cream cheese; (*b*) *F:* crook; pimp.
demi-sœur [dəmisœr] *n.f.* half sister.
demi-solde [dəmisɔld] **1.** *n.f. Mil:* half pay; **en d.-s.,** on half pay. **2.** *n.m. inv.* half-pay officer.
demi-sommeil [dəmisɔmɛj] *n.m.* drowsiness, somnolence.
demi-soupir [dəmisupir] *n.m. Mus:* quaver rest.
démission [demisjɔ̃] *n.f.* **1.** resignation; **donner sa d.,** to tender, send in, one's resignation; to resign. **2.** renunciation; **donner sa d.,** to give up.
démissionnaire [demisjɔnɛr] *a. & n.* (one) who has resigned (his office, etc.); resigning (officer, etc.).
démissionner [demisjɔne] **1.** *v.i.* (*a*) to resign (**de,** from); (*b*) *F:* **je démissionne!** I give up! **2.** *v.tr. F:* to sack (s.o.).
demi-tarif [dəmitarif] *n.m.* half price; **billet (à) d.-t.,** half fare (ticket).
demi-tasse [dəmitas] *n.f.* **1.** small coffee cup. **2.** half a cup; a small coffee; *U.S:* demitasse.
demi-teinte [dəmitɛ̃t] *n.f. Art: Phot:* halftone.
demi-ton [dəmitɔ̃] *n.m. Mus:* semitone.
demi-tonneau [dəmitɔno] *n.m. Av:* half roll.
demi-tour [dəmitur] *n.m.* half turn; *Mil:* about turn; *Aut:* U turn; **faire d.-t.,** to go back.
demi-voix (à) [ad(ə)mivwa] *adv.phr.* in an undertone; under one's breath.
demi-volée [dəmivɔle] *n.f. Ten:* half volley.
démobilisation [demɔbilizasjɔ̃] *n.f.* demobilization (of troops), *F:* demob.
démobiliser [demɔbilize] *v.tr.* to demobilize (troops); *F:* to demob.
démocrate [demɔkrat] **1.** *a.* democratic. **2.** *n.m. & f.* democrat.
démocrate-chrétien, -ienne [demɔkratkretjɛ̃, -jɛn] *a. & n.* Christian Democrat.
démocratie [demɔkrasi] *n.f.* democracy.
démocratique [demɔkratik] *a.* democratic.
démocratiquement [demɔkratikmɑ̃] *adv.* democratically.
démocratisation [demɔkratizasjɔ̃] *n.f.* democratization.
démocratiser [demɔkratize] *v.tr.* (*a*) to democratize; (*b*) **se d.,** to become (more) democratic.
démodé [demɔde] *a.* oldfashioned; out of fashion, outmoded; obsolete, out of date.
démoder (se) [sədemɔde] *v.pr.* (*of clothes, etc.*) to go out of fashion, to become oldfashioned.
démographe [demɔgraf] *n.m. & f.* demographer.
démographie [demɔgrafi] *n.f.* demography.
démographique [demɔgrafik] *a.* demographic; *Adm: Pol. Ec:* **statistiques démographiques,** vital statistics; **poussée démographique,** population growth.
demoiselle [dəmwazɛl] *n.f.* **1.** (*a*) spinster; single, unmarried, woman; (*b*) **d. d'honneur,** (i) maid of honour; (ii) bridesmaid; **d. de compagnie,** lady's companion. **2.** young lady. **3.** (*a*) *Orn:* **d. (de Numidie),** demoiselle; Numidian crane; (*b*) *Ent:* dragonfly. **4.** *Tchn:* paving beetle.
démolir [demɔlir] *v.tr.* **1.** to demolish, pull down (house, etc.); to break up (ship); to wreck, smash up (car, etc.). **2.** to overthrow (government, authority, etc.); to demolish (argument, theory, etc.); to ruin (reputation); to criticize (author, etc.) severely. **3.** *F:* (*a*) to beat (s.o.) up, to bash (s.o.) about; **il s'est fait d.,** he got beaten up; (*b*) to tire (s.o.); **tout ce travail l'a démoli,** he's exhausted, shattered, after all this work.
démolissage [demɔlisaʒ] *n.m.* severe criticism, *F:* slating (of author, etc.).
démolisseur, -euse [demɔlisœr, -øz] *n.* **1.** (*a*) demolition worker, contractor; (*b*) shipbreaker. **2.** demolisher, overthrower (of argument, etc.)
démolition [demɔlisjɔ̃] *n.f.* demolition; pulling down (of structure); **chantier de d.,** demolition yard.
démon [demɔ̃] *n.m.* **1.** *Myth:* daemon; (good, evil) genius. **2.** demon, devil, fiend; **le d.,** the Devil; **cette femme est un d.,** she's a wicked woman; **cet enfant est un petit d.,** that child is a little devil; **le d. de la jalousie,** the demon of jealousy.
démonétisation [demɔnetizasjɔ̃] *n.f.* **1.** demonetization; withdrawal from circulation (of coinage). **2.** *Fig:* discrediting (of s.o.).
démoniaque [demɔnjak] **1.** *a.* demoniac(al); possessed of the devil. **2.** *n.* demoniac.
démonstrateur, -trice [demɔ̃stratœr, -tris] *n.* demonstrator.
démonstratif, -ive [demɔ̃stratif, -iv] *a.* **1.** (logically) conclusive. **2.** *Gram:* demonstrative (adjective, etc.). **3.** demonstrative, expansive (person); **peu d.,** undemonstrative.
démonstration [demɔ̃strasjɔ̃] *n.f.* demonstration. **1.** (*a*) proof (of theorem, etc.); (*b*) *Box:* **assaut de d.,** sparring match; (*c*) *Com:* demonstration (of article); **appareil de d.,** demonstration model. **2.** (*a*) *Mil:* show of force; (*b*) *esp. pl.* **faire de grandes démonstrations d'amitié,** to make a great show of friendship.
démontable [demɔ̃tabl̩] *a.* (*of machine, etc.*) that can be dismantled; portable (building); collapsible (boat).
démontage [demɔ̃taʒ] *n.m.* dismantling; taking to pieces.
démonté [demɔ̃te] *a.* **1.** (*a*) dismounted (cavalry); (*b*) (*of rider*) thrown unseated. **2.** stormy, raging (sea). **3.** (*of pers.*) disconcerted. **4.** (*of mechanism, etc.*) taken to pieces, dismantled.
démonte-pneu [demɔ̃tpnø] *n.m.* tyre, *NAm:* tire, lever; *pl. démonte-pneus.*

démonter [demɔ̃te] *v.tr.* **1.** to throw (off), unseat (rider). **2. la nouvelle m'a démonté,** I was greatly upset, put out, by the news; **se laisser d.,** to get upset, flustered. **3.** to take down, take to pieces, take apart, dismantle; to dismount (gun); to unhinge (door); to remove (tyre). **4. se d.** (*a*) (*of mechanism*) to come apart; (*b*) *F:* **il ne se démonte pas pour si peu,** he's not so easily put out.

démontrable [demɔ̃trabḷ] *a.* demonstrable, provable.

démontrer [demɔ̃tre] *v.tr.* **1.** to demonstrate; **cela se démontre facilement,** that's easily proved. **2.** to give a clear indication of (sth.).

démoralisateur, -trice [demɔralizatœr, -tris] **1.** *n. Lit:* corrupter. **2.** *a.* demoralizing.

démoralisation [demɔralizasjɔ̃] *n.f.* demoralization.

démoraliser [demɔralize] *v.tr.* **1.** to demoralize; to dishearten. **2. se d.,** to become demoralized, to lose heart.

démordre [demɔrdr̥] *v.i.* (*a*) to let go one's hold (with the teeth); (*b*) (*usu. with negative*) **ne pas d. de ses opinions,** to stand by, to stick to, one's opinions; **il ne veut pas en d.,** he won't give up his point; he's sticking to his guns.

démoulage [demulaʒ] *n.m.* removal (of cast) from mould.

démouler [demule] *v.tr.* (*a*) to remove (cast) from the mould; (*b*) *Cu:* to turn out (jelly, cake).

démultiplicateur, -trice [demyltiplikatœr, -tris] *a. & n.m. Mec.E:* **1.** *a.* reducing; reduction (gear). **2.** *n.m.* reduction system; **d. de vitesse,** motor reduction unit.

démultiplication [demyltiplikasjɔ̃] *n.f. Mec.E:* **1.** gearing down; reduction. **2.** reduction ratio (of gears).

démultiplier [demyltiplije] *v.tr. Mec.E:* to reduce the gear ratio; to gear down.

démuni [demyni] *a.* **1.** unprovided **(de,** with); **d. d'argent,** without any money, penniless. **2.** *Com:* **être d. de qch.,** to be out of sth., sold out of sth.

démunir [demynir] *v.tr.* **1.** to strip (fortress, etc.) of munitions; to deprive (s.o. of sth.). **2. se d. de qch.,** (i) to allow oneself to run short of sth.; (ii) to part with sth.

démuseler [demyzle] *v.tr.* **(je démuselle; je démusellerai)** to unmuzzle (dog).

démystification [demistifikasjɔ̃] *n.f.* undeceiving; *F:* debunking.

démystifier [demistifje] *v.tr.* (*impf. & pr. sub.* **n. démystifiions, v. démystifiiez**) to undeceive, disabuse; *F:* to debunk.

dénantir [denɑ̃tir] *v.tr. Jur:* **1.** to deprive (creditor, etc.) of pledges, of his securities. **2. se d.,** to part with one's securities.

dénatalité [denatalite] *n.f.* fall in the birthrate.

dénationalisation [denasjɔnalizasjɔ̃] *n.f.* denationalization.

dénationaliser [denasjɔnalize] *v.tr.* to denationalize.

dénaturalisation [denatyralizasjɔ̃] *n.f.* denaturalization.

dénaturaliser [denatyralize] *v.tr.* to denaturalize (person).

dénaturant [denatyrɑ̃] *Ch:* **1.** *a.* denaturing. **2.** *n.m.* denaturant; denaturing agent.

dénaturation [denatyrasjɔ̃] *n.f.* denaturation, changing the nature (of sth.); **d. de l'alcool,** denaturing of alcohol.

dénaturé [denatyre] *a.* **1.** denatured. **2.** unnatural; negligent (parents); perverted (taste).

dénaturer [denatyre] *v.tr.* **1.** (*a*) to denature (alcohol, etc.); (*b*) to misrepresent, pervert, distort (words, actions); **d. les faits,** to garble the facts. **2.** to render (sth.) unnatural; to pervert (the soul).

dénazification [denazifikasjɔ̃] *n.f.* denazification.

dénazifier [denazifje] *v.tr.* to denazify.

dénégateur, -trice [denegatœr, -tris] *n.* denier.

dénégation [denegasjɔ̃] *n.f.* denial.

déneigement [denɛʒmɑ̃] *n.m.* clearing (away), removal, of snow.

déneiger [deneʒe] *v.tr.* to clear (away) the snow; to remove snow from (road, etc.).

dengue [dɛ̃g] *n.f. Med:* dengue (fever).

déni [deni] *n.m. Jur:* denial, refusal (of sth. which is due); **d. de justice,** denial of justice.

déniaiser [denjeze] *v.tr.* (*a*) to educate (s.o.) in the ways of the world; (*b*) *F:* to take away s.o.'s innocence; (*c*) **se d.,** (i) to get smart; (ii) *F:* to lose one's innocence.

dénichement [deniʃmɑ̃] *n.m.* **1.** robbing (of nest, eggs). **2.** finding (of sth.).

dénicher [deniʃe] **1.** *v.tr.* (*a*) to take (bird, eggs) out of the nest; (*b*) to find, discover, unearth (s.o., sth.); **nous avons déniché une maison superbe,** we've found a beautiful house; (*c*) to drive (animal) out of hiding. **2.** *v.i.* (*of bird*) to leave the nest.

dénicheur, -euse [deniʃœr, -øz] *n.m.* **1.** bird's nester. **2.** searcher; unearther (of objects); **d. de curiosités,** curio hunter.

dénicotiniser [denikɔtinize] *v.tr.* to denicotinize (tobacco).

denier [dənje] *n.m.* **1.** (*a*) *Rom.Ant:* denarius; (*b*) *A:* (*Fr.*) denier; (*Eng.*) penny; **le d. de la veuve,** the widow's mite; **d. à Dieu,** key money; tip (to *concierge* from new tenant); **le d. de saint Pierre,** Peter's pence; **payer jusqu'au dernier d.,** to pay to the last farthing. **2.** *A:* (rate of) interest. **3.** money, funds; **je l'ai payé de mes deniers,** I paid for it with my own money; *R.C.Ch:* **d. du culte,** church offering (given privately to parish priest). **4.** (*hosiery*) denier; **bas de 30 deniers,** 30 denier stockings.

dénier [denje] *v.tr.* **1.** to deny (crime, etc.); to disclaim (responsibility). **2. d. qch. à qn,** to refuse, deny, s.o. sth.

dénigrement [denigrəmɑ̃] *n.m.* disparagement.

dénigrer [denigre] *v.tr.* to disparage, denigrate; to run down (s.o., sth.).

dénigreur, -euse [denigrœr, -øz] *n.* disparager.

dénivelé [denivle] *a.* uneven, unlevel (surface).

dénivelée [denivle] *n.f.* difference, variation, in level, in height (*esp. bet.* firearm and target).

déniveler [denivle] *v.tr.* (*conj. like* NIVELER) to make (surface, etc.) uneven; to put out of level.

dénivellation [denivɛlasjɔ̃] *n.f.*, **dénivellement** [denivɛlmɑ̃] *n.m.* **1.** making uneven; lowering, lifting, of level. **2.** difference in level, in height; **d. d'une route,** (i) unevenness, (ii) gradients, ups and downs, of a road.

dénombrable [denɔ̃brabḷ] *a.* countable.

dénombrement [denɔ̃brəmɑ̃] *n.m.* enumeration, counting; census (of population); *Med:* **d. des hématies,** blood count.

dénombrer [denɔ̃bre] *v.tr.* to count, enumerate; to take a census of (population).

dénominateur [denɔminatœr] *n.m. Mth:* denominator; **d. commun,** common denominator.

dénominatif, -ive [denɔminatif, -iv] *a. & n.m. Ling:* denominative.

dénomination [denɔminasjɔ̃] *n.f.* denomination, designation, name.

dénommer [denɔme] *v.tr.* to denominate, name; *occ. Pej:* **un dénommé Charles,** someone called, who calls himself, Charles.

dénoncer [denɔ̃se] *v.tr.* **(je dénonçai(s); n. dénonçons) 1.** (*a*) *A:* to declare, proclaim (war, etc.); (*b*) **d. un**

traité, to denounce a treaty; (*c*) to indicate, to reveal; **son attitude dénonce sa méfiance des autres,** his attitude betrays his mistrust of others. **2.** (*a*) to denounce (s.o.); to inform against (s.o.); **se d.,** to give oneself up; (*b*) to expose (crime, etc.).
dénonciateur, -trice [denɔ̃sjatœr, -tris] **1.** *n.* informer, denouncer; exposer. **2.** *a.* accusatory.
dénonciation [denɔ̃sjasjɔ̃] *n.f.* **1.** notice of termination (of treaty, etc.). **2.** denunciation; information (**de qn,** against s.o.).
dénotation [denɔtasjɔ̃] *n.f.* denotation.
dénoter [denɔte] *v.tr.* to denote, show, indicate.
dénouement [denumɑ̃] *n.m.* issue, upshot, result, outcome, conclusion (of event); solution (of difficulty); ending (of plot, story); *Th:* dénouement.
dénouer [denwe] *v.tr.* **1.** to unknot; to untie, undo, loose (knot, etc.); **d. ses cheveux,** to undo, let down, one's hair. **2. d. une intrigue,** to clear up, unravel, resolve, a plot. **3. se d.** (*a*) to come undone; (*b*) (*of plot, etc.*) to be resolved, to wind up; (*c*) **sa langue se dénoue,** he's finding his tongue.
dénoyauter [denwajote] *v.tr.* to stone, *NAm:* pit (fruit).
dénoyauteur [denwajotœr] *n.m.* (*machine*) stoner.
denrée [dɑ̃re] *n.f.* (*a*) *usu. pl.* commodity; *esp.* foodstuff, produce; **denrées alimentaires,** food products; foodstuffs; (*b*) **une d. rare,** a rare object, thing.
dense [dɑ̃s] *a.* **1.** *Ph:* dense. **2.** dense, crowded; close (formation of troops); thick (atmosphere); concise, condensed (style).
densité [dɑ̃site] *n.f.* **1.** *Ph:* density; **d. moyenne,** mean specific weight; **flacon à d.,** specific gravity flask. **2.** density (of population, etc.).
dent [dɑ̃] *n.f.* **1.** (*a*) tooth; **d. du fond, du devant,** back, front, tooth; **d. de lait,** milk tooth, first tooth; **sans dents,** toothless; **faire, percer, ses dents,** to cut one's teeth; to be teething; **mal, rage, de dents,** toothache; **coup de d.,** bite; *F:* **avoir la d.,** to be hungry; **manger à belles dents,** to eat hungrily, with relish; **manger du bout des dents,** to pick at one's food; **rire du bout des dents,** to force a laugh; **avoir les dents longues,** (i) to be very hungry; (ii) to be greedy, grasping; **serrer les dents,** to grit one's teeth; **avoir, conserver, garder, une d. contre qn,** to have a grudge against s.o.; **ce bruit agace les dents,** this noise sets one's teeth on edge; **parler entre ses dents,** to mumble; to mutter; **être sur les dents,** (i) to be worn out; (ii) to be very busy, overworked; (*b*) **d. d'éléphant,** elephant's tusk. **2.** tooth (of comb, saw); cog (of wheel); prong (of fork); (jagged) peak (of mountain); **en dents de scie,** serrated, jagged; **roue à dents,** cogged wheel.
dentaire [dɑ̃tɛr] *a.* (*a*) *Anat:* dental, dentary (pulp, etc.); (*b*) **l'art d.,** dentistry; **prothèse d.,** denture.
dental, aux [dɑ̃tal, -o] *Ling:* **1.** *a.* dental (consonant). **2.** *n.f.* **dentale,** dental consonant.
dent-de-lion [dɑ̃d(ə)ljɔ̃] *n.f. Bot:* dandelion; *pl. dents-de-lion.*
dent-de-loup [dɑ̃dlu] *n.f. Aut:* ratchet tooth, catch; *pl. dents-de-loup.*
denté [dɑ̃te] *a.* cogged, toothed (wheel); dentate (leaf); **roue dentée,** cogwheel.
dentelé [dɑ̃tle] *a.* jagged, notched, indented; serrated (leaf); scalloped (design); perforated (stamp).
denteler [dɑ̃tle] *v.tr.* **(je dentelle; je dentellerai)** to notch, jag, indent; to pink (out) (leather); to perforate (postage stamp).
dentelle [dɑ̃tɛl] *n.f.* (*a*) lace; **d. à l'aiguille, au point,** point lace; **d. aux fuseaux,** pillow lace; (*b*) wrought ironwork, sculpture, etc. (that has the appearance of lace); (*c*) **crêpe d.,** very thin pancake, crêpe.
dentellerie [dɑ̃tɛlri] *n.f.* lacemaking; lace manufacture.
dentellier, -ière [dɑ̃tɛlje, -jɛr] **1.** *a.* lace (industry, etc.). **2.** (*a*) *n.* lacemaker; (*b*) *n.f.* **dentellière,** lacemaking machine.
dentelure [dɑ̃tlyr] *n.f.* denticulation, indentation; serration (of leaf); perforation (at edge of postage stamp); (jagged) mountain peaks.
dentier [dɑ̃tje] *n.m.* set of false teeth, denture.
dentifrice [dɑ̃tifris] **1.** *n.m.* toothpaste, toothpowder; mouthwash. **2.** *a.* **pâte d.,** toothpaste; **eau d.,** mouthwash.
dentine [dɑ̃tin] *n.f. Anat:* dentine.
dentiste [dɑ̃tist] *n.m. & f.* dentist; **chirurgien d.,** dental surgeon.
dentition [dɑ̃tisjɔ̃] *n.f.* dentition. **1.** (*a*) cutting of teeth; teething; (*b*) **d. définitive, permanente,** permanent teeth. **2.** arrangement of the teeth.
denture [dɑ̃tyr] *n.f.* **1.** set of (natural) teeth. **2.** set of false teeth, denture. **3.** *Mec.E:* teeth, cogs, gearing.
dénucléarisation [denyklearizasjɔ̃] *n.f.* denuclearization.
dénucléariser [denyklearize] *v.tr.* to denuclearize.
dénudation [denydasjɔ̃] *n.f.* denudation, laying bare, stripping.
dénudé [denyde] *a.* bare (countryside); stripped, bare (tree, etc.); bald (head); *Elcs:* bare (wire).
dénuder [denyde] *v.tr.* **1.** to denude, to lay bare, strip; (*of dress*) to leave bare; **d. un arbre de son écorce,** to strip the bark off a tree. **2. se d.** (*a*) to grow bare; (*b*) to strip (naked).
dénué [denɥe] *a.* (*a*) **d. d'argent,** without money, out of cash; (*b*) **d. de sens, de raison,** senseless; **d. d'intelligence,** unintelligent.
dénuement [denymɑ̃] *n.m.* destitution, penury, need; **être dans le d.,** to be destitute, poverty stricken; **d. moral,** moral deprivation.
dénuer (se) [sədenɥe] *Lit:* to deprive oneself (**de,** of); **se d. de ses biens,** to part with all one's possessions.
dénutrition [denytrisjɔ̃] *n.f. Med:* malnutrition.
déodorant [deɔdɔrɑ̃] *a. & n.m. Toil:* deodorant.
déodoriser [deɔdɔrize] *v.tr.* to deodorize.
dépannage [depanaʒ] *n.m.* (*a*) (emergency) repairs (to engine, etc.), *U.S:* troubleshooting; road repairs (to car); **service de d.,** breakdown service; (*b*) helping (s.o.) out.
dépanner [depane] *v.tr.* (*a*) to repair, do running repairs on (broken-down engine, car, etc.); *U.S:* to troubleshoot; **il m'a dépanné,** he got my car, T.V., etc. going again; (*b*) to help (s.o.) out, to get (s.o.) out of a hole.
dépanneur [depanœr] *n.m.* breakdown mechanic; (television) repairman; *U.S:* troubleshooter.
dépanneuse [depanøz] *n.f. Aut:* breakdown van, lorry, *U.S:* wrecker.
dépaquetage [depaktaʒ] *n.m.* unpacking (of goods).
dépaqueter [depakte] *v.tr.* (*conj. like* PAQUETER) to unpack (goods, etc.).
dépareillé [depareje] *a.* odd, incomplete, unpaired; *Com:* **articles dépareillés,** oddments, job lot.
déparier [deparje] *v.tr.* (*impf. & pr.sub.* **n. dépariions, v. dépariiez**) to remove one of a pair of, to spoil a pair of (objects); **gant déparié,** odd glove.
déparler [deparle] *v.i.* to talk nonsense; to become incoherent, inarticulate.
départ [depar] *n.m.* **1.** *O:* division, separation, sorting (out); **faire le d. entre qch. et qch.,** to sort out sth. from sth., to discriminate between sth. and sth. **2.** (*a*) departure (of person, vehicle, etc.); sailing (of ship); start (of race, etc.); **dès son d. j'ai rangé sa chambre,** as soon as he had gone I tidied his room; **au d.,** at the outset; **point de d.,** starting point; **être sur le d.,** to be on the point of leaving; **produit de d.,**

original material (of an experiment); **excursions au d. de Chamonix,** trips (leaving) from Chamonix; **exiger le d. d'un employé,** to insist on the dismissal of an employee; *Sp:* **d. arrêté,** standing start; **d. lancé,** flying start; **faux d.,** false start; **donner le d.,** to start the race; *Golf:* **(tertre de) d.,** tee; *Com:* **prix d. usine,** prices ex works; (*at auction*) **prix de d.,** upset price. **3.** (*a*) *Rail:* departure platform; (*b*) *Sp:* starting post; (*c*) **d. d'escalier,** foot of stairs.

départager [departaʒe] *v.tr.* (*conj. like* PARTAGER) to decide between, to settle (opinions, etc.); *Lit:* to separate; **d. les votes,** to give the casting vote.

département [departəmɑ̃] *n.m. Adm:* (*a*) department, ministry; *F:* **cela n'est pas dans mon d.,** that is not in my line, not within my province; (*b*) subdivision (of France) administered by a prefect; department.

départemental, -aux [departəmɑ̃tal, -o] *a.* departmental; *a. & n.f.* **(route) départementale** = secondary, B, road.

départir [departir] *v.tr.* (*conj. like* PARTIR, *occ. like* FINIR) **1.** to distribute, dispense, deal out (favours, etc.). **2. se d. de qch.,** to abandon, give up, sth.

dépassé [depase] *a.* out of date; obsolete.

dépassement [depasmɑ̃] *n.m.* **1.** surpassing (of oneself); overstepping (one's credit, etc.). **2.** *Aut:* overtaking; **d. interdit,** no overtaking.

dépasser [depase] *v.tr.* **1.** (*a*) to pass beyond, go beyond (s.o., sth.); to overrun (signal, etc.); **d. le but,** to overshoot the mark; **d. les bornes,** (i) to overstep the bounds, the mark, to overdo it; (ii) to be beyond all bounds; **il a dépassé la trentaine,** he has turned thirty, is over thirty; (*b*) **d. qn (à la course, etc.),** to overtake, outrun, outstrip, s.o.; *Aut:* **il est interdit de d. sur ce pont,** no overtaking on this bridge. **2. d. qch en hauteur,** to top sth.; **d. qn de la tête,** to stand a head taller than s.o.; **cette maison dépasse l'alignement,** this house projects beyond the building line; **votre jupon dépasse,** your petticoat is showing; **cela dépasse ma compétence,** it lies beyond, outside, my competence; **cela dépasse mon entendement, cela me dépasse,** it is beyond me; it goes over my head; **son mouchoir dépasse de sa poche,** his handkerchief is sticking out of his pocket; **je suis dépassé par les événements,** things are getting too much for me. **3.** to exceed; **d. son congé,** to overstay one's leave; **d. la limite de vitesse,** to exceed the speed limit; **le prix ne doit pas d. dix francs,** the price must not exceed ten francs; **toutes ces voitures dépassent nos moyens,** all these cars are beyond our means; **ne pas d. la dose prescrite,** do not exceed the stated dose. **4. se d.,** to surpass oneself.

dépaver [depave] *v.tr.* to take up the paving from (yard, street).

dépaysé [depeize] *a.* out of one's element; **je me sens d.,** I feel strange, like a fish out of water; I don't feel at home.

dépaysement [depeizmɑ̃] *n.m.* disorientation (of s.o.).

dépayser [depeize] *v.tr.* to remove (s.o.) from his usual surroundings, from his element; to disorientate (s.o.).

dépeçage [depəsaʒ], **dépècement** [depɛsmɑ̃] *n.m.* cutting up (of a slaughtered, hunted, animal); **le dépècement du pays fut complété par les barbares,** the barbarians completed the dismemberment of the country.

dépecer [depəse] *v.tr.* **(je dépèce, n. dépeçons; je dépècerai)** (*a*) to dismember, to cut up (carcass); to carve, cut up (fowl); to flense (whale); **le lion dépèce sa proie,** the lion tears its prey; (*b*) to dismember (territory).

dépeceur, -euse [depəsœr, -øz] *n.* cutter up (of carcass, etc.); **d. (de baleines),** flenser.

dépêche [depɛʃ] *n.f.* (*a*) (official) dispatch, message; (*b*) **d. (télégraphique),** telegram; *F:* wire.

dépêcher [depeʃe] *v.tr.* **1.** to dispatch; to do (sth.) quickly; **d. une besogne,** to dispatch, rush, a job. **2. d. un courrier, un messager,** to dispatch a messenger. **3. se d.,** to hurry; to be quick; **dépêchez-vous!** hurry up! get a move on! buck up! quick! **se d. de faire qch.,** to be quick to do sth.; **dépêchez-vous de guérir,** get well soon; **se d. de rentrer,** to hurry home.

dépeigner [depeɲe] *v.tr.* **d. qn,** to ruffle s.o.'s hair; to make s.o.'s hair untidy; **elle est toute dépeignée,** her hair's uncombed, she hasn't combed her hair.

dépeindre [depɛ̃dr̥] *v.tr.* (*conj. like* PEINDRE) to depict, picture, describe (s.o., sth.).

dépelotonner [deplɔtɔne] *v.tr.* to unwind (ball of wool, etc.).

dépenaillé [depnaje] *a.* ragged, tattered, torn; in rags, in tatters.

dépendance [depɑ̃dɑ̃s] *n.f.* **1.** dependence (of sth. on sth.). **2.** (*a*) dependency (of a country); (*b*) *pl.* outbuildings. **3.** dependence, subjection, subordination; **être sous la d. de qn,** to be under s.o.'s domination, control.

dépendant [depɑ̃dɑ̃] *a.* **1.** dependent; **fonctions dépendantes l'une de l'autre,** functions dependent on each other, interdependent functions. **2.** dependent, subordinate; **être d. de qn,** to be dependent on s.o.

dépendre¹ [depɑ̃dr̥] *v.tr.* to take down (hanging object).

dépendre² *v.i.* to depend. **1. d. de qn, de qch.,** to depend on s.o., on sth.; **tout dépend des circonstances,** everything depends on the circumstances; **ces événements ne dépendent pas de nous,** these events are not within our control; **il dépend de vous de le faire,** it lies, rests, with you to do it; **cela dépend,** that depends, we shall see; maybe; *F:* **ça dépend s'il est marié,** it depends whether he's married. **2.** (*a*) (*of land, etc.*) to be a dependency (**de,** of) to appertain to, belong to (the Crown); (*b*) (*of ship*) to hail (from a port). **3.** to be subordinate, subject (**de,** to); to be under (s.o.'s) domination; **je ne dépends pas de lui,** I don't take orders from him; **ne d. que de soi,** to be one's own boss.

dépens [depɑ̃] *n.m.pl.* **1.** *Jur:* costs; *Com:* cost, expenses; **être condamné aux d.,** to be ordered to pay costs. **2.** *prep. phr.* **aux d. de,** at the expense of (s.o., sth.); **s'amuser aux d. de ses études,** to enjoy oneself at the expense of one's studies; **il apprit à ses d. que . . .,** he learnt to his cost that . . ..

dépense [depɑ̃s] *n.f.* **1.** expenditure, expense, outlay (of money); **dépenses du ménage,** household expenses; **dépenses courantes,** current expenditures, expenses; **faire des dépenses,** to incur expenses; **faire qch. au prix de dépenses énormes,** to do sth. at enormous cost; **je n'aurais pas dû faire cette d.,** I shouldn't have spent that money; **faire trop de d.,** to spend too much (money); **se mettre en d.,** (i) to incur expense; (ii) *F:* to put oneself to a great deal of trouble; **on ne regardait pas à la d.,** there was no stinting; they didn't mind the cost, they spared no expense; **faire de folles dépenses,** to spend money extravagantly; **recettes et dépenses,** receipts and expenditure; **dépenses publiques,** public spending. **2.** *Tchn:* **d. d'essence,** petrol, *U.S:* gas, consumption; **d. à vide,** wasted energy. **3.** bursary.

dépenser [depɑ̃se] *v.tr.* **1.** to spend, lay out (money); **il dépense peu en livres,** he doesn't spend much on books; **d. sans compter,** to spend lavishly, to be free with one's money. **2.** to spend, consume (time, energy, etc.); **d. sa salive,** to talk a lot. **3. se d.,** to exert oneself; **se d. pour qn,** to spare no trouble on s.o.'s behalf; **se d. en démarches inutiles,** to waste one's energies in useless activities.

dépensier, -ière [depɑ̃sje, -jɛr] **1.** *n.* bursar (of convent). **2.** (*a*) *a.* extravagant, thriftless; (*b*) *n.* spendthrift.

déperdition [depɛrdisjɔ̃] *n.f.* waste, wastage, destruction (of tissue, etc.); loss (of heat, energy).

dépérir [deperir] *v.i.* to waste away, pine, dwindle; (*of health*) to decline; (*of flowers*) to wither, decay; (*of race*) to die out; (*of business*) to go downhill.

dépérissement [deperismɑ̃] *n.m.* declining, pining, wasting away; withering, decay (of tree, etc.); dying out (of race); decline (of business).

dépersonnalisation [depɛrsɔnalizasjɔ̃] *n.f.* depersonalization.

dépersonnaliser [depɛrsɔnalize] *v.tr.* **1.** to depersonalize. **2. se d.,** to lose one's personality, one's character.

dépêtrer [depetre] *v.tr.* **1.** to extricate, free (s.o.) (from entanglement); **d. qn d'une mauvaise affaire,** to get s.o. out of a scrape. **2. se d.,** get out of a scrape; **se d. de qn,** to get rid of s.o., to shake s.o. off.

dépeuplement [depœpləmɑ̃] *n.m.* depopulation (of country, etc.); unstocking (of pond); thinning, clearing (of forest).

dépeupler [depœple] *v.tr.* (*a*) to depopulate (country, etc.); to unstock (pond); (*b*) **se d.,** to thin, clear (forest); to become depopulated.

déphasage [defɑzaʒ] *n.m.* **1.** *El:* phase displacement; dephasing; difference in phase; **d. en avant,** (phase) lead; **d. en arrière,** lag. **2.** disorientation (of s.o.).

déphasé [defɑze] *a.* **1.** *El:* (*of current*) out of phase; **d. en arrière,** lagging (current); **d. en avant,** leading (current). **2.** (*of pers.*) disoriented; out of touch.

déphaser [defɑze] *v.tr.* **1.** *El:* to dephase (current). **2.** to disorientate (s.o.).

dépiauter [depjote] *v.tr.* *F:* to skin, flay (rabbit, etc.); **d. un texte,** to pull a text to pieces.

dépilation [depilasjɔ̃] *n.f.* (*a*) removal of (superfluous) hair; (*b*) loss of hair.

dépilatoire [depilatwar] *a.* *Toil:* depilatory; **crème d.,** hair removing cream.

dépiler [depile] *v.tr.* (*a*) to remove (superfluous) hair from (face, etc.); (*b*) to cause loss of hair; (*c*) *Leath:* to grain (skin).

dépiquage [depikaʒ] *n.m.* *Agr:* treading out (of corn).

dépiquer[1] [depike] *v.tr.* **1.** *Agr:* to tread out (corn). **2.** *Hort:* to transplant (shoots).

dépiquer[2] *v.tr.* to unstitch, unpick (dress, etc.).

dépistage [depistaʒ] *n.m.* tracking down, detection (of criminal, etc.); (early) detection, screening (of disease, virus, etc.).

dépister [depiste] *v.tr.* **1.** to track down (game, criminal); to detect (a disease). **2.** to put (hounds) off the scent; to throw (s.o.) off the scent; **il a dépisté la police,** he gave the police the slip.

dépit [depi] *n.m.* **1.** spite, resentment, chagrin; **par d.,** out of spite; **pleurer de d.,** to cry with vexation. **2. en d. de,** in spite of, in defiance of; **en d. du bon sens,** (i) contrary to common sense; (ii) very badly; **en d. de ce que** + *ind.*, in spite of the fact that . . ..

dépiter [depite] *v.tr.* **1.** to vex, upset (s.o.), to cause (s.o.) annoyance; **je l'ai dit pour la d.,** I said it to spite her. **2. se d.,** to take offence, to be annoyed.

déplacé [deplase] *a.* **1.** out of its place; displaced (heart, etc.). **2.** out of place, misplaced, ill-timed; **observation déplacée,** unwarranted, uncalled-for, remark. **3.** *Pol:* **personne déplacée,** displaced person.

déplacement [deplasmɑ̃] *n.m.* **1.** displacement, moving, shifting (of furniture, heart, etc.); transfer (of official); *Med:* **d. de vertèbre,** slipped disc. **2.** (*a*) change of location, of site, of position; *Mil:* change of station (of troops); (*b*) travelling; moving, movement; journey; **être en d.,** to be on a (business) trip; **frais de d.,** travelling expenses. **3.** (*a*) **d. d'un navire,** displacement of a ship; **d. en charge,** displacement loaded, load displacement; (*b*) **d. d'air,** air displacement.

déplacer [deplase] *v.tr.* **(je déplaçai(s); n. déplaçons) 1.** displace, shift (an object); to change the place of (s.o., sth.); **meubles difficiles à d.,** furniture difficult to move; **d. un fonctionnaire,** to transfer a civil servant; **d. la question,** to shift one's ground. **2.** to oust, take the place of (s.o.). **3. ce navire déplace dix mille tonneaux,** this ship has a displacement of ten thousand tons. **4. se d.** (*a*) to change one's place, to move (around); to walk; (*b*) to move about, to travel; (*c*) to get out of place, to shift; to be displaced.

déplafonner [deplafɔne] *v.tr.* to remove the upper limit, the ceiling (of prices).

déplaire [deplɛr] *v.i.* (*conj. like* PLAIRE) **1.** (*a*) to displease; **d. à qn,** (i) to displease, offend, s.o.; (ii) to fail to please s.o., to be displeasing to s.o.; **odeur qui déplaît,** offensive, disagreeable, smell; **tu lui déplais,** he dislikes you; **il me déplaît de le faire,** I don't like doing it; **cela ne me déplairait pas,** I wouldn't mind (it); (*b*) **il a tout fait pour nous déplaire,** he has been utterly disagreeable; (*c*) *impers.* **n'en déplaise à la compagnie,** with all due respect to those present; **n'en déplaise à votre Altesse!** may it please your Highness! **ne vous en déplaise,** whether you like it or not. **2. se d.,** to be displeased, dissatisfied; **il se déplaît à Paris,** he doesn't like Paris; he dislikes living in Paris.

déplaisant [deplɛzɑ̃] *a.* unpleasant, disagreeable.

déplaisir [deplezir] *n.m.* displeasure, annoyance.

déplantage [deplɑ̃taʒ] *n.m.*, **déplantation** [deplɑ̃tasjɔ̃] *n.f.* digging up (of plant); transplanting.

déplanter [deplɑ̃te] *v.tr.* to take up, dig up (plant); to transplant.

déplantoir [deplɑ̃twar] *n.m.* hand fork.

déplâtrage [deplɑtraʒ] *n.m.* **1.** stripping of plaster (from wall, etc.). **2.** taking (limb) out of plaster.

déplâtrer [deplɑtre] *v.tr.* **1.** to strip plaster from (wall, etc.). **2.** to take (limb) out of plaster.

dépliage [deplijaʒ] *n.m.* unfolding, opening out.

dépliant [deplijɑ̃] **1.** *a.* extendable (sofa, etc.) **2.** *n.m.* (*a*) folding album; (*b*) folder, brochure; (*c*) fold-out page.

dépliement [deplimɑ̃] *n.m.* = DÉPLIAGE.

déplier [deplije] *v.tr.* (*pr.sub.* & *impf.* **n. dépliions, v. dépliiez) 1.** to unfold, open out, spread out (newspaper, handkerchief, etc.); **d. sa marchandise,** to unpack, spread out, one's wares. **2. se d.,** to unfold, to open out.

déplissage [deplisaʒ] *n.m.* taking the pleats out, smoothing out (of material, etc.).

déplisser [deplise] *v.tr.* (*a*) to take the pleats out of, to smooth out (material, etc.); (*b*) (*of material, etc.*) **se d.,** to come unpleated, to lose its pleats.

déploiement [deplwamɑ̃] *n.m.* **1.** (*a*) spreading out, unfolding (of wings, etc.); unfurling (of flag); (*b*) deployment (of troops, ships, etc.). **2.** display (of forces, of courage); display, show (of goods, etc.).

déplombage [deplɔ̃baʒ] *n.m.* **1.** removal of seal (from electricity meter, parcel, etc.). **2.** removal of filling (from tooth).

déplomber [deplɔ̃be] *v.tr.* **1.** to remove the seal from (electricity meter, parcel, etc.). **2.** to remove the filling from (tooth).

déplorable [deplɔrabl̩] *a.* (*a*) deplorable, regrettable (incident, etc.); (*b*) deplorable, disgraceful (behaviour, etc.).

déplorablement [deplɔrabləmɑ̃] *adv.* deplorably; disgracefully.
déplorer [deplɔre] *v.tr.* to deplore, lament, regret deeply (sth.); **d. la mort de qn,** to grieve over, to mourn, s.o.'s death.
déployer [deplwaje] *v.tr.* **(je déploie, n. déployons; je déploierai) 1.** to unfold, open out (newspaper, etc.); to unfurl (flag); to spread (sails, wings); to deploy (troops); **rire à gorge déployée,** to roar with laughter. **2.** to display, show (goods, patience, etc.). **3. se d.** (*a*) (*of sail, flag*) to unfurl; (*b*) *Mil: Navy:* to deploy.
déplumé [deplyme] *a.* (*a*) featherless; (*b*) *F:* bald.
déplumer [deplyme] *v.tr.* **1.** to pluck (chicken, etc.) **2. se d.** (*a*) (*of bird*) to moult; (*b*) *F:* (*of pers.*) to go bald.
dépolarisant [depɔlarizɑ̃] *Ph:* **1.** *a.* depolarizing. **2.** *n.m.* depolarizer.
dépolarisation [depɔlarizasjɔ̃] *n.f. Ph:* depolarization.
dépolariser [depɔlarize] *v.tr. Ph:* to depolarize.
dépoli [depɔli] *a.* frosted (glass).
dépolir [depɔlir] *v.tr.* **1.** to dull, tarnish (surface). **2.** to frost (glass). **3. se d.,** to become dull; to tarnish.
dépolissage [depɔlisaʒ] *n.m.*, **dépolissement** [depɔlismɑ̃] *n.m.* **1.** dulling, tarnishing (of surface). **2.** frosting (of glass).
déponent [depɔnɑ̃] *a. & n.m. Gram:* deponent (verb).
dépopulation [depɔpylasjɔ̃] *n.f.* depopulation.
déportation [depɔrtasjɔ̃] *n.f.* **1.** (*a*) deportation (of undesirable alien, etc.); (*b*) transportation (of convict). **2.** internment (in concentration camp).
déporté, -ée [depɔrte] *n.* **1.** deportee. **2.** internee, prisoner (in concentration camp).
déportement [depɔrtəmɑ̃] *n.m.* **1. déportements,** misbehaviour, misconduct, excesses, dissolute life. **2.** *Aut:* skidding, swerving.
déporter[1] [depɔrte] *v.tr.* **1.** (*a*) to deport (undesirable alien); (*b*) to transport (convict). **2.** to send (prisoner) to concentration camp.
déporter[2] *v.tr.* to carry off course; **voiture déportée par la violence du vent,** car blown off the road by the violence of the wind.
déposant, -ante [depozɑ̃, -ɑ̃t] *n.* **1.** depositor (of money in bank, etc.). **2.** *Jur:* deponent, witness.
dépose [depoz] *n.f.* lifting, taking up (of carpet, etc.); removal (of engine, etc.).
déposer[1] [depoze] *v.tr.* **1.** to lift, take up (carpet etc.). **2. d. les rideaux,** to take down the curtains.
déposer[2] *v.tr.* **1.** (*a*) to lay, set, put (sth.) down; **ma voiture vous déposera à l'hotel,** my car will set you down, *F:* will drop you, at the hotel; **d. sa carte chez qn,** to leave one's card on s.o.; *P.N:* **défense de d. des ordures,** no tipping; **d. les armes,** to lay down one's arms, to surrender; (*b*) (*of liquid*) to deposit (sediment); *v.i.* **il faut laisser au liquide le temps de d.,** we must allow the liquid some time to settle. **2.** (*a*) to deposit, lodge (sth.) in a safe place; **d. son argent à la banque,** to deposit one's money at the bank; (*b*) *Com:* to register (a trademark); **marque déposée,** registered trademark; (*c*) *Jur:* **d. une plainte contre qn,** to prefer a charge, lodge a complaint, against s.o.; *Com:* **d. son bilan,** to file one's petition (in bankruptcy); (*d*) **d. un projet de loi,** to table, bring in, a bill; (*e*) *v.i. Jur:* **d. (en justice),** to give evidence (**contre,** against); to depose. **3.** to depose (monarch, etc.). **4.** (*of matter*) **se d.,** to settle, to form a deposit.
dépositaire [depozitɛr] *n.m. & f.* (*a*) depositary, trustee; possessor (of secret, etc.); **d. de valeurs,** holder of securities on trust; (*b*) *Com:* sole agent (for products); **d. de journaux,** newsagent.
déposition [depozisjɔ̃] *n.f.* **1.** *Jur:* deposition; statement (made by witness); **recueillir une d.,** to take s.o.'s evidence. **2.** deposing (of monarch). **3.** *Art:* **D. de croix,** Deposition.
déposséder [depɔsede] *v.tr.* **(je dépossède, n. dépossédons; je déposséderai)** to dispossess (**de,** of); to oust (**de,** from); **d. qn de sa place,** to deprive s.o. of, oust s.o. from, his seat.
dépossession [depɔsɛsjɔ̃] *n.f.* dispossession; deprivation.
dépôt [depo] *n.m.* **1.** (*a*) depositing; **d. d'une gerbe,** laying of a wreath; **banque de d.** = deposit bank; *Com:* **d. d'une marque de fabrique,** registration of a trademark; *Jur:* **d. légal,** registration of copyright; *Pol:* **d. d'un projet de loi,** bringing in, tabling, of a bill; (*b*) deposit; **d. sacré,** sacred trust; **d. bancaire,** bank deposit; **compte de d.,** deposit account; (*c*) **avoir, détenir, qch. en d.,** to hold sth. in trust; **marchandises en d.,** (i) *Cust:* goods in bond; (ii) *Com:* goods on sale or return. **2.** (*a*) depository, repository, store(house), depot; *Rail:* engine shed; **il a passé la nuit au d.,** he spent the night in jail; *Jur:* **mandat de d.,** committal, commitment (of prisoner); **d. de(s) marchandises,** goods depot; warehouse; **d. de bois,** timber yard; **d. d'essence,** petrol storage depot; *Rail: etc:* **d. de(s) bagages,** left-luggage office; (*b*) **d. d'ordures,** rubbish dump, tip. **3.** (*a*) deposition, settling (of precipitate, mud, etc.); (*b*) deposit, sediment; silt (of harbour, etc.); fur (in kettle); scale (in boiler).
dépotage [depɔtaʒ] *n.m.*, **dépotement** [depɔtmɑ̃] *n.m.* **1.** decanting (of liquid). **2.** repotting; planting out.
dépoter [depɔte] *v.tr.* **1.** to decant (liquid). **2.** to repot (plants); to plant out (seedlings).
dépotoir [depɔtwar] *n.m.* (*a*) rubbish tip, dump; (*b*) (refuse) disposal plant; sewage works.
dépouille [depuj] *n.f.* **1.** skin, hide (taken from animal); slough (of snake); **d. (mortelle),** (mortal) remains. **2.** (*a*) *pl.* spoils, booty (of war); (*b*) effects, clothes (of deceased person). **3.** *Mec.E:* relief, clearance (of drill, of machine tool).
dépouillé [depuje] *a.* bare; bald (style, etc.); **d. de,** lacking in, deprived of.
dépouillement [depujmɑ̃] *n.m.* **1.** deprivation (of s.o.) of his belongings; **d. volontaire de ses biens,** relinquishment, renouncement, of one's property. **2. d. d'un rapport,** examination, analysis, of a report; **d. des votes, d'un scrutin,** counting of the votes (at ballot, election); **d. du courrier,** going through the mail.
dépouiller [depuje] *v.* **I.** *v.tr.* **1.** (*a*) to skin (rabbit, etc.); **le vent a dépouillé les arbres de leurs feuilles,** the wind stripped the trees of their leaves; (*b*) to cast off, lay aside; **d. ses vêtements,** to take off one's clothes, to strip. **2.** to deprive, strip, despoil; **d. qn de ses habits,** to strip, divest, s.o. of his clothes; **d. qn de ses droits,** to deprive s.o. of his rights; **d. un pays,** to plunder a country. **3. d. un inventaire,** to examine, analyse, an inventory; **d. le scrutin,** to count the votes; **d. le courrier,** to open, go through, the mail. **4.** *Mec.E:* to back off, give clearance to (drill, etc.). **II. se dépouiller 1.** (*of insect, snake*) to cast (off) its skin, its slough; (*of tree*) to shed its leaves; (*of wine*) to lose colour. **2. se d. de qch.,** to deprive, divest, rid, oneself of sth.; **se d. de ses vêtements,** to strip off one's clothes; *F:* to strip.
dépourvu [depurvy] *a.* short, devoid (**de,** of); **d. d'intelligence,** lacking, devoid of, intelligence; **pays d. d'arbres,** treeless country; **être d. (d'argent),** to be without money, penniless, short of cash; **être pris au d.,** to be caught off one's guard.
dépoussiérage [depusjeraʒ] *n.m. Ind:* vacuum cleaning; freeing from dust; dust removal.
dépoussiérer [depusjere] *v.tr. Ind:* to vacuum clean; to free from dust, to remove the dust.

dépoussiéreur [depusjerœr] *n.m. Ind:* dust remover; vacuum cleaner.
dépravant [depravɑ̃] *a.* depraving.
dépravation [depravasjɔ̃] *n.f.* (moral) depravity.
dépravé, -ée [deprave] **1.** *a.* depraved. **2.** *n.* degenerate; depraved person.
dépraver [deprave] *v.tr.* to deprave; **se d.,** to become depraved.
dépréciateur, -trice [depresjatœr, -tris] *n.* disparager, belittler (of s.o.'s character, etc.).
dépréciatif, -ive [depresjatif, -iv] *a. Ling:* pejorative (expression, etc.); **mot d.,** derogatory word.
dépréciation [depresjasjɔ̃] *n.f.* **1.** depreciation; fall in value. **2.** (*a*) underrating, undervaluing; (*b*) disparagement.
déprécier [depresje] *v.tr.* (*impf. & pr.sub.* **n. dépréciions, v. dépréciiez) I. 1.** to depreciate (coinage, etc.). **2.** (*a*) to underrate, undervalue (goods, merits); (*b*) to disparage, belittle (s.o.); *F:* to run down (s.o., book). **II. se déprécier 1.** (*a*) (*of values*) to depreciate, to fall; (*b*) (*of goods*) to depreciate, to fall in value. **2.** (*of pers.*) to belittle oneself.
déprédateur, -trice [depredatœr, -tris] **1.** *n.* (*a*) depredator, pillager; (*b*) embezzler. **2.** *a.* depredatory.
déprédation [depredasjɔ̃] *n.f.* **1.** depredation, pillaging. **2.** misappropriation (of funds, etc.); embezzlement.
déprendre (se) [sədeprɑ̃dr̥] *v.pr.* (*conj. like* PRENDRE) to detach oneself, to get free; **se d. d'une habitude,** to get out of a habit.
dépressif, -ive [depresif, -iv] *a.* depressive.
dépression [depresjɔ̃] *n.f.* depression. **1.** hollow, dip (in floor, ground); *Oc:* trough; *Astr:* dip (of horizon); *Artil:* **angle de d.,** angle of depression (of gun). **2.** (*a*) fall (in value); **d. économique,** economic depression, slump; (*b*) *Meteor:* **d. (barométrique),** (barometric) depression; low; trough. **3.** (mental) depression, dejection; *Med:* **d. nerveuse,** nervous breakdown.
dépressionnaire [depresjɔnɛr] *a. Meteor:* **zone d.,** depression, trough of low pressure.
déprimant [deprimɑ̃] *a. Med:* depressing; enervating.
déprime [deprim] *n.f. F:* **la d.,** the blues.
déprimé [deprime] *a.* depressed; (*a*) low, flat, flattened (surface, etc.); **front d.,** low forehead; (*b*) (*of pers.*) depressed, low.
déprimer [deprime] *v.tr.* (*a*) to depress lower (surface, etc.); (*b*) to enervate, debilitate; to lower (morale).
depuis [dəpɥi] *prep.* **1.** (*a*) (*of time*) since; for; **je ne suis pas sorti d. hier,** I have not been out since yesterday; **d. quand êtes-vous ici?** how long have you been here? **je suis ici d. trois jours,** I have been here for three days; **d. ce temps-là, d. lors,** since then, since that time; **je suis là d. le déjeuner,** I have been here ever since lunch; **d. quand est-il permis d'entrer sans frapper?** since when can you come in without knocking? **d. toujours,** right from the start, from the very beginning; (*b*) *adv.* since (then), since that time; afterwards, later; **je l'ai connu d.,** I made his acquaintance later; (*c*) *conj.phr.* **d. que** + *ind.*, since . . .; **nous ne l'avons pas vu d. qu'il est marié,** we haven't seen him since he was married. **2.** (*a*) (*of time, place, etc.*) from; **d. le matin jusqu'au soir,** from morning till night; **il ne m'a pas parlé d. Rouen,** he hasn't spoken to me since (we left) Rouen; (*b*) (*of order, quantity*) **chemises d. 30 F jusqu'à 150 F,** shirts from 30 to 150 francs. **3.** *W.Tel:* **concert transmis d. Londres,** concert broadcast from London.
dépuratif, -ive [depyratif, -iv] *a. & n.m. Med:* depurative.
dépuration [depyrasjɔ̃] *n.f.* depuration; cleansing (of blood); purification (of metal, etc.).
dépurer [depyre] *v.tr.* to depurate, cleanse, clear (the blood); to purify (metal, water).
députation [depytasjɔ̃] *n.f.* **1.** (*a*) deputing, delegating (of s.o.); (*b*) deputation, delegation. **2.** *Pol:* membership (of parliament); **candidat à la d.,** parliamentary candidate; **se présenter à la d.,** to stand, *U.S:* run, for parliament.
député [depyte] *n.m.* **1.** deputy, delegate. **2.** *Pol:* = Member of Parliament; **La Chambre des députés,** the Chamber of Deputies.
députer [depyte] *v.tr.* to depute (s.o.), to appoint (s.o.) as deputy, as delegate (**à, vers,** to).
der [dɛr] *n. F:* (*short for* **dernier, -ère**) **la d. des d.,** the war to end all wars.
déraciné [derasine] **1.** *a.* uprooted. **2.** *n.* exile; uprooted person.
déracinement [derasinmɑ̃] *n.m.* **1.** uprooting (of stump); eradication (of fault). **2.** uprooting (of pers.).
déraciner [derasine] *v.tr.* **1.** to uproot; to tear (tree, etc.) up by the roots. **2.** to eradicate (fault, abuse). **3.** to tear, uproot, (s.o.) from his homeland.
déraidir [derɛdir] *v.tr.* **1.** to unstiffen, take the stiffness out of (limb, material, etc.); to soften (s.o.'s character). **2. se d.** (*a*) (*of limb, material, etc.*) to lose its stiffness; (*b*) (*of pers.*) to unbend, to thaw.
déraillement [derɑjmɑ̃] *n.m. Rail:* derailment.
dérailler [derɑje] *v.i.* **1.** (*a*) (*of train, tram*) to become derailed; to leave the rails; **faire d. un train,** to derail a train; (*b*) (*of stylus*) to jump, leave, the sound groove; (*c*) *F:* (*of machine, etc.*) to be on the blink. **2.** *F:* (*of pers.*) to rave, to talk drivel.
dérailleur [derɑjœr] *n.m.* (*a*) *Rail:* derailer, derailing stop; (*b*) *Cy:* derailleur (gears).
déraison [derɛzɔ̃] *n.f.* unreasonableness; folly.
déraisonnable [derɛzɔnabl̥] *a.* unreasonable, irrational; senseless, foolish.
déraisonnablement [derɛzɔnabləmɑ̃] *adv.* unreasonably.
déraisonner [derɛzɔne] *v.i.* to talk nonsense; *F:* to rave.
dérangé [derɑ̃ʒe] *a.* (*of mind*) deranged, unbalanced; (*of stomach*) upset.
dérangement [derɑ̃ʒmɑ̃] *n.m.* derangement; (*a*) disarrangement, disorder (of books, furniture, etc.); (*b*) disturbance, trouble; **excusez-moi pour le d.,** I'm sorry to disturb, trouble, you; (*c*) disturbed, unsettled, state; upset; **d. du cerveau, de l'esprit,** mental derangement; **d. de l'intestin,** upset stomach, diarrhoea; (*d*) *El:* fault (in line, etc.); *Tp:* **la ligne est en d.,** the line is out of order, *U.S:* is in trouble.
déranger [derɑ̃ʒe] *v.tr.* (**je dérangeai(s); n. dérangeons) 1.** (*a*) to disarrange (papers, books, etc.); (*b*) to disturb, trouble; **excusez-moi de vous d.,** I'm sorry to disturb, trouble, you; **si cela ne vous dérange pas,** if it's no trouble to you, if that's all right by you; (*c*) to put (sth.) out of order, to upset (s.o.); **d. l'esprit de qn,** to disturb s.o.'s mind; **quelque chose lui a dérangé l'estomac,** something upset his stomach. **2. se d.,** to move; **ne vous dérangez pas pour moi,** (i) please don't move, (ii) please don't put yourself out on my account.
dérapage [derapaʒ] *n.m.* **1.** *Nau:* dragging (of anchor). **2.** (*a*) *Aut: etc:* skid(ding); **d. contrôlé,** controlled skid; (*b*) *Av:* sideslip; *Ski:* sideslip(ping).
déraper [derape] *v.tr. & i.* **1.** *Nau:* (*of anchor*) to drag, to pull out; (*of ship*) to drag its anchor. **2.** *Aut: etc:* to skid; *Av: Ski:* to sideslip.
dératé [derate] *a. F:* **courir comme un d.,** to run flat out.
dératisation [deratizasjɔ̃] *n.f.* extermination of rats.
dératiser [deratize] *v.tr.* to clear of rats.
derby [dɛrbi] *n.m.* (*a*) *Turf:* **le d. d'Epsom,** the Derby; (*b*) *Fb:* local derby.

derechef [dərəʃɛf] *adv. A: & Lit:* a second time, yet again, once more.

déréglé [deregle] *a.* **1.** (*of machine, clock, compass, etc.*) out of order; out of adjustment. **2.** upset (stomach); disordered (mind); irregular (pulse). **3.** wild, dissolute (life, etc.); immoderate (desires).

dérèglement [derɛgləmɑ̃] *n.m.* **1.** disordered state (of house, imagination, etc.); unsettled state (of weather); irregularity (of pulse); **d. de l'esprit,** mental derangement. **2.** dissoluteness.

dérégler [deregle] *v.tr.* **(je dérègle, n. déréglons; je déréglerai) 1.** to disturb (mechanism, etc.); to put (mechanism, etc.) out of order; to put out of balance. **2.** (*a*) to upset (pulse, stomach); to unsettle (mind, habits); (*b*) to make dissolute. **3. se d.,** (*of clock, etc.*) to go out of order, to go wrong; (*of pulse, stomach*) to be upset; (*of mind*) to become unsettled; (*of morals*) to become dissolute.

dérider [deride] *v.tr.* to remove the lines, the wrinkles, from (brow); *F:* to cheer (s.o.) up; to brighten (s.o.) up; **se d.,** to brighten up, cheer up.

dérision [derizjɔ̃] *n.f.* derision, mockery; **dire qch. par d.,** to say sth. derisively, in mockery, mockingly; **geste de d.,** derisive gesture.

dérisoire [derizwar] *a.* ridiculous, laughable (offer, etc.); paltry (salary, etc.); **vendre qch. à un prix d.,** to sell sth. at an absurdly low price.

dérivatif, -ive [derivatif, -iv] *a. & n.m.* derivative; derived (word); relief, distraction (**à, de,** from); **c'est un d. à sa douleur,** it takes his mind off his grief.

dérivation [derivasjɔ̃] *n.f.* **1.** (*a*) diversion, tapping (of watercourse); **canal de d.,** headrace, penstock; (*b*) *Med:* derivation (of blood, etc., from inflamed part); (*c*) branching off; *El:* shunt(ing), branching, tapping (of current); **monté en d.,** shunt connected. **2.** *Ling:* (*a*) derivation (of word); (*b*) *Mth:* derivation. **3.** *Nau: Av:* drift.

dérive [deriv] *n.f.* (*a*) *Nau:* drift, leeway; *Av:* drift; **angle de d.,** drift angle; **à la d., en d.,** adrift; **(quille de) d.,** (i) drop keel; centre board; (ii) *Av:* fin; (*b*) *Fig:* **tout va à la d.,** everything has been left to drift; (*c*) *Geog:* **d. des continents,** continental drift.

dérivé [derive] **1.** *a.* (*a*) derived, secondary (meaning, etc.); *Mth:* derived (function, curve); *Ch:* derived (product); (*b*) *El:* **courant d.,** shunt current. **2.** *n.* (*a*) *n.m. Ling: etc:* derivative; *Ch: Ind:* derivative; by-product; (*b*) *n.f. Mth:* **dérivée,** derivative.

dériver¹ [derive] **1.** *v.tr.* (*a*) to divert, tap, the course of (running water); *El:* to shunt, branch (current); (*b*) *Ling: Mth:* to derive. **2.** *v.i.* (*a*) (*of stream*) to be diverted, to flow (**de,** from); (*b*) **ce mot dérive du grec,** this word is derived from Greek.

dériver² *v.tr.* to unrivet.

dériver³ *v.i.* **1.** *Nau: Av:* to drift; **d. à vau-l'eau,** to drift down stream. **2.** to drift away (from subject, etc.).

dériveur [derivœr] *n.m. Nau:* **1.** storm sail. **2.** sailing dinghy (with centre board).

dérivomètre [derivɔmɛtr̥] *n.m. Av:* drift meter.

dermatite [dɛrmatit] *n.f. Med:* dermatitis.

dermatologie [dɛrmatɔlɔʒi] *n.f.* dermatology.

dermatologique [dɛrmatɔlɔʒik] *a.* dermatological.

dermatologiste [dɛrmatɔlɔʒist], **dermatologue** [dɛrmatɔlɔg] *n.m. & f.* dermatologist.

dermatose [dɛrmatoz] *n.f. Med:* dermatosis.

derme [dɛrm] *n.m. Anat:* derm; cutis, true skin.

dermique [dɛrmik] *a. Anat:* dermic, dermal.

dermite [dɛrmit] *n.f. Med:* = DERMATITE.

dernier, -ière [dɛrnje, -jɛr] *a. & n.* **1.** last, latest; (*a*) **au d. moment,** at the last (moment); **faire un d. effort,** to make a final effort; **mettre la dernière main à qch.,** to give, put, the finishing, the final, touches to sth.; **j'ai dépensé jusqu'à mon d. sou,** I've spent my last farthing; **les derniers préparatifs,** the final preparations; **je m'en souviendrai jusqu'à mon d. jour, jusqu'à ma dernière heure,** I shall remember it to my dying day; **il veut toujours avoir le d. mot,** he must always have the last word; **il est arrivé le d., bon d.,** he was the last to arrive; **au cours des dernières années,** over the past few years; **le d. roman de cet auteur,** this author's latest novel; **dernières nouvelles,** latest news; **la dernière mode, le d. cri,** the latest fashion, the latest thing; *St.Exch:* **d. cours,** closing price; (*b*) **le mois d.,** last month; **ces derniers temps,** lately; **les six derniers,** the last six; **le d. rang,** the last row; **d. paiement,** final payment; **d. délai pour l'inscription,** last date, deadline, for registering; **c'est notre petit d.,** he's our youngest (child); **le d. élève de la classe,** the bottom pupil in the form; **cela vient en d.,** that comes last; (*c*) **ce d. répondit . . .,** the latter answered . . . . **2.** (*a*) utmost, highest; **de la dernière importance,** of the utmost, greatest, importance; **au d. degré,** to the utmost, highest, degree; **il me déplaît au d. point,** I dislike him intensely; **dans la dernière misère,** in utmost poverty; in dire distress; (*b*) lowest, worst; **de d. ordre,** very inferior; **ça, c'est le d. de mes soucis,** that's the least of my worries; **on le traite comme le d. des derniers,** they treat him like dirt.

dernièrement [dɛrnjɛrmɑ̃] *adv.* lately, of late, recently.

dernier-né [dɛrnjene] *n.m.*, **dernière-née** [dɛrnjɛrne] *n.f.* last-born child; *pl. derniers-nés, dernières-nées.*

dérobade [derɔbad] *n.f.* **1.** evasion, avoidance (of s.o., sth.); side stepping. **2.** swerve, jib (of horse).

dérobé [derɔbe] *a.* **1.** (*a*) *Agr:* **culture dérobée,** catch, snatch, crop; (*b*) hidden, concealed, secret (staircase, door, etc.); *adv.phr.* **à la dérobée,** stealthily, secretly, on the sly; **regarder qn à la dérobée,** to steal a glance at s.o.; **sortir à la dérobée,** to steal out.

dérober [derɔbe] *v.* **I.** *v.tr.* **1.** (*a*) to steal, to make away with (sth.); **d. qch. à qn,** to filch sth. from s.o.; **d. un baiser,** to steal a kiss; (*b*) **d. qn au danger,** to rescue, save, s.o. from danger. **2.** to hide, conceal; **d. qch. à qn,** to hide sth. from s.o.; **ce mur dérobe la vue,** this wall hides the view. **II. se dérober 1.** (*a*) to escape, steal away, slip away (**à,** from); **se d. à l'étreinte de qn,** to slip out of s.o.'s arms; **se d. aux regards,** to escape observation, to avoid notice; **se d. à la curiosité,** to escape curiosity; **se d. à son devoir,** to evade, shirk, one's duty; **je le lui ai demandé, mais il s'est dérobé,** I asked him, but he avoided the issue; (*b*) (*of horse*) to swerve (at a jump); to jib; to refuse. **2.** to give way (**sous,** under); **ses genoux se dérobèrent sous lui,** his knees gave way beneath him.

dérogation [derɔgasjɔ̃] *n.f.* derogation, impairment (**à une loi,** of a law); **faire d. à l'usage,** to make a departure from custom; **par, en, d. à cette règle,** this rule notwithstanding.

dérogatoire [derɔgatwar] *a. Jur:* derogatory (clause).

déroger [derɔʒe] *v.i.* **(je dérogeai(s); n. dérogeons)** (*a*) **d. à l'usage, à la loi,** to depart from custom, from the law; **d. à un principe,** to waive a principle; (*b*) to derogate; *Hist:* **d. à noblesse,** to lose rank; **d. à son rang,** to lower, demean, oneself.

dérouillée [deruje] *n.f. P:* belting, thrashing.

dérouiller [deruje] **1.** *v.tr.* (*a*) to take, rub, the rust off (sth.); (*b*) **se d. les jambes,** to stretch one's legs; **se d. la mémoire,** to refresh one's memory; (*c*) *P:* to give (s.o.) a thrashing, to beat (s.o.) up. **2.** *v.i. P:* to catch it; **qu'est-ce qu'il a dérouillé!** he really had a hard time.

déroulage [derulaʒ], **déroulement** [derulmɑ̃] *n.m.* (*a*) unrolling; unwinding, uncoiling (of cable, etc.); (*b*) unfolding, development, progress (of plot, events).

dérouler [derule] *v.tr.* **1.** (*a*) to unroll (blind, etc.); to unwind, unreel, wind off, uncoil (cable, etc.); **le serpent a déroulé ses anneaux,** the snake uncoiled itself; (*b*) **d. ses plans à qn,** to unfold, make known one's plans, to s.o. **2. se d.** (*a*) (*of blind, etc.*) to come unrolled, to unroll; (*of cable, etc.*) to come unwound; (*of snake*) to uncoil; (*b*) to unfold, to develop; **le paysage se déroule devant nous,** the landscape unfolds, stretches out, before us; **les événements qui se déroulent à Paris,** the events that are taking place in Paris; **la manifestation s'est déroulée dans le calme,** the demonstration went off peacefully.

déroutant [derutɑ̃] *a.* confusing; disconcerting.

déroute [derut] *n.f.* (*a*) rout, disorderly retreat; **l'ennemi fut mis en d.,** the enemy was put to flight, was routed; (*b*) ruin, downfall (of family, etc.); (*c*) confusion; **mettre qn en d.,** to confuse s.o.

déroutement [derutmɑ̃] *n.m. Nau: Av:* rerouting, diversion.

dérouter [derute] *v.tr.* **1.** (*a*) to lead astray; **d. la police,** to throw the police off the scent; **d. les soupçons,** to throw people off the scent; (*b*) to divert, reroute (ship, aircraft, etc.), **2.** to confuse, baffle; **la question a dérouté le candidat,** the question nonplussed the candidate. **3. se d.,** to lose one's head, become confused.

derrick [dɛrik] *n.m. Petr:* derrick.

derrière [dɛrjɛr] **1.** *prep.* (*a*) behind, at the back of, in the rear of (s.o., sth.); *U.S:* the back of (sth.); **il s'est caché d. le rideau,** he hid behind the curtain; **il faut toujours être d. elle,** you always have to keep an eye on her, be behind her; **ne vous inquiétez pas, je suis d. vous,** don't worry, I'll back you up; (*b*) *Nau:* (i) abaft; (ii) astern of (ship). **2.** *adv.* (*a*) behind, at the back, in the rear; **laisser qn d.,** to leave s.o. behind; **attaquer qn par d.,** to attack s.o. from behind, from the rear; **cette robe s'attache par d.,** this dress does up at the back; **il a dû passer par d.,** he had to go round the back; **porte de d.,** back door; **pattes de d.,** hind legs; (*b*) *Nau:* (i) aft; (ii) astern. **3.** *n.m.* (*a*) back, rear (of building, etc.); **le d. de la tête,** the back of the head; **ma chambre donne sur le d.,** my room looks out on the back; (*b*) behind, backside, bottom; (*of animal*) hindquarters; **tomber sur le d.,** to fall on one's behind, to sit down suddenly.

derviche [dɛrviʃ] *n.m.* dervish; **d. tourneur,** dancing, whirling, dervish.

dès [dɛ] *prep.* since, from, as early as, as long ago as (a certain time); **d. sa jeunesse . . .,** from childhood . . .; **d. l'abord,** from the outset, from the (very) first; **d. maintenant, d. à présent,** already, henceforth, from now on; **d. 1840,** as far back as 1840; **d. le matin,** first thing in the morning, in the day; **d. son arrivée,** the minute, the moment, he arrives; **d. mon retour,** immediately on my return; **d. la porte il commença à crier,** he had no sooner reached the door than he began to shout; *conj.phr.* **d. que** + *ind.,* as soon as; *adv.phr.* **d. lors,** (i) from that time onwards, ever since (then); (ii) consequently; therefore; *conj.phr.* **d. lors que vous refusez,** since, seeing that, you refuse.

désabonner [dezabɔne] **1.** *v.tr.* **1. d. qn à une revue,** to cancel s.o.'s subscription to a magazine. **2. se d.,** to stop subscribing, to withdraw one's subscription (**à,** to).

désabusé [dezabyze] *a.* disillusioned, disenchanted (person, etc.); *n.* **un d.,** a disappointed man.

désabusement [dezabyzmɑ̃] *n.m.* **1.** disabusing, undeceiving. **2.** disillusionment.

désabuser [dezabyze] *v.tr.* to disillusion, undeceive (s.o.); to open (s.o.'s) eyes; **esprit désabusé du monde,** disillusioned mind.

désacclimater [dezaklimate] *v.tr.* to remove (s.o., sth.) from his, its, normal climate.

désaccord [dezakɔr] *n.m.* (*a*) disagreement, dissension; **être, se trouver, en d. avec qn sur qch.,** to disagree, to be at odds, at issue, with s.o. about sth.; **sujet de d.,** bone of contention; (*b*) clash (of interests, etc.); **il y a d. entre ses paroles et sa conduite,** his words are inconsistent, not in keeping, with his conduct; **d. entre la théorie et les faits,** discrepancy between the theory and the facts.

désaccordé [dezakɔrde] *a.* out of tune.

désaccorder [dezakɔrde] *v.tr.* **1.** to set (persons) at variance. **2.** *Mus:* to put (instrument) out of tune; **se d.,** to go out of tune.

désaccoupler [dezakuple] *v.tr.* **1.** to slip, uncouple (hounds, etc.). **2.** to uncouple (trucks, etc.); *El: Mec:* to disconnect.

désaccoutumance [dezakutymɑ̃s] *n.f. Lit:* **d. de qch.,** loss of the habit of, of familiarity with, sth.

désaccoutumer [dezakutyme] *v.tr.* to disaccustom (s.o. to sth.); **se d. de qch., de faire qch.** to get out of the habit of doing sth.

désaffectation [dezafɛktasjɔ̃] *n.f.* putting (of public building, etc.) to another purpose; closing down (of building); deconsecration, secularization (of church).

désaffecter [dezafɛkte] *v.tr.* to put (public building, etc.) to another purpose; to close down (building); **église désaffectée,** deconsecrated, secularized, church.

désagréable [dezagreabl̥] *a.* disagreeable, unpleasant (**à,** to); (*of pers.*) grumpy, surly; **odeur d.,** unpleasant, nasty, smell.

désagréablement [dezagreabləmɑ̃] *adv.* disagreeably, unpleasantly.

désagrégation [dezagregasjɔ̃] *n.f.* disintegration; breaking up.

désagréger [dezagreʒe] *v.tr.* **(je désagrège, n. désagrégeons; je désagrégeai(s); je désagrégerai)** to disintegrate; to break up; **se d.,** to break up.

désagrément [dezagremɑ̃] *n.m.* (source of) annoyance; unpleasant occurrence; trouble; **causer à qn du d., des désagréments,** to cause s.o. unpleasantness; to get s.o. into a scrape, into trouble.

désaimanter [dezɛmɑ̃te] *v.tr.* to demagnetize.

désaligné [dezaliɲe] *a.* out of alignment, out of line, disaligned.

désaltérant [dezalterɑ̃] *a.* thirst-quenching.

désaltérer [dezaltere] *v.tr.* **(je désaltère, n. désaltérons; je désaltérerai)** (*a*) to quench (s.o.'s) thirst; *v.i.* **le thé désaltère mieux qu'une boisson glacée,** tea is more thirst-quenching than an ice-cold drink; (*b*) **se d.,** to quench one's thirst; to have sth. to drink.

désamorçage [dezamɔrsaʒ] *n.m.* unpriming (of cartridge, fuse, etc.); defusing (of bomb, shell, etc.); running down (of dynamo).

désamorcer [dezamɔrse] *v.tr.* **(je désamorçai(s); n. désamorçons) 1.** (*a*) to unprime (cartridge, fuse, siphon, etc.); to defuse (bomb, shell, etc.); to drain (pump); (*b*) to render (sth.) harmless; to take the sting out of (sth.). **2. se d.,** (*of pump, etc.*) to fail, to run dry; (*of dynamo*) to run down.

désapparier [dezaparje] *v.tr.* (*a*) to remove one of a pair, to spoil a pair (of objects); (*b*) to separate (pair of birds, animals).

désappointement [dezapwɛ̃tmɑ̃] *n.m.* disappointment.

désappointer [dezapwɛ̃te] *v.tr.* to disappoint.

désapprobateur, -trice [dezaprɔbatœr, -tris] *a.* disapproving; **regard d.,** look of disapproval.

désapprobation [dezaprɔbasjɔ̃] *n.f.* disapproval, disapprobation (**de,** of).

désapprouver [dezapruve] *v.tr.* to disapprove, disapprove of, object to (s.o., sth.); **elle désapprouve mon projet,** she doesn't approve of my plan; **il désapprouve que je vienne,** he objects to my coming.

désarçonner [dezarsɔne] *v.tr.* **1.** (*of horse*) to unseat, throw (rider). **2.** *Fig*: to floor (s.o.).

désargenté [dezarʒɑ̃te] *a.* **1.** (*of plated spoon, fork, etc.*) worn, rubbed; that has lost its silver. **2.** *F:* short of cash; broke.

désarmant [dezarmɑ̃] *a.* disarming (smile, etc.)

désarmé [dezarme] **1.** (*a*) disarmed; (*b*) (ship) laid up, out of commission. **2.** (*a*) unarmed, defenceless; (*b*) unloaded (gun).

désarmement [dezarməmɑ̃] *n.m.* **1.** disarming (of s.o.). **2.** disarmament. **3.** *Nau:* laying up (of ship).

désarmer [dezarme] **1.** *v.tr.* (*a*) to disarm (s.o.); **il montrait une franchise qui vous désarmait,** he was disarmingly frank; (*b*) *Mil:* (i) to unload (gun); (ii) to uncock (rifle); (*c*) *Nau:* to lay up (ship); to put (ship) out of commission. **2.** *v.i.* (*a*) to disarm; (*b*) to relent; **haine qui ne désarme pas,** unrelenting hatred.

désarrimage [dezarimaʒ] *n.m. Nau: etc:* shifting (of cargo).

désarrimer [dezarime] *v.tr. Nau: etc:* to unstow, to shift (cargo).

désarroi [dezarwa] *n.m.* disarray, confusion; **il est en plein d.,** he's in a state of utter confusion.

désarticulation [dezartikylasjɔ̃] *n.f.* (*a*) *Med:* disarticulation; (*b*) dislocation.

désarticuler [dezartikyle] *v.tr.* (*a*) to disarticulate, disjoint; (*b*) to dislocate.

désassemblage [dezasɑ̃blaʒ] *n.m.* dismantling; disconnecting (of joints, etc.).

désassembler [dezasɑ̃ble] *v.tr.* to dismantle (sth.); to take (sth.) apart; to disconnect (joints, etc.).

désassocier [dezasɔsje] *v.tr.* (*impf. & pr.sub.* **n. désassociions, v. désassociiez)** to disassociate, dissociate (**de,** from); **se d. de qn,** to sever one's connection with s.o.

désassortir [dezasɔrtir] *v.tr.* (*conj. like* ASSORTIR) (*a*) to spoil, break up (set, collection, etc.); **service de table désassorti,** dinner service made up of odd pieces; (*b*) to clear (shop) (of stock).

désastre [dezastr̥] *n.m.* disaster, calamity; **d. financier,** financial disaster, crash.

désastreusement [dezastrøzmɑ̃] *adv.* disastrously.

désastreux, -euse [dezastrø, -øz] *a.* disastrous; appalling.

désatomisation [dezatɔmizasjɔ̃] *n.f.* nuclear disarmament.

désatomiser [dezatɔmize] *v.tr.* to undertake the nuclear disarmament of (a country).

désavantage [dezavɑ̃taʒ] *n.m.* disadvantage, handicap, drawback; **avoir un d. sur qn,** to be at a disadvantage in comparison with s.o.; **avoir le d.,** (i) to be handicapped; (ii) to get the worst of it.

désavantager [dezavɑ̃taʒe] *v.tr.* **(je désavantageai(s); n. désavantageons)** to put (s.o.) at a disadvantage; **être désavantagé par rapport à qn,** to be at a disadvantage by comparison with s.o.

désavantageusement [dezavɑ̃taʒøzmɑ̃] *adv.* disadvantageously, unfavourably.

désavantageux, -euse [dezavɑ̃taʒø, -øz] *a.* disadvantageous, unfavourable (position, etc.).

désaveu [dezavø] *n.m.* disavowal, denial; disowning (of s.o.); *Jur:* **d. de paternité,** repudiation of paternity.

désavouer [dezavwe] *v.tr.* **1.** to disavow, disown, repudiate, deny (action, work, etc.); to deny (promise, etc.); to retract (opinion); to disclaim (paternity); **d. la conduite de qn,** to disapprove of s.o.'s behaviour. **2. se d.,** to go back on one's word; to retract.

désaxé [dezakse] *a.* **1.** *Mec.E:* (*a*) excentric (cam, etc.); (*b*) **roue désaxée,** wheel out of true. **2.** unbalanced (mind); *n.* unbalanced person.

désaxer [dezakse] *v.tr.* **1.** *Mec.E:* to set over (cylinder, etc.); to put (wheel) out of true. **2.** to unbalance (mind).

descellement [desɛlmɑ̃] *n.m.* **1.** unsealing, breaking the seal (of sth.). **2.** loosening, pulling out, of iron post (from stone).

desceller [desele] *v.tr.* **1.** to unseal, to break the seal of (document, etc.). **2.** to loosen, pull out (iron post from stone).

descendance [desɑ̃dɑ̃s] *n.f.* **1.** *Lit:* descent; lineage. **2.** descendants.

descendant, -ante [desɑ̃dɑ̃, -ɑ̃t] **1.** *a.* (*a*) descending; downward (motion); (*b*) (*of train, line*) down; (*c*) **ligne descendante,** (genealogical) line of descent; (*d*) *Mus:* **gamme descendante,** descending scale. **2.** *n.* descendant.

descendeur [desɑ̃dœr] *n.m.* **1.** *Ski:* downhill specialist. **2.** *Mount:* descender.

descendre [desɑ̃dr̥] **I.** *v.i.* (*the aux. is* **être,** *occ.* **avoir) 1.** (*a*) to descend; to come down, go down; **d. d'un arbre,** to come down from a tree; **le fleuve descend vers la mer,** the river flows down to the sea; **d. en glissant,** to slide down; **la marée descend,** the tide is falling, going out; *F:* **mon dîner ne descend pas,** my dinner won't go down; **le baromètre descend,** the glass is falling; **la police est descendue dans la boîte de nuit,** the police made a descent on, raided, the nightclub; *Av:* **d. en vol plané,** to glide down; (*b*) to come, go, downstairs; **il n'est pas encore descendu,** he is not down yet; **faites-le d.,** (i) send him down; (ii) call him down; *Fig:* **d. dans la rue,** to go on a demonstration; (*c*) to lower oneself, condescend; **d. jusqu'au mensonge,** to stoop to lying. **2.** (*a*) to alight (from vehicle); **d. de cheval,** to dismount; **c'est ici que je descends,** this is where I get off (the bus, etc.); **tout le monde descend!** all change! **d. à terre,** to go ashore, to land; (*b*) **d. à l'hôtel,** to put up, stay, at a hotel. **3.** to extend downwards; (*of road, street*) to go downhill; **ses cheveux descendent jusqu'à la taille,** her hair comes down to her waist; **la route descend en lacets,** the road winds down. **4.** to be descended (from); **ces gens-là descendent d'une ancienne famille,** these people are descended from an ancient family. **II.** *v.tr.* (*aux.* **avoir) 1. d. les marches, la rue,** to go down the steps, the street; **d. la rivière,** to row, swim, float, etc. down the river; *Mus:* **d. la gamme,** to run down the scale. **2.** (*a*) to take, bring (sth.) down; **d. les bagages,** to bring down the luggage; **d. un tableau,** to take down a picture; (*b*) *F:* to shoot down, kill (partridge, man); **d. un avion,** to bring down, shoot down, an aircraft; **il s'est fait d. par la police,** he was killed by the police; (*d*) *F:* **je vous descendrai à votre porte,** I will put you down, drop you, at your door.

descente [desɑ̃t] *n.f.* **1.** (*a*) descent; coming down, going down (from a height); *Ski:* run; downhill race; **d. de cheval,** dismounting; **d. en parachute,** parachute drop; *Av:* **d. en vol plané,** glide; **mouvement de d.,** descending motion; down stroke (of piston, etc.); (*b*) **accueillir qn à la d. du train,** to meet s.o. off the train; (*c*) raid; **faire une descente dans un pays,** to make an incursion into a country; *Jur:* **d. sur les lieux,** visit to the scene (of a crime, etc.); **d. de police,** police raid; *Fb:* **d. des avants,** raid by the forwards; (*d*) *Med:* falling, prolapse (of womb, rectum). **2.** taking down, letting down, lowering (of picture, etc.); *Art:* **D. de croix,** Deposition. **3.** (*a*) slope, incline; **une d. rapide,** a steep slope; **d. dangereuse,** dangerous hill; **d. de mine,** descending shaft; (*b*) **d. de lit,** bedside rug; (*c*) cellar steps; descending stair; (*d*) down pipe, rainwater pipe; (*e*)

F: **avoir une bonne d.,** to be a great eater and drinker.

descriptible [dɛskriptibl̥] *a.* describable.

descriptif, -ive [dɛskriptif, -iv] **1.** *a.* descriptive. **2.** *n.m. Civ.E:* specification (of work to be carried out).

description [dɛskripsjɔ̃] *n.f.* description; **faire la d. de qn, de qch.,** to describe s.o., sth.; **conforme à la d.,** as represented.

déséchouage [dezeʃwaʒ] *n.m.*, **déséchouement** [dezeʃumɑ̃] *n.m. Nau:* refloating (of ship).

déséchouer [dezeʃwe] *v.tr. Nau:* to refloat (ship).

désemballage [dezɑ̃balaʒ] *n.m.* unpacking (of goods).

désemballer [dezɑ̃bale] *v.tr.* to unpack (goods).

désembourber [dezɑ̃burbe] *v.tr.* to extricate (vehicle, etc.) from the mud.

désembuer [dezɑ̃bɥe] *v.tr.* to demist.

désemparé [dezɑ̃pare] *a.* (*a*) (ship) in distress; crippled, disabled (ship); (aircraft) out of control; (*b*) **être d.,** to be at a loss; to be distraught, bewildered.

désemparer [dezɑ̃pare] **1.** *v.tr. Nau:* to disable (ship). **2.** *v.i.* **sans d.,** without stopping; **ils travaillent des heures sans d.,** they work for hours on end.

désemplir [dezɑ̃plir] **1.** *v.tr.* to empty partially (bottle, etc.). **2.** *v.i. & pr. usu. in the negative;* **son magasin ne (se) désemplit pas,** his shop is always full (of customers).

désencadrer [dezɑ̃kadre] *v.tr.* to take (a picture) out of its frame.

désenchaîner [dezɑ̃ʃene] *v.tr.* to unchain, unfetter.

désenchantement [dezɑ̃ʃɑ̃tmɑ̃] *n.m.* (*a*) disenchantment; (*b*) disillusion.

désenchanter [dezɑ̃ʃɑ̃te] *v.tr.* (*a*) to disenchant; (*b*) to disillusion, undeceive (s.o.); **sourire désenchanté,** wistful smile.

désenchanteur, -eresse [dezɑ̃ʃɑ̃tœr -(ə)rɛs] *a.* (*a*) disenchanting; (*b*) disillusioning.

désencombrement [dezɑ̃kɔ̃brəmɑ̃] *n.m.* clearing, freeing (of passage, etc.).

désencombrer [dezɑ̃kɔ̃bre] *v.tr.* to clear, free (passage, etc.).

désencrasser [dezɑ̃krase] *v.tr.* to clean (sth. greasy).

désencroûter [dezɑ̃krute] *v.tr.* **1.** (*a*) to scale (boiler, etc.); (*b*) to broaden (s.o.'s) outlook; to get (s.o.) out of a rut. **2. se d.,** to get out of the, a, rut.

désendetter (se) [sədezɑ̃dete] *v.pr.* to get out of debt.

désenfiler [dezɑ̃file] *v.tr.* (*a*) to unthread (needle); to unstring (beads, etc.); (*b*) **se d.,** to come unthreaded; (*of beads*) to come unstrung.

désenflammer [dezɑ̃flame] *v.tr.* (*a*) *Med:* to reduce inflammation in (wound, etc.); (*b*) to quench (s.o.'s passion).

désenfler [dezɑ̃fle] **1.** *v.tr.* to reduce swelling of (ankle, etc.); to deflate (tyre, etc.). **2.** *v.i. & pr.* to become less swollen; **ma joue (se) désenfle,** the swelling (in my cheek) is going down.

désenflure [dezɑ̃flyr] *n.f.* reduction of swelling.

désengagement [dezɑ̃gaʒmɑ̃] *n.m.* disengagement.

désengager [dezɑ̃gaʒe] *v.tr.* **(je désengageai(s); n. désengageons)** (*a*) to free (s.o.) from an obligation; (*b*) **d. sa parole,** to obtain release from a promise; (*c*) **se d.,** to free oneself from an appointment.

désengorgement [dezɑ̃gɔrʒəmɑ̃] *n.m.* unblocking (of pipe, etc.).

désengorger [dezɑ̃gɔrʒe] *v.tr.* **(je désengorgeai(s); n. désengorgeons)** to unblock (pipe, etc.).

désengrenage [dezɑ̃grənaʒ] *n.m.* disengaging (of toothed wheels, etc.); throwing (of machine, etc.) out of gear.

désengrener [dezɑ̃grəne] *v.tr.* (*conj. like* ENGRENER) (*a*) to disengage (toothed wheels, etc.); to throw (machine) out of gear; (*b*) **se d.,** to get out of gear.

désenivrer [dezɑ̃nivre] **1.** *v.tr.* to sober (s.o.). **2.** *v.i.* **il ne désenivre pas,** he's never sober.

désennuyer [dezɑ̃nɥije] *v.tr.* **(je désennuie, n. désennuyons; je désennuierai)** (*a*) to amuse, divert (s.o.); to relieve (s.o.'s) boredom; (*b*) **se d.,** to amuse oneself; to relieve one's boredom.

désenrayer [dezɑ̃reje] *v.tr.* **1.** to release (brake, jammed part, mechanism). **2.** to unscotch (wheel).

désensabler [dezɑ̃sable] *v.tr.* (*a*) to get (ship) off the sand; to dig (car, etc.) out of the sand; (*b*) to dredge (channel, etc.) of sand.

désensevelir [dezɑ̃səvlir] *v.tr.* to disinter, exhume (corpse); to dig up (sth.).

désensibilisateur, -trice [desɑ̃sibilizatœr, -tris] *Phot: n.m.* desensitizer.

désensibilisation [desɑ̃sibilizasjɔ̃] *n.f. Med: Phot:* desensitization.

désensibiliser [desɑ̃sibilize] *v.tr. Med: Phot:* to desensitize.

désensorceler [dezɑ̃sɔrsəle] *v.tr.* **(je désensorcelle, n. désensorcelons; je desensorcellerai)** to free (sth.) from a magic spell; to disenchant.

désensorcellement [dezɑ̃sɔrsɛlmɑ̃] *n.m.* disenchantment.

désentortiller [dezɑ̃tɔrtije] *v.tr.* to untwist (thread, etc.); to disentangle, unravel (wool, etc.).

désentraver [dezɑ̃trave] *v.tr.* **1.** to unshackle (horse, etc.). **2.** to clear (matter, business) of difficulties.

désenvaser [dezɑ̃vaze] *v.tr.* **1.** to clean out (sewer, harbour). **2.** to extract, to get (sth.) out of the mud.

déséquilibre [dezekilibr̥] *n.m.* (*a*) *Ph: etc:* want, lack, of balance, imbalance; (*b*) *Psy:* unbalance, imbalance; **d. émotif,** emotional maladjustment.

déséquilibré [dezekilibre] *a.* **1.** (*of thg*) unbalanced. **2.** unbalanced (person, mind); *n.* **un(e) déséquilibré(e),** an unbalanced person.

déséquilibrer [dezekilibre] *v.tr.* to unbalance; to throw (sth.) out of balance; to throw (s.o.) off balance.

désert [dezɛr] **1.** *a.* (*a*) deserted, abandoned (place); (*b*) uninhabited (country, island, etc.); lonely (spot). **2.** *n.m.* desert, wilderness; **prêcher dans le d.,** to talk to the wind, to deaf ears.

déserter [dezɛrte] *v.tr.* to desert, abandon; **d. son poste,** to abandon, quit, one's post; **d. (l'armée),** to desert (from the army).

déserteur [dezɛrtœr] *n.m.* deserter.

désertion [dezɛrsjɔ̃, dɛ-] *n.f.* desertion (from the army, from a party).

désertique [dezɛrtik, dɛ-] *a. Geog:* of the desert; **région d.,** desert region.

désescalade [dezɛskalad] *n.f.* de-escalation.

désespérance [dezɛsperɑ̃s] *n.f. Lit:* loss of hope; despair.

désespérant [dezɛsperɑ̃] *a.* heartbreaking; **enfant d.,** child that drives one to despair; **temps d.,** appalling weather.

désespéré, -ée [dezɛspere] **1.** *a.* desperate; (*a*) hopeless, to be despaired of; **être dans un état d.,** to be in a hopeless, desperate, state; (*b*) prompted by despair; despairing (look, etc.); desperate (struggle); (*c*) driven to despair; **être d. de qch., d'apprendre qch.,** to be in despair, heartbroken, about sth., to hear sth. **2.** *n.* (*a*) desperate person; **agir en d.,** to act desperately; (*b*) suicide.

désespérément [dezɛsperemɑ̃] *adv.* **1.** despairingly, hopelessly. **2.** desperately.

désespérer [dezɛspere] *v.* **(je désespère, n. désespérons; je désespérai) 1.** *v.i.* to despair; to lose hope;

il ne faut pas d., we must hope for the best; **d. de qn,** to despair of s.o., to lose all hope in s.o., of s.o. **2.** *v.tr.* to reduce, drive, (s.o.) to despair. **3. se d.,** to be in despair, to give way to despair.

désespoir [dezɛspwar] *n.m.* **1.** despair; **être au d., dans le d.,** to be in despair; **enfant qui fait le d. de sa famille,** child who is the despair of his family; **cette cuisine fait mon d.,** this kitchen will drive me to despair. **2.** desperation; **réduire qn au d.,** to drive s.o. to desperation, to despair; **en d. de cause,** in desperation, when everything else fails. **3.** *Bot:* **d. des peintres,** London pride.

déshabiliter [dezabilite] *v.tr. Jur:* to disqualify.

déshabillage [dezabijaʒ] *n.m.* undressing.

déshabillé [dezabije] *n.m.* négligé(e); housecoat.

déshabiller [dezabije] *v.tr.* **1.** (*a*) to undress (s.o.); to reveal (sth., s.o.'s ideas, etc.). **2. se d.** (*a*) to undress (oneself); to take off one's clothes; to strip; (*b*) to take off one's coat, etc.

déshabituer [dezabitɥe] *v.tr.* (*a*) **d. qn de (faire) qch.,** to break s.o. of the habit of (doing) sth; (*b*) **se d.,** to lose, get out of, the habit (**de,** of).

désherbage [dezɛrbaʒ] *n.m.* weeding.

désherbant [dezɛrbɑ̃] *n.m.* weedkiller.

désherber [dezɛrbe] *v.tr.* to weed (garden, field).

déshérence [dezerɑ̃s] *n.f. Jur:* default of heirs, escheat; **tomber en d.,** to escheat.

déshérité [dezerite] *a.* (*a*) disinherited; (*b*) deprived; (*c*) *n.m.* **les déshérités,** the underprivileged.

déshéritement [dezeritmɑ̃] *n.m.* disinheritance, disinheriting.

déshériter [dezerite] *v.tr.* to disinherit (s.o.), to deprive (s.o.) of an inheritance.

déshonnête [dezɔnɛt] *a. Lit:* improper, immodest, unseemly.

déshonnêtement [dezɔnɛtmɑ̃] *adv. Lit:* improperly, immodestly.

déshonnêteté [dezɔnɛt(ə)te] *n.f. A:* & *Lit:* impropriety, immodesty, unseemliness.

déshonneur [dezɔnœr] *n.m.* dishonour, *NAm:* dishonor; disgrace; **faire d. à qn,** to disgrace s.o.

déshonorant [dezɔnɔrɑ̃], *a.* dishonourable, *NAm:* dishonorable; discreditable, disgraceful.

déshonorer [dezɔnɔre] *v.tr.* **1.** (*a*) to dishonour, *NAm:* dishonor; to disgrace; to bring dishonour, disgrace, on (s.o.); **d. une jeune fille,** to seduce a girl; (*b*) to maltreat, disfigure, spoil (picture, etc.). **2. se d.,** to disgrace oneself, to lose one's honour.

déshuiler [dezɥile] *v.tr.* to extract, separate, remove, oil, grease, from (sth.); to de-oil.

déshumaniser [dezymanize], *v.tr.* to dehumanize.

déshydratation [dezidratasjɔ̃] *n.f.* dehydration.

déshydrater [dezidrate] *v.tr.* (*a*) to dehydrate; to desiccate; **noix de coco déshydratée,** desiccated coconut; (*b*) **se d.,** to become dehydrated, desiccated.

déshydrogénation [dezidrɔʒenasjɔ̃] *n.f. Ch:* dehydrogenation.

déshydrogéner [dezidrɔʒene] *v.tr.* **(je déshydrogène, n. déshydrogénons; je déshydrogènerai)** *Ch:* to dehydrogenate.

déshypothéquer [dezipɔteke] *v.tr.* (*conj. like* HYPOTHÉQUER) to disencumber (estate).

desideratum [deziderato m] *n.m.* desideratum; *pl. desiderata.*

désignation [deziɲasjɔ̃] *n.f.* **1.** designation; description (of goods, etc.). **2. d. de qn pour un poste,** appointment, nomination, of s.o., to a post.

désigner [desiɲe] *v.tr.* **1.** to designate, show, indicate, point out; **d. qn par son nom,** to call s.o., refer to s.o., by name; **d. qch. du doigt,** to point sth. out, to point at sth.; **d. qch. à l'attention de qn,** to call s.o.'s attention to sth. **2.** (*a*) **d. un jour,** to appoint, set, fix, a day; **il a pris le siège qu'on lui avait désigné,** he took the seat indicated to him; **il est tout désigné pour le faire,** he is just the man to do it; he is cut out for it; (*b*) **d. qn à, pour, un poste,** to appoint, draft, nominate, s.o. to a post; **il a été désigné pour nous représenter,** he was chosen to represent us; (*c*) **se d.,** to call attention to oneself.

désillusion [dezilyzjɔ̃] *n.f.* disillusion.

désillusionnant [dezilyzjɔnɑ̃] *a.* disillusioning.

désillusionnement [dezilyzjɔnmɑ̃] *n.m.* disillusionment, disillusioning, undeceiving.

désillusionner [dezilyzjɔne] *v.tr.* to disillusion, undeceive.

désincarné [dezɛ̃karne] *a.* disincarnate.

désincarner (se) [sədezɛ̃karne] *v.pr. Psychics:* to become disembodied.

désincrustant [dezɛ̃krystɑ̃] **1.** *a.* scaling (substance). **2.** *n.m.* anti-scale composition, scale preventive.

désinncrustation [dezɛ̃krystasjɔ̃] *n.f.* scaling (of boiler, etc.).

désincruster [dezɛ̃kryste] *v.tr.* to scale (boiler, etc.).

désinence [dezinɑ̃s] *n.f. Gram:* termination (of word); flexional ending.

désinfectant [dezɛ̃fɛktɑ̃] *a.* & *n.m.* disinfectant.

désinfecter [dezɛ̃fɛkte] *v.tr.* to disinfect.

désinfection [dezɛ̃fɛksjɔ̃] *n.f.* disinfection.

désintégration [dezɛ̃tegrasjɔ̃] *n.f.* disintegration, breaking up; weathering (of rocks); *Atom.Ph:* (nuclear) disintegration; splitting, smashing (of the atom).

désintégrer [dezɛ̃tegre] *v.tr.* **(je désintègre, n. désintégrons; je désintegrerai) 1.** to disintegrate; to weather (rocks); *Atom.Ph:* to disintegrate (matter); to split, smash (the atom). **2. se d.,** to disintegrate; (*of rocks*) to weather; *Atom.Ph:* (*of matter*) to disintegrate; (*of atom*) to smash, split.

désintéressé [dezɛ̃terese] *a.* **1.** not involved, not implicated; **être d. dans une affaire,** to have no interest at stake in a business. **2.** (*a*) disinterested, impartial (opinion, advice, etc.); (*b*) unselfish (motive).

désintéressement [dezɛ̃terɛsmɑ̃] *n.m.* **1.** disinterestedness; (i) impartiality; (ii) unselfishness. **2.** buying out (of partner, etc.); paying off (of creditor, etc.).

désintéresser [dezɛ̃terese] *v.tr.* **1.** to buy out (partner); pay off (creditor). **2. se d. de qch.,** to take (i) no further interest, (ii) no part, in sth.; **se d. de qn,** to ignore (s.o.).

désintérêt [dezɛ̃terɛ] *n.m.* disinterest.

désintoxication [dezɛ̃tɔksikasjɔ̃] *n.f. Med:* detoxication, detoxification; **faire une cure de d.,** to undergo treatment for alcoholism, drug addition.

désintoxiquer [dezɛ̃tɔksike] *v.tr. Med:* to detoxicate; to treat for alcoholism, drug addiction.

désinviter [dezɛ̃vite] *v.tr.* to cancel an invitation to (s.o.).

désinvolte [dezɛ̃vɔlt] *a.* (*a*) easy, free (movements); (*b*) airy, unembarrassed, unselfconscious (manner); **d. à l'égard de qn,** casual, offhand, with s.o.

désinvolture [dezɛ̃vɔltyr] *n.f.* (*a*) unconstraint, unselfconsciousness (in manner, etc.); ease (of movement) (*b*) free and easy manner; offhand, airy, manner; **avec d.,** in an offhand, casual, way.

désir [dezir] *n.m.* (*a*) desire, wish; **avoir un d. de qch.,** to have a desire for something; **d. de plaire,** wish to please; **d. ardent,** craving, longing; **ardent d. de réussir,** eagerness to succeed; **selon le d. de son père,** at his father's wish; **prendre ses désirs pour des réalités,** to indulge in wishful thinking; (*b*) **d.(sexuel),** (sexual) desire.

désirable [dezirabl̩] *a.* desirable; **peu d.,** undesirable.

désirer [dezire] *v.tr.* **1.** to desire, want; to wish for (sth.); **d. ardemment qch.,** to yearn, long, for sth.; to crave for sth.; **d. qch. de qn,** to want sth. of, from, s.o.; **je désire le voir,** I want, wish, to see him; I am anxious to see him; **je désire qu'il vienne,** I would like him to come; **cela laisse à d.,** it's not satisfactory, not up to the mark; there's room for improvement; **je n'avais plus rien à d.,** I had nothing left to wish for; **que désirez-vous?** what would you like? **2.** to desire (s.o. sexually); **je te désire,** I want you.

désireux, -euse [dezirø, øz] *a.* desirous (**de,** of); **d. de plaire,** anxious to please.

désistement [dezistəmɑ̃] *n.m.* (*a*) *Jur:* waiver (of claim); withdrawal (of suit); (*b*) withdrawal of one's candidature; standing down; (*c*) recession.

désister (se) [sədeziste] *v.pr.* (*a*) *Jur:* **se d. d'une poursuite,** to withdraw an action; **se d. d'une demande,** to waive a claim; (*b*) to withdraw (one's candidature); to stand down.

désobéir [dezɔbeir] *v.i.* **d. (à qn, à un ordre),** to disobey (s.o., an order); **d. à une règle,** to break a rule; *may be used in the passive:* **mes ordres ont été désobéis,** my orders were disobeyed.

désobéissance [dezɔbeisɑ̃s] *n.f.* disobedience (**à qn,** to s.o., **à un ordre,** of an order; **d. à une règle,** disregard for, breaking of, a rule.

désobéissant [dezɔbeisɑ̃] *a.* disobedient (**à,** to).

désobligeance [dezɔbliʒɑ̃s] *n.f.* disagreeableness, unkindness (**envers,** to).

désobligeant, -ante [dezɔbliʒɑ̃ -ɑ̃t] *a.* disagreeable, unkind, ungracious, offensive (person, manner, words, etc.) (**envers,** to).

désobliger [dezɔbliʒe] *v.tr.* **(je désobligeai(s); n. désobligeons)** to offend.

désobstruer [dezɔpstrye], *v.tr.* to clear, free, (sth.) of obstructions; to clear (pipe, etc.).

désodorisant [dezɔdɔrizɑ̃] *a. & n.m. Toil:* deodorant.

désodoriser [dezɔdɔrize] *v.tr.* to deodorize.

désœuvré [dezœvre, -øvre] *a.* unoccupied, idle; **me trouvant d.,** finding myself with nothing to do, *F:* at a loose end; *n.* **les désœuvrés,** people with nothing to do.

désœuvrement [dezœvrəmɑ̃] *n.m.* idleness; **par d.,** to kill time, for want of something to do.

désolant [dezɔlɑ̃] *a.* distressing, sad, disheartening (news, etc.); **ce temps est d.,** this weather is very depressing.

désolation [dezɔlasjɔ̃] *n.f.* desolation. **1.** devastation, laying waste. **2.** grief, sorrow; **être plongé dans la d.,** to be grief-stricken.

désolé [dezɔle] *a.* **1.** desolate, dreary (region, etc.). **2.** very sorry; grieved; distressed; **je suis d. de vous avoir fait attendre**, I'm so sorry to have kept you waiting.

désoler [dezɔle] *v.tr.* to desolate. **1.** *A: & Lit:* to devastate, ravage, lay waste (country, etc.). **2.** to afflict, distress, grieve (s.o.); **son échec à l'examen le désole**, he's very upset, *F:* cut up, about failing the exam. **3. se d.,** to be distressed, upset.

désolidariser [desɔlidarize] *v.tr.* **1.** to break away from (party, etc.). **2. se d. de, d'avec, ses collègues,** to break (one's ties) with one's colleagues, to go one's own way; **se d. d'une cause,** to withdraw one's support from a cause.

désopilant [dezɔpilɑ̃] *a.* screamingly funny, hilarious.

désordonné [dezɔrdɔne] *a.* (*a*) disordered (ranks, etc.); disorganized, disorderly (life, etc.); uncoordinated (movements); reckless (expenditure); (*b*) untidy (room, etc.); (*c*) (*of person*) (i) disorganized; (ii) untidy; (iii) disorderly.

désordre [dezɔrdr̥] *n.m.* **1.** (*a*) disorder, confusion, chaos; untidiness; **quel d.!** what a mess! **cheveux en d.,** tangled, untidy hair; **mettre le d. dans les rangs,** to throw the ranks into disorder, into confusion; **d. de la pensée,** confusion of the mind; (*b*) *Med:* **d. nerveux,** nervous disorder. **2.** disorderliness, licentiousness. **3.** *pl.* disturbances, riots; **de graves désordres ont éclaté,** serious disturbances have broken out.

désorganisateur, -trice [dezɔrganizatœr, -tris] **1.** *a.* disorganizing. **2.** *n.* disorganizer, one who upsets (plans, etc.).

désorganisation [dezɔrganizasjɔ̃] *n.f.* disorganization.

désorganiser [dezɔrganize] *v.tr.* **1.** to disorganize (system, etc.); to upset (plans, etc.). **2. se d.,** to become disorganized, *F:* to go to pieces.

désorientation [dezɔrjɑ̃tasjɔ̃] *n.f.* **1.** disorientation. **2.** confusion, bewilderment.

désorienté [dezɔrjɑ̃te] *a.* puzzled, bewildered, at a loss; lost; **je suis tout d.,** I don't know where I am.

désorienter [dezɔrjɑ̃te] *v.tr.* **1.** (*a*) to make (s.o.) lose his bearings, to disorientate (s.o.); (*b*) to throw (compass, instrument) out of adjustment. **2.** to disconcert, bewilder; to put (s.o.) out. **3. se d.** (*a*) to lose one's bearings, (*b*) to get confused.

désormais [dezɔrmɛ] *adv.* henceforward, henceforth, from now on(wards); hereafter; in future.

désossé [dezɔse] **1.** *a.* (*a*) boned; (*b*) supple (person); flabby, flaccid (style, etc.).

désossement [dezɔsmɑ̃] *n.m.* boning (of meat, etc.).

désosser [dezɔse] *v.tr.* **1.** to bone (meat, fish). **2.** to dissect (sentence, book). **3. se d.,** to contort oneself.

désoxydant [dezɔksidɑ̃] *Ch:* **1.** *a.* deoxidizing. **2.** *n.m.* deoxidizer.

désoxyder [dezɔkside] *v.tr. Ch: Metall:* to deoxidize.

despote [dɛspɔt] *n.m.* despot, absolute ruler; *a.* **homme, femme, d.,** despotic man, woman.

despotique [dɛspɔtik] *a.* despotic (power, etc.)

despotiquement [dɛspɔtikmɑ̃] *adv.* despotically.

despotisme [dɛspɔtism] *n.m.* despotism.

desquamation [dɛskwamasjɔ̃] *n.f. Med:* desquamation; peeling (of skin).

desquels, desquelles [dekɛl]. *see* LEQUEL.

dessaisir [desezir] *v.tr. Jur:* **d. un tribunal d'une affaire,** to remove a case from a court. **2. se d. de qch.,** to relinquish sth.; to part with, give up, sth.

dessaisissement [desɛzismɑ̃, -se-] *n.m.* **1.** *Jur:* **d. d'un tribunal d'une affaire,** removal of case from a court. **2. d. de qch.,** relinquishing, relinquishment, of sth.

dessalage [desalaʒ] *n.m.,* **dessalaison** [desalɛzɔ̃], *n.f.* removal of salt (from fish, meat, etc.); soaking.

dessalé [desale] *a.* **1.** (*of meat, fish, etc.*) freed of salt. **2.** *F:* awake, sharp (person).

dessalement [desalmɑ̃] *n.m.* desalination, desalinization (of sea water).

dessaler [desale] *v.tr.* **1.** to remove the salt from (meat, fish); to put (meat, fish) to soak; to desalinate, desalinize (sea water). **2.** *F:* **d. qn,** to sharpen s.o.'s wits. **3. se d.** (*a*) to become less salty; (*b*) *F:* to learn a thing or two.

dessangler [desɑ̃gle] *v.tr.* to ungirth, take the girths off (horse).

dessaouler [desule] = DESSOÛLER.

desséchant [deseʃɑ̃] *a.* drying, desiccating; parching.

desséché [deseʃe] *a.* **1.** dry (pond, bed of torrent). **2.** dry, withered.

dessèchement [desɛʃmɑ̃] *n.m.* (*a*) drying up (of pond, etc.); (*b*) seasoning, drying (of wood); (*c*) withering (of plants); emaciation (of body); (*d*) hardness (of heart).

dessécher [deseʃe] *v.tr.* **(je dessèche, n. desséchons; je dessécherai) 1.** to dry up (ground). **2.** to season (wood); to desiccate (foodstuffs). **3.** (*a*) (*of wind, heat*) to wither (plant); to dry (skin); to parch (mouth); (*b*) (*of illness, etc.*) to emaciate (body); (*c*) **d. le cœur de qn,** to harden s.o.'s heart. **4. se d.** (*a*) to dry up, to become dry; (*of pond, etc.*) to go dry; (*b*) to wither; to waste away; (*c*) (*of pers.*) to become insensitive.

dessein [desɛ̃] *n.m.* **1.** design, plan, scheme, project. **2.** intention, purpose; **avoir le d. de faire qch.,** to have the intention of, to purpose, doing sth.; **former le d. de faire qch.,** to plan to do sth.; **dans ce d.,** with this intention; with this in mind; **à d.,** on purpose, purposely, intentionally; **à d. de faire qch.,** in order to do sth.; **c'est à d. que je n'ai pas répondu,** I deliberately didn't answer.

desseller [desele] *v.tr.* to unsaddle (horse).

desserrage [desɛraʒ] *n.m.* (*a*) loosening; (*b*) easing, slackening, releasing, release; (*c*) unscrewing.

desserre [desɛr] *n.f. F:* forking out; **être dur à la d.,** to be close-fisted, stingy.

desserrement [desɛrmɑ̃] *n.m.* loosening, slackening.

desserrer [desere] *v.tr.* **1.** to loosen (screw); to slacken (belt, knot); to unclamp; to unscrew (nut); to unclench (fist, teeth); to release (brake); **d. son étreinte,** to relax one's hold; **je n'ai pas desserré les dents,** I didn't open my mouth, didn't utter a word. **2. se d.,** to work loose; (*of grip, etc.*) to relax.

dessert [desɛr, dɛ-] *n.m.* dessert; pudding, sweet.

desserte¹ [desɛrt, dɛ-] *n.f.* **1.** *Ecc:* duties of an officiating clergyman; care (of parish). **2. d. d'un port par voie ferrée,** railway service to a port; **chemin de d.,** service road, *U.S:* frontage road.

desserte² *n.f.* (*a*) sideboard; (*b*) **d. roulante,** (dinner) trolley.

dessertir [desɛrtir] *v.tr.* to unset (precious stone).

desservant [desɛrvɑ̃] *n.m. Ecc:* priest in charge (of parish, etc.).

desservir¹ [desɛrvir], *v.tr.* (*conj. like* SERVIR) **1.** *Ecc:* to minister to (parish, etc.). **2.** (*a*) (*of railways, steamers, etc.*) to serve; **ce train ne dessert pas toutes les gares,** this train does not stop at every station; **ville bien desservie,** town with efficient public transport; (*b*) (*of door*) to lead into (room).

desservir² *v.tr.* (*conj. like* SERVIR) **1.** to clear (the table); *v.i.* to clear away. **2. desservir qn,** to be a bad friend to s.o.; to do s.o. a disservice; **il s'est desservi lui-même,** he has been his own worst enemy; **cela desservirait mes intérêts,** it would be detrimental to my interests.

dessiller [desije] *v.tr.* **d. les yeux à, de, qn,** to open s.o.'s eyes (to facts); to undeceive s.o.; **ses yeux se dessillèrent,** the scales fell from his eyes; his eyes were opened.

dessin [desɛ̃] *n.m.* **1.** (*a*) (art of) drawing, sketching; **d. à main levée,** freehand drawing; (*b*) drawing, sketch; **d. à la plume,** pen-and-ink sketch; *Cin:* **dessin(s) animé(s),** motion-picture cartoon; **d. humoristique,** cartoon; **d. publicitaire,** publicity drawing. **2.** design, pattern; **d. de mode,** fashion design. **3.** *Tchn:* (*a*) **(l'art du) d.,** draughtsmanship; **planche à d.,** drawing board; (*b*) draught, draft, drawing, plan (of building, machine, etc.); **d. d'ensemble,** general assembly drawing. **4.** outline (of face, etc.).

dessinateur, -trice [desinatœr, -tris] *n.* **1.** (*a*) sketcher, drawer; (*b*) black-and-white artist; (*c*) cartoonist. **2.** designer (of wallpapers, etc.); dress designer. **3.** *Tchn:* draughtsman, draftsman, -woman.

dessiner [desine] *v.tr.* **1.** to draw, sketch; **d. qch. d'après nature,** to draw sth. from nature; **d. à l'encre, à la craie,** to draw in ink, in chalk. **2.** to design (wall-paper, material, etc.). **3.** to show, outline (sth.); **les montagnes dessinent leur courbe sur le ciel,** the line of the mountains stands out against the sky; **vêtement qui dessine bien la taille,** garment that shows off the figure; **visage bien dessiné,** finely chiselled face. **4. se d.,** to stand out, take form; to be outlined; **les arbres se dessinent à l'horizon,** the trees stand out, are outlined, on the horizon; **nos projets se dessinent,** our plans are taking shape.

dessouder [desude] *v.tr.* to unsolder (sth.); **le tuyau s'est déssoudé,** the pipe has come unsoldered.

dessoûler [desule] *F:* **1.** *v.tr.* to sober (s.o.), to make (s.o.). sober. **2.** *v.i. & pr.* to become sober, to sober off; **il ne dessoûle pas,** he's never sober.

dessous [dəsu] **1.** *adv.* under(neath), below, beneath; **passez (par) d.,** go underneath (it); **marcher bras dessus bras d.,** to walk arm in arm; *adv.phr.* **en d.,** underneath; **regarder qn en d.,** to look at s.o. furtively, stealthily; **agir en d.,** to act in an underhand way. **2.** *n.m.* (*a*) lower part, underpart, underside, bottom; **les gens du d.,** the people on the floor below (us); **d. d'une assiette,** bottom of a plate; **d. de bouteille,** bottle mat; coaster; **verser un d. de table,** to pay (s.o.) a bribe; **avoir le d.,** to get the worst of it, to be defeated; **être dans le troisième, trente-sixième, d.,** to be in a very bad situation; *Cost:* **d. de robe,** slip; petticoat; **les d.,** (ladies') underwear; *F:* undies; (*b*) **les d. de la politique,** the shady side of politics. **3.** *prep.phr.* **de. d. de,** from under(neath).

dessous-de-bras [d(ə)sudbra] *n.m.inv.* dress shield.

dessous-de-plat [d(ə)sudpla] *n.m.inv.* table mat.

dessus [dəsy] **1.** *adv.* above, over; (up)on (it, them); **il a marché d.,** he trod on it; **j'ai failli lui tirer d.,** I nearly shot him; **mettre la main d.,** to lay hands on it, on them; **vous avez mis le doigt d.,** you've hit the nail on the head; *Nau:* **avoir le vent d.,** to be aback; *adv.phr.* **en d.,** at the top, on top, above; **mettre les meilleures pommes (en, au) d.,** to put the best apples on top. **2.** *n.m.* (*a*) top, upper part (of table, etc.); **d. de plateau,** traycloth; *Th:* **les d.,** the flies; *Fig:* **le d. du panier,** (i) the pick of the bunch; (ii) the upper crust; (*b*) **avoir le d.,** to have the upper hand, to be on top; **(re)prendre le d.,** (i) to get over (illness); (ii) to overcome one's feelings (of sorrow, etc.). **3.** *prep.phr.* **de d.,** from, off; **elle ne leva pas les yeux de d. son ouvrage,** she did not lift her eyes from, take her eyes off, her work.

dessus-de-lit [dəsydli] *n.m.inv.* coverlet, bedspread.

déstalinisation [destalinizasjɔ̃] *n.f. Pol:* destalinization.

destin [dɛstɛ̃], *n.m.* fate, destiny.

destinataire [dɛstinatɛr], *n.m. & f.* addressee, recipient (of letter, etc.); consignee (of goods); payee (of money order).

destination [dɛstinasjɔ̃] *n.f.* **1.** destination; **ce paquet est à votre d.,** this parcel is addressed to you; **trains à de. de Paris,** trains for, to, Paris; **articles à d. de la province et de l'étranger,** goods for the provinces and for export; **lignes aériennes à d. ou en provenance de l'Amérique,** airlines to and from America. **2.** destination, intended purpose (of building, sum of money, etc.).

destinée [dɛstine] *n.f.* **1.** (*a*) destiny; **unir sa d. à celle de qn,** to marry s.o.; (*b*) *pl.* destinies, fortunes. **2.** = DESTIN.

destiner [dɛstine] *v.tr.* **1.** *O:* to destine; **être destiné à mourir sur l'échafaud,** to be fated, doomed, to die on the scaffold. **2.** (*a*) **d. qch. à qn,** to intend, mean, sth. for s.o.; **la balle vous était destinée,** the bullet was aimed at you; (*b*) **il avait destiné son fils au barreau,** he had intended his son for the bar; (*c*) **d. une somme d'argent à un achat,** to allot, assign, a sum of money to a purchase. **3. se d. à qch.,** to intend to take up sth. (as a profession); **il se destine à la médecine,** he intends to be a doctor.

destituer [dɛstitɥe] *v.tr.* to dismiss, discharge (s.o.); to remove (official) from office; **d. un général de son commandement,** to relieve a general of his command.

destitution [dɛstitysjɔ̃] *n.f.* dismissal (of official, etc.).

destrier [dɛstrije], *n.m. Hist:* charger, war horse.

destroyer [dɛstrwajœr, -e] *n.m. Nav:* destroyer.

destructeur, -trice [dɛstryktœr, -tris] **1.** *a.* destroying (agent, etc.); destructive (child, war, etc.). **2.** *n.* destroyer, destructor.

destructible [dɛstryktibl̩] *a.* destructible.

destructif, -ive [dɛstryktif, -iv] *a.* destructive.

destruction [dɛstryksjɔ̃] *n.f.* **1.** destruction, destroying; extermination (of rats, etc.). **2.** *Mil:* demolition (by blasting, etc.).

destructivité [dɛstryktivite] *n.f.* destructiveness.

désuet, -uète [desɥɛ, -ɥɛt] *a.* obsolete (word); **théories désuètes,** antiquated, out-of-date, theories.

désuétude [desɥetyd] *n.f.* disuse; **tomber en d.,** to fall, pass, into disuse; (*of right, etc.*) to lapse; (*of law*) to fall into abeyance; **mot tombé en d.,** obsolete word.

désuni [dezyni] *a.* (*of people*) disunited, divided; (*of parts, etc.*) disjoined, disconnected; (*of manœuvre*) uncoordinated.

désunion [dezynjɔ̃] *n.f.* disunion (of people, etc.); dissension (in family, etc.).

désunir [dezynir] *v.* **1.** *v.tr.* to disunite, divide (people, etc.); to disjoin, disconnect (parts, etc.); **questions qu'on ne peut pas d.,** questions that cannot be treated apart. **2.** *v.pr.* (*of athlete*) to lose one's stride.

détachable [detaʃabl̩] *a.* detachable.

détachage [detaʃaʒ] *n.m.* removal of stains (from clothes, etc.).

détachant [detaʃɑ̃] **1.** *a.* stain-removing. **2.** *n.m.* stain remover.

détaché [detaʃe] *a.* **1.** loose, detached (part); untethered (horse, etc.); **pièces détachées,** spare parts. **2.** seconded (to another department). **3.** indifferent, casual, detached, unconcerned (manner, etc.); **d. de ce monde,** unworldly. **4.** *n.m. Mus:* détaché, detached (bowing).

détachement [detaʃmɑ̃] *n.m.* **1.** detaching, cutting off (of sth.). **2.** indifference (**de,** to); lack of interest (**de,** in); detachment (**de,** from); **d. de ce monde,** unworldliness. **3.** (*a*) secondment, seconding (of person); **il est en d. à l'université de Cambridge,** he has been seconded to the University of Cambridge; (*b*) *Mil:* detachment, draft (of troops), *U.S:* detail; **d. de corvée,** fatigue party.

détacher[1] [detaʃe] *v.* **I.** *v.tr.* to detach; (*a*) to loose, unfasten, untie, unbind, unlash; to uncouple (truck); to untether (horse); **d. un rideau,** to take down, unhook, a curtain; **je ne peux pas en d. mes yeux,** I can't take my eyes off it; (*b*) to separate, disjoin (**de,** from); to cut off, pull off, break off, bite off, saw off, chisel off (sth. from sth.); **d. un chèque du carnet,** to tear out a cheque from the book; **d. les pétales d'une fleur,** to pick, pluck, the petals off a flower; (*c*) **d. qn de qch.,** to turn s.o. away from sth.; (*d*) *Mil: etc:* to detach, attach, second; **d. un officier auprès de qn,** to detach an officer to serve with s.o.; **fonctionnaire détaché à un autre service,** official temporarily attached, seconded, to another department; (*e*) **d. une figure dans un tableau,** to make a figure stand out, to bring out a figure, in a picture; *Mus:* **d. les notes,** to detach the notes. **II. se détacher** **1.** (*a*) (*of knot, etc.*) to come undone, unfastened, untied, loose; (*b*) (*of animal*) to slip its chain, to break loose. **2.** to break off, break loose, become detached; to separate; (*of parts*) to come apart; (*of paint*) to flake away, off; **un bouton s'est détaché,** a button has come off; **l'écorce se détache,** the bark is peeling off the tree. **3.** (*a*) **se d. de sa famille,** to separate, break away, from one's family; (*b*) **un petit groupe de coureurs se détacha en avant,** a small group, bunch, pulled ahead (of the field). **4. se d. sur un fond, sur l'horizon,** to stand out against a background, against the horizon.

détacher[2] *v.tr.* to remove stains, spots, from (clothing, etc.).

détacheur, -euse [detaʃœr, -øz] **1.** *n.* (*pers.*) (dry) cleaner. **2.** *a. & n.m.* **(flacon) détacheur,** (bottle of) stain remover.

détail [detaj] *n.m.* **1.** (*a*) dividing up, cutting up (of cloth, meat, etc.); (*b*) *Com:* retail; **vendre au d.,** to sell (goods) retail; **marchand au d.,** retailer; **prix de d.,** retail price. **2.** detail; small point; **donner tous les détails,** to enter, go, into all the details, to give full particulars; **raconter qch. en d.,** to give a detailed account of sth.; **c'est un d.,** it's not important; **le d. d'un compte,** the items of an account; **le d. d'une facture,** the breakdown of an invoice. **3.** *Adm: Mil: etc:* internal economy; **service de d.,** executive duties; **officier de détail,** quartermaster officer (= supply and pay officer).

détaillant, -ante [detajɑ̃,-ɑ̃t] *n.* retailer.

détaillé [detaje] *a.* **1.** detailed, circumstantial (narrative, etc.). **2.** *Com:* **état d. de compte,** detailed, itemized, statement of account.

détailler [detaje] *v.tr.* **1.** (*a*) to divide up, cut up (cloth, meat, etc.); (*b*) *Com:* to retail (goods), to sell (goods) retail. **2.** (*a*) to detail, enumerate; to relate in detail; to itemize (account); (*b*) **d. qn,** to scrutinize s.o., to look s.o. up and down.

détaler [detale] *v.i. F:* (*of animal*) to bolt; (*of pers.*) to decamp, to take (oneself) off; **la souris détala vers son trou,** the mouse scuttled off, scurried off, to its hole.

détartrage [detartraʒ] *n.m.* (*a*) descaling (of boiler); (*b*) scaling (of teeth).

détartrant [detartrɑ̃] *n.m.* scaling substance.

détartrer [detartre] *v.tr.* (*a*) to scale, fur, descale (boiler); (*b*) to scale (teeth).

détartreur [detartrœr] *n.m.* scaler (for boilers).

détaxation [detaksasjɔ̃] *n.f.* reduction, removal, of tax.

détaxe [detaks] *n.f.* **1.** tax refund, rebate. **2.** decontrolling.

détaxer [detakse] *v.tr.* to take the tax off, to remove the tax on (sth.); to reduce the tax.

détecter [detɛkte] *v.tr.* to detect.

détecteur, -trice [detɛktœr, -tris] **1.** *a. Tchn:* detecting, sensing; *Elcs:* **lampe détectrice,** detector valve. **2.** *n.m. Tchn:* detector; (*a*) **d. de fumée,** smoke detector, indicator; **d. de mines,** mine detector; (*b*) *Elcs:* detector, sensor; **d. d'ondes,** wave detector.

détection [detɛksjɔ̃] *n.f.* detection, location; (*a*) **d. électromagnétique,** radio location; **d. sous-marine,** underwater detection; (*b*) *Mil: Navy:* **d. des mines,** mine detection.

détective [detɛktiv] *n.m.* (*a*) detective; (*b*) **d. privé,** private detective; *F:* private eye.

déteindre [detɛ̃dr̥] *v.* (*conj. like* TEINDRE) **1.** *v.tr.* to take the colour out of (sth.). **2.** *v.i.* (*a*) to fade, to lose colour; (*b*) *Dy:* (*of colour*) to bleed; **d. au lavage,** to run in the wash; **le ruban a déteint sur ma robe,** the colour of the ribbon has come off on my dress; (*c*) *Fig:* **cela déteint sur eux,** it rubs off on them.

dételage [detlaʒ] *n.m.* **1.** (*a*) unharnessing; (*b*) unhitching (of horses). **2.** uncoupling (of wag(g)ons).

dételer [detle] *v.tr.* (**je dételle, n. dételons; je dételler ai**) **1.** (*a*) to unharness; (*b*) to unhitch (horse(s)); to unyoke (oxen); (*c*) *v.i. F:* to ease off, to stop working. **2.** *Rail:* to uncouple (trucks, etc.).

détendeur [detãdœr] *n.m.* pressure reducer; relief valve.

détendre [detɑ̃dr̥] *v.tr.* **1.** to slacken, relax, loosen (sth. that is taut); to unbend (bow); **d. un ressort,** to release a spring; **d. l'esprit,** (i) to relax the mind; (ii) to calm the mind; **d. les nerfs,** to steady the nerves. **2. d. (un gaz),** to release the pressure (of a gas). **3. se d.,** to become slack, to slacken, relax; **se d. pendant une heure,** to relax for an hour; **son visage se détendit dans un sourire,** his face relaxed into a smile; **la situation se détend,** the situation is easing. **2.** (*of steam, etc.*) to be reduced in pressure.

détendu [detãdy] *a.* (*a*) slack; (*b*) relaxed (conversation, etc.).

détenir [detnir] *v.tr.* (*conj. like* TENIR) **1.** to hold, to be in possession of (sth.); **d. le record du monde,** to hold the world record. **2.** to detain (s.o.), to keep (s.o.) prisoner.

détente [detãt] *n.f.* **1.** (*a*) relaxation, loosening, slackening (of sth. that is taut); relaxing (of muscles); (*b*) easing (of political situation, etc.); détente; (*c*) **j'ai besoin de quelques instants de d.,** I need to relax for a moment, I need a moment's relaxation; (*d*) *Sm.a:* trigger; **dure à la d.,** (i) hard on the trigger; (ii) *F:* close-fisted, stingy (person). **2.** (*a*) expansion (of steam, of gases); **soupape de d.,** expansion valve; (*b*) *I.C.E:* explosion, power, stroke.

détenteur, -trice [detãtœr, -tris] *n.* (*a*) holder (of securities, of challenge cup, etc.); **d. de titres,** stockholder; (*b*) owner (of copyright, etc.).

détention [detãsjɔ̃] *n.f.* **1.** holding (of securities, etc.); possession (of firearms, etc.). **2.** detention, imprisonment (of s.o.); **d. préventive,** detention pending trial.

détenu, -e [detny] *n.* prisoner.

détergent [detɛrʒã] *a. & n.m.* detergent.

déterger [detɛrʒe] *v.tr.* (**détergeant**) to clean, remove (oil stains, etc.).

détérioration [deterjɔrasjɔ̃] *n.f.* deterioration, deteriorating; damage; *Med:* **d. mentale,** mental deterioration.

détériorer [deterjɔre] *v.* **1.** *v.tr.* to make (sth.) worse; to spoil, damage. **2. se d.,** to deteriorate, to become spoilt, to spoil; **sa santé se détériore,** his health is becoming worse, is worsening.

déterminable [detɛrminabl̥] *a.* determinable.

déterminant [detɛrminã] **1.** *a.* determinant, determining, deciding (factor, cause, etc.). **2.** *n.m.* (*a*) *Ling:* determiner; (*b*) *Mth:* determinant.

déterminatif, -ive [detɛrminatif, -iv] *Ling: Gram:* **1.** *a.* determinative, defining (word, etc.). **2.** *n.m.* determiner, determinative.

détermination [detɛrminasjɔ̃] *n.f.* **1.** determination (of species, noun, date, area, etc.); typing (of bacteria, of blood). **2.** determination, resolution; **agir avec d.,** to act resolutely. **3.** resolve, determination; **prendre une d.,** to make up one's mind.

déterminé [detɛrmine] *a.* **1.** determined, definite, well-defined (area, purpose, etc.); specific, particular (aim); **dans un sens d.,** in a given direction. **2.** (*a*) determined, resolute (person, manner, etc.); (*b*) **être d. à faire qch.,** to be resolved, determined to do sth.; to have set one's heart on doing sth.

déterminer [detɛrmine] *v.tr.* **1.** to determine (species, value, noun, area, etc.); **d. un lieu de rendez-vous,** to fix, decide on, a meeting place. **2.** to cause; to give rise to (sth.); to determine (one's actions). **3. d. qn à faire qch.,** to induce, move, impel, s.o. to do sth.; **qu'est-ce qui vous a déterminé à partir?** what made you leave? **4. se d. (à faire qch.),** to make up one's mind (to do sth.).

déterminisme [detɛrminism] *n.m. Phil:* determinism.

déterministe [detɛrminist] **1.** *n.m. & f. Phil:* determinist. **2.** *a.* determinist(ic).

déterré, -ée [detɛre] *n.* **il a un air, une mine, de d.,** he looks as if he had risen from the grave; *F:* he looks like death warmed up.

déterrer [detere] *v.tr.* to dig up, unearth (buried treasure, etc.); to uproot (tree); to exhume, disinter (corpse); to dig out (old book, etc.).

détersif, -ive [detɛrsif, -iv] **1.** *a. & n.m. Med:* detersive, detergent. **2.** *n.m. Dom.Ec:* detergent, cleaning product.

détersion [detɛrsjɔ̃] *n.f. Med:* detersion; cleansing (of wound, etc.); *Dom.Ec:* cleaning with a detergent.

détestable [detɛstabl̥] *a.* awful, hateful (person, etc.); very bad, execrable (work, etc.); foul, ghastly (weather, mood).

détestablement [detɛstabləmã] *adv.* extremely badly; **chanter d.,** to sing appallingly (badly).

détester [detɛste] *v.tr.* to detest, hate; **je déteste être dérangé,** I hate to be disturbed, I hate being disturbed; **il ne déteste pas les bonbons,** he rather likes sweets.

détonant [detɔnã] **1.** *a.* detonating explosive (substance); **explosif d.,** high explosive. **2.** *n.m.* explosive.

détonateur [detɔnatœr] *n.m. Exp:* detonator.

détonation [detɔnasjɔ̃] *n.f.* (*a*) detonation; explosion; (*b*) report, bang (of firearm).

détoner [detɔne] *v.i.* to detonate, explode; **faire d.,** to detonate (dynamite, etc.).

détonner [detɔne] *v.i.* (*a*) to be, play, sing, out of tune; to sing flat, sharp; (*b*) (*of colours*) to jar, clash; **ses bijoux détonnent dans ce milieu,** her jewels are out of place, out of keeping, in these surroundings.

détordre [detɔrdr̥] *v.tr.* (*a*) to untwist, unravel (yarn, etc.); to unlay (rope); (*b*) (*of yarn, etc.*) **se d.,** to come untwisted, to untwist.

détortiller [detɔrtije] *v.tr.* to untwist (yarn, etc.); to disentangle (hair, etc.).

détour [detur] *n.m.* **1.** turning, deviation (from direct way); detour; roundabout way; **faire un long d.,** to go a long way round. **2. user de détours pour arriver à un but,** to achieve one's end in a roundabout way; **répondre sans d.,** to give a plain, straightforward, answer. **3.** turn, curve, bend (in road, river); **la route fait un brusque d.,** the road takes a sharp turn.

détourné [deturne] *a.* indirect, circuitous, roundabout (road, route); **chemin d.,** by-road; **par des voies détournées,** indirectly, in a roundabout way.

détournement [deturnəmã] *n.m.* **1.** diversion, diverting (of river, etc.); diversion, rerouting (of traffic); **d. d'avion,** hijacking. **2.** (*a*) misappropriation (of funds); embezzlement; (*b*) *Jur:* **d. de mineur,** (i) abduction, (ii) seduction, of a minor.

détourner [deturne] *v.tr.* **1.** (*a*) to divert (river, etc.); to turn (weapon, etc.) aside; to divert (traffic); **d. l'attention de qn,** to divert, distract, s.o.'s attention; **d. qn de sa route,** to lead s.o. out of his way; **d. qn de la bonne voie,** to lead s.o. astray; **d. la conversation,** to change the conversation; **d. les soupçons,** to avert suspicion; (*b*) to turn away, avert (one's head, eyes, etc.); **elle détourna les yeux,** she looked away, in another direction. **2.** to misappropriate, embezzle (funds) (**à,** from). **3. d. un avion,** to hijack a plane. **4. se d.,** to turn away, turn aside (**de,** from).

détoxication [detɔksikasjɔ̃] *n.f.* detoxication.

détoxiquer [detɔksike] *v.tr.* to detoxicate.

détracteur, -trice [detraktœr, -tris] *n.* detractor, disparager.

détraqué [detrake] *a.* (*of mechanism, digestion, etc.*) out of order; (*of pers.*) deranged; **il a le cerveau d.,** his mind is unhinged; **avoir les nerfs détraqués,** to be a nervous wreck; **le temps est d.,** the weather is unsettled; *n.* **c'est un,** he's unbalanced, a headcase.

détraquement [detrakmɑ̃] *n.m.* (*a*) putting (of mechanism, etc.) out of order; (*b*) breakdown (of mechanism, health, etc.).

détraquer [detrake] *v.tr.* (*a*) to put (apparatus) out of order; to throw (mechanism) out of gear; *F:* **cette déception lui a détraqué le cerveau,** this disappointment has unhinged his mind; **se d. l'estomac, les nerfs,** to wreck one's digestion, one's nerves; (*b*) **se d.,** (*of mechanism, etc.*) to get out of order; (*of health*) to break down; (*of digestion*) to be upset; (*of weather*) to become unsettled.

détrempe[1] [detrɑ̃p] *n.f.* **1.** (*a*) *Art:* distemper, tempera (painting); (*b*) *Paint:* distemper, tempera.

détrempe[2] *n.f.* annealing, softening (of steel).

détremper[1] [detrɑ̃pe] *v.tr.* to dilute, moisten, soak (sth.); to slake (lime); **champ détrempé,** sodden, waterlogged, field.

détremper[2] *v.tr.* to anneal, soften (steel).

détresse [detrɛs] *n.f.* **1.** grief, anguish, distress. **2.** (*a*) (financial) straits, difficulties; (*b*) *esp. Nau:* danger; **navire en d.,** ship in distress, in difficulties; **signal de d.,** distress signal; S O S.

détriment [detrimɑ̃] *n.m.* detriment, loss; *prep.phr.* **au d. de qn, de qch.,** to the detriment, prejudice, of s.o., of sth.; **je l'ai appris à mon d.,** I found it out to my cost.

détritique [detritik] *a.* detrital (deposit, etc.).

détritus [detritys] *n.m.* (*a*) rubbish; (*b*) refuse.

détroit [detrwa] *n.m.* **1.** *Geog:* strait(s), sound. **2.** *Anat:* strait (of the pelvis).

détromper [detrɔ̃pe] *v.tr.* to undeceive (s.o.); to correct (s.o.'s) mistake; **détrompez-vous!** don't you believe it!

détrôner [detrone] *v.tr.* **1.** to dethrone. **2.** to supersede, overthrow (old method, etc.).

détrousser [detruse] *v.tr. A: or Hum:* to rob, to relieve (s.o.) of his valuables.

détrousseur [detrusœr] *n.m. A: or Hum:* highwayman, footpad.

détruire [detrɥir] *v.tr.* (*pr.p.* **détruisant;** *p.p.* **détruit;** *pr.ind.* **je détruis, n. détruisons;** *impf.* **je détruisais;** *p.h.* **je detruisis;** *fu.* **je détruirai**) **1.** (*a*) to demolish, pull down, raze (building, town, etc.); to overthrow (empire, etc.); (*b*) to break up, scrap (ship, etc.); to destroy, write off (aircraft, etc.). **2.** to destroy, ruin; **la pluie a détruit la moisson,** the rain has ruined the harvest; **le village a été complètement détruit,** the village was razed to the ground; **d. les espérances de qn,** to dash, blast, s.o.'s hopes. **3. se d.** (*a*) to fall into decay, to rot; (*b*) to do away with oneself; (*c*) **critiques qui se détruisent,** criticisms that cancel (each other) out.

dette [dɛt] *n.f.* debt; (*a*) **faire des dettes,** to run into debt; **avoir des dettes,** to be in debt; **être perdu, criblé, de dettes,** to be head over ears in debt; *Book-k:* **dettes actives,** accounts receivable; assets; **dettes passives,** accounts payable; liabilities; *Fin:* **la d. publique, de l'État,** the National Debt; (*b*) **avoir une d. de reconnaissance envers qn,** to owe a debt of gratitude, to be under an obligation, to s.o.

deuil [dœj] *n.m.* **1.** (*a*) mourning, sorrow (for the loss of s.o.); *F:* **faire son deuil de qch.,** to give sth. up as lost; (*b*) bereavement. **2.** (*a*) mourning (clothes, etc.); **grand d.,** deep mourning; **porter le d.,** to be in mourning; *F:* **il avait toujours les ongles en d.,** his fingernails were always dirty; (*b*) funeral procession; **conduire le d.,** to be chief mourner.

deutérium [døterjɔm] *n.m. Ch:* deuterium.

Deutéronome [døterɔnɔm] *n.m. B:* Deuteronomy.

deux [dø; *before a vowel sound in the same word group,* døz] *num.a.inv. & n.m.* (*a*) two; **d. enfants** [døzɑ̃fɑ̃] two children; **j'en ai d.** [dø] I have two; **d. ou trois** [døzutrwa] two or three; (*of date*) **aujourd'hui nous sommes le d.,** today is the second, it's the second today; **Charles D.,** Charles the Second; **il est arrivé d. ou troisième,** he arrived second or third; (*b*) *Cards:* two, deuce; (*in dicing*) **d. et un,** deuce-ace; (*c*) **chapitre d.,** chapter two; **c'est clair comme d. et d. font quatre,** it's clear as daylight; **d. fois,** twice; **d. fois d. font quatre,** twice two is four; **tous (les) d.,** both; **des d. côtés du fleuve,** on either side, on both sides, of the river; **tous les d. jours,** every other day; **casser qch. en d.,** to break sth. in two; **diviser, couper, une ligne en d.,** to bisect a line; **marcher par d.,** to walk in pairs; to march two abreast, *Mil:* in file; **entrer d. par d.,** to come in two by two; **entre d. âges,** middle-aged; **vivre à d.,** to live (i) as (married) couple, (ii) together; **à nous d.,** (i) let's get on with it (together); (ii) let's fight it out; *Ten:* **à d.,** deuce; **à d. de jeux,** five (games) all; *F:* **il fera ça en moins de d., en d. temps, trois mouvements,** he will do it in two ticks, in no time at all; **c'est à d. pas d'ici,** it's very close, it's only a short distance away; **nous d., vous d., eux d.,** (i) the two of us, you, them; (ii) us two, you two, those two; (iii) we two, you two, these two.

deuxième [døzjɛm] *num. a. & n.* second; **appartement au d. (étage),** second floor flat, *NAm:* third floor apartment; **elle est née la d.,** she is the second child; *Mth:* **équation du d. degré,** quadratic equation.

deuxièmement [døzjɛmmɑ̃] *adv.* secondly, in the second place.

deux-mâts [døma] *n.m.* two-master.

deux-pièces [døpjɛs] *n.m.inv.* **1.** *Cost:* (*a*) two-piece swimsuit; bikini; (*b*) two-piece (dress, suit). **2.** two-roomed flat, apartment.

deux-points [døpwɛ̃] *n.m. Typ:* colon.

deux-ponts [døpɔ̃] *n.m.inv.* double-decker (ship); double-decker (aircraft).

deux-roues [døru] *n.m.inv.* two-wheeled vehicle.

deux-temps [døtɑ̃] *n.m.* **1.** *Mus:* two-two time. **2.** two stroke (engine); **(mélange) d.-t.,** two-stroke mixture.

dévaler [devale] **1.** *v.i.* to descend, go down; (*of stream*) to rush down; **le jardin dévale jusqu'à la rivière,** the garden slopes down, extends down, to the river. **2.** *v.tr.* **d. la colline, l'escalier,** to hurry down the hill, the stairs; **d. la rue à toute vitesse,** to race down the street.

dévaliser [devalize] *v.tr.* to rob (s.o. of his money, etc.); **d. une maison,** to rifle, burgle, a house.

dévalorisation [devalɔrizasjɔ̃] *n.f.* **1.** devaluation (of currency); fall in value, depreciation. **2.** discrediting (of s.o., a policy).

dévaloriser [devalɔrize] *v.tr.* **1.** to devalue (currency); to depreciate, mark down (goods). **2. se d.,** to depreciate.

dévaluation [devalɥasjɔ̃] *n.f.* devaluation (of currency).

dévaluer [devalɥe] *v.tr.* to devalue, devaluate (currency).

devancement [dəvɑ̃smɑ̃] *n.m.* (*a*) preceding; (*b*) overtaking (of s.o., sth.); (*c*) forestalling (of s.o., sth.); *Mil:* **d. d'appel,** enlistment before call-up.

devancer [dəvɑ̃se] *v.tr.* (**je devançai(s); n. devançons**) **1.** to precede; to go, come, before (s.o., sth.). **2.** to leave (the others) behind; to out-distance, overtake, outstrip; **je vous ai devancé,** (i) I got here before you; (ii) I forestalled you; **d. son époque,** to be ahead of one's times. **3. d. les désirs de qn,** to anticipate s.o.'s wishes; *Mil:* **d. l'appel,** to enlist before call-up.

devancier, -ière [dəvɑ̃sje, -jɛr] *n* (*a*) precursor; (*b*) predecessor.

devant [dəvɑ̃] **1.** *prep.* before, in front of (s.o., sth.); **regardez d. vous,** look in front of you; **assis d. un verre de vin,** sitting over a glass of wine; **marchez tout droit d. vous,** go straight ahead, on; **être courageux d. le danger,** to show courage in the face of danger; **égaux d. la loi,** equal in the eyes of the law; **sa position d. ce problème,** his position with regard to this problem; **navire d. Calais,** ship off Calais; **d. cet état de choses, d. votre silence,** in view of this state of affairs, of your silence. **2.** *adv.* (*a*) before, in (the) front; **envoyer qn d.,** to send s.o. on (in front); **aller d.,** to go in front, to lead the way; **porter qch. sens d. derrière,** to wear sth. back to front; *Nau:* **un navire d.!** ship ahead! **être vent d.,** to be in stays, to be wind ahead; *adv.phr.* **saisir qch. par d.,** to seize sth. in front; (*b*) *A: & Lit:* **comme d.,** as before. **3.** *n.m.* front (part), forepart, **d. (de chemise)** (shirt) front; **chambre sur le d.,** front room; **dents de d.,** front teeth; **pattes de d. (d'un animal),** forelegs, front paws; **prendre les devants,** (i) to go on ahead; (ii) to make the first move; **gagner les devants,** to take the lead.

devanture [dəvɑ̃tyr] *n.f.* (*a*) façade, front (of building); (*b*) **d. de magasin,** shopfront, shop window.

dévastateur, -trice [devastatœr, -tris] *a.* devastating.

dévastation [devastasjɔ̃] *n.f.* devastation, destruction, havoc.

dévaster [devaste] *v.tr.* to devastate, lay waste, ravage (country, etc.); **les cultures ont été dévastées par les pluies,** the crops have been destroyed, ruined, by the rain.

déveine [devɛn] *n.f. F:* (run of) bad luck; **être dans la d.,** to be down on one's luck; **quelle d.!** (what) hard luck!

développé [devlɔpe] *n.m.* **1.** *Sp:* (*weight lifting*) press. **2.** *Danc:* developpé.

développement [devlɔpmɑ̃] *n.m.* **1.** (*a*) spreading out, opening out (of wings, etc.); (*b*) *Mth:* expansion, development (of contracted expression, etc.). **2.** (*a*) spread (of branches of tree, etc.); (*b*) **bicyclette avec un d. de 5 m. 25,** bicycle with a 66 inch gear, geared to 66 inches. **3.** development, growth (of the body); development (of muscles, flower, faculties, etc., *Phot:* of image); **d. d'une affaire,** growth of a business; *Pol.Ec:* **pays en voie de d.,** developing countries. **4.** *Mus: Lit: Art:* development (of a theme).

développer [devlɔpe] *v.* **I.** *v.tr.* **1.** (*a*) to spread out, open out (wings, etc.); to unroll (map, etc.); to unwrap (parcel, etc.); (*b*) *Mth:* to expand, develop (contracted expression, etc.); (*c*) **bicyclette qui développe . . .,** bicycle that has a gear of . . ., that is geared to . . .. **2.** to develop (muscles, faculties, trade, etc.; *Phot:* a negative); to evolve (theory, etc.); **d. ses dons naturels par l'étude,** to improve one's natural gifts by study; **d. un sujet,** to develop a subject, to treat a subject at greater length. **II. se développer 1.** to spread out, open out, expand, extend; **la plaine se développe à perte de vue,** the plain extends, stretches out, as far as the eye can see. **2.** (*of organs, flowers, the intelligence, etc.*) to develop; **l'enfant se développe rapidement,** the child is developing rapidly.

devenir¹ [dəvnir] **I.** *v.pred.* (*conj. like* VENIR; *the aux. is* **être**) (*a*) to become; **il devint général,** he became a general; **que devenez-vous ces temps-ci?** what are you doing these days? **qu'est-il devenu?** what has become of him? **que devient votre cousin?** how is your cousin getting on? (*b*) to grow into; **il était devenu homme,** he had grown into a man; (*c*) to grow, get, turn; **d. grand,** (i) to grow tall; (ii) to grow up; **d. vieux,** to grow, get, old; **c'est à d. fou!** it's enough to drive one, you, mad!

devenir², *n.m.* gradual change, development; **la langue est dans un perpétuel d.,** language is in a constant state of flux.

dévergondage [devɛrgɔ̃daʒ] *n.m.* **1.** licentiousness. **2.** extravagance (of style, imagination).

dévergondé, -ée [devɛrgɔ̃de] **1.** *a.* (*a*) licentious, shameless; (*b*) extravagant (style, imagination). **2.** *s.* profligate; loose living man, woman.

dévergonder (se) [sədevɛrgɔ̃de] *v.pr.* to fall into dissolute ways.

dévernir [devɛrnir] *v.tr.* to take the varnish, the polish, off (furniture, etc.).

déverrouillage [devɛrujaʒ] *n.m.* unbolting, unlocking (of door, etc.).

déverrouiller [devɛruje] *v.tr.* to unbolt, unlock (door, etc.); *Artil: Sm.a:* to unlock, unbolt; to release the bolt of (a gun).

devers [dəvɛr] *prep.* (*a*) *A:* towards; (*b*) *prep.phr.* **retenir ses papiers par(-)d. soi,** to keep papers in one's possession; **par(-)d. les juges,** in the presence of the judges.

dévers [devɛr] *n.m.* (*a*) inclination, slope (of wall, etc.); banking (of road at a bend); *Rail:* vertical slant, cant, (of outer rail at curve); (*b*) warp, twist (in timber, etc.).

déversé [devɛrse] *a.* **1.** sloping, banked. **2.** lopsided. **3.** warped.

déversement¹ [devɛrsəmɑ̃] *n.m.* (*a*) inclination, sloping (of wall, etc.); (*b*) warping; warp.

déversement² *n.m.* (*a*) discharge, overflow (of liquid); (*b*) pouring out (of liquid).

déverser¹ [devɛrse] **1.** *v.tr.* (*a*) to slope (wall, etc.); to bank (road); to raise the outer rail (of railway track); (*b*) to warp (timber). **2.** *v.i. & pr.* (*a*) (*of wall, etc.*) to incline, lean; (*b*) (*of wood*) to warp.

déverser² *v.* **1.** *v.tr.* to pour (water); to discharge (overflow of canal, etc.); to tip, dump (rubbish, etc.); **le train les déversa sur le quai,** the train deposited them on the platform; **d. le mépris sur qn,** to pour contempt on s.o. **2.** (*of river, etc.*) **se d.,** to empty, flow (**dans,** into).

déversoir [devɛrswar] *n.m.* **1.** overflow (of tank, basin, etc.); *Hyd.E:* spillway (of dam). **2.** outlet, safety-valve (for one's energies, etc.).

dévêtir [devetir] *v.* (*conj. like* VÊTIR) **1.** *v.tr.* to undress, strip (s.o.). **2. se d.** (*a*) to undress, strip; to take off one's clothes; (*b*) to leave off some of one's clothing (*e.g.* in warm weather).

déviation [devjasjɔ̃] *n.f.* deviation; variation (of compass); curvature (of the spine); displacement (of uterus); departure, deviation (from proper conduct, etc.); *Aut: P.N:* **d.,** diversion, *NAm:* detour; *Elcs: El:* **champ de d.,** deflecting field.

déviationnisme [devjasjɔnism] *n.m. Pol:* deviationism.

déviationniste [devjasjɔnist] *a. & n.m. or f. Pol:* deviationist.

dévidage [devidaʒ] *n.m. Tex: etc:* (*a*) unwinding; (*b*) reeling, spooling.

dévider [devide] *v.tr. Tex: etc:* (*a*) to unwind; (*b*) to reel, spool (thread, etc.); *F:* **il m'a dévidé son chapelet,** he reeled off his whole story to me.

dévideur, -euse [devidœr, -øz] *n. Tex:* (*pers.*) reeler, wind(st)er.

dévidoir [devidwar] *n.m.* (*a*) *Tex:* reeling machine, reel, winder, spool; (*b*) hose reel; (*c*) drum (for cable).

dévié [devje] *a.* **route déviée,** diversion; **rayon de lumière d.,** refracted ray of light.

dévier [devje] *v.* (*pr.sub. & impf.* **n. déviions, v. déviiez**) **1.** *v.i.* to deviate, swerve, diverge; (*of ball*) to veer (off course); *Mec.E:* to run out of true; **faire d. une balle,** to deflect a bullet; **il ne dévie jamais de ses principes,** he never deviates, never departs, from his principles; *Nau: Av:* **d. de sa route,** to be, turn, off course. **2.** *v.tr.* to turn (blow, etc.) aside; to deflect (ray, etc.); **l'accident lui a dévié la colonne vertébrale,** the accident gave him curvature of the spine.

devin, devineresse [dəvɛ̃, dəvinrɛs] *n.* diviner; soothsayer; *f.* fortune teller; *F:* **je ne suis pas d.,** I can't see into the future.

devinable [dəvinabl] *a.* guessable; forseeable.

deviner [dəvine] *v.i.* **1.** to divine, to practise divination. **2.** *v.tr.* to guess (riddle, secret, etc.); to predict (the future); to read (s.o.'s character); **d. la pensée de qn,** to read s.o.'s thoughts; **vous ne devinez pas?** can't you guess?

devinette [dəvinɛt] *n.f.* riddle, conundrum; guessing game.

dévirer [devire] *v.tr. Nau:* to veer (the capstan).

devis [dəvi] *n.m.* estimate (of work to be done, etc.); quotation; specification.

dévisager [devizaʒe] *v.tr.* (**je dévisageai(s); n. dévisageons**) to stare, look hard, at (s.o.).

devise [dəviz] *n.f.* **1.** (*a*) *Her:* device; (*b*) motto; (*c*) slogan. **2.** *Fin:* currency; *used esp. in* **devises étrangères,** foreign currency.

deviser [dəvize] *v.i.* to chat, gossip.

dévissage [devisaʒ] *n.m.* **1.** unscrewing (of bolt, etc.). **2.** *Mount:* fall.

dévisser [devise] **1.** *v.tr.* (*a*) to unscrew (bolt nut, etc.); *F:* **d. son billard,** to die, peg out. **2.** *v.i. Mount:* to fall. **3. se d.,** to come unscrewed, to unscrew.

dévitaliser [devitalize] *v.tr. Dent:* to devitalize (tooth); *F:* to kill the nerve (of a tooth).

dévoiement [devwamɑ̃] *n.m.* canting, tilting (of flue, etc.).

dévoilement [devwalmɑ̃] *n.m.* (*a*) unveiling; (*b*) revealing, disclosure (of name, secret, etc.).

dévoiler [devwale] *v.tr.* **1.** to unveil (face, statue). **2.** to reveal, disclose (name, secret, etc.); to unmask (conspiracy); to lay bare (fraud). **3.** (*of secret, etc.*) **se d.,** to come to light.

devoir¹ [dəvwar] **I.** *v.tr.* (*pr.p.* **devant;** *p.p.* **dû,** *f.* **due;** *pr.ind.* **je dois, n. devons, ils doivent;** *pr.sub.* **je doive, n. devions, ils doivent;** *impf.* **je devais;** *p.h.* **je dus;** *fu.* **je devrai) 1.** (*duty*) should, ought; (*a*) (*general precept*) **tu dois honorer tes parents,** you should, it is your duty to, honour your parents; **fais ce que dois, advienne que pourra,** do your duty come what may; (*b*) (*command*) **vous devez, devrez, vous trouver à votre poste à trois heures,** you must be at your post at three o'clock; **les commandes doivent être adressées à . . .,** orders should be sent to . . .; (*c*) **je ne savais pas ce que je devais faire,** I did not know what (I ought) to do; **il aurait dû m'avertir,** he should have warned me; **il a cru d. refuser,** he thought it advisable to refuse. **2.** (*compulsion*) must, have to; **tous les hommes doivent mourir,** all men must die; **enfin j'ai dû céder,** finally I had to yield, I was obliged to yield. **3.** (*futurity*) (*a*) **je dois partir demain,** I am to, have to, leave tomorrow; **je devais le rencontrer à Paris,** I was to meet him in Paris; **le train doit arriver à midi,** the train is due (to arrive) at twelve o'clock; **dût-il m'en coûter la vie,** were I to die for it; (*b*) **il ne devait plus les revoir,** he was (destined) never to see them again; **cela devait arriver!** it was bound, it had, to happen. **4.** (*opinion expressed*) must; **vous devez avoir faim,** you must be hungry; **il a dû, avait dû, me prendre pour un autre,** he must have taken me for someone else; **il doit être trois heures,** it must be three o'clock; **il ne doit pas avoir plus de 40 ans,** he can't be more than 40. **5. d. qch. à qn,** to owe s.o. sth.; **il me doit mille francs,** he owes me a thousand francs; **d. du respect à son père,** to owe respect to one's father; **je lui dois d'être en vie, la vie,** I owe my life to him; **je lui dois bien cela,** it's the least I can do for him; **je me dois de le faire,** it's my duty to do it; **sa réussite est due à ses parents,** it's thanks to his parents that he's so successful. **II. se devoir 1.** to have to devote oneself to s.o., sth.; **je me dois à ma famille,** I must devote myself to my family. **2. comme il se doit,** as is right and proper.

devoir² *n.m.* **1.** (*a*) duty; **manquer à son d.,** to fail in one's duty; **faire, remplir, son d. (envers qn, envers la patrie),** to do one's duty (by s.o., by one's country); **se faire un d. de (faire qch.),** to make a point of (doing sth.); **se mettre en d. de faire qch.,** to prepare to do sth.; **il est de mon d. de vous le dire,** it is my duty, my business, to tell you; **je sais ce qui est de mon d.,** I know where my duty lies; **je l'ai fait par d.,** I did it from a sense of duty; (*b*) obligation; **mes devoirs de citoyen, de père,** my duties, obligations, as a citizen, as a father; (*c*) *Sch:* exercise; *pl.* homework, prep; **un d. de latin,** a Latin exercise. **2.** *pl.* respects, duty; **rendre ses devoirs à qn,** to pay one's respects to s.o.; **rendre à qn les derniers devoirs,** to pay the last honours to s.o.

dévoltage [devɔltaʒ] *n.m.* reduction of voltage.

dévolter [devɔlte] *v.tr. El:* to reduce the voltage of (current).

dévolteur [devɔltœr] *n.m. El:* reducing, stepdown, transformer.

dévolu [devɔly] **1.** *a. Jur:* (*of inheritance, etc.*) devolved; devolving (**à,** to, upon); **part dévolue à la ligne paternelle,** share that falls to the heirs on the father's side; **être d. à qn de faire qch.,** to fall to s.o.'s lot to do sth. **2.** *n.m.* **jeter son dévolu sur qch.,** (i) to have designs on sth., to set one's heart on sth.; (ii) to choose sth.

dévolution [devɔlysjɔ̃] *n.f. Jur:* devolution; **d. d'un héritage à l'État,** escheat.

dévorant [devɔrɑ̃] *a.* **1.** ravenous; **faim dévorante,** gnawing hunger. **2.** consuming (fire, etc.); wasting (disease); devouring (passion).

dévorateur, -trice [devɔratœr, -tris] *a.* devouring, consuming.

dévorer [devɔre] *v.tr.* (*a*) to devour (prey); (*of human beings*) to devour, eat greedily, gobble up, wolf (food); (*b*) **d. un livre,** to devour a book; **d. qn des yeux,** to devour s.o. with one's eyes, to gaze intently on s.o.; **d. sa fortune,** to squander one's fortune; **les flammes ont dévoré le bâtiment,** the flames destroyed the building; **l'angoisse le dévore,** he's sick with worry; (*c*) **d. la route,** to tear along; to eat up the miles.

dévoreur, -euse [devɔrœr, -øz] *n.* devourer; **d. de livres,** avid reader, bookworm.

dévot, -ote [devo, -ɔt] **1.** (*a*) *a.* devout, religious, pious; **être d. à un saint,** to be a votary of a saint; (*b*) *n.* devout person. **2.** *a. & n. Pej:* sanctimonious (person); bigot; *A:* **faux d.,** hypocrite.

dévotement [devɔtmɑ̃] *adv.* devoutly.

dévotion [devosjɔ̃] *n.f.* **1.** devotion, *esp.* devoutness, piety; **faire ses dévotions,** to make one's devotions, say one's prayers; **fausse d.,** assumed piety. **2. avoir une grande d. pour qn, qch.,** to have a great devotion for, to be extremely attached to, s.o., sth.; **être à la d. de qn,** to give oneself up to the service of s.o., to be at s.o.'s disposal.

dévoué [devwe] *a.* devoted, staunch, loyal (friend, etc.); *Corr:* **votre (tout) d.** = yours sincerely.

dévouement [devumɑ̃] *n.m.* **1.** self sacrifice, devotion to duty; dedication (of scientist, etc.). **2.** devotion, devotedness, affection; **soigner qn avec d.,** to nurse, look after, s.o. devotedly.

dévouer [devwe] *v.tr.* **1.** (*a*) *A:* to dedicate, consecrate (s.o., sth.). (*b*) **d. son temps, son énergie, à une cause,** to devote, sacrifice, one's time, one's energy, to a cause. **2. se d.** (*a*) *O:* to devote oneself, dedicate oneself; **se d. au secours des pauvres,** to devote oneself to the poor; (*b*) **se d. pour qn,** to sacrifice oneself for s.o.; **il est toujours prêt à se d.,** he is always ready to sacrifice himself.

dévoyé [devwaje] *a.* astray; *n.* **un jeune d.,** a delinquent.

dévoyer [devwaje] *v.tr.* **(je dévoie, n. dévoyons; je dévoierai) 1.** *Lit:* to mislead; to lead (s.o.) astray. **2. se d.,** to go astray; to stray (*esp.* from path of duty).

déwatté [dewate] *a. El:* wattless (current).

dextérité [dɛksterite] *n.f.* dexterity, skill, skilfulness; **conduire ses affaires avec d.,** to manage one's business with tact, cleverness, skill.

dextrine [dɛkstrin] *n.f. Ch: Ind:* dextrin.

dia [dja] *int.* driver's signal to horse to turn to the left, *U.S:* haw!

diabète [djabɛt] *n.m. Med:* diabetes.

diabétique [djabetik] *a. & n.* diabetic.

diable [djɑbl̩] *n.m.* **1.** devil; **le d.,** the devil, Satan; *F:* Old Nick; **en d.,** extremely; *F:* **faire le d. (à quatre),** to kick up a row; **tirer le d. par la queue,** to be hard up; **c'est bien le d. si . . .,** it would be surprising if . . .; **allez au d.!** go to the devil! go to hell! **que le d. l'emporte!** the devil take him! **(que) le d. m'emporte si j'y comprends quelque chose!** I'll be hanged, damned if I understand (it)! **il demeure au d.,** he lives miles away; **au d. vauvert, au d. vert,** a long way (away), at the back of beyond; **c'est le d. pour lui faire entendre raison,** it's damned hard to make him see reason; **ce n'est pas le d.,** (i) it's not that difficult; (ii) it's nothing to worry about; **où d. est-il allé?** where the devil has he gone? *int.* **d.!** heavens! **bruit de tous les diables,** the devil, a hell, of a din; *adv.phr.* **à la d.,** anyhow; **pauvre d.!** poor beggar! **un drôle de petit d.,** a funny little chap; **un grand d.,** a big fellow; **c'est un bon d.,** he's not a bad type; **ce d. de parapluie,** that wretched umbrella; **un d. de temps, un temps du d.,** wretched, lousy, weather; *a.* **il est très d.,** he's full of spirit, of mischief; he's a real little devil. **2.** (*a*) (two-wheeled) trolley; (railway porter's) barrow, luggage truck; (*b*) *Toys:* Jack in the box; (*c*) *Ich:* **d. de mer,** angler (fish), frog fish.

diablement [djɑbləmɑ̃] *adv. F:* devilish(ly) (strong, good, funny, etc.); **il y a d. longtemps,** it's a hell of a long time ago; **il faisait d. froid,** it was hellishly cold.

diablerie [djɑbləri] *n.f.* **1.** *A:* (*a*) devilry, sorcery; (*b*) machination, (evil) intrigue. **2.** *F:* mischievousness, boisterousness; fun, devilry.

diablotin [djɑblɔtɛ̃] *n.f.* **1.** (*a*) little devil, imp; (*b*) mischievous child, imp. **2.** (Christmas) cracker.

diabolique [djɑbɔlik] *a.* diabolic(al), fiendish; **possession d.,** demoniacal possession.

diaboliquement [djɑbɔlikmɑ̃] *adv.* diabolically, fiendishly.

diabolo [djɑbɔlo] *n.m.* **1.** *Games:* diabolo. **2.** lemonade (drink) with syrup; **d. menthe,** lemonade and mint (cordial).

diachronie [djakrɔni] *n.f. Ling:* diachrony.

diachronique [djakrɔnik] *a. Ling:* diachronic.

diaconesse [djakɔnɛs] *n.f.* deaconess.

diacre [djakr̩] *n.m. Ecc:* deacon.

diacritique [djakritik] *a. Ling:* diacritic(al) (mark, sign); **signe d.,** diacritic(al).

diadème [djadɛm] *n.m.* (*a*) diadem; (*b*) tiara.

diagnose [djagnoz] *n.f.* **1.** *Med:* diagnostics, diagnosis. **2.** *Biol:* diagnosis; characterization of species.

diagnostic [djagnɔstik] *n.m. Med:* diagnosis (of disease).

diagnostique [djagnɔstik] *a. Med:* diagnostic (skill, sign, etc.).

diagnostiquer [djagnɔstike] *v.tr. Med:* to diagnose.

diagonal, -aux [djagɔnal, -o] **1.** *a. Mth: etc:* diagonal. **2.** *n.f.* **diagonale;** (*a*) diagonal (line); **en diagonale,** diagonally.

diagonalement [djagɔnalmɑ̃] *adv.* diagonally.

diagramme [djagram] *n.m.* diagram; chart; graph.

diagraphe [djagraf] *n.m.* diagraph.

dialectal, -aux [djalɛktal, -o] *a. Ling:* dialectal.

dialecte [djalɛkt] *n.m.* dialect.

dialecticien, -ienne [djalɛktisjɛ̃, -jɛn] *n.* dialectician.

dialectique [djalɛktik] **1.** *a.* dialectic(al) (argument). **2.** *n.f.* dialectics.

dialectiquement [djalɛktikmɑ̃] *adv.* dialectically.

dialogue [djalɔg] *n.m.* dialogue; *Pol:* talks; **c'est un d. de sourds,** we're, they're, not on the same wavelength.

dialoguer [djalɔge] **1.** *v.i.* (*a*) to hold a dialogue; to converse. **2.** *v.tr. Lit:* to write (literary work) in dialogue form.

dialoguiste [djalɔgist] *n.m. & f. Cin:* screenwriter.

dialyse [djaliz] *n.f. Ch:* dialysis.

diamant [djamɑ̃] *n.m.* **1.** diamond; **d. de première eau,** diamond of the first water; **d. brut,** rough diamond; *Tls:* **d. de vitrier,** glazier's diamond, diamond point.

diamantaire [djamɑ̃tɛr] **1.** *a.* diamond-like, sparkling. **2.** *n.m.* diamond (i) cutter, (ii) merchant.

diamanté [djamɑ̃te] *a.* set with diamonds.

diamanter [djamɑ̃te] *v.tr.* (*a*) to set (piece) with diamonds; (*b*) to make (sth.) shine like a diamond.

diamantifère [djamɑ̃tifɛr] *a. Geol: etc:* diamantiferous (region, etc.); diamond-yielding, -bearing (gravel, etc.).

diamétral, -aux [djametral, -o] *a.* diametric(al), diametral (line, etc.).

diamétralement [djametralmɑ̃] *adv.* diametr(ic)ally; **opinions d. opposées,** diametrically opposite, diametrically opposed, views.

diamètre [djamɛtr̩] *n.m. Mth: etc:* diameter; **la roue a 60 cm de d.,** the wheel is 60 cm in diameter, across.

diane[1] [djan] *n.f. Mil: etc: A: & Lit:* reveille; **battre, sonner, la d.,** to sound the reveille.

Diane[2] *Pr.n.f. Myth:* Diana.

diantre [djɑ̃tr̩] *int. A: & Lit:* (*euphemistic form of* DIABLE) **que d. désirez-vous?** what the devil do you want? **d., c'est cher!** hell, it's expensive!

diapason [djapazɔ̃] *n.m. Mus:* **1.** diapason, pitch; **se mettre au d. de la compagnie,** to adapt oneself to the company, to fall in with the mood of the company. **2.** (*a*) tuning fork; (*b*) pitch pipe. **3.** compass, range (of the voice).

diaphane [djafan] *a.* (*a*) diaphanous; translucent; (*b*) transparent.

diaphragme [djafragm] *n.m.* **1.** *Anat:* diaphragm. **2.** *Tchn:* (*a*) diaphragm (of telescope, electric cell, etc.); *Phot:* diaphragm stop (of lens); **d. iris,** iris diaphragm; (*b*) soundbox (of speaker, etc.); (*c*) *Med:* (*contraceptive*) diaphragm; *F:* (Dutch) cap.

diaphragmer [djafragme] *v.tr. Phot:* to stop down (lens).

diapo [djapo] *n.f. Phot: F:* slide, transparency.

diapositive [djapɔzitiv] *n.f. Phot:* transparency, slide; **d. en couleurs,** colour slide.

diapré [djapre] *a.* variegated, mottled, speckled.

diaprer [djapre] *v.tr.* to variegate, mottle, speckle.

diarrhée [djare] *n.f. Med:* diarrhoea.

diarrhéique [djareik] **1.** *a. Med:* diarrhoeic, diarrhoeal. **2.** *n.* diarrhoeic subject.

diastase [djastɑz] *n.f. Ch:* diastase.

diastasique [djastɑzik] *a. Ch:* diastatic, diastasic.
diastole [djastɔl] *n.f. Physiol:* diastole.
diathermie [djatɛrmi] *n.f. Med:* diathermy.
diathèse [djatɛz] *n.f. Med:* diathesis, predisposition (to disease).
diatomée [djatɔme] *n.f. Algae:* diatom.
diatomique [djatɔmik] *a. Ch:* diatomic.
diatonique [djatɔnik] *a. Mus:* diatonic (scale, interval).
diatoniquement [djatɔnikmɑ̃] *adv. Mus:* diatonically.
diatribe [djatrib] *n.f.* diatribe.
dichotomie [dikɔtɔmi] *n.f.* dichotomy.
dichotomique [dikɔtɔmik] *a.* dichotomous.
dichromatique [dikrɔmatik], *a.* dichromatic.
dico [diko] *n.m. F:* dictionary.
dicotylédone [dikɔtiledɔn] *Bot:* **1.** *a.* dicotyledonous. **2.** *n.f.* dicotyledon.
Dictaphone [diktafɔn] *n.m. R.t.m:* Dictaphone.
dictateur [diktatœr] *n.m.* dictator; **ton de d.,** dictatorial tone.
dictatorial, -iaux [diktatɔrjal, -jo] *a.* dictatorial.
dictatorialement [diktatɔrjalmɑ̃] *adv.* dictatorially.
dictature [diktatyr] *n.f.* dictatorship.
dictée [dikte] *n.f.* (*a*) dictation; dictating; **écrire qch. sous la d. de qn,** to write sth. at s.o.'s dictation; (*b*) *Sch:* dictation (exercise).
dicter [dikte] *v.tr.* to dictate (letter, etc.); **d. des conditions,** to dictate, lay down, conditions; **votre conscience vous dictera votre devoir,** you must follow the dictates of your conscience; **d. sa volonté à qn,** to impose one's will on s.o.
diction [diksjɔ̃] *n.f.* diction; **professeur de d.,** elocution teacher.
dictionnaire [diksjɔnɛr] *n.m.* dictionary; lexicon; **d. anglais-français,** English-French dictionary; **d. géographique,** gazetteer; **c'est un d. ambulant,** he's a walking encyclopaedia.
dicton [diktɔ̃] *n.m.* dictum, (common) saying.
didactique [didaktik] *a.* (*a*) didactic; (*b*) technical (term, etc.).
didactiquement [didaktikmɑ̃] *adv.* didactically.
didactyle [didaktil] *Z: a.* didactyl(e).
dièdre [djɛdr̥], *Mth:* **1.** *a.* dihedral (angle). **2.** *n.m.* dihedron.
diélectrique [dielɛktrik] *a. & n.m. El:* dielectric; insulating, non-conducting (medium).
diérèse [djerɛz] *n.f.* **1.** *Ling:* diaeresis. **2.** *Surg:* diaeresis.
dièse [djɛz] *n.m. Mus:* sharp; **fa d.,** F sharp.
diesel [djezɛl] *n.m.* diesel (engine).
diéser [djeze] *v.tr.* **(je dièse, n. diésons; je diéserai)** *Mus:* to sharpen, *NAm:* sharp (note).
diète[1] [djɛt] *n.f.* diet; **d. lactée,** milk diet; **être à la diète,** to be (i) on a low diet, (ii) on a starvation diet.
diète[2] *n.f. Hist: Pol:* diet.
diététicien, -ienne [djetetisjɛ̃, -jɛn] *n.* dietician.
diététique [djetetik] *Med:* **1.** *a.* dietetic. **2.** *n.f.* dietetics.
dieu, -ieux [djø] *n.m.* **1.** god; **les dieux d'Égypte,** the gods of Egypt; **grands dieux!** heavens! **faire de qch. son d.,** to turn sth. into a cult (object). **2.** (*a*) God; **la voix de Dieu,** the voice of God; **un homme de D.,** a holy man; **s'il plaît à D.,** please God, God willing; **D. merci!** thank God! (*b*) **le bon D.,** God; **recevoir le bon D.,** to receive the Holy Sacrament; **on lui donnerait le bon D. sans confession,** he looks as though butter wouldn't melt in his mouth; (*c*) *F:* **D. merci!** thank heaven! thank goodness! **pour l'amour de D.,** for goodness' sake; **D. sait si j'ai travaillé,** heaven knows I have worked hard enough; **cela va D. sait comme,** things are going none too well. **3.** *int.* (*a*) (*admitted*) **mon D.! grand D.!** heavens (above)! **mon D. oui!** why, well, yes; **mon D. je veux bien!** well, I don't mind! (*b*) (*profane*) **bon D.! D. de D.! bon D. de bon D.! (sacré) nom de D.!** for Christ's sake! God almighty! hell!
diffa [difa] *n.f.* (*in Algeria*) diffa; banquet.
diffamant [difamɑ̃] *a.* slanderous, libellous.
diffamateur, -trice [difamatœr, -tris] *n.* slanderer, libeller.
diffamation [difamasjɔ̃] *n.f.* defamation, slander, libel.
diffamatoire [difamatwar] *a.* defamatory, slanderous, libellous.
diffamer [difame] *v.tr.* to defame, slander, libel.
différé [difere] *a.* deferred (payment, call, annuity, etc.); *El:* **coupe-circuit à action différée,** time-lag cutout; *Phot:* **obturateur à action différée,** delayed action shutter; *W.Tel: T.V:* **émission en d.,** (pre-)recorded broadcast.
différemment [diferamɑ̃] *adv.* differently.
différence [diferɑ̃s] *n.f.* difference; **d. de goûts,** differences of taste; **la d. de A à B, entre A et B, de A et de B,** the difference between A and B; **il n'y a pas de d. entre eux,** there's nothing to choose between them; **cela ne fait pas de d.,** it makes no difference, no odds; **quelle d. avec . . .!** what a difference from . . .! **faire la d. d'une chose avec une autre, entre une chose et une autre,** to distinguish, discriminate, between two things; **à la d. de . . .,** unlike . . ., contrary to . . .; *conj.phr.* **à la de. que . . .,** with this difference that . . ., except that . . .
différenciateur, -trice [diferɑ̃sjatœr, -tris] *a.* differentiating.
différenciation [diferɑ̃sjasjɔ̃] *n.f.* differentiation.
différencier [diferɑ̃sje] *v.* **1.** *v.tr.* (*impf. & pr.sub.* **n. différenciions**) to differentiate (**de, d'avec,** from); (*a*) to distinguish, to mark the difference (**entre . . . et . . .,** between . . . and . . .); (*b*) *Mth:* to obtain the differential (coefficient) of (equation, etc.). **2. se d.** (*a*) to be different (from each other), to differ; (*b*) to differentiate oneself (from s.o., sth., else).
différend [diferɑ̃] *n.m.* difference, dispute, disagreement (**entre,** between); **avoir un d. avec qn,** to be at variance with s.o.; **régler un d.** to settle a difference, a dispute.
différent [diferɑ̃] *a.* different; (*a*) unlike; **mœurs différentes des nôtres,** habits different from ours; (*b*) not the same; **ils habitent des maisons différentes,** they live in different houses; (*c*) various; **différentes personnes l'ont vu,** different people saw him; **à différentes reprises,** at various times, off and on.
différentiation [diferɑ̃sjasjɔ̃] *n.f. Mth:* differentiation.
différentiel, -ielle [diferɑ̃sjɛl] **1.** *a.* differential (calculus, gear, etc.); discriminating, discriminatory, (duty, tariff). **2.** *n.m. Aut: etc:* differential. **3.** *n.f. Mth:* **différentielle,** differential.
différer [difere] *v.* **(je diffère, n. différons; je différerai) 1.** *v.tr.* to defer, postpone (judgment); to put off, hold over (payment); **d. de faire qch.,** to defer, put off, doing sth. **2.** *v.i.* to differ; (*a*) **ils diffèrent entre eux par la taille,** they differ from one another in height; **ils diffèrent de race et d'idiome,** they are different in race and speech; (*b*) **d. d'opinion,** to differ in opinion.
difficile [difisil] *a.* **1.** difficult (work, situation, etc.); **ce raisonnement est d. à suivre,** this argument is difficult, hard, to follow; **circonstances difficiles,** trying circumstances; **les temps sont difficiles,** times are hard; **le plus d. est fait,** we've done the hardest part; **il m'est d. d'accepter,** it is difficult for me to accept, I can't very well accept. **2.** difficult to get on with, hard to please, particular, choosy; **enfant d.,**

difficult, problem, child; **il est d. à vivre,** he is difficult to get on with; **il est d. sur la nourriture,** he's difficult, fussy, about his food; *n.* **faire le d.,** to be hard to please; **ne faites pas le d.,** don't be difficult; stop fussing.

difficilement [difisilmɑ̃] *adv.* with difficulty; not easily; **il apprend d.,** he is slow at learning.

difficulté [difikylte] *n.f.* difficulty; **il est en d.,** he's in trouble; **cela ne présente aucune d.,** there is no difficulty about it; **faire, élever, des difficultés,** to create obstacles, raise objections, make difficulties; **avoir de la d. à faire qch.,** to have difficulty in doing sth., to find it hard, difficult, to do sth.; **susciter des difficultés à qn,** to put difficulties in s.o.'s way; **cela ne fera pas de d. que je sache,** I'm sure that will be all right.

diffluence [diflyɑ̃s] *n.f.* diffluence.

diffluent [diflyɑ̃] *a.* diffluent (tumour, stream).

difforme [difɔrm) *a.* deformed, misshapen, twisted (person, limb); **troncs d'arbres difformes,** gnarled tree trunks.

difformité [difɔrmite] *n.f.* deformity; malformation.

diffracter [difrakte] *v.tr. Opt:* to diffract.

diffraction [difraksjɔ̃] *n.f. Opt:* diffraction.

diffus [dify] *a.* diffused (light); diffuse (matter, inflammation, etc.); vague (thought, etc.); **éclairs diffus,** sheet lightning; **style d.,** diffuse, prolix, style.

diffusément [difyzemɑ̃] *adv.* diffusedly; wordily; vaguely.

diffuser [difyze] *v.tr.* **1.** to diffuse, spread (light, heat, etc.). **2.** (*a*) to broadcast (programme, etc.); (*b*) to spread (ideas, news); (*c*) to distribute, circulate (books, newspapers).

diffuseur [difyzœr] *n.m.* **1.** diffuser (of light); *I.C.E:* mixer, diffuser; *Sug.-R:* diffusion battery. **2.** (*pers.*) (*a*) spreader (of ideas, news, etc.); (*b*) distributor (of books, newspapers).

diffusion [difyzjɔ̃] *n.f.* **1.** diffusion (of light, heat, etc.). **2.** (*a*) spreading (of news, etc.); broadcasting (of programme); (*b*) distribution (of books).

digérer [diʒere] *v.tr.* (**je digère, n. digérons; je digérerai**) **1.** to digest, think over, assimilate (what one reads, learns). **2.** (*a*) to digest (food); **je ne digère pas le porc,** pork does not agree with me; *v.i.* **je digère mal,** I have a bad digestion; (*b*) *F:* to swallow, stomach, put up with (insult, etc.); **vérités dures à d.,** unpalatable truths.

digest [daiʒɛst, diʒɛst] *n.m. Journ: F:* digest.

digeste [diʒɛst] *a. F:* easily digestible.

digestibilité [diʒɛstibilite] *n.f.* digestibility.

digestible [diʒɛstibl̥] *a.* digestible.

digestif, -ive [diʒɛstif, -iv] **1.** *a.* (*a*) digestive; **le tube d.,** the alimentary canal; (*b*) *Med:* digestive; which aids digestion. **2.** *n.m.* brandy; liqueur.

digestion [diʒɛstjɔ̃] *n.f.* digestion; **il a une d. difficile,** he has digestive problems.

digital, -ale, -aux [diʒital, -o] **1.** *a.* digital (nerve, etc.); **empreinte digitale,** fingerprint. **2.** *n.f. Bot:* **digitale,** digitalis; **digitale pourprée,** foxglove.

digitaline [diʒitalin] *n.f. Ch: Pharm:* digitalin.

digne [diɲ] *a.* **1.** (*a*) deserving, worthy (**de,** of); **cela est d. de récompense,** that deserves a reward; **il est d. qu'on le remercie,** he deserves thanks, to be thanked; **d. d'éloges,** praiseworthy; **d. de remarque,** noteworthy; **d. d'une mère,** motherly; **d. de ce nom,** worthy of the name; **il n'est pas d. de vivre,** he is not fit to live; (*b*) **un d. homme,** a worthy man. **2.** dignified (air, etc.).

dignement [diɲmɑ̃] *adv.* with dignity.

dignitaire [diɲitɛr] *n.m.* dignitary (of the Church).

dignité [diɲite] *n.f.* **1.** dignity; **air, ton, de d.,** dignified air, tone; **elle manque de d.,** she's undignified; **elle fit une entrée pleine de d.,** she came in with great dignity. **2.** high position, dignity; **être élevé à la d. de chancelier,** to be promoted, to rise, to the dignity of chancellor.

digramme [digram] *n.m. Ling:* digraph.

digraphie [digrafi] *n.f. Com:* double-entry bookkeeping.

digression [digrɛsjɔ̃] *n.f.* **1.** digression, departure from the subject; **faire une d.,** to digress, to wander from the point.

digue [dig] *n.f. Hyd.E:* (*a*) dyke, dam, causeway; embankment (of waterway, etc.); (*b*) breakwater (of stone); sea wall; (*c*) barrier (to passions, etc.); **opposer une d. aux eaux, à la colère,** to stem the waters, a flood of anger.

diktat [diktat] *n.m.* diktat, dictate.

dilapidateur, -trice [dilapidatœr, -tris] **1.** *a.* spendthrift; wasteful. **2.** *n.* (*a*) spendthrift, squanderer; (*b*) embezzler.

dilapidation [dilapidasjɔ̃] *n.f.* **1.** wasting, dilapidation, squandering (of fortune, etc.). **2.** embezzlement, misappropriation (of funds).

dilapider [dilapide] *v.tr.* **1.** to waste, squander (fortune, etc.). **2.** to misappropriate, embezzle (funds).

dilatable [dilatabl̥] *a.* dilatable, expansible.

dilatant [dilatɑ̃] **1.** *a.* dilating, dilative (force, etc.). **2.** *n.m. Surg:* dilator.

dilatateur, -trice [dilatatœr, -tris] **1.** *a.* dilating, dilative. **2.** *n.m. Surg:* dilator.

dilatation [dilatasjɔ̃] *n.f.* (*a*) dila(ta)tion, expansion; **d. des gaz,** expansion of gases; *Const:* **joint de d.,** expansion, dilatation, joint; (*b*) distension (of stomach, etc.).

dilater [dilate] *v.* **1.** *v.tr.* (*a*) to dilate, expand; *Fig:* **d. le cœur,** to cheer, gladden, the heart; (*b*) to distend (stomach). **2. se d.** (*a*) to dilate, expand; (*b*) (*of the stomach*) to become distended.

dilatoire [dilatwar] *a. Jur: etc:* dilatory; delaying (tactics, etc.).

dilemme [dilɛm] *n.m. Log: etc:* dilemma; **les termes d'un d.,** the horns of a dilemma.

dilettante [dilɛtɑ̃t] *n.* dilettante, amateur; **faire des sciences en d.,** to dabble in science.

dilettantisme [dilɛtɑ̃tism] *n.m.* dilettantism, amateurism.

diligemment [diliʒamɑ̃] *adv. A: & Lit:* **1.** diligently. **2.** promptly, quickly.

diligence [diliʒɑ̃s] *n.f.* **1.** *A: & Lit:* (*a*) diligence, industry, application; (*b*) haste, dispatch; **faire d.,** to hurry, to make haste. **2.** *Jur:* proceedings. **3.** *A.Veh:* (stage)coach.

diligent [diliʒɑ̃] *a. A: & Lit:* **1.** diligent, industrious; **soins diligents,** assiduous care. **2.** speedy, prompt (messenger, etc.).

diluer [dilɥe] *v.tr.* to dilute (**de,** with); to water down (drink, etc.); to thin down (paint); to weaken (power, etc.).

dilution [dilysjɔ̃] *n.f.* dilution; thinning down; watering down (of liquid).

diluvien, -ienne [dilyvjɛ̃, -jɛn] *a.* **1.** diluvian (fossils, etc.); diluvial (deposit, clay, etc.). **2. pluie diluvienne,** torrential rain, downpour.

dimanche [dimɑ̃ʃ] *n.m.* Sunday; **d. des Rameaux, de Pâques,** Palm Sunday, Easter Sunday; **venez me voir d.,** come and see me on Sunday; **il vient le d.,** he comes on Sundays; **habits du d.,** (one's) Sunday clothes, best; *F:* **chauffeur du d.,** weekend, Sunday, driver.

dîme [dim] *n.f. Hist:* tithe.

dimension [dimɑ̃sjɔ̃] *n.f.* (*a*) dimension, size; **à deux, à trois, dimensions,** two-, three-dimensional; **prendre les dimensions de qch.,** to take the measurements of sth.; **prendre les dimensions de qn,** to size s.o. up; **taillé à la d.,** cut to size; (*b*) **ce travail n'est pas à la d. de son talent,** this work is not equal to his talent.

diminué [diminɥe] **1.** *Mus:* diminished (interval). **2.** (*of clothes*) fully fashioned; *Knit:* (*of row*) decreased. **3. colonne diminuée,** tapering column. **4. c'est un homme diminué,** he is failing, he is not what he used to be; *n.m.* **diminué physique,** physically handicapped person.

diminuer [diminɥe] **1.** *v.tr.* to lessen; to diminish; reduce; to shorten; *Knit:* to decrease (number of stitches); to reduce, bring down (prices); to lessen (authority, etc.); to taper (column); **cela vous diminuerait aux yeux du public,** it would lower you in the eyes of the public; **d. le son,** to reduce the volume of sound. **2.** *v.i.* to diminish, decrease, lessen, grow less; (*of fever, etc.*) to abate; (*of profits*) to fall off, decline; (*of prices*) to fall; (*of column*) to taper; **d. de vitesse,** to slow down, to reduce speed; **les jours diminuent,** the days are drawing in, are growing shorter; **ses forces ont diminué,** his strength has declined, is declining; *Nau:* **d. de toile,** to shorten sail; (*of water*) **d. de profondeur, de fond,** to shoal. **3. se d.,** to lower, belittle, oneself.

diminutif, -ive [diminytif, -iv] *a. & n.m.* diminutive; **appeler qn par, de, son d.,** to call s.o. by his pet name, by his nickname.

diminution [diminysjɔ̃] *n.f.* diminution, lessening; reduction, decrease, lowering (of price, etc.); abatement (of fever, etc.); cutting down (of expenses); slackening (of speed); tapering (of column); *Knit:* **commencer les diminutions,** to begin decreasing, to decrease.

dimorphe [dimɔrf] *a. Biol: Cryst:* dimorphic, dimorphous.

dinanderie [dinɑ̃dri] *n.f.* copper, brass, kitchen utensils; brass ware, copper ware.

dinde [dɛ̃d] *n.f.* **1.** turkey hen; *Cu:* turkey. **2.** stupid woman.

dindon [dɛ̃dɔ̃] *n.m.* **1.** turkey (cock). **2. être le d. de la farce,** to be fooled, duped; to be made a fool of.

dindonneau, -eaux [dɛ̃dɔno] *n.m.* young turkey, turkey poult.

dîner¹ [dine] *v.i.* to dine, to have dinner; *Fr. C: Belg:* to (have) lunch; **d. en ville,** to dine out; **à quelle heure dînez-vous?** what time do you have dinner; **avoir, inviter, qn à d.,** to have, invite, s.o. for, to, dinner; *Prov:* **qui dort dîne,** he who sleeps forgets his hunger.

dîner² *n.m.* dinner; *Fr.C: Belg:* lunch; **je donne un d. ce soir,** I'm having a dinner party tonight.

dînette [dinɛt] *n.f. F:* **1.** (*a*) dolls' tea party; (*b*) doll's teaset. **2.** informal meal (between friends).

dîneur, -euse [dinœr, -øz] *n.* diner.

dingo¹ [dɛ̃go] *n.m. Z:* dingo (of Australia).

dingo² [dɛ̃go], **dingue** [dɛ̃g] *a. & n.m. & f. F:* (*a*) *a.* crazy, nuts, off his head; (*b*) *n.* idiot, nutcase, loony.

dinguer [dɛ̃ge] *v.i. F:* **s'en aller d.,** to go sprawling; **envoyer d. qch.,** to fling sth. away; **envoyer d. qn,** (i) to send s.o. packing; (ii) to send s.o. spinning (**contre,** against).

dinosaure [dinɔsɔr] *n.m. Paleont:* dinosaur.

diocésain, -aine [djɔsezɛ̃, -ɛn] *a. & n. Ecc:* diocesan.

diocèse [djɔsɛz] *n.m. Ecc:* diocese.

diode [djɔd] *a. & n.f. W.Tel:* diode; **d. en montage croisé,** cross-connected diode.

dionée [djɔne] *n.f. Bot:* Venus's fly trap.

dioptrie [djɔptri] *n.f. Opt:* dioptre.

dioptrique [djɔptrik] **1.** *a.* dioptric, refractive. **2.** *s.f.* refraction, dioptrics.

diorama [djɔrama] *n.m.* diorama.

dioxide [diɔksid] *n.m. Ch:* dioxide.

diphasé [difɑze] *a. El:* two-phase (system, etc.).

diphtérie [difteri] *n.f. Med:* diphtheria.

diphtérique [difterik] *a. Med:* diphther(it)ic, diphtherial.

diphtongue [diftɔ̃g] *n.f. Ling:* diphthong.

diphtonguer [diftɔ̃ge] *v.tr. Ling:* to diphthongize.

diplégie [dipleʒi] *n.f. Med:* diplegia, bilateral paralysis.

diplodocus [diplɔdɔkys] *n.m. Paleont:* diplodocus.

diplomate [diplɔmat] *n.m.* **1.** diplomat; diplomatist; *a.* **un air d.,** a diplomatic appearance. **2.** *Cu:* = trifle.

diplomatie [diplɔmasi] *n.f.* **1.** diplomacy; **user de d.,** to be diplomatic. **2. entrer dans la d.,** to enter the diplomatic service.

diplomatique [diplɔmatik] *a.* diplomatic (service, body, etc.); **valise d.,** diplomatic bag, *F:* the bag, *U.S:* (diplomatic) pouch; **réponse d.,** diplomatic answer.

diplomatiquement [diplɔmatikmɑ̃] *adv.* (*a*) diplomatically; (*b*) tactfully, discreetly.

diplôme [diplom] *n.m.* diploma (of teacher, doctor, etc.); **il a ses diplômes,** (i) he has his degree, he is a graduate; (ii) he is qualified.

diplômé, -ée [diplome] *a. & n.* = graduate; holder of diploma; **architecte d.,** fully qualified architect.

diplopie [diplɔpi] *n.f. Med:* diplopia, double vision.

dipsomane [dipsɔman], **dipsomaniaque** [dipsɔmanjak] *a. & n.* dipsomaniac.

dipsomanie [dipsɔmani] *n.f.* dipsomania.

diptère¹ [diptɛr] *Ent:* **1.** *a.* dipterous, two-winged. **2.** *n.m.* dipter(an); **les diptères,** the Diptera.

diptère² *a. Arch:* dipteral (temple).

diptyque [diptik] *n.m.* diptych.

dire¹ [dir] *v.tr.* (*pr.p.* **disant;** *p.p.* **dit;** *pr.ind.* **je dis, n. disons, vous dites, ils disent;** *impf.* **je disais;** *p.h.* **je dis;** *fu.* **je dirai**) **1.** to say, tell; (*a*) **d. qch. à qn,** to tell s.o. sth., to say sth. to s.o.; **vous ne m'en avez jamais rien dit,** you never mentioned it; **envoyer d. à qn que . . .,** to send word to s.o. that . . .; **ce disant . . ., ceci dit . . .,** with these words . . ., having said that . . .; **d. du mal de qn,** to speak ill of s.o.; **qu'en dira-t-on?** what will people say? **je n'ai rien à d. contre lui,** I have nothing to say against him, have no objection to him; **d. un secret,** to tell a secret; **d. ce qu'on pense,** to say what one thinks, to speak one's mind; **un ami, que dis-je! un frère,** a friend, no, a brother! **quand je vous le disais! je vous l'avais bien dit!** didn't I say so? **c'est justement ce que j'allais d.!** that's just what I was about to say! **d. bonjour à qn,** to say good day, good morning, good afternoon, to s.o.; **d. bonsoir à qn,** to say goodnight to s.o.; to wish s.o. goodnight; **comme dit l'autre, comme on dit,** as the saying does; as they say; **comment dites-vous cela en français?** how do you say that in French? what is the French for that? **cela ne se dit pas,** that isn't said, that expression isn't used; **qui vous dit qu'il viendra?** how do you know he will come? **puisque je vous le dis,** you can take it from *me*; *F:* **à qui le dites-vous?** who are you telling? you're telling me! (*at auction sale*) **qui dit mieux?** any advance? **dites toujours!** go on! say it! *F:* fire away! **d. que oui,** to say yes; **je vous dis que non,** I tell you, no; **je ne sais comment d.,** I don't know how to put it; **je me disais que tout était fini,** I thought all was over; **que dites-vous de ce tableau?** what do you think of this picture? **à vrai d.,** to tell the truth; **pour tout d.,** in a word; **c'est tout d.,** I need say no more; **tout n'est pas dit,** we haven't heard the last of it; **pour ainsi d.,** so to speak, as it were; *F:* **comme qui dirait . . .,** as you might say . . .; **à ce qu'il dit,** according to him; **j'ai dit ce que j'avais à d.,** I (have) had my say; *F:* **vous l'avez dit!** you've said it! **aussitôt dit, aussitôt fait,** no sooner said than done; **cela va sans dire,** that goes without saying;

tenez-vous cela pour dit, don't let me have to tell you that again; that's my last word; that's it! **alors c'est dit, voilà qui est dit,** (well then), that's settled, decided; **on dit que c'est lui le coupable,** he is said to be the culprit; **on dirait qu'il va pleuvoir,** it looks like rain; **on aurait dit que . . .,** it seemed as though . . .; **on se dirait en Suisse,** you might think you were in Switzerland; **il n'y a pas à d.,** there's no denying it, no doubt about it; **dites donc, dis donc,** (i) tell me now . . .; (ii) look here, I say (that's enough)! *P:* **non, mais, dis!** do you mind? that's a bit thick! **et d. qu'il n'a que vingt ans!** and to think that he's only twenty! **c'est beaucoup d.,** that's going rather far; **vous avez beau d.,** you can argue as much as you like; **on dirait qu'il pleut,** it looks as if it were raining; **on dirait du Mozart,** it sounds like Mozart; **on dirait du gin,** it tastes like gin; (*b*) **on le dit mort,** he is reported (to be) dead, they say he's dead. **2.** (*a*) **d. à qn de faire qch.,** to tell, order, s.o., to do sth.; **dites-lui d'entrer,** ask him to come in; **faites ce qu'on vous dit,** do as you are told; (*b*) **dites qu'on le fasse entrer,** ask them to show him in. **3. d. des vers,** to recite poetry; **d. son chapelet,** to tell one's beads. **4.** (*a*) to show, express; **horloge qui dit l'heure exacte,** clock that tells the right time; **cela en dit long sur son courage,** it speaks volumes for his courage; **ce nom ne me dit rien,** the name conveys, means, nothing to me; **cela ne me disait rien de bon,** I didn't like the look of it; (*b*) to suit (s.o.), appeal to (s.o.); **cette musique ne me dit rien,** this music does not appeal to me, I don't care for this music; **si cela te dit,** if you feel like it. **5.** (*a*) **je veux d. . . .,** that is to say . . ., I mean . . .; **que voulez-vous d. par là?** what do you mean by that? **que veut d. ce mot?** what does this word mean? (*b*) **qu'est-ce à d.?** what does this mean? **est-ce à d. qu'il ne viendra pas?** does this mean he won't come? (*c*) **faire d. qch. à qn,** to send word of sth. to s.o.; **je lui ai fait d. de venir,** I sent for him; **il ne se le fit pas d. deux fois,** he didn't wait to be told twice; (*d*) **faire d. qch. à qn,** to make s.o. say, tell, sth.; *F:* **je ne vous le fais pas d.,** I'm not telling you anything you don't know; you know that very well already; (*e*) **faire d. qch. par qn,** to send word of sth. through s.o.; (*f*) *with inf.* **vous m'avez dit adorer la musique,** you told me you loved music.

dire,[2] *n.m.* statement, assertion; *Jur:* allegation; **on ne peut pas se fier à leurs dires,** one cannot trust their statements, what they say; **au d. de l'expert,** according to expert opinion; **selon son d., à son d.,** according to him, by his own account.

direct [dirɛkt] (*a*) *a.* direct, straight; **descendre de qn en ligne directe,** to be a direct descendant of s.o.; **impôts directs,** direct taxes; **une personne directe,** a straightforward person; *Gram:* **complément d.,** direct object; *Rail:* **train d.,** through train, fast train; (*b*) *n.m. W.Tel:* **émission en d.,** live broadcast; (*c*) *n.m. Box:* **d. du droit,** straight right.

directement [dirɛktəmɑ̃] *adv.* directly, straight; **il est venu d. vers nous,** he came straight towards us; **se diriger d. au nord,** to go due north; **répondre d. à la question,** to give a direct, straight, answer to the question; **expédier des marchandises d. à qn,** to send goods direct to s.o.

directeur, -trice [dirɛktœr, -tris] **1.** *n.* director; manager, manageress; head (of industrial concern, etc.); headmaster, headmistress (of school); principal (of school); governor (of prison); conductor (of orchestra); editor (of paper); leader (of undertaking); **d. d'école,** headmaster of primary school; **d. gérant,** managing director; **(président) d. général,** general manager; *Adm:* **d. général (d'un ministère),** permanent under-secretary; *Ecc:* **d. (de conscience),** spiritual adviser, director. **2.** *a.* directing, managing, controlling (force, etc.); guiding (principle); *Cy:* **roue directrice,** front wheel.

directif, -ive [dirɛktif, -iv] **1.** *a.* directing, guiding (rule, etc.). **2.** *n.f.* **directive,** instruction, directive; *Pol:* guideline.

direction [dirɛksjɔ̃] *n.f.* **1.** (*a*) guidance, direction: conduct (of undertaking, war); management, control (of business, house, etc.); directorate (of firm, etc.); editorship (of newspaper); head(master)ship (of school); leadership (of party); **orchestre (placé) sous la d. de X,** orchestra conducted by X; (*b*) (i) board (of directors); directorate; (ii) administrative staff; management; (*c*) (i) offices (of the board); manager's office; (ii) head office (of firm, etc.). **2.** direction, driving, guiding (of engine, etc.); *Aut: Nau:* steering. **3.** direction, course; *Nau:* bearing; **changer de d.,** to change one's direction; to alter one's course, one's route; **quelle d. ont-ils prise?** which way did they go? **ce train va en d. de Paris,** this train goes to Paris; **le courant de l'opinion prend une nouvelle d.,** opinion is taking a new turn. **4.** advice; guidance.

directionnel, -elle [dirɛksjɔnɛl] *a.* directional (aerial, etc.).

directoire [dirɛktwar] *n.m. Fr:Hist:* **le D.,** the Directoire (1795–9); *Furn:* **chaise D.,** Directoire chair.

directorial[1]**, -aux** [dirɛktɔrjal, -o] *a. Fr.Hist:* directorial (constitution, government).

directorial[2]**, -aux** *a.* directorial, managerial.

dirigé [diriʒe] *a.* controlled, managed; **économie dirigée,** planned economy; *Sch:* **activités dirigées,** extra-curricular activities.

dirigeable [diriʒabl] **1.** *a.* dirigible. **2.** *n.m. Aer:* dirigible (balloon); airship.

dirigeant, -ante [diriʒɑ̃, -ɑ̃t] **1.** *a.* directing, guiding (power, principle, etc.); **classes dirigeantes,** ruling classes. **2.** *n.* leader; ruler.

diriger [diriʒe] *v.tr.* **(je dirigeai(s); n. dirigeons) 1.** to direct, control, manage; to run (business, school, etc.); to conduct (orchestra); to edit (newspaper); to superintend, conduct (proceedings, election, etc.); **d. la production,** to control production. **2.** (*a*) to direct, guide, lead (sth., s.o.); to drive (horse, car); to steer, navigate (ship); **d. un colis sur Paris,** to send a parcel off to Paris; (*b*) **d. ses pas vers . . .,** to go, move, towards . . .; **d. son attention sur qch.,** to turn one's attention to sth.; **d. ses accusations contre qn,** to level, aim, accusations at s.o.; (*c*) to aim (rifle, gun) **(sur,** at); to level, point (telescope) **(sur,** at). **3. se d.** (*a*) **se d. vers un endroit,** to turn, to make one's way, towards a place; to make for, head for, a place; **le navire se dirigea vers le port,** the ship steered, headed, for the harbour; (*b*) **se d. vers qn,** to go up to s.o.

dirigisme [diriʒism] *n.m. Pol.Ec:* planning; planned economy.

dirigiste [diriʒist] *Pol.Ec:* **1.** *a.* **système d.,** system of planned economy. **2.** *n.m. & f.* advocate, exponent, of planned economy.

discal [diskal] *a. Med:* **hernie discale,** slipped disc.

discernable [disɛrnabl̩] *a.* discernible, visible.

discernement [disɛrnəmɑ̃] *n.m.* **1.** perception, distinguishing (by sight); discrimination **(de . . . et de . . .,** between . . . and . . .); **faire le d. de deux choses,** to distinguish, discriminate, between two things. **2.** discernment, judgment; **agir sans d.,** to act without proper judgment; **âge de d.,** age of understanding.

discerner [disɛrne] *v.tr.* (*a*) to discern, distinguish (sth.); **on discernait une maison dans le lointain,** we could (just) see, make out, a house in the distance; (*b*) to distinguish (sth. from sth.); to discriminate (between sth. and sth.); **d. le bien du mal,** to tell right from wrong.

disciple [disipl̩] *n.m. & f.* disciple; follower.

disciplinable [disiplinabl] *a.* that can be disciplined.
disciplinaire [disipliner] *a.* disciplinary (punishment, etc.).
discipline [disiplin] *n.f.* **1.** scourge (for self flagellation). **2.** discipline; (*a*) **garder la d.,** to maintain discipline, order; **il ne sait pas maintenir la d.,** he cannot keep discipline; (*b*) branch of instruction; subject.
discipliné [disipline] *a.* disciplined.
discipliner [disipline] *v.tr.* to discipline (school); to bring (troops, etc.) under control, under discipline; **il faut se d.,** one must discipline oneself.
discobole [diskɔbɔl] *n.m.* **1.** (*a*) *Gr.Ant:* discobolus; (*b*) *Sp:* discus thrower.
discoïde [diskɔid], **discoïdal, -aux** [diskɔidal, -o] *a.* discoid(al); disc-shaped.
discontinu [diskɔ̃tiny] **1.** *a.* discontinuous. **2.** *n.m.* discontinuity.
discontinuer [diskɔ̃tinɥe] *A: & Lit: rarely used now except in the phrase* **sans d. 1.** *v.tr.* to discontinue, stop (sth.). **2.** *v.i.* to discontinue, stop, leave off; **parler pendant des heures sans d.,** to talk for hours on end, without a break.
discontinuité [diskɔ̃tinɥite] *n.f.* discontinuity.
disconvenance [diskɔ̃vnɑ̃s] *n.f. Lit:* **1.** unsuitableness, unfitness (of climate, occupation, etc.). **2.** disparity, dissimilarity (between persons, objects).
disconvenir [diskɔ̃vnir] *v.i.* (*conj. like* VENIR; *the aux. is* **avoir**) **1. d. à qn, à qch.,** to be unsuited to, unsuitable for, s.o., sth. **2. d. de qch.,** not to agree with sth.; **je n'en disconviens pas,** I admit it, I don't deny it; **d. que** + *sub.*, to deny that . . ..
discophile [diskɔfil] *n.m. & f.* record enthusiast; *U.S:* discophile.
discordance [diskɔrdɑ̃s] *n.f.* **1.** discordance, dissonance (of sounds); clashing (of colours); difference (of opinions); clash (of personalities). **2.** *Geol:* unconformability (of strata).
discordant [diskɔrdɑ̃] *a.* **1.** discordant, dissonant (sound); grating, jarring (noise); clashing (colours); conflicting (evidence, opinions, etc.). **2.** *Geol:* **stratifications discordantes,** uncomformable strata.
discorde [diskɔrd] *n.f.* discord, dissension, strife; **semer la d.,** to make trouble.
discothèque [diskɔtɛk] *n.f.* (*a*) record library; (*b*) record cabinet; (*c*) record collection; (*d*) discothèque; *F:* disco.
discoureur, -euse [diskurœr, -øz] *n. Pej:* (great) talker; speechifier.
discourir [diskurir] *v.i.* (*conj. like* COURIR) *usu. Pej:* to discourse, to air one's opinions (**sur,** on).
discours [diskur] *n.m.* **1.** talk; *O:* **ce sont des d. en l'air,** it's all (idle) talk. **2.** discourse, dissertation, treatise. **3.** speech, oration; **prononcer, faire, un d.,** to make a speech; **tenir un d. à qn,** to address s.o. at length. **4.** diction, language; *Gram:* **parties du d.,** parts of speech; **d. indirect,** indirect, reported, speech.
discourtois [diskurtwa] *a.* discourteous.
discourtoisement [diskurtwazmɑ̃] *adv.* discourteously.
discourtoisie [diskurtwazi] *n.f. A:* discourtesy.
discrédit [diskredi] *n.m.* discredit, loss of credit; disrepute; **être en d. auprès de qn,** to be in s.o.'s disfavour.
discréditer [diskredite] *v.* **1.** *v.tr.* to disparage, run down (s.o.); to discredit (theory, etc.); **d. l'autorité de qn,** to bring s.o.'s authority into disrepute. **2. se d.,** to become discredited (**auprès de qn,** in s.o.'s eyes); to (bring) discredit (upon) oneself.
discret, -ète [diskrɛ, -ɛt] *a.* **1.** (*a*) discreet, cautious, circumspect (behaviour, conversation, etc.); **être trop d.,** to be too reticent; *Post: etc:* **sous pli d.,** under plain cover; (*b*) quiet, unobtrusive, unassuming; sober, simple, plain (clothes); inconspicuous (appearance, etc.); modest (request, etc.); quiet, secluded (place). **2.** *Mth:* discrete (quantity); *Ph:* discontinuous (function).
discrètement [diskrɛtmɑ̃] *adv.* (*a*) discreetly, with discretion; **il lui a parlé d.,** he had a quiet word with him; (*b*) quietly, unobtrusively, modestly, simply.
discrétion [diskresjɔ̃] *n.f.* discretion. **1.** prudence, circumspection, judgment; **user de qch. avec d.,** to use sth. in moderation; **avoir de la d.,** to be discreet. **2. être à la d. de qn,** to be in s.o.'s hands; *adv. phr.* **à d.,** (i) at one's own discretion; (ii) unconditionally; **pain à d.,** unlimited bread, as much bread as one wants.
discrétionnaire [diskresjɔnɛr] *a.* discretionary (powers, etc.).
discrimination [diskriminasjɔ̃] *n.f.* discrimination; differentiation; **d. raciale,** racial discrimination.
discriminatoire [diskriminatwar] *a.* discriminatory, discriminating.
discriminer [diskrimine] *v.tr. Lit:* to discriminate, to distinguish.
disculper [diskylpe] *v.* **1.** *v.tr.* to exculpate, exonerate (**de,** from); to clear (s.o. of a crime). **2. se d.,** to exonerate oneself (**de,** from); to clear oneself (**de,** of).
discursif, -ive [diskyrsif, -iv] *a.* discursive.
discussion [diskysjɔ̃] *n.f.* **1.** discussion, debate; **question en d.,** the question under discussion, in debate, under debate, at issue; **aborder la d. d'une question,** to take up a matter; **sans d. possible,** indisputably; **il s'exécuta sans d.,** he complied without arguing (the point); **entrer en d. avec qn,** to enter into an argument with s.o. **2.** *Jur:* **d. de biens,** enquiry into the assets of a debtor (with a view to recovery of debt).
discutable [diskytabl] *a.* debatable, questionable, arguable, doubtful (point, etc.).
discutailler [diskytɑje] *v.i. F: Pej:* to natter away; to argue, to quibble.
discuté [diskyte] *a.* disputed (question); much discussed (book, subject).
discuter [diskyte] **1.** *v.tr.* (*a*) to discuss, debate; **d. un problème,** to examine a problem; **discutons la chose,** let's talk the matter over, let's talk it over; *F:* **d. le coup, le bout de gras,** to have a natter, a chat; (*b*) to question, dispute; **d. un droit,** to call a right into question. **2.** *Jur:* **d. un débiteur,** (i) to enquire into the assets of a debtor; (ii) to sell up a debtor. **3.** *v.i.* **d. avec qn sur qch.,** to argue with s.o. about sth.; **d. (de) politique,** to discuss politics; **ne discutez pas,** no arguing, don't argue.
discuteur, -euse [diskytœr, -øz] *n.* arguer.
disert [dizɛr] *a. Lit:* eloquent, fluent (orator).
disette [dizɛt] *n.f.* scarcity, dearth, shortage; **d. d'eau,** drought; **vivre dans la d.,** to live in poverty.
diseur, -euse [dizœr, -øz] *n.* (*a*) monologuist; diseur, diseuse; (*b*) **d., diseuse, de bonne aventure,** fortune teller.
disgrâce [disgrɑs] *n.f.* disfavour, disgrace; **encourir la d. de qn,** to incur s.o.'s displeasure.
disgracié [disgrasje] *a.* out of favour; disgraced.
disgracier [disgrasje] *v.tr.* (*impf. & pr.sub.* **n. disgraciions, v. disgraciiez**) to dismiss (s.o.) from favour; to disgrace.
disgracieux, -ieuse [disgrasjø, -jøz] *a.* **1.** awkward, ungraceful, inelegant (person). **2.** ungracious (answer). **3.** (*of face, etc.*) (i) ugly; (ii) plain, *U.S:* homely.
disjoindre [disʒwɛ̃dr] *v.* **1.** *v.tr.* (*conj. like* JOINDRE) to disjoint, separate, disconnect, take apart. **2. se d.,** to come apart, to separate.

disjoint [disʒwɛ̃] *a.* (*a*) disjoined, disjointed, disconnected (parts, etc); (*b*) *Mus:* disjunct (motion).

disjoncteur [disʒɔ̃ktœr] *n.m. El:* circuit breaker, cutout.

disjonctif, -ive [disʒɔ̃ktif, -iv] *a.* disjunctive.

disjonction [disʒɔ̃ksjɔ̃] *n.f.* disjunction, separation (of parts of whole); *Jur:* severance (of causes, etc.).

dislocation [dislɔkasjɔ̃] *n.f.* dislocation (of joint, business); taking to pieces, dismantling (of machine, etc.); dismemberment (of empire, etc.); *Geol:* fault; *Mil: etc:* dispersal, breaking up (of troops, etc.).

disloqué [dislɔke] **1.** *a.* (*of limb*) dislocated; out of joint; (*of machine*) dismantled; (*of empire, etc.*) dismembered, broken up.

disloquer [dislɔke] *v.* **1.** *v.tr.* to dislocate; to put (limb) out of joint; to take (machine) to pieces, to dismantle (machine); to break up, disperse (troops); to dismember (state). **2. se d.,** to break up, to fall to pieces; **son bras s'est disloqué,** he's dislocated his arm.

disparaître [disparɛtr̥] *v.i.* (*conj. like* PARAÎTRE) to disappear. **1.** to vanish; (*of pers.*) to go missing; **d. aux regards,** to vanish out of sight, disappear from view; **le soleil a disparu à l'horizon,** the sun sank below the horizon; **il a disparu sans laisser de traces,** he's disappeared without trace; **tous ses amis ont disparu,** all his friends have died, are dead; **faire d. qn, qch.,** (i) to make away with s.o., sth.; to remove (stain, etc.); (ii) to put s.o., sth., out of sight; to hide sth.; **j'ai pris un cachet pour faire d. la douleur,** I took a pill to relieve, get rid of, the pain; **cette mode disparaît,** this fashion is going out; **sa timidité disparaît peu à peu,** his shyness is wearing off. **2.** to be hidden; **la muraille disparaît sous le lierre,** the wall is hidden under the ivy.

disparate [disparat] *a.* (*a*) dissimilar; (*b*) ill matched, ill assorted; jarring; **couleurs disparates,** clashing colours.

disparité [disparite] *n.f.* disparity (of age, etc.).

disparition [disparisjɔ̃] *n.f.* **1.** disappearing, vanishing. **2.** disappearance; **remarquer la d. de qch.,** to miss sth.

disparu, -ue [dispary] **1.** *a.* (*a*) *Mil: etc:* missing; **être porté d.,** to be reported missing; **marin d. en mer,** sailor lost at sea; (*b*) extinct, bygone (race, etc.) vanished (world, etc.). **2.** *n.* (*a*) dead person, deceased; **nos chers disparus,** our dear departed; (*b*) *Mil:* missing soldier (believed dead).

dispendieusement [dispɑ̃djøzmɑ̃] expensively; extravagantly.

dispendieux, -ieuse [dispɑ̃djø, -jøz] *a.* expensive (process, etc.); expensive, extravagant (tastes).

dispensaire [dispɑ̃sɛr] *n.m.* = out-patients' department (of hospital); clinic; health centre.

dispensateur, -trice [dispɑ̃satœr, -tris] *n.* dispenser, distributor (of charity, justice, etc.).

dispense [dispɑ̃s] *n.f.* **1.** (*a*) exemption (from military service, etc.); **d. d'age,** waiving of age limit; (*b*) *Ecc:* dispensation. **2.** certificate of exemption.

dispenser [dispɑ̃se] *v.tr.* **1. d. qn de qch., de faire qch.,** to exempt, excuse, s.o. from sth., from doing sth.; **dispensez-moi de ce voyage,** spare me this journey; **d. qn du service militaire,** to exempt s.o. from military service; **je vous dispense de vos commentaires,** you can keep your remarks to yourself. **2.** to dispense, distribute (charity, favours, etc.). **3. se d. de (faire) qch.,** to excuse oneself from (doing) sth., to get out of (doing) sth.; **on peut s'en d.,** we, one, can do without it.

dispersé [dispɛrse] *a.* scattered (leaves, etc.); disorganized (work, etc.).

disperser [dispɛrse] *v.* **1.** *v.tr.* to disperse, scatter; to spread (far and wide); to disperse, break up (crowd); **d. une armée,** to rout an army. **2. se d.,** to disperse, scatter; (*of clouds, crowd, etc.*) to break up.

dispersion [dispɛrsjɔ̃] *n.f.* **1.** dispersion, dispersal (of people); breaking up (of crowd); scattering (of leaves, etc.); rout (of army); **2.** *Opt:* dispersion, decomposition (of light).

disponibilité [dispɔnibilite] *n.f.* **1.** availability (of seats, capital, etc.); **avoir la d. de qch.,** to have the disposal of sth.; *Mil:* **la d.,** the reserve; **mettre qn en d.,** to release s.o. temporarily from duty. **2.** *pl.* (*a*) available time, means; (*b*) *Fin:* available funds, liquid assets.

disponible [dispɔnibl̥] **1.** *a.* available; at (s.o's) disposal; **places disponibles,** vacant, unoccupied, seats (in bus, etc.); **êtes-vous d. ce soir?** are you free tonight? *Com:* **marché du d.,** spot market; **actif d.,** *n.m.* **le d.,** liquid assets; *Mil:* **officier d.,** unattached officer, half-pay officer. **2.** *n.m. Mil:* member of the reserve.

dispos [dispo] *a.* (*a*) fit, well, in good form, in good spirits; (*b*) **esprit d.,** fresh, alert, mind.

disposé [dispoze] *a.* (*a*) disposed; **être bien, mal, d.,** to be in a good, bad, mood; **être bien d. pour, envers, qn,** to be well disposed towards s.o.; **être, se sentir, d. à faire qch.,** to feel disposed, willing, in the mood, to do sth.; **je suis tout d. à pardonner,** I am fully prepared to forgive; (*b*) arranged, set out; **fleurs disposées avec goût,** tastefully arranged flowers.

disposer [dispoze] **1.** *v.tr.* (*a*) to dispose, set out, arrange (objects in order, in position); to lay, set (table); *Prov:* **l'homme propose, Dieu dispose,** man proposes, God disposes; (*b*) **d. qn à qch., à faire qch.,** to dispose, incline, s.o. to sth., to do sth. **2.** *v.i.* (*a*) **d. de qn, de qch.,** to dispose of s.o., of sth.; to have s.o., sth., at one's disposal; **disposez de moi,** I am at your service; **toutes les heures dont je puis d.,** every hour I can spare; **les renseignements dont je dispose,** the information in my possession; **d. de capitaux importants,** to have a large capital in hand; to command a large capital; **vous pouvez en d.,** you may use it; **vous pouvez d.,** you may go; (*b*) **d. de ses biens en faveur de qn,** to make over one's property to s.o. **3.** *v.i.* to prescribe, provide, enjoin; **la loi ne dispose que pour l'avenir,** the law applies only to the future. **4. se d. à qch., à faire qch.,** to get ready for sth., to get ready to do sth.; **se d. à partir,** to get ready to leave.

dispositif [dispozitif] *n.m.* **1.** *Jur:* purview, enacting terms (of statute, etc.). **2.** *Mil:* disposition, deployment (of troops in battle, etc.); plan of action; **d. d'attaque,** attack force; **d. de défense,** defence system. **3.** *Tchn:* apparatus, device, mechanism, appliance; **d. de commande, de manœuvre,** driving, controlling, gear, mechanism; **d. de sûreté,** safety device.

disposition [dispozisjɔ̃] *n.f.* disposition. **1.** arrangement, ordering (of house, etc.); laying out, layout (of garden, etc.); **d. du terrain,** lie of the land. **2.** (*a*) state (of mind, body); frame of mind; **être en bonne d. pour faire qch.,** to be disposed, inclined, in the mood, to do sth.; **être dans de bonnes dispositions à l'égard de qn,** to be favourably disposed towards s.o.; (*b*) predisposition; **avoir une d. au rhumatisme,** to have a tendency to rheumatism; (*c*) *pl.* natural ability, aptitude (for sth.); **dispositions naturelles pour la musique,** natural bent for music; **cet enfant a des dispositions,** he, she, is a (naturally) gifted child. **3.** *pl.* (*a*) arrangements; **prendre des dispositions pour faire qch.,** to prepare, arrange, make the necessary arrangements, for doing sth.; (*b*) provisions, conditions (of will, law, etc.); clauses (of law); **les dispositions contenues dans l'article 34,** the provisions of article 34. **4.** disposal; **avoir la libre d. de son bien,** to be free to dispose of one's property;

libre d. de soi-même, self determination; **fonds à ma d.,** funds at my disposal, under my control; **mettre qch. à la d. de qn,** to place sth. at s.o.'s disposal; **je suis à votre (entière) d.,** I am (entirely) at your service.

disproportion [disprɔpɔrsjɔ̃] *n.f.* disproportion, lack of proportion (**entre,** between).

disproportionné [disprɔpɔrsjɔne] *a.* disproportionate (**à, avec,** to); out of proportion (**à, avec,** with).

disputable [dispytabl̩] *a.* disputable, debatable.

dispute [dispyt] *n.f.* **1.** *A:* debate, controversy, dispute; **sujet en d.,** subject under discussion. **2.** altercation, quarrel; **chercher d. à qn,** to pick a quarrel with s.o.; **c'est un sujet de d. entre eux,** it is a bone of contention between them.

disputer [dispyte] *v.tr. & i.* **1.** *A: & Lit:* **disputer qch., de qch., sur qch.,** to dispute, debate, about sth.; to discuss sth. **2. disputer qch., de qch.,** to dispute, contest, sth.; **d. le terrain,** to fight every inch of the way; **d. qch. à qn,** to contend with s.o. for sth.; **deux chiens qui se disputent un os,** two dogs fighting over a bone; **d. un match,** to play a match; **d. une course sur mille mètres,** to run a thousand metre race. **3.** *v.i.* to quarrel, argue (**avec,** with); **4.** *F:* **d. qn,** to tick, tell, s.o. off; **il s'est fait d. par son père,** he got told off by, he got a telling off from, his father. **5. se d.,** to quarrel, wrangle, argue (**pour,** over, about; **avec,** with); **ils se disputent à qui aura le plus gros morceau,** they are arguing about who is to, shall, get the biggest piece.

disquaire [diskɛr] *n.m. Rec:* record dealer.

disqualification [diskalifikasjɔ̃] *n.f. Sp:* disqualification.

disqualifier [diskalifje] *v.tr.* (*pr.sub. & impf.* **n. disqualifiions, v. disqualifiiez**) (*a*) *Sp:* to disqualify; (*b*) to discredit (s.o.).

disque [disk] *n.m.* **1.** *Sp:* discus. **2.** disc, *occ.* disk; (*a*) disc (of moon, etc.); (*b*) *Tchn:* disc, plate; **d. d'embrayage,** clutch plate, disc; **frein à d.,** disc brake; (*c*) *Rec:* record, disc; **d. microsillon, (de) longue durée,** long-playing record, L.P.; *F:* **changer de d.,** to change the subject; *Cmptr:* **d. magnétique,** magnetic disc; (*d*) *Rail:* disc signal; (*e*) *Anat:* **d. intervertébral,** (intervertebral) disc; (*f*) *Adm: Aut:* **d. de stationnement,** parking disc.

disruptif, -ive [disryptif, -iv] *a.* disruptive (force, electric discharge, etc.).

dissection [disɛksjɔ̃] *n.f.* dissection (of body, literary work, etc.).

dissemblable [disɑ̃blabl̩] *a.* dissimilar, different (**de, à,** from); unlike.

dissemblance [disɑ̃blɑ̃s] *n.f.* dissimilarity, difference (**entre,** between).

dissemblant [disɑ̃blɑ̃] *a.* dissimilar, different, unlike.

dissémination [diseminasjɔ̃] *n.f.* **1.** scattering (of seeds, etc.); spreading (of germs, troops, etc.). **2.** dissemination, spreading (of ideas, etc.).

disséminer [disemine] *v.tr.* **1.** to scatter (seeds, etc.); to spread (germs); to spread out (troops, etc.). **2.** to disseminate (ideas, etc.). to spread.

dissension [disɑ̃sjɔ̃] *n.f.* dissension, discord.

dissentiment [disɑ̃timɑ̃] *n.m.* disagreement, dissent, difference of opinion.

disséquer [diseke] *v.tr.* (**je dissèque; je disséquerai**) to dissect (corpse, literary work, etc.).

dissertation [disɛrtasjɔ̃] *n.f.* (*a*) *O:* dissertation (**sur,** (up)on); (*b*) *Sch:* **d. (française),** (French) essay.

disserter [disɛrte] *v.i.* (*a*) **d. sur un sujet,** to discourse on a subject; (*b*) to talk at length, *F:* to hold forth.

dissidence [disidɑ̃s] *n.f. Ecc: etc:* dissidence, dissent; *coll.* **la d.,** dissidents.

dissident, -ente [disidɑ̃, -ɑ̃t] **1.** *a.* dissident, dissenting (sect, party, etc.). **2.** *n.* (*a*) *Pol:* dissident; (*b*) *Ecc:* dissenter, nonconformist.

dissimilation [disimilasjɔ̃] *n.f. Ling:* dissimilation.

dissimilitude [disimilityd] *n.f.* dissimilitude, dissimilarity.

dissimulateur, -trice [disimylatœr, -tris] **1.** *a.* dissembling. **2.** *n.* dissembler, deceiver.

dissimulation [disimylasjɔ̃] *n.f.* **1.** dissimulation, dissembling, deceit; **agir avec d.,** to act in an underhand way. **2.** concealment, covering up (of the truth, etc.); *Jur:* **d. d'actif,** (fraudulent) concealment of assets.

dissimulé [disimyle] *a.* **1.** hidden; secret. **2.** dissimulating, dissembling, secretive (man, character).

dissimuler [disimyle] *v.* **1.** *v.tr.* to dissemble, dissimulate, hide, conceal (feelings, etc.); to cover up (fault); **d. qch. à qn,** to hide sth., keep sth. back, from s.o.; **il m'avait dissimulé qu'il voulait partir,** he hadn't told me he wanted to leave; **je ne (vous) dissimule pas qu'il en est ainsi,** I cannot hide the fact, I have to tell you, that it is like this. **2. se d.,** to hide; **parmi tant de qualités se dissimule un défaut,** among so many qualities lurks a weakness.

dissipateur, -trice [disipatœr, -tris] **1.** *n.* spendthrift, squanderer, waster. **2.** *a.* wasteful (administration, etc.); prodigal.

dissipation [disipasjɔ̃] *n.f.* **1.** (*a*) dissipation, dispersion (of clouds, etc.); (*b*) dissipation, wasting (of money, time, etc.); squandering (of fortune). **2.** (*a*) dissipation, dissolute living; (*b*) misbehaviour, inattention (in school).

dissipé [disipe] *a.* (*a*) dissipated, dissolute; **mener une vie dissipée,** to lead a gay life; (*b*) *Sch:* inattentive (pupil).

dissiper [disipe] *v.tr.* **1.** (*a*) to dissipate, disperse, scatter, dispel (clouds, etc.); to clear up (misunderstanding); to dispel (fears, suspicions); (*b*) to dissipate, waste (fortune, time, etc.); to ruin (health, etc.). **2. d. qn,** to distract s.o.'s attention. **3. se d.** (*a*) (*of visions, suspicions, etc.*) to vanish, disappear; **le brouillard se dissipe,** the fog is lifting, clearing (away); **ses doutes se sont dissipés,** his doubts faded; (*b*) to be inattentive, to misbehave (in school, etc.).

dissociable [disɔsjabl̩] *a.* dissociable, separable.

dissociation [disɔsjasjɔ̃] *n.f.* dissociation, separation; *Ch:* decomposition, dissociation.

dissocier [disɔsje] *v.tr.* **1.** *Ch:* to dissociate (compound). **2.** to disunite, separate, dissociate (ideas, etc.).

dissolu [disɔly] *a.* dissolute, loose, corrupt, profligate (person, life).

dissolubilité [disɔlybilite] *n.f.* dissolubility.

dissoluble [disɔlybl̩] *a.* **1.** *A:* soluble. **2.** *Pol:* dissoluble, dissolvable (assembly, etc.).

dissolution [disɔlysjɔ̃] *n.f.* **1.** disintegration, dissolution, decomposition (of body, etc.). **2.** (*a*) *Ch:* dissolving (of substance in liquid); (*b*) rubber solution. **3.** dissolution (of parliament, marriage); breaking up (of meeting); winding up (of company). **4.** *Lit:* dissoluteness, licentiousness, profligacy.

dissolvant [disɔlvɑ̃] *a. & n.m.* (*a*) solvent; **d. (pour ongles),** nail varnish remover; (*b*) dissolvent; debilitating (climate, etc.); corrupt (doctrine, etc.).

dissonance [disɔnɑ̃s] *n.f.* **1.** dissonance; clash (of colours). **2.** *Mus:* discord.

dissonant [disɔnɑ̃] *a.* dissonant, discordant; clashing (colours).

dissoudre [disudr̥] *v.tr.* (*pr.p.* **dissolvant;** *p.p.* **dissous,** *f.* **dissoute;** *pr.ind.* **je dissous, il dissout, n. dissolvons;** *impf.* **je dissolvais;** *p.h. & p.sub. are lacking, fu.* **je dissoudrai**) **1.** to dissolve; to melt (substance) in a liquid. **2.** to dissolve (parliament); to dissolve, break (partnership); to annul (marriage). **3. se d.,** to dissolve; (*a*) (*of sugar, etc.*) **se d. dans l'eau,** to dissolve, melt, in water; (*b*) **colère qui se dissout en larmes,** anger that dissolves into tears; (*c*) (*of assembly*) to break up.

dissuader [disɥade] *v.tr.* **d. qn de (faire) qch.,** to dissuade s.o. from (doing) sth.; to talk s.o. out of (doing) sth.; **d. qn de partir,** to persuade s.o. not to go away.

dissuasif, -ive [disɥazif, -iv] *a.* dissuasive.

dissuasion [disɥazjɔ̃] *n.f.* dissuasion (**de,** from); *Mil: Pol:* **force de d.,** deterrent power.

dissyllabe [disilab] **1.** *a.* di(s)syllabic. **2.** *n.m.* di(s)syllable.

dissyllabique [disilabik] *a.* di(s)syllabic.

dissymétrie [disimetri] *n.f.* asymmetry, dissymmetry.

dissymétrique [disimetrik] *a.* asymmetric(al), dissymmetrical, unsymmetrical.

distance [distɑ̃s] *n.f.* distance; **on ne voyait rien à cette d.,** one couldn't see anything from that distance; **suivre qn à d., à peu de d.,** to follow s.o. at a distance, at a short distance; **à quelle d. sommes-nous de la ville?** how far are we from the town? **à une courte d.,** within easy reach (**de,** of); **c'est à une grande d.,** it's a long way off (**de,** from); **j'en juge mieux à d.,** I can judge better at, from, a distance; **d. de dix ans entre deux événements,** ten years' interval between two events; **d. entre générations,** generation gap; **de d. en d.,** at intervals; **tenir qn à d.,** to keep s.o. at a distance; **conserver, garder, ses distances, se tenir à d.,** to keep at a distance, to keep aloof; **prendre ses distances,** *Mil:* to dress; *Gym:* to space out; *Sp:* **tenir la d.,** to go the distance, to stay, last, the course; *Mec.E:* **commande à d.,** remote control; *Opt:* **d. focale,** focal length; *Artil: etc:* **à petite d., à faible d.,** at short range; *Nau:* **d. parcourue,** day's run.

distancement [distɑ̃smɑ̃] *n.m. Rac:* disqualifying, disqualification (of horse).

distancer [distɑ̃se] *v.tr.* **(je distançai(s); n. distançons)** *Rac: etc:* **1.** to outdistance, outrun, outstrip; **se laisser d.,** to drop away, to fall, lag, behind. **2.** to disqualify (horse).

distant [distɑ̃] *a.* **1.** distant; **nos deux maisons sont distantes d'un kilomètre l'une de l'autre,** our two houses are a kilometre apart. **2. il est très d.,** he is very standoffish, very aloof.

distendre [distɑ̃dr̥] *v.tr.* **1.** to distend (stomach, etc.), **2.** to strain (muscle, etc.); to stretch (rope, etc.) to breaking point. **3. se d.** (*a*) to become distended; to swell (out); (*b*) to relax, to slacken.

distension [distɑ̃sjɔ̃] *n.f.* **1.** distension (of stomach, etc.); straining (of muscle, etc.). **2.** slackening, loosening (of rope, etc.).

distillateur [distilatœr] *n.m.* distiller.

distillation [distilasjɔ̃] *n.f.* distillation; distilling; **d. fractionnée,** fractional distillation.

distiller [distile] **1.** *v.tr.* (*a*) to distil, *NAm:* distill, exude, secrete (poison, moisture, etc.); to exude (anger, etc.); (*b*) to distil (spirits, etc.); **eau distillée,** distilled water; (*c*) *Lit:* to refine (one's thoughts). **2.** *v.i.* to distil, exude (**de,** from).

distillerie [distilri] *n.f.* **1.** distillery. **2.** (*trade*) distilling.

distinct [distɛ̃(kt)] *a.* **1.** distinct, separate (**de,** from). **2.** distinct, clear (outline, voice, etc.); audible (voice).

distinctement [distɛ̃ktəmɑ̃] *adv.* distinctly, clearly.

distinctif, -ive [distɛ̃ktif, -iv] *a.* distinctive, characteristic, distinguishing (sign, feature, etc.); **trait d.,** characteristic, peculiarity.

distinction [distɛ̃ksjɔ̃] *n.f.* **1.** distinction; **faire une d. entre deux choses,** to make a distinction, differentiate, distinguish, between two things; **sans d.,** indiscriminately; **sans d. de race ou de couleur,** irrespective of race or colour. **2.** (*a*) distinction, honour, *NAm:* honor; (*b*) (*medal, etc.*) decoration. **3.** (*a*) distinction, eminence; **un personnage de haute d.,** a highly distinguished person; (*b*) **avoir de la d.,** to be distinguished.

distinctivement [distɛ̃ktivmɑ̃] *adv.* distinctively.

distinguable [distɛ̃gabl̥] *a.* distinguishable.

distingué [distɛ̃ge] *a.* distinguished. **1.** eminent, noted (writer, politician, etc.). **2.** (*a*) refined (taste, bearing, etc.); **avoir un air d.,** to look distinguished; (*b*) smart (costume, etc.). **3.** *Corr:* **agréez mes sentiments distingués,** yours truly.

distinguer [distɛ̃ge] *v.* **I.** *v.tr.* to distinguish. **1.** to mark (off), characterize; **sa mise soignée le distinguait de la foule,** his impeccable appearance made him stand out, set him apart, from the crowd. **2.** to honour; to single (s.o.) out (for distinction). **3. d. entre deux choses,** to distinguish between two things; **d. qch. de qch., d'avec qch.,** to distinguish, tell, sth. from sth.; **on peut à peine les d. l'un de l'autre,** you can hardly tell them apart. **4.** to discern, perceive; **je ne peux pas d. ses traits,** I cannot make out his features; **je l'ai distingué dans la foule,** I singled him out, spotted him, in the crowd. **II. se distinguer 1.** to distinguish oneself (**par ses talents,** by one's talents). **2. se d. des autres,** to be distinguishable from others (**par,** by); **il se distingue de son frère par son grand nez,** one can tell him from his brother by his big nose. **3.** to be noticeable, conspicuous; to stand out.

distique [distik] *n.m. Pros:* **1.** (*Gr. or Lt. verse*) distich. **2.** (*Fr. verse*) couplet.

distordre [distɔrdr̥] *v.tr.* to distort (features, etc.).

distorsion [distɔrsjɔ̃] *n.f.* (*a*) distortion (of face, optical image, of electrical impulse, etc.); (*b*) imbalance (between two factors).

distraction [distraksjɔ̃] *n.f.* **1.** *A: & Jur:* division, severance (of part from a whole, etc.). **2.** absentmindedness, lack of attention, abstraction; **par d.,** inadvertently, absentmindedly. **3.** diversion, amusement, distraction, recreation.

distraire [distrɛr] *v.tr.* (*conj. like* TRAIRE) **1.** *Lit:* to divert, separate (part from whole, etc.). **2.** to distract, divert (s.o.'s attention, etc.); **d. l'attention de qn,** to take s.o.'s attention, mind, off sth.; **d. qn de ses travaux,** to take s.o. from his work. **3.** to divert, entertain, amuse. **4. se d.,** to amuse oneself; **il a besoin de se d.,** he needs to relax a bit, to enjoy himself.

distrait [distrɛ] *a.* (*a*) absentminded; (*b*) inattentive, listless, abstracted; **air d.,** absent, vacant, look; **vous êtes d.,** you're not paying attention; **d'une oreille distraite,** abstractedly; inattentively; with only half an ear.

distraitement [distrɛtmɑ̃] *adv.* absentmindedly, absently, abstractedly.

distrayant [distrɛjɑ̃] *a.* diverting, entertaining (book, spectacle).

distribanque [distribɑ̃k] *n.m.* cash dispenser.

distribuer [distribɥe] *v.tr.* **1.** to distribute, deal out, give (orders, prizes, etc.); to issue, serve, share out (provisions, etc.); to deal (cards); (*of postman*) to deliver (letters); **d. les fleurs en plusieurs classes,** to classify flowers; *Th:* **d. les rôles,** to assign, cast, the parts (in a play); to cast a play. **2. d. un appartement,** to arrange (the furniture, etc., in) a flat.

distributaire [distribytɛr] *n.m. & f.* recipient (in distribution); *Jur:* distributee.

distributeur, -trice [distribytœr, -tris] **1.** (*a*) *n.* distributor, dispenser (of prizes, favours, etc.); (*b*) *n.m. Cin:* film distributor. **2.** *n.m. Tchn:* distributor; *Aut:* alternator; **d. d'essence,** petrol pump, *NAm:* gasoline pump; **d. automatique,** automatic vending machine, slot machine; **d. de billets,** (i) ticket machine; (ii) cash dispenser, cash point; *I.C.E:* **d. de courant,** distributor; *Mch:* **d. de vapeur,** steam distributor, regulator; steam valve; *Agr:* **d. d'engrais,** fertilizer spreader.

distributif, -ive [distribytif, -iv] *a.* **1.** *Log: Gram:* distributive (term, pronoun, etc.). **2. justice distributive,** distributive justice.

distribution [distribysjɔ̃] *n.f.* distribution; allotment (of duties, etc.); issue (of rations); delivery (of letters, goods); arrangement (of furniture, etc.); *Com:* handling; *I.C.E: Aut:* distribution; **d. des plantes,** classification of plants; *Sch:* **d. des prix,** prize giving; speech day; *Th:* **d. des rôles d'une pièce,** (i) casting, (ii) cast, of a play; *Th: Cin:* **d. par ordre d'entrée en scène,** characters, cast, in order of appearance; **d. des eaux,** water supply.

distributivement [distribytivmɑ̃] *adv.* distributively.

district [distrik(t)] *n.m.* district, region.

dit [di] **1.** *a.* (*a*) settled, fixed; **prendre qch. pour d.,** to take sth. for granted; **à l'heure dite,** at the appointed time, at the time indicated; (*b*) (so-)called; **la zone dite tempérée,** the so-called temperate zone. **2.** *n.m. A: & Lit:* traditional story (usually in verse); **le d. des trois larrons,** the story of the three thieves.

dithyrambe [ditirɑ̃b] *n.m.* (*a*) *Lit:* dithyramb; (*b*) eulogy.

dithyrambique [ditirɑ̃bik] *a.* (*a*) *Lit:* dithyrambic; (*b*) eulogistic (words, etc.).

dito [dito] *adv.* ditto.

diurétique [djyretik] *a. & n.m. Med:* diuretic.

diurne [djyrn] *a.* diurnal (motion of planet, etc.).

divagation [divagasjɔ̃] *n.f.* **1.** (*a*) *Jur:* straying (of cattle, etc.); (*b*) shifting (of river) from its course. **2.** (*a*) digression (in a speech, etc.); (*b*) **divagations d'un fou,** ravings, ramblings, of a madman.

divaguer [divage] *v.i.* **1.** (*a*) *Jur:* (*of cattle, etc.*) to stray; (*b*) (*of river*) to shift its course. **2.** (*a*) to digress, to wander away from the point; (*b*) **malade qui divague,** patient whose mind is wandering, who rambles (in his speech); **vous divaguez!** you're raving!

divan [divɑ̃] *n.m.* **1.** *Hist:* divan, (i) oriental council; (ii) council room. **2.** *Furn:* divan; couch.

divergence [divɛrʒɑ̃s] *n.f.* divergence, divarication (of lines, opinions, rays, etc.); differences (of opinion).

divergent [divɛrʒɑ̃] *a.* divergent (lines, opinions).

diverger [divɛrʒe] *v.i.* **(il divergea(it); n. divergeons)** (*a*) (*of lines, rays, etc.*) to diverge (**de,** from); (*b*) **nos opinions divergent sur certains points,** our opinions differ on certain points.

divers [divɛr] *a.* **1.** *A:* changing, varying (nature, etc.). **2.** (*a*) *pl.* diverse, different, varied; **des opinions très diverses,** very varied opinions; **(frais) d.,** sundry expenses, sundries; (*b*) *Journ:* **faits d.,** news items; **un fait d.,** an incident; (*c*) *indef. adj., always preceding the n.* various; **diverses personnes l'ont vu,** various people saw him.

diversement [divɛrsəmɑ̃] *adv.* diversely; in various, different, ways.

diversification [divɛrsifikasjɔ̃] *n.f.* diversification.

diversifier [divɛrsifje] *v.* **1.** *v.tr.* (*pr.sub. & impf.* **n. diversifiions, v. diversifiiez)** to diversify, vary (conversation, pursuits, etc.); to variegate (colours). **2.** (*of matter, interests, etc.*) **se d.,** to change; to vary; to become different.

diversion [divɛrsjɔ̃] *n.f.* **1.** *Mil:* diversion. **2.** diversion, change, distraction; **faire d. à la tristesse de qn,** to take s.o.'s mind off his sorrow, to cheer s.o. up.

diversité [divɛrsite] *n.f.* (*a*) diversity; variety; (*b*) difference.

divertir [divɛrtir] *v.tr.* **1.** *A:* (*a*) to divert, ward off (blow, etc.); to turn (s.o.) away (from project, etc.); (*b*) to misappropriate (sum of money); (*c*) to divert (attention, etc.). **2.** to divert, entertain, amuse. **3. se d.,** to enjoy oneself.

divertissant [divɛrtisɑ̃] *a.* diverting, amusing, entertaining.

divertissement [divɛrtismɑ̃] *n.m.* **1. d. de fonds,** misappropriation of funds. **2.** (*a*) diversion; entertainment, amusement, recreation, relaxation; (*b*) *Mus:* divertimento.

dividende [dividɑ̃d] *n.m. Mth: Fin:* dividend.

divin [divɛ̃] *a.* (*a*) divine (majesty, word, etc.); sacred (blood, etc.); **le d. Enfant** [divinɑ̃fɑ̃] the Holy Child; (*b*) heavenly, divine (music, weather, etc.); (*c*) *n.m.* **le d.,** the divine.

divinateur, -trice [divinatœr, -tris] **1.** *n. A:* diviner, soothsayer. **2.** *a.* foreseeing, prophetic.

divination [divinasjɔ̃] *n.f.* **1.** divination, soothsaying. **2.** instinctive foresight.

divinatoire [divinatwar] *a.* divinatory; **baguette d.,** divining rod, dowsing rod.

divinement [divinmɑ̃] *adv.* divinely.

divinisation [divinizasjɔ̃] *n.f.* deification.

diviniser [divinize] *v.tr.* to deify.

divinité [divinite] *n.f.* divinity. **1.** divine nature; godhead (of Christ, etc.). **2.** deity; god, goddess.

diviser [divize] *v.tr.* to divide. **1. d. le travail,** to share (out) the work; *Mth:* **d. un nombre par un autre,** to divide one number by another. **2.** (*a*) to part, separate; **les Pyrénées divisent la France d'avec l'Espagne,** the Pyrenees divide, separate, France from Spain; (*b*) to set (people, etc.) at variance; **maison divisée contre elle-même,** house divided against itself; **d. pour régner,** divide and rule. **3. se d.** (*a*) to divide, to break up (**en,** into); (*b*) **l'examen se divise en trois parties,** the examination is divided into three parts.

diviseur [divizœr] *n.m. & a.inv.* **1.** *Mth:* divisor; **plus grand commun d.,** highest common factor. **2.** divider; *El:* **d. de courant,** current divider.

divisibilité [divizibilite] *n.f.* divisibility.

divisible [divizibl̥] *a.* divisible.

division [divizjɔ̃] *n.f.* division. **1.** partition (**en,** into); dividing (of whole into parts); *Mth:* division; **d. du travail,** division of labour. **2.** part, portion, section (of whole); (administrative) department, branch; *Sch:* group, section; *Mil: Navy:* division; *Mil:* **d. blindée,** armoured division. **3.** discord, dissension, disagreement. **4.** *Typ:* hyphen.

divisionnaire [divizjɔnɛr] *a.* **1.** (*a*) *Mil: etc:* divisional; *Adm:* **commissaire d.** = (police) superintendent; (*b*) *n.m.* (i) *Mil:* major general; (ii) (police) superintendent. **2.** *Com:* **monnaie d.,** fractional coins.

divorce [divɔrs] *n.m.* **1.** divorce; **intenter une action en d. (contre qn),** to take divorce proceedings (against s.o.); **demander le d.,** to sue for a divorce, to file a petition for divorce. **2. le d. de la langue écrite avec la langue parlée,** the gulf between the written and the spoken language.

divorcé, -ée [divɔrse] **1.** *a.* divorced. **2.** *n.* divorced man, woman; divorcee.

divorcer [divɔrse] *v.i.* **(je divorçai(s); n. divorçons) d. (d')avec qn,** to divorce s.o.; **il veut d.,** he wants to be divorced, to obtain a divorce.

divulgateur, -trice [divylgatœr, -tris] *n.* discloser, betrayer (of secrets); informer.

divulgation [divylgasjɔ̃] *n.f.* divulging, divulgence, disclosure (**de,** of).

divulguer [divylge] *v.tr.* to divulge, reveal, disclose, to let out (secret, etc.).

dix *num.a.inv. & n.m.inv.* ten. **1.** *card. a.* (*at the end of the word group* [dis] *before n. or adj. beginning with a vowel sound* [diz] *before n. or adj. beginning with a consonant* [di]) **il est d. heures** (dizœr] it is ten o'clock; **j'en ai d.** [dis] I have ten. **2.** *n.m.inv. usu.* [dis] (*a*) **d. et demi** [disedmi] ten and a half; (*b*) (*ordinal uses, etc.*) **le d. mai** [lədimɛ] the tenth of May; **Charles D.,** Charles the Tenth; **le numéro d.,** number ten.

dix-huit [dizɥi(t)] *num.a.inv. & n.m.inv.* **1.** eighteen. **2.** [dizɥi] **le dix-huit mai,** the eighteenth of May.

dix-huitième [dizɥitjɛm] *num.a. & n.m. & f.* eighteenth.

dixième [dizjɛm] *num.a. & n.m. & f.* tenth.

dixièmement [dizjɛmmɑ̃] *adv.* tenthly, in the tenth place.

dix-neuf [diznœf] *num.a.inv. & n.m.inv.* **1.** nineteen. **2. le dix-neuf mai,** the nineteenth of May.

dix-neuvième [diznœvjɛm] *num.a. & n.m. & f.* nineteenth.

dix-sept [dis(s)ɛt] *num.a.inv. & n.m.inv.* **1.** seventeen. **2. le dix-sept mai,** the seventeenth of May.

dix-septième [diz(s)ɛtjɛm] *num.a. & n.m. & f.* seventeenth.

dizain [dizɛ̃] *n.m. Pros:* ten-line stanza.

dizaine [dizɛn] *n.f.* (*a*) *Mth:* ten; **compter par dizaines,** to count in tens; (*b*) about ten; **une d. de personnes,** ten or a dozen people, about ten people; **il y a une d. d'années,** some ten years ago.

djebel [dʒɛbɛl] *n.m.* (*in N. Africa*) jebel, mountain.

djellaba [dʒɛlaba] *n.f. Cost:* djellaba.

djinn [dʒin] *n.m. Myth:* djin(n), jinn.

do [do] *n.m. Mus:* **1.** (*the note*) C. **2.** (*in tonic sol-fa*) doh.

docile [dɔsil] *a.* docile, submissive, manageable, amenable (child); tractable (animal, etc.); manageable (hair).

docilement [dɔsilmɑ̃] *adv.* submissively, obediently, with docility.

docilité [dɔsilite] *n.f.* docility.

dock [dɔk] *n.m.* **1.** *Nau:* (*a*) dock; **d. de carénage, flottant,** dry, floating, dock; (*b*) dock(s), dockyard. **2.** *Com:* warehouse.

docker [dɔkɛr] *n.m.* docker.

docte [dɔkt] (*a*) *a. Lit: or* (*when it precedes noun*) *Iron:* learned; (*b*) *n.m.pl.* **les doctes,** scholars.

doctement [dɔktəmɑ̃] *adv. Lit: or Iron:* in a learned manner, learnedly.

docteur [dɔktœr] *n.m.* doctor. **1. les docteurs de l'Église,** the Doctors of the Church. **2.** *Sch:* **d. ès lettres** = Doctor of Literature; **Mlle X est docteur ès sciences,** Miss X is a doctor of science. **3. d. (en médecine),** doctor (of medicine); **leur fille est d.,** their daughter is a doctor; **le d. Thomas,** Dr Thomas.

doctoral, -aux [dɔktɔral, -o] *a.* **1.** doctoral. **2.** pompous (manner); bombastic (tone).

doctoralement [dɔktɔralmɑ̃] *adv.* pompously, bombastically.

doctorat [dɔktɔra] *n.m. Sch:* degree of doctor; doctorate; **d. d'État** = D.Litt., D.Sc., etc.; **d. d'université** = Ph.D.

doctoresse [dɔktɔrɛs] *n.f.* woman doctor.

doctrinaire [dɔktrinɛr] **1.** *a.* (*a*) doctrinary (school of thought); (*b*) pedantic, dogmatic, doctrinaire. **2.** *n.m.* doctrinarian; doctrinaire.

doctrinal, -aux [dɔktrinal, -o] *a.* doctrinal.

doctrine [dɔktrin] *n.f.* doctrine, tenet.

docudrame [dɔkydram] *n.m. T.V:* faction; docudrama; dramatized documentary.

document [dɔkymɑ̃] *n.m.* document; **nous avons des documents pour le prouver,** we have documentary evidence to prove it.

documentaire [dɔkymɑ̃tɛr] *a. & n.m.* **1.** *a.* documentary (proof, etc.); **à titre d.,** for (your) information; *Cin:* **film d.,** documentary. **2.** *n.m. Cin:* documentary.

documentaliste [dɔkymɑ̃talist] *n.m. or f.* (*a*) documentalist; archivist; *Adm:* keeper of records; (*b*) researcher.

documentariste [dɔkymɑ̃tarist] *n.m. & f.* director of documentary films.

documentation [dɔkymɑ̃tasjɔ̃] *n.f.* **1.** documentation; research. **2.** *coll.* documents; information; literature.

documenter [dɔkymɑ̃te] *v.* **1.** *v.tr.* to document (matter); to support (statement, etc.) with documentary evidence; **d. qn sur une question,** to brief s.o. on a question; **il est bien documenté,** he is well informed on the subject. **2. se d.,** to gather documentary evidence, information, material.

dodécaèdre [dɔdekaɛdr] *n.m. Mth:* dodecahedron.

dodécagone [dɔdekagɔn] *n.m. Mth:* dodecagon.

dodécaphonique [dɔdekafɔnik] *a. Mus:* twelve-tone, dodecaphonic.

dodécaphonisme [dɔdekafɔnism] *n.m. Mus:* twelve-tone system, dodecaphony.

dodelinement [dɔdlinmɑ̃] *n.m.* **1.** wagging, nodding, shaking (of head); shaking (of body).

dodeliner [dɔdline] *v.i.* **d. de la tête,** to wag one's head, to nod.

dodo [dodo] *n.m.* (*in nursery language*) (*a*) sleep, byebyes; **faire d.,** to sleep; (*b*) bed; **aller à d., au d.,** to go to bed, to bye-byes.

dodu [dɔdy] *a. F:* plump.

doge [dɔʒ] *n.m. Hist:* doge.

dogmatique [dɔgmatik] *a.* dogmatic.

dogmatiquement [dɔgmatikmɑ̃] *adv.* dogmatically.

dogmatiser [dɔgmatize] *v.i.* to dogmatize; to lay down the law.

dogmatisme [dɔgmatism] *n.m.* dogmatism.

dogmatiste [dɔgmatist] *n.m.* dogmatist.

dogme [dɔgm] *n.m.* dogma, tenet.

dogue [dɔg] *n.m.* **1.** large watchdog; mastiff; **d'une humeur de d.,** like a bear with a sore head.

doigt [dwa] *n.m.* **1.** finger; *Anat: Z:* digit; (*a*) **le petit d.,** the little finger; *F:* (*to child*) **mon petit d. me l'a dit,** a little bird told me so; (*in class, etc.*) **lever le d.** = to put one's hand up; **ne pas lever, remuer, le petit d.,** not to lift a finger; **compter sur ses doigts,** to count on one's fingers; **porter une bague au d.,** to wear a ring on one's finger; **promener ses doigts sur qch.,** to finger, feel, sth.; to run one's fingers over, along sth.; **elle a des doigts de fée,** she's got nimble fingers; she's good with her hands; **se faire taper sur les doigts,** to take the rap; **savoir qch. sur le bout du d.,** to have sth. at one's finger tips; **menacer qn du d.,** to shake, wag, one's finger at s.o.; **il lui fit signe du d. (de venir),** he beckoned to him (to come); **désigner, montrer, qn, qch., du d.,** to point at s.o., sth.; **mettre le d. dans l'engrenage,** to get involved, mixed up, in sth.; **vous avez mis le d. dessus,** you've hit the nail on the head; *F:* **se mettre, se fourrer, le d. dans l'œil (jusqu'au coude),** to be completely wrong; *F:* **mener qn au d. et à l'œil,** to keep a tight rein on s.o.; **se mordre les doigts,** to bite one's nails with impatience; **s'en mordre les doigts,** to repent (of) it, to regret it; *F:* **ce gâteau, je m'en lèche les doigts!** this cake is really delicious! **fourrer ses doigts partout,** to interfere with everything; **ils sont ensemble comme les doigts de la main,** they are hand in glove; (*b*) finger's breadth; **la robe est trop courte d'un d.,** the dress is a fraction too short; **un d. de cognac,** a nip, spot, of brandy; **être à deux doigts de la mort,** to be within an ace, an inch, of death; (*c*) **d. de pied,** toe. **2.** (*finger-shaped object*) **doigts d'un gant,** fingers of a glove; *Mec.E: etc:* **d. d'encliquetage,** iron finger, pawl, click (of ratchet-wheel, etc.); **d. d'entraînement,** driving-plate pin, driver, catch pin (of lathe).

doigté [dwate] *n.m.* **1.** *Mus:* fingering (of piece of music); **exercises de d.,** five-finger exercises. **2.** touch. **3.** tact, diplomacy, judgment; **manquer de d.,** to be tactless.

doigter [dwate] *v.tr.* (*a*) to finger (piece of music); (*b*) to mark (music) with the proper fingering.

doigtier [dwatje] *n.m.* fingerstall.

doit [dwa] *n.m. Com:* debit, liability; **d. et avoir,** debit and credit; debtor and creditor.

dol [dɔl] *n.m. Jur:* fraud, wilful misrepresentation.

doléances [dɔleɑ̃s] *n.f.pl.* complaints; **conter ses d.,** to tell one's tale of woe, to air one's grievances.

dolent [dɔlɑ̃] *a.* doleful, plaintive, complaining (voice, person, etc.).

doline [dɔlin] *n.f. Geol:* doline, sinkhole.

dollar [dɔlar] *n.m. Num:* dollar.

dolman [dɔlmɑ̃] *n.m. A.Mil.Cost:* dolman; short-skirted jacket (of hussars, etc.).

dolmen [dɔlmɛn] *n.m. Prehist:* dolmen.

doloire [dɔlwar] *n.f.* (cooper's) adze, *NAm:* adz; (mason's) larry.

dolomie [dɔlɔmi] *n.f.*, **dolomite** [dɔlɔmit] *n.f. Miner:* dolomite; *Geog:* **les Dolomites,** the Dolomites.

dolomitique [dɔlɔmitik] *a. Geol:* dolomitic.

dolosif, -ive [dɔlɔzif, -iv] *a. Jur:* fraudulent.

domaine [dɔmɛn] *n.m.* **1.** domain; (real) estate, property; *Jur:* demesne; **domaines de la Couronne,** Crown lands; **d. (de l'État),** State (administered) property; **d. public,** public property; **le d. forestier,** the national forests; **ouvrage tombé dans le d. public,** work the copyright of which has lapsed, run out; work out of copyright. **2. d. d'une science,** field, scope, of a science; **ce n'est pas de mon d.,** that is not within my province, not within my sphere; **le d. du possible,** the realm(s) of possibility.

domanial, -aux [dɔmanjal, -o] *a.* (*a*) domanial (property, rights, etc.); (*b*) (*of estates, forests, etc.*) national, (belonging to the) State.

dôme [dom] *n.m.* **1.** (*a*) *Arch:* dome, cupola; (*b*) *Lit:* vault, canopy (of heaven, trees); (*c*) *Geog:* dome. **2.** *Mch:* **d. de (prise de) vapeur,** steam dome.

domestication [dɔmɛstikasjɔ̃] *n.f.* domestication.

domesticité [dɔmɛstisite] *n.f.* **1.** (*a*) domestic service; (*b*) domesticity (of animal). **2.** *coll.* domestic staff; household.

domestique [dɔmɛstik] **1.** *a.* (*a*) domestic (animal, life, etc.); household (duties, etc.); family (quarrel, etc.); **économie d.,** domestic economy, housekeeping; (*b*) domestic (service). **2.** *n.m. & f.* (*a*) (domestic) servant; *f.* maid; (*in formal speech*) domestic.

domestiquer [dɔmɛstike] *v.tr.* (*a*) to domesticate (animal); (*b*) to bring (s.o.) to a state of subjection; to subjugate (s.o.); (*c*) to harness (atomic energy, etc.).

domicile [dɔmisil] *n.m.* (place of) residence, home; *Jur:* domicile; **sans d. fixe,** of no fixed abode, address; **à d.,** at one's private house; at home; **notre épicier livre à d.,** our grocer has a delivery service; **franco à d.,** carriage paid.

domiciliaire [dɔmisiljɛr] *a.* domiciliary (visit, etc.).

domiciliation [dɔmisiljasjɔ̃] *n.f. Com:* domiciliation (of bill of exchange).

domicilié [dɔmisilje] *a.* resident, domiciled (**à,** at).

domicilier [dɔmisilje] *v.tr.* (*pr.sub. & impf.* **n. domiciliions, v. domiciliiez**) *Com:* to domicile (bill at bank, etc.).

dominance [dɔminɑ̃s] *n.f. Biol:* dominance.

dominant, -ante [dɔminɑ̃, -ɑ̃t] *a.* **1.** dominating, dominant, ruling (power, passion, etc.). **2.** predominating, prevailing (colour, opinion, etc.); outstanding (feature, idea, etc.); *Biol:* **caractère d.,** dominant (characteristic). **3.** *n.f.* **dominante** (*a*) *Mus:* dominant (note); (*b*) chief characteristic.

dominateur, -trice [dɔminatœr, -tris] **1.** *n. Lit:* dominator, ruler. **2.** *a.* (*a*) dominating, ruling (power, country, etc.); (*b*) domineering, overbearing (person, tone, etc.).

domination [dɔminasjɔ̃] *n.f.* domination, rule; dominion; **d. morale,** moral influence; **d. de soi-même,** self control.

dominer [dɔmine] **1.** *v.i.* to rule (**sur,** over); **couleur qui domine,** predominating colour. **2.** *v.tr.* to dominate; (*a*) to rule; to master, overcome (shyness, etc.); **l'ambition le domine,** he is dominated by ambition; **sa voix dominait toutes les autres,** his voice rose, was heard, above all others; *Sp:* **d. la partie,** to have the best of the game; (*b*) to tower over, above (sth.); to overlook; **le château domine la vallée,** the castle looks down upon the valley. **3. se d.,** to have command of oneself, to control one's feelings.

dominicain, -aine [dɔminikɛ̃, -ɛn] *a. & n.* **1.** *Ecc:* dominican (friar, nun). **2.** *Geog:* Dominican; (native, inhabitant) of Santo Domingo; **la République Dominicaine,** the Dominican Republic, Santo Domingo.

dominical, -aux [dɔminikal, -o] *a.* dominical (letter, etc.); **l'oraison dominicale,** the Lord's prayer; **repos d.,** Sunday rest.

dominion [dɔminjɔ̃, -njɔn] *n.m. Pol:* Dominion.

domino [dɔmino] *n.m.* **1.** *Cost: Games:* domino; **jouer aux dominos,** to play (at) dominoes.

dommage [dɔmaʒ] *n.m.* **1.** (*a*) damage, injury; **causer du d. à qn,** to do s.o. harm, an injury; (*b*) **quel d.!** what a pity! what a shame! **c'est (bien) d., qu'elle ne soit pas venue,** it's a (great) pity that she didn't come. **2.** *usu. pl.* (*a*) damage (to property, etc.); **réparer les dommages,** to repair, make good, the damage; to make up the losses; (*b*) *Jur:* **dommages et intérêts, dommages-intérêts,** damages; **dommages de guerre,** war damages.

dommageable [dɔmaʒabl̩] *a.* detrimental, injurious; *Jur:* prejudicial; **acte d.,** tort.

domptable [dɔ̃tabl̩] *a.* capable of being tamed, subdued; tamable.

domptage [dɔ̃taʒ] *n.m.* taming (of animals, etc.).

dompter [dɔ̃te] *v.tr.* to tame, train (animal); to break in (horse); to subdue, overcome (one's feelings, etc.).

dompteur, -euse [dɔ̃tœr, -øz] *n.* tamer, trainer (of animals); subduer, vanquisher (of people, etc.); **d. de chevaux,** horse breaker.

don [dɔ̃] *n.m.* **1. d. de qch. à qn,** giving of sth. to s.o., bestowal of sth. on s.o. **2.** (*a*) gift, present; donation; **faire d. à qn de qch.,** to make a present, a donation, of sth. to s.o.; (*b*) gift, natural quality, talent; **le d. des langues,** the gift of languages, a talent for languages; **avoir le d. de faire qch.,** to have a talent, a genius, for doing sth.

donataire [dɔnatɛr] *n.m. & f. Jur:* donee.

donateur, -trice [dɔnatœr, -tris] *n.* giver; *Jur:* donor.

donation [dɔnasjɔ̃] *n.f.* donation, gift.

donc [dɔ̃k] **1.** *conj.* therefore, accordingly, then, hence, consequently, so; **je pense, donc je suis,** I think, therefore I am. **2.** *adv.* [dɔ̃, *but in oratory often* dɔ̃k] (*a*) (*emphatic*) **vous voilà d. de retour,** so you're back (again); **que voulez-vous d.?** what(ever) do you want? **mais taisez-vous d.!** do be quiet! *F:* do shut up! **allons d.!** nonsense! come on! come now! **comment d.?** how do you mean? **pensez d.!** (i) just think! (ii) that's what you think! that'll be the day! **tu as d. oublié?** have you forgotten? **dites d.!** (i) tell me now . . .; (ii) look here! I say! (*b*) (*after interruption or* *digression*) **donc** [dɔ̃k] **pour en revenir à notre sujet,** well, to come back to our subject.

dondon [dɔ̃dɔ̃] *n.f. F:* fat woman; **grosse d.,** great lump of a girl, of a woman.

donjon [dɔ̃ʒɔ̃] *n.m.* **1.** keep, donjon (of castle). **2.** turret mast (of warship).

don Juan [dɔ̃ʒɥɑ̃] *n.m.* Don Juan, seducer.

donnant [dɔnɑ̃] *a.* (*a*) *A:* generous, open-handed; (*b*) **d. d.,** give and take, tit for tat.

donne [dɔn] *n.f. Cards:* deal; **à vous la d.!** your deal! **fausse d.,** misdeal.

donné [dɔne] *a. & p.p.* **1.** (*a*) given; **propriété donnée en dot,** property given as a dowry; *F:* **c'est d.,** it's dirt cheap; it's a gift; (*b*) **à un point d., à une distance donnée,** at a given, certain, point, distance. **2.** (*a*) **étant d. deux triangles,** given two triangles; **étant d. l'heure tardive,** in view, in consideration, of the lateness of the hour; (*b*) **étant d. qu'il est mineur,** since, as, he is not of age.

donnée [dɔne] *n.f.* **1.** datum, given information (of problem, etc.); fundamental idea, subject (of novel, etc.). **2.** *pl.* data, particulars; facts.

donner [dɔne] *v.* **I.** *v.tr.* to give. **1.** (*a*) **d. un cadeau à qn,** to give a present to s.o., to give s.o. a present; **d. un bal, un dîner,** to give a ball, a dinner party; *abs.* **d. aux pauvres,** to give to the poor; **d. un coup de peigne à ses cheveux,** to give one's hair a quick comb; **il m'a donné son rhume,** he gave me his cold, I caught his cold; **d. des conseils,** to give advice; **d. à boire à qn,** to give s.o. something to drink; **d. une conférence,** to give a lecture; *F:* **d. aux poules,** to feed the hens; **je lui ai donné à entendre que . . .,** I gave him to understand that . . .; **cela me donne à croire que . . .,** it leads me to believe that . . .; **je vous en donne dix francs,** I will give you ten francs for it; **je vous le donne en mille,** you'll never guess; **d. un cheval pour, contre, un âne,** to give a horse in exchange for a donkey; **je donnerais beaucoup pour le savoir,** I would give a lot to know it; **s'en d. (à cœur joie),** to enjoy oneself (to the full), to have a good time; **il n'est pas donné à tout le monde d'être un écrivain,** not everybody can be a writer; **d. du sang,** to donate, give, blood; (*b*) to give up (sth.); **d. sa vie pour qn,** to give one's life for s.o.; (*c*) **d. à qn qch. à garder,** to entrust s.o. with sth., to give s.o. sth. to keep; **d. à qn sa fille en mariage,** to give one's daughter to s.o. in marriage; **d. la main à qn,** to shake hands with s.o.; (*d*) **d. les cartes,** to deal (the cards); **mal d.,** to misdeal. **2.** (*a*) to provide, furnish; (*of crops*) to yield; **arbre qui donne des fruits,** tree that yields, bears, fruit; **d. des preuves à qn,** to furnish s.o. with proofs; **d. du souci à qn,** to cause s.o. worry; **cela donne l'idée que . . .,** it conveys the idea that . . .; **d. un bon exemple,** to set a good example; **d. une pièce de théâtre,** to produce, perform, a play; **qu'est-ce qu'on donne au cinéma aujourd'hui?** what's on at the cinema today? *F:* **ça n'a rien donné,** nothing came of it; it didn't work out, turn out; **je me demande ce que cela va d.,** I wonder what will come of it, what the result of it will be; *v.i.* **si les blés donnent cette année,** if there is a good yield of wheat this year; (*b*) **d. faim, soif, sommeil, chaud, à qn,** to make s.o. hungry, thirsty, sleepy, hot; **cette odeur me donne mal à la tête,** this smell is giving me a headache; (*c*) *F:* to inform on (s.o.). **3.** to ascribe, attribute (sth. to s.o.); **on lui donne une grande fortune,** they say he has a large fortune; **je lui donne vingt ans,** I reckon he's about twenty; **d. tort, d. raison, à qn,** to disagree, agree, with s.o. **II.** *v.i.* (*a*) **la fenêtre donne sur la cour,** the window looks on to the yard; **cette porte donne sur le jardin,** this door leads out into the garden; **le soleil donne dans la pièce,** the sun is shining into the room; (*b*) **d. de la tête contre qch.,** to knock, strike, bump, run, one's head against sth.; *F:* **ne pas savoir où d. de la tête,** not to know which way to turn; **le navire a donné sur les rochers,** the ship ran on to, struck, the rocks; **d. dans le piège,** *F:* **dans le panneau,** to fall into the trap; **il donne dans les préjugés,** he is very prejudiced; *Mil:* **l'armée va d.,** the army's about to attack; **faire d. un bataillon,** to send a battalion into action; (*c*) (*of material*) to stretch; **le cordage a beaucoup donné,** the rope has given a good deal. **se donner 1.** (*a*) **se d. à une cause,** to devote oneself to a cause; **se d. des airs,** to put on airs, to give oneself airs; **se d. en spectacle,** to make an exhibition of oneself; (*b*) (*of woman*) to give oneself ((i) to a husband, (ii) to a lover). **2.** (*a*) **cela se donne,** it can be had for the asking; (*b*) *Hamlet* **se donne ce soir,** they are playing *Hamlet* tonight. **3. se d. du tourment,** to worry (oneself); **se d. du mal,** (i) to work hard; (ii) to take (great) trouble (over sth.).

donneur, -euse [dɔnœr, -øz] *n.* (*a*) giver, donor; *Med:* **d. de sang,** blood donor; *Com:* **d. d'ordre,** principal; **d. d'avis, de conseils,** busybody, know-all, *U.S:* wise guy; (*b*) *Cards:* dealer; (*c*) *P:* (police) informer, squealer.

donquichottisme [dɔ̃kiʃɔtism] *n.m.* quixotism.

dont [dɔ̃] **1.** *rel.adv.* [... **d'où**) whence; **la pièce d. elle sort,** the room out of which she is coming. **2.** *rel.-pron.* (= **de qui, duquel, desquels, etc.**) (*a*) from, by, with, whom, or which; **les aïeux d. je suis descendu,** the ancestors from whom I am descended; my ancestors; **la femme d. il est amoureux,** the woman he is in love with; **la façon d. il me regardait,** the way he looked at me; (*b*) (*of, about, concerning*) whom, which; **le livre d. j'ai besoin,** the book (which, that) I want, need; **voici ce d. il s'agit,** this is what it's all about; (*c*) whose, of whom, of which; **la dame d. je connais le fils,** the lady whose son I know; **la dame d. le fils vous connaît,** the lady whose son knows you; **la chambre d. la porte est fermée,** the room with the closed door; (*d*) **quelques-uns étaient là, d. votre frère,** there were a few people there, including your brother.

donzelle [dɔ̃zɛl] *n.f. F:* (i) fast girl; (ii) difficult, capricious, woman.

dopage [dɔpaʒ] *n.m.* doping.

dopant [dɔpɑ̃] *n.m.* dope.

doper [dɔpe] *v.tr. Rac: etc:* to dope; **se d.,** to take stimulants, to dope oneself.

doping [dɔpiŋ] *n.m.* **1.** doping. **2.** dope.

dorade [dɔrad] *n.f. Ich:* gilthead bream, sea bream.

doré [dɔre] *a.* **1.** gilded, gilt; *Bookb:* **d. sur tranche,** gilt-edged; **cheveux blond d.,** golden hair. **2.** *Cu:* (*a*) glazed (cake); (*b*) browned (meat, etc.). **3.** *n.m. Ich: Fr.C:* wall-eyed pike, yellow pike.

dorée [dɔre] *n.f. Ich:* (John) Dory.

dorénavant [dɔrenavɑ̃] *adv.* henceforth, from now on, hereafter.

dorer [dɔre] *v.tr.* **1.** to gild; **le soleil dorait les cimes,** the sun shed a golden light upon, cast a glow upon, the hilltops; *Fig:* **d. la pilule,** to sugar the pill. **2.** *Bookb:* **d. à froid,** to stamp (cover) in blind. **3.** *Cu:* (*a*) to glaze (cake); (*b*) to brown (meat, fish, etc.). **4. se d.,** to turn a golden colour; **elle se dore au soleil,** she's sunbathing, she's getting a suntan.

doreur, -euse [dɔrœr, -øz] *n.* gilder.

dorien, -ienne [dɔrjɛ̃, -jɛn] **1.** *a. Gr.Civ:* Dorian (people); Doric (dialect); *Mus:* Dorian (mode). **2.** *n.m. Ling:* Doric.

dorique [dɔrik] *a. Arch:* Doric.

dorlotement [dɔrlɔtmɑ̃] *n.m.* fondling; coddling (of child, etc.).

dorloter [dɔlɔte] *v.tr.* to fondle, to coddle; to pamper (s.o.); **se d.,** to coddle oneself.

dormant [dɔrmɑ̃] **1.** *a.* (*a*) sleeping; (*b*) (*of water*) still, stagnant; (*c*) *Her:* dormant; (*d*) fixed, immovable (frame, etc.); (window, etc.) that cannot be opened; **serrure dormante,** dead lock. **2.** *n.m.* frame, casing (of door, window).

dormeur, -euse [dɔrmœr, -øz] *n.* **1.** (*a*) sleeper; *a.* **poupée dormeuse,** sleeping doll; (*b*) sleepyhead. **2.** *n.f.* **dormeuse,** stud earring. **3.** *n.m. Crust:* edible crab.

dormir [dɔrmir] *v.i.* (*pr.p* **dormant;** *p.p.* **dormi;** *pr. ind.* **je dors, n. dormons;** *impf.* **je dormais;** *p.h.* **je dormis**) **1.** to sleep, to be asleep; **d. profondément, d'un profond sommeil,** to be fast asleep; **il dort d'un sommeil léger,** he's a light sleeper; **d. du sommeil du juste,** to sleep the sleep of the just; **je n'ai pas dormi de la nuit,** I haven't slept a wink all night, I didn't sleep all night; **il n'en dort pas,** he can't (get to) sleep for thinking of it; **le café m'empêche de d.,** coffee keeps me awake; **d. trop longtemps,** to oversleep; **d. à poings fermés, comme une souche, comme un loir,** to sleep soundly, like a log; **d. comme un sabot, une toupie,** to snore; **ne d. que d'un œil,** to sleep with one eye open; **vous pouvez d. sur les, vos, deux oreilles,** don't worry; rest assured; **avoir envie de d.,** to be, feel, sleepy, drowsy; **il dort debout,** he's falling asleep on his feet, he can't keep his eyes open; **une histoire, un conte, à d. debout,** a tall story; a cock-and-bull story. **2.** to remain inactive; to be, lie, dormant; **il dort sur son travail,** he's slack at his work; **ses capitaux dorment,** his capital is lying idle; **eau qui dort,** stagnant, still, water; *Prov:* **il n'est pire eau que l'eau qui dort,** still waters run deep.

dormitif, -ive [dɔrmitif, -iv] *a.* soporific.

dorsal, -aux [dɔrsal, -o] **1.** *a.* dorsal; **région dorsale de la main,** back of the hand; *Av:* **parachute d.,** back-type parachute. **2.** *n.f.* **dorsale** (*a*) *Ling:* dorsal consonant; (*b*) *Geog:* ridge (of mountains).

dortoir [dɔrtwar] *n.m.* dormitory; **ville-d., cité-d.,** dormitory town.

dorure [dɔryr] *n.f.* **1.** (*a*) gilding; (*b*) *Bookb:* **d. à froid,** blind tooling; (*c*) *Cu:* glazing (of cake) (with egg yolk). **2.** gilt, gilding; **uniforme couvert de dorures,** gold-braided uniform.

doryphore [dɔrifɔr] *n.m. Ent:* Colorado beetle.

dos [do] *n.m.* back. **1. avoir le d. voûté,** to be round-shouldered; **voir qn de d.,** to have a back view of s.o.; to see s.o.'s back; **robe décolletée dans le d.,** low-backed dress; **tourner le d. à qn,** to turn one's back on s.o.; to stand, sit, with one's back to s.o.; **dès qu'il a le d. tourné,** the moment as soon as, his back is turned; **faire qch. derrière le d. de qn,** to do sth. behind s.o.'s back; **il me tombe toujours sur le d.,** he's always jumping down my throat, cracking down on me; (*of cat*) **faire le gros d.,** to arch its back; **voyager à d. d'âne,** to ride, travel, on a donkey; **se mettre tout le monde à d.,** to set everybody against one; **d. à d.,** back to back; **je n'ai rien à me mettre sur le d.,** I haven't a thing to wear; **elle porte ses cheveux dans le d.,** she wears her hair loose; *F:* **ça fait froid dans le d.,** it's scary, creepy; it gives one the shivers; *F:* **avoir qn sur le d.,** to be saddled with s.o.; **il a bon d.,** he's got a broad back; he can take anything; *F:* **j'en ai plein le d.,** I'm sick of it, fed up with it. **2.** back (of chair, page, etc.); bridge (of the nose); spine (of book); **scie à d.,** back saw; **signer au d. d'un chèque,** to endorse a cheque; **voir au d.,** (please) turn over.

dosage [dozaʒ] *n.m.* **1.** *Ch: etc:* quantity determination, proportioning (of ingredients). **2.** dosage (of medicine).

dose [doz] *n.f.* **1.** *Ch: etc:* proportion, amount (of constituent in compound). **2.** dose (of medicine); **par petites doses,** in small quantities, doses; **une légère d. d'ironie,** a tinge of irony; **forcer la d.,** to overdo it.

doser [doze] *v.tr.* **1.** *Ch: etc:* (i) to determine the quantity of; (ii) to proportion (constituent in compound). **2.** to measure out dose (of medicine); *Fig:* **il faut savoir d. l'ironie,** one must be able to include just the right amount of irony.

doseur [dozœr] *n.m.* measure.

dossard [dosar] *n.m. Sp:* number (worn by player, competitor).

dossier [dosje] *n.m.* **1.** back (of seat, etc.); **chaise à d. droit,** straight-backed chair; *Aut: etc:* **d. réglable,** adjustable back. **2.** (*a*) dossier; file; record (of prisoner, etc.); **verser une pièce au d.,** to file a document; (*b*) folder, file.

dot [dɔt] *n.f.* **1.** dowry; marriage settlement; **coureur de d.,** fortune hunter. **2.** portion brought by postulate on entering a convent.

dotal, -aux [dɔtal, -o] *a.* dotal (property, etc.); *Jur:* **régime d.,** (marriage) settlement in trust.

dotation [dɔtasjɔ̃] *n.f.* endowment (of hospital, etc.); foundation; allowance (made to royal family, etc.).

doter [dɔte] *v.tr.* (*a*) to dower (bride); **être doté de toutes les vertus,** to be endowed with every virtue; (*b*) to endow (hospital, etc.); (*c*) **d. une usine d'un matériel neuf,** to equip a factory with new plant.

douaire [dwɛr] *n.m.* dower.

douairière [dwɛrjɛr] *a. & n.f.* dowager.

douane [dwan] *n.f. Adm:* customs; **passer à la d.,** to go through customs; **formalités de d.,** customs clearance; **marchandises en d.,** bonded goods; **(bureau de) d.,** customs house; **(droits de) d.,** customs dues; (customs) duty; **franc de d.,** duty paid.

douanier, -ière [dwanje, -jɛr] **1.** *a.* (of) customs; **tarif d.,** customs tariff; **union douanière,** customs union; **barrières douanières,** tariff walls. **2.** *n.m.* customs officer; *Nau:* tide-waiter, tidesman.

doublage [dublaʒ] *n.m.* **1.** (*a*) doubling (of quantity, etc.); (*b*) doubling, folding in half (of sheet of paper, etc.); (*c*) *Cin:* dubbing. **2.** (process of) lining (coat); sheathing (ship).

double [dubl̩] **1.** *a.* double, twofold (measure, quantity, etc.); **valise à d. fond,** suitcase with a false bottom; **mot à d. sens,** ambiguous word; **agent d.,** double agent; **jouer un d. jeu avec qn,** to play a double game with s.o.; **vêtement à d. face,** reversible garment; **faire qch. en d. exemplaire,** to do sth. in duplicate; **coup d.,** right and left (in shooting); *Fig:* **faire coup d.,** to kill two birds with one stone; **mot qui fait d. emploi (avec un autre),** redundant word; **sa canne à pêche a une longueur d. de la mienne,** his fishing rod is twice the length of mine; **fermer une porte à d. tour,** to double-lock a door; **à d. effet,** dual, double, action; **outil à d. usage,** dual-purpose tool; **comptabilité en partie d.,** double-entry book-keeping; *I.C.E:* **d. allumage,** dual ignition; **d. whisky,** double, large, whisky. **2.** *adv.* **voir d.,** to see double; **en d.,** in duplicate. **3.** *n.m.* (*a*) double; **j'ai le d. de votre âge,** I am twice your age; **ça m'a coûté le d.,** it cost me twice as much; **plier qch. en d.,** to fold sth. in two, in half; *Ten:* **d. messieurs, dames, mixte,** men's, ladies', mixed, doubles; (*b*) duplicate, counterpart; copy; *Typwr:* carbon copy; (*c*) (*pers.*) double.

doublé [duble] **1.** *a.* (*a*) doubled; (*b*) (*of garment*) lined; (*c*) *Cin:* dubbed. **2.** *n.m.* (*a*) **d. (or),** gold plate; rolled gold; gold-plated jewellery; **d. argent,** silver plate; silver-plated jewellery; (*b*) *Ven:* right and left; (*d*) *Sp:* double.

doubleau, -eaux [dublo] *n.m. Const:* (ceiling) beam; *Arch:* transverse rib.

double-blanc [dubləblɑ̃] *n.m.* (*at dominoes*) double blank; *pl. doubles-blancs.*

double-commande [dubləkɔmɑ̃d] *n.f. Av: Aut:* dual controls; *pl. doubles-commandes.*

double-corde [dubləkɔrd] *n.f. Mus:* double-stopping (on violin, etc.); *pl. doubles-cordes.*

double-crème [dubləkrɛm] *n.m.* (type of) cream cheese; *pl. double(s)-crème(s).*

double-décimètre [dublədesimɛtr̥] *n.m.* = ruler, foot rule; *pl. doubles-décimètres.*

doublement¹ [dubləmɑ̃] *adv.* doubly.

doublement² *n.m.* doubling (of number, etc.); folding in two, doubling (of piece of paper, etc.).

doubler [duble] **1.** *v.tr.* (*a*) to double (the amount, size, etc.); (*b*) **d. une feuille de papier,** to fold a sheet of paper in half, in two; *Mus:* **d. une partie,** to double a part; *Nau:* **d. un cap,** to double, make, weather, a cape; *Sch:* **d. une classe,** to repeat a year; to stay in the same form (for another year); *Th:* **d. un rôle, un acteur,** to understudy a part, an actor; *Cin:* to stand in for (s.o.); **d. le pas,** to quicken one's pace; **d. une voiture,** to overtake, pass, a car; *P.N:* **défense de d.,** no overtaking, *NAm:* no passing; (*c*) to line (coat, etc.); **haine qui se double de mépris,** hatred coupled with contempt; (*d*) *Cin:* to dub (a film); (*e*) *F:* to double-cross (s.o.). **2.** *v.i.* (*of population, etc.*) to double, to increase twofold.

doublet [dublɛ] *n.m. Lap: Ling:* doublet.

doublon¹ [dublɔ̃] *n.m. Typ:* double.

doublon² *n.m. Num:* doubloon.

doublure [dublyr] *n.f.* **1.** lining (of garment, etc.). **2.** *Th:* understudy; *Cin:* stand-in; *occ.* stunt man.

douce-amère [dusamɛr] *n.f. Bot:* woody nightshade, bittersweet; *pl. douces-amères.*

douceâtre [dusɑtr̥] *a.* sweetish; sickly sweet (taste).

doucement [dusmɑ̃] *adv.* (*a*) gently; (to speak, sing) softly; (to tread) lightly, delicately, carefully; (*b*) gently, carefully, slowly; **allez-y d.!** gently does it! easy does it! **les affaires vont d.,** business is so-so; *F:* **(allez-y) d. avec le vin,** go easy on the wine; *P:* **ça m'a fait d. rigoler,** I had a good laugh over it; **d. les basses!** take it easy!

doucereux, -euse [dusrø, -øz] *a.* **1.** sickly (sweet) (taste, etc.). **2.** smooth, smooth-tongued (person); smooth, sugary (voice, tone).

doucet, -ette [dusɛ, -ɛt] **1.** *a. A:* meek, mild, demure (person). **2.** *n.f. Bot:* **doucette,** corn salad, lamb's lettuce.

douceur [dusœr] *n.f.* **1.** (*a*) sweetness (of honey, perfume, etc.); (*b*) *pl.* sweets, sweet things; **aimer les douceurs,** to have a sweet tooth. **2.** softness (of sound, material, etc.); mildness (of climate). **3.** (*a*) pleasantness; (*b*) pleasant thing; **d. de vivre,** easy, gentle, way of life; **les douceurs de l'amitié,** comforts, pleasures, of friendship; **dire des douceurs à une femme,** to say sweet nothings to a woman. **4.** gentleness (of character, etc.); sweetness (of smile); **traiter qn avec d.,** to treat s.o. gently, with kindness; **en d.,** gently; **la voiture a démarré en d.,** the car started smoothly; **allez-y en d.!** gently does it! easy does it!

douche [duʃ] *n.f.* **1.** (*a*) shower (bath); **prendre une d.,** to take a shower; *pl.* **les douches,** the shower room(s); **d. écossaise,** (i) (alternately) hot and cold shower; (ii) succession of good and bad news, experiences, etc.; ups and downs; (*b*) shower (of rain, etc.); soaking, drenching; *F:* **administrer une d. à qn,** to give s.o. a telling-off, to blow s.o. up; **d. (froide),** terrible disappointment, let-down; (*c*) shower unit. **2.** *Med:* douche.

doucher [duʃe] *v.tr.* **1.** (*a*) to give (s.o.) a shower; **se d.,** to take a shower; (*b*) *F:* to tell (s.o.) off; **il s'est fait d.,** (i) he got soaked; (ii) he got a telling-off; (*c*) *F:* to disappoint (s.o.). **2.** *Med:* to douche.

doué [dwe] *a.* gifted; **il n'est guère d. pour les langues,** he has no gift for languages; he's no linguist.

douer [dwe] *v.tr.* to endow (s.o.) (with qualities, advantages); **il est doué d'une bonne mémoire,** he has a good memory.

douille [duj] *n.f.* tubular casing; (*a*) socket (of tool, etc.); handle of contact socket, lamp socket (of electric light bulb); **d. à (pas de) vis,** screw lamp holder; (*b*) case (of cartridge, etc.); (*c*) *Cu:* piping nozzle.

douillet, -ette [dujɛ, -ɛt] **1.** *a.* (*a*) soft, downy (cushion, etc.); cosy (bed); (*b*) (*of pers.*) soft; frightened of getting hurt; self-indulgent; over sensitive. **2.** *n.f.* **douillette** (i) quilted overcoat (of priest); (ii) quilted housecoat; (iii) (*for baby*) quilted coat.

douillettement [dujɛtmɑ̃] *adv.* softly, delicately; cosily; **élever un enfant d.,** to coddle a child.

douleur [dulœr] *n.f.* **1.** pain, ache; **d. aiguë,** sharp pain; **pousser un cri, des cris, de d.,** to cry out with pain; **se sentir des douleurs par tout le corps,** to ache all over; **sans d.,** painless (operation, etc.). **2.** sorrow, grief; **il a eu la d. de perdre sa mère,** he had the sorrow of losing his mother; **partager la d. de qn,** to share s.o.'s sorrow, grief; to feel with s.o.

douloureusement [dulurøzmɑ̃] *adv.* **1.** painfully. **2.** sorrowfully.

douloureux, -euse [dulurø, -øz] *a.* **1.** painful; aching (wound, etc.); sore, tender. **2.** sad, distressing, grievous (loss, event, etc.); pained, sorrowful (look); **des cris d.,** heart-rending, mournful, cries. **3.** *n.f. F:* **la douloureuse,** the bill; **apportez-moi la douloureuse,** let's see what the damage is.

doute [dut] *n.m.* doubt, uncertainty, misgiving; **être dans le d. (au sujet de qch.),** to be in doubt, doubtful, (about sth.); **avoir des doutes sur qn, qch., au sujet de qn,** to have misgivings, suspicions, about s.o., sth.; **mettre, révoquer, qch. en d.,** to question sth.; to cast doubts on sth.; **mettre en d. la parole de qn,** to challenge s.o.'s word; **c'est hors de d., il n'y a pas de d.,** it is beyond doubt, beyond (all) question; **cela ne fait plus aucun d.,** there is no longer any doubt about it; **nul d. qu'il (ne) soit mort,** there is no doubt that he is dead; **sans d.,** no doubt, probably; **sans aucun d.,** without (any) doubt; **vous ne me reconnaissez pas, sans d.,** I don't suppose you recognize me; **sans d. viendra-t-il; sans d. qu'il viendra,** I expect he'll come.

douter [dute] *v.* **1.** *v.i.* (*and tr. with noun clause as object*) to doubt; **d. du zèle de qn,** to doubt, to question, to have doubts about, s.o.'s enthusiasm; **il était à n'en point d. courageux,** his courage was beyond all question; **j'en doute fort,** I doubt it very much; **je ne doute pas de le voir bientôt,** I have no doubt I shall see him before long; **je doute qu'il soit assez fort,** I doubt whether he is strong enough; **je ne doute pas qu'il (ne) vous vienne en aide,** I am confident that he will help you; **il ne doute de rien,** he is full of self confidence. **2. se d. de qch.,** to suspect sth.; **je m'en doutais (bien),** I guessed, thought, as much; **il ne se doute de rien,** he suspects nothing; **je ne me doutais pas qu'il fût là,** I had no idea that he was there.

douteur, -euse [dutœr, -øz] *n. Lit:* doubter.

douteusement [dutøzmɑ̃] *adv.* doubtfully.

douteux, -euse [dutø, -øz] *a.* doubtful, uncertain, questionable; dubious (honour, company); **créance douteuse,** bad debt; **jour d.,** dubious, uncertain, light; **il est d. que** + *sub.*, it is doubtful whether . . .; **il n'est pas d. que . . . (ne)** + *sub., more usu.* **que** + *ind.*, there is no doubt that . . ..

douve [duv] *n.f.* **1.** (*a*) *Agr:* trench, ditch; (*b*) *usu. pl.* moat (of castle); (*c*) *Turf:* water jump. **2.** *Coop:* stave. **3.** *Bot:* **grande d.,** spearwort. **4.** *Vet:* fluke-(worm); **d. du foie,** liver fluke.

Douvres [duvr̥] *Pr.n. Geog:* Dover.

doux, douce [du, dus] **1.** *a.* (*a*) sweet; smooth, soft (to the touch); mild (to the taste); **eau douce,** (i) fresh water; (ii) soft water; **poisson d'eau douce,** freshwater fish; **peau douce,** smooth, soft, skin; (*b*) pleasant, agreeable (air, tone, etc.); **d. souvenir,** pleasant memory; **mener une vie douce,** to lead a calm, peaceful, life; *P:* **se la couler douce;** to take it easy; **faire les yeux d. à qn,** to make sheep's eyes at s.o.; *Iron:* **douce perspective!** charming prospect! (*c*) gentle (movement, voice); soft, subdued (light, colour, sound); mellow (light); mild (climate); **pente douce,** gentle slope; **chaleur douce,** moderate heat; *Cu:* **faire cuire à feu d.,** to cook on a low heat, on a low gas, in a low oven; **fer d.,** soft iron; **lime douce,** smooth file; **tabac d.,** mild tobacco; **consonne douce,** soft consonant; (*d*) meek, gentle (nature); **regard d.,** gentle, mild, look; **d. comme un agneau,** as gentle as a lamb; (*e*) *F:* **c'est de la folie douce!** it's sheer madness! (*f*) *adv. F:* **filer d.,** to give in; **en douce,** discreetly, quietly, on the Q.T. **2.** (*a*) *n.m.* **préférer le sec au d.,** to prefer dry (wine) to sweet; *F:* **c'est un d.,** he's a gentle creature; (*b*) *n.f. F:* **ma douce,** my fiancée; my girlfriend.

douzain [duzɛ̃] *n.m.* twelve-line poem.

douzaine [duzɛn] *n.f.* dozen; **trois douzaines d'œufs,** three dozen eggs; **une d. de personnes,** about a dozen, ten or a dozen, people; **à la d.,** by the dozen; **il y en a à la d.,** there are dozens, lots, of them.

douze [duz] *num.a.inv. & n.m.inv.* twelve; **le d. mai,** the twelfth of May; **Louis D.,** Louis the Twelfth; **d. heures,** twelve o'clock (noon).

douzième [duzjɛm] *num.a. & n.* twelfth.

douzièmement [duzjɛmmɑ̃] *adv.* twelfthly, in the twelfth place.

doyen, -enne [dwajɛ̃, -ɛn] *n.* **1.** (*a*) *Ecc: Sch:* dean (of chapter, of faculty); (*b*) doyen (of diplomatic corps, etc.). **2.** senior; **d. d'âge,** oldest member (of a club).

doyenné [dwajɛne] *n.m.* **1.** deanery; (*a*) office of dean; (*b*) dean's residence. **2.** *Hort:* comice (pears).

drachme [drakm] *n.f. Num:* drachma.

draconien, -ienne [drakɔnjɛ̃, -jɛn] *a.* Draconian; harsh, unduly severe (regulations); **régime d.,** very strict diet.

drag [drag] *n.m.* **1.** *A.Ven:* drag(hunt). **2.** *Veh:* drag.

dragage [dragaʒ] *n.m.* **1.** dredging (of river, harbour, etc.). **2.** (*a*) **d. des mines,** mine-sweeping; (*b*) dragging (of river for body, etc.).

dragée [draʒe] *n.f.* **1.** (*a*) sugar(ed) almond, dragée; **tenir la d. haute à qn,** (i) to keep s.o. waiting; (ii) to make s.o. pay dearly (for sth.); (*b*) *Pharm:* sugar-coated pill. **2.** *Ven:* small shot.

dragéifier [draʒeifje] *v.tr. Pharm:* to coat (pill) with sugar; to sugar (pill); **comprimé dragéifié,** sugar-coated tablet.

drageon [draʒɔ̃] *n.m. Arb: Hort:* sucker.

dragon [dragɔ̃] *n.m.* **1.** (*a*) *Myth:* dragon; (*b*) **d. de vertu,** dragon of virtue; (*c*) *Rept:* **d. volant,** flying lizard; (*d*) *Her:* (i) dragon; (ii) wyvern. **2.** *Mil:* dragoon.

dragonne [dragɔn] *n.f.* (*a*) sword knot; (*b*) strap, loop (for holding umbrella, etc.).

drague [drag] *n.f.* **1.** (*a*) *Hyd.E:* dredger; **d. suceuse,** pump dredger; **d. à godets,** bucket dredger; (*b*) drag, grappling hook; (*c*) *Fish:* dredge, dragnet. **2.** *Nau:* drogue, sea anchor.

draguer [drage] *v.tr.* **1.** to dredge (river, harbour, etc.). **2.** (*a*) to drag (pond, etc.); to sweep (channel); (*b*) to dredge for (oysters, etc.). **3.** *v.tr. & i. P:* to chat up, pick up (girls).

dragueur [dragœr] *n.m.* **1.** (*a*) *Hyd.E:* dredgerman; (*b*) dragman. **2.** (*a*) dredger; (*b*) **d. de mines,** mine-sweeper. **3.** *P:* skirt chaser.

drain [drɛ̃] *n.m.* **1.** drain(pipe). **2.** *Surg:* drainage tube.

drainage [drɛnaʒ] *n.m.* **1.** drainage, draining (of field, wound, etc.). **2.** drain (of money, capital).

drainer [drene] *v.tr.* (*a*) to drain (soil, abscess); (*b*) to tap (capital, talent, etc.); to draw, attract (trade, workers, etc.).

draisine [drɛzin] *n.f. Rail:* track motor car; *U.S:* gang car.

dramatique [dramatik] **1.** *a.* dramatic (art, situation, etc.); **l'art d.,** the drama; **auteur d.,** playwright; **je ne considère pas son départ comme d.,** I don't think his leaving is a tragedy. **2.** *n.f.* television play, drama.

dramatiquement [dramatikmɑ̃] *adv.* dramatically.

dramatisation [dramatizasjɔ̃] *n.f.* (*a*) dramatizing; (*b*) dramatization.

dramatiser [dramatize] *v.tr.* **1.** to dramatize (event, etc.). **2.** to dramatize, to adapt (novel) for the stage.

dramaturge [dramatyrʒ] *n.m.* dramatist, playwright.

dramaturgie [dramatyrʒi] *n.f.* dramatic art.

drame [dram] *n.m.* **1.** *Lit:* (*a*) drama (as a literary genre); (*b*) (i) *A:* (any) play; (ii) play (of a serious nature); **d. lyrique,** (comic) opera. **2.** catastrophic event; drama, tragedy; **la scène a tourné au d.,** the scene took a tragic turn; **il ne faut pas en faire un d.,** there's no need to dramatize it.

drap [dra] *n.m.* **1.** cloth; **d. fin,** broadcloth; **d. mortuaire,** pall; **d. d'or,** gold brocade; *Hist:* **le camp du D. d'or,** the Field of the Cloth of Gold. **2. d. (de lit),** sheet; **être dans de beaux, mauvais, vilains, draps,** to be in a fine mess, in a pickle, in a predicament. **3.** *Belg:* towel.

drapé [drape] **1.** *a.* (*a*) covered with a sheet, a cloth; (*b*) **robe drapée sur les épaules,** dress pleated on the shoulders. **2.** *n.m.* drape (of a garment).

drapeau, -eaux [drapo] *n.m.* (*a*) flag; (regimental) colour; **d. blanc,** white flag; **arborer, hisser, un d.,** to hoist a flag; *Mil:* **présentation du d.** = trooping the colour; (*b*) **être sous les drapeaux,** to serve in the (armed) forces; **porter le d.,** to be the first to uphold an opinion; *P:* **planter un d.,** to leave without paying (the bill); (*c*) *Av:* **mettre une hélice en d.,** to feather a propeller; (*d*) *Sp:* **abaisser le d. à l'arrivée du premier concurrent,** to flag in the winner.

drapement [drapmɑ̃] *n.m.* draping (of material).

draper [drape] *v.tr.* **1.** *Tex:* to process (wool). **2.** to drape (cloth into folds, etc.). **3. se d.** (*a*) to wrap oneself up, drape oneself (**dans, de,** in); (*b*) **se d. dans sa dignité,** to stand on one's dignity.

draperie [drapri] *n.f.* **1.** (*a*) cloth manufacture, factory; (*b*) drapery (trade). **2.** *Art:* drapery. **3.** curtains, *NAm:* drapes; hangings.

drap-housse [draus] *n.m.* fitted sheet; *pl. draps-housses.*

drapier, -ière [drapje, -jɛr] *n.* (*a*) draper; cloth merchant; (*b*) cloth manufacturer; (*c*) *a.* **marchand d.,** cloth merchant.

drastique [drastik] *a. & n.m.* drastic (remedy, etc.).

drave [drav] *n.f. Fr.C:* drive (of logs).

draver [drave] *v.tr. Fr.C:* to float, to drive (logs).

draveur [dravœr] *n.m. Fr.C:* driver, raftsman, rafter, wood floater.

drèche, drêche [drɛʃ] *n.f. Brew:* draff.

drelin [drəlɛ̃] *onomat. & n.m. F: O:* ting-a-ling; tinkle.

dressage [drɛsaʒ] *n.m.* **1.** erection, raising (of scaffolding, etc.); pitching (of tent). **2.** flattening, straightening (of sth.); trimming, dressing (of piece of wood, etc.); straightening (of rod, bar). **3.** (*a*) training (of animal); *Equit:* **d. (élémentaire),** breaking in (of horse); **d. (supérieur),** dressage; (*b*) *F:* (severe) disciplining (of child).

dresser [drese] *v.* **I.** *v.tr.* **1.** to erect, put up, raise (mast, monument, etc.); to put up (ladder); to set (trap); to pitch (tent); **d. la tête,** (i) to hold up, lift, one's head; (ii) to look up; **d. les oreilles,** to prick up, cock, one's ears. **2.** to prepare, draw up (plan, report, estimate, etc.); to make out, draw up (list). **3. d. une personne contre une autre,** to set one person against another. **4.** to flatten, straighten (sth.); to trim, dress, (piece of wood); to straighten out (piece of wire). **5.** (*a*) to train (animal); to break in (horse); (*b*) *A: or Pej:* to train, drill (a recruit); *F:* to discipline (s.o.) (severely); **ça le dressera!** that'll teach him, put him in his place! **II. se dresser** (*a*) to stand up, rise; to hold oneself erect, straight; to sit up, straighten up; **se d. sur la pointe des pieds,** to stand on tiptoe; **ses cheveux se dressaient (sur sa tête),** his hair stood on end; **les obstacles qui se dressent sur notre chemin,** the obstacles that stand, lie, in our way; (*b*) **se d. contre qch.,** to rise up (in protest) against sth.; to revolt against sth.; (*c*) (*of horse*) to rear; (*of dog*) to stand up (on its hind legs).

dresseur, -euse [drɛsœr, -øz] *n.* trainer (of animals); **d. de chevaux,** horse breaker; **d. de fauves,** wild animal tamer.

dressoir [drɛswar] *n.m.* dresser, sideboard.

dreyfusard, -arde [drɛfyzar, -ard] *n.m. & f. Hist:* supporter, defender, of Dreyfus.

dribble [dribl̥] *n.m. Fb: etc:* dribble.

dribbler [drible] *v.tr. Fb: etc:* to dribble.

dribbleur [driblœr] *n.m. Fb: etc:* dribbler.

dribbling [dribliŋ] *n.m. Fb: etc:* dribbling.

drill¹ [drij] *n.m. Z:* drill; West African baboon.

drill² [dril] *n.m. Mil: etc:* drill.

drille¹ [drij] *n.m. F:* **un bon, joyeux, d.,** a good sort; a cheerful character.

drille² *n.f. Tls:* hand drill.

driller [drije] *v.tr.* to drill, bore.

drink [drink] *n.m. F:* drink.

drisse [dris] *n.f. Nau:* halyard.

drive [drajv] *n.m. Ten: Golf:* drive.

driver¹ [drajvœr, driv-] *n.m.* **1.** *Rac:* (*in trotting races*) driver. **2.** *Golf:* (*club*) driver.

driver² [drajve, dri-] *v. Sp:* **1.** *v.i. & tr. Ten: Golf:* to drive (ball). **2.** *v.tr.* (*trotting races*) to drive (horse).

drogman [drɔgmɑ̃] *n.m.* dragoman.

drogue [drɔg] *n.f.* **1.** *A:* (*a*) pharmaceutical ingredient; (*b*) drug; nostrum; quack remedy. **2.** (*a*) (any) chemical product (found in food, etc.); (*b*) something unpleasant to swallow; **cette boisson est une vraie d.,** this drink tastes like medicine. **3.** *F:* narcotic, drug(s); **d. dure, douce,** hard, soft, drug; **la télévision est devenue une d. pour beaucoup de gens,** many people are now television addicts.

drogué, -ée [drɔge] *n.* drug addict.

droguer [drɔge] **1.** *v.tr.* (*a*) to dose (person) (with medicine); to dope, *P:* nobble (racehorse, etc.); **se d.,** (i) to be always taking medicine; (ii) to take drugs; **il se drogue,** he's a drug addict; (*b*) to drug (victim). **2.** *v.i. F: A:* to wait, to cool one's heels.

droguerie [drɔgri] *n.f.* (*a*) = ironmonger's, hardware store (selling paint, cleaning materials, etc.); (*b*) = hardware trade.

droguet [drɔgɛ] *n.m. Text:* (*a*) *O:* drugget; (*b*) material of real or artificial silk with design made out of extra warp.

droguiste [drɔgist] *n.m.* = ironmonger (dealing in paints, cleaning materials, etc.); **épicier d.,** grocer and general storekeeper.

droit¹, droite [drwa, drwat] *a., adv. & n.* **I** *a.* **1.** straight, upright; plumb (wall, etc.); **se tenir d.,** to hold oneself erect, to stand up straight; **col d.,** stand-up collar; **d. comme un i, comme un piquet,** as straight, stiff, as a poker, as a post; *Mth:* **angle d.,** *n.m.* **droit,** right angle; **section droite,** cross section. **2.** (*a*) direct, straight (road, etc.); **coup d.,** (i) *Fenc:* straight thrust; (ii) *Ten:* forehand drive; *Nau:* **mettre la barre droite,** to right the helm; **d. la barre!** helm amidships! (*b*) **ligne droite,** *n.f.* **droite,** straight line; **en ligne droite,** in a straight line, as the crow flies; **s'avancer en ligne droite vers qch.,** to make a beeline for sth. **3.** straightforward, upright, honest (person, conduct). **4.** (*a*) right (hand, side, etc.); **être le bras d. de qn,** to be s.o.'s right-hand man. **II.** *adv.* (in a) straight (line), directly; **c'est d. devant vous, tout d.,** it's straight ahead of you; **aller d. au fait,** to go straight to the point; *Nau:* **d. devant, d. debout,** right ahead. **III.** *n.f.* **droite** (*a*) right hand, right(-hand) side; **tourner à d.,** to turn (to the) right; **rouler à d.,** to drive on the right; **tenir la d.,** to keep to the right; *Aut: F:* **et votre d.!** move over! **j'entends dire à d. et à gauche, de d. et de gauche, que . . .,** I hear from all quarters that . . .; *Nau:* **à d. (la barre)!** starboard! (*b*) *Pol:* **la D.,** the right (wing); (*in Eng.*) the Conservatives; **candidat de d.,** right-wing candidate.

droit² *n.m.* **1.** right; (*a*) privilege; **droits civils,** civil rights; **d. de passage,** right of way; **d. de cité,** freedom of a city; **d. d'aînesse,** birthright; **d. d'auteur,** copyright; **tous droits réservés,** all rights reserved; (*b*) justification; fair claim; **faire valoir ses droits,** to vindicate one's rights; **droits acquis,** vested interests; **avoir d. à qch.,** to have a right to sth., to be entitled to sth.; **il a d. à mes excuses,** I owe him an apology; *F: Iron:* **il a eu d. aux inévitables recommandations,** he was treated to the inevitable good advice; **avoir le d., être en d., de faire qch.,** to have a right to do sth.; to be justified in doing sth.; to be entitled to do sth.; **je n'ai pas le d. de le faire,** I'm not allowed to do it; **s'adresser à qui de d.,** to apply to the proper quarter, to an authorized person; **être dans son d.,** to be within one's rights; **à bon d.,** (i) with good reason; (ii) legitimately; **de d. et de fait,** de facto and de jure; **de quel d. êtes-vous entré?** what right had you, what gave you the right, to come in? **faire d. à une demande,** to comply with, accede to, a request. **2.** charge, fee, due; **droits d'auteur,** royalties; **droits de port,** harbour dues; *Cust:* **d. de douane,** duty; **exempt de droits,** duty-free; *Adm:* **d. de timbre,** stamp duty; **d. d'inscription,** registration fee. **3.** law; **d. écrit,** statute law; **d. coutumier, commun,** common law; **d. pénal, criminel,** criminal law; **d. des obligations** = law of contract; **responsable en d.,** legally responsible; **faire son d.,** to study, read, law; **étudiant en d.,** law student.

droitement [drwatmɑ̃] *adv.* uprightly, righteously, honestly, justly.

droitier, -ière [drwatje, -jɛr] *a.* **1.** right-handed; *n.* right-handed person. **2.** *Pol: F:* right-wing; *n.* right winger.

droiture [drwatyr] *n.f.* uprightness, straightforwardness, rectitude, honesty.

drolatique [drɔlatik] *a. Lit:* comic, humorous, droll.

drôle¹ [drol] *n.m. A:* rascal, knave, scamp.

drôle² *a.* (*a*) funny, amusing; **je ne trouve pas ça très d.,** I don't think that's very funny; (*b*) funny, curious, queer, strange; **je l'ai trouvé d.,** he's behaving rather oddly, (he must be worrying about something); *F:* **se sentir tout d.,** to feel peculiar; *F:* **vous êtes d.! qu'auriez-vous fait à ma place?** don't be funny! you must be joking! what would you have done in my place? (*c*) **une d. d'odeur,** a strange, peculiar smell; **quelle d. d'idée!** what a funny idea! *F:* **un d. de type,** a queer fish; an odd type; *F:* **la d. de guerre,** the phoney war (1939–40); *F:* (*intensive*) **il faut une d. de patience,** it needs a heck of a lot of patience; (*d*) *adv. P:* **ça m'a fait tout d. de te voir là,** it gave me an odd feeling to see you there.

drôlement [drolmɑ̃] *adv.* **1.** funnily, strangely,

oddly. **2.** *F:* excessively; awfully; **elle est d. bien,** she's gorgeous; **il fait d. froid,** it's awfully, terribly, cold; **les prix ont d. augmenté,** prices have gone up a hell of a lot.

drôlerie [drolri] *n.f.* (*a*) joking; jesting; fun; (*b*) joke; funny remark.

drôlesse [droles] *n.f. A:* jade, hussy.

dromadaire [drɔmadɛr] *n.m. Z:* dromedary.

drome [drɔm] *n.f.* **1.** *Nau:* (*a*) spars, etc., lashed together; float, raft; (*b*) spare masts and yards, spare gear. **2.** main beam (of forge hammer).

drop (goal) [drɔp(gol)] *n.m. Rugby Fb:* drop goal.

droppage [drɔpaʒ] *n.m. Av:* parachuting; drop; **zone de d.,** dropping zone.

drosophile [drɔzɔfil] *n.f. Ent:* fruit fly.

drosse [drɔs] *n.f. Nau:* wheel, tiller, rope; rudder chain.

drosser [drɔse] *v.tr. Nau:* (*of wind, current*) to drive (ship).

dru [dry] **1.** *a.* thick, dense (grass, hair, etc.); heavy (rain). **2.** *adv.* **tomber d.,** to fall thick and fast; (*of grass, etc.*) **pousser d.,** to grow thickly.

druide, druidesse [drɥid, drɥidɛs] *n.* druid, druidess.

druidique [drɥidik] *a.* druidic(al).

druidisme [drɥidism] *n.m.* druidism.

drupe [dryp] *n.m. or f. Bot:* drupe.

dryade [drijad] *n.f.* **1.** dryad, wood nymph. **2.** *Bot:* dryas, mountain avens.

dû, due [dy] **1.** *a.* due; (*a*) owing, owed; **en port dû,** carriage forward; (*b*) proper; **en temps dû,** in due course; **contrat rédigé en bonne et due forme,** contract drawn up in due form, formal contract. **2.** *n.m.* due; **à chacun son dû,** give the devil his due.

dualisme [dɥalism] *n.m.* dualism.

dualiste [dɥalist] **1.** *a.* dualistic. **2.** *n.* dualist.

dualité [dɥalite] *n.f.* duality.

dubitatif, -ive [dybitatif, -iv] *a.* doubtful, dubious.

dubitativement [dybitativmɑ̃] *adv.* doubtfully, dubiously.

duc [dyk] *n.m.* **1.** duke. **2.** *Orn:* horned owl; **grand d.,** eagle owl.

ducal, -aux [dykal, -o] *a.* ducal.

duché [dyʃe] *n.m.* duchy, dukedom.

duchesse [dyʃɛs] *n.f.* **1.** duchess; **elle fait la d.,** she puts on airs. **2. (poire) d.,** duchess pear.

ductile [dyktil] *a.* ductile, tensile, malleable.

ductilité [dyktilite] *n.f.* ductility, malleability.

duègne [dɥɛɲ] *n.f. A:* duenna, chaperon.

duel[1] [dɥɛl] *n.m.* duel; **provoquer qn en d.,** to challenge s.o. to a duel; **d. oratoire,** battle of words.

duel[2] *n.m. Gram:* dual (number).

duelliste [dɥɛlist] *n.m.* duellist.

duettiste [dɥɛtist] *n.m. & f. Mus:* duettist.

duffel-coat, duffle-coat [dœfœlkot] *n.m. Cost:* duffel coat, duffle coat; *pl. duffel-coats, duffle-coats.*

dum-dum [dumdum] *n.f. & a.inv.* **(balle) d.-d.,** dumdum (bullet).

dûment [dymɑ̃] *adv.* duly, in due form.

dumping [dœmpiŋ] *n.m. Com:* dumping.

dune [dyn] *n.f.* dune; sandhill.

dunette [dynɛt] *n.f. Nau:* poop (deck).

Dunkerque [dœ̃kɛrk] *Pr.n.f. Geog:* Dunkirk.

duo [dɥo] *n.m. Mus:* duet; *Th:* duo; *F:* **d. d'injures,** slanging match.

duodécimal, -aux [dɥɔdesimal, -o] *a.* duodecimal.

duodénal, -aux [dɥɔdenal, -o] *a. Anat:* duodenal.

duodénite [dɥɔdenit] *n.f. Med:* duodenitis.

duodénum [dɥɔdenɔm] *n.m. Anat:* duodenum.

dupe [dyp] **1.** *n.f.* dupe; *F:* sucker; **prendre qn pour d.,** to fool s.o., to take s.o. in; **c'est un marché de dupes,** I've, he's, etc., been had, taken in, swindled. **2.** *a.* naïve, gullible, easily deceived; **il me ment, mais je ne suis pas d.,** I'm well aware that he's lying to me.

duper [dype] *v.tr.* to dupe, deceive, fool (s.o.); to take (s.o.) in; **se d.,** to deceive oneself.

duperie [dypri] *n.f.* (*a*) dupery, deception; (*b*) gullibility, credulity.

dupeur, -euse [dypœr, -øz] *n.* deceiver, trickster.

duplex [dyplɛks] *a.inv. & n.m.* (*a*) duplex (telegraphy, etc.); (*b*) *W.Tel: T.V:* **(émission en) d.,** link-up; (*c*) *n.m.* maison(n)ette, *NAm:* duplex (apartment).

duplexer [dyplɛkse] *v.tr. Tg:* to duplex.

duplicata [dyplikata] *n.m.inv.* duplicate (copy).

duplicateur [dyplikatœr] *n.m.* duplicator, duplicating machine; copier.

duplication [dyplikasjɔ̃] *n.f.* (*a*) *Mth:* duplication; (*b*) *Biol:* doubling; (*c*) *Tg:* duplexing.

duplicité [dyplisite] *n.f.* duplicity, double dealing.

dupliquer [dyplike] *v.tr. Tg:* to duplex.

dur [dyr] *a.* **1.** hard (substance); tough (meat, wood); **œuf d.,** hard-boiled egg; **pain d.,** stale bread; **être d. à cuire,** (i) (*of food*) to take a lot of cooking; (ii) (*of pers.*) to be a tough nut; **eau dure,** hard water. **2.** hard, difficult (work, etc.); **c'est d. à croire,** it's difficult to believe; **rendre la vie dure à qn,** to make s.o.'s life a misery; **avoir la vie dure,** (i) to be resilient to physical pain; (ii) to have a hard time of it; **la vie est dure,** it's a hard life; **enfant d.,** difficult, problem, child. **3.** (*a*) **être d. à la peine,** to be a tireless worker; **être d. d'oreille,** to be hard of hearing; **avoir la tête dure,** to be obstinate, pig-headed; **être d. à la détente,** (i) to be hard to convince; (ii) to be mean, tight-fisted; (*b*) hard, harsh, cruel, callous; **traits durs,** hard features; **avoir le cœur d.,** to be hard-hearted, callous; **être d. envers, pour, avec, à, qn,** to be hard, rough, on s.o.; to be unkind to s.o.; **hiver d.,** hard, severe, winter; (*c*) stiff; **commande dure,** stiff control lever. **4.** (*a*) *adv.* **travailler d.,** to work hard; **cogner d.,** to hit (out) hard; (*b*) *adv.phr.* **il a été élevé à la dure,** he's had a hard upbringing. **5.** *n.m.* (*a*) *Const:* **en d.,** in concrete; in stone; (*b*) *n.m. & f.* (*pers.*) **un d.,** (i) *F:* a tough guy, a hard nut; (ii) *Pol:* a hard liner; *F:* **un d., une dure, à cuire,** a hard nut to crack; (*c*) *P:* train. **6.** *n.f.* (*a*) **coucher sur la dure,** to sleep on the bare floor, on the bare ground; (*b*) *F:* **en dire de dures à qn,** to tell s.o. where he gets off; (*c*) *F:* **il en a vu de dures,** he's had a hard, tough, time (of it).

durabilité [dyrabilite] *n.f.* durability.

durable [dyrabl̩] *a.* durable, lasting, long-lasting.

durablement [dyrabləmɑ̃] *adv.* durably.

durant [dyrɑ̃] *prep.* (*may follow a n. sounded as one syllable*) during; **d. toute sa vie, sa vie d.,** during his whole life, throughout his life; **parler des heures d.,** to talk for hours on end, for hours at a time; **d. quelques instants,** for a few moments.

durcir [dyrsir] **1.** *v.tr.* to harden, to make hard. **2.** *v.i. & pr.* (*a*) to harden; to become, grow, hard, tough; (*b*) (*of cement, etc.*) (i) to set; (ii) to harden.

durcissement [dyrsismɑ̃] *n.m.* **1.** hardening; setting (of cement, etc.). **2.** stiffening (of enemy resistance); hardening (of attitude).

durée [dyre] *n.f.* **1.** lasting quality, wear (of material, building, etc.); life (of light bulb). **2.** (*a*) duration (of reign, war, etc.); *Mus:* length, value (of note); **bonheur de courte d.,** short-lived happiness; (*b*) **d. d'un bail,** duration, term, of a lease; **quelle est la d. de votre congé?** how long is your leave? **disque de longue d.,** long-playing record, disc, *F:* L.P.; *Cin:* **d. de projection,** running, projection, time.

durement [dyrmɑ̃] *adv.* **1.** hard, vigorously; **frapper d.,** to hit hard. **2.** with difficulty; **d. éprouvé,** severely tried. **3.** (to speak, treat s.o.) harshly, severely, unkindly.

durer [dyre] *v.i.* **1.** (*of thgs*) to last; to continue; (*a*)

voilà trois ans que cela dure, it's been going on for three years; **votre congé dure combien de temps?** how long is your leave? **ça va d. longtemps, cette plaisanterie?** haven't we had about enough of this? **ça ne peut pas d.,** this (i) can't go on, (ii) can't last long; (*b*) **la pierre dure plus que le bois,** stone lasts longer than wood; *F:* **ça durera ce que ça durera,** it won't, may not, last long; **ce costume a duré deux ans,** this suit has lasted two years; **tissu qui durera,** material which will wear well. **2.** (*of pers.*) (*a*) (i) *A:* to live; (ii) *F:* to remain alive; (*b*) *F:* (*usu. neg.*) to hold out; **il ne peut pas d. en place,** he can't stay put, keep still.

dureté [dyrte] *n.f.* **1.** hardness (of substance, of water); toughness (of meat). **2.** difficulty, hardness (of task, etc.); **d. d'oreille,** hardness of hearing. **3.** harshness, callousness, unkindness; severity; hardness (of features); harshness (of voice); **d. de cœur,** hard-heartedness; **parler avec d.,** to speak harshly.

durillon [dyrijɔ̃] *n.m.* callosity, callus (on hand, foot, etc.); corn (on foot).

durit(e) [dyrit] *n.f. Aut: Av: etc: R.t.m:* flexible connection piping; hose (connection).

duvet [dyve] *n.m.* (*a*) down (on chin, young bird, peach, etc.); **d. de l'eider, du cygne,** eider down, swan's down; (*b*) underfur (of animal); (*c*) sleeping bag; (*d*) *Sw.Fr:* duvet, continental quilt.

duveté [dyvte] *a.* downy.

duveter (se) [sədyvte] *v.pr.* to become downy.

duveteux, -euse [dyvtø, -øz] *a.* downy.

dyke [dik] *n.m. Geol:* dyke.

dynamique [dinamik] **1.** *a.* dynamic; *Aer:* **pression d.,** ram pressure; *F:* **c'est un type d.,** he's lively, dynamic, go-ahead. **2.** *n.f.* (*a*) dynamics; (*b*) **la d. de(s) groupe(s),** group dynamism.

dynamiquement [dinamikmɑ̃] *adv.* dynamically.

dynamisme [dinamism] *n.m.* (*a*) dynamism; (*b*) energy, vitality; drive.

dynamiste [dinamist] *n.m.* dynamist.

dynamitage [dinamitaʒ] *n.m.* dynamiting.

dynamite [dinamit] *n.f.* dynamite.

dynamiter [dinamite] *v.tr.* to dynamite, to blow up (building, etc.).

dynamiteur, -euse [dinamitœr, -øz] *n.* dynamiter.

dynamo [dinamo] *n.f. El:* dynamo.

dynamographe [dinamɔgraf] *n.m.* dynamograph.

dynamomètre [dinamɔmɛtr̥] *n.m.* dynamometer.

dynamométrique [dinamɔmetrik] *a.* dynamometric(al).

dynaste [dinast] *n.m.* dynast.

dynastie [dinasti] *n.f.* dynasty.

dynastique [dinastik] *a.* dynastic.

dyne [din] *n.f. Ph.Meas:* dyne.

dysenterie [disɑ̃tri] *n.f. Med:* dysentery.

dysentérique [disɑ̃terik] *a. Med:* dysenteric.

dyslexie [dislɛksi] *n.f. Med:* dyslexia.

dyslexique [dislɛksik] *a. & n. Med:* dyslexic.

dysménorrhée [dismenɔre] *n.f. Med:* dysmenorrhoea.

dyspepsie [dispɛpsi] *n.f. Med:* dyspepsia.

dyspepsique [dispɛpsik], **dyspeptique** [dispɛptik] *a. & n. Med:* dyspeptic.

dystrophie [distrɔfi] *n.f. Med:* dystrophy; **d. musculaire progressive,** muscular dystrophy.

dytique [ditik] *n.m. Ent:* water beetle.

E

E, e [œ] *n.m.* (the letter) E, e.

eau, eaux [o] *n.f.* water. **1. e. dure,** hard water; **e. douce,** (i) fresh water; (ii) soft water; *F:* **marin d'e. douce,** landlubber; **être comme l'e. et le feu,** to be as different as chalk from cheese; **laver le plancher à grande e.,** to swill down the floor; **e. de vaisselle, e. grasse,** washing-up water; **passer à l'e.,** to rinse; **e. potable,** drinking water; **e. non potable,** water unfit for drinking; *F:* **croyez ça et buvez de l'e.!** don't you believe it!; **e. rougie,** wine and water; **mettre de l'e. dans son vin,** (i) to reduce one's expenses; (ii) to draw in one's horns; (iii) to tone it down a bit; **whisky à l'e.,** whisky and water; **whisky sans e.,** neat whisky; **eaux thermales,** thermal springs, hot springs; **e. minérale,** (natural) mineral water; **ville d'eau(x),** spa; **prendre les eaux,** to take, drink, the waters; (*of locomotive, ship*) **faire de l'e.,** to water, take on water. **2.** (*a*) **e. de pluie,** rainwater; **il tombe de l'e.,** it's raining; **le temps est à l'e.,** it's wet, rainy, weather; (*b*) **cours d'e.,** waterway; stream; river; **jet d'e.,** fountain; **dimanche grandes eaux à Versailles,** the fountains will play at Versailles on Sunday; **pièce d'e.,** (ornamental) lake; pool; **sur l'e.,** afloat; **revenir sur l'e.,** to surface; **tomber à l'e.,** (i) to fall into the water; (ii) (*of plan*) to fall through; **porter de l'e. à la rivière, à la mer,** to bring, carry, coals to Newcastle; (*c*) **mortes eaux,** neap tides; **vives eaux,** spring tides; **hautes, basses, eaux,** high, low, water; **grandes eaux,** high water; **nager entre deux eaux,** (i) to swim under water; (ii) to hedge, to run with the hare and hunt with the hounds; (*of ship*) **faire e.,** to leak, to spring a leak; **chaussures qui prennent l'e.,** shoes that let in the water, the wet; **être dans les eaux d'un navire,** to be in the wake of a ship; **mettre un navire à l'e.,** to launch a ship; (*d*) **service des eaux,** water supply; **e. de la ville,** main(s) water; **château d'e.,** water tower; **conduite d'e.,** water main(s); **faire mettre l'e. courante,** to have the water laid on; **e. courante,** running water. **3.** (*a*) juice (of a melon, etc.); **cela me fait venir l'e. à la bouche,** it makes my mouth water; **être tout en e.,** to be dripping with perspiration; (*b*) **diamant de la première e.,** diamond of the first water. **4. e. de Cologne,** eau de Cologne; **e. de rose,** rose water; **socialisme à l'e. de rose,** milk-and-water socialism; **e. de toilette,** lotion, toilet water; **e. oxygénée,** hydrogen peroxide; **e. de Javel,** = bleach; *Atom.Ph:* **e. lourde,** heavy water.

eau-de-vie [odvi] *n.f.* (*a*) (plum, etc.) brandy; (*b*) spirits; *pl. eaux-de-vie.*

eau-forte [ofɔrt] *n.f.* **1.** *Ch:* aqua fortis, nitric acid. **2.** etching, etched engraving; *pl. eaux-fortes.*

eaux-vannes [ovan] *n.f.pl.* sewage (water).

ébahi [ebai] *a.* amazed, stupefied, flabbergasted, staggered, astounded, dumbfounded, tongue-tied; **un regard é.,** a look of blank astonishment.

ébahir [ebair] *v.* **1.** *v.tr.* to amaze, astound, flabbergast; to take (s.o.'s) breath away. **2. s'é.,** to gape, to stare; to stand amazed, to be dumbfounded (**de,** at).

ébahissement [ebaismã] *n.m.* amazement, astonishment.

ébarbage [ebarbaʒ] *n.m.*, **ébarbement** [ebarbəmã] *n.m.* trimming (of sth.); fettling (of casting); clipping (of hedge).

ébarber [ebarbe] *v.tr.* to trim; to remove rough edges from (sth.); to fettle (casting); to clip (hedge, etc.).

ébarbeuse [ebarbøz] *n.f. Metall: etc:* trimming machine.

ébarboir [ebarbwar] *n.m. Tls:* scraper, chipping chisel.

ébarbure [ebarbyr] *n.f.* burr, paring (of metal, etc.); trimming (from paper).

ébats [eba] *n.m.pl.* revels; playing (about).

ébattre (s') [sebatr̥] *v.pr.* (*conj. like* BATTRE) to gambol; to frolic, play (about).

ébaubi [ebobi] *a. F:* flabbergasted, struck all of a heap.

ébauchage [eboʃaʒ] *n.m.* roughing out; sketching out (of picture); outlining (of novel, etc.).

ébauche [eboʃ] *n.f.* rough shape; rough sketch (of picture); skeleton, outline, rough draft (of novel, etc.); rough model; *NAm:* roughcast; **e. d'un sourire,** suspicion, ghost, of a smile.

ébaucher [eboʃe] *v.tr.* to rough (sth.) out; to sketch out, outline (picture, plan); to rough-hew (statue, etc.); **é. un sourire,** to give a faint, wan, smile.

ébauchoir [eboʃwar] *n.m.* (sculptor's, mason's) boaster; roughing-chisel; (carpenter's) paring chisel.

ébène [ebɛn] *n.f.* ebony; **(d'un noir) d'é.,** jet-black.

ébénier [ebenje] *n.m.* **1.** ebony tree. **2. faux é.,** laburnum.

ébéniste [ebenist] *n.m.* cabinet maker.

ébénisterie [ebenist(ə)ri] *n.f.* (*a*) cabinet making; (*b*) cabinet work; (*c*) cabinet (for radio, etc.).

éberlué [ebɛrlɥe] *a. F:* flabbergasted.

éblouir [ebluir] *v.tr.* to dazzle; **ébloui par les phares d'une voiture,** dazzled by the headlights of a car.

éblouissant [ebluisã] *a.* dazzling, blinding.

éblouissement [ebluismã] *n.m.* **1.** (*a*) dazzling, dazzle, glare; (*b*) **avoir des éblouissements,** to have fits of dizziness. **2.** amazement.

éborgnement [ebɔrɲəmã] *n.m.* (i) blinding, (ii) blindness, in one eye.

éborgner [ebɔrɲe] *v.tr.* **1. é. qn,** to blind s.o. in one eye, to put s.o.'s eye out; **j'ai failli m'é.,** I nearly put my eye out. **2.** *Hort:* to disbud (fruit tree).

éboueur [ebuœr] *n.m.* dustman.

ébouillanter [ebujãte] *v.tr.* to scald.

éboulement [ebulmã] *n.m.* **1.** falling in, crumbling; caving in, collapsing. **2.** rock fall, (mass of) fallen rock; **é. de terre,** landslide, landslip.

ébouler (s') [sebule] *v.pr.* to fall down, fall in, crumble, collapse, cave in; (*of cliff*) to slip.

éboulis [ebuli] *n.m.* mass of fallen earth; debris; scree.

ébourgeonnage [eburʒɔnaʒ] *n.m.*, **ébourgeonnement** [eburʒɔnmã] *n.m. Hort:* disbudding.

ébourgeonner [eburʒɔne] *v.tr.* to disbud (fruit tree).

ébouriffant [eburifã] *a. F:* breathtaking, startling.

ébouriffé [eburife] *a.* **1.** dishevelled. **2.** amazed; startled.

ébouriffer [eburife] *v.tr.* **1.** to ruffle, tousle (s.o.'s hair). **2.** *F:* to amaze (s.o.); to take (s.o.'s) breath away.

ébranchage [ebrãʃaʒ] *n.m.*, **ébranchement** [ebrãʃmã] *n.m. Arb:* stripping, lopping.

ébrancher [ebrɑ̃ʃe] *v.tr.* lop off, strip, the branches from (tree).

ébranchoir [ebrɑ̃nʃwar] *n.m. Hort:* billhook.

ébranlement [ebrɑ̃l(ə)mɑ̃] *n.m.* **1.** shaking, shock. **2.** agitation; (nervous) shock; **é. de la raison,** unhinging of the mind.

ébranler [ebrɑ̃le] *v.* **1.** *v.tr.* (*a*) to shake; to loosen; to rock (building, etc.); **é. une cloche,** to set a bell ringing; (*b*) to shake, disturb (s.o.). **2. s'é.** (*a*) to shake, totter; (*b*) (*of train*) to start; (*of procession, etc.*) to move off.

ébrasement [ebrazmɑ̃] *n.m.*, **ébrasure** [ebrazyr] *n.f. Arch:* (*a*) splaying; (*b*) splay (of embrasure).

ébraser [ebraze] *v.tr. Arch:* to splay (embrasure).

Èbre (l') [lɛbbr̥] *Pr.n.m.* the (river) Ebro.

ébrécher [ebreʃe] *v.tr.* **(j'ébrèche; j'ébrécherai)** (*a*) to notch; to make a notch, a gap, in (sth.); to chip (a plate); to break (a tooth); (*b*) *F:* to damage, impair (reputation); to make a hole in (one's capital).

ébréchure [ebreʃyr] *n.f.* nick, notch, gap (in blade); chip(ped place) (in plate, etc.).

ébriété [ebriete] *n.f.* (state of) inebriation, intoxication, drunkenness.

ébrouement [ebrumɑ̃] *n.m.* (*a*) snorting, snort (of horse, etc.); (*b*) flap(ping).

ébrouer (s') [sebrue] *v.pr.* **1.** (*of horse, etc.*) to snort. **2.** to splash about.

ébruitement [ebrɥitmɑ̃] *n.m.* spreading (of rumour).

ébruiter [ebrɥite] *v.* **1.** *v.tr.* to make known; to spread (rumour). **2.** (*of news, etc.*) **s'é.,** to become known, to spread; *F:* to get (a)round.

ébullition [ebylisjɔ̃] *n.f.* **1.** (*a*) boiling; **entrer en é.,** to come to the boil; *F:* **être en é.,** to be boiling, seething, with rage; (*b*) **en é.,** in a state of agitation.

écaillage [ekajaʒ] *n.m.* **1.** scaling (of fish); opening (of oysters). **2.** flaking off, peeling off (of paint); scaling off, chipping (of enamel).

écaille [ekaj] *n.f.* **1.** (*a*) scale (of fish, etc.); (*b*) flake (of paint); chip (of marble, enamel); splinter (of wood); *Lit:* **les écailles lui tombèrent des yeux,** the scales fell from his eyes. **2.** shell (of tortoise); **lunettes à monture d'é.,** tortoiseshell-rimmed spectacles.

écaillement [ekajmɑ̃] *n.m.* scaling; peeling (off), flaking (off).

écailler¹ [ekaje] *v.* **1.** *v.tr.* (*a*) to scale (fish); to open (oyster); (*b*) to scale (boiler). **2. s'é.,** to scale off, peel off; to flake (off); to chip.

écailler², -ère [ekaje, -ɛr] *n.* **1.** oyster seller; oyster opener. **2.** *n.f.* **écaillère,** oyster knife.

écailleux, -euse [ekajø, -øz] *a.* scaly (animal, etc.); splintery (wood); flaky (paint).

écale [ekal] *n.f.* hull, husk (of walnut); shuck (of chestnut).

écaler [ekale] *v.tr.* to hull, husk (walnuts); to shuck (chestnuts).

écarlate [ekarlat] *n.f.* & *a.* scarlet; **devenir é.,** to blush, turn red.

écarquiller [ekarkije] *v.tr.* **é. les yeux,** to open one's eyes wide; to stare; *F:* to goggle.

écart¹ [ekar] *n.m.* **1.** (*a*) distance apart, gap; **é. entre le prix de vente et le coût,** margin between cost and selling price; **é. entre deux lectures,** difference, variation, between readings (of an apparatus); *Book-k:* **é. entre deux comptes,** discrepancy between two accounts; **réduire l'é. entre deux objets,** to reduce the gap between two objects; *Mec.E:* **é. admissible,** tolerance; (*b*) separation, spreading out; straddling (of the legs); **faire le grand é.,** to do the splits; (*c*) *Vet:* shoulder strain (of horse). **2.** deviation; (*a*) deflection (of compass needle); (*b*) swerve, step(ping) aside; **faire un é.,** to step aside; (*of horse*) to shy; **é. de l'imagination,** flight of the imagination; **écarts de conduite,** lapses of conduct; **écarts de jeunesse,** youthful indiscretions; **il ne fait pas des écarts de régime,** he keeps, *F:* sticks, to his diet; (*c*) digression (in speech, etc.). **3. à. l'é.,** aside, on one side, apart; **se tenir à l'é.,** to keep in the background; to keep oneself apart, aloof (from the crowd, etc.); **habiter à l'é.,** to live in a remote, lonely, spot; **mettre à l'é. tout sentiment personnel,** to set aside, banish, any personal feeling.

écart² *n.m. Cards:* **1.** discarding. **2.** discard.

écarté¹ [ekarte] *a.* **1.** isolated, lonely, remote (house, spot); **sentier é.,** bypath; *Cr:* **balle écartée,** wide (ball). **2.** (far) apart; widely spaced (eyes); **se tenir les jambes écartées,** to stand with one's feet apart.

écarté² *n.m. Cards:* (game of) écarté.

écartelé [ekartəle] *a. Her:* quartered, quarterly.

écarteler [ekartəle] *v.tr.* **(j'écartèle; j'écartèlerai)** to quarter (criminal, *Her:* shield).

écartement [ekartəmɑ̃] *n.m.* **1.** (*a*) separation, spreading out, spacing; **pièce d'écartement,** spacer; (*b*) setting aside (of obstacle). **2.** space, gap, clearance (between bars, etc.); *Rail:* gauge (of track); *Veh:* **é. des essieux,** wheelbase; **é. des roues,** track.

écarter¹ [ekarte] *v.* **1.** *v.tr.* (*a*) to separate, part (the fingers, branches, etc.); to draw aside (curtains); to open (one's arms); to spread (one's legs); to square (one's elbows); (*b*) to move, thrust, (s.o., sth.) aside; **é. les obstacles de son chemin,** to brush aside the obstacles in one's path; **é. un coup, un danger,** to ward off, avert, a blow, a danger; **é. une réclamation,** to turn down a claim; (*c*) to divert (suspicion, etc.). **2. s'é.** (*a*) to move, draw, step, stand, aside; (*b*) to move apart, diverge; (*of shot*) to spread; (*c*) to deviate, stray **(de,** from); **maison écartée du chemin,** house standing back from the road; **s'é. du sujet,** to deviate, wander (away), from the subject; **s'é. des règles,** to depart from the rules.

écarter² *v.tr. Cards:* to discard.

ecchymose [ekimoz] *n.f.* bruise.

Ecclésiaste (l') [leklezjast] *n.m. B:* (the book of) Ecclesiastes.

ecclésiastique [eklezjastik] **1.** *a.* ecclesiastical; clerical (hat, dress). **2.** *n.m.* (*a*) ecclesiastic, clergyman; (*b*) *B.Lit:* **l'E.,** Ecclesiasticus.

écervelé, -ée [esɛrvəle] **1.** *a.* thoughtless; harebrained, scatterbrained. **2.** *n.* scatterbrain.

échafaud [eʃafo] *n.m.* **1.** *O:* stand, platform. **2.** scaffold; **monter sur l'é., à l'é.,** to go to the scaffold, to mount the scaffold.

échafaudage [eʃafodaʒ] *n.m.* **1.** (*a*) erection of scaffolding; (*b*) building up (of reputation, etc.). **2.** (*a*) scaffolding; *Civ.E:* **é. volant,** hanging stage, travelling cradle; (*b*) structure, fabric (of argument); (*c*) pile (of objects).

échafauder [eʃafode] **1.** *v.i.* to erect (a) scaffolding. **2.** *v.tr.* to pile up (objects); to build up, construct (system, argument, plan).

échalas [eʃala] *n.m.* **1.** (*a*) cane, stake (to support plant). **2.** (*a*) **jambes en é.,** long, spindly, legs; (*b*) (*pers.*) **grand é.,** beanpole.

échal(l)ier [eʃalje] *n.m.* **échalis** [eʃali] *n.m.* **1.** barrier, hurdle (closing gap). **2.** stile.

échalote [eʃalɔt] *n.f.* shallot, scallion.

échancrer [eʃɑ̃kre] *v.tr.* to make a circular, a V-shaped, cut in (neck of dress, etc.); to indent, notch (plank, etc.); **littoral échancré,** indented coastline.

échancrure [eʃɑ̃kryr] *n.f.* cut-out part, opening (in garment, neckline); notch, cut, nick (in plank, etc.); indentation (in coastline, etc.).

échange [eʃɑ̃ʒ] *n.m.* (*a*) exchange (of prisoners, ideas, blows, etc.); **faire un é. de qch. pour, contre, qch.,** to exchange sth. for sth.; **recevoir qch. en é. de qch.,** to receive sth. in exchange, in return, for sth.; (*b*) *Com: Pol.Ec:* exchange; barter; **taux de l'é.,** rate of exchange.

échangeable [eʃɑ̃ʒabl̩] *a.* exchangeable.
échanger [eʃɑ̃ʒe] *v.tr.* **(j'échangeai(s); n. échangeons)** to exchange; to barter (sth. for sth).
échangeur [eʃɑ̃ʒœr] *n.m.* **1.** *Civ.E:* (*on motorway*) (clover leaf) intersection. **2.** *Ph:* (heat) exchanger.
échangiste [eʃɑ̃ʒist] *n.m. & f. Fin:* exchanger.
échanson [eʃɑ̃sɔ̃] *n.m.* cup-bearer.
échantillon [eʃɑ̃tijɔ̃] *n.m.* **1. brique, tuile, d'é.,** standard brick, tile. **2.** sample (of wine, etc.); sample, pattern (of cloth); specimen (of one's work); population sample (for opinion poll); **prendre, prélever, des échantillons de qch.,** to sample sth.; **livre d'échantillons,** pattern book; **conforme, pareil, à l'é.,** up to sample; *Post:* **échantillons sans valeur,** samples of no (commercial) value.
échantillonnage [eʃɑ̃tijɔnaʒ] *n.m.* **1.** *Com:* making up of samples (of wine, etc.), of patterns (of cloth, etc.). **2.** sampling; verifying, checking, by the samples; *Stat:* choice, selection (of people, etc., for survey).
échantillonner [eʃɑ̃tijɔne] *v.tr.* **1.** *Com:* to prepare patterns, samples, of (sth.). **2.** (*a*) to verify, check, (articles) by the samples; (*b*) to sample (wine, etc.); *Stat:* to sample (the population). **3.** to make (articles) according to sample.
échantillonneur, -euse [eʃɑ̃tijɔnœr, -øz] *n. Com: Stat:* (*pers.*) sampler.
échappatoire [eʃapatwar] *n.f.* **1.** subterfuge, way out, loophole (of escape from obligation); **chercher des échappatoires,** (i) to hedge; (ii) to try to find excuses; *a.* **clause é.,** escape clause. **2.** *Aut:* escape way.
échappée [eʃape] *n.f.* **1.** *Sp:* sudden spurt, burst (in race). **2.** space, interval; **é. de vue,** vista (**sur,** over); **é. de ciel,** patch of sky; **é. de soleil,** burst of sunshine; **é. de beau temps,** short spell of fine weather; **faire qch. par échappées,** to do sth. by fits and starts. **3.** (*a*) turning space (for vehicles); (*b*) headroom (of staircase).
échappement [eʃapmɑ̃] *n.m.* **1.** escape, leakage (of gas, water). **2.** *Mch:* (i) exhaust, release (of steam); eduction; (ii) exhaust stroke; **(tuyau d')é.,** (i) waste-steam pipe; (ii) *I.C.E:* exhaust (pipe); *I.C.E:* **pot d'é.,** silencer; *NAm:* muffler; **(soupape d')é. libre,** cut-out (to silencer); **gaz d'é.,** exhaust fumes; **clapet d'é.,** exhaust cut-out. **3.** (*a*) *Clockm:* escapement; **montre à é.,** lever watch; (*b*) hopper (of piano).
échapper [eʃape] *v.* **I.** *v.i.* (*aux.* **être** *or* **avoir**) to escape. **1.** (*a*) **é. à qn, à qch.,** to escape s.o., sth.; **le prisonnier nous a échappé,** the prisoner got away (from us); **il n'y a pas moyen d'y é.,** there is no escaping it; **ce fait a, est, échappé à mon attention, ce fait m'a échappé,** this fact escaped me, my attention; **pas un mot ne lui a échappé,** he did not miss a single word; **la vérité lui échappe parfois,** he sometimes blurts out the truth; **son nom m'échappe,** I can't remember his name; **é. à toute définition,** to defy definition; (*b*) (*aux.* **avoir**) to dodge (sth.); **é. à un coup,** to dodge a blow; *F:* **vous l'avez échappé belle,** you've had a narrow escape; (*c*) **laisser échapper,** to let (s.o., sth.) escape; to set (s.o.) free; to let out (air from balloon); to let off (steam); to give vent to (one's anger); to let fall (a tear); to let out (secret, sigh, cry); **laisser é. son stylo,** to let one's pen slip from one's fingers; **laisser é. l'occasion,** to let the opportunity slip. **2.** to escape (**de,** from, out of); **é. de prison,** to escape, make one's escape, from prison; **é. d'une maladie, d'un naufrage,** to survive an illness, a shipwreck. **II. s'échapper,** to escape; to break free, loose; **s'é. de prison,** to break prison; *F:* **il faut que je m'échappe,** I must be off; **le gaz s'échappe,** the gas is leaking; **un cri s'échappa de ses lèvres,** a cry burst from his lips.
écharde [eʃard] *n.f.* prickle, splinter, thorn (under the skin).
échardonner [eʃardɔne] *v.tr.* **1.** to clear (ground) of thistles. **2.** to pick (wool).
échardonnet [eʃardɔnɛ] *n.m.*, **échardonnette** [eʃardɔnɛt] *n.f.*, **échardonnoir** [eʃardɔnwar] *n.m.* *Agr:* thistle hook.
écharpe [eʃarp] *n.f.* **1.** (*a*) official sash; (*b*) (lady's) scarf; **é. de fourrure,** fur stole; (*c*) (arm) sling; **porter le bras en é.,** to have one's arm in a sling; (*d*) **en é.,** slantwise, aslant; **se prendre en é.,** to collide at an angle, obliquely; (*of trains*) to collide at the points; *Tchn:* **moise en é.,** diagonal brace.
écharper [eʃarpe] *v.tr.* (*a*) to slash, gash, hack (one's finger, etc.); (*b*) to hack (up) (meat); to cut (troops) to pieces; **vous allez vous faire é.!** you'll get torn to pieces!
échasse [eʃas] *n.f.* **1.** stilt; **marcher, être monté, sur des échasses,** (i) to be on stilts; (ii) to be stilted, pompous; (iii) *F:* to be long in the leg. **2. é. d'échafaud,** scaffolding pole. **3.** *Orn:* stilt.
échassier [eʃasje] *n.m. Orn:* wader.
échaudage [eʃodaʒ] *n.m.* scalding.
échaudé [eʃode] *a.* (*a*) scalded; (*b*) **blé é.,** wheat shrivelled by the sun.
échauder [eʃode] *v.tr.* to scald (one's foot, a saucepan, etc.); to scour (wool); *F:* **se faire é. dans une affaire,** to burn one's fingers over sth.
échaudoir [eʃodwar] *n.m.* **1.** (*in slaughterhouse*) (*a*) scalding room; (*b*) scalding tub. **2.** *Tex:* (*a*) scouring room; (*b*) scouring vat.
échauffant [eʃofɑ̃] *a.* **1.** heating (food, etc.). **2.** exciting (discussion).
échauffé [eʃofe] *a.* (*a*) overheated (room); hot (bearings); (*b*) fermented, heated (hay).
échauffement [eʃofmɑ̃] *n.m.* **1.** (*a*) heating (of soil, bearings); overheating (of engine); (*b*) fermenting (of hay); (*c*) chafing (of rope). **2.** (over) excitement; **dans l'é. de sa jeunesse,** in the heat of (his) youth.
échauffer [eʃofe] *v.* **1.** *v.tr.* (*a*) to overheat (room, blood); **frottement qui échauffe les roues,** friction that overheats the wheels; **é. la bile, les oreilles, de qn,** to irritate s.o.; to rub s.o. up the wrong way; (*b*) to cause fermentation in (cereals, hay). **2. s'é.** (*a*) to become, get, overheated; **ne vous échauffez pas,** don't get excited; **la dispute s'échauffait,** feelings were beginning to run high; (*b*) (*of athlete, etc.*) to warm up; (*c*) (*of bearings*) to run hot, heat; (*of cereals, etc.*) to ferment.
échauffourée [eʃofure] *n.f.* scuffle; clash (between mobs); *Mil:* affray, skirmish.
échéance [eʃeɑ̃s] *n.f.* **1.** (*a*) falling due, maturity (of bill); date of payment; **venir à é.,** to fall due; **payable à l'é.,** payable at maturity; **à trois mois d'é.,** at three months' date; **billet à longue, courte, é.,** long-dated, short-dated, bill; **politique à longue é.,** long-term policy; (*b*) bill (falling due); **é. à vue,** sight bill; **faire face à une é.,** to meet a bill. **2.** expiry (of tenancy, etc.).
échéancier [eʃeɑ̃sje] *n.m. Fin:* bill book.
échéant [eʃeɑ̃] **1.** *a. Fin:* falling due. **2. le cas é.,** should the occasion arise; if necessary.
échec [eʃɛk] *n.m.* **1.** (*a*) (*at chess*) check; **é. et mat,** checkmate; **tenir l'ennemi en é.,** to hold the enemy in check; (*b*) check, setback; **faire é. à (qch.),** to put a check on, to check (activities, etc.); **faire é., donner (un) é., à qn,** to checkmate, frustrate, s.o., to frustrate s.o.'s plans; **voué à l'é.,** bound to fail. **2.** *pl.* (*a*) chess; **une partie d'échecs,** a game of chess; **joueur, -euse, d'échecs,** chess player; (*b*) chessmen.
échelle [eʃɛl] *n.f.* **1.** (*a*) ladder; **é d'incendie, de sauvetage,** fire escape; **é. brisée,** folding steps; **é. de corde,** rope ladder; **é. à coulisse,** extension ladder; *Nau:* **é. de commandement, d'honneur,** companion ladder; **é. de revers,** Jacob's ladder: **faire la courte é. à qn,** to give s.o. (i) a leg up, (ii) a helping hand; *F:* **vous voulez me faire monter à l'é.,** you're having me

on; **il faut, il n'y a plus qu'à, tirer l'é.,** there's no point in trying any further; we'd better give up; (*b*) **é. à poissons,** fish ladder; salmon leap; (*c*) *Gym:* **é. suédoise,** rib stall. **2.** (*a*) **l'é. sociale,** the social scale; **être en haut, au sommet, de l'é.,** to be at the top of the tree, the ladder; (*b*) *Mus:* scale; (*c*) **é. des traitements,** salary scale; **é. mobile,** (i) sliding scale (of prices, etc.); (ii) escalator clause. **3.** (*a*) scale (of map, etc.); **carte à petite, à grande, é.,** small-scale, large-scale, map; **faire les choses sur une grande é.,** to do things on a large scale; (*b*) scale (of thermometer, etc.); *Nau:* **é. de tirant d'eau,** water marks, draft marks; *U.S:* immersion scale; **é. de marée,** tide gauge. **4.** *Hist:* **les échelles du Levant,** the (commercial) ports of the Levant.

échelon [eʃlɔ̃] *n.m.* **1.** (*a*) rung (of ladder); (*b*) step, grade, echelon; **monter par échelons,** to rise by degrees, by successive stages; **les échelons de l'administration,** the grades of the civil service; **à l'é. ministériel,** at ministerial level. **2.** *Mil:* **en é.,** in echelon, in stepped formation; *Av:* **vol en é.,** stepped-up formation.

échelonnement [eʃlɔnmɑ̃] *n.m.* **1.** *Mil:* echelonment, echeloning (of troops) **2.** (*a*) spreading out (of payments); staggering (of holidays); (*b*) *El:* staggering (of brushes).

échelonner [eʃlɔne] *v.tr.* **1.** *Mil:* to dispose (troops) in echelon, in depth. **2.** (*a*) to space out (objects); to place (objects) at intervals; to spread out (payments); **congés échelonnés,** staggered holidays; (*b*) *El:* to stagger (brushes).

écheniller [eʃnije] *v.tr.* (*a*) to clear (fruit trees, etc.) of caterpillars; (*b*) to clean up; to polish (style, etc.); to remove undesirable elements from (society, etc.).

écheveau, -eaux [eʃ(ə)vo] *n.m.* (*a*) hank, skein (of yarn, etc.); (*b*) **é. de rues,** maze of streets; **l'é. d'une intrigue,** the intricacies of a plot.

échevelé [eʃəvle] *a.* (*a*) dishevelled (hair, person); tousled (hair); (*b*) wild, disorderly (dance, etc.).

échevin [eʃvɛ̃] *n.m.* **1.** *A:* municipal magistrate. **2.** *Belg:* deputy mayor.

échidné [ekidne] *n.m.* *Z:* spiny anteater.

échinant [eʃinɑ̃] *a.* *P:* back-breaking (work).

échine [eʃin] *n.f.* **1.** spine, backbone; (*of animals*) chine; *F:* **crotté jusqu'à l'é.,** all over mud; **courber l'é. devant qn,** to kowtow, toady, to s.o.; to lick s.o.'s boots; **avoir l'é. souple, flexible,** to be obsequious. **2.** *Cu:* loin (of pork).

échiner (s') [seʃine] *v.pr.* **s'é. (à (faire) qch.),** to exhaust oneself, tire oneself out (at sth., doing sth.); to make a great effort (to do sth.); to slog (at sth.).

échinoderme [ekinɔdɛrm] *n.m.* echinoderm.

échiquier [eʃikje] *n.m.* **1.** chessboard; **en é.,** chequerwise, in chequer pattern, chequered. **2.** (*in Eng.*) **l'É.,** the Exchequer.

écho [eko] *n.m.* **1.** echo; (*a*) **faire é.,** to echo (back); **se faire l'é. des opinions de qn,** to echo, repeat, s.o.'s opinions; *Elcs:* **éliminateur, suppresseur, d'é.,** echo suppressor; **échos parasites,** clutter; (*b*) *T.V:* ghost(ing). **2.** *Journ:* **échos,** news items; gossip column.

échoir [eʃwar] *v.i.* (*pr.p* **échéant;** *p.p.* **échu;** *pr.ind.* **il échoit, ils échoient;** *impf.* **il échoyait;** *p.h.* **il échut;** *fu.* **il échoira;** *aux usu.* **être**) **1. é. (en partage) à qn,** to fall to s.o., to s.o.'s lot; **le devoir m'échut de lui apprendre la nouvelle,** it fell to me to break the news to him. **2.** (*a*) *Fin:* to fall due, to mature; **billets échus,** bills (over)due; **intérêts échus,** outstanding interest; **intérêts à é.,** accruing interest; (*b*) (*of tenancy*) to expire.

échométrie [ekometri] *n.f.* *Ph:* echometry, echo ranging.

échoppe¹ [eʃɔp] *n.f.* (*a*) booth, covered stall, street stall; (*b*) (cobbler's) small (work)shop.

échoppe² *n.f.* *Tls:* graver, burin.

échopper [eʃɔpe] *v.tr.* *Engr:* to grave, gouge, scoop; to rout (out).

écho-sondeur [ekosɔ̃dœr] *n.m.* *Nau:* echo sounder, sonic depth finder; *pl.* *écho-sondeurs.*

échotier [ekɔtje] *n.m.* *Journ:* gossip columnist.

échouage [eʃwaʒ] *n.m.* *Nau:* **1.** (*a*) stranding, running aground, grounding; (*b*) beaching. **2.** beaching strand, graving beach.

échouement [eʃumɑ̃] *n.m.* = ÉCHOUAGE 1.

échouer [eʃwe] **1.** *v.i.* (*a*) *Nau:* to run aground, to be stranded, to ground; **navire échoué,** ship aground; **échoué à sec,** high and dry; (*b*) to fail, miscarry, come to grief; **le projet a échoué,** the plan failed, came to nothing; **é. à un examen,** to fail an examination; **faire é. un projet,** to wreck a plan. **2.** *v.tr.* *Nau:* to beach; to run (ship) aground. **3. s'é.,** to run aground, to be driven ashore.

écimage [esimaʒ] *n.m.* *Arb:* topping, pollarding.

écimer [esime] *v.tr.* to top, pollard (tree).

éclaboussement [eklabusmɑ̃] *n.m.* splashing, spattering.

éclabousser [eklabuse] *v.tr.* (*a*) to splash, spatter (**de,** with); (*b*) to damage (s.o.'s) reputation.

éclaboussure [eklabusyr] *n.f.* (*a*) splash, spatter (of mud, etc.); splash (of colour); splinter (of metal); (*b*) blemish, blot, smirch (on reputation).

éclair [eklɛr] *n.m.* **1.** flash of lightning; **éclairs,** lightning; **éclairs en nappe,** sheet lightning; **é. arborescent, en zigzag,** (flash of) forked lightning; **il fait des éclairs,** it's lightening; **rapide comme l'é.,** quick as lightning; **la voiture passa comme un é.,** the car flashed by; **la pensée traversa mon esprit comme un é.,** the thought flashed through my mind; **visite é.,** lightning visit; **guerre é.,** blitzkrieg; **attaque é.,** lightning raid. **2.** flash (of gun, etc.); (*of diamond, eyes, etc.*) **lancer des éclairs,** to flash; **é. de génie,** flash of genius. **3.** *Cu:* éclair.

éclairage [eklɛraʒ] *n.m.* **1.** (*a*) lighting; illumination; **é. par projecteurs,** floodlighting; **é. des rues,** street lighting; *Aut:* **é. intérieur automatique,** courtesy light; **heure d'é.,** lighting-up time; (*b*) light; **sous cet é.,** seen in this light; **montrer qch. dans un autre é.,** to show sth. in a different light. **2.** *Mil:* *Navy:* scouting.

éclairagiste [eklɛraʒist] *n.m.* lighting technician.

éclairant [eklɛrɑ̃] *a.* lighting, illuminating (power, etc.); **fusée éclairante,** flare.

éclaircie [eklɛrsi] *n.f.* **1.** break, opening, rift (in clouds, etc.); *Meteor:* bright interval. **2.** clearing (in forest); glade.

éclaircir [eklɛrsir] *v.* **I.** *v.tr.* **1.** to clear (fog, etc.); **s'é. la voix,** to clear one's throat. **2.** (*a*) to lighten; to make (sth.) clear; **é. une couleur,** to lighten a colour; **é. le teint,** to clear the complexion; (*b*) to throw light on, clear up (mystery); to clarify (situation). **3.** to thin (forest, sauce); to thin out (seedlings, etc.). **II. s'éclaircir 1.** (*a*) (*of the weather*) to clear (up), to become bright(er); (*of complexion, voice*) to clear, become clear(er); **sa figure s'éclaircit,** his face brightened up, lit up; (*b*) **je veux m'é. sur ce point,** I want to get clear on this point; (*c*) **la vérité s'éclaircit,** the truth is coming out. **2.** (*of hair, plants, etc.*) to become thin, to thin; **enfin les arbres s'éclaircirent,** at length the trees thinned out, became fewer and farther between.

éclaircissage [eklɛrsisaʒ] *n.m.* **1.** polishing (of glass). **2.** thinning out (of plants).

éclaircissement [eklɛrsismɑ̃] *n.m.* (*a*) enlightenment; elucidation; (*b*) explanatory statement; **demander des éclaircissements sur qch.,** to ask for explanations about sth.

éclaire [eklɛr] *n.f.* *Bot:* celandine.

éclairé [eklere] *a.* enlightened, well informed, educated (person, mind).

éclairement [eklɛrmɑ̃] *n.m.* illumination, lighting.

éclairer [eklere] *v.* **I. 1.** *v.tr.* (*a*) to light, illuminate; to light the way for (s.o.); **je suis nourri, logé et éclairé,** I get my board, lodging and lighting; **é. un angle sombre,** to light up a dark corner; **cafés éclairés au néon,** cafés with neon lights; (*b*) to shed, throw, light on (a subject); (*c*) to enlighten (s.o.); **éclairez-moi sur ce sujet,** tell me what it's all about; (*d*) *Cards: etc:* **é. (le tapis),** to put down one's stake; (*e*) *Mil:* **é. le terrain, la marche,** to reconnoitre the ground; to scout. **2.** *v.i.* (*a*) *impers. A: & Dial:* **il éclaire,** it's lightening; (*b*) **cette lampe éclaire mal,** this lamp gives a poor light; (*c*) *P:* to pay up, foot the bill. **II. s'éclairer** (*a*) **il s'éclaire toujours au pétrole,** he still has oil lamps; (*b*) **sa figure s'est éclairée,** his face lit up, brightened; (*c*) **la situation s'éclaire,** the situation is becoming clear(er).

éclaireur, -euse [eklɛrœr, -øz] *n.* **1.** *n.m.* (*a*) *Mil:* scout; (*b*) *Navy:* scouting vessel, scout; *Av:* **avion é.,** reconnaissance aircraft. **2.** *n.m. & f.* (non-Catholic) (boy) scout, (girl) guide; **chef é.,** scoutmaster.

éclat [ekla] *n.m.* **1.** splinter, chip (of wood, stone, etc.); flake (of mica); **é. d'obus,** shell splinter; **voler en éclats,** to fly, burst, into pieces; **briser qch. en éclats,** to smash sth. to pieces, to smithereens; **éclats de verre,** (i) broken glass; (ii) flying glass. **2.** (*a*) burst (of noise, laughter, etc.); **é. de colère,** outburst of anger; **de grands éclats de voix,** (i) voices raised in anger, (ii) snatches of loud conversation; **partir d'un grand é. de rire,** to burst out laughing; **rire aux éclats,** to roar with laughter; (*b*) **cette nouvelle fera é., de l'é.,** this news will create a stir, a scandal; **sans é.,** quietly; without any fuss, any scandal. **3.** (*a*) flash (of light); **feu à éclats,** flashing light; (*b*) glare (of the sun); glitter, lustre (of diamond); brilliancy, vividness (of colours); **l'é. de ses yeux,** the sparkle in her eyes; **l'é. de la jeunesse,** the bloom, freshness, of youth; **le soleil brille de son plus vif é.,** the sun is (shining) at its brightest, most brilliant; **sans é.,** dull, lustreless; lack-lustre (eyes); (*c*) brilliance (of style, etc.); **action d'é.,** brilliant feat; **aimer l'é.,** to be fond of show, ostentation; **faux é.,** false glamour.

éclatant [eklatɑ̃] *a.* **1.** loud, ringing (sound, laughter); piercing (shriek); **bruit é.,** crash. **2.** glaring, dazzling brilliant (light, colour, success); bright, vivid (light, colour); sparkling, glittering, flashing (jewels); **mensonge é.,** thumping lie.

éclatement [eklatmɑ̃] *n.m.* bursting, explosion (of boiler, shell, gun); bursting, blow-out (of tyre); shattering, flying (of glass); dispersal (of convoy, etc.); *El:* **pont d'é.,** spark gap; **fréquence d'é.,** spark frequency; *Artil:* **é. en surface,** surface burst; *Pol:* **e. d'un parti,** splitting of a party.

éclater [eklate] **1.** *v.tr.* (*a*) to split, splinter (branch, mast); to burst (tyre); (*b*) *Hort:* to divide, partition (roots of plant, for propagation); (*c*) to disperse (cargo of crude oil). **2.** *v.i.* (*a*) (*of boiler, shell, gun*) to burst, explode; (*of mine*) to blow up; (*of tyre*) to burst; (*of glass*) to fly (into pieces); (*of mast*) to split, splinter; **faire é. qch.,** to burst, explode, shatter, split, sth.; **faire é. un pétard,** to detonate a fog signal; (*b*) (*of war, epidemic*) to break out; (*of storm*) to break; (*of anger*) to burst out; **quand la guerre éclata,** at the outbreak of the war; **le tonnerre éclata,** there was a clap of thunder; **é. de rire,** to burst out laughing; **é. en larmes,** to burst into tears; **é. de colère,** to fly into a rage. **3.** *v.i.* (*a*) (*of jewels*) sparkle, glitter; **l'indignation éclatait dans ses yeux,** his eyes were blazing with indignation; (*b*) to be obvious, evident; to stand out; **les préjugés de l'auteur éclatent à chaque page,** the author's prejudices stand out on every page.

éclateur [eklatœr] *n.m. El:* spark gap, discharger.

éclectique [eklɛktik] *a. & n.* eclectic.

éclipse [eklips] *n.f.* eclipse (of sun, moon); **é. totale de la raison,** total loss of reason; *Nau:* **feu à éclipses,** occulting, intermittent, light.

éclipser [eklipse] *v.* **1.** *v.tr.* (*a*) to eclipse; to surpass, outshine, overshadow; *F:* to put (s.o.) in the shade; (*b*) to obscure (beam of light). **2. s'é.,** to become eclipsed; to disappear; *Nau:* (*of light*) to occult; *F:* (*of pers.*) to make off, disappear, vanish.

écliptique [ekliptik] *a. & n.f. Astr:* ecliptic.

éclisse [eklis] *n.f.* **1.** (wooden) wedge. **2.** split wood. **3.** cheese tray. **4.** *Med:* splint. **5.** *Rail:* (*a*) fishplate; (*b*) bond (of live rail).

éclisser [eklise] *v.tr.* **1.** to put (limb) in splints, to splint. **2.** *Rail:* to fish (rails).

éclopé [eklɔpe] **1.** *a.* lame, limping, (temporarily) crippled. **2.** *n.m.* temporarily disabled soldier.

éclore [eklɔr] *v.i. def.* (*p.p.* **éclos;** *pr.ind.* **il éclôt, ils éclosent;** *impf.* **il éclosait;** no *p.h.*; *fu.* **il éclora;** *aux. usu.* **être,** *occ.* **avoir**) **1.** (*of eggs, chicks*) to hatch (out), to be hatched. **2.** (*of flowers*) to open, to bloom; (*of buds*) to burst; **roses fraîches écloses,** fresh-blown roses; **génie près d'é.,** budding genius; **le jour est près d'é.,** dawn is near; **faire é. un projet,** to realize a plan.

éclosion [eklozjɔ̃] *n.f.* **1.** hatching (of eggs, chicks). **2.** opening, blossoming, blooming (of flowers).

éclusage [eklyzaʒ] *n.m.* locking (of boat).

écluse [eklyz] *n.f.* **1.** (*a*) (canal) lock; **droit d'é.,** lockage; **(porte d')é.,** lock gate, sluice (gate); **é. de moulin,** mill dam; **lâcher une é.,** to open a sluice gate; (*b*) tide gate (of dock). **2.** *Geog:* **L'É.,** Sluys.

écluser [eklyze] *v.tr.* to lock; (*a*) to equip (canal) with locks; (*b*) to pass (barge) through a lock.

éclusier, -ière [eklyzje, -jɛr] *n.* lock keeper.

écœurant [ekœrɑ̃] *a.* (*a*) nauseating, sickening; disgusting, loathsome (food, conduct); (*b*) disheartening, discouraging, demoralizing (work).

écœurement [ekœrmɑ̃] *n.m.* (*a*) nausea; (*b*) disgust; loathing; (*c*) dejection, discouragement.

écœurer [ekœre] *v.tr.* (*a*) to nauseate; (i) to make (s.o.) feel sick; (ii) to disgust, revolt; (*b*) to dishearten.

écoinçon [ekwɛ̃sɔ̃] *n.m. Const:* corner piece, stone.

école [ekɔl] *n.f.* **1.** (*a*) school; **é. maternelle,** nursery school, kindergarten; **é. primaire,** primary school; **é. d'État,** state, *U.S:* public, school; **é. libre** = independent school; **maison d'é.,** schoolhouse; **maître d'é.,** (primary) schoolmaster; **vous êtes à bonne é.,** you're in good hands; (*b*) **les grandes écoles,** colleges of university level specializing in professional training; **é. normale,** college of education; **é. ménagère,** domestic training college; (*in Paris*) **le quartier des Écoles,** the Latin quarter; *Mil:* **É. (supérieure) de Guerre** = Staff College; (*c*) *Mil:* school, drill, training; **é. du soldat,** recruit drill; **é. de tir,** rifle drill; *Nau:* **é. de nœuds,** knotting and splicing; *Av:* **appareil d'é.,** training aircraft; (*d*) **é. d'équitation,** riding school; **haute é.,** haute école. **2.** (*a*) school (of thought, art, literature); **faire é.,** (i) to found a school; (ii) to set a fashion; (*b*) *Hist:* **l'É.,** the Schoolmen.

écolier, -ière [ekɔlje, -jɛr] *n.* (*a*) (primary) schoolboy, schoolgirl; **bévue d'é.,** (i) schoolboy howler; (ii) childish mistake; **le chemin des écoliers,** the longest way round; *a.* **papier é.,** exercise paper; (*b*) novice, beginner.

écologie [ekɔlɔʒi] *n.f.* ecology.

écologique [ekɔlɔʒik] *a.* ecological.

écologiste [ekɔlɔʒist] *n.m. & f.* ecologist.

éconduire [ekɔ̃dɥir] *v.tr.* (*conj. like* CONDUIRE) to get rid of (s.o.) (politely); to show (s.o.) to the door; **être éconduit,** to meet with a refusal; (*of lover*) to be rejected.

économat [ekɔnɔma] *n.m.* (*a*) stewardship; treasurership; bursarship; (*b*) steward's, treasurer's, bursar's, office; (*c*) staff (discount) store; (*d*) multiple store.

économe [ekɔnɔm] **1.** *n.m. & f.* treasurer, bursar (of college, institution, etc.); steward, housekeeper; agent; *B:* **l'é. infidèle,** the unjust steward. **2.** *a.* economical, thrifty; **é. de paroles,** sparing of words.

économétrie [ekɔnɔmetri] *n.f.* econometrics.

économie [ekɔnɔmi] *n.f.* **1.** (*a*) economy; management; **é. politique,** political economy; **é. dirigée,** planned economy; (*b*) arrangement, structure (of literary work). **2.** economy, saving, thrift; **vivre avec é.,** to live economically; **faire une é. de temps,** to save time; **faire une é. de vingt pour cent,** to save twenty per cent. **3.** *pl.* savings; **faire des économies,** to save money; **prendre sur ses économies,** to draw upon one's savings; *F:* **économies de bouts de chandelles,** cheeseparing (economy).

économique [ekɔnɔmik] *a.* **1.** economic (problem, doctrine, etc.); **sciences économiques,** economics. **2.** economical, inexpensive (method, apparatus, etc.); **vitesse é.,** economical speed (of car, etc.).

économiquement [ekɔnɔmikmɑ̃] *adv.* economically; **les é. faibles,** the underprivileged.

économiser [ekɔnɔmize] *v.tr.&i.* to economize, save (money, time); to husband (resources, etc.); **é. ses paroles,** to be sparing of one's words; **é. ses forces,** to conserve one's strength; **é. sur qch.,** to save, economize, on sth.

économiste [ekɔnɔmist] *n.m. & f.* economist.

écope [ekɔp] *n.f.* ladle; *Nau:* bailer, scoop.

écoper [ekɔpe] **1.** *v.tr.* (*a*) to bail (out); **é. l'eau d'une embarcation,** to bail out a boat; (*b*) *P:* to drink. **2.** *v.i. F:* (*a*) to be hit, wounded; to cop it; **é. de cinq ans de prison,** to cop five years' prison; (*b*) to get the blame, to catch, cop, it.

écoperche [ekɔpɛrʃ] *n.f.* **1.** standard (of scaffolding). **2.** derrick.

écorçage [ekɔrsaʒ] *n.m.* barking (of trees); peeling (of oranges); husking (of rice).

écorce [ekɔrs] *n.f.* (*a*) *Bot:* cortex; (*b*) bark (of tree); rind, peel (of orange); husk (of rice); (*c*) **l'é. terrestre,** the earth's crust; (*d*) outward appearance.

écorcer [ekɔrse] *v.tr.* **(j'écorçai(s); n. écorçons)** to bark (tree); peel (orange); husk (rice).

écorché [ekɔrʃe] *n.m.* (*a*) *Art:* anatomical model, écorché; (*b*) sectional view.

écorchement [ekɔrʃəmɑ̃] *n.m.* **1.** flaying, skinning. **2.** abrasion, grazing (of the skin); barking (of shin).

écorcher [ekɔrʃe] *v.tr.* **1.** to flay (large animal); to skin (rabbit, eel); *F:* **é. une langue,** to murder a language; **é. les clients,** to fleece the customers; **é. l'anguille par la queue,** to begin at the wrong end. **2.** (*a*) to graze, chafe (the skin); **s'é. le tibia,** to bark one's shin; (*b*) to scrape, scratch (furniture); to rasp (throat); **son qui écorche l'oreille,** sound that grates on the ear.

écorcheur, -euse [ekɔrʃœr, -øz] *n.* (*a*) flayer; skinner; (*b*) *F:* fleecer, extortioner.

écorchure [ekɔrʃyr] *n.f.* abrasion, scratch, graze; gall; *Vet:* **é. sous la selle,** saddle gall.

écorner [ekɔrne] *v.tr.* (*a*) to break, cut, the corner(s) off (sth.); **é. (les pages d')un livre,** to dog('s)-ear (the pages of) a book; (*b*) **é. son capital,** to break into one's capital; (*c*) to chamfer, trim (plank, stone).

écornifler [ekɔrnifle] *v.tr. F:* to cadge, scrounge (meal, money); *v.i.* to sponge.

écornifleur, -euse [ekɔrniflœr, -øz] *n. F:* sponger, cadger; scrounger.

écornure [ekɔrnyr] *n.f.* **1.** chip (from a corner). **2.** chipped corner.

écossais, -aise [ekɔsɛ, -ɛz] **1.** *a.* (*of thg*) Scotch; (*of pers.*) Scottish, Scots. **2.** *n.* Scot; Scotsman, Scotswoman. **3.** *a. & n.m.* **(tissu) é.,** tartan, plaid; check material. **4.** *n.m. Ling:* Scotch, Scots.

Écosse [ekɔs] *Pr.n.f. Geog:* Scotland; **la Haute É.,** the Highlands.

écosser [ekɔse] *v.tr.* to shell, hull, husk (peas).

écosystème [ekɔsistɛm] *n.m. Biol:* ecosystem.

écot [eko] *n.m.* **payer son é.,** to pay one's share.

écoulé [ekule] *a. Com:* of last month, ultimo; *F:* ult.

écoulement [ekulmɑ̃] *n.m.* **1.** (*a*) (out)flow, flowing, discharge (of liquid); *Hyd.E:* run-off; drainage; **fossé d'é.,** drain; **(tube d')é.,** outlet tube; waste pipe (of bath); **trou d'é.,** plughole (of a sink); *Av:* **é. (des filets) d'air,** air flow; (*b*) *Med:* discharge; (*c*) dispersal (of a crowd); **é. de la circulation,** flow of traffic. **2.** sale, disposal, (of goods); **marchandises d'é. facile,** goods with a ready sale.

écouler [ekule] *v.* **1.** *v.tr.* to sell (off), dispose of, get rid of (goods); **é. de faux billets,** to utter forged notes. **2. s'é.** (*a*) (*of liquid, etc.*) to flow out, run out; (*of crowd*) to pour out (of building), to disperse; **son argent s'écoule,** his money is melting away; **faire é. l'eau,** to run off, drain off, the water; (*b*) (*of goods*) to sell (fast, easily); (*c*) (*of time*) to pass, slip away.

écourter [ekurte] *v.tr.* (*a*) to shorten (dress, etc.); to curtail, to cut short (visit, speech); (*b*) to dock (dog's tail, dog); to crop (dog's ears, dog).

écoute[1] [ekut] *n.f.* **1. être, se tenir, aux écoutes,** (i) to eavesdrop; (ii) to keep one's ears open; *Mil:* **poste d'é.,** listening post. **2.** *Tp: W.Tel:* listening-in; **é. de contrôle,** monitoring; **se mettre, se porter, à l'é., prendre l'é.,** to listen in; **l'heure de grande é.,** peak listening time; *Tp:* **ne quittez pas l'é.! restez à l'é.!** hold the line!

écoute[2] *n.f. Nau:* sheet (of sail); **nœud d'é.,** sheet bend; **point d'é.,** clew.

écouter [ekute] *v.tr.* **1.** (*a*) to listen to (s.o., sth.); **savoir é.,** to be a good listener; **se faire é.,** to get a hearing; **é. qn jusqu'au bout,** to hear s.o. out; **é. à la porte, aux portes,** to eavesdrop; **écoutez!** look (here)! I say! (*b*) *W.Tel:* to listen in. **2.** to pay attention to (s.o., advice); **ne les écoutez pas!** don't mind them! **é. sa conscience,** to listen to one's conscience; **il s'écoute trop,** he coddles himself.

écouteur, -euse [ekutœr, -øz] *n.* **1.** (*a*) listener; **é. aux portes,** eavesdropper; (*b*) *W.Tel:* listener-in. **2.** *n.m.* (i) *Tp:* receiver; (ii) *W.Tel:* earphone, headphone.

écoutille [ekutij] *n.f. Nau:* hatchway.

écouvillon [ekuvijɔ̃] *n.m.* (baker's) oven mop; bottle brush, (gun) sponge; (rifle) cleaning brush; *Med:* swab.

écouvillonnage [ekuvijɔnaʒ] *n.m.* mopping out (of oven); *Med:* swabbing (of cavity); cleaning, brushing out (of tube, flue); swabbing out (of gun).

écouvillonner [ekuvijɔne] *v.tr.* to mop out, clean out (oven); to brush out (rifle, etc.); to sponge out, swab (gun); *Med:* to swab (cavity).

écrabouillage [ekrabujaʒ], **écrabouillement** [ekrabujmɑ̃] *n.m. F:* crushing, squashing.

écrabouiller [ekrabuje] *v.tr. F:* to crush; to squash; to reduce (s.o., sth.) to pulp.

écran [ekrɑ̃] *n.m.* **1.** screen; (*a*) **é. de fumée,** smoke screen; **é. de protection, é. protecteur,** shield; *Cin:* **é. de sûreté,** cut-off (of projector); **é. filtre, é. de ciel,** sky filter; (*b*) (*printing*) **procédé à l'é. de soie,** silk screen process. **2.** *Cin: Phot:* **é. (de projection),** screen; **l'é.,** the cinema; **la technique de l'é.,** film technique; *F:* **le petit é.,** television.

écrasant [ekrazɑ̃] *a.* crushing (weight, defeat, etc.); overwhelming (proof, majority).

écrasé [ekraze] *a.* **1.** crushed, squashed; *Journ: F:* **rubrique des chiens écrasés,** odd news items (especially accidents). **2. nez é.,** flat nose.

écrasement [ekrazmɑ̃] *n.m.* crushing, squashing (of fruit, etc.); oppression (of the people); crushing defeat (of army); collapse (of building); *Av:* **é. au sol,** crash (of plane).

écraser [ekraze] *v.* **1.** *v.tr.* (*a*) to crush, bruise (fruit, limb); to flatten out (can, etc.); to squash (fruit, beetle); to swat (fly); **se faire é.,** to get run over; *Aut: F:* **é. l'accélérateur,** to step on the gas; **é. d'impôts,** to overburden with taxes; **écrasé de travail,** overwhelmed, *F:* snowed under, with work; **é. ses adversaires,** to crush, squash, one's opponents; *Fin: F:* **é. le marché,** to glut, flood, the market; *Ten:* **é. la balle,** to kill, smash, the ball; **coup écrasé,** smash; (*b*) to dwarf (building); (*c*) *P:* **en é.,** to sleep like a log. **2.** *v.i. P:* **écrase!** shut up! **3. s'é.,** to collapse, break down, crumple up; **s'é. sur le sol,** (*of pers.*) to crash to the ground; (*of aircraft*) to crash; **la neige s'écrase sous nos pieds,** the snow crunches under our feet.

écraseur, -euse [ekrazœr, -øz] **1.** *n.* (*a*) crusher; (*b*) *Aut: F:* road hog. **2.** *n.m.* crusher; steam roller.

écrémage [ekremaʒ] *n.m.* creaming: skimming (of milk).

écrémer [ekreme] *v.tr.* **(j'écrème; j'écrémerai)** (*a*) to cream; (i) to separate; (ii) to skim (milk); **lait écrémé,** skim(med) milk; **lait non écrémé,** full cream milk; (*b*) to take the best, the cream, of, to cream (off) (a collection).

écrémeur [ekremœr] *n.m. Petr:* oil separator.

écrémeuse [ekremøz] *n.f.* (cream) separator; creamer.

écrémoir *n.m.*, **écrémoire** [ekremwar] *n.f.* creamer, (milk) skimmer.

écrêter [ekrete] *v.tr.* (*a*) to remove the comb of (cock); (*b*) to knock the tops off (flowers, etc.); (*c*) to lower the crest of (hill).

écrevisse [ekrəvis] *n.f.* **1.** (fresh-water) crayfish; *F:* **rouge comme une é.,** as red as a lobster; *F:* **marcher, comme une é.,** to walk (i) backwards, (ii) at a snail's pace.

écrier (s') [sekrije] *v.pr.* to cry (out), exclaim.

écrin [ekrɛ̃] *n.m.* (jewel) case.

écrire [ekrir] (*p.pr.* **écrivant;** *p.p.* **écrit;** *pr.ind.* **j'écris, n. écrivons, ils écrivent;** *p.h.* **j'écrivis;** *fu.* **j'écrirai**) to write; (*a*) **é. qch. à l'encre, avec de l'encre,** to write sth. in ink; **il écrit bien,** (i) he has good (hand)writing; (ii) he's a good writer (of fiction, etc.); **machine à é.,** typewriter; **é. une lettre à la machine,** to type a letter; **é. un mot à la hâte,** to scribble a note; **é. un mot à qn,** to drop s.o. a line; **je lui ai écrit de venir,** I have written asking him to come; (*b*) to write (sth.) down; **é. l'adresse de qn,** to write, jot, down, s.o.'s address; **ce mot s'écrit avec un g,** this word is written, spelt, with a g; *F:* **il est écrit que je ne peux pas y aller,** I am fated not to get there; **c'est écrit,** it is, was, bound to happen; (*c*) to write, compose (book, song, etc.); **é. dans les journaux,** to write for the papers.

écrit [ekri] **1.** *a.* written (word, law). **2.** *n.m.* (*a*) writing; **consigner, coucher, qch. par é.,** to set down sth. in writing; **convention en, par, é.,** written agreement; (*b*) written document; **faire, signer, un é.,** to draw up, to sign, a document; (*c*) **les écrits de Bossuet,** the writings, works, of Bossuet; (*d*) *Sch:* **échouer à l'é.,** to fail in the written examination.

écriteau, -eaux [ekrito] *n.m.* placard; notice, bill, announcement (posted up).

écritoire [ekritwar] *n.f.* **1.** writing case. **2.** desk (for public in post office).

écriture [ekrityr] *n.f.* **1.** (*a*) writing, script; (*b*) (hand)-writing; **é. à la machine,** typewriting, typing. **2.** (*a*) *pl.* (legal, commercial) papers, documents, records; **tenir les écritures,** to keep the accounts; (*b*) *Book-k:* entry, item; **écritures en partie double,** double entry; (*c*) **l'É. sainte,** Holy Scripture, Holy Writ. **3.** (literary) writing.

écrivailler [ekrivaje] *v.i. F:* to be a hack (writer); to scribble.

écrivailleur, -euse [ekrivajœr, -øz] *n.*, **écrivaillon** [ekrivajɔ̃] *n.m. F:* hack (writer), scribbler.

écrivain [ekrivɛ̃] *n.m.* **1.** (*a*) **é. public,** (public) letter writer; (*b*) *Nau:* writer. **2.** author, writer; **femme é.,** woman writer; authoress.

écrivasser [ekrivase] *v.i. F:* = ÉCRIVAILLER.

écrivassier, -ière [ekrivasje, -jɛr] *n. F:* hack (writer); scribbler.

écrou[1] [ekru] *n.m. Jur:* committal to gaol; **levée d'é.,** release, discharge (from prison).

écrou[2] *n.m.* (screw)nut, female screw; **é. à ailettes, à oreilles,** thumb, wing, butterfly, nut; **é. crénelé, à créneaux, à encoches,** castellated, castle, nut.

écrouelles [ekruɛl] *n.f.pl. A:* scrofula, king's evil.

écrouer [ekrue] *v.tr.* to consign (s.o.) to prison.

écrouir [ekruir] *v.tr. Metalw:* (*a*) to hammer harden, to cold hammer; (*b*) to cold draw; (*c*) to cold roll.

écrouissage [ekruisaʒ] *n.m.*, **écrouissement** [ekruismɑ̃] *n.m. Metalw:* (*a*) hammer hardening, cold hammering; (*b*) cold drawing; (*c*) cold rolling.

écroulement [ekrulmɑ̃] *n.m.* collapse, tumbling down, falling in; fall (of earth, rock); ruin, downfall (of hopes); **é. de la santé,** breakdown in health.

écrouler (s') [sekrule] *v.pr.* (*a*) (*of building, bridge*) to collapse, fall in, give way; **empire près de s'é.,** empire on the verge of collapse; (*b*) *F:* **s'é. sur une chaise,** to drop, flop, on to a chair.

écroûter [ekryte] *v.tr.* (*a*) to remove the crust from (bread, etc.); (*b*) *Agr:* to scarify (land).

écru [ekry] *a.* (*of material*) unbleached, écru, natural-coloured; **soie écrue,** raw silk; **toile écrue,** holland.

ectoderme [ɛktɔdɛrm] *n.m. Biol:* ectoderm.

ectoplasme [ɛktɔplasm] *n.m.* ectoplasm.

ectoplasmique [ɛktɔplasmik] *a.* ectoplasm(at)ic.

ectropion [ɛktrɔpjɔ̃] *n.m.* ectropion, ectropium; eversion (of eyelid).

écu [eky] *n.m.* **1.** (*a*) *Arm:* shield; (*b*) *Her:* escutcheon, coat of arms. **2.** *Num: A:* crown; *F:* **avoir des écus,** to have plenty, pots, of money. **3.** *Bot: F:* **herbe aux écus,** moneywort, creeping jenny. **4.** *Ent:* scutum. **5.** *Paperm: approx.* = large post.

écubier [ekybje] *n.m. Nau:* hawse hole.

écueil [ekœj] *n.m.* reef, shelf; (*of ship*) **donner sur les écueils,** to strike the rocks; **se heurter à un é.,** to strike a snag; **ce manque d'harmonie fut l'é. de l'entreprise,** this lack of harmony was the rock on which the undertaking came to grief.

écuelle [ekɥɛl] *n.f.* **1.** bowl, porringer; **manger à la même é.,** (i) to live on intimate terms together; (ii) to have the same interests. **2.** *Bot: F:* **é. d'eau,** marsh pennywort, water-cup.

éculé [ekyle] *a.* (*a*) (*of shoe*) down-at-heel; (*b*) well worn (trick, etc.).

écumage [ekymaʒ] *n.m.* skimming, scumming (of soup, jam, molten metal).

écumant [ekymɑ̃] *a.* foaming, frothing (sea, beer).

écume [ekym] *n.f.* **1.** (*a*) froth; foam; **il avait de l'é. à la bouche,** he was foaming at the mouth; **cheval couvert d'é.,** foam-covered horse; *Ent:* **é. printanière,** cuckoo spit; (*b*) scum (on jam, etc.); **é. de la société,** scum, dregs, of society. **2. é. (de mer),** meerschaum.

écumer [ekyme] **1.** *v.tr.* (*a*) to skim, scum (soup, molten metal, etc.); (*b*) to scour, pillage (countryside); **é. les mers,** to scour the seas; to buccaneer. **2.** *v.i.* (*a*) (*of wine, sea, etc.*) to foam, froth; **cheval qui écume,** foaming horse; (*of pers.*) **é. (de rage),** to foam with rage; (*b*) (*of jam, etc.*) to scum, froth.

écumeur [ekymœr] *n.m.* **é. de mer,** sea-rover, pirate; **é. littéraire,** plagiarist.

écumeux, -euse [ekymø, -øz] *a.* foamy, frothy (beer, etc.); scummy (jam).

écumoire [ekymwar] *n.f.* skimmer; skimming ladle, perforated ladle.
écureuil [ekyrœj] *n.m.* (*a*) squirrel; (*b*) **é. volant,** flying squirrel, flying phalanger.
écurie [ekyri] *n.f.* (*a*) stable; **mettre les chevaux à, dans, l'é.,** to stable the horses; (*b*) **é. (de courses),** (racing) stable (of horses, cars).
écusson [ekysɔ̃] *n.m.* **1.** *Her:* escutcheon, shield, coat of arms. **2.** keyhole scutcheon; key-plate. **3.** *Mil:* tab, badge, (collar) patch. **4.** *Hort:* (shield) bud; **greffe en é.,** budding. **5.** *Ent:* scutellum.
écussonnage [ekysɔnaʒ] *n.m. Hort:* shield grafting, budding.
écussonner [ekysɔne] *v.tr. Hort:* to bud (a tree).
écussonnoir [ekysɔnwar] *n.m.* budding knife.
écuyer, -ère [ekɥije, -ɛr] *n.* **1.** *n.m. A:* (*a*) squire, armour-bearer; (*b*) equerry; *Hist:* **grand é.,** Master of the Horse. **2.** (*a*) *n.m. & f.* rider; horseman, horsewoman; **être bon é., bonne écuyère,** to ride well, to be a good rider; **é. de cirque,** circus rider; equestrian, *f.* equestrienne; **bottes à l'écuyère,** riding boots; (*of woman*) **monter à l'écuyère,** to ride astride; (*b*) *n.m.* riding master.
eczéma [ɛgzema] *n.m.* eczema.
eczémateux, -euse [ɛgzematø, -øz] *a.* eczematous.
Éden (l') [ledɛn] *n.m. B:* (the Garden of) Eden.
édénique [edenik] *a.* edenic.
édenté [edɑ̃te] *a.* toothless (person); *Z:* edentate.
édenter [edɑ̃te] *v.tr.* (*a*) **é. qn,** to take out s.o.'s teeth; to break s.o.'s teeth; **la vieillesse l'a édenté,** old age has left him toothless; (*b*) to break the teeth of (a comb).
édicter [edikte] *v.tr.* to enact, decree (penalties).
édicule [edikyl] *n.m.* (*a*) kiosk, shelter; (*b*) *F:* public convenience.
édifiant [edifjɑ̃] *a.* edifying.
édification [edifikasjɔ̃] *n.f.* **1.** (*a*) erection, building (of monument, etc.); (*b*) building up (of empire, etc.). **2.** (*a*) edification, moral improvement; (*b*) **pour votre é.,** for your information.
édifice [edifis] *n.m.* (*a*) building, edifice; **édifices publics,** public buildings; (*b*) **tout l'é. social,** the whole fabric, structure, of society.
édifier [edifje] *v.tr.* **1.** (*a*) to erect, build (public building); (*b*) to construct, create; **é. un système,** to build up a system. **2.** (*a*) (*of sermon, etc.*) to edify; (*b*) to enlighten, inform; *Iron:* **alors je suis édifié,** well, now I know.
édile [edil] *n.m.* (*a*) *Rom.Ant:* aedile; (*b*) municipal official; town councillor.
Édimbourg [edɛ̃bur] *Pr.n. Geog:* Edinburgh.
édit [edi] *n.m.* edict.
éditer [edite] *v.tr.* **1.** to edit (text with notes, etc.). **2.** to publish (book, etc.).
éditeur, -trice [editœr, -tris] *n.* **1.** editor (of text). **2.** publisher.
édition [edisjɔ̃] *n.f.* **1.** edition, issue, impression; **é. scolaire,** school edition. **2.** publishing; **maison d'é.,** publishing house, firm.
éditorial, -iaux [editɔrjal, -jo] *Journ:* **1.** *a.* editorial. **2.** *n.m.* leading article, leader; editorial.
éditorialiste [editɔrjalist] *n.m. & f.* (*a*) *Journ:* leader writer; (*b*) *W.Tel:* programme editor.
Édouard [edwar] *Pr.n.m.* Edward.
édouardien, -ienne [edwardjɛ̃, -jɛn] *a.* Edwardian.
édredon [edrədɔ̃] *n.m.* **é. (piqué, américain),** eiderdown (quilt).
éducable [edykabl̩] *a.* educable (child); trainable (animal).
éducateur, -trice [edykatœr, -tris] **1.** *n.* (*a*) educator, instructor; (*b*) educationalist. **2.** *a.* educative (method); educational (book); **le rôle é. des parents,** the educational rôle of parents.
éducatif, -ive [edykatif, -iv] *a.* educative, instructive; **film é.,** educational film.
éducation [edykasjɔ̃] *n.f.* (*a*) education; **faire l'é. de qn,** to educate s.o.; **é. professionnelle,** vocational training; **é. physique,** physical training; (*b*) training (of animals); (*c*) upbringing, breeding; **sans é.,** ill bred; **il manque d'é.,** he has no manners.
édulcorant [edylkɔrɑ̃] **1.** *a.* sweetening. **2.** *n.m.* sweetener.
édulcorer [edylkɔre] *v.tr.* **1.** to sweeten (medicine, etc.). **2. é. une triste nouvelle,** to break a piece of bad news gently; **compte rendu édulcoré,** watered-down account, report.
éduquer [edyke] *v.tr.* **1.** to bring up, educate (child); **mal éduqué,** ill bred.**2.** to train (animal).
effaçage [efasaʒ] *n.m.* (*a*) rubbing out, erasing; (*b*) crossing out.
effacé [efase] *a.* unobtrusive; retiring (person, manner); small, insignificant (rôle); receding (chin).
effacement [efasmɑ̃] *n.m.* **1.** obliteration (of word, stain, etc.); wearing away (of inscription); fading (of memories). **2.** unobtrusiveness, self effacement.
effacer [efase] *v.tr.* **(j'effaçai(s); n. effaçons) 1.** (*a*) to efface, obliterate, delete; **e. un mot au crayon,** to rub, cross, out a word; **e. une tache,** to wash out, wipe out, a stain; **e. des imperfections,** to smooth out imperfections; **sculptures effacées par le temps,** carvings worn away in the course of time; **e. qch. de sa mémoire,** to blot sth. out of one's memory; (*b*) to put (s.o.) in the shade; (*c*) **e. le corps,** to stand sideways; **e. les épaules,** to throw back, set back, the shoulders. **2. s'e.** (*a*) to become obliterated; to wear away; to fade (away); **cela s'effacera à l'eau,** it will wash off; (*b*) to stand, draw, aside; **depuis quelque temps il s'était effacé,** for some time he had kept in the background.
effarant [efarɑ̃] *a.* frightening, bewildering, dismaying.
effarement [efarmɑ̃] *n.m.* fright; dismay; bewilderment.
effarer [efare] *v.* **1.** *v.tr.* to frighten, scare, dismay; to bewilder. **2. s'e.,** to be frightened, scared **(de,** at, by); to take fright (at); to be bewildered (by).
effarouchant [efaruʃɑ̃] *a.* frightening; startling.
effarouchement [efaruʃmɑ̃] *n.m.* startling, frightening (away) (of animal, etc.).
effaroucher [efaruʃe] *v.* **1.** *v.tr.* (*a*) to startle, scare away, frighten away (animal); (*b*) to shock (s.o.). **2. s'e.** (*a*) (*of animal*) to be frightened away **(de,** at, by); to be scared, take fright **(de,** at); (*b*) (*of pers.*) to be shocked.
effectif, -ive [efɛktif, -iv]. **1.** *a.* (*a*) effective, efficacious (treatment, etc.); (*b*) effective, actual; *Fin:* active (circulation), real (value). **2.** *n.m.* (*a*) *Mil:* strength, establishment, manpower; *Navy:* complement; **à e. réduit,** under, below, strength; *Sch:* **réduire l'e. des classes à 25,** to reduce the size of classes to 25; (*b*) *Mil:* **les effectifs,** the total strength; **crise d'effectifs,** shortage of manpower.
effectivement [efɛktivmɑ̃] *adv.* **1.** effectively, efficaciously. **2.** actually, in reality, really; in actual fact. **3.** (*as answer*) that is so; yes indeed!
effectuer [efɛktɥe] *v.tr.* to effect, carry out, bring into effect, accomplish; to execute (operation); to effect, make (payment); to accomplish (journey); to bring about (reconciliation); **e. une retraite,** to make good a retreat; *Mth:* **e. un calcul,** to make a calculation.
effémination [efeminasjɔ̃] *n.f.*, **efféminement** [efeminmɑ̃] *n.m.* (*a*) effemination; (*b*) effeminacy.
effeminé [efemine] *a.* effeminate.
efféminer [efemine] *v.tr.* to make effeminate.
effervescence [efɛrvɛsɑ̃s] *n.f.* **1.** effervescence; **être**

en e., faire e., to effervesce. **2.** agitation; restlessness; **ville en e.,** town seething with excitement.

effervescent [efɛrvɛsɑ̃] *a.* **1.** effervescent (drink, etc.). **2.** excitable, exuberant (disposition); excited (crowd).

effet [efɛ] *n.m.* **1.** effect, result; **faire de l'e.,** to be effective; **avoir de l'e. sur le résultat,** to affect the result; **produire l'e. voulu,** to produce the desired effect; **à cet e.,** for this purpose; with this end in view; **à l'e. de,** for the purpose of, in order to; **sans e.,** ineffective, ineffectual. **2.** action, operation, working; (*a*) **mettre un projet à l'e., en e.,** to put a plan into action; to carry out a plan; (*of law*) **prendre e.,** to become operative; (*b*) *Cr: Ten:* spin, break; **balle qui a de l'e.,** ball that breaks; *Bill:* **e. de côté,** side (screw); (*c*) *Mec.E:* **e. utile,** efficiency; **e. réactif,** backlash; **à simple, double, e.,** single-action, single-acting; double-action, double-acting; (*d*) *Elcs:* **e. Edison,** Edison effect; *Ph:* **e. corona, de couronne,** corona discharge; (*e*) **en e.,** as a matter of fact; indeed; **oui, je m'en souviens, en e.,** yes, I do remember; **vous oubliez vos paquets—en e.!** you are forgetting your parcels—so I am! **3.** (*a*) impression; **voilà l'e. que cela m'a produit,** that is how it impressed me, how it struck me; *F:* **ça m'a fait un e. de la voir si pâle,** it gave me quite a turn to see her so pale; **faire de l'e.,** to make a show, attract attention; **cela fait bon e.,** it looks, sounds, well; **manquer son e.,** to fail to attract attention; (*of joke*) to misfire, fall flat; **phrases à e.,** words used for effect; **scène à e.,** striking, effective, scene; (*b*) *Art:* **e. de lune,** moonlight effect; *Cin: etc:* **effets sonores,** sound effects. **4.** *Com:* **e. de commerce,** negotiable instrument; bill; **e. à vue,** sight draft; **effets publics,** government stock, securities. **5.** *pl.* possessions, belongings; **faites vos effets,** pack up your clothes, your things; **effets mobiliers,** personal effects; goods and chattels.

effeuillage [efœjaʒ] *n.m.* **1.** thinning out of leaves (of fruit trees, etc.). **2.** *F:* striptease.

effeuillaison [efœjɛzɔ̃] *n.f.*, **effeuillement** [efœjmɑ̃] *n.m.* leaf fall.

effeuiller [efœje] *v.* **1.** *v.tr.* to thin out the leaves of (fruit tree); to pluck off the petals of (flower). **2. s'e.,** (*of tree*) to lose, shed, its leaves; (*of flower*) to shed its petals.

effeuilleuse [efœjøz] *n.f.* strip-teaser, stripper.

efficace [efikas] *a.* efficacious, effectual, effective (action, remedy); efficient, capable (person); **prêter à qn un appui e.,** to give s.o. useful, helpful, support.

efficacement [efikasmɑ̃] *adv.* efficaciously, effectively; effectually; efficiently.

efficacité [efikasite] *n.f.* efficacy, effectiveness (of remedy, prayer, etc.); efficiency (of machine, etc.).

efficience [efisjɑ̃s] *n.f.* efficiency.

efficient [efisjɑ̃] *a.* **1.** *Phil:* efficient (cause). **2.** *F:* (*of pers.*) efficient.

effigie [efiʒi] *n.f.* **1.** effigy; **pendre qn en e.,** to hang s.o. in effigy. **2.** *Num:* effigy, head.

effilage [efilaʒ] *n.m.* fraying, ravelling out (of material).

effilé [efile] *a.* **1.** *Tex:* frayed, fringed (material); *n.m.* fringe, fringed trimming. **2.** tapered, pointed, sharp (tool); tapering (fingers), slight (figure).

effilement [efilmɑ̃] *n.m.* tapering.

effiler [efile] *v.* **1.** *v.tr.* (*a*) *Tex:* to fray, unravel, ravel out; (*b*) to taper; to cut (sth.) to a point; **e. les cheveux,** to taper hair. **2. s'e.** (*a*) (*of material*) to fray (out); (*b*) to taper, to become thin, sharp, pointed; to thin out.

effilochage [efilɔʃaʒ] *n.m.* (*a*) teasing out; (*b*) fraying; (*c*) *Tex:* breaking, tearing (of waste); **drap de laine d'e.,** shoddy.

effiloche [efilɔʃ] *n.f.* **1.** fringe (of threads left loose). **2.** *pl.* floss silk.

effilochement [efilɔʃmɑ̃] *n.m.* **1.** (*a*) ravelling; fraying; (*b*) *Tex:* teasing. **2.** ravelled, frayed, condition.

effilocher [efilɔʃe] *v.* **1.** *v.tr.* (*a*) to ravel out, tease out; (*b*) *Tex:* to break, tear (wool, cotton waste). **2.** (*of material*) **s'e.,** to fray.

efflanqué [eflɑ̃ke] *a.* lean, lean-flanked, raw-boned (animal); skinny, lanky (person).

effleurement [eflœrmɑ̃] *n.m.* **1.** (*a*) (light, gentle) touch; (*b*) skimming (of the water). **2.** graze (on skin).

effleurer [eflœre] *v.tr.* to touch lightly; to skim (surface of water); to graze, brush (object, skin); **e. un sujet,** to touch on a topic; **quelques soupçons l'avaient effleuré,** some misgivings had crossed his mind.

efflorescence [eflɔrɛsɑ̃s] *n.f.* **1.** *Ch:* efflorescence; bloom (on rubber). **2.** *Med:* rash, eruption.

efflorescent [eflɔrɛsɑ̃] *a.* *Ch:* efflorescent.

effluent [eflyɑ̃] **1.** *a.* effluent. **2.** *n.m.* (sewage) effluent; **e. radio-actif,** radioactive waste.

effluve [eflyv] *n.m.* **1.** effluvium, emanation. **2.** *El:* brush discharge.

effondrement [efɔ̃drəmɑ̃] *n.m.* **1.** *Agr:* subsoiling, trenching. **2.** breaking down, caving in; collapse (of bridge, etc.); falling in (of roof); falling through (of plan); downfall, collapse (of ministry); slump (in prices); **il est dans un état d'e. complet,** he is in a state of total collapse. **3.** *Geol:* subsidence.

effondrer [efɔ̃dre] *v.* **1.** *v.tr.* (*a*) *Agr:* to subsoil, trench (the ground); (*b*) (*of bomb, etc.*) to plough up (the ground). (*c*) to break (sth.) in, down; to break open (door); to stave in (barrel). **2. s'e.,** to fall in, cave in, break down, collapse; (*of prices*) to slump; *F:* (*of pers., government*) to collapse; *F:* **s'e. dans un fauteuil,** to sink, flop, into an armchair.

efforcer (s') [seforse] *v.pr.* **(je m'efforçai(s); n.n. efforçons) s'e. de faire qch.,** to strive, do one's utmost, one's best, to make every effort, to do sth.; **s'e. vers un but,** to strive towards, for, an end.

effort [efɔr] *n.m.* **1.** effort, exertion; **faire (un) e. pour faire qch.,** to make an effort to do sth.; **faire un e. sur soi-même,** to exercise self-control; **faire tous ses efforts pour réussir,** to strain every nerve, do one's utmost, to succeed; **e. financier,** financial outlay; **sans e.,** easily, without effort; **faire des efforts de mémoire,** to rack, cudgel, one's brains; *F:* **suivre la loi du moindre e.,** to take the line of least resistance. **2.** (*a*) *Mec.E:* strain, stress; **e. de tension,** tensile stress, pull; **e. de torsion,** torque; **e. de rupture,** breaking strain; **e. de traction,** pull; **e. de cisaillement,** shearing stress; (*b*) *Med:* (i) strain, rick; (ii) rupture; **se donner, attraper, un e.,** to rick one's back.

effraction [efraksjɔ̃] *n.f.* *Jur:* house breaking; **vol de nuit avec e.,** burglary; **à l'épreuve de l'e.,** burglar-proof.

effraie [efrɛ] *n.f.* *Orn:* *F:* barn owl, screech owl.

effranger [efrɑ̃ʒe] *v.* **(j'effrangeai(s); n. effrangeons) 1.** *v.tr.* to fray (out) (edges of material). **2. s'e.,** to fray (out), become frayed.

effrayant [efrɛjɑ̃] *a.* (*a*) terrifying, appalling; (*b*) *F:* tremendous, terrific (heat, appetite).

effrayer [efreje] *v.* **(j'effraie, j'effraye, n. effrayons; j'effraierai, j'effrayerai) 1.** *v.tr.* (*a*) to frighten, scare (s.o.); (*b*) **l'énormité de la besogne nous effraie,** the magnitude of the task appals us. **2. s'e.,** to get frightened; to take fright (at sth.).

effréné [efrene] *a.* unbridled, unrestrained (passion, curiosity); frantic (efforts).

effrénément [efrenemɑ̃] *adv.* unrestrainedly; frantically.

effritement [efritmɑ̃] *n.m.* crumbling (into dust), disintegration (of plaster, etc.); weathering (of rock).

effriter [efrite] *v.* **1.** *v.tr.* to cause (sth.) to crumble, to disintegrate; to make (sth.) friable; (*b*) (*of funds*) to dwindle. **2. s'e.** (*of plaster work, etc.*) to crumble; (*of rock*) to weather.

effroi [efrwa, -ɑ] *n.m.* fright, terror, fear, dread; **silence qui inspire un e. religieux,** awe-inspiring silence.

effronté [efrɔ̃te] *a.* shameless, bold, impudent, brazen, brash; cheeky (child); barefaced (lie, liar).

effrontément [efrɔ̃temɑ̃] *adv.* shamelessly, barefacedly, brazenly, impudently.

effronterie [efrɔ̃tri] *n.f.* effrontery, insolence, impudence; *F:* cheek; **payer d'e.,** to brazen it out.

effroyable [efrwajabl̩] *a.* (*a*) frightful, fearful, dreadful, appalling; **visage e.,** hideous face; (*b*) *F:* tremendous, terrific, awful (expense, crowd).

effroyablement [efrwajabləmɑ̃], *adv. F:* tremendously, terribly.

effusion [efyzjɔ̃] *n.f.* **1.** effusion, outpouring, overflowing; **e. de sang,** (i) haemorrhage; (ii) bloodshed. **2.** effusiveness; **avec e.,** effusively, gushingly.

égal, -aux [egal, -o] *a.* **1.** (*a*) equal (share, weight, etc.); **être é. à,** to be equal to, to equal; **à écartement é.,** equidistant ; **toutes choses égales (d'ailleurs),** other things being equal; **à travail é., salaire é.,** equal pay for equal work; *n.* **s'associer avec ses égaux,** to associate with one's equals; **traiter qn d'é. à é.,** to treat s.o. as an equal; **sans é.,** matchless; **à l'é. de,** as much as, equally with; **il me chérit à l'é. d'un fils,** he loves me like a son; (*b*) level, even, regular (line, breathing, etc.); steady (pace, pulse); **homme d'humeur égale,** even-tempered man. **2.** all the same; **cela m'est (bien) é.,** it's all the same, all one, to me; I don't mind; *F:* I couldn't care less.

également [egalmɑ̃] *adv.* **1.** equally, alike; **é. bon,** equally good; **servir tout le monde é.,** to serve everyone alike. **2.** also, likewise; **j'en veux é.,** I want some too.

égaler [egale] *v.tr.* **1.** to equalize; to make (s.o., sth.) equal; to put (people) on the same footing; to consider (people) as equal. **2.** to equal, be equal to, to match, come up to (s.o., sth.); **deux et deux égalent quatre,** two and two equal, make, four.

égalisateur, -trice [egalizatœr, -tris] *a.* equalizing, levelling (system); *Sp:* **but é.,** equalizer.

égalisation [egalizasjɔ̃] *n.f.* **1.** equalization, equalizing; *Mth:* **é. à zéro,** equating to zero; *Sp:* **but d'é.,** equalizer. **2.** levelling, smoothing (of ground, etc.).

égaliser [egalize] *v.tr.* **1.** to equalize (wages, pressure); to size (small shot, etc.); **é. les cheveux de qn,** to trim s.o.'s hair; *Mth:* **é. une expression à zéro,** to equate an expression to zero; *Sp:* **é. (la marque),** to equalize. **2.** to level, smooth (ground); to make (ground) even.

égaliseur [egalizœr] *n.m.* (*device*) equalizer, regulator.

égalitaire [egalitɛr] *a. & s.* egalitarian.

égalitarisme [egalitarism] *n.m.* egalitarianism.

égalité [egalite] *n.f.* **1.** (*a*) equality; **être sur un pied d'é. avec qn,** to be on an equal footing, on equal terms, with s.o.; *Sp:* **é. de points,** tie; **à é.,** (*of teams*) level; (*of result*) drawn, tied; *Golf:* all square; *Ten:* **é. à 40,** deuce; *Rac:* **course à é.,** dead heat; tie; *Turf:* **parier à é. sur un cheval,** to lay evens on a horse; (*b*) *Typ:* (sign of) equality. **2.** evenness, regularity, smoothness (of breathing, temper, etc.).

égard [egar] *n.m.* consideration, respect; (*a*) **avoir é. à qch.,** to take sth. into consideration, into account; to make allowance(s), to allow, for sth.; **eu é. aux circonstances,** in consideration of, due allowance being made for, the circumstances; **sans é. à,** regardless of, irrespective of; **à tous (les) égards,** in all respects, in every respect; **à certains égards,** in some respects; **n'ayez aucune crainte à cet é.,** don't worry about that; **à l'é. de,** with reference to, with regard to, with respect to; compared with; **être injuste à l'é. de qn,** to be unjust to(wards) s.o.; (*b*) **faire qch. par é. pour qn,** to do sth. (i) out of respect, consideration, for s.o., (ii) for s.o.'s sake; **être sans é. pour qn,** to have no consideration for s.o.

égaré [egare] *a.* **1.** stray, lost (sheep, traveller); **balles égarées,** stray bullets; **village é.,** remote, out-of-the-way, village. **2.** distraught, distracted, (face, etc.); wild (eyes).

égarement [egarmɑ̃] *n.m.* **1.** (*a*) mislaying (of object); (*b*) bewilderment; **é. (d'esprit),** (mental) aberration. **2.** deviation (from virtue, etc.); wildness (of conduct); **il est revenu de ses égarements,** he has seen the error of his ways.

égarer [egare] *v.* **1.** *v.tr.* (*a*) to lead (s.o.) astray, out of his way; to mislead, misguide (s.o.); **les mauvais exemples l'ont égaré,** he has been led astray by bad examples; (*b*) to mislay, lose (sth.); (*c*) to bewilder (s.o.); **égaré par tant de malheurs,** distraught by so many misfortunes. **2. s'é.** (*a*) to lose one's way, to go astray; **colis qui s'est égaré,** parcel that has got lost; *Lit:* **s'é. loin du droit chemin,** to wander from the straight path; (*b*) **son esprit s'égare,** his mind is wandering.

égayer [egeje] *v.* **(j'égaie, j'égaye, n. égayons; j'égaierai, j'égayerai) 1.** *v.tr.* to cheer up (patient); to amuse (the guests); to enliven (company, conversation); to brighten (up) (room, dress, s.o.'s life). **2. s'é.,** to be amused; **s'é. aux dépens de qn,** to make fun of s.o.

Égée [eʒe] **1.** *Pr.n.m. Gr.Myth:* Aegeus. **2.** *a. Geog:* **la mer É.,** the Aegean (Sea).

égéen, -éenne [eʒeɛ̃, -eɛn] *a.* Aegean.

égide [eʒid] *n.f.* (*a*) *Gr.Myth:* aegis, shield; (*b*) *Lit:* protection, defence; **sous l'é. de,** under the aegis, care, sponsorship, of; **prendre qn sous son é.,** to take s.o. under one's wing.

églantier [eglɑ̃tje] *n.m. Bot:* wild rose, dog rose (bush).

églantine [eglɑ̃tin] *n.f. Bot:* wild rose, dog rose (flower).

église [egliz] *n.f.* church. **1. l'É. (catholique romaine),** the (Roman) Catholic Church; **l'É. et l'État,** Church and State; **entrer dans l'É.,** to go into the church, to take holy orders. **2. une é.,** a church (building); **l'é. Saint-Pierre,** St. Peter's (church).

églogue [eglɔg] *n.f. Lit:* eclogue.

égocentrique [egɔsɑ̃trik] *a.* self-centred, egocentric.

égocentrisme [egɔsɑtrism] *n.m.* egocentricity, egocentrism.

égoïsme [egɔism] egoism, selfishness.

égoïste [egɔist] **1.** *n.m. & f.* egoist. **2.** *a.* egoistic, selfish, self-centred.

égoïstement [egɔistəmɑ̃] *adv.* egoistically.

égorgement [egɔrʒəmɑ̃] *n.m.* **1.** sticking, cutting the throat (of pig, etc.). **2.** butchery, slaughter.

égorger [egɔrʒe] *v.tr.* **(j'égorgeai(s); n. égorgeons) 1.** (*a*) to cut the throat of (animal); to stick (pig); (*b*) *O:* **é. qn,** to slit s.o.'s throat. **2.** to butcher, massacre, slaughter (persons).

égorgeur, -euse [egɔrʒœr, -øz] *n.* murderer, butcher, slaughterer.

égosiller (s') [segozije] *v.pr.* to bawl; to shout (oneself hoarse); (*of bird*) to sing away, *F:* to sing its head off; **mais je m'égosille à vous le dire!** I've told you so till I'm blue in the face.

égotisme [egɔtism] *n.m.* egotism.

égotiste [egɔtist] **1.** *n.m. & f.* egotist. **2.** *a.* egotistic(al).

égout [egu] *n.m.* **1.** (*a*) *A:* drip(ping) (of roof water); (*b*) (i) eaves, (ii) gutter (of roof); **toit à deux égouts,** ridge roof. **2.** (i) sewer; (ii) drain; **eaux d'é.,** sewage;

tuyau d'é., drainpipe; **é. collecteur,** main sewer; **jeter à l'é.,** (i) to flush away; (ii) to pour down the drain.
égoutier [egutje] *n.m.* sewerman.
égouttage [egutaʒ] *n.m.* drainage; draining (of cheese, ground, etc.).
égouttement [egutmɑ̃] *n.m.* **1.** dripping (of water, etc.). **2.** drainage, draining.
égoutter [egute] *v.* **1.** *v.tr.* to drain (cheese, lettuce). **2. s'é.,** to drain, drip.
égouttoir [egutwar] *n.m.* (*a*) draining board; (*b*) drainer, draining rack; (*c*) **(panier) é.,** basket (of deep fryer).
égrappage [egrapaʒ] *n.m.* picking off (of grapes, etc., from bunch).
égrapper [egrape] *v.tr.* to pick off (grapes, etc.) from bunch.
égratigner [egratiɲe] *v.tr.* **1.** to scratch (s.o., sth.). **2.** to nettle, ruffle (s.o.).
égratignure [egratiɲyr] *n.f.* **1.** scratch; **je n'ai pas reçu une é.,** I escaped without a scratch. **2.** gibe; dig (at s.o.).
égrenage [egrənaʒ] *n.m.*, **égrènement** [egrɛnmɑ̃] *n.m.* **1.** shelling (of peas, etc.); picking off (of grapes). **2. égrènement de lumières,** string of lights.
égrener [egrəne] *v.* **(j'égrène, n. égrenons; j'égrènerai) 1.** *v.tr.* (*a*) to shell (maize, peas); to pick off (grapes, etc., from the bunch); to gin (cotton); to ripple, boll (flax); (*b*) **é. son chapelet,** to tell one's beads; **é. des sujets de conversation,** to try one subject of conversation after another. **2. s'é.** (*a*) (*of seed, berries*) to fall, drop from the bunch; (*of wheat*) to seed; (*b*) **des lumières s'égrènent le long du quai,** a chain, string, of lights stretches along the quay.
égreneuse [egrənøz] *n.f.* sheller; **é. de coton,** cotton gin.
égrillard [egrijar] *a.* ribald; risqué, spicy (story).
égrisage [egrizaʒ] *n.m.* grinding (of glass, diamonds).
égriser [egrize] *v.tr.* to grind (glass, diamonds, etc.).
égrugeage [egryʒaʒ] *n.m.* bruising (of grain); pounding (of salt, sugar).
égrugeoir [egryʒwar] *n.m. Dom.Ec:* mortar; **é. de table,** (i) salt mill; (ii) pepper mill.
égruger [egryʒe] *v.tr.* **(j'égrugeai(s); n. égrugeons)** to bruise (grain); to pound (salt, sugar).
Égypte [eʒipt] *Pr.n.f. Geog:* Egypt.
égyptien, -ienne [eʒipsjɛ̃, -jɛn] **1.** *a. & n.* Egyptian. **2.** *n. A:* gipsy. **3.** *n.f. Typ:* clarendon.
égyptologie [eʒiptɔlɔʒi] *n.f.* Egyptology.
égyptologue [eʒiptɔlɔg] *n.m. & f.* Egyptologist.
eh [e] *int.* hey! **eh bien!** well! now then! **eh! que voulez-vous que je fasse?** why, what can I do? **eh, là-bas!** hello there!
éhonté [eɔ̃te] *a.* shameless, barefaced, unblushing.
eider [ɛdɛr] *n.m.* eider (duck).
eidétique [ɛjdetik] *a. Psy:* eidetic.
éjaculation [eʒakylasjɔ̃] *n.f. Physiol:* ejaculation.
éjaculer [eʒakyle] *v.tr. Physiol:* to ejaculate.
éjectable [eʒɛktabl̩] *a. Av:* **siège é.,** ejector seat.
éjecter [eʒɛkte] *v.tr.* to eject (fluid, cartridge, pilot); *F:* to throw out, expel (s.o.).
éjecteur [eʒɛktœr] *n.m.* ejector (of steam, water, cartridge, etc.); outlet works (of a reservoir); *Av:* **siège é.,** ejector seat.
éjection [eʒɛksjɔ̃] *n.f.* (*a*) ejection (of fluid, cartridge, pilot); **éjections volcaniques,** ejecta; (*b*) *F:* expulsion (of s.o.).
élaboration [elabɔrasjɔ̃] *n.f.* elaboration (of work); working out (of plan, idea); drawing up (of constitution, etc.).
élaborer [elabɔre] *v.tr.* to elaborate; to transform, work on (raw material); to work out, draw up (plan).
élagage [elagaʒ] *n.m.* (*a*) pruning (of tree); (*b*) cutting (down) (of play, etc.).
élaguer [elage] *v.tr.* (*a*) to prune (tree); (*b*) to curtail, prune, cut (down) (play, etc.).
élagueur [elagœr] *n.m.* pruner.
élan¹ [elɑ̃] *n.m.* **1.** (*a*) spring, bound, dash; **d'un seul é.,** at one bound; (*when jumping*) **prendre son é.,** to take off; **saut sans é., avec é.,** standing jump, running jump; (*b*) **travailler avec é.,** to work enthusiastically, with a will; (*c*) impetus; **perdre son é.,** to lose momentum; **é. vital,** life force. **2.** burst, outburst (of feeling); glow (of enthusiasm); impulse.
élan² *n.m.* (*a*) (Scandinavian) elk; (*b*) **é. du Canada,** moose.
élancé [elɑ̃se] *a.* tall and slim; slender (figure, person, tree); lank, lean (horse); **(navire, voiture) aux formes élancées,** streamlined.
élancement [elɑ̃smɑ̃] *n.m.* shooting pain, twinge.
élancer [elɑ̃se] *v.* **(j'élançai(s); n. élançons) 1.** *v.i.* (*of finger, etc.*) to throb, shoot (with pain), to give a twinge. **2.** (*a*) **s'é. en avant,** to spring, bound, dash, shoot, forward; **s'é. sur qn,** to rush, make a rush, at s.o.; *F:* to go for s.o.; **le chat s'élança sur moi,** the cat flew at me; **s'é. à l'assaut,** to throw oneself into the fray; (*b*) (*of child, plant*) to shoot up, grow taller; (*c*) **s'é. vers le ciel,** to soar skywards.
élargir [elarʒir] *v.* **1.** *v.tr.* (*a*) (i) to widen (road); to let out (dress); to stretch (shoes); to expand (tube); enlarge (hole); **é. des règles,** to stretch rules; (ii) to enlarge, extend, add to (one's estate, knowledge); to widen (horizon, debate); (*b*) to set (prisoner) free; (*c*) *v.i. F:* **il a élargi,** he has broadened out. **2. s'é.** (*a*) to widen (out); broaden (out); (*of shoes, etc.*) to stretch; (*b*) (*of ideas, group*) to grow, extend.
élargissage [elarʒisaʒ] *n.m. Tex:* tentering.
élargissement [elarʒismɑ̃] *n.m.* **1.** (*a*) widening, broadening (of road); letting out (of dress); stretching (of shoes); (*b*) extension, expansion (of estate, group, knowledge). **2.** release, liberation, discharge (of prisoner).
élasticité [elastisite] *n.f.* elasticity (of body, gas, etc.); springiness, spring (of step); resilience (of person).
élastique [elastik] **1.** *a.* (*a*) (*of rubber, conscience, etc.*) elastic; (*b*) elastic, (made of) rubber; **gomme é.,** indiarubber; **balle é.,** rubber ball; (*c*) resilient; springy; **d'un pas é.,** with a springy, buoyant, step. **2.** *n.m.* (*a*) (india) rubber; (*b*) *Dressm: etc:* elastic; **bretelles en é.,** elastic braces; (*c*) elastic band, rubber band.
élastomère [elastɔmɛr] *n.m. Ch: Ind:* elastomer.
Elbe [ɛlb] **1.** *Pr.n.f.* **(l'île d')E.,** (the island of) Elba. **2.** *Pr.n.m.* (the river) Elbe.
électeur, -trice [elɛktœr, -tris] *n.* **1.** *Hist:* Elector, *f.* Electress. **2.** elector, voter; **mes électeurs,** my constituents.
électif, -ive [elɛktif, -iv] *a.* elective.
élection [elɛksjɔ̃] *n.f.* **1.** election, polling; **élections (législatives),** (parliamentary) elections; **é. partielle,** by-election; **jour des élections,** polling day; **annuler l'é. de qn,** to unseat s.o. **2.** (*a*) election, choice, preference; **mon pays d'é.,** the country of my choice; *Jur:* **faire é. de domicile,** to elect domicile; (*b*) *Theol:* **vase d'é.,** chosen vessel.
électoral, -aux [elɛktɔral, -o] *a.* electoral; **circonscription électorale,** constituency; **corps é.,** electorate; **comité é.,** election committee.
électorat [elɛktɔra] *n.m.* **1.** *Hist:* electorate. **2.** *Pol:* (*a*) electorate; **consulter l'é.,** to go to the country; (*b*) franchise.
électricien, -ienne [elɛktrisjɛ̃, -jɛn] *a. & n.* electrician; **(ingénieur) é.,** electrical engineer.
électricité [elɛktrisite] *n.f.* electricity; **allumer, donner, l'é.,** to switch on the light; **éteindre, couper, l'é.,** to switch off the light; **panne d'é.,** power failure.

électrification [elɛktrifikasjɔ̃] *n.f.* electrification.
électrifier [elɛktrifje] *v.tr.* (*a*) to electrify (railway, etc.); (*b*) to bring electric light to (village).
électrique [elɛktrik] *a.* **1.** electric (current, train). **2.** electrical (engineering, etc.).
électriquement [elɛtrikmɑ̃] *adv.* electrically.
électrisant [elɛktrizɑ̃] *a.* electrifying.
électrisation [elɛktrizasjɔ̃] *n.f.* electrification (of substance, audience); **à é. positive,** positively charged, charged with positive electricity.
électriser [elɛktrize] *v.tr.* to electrify (substance, audience); to thrill (audience); **fil électrisé,** live wire.
électro-aimant [elɛktrɔɛmɑ̃] *n.m.* (electro)magnet; *pl. électro-aimants.*
électrocardiogramme [elɛktrɔkardjɔgram] *n.m.* electrocardiogram.
électrocardiographie [elɛktrɔkardjɔgrafi] *n.f.* electrocardiography.
électrochimie [elɛktrɔʃimi] *n.f.* electrochemistry.
électrochimique [elɛktrɔʃimik] *a.* electrochemical.
électrochirurgie [elɛktrɔʃiryrʒi] *n.f.* electrosurgery.
électrochoc [elɛktrɔʃɔk] *n.m. Med:* **traitement par électrochocs,** electric shock treatment.
électrocuter [elɛktrɔkyte] *v.tr.* to electrocute.
électrocution [elɛktrɔkysjɔ̃] *n.f.* electrocution.
électrode [elɛktrɔd] *n.f.* electrode.
électrodiagnostic [elɛktrɔdjagnɔstik] *n.m.* electrodiagnosis.
électrodynamique [elɛktrɔdinamik] **1.** *a.* electrodynamic(al). **2.** *n.f.* electrodynamics.
électrogène [elɛktrɔʒɛn] *a. El:* generating (plant).
électrolyse [elɛktrɔliz] *n.f.* electrolysis.
électrolyser [elɛktrɔlize] *v.tr.* to electrolyse.
électrolyte [elɛktrɔlit] *n.m. El:* electrolyte.
électrolytique [elɛktrɔlitik] *a.* electrolytic.
électromagnétique [elɛktrɔmaɲetik] *a.* electromagnetic.
électromagnétisme [elɛktrɔmaɲetism] *n.m.* electromagnetism.
électromécanicien [elɛktrɔmekanisjɛ̃] *n.m.* electrical engineer.
électromécanique [elɛktrɔmekanik] **1.** *a.* electromechanical. **2.** *n.f.* electromechanics.
électroménager [elɛktrɔmenaʒe] *a.* & *n.m.* **(appareils) électroménagers,** electric household appliances, *U.S:* household electricals.
électrométallurgie [elɛktrɔmetalyrʒi] *n.f.* electrometallurgy.
électromètre [elɛktrɔmɛtr̥] *n.m.* electrometer.
électromobile [elɛktrɔmɔbil] *a.* electrically driven, operated (vehicle).
électromoteur, -trice [elɛktrɔmɔtœr, -tris] **1.** *a.* electromotive. **2.** *n.m.* electromotor.
électron [elɛktrɔ̃] *n.m. Ph:* electron.
électronicien, -ienne [elɛktrɔnisjɛ̃, -jɛn] *n.* electronics specialist.
électronique [elɛktrɔnik] **1.** *a.* electronic; **faisceau, flux, é.,** electron beam, flow; **valve é.,** thermionic, electron, valve; **ensemble é.,** computer. **2.** *n.f.* electronics.
électroniquement [elɛktrɔnikmɑ̃] *adv.* electronically.
électron-volt [elɛktrɔ̃vɔlt] *n.m.* electron-volt; *pl. électrons-volts.*
électrophone [elɛktrɔfɔn] *n.m.* record player.
électroponcture [elɛktrɔpɔ̃ktyr] *n.f.*, **électropuncture** [elɛktrɔpœ̃ktyr] *n.f. Med:* electropuncture.
électropositif, -ive [elɛktrɔpɔzitif, -iv] *a.* electropositive.
électroscope [elɛktrɔskɔp] *n.m.* electroscope.
électrostatique [elɛktrɔstatik] **1.** *a.* electrostatic(al). **2.** *n.f.* electrostatics.
électrotechnique [elɛktrɔtɛknik] **1.** *a.* electrotechnic(al). **2.** *n.f.* (*a*) electrotechnology; (*b*) electrical engineering.
électrothérapie [elɛktrɔterapi] *n.f.* electrotherapy, electrotherapeutics.
électrotrain [elɛktrɔtrɛ̃] *n.m. Rail:* electric multiple unit (EMU).
électrotype [elɛktrɔtip] *n.m. Typ:* electrotype; *F:* electro.
électrotyper [elɛktrɔtipe] *v.tr. Typ:* to electrotype.
électrotypie [elɛktrɔtipi] *n.f. Typ:* electrotyping.
électrum [elɛktrɔm] *n.m.* electrum.
élégamment [elegamɑ̃] *adv.* elegantly.
élégance [elegɑ̃s] *n.f.* elegance; (*a*) **l'é. du chat siamois,** the elegance, grace, of a Siamese cat; **femme qui a de l'é.,** (i) elegant, graceful, (ii) well-dressed, woman; (*b*) neatness (of method, etc.); (*c*) **les élégances de la vie,** the refinements of life.
élégant [elegɑ̃] **1.** *a.* elegant; (*a*) graceful (figure); shapely (hands); smart, fashionable (dress, restaurant); **femme élégante,** (i) graceful, elegant, (ii) well-dressed, woman; (*b*) distinguished, polished (style); (*c*) neat (method, solution); **mensonge é.,** diplomatic lie. **2.** *n.* (*a*) *n.m. A:* **un é.,** a man of fashion; a dandy; (*b*) *n.f.* **une élégante,** a well dressed, fashionably dressed, woman.
élégiaque [eleʒjak] *a.* elegiac.
élégie [eleʒi] *n.f.* elegy.
élément [elemɑ̃] *n.m.* element. **1.** (*a*) **les quatre éléments,** the four elements; *Fig:* **être dans son é.,** to be in one's element; (*b*) *Ch:* **les éléments qui forment un composé,** the elements in a compound; *Ph:* **é. radioactif,** radioactive element. **2.** (*a*) component, constituent (of sth.); ingredient (of medicine); standardized part (of sectional structure); **les éléments d'un ensemble,** the elements, parts, of a whole; **les élements indésirables de la population,** the undesirable elements of the population; **l'e. décisif,** the deciding factor; *Tchn:* **é. chauffant,** heating unit, element; *Elcs:* **é. de calculateur, de calculatrice, électronique,** computer unit; **mobilier formé d'éléments,** unit furniture; (*b*) *El:* cell (of battery, accumulator); **batterie de cinq éléments,** five-cell battery. **3.** *pl.* (*a*) elements, rudiments, first principles (of science, etc.); **bien connaître ses éléments,** to have a good grounding; (*b*) data (of problem, etc.).
élémentaire [elemɑ̃tɛr] *a.* **1.** (*a*) elementary (chemical analysis, atomic particle); (*b*) elementary knowledge, etc.); *Sch:* **classes élémentaires,** junior forms. **2.** rudimentary (dwelling, etc.).
éléphant [elefɑ̃] *n.m.* elephant; (*a*) **é. mâle, femelle,** bull, cow, elephant; (*b*) **é. de mer, é. marin,** sea elephant, elephant seal.
éléphanteau, -eaux [elefɑ̃to] *n.m.* elephant calf.
éléphantesque [elefɑ̃tɛsk] *a. F:* elephantine, gigantic, enormous.
éléphantiasis [elefɑ̃tjazis] *n.f. Med:* elephantiasis.
élevage [ɛlvaʒ, e-] *n.m.* **1.** breeding, rearing (of stock); animal husbandry; stock farming; grazing (of sheep); raising (of plants); **é. des animaux à fourrure,** fur farming; **poulet d'é.,** battery-reared chicken. **2.** (stock) farm; *NAm:* ranch; *Austr:* station.
élévateur, -trice [elevatœr, -tris] **1.** *a.* & *n.m.* (*a*) elevator (muscle); (*b*) **(chariot) é. (à fourche),** fork-lift truck. **2.** *n.m.* (*a*) elevator, lift, hoist; **é. à bascule,** tip; **é. à augets, à godets,** bucket elevator; (*b*) *El:* **é. de tension,** step-up transformer.
élévation [elevasjɔ̃] *n.f.* **1.** (*a*) elevation, lifting, raising (of s.o., sth.); elevation (of the Host); pumping (up) (of water); **é. des prix,** raising, putting up, of prices; **é. de la voix,** raising of the voice; (*b*) erection, setting up (of statue, etc.). **2.** (*a*) rise (in temperature,

price, etc.); **é. du niveau des eaux,** rise in water level; (*b*) **é. du pouls,** quickening of the pulse. **3. é. de style,** grandeur, nobility, of style. **4.** *Arch:* elevation, vertical section. **5.** rise in the ground; height, eminence.

élévatoire [elevatwar] *a.* lifting, hoisting (apparatus); **usine é.,** waterworks.

élève [elɛv] *n.m. & f.* **1.** pupil; student; apprentice; trainee; *Mil:* **é. officier,** cadet; **é. pilote,** pilot trainee, student pilot. **2.** *n.f.* (*a*) *Husb:* young stock animal; (*b*) seedling.

élevé [elve] *a.* **1.** (*a*) high (mountain, price); noble, elevated (style, mind); exalted (position, rank); **l'officier le plus é. en grade,** the senior officer; **occuper un rang é.,** to rank high; (*b*) **pouls é.,** quick pulse. **2. bien é.,** well brought up, well-bred; **mal é.,** ill bred.

élever [elve] *v.* **(j'élève, n. élevons; j'élèverai) I.** *v.tr.* **1.** (*a*) to raise (the height of a wall, the temperature, one's voice, prices); to lift up, hoist (load); (*b*) to promote (employee); (*c*) to elevate (the mind); (*d*) *Nau:* **é. une côte, un phare,** to raise a coast, a lighthouse. **2.** (*a*) to erect, set up (machine, statue, etc.); (*b*) to raise (objection, difficulties); (*c*) **é. (qch.) sur qch.,** to found (a fortune), establish (a doctrine), on sth. **3.** to bring up, rear (child); to rear (stock); to breed (cattle, horses, rabbits); to keep (bees, poultry); to grow (plants); **bébé élevé au sein, au biberon,** breast-fed, bottle-fed, baby. **II. s'élever 1.** (*a*) to rise (up); (*b*) **le château s'élève sur la colline,** the castle stands on the hill; (*c*) (*of doubts, difficulties, objection*) to arise; **un cri s'éleva,** a shout was heard; **le vent s'élève,** the wind is rising; (*d*) **s'é. contre qch.,** to protest, make a stand, against sth. **2.** to raise oneself; **s'é. sur les pointes des pieds,** to stand on tiptoe; **s'é. à force de travail,** to work one's way up; **s'é. au-dessus de ses préjugés,** to rise above one's prejudices. **3.** (*a*) (*of temperature, prices*) to rise; (*b*) **le compte s'élève à mille francs,** the bill comes, amounts, to a thousand francs.

éleveur, -euse [elvœr, -øz] *Husb:* **1.** *n.* stock breeder; grazier; horse breeder; **é. de chiens,** dog breeder. **2.** *n.f.* battery, brooder (for chicks).

elfe [ɛlf] *n.m.* elf.

élider [elide] *v.tr. Ling:* to elide (vowel).

Élie [eli] *Pr.n.m.* Elijah, Elias.

éligibilité [eliʒibilite] *n.f.* eligibility.

éligible [eliʒibl̩] *a.* eligible.

élimé [elime] *a.* (*of material*) worn, threadbare.

élimer [elime] *v.tr.* to wear the nap off (material).

élimination [eliminasjɔ̃] *n.f.* elimination; **en procédant par é.,** by a process of elimination; *Sp: etc:* **concours sur le principe d'é.,** knock-out competition; *Ind: etc:* **é. des déchets,** waste disposal; *W.Tel:* **é. des parasites,** suppression of noise, interference.

éliminatoire [eliminatwar] *a.* eliminatory (examination, etc.) *Sp:* **épreuve é.,** *n.f.* **é.,** preliminary, eliminating, heat.

éliminer [elimine] *v.tr.* to eliminate (candidate, suspect); to get rid of, eliminate (body wastes); to rule out (theory); to exclude (s.o., sth.); *Sp:* **être éliminé,** to be knocked out (in a tournament); *Mth:* **é. une inconnue,** to eliminate an unknown quantity; (*of quantities*) **s'é.,** to cancel out.

élingue [elɛ̃g] *n.f. Nau: etc:* sling; **é. en filet, filet d'é.,** cargo net, loading net.

élinguer [elɛ̃ge] *v.tr.* to sling; to raise by a sling.

élire [elir] *v.tr.* (*conj. like* LIRE). **1.** to elect, choose (s.o.); to elect, return (member of parliament); **é. qn président,** (i) to elect s.o. president; (ii) to vote s.o. into the chair. **2. é. domicile (dans un endroit),** to take up one's residence; *Jur:* to elect domicile (in a place).

élision [elizjɔ̃] *n.f. Ling:* elision, eliding.

élite [elit] *n.f.* élite; **les élites,** the élite; **personnel d'é.,** picked personnel; **régiment, tireur, d'é.,** crack regiment, shot.

élixir [eliksir] *n.m.* elixir.

elle, elles [ɛl] *pers.pron. f.* **1.** (*unstressed*) (*of pers.*) she, they; (*of thg*) it, they; **e. chante, elles dansent,** she sings, they dance; **qu'elle est jolie, cette broche!** how pretty that brooch is! **2.** (*stressed*) (*a*) (*subject*) she, it, they; **c'est e., ce sont elles,** it is she, they; **je fais comme e.,** I do what she does; **e.-même l'a vu,** she saw it herself; (*b*) (*object*) her, it, them; **je suis content d'elle(s),** I am pleased with her, with them; **e. ne pense qu'à e.,** she thinks only of herself; **chacune d'elles travaille pour e.-même,** each of them works for herself; **il aimait sa patrie et mourut pour e.,** he loved his country and died for it.

ellébore [ɛlebɔr] *n.m.* hellebore.

ellipse [elips] *n.f.* **1.** *Gram:* ellipsis. **2.** *Mth:* ellipse.

ellipsoïdal, -aux [elipsɔidal, -o] *a. Mth:* ellipsoidal.

ellipsoïde [elipsɔid] *Mth:* **1.** *a.* ellipsoidal. **2.** *n.m.* ellipsoid.

elliptique [eliptik] *a. Gram: Mth:* elliptic(al).

elliptiquement [eliptikmɑ̃] *adv.* elliptically.

élocution [elɔkysjɔ̃] *n.f.* elocution.

éloge [elɔʒ] *n.m.* **1.** eulogy; **é. funèbre,** funeral oration. **2.** praise; **faire l'é. de qn,** to speak highly of, in praise of, s.o.; **faire son propre é.,** to blow one's own trumpet; **digne d'éloges,** praiseworthy.

élogieux, -ieuse [elɔʒjø, -jøz] *a.* eulogistic, laudatory (speech, etc.); **parler de qn en termes é.,** to speak (very) highly, flatteringly, of s.o.

éloigné [elwaɲe] *a.* far (away), distant, remote (place, time); **la ville est éloignée de cinq kilomètres,** the town is five kilometres away; **maison éloignée de la gare,** house a long way from the station; **une date plus éloignée,** a later date; **avenir peu é.,** near future; **parent é.,** distant relation; **rien n'est plus é. de ma pensée,** nothing is further from my thoughts; **se tenir é. de qch.,** to hold (oneself) aloof from sth.

éloignement [elwaɲmɑ̃] *n.m.* **1.** removal, removing (of s.o., sth.); postponement (of departure, etc.); deferment (of payment, etc.). **2.** (*a*) absence; (*b*) distance, remoteness (in place, time); **voir qch. en é.,** to have a distant view of sth.; **vivre dans l'é. du monde,** to live apart from the world.

éloigner [elwaɲe] *v.* **1.** *v.tr.* (*a*) to (re)move, move away (s.o., sth.) to a distance, further off; to get (s.o., sth.) out of the way; **é. qch. de qch.,** to move sth. away from sth.; **ils sont éloignés d'un kilomètre,** they are one kilometre apart; **é. une crainte, une pensée, des soupçons,** to banish a fear, dismiss a thought, avert suspicion; **é. qn de son travail,** to keep s.o. away from his work; (*b*) to postpone, put off (departure, etc.); to defer (payment); (*c*) to alienate, estrange (s.o.) **2. s'é.** (*a*) to move off, retire, withdraw, to go away; **ne vous éloignez pas!** don't go away! **s'é. de son devoir,** to neglect one's duty; **s'é. du sujet,** to wander from the subject; (*b*) **voudriez-vous vous é. un peu?** would you please stand further away, further back? **s'é. de tout le monde,** to keep aloof from, lose touch with, everybody.

élongation [elɔ̃gasjɔ̃] *n.f.* elongation; pulled muscle.

élonger [elɔ̃ʒe] *v.tr.* **(j'élongeai(s); n. élongeons)** *Nau:* **1.** to lay out, run out (cable); to shoot (the lines). **2.** to come alongside (wharf); to skirt (coast).

éloquemment [elɔkamɑ̃] *adv.* eloquently.

éloquence [elɔkɑ̃s] *n.f.* (*a*) eloquence; (*b*) oratory.

éloquent [elɔkɑ̃] *a.* eloquent (person, silence); expressive (gesture); **ces chiffres sont éloquents,** these figures speak volumes.

élu, -e [ely] **1.** *a.* chosen; elected; successful (candidate); **président é.,** president elect; *B:* **le peuple é.,** the chosen people. **2.** *n.* (*a*) *Ecc:* **les élus,** the elect; (*b*) **les élus du peuple,** the people's representatives; **nouvel é.,** newly elected member.

élucidation [elysidasjɔ̃] *n.f.* elucidation.

élucider [elyside] *v.tr.* to elucidate, clear up, clarify (mystery, etc.).

éluder [elyde] *v.tr.* to elude, evade (law, difficulty, etc.); *F:* to dodge (question).

Élysée [elize] **1.** *Pr.n.m.* (*a*) *Myth:* **L'É.,** Elysium; (*b*) **(le palais de) l'É.,** the official residence of the President of the French Republic. **2.** *a.* **les Champs Élysées,** (i) *Myth:* the Elysian Fields; (ii) the Champs Élysées (avenue in Paris).

émaciation [emasjasjɔ̃] *n.f.* emaciation.

émacié [emasje] *a.* emaciated, wasted (figure, face).

émacier (s') [semasje] *v.pr.* to become emaciated, to waste away.

émail, émaux [emaj, emo] *n.m.* **1.** (*a*) *Art: etc:* enamel; **émaux de niellure,** niello enamels; (*b*) *Her:* tincture; (*c*) enamel (of the teeth). **2.** (*pl.* **émails**) enamelling material, enamel; *Cer: Phot:* glaze.

émaillage [emajaʒ] *n.m.* **1.** enamelling (of precious metals, etc.). **2.** *Cer: Phot:* glazing.

émailler [emaje] *v.tr.* **1.** to enamel (metal, etc.); **émaillé au four,** stove-enamelled. **2.** *Cer: Phot:* to glaze (porcelain, print). **3.** (*of flowers, etc.*) to fleck, spangle (fields, etc.); **style émaillé de métaphores,** style studded with metaphors.

émailleur, -euse [emajœr, -øz] *n.* enameller.

émaillure [emajyr] *n.f.* enamelling; enamel work.

émanateur [emanatœr] *n.m.* vaporizer, atomizer.

émanation [emanasjɔ̃] *n.f.* emanation; **é. fétide,** foul smell; **é. du radium,** radium emanation, radon.

émancipateur, -trice [emɑ̃sipatœr, -tris] **1.** *a.* emancipatory. **2.** *n.* emancipator.

émancipation [emɑ̃sipasjɔ̃] *n.f.* emancipation.

émancipé [emɑ̃sipe] *a. F:* uninhibited.

émanciper [emɑ̃sipe] *v.* **1.** *v.tr.* to emancipate (people, slave). **2.** **s'é.,** to free oneself (from control); to become independent.

émaner [emane] *v.i.* (*a*) (*of fumes, etc.*) to emanate (**de,** from); (*b*) **ordres émanant de qn,** orders from s.o.

émargement [emarʒəmɑ̃] *n.m.* **1.** *Bookb:* trimming (of pages). **2.** (*a*) marginal note; (*b*) initialling in the margin; **feuille, état, d'é.,** pay sheet.

émarger [emarʒe] *v.tr.* **(j'émargeai(s); n. émargeons) 1.** *Bookb:* to cut down, trim, the margins of (sheets, etc.). **2.** (*a*) **é. un livre,** to make marginal notes in a book; (*b*) *Adm:* **é. un compte,** to receipt, initial, an account (in the margin); (*c*) *v.i.* to sign for, draw, one's salary; **il émarge aux fonds secrets,** he's paid, subsidized, out of the secret funds.

émasculation [emaskylasjɔ̃] *n.f.* emasculation; (*a*) castration; gelding; (*b*) weakening.

émasculer [emaskyle] *v.tr.* to emasculate; (*a*) to castrate, to geld; (*b*) to weaken; to make effeminate.

embâcle [ɑ̃bakl] *n.m.* (*in river, etc.*) (*a*) blockage; (*b*) ice block, jam.

emballage [ɑ̃balaʒ] *n.m.* **1.** (*a*) packing, wrapping (of parcels, goods); **papier d'e.,** packing paper; (*b*) packing material; boxes, crates, etc.; **emballages vides,** (returned) empties. **2.** *Rac:* spurt.

emballé [ɑ̃bale] *a. F:* enthusiastic, carried away.

emballement [ɑ̃balmɑ̃] *n.m.* **1.** (*of machine, engine*) racing. **2.** excitement; burst of enthusiasm, of energy; *St.Exch:* boom; **prompt aux emballements,** easily carried away.

emballer [ɑ̃bale] *v.* **1.** *v.tr.* (*a*) to pack (goods); to wrap (sth.) up; *F:* **e. qn dans un train,** to bundle s.o. into a train; *P:* **e. qn,** to arrest s.o., to run s.o. in; (*b*) (i) *I.C.E:* **e. le moteur,** to race the engine; (ii) *v.i. Sp:* to (put on a) spurt; (*c*) *F:* to fire s.o. with enthusiasm, to excite s.o.; **être emballé par qn, qch.,** to be (mad) keen on s.o., sth. **2.** **s'e.** (*a*) (*of horse*) to bolt, run away; (*b*) (*of engine*) to race; (*c*) *F:* to be carried away (by enthusiasm); **ne vous emballez pas!** keep your head! keep cool! *F:* cool it!

emballeur, -euse [ɑ̃balœr, -øz] *n.* packer.

embarbouiller [ɑ̃barbuje] *v.* **1.** *v.tr.* (*a*) to dirty (one's hands, etc.); (*b*) to muddle (s.o.), to put (s.o.) out. **2.** **s'e.,** to get muddled, into a muddle.

embarcadère [ɑ̃barkadɛr] *n.m.* landing stage; wharf, quay; loading dock.

embarcation [ɑ̃barkasjɔ̃] *n.f.* boat; small craft; **e. à moteur,** motor boat, motor launch.

embardée [ɑ̃barde] *n.f.* *Nau:* yaw, lurch; *Aut:* swerve; **faire une e.,** (*of boat*) to yaw; (*of car*) to swerve (across the road); *F:* (*of pers.*) to lurch across the road.

embarder [ɑ̃barde] *v.i.* (*of ship*) to yaw; (*of car*) to swerve.

embargo [ɑ̃bargo] *n.m. Nau: etc:* embargo.

embarquement [ɑ̃barkəmɑ̃] *n.m.* **1.** embarking, embarcation (of passengers); shipping (of goods); loading (of goods on train, truck); *Rail: Mil:* entrainment (of troops); **quai d'e.,** (i) departure platform; (ii) loading platform. **2.** boarding, going on board (ship, aircraft, etc.).

embarquer [ɑ̃barke] **1.** *v.tr.* (*a*) to embark (passengers); to ship (goods); to put (passengers) on (train, bus); *Rail: Mil:* to entrain (troops); *Av:* to emplane (passengers); *Fig:* **e. qn dans un procès,** to involve s.o. in a lawsuit; *P:* **e. un voleur,** to arrest, run in, a thief; (*b*) *Nau:* **e. (de l'eau),** to ship water; (*c*) to start on (sth.); **e. très mal un projet,** to make a bad start on a scheme. **2.** *v.i. & pr.* to embark; (*a*) **(s')e. (sur un navire),** to go on board, to board (ship); **s'e. dans un train, un autobus,** to board, get on, a train, bus; **s'e. en avion,** to board an aircraft; (*b*) **s'e. dans une entreprise, une discussion,** to embark on an undertaking, a discussion.

embarras [ɑ̃bara] *n.m.* **1.** (*a*) *A:* obstruction; **e. de voitures,** traffic block; (*b*) **e. gastrique,** bilious attack. **2.** (*a*) difficulty, trouble; **se trouver dans l'e.,** to be in (financial) difficulties; **tirer qn d'e.,** to help s.o. out of a difficulty; **je vous donne beaucoup d'e.,** I'm giving you a lot of trouble; (*b*) *F:* **faire des e., de l'e.,** (i) to be fussy; to make a fuss, a song and dance; (ii) to show off; **sans plus d'e.,** without more ado. **3.** embarrassment; (*a*) perplexity, hesitation; **n'avoir que l'e. du choix,** to have far too much to choose from; **je suis dans l'e.,** I'm in a fix; (*b*) confusion, discomposure.

embarrassant [ɑ̃barasɑ̃] *a.* awkward. **1.** cumbersome (parcel, etc.). **2.** (*a*) perplexing, puzzling (question); (*b*) embarrassing (question, situation).

embarrassé [ɑ̃barase] *a.* **1.** hampered (movements); involved (style); **avoir les mains embarrassées,** to have one's hands full; **être dans une situation (financière) embarrassée,** to be in (financial) difficulties; **explications embarrassées,** involved, confused, explanations; **avoir l'estomac e.,** to feel bilious. **2.** embarrassed; (*a*) perplexed, puzzled; **il n'est jamais e.,** he's never at a loss; (*b*) bashful, diffident.

embarrasser [ɑ̃barase] *v.* **1.** *v.tr.* (*a*) to encumber, hamper (s.o.); to clutter up (a room); **est-ce que ma valise vous embarrasse?** is my case in your way? (*b*) to embarrass; (i) to trouble, bother (s.o.) (ii) to perplex, puzzle (s.o.); (iii) to make (s.o.) feel awkward. **2.** **s'e.** (*a*) to burden, encumber, hamper, oneself (**de,** with); (*b*) (i) to trouble oneself, be concerned (about sth.); (ii) to feel embarrassed, awkward.

embauchage [ɑ̃boʃaʒ] *n.m.* engaging, taking on (of

workmen); hiring (of farm hands).
embauche [ɑ̃boʃ] *n.f.* **1.** = EMBAUCHAGE. **2. chercher de l'e.,** to look for a job.
embaucher [ɑ̃boʃe] *v.tr.* to engage, take on, sign on (workmen); to hire (farm hands).
embauchoir [ɑ̃boʃwar] *n.m.* boot tree, shoe tree.
embaumement [ɑ̃bommɑ̃] *n.m.* embalming (of corpse).
embaumer [ɑ̃bome] *v.tr.* **1.** to embalm (corpse). **2.** (*a*) to perfume, scent; **air embaumé,** balmy air; (*b*) *v.i.* to be fragrant; (*c*) to smell of (sth.); **l'église embaume l'encens,** the church is heavy with incense.
embaumeur [ɑ̃bomœr] *n.m.* embalmer (of corpses).
embéguiner (s') [sɑ̃begine] *v.pr.* **s'e. de qn,** to become infatuated with s.o.
embellie [ɑ̃beli] *n.f. Nau:* clearing (in sky, weather); lull (in wind); **courte e.,** bright interval.
embellir [ɑ̃belir] **1.** *v.tr.* to embellish; to beautify (sth.); to improve the looks of (s.o.); **e. une histoire,** to improve on a story. **2.** *v.i.* to improve (in looks).
embellissement [ɑ̃bɛlismɑ̃] *n.m.* **1.** embellishing, improving, beautifying. **2.** improvement (in looks). **3.** embellishing touch; ornament, adornment.
emberlificoter [ɑ̃bɛrlifikɔte] *v.tr. F:* **1.** to entangle (s.o.), to tangle (s.o.) up. **2.** to trick (s.o.); to take (s.o.) in.
embêtant [ɑ̃bɛtɑ̃] *a. F:* annoying.
embêtement [ɑ̃bɛtmɑ̃] *n.m. F:* annoyance; unpleasantness; worry.
embêter [ɑ̃bete] *v. F:* **1.** *v.tr.* to annoy; **ça m'embête d'y aller,** (i) I can't be bothered, (ii) I wish I didn't have, to go there; **ça m'embête d'arriver en retard,** I hate being late. **2. s'e.,** to be, get, bored (stiff).
emblée (d') [dɑ̃ble] *adv.phr.* directly, right away, straight off; (to succeed) at the first attempt, go.
emblématique [ɑ̃blematik] *a.* emblematic(al).
emblème [ɑ̃blɛm] *n.m.* **1.** (*a*) emblem, device; (*b*) badge, crest. **2.** symbol, sign.
embobeliner [ɑ̃bɔbline] = EMBOBINER.
embobiner [ɑ̃bɔbine] *v.tr. F:* to deceive (s.o.), to take (s.o.) in; **ne vous laissez pas e.,** don't let yourself be had.
emboire (s') [sɑ̃bwar] *v.pr.* (*of paint*) to soak in; to become flat, dull.
emboîtage [ɑ̃bwataʒ] *n.m.* **1.** (*a*) packing (of articles) into boxes; (*b*) box, casing. **2.** *F:* hooting, booing (of speaker).
emboîtement [ɑ̃bwatmɑ̃] *n.m.* **1.** (*a*) encasing; (*b*) fitting, jointing (of pipes, timbers, etc.). **2.** fitment; joint; housing (of tenon, etc.); socket (of pipe).
emboîter [ɑ̃bwate] *v.tr.* **1.** (*a*) to encase; *El:* **fusible emboîté,** enclosed fuse; (*b*) *Bookb:* to case (book) on mull. **2.** (*a*) to pack (sardines, etc.) in boxes, cans, tins; (*b*) to fit (things) together, to joint; to house, box (tenon, etc.); to nest (boxes, tables); **les pièces s'emboîtent,** the pieces fit together, interlock; (*c*) **e. le pas à qn,** (i) to follow, tread, in s.o.'s footsteps, on s.o.'s heels; (ii) to join in with s.o., to follow suit.
emboîture [ɑ̃bwatyr] *n.f.* **1.** fit, interlock(ing) (of two things). **2.** socket.
embolie [ɑ̃bɔli] *n.f. Med:* embolism.
embonpoint [ɑ̃bɔ̃pwɛ̃] *n.m.* stoutness, plumpness; **avoir de l'e.,** to be stout, corpulent, fat.
embossage [ɑ̃bɔsaʒ] *n.m. Nau:* mooring fore and aft.
embouché [ɑ̃buʃe] *a. F:* **mal e.,** foul-mouthed.
emboucher [ɑ̃buʃe] *v.tr.* **1.** to put (trumpet) to one's mouth; to blow (trumpet); *F:* **e. la trompette,** to announce (sth.) with a flourish; to trumpet the news. **2. e. un cheval,** to put the bit in a horse's mouth.
embouchoir [ɑ̃buʃwar] *n.m.* mouthpiece (of wind instrument).
embouchure [ɑ̃buʃyr] *n.f.* **1.** mouthpiece (of trumpet, blowpipe, etc.). **2.** (*a*) opening, mouth (of sack, vessel, etc.); (*b*) mouth (of river, etc.).
embouquer [ɑ̃buke] *v.tr. & i. Nau:* **e. (dans) la passe,** to enter the channel.
embourbement [ɑ̃burbəmɑ̃] *n.m.* sinking, sticking, in the mud.
embourber (s') [sɑ̃burbe] *v.pr.* (*a*) to stick in the mud; (*b*) to flounder, get tied up (in explanation).
embourgeoisement [ɑ̃burʒwazmɑ̃] *n.m.* attainment of middle-class respectability.
embourgeoiser (s') [sɑ̃burʒwaze] *v.pr.* to become bourgeois, middle class.
embourrer [ɑ̃bure] *v.tr.* to stuff (chair, etc.).
embout [ɑ̃bu] *n.m.* ferrule, tip (of umbrella, stick, etc.); nipple, terminal (of cable); nozzle (of hose); connector (of tie-rod, wire, etc.).
embouteillage [ɑ̃butɛjaʒ] *n.m.* **1.** bottling up (of fleet). **2.** (*a*) bottleneck (in street); (*b*) traffic jam, congestion (of traffic); **l'heure de l'e. du métro,** the rush hour on the tube, *NAm:* subway.
embouteiller [ɑ̃buteje] *v.tr.* to bottle up, block (up) (harbour mouth, entrance, etc.); **circulation embouteillée,** congested traffic; **route embouteillée,** road blocked with traffic.
emboutir [ɑ̃butir] *v.tr.* **1.** *Metalw:* (*a*) to stamp, press, swage (metal); **châssis en tôle emboutie,** pressed steel frame; (*b*) to emboss. **2.** to sheathe with metal; to tip, cap (rod, etc.) with a metal ferrule. **3.** *F:* to bash (sth.) in; **e. un arbre, s'e. sur un arbre,** to crash (one's car) into a tree.
emboutissage [ɑ̃butisaʒ] *n.m.* (*a*) (drop-)stamping, pressing, swaging (of metals); (*b*) embossing; (*c*) *F:* (*of cars*) collision.
embranchement [ɑ̃brɑ̃ʃmɑ̃] *n.m.* **1.** branching (off) (of tree, road, etc.). **2.** (road, rail, pipe) junction; fork (in road). **3.** (*a*) side road; branch (of motorway, etc.); (*b*) *Rail:* (i) branch line; (ii) siding; (*c*) branch (of a science); *Nat.Hist:* sub-kingdom, phylum.
embrancher [ɑ̃brɑ̃ʃe] *v.tr.* to connect up, join up (with main road, pipe, etc.); **route qui s'embranche sur la grande route,** road that (i) forms a junction with, (ii) branches off, the main highway.
embraquer [ɑ̃brake] *v.tr. Nau:* to haul, (rope) taut; to tighten (a rope).
embrasé [ɑ̃braze] *a.* (*a*) blazing (forest, etc.,); glowing (coals, etc.); (*b*) sultry, sweltering (heat).
embrasement [ɑ̃brazmɑ̃] *n.m. A:* burning, conflagration.
embraser [ɑ̃braze] *v.* **1.** *v.tr. Lit:* (*a*) to set (sth.) ablaze; (*b*) (*of sun*) to scorch (ground); (*c*) (*of sunset*) to set (sth.) aglow; (*d*) to fire, inflame (imagination). **2. s'e.** (*a*) to catch fire; (*b*) to glow.
embrassade [ɑ̃brasad] *n.f.* embrace; hug.
embrasse [ɑ̃bras] *n.f.* curtain loop.
embrasser [ɑ̃brase] *v.tr.* to embrace. **1.** (*a*) to put one's arms round (s.o., sth.); to clasp (s.o.) (in one's arms); to hug (s.o., sth.); (*b*) to kiss; **ils s'embrassèrent,** they kissed; *Corr:* **je t'embrasse de tout mon cœur,** with fondest love; (*c*) to take up (career, cause, etc.); to seize (an opportunity). **2.** to contain, include, take in; **l'explication n'embrasse pas tous les faits,** the explanation does not cover all the facts.
embrasure [ɑ̃brazyr] *n.f.* **1.** (*a*) embrasure; window, door, recess; (*b*) *Fort:* embrasure; *Nau:* gun port.
embrayage [ɑ̃brɛjaʒ] *n.m.* **1.** connecting, coupling; engaging (of the clutch); throwing into gear (of engine parts). **2.** clutch, coupling, connecting gear; **e. à disques multiples,** multi(ple)-disc clutch, coupling; **pédale d'e.,** clutch pedal.
embrayer [ɑ̃breje] *v.tr.* **(j'embraie, j'embraye, n. embrayons; j'embraierai, j'embrayerai)** *Mec.E:* to

connect, couple; to engage; to throw (parts) into gear; *v.i.* (i) to engage the gear; *Aut:* to let in the clutch; (ii) *F:* to start work.

embrayeur [ɑ̃brɛjœr] *n.m. Mec.E:* (*a*) clutch lever, fork; (*b*) belt shifter.

embrigadement [ɑ̃brigadmɑ̃] *n.m.* enrolling (of a group of workers); recruitment (of supporters).

embrigader [ɑ̃brigade] *v.tr.* to enrol (a group of workers); **il m'a embrigadé dans son club,** he made me join his club.

embrocation [ɑ̃brɔkasjɔ̃] *n.f. Med:* embrocation.

embrochement [ɑ̃brɔʃmɑ̃] *n.m. Cu:* spitting (of meat, etc.).

embrocher [ɑ̃brɔʃe] *v.tr.* **1.** *Cu:* to spit, to put (meat) on the spit. **2.** *Surg:* to pin (fracture).

embrouillage [ɑ̃brujaʒ] *n.m. F:* chaos, mess.

embrouillamini [ɑ̃brujamini] *n.m. F:* confusion, muddle.

embrouillé [ɑ̃bruje] *a.* tangled, (skein, etc.); complicated, involved (style, business).

embrouillement [ɑ̃brujmɑ̃] *n.m.* **1.** entanglement, ravelling (of threads, etc.). **2.** confusion (of ideas, etc.); jumbled state (of things); intricacy (of question).

embrouiller [ɑ̃bruje] *v.* **1.** *v.tr.* (*a*) to ravel, tangle (threads, etc.); (*b*) to tangle up, muddle; to mix up (papers); to confuse, muddle (s.o.); **e. la question,** to confuse, cloud, the issue. **2. s'e.** (*a*) (*of threads, etc.*) to get tangled, into a tangle; (*b*) (*of pers.*) to get muddled, confused, to lose track; **ses affaires s'embrouillent,** his business is getting into a muddle.

embroussaillé [ɑ̃brusaje] *a.* covered with bushes, brushwood; *F:* **cheveux embroussaillés,** tousled hair.

embrumé [ɑ̃bryme] *a.* misty (weather); hazy (horizon); clouded (countenance).

embrumer [ɑ̃bryme] *v.* **1.** *v.tr.* to cover (landscape, etc.) with mist, haze, fog; **craintes qui embrument l'avenir,** fears that darken the future. **2. s'e.,** to become misty, hazy (*of sky*) to cloud over.

embrun [ɑ̃brœ̃] *n.m. usu. pl.* spray, spindrift.

embrunir [ɑ̃brynir] *v.tr.* to darken, to turn brown.

embryologie [ɑ̃brijɔlɔʒi] *n.f. Biol:* embryology.

embryologiste [ɑ̃brijɔlɔʒist] *n.m. & f.*, **embryologue** [ɑ̃brijɔlɔg] *n.m. & f.* embryologist.

embryon [ɑ̃brijɔ̃] *n.m.* embryo; **œuvre encore en e.,** work still in embryo.

embryonnaire [ɑ̃brijɔnɛr] *a.* embryonic; (*a*) (chick, etc.), in embryo; (*b*) **sac e.,** embryo sac.

embryotomie [ɑ̃brijɔtɔmi] *n.f. Obst:* embryotomy.

embu [ɑ̃by] **1.** *a.* flat, dull (paint, painting). **2.** *n.m.* flatness, dullness (of paint).

embûche [ɑ̃byʃ] *n.f. usu. pl.* plot (against s.o.); trap; **tendre, dresser, des embûches à qn,** to set a trap for s.o.; **sujet plein d'embûches,** tricky subject.

embuer [ɑ̃bɥe] *v.tr.* (*of steam, etc.*) to dim, cloud (glass, etc.); **yeux embués de larmes,** eyes dimmed with tears; **pare-brise embué,** misted (up) windscreen.

embuscade [ɑ̃byskad] *n.f.* ambush; **dresser, tendre, une e. à qn,** to lay an ambush for s.o.; **attirer qn dans une e.,** to ambush, waylay, s.o.; **se tenir en e.,** to lie in ambush, in wait.

embusqué [ɑ̃byske] *n.m.* **1.** *Mil:* shirker, dodger. **2.** *Rugby Fb:* **les embusqués,** the back row of forwards.

embusquer [ɑ̃byske] *v.* **1.** *v.tr.* (*a*) to place (troops, etc.) (i) in ambush, (ii) under cover; (*b*) to find (s.o.) a safe job (in wartime). **2. s'e.** (*a*) to lie in ambush; (*b*) to take cover; (*c*) to shirk active service.

éméché [emeʃe] *a. F:* slightly the worse for drink; a bit screwed.

émeraude [ɛmrod] **1.** *n.f.* emerald. **2.** *a.inv. & n.f.* emerald green.

émergence [emɛrʒɑ̃s] *n.f.* (*a*) emergence; (*b*) point of emergence.

émergent [emɛrʒɑ̃] *a.* emergent.

émerger [emɛrʒe] *v.i.* **(j'émergeai(s); n. émergeons) 1.** to emerge (from the sea, etc.). **2.** to come into view; (*from background*) to come to light.

émeri [ɛmri] *n.m.* emery; **papier (d')é.,** emery paper; **bouchon à l'é.,** (ground glass) stopper; **bouché à l'é.,** (*of flask*) stoppered; *F:* (*of pers.*) narrow-minded.

émerillon [ɛmrijɔ̃] *n.m.* **1.** *Orn:* merlin. **2.** swivel (hook).

émeriser [ɛmrize] *v.tr.* to coat (paper, etc.) with emery.

émérite [emerit] *a.* **1.** *A:* emeritus (professor). **2.** skilled, experienced; **chirurgien é.,** eminent surgeon.

émersion [emɛrsjɔ̃] *n.f. Astr:* emersion (of moon).

émerveillement [emɛrvɛjmɑ̃] *n.m.* (i) amazement; (ii) wonder; **c'était un é.,** it was amazing, wonderful.

émerveiller [emɛrveje] *v.* **1.** *v.tr.* to amaze; to fill (s.o.) with (i) wonder, (ii) admiration. **2. s'é.,** to be struck with (i) amazement, (ii) admiration.

émétique [emetik] *a. & n.m.* emetic.

émetteur, -trice [emɛtœr, -tris] **1.** *a.* (*a*) issuing (banker, etc.); (*b*) *W.Tel:* **poste é., station émettrice,** (i) transmitting, (ii) broadcasting, station. **2.** *n.* issuer (of bank notes, shares). **3.** *n.m. W.Tel:* transmitter; *Atom. Ph:* emitter, radiator.

émetteur-récepteur [emɛtœrresɛptœr] *n.m. W.Tel:* transmitter-receiver, transceiver; **é.-r. (portatif),** *F:* walkie-talkie; *pl. émetteurs-récepteurs.*

émettre [emɛtr̥] *v.tr.* (*conj. like* METTRE) **1.** (*a*) to emit (sound, heat, ray of light, etc.); to give, utter (sound); to give off (fumes); to give out (heat); (*b*) to express (opinion); to raise, put forward (objection); (*c*) *W.Tel:* (i) to send out, to transmit; (ii) *v.tr. & i.* to broadcast. **2.** to issue (cheque, etc.); to float (loan); to utter (counterfeit money).

émeu [emø] *n.m.* emu; *pl. émeus.*

émeute [emøt] *n.f.* riot, outbreak, disturbance; **faire é.,** to riot; **chef d'é.,** ringleader.

émeutier, -ière [emøtje, -jɛr] *n.* (*a*) rioter; (*b*) riot leader.

émietter [emjɛte] *v.* **1.** *v.tr.* (*a*) to crumb (bread), crumble (up) (biscuit); (*b*) to fritter away (fortune). **2. s'é.,** (*of biscuit, etc.*) to crumble; (*of empire, etc.*) to crumble, disintegrate, break up.

émigrant, -ante [emigrɑ̃, -ɑ̃t] **1.** *a.* emigrating (population, etc.); migratory (birds). **2.** *n.* emigrant.

émigration [emigrasjɔ̃] *n.f.* **1.** migration (of birds, fishes). **2.** emigration (of people); **é. des savants,** brain drain.

émigré, -ée [emigre] *n.* (political) exile, refugee.

émigrer [emigre] *v.i.* **1.** (*of pers.*) to emigrate. **2.** (*of birds*) to migrate.

émincer [emɛ̃se] *v.tr.* **(j'éminçai(s); n. éminçons)** to slice (meat) finely; to shred (vegetables).

éminemment [eminamɑ̃] *adv.* eminently; highly; to, in, a high degree; outstandingly.

éminence [eminɑ̃s] *n.f.* eminence. **1.** (*a*) rise, hill, height; (*b*) *Anat:* protuberance, process; ball (of the thumb); (*c*) *A:* (moral, intellectual) superiority. **2.** *Ecc:* **son É. le Cardinal,** his Eminence the Cardinal; **l'É. grise,** the power behind the throne.

éminent [eminɑ̃] *a.* eminent, distinguished; outstanding.

émir [emir] *n.m.* emir.

émirat [emira] *n.m.* emirate.

émissaire [emisɛr] *a. & n.m.* **1.** (*a*) emissary, messenger; (*b*) **bouc é.,** scapegoat. **2.** (*a*) *Anat:* **(veine) é.,** emissary vein; (*b*) outlet, drainage channel (of lake).

émission [emisjɔ̃] *n.f.* **1.** (*a*) emission (of sound, fluid, etc.); utterance (of sound); sending out (of signals); **tuyau d'é.,** discharge pipe; (*b*) *W.Tel:* (i) transmission; sending out; (ii) broadcasting; **poste d'é.,** transmitter; **station d'é.,** transmitting, sending, station; broadcasting station; (*c*) *Elcs:* **é. électronique,** electron emission; *Atom.Ph:* **é. de particules,** particle emission. **2.** issue, issuing (of banknotes, tickets); uttering (of counterfeit money). **3.** broadcast (programme); **é. en différé, en direct,** recorded, live, broadcast.

emmagasinage [ɑ̃magazinaʒ] *n.m.* storage, warehousing (of goods); storing up, storage (of electrical energy).

emmagasiner [ɑ̃magazine] *v.tr.* **1.** to store, warehouse (goods); to house (aircraft, etc.); to store (information in the memory). **2.** to store up, to accumulate (electrical energy, etc.).

emmailloter [ɑ̃majɔte] *v.tr.* (*a*) *A:* to swaddle (infant); (*b*) to bind (up), swathe (limb, etc.).

emmanchement [ɑ̃mɑ̃ʃmɑ̃] *n.m.* (*a*) fitting a handle (to tool, etc.); hafting, helving (of tool, etc.); (*b*) jointing (of pipes, etc.); coupling, mounting.

emmancher [ɑ̃mɑ̃ʃe] *v.tr.* **1.** to fix a handle to, to haft, to helve (tool, etc.). **2.** (*a*) to fit together, joint (pipes, etc.); to fix (pulley on shaft, etc.); (*b*) *F:* to start, set about (scheme, job).

emmanchure [ɑ̃mɑ̃ʃyr] *n.f.* armhole.

emmêlement [ɑ̃mɛlmɑ̃] *n.m.* **1.** (*a*) tangling (of threads, etc.); (*b*) mixing up (of facts). **2.** (*a*) tangle; (*b*) mix-up, muddle.

emmêler [ɑ̃mele] *v.* **1.** *v.tr.* (*a*) to (en)tangle (thread, hair, etc.); (*b*) to mix up (facts); to muddle (story). **2. s'e.,** to become (i) tangled, (ii) mixed up; to get into a (i) tangle, (ii) muddle.

emménagement [ɑ̃menaʒmɑ̃] *n.m.* **1.** (*a*) moving in (house); (*b*) installation (of furniture, etc.). **2.** *pl.* accommodation, appointments (in ship, aircraft).

emménager [ɑ̃menaʒe] *v.* **(j'emménageai(s)) 1.** *v.tr.* (*a*) to move (s.o.) into a house; to install (s.o., furniture); (*b*) to fit up the accommodation in (ship, aircraft). **2.** *v.i.* to move in.

emmener [ɑ̃mne] *v.tr.* **(j'emmène, j'emmènerai)** (*a*) to lead, take, (s.o.) away, out; **emmené en prison,** taken off to prison; **je vous emmène avec moi,** I'm taking you with me; **emmenez-le!** take him away! (*b*) to lead (troops, sports team).

emmerdant [ɑ̃mɛrdɑ̃] *a. P:* (bloody) annoying; **c'est e.,** it's a bloody nuisance; **tu es e.,** you're a pain in the neck.

emmerder [ɑ̃mɛrde] *v.tr. P:* (*a*) to plague (s.o.); **tu m'emmerdes,** you get on my wick; you're a pain in the neck; (*b*) **je l'emmerde,** he can go and get stuffed.

emmerdeur, -euse [ɑ̃mɛrdœr, -øz] *n. P:* bloody nuisance; pain in the neck.

emmitoufler [ɑ̃mitufle] *v.tr.& pr.* to muffle (s.o., oneself) up (**dans, de,** in).

emmurer [ɑ̃myre] *v.tr.* to immure, wall in (victim); (*of rockfall*) to trap (miners etc.).

émoi [emwa] *n.m.* emotion, agitation, excitement, anxiety, trepidation; **être (tout) en é.,** to be in a state of excitement, all in a flutter; **toute la ville était en é.,** the town was in a commotion; **au grand é. de sa mère,** to his mother's great anxiety.

émollient [emɔljɑ̃] *a. & n.m.* emollient; counter-irritant.

émoluments [emɔlymɑ̃] *n.m.pl.* emoluments, remuneration, salary.

émondage [emɔ̃daʒ], **émondement** [emɔ̃dmɑ̃] *n.m.* **1.** pruning, trimming. **2.** cleaning (of seed, etc.); blanching (of almonds).

émonder [emɔ̃de] *v.tr.* **1.** to prune, trim (tree); *Fig:* **é. un livre,** to cut down, prune, a book. **2.** to clean (seed, etc.); to blanch (almonds).

émondeur, -euse [emɔ̃dœr, -øz] *n.* pruner.

émondoir [emɔ̃dwar] *n.m.* pruning hook, knife; trimming axe.

émotif, -ive [emɔtif, -iv] (*a*) *a.* (*of memories, words, etc.*) emotive; (*b*) *a. & n.* **(homme) é., (femme) émotive,** emotional man, woman.

émotion [emosjɔ̃] *n.f.* emotion; **vive é.,** excitement; thrill; **ressentir une vive é.,** (i) to be greatly moved, (ii) to be thrilled; **parler avec é.,** to speak feelingly; *F:* **j'ai eu une é.,** I've had a shock.

émotionnable [emosjɔnabl̩] *a. F:* (*of pers.*) emotional, excitable.

émotionnel, -elle [emosjɔnɛl] *a. Psy:* emotional (reaction, etc.)

émotionner [emosjɔne] *v.tr. F:* to touch, move (s.o.); **s'é. au sujet de qch.,** to get excited about sth.

émou [emu] *n.m. Orn:* emu; *pl. émous.*

émoulu [emuly] *a.* **1.** *A:* sharpened, newly ground (weapon). **2.** *F:* **jeune homme frais é. du collège,** young man fresh from school.

émoussement [emusmɑ̃] *n.m.* (*a*) blunting (of blade, tool); (*b*) dulling (of senses).

émousser [emuse] *v.* **1.** *v.tr.* (*a*) to blunt (edge, pencil, angle); (*b*) to dull, deaden, blunt (the senses, etc.); to take the edge off (appetite). **2. s'é.:** (*a*) (*of tool*) to lose its edge, its point; (*b*) (*of senses, passions*) to become blunted, dull.

émoustillant [emustijɑ̃] *a.* exhilarating, enlivening, cheering; heady (wine).

émoustiller [emustije] *v.tr.* to exhilarate; to animate (s.o.); to put (s.o.) in a good humour.

émouvant [emuvɑ̃] *a.* moving; touching (scene, etc.); stirring, thrilling (incident).

émouvoir [emuvwar] *v.* (*p.p.* **ému;** *otherwise conj. like* MOUVOIR). **1.** *v.tr.* (*a*) to excite, stir up, rouse (mob, etc.); (*b*) to affect, touch; **é. qn (jusqu')aux larmes,** to move s.o. to tears; **facile à é.,** emotional, easily moved. **2. s'é.** (*a*) to get excited, to be roused; **le pays s'émeut,** the country is in a state of excitement; (*b*) to be touched, affected, moved.

empaillage [ɑ̃pajaʒ] *n.m.* **1.** packing (of goods, etc.) in straw; covering (of plants) with straw (litter). **2.** bottoming (of chairs) with straw. **3.** stuffing (of dead animals).

empaillé, -ée [ɑ̃paje] **1.** *a.* stuffed (bird); *F:* **avoir l'air e.,** to look like a stuffed owl. **2.** *a. & n.* lazy (person); stupid (person).

empailler [ɑ̃paje] *v.tr.* **1.** to pack (goods, etc.) in straw; to cover up (plants) with straw (litter). **2.** to bottom (chair) with straw. **3.** to stuff (dead animal).

empailleur, -euse [ɑ̃pajœr, -øz] *n.* **1.** chairbottomer. **2.** taxidermist.

empalement [ɑ̃palmɑ̃] *n.m.* impalement (of criminal, etc.).

empaler [ɑ̃pale] *v.tr.* to impale.

empanaché [ɑ̃panaʃe] *a.* plumed; decorated with plumes; **style e.,** pompous, flowery, style.

empaquetage [ɑ̃paktaʒ] *n.m.* **1.** packing (of goods); doing up into parcels. **2.** packing (material).

empaqueter [ɑ̃pakte] *v.tr.* **(j'empaquette; j'empaquetterai)** to pack (sth.) up, to make (sth.) into a parcel; to wrap (sth.) up (in paper).

empaqueteur, -euse [ɑ̃paktœr, -øz] *n.* packer.

emparer (s') [sɑ̃pare] *v.pr.* **s'e. de qch.,** take hold of, lay hands on, seize, secure, take possession of, get hold of, sth.; **s'e. de la conversation,** to monopolize the conversation.

empâté [ɑ̃pɑte] *a.* coated, sticky (tongue); thick (voice); fleshy, bloated (face).

empâtement [ɑ̃pɑtmɑ̃] *n.m.* **1.** (*a*) pasting (of covers of book, accumulator plate); (*b*) *Art:* impasto. **2.** stickiness (of hands); thickness, huskiness (of voice). **3.** fattening, cramming (of fowls).

empâter [ɑ̃pɑte] *v.* **1.** *v.tr.* (*a*) to paste (covers of book, accumulator plate); (*b*) to clog, choke up

(file); to make (hands) sticky; **boissons qui empâtent la bouche,** drinks that coat the palate; (*c*) to fatten up, cram (fowls). **2. s'e.,** to put on flesh.
empathie [ɑ̃pati] *n.f.* empathy.
empattement [ɑ̃patmɑ̃] *n.m.* **1.** tenoning (of timbers). **2.** (*a*) footing (of wall); base plate (of crane); (*b*) wheelbase (of car, engine); (*c*) *Typ:* serif.
empatter [ɑ̃pate] *v.tr.* **1.** to foot, tenon, (timbers); **e. les raies d'une roue,** to let in the spokes of a wheel. **2.** to fix on a foundation; to give footing to (wall).
empaumer [ɑ̃pome] *v.tr.* (*a*) to catch (ball, etc.) in the palm of the hand; to strike (ball, etc.) with the palm of the hand; (*b*) *F:* **se laisser, se faire, e.,** to be tricked, taken in; to be swindled.
empêché [ɑ̃peʃe] *a.* **1.** puzzled, at a loss; embarrassed. **2.** (*of rope, etc.*) fouled. **3.** *F:* **être e. de sa personne,** to be awkward, not to know what to do with oneself.
empêchement [ɑ̃pɛʃmɑ̃] *n.m.* (*a*) obstacle, hindrance, impediment (**à,** to); **je n'ai pas pu venir car j'ai eu un e.,** I couldn't come as something turned up (at the last minute); **excusez-moi de mon retard, j'ai eu un e.,** I'm sorry I'm late, I got held up; **sans e.,** without (let or) hindrance; **en cas d'e.,** should you be prevented from coming; (*b*) **e. de la langue,** impediment of speech.
empêcher [ɑ̃peʃe] *v.* **1.** *v.tr.* to prevent, hinder, impede, preclude; (*a*) **cette muraille empêche la vue,** this wall obstructs the view; **ce vent empêchera la pluie,** this wind will keep the rain off; (*b*) **e. qn de faire qch.,** to prevent, keep, s.o. from doing sth.; **empêché, il a envoyé ses excuses,** unavoidably absent, he sent his apologies; **que rien ne vous en empêche!** do it by all means! (*c*) **la pluie empêche que nous (ne) sortions,** the rain prevents us from going out; (*d*) *impers.* **il n'empêche que cela nous a coûté cher,** all the same, nevertheless, it has cost us dear; **cela n'empêche qu'il soit sévère,** that doesn't prevent him from being, his being, strict; *F:* **n'empêche,** (i) all the same; (ii) so what? **2. s'e.,** (*usu. neg.*) to refrain (**de,** from); **je ne pouvais m'e. de rire,** I couldn't help laughing, I had to laugh.
empêcheur, -euse [ɑ̃pɛʃœr, -øz] *n. F:* **e. de danser en rond,** spoilsport, wet blanket.
empeigne [ɑ̃pɛɲ] *n.f.* vamp, upper (of shoe); *P:* **gueule d'e.,** ugly mug.
empennage [ɑ̃pɛnaʒ] *n.m.* feathering, feathers (of arrow); fins, vanes (of bomb); fins (of torpedo); empennage, tail (of aircraft).
empenner [ɑ̃pene] *v.tr.* to feather (arrow); to fit the fins, vanes, on (bomb, etc.); to fit the empennage onto (aircraft).
empereur [ɑ̃prœr] *n.m.* emperor.
empesage [ɑ̃pəzaʒ] *n.m.* starching (of linen).
empesé [ɑ̃pəze] *a.* (*a*) starched (collar); **chemise empesée,** starched, *F:* boiled, shirt; (*b*) stiff, starchy, unbending (manner); stiff, affected (style).
empeser [ɑ̃pəze] *v.tr.* **(j'empèse; j'empèserai)** to starch (linen, etc.).
empesté [ɑ̃pɛste] *a.* foul, pestilential.
empester [ɑ̃pɛste] *v.tr.* **1.** to make (sth.) stink; **air empesté par le tabac,** air reeking of tobacco. **2.** *v.i.* to stink.
empêtrer [ɑ̃petre] *v.* **1.** *v.tr.* (*a*) to hobble (animal); (*b*) to entangle; **s'e. les pieds dans les broussailles,** to get one's feet caught in the undergrowth; **être empêtré de bagages,** to be hampered with luggage. **2. s'e.,** to become entangled; **s'e. dans une mauvaise affaire,** to get involved, mixed up, in a bad business.
emphase [ɑ̃fɑz] *n.f.* bombast, turgidity, grandiloquence, pomposity; **écrire avec e.,** to write in a bombastic, high-flown, style.
emphatique [ɑ̃fatik] *a.* bombastic, pompous, grandiloquent, turgid (style).
emphatiquement [ɑ̃fatikmɑ̃] *adv.* grandiloquently; pompously.
emphysème [ɑ̃fizɛm] *n.m. Med:* emphysema.
empiècement [ɑ̃pjɛsmɑ̃] *n.m.* yoke (of dress).
empierrement [ɑ̃pjɛrmɑ̃] *n.m.* **1.** metalling, macadamization (of road); *Rail:* ballasting (of track). **2.** macadam, (road) metal; *Rail:* ballast.
empierrer [ɑ̃pjere] *v.tr.* to metal, macadamize (road); *Rail:* to ballast (track).
empiétement [ɑ̃pjɛtmɑ̃] *n.m.* encroachment, trespass (**sur,** on); **e. sur les droits de qn.,** infringement of s.o.'s rights.
empiéter [ɑ̃pjete] *v.i.* **(j'empiète, j'empiéterai) e. sur le terrain de qn,** to encroach (up)on s.o.'s land; **e. sur les droits de qn,** to infringe s.o.'s rights; **e. sur le domaine de qn,** to trespass on s.o.'s domain.
empiffrer (s') [ɑ̃pifre] *v.pr. P:* to stuff, gorge oneself.
empilage [ɑ̃pilaʒ] *n.m.*, **empilement** [ɑ̃pilmɑ̃] *n.m.* (*a*) stacking, piling (up) (of wood, etc.); (*b*) pile, stack.
empiler [ɑ̃pile] *v.* **1.** *v.tr.* (*a*) to stack, to pile (up) (books, etc.); (*b*) to cram (passengers into vehicle, etc.); (*c*) *F:* to cheat, rook (s.o.). **2.** (*of books, etc.*) **s'e.,** to pile up.
empire [ɑ̃pir] *n.m.* **1.** (*a*) sovereign authority, dominion; sway; **e. des mers,** command of the sea; **sous l'e. d'un tyran,** under the rule, sway, of a tyrant; (*b*) influence, control, sway; **exercer un e. sur qn,** to have an influence, power, over s.o.; **faire qch. sous l'e. de la nécessité, de la boisson, de la colère,** to do sth. under the pressure of necessity, under the influence of drink, in a fit of anger. **2.** empire; *Hist:* **le Saint-E. romain (germanique),** the Holy Roman Empire; *Fr.Hist:* **le premier E., l'E.,** the First Empire; **style, meubles, E.,** Empire style, furniture.
empirer [ɑ̃pire] *v.* to worsen. **1.** *v.tr.* to make (sth.) worse, to aggravate (an ill, etc.); **pour e. les choses,** to make matters worse. **2.** *v.i.* to become, get, grow, worse; to deteriorate.
empirique [ɑ̃pirik] *a.* empiric(al).
empirisme [ɑ̃pirism] *n.m.* empiricism.
empiriste [ɑ̃pirist] *n.m.* empiricist.
emplacement [ɑ̃plasmɑ̃] *n.m.* site (of, for, building, etc.); location (of works, etc.); *Mil:* emplacement (of gun), position (of troops on battlefield); *Nau:* **e. de chargement,** loading berth.
emplanture [ɑ̃plɑ̃tyr] *n.f.* step (of mast); *Av:* root, socket (of wing).
emplâtre [ɑ̃plɑtr̥] *n.m.* **1.** (*a*) *Pharm:* (i) plaster; (ii) sticking, adhesive, plaster; **e. contre, pour, les cors,** corn plaster; *F:* **c'est mettre un e. sur une jambe de bois,** it's no earthly use; (*b*) *F:* spineless person; **c'est un e.,** he's got no backbone. **2.** gaiter (for repair of tyre).
emplette [ɑ̃plɛt] *n.f.* **1.** purchase, purchasing, shopping; **aller faire ses emplettes,** to go shopping; **faire e. de qch.,** to purchase sth.; **être de bonne e.,** to be worth buying, to be a bargain, a good buy. **2.** *pl.* purchases; shopping.
emplir [ɑ̃plir] *v.* **1.** *v.tr.* to fill (up); **la foule emplissait les rues,** the crowd filled the streets; **nouvelle qui m'emplit de joie,** news that fills me with delight. **2. s'e.,** to fill up, to become full.
emploi [ɑ̃plwa] *n.m.* **1.** use, employment (of sth.); **mode d'e.,** directions for use; **e. du temps,** timetable (of work), allotment of time; **mot qui fait double e.,** word that is a useless repetition; **faire un bon e. de qch.,** to make good use of sth., to put sth. to good use. **2.** employment, occupation, post, job; **être sans e.,** to be out of work, out of a job, to be unemployed, *F:* jobless; **quel est son e.?** what does he do (for a

living)? **e. public,** public office; *Journ:* **demandes d'e.,** situations wanted; **offres d'e.,** situations vacant; *Th:* **tenir l'e. de père noble,** to play heavy father parts; *Pol. Ec:* **plein e.,** full employment.

employé, -ée [ɑ̃plwaje] *n.* employee; **e. de magasin,** shop assistant; *NAm:* clerk; **e. à la vente,** salesman; **e. de banque,** bank clerk; **e. (de bureau),** office worker; **e. d'administration,** government employee, civil servant.

employer [ɑ̃plwaje] *v.* **(j'emploie; j'emploierai) 1.** *v.tr.* (*a*) to employ, use, make use of (sth.); **e. toute son industrie à faire qch.,** to devote all one energies to doing sth.; **bien e. son temps,** to make good use of, the most of, one's time; **ne savoir à quoi e. son temps,** to have no idea how to spend one's time; **vêtement qui emploie trois mètres d'étoffe,** garment that requires three metres of material; **machine à écrire qui emploie de grands formats,** typewriter that takes large sizes; (*b*) *Book-k:* **e. une somme en recette,** to put, enter, an amount in the receipts; (*c*) (i) to employ (workmen, staff); **e. qn comme secrétaire,** to employ s.o. as secretary; (ii) **e. qn,** to make use of s.o.'s services. **2. s'e.** (*a*) **s'e. à faire qch.,** to occupy oneself, spend one's time, (in) doing sth.; (*b*) **s'e. pour qn,** to exert oneself on s.o.'s behalf; (*c*) **mot qui s'emploie au figuré,** word used in the figurative.

employeur, -euse [ɑ̃plwajœr, -øz] *n.* employer.

emplumé [ɑ̃plyme] *a.* feathered.

empocher [ɑ̃pɔʃe] *v.tr.* (*a*) to pocket, receive (money); (*b*) to pocket, put up with (an insult).

empoignade [ɑ̃pwaɲad] *n.f. F:* quarrel, row, set-to.

empoigne [ɑ̃pwaɲ] *n.f. F:* **acheter qch. à la foire d'e.,** to get sth. dishonestly; **la vie n'est qu'une foire d'e.,** life's just a rat race.

empoigner [ɑ̃pwaɲe] *v.tr.* **1.** (*a*) to grasp, seize, grip, grab, to lay hold of (s.o., sth.); *F:* to collar (s.o.); (*b*) **ils se sont empoignés,** they quarrelled, had a set-to. **2.** to thrill, grip, to take hold of (reader, spectator).

empois [ɑ̃pwa] *n.m.* (laundry) starch; *Tex:* dressing.

empoisonnant [ɑ̃pwazɔnɑ̃] *a. F:* annoying, irritating.

empoisonnement [ɑ̃pwazɔnmɑ̃] *n.m.* (*a*) poisoning (of s.o., food); (*b*) **quel e.!** what a nuisance! what a pest!

empoisonner [ɑ̃pwazɔne] *v.tr.* **1.** to poison (s.o.); *v.i.* (*of plant*) to be poisonous. **2.** to poison (food, etc.); **odeur qui empoisonne l'air,** smell that infects the air; **e. la vie de qn,** to embitter, poison, s.o.'s life. **3.** *F:* to bore (s.o.) to death; to plague, pester (s.o.); **s'e.,** to get bored.

empoisonneur, -euse [ɑ̃pwazɔnœr, -øz] *n.* (*a*) poisoner; (*b*) bore.

empoissonner [ɑ̃pwasɔne] *v.tr.* to stock (pond, etc.) with fish.

emporté, -ée [ɑ̃pɔrte] *a.* & *n.* irascible, quick-tempered, hot-headed (person); *n.* hot-head.

emportement [ɑ̃pɔrtəmɑ̃] *n.m.* (*a*) transport (of anger); **dans l'e. de la discussion,** in the heat of debate; (*b*) anger; **répondre avec e.,** to make a heated reply, to reply angrily.

emporte-pièce [ɑ̃pɔrtəpjɛs] *n.m.inv. Tls:* punch; pastry cutter; **découper qch. à l'e.-p.,** to stamp sth. out; **style (à l') e.-p.,** clear, incisive, style; **mots à l'e.-p.,** biting, cutting, words; words that tell; **répondre à l'e.-p.,** to reply neatly, trenchantly.

emporter [ɑ̃pɔrte] *v.* **I.** *v.tr.* **1.** to carry, take (s.o., sth.) away; **e. un blessé sur un brancard,** to carry off, bear away, a wounded man on a stretcher; **ils ont emporté de quoi manger,** they took some food with them; **mets à e.,** take-away food; *F:* **il ne l'emportera pas en paradis,** I'll get my own back sooner or later; **(que) le diable l'emporte!** the devil take him! **2.** (*a*) to carry, tear, sweep, (s.o., sth.) away; **le choléra l'emporta,** cholera carried him off; **le vent emporta son chapeau,** the wind blew off his hat; *F:* **autant en emporte le vent,** it's all idle talk; *F:* **cette moutarde vous emporte la bouche,** this mustard takes the roof off your mouth; (*b*) to take (fort) (by assault); **e. la victoire, la journée,** to carry off the victory, to win the day; (*c*) (*of tool*) to cut out, stamp out, punch out (piece); *F:* **e. le morceau,** to succeed, to get one's own way. **3.** to carry (s.o., sth.) along; **se laisser e. par, à, la colère,** to give way to, let oneself be carried away by, anger. **4. l'e. sur qn, qch.,** to get the better of s.o., sth.; to prevail over s.o.; **considérations qui l'emportent sur toutes les autres,** overriding considerations. **II. s'emporter 1.** to be carried away (by passion); to lose one's temper, to fly into a rage (**contre qn,** with s.o.). **2.** (*of horse*) to bolt.

empoté [ɑ̃pɔte] *a.* & *n. F:* awkward, clumsy (person).

empoter [ɑ̃pɔte] *v.tr.* to pot (plants).

empourprer [ɑ̃purpre] *v.* **1.** *v.tr.* to tinge (sth.) with crimson. **2. s'e.,** to flush; to turn crimson.

empoussiéré [ɑ̃pusjere] *a.* covered with dust; dusty.

empreindre [ɑ̃prɛ̃dr] *v.tr.* (*pr.p.* **empreignant;** *p.p.* **empreint;** *pr.ind.* **j'empreins, il empreint, n. empreignons, ils empreignent;** *impf.* **j'empreignais;** *p.h.* **j'empreignis;** *fu.* **j'empreindrai)** to impress, imprint, stamp (sth. on wax, on the mind); **visage empreint de mélancolie, de terreur,** face marked, stamped, with sadness, full of terror.

empreinte [ɑ̃prɛ̃t] *n.f.* (*a*) impression, (im)print, stamp; **e. en plâtre,** plaster cast; **e. des roues,** track of the wheels; **e. de pas,** footprint; **e. de doigt,** finger-mark; **e. digitale,** fingerprint; **e. du génie,** stamp, mark, impress, of genius; **prendre l'e. de qch.,** to take an impression of sth.; (*b*) *Typ:* mould (from standing type); **e. pour prothèse (dentaire),** denture impression.

empressé, -ée [ɑ̃prese] *a.* eager, zealous; **des soins empressés,** assiduous attentions; *Corr:* **agréez mes salutations empressées,** yours faithfully; *n.* **faire l'e. auprès de qn,** to dance attendance on s.o.

empressement [ɑ̃prɛsmɑ̃] *n.m.* (*a*) eagerness, readiness, willingness (**à faire qch.,** to do sth.); **faire qch. avec e.,** to do sth. readily, with alacrity, *F:* like a shot; **mettre beaucoup d'e. à faire qch.,** to show great keenness in doing sth.; (*b*) **témoigner de l'e. auprès de qn,** to pay marked attention(s) to s.o.; to make a fuss of s.o.

empresser (s') [sɑ̃prese] *v.pr.* **1.** to hurry; **s'e. de faire qch.,** to make haste to do sth.; **il s'empressa de répondre à ma lettre,** he lost no time in answering my letter. **2. s'e. à faire qch.,** to show eagerness, zeal, in doing sth.; **s'e. auprès de qn,** (i) to dance attendance on s.o.; (ii) to pay marked attention(s) to s.o.

emprise [ɑ̃priz] *n.f.* **1.** *Jur:* expropriation, acquisition (of land for public purposes). **2.** ascendancy (over person, mind); hold (on s.o.); **sous l'e. de (qn, qch.),** under the influence of (s.o., sth.).

emprisonnement [ɑ̃prizɔnmɑ̃] *n.m.* imprisonment; **e. cellulaire,** solitary confinement.

emprisonner [ɑ̃prizɔne] *v.tr.* (*a*) to imprison (s.o.); to put (s.o.) in prison; (*b*) to box up, confine (s.o., sth.).

emprunt [ɑ̃prœ̃] *n.m.* **1.** borrowing; **faire un e. à qn,** to borrow (money) from s.o.; **offrir qch. à qn à titre d'e.,** to offer sth. to s.o. as a loan, on loan; **nom d'e.,** assumed name; **route d'e.,** alternative road. **2.** loan; **e. d'État,** government loan; **procéder à un nouvel e.,** to make a new loan issue.

emprunté [ɑ̃prœ̃te] *a.* selfconscious, stiff, awkward (manner).

emprunter [ɑ̃prœ̃te] *v.tr.* to borrow; **e. (de l'argent) à qn,** to borrow (money) from s.o.; **e. un nom,** to assume a name; **le cortège emprunta la rue de Rivoli,** the procession took, went down, the Rue de Rivoli.

emprunteur, -euse [ɑ̃prœ̃tœr, -øz] *n.* borrower.

empuantir [ɑ̃pɥɑ̃tir] *v.tr.* to infect (the air); to make (sth.) stink.

ému [emy] *a.* affected (by emotion), moved; **voix émue,** voice touched with emotion; **nous étions tous très émus,** we were all (i) deeply moved, deeply affected, (ii) greatly excited; **se sentir un peu é.,** to feel a bit nervous.

émulation [emylasjɔ̃] *n.f.* emulation, rivalry.

émule [emyl] *n.m. & f.* emulator, rival.

émulseur [emylsœr] *n.m.* emulsifier.

émulsif, -ive [emylsif, -iv] *a.* emulsive.

émulsifiable [emylsifjabl̥] *a.* emulsifiable.

émulsifier [emylsifje] *v.tr.* to emulsify.

émulsion [emylsjɔ̃] *n.f.* emulsion.

émulsionner [emylsjɔne] *v.tr.* to emulsify.

en¹ [ɑ̃] *prep.* **1.** (*place*) (*a*) (*without def. art.*) in, (in)to; **être, aller, en ville,** to be in town, to go (in)to town; **en province,** in the country, in the provinces; **il est parti en mer,** he's gone to sea; **venir en taxi, en avion,** to come by taxi, by air; **en tête, en queue,** at the head, in the rear; **la suite en quatrième page,** continued on page four; **professeur en Sorbonne,** professor at the Sorbonne; (*with f. names of countries*) **aller en France, en Amérique,** to go to France, America; (*b*) (*with pers. pron.*) **il y a quelque chose en lui que j'admire,** there is something I admire about him; **un homme en qui, en lequel, j'ai confiance,** a man whom I trust; **ils créent le bonheur en eux,** they create happiness within themselves; (*c*) (*with def. art., poss. adj., etc.*) **en votre honneur,** in your honour; **regarder en l'air,** to look up at the sky; **s'épuiser en d'inutiles efforts,** to exhaust oneself in useless efforts; **le mariage aura lieu en l'église Saint-Jean,** the marriage will be celebrated at St. John's (church). **2.** (*time*) in; (*a*) **en été, automne, hiver,** in (the) summer, autumn, winter; **né en 1905,** born in 1905; **en avril,** in April; **d'aujourd'hui en huit,** today week; (*b*) **on peut y aller en cinq heures,** one can get there in five hours; (*c*) (*with def. art., poss. adj.*) **en l'an 1800,** in (the year) 1800; **en ce temps-là,** in those days, at that time; **en l'absence du chef,** in the absence of the chief. **3.** (*a*) (*state*) in; **être en deuil, en loques, en tenue de sport,** to be in mourning, in rags; in, wearing, sports clothes; **arbres en fleur,** trees in blossom; **être en guerre,** to be at war; **en vacances,** on holiday; **peindre qch. en bleu,** to paint sth. blue; (*b*) (*material*) **montre en or,** gold watch; **c'est en or,** it's made of gold; (*c*) (*manner*) **escalier en spirale,** spiral staircase; **chemin en pente,** inclined road; **faire cent à l'heure en palier,** to do 100 an hour on the level; **docteur en médecine,** doctor of medicine; **peintre en bâtiment,** house painter; **fort, faible, en mathématiques,** good, bad, at mathematics; **parler en français,** to speak in French; (*d*) (*change, division*) into; **changé en serpent,** changed into a serpent; **traduire une lettre en français,** to translate a letter into French; **briser qch. en morceaux,** to break sth. (in)to bits; **casser qch. en deux,** to break sth. in two; **pièce en trois actes,** play in three acts; (*e*) **de mal en pis,** from bad to worse; **d'année en année,** from year to year, year by year; (*f*) **vendre en paquets, en feuilles,** to sell in packets, in sheets. **4. envoyer qch. en cadeau,** to send sth. as a present; **donner qch. à qn en compensation,** to give s.o. sth. by way of compensation; **il mourut en brave,** he died like the brave man that he was; **agir en honnête homme,** to act like an honest man; **prendre la chose en philososophe,** to take the thing philosophically. **5.** (*with gerund*) **il marchait en lisant son journal,** he walked along reading his paper; **il répondit en riant,** he answered with a laugh; **elle entra, sortit, en dansant,** she danced into, out of, the room; **on apprend en vieillissant,** we learn as we grow older; **en faisant cela vous l'offenserez,** by doing that you will offend him; **en arrivant à Paris,** on arriving in Paris; **en vous écrivant hier j'avais oublié de vous le dire,** when writing to you yesterday, I forgot to mention it; **en attendant,** while waiting; in the meantime; **tout en tricotant elle nous racontait des histoires,** as she knitted she told us stories; **s'enrhumer en marchant sous la pluie,** to catch a cold (through) walking in the rain.

en² *unstressed adv. and pron.* **I.** *adv.* **1.** from there, thence; **vous avez été à Londres?—oui, j'en arrive,** you've been to London?—yes, I've just come from there. **2.** on that account; **si vous étiez riche, en seriez-vous plus heureux?** if you were rich, would you be happier for it, any the happier? **II.** *pron.inv.* **1.** (*a*) (*standing for a n. governed by* **de**) of (from, by, with, about) him, her, it, them; **j'aime mieux n'en pas parler, ne pas en parler,** I would rather not speak about it; **qu'en pensez-vous?** what do you think of it, about it? **les rues en sont pleines,** the streets are full of it, of them; **il reçut une blessure et en mourut,** he received a wound and died of from it; **il en devint amoureux,** he fell in love with her; (*b*) (*with expressions of quantity*), **combien avez-vous de chevaux?—j'en ai un, trois, plusieurs,** how many horses have you (got)?—I have one, three, several; **combien en voulez-vous?** how many, much, do you want? (*c*) (*replacing the possessive, of things*) **j'ai la valise mais je n'en ai pas la clef,** I have the suitcase but I haven't (got) the key (for it); (*d*) (*standing for a clause*) **il ne l'a pas fait, mais il en est capable,** he did not do it but he is (quite) capable of it. **2.** some, any; **j'en ai,** I have some; **je n'en ai pas,** I have none, I haven't any; **en avez-vous?** have you any? **parmi ses livres il y en a d'excellents,** among his books are some excellent ones. **3. je n'en ai pas encore fini avec lui,** I haven't done with him yet; **si le cœur vous en dit,** if you feel so inclined, if you feel like it; **il en est ainsi,** that's the way it is. **4.** (*after imperative*) **prenez-en,** take some; **prenez-en dix,** take ten (of them); **va-t'en,** go away.

enamouré [ɑ̃namure] *a.* **être e. de qn,** to be enamoured of, in love with, s.o.

enamourer (s') [sɑ̃namure] *v.pr.* to fall in love (**de,** with).

en-arrière [ɑ̃narjɛr] *n.m.inv.* (*skating*) backward glide.

énarthrose [enartroz] *n.f.* enarthrosis, ball-and-socket joint.

en-avant [ɑ̃navɑ̃] *n.m.inv.* **1.** *Fb:* forward pass; (*Rugby*) knock-on. **2.** (*skating*) forward glide.

en-but [ɑ̃by] *n.m.inv. Rugby Fb:* in-goal.

encabaner (s') [sɑ̃kabane] *v.pr. Fr.C:* to shut oneself up; to see nobody; *F:* to hole up, dig in.

encadrement [ɑ̃kɑdrəmɑ̃] *n.m.* **1.** (*a*) framing; (*b*) *Mil:* officering (of unit). **2.** (*a*) framework; frame (of picture, window, etc.); **dans l'e. de la porte,** in the doorway; (*b*) setting (of story, etc.).

encadrer [ɑ̃kadre] *v.tr.* **1.** (*a*) to frame (picture, etc.); **jardin encadré de haies,** garden enclosed by hedges; *F:* **il a encadré un arbre,** he wrapped his car round a tree; (*b*) **prévenu encadré par deux gendarmes,** accused man flanked by two policemen; (*c*) *Artil:* to bracket, straddle (target). **2.** *Mil:* **e. un bataillon,** to officer a battalion.

encadreur [ɑ̃kadrœr] *n.m.* picture framer.

encagement [ɑ̃kaʒmɑ̃] *n.m.* caging (of bird, etc.).

encager [ɑ̃kaʒe] *v.tr.* **(j'encageai(s); n. encageons)**

to cage (bird); **tenir qn encagé,** to keep s.o. caged up.

encaisse [ãkɛs] *n.f.* cash (in hand); **e. de 1000 francs,** cash balance of 1000 francs; **e. or et argent d'un pays,** gold and silver holding of a country; *Bank:* **pas d'e.,** no funds.

encaissé [ãkese] *a.* boxed in; deeply embanked (river); sunken (road); **tournant e.,** blind corner.

encaissement [ãkɛsmã] *n.m.* **1.** (*a*) encashment, collection (of money or bills); (*b*) paying in (of cheque); **donner un chèque à l'e.,** to pay in a cheque. **2.** (i) embanking; (ii) embankment (of river).

encaisser [ãkese] *v.tr.* **1.** (*a*) to encash, receive, collect (money); to cash, collect (bill); (*b*) *F:* (*of boxer, etc.*) **e. un coup,** to take a blow; **il sait e.,** he can take punishment, *F:* take it; **e. sans broncher,** to grin and bear it; **je ne peux pas l'e.,** I can't stand him. **2.** to embank (river).

encaisseur [ãkɛsœr] *n.m.* bank messenger.

encan [ãkã] *n.m.* (public) auction; **vendre qch. à l'e.,** to sell sth. by, at, auction; **mettre qch. à l'e.,** to put sth. up for auction.

encanailler (s') [sãkanaje] *v.pr.* to get into, keep, bad company.

encapuchonner [ãkapyʃɔne] *v.* **1.** *v.tr.* to put a hood, cowl, on (s.o.); to hood, cover (machine, etc.). **2. s'e.** to put on a hood, a cowl; to wrap up one's head.

encart [ãkar] *n.m.* (*a*) *Bookb:* inset; (*b*) (loose) insert.

encartage [ãkartaʒ] *n.m.* **1.** (*a*) *Bookb:* insetting; (*b*) inserting (of leaflet, etc.). **2.** = ENCART.

encarter [ãkarte] *v.tr.* **1.** (*a*) *Bookb:* to inset (pages); (*b*) to insert (leaflet in book); **supplément littéraire encarté dans chaque numéro,** literary supplement folded in with each number. **2.** to card (pins, etc.). **3.** to card-index.

en-cas [ãka] *n.m.inv.* emergency supply; snack meal; **en-c. de première nécessité,** first-aid outfit.

encastré [ãkastre] *a.* embedded; inserted, sunk; built in; **serrure encastrée,** mortise lock.

encastrement [ãkastrəmã] *n.m.* **1.** embedding, housing (of sth.) (in recess). **2.** (*a*) bed, recess, housing; (*b*) frame, casing.

encastrer [ãkastre] *v.tr.* to embed, to set in, house, (beam, etc.); to recess (rivet head, etc.).

encaustiquage [ãkɔstikaʒ, -ko-] *n.m.* beeswaxing, wax-polishing (of floor, furniture).

encaustique [ãkɔstik, -ko-] *n.f.* **1.** *Art:* encaustic (painting). **2.** wax, furniture, floor, polish.

encaustiquer [ãkɔstike, -ko-] *v.tr.* to beeswax, polish (floor, etc.)

encavement [ãkavmã] *n.m.* cellaring (of wine).

encaver [ãkave] *v.tr.* to cellar (wine, etc.).

enceindre [ãsɛ̃dr̥] *v.tr.* (*conj. like* CEINDRE) to surround, encompass.

enceinte¹ [ãsɛ̃t] *n.f.* **1.** (*a*) surrounding wall; fence; (*b*) **parc qui a dix kilomètres d'e.,** park ten kilometres in circumference. **2.** enclosure; precinct(s); *Box: Turf:* ring. **3. e. (acoustique),** loudspeaker.

enceinte² *a.f.* with child; pregnant; **femme e.,** expectant mother; **e. de cinq mois,** five months pregnant, *F:* gone.

encens [ãsã] *n.m.* incense; **e. mâle,** frankincense.

encensement [ãsãsmã] *n.m.* *Ecc:* censing (of the altar, etc.).

encenser [ãsãse] *v.tr.* (*a*) to cense (altar, etc.); (*b*) to burn incense to, before (idol); *O:* **e. qn,** to shower fulsome praise, flattery, on s.o.; (*c*) *v.i.* (*of horse*) to toss its head up and down.

encenseur, -euse [ãsãsœr, -øz] *n.* (*a*) *Ecc:* thurifer, censer bearer; (*b*) *O:* flatterer, sycophant.

encensoir [ãsãswar] *n.m.* *Ecc:* censer.

encéphale [ãsefal] *n.m.* encephalon.

encéphalite [ãsefalit] *n.f.* *Med:* encephalitis; **e. léthargique,** sleeping sickness.

encéphalogramme [ãsefalɔgram] *n.m.* (electro)-encephalogram.

encéphalographie [ãsefalɔgrafi] *n.f.* (electro)-encephalography.

encéphalopathie [ãsefalɔpati] *n.f.* encephalopathy.

encerclement [ãsɛrkləmã] *n.m.* encircling.

encercler [ãsɛrkle] *v.tr.* to encircle; to shut in.

enchaîné [ɑʃene] *n.m.* **1.** chained book (in library, etc.). **2.** *Cin:* (lap) dissolve, mix.

enchaînement [ãʃɛnmã] *n.m.* **1.** chaining (up) (of animals, prisoners). **2.** (*a*) chain, series, train (of ideas, events); (*b*) *Cin:* mix, (lap) dissolve.

enchaîner [ãʃene] *v.tr.* **1.** to chain up (s.o., dog, etc.); to put (prisoner) in chains, in irons; to fetter (prisoner); *Fig:* to curb (passions); to rivet (the attention). **2.** (*a*) to link (up), connect (machinery, ideas); **e. la conversation,** to resume the conversation; **on voit comme les choses s'enchaînent,** one can see how things hang, are linked, together; (*b*) *v.i.* (*in conversation*) to resume, go on, carry on; (*c*) *Cin:* to fade in; **fondu enchaîné,** mix, (lap) dissolve.

enchanté [ãʃãte] *a.* **1.** enchanted, under a spell, bewitched; **la Flûte enchantée,** the Magic Flute. **2. être e. de qch.,** to be delighted, charmed, at, with, sth.; **e. (de faire votre connaissance),** (i) delighted to meet you; (ii) = how do you do?

enchantement [ãʃãtmã] *n.m.* **1.** enchantment, magic; (magic) spell. **2.** charm; glamour. **3.** delight; **être dans l'e.,** to be delighted.

enchanter [ãʃãte] *v.tr.* **1.** to enchant, bewitch (s.o., sth.); to lay (s.o., sth.) under a spell. **2.** to charm, delight, enrapture (s.o.); **cette idée ne l'enchante pas,** he is not taken with the idea.

enchanteur, -eresse [ãʃãtœr, -rɛs] **1.** *n* enchanter, *f.* enchantress; *F:* **c'est un e.,** he's a charmer. **2.** *a.* bewitching, captivating (smile); enchanting, delightful, charming (speech, etc.).

enchâssement [ãʃɑsmã] *n.m.* setting, mounting (of jewel).

enchâsser [ãʃɑse] *v.tr.* **1.** to enshrine (relic). **2.** (*a*) to set, mount (jewel); (*b*) *Mec.E:* to house (axle).

enchâssure [ãʃɑsyr] *n.f.* (*a*) setting, mount (of jewel; (*b*) housing (for axle).

enchatonner [ãʃatɔne] *v.tr.* to set, mount (jewel in a bezel).

enchausser [ãʃose] *v.tr.* to earth up, straw up (vegetables, etc.).

enchère [ãʃɛr] *n.f.* **une e.,** a bid; **les enchères, l'e.,** the bidding; **faire, porter, une e.,** to make a bid; **vente aux enchères,** sale by auction; **e. au rabais,** Dutch auction; *Cards:* **bridge aux enchères,** auction bridge.

enchérir [ãʃerir] **1.** *v.i.* (*a*) *O:* to rise, go up, in price; to grow dearer; (*b*) to make a higher bid; **e. de dix francs,** to bid another ten francs; **e. sur qn,** (i) to outbid s.o.; (ii) to go one better than s.o.; **e. sur les idées de qn,** to improve on s.o.'s ideas. **2.** *v.tr.* to raise, put up, the price of (goods); **sans rien e.,** without exaggeration.

enchérissement [ãʃerismã] *n.m.* rise, increase (in price).

enchérisseur, -euse [ãʃerisœr, -øz] *n.* bidder; **au dernier e., au plus offrant e.,** to the highest bidder.

enchevaucher [ãʃ(ə)voʃe] *v.tr.* to fix, lay (tiles, etc.) with an overlap; to lap (tiles).

enchevauchure [ãʃ(ə)voʃyr] *n.f.* (*a*) overlapping (of tiles, etc.); (*b*) overlap.

enchevêtré [ãʃ(ə)vetre] *a.* tangled (skein); confused, involved (style).

enchevêtrement [ãʃ(ə)vɛtrəmã] *n.m.* **1.** tangling

(up). **2.** tangle (of string, traffic), jumble (of objects, words); **e. de fils de fer,** criss-cross of wires.

enchevêtrer [ɑ̃ʃ(ə)vetre] *v.* **1.** *v.tr.* (*a*) to join (joists) by a trimmer. (*b*) to mix up, muddle up (objects) tangle up (wires). **2. s'e.,** to get mixed up, confused, entangled; (*of horse*) to get tangled up (in rope, etc.).

enchifrené [ɑ̃ʃifrəne] *a.* **il est e.,** his nose is blocked (with a cold).

enclave [ɑ̃klav] *n.f.* (*a*) (i) enclave; (ii) piece of land without access; (*b*) **l'escalier fait e. dans la pièce,** the staircase leads directly from, into, the room.

enclaver [ɑ̃klave] *v.tr.* **1.** to wedge in, fit in (timbers, etc.). **2.** to make an enclave of (territory); **domaine qui enclave deux petites terres,** estate which encloses two small properties.

enclenchement [ɑ̃klɑ̃ʃmɑ̃] *n.m. Mec.E:* throwing into gear; interlocking (of parts).

enclencher [ɑ̃klɑ̃ʃe] *v.* **1.** *v.tr. Mec.E:* to lock, engage; to throw (parts) into gear. **2. s'e.,** to engage; to come into gear (**avec,** with).

enclin [ɑ̃klɛ̃] *a.* inclined, disposed (**à qch., à faire qch.,** to sth., to do sth.); **e. aux accidents,** accident prone.

encliquetage [ɑ̃kliktaʒ] *n.m.* (pawl-and-)ratchet mechanism; **doigt d'e.,** pawl.

encliqueter [ɑ̃klikte] *v.tr.* (**j'encliquette; j'encliquetterai**) to cog, ratch (wheel, etc.); **roue encliquetée,** ratchet wheel, cog wheel.

enclitique [ɑ̃klitik] *a. & n.m. or f.* enclitic.

enclore [ɑ̃klɔr] *v.tr.* (*conj. like* CLORE) to enclose, fence in, wall in.

enclos [ɑ̃klo] *n.m.* **1.** enclosure, close; paddock. **2.** ring fence, (enclosing) wall.

enclouage [ɑ̃kluaʒ] *n.m.* **1.** *A:* spiking (of gun). **2.** *Surg:* pinning (of bone).

enclouer [ɑ̃klue] *v.tr.* **1.** to prick (horse) (in shoeing). **2.** *A:* to spike (gun). **3.** *Surg:* to pin (bone).

enclume [ɑ̃klym] *n.f.* **1.** anvil; **e. de cordonnier,** shoemender's block; **être entre l'e. et le marteau,** to be between the devil and the deep (blue) sea. **2.** incus, anvil (of inner ear).

encoche [ɑ̃kɔʃ] *n.f.* notch, nick (in stick, etc.); nock (of arrow); *Bookb:* notch (for thumb index); *El.E:* **armature à encoches,** slotted armature; *Bookb:* **avec encoches,** with thumb index.

encochement [ɑ̃kɔʃmɑ̃] *n.m.* notching, nicking.

encocher [ɑ̃kɔʃe] *v.tr.* **1.** to notch, nick (stick, etc.); *Bookb:* to notch (for thumb index). **2.** to nock (arrow on bowstring).

encoffrer [ɑ̃kɔfre] *v.tr.* to lock (sth.) up; to hoard (money).

encoignure [ɑ̃kwaɲyr] *n.f.* **1.** corner, angle (of room, street). **2.** corner cupboard.

encollage [ɑ̃kɔlaʒ] *n.m.* **1.** (*a*) gluing (of wood, etc.); (*b*) gumming, pasting (of paper, etc.); (*c*) sizing. **2.** (*a*) glue; (*b*) gum; (*c*) size.

encoller [ɑ̃kɔle] *v.tr.* (*a*) to glue (wood, etc.); (*b*) to gum, paste (paper, etc.); (*c*) to size (paper, etc.).

encolure [ɑ̃kɔlyr] *n.f.* **1.** (*a*) neck and withers (of horse); neck (of camel, ostrich); *Turf:* **gagner d'une, par une, e.,** to win by a neck; (*b*) *F:* **homme de forte e.,** thickset, stocky, man. **2.** (*a*) neck opening, neckline (of dress); **e. carrée,** square neck; (*b*) size in (men's shirt) collars. **3.** *Nau:* crown (of anchor).

encombrant [ɑ̃kɔ̃brɑ̃] *a.* cumbersome; clumsy (furniture); **colis encombrants,** bulky packages; *F:* **c'est un personnage e.,** he's always in the way.

encombre [ɑ̃kɔ̃br̥] *n.m.* **sans e.,** without mishap, without difficulty, without (let or) hindrance.

encombrement [ɑ̃kɔ̃brəmɑ̃] *n.m.* **1.** litter (of articles); congestion (of traffic, etc.), traffic jam; glut (of goods); overcrowding (of streets, the air space). **2.** floor, ground, space (required); room occupied (by engine, etc.); width of track (of car); **e. hors tout,** overall dimensions.

encombrer [ɑ̃kɔ̃bre] *v.* **1.** *v.tr.* to encumber; to clutter up (room); **e. les rues,** to congest, overcrowd, the streets; **table encombrée de papiers,** table littered with papers; **sentier encombré de ronces,** path overgrown with brambles; **e. le marché, une profession,** to glut, to overstock, the market; to overcrowd a profession. **2. s'e.,** to burden oneself, saddle oneself, load oneself up (**de,** with).

encontre (à l') [alɑ̃kɔ̃tr̥] *adv.phr.* in opposition, to the contrary; **je n'ai rien à dire à l'e.,** I have nothing to say against it; *prep.phr.* **à l'e. de,** against, in opposition to, contrary to; **aller à l'e. de la loi,** to run counter to the law.

encorbellement [ɑ̃kɔrbɛlmɑ̃] *n.m.* (*a*) *Arch:* corbelling (out) (of wall, etc.); overhang (of upper storey); **fenêtre en e.,** oriel window; **trottoir en e.,** overhanging footway, cantilever footway (of bridge).

encorder (s') [sɑ̃kɔrde] *v.pr. Mount:* to rope (up).

encore [ɑ̃kɔr] *adv.* **1.** (*a*) still; **je suis e. à chercher une explication,** I am still looking for an explanation; (*b*) yet; **je ne suis e. qu'étudiant,** I am only a student yet, so far; **pas e.,** not yet; **un homme que je n'avais e. jamais vu,** a man I had never seen before; (*c*) more, again; **e. un mot,** (just) one word more; **en voulez-vous e.?** would you like some more? **e. du mouton, s'il vous plaît!** some more mutton, please! **e. une tasse de café,** another, one more, cup of coffee; **quoi e.?** what else? **pendant trois mois e., pendant e. trois mois,** for three months longer; **réduire e. le prix,** to reduce the price still further; **e. une fois,** once more, once again; **voilà la pluie e.!** here's that rain again! **nous l'avons e. vu hier,** we saw him again yesterday; **e. autant,** as much again; **e. pis,** still worse; **e. vous!** (what) you again? **e. s'il vous plaît,** would you say that again please? **comment s'appelle-t-il e.?** what's his name again? **2.** moreover, furthermore; **non seulement stupide, mais e. têtu,** not only stupid, but also pigheaded. **3.** (*restrictive*) (*a*) **hier e. je lui ai parlé,** I spoke to him only yesterday; **e. s'il était reconnaissant!** if only he was at least grateful; (*b*) (*with inversion of subj. and vb.*) **je n'ai qu'un ciseau, e. est-il émoussé,** I have only one chisel and even that is blunt; **e. vous aurait-il fallu me prévenir,** all the same you should have let me know; (*c*) **il vous en donnera dix francs et e.!** he will give you ten francs for it, if that! (*d*) *conj.phr.* **e. (bien) que** + *sub.*, (al)though, even though; **e. qu'il ne me soit rien,** although he is nothing to me; **temps agréable e. qu'un peu froid,** pleasant weather if rather cold. **4. il s'est montré très discret—mais e.!** he was very reticent—but what *did* he say?

encorné [ɑ̃kɔrne] *a.* horned (animal).

encorner [ɑ̃kɔrne] *v.tr.* (*of bull*) to gore, toss (s.o.).

encornet [ɑ̃kɔrnɛ] *n.m. Moll:* squid; calamary.

encourageant [ɑ̃kuraʒɑ̃] *a.* encouraging, cheering; cheerful (news).

encouragement [ɑ̃kuraʒmɑ̃] *n.m.* encouragement; **e. à la vertu,** incentive to virtue; **recevoir peu d'e., d'encouragements, à faire qch.,** to receive little encouragement, little inducement, to do sth.

encourager [ɑ̃kuraʒe] *v.tr.* (**j'encourageai(s)**) **1.** to encourage, hearten (s.o.); **e. qn à faire qch.,** to encourage s.o. to do sth.; **e. qn au bien,** to encourage s.o. in well-doing. **2.** to encourage, foster, promote (the arts); to promote, countenance (scheme).

encourir [ɑ̃kurir] *v.tr.* (*conj. like* COURIR) to incur (reproaches, expense); to bring (punishment, reproaches) upon oneself.

encrage [ɑ̃kraʒ] *n.m. Typ:* inking (up).

encrassement [ãkrasmã] *n.m.* dirtying (of clothes); fouling (of fire-arms); fouling, sooting (up), oiling up (of sparking plug); clogging, choking (of machine); gumming up (of piston).

encrasser [ãkrase] *v.* **1.** *v.tr.* to dirty, grease (one's clothes); to foul (gun); to oil up; to soot up (sparking plug); to clog, choke (machine). **2. s'e.,** to get dirty, greasy; to get foul; to soot up, oil up, gum up.

encre [ãkr̥] *n.f.* (*a*) ink; **e. de Chine,** Indian ink; **e. d'impression,** printing ink; **e. sympathique,** invisible ink; **écrit à l'e.,** written in ink; **dessinateur à l'e.,** black and white artist; **doigts couverts d'e.,** inky fingers; *F:* **c'est la bouteille à l'e.,** there's no making head or tail of it; **noir comme de l'e.,** inky black, murky; (*b*) ink (of cuttlefish).

encrer [ãkre] *v.tr.* to ink.

encreur [ãkrœr] *a.* **ruban e.,** (typewriter) ribbon; *Typ:* **rouleau e.,** inker.

encrier [ãkrije] *n.m.* **1.** ink pot, inkstand; inkwell. **2.** *Typ:* ink trough.

encroûtant [ãkrutã] *a.* (*a*) encrusting; (*b*) *F:* soul-destroying (occupation, etc.).

encroûté [ãkrute] *a.* (*a*) (en)crusted, crusted over; (*b*) **vieux bonhomme e.,** old fogey, stick-in-the-mud.

encroûtement [ãkrutmã] *n.m.* **1.** (*a*) encrusting, crusting over (of sth.); (*b*) *F:* sinking into the rut. **2.** crust; scale (in boiler); fur, deposit (in kettle).

encroûter [ãkrute] *v.* **1.** *v.tr.* to encrust (sth.); to cover (sth.) with a crust; to cake (sth.) with mud, etc. **2. s'e.** (*a*) to become encrusted, crusted over, caked over (**de,** with); (*b*) *F:* to sink into a rut; to become hidebound, *F:* fossilized.

encuver [ãkyve] *v.tr.* to vat (hides, grapes).

encyclique [ãsiklik] *a. & n.f.* encyclical (letter).

encyclopédie [ãsiklɔpedi] *n.f.* encyclop(a)edia; *F:* **e. vivante,** walking encyclopaedia.

encyclopédique [ãsiklɔpedik] *a.* encyclop(a)edic.

encyclopédiste [ãsiklɔpedist] *n.m.* encyclop(a)edist.

endémie [ãdemi] *n.f.* endemic (disease).

endémique [ãdemik] *a.* endemic.

endenté [ãdãte] *a.* **1.** having teeth; **mâchoires vigoureusement endentées,** jaws with strong rows of teeth. **2.** (*a*) cogged, toothed (wheel); (*b*) scarf (joint); (*c*) indented (line, etc.).

endenter [ãdãte] *v.tr.* **1.** (*a*) to furnish (s.o., sth.) with teeth; (*b*) to tooth, cog, ratch (wheel, etc.); (*c*) to mesh (wheels). **2.** to indent (line, etc.). **3.** *Carp:* to scarf (timbers).

endetté [ãdɛte] *a.* in debt.

endettement [ãdɛtmã] *n.m.* running into debt.

endetter (s') [sãdete] *v.pr.* to get, run, into debt.

endeuiller [ãdœje] *v.tr.* to put, plunge, (s.o., sth.) into mourning; to cast gloom over (event); **maison endeuillée,** house of mourning.

endiablé [ãdjable] *a.* (*a*) reckless, devil-may-care (courage, etc.); wild, frenzied (music, etc.); (*b*) devilish (wind, etc.).

endiamanté [ãdjamãte] *a.* studded with diamonds; (hands) covered with diamonds.

endiguement [ãdigmã] *n.m.* **1.** (*a*) damming (up); (*b*) embanking (of river, etc.). **2.** (*a*) dam; (*b*) sea wall; (*c*) embankment, dyke.

endiguer [ãdige] *v.tr.* **1.** to dam up (river, etc.). **2.** to (em)bank (river, etc.); to dyke (land). **3.** to impound (water).

endimanché [ãdimãʃe] *a.* all dressed up, in one's Sunday best.

endimancher (s') [sãdimãʃe] *v.pr.* to put on one's best clothes, one's Sunday best.

endive [ãdiv] *n.f.* **1.** endive. **2.** witloof, broad-leaved chicory.

endocarde [ãdɔkard] *n.m.* *Anat:* endocardium.

endocardite [ãdɔkardit] *n.f.* *Med:* endocarditis.

endocarpe [ãdɔkarp] *n.m.* *Bot:* endocarp.

endocrine [ãdɔkrin] *a.f.* endocrine (gland).

endocrinien, -ienne [ãdɔkrinjɛ̃, -jɛn] *a.* endocrine, endocrinal (glands, etc.).

endocrinologie [ãdɔkrinɔlɔʒi] *n.f.* endocrinology.

endoctrinement [ãdɔktrinmã] *n.m.* indoctrination.

endoctriner [ãdɔktrine] *v.tr.* to indoctrinate; *F:* to brainwash.

endogamie [ãdɔgami] *n.f.* endogamy; inbreeding.

endolori [ãdɔlɔri] *a.* painful, sore; tender.

endolorir [ãdɔlɔrir] *v.* **1.** *v.tr.* to make (limb, etc.) ache. **2. s'e.,** to become painful.

endolorissement [ãdɔlɔrismã] *n.m.* ache, pain (in limb, etc.); tenderness.

endométrite [ãdɔmetrit] *n.f.* endometritis.

endommagement [ãdɔmaʒmã] *n.m.* damage, injury (**de,** to).

endommager [ãdɔmaʒe] *v.tr.* **(j'endommageai(s))** to damage, injure; to do damage to (sth.).

endormant [ãdɔrmã] *a.* **1.** soporific. **2.** *F:* boring, wearisome (speech); humdrum (task).

endormi, -ie [ãdɔrmi] *a.* **1.** (*a*) asleep, sleeping; (*b*) *F:* **être e.,** to be a slowcoach; *n.* **c'est un e.,** he's a sleepy-head; (*c*) dormant (passion, etc.) **2. j'ai la jambe endormie,** my leg has gone to sleep, is numb.

endormir [ãdɔrmir] *v.* (*conj. like* DORMIR) **1.** *v.tr.* (*a*) to put, send, lull (s.o.) to sleep; to bore (s.o.); to hypnotize; to anaesthetize (patient); (*b*) to deaden (pain); (*c*) **e. les soupçons,** to allay suspicion. **2. s'e.,** to fall asleep; to go, drop off, to sleep.

endos [ãdo] *n.m.* endorsement (on cheque).

endoscope [ãdɔskɔp] *n.m.* *Med:* endoscope.

endosmose [ãdɔsmoz] *n.f.* endosmosis.

endossable [ãdosabl̥] *a.* endorsable (cheque).

endossataire [ãdosatɛr] *n.m. & f.* endorsee.

endossement [ãdosmã] *n.m.* **1.** (*a*) putting on, slipping on (of jacket, etc.); (*b*) *F:* shouldering (of responsibility). **2.** *Com:* (*a*) endorsing; (*b*) = ENDOS. **3.** *Bookb:* = ENDOSSURE.

endosser [ãdose] *v.tr.* **1.** to put on (jacket, etc.); (*b*) to assume, shoulder (a responsibility). **2.** to endorse (cheque); to back (bill). **3.** *Bookb:* to back (book).

endosseur, -euse [ãdosœr, -øz] *n.* endorser (of bill, etc.).

endossure [ãdosyr] *n.f.* *Bookb:* backing, rounding (of back).

endroit [ãdrwa] *n.m.* **1.** place, spot; **par endroits,** here and there, in places; **j'ai perdu l'e.,** I've lost my place (in the book); **rire au bon e.,** to laugh in the right place; *F:* **le petit e.,** the loo, *NAm:* the john. **2.** side, aspect; **prendre qn par son e. faible,** to get on the soft side of s.o. **3.** right side (of material); **à l'e.,** right way out, round, up; **tissu à deux endroits,** reversible material; *Knit:* **maille à l'e.,** plain stitch.

enduire [ãdɥir] *v.tr.* (*pr.p.* **enduisant;** *p.p.* **enduit;** *pr.ind.* **j'enduis, il enduit;** *impf.* **j'enduisais;** *p.h.* **j'enduisis;** *fu.* **j'enduirai**) to smear, besmear, cover, coat (surface); **e. un mur de chaux, de ciment,** to plaster a wall; to render a wall with cement; **e. la peau de vaseline,** to smear the skin with vaseline.

enduit [ãdɥi] *n.m.* **1.** (*a*) coat, coating (of tar, paint, etc.); (*b*) *Const:* plastering, coat of plaster; **e. de ciment,** cement rendering. **2.** (water)proofing (of cloth, etc.). **3.** *Cer:* glaze, glazing. **4.** *Phot:* **e. anti-halo,** backing.

endurable [ãdyrabl̥] *a.* endurable.

endurance [ãdyrãs] *n.f.* endurance. **1.** long-suffering, patience. **2.** resistance to wear and tear; *Aut: etc:* **épreuve, course, d'e.,** reliability trial, run. **3.** stamina; staying-power.

endurant [ɑ̃dyrɑ̃] *a.* (*a*) *O:* enduring, long-suffering; (*b*) resistant; tough.

endurci [ɑ̃dyrsi] *a.* tough; hard, callous (heart); hardened (sinner); confirmed (bachelor); inveterate (hatred).

endurcir [ɑ̃dyrsir] *v.* **1.** *v.tr.* (*a*) **e. le cœur de qn,** to harden s.o.'s heart; (*b*) **être endurci à la fatigue,** to be inured, hardened, to fatigue. **2. s'e.** (*a*) to harden, become hard; (*b*) to become hardened, fit, tough.

endurcissement [ɑ̃dyrsismɑ̃] *n.m.* **1. e. à la fatigue,** inuring (of s.o.) to fatigue; toughening (up). **2.** hardness (of heart); callousness.

endurer [ɑ̃dyre] *v.tr.* to endure, bear (hardship, ill-treatment; **e. des railleries,** to put up with joking.

Énéide (l') [leneid] *Pr.n.f. Lt.Lit:* the Aeneid.

énéma [enema] *n.m. Med:* enema.

énergétique [enɛrʒetik] **1.** *a.* (*a*) energizing (medicine, food, etc.); (*b*) **dépense e.,** expenditure of energy, power. **2.** *n.f.* energetics.

énergie [enɛrʒi] *n.f.* **1.** energy; force, vigour; **apporter, appliquer, toute son é. à une tâche, à faire qch.,** devote, direct, all one's energies to a task, to doing sth.; **avec é.,** energetically; **sans é.,** listless(ly). **2.** (*a*) **é. cinétique,** kinetic energy; **é. potentielle,** potential energy; **é. atomique,** atomic energy, nuclear power; (*b*) *Ind:* energy, (fuel and) power.

énergique [enɛrʒik] *a.* energetic; (*a*) **travailleur e.,** strenuous worker; (*b*) strong, drastic (measures); forcible (language); emphatic (gesture); forceful (kick); powerful (medicine).

énergiquement [enɛrʒikmɑ̃] *adv.* energetically; forcefully; strenuously; **s'y mettre é.,** to put one's back into it.

énergumène [enɛrgymɛn] *n.m. & f.* **1.** energumen; **crier comme un é.,** to scream like one possessed. **2.** *F:* fanatic; ranter.

énervant [enɛrvɑ̃] *a.* **1.** enervating (climate). **2.** irritating (person, habit, etc.); nerve-racking (noise).

énervé [enɛrve] *a. F:* (*of pers.*) fidgety, nervy; nervous (giggle).

énervement [enɛrvəmɑ̃] *n.m.* nervous irritation; restiveness.

énerver [enɛrve] *v.* **1.** *v.tr.* (*a*) to enervate, weaken; (*b*) to hamstring (horse); (*c*) **é. qn,** to get on s.o.'s nerves, to set s.o.'s nerves on edge, to fray s.o.'s nerves, to irritate s.o. **2. s'e.,** to become irritable, fidgety, nervy, restive; to get excited; to get (all) worked up.

enfaîteau, -eaux [ɑ̃fɛto] *n.m.* ridge tile.

enfaîtement [ɑ̃fɛtmɑ̃] *n.m.* ridge tiling, ridging.

enfaîter [ɑ̃fete] *v.tr. Const:* to ridge (roof); to finish off (roof) with ridge tiles, galvanized iron.

enfance [ɑ̃fɑ̃s] *n.f.* **1.** (*a*) childhood; **première e.,** infancy; **l'e. de la civilisation,** the dawn, beginning, of civilization; *F:* **c'est l'e. de l'art,** it's (mere) child's play; **industrie encore dans son e.,** industry still in its infancy; (*b*) boyhood; girlhood. **2.** childishness; **retomber en e.,** to sink into one's second childhood, into one's dotage. **3.** *coll.* children.

enfant [ɑ̃fɑ̃] *n.m. & f.* **1.** (*a*) child; boy or girl; *F:* youngster; *Jur:* infant; **e. en bas âge, du premier âge,** infant; **c'est une belle e.,** she is a beautiful child; **e. trouvé,** foundling; *F:* **ce n'est qu'un jeu d'e.,** it is child's play; **babil d'e.,** childish prattle; **se conduire en e., faire l'e.,** to behave childishly; **contes pour les enfants,** nursery tales; (*b*) *a.* childlike; babyish (smile, etc.); **ne soyez pas si e.,** don't be so childish; (*c*) *F:* lad, fellow, man; **allons-y, mes enfants!** come on, lads! (*d*) **manière bon e.,** kindly, good-natured, manner; **il est trop bon e. pour garder rancune,** he is too decent a chap to bear a grudge. **2.** (*a*) offspring; **elle attend un e.,** she's expecting a child; *F:* **c'est son e.,** it's his baby, his brainchild; **mourir sans enfants,** to die childless, *Jur:* without issue; (*b*) descendant; **les enfants d'Israël,** the children of Israel; (*c*) **un e. de Paris,** a native of Paris.

enfantement [ɑ̃fɑ̃tmɑ̃] *n.m.* **1.** childbirth. **2.** giving birth (to a literary work).

enfanter [ɑ̃fɑ̃te] *v.tr.* to bear, to give birth to (child); **la discorde enfante le crime,** discord begets crime.

enfantillage [ɑ̃fɑ̃tijaʒ] *n.m.* **1.** childishness. **2.** childish act, saying; baby trick.

enfantin [ɑ̃fɑ̃tɛ̃] *a.* **1.** childish (voice, game, etc.); **littérature enfantine,** children's, juvenile, literature; **babil e.,** baby talk. **2.** elementary; **c'est e.,** it's just too easy; it's child's play.

enfariné [ɑ̃farine] *a.* floured, covered with flour; *F:* (face) smothered in powder.

enfer [ɑ̃fɛr] *n.m.* **1.** hell; **les enfers,** the underworld; Hades; **l'E. de Dante,** Dante's Inferno; **aller en e.,** to go to hell; **il fait de ma vie un e.,** he has made my life hell; **aller un train d'e.,** to go at top speed; to ride hell for leather; (*of car, etc.*) to scorch along; **bruit d'e.,** hellish noise. **2.** library department containing books not available to the public.

enfermer [ɑ̃fɛrme] *v.* **1.** *v.tr.* (*a*) to shut (s.o., sth.) up; **e. qch., qn, à clef,** to lock sth., s.o., up; **tenir qn enfermé,** to keep s.o. in confinement; **j'ai été enfermé dans une pièce toute la journée,** I have been cooped up in a room all day; (*of room*) **sentir l'enfermé,** to smell stuffy; *F:* **il est bon à e.,** he ought to be locked up; (*b*) to shut, hem, (sth.) in; to enclose, surround; *Rac:* to hem, box, in (competitor). **2. s'e.,** to lock oneself in, to shut, coop, oneself up; **enfermé dans ses pensées,** wrapped up in his thoughts; **vivre trop enfermé,** to live too much indoors.

enfeu [ɑ̃fø] *n.m. Arch:* recess (tomb).

enfieller [ɑ̃fjɛle] *v.tr.* to embitter, sour (s.o.).

enfiévré [ɑ̃fjevre] *a.* fevered (brow); feverish (activity).

enfièvrement [ɑ̃fjɛvrəmɑ̃] *n.m.* fever (of excitement).

enfiévrer [ɑ̃fjevre] *v.* **(j'enfièvre; j'enfiéverai). 1.** *v.tr.* (*a*) to give (s.o.) fever; to make (s.o.) feverish; (*b*) to excite, fire, animate (s.o.). **2. s'e.** (*a*) to grow feverish; (*b*) to get excited, *F:* (all) worked up.

enfilade [ɑ̃filad] *n.f.* **1.** succession, series (of doors, etc.); suite (of rooms, etc.); **maisons en e.,** row of houses. **2.** *Mil:* enfilade; **tir d'e.,** raking, enfilading, fire.

enfiler [ɑ̃file] *v.tr.* **1.** to thread (needle); to file (papers on spike file); to string (beads); to string (words) together; **e. qn,** to run s.o. through (with a sword, etc.). **2.** to take, go along (a street).**3.** to slip on (clothes); to pull on, draw on (trousers, stockings); **blouse à e.,** slip-on blouse. **4.** *F:* **s'e.** (*a*) to down (a drink); **s'e. un bon dîner,** to get outside a good dinner; (*b*) to plod through, *F:* be stuck with (task). **5.** *Mil:* to enfilade, rake (troops).

enfin [ɑ̃fɛ̃] **1.** *adv.* (*a*) finally, lastly, after all; **e. et surtout,** last but not least; (*b*) in fact, in a word, in short; (*c*) at last, at length; **e. vous voilà! vous voilà e.!** here you are at last! **2.** *int.* (*a*) that's that! (*b*) **mais e., s'il acceptait!** but still, if he did accept! (*c*) **e.! ce qui est fait est fait,** anyhow, after all, what is done is done.

enflammé [ɑ̃flame] *a.* **1.** burning, blazing (wood, etc.); fiery (sun, sunset). **2.** (*a*) blazing, glowing (cheeks); (*b*) inflamed (wound). **3.** fiery (speech).

enflammement [ɑ̃flɑm(ə)mɑ̃] *n.m.* **1.** blazing (of fire, etc.). **2.** *F:* exciting, stirring up (of passions).

enflammer [ɑ̃flɑme] *v.* **1.** *v.tr.* to inflame. (*a*) to ignite; to set (sth.) on fire, ablaze; **e. une allumette,** to strike a match; (*b*) to inflame (wound); (*c*) to excite, fire, stir up (s.o.). **2. s'e.** (*a*) to catch fire, to ignite, to burst into flame, to blaze up, to flare up; (*b*) (*of wound, etc.*) to become inflamed; (*c*) (*of pers.*) to be stirred up; **s'e. de colère,** to flare up.

enflé [ɑ̃fle] *a.* swollen (river, limb, etc.); turgid, bombastic (style); *n.m. F:* **espèce d'e.!** you idiot!
enfléchure [ɑ̃fleʃyr] *n.f. Nau:* ratline.
enfler [ɑ̃fle] **1.** *v.tr.* (*a*) to swell; to cause (sth.) to swell; **e. les joues,** to puff out, blow out, one's cheeks; (*of wind*) **e. les voiles,** to fill the sails; **e. la voix,** to raise one's voice; **e. le nombre, la dépense,** to swell, add to, the number, the expenditure; (*b*) **e. son style,** to inflate one's style. **2.** *v.i. & pr.* to swell; **son bras (s')enfle,** his arm is swelling; **la rivière (s')enfle,** the river is rising.
enflure [ɑ̃flyr] *n.f.* (*a*) swelling (of cheek, limb); (*b*) turgidity (of style).
enfoncé [ɑ̃fɔ̃se] *a.* (*a*) sunken, deep (cavity, ravine, etc.); deep-set (eyes); (*b*) low-lying (ground, village).
enfoncement [ɑ̃fɔ̃smɑ̃] *n.m.* **1.** (*a*) driving (in) (of pile, nail); breaking open (of door, etc.); (*b*) sinking in; (*c*) staving in (of metal, wall, etc.). **2.** (*a*) hollow, depression (in the ground); (*b*) *Arch:* alcove, recess; (*c*) *Nau:* bay, bight.
enfoncer [ɑ̃fɔ̃se] *v.* **(j'enfonçai(s)) 1.** *v.tr.* (*a*) to drive (in) (pile, nail); **e. la main dans sa poche,** to thrust one's hand into one's pocket; *F:* to dive into one's pocket; **e. son chapeau sur sa tête,** to cram one's hat on one's head; **e. la clef dans la serrure,** to insert the key in the lock; *F:* **je ne peux pas lui e. cela dans la tête,** I can't get, drive, it into his head; (*b*) to break open, burst in (door, etc.); to stave in (cask); **e. un carreau,** to break a window pane; *Fig:* **e. une porte ouverte,** to flog a dead horse; **e. tous les obstacles,** to break through all obstacles; (*c*) *F:* to get the better of (s.o.). **2.** *v.i.* to sink (into mud, sea); **le navire enfonçait,** the ship was settling; **nous y avons enfoncé jusqu'aux genoux,** we sank into it up to our knees. **3. s'e.,** to penetrate, plunge, go deep (into sth.); (*of ship*) to sink, settle; (*of floor*) to subside, give way; **la balle s'enfonça dans le mur,** the bullet embedded itself in the wall; **s'e. dans l'ombre,** to disappear in, be swallowed up by, the darkness; **s'e. dans une rue,** to turn into a street; **s'e. dans l'étude,** to bury oneself in study; **s'e. dans le crime,** to sink deep(er) into crime.
enfonceur, -euse [ɑ̃fɔ̃sœr, -øz] *n.* **c'est un e. de portes ouvertes,** he's got a gift for stating the obvious.
enfonçure [ɑ̃fɔ̃syr] *n.f.* cavity; depression, hollow; recess.
enfouir [ɑ̃fwir] *v.* **1.** *v.tr.* to hide, cover up, (sth.) in the ground; to bury (treasure); to plough in (manure). **2. s'e.,** to retire, to hide oneself; **s'e. dans la campagne,** to bury oneself in the country.
enfouissement [ɑ̃fwismɑ̃] *n.m.* burying (of treasure); ploughing in (of manure).
enfourcher [ɑ̃furʃe] *v.tr.* to get astride, mount (horse, bicycle).
enfourchure [ɑ̃furʃyr] *n.f.* fork (of tree, legs); crotch (of tree).
enfournage [ɑ̃furnaʒ] *n.m.*, **enfournement** [ɑ̃furnəmɑ̃] *n.m.* placing (of bread) in the oven, (of pottery) in the kiln.
enfourner [ɑ̃furne] *v.tr.* to put (bread, etc.) in an oven, (pottery, bricks) in a kiln; *F:* to gobble (sth.) up.
enfourneur [ɑ̃furnœr] *n.m.* oven man; kiln man; charger.
enfreindre [ɑ̃frɛ̃dr̥] *v.tr.* (*pr.p.* **enfreignant;** *p.p.* **enfreint;** *pr.ind.* **j'enfreins, il enfreint, ils enfreignent;** *impf.* **j'enfreignais;** *p.h.* **j'enfreignis;** *fu.* **j'enfreindrai)** to infringe, transgress, break (the law); to act contrary to (rules, orders); **e. les dispositions d'un traité,** to violate a treaty.
enfuir (s') [sɑ̃fɥir] *v.pr.* (*conj. like* FUIR) **1.** to flee, fly; to run away; to slip away; (*of embezzler*) to abscond; (*of lovers*) to elope; **s'e. de prison,** to escape from prison; **à mesure que les jours s'enfuyaient,** as the days flew by; **les côtes s'enfuient,** the coast recedes. **2.** (*of liquid*) to leak out, run out.
enfumé [ɑ̃fyme] *a.* (*a*) smoky (room, etc.); (*b*) smoke-blackened (walls, etc.).
enfumer [ɑ̃fyme] *v.tr.* (*a*) to fill (room, etc.) with smoke; (*b*) to blacken (sth.) with smoke; (*c*) to smoke out (bees, etc.).
enfûtage [ɑ̃fytaʒ] *n.m.* barrelling (of wine).
enfutailler [ɑ̃fytaje], **enfûter** [ɑ̃fyte] *v.tr.* to barrel, cask (wine).
engagé [ɑ̃gaʒe] **1.** *a.* (*a*) *Arch:* engaged; (*b*) (*of ship*) gunwale under; on her beam-ends; (*c*) committed (literature, etc.) **2.** *n.m. Mil:* **e. (volontaire),** volunteer; *Turf:* **la liste des engagés,** the list of entries.
engageant [ɑ̃gaʒɑ̃] *a.* engaging, prepossessing (manner, etc.).
engagement [ɑ̃gaʒmɑ̃] *n.m.* **1.** (*a*) pawning, pledging (of jewels, etc.); mortgaging (of estate); (*b*) tying up, locking up (of capital). **2.** (*a*) engagement, promise, contract; commitment; **tenir ses engagements, faire honneur, faire face, à ses engagements,** to keep, observe, carry out, one's engagements; to meet one's obligations, one's liabilities; **contracter, prendre, un e.,** to enter into a contract, an engagement; **sans e.,** without obligation; (*b*) engagement, appointment (of employee); booking (of pianist, etc.); *Mil:* voluntary enlistment; **se trouver sans e.,** to be out of a job; *Th: F:* to be resting; (*c*) *Sp:* (i) entering, (ii) entry (for sporting event); (iii) fixture. **3.** (*a*) *Mil: Navy:* engagement, action; (*b*) (*hockey*) **e. du jeu,** bully. **4.** commitment (to), alignment (with) (a cause).
engager [ɑ̃gaʒe] *v.* **(j'engageai(s)) I.** *v.tr.* **1.** (*a*) to pledge, pawn (jewellery, etc.); to mortgage (property); **e. sa parole,** to pledge one's word; **cette lettre ne vous engage pas,** this letter does not bind you, commit you; (*b*) *Rac:* to enter (a horse). **2.** to engage (cook, etc.); to take on (hands), to sign on (crew); to enlist (recruit). **3.** (*a*) to catch, foul, entangle (rope, etc.); to jam (machinery); **e. une ancre,** to foul an anchor; **e. un aviron,** to catch a crab; **e. un vaisseau,** to run a ship aground; **e. qn dans une querelle,** to involve s.o. in, draw s.o. into, a quarrel; (*b*) *Fin:* to lock up, tie up (money); (*c*) to engage (machinery), to put (machinery) into gear; (*d*) **e. le pied dans l'étrier,** to put one's foot in the stirrup; **e. la clef dans la serrure,** to fit, insert, the key in the lock. **4.** to begin, start; to set (sth.) going; to open (conversation, fight); to enter, start upon (negotiations); *Jur:* to institute (proceedings); **e. le combat,** to join battle; to engage; **e. des troupes,** to bring troops into action, to engage troops; *Hockey:* **e. le jeu,** to bully off. **5. e. qn à faire qch.,** to invite, urge, advise, s.o. to do sth.; **le beau temps nous engage à sortir,** the fine weather makes us go out. **6.** *v.i.* (*a*) (*of machinery*) to come into gear; (*b*) (*of ship*) to roll gunwale under. **II. s'engager 1. s'e. à faire qch.,** to undertake, commit oneself, to do sth.; **s'e. par traité à faire qch.,** to contract to do sth.; **sans s'e. à rien,** without pinning oneself down (to anything); **je suis trop engagé pour reculer,** I have gone too far to draw back. **2.** (*a*) **s'e. chez qn,** to enter s.o.'s service; (*b*) *Mil:* to enlist; join up; (*c*) **s'e. pour une course,** to enter for a race. **3.** (*of rope, propeller*) to foul; to become fouled; (*of machine*) to jam; (*of aircraft*) to get out of control. **4.** (*a*) **un tube s'engage dans l'ouverture,** a pipe fits into the opening; (*b*) **s'e. dans une rue, forêt,** to turn into a street, enter a forest; (*c*) (*of battle, etc.*) to begin.
engainer [ɑ̃gene] *v.tr.* to sheathe (dagger).
engazonnement [ɑ̃gazɔnmɑ̃] *n.m.* **1.** turfing (of ground). **2.** sowing with grass seed.

engazonner [ãgazɔne] *v.tr.* **1.** to turf (ground). **2.** to sow with grass seed.

engeance [ãʒãs] *n.f. F:* **e. de scélérats,** bunch of scoundrels; **quelle e.!** what a crew!

engelure [ãʒlyr] *n.f.* chilblain.

engendrement [ãʒãdrəmã] *n.m.* **1.** begetting (of children). **2.** production; generation (of heat, etc.); breeding (of disease, etc.).

engendrer [ãʒãdre] *v.tr.* **1.** to beget (child); (*of stallion, etc.*) to sire. **2.** (*a*) to engender, give rise to (strife); to breed (disease); (*b*) to generate, develop (heat, etc.).

engerbage [ãʒɛrbaʒ] *n.m.* binding (of sheaves).

engerber [ãʒɛrbe] *v.tr. Agr:* to sheaf; to bind (wheat) in sheaves.

engin [ãʒɛ̃] *n.m.* **1.** (*a*) engine, machine; device, contrivance; **engins de pêche,** fishing tackle; **e. de sauvetage,** rescue appliance; life-saving apparatus; (*b*) *P.N:* **passage d'engins,** heavy plant crossing. **2.** **engins de guerre,** engines, appliances, of war; **e. amphibie,** amphibian, amphibious, craft, vehicle; **e. téléguidé,** guided missile; **e. air-air,** air-to-air missile; **e. à moteur interne,** hot missile.

englober [ãglɔbe] *v.tr.* to include; to take (sth.) in; **e. les innocents parmi les coupables,** to include the innocent with the guilty; **ces états furent englobés dans l'Empire,** these states were merged in the Empire.

engloutir [ãglutir] *v.* **1.** *v.tr.* (*a*) to swallow; to gulp (sth.) down; to wolf down (food); (*b*) to engulf (sth.), to swallow (ship, etc.) up; **e. une fortune dans une entreprise,** to sink a fortune in an undertaking. **2.** **s'e.,** (*of ship*) to be engulfed; to sink.

engloutissement [ãglutismã] *n.m.* **1.** swallowing, gulping down (of food). **2.** sinking (of ship, by sea); swallowing up (of fortune).

engluage [ãglyaʒ] *n.m.*, **engluement** [ãglymã] *n.m.* (*a*) liming (of twigs, birds); (*b*) birdlime.

engluer [ãglye] *v.tr.* (*a*) to lime (twigs, bird); *F:* to trap (s.o.); **se laisser e.,** to allow oneself to to be taken in.

engorgement [ãgɔrʒəmã] *n.m.* **1.** choking, stopping (up), blocking, clogging (of passage, pipe, etc.); **l'e. des marchés,** glutting of the markets. **2.** obstruction, stoppage; *Med:* engorgement, congestion.

engorger [ãgɔrʒe] *v.* **(j'engorgeai(s)) 1.** *v.tr.* to choke (up), stop (up), to block, clog (passage, pipe, etc.); to glut (market). **2.** **s'e.,** to become choked (up), blocked (up), clogged; *Med:* (*of gland*) to become engorged, congested.

engouement [ãgumã] *n.m.* **1.** *Med:* obstruction, choking up (of hernia). **2.** infatuation, craze (**pour qn, qch.,** for s.o., sth.).

engouer (s') [sãgwe] *v.pr.* **1.** *Med:* (*of hernia*) to become obstructed. **2.** **s'e. de qn, de qch.,** to become infatuated with s.o., to go crazy over s.o., sth.

engouffrement [ãgufrəmã] *n.m.* engulfment, engulfing, swallowing up (of vessel by the sea, etc.);

engouffrer [ãgufre] *v.* **1.** *v.tr.* to engulf; **e. une fortune,** to swallow up a fortune; **e. sa nourriture,** to devour, gulp down, wolf, one's food. **2.** **s'e.,** to be engulfed, swallowed up, lost to sight; **il s'engouffra dans le hall de la gare,** he disappeared into the station; **le vent s'engouffra par la porte,** the wind swept in.

engoulevent [ãgulvã] *n.m. Orn:* nightjar.

engourdi [ãgurdi] *a.* **1.** numb(ed); **j'ai le pied e.,** my foot has gone to sleep. **2.** dull, sluggish (mind).

engourdir [ãgurdir] *v.* **1.** *v.tr.* to (be)numb (limb). **2.** **s'e.** (*a*) (*of limb, etc.*) to grow numb, *F:* to go to sleep; (*b*) (*of the mind*) to become dull, sluggish, torpid; (*c*) (*of hibernating animal*) to become dormant.

engourdissement [ãgurdismã] *n.m.* **1.** numbness (of limb, etc.). **2.** dullness, torpor (of mind, etc.); sluggishness (of the market). **3.** torpor (of hibernating animal).

engrais [ãgrɛ] *n.m.* **1.** *Husb:* fattening food, pasture; food; **mettre des bœufs à l'e.,** to put cattle to fatten. **2.** manure; **e. chimiques,** chemical fertilizers.

engraissage [ãgrɛsaʒ] *n.m.*, **engraissement** [ãgrɛsmã] *n.m.* fattening (of animals).

engraisser [ãgrese] **1.** *v.tr.* (*a*) to fatten (animals); (*b*) to make (s.o.) fat; (*c*) to fertilize (land). **2.** *v.i. & pr.* (*of pers., animal*) to get fat, put on flesh; (*of pers.*) to grow stout.

engrangement [ãgrãʒmã] *n.m.* getting in, garnering (of cereals).

engranger [ãgrãʒe] *v.tr.* **(j'engrangeai(s); n. engrangeons)** to get in, garner (cereals).

engravement [ãgravmã] *n.m.* **1.** grounding, stranding (of boat). **2.** silting up (of harbour).

engraver [ãgrave] **1.** *v.tr.* to strand (ship). **2.** *v.i. & pr.* (*a*) (*of boat*) to ground; to run on to the sand; (*b*) (*of harbour*) to silt up.

engrenage [ãgrənaʒ] *n.m.* (toothed) gearing; gear; gear wheels; **e. hélicoïdal,** helical gear, screw gear; **système, jeu, d'engrenages,** train, set, of gear wheels; gearing; *Fig:* **être pris dans l'e.,** to get caught (up) in the mesh, the machine.

engrènement [ãgrɛnmã] *n.m.* **1.** feeding (of threshing machine) with wheat, corn. **2.** *Mec.E:* coming into gear, meshing, engaging.

engrener [ãgrəne] *v.tr.* **(j'engrène; j'engrènerai) 1.** to feed wheat, corn (into threshing machine). **2.** (*a*) *Mec.E:* to gear, put into gear, engage, mesh (toothed wheels); *F:* **e. une affaire,** to set a thing going; (*b*) *v.i. & pr.* **roues qui (s')engrènent,** wheels that gear, engage, into one another, that mesh with one another.

engrenure [ãgrənyr] *n.f.* **1.** *Mec.E:* (*a*) engaging, meshing (of toothed wheels); (*b*) gear ratio. **2.** *Anat:* serrated suture.

engrosser [ãgrose] *v.tr. P:* to make (woman) pregnant.

engueulade [ãgœlad] *n.f.*, **engueulement** [ãgœlmã] *n.m. P:* scolding, slanging; blowing up; **recevoir une e.,** to be hauled over the coals.

engueuler [ãgœle] *v.tr. P:* to abuse, slang (s.o.); to blow (s.o.) up; **ils se sont engueulés,** they had a row.

enguirlander [ãgirlãde] *v.tr.* **1.** to (en)garland, wreathe. **2.** *F:* = ENGUEULER.

enhardir [ãardir] *v.* **1.** *v.tr.* to embolden; to put courage into (s.o.); to give (s.o.) courage. **2.** **s'e.,** to pluck up courage; **s'e. (jusqu') à faire qch.,** to venture to do sth.

enharmonie [ãnarmɔni] *n.f. Mus:* enharmonic change.

enharnacher [ãarnaʃe] *v.tr.* to harness (horse).

enherber [ãnɛrbe] *v.tr.* to put (land) under grass.

énième [enjɛm] *a. & n.m.* n^{th}; **pour la é. fois,** for the nth, umpteenth, time.

énigmatique [enigmatik] *a.* enigmatic.

énigmatiquement [enigmatikmã] *adv.* enigmatically.

énigme [enigm] *n.f.* enigma, riddle; **proposer une é. (à qn),** to ask (s.o.) a riddle; **trouver le mot de l'é.,** to find the answer to the riddle; to guess, solve, the riddle; **parler par énigmes,** to speak in riddles; **ce garçon est une é. pour moi,** I can't make the boy out.

enivrant [ãnivrã] *a.* intoxicating, heady.

enivrement [ãnivrəmã] *n.m.* **1.** intoxication, inebriation. **2.** ecstasy (of joy); elation.

enivrer [ãnivre] *v.* **1.** *v.tr.* to intoxicate; (*a*) to inebriate; to make (s.o.) drunk; (*b*) to elate, exalt. **2.** **s'e.** (*a*) to become intoxicated, inebriated (**de,** with); to get drunk, *F:* fuddled; (*b*) **s'e. de mots,** to revel in words.

enjambée [ɑ̃ʒɑ̃be] *n.f.* stride; **marcher à grandes enjambées,** to stride along, stalk along.
enjambement [ɑ̃ʒɑ̃bmɑ̃] *n.m.* **1.** *Pros:* enjambment. **2.** flyover, overpass.
enjamber [ɑ̃ʒɑ̃be] **1.** *v.tr.* to step over, stride over (obstacle); (*of bridge*) to span (river). **2.** *v.i.* (*a*) to stride; to step out; (*b*) **e. sur qch.,** (i) to jut, project, over sth.; (ii) to encroach on sth.; (*c*) *Pros:* to run on (to next line).
enjaveler [ɑ̃ʒavle] *v.tr.* **(j'enjavelle; j'enjavellerai)** to sheaf (wheat, etc.).
enjeu, -eux [ɑ̃ʒø] *n.m. Gaming:* stake.
enjoindre [ɑ̃ʒwɛ̃dr̥] *v.tr.* (*conj. like* JOINDRE) to enjoin; **e. (strictement) à qn de faire qch.,** to enjoin, call upon, charge, direct, s.o. to do sth.
enjôlement [ɑ̃ʒolmɑ̃] *n.m.* **1.** cajoling, wheedling, inveigling. **2.** cajolery, blandishment, blarney.
enjôler [ɑ̃ʒole] *v.tr.* to coax, inveigle, wheedle; to get round (s.o.).
enjôleur, -euse [ɑ̃ʒolœr, -øz] **1.** *n.* coaxer, cajoler, wheedler. **2.** *a.* coaxing, cajoling, wheedling.
enjolivement [ɑ̃ʒɔlivmɑ̃] *n.m.* **1.** beautifying, embellishing (of s.o., sth.); embroidering (of a tale). **2.** embellishment, ornamental piece; scroll.
enjoliver [ɑ̃ʒɔlive] *v.tr.* to beautify, embellish; to make (sth.) look attractive; **e. un récit,** to embroider a tale.
enjoliveur, -euse [ɑ̃ʒɔlivœr, -øz] *n.* **1. c'est un e.,** he likes to embroider his stories. **2.** *n.m. Aut:* hub cap; wheel disc.
enjolivure [ɑ̃ʒɔlivyr] *n.f.* small embellishment.
enjoué [ɑ̃ʒwe] *a.* vivacious, lively, sprightly.
enjouement [ɑ̃ʒumɑ̃] *n.m.* sprightliness; playfulness.
enkystement [ɑ̃kistəmɑ̃] *n.m. Med:* encystation, encystment.
enkyster (s') [sɑ̃kiste] *v.pr. Med:* (*of tumour*) to become encysted.
enlacement [ɑ̃lasmɑ̃] *n.m.* **1.** intertwining, interlacing. **2.** enlacing, entwining.
enlacer [ɑ̃lase] *v.tr.* **(j'enlaçai(s)) 1.** to intertwine, interlace (ribbons, branches). **2.** (*a*) to entwine, enlace, twine round (sth.); to tie up (papers); (*b*) to clasp (s.o.) in one's arms, to hug (s.o.).
enlaidir [ɑ̃ledir] **1.** *v.tr.* to make (s.o.) ugly; to disfigure (landscape). **2.** *v.i.* to grow ugly, plain.
enlaidissement [ɑ̃ledismɑ̃] *n.m.* **1.** disfigurement. **2.** growing ugly; loss of good looks.
enlevage [ɑ̃lvaʒ] *n.m. Row:* spurt.
enlevé [ɑ̃lve] *a.* (*of sketch, etc.*) lively.
enlèvement [ɑ̃lɛvmɑ̃] *n.m.* **1.** removal, removing; carrying off, away; clearing away; collection (of luggage, refuse). **2.** kidnapping, carrying off; *Jur:* abduction (of minor); **l'e. des Sabines,** the rape of the Sabine women; **mariage par e.,** runaway match; **e. d'enfant,** baby-snatching. **3.** *Mil:* storming, carrying (of position).
enlever [ɑ̃lve] *v.* **(j'enlève; j'enlèverai) I.** *v.tr.* **1.** (*a*) to remove; to take off (clothes); to carry away, take away; to carry off; to take up (carpet), take down (curtains); to peel off, strip (rind); **e. le couvert,** to clear away, clear the table; **e. une tache,** to remove, take out, a stain; **enlevé par la mer,** carried away, washed away, by the sea; **la mort l'enleva à vingt ans,** death carried him off at twenty; (*b*) **e. qch. à qn,** to take sth. (away) from s.o.; to snatch sth. (away) from s.o.; **une bombe lui a enlevé ses jambes,** a bomb took, blew, off his legs; **on m'a enlevé mon pardessus,** someone has made off with my overcoat; **il m'a enlevé mes cors,** he removed my corns. **2.** to carry off, steal (s.o., sth.); to kidnap (s.o.); to abduct (a girl); (*of girl*) **se faire e.,** to elope; **e. une course,** to win, carry off, a race. **3.** *Mil:* to carry, storm (position). **4.** to raise, lift (up) (weight, lid); to send up (balloon); **le vent enlève la poussière,** the wind raises the dust; **e. son cheval,** (i) to lift one's horse (to a fence); (ii) to set one's horse at full speed; **la foule fut enlevée par ces paroles,** the crowd was carried away by these words; **e. un morceau (de musique),** to play a piece of music brilliantly, with brio. **II. s'enlever 1.** (*a*) (*of paint, etc.*) to come off; (*of bark, etc.*) to strip (off); (*of skin*) to peel (off); (*b*) (*of goods*) to sell quickly, be snapped up. **2.** (*of balloon, etc.*) to rise.
enlisement [ɑ̃lizmɑ̃] *n.m.* sinking (into quicksand).
enliser [ɑ̃lize] *v.* **1.** *v.tr.* (*of quicksand*) to suck in, swallow up. **2. s'e.,** to sink, be sucked down (into bog); (*of car, etc.*) to get bogged; **s'e. dans ses explications,** to get bogged down in one's explanations.
enluminer [ɑ̃lymine] *v.tr.* (*a*) to illuminate (MS.); (*b*) to colour (print, map); **visage enluminé,** flushed, glowing, face.
enluminure [ɑ̃lyminyr] *n.f.* **1.** (*a*) illumination, illuminating (of MSS.); (*b*) colouring (of prints, maps, etc.); (*c*) *F:* high colour (of face). **2.** illuminated design, illumination.
enneigé [ɑ̃neʒe] *a.* snowclad, -covered (mountain).
enneigement [ɑ̃nɛʒmɑ̃] *n.m.* snowing up; **bulletin d'e.,** snow report.
ennemi, -ie [ɛnmi] **1.** *n.* enemy; **se faire un e. de qn,** to make an enemy of s.o.; **passer à l'e.,** to go over to the enemy; **je suis e. de la bouffonnerie,** I hate, won't have, buffoonery. **2.** *a.* **le camp e.,** the enemy('s) camp; **en pays e.,** in enemy country.
ennoblir [ɑ̃nɔblir] *v.tr.* to ennoble, elevate, (mind, etc.).
ennui [ɑ̃nɥi] *n.m.* **1.** worry, annoyance, anxiety; **avoir des ennuis,** to be worried; to have problems; **petits ennuis,** petty annoyances; **créer, susciter, des ennuis à qn,** to make trouble for s.o.; **quel e.!** what a nuisance, bother, bind! **2.** boredom, tedium, ennui; **ils me font mourir d'e.,** they bore me to death.
ennuyer [ɑ̃nɥije] *v.* **(j'ennuie; j'ennuierai) 1.** *v.tr.* (*a*) to annoy, worry, vex; **cela vous ennuierait-il d'attendre?** would you mind waiting? (*b*) to bore (s.o.); **il m'ennuie à mourir,** he bores me stiff. **2. s'e.** (*a*) to be bored; **je m'ennuie à ne rien faire,** (i) I'm bored, *F:* fed up, with doing nothing; (ii) I get bored if I have nothing to do; **s.'e. de faire qch.,** to get tired of doing sth.; (*b*) *O:* **s'e. de qn,** to miss, long for, s.o.
ennuyeux, -euse [ɑ̃nɥijø, -øz] *a.* (*a*) boring, tedious, tiresome, wearisome, dull; **mortellement e.,** deadly dull; (*b*) annoying, irritating; **comme c'est e.!** what a nuisance!
énoncé [enɔ̃se] *n.m.* statement (of facts); terms (of a problem); text, wording (of an act).
énoncer [enɔ̃se] *v.* **(j'énonçai(s)) 1.** *v.tr.* to state (opinion, fact). **2. s'é.,** to express oneself (clearly, etc.).
énonciation [enɔ̃sjasjɔ̃] *n.f.* stating, statement (of fact, etc.).
enorgueillir [ɑ̃nɔrgœjir] *v.* **1.** *v.tr.* to make (s.o.) proud. **2. s'e.,** to become proud, elated; **s'e. de qch., d'avoir fait qch.,** to be proud of (having done) sth.; to pride oneself on (having done) sth.
énorme [enɔrm] *a.* enormous, huge, inordinate; **crime é.,** shocking, outrageous, crime; **perte é.,** grievous, tremendous, loss; **majorité é.,** overwhelming majority; **mensonge é.,** thumping lie.
énormément [enɔrmemɑ̃] *adv.* **1.** enormously, hugely; *F:* tremendously; **je le regrette é.,** I'm extremely, *F:* awfully, sorry. **2. é. de bien,** an enormous amount, a great deal, of good; **é. de gens,** a great many, any number of, *F:* lots of, people.

énormité [enɔrmite] *n.f.* **1.** (*a*) enormity, outrageousness (of demand, sin, etc.); heinousness (of crime); (*b*) enormousness, vastness, hugeness. **2.** *F:* **commettre une é.,** to put one's foot in it badly; **dire des énormités,** to say the most awful things.

énoyautage [enwajotaʒ] *n.m.* stoning, *U.S:* pitting (of fruit).

enquérir (s') [sɑ̃kerir] *v.pr.* (*conj. like* ACQUÉRIR) to inquire, make inquiries (**de,** after); **s'e. du prix,** to ask the price; **il s'est enquis de vous,** he inquired, asked, after you.

enquête [ɑ̃kɛt] *n.f.* inquiry, investigation; **e. scientifique,** scientific investigation; piece of research; **e. par sondage,** sample survey; **faire, procéder à, une e. sur qch.,** to hold, set up, conduct, an inquiry, to inquire, into sth.; **commission d'e.,** court of inquiry; *Parl:* select committee.

enquêter [ɑ̃kete] *v.i.* to hold an inquiry, to make investigations; **e. sur une affaire,** to inquire into a matter.

enquêteur, -euse [ɑ̃kɛtœr, -øz] **1.** *a. Jur:* **commissaire e.,** investigating commissioner. **2.** *n* investigator; *Journ:* interviewer.

enquiquinant [ɑ̃kikinɑ̃] *a. F:* infuriating; irritating.

enquiquiner [ɑ̃kikine] *v.tr. F:* to aggravate, bore, annoy.

enraciné [ɑ̃rasine] *a.* deep-rooted, deep-seated.

enracinement [ɑ̃rasinmɑ̃] *n.m.* (*a*) digging in (of sapling); (*b*) rooting, taking root.

enraciner [ɑ̃rasine] *v.* **1.** *v.tr.* (*a*) to dig in, root (tree, etc.); (*b*) to establish, implant (principles, etc.). **2.** **s'e.** (*a*) (*of tree*) to take root; (*b*) (*of feelings, habits*) to become established, deeply rooted.

enragé, -ée [ɑ̃raʒe] **1.** *a.* (*a*) mad (dog, etc.); (*b*) *F:* rabid, out-and-out (socialist, etc.); keen (angler). **2.** *n.* **un e. de golf,** a golf enthusiast, a keen golfer.

enrager [ɑ̃raʒe] *v.i.* **(j'enrageai(s); n. enrageons)** to (fret and) fume; **faire e. qn,** to make s.o. wild; to tease s.o.

enrayage [ɑ̃rɛjaʒ] *n.m.* **1.** (*a*) locking, braking (of wheel); arresting, checking (of disease); (*b*) jamming (of mechanism). **2.** spoking (of wheel).

enrayer¹ [ɑ̃reje] *v.tr.* **(j'enraye, j'enraie; j'enrayerai, j'enraierai) e. un champ,** to plough the first furrow of a field.

enrayer² *v.* **1.** *v.tr.* (*a*) to lock, skid (wheel); to put (i) the brake, (ii) the drag, on (wheel); **e. une maladie,** to arrest, check (disease); (*b*) **e. une machine,** to jam, stop (machinery); (*c*) to spoke (wheel). **2.** **s'e.** (*a*) (*of firearm*) to jam; (*b*) (*of epidemic*) to abate.

enrayure [ɑ̃rɛjyr] *n.f. Veh:* **1.** drag, shoe, skid, trig. **2.** spokes (of wheel).

enrégimenter [ɑ̃reʒimɑ̃te] *v.tr.* **1.** to form into regiments. **2.** (*a*) to enrol (body of helpers, etc.); (*b*) to regiment (staff).

enregistrement [ɑ̃r(ə)ʒistrəmɑ̃] *n.m.* **1.** registration, registry; recording; booking, entering (up) (of an order); **bureau d'e.,** (i) registry office; (ii) booking office (for luggage); **e. d'une compagnie,** incorporation of a company; *Adm:* **droit d'e.,** stamp duty. **2.** (sound) recording; **e. sur bande, sur cassette,** tape, cassette, recording; *T.V:* **camion d'e. (du son),** sound van; **passer un e.,** to play a recording.

enregistrer [ɑ̃r(ə)ʒistre] *v.tr.* **1.** (*a*) to record (facts); to register (a birth, a deed); to book, enter up (an order); to book, register (luggage); **société enregistrée,** incorporated company; (*b*) *F:* to memorize. **2.** to record (for sound reproduction); **e. sur bande,** to tape, to record on tape; **musique enregistrée,** recorded, *F:* canned, music; (*of actor*) **e. la joie,** to register joy; *Cmptr:* **programme enregistré,** stored programme. **3.** *Fb:* to score (goal).

enregistreur, -euse [ɑ̃r(ə)ʒistrœr, -øz] **1.** *a.* (self-) recording, registering (apparatus, device); **bande enregistreuse,** recording chart; **stylet e.,** recording pen. **2.** *n.m.* (*a*) registrar; (*b*) (automatic) recording instrument; recorder; **e. du son, e. sonore,** sound recorder; **e. à bande,** (strip) chart recorder; **e. à tambour,** drum recorder; *Av:* **e. de vol,** flight recorder; *F:* black box; *Ind:* **e. de temps,** time clock, recorder.

enrhumer [ɑ̃ryme] *v.* **1.** *v.tr.* to give (s.o.) a cold. **2.** **s'e,** to catch (a) cold; **être enrhumé du cerveau, de la poitrine,** to have a cold in the head, on the chest.

enrichi, -ie [ɑ̃riʃi] *a. & n.* newly rich (person); parvenu.

enrichir [ɑ̃riʃir] *v.* **1.** *v.tr.* (*a*) to enrich; to make (s.o.) wealthy; (*b*) to enrich (art collection, etc.); (*c*) *Ph:* to enrich (uranium, etc.). **2.** **s'e.** (*a*) to grow rich, to make money; (*b*) (*of language, etc.*) to grow, become, richer (**de,** with, **en,** in).

enrichissement [ɑ̃riʃismɑ̃] *n.m.* **1.** enriching, enrichment (of pers., museum) **2.** *Ph:* enrichment (of uranium, etc.).

enrobage [ɑ̃rɔbaʒ], **enrobement** [ɑ̃rɔbmɑ̃] *n.m.* coating, covering (of sth. with sth.); **e. de sucre, de chocolat,** sugar, chocolate, coating.

enrober [ɑ̃rɔbe] *v.tr.* to coat, cover (sth. with sth.); to wrap (sth. in sth.).

enrôlé [ɑ̃role] *n.m.* person on the rolls.

enrôlement [ɑ̃rolmɑ̃] *n.m.* enrolment; *Mil:* enlistment.

enrôler [ɑ̃role] *v.* **1.** *v.tr.* (*a*) to enrol, recruit (members, workers); *Mil:* to enlist; *Hist:* **e. de force,** to impress (for the Navy). **2.** **s'e.,** to enrol (oneself); *Mil:* to enlist.

enroué [ɑ̃rwe] *a.* hoarse, husky (person, voice).

enrouement [ɑ̃rumɑ̃] *n.m.* hoarseness, huskiness.

enrouer [ɑ̃rwe] *v.* **1.** *v.tr.* to make (voice) hoarse, husky. **2.** **s'e.,** to get hoarse; **s'e. à force de crier,** to shout oneself hoarse.

enroulement [ɑ̃rulmɑ̃] *n.m.* **1.** rolling up; winding. **2.** (*a*) *El:* coil; (*b*) volute, scroll.

enrouler [ɑ̃rule] *v.* **1.** *v.tr.* (*a*) to roll up (map, etc.); to wind (cable, etc.); (*b*) to wrap up (**dans,** in). **2.** **s'e.,** to wind, coil; to be wound (**autour de,** round).

ensablement [ɑ̃sɑbləmɑ̃] *n.m.* **1.** running aground, stranding (of ship). **2.** silting up (of harbour); choking up (of pipes). **3.** sandbank; harbour bar.

ensabler [ɑ̃sɑble] *v.* **1.** *v.tr.* (*a*) to strand; to run (boat) aground; (*b*) (*of flood*) to cover (land) with sand; to silt up, sand up, (harbour). **2.** **s'e.** (*a*) (*of ship, fish*) to settle in the sand; (*b*) (*of harbour, river*) to silt up; (*of pipes*) to get choked up.

ensachage [ɑ̃saʃaʒ] *n.m.* bagging, sacking (of cereals, etc.).

ensacher [ɑ̃saʃe] *v.tr.* to put into sacks; to bag (fruit, corn).

ensanglanter [ɑ̃sɑ̃glɑ̃te] *v.tr.* to cover, stain, (sth.) with blood; **mains ensanglantées,** bloodstained, bloody, hands.

enseignant, -ante [ɑ̃sɛɲɑ̃, -ɑ̃t] (*a*) *a.* teaching; **corps e.,** teaching profession; (*b*) *n.* teacher.

enseigne [ɑ̃sɛɲ] **1.** *n.f.* (*a*) sign, token (of quality, etc.); (*b*) sign(board), shop sign; **e. au néon,** neon sign; **à l'e. du Lion d'or,** at the (sign of the) Golden Lion; *F:* **nous sommes tous logés à la même e.,** we are all in the same boat; *Prov:* **à bon vin point d'e.,** good wine needs no bush; (*c*) *Mil:* ensign, colour(s). **2.** *n.m.* (*a*) *Mil: A:* standard bearer, ensign; (*b*) *Navy:* **e. (de vaisseau),** sub-lieutenant; *U.S:* ensign.

enseignement [ɑ̃sɛɲmɑ̃] *n.m.* **1.** (*a*) teaching; **l'e. de l'anglais,** the teaching of English; **méthode d'e.,** teaching method; **il est dans l'e.,** he is a teacher; he teaches; (*b*) **e. supérieur,** higher education; **e. par**

correspondance, postal tuition. **2.** *O:* **tirer un e. de qch.,** to draw a lesson from sth.

enseigner [ɑ̃sɛɲe] *v.tr.* **1.** to teach; *(a)* **e. la grammaire à qn,** to teach s.o. grammar; **e. à qn à faire qch.,** to teach s.o., show s.o. how, to do sth.; **e. l'anglais,** to teach English; *(b)* **e. les enfants,** to teach children; **il enseigne,** he's a teacher, *NAm:* he teaches school. **2.** *O:* to show, point out; **e. à qn son devoir,** to point out his duty to s.o.

ensemble [ɑ̃sɑ̃bl̥] **1.** *adv.* together; *(a)* in company, one with another; **ils se marièrent e.,** they married (each other); **vivre e.,** to live together; **être bien e.,** to be good friends; **ils vont mal e.,** they don't get on, don't hit it off; **choses qui vont e.,** things that belong, go, together; **le tout e.,** the general effect; **agir d'e.,** to act in concert, as a body; *(b)* at the same time; **vendre tous ses meubles e.,** to sell all one's furniture at once. **2.** *n.m.* *(a)* whole, entirety; **l'e. du travail est bon,** the work as a whole is good; **l'e. d'un tableau,** the general effect of a picture; **vue d'e.,** comprehensive, general, view; overall picture; **idée d'e.,** broad, general, idea (of a subject); **dans l'e.,** on the whole, taken all round, by and large; **les juges, pris dans leur e., étaient intègres,** the judges, taken as a body, were honest; *(b)* cohesion, unity; **mouvement d'e.,** combined movement; **l'exécution manque d'e.,** the execution is ragged; **avec e.,** all together, harmoniously, as one; *(c)* **e. vocal,** vocal ensemble; **e. de couleurs,** harmonious (group of) colours; *(d)* set (of tools); suite (of furniture); *Cost:* ensemble; suit; **e. de bâtiments,** block of buildings; *Town P:* **grand e.,** new residential estate; new town.

ensemblier [ɑ̃sɑ̃blije] *n.m.* interior decorator.

ensemencement [ɑ̃s(ə)mɑ̃smɑ̃] *n.m.* **1.** *Agr:* sowing. **2.** *Biol:* seeding.

ensemencer [ɑ̃smɑ̃se] *v.tr.* **(j'ensemençai(s)) 1.** to sow (field). **2.** *Biol:* to seed (culture medium).

enserrer [ɑ̃sere] *v.tr.* *(a)* to enclose, encompass (sth.); to hem in (army, etc.); *(b)* to grip tightly.

ensevelir [ɑ̃səvlir] *v.* **1.** *v.tr.* *(a)* to bury, entomb (corpse); to hide away (secret); *(b)* to shroud (corpse). **2. s'e.,** to bury oneself (in a book, in the country); **enseveli dans la méditation,** lost, sunk, wrapped, in thought.

ensevelissement [ɑ̃səvlismɑ̃] *n.m.* **1.** burial, entombment. **2.** shrouding (of corpse).

ensilage [ɑ̃silaʒ] *n.m.* ensilage (of crops).

ensiler [ɑ̃sile] *v.tr.* to ensile, silo (crop).

ensoleillé [ɑ̃sɔleje] *a.* sunny, sunlit.

ensoleiller [ɑ̃sɔleje] *v.tr.* *(a)* to give sunlight to (sth.); to shine on (sth); to sun; *(b)* to brighten, light up (s.o.'s life, etc.).

ensommeillé [ɑ̃sɔmeje] *a.* sleepy, drowsy.

ensorcelant [ɑ̃sɔrsəlɑ̃] *a.* bewitching (smile, etc.).

ensorcelé [ɑ̃sɔrsəle] *a.* bewitched; under a spell; spellbound.

ensorceler [ɑ̃sɔrsəle] *v.tr.* **(j'ensorcelle; j'ensorcellerai)** *(a)* to bewitch; to cast a spell, put a spell, (up)on (s.o., sth.); *(b)* to captivate (s.o.).

ensorceleur, -euse [ɑ̃sɔrsəlœr, -øz] *n.* *(a)* sorcerer, *f.* sorceress; *(b)* charmer.

ensorcellement [ɑ̃sɔrsɛlmɑ̃] *n.m.* **1.** sorcery, witchcraft. **2.** charm, spell.

ensuite [ɑ̃sɥit] *adv.* after(wards), then; next, after that; **et e.?** what then? what next? *F:* **e. de quoi, e. de cela, il s'est enragé,** after which, after that, he lost his temper; **les pompiers marchaient en tête, e. venait la musique,** the firemen led the procession, next came the band.

ensuivre (s') [sɑ̃sɥivr̥] *v.pr.* (*conj like* SUIVRE; *used only in the third pers.*) to follow, ensue, result; **il s'ensuit qu'il est sans emploi,** the consequence is he's out of a job; *F:* **et tout ce qui s'ensuit,** and what not, and all the rest of it, and whatever.

entablement [ɑ̃tabləmɑ̃] *n.m.* **1.** entablature (of building). **2.** coping (of wall).

entacher [ɑ̃taʃe] *v.tr.* **1.** to sully, besmirch, to cast a slur on (s.o.'s honour); **religion entachée de superstition,** religion tainted with superstition. **2.** *Jur:* to vitiate (contract, etc.); **entaché de nullité,** voidable.

entaille [ɑ̃tɑj] *n.f.* *(a)* notch, jag, nick (in piece of wood, etc.); groove; slot; **à entailles,** slotted; notched; *(b)* gash, cut, slash; **se faire une e. au menton,** to cut one's chin; **une e. dans la confiance publique,** a blow to public confidence.

entailler [ɑ̃taje] *v.tr.* *(a)* to notch, nick (piece of wood, etc.); to groove, slot; *(b)* to gash, cut, slash; **s'e. le doigt,** to cut one's finger.

entame [ɑ̃tam] *n.f.* **1.** first cut, outside slice (of loaf, etc.). **2.** *Cards:* opening (of a suit).

entamer [ɑ̃tame] *v.tr.* **1.** to cut into, make the first cut in (loaf, etc.); to broach (cask); to open (bottle, pot of jam); to penetrate, breach (defence); **e. la peau,** to break the skin; **doutes qui entament la foi,** doubts that undermine, shake, one's faith; **e. son capital,** to break into one's capital. **2.** to begin, commence, start (conversation, etc.); to initiate (deal); **e. des relations avec qn,** to enter into relations with s.o.; **e. des poursuites contre qn,** to initiate, institute, proceedings against s.o.; **e. un sujet,** to broach a subject; *Cards:* **e. trèfle,** to open clubs.

entartrage [ɑ̃tartraʒ] *n.m.* furring, incrustation, scaling (of boiler, etc.).

entartrer [ɑ̃tartre] *v.* **1.** *v.tr.* to incrust, fur, scale (boiler, etc.); to foul up (boiler tubes). **2.** (*of boiler*) **s'e.,** to fur; to become furred, fouled up.

entassement [ɑ̃tɑsmɑ̃] *n.m.* **1.** *(a)* piling (up), heaping (up) (of stones, etc.); stacking (of cases, etc.); *(b)* crowding (up), packing together, overcrowding (of passengers, cattle, etc.); congestion. **2.** pile (of goods, etc.); clutter (of furniture).

entasser [ɑ̃tɑse] *v.* **1.** *v.tr.* *(a)* to accumulate; to pile (up), heap (up) (stones, etc.); to stack (up) (cases); to heap (up) (insults); to amass, pile up (money); *(b)* to pack, crowd, cram, (passengers, cattle, etc.) together. **2. s'e.** *(a)* (*of thgs*) to accumulate; to pile up; *(b)* (*of persons*) to crowd, huddle, together.

ente [ɑ̃t] *n.f.* **1.** *Hort:* *(a)* scion, graft; *(b)* stock. **2.** handle (of paintbrush, etc.).

entendement [ɑ̃tɑ̃dmɑ̃] *n.m.* understanding; **homme d'e.,** man of sense, of intelligence.

entendeur [ɑ̃tɑ̃dœr] *n.m.* *used only in the phr.* **à bon e. salut!** (i) a word to the wise (is enough); (ii) if the cap fits, wear it.

entendre [ɑ̃tɑ̃dr̥] *v.* **I.** *v.tr.* **1.** to intend, mean; **e. faire qch.,** to intend, mean, propose, to do sth.; **qu'entendez-vous par là?** what do you mean by that? **il n'y entend pas malice,** (i) he means no harm; (ii) he takes what you say at its face value; **faites comme vous l'entendez,** do as you think best, do as you please; **j'entends que vous veniez,** I expect you to come; **je n'entends pas qu'on le vende,** I won't have it sold. **2.** *(a)* to hear; **e. un concert,** to listen to a concert; **j'entendis un cri,** I heard a cry; **on l'entend à peine,** it is scarcely audible; **je pouvais à peine me faire e.,** I could hardly make myself heard; **on ne s'entend plus ici,** one can't hear oneself speak here; **je l'entendis rire,** I heard him laugh; **e. parler de qn, de qch.,** to hear of, about, s.o., sth.; **je ne veux plus e. parler de lui,** I don't want to hear him mentioned again; **e. dire que** + *ind.*, to hear (it said) that . . .; **on entend dire que sa femme l'a quitté,** it is rumoured that his wife has left him; **je le sais par ce qu'on entend dire,** I know it by hearsay; **e. dire qch. à qn,** (i) to hear sth. said to s.o.; (ii) to hear s.o. say sth.; *v.i.* **il entend mal,** he is hard of hearing; *(b)* to hear, to listen to; **on le congédia sans l'e.,** he was dismissed without a hearing; **l'affaire sera entendue demain,** the case comes up for hearing tomorrow; **à vous e., il a eu tort,** judging from what you say, according to you, he was in the wrong; **refuser d'e. une requête,** to turn a deaf ear to a request; **e. raison,** to listen to reason; **il n'a rien voulu e.,** he would not listen. **3.** (*a*) to understand; **il ne l'entend pas ainsi,** he doesn't see it that way, doesn't agree; **e. une langue,** to understand a language; **intérêt bien entendu,** enlightened self-interest; **donner à e. à qn,** (i) to lead s.o. to believe sth.; (ii) to give s.o. to understand sth.; **laisser e. qch.,** to insinuate, imply, sth.; **il n'entend pas la plaisanterie,** he can't take a joke; **cela s'entend,** of course; that goes without saying; **c'est entendu,** agreed, all right; very well; **c'est une affaire entendue,** it's all settled; **bien entendu!** of course! certainly! **entendu!** very well! all right! agreed! (*b*) to know (all about sth.); to be good at (sth.); **je n'y entends rien,** I don't know the first thing about it. **II. s'entendre 1.** to understand one another, to agree; **ils s'entendent bien,** they get on (well); **nous ne sommes pas faits pour nous e.,** we are not suited to each other; **s'e. directement avec qn,** to come to a direct understanding with s.o.; **s'e. pour commettre un crime,** to conspire to commit a crime; **ils s'entendent comme larrons en foire,** they are as thick as thieves. **2.** to be skilled (**à,** in); **s'e. aux affaires,** to be a good business man; **s'e. aux chevaux,** to understand, know about, horses; **s'e. mal à mentir,** to be a poor liar.

entendu [ɑ̃tɑ̃dy] *a.* (*a*) businesslike, sensible, capable (person); (*b*) knowing, shrewd (look); *n. O:* **faire l'e.,** to pretend to know all about it.

enténébrer [ɑ̃tenebre] *v.tr.* **(il enténèbre; il enténébrera)** *Lit:* to envelop, plunge, in darkness, gloom.

entente [ɑ̃tɑ̃t] *n.f.* **1.** (*a*) understanding (**de,** of); skill (**de,** in); (*b*) **mot à double e.,** word with a double meaning; double entendre. **2.** agreement, understanding (**entre,** between); **bonne e.,** good feeling; **arriver à une e.,** to reach an agreement; **terrain d'e.,** common ground; **après e. avec les autorités,** after consultation with the authorities; **e. industrielle,** combine.

enter [ɑ̃te] *v.tr.* to graft, engraft (tree).

entérinement [ɑ̃terinmɑ̃] *n.m. Jur:* ratification, confirmation.

entériner [ɑ̃terine] *v.tr. Jur:* to ratify, confirm.

entérique [ɑ̃terik] *a.* enteric, intestinal.

entérite [ɑ̃terit] *n.f.* enteritis.

enterrement [ɑ̃tɛrmɑ̃] *n.m.* (*a*) burial, interment; (*b*) funeral; *F:* **figure d'e.,** funereal expression.

enterrer [ɑ̃tɛre] *v.tr..* **1.** to put (sth.) in the earth; to plant (bulbs). **2.** to bury, inter (corpse); *F:* **il nous enterrera tous,** he will outlive us all; **elle désire e. toute cette affaire,** she wants the whole thing buried and forgotten. **3. il s'est enterré au fond de la campagne,** he buried himself in the depths of the country.

en-tête [ɑ̃tɛt] *n.m.* **1.** heading (of letter, document); **en-t. de facture,** billhead; **papier à en-t.,** headed notepaper. **2.** *Typ:* headline (of page, etc.); *N.Am:* caption; *pl. en-têtes.*

entêté, -ée [ɑ̃tɛte] *a. n.* obstinate, headstrong, stubborn, *F:* pigheaded (person).

entêtement [ɑ̃tɛtmɑ̃] *n.m.* obstinacy, stubbornness; *F:* pig-headedness, mulishness; **e. à faire qch.,** persistency in doing sth.

entêter [ɑ̃tete] *v.* **1.** *v.tr.* (*of odour, etc.*) to give (s.o.) a headache; to make (s.o.) giddy; to intoxicate; **ces louanges l'entêtaient,** this praise went to his head, turned his head. **2. s'e. dans une opinion,** to persist in an opinion; **s'e. à faire qch.,** to persist in doing sth.

enthousiasme [ɑ̃tuzjasm] *n.m.* enthusiasm; **parler avec e.,** to speak with warmth, feeling; **faire qch. sans e.,** to do sth. half-heartedly; **accepter d'e.,** to accept enthusiastically.

enthousiasmer [ɑ̃tuzjasme] *v.* **1.** *v.tr.* to fire (s.o.) with enthusiasm; to enrapture. **2. s'e.,** to become enthusiastic; **s'e. pour, de, sur, qn, qch.,** to be enthusiastic, go into raptures, over s.o., sth.; to become keen on s.o., sth.

enthousiaste [ɑ̃tuzjast] **1.** *n.m. & f.* enthusiast. **2.** *a.* enthusiastic.

entiché [ɑ̃tiʃe] *a.* infatuated (**de qn,** with s.o.); crazy (**de qn, qch.,** about s.o., sth.)

enticher (s') [sɑ̃tiʃe] *v.pr.* **s'e. de qn, de qch.,** to become infatuated with, to take a fancy to, s.o., sth.

entier, -ière [ɑ̃tje, -jɛr] *a.* **1.** entire, whole; **lait e.,** full-cream milk; **la France entière,** the whole of France; **l'œuvre est tout entière à recommencer,** the whole work must be done again; **pendant des heures entières,** for hours on end; **conserver sa réputation entière,** to keep one's reputation intact; **(nombre) e.,** integer, whole number; **cheval e.,** stallion; **payer place entière,** to pay full fare. **2.** complete, full (authority, etc.); **l'entière direction de qch.,** the entire, sole, management of sth.; **elle est tout(e) entière à ce qu'elle fait,** she is engrossed in, intent on, what she is doing; **tout e. pour une ligne de conduite,** all in favour of a course of action. **3.** (*of pers.*) unyielding, uncompromising. **4.** *n.m.* entirety; **raconter une histoire dans son e.,** to relate a story in its entirety; **en e.,** wholly, entirely, fully, in full; **nom en e.,** name in full.

entièrement [ɑ̃tjɛrmɑ̃] *adv.* entirely, wholly, fully, completely; **il n'est pas e. mauvais,** he's not all bad.

entité [ɑ̃tite] *n.f.* entity.

entoilage [ɑ̃twalaʒ] *n.m.* **1.** mounting (of maps, etc.) on linen, canvas; *Tail:* stiffening with canvas. **2.** canvas mount.

entoiler [ɑ̃twale] *v.tr.* to mount (map, etc.) on linen, canvas; **carte entoilée,** map mounted on cloth.

entôler [ɑ̃tole] *v.tr. P:* (*esp. of prostitute*) to (inveigle and) rob.

entomologie [ɑ̃tɔmɔlɔʒi] *n.f.* entomology.

entomologique [ɑ̃tɔmɔlɔʒik] *a.* entomological.

entomologiste [ɑ̃tɔmɔlɔʒist] *n.m. & f.* entomologist.

entonner¹ [ɑ̃tɔne] *v.tr.* to barrel, cask (wine); *F:* **s'e. du vin dans le gosier,** to swig wine.

entonner² *v.tr.* to strike up, start (song); **e. les louanges de qn,** to sing s.o.'s praises.

entonnoir [ɑ̃tɔnwar] *n.m.* **1.** funnel; **en (forme d')e.,** funnel-shaped. **2.** (*a*) bomb hole, crater; (*b*) hollow (among hills).

entorse [ɑ̃tɔrs] *n.f.* sprain, wrench, twist, strain (*esp.* of the ankle); **se donner une e.,** to sprain, twist, wrench, one's ankle; **faire une e. à la loi,** to go beyond, to stretch, the law; **donner une e. à la vérité,** to twist, distort, the truth.

entortillé [ɑ̃tɔrtije] *a.* involved (style).

entortillement [ɑ̃tɔrtijmɑ̃] *n.m.* **1.** (*a*) winding, twisting, wrapping; (*b*) twisting, twining, coiling (of snake, convolvulus). **2.** entanglement.

entortiller [ɑ̃tɔrtije] *v.* **1.** *v.tr.* (*a*) **e. qch. dans qch., autour de qch.,** to wind, twist, twine, wrap, sth. in sth., round sth.; (*b*) to wheedle; to get round (s.o.); to inveigle. **2. s'e.,** to twist, twine, coil (**autour de,** round); to get entangled (**dans,** in).

entour [ɑ̃tur] *n.m.* (*used in*) **à l'entour,** around, round about; **à l'entour de,** round (about) (town, etc.)

entourage [ɑ̃turaʒ] *n.m.* **1.** setting, framework, border (of sth.); **miniature avec un e. de perles,** miniature set in pearls. **2.** set, circle (of friends, etc.); associates; attendants; entourage, suite (of monarch).

entourer [ɑ̃ture] *v.tr.* to surround (**de,** with); to fence in (field); to encircle (army); **s'e. d'amis,** to surround oneself with friends; **il était très entouré,** he was the centre of attraction; **entouré de mystère,** wrapped in mystery; **e. qn de soins, de respect,** to lavish attentions on s.o.; to show respect to s.o.; **entouré de difficultés,** beset with difficulties.

entourloupette [ɑ̃turlupɛt] *n.f. F:* dirty trick.

entournure [ɑ̃turnyr] *n.f.* armhole; *F:* **être gêné aux entournures,** (i) to be awkward, ill at ease; (ii) to feel the pinch.

entracte [ɑ̃trakt] *n.m. Th:* **1.** interval, intermission; **à l'e.,** between the acts. **2.** entracte, interlude.

entraide [ɑ̃trɛd] *n.f.* (*no pl.*) mutual aid.

entraider(s') [sɑ̃trede] *v.pr.* to help one another.

entrailles [ɑ̃trɑj] *n.f.pl.* **1.** entrails, intestines, bowels; **les e. de la terre,** the bowels of the earth. **2.** compassion; **être sans e.,** to be heartless.

entrain [ɑ̃trɛ̃] *n.m.* liveliness, briskness; high spirits; spirit; **être plein d'e.,** to be full of life, of go; **musique pleine d'e.,** lively music; **manger avec e.,** to eat with gusto; **travailler avec e.,** to work with a will; **donner plus d'e. à la conversation,** to liven up the conversation; **faire qch. sans e.,** to do sth. half-heartedly.

entraînant [ɑ̃trɛnɑ̃] *a.* inspiriting, stirring (speech, tune, etc.); lively, catchy (tune).

entraînement [ɑ̃trɛnmɑ̃] *n.m.* **1.** (*a*) dragging, being dragged, along; carrying away; (*b*) feed (of machine tool); drive (of machine). **2.** leading, being led, astray; allurement. **3.** training (of racehorses, athletes); coaching (of team); **être à l'e.,** to be in training; **partie d'e.,** practice match.

entraîner [ɑ̃trene] *v.tr.* **1.** (*a*) to drag, draw, carry, along; (*of river*) to carry away; to wash away, wash down; **e. qn quelque part,** to drag s.o. off somewhere; **il m'a entraîné chez lui,** he took me along to his home; **entraîné par le courant,** swept along by the current; **il vous entraînera dans sa perte,** he will drag you down with him; (*b*) to drive (part of machine, etc.). **2.** to seduce, inveigle (s.o.); **e. qn à faire qch.,** to lead s.o. to do sth.; **être entrainé dans un piège,** to be lured into a trap; **entraîné par l'éloquence de l'orateur,** carried away by the speaker's eloquence; **se laisser e.,** to allow oneself to be led astray; **se laisser e. à faire qch.,** to be drawn into doing sth. **3.** to result in (sth.); to entail, involve; **cela entraînera un retard,** it will involve, lead to, delay; **cela entraîne de la dépense,** that entails, runs one into, expense; **décision qui peut e. des inconvénients,** decision that may land one in difficulties, give rise to difficulties. **4.** (*a*) to train (racehorse, athlete); to coach (team); (*b*) *Sp:* to pace (a cyclist).

entraîneur [ɑ̃trɛnœr] *n.m.* **1.** *Sp:* (*a*) trainer (of horses, etc.); coach (of team); (*b*) **e. (de coureur),** pacemaker, pacer. **2.** *Mec.E:* driving device. **3.** *Atom.Ph:* carrier.

entraîneuse [ɑ̃trɛnøz] *n.f.* dance hostess.

entrant, ante [ɑ̃trɑ̃, -ɑ̃t] **1.** *a.* incoming, ingoing; newly appointed (officials); **les élèves entrants,** the new pupils. **2.** *n.* incomer, ingoer; (*at cards*) player cutting in.

entr'apercevoir [ɑ̃trapɛrsəvwar] *v.tr.* (*conj. like* APERCEVOIR) to catch a fleeting glimpse of (sth.).

entrave [ɑ̃trav] *n.f.* **1.** (*a*) shackle, fetter; (*b*) hobble. **2. e. à qch.,** hindrance, impediment, to sth.; **e. à la liberté,** interference with freedom.

entravé [ɑ̃trave] *a.* impeded, hampered.

entraver [ɑ̃trave] *v.tr.* **1.** to shackle, fetter; to hobble (horse). **2.** to hinder, hamper, impede; **e. la circulation,** to hold up, block, the traffic.

entre [ɑ̃tr̥] *prep.* **1.** (*a*) between; **e. deux haies,** between two hedges; **e. les arbres,** (in) between the trees; **distance de 10 kilomètres e. deux villes,** distance of 10 kilometres between two towns; **e. deux et trois (heures),** between two and three; (*b*) **e. les deux,** betwixt and between, neither one thing nor the other; **être e. la vie et la mort,** to be between life and death. **2.** (*a*) among(st); **nous sommes e. amis,** we are among friends; **nous dînerons e. nous,** there won't be anyone else at dinner; **un homme dangereux e. tous,** a most dangerous man; **un homme qu'il admirait entre tous,** a man he admired above all others; **un jour e. mille,** a day in a thousand; **ce jour e. tous,** this day of all days; (*b*) **tomber e. les mains de l'ennemi,** to fall into the enemy's hands; **tenir qch. e. les mains,** to hold sth. in one's hands; (*c*) **d'e.,** (from) among; **plusieurs d'e. nous,** several of us. **3.** in relation to (one another); **ils s'accordent e. eux,** they agree among themselves; **soit dit e. nous,** (be it said) between ourselves.

entrebâillement [ɑ̃trəbɑjmɑ̃] *n.m.* narrow opening, chink (of door, etc.); slit, gap (between curtains, etc.).

entrebâiller [ɑ̃trəbɑje] *v.tr.* to half-open (door, curtain, etc.); **la porte était entrebâillée,** the door was ajar.

entrebâilleur [ɑ̃trəbɑjœr] *n.m.* door stop, chain.

entrechat [ɑ̃trəʃa] *n.m.* (*a*) *Danc:* entrechat; (*b*) *pl. F:* **faire des entrechats,** to cut capers.

entrechoquer (s') [sɑ̃trəʃɔke] *v.pr.* (*a*) to collide, clash; (*b*) to knock against one another; (*of glasses*) to chink.

entrecôte [ɑ̃trəkot] *n.f. Cu:* steak cut from the ribs (of beef); **e. minute,** thin grilled steak.

entrecoupé [ɑ̃trəkupe] *a.* interrupted, broken (speech, sleep, etc.); **d'une voix entrecoupée,** with a catch in one's voice.

entrecouper [ɑ̃trəkupe] *v.tr.* **1.** to interrupt, break into (speech, etc.). **2.** to intersect.

entrecroisement [ɑ̃trəkrwazmɑ̃] *n.m.* intersection; criss-cross (of lines); interlacing (of threads).

entrecroiser [ɑ̃trəkrwaze] *v.* **1.** *v.tr.* to intersect, cross (lines); to interlace (threads). **2. s'e.,** to intersect, interlace, interlock; to criss-cross.

entre-deux [ɑ̃trədø] *n.m.inv.* **1.** space between; interspace, interval; **la vérité est dans l'e.-d.,** the truth is between the two. **2.** *Needlew:* insertion.

entre-deux-guerres [ɑ̃trədøgɛr] *n.m. or f.inv.* the inter-war years (1918–1939).

entrée [ɑ̃tre] *n.f.* **1.** entry, entering, entrance; **e. en scène d'un acteur,** actor's entrance (on the stage); **faire son e.,** to make one's entrance; (*of girl*) **faire son e. dans le monde,** to come out (into society); **l'e. des États-Unis dans la politique mondiale,** the entry of the United States into world politics; *Sch:* **e. en vacances,** break(ing) up. **2.** (*a*) admission, admittance (to club, college); **avoir son e., ses entrées dans un lieu,** to have one's entrée to, have the run of, a place; **avoir ses entrées libres chez qn,** to have free access to s.o.; **e. interdite,** no admittance; **payer ses entrées,** to pay one's admission fee, entrance fee; **e. libre,** open to the public; *Com:* no obligation to buy; (*b*) *Com:* import(ation); *Cust:* entry; **droit d'e.,** import duty. **3.** (*a*) way in, entrance (to building, etc.); (entrance) hall; lobby; mouth of (river, sack); **e. de clef,** keyhole; **à l'e. de l'hiver,** at the beginning of winter; **l'e. ouest de la Manche,** the chops of the Channel; (*b*) *Mch:* admission, inlet (of cylinder, etc.); **(orifice d')e.,** inlet; *I.C.E:* **e. d'air,** air intake; *W.Tel:* **e. de poste,** lead-in; (*c*) *Elcs*: input. **4.** *Cu:* entrée.

entrefaite [ɑ̃trəfɛt] *n.f. used only in* **sur ces entrefaites,** meanwhile, while this was going on.

entrefilet [ɑ̃trəfilɛ] *n.m.* paragraph (in newspaper); *F:* par.

entregent [ɑ̃trəʒɑ̃] *n.m.* tact; discretion.

entrejambe [ɑ̃trəʒɑ̃b] *n.m. Tail:* (*a*) crutch; (*b*) **(lon-**

gueur d')e., inside leg length.

entrelacement [ɑ̃trəlasmɑ̃] *n.m.* interlacing (of ribbon); interweaving (of threads); intertwining, network (of branches); *T.V:* interlacing, interlaced scanning.

entrelacer [ɑ̃trəlase] *v.* (*conj. like* LACER) **1.** *v.tr.* to interlace (ribbons); to interweave (threads); to intertwine (branches); *Typ:* to ligature (letters); **mains entrelacées,** hand in hand. **2. s'e.,** to intertwine.

entrelacs [ɑ̃trəlɑ] *n.m.* interlaced design, tracery; knotwork, strapwork (in embroidery, architecture).

entrelardement [ɑ̃trəlardəmɑ̃] *n.m.* (*a*) *Cu:* larding; (*b*) interlarding.

enterlarder [ɑ̃trəlarde] *v.tr.* to lard (meat); **e. un discours de citations,** to interlard a speech with quotations.

entremêlement [ɑtrəmɛlmɑ̃] *n.m. A:* **1.** (inter)mingling. **2.** (inter)mixture, jumble, medley.

entremêler [ɑ̃trəmele] *v.* **1.** *v.tr.* **e. qch. (de, parmi, qch.),** to (inter)mix, (inter)mingle, sth. (with sth.); **e. des couleurs,** to mix, blend, colours; **ordres entremêlés de jurons,** orders interspersed with oaths. **2. s'e.,** to (inter)mix, (inter)mingle.

entremets [ɑ̃trəmɛ] *n.m.* side dish, second course; **e. sucré,** sweet (as dinner course).

entremetteur, -euse [ɑ̃trəmɛtœr, -øz] *n.* **1.** *A:* intermediary, mediator. **2.** procurer, procuress; *m.* pimp; *f.* bawd.

entremettre (s') [sɑ̃trəmɛtr̥] *v.pr.* (*conj. like* METTRE) to interpose, intervene; to act as go-between.

entremise [ɑ̃trəmiz] *n.f.* (*a*) intervention; (*b*) mediation; **agir par l'e. de qn,** to act through s.o.

entre-nœud [ɑ̃trənø] *n.m.* internode; *pl. entre-nœuds.*

entrepont [ɑ̃trəpɔ̃] *n.m.* between decks; **passager d'e.,** steerage passenger.

entreposage [ɑ̃trəpozaʒ] *n.m.* warehousing, storing; *Cust:* bonding.

entreposer [ɑ̃trəpoze] *v.tr.* to warehouse, store; *Cust:* to bond.

entreposeur [ɑ̃trəpozœr] *n.m.* warehouse keeper, warehouseman.

entrepositaire [ɑ̃trəpozitɛr] *n.m. Cust:* bonder.

entrepôt [ɑ̃trəpo] *n.m.* **1.** warehouse, store; repository; **e. maritime,** wharf; **e. de la douane,** bonded warehouse; **e. frigorifique,** cold store; **marchandises en e.,** goods in bond. **2.** *Mil:* (repair, etc.) depot.

entreprenant [ɑ̃trəprənɑ̃] *a.* enterprising, go-ahead.

entreprendre [ɑ̃trəprɑ̃dr̥] *v.tr.* (*conj. like* PRENDRE) **1.** to undertake; to take (sth.) in hand; **e. un commerce,** to open shop, start a business; **e. une étude,** to begin a study; **e. de faire qch.,** to undertake to do sth. **2.** to contract for (piece of work).

entrepreneur, -euse [ɑ̃trəprənœr, -øz] *n.* contractor; **e. (en bâtiments),** (i) building contractor; (ii) master builder; **e. de déménagements,** furniture remover; **e. de transports,** carrier, forwarding agent; **e. de pompes funèbres,** undertaker, *U.S:* mortician.

entreprise [ɑ̃trəpriz] *n.f.* **1.** enterprise; (*a*) undertaking, venture; **e. hardie,** bold enterprise; (*b*) *Com: Ind:* firm; **e. publique,** public corporation; **e. de transports,** carrying company, forwarding agency. **2.** contracting; **travail à l'e.,** work by, on, contract; **mettre qch. à l'e.,** to put sth. out to contract.

entrer [ɑ̃tre] *v.i.* (*aux.* **être**) **1.** (*a*) to enter; to go in, to come in; to step in; **e. dans une salle,** to enter, go into, come into, walk into, a room; **entrez!** come in! *P.N:* **défense d'e.,** no admittance, private; **faire e. qn,** (i) to show s.o. in; (ii) to call s.o. in; **laisser e. qn, qch.,** to let s.o., sth., in; to admit s.o.; **e. en passant,** to drop in, look in (on s.o.); **je n'ai fait qu'e. et sortir,** I just dropped in for a moment; **empêcher qn d'entrer,** to keep s.o. out; **la clef n'entre pas dans la serrure,** the key does not go into the lock; **faire entrer qch. dans qch.,** to insert, put, sth. in sth.; **une pareille idée ne lui est jamais entrée dans la tête,** such an idea never entered his head; *Th:* **Hamlet entre (en scène),** enter Hamlet; **e. en courant, en dansant,** to run, dance, in; **e. furtivement,** to steal in; (*b*) **e. dans l'armée,** to join the army; **e. dans une carrière,** to take up a career; **e. dans la finance,** to go in for finance; **e. en fonction,** to enter upon one's duties; *Mil:* **e. en compagne,** to take the field; *Sch:* **e. en vacances,** to break up (for holidays); (*c*) **e. dans de longues explications,** to go into long explanations; (*d*) **e. en colère,** to get angry; **e. en ébullition,** to begin to boil, to come to the boil. **2.** to enter into, take part in (sth.); **je n'entrerai pas dans l'affaire,** I will have nothing to do with the matter; **e. dans les idées de qn,** to agree with s.o.; **e. dans le jeu,** to enter into the spirit of the game; **e. dans une catégorie,** to fall into a category; **dans tout ceci l'imagination entre pour beaucoup,** in all this imagination plays a large part. **3.** *v.tr.* (*aux.* **avoir**) to bring, let, put (sth.) in; **e. des marchandises en fraude,** to smuggle in goods.

entre-rail [ɑ̃trərɑj] *n.m. Rail:* gauge (of track); *pl. entre-rails.*

entresol [ɑ̃trəsɔl] *n.m.* entresol; mezzanine (floor).

entre-temps [ɑ̃trətɑ̃] **1.** *adv.* meanwhile, in the meantime. **2.** *n.m.inv. A:* **dans l'e.,** meanwhile.

entretenir [ɑ̃trətnir] *v.* (*conj. like* TENIR) **I.** *v.tr.* **1.** to maintain; to keep (sth.) up; **e. qch. en bon état,** to keep sth. in repair; **j'entretiens la voiture moi-même,** I look after the car myself; **e. son français,** to keep up one's French; **e. une correspondance avec qn,** to keep up a correspondence with s.o.; **e. l'espoir de qn,** to keep s.o.'s hopes alive; **e. le feu,** to keep the fire going. **2.** (*a*) to maintain, support, keep (family, mistress, fleet, etc.); **il ne gagne pas de quoi s'e.,** he does not earn enough to live on, to keep himself; (*b*) **e. des soupçons,** to entertain, harbour, suspicions. **3. e. qn (de qch.),** to converse with, talk to, s.o. (about sth.). **II. s'entretenir 1. s'e. avec qn (de qch.),** to converse, talk, with s.o. (about sth.), to discuss (sth.) with s.o. **2.** *Sp:* to keep fit.

entretenu [ɑ̃trətny] *a.* **1. femme entretenue,** kept woman. **2.** *W.Tel:* sustained (oscillations); undamped, continuous (waves).

entretien [ɑ̃trətjɛ̃] *n.m.* **1.** upkeep, maintenance (of roads, etc.); maintenance (of machines, etc.); **personnel d'e.,** maintenance staff; **e. (par les fournisseurs),** servicing (of car, radio); **manuel d'e.,** service manual; **produits d'e.,** (household) cleaning materials. **2.** support, maintenance (of family, army, etc.). **3.** conversation, interview; **j'ai eu un e. avec lui,** I had a talk with him; **avoir des entretiens avec le patronat,** to hold talks with the employers.

entretoile [ɑ̃trətwal] *n.f.* (lace) insertion.

entretoise [ɑ̃trətwaz] *n.f. Const: etc:* brace, strut, crossbar, tie, stay.

entretoisement [ɑ̃trətwazmɑ̃] *n.m. Const:* **1.** bracing, staying, strutting. **2.** = ENTRETOISE.

entretoiser [ɑ̃trətwaze] *v.tr. Const: etc:* to (cross-)brace, stay, strut, tie.

entre-tuer (s') [sɑ̃trətɥe] *v.pr.* to kill one another.

entre-voie [ɑ̃trəvwa] *n.f. Rail:* space between tracks. *pl. entre-voies.*

entrevoir [ɑ̃trəvwar] *v.tr.* (*conj. like* VOIR) to catch sight, catch a glimpse, of (s.o., sth.); **je n'ai fait que l'e.,** I caught only a glimpse of him; **il entrevoyait la vérité,** he had an inkling of the truth; **j'entrevois des difficultés,** I foresee difficulties.

entrevue [ɑ̃trəvy] *n.f.* interview.

entrouvert [ɑ̃truvɛr] *a.* **1.** half-open (window, flower, etc.); **laissez la porte entrouverte,** leave the door ajar. 2. gaping, yawning (chasm).

entrouvrir [ɑ̃truvrir] *v.* 1. *v.tr.* (*conj. like* OUVRIR) to half open (door, eyes, etc.); **e. la porte,** to set the door ajar. 2. **s'e.** (*a*) to half open; (*b*) (*of chasm*) to open up, gape, yawn.

énucléation [enykleasjɔ̃] *n.f. Surg:* enucleation.

énucléer [enyklee] *v.tr. Surg:* to enucleate (tumour, eye).

énumératif, -ive [enymeratif, -iv] *a.* enumerative.

énumération [enymerasjɔ̃] *n.f.* enumeration; recital (of facts); counting (of votes).

énumérer [enymere] *v.tr.* **(j'énumère, n. énumérons; j'énumérerai)** to enumerate; to count up; **é. les voix,** to count the votes.

envahir [ɑ̃vair] *v.tr.* 1. to invade, to overrun (country, etc.); **envahi par les mauvaises herbes,** overgrown with weeds; **envahi par l'eau,** flooded; **quand le doute nous envahit,** when we are seized with doubt; **la politique envahit tout,** politics invade everything. 2. to encroach on (s.o.'s territory).

envahissant [ɑ̃vaisɑ̃] *a.* intrusive (neighbours); invasive (plants).

envahissement [ɑ̃vaismɑ̃] *n.m.* invasion, overrunning; encroachment; inrush (of water, etc.).

envahisseur [ɑ̃vaisœr] *n.m.* invader.

envasement [ɑ̃vɑzmɑ̃] *n.m.* silting.

envaser [ɑ̃vɑze] *v.* 1. *v.tr.* to run (boat) on the mud. 2. **s'e.** (*a*) (*of harbour, etc.*) to silt up; (*b*) (*of pers.*) to get stuck in the mud.

enveloppant, -ante [ɑ̃vlɔpɑ̃, -ɑ̃t] *a.* enveloping, enclosing; *Aut:* **pare-choc(s) e.,** wrap-round bumper.

enveloppe [ɑ̃vlɔp] *n.f.* 1. (*a*) wrapper, wrapping (of parcel, etc.); (*b*) envelope; **envoyer qch. sous e.,** to send sth. under cover; **e. à panneau transparent,** window envelope; **e. à panneau découpé,** aperture envelope; **e. premier jour,** first-day cover; *F:* **recevoir une e.,** to receive a bribe. 2. **un bon cœur sous une rude e.,** a kind heart beneath a rough exterior, external appearance. 3. sheathing, casing, jacket (of boiler); **e. calorifuge,** (insulating) lagging; *Aut:* outer cover (of tyre); **e. d'induit,** armature casing.

enveloppement [ɑ̃vlɔpmɑ̃] *n.m.* 1. envelopment, wrapping (up); *Mil:* **manœuvre d'e.,** enveloping, encircling, movement. 2. (*a*) sheath (of seed, etc.); (*b*) *Med:* **e. froid,** cold pack.

envelopper [ɑ̃vlɔpe] *v.tr.* 1. to envelop; (*a*) to wrap (s.o., sth.) up; **e. un paquet,** to wrap up, do up, a parcel; **enveloppé de bandages,** swathed in bandages; **enveloppé de mystère, de brume,** shrouded in mystery, in mist; (*b*) to cover, case (tube, etc.); to jacket, lag, (boiler); (*c*) to surround, encircle, close in on (s.o.); **la nuit nous enveloppa,** darkness closed in on us. 2. **e. qn dans un désastre,** to involve s.o. in a disaster.

envenimement [ɑ̃vnimmɑ̃] *n.m.* 1. poisoning (of finger, etc.). 2. irritation, aggravation (of quarrel).

envenimer [ɑ̃vnime] *v.* 1. *v.tr.* (*a*) poison (wound, etc.); **e. une querelle,** to envenom a quarrel; (*b*) to irritate, aggravate (wound). 2. (*of wound*) **s'e.,** to fester; **la discussion s'envenimait,** the discussion was growing acrimonious.

envergure [ɑ̃vɛrgyr] *n.f.* spread, breadth, span (of bird's wings, etc.); wingspread, wingspan (of bird, aircraft); full span (of the arms); **de grande e., d'e.,** far-reaching, wide-spreading; on a large scale; **esprit de grande e.,** wide-ranging mind; **homme d'e.,** man of great ability.

envers¹ [ɑ̃vɛr] *n.m.* reverse, back; **l'endroit et l'e. d'un tissu,** the right and the wrong side of a material; **tissu sans e. (ni endroit),** reversible material; **l'e. de la vie,** the seamy side of life; **l'e. de la médaille,** the reverse of the medal; **l'e. du décor,** the other side of the picture; **à l'envers,** (i) on the wrong side, inside out; (ii) the wrong way up; upside down; (iii) the wrong way round; back to front; **le monde à l'e.,** the world turned upside down; **j'ai la tête à l'e.,** my brain is in a whirl.

envers² *prep:* toward(s); **juste e. tous,** just to(wards), with, everyone; **son devoir e. sa patrie,** his duty to his country; **e. et contre tous,** against the whole world.

envi [ɑ̃vi] *n.m.* **ils étudient à l'e. (les uns des autres, l'un de l'autre),** they vie with one another, try to outdo each other, in their work.

enviable [ɑ̃vjabl̩] *a.* enviable.

envie [ɑ̃vi] *n.f.* 1. desire, longing; inclination; **avoir (l')e. de qch., de faire qch.,** to want sth., to do sth.; **j'avais e. de dormir,** I felt sleepy; **avoir bien e. de faire qch.,** to want very much to do sth.; **brûler d'e. de faire qch.,** to long to do sth.; **il a e. que je fasse cela,** he wants me to do that; **regarder qch. avec e.,** to look longingly at sth. 2. envy; **être dévoré d'e.,** to be eaten up, green, with envy; **faire e. à qn,** to make s.o. envious; **porter e. à qn,** to envy s.o. 3. (*a*) agnail, hangnail; (*b*) birthmark.

envier [ɑ̃vje] *v.tr.* (*impf. & pr.sub.* **n. enviions**) to envy. 1. to covet, want, hanker after (sth.); to wish for (sth.). 2. to be envious of (s.o., sth.); **e. qch. à qn,** (i) to envy s.o. sth.; (ii) to begrudge s.o. sth.

envieux, -ieuse [ɑ̃vjø, -jøz] *a.* envious (**de,** of); *n.* **faire des envieux,** to make people envious.

environ [ɑ̃virɔ̃] 1. *adv.* about; **il a e. quarante ans,** he is about forty. 2. *n.m.pl.* surroundings, outskirts, neighbourhood; **habiter aux, dans les, environs de Paris,** to live in the vicinity of, near, Paris.

environnant [ɑ̃virɔnɑ̃] *a.* surrounding (country).

environnement [ɑ̃virɔnmɑ̃] *n.m.* surroundings; environment.

environner [ɑ̃virɔne] *v.tr.* to surround.

envisagement [ɑ̃vizaʒmɑ̃] *n.m* facing, envisagement (of s.o., sth.).

envisager [ɑ̃vizaʒe] *v.tr.* **(j'envisageai(s))** (*a*) *A:* to look (s.o.) in the face; (*b*) to consider, envisage, contemplate (possibility, etc.); **e. l'avenir,** to look to the future; **le cas que nous envisageons,** the case under consideration; **cas non envisagé,** unforeseen case; **comment envisagez-vous la question?** what are your views on the matter? **il n'envisageait pas de partir,** he wasn't thinking of leaving.

envoi [ɑ̃vwa] *n.m.* 1. (*a*) sending, dispatch, forwarding, consignment (of goods); dispatch (of troops, etc.); **e. par mer,** shipment; **faire un e. tous les mois,** to send, dispatch, goods every month; *Com:* **lettre d'e.,** letter of advice; **e. de fonds,** remittance of funds; **faire un e. de fonds à qn,** to remit funds to s.o.; (*b*) *Fb:* **coup d'envoi,** kick-off. 2. consignment, parcel; shipment; **e. de l'auteur,** presentation copy, with the compliments of the author. 3. (*of poem*) envoi, envoy.

envol [ɑ̃vɔl] *n.m.* (*a*) (*of birds*) taking flight, taking wing; (*b*) (*of aircraft*) takeoff; **piste d'e.,** tarmac, airstrip, runway; *Navy: Av:* **pont d'e.,** flight deck.

envolée [ɑ̃vɔle] *n.f.* (*a*) (i) flight (of birds); (ii) *Av:* takeoff; (*b*) **e. d'éloquence,** flight of oratory.

envoler (s') [sɑ̃vɔle] *v.pr.* (*a*) (*of bird*) to fly away, to fly off; to take flight, wing; **faire e. des oiseaux,** to put birds to flight, to flush (game) birds; (*b*) (*of aircraft*) to take off; *F:* (*of pers.*) to disappear, make off; (*c*) (*of hat, etc.*) to blow off; (*of papers*) to blow away; **le temps s'envole,** time is flying.

envoûtant [ɑ̃vutɑ̃] *a.* captivating.

envoûtement [ɑ̃vutmɑ] *n.m.* (*a*) sympathetic magic; hoodoo; (*b*) charm, appeal.

envoûter [ɑ̃vute] *v.tr.* to practise sympathetic magic on (s.o.); to hoodoo; **comme envoûté,** as if spellbound, infatuated.

envoûteur, -euse [ɑ̃vutœr, -øz] *n.* worker of spells.

envoyé, -ée [ɑ̃vwaje] *n.* messenger, representative; (government) envoy; *Journ:* **e. spécial,** special correspondent.

envoyer [ɑ̃vwaje] *v.* **(j'envoie, n. envoyons;** *fu.* **j'enverrai) 1.** *v.tr.* (*a*) to send (s.o., sth.); to remit (money); to dispatch (goods, telegram); to forward (goods); **e. qn à Paris,** to send s.o. to Paris; **e. une lettre à qn,** to send s.o. a letter; **envoyez-moi un petit mot,** drop me a line; **e. sa démission,** to send in, tender, one's resignation; **e. un baiser à qn,** to blow s.o. a kiss; **e. chercher qn,** to send for s.o.; **j'ai envoyé (qn) prendre de ses nouvelles,** I sent (s.o.) to ask after him; *F:* **je ne le lui ai pas envoyé dire,** I told him straight, to his face; *F:* **e. promener qn,** to send s.o. packing; *Nau:* **e. les couleurs, une vergue,** to hoist the colours, send up a yard; (*b*) *Nau:* **envoyez!** about ship! **2.** *P:* **s'e.,** to stand oneself (a treat); **s'e. un verre de vin,** to knock back a glass of wine; **s'e. une corvée,** to take on a tedious job.

envoyeur, -euse [ɑ̃vwajœr, -øz] *n.* sender; remitter (of money).

enzyme [ɑ̃zim] *n.f.* enzym(e).

enzymologie [ɑ̃zimɔlɔʒi] *n.f.* enzymology.

éocène [eɔsɛn] *a. & n.m. Geol:* eocene (period).

éolien, -ienne [eɔljɛ̃, -jɛn] **1.** *a.* **harpe éloienne,** Aeolian harp; **érosion éolienne,** wind erosion; **moteur é.,** wind engine. **2.** *n.f.* **éolienne,** windmill (for pumping).

éon [eɔ̃] *n.m.* aeon, eon.

épagneul, -eule [epaɲœl] *n.* spaniel.

épais, -aisse [epɛ, -pɛs] **1.** *a.* thick (hair, wall, sauce); dense (foliage); bulky (book); **é. de deux mètres,** two metres thick; **couper dans l'é.,** to cut into the thick part; **fourré é.,** close thicket; **brouillard é.,** heavy, dense, thick, fog; **avoir la taille épaisse,** to be thickset; *F:* **avoir l'esprit é.,** to be dense, dull-witted; **avoir la langue épaisse,** to have a furred tongue; **peu é.,** thin. **2.** *adv.* thick(ly); **semer é.,** to sow thick.

épaisseur [epɛsœr] *n.f.* **1.** thickness (of wall, etc.); depth (of layer); **le mur a deux pieds d'é.,** the wall is two foot thick; **courroie en trois épaisseurs,** three-ply belt; *Mec.E:* **feuilles d'é.,** feelers; **le peu d'é. d'une planche,** the thinness of a board. **2.** density, thickness (of foliage, fog, etc.); thickness (of sauce); depth (of thought).

épaissir [epesir] *v.* **1.** *v.tr.* to thicken ((i) wall, board, etc.; (ii) sauce, etc.). **2. s'é.,** to thicken, to become (i) thick, (ii) dense; (*of darkness*) to deepen; (*of pers.*) to grow stout.

épaississant [epɛsisɑ̃] *n.m. Phot:* thickener.

épaississement [epɛsismɑ̃] *n.m.* thickening.

épanchement [epɑ̃ʃmɑ̃] *n.m.* (*a*) pouring out, discharge (of liquid); *Med:* **é. de synovie,** synovial extravasation; (*b*) outpouring (of thoughts, feelings); effusion; **en veine d'é.,** in an expansive mood.

épancher [epɑ̃ʃe] *v.* **1.** *v.tr.* (*a*) to pour out (liquid); **é. sa bile,** to vent one's spleen; (*b*) **é. son cœur,** to pour out one's heart, to unbosom oneself. **2. (s')é.** (*a*) (*of liquid*) to pour out, overflow; *Med:* to extravasate; (*b*) to unbosom oneself.

épandage [epɑ̃daʒ] *n.m.* spreading (of manure, etc.); **champs d'é.,** sewage farm.

épandeur, -euse [epɑ̃dœr, -øz] *n.* spreader (of muck, asphalt).

épandre [epɑ̃dr] *v.* **1.** *v.tr.* to spread, scatter (manure, etc.). **2. s'é.,** to spread.

épanoui [epanwi] *a.* in full bloom; full-blown (rose); beaming (face, smile).

épanouir [epanwir] *v.* **1.** *v.tr.* to cause (flower, etc.) to open; to open out (petals); to spread (sails, feathers); **un large sourire lui épanouit le visage,** his face broadened into a grin. **2. s'é.** (*a*) (*of flower*) to open out, bloom, blow; (*b*) (*of face*) to beam, to light up; **chez nous elle s'épanouit,** she opens out with us.

épanouissement [epanwismɑ̃] *n.m.* **1.** (*b*) opening (out), blooming (of flowers); (*b*) brightening up (of the face); flowering (of art, etc.). **2.** (full) bloom.

épargnant, -ante [eparɲɑ̃ -ɑ̃t]. **1.** *a.* thrifty. **2.** *n.* saver.

épargne [eparɲ] *n.f.* **1.** saving, economy, thrift; **caisse d'é.,** savings bank; **l'é. privée,** private investors. **2. vivre de ses épargnes,** to live on one's savings.

épargner [eparɲe] *v.tr.* **1.** to save (up), put by (money, provisions); to economize, be sparing with (the butter, etc.); **é. ses forces,** to husband one's strength. **2.** to save, spare (energy, time); **é. à qn la peine de faire qch.,** to save s.o. the trouble of doing sth. **3.** to spare, have mercy on (prisoner, etc.).

éparpillement [eparpijmɑ̃] *n.m.* **1.** scattering, dispersal. **2.** scatter (of papers).

éparpiller [eparpije] *v.* **1.** *v.tr.* to disperse, scatter; to spread, strew (sth.) about. **2. s'é.,** (*of crowd, etc.*) to scatter, disperse.

épars [epar] *a.* scattered (houses); straggly (hair).

éparvin [eparvɛ̃] *n.m.* spavin (of horse).

épatamment [epatamɑ̃], *adv. F:* stunningly, splendidly.

épatant [epatɑ̃] *a. F:* wonderful; stunning; fine, great, splendid; gorgeous; **c'est un type é.,** he's a wonderful, grand, chap; **elle est épatante,** she's stunning.

épate [epat] *n.f. F:* swank, swagger; **faire de l'é.,** to show off, cut a dash.

épaté [epate] *a.* **1.** splay-footed (table, etc.); flat (nose). **2.** *F:* dumbfounded, flabbergasted.

épater [epate] *v.tr.* **1.** *F:* to astound, flabbergast, amaze; to bowl (s.o.) over; **rien ne l'épate, il ne se laisse pas é.,** nothing surprises him; he isn't easily impressed. **2.** to flatten out the base of (sth.).

épaulard [epolar] *n.m.* grampus, orc; killer whale.

épaule [epol] *n.f.* shoulder; **large d'épaules,** broad-shouldered; **hausser les épaules,** to shrug one's shoulders; **é d'agneau,** shoulder of lamb; **donner un coup d'é. à qn,** to lend s.o. one's help; to give s.o. a leg-up; **regarder qn par-dessus l'é.,** to look down one's nose at s.o.; **charger un fardeau sur son é.,** to shoulder a burden; *Mil:* **l'arme sur l'é.,** with rifle at the slope; **rouler les épaules,** to swagger.

épaulement [epolmɑ̃] *n.m.* **1.** revetment wall; *Fort:* breastwork. **2.** shoulder (of hill). **3.** shoulder(ing) of tenon, axle); bolster (of penknife, etc.).

épauler [epole] *v.tr.* **1.** to bring (gun) to the shoulder; *v.i.* to take aim. **2. é. qn.** to give s.o. a leg-up, to back s.o. up.

épaulette [epolɛt] *n.f.* (*a*) shoulder-strap (of slip, etc.); (*b*) *Mil:* epaulette; (*c*) shoulder pad.

épave [epav] *n.f.* (*a*) unclaimed object; (*b*) (i) waif, stray; (ii) down-and-out; (*c*) **é. (maritime),** wreck, derelict; **épaves d'un naufrage,** wreckage; **épaves flottantes,** flotsam; **épaves rejetées,** jetsam.

épée [epe] *n.f.* (straight) sword; rapier; **homme d'é.,** soldier; **coup d'é.,** swordthrust; **coup d'é. dans l'eau,** wasted effort.

épeiche [epɛʃ] *n.f. Orn:* **(pic) é.,** great spotted woodpecker.

épeichette [epɛʃɛt] *n.f. Orn:* **(pic) é.,** lesser spotted woodpecker.

épeler [eple] *v.tr.* **(j'épelle; j'épellerai). 1.** to spell; **mot mal épelé,** misspelt word. **2.** to spell out (text).

épellation [epɛlasjɔ̃] *n.f.* spelling.

épépinage [epepinaʒ] *n.m.* stoning (of raisins); coring (of apples); seeding (of melons).

épépiner [epepine] *v.tr.* to remove seeds, pips, from (fruit); to stone (raisins); to core (apples).
éperdu [epɛrdy] *a.* distracted, bewildered; desperate (resistance); **é. de joie,** wild with delight.
éperdument [epɛrdymɑ̃] *adv.* distractedly, madly, desperately; **é. amoureux,** head over heels in love; *F:* **je m'en fiche é.,** I couldn't care less, I don't give a damn.
éperlan [epɛrlɑ̃] *n.m. Ich:* smelt, sparling.
éperon [eprɔ̃] *n.m.* **1.** spur; **donner de l'é. à son cheval, piquer de l'é.,** to spur one's horse; **gagner ses éperons,** to win one's spurs. **2.** (*a*) spur (of violet, mountain range, cock's leg); (*b*) ram (of warship). **3.** buttress (of wall); cutwater (of bridge).
éperonner [eprɔne] *v.tr.* **1.** (*a*) to spur, put spurs to (horse); **é. qn,** to spur, urge, s.o. on; (*b*) to ram (enemy ship). **2.** to spur, put spurs on (boot, etc.).
épervier [epɛrvje] *n.m.* **1.** sparrowhawk. **2.** *Fish:* castnet.
éphémère [efemɛr] **1.** *a.* ephemeral; short-lived, passing, fleeting (happiness, etc.). **2.** *n.m. Ent:* ephemera, mayfly.
éphéméride [efemerid] *n.f.* **1.** *Astr:* ephemeris; *F:* **calendrier é.,** tear-off calendar. **2.** *pl.* ephemerides; astronomical tables; **éphémérides nautiques,** nautical almanac.
Éphèse [efɛz] *Pr.n.f. A. Geog:* Ephesus.
épi [epi] *n.m.* **1.** ear (of grain); spike (of flower); **blés en é.,** corn in the ear; (*of cereals*) **monter en é.,** to ear. **2.** cluster (of diamonds); *Arch:* finial; *Med:* spica (bandage); *Rail:* **é. de voies,** spur tracks; *Aut:* **stationnement en é.,** angle parking; *Const:* **appareil en é.,** herringbone work. **3.** *Hyd.E:* groyne.
épicarpe [epikarp] *n.m. Bot:* epicarp.
épice [epis] *n.f.* spice; **pain d'é.,** gingerbread.
épicé [epise] *a.* highly spiced; hot (seasoning); *F:* **conte é.,** spicy story.
épicéa [episea] *n.m.* picea, spruce.
épicentre [episɑ̃tr̥] *n.m.* epicentre (of earthquake).
épicer [epise] *v.tr.* **(j'épiçai(s))** to spice (cake, drink); *F:* to add a bit of spice to (a story).
épicerie [espisri] *n.f.* **1.** *A:* spices. **2.** groceries; **être dans l'é.,** to be in the grocery business. **3.** grocer's shop; grocery; **é. fine,** delicatessen.
épicier, -ière [episje, -jɛr] *n.* grocer; *Pej:* **c'est un é.,** (i) he's a philistine; (ii) he cares only about making money.
épicurien, -ienne [epikyrjɛ̃, -jɛn] **1.** *a.* & *n.* *Gr.Phil:* Epicurean. **2.** *n.* epicure, sybarite.
épicurisme [epikyrism] *n.m.* **1.** *Gr.Phil:* epicureanism. **2.** epicurism.
épidémie [epidemi] *n.f.* epidemic; outbreak (of disease, burglaries).
épidémique [epidemik] *a.* epidemic.
épiderme [epidɛrm] *n.m.* epiderm(is), skin; cuticle; *Fig:* **avoir l'é. sensible, délicat,** to be thin-skinned, touchy.
épidermique [epidɛrmik] *a.* epidermal, epidermic (tissue, etc.).
épidiascope [epidjaskɔp], *n.m.* epidiascope.
épié [epje] *a.* spicate (flower).
épier [epje] *v.tr.* (*impf.* & *pr.sub.* **n. épiions, v. épiiez).** **1.** to watch (s.o.); to spy on (s.o.); to keep watch on (s.o.). **2.** to be on the lookout, on the watch, for sth.
épierrer [epjere] *v.tr.* to clear (field) of stones.
épigastre [epigastr̥] *n.m. Anat:* epigastrium.
épigastrique [epigastrik] *a. Anat:* epigastric.
épiglotte [epiglɔt] *n.f.* epiglottis.
épigramme [epigram] *n.f.* epigram.
épigraphe [epigraf] *n.f.* epigraph.
épigraphie [epigrafi] *n.f.* epigraphy.
épilage [epilaʒ] *n.m.*, **épilation** [epilasjɔ̃] *n.f.* depilation; removal of superfluous hair; plucking (of eyebrows).
épilatoire [epilatwar] *a.* & *n.m.* depilatory; **crème é.,** hair removing cream.
épilepsie [epilɛpsi] *n.f.* epilepsy.
épileptique [epilɛptik] *a.* & *n.m.* & *f.* epileptic.
épiler [epile] *v.tr.* to depilate; to remove superfluous hairs; to pluck (eyebrows).
épilogue [epilɔg] *n.m.* epilogue.
épiloguer [epilɔge]. **1.** *v.tr.* *A:* to pass censure on (s.o., sth.) **2.** *v.i.* **é. sur qch., qn,** to carp at, cavil at, about, sth., s.o.; **ce n'est pas la peine d'é.,** no need to go on commenting.
épilogueur, -euse [epilɔgœr, -øz] *n.* caviller, fault-finder.
épinard [epinar] *n.m.* spinach; *Cu:* **épinards en branches,** leaf spinach.
épine [epin] *n.f.* **1.** thornbush; **é. blanche,** hawthorn; **é. noire,** blackthorn; **é. de rat,** butcher's broom. **2.** (*a*) thorn, prickle; *Fig:* **la vie est hérissée d'épines,** life bristles with difficulties; **être, marcher, sur des épines,** to be on pins and needles; **une é. au pied,** a thorn in the flesh; **tirer à qn une é. du pied,** (i) to get s.o. out of a mess; (ii) to relieve s.o.'s mind; (*b*) spine (of hedgehog, fish). **3. é. dorsale,** backbone.
épinette [epinɛt] *n.f.* **1.** *Bot:* spruce. **2.** *Mus:* spinet, virginal. **3.** hen coop.
épinettière [epinɛtjɛr] *n.f. Fr. C:* spruce grove.
épineux, -euse [epinø, -øz] **1.** *a.* (*a*) thorny, prickly, spiky (bush, stem); spiny (fish); **être dans une situation épineuse,** to be in a ticklish situation; (*b*) *Anat:* spinous (process). **2.** *n.m.* thornbush.
épinglage [epɛ̃glaʒ] *n.m.* pinning.
épingle [epɛ̃gl] *n.f.* pin; **é. de cravate,** tiepin; **de sûreté, de nourrice,** safety pin; **é. à cheveux,** hairpin; **virage en é. à cheveux,** hairpin bend; **é. à linge,** clothes peg; **attacher qch. avec des épingles,** to pin sth. (up, down); **tiré à quatre épingles,** spick and span; **tirer son é. du jeu,** to get out of a ticklish situation; **coups d'é.,** pinpricks; petty annoyances; **chercher une é. dans une botte de foin,** to look for a needle in a haystack; **monter qch. en é.,** to make (too) much of sth.
épingler [epɛ̃gle] *v.tr.* **1.** to pin; to fasten (sth.) with a pin; **é. ses cheveux,** to pin up one's hair. **2.** *F:* (i) to arrest, to pinch (s.o.); (ii) to catch (s.o.) out.
épinière [epinjɛr] *a.f.* **moelle é.,** spinal cord.
épinoche [epinɔʃ] *n.f.* stickleback.
Épiphanie [epifani] *n.f.* Epiphany, Twelfth Night.
épiphyse [epifiz] *n.f. Anat:* epiphysis.
épique [epik] *a.* epic; **poème é.,** epic (poem).
épiscopal, -aux [episkɔpal, -o] *Ecc:* **1.** *a.* episcopal. **2.** *a.* & *n.* Episcopalian.
épiscopat [episkɔpa] *n.m.* episcopate.
épiscope [episkɔp] *n.m.* episcope.
épisode [epizɔd] *n.m.* (i) episode; (ii) instalment; **film à épisodes,** serial film.
épisodique [epizɔdik] *a.* episodic.
épisser [epise] *v.tr.* to splice (rope, cable).
épistolaire [epistɔlɛr] *a.* epistolary.
épistolier, -ière [epistɔlje, -jɛr] *n.* letter writer.
épitaphe [epitaf] *n.f.* epitaph.
épithète [epitɛt] *n.f.* epithet.
épitoge [epitɔʒ] *n.f.* (*a*) *Rom.Ant:* cloak; (*b*) *Sch:* = (graduate's) hood.
épitomé [epitɔme] *n.m.* epitome.
épître [epitr̥] *n.f.* epistle; *Ecc:* **côté de l'é.,** south, epistle, side (of altar).
éploré [eplɔre] *a.* & *n.* tearful, weeping.
épluchage [eplyʃaʒ] *n.m.* **1.** (*a*) cleaning (of feathers, etc.); picking (over) (of salad, wool,); shelling (of shrimps); (*b*) peeling, paring (of fruit, potatoes). **2.** hypercritical examination (of work).

éplucher [eplyʃe] *v.tr.* **1.** (*a*) to clean, pick (feathers, salad); *Tex:* to pick, pluck (wool); (*b*) to peel (fruit, potatoes). **2.** to examine, criticize (work) in detail.
épluchette [eplyʃɛt] *n.f. Fr.C:* **é. de blé d'Inde,** corn-husking party.
éplucheur, -euse [eplyʃœr, -øz] *n.* (*a*) (*pers.*) cleaner; **é de laine,** wool picker; (*b*) (*pers., device*) **é. de pommes de terre,** potato peeler.
épluchure [eplyʃyr] *n.f. usu. pl.* peeling(s), paring(s) (of potatoes, etc.); refuse.
épointage [epwɛ̃taʒ] *n.m.* breaking the point (of needle, pencil, etc.).
épointé [epwɛ̃te] *a.* blunt (needle, pencil.).
épointer [epwɛ̃te] *v.tr.* to break, blunt, the point of (needle, pencil, etc.).
éponge [epɔ̃ʒ] *n.f.* (*a*) *Nat.Hist:* sponge; (*b*) *Com:* sponge; **é. métallique,** (pot) scourer; **effacer une tache d'un coup d'é.,** to sponge out a stain; **passons l'é. là-dessus,** let's forget it; *Box:* **jeter l'é.,** to throw in the sponge; *Tex:* **tissu é.,** (Turkish) towelling; **serviette é.,** Turkish towel; (*c*) **é. végétale,** vegetable sponge; loofah.
épongeage [epɔ̃ʒaʒ] *n.m.* sponging; mopping (up).
éponger [epɔ̃ʒe] *v.tr.* **(j'épongeai(s), n. épongeons). 1.** to sponge up, mop up (liquid). **2.** to sponge, mop (surface); to sponge down (horse, etc.); **s'é. le front,** to mop one's brow. **3.** *Fin:* to absorb (deficit, etc.).
épontille [epɔ̃tij] *n.f. Nau:* (i) pillar, stanchion; (ii) shore, prop.
épontiller [epɔ̃tije] *v.tr. Nau:* to prop, shore (up).
épopée [epɔpe] *n.f.* epic (poem).
époque [epɔk] *n.f.* **1.** epoch, era, age; **l'é. glaciaire,** the ice age; **la belle é.,** the Edwardian era; **meubles d'é.,** period, (genuine) antique, furniture; **faire é.,** to mark an epoch; **découverte qui fait é.,** epoch-making discovery. **2.** time, period, date; **à l'é. de sa naissance,** at the time of his birth.
épouillage [epujaʒ] *n.m.* delousing.
épouiller [epuje] *v.tr.* to delouse.
époumoné [epumɔne] *a.* puffed, breathless.
époumoner (s') [sepumɔne] *v.pr.* to shout oneself hoarse.
épousailles [epuzɑj] *n.f.pl. A:* nuptials, wedding.
épousée [epuze] *n.f.* bride.
épouser [epuze] *v.tr.* **1.** to marry, wed; **é. une grosse dot,** to marry money. **2.** to espouse, take up, adopt (cause, doctrine, etc.). **3. é. la forme de qch.,** to take the exact shape of sth.; to fit sth. exactly.
époussetage [epustaʒ] *n.m.* dusting (of furniture).
épousseter [epuste] *v.tr.* **(j'époussette** [epusɛt]; **j'époussetterai)** to dust (furniture, etc.); to brush (the dust from) (clothes, etc.); to rub down (horse).
époustouflant [epustuflɑ̃] *a. F:* amazing, startling.
époustoufler [epustufle] *v.tr. F:* to astound, to flabbergast.
épouvantable [epuvɑ̃tabl̩] *a.* dreadful, frightful; appalling.
épouvantablement [epuvɑ̃tabləmɑ̃] *adv.* dreadfully, frightfully; appallingly.
épouvantail [epuvɑ̃taj] *n.m.* **1.** scarecrow. **2.** (*a*) bugbear, bogy; (*b*) **quel é.!** isn't she a fright!
épouvante [epuvɑ̃t] *n.f.* terror, fright; **jeter, porter, l'é. dans un pays,** to spread terror in a country; **saisi d'é.,** terror-stricken, frightened to death; **film d'é.,** horror film.
épouvanté [epuvɑ̃te] *a.* terror-stricken.
épouvanter [epuvɑ̃te] *v.* **1.** *v.tr.* to terrify, scare (s.o.); to frighten (s.o.) to death. **2. s'é.,** to take fright, to panic.
époux, -ouse [epu, -uz] *n.* husband, wife; spouse; **les é.,** the married couple, the husband and wife; **les é. Thomas,** Mr and Mrs Thomas.
éprendre (s') [seprɑ̃dr̩] *v.pr.* (*conj. like* PRENDRE). to become attached (**de,** to); **s'é. de qn, qch.,** to fall in love with s.o.; to take a fancy to sth.
épreuve [eprœv] *n.f.* **1.** (*a*) proof, test, trial; **é. d'un pont,** test(ing) of a bridge; **é. d'outrance,** resistance test; **faire l'é. de qch., mettre qch. à l'é.,** to try, test, prove, sth., to put sth. to the test; **à l'é. du feu, de l'eau,** fireproof, waterproof; **mécanisme à toute é.,** foolproof mechanism; **bonté à toute é.,** never-failing kindness; (*b*) (examination) test, paper; (*c*) *Sp:* event (at athletic meeting); **é. éliminatoire,** (preliminary) heat; **épreuves sur terrain,** field events; **épreuves sur piste,** track events; (*d*) *A:* **l'e. du feu,** ordeal by fire. **2.** trial, affliction, ordeal; **passer par de rudes épreuves,** to go through a bad time. **3.** *Typ: Engr:* proof; *Phot:* print; *Cin:* **épreuves (de tournage),** rushes.
épris [epri] *a.* **1. é. de qn,** in love with s.o.. **2. é. de qch.,** devoted to, passionately fond of, sth.
éprouvant [epruvɑ̃] *a.* trying, distressing; tiring.
éprouvé [epruve] *a.* **1.** tested, tried; **remède é.,** well tried remedy. **2.** stricken (family); hard-hit (district); **troupes très éprouvées,** troops that have suffered severely.
éprouver [epruve] *v.tr.* **1.** to test, try (s.o., sth.); to put (s.o., sth.) to the test. **2.** (*a*) to feel, experience (sensation, pain, etc.); (*b*) to sustain, suffer, (a loss); to meet with (difficulties).
éprouvette [epruvɛt] *n.f.* **1.** test tube; **bébé é.,** test-tube baby. **2.** *Metall:* test piece, bar.
épucer [epyse] *v.tr.* **(j'épuçai(s); n. épuçons);** to clean (dog, etc.) of fleas.
épuisant [epɥizɑ̃], *a.* exhausting.
épuisé [epɥize] *a.* exhausted; (*a*) worked-out (soil, mine); **édition épuisée,** edition out of print; *El:* **pile épuisée,** dead cell; *Atom.Ph:* **uranium é.,** depleted, impoverished uranium; (*b*) tired out, worn out; *F:* dead-beat.
épuisement [epɥizmɑ̃] *n.m.* **1.** exhausting, using up (of provisions, etc.); emptying, draining (of cask, cistern); depletion (of resources); *Atom. Ph:* depletion, impoverishment (of uranium); **é. d'une mine,** (i) exhausting, working out, (ii) drainage, pumping out, of a mine; *Com:* **jusqu'à é. des stocks,** as long as supplies last. **2.** exhaustion; **é. cérébral,** brain fag.
épuiser [epɥize] *v.* **1.** *v.tr.* to exhaust; (*a*) to use up, consume (provisions, ammunition, etc.); to drain, empty (tank); to sell out (goods); **é. une mine,** (i) to work out, exhaust, (ii) to drain, pump out, a mine; **é. un sujet,** to exhaust a subject; (*b*) to wear, tire, (s.o.) out. **2. s'é.,** to become exhausted; (*a*) (*of spring, etc.*) to dry up, to run dry; (*of stock, money, provisions*) (i) to run out, give out; (ii) to run low; (*b*) to tire, wear, oneself out; **mais je m'épuise à vous le dire,** I've told you so until I'm blue in the face.
épuisette [epɥizɛt] *n.f.* **1.** *Nau:* scoop, bailer. **2.** *Fish:* landing net.
épurateur [epyratœr] *n.m.* purifier; **é. de gaz,** gas-cleaning plant; **é. d'air,** air filter; air scrubber, cleaner.
épuration [epyrasjɔ̃] *n.f.* (*a*) purification, purifying, cleansing; filtering, scrubbing (of gas); purging (of morals); expurgation (of a text); (*b*) *Pol:* purge.
épure [epyr] *n.f.* **1.** diagram; working drawing. **2.** finished design, plan (of building, engine).
épurement [epyrmɑ̃] *n.m.* purity (of style).
épurer [epyre] *v.tr.* to purify, filter (gas, water, etc.); to refine (oil, metals); to scrub, clean (gas); to purify, purge (morals); **é. une administration,** to weed out, purge, a branch of the service.
équarrir [ekarir] *v.tr.* **1.** to square (timber, stone); **bois équarri,** scantling(s). **2.** to quarter, cut up the carcass of (animal).

équarrissage [ekarisaʒ] *n.m.*, **1.** squaring (of timber, stone); **bois d'é.,** scantling(s). **2.** quartering, cutting up (of animal carcasses); **chantier d'é.,** knacker's yard.

équarrisseur [ekarisœr] *n.m.* **1.** squarer (of timber, etc.). **2.** knacker.

équarrissoir [ekariswar] *n.m.* **1.** broach, reamer. **2.** (*a*) knacker's knife; (*b*) knacker's yard.

équateur [ekwatœr] *n.m.* **1.** equator; **sous l'é.,** at the equator; **é. magnétique,** magnetic equator; *Astr:* **é. céleste,** celestial equator. **2.** *Pr.n.m. Geog:* Ecuador.

équation [ekwasjɔ̃] *n.f.* equation; *Mth:* **é. du premier, du deuxième, degré,** simple, quadratic, equation.

équatorial, -iaux [ekwatɔrjal, -jo] **1.** *a.* equatorial. **2.** *n.m.* equatorial (telescope).

équatorien, -ienne [ekwatɔrjɛ̃, -jɛn] *a. & n. Geog:* Ecuadorian.

équerrage [ekɛraʒ] *n.m. Carp:* square, bevel, angle; **é. en gras,** obtuse angle (of timber); standing bevelling.

équerre [ekɛr] *n.f.* **1.** *Tls:* square; **é. à dessin,** set square; **e. à coulisse,** (sliding) caliper gauge; **fausse é.,** bevel square; **é. à onglet,** mitre square; *Surv:* **é. d'arpenteur,** cross-staff; optical square. **2. en é., d'é.,** at right angles; **hors d'é.,** out of square, out of perpendicular; **couper qch. à fausse é.,** to cut sth. askew, on the bevel; **mettre qch. d'é.,** to square sth. **3.** angle iron, iron knee, corner plate.

équerrer [ekere] v.tr. (a) to square; (*b*) to bevel (timber, etc.).

équestre [ekɛstr̥] *a.* equestrian.

équeuter [ekøte] *v.tr.* to stalk, tail (fruit).

équiangle [ekɥiɑ̃gl̥] *a.* equiangular.

équidés [ekɥide] *n.m.pl. Z:* Equidae.

équidistant [ekɥidistɑ̃] *a.* equidistant.

équilatéral, -aux [ekɥilateral, -o] *a.* equilateral.

équilibrage [ekilibraʒ] *n.m.* **1.** (*a*) counterbalancing, counterpoising; *Mch:* balancing (of slide valve, etc.); **masse d'é.,** counterpoise; (*b*) *El.E:* balancing (of circuit); correction (of phases); **é. d'impédance,** impedance match(ing). **2.** trim (of aircraft, etc.).

équilibration [ekilibrasjɔ̃] *n.f.* **1.** equilibration, counterbalancing. **2.** balancing (of the budget).

équilibre [ekilibr̥] *n.m.* equilibrium, balance, (equi)-poise; stability (of aircraft); poise (of mind); **il a un bon é.,** he's well balanced; **mettre qch. en é.,** to balance sth.; **budget en é.,** balanced budget; **tenir qch. en é. sur son nez,** to balance sth. on one's nose; **perdre l'é.,** to lose (i) one's balance, (ii) one's (mental) equilibrium; **faire perdre l'é. à qn,** to throw s.o. off his balance; **faire de l'é.,** to do balancing tricks; **é. européen,** balance of power in Europe; *El:* **fil d'é.,** equalizing conductor.

équilibré [ekilibre] *a.* in equilibrium; balanced; **esprit bien é.,** well balanced mind, **mal é., non é.,** ill balanced, unbalanced.

équilibrer [ekilibre] *v.tr.* to balance, (counter) poise, equilibrate; *Nau: Av:* to trim (craft); **é. qch. par un contrepoids,** to counterbalance sth.; **é. le budget,** to balance the budget; *Aut:* **é. les roues,** to balance the wheels.

équilibreur, -euse [ekilibrœr, -øz] **1.** *a.* balancing (action, etc.). **2.** *n.m. Av:* stabilizer.

équilibriste [ekilibrist] *n.m. & f.* equilibrist; tightrope walker.

équin [ekɛ̃] *a.* equine; **pied é.,** club foot.

équinisme [ekinism] *n.m. Med:* clubfoot.

équinoxe [ekinɔks] *n.m.* equinox; **vent d'é.,** equinoctial gale.

équinoxial, -iaux [ekinɔksjal, -jo] *a.* equinoctial.

équipage [ekipaʒ] *n.m.* **1.** *Nau:* crew, ship's company; *Av:* aircrew; **maître d'é.,** boatswain; **é. d'un camion,** crew of a lorry; *Mil:* **é. de char,** tank crew. **2.** *Mil:* (i) train, equipment; (ii) = Royal Transport Corps. **3.** equipage; (*a*) retinue, suite, train; *F:* **arriver en grand é.,** to arrive in state; (*b*) *A:* carriage and horses. **4.** pack of (stag) hounds; hunt; **maître d'é.,** master of the hounds. **5.** *O:* attire. **6.** equipment, apparatus; set (of tools); **é. de construction,** builder's paraphernalia, gear.

équipe [ekip] *n.f.* **1.** *O:* train of barges. **2.** gang (of workmen); *Mil:* working party; *Rail:* **é. de conduite, de locomotive,** engine crew; **é. de nuit,** night shift; **travailler par équipes,** to work in shifts; **homme d'é.,** gangman, navvy; **chef d'é.,** foreman (of gang); ganger; charge hand; **é. de secours,** rescue squad; **esprit d'é.,** team spirit. **3.** *Sp:* (*a*) team; **é. de cricket,** cricket eleven; **les deux équipes,** the two sides; (*b*) crew (of rowing boat).

équipée [ekipe] *n.f. F:* escapade, lark.

équipement [ekipmɑ̃] *n.m.* **1.** (*a*) equipment; fitting out; **é. en hommes,** manning; (*b*) *Nau:* rigging, fitting up (of sheers, etc.); (*c*) **é. électrique,** electrical fittings; **industrie de l'é. électrique,** electrical engineering industry. **2.** outfit (of ship, soldier, etc.); gear, appurtenances; **petit é.,** kit; **é. de survie,** survival kit.

équiper [ekipe] *v.tr.* to equip, fit out (**de,** with); **é. un navire,** (i) to equip, fit out, (ii) to man, a ship; **é. un atelier,** to fit out a workshop; *F:* **comme vous voilà équipé!** what a get-up!

équipier, -ière [ekipje, -jɛr] *n.* member of a team; team mate; **les équipiers,** (i) the players, the team; (ii) the crew (of rowing boat).

équitable [ekitabl̥] *a.* (*a*) equitable, fair, just, (dealing, etc.); (*b*) impartial, fair-minded (person).

équitablement [ekitabləmɑ̃] *adv.* equitably, fairly, impartially.

équitation [ekitasjɔ̃] *n.f.* equitation ((i) riding; (ii) horsemanship); **école d'é.,** riding school.

équité [ekite] *n.f.* equity, equitableness, fairness.

équivalence [ekivalɑ̃s] *n.f.* equivalence.

équivalent [ekivalɑ̃] *a. & n.m.* equivalent (**à,** to).

équivaloir [ekivalwar] *v.i.* (*conj. like* VALOIR) to be equivalent, equal in value (**à,** to); **cela équivaut à un refus,** that amounts to a refusal.

équivoque [ekivɔk] **1.** *a.* (*a*) equivocal, ambiguous (words, etc.); (*b*) questionable, doubtful, dubious (conduct, etc.). **2.** *n.f.* (*a*) ambiguity; **sans é.,** unequivocal(ly); **user d'é.,** to quibble; (*b*) ambiguous expression; (*c*) misunderstanding (**sur,** about).

érable [erabl̥] *n.m.* maple (tree, wood); **é. à sucre,** sugar maple; **sucre d'é.,** maple sugar.

érablière [erablijɛr] *n.f. Fr.C:* maple grove.

éradication [eradikasjɔ̃] *n.f. esp. Med:* eradication.

érafler [erɑfle] *v.tr.* (*a*) to scratch, graze, to scuff (leather); **s'é. les tibias,** to bark one's shins; (*b*) to score (inside of gun, etc.).

éraflure [erɑflyr] *n.f.* slight scratch, abrasion.

éraillé [erɑje] *a.* **1.** frayed (material); scratched (surface); fretted (rope). **2. yeux éraillés,** (i) bloodshot, (ii) red-rimmed, eyes. **3.** raucous, hoarse (voice).

éraillement [erɑjmɑ̃] *n.m.* **1.** (*a*) fraying (of material, etc.); fretting (of rope); (*b*) grazing, chafing (of surface). **2.** scratch. **3.** raucousness (of voice).

érailler [erɑje] *v.* **1.** (*a*) *v.tr.* to unravel, fray out (material); to fret (rope); (*b*) to graze, chafe, scratch (the skin, etc.); (*c*) to make (voice) hoarse. **2. s'é.** (*a*) to unravel, come unravelled; to fray; (*of rope*) to fret; (*b*) (*of skin, voice*) to grow rough.

ère [ɛr] *n.f.* (*a*) era, epoch; **en l'an 1550 de notre è.,** in 1550 A.D.; **è. de prospérité,** a period of prosperity.

érecteur, -trice [erɛktœr, -tris] *a. & n.m.* erector (muscle, etc.).

érectile [erɛktil] *a.* erectile (tissue).

érection [erɛksjɔ̃] *n.f.* **1.** erection, setting up, raising (of statue, mast). **2.** *Physiol:* erection.

éreintage [erε̃taʒ] *n.m.* = ÉREINTEMENT 2.
éreintant [erε̃tɑ̃] *a. F:* back-breaking, exhausting (work, etc.).
éreinté [erε̃te] *a. F:* exhausted, whacked.
éreintement [erε̃tmɑ̃] *n.m.* **1.** exhaustion, great fatigue. **2.** savage criticism; slating.
éreinter [erε̃te] *v.* **1.** *v.tr.* (*a*) to break the back of (horse, etc.); *F: A:* to thrash (s.o.); (*b*) to exhaust; to tire (s.o.) out; (*c*) to criticize unmercifully; to slate, slash (literary work, etc.); to pull (performance) to pieces. **2. s'é.** (*a*) to exhaust oneself; to tire oneself out; (*b*) to drudge, toil (**à,** at).
éreinteur [erε̃tœr] *n.m. F:* slashing critic.
erg¹ [εrg] *n.m. Ph.Meas:* erg.
erg² *n.m. Geog:* erg (of the Sahara).
ergot [εrgo] *n.m.* **1.** (*a*) spur (of cock, etc.); *F:* **monter, se dresser, sur ses ergots,** to get on one's high horse; (*b*) dewclaw (of dog, etc.). **2.** *Agr: Pharm:* ergot. **3.** *Mec.E: etc:* catch, lug, stop; **e. d'arrêt,** stop pin.
ergotage [εrgɔtaʒ] *n.m.*, **ergoterie** [εrgɔtri] *n.f. F:* quibbling, cavilling.
ergoté [εrgɔte] *a.* **1.** (*of bird*) spurred; (*of dog, etc.*) dew-clawed. **2.** *Agr:* ergotted, spurred (rye).
ergoter [εrgɔte] *v.i. F:* to quibble, cavil (**sur,** about); to split hairs.
ergoteur, -euse [εrgɔtœr, -øz] *F:* **1.** *a.* cavilling, quibbling, pettifogging. **2.** *n.* quibbler.
Érié [erje] *Pr.n.m. Geog:* **le Lac É.,** Lake Erie.
ériger [eriʒe] *v.tr.* **(j'érigeai(s)) 1.** to erect, set up, raise (statue, temple, etc.). **2.** to establish, set up (office, tribunal). **3.** to elevate, exalt; **é. une église en cathédrale,** to raise a church to (the dignity of) a cathedral.
ermitage [εrmitaʒ] *n.m.* hermitage.
ermite [εrmit] *n.m.* hermit; **vivre en e.,** to live the life of a recluse.
éroder [erɔde] *v.tr.* to erode, wear away (coast, etc.); to corrode, eat away (metals, etc.).
érosif, -ive [erozif, -iv] *a.* erosive.
érosion [erozjɔ̃] *n.f.* erosion; wearing away; **é. dentaire,** dental erosion.
érotique [erɔtik] *a.* erotic.
érotiquement [erɔtikmɑ̃] *adv.* erotically.
érotisme [erɔtism] *n.m.* (i) erotism; (ii) eroticism.
errant [εrɑ̃] *a.* rambling, roaming, roving, wandering (traveller, life, etc.); **chevalier e.,** knight errant; **le Juif e.,** the Wandering Jew; **chien e.,** stray dog; **pensées errantes,** wandering thoughts.
errata [εrata] *n.m.inv. Typ:* errata slip.
erratique [εratik] *a.* erratic (rocks, pulse, etc.).
erratum [εratɔm] *n.m. Typ:* erratum; misprint; *pl. errata.*
erre [εr], *n.f.* **1.** *Nau:* (head)way of (ship); **e. pour gouverner,** steerage way; **avoir de l'e.,** to have headway, to have way on; **perdre de l'e., son e.,** to lose way. **2.** *pl.* track, spoor, slot (of stag, etc.); **suivre les erres de qn,** to walk in s.o.'s footsteps.
errements [εrmɑ̃] *n.m.pl.* **1.** *A:* procedure, ways. **2.** erring ways; **retomber dans, revenir à, ses anciens e.,** to fall back into the bad old ways.
errer [εre] *v.i.* **1.** to ramble, roam, rove, wander, stroll (about); **e. par les rues,** to wander about the streets; **laisser e. ses pensées,** to let one's thoughts wander, stray. **2.** to err; to be mistaken.
erreur [εrœr] *n.f.* **1.** error; mistake, blunder; **e. de plume,** slip of the pen; **e. de date,** mistake in the date; **e. de jugement,** error of judgment; **e. judiciaire,** miscarriage of justice; **e. typographique,** misprint; **faire, commettre, une e.,** to make a mistake, **par e.,** by mistake; **sauf e.,** if I am not mistaken; *Com:* **sauf e. ou omission,** errors and omissions excepted; **faire e.,** to be mistaken; *F:* **c'est un malin, pas d'e.,** he's a smart one and no mistake. **2.** error; delusion; fallacy; **être dans l'e.,** to be under a misapprehension, to be mistaken; **une e. courante,** a current fallacy; **induire qn en e.,** to mislead, delude, s.o. **3. les erreurs de la jeunesse,** the errors of youth; **revenir de ses erreurs,** to turn over a new leaf.
erroné [εrɔne] *a.* erroneous, wrong, mistaken (statement, etc.).
erronément [εrɔnemɑ̃] *adv.* erroneously.
ersatz [εrzats] *n.m.inv.* substitute; **e. de café,** ersatz coffee.
erse¹ [εrs] *a. & n.m. Ling:* Gaelic (of the Highlands).
erse² *n.f. Nau:* grummet, grommet.
éructation [eryktasjɔ̃] *n.f.* eructation, belch(ing).
éructer [erykte] **1.** *v.i.* to eruct, to belch. **2.** *v.tr.* **é. des injures,** to belch forth abuse.
érudit [erydi] **1.** *a.* erudite, scholarly, learned. **2.** *n.m.* scholar.
érudition [erydisjɔ̃] *n.f.* erudition, learning, scholarship; **discourir avec é.,** to talk learnedly.
éruptif, -ve [eryptif, -iv] *a.* eruptive (disease, rock, etc.).
éruption [erypsjɔ̃] *n.f.* **1.** eruption (of volcano, etc.); **faire, entrer en, é.,** to erupt. **2. é. dentaire, des dents,** cutting of the teeth. **3.** *Med:* eruption, rash.
érysipèle [erizipεl] *n.m. Med:* erysipelas.
ès [εs] *contracted article* = **en les; docteur ès lettres** = D.Litt; **licencié(e) ès lettres** = Bachelor of Arts (B.A.).
esbroufe [εzbruf] *n.f. F:* showing off, swagger; *Box:* hustling tactics; **faire de l'e.,** to show off, to bluster; **vol à l'e.,** hustling; snatch-and-grab robbery.
esbroufer [εzbrufe] *v.tr. F:* to impress (s.o.), to take (s.o.) in, to bluff (s.o.).
esbroufeur, -euse [εzbrufœr, -øz] *n. F:* (*a*) swank; swaggerer; (*b*) snatch-and-grab thief.
escabeau, -eaux [εskabo] *n.m.* **1.** (wooden) stool. **2.** step ladder, pair of steps.
escadre [εskadr̥] *n.f. Navy:* fleet; squadron; **l'e. de la Méditerranée,** the Mediterranean fleet; *Av:* **e. aérienne,** wing; *U.S:* combat wing; **chef d'e.,** commodore; squadron commander; *Av:* wing commander.
escadrille [εskadrij] *n.f.* **1.** *Navy:* flotilla. **2.** *Av:* flight (of aircraft).
escadron [εskadrɔ̃] *n.m.* (*a*) *Mil:* squadron; **e. de chars,** armoured squadron, *U.S:* tank company; **chef d'escadron(s),** major; (*b*) *Av:* **e. de chasse, de bombardement,** fighter, bomber, squadron; (*c*) band, group; bevy (of girls).
escalade [εskalad] *n.f.* **1.** (*a*) scaling, climbing (of wall, cliff); (*b*) climb; (*c*) housebreaking; **cambrioleur à l'e.,** cat burglar. **2.** escalation (of war, prices, etc.).
escalader [εskalade] *v.tr.* to scale, climb; *Mil:* to escalade.
escale [εskal] *n.f. Nau: Av:* **1.** port, place, of call. **2.** call; *Av:* stop(over); **faire e.,** *Nau:* to put into port; *Av:* to touch down; *Av:* **escales prévues,** scheduled stops; **vol sans e.,** non-stop flight; **une e. de quatre heures,** a four-hour stop.
escalier [εskalje] *n.m.* staircase; (flight of) stairs; **e. de service, de dégagement,** backstairs; **e. de secours,** fire escape; *Nau:* **e. des cabines,** companion (way); **e. tournant, en vis, en colimaçon,** spiral staircase; **e. roulant, mécanique,** *Fr.C:* **e. mobile,** escalator, moving staircase; **rencontrer qn dans l'escalier,** to meet s.o. on the stairs; **j'ai l'esprit de l'e.,** I always think of a retort when it's too late.
escalope [εskalɔp] *n.f. Cu:* escalope (of veal).
escamotable [εskamɔtabl̥] *a.* concealable, disappearing (handle, etc.); retractable (aerial, *Av:* undercarriage).
escamotage [εskamɔtaʒ] *n.m.* (*a*) conjuring, sleight

of hand; (*b*) conjuring away (of card); **e. d'une tâche, difficulté,** skipping of a task, dodging of a difficulty; (*c*) *Av:* retraction (of undercarriage); (*d*) stealing, filching.

escamoter [ɛskamɔte] *v.tr.* (*a*) to conjure (sth.) away, make (sth.) disappear; (*b*) to skip (task), dodge (the issue); (*c*) *Av:* to retract (the undercarriage); (*d*) to steal, filch; **on m'a escamoté ma montre,** my watch has been pinched.

escamoteur, -euse [ɛskamɔtœr, -øz] *n.* (*a*) conjuror; (*b*) sneak thief.

escampette [ɛskɑ̃pɛt] *n.f. F: only in* **prendre la poudre d'e.,** to make off, do a bunk.

escapade [ɛskapad], *n.f.* escapade; (boy's) prank.

escarbot [ɛskarbo] *n.m. Ent:* **1. e. doré,** rosechafer; **e. de la farine,** meal beetle. **2.** *F:* (*a*) cockchafer; (*b*) dung beetle.

escarboucle [ɛskarbukl̥] *n.f. Lap:* carbuncle.

escargot [ɛskargo] *n.m.* snail; *Cu:* escargot; **allure d'e.,** snail's pace.

escargotière [ɛskargɔtjɛr] *n.f.* **1.** snailery. **2.** dish for snails.

escarmouche [ɛskarmuʃ] *n.f.* skirmish.

escarmoucher [ɛskarmuʃe] *v.i.* to skirmish.

escarpe[1] [ɛskarp] *n.f. Fort:* (e)scarp.

escarpe[2] *n.m.* cut-throat.

escarpé [ɛskarpe] *a.* steep (road); precipitous, abrupt (slope); sheer (cliff).

escarpement [ɛskarpəmɑ̃] *n.m.* **1.** steepness. **2.** steep slope; *Fort: Geog:* escarpment; *Geog:* **e. de faille,** fault scarp.

escarpin [ɛskarpɛ̃] *n.m.* (*a*) dancing shoe; pump; (*b*) court shoe.

escarpolette [ɛskarpɔlɛt] *n.f.* (child's) swing.

escarre, eschare [ɛskar] *n.f.* (*a*) scab; (*b*) bedsore.

Escaut (l') [lɛsko] *Pr.n.m. Geog:* the (river) Scheldt.

escient [ɛsjɑ̃] *n.m.* knowledge; *used in* **à bon e.,** deliberately, wittingly; **à mon escient,** to my (certain) knowledge; **dépenser son argent à bon e.,** to spend one's money judiciously.

esclaffer (s') [sɛsklafe] *v.pr.* **s'e. (de rire),** to burst out laughing; to roar with laughter; to guffaw.

esclandre [ɛsklɑ̃dr̥] *n.m.* (*a*) *A:* misadventure; (*b*) scandal; scene; row; **faire, causer, un e., faire de l'e.,** to cause a scandal; to make a scene.

esclavage [ɛsklavaʒ] *n.m.* slavery; **réduire qn en e.,** to enslave s.o., to reduce s.o. to slavery; **l'e. du bureau,** the drudgery of the office.

esclavagiste [ɛsklavaʒist] *n.m. U.S: Hist:* advocate of negro slavery.

esclave [ɛsklɑv] *n.m. & f.* slave; **marchand d'esclaves,** slave trader; **il fut vendu comme e.,** he was sold into slavery; **elle est l'e. de sa famille,** she is the family drudge; **être (l')e. de la mode, de son travail,** to be a slave to, the slave of, fashion, one's work.

escogriffe [ɛskɔgrif] *n.m.* **(grand) e.,** lanky, gawky, man.

escompte [ɛskɔ̃t] *n.m.* **1.** *Com:* discount, rebate; **accorder un e. sur les prix,** to allow a discount off the prices; **maison d'e.,** cut-price stores; **à e.,** at a discount. **2.** *Fin:* **e. (de banque),** discount; **e. officiel, taux d'e.,** discount rate; **prendre à l'e. un effet de commerce,** to discount a bill of exchange.

escompter [ɛskɔ̃te] *v.tr.* **1.** to discount (bill). **2. e. les variations du marché,** to anticipate, allow for, variations in prices; **e. un succès,** to take success for granted, to reckon on success.

escorte [ɛskɔrt] *n.f. Mil: etc:* escort; **faire e., servir d'e., à qn,** to escort s.o.; **conduire un prisonnier sous e.,** to escort a prisoner; *Navy:* **sous l'e. d'une corvette,** convoyed by a corvette.

escorter [ɛskɔrte] *v.tr.* to escort; *Navy:* to convoy, escort; **e. qn. jusqu'à la porte,** to show s.o. out.

escorteur [ɛskɔrtœr] *n.m. Navy:* escort (vessel).

escouade [ɛskwad] *n.f.* **1.** squad, gang (of workmen); group (of people). **2.** *A:* section (of infantry).

escrime [ɛskrim] *n.f.* fencing; swordsmanship; **faire de l'e.,** (i) to fence; (ii) to go in for fencing; **e. à la baïonnette,** bayonet drill.

escrimer (s') [sɛskrime] *v.pr.* to fight, struggle; to spar; **s'e. des dents, des mâchoires,** to eat heartily; **s'e. des pieds et des mains,** to fight tooth and nail; **s'e. à faire qch.,** to try hard to do sth.

escrimeur, -euse [ɛskrimœr, -øz] *n.* fencer.

escroc [ɛskro] *n.m.* swindler, sharper, crook.

escroquer [ɛskrɔke] *v.tr.* **1. e. qch. à qn,** to cheat, rob, s.o. of sth., to trick s.o. out of sth. **2. e. qn,** to swindle, defraud, s.o.

escroquerie [ɛskrɔkri] *n.f.* **1.** (obtaining by) false pretences; swindling. **2.** swindle, fraud.

eskimo, -os [ɛskimo] *a. & n. Geog:* Eskimo.

Ésope [ezɔp] *Pr.n.m. Gr.Lit:* Aesop.

ésotérique [ezɔterik] *a.* esoteric.

espace [ɛspas] **I.** *n.m.* space. **1.** (*a*) **laisser de l'e.,** to leave space, room; **e. vital,** lebensraum; **e. aérien,** airspace; *Town P:* **espaces verts,** open spaces; (*b*) **un e. de dix mètres entre deux choses,** a distance, space, of ten metres between two things; (*c*) **pendant le même e. de temps,** in the same space of time; **en l'e. d'une semaine,** within a week; (*d*) *Mus:* space. **2.** (*a*) (*void*) **regarder dans l'e.,** to stare into space; **e. lointain, extra-atmosphérique,** outer space; **vol, voyage, dans l'e.,** space flight, space travel; (*b*) *Mth:* **e. à trois, à quatre, dimensions,** three-dimensional, four-dimensional, space. **II.** *n.f. Typ:* space; **e. fine,** hair space; **e. moyenne, forte,** middle, thick, space.

espacé [ɛspase] *a.* far between, far apart; at wide intervals.

espacement [ɛspasmɑ̃] *n.m.* spacing (of columns, trees, etc.); *Typ:* spacing, leading (of lines); spacing out (of letters); *Typewr:* spacing, escapement; **barre d'e.,** spacebar, spacer.

espacer [ɛspase] *v.* **(j'espaçai(s)) 1.** *v.tr.* (*a*) to space; to leave a space between (objects); *Typ:* to lead, space, white out (lines); to space out, set out, (type); (*b*) **il faut e. nos rencontres,** we must meet less often. **2. s'e.** (*a*) to get farther apart, spaced out; (*b*) **ses visites s'espacent,** his visits are becoming less frequent.

espace-temps [ɛspastɑ̃] *n.m.inv. Mth: Ph:* space-time.

espadon [ɛspadɔ̃] *n.m. Ich:* swordfish.

espadrille [ɛspadrij] *n.f.* alpargata, espadrille, rope-soled sandal.

Espagne [ɛspaɲ] *Pr.n.f.* Spain.

espagnol, -ole [ɛspaɲɔl] **1.** *a.* Spanish. **2.** *n.* Spaniard. **3.** *n.m. Ling:* Spanish.

espagnolette [ɛspaɲɔlɛt] *n.f.* espagnolette, fastening (of French window).

espalier [ɛspalje] *n.m.* **1.** (*a*) **(arbre en) e.,** espalier; (*b*) wall (for espaliers). **2.** *Gym:* rib stalls.

espar [ɛspar] *n.m. Nau:* spar.

espèce [ɛspɛs] *n.f.* **1.** (*a*) kind, sort; **gens de toute e.,** people of all kinds, of every description; **il portait une e. d'uniforme brun,** he wore a kind, sort, of brown uniform; *F:* **cette e. d'idiot,** that silly fool! **e. d'idiot!** you idiot! (*b*) *Jur: etc:* **dans chaque cas d'e.,** in each specific case; **loi applicable en l'e.,** law applicable to the case in point; *F:* **mais je suis un cas d'e.,** but I'm a special case; (*c*) *pl.* specie, coin; **payer en espèces,** to pay in cash; **espèces sonnantes,** hard cash. **2.** species (of plants, animals); **l'e. humaine,** mankind. **3.** (eucharistic) species.

espérance [ɛsperɑ̃s] *n.f.* hope; **vivre dans l'e.,** to live in hope; **fonder son e. sur qn, qch.,** to found one's hopes on s.o., sth.; **mettre ses espérances en qch.,** to pin one's faith on sth.; **l'affaire n'a pas répondu à nos espérances,** the business did not come up to our expectations; **avoir des espérances,** to have expectations (of inheritance); **e. de vie,** expectation of life.

espérantiste [ɛsperɑ̃tist] *Ling:* **1.** *n.m. & f.* Esperantist. **2.** *a.* Esperanto (society, etc.).

espéranto [ɛsperɑ̃to] *n.m. Ling:* Esperanto.

espérer [ɛspere] *v.tr.* **(j'espère; j'espérerai) 1.** to hope for (sth.); **j'espère vous revoir,** I hope I'll see you again; **j'espère qu'il viendra,** I hope he comes, will come; **je n'espère pas qu'il vienne,** I don't expect him to come; *v.i.* **e. en Dieu,** to trust in God; **e. contre toute espérance, e. quand même,** to hope against hope. **2.** to expect (s.o., sth.); **je ne vous espérais plus,** I had given you up.

espiègle [ɛspjɛgl] *a. & n.* mischievous (child, reply, etc.); **petit(e) e.,** little monkey.

espièglerie [ɛspjɛgləri] *n.f.* **1.** mischievousness; **par pure e.,** out of pure mischief. **2.** prank.

espion, -ionne [ɛspjɔ̃, -jɔn] *n.* **1.** (*a*) spy; (*b*) secret agent; **avion e.,** spy plane. **2.** *n.m.* (*a*) concealed microphone; bug; (*b*) window mirror; (*c*) peephole (in door).

espionnage [ɛspjɔnaʒ] *n.m.* espionage, spying; **e. et contre-e.** = the secret service.

espionner [ɛspjɔne] *v.tr.* to spy on (s.o., s.o.'s movements, etc.); *v.i.* to spy.

esplanade [ɛsplanad] *n.f.* esplanade; promenade, parade.

espoir [ɛspwar] *n.m.* **1.** hope; **avoir l'e. de faire qch.,** to have hopes of doing sth.; **dans l'e. de vous revoir,** in the hope of seeing you again; **avoir bon e.,** to be full of hope; **mettre son e. en qch., qn,** to trust in sth., in s.o.; **nourrir l'e. de faire qch.,** to live in hope of doing sth.; **cas sans e.,** hopeless case. **2. vous êtes leur seul e.,** you are their only hope.

esprit [ɛspri] *n.m.* **1.** spirit; (*a*) **le Saint-E., l'E. saint,** the Holy Ghost, the Holy Spirit; **rendre l'e.,** to give up the ghost; **l'e. malin,** the Evil One; (*b*) ghost, phantom; spirit (of the dead); **il revient des esprits dans cette maison,** this house is haunted; (*c*) sprite; **e. follet,** elfish spirit, hobgoblin. **2.** (*a*) vital spirit; **esprits animaux,** animal spirits; **perdre ses esprits,** to lose consciousness; (*b*) *Ch: etc:* (volatile) spirit; **e. brut,** raw spirits; **e. de vin,** spirit(s) of wine. **3.** *Gr.Gram:* **e. rude,** rough breathing. **4.** (*a*) mind; **d'e. lent,** slow-witted; **d'e. vif,** quick-witted; **avoir l'e. tranquille,** to be easy in one's mind; **perdre l'e.,** to go out of one's mind; **elle avait l'e. ailleurs,** her thoughts were elsewhere; **où aviez-vous l'e.?** what were you thinking of? **présence d'e.,** presence of mind; **une pareille idée ne me serait jamais venue à l'e.,** such an idea would never have occurred to me, entered my head; **avoir l'e. de se taire,** to have the sense to be silent; (*b*) wit; **mots d'e., traits d'e.,** witticisms; witty remarks. **5.** (*a*) spirit; feeling; **e. de corps,** esprit de corps; **e. d'équipe,** team spirit; **e. de famille,** family feeling; **avoir bon e.,** to be well meaning, good natured; (*b*) spirit, (inner) meaning, sense; **s'attacher à l'e. de la loi plutôt qu'à la lettre,** to go by the spirit of the law rather than the letter. **6. les esprits sérieux,** serious-minded people; *Prov:* **les grands esprits se rencontrent,** great minds think alike; **un e. fort,** a freethinker; **un e. dangereux,** a dangerous man.

esquif [ɛskif] *n.m.* small boat; skiff.

esquille [ɛskij] *n.f.* splinter (of bone).

esquilleux, -euse [ɛskijø, -øz], *a.* comminuted (fracture); splintered (bone).

esquimau, -aude, -aux [ɛskimo, -od, -o] *n. & a.* (*occ. inv. in f.*) **1.** (*a*) Eskimo, Esquimau. (*b*) **chien e.,** husky. **2.** *n.m.* (*a*) chocolate ice (stick); (*b*) child's woolly suit.

esquimautage [ɛskimotaʒ] *n.m. Sp:* (canoe) rolling.

esquintant [ɛskɛ̃tɑ̃] *a. F:* exhausting, killing (work).

esquinter [ɛskɛ̃te] *v.tr. F:* **1.** to exhaust; to tire, wear (s.o.) out. **2.** (*a*) to spoil, damage (sth.); to ruin (one's health); (*b*) to slate (author, etc.).

esquisse [ɛskis] *n.f.* (rough) sketch; draft, outline (of portrait, novel, etc.); rough plan (of building).

esquisser [ɛskise] *v.tr.* to sketch, outline (portrait, design, essay); **e. un sourire,** to give a slight smile.

esquive [ɛskiv] *n.f. Sp:* dodging; **e. de la tête,** duck(ing); *Mil:* **manœuvre d'e.,** evasive action.

esquiver [ɛskive]. **1.** *v.tr.* to avoid, dodge, evade (blow, s.o.); *v.i. Box:* **e. de la tête,** to duck. **2. s'e.,** to slip away, off; to steal off; to make oneself scarce.

essai [esɛ] *n.m.* **1.** (*a*) trial, test(ing); **e. d'usine,** shop trial, bench test; **e. de vitesse,** speed trial; **terrain d'e.,** testing ground; **en (cours d')e.,** undergoing trials; **faire l'e. de qch.,** to test sth., to try sth. out; **mettre qn, qch., à l'e.,** to put s.o., sth., to the test; **prendre qch., qn, à l'e.,** to take sth., s.o., on trial, s.o. on probation, sth. on approval; **à titre d'e.,** experimentally; as an experiment; **vente à l'e.,** sale on approval; **commande d'e.,** trial order; **pilote d'e.,** test pilot; *Aut:* **essais sur route, e. routier,** road test; (*b*) *Metall:* assay(ing) (of ore); **fourneau d'e.,** assay furnace. **2.** (*a*) attempt, try; **au premier e.,** at the first attempt, try; **coup d'e.,** trial shot; (*b*) *Lit:* essay; (*c*) *Rugby Fb:* try; **transformer un e. (en but),** to convert a try.

essaim [esɛ̃] *n.m.* (*a*) swarm (of bees); (*of hive*) **jeter un e.,** to send out, throw off, a swarm; (*b*) crowd, swarm (of students); bevy (of girls).

essaimage [esɛmaʒ] *n.m.* **1.** swarming (of bees); hiving off (of population). **2.** swarming time.

essaimer [eseme] *v.i.* (*of bees*) to swarm; (*of population*) to hive off.

essart [esar] *n.m. Agr:* freshly cleared ground.

essarter [esarte] *v.tr.* to grub, clear (ground).

essayage [esɛjaʒ] *n.m.* trying on, fitting (of clothes); **salon d'e.,** fitting room.

essayer [eseje] *v.* **(j'essaie, j'essaye; n. essayons; j'essaierai, j'essayerai) 1.** *v.tr.* (*a*) to test, try (machine, etc.); to taste (wines); to try on (garment, etc.); *Metall:* to assay (ore); (*b*) **e. de qch.,** to try, taste, (wine, dish, etc.); (*c*) **e. de faire qch.,** to try, attempt, endeavour, to do sth.; **essayez de l'attraper,** try and catch him; **laissez-moi e.,** let me have a try. **2. s'e. à qch., à faire qch.,** to try one's hand, one's skill, at sth., at doing sth.

essayeur, -euse [esɛjœr, -øz] *n.* **1.** *Ind:* assayer; tester. **2.** *Tail: etc.* fitter; trier-on.

esse [ɛs] *n.f.* **1.** (the letter) s. **2.** S-shaped hook, pin; S-hook, snake-fastener. **3.** sound hole, *f*-hole (of violin).

essence [esɑ̃s] *n.f.* **1.** *Phil:* essential being; essence. **2.** (*a*) (essential) oil; attar (of roses); (*b*) motor spirit; petrol; *NAm:* gasoline; **poste d'e.,** petrol pump; filling, *NAm:* gas, station; (*c*) (concentrated) essence, extract (of beef, etc.). **3.** (*a*) nature, spirit; **l'e. de l'affaire,** the gist, essence, of the matter; **par e.,** essentially; (*b*) species (of tree); **essences résineuses,** resinous trees; conifers.

essentiel, -ielle [esɑ̃sjɛl]. **1.** *a.* (*a*) essential (truth, character, oil, etc.); **les organes essentiels,** the vital organs; (*b*) essential, necessary (condition, etc.). **2.** *n.m.* **l'e.,** the essential thing, the main point.

essentiellement [esɑ̃sjɛlmɑ̃] *adv.* (*a*) essentially, fundamentally; (*b*) primarily.

esseulé [esœle], *a.* left alone; lonely (person).

essieu, -ieux [esjø ɛ-] *n.m.* axle(-tree) (of wheel); **e. moteur,** driving axle; **e. tournant,** live axle.

essor [esɔr] *n.m.* flight, soaring (of bird); **donner l'e. à un oiseau,** to release a bird; **donner libre e. à son génie,** to give full scope to one's genius; **prendre son e.,** (i) to take wing, to soar; (ii) to spring into life; **e. d'une industrie,** rise of an industry; **prendre un grand e.,** to make great strides.

essorage [esɔraʒ] *n.m.* drying (of herbs, etc.); wringing (of linen); spin drying (of clothes).

essorer [esɔre] *v.tr.* to dry (herbs, etc.); to wring (linen) dry, to spin dry (clothes).

essoreuse [esɔrøz] *n.f.* **1.** drying machine, centrifugal drier; *Dom.Ec:* spin drier. **2. e. à rouleaux,** wringer; mangle.

essoucher [esuʃe] *v.tr.* to stub (land), clear (land) of tree stumps.

essoufflé [esufle] *a.* out of breath, short of breath; winded; *F:* puffed.

essoufflement [esufləmɑ̃] *n.m.* shortness of breath; breathlessness.

essouffler [esufle] *v.* **1.** *v.tr.* to blow, wind (horse, man). **2. s'e.,** to get out of breath, *F:* puffed.

essuie-glace [esɥiglas] *n.m. Aut:* windscreen wiper; *NAm:* windshield wiper; *pl. essuie-glaces.*

essuie-main(s) [esɥimɛ̃] *n.m.inv.* hand towel; **e.-m. à rouleau,** roller towel.

essuie-meubles [esɥimœbl̩] *n.m.inv.* duster.

essuie-pieds [esɥipje] *n.m.inv.* doormat.

essuie-verres [esɥivɛr] *n.m.inv.* glass cloth; tea towel.

essuyage [esɥijaʒ] *n.m.* wiping (up) (of dishes, etc.); wiping up, mopping up (of water, etc.).

essuyer [esɥije] *v.tr.* **(j'essuie; j'essuierai) 1.** to wipe, dry (dishes, etc.); to wipe (sth.) clean; to dust (furniture); to wipe up, mop up (water); **e. la vaisselle,** to wipe up. **2.** to suffer, endure, be subjected to (defeat, insults, etc.); **e. un refus,** to meet with a refusal; **e. une perte,** to suffer a loss; **e. le feu de l'ennemi,** to come under enemy fire.

est [ɛst] **1.** *n.m. no pl.* east; **un vent (d')e.,** an easterly wind; **le vent d'e.,** the east wind; **à l'e. de Suez,** eastward, (to the) east, of Suez; **vers l'e.,** eastward, towards the east. **2.** *a.inv.* **les régions e. de la France,** the eastern parts of France.

estacade [ɛstakad] *n.f.* **1.** barricade of piles; (*a*) stockade; (*b*) (i) breakwater; (ii) pier (on piles). **2. e. flottante,** (harbour) boom.

estafette [ɛstafɛt] *n.f.* (*a*) *A:* courier; (*b*) *Mil:* liaison officer; dispatch rider.

estafilade [ɛstafilad] *n.f.* gash in the face (from razor, sword).

estaminet [ɛstaminɛ] *n.m.* (*esp. in N.Fr.*) (small) public house; *F:* pub.

estampage [ɛstɑ̃paʒ] *n.m.* **1.** stamping, embossing (of silver, etc.); impressing (of pattern). **2.** *Metalw:* stamping, punching. **3.** *F:* (*a*) swindling, fleecing; (*b*) swindle.

estampe [ɛstɑ̃p] *n.f.* **1.** *Tls:* punch. **2.** print, engraving; **e. sur bois,** woodcut; **e. sur acier,** steel engraving; **cabinet des estampes,** print room (of library).

estamper [ɛstɑ̃pe] *v.tr.* **1.** to stamp, emboss (silver, coin, etc.); to impress (pattern). **2.** to stamp (sheet metal, etc.); to punch; **pièce estampée,** punched piece. **3.** *F:* to swindle, fleece (s.o.).

estampeur, -euse [ɛstɑ̃pœr, -øz] *n.* **1.** stamper, embosser. **2.** *F:* swindler.

estampillage [ɛstɑ̃pijaʒ] *n.m.* stamping, marking.

estampille [ɛstɑ̃pij] *n.f.* (official) stamp; identification mark; trademark.

estampiller [ɛstɑ̃pije] *v.tr.* to stamp document, etc.); to mark (goods); to hallmark (gold, silver).

esthète [ɛstɛt] *n.m. & f.* (a)esthete.

esthéticien, -ienne [ɛstetisjɛ̃, -jɛn] *n.* **1.** (a)esthetician. **2.** beauty specialist; beautician.

esthéticisme [ɛstetisism] *n.m.* (a)estheticism.

esthétique [ɛstetik] **1.** *a.* (a)esthetic; **chirurgie e.,** plastic surgery. **2.** *n.f.* aesthetics.

esthétiquement [ɛstetikmɑ̃] *adv.* aesthetically.

esthétisme [ɛstetism] *n.m.* (a)estheticism.

estimable [ɛstimabl̩] *a.* **1.** estimable. **2.** fairly good (work, etc.).

estimatif, -ive [ɛstimatif, -iv] *a.* estimated (cost, etc.); **devis e.,** estimate.

estimation [ɛstimasjɔ̃] *n.f.* (*a*) estimation (of value, price); valuing, appraising (of goods); assessment (of damage); (*b*) estimate, valuation.

estime [ɛstim] *n.f.* **1.** guesswork; *Nau:* reckoning; **à l'e.,** by guesswork; *Nau:* by dead reckoning; **navigation à l'e.,** dead-reckoning (navigation). **2.** (*a*) estimation, opinion; (*b*) esteem, regard; **témoigner de l'e. pour qn,** to show regard for s.o.; **tenir qn en grande, en médiocre, e.,** to think highly, little, of s.o.

estimer [ɛstime] *v.tr.* **1.** (*a*) to estimate; to value, appraise (goods); to assess (damage); **e. la gloire à sa valeur,** to rate glory at its true value; (*b*) to calculate (distance, etc.); *Nau:* to reckon; **longitude estimée,** longitude by dead reckoning. **2.** (*a*) to consider; **s'e. heureux,** to think, count, oneself lucky; **j'estime qu'il est de mon devoir de parler,** I consider it my duty to speak; (*b*) to esteem (s.o.); to have a high opinion of (s.o., sth.); to prize, value (sth.).

estivage [ɛstivaʒ] *n.m.* **1.** summering (of cattle) in mountain pastures. **2.** spending the summer (at a resort).

estival, -aux [ɛstival, -o] *a.* (a)estival (plant, illness, etc.); summer (residence, resort).

estivant, -ante [ɛstivɑ̃, ɑ̃t] *n.* summer visitor; (summer) holiday maker.

estiver [ɛstive] **1.** *v.tr.* to move (cattle, etc.) to summer pastures. **2.** *v.i.* (*of pers.*) **e. à la campagne,** to spend the summer in the country.

estoc [ɛstɔk] *n.m. A:* rapier *Fenc:* **coup d'e.,** (rapier) thrust; **frapper d'e. et de taille,** to cut and thrust.

estocade [ɛstɔkad] *n.f.* stab; *Fenc:* thrust.

estomac [ɛstɔma] *n.m.* stomach; **creux de l'e.,** pit of the stomach; **mal d'e.,** stomach ache; **avoir l'e. dans les talons,** to be ravenously hungry; **avoir de l'e.,** to have plenty of (i) pluck, (ii) cheek.

estomaquer [ɛstɔmake] *v.tr. F:* to stagger, astound, flabbergast.

estompage [ɛstɔ̃paʒ] *n.m.* shading (off).

estompe [ɛstɔ̃p] *n.f. Art:* stump; **dessin à l'e.,** stump drawing.

estompé [ɛstɔ̃pe] *a.* soft, indistinct, blurred (outline); blurred, dim (memories).

estomper [ɛstɔ̃pe] *v.tr. Art:* to stump; to shade off (drawing) with a stump; to blur, dim (landscape); to tone down (contrast).

estoquer [ɛstɔke] *v.tr.* (*of matador*) to kill (the bull).

estourbir [ɛsturbir] *v.tr. F:* (*a*) to kill (s.o.); to do (s.o.) in; (*b*) to astound (s.o.), knock (s.o.) flat.

estrade [ɛstrad] *n.f.* dais, rostrum; platform, stage.

estragon [ɛstragɔ̃] *n.m. Bot: Cu:* tarragon.

estrapade [ɛstrapad] *n.f.* **1.** *A:* strappado (punishment); *Nau:* dipping from the yard arm. **2.** *Gym:* skinning the cat; **faire l'e.,** to skin the cat.

estropié, -ée [ɛstrɔpje] **1.** *a.* crippled, disabled, maimed; **être e. de la jambe,** to have a lame, game, leg. **2.** *n.* **les estropiés,** the maimed.

estropier [ɛstrɔpje] *v.tr.* (*impf. & pr.sub.* **n. estropiions)** (*a*) to cripple, lame, disable, maim; (*b*) to murder (waltz, etc.); to mispronounce (word); to mutilate (text).

estuaire [ɛstɥɛr] *n.m.* estuary.

estudiantin [ɛstydjɑ̃tɛ̃] *a.* student (life, etc.).

esturgeon [ɛstyrʒɔ̃] *n.m.* sturgeon.

et [e] **1.** *conj.* and; **c'est un homme de grande énergie,**

et qui arrivera, he is a man of great energy, who will succeed; **et son frère et sa sœur,** both his brother and his sister; **j'aime le café; et vous?** I like coffee; do you? **et les dix francs que je vous ai prêtés?** and (what about) the ten francs I lent you? (NOTE: *there is no liaison with* **et; j'ai écrit et écrit** [ʒeekrieekri]). **2.** *n.m.* **et commercial,** ampersand.

étable [etabl̩] *n.f.* cowshed, byre; **é. à pourceaux,** pigsty.

établi [etabli] *n.m.* (work)bench.

établir [etablir] *v.* **1.** *v.tr.* (*a*) to establish (form of government, business house, peace, etc.); to set up (statue, agency); to put up (building); to construct (dam, railway); to settle, fix (place of residence); to install (machinery); to set (a sail); to pitch (a camp); to quote, fix (price); **é. un record,** to set up a record; (*b*) to establish, prove (fact, s.o.'s innocence); **é. une accusation,** to establish, substantiate, a charge; (*c*) to work out (plan, proposition, etc.); to draw up (plan); **considérer qch. comme chose établie,** to take sth. for granted; **é. un devis,** to make an estimate; **é. un compte, un bilan, un budget,** to draw up an account, a balance sheet, a budget; **é. une balance,** to strike a balance; (*d*) to institute, create (tax, tribunal, etc.); to prescribe, lay down (rule); to lay down (principle); to set (s.o.) up in business. **2.** **s'é.** (*a*) to settle (in a place); to set up house; (*b*) **s'é. épicier,** to set up as a grocer; (*c*) (*of custom, etc.*) to become established.

établissement [etablismɑ̃] *n.m.* **1.** (*a*) establishment; setting up, putting up, fixing, installing (of machinery, etc.); setting (of a sail); establishing, building up (of reputation, fortune, etc.); (*b*) establishment, proving (of innocence, guilt). **2.** working out (of design, etc.); drawing up, making up (of accounts, schedule, etc.); striking (of balance). **3.** instituting, creating, forming (of government, etc.); laying down (of rules); founding (of colony, industry). **4.** (*a*) establishment, settling (of one's children, etc.); (*b*) establishment, setting up (of a business); **frais d'é., coût de premier é.,** initial outlay, expenditure. **5.** (*a*) institution; **é. de charité,** charitable institution; **é. scolaire,** school, educational establishment; **é. de crédit,** bank; (*b*) *Hist:* (colonial) trading centre; settlement; (*c*) (i) factory; business; firm; **les établissements Martin,** Martin & Co.; **é. principal,** main branch; (ii) (business, etc.) premises.

étage [etaʒ] *n.m.* **1.** stor(e)y, floor (of building); **maison à un e., sans e.,** single-storeyed house; bungalow; **à deux étages, avec é.,** two-storeyed; **au troisième é.,** on the third floor; *NAm:* on the fourth story. **2.** (*a*) tier, range, step; **gâteau à quatre étages,** four-tiered cake; *F:* **menton à deux étages,** double chin; (*b*) *Geol:* stage, formation; (*c*) *Tchn:* stage; **compression par étages,** compression by stages; **fusée à trois étages,** three-stage rocket.

étagement [etaʒmɑ̃] *n.m.* arrangement in tiers; terracing (of vines on hillsides); staging (of turbine).

étager [etaʒe] *v.tr.* **(j'étageai(s)). 1.** to range (seats, etc.) in tiers; **jardin étagé,** terraced garden; **poulie étagée,** cone pulley. **2.** to perform (operation) by stages; **compression étagée,** compression by stages, staged compression.

étagère [etaʒɛr] *n.f.* (*a*) rack; (set of) shelves; whatnot; (*b*) shelf.

étai¹ [etɛ] *n.m. Nau:* stay; **voile d'é.,** staysail.

étai² *n.m.* stay, prop, strut; **é. de mine,** pit prop.

étaiement [etɛmɑ̃] *n.m.* staying, shoring, propping (up); buttressing.

étain [etɛ̃] *n.m.* **1.** (*a*) tin; **é. battu, é. en feuilles,** tinfoil, thin sheet tin; (*b*) **papier d'é.,** tinfoil, silver paper. **2.** pewter; **vaisselle d'é.,** pewter (plate).

étal, -aux, *occ.* **-als** [etal, -o] *n.m.* (*a*) butcher's stall, meat stall; (*b*) (market) stall.

étalage [etalaʒ] *n.m.* (*a*) display, show (of goods, etc.); **é. de bouquiniste,** secondhand bookstall; **faire l'é.,** (i) to set out one's wares; (ii) to dress the window(s); **mettre qch. à l'é.,** (i) to display sth. for sale; (ii) to put sth. in the window; **article qui a fait l'é.,** shop-soiled article; (*b*) showing off; show, parade (of learning); **faire é. de ses bijoux, son savoir,** to show off, parade, one's jewels, knowledge.

étalager [etalaʒe] *v.tr.* **(j'étalageai(s))** to display (goods) for sale.

étalagiste [etalaʒist] *n.m. & f.* (*a*) stallkeeper, stallholder; (*b*) window dresser.

étale [etal] *Nau:* **1.** *a.* slack (sea, tide); steady (breeze); **2.** *s.m.* **é. du flot,** slack water.

étalement [etalmɑ̃] *n.m.* **1.** (*a*) displaying (of goods, etc.); (*b*) spreading out (of linen to dry); spreading (of tablecloth); (*c*) *Cards:* laying down (of one's hand); (*d*) staggering (of holidays). **2.** *F:* showing off.

étaler [etale] *v.* **1.** *v.tr.* (*a*) *Nau:* (i) to stem (the current); to weather out, ride out (gale); (ii) to check (the way); (*b*) to display (goods), expose (goods) for sale; (*c*) to spread out, lay out (linen to dry, papers on the table, etc.); to spread (tablecloth, butter, paint, etc.); (*d*) *Cards:* to lay down (one's cards); (*e*) to parade, show off (one's wealth); (*f*) to stagger (holidays, payments). **2.** **s.'é** (*a*) (*of village, etc.*) to spread out; **arbre à cime étalée,** large-crowned tree; (*b*) to stretch oneself out; to sprawl; **s'é. sur un sujet,** to hold forth, to spread oneself, on a topic; **s'é. par terre,** (i) to lie down full length on the ground; (ii) to come a cropper.

étalinguer [etalɛ̃ge] *v.tr. Nau:* to bend (cable) to the anchor.

étalingure [etalɛ̃gyr] *n.f. Nau:* clinch (of cable to anchor).

étalon¹ [etalɔ̃] *n.m.* stallion.

étalon² *n.m.* standard (of measures); **mètre é.,** standard metre; *Fin:* **l'é (d')or,** the gold standard.

étalonnage [etalɔnaʒ], **étalonnement** [etalɔnmɑ̃] *n.m.* **1.** standardization (of weights, etc.); calibration (of tubes, etc.); testing, gauging (of instruments); rating (of light); *W.Tel:* logging (of stations). **2.** stamping, marking (of standardized weights, etc.).

étalonner [etalɔne] *v.tr.* **1.** to standardize (weights, etc.); to calibrate (tubes, etc.); to test, gauge, adjust (instruments); to rate (light); *Psy:* to standardize (test); *W.Tel:* to log (stations). **2.** to stamp, mark (standardized weights, etc.).

étamage [etamaʒ] *n.m.* **1.** tinning (of copper, etc.); tinplating (of sheet iron). **2.** silvering (of mirror).

étambot [etɑ̃bo] *n.m. Nau:* stern post.

étamer [etame] *v.tr.* **1.** to tin (copper, etc.); to tinplate (iron). **2.** to silver (mirror).

étameur [etamœr] *n.m.* **1.** tinner, tinsmith; **é. ambulant,** tinker. **2.** silverer (of mirrors).

étamine¹ [etamin] *n.f.* **1.** (*a*) coarse muslin; bolting cloth; butter muslin, cheesecloth; **é. de crin,** haircloth; (*b*) **é. à pavillon,** bunting. **2.** sieve, strainer; **passer à, par, l'é.,** (i) to sift, bolt, (flour, etc.); (ii) to sift, (evidence, etc.).

étamine² *n.f. Bot:* stamen.

étampage [etɑ̃paʒ] *n.m.* **1.** stamping, punching. **2.** (*a*) swaging; (*b*) drop forging.

étampe [etɑ̃p] *n.f.* **1.** stamp, die. **2.** (*a*) punch; (*b*) swage.

étamper [etɑ̃pe] *v.tr.* **1.** to stamp (sheet metal, etc.); to punch (horseshoe, etc.); (*a*) to swage, shape with a swage; (*b*) to drop-forge; **pièce étampée,** drop forging.

étanche [etɑ̃ʃ] *a.* impervious; (water)tight; **é. à l'eau,**

à l'air, à la poussière, watertight, airtight, dustproof; *N.Arch:* **cloison é.,** watertight bulkhead; *Fig:* impenetrable barrier (between departments, etc.); *Av:* **cabine é.,** pressure cabin; *n.f.* **entretenir une toiture à é. d'eau,** to keep a roof watertight.

étanchéité [etɑ̃ʃeite] *n.f.* **é. à l'eau, à l'air,** watertightness, airtightness; **vérifier l'é.,** to check for leaks.

étancher [etɑ̃ʃe] *v.tr.* **1.** (*a*) to check the flow of (liquid); to sta(u)nch (blood); to check, dry (s.o.'s tears); **é. une voie d'eau,** to stop a leak; (*b*) to quench, slake (one's thirst); (*c*) to clear of water; to dry up. **2.** to make watertight, airtight; to seal.

étançon [etɑ̃sɔ̃] *n.m.* prop, stay; *Nau:* stanchion.

étançonnement [etɑ̃sɔnmɑ̃] *n.m.* staying, propping, shoring (up) (of wall, etc.); underpinning (of building).

étang [etɑ̃] *n.m.* pond, pool.

étape [etap] *n.f.* (*a*) stopping place; **faire é.,** to stop; **nous avons fait é. à Bordeaux,** we stopped overnight at Bordeaux; **brûler une é.,** (i) *Rail: etc:* to fail to stop at a scheduled stop; (ii) to press on; **brûler les étapes,** to get ahead of schedule; *Mil:* **zone des étapes,** area behind the lines; (*b*) day's run, march, flight; **à, par, petites étapes,** by easy stages; **nous avons fait hier une é. de 500 kilomètres,** we covered, did, 500 kilometres yesterday; (*c*) **d'é. en é.,** progressively, stage by stage.

état [eta] *n.m.* **1.** state, condition; **dans l'é. (actuel) des choses,** in the present circumstances, state of things; **en (bon) é.,** in good condition, in good order; undamaged; (*house*) in good repair; (*athlete*) in good shape, good trim; **navire en bon é. (de navigabilité),** seaworthy ship; **en mauvais é., hors d'é.,** in need of repair, out of order, in poor condition; **mettre ses affaires en é.,** to put one's affairs in order; **remettre qch. en é.,** to put sth. to rights; to overhaul, recondition (engine, etc.); **laisser les choses en l'é.,** to leave things as they stand; **en é. d'ivresse,** in a state of intoxication; **é. d'esprit,** state, frame, of mind; **é de guerre,** (i) state of war; (ii) war footing; **être en é. de faire qch.,** to be (i) fit, in a fit state, (ii) able, ready, in a position, to do sth.; **n'être plus en é. de travailler,** to be past (one's) work; **hors d'é. de faire qch.,** unable, not in a position, to do sth.; **hors d'é. de rendre aucun service,** totally unfit for use; *F:* **être dans tous ses états,** to be upset, in a great state. **2.** (*a*) statement, report, list, return; **é. néant,** nil return; **é. des dépenses, é. de compte,** statement of expenses, statement of account; *Jur:* **é. de frais,** bill of costs; **é. des lieux,** inventory of fixtures (in rented premises); *Adm: Mil:* **é. de services,** record of service; **é. nominatif,** list of names, (nominal) roll; **rayer qn des états,** to strike s.o. off the rolls; (*b*) **faire é de qch.,** (i) to take sth. into account, to note a fact; (ii) to depend, count, on sth.; **faire grand é. de qn,** to think highly of s.o.; (*c*) *Adm:* **é. civil,** (i) civil status; (ii) registry office; **actes de l'é. civil,** certificates of births, marriages, deaths; **informer l'é. civil d'un décès,** to register a death. **3.** profession, trade; **militaire, épicier, de son é.,** soldier by profession, grocer by trade. **4.** *Pol:* (*a*) estate (of the realm); **le tiers é.,** the third estate, the commonalty; *Hist:* **les États généraux,** the States General; (*b*) state, body politic, (form of) government; **coup d'É.,** coup (d'état); **homme d'É.,** statesman; **pour des raisons d'É.,** for reasons of state; **é. providence,** welfare state; (*c*) nation, state.

étatique [etatik] *a.* (of the) state; **l'appareil é.,** the state machine.

étatisation [etatizasjɔ̃] *n.f.* nationalization.

étatisé [etatize] *a.* state-controlled; nationalized.

étatiser [etatize] *v.tr.* to nationalize.

étatisme [etatism] *n.m.* state management, control; state socialism.

étatiste [etatist] *n.m.* partisan of state control.

état-major [etamaʒɔr] *n.m.* **1.** *Mil: etc:* (*a*) (general) staff; **officier d'é.-m.,** staff officer; **carte d'é-m.** = ordnance survey map. (*b*) headquarters. **2.** management (of firm, etc.); *pl. états-majors.*

États-Unis (les) [lezetazyni] *Pr.n.m.pl.* the United States (of America); *F:* the States.

étau, -aux [eto] *n.m. Tls:* vice, *NAm:* vise; **é. d'établi,** bench vice.

étayage [etɛjaʒ] *n.m.* staying, shoring, propping (up).

étayer [eteje] *v.tr.* (**j'étaie, j'étaye; j'étaierai, j'etayerai**) (*a*) to stay, prop (up), shore (up), support; to buttress, to underpin; (*b*) to support, back up (statement, etc.); **pour é. ses allégations,** in support of his allegations; **s'é. contre un choc,** to steady oneself against a shock; **il s'étaie sur ses amis,** he leans on his friends.

été [ete] *n.m.* summer; **en é.,** in summer; **un jour d'é.,** a summer('s) day; **heure d'é.,** summer time; **é. de la Saint-Martin,** St Martin's summer, Indian summer.

éteignoir [etɛɲwar] *n.m.* (*a*) (candle) extinguisher; **en é.,** conical; (*b*) *F:* killjoy, wet blanket.

éteindre [etɛ̃dr̥] *v.* (*conj. like* TEINDRE) **1.** *v.tr.* (*a*) to extinguish, put out (fire, light); to turn off (the gas); to switch off (electric light, radio); **laisser é. le feu,** to let the fire go out; **é. les feux d'un fourneau,** to draw the fires of a furnace; *v.i.* **éteignez,** turn out, switch off, the light; (*b*) to extinguish (hope), kill (ambition); to annul, pay off (a debt); to abolish (a right); to put an end to (a quarrel); **é. la soif,** to slake, quench, thirst; **é. le feu de l'ennemi,** to silence the enemy's guns; (*c*) (i) to slake, slack, kill (lime); (ii) to quench (red-hot iron, etc.); (*d*) to fade, soften (colours); to muffle, smother, deaden (sound); to appease, allay (passions); to dim (light, eyes, etc.). **2. s'é.** (*a*) (*of fire, light*) to go out, to die out; (*of fire*) to burn out; (*b*) (*of colour, etc.*) to fade, grow dim; (*of sound*) to die down, die away; to subside; (*of passion*) to die down; **le jour s'éteint,** daylight is failing, fading; (*c*) (*of pers.*) to die; (*of race, family*) to become extinct, to die out; **il s'éteignit dans mes bras,** he passed away in my arms.

éteint [etɛ̃] *a.* (*a*) extinguished; **le feu est é.,** the fire is out; (*b*) extinct (race, family, volcano); (*c*) dull, dim, faint (colour, sound); dull, lacklustre (eyes); faint, toneless, faraway (voice).

étendage [etɑ̃daʒ] *n.m.* **1.** (*a*) hanging out (of washing, etc.), spreading (of butter, etc.); (*b*) stretching (of skin, etc.). **2.** (*a*) clothes lines; (*b*) drying yard.

étendard [etɑ̃dar] *n.m.* **1.** (*a*) *Mil:* standard (of mounted arms); colour(s); (*b*) **lever l'é. de la révolte,** to raise the flag of rebellion. **2.** *Bot:* vexillum, standard.

étendoir [etɑ̃dwar] *n.m.* (*a*) clothes lines; (*b*) drying yard, room.

étendre [etɑ̃dr̥] *v.* **1.** *v.tr.* to spread, extend; (*a*) to spread, stretch, (s.o., sth.) out to full length; to lay (tablecloth); to spread (butter on bread); to hang out (washing); to spread (straw); **é. une couche de peinture sur qch.,** to give sth. a coat of paint; **é. le bras,** to stretch out, reach out, one's arm; (*of bird*) **é. ses ailes,** to spread its wings; **é. qn (par terre) d'un coup de poing,** to knock s.o. down; *F:* to lay s.o. out; *Box:* **se faire é.,** to be knocked out; *F:* **se faire é. à un examen,** to fail an exam; (*b*) (i) to stretch (sth.) out (to more than original size); **é. une peau,** to stretch a skin; **é. l'or,** (i) to beat out, hammer out, gold; (ii) to wire-draw gold; **é. la pâte,** to roll out the dough; **é. ses connaissances,** to extend one's knowledge; **é. les termes d'une loi,** to widen, broaden, the terms of a law; (*b*) to dilute (wine, milk, etc.); **é. d'eau une boisson,** to water (down) a drink. **2. s'é.**

(*a*) (i) to stretch oneself out, to lie down (at) full length; (ii) **s'é. sur un sujet,** to dwell, enlarge, expatiate, (up)on a subject; (*b*) (i) to extend, stretch; **la ligne s'étend depuis Ivry jusqu'à Charenton,** the line stretches, runs, from Ivry to Charenton; **aussi loin que le regard peut s'é.,** as far as the eye can reach; (ii) (*of fire, etc.*) to spread; (*of dye, ink*) to run; (iii) to expand, grow larger.

étendu, -ue [etɑ̃dy] **1.** *a.* (*a*) extensive (knowledge, memory); far-reaching (influence); wide (plain, knowledge); (*b*) outspread (wings); outstretched (hands); (*c*) diluted (**de**, with). **2.** *s.f.* **étendue;** extent, size, dimensions, area; scale (of calamity, etc.); stretch (of water, etc.); tract (of land, etc.); reach (of the mind); sweep (of country); expanse (of sea); compass, range (of a voice); extent, scope (of s.o.'s knowledge); **l'é. de la vie,** the duration of life.

éternel, -elle [etɛrnɛl] *a.* eternal; (*a*) **le père é.,** the Father Eternal; *n.m.* **L'É.,** God, the Lord; (*b*) everlasting, perpetual (life, joy, etc.); (*c*) **un é. causeur,** an inveterate chatterer; **fumant son éternelle cigarette,** smoking the inevitable cigarette.

éternellement [etɛrnɛlmɑ̃] *adv.* (*a*) eternally, for ever(more); (*b*) everlastingly, perpetually, endlessly.

éterniser [etɛrnize] *v.* **1.** *v.tr.* to etern(al)ize, perpetuate; (*a*) **é. la mémoire de qn,** to immortalize s.o.'s memory; **si nous pouvions é. cette heure,** if only we could make this hour last for ever; (*b*) to drag on (a discussion) interminably. **2. s'é.,** to last for ever; (*of lawsuit, etc.*) to drag on, go on and on; **s'é. chez qn,** to outstay one's welcome.

éternité [etɛrnite] *n.f.* eternity; **de toute é.,** from time immemorial; **il y a une é. que je ne vous ai vu,** it's ages since I saw you.

éternuement [etɛrnymɑ̃] *n.m.* **1.** sneezing. **2.** sneeze.

éternuer [etɛrnɥe] *v.i.* to sneeze.

étêtage [etɛtaʒ] *n.m.*, **étêtement** [etɛ̃tmɑ̃] *n.m.* pollarding, topping (of trees).

étêter [etete] *v.tr.* (*a*) to remove the head from (fish, nail, etc.); (*b*) to pollard, top (tree).

éteule [etœl] *n.f. Agr:* stubble.

éthane [etan] *n.m. Ch:* ethane.

éther [etɛr] *n.m.* ether.

éthéré [etere] *a.* ethereal (region, *Ch:* salt).

éthéromane [eterɔman) *n.m. & f.* ether addict.

Éthiopie [etjɔpi] *Pr.n.f. Geog:* Ethiopia.

éthiopien, -ienne [etjɔpjɛ̃, -jɛn] *a. & n.* Ethiopian.

éthique [etik] **1.** *a.* (*a*) ethical (problem, etc.); (*b*) **datif é.,** ethic dative. **2.** *n.f.* ethics.

ethnie [ɛtni] *n.f.* ethnos, ethnic group.

ethnique [ɛtnik] *n.* ethnic(al) (group, etc.).

ethnographe [ɛtnɔgraf] *n.m. & f.* ethnographer.

ethnographie [ɛtnɔgrafi] *n.f.* ethnography.

ethnographique [ɛtnɔgrafik] *a.* ethnographic(al).

ethnologie [ɛtnɔlɔʒi] *n.f.* ethnology.

ethnologique [ɛtnɔlɔʒik] *a.* ethnological.

ethnologue [ɛtnɔlɔg] *n.m. & f.* ethnologist.

éthyle [etil] *n.m. Ch:* ethyl.

éthylène [etilɛn] *n.m. Ch:* ethylene.

éthylique [etilik] **1.** *a. Ch:* ethyl(ic); **alcool é.,** ethyl alcohol. **2.** *n.m. & f. Med:* alcoholic.

éthylisme [etilism] *n.m.* alcoholism.

étiage [etjaʒ] *n.m.* lowest water level (of river); **échelle d'é.,** water gauge.

étincelage [etɛ̃slaʒ] *n.m.* (*a*) **soudure par é.,** flash welding; (*b*) electrotherapy.

étincelant [etɛ̃slɑ̃] *a.* sparkling, glittering, glistening, flashing (jewels, eyes, etc.); sparkling (wit).

étinceler [etɛ̃sle] *v.i.* (**il étincelle; il étincelait; il étincellera**) **1.** to throw out sparks. **2.** (*of diamonds, stars, etc.*) to sparkle, glitter, gleam; (*of wit*) to sparkle; **ses yeux étincelaient de joie, de colère,** his eyes sparkled with joy, flashed with anger.

étincelle [etɛ̃sɛl] *n.f.* spark; (*a*) **lancer des étincelles,** to throw out sparks, to sparkle, flash; *El:* **é. éclatante,** jump spark; **é. bien nourrie,** fat spark; *I.C.E:* **allumage par é.,** spark ignition; (*b*) spark, flash (of genius); spark (of life).

étincellement [etɛ̃sɛlmɑ̃] *n.m.* sparkling, glittering, scintillation (of gem, etc.); twinkling (of star).

étiolement [etjɔlmɑ̃] *n.m.* (*a*) *Bot: Med:* chlorosis, etiolation; *Hort:* blanching (of celery); (*b*) **é. de l'esprit, de l'intelligence,** atrophy of the mind; weakening of the intellect.

étioler [etjɔle] *v.* **1.** *v.tr.* (*a*) to etiolate, blanch (celery, etc.); (*b*) to make (s.o.) sickly, pale; to enfeeble (s.o.). **2. s'é.** (*a*) to etiolate, blanch; (*b*) (*of plant*) to starve, (*of mind*) to become atrophied.

étiologie [etjɔlɔʒi] *n.f.* aetiology, etiology.

étique [etik] *a.* emaciated, wasted; *F:* skinny.

étiquetage [etiktaʒ] *n.m.* labelling (of luggage, etc.); docketing (of manuscripts, etc.); ticketing (of goods).

étiqueter [etikte] *v.tr.* (**j'étiquète, j'étiquèterai**) (*a*) to label (luggage); to docket (manuscripts); to ticket (goods); (*b*) to label, classify (politician, writer).

étiquette [etikɛt] *n.f.* **1.** (*a*) label, docket, ticket; **é. à bagages, de direction,** luggage label; **é. à œillets,** tie-on label; tag; **é. gommée,** gummed label, stick-on label; **é. de vitrine,** show card; **apposer une é. à un paquet,** to label, stick a label on, a parcel; (*b*) (political) label. **2.** etiquette, formality, ceremony; **l'é. de la cour,** Court ceremonial; **il est contraire à l'é. de s'asseoir,** it is bad form to sit down.

étirage [etiraʒ] *n.m.* stretching; **é. des métaux,** drawing (out) of metals; **é. à chaud, à froid,** hot, cold, drawing; **é. du fil,** wire drawing; *Tex:* **banc d'é.,** drawing frame.

étirer [etire] *v.* **1.** *v.tr.* to stretch; to draw out (sth.); to draw (wire); **é. les métaux,** to draw (out) metals; **2. s'é.** (*a*) to stretch oneself, one's limbs; (*b*) (*of jersey, etc.*) to stretch.

étoffe [etɔf] *n.f.* **1.** material (for making sth.); **l'é. dont sont faits les héros,** the stuff heroes are made of; **il a de l'é.,** there's good stuff in him; **il y a en lui l'é. d'un écrivain,** he has the makings of a writer. **2.** *Tex:* material, fabric; **étoffes de soie,** silk fabrics.

étoffé [etɔfe] *a.* **1.** ample, full (garment); rich, full (voice); **homme bien é.,** (i) stout, thickset, (ii) well-to-do, man; **discours é.,** speech full of substance.

étoffer [etɔfe] *v.* **1.** *v.tr.* to use ample material in making (sth.); **é. un discours,** to give substance to a speech. **2.** (*of pers.*) **s'é.,** to fill out.

étoile [etwal] *n.f.* star. **1. é. filante,** shooting star; **à la clarté des étoiles,** in the starlight; **coucher, dormir, à la belle é.,** to sleep in the open; **né sous une bonne, mauvaise, é.,** born under a lucky, an unlucky star. **2.** (*a*) star (of a decoration); (*b*) *Typ:* asterisk, star; **hôtel à cinq étoiles,** five-star hotel; (*c*) circus (where several roads meet); roundabout; (*d*) **é. de mer,** starfish. **3.** (film, operatic) star; **é. montante,** rising star.

étoilé [etwale] *a.* **1.** starry, starlit (sky); studded with stars; **la Bannière étoilée,** the Star-spangled Banner, the Stars and Stripes (of the U.S.A.). **2.** star-shaped (crack, etc.).

étoiler [etwale] *v.* **1.** *v.tr.* (*a*) to stud, spangle, (sth.) with stars; (*b*) to make a star-shaped crack in (glass, etc.). **2.** (*of the sky*) **s'é.,** to light up with stars.

étole [etɔl] *n.f. Ecc: Cost:* stole.

étonnamment [etɔnamɑ̃] *adv.* astonishingly, surprisingly.

étonnant [etɔnɑ̃] *a.* astonishing, surprising; **rien d'é. à cela,** that's no wonder; **ce n'est pas é. qu'il soit**

malade, it's no wonder, not to be wondered at, that he's ill; *F:* **vous êtes é.!** you're the limit! *n.* **l'é. est qu'il soit venu,** the surprising thing is that he came.

étonné, -ée [etɔne] *a.* astonished, surprised.

étonnement [etɔnmɑ̃] *n.m.* astonishment, surprise; wonder; amazement; **frappé, saisi, d'é.,** taken aback; **à mon grand é.,** to my great surprise; **faire l'é. de tout le monde,** to be the talk of the town.

étonner [etɔne] *v.* **1.** *v.tr.* to astonish, amaze, surprise; **cela ne m'étonnerait pas,** I shouldn't be surprised (at it); **ce qui m'étonne, c'est qu'il a menti,** what surprises me is that he lied. **2. s'é.,** to be astonished, surprised, to wonder (**de,** at); **je m'étonne de vous voir,** I'm surprised to see you; **je m'étonne qu'il ne voie pas le danger,** it amazes me that he does not see the danger; **comment s'é. qu'il ait refusé?** can you wonder that he refused? **je ne m'étonne plus de rien,** nothing surprises me any more.

étouffant [etufɑ̃] *a.* stifling, suffocating, stuffy (atmosphere, etc.); oppressive, sultry (weather).

étouffée [etufe] *n.f.* **cuire à l'é.,** to braise (meat).

étouffement [etufmɑ̃] *n.m.* **1.** suffocation, stifling (of s.o.); smothering (of fire); hushing-up (of scandal). **2.** choking sensation.

étouffer [etufe] **1.** *v.tr.* (*a*) to suffocate, choke, smother (s.o.); **plantes qui s'étouffent,** plants that choke one another; **on s'étouffait pour entrer,** people crushed in; (*b*) to stifle (cry, passion, industry); to smother (fire); to stamp out (epidemic); to quell, suppress (revolt); to damp, muffle (sound); *El:* to quench (spark); **é. une affaire,** to hush up a matter; **é. un sanglot,** to choke back a sob; (*c*) *Cu:* to stew, to braise. **2.** *v.i. & pr.* (*a*) to suffocate, choke; **é. de rire,** to choke with laughter; (*b*) **on étouffe ici,** it's stifling here.

étouffoir [etufwar] *n.m.* **1.** charcoal extinguisher. **2.** damper (of piano). **3.** stuffy room.

étoupe [etup] *n.f.* **1.** (*a*) **é. blanche,** tow; (*b*) **é. noire,** oakum; (*c*) **é. de coton,** cotton waste. **2.** packing, stuffing (of piston rod, etc.).

étouper [etupe] *v.tr.* to stop up (crevice) with tow, oakum; to caulk (boat). **2.** *Mec.E:* to stuff, pack (gland, etc.).

étoupille [etupij] *n.f.* **1.** *Artil:* firing tube. **2.** *Min:* fuse.

étourderie [eturdəri] *n.f.* **1.** thoughtlessness; **par é.,** inadvertently; in an unthinking moment. **2.** thoughtless action; blunder; careless mistake.

étourdi, -ie [eturdi] **1.** *a.* thoughtless, scatterbrained, harebrained; flighty (girl); foolish (answer, etc.). **2.** *n.* scatterbrain, harum-scarum. **3.** *adv.phr.* **à l'étourdie,** thoughtlessly, heedlessly.

étourdiment [eturdimɑ̃] *adv.* thoughtlessly; without thinking.

étourdir [eturdir] *v.* **1.** *v.tr.* (*a*) to stun, daze; to make (s.o.) dizzy; to make (s.o.'s) head swim; **bruit qui étourdit les oreilles,** deafening noise; (*b*) to ease, deaden (pain); to allay (grief, hunger). **2. s'é.,** to try to forget; **s'é. dans la boisson,** to drown one's sorrows.

étourdissant [eturdisɑ̃] *a.* **1.** deafening, ear-splitting (noise). **2.** staggering, stunning, astounding (news, etc.).

étourdissement [eturdismɑ̃] *n.m.* **1.** giddiness, dizziness; **avoir un é.,** to feel giddy; **cela me donne des étourdissements,** it makes my head swim. **2.** numbing, deadening (of pain); dazing (of the mind).

étourneau, -eaux [eturno] *n.m.* **1.** *Orn:* starling. **2.** *F:* scatterbrain.

étrange [etrɑ̃ʒ] *a.* strange, peculiar, odd, queer; **chose é., il est revenu,** strange to say, he came back.

étrangement [etrɑ̃ʒmɑ̃] *adv.* strangely, queerly, oddly, peculiarly; **cela ressemble é. à la rougeole,** it looks suspiciously like measles.

étranger, -ère [etrɑ̃ʒe, -ɛr] *a. & n.* **1.** (*a*) *a.* foreign; **Ministère des affaires étrangères** = Foreign (and Commonwealth) Office; (*b*) *n.* foreigner, alien; (*c*) *n.m.* foreign parts; **vivre à l'é.,** to live abroad; **voyages à l'é.,** foreign travel. **2.** (*a*) *a.* strange, unknown; **sa voix m'est étrangère,** I've never heard his voice; never heard him speak; (*b*) *n.* stranger; **société fermée aux étrangers,** society not open to outsiders. **3.** *a.* extraneous, foreign; not belonging (to sth.); **corps é.,** foreign body (in an organism, etc.); **cela est é. à la question,** that is beside the point, irrelevant (to the subject); **la haine lui est étrangère,** he doesn't know what hatred is; **il est é. à la musique,** he has no knowledge of music.

étrangeté [etrɑ̃ʒte] *n.f.* strangeness, quaintness, oddness, peculiarity (of conduct, dress, etc.).

étranglé [etrɑ̃gle] *a.* constricted, narrow (passage, etc.); nipped-in (waist); choked, choking (voice); strangulated (hernia).

étranglement [etrɑ̃gləmɑ̃] *n.m.* **1.** (*a*) strangling, strangulation (of s.o.); (*b*) constriction, narrowing (of sth.); *Mch:* throttling; **soupape d'é.,** throttle valve; *Med:* **é. herniaire,** strangulated hernia. **2.** narrow part, narrows (of river); bottleneck (in road).

étrangler [etrɑ̃gle] *v.* **1.** *v.tr.* (*a*) to strangle, throttle (s.o.); **sa cravate l'étrangle,** his tie is choking him; **é. un complot au berceau,** to nip a plot in the bud; *v.i.* **é. de soif,** to be parched with thirst; (*b*) to constrict, compress (sth.); to strangulate (blood vessel); *Mch:* to throttle (steam, etc.); *I.C.E:* **é. le moteur,** to throttle down the engine. **2. s'é.,** to choke, suffocate; **s'é. de colère,** to choke with rage; **s'é. avec une arête de poisson,** to choke on a fishbone.

étrangleur, -euse [etrɑ̃glœr, -øz] **1.** *n.* strangler, thug. **2.** *n.m.* (*a*) *Mch:* throttle(-valve); (*b*) *I.C.E:* strangler, choke.

étrave [etrav] *n.f.* *Nau:* stem (of ship); **de l'é. à l'étambot,** from stem to stern; **lame d'é.,** bow wave.

être[1] [ɛtr̥] *v.i. & pred.* (*pr.p.* **étant;** *p.p.* **été;** *pr.ind.* **je suis, tu es, il est, n. sommes, v. êtes, ils sont;** *pr.sub.* **je sois, tu sois, il soit, n. soyons, v. soyez, ils soient;** *imp.* **sois, soyons, soyez;** *impf.* **j'étais;** *p.h.* **je fus, tu fus, il fut, n. fûmes, v. fûtes, ils furent;** *p.sub.* **je fusse;** *fu.* **je serai**) **1.** to be, to exist; **je pense, donc je suis,** I think, therefore I am; **l'ancien projet n'est plus,** the old plan is a thing of the past; **elle n'est plus,** she is no more, is dead; **cela étant,** that being the case; **cela n'est pas,** that is not so; **la plus belle voiture qui soit,** the finest car there is; **eh bien, soit!** well, so be it! **ainsi soit-il,** so be it; *Ecc:* amen; **on ne peut pas ê. et avoir été,** you can't have your cake and eat it. **2.** (*as copula*) (*a*) **c'est le chef de gare,** he's the stationmaster; **il est, c'est un, chef de gare,** he's a stationmaster; **soit** *a* **la base d'un triangle,** let *a* be the base of a triangle; **soit un triangle ABC,** given a triangle ABC; (*b*) **l'homme est mortel,** man is mortal; **nous étions deux, plusieurs,** there were two, several, of us; (*c*) **elle est très mal, beaucoup mieux,** she is very ill, much better; **ê. bien avec qn,** to be on good terms, to stand well, with s.o.; **nous sommes le dix,** it's the tenth (today); **la vérité est entre ces extrêmes,** the truth lies between these extremes; **il est à Paris,** he is in Paris; **quand il fut pour sortir,** just as he was about to leave; (*d*) **ê. au travail,** to be at work; **ê. à l'agonie,** to be dying; **vous n'êtes pas à ce que je dis,** you are not paying attention to what I say, are not with me; **il est tout à son travail,** he is entirely engrossed in his work; (*e*) **ce tableau est de Gauguin,** this picture is by Gauguin; **il est d'un bon caractère,** he's good-tempered; **il est de Londres,** he is from London; **il était du conseil municipal,** he belonged to the municipal council; **il n'est pas des nôtres,** he isn't a member of our party, he isn't with us; he isn't one of us; **il est de mes amis,** he's a friend of mine, one of my friends; **ê. de service,** to be on duty; (*f*) **il est à travailler, à jouer,** he is at work, at play; **j'étais là à l'attendre,** I was there waiting for her; **la maison est à louer,** the house is to be let; (*g*) (*with* **ce** *as neuter subject*) **je sais ce qui est arrivé,** I know what happened; **est-ce vrai?** is it true? **serait-ce vrai?** can it be, could it (possibly) be, true? **ne fût-ce que, ne serait-ce que,** if only; **vous venez, n'est-ce pas?** you're coming, aren't you? **vous ne venez pas, n'est-ce pas?** you're not coming, are you? **n'est-ce pas qu'il a de la chance?** isn't he lucky? **je le ferais (si ce) n'était que je vais partir,** I should do it if I weren't leaving; **n'était mon rhumatisme,** if it weren't, wasn't, for my rheumatism; (*h*) *impers. uses* (i) **il est midi,** it is twelve o'clock; **il est temps de partir,** it is time to go; **il est de mon devoir de rester,** it is my duty to stay; **il n'est que de faire preuve d'énergie,** we, you, need only show energy; **comme si de rien n'était,** as if nothing had happened; **trois tours de piste, soit deux kilomètres,** three times round the track, that is, (let us) say, two kilometres; **soit dit sans offense,** if you don't mind my saying so; (ii) **il est un Dieu,** there is a God; **il était une fois une fée,** once upon a time there was a fairy; **un héros, s'il en fut (jamais),** a hero, if ever there was one; (*i*) (*with indeterminate* **en**) (i) **où en sommes-nous?** how far have we got? where are we? **l'affaire en est là,** so the matter rests; **vous n'en êtes pas encore là,** you haven't come to that yet! **il n'en est pas à son coup d'essai,** this is not his first attempt; **je ne sais plus où j'en suis,** I don't know where I am, what I'm doing; **nous n'en sommes pas à le renvoyer,** we haven't reached the point of sacking him yet; (ii) **j'en suis pour mon argent,** I've spent my money to no purpose; **j'en suis pour mille francs,** I am the poorer by a thousand francs; (iii) **j'en suis pour ce que j'ai dit,** I stick to what I said; **il en est pour les changements,** he's all for change; (iv) **j'en suis!** I'm game! I'm on! **je n'en suis pas,** count me out! (v) **c'en est trop!** this is past bearing; **c'en est assez!** enough! (vi) (*impers.*) **il en est de l'homme comme de la nature,** it's the same with man as with nature; **puisqu'il en est ainsi,** since that is how things are; **il n'en est rien!** nothing of the kind! (*j*) (*with indeterminate* **y**) **il y est pour quelque chose,** he's got something to do with it; **j'y suis pour un tiers,** I'm in for a third share; **ça y est!** that's it! **vous y êtes?** are you with me? have you got it? **3.** (*a*) **ê. à qn,** to belong to s.o.; **à qui sont ces livres?** whose books are these? **ma vie est-elle à moi?** is my life my own? **je suis à vous dans un moment,** I shall be at your service in a moment; (*b*) **c'est à vous de jouer,** it's your turn to play; **c'est à vous de veiller sur l'enfant,** it's your job to look after the child. **4.** (*aux. use*) (*a*) (*with v.i. denoting change of place or state, etc.*) **il est arrivé,** he has arrived; **il est arrivé hier,** he arrived yesterday; **elle est née en 1950,** she was born in 1950; (*b*) (*with v.pr*) **nous nous sommes trompés,** we (have) made a mistake; **elle s'est fait mal,** she (has) hurt herself. **5.** (*as aux. of the passive voice*) **il fut puni par son père,** he was punished by his father; **il est aimé de tout le monde,** he is loved by everyone; **j'entends ê. obéi,** I mean to be obeyed. **6.** (*a*) = ALLER (*in compound tenses and in p.h.*); **j'avais été à Paris,** I had been to Paris; **j'ai été voir Martin,** I've been, I went, to see Martin; **on a été jusqu'à démissionner,** people have gone so far as to resign; (*b*) = S'EN ALLER (*in p.h. only*) **il s'en fut ouvrir la porte,** he went off to open the door.

être² *n.m.* being; (*a*) **ceux qui vous ont donné l'ê.,** those to whom you owe your being, existence; (*b*) **tout mon ê. se révolte à l'idée,** my whole being revolts at the idea; (*c*) **L'Ê. suprême,** the Supreme Being; **un ê. humain,** a human being; **pauvres petits êtres!** poor little creatures! poor little things! **quel ê.!** what a fellow!

étreindre [etrɛ̃dr̥] *v.tr.* (*pr.p.* **étreignant;** *p.p.* **étreint;** *pr.ind.* **j'étreins, il étreint, n. étreignons;** *impf.* **j'étreignais;** *p.h.* **j'étreignis;** *fu.* **j'étreindrai)** to embrace, hug; to clasp (s.o.) in one's arms; **é. qch. dans la main,** to grasp, grip, clutch (sth.); **é. la main de qn,** to wring s.o.'s hand; **spectacle qui vous étreint le cœur,** sight that wrings one's heart; moving sight; **la peur l'étreignait,** he was in the grip of fear; *Prov:* **qui trop embrasse mal étreint,** grasp all, lose all.

étreinte [etrɛ̃t] *n.f.* **1.** (*a*) embrace, hug; (*b*) grasp, grip; (*c*) *Wr:* lock. **2.** (exertion of) pressure; **sous l'é. de la misère,** under the pressure of poverty.

étrenne [etrɛn] *n.f.* **1.** *usu. pl.* New Year's gift; **les étrennes du facteur** = the postman's Christmas box. **2. avoir l'é. de qch.,** to have the first use of sth.; **ne pas avoir l'é. de qch.,** to get sth. secondhand.

étrenner [etrene] **1.** *v.tr.* to use (sth.), wear (dress), for the first time; to christen (object). **2.** *v.i. P:* **tu vas étrenner!** you're going to catch it!

êtres [ɛtr̥] *n.m.pl.* arrangement of a house; **connaître les ê.,** to know one's way about a house.

étrésillon [etrezijɔ̃] *n.m.* (cross) shore, strut, brace.

étrésillonner [etrezijɔne] *v.tr.* to shore (across) (trench); to strut, brace (wall).

étrier [etrije] *n.m.* **1.** (*a*) stirrup; **à franc é.,** at full gallop; **vider les étriers,** (i) to be thrown, unhorsed; (ii) to be disconcerted; **avoir le pied à l'é.,** (i) to be on the point of leaving; (ii) to be off to a good start; **tenir l'é. à qn,** (i) to help (rider) to mount; (ii) to give s.o. a helping hand; **coup de l'é.,** stirrup cup; (*b*) *Med:* **é. de soutien,** stirrup, leg rest; **é. de traction, de réduction,** calliper. **2.** *Anat:* stirrup bone (of ear). **3.** *Tchn:* stirrup piece; clip, yoke; *Tp:* **é. du récepteur,** receiver rest, cradle.

étrille [etrij] *n.f.* **1.** currycomb. **2.** velvet swimming crab.

étriller [etrije] *v.tr.* **1.** to curry(comb) horse. **2.** (*a*) to tick (s.o.) off; to haul (s.o.) over the coals; (*b*) to fleece, sting (s.o.).

étripage [etripaʒ] *n.m.* gutting (of fish); drawing (of chicken, etc.).

étriper [etripe] *v.tr.* to gut (fish); to draw (chicken, etc.); to disembowel (horse, etc.).

étriqué [etrike] *a.* (*a*) skimpy, tight (garment); (*b*) narrow, limited, (outlook, life).

étriquer [etrike] *v.tr.* **1.** to thin (plank, etc.). **2.** to skimp (garment); to make (garment) too tight.

étrivière [etrivjɛr] *n.f.* stirrup leather.

étroit [etrwa] *a.* **1.** narrow (space, ribbon, etc.); confined (space); **la voie étroite,** the straight and narrow way; **esprit é.,** narrow mind. **2.** tight, close (knot, bond, etc.); tight(-fitting) (coat, etc.); **alliance étroite,** close, intimate, alliance; **règlements étroits,** strict rules; **le sens é. d'un mot,** the strict meaning of a word. **3.** *adv.phr.* **être à l'é.,** (i) to be cramped for room; (ii) to be in straitened circumstances.

étroitement [etrwatmɑ̃] *adv.* tightly, closely (bound, knotted, etc.); **ils sont é. liés d'amitié,** they are close friends; **surveiller qn é.,** to keep a close watch over s.o.

étroitesse [etrwatɛs] *n.f.* **1.** narrowness (of path, etc.); **é. d'esprit,** narrow-mindedness. **2.** tightness, closeness (of bond, etc.).

étrusque [etrysk] *a. & n.* Etruscan.

étude [etyd] *n.f.* **1.** (*a*) study, studying; **l'é. des langues,** the study of languages; **programme d'études,** curriculum; syllabus; **faire des études de français,** to study French; **il a fait ses études à Eton, à Oxford,** he was educated at Eton; he went to Oxford; **faire**

ses études sans maître, to be self-educated; **payer les études de qn,** to pay for s.o.'s education; **faire de bonnes études,** to have a successful school career; *Sch:* **l'é. du soir,** (evening) preparation; *F:* prep; **(salle d')é.,** prep. room; **faire son é. de qch., mettre son é. à qch.,** to make sth. one's study; **cela sent l'é.,** it's painstaking work; (*b*) research (work); investigation; *Civ.E:* survey; **bureau d'études,** (i) research department; (ii) drawing office (of factory, etc.); **é. d'un canal,** scheme, project, for a canal; **moteur, voiture, d'é.,** test engine, car; **ingénieur d'études,** design engineer; **comité d'é.,** committee of enquiry; **procéder à l'é. d'une question, mettre une question à l'é.,** to study, go into, a question. **2.** *Mus:* **é. pour violon,** violin study; *Art:* **é. de tête,** study of a head; **é. de bétail,** cattle piece. **3.** (*a*) office (of solicitor); chambers (of barrister); (*b*) (lawyer's) practice.

étudiant, -iante [etydjɑ̃, -jɑ̃t] **1.** *n.* student; undergraduate; **é. en médecine,** medical student; **é. de première année,** freshman.

étudié [etydje] *a.* studied (calm); studied, elaborate, deliberate (effect); set (speech); **manières étudiées,** artificial, affected, manners; **prix très étudiés,** cheapest possible, keenest, prices.

étudier [etydje] *v.* (*impf.* & *pr.sub.* **n. étudiions**) **1.** *v.tr.* (*a*) to study (language, music, person's character); to prepare (lessons, etc.); to read (law, medicine); **é. une matière en vue d'un examen,** to read up a subject for an examination; **é. son piano,** to practise on the piano; (*b*) to study (one's effect, appearance); (*c*) to investigate, enquire into, look into (question, plan, theory); to make a study of (case); **machine étudiée dans un but spécial,** purpose-built machine. **2. s'é. à faire qch.,** to take pains to do sth., make a point of doing sth.; **il s'étudiait à m'éviter,** he studiously avoided me.

étui [etɥi] *n.m.* case, box, cover; **é. de voile,** sail cover; **é. de cartouche,** cartridge case; **é. à lunettes,** spectacle case; **é. de revolver,** holster.

étuvage [etyvaʒ] *n.m.* drying; stoving, baking.

étuve [etyv] *n.f.* **1.** sweating room (of baths); **é. sèche,** hot-air bath cabinet; **é. humide,** vapour bath. **2.** *Ch: Ind. etc:* drying oven, cupboard; *Med:* sterilizer; *Bac:* **é. à incubation, à cultures,** incubator; *F:* **quelle é.!** what an oven!

étuvée [etyve] *n.f. Cu:* **à l'é.,** braised.

étuver [etyve] *v.tr.* **1.** *Ind: etc:* to dry; to heat; to steam; to stove, bake (contaminated clothing). **2.** *Cu:* to braise (meat); to steam (potatoes).

étymologie [etimɔlɔʒi] *n.f.* etymology.

étymologique [etimɔlɔʒik] *a.* etymological.

étymologiste [etimɔlɔʒist] *n.m.* & *f.* etymologist.

eucalyptus [økalyptys] *n.m.* eucalyptus; gum(tree); **essence d'e.,** eucalyptus oil.

Eucharistie (l') [løkaristi] *n.f. Ecc:* the eucharist.

eucharistique [økaristik] *a.* eucharistic(al).

euclidien, -ienne [øklidjɛ̃, -jɛn] *a.* Euclidean.

eudiomètre [ødjɔmɛtr̥] *n.m. Ph:* eudiometer.

eugénique [øʒenik] *n.f.*, **eugénisme** [øʒenism] *n.m.* eugenics.

euh [ø] *int.* er!

eunuque [ønyk] *n.m.* eunuch.

euphémique [øfemik] *a.* euphemistic.

euphémisme [øfemism] *n.m.* euphemism.

euphonie [øfɔni] *n.f.* euphony.

euphonique [øfɔnik] *a.* euphonic, euphonious.

euphorbe [øfɔrb] *n.f. Bot:* euphorbia, spurge.

euphorie [øfɔri] *n.f.* euphoria, wellbeing.

euphorique [øfɔrik] *a.* & *n.m.* euphoric.

euphorisant [øfɔrizɑ̃] *n.m.* euphoriant (drug).

eurafricain, -aine [ørafrikɛ̃, -ɛn], *a.* & *n.* Eurafrican.

Eurasie [ørazi] *Pr.n.f. Geog:* Eurasia.

eurasien, -ienne [ørazjɛ̃, -jɛn] *a.* & *n.* Eurasian.

eurocrate [ørɔkrat] *n.m.* Eurocrat.

Europe [ørɔp] *Pr.n.f.* Europe.

européaniser [ørɔpeanize], *v.tr.* to Europeanize.

européen, -enne [ørɔpeɛ̃, -ɛn], *a.* & *n.* European.

Eurovision [ørovizjɔ̃] *Pr.n.f.* Eurovision.

eurythmie [øritmi] *n.f.* eurhythmy.

eurythmique [øritmik] *a.* eurhythmic.

euthanasie [øtanazi] *n.f.* euthanasia.

eux [ø]. *see* LUI[2].

évacuation [evakɥasjɔ̃] *n.f.* **1.** evacuation, voiding, discharge (of matter from the body, etc.); draining off, emptying (of water); draining (of abscess); *I.C.E:* **course d'é.,** exhaust stroke. **2.** (*a*) removal, clearing out (of goods, people, etc.); evacuation (of population); emptying, clearing (of a theatre); (*b*) *Mil:* evacuation, withdrawal (of troops, wounded); **hôpital d'é.,** clearing hospital; (*c*) evacuation (of fortress, town); *Nau:* abandoning (of ship).

évacué, -ée [evakɥe] *n.* evacuee.

évacuer [evakɥe] *v.tr.* **1.** to evacuate, discharge, void (matter from the body); to exhaust (steam); to drain (off) (water); **é. l'eau d'une chaudière,** to empty a boiler. **2.** (*a*) **é. des locataires,** to evict tenants; (*b*) to evacuate, withdraw (troops); to evacuate (inhabitants). **3.** to evacuate (fortress, town); **faire é. une salle,** to clear a hall; *Nau:* **é. le bâtiment,** to abandon ship.

évadé, -ée [evade] *a.* & *n.* escaped (prisoner).

évader (s') [sevade] *v.pr.* to escape; to run away; **s'é. de prison,** to escape from prison, to break gaol.

évaluateur, -trice [evalɥatœr, -tris] *n.* valuer, appraiser.

évaluation [evalɥasjɔ̃] *n.f.* valuation, appraisement (of property, etc.); assessment (of damages); estimate (of weight, etc.); *Typ:* cast(ing) off (of MS).

évaluer [evalɥe] *v.tr.* to value, appraise (property, etc.); to assess (damages); to estimate, reckon (weight, etc.).

évanescent [evanesɑ̃] *a.* evanescent.

évangélique [evɑ̃ʒelik] *a. Ecc:* evangelical.

évangélisateur [evɑ̃ʒelizatœr] *n.m.* evangelist.

évangélisation [evɑ̃ʒelizasjɔ̃] *n.f.* evangelization, evangelizing.

évangéliser [evɑ̃ʒelize] *v.tr.* to evangelize.

évangéliste [evɑ̃ʒelist] *n.m.* evangelist.

évangile [evɑ̃ʒil] *n.m.* **1. l'É.,** the Gospel; **l'É. selon saint Jean,** the Gospel according to St. John; **prendre qch. pour parole d'é.,** to take sth. for gospel (truth). **2. l'é.,** the gospel (for the day).

évanouir (s') [sevanwir] *v.pr.* **1.** to vanish, disappear; (*of sound*) to die away; *W.Tel:* to fade; *Mth:* **faire é. *y*,** to eliminate *y*. **2.** to faint; **tomber évanoui,** to fall down in a faint; **on l'a trouvé évanoui,** he was found unconscious, in a dead faint.

évanouissement [evanwismɑ̃] *n.m.* **1.** vanishing, disappearance (of ghost, etc.); dying away (of sound); *W.Tel:* fading. **2.** faint(ing fit).

évaporateur [evapɔratœr] *n.m. Ch: Ind:* evaporator.

évaporation [evapɔrasjɔ̃] *n.f.* evaporation.

évaporé, -ée [evapɔre]. **1.** *a.* featherbrained, irresponsible, flighty. **2.** *n.* featherbrain.

évaporer [evapɔre] *v.* **1.** *v.tr.* *A:* to evaporate (liquid). **2. s'é.** (*a*) (*of liquid, perfume, etc.*) to evaporate; **faire é. un liquide,** to evaporate, dry off, a liquid; (*b*) *F:* to vanish (into thin air).

évasé [evɑze] *a.* bell-mouthed, wide-mouthed (vessel, etc.); flared (skirt, etc.); splayed (window opening).

évasement [evɑzmɑ̃] *n.m.* **1.** widening out, splaying. **2.** bell mouth (of vessel, etc.); flare (of skirt, etc.); splay (of window opening, etc.).

évaser [evɑze] *v.* **1.** *v.tr.* to widen (out) the opening of (vessel); to open out (pipe, etc.); to flare (skirt); to splay (window opening, etc.). **2. s'é.,** to widen, open out; *Dressm:* to flare (out).

évasif, -ive [evazif, -iv] *a.* evasive.

évasion [evazjɔ̃] *n.f.* **1.** escape, flight (from prison, etc.); **é. des capitaux,** exodus of capital; **é. fiscale,** tax avoidance. **2.** escapism; **littérature d'é.,** escapist literature.

Ève [ɛv] *Pr.n.f.* Eva; *B.Lit:* Eve; *F:* **je ne le connais ni ni d'Adam, ni d'È.,** I don't know him from Adam.

évêché [eveʃe] *n.m.* **1.** (*a*) bishopric, see; (*b*) diocese. **2.** bishop's palace.

éveil [evɛj] *n.m.* **1.** (*a*) awakening; (*b*) **être en é.,** to be wide awake; to be on the alert. **2.** warning (**contre,** against); **donner l'é.,** to raise the alarm; **donner l'é. à qn,** to warn s.o.; to put s.o. on his guard.

éveillé [eveje] *a.* **1.** awake, waking; **rêve é.,** waking dream; **tenir qn é.,** to keep s.o. awake; **é. ou endormi,** waking or sleeping. **2.** wide-awake, alert, lively; **garçon (à l'esprit) é.,** bright boy.

éveiller [eveje] *v.* **1.** *v.tr.* to awake(n), wake (s.o.) up; to arouse, awaken (curiosity, suspicion). **2. s'é.,** to wake (up); **il s'éveilla en sursaut,** he woke with a start.

événement [evɛnmɑ̃] *n.m.* event. **1.** (*a*) *A:* consequence, outcome; *still so used in* **dans, en, l'é.,** as things turned out; in the event; (*b*) *Th:* climax. **2.** occurrence, incident; **la suite des événements,** the course of events; further developments; **faire é.,** to cause a stir; **semaine pleine d'événements,** eventful week; **en cas d'é.,** in case of emergency.

évent [evɑ̃] *n.m.* **1.** mustiness (of food); flatness (of beer); **sentir l'évent,** to smell stale, musty. **2.** (*a*) blowhole, spout (of whale); (*b*) *Tchn:* vent(hole).

éventage [evɑ̃taʒ] *n.m.* airing.

éventail [evɑ̃taj] *n.m.* **1.** fan; **en é.,** fan-shaped; **voûte en é.,** fan vaulting; **(fenêtre en) é.,** fanlight. **2.** range (of goods for sale, salaries, etc.).

éventaire [evɑ̃tɛr] *n.m.* (*a*) (hawker's) flat basket, tray; (*b*) (street) stall.

éventé [evɑ̃te] *a.* stale, musty (food, etc.); flat (beer).

éventement [evɑ̃tmɑ̃] *n.m.* **1.** airing, ventilation. **2.** (*of food*) spoiling, going stale; (*of drink*) going flat.

éventer [evɑ̃te] *v.tr.* **1.** (*a*) to air; to expose (grain, etc.) to the air; to ventilate (coal pit); (*b*) to damage, spoil (scent, wine, etc.) by exposure to the air; (*c*) **é. la mèche,** to reveal the secret; *F:* to let the cat out of the bag; (*d*) to fan (s.o.); (*e*) (*of hounds*) to scent, get the scent of (game); *F:* **é. un complot,** to get wind of a plot. **2. s'é.,** (*of food, etc.*) to spoil (from exposure to the air); (*of beverage*) to go flat, stale.

éventrer [evɑ̃tre] *v.tr.* to disembowel, eviscerate; to gut (fish); to draw (poultry); to rip, tear open (parcel, envelope); to break, smash, open (cask, box); to burst open (door); to slit open (sack).

éventreur [evɑ̃trœr] *n.m.* disemboweller; **Jack l'É.,** Jack the Ripper.

éventualité [evɑ̃tɥalite] *n.f.* possibility, contingency, eventuality; **parer à toute é.,** to provide for all contingencies.

éventuel, -elle [evɑ̃tɥɛl] **1.** *a.* (*a*) possible, that may happen; **à titre é.,** as a possible event; **client é.,** potential, prospective, customer; (*b*) eventual (profits). **2.** *n.m.* eventuality, contingency, possible event.

éventuellement [evɑ̃tɥɛlmɑ̃] *adv.* possibly; if necessary; should the occasion arise; **j'aurais é. besoin de votre concours,** I may need your help (later).

évêque [evɛk] *n.m.* bishop; *Prov:* **un chien regarde bien un é.,** a cat may look at a king; **bonnet d'é.,** (i) bishop's mitre; (ii) *F:* parson's nose (of fowl); *attrib.* **violet é.,** episcopal purple.

évertuer (s') [sevɛrtɥe] *v.pr.* to do one's utmost, to exert oneself; **s'é. à, pour, faire qch.,** to make every effort to do sth.

éviction [eviksjɔ̃] *n.f.* eviction, dispossession (of tenant).

évidage [evidaʒ] *n.m.* (*a*) hollowing out, scooping out (of stone, flute, etc.); *Surg:* scraping out; (*b*) grooving, channelling, fluting.

évidé [evide] *a.* hollow; hollow-ground (razor); gaunt (face).

évidement [evidmɑ̃] *n.m.* **1.** = ÉVIDAGE. **2.** hollow, recess, cavity.

évidemment [evidamɑ̃] *adv.* **1.** evidently, obviously, clearly. **2.** certainly, of course; naturally.

évidence [evidɑ̃s] *n.f.* (*a*) obviousness, clearness (of fact); **se rendre à l'é.,** to yield to the facts, to acknowledge oneself in the wrong; **se refuser à l'é.,** to fly in the face of facts; **de toute é., d'é. même,** clearly, evidently, obviously; (*b*) conspicuousness; **être en é.,** to be in a prominent position, in evidence; **mettre des marchandises en é.,** to display goods.

évident [evidɑ̃] *a.* evident, obvious, clear, plain; **erreur évidente,** palpable error, glaring mistake; **c'est é.,** that's evident, it stands to reason.

évider [evide] *v.tr.* **1.** to hollow out, scoop out; **é. un os,** to scrape the cavity of a bone. **2.** to groove, channel, flute (sword blade, etc.). **3.** to cut away, slope out (neck of dress).

évidoir [evidwar] *n.m.* groover; gouge.

évier [evje] *n.m.* (kitchen) sink.

évincer [evɛ̃se] *v.tr.* (**j'évinçai(s)**) **1.** to evict, turn out (tenant). **2.** to oust, supplant (s.o.).

éviscération [eviserasjɔ̃] *n.f.* evisceration.

éviscérer [evisere] *v.tr.* (**j'éviscère, n. éviscérons**) to eviscerate, disembowel.

évitable [evitabl̩] *a.* avoidable, preventable.

évitage [evitaʒ] *n.m.,* **évitée** [evite] *n.f.* *Nau:* **1.** swinging (of ship); **bassin d'é.,** turning basin. **2.** room to swing, sea room.

évitement [evitmɑ̃] *n.m.* **1.** avoidance (of s.o., sth.); **faire une manœuvre d'é.,** to take evasive action; *Biol:* **réaction d'é.,** avoiding reaction. **2.** (*a*) *Rail:* shunting (of train); **voie, gare, d'é.,** siding; **ligne d'é.,** loop line; (*b*) **route d'é.,** bypass.

éviter [evite] **1.** *v.tr.* (*a*) to avoid, shun; to give (s.o., sth.) a wide berth; to keep out of (s.o.'s) way; to keep clear of (s.o.); **é. un coup,** to avoid, dodge, a blow; **é. de la tête,** to duck; **é. de faire qch.,** to avoid doing sth.; **é. la question,** to dodge the issue; (*b*) **é. une peine à qn,** to save s.o. trouble. **2.** *v.i.* *Nau:* **é. sur l'ancre,** to swing at anchor; **évité au vent,** riding to the wind.

évocable [evɔkabl̩] *a.* evocable (spirit, memory, etc.); *Jur:* **cause é.,** case that may be transferred to a higher court.

évocateur, -trice [evɔkatœr, -tris] *a.* evocative, suggestive (**de,** of).

évocation [evɔkasjɔ̃] *n.f.* (*a*) evocation, calling forth, conjuring up, raising (of spirits, etc.); (*b*) conjuring up, calling up (of the past).

évocatoire [evɔkatwar] *a.* evocatory.

évolué [evɔlɥe] *a.* (highly) developed, advanced (race); mature, broadminded (person).

évoluer [evɔlɥe] *v.i.* **1.** (*a*) (*of ship, troops, etc.*) to perform evolutions, to manœuvre; (*b*) (i) to move around; (ii) to move (in society). **2.** to evolve, develop; (*of science*) to advance; (*of illness*) to take its course.

évolutif, -ive [evɔlytif, -iv] *a.* (*a*) evolutionary; (*b*) (*of disease*) developing by stages.

évolution [evɔlysjɔ̃] *n.f.* **1.** (*a*) evolution, manœuvre

ship, troops, etc.); **évolutions tactiques,** tactical exercises; (*b*) movement, circling, wheeling (of dancer, etc.). **2.** (*a*) *Biol:* evolution; development; (*b*) evolvement (of plan, etc.); course (of disease).
évolutionnisme [evɔlysjɔnism) *n.m. Biol:* evolutionism.
évolutionniste [evɔlysjɔnist] *Biol:* **1.** *a.* evolutionist(ic). **2.** *n.m. & f.* evolutionist.
évoquer [evɔke] *v.tr.* (*a*) to evoke, summon, conjure up, raise (spirit); (*b*) to recall, call to mind, conjure up, evoke (memory); to be reminiscent of (sth.).
ex- [ɛks] *pref.* ex-; **ex-femme,** ex-wife; *F:* **mon ex,** my ex.
exacerbation [ɛgzasɛrbasjɔ̃] *n.f.* exacerbation.
exacerber [ɛgzasɛrbe] *v.tr.* to exacerbate, aggravate (pain, irritation).
exact [ɛgza(kt)] *a.* exact; (*a*) accurate, true, right, correct, precise (calculation, etc.); **sciences exactes,** exact sciences; **l'heure exacte,** the right, correct, time; **e. à un millimètre près,** correct to a millimetre; **c'est e.,** it's quite true, it's a fact; (*b*) strict, rigorous (diet, etc.); (*c*) punctual; **e. à payer son loyer,** punctual in paying his rent.
exactement [ɛgzaktəmɑ̃] *adv.* exactly; (*a*) accurately, correctly; **reproduire e. un texte,** to reproduce a text faithfully; (*b*) just, precisely; **il avait e. l'air d'un spectre,** he looked just, for all the world, like a ghost; **effet e. contraire,** directly opposite effect; (*c*) punctually.
exaction [egzaksjɔ̃] *n.f.* **1.** exaction (of tax, etc.). **2.** extortion.
exactitude [ɛgzaktityd] *n.f.* (*a*) exactness, exactitude, correctness, accuracy (of statement, calculation, etc.); (*b*) punctuality; **avec e.,** (i) accurately; (ii) punctually.
ex æquo [ɛgzeko] *Lt.adj.phr.* of equal merit; **classés ex a.,** bracketed equal (in competition); **être troisième ex a.,** to tie for third place.
exagération [ɛgzaʒerasjɔ̃] *n.f.* exaggeration; overstatement; **e. de la sensibilité,** hypersensitivity.
exagéré [ɛgzaʒere] *a.* exaggerated; **prix e.,** exorbitant price; **confiance exagérée,** overconfidence.
exagérément [ɛgzaʒeremɑ̃] *adv.* exaggeratedly.
exagérer [ɛgzaʒere] *v.tr.* (**j'exagère**) to exaggerate (facts, dangers, etc.); to overstate (truth, etc.); to overestimate, overrate (s.o.'s qualities); **n'exagérez pas!** *F:* come off it! **vous exagérez!** you're going too far!
exaltant [ɛgzaltɑ̃] *a.* exciting, stirring (speech, etc.).
exaltation [ɛgzaltasjɔ̃] *n.f.* **1.** (*a*) exaltation (of the Cross); (*b*) exalting, extolling (of virtue, etc.). **2.** (*a*) exaltation; elation; (*b*) *Med:* over-excitement.
exalté, -ée [ɛgzalte] **1.** (*a*) excited, impassioned (speech, etc.); (*b*) hotheaded; quixotic (person); (*c*) uplifted (state of mind, etc.). **2.** *n.* excitable person; hothead; fanatic.
exalter [ɛgzalte] *v.* **1.** *v.tr.* (*a*) to exalt, praise, glorify, magnify, extol; (*b*) to excite, inflame, stir (imagination, etc.); (*c*) to exalt, dignify. **2. s'é.,** to grow excited, enthusiastic; to enthuse.
examen [ɛgzamɛ̃] *n.m.* examination; (*a*) investigation; overhauling (of a machine); inspection (of accounts); **après un e. attentif de l'horizon,** after a careful scrutiny of the horizon; **e. de la vue,** sight testing; **cette assertion ne supporte pas l'e.,** this assertion will not bear examination; **question à l'e.,** matter under examination, under consideration; **e. de conscience,** self examination; (*b*) *Sch:* **passer un e.,** to go in, sit, for an examination, *F:* an exam; **être reçu, refusé, à un e.,** to pass, fail in, an examination; **jury d'e.,** the examining body, the examiners; *Aut:* **e. pour permis de conduire,** driving test.
examinateur, -trice [ɛgzaminatœr, -tris] *n.* (*a*) investigator, inspector; (*b*) examiner.
examiner [ɛgzamine] *v.* **1.** *v.tr.* to examine; (*a*) to scrutinize, study carefully; to inspect, go through (accounts); to overhaul (machinery); **se faire e. par un médecin,** to have oneself examined by a doctor; **e. attentivement l'horizon,** to scan, survey, the horizon; **e. une question,** to look into, go into, consider, a matter; (*b*) *Sch:* **e. qn en algèbre,** to examine s.o. in algebra. **2. s'e.,** to examine one's conscience.
exaspérant [ɛgzasperɑ̃] *a.* exasperating, irritating, aggravating.
exaspération [ɛgzasperasjɔ̃] *n.f.* exasperation, irritation, aggravation.
exaspérer [ɛgzaspere] *v.* **1.** *v.tr.* (**j'exaspère; j'exaspérerai**) (*a*) to aggravate (pain); (*b*) to exasperate, irritate (s.o.). **2. s'e.,** to become exasperated.
exaucement [ɛgzosmɑ̃] *n.m.* **1.** granting of the prayer (of s.o.). **2.** granting, fulfilment (of wish).
exaucer [ɛgzose] *v.tr.* (**j'exauçai(s); n. exauçons**) **1. e. qn,** to grant, give ear to, answer, the prayer of s.o. **2.** to grant, fulfil (wish, desire); **exauce ma prière!** hear my prayer!
excavateur, -trice [ɛkskavatœr, -tris] *n.* digging machine, digger.
excavation [ɛkskavasjɔ̃] *n.f.* (*a*) excavation; excavating; (*b*) excavation, hollow, pit.
excaver [ɛkskave] *v.tr.* to excavate, to dig out.
excédant [ɛksedɑ̃] *a.* **1.** surplus (sum, etc.); excess(ive) (luggage, etc.). **2.** tiresome, exasperating (visitor).
excédent [ɛksedɑ̃] *n.m.* excess, surplus; **somme en e.,** sum in excess; **vous garderez l'e.,** you will keep what is over; **e. de poids,** excess weight; **e. de dépenses,** deficit; **e. de bagages,** excess luggage.
excédentaire [ɛksedɑ̃tɛr] *a.* excess, surplus.
excéder [ɛksede] *v.tr.* (**j'excède, n. excédons; j'excéderai**) **1.** to exceed, go beyond (a certain limit); **le résultat a excédé mes espérances,** the result has surpassed my hopes; **e. ses pouvoirs,** to exceed one's powers. **2.** (*a*) *O:* to tire, wear, (s.o.) out; **excédé de fatigue,** worn out, fagged out; (*b*) to exasperate (s.o.); **j'étais excédé,** I had lost all patience.
excellemment [ɛksɛlamɑ̃] *adv.* excellently.
excellence [ɛksɛlɑ̃s] *n.f.* **1.** excellence, pre-eminence; *Sch:* **prix d'e.,** first prize (for a general all-round standard); **par e.,** (i) par excellence, pre-eminently, in the highest sense of the word; (ii) supremely, above all. **2. votre E.,** your Excellency.
excellent [ɛksɛlɑ̃] *a.* excellent, first-rate; **en excellente santé,** in the best of health; **une idée excellente,** an excellent, splendid, idea.
exceller [ɛksele] *v.i.* to excel (**à faire qch.,** in doing sth.).
excentration [ɛksɑ̃trasjɔ̃] *n.f. Mec.E:* setting over, offsetting; off-cent(e)ring.
excentrer [ɛksɑ̃tre] *v.tr. Mec.E:* to throw off centre; to offset, to set over.
excentricité [ɛksɑ̃trisite] *n.f.* **1.** (*a*) eccentricity (of orbit, etc.); *Mec.E:* throw (of eccentric); (*b*) remoteness (of suburb, etc.). **2.** eccentricity, peculiarity, oddity (of manner).
excentrique [ɛksɑ̃trik] **1.** *a.* (*a*) eccentric (orbit, pulley, etc.); (*b*) remote, outlying (suburb, etc.); (*c*) eccentric, odd (person). **2.** *n.* odd, eccentric, person. **3.** *n.m. Mec.E:* (*a*) eccentric (gear); (*b*) cam.
excentriquement [ɛksɑ̃trikmɑ̃] *adv.* eccentrically.
excepté [ɛksepte] *prep.* except(ing), but, besides, with the exception of; **personne e. lui,** nobody except him; **la maison nous convient e. qu'elle manque de garage,** the house suits us except (for the fact) that there's no garage.
excepter [ɛksɛpte] *v.tr.* to except, exclude (s.o., sth.) (**de,** from); **si l'on excepte une seule rue,** with the

exception of one street; **les femmes exceptées,** except, apart from, the women.

exception [ɛksɛpsjɔ̃] *n.f.* **1.** exception; **faire une e. à une règle,** to make an exception to a rule; **faire e. à une règle,** to be an exception to a rule; **l'e. confirme la règle,** the exception proves the rule; **à quelques exceptions près,** with a few exceptions; **tous, à l'e. du docteur, e. faite du docteur,** all, except, but, the doctor. **2.** *Jur:* exception, incidental plea (of defence). **3. mesures d'e.,** emergency regulations; **tribunal d'e.,** emergency court.

exceptionnel, -elle [ɛksɛpsjɔnɛl] *a.* exceptional; (i) special (leave, etc.); (ii) uncommon, out of the ordinary; outstanding (talent); **taille exceptionnelle,** outsize (in clothes).

exceptionnellement [ɛksɛpsjɔnɛlmɑ̃] *adv.* exceptionally.

excès [ɛksɛ] *n.m.* (*a*) excess; **e. de l'offre sur la demande,** excess of supply over demand; **pécher par e. de zèle,** to be overzealous; *Mec.E:* **clapet d'e. de pression,** relief valve; *Phot:* **e. de pose,** over-exposure; *Aut:* **e. de vitesse,** exceeding the speed limit; **manger avec e.,** to eat too much; **manger sans e.,** to eat moderately, reasonably; **(jusqu') à l'e.,** to excess, too much; **se dépenser à l'e.,** to overexert oneself; **scrupuleux à l'e.,** scrupulous to a fault, over-scrupulous; (*b*) **commettre des e.,** to commit excesses, to go too far; **e. (de table),** overeating; **e. de conduite,** loose living; (*c*) *Jur:* **e. de pouvoir,** action ultra vires.

excessif, -ive [ɛksɛsif, -iv] *a.* (*a*) excessive, extreme; undue (optimism, etc.); exorbitant (price); immoderate (eating, drinking); inordinate (pride); **un travail e. l'a rendu malade,** he has become ill through overwork; (*b*) **il est e.,** he goes to extremes.

excessivement [ɛksɛsivmɑ̃] *adv.* excessively, exceedingly; extremely; **manger e.,** to eat too much.

exciper [ɛksipe] *v.i. Jur:* to put in a plea; **e. de sa bonne foi,** to plead one's good faith.

excipient [ɛksipjɑ̃] *n.m. Pharm:* vehicle.

exciser [ɛksize] *v.tr. Surg:* to excise, cut out.

excision [ɛksizjɔ̃] *n.f. Surg:* excision.

excitabilité [ɛksitabilite] *n.f.* excitability.

excitable [ɛksitabl̩] *a.* excitable.

excitant [ɛksitɑ̃] **1.** *a.* exciting, stimulating (news, etc.). **2.** *n.m.* excitant, stimulant.

excitateur, -trice [ɛksitatœr, -tris] **1.** (*a*) *a.* exciting (cause, etc.); provocative (**de,** of); (*b*) *n.* exciter, instigator (**de,** of). **2.** *El:* (*a*) *n.m.* discharger, (static) exciter; (*b*) *n.f.* **excitatrice,** exciter, exciting dynamo.

excitation [ɛksitasjɔ̃] *n.f.* **1.** excitation (of the senses, etc.); **e. à la révolte,** instigation, incitement, to rebellion. **2.** (state of) excitement. **3.** *El:* excitation.

excité, -ée [ɛksite] *a. & n.* excited (person).

exciter [ɛksite] *v.* **1.** *v.tr.* to excite; (*a*) to arouse, stir up (curiosity, etc.); **e. la pitié de qn,** to move s.o. to pity; (*b*) to urge (s.o.) on; **e. qn à la révolte, à se révolter,** to incite s.o. to revolt; **e. qn contre qn,** to set s.o. against s.o.; (*c*) to stimulate (nerve, etc.); (*d*) *El:* to energize (dynamo). **2. s'e.,** to get excited, worked up.

exclamatif, -ive [ɛksklamatif, -iv] *a.* exclamatory.

exclamation [ɛksklamasjɔ̃] *n.f.* exclamation; **point d'e.,** exclamation mark, *NAm:* point.

exclamer (s') [sɛksklame] *v.pr.* to exclaim.

exclure [ɛksklyr] *v.tr.* (*pr.p.* **excluant;** *p.p.* **exclu;** *pr.ind.* **j'exclus, n. excluons;** *impf.* **j'excluais;** *p.h.* **j'exclus;** *fu.* **j'exclurai**) (*a*) to exclude, shut out, leave out (s.o., sth.); **e. qn de qch.,** to exclude s.o. from sth.; **candidat exclu,** unsuccessful candidate; **le mois d'août jusqu'au 31 exclu,** the month of August excluding the 31st; (*b*) **deux choses qui s'excluent,** two things that are incompatible, mutually exclusive; **e. la possibilité d'un accord,** to rule out the possibility of an agreement.

exclusif, -ive [ɛksklyzif, -iv] *a.* **1.** exclusive, sole (right, agent); **article e.,** exclusive article, speciality. **2.** self-opinionated. **3.** *n.f.* **exclusive,** veto.

exclusion [ɛksklyzjɔ̃] *n.f.* exclusion, excluding, debarring (of s.o., sth., from sth.); *Sp:* suspension (of player); **à. l'e. d'autres intérêts,** to the exclusion of other interests.

exclusivement [ɛksklyzivmɑ̃] *adv.* exclusively, solely; **depuis lundi jusqu'à vendredi e.,** from Monday to Friday exclusive.

exclusivisme [ɛksklyzivism] *n.m.* exclusivism.

exclusiviste [ɛksklyzivist] *n.* exclusivist.

exclusivité [ɛksklyzivite] *n.f.* sole, exclusive, rights (**de,** in); **film en e.,** exclusive film; *Journ:* **article en e.,** exclusive.

excommunication [ɛkskɔmynikasjɔ̃] *n.f.* excommunication.

excommunier [ɛkskɔmynje] *v.tr.* (*impf. & pr.sub.* **n. excommuniions)** to excommunicate.

excrément [ɛkskremɑ̃] *n.m. often pl.* **excrément(s),** excrement; **e. de la terre!** scum (of the earth)!

excréter [ɛkskrete] *v.tr.* (**j'excrète; j'excréterai**) to excrete.

excréteur, -euse, -trice [ɛkskretœr, -øz, -tris] **excrétoire** [ɛkskretwar], *a.* excretive, excretory.

excrétion [ɛkskresjɔ̃] *n.f.* excretion; (*a*) excreting; (*b*) excreted matter; **excrétions,** excreta.

excroissance [ɛkskrwasɑ̃s] *n.f.* excrescence.

excursion [ɛkskyrsjɔ̃] *n.f.* **1.** excursion; tour; trip; outing; ramble; **e. à pied,** walking tour; hike; **e. scientifique,** scientific expedition. **2.** digression, excursion (in speech, etc.).

excursionniste [ɛkskyrsjɔnist] *n.* excursionist, tourist, tripper; **e. à pied,** hiker.

excusable [ɛkskyzabl̩] *a.* excusable, pardonable.

excuse [ɛkskyz] *n.f.* **1.** (*a*) excuse; **trouver une e. à qch.,** to find an excuse for sth.; **je prends mon travail comme e.,** I make my work the excuse; (*b*) *P:* **faites e.!** sorry! **2.** *pl.* apology; **faire, présenter, ses excuses à qn,** to make one's apologies, to apologize, to s.o.; **lettre d'excuses,** letter of apology.

excuser [ɛkskyze] *v.* **1.** *v.tr.* (*a*) to make excuses, to apologize, for (s.o.); **e. qn auprès de qn,** to apologize for s.o. to s.o.; (*b*) to excuse (s.o.); **e. qch. à qn,** to excuse s.o. sth.; **e. qn de faire qch.,** to excuse s.o. (i) for doing sth., (ii) from doing sth.; **e. un juré,** to excuse a juryman (from attendance); **l'ignorance n'excuse personne,** ignorance is no excuse. **2. s'e.,** to apologize; **s'e. auprès de qn,** to make, send, one's apologies to s.o.; **s'e. de faire qch.,** to apologize for doing sth.; *F:* **je m'excuse,** excuse me; **s'e. de, sur, sa tenue,** to apologize for one's dress; *Prov:* **qui s'excuse s'accuse,** he who excuses himself accuses himself.

exécrable [ɛgzekrabl̩] *a.* execrable; abominable, loathsome (crime); deplorable (taste, verse).

exécrablement [ɛgzekrabləmɑ̃] *adv.* execrably, abominably.

exécration [ɛgzekrasjɔ̃] *n.f.* execration, detestation (of crime, etc.); **avoir qn en e.,** to loath s.o.

exécrer [ɛgzekre] *v.tr.* (**j'exècre; j'exécrerai**) to execrate, loathe, detest.

exécutable [ɛgzekytabl̩] *a.* practicable, feasible.

exécutant, -ante [egzekytɑ̃, -ɑ̃t] *n.* executant.

exécuter [ɛgzekyte] *v.* **1.** *v.tr.* (*a*) to execute; to carry out, achieve (work, plan); to follow out, carry out, act upon (orders); to perform, fulfil (promise); to carry out, give effect to (decree); to play (piece of music); to perform (dance); (*b*) (i) to execute, to put (criminal, etc.) to death; (ii) *Jur:* to distrain upon (debtor); (iii) (*of critic*) to slaughter (author, work). **2. s'e.,** to submit; to comply; **il faudra bien vous e.,**

you'll have to bring yourself to do it.
exécuteur, -trice [ɛgzekytœr, -tris] **1.** (*a*) *A:* executant, performer (of undertaking); (*b*) *Jur:* **exécuteur, -trice, testamentaire,** executor, -trix. **2.** executioner.
exécutif, -ive [ɛgzekytif, -iv] *a.* executive; **le pouvoir e.,** *n.m.* **l'exécutif,** the Executive.
exécution [ɛgzekysjɔ̃] *n.f.* **1.** execution, performance, carrying out (of plan, orders); fulfilment (of promise); enforcement (of law, judgment); performance (of opera, piece of music); **droit d'e.,** (i) right of performance; (ii) performing rights, author's fee; **difficultés d'e. d'un morceau de musique,** difficulties in the execution of a piece of music; **mettre un projet à e.,** to put a plan into execution; to carry out a plan; **travaux en voie d'e.,** work in progress. **2.** (*a*) **e. capitale,** carrying out the death sentence; execution; **ordre d'e.,** death warrant; *Mil:* **peloton d'e.,** firing party; (*b*) *Jur:* distraint, distress.
exécutoire [ɛgzekytwar] *Jur:* **1.** *a.* (*a*) **jugement (de force) e.,** enforceable decision (of the court); (*b*) executory (formula, etc.). **2.** *n.m.* writ of execution; **e. de dépens,** order to pay costs.
exégèse [ɛgzeʒɛz] *n.f.* exegesis.
exemplaire[1] [ɛgzɑ̃plɛr] *a.* exemplary.
exemplaire[2] *n.m.* **1.** exemplar, pattern, model. **2.** (*a*) sample, specimen (of work); (*b*) copy (of book, engraving); **édition tirée à dix mille exemplaires,** edition of ten thousand copies; **dactylographié en double e.,** typed in duplicate.
exemplairement [ɛgzɑ̃plɛrmɑ̃] *adv.* exemplarily.
exemple [ɛgzɑ̃pl̩] *n.m.* example. **1. donner l'e.,** to set an, the, example; **suivre l'e. de qn, prendre e. sur qn,** to follow s.o.'s example; **supposons à titre d'e. qu'il n'y a point de candidats,** let us suppose for argument's sake, for example, that no one applies; **prêcher d'e.,** to practise what one preaches. **2.** lesson, warning, caution; **faire un e. de qn,** to make an example of s.o.; **servir d'e. à qn,** to be a lesson, a warning, to s.o.; **infliger une punition pour l'e.,** to punish s.o. as a warning to others. **3.** instance, precedent; **sans e.,** without parallel; **par e.,** for instance, for example; **un de ces jours, par e. dimanche,** one of these days, say on Sunday; **par e.!** well! who'd have thought it! **ah non, par e.!** I should think not! **c'est utile, mais c'est cher, par e.,** it's useful but it is, indeed, very expensive.
exemplifier [ɛgzɑ̃plifje] *v.tr.* to exemplify.
exempt, -empte [ɛgzɑ̃, -ɑ̃t] **1.** *a.* exempt (from service, tax, etc.); free (from anxiety, disease, etc.); **e. de soucis,** carefree; *Cust:* **e. de droits,** free of duty, duty-free; **e. de port,** carriage free. **2.** *n. Sp:* player who has a bye.
exempter [ɛgzɑ̃te] *v.* **1.** *v.tr.* **e. qn de qch.,** to exempt, free, excuse, s.o. from sth.; **e. qn de faire qch.,** to exempt, excuse, s.o. from doing sth. **2. s'e. de faire qch.,** to get off, out of, doing sth.
exemption [ɛgzɑ̃psjɔ̃] *n.f.* exemption (**de,** from); freedom (from anxiety, etc.); *Cust:* **liste d'exemptions,** free list.
exerçant [ɛgzɛrsɑ̃] *a.* practising (doctor, etc.).
exercé [ɛgzɛrse] *a.* experienced, practised, trained.
exercer [ɛgzɛrse] *v.* (**j'exerçai(s)**) **1.** *v.tr.* (*a*) (i) to exercise (one's body, mind); (ii) *Mil:* to drill, train (soldiers); **e. qn à qch., à faire qch.,** to give s.o. practice in sth., at doing sth.; to train s.o. for sth., to do sth.; (*b*) to exercise; **e. son influence sur qn,** to exert, exercise, one's influence, bring one's influence to bear, on s.o.; **e. une pression sur qch.,** to exert pressure on sth.; **e. ses droits,** to exercise one's rights; (*c*) **médecine qui exerce une action sur le foie,** medicine that acts, has an action, upon the liver; (*d*) to exercise, practise, follow (profession); to follow, carry on (business, trade); *v.i.* **médecin qui n'exerce plus,** doctor no longer in practice. **2. s'e.** (*a*) to drill; to do exercises; (*b*) to practise; **s'e. à qch., à faire qch.,** to practise sth., doing sth..
exercice [ɛgzɛrsis] *n.m.* **1.** (*a*) exercise; **prendre de l'e.,** to take exercise; **e. physique,** physical exercise; (*b*) *Mil: etc:* drill(ing), training; **être à l'e.,** to be on parade; **faire l'e.,** to drill; (*c*) **exercices scolaires,** school exercises; **jouer des exercices au piano,** to practise exercises (on the piano). **2.** (*a*) exercise (of power, privilege, etc.); carrying out (of mandate, etc.); practice (of profession); **dans l'e. de ses fonctions,** in the exercise, discharge, of one's duties; **avocat en e.,** practising barrister; **le président en e.,** the president in office; (*b*) **l'e. du culte,** public worship. **3.** financial year, year's trading.
exfoliation [ɛksfɔljasjɔ̃] *n.f.* exfoliation.
exfolier (s') [sɛksfɔlje], *v.pr.* to exfoliate, scale off.
exhalaison [ɛgzalɛzɔ̃] *n.f.* exhalation, effluvium; *pl.* fumes.
exhalation [ɛgzalasjɔ̃] *n.f.* exhalation, exhaling.
exhaler [ɛgzale] *v.* **1.** *v.tr.* to exhale, emit, give out (smell, vapour, etc.); to breathe (a sigh); to give vent to, to vent (one's wrath). **2. s'e.,** (*of gas, vapour, etc.*) to exhale, be given off.
exhaussement [ɛgzosmɑ̃] *n.m.* **1.** raising, increasing the height (of wall, etc.). **2. e. du terrain,** rise in the ground; mound, elevation.
exhausser [ɛgzose] *v.* **1.** *v.tr.* to heighten, increase the height of (wall, etc.); **e. une maison d'un étage,** to add a storey to a house. **2. s'e.,** (*of ground, etc.*) to rise.
exhausteur [ɛgzostœr] *n.m. Aut:* suction pipe (of vacuum-feed tank).
exhaustif, -ive [ɛgzostif, -iv] *a.* exhaustive.
exhaustion [ɛgzostjɔ̃] *n.f. Log:* exhaustion.
exhaustivement [ɛgzostivmɑ̃] *adv.* exhaustively.
exhérédation [ɛgzeredasjɔ̃] *n.f. Jur:* disinheritance.
exhéréder [ɛgzerede] *v.tr.* (**j'exhérède; j'exhéréderai**) *Jur:* to disinherit.
exhiber [ɛgzibe] *v.* **1.** *v.tr.* (*a*) to produce (documents, etc.); to present, show (passport, etc.); (*b*) to exhibit, show (animals, etc.); to show off, display (one's knowledge). **2. s'e.,** to make an exhibition of oneself.
exhibition [ɛgzibisjɔ̃] *n.f.* **1.** *Jur:* production (of documents). **2.** (cattle, etc.) show; exhibition (of pictures, etc.).
exhibitionnisme [ɛgzibisjɔnism] *n.m.* exhibitionism.
exhibitionniste [ɛgzibisjɔnist] *n* exhibitionist.
exhortation [ɛgzɔrtasjɔ̃] *n.f.* exhortation (**à qch., à faire qch.,** to sth., to do sth.).
exhorter [ɛgzɔrte] *v.tr.* to exhort, urge (**à faire qch.,** to do sth.).
exhumation [ɛgzymasjɔ̃] *n.f.* (*a*) exhumation, disinterment (of corpse); digging up (of buried city); (*b*) unearthing (of old documents, etc.).
exhumer [ɛgzyme] *v.tr.* (*a*) to exhume, disinter (body); to dig up, excavate (treasure, etc.); (*b*) to unearth, bring to light (old documents, etc.); to dig up (old grudges, etc.).
exigeant [ɛgziʒɑ̃] *a.* exacting, demanding (person, job); (*of pers.*) **être trop e.,** to expect too much.
exigence [ɛgziʒɑ̃s] *n.f.* **1. elle est d'une e. insupportable,** she's intolerably demanding. **2.** (*a*) (unreasonable) demand; whim; (*b*) demand, requirement; **l'e., les exigences, de l'étiquette,** the demands of etiquette; **selon l'e. du cas,** as may be required.
exiger [ɛgziʒe] *v.tr.* (**j'exigeai(s)**) **1.** to exact (tax); to demand, require (**de,** from); to insist on (sth.); **e. qu'une chose soit faite,** to insist on something being done; **trop e. des forces de qn,** to overtax s.o.'s

strength. **2.** to require, necessitate, call for (care, etc.); **prendre les mesures qu'exigent les circonstances,** to take the necessary measures.

exigible [ɛgziʒibl̩] *a.* exactable; (payment) due.

exigu, -uë [ɛgzigy] *a.* exiguous, tiny (dwelling, etc.); diminutive (stature); slender (income).

exiguïté [ɛgzigɥite] *n.f.* exiguity, smallness (of dwelling, etc.); slenderness (of income).

exil [ɛgzil] *n.m.* exile, banishment; **envoyer qn en e.,** to send s.o. into exile, to banish s.o.

exilé, -ée [ɛgzile] *n.* (*pers.*) exile.

exiler [ɛgzile] *v.* **1.** *v.tr.* to exile, banish. **2. s'e.,** to go into (voluntary) exile; **s'e. du monde,** to withdraw from the world.

existant [ɛgzistɑ̃] **1.** *a.* (*a*) existing, living, existent; **lois existantes,** existing laws, laws in force; (*b*) extant (species, etc.); (*c*) (supplies, etc.) in hand. **2.** *n.m.* **e. en caisse, en magasin,** cash, stock, in hand.

existence [ɛgzistɑ̃s] *n.f.* **1.** (*a*) existence, (state of) being; (*b*) life; **mener une e. agréable,** to lead a pleasant existence. **2.** *Com:* **e. (en magasin),** stock (in hand).

existentialisme [ɛgzistɑ̃sjalism] *n.m. Phil:* existentialism.

existentialiste [ɛgzistɑ̃sjalist] *a. & n.m. & f. Phil:* existentialist.

existentiel, -elle [ɛgzistɑ̃sjɛl] *a.* existential.

exister [ɛgziste] *v.i.* (*a*) to exist, be; to live; **la maison existe toujours,** (i) the house is still standing; (ii) the firm is still in existence; **rien n'existe pour lui que l'art,** nothing but art matters to him; (*b*) to be extant.

ex-libris [ɛkslibris] *n.m.* book plate, ex libris.

exocrine [ɛgzɔkrin] *a.* exocrine (gland).

exode [ɛgzɔd] *n.m.* (*a*) **l'E.,** Exodus; (*b*) exodus; emigration; **l'e. des cerveaux,** the brain drain; **e. rural,** rural depopulation.

exogame [ɛgzɔgam] *a.* exogamous (tribe).

exogamie [ɛgzɔgami] *n.f.* exogamy.

exonération [ɛgzɔnerasjɔ̃] *n.f.* exoneration; **e. d'impôts,** tax relief.

exonérer [ɛgzɔnere] *v.tr.* (**j'exonère, j'exonérerai**) (*a*) to exonerate (**de,** from); to free, relieve (s.o. from duty, etc.); to exempt (s.o. from income tax); (*b*) to exempt (goods) from import duty.

exophtalmie [ɛgzɔftalmi] *n.f. Med:* exophthalmus, exophthalmos.

exophtalmique [ɛgzɔftalmik] *a.* exophthalmic (goitre).

exorbitant [ɛgzɔrbitɑ̃] *a.* exorbitant, outrageous.

exorbité [ɛgzɔrbite] *a.* **ils regardaient, les yeux exorbités,** they were looking on, with their eyes starting out of their heads.

exorciser [ɛgzɔrsize] *v.tr.* to exorcize (demon, one possessed); to cast out (devil); to lay (ghost).

exorciseur, -euse [ɛgzɔrsizœr, -øz], **exorciste** [ɛgzɔrsist], exorcizer, exorcist.

exorcisme [ɛgzɔrsism] *n.m.* **1.** exorcizing. **2.** exorcism.

exorde [ɛgzɔrd] *n.m.* exordium.

exosmose [ɛgzɔsmoz] *n.f. Ph:* exosmosis.

exotique [ɛgzɔtik] *a.* exotic.

exotisme [ɛgzɔtism] *n.m.* exot(ic)ism.

expansibilité [ɛkspɑ̃sibilite] *n.f.* **1.** expansibility (of gas, etc.). **2.** expansiveness (of disposition).

expansible [ɛkspɑ̃sibl̩] *a.* expansible (gas, etc.).

expansif, -ive [ɛkspɑ̃sif, -iv] *a.* **1.** expansive (force, etc.). **2.** (*of pers.*) expansive, exuberant, effusive.

expansion [ɛkspɑ̃sjɔ̃] *n.f.* **1.** expansion; (*a*) expansion (of gases, etc.); **machine à triple e.,** triple-expansion engine; **l'univers en e.,** the expanding universe; (*b*) spread (of ideas, etc.); **e. coloniale,** colonial expansion; **taux d'e. économique,** economic growth rate. **2.** (*a*) expansiveness; **avec e.,** effusively; (*b*) effusion.

expansionnisme [ɛkspɑ̃sjɔnism] *n.m.* (*a*) *Pol:* colonialism; (*b*) *Pol.Ec:* expansionism.

expansionniste [ɛkspɑ̃sjɔnist] *a. & n.* expansionist.

expansivité [ɛkspɑ̃sivite] *n.f.* expansiveness.

expatriation [ɛkspatrijasjɔ̃] *n.f.* expatriation.

expatrié, -ée [ɛkspatrije] *a. & n.* expatriate.

expatrier [ɛkspatrije] *v.* (*impf. & pr.sub.* **n. expatriions**) **1.** *v.tr.* to expatriate; to invest (capital) abroad. **2. s'e.,** to settle abroad.

expectative [ɛkspɛktativ] *n.f.* expectation, expectancy; **nous vivons dans l'e.,** we are living in hopes; **rester dans l'e.,** to wait and see; **triste e.,** gloomy prospect.

expectorant [ɛkspɛktɔrɑ̃] *a. & n.m. Med:* expectorant.

expectoration [ɛkspɛktɔrasjɔ̃] *n.f.* expectoration; (i) expectorating; (ii) sputum.

expectorer [ɛkspɛktɔre] *v.tr.* to expectorate.

expédient [ɛkspedjɑ̃] **1.** *a.* expedient; **il est e. de prendre les devants,** it is advisable to take the initiative. **2.** *n.m.* expedient, device; makeshift; **vivre d'expédients,** to live by one's wits.

expédier [ɛkspedje] *v.tr.* (*impf. & pr.sub.* **n. expédiions**) to dispatch, despatch. **1.** to get rid of, dispose of (s.o.); to get (s.o.) out of the way. **2.** (*a*) to expedite, hurry through (task), deal (promptly) with (business); **e. son déjeuner,** to make short work of one's lunch; (*b*) *Cust:* **e. des marchandises en douane,** to clear goods. **3.** *Jur:* to draw up (contract, deed). **4.** to forward, send off (letter, goods); **e. des marchandises par navire,** to ship goods; *F:* **expédiez-le-moi!** send him along (to me)!

expéditeur, -trice [ɛkspeditœr, -tris] **1.** *n.* (*a*) sender (of letter, etc.); (*on letter, etc.*) **expéditeur, -trice, J. Martin,** sender, from, J. Martin; (*b*) shipper, consigner, consignor (of goods); (*c*) forwarding agents. **2.** *a.* dispatching (office, etc.).

expéditif, -ive [ɛkspeditif, -iv] *a.* expeditious.

expédition [ɛkspedisjɔ̃] *n.f.* **1.** (*a*) expedition, dispatch, disposal (of business, etc.); (*b*) **e. en douane,** (customs) clearance. **2.** (authentic) copy (of deed, contract, etc.). **3.** (*a*) dispatch(ing), forwarding, sending (of parcel, etc.); **e. par mer,** shipping, shipment; **bulletin d'e.,** waybill; (*b*) consignment. **4.** (military, scientific) expedition.

expéditionnaire [ɛkspedisjɔnɛr] **1.** *a. & n.* **(commis) e.,** (i) copying clerk; (ii) shipping clerk. **2.** *a. Mil:* **corps e.,** expeditionary force.

expérience [ɛksperjɑ̃s] *n.f.* **1.** experience; **avoir l'e. de qch.,** to have experience of, to be experienced in, sth.; **faire l'e. de qch.,** to experience sth.; **connaître qch. par e.,** to know sth. from experience; **sans e.,** inexperienced (**de,** in). **2.** experiment, test; **faire une e.,** to carry out an experiment; **faire une e. sur qn, sur qch.,** to experiment on s.o., on sth.

expérimental, -aux [ɛksperimɑ̃tal, -o] *a.* experimental; **les sciences expérimentales,** the applied sciences.

expérimentalement [ɛksperimɑ̃talmɑ̃] *adv.* experimentally.

expérimentateur, -trice [ɛksperimɑ̃tatœr, -tris] *n.* (*a*) experimenter; (*b*) (scientific) research worker.

expérimentation [ɛksperimɑ̃tasjɔ̃] *n.f.* experimentation, experimenting.

expérimenté [ɛksperimɑ̃te] *a.* experienced; skilled (workman).

expérimenter [ɛksperimɑ̃te] *v.tr.* **1.** to test, try (remedy, model, etc.); *v.i.* to make experiments. **2.** to know (sth.) by experience.

expert [ɛkspɛr] **1.** *a.* expert, skilled (**en, dans,** in; **à**

faire qch., in doing sth.). **2.** *n.m.* (*a*) expert; connoisseur; (*b*) valuer, appraiser; *Nau:* surveyor.
expert-comptable [ɛkspɛrkɔ̃tabl̩] *n.m.* = chartered accountant; *pl. experts-comptables.*
expertise [ɛkspɛrtiz] *n.f.* **1.** expert appraisement, valuation; *Nau:* **e. d'avarie,** damage survey. **2.** expert's report, expert opinion.
expertiser [ɛkspɛrtize] *v.tr.* to value, estimate; *Nau:* to survey (ship for damage).
expiation [ɛkspjasjɔ̃] *n.f.* expiation; *Theol:* atonement.
expiatoire [ɛkspjatwar] *a.* expiatory.
expier [ɛkspje] *v.tr.* (*impf.* & *pr.sub.* **n. expiions**) to expiate, atone for, pay the penalty of (sin, etc.).
expirant [ɛkspirɑ̃] *a.* expiring, dying; **voix expirante,** faint, barely audible, voice.
expiration [ɛkspirasjɔ̃] *n.f.* **1.** expiration; breathing out (of air); *Mch:* discharge (of steam). **2.** expiry, termination, end (of lease, etc.).
expirer [ɛkspire] *v.* to expire. **1.** *v.tr.* to breathe out (air). **2.** *v.i.* (*a*) to die; (*b*) to come to an end; (*of lease*) to run out; **mon congé est expiré,** my leave is up.
explétif, -ive [ɛkspletif, -iv] *a.* & *n.m.* expletive.
explicable [ɛksplikabl̩] *a.* explicable, explainable.
explicatif, -ive [ɛksplikatif, -iv] *a.* explanatory; **notice explicative,** *Lit:* prefatory note; *Com:* directions for use.
explication [ɛksplikasjɔ̃] *n.f.* explanation; **donner l'e. de qch.,** to account for, explain, sth.; **avoir une e. avec qn,** to have it out with s.o.; *Sch:* **e. de textes,** literary appreciation (of texts).
explicite [ɛksplisit] *a.* explicit, clear, plain.
explicitement [ɛksplisitmɑ̃] *adv.* explicitly, clearly, plainly.
expliciter [ɛksplisite] *v.tr.* to make (clause of contract, etc.) clear; to clarify (text).
expliquer [ɛksplike] *v.* **1.** *v.tr.* to explain, make clear (one's ideas, plans, etc.); (*b*) to explain, expound, elucidate (doctrine, theorem, etc.); to explain, account for (action, etc.); **je ne m'explique pas pourquoi,** I can't understand why. **2. s'e.,** to explain oneself; **je m'explique,** this is what I mean; *F:* **s'e. avec qn,** to have it out with s.o.
exploit [ɛksplwa] *n.m.* **1.** exploit, feat (of arms, etc.); achievement. **2.** *Jur:* writ, process, summons.
exploitant [ɛksplwatɑ̃] **1.** *a.* (*a*) *Ind:* operating (company, etc.); (*b*) *Jur:* **huissier e.,** process server. **2.** *n.m.* (*a*) owner, operator (of mine, etc.); cultivator (of land); **e. agricole,** farmer; (*b*) *Cin:* exhibitor.
exploitation [ɛksplwatasjɔ̃] *n.f.* **1.** (*a*) exploitation, exploiting; working (of mine); running (of railway, newspaper); utilization (of invention, patent, etc.); tapping (of natural resources); **société d'e.,** development company; **e. agricole,** farming; **e. du sel,** salt mining; (*b*) exploitation, taking (unfair) advantage of (tourists, etc.); making capital out of (s.o.'s ignorance, etc.). **2.** (*a*) workings; mine; works; (*b*) farm (estate); holding.
exploiter [ɛksplwate] **1.** *v.tr.* (*a*) to exploit; to work (mine, patent, etc.); to operate (railway, etc.); to get, win (coal); to farm (land); to run (farm); to make the most of (one's talent); **e. un succès,** to make capital out of a success; (*b*) to exploit; to take (unfair) advantage of (s.o.); to trade upon (s.o.'s ignorance, etc.). **2.** *v.i. Jur:* to serve a writ.
exploiteur, -euse [ɛksplwatœr, -øz) *n.* exploiter (of labour, s.o.'s ignorance).
explorateur, -trice [ɛksplɔratœr, -tris] **1.** *n.* (*a*) explorer; (*b*) *n.m. Surg:* exploring needle. **2.** *a.* exploring; *T.V:* scanning (cell, etc.).
exploration [ɛksplɔrasjɔ̃] *n.f.* **1.** exploration; **voyage d'e.,** voyage of discovery. **2.** *Min: etc:* fieldwork; prospecting. **3.** *T.V:* scanning. **4.** *Med:* examination; exploration.
explorer [ɛksplɔre] *v.tr.* **1.** (*a*) to explore (country); (*b*) *Med:* to explore, probe (wound); (*c*) *Cin: T.V:* to scan (sound track, image). **2.** *Min:* to prospect.
exploser [ɛksploze] *v.i.* (*a*) (*of boiler*) to explode, to blow up; (*of bomb*) to explode; *I.C.E:* (*of mixture*) to fire, burn; (*b*) (*of pers.*) to explode, blow up; (*of anger*) to burst out, explode; **e. en injures,** to burst out into abuse.
explosible [ɛksplozibl̩] *a.* explosive (gas, etc.).
explosif, -ive [ɛksplozif, -iv] **1.** *a.* (*a*) explosive, detonating; *El:* **distance explosive,** spark(ing) gap; (*b*) explosive (situation, temper); (*c*) *Phon:* (ex)plosive (consonant). **2.** *n.m.* explosive; **e. à grande puissance,** high explosive; **e. propulsif,** propellant explosive.
explosion [ɛksplozjɔ̃] *n.f.* explosion, bursting; **e. atomique,** atomic explosion; **e. aérienne,** air burst; **faire e.,** to explode, blow up; (*of boiler*) to burst; **moteur à e.,** internal combustion engine; **e. de fureur, rires,** (out)burst of fury, of laughter; **e. démographique,** population explosion.
exponentiel, -ielle [ɛkspɔnɑ̃sjɛl] *a. Mth:* exponential.
exportable [ɛkspɔrtabl̩] *a.* exportable.
exportateur, -trice [ɛkspɔrtatœr, -tris] **1.** *n.* exporter. **2.** *a.* exporting.
exportation [ɛkspɔrtasjɔ̃] *n.f.* export(ation); **articles d'e.,** exports; **faire l'e.,** to export; **les exportations,** (i) the export trade; (ii) exports; **commerce d'e.,** export trade.
exporter [ɛkspɔrte] *v.tr.* to export.
exposant, -ante [ɛkspozɑ̃, -ɑ̃t] *n.* **1.** (*a*) *Jur:* petitioner, deponent; (*b*) exhibitor (of work of art, etc.). **2.** *n.m. Mth:* exponent; (power) index.
exposé [ɛkspoze] *n.m.* statement, account, report, exposition (of facts, affairs, etc.); **e. verbal (de mission),** briefing; **donner un e. d'un projet,** to sketch out a plan; **faire un e.,** to read a paper.
exposer [ɛkspoze] *v.tr.* **1.** (*a*) to exhibit, show, display (goods, works of art); **objet exposé,** exhibit; **être exposé (sur un lit de parade),** to lie in state; **e. des marchandises en vente, à la devanture,** to display goods for sale; (*b*) to set out, unfold, expound (plans, reasons, etc.); **je leur ai exposé ma situation,** I explained to them how I was placed. **2.** (*a*) to expose; to lay (s.o., sth.) open (to sth.); **exposé à tous les vents,** open to every wind; **après avoir été exposé au soleil,** after exposure to the sun; *Phot:* **e. un film,** to expose a film; **maison exposée au nord,** house with a north aspect, facing north; **e. sa vie,** to imperil one's life; **s'e. à des critiques,** to lay oneself open to criticism; **il s'expose à des poursuites,** he is rendering himself liable to proceedings; **il s'expose à devenir ridicule,** he is in danger of becoming ridiculous; (*b*) (i) to expose, (ii) to abandon (newborn child).
exposition [ɛkspozisjɔ̃] *n.f.* **1.** (*a*) exhibition, show (of goods, works of art, flowers); exposition (of Sacrament); lying in state (of body); **salle d'e.,** (i) exhibition room; (ii) show room; (*b*) exposure (to danger, cold); (*c*) exposition, statement (of facts, reasons, etc.); *Lit:* introduction; (*e*) *Mus:* exposition. **2.** aspect, exposure (of house). **3.** *Phot:* exposure.
exprès¹, -esse [ɛksprɛs] **1.** *a.* express, distinct, explicit (order, warning, etc.); **défense expresse de fumer,** smoking strictly prohibited. **2.** (*a*) *a.* & *n.m. A:* express (messenger); (*b*) *a. inv.* & *n.m.* **(lettre, paquet) e.,** express letter, parcel.
exprès² [ɛksprɛ] *adv.* designedly, on purpose, intentionally, deliberately; **outil façonné e.,** specially designed tool; **je ne l'ai pas fait e.,** I didn't mean to

do it, I didn't do it on purpose; **il fait e. de vous contredire,** he makes a point of contradicting you; **c'est fait e.,** it's (quite) intentional; I meant (to do) it; **on dirait un fait e.,** of course it *would* happen; you'd think it was done on purpose.

express [ɛksprɛs] *a. & n.m.* **1.** express (train). **2.** espresso (coffee).

expressément [ɛksprɛsemɑ̃] *adv.* **1.** expressly (forbidden); explicitly. **2.** expressly, especially; on purpose.

expressif, -ive [ɛksprɛsif, -iv] *a.* expressive (language, glance, face); *Mus:* **clavier e.,** swell organ.

expression [ɛksprɛsjɔ̃] *n.f.* **1.** expression, voicing (of opinion, etc.); show (of feelings); **au delà de toute e.,** inexpressible, beyond expression; **visage d'une e. triste,** face with a sad expression; **sans e.,** expressionless; *Mus:* **jouer avec e.,** to play with expression; **signe d'e.,** expression mark; **boîte d'e.,** swell box (of organ). **2.** term, phrase; **e. familière,** colloquial expression. **3.** *Mth:* **e. algébrique,** algebraic expression. **4.** squeezing out (of juice, etc.).

expressionnisme [ɛksprɛsjɔnism] *n.m.* expressionism.

expressionniste [ɛksprɛsjɔnist] *a. & n.* expressionist.

exprimable [ɛksprimabl̩] *a.* expressible.

exprimer [ɛksprime] *v.* **1.** *v.tr.* to express; (*a*) **e. les jus d'un citron,** to squeeze (out), press, the juice from a lemon; (*b*) to voice, put into words, to convey (one's feelings, opinion, etc.); (*of looks, gestures, etc.*) to show, manifest, reveal (pain, pleasure, etc.). **2. s'e.,** to express oneself; **si l'on peut s'e. ainsi,** if one may put it this way, if one may say so.

expropriation [ɛksprɔprijasjɔ̃] *n.f. Jur:* expropriation (of property, owner); compulsory purchase.

exproprier [ɛksprɔprije] *v.tr.* (*impf. & pr.sub.* **n. expropriions,** to expropriate ((i) proprietor, (ii) property).

expulser [ɛkspylse] *v.tr.* to expel; to eject (s.o.); to turn (s.o.) out; to evict (tenant); to deport (alien); to send down (student); to expel (pupil); to expel (air, body waste).

expulsif, -ive [ɛkspylsif, -iv] *a.* expulsive (force, etc.).

expulsion [ɛkspylsjɔ̃] *n.f.* expulsion; deportation (of alien); ejection, eviction (of tenant); ejection (of heckler); *Med:* evacuation.

expurgation [ɛkspyrgasjɔ̃] *n.f.* expurgation; bowdlerizing (of book).

expurgatoire [ɛkspyrgatwar] *a.* expurgatory (index, etc.).

expurger [ɛkspyrʒe] *v.tr.* (**j'expurgeai(s)**) to expurgate; to bowdlerize (book).

exquis [ɛkski] *a.* exquisite (beauty, manners, taste, etc.).

exsangue [ɛksɑ̃g, ɛgz-] *a.* an(a)emic, bloodless; deathly pale.

exsudation [ɛksydasjɔ̃] *n.f.* exudation.

exsuder [ɛksyde] *v.tr. & i.* to exude.

extase [ɛkstɑz] *n.f.* ecstasy. **1.** *Psy: Med:* trance. **2.** rapture; **être en e. devant qch.,** to be enraptured by, in ecstasies over, sth.

extasier (s') [sɛkstɑzje] *v.pr.* (*impf. & pr.sub.* **n. n. extasiions**) to be in, go into, ecstasies.

extatique [ɛkstatik] *a.* **1.** *Med:* **état e.,** ecstatic state, (state of) trance. **2.** ecstatic, rapturous, enraptured.

extenseur [ɛkstɑ̃sœr] **1.** *a. & n.m. Anat:* extensor (muscle). **2.** *n.m. Gym:* (chest) expander.

extensible [ɛkstɑ̃sibl̩] *a.* **1.** extensible; stretchable; extending (table, etc.); expanding (bracelet, etc.). **2.** tensile (metal).

extensif, -ive [ɛkstɑ̃sif, -iv] *a.* **1.** tensile (force, etc.). **2.** (*a*) extensive (agriculture); (*b*) **sens e.,** extended meaning (of word).

extension [ɛkstɑ̃sjɔ̃] *n.f.* **1.** extension; (*a*) stretching (of muscle, etc.); *Mec:* **travail à l'e.,** tensile stress; (*b*) straining (of muscle, etc.); (*c*) spreading, enlargement (of territory, etc.); spread (of a disease); **donner de l'e. à qch.,** to extend, enlarge, sth.; **prendre de l'e.,** to spread, grow, increase. **2.** extended meaning (of word); **par e.,** in a wider sense.

exténuant [ɛkstenɥɑ̃] *a.* exhausting (work, etc.).

exténuation [ɛkstenɥasjɔ̃] *n.f.* exhaustion (of body, mind).

exténuer [ɛkstenɥe] *v.tr.* to exhaust; **s'e.,** to tire oneself out; **être exténué (de fatigue),** to be tired out, worn out.

extérieur [ɛksterjœr] **1.** *a.* (*a*) exterior, outer, external; outside (staircase, interests, etc.); **port e.,** outer harbour; **le côté e. de qch.,** the outer side, outside, of sth.; **le monde e.,** the outside world; (*b*) foreign (trade, policy, etc.). **2.** *n.m.* (*a*) exterior, outside (of building, etc.); **vu de l'e.,** seen from the outside; **à l'e.,** (i) out of doors; (ii) (on the) outside; (iii) abroad; **à l'intérieur et à l'e.,** inside and out; *Sp:* **match à l'e.,** away match; **à l'e. de la gare,** outside the station; (*b*) abroad; **de l'e.,** from abroad; **nos rapports avec l'e.,** our relations with (i) other people, other firms, (ii) foreign countries; (*c*) (outward) appearance, looks; **juger par l'e.,** to judge by externals, by appearances; **avoir un e. imposant,** to have an imposing appearance, to look imposing; (*d*) *Cin:* location shot; **il tourne en e.,** he's on location.

extérieurement [ɛksterjœrmɑ̃] *adv.* **1.** externally, on the outside, outwardly. **2.** on the surface, in appearance.

extérioration [ɛksterjɔrasjɔ̃] *n.f. Physiol:* exterioration (of sensation).

extériorisation [ɛksterjɔrizasjɔ̃] *n.f. Psy:* exteriorization, externalization.

extérioriser [ɛksterjɔrize] *v.tr.* (*a*) *Psy:* to exteriorize, to externalize; (*b*) to manifest outwardly, to show (one's feelings, etc.).

exterminateur, -trice [ɛkstɛrminatœr, -tris] **1.** *a.* exterminating, destroying (angel, etc.). **2.** *n.* exterminator, destroyer.

extermination [ɛkstɛrminasjɔ̃] *n.f.* extermination, destruction (of race, etc.); **camp d'e.,** extermination camp.

exterminer [ɛkstɛrmine] *v.tr.* to exterminate, destroy; *F:* to wipe out (race, army, etc.); *F:* **s'e. à faire qch.,** to kill oneself doing sth.

externat [ɛkstɛrna] *n.m.* **1.** (*a*) day school; (*b*) day pupils. **2.** *Med:* non-resident medical studentship.

externe [ɛkstɛrn] **1.** *a.* (*a*) external, outside, outer; **côté e.,** outside; **angle e.,** exterior angle; *Pharm:* **pour l'usage e.,** for external use; (*b*) **élève e.,** day pupil. **2.** *n.* (*a*) day pupil; (*b*) non-resident medical student.

exterritorial, -aux [ɛkstɛritɔrjal, -o] *a.* ex(tra)-territorial.

exterritorialité [ɛkstɛritɔrjalite] *n.f.* ex(tra)-territoriality.

extincteur, -trice [ɛkstɛ̃ktœr, -tris] **1.** *a.* extinguishing (material, etc.). **2.** *n.m.* **e. d'incendie,** fire extinguisher.

extinction [ɛkstɛ̃ksjɔ̃] *n.f.* extinction. **1.** (*a*) extinguishing, putting out (of fire, etc.); quenching (of red-hot iron); slacking, slaking (of lime); *Mil:* **e. des feux,** lights out; (*b*) abolition, suppression; paying off, wiping out (of debt, etc.); termination (of contract). **2.** (*a*) dying out, extinction (of race, species); (*b*) **e. de voix, vue,** loss of voice, sight; **attraper une e. de voix,** to lose one's voice.

extirpateur [ɛkstirpatœr] *n.m.* weeding machine, weeder; grubber.

extirpation [ɛkstirpasjɔ̃] *n.f.* eradication; extirpation; uprooting; removal (of corns, etc.).

extirper [ɛkstirpe] *v.tr.* to extirpate, eradicate, root out (plant, evil, etc.); to remove (a corn); *F:* **e. qn de son lit,** to drag s.o. out of bed.
extorquer [ɛkstɔrke] *v.tr.* to extort, wring (money, promise) (**à qn,** from s.o.).
extorqueur, -euse [ekstɔrkœr, -øz] *n.* extortioner.
extorsion [ɛkstɔrsjɔ̃] *n.f.* extortion, exaction.
extra [ɛkstra] **1.** *n.m. inv.* something extra; (*a*) extra dish; extra-special meal, etc.; **faire un e.,** to do sth. special; (*b*) occasional job; **faire des e. chez qn,** to help s.o. out from time to time; **engager des e.,** to hire occasional help, extra hands. **2.** *a.inv.* extra-special; first-class, first-rate (wine, etc.). **3.** *pref.* extra-.
extracteur [ɛkstraktœr] *n.m.* **1.** drawer, extractor (of teeth, etc.). **2.** *Tls:* extractor.
extractif, -ive [ɛkstraktif, -iv] *a.* extractive (industry).
extraction [ɛkstraksjɔ̃] *n.f.* **1.** (*a*) extraction, extracting (of teeth); removal (of appendix, etc.); extraction, mining (of coal, etc.); quarrying (of stone); (*b*) hoisting, drawing up; *Min:* **machine d'e.,** winding gear; (*c*) *Mth:* extraction (of root). **2. de haute, basse, e.,** of noble, humble, extraction, birth.
extrader [ɛkstrade] *v.tr.* to extradite.
extradition [ɛkstradisjɔ̃] *n.f.* extradition.
extrados [ɛkstrado] *n.m.* **1.** *Arch:* extrados, back (of arch). **2.** *Av:* upper surface (of wing).
extra-fin [ɛkstrafɛ̃] *a.* superfine; of a special brand, vintage, etc.
extra-fort [ɛkstrafɔr] (*a*) *a.* extra-strong; (*b*) *n.m. Dressm:* bias binding.
extraire [ɛkstrɛr] *v.tr.* (*conj. like* TRAIRE) to extract, draw out, take out, pull out; to extract, pull out (tooth); to extract, mine (coal, ore); to quarry (stone); to extract (metal from ore); **e. des plants,** to lift seedlings; *Mth:* **e. une racine,** to extract a root; **s'e. d'une position difficile,** to get out, wriggle out, of an awkward position.
extrait [ɛkstrɛ] *n.m.* **1.** extract; **e. de viande,** meat extract, meat essence. **2.** extract, excerpt (from book); abstract (of deed, account); **e. de naissance,** birth certificate.
extrajudiciaire [ɛkstraʒydisjɛr] *a.* extrajudicial; out of court.
extraordinaire [ɛkstraɔrdinɛr] **1.** *a.* (*a*) extraordinary (meeting, etc.); special (messenger, etc.); **ambassadeur e.,** ambassador extraordinary; **frais, dépenses, extraordinaires,** (i) extras; (ii) non-recurring expenditure; (*b*) extraordinary, unusual, astonishing, fantastic; **cela n'a rien d'e.,** that's nothing out of the ordinary; (*c*) remarkable, outstanding (beauty, success); (*d*) *F:* extraordinarily good; first rate. **2.** *adv.phr.* **par e.,** exceptionally; strange to say, to relate; strangely enough; for once.
extraordinairement [ɛkstraɔrdinɛrmɑ̃] *adv.* extraordinarily.
extra-parlementaire [ɛkstraparləmɑ̃tɛr] *a.* extra-parliamentary.
extrapolation [ɛkstrapɔlasjɔ̃] *n.f. Mth:* extrapolation.
extrapoler [ɛkstrapɔle] *v.tr.* (*a*) *Mth:* to extrapolate.
extra-scolaire [ɛkstraskɔlɛr] *a.* out-of-school (activities, etc.).
extra(-)sensoriel, -ielle [ɛkstrasɑ̃sɔrjɛl] *a. Psy:* extrasensory (perception, etc.).
extraterritorialité [ɛkstratɛritɔrjalite] *n.f.* extraterritoriality.
extravagamment [ɛkstravagamɑ̃] *adv.* extravagantly; exaggeratedly.
extravagance [ɛkstravagɑ̃s] *n.f.* extravagance. **1.** absurdity, folly (of action, request, etc.); exorbitance (of price); immoderateness (of desires). **2. se livrer à des extravagances,** to do, say, absurd, foolish, things; **il a dit un tas d'extravagances,** he talked a lot of nonsense.
extravagant [ɛkstravagɑ̃] *a.* extravagant; absurd, foolish (person, action, etc.); wild (idea); exorbitant (price, demand); immoderate (desire).
extravaguer [ɛkstravage] *v.i.* to rave; to talk nonsense; to act wildly, extravagantly.
extravasation [ɛkstravɑzasjɔ̃] *n.f.* extravasation (of blood, etc.).
extravaser (s') [sɛkstravɑze] *v.pr.* (*of blood, etc.*) to extravasate.
extraversion [ɛkstravɛrsɔ̃] *n.f. Psy:* extraversion.
extraverti, -ie [ɛkstravɛrti] *a. & n. Psy:* extravert.
extrême [ɛkstrɛm] **1.** *a.* extreme; (*a*) farthest, utmost (point, limit, etc.); **dans l'e. lointain,** in the extreme distance; (*b*) intense, excessive (cold, pleasure); (*c*) drastic, severe (measure); **être e. dans ses opinions,** to hold extreme opinions. **2.** *n.m.* extreme limit; **les extrêmes,** the extremes (of heat and cold, *Mth:* of a proportion); **scrupuleux à l'e.,** scrupulous in the extreme, to a degree; **pousser les choses à l'e.,** to carry matters to extremes; *Prov:* **les extrêmes se touchent,** extremes meet.
extrêmement [ɛkstrɛmmɑ̃] *adv.* extremely, exceedingly.
extrême-onction [ɛkstrɛmɔ̃ksjɔ̃] *n.f. Ecc:* extreme unction.
Extrême-Orient (l') [lɛkstrɛmɔrjɑ̃] *n.m.* the Far East.
extrémisme [ɛkstremism] *n.m.* extremism.
extrémiste [ɛkstremist] *a. & n.* extremist.
extrémité [ɛkstremite] *n.f.* (*a*) extremity, end (of lake, etc.); tip (of finger, wing, etc.); point (of needle, etc.); **aux extrémités de la ligne,** at the ends of the line; **les extrémités de la terre,** the uttermost ends of the earth; **les extrémités,** the extremities, the hands and feet; (*b*) extremity, extreme, last degree (of misery, etc.); **pousser qch. à l'e.,** to carry sth. to extremes; **pousser qn à des extrémités,** to drive s.o. to extremes, extremities; **en venir à des extrémités,** to resort to violence; **l'e. d'un besoin,** the urgency of a need; **dans cette e.,** in this extremity; **réduit à l'e.,** in dire distress; (*c*) **être à la dernière, à toute, e.,** to be at the point of death, in the last extremity.
extrinsèque [ɛkstrɛ̃sɛk] *a.* extrinsic; *Num:* **valeur e.,** face value.
extroverti, -ie [ɛkstrɔvɛrti] *n. Psy:* extrovert, extravert.
extrusion [ɛkstryzjɔ̃] *n.f. Techn:* extrusion.
exubérance [ɛgsyberɑ̃s] *n.f.* exuberance (of vegetation, spirits, etc.).
exubérant [ɛgzyberɑ̃] *a.* exuberant (growth, person); **e. de santé,** bursting with health.
exultation [ɛgzyltasjɔ] *n.f.* exultation.
exulter [ɛgzylte] *v.i.* to exult, rejoice.
exutoire [ɛgzytwar] *n.m.* outlet (for anger, etc.).
ex-voto [ɛksvɔto] *n.m.inv.* ex-voto; votive offering.
Ézéchiel [ezekjɛl] *Pr.n.m. B.Hist:* Ezekiel.

F

F, f [ɛf] *n.m. & f.* (the letter) F, f.

fa [fɑ] *n.m.inv. Mus:* (the note) F; **clef de fa,** bass clef, F clef.

fable [fɑbl̥] *n.f.* (*a*) fable; (*b*) story; **c'est pure f.,** it's pure invention; **être la f. de toute la ville,** to be the laughing stock of the town; **célèbre dans la f.,** famous in story, in fable.

fablier [fɑblije] *n.m.* book of fables.

fabricant, -ante [fabrikɑ̃, -ɑ̃t] *n.* maker, manufacturer; **f. de chapeaux,** hat maker, manufacturer.

fabricateur, -trice [fabrikatœr, -tris] *n.* fabricator (of lies, etc.); **f. de fausse monnaie,** coiner; **f. d'un document,** forger of a document.

fabrication [fabrikasjɔ̃] *n.f.* **1.** manufacture, making (of sth.); **n'employer que la meilleure f.,** to employ only the best workmanship; **article de f. française,** article made in France. **2.** forging (of document); coining (of counterfeit money); **c'est de la f.,** it's pure fabrication.

fabrique [fabrik] *n.f.* **1.** making, manufacture; **prix de f.,** cost price, manufacturer's price; **marque de f.,** trademark; **secret de f.,** trade secret. **2.** factory, works; (cloth, paper, oil) mill; **valeur en f.,** cost price. **3. (conseil de) f.** = (parochial) church council; vestry.

fabriquer [fabrike] *v.tr.* **1.** (*a*) to manufacture (cloth, bicycles, etc.); (*b*) to make (sth.); **qu'est-ce que tu fabriques?** (i) what's that you're making? (ii) what are you doing? what on earth are you up to? **2.** to fabricate (story), trump up (charge).

fabulation [fabylasjɔ̃] *n.f. Psy:* fabrication, confabulation.

fabuler [fabyle] *v.i. Psy:* to confabulate.

fabuleusement [fabyløzmɑ̃] *adv.* fabulously.

fabuleux, -euse [fabylø, -øz] *a.* **1.** fabulous, legendary (exploits). **2.** incredible; prodigious; **une somme fabuleuse,** a fabulous sum, a mint of money.

fabuliste [fabylist] *n.m.* fabulist.

fac [fak] *n.f. F:* university; **quand j'étais à la f.,** when I was a student, at university.

façade [fasad] *n.f.* façade, front(age); **hôtel en f. sur la place,** hotel facing the square; **patriotisme de f.,** sham patriotism; **ce n'est qu'une f.,** it's all window dressing; *F:* **refaire sa f.,** to make up (one's face).

face [fas] *n.f.* face. **1. jeter la vérité à la f. de qn,** to cast the truth in s.o.'s face; **sauver la f.,** to save (one's) face; **perdre la f.,** to lose face. **2.** (*a*) **la f. des eaux, de la terre,** the face of the waters, of the earth; (*b*) flat (of sword blade); side (of lens, gramophone record); obverse (of medal); head side (of coin); **f. avant,** front; **f. arrière,** back; **polyèdre à douze faces,** twelve-sided polyhedron; **tissu (à) double f.,** reversible fabric; **considérer qch. sous toutes ses faces,** to consider sth. from all sides, from all aspects. **3.** (*a*) **faire f. (à qn, à qch.),** to face (s.o., sth); to meet (liabilities, expenses, needs); to cope with (difficulties); **sa maison fait f. à l'église,** his house stands opposite to, faces, the church; (*b*) **portrait de f.,** full-face portrait; **vue de f.,** front view; **se présenter de f.,** to face (the observer, etc.); **la maison (d')en f.,** the house opposite; **regarder qn (bien) en f.,** to look s.o. full, straight, in the face; **regarder les choses en f.,** to face facts; **f. à f.,** face to face (**avec,** with); **mettre deux témoins f. à f.,** to confront two witnesses. **4.** *prep.phr.* **f. à,** facing; *Rail:* **place f. à l'arrière,** seat with back to the engine; **en f. de,** opposite; **les maisons en f. de l'école,** *F:* **en f. l'école,** the houses opposite the school; **en f. l'un de l'autre, l'un en f. de l'autre,** opposite each other, facing each other.

face-à-face [fasafas] *n.m.inv. T.V: etc:* dialogue.

face-à-main [fasamɛ̃] *n.m.* lorgnette; *pl. faces-à-main.*

facétie [fasesi] *n.f.* facetious remark; joke; **dire des facéties,** to crack jokes; **faire des facéties à qn,** to play pranks on s.o.

facétieux, -ieuse [fasesjø, -jøz] *a.* facetious.

facette [fasɛt] *n.f.* facet (of diamond, insect's eye); **(taillé) à facettes,** (cut) in facets; facetted.

facetter [fasete] *v.tr.* to facet (diamond, etc.).

fâché [fɑʃe] *a.* **1.** sorry; **être f. de qch., pour qn,** to be sorry about sth., for s.o. **2.** angry, annoyed; **être f. contre qn,** to be annoyed, vexed, with s.o. **3. être f. avec qn,** to have fallen out with s.o.

fâcher [fɑʃe] **1.** *v.tr.* (*a*) to grieve; (*b*) to anger, annoy; to make (s.o.) angry. **2. se f.** (*a*) to get angry, annoyed; to lose one's temper; to take offence; **se f. contre qn,** to get annoyed with s.o.; (*b*) **se f. avec qn,** to quarrel, fall out, with s.o.

fâcherie [fɑʃri] *n.f.* bad feeling; quarrel, tiff.

fâcheusement [fɑʃøzmɑ̃] *adv.* tiresomely, annoyingly.

fâcheux, -euse [fɑʃø, -øz] **1.** *a.* troublesome, tiresome, trying, annoying, unfortunate (event); awkward (position); disturbing, distressing (news). **2.** *n.* intruder (in conversation, etc.); nuisance.

facial, -iaux [fasjal, -jo] *a.* facial (muscle, angle); **massage f.,** facial, face, massage.

faciès [fasjɛs] *n.m.* **1.** *Bot: Med:* facies, aspect, appearance (of plant, person). **2.** cast of features.

facile [fasil] *a.* **1.** easy; (*a*) **chose f. à faire,** thing easy to do, easily done; **c'est f. à dire,** it's more easily said than done; **il lui est f. de le faire,** it's easy for him to do it; **d'une mise en place f.,** easily installed; **besognes faciles,** light tasks; (*b*) (i) easy-going; **homme f. à vivre, f. en affaires,** man easy to live with, to deal with; **f. à émouvoir,** easily moved; **mari f.,** complaisant husband; **femme f.,** woman of easy virtue; (ii) pliable, easily influenced. **2.** facile (genius, etc.); fluent (style); ready, quick (writer); **je n'ai pas la parole f.,** words do not come easily to me; **elle a les larmes faciles,** she is easily moved to tears.

facilement [fasilmɑ̃] *adv.* easily, readily.

facilité [fasilite] *n.f.* **1.** (*a*) easiness (of task, etc.); ease (with which a thing is done); **avec f.,** easily, with ease; (*b*) **avoir la f. de faire qch.,** to enjoy facilities for, the opportunity of, doing sth.; **facilités de paiement,** facilities for payment; easy terms; *Bank:* **facilités de caisse,** overdraft facilities. **2.** aptitude, talent (**pour qch.,** for sth.); **f. à faire qch.,** gift, aptitude, for doing sth.; **f. de parole,** fluency. **3.** pliancy, complaisance.

faciliter [fasilite] *v.tr.* to facilitate; to make (sth.) easier, easy (**à qn,** for s.o.).

façon [fasɔ̃] *n.f.* **1.** (*a*) (i) making, fashioning; workmanship; (ii) style; **f. d'un manteau,** (i) making (up), (ii) cut, of a coat; **matière et f.,** material and labour, *NAm:* labor; **on travaille à f.,** customers' own materials made up; **poème de sa f.,** poem of his own composition; **robe qui a bonne f.,** well cut dress; *Agr:* **donner une f. à la terre,** to cultivate the soil; (*b*) **cuir f. porc,** imitation pigskin. **2.** (*a*) manner, mode, way (of acting, speaking, etc.); **vivre à la f. des sauvages,** to live like savages; **avoir une f. à soi de faire qch.,** to have one's own way of doing sth.; **je le ferai à ma f.,** I shall do it (in) my own way; **f. de parler,** manner of speaking; form of speech; **ils agissent tous de la même f.,** they all act alike; **de la bonne f.,** properly, nicely; (*b*) *pl.* manners, ways; **en voilà des façons!** what a way to behave! (*c*) **sans façons,** (i) (*of pers.*) unceremonious; free-and-easy; (ii) (*of manners*) rough and ready; **traiter qn sans f.,** to treat s.o. in an offhand manner; **sans plus de façons,** without any more ado; **faire des façons,** to stand on ceremony, make a fuss; (*d*) **de cette f.,** thus, in this way; **venez avec nous, de cette f. cela ne vous coûtera rien,** come with us; (in) that way it won't cost you anything; **de f. ou d'autre, d'une f. ou d'une autre,** (i) (in) one way or another; (ii) by some means or other, by hook or by crook; **de toute f. j'irai,** anyhow, in any case, I shall go; **en aucune f.!** not at all! by no means! **3.** (*a*) **de f. à,** so as to; **parlez de f. à vous faire comprendre,** speak so that you can be understood; (*b*) **de (telle) f. que,** so that; **parlez de f. qu'on vous comprenne,** speak so as to be understood; **il pleuvait de telle f. que je fus obligé de rentrer,** it was raining so hard that I had to go home; **il pleuvait, de f. que je fus obligé de rentrer,** it was raining, (and) so I had to go home; as it was raining I had to go home.

faconde [fakɔ̃d] *n.f.* (*often Pej:*) fluency (of speech), ready flow of language, *F:* gift of the gab.

façonnage [fasɔnaʒ] *n.m.*, **façonnement** [fasɔnmɑ̃] *n.m.* shaping, working.

façonné [fasɔne] *a. Tex:* figured (fabric).

façonner [fasɔne] *v.tr.* to work, shape (wood, metal, etc.); to turn (sth. on lathe); to fashion (clay, etc.); **f. une robe,** to make (up) a dress; *Agr:* **f. la terre,** to work the soil; **f. un enfant,** to mould, form, a child's character.

façonneur, -euse [fasɔnœr, -øz] *n.* maker, shaper, fashioner.

fac-similé [faksimile] *n.m.* facsimile, exact copy; *pl. fac-similés.*

factage [faktaʒ] *n.m.* (*a*) carriage (and delivery); transport (of goods); (*b*) **payer le f.,** to pay the carriage; (*c*) delivery (of letters).

facteur, -trice [faktœr, -tris] *n.* **1.** (musical) instrument maker; **f. d'orgues,** organ-builder. **2.** postman, *f.* postwoman. **3.** agent, middleman, factor. **4.** *n.m.* factor; *Mth:* **décomposer en facteurs,** to factorize; **f. premier,** prime factor; **le f. humain,** the human factor; **le f. temps,** the time factor; *Mec.E:* **f. de sûreté,** safety factor.

factice [faktis] *a.* factitious; artificial, imitation (rocks, gems, etc.); dummy (box of chocolates); feigned (emotion).

factieux, -ieuse [faksjø, -jøz] **1.** *a.* factious, partisan (spirit, etc.). **2.** *n.* troublemaker.

faction [faksjɔ̃] *n.f.* **1.** sentry duty, guard; **être de, en, f.,** to be on guard, on sentry duty; **mettre (qn) en f.,** to post (a sentry); *Ind:* to place (striker) on picket duty. **2.** faction; factious party; **la Constituante était divisée en factions,** the Constituent Assembly was broken up into factions.

factionnaire [faksjɔnɛr] *n.m.* (*a*) sentry; **poser, relever, un f.,** to post, relieve, a sentry; (*b*) *Ind:* picket.

factitif, -ive [faktitif, -iv] *a.* causative, factitive.

factorerie [faktɔrəri] *n.f.* foreign (trading) post.

factoriel, -ielle [faktɔrjɛl] *a.* & *n.f. Mth:* factorial.

factotum [faktɔtɔm] *n.m.* factotum.

facturation [faktyrasjɔ̃] *n.f.* invoicing; **(service de) f.,** invoice department.

facture¹ [faktyr] *n.f.* **1.** composition (of music, work of art); workmanship; style; **pardessus f. soignée,** carefully tailored overcoat. **2.** manufacturing (of musical instruments); building (of organs).

facture² *n.f.* invoice, bill (of sale); **faire, dresser, établir, une f.,** to make out an invoice; **selon, suivant, f.,** as per invoice.

facturer [faktyre] *v.tr.* to invoice (goods).

facturier, -ière [faktyrje, -jɛr] *n.* **1.** *n.m.* sales book. **2.** *n.m.* & *f.* invoice clerk.

facultatif, -ive [fakyltatif, -iv] *a.* optional, facultative; *P.N:* **arrêt f.,** request stop.

facultativement [fakyltativmɑ̃] *adv.* optionally.

faculté [fakylte] *n.f.* **1.** (*a*) option, right, faculty; **avoir la f. de faire qch.,** to have (i) the option of doing sth., (ii) power to do sth.; (*b*) faculty, ability, power; **facultés de l'esprit,** intellectual faculties; **jouir de toutes ses facultés,** to be in possession of all one's faculties; **homme doué de grandes facultés,** man of great abilities; (*c*) *pl.* resources, means. **2.** *Sch:* faculty (of arts, law, etc); **professeur de f.,** (university) professor; **la F.,** (i) the Faculty of Medicine; (ii) the medical profession.

fada [fada] *n.m. F:* fool; simpleton; clot.

fadaise [fadɛz] *n.f.* piece of nonsense, silly remark; **débiter des fadaises,** to talk rot, nonsense, twaddle.

fadasse [fadas] *a. F:* insipid, sickly, cloying (taste, etc.); pale, washed out (colour); sloppy (novel, etc.).

fade [fad] *a.* insipid; tasteless, flavourless, *NAm:* flavorless (dish, etc.); pointless, tame (joke); drab, washed-out (colour); stale (smell).

fadement [fadmɑ̃] *adv.* insipidly.

fadeur [fadœr] *n.f.* (*a*) insipidity; dullness, drabness (of colour); sickliness (of taste, etc.); (*b*) **dire des fadeurs à qn,** to make dull, uninspired, remarks to s.o.

fading [fediŋ] *n.m. W.Tel:* fading (effect).

fafiot [fafjo] *n.m. P:* banknote.

fagot [fago] *n.m.* faggot, bundle of firewood; **sentir le f.,** to savour of heresy; **bouteille de vin de derrière les fagots,** bottle of wine from the hidden store, kept for special occasions.

fagotage [fagɔtaʒ] *n.m.* **1.** putting, tying, (of sticks) in bundles; faggoting **2.** *F:* ridiculous get-up.

fagoter [fagɔte] *v.tr.* **1.** to tie up (wood, etc.) in bundles; to faggot (firewood). **2.** *F:* to dress (a child, oneself) like a scarecrow; **(mal) fagoté,** badly dressed (child); dowdy (woman).

faiblard [fɛblar] *a. F:* weakish; a bit weak.

faible [fɛbl̥] **1.** *a.* (*a*) feeble, weak (body, legs); **le sexe f.,** the weaker sex; **f. d'esprit,** weak-, feeble-minded; *n.* **les faibles d'esprit,** the feeble-minded; **protéger les faibles,** to protect the weak; **points faibles chez qn,** shortcomings in s.o.; **son point f.,** his weak spot; **c'est là son côté f.,** that is his weak side; (*b*) weak, thin (coffee, wine); faint (sound, odour); weak, faint (voice); poor, slender (chance); **prix f.,** low price; **f. vitesse,** low speed, slow speed; **boisson f. en alcool,** drink with low alcoholic content; weak drink; **f. quantité,** small quantity; **f. différence,** slight difference; *Mus:* **temps f.,** unaccented beat; *Nau:* **f. tirant,** shallow draught; small tonnage; *Phot:* **cliché f.,** thin negative; (*c*) **élève f. en chimie,** pupil weak in chemistry; **c'est un étudiant f.,** he's a poor scholar; his work is poor. **2.** *n.m.* weakness, failing (**de qn, qch.,** in s.o., sth.); failing, foible (of s.o.); **avoir un f. pour qn, qch.,** to have a weakness, a partiality, for s.o., sth., to be partial to s.o., sth., to have a soft spot for s.o.; **c'est là son f.,** that's his weak point; **son f. c'est la boisson,** his failing, weakness, is drink.

faiblement [fɛbləmɑ̃] *adv.* feebly, weakly.

faiblesse [fɛblɛs] *n.f.* **1.** (*a*) feebleness, weakness; **je**

tombais de f., I was ready to drop with exhaustion; (*b*) faintness; **il lui a pris une f.,** she (nearly) fainted; (*c*) **la f. humaine,** human weakness, frailty; **f. d'une mère,** a mother's indulgence; (*d*) smallness (of sum, number); slightness (of difference). **2. je l'aime avec toutes ses faiblesses,** I love him in spite of all his failings.

faiblir [fɛblir] *v.i.* to weaken; to grow weak(er), lose strength; (*of sight*) to fail; (*of wind*) to abate, drop; (*of courage*) to fail, flag.

faïence [fajɑ̃s] *n.f.* faience, crockery, earthenware; stoneware; **f. fine,** china.

faïencerie [fajɑ̃sri] *n.f.* **1.** crockery, earthenware. **2.** (*a*) china shop; (*b*) pottery (works, trade).

faïencier, -ière [fajɑ̃sje, -jɛr] *n.* crockery, earthenware, maker, dealer.

faille [faj] *n.f.* (*a*) *Geol: Min:* break (in lode); (*b*) flaw (in argument).

failli, -ie [faji] *a. & n. Jur:* bankrupt.

faillibilité [fajibilite] *n.f.* fallibility.

faillible [fajibl̥] *a.* fallible; **tout le monde est f.,** anybody can make a mistake.

faillir [fajir] *v.i.* (*pr.p.* **faillant;** *p.p.* **failli;** *pr.ind.* **je faux, il faut, n. faillons;** *p.h.* **je faillis;** *fu.* **je faillirai;** *used mostly in p.h. and compound tenses*) **1.** to fail; **f. à son devoir,** to fail in, fall short of, one's duty; **f. à une promesse,** to fail to keep a promise; **la mémoire me faut,** my memory fails me. **2. j'ai failli manquer le train,** I nearly, almost, missed the train; **il faillit être écrasé,** he narrowly missed being run over; **j'ai bien failli me noyer,** I was very nearly drowned, had a narrow escape from drowning.

faillite [fajit] *n.f.* (*a*) *Com:* failure; insolvency; *Jur:* bankruptcy; **être en (état) de f.,** to be bankrupt, insolvent; **faire f.,** to go bankrupt; **déclarer, mettre, qn en f.,** to adjudicate, adjudge, s.o. bankrupt; (*b*) failure (of project, etc.).

faim [fɛ̃] *n.f.* hunger; **avoir f.,** to be, feel, hungry; **avoir une f. de loup,** to be ravenous; **mourir de f.,** (i) to die of starvation; (ii) *F:* to be starving; **manger à sa f.,** to eat one's fill, have enough to eat; **rester sur sa f.,** (i) to remain hungry; (ii) *Fig:* to be left wanting, unsatisfied; **avoir f. de gloire,** to hunger, thirst, for glory.

faîne [fɛn] *n.f.* **1.** beechnut. **2.** *pl.* beechmast.

fainéant, -ante [fɛneɑ̃, -ɑ̃t] **1.** *a.* idle, lazy. **2.** *n.* idler, sluggard, lazybones.

fainéanter [fɛneɑ̃te] *v.i.* to idle; to loaf (about).

fainéantise [fɛneɑ̃tiz] *n.f.* idleness, laziness.

faire[1] [fɛr] *v.tr.* (*pr.p.* **faisant** [fəzɑ̃]; *p.p.* **fait** [fɛ]; *pr.ind.* **je fais, il fait; n. faisons** [fəzɔ̃], **v. faites** [fɛt], **ils font;** *pr.sub.* **je fasse;** *imp.* **fais, faisons, faites;** *p.h.* **je fis;** *fu.* **je ferai**) **I.** to make. **1. Dieu a fait l'homme à son image,** God made, created, man in his own image; **ils ne veulent pas f. d'enfants,** they don't want to have children; **les vieilles gens sont ainsi faits,** old people are like that; **comment est-il fait?** (i) what sort of man is he? (ii) what does he look like? **il n'est pas fait pour cela,** he is not the man, not fitted, not cut out, for that; **jambe bien faite,** shapely leg. **2.** (*a*) **f. un gâteau, du cidre,** to make a cake, cider; **statue faite en, de, marbre,** statue sculpted in, made out of, marble; **vêtements tout faits, expressions toutes faites,** ready-made clothes, phrases; set phrases; **f. un poème, un tableau,** to write a poem, paint a picture; **f. un chèque de cent francs,** to make out, write, a cheque for 100 francs; **f. la guerre,** to wage war; **f. un miracle,** to work a miracle; **ferme où on fait de la betterave,** farm that grows beet; (*b*) **f. un geste,** to make a gesture; **f. de l'œil à qn,** to ogle s.o. **3.** (*a*) **f. sa fortune,** to make one's fortune; **se f. tant par mois,** to make, earn, so much a month; **se f. des amis,** to make friends; (*b*) **f. des provisions,** to lay in provisions; **f. de l'eau, du charbon,** to take in water, coal; *F:* **on m'a fait ma montre,** someone's pinched my watch; (*c*) **on vous a fait,** you've been done, had; *P:* **tu es fait, mon vieux!** you've had it, chum! **II.** to do. **1.** (*a*) **qu'est-ce que vous faites?** (i) what are you doing? (ii) what are you up to? **qu'est-ce qu'il y a à f.?** what is there to do? **il n'y a rien à f.,** there is nothing to be done, there's no help for it; **je n'ai rien à f. avec eux,** I have nothing to do with them; **il n'a rien à f. ici,** he has no business here; **que f.?** what is, was, to be done? what can, could, he, we, I, do? **je ne sais que f.,** I don't know what to do; **si f. se peut,** if it's possible; **je le regardais f.,** I watched him at it, doing it; **est-ce que je peux ouvrir la fenêtre?—faites donc!** may I open the window?—do! by all means! **faites vite!** look sharp! **nous avons fort à f. pour joindre les deux bouts,** we are hard put to make ends meet; **homme à tout f.,** handyman; **ces choses-là ne se font pas,** those things are not done; **grand bien vous fasse!** much *good* may it do you! **c'est bien fait!** it serves you right! **c'est toujours ça de fait,** that's a good job done; **voilà qui est fait,** that's done, settled; (*b*) to say; **"vous partez demain!" fit-il,** "you leave tomorrow!" he said, exclaimed; **il fit un petit "oh" de surprise,** he gave a little "oh" of surprise. **2.** (to perform, practise) (*a*) **f. son devoir,** to do one's duty; **f. la ronde,** to go one's rounds; *F:* **f. (ses besoins),** to relieve oneself; **un chien a fait sur le trottoir,** a dog has made a mess on the pavement; (*b*) **f. un métier,** to practise a trade; **f. les cuirs, la laine,** to deal in leather, wool; **nous ne faisons que le gros,** we are wholesalers only; **quel article faites-vous?** what's your line? (*c*) **f. du sport, de la politique,** to go in for sport, politics; **j'ai fait de l'anglais à l'école,** I did English at school; **il fait sa médecine, son droit,** he is reading, studying, medicine, law; **f. une maladie,** to have an illness; **f. son apprentissage,** to serve one's apprenticeship; **f. les magasins,** to go round, do, the shops. **3.** (*to proceed, go*) **f. quelques pas dans le sentier,** to go, take, a few steps along the path; **f. une promenade,** to go for a walk; *F:* **f. du cent à l'heure,** to go, do, a hundred kilometres an hour. **4.** to cause; **f. pitié, peur,** to arouse pity, fear. **5.** (*a*) to amount to; **combien cela fait-il?** how much does that come to? **deux fois deux font quatre,** twice two is four; **ça fait trois jours qu'il est parti,** it's three days since he left; **ce poulet fait trois kilos,** this chicken weighs three kilos; **combien faites-vous la livre de chocolat?** how much do you charge for a pound of chocolate? (*b*) **"cheval" fait "chevaux" au pluriel,** *cheval* becomes *chevaux* in the plural. **6.** to be, constitute; **f. l'admiration de tous,** to be the admiration of all; **cela fera mon affaire,** (i) that will suit me; (ii) that's just what I'm looking for; **quel taquin vous faites!** what a tease you are! *Prov:* **l'habit ne fait pas le moine,** it is not the cowl that makes the monk. **7.** to matter; **qu'est-ce que ça fait?** what does it matter? who cares? **qu'est-ce que cela vous fait?** what's that to you? **si cela ne vous fait rien,** if you don't mind; **cela ne fait rien,** that makes no difference; never mind; it doesn't matter. **8.** (*replacing previous verb*) **pourquoi agir comme vous le faites?** why do you act as you do? **il m'a traité comme il aurait fait d'un, pour un, animal,** he treated me as he would an animal. **III. 1.** to form; **ce professeur fait de bons élèves,** this master turns out good pupils; **se f. une opinion sur qch.,** to form an opinion on sth.; **f. des chaussures à son pied,** to break in a pair of shoes. **2.** to arrange; **f. la chambre,** to clean, do, the room; **f. sa valise,** to pack one's suitcase; **f. ses ongles,** to do one's nails; **f. les cartes,** to deal the cards; **à qui de f.?** whose deal is it? **3. qu'allez-vous f. de votre fils?** what are you going to do with your son? **qu'avez-vous fait de mon parapluie?** what have you done with my umbrella? **n'avoir que f. de qch.,** to have no need, use, for sth.; *F:* **ça fait riche,** it looks expensive, stylish; **vases qui font bien sur la cheminée,** vases that look well on the mantelpiece; **il ne fait pas quarante ans,** he doesn't look forty; **il se fait plus pauvre qu'il ne l'est,** he makes himself out to be poorer than he is. **4.** (*to act a part*) **il fait Hamlet,** he acts Hamlet; **un des invités faisait le croupier,** one of the guests acted as croupier; **elle ne va pas f. la reine ici,** she isn't going to queen it here; **f. le pauvre,** to pretend to be poor; **il fait le mort,** he is shamming dead; **f. l'imbécile,** to play the fool. **IV. 1. en f.** (*a*) **il n'en fait qu'à sa tête,** he does what he likes; **n'en faites rien,** don't do any such thing; (*b*) **c'(en) est fait de lui,** it's all up with him; he's done for; (*c*) *P:* **(ne) t'en fais pas,** don't worry. **2. y f.: rien n'y fit,** nothing availed, it was all of no use; **que voulez-vous que j'y fasse?** how can I help it? **il sait y f.,** he knows what he's doing, he can fend for himself. **3.** *F:* **la f. à qn,** to take s.o. in; **on ne me la fait pas!** nothing doing! I'm not going to be had! **V.** *v. impers.* **1. il fait beau (temps),** it is fine (weather); **il fait du soleil, de la neige,** it's sunny, snowing; **par le froid qu'il fait,** in this cold weather. **2. il fait mauvais voyager par ces routes,** it is hard travelling on these roads. **VI.** (*syntactical constructions*) **1. il ne fait que lire toute la journée,** he does nothing but read all day; **je n'ai fait que le toucher,** I only touched it. **2. je ne fais que d'arriver,** I have only just arrived. **3. vous n'aviez que f. de parler,** you had no business to speak. **4.** (*a*) **c'est ce qui fait que je suis venu si vite,** that is why, this is how it happens that, I came so quickly; **les événements qui font que les choses sont comme elles sont,** the events that make things what they are; (*b*) **faites qu'il vienne demain,** arrange, see to it, that he comes tomorrow. **VII.** (*causative*) **1.** (*the noun or pron. object is the subject of the inf.*) (*a*) **le soleil fait fondre la neige,** the sun makes the snow melt, melts the snow; **on le fit chanter,** he was made to sing; **il nous a fait venir,** he sent for us; **faites-le entrer,** show him in; **f. attendre qn,** to keep s.o. waiting; (*b*) (*with v.pr.*) (i) (*reflexive pron. omitted*) **faire asseoir qn,** to make s.o. sit down; **f. coucher un enfant,** to put a child to bed; (ii) (*reflexive pron. retained*) **nous l'avons fait se cacher dans une armoire,** we made him hide in a cupboard; **je le fis s'arrêter,** I made him stop. **2.** (*the noun or pron. is the object of the inf.*) (*a*) **f. bâtir une maison,** to have, to get, a house built; **f. f. deux exemplaires,** to have two copies made; **faites-le réparer,** get it mended; (*b*) **se f.** + *inf.*: **se f. photographier,** to have, get, oneself photographed, to have one's photograph taken; **un bruit se fit entendre,** a noise was heard; **ne vous faites pas tant prier,** don't take so much asking; **il ne se le fit pas dire deux fois,** he didn't need to be told twice; **il s'est fait punir,** he's got himself punished. **3. f. f. qch. à qn,** to cause, get, s.o. to do sth.; to have s.o. do sth.; **il fit lâcher prise à son adversaire,** he made his opponent let go; **faites-lui lire cette lettre,** get him to read, make him read, this letter; **je lui ai fait observer qu'il se faisait tard,** I called his attention to the fact that it was getting late; **faites-lui comprendre qu'il n'est pas le bienvenu,** make him understand that he is not welcome; **je le ferai examiner par un médecin,** I shall have him examined by a doctor. **VIII. se f. 1.** to become; (*a*) to develop, mature; **ce fromage se fera,** this cheese will ripen; **son style se fait,** his style is forming; (*b*) to become; **se f. vieux,** to become, grow, get, old; **se f. soldat,** to become a soldier; **la nuit se fait,** night is falling; (*c*) to adapt oneself; **se f. à qch.,** to get used, accustomed, to sth.; **se f. à la fatigue,** to become inured to fatigue; **vous y ferez,** you will get into the way of it; *Mec.E:* **permettre aux engrenages de se f.,** to run in the gears; (*d*) **la mer, le vent, se fait,** the sea, the wind, is getting up. **2.** *impers.* (*a*) **il se fait tard,** it's getting late; (*b*) **il se fit un long silence,** a long silence followed; **comment se fait-il que vous soyez en retard?** how is it that you're late? **3. il est venu voir ce qui se faisait,** he came to see what was happening, doing; **le miracle s'est fait tout seul,** the miracle came about by itself; **le mariage ne se fera pas,** the marriage will not take place.

faire² *n.m.* **1.** doing, making; **il y a loin du dire au f.,** saying is one thing, doing another. **2.** *Art: Lit:* technique; handling; execution.

faire-part [fɛrpar] *n.m.inv.* card, notice (announcing birth, death, marriage); **f.-p. de mariage,** wedding card; **le présent avis tiendra lieu de f.-p.,** friends will accept this, the only intimation.

faire-valoir [fɛrvalwar] *n.m.inv.* **1.** farming; **exploitation en f.-v. direct,** farm run by owner. **2.** foil (to s.o.); (comedian's) stooge.

faisabilité [fəzabilite] *n.f.* feasibility.

faisable [fəzabl̩] *a.* practicable, feasible.

faisan [fəzɑ̃] *n.m.* **1. (coq) f.,** (cock) pheasant; **f. bruyant,** grouse. **2.** *P:* crook.

faisandage [fəzɑ̃daʒ] *n.m. Cu:* hanging (of game).

faisandé [fəzɑ̃de] *a.* (*a*) high, gamy (meat); (*b*) *F:* decadent (literature, etc.).

faisandeau, -eaux [fəzɑ̃do] *n.m.* young pheasant.

faisander [fəzɑ̃de,] *v.tr. Cu:* to hang (game).

faisanderie [fəzɑ̃dri] *n.f.* pheasantry, pheasant preserve.

faisane [fəzan] *n.f.* **(poule) f.,** hen pheasant.

faisceau, -eaux [fɛso] *n.m.* (*a*) bundle (of sticks, etc.); *Anat:* fasciculus, bundle, bunch (of fibres); cluster (of electric bulbs); *Rail:* group (of sidings); **un f. de preuves,** a body of proof; *Rom.Ant:* **les faisceaux,** the fasces (of lictor); *Arch:* **colonne en f.,** clustered column; *Mil:* **former les faisceaux,** to pile arms; **rompre les faisceaux,** to unpile arms; (*b*) *Opt:* beam; **f. lumineux, de lumière,** pencil of rays; **f. d'un phare,** beam of a lighthouse, headlight; (*c*) *Elcs:* **f. hertzien,** radio beam, microwave link; *T.V:* **f. cathodique explorateur,** scanning electron beam; **f. radar,** radar beam.

faiseur, -euse [fəzœr, -øz] *n.* **1.** maker; **f. de dentelles,** lacemaker; **costume du bon f.,** suit from a good tailor; **f. de miracles,** miracle worker; **f. de tours,** mountebank; **f. de projets,** schemer; **f. de mariages,** matchmaker. **2.** *F:* thruster, pusher.

fait¹ [fɛ] *a.* fully developed; **homme f.,** (i) (full-)grown man; (ii) man of ripe experience; **fromage f.,** ripe cheese.

fait² [fɛ *and sometimes* fɛt] *n.m.* **1.** act, deed, feat, achievement; **faits et dits,** sayings and doings; **f. d'armes,** feat of arms; **cela est du f. d'un tel,** this is so-and-so's doing; **prendre qn sur le f.,** to catch s.o. in the act, red-handed; **se porter à des voies de f.,** to resort to force, to violence; **parler n'était pas son f.,** he was no talker; talking was not his line; **dire son f. à qn,** to talk straight to s.o., to give s.o. a piece of one's mind; **elle lui a dit son f.,** she told him what she thought of him. **2.** (*a*) fact; **f. accompli,** accomplished fact, definite situation; **les faits d'une cause,** the facts of a case; **prendre f. et cause pour qn,** to stand up for s.o.; **ceci est un f.,** this is a (matter of) fact; **roi de nom plutôt que de f.,** king in name rather than in fact; **possession de f.,** actual possession; **il est de f. que c'était un traître,** it is a fact that he was a traitor; **aller droit au f.,** to go straight to the point; **en venir au f.,** to come to the point; **être au f. de la question,** to know how things stand; **mettre qn au f.,**

to give s.o. full information, to make s.o. acquainted with the facts; **mettre, poser, qch. en f.**, to lay sth. down as a fact; **au f.**, in fact, after all; **au f., que venez-vous faire ici?** by the way, what have you come here for? **en f., par le f., dans le f., de f.**, as a matter of fact, in point of fact, in actual fact; actually; **de f. cela est un refus,** that is in effect a refusal; **de ce f.**, thereby, on that account; **du f., par le f., qu'il boîte,** owing to the fact that, because, he's lame; **par le seul f. d'y être,** by the mere fact of, simply by, being there; **en f. de,** as regards; **qu'est-ce que vous avez en f. de rôti?** what have you in the way of a joint? (*b*) occurrence, happening; **un f. nouveau s'est produit,** there was a new development; *Journ:* **faits divers,** news in brief; **f. divers,** news item.

faîtage [fɛtaʒ] *n.m. Const:* **1.** rooftree. **2.** ridge tiling, sheathing.

faîte [fɛt] *n.m.* **1.** (*a*) *Const:* ridge (of roof); (*b*) *Geog:* **ligne de f.**, watershed, crest line. **2.** top (of house, tree, etc.); **le f. de la gloire,** the pinnacle of glory.

faîtière [fɛtjɛr] *a.f. & n.f. Const:* **(tuile) f.**, ridge tile; **(lucarne) f.**, skylight.

faitout, *n.m.*, **fait-tout,** *n.m.inv.* [fɛtu] stewpan.

faix [fɛ] *n.m.* (*a*) burden, load; **le f. des années,** the weight of years; **le f. des impôts,** the burden of taxation; (*b*) *Obst:* fœtus (in the womb).

falaise [falɛz] *n.f.* cliff; **f. littorale,** sea cliff.

falbalas [falbala] *n.m.pl.* furbelows, flounces.

fallacieusement [falasjøzmɑ̃] *adv.* fallaciously.

fallacieux, -ieuse [falasjø, -jøz] *a.* fallacious, deceptive, misleading.

falloir [falwar] *v.impers. def.* (*no pr.p.; p.p.* **fallu;** *pr.ind.* **il faut;** *pr.sub.* **il faille;** *impf.* **il fallait;** *p.h.* **il fallut;** *fu.* **il faudra**) **1.** (*a*) to be necessary, required; **il lui faut un nouveau pardessus,** he needs a new overcoat; **avez-vous tout ce qu'il (vous) faut?** have you got all you want, require, need? **faut-il de tout cela?** is all that necessary? **c'est juste ce qu'il (me) faut,** that's the very thing (I want); that's just the right thing; **nous en avons plus qu'il ne nous en faut,** we have more than enough, than we need; **il m'a fallu trois jours pour le faire,** it took me three days to do it; **il a tout ce qu'il faut pour réussir,** he has everything he needs, *F:* he's got what it takes, to succeed; (*b*) **s'en f.**, to be lacking, wanting; **il s'en faut de deux francs,** it is two francs short; **je ne suis pas satisfait, il s'en faut de beaucoup, tant s'en faut,** I am not satisfied, far from it, not by a long way; **il s'en faut de beaucoup que l'autobus (ne) soit plein,** the bus is far from being full; **il s'en est fallu de peu, peu s'en faut, qu'il ne mourût,** he very nearly died, it was touch and go whether he died; **cinq livres ou peu s'en faut,** the best part of £5; **il s'en est fallu de rien qu'il (ne) fût écrasé,** he was within an ace of being run over; **il s'en faut de peu qu'il accepte,** he is more than half inclined to accept; **vous êtes satisfait?—peu s'en faut!** are you satisfied?—not a bit! (*c*) **comme il faut,** proper(ly); **se conduire comme il faut,** to behave in a civilized manner, in the right way; **il, elle, est très comme il faut,** he's very gentlemanly, she's very ladylike; **ce sont des gens très comme il faut,** they're very decent people; **votre toilette est tout à fait comme il faut,** your dress is just right. **2.** (*a*) to be necessary; **il faut partir,** I, we, you, etc., must start; **il faut dire qu'il s'est bien comporté,** it must be said, I am bound to say, he behaved well; **il nous faut le voir, il faut que nous le voyions,** we must see him; **il lui faut se dépêcher,** he must hurry; **il faudra marcher plus vite,** we shall have to walk faster; **il fallait porter plainte,** you should, ought to, have made a complaint; **il fallait le dire!** why didn't you say so? **il n'aurait pas fallu attendre,** you shouldn't have, ought not to have, waited; **il faut qu'il ait été fâché pour avoir dit cela,** he must have been angry to have said that; **c'est ce qu'il faudra voir!** we must see about that! **la police a arrêté l'homme qu'il ne fallait pas,** the police have arrested the wrong man; *P:* **faut voir!** you should see it! **c'est simple, mais il fallait y penser,** it's simple once you've thought of it; **il a fallu qu'elle apprenne cet accident!** she *had* to hear, she *would* hear, of that accident! **il faut les féliciter tous les deux,** they are both to be congratulated; **il ne faudrait pas que je les rencontre,** it would never do for me to meet them; **il ne faut pas y aller,** (i) you must not go there; (ii) you are not supposed to go there; (*b*) (*with* **le** = *noun clause*); **il viendra s'il le faut,** he will come if need be, if necessary, if he has to; **vous êtes revenu à pied?—il l'a bien fallu,** *occ.* **il a bien fallu,** you walked back?—there was nothing else for it.

falot¹ [falo] *n.m.* **1.** (hand) lantern; (stable) lamp. **2.** *P:* court martial.

falot², -ote [falo, -ɔt] *a.* (*a*) *O:* odd (person, idea); (*b*) insignificant, *F:* dim (person).

falsificateur, -trice [falsifikatœr, -tris] *n.* falsifier; forger (of documents); adulterator (of food, etc.).

falsification [falsifikasjɔ̃] *n.f.* falsification; forgery, faking (of documents, etc.); adulteration (of food, etc.).

falsifier [falsifje] *v.tr.* (*impf. & pr.sub.* **n. falsifiions**) to falsify, tamper with (text, etc.); to forge, fake (document, etc.); to adulterate (wine, etc.); **f. les comptes,** to falsify, *F:* cook, the accounts; **monnaie falsifiée,** spurious coins.

famé [fame] *a.* **bien, mal, f.**, of good, evil, repute.

famélique [famelik] *a.* famished; half-starved.

fameusement [faməzmɑ̃] *adv.* famously; *F:* **on s'est f. amusé,** we had a whale of a time.

fameux, -euse [famø, -øz] *a.* **1.** famous; **rocher f. par cent naufrages,** rock notorious for (many) wrecks. **2.** *F:* **fameuse idée,** splendid idea; **vous commettez une fameuse erreur,** you're making a (mighty) big mistake; **ce n'est pas f.**, it isn't up to much.

familial, -iaux [familjal, -jo] **1.** *a.* family (life, etc.); **allocation familiale,** family allowance; **maladie familiale,** hereditary disease; **en pot f.**, in a family-size jar; **placement f. des enfants,** placing of children in fosterhomes. **2.** *n.f. Aut:* **familiale,** seven-seater saloon; estate car, *NAm:* station wagon.

familiariser [familjarize] **1.** *v.tr.* to familiarize; **f. qn à, avec, qch.**, to make s.o. used to, accustomed to, familiar with, sth. **2. se f.;** (*a*) to familiarize oneself, make oneself familiar **(avec,** with); **se f. avec une langue,** to master a language; (*b*) to grow familiar, too free (in manner).

familiarité [familjarite] *n.f.* familiarity; (*a*) **être d'une grande f. avec qn,** to be on terms of great familiarity, intimacy, with s.o.; (*b*) **prendre trop de familiarités avec qn,** to be too familiar, to take liberties, with s.o.

familier, -ière [familje, -jɛr] *a.* **1.** domestic, of the family; **dieux familiers,** household gods. **2.** familiar; (*a*) **être f. avec qn,** to be on familiar terms, to be intimate, with s.o.; **prendre des airs trop familiers,** to be over-familiar; **expression familière,** colloquial expression; colloquialism; **animal f.**, pet (animal); *n.m.* **un des familiers de la maison,** a regular visitor to the house; an intimate friend of the family; (*b*) **visage qui lui est f.**, face which is well-known to him; **cette question lui est familière,** he is familiar with, he is at home in, this subject; **le mensonge lui est f.**, he is a habitual liar.

familièrement [familjɛrmɑ̃] *adv.* familiarly.

familistère [familistɛr] *n.m.* workers' co-operative association.

famille [famij] *n.f.* **1.** family; household; relatives; **elle a une f. de six enfants,** she has a family of six; **il faut que je vous présente à ma f.,** I must introduce you to (i) my people, my parents, (ii) my wife and children; **charges de famille,** dependants; **chef de f.,** (i) head of the family; (ii) householder, head of the household; **soutien de f.,** breadwinner; **fils de f.,** young man of good social position; **dîner en f.,** to dine at home with one's family; **avec eux je me sens en f.,** I feel quite at home with them; **cela tient, vient, de f.,** it runs in the family, in the blood; **la f. des Bourbons,** the house of Bourbon; **pension de f.,** (small) boarding house; *Jur:* **prévenir la f.,** to inform the next of kin. **2. f. de mots, de plantes,** family of words, of plants.
famine [famin] *n.f.* famine, starvation; **crier f.,** to complain of hunger, of hard times; **salaire de f.,** starvation wages.
fan [fan] *n.m. F:* (football, etc.) fan.
fana [fana] *a. & n. P:* enthusiast(ic), *n.* fan.
fanage [fanaʒ] *n.m.* tedding, tossing (of hay).
fanal, -aux [fanal, -o] *n.m.* lantern, lamp, light (for signalling); (ship's) navigation light; *Rail:* **f. de tête,** headlight (of locomotive).
fanatique [fanatik] **1.** *a.* fanatic(al); **être f. de qn, de qch.,** to be an enthusiastic admirer, supporter, of s.o., of sth.; to be keen, mad, on s.o., sth. **2.** *n.* fanatic, zealot, enthusiast; **f. du football,** football fan.
fanatiquement [fanatikmɑ̃] *adv.* fanatically.
fanatisme [fanatism] *n.m.* fanaticism, zealotry.
fanchon [fɑ̃ʃɔ̃] *n.f.* kerchief, headscarf.
fandango [fɑ̃dɑ̃go] *n.m.* fandango.
fane [fan] *n.f.* haulm (of potatoes); **fanes de navets,** turnip tops.
faner [fane] **1.** *v.tr.* (*a*) to ted, toss (hay); (*b*) to fade, make (flowers, colours) fade. **2. se f.** (*of plants*) to droop, wither, wilt, fade; (*of colours, etc.*) to fade.
faneur, -euse [fanœr, -øz] *n. Agr:* **1.** (*pers.*) tedder. **2.** *n.f.* tedding machine; tedder.
fanfare [fɑ̃far] *n.f.* **1.** (*a*) flourish, fanfare (of trumpets, etc.); *F:* **réveil en f.,** sudden, rude, awakening. **2.** brass band; military band.
fanfaron, -onne [fɑ̃farɔ̃, -ɔn] **1.** *a.* boasting, bragging. **2.** *n.* braggart, boaster.
fanfaronnade [fɑ̃farɔnad] *n.f.* (piece of) bragging, boasting.
fanfaronner [fɑ̃farɔne] *v.i.* to brag, boast.
fange [fɑ̃ʒ] *n.f.* mud, mire, filth, muck; **élevé dans la f.,** brought up in the gutter.
fangeux, -euse [fɑ̃ʒø, -øz] *a.* muddy (ground, etc.).
fanion [fanjɔ̃] *n.m.* (*a*) (distinguishing) flag (of general, company, etc.); (*b*) lance pennon.
fanon [fanɔ̃] *n.m.* **1.** *Ecc:* lappet (of mitre). **2.** dewlap (of ox); wattle (of bird); fetlock (of horse). **3.** whalebone, baleen.
fantaisie [fɑ̃tezi] *n.f.* **1.** (*a*) imagination, fancy, fantasy; **de f.,** (i) imaginary (tale); (ii) fanciful (portrait); (*b*) *Mus:* fantasia. **2.** (*a*) fancy, desire; **il a eu, il lui a pris, la f. de se baigner,** he had a sudden idea he'd like a swim; **chacun s'amusait à sa f.,** everyone amused himself as the fancy took him, as he pleased; **articles (de) f.,** fancy goods; **pain (de) f.,** fancy bread (not sold by weight); **bijoux (de) f.,** costume jewellery; **rayon de fantaisies,** fancy goods counter; (*b*) freak, vagary, whim.
fantaisiste [fɑ̃tezist] *a. & n.* **1.** capricious (person). **2.** entertainer; cabaret artiste.
fantasmagorie [fɑ̃tasmagɔri] *n.f.* (*a*) phantasmagoria; (*b*) weird spectacle.
fantasmagorique [fɑ̃tasmagɔrik] *a.* (*a*) phantasmagoric(al); (*b*) weird, fantastic.
fantasme [fɑ̃tasm] *n.m.* phantasm, hallucination; *Psy:* fantasy.
fantasque [fɑ̃task] *a.* odd, whimsical.
fantassin [fɑ̃tasɛ̃] *n.m.* foot soldier, infantryman.
fantastique [fɑ̃tastik] **1.** *a.* fantastic; (*a*) fanciful, imaginary; weird (light, etc.); (*b*) **paysage d'une beauté f.,** fantastically beautiful country; **histoire f.,** incredible story, fantastic yarn. **2.** *n.m.* **le f.,** the uncanny, the fantastic.
fantastiquement [fɑ̃tastikmɑ̃] *adv.* fantastically.
fantoche [fɑ̃tɔʃ] *n.m.* puppet; *a.* **gouvernement f.,** puppet government.
fantôme [fɑ̃tom] *n.m.* phantom, ghost, apparition, spirit; spectre, *NAm:* specter; *Mus:* **le Vaisseau F.,** the Flying Dutchman; **ce n'est plus qu'un f.,** he's just a skeleton; *Pol:* **gouvernement, cabinet, f.,** shadow government.
faon [fɑ̃] *n.m.* fawn; roe calf; **f. femelle,** hind calf.
farad [farad] *n.m. El:* farad.
faradique [faradik] *a. El:* faradic (current, etc.).
faramineux, -euse [faraminø, -øz] *a. F:* phenomenal, colossal.
faraud [faro] *a. A:* pleased with oneself; **faire le f.,** to preen oneself; to show off.
farce [fars] *n.f.* **1.** *Cu:* stuffing; forcemeat. **2.** (*a*) *Th:* farce; (*b*) practical joke; prank; **faire des farces à qn,** to play tricks on s.o.; *Com:* **farces et attrapes,** tricks and jokes. **3.** *a. F:* funny, comical.
farceur, -euse [farsœr, -øz] *n.* **1.** practical joker. **2.** wag, joker; **c'est un f. qui vous aura dit cela,** somebody's been pulling your leg.
farcir [farsir] *v.tr.* **1.** *Cu:* to stuff (poultry, etc.). **2.** to cram; **se f. la tête d'idées romanesques,** to fill one's head with romantic ideas. **3.** *P:* **se f. qch.,** (i) to treat oneself to sth.; (ii) to put up with sth.
fard [far] *n.m.* paint, rouge, makeup (for the face); **f. à paupières,** eye shadow; **la vérité sans f.,** the plain unvarnished truth; *F:* **piquer un f.,** to blush.
fardage [fardaʒ] *n.m.* (*a*) making up; rougeing; (*b*) *F:* camouflage (of inferior goods, produce).
fardeau, -eaux [fardo] *n.m.* burden, load; **le f. des impôts,** the burden of taxation; **c'est un lourd f. qu'il traîne,** it's a millstone round his neck.
farder [farde] **1.** *v.tr.* (*a*) to paint; to make (s.o., one's face) up; **f. la vérité, les faits,** to gloss over the truth, facts; (*b*) *F:* to camouflage (inferior goods, produce). **2. se f.,** to make up, put on one's makeup.
fardier [fardje] *n.m.* trolley, truck (for logs, etc.).
farfadet [farfadɛ] *n.m.* (hob)goblin; sprite.
farfelu [farfəly] *a. & n.* odd, crazy, comical (person).
farfouiller [farfuje] *v.i. F:* to rummage.
faribole [faribɔl] *n.f.* nonsense.
farinacé [farinase] *a.* farinaceous, floury.
farine [farin] *n.f.* **1.** flour, meal; **fleur de f.,** pure wheaten flour; whites; **folle f.,** flour dust, mill dust; **f. d'avoine,** oatmeal; **f. de maïs,** cornflour; *F:* **ce sont gens de (la) même f.,** they are birds of a feather; *F:* **rouler qn dans la f.,** to make a fool of s.o. **2.** *Mec.E:* **f. de forage,** bore dust.
fariner [farine] *v.tr. Cu:* to dredge, coat, (sth.) with flour; to flour.
farineux, -euse [farinø, -øz] **1.** *a. & n.m.* farinaceous (food). **2.** *a.* (*a*) **pomme de terre farineuse,** floury, mealy, potato; (*b*) floury, powdery.
farlouse [farluz] *n.f. Orn:* meadow pipit.
farniente [farnjɛnte] *n.m.* (sweet) idleness.
farouche [faruʃ] *a.* fierce, untamed (animal); savage, cruel (enemy).
farouchement [faruʃmɑ̃] *adv.* fiercely, savagely.
fart [far(t)] *n.m.* wax (for skis).
fartage [fartaʒ] *n.m.* waxing (of skis).
farter [farte] *v.tr.* to wax (skis).
fasciculaire [fasikylɛr], **fasciculé** [fasikyle] *a.* fascicular, fasciculate, growing in bunches.

fascicule [fasikyl] *n.m.* **1.** instalment, part, section (of publication); **publier un livre par fascicules,** to publish a book in parts. **2.** *Mil:* **f. de mobilisation,** (reservist's) call-up instructions.
fascinant [fasinɑ̃], **fascinateur, -trice** [fasinatœr, -tris] *a.* fascinating.
fascination [fasinasjɔ̃] *n.f.* fascination; charm; witchery.
fascine [fasin] *n.f.* fascine, faggot (of brushwood).
fasciner[1] [fasine] *v.tr.* (*a*) (*of snake*) to fascinate, hypnotize (prey); (*b*) to entrance, bewitch (s.o.).
fasciner[2] *v.tr.* to line (river bank, etc.) with fascines; **route fascinée,** corduroy road.
fascisme [faʃism] *n.m. Pol:* Fascism.
fasciste [faʃist] *n. Pol:* Fascist.
faste[1] [fast] *n.m. no pl.* ostentation, display; pomp; **mariage sans f.,** quiet wedding.
faste[2] *a.* **jour f.,** (i) *Rom.Ant:* lawful day; (ii) auspicious, lucky, day.
fastidieusement [fastidjøzmɑ̃] *adv.* tediously; in a dull, wearying, manner.
fastidieux, -ieuse [fastidjø, -jøz] *a.* dull, tedious, irksome; **besognes fastidieuses,** drudgery; **discours f.,** dull, boring, speech.
fastueusement [fastɥøzmɑ̃] *adv.* ostentatiously.
fastueux, -euse [fastɥø, -øz] *a.* ostentatious, fond of show; sumptuous (furnishings).
fat [fa(t)] *a. & n.m.* conceited, self-satisfied (person).
fatal, -als [fatal] *a.* **1.** fatal; **heure fatale,** fatal hour, hour of death; **coup f.,** deadly, mortal, blow; **cancer f.,** terminal cancer; **f. à qn,** fatal, disastrous, to s.o.; **femme fatale,** *femme fatale.* **2.** fated, inevitable; **c'est f.,** it is bound to come, sure to happen.
fatalement [fatalmɑ̃] *adv.* fatally; inevitably.
fatalisme [fatalism] *n.m.* fatalism.
fataliste [fatalist] **1.** *n.* fatalist. **2.** *a.* fatalistic.
fatalité [fatalite] *n.f.* **1.** fate, fatality; **poursuivi par la f.,** pursued by fate; **c'est la f.!** it's just bad luck! **c'est comme une f.!** it is, was, bound to happen! **2.** mischance, misfortune.
fatidique [fatidik] *a.* fated; fateful.
fatigant [fatigɑ̃] *a.* **1.** tiring, fatiguing. **2.** tiresome, wearisome; tedious; boring.
fatigue [fatig] *n.f.* **1.** (*a*) fatigue; tiredness, weariness; **tomber, être mort, de f.,** to be tired out, dead beat; **f. nerveuse,** nervous exhaustion; **f. oculaire,** eyestrain; **la f. des affaires,** the strain of business; (*b*) **souliers de f.,** strong shoes; **habits de f.,** working clothes. **2.** stress, fatigue (of metal); heavy duty (of transmission gear, etc.). **3.** wear and tear (of machines, clothes).
fatigué [fatige] *a.* **1.** (*a*) tired, fatigued; jaded; weary; **cœur f.,** strained heart; **être f. de qch., de faire qch.,** to be tired of sth., of doing sth.; **f. par le voyage,** travel-worn; (*b*) (i) *Dial:* ill; (ii) *F:* loony. **2.** worn, shabby (clothes, etc.).
fatiguer [fatige] **1.** *v.tr.* (*a*) to fatigue, tire; to make (s.o.) tired, weary; **f. l'ennemi,** to harass the enemy; **se f. les yeux a faire qch.,** to strain one's eyes doing sth.; *F:* **il me fatigue!** he bores me! (*b*) to overwork (animal, etc.); to impose a strain on (machine); to strain (ship); to exhaust, impoverish (a field); **f. un livre,** to give a book hard use; **f. la salade,** to mix the salad. **2.** *v.i.* (*of ship, engine*) to labour. **3. se f.,** to tire; to get tired; (*of voice, etc.*) to get strained; **se f. de qch.,** to tire, get tired, of sth.; **se f. à faire qch.,** to tire oneself out doing sth.
fatras [fatra] *n.m.* (*a*) jumble, medley, hotchpotch (of ideas, papers, etc.); (*b*) lumber, rubbish.
fatuité [fatɥite] *n.f.* self-conceit, self-satisfaction.
fauberder [fobɛrde], **fauberter** [fobɛrte] *v.tr. Nau:* to swab, mop (the decks, etc.).
fauber(t) [fobɛr] *n.m. Nau:* (deck) swab, mop.
faubourg [fobur] *n.m.* suburb; outlying district (of town); **accent des faubourgs,** working-class accent.
faubourien, -ienne [foburjɛ̃, -jɛn] *a.* suburban; **accent f.,** working class, common, accent.
fauchage [foʃaʒ] *n.m.* **1.** mowing, reaping (of corn, etc.). **2.** (*a*) mowing down (of troops); (*b*) sweeping of ground (with machine-gun fire).
fauchaison [foʃɛzɔ̃] *n.f.* mowing, reaping, time.
fauchard [foʃar] *n.m.* double-edged slasher.
fauche [foʃ] *n.f. P:* (*a*) petty theft; (*b*) loot.
fauché [foʃe] *a. F:* **f. (comme les blés),** (stony) broke.
faucher [foʃe] *v.tr.* **1.** (*a*) to mow, cut, reap (grass, etc.); *F:* **f. l'herbe sous les pieds de qn,** to cut the ground from under s.o.'s feet; **la voiture a fauché le poteau télégraphique,** the car brought down the telegraph pole; *Rugby Fb:* **f. son homme,** to bring down one's man; (*b*) *F:* to steal; to pinch, swipe. **2.** (*a*) to mow down (troops); (*b*) to sweep (ground) (with machine-gun fire).
faucheur, -euse [foʃœr, -øz] *n.* **1.** mower, reaper. **2.** *n.m.* harvest spider. **3.** *n.f.* (mechanical) reaper, mower.
faucheux [foʃø] *n.m.* harvest spider.
faucille [fosij] *n.f.* sickle, reaping hook.
faucon [fokɔ̃] *n.m.* **1.** *Orn:* falcon; hawk; **f. mâle,** tercel, tiercel; **f. pèlerin,** peregrine falcon; **chasser au f.,** to hawk; **chasse au f.,** hawking. **2.** *Pol:* hawk.
fauconneau, -eaux [fokɔno] *n.m.* young falcon.
fauconnerie [fokɔnri] *n.f.* **1.** hawk house, falcon house. **2.** falconry; hawking.
fauconnet [fokɔnɛ] *n.m. Orn:* falconet.
fauconnier [fokɔnje] *n.m.* falconer.
faufil [fofil] *n.m.* (*a*) tacking thread, basting thread; (*b*) = FAUFILAGE.
faufilage [fofilaʒ] *n.m.* tacking, basting.
faufiler [fofile] **1.** *v.tr.* to tack, baste (seam, etc.). **2. se f.,** to thread one's way; **se f. dans la faveur de qn,** to insinuate oneself into s.o.'s favour; **il s'était faufilé avec les invités,** he had slipped in, sneaked in, among the guests; **se f. entre les voitures,** to nip in and out of the traffic.
faufilure [fofilyr] *n.f.* tacked seam; tacking, basting.
faune[1] [fon] *n.m. Myth:* faun.
faune[2] *n.f.* fauna, animal life (of region, etc.); **la f. des boîtes de nuit,** the regular crowd in the night clubs.
faunesque [fonɛsk] *a.* faun-like.
faussage [fosaʒ] *n.m.* warping, buckling.
faussaire [fosɛr] *n.* forger (of document).
faussement [fosmɑ̃] *adv.* falsely, erroneously.
fausser [fose] **1.** *v.tr.* (*a*) to falsify; to pervert (the truth), distort (meaning); **f. les faits,** to present the facts in a wrong light; **esprit faussé,** warped mind; (*b*) to force (lock); to bend, buckle; to wrench (key); (*c*) to put (instrument) out of tune; to strain (voice). **2. se f.** (*a*) (*of instrument, etc.*) to get out of true; (*b*) (*of axle, etc.*) to bend, buckle; (*c*) (*of voice*) to go out of tune.
fausset[1] [fosɛ] *n.m.* falsetto; **chanter en f.,** to sing falsetto; **voix de f.,** high-pitched voice.
fausset[2] *n.m.* spigot, vent peg (of barrel); **trou de f.,** vent hole.
fausseté [foste] *n.f.* **1.** falseness, falsity (of statement, etc.). **2.** falsehood, untruth. **3.** duplicity; **f. de conduite,** double dealing.
faute [fot] *n.f.* **1.** lack, need, want; **faire f.,** to be lacking; **la main-d'œuvre nous fait f.,** we're short of labour; **ne se faire f. de rien,** to deny oneself nothing; **nous ne nous faisons jamais f. de lui écrire,** we never fail to write to him; **sans f.,** without fail; **f. de,** for want of, for lack of; **f. de réponse satisfaisante,** failing a satisfactory reply; **f. d'argent,** for want of

money; **f. d'ordres précis,** in the absence of, in default of, definite instructions; **f. de quoi,** failing which; otherwise; **f. d'essayer,** for want of trying; **f. de paiement,** non-payment. **2.** (*a*) fault, mistake; **être en f.,** to be at fault; **trouver, prendre, qn en f.,** to catch s.o. in the act; **il n'y a pas (de) f. de ma part, ce n'est pas (de) ma f.,** it's not my fault; **à qui la f.?** whose fault is it? who's to blame? **c'est un peu de ma f.,** I'm partly to blame; **il a été tué par ma f.,** it's my fault he was killed; **f. d'orthographe,** spelling mistake; **f. de jugement,** error of judgment; **commettre une f. grave,** to make a serious mistake; **f. d'impression,** misprint; (*b*) misconduct, moral lapse; transgression, offence; **f. grave,** serious offence; (*c*) *Fb: etc:* foul; *Ten:* fault; **f. de pied,** foot fault.

fauter [fote] *v.i. F:* (*of woman*) to go astray, wrong.

fauteuil [fotœj] *n.m.* **1.** armchair, easy chair; **f. à oreillettes,** wing chair; **f. à bascule,** rocking chair; **f. pliant,** folding chair; **f. roulant,** wheelchair; *Th:* **f. d'orchestre,** seat in the stalls, orchestra stall; **f. de premier balcon,** dress-circle seat; **arriver dans un f.,** (i) *Rac:* to win in a canter; (ii) to win hands down; *Jur:* **f. électrique,** electric chair. **2.** (*a*) chair (of meeting); **occuper le f.,** to be in the chair; (*b*) **f. (d'académicien),** seat in the French Academy.

fauteur [fotœr] *n.m.* instigator (of a rising); **f. de troubles, de désordre,** agitator, troublemaker.

fautif, -ive [fotif, -iv] *a.* **1.** faulty, incorrect; **monnaie fautive,** flawed currency; **calcul f.,** miscalculation; **mémoire fautive,** defective memory. **2.** sinning, offending, at fault; (child) who has been naughty.

fautivement [fotivmɑ̃] *adv.* faultily, incorrectly.

fauve [fov] **1.** *a.* (*a*) fawn-coloured; tawny (hair, etc.); (*of deer*) fallow; (*b*) **odeur f.,** musky smell. **2.** *n.m.* (*a*) fawn (colour); (*b*) **le f., les (bêtes) fauves,** deer; (*c*) **les (grands) fauves,** big game; (*d*) *Art:* **les Fauves,** the Fauves, Fauvists.

fauverie [fovri] *n.f.* lion house.

fauvette [fovɛt] *n.f. Orn:* warbler; **f. d'hiver,** hedge sparrow; dunnock; **f. des roseaux,** reed warbler.

fauvisme [fovism] *n.m. Art:* Fauvism.

faux¹, fausse [fo, fos] **I.** *a.* false. **1.** untrue; **fausse nouvelle,** false report; **f. témoin,** false witness; **f. témoignage,** perjury. **2.** not genuine; (*a*) false (hair, teeth, jewellery); bogus (doctor); **fausse monnaie,** false, spurious, counterfeit, base, coin(age); **fausse clef,** skeleton key; **fausse cartouche,** dummy cartridge; **fausse fenêtre,** blind window; **f. chèque,** forged cheque; **fausse déclaration,** misrepresentation; **f. nom,** false, assumed, name; *Anat:* **fausses côtes,** floating ribs; *Bot:* **f. persil,** false parsley, fool's parsley; *Typ:* **f. titre,** half, bastard, title; **fausse sortie,** *Mil:* feint sortie; *Th:* sham exit; (*b*) (*usu. after noun*) treacherous; **il est f. comme un jeton, c'est un f. jeton,** he's a hypocrite, *F:* a phoney; **f. bonhomme,** shifty, sly, character. **3.** wrong, mistaken; erroneous; **fausse date,** wrong date; **raisonnement f.,** unsound reasoning; **présenter la conduite de qn sous un f. jour,** to misrepresent s.o.'s conduct; **situation fausse,** equivocal situation; **balance fausse,** inaccurate balance; **f. poids,** unjust weight; **faire un f. pas,** (i) to take a false step; (ii) to blunder, to make a faux pas; **faire fausse route,** (i) to take the wrong road, go astray; (ii) to be on the wrong tack, track; **f. calcul,** miscalculation; *Cr:* **fausse balle,** no ball; *Mus:* **fausse note,** wrong note. **II. 1.** *adv.* falsely; wrongly; **chanter f.,** to sing out of tune; **cela sonne f.,** that doesn't sound right; **rire qui sonne f.,** hollow laugh(ter). **2.** *adv. phr.* **à f.,** wrongly; **poser le pied à f.,** to miss one's footing; **accuser qn à f.,** to make a false accusation against s.o.; **porter à f.,** to be out of true; **mur qui porte à f.,** wall out of plumb. **III.** *n.m.* **1.** (*a*) **le f.,** the false, the untrue; **distinguer le vrai du f.,** to distinguish truth from falsehood; (*b*) imitation (of work of art, etc.); **(bijouterie en) f.,** costume jewellery. **2.** forgery; **s'inscrire en f. contre qch.,** to dispute the validity of sth.

faux² *n.f.* **1.** *Agr:* scythe. **2.** *Anat:* falx.

faux-bourdon [foburdɔ̃] *n.m.* **1.** *Mus:* fauxbourdon. **2.** *Ent:* drone; *pl. faux-bourdons.*

faux-filet [fofilɛ] *n.m. Cu:* sirloin; *pl. faux-filets.*

faux-fuyant [fofɥijɑ̃] *n.m.* **1.** *A:* byway, bypath. **2.** subterfuge, evasion, dodge; **chercher des f.-fuyants,** to hedge.

faux-monnayeur [fomɔnɛjœr] *n.m.* coiner, counterfeiter; *pl. faux-monnayeurs.*

faveur [favœr] *n.f.* favour, *NAm:* favor. **1.** (*a*) **gagner, obtenir, la f. de qn,** to obtain s.o.'s favour, interest; **recevoir des marques de f. de qn,** to receive marks of favour from s.o.; **être en (grande) f. auprès de qn,** to be in (high) favour with s.o.; **perdre la f. de qn,** to fall out of favour with s.o.; **prendre f.,** to come into vogue, into favour; **prix de f.,** preferential, special, price; **traitement de f.,** *F:* V.I.P. treatment; **jours de f.,** days of grace; **billet de f.,** complimentary ticket; **à la f. de qch.,** with the help of, by means of, sth.; **à la f. de la nuit,** under cover of darkness; **plaider en f. de qn,** to plead on s.o.'s behalf, in s.o.'s favour; **on lui fit grâce en f. de sa jeunesse,** he was let off in consideration of his youth; **quête en f. de qn,** collection in aid of s.o.; (*b*) **faire une f. à qn,** to do s.o. a favour, a kindness; **elle lui accorde ses faveurs,** she encourages him. **2.** favour, ribbon.

favorable [favɔrabl̥] *a.* **1.** (*of pers., opinion*) favourable, *NAm:* favorable **(à, pour,** to); **il est f. à cette idée,** he is in favour, *NAm:* favor, of this idea; **mon impression lui fut f.,** he impressed me favourably, *NAm:* favorably. **2.** favourable, propitious (wind, occasion); auspicious (occasion); fair (wind); **le moment était f. pour lui parler,** it was a good moment to speak to him; **peu f.,** unpropitious, unfavourable, *NAm:* unfavorable.

favorablement [favɔrabləmɑ̃] *adv.* favourably, *NAm:* favorably; **recevoir f. qn, qch.,** to give s.o., sth., a kind, favourable, *NAm:* favorable, reception.

favori, -ite [favɔri, -it] **1.** *a.* favourite, *NAm:* favorite (person, object, racehorse). **2.** *n.* favourite. **3.** *n.m.pl.* (side)whiskers.

favoriser [favɔrize] *v.tr.* (*a*) to favour, *NAm:* to favour; to be partial to (s.o., sth.); to show favouritism, *NAm:* favoritism, to (s.o.); **f. une entreprise,** to be in favour of an enterprise; **f. les arts,** to patronize, encourage, the arts; (*b*) (*of thg*) to be favourable, *NAm:* favorable, to (s.o.); to help, encourage (sth.); **les événements l'ont favorisé,** events were in his favour.

favoritisme [favɔritism] *n.m.* favouritism, *NAm:* favoritism.

fayot [fajo] *n.m. P:* **1.** haricot bean, kidney bean. **2.** eager beaver.

féal, -aux [feal, -o] *a. A:* faithful, trusty (vassal).

fébrifuge [febrifyʒ] *a. & n.m. Med:* febrifuge.

fébrile [febril] *a.* febrile, feverish (pulse, patient); feverish (activity).

fébrilement [febrilmɑ̃] *adv.* feverishly.

fébrilité [febrilite] *n.f.* feverishness.

fécal, -aux [fekal, -o] *a.* faecal, *NAm:* fecal; **matières fécales,** faeces, *NAm:* feces.

fèces [fɛs] *n.f.pl.* faeces, *NAm:* feces. **1.** *Ch:* sediment, precipitate. **2.** *Physiol:* stool.

fécond [fekɔ̃] *a.* fecund; fertile (animal, egg); fruitful (earth, etc.); productive (soil, writer); fertile, rich (soil, imagination); prolific (author, etc.); **chaleur féconde,** life-giving heat.

fécondabilité [fekɔ̃dabilite] *n.f.Pol.Ec:* **taux de f.,** fertility rate.

fécondateur, -trice [fekɔ̃datœr, -tris] *a.* fertilizing.

fécondation [fekɔ̃dasjɔ̃] *n.f. Biol:* fecundation, fertilization; impregnation; **f. artificielle,** artificial insemination.
féconder [fekɔ̃de] *v.tr.* to fecundate; to fertilize; to impregnate.
fécondité [fekɔ̃dite] *n.f.* fecundity. **1.** fruitfulness; *Pol.Ec:* **taux de f.,** reproduction rate. **2.** fertility (of land, imagination, etc.).
fécule [fekyl] *n.f.* starch; **f. de pommes de terre,** potato starch, flour.
féculent [fekylɑ̃] **1.** *a.* starchy (food). **2.** *n.m.* starchy substance, food.
fédéral, -aux [federal, -o] *a. & n.m.* federal.
fédéraliser [federalize] *v.tr.* to federalize.
fédéralisme [federalism] *n.m.* federalism.
fédéraliste [federalist] *a. & n.* federalist.
fédération [federasjɔ̃] *n.f.* federation (of states, etc.); **f. de syndicats (ouvriers),** amalgamated unions.
fédéré [federe] **1.** *a.* federate (states). **2.** *n.m.* federate (of 1871, etc.).
fédérer [federe] **1.** *v.tr.* **(je fédère; je fédérerai)** to federate, federalize (states, etc.). **2. se f.,** to federate.
fée [fe] **1.** *n.f.* fairy; **conte de fées,** fairytale; **pays des fées,** fairyland; **doigts de f.,** nimble fingers; **vieille f.,** old hag. **2.** *a.* fairy, magic, enchanted.
feeder [fidœr] *n.m.* (*a*) *El:* feeder (cable); (*b*) (gas) pipeline.
féerie [fe(e)ri] *n.f.* **1.** (power of) enchantment. **2.** fairyland. **3.** *Th:* fairy play (of the pantomime type).
féerique [fe(e)rik] *a.* **1.** fairy, magic (castle, etc.). **2.** fairylike, enchanting (sight, etc.).
feignant [fɛɲɑ̃], **feignasse** [fɛɲas] *a. & n. P:* lazy, bone idle (person).
feindre [fɛ̃dr̥] *v.tr.* (*pr.p.* **feignant;** *p.p.* **feint;** *pr.ind.* **je feins, n. feignons;** *pr.sub.* **je feigne;** *impf.* **je feignais;** *p.h.* **je feignis;** *fu.* **je feindrai**) to feign, simulate, sham (illness, surprise); **f. de faire qch.,** to pretend to do sth., to make a pretence of doing sth.; **inutile de f.,** it's no use pretending.
feint [fɛ̃] *a.* (*a*) feigned, assumed, sham; (*b*) **porte feinte,** blind, dummy, door.
feinte [fɛ̃t] *n.f.* (*a*) feint, sham, pretence; **sans f.,** frankly, without pretence; **c'était une f. pour le surprendre,** it was a dodge to catch him out; (*b*) *Box: Fenc:* feint; *Rugby Fb:* **faire une f. de passe,** to give, sell, the dummy.
feinter [fɛ̃te] **1.** *v.i. Box: Fenc:* to feint, make a feint; *Rugby Fb:* to dummy. **2.** *v.tr.* to deceive (s.o.), take (s.o.) in.
feldspath [fɛldspat] *n.m. Miner:* fel(d)spar.
fêlé [fele] *a.* cracked (glass, voice, etc.); **à l'esprit f.,** crackbrained; **il a le cerveau f.,** he's a bit cracked.
fêler [fele] **1.** *v.tr.* to crack (glass, china, etc.). **2.** (*of glass, etc.*) **se f.** to crack.
félicitation [felisitasjɔ̃] *n.f.* congratulation; **adresser des félicitations, faire ses félicitations, à qn,** to congratulate s.o.; **félicitations!** congratulations!
félicité [felisite] *n.f.* felicity, bliss(fulness), happiness, joy.
féliciter [felisite] **1.** *v.tr.* to congratulate (s.o.); **f. qn. de, sur, qch., d'avoir fait qch.,** to congratulate, compliment, s.o. on sth., on having done sth.; **je vous en félicite!** I wish you joy! much good may it do you! **2. se f. de qch.,** to be pleased, satisified, with sth.; **félicitons-nous de ce que nous avons la vie sauve,** let us be thankful we came out alive.
félidés [felide] *n.m.pl. Z:* Felidae; the cat family; **un félidé,** a felid.
félin, -ine [felɛ̃, -in] *a.* feline; (*a*) cat (family, show, etc.); *n.* **les grands félins,** the great felines; *F:* the big cats; (*b*) cat-like (grace, etc.).
fellah [fella] *n.m.* fellah, Egyptian peasant.
félon, -onne [felɔ̃, -ɔn] *A:* **1.** *a.* disloyal, false, felon. **2.** *n.m.* felon, traitor.
félonie [felɔni] *n.f. A:* disloyalty.
fêlure [felyr] *n.f.* crack (in china); split (in wood), flaw (in diamond); **f. du crâne,** fracture of the skull; **une f. dans notre amitié,** a rift between us.
femelle [fəmɛl] **1.** (*a*) *a.* female (animal, sex, etc.); she (animal); cow (elephant, etc.); hen (bird); (*b*) *n.f.* (*animal*) female; *Pej:* woman, female. **2.** *a.* (*a*) *Tchn:* female (screw, etc.); (*b*) *Bot:* female, pistillate.
féminin, -ine [feminɛ̃, -in] **1.** *a.* feminine; **le sexe f.,** the female sex; **vêtements féminins,** women's clothes, clothes for women. **2.** *n.m. Gram:* feminine (gender); **ce mot est du f.,** this word is feminine.
féminiser [feminize] *v.tr.* (*a*) to feminize; to make feminine, womanish; (*b*) to make (word) feminine.
féminisme [feminism] *n.m.* feminism.
féministe [feminist] *a. & n.* feminist.
féminité [feminite] *n.f.* femineity, femininity.
femme [fam] *n.f.* **1.** woman; **les femmes,** women, womankind; **l'instinct de la f.,** a woman's instinct; **l'émancipation de la f.,** the emancipation of women; **cherchez la f.,** there's a woman in the case; **elle est très f.,** she's very feminine; **f. auteur,** woman author; authoress; **f. médecin,** woman doctor; **elle n'est pas f. à se plaindre,** she's not the sort of woman to complain. **2.** wife; **une jeune f.,** a young married woman; **chercher f.,** to look for a wife; **prendre f.,** to get married. **3. f. de chambre,** (i) housemaid; (ii) lady's maid; (iii) chambermaid; *Nau:* stewardess; **f. de charge,** housekeeper; **f. de journée,** charwoman, daily help. **4.** (*a*) **une bonne f.,** a simple, good-natured, (old) woman; **sa bonne f. de mère,** his old mother; (*b*) **une vieille bonne f.,** a little old woman; **contes, remèdes, de bonne f.,** old wives' tales, remedies.
femme-agent [famaʒɑ̃] *n.f.* policewoman; *pl. femmes-agents.*
femmelette [famlɛt] *n.f. F:* (*a*) little woman; weak, silly, woman; (*b*) (*of man*) weakling.
femme-soldat [famsɔlda] *n.f.* servicewoman; *pl. femmes-soldats.*
fémoral, -aux [femɔral, -o] *a. Anat:* femoral.
fémur [femyr] *n.m. Anat:* femur, thighbone.
fenaison [fənɛzɔ̃] *n.f.* **1.** haymaking, hay harvest. **2.** haymaking season.
fendage [fɑ̃daʒ] *n.m.* splitting, cleaving, slitting (of wood, etc.).
fendeur, -euse [fɑ̃dœr, -øz] *n.* splitter, slitter (of slates, wood, etc.).
fendillé [fɑ̃dije] *a.* fissured; cracked; crackled.
fendillement [fɑ̃dijmɑ̃] *n.m.* cracking (of paint, wood, skin, etc.); crackling (of glaze).
fendiller [fɑ̃dije] *v.* **1.** *v.tr.* to fissure; to crack (wood, etc.); to crackle (glaze). **2. se f.** (*of wood, paint, etc.*) to crack; (*of china, glaze*) to crackle.
fendre [fɑ̃dr̥] **1.** *v.tr.* (*a*) to cleave (lengthwise); to split, slit, rive (wood, slate, etc.); (*b*) to fissure; to crack (the ground, etc.); **f. les eaux,** to plough through the waters; **f. l'air,** to cleave the air; (*of sound*) to rend the air; **f. la foule,** to force, elbow, one's way through the crowd; **il gèle à pierre f.,** it's freezing hard; **c'était à f. l'âme, le cœur,** it was heartbreaking, heartrending; **bruit à f. la tête, à vous f. les oreilles,** ear-splitting noise. **2. se f.** (*a*) (*of wood, etc.*) to split, crack; (*b*) *Fenc:* to lunge; (*c*) *P:* **se f. de 200 francs,** to fork out 200 francs.
fendu [fɑ̃dy] *a.* split (ring, pin); slit, slashed (skirt, etc.); cloven (hoof); **bouche fendue jusqu'aux oreilles,** mouth that stretches from ear to ear; **yeux bien fendus,** large, wide-open, eyes.
fenêtrage [fənɛtraʒ] *n.m.* windows; fenestration (of building).
fenêtre [fənɛtr̥] *n.f.* **1.** window; **f. à coulisse, à guil-**

lotine, sash window; **f. croisée, à battants,** casement window; **f. en saillie,** bay window, bow window; **regarder par la f.,** to look out of the window; **il faut passer par là ou par la f.,** there's no choice, nothing else for it. **2.** blank, space (in document). **3.** aperture; window (in envelope).

fenêtrer [fənetre] *v.tr.* to put windows in (house); to fenestrate (bandage, etc.).

fenil [fəni(l)] *n.m.* hayloft.

fenouil [fənuj] *n.m. Bot:* fennel.

fente [fɑ̃t] *n.f.* **1.** (*a*) crack, crevice, split, slit, fissure, chink (in door, etc.); (*b*) slot, cut (in head of screw, etc.); *Tail:* **f. de poche,** pocket hole. **2.** *Fenc:* lunge.

féodal, -aux [feɔdal, -o] *a.* feudal.

féodalisme [feɔdalism] *n.m.* feudalism.

féodalité [feɔdalite] *n.f.* feudality; feudal system.

fer [fɛr] *n.m.* iron. **1. minerai de f.,** iron ore; **f. coulé, de fonte,** cast iron; **f. en saumon, en gueuse,** pig (iron); **f. forgé,** wrought iron; **fil de f.,** wire; **corps, discipline, de f.,** iron constitution, discipline; **dur comme (le) f.,** as hard as iron; **avoir une volonté, une tête, de f.,** to have an iron will, a will of iron. **2.** (*a*) head (of axe, arrow); tag (of lace); **f. de lance,** spearhead; *Bot:* **en f. de lance,** lanceolate; **f. de rabot,** plane iron; (*b*) shoe, band, cap (of pile, etc.); *Bookb:* tool; brass; (*c*) sword; **croiser, engager, le f. avec qn,** to cross swords with s.o.; **battre le f.,** to fence; **porter le feu et le f. dans un pays,** to put a country to fire and sword. **3. f. à souder,** soldering iron; **f. à marquer,** branding iron; **marquer au f. rouge,** to brand; **f. à repasser,** (laundry) iron; **f. électrique,** electric iron; **donner un coup de f. à qch.,** to press, iron, sth.; **f. à friser,** curling tongs; *Golf:* **grand f.,** driving iron. **4.** *pl.* (*a*) irons, chains, fetters; **être aux fers,** to be in irons; **briser les fers à qn,** to set s.o. free; (*b*) *Obst:* forceps. **5. fer à, de, cheval,** horseshoe; **en f. à cheval,** horseshoe(-shaped); **mettre un f. à un cheval,** to shoe a horse; **perdre un f.,** to cast a shoe; *F:* (*of pers.*) **tomber les quatre fers en l'air,** to go sprawling.

fer-blanc [fɛrblɑ̃] *n.m.* tinplate; **boîte en f.-b.,** tin, can; **articles en f.-b.,** tinware; *pl. fers-blancs.*

ferblanterie [fɛrblɑ̃tri] *n.f.* **1.** (*a*) tinplate industry, trade; (*b*) ironmonger's shop, hardware store. **2.** tinware; ironmongery, hardware.

ferblantier [fɛrblɑ̃tje] *n.m.* (*a*) tinman, tinsmith; (*b*) ironmonger.

férié [ferje] *a.* **jour f.,** (public) holiday; *Adm:* = bank holiday, *U.S:* legal holiday.

férir [ferir] *v.tr.* to strike; *used only in* **sans coup f.,** (i) without striking a blow; without firing a shot; (ii) without meeting any resistance, obstacle.

ferlage [fɛrlaʒ] *n.m.* furling (of sails).

ferler [fɛrle] *v.tr.* to furl (sail).

fermage [fɛrmaʒ] *n.m.* **1.** (tenant) farming. **2.** rent (of farm).

fermail,-aux [fɛrmaj, -o] *n.m.* (ornamental) clasp.

ferme[1] [fɛrm] **1.** *a.* (*a*) firm, steady; **poutre f.,** firm, rigid, beam; **terre f.,** (i) firm, solid, land; (ii) mainland; terra firma; **il répondit d'une voix f.,** he replied in a firm, steady, voice; **le marché reste très f.,** the market continues very strong; **être f. dans ses desseins,** to be firm, steadfast, in one's intentions; **attendre qn de pied f.,** to be quite ready for s.o.; (*b*) **prendre un engagement f.,** to enter into a firm contract; **vente f., offre f.,** firm, definite, sale, offer. **2.** *adv.* firmly; **tenir f.,** (i) to stand fast, hold one's own; (ii) (*of nail*) to hold fast; **f.!** (i) steady! (ii) pull! **frapper f.,** to hit hard; **j'y travaille f.,** I'm hard at it; **croire fort et f. aux esprits,** to be a firm believer in spirits; **vendre f.,** to make a firm sale.

ferme[2] *n.f.* **1.** (*a*) **bail à f.,** farming lease; **prendre une terre à f.,** to take a lease of, to lease, a piece of land; **donner une terre à f.,** to farm out, lease out, a piece of land; (*b*) farm; farmhouse; farmstead; **f. d'élevage,** stud farm; **petite f.,** smallholding. **2.** *Adm: A:* farming (out) (of taxes). **3.** truss (of roof, bridge). **4.** *Th:* rigid flat, set piece.

fermé [fɛrme] *a.* **1.** closed; landlocked (sea); **bout f.,** dead end (of pipe, etc.); **dormir à poings fermés,** to sleep soundly, like a log; **je pouvais y aller les yeux fermés,** I could go there blindfold, with my eyes shut; **être f. à qch.,** to have no taste for, no appreciation of, sth.; **il a l'esprit f. aux mathématiques,** mathematics are a closed book to him; *Ling:* **voyelle, fermée,** closed vowel; *Tchn:* **position f.,** off position; *Ven:* **chasse fermée,** close season. **2.** irresponsive; impassive (expression). **3.** exclusive (society, club).

fermement [fɛrməmɑ̃] *adv.* firmly, steadily.

ferment [fɛrmɑ̃] *n.m.* ferment (of wine, etc.); leaven (of discontent).

fermentation [fɛrmɑ̃tasjɔ̃] *n.f.* **1.** fermentation; rising (of dough). **2.** agitation; unrest; ferment.

fermenter [fɛrmɑ̃te] *v.i.* **1.** (*of wine*) to ferment, *F:* work; (*of dough*) to rise. **2.** (*of mind*) to be in a ferment.

fermer [fɛrme] **1.** *v.tr.* (*a*) to close, shut (door, window); **f. violemment la porte,** to slam, bang, the door; **f. sa porte à qn,** to close one's door to s.o.; **f. la porte à clef, au verrou,** to lock, bolt, the door; **f. les rideaux, le store,** to draw, close, the curtains; to pull down the blind; **f. une maison,** to shut up a house; **f. boutique,** to shut up shop; **on ferme!** closing time! **f. un trou,** to stop up, block up, a hole; **f. une liste, un débat,** to close a list, a debate; **f. la frontière,** to close the frontier; **f. un robinet, l'eau, le gaz,** to turn off a tap, *NAm:* a faucet, the water, the gas; **f. l'électricité, la radio,** to turn, switch, off the light, the radio; *El:* **f. un circuit,** to close a circuit; *Rail:* **f. la voie,** to block the line; *Knit:* **f. cinq mailles,** to cast off five stitches; *P:* **ferme ta gueule! ferme-la! la ferme!** shut up! shut it! shut your trap! (*b*) **f. la marche,** to bring up the rear. **2.** *v.i.* (*of door, shop, etc.*) to close, shut. **3. se f.** (*of door, etc.*) to close, shut; (*of eyes*) to close; (*of wound*) to heal, close up; **à cette demande son visage se ferma,** at this request his face froze.

fermeté [fɛrməte] *n.f.* firmness; steadfastness (of purpose); strength (of mind); **agir avec f.,** to act firmly, resolutely.

fermette [fɛrmɛt] *n.f.* (*a*) small farm; (*b*) (country) weekend cottage.

fermeture [fɛrmətyr] *n.f.* **1.** (*a*) closing, shutting (of gates, door, etc.); closure; **f. à clef,** locking; **f. des ateliers,** (i) knocking off (work); (ii) closing down of the workshops; **heure de f.,** closing time (of shop); knocking-off time (of works); **f. de la pêche,** close of the fishing season; **f. d'un compte,** closing of an account; *El:* **f. du circuit,** closing, making, of the circuit; *Mch:* **f. de l'admission,** cut-off (of steam); (*b*) **f. d'esprit,** narrow-mindedness. **2.** (*a*) (*apparatus*) **f. à glissière,** *R.t.m:* **f. éclair,** zip (fastener); *esp. NAm:* zipper; **f. à rouleau,** revolving shutter (of shop).

fermier, -ière [fɛrmje, -jɛr] *n.* **1.** (*a*) tenant (of farm); tenant farmer; (*b*) farmer; *f.* farmer's wife; woman farmer; *a.* **poulet f.,** farm, free-range, chicken. **2.** (*a*) *Hist:* farmer of taxes, tax farmer; **f. général,** farmer general; (*b*) **f. d'entreprise,** contractor.

fermoir [fɛrmwar] *n.m.* clasp, hasp, snap, catch, fastener (of handbag, etc.); **bouton f. à pression,** snap fastener; **f. de sûreté,** safety catch.

féroce [ferɔs] *a.* ferocious, savage, fierce; **bêtes féroces,** wild beasts; **appétit f.,** ravenous appetite.

férocement [ferɔsmɑ̃] *adv.* ferociously, savagely, fiercely.

férocité [ferɔsite] *n.f.* ferocity, ferociousness; savagery, fierceness.

Féroé [ferɔe] *Pr.n.* **les îles F.,** the Faroe Islands.
ferrage [fɛraʒ] *n.m.* providing (sth.) with iron fittings; shoeing (of wheel, horse); tagging (of lace); putting (of man) in irons.
ferraille [fɛrɑj] *n.f.* (*a*) old iron, scrap iron; **tas de f.,** scrap heap; **mettre qch. à la f.,** to put sth. on the scrap heap; **faire un bruit de f.,** to rattle, clank; **marchand de f.,** scrap merchant; (*b*) *F:* small change.
ferraillement [fɛrɑjmɑ̃] *n.m.* **1.** hammer-and-tongs fighting. **2.** rattling, clanking (of car, etc.).
ferrailler [fɛrɑje] *v.i.* **1.** *Pej:* to clash swords; to slash about with swords. **2.** to clank, rattle.
ferrailleur [fɛrɑjœr] *n.m.* **1.** *Pej:* sword rattler, swashbuckler. **2.** scrap merchant.
ferrate [fɛrat] *n.m. Ch:* ferrate.
ferré [fɛre] *a.* (*a*) fitted, mounted, with iron; iron-shod (stick, lever, etc.); **souliers ferrés,** hob-nailed shoes; **voie ferrée,** (i) (railway) track, permanent way; (ii) railway (line); *NAm:* railroad; **réseau f.,** railway system; **cheval f. à glace,** roughshod horse; *F:* **être f. (à glace) sur un sujet,** to be well up in a subject; (*b*) metalled (road).
ferrer [fɛre] *v.tr.* **1.** to fit, mount, (sth.) with iron; to tyre, shoe (wheel); to shoe (horse); to tag (shoelace); **f. une porte,** to fit locks and hinges to a door. **2.** to metal (road). **3.** *Fish:* to strike (fish).
ferret [fɛrɛ] *n.m.* tag, tab (of shoelace).
ferreur [fɛrœr] *n.m.* **f. de chevaux,** farrier, shoeing smith; **f. de porte,** lock fitter.
ferreux, -euse [fɛrø, -øz] *a. Ch: Miner:* ferrous; **alliages ferreux,** iron alloys, ferro-alloys.
ferricyanure [fɛrisjanyr] *n.m. Ch:* ferricyanide.
ferrique [fɛrik] *a. Ch:* ferric (salt, etc.).
ferrite [fɛrit] *n.m. Metall:* ferrite; *Elcs:* **mémoire à f.,** ferrite core memory.
ferrochrome [fɛrɔkrom] *n.m. Metall:* ferrochrome, -chromium; chrome iron.
ferrocyanure [fɛrɔsjanyr] *n.m. Ch:* ferrocyanide.
ferro-électrique [fɛrɔelɛktrik] *a.* ferroelectric.
ferromagnétique [fɛrɔmaɲetik] *a.* ferromagnetic.
ferronnerie [fɛrɔnri] *n.f.* **1.** ironworks, iron foundry. **2.** ironmongery, hardware; **f. (d'art),** art metalwork; **f. au marteau,** wrought-iron work.
ferronnier, -ière [fɛrɔnje, -jɛr] *n.* **1.** ironworker; blacksmith; **f. (d'art),** wrought-iron worker, art metalworker. **2.** ironmonger; hardware dealer.
ferrotypie [fɛrɔtipi] *n.f. Phot:* ferrotype.
ferrotypique [fɛrɔtipik] *a. Phot:* ferrotype (plate, etc.).
ferroviaire [fɛrɔvjɛr] *a.* pertaining to railways, *NAm:* railroads; **trafic f.,** rail(way) traffic; **les grandes lignes ferroviaires,** the main railway lines.
ferrugineux, -euse [fɛryʒinø, -øz] *a.* ferruginous; **source ferrugineuse,** chalybeate spring.
ferrure [fɛryr] *n.f.* **1.** piece of ironwork; iron fitting, mounting; **ferrures de porte,** door fittings; **ferrures en cuivre,** brass fittings, mounts. **2.** shoeing (of horse).
ferry-boat [fɛrebot] *n.m.* (train, car) ferry; *pl. ferry-boats.*
fertile [fɛrtil] *a.* fertile, fruitful (land, imagination); **semaine f. en événements,** eventful week.
fertilisant [fɛrtilizɑ̃] **1.** *a.* fertilizing. **2.** *n.m.* fertilizer.
fertilisation [fɛrtilizasjɔ̃] *n.f.* fertilization, fertilizing.
fertiliser [fɛrtilize] *v.tr.* to fertilize; to manure (land); to make (sth.) fertile, fruitful.
fertilité [fɛrtilite] *n.f.* fertility; fruitfulness, richness (of soil, imagination, etc.).
féru [fery] *a.* **f. (d'amour) pour qn,** (madly) in love with s.o.; **être f. d'une idée,** to be set on an idea.
férule [feryl] *n.f. Sch:* ruler, cane (for punishment on the hands); **être sous la f. de qn,** to be ruled by s.o. with a rod of iron.
fervent, -ente [fɛrvɑ̃, -ɑ̃t] **1.** *a.* fervent, ardent, earnest (devotion, etc.); enthusiastic (approval, etc.). **2.** *n.* enthusiast, devotee; *F:* (bridge) fiend; (football) fan.
ferveur [fɛrvœr] *n.f.* fervour, devotion; **avec f.,** (to pray) fervently, earnestly; (to work) with enthusiasm; (to love) with devotion, ardently.
fesse [fɛs] *n.f.* **1.** buttock; *F:* **donner sur les fesses d'un enfant,** to give a child a spanking; **donner à qn un coup de pied aux fesses,** to give s.o. a kick in the pants; *P:* **serrer les fesses,** to have cold feet, to have the wind up. **2.** *pl. Nau:* buttocks, tuck (of a ship).
fessée [fese] *n.f.* spanking, smacking.
fesse-mathieu [fɛsmatjø] *n.m.* skinflint, scrooge; *pl. fesse-mathieux.*
fesser [fese] *v.tr.* to spank (s.o.), smack (s.o.'s) bottom.
fesseur, -euse [fesœr, -øz] *n.* spanker, flogger.
fessier, -ière [fesje, -jɛr] **1.** *a. Anat:* gluteal (muscle, etc.); **poche fessière,** hip pocket (of trousers). **2.** *n.m.* gluteal muscle.
festin [fɛstɛ̃] *n.m.* feast, banquet; **quel f.!** what a feast! what a spread! **salle de f.,** banqueting hall; **faire (un) f.,** to feast, banquet.
festival, -als [fɛstival] *n.m.* (musical) festival; **f. du film,** film festival.
festivité [fɛstivite] *n.f. usu. pl.* festivity, rejoicing.
feston [fɛstɔ̃] *n.m.* **1.** festoon (of flowers, etc.). **2.** *Needlew:* scallop; **point de f.,** buttonhole stitch.
festonner [fɛstɔne] *v.tr.* **1.** to festoon. **2.** to scallop (hem, etc.).
festoyer [fɛstwaje] *v.i.* **(je festoie; je festoierai)** to feast, carouse.
fêtard, -arde [fɛtar, -ard] *n. F:* reveller, roisterer.
fête [fɛt] *n.f.* **1.** (*a*) feast, festival; **la f. des Morts,** All Souls' Day; **jour de f.,** (i) *Ecc:* feast day; (ii) public holiday; **f. légale** = bank holiday, *U.S:* legal holiday; **c'est f. demain,** tomorrow is a holiday; **ce n'est pas tous les jours f.,** Christmas comes but once a year; (*b*) **c'est demain ma f.,** it's my saint's day, name day, tomorrow; **souhaiter la f., une bonne f., à qn** = to wish s.o. many happy returns. **2.** (*a*) fete; fête; **f. champêtre, de village,** village fete, fair; **f. foraine,** fun fair; **f. de charité, de bienfaisance,** charity fete, bazaar; **f. d'aviation, aéronautique,** air display, show; (*b*) entertainment; **donner une f.,** to give an entertainment; **une petite f.,** a party. **3.** festivity, gaiety, merrymaking, rejoicings; **air de f.,** festive air; **le village était en f.,** the village was on holiday; **faire la f.,** to lead a gay life; **faire f. à qn,** to welcome s.o. with open arms; **être de la f.,** to be one of the party; **se faire une f. de (faire) qch.,** to look forward to (doing) sth.; **il ne s'était jamais vu à pareille f.,** he had never had such a good time; *F:* **il n'était pas à la f.,** he was having a bad time.
Fête-Dieu [fɛtdjø] *n.f. Ecc:* Corpus Christi; *pl. Fêtes-Dieu.*
fêter [fete] *v.tr.* **1.** (*a*) to keep (day, etc.) as a holiday, as a festival; **f. la naissance de qn,** to celebrate s.o.'s birthday; (*b*) **f. un saint,** to keep a saint's day. **2. f. qn,** (i) to fete s.o.; (ii) to entertain s.o.; **dîner pour f. le nouveau membre,** dinner to welcome the new member.
fétiche [fetiʃ] *n.m.* fetish; *Aut:* mascot.
fétichisme [fetiʃism] *n.m.* fetishism.
fétide [fetid] *a.* fetid, rank, stinking, foul.
fétidité [fetidite] *n.f.* fetidness.
fétu [fety] *n.m.* straw; **être emporté comme un f.,** to be blown along like a straw in the wind; **je m'en soucie comme d'un f.,** I don't care a rap about it.
fétuque [fetyk] *n.f. Bot:* fescue.

feu¹, feux [fø] *n.m.* fire. **1.** (*a*) **le f. et l'eau,** fire and water; **craindre qch. comme le f.,** to stand in dread of sth.; **jouer avec le f.,** to play with fire; **soleil de f.,** fiery sun; **faire f. des quatre pieds,** (i) (*of horse*) to make the sparks fly; (ii) (*of pers.*) to go all out; **il fait f. de tout bois,** he makes the most of his opportunities; he can turn anything to account; *F:* **avoir le f. au derrière,** to be in a tearing hurry; to have ants in one's pants; **mettre (le) f. à qch.,** to set fire to sth., to set sth. on fire; **mettre une ville à f. et à sang,** to put a town to fire and sword; **enlever de la peinture au f.,** to burn off paint; **en f.,** on fire; **le visage en f.,** flushed face; **prendre f.,** (i) to catch fire; (ii) to fly into a rage; **"au f.!"** "fire!"; **faire la part du f.,** (i) to make a fire break; (ii) to cut one's losses; *F:* **il n'y a pas le f. à la maison,** there's no particular hurry; **jeter f. et flamme (contre qn),** to rage (at s.o.); **est-ce que vous avez du f.?** have you got a light, a match? *a.inv.* **rouge f.,** flame-coloured; **chien noir et f.,** black and tan dog; (*b*) ardour, heat, passion; *A:* love; **tout f. tout flamme,** heart and soul; **dans le f. de la discussion,** in the heat of the debate. **2.** (*a*) **f. nu,** open fire; **faire du f.,** to light a fire; **garniture de f.,** fire irons; **f. de joie,** bonfire; beacon; **feux d'artifice,** fireworks; **leur amitié ne fera pas long f.,** their friendship won't last long; (*b*) *Mch:* **mettre une chaudière en f.,** to fire up a boiler; (*c*) **condamner qn au f.,** to condemn s.o. to be burnt at the stake; **j'en mettrais la main au f.,** I would swear to it; **épreuve du f.,** ordeal by fire; **mourir à petit f.,** to die by inches; **faire mourir qn à petit f.,** (i) to kill s.o. by inches; (ii) to keep s.o. on tenterhooks; (*d*) *Cu:* **faire cuire à f. doux, à petit f.,** to cook gently, over a slow heat, in a slow oven; **à grand f., à f. vif,** over a brisk heat, in a quick, hot, oven; **ustensiles qui vont au f.,** fireproof utensils; **cuisinière à quatre feux,** four-burner cooker; (*e*) (i) *A:* **hameau de 50 feux,** hamlet of 50 homes; (ii) **n'avoir ni f. ni lieu,** to be homeless, to have neither hearth nor home. **3. armes à f.,** firearms; **bouche à f.,** piece of ordnance, of artillery; **faire f. sur qn,** to fire, shoot, at s.o.; **commencer, déclencher, ouvrir, le f.,** to open fire; **f.!** fire! **sous le f.,** under fire; (*of pistol, plan, etc.*) **faire long f.,** to hang fire; **aller au f.,** to go into action, be under fire; **il n'a jamais vu le f.,** he has never heard a gun fired; **f. roulant,** running fire, drumfire; **un f. roulant de questions,** a running fire of questions; **être entre deux feux,** to be between two fires. **4.** (*a*) *Nau:* light (of lighthouse, beacon); **feux (d'entrée) de port,** harbour lights; **droits de feux,** light dues; **f. à occultations, à éclipses,** occulting light; **feux de route,** navigation lights; **feux de mouillage,** anchor lights (of ship); **f. de tribord,** starboard light; (*b*) *Av:* **feux de balisage,** boundary lights; **feux de piste,** course lights, runway lights; **feux de bord, de navigation,** navigation lights; (*c*) *Adm:* **feux de circulation,** *F:* **f. rouge,** traffic lights; **donner le f. vert à qn, qch.,** to give s.o., sth., the green light, the go-ahead; *Aut: etc:* **feux de route,** headlights; **feux de croisement,** dipped headlights; **feux de stationnement,** sidelights, parking lights; *Rail:* **f. d'avant,** headlight (of locomotive); **f. d'arrière,** tail light, rear light (of train); (*d*) **feux d'un diamant,** sparkle of a diamond; **yeux pleins de f.,** flashing eyes; **n'y voir que du f.,** (i) to be dazzled; (ii) to make neither head nor tail of sth. **5. coup de f.** (*a*) (i) browning (of joint, etc.); (ii) burning (of bread, etc.); (iii) *F:* rush hour; **être dans son coup de f.,** to be at one's busiest; (*b*) gun shot, pistol shot; **nous avons reçu des coups de f.,** we were fired on.

feu² *a.*(*inv. if preceding article or poss.adj.*) late; **la feue reine, f. la reine,** the late queen; **f. mon père,** my late father; **fils de feue Berthe Dupont,** son of the late Berthe Dupont, of Berthe Dupont deceased.

feudataire [fødatɛr] *n.m.* feudatory.

feuillage [fœjaʒ] *n.m.* foliage, leaves.

feuillaison [fœjɛzɔ̃] *n.f.* (time of) coming into leaf.

feuille [fœj] *n.f.* **1.** leaf (of plant); (*of tree*) **mettre, prendre, ses feuilles,** to come into leaf; **f. morte,** dead leaf; *Av:* **descente en f. morte,** dead leaf dive; **f. de chou,** (i) cabbage leaf; (ii) *F:* (*newspaper*) rag. **2.** (*a*) **f. de métal,** sheet of metal; **fer en feuilles,** sheet iron; **f. d'or,** gold leaf, foil; **f. d'étain,** tinfoil; (*b*) **f. de bois,** thin board. **3.** sheet (of paper); **f. volante, f. mobile,** loose sheet, fly sheet; leaflet; **feuilles d'un livre,** leaves of a book; *Bookb:* **f. de garde,** fly leaf, end paper (of book); **f. (quotidienne),** (daily) paper; *Publ:* **bonnes feuilles (de publicité),** advance proofs; **lire sous la f.,** to read between the lines; **f. de paie,** *Mil:* **de soldes,** payroll; **f. de présence,** time sheet; attendance list; **f. d'impôt,** (i) tax return (sheet); (ii) notice of assessment; **f. de température,** temperature chart; *Mil:* **f. de service,** (duty) roster; **f. de route,** *Com:* waybill; *Mil:* travel warrant.

feuillées [fœje] *n.f.pl. Mil:* latrines (in camp).

feuille-morte [fœjmɔrt] *a. & n.m.inv.* dead-leaf colour(ed).

feuiller [fœje] *v.tr. Carp:* to rabbet, groove (board).

feuilleret [fœjrɛ] *n.m. Tls:* rabbet plane, grooving plane.

feuillet [fœjɛ] *n.m.* **1.** (*a*) leaf (of book); **f. de garde,** fly leaf (of unbound book); end paper (of bound book); (*b*) *Adm:* form (for a return); return sheet. **2.** thin sheet, plate (of wood, etc.). **3.** omasum, third stomach (of ruminant). **4.** *pl. Geol:* folia.

feuilletage [fœjtaʒ] *n.m. Cu:* (*a*) rolling (of dough for flaky pastry); (*b*) flaky pastry.

feuilleté [fœjte] **1.** *a.* foliated, laminated, lamellar (rocks, etc.); *El:* laminated (core); *Cu:* **pâte feuilletée,** flaky pastry.

feuilleter [fœjte] *v.* **(je feuillette; je feuilletterai) 1.** *v.tr.* (*a*) *Cu:* to roll and fold (pastry); (*b*) **f. un livre,** to turn over the pages of a book; to dip into a book; **livre bien feuilleté,** well-thumbed book. **2.** (*of mineral, etc.*) **se f.,** to split up, flake, cleave.

feuilleton [fœjtɔ̃] *n.m.* (*a*) *Journ:* (literary, scientific) article; feature; (*b*) *Journ: W.Tel: T.V:* (i) instalment (of serial); **publier un roman en feuilletons,** to serialize a novel; (ii) serial (story).

feuilletoniste [fœjtɔnist] *n.* (*a*) feature writer; (*b*) serial writer.

feuillu [fœjy] *a.* leafy; broad-leaved, deciduous (tree).

feuillure [fœjyr] *n.f. Carp:* groove, rabbet.

feulement [følmɑ̃] *n.m.* (*of tiger*) snarl; (*of cat*) growl, growling.

feuler [føle] *v.i.* (*of tiger*) to snarl; (*of cat*) to growl.

feutrage [føtraʒ] *n.m.* **1.** felting (of hair, wool, fabric). **2.** (*a*) felting; covering with felt; (*b*) stuffing, padding (of saddle, etc.).

feutre [føtr̥] *n.m.* **1.** felt; **chaussons de f.,** felt slippers. **2.** (*a*) felt hat; (*b*) felt pen. **3.** stuffing, padding (of saddle, etc.).

feutré [føtre] *a.* **1.** covered, lined, with felt; **porte feutrée,** baize door. **2.** muffled (sound); **à pas feutrés,** with noiseless tread; **s'éloigner à pas feutrés,** to steal away, slip quietly away.

feutrer [føtre] **1.** *v.tr.* (*a*) to felt; to make (hair, wool) into felt; (*b*) to felt, pack; to cover (boiler, etc.). with felt; (*c*) to stuff, pad (saddle, etc.). **2.** *v.pr. & i.* **(se) f.,** to become matted, to felt.

feutrine [føtrin] *n.f.* baize; imitation felt.

fève [fɛv] *n.f.* (*a*) bean; **f. (des marais),** broad bean; *Fr.C:* **f. verte,** string bean; **petite f. (jaune),** wax bean; **gâteau de la f.,** Twelfth-night cake; (*b*) **f. de cacao,** cocoa nib.

février [fevrije] *n.m.* February; **en f., au mois de f.,** in (the month of) February; **le sept f.,** (on) the seventh of February; (on) February (the) seventh.

fez [fɛz] *n.m. Cost:* fez.

fi [fi] *int.* (*a*) *O:* fie! for shame! (*b*) **faire fi de qch.,** to despise, scorn, sth.

fiabilité [fjabilite] *n.f.* reliability (of machine, etc.).

fiable [fjabl̥] *a.* (*of machine, etc.*) reliable; dependable.

fiacre [fjakr̥] *n.m.* (horse-drawn) hackney carriage, cab.

fiançailles [fjɑ̃sɑj] *n.m.pl.* engagement.

fiancé, -ée [fjɑ̃se] *n.* fiancé, fiancée.

fiancer (se) [səfjɑ̃se] *v.p.r.* to become, get, engaged.

fiasco [fjasko] *n.m.inv.* fiasco; *F:* flop; **faire f.,** (*of plan*) to come to nothing; (*of film*) to be a flop.

fibranne [fibran] *n.m. Tex:* staple fibre, *NAm:* fiber.

fibre [fibr̥] *n.f.* fibre, *NAm:* fiber; (*a*) grain (of wood); **coton à fibres longues,** long-staple cotton; **f. de verre,** glass fibre, fibreglass, *NAm:* fiberglass; (*b*) **avoir la f. sensible,** to be susceptible, impressionable.

fibreux, -euse [fibrø, -øz] *a.* fibrous; stringy.

fibrille [fibrij] *n.f. Physiol: Bot:* fibril(la).

fibrine [fibrin] *n.f. Physiol:* fibrin.

fibrineux, -euse [fibrinø, -øz] *a.* fibrinous.

fibroïde [fibrɔid] *a. & n.m.* fibroid (tumour).

fibrome [fibrom] *n.m.* fibroma, fibrous tumour; *F:* fibroid.

ficaire [fikɛr] *n.f. Bot:* lesser celandine; pilewort.

ficelé [fisle] *a.* **mal f.,** (i) badly tied up; (ii) *F:* badly dressed.

ficeler [fisle] *v.tr.* **(je ficelle; je ficellerai)** to tie up, do up, (parcel, etc.) with string.

ficelle [fisɛl] *n.f.* **1.** (*a*) (i) string, twine; (ii) pack thread; **f. à fouet,** whipcord; (*b*) **c'est lui qui tient, tire, les ficelles,** he's the one who pulls the strings; **connaître les ficelles,** to know the ropes, all the tricks of the trade. **2.** long, very thin loaf (of bread).

fiche [fiʃ] *n.f.* **1.** (*a*) peg, pin (of iron, wood, etc.); stake; *Surv:* arrow, chain pin; (*b*) *El:* plug; **mettre la f. dans la prise de contact,** to plug in the connection; *Tp:* **f. d'appel,** calling plug; jack. **2.** (*a*) docket; slip (of paper); memorandum slip, sheet; voucher; **f. scolaire,** school record card; *Ind:* **f. de contrôle,** checking form, docket; **f. dentaire,** dental chart; *Adm:* **f. anthropométrique** = (criminal's) dossier; (*b*) (index) card; **jeu de fiches,** card index; **mettre des informations sur fiches,** to card(-index) data; (*c*) tie-on label. **3.** *Cards: etc:* (bone, ivory) counter, marker; fish; *F:* **f. de consolation,** crumb of comfort.

ficher [fiʃe] **I.** *v.tr.* **1.** to drive in (nail, etc.); **f. une épingle dans qch.,** to stick a pin into sth.; *F:* **f. les yeux sur qch.,** to fix, fasten, one's eyes on sth. **2.** to card(-index). **3.** *F:* (*inf. usu.* **fiche;** *p.p.* **fichu**) (*a*) (= METTRE) **fiche(r) qn à la porte, son chapeau par terre,** to throw, chuck, s.o. out, one's hat on the ground; to sack, fire, s.o.; **fiche(r) qn dedans,** to cheat s.o., take s.o. in; (*b*) (= FAIRE) **il n'a rien fichu de la journée,** he hasn't done a stroke all day; (*c*) (= DONNER) **f. une gifle à qn,** to slap s.o. in the face; **fiche-moi la paix!** shut up! (*d*) **fiche(r) le camp,** to escape, get away, make off, *F:* buzz off; *P:* **va te faire fiche!** get to hell out of here! scram! **II. se f.,** *F:* (*inf., usu.* **se fiche;** *p.p.* **fichu**) **1.** (*a*) **se f. par terre,** to fall, go sprawling; (*b*) **se f. dedans,** to make a mistake. **2.** (*a*) **se fiche(r) de qn, de qch.,** to make fun of s.o., sth.; **vous vous fichez de moi,** you must be joking; (*b*) **je m'en fiche pas mal!** I don't give a damn! I couldn't care less!

fichet [fiʃɛ] *n.m.* peg (used for backgammon).

fichier [fiʃje] *n.m.* (*a*) card index; *Cmptr:* file; (*b*) card-index cabinet, box.

fichiste [fiʃist] *n.* filing clerk; card indexer.

fichtre [fiʃtr̥] *int. F:* (*a*) (*admiration*) good heavens! well . . .! (*b*) (*annoyance*) blast! hell! (*c*) (*intensive*) **f. oui!** of course! I should say so! **f. non!** not likely! no fear!

fichtrement [fiʃtrəmɑ̃] *adv. F:* extremely, awfully; **c'est f. bien,** it's damn good.

fichu¹ [fiʃy] *a. F:* **1.** rotten, awful; **quel f. pays!** what a god-forsaken country! **quel f. temps!** what filthy weather! **2. il est f.,** he's done for; it's all up with him; he's had it; **ma robe est fichue,** my dress is ruined. **3. être bien f.,** to be well dressed, well turned out; **être mal f.,** to be off colour, out of sorts. **4. f. de faire qch.,** capable of doing sth., able to do sth.

fichu² *n.m.* small shawl; fichu.

fictif, -ive [fiktif, -iv] *a.* **1.** fictitious, imaginary (person, etc.); *n.m.* **le réel et le f.,** truth and fiction. **2.** (*a*) false, fictitious; sham (fight); (*b*) *Fin:* **valeur fictive,** face value (of notes).

fiction [fiksjɔ̃] *n.f.* fiction; **f. légale,** legal fiction.

fictivement [fiktivmɑ̃] *adv.* fictitiously.

fidéicommis [fideikɔmi] *n.m. Jur:* trust.

fidéicommissaire [fideikɔmisɛr] *n.m. Jur:* beneficiary (of a trust).

fidèle [fidɛl] **1.** *a.* (*a*) faithful, loyal (friend, etc.); staunch (supporter); **lecteur f.,** regular reader (of newspaper); **rester f. à une promesse,** to stand by, keep, a promise; **peu f.,** unreliable; (*b*) faithful, accurate (copy, etc.); **mémoire f.,** reliable memory; **témoin f.,** accurate witness. **2.** *n.* (loyal) supporter; *Com:* regular customer; *Ecc:* **les fidèles,** (i) the faithful; (ii) the congregation.

fidèlement [fidɛlmɑ̃] *adv.* faithfully; (*a*) loyally; (*b*) accurately.

fidélité [fidelite] *n.f.* (*a*) faithfulness; fidelity; trustworthiness (of employee); **serment de f.,** oath of allegiance; (*b*) accuracy, closeness (of translation); accuracy (in reporting); reliability (of memory); *Rec:* **haute f.,** high fidelity, hi-fi.

fiduciaire [fidysjɛr] **1.** *a.* fiduciary (loan, etc.); (legacy, etc.) held in trust; **circulation f., monnaie f.,** fiduciary currency, paper money. **2.** *n.m.* fiduciary, trustee.

fiduciairement [fidysjɛrmɑ̃] *adv.* in trust.

fief [fjɛf] *n.m.* (*a*) *Jur: A:* fief, feoff, fee; **franc f.,** freehold; (*b*) **f. électoral,** (loyal) constituency.

fieffé [fjefe] *a.* arrant (liar, etc.); rank (impostor); out-and-out (scoundrel).

fiel [fjɛl] *n.m.* (*a*) gall (of ox, etc.); (*b*) bitterness, venom, malice; **épancher son f.,** to vent one's spleen.

fielleux, -euse [fjɛlø, -øz] *a.* rancorous, bitter.

fiente [fjɑ̃t] *n.f.* droppings (of birds); dung (of cattle).

fienter [fjɑ̃te] *v.i.* (*of cattle, etc.*) to dung.

fier¹, -ère [fjɛr] *a.* **1.** proud; high-minded; **courage f.,** lofty courage; **être trop f. pour mendier,** to be too proud to beg; **être f. de qch., d'avoir fait qch.,** to be proud of sth., of having done sth. **2.** proud, haughty, **air f.,** lordly air; **faire le f.,** to show off; **il n'y a pas là de quoi être f.,** that's nothing to boast about; **f. comme Artaban,** as proud as a peacock. **3.** fine, famous; **tu m'as fait une fière peur,** a fine, rare, fright you gave me.

fier² (se) [səfje] *v.pr.* (*impf. & pr.sub.* **n. n. fiions**) to trust; **se f. à qn,** to rely on s.o., to trust s.o.; **fiez-vous à moi,** leave it to me; **ne pas se f. à ses yeux,** not to believe one's eyes; **je me fie à lui pour décider,** I am depending on him for a decision; **ne vous y fiez pas,** (i) beware! (ii) don't count on it.

fièrement [fjɛrmɑ̃] *adv.* **1.** proudly. **2.** *A:* haughtily. **3.** *O:* famously, properly.

fierté [fjɛrte] *n.f.* pride (in sth., of pers.). **1.** (*a*) haughtiness; (*b*) *O:* vanity **2.** *Lit:* self respect.

fièvre [fjɛvr̥] *n.f.* **1.** fever; **avoir une f. de cheval,** to have a raging fever; **avoir (de) la f.,** to be feverish, have a (high) temperature; **f. des foins,** hay fever; **f. paludéenne,** malaria. **2.** (*a*) excitement, restlessness; **sans f.,** calmly; **dans la f. de la campagne électorale,** in the heat of the electoral campaign; **travailler avec f.,** to work feverishly; (*b*) passion (**de qch.,** for sth.); urge (**de faire qch.,** to do sth.).

fiévreusement [fjevrøzmɑ̃] *adv.* feverishly; frantically.

fiévreux, -euse [fjevrø, -øz] *a.* (*a*) feverish (pulse, etc.); *b*) feverish (activity, etc.); (*of pers.*) excited; frantic; *F:* worked up.

fifre [fifr̥] *n.m.* **1.** fife. **2.** fife (player).

figer [fiʒe] **1.** *v.tr.* (**figeant, il figeait**) (*a*) (*of blood, oil*) to coagulate, congeal; **cris qui vous figent le sang,** blood-curdling cries; **figé sur place,** rooted to the spot; spellbound; **locution figée,** set phrase. **2. se f.,** to stand still; (*of oil, blood*) to coagulate, congeal; (*of blood*) to clot; (*of the features*) to set; **son sang se figea,** his blood ran cold.

fignolage [fiɲɔlaʒ] *n.m. F:* (*a*) fiddling (over a job); (*b*) finickiness.

fignoler [fiɲɔle] *v.tr. F:* to fiddle, be finicky, too thorough, over (a job).

fignoleur, -euse [fiɲɔlœr, -øz] *a. & n.* finical, finicky (worker).

figue [fig] *n.f.* **1.** fig; **mi-f., mi-raisin,** half one thing and half another; wavering; **un petit sourire mi-f., mi-raisin,** a wry, forced smile; **ton mi-f., mi-raisin,** tone (of voice), half in jest half in earnest; **ce n'est ni f. ni raisin,** it's neither one thing nor the other. **2. f. de Barbarie,** prickly pear.

figuier [figje] *n.m.* **1.** fig tree. **2. f. de Barbarie,** prickly pear (tree).

figurant, -ante [figyrɑ̃, -ɑ̃t] *n. Th: Cin:* walker-on, extra, supernumerary; *F:* super; **les figurants,** the crowd; **rôle de f.,** walk-on part, bit part; **n'être qu'un f. dans qch.,** to take no active part, be just an on-looker, in sth.

figuratif, -ive [figyratif, -iv] *a.* (*a*) figurative; emblematic; (*b*) **art f.,** representational art.

figuration [figyrasjɔ̃] *n.f.* **1.** (*a*) figuration, representation; **f. d'un son par un symbole,** notation of a sound by a symbol; (*b*) *Elcs:* **figurations de grandes dimensions,** large-size displays. **2.** *Th:* supers, extras.

figurativement [figyrativmɑ̃] *adv.* figuratively.

figure [figyr] *n.f.* **1.** figure; (*a*) **portrait de demi-f.,** half-length portrait; **figures de cire,** waxworks; **f. de proue,** figurehead (of ship); *Cards:* **les figures,** the court cards; **prendre f.,** to take shape; **les grandes figures de la Guerre,** the great figures of the War; **faire f. de richesse,** to give an impression, keep up an appearance, of wealth; **faire pauvre, piètre, f.,** to cut a sorry figure; **faire grande f. dans une entreprise,** to play an important role in a business; (*b*) **figures géométriques,** geometrical figures; **livre avec figures dans le texte,** book with figures, diagrams, in the text; **f. de dance,** dance figure; (*c*) **f. de mots, de rhétorique,** figure of speech. **2.** face, countenance; **jeter qch. à la f. de qn,** to throw sth. in s.o.'s face; **faire bonne f. à qn,** to give s.o. a warm welcome; **faire longue f.,** to pull a long face.

figuré [figyre] *a.* **1.** bearing, using, figures, diagrams; figured (material). **2. sens f.,** figurative meaning; **au f.,** in the figurative sense; figuratively.

figurément [figyremɑ̃] *adv.* figuratively.

figurer [figyre] **1.** *v.tr.* to represent; **une croix figure une église,** a cross stands for, indicates, a church; **la scène figure le camp des brigands,** the scene shows the brigands' camp; **f. un personnage sur la scène,** to act, take the part of, a character. **2.** *v.i.* **je ne veux pas que mon nom figure dans l'affaire,** I don't want my name to appear, figure, in the matter; **f. dans un catalogue,** to be listed in a catalogue; *Th:* **f. sur la scène,** to walk on. **3. se f. qch.,** to imagine, fancy, sth.; **figurez-vous la situation,** picture the situation to yourself; **ne vous figurez pas que je sois satisfait,** do not imagine that I'm satisfied; **je suis à sec, figure-toi,** believe it or not, I'm broke.

figurine [figyrin] *n.f.* figurine, statuette.

fil [fil] *n.m.* **1.** (*a*) thread; yarn; **f. de coton, de nylon,** cotton, nylon, yarn; **f. de lin,** linen yarn, thread; **des draps pur f.,** (pure) linen sheets; **f. d'emballage,** pack(ing) thread; **f. d'Écosse,** lisle thread; **bas de f.,** lisle stockings; **gants de f.,** cotton gloves; **laine trois, quatre, fils,** three-ply, four-ply, wool; **f. à coudre,** sewing thread; cotton; **f. à boutons, gros f.,** button thread; **finesse cousue de f. blanc,** obvious trick; **de f. en aiguille,** little by little; gradually; **brouiller les fils,** to muddle things up; **démêler les fils d'une intrigue,** to unravel the threads of a plot; **avoir un f. sur la langue,** to have a lisp; **trouver le f. d'Ariane, le f. conducteur,** to find the clue (to the mystery); (*b*) strand (of cable, rope); **fils de marionnette,** puppet strings; **c'est lui qui tient les fils,** he's the one who can pull the strings; **être dans le droit f. de qch.,** to be in line with sth.; *Fish:* **donner du f. au poisson,** to give the fish some line; **sa vie ne tenait qu'à un f.,** his life hung by a thread; *F:* **avoir un f. à la patte,** to be tied up (with s.o.); (*c*) **f. d'araignée,** spider's thread; **fils de la vierge,** gossamer. **2. f. métallique, de fer,** wire; *F:* **il n'a pas inventé le f. à couper le beurre** = he'll never set the Thames on fire; *El:* **f. souple,** flexible wire, flex; **f. d'arrivée (de courant),** (electric) lead; **f. de masse, de terre,** earth (wire), *NAm:* ground wire; *Tp:* **donner un coup de f. à qn,** to give s.o. a ring, ring s.o. up; to call s.o.; **être au bout du f.,** to be on the line, on the phone; **je viens d'avoir Martin au bout du f.,** I've just had Martin on the line; I've just (i) been through to, called, (ii) had a call from, Martin; **télégraphie, téléphonie, sans f.,** wireless telegraphy, telephony. **3.** grain (of wood, meat); **contre le f., à contre-f.,** against, across, the grain; **couper (qch.) de droit f.,** to cut (wood) along the grain, (cloth) on the straight. **4.** (*a*) **au f. de l'eau,** with the current, downstream; **se laisser aller au f. de l'eau,** to let oneself drift (with the current); **au f. des jours,** day after day; (*b*) **le f. des événements,** the chain of events; **perdre, reprendre, le f. de la conversation,** to lose, pick up, the thread of the conversation. **5.** edge (of knife, sword); **donner le f. à un rasoir,** to put an edge on a razor; *Lit:* **passer des prisonniers au f. de l'épée,** to put prisoners to the sword.

filage [filaʒ] *n.m.* spinning (of wool, etc.).

filament [filamɑ̃] *n.m.* filament, fibre, *NAm:* fiber (of plant, meat); filament (of electric lamp).

filamenteux, -euse [filamɑ̃tø, -øz] *a.* filamentous; fibrous; *F:* stringy (meat, etc.).

filandière [filɑ̃djɛr] *n.f. A:* spinner.

filandreux, -euse [filɑ̃drø, -øz] *a.* (*a*) (*of meat, etc.*) tough, stringy; (*b*) involved, confused (explanation).

filant [filɑ̃] *a.* **1.** fluid. **2. étoile filante,** shooting star, falling star.

filasse [filas] *n.f.* **1.** tow; **aux cheveux blond f.,** tow-headed. **2.** oakum.

filateur, -trice [filatœr, -tris] *n.* spinner; owner of a spinning mill.

filature [filatyr] *n.f.* **1.** spinning. **2.** spinning mill, factory; **f. de coton,** cotton mill. **3.** shadowing, trailing (by detective, etc.).

file [fil] *n.f.* file (of soldiers, etc.); **chef de f.,** (i) front-rank man, file leader; (ii) leader (of a party, etc.); **aller à la f.,** to go in file, one behind another; **en, à**

la, f. indienne, in Indian, single, file; **deux heures à la f.,** two hours on end; **fumeur de cigarettes à la f.,** chain-smoker; **sortir, entrer, à la f.,** to file out, in; **prendre la, sa, f.,** to line up, queue up; **stationner en double f.,** to double-park; *Navy:* **en ligne de f.,** (single) line ahead; *Mil:* **par f. à droite! à gauche!** right, left, wheel!

filé [file] *n.m.* thread; **f. (de coton),** yarn; **f. d'or,** gold thread.

filer [file] **I.** *v.tr.* **1.** to spin (cotton, etc.). **2.** (*a*) *Nau:* to pay out, run out (cable); to slip (moorings); to heave (the lead); (*b*) to prolong, spin out, draw out (story, etc.); to pour out (oil) in a trickle; **f. des jours heureux,** to spend, pass, happy days; *Cards:* **f. les cartes,** to lay the cards down slowly. **3.** (*of detective, etc.*) to shadow, tail, trail (s.o.). **4.** *F:* **f. qch. à qn,** to slip, give, s.o. sth.; to land s.o. (a blow). **II.** *v.i.* **1.** (*a*) to flow smoothly; (*of oil, etc.*) to run; (*of wine*) to rope; (*b*) **la lampe file,** the lamp is smoking; (*c*) *F:* **f. doux,** to sing small, to obey without a word; (*d*) **j'ai une maille qui file,** I've got a ladder, run, (in my stocking). **2.** (*a*) to slip by, move past; **le temps file,** time flies; **laisser f. un câble,** to pay out a cable; **train qui file à toute vitesse,** train rushing along at full speed; **les voitures filaient sur la route,** cars were speeding along the road; *Nau:* **f. (à) vingt nœuds,** to proceed at twenty knots; (*b*) **il a filé,** he made a bolt for it, he made tracks; **f. (en vitesse),** to cut and run; **allez, filez!** buzz off! go on! scram! **f. à l'anglaise,** to take French leave; **f. (en douceur),** to slip away.

filet¹ [filɛ] *n.m.* **1.** small, fine, thread; (*a*) thin streak (of light); thin stream (of air); thin trickle, thin jet, (of water); **f. de voix,** thin, weak, voice; (*b*) **ajoutez-y un f. de citron,** add a dash of lemon; **f. d'une vis,** thread, worm, of a screw; (*c*) *Anat:* frenum; string (of the tongue); (*d*) *Bot:* filament (of stamen); (*e*) *Bookb: Arch:* fillet; (*f*) *Typ:* (brass) rule. **2.** *Cu:* fillet (of fish, beef, etc.). **3.** *Harn:* snaffle.

filet² *n.m.* net(ting); (*in a circus*) safety net; **f. de pêche,** fishing net; **f. à papillons,** butterfly net; **être pris au f.,** to be caught in the net; **faire tomber qn dans un f.,** to ensnare s.o.; **f. à provisions,** string bag; **f. pour cheveux,** hairnet; *Rail:* **f. à bagages,** luggage rack; *Ten:* **jeu au f.,** net play; **balle de f.,** let ball.

filetage [filtaʒ] *n.m.* (*a*) threading (of screw), screw cutting; (*b*) thread, pitch (of screw).

fileter [filte] *v.tr.* (**je filète; je filèterai**) **1.** to wire-(draw) (metal); to draw (wire). **2.** to worm, thread, screw (bolt, rod).

fileur, -euse [filœr, -øz] *n. Tex:* (*a*) spinner; (*b*) (silk) thrower, throwster.

filial, -aux [filjal, -o] **1.** *a.* filial; daughterly; **peu f.,** unfilial. **2.** *n.f.* (*a*) *Com:* subsidiary company; (*b*) provincial branch, offshoot (of association); (*c*) *Ecc:* daughter house.

filiation [filjasjɔ̃] *n.f.* **1.** (*a*) (af)filiation; **en f. directe,** in direct line; (*b*) descendants. **2.** dependence, relationship (between events, words).

filière [filjɛr] *n.f.* **1.** (*a*) (stock and) die; **f. simple, f. à truelle,** die plate, screw plate; (*b*) **f. (à étirer),** draw(ing) plate; **travailler un métal à la f.,** to draw a metal; *F:* **il a passé par la f.,** he has worked his way up; **la f. administrative,** the usual official channels. **2.** ridge rope (of tent); *Nau:* (man) rope; **f. d'envergure,** jackstay. **3.** spinneret (of spider, silkworm). **4.** *Com:* transfer note. **5.** *Atom.Ph:* line (of reactors).

filiforme [filifɔrm] *a.* filiform, threadlike.

filigrane [filigran] *n.m.* **1.** filigree (work). **2.** watermark (of banknotes, etc.); **f. ombré,** embossement; **lire en f.,** to read between the lines.

filigrané [filigrane] *a.* **1.** filigreed (brooch, etc.). **2.** watermarked (paper).

filin [filɛ̃] *n.m.* rope; **vieux f.,** junk.

fille [fij] *n.f.* **1.** daughter. **2.** (*a*) girl; **petite f.,** little girl; child; **jeune f.,** girl, young woman; **nom de jeune f.,** maiden name; **école de filles,** girls' school; **vieille f.,** old maid, spinster; **habitudes de vieille f.,** old-maidish habits; *O:* **rester f.,** to remain single, unmarried; (*b*) **f. d'honneur,** maid of honour (at Court); (*c*) **f. publique, de joie,** *F:* **f.,** prostitute. **3.** *Ecc:* **les filles de Port-Royal,** the sisters, nuns, of Port-Royal. **4. f. de service,** maidservant; **f. de cuisine,** kitchen-maid; **f. de salle,** (i) (*in hotel*) waitress; (ii) (*in hospital*) ward maid; **f. de comptoir,** barmaid. **5.** *P:* bottle of wine.

fille-mère [fijmɛr] *n.f. O:* unmarried mother; *pl. filles-mères.*

fillette [fijɛt] *n.f.* **1.** little girl. **2.** *F:* half-bottle (of wine).

filleul, -eule [fijœl] *n.* godchild; godson, *f.* goddaughter; **f. de guerre,** adopted godson, protégé (during the war).

film [film] *n.m.* **1.** (*a*) *Phot:* film; (*b*) *Cin:* film; picture; *NAm:* motion picture, *F:* movie; **f. d'actualité,** newsreel, news film; **f. annonce,** trailer; **f. supplémentaire,** supporting film; **f. fixe (d'enseignement),** filmstrip. **2.** film (of oil, etc.).

filmage [filmaʒ] *n.m. Cin:* filming, shooting.

filmer [filme] *v.tr.* **1.** to cover (sth.) with a film. **2.** *Cin:* to film, shoot (scene); to film (novel).

filmographie [filmɔgrafi] *n.f. Cin:* catalogue of films (made by producer, actor).

filmologie [filmɔlɔʒi] *n.f.* study of the cinema.

filmothèque [filmɔtɛk] *n.f.* film library.

filon [filɔ̃] *n.m.* (*a*) *Min:* vein, seam, lode (of metal, etc.); reef (of gold); (*b*) *P:* cushy job; **il tient le f., il a déniché, trouvé, le (bon) f.,** he's struck it rich.

filou [filu] *n.m.* (*a*) pickpocket, thief; (*b*) rogue, swindler; cheat; cardsharp.

filoutage [filutaʒ] *n.m.* (*a*) pocket picking; stealing; (*b*) swindling, cheating.

filouter [filute] *v.tr.* **1. f. qch. à qn,** to steal, *F:* pinch, sth. from s.o. **2. f. qn,** to swindle, cheat, s.o.

filouterie [filutri] *n.f.* **1.** = FILOUTAGE. **2.** swindle, fraud.

fils [fis] *n.m.* son; **ses deux f.,** her two boys; **f. à papa,** daddy's boy; young man with an influential father; **c'est bien le f. de son père,** he's a chip off the old block; **être le f. de ses œuvres,** to be a self-made man; **M. Duval f.,** Mr Duval junior; **le f. Duval,** young Duval.

filtrable [filtrabl̩] *a.* filt(e)rable (virus).

filtrage [filtraʒ] *n.m.* (*a*) filtering, straining (of liquid); (*b*) *El:* filtering, smoothing (of current); filtering, suppression (of sound); **chargement par f.,** trickle charging.

filtrant [filtrɑ̃] *a.* **1.** filtering; **bout f.,** filter tip (of cigarette). **2. virus f.,** filt(e)rable virus, filter passer.

filtration [filtrasjɔ̃] *n.f.* filtration, percolation.

filtre [filtr̩] *n.m.* filter, strainer; **(bout) f.,** filter tip (of cigarette); **f. à café,** coffee filter; **(café) f.,** drip coffee; **papier f.,** filter paper; **f. à air,** air filter, strainer, scrubber; *Phot:* **f. de couleur, coloré,** colour filter, screen; *W.Tel: T.V:* **f. anti-parasites,** interference filter, suppressor; bypass.

filtrer [filtre] **1.** *v.tr.* (*a*) to filter, strain; (*b*) *El:* to filter, smooth (current); *W.Tel:* to bypass (station); (*c*) *F:* to screen (visitors). **2.** *v.i. & pr.* (*of liquid*) **(se) f.** to filter, percolate, seep (**à travers,** through); **la lumière filtrait à travers, par, les branches,** the light filtered, stole, through the branches; **laisser f. une nouvelle,** to let a piece of news leak, filter, out.

fin¹ [fɛ̃] *n.f.* **1.** end, close, termination; expiration (of contract, etc.); **le cinquième avant, en commençant par, la f.,** the fifth from the end, the last but four; **la**

f. du jour, the close of day; **f. du mois,** end of the month; *Com:* **f. de mois,** monthly statement; **payable f. prochain,** payable at the end of next month; **en f. de soirée,** towards the end of the evening; **il est venu vers la f. de l'après-midi,** he came late in the afternoon; **l'année touche, tire, à sa f.,** the year is drawing to an end, a close; **en f. d'année,** at the end of the year; **jusqu'à la f. des temps, des siècles,** till the end of time; **style f. de siècle,** fin de siècle, decadent, style; **le vocabulaire est à la f. du livre,** the vocabulary is at the back of the book; **vis sans f.,** endless screw; **des activités sans f.,** never-ending, endless, activities; **il parle sans f.,** he never stops talking; **f. prématurée,** untimely death, end; **il est sur sa f.,** he hasn't much longer to live; **la maison est sur ses fins,** the firm is on its last legs; **mettre f. à qch.,** to put an end, a stop, to sth.; **mettre une entreprise à f.,** to bring an undertaking to an end, to complete an undertaking; (*of pers.*) **faire une f.,** to settle down; **prendre f., avoir une f.,** to come to an end; **mener une affaire à bonne f.,** to bring a matter to a successful conclusion; to deal successfully with a matter; **c'est la f.,** (i) this is the end; (ii) this is the last of it, of him, etc.; **c'est la f. de tout,** this is the last straw; **à la f. il répondit,** in the end, finally, at last, he answered; *F:* **tu es stupide à la f.!** you really are very stupid; **à la f. du compte, en f. de compte,** in the end; in the last resort; to cut a long story short; to sum up; *F:* **à la f. des fins,** when all's said and done. **2.** end, aim, purpose, object; (*a*) **la f. justifie les moyens,** the end justifies the means; **en venir, arriver, à ses fins,** to achieve one's aim, purpose; to get what one wants; **à cette f. il faut avoir beaucoup de patience,** in order to attain, achieve, this one must have a lot of patience; **à quelle f.?** for what purpose? with what end in view? **à deux fins,** dual-purpose; **à toutes fins,** for all purposes; all-purpose; **à toutes fins utiles,** (i) for whatever purpose it may serve; (ii) to whom it may concern; **aux fins de faire qch.,** with a view to doing sth.; **à seule(s) fin(s) de l'aider,** for the sole purpose of helping him; **aller à ses fins,** to pursue one's point; *Jur:* **aux fins de débauche,** for immoral purposes; (*b*) *Jur:* **renvoyer qn des fins de sa plainte,** to nonsuit s.o.; **renvoyé des fins de la plainte,** discharged, acquitted.

fin², fine [fɛ̃, fin] **1.** *a.* **dans le f. fond du hangar, du panier,** right at the back of the shed, at the very bottom of the basket; **au f. fond de la Sibérie,** in farthest Siberia. **2.** *a.* (*a*) fine; first-class; **vins fins,** choice wines; **or f.,** pure, fine, gold; **linge f.,** fine linen; (*b*) fine, subtle, discriminating; **f. connaisseur de vins,** fine judge of wine; **f. tireur,** crack shot; **fine ironie,** subtle irony; **avoir l'oreille fine,** to have sharp ears, an acute, a keen, ear; **f. comme l'ambre,** sharp as a needle; **il est trop f. pour vous,** he's too quick for you; **bien f. qui le prendra,** it would take a smart man to catch him; **plus f. que lui n'est pas bête,** *he's* no fool; (*c*) fine, small (rain, grains, etc.); fine (needle); delicate (features); slender (figure); neat (ankle, etc.). **3.** *n.m.* (*a*) **savoir le fort et le f. d'une affaire,** to know the ins and outs of sth.; **le f. de l'affaire,** the crux of the matter; **le f. du f.,** the ultimate, the ne plus ultra; (*b*) **jouer au (plus) f.,** to have a battle of wits; **f. contre f.,** diamond cut diamond; (*c*) fineness (of gold); (*d*) *Tex:* fine linen. **4.** *n.f.* **fine,** liqueur brandy; **une fine à l'eau** = a brandy and soda. **5.** *adv.* (*a*) **tout était f. prêt,** everything was absolutely ready; (*b*) finely; **café moulu f.,** finely ground coffee; **des crayons taillés f.,** sharp-pointed pencils.

final, -als [final] *a.* final. **1.** (*a*) last (letter, etc.); *Sp:* **les épreuves finales,** the finals; (*b*) ultimate; eventual. **2.** *Phil: Gram:* final (cause, clause).

finale [final] **1.** *n.f.* (*a*) end syllable (of word); (*b*) *Mus:* keynote, tonic; (*c*) *Sp:* final; **f. de coupe,** cup final. **2.** *n.m. Mus:* finale (of opera, etc.).

finalement [finalmɑ̃] *adv.* finally, at last, in the end; ultimately.

finaliste [finalist] *n. Sp:* finalist.

finalité [finalite] *n.f. Phil:* finality; *Biol:* adaptation.

finance [finɑ̃s] *n.f.* **1.** *A:* ready money; *F:* **faire qch. moyennant f.,** to do sth. for a consideration, for cash. **2.** finance; **monde de la f.,** financial world; **la haute f.,** (i) high finance; (ii) the financiers, the bankers. **3.** *pl.* finances, resources; **être mal dans ses finances,** to be hard up; **ministre des Finances,** minister of Finance = Chancellor of the Exchequer; **le Ministère des Finances** = the Treasury.

financer [finɑ̃se] *v.tr.* (**je finançai(s); n. finançons**) to finance (undertaking, etc.); to put up the money for (sth.), to back (s.o., sth.).

financier, -ière [finɑ̃sje, -jɛr] **1.** *a.* financial; **embarras financiers,** pecuniary difficulties; **le marché f.,** the money market. **2.** *n.m.* financier.

financièrement [finɑ̃sjɛrmɑ̃] *adv.* financially.

finasser [finase] *v.i.* to resort to trickery.

finasserie [finasri] *n.f.* **1.** trickery, artifice, cunning; *F:* hanky-panky. **2.** cunning move; **les finasseries du métier,** the tricks of the trade.

finasseur, -euse [finasœr, -øz], **finassier, -ière** [finasje, -jɛr] *n.* trickster.

finaud, -aude [fino, -od] **1.** *a.* wily, cunning (peasant, etc.). **2.** *n.* crafty type; wangler.

finauderie [finodri] *n.f.* trickery; cunning trick, dodge, wangle.

finement [finmɑ̃] *adv.* **1.** finely, delicately, well (executed, etc.). **2.** smartly, subtly; with finesse.

finesse [finɛs] *n.f.* **1.** fineness (of material, etc.); delicacy (of execution). **2.** (*a*) subtlety, shrewdness; **f. d'ouïe,** quickness, keenness, acuteness, of hearing; **f. de goût,** nicety, delicacy, of taste; **f. d'esprit,** shrewdness; **discours plein de f.,** speech full of finesse; **parodie pleine de f.,** clever, subtle, parody; **finesses d'un métier,** fine points, niceties, of a craft; (*b*) cunning, guile; **chercher f. (à qch.),** to look for snags; (*c*) trick. **3.** (*a*) fineness (of dust, etc.); slenderness, slimness (of waist, etc.); (*b*) sharpness (of point, optical image, etc.); keenness (of cutting edge).

fini [fini] **1.** *a.* (*a*) finished, over, done with; **c'est f. (tout cela), tout est f.,** that's all over (and done with); **c'est f. entre nous,** it's all over between us; **c'est f. de rire,** nobody is laughing now; **c'est un homme f.,** he's done for; (*b*) well finished (piece of work); accomplished (actor); **un idiot f.,** a complete idiot; (*c*) finite (space, tense, number). **2.** *n.m.* (*a*) finish (of manufactured article, etc.); (*b*) **le f. et l'infini,** the finite and the infinite.

finir [finir] **1.** *v.tr.* to finish, end (task, etc.); **f. un tableau, une sculpture,** to finish off a picture, sculpture. **2.** *v.i.* to end, come to an end, finish; **voir f. qch.,** to see sth. out, through; **f. en pointe,** to end, terminate, in a point; **il finira mal,** he will come to a bad end; **en f. avec qn, qch.,** to be, have, done with s.o., sth.; **je voudrais en f.,** I want to get it over (with); **cela n'en finit pas,** there's no end to it; **pour en f.,** to cut the matter short; **histoires à n'en plus f.,** (i) never-ending, interminable, stories; (ii) no end of stories; **f. de faire qch.,** to finish, leave off, stop, doing sth.; **cette route n'en finit pas,** this road seems to go on (and on) for ever; **f. par faire qch.,** to end in, by, doing sth.; **la justice finit par triompher,** justice triumphs in the end, in the long run, eventually.

finish [finiʃ] *n.m. Sp:* (*a*) finish; (*b*) final burst; **il a un bon f.,** he has a fast finish.

finissage [finisaʒ] *n.m. Ind:* finishing (off).

finissant [finisɑ̃] *a.* ending, finishing; (society) in decline; **le jour f.,** dusk, twilight, gloaming.

finisseur, -euse [finisœr, -øz] *n. Ind: Sp:* finisher.
finition [finisjɔ̃] *n.f. Ind:* finish; finishing; finishing touches.
finlandais, -aise [fɛ̃lɑ̃dɛ, -ɛz] *Geog:* **1.** *a.* Finnish. **2.** *n.* Finlander, Finn.
Finlande [fɛ̃lɑ̃d] *Pr.n.f. Geog:* Finland.
finnois, -oise [finwa, -waz]. **1.** *a.* Finnish. **2.** *n.m. Ling:* Finnish.
fiole [fjɔl] *n.f.* (*a*) phial, flask; (*b*) *P:* head, mug; **se payer la f. de qn,** to make a fool of s.o.
Fionie [fjɔni] *Pr.n. Geog:* Fyn.
fiord [fjɔr] *n.m. Geog:* fjord.
fioriture [fjɔrityr] *n.f.* (*a*) *Mus:* grace note(s); (*b*) flourish (to handwriting, etc.); embellishment (of style).
firmament [firmamɑ̃] *n.m. Lit:* firmament, sky.
firme [firm] *n.f.* (business) firm.
fisc [fisc] *n.m.* (*a*) the Treasury, the Exchequer; (*b*) the Inland Revenue; *F:* **les gens du f.,** income tax people.
fiscal, -aux [fiskal, -o] *a.* fiscal; **dans un but f.,** for purposes of revenue; **l'administration fiscale,** the taxation authorities; **timbre f.,** (Inland) Revenue stamp; **fraude fiscale,** tax evasion.
fiscalement [fiskalmɑ̃] *adv.* fiscally.
fiscaliser [fiskalize] *v.tr.* to tax.
fiscalité [fiskalite] *n.f.* fiscal system, policy.
fissible [fisibl̥] *a. Ph:* fissionable, fissile.
fissile [fisil] *a.* (*a*) fissile (rock); tending to split; (*b*) = FISSIBLE.
fission [fisjɔ̃] *n.f. Atom.Ph:* fission; **f. de l'atome,** atomic fission, splitting of the atom.
fissuration [fisyrasjɔ̃] *n.f.* cracking, fissuring.
fissure [fisyr] *n.f.* fissure, crack (in rock, etc.); split (between friends).
fissurer [fisyre] *v.tr.* to fissure, split, crack.
fiston [fistɔ̃] *n.m. F:* son, youngster; **allons (mon) f.!** now then, young fellow, my lad, sonny!
fistule [fistyl] *n.f. Med:* fistula.
fistuleux, -euse [fistylø, -øz] *a. Med:* fistulous.
fixage [fiksaʒ] *n.m.* fixing (of drawing, etc.); *Phot:* **bain de f.,** fixing bath.
fixateur [fiksatœr] *n.m.* fixer (of dyes, etc.); *Phot:* fixing solution, bath; *Biol:* fixative.
fixatif [fiksatif] *n.m.* (*a*) fixative (for drawings, etc.); (*b*) hair cream.
fixation [fiksasjɔ̃] *n.f.* **1.** fixing (of date, price, etc.). **2.** (*a*) fixing, attaching (of shelf, etc.); **f. par bride, par collier,** clamping; **vis de f.,** fixing screw, set screw; **patte de f.,** anchor(ing) clip; (*b*) fixation (of drifting sands, *Ch:* of nitrogen). **3.** (*a*) *Mec.E:* attachment, anchor; (*b*) (ski) binding. **4.** *Psy:* fixation (**à qn,** on s.o.).
fixe [fiks] *a.* **1.** fixed, firm; **grue f.,** fixed, stationary, crane; **idée f.,** fixed idea, obsession; **regard f.,** intent gaze; **essieu f.,** dead axle; *Mil:* **f.!** eyes front! **2.** fixed, regular, settled; **prix f.,** set price; **à prix f.,** at fixed prices; **traitement f.,** *n.m.* **f.,** fixed salary; **résidence f.,** permanent abode; **prendre ses repas à heure f.,** to eat at fixed, set, hours; **beau (temps) f.,** set fair (weather); *P.N:* **arrêt f.,** all buses stop here.
fixé [fikse] *a.* **1.** set, fixed, stated (time, etc.). **2.** (*a*) **être f. sur qch.,** to entertain no further doubts, have made up one's mind, about sth.; **ne pas être f.,** to have no fixed plans; (*b*) *Psy:* suffering from a fixation.
fixe-chaussettes [fiks(ə)ʃosɛt] *n.m.inv.* sock suspender(s); *NAm:* garter(s).
fixe-cravate [fiks(ə)kravat] *n.m.* tieclip; tie pin; *pl. fixe-cravates.*
fixement [fiksəmɑ̃] *adv.* fixedly; **regarder f. qch.,** to stare at sth.; to look hard, intently, at sth.
fixer [fikse] **1.** *v.tr.* (*a*) to fix; to make (sth.) firm, rigid, fast; to fasten, stabilize; **les vis qui fixent la serrure,** the screws that hold the lock; **f. qch. dans sa mémoire,** to fix sth. in one's memory; **f. l'attention de qn,** to engage, hold, arrest, s.o.'s attention; **f. les yeux sur qch.,** to fix one's eyes on sth.; to gaze, stare, at sth.; to look hard, intently, at sth.; to keep one's eye on sth.; **f. qn,** to stare at s.o.; (*b*) *Ch: Phot:* to fix; (*c*) to fix, determine; to set, appoint (time); to assess (damages, taxes); to lay down (conditions, rules); (*d*) **f. qn sur qch.,** to give s.o. definite information about sth. **2. se f.** (*a*) to settle down; **se f. dans un pays,** to settle in a country; (*b*) **se f. à une opinion,** to stick to an opinion.
fixisme [fiksism] *n.m. Biol:* creationism.
fixité [fiksite] *n.f.* fixity; steadiness (of gaze).
fjord [fjɔr] *n.m. Geog:* fjord.
flac [flak] *n.m. & int.* plop, slap; **faire f.,** to plop.
flaccidité [flaksidite] *n.f.* flaccidity, flabbiness, limpness.
flache [flaʃ] *n.f.* (*a*) (pot)hole; depression (in pavement, road); (*b*) **f. (d'eau),** puddle.
flacon [flakɔ̃] *n.m.* small (stoppered) bottle; flask; **f. à parfum,** scent bottle; **f. à liqueur,** liqueur decanter.
fla-fla [flafla] *n.m. F:* ostentation, show; *Cost:* trimmings; **faire du f.-f.,** to show off, make a show.
flagellation [flaʒɛlasjɔ̃] *n.f.* flagellation, scourging, whipping, flogging.
flagellé [flaʒɛle] *a. & n.m. Biol:* flagellate.
flageller [flaʒɛle] *v.tr.* to scourge, flog, whip.
flageoler [flaʒɔle] *v.i.* (*of legs*) to shake, tremble, give way.
flageolet[1] [flaʒɔlɛ] *n.m. Mus:* flageolet.
flageolet[2] *n.m.* flageolet, (small) kidney bean.
flagorner [flagɔrne] *v.tr.* to flatter; to toady, suck up, to (s.o.).
flagornerie [flagɔrnəri] *n.f.* flattery, toadyism.
flagorneur, -euse [flagɔrnœr, -øz] *n.* flatterer, toady, creep.
flagrant [flagrɑ̃] *a.* flagrant, glaring (injustice, etc.); **pris en f. délit,** caught in the act, red-handed; *F:* **c'est f.!** it's (glaringly) obvious!
flair [flɛr] *n.m.* (*a*) (*of dogs*) scent, (sense of) smell; nose; (*b*) (*of pers.*) intuition; **avoir du f.,** to have a gift for nosing things out.
flairer [flere] *v.tr.* (*a*) (*of dog*) to scent, smell (out), nose out (game); **f. le danger,** to scent, smell, suspect, danger; (*b*) to smell, sniff (at) (sth.).
flamand, -ande [flamɑ̃, -ɑ̃d] **1.** *a.* Flemish. **2.** *n.* Fleming. **3.** *n.m. Ling:* Flemish.
flamant [flamɑ̃] *n.m. Orn:* flamingo.
flambage [flɑ̃baʒ] *n.m.* **1.** (*a*) singeing (of hair, chicken, etc.); sterilization (of needle); charring (of stake, etc.). **2.** buckling, collapse (of metal plate, etc.).
flambant [flɑ̃bɑ̃] *a.* **1.** blazing, flaming (log, sun); *adv.* **manteau f. neuf, robe f. neuve,** brand new coat, dress. **2. houille flambante,** *n.m.* **f.,** bituminous, soft, coal.
flambard [flɑ̃bar] *n.m.* **faire le f.,** to show off.
flambé [flɑ̃be] *a.* (*a*) *Cu:* flambé; (*b*) *F:* **il est f.,** he's done for; his goose is cooked.
flambeau, -eaux [flɑ̃bo] *n.m.* **1.** torch; **à la lueur des flambeaux, aux flambeaux,** by torchlight. **2.** candlestick, candelabra.
flambée [flɑ̃be] *n.f.* **1.** blaze, blazing fire. **2.** outbreak (of violence); rocketing (of prices).
flambement [flɑ̃bmɑ̃] *n.m.* buckling, collapse (of metal plate, etc.).
flamber [flɑ̃be] **1.** *v.i.* (*a*) to flame, blaze; to be ablaze; **faire f. le feu,** to make the fire burn up, to stir the fire into a blaze; **f. comme une allumette,** to burn like matchwood; (*b*) (*of metal bar, etc.*) to buckle, yield. **2.** *v.tr.* to singe (hair, fowl, etc.); to

char (stake, etc.); **f. une aiguille,** to sterilize a needle (in a flame).

flamboiement [flɑ̃bwamɑ̃] *n.m.* flaming; blazing, blaze.

flamboyant [flɑ̃bwajɑ̃] *a.* **1.** flaming, blazing (fire); blazing (eyes). **2.** (*a*) *Arch:* flamboyant; (*b*) *Journ:* **des titres flamboyants,** banner headlines.

flamboyer [flɑ̃bwaje] *v.i.* **(il flamboie)** (*of fire*) to blaze; (*of eyes*) **f. de colère,** to blaze, flash, with anger.

flamingant, -ante [flamɛ̃gɑ̃, -ɑ̃t] **1.** *a.* Flemish-speaking (town, person). **2.** *n. Pol:* Flemish nationalist.

flamme [flam] *n.f.* **1.** (*a*) flame; **en flammes,** on fire, ablaze; **par le fer et la f.,** with fire and sword; **jeter feu et f.,** to fly into a rage; **retour de f.,** (i) back flash (from gun); (ii) *I.C.E:* backfire, backfiring; **donner des retours de f.,** to backfire; (*of gas stove*) **avoir des retours de f.,** to flash back; **pointe de f.,** flashpoint (of petrol); **passer à la f.,** to singe; (*b*) *Lit:* passion, love; (*c*) fire, enthusiasm; **discours plein de f.,** fiery speech. **2.** *Mil: etc:* pennant, pendant, pennon, streamer. **3.** *Post:* slogan (accompanying postmark).

flammèche [flamɛʃ] *n.f.* spark (of fire).

flan [flɑ̃] *n.m.* **1.** *Cu:* baked custard; *P:* **c'est du f.,** it's a lot of eyewash! **rester, être, comme deux ronds de f.,** to be flabbergasted. **2.** blank (of coin, gramophone record, etc.). **3.** *Typ:* mould, *NAm:* mold. **4.** *P:* **travail (fait) à la f.,** work done anyhow, in a happy-go-lucky fashion; **j'ai dit ça au f.,** I said that for the sake of saying something.

flanc [flɑ̃] *n.m.* flank, side; wall (of tyre); **route à f. de coteau,** road following the hillside; **être sur le f.,** (i) to be laid up (in bed); (ii) to be quite worn out; **se battre les flancs,** (i) (*of tiger, etc.*) to lash its tail; (ii) to waste one's energy; (*of horse*) **battre des flancs,** to heave, pant; *Mil:* **par le f. droit!** by the right! **attaquer de f.,** to attack on the flank; **le navire se présentait de f.,** the ship was broadside on (to us); **prêter le f. à la critique,** to lay oneself open to criticism; *Mil: P:* **tirer au f.,** to malinger, swing the lead.

flancher [flɑ̃ʃe] *v.i. F:* **1.** (*a*) to flinch; to give in; (*b*) to rat; to quit. **2.** (*a*) (*of car, etc.*) to break down; (*b*) **j'ai flanché en histoire,** I did badly, came a cropper, in history.

flanchet [flɑ̃ʃɛ] *n.m. Cu:* flank (of beef).

Flandre [flɑ̃dr̥] *Pr.n.f. Geog:* Flanders.

flandrin [flɑ̃drɛ̃] *n.m. F:* **grand f.,** tall, lanky, fellow; great lout of a fellow.

flanelle [flanɛl] *n.f.* flannel; **f. (de) coton,** flannelette; **pantalon de f. gris(e),** grey flannels.

flâner [flɑne] *v.i.* (*a*) to stroll, dawdle, saunter; (*b*) **perdre son temps à f.,** to idle away one's time.

flânerie [flɑnri] *n.f.* (*a*) dawdling, strolling; (*b*) idling.

flâneur, -euse [flɑnœr, -øz] *n.* (*a*) stroller, saunterer; (*b*) loafer, idler.

flanquer[1] [flɑ̃ke] *v.tr.* to flank (building, etc.; *Mil:* a column, the enemy); **flanqué de deux agents,** between, flanked by, two policemen.

flanquer[2] *v.tr. F:* to throw, pitch, chuck; **f. une gifle, un coup de pied, à qn,** to give s.o. a slap, land s.o. a kick; **f. qn à la porte,** (i) to throw s.o. out; (ii) to fire, sack, s.o.; **f. la trouille à qn,** to give s.o. the jitters; **se f. par terre,** to fall flat, come a cropper.

flapi [flapi] *a. F:* tired, fagged out, jaded.

flaque [flak] *n.f.* puddle, pool.

flash, *pl.* **flashes** [flaʃ] *n.m.* **1.** *Phot:* flash(light). **2.** *Cin:* shot, flash. **3.** (news)flash.

flasque[1] [flask] *a.* flaccid (flesh); flabby (hand, style); limp (cloth, style); floppy (hat); **se sentir f.,** to feel limp.

flasque[2] *n.f.* flask.

flasque[3] *n.m.* **1.** cheek (of gun carriage); cheek web (of crank). **2.** *pl. Nau:* whelps (of capstan). **3.** *Aut:* wheel disc.

flatter [flate] **1.** *v.tr.* (*a*) to stroke, caress; **f. un cheval,** to pat a horse; (*b*) to delight, please, charm; **spectacle qui flatte les yeux,** sight that is pleasant to the eye; **vers qui flatte l'oreille,** verse that falls pleasingly on the ear; **f. les caprices de qn,** to humour, indulge, s.o.'s fancies; (*c*) to delude; **f. qn de l'espoir de qch.,** to hold out the hope, false hopes, of sth. to s.o; (*d*) to flatter, compliment; **f. qn sur son bel esprit,** to flatter s.o. on his wit; **être flatté de qch.,** to feel flattered by sth.; **peintre qui flatte ses modèles,** painter who flatters his sitters. **2. se f.,** to flatter oneself, delude oneself; **elle se flattait de réussir,** she flattered herself, felt sure, that she would succeed; **il se flatte qu'on a besoin de lui,** he flatters himself that he is indispensable; **se f. de son habileté,** to congratulate oneself on one's cleverness; **se f. d'avoir fait qch.,** to take the credit, *F:* pat oneself on the back, for having done sth.

flatterie [flatri] *n.f.* flattery.

flatteur, -euse [flatœr, -øz] **1.** *a.* (*a*) pleasing, pleasant (taste, etc.); (*b*) flattering (remark, portrait); (*of pers*) full of flattery; **peu f.,** unflattering. **2.** *n.* flatterer.

flatteusement [flatøzmɑ̃] *adv.* flatteringly.

flatulence [flatylɑ̃s] *n.f. Med:* flatulence; *F:* wind.

flatulent [flatylɑ̃] *a. Med:* flatulent.

flatuosité [flatɥozite] *n.f. Med:* flatus; *F:* wind.

fléau, -aux [fleo] *n.m.* **1.** flail. **2.** scourge; plague, pest, curse, bane; *F:* **c'est un vrai f.!** he's a real pest! **3.** beam, arm (of balance).

fléchage [fleʃaʒ] *n.m.* arrowing (of direction).

flèche[1] [flɛʃ] *n.f.* **1.** (*a*) arrow; shaft (of satire); **fer de f.,** arrowhead; **faire f. de tout bois,** to leave no stone unturned; (*of pers.*) **partir en f., comme une f.,** to shoot off; **monter en f.,** (*of aircraft, etc.*) to shoot (straight) up; (*of prices*) to rocket; (*b*) direction sign, arrow; *A. Aut:* **f. de direction,** trafficator; (*c*) **chevaux en f.,** horses driven tandem; **cheval de f.,** leader; (*of pers.*) **se trouver en f.,** to be prominent (in a group); (*d*) spit (of land). **2.** (*a*) spire (of church); (*b*) jib, boom (of crane); (*c*) *Nau:* pole (of mast); topsail (of cutter). **3.** (*a*) *Arch:* rise (of arch); *Av:* camber (of aerofoil); (*b*) sag, dip (of cable, etc.); **faire f.,** to sag, dip.

flèche[2] *n.f.* flitch (of bacon).

flécher [fleʃe] *v.tr.* to arrow (route, direction).

fléchette [fleʃɛt] *n.f. Games:* dart.

fléchir [fleʃir] **1.** *v.tr.* (*a*) to bend, flex (arm, etc.); **f. le genou devant qn,** to bend, bow, the knee to s.o.; (*b*) to move (s.o.) (to pity, mercy); **se laisser f.,** to let oneself be swayed; to relent. **2.** *v.i.* (*a*) to give way, bend; (*of legs, troops, etc.*) to give way; (*of cable, beam*) to sag; (*b*) (*of sound, current, etc.*) to grow weaker; **les prix fléchissent,** prices are coming down.

fléchissement [fleʃismɑ̃] *n.m.* **1.** bending (of the knee, etc.). **2.** (*a*) yielding, bending (of girder, etc.); sagging (of cable, etc.); (*b*) weakening (of sound, current); (*c*) falling, easing (of prices).

fléchisseur [fleʃisœr] *a. & n.m. Anat:* **(muscle) f.,** flexor.

flegmatique [flɛgmatik] *a.* phlegmatic; calm, imperturbable, stolid.

flegmatiquement [flɛgmatikmɑ̃] *adv.* phlegmatically, imperturbably, stolidly.

flegme [flɛgm] *n.m.* **1.** *Med:* phlegm. **2.** coolness, stolidness, imperturbability.

flémard, flemmard, -arde [flemar, -ard] *F:* **1.** *a.* idle, indolent, lazy. **2.** *n.* idler, slacker.

flemmarder [flemarde] *v.i. F:* to laze, idle, slack.

flemme [flɛm] *n.f. F:* laziness, idleness; slacking; **j'ai la f. de le faire,** I can't be bothered with it, to do it.
flet [flɛ] *n.m. Ich:* flounder.
flétan [fletɑ̃] *n.m. Ich:* halibut.
flétrir[1] [fletrir] **1.** *v.tr.* to fade, wilt; to make (colours, etc.) fade; to wither (up) (plants). **2. se f.,** (*of colours, etc.*) to fade; (*of plants*) to wither, wilt; (*of skin*) to shrivel.
flétrir[2] *v.tr.* **1.** to brand (criminal); to stigmatize (crime, etc.). **2.** to sully, stain, cast a slur on (s.o.'s character).
flétrissure [fletrisyr] *n.f.* fading; withering.
fleur [flœr] *n.f.* **1.** flower; (*a*) blossom, bloom; **arbre en fleur(s),** tree in blossom, in flower; **fleurs des champs,** wild flowers; **ni fleurs, ni couronnes,** no flowers by request; **tissu à fleurs,** flowered, flowery, material; **faire une f. à qn,** to do s.o. a favour (unexpectedly); **être f. bleue,** to be romantic; (*b*) **dans, à, la f. de l'âge,** in the prime, heyday, of life; **dans la première f. de la jeunesse,** in the first flush, flower, of youth; **être dans la f. de la santé,** to be blooming with health; **la fine f. de la race,** the flower of the race; (*c*) bloom (on peaches, grapes); (*d*) flowers (of antimony, wine, etc.). **2. à f. de,** on the surface of, on a level with; **à f. d'eau,** at water level; **rocher à f. d'eau,** rock that is awash; **voler à f. d'eau,** to skim the water; *Ten:* **balle à f. de corde,** ball that just grazes, skims, the net; **émotions, beauté, à f. de peau,** skin-deep emotions, beauty; **avoir les nerfs à f. de peau,** to be on edge; **yeux à f. de tête,** prominent eyes. **3.** *Tan:* hair side, grain side (of skin).
fleurage [flœraʒ] *n.m.* floral pattern (on cloth, carpet).
fleurdelisé [flœrdəlize] *a.* lilied; decorated with fleurs-de-lis; *Her:* fleury.
fleurer [flœre] *v.i. Lit:* to smell, to be fragrant; **f. la violette,** to smell of violets.
fleuret [flœrɛ] *n.m.* **1.** (*a*) (fencing) foil; (*b*) *Min:* borer. **2.** *Tex:* floss silk.
fleurette [flœrɛt] *n.f.* **conter f. à qn,** to say sweet nothings to s.o.
fleuri [flœri] *a.* **1.** (*a*) in bloom; in flower, in blossom; (*b*) decorated with flowers; flowered; **avoir la boutonnière fleurie,** (i) to have a flower in one's buttonhole; (ii) to wear a decoration. **2.** flowery (path, style, etc.); florid (style, complexion).
fleurir [flœrir] **1.** *v.i.* (*a*) (*of plants*) to flower, bloom, blossom; (*of pers.*) to come out in spots, pimples; (*b*) (*pr.p.* **florissant;** *impf.* **il fleurissait,** *Lit:* **il florissait**) (*of art, etc.*) to flourish, prosper. **2.** *v.tr.* to decorate (table) with flowers; to deck with flowers; to put a flower in (buttonhole); to lay flowers on (grave).
fleuriste [flœrist] *n.* **1.** florist, flower grower. **2.** florist, flower seller. **3.** artificial-flower maker.
fleuron [flœrɔ̃] *n.m.* **1.** *Bot:* floret. **2.** flower-shaped ornament; rosette; fleuron; *Arch:* finial; **c'est encore un f. à sa couronne,** that's another feather in his cap, another precious item for his collection.
fleuve [flœv] *n.m.* river (*as opposed to* **tributary**); **f. côtier,** short coastal river; **un f. de sang, de larmes,** a river of blood, a flood of tears; *a.* **roman f.,** saga (novel); **discours f.,** lengthy speech.
flexibilité [flɛksibilite] *n.f.* flexibility; pliability (of disposition); suppleness, litheness (of body).
flexible [flɛksibl̥] **1.** *a.* (*a*) flexible, supple, pliable; **tuyau f.,** hosepipe; (*b*) pliable, pliant, accommodating (disposition); adaptable (mind). **2.** *n.m.* (*a*) hosepipe; (*b*) *El:* flexible lead, flex.
flexion [flɛksjɔ̃] *n.f.* **1.** (*a*) flexion, bending, sagging; *Gym:* **f. du corps,** trunk exercise; *Mec.E:* **effort de f.,** bending, stress; (*b*) buckling, collapse (of rod, etc.). **2.** *Ling:* inflexion (of word); **langue à flexions,** inflected language.
flibuste [flibyst] *n.f. A:* (*a*) buccaneering, freebooting, piracy; (*b*) *coll.* pirates.
flibuster [flibyste] **1.** *v.i. A:* to freeboot, buccaneer. **2.** *v.tr. P:* to pinch, steal (sth.).
flibustier [flibystje] *n.m.* **1.** *A:* (*a*) pirate, freebooter, buccaneer, filibuster; (*b*) privateer; (*c*) gun runner. **2.** (*a*) cheat, crook.
flic [flik] *n.m. F:* (*a*) policeman, cop, bobby; (*b*) detective.
flic flac [flikflak] *n.m.* crack (of whip); slap, smack.
flirt [flœrt] *n.m.* **1.** flirtation, flirting. **2.** *O:* **mon f.,** my boyfriend, girlfriend; **un de mes anciens flirts,** an old flame of mine.
flirter [flœrte] *v.i.* to flirt.
flirteur, -euse [flœrtœr, -øz] (*a*) *a.* flirtatious; (*b*) *n.* flirt, *m.* philanderer.
floc [flɔk] **1.** *int.* plop! flop! **2.** *n.m.* splash.
floche [flɔʃ] *a.* flossy; **soie f.,** floss silk.
flocon [flɔkɔ̃] *n.m.* (*a*) flake (of snow, foam, cereal); *Fr.C:* **flocons de maïs,** cornflakes; (*b*) tuft, flock (of wool, cotton).
floconneux, -euse [flɔkɔnø, -øz] *a.* fleecy, fluffy.
flondre [flɔ̃dr̥] *n.m. Ich:* flounder.
flonflon [flɔ̃flɔ̃] *n.m.* pom pom pom (of big drum).
flopée [flɔpe] *n.f. P:* large quantity, lashings (of sth.); crowd, bevy (of people).
floraison [flɔrɛzɔ̃] *n.f.* flowering, blossoming (time).
floral, -aux [flɔral, -o] *a.* floral; **exposition florale,** flower show.
floralies [flɔrali] *n.f.pl.* floral festival; flower show, festival.
flore [flɔr] *n.f. Bot:* flora.
floréal [flɔreal] *n.m. Fr.Hist:* eighth month of the French Republican calendar (April-May).
florès [flɔrɛs] *n.m.* **faire f.,** to prosper; to shine (in society).
florifère [flɔrifɛr] *a.* floriferous, flower-bearing; **plante très f.,** prolific flowerer.
florilège [flɔrilɛʒ] *n.m.* florilegium, anthology of verse.
florin [flɔrɛ̃] *n.m. Num:* florin.
florissant [flɔrisɑ̃] *a.* flourishing, prosperous (business, etc.); **d'une santé florissante,** in the best of health, flourishing.
flot [flo] *n.m.* **1.** (*a*) wave; (*b*) **f. de dentelle, de rubans,** cascade of lace, of ribbons; (*c*) **(marée de) f.,** flood (tide); (*d*) flood (of tears); torrent, stream (of blood, abuse); crowd (of people); stream (of traffic); (*of people, sun*) **entrer à flots,** to stream in; **couler à flots,** to pour out. **2.** (*a*) **à f.,** (i) (*of ship*) afloat; (ii) (*of pers.*) solvent; **mettre un navire à f.,** to launch a ship; **remettre un navire à f.,** to refloat, float off, a ship; **remettre qn à f.,** to make s.o. solvent; (*b*) **choses de mer et de f.,** flotsam and jetsam.
flottabilité [flɔtabilite] *n.f.* buoyancy; **caisson, réservoir, de f.,** buoyancy tank.
flottable [flɔtabl̥] *a.* **1.** (*of river*) navigable, floatable (for rafts of wood). **2.** (*of wood, etc.*) floatable, buoyant.
flottage [flɔtaʒ] *n.m.* floating, running, (of timber) down a river; **bois de f.,** raft wood; **train de f.,** timber raft.
flottaison [flɔtɛzɔ̃] *n.f.* floating; *Nau:* **(ligne de) f.,** floating line; waterline; **f. en charge,** load line; **f. lège,** light waterline.
flottant [flɔtɑ̃] *a.* (*a*) floating (island, debt, engine, etc.); flowing, loose (robe, hair); **filet f.,** drift net; (*b*) irresolute, undecided, wavering.
flottard[1] [flɔtar] *n.m. F:* naval cadet.
flottard[2] *a. F:* watery; **sauce flottarde,** thin gravy.
flotte[1] [flɔt] *n.f.* **1.** (*a*) fleet; **f. de ligne, de combat,**

battle fleet; **f. aérienne,** air fleet; (*b*) **être dans la f.,** to be in the navy. **2.** *F:* water, rain; **il tombe de la f.,** it's pouring with rain.

flotte² *n.f.* float (of net, etc.); (mooring) buoy.

flottement [flɔtmɑ̃] *n.m.* undulation; wavering, swaying (of line of troops, etc.); flapping (of flag); wobble (of chain, wheel); fluctuation (of floating currency); **il y eut un moment de f.,** there was a moment's hesitation.

flotter [flɔte] **1.** *v.i.* (*a*) to float; (*b*) to float, stream, wave (in the wind); (*of hair, clothes*) to hang loosely; (*c*) to waver, hesitate; (*of thoughts*) to wander; (*of prices*) to fluctuate; (*d*) *F:* **il flotte,** it's raining. **2.** *v.tr.* **f. du bois,** to float, drive, run, timber (down a stream); **bois flotté,** (i) driftwood; (ii) raft wood.

flotteur [flɔtœr] *n.m.* **1.** raftsman (in charge of timber raft). **2.** (*a*) float (of fishing line, seaplane, carburettor, etc.); (*b*) *Plumb:* ball (of ball tap, etc.); **robinet à f.,** ballcock.

flotille [flɔtij] *n.f.* flotilla (of ships); squadron (of aircraft); **f. de pêche,** fishing fleet.

flou [flu] **1.** *a.* blurred (outline, painting, sound); fuzzy (image); hazy (horizon); vague (idea); soft, fluffy (hair); loose-fitting (dress). **2.** *n.m.* (*a*) blur, softness, woolliness, fuzziness (of outline); *Phot:* **f. artistique,** soft-focus effect; (*b*) dressmaking (as opposed to tailoring).

flouer [flue] *v.tr.* *F:* to swindle (s.o.).

fluctuant [flyktɥɑ̃] *a.* fluctuating, varying; **un esprit f.,** a weathercock.

fluctuation [flyktɥasjɔ̃] *n.f.* fluctuation.

fluctuer [flyktɥe] *v.i.* to fluctuate.

fluent [flyɑ̃] *a.* flowing; loose (soil); *Med:* **hémorroïdes fluentes,** bleeding piles.

fluer [flye] *v.i.* **1.** to flow. **2.** *Med:* (*of pus*) to run; (*of haemorrhoids*) to bleed.

fluet, -ette [flyɛ, -ɛt] *a.* thin, slender (person, etc.); thin (voice).

fluide [flɥid] **1.** *a.* fluid (oil, situation); flowing (style); **la circulation était f.,** the traffic kept moving. **2.** *n.m.* fluid; *Aut:* **f. de frein,** brake fluid.

fluidité [flɥidite] *n.f.* fluidity; **f. de la circulation,** steady flow of the traffic.

fluor [flyɔr] *n.m.* *Ch:* fluorine; *Miner:* **spath f.,** fluorspar.

fluoration [flyɔrasjɔ̃] *n.f.* fluoridation (of water supply, etc.).

fluorescence [flyɔresɑ̃s] *n.f.* fluorescence; **éclairage par f.,** fluorescent, strip, lighting.

fluorescent [flyɔresɑ̃] *a.* fluorescent; **éclairage f.,** fluorescent, strip, lighting.

fluorine [flyɔrin] *n.f.* *Miner:* fluorspar.

fluorure [flyɔryr] *n.m.* *Ch:* fluoride.

flûte [flyt] *n.f.* **1.** (*a*) flute; **grande f.,** concert flute; **petite f.,** piccolo; **f. à bec,** fipple flute; recorder; **ce qui vient de la f. s'en va par le tambour,** easy come easy go; (*b*) flautist, flute; *NAm:* flutist. **2.** (*a*) long thin loaf of French bread; (*b*) tall champagne glass; flute; (*c*) *pl.* *F:* (thin) legs; **jouer des flûtes, se tirer des flûtes,** to show a clean pair of heels. **3.** *int:* *F:* damn!

flûté [flyte] *a.* **voix flûtée,** (i) soft, flute-like, voice; (ii) piping voice.

flûter [flyte] *v.i.* to play the flute.

flûtiste [flytist] *n.* flautist, flute player; *NAm:* flutist.

fluvial, -iaux [flyvjal, -jo] *a.* fluvial; **police fluviale,** river police.

fluviatile [flyvjatil] *a.* fluviatile; **mollusques fluviatiles,** river, freshwater, molluscs.

flux [fly] *n.m.* **1.** flow; (*a*) flow, stream (of words); (*b*) flow, flood (of the tide); **le f. et le reflux,** the ebb and flow; *Pol:* *F:* the swing of the pendulum; (*c*) *Med:* flux. **2.** *Ch:* *Metall:* flux. **3.** *Ph:* *El:* **f. magnétique,** magnetic flux; **f. lumineux,** luminous, light, flux; **f. électronique,** electron flow, stream.

fluxion [flyksjɔ̃] *n.f.* *Med:* fluxion, inflammation; **f. à la joue,** swollen cheek; **f. de la gencive,** gumboil; **f. de poitrine,** inflammation of the lungs; pneumonia.

foc [fɔk] *n.m.* *Nau:* jib; **grand f.,** main jib, outer jib; **petit f.,** fore staysail; inner jib; **bâton de f.,** jib boom.

focal, -aux [fɔkal, -o] *a.* *Mth:* *Opt:* focal.

focalisation [fɔkalizasjɔ̃] *n.f.* *Opt:* *Elcs:* focusing.

focaliser [fɔkalize] *v.tr.* *Opt:* *Elcs:* to focus.

foène [fwɛn] *n.f.* fishgig, pronged harpoon.

fœtal, -aux [fetal, -o] *a.* f(o)etal.

fœtus [fetys] *n.m.* f(o)etus.

fofolle [fɔfɔl] *a.f.* *F:* foolish, silly; flighty.

foi [fwa] *n.f.* faith. **1.** (*a*) **acheteur de bonne f.,** genuine, bona fide, purchaser; **il est de bonne f.,** he is completely sincere; **mauvaise f.,** dishonesty, insincerity; **témoin de bonne, mauvaise, f.,** truthful, dishonest, witness; **jurer sur, par, sa f.,** to swear on one's honour, *NAm:* honor; **manquer de f. à qn,** to break faith with s.o.; **ma f., oui!** yes indeed!; **f. d'honnête homme,** on my word as a gentleman; **sur la f. de sa lettre,** on the strength of his letter; (*b*) *Hist:* fealty; **homme de f.,** vassal. **2.** belief, trust, confidence; **avoir f. en qn, en qch.,** to have faith, to believe, in s.o., in sth.; **avoir f. en l'avenir,** to have confidence in the future; **ajouter f., attacher f., à une nouvelle,** to credit, to believe (in), a piece of news; **témoin digne de f.,** trustworthy, reliable, credible, witness; **texte qui fait f.,** authentic text; *Jur:* **en f. de quoi,** in witness whereof; **ligne de f.,** (i) *Opt:* zero alignment; (ii) *Nau:* *Av:* lubber line. **3.** (religious) faith, belief; **acte, article, de f.,** act, article, of faith; **profession de f.,** (i) profession of faith; *R.C.Ch:* confirmation; (ii) *Pol:* (candidate's) statement of policy; **il n'a ni f. ni loi,** he fears neither God nor man.

foie [fwa] *n.m.* liver; **huile de f. de morue,** cod-liver oil; **se ronger, se manger, les foies,** to be very worried, eat one's heart out; *P:* **avoir les foies,** to be scared, in a funk.

foin [fwɛ̃] *n.m.* **1.** hay; **faire les foins,** to make hay; **tas de f.,** haycock; **meule de f.,** haystack; **rhume des foins,** hay fever; *P:* **faire du f.,** to make a fuss, kick up a row. **2.** choke (of artichoke).

foire [fwar] *n.f.* fair; **f. aux plaisirs,** funfair; **champ de f.,** fairground; **c'est une f. ici,** this place is a beargarden.

foirer [fware] *v.i.* **1.** *P:* (*a*) to have diarrhoea, the squitters; (*b*) to fail, flop. **2.** (*a*) **vis qui foire,** screw that won't bite; (*b*) *Artil:* **fusée qui foire,** fuse that hangs fire.

foireux, -euse [fwarø, -øz] *a.* *P:* (*a*) suffering from diarrhoea; (*b*) scared, in a funk; (*c*) **film f.,** bad, dud film; flop.

fois [fwa] *n.f.* **1.** time, occasion; **une fois,** once; **une f. et une seule f.,** once and once only; **il y avait, il était, une f. un roi,** once upon a time there was a king; **deux f.,** twice; **trois f. quatre font douze,** three times four is twelve; **trois f. plus grand,** three times as big; **encore une f.,** once more, once again; **y regarder à deux f. pour faire qch.,** to think twice before doing sth.; **une (bonne) f. (pour toutes),** once (and) for all; **une dernière f., cessez de le faire!** for the last time, stop it! **cette f.,** on this occasion; this time; **pour cette f.,** this once; **une autre f.,** another time, on another occasion; **d'autres f.,** at other times; **de f. à autre,** from time to time; **bien des f.,** many times, often; **par deux f.,** not (only) once, but twice; **combien de f.?** how many times? how often? **il faut le boire en une f.,** you must drink it at one go; **toutes les f., chaque f., que j'y pense,** every time that, whenever, I think about it; **pour une f. tu as raison,** you're right for once; **une f. que vous aurez des informations,** once, as soon as, you have some information; **à la f.,** at one and the same time; at once. **2.** *P:* **des f.** sometimes, now and then; **vous n'auriez pas des f. une remorque?** you haven't by any chance got a towrope? **des f. qu'il viendrait,** in case he should come; **non, mais des f.!** that's a bit thick!

foison [fwazɔ̃] *n.f.* (*a*) *A:* abundance, plenty; (*b*) **à f.,** plentifully, in abundance; **des pommes à f.,** plenty of apples.

foisonnant [fwazɔnɑ̃] *a.* abundant, plentiful.

foisonnement [fwazɔnmɑ̃] *n.f.* **1.** multiplying, swarming. **2.** swelling, expansion (of lime, etc.).

foisonner [fwazɔne] *v.i.* **1.** to abound (**de, en,** in, with); to swarm, teem (with vermin); **le gibier foisonne ici,** game is plentiful here. **2.** (*a*) (*of animals*) to multiply, swarm; (*b*) (*of lime, etc.*) to swell, expand.

folâtre [fɔlɑtr̥] *a.* playful, lively (child); frisky.

folâtrement [fɔlɑtrəmɑ̃] *adv.* playfully.

folâtrer [fɔlɑtre] *v.i.* to romp, frolic; (*of lamb*) to frisk about, gambol.

folâtrerie [fɔlɑtrəri] *n.f.* **1.** playfulness; friskiness (of kitten). **2.** frolic, romp.

folichon, -onne [fɔliʃɔ̃, -ɔn] *a.* playful, light-hearted; *F:* **ce n'est pas f.,** it's not much fun.

folichonner [fɔliʃɔne] *v.i. O:* to play, lark, about.

folie [fɔli] *n.f.* **1.** madness; **accès de f.,** fit of madness; **f. du suicide,** suicidal mania; **f. des grandeurs,** delusions of grandeur; megalomania; **être pris de f.,** to go mad; **avoir un grain de f.,** to be a bit touched; **aimer qn à la f.,** to be madly in love with s.o., to love s.o. to distraction; **aimer qch. à la f.,** to be mad on, have a mania for, sth. **2.** folly; **il a eu la f. de céder,** he was silly enough to give in; **dire des folies,** to talk wildly, extravagantly; **faire des folies,** to act irrationally, to be extravagant. **3.** (*building*) folly.

folio [fɔljo] *n.m. Typ: etc:* folio.

folioter [fɔljɔte] *v.tr.* (i) to folio; (ii) to paginate.

folklore [fɔlklɔr] *n.m.* (*a*) folklore; (*b*) folk songs, country dancing, local traditions.

folklorique [fɔlklɔrik] *a.* traditional (costume, etc.); **danses folkloriques,** folk, country, dancing..

folkloriste [fɔlklɔrist] *n.* folklorist, student of folklore.

follement [fɔlmɑ̃] *adv.* madly. **1.** foolishly, rashly, desperately. **2.** extravagantly; **s'amuser f.,** to have a wonderful time.

follet, -ette [fɔlɛ, -ɛt] *a.* **1.** merry, lively; **esprit f.,** elfish spirit; sprite; (hob)goblin; **feu f.,** will-o'-the-wisp, Jack-o'-lantern. **2. poil f.,** down (of bird, boy's face); **cheveux follets,** stray lock(s).

follicule [fɔlikyl] *n.m. Bot: Anat:* follicle.

fomentateur, -trice [fɔmɑ̃tatœr, -tris] *n.* fomenter, troublemaker.

fomentation [fɔmɑ̃tasjɔ̃] *n.f.* fomentation.

fomenter [fɔmɑ̃te] *v.tr.* to foment (wound, sedition); to stir up (strife).

fonçage [fɔ̃saʒ] *n.m.* **1.** bottoming, heading (of cask). **2.** boring, sinking (of well).

foncé [fɔ̃se] *a.* dark (colour); **bleu f.,** dark blue.

foncer [fɔ̃se] *v.* **(je fonçai(s); n. fonçons) 1.** *v.tr.* (*a*) to bottom, head (a cask); (*b*) to sink, drive (in) (pile); to sink, bore (well); (*c*) to deepen, darken, the colour of (sth.); (*d*) *Cu:* to line (mould). **2.** *v.i.* (*a*) **f. sur qn,** to rush at, swoop (down) on, s.o.; (*of bull, footballer*) to charge s.o.; (*b*) *F:* to speed along; to forge ahead; (*c*) to deepen, darken (in colour).

foncier, -ière [fɔ̃sje, -jɛr] *a.* **1.** of land; **propriété foncière,** landed property; real estate; **le propriétaire f.,** the ground landlord; **rente foncière,** ground rent; **impôt f.,** *n.m.* **f.,** land tax; **crédit f.,** land bank. **2.** deep-seated, fundamental (commonsense).

foncièrement [fɔ̃sjɛrmɑ̃] *adv.* fundamentally, at bottom, thoroughly.

fonction [fɔ̃ksjɔ̃] *n.f.* **1.** function; office; (*a*) **fonctions publiques,** public offices; **entrer en fonctions,** to take up one's duties; **faire f. de gérant,** to act as manager; **adjectif qui fait f. d'adverbe,** adjective that is used as an adverb; (*b*) **fonctions de l'estomac, du cœur,** functions of the stomach, of the heart. **2.** *Mth: etc:* function; **f. inverse,** inverse function; **exprimer une quantité en f. d'une autre,** to express one quantity in terms of, as a function of, another; **les prix varient en f. de la demande,** prices vary in accordance with, according to, demand; **le bon marché est f. de l'abondance,** cheapness is conditional upon abundance.

fonctionnaire [fɔ̃ksjɔnɛr] *n.* official, *esp.* civil servant; **haut, moyen, petit, f.,** higher, senior, minor, official, civil servant.

fonctionnalisme [fɔksjɔnalism] *n.m.* functionalism.

fonctionnaliste [fɔksjɔnalist] *a.* functionalist.

fonctionnariser [fɔ̃ksjɔnarize] *v.tr.* **1.** to bring (employees, profession) into the civil service. **2.** to deal with in the official manner.

fonctionnarisme [fɔ̃ksjɔnarism] *n.m.* officialdom; bureaucracy; *F:* red tape.

fonctionnel, -elle [fɔ̃ksjɔnɛl] *a.* functional.

fonctionnellement [fɔ̃ksjɔnɛlmɑ̃] *adv.* functionally.

fonctionnement [fɔ̃ksjɔnmɑ̃] *n.m.* (*a*) functioning, working (of government, plan, etc.); (*b*) operation, running, working (of a machine, etc.); **entrer en f.,** to begin working; **en (bon) état de f.,** in (good) running, working, order; **cycle de f.,** operating cycle.

fonctionner [fɔ̃ksjɔne] *v.i.* **1.** (*of committee, etc.*) to function. **2.** to act, work; **les trains ne fonctionnent plus,** the trains are no longer running; **les freins n'ont pas fonctionné,** the brakes failed; **faire f. une machine,** to run, work, a machine; *El:* **f. sur courant continu,** to operate on direct current.

fond [fɔ̃] *n.m.* **1.** (*a*) bottom; crown (of hat); seat (of chair, trousers); bottom, head (of cask); heart, bottom (of artichoke); back (of the throat); **abîme sans f.,** bottomless chasm; **boîte à double f.,** box with a false bottom; **bateau à f. plat,** flat-bottomed boat; **f. de cale,** bilge; *Mch:* **f. de cylindre, de chaudière,** cylinder head, boiler head; **f. de bouteille,** dregs; **f. de café,** coffee grounds; **au f. du cœur,** at the bottom of one's heart, deep down; **au f. il était très flatté,** in his heart of hearts he was extremely gratified; **aller au f. d'une affaire,** to get to the bottom, root, of a matter; **il possède le f. de cette matière,** he has sound knowledge of the subject; (*b*) bottom, bed (of the ocean); **f. de sable,** sandy bottom; (*of anchor*) **prendre f.,** to bite, grip; **envoyer un navire par le f.,** to send a ship to the bottom; **grands fonds,** ocean deeps; **hauts, petits, fonds,** shallows; **courant de f.,** undertow; **mer du f.,** ground swell; **trouver, prendre, le f.,** to sound, to take soundings; **le grand, petit, f.,** the deep, shallow, end (of swimming pool); **à fond,** thoroughly; **visser une pièce à f.,** to screw a piece home; **connaître un sujet à f.,** to have a thorough knowledge of a subject; **à f. (de train),** at top speed. **2.** foundation; **rebâtir une maison de f. en comble,** to rebuild a house from top to bottom; **être ruiné de f. en comble,** to be completely ruined; **il a un bon f.,** he's good at heart, basically good; **f. de teint,** makeup foundation (cream); **f. de robe,** full-length slip; **accusation sans f.,** unfounded accusation; **faire f. sur qn, sur qch.,** to rely, depend, on s.o., sth.; **le f. et la forme,** the form and the substance; **le f. de cette politique,** the essential features of this policy; **cheval qui a du f.,** horse with staying power; **course de (grand) f.,** long distance race; *Ski:* cross-country race; **coureur de f.,**

long-distance runner; **question de f.,** fundamental question; *Journ:* **article de f.,** leading article; leader; *Mus:* **jeu de f.,** pipe stop (of organ), foundation stop; **bruit de f.,** (i) scratching (of gramophone needle); (ii) *Cin: W.Tel:* background noise; **f. sonore, musical,** background music; **au f., dans le f.,** fundamentally, basically; at bottom. **3.** back, furthermost part, far end (of enclosed space); background (of picture); *F:* **fonds de boutique,** oddments, old stock; **au (fin) f. du désert,** in the heart of the desert; *Th:* **toile de f.,** backdrop, backcloth; *Ten:* **ligne de f.,** baseline.

fondamental, -aux [fɔ̃damɑ̃tal, -o] *a.* fundamental; basic, underlying (principle); **pierre fondamentale,** foundation stone; **couleurs fondamentales,** primary colours; *Mus:* **son f.,** root, generator (of chord).

fondamentalement [fɔ̃damɑ̃talmɑ̃] *adv.* fundamentally; basically.

fondant [fɔ̃dɑ̃] **1.** *a.* melting; **poire fondante,** pear that melts in the mouth; **tons fondants,** graduated shades, colours that shade off. **2.** *n.m.* (*a*) fondant; bonbon; (*b*) *Metall:* flux.

fondateur, -trice [fɔ̃datœr, -tris] *n.* founder (of business, etc.); **membre f.,** founder member.

fondation [fɔ̃dasjɔ̃] *n.f.* **1.** (*a*) founding, foundation (of city, hospital, etc.); (*b*) (fund for) endowment, foundation; (*c*) (endowed) institution; foundation. **2.** *Const:* foundation (of house).

fondé [fɔ̃de] **1.** *a.* founded, grounded, reasonable, justified; **doutes (bien) fondés,** well founded, well grounded, (fully) justified, suspicions; **mal f.,** groundless, unjustified (suspicions); **qu'est-ce qu'il y a de f. dans ces bruits?** what grounds are there for these reports? **2.** *n.m.* **f. de pouvoir,** (i) *Jur:* agent (holding power of attorney); proxy; (ii) manager, managing director; (iii) chief clerk.

fondement [fɔ̃dmɑ̃] *n.m.* **1.** (*a*) *A:* = FONDATION 2; (*b*) **soupçons sans f.,** groundless, unfounded, suspicions. **2.** *F:* buttocks, bottom.

fonder [fɔ̃de] *v.tr.* **1.** to found (city, business, etc.); to start, set up (business, newspaper); to float (company); **f. ses espérances sur qch.,** to base, build, one's hopes on sth. **2.** (*a*) **se f. sur qch.,** to place one's reliance on sth.; to build upon (promise, etc.); **sur quoi se fonde-t-il pour le nier?** what are his grounds for denying it? (*b*) **un espoir qui se fondait sur une information fausse,** a hope that was based, founded, on misinformation.

fonderie [fɔ̃dri] *n.f.* **1.** (*a*) smelting; (*b*) founding, casting (of metals). **2.** (*a*) smelting works; (*b*) foundry.

fondeur [fɔ̃dœr] *n.m.* (*a*) smelter; (*b*) (metal) founder, caster; **f. en cuivre,** brass founder; **f. en caractères, f. typographe,** type founder.

fondre [fɔ̃dr̥] **1.** *v.tr.* (*a*) to smelt (ore); (*b*) to melt (snow, wax, etc.); to melt down (metal); **f. deux fils ensemble,** to fuse two wires together; (*c*) to cast, found (bell, gun, etc.); (*d*) to dissolve, melt (sugar, etc.); (*e*) **f. des teintes,** to blend colours; (*f*) *Com:* to amalgamate (companies). **2.** *v.i.* (*a*) to melt; **le beurre fond au soleil,** butter melts in the sun; *El:* **faire f. un fusible,** to blow a fuse; **mon cœur fondit de pitié,** my heart melted with pity; **l'argent lui fond entre les mains,** he spends money like water; **il fond à vue d'œil,** he's getting thinner every day; (*b*) (*of sugar, etc.*) to melt, dissolve; **f. en larmes,** to dissolve in(to) tears. **3.** *v.i.* to pounce; to swoop down (upon the prey, etc.). **4. se f.** (*a*) to melt; (*b*) to mix, merge; (*of companies*) to amalgamate.

fondrière [fɔ̃drijɛr] *n.f.* (*a*) hollow (in ground); muddy, slushy, hole (in road); (*b*) bog; *Fr.C:* **f. de mousse,** muskeg.

fonds [fɔ̃] *n.m.* **1.** (*a*) **f. de terre,** estate, (piece of) land; (*b*) (*in museum*) bequest. **2.** (*a*) **f. de commerce,** business (with goodwill); **f. de commerce à vendre,** business for sale (as a going concern); *Publ:* **livres de f.,** books belonging to the publisher's goodwill; (*b*) stock(-in-trade); **avoir un f. de science,** to have a stock, fund, of knowledge. **3.** (*a*) funds; **fournir les f. d'une entreprise,** to supply the capital for an undertaking; **mise de f.,** paid-in capital; **rentrer dans ses f.,** to see one's money back; **appel de f.,** call upon shareholders; **mangez vos revenus, mais ne touchez pas au f.,** spend your income, but don't touch your capital; **placer son argent à f. perdu,** to purchase an annuity; **prêt à f. perdu,** loan without security; (*b*) fund (for special purpose); **F. monétaire international,** International Monetary Fund; **f. commun,** pool; (*c*) means, resources; *F:* cash, ready money; **être en f.,** to be in funds; (*d*) *pl. Fin:* stocks, securities; **f. d'État, f. publics,** Government stock(s).

fondu, -ue [fɔ̃dy] **1.** *a.* melted (butter, etc.); molten (lead, lava). **2.** *n.m.* (*a*) blending (of colours); (*b*) *Cin:* dissolve; **ouverture en f.,** fade-in, fading in; **fermeture en f.,** fade-out. **3.** *n.f. Cu:* **fondue,** fondue.

fongicide [fɔ̃ʒisid] **1.** *a.* fungicidal. **2.** *n.m.* fungicide.

fongosité [fɔ̃gɔzite] *n.f. Med:* fungosity.

fongueux, -euse [fɔ̃gø, -øz] *a. Med:* fungous.

fontaine [fɔ̃tɛn] *n.f.* **1.** spring; pool (of running water); **f. de boue,** mud spring. **2.** fountain. **3.** cistern; **f. filtrante, de ménage,** (household) filter.

fontainier [fɔ̃tenje] *n.m.* **1.** water engineer; *Adm:* turncock. **2.** well borer, sinker.

fonte[1] [fɔ̃t] *n.f.* **1.** melting; **f. des neiges,** melting, thawing, of the snow. **2.** (*a*) smelting (of ore); (*b*) casting, founding; **jeter du métal en f.,** to cast metal; **pièces de f.,** castings. **3. (fer de) f., f. de fer,** cast iron; **f. d'acier,** cast steel; **poêle en f.,** cast-iron stove. **4.** *Typ:* fount.

fonte[2] *n.f.* (saddle) holster.

fonts [fɔ̃] *n.m.pl.* **f. (baptismaux),** font; **tenir un enfant sur les f.,** to stand godfather, godmother, to a child.

football [futbol] *n.m.* (association) football; *F:* soccer.

footballer, footballeur, -euse [futbolœr, -øz] *n.* footballer.

footing [futiŋ] *n.m.* walking (for exercise).

for [fɔr] *n.m.* **le f. intérieur,** the conscience; **dans, en, son f. intérieur,** in one's heart of hearts.

forage [fɔraʒ] *n.m.* **1.** drilling, boring; sinking (of well). **2.** borehole, drill hole; **f. de reconnaissance,** wildcat (well).

forain, -aine [fɔrɛ̃, -ɛn] **1.** *a. Nau:* **mouillage f.,** open berth. **2.** *a. & n.* itinerant; **spectacle f.,** travelling show (at a fair); **(acteur) f.,** strolling player; **fête foraine,** funfair; **(marchand) f.,** stallkeeper (at fair).

forban [fɔrbɑ̃] *n.m.* corsair, pirate, buccaneer; *P:* rogue.

forçage [fɔrsaʒ] *n.m.* forcing (of plants).

forçat [fɔrsa] *n.m.* **1.** *A:* galley slave. **2.** convict; *F:* **mener une vie de f.,** to slave.

force [fɔrs] *n.f.* **1.** strength, force, vigour; (*a*) **f. d'âme,** strength (in adversity); fortitude; **dans la f. de l'âge,** in the prime of life; **être à bout de f.,** to be exhausted, at the end of one's tether; **travailler de toutes ses forces, de toute sa f.,** to work with all one's might, to work all out; **elle n'avait plus la f. de répondre,** she had no strength left to answer; **tour de f.,** feat of strength, of skill; **travailleur de f.,** heavy worker; *Const:* **(jambe de) f.,** force piece, strut; *Mec:* **f. de résistance à la tension,** tensile strength; (*b*) **ils sont de f. (égale),** they are equally matched, well matched; **boxeur de première f.,** first-class boxer; **je ne me sens pas de f. à faire cela,** I don't feel up to, equal to, doing it; (*c*) force, violence; **f. majeure,** circumstances outside one's control; force majeure; **faire appel à la f.,** to resort to force; **faire qch. de vive f.,** to do sth. by sheer force; **entrer, pénétrer, de f. dans une maison,** to force one's way into a house; **faire entrer qch. de f. dans qch.,** to force sth. into sth.; *Nau:* **faire f. de voiles,** to crowd on (all) sail; **faire f. de rames,** to row, pull, hard; **f. lui fut d'obéir,** he was obliged to obey, he had no option but to obey; **céder à la f.,** to act under duress; **faire qch. par f.,** to do sth. under compulsion, to be forced to do sth; *Prov:* **la f. prime le droit; f. passe droit,** might is right; **de gré ou de f.,** willy-nilly; **de toute f. il nous faut y assister,** we absolutely must be present; **à toute f.,** in spite of all opposition; **il veut à toute f. entrer,** he is determined to get in. **2.** (*a*) force (of blow, the wind); force, cogency (of an argument); **les forces de la nature,** the forces of nature; **par la f. des choses,** through the force of circumstances; **dans toute la f. du mot,** in every sense of the word; (*b*) **f. motrice,** motive power; **f. d'inertie,** inertia; **f. vive,** kinetic energy; momentum; (*c*) **f. (électrique),** (electric) power; **prise de f.,** power point. **3. la f. armée,** the military; the troops; **les forces armées,** the armed forces; the services; **f. tactique, d'intervention,** task force; **la force publique, les forces de police, de l'ordre,** the police (force); **nous étions là en force(s),** we turned out in (full) force. **4.** *a.inv. A: & Lit:* **f. gens,** a great number of, a lot of, (very) many, people; **f. bière,** large amounts of beer. **5. à f. de,** by (dint of), by means of; **à f. de travailler,** by dint of hard work; **à f. de volonté,** by sheer force of will; **à f. de répéter,** by constant repetition; **il s'est enroué à f. de crier,** he shouted himself hoarse.

forcé [fɔrse] *a.* **1.** forced; compulsory; *Av:* **atterrissage f.,** forced landing; *Jur:* **travaux forcés,** hard labour; **mariage f.,** *F:* shotgun wedding. **2.** strained (heart, etc.); **exemple f.,** far-fetched example; **rire f.,** forced, unnatural, laugh; **sourire f.,** forced, wry, smile. **3.** *F:* **c'est f.!** it's inevitable!

forcement [fɔrsəmɑ̃] *n.m.* forcing open, breaking open; **f. de blocus,** blockade running.

forcément [fɔrsemɑ̃] *adv.* perforce. **1.** under compulsion. **2.** necessarily, inevitably.

forcené, -ée [fɔrsəne] **1.** *a.* frantic, mad, frenzied. **2.** *n.* madman, *f.* madwoman.

forceps [fɔrsɛps] *n.m. Obst:* forceps.

forcer [fɔrse] *v.* **(je forçai(s)) 1.** *v.tr.* (*a*) to force, compel; **f. la main à qn,** to force s.o.'s hand; **f. le respect de qn,** to compel respect from s.o.; **f. qn à faire qch.,** to force, compel, s.o. to do sth.; **être forcé de faire qch.,** to be forced to do sth.; (*b*) **f. qn, qch.,** to deal violently with, to do violence to, s.o., sth.; **f. une femme,** to violate, rape, a woman; **f. la consigne,** to force one's way in; **f. un poste,** to take a post by storm, by force; **f. une serrure,** to force a lock; **f. la caisse,** to break into the till; **f. une porte,** to break open a door; **f. la porte de qn,** to force one's way in; **f. sa prison,** to break jail; (*c*) to force (voice, pace, etc.); to strain (mast); to buckle (plate); **se f. l'épaule,** to wrench, strain, one's shoulder; *F:* **f. la note,** to overdo it; **f. le sens,** to strain, twist, the meaning; **f. un cheval,** to override a horse; **f. des fleurs,** to force flowers; **f. un cerf,** to run down a stag, bring a stag to bay; (*d*) **f. la dose d'un médicament,** to take, give, too large a dose of a medicine. **2.** *v.i.* **f. de voiles,** to crowd on sail; **f. sur les avirons,** to strain at the oars; **le vent force,** the wind is rising; *Cards:* **f. sur l'annonce de qn,** to overcall, to overbid, s.o. **3. se f.** (*a*) to overstrain oneself; (*b*) to restrain oneself, one's feelings.

forcerie [fɔrsəri] *n.f. Hort:* forcing house.

forcing [fɔrsiŋ] *n.m. Sp:* sustained pressure.

forcir [fɔrsir] *v.i. F:* to get fat; to put on weight.

forer [fɔre] *v.tr.* to drill, bore, perforate; to sink (a well).

forestier, -ière [fɔrɛstje, -jɛr] **1.** *a.* forested (area); **chemin f.,** forest road; **exploitation forestière,** lumbering; **garde f.,** forester, (forest) ranger. **2.** *n.m.* forester.

foret [fɔrɛ] *n.m.* (*a*) drill, bit; **f. à hélice, f. hélicoïdal,** twist drill; **f. aléseur,** reamer bit; (*b*) **f. à bois,** gimlet; **f. de charpentier,** auger; (*c*) (brace) bit; **f. à centre, à téton,** centre bit.

forêt [fɔrɛ] *n.f.* forest; **région couverte de forêts,** forested region; *Adm:* **le service des Eaux et Forêts** = the Forestry Commission; *Prov:* **l'arbre vous cache la f.,** you can't see the wood for the trees.

foreur [fɔrœr] *n.m.* borer, driller; *Petr:* **f. d'exploration,** wildcatter.

foreuse [fɔrøz] *n.f.* **1.** *Tls:* drill; **f. à appui,** breast drill; **f. à main,** hand drill. **2.** *Min: etc:* rock drill; **f. à câble,** churn drill.

forfaire [fɔrfɛr] *v.ind.tr.* (*conj. like* FAIRE) *A: & Lit:* **f. à son devoir,** to fail in one's duty; **f. à l'honneur,** to forfeit one's honour, *NAm:* honor; **f. à sa parole,** to break one's word.

forfait[1] [fɔrfɛ] *n.m.* heinous crime.

forfait[2] *n.m.* contract; **travail à f.,** (i) contract work; (ii) (*for workman*) job work; **prix à f.,** price as per contract; **vente à f.,** outright sale.

forfait[3] *n.m. Turf:* fine, forfeit (paid for scratching a horse); **déclarer f. pour un cheval,** to scratch a horse; (*of athlete, competitor*) **déclarer f.,** to scratch.

forfaitaire [fɔrfɛtɛr] *a.* contractual; **marché f.,** (transaction by) contract, outright purchase; **paiement f.,** lump sum; **prix f.,** contract price; price of a job lot; all-in price; **voyage à prix f.,** package tour.

forfaiture [fɔrfɛtyr] *n.f.* **1.** abuse (of authority); maladministration. **2. f. au devoir, à l'honneur,** breach of duty, honour.

forfanterie [fɔrfɑ̃tri] *n.f.* impudent boast(ing); bragging.

forge [fɔrʒ] *n.f.* **1.** (*a*) forge, smith's hearth; **pièce de f.,** forging; (*b*) **f. (maréchale),** smithy; **mener un cheval à la f.,** to take a horse to the blacksmith's; **f. de serrurier,** locksmith's workshop. **2.** *usu.pl.* ironworks; **maître de forges,** ironmaster.

forgeable [fɔrʒabl] *a.* forgeable (metal).

forgeage [fɔrʒaʒ] *n.m.* forging, smithing.

forger [fɔrʒe] *v.tr.* **(je forgeai(s))** (*a*) to forge; **fer forgé,** wrought iron; *Prov:* **c'est en forgeant qu'on devient forgeron,** practice makes perfect; (*b*) to fabricate, make up (story, excuse); to coin (word); to trump up (charge); to conjure up (vision).

forgeron [fɔrʒərɔ̃] *n.m.* (black)smith.

forgeur, -euse [fɔrʒœr, -øz] *n.* **1.** inventor, fabricator (of news, lies); coiner (of words). **2.** *n.m.* (black)smith.

formaldéhyde [fɔrmaldeid] *n.m. occ. n.f. Ch:* formaldehyde.

formaliser [fɔrmalize] **1.** *v.tr.* to formalize; **logique formalisée,** formal logic. **2. se f.,** to take offence (**de,** at); to take exception (**de,** to).

formalisme [fɔrmalism] *n.m.* formalism; **f. administratif,** bureaucracy, *F:* red tape.

formaliste [fɔrmalist] **1.** *a.* formalistic, punctilious, precise. **2.** *n.* formalist, stickler for formalities.

formalité [fɔrmalite] *n.f.* **1.** formality, formal procedure; **c'est une pure f.,** it's a mere matter of form; **sans autre f.,** without further ado. **2.** ceremoniousness; **sans formalité(s),** without ceremony.

format [fɔrma] *n.m.* format (of book); size (of paper, *Phot:* of plate); **f. de poche,** pocket size; **appareil de petit f.,** miniature camera.

formateur, -trice [fɔrmatœr, -tris] *a.* formative.

formation [fɔrmasjɔ̃] *n.f.* formation. **1.** (*a*) forming;

development, moulding, *NAm:* molding (of character); **nation en voie de f.,** nation in the making; **mot de f. savante,** word of learned origin; (*b*) education; training. **2.** (*a*) makeup (of train, etc.); structure (of rock, etc.); *Mil:* **f. serrée,** close formation; (*b*) *Mil:* unit; *Mus:* group.

forme [fɔrm] *n.f.* **1.** form, shape; *pl.* lines (of ship); (*of pers.*) build; *F:* curves (of woman); **vêtement qui épouse les formes,** close-fitting garment; **en f. d'œuf,** egg-shaped; **sous la f. d'une nymphe,** in the form, shape, of a nymph; **statistiques sous f. de tableau,** statistics in tabular form; **sans f.,** shapeless; **prendre f.,** to take shape; to materialize. **2.** form; method of procedure; (*a*) **quittance en bonne (et due) f.,** receipt in order, in proper form; **arrêt cassé pour vice de f.,** judgement quashed on a technical point, on a point of law; **renvoyer qn sans autre f. de procès,** to dismiss s.o. without ceremony; **avertir qn dans les formes,** to give s.o. formal, due, warning; **faire qch. dans les formes,** to do sth. in the accepted way; **pour la f.,** as a matter of form; **de pure f.,** purely formal; (*b*) *pl.* manners; tact; **avoir des formes,** to be polite, to use tact; (*c*) **être en f.,** to be on form, in condition; **ne pas être en f., être en mauvaise f.,** to be in poor form; **équipe bien en f.,** team at the top of its form. **3.** *Ind:* former, forming block; mould, *NAm:* mold (for cheese, etc.); *Bootm:* (i) last; (ii) shoe tree; *Hatm:* (i) block; (ii) crown; **chapeau haut de f.,** top hat. **4. lièvre en f.,** hare in its form. **5.** *Nau:* dock. **6.** *Typ:* form(e).

formé [fɔrme] *a.* formed, full grown; fully developed; (*of fruit*) set.

formel, -elle [fɔrmɛl] *a.* **1.** formal, express, precise (order, etc.); flat, categorical (denial); absolute (veto); **défense formelle,** strict prohibition. **2.** (*a*) formal, superficial; (*b*) *Phil:* formal (cause).

formellement [fɔrmɛlmɑ̃] *adv.* formally; absolutely, strictly, expressly (forbidden); **promettre f.,** to promise faithfully.

former [fɔrme] **1.** *v.tr.* to form; (*a*) to make, create; to form, draw up (plan); to raise (objections); *Rail:* to make up (train); **les murs forment un carré,** the walls form a square; (*b*) to shape, fashion; **lettres mal formées,** badly formed, shaped, letters; (*c*) to school (child, horse); to train (pilot, etc.); to mould, *NAm:* mold (character); **cette université a formé des hommes remarquables,** this university has turned out some remarkable men. **2. se f.,** to form, develop; (*of plan*) to take shape; (*of fruit*) to set; **se f. aux affaires,** to acquire a business training.

formidable [fɔrmidabl̩] *a.* (*a*) *O:* fearsome, formidable; (*b*) *F:* tremendous; fantastic.

formidablement [fɔrmidabləmɑ̃] *adv.* (*a*) *A:* formidably; (*b*) *F:* tremendously, fantastically.

formique [fɔrmik] *a. Ch:* formic (acid).

formulaire [fɔrmylɛr] *n.m.* **1.** (*a*) collection of formulae; formulary; (*b*) pharmacopoeia. **2.** (printed) form.

formulation [fɔrmylasjɔ̃] *n.f.* formulation, expressing (of one's feelings, etc.).

formule [fɔrmyl] *n.f.* **1.** (*a*) *Mth: Ch: etc:* formula; (*b*) (set) form of words; (turn of) phrase; formula; **f. finale, f. de politesse,** formal ending (of letter); (*c*) formula (for agreement); method. **2.** *Adm:* (printed) form; *Post:* telegraph form.

formuler [fɔrmyle] *v.tr.* (*a*) to formulate (doctrine); to draw up (document) in due form; *Med:* to write out (prescription); (*b*) to express (wish); to formulate (proposal), put (proposal) into words; to lodge (complaint); to lay down (rule).

fornication [fɔrnikasjɔ̃] *n.f.* fornication.

forniquer [fɔrnike] *v.i.* to fornicate.

fors [fɔr] *prep. Lit:* except, save; **tout est perdu f. l'honneur,** all is lost save honour, *NAm:* honor.

fort [fɔr] **I.** *a.* **1.** (*a*) strong; **f. comme un Turc, comme un bœuf,** as strong as a horse; **partisans de la manière forte,** believers in strong measures, violent action; **je suis plus f. des bras que vous,** I'm stronger in the arms than you; **trouver plus f. que soi,** to meet one's match; **être f. de qch.,** to get one's strength from, be supported by, sth.; **c'est une forte tête,** (i) he has a good head on his shoulders; (ii) he's very independent; **être f. en mathématiques, à tous les jeux,** to be good at mathematics, at games; (*b*) strong (rope, drink, etc.); high (fever, wind); intense (heat); heavy (rain, soil); loud (voice); **avoir une forte odeur,** to have a strong smell; **c'est plus f. que moi!** I can't help it! *F:* **c'est (par) trop f.!** that's a bit thick! *F:* **en voilà une forte!** that's a good one! **ce qu'il y a de plus f., c'est qu'on n'y peut rien,** the worst of it is that one can do nothing about it; (*c*) **ville, place, forte,** fortified town; fortress; (*d*) **se faire f. de faire qch.,** to engage, undertake, to do sth.; **elles se font f., fortes, de le retrouver,** they undertake to find it; *Jur:* **se porter f.** (*inv.*) **pour qn,** to stand as security for s.o., to answer for s.o. **2.** large, stout (person); thick, full (lips); heavy (beard); stout (timber); **elle est forte des hanches,** she's big round the hips; **forte somme,** large sum of money; **forte différence,** great difference; **forte hausse des prix,** sharp, big, rise in prices; **forte pente,** steep gradient; **armée forte de cinq mille hommes,** army five thousand strong; *Com:* **prix f.,** full price. **II.** *adv.* **1.** strongly, hard; **frapper f.,** to strike hard; **tirer f. la sonnette,** to pull the bell hard; **y aller f.,** (i) to go hard at it; (ii) to exaggerate; **crier f.,** to shout loudly; **sentir f.,** to smell strong, high. **2.** very, extremely; **il a été f. mécontent,** he was extremely displeased, very annoyed; **vous vous trompez f.,** you are greatly mistaken; **j'ai f. à faire,** I have a great deal to do. **III.** *n.m.* **1.** strong part; **le f. et le faible de l'affaire,** the strong and weak points of the matter; **du f. au faible,** altogether, by and large; **le f. d'un bois,** the heart of a wood; **le f. de l'hiver,** the depth of winter; **au (plus) f. du combat,** in the thick of the fight; **au f. de l'été, de l'épidémie,** in the height of summer, of the epidemic; **le plus f. est fait,** the most difficult part is done; **la politesse n'est pas son f.,** politeness is not his strong point, his forte. **2.** strong man; **les forts des Halles,** the market porters; *Prov:* **la raison du plus f. est toujours la meilleure,** might is right. **3.** fort, stronghold.

fortement [fɔrtəmɑ̃] *adv.* strongly; stoutly; vigorously; hard; **insister f. sur qch.,** to insist firmly, strongly, on sth.; **f. épicé,** highly spiced; **f. irrité,** greatly, extremely irritated.

forteresse [fɔrtərɛs] *n.f.* fortress, fortified place; stronghold.

fortifiant [fɔrtifjɑ̃] **1.** *a.* fortifying, strengthening; invigorating. **2.** *n.m. Med:* tonic.

fortification [fɔrtifikasjɔ̃] *n.f.* **1.** fortification; fortifying (of town, etc.). **2.** defence work(s); **les fortifications,** the fortifications (of a town).

fortifier [fɔrtifje] *v.* (*impf.* & *pr.sub.* **n. fortifiions**) **1.** *v.tr.* (*a*) to fortify; to strengthen (wall, muscles); to invigorate (the body); to confirm, support (suspicion, etc.); **f. qn dans une résolution,** to support s.o. in a resolution; (*b*) to fortify (town, etc.). **2. se f.** (*a*) to become stronger; (*b*) *Mil:* to raise a line of defences; to entrench oneself.

fortifs (les) [lefɔrtif] *n.f.pl. P:* the fortifications (of Paris).

fortuit [fɔrtɥi] *a.* fortuitous; chance, casual (encounter); **cas f.,** (i) accident; (ii) *Jur:* act of God, fortuitous event.

fortuité [fɔrtɥite] *n.f.* fortuitousness, fortuity.

fortuitement [fɔrtɥitmɑ̃] *adv.* fortuitously, by chance, accidentally.

fortune [fɔrtyn] *n.f.* **1.** fortune, chance, luck; **coup de f.,** stroke of luck; **tenter (la) f.,** to try one's luck; **s'attacher à la f. de qn,** to throw in one's lot with s.o.; **venez dîner à la f. du pot,** come and take pot luck; **installation de f.,** temporary, makeshift, rough and ready, installation; **lit de f.,** shakedown; **réparations de f.,** emergency repairs; **disposez-vous de moyens de f.?** have you anything you can make shift, make do, with? *Nau:* **mât de f.,** jury mast; **(voile de) f.,** cross-jack (foresail); *M.Ins:* **f. de mer,** perils of the sea, sea risks. **2.** (*a*) **il n'a pas de f.,** he's unlucky; (*b*) **mauvaise f.,** misfortune; **revers de f.,** reverse, setback; **avoir la bonne, la mauvaise, f. de rencontrer qn,** to have the good, bad, luck to meet s.o.; **faire contre mauvaise f. bon cœur,** to make the best of a bad job. **3.** fortune, wealth; **faire f.,** (i) to make one's fortune, a fortune; (ii) to be successful, make a hit; **avoir de la f.,** to be well off; **être l'artisan de sa f.,** to be a self-made man; **chercher f.,** to seek one's fortune.

fortuné [fɔrtyne] *a.* **1.** *A: & Lit:* fortunate, happy. **2.** rich, well off, well-to-do.

forum [fɔrɔm] *n.m. Rom.Ant: etc:* forum.

forure [fɔryr] *n.f.* bore(hole); pipe (of key).

fosse [fos] *n.f.* **1.** pit, hole; *Oc:* trough; *Sp:* (jumping) pit; *Ven:* pit (trap); *Aut:* **f. (de réparation),** inspection pit; **f. de scieur,** sawpit; **f. aux lions,** lions' den; *Hyg:* **f. d'aisances,** cesspool; **f. septique,** septic tank; *Th:* **f. d'orchestre,** orchestra pit; *Geol:* **f. d'effondrement,** trough fault. **2.** grave; *A:* **f. commune,** paupers' grave; *F:* **avoir un pied dans la f.,** to have one foot in the grave. **3.** *Anat:* fossa. **4.** *Min:* pit.

fossé [fose] *n.m.* **1.** (*a*) ditch, trench, drain; **entretien des haies et fossés,** hedging and ditching; **creuser des fossés,** to trench, to ditch; (*b*) moat, fosse. **2.** *Geol:* trough; **f. d'effondrement,** rift valley. **3.** rift (between persons).

fossette [fosɛt] *n.f.* dimple; **joues à fossettes,** dimpled cheeks.

fossile [fosil] *a. & n.m.* fossil; *F:* **un vieux f.,** an old fossil.

fossiliser [fosilize] *v.* **1.** *v.tr.* to fossilize. **2. se f.,** to fossilize; to become fossilized.

fossoyeur [foswajœr] *n.m.* gravedigger.

fou [fu], **fol, folle** [fɔl] (*the form* **fol** *is used in the m. before a vowel or* **h** *mute*) **1.** *a.* (*a*) mad, insane; **f. à lier,** raving mad, out of one's mind; **il y a de quoi devenir f.,** it's enough to drive you mad; **f. de joie, de terreur,** beside oneself with joy, with fear; **être f. de qn,** to be madly in love with s.o.; to dote on s.o.; **f. de peinture,** mad about painting; (*b*) foolish, extravagant, silly; **illusions folles,** wild delusions; **les vierges folles,** the foolish virgins; **il n'est pas f.,** he's no fool; **un fol espoir,** a foolish, mad, hope; (*c*) excessive, enormous; **succès f.,** tremendous, wild, success; **mal de tête f.,** splitting headache; **il gagne un argent f.,** he makes no end of money; **à une allure folle,** at breakneck speed; **il y avait un monde f.,** there was a fearful crowd; **un prix f.,** an exorbitant price; *F:* **c'est f. ce que c'est cher!** it's madly expensive! **d'une gaieté folle,** wildly happy; in very high spirits; (*d*) out of control; loose (lock of hair); runaway (truck); crazy (compass needle); idle, free (wheel); loose (pulley); **f. rire,** uncontrollable laughter; **herbes folles,** rank weeds; *Bot:* **folle avoine,** wild oats. **2.** *n.* (*a*) madman, *f* madwoman; lunatic; **f. furieux,** raving lunatic, maniac; *F:* **maison de fous,** madhouse; **f. du volant,** reckless driver; *Lit:* **la folle du logis,** the imagination; (*b*) (court) fool; jester; **faire le f.,** to play the fool; **plus on est de fous plus on rit,** the more the merrier. **3.** *n.m.* (*a*) *Chess:* bishop; (*b*) *Orn: F:* gannet.

foucade [fukad] *n.f. A: & Lit:* passing whim.

foudre¹ [fudr] *n.* **1.** (*a*) *f.* thunderbolt, lightning; **maison frappée par la f.,** house struck by lightning; **coup de f.,** (i) *A:* unexpected event; bolt from the blue; (ii) love at first sight; (*b*) *m.pl.* wrath. **2.** *m.* **un f. de guerre,** a great warrior; **f. d'éloquence,** powerful orator.

foudre² *n.m.* tun, hogshead, large cask.

foudroyant [fudrwajɑ̃] *a.* terrifying; crushing (attack, news); withering (look); staggering (success); **progrès foudroyants,** lightning progress.

foudroyer [fudrwaje] *v.tr.* **(je foudroie; je foudroierai)** to strike (down) (by lightning); to blast; **arbre foudroyé,** blasted tree; **l'apoplexie l'a foudroyé,** he was struck down by apoplexy; **elle le foudroya d'un regard,** she gave him a withering look; **cette nouvelle m'a foudroyé,** I was thunderstruck by the news; **f. ses adversaires,** to crush one's opponents.

fouet [fwɛ] *n.m.* **1.** birch(rod); **donner le f. à qn,** to birch s.o. **2.** (*a*) whip; **donner le f. à qn,** to whip, flog, s.o.; **coup de f.,** (i) cut, lash (of whip); (ii) fillip, stimulus; (iii) whip(ping), lashing, surging (of cable); flapping (of sail); **faire claquer son f.,** to crack one's whip; *Artil:* **coup de plein f.,** direct hit; **collision de plein f.,** head-on collision; (*b*) *Dom.Ec:* whisk. **3.** tip (of bird's wing, dog's tail); *Nau:* tail (of pulley).

fouettement [fwɛtmɑ̃] *n.m.* whipping; flapping (of sail); lashing, (of rope, rain, etc.).

fouetter [fwete]. **1.** (*a*) *v.tr.* to whip, spank (a child); to beat, whisk (eggs); to whip (cream); **il n'y a pas là de quoi f. un chat,** there's nothing to make such a fuss about; **avoir d'autres chats à f.,** to have other fish to fry; (*b*) *v.tr. & i.* **la pluie fouette (contre) les vitres,** the rain is lashing against the panes; (*c*) *v.tr.* to excite, stimulate; **brise qui fouette le sang,** breeze that makes the blood tingle; **être fouetté par le désir,** to be spurred on, stimulated, by desire. **2.** *v.i.* (*a*) (*of moving part*) to lash, whip; (*of cable*) to surge; (*of sail*) to flap; (*b*) *P:* to be scared.

fou-fou [fufu] *a.m. F:* foolish, silly; flighty.

fougeraie [fuʒrɛ] *n.f.* fern patch, fernbrake.

fougère [fuʒɛr] *n.f.* fern; **f. aigle,** bracken; **f. arborescente,** tree fern.

fougue¹ [fug] *n.f.* fire, spirit, passion; ardour, *NAm:* ardor; **cheval plein de f.,** high-mettled, mettlesome, horse.

fougue² *n.f. Nau:* **perroquet de f.,** mizzen topsail.

fougueusement [fugøzmɑ̃] *adv.* ardently.

fougueux, -euse [fugø, -øz] *a.* fiery, ardent, spirited; high-spirited (person), spirited (horse).

fouille [fuj] *n.f.* **1.** (*a*) excavation; digging, excavating; (*b*) excavation, pit; **f. à ciel ouvert,** open pit; (*c*) *usu. pl. Archeol:* dig, excavations. **2.** search(ing) (of suspect, traveller).

fouillé [fuje] *a.* well researched, elaborate (work).

fouiller [fuje] **1.** *v.tr.* (*a*) to dig, excavate; (*b*) (*of animal*) to burrow into (*of pig*) to root, rout, in (the ground); (*c*) to search (house); to ransack (drawer); to go through (suitcase); to scour, comb (woods); **f. qn,** to search s.o., go through s.o.'s pockets; **ses yeux fouillaient la salle,** he scanned the room; **f. un problème,** to go thoroughly into a problem. **2.** *v.i.* (*a*) (*of animal*) to burrow; (*of pig*) to root, rout; (*b*) **f. dans une armoire, dans sa poche,** to search, rummage, in a cupboard, in one's pocket; **f. dans les librairies pour trouver un livre,** to ransack the bookshops for a book; **f. dans le passé,** to rake up the past. **3. se f.,** to go through one's pockets; *P:* **tu peux te f.!** nothing doing!

fouilleur, -euse [fujœr, -øz] *n.* **1.** (*a*) excavator, digger; (*b*) rummager; searcher. **2.** *n.f.* **fouilleuse,** subsoil plough.

fouillis [fuji] *n.m.* jumble, mess, muddle (of papers, etc.).

fouinard, -arde [fwinar, -ard] *a. & n. F:* (*a*) inquisitive, nosy; *n.* nosy parker; (*b*) sly, sneaking.
fouine [fwin] *n.f. Z:* stone marten; *F:* **à tête de f.,** weasel-faced, ferret-faced.
fouiner [fwine] *v.i. F:* to ferret, to nose about; **f. dans les affaires d'autrui,** to poke one's nose into other people's business.
fouineur, -euse [fwinœr, -øz] *a. & n. F:* = FOUINARD.
fouir [fwir] *v.tr.* to dig (underground); (*of animal*) to burrow.
fouisseur, -euse [fwisœr, -øz] *a. & n.m.* burrowing (animal); *n.* burrower.
foulage [fulaʒ] *n.m.* **1.** pressing, crushing, treading (of grapes). **2.** fulling, milling (of cloth). **3.** *Typ:* impression.
foulant [fulɑ̃] *a.* (*a*) pressing, crushing; **pompe foulante,** force pump; (*b*) *P:* **ce n'est pas bien f.,** it's not hard work.
foulard [fular] *n.m.* **1.** *Tex:* foulard, silk. **2.** (silk) scarf; headscarf.
foule [ful] *n.f.* **1.** crowd; host (of people, ideas); **psychologie des foules,** mob psychology; **entrer en f.,** to crowd in, come crowding in; **faire f. autour de qn,** to crowd round s.o. **2.** *Fr.C:* migration (of caribou).
foulée [fule] *n.f.* (*a*) tread (of horse's hoof); (*b*) *usu. pl.* stride; **parcourir les champs à longues foulées,** to stride over the fields; *Rac:* **courir, rester, dans la f. d'un concurrent,** to follow close behind another competitor; *Fig:* **marcher sur la f. de qn,** to follow in s.o.'s footsteps; (*c*) *pl. Ven:* foil, spoor, track (of game).
fouler [fule] **1.** *v.tr.* (*a*) to trample (down), tread down (grass); *Winem:* to tread, press, crush (grapes); **f. qch. aux pieds,** to tread, trample, sth. underfoot; (*b*) *Tex:* to full (cloth). **2. se f.** (*a*) **se f. la cheville, etc.,** to sprain, strain, twist, wrench, one's ankle, etc.; (*b*) *F:* **se f. (la rate),** to take a lot of trouble; **ne pas se f. (la rate),** to take things, it, easy.
fouleur, -euse [fulœr, -øz] *n.* **1.** *Tex:* fuller. **2.** wine presser.
fouloir [fulwar] *n.m.* **1.** *Tex:* (*a*) beater, fulling stock; (*b*) fulling mill. **2.** wine press.
foulon [fulɔ̃] *n.m. Tex:* fuller; **chardon à f.,** fuller's teasel; **terre à f.,** fuller's earth.
foulonnier [fulɔnje] *n.m. Tex:* fuller; (i) fulling-mill worker; (ii) owner of fulling mill.
foulque [fulk] *n.f. Orn:* coot.
foulure [fulyr] *n.f.* sprain, wrench; **f. au genou,** sprained knee.
four [fur] *n.m.* **1.** (*a*) (kitchen, baker's) oven; **f. à gaz,** gas cooker, oven, stove; **fair cuire au f.,** to bake; to roast (meat); **noir comme dans un f.,** pitch black; **vaisselle allant au f.,** ovenware; **plat allant au f.,** ovenproof dish; (*b*) *Cu:* **petits fours,** petits fours. **2.** (*a*) *Ind:* kiln; furnace; **f. à chaux,** lime kiln; **f. à briques,** brick kiln; **f. à houblon,** oast; **f. à recuire,** annealing furnace. **3.** *Th: F:* failure, flop; **la pièce a fait (un) f.,** the play was a flop.
fourbe [furb] **1.** *a.* cheating, double-dealing, two-faced. **2.** *n.O:* cheat, rogue, double-dealer.
fourberie [furbəri] *n.f.* **1.** deceit, cheating, double-dealing. **2.** *Lit:* underhand trick.
fourbi [furbi] *n.m. F:* (*a*) (soldier's) kit; gear; paraphernalia; **tout le f.,** the whole lot, whole bag of tricks; (*b*) thingummy, gadget.
fourbir [furbir] *v.tr.* to polish up, shine up, furbish (metal).
fourbissage [furbisaʒ] *n.m.* rubbing up, polishing, furbishing (of metal).
fourbu [furby] *a.* (*of horse*) foundered, broken-down; (*of pers.*) tired out, dead tired, dead beat, fagged (out).
fourbure [furbyr] *n.f. Vet:* founder.
fourche [furʃ] *n.f.* fork. **1.** (*a*) **f. à foin,** hayfork, pitchfork; **remuer le sol à la f.,** to fork the ground; **chariot (élévateur) à f.,** forklift (truck); (*b*) fork (of bicycle, clutch). **2.** fork (of tree); fork(ing) (of road); fork (of legs); crotch, crutch (of trousers); **à f.,** Y-shaped.
fourchée [furʃe] *n.f.* pitchforkful (of hay).
fourcher [furʃe] **1.** *v.i.* (*a*) *A:* to fork, divide, branch; (*b*) **la langue lui a fourché,** he made a slip of the tongue. **2.** *v.tr.* to fork (the ground).
fourchet [furʃɛ] *n.m. Vet:* foot rot.
fourchette [furʃɛt] *n.f.* **1.** (table) fork; *F:* **il a un joli coup de f., c'est une bonne f.,** he's a good trencherman; *F:* **la f. du père Adam** = one's fingers. **2.** *Artil: Stat:* bracket; *Cards:* tenace; **prendre une cible en f., à la f.,** to bracket a target; **tirer à la f.,** to straddle; *Stat:* **f. de salaire,** wage bracket. **3.** (*a*) wishbone (of fowl); (*b*) frog (of horse's hoof). **4.** (*a*) beam support (of balance); (*b*) *Mec.E:* belt guide, shifter; **f. de débrayage,** clutch throw-out fork.
fourchon [furʃɔ̃] *n.m.* prong, tine (of fork).
fourchu [furʃy] *a.* forked; Y-shaped; cleft (stick, chin); **pied f.,** cloven hoof.
fourgon[1] [furgɔ̃] *n.m.* (i) poker; (ii) (fire) rake.
fourgon[2] *n.m.* van; (*a*) **f. automobile,** (motor) van; **f. mortuaire, funéraire, funèbre,** hearse; **f. bancaire,** bullion van; **f. de déménagement,** furniture, removal, van; **f. de livraison,** delivery van; (*b*) *Rail:* **f. à frein,** brake van; **f. de queue,** rear (brake) van, guard's van, *NAm:* caboose; **f. à bagages,** luggage van, *NAm:* baggage car; **f. à marchandises,** (covered) goods wagon; *NAm:* freight car; **f. à bestiaux,** cattle truck.
fourgonner [furgɔne] *v.tr. & i.* to poke, rake (the fire); **f. dans un tiroir,** to poke about, rummage about, in a drawer.
fourgonnette [furgɔnɛt] *n.f. Aut:* light van.
fourmi [furmi] *n.f.* ant; **avoir des fourmis dans les jambes,** to have pins and needles in one's legs.
fourmilier [furmilje] *n.m. Z:* anteater.
fourmilière [furmiljɛr] *n.f.* anthill, ant's nest.
fourmi-lion [furmiljɔ̃] *n.m. Ent:* ant-lion; *pl. fourmis-lions.*
fourmillement [furmijmɑ̃] *n.m.* **1.** swarming (of ants, etc.). **2.** pricking, tingling, sensation; pins and needles.
fourmiller [furmije] *v.i.* **1.** to swarm; to teem; **les vers fourmillaient dans ce fromage,** the cheese was alive with maggots; **ouvrage qui fourmille de fautes,** work full of, teeming with, mistakes. **2. le pied me fourmille,** I've got pins and needles in my foot.
fournaise [furnɛz] *n.f.* furnace; **cette chambre est une (vraie) f.,** this room's like an oven.
fourneau, -eaux [furno] *n.m.* **1.** (*a*) furnace (of boiler, etc.); **f. d'une pipe,** bowl of a pipe; (*b*) **f. de cuisine,** (kitchen) range; **f. à gaz,** gas stove, cooker; (*c*) *Metall:* furnace; **haut f.,** blast furnace. **2.** *Min:* **f. de mine,** mine chamber, blast hole.
fournée [furne] *n.f.* batch (of loaves, etc.); *F:* batch, contingent (of tourists, etc.).
fourni [furni] *a.* **1.** well stocked (shop, etc.). **2.** thick (hair, etc.). **3.** *Sp:* **champ f.,** big field of starters.
fournil [furni] *n.m.* bakehouse.
fourniment [furnimɑ̃] *n.m.* gear, paraphernalia.
fournir [furnir] **1.** *v.tr.* (*a*) to supply, furnish, provide, produce; **f. qch. à qn, f. qn de qch.,** to supply s.o. with sth.; **tant par mois, tout fourni,** so much a month, all found; **bibliothèque bien fournie,** well stocked library; **f. une maison en vin,** to supply a house with wine; (*b*) **vignoble qui fournit un bon vin,** vineyard that yields, produces, a good wine; **f. un effort considérable,** to make a considerable effort;

Cards: **f. du trèfle,** to follow a club lead; *Sp:* **f. un jeu remarquable,** to play an outstanding game; *Rac:* **f. toute la carrière,** to complete the course. **2.** *v.ind.tr.* **f. aux dépenses,** to defray the expenses; **f. aux besoins de qn,** to supply s.o.'s wants; *Cards:* **f. à la couleur demandée,** to follow suit. **3. se f.** (*a*) (*of beard, etc.*) to grow thick; (*b*) **se f. de qch.,** to provide oneself with sth.; to get supplies of sth. (**chez,** from).

fournissement [furnismɑ̃] *n.m. Fin:* contribution, holding, in shares.

fournisseur, -euse [furnisœr, -øz] *n.* (*a*) supplier, purveyor, caterer; **f. de navires, de la marine,** ships' chandler; (*b*) **les fournisseurs,** the tradesmen.

fourniture [furnityr] *n.f.* **1.** supplying, providing. **2.** *Cu:* seasoning (of dish). **3.** *pl.* supplies, requisites; **façon et fournitures,** making and materials; **fournitures de navires,** ships' chandlery; **fournitures de bureau,** office equipment; stationery.

fourrage [furaʒ] *n.m.* **1.** forage, fodder. **2.** foraging.

fourrager¹ [furaʒe] *v.* (**n. fourrageons; je fourrageai(s)**) **1.** *v.i.* (*a*) to forage; (*b*) to rummage, forage. **2.** *v.tr.* (*a*) to pillage, ravage (country); (*b*) to jumble up (papers).

fourrager², -ère [furaʒe, -ɛr] **1.** *a.* **plantes fourragères,** fodder crops. **2.** *n.f.* (*a*) field sown with fodder crop; (*b*) *Mil:* shoulder braid.

fourrageur [furaʒœr] *n.m.* **1. cavaliers dispersés en fourrageurs,** cavalry in open, extended, order. **2.** *A:* pillager, marauder.

fourré [fure] **1.** *a.* (*a*) lined (coat, gloves, etc.); fur-lined; thick (wood); **chocolats fourrés à la crème,** chocolate creams; **bonbon f.,** sweet, *NAm:* candy, with a soft centre; (*b*) **paix fourrée,** hollow peace, mock peace; *Fenc:* **coup f.,** exchanged hit, double hit; **porter un coup f. à qn,** to deal s.o. a backhanded blow. **2.** *n.m.* thicket; *Ven:* cover.

fourreau, -eaux [furo] *n.m.* (*a*) sheath, cover, case; scabbard (of sword); *Cost:* sheath dress; **remettre l'épée au f.,** to sheathe one's sword; (*b*) *Mec.E:* sleeve; quill (for shaft, etc.); *I.C.E:* **soupapes à fourreaux,** sleeve valves.

fourrer [fure] *v.tr.* **1.** (*a*) to cover, line, with fur; (*b*) *Mec.E:* to pack (joint); *Nau:* to serve, keckle (cable). **2.** *F:* to stuff, cram; **f. ses mains dans ses poches,** to stuff, bury, one's hands in one's pockets; **je les avais fourrés dans le coin,** I had stuck them in the corner; **où est-il allé se f.?** where ever has he hidden himself? **f. son nez partout,** to poke one's nose into everything; **f. qn au trou,** to chuck s.o. into jail, run s.o. in.

fourre-tout [furtu] *n.m.inv.* **1.** lumber room. **2.** holdall (for travelling).

fourreur [furœr] *n.m.* furrier.

fourrier [furje] *n.m.* (*a*) *Mil:* quartermaster sergeant; (*b*) *Navy:* writer.

fourrière [furjɛr] *n.f.* (animal, car) pound; **mettre un chien, une voiture, en f.,** to impound a dog, a car.

fourrure [furyr] *n.f.* **1.** (*a*) fur, skin; **f. plate,** short-haired fur; **manteau de f.,** fur coat; **f. de peau de mouton,** (fleecy) sheepskin; (*b*) hair, coat (of animal). **2.** packing (of joint); **f. d'antifriction,** antifriction lining, bushing; *Aut:* **f. de frein,** brake lining.

fourvoyer [furvwaje] *v.tr.* (**je fourvoie; je fourvoierai**) to mislead; to lead (s.o.) astray; **être fourvoyé,** to be on the wrong track; to have lost one's way, gone astray.

foutaise [futɛz] *n.f. P:* rot, rubbish.

foutoir [futwar] *n.m. P:* bloody shambles.

foutre [futr̥] *v.* (*p.p.* **foutu;** *pr.ind.* **je fous, n. foutons**) *V:* **1.** *v.tr.* (*a*) **f. qch. par terre,** to chuck, fling, sth. on the ground; (*b*) **il ne fout rien,** he does damn all; **f. le camp,** to scram, piss off; **fous-moi la paix! va te faire f.!** bugger off! fuck off! **2. se f. de qn, qch.,** to make fun of, take the mickey out of, s.o., sth.; **je m'en fous,** I don't give a damn, a fuck.

foutriquet [futrikɛ] *n.m. P:* little squirt.

foutu [futy] *a. V:* (*a*) bloody awful; (*b*) ruined, done for; **il est f.,** he's had it.

fox(-terrier) [fɔks(terje)] *n.m.* fox terrier.

fox(-trot) [fɔks(trɔt)] *n.m. Danc:* foxtrot.

foyer [fwaje] *n.m.* **1.** fire(place), hearth, grate; firebox (of steam engine); **f. de chaudière,** boiler furnace; **f. mécanique,** mechanical stoker. **2.** source (of heat); seat (of a fire); centre (of learning, infection); **f. d'intrigue,** hotbed of intrigue. **3.** (*a*) hearth, home; **le f. familial,** the home; **rentrer dans ses foyers,** to come (back) home; **f. d'étudiants,** students' union, club, centre; (*b*) *Th:* foyer; **f. des artistes,** green room. **4.** focus (of lens, curve, etc.); **verres à double f.,** bifocal lenses, bifocals.

frac [frak] *n.m.* dress coat; tailcoat, *F:* tails.

fracas [fraka] *n.m.* din; crash (of broken glass, thunder); clash (of arms); **faire du f.,** (i) to kick up a dust, row, shindy; (ii) (*of event*) to create a sensation; **à grand f.,** ostentatiously.

fracasser [frakase] *v.tr.* to smash (sth.) to pieces; to shatter (sth.).

fraction [fraksjɔ̃] *n.f.* **1.** *Ecc:* breaking (of the bread). **2.** (*a*) *Mth:* fraction; **f. ordinaire,** vulgar fraction; **f. décimale,** decimal fraction; **f. périodique,** recurring decimal; (*b*) part, portion; proportion.

fractionnaire [fraksjɔnɛr] *a.* fractional; **nombre f.,** improper fraction.

fractionnel, -elle [fraksjɔnɛl] *a.* divisive (tactics).

fractionnement [fraksjɔnmɑ̃] *n.m.* **1.** dividing up; splitting up (of estate, group). **2.** *Ch: etc:* fractional distillation, fractionation; cracking (of oil).

fractionner [fraksjɔne] **1.** *v.tr.* (*a*) to divide into (fractional) parts; to split (up) (shares); *Mth:* to fractionize; **f. le paiement,** to pay in instalments; (*b*) *Ch: etc:* to fractionate (distillation); to crack (mineral oils). **2. se f.,** to split up; to divide into groups.

fractionnisme [fraksjɔnism] *n.m. Pol:* divisive tactics, splinter tactics.

fracture [fraktyr] *n.f.* **1.** breaking open, forcing (of lock, door). **2.** *Med: Geol:* fracture; *Med:* **réduire une f.,** to set a fracture.

fracturer [fraktyre] **1.** *v.tr.* (*a*) to force (lock); to break open (door, safe); (*b*) to fracture (bone). **2. se f.,** to fracture, break.

fragile [fraʒil] *a.* **1.** fragile; flimsy; brittle (glass). **2.** frail, delicate (person, health); weak (stomach); weak, unstable (authority); precarious (happiness).

fragilement [fraʒilmɑ̃] *adv.* fragilely, weakly.

fragilité [fraʒilite] *n.f.* **1.** fragility; brittleness (of glass). **2.** frailty, weakness.

fragment [fragmɑ̃] *n.m.* fragment; chip (of stone); splinter (of bone); snatch (of song); extract (from book).

fragmentaire [fragmɑ̃tɛr] *a.* fragmentary.

fragmentairement [fragmɑ̃tɛrmɑ̃] *adv.* in fragments; partially.

fragmentation [fragmɑ̃tasjɔ̃] *n.f.* fragmentation.

fragmenter [fragmɑ̃te] *v.tr.* to divide into fragments; to fragment, split up; **f. la publication d'un ouvrage,** to publish a work in parts.

frai [frɛ] *n.m.* **1.** abrasion, wear (of coins). **2.** (*a*) spawning (of fish); (*b*) spawn; (*c*) *Pisc:* fry.

fraîchement [frɛʃmɑ̃] *adv.* **1.** coolly. **2.** freshly, recently; newly.

fraîcheur [frɛʃœr] *n.f.* freshness. **1.** coolness, chilliness; **dans la f. du soir,** in the cool of the evening. **2.** freshness (of flowers, colours, ideas); bloom (of youth). **3.** *Nau:* catspaw, light air.

fraîchir [freʃir] *v.i. Meteor:* **1.** to freshen; to grow colder, cooler. **2.** (*of wind*) to freshen.

frais¹, fraîche [frɛ, frɛʃ] **1.** *a.* fresh; (*a*) cool (wind, dress); chilly (breeze, reception); **il fait f.,** it's cool, fresh; (*b*) *Nau:* **vent f.,** fresh wind; (*c*) new, recent; **œufs frais,** new-laid eggs; **pain f.,** fresh, new, bread; **encre encore fraîche,** ink still wet; *Lit:* (*with adv. force*) **roses toutes fraîches cueillies,** freshly gathered roses; (*d*) **teint f.,** fresh complexion; **f. comme l'œil,** as fresh as a daisy; **f. et dispos,** hale and hearty, ready for anything; *P:* **me voilà f.!** I'm in a (nice) mess, a pretty fix! **2.** (*a*) *n.m.* **prendre le f.,** to take the air, to enjoy the cool of the evening; **à mettre au f.,** to be kept cool, in a cool place; **peint de f.,** freshly painted; (*b*) *n.f.* **à la fraîche,** in the cool (of the day).

frais² *n.m.pl.* expenses, cost; **faux f.,** incidental expenses; **f. d'un procès,** costs of a lawsuit; **être condamné aux f.,** to be ordered to pay costs; **faire les f. de qch.,** to bear the cost, the expense, of sth.; **supporter tous les f. d'une entreprise,** to finance an undertaking; **faire ses f.,** to cover one's expenses; (*of enterprise*) to pay its way; **faire les f. de la conversation,** to keep the conversation going; **faire qch. à ses f.,** to do sth. at one's own expense; **à grands f., à peu de f.,** at great, at little, cost; **rentrer dans ses f.,** to get one's money back; **se mettre en f.,** to go to expense; to put oneself out; **j'en suis pour mes f.,** I've had all my trouble for nothing; *Com:* **f. généraux,** overhead expenses; overheads; charges; expenses incurred; **exempt de f., sans f.,** free of charge; (*on bill of exchange*) no expenses; **f. d'exploitation,** operating costs; **f. de pilotage,** pilotage; **f. de représentation,** expense account; entertainment allowance; *F:* **aux f. de la princesse,** at the expense of the government, the firm; on the house; **f. scolaires,** school fees.

fraisage [frɛzaʒ] *n.m.* **1.** *Metalw:* (*a*) milling (of surface); (*b*) countersinking (of hole). **2.** *Dent:* drilling.

fraise¹ [frɛz] *n.f.* (*a*) strawberry; **f. des bois,** wild, *NAm:* field, strawberry; *a.inv.* **f. (écrasée),** (crushed) strawberry; (*b*) strawberry mark; naevus, *NAm:* nevus.

fraise² *n.f.* **1.** *Cu:* crow (of calf, lamb). **2.** (*a*) *A.Cost:* ruff; (*b*) wattle (of turkey). **3.** *Mec.E: etc:* (*a*) milling cutter; mill; (*b*) **f. (conique),** countersink; (*c*) *Dent:* drill.

fraiser [freze] *v.tr.* **1.** *A:* to frill, goffer. **2.** *Mec.E:* (*a*) to mill; (*b*) to countersink (hole); (*c*) *Dent:* to drill.

fraiseraie [frɛzrɛ] *n.f.* strawberry field, bed.

fraiseuse [frɛzøz] *n.f. Mec.E:* milling machine.

fraisier [frezje] *n.m.* strawberry plant.

fraisiériste [frezjerist] *n.m.* strawberry grower.

fraisil [frezi(l)] *n.m.* coal cinders.

fraisure [frezyr] *n.f.* countersunk hole.

framboise [frɑ̃bwaz] *n.f.* (*a*) raspberry; (*b*) raspberry liqueur.

framboisé [frɑ̃bwaze] *a.* raspberry-flavoured.

framboisier [frɑ̃bwazje] *n.m.* raspberry cane.

franc¹ [frɑ̃] *n.m.* franc.

franc², franche [frɑ̃, frɑ̃ʃ] *a.* **1.** free; **f. arbitre,** free will; **f. de tout droit,** duty-free; **f. d'impôts,** exempt from taxation; **f. de port,** post-free; carriage paid; *Cust:* **zone franche,** free zone; **port f.,** free port; *Fb:* **coup f.,** free kick; *Mil:* **corps f.,** commando (unit). **2.** (*a*) frank; open; candid; **situation franche,** clear, unequivocal, position; **c'est net et f.,** it's all open and aboveboard; **y aller de f. jeu,** to be quite straightforward about it; **jouer jeu f., f. jeu (avec, contre, qn),** (i) to play a straightforward game; (ii) to play fair (with s.o.); *adv.* **pour parler f.,** frankly, candidly, speaking; (*b*) real, true; pure (colour, wine); clean (break); downright, out-and-out (scoundrel); **c'est un f. Breton,** he's a true Breton; **vin f. de goût,** wine clean to the taste; **terre franche,** loam; (*c*) **huit jours francs,** eight clear days.

franc³, franque [frɑ̃, frɑ̃k] *Hist:* **1.** *a.* Frankish. **2.** *n.* Frank.

français, -aise [frɑ̃sɛ, -ɛz] **1.** *a.* French. **2.** *n.* Frenchman, *f.* Frenchwoman; **les F.,** the French. **3.** *n.m. Ling:* French; **parler f.,** (i) to speak French; (ii) to express oneself clearly. **4.** *Cu:* **à la française,** à la française; **jardin à la française,** formal garden.

franc-bord [frɑ̃bɔr] *n.m. Nau:* **1.** freeboard. **2. bordé à f.-b.,** carvel built; *pl. francs-bords.*

franc-bourgeois [frɑ̃burʒwa] *n.m. Hist:* freeman; *pl. francs-bourgeois.*

France [frɑ̃s] *Pr.n.f. Geog:* France; **en F.,** in France; **les vins de F.,** French wines.

Francfort [frɑ̃kfɔr] *Pr.n. Geog:* Frankfurt; **saucisse de F.,** frankfurter.

franchement [frɑ̃ʃmɑ̃] *adv.* **1.** frankly, candidly, openly, readily. **2.** really, quite; **c'était f. stupide,** it was sheer stupidity; **j'en suis f. dégoûté,** I'm heartily sick of it.

franchir [frɑ̃ʃir] *v.tr.* (*a*) to clear (obstacle); to jump (over) (ditch); to shoot (rapids); to run past (danger signal); to exceed (limit); to get over (difficulty); (*b*) to pass through; to cross (river, frontier); **f. le seuil,** to step over, to cross, the threshold; **f. le mur du son,** to break (through) the sound barrier; **il a franchi la quarantaine,** he has turned forty.

franchise [frɑ̃ʃiz] *n.f.* **1.** (*a*) *Hist:* **charte de f.,** charter (of freedom) (of city); (*b*) exemption; **faire entrer qch. en f.,** to import sth. duty free; **entrée en f.,** free import; **bagages en f.,** free allowance of luggage; **en f. (postale)** = O.H.M.S., official paid; (*c*) *Ins:* accidental damage excess. **2.** frankness, openness, candour; plain speaking, outspokenness; **parler avec f.,** to speak frankly.

franchissable [frɑ̃ʃisabl̥] *a.* that can be crossed, passed; passable; negotiable (hill).

franchissement [frɑ̃ʃismɑ̃] *n.m.* clearing (of obstacle); jumping (of ditch, etc.); crossing, passing (of river, etc.).

francisation [frɑ̃sizasjɔ̃] *n.f.* **1.** gallicizing (of foreign word, etc.). **2.** *Nau:* registry as a French ship.

franciscain, -aine [frɑ̃siskɛ̃, -ɛn] *Ecc:* **1.** *a. & n.m.* Franciscan. **2.** *n.f.* (Poor) Clare.

franciser [frɑ̃size] *v.tr.* **1.** to gallicize (foreign word, etc.). **2.** *Nau:* to register (ship) as French.

franc-maçon [frɑ̃masɔ̃] *n. m.* freemason; *pl. francs-maçons.*

franc-maçonnerie [frɑ̃masɔnri] *n.f.* freemasonry.

franco [frɑ̃ko] *adv.* (*a*) free, carriage free; **f. (de port),** carriage paid, postage paid; **livré f.,** delivery free (of charge), post(age) paid; **catalogue f. sur demande,** catalogue sent free on request; **f. (à, de) bord,** free on board, F.O.B.; (*b*) *F:* readily, unhesitatingly; **vas-y f.!** go ahead!

franco-allemand [frɑ̃koalmɑ̃] *a.* Franco-German.

franco-américain, -aine [frɑ̃koamerikɛ̃, -ɛn] *a. & n.* Franco-American.

franco-canadien [frɑ̃kokanadjɛ̃] **1.** *a.* French Canadian. **2.** *n.m. Ling:* Canadian French.

François [frɑ̃swa] *Pr.n.m.* Francis, Frank.

Françoise [frɑ̃swaz] *Pr.n.f.* Frances.

francophile [frɑ̃kɔfil] *a. & n.* francophile.

francophobe [frɑ̃kɔfɔb] *a. & n.* francophobe.

francophobie [frɑ̃kɔfɔbi] *n.f.* francophobia.

francophone [frɑ̃kɔfɔn] *a. & n.* French-speaking (person).

franc-parler [frɑ̃parle] *n.m.* frankness, candour, *NAm:* candor; plain speaking; **avoir son f.-p.,** to speak one's mind; **aimer son f.-p.,** to be outspoken.

franc-tireur [frɑ̃tirœr] *n.m. Mil:* franc-tireur, irregular (soldier); guerrilla; *Fig:* freelance; *pl. francs-tireurs.*

frange [frɑ̃ʒ] *n.f.* fringe (of rug, hair, etc.).
franger [frɑ̃ʒe] *v.tr.* **(je frangeai(s))** to fringe, to border.
frangin, -ine [frɑ̃ʒɛ̃, -in] *n. P:* brother, sister.
frangipanier [frɑ̃ʒipanje] *n.m. Bot:* frangipani (tree).
franglais [frɑ̃glɛ] *n.m. F:* Franglais.
franquette [frɑ̃kɛt] *n.f. used only in* **à la bonne f.,** simply, without ceremony; in a homely way.
franquiste [frɑ̃kist] *Hist:* **1.** *a.* pro-Franco. **2.** *n.* supporter of Franco.
frappant [frapɑ̃] *a.* striking (picture, likeness, etc.).
frappe [frap] *n.f.* (*a*) striking, minting (of coins); (*b*) *Typew:* striking (of the keys); touch; **erreur, faute, de f.,** typing error; (*c*) (*baseball*) hit; (*d*) *Mil:* **force de f.,** strike force.
frappement [frapmɑ̃] *n.m.* (action of) striking; blow.
frapper [frape] *v.* to strike, hit. **I.** *v.tr.* **1.** (*a*) **f. légèrement,** to tap; **f. la table du poing,** to bang one's fist on the table; **f. qn avec la main,** to slap s.o.; **se f. les cuisses,** to slap one's thighs; **f. un coup,** to strike a blow; **f. des marchandises d'un droit,** to impose a duty on goods; **être frappé d'une maladie,** to be struck down by a disease; **être frappé de mutisme,** to be struck dumb; **f. qn d'étonnement,** to strike s.o. with amazement; **ce qui m'a frappé le plus c'était son sang-froid,** what struck, impressed, me most was his coolness; (*b*) to stamp; to strike (medal, coin); to mint (coins); to stamp, emboss (wallpaper); to block (leather); (*c*) to punch (out), cut out (paper pattern); (*d*) to type (letter). **2.** *Nau:* to bend (halyard); to bend on (signal). **3.** to ice; to chill (wine, etc.); **f. le champagne,** to put the champagne on ice; **whisky frappé,** whisky on the rocks. **II.** *v.i.* **1. f. sur la table** (i) **au poing,** to bang, (ii) **avec un crayon,** to tap, on the table; **f., f. doucement, à la porte,** to knock, to tap, on, at, the door; **on frappe,** there's a knock (at the door). **2. f. des mains, dans ses mains,** to clap (one's hands); **f. du pied,** to stamp (one's foot). **III. se f.,** *F:* to get demoralized, panicky; **ne vous frappez pas,** don't panic; don't flap.
frappeur, -euse [frapœr, -øz] *n.* (*a*) hitter, striker; *Metalw:* hammerman, striker; *Psychics:* **esprit f.,** rapping spirit; (*b*) stamper; embosser; (*c*) cutter-out.
frasque [frask] *n.f.* prank, escapade.
fraternel, -elle [fratɛrnɛl] *a.* fraternal, brotherly.
fraternellement [fratɛrnɛlmɑ̃] *adv.* fraternally.
fraternisation [fratɛrnizasjɔ̃] *n.f.* fraternization.
fraterniser [fratɛrnize] *v.i.* to fraternize.
fraternité [fratɛrnite] *n.f.* fraternity; brotherhood; fellowship.
fratricide[1] [fratrisid] **1.** *n.* (*pers.*) fratricide. **2.** *a.* fratricidal.
fratricide[2] *n.m.* (crime of) fratricide.
fraudatoire [frodatwar] *a.* fraudulent.
fraude [frod] *n.f.* **1.** fraud, deception, cheating; **f. fiscale,** tax evasion; **en f.,** (i) fraudulently, unlawfully; (ii) secretly; **passer qch. en f.,** to smuggle sth. through the customs. **2.** fraudulence, deceit; **par f.,** under false pretences.
frauder [frode] **1.** *v.tr.* (*a*) to defraud, cheat, swindle (s.o.); **f. la douane,** to defraud the customs, to smuggle; (*b*) **vin fraudé,** adulterated wine. **2.** *v.i.* to cheat.
fraudeur, -euse [frodœr, -øz] *n.* **1.** defrauder, cheat, swindler. **2.** smuggler.
frauduleusement [frodyløzmɑ̃] *adv.* fraudulently.
frauduleux, -euse [frodylø, -øz] *a.* fraudulent; **édition frauduleuse,** pirated edition.
frayer [freje] *v.* **(je fraye, fraie, n. frayons; je frayerai, fraierai) 1.** *v.tr.* (*a*) to scrape, rub; to gall (horse); (*b*) **f. un chemin,** to trace, clear, a path; to blaze a trail; **le chemin frayé,** the beaten track; **se f. un passage,** (i) to clear a way (for oneself); (ii) to effect an entrance; **se f. un chemin à travers la foule,** to force, push, elbow, one's way through the crowd; **f. la voie à qn,** to clear, pave, the way for s.o. **2.** *v.i.* (*a*) (*of fish*) to spawn; (*b*) **f. avec qn,** to associate with, frequent, s.o.; **je ne fraye pas avec eux,** I don't mix with them.
frayeur [frɛjœr] *n.f.* fright; fear, dread (**de,** of).
fredaine [frədɛn] *n.f.* prank, escapade.
fredonnement [frədɔnmɑ̃] *n.m.* humming (of tune).
fredonner [frədɔne] *v.tr.* to hum (tune).
frégate [fregat] *n.f.* **1.** *Navy:* frigate; **capitaine de f.,** commander. **2.** *Orn:* frigate bird.
frein [frɛ̃] *n.m.* **1.** (*a*) bit; (*of horse, pers.*) **ronger son f.,** to champ at the bit; **mettre un f. aux désirs de qn,** to curb, bridle, s.o.'s desires; **curiosité sans f.,** unbridled curiosity; (*b*) *Anat:* fr(a)enum; string(s) (of the tongue). **2.** brake; *Rail: etc:* **f. à vide,** vacuum brake; **f. à air (comprimé),** airbrake; *Aut:* **f. à main,** handbrake; **f. à pédale, au pied,** foot brake; **f. à disque,** disc brake; **f. à tambour,** drum brake; **mettre le f.,** to apply, put on, the brake(s), to brake; **donner un coup de f. à qn, à une entreprise,** to pull s.o. up short; to put a brake on an undertaking.
freinage [frɛnaʒ] *n.m.* **1.** braking; *Av:* **parachute de f.,** brake parachute. **2.** brake system; brakes.
freiner [frene] **1.** *v.tr.* (*a*) to brake, apply the brake(s) to (vehicle); (*b*) to curb (inflation, etc.); to check (production). **2.** *v.i.* to brake, apply the brake(s); **f. brusquement,** to jam on the brake(s).
freinte [frɛ̃t] *n.f. Com:* loss in volume, in weight (during transit, manufacture).
frelatage [frəlataʒ] *n.m.* adulteration.
frelater [frəlate] *v.tr.* to adulterate (food).
frêle [frɛl] *a.* frail, weak (health, person); fragile.
frelon [frəlɔ̃] *n.m. Ent:* hornet.
freluche [frəlyʃ] *n.f.* tuft (of tassel, etc.).
freluquet [frəlykɛ] *n.m. F:* whippersnapper.
frémir [fremir] *v.i.* **1.** to vibrate, quiver; (*of leaves*) to rustle; (*of wind*) to sigh; (*of hot water*) to simmer. **2.** to tremble, shake, quake, shudder; **f. de crainte,** to shake, quiver, with fear.
frémissement [fremismɑ̃] *n.m.* **1.** rustle (of leaves, etc.); simmering (of water); sighing, soughing (of wind). **2.** (*a*) shuddering, quaking, quivering; (*b*) shudder, tremor, quiver.
frênaie [frɛnɛ] *n.f.* ash plantation.
frêne [frɛn] *n.m.* ash (tree, timber).
frénésie [frenezi] *n.f.* frenzy; agitation; **applaudir avec f.,** to applaud frantically, enthusiastically.
frénétique [frenetik] *a.* frantic; frenzied; passionate; violent.
frénétiquement [frenetikmɑ̃] *adv.* frantically, frenetically.
fréquemment [frekamɑ̃] *adv.* frequently.
fréquence [frekɑ̃s] *n.f.* **1.** frequency; **f. du pouls,** pulse rate. **2.** *Ph: W.Tel: etc:* **basse, haute, f.,** low, high, frequency; **très haute f.,** very high frequency (V.H.F.); **bande de fréquences,** frequency band.
fréquent [frekɑ̃] *a.* frequent.
fréquentable [frekɑ̃tabl̩] *a.* pleasant to meet, to visit.
fréquentatif, -ive [frekɑ̃tatif, -iv] *a. Gram:* frequentative.
fréquentation [frekɑ̃tasjɔ̃] *n.f.* (*a*) frequenting; **f. des théâtres,** frequent visits to the theatre; **f. assidue des conférences,** regular attendance at lectures; (*b*) association (**de,** with); **mauvaises fréquentations,** bad company.
fréquenté [frekɑ̃te] *a.* much visited; crowded, popular (place); busy (road); **hôtel bien f.,** hotel with a good clientele; **endroit mal f.,** place with a bad reputation.

fréquenter [frekɑ̃te] *v.tr.* (*a*) to frequent; to visit frequently; (*b*) **f. qn,** (i) to associate with s.o.; (ii) to see s.o. regularly; **quels gens fréquente-t-il?** what company does he keep? who does he go around with?
frère [frɛr] *n.m.* **1.** brother; **f. de lait,** foster brother; **frères d'armes,** brothers-in-arms; *Ecc:* **mes très chers frères,** dearly beloved brethren; *F:* **f. trois-points,** freemason; *F:* **tu es un f.,** you're a real friend; **faux f.,** false friend; **vieux f.,** old chap. **2.** *Ecc:* friar; **f. lai,** lay brother.
frérot [frero] *n.m. F:* little brother.
fresque [frɛsk] *n.f.* fresco; **peinture à f.,** painting in fresco.
fresquiste [frɛskist] *a. & n.* **(peintre) f.,** fresco painter.
fressure [fresyr] *n.f.* pluck (of calf, sheep, etc.); *Cu:* (lamb's, pig's) fry.
fret [frɛ] *n.m.* freight. **1.** freightage; **payer le f.,** to pay the freight. **2.** chartering; **prendre un navire à f.,** to charter a ship; **donner un navire à f.,** to freight (out) a ship. **3.** cargo (of ship, aircraft); load (of lorry).
fréter [frete] *v.tr.* **(je frète; je fréterai) 1.** to freight (out) (ship). **2.** to hire (car). **3.** to equip, fit out (ship, lorry).
fréteur [fretœr] *n.m.* shipowner.
frétillant [fretijɑ̃] *a.* **1.** wriggling, wriggly (fish, etc.). **2.** (*pers.*) lively.
frétillement [fretijmɑ̃] *n.m.* **1.** wriggling (of fish, etc.); wagging (of tail). **2.** fidgeting, quivering.
frétiller [fretije] *v.i.* (*of fish, etc.*) to wriggle; **le chien frétille de la queue,** the dog is wagging its tail; **l'enfant frétille d'impatience,** the child is fidgeting, quivering, with impatience.
fretin [frətɛ̃] *n.m. Fish: Fig:* **(menu) f.,** small fry.
frettage [frɛtaʒ] *n.m.* binding, hooping.
frette[1] [frɛt] *n.f.* (binding) hoop, collar, ferrule; band (of axle); **f. de moyeu,** nave ring (of wheel).
frette[2] *n.f. Arch: Her:* fret.
fretter [frete] *v.tr.* to bind with a ring, ferrule; to band, hoop.
freudien, -ienne [frødjɛ̃, -jɛn] *a. Psy:* Freudian.
freudisme [frødism] *n.m. Psy:* Freud(ian)ism.
freux [frø] *n.m. Orn:* rook; **colonie de f.,** rookery.
friabilité [frijabilite] *n.f.* friability.
friable [frijabl̥] *a.* friable, crumbly.
friand, -ande [frijɑ̃, -ɑ̃d] **1.** *a.* fond of delicacies; **être f. de sucreries,** to have a sweet tooth; **f. de louanges,** fond of praise. **2.** *n.m. Cu:* (*a*) = sausage roll; (*b*) small almond cake.
friandise [frijɑ̃diz] *n.f.* dainty, delicacy, titbit.
Fribourg [fribur] *Pr.n. Geog:* **1.** Freiburg. **2.** Fribourg.
fric [frik] *n.m. P:* money, dough, lolly.
fricassée [frikase] *n.f.* (*a*) *Cu:* fricassee; *Belg:* bacon omelette; (*b*) *P:* **f. de museaux,** necking.
fricasser [frikase] *v.tr. Cu:* to fricassee.
fricatif, -ive [frikatif, -iv] *Ling: a. & n.f.* fricative.
fric-frac [frikfrak] *n.m. P:* burglary; *pl. fric-frac(s).*
friche [friʃ] *n.f.* waste land, fallow land; **rester, être, en f.,** to lie fallow, remain uncultivated.
frichti [friʃti] *n.m. P:* food, grub.
fricot [friko] *n.m. F:* made-up dish; stew; **faire le f.,** to do the cooking.
fricotage [frikɔtaʒ] *n.m. F:* fiddling; underhand dealing.
fricoter [frikɔte] *v.tr. F:* (*a*) to stew; to cook; (*b*) to plot; **je me demande ce qu'il fricote,** I wonder what he's up to, what he's cooking up.
fricoteur, -euse [frikɔtœr, -øz] *n. F:* (*a*) dishonest dealer, fiddler; (*b*) profiteer.
friction [friksjɔ̃] *n.f.* friction. **1.** rubbing, chafing (of the limbs, etc.); *Sp:* rub down; *Hairdr:* scalp massage. **2.** *Mec:* **embrayage à f.,** friction clutch. **3.** disagreement.
frictionner [friksjɔne] *v.tr.* to rub, chafe (limb); **f. qn,** to give s.o. a rub down; **f. la tête de qn,** to give s.o. a scalp massage.
Fridolin [fridɔlɛ̃] *n.m. P:* German, Jerry, Kraut.
frigidaire [friʒidɛr] *n.m. R.t.m:* refrigerator, fridge; *F:* **mettre un projet au f.,** to put a plan into cold storage.
frigide [friʒid] *a.* frigid; *Lit:* cold, icy.
frigo [frigo] *n.m. F:* **1.** fridge, refrigerator. **2.** frozen meat.
frigorification [frigɔrifikasjɔ̃] *n.f.* refrigerating, chilling (of meat).
frigorifié [frigɔrifje] *a.* frozen; chilled (meat, etc.); *F:* (*of pers.*) frozen stiff.
frigorifier [frigɔrifje] *v.tr.* to refrigerate.
frigorifique [frigɔrifik] *a.* refrigerating, *U.S:* frigorific; **appareil f.,** refrigerator; **mélange f.,** freezing mixture; **wagon f.,** refrigerator van; **entrepôt f.,** *n.m.* **f.,** cold store.
frigoriste [frigɔrist] *n.m.* refrigerating engineer.
frileusement [friløzmɑ̃] *adv.* with a shiver.
frileux, -euse [frilø, -øz] *a.* (*of pers.*) chilly; **je suis très f.,** I feel the cold terribly.
frimaire [frimɛr] *n.m. Hist:* third month of Fr. Republican calendar (Nov–Dec).
frimas [frimɑ] *n.m. Lit:* (hoar)frost; rime.
frime [frim] *n.f. F:* sham, pretence, make-believe; **tout ça c'est de la f.,** that's bunkum, all eyewash.
frimousse [frimus] *n.f. F:* (sweet, pretty little) face.
fringale [frɛ̃gal] *n.f. F:* hunger; **avoir la f.,** to be ravenous, starving; **avoir une f. de divertissements,** to hanker after pleasure.
fringant [frɛ̃gɑ̃] *a.* spirited, lively, frisky (horse); smart, dashing (person).
fringuer [frɛ̃ge] **1.** *v.i. A:* to prance, skip about. **2.** *v.tr. P:* to dress (s.o.); **bien fringué,** well dressed. **3.** **se f.,** to get dressed (up).
fringues [frɛ̃g] *n.f.pl. P:* clothes, togs.
friper [fripe] **1.** *v.tr.* to crumple, crush, crease (dress, etc.). **2.** (*of garment*) **se f.** to get crushed, crumpled; **visage fripé,** worn, tired, face.
friperie [fripri] *n.f.* **1.** (*a*) secondhand clothes; (*b*) rubbish, frippery. **2.** secondhand clothes shop.
fripier, -ière [fripje, -jɛr] *n.* secondhand clothes dealer.
fripon, -onne [fripɔ̃, -ɔn] *F:* **1.** *n.* **petit f.! petite friponne!** you naughty little thing! you little rascal! **2.** *a.* mischievous, roguish (smile, etc.).
friponnerie [fripɔnri] *n.f. A:* **1.** roguery, knavery. **2.** knavish trick.
fripouille [fripuj] *n.f.* (*a*) *A:* rabble; riff-raff; (*b*) *F:* rogue; cad, rotter.
friquet [frikɛ] *n.m.* tree sparrow.
frire [frir] *v.tr. & i. def.* (*p.p.* **frit;** *pr.ind.* **je fris, tu fris, il frit;** *no pl.*; *fu.* **je frirai;** *for the v.tr. the parts wanting are supplied by* **faire f.**) to fry; **je fris, fais f., du poisson,** I'm frying fish.
frisant [frizɑ̃] *a.* **lumière frisante,** oblique light.
frise[1] [friz] *n.f.* **1.** *Arch:* frieze. **2.** *Th: pl.* borders, sky pieces.
Frise[2] *Pr.n.f. Geog:* Friesland; *Mil:* **chevaux de f.,** (i) *A:* chevaux de frise; (ii) portable wire entanglement.
frisé [frize] *a.* curly; crisp (hair); **laitue frisée,** curly lettuce; **velours f.,** uncut velvet; terry.
friselis [frizli] *n.m. Lit:* rustle (of leaves).
friser [frize] **1.** (*a*) *v.tr.* to curl, wave; **f. (les cheveux de) qn,** to curl s.o.'s hair; **fer à f.,** curling tongs; (*b*) *v.i.* (*of hair*) to curl. **2.** *v.tr.* to touch, skim; **la balle lui a frisé le visage,** the bullet grazed his face; **f. un accident,** to have a narrow escape; **il frisait la soixantaine,** he was close on sixty.

frisette [frizɛt] *n.f.* ringlet, small curl.

frison¹ [frizɔ̃] *n.m.* **1.** curl (of hair). **2.** shaving (of wood, paper, etc.).

frison², -onne [frizɔ̃, -ɔn] *a. & n. Geog:* Frisian; **vache frisonne,** Friesian cow.

frisotter [frizɔte] **1.** *v.tr.* **f. (les cheveux de) qn,** to crimp, frizz, s.o.'s hair. **2.** *v.i.* (*of hair*) to curl; to be frizzy.

frisquet, -ette [friskɛ, -ɛt] *a. F:* chill(y); **il fait f.,** it is a bit chilly, *F:* parky.

frisson [frisɔ̃] *n.m.* (*a*) shiver (from cold); **avoir le f.,** to shiver; *F:* to have the shivers; (*b*) shudder; thrill (of fear, pleasure); **j'en ai le f.,** it makes me shudder.

frissonnement [frisɔnmɑ̃] *n.m.* **1.** shivering; shuddering; quivering. **2.** slight shiver, shudder, quiver.

frissonner [frisɔne] *v.i.* (*a*) to shiver, shudder (with cold, fear); (*b*) **f. de joie,** to be thrilled (with delight); (*c*) (*of foliage*) *Lit:* to quiver.

frisure [frizyr] *n.f.* (*a*) curling (of the hair, etc.), curliness; (*b*) *pl.* curly hair; curls.

frit, frite [fri, frit] *a.* **1.** fried; **pommes de terre frites,** *n.f.pl.* **frites,** chipped potatoes, chips, French fried potatoes; French fries. **2.** *F:* **il est f.,** he's had it.

friteuse [fritøz] *n.f. Dom.Ec:* deep fryer; chip pan.

fritillaire [fritilɛr] *n.f. Bot:* fritillary.

friture [frityr] *n.f.* **1.** (*a*) frying (of food); **panier à f.,** frying basket; (*b*) *W.Tel:* **(bruits de) f.,** crackling (noise). **2.** fried food, crackle, *esp.* fried fish. **3.** *Cu:* (deep) fat; oil (for frying). **4.** *Belg:* chip stall.

Fritz [frits] *n.m.inv. Hist:* German soldier; *F:* Jerry.

frivole [frivɔl] *a.* frivolous; (*a*) futile (occupation); (*b*) shallow (person); flighty (girl).

frivolement [frivɔlmɑ̃] *adv.* frivolously.

frivolité [frivɔlite] *n.f.* **1.** frivolity; (*a*) frivolousness; shallowness (of mind); (*b*) trifle. **2.** (*a*) *Needlew:* tatting; (*b*) **frivolités,** (fancy) trimmings.

froc [frɔk] *n.m.* (monk's) frock, gown; **prendre le f.,** to become a monk; **jeter le f. aux orties,** to unfrock oneself.

froid [frwa] **I.** *a.* **1.** (*a*) cold (wind, weather, bath); **chambre froide,** cold room; **viandes froides,** cold meat. **2.** (*a*) cold, unresponsive, (person); chilly (manner); frigid (reception); stiff (style); **se montrer, être, f. avec, pour, qn,** to treat s.o. coldly, coolly; **battre f. pour qn,** to cold-shoulder s.o.; **garder la tête froide,** to keep cool (and collected); **cela me laisse f.,** it leaves me cold; **tons froids,** cold tints; (*b*) *Physiol:* frigid. **II. à f.,** *adv.phr.* in the cold state; (*a*) **soluble à f.,** soluble when cold; *Aut:* **démarrer à f.,** to start from cold; (*b*) **parler à f. d'une catastrophe,** to speak calmly, unemotionally, about a catastrophe. **III.** *n.m.* **1.** cold; **coup de f.,** *Meteor:* cold snap; *Med:* chill; **prendre f.,** to catch a chill, a cold; **il fait f.,** it's cold; **cela m'a fait, donné, f. (dans le dos),** it sent cold shivers down my spine; **avoir f.,** to be, feel, cold; **avoir f. aux mains,** to have cold hands; **elle n'a pas f. aux yeux,** (i) she's very determined; (ii) she's got plenty of nerve. **2. l'industrie du f.,** (the) refrigerating (industry). **3.** coldness; **il y a du f. entre eux, ils sont en f.,** there's a coolness between them.

froidement [frwadmɑ̃] *adv.* **1.** coldly, frigidly. **2.** calmly.

froideur [frwadœr] *n.f.* **1.** coldness; (*a*) chilliness, frigidity (of manner); **il y a de la f. entre eux,** there is a coolness between them; (*b*) indifference; **contempler le spectacle avec f.,** to look coldly on. **2.** *Physiol:* (sexual) frigidity.

froissant [frwasɑ̃] *a.* hurtful, wounding.

froissement [frwasmɑ̃] *n.m.* **1.** bruising (of muscle, etc.). **2.** (*a*) rumpling, crumpling (of paper, cloth, etc.); (*b*) rustle, rustling (of silk, etc.); (*c*) conflict, clash (of interests). **3.** giving or taking offence; **éviter tous froissements,** to avoid wounding any susceptibilities.

froisser [frwase] **1.** *v.tr.* (*a*) to bruise (muscle, etc.); (*b*) to crease (material); to crumple (paper, material); (*c*) **f. qn,** to offend, give offence to, s.o.; to hurt, wound, s.o.'s feelings. **2. se f.,** to take offence, umbrage (**de,** at); to take exception (**de,** to).

frôlement [frolmɑ̃] *n.m.* (*a*) slight rubbing, brushing (**contre,** against); touch(ing); (*b*) rustle (of silk, etc.).

frôler [frole] *v.tr.* to touch lightly; to brush, graze; (*of bird, etc.*) to skim (tree tops); **il a frôlé la mort,** he came close to death.

fromage [frɔmaʒ] *n.m.* **1.** cheese; **f. bien fait,** ripe cheese; **f. blanc, f. gras,** cream cheese; **f. fondu, industriel,** processed cheese, *NAm:* process cheese; **un gentil petit f.,** a nice easy job. **2.** *Cu:* **f. de tête,** brawn, *NAm:* headcheese.

fromager, -ère [frɔmaʒe, -ɛr] **1.** *a.* concerning cheese; **industrie fromagère,** cheese industry. **2.** *n.* (i) cheesemonger; (ii) cheesemaker.

fromagerie [frɔmaʒri] *n.f.* cheese dairy; cheesemonger's (shop); cheese shop.

froment [frɔmɑ̃] *n.m.* wheat; **pain de f.,** (finest) wheaten bread.

fromental, -aux [frɔmɑ̃tal, -o] *n.m.* false oat.

fronce [frɔ̃s] *n.f.* (*a*) pucker; crease; (*b*) *Needlew:* gather; **jupe à fronces,** gathered skirt.

froncement [frɔ̃smɑ̃] *n.m.* wrinkling, puckering; **f. de(s) sourcils,** frown; scowl.

froncer [frɔ̃se] *v.tr.* **(je fronçai(s))** (*a*) to wrinkle, pucker; **f. les sourcils,** to knit one's brows, to frown; (*b*) *Needlew:* to gather.

frondaison [frɔ̃dɛzɔ̃] *n.f.* **1.** foliation. **2.** foliage.

fronde¹ [frɔ̃d] *n.f. Bot:* frond.

fronde² *n.f.* **1.** (*a*) sling; (*b*) (toy) catapult. **2.** *Hist:* **la F.,** the Fronde.

fronder [frɔ̃de] **1.** *v.tr.* (*a*) *A:* to sling (stone, etc.); (*b*) to criticize irreverently. **2.** *v.i. Hist:* to belong to the Fronde.

frondeur, -euse [frɔ̃dœr, -øz] **1.** *n.* (*a*) *Hist:* member of the Fronde; (*b*) critic of the authorities; rebel. **2.** *a.* critical (of the authorities); irreverent.

front [frɔ̃] *n.m.* **1.** forehead, brow; **marcher le f. haut,** to walk with one's head high; **montrer un f. serein,** to show an unruffled countenance; **et vous avez le f. de me dire cela!** you have the face to tell me that! **2.** face, front (of building, etc.); brow (of hill); **f. de bataille,** battle front; **le f.,** the front (line); *Min:* **f. de taille,** working face; coal face; *Meteor:* **f. chaud, froid,** warm, cold, front; **f. de mer,** (sea)front; *Pol:* **f. commun,** united, common, front; **faire f. à qn, qch.,** to face, resist, s.o., sth.; **faire f.,** to stand fast. **3.** (*a*) **de f.,** abreast; **mener plusieurs choses de f.,** to have several things on hand at once; *Mil:* **marche de f.,** march in line; *Navy:* **en ligne de f.,** line abreast; (*b*) **vue de f.,** front view; **attaque de f.,** frontal attack; **heurter qn, qch., de f.,** to run head-on into s.o., sth.

frontal, -aux [frɔ̃tal, -o] *a.* frontal, front; **os f.,** *n.m.* **f.,** frontal bone; **lampe frontale,** (miner's) cap lamp.

frontalier, -ière [frɔ̃talje, -jɛr] **1.** *a.* **régions frontalières,** frontier, border, regions. **2.** *n.* (i) inhabitant of frontier zone; (ii) frontier worker.

fronteau, -eaux [frɔ̃to] *n.m.* **1.** *Ecc:* frontlet (of nun, etc.); phylactery (of Jew). **2.** *Arch:* small pediment. **3.** *Artil:* **f. de mire,** foresight (of gun). **4.** *N.Arch:* (*a*) breast beam; (*b*) breastwork; (*c*) break bulkhead; (*d*) **f. d'écoutille,** headledge; (*e*) **f. de dunette,** poop.

frontière [frɔ̃tjɛr] **1.** *n.f.* frontier (line); border(line); boundary; **aux frontières de la vie et de la mort,** between life and death; **les frontières de la bienséance,** the limits of decency. **2.** *a.* frontier (town); boundary (stone).

frontispice [frɔ̃tispis] *n.m.* (*a*) frontispiece (of book); (*b*) title page.
fronton [frɔ̃tɔ̃] *n.m. Arch:* fronton, pediment.
frottage [frɔtaʒ] *n.m.* rubbing; friction, chafing (of limb, etc.); polishing (of floors, etc.).
frottée [frɔte] *n.f.* (*a*) beating, thrashing; (*b*) **f. d'ail,** garlic bread.
frottement [frɔtmɑ̃] *n.m.* **1.** rubbing; chafing; *Med:* **bruit de f.,** pleural rub; *Phot:* **marques de f.,** stress marks. **2.** *Mec.E:* (*a*) friction; **f. de glissement,** sliding friction; **usure par le f.,** abrasion; (*b*) fit (of parts); **f. doux,** easy fit.
frotter [frɔte] **1.** *v.tr.* to rub; to chafe (limb); to polish (floor, copper); **se f. les mains,** to rub one's hands; **f. une allumette,** to strike a match; *v.i.* **la roue frotte contre le frein,** the wheel is rubbing against the brake; *O:* **être frotté de latin,** to have a smattering of Latin. **2. se f.** (*a*) **se f. contre qch.,** to rub against sth.; (*b*) **se f. à qn, à qch.,** to come up against s.o., sth.; **ne vous y frottez pas!** don't get involved! don't meddle!
frotteur, -euse [frɔtœr, -øz] *n.* **1.** (*pers.*) floor polisher. **2.** *n.m.* sliding contact; (collecting) shoe (of electric train).
frottis [frɔti] *n.m.* **1.** (*a*) *Art:* scumble; (*b*) *Biol:* smear (for microscopic examination). **2. prendre un f. d'une inscription,** to take a rubbing of an inscription.
frottoir [frɔtwar] *n.m.* **1.** (*a*) rubber, polisher; (*b*) scrubbing brush; (*c*) friction strip (of matchbox). **2.** brush (of dynamo).
frou(-)frou [frufru] *n.m.* rustle, rustling (of silk dress, leaves); *pl. frou(-)frous.*
froufrouter [frufrute] *v.i.* (*of silk, etc.*) to rustle.
froussard, -arde [frusar, -ard] *a. P:* **1.** *a.* cowardly, chicken. **2.** *n.* coward, chicken.
frousse [frus] *n.f. P:* fear, funk; **avoir la f.,** to be scared, to have the wind up.
fructidor [fryktidɔr] *n.m. Hist:* twelfth month of the Fr. Republican calendar (August–September).
fructifère [fryktifɛr] *a.* fruitbearing.
fructification [fryktifikasjɔ̃] *n.f.* **1.** fructification. **2.** fruition (of idea, etc.).
fructifier [fryktifje] *v.i.* to fructify, to bear fruit; **ses placements commencent à f.,** his investments are beginning to show a profit.
fructueusement [fryktɥøzmɑ̃] *adv.* fruitfully, profitably.
fructueux, -euse [fryktɥø, -øz] *a.* fruitful, profitable.
frugal, -aux [frygal, -o] *a.* frugal (person, meal).
frugalement [frygalmɑ̃] *adv.* frugally.
frugalité [frygalite] *n.f.* frugality.
frugivore [fryʒivɔr] **1.** *a.* fruit-eating (animal). **2.** *n.* fruit-eater.
fruit¹ [frɥi] *n.m.* fruit; *n.* **arbre à f.,** fruit tree; **producteur de fruits,** fruit grower; **fruits secs,** dried fruit; *F:* (*pers.*) **f. sec,** failure (as a student, etc.); dud; (*of tree, action, etc.*) **porter (ses) f.,** to bear fruit; **quel f. espérez-vous en tirer?** what do you expect to get from it? **étudier avec f.,** to study to good purpose; **sans f.,** fruitlessly; *Cu:* **fruits de mer** = seafood.
fruit² *n.m. Civ.E:* batter (of wall, abutment, etc.).
fruité [frɥite] *a.* fruity (wine, etc.).
fruiterie [frɥitri] *n.f.* **1.** storeroom for fruit. **2.** fruiterer's, greengrocer's, shop, business.
fruitier, -ière [frɥitje, -jɛr] **1.** *a.* **arbre f.,** fruit tree. **2.** *n.* fruiterer, greengrocer. **3.** *n.m.* (*a*) (i) fruit storeroom; (ii) stand of fruit trays; (*b*) orchard.
frusques [frysk] *n.f.pl. P:* clothes; **apportez vos f. de football,** bring your football things, togs.
fruste [fryst] *a.* (*a*) worn, defaced (coin, statue); (*b*) rough, unpolished (style, person).
frustration [frystrasjɔ̃] *n.f.* **1.** frustration. **2.** cheating, defrauding (of legatee, etc.).
frustrer [frystre] *v.tr.* **1.** to frustrate, disappoint, thwart. **2. f. qn de qch.,** to defraud s.o. of sth.; **on m'a frustré de mes biens,** I have been cheated out of my property.
fuchsia [fyʃja] *n.m. Bot:* fuchsia.
fucus [fykys] *n.m. Algae:* fucus; sea wrack.
fuel(-oil) [fjul(ɔjl)] *n.m.* fuel oil.
fugace [fygas] *a.* fleeting, fugitive, transient; **lubie f.,** passing whim.
fugacité [fygasite] *n.f. Lit:* fugacity, transience.
fugitif, -ive [fyʒitif, -iv] **1.** *a. & n.* fugitive, runaway. **2.** *a.* transitory, fleeting, ephemeral; short-lived, passing (desire).
fugitivement [fyʒitivmɑ̃] *adv.* fleetingly.
fugue [fyg] *n.f.* **1.** *Mus: Psy:* fugue. **2. faire une f.,** to run away from home.
fuir [fɥir] *v.* (*pr.p.* **fuyant;** *p.p.* **fui;** *pr.ind.* **je fuis, n. fuyons, ils fuient**) **1.** *v.i.* (*a*) to flee, run away (**devant,** from); **faire f.,** to put to flight; **le temps fuit,** time flies, is slipping by; *Nau:* **f. devant le vent,** to scud, run, before the wind; (*b*) (*of horizon, forehead*) to recede; (*c*) to evade the issue; (*d*) (*of tap, cask, etc.*) to leak; (*of water*) to run out, escape. **2.** *v.tr.* to shun, avoid.
fuite [fɥit] *n.f.* **1.** (*a*) flight, running away (**devant,** from); **prendre la f.,** to take to flight, to turn tail; **être en f.,** to be on the run; **mettre l'ennemi en f.,** to put the enemy to flight; *F:* **la f. des cerveaux,** the brain drain; **écrasé par une voiture qui a pris la f.,** run over by a hit-and-run driver; (*b*) evasion, avoidance (of difficulties, etc.); (*c*) **la f. du temps,** the passage of time; (*d*) *Art:* **point de f.,** vanishing point. **2.** leak; escape (of gas, etc.); leakage (of information).
fulgurant [fylgyrɑ̃] *a.* lashing (like lightning); *Med:* lightning (pains); **lancer un regard f. à qn,** to look daggers at s.o.
fulguration [fylgyrasjɔ̃] *n.f.* **1.** lightning. **2.** *Med:* fulguration.
fulgurer [fylgyre] *v.i.* to flash (like lightning).
fuligineux, -euse [fyliʒinø, -øz] *a.* fuliginous, smoky, sooty; murky (sky).
fulmicoton [fylmikɔtɔ̃] *n.m.* gun cotton.
fulminant [fylminɑ̃] *a.* fulminating (powder); fulminant (pain); menacing (tone).
fulminer [fylmine] **1.** *v.tr.* to fulminate (Papal bull). **2.** *v.i.* **f. contre qn, qch.,** to fulminate, inveigh, against sth.
fumage¹ [fymaʒ] *n.m.,* **fumaison¹** [fymɛzɔ̃] *n.f.* dunging, dressing, manuring (of land).
fumage² *n.m.,* **fumaison²** *n.f.* smoking, smoke-curing (of fish, meat).
fumant [fymɑ̃] *a.* (*a*) smoking; *F:* **f. de colère,** fuming with anger; (*b*) steaming (soup, etc.); (*c*) *F:* terrific, sensational.
fumé [fyme] *a.* (*a*) smoked, smoke-cured (fish, meat, etc.); (*b*) **verre f.,** smoked glass; **verres fumés,** dark glasses, sunglasses.
fume-cigare [fymsigar] *n.m.inv.* cigar holder.
fume-cigarette [fymsigarɛt] *n.m.inv.* cigarette holder.
fumée [fyme] *n.f.* **1.** (*a*) smoke; **rideau de f.,** smoke-screen; **noir de f.,** lampblack; **la f. (de tabac) vous gêne-t-elle?** do you mind my smoking? **partir, s'en aller, en f.,** to come to nothing, end in smoke; *Prov:* **il n'y a pas de f. sans feu,** there's no smoke without fire; (*b*) steam (of soup, etc.); vapour, *NAm:* vapor (of marsh); fumes (of charcoal, wine, etc.). **2.** *a.inv.* **gris f.,** smoke-grey, *NAm:* -gray.
fumer¹ [fyme] *v.tr.* to dung, manure (land).
fumer² **1.** *v.i.* (*a*) to smoke; **lampe qui fume,** smoking lamp; (*b*) (*of soup, etc.*) to steam; (*c*) *F:* to fume, rage. **2.** *v.tr.* (*a*) to smoke; to smoke-cure (fish); (*b*)

to smoke (a pipe, tobacco, etc.); **f. tranquillement,** to have a quiet smoke; **défense de f.,** no smoking.

fumerie [fymri] *n.f.* **f. d'opium,** opium den.

fumerolle [fymrɔl] *n.f.* **1.** fumarole, smokehole (of volcano). **2.** smoke, exhalation, vapour, *NAm:* vapor (from the fumarole).

fumet [fymɛ] *n.m.* **1.** (pleasant) smell (of food cooking); bouquet (of wine). **2.** *Ven:* scent.

fumeterre [fymtɛr] *n.f. Bot:* fumitory.

fumeur, -euse[1] [fymœr, -øz] *n.* smoker; *Rail:* **compartiment fumeurs,** smoking compartment; *F:* smoker.

fumeux, -euse[2] [fymø, -øz] *a.* smoky, smoking (lamp, etc.); hazy (sky, ideas).

fumier [fymje] *n.m.* **1.** stable litter, manure, dung. **2.** dunghill, manure heap. **3.** *P:* **espèce de f.!** you bastard!

fumigation [fymigasjɔ̃] *n.f.* fumigation; *Med:* inhaling.

fumigène [fymiʒɛn] *a.* & *n.m. Mil: Hort:* smoke-producing (device); **bombe f.,** smoke bomb.

fumiger [fymiʒe] *v.tr.* **(je fumigeai(s))** to fumigate.

fumiste [fymist] *n.m.* **1.** heating engineer. **2.** *F:* (*a*) practical joker; (*b*) humbug, fraud.

fumisterie [fymistəri] *n.f.* **1.** heating engineering. **2.** *F:* practical joke; hoax; fraud; **c'est une vaste f.,** it's nothing but eyewash.

fumivore [fymivɔr] *a.* smoke-absorbing.

fumoir [fymwar] *n.m.* **1.** smoking room (of hotel, etc.). **2.** smokehouse (for meat, fish, etc.).

fumure [fymyr] *n.f.* dunging, manuring (of field).

funambule [fynɑ̃byl] *n.* funambulist, tightrope walker.

funambulesque [fynɑ̃bylɛsk] *a.* fantastic, grotesque (story, etc.).

funèbre [fynɛbr̥] *a.* **1.** funeral (ceremony, etc.); **hymne, chant, f.,** dirge; **marche f.,** funeral, dead, march. **2.** funereal, dismal, gloomy.

funérailles [fyneraj] *n.f.pl.* funeral (ceremony).

funéraire [fynerɛr] *a.* funeral (expenses); funerary (urn); **pierre f.,** tombstone; **drap f.,** pall.

funeste [fynɛst] *a.* (*a*) *Lit:* deadly, fatal (accident); (*b*) fatal, disastrous, catastrophic (mistake); **influence f.,** disastrous influence; (*c*) *A:* funereal, sombre, gloomy.

funiculaire [fynikylɛr] *a.* & *n.m.* funicular (railway).

fur [fyr] *n.m. used only in* **au f. et à mesure,** (in proportion) as, progressively; **au f. et à mesure des besoins,** as and when required; **payer qn au f. et à mesure de l'ouvrage,** to pay by instalments (as the work proceeds); *esp. US:* to make progress payments.

furet [fyrɛ] *n.m.* **1.** ferret; **chasse au f.,** ferreting; **chasser au f.,** to go ferreting; **jeu du f.** = hunt-the-slipper. **2.** inquisitive person; *F:* nosy parker.

furetage [fyrtaʒ] *n.m.* **1.** ferreting (for rabbits). **2.** searching, prying; rummaging, ferreting (about).

fureter [fyrte] *v.i.* **(je furette; je furetterai) 1.** (*a*) to ferret, go ferreting. **2.** to pry, to nose around; **f. dans les armoires,** to ferret (about), rummage, in the cupboards.

fureteur, -euse [fyrtœr, -øz] **1.** *n.* (*a*) ferreter; (*b*) searcher, rummager; *F:* nosy parker. **2.** *a.* prying, *F:* nosy.

fureur [fyrœr] *n.f.* **1.** fury, rage, wrath; **être en f.,** to be in a rage. **2.** fury, passion; **aimer qn, qch., avec f., à la f.,** to be passionately fond of s.o., sth.; **avoir la f. de bâtir,** to be mad on building; **chanson qui fait f.,** song that's all the rage.

furibard [fyribar] *a. F:* furious.

furibond [fyribɔ̃] *a.* furious, full of fury; **elle lui a lancé un regard f.,** she glared at him.

furie [fyri] *n.f.* **1.** *Myth:* **les Furies,** the Furies; **c'est une f.,** she's a termagant. **2.** fury, rage; **se battre avec f.,** to fight furiously; **applaudir avec f.,** to applaud frantically; **en f.,** infuriated, enraged; **se mettre en f.,** to become furious, fly into a rage.

furieusement [fyrjøzmɑ̃] *adv.* **1.** furiously, passionately. **2.** extremely, tremendously.

furieux, -ieuse [fyrjø, -jøz] *a.* **1.** (*a*) furious, raging; in a passion; **être f. contre qn,** to be furious, wild, with s.o.; **rendre qn f.,** to enrage, infuriate, s.o.; **tempête furieuse,** raging, howling, storm; (*b*) mad; *n.* madman, *f.* madwoman. **2.** *F:* **c'est un f. mangeur,** he has a tremendous appetite.

furoncle [fyrɔ̃kl̥] *n.m. Med:* furuncle; boil.

furonculose [fyrɔ̃kyloz] *n.f. Med:* furunculosis.

furtif, -ive [fyrtif, -iv] *a.* furtive, stealthy.

furtivement [fyrtivmɑ̃] *adv.* furtively, stealthily; **entrer, sortir, f.,** to steal in, out.

fusain [fyzɛ̃] *n.m.* **1.** spindle tree. **2.** (*a*) charcoal (pencil); (*b*) charcoal sketch.

fusant [fyzɑ̃] *a. Exp:* fusing; **obus fusant,** time shell.

fuseau, -eaux [fyzo] *n.m.* **1.** spindle; (*for lace*) bobbin; **f. de quenouille,** distaff; **en f.,** tapered, tapering; **jambes en f.,** spindly legs. **2.** (*a*) *Mth:* **f. sphérique,** spherical lune; (*b*) **f. horaire,** time zone; (*c*) *Cost:* **(pantalon) f., fuseaux,** tapered trousers, *esp.* ski slacks.

fusée [fyze] *n.f.* **1.** spindle (of shaft, axle); barrel (of capstan); *Aut:* stub axle; *Nau:* **f. de vergue,** yard arm. **2.** rocket; **f. éclairante,** flare; **f. volante,** sky rocket; **f. à pétard,** maroon; *Ball:* **f. à un étage,** one-stage rocket; **lancer une f.,** to launch a rocket; **f. d'appoint,** booster; **f. sonde,** sounding rocket, probe; **avion (à) f.,** rocket-propelled aircraft; **f. engin,** missile; *Nau:* **f. porte-amarre,** life(-saving) rocket. **3.** fuse (of bomb, etc.); **f. percutante,** percussion fuse; **f. à temps,** time fuse.

fuselage [fyzlaʒ] *n.m.Av:* fuselage.

fuselé [fyzle] *a.* spindle-shaped; tapering (column, fingers); *Aut:* streamlined.

fuseler [fyzle] *v.tr.* **(je fuselle; je fusellerai)** to shape like a spindle, to taper; *Aut:* to streamline.

fuser [fyze] *v.i.* **1.** (*of hot wax, etc.*) to spread, run; to melt. **2.** *Ch:* (*of salt*) to deflagrate, crackle. **3.** *Pyr:* (*of fuse*) to burn slowly.

fusibilité [fyzibilite] *n.f.* fusibility.

fusible [fyzibl̥] **1.** *a.* fusible, easily melted. **2.** *n.m. El:* fuse; fuse wire; **f. de sûreté,** safety fuse; cut-out.

fusiforme [fyzifɔrm] *a.* spindle-shaped.

fusil [fyzi] *n.m.* **1.** steel (of tinder box). **2.** (sharpening) steel. **3.** (*a*) gun; **f. de chasse,** sporting gun, shotgun; **f. à bascule,** hinged breech loader; **f. à deux coups,** double-barrelled gun; **f. à air comprimé,** air gun; **f. harpon,** harpoon gun; **f. rayé,** rifle; **f. automatique,** automatic gun, rifle; **f. à chargeur,** magazine rifle; *Fig:* **changer son f. d'épaule,** to change one's opinions; **coup de f.,** (i) gunshot, rifle shot; (ii) *F:* overcharging, fleecing (in hotel, etc.); **entendre un coup de f.,** to hear a shot; (*b*) **c'est un de nos meilleurs fusils,** he's one of our best shots.

fusilier [fyzilje] *n.m.* fusilier; **f. marin** = marine.

fusillade [fyzijad] *n.f.* **1.** fusillade, rifle fire. **2.** (execution by) shooting.

fusiller [fyzije] *v.tr.* (*a*) to execute (by shooting); to shoot; **f. qn d'un regard,** to look daggers at s.o.; (*b*) *P:* to mess up, ruin (car, etc.).

fusil-mitrailleur [fyzimitrajœr] *n.m.* automatic rifle; light machine gun; *pl. fusils-mitrailleurs.*

fusion [fyzjɔ̃] *n.f.* **1.** (*a*) fusion, melting (by heat); *Metall:* smelting; **point de f.,** melting point; **fer en f.,** molten iron; (*b*) *Atom.Ph:* fusion. **2.** coalescing (of ideas, etc.); merger, merging (of companies).

fusionnement [fyzjɔnmɑ̃] *n.m. Com:* amalgamation, merging (of companies).

fusionner [fyzjɔne] *v.tr.& i. Com:* (*of companies*) to amalgamate, unite, merge.
fustigation [fystigasjɔ̃] *n.f.Lit:* thrashing, beating.
fustiger [fystiʒe] *v.tr.* **(je fustigeai(s))** (*a*) *A:* to thrash, beat; (*b*) *Lit:* to give (s.o.) a dressing down.
fût [fy] *n.m.* **1.** stock (of rifle, plane, etc.); handle (of saw, racquet); brace (for bit). **2.** (*a*) shaft (of column, chimney); stem (of candelabra); shank (of rivet); (*b*) bole (of tree). **3.** cask, barrel; drum (for oil); **tirer de la bière du f.,** to draw beer from the wood.
futaie [fytɛ] *n.f.* wood, forest; **arbre de haute f.,** full-grown tree, timber tree.
futaille [fytɑj] *n.f.* cask; drum.
futaine [fytɛn] *n.f. Tex:* fustian.
futé [fyte] *a.* sharp, smart, astute, crafty; *n.* **c'est une petite futée,** she's a sharp little thing.
futile [fytil] *a.* futile; trivial, trifling; frivolous (person); idle (pretext).
futilement [fytilmɑ̃] *adv.* futilely.
futilité [fytilite] *n.f.* **1.** futility. **2. s'occuper à des futilités,** to play about.
futur [fytyr] **1.** *a.* (*a*) future; **la vie future,** the life to come; **f. acheteur,** intending purchaser; (*b*) *n.* **mon f., ma future,** my fiancé(e), my intended. **2.** *n.m. Gram:* future (tense).
futurisme [fytyrism] *n.m. Art:* futurism.
futuriste [fytyrist] *Art:* **1.** *a.* futurist(ic). **2.** *n.* futurist.
fuyant [fɥijɑ̃] *a.* **1.** *Lit:* fleeing; fleeting (moment). **2.** receding (forehead, line); *Art:* **lignes fuyantes,** *n.m.* **fuyants,** perspective lines (of picture). **3.** (*of pers.*) evasive; shifty (eyes, person).
fuyard, -arde [fɥijar, -ard] **1.** *a. A:* shy, timid. **2.** *n.* fugitive (soldier); runaway.

G

G, g [ʒe] *n.m.* the letter G, g; *Meteor:* **couche G,** G region (of ionosphere).
gabardine [gabardin] *n.f.* **1.** *Tex:* gabardine. **2.** *Cost:* (gabardine) raincoat.
gabare [gabar] *n.f.* **1.** *Nau:* (*a*) sailing barge; lighter; (*b*) transport vessel, store ship, scow. **2.** dragnet.
gabaret [gabarɛ] *n.m. Fish:* (small) dragnet.
gabarit [gabari] *n.m.* **1.** (*a*) *N.Arch:* model (of ship); mould, *NAm:* mold (of ship's part); (*b*) *Const:* outline (of building). **2.** (*a*) *Mec.E: etc:* template, templet, former; **g. d'assemblage,** assembly jig, assembling gauge; **tour à g.,** copying lathe; (*b*) *Rail:* clearance (under bridge); **g. de chargement,** loading gauge; **g. d'écartement (des voies),** rail, track, gauge; (*c*) *F: usu. Pej:* **des gens de son g.,** people of his sort, people like him.
gabbro [gabro] *n.m. Geol: Art:* gabbro.
gabegie [gabʒi] *n.f.* waste; muddle; disorder.
gabelle [gabɛl] *n.f. Hist:* salt tax, excise.
gabelou [gablu] *n.m. Pej:* customs officer.
gabier [gabje] *n.m. Nau:* topman; **g. breveté,** able(-bodied) seaman.
gable, gâble [gɑbl̥] *n.m. Arch:* **1.** gable. **2.** (triangular) window canopy.
Gabon (le) [ləgabɔ̃] *Pr.n.m. Geog:* Gabon.
gabonais, -aise [gabɔnɛ, -ɛz] *a. & n. Geog:* Gabonese.
gâchage [gɑʃaʒ] *n.m.* **1.** mixing (of mortar, etc.). **2.** spoiling, bungling; wasting.
gâche¹ [gɑʃ] *n.f.* **1.** trowel. **2.** (cook's) spatula.
gâche² *n.f.* **1.** *Locksm:* (*a*) (box) staple, keeper (of lock); (latch) catch; (*b*) striking box, plate; strike box (of spring bolt). **2.** notch (for pawl).
gâchée [gɑʃe] *n.f. Const:* batch (of cement, etc.).
gâcher [gɑʃe] *v.tr.* **1.** to mix, wet, temper; **g. du mortier,** to mix mortar; **g. la chaux,** to slack lime; **g. serré,** to temper (clay, etc.) hard. **2.** (*a*) to spoil (sheet of paper, etc.); to bungle, botch, mess up (job); **g. le métier,** (i) to undercut; (ii) to do more than is strictly necessary; (*b*) to waste; to squander (fortune); **g. sa vie,** (i) to waste one's life; (ii) to make a mess of one's life, to go to the dogs.
gâchette [gɑʃɛt] *n.f.* **1.** *Sm.a:* trigger; *F:* **avoir la g. facile,** to be trigger-happy. **2.** spring catch (of lock). **3.** *Mec.E:* pawl. **4.** *Elcs:* gate.
gâcheur, -euse [gɑʃœr, -øz] *a. & n.* **1.** *a.* (*a*) bungling; (*b*) undercutting. **2.** *n.* (*a*) bungler, botcher; (*b*) undercutter. **3.** *n.m.* (mason's, carpenter's) mate.
gâchis [gɑʃi] *n.m.* **1.** wet mortar. **2.** (*a*) mud; slush; (*b*) mess; muddle; **quel g.!** what a mess!
gadarénien, -ienne [gadarenjɛ̃, -jɛn] *a. & n. B.Hist:* Gadarene.
gadelle [gadɛl] *n.f. Bot: Fr.C:* redcurrant.
gadget [gadʒɛt] *n.m. F:* gadget.
gaditan, -ane [gaditɑ̃, -an] *a. & n. Geog:* (native, inhabitant) of Cadiz.
gadoue [gadu] *n.f.* **1.** (*a*) sewage sludge; (*b*) mud, slush, slime; (*c*) *P:* **je suis dans une belle g.,** I'm in a mess. **2.** *P:* (*a*) shit; (*b*) prostitute, tart.
Gaël [gaɛl] *n.m. Ethn:* Gael.
gaélique [gaelik] *a. & n. Ethn: Ling:* Gaelic.
gaffe [gaf] *n.f.* **1.** (*a*) boathook; (*b*) *Fish:* gaff; *P:* **avaler sa g.,** to die, kick the bucket. **2.** *F:* blunder, clanger; **faire une g.,** to put one's foot in it. **3.** *P:* **faire g.,** to be on the lookout; **fais g.!** look out! watch it! **4.** *P:* prison warder, screw.
gaffer [gafe] **1.** *v.tr.* (*a*) to hook (floating object, etc.); (*b*) *Fish:* to gaff (salmon, etc.). **2.** *v.i. F:* (*a*) *Row:* to catch a crab; (*b*) to make a faux pas; to put one's foot in it, drop a brick. **3.** *v.i. P:* to look; **gaffe un peu!** have a dekko!
gaffeur, -euse [gafœr, -øz] *n. F:* blunderer; blundering fool; **c'est un g.,** he's always putting his foot in it.
gag [gag] *n.m. Th: Cin: F:* gag.
gaga [gaga] *F:* **1.** *n.* old person; old dodderer. **2.** *a.inv.* gaga, doddering, senile.
gage [gaʒ] *n.m.* **1.** *Com: Jur:* (*a*) pledged chattels; pawned article; pledge, pawn, security; **laisser qch. pour g.,** to leave sth. as security, on deposit; **mettre qch. en g.,** to pawn, pledge, sth.; **mise en g.,** pawning, pledging; **prêteur sur gages,** pawnbroker; **ma montre est en g.,** my watch is in pawn; **lettre de g.,** (i) mortgage bond; (ii) debenture bond; (*b*) (*of pers.*) surety; **rester en g.,** to remain as surety. **2.** token, sign; **g. d'amour,** love token. **3.** forfeit; **jouer aux gages,** to play at forfeits. **4.** *pl.* wages, pay; **tueur à gages,** hired assassin; *Cin: etc:* **auteur à gages fixes,** staff writer; *esp. U.S:* staffer.
gagé [gaʒe] *a. Jur:* secured (loan); **meubles gagés,** furniture under distraint; **recettes non gagées,** unassigned, unpledged, revenue.
gager [gaʒe] *v.tr.* (**je gageai(s); n. gageons**) **1.** *Lit:* **je gagerais que . . .,** I'd bet that . . . . **2.** to guarantee, secure (loan, etc.).
gageure [gaʒyr] *n.f. A: & Lit:* wager.
gagiste [gaʒist] *n.m. Jur:* pledger, pawner.
gagnant, -ante [gaɲɑ̃, -ɑ̃t] **1.** *a.* winning (ticket, etc.); **partir g.,** (i) to start favourite; (ii) to be a sure winner; **jouer g.,** to bet on a certainty. **2.** *n.* winner.
gagne-pain [gaɲ(ə)pɛ̃] *n.m.inv.* (means of) living; livelihood.
gagne-petit [gɑɲ(ə)pəti] *n.m.inv.* person earning a pittance, a low wage; **le g.-p.,** the low-paid.
gagne-place [gɑɲ(ə)plas] *n.m. F:* spacesaver; *pl. gagne-places.*
gagner [gɑɲe] *v.tr.* **1.** (*a*) to earn; **g. de l'argent,** to earn money; **g. mille francs par mois,** to earn a thousand francs a month; **g. gros,** (i) to make big money; (ii) to make large profits; **g. sa vie, g. de quoi vivre,** to earn one's living; **ce que je gagne suffit à nos besoins,** I earn enough to keep us; **il l'a bien gagné,** (i) he's earned it; (ii) *F:* it serves him (damn well) right; (*b*) to gain; to benefit, profit (**à,** by); **g. du temps,** (i) to save time; (ii) to gain time; **chercher à g. du temps,** to play for time; **c'est autant de gagné, c'est toujours ça de gagné,** (i) that's so much to the good; (ii) at least that's settled; **g. à être connu,** to improve on acquaintance; **nous ne gagnerons rien à attendre,** there is nothing to be gained by waiting; **et moi, qu'est-ce que j'y gagne?** and what do I get out of it? what's in this for me? and where do I come in? **2.** (*a*) to win, gain (a victory); *Mil:* to take (a town); (*b*) to win (game, race); **g. dans un fauteuil,** to have a walkover; **g. haut la main,** to win in a canter; to win hands down; (*c*) **g. qn à une cause,** to win s.o. over to a cause; **g. qn à une idée,** to sell s.o. an idea;

g. la confiance de qn, to win, gain, s.o.'s confidence; (*d*) to get, catch (disease, etc.). **3.** to reach, arrive at, get to; **g. le haut,** to reach the top; *Nau:* **g. le port,** to fetch into port. **4.** (*a*) to gain on, overtake; **g. un navire,** to gain on, overhaul, a ship; **g. le devant,** to forge ahead, take the lead; **la nuit nous gagna,** darkness overtook us; **le feu, l'épidémie, gagne,** the fire, the epidemic, is spreading; **g. du terrain,** (i) to gain ground; (ii) to reclaim land (from the sea, etc.); **la mer gagne du terrain,** the sea is encroaching on the land; **g. une marche sur qn,** to steal a march on s.o.; **le mécontentement gagne de force,** there is increasing discontent; **la faim nous gagnait,** we were getting hungry; **gagné par le sommeil, par les larmes,** overcome by sleep, with tears; *Nau:* **g. le vent, au vent,** to make, fetch, to windward; **g. le vent d'une pointe,** to weather a headland; **g. de l'avant,** to forge ahead; (*b*) *Med:* to spread; **l'enflure a gagné la gorge,** the swelling has spread to the throat.

gagneur, -euse [gaɲœr, -øz] *n.* **1.** earner (of money). **2.** winner. **3.** *n.f. P:* prostitute, tart.

gai [ge] *a.* **1.** (*a*) cheerful, gay; merry, lively (person, song); (person) in good spirits; cheery (voice); **g. comme un pinson,** happy as a lark, a sandboy; **avoir l'esprit g.,** to be of a cheerful disposition; *F:* **être un peu g.,** to be tipsy, tight; **avoir le vin g.,** to be merry in one's cups; *Iron:* **ça va être g.!** that *will* be nice! (*b*) bright, cheerful (room, etc.); gay (colour, *NAm:* color, etc.); **vert g.,** light green; (*c*) amusing (talk, stories). **2.** (*of bolt, key, etc.*) free, easy, having play; loose; *Fish:* **hareng g.,** shotten herring.

gaiement [gemɑ̃] *adv.* gaily, cheerfully; merrily, brightly.

gaieté [gete] *n.f.* gaiety, cheerfulness; **vous n'êtes pas d'une g. folle!** (i) you're very depressed; (ii) you're getting me down! **déborder de g.,** to be bubbling over with high spirits; **reprendre sa g.,** to recover one's spirits; to perk up, buck up.

gaillard, -arde [gajar, -ard] **1.** *a.* (*a*) strong, well, vigorous; **frais et g.,** hale and hearty; **il se sentait g.,** he felt in good form; (*b*) *O:* merry, lively, cheery; (*c*) spicy, risqué, *NAm:* off-color (story, remark); (*d*) fresh (wind), cool (weather). **2.** (*a*) *n.m.* hearty, vigorous, type; **un grand et solide g.,** a great strapping young man; *A:* **un vert g.,** a rip; (*b*) *n.f.* **une grande gaillarde,** a strapping young woman. **3.** *n.m. Nau:* **g. d'avant,** forecastle; **g. d'arrière,** poop; **haut de g.,** deep-waisted. **4.** *n.f.* (*a*) *Danc:* galliard; (*b*) *Typ:* eight-point type; brevier.

gaillardement [gajardəmɑ̃] *adv.* **1.** gaily, good-humouredly. **2.** boldly, bravely, gallantly.

gaillardise [gajardiz] *n.f.* **conter des gaillardises,** to tell dirty, *NAm:* off-color, stories; to crack broad jokes.

gaillette [gajɛt] *n.f.* cobbles (of coal).

gaîment [gemɑ̃] *adv.* = GAIEMENT.

gain [gɛ̃] *n.m.* **1.** winning (of contest, war, etc.); *Jur:* **avoir g. de cause,** to win one's case; **donner g. de cause à qn,** to decide in favour of s.o.; **il y a chances égales de g. et de perte,** it's an even chance, there's a fifty-fifty chance. **2.** (*a*) gain, profit; **avoir l'amour du g.,** to be obsessed with making profits, money; (*b*) earnings; *Jur:* **g. de la femme mariée,** wife's earned income; **g. fortuit,** capital gain; (*c*) winnings; **les gains de la soirée,** the evening's winnings; **être en g.,** to be in pocket; (*d*) **un g. de temps,** a saving of time; **g. retiré d'une lecture,** profit acquired from reading. **3.** *El: etc:* gain; **g. en courant,** current gain; **g. en tension,** voltage magnification; *Elcs:* **g. d'étage,** stage gain; *Atom.Ph:* **g. de régénération,** breeding gain.

gainage [gɛnaʒ] *n.m.* (*a*) *Mec.E: Civ.E: etc:* casing, sheathing, sleeving; (*b*) *Atom.Ph:* canning, casing, cladding (of fuel, etc.).

gaine [gɛn] *n.f.* **1.** (*a*) cover, case; casing, wrapping, jacket; **g. d'une momie,** mummy case; **g. en cuir,** leather case; **g. métallique,** metallic sheath, sleeve; **câble sous g.,** sheathed cable; **g. souple,** flexible sheath; *Atom.Ph:* **g. d'électrons, d'ions,** electron, ion, sheath; (*b*) *Anat: Bot:* sheath; (*c*) *Cost:* foundation (garment); corset; roll-on; girdle; (*d*) *Geol:* gangue, matrix. **2.** *Const: Min: etc:* (ventilation) shaft, passage, duct.

gaine-combinaison [gɛnkɔ̃binɛzɔ̃] *n.f. Cost:* corselet; *pl. gaines-combinaisons.*

gaine-culotte [gɛnkylɔt] *n.f. Cost:* pantie girdle; *pl. gaines-culottes.*

gainer [gene] *v.tr.* to sheath; to cover, case (in leather, etc.).

gal [gal] *n.m. Ph:* gal.

gala [gala] *n.m.* gala, fête; **en habit, toilette, de g.,** (i) in gala dress, in full dress; (ii) in one's Sunday best; **dîner en grand g.,** to dine in state; to dine with great ceremony.

Galaad¹ [galaad] *Pr.n.m. B.Geog:* Gilead.

Galaad² *Pr.n.m. Lit:* Galahad.

galactique [galaktik] *a.* galactic.

galamment [galamɑ̃] *adv.* gallantly, like a gentleman; (*a*) politely, courteously; (*b*) *Lit:* bravely, honourably, *NAm:* honorably; **se tirer g. d'une affaire,** to come out of an affair with honour, *NAm:* with honor.

galandage [galɑ̃daʒ] *n.m.* (*a*) *Const:* brick partition; (*b*) half-timbered construction (with brickwork in between the beams).

galant¹ [galɑ̃] **1.** *a.* (*a*) *A:* gay, elegant; **costume g.,** stylish, elegant, costume; (*b*) attentive to women, gallant [gə'lænt]; **homme g.,** ladies' man; **vers galants,** love poems; (*c*) **femme galante,** (i) woman of loose morals; (ii) kept prostitute, woman; *Art: Lit:* **fête galante,** fête galante; **intrigue galante,** love affair; (*d*) *O:* **g. homme,** man of honour, *NAm:* of honor; gentleman; **se conduire en g. homme,** to behave like a gentleman. **2.** *n.m. O: & Lit:* lover, gallant, ladies' man; philanderer; **faire le g. auprès d'une dame,** to court, pay court to, a lady; to flirt with a lady.

Galant² *Pr.n.m. Lit:* Wa land.

galanterie [galɑ̃tri] *n.f.* politeness; attentiveness (*esp.* to ladies). **2.** *usu. pl.* (*a*) love affair, intrigue; (*b*) **dire des galanteries,** to pay compliments.

galantine [galɑ̃tin] *n.f. Cu:* galantine.

galate [galat] *a. & n. B.Hist:* Galatian.

Galatée [galate] *Pr.n.f. Myth:* Galatea.

Galatie [galasi] *Pr.n.f. A.Geog:* Galatia.

galaxie [galaksi] *n.f. Astr:* galaxy; the Milky Way.

galbe [galb] *n.m.* **1.** *Arch:* entasis (of column). **2.** curve (of furniture, baluster, etc.); curve(s), contour (of the human figure); sweep, outline, lines (of car).

galbé [galbe] *a.* (*a*) *Arch:* (*of column*) with entasis; (*b*) shapely; curved; well-proportioned.

galber [galbe] *v.tr.* (*a*) to construct (column) with entasis; (*b*) to give curves to (vase, chest of drawers, etc.); (*c*) *Tchn:* to curve, bend (lightly) (sheet metal).

galbord [galbɔr] *n.m. Nau:* garboard (strake).

gale [gal] *n.f.* **1.** (*a*) *Med:* scabies; **g. bédouine,** prickly heat; **arbre à la g.,** poison ivy, poison oak; (*b*) *F:* scold, shrew (of a woman). **2.** *Vet:* scab, mange. **3.** *Bot:* scurf, scale.

galé [gale] *n.m. Bot:* sweet gale, bog myrtle.

galée [gale] *n.f. Typ:* composing galley.

galéjade [galeʒad] *n.f. Dial:* tall story; **débiter, dire, des galéjades à qn,** to pull s.o.'s leg.

galéjer [galeʒe] *v.i. Dial:* to tell tall stories.

galène [galɛn] *n.f. Miner:* galena, sulphide of lead.

galéopithèque [galeɔpitɛk] *n.m. Z:* flying lemur.

galère [galɛr] *n.f.* **1.** (*a*) galley, slave ship; **vogue la g.!** let things rip! **mais que diable allait-il faire dans**

cette g.? but what the hell was he doing there? whatever took him there? *Nau:* **avirons en g.!** rest on your oars! (*b*) *A:* convict ship; *pl.* hulks; **condamné aux galères,** sentenced to penal servitude; **c'est une vraie g.,** it's hell on earth. **2.** *Coel:* Portuguese man-of-war.

galerie [galri] *n.f.* **1.** (*a*) gallery; **g. de portraits,** portrait gallery; (*b*) arcade, covered walk; (*c*) **g. marchande,** shopping centre; (*d*) *Fr.C:* porch. **2.** balcony, gallery; *Th:* **première g.,** dress circle; **seconde g.,** upper circle; **troisième g.,** gallery, *F:* the gods; **jouer pour la g.,** to play to the gallery; *Nau:* **g. de poupe,** stern gallery, stern walk. **3.** (*a*) *Min:* gallery, drift, level; **g. d'avancement,** heading; *Mil: etc:* **g. d'écoute,** listening gallery; *El:* **g. des câbles,** cable tunnel; (*b*) run (of mole). **4.** (*a*) cornice, moulding, beading (on furniture); (*b*) fender, curb; (*c*) *Aut:* roof rack; (*d*) shelf rail.

galérien [galerjɛ̃] *n.m.* (*a*) galley slave; **travailler comme un g.,** to work like a galley slave; (*b*) convict; *F:* **mener une vie de g.,** to lead a dog's life.

galet [galɛ] *n.m.* **1.** (*a*) pebble; **galets de chaussée,** cobblestones; *Anthr:* **civilisation du g. aménagé,** pebble culture; (*b*) *pl.* shingle; **plage de galets,** shingly, shingle, beach. **2.** *Mec.E:* roller, runner, pulley, (rail)wheel; **g. de roulement,** travelling, running, wheel; railwheel; runner. **3.** *Fish:* float (of net).

galetas [galtɑ] *n.m.* (*a*) garret, attic; (*b*) hovel.

galetouse [galtuz] *n.f. P:* bowl; mess tin, dixie.

galette [galɛt] *n.f.* (*a*) *Cu:* buckwheat pancake; **g. des Rois,** Twelfth Night cake; **g. aux pommes,** apple tart; *F:* **plat comme une g.,** flat as a pancake; (*b*) (ship's) biscuit; (*c*) *P:* money, lolly.

galetteux, -euse [galɛtø, -øz] *a. P:* rich, rolling.

galeux, -euse [galø, -øz] *a.* mangy (dog); scurfy (tree); **plaie galeuse,** sore caused by scabies; **société galeuse,** rotten society.

galgal, *pl.* **-als** [galgal] *n.m. Archeol:* cairn, barrow.

galibot [galibo] *n.m. Min:* (*N. France*) pit boy.

Galice [galis] *Pr.n.f. Geog:* Galicia (Spain).

Galicie [galisi] *Pr.n.f. Geog:* Galicia (Poland).

galicien, -ienne [galisjɛ̃, -jɛn] *a. & n. Geog:* Galician (of Spain or Poland).

Galien [galjɛ̃] *Pr.n.m.* Galen.

Galilée[1] [galile] *Pr.n.f. B.Geog:* Galilee.

Galilée[2] *Pr.n.m. Hist:* Galileo.

galiléen, -enne [galileɛ̃, -ɛn] *a. & n. B.Hist:* Galilean.

galimatias [galimatjɑ] *n.m.* gibberish.

galine [galin] *n.f. Sp:* (*ice hockey*) puck.

galion [galjɔ̃] *n.m. Nau:* galleon.

galipette [galipɛt] *n.f. F:* somersault; **faire la g.,** to turn a somersault.

galipot [galipo] *n.m.* **1.** *Com:* galipot, white resin. **2.** *Fr.C:* **courir le g.,** to go on a spree; to gad about.

galle [gal] *n.f. Bot:* gall(nut); **g. de chêne,** oak apple.

Galles [gal] *Pr.n.f. Geog:* **le pays de G.,** Wales; **la G. du Nord,** North Wales; **Prince de G.,** (i) Prince of Wales; (ii) *Tex:* Prince of Wales check.

gallican, -ane [galikɑ̃, -an] *a. & n. Ecc:* Gallican.

gallicanisme [galikanism] *n.m. Ecc:* Gallicanism.

gallicisme [galisism] *n.m.* French turn of phrase; gallicism.

gallinacé [galinase] *Orn:* **1.** *a.* gallinaceous. **2.** *n.m.pl.* Gallinaceae.

gallique[1] [galik] *a. Hist:* Gallic, of Gaul.

gallique[2] *a. Ch:* gallic (acid).

gallium [galjɔm] *n.m. Ch:* gallium.

gallois, -oise [galwa, -waz] **1.** *a.* Welsh. **2.** *n.* Welshman, *f.* Welshwoman; **les G.,** the Welsh. **3.** *Ling:* Welsh.

gallomanie [galɔmani] *n.f.* gallomania.

gallon [galɔ̃] *n.m. Meas:* gallon.

gallo-romain [galɔrɔmɛ̃] *a.* Gallo-Roman; *pl. gallo-romain(e)s.*

gallup [galœp] *n.m.* Gallup poll.

galoche [galɔʃ] *n.f.* (*a*) clog (with leather upper); *F:* **menton en g.,** nutcracker chin; *P:* **vieille g.,** old fogey; (*b*) overshoe, galosh, *NAm:* rubber.

galon [galɔ̃] *n.m.* **1.** braid, galloon; **g. de finition,** upholstery binding. **2.** *pl. Mil:* (N.C.O.'s) stripes; (officer's) bands, gold braid; *Navy:* (officer's) stripes; (*in Merchant Service*) bands; **priver qn de ses galons,** to reduce s.o. to the ranks; *F:* **prendre du g.,** (i) to be promoted; (ii) to move up in the world; *F:* **arroser ses galons,** to celebrate one's promotion.

galonné [galɔne] *n.m. P:* (non-commissioned) officer.

galonner [galɔne] *v.tr.* to (trim, ornament, with) braid, lace; **habit galonné d'or,** gold-laced coat.

galop [galo] *n.m.* gallop; **prendre le g.,** to break into a gallop; **au g. (allongé),** at a gallop; **grand g.,** full gallop; **g. de manège,** hand gallop; **petit g.,** canter; **partir au g.,** to gallop away; **faire qch. au g.,** to gallop, rush, through sth.; to scamp sth.

galopade [galɔpad] *n.f. Equit:* (*a*) galloping, gallop; canter; **son imagination prend la g.,** his imagination runs away with him; **expédier son repas à la g.,** to bolt one's meal; **traverser la France à la g.,** to rush across France; (*b*) **il n'y a qu'une g.,** it's only a short trot from here.

galopant [galɔpɑ̃] *a.* runaway; **démographie galopante,** spurt in population.

galoper [galɔpe] **1.** *v.i.* (*a*) to gallop; **se mettre à g.,** to break into a gallop; (*b*) to gallop, rush, around; (*c*) **g. en lisant,** to gallop, skim, through a book. **2.** *v.tr.* (*a*) to gallop (horse); (*b*) **g. les rues, la campagne,** to scour the streets, the countryside (in search of sth.). **3.** *v.ind.tr.* **g. après qn, qch.,** to run after s.o., sth.

galopeur, -euse [galɔpœr, -øz] **1.** *a.* galloping. **2.** *n.* (*horse*) galloper.

galopin, -ine [galɔpɛ̃, -in] *n.* **1.** (*a*) errand boy, *f.* girl; (*b*) *F:* (i) (street) urchin; (ii) child, brat; (*c*) *n.m.* young scamp. **2.** *n.m. Mec.E:* (*a*) idler, loose pulley; (*b*) jockey wheel.

galure [galyr], **galurin** [galyrɛ̃] *n.m. P:* hat, titfer.

galvanique [galvanik] *a.* galvanic (cell, etc.); **plaqué g.,** electroplate; **dorure g.,** electrogilding.

galvanisation [galvanizasjɔ̃] *n.f.* (*a*) galvanization, galvanizing; (*b*) *El:* galvanism.

galvaniser [galvanize] *v.tr.* **1.** to galvanize (corpse, etc.); to give new life to (undertaking, etc.); to stimulate, galvanize (a crowd, etc.). **2.** *Metall:* to galvanize; (i) to (electro)plate; (ii) to zinc; **tôle galvanisée,** galvanized (sheet) iron.

galvano- [galvano] **1.** *pref.* galvano-. **2.** *n.m.* **galvano,** *Typ: F:* electrotype plate; electro.

galvanomètre [galvanɔmɛtr̥] *n.m. El:* galvanometer.

galvanoplastie [galvanɔplasti] *n.f.* galvanoplasty; electrodeposition; *Ind:* electroplating; *Typ:* electrotyping.

galvanoplastique [galvanɔplastik] *a.* galvanoplastic.

galvanoscope [galvanɔskɔp] *n.m.* galvanoscope; *Tg:* (linesman's) detector.

galvanotype [galvanɔtip] *n.m. Typ:* electrotype.

galvanotypie [galvanɔtipi] *n.f. Typ:* electrotyping.

galvauder [galvode] *v.tr.* to bring into disrepute; to prostitute (one's talents); **se g.,** to damage one's reputation.

gambade [gɑ̃bad] *n.f.* leap, gambol; *Equit:* gambade; *pl.* capers, antics; **faire des gambades,** to gambol, to cut capers.

gambader [gɑ̃bade] *v.i.* to leap, caper; to frisk (about); to gambol.

gambette[1] [gɑ̃bɛt] *n.m. Orn:* redshank.
gambette[2] *n.f. P:* leg; **jouer, se tirer, des gambettes,** to run away, to beat it.
Gambie [gɑ̃bi] *Pr.n.f. Geog:* the Gambia.
gambille [gɑ̃bij] *n.f. P:* **1.** *pl.* legs, pins. **2.** (*a*) dance, hop; (*b*) dance hall.
gambiller [gɑ̃bije] *v.i. P:* to dance (to a lively rhythm); to jig about; to shake a leg.
gambit [gɑ̃bi] *n.m. Chess:* (*a*) gambit; (*b*) **(pion de) g.,** gambit pawn.
gamelle [gamɛl] *n.f.* **1.** *Mil: etc:* (*a*) *A:* (communal) mess bowl; (*b*) (i) mess kettle, dixie, dixy; (ii) mess tin; **manger à la g.,** to eat in the mess; (*c*) *P:* **ramasser une g.,** to come a cropper. **2.** *Min:* pan.
gamète [gamɛt] *n.m. Biol:* gamete.
gamétocide [gametɔsid] *n.m. Med:* gametocide.
gamétocyte [gametɔsit] *n.m. Biol:* gametocyte.
gamétogénèse [gametɔʒenɛz] *n.f. Biol:* gametogenesis.
gamétophyte [gametɔfit] *n.m. Bot:* gametophyte.
gamin, -ine [gamɛ̃, -in] **1.** *n.* (*a*) street urchin; (*b*) child, brat; **une gamine de dix ans,** a girl of ten; **mon g.,** my boy, my son; (*of man*) **ce n'est qu'un grand g.,** he's just a big schoolboy. **2.** *a.* (*a*) lively, mischievous; (*b*) **elle est encore gamine,** she's still just a child.
gaminerie [gaminri] *n.f.* childish prank, trick; childish behaviour; **il a passé l'âge de ces gamineries,** he's too old to behave in such a childish way.
gamma [gama] *n.m.* (*a*) *Gr.Alph:* gamma; (*b*) *Phot:* (development factor) gamma; (*c*) *Atom.Ph:* **rayons g.,** gamma rays.
gammaglobuline [gamaglɔbylin] *n.f. Biol:* gamma globulin.
gammamètre [gamamɛtr̥] *n.m.* gamma (radiation) meter.
gamme [gam] *n.f.* **1.** *Mus:* scale, gamut; **faire des gammes,** to practise scales; **changer de g.,** to alter one's tone, to change one's tune, to climb down. **2.** range, series, scale (of colours, etc.); **toute la g. des sensations,** the whole gamut, range, of sensations; *F:* **toute la g.!** the whole (damn) lot (of them)!
gammée [game] *a.f.* **croix g.,** swastika.
gamopétale [gamɔpetal] *a. Bot:* gamopetalous.
ganache [ganaʃ] *n.f.* **1.** (lower) jaw, jowl. **2.** *F:* (*a*) fool, idiot; (*b*) **vieille g.,** old fogey, buffer.
Gand [gɑ̃] *Pr.n.m. Geog:* Ghent.
gandin [gɑ̃dɛ̃] *n.m. A:* dandy.
gang [gɑ̃g] *n.m.* gang (of criminals, etc.).
ganga [gɑ̃ga] *n.m. Orn:* pintailed (sand) grouse.
Gange (le) [ləgɑ̃ʒ] *Pr.n.m. Geog:* the (river) Ganges.
gangétique [gɑ̃ʒetik] *a. Geog:* Gangetic (delta, etc.).
gangliforme [gɑ̃glifɔrm] *a.* gangliform.
ganglion [gɑ̃glijɔ̃] *n.m.* **1.** *Anat:* ganglion; **g. nerveux,** ganglion cell; **ganglions lymphatiques,** lymphatic glands, lymph glands. **2.** (*a*) *Med:* **g. synovial,** ganglion; (*b*) *Vet:* spavin.
ganglionnaire [gɑ̃glijɔnɛr] *a. Anat:* ganglionic; **fièvre g.,** glandular fever.
gangrène [gɑ̃grɛn] *n.f.* **1.** *Med:* gangrene; **g. gazeuse,** gas gangrene; **g. des os,** necrosis. **2.** *Bot:* canker. **3.** rot, corruption.
gangrené [gɑ̃grəne] *a.* **1.** *Med:* gangrenous, gangrened. **2.** corrupt.
gangrener [gɑ̃grəne] *v.* **(il gangrène; il gangrènera)** **1.** *v.tr.* (*a*) *Med:* to gangrene; to corrupt. **2. se g.,** to become, go, gangrenous.
gangreneux, -euse [gɑ̃grənø, -øz] *a.* **1.** *Med:* gangrenous, gangrened. **2.** *Bot:* cankerous.
gangster [gɑ̃gstɛr] *n.m.* gangster; hooligan.
gangstérisme [gɑ̃gsterism] *n.m.* gangsterism.
gangue [gɑ̃g] *n.f. Miner:* gang(ue), matrix (of precious stone, etc.).
gannet [ganɛ] *n.m. Orn:* gannet.
ganse [gɑ̃s] *n.f.* **1.** (*a*) braid, (plaited) cord, edging; piping (cord); (*b*) **g. de cheveux,** plait of hair. **2.** rope handle; loop.
gant [gɑ̃] *n.m.* **1.** glove; *Arm:* gauntlet; (*a*) **mettre ses gants,** to put on one's gloves; **gants en suède, en tissu,** suède, fabric, gloves; **gants fourrés,** lined gloves; **gants de caoutchouc,** rubber gloves; **cela vous va comme un g.,** it fits you like a glove; **il faut prendre des gants pour l'approcher,** one has to handle him with kid gloves (on); **jeter le g. à qn,** to throw down the gauntlet to s.o.; **relever le g.,** to take up the gauntlet, to accept the challenge; **souple comme un g.,** good-natured, easygoing; (*b*) **gants de boxe,** boxing gloves; *Mil:* **gants moufles,** mittens; (*c*) *Toil:* **g. de toilette** = facecloth, flannel, *NAm:* washcloth, washrag; **g. de crin,** friction glove. **2.** (*a*) *Bot:* **g. de bergère, (de) Notre-Dame,** (i) foxglove; (ii) columbine; (*b*) *Spong:* **g. de Neptune,** glove sponge.
gantelé [gɑ̃tle] *a.* gauntleted; **la main gantelée,** the mailed fist.
gantelée [gɑ̃tle] *n.f. Bot:* (*a*) foxglove; (*b*) throatwort.
gantelet [gɑ̃tlɛ] *n.m.* gauntlet.
ganter [gɑ̃te] **1.** *v.tr.* to glove; **être bien ganté,** to be well gloved. **2.** *v.i.* **g. du sept,** to take sevens, size seven, in gloves. **3. se g.,** to put on one's gloves.
ganterie [gɑ̃tri] *n.f.* **1.** (*a*) glovemaking, gloving; (*b*) glove trade. **2.** (*a*) glove factory; (*b*) glove shop; (*c*) (*in store*) glove counter, department.
gantier, -ière [gɑ̃tje, -jɛr] *n.* glover.
gantois, -oise [gɑ̃twa, -waz] *a. & n. Geog:* [native, inhabitant] of Ghent.
garage [garaʒ] *n.m.* **1.** (*a*) docking (of boats); (*b*) dock, basin (of canal, river); **g. à sec,** dry basin. **2.** *Rail:* shunting, side tracking; **voie de g.,** siding; *F:* **mettre, ranger (qn, qch.) sur une voie de g.,** to shelve (s.o., sth.). **3.** (*a*) garage; **g. à plusieurs étages,** multistorey car park, *U.S:* tiered parking lot; **g. de canots,** boathouse, *U.S:* boat shed; **g. d'autobus,** bus depot; **g. d'avions,** (aircraft) hangar; *Rail:* **g. de machines,** engine shed; (*b*) passing place (on narrow road).
garagiste [garaʒist] *n.m. Aut:* (*a*) garage keeper, proprietor; (*b*) garage mechanic.
garance [garɑ̃s] *n.f.* **1.** *Bot:* (*a*) madder(wort); (*b*) *F:* **petite g., g. de chien,** squinancy wort. **2.** madder (dye).
garant, -ante [garɑ̃, -ɑ̃t] *n.* (*a*) guarantor, surety, bail; **se rendre, se porter, g. de qn,** (i) to answer for s.o.; (ii) to go bail for s.o.; **je m'en porte g.,** I can vouch for it; **elle vous en est garante,** she gives you her word for it; **prendre qn à g. de qch.,** to call s.o. to witness sth.; **être g. de ses faits,** to be answerable for one's actions; (*b*) *nm* authority, guarantee.
garantie [garɑ̃ti] *n.f.* **1.** (*a*) guarantee, safeguard (**contre,** against); **prendre des garanties contre les abus,** to insure against abuses; (*b*) guarantee, pledge (of execution of contract); guaranty (of payment); **g. d'exécution,** contract bond; **fonds déposés, détenus, en g.,** funds lodged, held, as security; **verser une somme en g.,** to leave a deposit; **donner sa montre en g.,** to pledge one's watch; **donner une g. pour qn,** to stand security for s.o.; **g. accessoire,** collateral security; (*c*) *Com:* warranty, guarantee (of quality, etc.); **sans g.,** unwarranted; **lettre de g. d'indemnité,** letter of indemnity. **2.** *Fin:* underwriting; **syndicat de g.,** underwriters.
garantir [garɑ̃tir] *v.tr.* **1.** (*a*) to warrant, guarantee; **g. une dette,** to guarantee a debt; **créance garantie,** secured debt; **pendule garantie (pour) deux ans,** clock guaranteed for two years; **g. un fait,** to vouch for a fact; **je vous garantis qu'il viendra,** I'm sure he'll come; (*b*) *Fin:* to underwrite (issue of shares, etc.).

2. to shelter, protect; **se g. contre le froid,** to protect oneself against the cold. **3.** (*a*) *Jur:* **g. qn contre . . .,** to indemnify s.o. from, against . . .; (*b*) **g. une maison contre l'incendie,** to secure, insure, a house against fire.

garce [gars] *n.f.* (*a*) *A:* (*f. of* **gars**) girl; (*b*) *P:* prostitute, tart; **fils de g.,** son of a bitch; (*c*) *P:* disagreeable girl, woman; bitch; (*d*) *P:* **une belle g.,** a smasher; (*e*) *P:* **cette g. de vie,** this bloody (awful) life.

garçon [garsɔ̃] *n.m.* **1.** (*a*) boy; **elle est accouchée d'un g.,** she gave birth to a son; **école de garçons,** boys' school; **tu es un grand g.,** you're a big boy now; **c'est un g. manqué,** she's a tomboy; (*b*) son; **il est venu avec ses deux garçons,** he came with his two sons, boys. **2.** young man; **g. d'honneur,** best man, groomsman; **garçons (de la fête),** stewards; **un bon, brave, g.,** a good sort; **un beau, un joli, g.,** a handsome young man; **un mauvais g.,** a bad lot. **3.** bachelor; **il est encore g.,** he's still single, still a bachelor; **vieux g.,** old bachelor; confirmed bachelor; **appartement de g.,** bachelor flat, *NAm:* apartment. **4.** (assistant) caretaker; cleaner; messenger; **g. de salle,** auctioneer's messenger; **g. de bureau,** office boy, (office) messenger; **g. de courses,** errand boy; **g. de recette,** bank messenger; **g. boucher,** butcher's boy; **g. coiffeur,** hairdresser's assistant; **g. (de restaurant),** waiter; **g. (de comptoir),** barman; (*in restaurant*) **g.!** waiter! **g. d'écurie,** groom; (*in hotel*) **g. d'étage,** boots; floor waiter; **g. d'ascenseur,** lift boy, liftman, *NAm:* elevator operator; **g. de cuisine,** kitchen boy, kitchen porter; *Nau:* **g. de cabine,** (cabin) steward; **g. de pont,** deck steward.

garçonne [garsɔn] *n.f.* bachelor girl.

garçonnet [garsɔnɛ] *n.m.* **1.** little boy. **2.** *Com:* **taille g.,** small boys (size).

garçonnier, -ière [garsɔnje, -jɛr] **1.** *a.* **habitudes garçonnières,** (i) bachelor habits; (ii) (woman's) masculine, mannish, habits. **2.** *n.f.* bachelor flat, *NAm:* apartment.

garde¹ [gard] *n.m. & f.* (*a*) keeper; *Hist: Adm:* **G. des Sceaux** = Lord Chancellor; *Hist:* **G. des Archives** = Master of the Rolls; (*b*) guard; watchman; *Mil:* sentry; **g. de nuit,** night watchman; **g. champêtre,** rural policeman; **g. du corps,** bodyguard; **g. forestier,** forester, ranger, forest warden; (*c*) *n.f.* (i) nurse; (ii) nanny; **g. de nuit,** (privately employed) night nurse; (*d*) *n.m. Mil:* guardsman; **gardes du corps,** lifeguards; **g. (républicaine) mobile,** mobile guard = member of security police.

garde² *n.f.* **1.** (*a*) guardianship, care, protection, custody (of a person); care (of thing); **chien de g.,** watchdog; **commettre qch. à la g. de qn,** to entrust s.o. with (the care of) sth.; **être sous bonne g.,** to be in safe custody, keeping; **avoir qch. en g.,** to have charge of sth.; **que Dieu nous ait en g.,** may God protect us; **je laisse les enfants à, sous, votre g.,** I'm leaving the children in your charge; *Jur:* **g. des enfants,** custody of the children (after divorce); (*b*) guarding, protection (of frontier, machinery, etc.); *Rail:* **plaque de g.,** axle guard (of locomotive); (*c*) *Aut: etc:* clearance; **g. (au sol),** ground clearance; (*d*) **vin de g.,** good keeping wine; **de bonne g.,** worth keeping. **2.** (*a*) watch(ing); **g. à vue,** close watch; **faire la g.,** to keep watch; (*b*) care, guard; **mettre qn en g. contre qch.,** to put s.o. on his guard against sth.; **en g.!** on guard! *Fenc:* en garde! **être, se tenir, sur ses gardes,** to be on one's guard; to look out. **3.** (*a*) **prendre g. à qn, à qch.,** to beware of s.o., of sth.; **prenez g. aux orties!** mind the nettles! **prenez g.!** look out! take care! (*b*) **prendre g. à qch.,** to attend to, be careful of, to notice, sth.; **un fait auquel on n'a pas pris g.,** a fact that has been left out of consideration; **je n'y prendrais pas g.,** I should take no notice of it; I shouldn't take any notice of it; **faire qch. sans y prendre g.,** to do sth. without meaning to; (*c*) (i) *O:* **prendre g. à faire qch.,** to be careful to do sth.; to take good care to do sth.; (ii) **prendre g. de ne pas faire qch.,** to be careful not to do sth.; **prenez g. à, de, ne pas vous perdre,** mind you don't get lost; (*d*) *O:* **prendre g. de faire qch.,** to be careful not to do sth.; **prenez g. de tomber,** mind you don't fall; (*e*) **prendre g. que . . . (ne)** + *sub.*, to be careful, to take care that (sth. does not happen); **prenez g. qu'il (ne) vous voie,** take care he doesn't see you. **4.** guard; (*a*) **soldat de g. à la porte,** soldier on guard at the door; **être de g.,** to be on guard, *Nau:* on duty; **descendre de g.,** to come off guard, off duty; **monter la g.,** (i) to mount guard; (ii) to go on guard; **à la g.!** guard turn out! (*b*) **le corps de g., la g.,** the guard; **g. montante,** new guard, relieving guard; **g. descendante,** old guard; **g. du drapeau,** colour party, colour guard, *NAm:* color guard; **g. d'honneur,** guard of honour, *NAm:* of honor; (*c*) **la g.,** the Guards; **la g. à cheval,** the Horseguards; **la g. à pied,** the Footguards; **la g. du corps,** the Lifeguards; **la G. républicaine,** the Republican Guard (of Paris); **la G. mobile** = security (state) police; *Hist:* **la G. impériale,** (Napoleon's) Imperial Guard; (*d*) *Mil:* **(salle de) g.,** guardroom. **5.** *Cards:* covering card, guard. **6.** (*a*) (hilt) guard (of sword, foil); **jusqu'à la g.,** up to the hilt; (*b*) ward (of lock). **7.** *Bookb:* **(feuille, page, de) g.,** (i) flyleaf; (ii) end paper.

gardé [garde] *a.* guarded; *Cards:* **roi g., dame gardée,** guarded king, queen; **toute(s) proportion(s) gardée(s),** all things considered.

garde-à-vous [gardavu] *n.m. inv. Mil:* (position of) attention; **être, se tenir, au g.-à-v.,** to stand at attention; **au g.-à-v.,** at attention; **se mettre vivement au g.-à-v.,** to spring to attention; **g.-à-v.!** attention!

garde-barrière [gard(ə)barjɛr] *n.* gatekeeper (at level crossing, *U.S:* grade crossing); *pl. gardes-barrière(s).*

garde-boue [gard(ə)bu] *n.m.inv.* mudguard (of bicycle, etc.).

garde-boutique [gard(ə)butik] *n.m.inv. Com:* unsaleable article.

garde-canal [gard(ə)kanal] *n.m.* lock keeper; *pl. gardes-canal, -canaux.*

garde-chasse [gard(ə)ʃas] *n.m.* gamekeeper; *pl. gardes-chasse(s).*

garde-chiourme [gard(ə)ʃjurm] *n.m.* (*a*) *A:* warder (of convict gang); (*b*) **un vrai g.-c.,** a real slavedriver; *pl. garde(s)-chiourme(s).*

garde-corps [gard(ə)kɔr] *n.m.inv.* **1.** parapet, balustrade. **2.** railing, side rail, guard rail, handrail (of bridge, etc.); *Nau:* **g.-c. arrière,** stern rail.

garde-côte [gard(ə)kot] *n.m.* **1.** coastguard. **2.** (*a*) coastguard vessel; (*b*) coast-defence ship; *pl. garde-côte(s).*

garde-feu [gard(ə)fø] *n.m. inv.* (*a*) fender; (*b*) fireguard; (*c*) fire screen; (*d*) *For:* **tranchée g.-f.,** firebreak.

garde-fou [gard(ə)fu] *n.m.* **1.** parapet, balustrade. **2.** railing, handrail (of bridge, etc.); *pl. garde-fous.*

garde-frein [gard(ə)frɛ̃] *n.m. Rail:* brakesman, *NAm:* brakeman; *pl. gardes-frein(s).*

garde-frontière [gard(ə)frɔ̃tjɛr] *n.f.* frontier guard; *pl. gardes-frontière.*

garde-ligne [gard(ə)liɲ] *n.m. Rail:* track watchman; *pl. gardes-ligne(s).*

garde-magasin [gardmagazɛ̃] *n.m.* (*a*) warehouseman; (*b*) *Mil:* storekeeper, barrack sergeant; *Navy:* yeoman; *pl. gardes-magasin(s).*

garde-malade [gard(ə)malad] *n.* nurse; *pl. gardes-malade(s).*

garde-manger [gardmɑ̃ʒe] *n.m.inv.* **1.** *A:* pantry, larder. **2.** meat safe.
garde-meuble [gard(ə)mœbl] *n.m.* (*a*) furniture repository, warehouse; (*b*) lumber room; *pl. garde-meuble(s).*
gardénia [gardenja] *n.m. Bot:* gardenia.
garde-pêche [gard(ə)pɛʃ] *n.m.* **1.** water bailiff; river keeper, watcher; *pl. gardes-pêche.* **2.** *inv.* (*a*) (river) conservancy boat; (*b*) fishery protection vessel.
garde-place [gard(ə)plas] *n.m. Rail:* holder (for reservation ticket); **(ticket) g.-p.,** reservation ticket; *pl. garde-place(s).*
garde-port [gard(ə)pɔr] *n.m.* wharfmaster (on river); *pl. gardes-port(s).*
garder [garde] **I.** *v.tr.* to keep. **1.** to guard, protect; to keep watch over (s.o., sth.); **g. qn d'un danger,** to protect s.o. from a danger; **g. la boutique,** to look after, mind, the shop; **g. un troupeau,** to tend a flock; *F:* **dites donc, nous n'avons pas gardé les cochons ensemble!** don't be so familiar! don't take liberties! **g. les enfants,** to mind the children; **g. qn à vue,** to keep a close watch on s.o. **2.** (*a*) to retain; **g. un vêtement,** (i) to keep a garment; (ii) to keep on a garment; **g. qn à diner,** to keep s.o. to dinner; **g. qn en otage,** to keep, detain, s.o. as a hostage; (*b*) to preserve; to put by, keep (a sum of money); **g. les apparences,** to keep up appearances; **g. ses illusions, son innocence,** to keep one's illusions, one's innocence; **g. son sang-froid,** to keep cool (and collected); **g. rancune à qn,** to harbour, *NAm:* harbor, resentment against s.o.; **g. le sourire,** to keep smiling; **g. son sérieux,** to keep a straight face; **viande qui ne se garde pas bien,** meat that does not keep well. **3.** to remain in (a place); **g. la chambre,** to keep, stay, in one's room; **être obligé de g. le lit,** to have to stay in bed, to be laid up. **4.** to observe, respect; **g. les commandements,** to keep the commandments; **g. un secret, sa parole,** to keep a secret, one's word; **il n'a pas gardé sa parole,** he has broken his word. **II. se g. 1.** to protect oneself; **garde-toi!** look out (for yourself)! *Cards:* **se g. à trèfle,** to keep a guard in clubs; *F:* **se g. à carreau,** to take every precaution, to be on one's guard. **2.** (*a*) **se g. de qn, de qch.,** to beware of s.o., sth.; (*b*) **se g. de faire qch.,** to take care not to do sth.; **gardez-vous (bien) de le perdre,** mind you don't lose it! **je m'en garderai bien!** I shall do no such thing! *F:* no fear!
garderie [gard(ə)ri] *n.f.* **1.** beat, domain, of one ranger, keeper. **2.** day nursery.
garde-rivière [gard(ə)rivjɛr] *n.m.* river policeman; *pl. gardes-rivière(s).*
garde-robe [gard(ə)rɔb] *n.f.* **1.** wardrobe (= (i) piece of furniture; (ii) clothes). **2.** *A:* (*a*) water closet, privy, w.c.; (*b*) commode, nightstool; *pl. garde-robes.*
gardeur, -euse [gardœr, -øz] *n.* keeper, tender (of animals); herdsman; **g. de cochons,** swineherd; **gardeuse d'enfant,** (i) baby farmer; (ii) mother's help.
garde-voie [gard(ə)vwa] *n.m. Rail:* track watchman; *pl. gardes-voie.*
gardian [gardjɑ̃] *n.m.* cowherd (in the Camargue).
gardien, -ienne [gardjɛ̃, -jɛn] *n.* (*a*) guardian, keeper; watchman; caretaker, *esp. NAm:* janitor (of public building, etc.); (museum, car park) attendant; warder, *NAm:* guard (of prison); **g. de plage,** lifeguard; **g. de la paix,** policeman (in a town); *Sp:* **g. (de but),** goalkeeper; *Ecc:* **(père) g.,** (Father) Superior (of religious community); **g. des intérêts publics,** protector of the public interest; **se poser g. de l'ordre,** to set oneself up as an upholder of public order; (*b*) *a.* **ange g.,** (i) guardian angel; (ii) *F:* bodyguard.
gardiennage [gardjɛnaʒ] *n.m.* guarding (of bridges, etc.); caretaking (of building); conservancy (of port, etc.).
gardon [gardɔ̃] *n.m. Ich:* roach.
gare[1] [gar] *int.* look out! out of the way! mind yourself! **g. dessous!** look out below! down there! **g. à lui . . .,** woe betide him . . ., he's got it coming to him . . .; *A:* **g. l'eau!** mind the slops! look out below! *esp. Scot:* gardy loo! **sans crier g.,** without warning.
gare[2] *n.f.* **1.** *Nau:* (*a*) siding (of river, canal); (*b*) (canal) wharf; basin, dock (in river, canal). **2.** (*a*) (railway, *NAm:* railroad) station; **g. (de voyageurs),** passenger station; **g. de marchandises,** goods, freight, station, depot; **g. maritime,** harbour, *NAm:* harbor station; maritime station; **(colis à prendre) en g.,** (parcel) to be (left till) called for; **g. de triage,** marshalling yard; **chef de g.,** stationmaster, station manager; (*b*) **g. routière,** bus, coach, station; **g. routière (de marchandises),** road haulage depot; **g. dépôt de matériaux,** (contractor's) yard, store; **g. aérienne,** air terminal.
garenne [garɛn] *n.f.* **1.** (rabbit) warren; **lapin de g.,** wild rabbit. **2.** (fishing) preserve.
garer [gare] **1.** *v.tr.* (*a*) to get in (the harvest); *Lit:* to garner; (*b*) to dock (vessel); (*c*) to shunt (train) on to a siding; (*d*) to garage (car); to put (aircraft) into the hangar; (*e*) to park (car). **2. se g.** (*a*) to park (a car); **j'ai eu de la peine à me g.,** I've had trouble parking; (*b*) **se g. de qch.,** to avoid sth., get out of the way of sth., steer clear of sth.
Gargantua [gargɑ̃tɥa] *n.m. F:* glutton, guzzler; **un appétit, un repas, de G.,** a gargantuan appetite, meal.
gargantuesque [gargɑ̃tɥɛsk] *a.* gargantuan.
gargariser (se) [səgargarize] *v.pr.* to gargle; *P:* **se g. le sifflet,** to w(h)et one's whistle.
gargarisme [gargarism] *n.m.* **1.** gargle. **2.** gargling.
gargote [gargɔt] *n.f.* cheap restaurant.
gargotier, -ière [gargɔtje, -jɛr] *n.* **1.** keeper of poor restaurant. **2.** poor cook.
gargouille [garguj] *n.f.* **1.** (*a*) (water)spout (of roof gutter, of pump); (*b*) *Arch:* gargoyle. **2.** (*a*) (street) gutter; (*b*) culvert, drain (of embankment).
gargouillement [gargujmɑ̃] *n.m.* **1.** (*a*) gurgling, bubbling (of water); (*b*) squelch(ing) (of wet shoes). **2.** rumbling (of stomach); *F:* tummy rumbles.
gargouiller [garguje] *v.i.* **1.** (*a*) (*of water*) to gurgle, bubble; (*b*) *F:* (*of wet shoes*) to squelch; **sol qui gargouille sous les pas,** squelchy, squishy, ground. **2.** (*of the stomach*) to rumble.
gargouillis [garguji] *n.m.* (*a*) bubbling, gurgling (of water); (*b*) squelch(ing) (of wet shoes).
garnement [garnəmɑ̃] *n.m.* **(mauvais) g.,** scamp; wretch (of a child); rascal.
garni [garni] **I.** *a.* **1.** (*a*) **bien garni(e),** well lined (purse); well stocked (shop); well appointed (house); **chevelure bien garnie,** thick head of hair; *F:* **elle est bien garnie,** she's well upholstered; (*b*) *Cu:* **plat g.,** meat with vegetables; **choucroute garnie,** sauerkraut with sausages; (*c*) *Metall:* **g. d'anti-friction,** Babbit-lined. **2.** *O:* furnished (flat, *NAm:* apartment). **II.** *n.m.* **1.** filling (piece); (*a*) *Const:* packing; (*b*) *Carp:* sliver, splinter; (*c*) *Nau:* rounding (of rope). **2.** *O:* furnished room(s); bedsitter(s).
garnir [garnir] *v.tr.* **1.** to strengthen, protect; **bien garni contre le froid,** well protected against the cold; **g. une position, une place de guerre,** to occupy, man, a position; to garrison a stronghold. **2.** to furnish, provide (**de,** with); **g. qch. à l'intérieur,** to line sth.; **garni de feutre,** felt-lined; **salle garnie de monde,** (i) room full of people; (ii) *Th:* large audience; **la salle se garnit,** the hall, *Th:* the house, is beginning to fill (up); **g. un feu,** to stoke a fire. **3.** to trim (dress, hat, etc.); *Cu:* to garnish (a dish); *Harn:* to harness (horse). **4.** *Tchn:* (*a*) to garret (joints); to stuff (chair, etc.); to lag (boiler); to pack (piston); to line (brake);

Fish: to bait (hook); (*b*) *Tex:* to nap, teasel, teazle, raise (cloth).

garnison [garnizɔ̃] *n.f. Mil:* garrison; **mettre une g. dans une ville,** to garrison a town; **ville de g.,** garrison town; **être en g., tenir g., dans une ville,** to be garrisoned, in garrison, stationed, in a town; **changer de g.,** to change station.

garnissage [garnisaʒ] *n.m.* **1.** (*a*) garnishing, furnishing; trimming, facing (of coat); filling in (of flaws in wood); packing (of piston); lagging (of boiler); (*b*) (*material*) packing, stuffing; *Metall:* lining (of furnace). **2.** *Tex:* napping, teaseling, teazling, raising (of cloth).

garnisseur, -euse [garnisœr, -øz] *n.* **1.** garnisher, trimmer (of hats, dresses, etc.); fitter (of cases, etc.). **2.** *Tex:* napper, teaseler.

garniture [garnityr] *n.f.* **1.** furniture, fittings; (*a*) mountings (of a rifle); rigging (of a ship); (metal) furnishings (of chest of drawers, etc.); **g. de lit,** bedding; **garnitures d'une serrure,** wards of a lock; **g. d'une pompe à incendie,** hose of a fire engine; **g. intérieure d'une voiture,** upholstery of a car; (*b*) *Typ:* furniture. **2.** (*a*) trimming, decoration (of hat, dress, etc.); (*b*) trimming(s). **3.** (complete) set (of buttons, diamonds, ornaments, etc.); **g. de feu, de foyer,** fire irons; **g. de bureau,** desk set, writing set; **g. de toilette,** toilet set. **4.** *Cu:* garnish(ing) (of dish). **5.** (*a*) *Mch:* packing (of stuffing box); stuffing (piece); (packing) ring (of piston); **g. de métal blanc,** babitting; (*b*) lagging (of boiler); (*c*) *Aut: etc:* **g. de frein,** brake lining; brake pad (of disc brake); **g. d'embrayage,** clutch lining.

garrigue [garig] *n.f. Geog:* garrigue.

garrocher [garɔʃe] *v.tr. Fr.C: P:* to throw (stones, etc.).

garrot[1] [garo] *n.m.* **1.** *Med:* tourniquet. **2. (supplice du) g.,** gar(r)otting, gar(r)otte.

garrot[2] *n.m.* withers (of horse).

garrot[3] *n.m. Orn:* **g. arlequin,** harlequin duck.

garrotte [garɔt] *n.f. A:* gar(r)otte, gar(r)otting.

garrotter [garɔte] *v.tr.* to pinion (prisoner, etc.).

gars [gɑ] *n.m. F:* boy; (young) man; **un petit g.,** a little boy; **un beau g.,** a fine, handsome, young man; **un brave g.,** a good sort; **un drôle de g.,** an odd type; **allons-y, les gars!** come on, boys! (*to child*) **bonjour, mon petit g.!** hullo young man!

Gascogne [gaskɔɲ] *Pr.n.f. Geog:* Gascony; **le Golfe de G.,** the Bay of Biscay.

gascon, -onne [gaskɔ̃, -ɔn] *a. & n. Geog:* Gascon; **faire le G.,** to boast, brag; **offre de G.,** hollow promise.

gasconnade [gaskɔnad] *n.f.* boasting, bragging.

gas(-)oil [gɑzɔjl] *n.m.* diesel oil, diesel fuel; *esp. U.S:* gas oil.

Gaspard [gaspar] **1.** *Pr.n.m.* Jasper. **2.** *n.m. P:* rat.

gaspillage [gaspijaʒ] *n.m.* squandering, wasting (of money, etc.); **pas de gaspillages!** don't be wasteful!

gaspiller [gaspije] *v.tr.* to waste, squander (money); **g. son temps,** to waste one's time; **g. sa vie,** to make a mess of one's life.

gaspilleur, -euse [gaspijœr, -øz] (*a*) *n.* spendthrift, waster; (*b*) *a.* **il est tres g.,** he's very wasteful.

gastéropode [gasterɔpɔd] *n.m. Moll:* gast(e)ropod.

gastralgie [gastralʒi] *n.f. Med:* gastralgia.

gastralgique [gastralʒik] *a.* (*a*) *Med:* gastralgic; (*b*) dyspeptic.

gastrectomie [gastrɛktɔmi] *n.f. Surg:* gastrectomy.

gastrique [gastrik] *a.* gastric; **embarras g.,** stomach upset, bilious attack.

gastrite [gastrit] *n.f. Med:* gastritis.

gastro-entérite [gastrɔɑ̃terit] *n.f. Med:* gastroenteritis; *pl. gastro-entérites.*

gastro-entérologie [gastrɔɑ̃terɔlɔʒi] *n.f. Med:* gastro-enterology.

gastro-entérologue [gastrɔɑ̃terɔlɔg] *n. Med:* gastro-enterologist; *pl. gastro-entérologues.*

gastronome [gastrɔnɔm] *n.m.* gastronome; gourmet.

gastronomie [gastrɔnɔmi] *n.f.* gastronomy.

gastronomique [gastrɔnɔmik] *a.* gastronomic(al).

gastropode [gastrɔpɔd] *n.m. Moll:* gast(e)ropod.

gate [geit] *n.f. Elcs:* gate.

gâté [gɑte] *a.* spoilt; (*a*) damaged (fruit, etc.); **œufs gâtés,** rotten, addled, eggs; **viande gâtée,** tainted meat; **dents gâtées,** decayed teeth; (*b*) **enfant g.,** (i) spoilt, pampered, child; (ii) pet, favourite, *NAm:* favorite; **l'enfant g. de la famille,** the blue-eyed boy (of the family).

gâteau, -eaux [gɑto] *n.m.* **1.** cake; (open) tart; (cold, sweet) pudding; **gros g. à la crème,** gâteau; **g. sec,** (i) (sweet) biscuit; (ii) plain cake; **g. de riz** = rice pudding; **g. des Rois,** Twelfth Night cake; *F:* **papa g.,** (i) easy-going, over-indulgent, daddy; (ii) friend of the family who spoils the children; (iii) (*girl's wealthy older male friend*) sugar daddy; *F:* **marraine g.,** fairy godmother; *F:* **c'est du g.,** it's a piece of cake; *F:* **partager le g., avoir part au g.,** to share the profit, the loot; to have one's slice of the cake. **2.** (*a*) lump (of any material); disc (of gun cotton, etc.); *Surg:* pledget; (*b*) **g. de miel,** honeycomb; (*c*) **g. de bouse,** cow pat(ch).

gâter [gɑte] **1.** *v.tr.* to spoil; (*a*) to damage; **g. un vêtement,** to spoil a garment; **la grêle gâte le blé,** hail damages wheat; **les mouches gâtent la viande,** flies taint meat; **cela ne gâte rien,** that won't do any harm; **il a tout gâté,** he's spoiled everything, made a hash of everything; *Com:* **g. le métier,** to spoil the market; (*b*) to pamper; **g. ses enfants,** to spoil, pamper, over-indulge, one's children. **2. se g.,** to deteriorate; **le poisson se gâte facilement,** fish easily goes bad; **le temps se gâte,** the weather is breaking up; it's turning wet; **les affaires se gâtent,** things are going wrong.

gâterie [gɑtri] *n.f.* **1.** overindulgence, spoiling (of children). **2.** *pl.* treats, goodies (for children).

gâteux, -euse [gɑtø, -øz] **1.** *n.* dotard. **2.** *a.* senile, gaga; in one's second childhood.

gâtisme [gɑtism] *n.m.* senility, senile decay.

gauche [goʃ] *a.* **1.** warped, crooked; out of true; skew (surface, etc.). **2.** awkward, clumsy (person, manner); bungling (attempt). **3.** left; (*a*) **main g.,** left hand; **rive g.,** left bank (of river); *Equit: Aut:* **côté g.,** near side; (*b*) *n.f.* **assis à ma g.,** seated on my left; **mon voisin de g.,** my lefthand neighbour; **le tiroir de g.,** the lefthand drawer; *Nau:* **changer de route sur la g.,** to alter course to port; (*c*) *n.m. Box:* **feinter du g.,** to feint with the left; (*d*) *Pol:* (i) *n.f.* **la G.** the Left; (ii) **(politique) de g.,** leftwing (politics); **homme de g.,** leftist. **4.** (*a*) **à g.,** (i) on the left(hand side), to the left; **tournez à g.,** turn left; **la première rue à g.,** the first street on the left; *F:* **passer l'arme à g.,** to die, go west, peg out; (ii) (in a) counter-clockwise (direction); **vis, hélice, à pas de g.,** lefthanded screw; lefthand propeller; (iii) wrongly; (*b*) **jusqu'à la g.,** (i) to the end, to the last; (ii) right up to the hilt; **ils nous ont eu jusqu'à la g.,** they cheated us right, left and centre.

gauchement [goʃmɑ̃] *adv.* awkwardly, clumsily.

gaucher, -ère [goʃe, -ɛr] **1.** *a.* lefthanded. **2.** *n.* lefthander.

gaucherie [goʃri] *n.f.* **1.** lefthandedness. **2.** awkwardness, clumsiness, gaucherie.

gauchi [goʃi] *a. Tchn:* out of true.

gauchir [goʃir] **1.** *v.i. & pr.* (*of wood, etc.*) to warp, wind; to shrink out of true; (*of iron*) to buckle. **2.** *v.tr.* to camber (sth.). **3.** *v.tr. Av:* **g. l'aileron,** to bank.

gauchisant, -ante [goʃizɑ̃, -ɑ̃t] *a. & n. Pol:* leftish, leftist.
gauchisme [goʃism] *n.m. Pol:* leftism.
gauchissement [goʃismɑ̃] *n.m.* **1.** warping, winding, buckling. **2.** *Av:* banking.
gauchiste [goʃist] *a. & n. Pol:* leftist.
gaufrage [gofraʒ] *n.m.* **1.** embossing (of leather, etc.); goffering, fluting (of linen); crinkling, puckering (of paper); *Bookb:* blocking (of cover). **2.** embossed work; corrugation(s); goffers, fluting.
gaufre [gofr̥] *n.f.* **1. g. de miel,** honeycomb. **2.** *Cu:* waffle; **moule à gaufres,** waffle iron.
gaufrer [gofre] *v.tr.* (*a*) to figure, emboss (leather, velvet, etc.); *Bookb:* to block (cover); (*b*) to goffer, flute (linen); **fer à g.,** goffering iron; (*c*) to corrugate (iron, paper); to crinkle (paper).
gaufrette [gofrɛt] *n.f. Cu:* wafer (biscuit).
gaufrier [gofrije] *n.m. Cu:* waffle iron.
gaufrure [gofryr] *n.f.* **1.** stamped design (on leather, etc.). **2.** goffering (on linen).
gaule¹ [gol] *n.f.* (long thin) pole, stick.
Gaule² *Pr.n.f. A.Geog:* Gaul.
gauler [gole] *v.tr.* to beat, thrash (fruit, walnut, tree).
gaulis [goli] *n.m.* **1.** plantation (of young trees); sapling wood. **2.** coppice, copse, thicket. **3.** brush(wood).
gaullien,-ienne [goljɛ̃,-jɛn] *a. Hist:* concerning General de Gaulle.
gaullisme [golism] *n.m. Pol:* Gaullism.
gaulliste [golist] *a. & n. Pol:* Gaullist.
gaulois, -oise [golwa, -waz] **1.** *a.* Gallic, of Gaul; **esprit g.,** (broad) Gallic humour, *NAm:* humor; **contes g.,** spicy stories. **2.** *n.* (*a*) **les G.,** the Gauls; (*b*) **le g.,** (the) Gallic (tongue). **3.** *n.f. R.t.m:* popular brand of cigarette.
gauloiserie [golwazri] *n.f.* broad joke; spicy story.
gausser (se) [səgose] *v.pr. Lit:* **se g. de qn,** to laugh at, make fun of, s.o.; to sneer at s.o.
Gautier [gotje] *Pr.n.m.* Walter.
gavage [gavaʒ] *n.m.* (*a*) cramming (of poultry); (*b*) *Med:* forcible feeding; (*c*) *F:* gorging, stuffing.
gave¹ [gav] *n.f. F:* crop (of birds).
gave² *n.m. Geog:* (mountain) torrent (in the Pyrenees).
gaver [gave] **1.** *v.tr.* to cram (poultry); *Med:* to force-feed (s.o.); to fill (s.o.) up, stuff (s.o.) (with food). **2. se g.,** to gorge oneself.
gavotte [gavɔt] *n.f. Danc: Mus:* gavotte.
gaz [gɑz] *n.m.* gas; **gisement de g.,** gas field; **g. des marais,** marsh gas; **g. électronique,** electron gas; **bouteille à g., tube de g. comprimé,** gas cylinder; **g. d'éclairage,** lighting gas; coal gas; **g. de ville,** town gas; mains gas; **faire la cuisine au g.,** to cook by gas; **cuisinière à g.,** gas cooker; **réchaud à g.,** gas ring; **usine à g.,** gasworks; **g. hilarant, g. nitreux,** laughing gas; **g. asphyxiant, g. toxique,** asphyxiating gas; *F:* poison gas; **g. lacrymogène,** tear gas; **chambre à g.,** gas chamber; *F:* **mettre les g.,** to open the throttle; to put one's foot down, *NAm:* step on the gas; **à pleins g.,** with the throttle full open; flat out; **g. d'échappement,** exhaust fumes; *Med:* **avoir des g.,** to suffer from flatulence, to have wind; **lâcher un g.,** to break wind.
gaze [gɑz] *n.f.* (*a*) (i) gauze; (ii) butter muslin; **g. métallique,** wire gauze; *Med:* **g. oxygénée,** antiseptic gauze, sterilized gauze; (*b*) *Fig:* thin veil.
gazéification [gazeifikasjɔ̃] *n.f.* **1.** *Ch:* gasification. **2.** aeration (of mineral waters).
gazéifier [gazeifje] *v.tr.* (*pr.sub. & impf.* **n. gazéifiions, v. gazéifiiez**) **1.** *Ch:* to gasify, volatilize. **2.** to aerate (mineral waters).
gazelle [gazɛl] *n.f. Z:* gazelle.
gazer¹ [gɑze] *v.tr. Lit:* to veil, hide (opinion, etc.).
gazer² **1.** *v.tr. Mil:* to gas (troops). **2.** *v.i. F:* (*a*) to go at top speed; to step on the gas; (*b*) **ça gaze!** everything's O.K.! we're doing fine! **ça gaze?** all right? everything O.K.?
gazetier [gaztje] *n.m. A:* gazette writer; journalist.
gazette [gazɛt] *n.f.* gazette, news sheet.
gazeux, -euse [gɑzø, -øz] *a.* **1.** gaseous. **2.** aerated (water, etc.); fizzy (drink); **limonade gazeuse,** sparkling lemonade.
gazier, -ière [gɑzje, -jɛr] **1.** *a.* **l'industrie gazière,** the gas industry. **2.** *n.m.* (*a*) employee at gas works; (*b*) gas fitter, gasman.
gazoduc [gɑzɔdyk] *n.m.* gas pipeline.
gazogène [gɑzɔʒɛn] **1.** *a.* (*a*) gas-producing; (*b*) aerating. **2.** *n.m.* (*a*) gas producer, gas generator; **gaz de g.,** producer gas; (*b*) aerator (of mineral water, etc.).
gazoline [gɑzɔlin] *n.f.* gasolene, gasoline.
gazomètre [gɑzɔmɛtr̥] *n.m.* gasometer, gas holder.
gazon [gɑzɔ̃] *n.m.* **1.** (*a*) (fine, short) grass; turf; (*b*) lawn; *P.N:* **défense de marcher sur le g.,** keep off the grass. **2.** turf, sod. **3.** *Bot:* **g. mousse,** mossy saxifrage.
gazonnage [gɑzɔnaʒ] *n.m.,* **gazonnement** [gazɔnmɑ̃] *n.m.* **1.** turfing, sodding. **2.** edging with turf.
gazonné [gɑzɔne] *a.* grass-covered, turfed.
gazonner [gɑzɔne] **1.** *v.tr.* to cover with turf, to turf. **2.** *v.i.* (*of land*) to become covered with grass.
gazonneux, -euse [gɑzɔnø, -øz] *a.* turfy, covered with turf; grassy.
gazouillant [gazujɑ̃] *a.* warbling, chirping, twittering (bird); **ruisseau g.,** babbling, *Lit:* purling, brook.
gazouillement [gazujmɑ̃] *n.m.* twittering, warbling, chirping (of birds); babbling, murmuring (of running water); prattle, prattling (of children).
gazouiller [gazuje] *v.i.* (*of bird*) to twitter, warble, chirp; (*of water*) to babble, murmur, *Lit:* purl; (*of child*) to prattle.
gazouilleur, -euse [gazujœr, -øz] *a. & n.* warbling, twittering (bird); babbling (stream); prattling (child).
gazouillis [gazuji] *n.m.* twittering (of birds); murmuring (of running water).
geai [ʒɛ] *n.m. Orn:* jay.
géant, -ante [ʒeɑ̃, -ɑ̃t] **1.** *n.* (*a*) giant, *f.* giantess; *Gym:* **pas de g.,** giant's stride; **avancer à pas de g.,** to make great strides forward; to make spectacular progress; *Geog:* **la Chaussée des Géants,** the Giant's Causeway; (*b*) **les géants de l'art,** the great masters; **les géants du football,** the football stars. **2.** *a.* gigantic; **arbre g.,** giant tree; *Com:* **carton g.,** giant (-size) packet; *T.V:* **écran g.,** large screen.
gecko [ʒeko] *n.m. Rept:* gecko.
Gédéon [ʒedeɔ̃] *Pr.n.m. B.Hist:* Gideon.
géhenne [ʒeɛn] *n.f.* Gehenna, Hell; **sa vie est une g.,** his life is a hell on earth.
geignant [ʒɛɲɑ̃] *a.* whimpering, whining, fretful.
geignard,-arde [ʒɛɲar, -ard] *F:* **1.** *a.* fretful, (given to) whining; grumbling, peevish. **2.** *n.* whiner, grizzler.
geignement [ʒɛɲmɑ̃] *n.m.* **1.** whining, whimpering, grumbling. **2.** whine, whimper; (feeble) groan.
geigneur, -euse [ʒɛɲœr, -øz] *n.* (habitual, everlasting) whiner, (eternal) grizzler.
geindre¹ [ʒɛ̃dr̥] *v.i.* (*pr.p.* **geignant;** *p.p.* **geint;** *pr.ind.* **je geins, il geint, n. geignons, ils geignent;** *impf.* **je geignais;** *p.h.* **je geignis;** *fu.* **je geindrai**) to whine, whimper; to complain; to grizzle.
geindre² *n.m.* baker's assistant.
gel [ʒɛl] *n.m.* **1.** frost, freezing. **2.** *Ch:* gel; colloid.
gélatine [ʒelatin] *n.f.* gelatin(e); **g. détonante, g. explosive,** blasting gelatine, gum dynamite.
gélatiné [ʒelatine] *a.* gelatinized.

gélatineux, -euse [ʒelatinø, -øz] *a.* gelatinous.
gélatinisant [ʒelatinizɑ̃] *n.m.* **1.** *Exp:* gelatinizing agent. **2.** *Tchn:* plasticizer.
gélatiniser [ʒelatinize] *v.tr.* **1.** to gelatinize (dynamite). **2.** to coat (glass plate, etc.) with gelatine.
gelé [ʒ(ə)le] *a.* **1.** frozen; *F:* **je suis absolument g.,** I'm absolutely frozen. **2.** (*a*) frost-bitten (nose, toe); (*b*) frost-nipped (plant, fruit); (*c*) cold, indifferent (audience, etc.). **3.** *Fin:* frozen (debts, etc.). **4.** *P:* (*a*) drunk; canned; (*b*) bowled over; struck all of a heap.
gelée [ʒ(ə)le] *n.f.* **1.** frost; **forte g.,** hard frost; **g. blanche,** hoar frost, hoar; white frost; rime; **temps à la g.,** frosty weather. **2.** (*a*) *Cu:* jelly; **g. de veau, de poulet,** veal, chicken, jelly; **g. de cassis,** blackcurrant jelly; (*b*) *Ap:* **g. royale,** royal jelly.
geler [ʒ(ə)le] *v.* **(je gèle, n. gelons; je gèlerai) 1.** *v.tr.* (*a*) to convert into ice; to freeze; **froid qui gèle les conduites d'eau,** cold that freezes the water pipes; (*b*) *Fin:* to freeze (credits, capital). **2.** *v.i.* (*a*) to become frozen; to freeze; **l'étang a gelé d'un bout à l'autre,** the pond has, is, frozen over; **plantes qui gèlent facilement,** plants easily damaged by frost; **on gèle dans cette salle,** this room is like an icehouse, is icy cold; (*b*) *impers.* **il gèle dur, à pierre fendre,** it's freezing hard; **il a gelé blanc cette nuit,** there was a white frost last night; **il a gelé à dix degrés,** there were ten degrees of frost.
gélifier (se) [səʒelifje] *v.pr. Ch:* to gel.
gélignite [ʒeliɲit] *n.f. Exp:* gelignite.
gelinotte [ʒ(ə)linɔt] *n.f. Orn:* **g. (des bois),** hazel grouse; **g. des prairies,** prairie chicken.
gélivation [ʒelivasjɔ̃] *n.f. Geog:* congelifraction, frost weathering (of rocks).
gélivure [ʒelivyr] *n.f.* frost crack, cleft (in stone, earth); heart shake (in wood).
gélose [ʒeloz] *n.f. Ch:* agar-agar.
gélule [ʒelyl] *n.f. Pharm:* capsule.
gelure [ʒ(ə)lyr] *n.f.* frostbite.
Gémeaux (les) [leʒemo] *n.m.pl. Astr:* Gemini.
gémellaire [ʒemelɛr] *a.* twin (pregnancy, etc.).
gémination [ʒeminasjɔ̃] *n.f.* **1.** *Biol: etc:* gemination. **2.** *Sch:* **g. de classes,** grouping, combination, of forms.
géminé [ʒemine] *a.* **1.** *Biol:* geminate, twin (leaves, etc.); *Ch:* geminate; *Arch:* **colonnes géminées,** twin columns. **2.** *Ling:* **consonnes, voyelles, géminées,** doubled consonants, vowels; geminates.
gémir [ʒemir] *v.i.* to groan, moan, wail; **g. de douleur,** to groan with pain; **je gémissais de les voir (faire cela),** I could have wept to see them (doing that); **g. sous le joug de la tyrannie,** to groan under the yoke of tyranny.
gémissant [ʒemisɑ̃] *a.* moaning, wailing; **essieu g.,** creaking axle.
gémissement [ʒemismɑ̃] *n.m.* groan(ing), moan(ing); wail(ing).
gemmage [ʒɛmaʒ] *n.m.* tapping (of trees for resin).
gemme [ʒɛm] *n.f.* **1.** *Miner:* (*a*) gem; precious stone; (*b*) *a.* **pierre g.,** gem stone; **sel g.,** rock salt. **2.** *Arb:* pine resin. **3.** *Bot: A:* (leaf) bud.
gemmé [ʒeme] *a. Lit:* gemmed, jewelled.
gemmer [ʒeme] **1.** *v.i.* (*of trees*) to bud. **2.** *v.tr.* to tap (trees for resin).
gemmeur [ʒɛmœr] *n.m. Arb:* tapper.
gémonies [ʒemɔni] *n.f.pl. Lit:* **traîner, vouer, qn aux g.,** to hold s.o. up to public obloquy.
gênant [ʒɛnɑ̃] *a.* **1.** in the way; cumbersome; **les jupes longues sont gênantes,** long skirts are awkward, are a nuisance, get in one's way. **2.** embarrassing, awkward (situation, silence); (*of pers.*) annoying.
gencive [ʒɑ̃siv] *n.f.* (*a*) *Anat:* gum; **abcès à la g.,** gumboil; (*b*) *pl. P:* jaw(s); **un coup dans les gencives,** a punch on the jaw.
gendarme [ʒɑ̃darm] *n.m.* **1.** (*a*) gendarme, member of the state police force, *approx.* = police constable; **gendarmes à cheval** = mounted police; **gendarmes motocyclistes,** motorcycle police; (*of children*) **jouer aux gendarmes et aux voleurs,** to play at cops and robbers; (*b*) *F:* (*of women*) martinet; **faire le g.,** to boss people about; (*c*) **chapeau de g.** = paper hat. **2.** flaw (in jewel). **3.** *Geol:* rock pinnacle, gendarme. **4.** *Cu: F:* (*a*) red herring; (*b*) flat, dry sausage.
gendarmer (se) [səʒɑ̃darme] *v.pr.* to be up in arms (against s.o., a proposal, etc.); **il n'y a pas de quoi se g.,** there's nothing to get worked up about.
gendarmerie [ʒɑ̃darməri] *n.f.* **1.** (*a*) (*in Fr.*) state police force; (*b*) **la G. royale du Canada,** the Royal Canadian Mounted Police. **2.** barracks, headquarters (of the *gendarmes*).
gendre [ʒɑ̃dr] *n.m.* son-in-law.
gène [ʒɛn] *n.m. Biol:* gene.
gêne [ʒɛn] *n.f.* **1.** *A:* (physical or moral) torture. **2.** discomfort, constraint, embarrassment; **ressentir de la g. en la présence de qn,** to feel ill at ease in s.o.'s presence; **vous ne me causerez aucune g.,** you won't inconvenience me in the least; **sans g.,** unconventional, free and easy; **il est sans g.!** he's a cool customer! **3. être dans la g.,** to be in financial difficulties; to be badly off.
gêné [ʒene] *a.* **1.** embarrassed, ill at ease; **il n'est jamais g.,** he's never embarrassed; he's got no inhibitions; **silence g.,** awkward, uneasy, silence. **2.** in financial difficulties; badly off.
généalogie [ʒenealɔʒi] *n.f.* **1.** genealogy, pedigree, descent; pedigree (of horse, etc.). **2.** (science of) genealogy.
généalogique [ʒenealɔʒik] *a.* genealogical; **arbre g.,** family tree, genealogical tree; pedigree; **livre g.,** stud book (of horses); herd book (of cattle).
généalogiquement [ʒenealɔʒikmɑ̃] *adv.* genealogically.
généalogiste [ʒenealɔʒist] *n.* genealogist.
gêner [ʒene]. **I.** *v.tr.* **1.** to constrict, cramp; (*of garment*) to pull, drag, pinch; **mes souliers me gênent,** my shoes pinch, are too tight; **on est gêné ici,** it's cramped, too crowded, here. **2.** to hinder, obstruct; to be in (s.o.'s) way; to interfere with (an activity); to impede; **g. la circulation,** to hold up the traffic; **g. la vue,** to obstruct, block, the view; **cette valise vous gêne-t-elle?** is this bag in your way? **3.** to inconvenience, embarrass; **cela vous gênerait-il que je revienne demain?** I hope it won't disturb you, bother you, put you out, if I come back tomorrow; **le froid ne me gêne pas,** I don't mind the cold; **la fumée (de tabac) vous gêne-t-elle?** do you mind my smoking? **cela me gênerait de le rencontrer,** it would be awkward for me to meet him. **II. se g. 1.** to put oneself under some restraint; to put oneself out; **je ne me suis pas gêné pour le lui dire,** I didn't hesitate to tell him so; I made no bones about telling him so; **il ne se gêne pas avec nous,** he doesn't stand on ceremony with us, he makes himself at home; *Iron:* **il ne se gêne pas!** he's not backward in coming forward! *Iron:* **ne vous gênez pas!** that's right! make yourself at home! **2.** (*a*) to put oneself out; **en vous gênant un peu vous pourrez tous vous asseoir,** by squeezing up a little you will all be able to sit down; (*b*) **nous avons dû nous g. un peu,** we had to economize, tighten our belt, a bit.
général, -ale, -aux [ʒeneral, -o] **1.** *a.* general (rule, appearance, etc.); **le consentement g.,** common consent; **en règle générale,** as a general rule, in general; **d'une façon générale,** generally speaking, broadly speaking; **inspecteur g.,** inspector general; *Th:* **répétition générale,** dress rehearsal; **quartier g.,** headquarters; (*Fr.Hist: & Channel Islands*) **états géné-**

raux, states general; **officier g.,** (i) *Mil: etc:* general officer; (ii) *Navy:* flag officer; **en g.,** in general, generally (speaking); taken all round; as a rule. **2.** *n.m.* (*a*) the general; **procéder du g. au particulier,** to go from the general to the particular; (*b*) (i) *Mil:* general; **g. de brigade,** brigadier, *NAm:* brigadier general; **g. de division,** major general; **g. de corps d'armée,** lieutenant general; **g. d'armée,** (army) general; (ii) *Mil.Av:* **g. de brigade aérienne,** air commodore, *U.S:* brigadier general; **g. de division aérienne,** air vice-marshal, *U.S:* major general; **g. de corps d'armée aérienne,** air marshal, *U.S:* lieutenant general; **g. d'armée aérienne,** air chief marshal, *U.S:* major general. **3.** *n.f.* (*a*) **madame la générale,** the general's wife; (*b*) alarm call; **battre la générale,** to call to arms; to sound the alarm; *Navy:* to beat to quarters; (*c*) *Th:* dress rehearsal.

généralement [ʒeneralmɑ̃] *adv.* generally; **g. parlant,** generally speaking, on the whole, broadly speaking.

généralisant [ʒeneralizɑ̃] *a.* generalizing.

généralisateur, -trice [ʒeneralizatœr, -tris] **1.** *a.* generalizing (mind, method). **2.** *n.* generalizer.

généralisation [ʒeneralizasjɔ̃] *n.f.* **1.** generalizing. **2.** generalization.

généraliser [ʒeneralize] **1.** *v.tr.* to generalize. **2.** **se g.,** to become general; (*of custom, etc.*) to spread.

généralissime [ʒeneralisim] *n.m.* generalissimo, commander-in-chief.

généraliste [ʒeneralist] *n. Med:* general practitioner.

généralité [ʒeneralite] *n.f.* **1.** **dans la g. des cas,** in the majority of cases, in most cases. **2.** **s'en tenir à des généralités,** to confine oneself to generalities, to general remarks.

générateur, -trice [ʒeneratœr, -tris] **1.** *a.* generating (machine, etc.); generative (force, organ); productive (**de,** of); *El:* **station, usine, génératrice,** generating station, plant; *Mch:* **chaudière génératrice,** *n.m.* **g.,** steam boiler. **2.** *n.m.* generator; *Mch:* **g. (de vapeur),** (steam) boiler, steam generator; *El:* **g. d'électricité,** electric generator; *Elcs:* **g. d'impulsions,** pulse generator; **g. de signaux,** *Elcs:* signal(ling) generator; *T.V:* colour coder. **3.** *n.f.* generator, generating set; *Atom.Ph:* **génératrice nucléaire,** nuclear power reactor.

génératif, -ive [ʒeneratif, -iv] *a.* generative.

génération [ʒenerasjɔ̃] *n.f.* **1.** (act of) generation, generating; production (of steam, etc.); formation (of metals); **la g. d'une idée,** the originating of an idea; *Nat.Hist:* **g. spontanée,** spontaneous generation. **2.** (*a*) **la g. de Noé,** the descendants of Noah; (*b*) **la g. actuelle,** the present generation; **la jeune g.,** the younger generation.

générer [ʒenere] *v.tr.* (**je génère, n. générons; je générerai**) **1.** to generate, engender. **2.** to generate, produce (electricity, steam, etc.).

généreusement [ʒenerøzmɑ̃] *adv.* generously; nobly (treated); liberally (rewarded); munificently.

généreux, -euse [ʒenerø, -øz] **1.** *a.* (*a*) noble, generous (soul); **cœur g.,** warm heart; **vin g.,** generous wine, wine with a fine bouquet; (*b*) generous, openhanded; **terre généreuse,** fertile soil; (*c*) **elle a des formes généreuses,** she is built on generous lines. **2.** *n.* generous person.

générique [ʒenerik] **1.** *a.* generic (term, etc.). **2.** *n.m. Cin:* credit titles, credits.

génériquement [ʒenerikmɑ̃] *adv.* generically.

générosité [ʒenerozite] *n.f.* **1.** (*a*) generosity; openhandedness; **avec g.,** generously; (*b*) body (of a wine). **2.** *pl.* acts of generosity.

Gênes [ʒɛn] *Pr.n.f. Geog:* Genoa.

genèse [ʒənɛz] *n.f.* genesis, origin, birth; *B:* **la G.,** (the Book of) Genesis.

génésique [ʒenezik] *a. Physiol:* genetic.

genet [ʒ(ə)nɛ] *n.m. A:* jennet (horse).

genêt [ʒ(ə)nɛ] *n.m. Bot:* broom.

généticien, -ienne [ʒenetisjɛ̃, -jɛn] *n.* geneticist.

génétique [ʒenetik] (*a*) *a.* genetic; (*b*) *n.f.* genetics.

génétiquement [ʒenetikmɑ̃] *adv.* genetically.

genette [ʒ(ə)nɛt] *n.f. Z:* genet (civet).

gêneur, -euse [ʒɛnœr, -øz] *n.* intruder; nuisance; spoilsport.

Genève [ʒ(ə)nɛv] *Pr.n.f. Geog:* Geneva.

Geneviève [ʒənvjɛv] *Pr.n.f.* Genevieve, Winifred.

genevois, -oise [ʒənvwa, -waz] *a. & n.* Genevese, Genevan.

genévrier [ʒənevrije] *n.m. Bot:* juniper (tree).

génial, -aux [ʒenjal, -o] *a.* inspired, full of genius; brilliant (idea); **œuvre géniale,** work of genius.

génialement [ʒenjalmɑ̃] *adv.* brilliantly; in a brilliant manner; with genius.

génialité [ʒenjalite] *n.f.* (quality of) genius; brilliancy (of invention, etc.).

génie [ʒeni] *n.m.* **1.** (*a*) (guardian) spirit; (presiding) genius; **son mauvais g.,** his evil genius; (*b*) genie; **les génies des contes arabes,** the genii, the jinn, of the Arabian Nights. **2.** (*a*) (*quality*) genius; **homme de g.,** man of genius; **g. très marqué pour les mathématiques,** genius for mathematics; (*b*) (*pers.*) genius; (*c*) **g. d'une langue,** essence, spirit, of a language. **3.** *Tchn:* (*a*) **g. civil,** (i) civil engineering (industry); (ii) civil engineers (as a body); **g. atomique,** atomic, nuclear, (i) engineering, (ii) engineers; **g. maritime,** (i) marine, naval, architecture; naval construction; (ii) marine, naval, architects; (*b*) *Mil:* **le (Corps du) G.** = the Royal Engineers, the Engineers; *U.S:* the Corps of Engineers, the Engineer Corps; **g. aéroporté,** airborne engineers; **g. de l'air,** aviation, air, engineers; **officier du g.,** engineer officer; **soldat du g.,** engineer.

genièvre [ʒənjɛvr̥] *n.m.* **1.** *Bot:* (*a*) juniper berry; *Pharm:* **essence de g.,** juniper oil. (*b*) juniper (tree). **2.** gin.

génisse [ʒenis] *n.f.* heifer.

génital, -aux [ʒenital, -o] *a.* genital; **les organes génitaux,** the genitals.

géniteur, -trice [ʒenitœr, -tris] **1.** *n.m. Z:* sire; dam. **2.** *n. Hum:* father, mother; **nos géniteurs,** our parents.

génitif [ʒenitif] *n.m. Gram:* genitive (case); **au g.,** in the genitive.

génito-urinaire [ʒenitɔyrinɛr] *a. Anat:* genito-urinary.

génocide [ʒenɔsid] *n.m.* genocide.

génois, -oise [ʒenwa, -waz] **1.** *a. & n. Geog:* Genoese. **2.** *n.f.* Genoese cake, pastry.

genou, -oux [ʒ(ə)nu] *n.m.* **1.** knee; **enfoncé jusqu'aux genoux dans la boue,** knee-deep in mud; **avoir les genoux en dedans,** to be knock-kneed; **se mettre à genoux,** to kneel (down); **à genoux,** kneeling, on one's knees; **se jeter aux genoux de qn,** to go down on one's knees to s.o.; **tenir un enfant sur ses genoux,** to hold a child on one's knees, in one's lap; **sur les genoux des dieux,** in the lap of the gods; *F:* **ronds de genoux,** knee patches (in trousers). **2.** *Mec.E:* **(joint à) g.,** (i) elbow (joint); (ii) ball-and-socket joint; (iii) toggle joint.

genouillère [ʒ(ə)nujɛr] *n.f.* **1.** kneepad, knee guard, kneecap; knee bandage. **2.** *Mec.E:* **articulation à g.,** knuckle joint, ball-and-socket joint; toggle joint.

genre [ʒɑ̃r̥] *n.m.* **1.** genus, family, race, kind; **le g. humain,** the human race, humanity, mankind. **2.** kind, sort, type; manner, way; **quel g. de vie mène-t-il?** what kind of a life does he lead? **toutes les tentatives de ce g. ont échoué,** all such attempts have failed; **c'est plus dans son g.,** that's more in his line;

c'est un artiste dans son g., he is an artist in his way; **très bon dans son g.,** very good of its kind; **vin blanc g. sauternes,** white wine of the Sauterne type; **étui g. maroquin,** case in imitation morocco; **c'est dans le g. de . . .,** (it's) like . . .; **un peu dans le g. de . . .,** rather like . . .; **ce n'est pas mon g.,** (i) he, she, is not the kind of person I like, is not my sort; it's not the sort of thing I like; (ii) it's just not me; **ce n'est pas son g.,** that's not like him, her. **3.** (artistic, literary) style, manner; **le g. comique,** comedy; **le g. tragique,** tragedy; **peinture de g.,** genre painting; *Art:* **tableau de g.,** subject picture. **4.** manners, fashion, taste; **c'est bon, mauvais, g.,** it is good, bad, form, in good, bad, taste; **elle a du g.,** she's got a style about her. **5.** *Gram:* gender.

gens [ʒɑ̃] *n.m.pl.* (*was originally feminine and most attrib. adjectives preceding* **gens** *still take the feminine form, the word group being nevertheless felt as masculine*—**ces bonnes gens sont venus me trouver; heureux les petites gens éloignés des grandeurs! quels sont ces gens? quels** *or* **quelles sont ces bonnes gens? tout** *varies according as the attrib. adjective has a distinct feminine ending or not:* **toutes ces bonnes gens,** *but* **tous ces pauvres gens; jeunes gens,** *and the compounds of group* 2(*b*) *below, never have a feminine adjective;* **de bons petits jeunes gens; les malheureux gens de lettres.**) **1.** people, folk(s), men and women; **il y avait peu de g. dans la salle,** there were not many people in the hall; *Th:* there was a poor house; **beaucoup de g., bien des g., l'ont vu,** many people have seen it; **qui sont ces gens-là?** who are these people? **il y a des g. qui . . .,** there are people who . . ., some people . . .. **2.** (*a*) **jeunes g.,** (i) young people; adolescents; (ii) young men; (*b*) **g. du monde,** society people; **g. de lettres,** men of letters; **g. de théâtre,** the acting profession; **les g. du pays,** the locals; (*c*) **petites gens,** (i) humble people; (ii) petty(-minded) people; (*d*) *O:* servants, domestics; retinue; attendants, retainers, people. **3.** nations, peoples; **le droit des g.,** the law of nations.

gent [ʒɑ̃] *n.f. A: & Hum:* tribe, race; **la g. moutonnière,** the woolly race, sheep.

gentiane [ʒɑ̃sjan] *n.f.* **1.** *Bot:* gentian. **2.** gentian bitters.

gentil[1], -ille [ʒɑ̃ti, -ij] *a.* (*a*) pretty, pleasing, nice; **un g. enfant** (*no liaison* [ʒɑ̃tiɑ̃fɑ̃]), a pretty child; **elle a été très gentille pour, avec, moi,** she was very kind to me; **il est g. de votre part de m'écrire,** it is very kind, good, of you to write to me; (*b*) **sois gentil(le),** (i) be a good boy, a good girl; (ii) (*to older people*) be an angel, be a dear; (*c*) **une gentille somme,** a considerable sum of money.

gentil[2] *n.m. Hist:* gentile.

gentilhomme [ʒɑ̃tijɔm] *n.m.* man of gentle birth, gentleman; *Hist:* **g. de la Chambre du Roi,** gentleman of the Privy Chamber; *pl. gentilshommes* [ʒɑ̃tizɔm].

gentilhommière [ʒɑ̃tijɔmjɛr] *n.f.* (*a*) country seat, manor house; (*b*) *Belg:* boarding house for men.

gentilité [ʒɑ̃tilite] *n.f. coll.* the gentiles.

gentillesse [ʒɑ̃tijɛs] *n.f.* (*a*) prettiness; graciousness, engaging manner; pleasant disposition; (*b*) kindness; **auriez-vous la g. de . . .,** would you be so kind as to . . .; (*c*) *pl.* **dire des gentillesses à qn,** to say nice, kind, things to s.o.

gentillet, -ette [ʒɑ̃tijɛ, -ɛt] *a.* (*a*) (rather) nice; (quite) pretty, pleasing; engaging; (*b*) **romans gentillets,** pleasant light reading.

gentiment [ʒɑ̃timɑ̃] *adv.* pleasantly; **elle me fait g. compagnie,** she's kind enough to keep me company; *Iron:* **vous voilà g. arrangé!** that's a nice mess you're in!

gentleman [dʒɛntləman] *n.m.* (*a*) gentleman; (*b*) amateur jockey; *pl. gentlemen.*

gentleman-farmer [dʒɛntləmanfarmœr] *n.m.* gentleman farmer; *pl. gentlemen-farmers.*

génuflexion [ʒenyflɛksjɔ̃] *n.f. Ecc:* genuflexion; **faire une g.,** to genuflect.

geó [ʒeo] *n.f. Sch: F:* geography.

géocentrique (ʒeɔsɑ̃trik] *a. Astr:* geocentric.

géodésie [ʒeɔdezi] *n.f.* geodesy, surveying.

géodésique [ʒeɔdezik] geodesic, geodetic; *Surv:* **point g.,** triangulation point.

géodynamique [ʒeɔdinamik] **1.** *a.* geodynamic. **2.** *n.f.* geodynamics.

géographe [ʒeɔgraf] *n.* geographer; **ingénieur g.,** surveyor.

géographie [ʒeɔgrafi] *n.f.* geography; **g. économique,** economic geography; **g. humaine,** human geography.

géographique [ʒeɔgrafik] *a.* geographic(al); **carte g.,** map; **dictionnaire g.,** gazetteer.

géographiquement [ʒeɔgrafikmɑ̃] *adv.* geographically.

geôle [ʒol] *n.f. A: & Lit:* gaol, jail, prison.

geôlier, -ière [ʒolje, -jɛr] *n. A: & Lit:* gaoler, jailer.

géologie [ʒeɔlɔʒi] *n.f.* geology.

géologique [ʒeɔlɔʒik] *a.* geological.

géologiquement [ʒeɔlɔʒikmɑ̃] *adv.* geologically.

géologue [ʒeɔlɔg] *n.* geologist.

géomagnétique [ʒeɔmaɲetik] *a.* geomagnetic.

géomagnétisme [ʒeɔmaɲetism) *n.m.* geomagnetism.

géométral, -aux [ʒeɔmetral, -o] **1.** *a.* flat (projection, elevation) (as opposed to perspective view). **2.** *n.m.* flat projection.

géomètre [ʒeɔmɛtr̥] **1.** *n.m.* geometer, geometrician; **(arpenteur) g.,** (land) surveyor. **2.** *n.f. Ent:* geometer (moth).

géométrie [ʒeɔmetri] *n.f.* geometry; **g. plane,** plane geometry; **g. analytique,** analytical, co-ordinate, geometry; **g. dans l'espace, à trois dimensions,** solid, three-dimensional, geometry; *Aut:* **g. de la direction,** steering geometry; *Atom.Ph:* **g. du réseau (du réacteur),** lattice design, lattice pitch (of reactor); *Av:* **avion à g. fixe, variable,** fixed-geometry, variable-geometry, aircraft.

géométrique [ʒeɔmetrik] *a.* geometric(al); **progression g.,** geometrical progression.

géométriquement [ʒeɔmetrikmɑ̃] *adv.* geometrically.

géomorphologie [ʒeɔmɔrfɔlɔʒi] *n.f.* geomorphology.

geophone [ʒeɔfɔn] *n.m.* geophone, sound detector.

géophysique [ʒeɔfizik] **1.** *a.* geophysical. **2.** *n.f.* geophysics.

géopolitique [ʒeɔpɔlitik] *n.f.* geopolitics.

Georges [ʒɔrʒ] **1.** *Pr.n.m.* George. **2.** *n.m. Av: F:* George = automatic pilot.

Georgette [ʒɔrʒɛt] *Pr.n.f.* Georgina; *Tex:* **crêpe g.,** georgette.

Géorgie [ʒeɔrʒi] *Pr.n.f. Geog:* Georgia (i) in U.S.S.R.; (ii) in U.S.A.; **G. du Sud,** South Georgia (Tierra del Fuego).

géorgien, -ienne [ʒeɔrʒjɛ̃, -jɛn] *a. & n. Geog:* Georgian.

Géorgiques (les) [leʒeɔrʒik] *n.f.pl. Lt.Lit:* the Georgics (of Virgil).

géosynclinal, -aux [ʒeɔsɛ̃klinal, -o] *Geol: n.m.* geosyncline.

géothermie [ʒeɔtɛrmi] *n.f.* geothermics.

géothermique [ʒeɔtɛrmik] *a.* geothermal.

gérance [ʒerɑ̃s] *n.f.* **1.** (*a*) management, direction (of business, etc.); (*b*) managership, administratorship. **2.** board of governors, of directors.

géranium [ʒeranjɔm] *n.m.* **1.** *Bot:* geranium, crane's bill. **2.** *Hort:* pelargonium, *F:* geranium.

gérant, -ante [ʒerɑ̃, -ɑ̃t] *n.* manager, *f.* manageress; director; managing director (of company); *a. Journ:* **rédacteur g.,** managing editor.

Gérard [ʒerar] *Pr.n.m.* Gerald, Gerard.

gerbage [ʒɛrbaʒ] *n.m.* **1.** binding (of sheaves); sheaving. **2.** stacking, piling (of casks, bales).

gerbe [ʒɛrb] *n.f.* **1.** sheaf (of corn); **mettre le blé en gerbes,** to sheave, sheaf, the wheat; **g. d'étincelles,** shower of sparks; **g. d'eau,** spray, shower, of water; splash; **g. de fleurs,** sheaf, spray, of flowers (at funeral). **2.** *Mil:* cone of fire.

gerber [ʒɛrbe] *v.tr.* **1.** to bind, sheave, sheaf (corn, etc.). **2.** to stack, pile (barrels, crates, shells). **3.** *P:* to vomit, throw up.

gerbeuse [ʒɛbøz] *n.f.* stacker, stacking machine (for barrels).

gerbier [ʒɛrbje] *n.m.* stack (of corn).

gerbille [ʒɛrbij] *n.f. Z:* gerbil.

gerboise [ʒɛrbwaz] *n.f. Z:* jerboa.

gerce [ʒɛrs] *n.f.* **1.** crack, fissure (in wood). **2.** *Ent:* clothes moth.

gercé [ʒɛrse] *a.* cracked, cleft; shaky (wood); chapped (hands).

gercement [ʒɛrs(ə)mɑ̃] *n.m.* cracking (of wood); chapping (of hands).

gercer [ʒɛrse] *v.tr. & i.* **(il gerçait; il gerça)** to crack (wood, soil); to chap (the hands, etc.).

gerçure [ʒɛrsyr] *n.f.* crack, cleft, fissure, flaw; chap (in skin); *Tchn:* shake, flaw (in wood); hair crack, hair line (in metal); **avoir des gerçures aux mains,** to have chapped hands.

gérer [ʒere] *v.* **(je gère, n. gérons; je gérerai) 1.** *v.tr.* to manage, run (newspaper, hotel, etc.); to administer (estate, etc.); **mal g. ses finances,** to mismanage one's finances. **2.** *Jur:* **se g. créancier,** to come forward as creditor.

gerfaut [ʒɛrfo] *n.m. Orn:* gyrfalcon, gerfalcon.

gériatrie [ʒerjatri] *n.f. Med:* geriatrics.

germain¹, -aine [ʒɛrmɛ̃, -ɛn] *Hist:* **1.** *a.* Germanic, Teutonic. **2.** *n.* German, Teuton.

germain² *a. Jur:* **frère g.,** full brother; **sœur germaine,** full sister; **cousin g.,** first cousin.

germandrée [ʒɛrmɑ̃dre] *n.f. Bot:* germander.

germanique [ʒɛrmanik] **1.** *a.* Germanic, Teutonic; *Hist:* **l'Empire g.,** the German(ic) Empire. **2.** *n.m. Ling:* Germanic.

germanisant, -ante [ʒɛrmanizɑ̃, -ɑ̃t] *n.* student of Germanic, of German.

germanisation [ʒɛrmanizasjɔ̃] *n.f.* Germanization.

germaniser [ʒɛrmanize] *v.tr.* to Germanize.

germanisme [ʒɛrmanism] *n.m. Ling:* Germanism; German phrase, idiom.

germaniste [ʒɛrmanist] *n. Ling:* Germanist, student of German.

germanium [ʒɛrmanjɔm] *n.m. Ch:* germanium.

germanophile [ʒɛrmanɔfil] *a. & n.* Germanophile.

germanophobe [ʒɛrmanɔfɔb] **1.** *a.* Germanophobic. **2.** *n.* Germanophobe.

germanophobie [ʒɛrmanɔfɔbi] *n.f.* Germanophobia.

germe [ʒɛrm] *n.m. Biol:* germ; eye (of potato); (*of potatoes*) **pousser des germes,** to sprout; **g. d'un œuf,** t(h)read of an egg; **les germes de la corruption,** the seeds of corruption; **étouffer une rébellion dans le g.,** to nip a rebellion in the bud.

germer [ʒɛrme] *v.i.* to germinate; to shoot, spring (up); (*of potatoes*) to sprout.

germicide [ʒɛrmisid] **1.** *n.m.* germicide. **2.** *a.* germicidal.

germinal, -aux [ʒɛrminal, -o] **1.** *a. Biol:* germinal. **2.** *n.m. Hist:* seventh month of Fr. Republican calendar (March-April).

germinateur, -trice [ʒɛrminatœr, -tris] *a.* germinative.

germinatif, -ive [ʒɛrminatif, -iv] *a. Biol:* germinative, germinal; **plasma g.,** germ plasm.

germination [ʒɛrminasjɔ̃] *n.f. Biol:* germination.

germoir [ʒɛrmwar] *n.m.* (*a*) *Hort:* hot bed, seed bed; (*b*) seed tray.

gérondif [ʒerɔ̃dif] *n.m. Gram:* **1.** gerund. **2.** gerundive; **au g.,** in the gerund(ive).

gérontocratie [ʒerɔ̃tɔkrasi] *n.f. Pol:* gerontocracy.

gérontologie [ʒerɔ̃tɔlɔʒi] *n.f. Med:* gerontology.

gérontologue [ʒerɔ̃tɔlɔg] *n. Med:* gerontologist.

gésier [ʒezje] *n.m.* (*a*) *Orn:* gizzard; (*b*) *P:* stomach, guts.

gésir [ʒezir] *v.i. def.* (*used only in the following forms: pr.p.* **gisant;** *pr.ind.* **il gît, n. gisons, vous gisez, ils gisent;** *impf.* **je gisais,** *etc.*) *Lit:* (*of pers.*) to lie (helpless or dead); (*of thg*) to lie; **il gisait dans son sang,** he was lying, weltering, in his blood; (*on gravestone*) **ci-gît, ci-gisent . . .,** here lies, here lie . . .; **c'est là que gît le lièvre,** that's the point, there's the rub.

gesse [ʒɛs] *n.f. Bot:* vetch, everlasting pea; **g. odorante,** sweet pea.

gestapo [gɛstapo] *n.f. Hist:* Gestapo.

gestation [ʒɛstasjɔ̃] *n.f. Physiol:* (period of) gestation; pregnancy; **projet en g.,** plan in embryo.

geste¹ [ʒɛst] *n.m.* **1.** gesture, motion, movement; **d'un g. large il nous a fait entrer,** he waved us in, showed us in, with a flourish; **d'un g. de la main,** with a wave of the hand; **écarter qn d'un g.,** to wave s.o. aside; **faire un g.,** to make a gesture; **g. de résignation,** shrug of resignation; **joindre le g. à la parole,** to suit the action to the word. **2. beau g.,** handsome gesture, gesture of sympathy.

geste² *n.f.* **1.** *Lit:* **(chanson de) g.,** chanson de geste, mediaeval verse chronicle (of heroic exploits). **2. rendre compte de ses faits et gestes,** to give an account of oneself, one's exploits, one's movements.

gesticulation [ʒɛstikylasjɔ̃] *n.f.* gesticulating, gesticulation.

gesticuler [ʒɛstikyle] *v.i.* to gesticulate.

gestion [ʒɛstjɔ̃] *n.f.* management (of business, works, etc.); conduct (of affairs); administration, control; **g. administrative,** administration; **mauvaise g.,** maladministration, bad management, mismanagement; *Ind:* **g. de la production, de stock,** production, stock, control; *Cmptr:* **g. de fichiers,** file maintenance.

gestionnaire [ʒɛstjɔnɛr] **1.** *a.* administrative; **compte g.,** management account. **2.** *n.* administrator.

Gethsémani [ʒɛtsemani] *Pr.n. B.Hist:* Gethsemane.

geyser [ʒɛzɛr] *n.m. Geog:* geyser.

Ghana [gana] *Pr.n.m. Geog:* Ghana.

ghanéen, -éenne [ganeɛ̃, -eɛn] *a. & n. Geog:* Ghanaian.

ghetto [gɛto] *n.m.* ghetto.

gibbeux, -euse [ʒibø, -øz] *a.* gibbous.

gibbon [ʒibɔ̃] *n.m. Z:* gibbon (ape).

gibbosité [ʒibozite] *n.f.* gibbosity; hump.

gibecière [ʒibsjɛr] *n.f.* game bag, pouch.

giberne [ʒibɛrn] *n.f. A:* cartridge pouch; *Prov:* **chaque soldat a son bâton de maréchal dans sa g.,** every soldier carries a marshal's baton in his knapsack.

gibet [ʒibɛ] *n.m.* gibbet, gallows.

gibier [ʒibje] *n.m.* game (= wild animals); **gros g., menu g.,** big, small, game; **g. à poil,** ground game; game animals; **g. à plumes,** game birds; **g. d'eau,** wildfowl; **g. de potence,** gallows bird, jailbird.

giboulée [ʒibule] *n.f.* sudden shower (*usu.* with snow or hail); **giboulées de mars** = April showers.

giboyeux, -euse [ʒibwajø, -øz] *a.* abounding in, well stocked with, game.
gibus [ʒibys] *n.m.* crush hat, opera hat.
giclée [ʒikle] *n.f.* spurt, squirt (of water, blood).
giclement [ʒikləmɑ̃] *n.m.* splashing up, squelching (of mud, etc.); spurting (of blood, etc.).
gicler [ʒikle] *v.i.* **1.** to squirt (out); to spout; (*of blood, etc.*) to spurt (up, out) **2.** to splash up.
gicleur [ʒiklœr] *n.m. I.C.E:* jet; **g. de ralenti,** idling jet.
gifle [ʒifl̥] *n.f.* (*a*) slap in the face; box on the ear; **donner, appliquer,** *F:* **flanquer, une g. à qn,** to slap s.o.'s face; *F:* **tête à gifles,** unpleasant, sullen, face; (*b*) insult, (public) humiliation.
gifler [ʒifle] *v.tr.* (*a*) to slap, smack, (s.o.'s) face; to box (s.o.'s) ears; **visage giflé par le vent,** face lashed by the wind; (*b*) **mots qui giflent,** humiliating words.
gigahertz [ʒigaɛrts] *n.m. Meas:* gigahertz.
gigantesque [ʒigɑ̃tɛsk] *a. & n.m.* gigantic.
gigantesquement [ʒigɑ̃tɛskəmɑ̃] *adv.* gigantically.
gigantisme [ʒigɑ̃tism] *n.m. Med:* gi(g)antism.
Gigogne [ʒigɔɲ] *n.f.* **la mère G.** = the Old Woman who lived in a shoe; **une mère G.,** the mother of a large and ever-increasing family; **table g.,** nest of tables; **lit g.,** trundle, truckle, bed; **poupée g.,** nest of (Russian) dolls; *Ball:* **fusée g.,** multistage rocket.
gigolo [ʒigɔlo] *n.m. F:* gigolo.
gigot [ʒigo] *n.m.* **1.** *Cu:* leg of lamb; *Cost:* **manche g.,** leg-of-mutton sleeve. **2.** (*a*) hind leg (of horse); (*b*) *F:* leg, thigh (of pers.).
gigoter [ʒigɔte] *v.i. F:* **1.** to shake, jerk around (one's legs, arms); to wriggle, fidget. **2.** (*of dying animal*) to give a convulsive jerk.
gigue[1] [ʒig] *n.f. Danc:* jig.
gigue[2] *n.f.* (*a*) haunch (of venison); (*b*) *pl. F:* legs, stumps, pins; (*c*) **une grande g.,** a lanky, gawky, young woman; a beanpole.
gilde [gild] *n.f. Hist:* g(u)ild.
gilet [ʒilɛ] *n.m.* (*a*) waistcoat, *NAm:* vest; (*b*) **g. de sauvetage,** life jacket; **g. d'armes,** fencing jacket; (*c*) **g. (de corps, de peau, de dessous),** vest, singlet, *NAm:* undershirt; (*d*) (woman's) cardigan.
giletier, -ière [ʒiltje, -jɛr] **1.** *n.* waistcoat, *NAm:* vest, maker. **2.** *n.f.* watch chain.
Gilles [ʒil] *Pr.n.m.* Giles.
gin [dʒin] *n.m.* gin.
gindre [ʒɛ̃dr̥] *n.m.* baker's assistant.
gingembre [ʒɛ̃ʒɑ̃br̥] *n.m.* ginger; **racine de g.,** root ginger, ginger race.
gingival, -aux [ʒɛ̃ʒival, -o] *a. Anat:* gingival.
gingivite [ʒɛ̃ʒivit] *n.f. Med:* gingivitis; **g. expulsive,** pyorrhoea, *NAm:* pyorrhea.
ginseng [ʒɛ̃sɑ̃] *n.m. Bot: etc:* ginseng.
girafe [ʒiraf] *n.f.* **1.** (*a*) *Z:* giraffe; *F:* **peigner la g.,** to waste one's time; to do damn all; (*b*) *F:* tall, thin, lanky, person; beanpole. **2.** *Cin:* boom (of microphone).
girafeau, -eaux [ʒirafo], **girafon** [ʒirafɔ̃] *n.m.* baby giraffe.
girandole [ʒirɑ̃dɔl] *n.f.* **1.** girandole, chandelier; *Pyr:* girandole. **2.** centrepiece (for table). **3.** cluster (of blooms); girandole (of jewels).
girasol [ʒirasɔl] *n.m. Miner:* girasol, fire opal.
giration [ʒirasjɔ̃] *n.f.* gyration; *Nau:* **cercle de g.,** turning circle (of ship).
giratoire [ʒiratwar] *a.* gyratory (movement, etc.); **sens g.,** roundabout, *NAm:* rotary, traffic circle.
giravion [ʒiravjɔ̃] *n.m. Av:* gyroplane; rotary wing aircraft; rotorcraft.
girelle [ʒirɛl] *n.f.* revolving table (of potter's wheel).
girl [gœrl] *n.f.* chorus girl; showgirl.
girofle [ʒirɔfl̥] *n.m. Bot:* clove; **un clou de g.,** a clove; **huile de g.,** oil of cloves.
giroflée [ʒirɔfle] *n.f. Bot:* stock; **g. jaune, des murailles,** wallflower; *F:* **une g. (à cinq feuilles),** a slap in the face.
giroflier [ʒirɔflije], *n.m. Bot:* clove tree.
girolle [ʒirɔl] *n.f. Fung:* chanterelle (mushroom).
giron [ʒirɔ̃] *n.m.* **1.** lap; **tenir un enfant dans son g.,** to hold a child in one's lap; **le g. de l'Église,** the bosom of the Church. **2.** *Const:* tread (board) (of step).
girond [ʒirɔ̃] *a. P:* (*usu. of woman*) nice and plump; easy on the eye; **ce qu'elle est gironde!** she's a bit of all right!
Gironde [ʒirɔ̃d] *Pr.n.f. Geog:* the (river) Gironde.
girondin, -ine [ʒirɔ̃dɛ̃, -in] (*a*) *Hist: a. & n.* Girondin; (*b*) *a.* **le vignoble g.,** the vineyards of the Gironde.
girouette [ʒirwɛt] *n.f.* (*a*) weathercock; (weather)-vane; (*b*) (*pers.*) weathercock.
gisant [ʒizɑ̃] **1.** *a.* (*of pers.*) lying (helpless or dead); *For:* felled (timber); fallen (trunks); *Nau:* **navire g.,** stranded vessel; *Mill:* **meule gisante,** lower millstone. **2.** *n.m.* recumbent figure (on tomb).
gisement [ʒizmɑ̃] *n.m.* **1.** (*a*) *Geol:* layer, bed, deposit, stratum; **g. pétrolifère,** oilfield; (*b*) *Min:* (i) lode, vein; (ii) lie of the lodes; **gisements houillers,** coal measures; (*c*) *Archeol:* **g. préhistorique,** prehistoric site. **2.** *Nau: etc:* bearing; **g. à la boussole,** compass bearing; **connaître le g. de la côte,** to know the lie of the coast.
gitan, -ane [ʒitɑ̃, -an] **1.** *n.* (Spanish) gipsy. **2.** *n.f. R.t.m:* popular brand of cigarette.
gîte[1] [ʒit] *n.m.* **1.** (*a*) resting place, lodging; **ne pas avoir de g.,** to be homeless; **revenir au g.,** to return to one's old home; (*b*) lair (of deer); form, seat (of hare); **trouver un lièvre au g.,** to find a hare sitting. **2.** stratum, bed, deposit (of ore, etc.); **gîtes houillers,** coal measures. **3.** leg of beef; **g. à la noix,** silverside.
gîte[2] *n.f. Nau:* list(ing); (*of ship*) **avoir, prendre, de la g.,** to have, take, a list; to list, heel (over); **donner de la g. sur tribord,** to list to starboard.
gîter [ʒite] **1.** *v.i. & pr. A: & Lit:* (*a*) (*of pers.*) to lodge, live; (*b*) (*of animal*) to find shelter; to bed; (*of bird*) to perch. **2.** *v.i.* (*of ship*) (i) to run aground; (ii) to list, heel.
givrage [ʒivraʒ] *n.m. Av: etc:* icing.
givre [ʒivr̥] *n.m.* **1.** hoar frost, rime. **2.** (*a*) frost (forming in refrigerator, etc.); (*b*) sugar crystals (on crystallized fruit, etc.).
givré [ʒivre] *a.* **1.** frosty; covered with hoar frost; *Av:* iced up. **2.** (*of cake, etc.*) frosted; (*of preserved fruit, etc.*) covered with sugar crystals; *Cu:* **orange givrée,** orange filled with sorbet. **3.** *P:* (*a*) drunk, canned, stoned; (*b*) mad, nuts, batty.
givrer [ʒivre] **1.** *v.tr.* (*a*) to cover with hoar frost; (*b*) to frost (cake, etc.). **2.** *v.tr. & pr. Av:* to ice up.
givreux, -euse [ʒivrø, -øz] *a.* (*of diamonds, etc.*) with icy flecks.
givrure [ʒivryr] *n.f.* icy fleck (in diamond, etc.).
glabre [glɑbr̥] *a. Nat.Hist:* glabrous, smooth; **visage g.,** (i) hairless face; (ii) clean-shaven face.
glaçage [glasaʒ] *n.m.* (*a*) glazing, glossing; surfacing (of paper); (*b*) *Cu:* icing, frosting (of cake, etc.); glazing (of pastry, etc.).
glaçant [glasɑ̃] *a.* (*a*) *O:* freezing (cold); icy (coldness, wind); (*b*) chilling, frigid (manner, reception).
glace [glas] *n.f.* **1.** ice; **cube de g.,** ice cube; *Fr.C:* (*of drink*) **sur g.,** on the rocks; **glaces de fond,** bottom ice, anchor ice; **g. flottante,** floating ice, drift ice; **navire retenu, pris, par les glaces,** icebound ship; **un accueil de g.,** a frigid, icy, reception. **2.** (*a*) glass; **g. (de vitrine),** plate glass; (*b*) (looking) glass, mirror; **g. à main,** hand mirror; (*c*) *Aut: etc:* window. **3.** *Cu:* (*a*) glaze; (*b*) (sugar) icing; (*c*) ice cream; **g. à la vanille, aux fraises,** vanilla, strawberry, ice (cream). **4.** *Lap:* flaw (in diamond).

glacé [glase] *a.* **1.** (*a*) frozen (river, etc.); (*b*) chilled, freezing, icy, cold; **j'ai les pieds glacés,** my feet are (as) cold as ice; **g. jusqu'aux os,** chilled to the bone; **politesse glacée,** frosty, icy, politeness; **regard g.,** cold stare; (*c*) iced (coffee, etc.). **2.** glazed, glossy (paper, etc.); **gants glacés,** glacé kid gloves; **soie glacée,** watered silk; **fil g.,** glazed thread; *Phot:* **épreuve glacée,** glossy print; *Cu:* **cerises glacées,** glacé cherries.

glacer [glase] *v.* **(je glaça(i)s); n. glaçons) 1.** *v.tr.* (*a*) to freeze; to chill; **cela me glace le sang,** it makes my blood run cold; (*b*) to ice (water, etc.); (*c*) *Cu:* to ice, frost (cake, etc.); (*d*) to glaze (thread, pastry, etc.); to surface (paper). **2.** (*of water, etc.*) **se g.** to freeze (over); **son sang se glaça,** his blood ran cold.

glacerie [glasri] *n.f.* **1.** (*a*) glass works; mirror factory; (*b*) glass trade. **2.** (*a*) ice cream factory; (*b*) ice cream trade.

glaceur [glasœr] *n.m.* glazer (of material, etc).

glaceux, -euse [glasø, -øz] *a. Lap:* flawed (diamond, etc.).

glaciaire [glasjɛr] *a. Geol:* glacial; glaciated (valley, etc.); **période g.,** ice age.

glacial, -als *or* **-aux** [glasjal, -o] (*pl. rarely used*) *a.* icy (temperature); frosty (air); frigid; **vent g.,** icy, cutting, bitter, wind; **zone glaciale,** arctic region; **politesse glaciale,** icy, chilly, politeness.

glacialement [glasjalmɑ̃] *adv.* icily, frigidly.

glaciation [glasjasjɔ̃] *n.f.* glaciation.

glacier¹ [glasje] *n.m. Geol:* glacier.

glacier² *n.m.* ice cream (i) manufacturer, (ii) retailer, man; **pâtissier g., g. confiseur,** confectioner (who also sells ice cream).

glacière [glasjɛr] *n.f.* **1.** (*a*) *A:* ice cave; (*b*) ice box; (*c*) *F:* refrigerator, fridge; (*d*) insulated picnic bag, box. **2.** *F:* **cette chambre est une vraie g.!** this room's like an ice box, ice house!

glacis [glasi] *n.m.* **1.** slope, bank; *Const:* (i) ramp; (ii) weathering; *Geog: Fort:* glacis. **2.** *Art:* scumble, glaze.

glaçon [glasɔ̃] *n.m.* (*a*) block of ice; ice floe; *pl.* drift ice, broken ice (on river); (*b*) icicle; (*c*) ice cube; **whisky aux glaçons,** whisky on the rocks; (*d*) *F:* **c'est un g.!** he's, she's, a cold fish!

glaçure [glasyr] *n.f. Cer: etc:* glaze.

gladiateur [gladjatœr] *n.m.* gladiator.

glaïeul [glajœl] *n.m. Bot:* gladiolus; **g. des marais,** (sword) flag.

glaire [glɛr] *n.f.* glair; (*a*) white of egg; (*b*) mucus, phlegm.

glaireux, -euse [glɛrø, -øz] *a.* glaireous, glairy.

glaise [glɛz] *n.f.* **(terre) g.,** clay, loam; *Hyd.E:* puddled clay, puddle clay.

glaiser [gleze] *v.tr.* **1.** *Agr:* to clay; to dress (soil) with clay. **2.** to line (sth.) with clay; to loam; *Hyd.E:* to puddle, pug (reservoir).

glaiseux, -euse [glɛzø, -øz] *a.* clayey, loamy.

glaisière [glɛzjɛr] *n.f.* clay pit.

glaive [glɛv] *n.m. A: & Lit:* sword, blade.

glanage [glanaʒ] *n.m.* gleaning.

gland [glɑ̃] *n.m.* **1.** (*a*) *Bot:* acorn; (*b*) *pl. Agr:* mast. **2.** tassel (of curtain, etc.); acorn (of sword knot). **3.** *Anat:* glans. **4.** *Mch:* **g. de presse-étoupe,** stuffing gland.

glande [glɑ̃d] *n.f. Anat: Bot:* gland; *F:* **avoir des glandes (au cou),** to have swollen glands.

glanduleux, -euse [glɑ̃dylø, -øz], **glandulaire** [glɑ̃dylɛr] *a.* glandular.

glane [glan] *n.f.* **1.** (*a*) gleaning; (*b*) *pl.* gleanings. **2.** string, rope (of onions); cluster (of pears).

glaner [glane] *v.tr.* to glean.

glaneur, -euse [glanœr, -øz] *n.* gleaner.

glanure [glanyr] *n.f.* gleaning(s).

glapir [glapir] *v.i.* to yelp, yap; (*of fox*) to bark.

glapissant [glapisɑ̃] *a.* yapping, yelping (dog); **voix glapissante,** shrill voice.

glapissement [glapismɑ̃] *n.m.* yapping, yelping (of puppies); barking (of foxes).

glas [glɑ] *n.m.* (*a*) knell; **sonner le g.,** to toll the knell, the passing bell; **sonner le g. de . . . ,** to sound, ring, the knell of . . . ; (*b*) salvo of guns (at military or State funeral).

glaucome [glokom] *n.m. Med:* glaucoma.

glauque [glok] *a.* glaucous; blue-green; sea-green.

glèbe [glɛb] *n.f.* **1.** *A:* clod (of earth), sod. **2.** (*a*) *A: & Lit:* soil, land (under cultivation); glebe.

glène¹ [glɛn] *n.f. Anat:* glene, socket.

glène² *n.f. Fish:* creel.

glissade [glisad] *n.f.* **1.** slip; (*a*) **faire une g.,** (i) to slip; (ii) to make a faux pas; (*b*) *Av:* **g. sur l'aile,** side slip; **g. sur la queue,** tail slide. **2.** (*a*) sliding; **faire une g.,** to slide; (*b*) *Danc:* glissade; (*c*) *Mus:* (i) portamento; (ii) rapid scale passage (produced by running finger along the keys of the piano).

glissage [glisaʒ] *n.m.* sliding down (of cut timber in the mountains).

glissant [glisɑ̃] *a.* **1.** slippery (eel, pavement, etc.). **2.** sliding; **porte glissante,** sliding door; *Mec.E:* **joint g.,** sliding joint, slip joint.

glissé [glise] *a. & n.m. Danc:* **(pas) g.,** glissade, glide.

glissement [glismɑ̃] *n.m.* (*a*) sliding, slipping; slip; (*b*) gliding, glide; *Av:* sideslipping; *Elcs:* **g. de fréquence,** frequency variation; *Geol:* **g. de terrain,** landslide; landslip; *Ling:* **g. de sens,** shift in meaning; *Pol:* **g. à gauche, vers la gauche,** swing to the left.

glisser [glise] **I.** *v.i.* **1.** (*a*) to slip; **le couteau lui a glissé des mains,** the knife slipped from his hands; (*b*) (*of wheel*) to skid; *Av:* **g. sur l'aile,** to sideslip. **2.** to slide (on ice, etc.); **faire g.,** to slide (part of machine, etc.); **se laisser g. le long d'une corde,** to slide down a rope. **3.** to glide (over the water, etc.); **un sourire ironique glissa sur ses lèvres,** he gave a brief ironic smile. **4. g. sur qch.** (*a*) to make little impression on sth.; **l'épée lui glissa sur les côtes,** the sword glanced off his ribs; (*b*) to touch lightly on (subject); **glissons (là-dessus)!** let's not dwell on that; let that pass. **II.** *v.tr.* **1. g. qch. dans la poche de qn,** to slip sth. into s.o.'s pocket; **g. un œil vers qn,** to sneak a glance at s.o.; **g. un mot à l'oreille de qn,** to drop a word in s.o.'s ear. **2.** *Knit:* to slip (a stitch). **III. se g.,** to glide, creep, steal (**dans,** into); **se g. dans son lit,** to slip, creep, into bed.

glisseur, -euse [glisœr, -øz] *n.m.* (*a*) *Mch:* slide block; (*b*) *Av:* glider; (*c*) *Mth:* sliding vector.

glissière [glisjɛr] *n.f.* **1.** groove, slide; **porte à glissières,** sliding door; **à g.,** skid-mounted; *Row:* **banc à glissières,** sliding seat. **2.** (*a*) *Mch:* (slipper) guide, slipper, slide bar, guide rod; *Artil:* recoil slide; (*b*) (*alongside road*) crash barrier. **3.** *Ind:* shoot (for coal, etc.).

glissoir [gliswar] *n.m.* **1.** *Mch:* slide, sliding block. **2.** *For:* timber slide, shoot.

glissoire [gliswar] *n.f.* slide (on ice or snow).

global, -aux [glɔbal, -o] *a.* total, aggregate, inclusive, gross, global (sum, etc.); lump (payment).

globalement [glɔbalmɑ̃] *adv.* in the aggregate, globally.

globe [glɔb] *n.m.* **1.** (*a*) globe, sphere; **faire le tour du g.,** to go round the world; **le g. du soleil,** the orb of the sun; (*b*) orb (of regalia). **2.** glass cover, shade (of clock, etc.); **g. électrique,** electric light globe; **statuette sous g.,** statuette under glass; **c'est à conserver sous g.,** it ought to be in a glass case. **3.** *Anat:* **g. de l'œil,** eyeball. **4.** *Meteor:* **g. de feu,** fireball, globe lightning.

globe-trotter [glɔbtrɔtœr] *n.m.* globetrotter; *pl. globe-trotters.*

globulaire [glɔbylɛr] *a.* (*a*) globular; (*b*) *Med:* **numération g.,** blood count.

globule [glɔbyl] *n.m.* (*a*) globule (of air, water); drop (of water); (*b*) *Physiol:* (blood) corpuscle; **g. blanc,** white corpuscle; **g. rouge,** red corpuscle; (*c*) *Pharm:* globule, small pill.

globuleux, -euse [glɔbylø, -øz] *a.* globular; **yeux g.,** protruding eyes.

glockenspiel [glɔkɛnʃpil] *n.m. Mus:* glockenspiel.

gloire [glwar] *n.f.* **1.** glory; **il fut la g. de son siècle,** he was the glory of his age; **g. à Dieu!** glory (be) to God; **travailler pour la g.,** to work for nothing. **2.** boast, pride; **se faire g. de qch.,** to glory in sth., to pride oneself on sth.; **mettre sa g. à, en, qch.,** to boast of, glory in, sth. **3.** glory, halo, aureola, nimbus.

gloria [glɔrja] *n.m.* **1.** *Ecc:* Gloria. **2.** *F: O:* coffee served with spirits.

glorieusement [glɔrjøzmɑ̃] *adv.* gloriously.

glorieux, -euse [glɔrjø, -øz] *a.* **1.** glorious; **les g.,** the saints in glory. **2.** *A: & Lit:* proud; **g. de qch.,** vain, conceited, about, sth.

glorification [glɔrifikasjɔ̃] *n.f.* glorification.

glorifier [glɔrifje] *v.* (*impf. & pr.sub.* **n. glorifiions, v. glorifiiez**) **1.** *v.tr.* to praise, glorify; *Ecc:* **que ton nom soit glorifié!** hallowed be thy name. **2. se g.,** to boast; **se g. de qch., de faire qch.,** to glory in sth., in doing sth.; to boast of sth., of doing sth.

gloriole [glɔrjɔl] *n.f.* vainglory; **pour la g.,** for the sake of kudos; **faire de la g.,** to talk big.

glose [gloz] *n.f.* **1.** gloss, commentary; **g. marginale,** marginal note. **2.** comment, criticism; **dire la vérité sans g.,** to speak the plain, unvarnished truth.

gloser [gloze] **1.** *v.tr.* to gloss, expound (text). **2.** *v.i.* (*a*) to gossip (**sur,** about); (*b*) *O:* **g. sur qch.,** to find fault with sth., carp at sth.

glossaire [glɔsɛr] *n.m.* **1.** glossary. **2.** vocabulary.

glossine [glɔsin] *n.f. Ent:* tsetse fly.

glottal, -aux [glɔtal, -o] *a. Ling: Anat:* glottal.

glotte [glɔt] *n.f. Anat:* glottis; *Ling:* **coup de g.,** glottal stop.

glouglou [gluglu] *n.m.* **1.** glug-glug, gurgle, bubbling (of liquid poured from bottle); **faire g.,** to gurgle, to bubble. **2.** gobble (of turkey); coo (of pigeon).

glouglouter [gluglute] *v.i.* **1.** (*of liquid*) to gurgle, bubble. **2.** (*of turkey*) to gobble.

gloussement [glusmɑ̃] *n.m.* clucking, cluck (of hen); gobbling, gobble (of turkey); chuckling, chuckle, chortle (of person).

glousser [gluse] *v.i.* (*of hen*) to cluck; (*of turkey*) to gobble; (*of pers.*) to chuckle, chortle.

glouteron [glutrɔ̃] *n.m. Bot:* burdock, burr.

glouton, -onne [glutɔ̃, -ɔn] **1.** *a.* greedy, gluttonous. **2.** (*a*) *n.* glutton; **c'est un petit g.,** he's a regular little pig; (*b*) *n.m. Z:* glutton, wolverine.

gloutonnement [glutɔnmɑ̃] *adv.* gluttonously; ravenously, greedily; *F:* like a pig.

gloutonnerie [glutɔnri] *n.f.* gluttony.

gloxinie [glɔksini] *n.f. Bot:* gloxinia.

glu [gly] *n.f.* (*a*) bird lime; **prendre des oiseaux à la g.,** to lime birds; **être pris à la g.,** to be caught in a trap; **il a de la g. aux mains,** money sticks to his fingers; (*b*) glue, gum.

gluant [glyɑ̃] *a.* sticky, gummy, gluey.

gluau, -aux [glyo] *n.m.* lime twig, snare.

glucide [glysid] *n.m. Bio-Ch:* glucide.

glucose [glykoz] *n.m.* glucose; **g. sanguin,** blood sugar.

glume [glym] *n.f.* (*a*) *Bot:* glume; (*b*) *Agr:* chaff.

gluten [glytɛn] *n.m.* gluten.

glutineux, -euse [glytinø, -øz] *a.* glutinous.

glycémie [glisemi] *n.f. Med:* glycaemia.

glycérine [gliserin] *n.f. Ch:* glycerin(e), glycerol.

glycériner [gliserine] *v.tr.* to rub (sth.) over, treat (sth.), with glycerin(e).

glycérol [gliserɔl] *n.m. Ch:* glycerol, glycerin(e).

glycine[1] [glisin] *n.f. Bot:* wisteria, wistaria.

glycine[2] *n.f. Bio-Ch:* glycine.

glycogène [glikɔʒɛn] *n.m. Ch:* glycogen.

glycol [glikɔl] *n.m. Ch:* glycol.

glyphe [glif] *n.m. Arch:* glyph, groove, channel.

glyptique [gliptik] *n.f. Engr:* glyptics.

gnangnan [ɲɑ̃ɲɑ̃] *F:* **1.** *a.inv.* flabby, spineless, wet. **2.** *n.* spineless person, wet.

gnaule [ɲol] *n.f. P:* brandy, spirits, rotgut.

gneiss [gnɛs] *n.m. Geol:* gneiss.

gniole, gnole, gnôle [ɲol] *n.f. P:* brandy, spirits, rotgut.

gnome [gnom] *n.m.* gnome.

gnomique [gnɔmik] *a.* gnomic (poetry, etc.).

gnon [ɲɔ̃] *n.m. P:* blow, biff, punch.

gnose [gnoz], **gnosie** [gnozi] *n.f.* **1.** *A:* gnosis. **2.** *Rel.H:* gnosticism.

gnosticisme [gnɔstisism] *n.m. Rel.H:* gnosticism.

gnostique [gnɔstik] *a. & n. Rel:* gnostic.

gnou [gnu] *n.m. Z:* gnu, wildebeest.

go [go] *used in the adv.phr. F:* **tout de go,** (i) easily, without a hitch; (ii) without ceremony, all of a sudden; **avaler qch. tout de go,** to swallow sth. at a gulp; **répondre tout de go,** to answer straight off.

goal [gol] *n.m. Fb: etc: F:* goalkeeper, goalie.

gobelet [gɔblɛ] *n.m.* goblet, cup; beaker; **(verre) g.,** tumbler; **g. gradué,** graduated measure; **joueur de gobelets,** thimblerigger; **tour de g.,** conjuring trick (with glasses).

gobeleterie [gɔbletri] *n.f.* hollow (i) glass trade, (ii) glassware.

gobeletier [gɔblətje] *n.m.* manufacturer of, dealer in, glassware.

gobe-mouches [gɔbmuʃ] *n.m.inv.* **1.** *Orn:* flycatcher. **2.** *Bot:* **dionée g.-m.,** Venus flytrap. **3.** *F: O:* simpleton, dope.

gober [gɔbe] **1.** *v.tr.* (*a*) to swallow, gulp down; to bolt (food); **g. l'appât, le morceau, la mouche,** to swallow, rise to, the bait; *F:* **g. des mouches,** to stand gaping; **il gobe tout ce qu'on lui dit,** he believes everything he's told, takes it all in; he'll swallow anything; (*b*) *F:* to have a strong liking for (s.o.); **les élèves le, la, gobent,** the pupils think no end of him, adore her. **2.** *F:* **se g.,** to think a lot of, to fancy, oneself.

goberger (se) [səgɔbɛrʒe] *v.pr.* **(je me gobergeai(s); n.n. gobergeons)** *F:* to do oneself well, proud.

gobeur, -euse [gɔbœr, -øz] *n.* **1.** gulper, swallower. **2.** *F:* **c'est un g.,** he's very gullible; he'll swallow anything.

gobie [gɔbi] *n.m. Ich:* (common sand) goby.

godailler [gɔdaje] *v.i.* = GODER.

godasse [gɔdas] *n.f. P:* shoe, boot.

Godefroi [gɔdfrwa] *Pr.n.m.* Godfrey.

godelureau, -eaux [gɔdlyro] *n.m. Pej:* young; *NAm:* dude; dandy.

goder [gɔde] *v.i.* (*of cloth*) to pucker, ruck (up); (*of trousers*) **g. aux genoux,** to bag at the knees.

godet [gɔdɛ] *n.m.* **1.** (*a*) bowl; pot; (drinking) cup, mug; *P:* **viens boire un g.,** come and have a drink, a pint; (*b*) **g. à couleur,** saucer for mixing water colours; **g. à huile,** waste oil cup (of machine); drip receiver; **g. d'une pipe,** bowl of a pipe; (*c*) *Mec.E: etc:* socket (for foot of machine, etc.); (*d*) *Min:* skip; (*e*) *Hyd.E:* (noria) scoop; bucket (of dredger, excavator, waterwheel); **roue à godets,** overshot wheel. **2.** (*a*) pucker, ruck (in cloth); (*b*) *Dressm:* flare; gore; **à godets,** flared; gored.

godiche [gɔdiʃ], **godichon, -onne** [gɔdiʃɔ̃, -ɔn]

F: **1.** *a.* (*a*) stupid, silly; (*b*) awkward, clumsy, ham-fisted. **2.** *n.* (*a*) simpleton, clot, dope; (*b*) lout; **quelle godiche, cette fille!** what a lump (of a girl)!

godille [gɔdij] *n.f.* **1.** stern oar; scull; **aller à la g.,** to (single-)scull; **(faire qch.) à la g.,** (to do sth.) without rhyme or reason. **2.** *Ski:* wedeln.

godiller [gɔdije] *v.i.* to (single-)scull.

godilleur [gɔdijœr] *n.m.* sculler.

godillot [gɔdijo] *n.m.* (*a*) (military) boot; (*b*) hob-nailed boot; (*c*) *F:* shapeless old shoe.

godron [gɔdrɔ̃] *n.m.* **1.** *Arch:* gadroon. **2.** *pl. Metalw:* boss beading. **3.** *A.Cost:* pleat, goffer; *pl.* fluting.

godronnage [gɔdrɔnaʒ] *n.m.* **1.** *Metalw:* milling (of the head of a screw). **2.** *Dressm:* goffering, fluting.

godronner [gɔdrɔne] *v.tr.* **1.** *Metalw:* to mill (head of screw, etc.). **2.** *Dressm:* to goffer, flute.

goéland [gɔelɑ̃] *n.m. Orn:* (sea)gull.

goélette [gɔelɛt] *n.f. Nau:* (*a*) schooner; (*b*) **(voile) g.,** trysail.

goémon [gɔemɔ̃] *n.m.* seaweed; wrack.

goglu [gɔgly] *n.m. Fr.C: Orn:* bobolink.

gogo¹ (à) [agogo] *adv. phr. F:* **livres à g.,** books galore; **avoir de l'argent à g.,** to have money to burn.

gogo² *n.m. F:* easy dupe, gullible fool, sucker.

goguenard, -arde [gɔgnar, -ard] **1.** *a.* mocking; bantering; joking; sarcastic; jeering. **2.** *n.* joker; sarcastic person; **c'est un g.,** he likes to make fun of people.

goguenardise [gɔgnardiz] *n.f.* banter(ing); sarcasm; sarcastic remarks; jeering.

goguenot [gɔgno] *n.m. P:* (i) chamber pot, po, jerry; (ii) *pl.* toilet, bog, *NAm:* john.

goguette [gɔgɛt] *n.f. F:* **être en g.,** to be (a bit) tight, merry.

goï, *pl.* **goïm** [gɔj, gɔim] *n.m. Jewish Rel:* goy, *pl.* goyim.

goinfre [gwɛ̃fr̥] *n.m. F:* guzzler, greedyguts, pig.

goinfrer (se) [səgwɛ̃fre] *v.pr. F:* to guzzle, gorge.

goinfrerie [gwɛ̃frəri] *n.f.* gluttony, guzzling.

goitre [gwatr̥] *n.m. Med:* goitre, *NAm:* goiter.

goitreux, -euse [gwatrø, -øz] **1.** *a.* goitrous (neck, swelling, person). **2.** *n.* goitrous person.

golden [gɔlden] *n.f.inv.* golden delicious (apple).

golf [gɔlf] *n.m.* golf; **g. miniature,** miniature golf; **(terrain de) g.,** golf course, links.

golfe [gɔlf] *n.m.* gulf, bay; **le Courant du G.,** the gulf stream.

golfeur, -euse [gɔlfœr, -øz] *n.* golfer.

gomina [gɔmina] *n.f. R.t.m:* solid brilliantine, hair cream.

gominer (se) [səgɔmine] *v.pr.* to plaster down one's hair (with brilliantine, etc.).

gommage [gɔmaʒ] *n.m.* **1.** gumming. **2.** *Mch: I.C.E:* sticking, gumming (of valves, pistons). **3.** toning down, smoothing out.

gomme [gɔm] *n.f.* **1.** (*a*) gum; **g. arabique,** gum arabic; **g. laque,** shellac; (*b*) *Comest:* **pastille, boule, de g.,** gum; **g. à mâcher,** chewing gum. **2.** (*a*) **g. (à crayon, à effacer),** (india) rubber, eraser; **g. à encre,** ink eraser; (*b*) *F:* **histoire à la g.,** pointless tale; **individu à la g.,** useless individual. **3.** *F:* **mettre la g.,** to get a move on; to go all out; *Aut:* to put one's foot down.

gomme-gutte [gɔmgyt] *n.f. Paint: Med:* gamboge; *pl. gommes-guttes.*

gomme-laque [gɔmlak] *n.f.* shellac, lac; *pl. gommes-laques.*

gommer [gɔme] *v.tr.* **1.** to gum. **2.** to erase, rub out. **3.** *v.i. Mec.E:* to stick, jam; **piston gommé,** gummed piston.

gomme-résine [gɔmrezin] *n.f.* gum resin; *pl. gommes-résines.*

gommeux, -euse [gɔmø, -øz] **1.** *a.* gummy, sticky; **plante gommeuse,** gum-yielding plant. **2.** *A:* (*a*) overdressed; (*b*) *n.m.* dandy, fop, *N.Am:* dude.

gommier [gɔmje] *n.m. Bot:* gum tree.

gonade [gɔnad] *n.f. Biol:* gonad.

gond [gɔ̃] *n.m.* hinge (pin) (of door); **mettre une porte sur ses gonds,** to hang a door; *F:* **sortir (hors) de ses gonds,** to lose one's temper, fly off the handle.

gondolage [gɔ̃dɔlaʒ] *n.m.* warping (of wood); curling (of paper); buckling (of sheet iron, etc.).

gondolant [gɔ̃dɔlɑ̃] *a. F:* side-splitting, uproariously funny (story, etc.).

gondole [gɔ̃dɔl] *n.f.* **1.** gondola. **2.** (*in supermarket, etc.*) island, gondola.

gondolement [gɔ̃dɔlmɑ̃] *n.m.* = GONDOLAGE.

gondoler [gɔ̃dɔle] **1.** *v.i. & pr.* (*of wood*) to warp; (*of paper*) to curl; (*of sheet iron*) to buckle; (*of car bumper, etc.*) to crumple up. **2.** *F:* **se g.,** to split one's sides laughing.

gondolier, -ière [gɔ̃dɔlje, -jɛr] *n.* gondolier.

gonfalon [gɔ̃falɔ̃] *n.m.*, **gonfanon** [gɔ̃fanɔ̃] *n.m. A:* gonfalon (banner, streamer).

gonflage [gɔ̃flaʒ] *n.m. Aut: etc:* inflation; **vérifier le g. (des pneus),** to check the tyre pressures, *NAm:* tire pressures.

gonflé [gɔ̃fle] *a.* **1.** (*of sail*) full. **2.** swollen, puffy (eyes); bloated (face); **riz g.,** puffed rice; **g. d'orgueil,** puffed up with pride; **avoir le cœur g.,** to be sad. **3.** (*a*) sure of oneself; full of oneself; *F:* **t'es g.,** you've got a nerve; **g. à bloc,** (i) keyed-up; (ii) sure of oneself; (*b*) *Aut: F:* **moteur g.,** hotted-up, souped-up, engine. **4. prix gonflés,** exaggerated prices.

gonflement [gɔ̃fləmɑ̃] *n.m.* inflating, inflation (of tyres, balloon); distension (of stomach); swelling.

gonfler [gɔ̃fle] **1.** *v.tr.* (*a*) to inflate, distend; to blow up, pump up (tyre); to puff out, blow out, bulge (one's cheeks); to puff (rice); **le vent gonfle les voiles,** the wind fills the sails; (*b*) to swell; **torrent gonflé par les pluies,** torrent swollen by the rains; (*c*) *Aut: F:* to hot up, soup up (an engine). **2.** *v.i. & pr.* to become inflated; to swell; (*of stomach*) to become distended.

gonfleur [gɔ̃flœr] *n.m.* (air) pump, air line; *Aut:* (tyre) inflator.

gong [gɔ̃(g)] *n.m.* **1.** gong. **2.** *Box:* bell.

gonio [gɔnjo] *n.m. Nau: Av: F:* direction finder, radiogoniometer.

goniomètre [gɔnjɔmɛtr̥] *n.m. Surv: etc:* goniometer, position finder, direction finder; *Artil:* dial sight.

goniométrie [gɔnjɔmetri] *n.f.* goniometry, position finding, direction finding.

gonocoque [gɔnɔkɔk] *n.m. Bac:* gonococcus.

gonze [gɔ̃z] *n.m. P:* man, bloke, type, guy.

gonzesse [gɔ̃zɛs] *n.f. P:* woman, girl, bird, bit of skirt, *NAm:* broad.

gordien [gɔrdjɛ̃] *a.m.* Gordian (knot).

goret [gɔrɛ] *n.m.* (*a*) piglet; (*b*) *F:* dirty little child, pig.

gorge [gɔrʒ] *n.f.* **1.** (*a*) throat; neck; **couper la g. à qn,** to cut s.o.'s throat; **je le tiens à la g.,** I've got him by the throat; I've got a stranglehold on him; (*b*) bosom, bust (of woman); **g. d'un pigeon,** pigeon's breast. **2.** throat; **avoir mal à la g., avoir un mal de g.,** to have a sore throat; **avoir un serrement de g.,** to gulp; **avoir la gorge serrée,** to have a lump in one's throat; **crier à pleine g.,** to shout at the top of one's voice; **avaler qch. à pleine g.,** to gulp sth. down; **rire à g. déployée,** to roar with laughter. **3.** *Ven:* gorge; **rendre g.,** (i) (*of bird*) to bring up food, to vomit; (ii) *Fig:* to make restitution, to have to cough up. **4.** *Geog:* gorge. **5.** *Tchn:* groove; *Arch:* quirk, gorge; furrow (of screw); neck, (of gun, cartridge case); tumbler (of lock); *Arch:* **moulure à g.,** grooved moulding, *NAm:* molding.

gorgé [gɔrʒe] *a.* gorged, replete.
gorge-de-pigeon [gɔrʒdəpiʒɔ̃] *a.inv. & n.m.* dove-coloured shot (silk).
gorgée [gɔrʒe] *n.f.* mouthful (of wine, etc.); gulp; **petite g.,** sip; **avaler qch. d'une g.,** to swallow sth. in one draught, gulp.
gorger [gɔrʒe] *v.* **(je gorgeai(s); n. gorgeons) 1. se g.,** to stuff, gorge (oneself). **2.** *v.tr. Husb:* to cram (fowls).
Gorgone [gɔrgɔn] *n.f. Myth:* Gorgon.
gorille [gɔrij] *n.m.* **1.** *Z:* gorilla. **2.** *F:* bodyguard.
gosier [gozje] *n.m.* throat; (i) gullet, (ii) windpipe; **s'éclaircir le g.,** to clear one's throat; **rire à plein g.,** to laugh loudly, heartily; **avoir une arête dans le g.,** to have a fishbone stuck in one's throat.
gosse [gɔs] *n. F:* youngster, kid, nipper.
gosser [gɔse] *v.tr. Fr.C: F:* to whittle.
Goth [gɔt] *Hist:* Goth.
gothique [gɔtik] **1.** *a.* Gothic. **2.** *n.m. Arch: Ling:* Gothic. **3.** *n.f. Typ:* black letter.
gotique [gɔtik] *n.m. Ling:* Gothic.
gouache [gwaʃ] *n.f. Art:* gouache.
gouailler [gwaje] *v.i.* to joke.
gouailleur, -euse [gwɑjœr, -øz] **1.** *a.* joking, mocking, bantering (tone). **2.** *n.* joker.
goualante [gwalɑ̃t] *n.f. F:* song.
gouape [gwap] *n.f. P:* rogue; louse.
goudron [gudrɔ̃] *n.m.* tar; **g. de gaz, de houille,** coal tar; **g. de bois,** wood tar; **g. minéral,** asphalt; bitumen.
goudronnage [gudrɔnaʒ] *n.m.* tarring.
goudronner [gudrɔne] *v.tr.* to tar; *Nau:* to pay; **toile goudronnée,** tarpaulin; **papier goudronné,** tar-lined paper.
goudronneur [gudrɔnœr] *n.m.* (*pers.*) tar sprayer, spreader.
goudronneuse[1] [gudrɔnøz] *n.f.* (*machine*) tar sprayer; asphalt spreader.
goudronneux, -euse[2] [gudrɔnø, -øz] *a.* (*a*) tarry; (*b*) gummy (oil).
gouffre [gufr̥] *n.m.* (*a*) gulf, pit, abyss; **g. béant,** yawning chasm; **c'est un g. (que cet homme-là)!** money just slips through his fingers! **un g. de tous les vices,** a sink of iniquity; (*b*) whirlpool, vortex; (*c*) *Geol:* swallow hole; (*d*) *Oc:* cauldron.
gouge [guʒ] *n.f. Tls:* gouge, hollow chisel.
gouine [gwin] *n.f. P:* lesbian.
goujat [guʒa] *n.m.* boor, lout, churl.
goujaterie [guʒatri] *n.f.* boorishness, churlishness.
goujon[1] [guʒɔ̃] *n.m. Ich:* gudgeon.
goujon[2] *n.m.* **1.** (*a*) *Const:* gudgeon, joggle (in stonework); (*b*) projecting stud; *Carp:* tenon, joggle (on foot of post, etc.). **2.** (*a*) *Carp:* **g. perdu, g. prisonnier,** dowel (pin); (*b*) *Mec.E:* **g. de jonction,** assembling pin, bolt; **g. de charnière,** pin, pintle, of a hinge; **g. d'arbre,** gudgeon of a shaft.
goujonner [guʒɔne] *v.tr. Carp:* to dowel; *Const:* to joggle; *Mec.E:* to pin, to bolt.
goulache, goulasch [gulaʃ] *n.f. Cu:* (Hungarian) goulash.
goulée [gule] *n.f.* **1.** *F:* big mouthful, gulp.
goulet [gulɛ] *n.m.* gully (in mountains); *Nau:* gut, bottleneck, narrows (of harbour); **le G. de Brest,** the Brest Channel.
goulot [gulo] *n.m.* **1.** neck (of bottle); spout (of watering can); **boire au g.,** to drink (straight) from the bottle; *Aut: etc:* **g. d'étranglement,** bottleneck. **2.** *P:* gullet, mouth.
goulotte [gulɔt] *n.f.* spout (of coal hopper, etc.); shoot, chute.
goulu, -ue [guly] **1.** *a.* (*a*) greedy, gluttonous; (*b*) **pois g.,** sugar pea. **2.** *n.* glutton.
goulûment [gulymɑ̃] *adv.* greedily, voraciously.
goupil [gupi] *n.m. A:* fox; *Lit:* Reynard the Fox.
goupille [gupij] *n.f. Tchn:* (linch)pin; gudgeon; **g. fendue,** split pin, cotter; **g. d'arrêt,** stop bolt.
goupiller [gupije] *v.tr.* **1.** *Tchn:* to pin, key; to cotter (bolt). **2.** *F:* to contrive, wangle (sth.); **bien, mal, goupillé,** well, badly, worked out.
goupillon [gupijɔ̃] *n.m.* **1.** *Ecc:* aspergillum, sprinkler (for holy water). **2.** brush (for gum, bottle, etc.).
gourance [gurɑ̃s] *n.f. P:* boob, bloomer.
gourbi [gurbi] *n.m.* (*a*) (Arab) hut, shack; (*b*) hovel.
gourd [gur] *a.* numb(ed) (with cold); stiff, swollen (with cold).
gourde [gurd] **1.** *n.f.* (*a*) *Bot:* gourd; (*b*) calabash, gourd, water bottle; flask (of brandy, etc.); (*c*) *F:* idiot, dimwit, dope. **2.** *a. F:* stupid, dimwitted.
gourdin [gurdɛ̃] *n.m.* club, cudgel, bludgeon.
gourer (se) [səgure] *v.pr. P:* to make a mistake, a bloomer; **se g. de route,** to lose one's way.
gourmand, -ande [gurmɑ̃, -ɑ̃d] **1.** *a.* (*a*) **être g.,** to appreciate good food; *Fig:* **être g. de qch.,** to be greedy for, hanker after, sth.; (*b*) *Agr:* **herbes gourmandes,** parasitical weeds; *Hort:* **pois g.,** sugar pea. **2.** (*a*) *n.* gourmand; gourmet; (*b*) *n.m. Hort:* sucker.
gourmander [gurmɑ̃de] *v.tr.* (*a*) *Lit:* to rebuke, chide; (*b*) *A:* to saw at (horse's mouth).
gourmandise [gurmɑ̃diz] *n.f.* **1.** greediness, gluttony; **manger avec g.,** to eat greedily. **2.** *pl.* sweetmeats, dainties.
gourme [gurm] *n.f.* **1.** *Med:* (*a*) impetigo; (*b*) teething rash. **2.** (*a*) *Vet:* strangles; (*b*) (*of pers.*) **jeter sa g.,** to sow one's wild oats.
gourmé [gurme] *a.* stiff, starched, affected.
gourmet [gurmɛ] *n.m.* gourmet; epicure.
gourmette [gurmɛt] *n.f.* **1.** *Harn:* curb (chain); **lâcher la g. à qn,** to give s.o. a free rein, a free hand. **2.** (*a*) curb watch chain; (*b*) chain bracelet.
gourou [guru] *n.m. Hindu Rel:* guru.
gousse [gus] *n.f.* pod, shell, husk (of peas, etc.); **g. d'ail,** clove of garlic.
gousset [gusɛ] *n.m.* **1.** (*a*) fob pocket; waistcoat pocket; trouser pocket; **avoir le g. bien garni,** to have one's pockets well lined; (*b*) gusset (of knickers). **2.** *Mec.E: etc:* (shoulder) bracket, stay plate, gusset (plate).
goût [gu] *n.m.* **1.** (sense of) taste; **avoir le g. fin,** to have a fine palate; *F:* **faire passer le g. du pain à qn,** (i) to murder s.o.; to do away with s.o.; (ii) to make s.o. want to give up. **2.** flavour, *NAm:* flavor; taste; bouquet (of wine); **g. de terroir,** native tang; **cela a le g. de . . .,** it tastes like . . .; **donner du g. à un mets,** to flavour, *NAm:* flavor, a dish; **sans g.,** tasteless(ly); **manque de g.,** tastelessness. **3.** (*pleasure in, preference for, sth.*) *Cu:* **ajouter du sucre et du citron selon son g.,** add sugar and lemon to taste; **le g. des affaires,** a liking for business; **g. passager,** passing fancy; **avoir du g. pour, le g. de, qch.,** to have a taste for sth.; **chacun (à) son g., à chacun son g., des goûts et des couleurs on ne discute pas,** everyone to his taste; there's no accounting for taste; **avoir des goûts de luxe,** to have expensive tastes; **une maison à mon g.,** a house to my liking; **elle n'est pas à mon g.,** I don't care for her; **faire qch. par g.,** to do sth. from inclination; **je n'habite pas ici par g.,** I don't live here from choice; **affaire de g.,** matter of taste. **4.** (*discernment, right judgement*) **g. parfait,** perfect taste; **parole d'un g. douteux,** remark in doubtful taste; **il a du g.,** he has (good) taste; **mauvais g.,** (i) bad taste; (ii) lack of taste; (iii) bad form ; **elle s'habille avec g.,** she has (a) good dress sense, a flair for clothes; *Mus:* **notes de g.,** grace notes. **5.** style, manner; **peint dans le g. de Watteau,** painted in the Watteau manner; **quelque chose dans ce g.-là,** something of that sort, style.
goûter[1] [gute] *v.tr.* **1.** (*a*) to taste (food); (*b*) (*of cook,*

etc.) to taste, try, sample (food, drink). **2.** to enjoy, appreciate, relish; **g. la musique,** to enjoy music. **3. g. de qch.,** (i) to taste sth. for the first time, (ii) to taste, enjoy (s.o.'s hospitality, etc.); *Prov:* **qui goûte de tout se dégoûte de tout,** he who tastes of everything tires of everything. **4. g. à qch.,** to taste sth.; to take a little of sth.; **goûtez donc à ce vin!** just try this wine! **5.** *v.i.* **g. à quatre heures,** to have tea, a snack, at four o'clock.

goûter² *n.m.* = (afternoon) tea; **g. d'enfants,** children's party.

goûteur, -euse [gutœr, -øz] *n.* taster.

goutte [gut] *n.f.* **1.** drop (of liquid); **g. à g.,** drop by drop; (*of liquid*) **tomber g. à g.,** to drip; **c'est une g. d'eau dans la mer,** it's a drop in the ocean; **il suait à grosses gouttes,** he had beads of perspiration on his forehead; **il tombait quelques gouttes,** it was spitting with rain; *F:* **avoir la g. au nez,** to have a runny, dripping, nose; **g. d'eau,** (i) drop of water; drip; (ii) *Jewel:* teardrop. **2.** spot, splash (of colour); speck; fleck. **3.** (*a*) small quantity, sip; **prendre une g. de bouillon,** to take a sip, just a mouthful, of soup; **g. de cognac,** dash of brandy (in sauce); (*b*) drop, nip (of brandy, etc.); **encore une g. de café?** a drop more coffee? *F:* **boire la g.,** to have a nip. **4.** *adv.phr. A: & Hum:* **ne . . . g.,** not at all; **je n'entends g. à ce que vous dites,** I don't understand a word of what you're saying; **je n'y vois g.,** (i) I can't see a thing; (ii) I can't make anything of it. **5.** *pl. Pharm:* drops; **gouttes pour le nez,** nasal drops. **6.** *Med:* gout.

goutte-à-goutte [gutagut] *n.m.inv. Med:* drip; **g.-à.-g. intraveineux,** intravenous drip.

gouttelette [gutlɛt] *n.f.* droplet, tiny drop, globule.

goutter [gute] *v.i.* to drip.

goutteux, -euse [gutø, øz] *a. & n. Med:* gouty (person).

gouttière [gutjɛr] *n.f.* **1.** *Const:* (*a*) (roof) gutter; (rainwater) guttering; (*b*) *pl.* eaves; **chat de g.,** common domestic cat; alley cat. **2.** (*a*) spout, rain pipe; (*b*) shoot, chute. **3.** groove (of bone, sword). **4.** (*a*) *Med:* cradle, (cradle-like) splint; (*b*) trough (for rocket, etc.). **5.** fore edge (of book).

gouvernable [guvɛrnabl] *a.* governable, manageable; **peu g.,** unmanageable.

gouvernail [guvɛrnaj] *n.m.* (*a*) *Nau:* rudder, helm; **roue du g.,** (steering) wheel; **tenir le g.,** to be at the wheel, at the helm; to steer; **g. de plongée,** horizontal rudder (of submarine); **g. de profondeur,** diving rudder, plane, hydroplane; (*b*) *Av:* **g. de direction,** rudder; **g. de profondeur,** elevator.

gouvernant [guvɛrnɑ̃] *a.* (*a*) governing, ruling; (party) in power; (*b*) *n.* **les gouvernants,** the party in power; the executive.

gouvernante [guvɛrnɑ̃t] *n.f.* **1.** housekeeper (of bachelor, priest). **2.** *A:* governess.

gouverne [guvɛrn] *n.f.* **1.** (*a*) **pour vous servir de g.,** to serve as your guiding principle; **pour votre g.,** for your guidance; (*b*) *Nau:* steering. **2.** *Av:* **gouvernes,** control surfaces; **g. de direction,** rudder; **g. de profondeur,** elevator; **g. compensée,** balanced surface.

gouvernement [guvɛrnəmɑ̃] *n.m.* **1.** (*a*) government, management, direction, administration (of household, business, state, etc.); **g. monarchique,** monarchic(al) government; (*b*) governorship; *Mil:* command (of fortified position); (*c*) *Nau:* steering, handling (of boat). **2.** (the) government; (the) Cabinet; **le g. français, britannique,** the French, British, government.

gouvernemental, -aux [guvɛrnəmɑ̃tal, -o] *a.* governmental; **le parti g.,** the government party.

gouverner [guvɛrne] *v.tr.* **1.** *Nau:* to steer, handle (ship); **faire g.,** to con; **g. sur un port,** to steer, stand, head, for a port; to bear in with a port; **g. à la lame,** to steer by the sea; **gouvernez droit!** steady! **2.** (*a*) to govern, rule, control, direct; **Dieu gouverne l'univers,** God is the ruler of the universe; **g. ses passions,** to control, govern, one's passions; *Tchn:* **mouvement governé par un pendule,** movement regulated, governed, controlled, by a pendulum; (*b*) to manage, administer; **bien g. ses ressources,** to make the most of one's resources; (*c*) to govern (country). **3.** *Gram:* **verbe qui gouverne l'accusatif,** verb that governs, takes, the accusative. **4.** *v.i. Nau:* **navire qui ne gouverne plus,** ship that no longer answers to her helm.

gouverneur [guvɛrnœr] *n.m.* governor (of province, bank, etc.; *U.S:* of State); commanding officer (of fortified position); **g. général,** governor-general; *Fr.C:* **lieutenant g.,** lieutenant governor.

goyave [gɔjav] *n.f. Bot:* guava (fruit).

goye, *pl.* **goyim** [gɔj, gɔim] *n. Jewish Rel:* goy; *pl. goyim.*

Graal (le) [ləgral] *n.m. Lit:* the (Holy) Grail.

grabat [graba] *n.m.* mean bed, litter (of straw, rags, etc.); pallet; **mourir sur un g.,** to die in abject poverty.

grabuge [grabyʒ] *n.m. F:* quarrel, (noisy) squabble, row, rumpus; **il y aura du g.,** there'll be ructions.

grâce [grɑs] *n.f.* **1.** (*a*) grace, gracefulness, charm; **avoir de la g.,** to be graceful; **avec g.,** gracefully; **elle fait des grâces devant le miroir,** she's preening herself in front of the mirror; (*b*) **de bonne g.,** willingly, readily; **de mauvaise g.,** unwillingly, ungraciously; **il serait de mauvaise g. de refuser,** it would be ungracious, in bad taste, to refuse; (*c*) *Myth:* **les trois Grâces,** the three Graces. **2.** favour, *NAm:* favor; **trouver g. devant qn, auprès de qn,** to find favour in s.o.'s eyes; **se mettre dans, entrer dans, obtenir, les bonnes grâces de qn,** to get into s.o.'s favour, *F:* into s.o.'s good books; **de g.!** please! for pity's sake! **g.!** mercy! **3.** (*a*) (act of) grace; **faire une g. à qn,** to do s.o. a favour, a kindness; **les grâces de Dieu,** God's blessings; **demander une g. à qn,** to ask a favour of s.o.; **coup de g.,** finishing stroke, quietus, coup de grâce; **donner le coup de g. à un animal,** to put an animal out of its pain; **c'est trop de grâces que vous me faites!** you really are too kind! *Com:* **jours, terme, de g.,** days of grace; (*b*) *Theol:* **en état de g.,** in a state of grace; **l'an de g. 1802,** the year of grace 1802. **4.** (*a*) *Jur:* free pardon; **lettre(s) de g.,** reprieve; **je vous fais g. cette fois-ci,** I'll let you off this time; (*b*) **demander g., crier g.,** to cry for mercy; **je vous fais g. du reste,** (i) you needn't do, say, any more; (ii) I'll spare you the rest. **5.** (*a*) thanks; (*after meal*) **dire les graces,** to say grace, give thanks; **action de grâce(s),** thanksgiving; *Fr.C:* **Jour d'action de g.,** Thanksgiving Day; (*b*) **g. à,** thanks to, owing to; **g. à votre aide,** thanks to your help; **g. à Dieu,** (i) thanks be to God; (ii) with God's help, by God's grace.

gracier [grasje] *v.tr.* (*impf. & pr.sub.* **n. graciions, v. graciiez**) to pardon, reprieve.

gracieusement [grasjøzmɑ̃] *adv.* **1.** gracefully, becomingly. **2.** graciously, kindly. **3.** gratuitously, without payment, free of charge.

gracieuseté [grasjøzte] *n.f.* **1.** graciousness, affability, kindness. **2. faire une g. à qn,** to do s.o. a kindness, a favour, *NAm:* favor. **3.** *A:* gratuity.

gracieux, -euse [grasjø, -øz] *a.* **1.** graceful, pleasing (figure, style, etc.). **2.** (*a*) gracious (manner, etc.); **sourire g.,** charming smile; (*b*) free (of charge); **à titre g.,** as a favour, *NAm:* favor; gratis, free of charge; **exemplaire envoyé à titre g.,** complimentary, presentation, copy. **3. notre g. souverain,** our gracious Sovereign.

gracile [grasil] *a.* slender (stalk, etc.); slim.

gracilité [grasilite] *n.f.* slenderness, slimness.

Gracques (les) [legrak] *Pr.n.m.pl. Rom.Hist:* the Gracchi.

gradation [gradasjɔ̃] *n.f.* gradation, gradual process; **avec une g. lente,** by slow degrees; **par g.,** gradually.

grade [grad] *n.m.* **1.** rank, dignity, degree, grade; **détenir un g.,** to hold a rank. **2.** (university) degree; **être admis au g. de docteur ès lettres** = to obtain one's D.Litt. **3.** *Mil: etc:* rank; **g. honoraire,** brevet rank; **g. honorifique,** honorary rank; **g. (à titre) définitif,** substantive, permanent, rank; **monter en g.,** to be promoted; *F:* **en prendre pour son g.,** to be told off, hauled over the coals. **4.** *Mth:* grade. **5.** grade (of engine oil).

gradé [grade] *n.m.* **1.** *Mil: etc:* non-commissioned officer, N.C.O.; **tous les gradés,** all ranks (commissioned and non-commissioned). **2.** *Navy:* **les gradés,** the petty officers.

grader [gradœr] *n.m. Civ.E:* grader.

gradient [gradjɑ̃] *n.m.* gradient.

gradin [gradɛ̃] *n.m.* **1.** step, tier; stepped row of seats; *F: O:* **quand j'étais sur les gradins,** when I was at school. **2.** *Tchn:* **poulie à gradins,** cone pulley, stepped pulley; *El:* **disposer les balais en gradins,** to stagger the brushes (of a dynamo).

graduation [gradɥasjɔ̃] *n.f.* **1.** graduating (of scale). **2.** graduation. **3.** scale.

gradué [gradɥe] *a.* (*a*) graduated; **verre g.,** measuring glass; *NAm:* graduate; (*b*) graded, progressive (exercises, etc.).

graduel, -elle [gradɥɛl] **1.** *a.* gradual, progressive. **2.** *n.m. Ecc:* gradual.

graduellement [gradɥɛlmɑ̃] *adv.* gradually.

graduer [gradɥe] *v.tr.* **1.** to graduate, calibrate (thermometer, etc.). **2.** to grade (studies, etc.).

graffiti [grafiti] *n.m. pl.* graffiti.

grailler [grɑje] *v.i.* **1.** to speak huskily. **2.** *P:* to eat, nosh.

graillon [grɑjɔ̃] *n.m.* **sentir le g.,** to smell of burnt fat; to taste greasy.

grain[1] [grɛ̃] *n.m.* **1.** (*a*) grain; **g. de blé,** grain of wheat; **g. d'orge,** (i) barleycorn; (ii) *Med:* sty(e) (on the eyelid); (iii) *Carp:* barleycorn; **g. de moutarde, de grenade,** mustard, pomegranate, seed; **le bon g. finit toujours par lever,** quality will tell in the end; (*b*) cereals, grain, corn; *Husb:* hard food (for poultry); **entrepôt de g.,** granary; **poulet de g.,** corn-fed chicken. **2. g. de café,** coffee bean; **g. de poivre,** peppercorn; **g. de raisin,** grape; **g. de beauté,** beauty spot, mole. **3.** particle, atom; (*a*) grain (of salt, sand, powder); speck (of dust); (*b*) **g. de coquetterie, de jalousie,** touch, hint, of coquetry, jealousy; **pas un g. de bon sens,** not a grain, not an atom, of common sense; **il a un g.,** he's not quite right in the head, not all there; *F:* **avoir son g.,** to be drunk, tight. **4.** (*a*) bead; (*b*) *Sm.a:* **g. d'orge,** bead; *Ball:* **g. de plomb,** pellet; (*c*) *I.C.E: El:* **grains platinés,** platinum points; (*d*) *Pharm:* pellet. **5.** grain, texture (of substance); rough side (of skin, etc.); **côté g. du cuir,** grain side of leather; **contre le g.,** against the grain; **à gros grains,** coarse-grained; **à grains fins, serrés,** close-grained; fine-grained; **cassure à grains,** granular fracture; **ruban gros g.,** petersham. **6.** *Meas:* (*a*) *A:* grain;(*b*) *Fr.C.* grain (=0.0647 gm).

grain[2] *n.m. Nau:* squall; gust of wind; **essuyer un g.,** to meet with a squall; **veiller au g.,** to look out for squalls.

graine [grɛn] *n.f.* seed; **g. de lin,** linseed; **g. de moutarde,** mustard seed; **g. d'anis,** aniseed; **monter en g.,** (i) (*of plant*) to run to seed, bolt to seed; (*of woman*) to be (left) on the shelf; *F:* **en prendre de la g.,** to profit from s.o.'s example; **c'est une mauvaise g.,** he's a bad lot.

grainer [grene] *v.tr.* (*a*) to granulate (gunpowder); to shred (wax); to grain (salt).

graineterie [grɛntri] *n.f.* seed trade; seed shop.

grainetier, -ière [grɛntje, -jɛr] *n.* corn chandler.

grainier, -ière [grɛnje, -jɛr] *n.* seedsman, seed merchant.

graissage [grɛsaʒ] *n.m.* greasing, oiling, lubrication; **g. par gravité,** gravity-feed lubrication; **g. sous pression,** pressure greasing; **huile de g.,** lubricating oil; **circuit de g.,** lubrication system; *F:* **g. de patte,** bribery, palm greasing.

graisse [grɛs] *n.f.* **1.** (*a*) grease, fat; **g. de rognon,** suet; **g. de rôti,** dripping; **g. de porc,** lard; **g. de baleine,** blubber; **prendre de la g.,** to put on fat; (*b*) **g. pour essieux,** axle grease; **g. pour engrenages,** gear lubricant; **pistolet, pompe, injecteur, à g.,** grease gun; (*c*) **g. minérale,** crude paraffin, mineral jelly; *Typ:* thickness of type. **3. tourner à la g.,** to get ropy.

graisser [grese] **1.** *v.tr.* (*a*) to grease, oil, lubricate; to oil, dub (boots); **g. la patte à qn,** to bribe s.o.; to grease s.o.'s palm; (*b*) to get grease on (one's clothes); to make (one's clothes) greasy. **2.** *v.i.* (*a*) (*of wine*) to become ropy; (*b*) **onguent qui ne graisse pas,** non-greasy ointment.

graisseur, -euse [grɛsœr, -øz] *Mec.E:* **1.** (*a*) *n.* (*pers.*) greaser, oiler; (*b*) *n.m.* greaser, lubricator; grease cup; nipple; **g. à graisse,** grease gun. **2.** *a.* **godet g.,** grease box; **pistolet g.,** grease gun.

graisseux, -euse [grɛsø, -øz] *a.* **1.** (*a*) greasy, oily, unctuous; (*b*) fatty, adipose (tissue). **2.** ropy (wine).

graminacées [graminase] *n.f.pl. Bot:* Graminaceae.

graminé [gramine] **1.** *a. Bot:* graminaceous. **2.** *n.f.pl.* **graminées,** Graminaceae.

grammaire [gramɛr] *n.f.* (*a*) grammar; **faute de g.,** grammatical error; (*b*) grammar (book).

grammairien, -ienne [gramɛrjɛ̃, -jɛn] *n.* grammarian.

grammatical, -aux [gramatikal, -o] *a.* grammatical.

grammaticalement [gramatikalmɑ̃] *adv.* grammatically.

gramme [gram] *n.m. Meas:* gram(me) (= 0·0353 oz.).

gramme-force [gramfɔrs] *n.m. Ph:* gram weight; *pl. grammes-force.*

gramme-poids [grampwa] *n.m. Ph:* gram weight; *pl. grammes-poids.*

gramophone [gramɔfɔn] *n.m. O:* gramophone.

grand, grande [grɑ̃, grɑ̃d] *a.* **1.** (*a*) tall (in stature), large, big (in size); **homme g.,** tall man; **un g. homme blond,** a tall, fair man; **pas plus g. que ça,** only so high; **grande ville,** large town; **grande échelle,** tall, long, ladder; **grands bras, grandes jambes,** long arms, legs; **grands pieds,** big feet; **grande distance,** great distance; **plus g. que nature,** larger than life; **une grande heure,** a full, good, hour; *Opt:* **objectif g. angle,** wide angle lens; **un g. A,** a capital A; **le G. Montréal,** Greater Montreal; (*b*) chief, main; **g. chemin,** main road, highway, high road; **la grande rue,** the high street, *NAm:* main street; **grandes marées,** spring tides; *Nau:* **le g. mât,** the mainmast; **la grande messe,** high mass; **g. ressort,** mainspring; **les grandes vacances,** the long vacation, the summer holidays; (*c*) **quand tu seras g.,** when you're grown up, when you're old enough; **elle se fait grande,** (i) she's growing up; (ii) she's growing tall; **les grandes personnes,** the grown-ups; *Sch:* **les grandes classes,** the upper forms; **un g. garçon,** a big boy; **son g. frère,** his big brother; (*d*) *adv.* **faire g.,** to do things in a big way, on a large scale; **voir g.,** to have big ideas; **ouvrir la fenêtre toute grande,** to open the window wide; **yeux grands ouverts,** wide-open eyes; **en g.,** (i) on a large scale; (ii) full size; **faire les choses en g.,** to do things on a grand scale; **statue en g.,** life-size statue; **reproduction en g.,** enlarged copy;

ouvrir toutes les fenêtres en g., to open all the windows wide; **ouvrir un robinet en g.,** to turn a tap *NAm:* a faucet, full on. **2. pas g. monde,** not many people; **le g. public,** the general public; **dans le plus g. détail,** in the fullest detail; **en grande partie,** largely, to a great extent. **3.** (*of worth, rank, fame*) **les grands hommes,** great men; **le g. monde,** (high) society; **grands vins,** vintage wines; **Alexandre le G.,** Alexander the Great; **se donner de grands airs,** to give oneself airs; **une grande dame,** a great lady, a grand lady. **4.** (*of moral, intellectual, qualities*) **grandes pensées,** great, noble, thoughts; **se montrer g.,** to show oneself magnanimous; **la grande manière,** the grand manner. **5.** great; **une grande découverte,** a great discovery; **ils sont grands amis,** they are great friends; **avec le plus g. plaisir,** with the greatest pleasure; **g. froid,** severe cold; **il fait g. jour,** it's broad daylight; **il est g. temps de partir,** it's high time we left; **grandes pluies,** heavy rains; **g. vent,** high wind; **g. bruit,** loud noise; **g. buveur,** heavy, hard, drinker; **les grands blessés,** the seriously wounded; **les grands infirmes,** the badly disabled; *Tex:* **couleur g. teint,** fast dye. **6.** *n.* (*a*) *n.m.* **g. (d'Espagne),** grandee; (*b*) **grands et petits,** old and young; grown-ups and children; *Sch:* **les grand(e)s,** the senior boys, girls; (*c*) **les grands de la terre,** the great of the earth, of this world; **les grands,** great men; (*d*) *Pol:* **les Grands,** the Great Powers; **les Quatre Grands,** the Big Four.

grand-angulaire [grɑ̃tɑ̃gylɛr] *a. & n.m. Opt:* wide-angle (lens, etc.); *pl. grand(e)s-angulaires.*

grand-chose [grɑ̃ʃoz] **1.** *indef.pron. m.inv.* (*usu. coupled with* **pas** *or* **sans**) **il ne fait pas g.-c.,** he doesn't do much; **il ne sera, ne fera, jamais g.-c.,** he'll never amount to much; **cela ne fait pas g.-c.,** it's of no great importance, it doesn't matter much; **cela ne vaut pas g.-c.,** it's not worth much. **2.** *n. F:* **un, une, pas g.-c.,** a good-for-nothing; a dead loss; a wet.

grand-croix [grɑ̃krwa] **1.** *n.f.inv.* Grand Cross (of the Legion of Honour). **2.** *n.m.* Knight Grand Cross; *pl. grands-croix.*

grand-duc [grɑ̃dyk] *n.m.* **1.** grand duke. **2.** *Orn:* great horned owl, eagle owl. **3.** *F:* **faire la tournée des grands-ducs,** to go out on the town, round the night clubs; *pl. grands-ducs.*

grand-ducal, -aux [grɑ̃dykal, -o] *a.* grand-ducal.

grand-duché [grɑ̃dyʃe] *n.m.* grand duchy; *pl. grands-duchés.*

Grande-Bretagne [grɑ̃dbrətaɲ] *Pr.n.f. Geog:* Great Britain.

grande-duchesse [grɑ̃ddyʃɛs] *n.f.* grand duchess; *pl. grandes-duchesses.*

grandelet, -ette [grɑ̃dlɛ, -ɛt] *a. F:* tallish; quite, fairly, big.

grandement [grɑ̃dmɑ̃] *adv.* **1.** grandly, nobly; **faire les choses g.,** to do things lavishly, on a grand scale. **2.** greatly, largely; **se tromper g.,** to be greatly mistaken; **avoir g. raison,** to be completely, absolutely, right; **avoir g. le temps,** to have ample time; **il est g. temps de . . .,** it is high time to . . .; **avoir g. de quoi vivre,** to have plenty to live on.

grandeur [grɑ̃dœr] *n.f.* **1.** (*a*) size; height (of tree); bulk (of parcel); **échelle de grandeurs,** scale of sizes; **g. nature,** full-size(d); life-size(d); (*b*) loudness (of noise); (*c*) extent (of voyage); scale (of undertaking). **2.** greatness; (*a*) importance; magnitude (of offence); grandeur (of conception); (*b*) grandeur; majesty, splendour, *NAm:* splendor; **la g. de Rome,** the greatness of Rome; **regarder qn du haut de sa g.,** to look down on s.o.; (*c*) nobility (of character, etc.). **3. sa G.,** his Highness; **sa G. l'archevêque,** his Grace the Archbishop; **votre G.,** your Highness; your Grace; your Lordship.

grandiloquence [grɑ̃dilɔkɑ̃s] *n.f.* grandiloquence.

grandiloquent [grɑ̃dilɔkɑ̃] *a.* grandiloquent.

grandiose [grɑ̃djoz] (*a*) *a.* grand, imposing; grandiose; (imposing, awe-inspiring) spectacle.

grandir [grɑ̃dir] **1.** *v.i.* (*a*) (i) to grow tall; (ii) to grow up; **il a grandi,** he has grown, he is taller; **il a grandi l'année dernière,** he shot up last year; **en grandissant,** as one grows up, as one grows older; (*b*) **g. en sagesse,** to grow in wisdom; **son influence grandit,** his influence is increasing, growing. **2.** *v.tr.* (*a*) to make (sth.) greater, to increase; **ses talons la grandissent,** her heels make her look taller; **se g. en se haussant sur la pointe des pieds,** to make oneself taller by standing on tiptoe; (*b*) **ses malheurs l'ont grandi,** he is all the greater for his misfortunes; (*c*) to magnify, exaggerate (an incident).

grandissant [grɑ̃disɑ̃] *a.* growing, increasing; **tempête grandissante,** rising storm.

grandissement [grɑ̃dismɑ̃] *n.m.* (*a*) *O:* growth, increase; (*b*) *Opt:* magnification.

grand(-)livre [grɑ̃livr̥] *n.m. Com:* ledger; *pl. grands(-)livres.*

grand-maman [grɑ̃mamɑ̃] *n.f. F:* grandma, granny, nan, grandmamma; *pl. grand(s)-mamans.*

grand-mère [grɑ̃mɛr] *n.f.* (*a*) grandmother; (*b*) *F:* old woman; *pl. grand(s)-mères.*

grand-messe [grɑ̃mɛs] *n.f. Ecc:* high mass; *pl. grand(s)-messes.*

grand-oncle [grɑ̃tɔ̃kl̥] *n.m.* great-uncle; *pl. grands-oncles.*

grand-papa [grɑ̃papa] *n.m. F:* grandpa, grandad; grandpapa; *pl. grands-papas.*

grand-peine (à) [agrɑ̃pɛn] *adv.phr.* with great difficulty.

grand-père [grɑ̃pɛr] *n.m.* grandfather; *pl. grands-pères.*

grand-prêtre [grɑ̃prɛtr̥] *n.m.* high priest; *pl. grands-prêtres.*

grand-route [grɑ̃rut] *n.f.* highway, highroad, main road; *pl. grand-routes.*

grand-rue [grɑ̃ry] *n.f.* high street, main street; *pl. grand-rues.*

grands-parents [grɑ̃parɑ̃] *n.m.pl.* grandparents.

grand-tante [grɑ̃tɑ̃t] *n.f.* great aunt; *pl. grand(s)-tantes.*

grand-vergue [grɑ̃vɛrg] *n.f. Nau:* mainyard; *pl. grand(s)-vergues.*

grand-voile [grɑ̃vwal] *n.f. Nau:* mainsail; *pl. grand(s)-voiles.*

grange [grɑ̃ʒ] *n.f.* barn.

granit(e) [granit] *n.m.* granite; **cœur de g.,** heart of stone.

granité [granite] **1.** *a.* granite-like. **2.** *n.m. Tex:* pebble weave.

graniteux, -euse [granitø, -øz], **granitique** [granitik] *a.* granitic; granite (formation).

granivore [granivɔr] **1.** *a.* granivorous. **2.** *n.* granivore.

granulaire [granylɛr] *a.* granular.

granulation [granylasjɔ̃] *n.f.* granulation.

granule [granyl] *n.m.* granule.

granulé [granyle] **1.** *a.* granulated. **2.** *n.m.* (*a*) *Pharm:* pellet; (*b*) granule; **g. chocolaté,** granulated chocolate.

granuler [granyle] *v.tr.* **1.** to granulate. **2.** *Engr:* to stipple.

granuleux, -euse [granylø, -øz] *a.* granular, granulous; *Biol:* **cellule granuleuse,** granule cell.

grape(-)fruit [grɛpfrut] *n.m. Bot: F:* grapefruit.

graphe [graf] *n.m.* graph.

graphie [grafi] *n.f.* **1.** method of writing. **2.** *Ling:* graph.

graphique [grafik] **1.** *a.* graphic (sign, method etc.); graphical (method). **2.** *n.m.* diagram; graph; (patient's) temperature chart; **g. à barres, à bandes,** bar chart; **g. à secteurs,** pie chart. **3.** *n.f.* graphics; graphic arts.

graphiquement [grafikmɑ̃] *adv.* graphically.

graphitage [grafitaʒ] *n.m. Tchn:* graphitizing, graphitization.

graphite [grafit] *n.m.* graphite.

graphité [grafite] *a.* **huile graphitée,** graphite oil.

graphiter [grafite] *v.tr.* to graphitize; *Cmptr:* to mark-sense.

graphiteux, -euse [grafitø,-øz], **graphitique** [grafitik] *a.* graphitic.

graphologie [grafɔlɔʒi] *n.f.* graphology.

graphologique [grafɔlɔʒik] *a.* graphological.

graphologue [grafɔlɔg] *n.* graphologist.

grappe [grap] *n.f.* **1.** (*a*) cluster, bunch (of grapes, etc.); **g. de (deux ou trois) cerises,** cherry bob; **g. d'oignons,** string of onions; (*b*) cluster, group (of people). **2.** *Bot:* raceme.

grappillage [grapijaʒ] *n.m.* **1.** gleaning (of grapes). **2.** (*a*) making of petty profits; (*b*) scrounging.

grappiller [grapije] *v.tr. & i.* **1.** to glean (in vineyard). **2.** (*a*) to make petty (illicit) profits; to make sth. on the side; (*b*) to pilfer, cadge, scrounge.

grappin [grapɛ̃] *n.m.* **1.** (*a*) *Nau:* grapnel, hook, grappling anchor; *F:* **mettre le g. sur qch., qn,** to hook, lay hands on, get hold of, sth., s.o.; (*b*) **g. à main,** drag, creeper; (*c*) *Hyd.E:* grab (dredger); (*d*) clutch (of crane). **2.** *pl.* climbing irons.

gras, grasse [grɑ, grɑs] *a.* **1.** (*a*) fat (meat); fatty (tissues); **matières grasses,** fats; (*b*) rich (food, pastures, etc.); **mardi g.,** Shrove Tuesday; **faire g., manger g.,** to eat meat (*esp.* on a fast day); **fromage g.,** full cream cheese; (*c*) *n.m.* fat (of meat). **2.** (*a*) fat, stout (person); *n.* **les g. et les maigres,** fat and thin people; **g. comme un porc,** as fat as a pig; **être g. comme un cent de clous,** to be as thin as a lath; (*b*) fatted, fat (animal); plump (chicken); **tuer le veau g.,** to kill the fatted calf. **3.** greasy, oily (rag, hair, etc.); **eaux grasses,** swill, swillings; *Th:* **crayon g.,** stick of greasepaint; *Ch:* **acide g.,** fatty acid; *Toil:* **crème grasse,** cream for dry skin. **4.** thick; (*a*) heavy, clayey (soil); **boue grasse,** thick, slimy, mud; **il fait g. à marcher,** it is slippery under foot; **vin g.,** ropy wine; **toux grasse,** loose, phlegmy, cough; **voix grasse,** oily voice; **avoir le parler g., parler g.,** (i) = GRASSEYER; (ii) to have a thick voice; *adv.* **rire g.,** to give a deep chuckle; **temps g.,** thick, foggy, weather; (*b*) **poutre grasse,** thick beam; **plante grasse,** succulent (plant); *Typ:* **caractères g.,** heavy, bold(-faced), type; *P:* **il n'y en a pas g.,** there's not much of it; *n.m.* **le g. de la jambe,** the calf of the leg; (*c*) *O:* dirty, smutty (story, etc.). **5.** soft; **contours g.,** softened, woolly, outlines; **pierre grasse,** soft stone.

gras-double [grɑdubl] *n.m. Cu:* tripe.

grassement [grɑsmɑ̃] *adv.* **1. vivre g.,** to live in plenty, on the fat of the land; **rire g.,** to give a deep chuckle. **2. récompenser qn g.,** to reward s.o. handsomely, generously.

grasseyement [grasɛjmɑ̃] *n.m.* (*a*) strongly marked r (in speech); (*b*) exaggerated rolling of uvular r.

grasseyer [graseje] *v.i.* (*a*) to speak with a strongly marked r; (*b*) to speak with a strong uvular r, to roll one's r's.

grassouillet, -ette [grɑsujɛ, -ɛt] *a.* plump (person); chubby (child).

grateron [gratrɔ̃] *n.m. Bot:* goose-grass, cleavers.

graticuler [gratikyle] *v.tr.* to divide (drawing, etc.) into squares.

gratification [gratifikasjɔ̃] *n.f.* **1.** (*a*) gratuity; tip; (*b*) bonus, bounty; **g. du jour de l'an** = Christmas (i) box, (ii) bonus. **2.** *Psy:* gratification.

gratifier [gratifje] *v.tr.* (*impf. & pr.sub.* **n. gratifiions, v. gratifiiez**) (*a*) to present (**qn de qch.,** s.o. with sth.); *Iron:* **être gratifié d'une amende,** to be landed with a fine; (*b*) *Psy:* to gratify (s.o.).

gratin [gratɛ̃] *n.m.* **1.** *Cu:* (*a*) (seasoned) breadcrumbs; cheese topping; **au g.,** (cooked) with (breadcrumbs and) grated cheese; **chou-fleur au g.** = cauliflower cheese; (*b*) dish cooked *au gratin.* **2.** *F:* **le g.,** the upper crust (of society); the pick of the basket.

gratiné, -ée [gratine] **1.** *a.* (*a*) *Cu:* sprinkled with (breadcrumbs and) cheese; *au gratin*; (*b*) *F:* **une addition gratinée,** a bill to beat all bills, an enormous bill; **c'est g.!** it's a bit much! **2.** *n.f. Cu:* (onion) soup *au gratin.*

gratiner [gratine] *v.tr.* to cook (sth.) *au gratin.*

gratis [gratis] **1.** *adv.* gratis, for nothing, free of charge; **entrée g.,** admission free. **2.** *a.* free (ticket, etc.).

gratitude [gratityd] *n.f.* gratitude, gratefulness.

grattage [grataʒ] *n.m.* **1.** *Tex:* teaseling, napping, raising. **2.** (*a*) scraping (off); (*b*) erasure (of writing); scratching out; (*c*) *Surg:* scraping (of a bone).

gratte [grat] *n.f. F:* pickings, rake-off; perks; fringe benefits; profits on the side; **faire de la g.,** to get a rake-off; to make a bit on the side. **2.** *Fr.C:* (snow) plough.

gratte-ciel [gratsjɛl] *n.m.inv.* skyscraper; high rise building.

gratte-dos [gratdo] *n.m.inv.* backscratcher.

grattement [gratmɑ̃] *n.m.* **1.** scratching. **2.** *F:* itching.

gratte-papier [gratpapje] *n.m.inv. Pej:* **1.** penpusher. **2.** (junior) clerk; (lawyer's) copying clerk.

gratte-pieds [gratpje] *n.m.inv.* (metal) doormat.

gratter [grate] **1.** *v.tr.* (*a*) to scrape, scratch; (*of horse*) **g. (la terre) du pied,** to paw the ground; **se g. la tête, l'oreille,** to scratch one's head, one's ear; *P:* **tu peux toujours te g.!** you can whistle for it! nothing doing! *F:* **ça me gratte terriblement,** it makes me itch like mad; **vin qui gratte le gosier,** wine that rasps the throat; *F:* **g. les fonds de tiroir,** to scrape the barrel; **c'est une affaire ou il n'y a pas grand-chose à g.,** you can't make much out of that; (*b*) *Tex:* to teasel, raise, nap (of cloth); **laine grattée,** brushed wool; (*c*) to erase, scratch out (a word, etc.); (*d*) *F:* to overtake, pass (a competitor, another car). **2.** *v.i.* (*a*) **g. à la porte,** to scratch at the door; (*b*) **g. du violon, g. de la guitare,** to scrape on the fiddle, to strum away on the guitar; (*c*) **plume qui gratte,** scratchy nib.

gratteron [gratrɔ̃] *n.m. Bot:* goose grass, cleavers.

gratteur, -euse [gratœr, -øz] *n.* scratcher.

grattoir [gratwar] *n.m.* scraper; *Typ:* slice; **g. de bureau,** erasing knife, scraper eraser.

gratuit [gratɥi] *a.* (*a*) free (of charge); **à titre g.,** gratis, free of charge; (*b*) gratuitous (insult, etc.).

gratuité [gratɥite] *n.f.* (*a*) exemption from payment; **la g. de l'enseignement,** free education; (*b*) gratuitousness (of insult, etc.).

gratuitement [gratɥitmɑ̃] *adv.* (*a*) for nothing, free of charge; (*b*) gratuitously; without provocation.

gravats [gravɑ] *n.m.pl.* **1.** screenings (of plaster). **2.** (plaster) rubbish, rubble.

grave [grav] **I.** *a.* **1.** (*a*) *A:* heavy; (*b*) *Ph:* **corps g.,** heavy body. **2.** (*a*) grave, serious (mistake, face); grave, solemn (tone); sober (expression); (*b*) important, weighty (business); (*c*) severe, serious (wound); **subir une g. opération,** to undergo a serious operation; **hélas! il y avait plus g.,** alas! there was worse to come. **3.** *Mus: etc:* low(-pitched), deep (note, voice); **sons graves,** bass tones. **4.** *Gram:* **accent g.,** grave accent. **II.** *n.m.* **1. le g.,** serious matters, things. **2.** low(-pitched), deep, note; bass.

gravé [grave] *a.* (*a*) **pierre gravée,** engraved stone; **image gravée,** graven image; (*b*) (*of metals, skin, etc.*) pitted.
gravelé [gravle] (*a*) *a.* **allée gravelée,** gravel path; (*b*) *a. & n.f. Com:* **(cendre) gravelée,** pearl ash.
graveleux, -euse [gravlø, -øz] *a.* **1.** gravelly (soil); gritty (pencil, pear). **2.** smutty, rude (story, song).
gravelle [gravɛl] *n.f. Med: A:* gravel.
gravelure [gravlyr] *n.f.* smutty talk, story.
gravement [gravmɑ̃] *adv.* **1.** gravely, solemnly, soberly. **2.** seriously (ill); **il s'est g. trompé,** he was seriously, greatly, mistaken. **3.** *Mus:* in slow tempo.
graver [grave] *v.tr.* to cut, engrave, carve (material, design); *Rec:* to cut (record); **g. à l'eau-forte,** to etch; **gravé par le feu,** burnt in; **cela reste gravé dans ma mémoire,** it remains graven on my memory.
graveur [gravœr] **1.** *n.m.* engraver; carver (on stone, etc.); **g. à l'eau-forte,** etcher; **g. sur bois,** wood engraver, woodcutter. **2.** *a.* **bain g.,** etching bath.
gravide [gravid] *a.* gravid, pregnant.
gravier [gravje] *n.m.* gravel, grit; **terrain de g.,** gravelly soil; **couvrir un chemin de g.,** to gravel a path.
gravillon [gravijɔ̃] *n.m.* fine gravel; grit; *P.N:* **gravillons,** loose chippings, *NAm:* gravel.
gravillonnage [gravijɔnaʒ] *n.m.* fine gravelling; gritting.
gravillonner [gravijɔne] *v.tr.* to (fine-)gravel (path, etc.); to grit (a road).
gravillonneuse [gravijɔnøz] *n.f.* (*machine*) gravel spreader; grit spreader; gritter.
gravimétrie [gravimetri] *n.f. Ph:* gravimetry.
gravimétrique [gravimetrik] *a. Ph:* gravimetric.
gravir [gravir] **1.** *v.i.* **g. sur qch.,** to climb, clamber, on to sth. **2.** *v.tr.* to climb (mountain, stairs); to climb, mount (ladder).
gravitation [gravitasjɔ̃] *n.f.* gravitation.
gravité [gravite] *n.f.* **1.** *Ph:* gravity; **g. spécifique,** specific gravity; **centre de g.,** centre of gravity; **alimentation par g.,** gravity feed. **2.** (*a*) gravity, seriousness; soberness (of bearing); (*b*) severity, seriousness (of illness); seriousness (of operation); **blessure sans g.,** slight wound. **3.** *Mus:* low pitch, deepness (of note).
graviter [gravite] *v.i.* **1.** to gravitate (**vers,** towards). **2.** to revolve (**autour de,** round); **g. autour de la terre,** to orbit the earth.
gravois [gravwa] *n.m.pl. O:* =GRAVATS.
gravure [gravyr] *n.f.* **1.** engraving; **g. sur bois** woodcutting; wood engraving; **g. en taille-douce,** copperplate engraving; **g. en creux,** (i) intaglio engraving; (ii) die sinking; (iii) etching; **g. à l'eau-forte,** etching. **2.** print; engraving; etching; **g. en taille-douce, g. sur cuivre,** copperplate; **g. sur bois,** woodcut; wood engraving; **g. en couleurs,** colour print; **g. hors texte,** full-page plate; **g. avant la lettre,** proof before letters. **3.** carving (on stone, wood, etc.). **4.** *Rec:* cutting (of record).
gré [gre] *n.m.* **1.** liking, taste; **à mon g., selon mon g.,** (i) to my liking, to my taste; (ii) in my opinion; **je m'habille à mon g.,** I dress to please myself; **une chambre à mon g.,** a room that I like, that suits me. **2.** will, pleasure; **se marier contre le g. de son père,** to get married against one's father's wishes; **bail renouvelable au g. du locataire,** lease renewable at the option of the tenant; **de mon propre g., de mon plein g.,** of my own free will, of my own accord; **de bon g.,** willingly; gladly; **de mauvais g.,** reluctantly; **elle va et vient à son (bon) g.,** she comes and goes as she pleases; **bon g. mal g.,** whether we like it or not; willy-nilly; **de g. ou de force,** willy-nilly; by fair means or foul; **au g. des flots,** at the mercy of the waves; **de g. à g.,** by (mutual) agreement. **3. savoir (bon) g. à qn de (faire) qch.,** to be grateful to s.o. for (doing) sth.; **savoir mauvais g. à qn de qch.,** to be annoyed with s.o. about sth.
grèbe [grɛb] *n.m. Orn:* grebe.
grébiche [grebiʃ], **grébige** [grebiʒ] *n.f.* **1.** file number (of MS, etc.). **2.** looseleaf binder. **3.** printer's imprint.
grec, grecque [grɛk] **1.** *a.* (*a*) Greek; Grecian; **les orateurs grecs,** the Greek orators; **coiffure à la grecque,** hair done in the Grecian style; **profil g.,** Grecian profile; (*b*) **Église grecque,** Greek Orthodox church. **2.** *n.* Greek. **3.** *n.m. Ling:* Greek. **4.** *n.f. Arch: Art:* Greek key pattern, Greek border.
Grèce [grɛs] *Pr.n.f. Geog:* Greece.
gréciser [gresize] *v.tr.* to Hellenize, to Gr(a)ecize; **g. une phrase,** to give a Greek turn to a phrase.
gréco-latin, -ine [grekɔlatɛ̃, -in] *a. Ling:* Gr(a)eco-Latin; *pl. gréco-latin(e)s.*
gréco-romain, -aine [grekɔrɔmɛ̃, -ɛn] *a.* Gr(a)eco-Roman; *pl. gréco-romain(e)s.*
gredin, -ine [grədɛ̃, -in] *n.* (*a*) rogue, scoundrel; (*b*) *F:* rascal, wretch; **petit g.!** you little horror!
gredinerie [grədinri] *n.f. O:* low, mean, underhand, unscrupulous, (i) behaviour, (ii) action.
gréement [gremɑ̃] *n.m. Nau:* **1.** rigging. **2.** rig (of ship); *Y:* **g. Marconi,** Bermuda rig. **3.** gear (of boat, etc.).
gréer [gree] *v.tr. Nau:* (*a*) to rig (mast, vessel, etc.); **gréé en carré,** square-rigged; (*b*) to sling (hammock, nets); (*c*) **g. une vergue,** to send up a yard.
gréeur [greœr] *n.m. Nau:* rigger.
greffage [grɛfaʒ] *n.m. Hort: Surg:* grafting.
greffe[1] [grɛf] *n.f.* **1.** (*a*) *Hort:* graft, scion, slip; (*b*) *Surg:* graft (of skin, tissue, etc.); transplant (of organ); **g. cutanée,** skin graft; **g. du cœur, du rein,** heart, kidney, transplant. **2.** grafting; (*a*) *Hort:* **g. par œil détaché,** budding; **g. en écusson,** shield grafting, budding; (*b*) *Surg:* **g. épidermique,** skin grafting.
greffe[2] *n.m.* **1.** *Jur:* office of the clerk of the court. **2.** *Fin:* registry (of joint stock company).
greffer [grefe] *v.tr. Hort: Surg:* to graft; **g. un rein,** to transplant a kidney.
greffeur [grefœr] *n.m. Arb: Hort:* grafter, budder.
greffier [grefje] *n.m.* **1.** *Jur:* clerk (of the court). **2.** *Adm: Fin:* registrar.
greffoir [grɛfwar] *n.m.* grafting knife.
greffon [grɛfɔ̃] *n.m.* (*a*) *Arb: Hort:* graft, scion, slip; (*b*) *Surg:* graft, transplant.
grégaire [gregɛr] *a.* gregarious.
grégarisme [gregarism] *n.m.* gregariousness.
grège [grɛʒ] *a.* raw (silk).
grégeois [greʒwa] *a.m. A:* (= GREC) **feu g.,** Greek fire.
Grégoire [gregwar] *Pr.n.m.* Gregory.
grégorien, -ienne [gregɔrjɛ̃, -jɛn] *a.* Gregorian (chant, etc.).
grêle[1] [grɛl] *a.* slender, thin (leg, stalk, etc.); thin, high-pitched (voice); *Anat:* **intestin g.,** small intestine.
grêle[2] *n.f.* hail; **orage accompagné de g.,** hailstorm; **g. de coups, de balles,** hail, shower, of blows, of bullets.
grêlé [grele] *a.* pockmarked.
grêler [grele] **1.** *v.impers.* **il grêle,** it's hailing. **2.** *v.tr.* to damage, destroy (crops, etc.) by hail.
grelin [grəlɛ̃] *n.m. Nau:* hawser; rope.
grêlon [grɛlɔ̃] *n.m.* hailstone.
grelot [grəlo] *n.m.* (small globular) bell; sleigh bell; *Fig:* **attacher le g.,** to bell the cat; *P:* **avoir les grelots,** to be scared, have the wind up.
grelottement [grəlɔtmɑ̃] *n.m.* (*a*) shivering; (*b*) tinkling, jingling (like bells).
grelotter [grəlɔte] *v.i.* **1.** to tremble, shake, shiver (with cold, fear, etc.). **2.** to jingle, tinkle.

grenade[1] [grənad] *n.f.* **1.** *Bot:* pomegranate (fruit). **2.** (*a*) *Mil:* grenade; **g. à main,** hand grenade; **g. fumigène,** smoke grenade; (*b*) *Navy:* **g. sous-marine,** depth charge.

Grenade[2] *Pr.n.f. Geog:* **1.** Granada (Spain). **2.** Grenada (Windward Islands).

grenadier[1] [grənadje] *n.m. Bot:* pomegranate (tree).

grenadier[2] *n.m.* (*a*) *Mil:* grenadier; **boire comme un g.,** to drink like a fish; (*b*) tall, masculine woman; amazon.

grenadière [grənadjɛr] *n.f. Mil:* band (of rifle).

grenadine [grənadin] *n.f.* **1.** *Tex:* grenadine. **2.** grenadine; pomegranate (syrup).

grenaillage [grənɑjaʒ] *n.m. Tchn:* shot blasting.

grenaille [grənɑj] *n.f.* **1.** *Agr:* refuse grain, tailings. **2.** granular metal; shot; **g. de plomb,** lead shot. **3.** *P.N: Belg:* **grenailles errantes,** loose chippings, *NAm:* gravel.

grenailler [grənɑje] *v.tr.* to granulate (metal, etc.).

grenaison [grənɛzɔ̃] *n.f.* seeding (of cereals, etc.).

grenat [grəna] **1.** *n.m. Lap:* garnet. **2.** *a.inv.* garnet-red.

grené [grəne] **1.** *a.* stippled. **2.** *n.m.* stipple.

greneler [grənle] *v.tr.* **(je grenelle, n. grenelons; je grenellerai)** to grain (paper, leather).

grener [grəne] *v.* **(je grène, n. grenons; je grènerai) 1.** *v.i.* (*of cereals, etc.*) to seed. **2.** *v.tr.* (*a*) to granulate (gunpowder); to shred (wax); to grain (salt); (*b*) to grain (paper, leather).

grènetis [grɛnti] *n.m.* milled edge (of coin).

greneur [grənœr] *n.m. Engr: Typ:* (*pers.*) grainer; stippler.

grenier [grənje] *n.m.* **1.** granary, storehouse; **l'Égypte était le g. de l'ancien monde,** Egypt was the granary of the ancient world; **g. à foin, à blé,** hayloft, cornloft. **2.** attic, garret; **chercher qch. de la cave au g.,** to hunt for sth. from cellar to garret, high and low. **3.** *Nau:* dunnage.

grenouillage [grənujaʒ] *n.m. F:* shady dealing, wangling.

grenouille [grənuj] *n.f.* **1.** frog; **g. bœuf, g. mugissante,** bullfrog; *F:* **g. de bénitier,** bigoted churchwoman, church hen. **2.** *F:* = piggy bank; **manger la g.,** to make off with the cash.

grenu [grəny] **1.** (*of wheat, etc.*) grainy, full of grain. **2.** (*a*) granular (fracture, etc.); (*b*) grained (leather, etc.); (*c*) coarse-grained, crystalline (salt). **3.** *n.m.* granularity (of marble, etc.).

grenure [grənyr] *n.f.* **1.** *Art:* stippling, stipple. **2.** *Leath:* grain(ing).

grès [grɛ] *n.m.* **1.** sandstone; **g. rouge,** red sandstone; **g. bigarré,** Bunter, new red, sandstone; **g. à bâtir, de construction,** freestone, brownstone; **g. à meule,** millstone grit; **g. à pavés,** paving stone. **2. poterie de g., g. cérame,** stoneware; **cruche de g.,** stone jug.

gréseux, -euse [grezø, -øz] *a.* **1.** gritty, sandy. **2. roches gréseuses,** sandstones.

grésil [grezi(l)] *n.m.* sleet; hail; frozen rain.

grésillement[1] [grezijmɑ̃] *n.m.* pattering (of sleet).

grésillement[2] *n.m.* crackling (of fire); sputtering of flame); sizzling (of frying pan).

grésiller[1] [grezije] *v.impers.* to sleet, hail.

grésiller[2] *v.i.* (*a*) (*of fire*) to crackle; (*of flame*) to sputter; (*of frying pan*) to sizzle.

gressin [gresɛ̃] *n.m. Cu:* bread stick.

grève [grɛv] *n.f.* **1.** (*a*) (sea)shore, (sandy) beach; *Lit:* strand; (*b*) (sandy) bank, *Lit:* strand (of river); **les grèves de la Loire,** the sandbanks of the Loire; *Hist:* **la (place de) G.,** the Strand (open space on the banks of the Seine where dissatisfied workmen used to assemble). **2.** (*from* 1 (*b*)) strike; walkout; **se mettre en g.,** to go, come out, on strike; to strike; to take strike action, industrial action; **être en., faire g.,** to be on strike; **g. d'avertissement, g. symbolique,** token strike; **g. générale,** general strike; **g. perlée,** go-slow (strike); **g. sauvage,** wildcat strike; **g. de solidarité,** sympathy strike; **g. surprise,** lightning strike; **g. sur le tas,** sit-down strike; **g. tournante,** staggered strike; **g. du zèle,** work(ing) to rule; **briseur de g.,** strike breaker; **g. de la faim,** hunger strike.

grever [grəve] *v.tr.* **(je grève, n. grevons; je grèverai) 1.** to burden, encumber (estate); **grevé d'un impôt,** saddled with a tax. **2.** *Jur:* (*a*) to entail (estate); (*b*) to mortgage (property). **3.** *Adm:* to lay, impose, a rate on (a building).

gréviste [grevist] **1.** *n.* striker; **g. de la faim,** hunger striker. **2.** *a.* **mouvement g.,** strike movement.

gribouillage [gribujaʒ] *n.m.* scrawl; scribble; doodle.

gribouille [gribuj] *n.m.* simpleton, nitwit, clot.

gribouiller [gribuje] *v.i. & tr.* to scribble, scrawl; to doodle.

gribouilleur, -euse [gribujœr, -øz] *n.* scribbler, scrawler.

gribouillis [gribuji] *n.m.* = GRIBOUILLAGE.

grief [grijɛf] *n.m.* grievance, ground for complaint; **faire g. à qn de qch.,** to harbour resentment against s.o. on account of sth., to hold sth. against s.o.

grièvement [grijɛvmɑ̃] *adv.* seriously, severely, badly (wounded).

griffade [grifad] *n.f.* scratch (of the claw).

griffe [grif] *n.f.* **1.** (*a*) claw (of tiger, etc.); talon (of hawk); (*of cat*) **faire ses griffes,** to sharpen its claws; **coup de g.,** scratch; **donner un coup de g. à qn,** (i) to claw, scratch, s.o.; (ii) *Fig:* to have a dig at s.o.; **tomber sous les griffes de qn,** to fall into s.o.'s clutches; (*b*) *Mec.E: etc:* claw, clip, clamp; *Tls:* dog; **accouplement, embrayage, à griffes,** claw coupling, claw clutch; **griffes de monteur,** climbing irons; (*c*) *Bot:* tendril (of vine); crown (of asparagus). **2.** (*a*) stamped signature; (*b*) (signature) stamp; (*c*) (*on clothes*) label.

griffer [grife] *v.tr.* **1.** to scratch, claw. **2.** to stamp (circular, etc.) with a signature.

griffon [grifɔ̃] *n.m.* **1.** *Myth:* griffon, gryphon, griffin. **2.** griffon (terrier). **3.** *Orn:* griffon (vulture).

griffonnage [grifɔnaʒ] *n.m.* **1.** scribbling. **2.** (*a*) scrawl, scribble; doodle; (*b*) rough sketch.

griffonnement [grifɔnmɑ̃] *n.m. Art:* (*a*) preliminary, rough, sketch; (*b*) wax, clay, model.

griffonner [grifɔne] *v.tr. & i.* **1.** to scrawl, scribble (off) (letter, etc.); to scrawl; to doodle. **2.** to sketch (sth.) roughly.

griffu [grify] *a.* **patte griffue,** clawed foot; **main griffue,** claw of a hand, talon.

griffure [grifyr] *n.f.* scratch.

grigner [griɲe] *v.i.* (*of felt*) to pucker, crinkle up.

grignotage [griɲɔtaʒ] *n.m. Fig:* wearing down, away (of resistance, etc.).

grignotement [griɲɔtmɑ̃] *n.m.* nibbling.

grignoter [griɲɔte] *v.tr.* to nibble (at) sth., to pick at (food); **g. son capital,** to eat into one's capital; *F:* **il trouve toujours à g. qch.,** he always manages to make a bit on the side.

grignoteur, -euse [griɲɔtœr, -øz] *n.* **1.** (*pers.*) nibbler. **2.** *n.f. Tls:* nibbling machine.

grigou [grigu] *n.m. F:* miser, old screw; skinflint.

gri-gri [grigri] *n.m.* (West African) amulet.

gril [gri(l)] *n.m.* **1.** *Dom. Ec:* grid(iron), grill (pan), *N.Am:* broiler; **faire cuire qch. sur le g.,** to grill sth.; *F:* **être sur le g.,** to be on tenterhooks. **2.** *Hyd.E:* grating (protecting sluice gate); *Rail: Nau:* gridiron; *Th:* **le g.,** the upper flies. **3.** *Anat:* **g. costal,** rib cage.

grillade [grijad] *n.f. Cu:* grill; grilled meat, *esp.* steak; *NAm:* broil; *Fr.C:* grilled chop, cutlet.

grillage¹ [grijaʒ] *n.m.* **1.** *Cu:* (*a*) grilling, *NAm:* broiling (of meat); toasting (of bread); (*b*) roasting, (of nuts, etc.). **2.** calcining, roasting (of ores). **3.** *Tex:* singeing. **4.** *El:* (*a*) short circuit; (*b*) burning out (of bulb, etc.).

grillage² *n.m.* (*a*) (metal) grating, grill(e), latticework; **g. en fil de fer,** wire netting; (*b*) *El:* grid, frame (of accumulator plate).

grillager [grijaʒe] *v.tr.* **(je grillageai(s); n. grillageons) 1.** to fit latticework, a grill(e), on to (window, etc.); **fenêtre grillagée,** latticed window; **verre grillagé,** wired glass. **2.** to surround (court, etc.) with wire netting.

grille [grij] *n.f.* **1.** (*a*) (iron) bars; grill(e) (of convent parlour); trellis; grating, grid; screen, netting; **sous les grilles (d'une prison),** behind (prison) bars; **g. de comptoir,** counter grille (of bank, etc.); (*b*) iron gate, entrance gate (to grounds, etc.); (*c*) railings (round monument, etc.); **séparé de la rue par une g.,** railed off from the road; (*d*) grating, grate (of sink, drain, etc.); (*e*) **g. du foyer,** the bars of the grate; fire grate. **2.** *Aut:* gate (quadrant); **g. de radiateur,** radiator grille. **3.** *El:* grid ((i) of accumulator, (ii) of electron tube; **courant de g.,** grid current. **4.** (cipher) stencil. **5.** grid (of crossword).

grille-pain [grijpɛ̃] *n.m.inv.* toaster.

griller¹ [grije] **1.** *v.tr.* (*a*) to grill, *NAm:* broil (meat); to toast (bread); to roast (coffee, chestnuts); (*b*) to roast, calcine (ore); (*c*) *Tex:* to singe. **2.** *v.tr.* (*a*) to scorch, burn; **se g. les cheveux,** to singe one's hair; *F:* **g. une cigarette,** to smoke a cigarette; (*b*) *El:* to burn out (bulb, etc.); *P:* **il est grillé,** his game's up; (*c*) (*of sun, frost, etc.*) to scorch (vegetation); *Sp: F:* **g. un concurrent,** to race past a competitor; to leave a competitor standing; *Aut:* **g. un signal, le feu rouge,** to jump the lights; (*of bus, train*) **g. une étape, une station,** to go past a stop (without stopping). **3.** *v.i.* (*a*) *Cu:* (*of meat*) to grill; (*of bread*) to toast; (*of chestnuts*) to roast; (*b*) **g. d'impatience,** to be burning with impatience; **g. d'envie de faire qch.,** to be bursting, itching, to do sth.; (*c*) (*in guessing games, etc.*) to be warm.

griller² *v.tr.* **1.** (*a*) to rail in, rail off (garden, etc.); (*b*) to bar (window, etc.). **2.** *A:* to imprison (s.o.).

grilloir [grijwar] *n.m. Dom.Ec:* grill.

grillon [grijɔ̃] *n.m. Ent:* cricket.

grill-room [grilrum] *n.m.* grill (room); *pl. grill-rooms.*

grimaçant [grimasɑ̃] *a.* grimacing, grinning.

grimace [grimas] *n.f.* (*a*) grimace; wry face; **faire la g.,** to make, pull, a face; **faire une g. de douleur,** to wince; *Prov:* **on n'apprend pas à un vieux singe à faire des grimaces,** you can't teach an old dog new tricks; (*b*) **faire des grimaces,** to put on airs.

grimacer [grimase] *v.i.* **(je grimaçai(s); n. grimaçons)** to grimace; to make, pull, a face; **g. un sourire,** to force a smile; to give a wry smile.

grimacier, -ière [grimasje, -jɛr] **1.** *a.* (*a*) grimacing; grinning; (*b*) *O:* affected. **2.** *n.* (*a*) affected person; (*b*) hypocrite, humbug.

grimage [grimaʒ] *n.m. Th:* (*a*) making up; (*b*) makeup.

grimer [grime] *v.tr. & pr. Th:* to make up (an actor, one's face.

grimoire [grimwar] *n.m.* **1.** wizard's book of spells. **2.** gibberish, mumbo-jumbo. **3.** scrawl, illegible scribble.

grimpant [grɛ̃pɑ̃] **1.** *a.* climbing (animal); climbing, trailing, creeping (plant); **rose grimpante,** climbing rose; **plante grimpante,** creeper, climbing plant, *NAm:* vine. **2.** *n.m. P:* trousers, *NAm:* pants.

grimpée [grɛ̃pe] *n.f.* (stiff) climb.

grimper [grɛ̃pe] **1.** (*a*) *v.i.* to climb (up), clamber (up); **il a, est, grimpé sur la muraille,** he climbed (up) the wall; **g. au pouvoir,** to climb to power; (*b*) *v.tr.* to climb (a mountain); **g. l'escalier,** to go up the stairs. **2.** *v.i.* (*of plants, liquids*) to creep; (*of plants*) to climb; to trail.

grimpette [grɛ̃pɛt] *n.f. F:* steep climb; steep path.

grimpeur, -euse [grɛ̃pœr, -øz] **1.** *a.* climbing, scansorial (bird). **2.** *n.m.* climber; *Cy:* hill climber.

grinçant [grɛ̃sɑ̃] *a.* (*a*) creaking; grating; that sets one's teeth on edge; (*b*) caustic (remark).

grincement [grɛ̃smɑ̃] *n.m.* grinding, creaking, grating (of door, wheels, etc.); **g. de dents,** grinding, gnashing, of teeth.

grincer [grɛ̃se] *v.i.* **(je grinçai(s); n. grinçons)** (*a*) (*of door, wheels, etc.*) to grate; to grind; to creak; **g. des dents,** to grind, gnash, one's teeth; **cela fait g. les dents,** it sets one's teeth on edge; **porte qui grince sur ses gonds,** creaking door; **plume qui grince sur le papier,** scratchy pen; (*b*) (*of bat*) to squeak.

grincheux, -euse [grɛ̃ʃø, -øz] **1.** *a.* grumpy, bad-tempered. **2.** *n.* grumbler, grouser, moaner.

gringalet [grɛ̃galɛ] (*a*) *n.m.* (little) shrimp (of a man, boy); (*b*) *a.* puny.

griotte [grijɔt] *n.f.* **1.** *Bot:* morello (cherry). **2.** *Miner:* griotte (marble).

grippage [gripaʒ], **grippement** [gripmɑ̃] *n.m. Mch:* seizing, jamming, binding (of bearing, piston, etc.).

grippal, -aux [gripal, -o] *a. Med:* influenzal.

grippe [grip] *n.f.* **1.** (*a*) *A:* dislike, aversion; (*b*) **prendre qn en g.,** to take a dislike to s.o. **2.** *Med:* influenza; *F:* flu; *esp. NAm:* grippe; **g. gastro-intestinale,** gastric flu.

grippé [gripe] *a.* **1.** suffering from influenza, *esp. NAm:* from grippe. **2.** *Med:* pinched, drawn (face). **3.** seized(up) (engine, etc.).

gripper [gripe] **1.** *v.tr. Mec.E:* to seize up, jam (mechanism). **2.** *v.i. & pr.* (*a*) (*of material*) to crinkle (up), wrinkle, pucker; (*b*) *Mec.E:* (*of bearings*) (i) to run hot; (ii) to seize (up); to bind, jam.

grippe-sou [gripsu] *n.m.* miser, skinflint, money-grubber; *pl. grippe-sou(s).*

gris [gri] **1.** *a.* (*a*) grey, *NAm:* gray; **g. de poussière,** grey with dust; **papier g.,** (coarse) brown paper; **g. perle,** pearl grey; **g. (de) fer, g. acier,** iron grey, steel grey; **g. ardoise,** slate grey; **g.-bleu,** blue-grey; **g.-vert,** grey-green; **g. anthracite,** charcoal grey; (*of horse*) **g. pommelé,** dapple-grey; **robe g. clair,** light grey dress; *Hairdr:* **g. fumé, g. argent,** smoke grey; **aux cheveux g.,** silver grey (tint); grey-haired; *Anat:* **matière, substance, grise,** grey matter; (*b*) **vin g.,** rosé wine; (*c*) grey, cloudy, dull, overcast (weather); (*d*) **l'éminence grise,** the power behind the throne; (*e*) **faire grise mine,** to look anything but pleased; **faire grise mine à qn,** to give s.o. a poor welcome, the cold shoulder; **pensées grises,** grey, sombre, *NAm:* somber, thoughts; (*f*) (slightly) drunk, tipsy. **2.** *n.m.* (*a*) grey (colour); (*b*) grey horse; (*c*) (= **tabac g.**) = shag.

grisaille [grizɑj] *n.f.* (*a*) *Art:* grisaille; (*b*) *Engr:* tint drawing; *Lit:* **au soleil couchant la salle se remplit de grisaille(s),** at sunset the room is filled with grey shadows.

grisailler [grizɑje] **1.** *v.tr. Art:* to paint (sth.) (i) grey, *NAm:* gray, (ii) in grisaille. **2.** *v.i.* to (turn, become) grey.

grisant [grizɑ̃] *a.* intoxicating; heady; exhilarating.

grisâtre [grizɑtr̥] *a.* greyish, *NAm:* grayish.

grisbi [grizbi] *n.m. P:* money, dough, lolly.

griser [grize] **1.** *v.tr.* (*a*) to paint, tint, with grey, *NAm:* gray; (*b*) to make (s.o.) drunk, tipsy; **grisé par le succès,** intoxicated by, with, carried away by, success. **2. se g.,** to get drunk, tipsy.

griserie [grizri] *n.f.* **1.** tipsiness, intoxication. **2.** intoxication, exhilaration, excitement.

grisette [grizɛt] *n.f. A:* young dressmaker, milliner (of easy virtue); grisette.

gris-gris [grigri] *n.m.* (West African) amulet.

grisonnant [grizɔnɑ̃] *a.* greying, *NAm:* graying; touched with grey, *NAm:* gray.

grisonner [grizɔne] *v.i.* (*of pers., of hair*) to (grow, go, be going) grey, *NAm:* gray.

grisou [grizu] *n.m. Min:* firedamp; **coup de g.,** firedamp explosion.

grive [griv] *n.f. Orn:* thrush; *Prov:* **faute de grives on mange des merles,** beggars can't be choosers; half a loaf is better than no bread; **soûl comme une g.,** dead drunk.

grivelé [grivle] *a. A:* speckled (plumage).

grivèlerie [grivɛlri] *n.f. Jur:* (offence consisting of) ordering a meal in a restaurant without having the money to pay for it.

grivois, -oise [grivwa, -waz] *a.* risqué, rude, licentious (story, song, joke).

grivoiserie [grivwazri] *n.f.* risqué joke; licentious story; rude gesture.

grizzli, grizzly [grizli] *n.m. Z:* grizzly (bear).

Groenland [grɔɛnlɑ̃(d) *Pr.n.m. Geog:* Greenland; **au G.,** in Greenland.

groenlandais, -aise [grɔɛnlɑ̃dɛ, -ɛz] **1.** *Geog:* (*a*) *a.* from Greenland; (*b*) *n.* Greenlander. **2.** *n.m. Ling:* Greenlandic.

grog [grɔg] *n.m.* grog; toddy.

groggy [grɔgi] *a. Box: etc: F:* groggy.

grognard, -arde [grɔɲar, -ard] **1.** *O:* (*a*) *a.* grumbling; (*b*) *n.* grumbler. **2.** *n.m. Hist:* soldier of Napoleon's Old Guard.

grognement [grɔɲmɑ̃] *n.m.* **1.** grunt(ing) (of pig, etc.); growl(ing) (of dog, etc.); **pousser un g.,** to grunt, growl; to give a grunt, a growl. **2.** (*of pers.*) grumbling, grousing, moaning.

grogner [grɔɲe] *v.i.* **1.** (*of pig, etc.*) to grunt; (*of dog, etc.*) to growl. **2.** (*of pers.*) to grumble, grouse, moan; **g. un refus,** to growl out a refusal.

grognerie [grɔɲri] *n.f.* grumbling, growling, grousing, moaning.

grogneur, -euse [grɔɲœr, -øz] *a.* grumbling, grousing; **figure grogneuse,** sulky, disagreeable, face.

grognon [grɔɲɔ̃] **1.** *n.* grumbler, grouser, moaner. **2.** *a.* (*f.* **grognon** *or* **grognonne**) grumbling, peevish; **c'est une femme g., grognonne,** she's always moaning.

grognonner [grɔɲɔne] *v.i.* **1.** (*of pig, etc.*) to grunt. **2.** (*of pers.*) (*a*) to grouse, grumble, moan; (*b*) to be peevish.

groin [grwɛ̃] *n.m.* (*a*) snout (of pig, etc.); (*b*) ugly face.

grommeler [grɔmle] *v.i.* **(je grommelle, n. grommelons; je grommellerai)** to grumble, mutter; **g. un juron,** to mutter an oath.

grommellement [grɔmɛlmɑ̃] *n.m.* grumbling, muttering; rumbling (of thunder, etc.).

grondement [grɔ̃dmɑ̃] *n.m.* **1.** growl(ing), snarl(ing) (of dog, etc.). **2.** rumble, rumbling (of thunder); roar(ing) (of mountain torrent, engine, etc.); booming (of waves, guns, etc.).

gronder [grɔ̃de] **1.** *v.i.* (*a*) (*of dog, etc.*) to growl, snarl; (*b*) (*of thunder, etc.*) to rumble, roar; (*of guns, etc.*) to boom; (*of waves*) to roar; (*c*) *A: & Lit:* **g. contre qn,** to grumble at s.o., find fault with s.o. **2.** *v.tr.* **g. qn d'avoir fait qch.,** to scold s.o., tell s.o. off, for having done sth.

gronderie [grɔ̃dri] *n.f.* (severe) scolding.

grondeur, -euse [grɔ̃dœr, -øz] **1.** *a.* (*a*) grumbling, scolding, nagging (voice, etc.); (*b*) rumbling, roaring (storm, etc.). **2.** *n. O:* grumbler; *f.* scold, shrew.

grondin [grɔ̃dɛ̃] *n.m. Ich:* gurnard, gurnet.

groom [grum] *n.m.* **1.** *Equit: A:* groom. **2.** (*in hotel*) page, bellboy, *NAm:* bellhop.

gros, grosse [gro, gros] **1.** *a.* (*a*) big, bulky; large; stout; coarse; heavy; **grosse femme,** big, stout, woman; **g. morceau,** large piece; lump; **grosse corde,** thick, stout, rope; **g. pullover,** chunky sweater; **g. bout,** thick end (of stick, etc.); **g. murs,** main walls (of building); **g. moteur,** high-powered, heavy, engine; **g. doigt du pied,** big toe; **grosses lèvres,** thick lips; **g. souliers,** stout, strong, shoes; **grosse toile,** coarse linen; **g. sel,** cooking salt; **un peu g.,** not very subtle; a bit too obvious; **c'est un peu g.!** that's a bit much! **g. rire,** (i) loud laugh, (ii) coarse laugh; **grosse voix,** gruff voice; **g. mot,** coarse expression, swearword; **grosse indélicatesse,** gross impropriety; **grosse cavalerie,** heavy cavalry; **grosse somme,** large sum (of money); **ce n'est pas une grosse affaire,** (i) it's only a small business, deal; (ii) it's not very difficult; *Cards: etc:* **jouer g. (jeu),** to play for high stakes; **la plus grosse partie de nos affaires,** the bulk of our business; **g. mangeur,** big, hearty, eater; **g. appétit,** big, hearty, appetite; **g. rhume,** heavy cold; **grosse fièvre,** high fever; **un g. kilo,** a good kilo; **grosse faute,** gross, serious, mistake; **faire la grosse besogne,** to do the heavy work; **grosse mer,** heavy, high, sea; **g. temps,** stormy, bad, weather; **grosse averse, grosse pluie,** heavy shower, rain; **g. vent,** high wind; **g. propriétaire,** big landowner; **grosse héritière,** wealthy heiress; *F:* **les g. bonnets,** *P:* **les grosses légumes,** the top brass, brass hats; **yeux g. de larmes,** eyes swollen with tears; *O:* **femme grosse,** pregnant woman; (*b*) *adv.* **gagner g.,** to earn a great deal, to make big money; **il y a g. à parier qu'il ne viendra pas,** a hundred to one he won't come! **2.** *n.* (*a*) large, fat, person; **eh bien, mon g.!** well, old man! old chap! (*b*) *P:* rich, influential, person; bigwig. **3.** *n.m.* (*a*) bulk, mass, chief part; biggest, thickest, part; **g. d'un mât,** thick end of a mast; **le g. de la cargaison,** the bulk of the cargo; **le g. de l'armée,** the main body of the army; **le g. du peuple,** the mass, bulk, of the people; **le plus g. est fait,** the worst part of the job is done; **g. de l'été, de l'hiver,** height of summer, depth of winter; (*b*) **en g.,** roughly, broadly, approximately, on the whole, in the main; **évaluation en g.,** rough estimate; (*c*) *Com:* wholesale (trade); **acheter en g.,** to buy (i) wholesale, (ii) in bulk; **marchand en g.,** wholesaler; **boucher en g.,** wholesale butcher. **4.** *n.f.* **grosse** (*a*) *A:* roundhand (writing); (*b*) *Com:* gross; twelve dozen; (*c*) *Jur:* engrossed document, engrossment.

gros-bec [grobɛk] *n.m. Orn:* hawfinch, grosbeak; *pl. gros-becs.*

groseille [grozɛj] *n.f.* **1. g. (rouge),** redcurrant; **g. (blanche),** white currant; **gelée de groseille(s),** redcurrant jelly. **2. g. à maquereau,** gooseberry.

groseillier [grozeje] *n.m.* **1.** (red)currant bush. **2. g. à maquereau,** gooseberry bush.

gros-grain [grogrɛ̃] *n.m. Tex:* grosgrain, grogram; *pl. gros-grains.*

Gros-jean [groʒɑ̃] *n.m. Prov:* **être G.-j. comme devant,** to be disillusioned; to come down to earth again.

grossesse [grosɛs] *n.f.* pregnancy; **g. gémellaire,** twin pregnancy; **robe de g.,** maternity dress.

grosseur [grosœr] *n.f.* **1.** (*a*) size, bulk, volume; thickness (of lips, etc.); (*b*) (*of pers.*) fatness, weight. **2.** *Med:* swelling, growth, tumour, *NAm:* tumor.

grossier, -ière [grosje, -jɛr] *a.* (*a*) coarse, rough (food, cloth, etc.); uncivilized; crude (method, etc.); (*b*) **stupidité grossière,** rank stupidity; **ignorance grossière,** gross, crass, ignorance; **faute grossière,** blunder; (*c*) rude, unmannerly **(envers,** to); vulgar, coarse, gross; ill-mannered; **air g.,** uncouth appearance; **il a été on ne peut plus g.,** he was most rude; **langage g.,** coarse language; **plaisanterie grossière,** coarse, rude, joke; (*d*) unrefined; coarse (tastes, features, etc.).

grossièrement [grosjɛrmɑ̃] *adv.* **1.** coarsely, roughly; crudely; **table g. façonnée,** roughly made table. **2.** uncouthly; rudely; coarsely. **3. se tromper g.,** to be grossly mistaken. **4. répondre g.,** to answer rudely; to be rude (to s.o.).

grossièreté [grosjɛrte] *n.f.* **1.** (*a*) coarseness, roughness (of object); (*b*) rudeness, vulgarity, coarseness (of manner, etc.); (*c*) grossness (of mistake). **2. dire des grossièretés à qn,** to say rude things to s.o.; to be rude, offensive, to s.o.

grossir [grosir] **1.** *v.tr.* to enlarge, increase, swell, magnify; **torrent grossi par les pluies,** torrent swollen by the rain; **objet grossi trois fois,** object magnified three times; **g. sa voix,** to raise one's voice. 2. *v.i.* to increase, swell; to grow bigger, larger; **il grossit chaque jour,** he's getting fatter, putting on more weight, every day; **le vent, la mer, grossit,** the wind, sea, is rising.

grossissant [grosisɑ̃] *a.* **1.** growing, swelling (crowd, etc.). **2.** enlarging (lens, etc.); **verre g.,** magnifying glass.

grossissement [grosismɑ̃] *n.m.* **1.** increase in size, swelling. **2.** (*a*) magnifying, enlargement (of object through lens, etc.); (*b*) magnification, amplification, magnifying power (of lens, etc.).

grossiste [grosist] *n.* wholesaler.

grosso modo [grosomɔdo] *adv.* roughly (speaking); **raconter l'affaire g. m.,** to give a rough summary, account, of the matter.

grossoyer [groswaje] *v.tr.* **(je grossoie, n. grossoyons; je grossoierai)** *Jur:* to engross (document).

grotesque [grɔtɛsk] *a. & n.* grotesque, ludicrous (person, etc.); *n.* freak, figure of fun; *Art:* grotesque (figure).

grotesquement [grɔtɛskəmɑ̃] *adv.* grotesquely, ridiculously, absurdly.

grotte [grɔt] *n.f.* grotto, (underground) cave.

grouillant [grujɑ̃] *a.* crawling, alive, seething (**de,** with); **rue grouillante (de monde),** street swarming with people; **foule grouillante,** teeming crowd.

grouillement [grujmɑ̃] *n.m.* swarming, crawling; **g. de piétons,** swarming mass of pedestrians.

grouiller [gruje] **1.** *v.i.* (*a*) to crawl, swarm, be alive (**de,** with); **fromage qui grouille de vers,** cheese crawling, alive, with maggots; **la foule grouillait dans la rue,** the street was teeming, swarming, with people; (*b*) *A:* to move. **2.** *P:* **se g.,** to hurry up, get a move on; **grouille(-toi)!** get cracking!

grouillot [grujo] *n.m. St Exch:* messenger (boy).

group [grup] *n.m. Bank:* sealed bag of cash.

groupage [grupaʒ] *n.m.* **1.** *Com:* collecting, bulking (of parcels).

groupe [grup] *n.m.* **1.** (*a*) group (of people, things); clump (of trees, etc.); battery (of lights); cluster (of stars, etc.); party (of people); **en groupes de trois,** in groups of three; **ils arrivaient par groupes de deux ou trois,** they arrived in twos and threes; **g. de travail,** working party; **g. d'étude,** study group; seminar; *Pol:* **g. de pression,** pressure group; *Med:* **g. sanguin,** blood group; (*b*) **g. scolaire,** (multilateral) school block; (*c*) *Nat.Hist:* division. **2.** (*a*) *Mec.E:* bank (of machines, instruments, etc.); unit, block (of mechanical elements); *I.C.E:* **g. de(s) cylindres,** cylinder block; *Trans:* **g. mobile,** mobile unit; (*b*) *El:* set; **g. électrogène,** generating set; *Atom.Ph:* **g. de séparation (des isotopes, etc.),** (isotope, etc.) separation unit; *Cmptr:* **g. de bits consécutifs,** byte; **g. de deux bits,** dibit; **g. d'erreurs,** error burst; *Rail:* **g. de changements de voie,** set of points. **3.** *Mil: etc:* **g. de combat,** squad; **demi-g.,** section, *U.S:* half squad; **g. d'artillerie,** battery, *U.S:* battalion; **g. d'intervention,** mobile force, task force; **g. d'aviation,** squadron (of transport aircraft).

groupement [grupmɑ̃] *n.m.* **1.** (*a*) grouping; **g. des enfants d'après l'âge,** classification of children by age groups; (*b*) *Ind: Com:* pooling (of interests, etc.); (*c*) *El:* connection, connecting up, coupling (of cells, etc.). **2.** (*a*) group; **g. de consommateurs,** consumers' group; (*b*) *Ind:* pool; (*c*) *Mil:* group, formation; **g. tactique,** task force; **g. d'infanterie,** brigade group, *U.S:* battle group.

grouper [grupe] **1.** *v.tr.* to group; to arrange (in groups); **g. des moyens,** to pool resources; (*b*) *Com:* to bulk parcels; (*c*) *El:* to connect up, group, couple (cells, etc.). **2. se g.,** to form a group; **se g. autour du feu,** to gather round the fire; **se g. autour d'un chef,** to gather, rally, round a leader.

gruau [gryo] *n.m.* **1.** (finest) wheat flour; **pain de g.,** fine wheaten bread; **g. d'avoine,** (i) groats; (ii) oatmeal. **2.** *Cu:* gruel.

grue [gry] *n.f.* **1.** (*a*) *Orn:* crane; *F:* **faire le pied de g. (à attendre qn),** to hang about, to kick, cool, one's heels (waiting for s.o.); **cou de g.,** long scraggy neck; (*b*) *P:* prostitute, tart. **2.** *Mec.E: etc:* crane; **g. à volée, à flèche,** jib crane; **g. à pivot,** revolving crane; **g. à flotteur,** pontoon crane; *Rail:* **g. d'alimentation,** (water) crane.

gruger [gryʒe] *v.tr.* **(je grugeai(s); n. grugeons)** to swindle, exploit (s.o.).

grume [grym] *n.f.* **1.** bark (left on felled tree); **bois en g.,** rough timber; undressed timber. **2.** log.

grumeau, -eaux [grymo] *n.m.* **1.** (finely divided) curd (of milk, soap, etc.); **grumeaux de sel,** specks of salt; salty deposit. **2.** lump (in sauce, etc.).

grumeler (se) [səgrymle] *v.pr.* **(il se grumelle; il se grumellera) 1.** to clot, curdle. **2.** (*of sauce, etc*) to go lumpy.

grumeleux, -euse [grymlø, -øz] *a.* **1.** curdled. **2.** gritty (pear). **3.** lumpy (sauce, etc.).

grutier [grytje] *n.m.* crane driver, operator.

Guadeloupe [gwadlup] *Pr.n.f.* Guadeloupe.

guano [gwano] *n.m.* guano.

Guatemala [gwatemala] *Pr.n.m. Geog:* Guatemala.

guatémaltèque [gwatemaltɛk] *a. & n. Geog:* Guatemalan.

gué [ge] *n.m.* ford; **passer une rivière à g.,** to ford a river; to wade through a river.

guéable [geabl̩] *a.* fordable (river).

guède [gɛd] *n.f. Bot:* woad, pastel.

guéer [gee] *v.tr.* to ford (stream).

guelfe [gɛlf] *n.m. Hist:* Guelph.

guelte [gɛlt] *n.f. Com:* commission, percentage (on sales).

guenille [gənij] *n.f.* **1.** tattered garment, old rag; **en guenilles,** in rags (and tatters). **2.** worthless object.

guenon [gənɔ̃] *n.f.* **1.** *Z:* she-monkey. **2.** *F:* ugly woman, fright.

guépard [gepar] *n.m. Z:* cheetah.

guêpe [gɛp] *n.f.* **1.** *Ent:* wasp; **taille de g.,** wasp waist. **2.** artful, crafty, woman; *F:* **pas folle, la g.!** you won't get the better of her!

guêpier [gepje] *n.m.* **1.** wasps' nest; *Fig:* **donner, tomber, dans un g.,** to stir up a hornets' nest. **2.** *Orn:* bee eater.

guêpière [gɛpjɛr] *n.f. Cost:* wasp-waisted corset.

guère [gɛr] *adv.* (*always with neg. expressed or understood*) hardly (any), not much, not many, only a little, only a few; **je ne l'aime g.,** I don't care much for him; **le voyez-vous?—g.!** do you see him?—hardly ever! **cet appel n'a eu g. de succès,** the appeal met with very little success; **il n'a g. d'argent,** he hasn't much money; he has hardly any, scarcely any, money; **vous n'en avez g. non plus,** you haven't much either; **il ne mange g. que du pain,** he eats hardly anything but bread; **il ne tardera g. à venir,** he'll not be long in coming; **ne plus g.,** (i) hardly any more; (ii) not much longer; **il n'en reste plus g.,** there's hardly any left; **il n'y a g. plus de six ans,** it's barely more than six years ago; **il ne s'en faut (de) g.,** it's not far short; **sans g. avoir d'amis, il était respecté,** although he had very few friends, he was respected.

guéret [gerɛ] *n.m. Agr:* fallow land.

guéridon [geridɔ̃] *n.m.* pedestal table.

guérilla [gerija] *n.f.* **1.** guer(r)illa warfare. **2.** band, troop, of guer(r)illas.

guérillero [gerijero] *n.m.* guer(r)illa.

guérir [gerir] **1.** *v.tr.* to cure (s.o., an illness); to heal (wound); **g. qn d'une habitude,** to cure, break, s.o. of a habit; **cela ne guérit rien,** that doesn't help much. **2.** *v.i.* (*a*) to get better, be cured; to recover; **il n'en guérira pas,** he won't get over it; (*b*) (*of wound, etc.*) to heal. **3. se g.,** to get better, be cured; to cure oneself; **se g. de ses préjugés,** to overcome one's prejudices.

guérison [gerizɔ̃] *n.f.* **1.** recovery; **en voie de g.,** on the way to recovery. **2.** (*a*) cure (of disease); (*b*) healing (of wound).

guérissable [gerisabl̥] *a.* (*a*) curable; (*b*) (wound, etc.) that can be healed.

guérisseur, -euse [gerisœr, -øz] *n.* (*a*) healer; (*b*) quack (doctor); (*c*) faith healer.

guérite [gerit] *n.f.* **1.** *Mil:* sentry box. **2.** cabin, shelter (for watchman, etc.); *Fort:* lookout turret; cab (of crane, etc.).

guerre [gɛr] *n.f.* war, warfare. **1.** (*a*) **g. classique,** conventional warfare; **g. chaude, froide,** hot, cold, war; **g. sur terre,** land warfare; **g. aérienne,** air warfare; **g. atomique,** atomic warfare; **g. des nerfs,** war of nerves; **g. planétaire,** global war; **g. totale,** total war(fare); **g. éclair,** lightning war, blitzkrieg, *F:* blitz; **g. d'embuscade,** bush warfare, guerilla warfare; **g. de rues,** street fighting; **g. de positions,** static warfare; **g. de tranchées,** trench warfare; **g. civile,** civil war; **se mettre en g.,** to go to war; **en temps de g.,** in wartime; **faire la g. à, contre, un pays,** to wage war, make war, on, against, a country; **faire la g. avec qn,** to be in the war with s.o.; to serve (i) with, (ii) under, s.o.; **à la g. comme à la g.,** (i) one must take the rough with the smooth; (ii) we, you, have got to rough it; *A:* **le Ministère de la G.,** *F:* **la G.,** the War Department, the War Office; (*b*) *Hist:* **la g. de Trente ans,** the Thirty Years War; **la Grande G.,** the Great War; **la première, la deuxième, g. mondiale,** the first, the second, world war; World War I, II; **la drôle de g.,** the phoney war (1939–40). **2.** strife, quarrel, feud; **g. à outrance, à mort,** deadly feud; war to the knife; **être en g. ouverte avec, contre, qn,** to be openly at war with s.o.; *Com:* **g. des prix,** price war; **de g. lasse j'y consentis,** for the sake of peace and quiet I gave in.

guerrier, -ière [gɛrje, -jɛr] **1.** *a.* warlike, martial; **danse guerrière,** war dance. **2.** *n.m.* warrior. **3.** *n.f.* amazon.

guerroyer [gɛrwaje] *v.i.* **(je guerroie, n. guerroyons; je guerroierai)** to war, to wage war (**contre,** against).

guet [gɛ] *n.m.* **1.** watch(ing); lookout; **être au g.,** to be on the watch; **avoir l'œil au g.,** to keep a sharp lookout; **avoir l'œil et l'oreille au g.,** to keep one's eyes and ears open; *Mil: etc:* **poste de g.,** lookout post; **faire le g.,** (i) to be on the watch; (ii) to go the rounds; **chien de bon g.,** good watchdog. **2.** *A:* **le g.,** the watch.

guet-apens [gɛtapɑ̃] *n.m.* **1.** ambush; snare, trap; *Mil:* ambuscade; **attirer qn dans un g.-a.,** to ambush s.o.; **tomber dans un g.-a.,** to fall into an ambush, into a trap; to be ambushed. **2.** *Jur:* lying in wait; **de g.-a.,** with premeditation; *pl. guets-apens* [gɛtapɑ̃].

guêtre [gɛtr̥] *n.f.* gaiter; **demi-guêtres,** spats.

guetter [gete] *v.tr.* (*a*) to lie in wait for, to be on the lookout for, to watch for (s.o.); (*b*) to watch for (an opportunity).

guetteur [gɛtœr] *n.m.* **1.** *Mil: Nau:* lookout (man); **poste de guetteurs,** lookout post. **2.** fire watcher.

gueulante [gœlɑ̃t] *n.f. Sch: P:* uproar, din.

gueulard, -arde [gœlar, -ard] *F:* **1.** *a.* loudmouthed (person). **2.** (*a*) *n.* loudmouth; (*b*) *n.m. Nau:* loudhailer.

gueule [gœl] *n.f.* **1.** (*a*) mouth (of carnivorous animal, some large fish, etc.); (*b*) *P:* mouth (of pers.); **c'est un fort en g.,** he's got far too much to say for himself; **jeter des injures à pleine g.,** to bawl out abuse; **coups de g.,** slanging match; **(ferme) ta g.!** shut up! belt up! **s'en mettre plein la g.,** to stuff oneself; **avoir la g. de bois,** to have a hangover; **une fine g.,** a gourmet; (*c*) *P:* face, mug; **avoir une sale g.,** (i) to have an ugly mug; (ii) to look rotten, down in the mouth; (iii) to look a nasty customer; **faire la g.,** to sulk; to look sulky; **casser la g. à qn,** to bash s.o.'s face in; **se casser la g.,** to fall flat on one's face, come a cropper; *Mil:* **les Gueules cassées,** soldiers with serious facial injuries; (*d*) *F:* **avoir de la g.,** to have an air about one; **ce tableau a de la g.,** that's some picture; **ce chapeau a une drôle de g.,** that's a queer sort of hat. **2.** mouth (of sack, well, tunnel, etc.); muzzle (of gun); *Hyd.E:* **g. bée,** open sluice, (cylindrical) opening.

gueule-de-loup [gœldəlu] *n.f.* **1.** *Bot:* snapdragon. **2.** (*a*) *Const:* (chimney) cowl, chimney jack; (*b*) *Mch:* (exhaust) muffler; *pl. gueules-de-loup.*

gueulement [gœlmɑ̃] *n.m. F:* shout, yell; **il a poussé un g. de souffrance,** he let out a yell of pain.

gueuler [gœle] *P:* **1.** *v.i.* to bawl, shout; **faire g. la radio,** to turn the radio on full blast. **2.** *v.tr.* to bawl out (song, orders, etc.).

gueules [gœl] *n.m. Her:* gules.

gueuleton [gœltɔ̃] *n.m. F:* feast, spread, blowout.

gueuletonner [gœltɔne] *v.i. F:* to have a good blowout.

gueuse¹ [gøz] *n.f. Metall:* **g. (de fonte), fer en g.,** pig (iron).

gueuserie [gøzri] *n.f. A: & Lit:* **1.** beggary. **2.** foul deed.

gueux, -euse² [gø, -øz] **1.** *n. A: & Lit:* (*a*) beggar, tramp; (*b*) rascal, rogue. **2.** *n.f. F:* **courir la gueuse,** to go wenching, to chase the skirts.

gui¹ [gi] *n.m. Bot:* mistletoe.

gui² *n.m. Nau:* **1.** boom. **2.** guy(rope).

Gui³ *Pr.n.m.* Guy.

guibol(l)e [gibɔl] *n.f. P:* leg; pin; **jouer des guibolles,** to stir one's stumps.

guibre [gibr̥] *n.f. N.Arch:* cutwater.

guiches [giʃ) *n.f.pl.* kiss curls.

guichet [giʃɛ] *n.m.* **1.** (*a*) wicket (gate) (of prison, etc.); (*b*) spy hole, grille, grating (in door); (service) hatch (in restaurant, etc.). **2.** (*a*) *Bank: Post:* position, *NAm:* wicket; **g. fermé,** position closed; (*b*) booking office; *Th:* box office (window). **3.** *Cr:* wicket; **gardien de g.,** wicket keeper.

guichetier [giʃtje] *n.m.* booking clerk; box-office assistant; counter clerk, assistant.

guidage [gidaʒ] *n.m. Mec.E:* **1.** (*a*) guiding (of moving part); (*b*) centring, *NAm:* centering (on boring lathe). **2.** guides, guide rails, bars (of piledriver monkey, etc.). **3.** *Elcs: etc:* guidance; **tête de g.,** homing head; *Av:* **g. par radio-maillage, par radiomailles,** grid guidance.

guide¹ [gid] *n.m.* **1.** (*pers.*) (*a*) (tourist, museum) guide; **en tout sa sœur était son g.,** his sister was his guide in everything; (*b*) *n.f.* (girl) guide, *NAm:* girl scout; **g. aînée,** ranger; **Guides de France,** Catholic girl guides. **2.** guide (book). **3.** *Tchn:* **g. de courroie,** belt guide; *Elcs:* **g. d'ondes,** wave guide.

guide[2] *n.f. Equit:* rein; *Fig:* **mener la vie à grandes guides,** to live in lavish style.

guide-âne [gidɑn] *n.m.* **1.** (*a*) book of standing instructions (in office, etc.); (*b*) (elementary) handbook of instructions. **2.** writing lines (supplied with writing pad, etc.); *pl. guide-âne(s).*

guide-courroie [gidkurwa] *n.m. Mch:* strap guide, belt guide; *pl. guide-courroie(s).*

guider [gide] *v.tr.* to guide, conduct, direct, lead (s.o.); to drive (car, horse); to steer (boat); **g. un enfant dans le choix d'une carrière,** to advise a child in the choice of a career; **guidé par radio,** radio-controlled.

guidon [gidɔ̃] *n.m.* **1.** *Cy:* handlebar; *F:* **moustaches en g. de bicyclette,** handlebar moustache. **2.** *Mil:* (*a*) guidon, pennant; (*b*) foresight, bead (of gun, rifle). **3.** *Nau:* (*a*) pendant (of senior officer, etc.); (*b*) burgee.

guignard, -arde [giɲar, -ard] **1.** *n. F:* unlucky person, Jonah. **2.** *n.m. Orn:* **pluvier g.,** dotterel.

guigne[1] [giɲ] *n.f. Bot:* heart cherry; *F:* **se soucier de qch. comme d'une g.,** not to care a fig, a damn, a button, about sth.

guigne[2] *n.f. F:* bad luck; **porter la g. à qn,** to bring s.o. bad luck; **avoir la g.,** to be out of luck.

guigner [giɲe] *v.tr.* (*a*) to give a surreptitious, sidelong, glance at (sth.); *Cards:* **g. le jeu du voisin,** to look over one's opponent's hand; (*b*) to covet, look enviously at (sth.).

guignol [giɲɔl] *n.m.* **1.** (*a*) = Punch; (*b*) = Punch and Judy show; puppet show; *F:* **faire le g.,** to play, act, the fool. **2.** *Av: etc:* (*a*) kingpost (of aircraft); (*b*) **g. d'aileron,** aileron lever.

guignolet [giɲɔlɛ] *n.m.* cherry brandy.

guignon [giɲɔ̃] *n.m. F: O:* bad luck.

guilde [gild] *n.f.* **1.** *Hist:* g(u)ild; **g. de commerçants,** merchant guild. **2.** (record, book, etc.) club.

Guillaume [gijom] **1.** *Pr.n.m.* William. **2.** *n.m. Tls:* rabbet(ing) plane; rabbet; **g. à onglet,** mitre plane, *NAm:* miter plane.

guilledou [gijdu] *n.m. F:* **courir le g.,** to go wenching, to chase the skirts.

guillemeter [gijmete] *v.tr.* **(je guillemette, n. guillemetons; je guillemetterai)** to put (word, passage) in inverted commas, in quotation marks; to quote.

guillemets [gijmɛ] *n.m.pl.* inverted commas, quotation marks; *F:* quotes; **mot entre g.,** word in inverted commas; (*when dictating*) **ouvrez, fermez, les g.,** quote; unquote.

guillemot [gijmo] *n.m. Orn:* guillemot.

guilleret, -ette [gijrɛ, -ɛt] *a.* lively, gay, brisk (person, tune); broad, risqué (joke).

guillotine [gijɔtin] *n.f.* guillotine; **fenêtre à g.,** sash window; **cisailles à g.,** guillotine shears.

guillotiner [gijɔtine] *v.tr.* to guillotine.

guimauve [gimov] *n.f.* (*a*) *Bot:* marshmallow; **g. rose,** hollyhock; (*b*) *Cu:* **(pâte de) g.,** marshmallow; (*c*) **sentimentalité de, à la, g.,** insipid sentimentality.

guimbarde [gɛ̃bard] *n.f.* **1.** Jew's harp. **2.** *F:* ramshackle old vehicle; old banger, jalopy. **3.** *Tls:* router plane, grooving plane.

guimpe [gɛ̃p] *n.f.* **1.** (nun's) wimple. **2.** chemisette.

guincher [gɛ̃ʃe] *v.i. P:* to dance.

guindage [gɛ̃daʒ] *n.m.* hoisting.

guindé [gɛ̃de] *a.* stiff, strained; *F:* starchy (person); affected (language, etc.); stilted, stiff (style).

guindeau, -eaux [gɛ̃do] *n.m. Nau:* windlass.

guinder [gɛ̃de] **1.** *v.tr.* (*a*) to hoist; to windlass; (*b*) *Nau:* to send up, sway up (mast); (*c*) to make (sth.) stiff, stilted. **2. se g.,** to become stiff, stilted, strained, affected.

Guinée [gine] **1.** *Pr.n.f. Geog:* Guinea. **2.** *n.f. A.Num:* guinea.

guinéen, -enne [ginẽɛ, -ɛn] *a. & n. Geog:* Guinean.

guingois [gɛ̃gwa] *adv.phr.* **de g.,** askew, lopsided; **tout va de g.,** everything's going wrong.

guinguette [gɛ̃gɛt] *n.f.* (suburban) café (with music and dancing, *usu.* in the open).

guipage [gipaʒ] *n.m.* winding, taping, wrapping, lapping, covering; *El:* sleeve, sheath.

guiper [gipe] *v.tr. Tchn:* to tape, wrap, lap; *El: etc:* **g. un fil,** to cover a wire.

guipure [gipyr] *n.f.* point lace, pillow lace.

guirlande [girlɑ̃d] *n.f.* garland, festoon, wreath; **g. de perles,** rope of pearls.

guise [giz] *n.f.* manner, way, fashion; **faire qch. à sa g.,** to do sth. in one's own way; **faire, agir, à sa g.,** to have one's (own) way; to do as one pleases; **en g. de,** (i) by way of; (ii) instead of; **des caisses en g. de chaises,** boxes used as chairs.

guitare [gitar] *n.f. Mus:* guitar; **g. électrique,** electric guitar; **g. hawaïenne,** Hawaiian guitar.

guitariste [gitarist] *n.* guitarist, guitar player.

guitoune [gitun] *n.f. F:* (*a*) *Mil:* dugout, shelter; (*b*) tent; **coucher sous la g.,** to sleep under canvas.

guppy [gypi] *n.m. Ich:* guppy.

gustatif, -ive [gystatif, -iv] *a.* gustative; gustatory.

gustation [gystasjɔ̃] *n.f.* gustation, tasting.

gutta-percha [gytapɛrka] *n.f.* gutta-percha.

guttural, -aux [gytyral, -o] **1.** *a.* guttural; throaty (voice). **2.** *n.f. Ling:* guttural.

guyanais, -aise [gɥijanɛ, -ɛz] *a. & n. Geog:* Guianese; Guyanese.

Guyane [gyijan] *Pr.n.f Geog: Pol:* Guyana; **G. française,** French Guiana; *Hist:* **G. britannique,** British Guiana.

gym [ʒim] *n.f.* (= GYMNASTICS) gym.

gymkhana [ʒimkana] *n.m.* gymkhana.

gymnase [ʒimnaz] *n.m.* gymnasium.

gymnaste [ʒimnast] *n.* gymnast.

gymnastique [ʒimnastik] **1.** *a.* gymnastic. **2.** *n.f.* gymnastics; **g. rythmique,** eurhythmics; *Med:* **g. passive,** passive movements; **g. corrective,** remedial gymnastics; **g. respiratoire,** breathing exercises; **g. d'esprit,** mental gymnastics; *F:* **g. matinale,** morning exercises; *F:* daily dozen.

gymnosophiste [ʒimnɔsfist] *n.m. A.Phil:* gymnosophist, yogi.

gymnote [ʒimnɔt] *n.m. Ich: F:* electric eel.

gynécée [ʒinese] *n.m. Cl.Ant: Bot:* gynaeceum.

gynécologie [ʒinekɔlɔʒi] *n.f.* gyn(a)ecology.

gynécologique [ʒinekɔlɔʒik] *a.* gyn(a)ecological.

gynécologiste [ʒinekɔlɔʒist], **gynécologue** [ʒinekɔlɔg] *n.* gyn(a)ecologist.

gypaète [ʒipaɛt] *n.m. Orn:* bearded vulture; lammergeyer.

gypse [ʒips] *n.m.* **1.** *Miner:* gypsum, plasterstone. **2.** *Com:* plaster of Paris.

gypseux, -euse [ʒipsø, -øz] *a. Miner:* gypseous.

gyrocompas [ʒirɔkɔ̃pɑ] *n.m. Nau:* gyrocompass.

gyromètre [ʒirɔmɛtr̥] *n.m. Av:* gyrometer.

gyropilote [ʒirɔpilɔt] *n.m. Av:* gyropilot, automatic pilot.

gyroscope [ʒirɔskɔp] *n.m.* gyroscope; *Av:* **g. directionnel,** directional gyroscope.

gyroscopique [ʒirɔskɔpik] *a.* gyroscopic (top, etc.); **compas g.,** gyrocompass.

gyrostabilisateur [ʒirɔstabilizatœr] *n.m.* gyrostabilizer.

gyrostat [ʒirɔsta] *n.m.* gyrostat.

gyrostatique [ʒirɔstatik] *a.* gyrostatic.

H

Words beginning with an aspirate h *are shown by an asterisk.*

H, h [aʃ] *n.m. & f.* (the letter) H, h; **h muet(te),** mute h; **h aspiré(e),** aspirate h; *Mil: etc:* **l'heure H,** zero hour; **bombe H,** H bomb.

***ha** [ɑ] *int* **1.** ah! **2.** (*laughter*) **ha, ha!** ha! ha!

habile [abil] *a.* (*a*) clever, skilful, able, capable (workman, etc.); cunning, smart, artful, (politician etc.); **mains habiles,** skilled hands; **façonner qch. d'une main h.,** to make sth. skilfully; **h. à faire qch.,** clever at doing sth.; (*b*) *Jur:* **h. à succéder,** able, competent, to inherit.

habilement [abilmɑ̃] *adv.* cleverly, skilfully.

habileté [abilte] *n.f.* (*a*) ability, skill, skilfulness; (*b*) cleverness, smartness; (*c*) *pl.* skilful manœuvres; (*d*) *Jur:* = HABILITÉ.

habilitation [abilitasjɔ̃] *n.f. Jur:* **h. de qn à faire qch.,** enabling of s.o. to do sth.

habilité [abilite] *n.f. Jur:* ability, title; **avoir h. à hériter,** to be entitled to succeed.

habiliter [abilite] *v.tr. Jur:* **h. qn à faire qch.,** to enable, entitle, s.o. to do sth.

habillage [abijaʒ] *n.m.* **1.** preparing, preparation; (*a*) *Cu:* dressing; drawing and trussing (of poultry); cleaning (of fish); trimming (of meat); (*b*) *Arb:* pruning, trimming (of trees); (*c*) assembly, putting together (of watch, etc.); (*d*) *Tchn:* (*of boiler, etc.*) lagging. **2.** (*a*) *Com:* packaging (of goods). **3.** dressing (of child, etc.).

habillé [abije] *a.* **1.** dressed; **h. en femme,** dressed up as a woman; **h. de bleu, d'un complet,** dressed in blue, in a suit; **h. chaudement,** warmly clad, dressed. **2.** (*of clothes*) smart; **soirée habillée,** formal occasion, reception.

habillement [abijmɑ̃] *n.m.* **1.** clothing, dressing; **effets d'h.,** clothing, clothes. **2.** clothes, dress.

habiller [abije] **1.** *v.tr.* to prepare; (*a*) *Cu:* to dress (meat, fowl); to draw and truss (poultry); to clean (fish); to trim (meat); (*b*) *Arb:* to prune, trim (tree); (*c*) to put (watch, etc.) together; to assemble (parts); *Typ:* **h. une gravure,** to run type round a block; (*d*) to dress; **h. un enfant en soldat,** to dress a child up as a soldier; *F:* **h. qn,** to speak ill of, slate, s.o.; (*e*) to clothe; to provide (s.o.) with clothes; (*f*) to cover (up), wrap up; to lag (boiler, etc.); *Com:* to label, package (goods); **h. des meubles de housses,** to put loose covers on furniture. **2. s'h.** (*a*) to dress (oneself); to get dressed; (*of priest, etc.*) to robe; **s'h. en femme,** to dress up as a woman; (*b*) **s'h. sur mesure,** to have one's clothes made to measure; (*c*) to dress (for dinner, etc.).

habilleur, -euse [abijœr, -øz] *n. Th:* dresser.

habit [abi] *n.m.* **1.** dress, costume; *pl.* clothes; **mettre ses habits,** to put on one's clothes; **marchand d'habits,** old clothes man; **h. du dimanche,** Sunday best; **h. de cour,** court dress; **en h. ecclésiastique,** in clerical attire, garb. **2.** (*a*) *A:* coat; **h. de cheval,** riding habit; (*b*) **h. vert,** member of the *Académie française*; (*c*) **h. (de soirée),** evening dress, tails; **être en h.,** to be in evening dress, in tails. **3.** (monk's, nun's) habit; (monk's) frock; **prendre l'h.,** (i) (*of man*) to become a monk; (ii) (*of woman*) to take the veil.

habitabilité [abitabilite] *n.f.* habitability, fitness for habitation.

habitable [abitabḷ] *a.* (in)habitable, fit for habitation.

habitacle [abitakḷ] *n.m.* **1.** *Lit:* habitation, dwelling place. **2.** *Nau:* binnacle. **3.** *Av:* cockpit.

habitant, -ante [abitɑ̃, -ɑ̃t] *n.* **1.** (*a*) inhabitant; resident; **ville de 10.000 habitants,** town of 10,000 inhabitants; (*b*) occupier, occupant (of house); (*c*) inmate (of house); **loger chez l'h.,** (i) *Mil:* to be billeted with the locals; (ii) to rent a room in s.o.'s house. **2.** *Fr.C:* habitant; small-scale farmer.

habitat [abita] *n.m.* **1.** habitat (of animal, plant). **2.** accommodation (of people).

habitation [abitasjɔ̃] *n.f.* **1.** habitation; inhabiting; **le problème de l'h.,** the housing problem. **2.** dwelling (place), residence, abode; house; **ne pas avoir d'h.,** to have no fixed abode, no permanent home; **avoir son h. à . . .,** to reside, live, at . . .; **h. à loyer modéré, H.L.M.** = council house; council flat.

habiter [abite] **1.** *v.tr.* (*a*) to inhabit, dwell in, live in (a place); **elle habite une petite maison à la campagne,** she lives in a little house in the country; **cette pièce n'a jamais été habitée,** this room has never been lived in; **pays peu habité,** sparsely inhabited country; **vaisseau spatial habité,** manned spacecraft; (*b*) to occupy (house). **2.** *v.i.* to live, reside, dwell; to have one's home (**à,** at); **h. à la campagne,** to live in the country; **h. en Italie, chez son frère,** to live in Italy, at one's brother's, with one's brother.

habitude [abityd] *n.f.* (*a*) habit, custom, practice, use; **faire qch. par h.,** to do sth. from, out of, habit, from force of habit; *Prov:* **l'h. est une seconde nature,** use is second nature; **prendre l'h. de faire qch.,** to get into the habit of doing sth.; **se faire une h. de . . .,** to make it one's practice to . . .; **avoir l'h., avoir pour h., de faire qch.,** to be in the habit of doing sth.; **prendre de mauvaises habitudes,** to get into bad habits; **ce n'est pas une h. chez moi, ce n'est pas dans mes habitudes,** I don't make a habit of it; **à, selon, suivant son h.,** as is, was, his, her, custom; **se défaire d'une h., perdre une h.,** to get out of a habit; **faire perdre une h. à qn,** to break s.o. of a habit; **d'h.,** usually, ordinarily; **comme d'h.,** as usual; **plus tôt que d'h.,** earlier than usual; (*b*) knack; **je n'en ai plus l'h.,** I'm out of practice.

habitué, -ée [abitɥe] *n.* frequenter; regular visitor, customer; regular; habitué.

habituel, -elle [abitɥɛl] *a.* usual, customary, regular; habitual (**à,** to).

habituellement [abitɥɛlmɑ̃] *adv.* habitually, usually, regularly.

habituer [abitɥe] **1.** *v.tr.* to accustom, habituate, make familiar; **h. qn à qch.,** to accustom s.o., get s.o. used, to sth.; **h. qn à faire qch.,** to get s.o. into the habit of, used to, doing sth.; **h. qn à la fatigue,** to inure s.o. to fatigue. **2. s'h,** to get used, to get, grow, accustomed (**à,** to).

***hâblerie** [ɑbləri] *n.f.* **1.** bragging, boasting. **2.** boast.

***hâbleur, -euse** [ɑblœr, -øz] (*a*) *a.* bragging, boasting; (*b*) *n.* boaster, braggart.

***Habsbourg** [apsbur] *Pr.n.m. Hist:* **la maison de H.,** the House of Hapsburg.

***hachage** [aʃaʒ] *n.m.* chopping (up), mincing (of meat, etc.); cutting (of chaff, etc.).

***hache** [aʃ] *n.f.* axe, *esp. NAm:* ax; **h. à main,** hatchet; **fait, taillé, à coups de h.,** rough-hewn, hacked out; *A.Arms:* **h. d'armes,** battleaxe; **h. de guerre,** tomahawk; *Fig:* **enterrer la h. de guerre,** to bury the hatchet; **porter la h. dans les dépenses publiques,** to axe, cut, public spending.

***haché** [aʃe] **1.** *a.* (*a*) minced, chopped; **bifteck h.,** minced beef, mince; *NAm:* ground beef; (*b*) staccato, jerky (style, etc.); (*c*) (cross)hatched (drawing); hachured (map). **2.** *n.m. Cu:* minced meat, *esp.* minced beef; mince; *NAm:* ground beef.

***hache-légumes** [aʃlegym] *n.m.inv. Cu:* vegetable cutter, chopper.

***hachement** [aʃmɑ̃] *n.m.* = HACHAGE.

***hache-paille** [aʃpaj] *n.m.inv. Agr:* chaffcutter.

***hacher** [aʃe] *v.tr.* **1.** (*a*) to chop (up); to mince, *NAm:* grind (meat, etc.); **h. menu,** to mince finely, chop up small; **h. qn menu comme chair à pâté,** to make mincemeat of s.o.; **se faire h.,** to be cut to pieces; (*b*) to hack (up), mangle (joint, manuscript, etc.); to interrupt (speech, etc.). **2.** = HACHURER.

***hachette** [aʃɛt] *n.f.* hatchet.

***hache-viande** [aʃvjɑ̃d] *n.m.inv. Cu:* mincing machine; mincer.

***hachis** [aʃi] *n.m. Cu:* minced, *NAm:* ground, meat; forcemeat; mince; **h. de veau,** minced veal; **h. Parmentier** = cottage pie, shepherd's pie; **h. d'herbes,** chopped herbs.

***hachisch** [aʃiʃ] *n.m.* hashish.

***hachoir** [aʃwar] *n.m. Cu:* **1.** (*a*) chopping knife, chopper; (*b*) chopping board. **2.** mincing machine; mincer.

***hachure** [aʃyr] *n.f. Draw: etc:* (cross)hatching; (*on map*) hachures; **carte en hachures,** hachured map.

***hachurer** [aʃyre] *v.tr. Draw: etc:* to (cross)hatch; *Mapm:* to hachure.

***haddock** [adɔk] *n.m. Cu:* smoked haddock.

***hagard** [agar] *a.* haggard, wild(-looking) (appearance, etc.); drawn (face).

hagiographe [aʒjɔgraf] *n.* hagiographer.

hagiographie [aʒjɔgrafi] *n.f.* hagiography.

hagiographique [aʒjɔgrafik] *a.* hagiographic(al).

***haie** [ɛ] *n.f.* (*a*) hedge(row); **h. vive,** quickset hedge; (*b*) hurdle; *Sp:* **course de haies,** (short-distance) hurdle race; *F:* the hurdles; (*c*) line, row (of trees, etc.); **faire, former, la h,** to line the streets; **h. d'honneur,** guard of honour, *NAm:* of honor.

***haillon** [ɑjɔ̃] *n.m.* rag (of clothing); **être en haillons,** to be in rags and tatters.

***haillonneux, -euse** [ɑjɔnø, -øz] *a.* ragged, tattered.

***haine** [ɛn] *n.f.* hatred (**de, pour, contre,** of, for); detestation; hate; **avoir la h. de qch., de qn, avoir de la h. pour qch., qn,** to hate, detest, sth., s.o.; **prendre qch., qn, en h.,** to take a strong aversion to sth., s.o.; **en h., par h., de qch.,** out of hatred of, for, sth.

***haineusement** [ɛnøzmɑ̃] *adv.* with (bitter) hatred.

***haineux, -euse** [ɛnø, -øz] *a.* full of hatred, hate.

***haïr** [air] *v.tr.* (**je hais** [ɛ], **tu hais, il hait, n. haïssons,** etc.; *imp.* **hais;** *otherwise regular*) to hate, detest, loathe; **h. qn d'avoir fait qch.,** to hate s.o. for doing, having done, sth.

***haire** [ɛr] *n.f.* **1.** hairshirt. **2.** *Tex:* haircloth.

***haïssable** [aisabl̩] *a.* hateful, detestable.

***Haïti** [aiti] *Pr.n.m. or f. Geog:* Haiti.

***haïtien, -ienne** [aisjɛ̃, -jɛn] *a. & n. Geog:* Haitian.

***halage** [alaʒ] *n.m.* (*a*) warping, hauling (of ship); (*b*) towing; **chemin, corde, de h.,** towpath; towing line.

***hâle** [ɑl] *n.m.* (sun)tan, sunburn.

***hâlé** [ɑle] *a.* (sun)tanned, sunburnt, weatherbeaten.

haleine [alɛn] *n.f.* breath; **avoir mauvaise h., avoir l'h. forte,** to have bad breath; **retenir son h.,** to hold one's breath; **tout d'une h.,** (i) all in one breath, in the same breath; (ii) at one go; **avoir l'h. courte,** to be short-winded, short of breath; **reprendre h.,** to get, catch, one's breath; to get one's second wind; **perdre h.,** to get out of breath, lose one's breath; **courir à perdre h.,** to run until one is out of breath; **discuter à perdre h.,** to argue nonstop; **hors d'h.,** out of breath, breathless; **travail de longue h.,** long and exacting task; **tenir qn en h.,** to hold s.o. breathless, hold s.o.'s attention, keep s.o. in suspense.

***haler** [ale] *v.tr.* **1.** (*a*) to warp (ship); (*b*) to tow (barge, etc.); (*c*) **h. une embarcation au sec,** to haul up a boat (on the beach). **2.** *Nau:* to pull, haul in, heave (rope, etc.); *v.i.* **h. sur une manœuvre,** to haul, pull, on a rope; to heave at a rope. **3.** *Nau:* **h. le vent,** to sail closer to the wind.

***hâler** [ɑle] *v.tr.* (*of sun, etc.*) to tan, burn, brown.

***haletant** [altɑ̃] *a.* panting, breathless, out of breath; gasping (for breath).

***halètement** [alɛtmɑ̃] *n.m.* panting; gasping (for breath); puffing (and blowing).

***haleter** [alte] *v.i.* (**je halète; je halèterai**) to pant; to gasp (for breath); to puff (and blow).

***haleur, -euse** [alœr, -øz] *n.* hauler, tower (of boats).

***hall** [ol] *n.m.* entrance hall; (hotel) foyer; **h. de gare,** station concourse.

***hallage** [alaʒ] *n.m. Com:* market dues.

hallali [alali] *n.m. Ven:* mort; **assister à l'h.,** to be in at the death, at the finish, at the kill.

***halle** [al] *n.f.* (covered) market; **h. aux poissons,** fish market; **h. au blé,** corn exchange; **les Halles (centrales),** the Central Market (in Paris).

***hallebarde** [albard] *n.f. A.Arms:* halberd, halbert; bill; *F:* **il pleut, tombe, des hallebardes,** it's raining cats and dogs.

***hallebardier** [albardje] *n.m. A.Mil:* halberdier.

***hallier** [alje] *n.m.* (*a*) thicket, copse, brake; (*b*) *pl.* brushwood.

hallucinant [alysinɑ̃] *a.* hallucinating (drug, etc.); haunting (thought); striking (likeness, etc.).

hallucination [alysinasjɔ̃] *n.f.* hallucination, delusion.

hallucinatoire [alysinatwar] *a.* hallucinatory.

halluciné, -ée [alysine] *a. & n.* hallucinated, *F:* mad, loony (person).

halluciner [alysine] *v.tr.* to hallucinate.

hallucinogène [alysinɔʒɛn] *Pharm:* **1.** *n.m.* hallucinogen. **2.** *a.* hallucinogenic.

***halo** [alo] *n.m.* **1.** *Meteor: etc:* halo. **2.** (*a*) *Opt:* blurring; (*b*) *Phot:* halation.

halogène [alɔʒɛn] **1.** *a.* halogenous. **2.** *n.m.* halogen.

***halte** [alt] *n.f.* **1.** stop, halt; **faire h.,** to (make a) halt, (come to a) stop; **h.(-là)!** stop! halt! **2.** (*a*) stopping place, resting place; (*b*) *Rail:* halt.

haltère [altɛr] *n.m.* dumb-bell; barbell; **faire des haltères,** to do weightlifting, weight training.

haltérophile [alterɔfil] *n.* weightlifter.

haltérophilie [alterɔfili] *n.f.* weightlifting.

***hamac** [amak] *n.m.* hammock; **crocher, décrocher, un h.,** to sling, unsling, a hammock.

hamadryade [amadrijad] *n.f. Gr.Myth:* hamadryad, dryad, wood nymph.

hamamélis [amamelis] *n.m. Bot:* hamamelis, witch hazel.

***Hambourg** [ɑ̃bur] *Pr.n.m. Geog:* Hamburg.

***hambourgeois, -oise** [ɑ̃burʒwa, -waz] *a. & n. Geog:* (native, inhabitant) of Hamburg; Hamburger.

hamburger [ɑ̃burgœr] *n.m. Cu:* hamburger.

***hameau, -eaux** [amo] *n.m.* hamlet.

hameçon [amsɔ̃] *n.m.* (fish-)hook; **h. sans œillet,** blind hook; **mordre à l'h.,** to swallow, rise to, the bait.

hameçonner [amsɔne] *v.tr.* **1.** to hook (fish). **2.** to put hooks on (fishing line).

***hammam** [amam] *n.m.* Turkish baths.

***hammerless** [amɛrlɛs] *n.m.* hammerless (sporting gun); shotgun.

***hampe¹** [ɑ̃p] *n.f.* **1.** staff, pole (of flag, etc.); stave, shaft (of spear, etc.); shank (of fish-hook). **2.** *Bot:* scape, stem; **h. (florale),** spike.

***hampe²** *n.f. Cu:* (*a*) thin flank (of beef); (*b*) breast (of venison).

***hamster** [amstɛr] *n.m. Z:* hamster.

***han** [ɑ̃] *int.* (*sound of breath accompanying violent effort*) oof! **pousser un h. à chaque coup,** to give a grunt at every stroke.

***hanap** [anap] *n.m. A:* goblet, tankard.

***hanche** [ɑ̃ʃ] *n.f.* **1.** hip; **les poings sur les hanches,** (with his) hands on (his) hips; (with) arms akimbo; **tour de hanches,** hip measurement. **2.** haunch (of horse); *pl.* hindquarters. **3.** *Nau:* quarter (of ship); **par la h.,** on the quarter.

***hand-ball** [ɑ̃dbal] *n.m. Sp:* handball.

***handicap** [ɑ̃dikap] *n.m.* handicap.

***handicapé, -ée** [ɑ̃dikape] *a. & n.* handicapped (person); **h. physique,** physically handicapped; **les handicapés,** the handicapped, the disabled.

***handicaper** [ɑ̃dikape] *v.tr.* to handicap.

***handicapeur** [ɑ̃dikapœr] *n.m. Turf:* handicapper.

***hangar** [ɑ̃gar] *n.m.* **1.** (open) shed, shelter; depot; **h. à bateaux,** boathouse. **2.** *Av:* hangar.

***hanneton** [antɔ̃] *n.m. Ent:* cockchafer, maybug; *NAm:* June beetle, bug; *F:* **un froid qui n'est pas piqué des hannetons,** intense cold.

***Hanovre** [anɔvr̥] *Pr.n.m. Geog:* Hanover.

***hanovrien, -enne** [anɔvrijɛ̃, -ɛn] *a. & n. Geog: Hist:* Hanoverian.

***hanse** [ɑ̃s] *n.f. Hist:* Hanse; **la H.,** the Hanseatic league, the Hanse towns.

***hanséatique** [ɑ̃seatik] *a. Hist:* Hanseatic.

***hanter** [ɑ̃te] *v.tr.* (*of ghost*) to haunt (house, etc.); **l'idée du suicide le hante,** he is obsessed, haunted, by the idea of suicide.

***hantise** [ɑ̃tiz] *n.f.* haunting memory; obsession.

***happe** [ap] *n.f.* **1.** *Carp: Const: etc:* cramp (iron). **2.** staple; **anneau à h.,** ring and staple.

***happement** [apmɑ̃] *n.m.* snapping (up), snatching, seizing.

***happer** [ape] *v.tr.* (*of birds, etc.*) to snap up, snatch, seize, catch (insects, etc.); **la voiture a été happée par un train,** the car was caught, hit, by a train.

***haquenée** [akne] *n.f. A:* palfrey.

hara-kiri [arakiri] *n.m.* hara-kiri.

***harangue** [arɑ̃g] *n.f.* harangue; speech.

***haranguer** [arɑ̃ge] *v.tr.* (*a*) to harangue; (*b*) to hold forth at, lecture (s.o.).

***haras** [ara] *n.m.* stud farm.

***harassant** [arasɑ̃] *a.* tiring, exhausting.

***harassé** [arase] *a.* tired, worn out, exhausted.

***harassement** [arasmɑ̃] *n.m.* fatigue, exhaustion.

***harasser** [arase] *v.tr.* to tire (out), exhaust.

***harcelant** [arsəlɑ̃] *a.* harassing, worrying, tormenting; harrying; badgering, pestering.

***harcèlement** [arsɛlmɑ̃] *n.m.* harassing, worrying, tormenting; harrying; badgering, pestering, plaguing.

***harceler** [arsəle] *v.tr.* **(je harcèle; je harcèlerai)** to harass, worry, torment; to harry (enemy); to bait (an animal); **h. qn de questions,** to badger, pester, plague, s.o. with questions; **h. qn pour obtenir qch.,** to pester s.o. in order to obtain sth.

***harceleur, -euse** [arsəlœr, -øz] *n.* tormentor, worrier.

***harde¹** [ard] *n.f. Ven:* herd, bevy (of deer).

***harde²** *n.f. Ven:* leash (for hounds).

***hardes** [ard] *n.f.pl.*, worn, old, clothes.

***hardi** [ardi] *a.* bold, audacious; (*a*) daring, fearless; **écriture hardie,** bold hand(writing); **h. à agir,** bold to act; (*b*) rash, venturesome (undertaking, etc.); (*c*) impudent, brazen; (*d*) *int.* go on! go it!

***hardiesse** [ardjɛs] *n.f.* boldness; (*a*) daring, pluck; **avoir la h. de faire qch.,** to be so bold as to do sth.; (*b*) impudence, effrontery; **il a eu la h. de m'écrire,** he had the audacity, the cheek, to write to me.

***hardiment** [ardimɑ̃] *adv.* boldly, audaciously; (*a*) daringly, fearlessly; (*b*) rashly; (*c*) impudently.

***hardware** [ardwɛr] *n.m. Cmptr:* hardware.

***harem** [arɛm] *n.m.* harem.

***hareng** [arɑ̃] *n.m.* herring; **h. bouffi,** bloater; **h. (salé et) fumé,** kipper; **h. saur,** red, smoked, herring; *F:* **être sec comme un h.,** to be as skinny, thin, as a rake.

***harengaison** [arɑ̃gɛzɔ̃] *n.f.* (*a*) herring season; (*b*) herring fishing.

***harengère** [arɑ̃ʒɛr] *n.f. Pej:* fishwife.

***harenguet** [arɑ̃gɛ] *n.m. Ich:* sprat.

***harengueux** [arɑ̃gø] *n.m.*, ***harenguier** [arɑ̃gje] *n.m.* herring boat.

***hargne** [arɲ] *n.f.* bad temper, surly disposition; peevishness.

***hargneusement** [arɲøzmɑ̃] *adv.* peevishly, cantankerously; viciously.

***hargneux, -euse** [arɲø, -øz] *a.* snarling, vicious (dog); bad-tempered, peevish, cantankerous (person); nagging (woman).

***haricot** [ariko] *n.m.* **1.** *Cu:* **h. de mouton,** Irish stew, haricot mutton. **2. h. blanc,** haricot bean, *U.S:* bush bean; **h. rouge,** red kidney bean; **h. beurre,** butter bean; **h. vert,** French, *NAm:* string, bean; **h. d'Espagne,** scarlet runner; **h. à rames,** runner bean; *P:* **des haricots!** not a sausage! *P:* **la fin des haricots,** the bloody limit; *P:* **courir sur le h. à qn,** to pester s.o.

***haridelle** [aridɛl] *n.f.* old horse, screw.

***harle** [arl] *n.m. Orn:* merganser.

harmonica [armɔnika] *n.m. Mus:* harmonica, mouth organ.

harmonie [armɔni] *n.f.* **1.** (*a*) harmony; accord, agreement; **être en h. avec qch.,** to be in keeping, in harmony, in accordance with sth.; to fit in with sth.; **vivre en h.,** to live in harmony, harmoniously; (*b*) harmoniousness. **2.** *Mus:* (*a*) harmony; **table d'h.,** sounding board (of piano, etc.); (*b*) brass and reed band; (*c*) wind section (of orchestra).

harmonieusement [armɔnjøzmɑ̃] *adv.* harmoniously.

harmonieux, -euse [armɔnjø, -øz] *a.* (*a*) harmonious, melodious, tuneful (sound); (*b*) harmonious (arrangement, etc.); **couleurs harmonieuses,** colours that harmonize, that blend well.

harmonique [armɔnik] *a. & n.m. Mus:* harmonic.

harmoniquement [armɔnikmɑ̃] *adv.* harmonically.

harmonisation [armɔnizasjɔ̃] *n.f.* harmonization, harmonizing; *Ling:* **h. vocalique,** vowel harmony.

harmoniser [armɔnize] **1.** *v.tr.* to harmonize, attune (ideas); to match (colours); (*b*) *Mus:* to harmonize (melody, etc.); (*c*) *Mus:* to voice (pipe or stop of an organ). **2. s'h.,** to be in keeping, in harmony, to harmonize, agree (**avec,** with); (*of colours*) **s'h. avec qch.,** to match, to tone in with, sth.

harmonium [armɔnjɔm] *n.m.* harmonium.

***harnachement** [arnaʃmɑ̃] *n.m.* **1.** harnessing (of horse, etc.). **2.** (*a*) harness, trappings; (*b*) saddlery. **3.** *F:* (absurd) rig-out.

***harnacher** [arnaʃe] *v.tr.* (*a*) to harness (horse, etc.); (*b*) *F:* **h. qn,** to dress s.o. up, rig s.o. out.
***harnais** [arnɛ] *n.m.* **1.** (*a*) harness; (*b*) saddlery. **2.** (*a*) *A:* harness; armour, *NAm:* armor; military equipment; **blanchi sous le h.,** grown grey in service; **reprendre le h.,** to get into harness again, go back to work again. **3.** *Mec.E:* **h. d'engrenage,** train of gear wheels; gearing.
***haro** [aro] *int. & n.m.* **(clameur de) h.,** outcry, hue and cry; **crier h.,** to raise a hue and cry.
harpagon [arpagɔ̃] *n.m.* miser, skinflint; scrooge.
***harpe** [arp] *n.f. Mus:* harp; **jouer, pincer, de la h.,** to play the harp; **h. éolienne,** Aeolian harp.
***harpie** [arpi] *n.f.* **1.** (*a*) *Myth:* harpy; (*b*) *Fig:* harpy, shrew. **2.** *Orn:* harpy (eagle); crested eagle.
***harpiste** [arpist] *n.* harpist.
***harpon** [arpɔ̃] *n.m.* **1.** harpoon; **pêche, chasse (sous-marine), au h.,** (underwater) spear fishing. **2.** *Const:* (*a*) toothing stone; (*b*) wall staple.
***harponnage** [arpɔnaʒ] *n.m.*, ***harponnement** [arpɔnmɑ̃] *n.m.* harpooning.
***harponner** [arpɔne] *v.tr.* **1.** to harpoon. **2.** *P:* (*a*) to arrest, collar (s.o.); (*b*) to stop, corner (s.o.).
***harponneur** [arpɔnœr] *n.m.* harpooner.
***hasard** [azar] *n.m.* **1.** (*a*) chance, luck, accident; fortune; **coup de h.,** (i) stroke of luck, (ii) fluke; **par un coup de h.,** by a mere chance; **jeu de h.,** game of chance; **ne rien laisser au h.,** to leave nothing to chance; **le h. fit que** + *ind. or sub.*, (as) luck would have it . . .; **au h.,** haphazardly, at random; **choix fait au h.,** random choice; **par h.,** by accident, by chance; **par pur h.,** quite by chance, entirely by accident; **si par h. vous le voyez,** if you (should) happen to see him; **sauriez-vous son adresse par h.?** do you happen to know his address? (*b*) risk, danger, hazard; **à tout h.,** on the off chance; just in case; to make (doubly) sure; **les hasards de la guerre,** the hazards of war. **2.** *Games:* hazard.
***hasardé** [azarde] *a.* hazardous, risky, rash, foolhardy (undertaking, etc.); indiscreet (words, etc.)
***hasarder** [azarde] **1.** *v.tr.* to risk, venture, hazard (one's life, etc.); **h. une opinion,** to venture an opinion. **2. se h.,** to take risks; **se h. à faire qch.,** to venture to do sth.; **se h. dans la jungle,** to venture (out) into the jungle.
***hasardeux, -euse** [azardø, -øz] *a.* hazardous, perilous, risky, rash.
***hasch** [aʃ] *n.m. F:* hashish, hash, pot.
***haschisch** [aʃiʃ] *n.m.* hashish.
***hase** [ɑz] *n.f. Z:* (*a*) doe hare; (*b*) doe (of wild rabbit).
hast [ast] *n.m. A:* shaft; **arme d'h.,** shafted weapon; pike, spear.
***hasté** [aste] *a. Bot:* hastate (leaf, etc.).
***hâte** [ɑt] *n.f.* haste, hurry; **avoir h. de faire qch.,** (i) to be in a hurry to do sth.; (ii) to be eager, to long, to do sth.; **avoir trop h., mettre trop de h., à faire qch.,** to be in too great a hurry, in too much of a hurry, to do sth.; **à la h.,** in a hurry, in haste, hastily, hurriedly; **déjeuner à la h.,** to hurry over one's breakfast; **en h.,** hastily, in haste, hurriedly; **en toute h.,** with all possible speed, posthaste; **sans h.,** without haste, deliberately, in a leisurely way.
***hâter** [ɑte] **1.** *v.tr.* to hasten; to hurry (sth.) on; to bring, put, (sth.) forward; to accelerate (proceedings); to expedite (work); to force (fruit, etc.); **h. le pas,** to quicken one's pace. **2. se h.,** to hasten, hurry; **se h. de faire qch.,** to make haste, to hurry, to do sth.; to lose no time in doing sth.; *Prov:* **hâtez-vous lentement,** more haste, less speed.
***hâtif, -ive** [ɑtif, -iv] *a.* (*a*) forward, early (spring, fruit, etc.); premature (decision); precocious (fruit); (*b*) hasty, hurried, ill-considered (measure, etc.).
***hâtivement** [ɑtivmɑ̃] *adv.* hastily, in a hurry; hurriedly.
***hauban** [obɑ̃] *n.m. Nau:* (*a*) shrouds, rigging; (*b*) guy, stays.
***haubaner** [obane] *v.tr. Nau:* to guy, stay, brace.
***haubert** [obɛr] *n.m. A.Mil.Cost:* hauberk, shirt of mail, coat of mail.
***hausse** [os] *n.f.* **1.** rise, rising; increase (in prices); **barometre en h.,** rising barometer; *F:* **les affaires sont en h.,** things are looking up; *Com: Fin:* **marché à la h.,** rising market; **marchandises en h.,** goods on the rise; **les blés ont subi une h. considérable,** wheat has gone up considerably (in price); **jouer à la h.,** to speculate on a rising market, to bull the market; **spéculateur à la h.,** bull. **2.** (*a*) prop, block, stand; (*b*) *Hyd.E:* flush board, shutter. **3.** *Mil:* (*a*) *Sm.a:* (back)sight (of rifle); (*b*) *Artil:* tangent scale, sighting gear; (*c*) elevation, range.
***haussement** [osmɑ̃] *n.m.* raising, lifting; **h. d'épaules,** shrug(ging) (of the shoulders).
***hausser** [ose] **1.** *v.tr.* to raise, lift, make higher; to heighten (wall); to put up (prices); **h. la voix,** to raise one's voice; **h. les épaules,** to shrug (one's shoulders). **2.** *v.i. Nau:* (*of land, lighthouse*) to raise (over the horizon). **3. se h.,** to raise oneself (up); **se h. sur la pointe des pieds,** to stand on tiptoe; **se h. jusqu'à qn,** to raise oneself, to rise, to s.o.'s level.
***haussier** [osje] *n.m. St. Exch: F:* bull.
***haut** [o] **I.** *a.* **1.** high; (*a*) tall (grass, etc.); lofty (building, etc.); towering (cliff); **homme h. de taille, de haute taille,** tall man; **mur h. de six mètres,** wall six metres, *NAm:* meters, high; **hautes terres,** highlands, uplands; **hautes eaux,** high water; **haute mer,** open sea, high seas; **à mer haute,** at high water, at high tide; (*b*) exalted, important, great; **de h. rang,** of high rank; **h. fonctionnaire,** high-ranking official; **hauts faits,** deeds of valour, *NAm:* of valor; **haute finance,** high finance; **haute cuisine,** haute cuisine; **h. comique,** high comedy; **les hautes cartes,** the high cards, the picture cards; (*c*) raised; **marcher la tête haute,** to hold one's head high; **voix haute,** (i) loud voice; (ii) high(-pitched) voice; **lire à haute voix,** to read aloud; **pousser de hauts cris,** to shout out loud; (*d*) **haute trahison,** high treason; **être h. en couleur,** (i) to have a high colour, *NAm:* color; to have a florid complexion; (ii) to be colourful, *NAm:* colorful; **les hauts temps,** remote antiquity; *Mch:* **haute pression,** high, heavy, pressure; *W.Tel:* **haute fréquence,** high frequency. **2.** upper, higher; **les hauts étages,** the upper storeys; **les hautes branches,** the upper branches, the top branches; **le plus h. étage,** the top floor; **la plus haute branche,** the topmost branch; **les hautes classes,** (i) the upper classes (of society); (ii) the higher, upper, forms (of school); *P:* **la haute,** the smart set, the upper crust; **les hautes mathématiques,** higher mathematics; *Geog:* **le h. Canada,** Upper Canada; **le h. Rhin,** the upper Rhine; **la Haute Écosse,** the Highlands (of Scotland); *Nau:* **les hautes voiles,** the upper sails. **II.** *adv.* **1.** high (up), above, up; **h. les mains!** hands up! **h. le pied,** (i) *O:* (*of horse, etc.*) spare, in reserve; (ii) *Rail:* (*of engine*) running light; **parler h.,** to speak loudly; **parlez plus h.!** speak up! **parler, penser, tout h.,** to talk, think, aloud, out loud; **homme h. placé,** man in a high position; **viser h.,** to aim high; *Nau:* **l'ancre est h.,** the anchor is up. **2.** back; **remonter plus h. (dans le temps),** to go further back; **comme il est dit plus h.,** as aforesaid; as has been indicated above, earlier. **III.** *n.m.* **1.** height; **le mur a six mètres de h.,** the wall is six metres, *NAm:* meters, high; **regarder qn du h. de sa grandeur,** to look down on s.o.; **tomber de (son) h.,** (i) to fall flat on the ground; (ii) to fall from one's high position; (iii) to be very much taken

aback; to be dumbfounded. **2.** top, upper part; (*on packing cases*) **h.,** this side up; **h. de la table,** head of the table; **les hauts et les bas,** the ups and downs (of life, etc.); **h. de l'eau,** high water, top of the flood; **les hauts (d'un navire),** the topsides, upper works (of a ship); *Typ:* **h. de casse,** upper case, *F:* caps; **l'étage du h.,** the top floor; **le monsieur du h.,** the gentleman upstairs; **du h. de la falaise,** (down) from the cliff; **gloire à Dieu au plus h. des cieux,** Glory to God in the Highest; **de h. en bas,** (i) downwards, (ii) from top to bottom; **regarder qn de h. en bas,** to look s.o. up and down; **regarder qn de h.,** to look down on s.o.; **traiter qn de h. en bas,** to patronize s.o.; **du h. en bas,** from top to bottom; **en h.,** (i) above, at the top; *Nau:* aloft; (ii) upstairs; *Nau:* **en h. tout le monde!** all hands on deck! **en h., au h., de l'échelle,** at the top of the ladder; **d'en h.,** (i) from above, from on high; (ii) from upstairs.

***hautain** [otɛ̃] *a.* haughty; lofty.

***hautainement** [otɛnmɑ̃] *adv.* haughtily, loftily.

***hautbois** [obwa] *n.m. Mus:* oboe.

***hautboïste** [obɔist] *n. Mus:* oboe player, oboist.

***haut-de-chausse(s)** [odʃos] *n.m. A.Cost:* breeches, trunk hose; *pl. hauts-de-chausse(s).*

***haut-de-forme** [odfɔrm] *n.m.* top hat; *pl. hauts-de-forme.*

***haute-contre** [otkɔ̃tr̥] *Mus.* **1.** *n.f.* counter tenor (voice). **2.** *a.& n.m.* counter tenor; *pl. hautes-contre.*

***hautement** [otmɑ̃] *adv.* **1.** highly (esteemed, etc.). **2.** (*a*) *A:* loudly; (*b*) openly, boldly.

***hauteur** [otœr] *n.f.* **1.** (*a*) height, elevation; altitude (of star, triangle, etc.); (*of aircraft, etc.*) **prendre de la h.,** to climb; **à h. d'appui,** elbow-high; **le peu de h. du plafond,** the lowness of the ceiling; **tomber de (toute) sa h.,** to fall flat; **à la h. de qch.,** abreast of, level with, sth.; **arriver à la h. de qn, qch.,** to draw level with s.o., sth.; **à la h. de l'œil,** at eye level; **être, se montrer, à la h. d'une tâche,** to be, to prove, equal to a task, *F:* to be up to a job; *F:* **être à la h.,** to be up to scratch, up to it; *Nau:* **à la h. du cap Horn,** off, abreast of, Cape Horn; *Dressm:* **h. du dos** = length of back; *Sp:* **saut en h.,** high jump; (*b*) depth; **h. sous clef,** rise (of arch); **h. libre, de passage,** headroom (of bridge, etc.); **le pont manque de h. pour laisser passer les camions,** there isn't enough clearance for lorries under the bridge; (*c*) *Mus:* pitch (of note); (*d*) loftiness (of ideas, etc.). **2.** haughtiness, arrogance; **avec h.,** haughtily, arrogantly. **3.** height; eminence, rising ground, hill(top).

***haut-fond** [ofɔ̃] *n.m.* shoal, shallow (in sea, river); *pl. hauts-fonds.*

***haut(-)fourneau** [ofurno] *n.m. Metall:* blast furnace; *pl. hauts(-)fourneaux.*

***haut-le-cœur** [olkœr] *n.m.inv.* heave (of stomach); **avoir un, des, h.-le-c.,** to retch, heave.

***haut-le-corps** [olkɔr] *n.m.inv.* (sudden) start, jump; **faire un h.-le-c.,** to start, jump.

***haut-mal** [omal] *n.m. inv. Med: A:* epilepsy, falling sickness.

***haut-parleur** [oparlœr] *n.m. W.Tel:* (loud)-speaker; **h.-p. de cabine, de contrôle,** projection room monitor; *pl. haut-parleurs.*

***haut-relief** [orəljɛf] *n.m. Art:* high relief, alto-relievo; *pl. hauts-reliefs.*

***hauturier, -ière** [otyrje, -jɛr] *a.* of the high seas; **navigation hauturière,** ocean navigation; **pilote h.,** deep-sea pilot.

***havage** [avaʒ] *n.m. Min:* (under)cut(ting).

***havanais, -aise** [avanɛ, -ɛz] *a. & n. Geog:* Havanan.

***Havane** [avan] **1.** *Pr.n.f. Geog:* Havana. **2.** (*a*) *n.m.* Havana (cigar); (*b*) *a.inv.* **cuir h.,** (light) brown, tan, leather.

***hâve** [ɑv] *a.* haggard, emaciated, gaunt (face); sunken (cheeks); pale (skin).

***haveneau, -eaux** [avno] *n.m.* shrimping net.

***haver** [ave] *v.tr. Min:* to (under)cut, (under)hole.

***haveuse** [avøz] *n.f. Min:* coalcutter, coalcutting machine, undercutter.

***havir** [avir] *Cu: v.tr.* to burn (meat, etc.).

***havrais, -aise** [ɑvrɛ, -ɛz] *a. & s. Geog:* (native, inhabitant) of Le Havre.

***havre** [ɑvr̥] *n.m. Lit:* haven, port; habour, *NAm:* habor.

***havresac** [avrəsak] *n.m.* (*a*) *Mil: A:* knapsack, pack; (*b*) haversack; (workman's) tool bag.

Hawaï [awai] *Pr.n. Geog:* Hawaii.

hawaïen, -ïenne [awajɛ̃, -jɛn] *a. & n. Geog:* Hawaiian.

***Haye (la)** [laɛ] *Pr.n.f. Geog:* the Hague.

***hayon** [ajɔ̃] *n.m.* (*a*) tailboard (of cart); (*b*) rear door, back door (of van, lorry); (*c*) hatchback (of car).

***hé** [e] *int.* **1.** (*to call attention*) hullo! I say! hey! **2. hé! hé!** well, well! **hé oui!** yes indeed!

***heaume** [om] *n.m. Arm:* helm(et).

hebdomadaire [ɛbdɔmadɛr] *a. & n.m.* weekly.

hebdomadairement [ɛbdɔmadɛrmɑ̃] *adv.* weekly, once a week.

hébergement [ebɛrʒ(ə)mɑ̃] *n.m.* lodging, sheltering; putting (s.o.) up, taking (s.o.) in; habouring, *NAm:* haboring.

héberger [ebɛrʒe] *v.tr.* **(j'hébergeai(s); n. hébergeons)** to lodge, shelter (and feed); to put (s.o.) up, take (s.o.) in; to habour, *NAm:* habor.

hébété [ebete] *a.* dazed, vacant, bewildered (expression, etc.); **h. de douleur,** stupefied with grief.

hébétement [ebɛtmɑ̃] *n.m.* stupefaction.

hébéter [ebete] *v.tr.* **(j'hébète; j'hébéterai)** to dull, stupefy (the senses, etc.); to daze.

hébétude [ebetyd] *n.f.* **1.** *Med:* hebetude. **2.** *Lit:* stupor.

hébraïque [ebraik] *a.* Hebraic, Hebrew.

hébraïsant, -ante [ebraizɑ̃, -ɑ̃t] *n.* Hebraist; Hebrew scholar.

hébraïser [ebraize] **1.** *v.tr. & i.* to hebraize. **2.** *v.i.* (*a*) to study Hebrew; (*b*) to use Hebraisms.

hébraïsme [ebraism] *n.m.* Hebraism.

hébraïste [ebraist] *n.* Hebraist; Hebrew scholar.

hébreu, -eux [ebrø] **1.** *a.m. & n.m.* (**hébraïque** *is used for the f.*) Hebrew. **2.** *n.m. Ling:* Hebrew; *F:* **c'est de l'h. pour moi,** it's all Greek to me.

Hébrides (les) [lezebrid] *Pr.n.f.pl. Geog:* the Hebrides.

hécatombe [ekatɔ̃b] *n.f.* hecatomb; slaughter, massacre.

hectare [ɛktar] *n.m.* hectare (= 2.47 acres).

hectique [ɛktik] *a. Med:* hectic (fever).

hecto [ɛkto] *n.m.* (*a*) hectogram(me); (*b*) hectolitre, *NAm:* hectoliter.

hectogramme [ɛktɔgram] *n.m.* hectogram(me).

hectolitre [ɛktɔlitr̥] *n.m.* hectolitre, *NAm:* hectoliter.

hectomètre [ɛktɔmɛtr̥] *n.m.* hectometre, *NAm:* hectometer.

hectométrique [ɛktɔmetrik] *a.* hectometric.

hectowatt [ɛktɔwat] *n.m. El:* hectowatt.

hédonisme [edɔnism] *n.m.* hedonism.

hédoniste [edɔnist] **1.** *n.* hedonist. **2.** *a.* hedonist(ic).

hégélianisme [egeljanism] *n.m. Phil:* Hegelianism.

hégélien, -ienne [egeljɛ̃, -jɛn] *a. & n. Phil:* Hegelian.

hégémonie [eʒemɔni] *n.f.* hegemony.

hégire [eʒir] *n.f. Moham.Rel:* Hegira.

***hein** [ɛ̃] *int.* (*a*) eh? what? (*b*) **il fait beau aujourd'hui, h.?** fine day, isn't it?
hélas [elɑs] *int.* alas!
Hélène [elɛn] *Pr.n.f.* Helen, Helena; Ellen.
***héler** [ele] *v.tr.* **(je hèle, je hélerai)** to hail, call (s.o., a taxi); *Nau:* to hail, speak (a ship).
hélianthe [eljɑ̃t] *n.m. Bot:* helianthus, sunflower.
hélianthine [heljɑ̃tin] *n.f. Ch:* helianthin(e); methyl orange.
héliaque [eljak] *a. Astr:* heliac(al).
hélice [elis] *n.f.* **1.** *Mth: Arch:* helix; **escalier en h.,** spiral staircase. **2.** (*a*) *Mec.E:* Archimedean screw; conveyance worm; (*b*) *Nau: Av:* propeller, *F:* prop; *Nau:* screw; **vapeur à deux hélices,** twin-screw steamer; *Av:* **h. propulsive,** pusher propeller. **3.** *Moll:* helix.
hélicoïdal, -aux [elikɔidal, -o] *a.* helicoid(al), helical; *Tls:* **mèche hélicoïdale,** twist drill.
hélicoïde [elikɔid] *a. & n.m. Mth:* helicoid.
hélicon [elikɔ̃] *n.m. Mus:* helicon.
hélicoptère [elikɔptɛr] *n.m. Av:* helicopter.
héligare [eligar] *n.f.* heliport.
héliocentrique [eljɔsɑ̃trik] *a. Astr:* heliocentric.
héliographe [eljɔgraf] *n.m.* heliograph.
héliographie [eljɔgrafi] *n.f.* heliography.
héliograveur [eljɔgravœr] *n.m.* photogravure worker.
héliogravure [eljɔgravyr] *n.f.* photogravure.
héliomarin [eljɔmarɛ̃] *a. Med:* **centre h.,** seaside convalescent home where heliotherapy is used.
héliothérapie [eljɔterapi] *n.f. Med:* heliotherapy; sunray treatment.
héliotrope [eljɔtrɔp] *n.m. Bot:* heliotrope, turnsole.
héliport [elipɔr] *n.m.* heliport.
héliporté [elipɔrte] *a.* transported by helicopter.
hélium [eljɔm] *n.m. Ch:* helium.
hélix [eliks] *n.m. Anat:* helix (of the ear).
hellébore [elebɔr] *n.m. Bot:* hellebore.
hellène [elɛn] **1.** *a.* Hellenic. **2.** *n.* Hellene.
hellénique [elenik] *a.* Hellenic.
hellénisant, -ante [elenizɑ̃, -ɑ̃t] **1.** *a.* Hellenistic. **2.** *n.* Hellenist.
hellénisation [elenizasjɔ̃] *n.f.* Hellenization.
helléniser [elenize] *v.tr. & i.* to Hellenize.
hellénisme [elenism] *n.m.* Hellenism.
helléniste [elenist] *n.* Hellenist.
helvète [ɛlvɛt] **1.** *a. & n. Ethn:* Helvetian. **2.** *n.m.pl. Hist:* **les Helvètes,** the Helvetii.
Helvétie [ɛlvesi] *Pr.n.f. Geog: A: & Lit:* Helvetia.
helvétique [ɛlvetik] *a.* Helvetic, Swiss; **le gouvernement h.,** the Swiss government.
helvétisme [ɛlvetism] *n.m. Ling:* Swiss French expression.
***hem** [ɛm] *int.* (*to call attention*) hey! (*as question*) eh? what? (*expressing doubt, etc.*) h'm! (*clearing throat*) ahem!
hématie [emati] *n.f. Physiol:* red blood corpuscle.
hématite [ematit] *n.f. Miner:* h(a)ematite.
hématologie [ematɔlɔʒi] *n.f. Med:* h(a)ematology.
hématologiste [ematɔlɔʒist], **hématologue** [ematɔlɔg] *n.* h(a)ematologist.
hématome [ematom] *n.m. Med:* h(a)ematoma.
hémicycle [emisikl̥] *n.m. Arch:* hemicycle; **en h.,** semicircular (vault, etc.).
hémione [emjɔn] *n.m. Z:* hemione, dziggetai.
hémiplégie [emipleʒi] *n.f. Med:* hemiplegia.
hémiplégique [emipleʒik] *a. & n. Med:* hemiplegic.
hémiptère [emiptɛr] *Ent:* **1.** *a.* hemipterous, hemipteral. **2.** *n.m.* hemipter.
hémisphère [emisfɛr] *n.m.* hemisphere; **l'h. nord, sud,** the northern, southern, hemisphere.
hémisphérique [emisferik] *a.* hemispheric(al).
hémistiche [emistiʃ] *n.m. Pros:* hemistich.
hémoculture [emɔkyltyr] *n.f.* h(a)emoculture, blood culture.
hémoglobine [emɔglɔbin] *n.f.* h(a)emoglobin.
hémophile [emɔfil] *Med:* **1.** *a.* h(a)emophilic. **2.** *n.* h(a)emophiliac.
hémophilie [emɔfili] *n.f. Med:* h(a)emophilia.
hémoptysie [emɔptizi] *n.f. Med:* h(a)emoptysis, spitting of blood (from lungs).
hémorragie [emɔraʒi] *n.f. Med:* h(a)emorrhage; bleeding; **l'h. des réserves d'or,** the heavy drain on the gold reserve.
hémorragique [emɔraʒik] *a. Med:* h(a)emorrhagic.
hémorroïdaire [emɔrɔidɛr] *a. & n. Med:* **(personne) h.,** person suffering from h(a)emorrhoids.
hémorroïdal, -aux [emɔrɔidal, -o] *a. Med:* h(a)emorrhoidal.
hémorroïdes [emɔrɔid] *n.f.pl. Med:* h(a)emorrhoids, piles.
hémostatique [emɔstatik] *Med:* **1.** *a.* h(a)emostatic. **2.** *n.m.* h(a)emostat(ic).
hendécagone [ɛ̃dekagɔn] *n.m.* hendecagon.
hendécasyllabe [ɛ̃dekasilab] *Pros:* **1.** *a.* hendecasyllabic. **2.** *n.m.* hendecasyllable.
***henné** [ɛne] *n.m. Bot: Toil:* henna.
***hennin** [ɛnɛ̃] *n.m. A.Cost:* hennin.
***hennir** [ɛnir] *v.i.* to whinny, neigh.
***hennissement** [ɛnismɑ̃] *n.m.* (*a*) whinnying, neighing; (*b*) whinny, neigh.
Henri [ɑ̃ri] *Pr.n.m.* Henry.
Henriette [ɑ̃rjɛt] *Pr.n.f.* Henrietta.
henry [ɑ̃ri] *n.m. El:* henry; *pl. henrys.*
***hep** [ɛp] *int.* hey (there)!
hépatique [epatik] **1.** *a.* hepatic. **2.** *n.* person suffering from a liver complaint. **3.** *n.f. Bot:* hepatica; liverwort.
hépatisme [epatism] *n.m. Med:* liver ailments (in general).
hépatite [epatit] *n.f. Med:* hepatitis.
heptacorde [ɛptakɔrd] *Mus:* **1.** *a.* seven-stringed. **2.** *n.m.* heptachord (instrument, scale).
heptaèdre [ɛptaɛdr̥] *n.m.* heptahedron.
heptagonal, -aux [ɛptagɔnal, -o] *a.* heptagonal.
heptagone [ɛptagɔn] *n.m.* heptagon.
heptamètre [ɛptamɛtr̥] *n.m. Pros:* heptameter.
heptarchie [ɛptarʃi] *n.f. Hist:* heptarchy.
heptasyllabe [ɛptasilab] *a. Pros:* heptasyllabic.
Heptateuque (l') [lɛptatøk] *n.m. B:* the Heptateuch.
héraldique [eraldik] **1.** *a.* heraldic; armorial. **2.** *n.f.* heraldry.
héraldiste [eraldist] *n.* heraldist.
***héraut** [ero] *n.m.* (*a*) **h. (d'armes),** herald; (*b*) *Lit:* herald, harbinger (of spring, etc.).
herbacé [ɛrbase] *a. Bot:* herbaceous.
herbage [ɛrbaʒ] *n.m.* **1.** grassland; pasture. **2.** grass, herbage.
herbagement [ɛrbaʒmɑ̃] *n.m.* putting (of animals) out to grass.
herbager[1] [ɛrbaʒe] *v.tr.* **(j'herbageai(s); n. herbageons)** to put (animals) out to grass.
herbager[2], **-ère** [-ɛr] *n.* grazier.
herbe [ɛrb] *n.f.* **1.** herb, plant, weed; *Cu:* **fines herbes,** mixed herbs; **herbes marines,** seaweed; **mauvaise h.,** weed. **2.** grass; **brin d'h.,** blade of grass; **faire de l'h.,** to cut grass (for rabbit, etc.); **couper l'h. sous les pieds de qn,** to cut the ground from under s.o.'s feet; **déjeuner sur l'h.,** to picnic, have a picnic (lunch); *Golf:* **être dans l'h. longue,** to be in the rough. **3. en h.,** (i) green, unripe (corn, etc.); (ii) budding (poet, etc.). **4.** *Bot:* (*common names*) **h. aux chats,** catmint, *NAm:* catnip; **h. au cœur, aux poumons,** lungwort; **h.**

à éternuer, sneezewort; **h. sacrée, à tous les maux,** wild vervain; **h. aux écus,** moneywort; **h. aux puces,** fleawort; *Fr.C:* **h. à la puce,** poison ivy.
herbeux, -euse [ɛrbø, -øz] *a.* grassy.
herbicide [ɛrbisid] *n.m.* weedkiller.
herbier [ɛrbje] *n.m.* **1.** (*a*) *A:* herbal; (*b*) herbarium; hortus siccus. **2.** *Bot:* water plant community.
herbivore [ɛrbivɔr] *Z:* **1.** *a.* herbivorous. **2.** *n.m.* herbivore.
herborisation [ɛrbɔrizasjɔ̃] *n.f.* herborizing, botanizing; gathering plants.
herboriser [ɛrbɔrize] *v.i.* to herborize, botanize; to gather plants.
herboriste [ɛrbɔrist] *n.* herbalist.
herboristerie [ɛrbɔristəri] *n.f.* **1.** herbalist's shop. **2.** herb trade.
herbu [ɛrby] *a.* grassy.
***hercher** [ɛrʃe] *v.i. Min:* to haul (coal, ore).
***hercheur** [ɛrʃœr] *n.m. Min:* haulage man, boy.
Herculanum [ɛrkylanɔm] *Pr.n.m. A.Geog:* Herculaneum.
Hercule [ɛrkyl] *Pr.n.m.* Hercules; **travail d'H.,** Herculean task; **h. de foire,** (professional) strong man.
herculéen, -enne [ɛrkyleɛ̃] *a.* Herculean.
***hère** [ɛr] *n.m.* **pauvre h.,** poor, unlucky, creature; poor blighter, poor devil.
héréditaire [ereditɛr] *a.* hereditary; (disease) that runs in the family.
héréditairement [ereditɛrmɑ̃] *adv.* hereditarily.
hérédité [eredite] *n.f.* **1.** *Jur: Biol:* hereditary principle; heredity; heritage. **2.** right of inheritance.
hérésie [erezi] *n.f.* heresy.
hérétique [eretik] **1.** *a.* heretical. **2.** *n.* heretic.
***hérissé** [erise] *a.* **1.** bristling (**de,** with). **2.** (*of hair*) (standing) on end; spiky; bristly (moustache, person); prickly (stem, fruit).
***hérissement** [erismɑ̃] *n.m.* bristling.
***hérisser** [erise] **1.** *v.tr.* (*a*) to bristle (up); (*of bird*) **h. ses plumes,** to ruffle up, put up, its feathers; (*b*) to make (sth.) bristle; to cover, surround (sth.), with spikes; to make (hair) stand on end; **il a été hérissé par cette remarque,** this remark got his back up, made him bristle; **h. sa conversation de malices,** to lard, pepper, one's conversation with sly digs. **2. se h.,** to bristle (up); (*of hair*) to stand on end; (*of pers.*) to get one's back up, to bristle.
***hérisson** [erisɔ̃] *n.m.* **1.** (*a*) *Z:* hedgehog; (*b*) **h. de mer,** (i) *Echin:* sea urchin; (ii) *Ich:* porcupine fish; (*c*) cross-grained, bristly, person. **2.** (*a*) row of spikes (on wall, etc.); (*b*) bottle drainer. **3.** (*a*) (sweep's) flue brush; (*b*) *Agr:* toothed cylinder, toothed roller.
héritage [eritaʒ] *n.m.* inheritance, heritage; **part d'h.,** portion; **faire, recueillir, un h.,** to receive a legacy, come into money; *Fig:* **h. de honte,** legacy of shame.
hériter [erite] *v.* to inherit. **1.** *v.i.* (*a*) **h. d'une fortune,** to inherit, succeed to, come into, a fortune; (*b*) *F:* **il a hérité de dix jours de prison,** he got ten days in prison. **2.** *v.tr.* **h. qch. de qn,** to inherit sth. from s.o.
héritier, -ière [eritje, -jɛr] *n.* heir, *f.* heiress; **h. de qch., de qn,** heir to sth., to s.o.; **h. présomptif,** (i) *Jur:* next of kin; (ii) heir apparent; **h. légitime, naturel,** heir-at-law, rightful heir.
hermaphrodisme [ɛrmafrɔdism] *n.m. Biol:* hermaphroditism.
Hermaphrodite [ɛrmafrɔdit] **1.** *Pr.n.m. Gr.Myth:* Hermaphroditus. **2.** *n.m.* hermaphrodite. **3.** *a.* hermaphrodite, hermaphroditic.
hermétique [ɛrmetik] *a.* **1.** hermetic (philosophy, alchemy). **2.** tight (closed), hermetically sealed; hermetic (seal); **joint h.,** airtight, watertight, joint. **3.** abstruse, obscure (text, etc.).
hermétiquement [ɛrmetikmɑ̃] *a.* hermetically (sealed, etc.); tight(-shut), close(-shut).
hermétisme [ɛrmetism] *n.m.* **1.** hermetism. **2.** abstruseness, obscurity (of text, etc.).
hermine [ɛrmin] *n.f.* **1.** *Z:* stoat, ermine. **2.** *Com:* ermine (fur).
herminette [ɛrminɛt] *n.f. Tls:* adze.
***herniaire** [ɛrnjɛr] **1.** *a.* hernial (tumour, etc.); **bandage h.,** truss. **2.** *n.f. Bot:* rupture wort.
***hernie** [ɛrni] *n.f.* **1.** *Med:* (*a*) hernia, rupture; **h. étranglée,** strangulated hernia; (*b*) **h. discale,** slipped disc. **2.** *Aut: Cy:* bulge, swelling (in tyre).
***hernié** [ɛrnje] *a. Med:* herniated (intestine, etc.).
***hernieux, -euse** [ɛrnjø, -øz] *a. Med:* suffering from a hernia; ruptured.
Hérode [erɔd] *Pr.n.m.* Herod.
Hérodote [erɔdɔt] *Pr.n.m. Gr.Lit:* Herodotus.
héroï-comique [erɔikɔmik] *a.* mock-heroic; *pl. heroï-comiques.*
héroïne[1] [erɔin] *n.f.* heroine.
héroïne[2] *n.f. Ch:* heroin.
héroïque [erɔik] *a.* heroic.
héroïquement [erɔikmɑ̃] *adv.* heroically.
héroïsme [erɔism] *n.m.* heroism.
***héron** [erɔ̃] *n.m. Orn:* heron.
***héronneau, -eaux** [erɔno] *n.m. Orn:* young heron.
***héros** [ero] *n.m.* hero.
herpès [ɛrpɛs] *n.m. Med:* herpes; cold sore.
herpétique [ɛrpetik] *a. Med:* herpetic.
herpétologie [ɛrpetɔlɔʒi] *n.f.* herpetology.
***hersage** [ɛrsaʒ] *n.m. Agr:* harrowing.
***herscher** [ɛrʃe] *v.i. Min:* to haul (coal, ore).
***herse** [ɛrs] *n.f.* **1.** *Agr:* harrow. **2.** *A.Fort:* portcullis. **3.** (*a*) *Ecc:* (taper) hearse; (*b*) *Th:* stage light, batten.
***herser** [ɛrse] *v.tr. Agr:* to harrow.
***herseur** [ɛrsœr] *n.m. Agr:* harrower.
hertz [ɛrts] *n.m. El:* hertz.
hertzien, -ienne [ɛrtsjɛ̃, -jɛn] *a. El:* hertzian; *W.Tel:* **réseau h.,** radio relay system.
hésitant [ezitɑ̃] *a.* hesitant, wavering, undecided (character, etc.); faltering (voice, footsteps, etc.).
hésitation [ezitasjɔ̃] *n.f.* hesitation, hesitancy, wavering; **parler avec h.,** to speak hesitatingly; **sans h.,** unhesitatingly, without faltering.
hésiter [ezite] *v.i.* **1.** to hesitate, waver; **h. sur qch., entre deux choses,** to hesitate over sth, between two things; **h. sur ce qu'on fera,** to hesitate as to what one will do; **h. à faire qch.,** to hesitate, be reluctant, to do sth.; **il n'hésite devant rien,** he hesitates at nothing, nothing daunts him; **il n'y a pas à h.,** there's no room, no time, for hesitation. **2.** to hesitate, falter (in speaking, etc.).
hétéroclite [eterɔklit] *a.* **1.** heterogeneous, ill assorted (collection, etc.); **mélange h.,** incongruous medley. **2.** unusual, strange, odd, eccentric.
hétérodoxe [eterɔdɔks] *a.* heterodox.
hétérodoxie [eterɔdɔksi] *n.f.* heterodoxy.
hétérodyne [eterɔdin] *a. & n.f. W.Tel:* heterodyne (receiver).
hétérogène [eterɔʒɛn] *a.* (*a*) heterogeneous, dissimilar; (*b*) incongruous (collection, etc.); mixed (society).
hétérogénéité [eterɔʒeneite] *n.f.* heterogeneousness, heterogeneity.
hétéroplastie [eterɔplasti] *n.f. Surg:* heteroplasty.
hétérosexuel, -elle [eterɔsɛksɥɛl] *a.* heterosexual.
***hêtraie** [ɛtrɛ] *n.f.* beech grove, plantation.
***hêtre** [ɛtr̥] *n.m.* beech (tree, wood); **h. rouge, pourpre,** copper beech.
***heu** [ø] *int.* (*a*) (*doubt*) h'm! (*b*) (*in hesitating speech*) . . . er . . . .
heur [œr] *n.m.* (*a*) *A:* (good) luck; (*b*) *Iron:* **je n'ai pas l'h. de la connaître,** I have not the pleasure of her acquaintance.

heure [œr] *n.f.* hour; (*a*) **à toutes heures du jour,** at all hours of the day; **heures d'affluence, de pointe,** rush hour, peak period; **heures creuses,** off-peak hours, slack period; **d'h. en h.,** hour by hour; hourly; *Journ:* **la dernière h.,** (i) the latest news; (ii) stop press (news); **j'ai attendu une bonne h.,** I waited a full, good, solid, hour; **cent kilomètres à l'h.,** a hundred kilometres, *NAm:* kilometers, an hour; **être payé à l'h.,** to be paid by the hour; **toucher 30 francs l'h.,** *F:* **de l'h.,** to get 30 francs an hour; **semaine de 40 heures,** 40-hour week; **heures supplémentaires,** overtime; **tous les frais de travail hors d'heures seront payés par . . .,** all overtime to be paid by . . .; (*b*) (*time of day*) **l'h. de Greenwich,** Greenwich mean time; **h. astronomique,** sidereal time; **h. légale,** official, standard time; **h. d'été,** *Fr.C:* **h. avancée,** summer time, *NAm:* daylight saving time; **le parti communiste est à l'h. de la Russie,** the Communist party is under Russian influence; **quelle h. est-il?** what time is it? what's the time? **quelle h. avez-vous?** what time do you make it? **il est deux heures,** it's two o'clock; **cinq heures moins dix,** ten (minutes) to five; **dix-huit heures,** eighteen hundred (hours); **vingt heures quarante,** twenty forty; **le train de neuf heures,** the nine o'clock train; **où serai-je demain à cette h.-ci?** where will I be this time tomorrow? **à une h. avancée (de la journée),** late in the day; **à cinq heures juste(s), sonnant(es), tapant(es),** (right, exactly) on the stroke of five; at five on the dot, at five o'clock sharp; **mettre sa montre à l'h.,** to set one's watch (right); **ma montre n'est pas à l'h.,** my watch is wrong; **les trains partent à l'h.,** the trains leave (i) on the hour, (ii) on time; *Ecc:* **livre d'heures,** Book of Hours; (*c*) (*appointed time*) **l'h. du dîner,** dinner time; **l'h. d'aller se coucher,** bedtime; **son h. est venue,** his time has come; **à l'h. dite,** at the appointed, agreed, time; **être à l'h.,** to be punctual, on time; **arriver à l'h. exacte,** to arrive dead on time; **être, arriver, avoir fini, avant l'h.,** to be ahead of time; **à ses heures, il était charmant,** when he liked, felt like it, was in the mood, he could be charming; **il est, c'est, l'h.,** (i) the hour has come, it's time; (ii) time is up; (*d*) (*present time*) **pour l'h.,** for the present, for the time being; **la question de l'h.,** the question of the moment, the current question; **à l'h. qu'il est,** (i) by this time, by now; (ii) nowadays; now; currently; *esp. NAm:* presently; (*e*) time, period; *Sch:* **h. de cours,** period; **cette mode a eu son h.,** this fashion has had its day; **j'attends mon h.,** I'm biding my time; (*f*) **de bonne h.,** (i) early, in good time; (ii) at an early period; **il est de trop bonne h. pour rentrer,** it's too early to go home; **de meilleure h.,** earlier; **faire qch. sur l'h.,** to do sth. at once, right away; **je vais le faire dès cette h.,** I'll do it at once; **à toute h.,** at any time; at all hours of the day; round the clock; **tout à l'h.,** (i) just now, a few minutes ago; (ii) soon, presently, in a few minutes; **à tout à l'h.!** so long! see you soon, later! (*g*) *int.* **à la bonne h.!** well done! good (for you)! all right! fine!

heureusement [œrøzmɑ̃] *adv.* happily; (*a*) successfully; (*b*) luckily, fortunately; **h. que j'étais là,** it's a good thing I was there, fortunately I was there; (*c*) **commencer h.,** to begin auspiciously; (*d*) **h. exprimé,** well expressed.

heureux, -euse [œrø, -øz] *a.* **1.** happy; **h. comme un poisson dans l'eau,** as happy as a sandboy; **vivre h.,** to live happily; **heureuse ignorance,** blissful ignorance; **je suis très h. de ce cadeau,** I'm very happy, pleased, with, about, this gift; **je suis très h. de vous faire savoir que . . .,** I'm very happy, pleased, to inform you, that . . .; **nous serions h. que vous acceptiez,** we should be glad if you would accept; *n.* **vous avez fait un h.,** you have made one man very happy. **2.** (*a*) successful; **voyage h.,** good, prosperous, journey; **l'issue heureuse des négociations,** the successful outcome, happy issue, of the negotiations; (*b*) (*of pers.*) fortunate, favoured; **h. au jeu, en amour,** lucky at cards, in love; *B:* **h. sont les pauvres en esprit,** blessed are the poor in spirit. **3.** (*a*) favourable, *NAm:* favorable; lucky, fortunate; **c'est fort h. pour vous,** that's very lucky for you; **c'est h. que vous soyez libre,** it's a good thing, a good job, that you're free; **par un h. hasard,** by a fortunate, happy, coincidence; (*b*) **début h.,** auspicious beginning. **4.** felicitous, happy, apt (phrase, etc.).

heuristique [œristik] (*a*) *a.* heuristic; (*b*) *n.f.* heuristics.

***heurt** [œr] *n.m.* shock, blow, knock, bump; collision (of vehicles, etc.); clash (of interests, colours, etc.); **tout s'est fait sans h.,** everything went smoothly.

***heurté** [œrte] *a.* **1.** *Art: Phot:* contrasty, hard (negative, etc.). **2.** abrupt, halting (style).

***heurter** [œrte] **1.** *v.tr. & i.* (*a*) to knock (against), run against, run into, bang into, bump into (s.o., sth.); to jostle, collide with (s.o.); **h. sa tête à, contre, qch.,** to knock, bump, one's head against sth.; *Nau:* to hit, strike (a rock); (*b*) **h. à la porte,** to knock at, on, the door; (*c*) to shock, offend (s.o.'s feelings, etc.); **h. toutes les idées reçues,** to go against, run counter to, all conventions. **2. se h.** (*a*) **se h. à, contre, qn, qch.,** to run (slap) into, collide with, bang into, bump into, s.o., sth.; **se h. à une difficulté,** to come up against a difficulty; (*b*) (*of vehicles, etc.*) to collide (with each other); (*of colours, interests, etc.*) to clash.

***heurtoir** [œrtwar] *n.m.* **1.** (door) knocker. **2.** (*a*) *Mec.E:* (i) catch, stop; (ii) driver, tappet; (*b*) *Rail:* (i) buffer; (ii) bumping post (of siding). **3.** *Hyd.E:* sill (of lock gate).

hévéa [evea] *n.m. Bot:* hevea.

hexacorde [ɛgzakɔrd] *n.m. Mus:* hexachord.

hexaèdre [ɛgzaɛdr̥] **1.** *a.* hexahedral. **2.** *n.m.* hexahedron.

hexagonal, -aux [ɛgzagɔnal, -o] *a.* hexagonal.

hexagone [ɛgzagɔn] *n.m.* hexagon; **l'H. (français),** France.

hexamètre [ɛgzamɛtr̥] *Pros.* **1.** *a.* hexametric(al). **2.** *n.m.* hexameter.

hiatal, -aux [jatal, -o] *a. Med:* hiatal; **hernie hiatale,** hiatus hernia.

hiatus [jatys] *n.m.* **1.** gap, break (in narrative, etc.). **2.** *Pros: Anat:* hiatus.

hibernal, -aux [ibɛrnal, -o] *a.* hibernal (germination, etc.); wintry, winter (temperature, etc.).

hibernant [ibɛrnɑ̃] *a.* hibernating (animal).

hibernation [ibɛrnasjɔ̃] *n.f.* hibernation.

hiberner [ibɛrne] *v.i.* to hibernate.

hibiscus [ibiskys] *n.m. Bot:* hibiscus.

***hibou, -oux** [ibu] *n.m. Orn:* owl; **jeune h.,** owlet.

***hic** [ik] *n.m. F:* **voilà le h.!** that's the snag, the trouble; there's the rub!

hickory [ikɔri] *n.m. Bot:* hickory.

***hideur** [idœr] *n.f.* (*a*) hideousness; (*b*) hideous sight.

***hideusement** [idøzmɑ̃] *adv.* hideously.

***hideux, -euse** [idø, -øz] *a.* hideous; **h. à voir,** hideous-looking.

***hie** [i] *n.f.* **1.** (paviour's) beetle, (earth)rammer. **2.** pile driver.

hiémal, -aux [jemal, -o] *a. Lit:* hiemal; winter (solstice, etc.).

hier [jɛr] **1.** *adv.* yesterday; **h. (au) matin,** yesterday morning; **h. (au) soir,** yesterday evening, last night; **le journal d'h.,** yesterday's paper; *F:* **je ne suis pas né d'h.,** I wasn't born yesterday. **2.** *n.m.* **vous aviez tout**

h., toute la journée d'h., pour vous décider, you had all (day) yesterday to make up your mind.
***hiérarchie** [jerarʃi] *n.f.* hierarchy.
***hiérarchique** [jerarʃik] *a.* hierarchical; **par (la) voie h.,** through (the) official channels.
***hiérarchiquement** [jerarʃikmɑ̃] *adv.* hierarchically; through the official channels.
***hiérarchiser** [jerarʃize] *v.tr.* (*a*) to form, manage (state, etc.) on the hierarchical system; to hierarchize; (*b*) to grade (personnel).
hiératique [jeratik] *a.* hieratic (style, etc.).
***hiéroglyphe** [jerɔglif] *n.m.* hieroglyph(ic).
***hiéroglyphique** [jerɔglifik] *a.* hieroglyphic(al).
***hi-fi** [ifi] *a. & n.f. W.Tel: etc: F:* hi-fi, high-fidelity.
***hi-han** [iɑ̃] *int. & n.m. onomat.* (donkey's) hee-haw; *pl. hi-hans.*
hi hi [ii] *int. onomat.* (*sound of tittering*) tehee! teehee!
hilarant [ilarɑ̃] *a.* hilarious; *Ch:* **gaz h.,** laughing gas.
hilare [ilar] *a.* hilarious, mirthful.
hilarité [ilarite] *n.f.* hilarity, mirth, laughter.
***hile** [il] *n.m. Anat: Bot:* hilum; *Anat:* transverse fissure, porta (of the liver).
hiloire [ilwar] *n.f. N.Arch:* coaming.
himalayen, -enne [imalajɛ̃, -ɛn] *a. & n. Geog:* Himalayan.
***hindi** [indi] *n.m. Ling:* Hindi.
hindou, -oue [ɛ̃du] *a. & n. Ethn:* Hindu.
hindouisme [ɛ̃duism] *n.m.* Hinduism.
hindouiste [ɛ̃duist] *a. & n. Ethn:* Hindu.
Hindoustan [ɛ̃dustɑ̃] *Pr.n.m. Geog:* Hindustan.
hindoustani [ɛ̃dustani] *n.m. Ling:* Hindustani.
hinterland [intɛrlɑ̃d] *n.m.* hinterland.
***hippie** [ipi] *a. & n. F:* hippie.
hippique [ipik] *a.* relating to horses; equine; **concours h.,** (i) horse show; (ii) race meeting.
hippisme [ipism] *n.m.* horse racing, riding.
hippocampe [ipɔkɑ̃p] *n.m.* **1.** *Gr.Myth:* hippocampus. **2.** *Ich:* hippocampus, sea horse.
Hippocrate [ipɔkrat] *Pr.n.m. Gr.Ant:* Hippocrates.
hippocratique [ipɔkratik] *a.* Hippocratic.
hippodrome [ipɔdrom] *n.m.* **1.** *Ant:* hippodrome, circus. **2.** racecourse.
hippologie [ipɔlɔʒi] *n.f.* care and management of horses.
hippomobile [ipɔmɔbil] *a.* horse-drawn.
hippophagie [ipɔfaʒi] *n.f.* hippophagy.
hippophagique [ipɔfaʒik] *a.* **boucherie h.,** horse butcher('s).
hippopotame [ipɔpɔtam] *n.m. Z:* hippopotamus.
hippotechnie [ipɔtɛkni] *n.f.* technique of horse breeding and training; horsemanship.
***hippy** [ipi] *a. & n. F:* hippie.
hircin [irsɛ̃] *a.* hircine, goatish.
hirondelle [irɔ̃dɛl] *n.f.* **1.** *Orn:* swallow; **h. de fenêtre,** house martin; **h. de rivage,** sand martin; *Prov:* **une h. ne fait pas le printemps** = one swallow doesn't make a summer; *Cu:* **nid d'h.,** bird's nest. **2.** *F:* cycle cop.
hirsute [irsyt] *a.* hirsute, hairy, shaggy, unkempt.
hispanique [ispanik] *a.* Hispanic, Spanish.
hispanisant, -ante [ispanizɑ̃, -ɑ̃t] *n.* student of, expert on, Spanish.
hispanisme [ispanism] *n.m. Ling:* Hispanicism.
hispano-américain, -aine [ispanɔamerikɛ̃, -ɛn] *a. & n. Geog:* Hispano-American, Spanish-American; *pl. hispano-américain(e)s.*
hispano-arabe [ispanɔarab], **hispano-moresque** [ispanɔmɔrɛsk] *a.* Hispano-Moresque, Hispano-Moorish; *pl. hispano-arabes, -moresques.*
hispide [ispid] *a.* hispid; hairy, rough.
***hisser** [ise] **1.** *v.tr.* to hoist (up), pull up; *Nau:* to trice (up) (sail), hoist in (boat), run up (signal); **hissez!** up with it! hoist away! *Nau:* up sails! sway away! **oh! hisse!** (yo-)heave-ho! **2. se h. jusqu'à la fenêtre,** to pull, hoist, oneself up to the window; **se h. sur la pointe des pieds,** to stand on tiptoe.
histoire [istwar] *n.f.* **1.** (*a*) history; **h. du moyen âge,** medi(a)eval history; **peintre d'h.,** historical painter; **livre d'h.,** history book; **l'H. sainte,** Bible history; **la petite h.,** sidelights on history; (*b*) **h. naturelle,** natural history; (*c*) *Sch:* history book; **j'ai acheté une h. d'Allemagne,** I've bought a history of Germany. **2.** story, tale, narrative; **h. de marin,** sailor's yarn; **livre d'histoires,** story book; **h. de fous,** shaggy dog story; *F:* **c'est toujours la même h.,** it's always the same old story; **le plus beau de l'h., c'est que . . .,** the best part of the story, of the business, is that . . .; *F:* **il est sorti, h. de prendre un peu l'air,** he went out merely, just, to get a breath of fresh air; *F:* **en voilà une h.!** what a fuss! what a song and dance! **c'est toute une h.,** (i) it's a long story; (ii) it's no end of a job. **3.** *F:* lie, fib, story; **tout ça ce sont des histoires,** that's all bunkum; it's all eyewash, rubbish! **4.** *F:* **faire des histoires, un tas d'histoires,** to make a fuss, a to-do; **faire des histoires à qn,** to make trouble for s.o.; **il faut éviter d'avoir des histoires,** you, we, must keep out of trouble; *F:* **pas d'histoires!** no fuss! **5.** *F:* thing(ummy).
histologie [istɔlɔʒi] *n.f.* histology.
histologique [istɔlɔʒik] *a.* histological.
historié [istɔrje] *a.* historiated (initials, etc.); illuminated (Bible, etc.).
historien, -ienne [istɔrjɛ̃, -jɛn] *n.* historian.
historiette [istɔrjɛt] *n.f.* anecdote; short story.
historiographe [istɔrjɔgraf] *n.m.* historiographer, chronicler.
historiographie [istɔrjɔgrafi] *n.f.* historiography.
historique [istɔrik] **1.** *a.* historic(al); *Gram:* **présent h.,** historic present; (*of building*) **être classé (comme) monument h.,** to be scheduled as an ancient monument, as a place of historic interest. **2.** *n.m.* historical record, account; **faire l'h. des événements,** to give a chronological account of events.
historiquement [istɔrikmɑ̃] *adv.* historically.
histrion [istriɔ̃] *n.m.* (*a*) *Th: A:* histrion, play actor; (*b*) *Lit:* second-rate actor.
hitlérien, -ienne [itlerjɛ̃, -jɛn] *a. & n.* Hitlerite; **le gouvernement h.,** the Hitler government.
hitlérisme [itlerism] *n.m.* Hitlerism.
hittite [itit] *a. & n. A.Hist:* Hittite.
hiver [ivɛr] *n.m.* winter; **en h.,** in winter; **temps d'h.,** wintry weather; **vêtements, sports, d'h.,** winter clothes, sports; **jardin d'h.,** winter garden; *F:* **le bonhomme H.,** Jack Frost.
hivernage [ivɛrnaʒ] *n.m.* **1.** (*a*) wintering (of cattle, etc.); (*b*) laying up (of ships) for the winter. **2.** (*a*) winter season; (*b*) rainy season (in tropics). **3.** winter quarters, *Nau:* winter harbour. **4.** *Husb:* winter fodder.
hivernal, -aux [ivɛrnal, -o] *a.* winter (cold, etc.); wintry (weather); hibernal (sleep, etc.).
hivernant, -ante [ivɛrnɑ̃, -ɑ̃t] *n.* winter visitor, tourist (in holiday resort, etc.).
hiverner [ivɛrne] *v.i.* (*a*) to winter; (*of ship*) to lie up (for the winter); (*b*) (*of animal*) to hibernate.
***ho** [o] *int.* **1.** (*call*) hey! **2.** (*surprise*) oh!
***hobereau, -eaux** [ɔbro] *n.m.* **1.** *Orn:* hobby. **2.** (country) squire.
***hochement** [ɔʃmɑ̃] *n.m.* **h. de tête,** (i) shake of the head; (ii) nod (of the head); (iii) (*of pers. or horse*) toss of the head.
***hochepot** [ɔʃpo] *n.m. Cu:* meat and vegetable stew; hotchpotch.
***hochequeue** [ɔʃkø] *n.m. Orn:* wagtail.
***hocher** [ɔʃe] *v.tr.* **h. la tête,** (i) to shake one's head;

(ii) to nod (one's head); (iii) (*of pers. or horse*) to toss the head.

***hochet** [ɔʃɛ] *n.m.* (*a*) (child's) rattle; (*b*) bauble, toy.

***hockey** [ɔkɛ] *n.m. Sp:* (*a*) hockey, *Fr.C:* ice hockey; **h. sur glace,** ice hockey, *NAm:* hockey; **partie de h.,** hockey game, match; (*b*) *Fr.C:* (ice) hockey stick.

***hockeyeur, -euse** [ɔkɛjœr, -øz] *n.* (ice) hockey player.

hoir [war] *n.m. A.Jur:* heir.

hoirie [wari] *n.f. Jur:* (*a*) *A:* inheritance, succession; (*b*) **avance, avancement, d'h.,** advancement.

***holà** [ɔla] *int.* **1.** hey! **2.** stop! hold on! enough! whoa! **mettre le h. à qch.,** to check, put a stop to, sth.

***holding** [ɔldiŋ] *n.m. Fin:* holding company; holding.

***hold-up** [ɔldœp] *n.m.inv. F:* hold-up, *esp. NAm:* stick-up.

***hollandais, -aise** [ɔlɑ̃dɛ, -ɛz] **1.** *a.* Dutch. **2.** *n.* Dutchman, *f.* Dutchwoman; **les H.,** the Dutch. **3.** *n.m. Ling:* Dutch.

***Hollande** [ɔlɑ̃d] **1.** *Pr.n.f. Geog:* Holland. **2.** *n.m.* (*a*) **h., fromage de H.,** Dutch cheese; (*b*) *Paperm:* Dutch paper. **3.** *n.f. Tex:* holland (cambric).

holocauste [ɔlɔkost] *n.m.* holocaust; (i) burnt offering; (ii) sacrifice.

holothurie [ɔlɔtyri] *n.f. Echin:* holothurian, sea slug, sea cucumber.

***homard** [ɔmar] *n.m.* lobster.

hombre [ɔ̃bṛ] *n.m. A.Cards:* (game of) ombre.

***home** [om] *n.m.* home.

homélie [ɔmeli] *n.f.* homily.

homéopathe [ɔmeɔpat] *Med:* **1.** *a.* hom(o)eopathic. **2.** *n.* hom(o)eopath.

homéopathie [ɔmeɔpati] *n.f.* hom(o)eopathy.

homéopathique [ɔmeɔpatik] *a.* hom(o)eopathic.

Homère [ɔmɛr] *Pr.n.m. Gr.Lit:* Homer.

homérique [ɔmerik] *a.* Homeric.

homicide¹ [ɔmisid] **1.** *n.m. & f. Lit:* (*pers.*) homicide. **2.** *a. A: & Lit:* homicidal; murderous (weapon).

homicide² *n.m. Jur:* homicide (as a crime); **h. volontaire,** wilful homicide; murder; **h. excusable,** justifiable homicide; **h. par imprudence, h. involontaire,** manslaughter (through negligence); **h. sans préméditation,** (i) culpable homicide; (ii) manslaughter.

hommage [ɔmaʒ] *n.m.* **1.** homage; **rendre h. à qn,** (i) to do, render, pay, homage; to do, make, pay, obeisance, to s.o.; (ii) to pay (a) tribute to s.o. **2.** *pl.* respects, compliments; **présenter ses hommages à une dame,** (i) to pay one's respects, (ii) to send one's compliments, to a lady. **3.** tribute, token (of respect, esteem); **faire h. de qch. à qn,** to offer sth. to s.o. as a token of esteem; **h. de l'éditeur,** complimentary copy, presentation copy; **h. de l'auteur,** with the author's compliments.

hommasse [ɔmas] *a.* (*of woman*) masculine, mannish.

homme [ɔm] *n.m.* (*a*) man, mankind; **l'h. propose, Dieu dispose,** man proposes, God disposes; **tous les hommes,** all men, all mankind; **de mémoire d'h.,** within living memory; **les droits de l'h.,** the rights of man, human rights; (*b*) (*opposed to woman or boy*) **soyez un h.!** be a man! **h. fait,** grown man; *Com:* **rayon hommes,** men's department, menswear; **parler à qn d'h. à h.,** to speak to s.o. man to man; *P:* **mon h.,** my husband, the old man; **h. à femmes,** ladykiller; (*c*) (*individual, pl.* **hommes** *or* **gens,** *q.v.*) **il n'est pas, ce n'est pas, mon h.,** he's not the man for me; **trouver son h.,** to meet one's match; **h. à tout faire,** odd-job man; *esp. NAm:* handyman; **il n'est pas h. à souffrir un affront,** he's not a man to stand being insulted; **h. d'État,** statesman; **h. de mer,** seafaring man; **h. de journée, de peine,** (day) labourer; *Mil:* **les officiers et les hommes,** the officers and (the) men; *Nau:* **les hommes (d'équipage),** the crew, the ship's company; (*d*) **l'abominable h. des neiges,** the abominable snowman.

homme-Dieu (l') [lɔmdjø] *n.m. Theol:* God-made-man; God-man.

homme-grenouille [ɔmgrənuj] *n.m.* frogman; *pl. hommes-grenouilles.*

homme-orchestre [ɔmɔrkɛstṛ] *n.m.* one-man band; *pl. hommes-orchestres.*

homme-sandwich [ɔmsɑ̃dwitʃ] *n.m.* sandwich man; *pl. hommes-sandwich(e)s.*

homocentrique [ɔmɔsɑ̃trik] *a. Mth:* homocentric.

homogène [ɔmɔʒɛn] *a.* homogeneous.

homogénéisation [ɔmɔʒeneizasjɔ̃] *n.f.* homogenization.

homogénéiser [ɔmɔʒeneize] *v.tr.* to homogenize.

homogénéité [ɔmɔʒeneite] *n.f.* homogeneousness, homogeneity.

homographe [ɔmɔgraf] (*a*) *n.m.* homograph; (*b*) *a.* homographic.

homologation [ɔmɔlɔgasjɔ̃] *n.f. Jur:* confirmation (of deed, etc.); probate (of will); official approval; *Sp:* ratification (of record, etc.).

homologie [ɔmɔlɔʒi] *n.f.* homology.

homologue [ɔmɔlɔg] *Biol: etc:* **1.** *a.* homologous. **2.** (*a*) *n.m.* homologue; (*b*) *n.m. & f.* opposite number.

homologuer [ɔmɔlɔge] *v.tr.* **1.** *Jur:* to confirm, endorse (deed, etc.); to ratify (decision); to grant probate of (will). **2.** (*a*) *Jur:* to prove (will); (*b*) *Adm:* **prix homologués,** authorized charges. **3.** *Sp:* to ratify (record); **record homologué,** official record.

homoncule [ɔmɔ̃kyl] *n.m.* = HOMUNCULE.

homonyme [ɔmɔnim] *Ling:* **1.** *a.* homonymous. **2.** *n.m.* (*a*) homonym; (*b*) namesake.

homonymie [ɔmɔnimi] *n.f. Ling:* homonymy.

homophone [ɔmɔfɔn] **1.** *a. Ling: Mus:* homophonous, homophonic. **2.** *n.m. Ling:* homophone.

homosexualité [ɔmɔsɛksɥalite] *n.f.* homosexuality.

homosexuel, -elle [ɔmɔsɛksɥɛl] *a. & n.* homosexual.

homuncule [ɔmɔ̃kyl] *n.m. A:* **1.** homunculus. **2.** manikin, dwarf.

***hondurien, -ienne** [ɔ̃dyrjɛ̃, -jɛn] *a. & n. Geog:* Honduran.

***hongre** [ɔ̃gṛ] **1.** *a.m.* gelded, castrated (horse). **2.** *n.m.* gelding.

***hongrer** [ɔ̃gre] *v.tr. Vet:* to geld, castrate.

***Hongrie** [ɔ̃gri] *Pr.n.f. Geog:* Hungary.

***hongrois, -oise** [ɔ̃grwa, -waz] **1.** *a. & n. Geog:* Hungarian. **2.** *n.m. Ling:* Hungarian.

honnête [ɔnɛt] *a.* **1.** honest, upright, honourable, *NAm:* honorable (person, etc.); **homme h., h. homme,** honest man, man of honour, *NAm:* of honor; **peu h.,** dishonourable, *NAm:* dishonorable. **2.** (*a*) *A:* courteous, well bred, civil, polite; **h. homme,** gentleman; (*b*) *O:* **vous êtes vraiment trop h.,** you really are too kind. **3.** decent, seemly, becoming (behaviour, etc.); **attitude peu h.,** unseemly, unbecoming, attitude. **4.** reasonable, moderate, fair (price, etc.); **moyens honnêtes,** fair means.

honnêtement [ɔnɛtmɑ̃] *adv.* **1.** honestly, honourably, *NAm:* honorably. **2.** *O:* courteously, civilly, politely. **3.** reasonably, fairly.

honnêteté [ɔnɛtte] *n.f.* **1.** honesty, integrity. **2.** *A:* courtesy, civility, politeness. **3.** decency, propriety, decorum. **4.** fairness, fair dealing.

honneur [ɔnœr] *n.m.* honour, *NAm:* honor. **1.** **homme d'h.,** man of honour; honourable, *NAm:* honorable, man; **être engagé d'h., mettre son h., à faire qch.,** to be in honour bound, to make it a point of honour, to do sth.; **déclarer sur l'h. que . . .,** to state on one's honour that . . .; **(ma) parole d'h.!** (on) my word of honour! **se faire h. de qch., de faire qch.,** to be proud of sth., proud to do sth.; **en tout bien tout h.,** fair and square, fair and above-board; **affaire d'h.,** affair of honour; duel; **dette d'h.,** debt of honour; **assis à la place d'h.,** in the seat of honour; **cour d'h.,** main quadrangle, main courtyard; **table d'h.** = high table (at university); **escalier d'h.,** main, grand, staircase; *Mil: etc:* **garde d'h.,** guard of honour. **2.** (*a*) **réception en l'h. de qn,** reception in honour of s.o.; **hôte d'h.,** chief guest, principal guest; **président d'h.,** honorary president; **faire h. à qn,** to do honour to, to honour, *Nam:* honor, s.o.; *F:* **faire h. au dîner,** to do justice to the dinner; **à qui ai-je l'h. (de parler)?** to whom have I the honour, the pleasure, of speaking? **j'ai l'h. de vous faire savoir que . . .,** I beg to inform you that . . .; *F:* **en quel h. vous voit-on ici?** (i) what brings you here? (ii) what right have you to be here? *Games:* **à vous l'h.,** after you; **jouer pour l'h.,** to play for love; **le cricket est à l'h. en Angleterre,** cricket holds a place of honour, pride of place, in England; *Golf:* **avoir l'h.,** to have the honour; (*b*) credit; **faire h. à, être l'h. de, son pays,** to be an honour, a credit, to do credit, to one's country; **on doit dire à leur h. que . . .,** it must be said to their credit that . . .; **il en est sorti à son h.,** he came out of it with flying colours; **son refus est tout à son h.,** it speaks well for him, it is greatly to his credit, that he did not accept; **avec h.,** creditably; **h. à lui!** all honour to him! **3.** *pl.* (*marks of esteem*) **rendre les derniers honneurs, les honneurs suprêmes, à qn,** to pay the last tribute to s.o.; **faire (à qn) les honneurs de la maison,** to do (s.o.) the honours of the house; *Mil:* **rendre les honneurs à qn,** to present arms, give, pay, (military) honours, to s.o.; **avec tous les honneurs de la guerre,** with all the honours of war. **4. faire h. à sa signature,** to honour one's signature; *Com:* **faire h. à une traite,** to honour, meet, a bill. **5.** *Cards:* **les honneurs,** honours; **quatre d'honneurs,** four by honours; **honneurs partagés,** honours even.

***honnir** [ɔnir] *v.tr. A:* to disgrace, dishonour, *NAm:* dishonor; **hon(n)i soit qui mal y pense,** evil be to him who evil thinks; **honni de tous,** spurned by all.

honorabilité [ɔnɔrabilite] *n.f.* (*a*) honourable, *NAm:* honorable, character; (*b*) respectability.

honorable [ɔnɔrabl̥] *a.* (*a*) honourable, *NAm:* honorable; **vieillesse h.,** respected old age; (*b*) respectable, reputable (family, profession, etc.); creditable (performance, etc.).

honorablement [ɔnɔrabləmɑ̃] *adv.* (*a*) honourably, *NAm:* honorably; with honour, *NAm:* with honor; **famille h. connue,** family of good reputation; (*b*) **s'acquitter h.,** to acquit oneself creditably.

honoraire [ɔnɔrɛr] **1.** *a.* honorary (duty, member, etc.); **professeur h.,** emeritus professor. **2.** *n.m.pl.* fee(s) (of professional man); honorarium; (lawyer's) retainer.

honorariat [ɔnɔrarja] *n.m.* honorary membership.

honorer [ɔnɔre] **1.** *v.tr.* (*a*) to honour, *NAm:* honor (s.o.); to respect (s.o.'s good qualities, etc.); *Corr:* **votre honorée du . . .,** your communication, letter, of the . . .; **mon honoré confrère,** my respected colleague; (*b*) to do honour, *NAm:* honor, to (s.o.); **h. qn de sa confiance,** to honour s.o. with one's confidence; **h. une cérémonie de sa présence,** to grace a ceremony with one's presence; (*c*) *Com:* to honour, meet (bill); *Com: Jur:* **refuser d'h. (un contrat),** to repudiate (a contract); (*d*) to be an honour to, do credit to, be a credit to (s.o., sth.). **2. s'h.** (*a*) to gain distinction; (*b*) **s'h. de qch., d'avoir fait qch.,** to be proud of sth., of having done sth.

honorifique [ɔnɔrifik] *a.* **1.** honorary (title, rank, etc.); **président à titre h.,** honorary president. **2.** honorific.

***honte** [ɔ̃t] *n.f.* **1.** (*a*) (sense of) shame; **avoir perdu toute h., tout sentiment de h., avoir toute h. bue,** to be lost, dead, to all sense of shame; **h. à vous!** shame (on you)! **sans h.,** shameless(ly); **avoir h.,** to be ashamed (of oneself); **avoir h. de faire qch.; avoir, éprouver, de la h. à faire qch.,** to be, feel, ashamed to do sth., of doing sth.; **faire h. à qn,** to make s.o. ashamed, put s.o. to shame; (*b*) **fausse h., mauvaise h.,** selfconsciousness, bashfulness. **2.** (cause of) shame, disgrace, dishonour, *NAm:* dishonor; **couvrir qn de h.,** to bring shame, disgrace, on s.o.; **faire, être, la h. de qn,** to be a disgrace to s.o.; **quelle h.! c'est une h.,** what a disgrace! it's a disgrace.

***honteusement** [ɔ̃tøzmɑ̃] *a.* shamefully, disgracefully, ignominiously.

***honteux, -euse** [ɔ̃tø, -øz] *a.* **1.** ashamed; **être h. d'avoir fait qch.,** to be ashamed of having done sth. **2.** (*a*) *O:* bashful, shamefaced, sheepish; (*b*) **les pauvres h.,** the uncomplaining poor. **3.** shameful, disgraceful, ignominious (conduct, etc.); **c'est h.!** it's a disgrace!

***hop** [ɔp] *int.* **allez h.!** now then, jump! out you go! **h.-là!** oops(-a-daisy)!

hôpital, -aux [ɔpital, -o] *n.m.* (*a*) hospital; infirmary; (*b*) *Navy:* **navire h.,** hospital ship.

***hoquet** [ɔkɛ] *n.m.* **1.** hiccup, hiccough; **avoir le h.,** to have (the) hiccups. **2.** gasp (of surprise, terror, etc.); **avoir un h. de surprise,** to catch one's breath.

***hoqueter** [ɔkte] *v.i.* **(je hoquette, n. hoquetons; je hoquetterai)** to hiccup, hiccough; to have (the) hiccups.

horaire [ɔrɛr] **1.** *a.* (*a*) horary; **signal h.,** time signal; *Astr:* **cercle h.,** horary circle, hour circle; **fuseau h.,** time zone; (*b*) hourly; *Ind:* **débit h.,** hourly output, output per hour. **2.** *n.m.* timetable; schedule; *Rac:* **arriver à un contrôle selon l'h.,** to arrive at a check point on schedule (in long-distance road race).

***horde** [ɔrd] *n.f.* horde.

***horion** [ɔrjɔ̃] *n.m.* blow, punch, knock.

horizon [ɔrizɔ̃] *n.m.* horizon, skyline; *Art:* **la ligne d'h.,** the horizon; **à l'h., sur l'h., au-dessus de l'h.,** on the horizon, on the skyline; **tour d'h. politique,** political survey; **ouvrir des horizons nouveaux,** to open up new horizons, new vistas.

horizontal, -aux [ɔrizɔ̃tal, -o] **1.** *a.* horizontal; level. **2.** *n.f.* **horizontale** (*a*) horizontal; **à l'h.,** in the horizontal; (*b*) horizontal line.

horizontalement [ɔrizɔ̃talmɑ̃] *adv.* horizontally; (*in crosswords*) across.

horizontalité [ɔrizɔ̃talite] *n.f.* horizontality.

horloge [ɔrlɔʒ] *n.f.* **1.** clock (*esp.* town or church clock); **h. normande, de parquet,** grandfather clock; **l'h. parlante,** the speaking clock; **h. à quartz,** quartz crystal clock; **il est deux heures à l'h.,** it's two by the clock; **j'ai attendu une bonne heure d'h.,** I waited a full, solid, hour by the clock. **2.** *Ent:* **h. de la mort,** deathwatch (beetle).

horloger, -ère [ɔrlɔʒe, -ɛr] **1.** *a.* **l'industrie horlogère,** the clock- and watchmaking industry. **2.** *n.* clock- and watchmaker.

horlogerie [ɔrlɔʒri] *n.f.* **1.** clock- and watchmaking; **mouvement d'h.,** clockwork. **2.** clockmaker's, watchmaker's (shop). **3.** *coll.* clocks and watches.

***hormis** [ɔrmi] *prep. Lit:* (*no liaison:* **h. elle** [ɔrmiɛl]) except, but, save; **personne h. vous,** no one but you; no one besides yourself.

hormonal, -aux [ɔrmɔnal, -o] *a. Med:* hormonal; **insuffisance hormonale,** hormone deficiency.

hormone [ɔrmɔn] *n.f.* hormone.

hormonothérapie [ɔrmɔnɔterapi] *n.f. Med:* hormonotherapy, hormone treatment.

***hornblende** [ɔrnblɛ̃d] *n.f. Miner:* hornblende.

horoscope [ɔrɔskɔp] *n.m.* horoscope; **tirer l'h. de qn,** to cast s.o.'s horoscope.
horreur [ɔrœr] *n.f.* horror. **1. à ma grande h.,** to my unspeakable horror; **frappé, glacé, d'h.,** horror-stricken, horrorstruck. **2.** repugnance, disgust, abhorrence; **faire h. à qn,** to horrify s.o., fill s.o. with horror, be repulsive to s.o.; **avoir qn, qch., en h., avoir h. de qn, de qch.,** to have a horror of s.o., sth.; to hate, detest, abhor, loathe, s.o., sth. **3.** awfulness; **silence plein d'h.,** awful silence. **4.** (*a*) (cause, object, of) horror; hideousness; **quelle h.!** (i) what a shocking thing! how revolting! how horrid! (ii) what an awful, frightful, object! (*b*) **les horreurs de la guerre,** the horrors of war; **commettre des horreurs,** to commit atrocities; **dire des horreurs de qn,** to say horrid, horrible, dreadful, things about s.o.
horrible [ɔribl] *a.* horrible, awful, dreadful; shocking; horrid; **spectacle h.,** ghastly, gruesome, hideous, sight.
horriblement [ɔribləmɑ̃] *adv.* horribly, awfully, dreadfully; shockingly.
horrifiant [ɔrifjɑ̃] *a.* horrifying, shocking, appalling.
horrifier [ɔrifje] *v.tr.* to horrify; **être horrifié de qch.,** to be horrified at sth.
horrifique [ɔrifik] *a. F:* horrific, hair-raising.
horripilant [ɔripilɑ̃] *a.* exasperating, maddening.
horripilation [ɔripilasjɔ̃] *n.f.* **1.** *Med:* horripilation, gooseflesh. **2.** *F:* exasperation.
horripiler [ɔripile] *v.tr.* **1.** *Med:* to give (s.o.) gooseflesh. **2.** to exasperate.
***hors** [ɔr] *prep.* (*liaison with* **r: h. elle** [ɔrɛl]) **1.** (*a*) **longueur h. tout,** overall length; **h. taxe,** exclusive of tax, tax free; duty-free; **h. d'usage,** out of action, unserviceable; obsolete; *Fb:* (*of player*) **h. jeu,** offside; (*b*) *Lit:* except; **tous h. un seul,** all but one; **h. que** + *ind.*, except that, save that. **2. h. de,** out of, outside; **h. de la ville,** outside the town; **dîner h. de chez soi,** to dine out; **h. d'ici!** get out (of here)! **h. d'haleine,** out of breath; **h. de combat,** (i) (*of gun, ship, etc.*) out of action; (ii) (*of man*) disabled; **être h. d'affaire,** to have got through one's difficulties; (*of sick pers.*) to be out of danger; **h. de portée,** out of reach; beyond reach; **h. de là,** apart from that, otherwise; **être h. de soi,** to be beside oneself (with rage, etc.); **c'est h. de prix,** it's prohibitive; *Arch:* **h. d'œuvre,** out of the alignment, projecting.
***hors-bord** [ɔrbɔr] *n.m.inv.* (outboard) motor boat; speedboat; **moteur h.-b.,** outboard motor.
***hors-concours** [ɔrkɔ̃kur] **1.** *adv.* not competing, out of competition; **être (mis) h.-c.,** to be disqualified. **2.** *a.inv.* (*a*) ineligible to compete; (*b*) above competition, unrivalled, outstanding. **3.** *n.m.inv.* person, exhibit, ineligible for competition (because of superiority).
***hors-d'œuvre** [ɔrdœvr̥] *n.m.inv.* **1.** *Arch:* annexe, outwork **2.** *Cu:* hors d'œuvre; starter.
***hors-jeu** [ɔrʒø] *n.m.inv. Sp:* offside.
***hors-la-loi** [ɔrlalwa] *n.m.inv.* outlaw.
***hors-texte** [ɔrtɛkst] *n.m.inv. Bookb:* (inset) plate.
hortensia [ɔrtɑ̃sja] *n.m. Bot:* hydrangea.
horticole [ɔrtikɔl] *a.* horticultural; **exposition h.,** flower show.
horticulteur [ɔrtikyltœr] *n.m.* horticulturist.
horticulture [ɔrtikyltyr] *n.f.* horticulture, gardening.
hosanna [ozana] **1.** *int.* hosanna! **2.** *n.m.* (cry of) hosanna; song of praise.
hospice [ɔspis] *n.m.* **1.** hospice (on the Saint-Bernard, etc.). **2.** (*a*) (old people's, children's) home; (*b*) *A:* almshouse; **mourir à l'h.,** to die in the poorhouse.
hospitalier¹, -ière [ɔspitalje, -jɛr] *a.* hospitable.
hospitalier², -ière 1. *a. & n.* (**(religieux) h.,** hospitaller; **(sœur) hospitalière,** Sister of Charity. **2.** *a.* pertaining to hospitals; **personnel h.,** hospital staff.
hospitalisation [ɔspitalizasjɔ̃] *n.f.* hospitalization; admission to a nursing home or hospital.
hospitalisé, -ée [ɔspitalize] *n.* **1.** inmate (of home, etc.). **2.** (in-)patient (in hospital).
hospitaliser [ɔspitalize] *v.tr.* to send, admit (s.o.) to a nursing home, a hospital; to hospitalize (s.o.).
hospitalité [ɔspitalite] *n.f.* hospitality.
hostellerie [ɔstɛlri] *n.f.* fashionable country inn.
hostie [ɔsti] *n.f.* **1.** *Ant:* victim, offering (for sacrifice). **2.** *Ecc:* (eucharistic) host.
hostile [ɔstil] *a.* hostile; unfriendly (action); **être h. à qn, qch.,** to be hostile, opposed, adverse, to s.o., sth.
hostilement [ɔstilmɑ̃] *adv.* in a hostile manner.
hostilité [ɔstilite] *n.f.* **1.** hostility **(contre, envers,** to(wards)); enmity, ill will; **acte d'h.,** act of war. **2.** *pl.* hostilities.
hôte, hôtesse [ot, otɛs] *n.* **1.** (*a*) host, *f.* hostess; (*b*) *O:* innkeeper, host; landlord, *f.* landlady (of tavern, etc.); (*c*) **dîner à la table d'h.,** to have a table d'hôte dinner; to have the set menu; (*d*) *Av:* **hôtesse de l'air,** air hostess. **2.** (*a*) (*f.* **hôte**) guest, visitor; **h. payant,** paying guest; (*b*) *Lit:* dweller, denizen.
hôtel [otɛl] *n.m.* **1. h. (particulier),** mansion, town house. **2.** public building; **h. de ville,** town hall; **l'H. de la Monnaie** = the Mint; **L'H. des ventes,** the general auction rooms, salerooms (in Paris). **3.** (*a*) hotel; **descendre à l'h.,** to put up at a hotel; **h. de passe,** (hotel used as a) brothel; (*b*) **h. meublé,** residential hotel (providing lodging but not board); *often Pej:* apartments, lodgings; *NAm:* lodging house, rooming house.
hôtel-Dieu [otɛldjø] *n.m.* hospital; *pl. hôtels-Dieu.*
hôtelier, -ière [otəlje, -jɛr]. **1.** *n.* innkeeper; hotel keeper; landlord, *f.* landlady; hotelier (of large hotel). **2.** *a.* **l'industrie hôtelière,** the hotel trade.
hôtellerie [otɛlri] *n.f.* **1.** inn, hotel; hostelry. **2.** guest quarters (of convent). **3. l'h.,** the hotel trade.
hôtesse. *see* HÔTE.
***hotte** [ɔt] *n.f.* **1.** basket (carried on the back); pannier; (bricklayer's) hod. **2.** hood (in forge, laboratory, over cooker).
***hottentot, -ote** [ɔtɑ̃to, -ɔt] *a. & n. Ethn:* Hottentot.
***hou** [u] *int.* **1.** boo! **2. h.! la vilaine!** shame on you, you naughty girl!
***houache** [waʃ] *n.f. Nau: A:* wake, wash (of ship).
***houblon** [ublɔ̃] *n.m. Bot: Brew:* hop(s); **perche à h.,** hop pole.
***houblonner** [ublɔne] *v.tr.* to hop (beer).
***houblonnier, -ière** [ublɔnje, -jɛr] **1.** pertaining to hops; **région houblonnière,** hop(-growing) district. **2.** *n.m.* hop grower. **3.** *n.f.* hop field.
***houe** [u] *n.f. Tls:* hoe.
***houer** [we] *v.tr. A:* to hoe.
houille [uj] *n.f.* **1.** coal; **mine de h.,** coalmine, coal pit; colliery. **2. h. blanche,** hydroelectric power.
***houiller, -ère** [uje, -ɛr]. **1.** *a.* (*a*) carboniferous, coal-bearing; **dépôt, bassin, h.,** coal bed, basin; (*b*) **production houillère,** coal output. **2.** *n.f.* coalmine, coal pit; colliery.
***houle** [ul] *n.f.* swell, surge (of sea); **grosse h.,** heavy swell.
***houlette** [ulɛt] *n.f.* **1.** (*a*) (shepherd's) crook; (*b*) (bishop's) crosier. **2.** *Tls:* trowel, spud.
***houleux, -euse** [ulø, -øz] *a.* (*a*) swelling, surging, (sea); (*b*) surging, tumultuous (crowds); **réunion houleuse,** stormy meeting.
***houp** [up] *int.* **allons h.!** now then, jump! **h-là!** oops(-a-daisy)!
***houppe** [up] *n.f.* **1.** (*a*) bunch, tuft (of feathers, wool, etc.); pompon; **h. à poudrer,** powder puff; (*b*)

tassel, bob. **2.** (*a*) tuft, crest (of hair); topknot; (*b*) (bird's) tuft, crest (of feathers); (*c*) crest (of tree). **3.** *Cryst: Opt:* brush; absorption figure.

***houppelande** [uplɑ̃d] *n.f.* greatcoat; cloak; (coachman's) box coat.

***houpper** [upe] *v.tr.* to tuft; to comb (wool).

***houppette** [upɛt] *n.f.* **1.** small tuft (of wool, feathers). **2.** powder puff.

***hourdage** [urdaʒ] *n.m. Const:* (*a*) roughcasting; (*b*) rough masonry, plasterwork; rubble work.

***hourder** [urde] *v.tr. Const:* to roughcast.

***hourdis** [urdi] *n.m.* = HOURDAGE 2.

***houri** [uri] *n.f. Moham.Rel:* houri.

***hourra** [ura] *int. & n.m.* hurrah! **pousser trois hourras,** to give three cheers.

***hourvari** [urvari] *n.m.* **1.** *Ven:* huntsman's call to hounds to cast back. **2.** *Lit:* uproar, tumult.

***houspiller** [uspije] *v.tr.* **1.** *O:* to hustle, jostle (s.o.); to knock (s.o.) about. **2.** to abuse, rate (s.o.); to tell (s.o.) off.

***houssaie** [usɛ] *n.f.* holly plantation, grove.

***housse** [us] *n.f.* **1.** (*a*) covering; (furniture) cover; (protecting) bag; loose cover; *Aut:* seat cover; **h. à vêtements,** protective bag (for clothing); **drap h.,** fitted sheet; (*b*) dust sheet. **2.** *Harn:* housing.

***housser** [use] *v.tr.* to cover up, put covers on (furniture, etc.).

***houx** [u] *n.m. Bot:* holly.

hovercraft [ovœrkraft] *n.m.* hovercraft.

***hoyau, -aux** [wajo] *n.m.* **1.** *Agr:* mattock, grubbing hoe. **2.** *Min:* pickaxe, *NAm:* pickax.

***huard, *huart** [yar] *n.m. Orn:* **1.** osprey. **2.** *Fr.C:* black-throated diver; loon.

***hublot** [yblo] *n.m.* porthole, scuttle (in ship); window (in aircraft).

***huche** [yʃ] *n.f.* **1.** kneading trough. **2.** bin; **h. à, au, pain,** bread bin. **3.** hopper (of flour mill).

***hucher** [yʃe] *v.tr. A: & Ven: & Fr.C:* to call, shout (s.o., the hounds).

***hue** [y] *int.* (*to horse*) gee up! **l'un tire à h. et l'autre à dia,** they're not all pulling together.

***huée** [ɥe] *n.f.* **1.** *Ven:* hallooing. **2.** (*a*) boo, hoot; (*b*) *pl.* booing, hooting; jeering, jeers; **quitter la scène sous les huées,** to be booed off the stage.

***huer** [ɥe] **1.** *v.i.* (*of owl*) to hoot. **2.** *v.tr.* to boo (actor, etc.); to barrack (speaker, etc.).

***huguenot, -ote** [ygno, -ɔt] *a. & n.* **1.** *Hist:* Huguenot. **2.** *A.Dom.Ec:* **(marmite) huguenote,** pipkin.

***Hugues** [yg] *Pr.n.m.* Hugh.

***huhau** [yo] *int. O:* (*to horse*) gee up!

hui [ɥi] *adv. A:* today; *Jur:* **ce jour d'h.,** this day.

huilage [ɥilaʒ] *n.m.* oiling, lubrication, greasing.

huile [ɥil] *n.f.* oil. **1. h. comestible, de table,** edible oil, salad oil; **h. végétale,** vegetable oil; **h. de tournesol,** sunflower (seed) oil; **frit à l'h.,** fried in oil; **h. de lin,** linseed oil; **h. solaire,** suntan oil; **h. de foie de morue,** cod liver oil; **h. de baleine,** sperm oil, train oil; **h. minérale,** mineral oil; **h. de paraffine,** paraffin oil; **h. de graissage,** lubricating oil; **h. de machine,** engine oil; **moteur à h. lourde,** heavy-oil engine; **peinture à l'h.,** oil painting; **portrait à l'h.,** portrait in oils; **une de ses huiles,** one of his oil paintings; **tache d'h.,** oil stain; **mauvais exemple qui fait tache d'h.,** bad example that's spreading; **jeter, verser, de l'h. sur le feu,** to add fuel to the fire; *Lit:* **ouvrage qui sent l'h.,** painstaking work; *F:* **h. de bras, de coude,** elbow grease; *P:* **les huiles,** the big shots, the top brass. **2. h. essentielle,** essential oil; **h. de ricin,** castor oil; **h. de girofle,** oil of cloves.

huiler [ɥile] *v.tr.* to oil; to lubricate, grease.

huilerie [ɥilri] *n.f.* (*a*) *O:* oil mill; (*b*) oil works.

huileux, -euse [ɥilø, -øz] *a.* oily, greasy.

huilier [ɥilje] *n.m.* **1.** oil and vinegar cruet. **2.** oil manufacturer.

huis [ɥi] *n.m.* (*a*) *A:* door; (*b*) **entretien à h. clos,** conversation behind closed doors; *Jur:* **entendre une cause à h. clos,** to hear a case in camera; *the h is aspirate in* **ordonner le h. clos,** (i) to clear the court; (ii) to order a case to be heard in camera.

huisserie [ɥisri] *n.f. Const:* door frame, casing.

huissier [ɥisje] *n.m.* **1.** (gentleman) usher. **2.** *Jur:* (*a*) process server; = sheriff's officer, bailiff; (*b*) **h. audiencier,** court usher.

***huit** [ɥit] *num. a.inv. & n.m.inv.* (*as card. adj. before a noun or adj. beginning with a consonant sound* [ɥi]) (*a*) eight; **h. (petits) garçons** [ɥi(pti)garsɔ̃] eight (little) boys; **h.** [ɥit] **hommes,** eight men; **j'en ai h.** [ɥit], I have eight; **le h. mai** [ɥimɛ], the eighth of May; **h. jours,** a week; **(d')aujourd'hui en h.,** a week today, today week; **donner ses h. jours à qn,** to give s.o. a week's notice; (*b*) figure of eight.

***huitain** [ɥitɛ̃] *n.m. Pros:* octave, octet.

***huitaine** [ɥitɛn] *n.f.* **1.** (about) eight. **2.** week; **dans une h. (de jours),** in a week or so; **affaire remise à h.,** case adjourned for a week.

***huitante** [ɥitɑ̃t] *num.a.inv. Sw.Fr:* eighty.

***huitantième** [ɥitɑ̃tjɛm] *num.a. & n. Sw.Fr:* eightieth.

***huitième** [ɥitjɛm] **1.** *num. a. & n.* eighth. **2.** *n.m.* eighth (part); *Sp:* **être en h. de finale,** to be in the last eight. **3.** *n.f. Sch:* **(classe de) h.** = third form of junior school; *NAm:* eighth grade.

***huitièmement** [ɥitjɛmmɑ̃] *adv.* eighthly, in (the) eighth place.

huître [ɥitr̥] *n.f.* **1.** oyster; **h. perlière,** pearl oyster. **2.** *F:* fool, mug.

***huit-reflets** [ɥir(ə)flɛ] *n.m.inv.* top hat.

huîtrier, -ère [ɥitrije, -ɛr] **1.** *a.* **industrie huîtrière,** oyster farming. **2.** *n.m. Orn:* oyster catcher. **3.** *n.f.* **huîtrière,** oyster bed.

***hulotte** [ylɔt] *n.f. Orn:* wood owl, brown owl, tawny owl.

***hululement** [ylylmɑ̃] *n.m.* ululation (of owls); hoot(ing).

***hululer** [ylyle] *v.i.* (*of owl*) to ululate; to hoot.

***hum** [œm] *int.* hem! h'm!

humain [ymɛ̃] **1.** *a. & n.m.* human; **le genre h., les (êtres) humains,** human beings, humans; mankind; **sciences humaines,** social sciences; *Mus:* (*of organ*) **voix humaine,** vox humana. **2.** *a.* humane.

humainement [ymɛnmɑ̃] *adv.* **1.** humanly. **2.** humanely.

humanisation [ymanizasjɔ̃] *n.f.* humanization, humanizing.

humaniser [ymanize] **1.** *v.tr.* to humanize; (*a*) to make human; (*b*) to make (s.o.) more humane. **2. s'h.** (*a*) to become more humane; (*b*) to become more sociable, more human.

humanisme [ymanism] *n.m. Lit: Phil:* humanism.

humaniste [ymanist] **1.** *n.* humanist; classical scholar. **2.** *a.* humanist(ic).

humanitaire [ymanitɛr] *a.* humanitarian; **œuvre h.,** humane task.

humanitarisme [ymanitarism] *n.m.* humanitarianism.

humanité [ymanite] *n.f.* **1.** humanity; (*a*) human nature; (*b*) mankind; (*c*) kindness, humaneness. **2.** *pl.* humanities, classics; *Sch:* **les classes d'humanités,** the classical side (of school).

humble [œ̃bl̥] *a.* humble, lowly; meek; **à mon h. avis,** in my humble opinion.

humblement [œ̃bləmɑ̃] *adv.* humbly.

humectage [ymɛktaʒ] *n.m.* dampening, moistening.

humecter [ymɛkte] *v.tr.* to damp(en), moisten; **s'h.**

les lèvres, to moisten one's lips; *F:* **s'h. le gosier,** to wet one's whistle.

***humer** [yme] *v.tr.* **1.** *A: & Lit:* to suck in, up (liquid). **2.** to inhale, sniff; **h. l'air frais,** to inhale, breathe in, the fresh air; **h. le parfum d'une fleur,** to smell a flower.

huméral, -aux [ymeral, -o] *a. Anat:* humeral.

humérus [hymerys] *n.m. Anat:* humerus.

humeur [ymœr] *n.f.* **1.** (*a*) *A.Med:* humour, *NAm:* humor; (*b*) *pl. A.Med:* tissue fluids, body fluids; **humeurs froides,** scrofula; (*c*) *Anat:* **h. aqueuse, h. vitrée,** aqueous humour, vitreous humour (of the eye). **2.** (*a*) humour, mood, spirits; **être de bonne h.,** to be in a good mood, in high spirits; **être de mauvaise h., d'une h. de chien,** to be in a bad, foul, mood, temper; **de méchante h.,** in a (bad) temper, grumpy; cross; **être d'une h. noire,** (i) to feel depressed; (ii) to be in a (bad) temper; **être, se sentir, d'h. à refuser,** to be in the mood to refuse; (*b*) temper; temperament; **avoir l'h. vive,** to be quick-tempered; **homme d'h. égale,** even-tempered man; (*c*) *Lit:* ill humour, bad mood; **mouvement d'h.,** outburst of temper; **montrer de l'h.,** to show (ill) temper; **avec h.,** testily, irritably; **épancher son h. sur qn,** to vent one's spleen on s.o.

humide [ymid] *a.* damp, moist, humid; watery, wet; **draps humides,** damp sheets; **couloir sombre et h.,** dark, dank passage; **temps h. et chaud,** muggy weather; **temps h. et froid,** raw weather.

humidificateur [ymidifikatœr] *n.m.* humidor (in a spinning mill); *Dom.Ec:* humidifier.

humidification [ymidifikasjɔ̃] *n.f.* humidification; dampening, moistening.

humidifier [ymidifje] *v.tr.* to humidify; to dampen, moisten.

humidité [ymidite] *n.f.* humidity, damp(ness), moisture, moistness, wet(ness); (*on packet*) **craint l'h.,** to be kept dry; **taches d'h.,** damp patches, mildew; **teneur en h.,** moisture content.

humiliant [ymiljɑ̃] *a.* humiliating, mortifying.

humiliation [ymiljasjɔ̃] *n.f.* humiliation, mortification; affront.

humilier [ymilje] **1.** *v.tr.* to humiliate, humble. **2. s'h.,** to humble oneself; **s'h. jusqu'à faire qch.,** to stoop to doing sth.

humilité [ymilite] *n.f.* humility, humbleness.

humoral, -aux [ymɔral, -o] *a. A.Med:* humoral.

humoriste [ymɔrist] **1.** *a.* humorous (writer, etc.). **2.** *n.* humorist.

humoristique [ymɔristik] *a.* humorous, humoristic (talker, writer, etc.); **dessin h.,** cartoon.

humour [ymur] *n.m.* humour, *NAm:* humor; **avoir (le sens) de l'h.,** to have a (good) sense of humour; **h. noir,** (i) sick humour; (ii) bitter, sardonic, humour.

humus [ymys] *n.m.* humus; leaf mould, *NAm:* mold.

***Hun** [œ̃] *n.m. Hist:* Hun.

***hune** [yn] *n.f. Nau:* top; **h. de vigie,** crow's nest; **grande h.,** maintop; **mât de h.,** topmast; **oh(é) de la h.!** aloft there! **h. de direction de tir,** fire control top.

***hunier** [ynje] *n.m. Nau:* topsail.

***huppe**[1] [yp] *n.f. Orn:* hoopoe.

***huppe**[2] *n.f.* tuft, crest (of bird).

***huppé** [ype] *a.* **1.** *Orn:* tufted, crested. **2.** *F:* smart, well-dressed; high-class.

***hure** [yr] *n.f.* **1.** head (of boar, etc.); jowl (of salmon). **2.** *Cu:* brawn, *NAm:* headcheese.

***hurlement** [yrləmɑ̃] *n.m.* howl(ing) (*esp.* of wolf, dog); yell(ing), roar(ing), bellow(ing,) scream(ing) (of pers.); **pousser un h.,** to give a howl.

***hurler** [yrle] **1.** *v.i.* (*of dog, wolf*) to howl; (*of wind, storm*) to roar; (*of pers.*) to howl, roar, yell, bellow; **h. de douleur,** to howl, scream (out), with pain; **h. à la lune,** to bay at the moon; **h. avec les loups,** when in Rome, do as the Romans do; **couleurs qui hurlent,** colours, *NAm:* colors, that clash (with one another), swear (at one another). **2.** *v.tr.* to roar out, bawl out (song, speech, etc.).

***hurleur, -euse** [yrlœr, -øz] **1.** *a.* howling, yelling. **2.** *n.* howler, yeller. **3.** *n.m. Z:* howler (monkey).

hurluberlu [yrlybɛrly] *n.m.* eccentric (person); harum-scarum person.

***hurrah** [ura] *int. & n.m.* hurrah.

***hussard** [ysar] *n.m. Mil:* hussar.

***hussarde** [ysard] *n.f.* **à la h.,** cavalierly, brusquely.

***hussite** [ysit] *n.m. Rel.H:* Hussite.

***hutte** [yt] *n.f.* hut, shed, shanty.

hyacinthe [jasɛ̃t], *n.f.* (*a*) *Bot: A:* hyacinth; (*b*) *Miner:* hyacinth, jacinth.

hyalin [jalɛ̃] *a. Miner:* hyaline, glassy; **quartz h.,** rock crystal.

hyaloïde [jalɔid] *a. Anat: etc:* hyaloid.

hybridation [ibridasjɔ̃] *n.f. Biol:* hybridization; cross-breeding.

hybride [ibrid] *a. & n.m. Biol: Ling:* hybrid.

hybrider [ibride] *v.tr. Biol:* to hybridize, to cross.

hybridisme [ibridism] *n.m. Biol:* hybridism.

hybridité [ibridite] *n.f. Biol:* hybridity.

hydarthrose [idartroz] *n.f. Med:* hydrarthrosis; **h. du genou,** water on the knee.

hydracide [idrasid] *n.m. Ch:* hydracid.

hydratant [idratɑ̃] *Toil:* **1.** *a.* moisturizing (cream). **2.** *n.m.* moisturizer.

hydratation [idratasjɔ̃] *n.f. Ch:* hydration.

hydrate [idrat] *n.m. Ch:* hydrate; **h. de potasse,** caustic potash; **h. de carbone,** carbohydrate.

hydraté [idrate] *a. Ch:* hydrated, hydrous.

hydrater [idrate] *Ch:* **1.** *v.tr.* to hydrate. **2. s'h.,** to hydrate, become hydrated.

hydraulicien [idrolisjɛ̃] *n.m.* hydraulic engineer.

hydraulique [idrolik] **1.** *a.* hydraulic; **roue h.,** waterwheel; **usine h.,** waterworks; **énergie h.,** hydroelectric power. **2.** *n.f.* (*a*) hydraulics; (*b*) hydraulic engineering.

hydravion [idravjɔ̃] *n.m.* seaplane, hydroplane; **h. à coque,** flying boat.

hydre [idr̥] *n.f.* hydra.

hydrique [idrik] *a.* hydrous.

hydrocarbure [idrɔkarbyr] *n.m. Ch:* hydrocarbon.

hydrocéphale [idrɔsefal] *a. & n. Med:* hydrocephalic, hydrocephalous (subject).

hydrocéphalie [idrɔsefali] *n.f. Med:* hydrocephalus; water on the brain.

hydrocortisone [idrɔkɔrtizɔn] *n.f.* hydrocortisone.

hydrodynamique [idrɔdinamik] **1.** *a.* hydrodynamic. **2.** *n.f.* hydrodynamics.

hydro-électricité [idrɔelɛktrisite] *n.f.* hydroelectricity.

hydro-électrique [idrɔelɛktrik] *a.* hydroelectric.

hydrofoil [idrɔfɔil] *n.m. Nau:* hydrofoil.

hydrofuge [idrɔfyʒ] *a.* waterproof, damp-proof; (*of coat, etc.*) rainproof.

hydrofuger [idrɔfyʒe] *v.tr.* **(j'hydrofugeai(s); n. hydrofugeons)** to waterproof (garment, etc.).

hydrogénation [idrɔʒenasjɔ̃] *n.f.* hydrogenation.

hydrogène [idrɔʒɛn] *n.m. Ch:* hydrogen; **h. lourd,** heavy hydrogen.

hydrogéné [idrɔʒene] *a.* hydrogenated.

hydrogéner [idrɔʒene] *v.tr.* to hydrogenate, hydrogenize.

hydroglisseur [idrɔglisœr] *n.m.* hydroplane (speedboat).

hydrographe [idrɔgraf] *a. & n.m.* **(ingénieur) h.,** hydrographer.

hydrographie [idrɔgrafi] *n.f.* hydrography.

hydrographique [idrɔgrafik] *a.* hydrographic(al); *Navy:* **service h.,** survey department.

hydrologie [idrɔlɔʒi] *n.f.* hydrology.

hydrologique [idrɔlɔʒik] *a.* hydrological.
hydrologiste [idrɔlɔʒist], **hydrologue** [idrɔlɔg] *n.* hydrologist.
hydrolyse [idrɔliz] *n.f. Ch:* hydrolysis.
hydrolyser [idrɔlize] *v.tr.* to hydrolize, hydrolyse.
hydromel [idrɔmɛl] *n.m.* hydromel; mead.
hydromètre [idrɔmɛtr̥] **1.** *n.m.* hydrometer. **2.** *n.m. Oc: etc:* depth gauge. **3.** *n.f. Ent:* water spider.
hydrométrie [idrɔmetri] *n.f. Ph:* hydrometry.
hydrométrique [idrɔmetrik] *a.* hydrometric(al).
hydrophile [idrɔfil] *a.* absorbent (cotton wool, etc.).
hydrophobe [idrɔfɔb] *a. & n. Med:* hydrophobic (subject).
hydrophobie [idrɔfɔbi] *n.f. Med:* hydrophobia.
hydropique [idrɔpik] *a. & n. Med:* hydropic, dropsical (subject).
hydropisie [idrɔpizi] *n.f. Med:* dropsy.
hydroponique [idrɔpɔnik] *a.* hydroponic; **culture h.,** hydroponics, soilless gardening.
hydroptère [idrɔptɛr] *n.m.* hydrofoil.
hydroquinone [idrɔkinɔn] *n.f. Ch: Phot:* hydroquinone, quinol.
hydrosol [idrɔsɔl] *n.m. Ch:* hydrosol.
hydrosoluble [idrɔsɔlybl̥] *a.* water-soluble.
hydrosphère [idrɔsfɛr] *n.f.* hydrosphere.
hydrostatique [idrɔstatik] **1.** *a.* hydrostatic. **2.** *n.f.* hydrostatics.
hydrothérapie [idrɔterapi] *n.f.* hydrotherapy, hydrotherapeutics; water cure.
hydrothérapique [idrɔterapik] *a.* hydrotherapeutic.
hydrothermal, -aux [idrɔtɛrmal, -o] *a.* hydrothermal.
hydroxyde [idrɔksid] *n.m. Ch:* hydroxide.
hydrure [idryr] *n.m. Ch:* hydride.
hyène [jɛn] *n.f. Z:* hyena.
hygiène [iʒjɛn] *n.f.* hygiene; **h. publique,** public health; **mauvaise h. alimentaire,** malnutrition.
hygiénique [iʒjenik] *a.* hygienic; healthy; sanitary; **peu h.,** unhealthy (work, etc.) ; unsanitary (building); **papier h.,** toilet paper; **serviette h.,** sanitary towel, *U.S:* sanitary napkin.
hygiéniquement [iʒjenikmɑ̃] *adv.* hygienically, healthily.
hygiéniste [iʒjenist] *n.* hygienist; public health specialist.
hygroma [igrɔma] *n.m. Med:* hygroma; **h. du genou,** housemaid's knee.
hygromètre [igrɔmɛtr̥] *n.m. Ph:* hygrometer.
hygrométrie [igrɔmetri] *n.f. Ph:* hygrometry.
hygrométrique [igrɔmetrik] *a. Ph:* hygrometric(al).
hygroscope [igrɔskɔp] *n.m. Ph:* hygroscope.
hygroscopique [igrɔskɔpik] *a.* (*a*) hygroscopic(al); (*b*) slightly deliquescent (salt).
hymen [imɛn] *n.m.* (*a*) *Lit:* marriage; (*b*) *Anat:* hymen.
hyménée [imene] *n.m. Lit:* marriage.
hyménoptère [imenɔptɛr] *Ent:* **1.** *a.* hymenopterous. **2.** *n.m.pl.* Hymenoptera.
hymne [imn] **1.** *n.m.* song (of praise), patriotic song; **h. national,** national anthem. **2.** *n.m. & f. Ecc:* hymn.
hyoïde [jɔid] *a. & n.m. Anat:* hyoid (bone).
hyperacidité [ipɛrasidite] *n.f. Med:* hyperacidity.
hyperbole [ipɛrbɔl] *n.f.* **1.** *Rh:* hyperbole, exaggeration. **2.** *Mth:* hyperbola.
hyperbolique [ipɛrbɔlik] *a. Rh: Mth* hyperbolic(al).
hyperboliquement [ipɛrbɔlikmɑ̃] *adv. Rh:* hyperbolically.
hyperboloïde [ipɛrbɔlɔid] *Mth:* **1.** *a.* hyperboloidal. **2.** *n.m.* hyperboloid.
hypercritique [ipɛrkritik] **1.** *a.* hypercritical, overcritical. **2.** *n.m.* hypercritic, severe critic.
hyperémotivité [ipɛremɔtivite] *n.f. Psy:* hyperemotivity.
hyperesthésie [ipɛrɛstezi] *n.f. Med:* hyperaesthesia, *NAm:* hyperesthesia.
hyperfréquence [ipɛrfrekɑ̃s] *n.f. W.Tel:* ultra high frequency, very high frequency.
hyperglycémie [ipɛrglisemi] *n.f. Med:* hyperglyc(a)emia.
hypermarché [ipɛrmarʃe] *n.m.* hypermarket.
hypermétrope [ipɛrmetrɔp] *a. Med:* hypermetropic.
hypermétropie [ipɛrmetrɔpi] *n.f. Med:* hypermetropia.
hypernerveux, -euse [ipɛrnɛrvø, -øz] *a.* highly strung.
hypersensibilité [ipɛrsɑ̃sibilite] *n.f.* hypersensitivity, oversensitiveness, supersensitiveness.
hypersensible [ipɛrsɑ̃sibl̥] *a.* hypersensitive, oversensitive; supersensitive.
hypertendu [ipɛrtɑ̃dy] *a. & n. Med:* hypertensive (patient); (person) suffering from high blood pressure.
hypertension [ipɛrtɑ̃sjɔ̃] *n.f. Med:* hypertension; high blood pressure.
hypertrophie [ipɛrtrɔfi] *n.f. Med:* hypertrophy; **h. des amygdales,** enlarged tonsils.
hypertrophier (s') [sipɛrtrɔfje] *v.tr. & pr. Med:* to hypertrophy; **amygdales hypertrophiées,** enlarged tonsils.
hypertrophique [ipɛrtrɔfik] *a. Med:* hypertrophic.
hypnose [ipnoz] *n.f.* hypnosis; (hypnotic) trance.
hypnotique [ipnɔtik] *a. & n.* hypnotic.
hypnotiser [ipnɔtize] *v.tr.* to hypnotize.
hypnotiseur [ipnɔtizœr] *n.m.* hypnotist.
hypnotisme [ipnɔtism] *n.m.* hypnotism.
hypocondre [ipɔkɔ̃dr̥] **1.** *n.m. Anat:* hypochondrium. **2.** *n.* hypochondriac.
hypocondriaque [ipɔkɔ̃drijak] **1.** *a.* hypochondriac(al). **2.** *n.* hypochondriac.
hypocondrie [ipɔkɔ̃dri] *n.f.* hypochondria.
hypocras [ipɔkras] *n.m. A:* hippocras.
hypocrisie [ipɔkrizi] *n.f.* hypocrisy.
hypocrite [ipɔkrit] **1.** *a.* hypocritical. **2.** *n.* hypocrite.
hypocritement [ipɔkritmɑ̃] *adv.* hypocritically.
hypodermique [ipɔdɛrmik] *a.* hypodermic.
hypogastre [ipɔgastr̥] *n.m. Anat:* hypogastrium.
hypogastrique [ipɔgastrik] *a. Anat:* hypogastric; *Med:* **ceinture h.,** abdominal belt.
hypogée [ipɔʒe] *n.m. Archeol:* hypogeum.
hypoglycémie [ipɔglisemi] *n.f. Med:* hypoglyc(a)emia.
hypophosphite [ipɔfɔsfit] *n.m. Ch:* hypophosphite.
hypophyse [ipɔfiz] *n.f. Anat:* hypophysis; pituitary gland.
hypostase [ipɔstaz] *n.f.* hypostasis.
hypostatique [ipɔstatik] *a. Phil: Theol:* hypostatic.
hypostyle [ipɔstil] *a. Arch:* hypostyle, pillared.
hypotendu [ipɔtɑ̃dy] *a. & n. Med:* hypotensive (patient); (person) suffering from low blood pressure.
hypotension [ipɔtɑ̃sjɔ̃] *n.f. Med:* hypotension; low blood pressure.
hypoténuse [ipɔtenyz] *n.f.* hypotenuse.
hypothécable [ipɔtekabl̥] *a.* mortgageable.
hypothécaire [ipɔtekɛr] *a.* **prêt h.,** mortgage (loan);

contrat h., mortgage deed; **créancier h.**, mortgagee; **débiteur h.**, mortgager.

hypothécairement [ipɔtekɛrmɑ̃] *adv. Jur:* by, on, mortgage.

hypothèque [ipɔtɛk] *n.f.* mortgage; **franc, libre, d'hypothèques,** unencumbered, unmortgaged; **prendre une h.**, to raise a mortgage; **prêt sur h.**, mortgage loan; **purger une h.**, to pay off, clear off, redeem, a mortgage.

hypothéquer [ipɔteke] *v.tr.* **(j'hypothèque; j'hypothéquerai) 1.** to mortgage (estate, etc.). **2.** to secure (debt) by mortgage.

hypothermie [ipɔtɛrmi] *n.f. Med:* hypothermia.

hypothèse [ipɔtɛz] *n.f.* hypothesis; assumption; **selon cette h.**, on this assumption.

hypothétique [ipɔtetik] *a.* hypothetic(al).

hypothétiquement [ipɔtetikmɑ̃] *adv.* hypothetically.

hypothyroïdie [ipɔtirɔidi] *n.f. Med:* hypothyroidism, thyroid deficiency.

hypsomètre [ipsɔmɛtr̥] *n.m.* hypsometer; thermobarometer.

hypsométrie [ipsɔmetri] *n.f.* hypsometry, altimetry.

hypsométrique [ipsɔmetrik] *a.* hypsometric(al); **courbe h.**, contour line; **carte h.**, contour map.

hysope [izɔp] *n.f. Bot:* hyssop.

hystérectomie [isterɛktɔmi] *n.f. Surg:* hysterectomy.

hystérèse [isterɛz] *n.f.*, **hystérésis** [isterezis] *n.f. Magn:* hysteresis; magnetic lag.

hystérie [isteri] *n.f. Med:* hysteria; **h. collective,** mass hysteria.

hystérique [isterik] *Med:* **1.** *a.* hysterical. **2.** *n.* hysterical person; hysteric.

hystérotomie [isterɔtɔmi] *n.f. Surg:* hysterotomy; **h. abdominale,** caesarean, *NAm:* cesarean (section).

I

I, i [i] *n.m.* **1.** (the letter) I, i; **droit comme un i,** bolt upright; **mettre les points sur les i,** to speak plainly, unambiguously. **2. i grec,** (the letter) Y, y.

iambe [jɑ̃b] *n.m.* **1.** *Pros:* (*a*) iamb, iambus; (*b*) iambic. **2.** satirical poem.

iambique [jɑ̃bik] *a. Pros:* iambic (line, verse).

ibère [ibɛr] *a. & n. Ethn:* Iberian.

Ibérie [iberi] *Pr.n.f. A.Geog:* Iberia.

ibérien, -ienne [iberjɛ̃, -jɛn] *a. Ethn:* Iberian.

ibérique [iberik] *a. Geog:* Iberian; **la péninsule i.,** the Iberian peninsula.

ibidem, ibid., ib. [ibidɛm] *adv.* ibidem, ibid., ib.

ibis [ibis] *n.m. Orn:* ibis.

Icare [ikar] *Pr.n.m. Gr.Myth:* Icarus.

iceberg [ajsbɛrg] *n.m.* iceberg.

icelui [isəlɥi], **icelle** [isɛl], **iceux** [isø], **icelles** [isɛl] *dem. pron. & a. A: & Jur:* = CELUI(-CI), CELLE(-CI), CEUX(-CI), CELLES(-CI).

ichneumon [iknømɔ̃] *n.m.* **1.** *Z: A:* ichneumon, Pharaoh's rat. **2.** *Ent:* ichneumon (fly).

ichtyocolle [iktjɔkɔl] *n.f.* fish glue, isinglass.

ichtyologie [iktjɔlɔʒi] *n.f.* ichthyology.

ichtyologique [iktjɔlɔʒik] *a.* ichthyologic(al).

ichtyologiste [iktjɔlɔʒist] *n.* ichthyologist.

ichtyophage [iktjɔfaʒ] **1.** *a.* ichthyophagous, fish-eating. **2.** *n.* ichthyophagist.

ichtyosaure [iktjɔsɔr] *n.m. Paleont:* ichthyosaurus.

ici [isi] *adv.* **1.** here; **i. et là,** here and there; **les gens d'i.,** the people (who live) here, the locals; **je ne suis pas d'i.,** I'm a stranger here; I'm not from here; **i.-bas,** here below, on earth; **il y a vingt kilomètres d'i. à Paris,** it's twenty kilometres, *NAm:* kilometers, from here to Paris; **c'est à dix minutes d'i.,** it's ten minutes away; **par i.,** in here, out here, over here; **il habite par i., près d'i.,** he lives near here, around here; **passez par i.,** this way, please; **c'est i.,** it's here; this is the place; **le car vient jusqu'i.,** the bus comes as far as here, as far as this; *Tp:* **i. Thomas,** (it's) Thomas speaking, Thomas here; **i. Radio Luxembourg,** this is Radio Luxembourg. **2. jusqu'i.,** until now, up to now; **d'i.,** from today; from now on; **d'i. lundi,** between now and Monday, by Monday; **d'i. là,** by that time, by then; **d'i. peu,** before long; **d'i. à ce que vous ayez fini, je serai parti,** by the time you've finished, I'll have gone.

icône [ikon] *n.f. Ecc:* icon, ikon.

iconoclasme [ikɔnɔklasm] *n.m.* iconoclasm.

iconoclaste [ikɔnɔklast] **1.** *a.* iconoclastic. **2.** *n.m.* iconoclast.

iconogène [ikɔnɔʒɛn] *n.m. Phot:* eikonogen.

iconographe [ikɔnɔgraf] *n.m. & f.* iconographer.

iconographie [ikɔnɔgrafi] *n.f.* iconography.

iconographique [ikɔnɔgrafik] *a.* iconographic(al).

iconoscope [ikɔnɔskɔp] *n.m. T.V:* iconoscope.

ictère [iktɛr] *n.m. Med:* icterus, jaundice.

ictérique [ikterik] *Med:* **1.** *a.* (*a*) icteric(al) (disorder); (*b*) jaundiced (pers., eyes, etc.). **2.** *n.* sufferer from jaundice.

ictus [iktys] *n.m.* ictus. **1.** *Pros: etc:* stress. **2.** *Med:* (apoplectic) stroke; (epileptic) fit.

idéal, -als, -aux [ideal, -o] *a. & n.m.* ideal; **le beau i.,** the ideal of beauty.

idéalement [idealmɑ̃] *adv.* ideally.

idéalisation [idealizasjɔ̃] *n.f.* idealization, idealizing.

idéaliser [idealize] *v.tr.* to idealize.

idéalisme [idealism] *n.m.* idealism.

idéaliste [idealist] **1.** *a.* idealistic. **2.** *n.* idealist.

idée [ide] *n.f.* **1.** idea; (*a*) (mental) conception; notion; **je n'en ai pas la moindre i.,** I haven't the least, the faintest, idea; I haven't a clue; **on n'a pas i. de cela,** you can't imagine it; **quelle i.!** what an idea! what a thought! the very idea! **i. de génie, i. lumineuse,** brilliant idea, brainwave; **bonne i.!** good idea! **qu'est-ce qui vous a donné l'i. de venir?** what gave you the idea, made you think, of coming? **avoir une i. de derrière la tête,** to have an idea at the back of one's mind; **j'ai (comme une) i. qu'il va venir ce soir,** I've an idea he'll come tonight; **donner des idées à qn,** to put ideas into s.o.'s head, give s.o. ideas; (*b*) imagination; **essayez de vous faire une i. de notre situation,** try to imagine our position; **voir qch. en i.,** to see sth. in the mind's eye; **se faire des idées,** to imagine things; **i. fixe,** obsession, idée fixe; (*c*) view, opinion; **avoir une haute i. de qn, qch.,** to have a high opinion of s.o., sth.; **avoir des idées arrêtées sur qch.,** to have set ideas, very decided views, on sth.; **agir à son i.,** to act according to one's own ideas; **changer d'i.,** to change one's mind; (*d*) whim, fancy; **comme l'i. m'en prend,** just as the fancy takes me; **avoir des idées noires,** to be worried, depressed. **2.** mind; **j'ai dans l'i. que . . .,** I have an idea that . . .; **il me vient à l'i. que . . .,** it occurs to me that . . .; **je ne peux pas lui ôter cela de l'i.,** I can't get it out of his mind, head; **cela m'est sorti de l'i.,** it's gone right out, clean out, of my mind, head; **il me revient à l'i. que . . .,** now I remember that . . . .

idem [idɛm] *adv.* idem, id.; ditto.

identifiable [idɑ̃tifjabl̩] *a.* identifiable.

identification [idɑ̃tifikasjɔ̃] *n.f.* identification; *Med:* **i. des types (de bactéries, de virus),** typing.

identifier [idɑ̃tifje] **1.** *v.tr.* (*a*) to identify (**avec, à,** with); (*b*) to identify (s.o.). **2. s'i.,** to identify (oneself), become identified (**avec, à,** with).

identique [idɑ̃tik] *a.* identical.

identiquement [idɑ̃tikmɑ̃] *adv.* identically.

identité [idɑ̃tite] *n.f.* identity; **bracelet d'i.,** identity bracelet; *Adm:* **carte d'i.,** identity card; **pièces d'i.,** identification papers; **l'I. judiciaire** = the Criminal Records Office.

idéogramme [ideɔgram] *n.m.* ideogram, ideograph.

idéographie [ideɔgrafi] *n.f.* ideography.

idéographique [ideɔgrafik] *a.* ideographic(al).

idéologie [ideɔlɔʒi] *n.f.* ideology.

idéologique [ideɔlɔʒik] *a.* ideological.

idéologue [ideɔlɔg] *n.* ideologist; ideologue.

idiomatique [idjɔmatik] *a.* idiomatic; **expression i.,** idiom, idiomatic expression.

idiome [idjom] *n.m.* idiom.

idiosyncrasie [idjɔsɛ̃krazi] *n.f.* idiosyncrasy.

idiot, -ote [idjo, -ɔt] **1.** *a.* (*a*) *Med:* idiot (child, etc.); (*b*) idiotic, absurd; senseless (joke, etc.); **si tu es assez i. pour le croire,** if you're stupid enough to believe it. **2.** *n.* (*a*) *Med:* idiot, imbecile; *F:* **l'i. du village,** the village idiot; (*b*) idiot, fool, *F:* clot, dope; **faire l'i.,** to act, play, the fool.

idiotement [idjɔtmɑ̃] *adv.* idiotically, stupidly.
idiotie [idjɔsi] *n.f.* **1.** *Med:* (*a*) idiocy, imbecility; (*b*) mental deficiency. **2.** (*a*) stupidity, idiocy; (*b*) idiotic, stupid, thing; **ne dites pas d'idioties!** don't talk rubbish, nonsense! **faire une i.,** to do sth. stupid, idiotic.
idiotisme [idjɔtism] *n.m.* idiom; idiomatic expression.
idoine [idwan] *a. A: & Jur:* fit, able; suitable; *Jur:* **apte et i. à tester,** fit and competent to make a will.
idolâtre [idɔlɑtr̥] **1.** *a.* idolatrous. **2.** *n.* idolater, *f.* idolatress.
idolâtrer [idɔlɑtre] *v.tr.* to be passionately fond of (s.o., sth.); to idolize (s.o.).
idolâtrie [idɔlɑtri] *n.f.* idolatry.
idolâtrique [idɔlɑtrik] *a.* idolatrous.
idole [idɔl] *n.f.* idol, image; **faire une i. de qn,** to idolize s.o.; **faire son i. de l'argent,** to make a god of money.
idylle [idil] *n.f.* (*a*) *Lit:* idyll; (*b*) idyll, romance.
idyllique [idilik] *a.* idyllic.
if [if] *n.m.* **1.** yew (tree). **2.** draining rack (for bottles).
igame [igam] *n.m.* = **inspecteur général de l'Administration en mission extraordinaire,** administrator in charge of the prefects of a large district.
igloo, iglou [iglu] *n.m.* igloo.
Ignace [iɲas] *Pr.n.m.* Ignatius.
igname [iɲam] *n.f. Bot:* yam; Indian potato.
ignare [iɲar] **1.** *a.* ignorant. **2.** *n.* ignoramus.
igné [igne] *a. Geol:* igneous (rock, etc.).
ignifugation [ignifygasjɔ̃] *n.f.* fireproofing.
ignifuge [ignifyʒ] **1.** *a.* non-(in)flammable, fireproof; fire-resistant, -resisting. **2.** *n.m.* fireproof.
ignifugé [ignifyʒe] *a.* fireproofed (material).
ignifuger [ignifyʒe] *v.tr.* **(j'ignifugeai(s); n. ignifugeons)** to fireproof.
ignoble [iɲɔbl̥] *a.* (*a*) ignoble; base (person); vile, disgraceful, unspeakable (conduct, etc.); (*b*) wretched, filthy (dwelling, etc.).
ignoblement [iɲɔbləmɑ̃] *adv.* ignobly; basely, disgracefully.
ignominie [iɲɔmini] *n.f.* ignominy, shame, disgrace.
ignominieusement [iɲɔminjøzmɑ̃] *adv.* ignominiously.
ignominieux, -ieuse [iɲɔminjø, -jøz] *a.* ignominious, shameful, disgraceful.
ignorance [iɲɔrɑ̃s] *n.f.* **1.** ignorance; **par i.,** through, out of, ignorance; **tenir qn dans l'i. de qch.,** to keep s.o. in ignorance of sth., in the dark about sth.; **les siècles d'i.,** the dark ages; *Jur:* **prétendre cause d'i.,** to plead ignorance. **2.** *pl.* errors, mistakes.
ignorant, -ante [iɲɔrɑ̃, -ɑ̃t] **1.** *a.* (*a*) ignorant; **être i. en latin,** not to know (any) Latin; (*b*) ignorant, unaware **(de,** of); **il était i. des événements récents,** he did not know what had happened recently. **2.** *n.* ignoramus.
ignoré [iɲɔre] *a.* unknown; **vivre i.,** to live in obscurity; **i. de, par, ses contemporains,** (i) unknown to, (ii) ignored by, his contemporaries.
ignorer [iɲɔre] **1.** *v.tr.* (*a*) not to know (about) (sth.); to be ignorant, unaware, of (sth.); **il ignore tout de . . .,** he knows nothing whatever about . . .; **nul n'est censé i. la loi,** ignorance of the law is no excuse; **je n'ignore pas les difficultés,** I am not unaware of the difficulties; **il ignore qui je suis,** he doesn't know who I am; **ne pas i. qch.,** to be well aware of sth.; (*b*) to ignore (s.o.); (*c*) **i. que** + *sub. or* + *ind.*, not to know, to be unaware, that; **personne n'ignore que . . .,** everybody knows, nobody is unaware, that . . .; **j'ignorais si vous viendriez,** I didn't know whether you would come; **un fusil qu'il ignorait être chargé,** a gun which he did not know to be loaded. **2. s'i.,** not to know oneself; **charme qui s'ignore,** unconscious charm.
iguane [igwan] *n.m. Rept:* iguana.
il, ils [il] **1.** *pers. pron. nom. m.* (*of pers.*) he, they; (*of thg*) it, they; (*of ship*) she, they; **sont-ils arrivés?** have they come? **ton père a-t-il ouvert la bouteille?** has your father opened the bottle? **2.** *inv.* it, there; (*a*) **il est, il doit être, six heures,** it is, it must be, six o'clock; **il est facile de s'en assurer,** it's easy to make sure; **il est vrai que j'étais là,** it's true that I was there; **il était une fois une fée,** once upon a time there was a fairy; (*b*) (*with impers. vbs*) **il pleut, il neige,** it's raining, it's snowing; **il faut partir,** it's time to go, we must go; **il y a quelqu'un à la porte,** there's someone at the door.
île [il] *n.f.* island, isle; **habiter dans une î.,** to live on an island; **î. coralienne,** coral island; **l'î. de Man,** the Isle of Man; **les îles Anglo-Normandes,** the Channel Islands; **les îles du Vent,** the Windward Islands; **les îles sous le Vent,** the Leeward Islands; *A:* **les Îles,** the (French) West Indies; *Cu:* **î. flottante,** floating island.
iléon [ileɔ̃] *n.m. Anat:* ileum.
Iliade (l') [liljad] *n.f. Gr.Lit:* the Iliad.
iliaque [iljak] *a. Anat:* iliac; **os i.,** hip bone.
illégal, -aux [ilegal, -o] *a.* illegal, unlawful.
illégalement [ilegalmɑ̃] *adv.* illegally, unlawfully.
illégalité [ilegalite] *n.f.* illegality; unlawfulness.
illégitime [ileʒitim] *a.* illegitimate (child, etc.); unlawful (marriage, etc.); unwarranted (claim, etc.).
illégitimement [ileʒitim(ə)mɑ̃] *adv.* illegitimately, unlawfully.
illégitimité [ileʒitimite] *n.f.* illegitimacy (of child); unlawfulness (of marriage); unwarranted nature (of claim).
illettré, -ée [iletre] *a. & n.* illiterate.
illicite [ilisit] *a.* illicit, unlawful; *Sp:* **coup i.,** foul.
illicitement [ilisitmɑ̃] *adv.* illicitly, unlawfully.
illico [iliko] *adv. F:* at once, then and there; pronto.
illimité [ilimite] *a.* unlimited, limitless, boundless, unbounded; **congé i.,** indefinite leave.
illisibilité [ilizibilite] *n.f.* illegibility.
illisible [ilizibl̥] *a.* **1.** illegible, unreadable (writing, etc.). **2.** unreadable (book, etc.).
illisiblement [iliziblәmɑ̃] *adv.* illegibly.
illogique [ilɔʒik] *a.* illogical.
illogiquement [ilɔʒikmɑ̃] *adv.* illogically.
illogisme [ilɔʒism] *n.m.* illogicality, illogicalness.
illumination [ilyminasjɔ̃] *n.f.* illumination. **1.** (*a*) lighting (of room, etc.); **i. (par projecteurs),** floodlighting; (*b*) *pl.* lights, illuminations. **2.** enlightenment; inspiration.
illuminé, -ée [ilymine] **1.** *a.* illuminated; floodlit. **2.** *n.* visionary, fanatic; crank.
illuminer [ilymine] **1.** *v.tr.* (*a*) to illuminate (for festivity); to light up; (*b*) *Rel: Phil:* to enlighten. **2. s'i.,** to light up **(de,** with).
illusion [ilyzjɔ̃] *n.f.* **1.** illusion; **i. d'optique,** optical illusion; **se nourrir d'illusions,** to cherish illusions; **se bercer d'illusions, se faire des illusions,** to delude oneself; to live in a fool's paradise. **2.** delusion; **se faire i.,** to deceive oneself, to be, labour, *NAm:* labor, under a delusion.
illusionner [ilyzjɔne] **1.** *v.tr.* to delude (s.o.). **2. s'i.,** to labour, *NAm:* labor, under a delusion; to delude oneself, deceive oneself.
illusionnisme [ilyzjɔnism] *n.m.* art of the illusionist; conjuring.
illusionniste [ilyzjɔnist] *n.* illusionist, conjurer.
illusoire [ilyzwar] *a.* illusory; illusive.
illusoirement [ilyzwarmɑ̃] *adv.* illusively; illusorily.
illustrateur [ilystratœr] *n.m.* illustrator (of books, etc.).

illustration [ilystrasjɔ̃] *n.f.* illustration; (*a*) illustrating; (*b*) picture; **i. en couleur,** coloured, *NAm:* colored, illustration.

illustre [ilystr̥] *a.* illustrious, famous, renowned.

illustré [ilystre] **1.** *a.* illustrated; **abondamment i.,** profusely illustrated. **2.** *n.m.* illustrated magazine.

illustrer [ilystre] *v.tr.* (*a*) *A: & Lit:* to render illustrious; (*b*) to illustrate (book, etc.).

îlot [ilo] *n.m.* **1.** islet, small island. **2.** (*a*) block (of houses); (*b*) **î. de calme,** island of calm; **î. de résistance,** pocket of resistance.

ilote [ilɔt] *n. Gr.Hist:* helot.

image [imaʒ] *n.f.* image. **1.** (*a*) reflection (in water, etc.); (*b*) *Opt:* **i. réelle,** real image; **i. virtuelle,** virtual image; (*c*) *Cin: T.V:* frame; **i. de télévision,** television picture; **émission à 25 images par seconde,** emission at 25 frames per second. **2.** (*a*) **l'i. de son père,** the image of his father; **Dieu créa l'homme à son i.,** God created man in his own image; (*b*) picture; figure; **livre d'images,** picture book; **récit en images,** pictorial record. **3.** (*a*) (mental) picture, idea, impression; **expression qui évoque une i.,** evocative expression; (*b*) **i. de marque,** (i) brand image (of product); (ii) (public) image (of politician, etc.). **4.** *Lit:* image; simile; metaphor; *pl.* imagery.

imagé [imaʒe] *a.* vivid, picturesque (style, etc.); full of imagery.

imager [imaʒe] *v.tr.* **(j'imageai(s); n. imageons)** *Lit:* to colour, *NAm:* color (style, speech).

imagerie [imaʒri] *n.f.* **1.** *Lit:* imagery. **2.** colour, *NAm:* color, print (i) trade, (ii) works.

imagier [imaʒje] *n.m.* **1.** *A:* image maker; (*a*) painter; (*b*) sculptor, carver. **2.** (*a*) drawer of pictures; (*b*) colour, *NAm:* color, print maker; (*c*) colour print seller.

imaginable [imaʒinabl̥] *a.* imaginable, conceivable.

imaginaire [imaʒinɛr] *a.* imaginary; make-believe; *Mth:* imaginary (quantity); **malade i.,** hypochondriac.

imaginatif, -ive [imaʒinatif, -iv] *a.* imaginative.

imagination [imaʒinasjɔ̃] *n.f.* imagination; (*a*) **voir qch. en i.,** to see sth. in one's mind's eye, in one's imagination; (*b*) fancy, invention; **de pure i.,** baseless, unfounded.

imaginer [imaʒine] **1.** *v.tr.* to imagine; (*a*) to conceive, invent, devise; **i. une méthode,** to devise, think out, a method; **i. un dispositif,** to think up a device; **bien imaginé,** well thought out; (*b*) to picture; **imaginez un peu son étonnement,** just imagine his surprise; **tout ce qu'on peut i. de plus beau,** the finest thing imaginable; **vous plaisantez, j'imagine,** you must be joking; **i. que . . .,** to imagine that . . .. **2. s'i.** (*a*) to delude oneself (with the thought) (that . . .); to imagine, think, suppose (that . . .); **elle s'imagine que tout le monde l'admire,** she thinks everyone admires her; **elle s'est imaginé que . . .,** she got it into her head that . . .; **il s'imagine tout savoir,** he thinks he knows everything; (*b*) to imagine, picture; **comme on peut se l'i.,** as you can (well) imagine.

imago [imago] *n.m. or f. Ent: Psy:* imago.

imam [imam], **iman** [imɑ̃] *n.m. Moham.Rel:* imam.

imbattable [ɛ̃batabl̥] *a.* invincible; unbeatable (champion, prices, etc.); *Sp:* unbreakable (record).

imbécile [ɛ̃besil] **1.** *a.* (*a*) *Med:* imbecile; (*b*) silly, idiotic. **2.** *n.* (*a*) *Med:* imbecile; (*b*) idiot, fool; imbecile; **le premier i. venu vous dira cela,** any fool will tell you that; **faire l'i.,** to play, act, the fool.

imbécilement [ɛ̃besilmɑ̃] *adv.* idiotically, foolishly.

imbécillité [ɛ̃besilite] *n.f.* **1.** imbecility; (*a*) *Med:* feebleness of mind; (*b*) silliness, idiocy. **2.** silly, idiotic, thing; **dire des imbécillités,** to talk nonsense, rubbish.

imberbe [ɛ̃bɛrb] *a.* beardless.

imbiber [ɛ̃bibe] **1.** *v.tr.* **i. qch. (de qch.),** to soak, steep, sth. (in sth.); to saturate, moisten, impregnate, sth. (with sth.); **imbibé d'eau,** waterlogged, wet; saturated (with water); **chiffon imbibé d'huile,** oil-soaked rag. **2. s'i.** (*a*) to become saturated (**de,** with); to absorb; (*b*) (*of liquids*) to become absorbed, to sink in; (*c*) **s'i. d'alcool,** to drink too much, to drink like a fish.

imbibé [ɛ̃bibe] *a. F:* drunk, tipsy.

imbrication [ɛ̃brikasjɔ̃] *n.f.* imbrication; overlap(ping) (of tiles, scales, etc.).

imbriquer [ɛ̃brike] **1.** *v.tr.* to imbricate, overlap. **2. s'i.,** to overlap, fit in.

imbroglio [ɛ̃brɔljo] *n.m.* imbroglio.

imbrûlable [ɛ̃brylabl̥] *a.* unburnable, fireproof.

imbu [ɛ̃by] *a.* **i. de,** full of, steeped in, imbued with (prejudice, etc.); **i. de sa personne,** full of one's own importance.

imbuvable [ɛ̃byvabl̥] *a.* (*a*) undrinkable; (*b*) *F:* (*of pers.*) insufferable.

imitable [imitabl̥] *a.* imitable.

imitateur, -trice [imitatœr, -tris] **1.** *n.* imitator; *Th:* impersonator. **2.** *a.* imitative, imitating.

imitatif, -ive [imitatif, -iv] *a.* imitative.

imitation [imitasjɔ̃] *n.f.* imitation. **1.** (*a*) imitating, copying; **à l'i. de qn, de qch.,** in imitation, on the model, of s.o., of sth.; (*b*) mimicking, mimicry; *Th:* impersonation; (*c*) forgery, forging (of signature, etc.); counterfeiting (of money). **2.** (*a*) copy; **bijoux en i.,** imitation, costume, jewellery; **manteau (en) i. loutre,** imitation sealskin coat; (*b*) forgery, counterfeit.

imiter [imite] *v.tr.* to imitate; (*a*) to copy; to model (**de,** on); **il leva son verre et tout le monde l'imita,** he raised his glass and everyone followed suit, did likewise; (*b*) to mimic; to take (s.o.) off; *Th:* to impersonate (s.o.); (*c*) to forge (signature); to counterfeit (money).

immaculé [imakyle] *a.* immaculate; spotless, stainless; undefiled; *Theol:* **l'Immaculée Conception,** the Immaculate Conception.

immanence [imanɑ̃s] *n.f.* immanence.

immanent [imanɑ̃] *a.* immanent; **ce n'est que justice immanente,** it's only a just retribution.

immangeable [ɛ̃mɑ̃ʒabl̥] *a.* uneatable; inedible.

immanquable [ɛ̃mɑ̃kabl̥] *a.* **1.** (target, etc.) that cannot be missed. **2.** certain, inevitable (event, etc.).

immanquablement [ɛ̃mɑ̃kabləmɑ̃] *adv.* inevitably, without fail, for certain.

immatérialité [imaterjalite] *n.f.* immateriality.

immatériel, -ielle [imaterjɛl] *a.* **1.** immaterial, unsubstantial. **2.** intangible (assets, etc.).

immatriculation [imatrikylasjɔ̃] *n.f.* **1.** registering, registration (of deed, car, etc.); *Aut:* **plaque d'i.,** number plate, *NAm:* license plate; **numéro d'i.,** registration number. **2.** registration, enrolment (of student, etc.).

immatriculer [imatrikyle] *v.tr.* to register (document, car, student, etc); **voiture immatriculée SPF 342 T,** car with the registration number SPF 342 T.

immaturité [imatyrite] *n.f.* immaturity.

immédiat [imedja] *a.* immediate. **1.** (*a*) direct (cause, successor, etc.); *Ch:* **analyse immédiate,** proximate analysis; (*b*) close (proximity); near. **2.** without delay; **changement i.,** instant change; **(mécanisme) à action immédiate,** quick-acting (mechanism). **3.** *n.m.* **dans l'i.,** in the immediate future, for the time being.

immédiatement [imedjatmɑ̃] *adv.* immediately. **1.** without interval. **2.** directly, at once.

immédiateté [imedjat(ə)te] *n.f. Phil:* immediacy.
immémorial, -iaux [imemɔrjal, -jo] *a.* immemorial; **de temps i.,** from, since, time immemorial; from time out of mind.
immense [imɑ̃s] *a.* **1.** immeasurable, boundless. **2.** immense, vast, huge; tremendous.
immensément [imɑ̃semɑ̃] *adv.* immensely, vastly, hugely.
immensité [imɑ̃site] *n.f.* **1.** immensity, infinity; boundlessness. **2.** vastness, immenseness, hugeness.
immensurable [imɑ̃syrabl̥] *a.* immensurable, immeasurable.
immerger [imɛrʒe] **(j'immergeai(s); n. immergeons) 1.** *v.tr.* (*a*) to immerse, plunge, dip; to submerge; to lay (cable) underwater; to get rid of, dispose of, (waste) in the sea; (*b*) to bury (s.o.) at sea; (*c*) *Astr:* to occult. **2. s'i.,** (*of submarine*) to submerge, dive.
immérité [imerite] *a.* unmerited, undeserved.
immersion [imɛrsjɔ̃] *n.f.* **1.** immersion, dipping; laying (of cable) underwater; disposal (of waste) in the sea; *Astr:* occultation. **2.** submergence, submersion (of submarine). **3.** burial, funeral, at sea.
immettable [ɛ̃mɛtabl̥] *a.* unwearable.
immeuble [imœbl̥] **1.** *a. Jur:* real, fixed; **biens immeubles,** real estate. **2.** *n.m.* (*a*) *Jur:* real estate, landed property; (*b*) (large, urban) building, block; office block; block of flats, *NAm:* apartment house.
immigrant, -ante [imigrɑ̃, -ɑ̃t] *a. & n.* immigrant.
immigration [imigrasjɔ̃] *n.f.* immigration; **agent du service de l'i.,** immigration officer.
immigré, -ée [imigre] *a. & n.* immigrant.
immigrer [imigre] *v.i.* to immigrate.
imminence [iminɑ̃s] *n.f.* imminence.
imminent [iminɑ̃] *a.* imminent, impending.
immiscer (s') [simise] *v.pr.* **(je m'immisçai(s); n. n. immisçons)** to interfere, meddle (**dans,** in, with).
immixtion [imikstjɔ̃] *n.f.* interference, meddling.
immobile [imɔbil] *a.* **1.** motionless, still, unmoved; immobile; fixed, set (face, etc.); **rester complètement i.,** to stand stock-still. **2.** immovable; firm, steadfast.
immobilier, -ière [imɔbilje, -jɛr] *a. Jur:* real; **biens immobiliers,** *n.m.* **i.,** real estate, landed estate, realty; **vente immobilière,** sale of property; **société immobilière** = building society; **agence immobilière,** estate agency, *NAm:* real estate office; **agent i.,** estate agent, *NAm:* real estate agent, realtor.
immobilisation [imɔbilizasjɔ̃] *n.f.* **1.** immobilization, immobilizing; standstill. **2.** *Jur:* conversion into real estate. **3.** *Com:* (*a*) locking up, tying up, immobilization (of capital); (*b*) *pl.* fixed assets, capital assets.
immobiliser [imɔbilize] **1.** *v.tr.* (*a*) to immobilize, bring to a standstill; (*b*) to immobilize (sth.), fix (sth.) in position; (*c*) *Jur:* to convert into realty; (*d*) *Com:* to lock up, tie up, immobilize (capital). **2. s'i.,** to come to a stop, a standstill; *Mec:* (*of moving body*) to come to rest.
immobilisme [imɔbilism] *n.m.* opposition to progress; ultra-conservatism.
immobiliste [imɔbilist] **1.** *a.* opposed to progress. **2.** *n.* ultra-conservative.
immobilité [imɔbilite] *n.f.* immobility, motionlessness; fixity.
immodération [imɔderasjɔ̃] *n.f.* immoderation, immoderateness.
immodéré [imɔdere] *a.* immoderate, excessive, inordinate.
immodérément [imɔderemɑ̃] *adv.* immoderately, excessively, inordinately.
immodeste [imɔdɛst] *a. O:* immodest.
immodestement [imɔdɛstəmɑ̃] *adv. O:* immodestly, shamelessly.
immodestie [imɔdɛsti] *n.f. O:* immodesty.
immolateur [imɔlatœr] *n.m. A: & Lit:* immolator, sacrificer.
immolation [imɔlasjɔ̃] *n.f. Lit:* immolation, sacrifice.
immoler [imɔle] *v.tr. Lit:* to immolate, sacrifice.
immonde [imɔ̃d] *a.* **1.** *Rel:* unclean. **2.** foul; filthy; vile.
immondices [imɔ̃dis] *n.f.pl.* refuse, rubbish.
immoral, -aux [imɔral, -o] *a.* immoral.
immoralement [imɔralmɑ̃] *adv.* immorally.
immoralisme [imɔralism] *n.m. Phil:* immoralism.
immoraliste [imɔralist] *a. & n. Phil:* immoralist.
immoralité [imɔralite] *n.f.* immorality.
immortaliser [imɔrtalize] **1.** *v.tr.* to immortalize. **2. s'i.,** to win everlasting fame.
immortalité [imɔrtalite] *n.f.* immortality.
immortel, -elle [imɔrtɛl] **1.** *a.* immortal (life, etc.); everlasting, undying (fame, etc.). **2.** *n.m.* immortal, *esp.* member of the *Académie Française.* **3.** *n.f. Bot:* **immortelle,** everlasting (flower); immortelle.
immotivé [imɔtive] *a.* unmotivated, groundless.
immuabilité [imɥabilite] *n.f.* immutability.
immuable [imɥabl̥] *a.* immutable, unalterable; fixed, unchanging.
immuablement [imɥabləmɑ̃] *adv.* immutably, unalterably.
immunisation [imynizasjɔ̃] *n.f. Med: etc:* immunization.
immuniser [imynize] *v.tr. Med:* to immunize; **être immunisé contre qch.,** (i) *Med:* to be immunized against sth.; (ii) to be immune to, from, sth.
immunité [imynite] *n.f.* immunity; **i. parlementaire,** parliamentary privilege, immunity.
immutabilité [imytabilite] *n.f.* immutability.
impact [ɛ̃pakt] *n.m.* impact; shock; **point d'i.,** point of impact.
impair [ɛ̃pɛr] **1.** *a.* (*a*) odd, uneven (number, etc.); *Rail:* **voie impaire,** down line; (*b*) *Anat: A:* **organe i.,** unpaired organ. **2.** *n.m.* blunder, bloomer; **commettre un i.,** to drop a brick, put one's foot in it.
impalpable [ɛ̃palpabl̥] *a.* impalpable, intangible.
imparable [ɛ̃parabl̥] *a.* unstoppable (shot, etc.).
impardonnable [ɛ̃pardɔnabl̥] *a.* unpardonable, unforgivable.
imparfait [ɛ̃parfɛ] **1.** *a.* (*a*) unfinished, uncompleted (book, etc.); (*b*) imperfect, defective. **2.** *n.m. Gram:* imperfect (tense).
imparfaitement [ɛ̃parfɛtmɑ̃] *adv.* imperfectly.
impartial, -iaux [ɛ̃parsjal, -jo] *a.* impartial, unbias(s)ed, fair-minded, unprejudiced.
impartialement [ɛ̃parsjalmɑ̃] *adv.* impartially.
impartialité [ɛ̃parsjalite] *n.f.* impartiality.
impartir [ɛ̃partir] *v.tr. Jur: & Lit:* to grant (right, favour), assign (task) (**à,** to); to bestow (gift) (**à,** on); **délai imparti,** time limit.
impasse [ɛ̃pas] *n.f.* **1.** dead end, cul-de-sac; blind alley; *P.N:* no through road. **2.** impasse; deadlock; **se trouver dans une i.,** to find oneself in a dilemma, *F:* in a fix; **aboutir à une i.,** to come to a deadlock; *Fin:* **i. budgétaire,** budget deficit. **3.** *Cards:* **faire une i.,** to finesse.
impassibilité [ɛ̃pasibilite] *n.f.* impassibility, impassiveness, impassivity.
impassible [ɛ̃pasibl̥] *a.* impassive, impassible. **1.** unmoved; unconcerned. **2.** unimpressionable.
impassiblement [ɛ̃pasibləmɑ̃] *adv.* impassively, impassibly.

impatiemment [ɛ̃pasjamɑ̃] *adv.* impatiently.
impatience [ɛ̃pasjɑ̃s] *n.f.* **1.** *Lit:* intolerance (**de,** of). **2.** (*a*) impatience; **avec i.,** impatiently; (*b*) eagerness; **avoir une grande i., être dans l'i., de faire qch.,** to be most eager to do sth. **3.** *pl.* fits of impatience.
impatient [ɛ̃pasjɑ̃] **1.** *a.* (*a*) *Lit:* intolerant (**de,** of); (*b*) impatient; **d'un air i.,** impatiently; (*c*) **être i. de faire qch.,** to be eager, anxious, impatient, to do sth. **2.** *n.f. Bot:* **impatiente,** balsamine, busy Lizzie.
impatientant [ɛ̃pasjɑ̃tɑ̃] *a.* annoying, provoking.
impatienter [ɛ̃pasjɑ̃te] **1.** *v.tr.* to annoy, provoke (s.o.). **2. s'i.,** to lose patience, get impatient (**de, contre,** at, with).
impayable [ɛ̃pɛjabl̥] *a.* **1.** *A:* inestimable, invaluable, priceless. **2.** *F:* highly amusing, priceless (joke, etc.).
impayé [ɛ̃peje] *a.* (*a*) unpaid (debt, etc.); (*b*) *a. & n.m.* outstanding (payment), dishonoured, *NAm:* dishonored (bill).
impeccable [ɛ̃pɛkabl̥] *a.* impeccable; (*a*) *Lit:* infallible; (*b*) faultless (style, taste, etc.); flawless (technique).
impeccablement [ɛ̃pɛkabləmɑ̃] *adv.* impeccably, faultlessly, flawlessly.
impécunieux, -euse [ɛ̃pekynjø, -øz] *a. Lit:* impecunious.
impédance [ɛ̃pedɑ̃s] *n.f. El:* impedance.
impédimenta [ɛ̃pedimɛ̃ta] *n.m.pl.* impedimenta.
impénétrabilité [ɛ̃penetrabilite] *n.f.* **1.** impenetrability; imperviousness. **2.** inscrutability.
impénétrable [ɛ̃penetrabl̥] *a.* **1.** impenetrable (forest, etc.); **i. à l'eau,** impervious to water. **2.** inscrutable (face); unfathomable (mystery, etc.); close (secret).
impénitence [ɛ̃penitɑ̃s] *n.f.* impenitence.
impénitent [ɛ̃penitɑ̃] *a.* impenitent, unrepentant.
impensable [ɛ̃pɑ̃sabl̥] *a.* unthinkable.
imper [ɛ̃pɛr] *n.m. Cost: F:* (=IMPERMÉABLE 2) mac.
impératif, -ive [ɛ̃peratif, -iv] **1.** *a.* imperious, imperative, peremptory (tone, etc.); *Jur:* mandatory (law). **2.** *n.m.* (*a*) imperative; requirement; (*b*) *Gram:* imperative (mood).
impérativement [ɛ̃perativmɑ̃] *adv.* imperatively.
impératrice [ɛ̃peratris] *n.f.* empress.
imperceptibilité [ɛ̃pɛrsɛptibilite] *n.f.* imperceptibility.
imperceptible [ɛ̃pɛrsɛptibl̥] *a.* imperceptible, unperceivable, undiscernible; intangible.
imperceptiblement [ɛ̃pɛrsɛptibləmɑ̃] *adv.* imperceptibly.
imperfectible [ɛ̃pɛrfɛktibl̥] *a.* imperfectible.
imperfectif, -ive [ɛ̃pɛrfɛktif, -iv] *a. Gram:* imperfective.
imperfection [ɛ̃pɛrfɛksjɔ̃] *n.f.* imperfection. **1.** incompletion, incompleteness. **2.** (*a*) defectiveness; (*b*) defect, fault, flaw, blemish; shortcoming.
impérial, -aux [ɛ̃perjal, -o] **1.** *a.* imperial. **2.** *n.f.* **impériale** (*a*) top (deck) (of bus, etc.); **autobus à i.,** doubledecker (bus); (*b*) imperial; tuft (under lower lip) (as worn by Napoleon III).
impérialement [ɛ̃perjalmɑ̃] *adv.* imperially.
impérialisme [ɛ̃perjalism] *n.m.* imperialism.
impérialiste [ɛ̃perjalist] **1.** *a.* imperialist(ic). **2.** *n.* imperialist.
impérieusement [ɛ̃perjøzmɑ̃] *adv.* imperiously; (*a*) haughtily; (*b*) urgently.
impérieux, -euse [ɛ̃perjø, -øz] *a.* imperious; (*a*) domineering; (*b*) urgent, pressing (necessity, etc.).
impérissable [ɛ̃perisabl̥] *a.* imperishable, undying.
imperméabilisation [ɛ̃pɛrmeabilizasjɔ̃] *n.f.* (water)proofing.
imperméabiliser [ɛ̃pɛrmeabilize] *v.tr.* to (water)-proof.
imperméabilité [ɛ̃pɛrmeabilite] *n.f.* impermeability; imperviousness (**à,** to).
imperméable [ɛ̃pɛrmeabl̥] **1.** *a.* impervious (**à,** to); impermeable; water-repellent; **i. à l'eau,** waterproof; **i. à la poussière,** dustproof. **2.** *n.m. Cost:* raincoat, mackintosh.
impersonnalité [ɛ̃pɛrsɔnalite] *n.f.* impersonality.
impersonnel, -elle [ɛ̃pɛrsɔnɛl] *a.* impersonal.
impersonnellement [ɛ̃pɛrsɔnɛlmɑ̃] *adv.* impersonally.
impertinemment [ɛ̃pɛrtinamɑ̃] *adv.* impertinently.
impertinence [ɛ̃pɛrtinɑ̃s] *n.f.* impertinence. **1.** *A:* irrelevance. **2.** rudeness; **dire des impertinences à qn,** to speak impertinently to s.o.
impertinent, -ente [ɛ̃pɛrtinɑ̃, -ɑ̃t] **1.** *a. A:* impertinent, irrelevant. **2.** *a. & n.* impertinent, rude (person).
imperturbabilité [ɛ̃pɛrtyrbabilite] *n.f.* imperturbability.
imperturbable [ɛ̃pɛrtyrbabl̥] *a.* imperturbable, unruffled.
imperturbablement [ɛ̃pɛrtyrbabləmɑ̃] *adv.* imperturbably.
impétigo [ɛ̃petigo] *n.m. Med:* impetigo.
impétueusement [ɛ̃petɥøzmɑ̃] *adv. Lit:* impetuously.
impétueux, -euse [ɛ̃petɥø, -øz] *a.* (*a*) impetuous; hotheaded, impulsive; (*b*) *Lit:* rushing, raging (torrent, etc.).
impétuosité [ɛ̃petɥozite] *n.f.* impetuosity; impulsiveness.
impie [ɛ̃pi] *a.* impious; blasphemous.
impiété [ɛ̃pjete] *n.f.* **1.** (*a*) impiety; godlessness; ungodliness; (*b*) impiousness (of wish, etc.). **2.** blasphemy.
impitoyable [ɛ̃pitwajabl̥] *a.* (*a*) pitiless (**à, envers, pour,** towards); ruthless, merciless; (*b*) relentless.
impitoyablement [ɛ̃pitwajabləmɑ̃] *adv.* (*a*) pitilessly, ruthlessly, mercilessly; (*b*) relentlessly.
implacabilité [ɛ̃plakabilite] *n.f.* implacability.
implacable [ɛ̃plakabl̥] *a.* implacable, relentless, unrelenting (**à, pour, à l'égard de,** towards).
implacablement [ɛ̃plakabləmɑ̃] *adv.* implacably.
implant [ɛ̃plɑ̃] *n.m. Med:* implant.
implantation [ɛ̃plɑ̃tasjɔ̃] *n.f.* (*a*) planting, implantation; introduction; settling, establishment (of immigrants, etc.); setting up (of industry, etc.); (*b*) layout (of factory, etc.); (*c*) *Med:* implantation.
implanter [ɛ̃plɑ̃te] **1.** *v.tr.* to plant; to introduce, establish; to implant (idea, etc.); to set up (factory, etc.). **2. s'i.,** to take root; to be introduced, established, implanted, set up.
implication [ɛ̃plikasjɔ̃] *n.f.* **1.** (*a*) *Jur:* implication (**dans,** in); (*b*) involvement, entanglement.
implicite [ɛ̃plisit] *a.* implicit; (*a*) implied (intention, etc.); (*b*) absolute (faith, etc.).
implicitement [ɛ̃plisitmɑ̃] *adv.* implicitly.
impliquer [ɛ̃plike] *v.tr.* **1.** to implicate, involve; **véhicule impliqué (dans un accident),** vehicle involved (in an accident). **2. i. que . . .,** to imply that . . ..
implorant [ɛ̃plɔrɑ̃] *a.* imploring; **d'un ton i.,** imploringly.
imploration [ɛ̃plɔrasjɔ̃] *n.f.* imploring, entreaty.
implorer [ɛ̃plɔre] *v.tr.* to implore, beseech, entreat.
imploser [ɛ̃ploze] *v.i.* to implode.
implosion [ɛ̃plozjɔ̃] *n.f.* implosion.
impolarisable [ɛ̃pɔlarizabl̥] *a. El:* impolarizable.
impoli [ɛ̃pɔli] *a.* impolite, uncivil, rude, discourteous.
impoliment [ɛ̃pɔlimɑ̃] *adv.* impolitely, uncivilly, rudely, discourteously.
impolitesse [ɛ̃pɔlitɛs] *n.f.* **1.** impoliteness, rudeness; lack of manners. **2.** act of rudeness.

impolitique [ɛ̃pɔlitik] *a.* impolitic, ill-advised.

impondérabilité [ɛ̃pɔ̃derabilite] *n.f.* imponderability.

impondérable [ɛ̃pɔ̃derabl̩] **1.** *a.* imponderable. **2.** *n.m.pl.* imponderables.

impopulaire [ɛ̃pɔpylɛr] *a.* unpopular.

impopularité [ɛ̃pɔpylarite] *n.f.* unpopularity.

importable¹ [ɛ̃pɔrtabl̩] *a.* importable (goods, etc.).

importable² *a.* unwearable (dress, etc.).

importance [ɛ̃pɔrtɑ̃s] *n.f.* importance; (*a*) consequence, moment; **affaire d'i.**, important matter; **l'affaire est d'i.**, the matter is of some importance; **de peu d'i.**, of little importance, of no great significance; **sans i.**, unimportant; trifling (matter); insignificant (person, matter); **événement de la première i., de haute i.**, event of outstanding importance, all-important event; **avoir de l'i.**, to be important, of importance; **cela n'a pas d'i.**, it's of no importance, of no consequence; **cela n'a aucune i.**, it doesn't matter a bit; **le mouvement prend de l'i.**, the movement is gaining ground; **attacher de l'i. à qch.**, to attach importance to sth.; **tancer qn d'i.**, to give s.o. a good, thorough, scolding; (*b*) size (of town, etc.); extent (of damage, etc.); **i. d'une blessure**, extent, gravity, of a wound; (*c*) social importance; position, standing.

important, -ante [ɛ̃pɔrtɑ̃, -ɑ̃t] **1.** *a.* (*a*) important, significant; **peu i.**, unimportant; immaterial; **rien d'i.**, nothing important, nothing of significance; **personnage i.**, important, influential, person; (*b*) large (town, etc.); considerable (sum of money, etc.); **la recette a atteint un chiffre i.**, the takings reached a high, a considerable, figure; **un retard i.**, a considerable delay. **2.** *a.* & *n.* self-important (person); *n.* busybody; **faire l'i.**, to act big, put on airs. **3.** *n.m.* **l'i.**, the important thing, the main point.

importateur, -trice [ɛ̃pɔrtatœr, -tris] **1.** *n.* importer. **2.** *a.* importing (firm, etc.).

importation [ɛ̃pɔrtasjɔ̃] *n.f.* **1.** importation, import, importing (of goods); **articles d'i.**, imports; **licence d'i.**, import licence. **2.** (*thg imported*) import.

importer¹ [ɛ̃pɔrte] *v.tr.* (*a*) to import (goods); (*b*) to introduce (custom, etc.) (into a country).

importer² *v.i.* (*used only in the third pers., participles and inf.*) **1.** to be of importance, of consequence; to matter, to signify; **les choses qui importent**, (the) things that matter; **que m'importe la vie!** what is life to me! **2.** *impers.* **il importe que** + *sub.*, it is important, essential, that . . .; **peu importe que . . .**, it doesn't matter much whether . . .; **peu m'importe**, I don't mind; it's all the same to me; **n'importe**, never mind; **qu'importe?** what does it matter? **qu'importe qu'il vienne ou non?** what does it matter whether he comes or not? **que m'importe?** what do I care? **faire qch. n'importe comment, où, quand**, to do something no matter how, where, when; to do sth. anyhow, anywhere, (at) any time; **n'importe quelle autre personne**, anybody else; **venez n'importe quel jour**, come any day; **donnez-moi n'importe lequel**, give me any of them, whichever you like; **n'importe qui**, anyone, anybody; no matter who; **n'importe quoi**, anything; no matter what; *F:* **ce n'est pas n'importe qui**, he isn't just anybody.

import-export [ɛ̃pɔrɛkspɔr] *n.f.* *Com:* import-export (business).

importun, -une [ɛ̃pɔrtœ̃, -yn] **1.** *a.* importunate; obtrusive, troublesome, tiresome (person); unwelcome (visitor); ill timed (arrival); **je crains de vous être i.**, I'm afraid I'm disturbing you. **2.** *n.* (*pers.*) intruder; nuisance.

importunément [ɛ̃pɔrtynemɑ̃] *adv.* importunately.

importuner [ɛ̃pɔrtyne] *v.tr.* to importune; (*a*) to bother, pester, badger (s.o.); (*b*) to annoy, trouble, inconvenience (s.o.); **j'espère que je ne vous importune pas**, I hope I'm not disturbing you.

importunité [ɛ̃pɔrtynite] *n.f.* importunity.

imposable [ɛ̃pozabl̩] *a.* (*a*) taxable (person, income); (*b*) rateable, assessable (property).

imposant [ɛ̃pozɑ̃] *a.* imposing (figure, ceremony); commanding, stately, dignified.

imposé, -ée [ɛ̃poze] **1.** *a.* *Com:* **prix i.**, fixed price. **2.** *n.* (*a*) taxpayer; (*b*) ratepayer.

imposer [ɛ̃poze] **1.** *v.tr.* (*a*) *Ecc:* to lay on (hands); (*b*) *Typ:* to impose (sheet); (*c*) to give, assign (name); (*d*) to impose, prescribe; to set (task); **i. des conditions**, to impose, dictate, conditions; **i. une règle**, to lay down, enforce, a rule; **i. silence à qn**, to enjoin silence on s.o.; **i. sa manière de voir**, to carry one's point, force one's opinions on s.o.; **i. du respect à qn**, to inspire s.o. with respect; **i. le respect**, to command, compel, respect; **s'i. un labeur**, to set oneself, undertake, a task; **s'i. de faire qch.**, to make it a duty, a rule, to do sth.; (*e*) *Adm:* **i. des droits sur qch.**, to impose, put, a tax on sth., to tax sth.; **être lourdement imposé**, to be heavily taxed; **i. qn**, (i) to tax s.o., (ii) to rate s.o.; **i. qch.**, to make sth. taxable; **i. un immeuble**, to levy a rate on, to assess, a building. **2.** *v.i.* **en i.**, to inspire respect, awe; **en i. à qn**, to impress s.o. **3.** **s'i.** (*a*) to assert oneself; **s'i. à l'attention**, to command attention; **la conviction s'imposa à mon esprit que . . .**, the conviction forced itself upon me that . . .; (*b*) **s'i. à qn**, to foist, thrust, force, oneself upon s.o.; to impose on s.o.; (*c*) to be indispensable; **la discrétion s'impose**, discretion is imperative, is essential; **une visite au Louvre s'impose**, you, we, must visit the Louvre; *F:* a visit to the Louvre is a must.

imposition [ɛ̃pozisjɔ̃] *n.f.* **1.** (*a*) *Ecc:* laying on, imposition (of hands); (*b*) *Typ:* imposing, imposition. **2.** imposing, laying down (of conditions); setting, prescribing (of task). **3.** (*a*) imposition (of tax); taxation; (*b*) assessment (of property).

impossibilité [ɛ̃pɔsibilite] *n.f.* impossibility. **1.** **il y a i. à cela**, it is impossible that it should be so, this is impossible; **être dans l'i. matérielle de faire qch.**, (i) to find it impossible to do sth.; (ii) to be unavoidably prevented from doing sth. **2.** **accomplir des impossibilités**, to do the impossible.

impossible [ɛ̃pɔsibl̩] *a.* impossible. **1.** **cela m'est i.**, it's not possible for me; I can't; **il m'est i. de le faire**, I can't (possibly) do it; **il m'est i. de ne pas croire que . . .**, I can't help believing that . . .; **c'est i. à faire**, it can't be done; **il a fait l'i. pour nous secourir**, he did his utmost, did everything possible, to help us; **il est i. qu'il revienne avant lundi**, he can't possibly be back before Monday; **vous lui rendez la vie i.**, you're making life impossible for him; you're making his life a misery; *Prov:* **à l'i. nul n'est tenu**, one can't do the impossible; **par i.**, against all possibility; **si par i. il est encore vivant**, if, by some remote chance, he is still alive. **2.** *F:* extravagant, absurd; ridiculous (hat, etc.); **il a fallu nous lever à une heure i.**, we had to get up at an unearthly hour.

imposte [ɛ̃pɔst] *n.f.* *Arch:* (*a*) impost (of bearing arch); springer; (*b*) transom (window); fanlight.

imposteur [ɛ̃pɔstœr] *n.m.* impostor.

imposture [ɛ̃pɔstyr] *n.f.* imposture; deception, trickery.

impôt [ɛ̃po] *n.m.* **1.** tax; **i. foncier**, land tax; **impôts locaux**, rates; **i. sur le revenu**, income tax; **i. retenu à la source**, tax deducted at source = pay as you earn, PAYE, *NAm:* pay as you go; **i. sur les plus-values**, capital gains tax; **i. direct, indirect**, direct, indirect, tax; **payer mille francs d'impôts**, to pay a thousand francs in tax(es); **frapper qch. d'un i.**, to tax sth.; to put, levy, a tax on sth. **2.** taxes, taxation.

impotence [ɛpɔtɑ̃s] *n.f.* disability; infirmity.

impotent, -ente [ɛ̃pɔtɑ̃, -ɑ̃t] **1.** *a.* disabled; crippled; **être i. de la jambe gauche,** to be lame in, to have lost the use of, the left leg. **2.** *n.* cripple; invalid; **les impotents,** the disabled.

impraticabilité [ɛ̃pratikabilite] *n.f.* impracticability; unpracticalness.

impraticable [ɛ̃pratikabl̩] *a.* **1.** impracticable, unfeasible, unworkable; impractical, unpractical (plan). **2.** (*a*) impassable; **chemin i. aux, pour les, automobiles,** road unfit for motor vehicles; (*b*) *Sp:* (*of ground*) unplayable, unfit for play.

imprécation [ɛ̃prekasjɔ̃] *n.f.* imprecation, curse.

imprécatoire [ɛ̃prekatwar] *a.* imprecatory.

imprécis [ɛ̃presi] *a.* lacking in precision. **1.** vague, imprecise, indefinite; inexplicit. **2.** inaccurate (fire).

imprécision [ɛ̃presizjɔ̃] *n.f.* imprecision. **1.** looseness (of terminology, etc.); vagueness (of statement, etc.). **2.** inaccuracy (of fire).

imprégnation [ɛ̃preɲasjɔ̃] *n.* impregnation; permeation.

imprégné [ɛ̃preɲe] *a.* impregnated; **regard i. de tristesse,** look full of sadness.

imprégner [ɛ̃preɲe] **1.** *v.tr.* **(j'imprègne; j'imprégnerai)** to impregnate (**de,** with); to permeate. **2. s'i.,** to become impregnated, permeated (**de,** with); **s'i. d'eau,** to be saturated, soaked, with water.

imprenable [ɛ̃prənabl̩] *a.* impregnable; (*from house*) **vue i.,** view that cannot be obstructed.

impréparation [ɛ̃preparasjɔ̃] *n.f.* unpreparedness.

impresario [ɛ̃presarjo] *n.m.* impresario; business manager (for filmstar, etc.).

imprescriptibilité [ɛ̃prɛskriptibilite] *n.f. Jur:* imprescriptibility, indefeasibility (of a right, etc.).

imprescriptible [ɛ̃prɛskriptibl̩] *a. Jur:* imprescriptible, indefeasible (right, etc.).

impression [ɛ̃prɛsjɔ̃] *n.f.* **1.** impressing; *Typ: Tex:* printing; **livre à l'i.,** book in the press; **faute d'i.,** misprint; **i. en couleurs,** colour, *NAm:* color, printing; *Phot:* **double i.,** double exposure. **2.** (*a*) *O:* impression, imprint (on wax, ground, etc.); **i. de pas,** footprint; (*b*) **troisième i. d'un livre,** third impression, printing, of a book; (*c*) *Engr: etc:* print; **i. en couleurs,** colour print; (*d*) *Paint:* priming coat; (*e*) **tissu à impressions,** printed, patterned, figured, material. **3.** (mental) impression; **il nous a fait, a donné, l'i. que . . .,** he gave us the impression that . . .; **faire i.,** to make an impression, create a sensation; **j'ai l'i. de l'avoir déjà vu, que je l'ai déjà vu,** I've an idea, a feeling, I've seen him before.

impressionnabilité [ɛ̃prɛsjɔnabilite] *n.f.* **1.** impressionability. **2.** *Phot:* sensitivity.

impressionnable [ɛ̃prɛsjɔnabl̩] *a.* **1.** impressionable. **2.** *Phot:* sensitive (plate, etc.).

impressionnant [ɛ̃prɛsjɔnɑ̃] *a.* impressive; moving (sight, voice); sensational (news); spectacular (effect).

impressionner [ɛ̃prɛsjɔne] *v.tr.* **1.** to impress, affect, move; to make an impression (up)on (s.o.); to upset; **spectacle qui impressionne,** impressive sight. **2.** to act on (the retina); *Phot:* to produce an image on (sensitized paper, etc.); to expose (film).

impressionnisme [ɛ̃prɛsjɔnism] *n.m. Art:* impressionism.

impressionniste [ɛ̃prɛsjɔnist] *Art:* **1.** *a.* impressionist(ic). **2.** *n.* impressionist.

imprévisibilité [ɛ̃previzibilite] *n.f.* unpredictability.

imprévisible [ɛ̃previzibl̩] *a.* unforeseeable, unpredictable.

imprévoyance [ɛ̃prevwajɑ̃s] *n.f.* lack of foresight, improvidence.

imprévoyant [ɛ̃prevwajɑ̃] *a.* lacking in foresight; improvident.

imprévu [ɛ̃prevy] **1.** *a.* unforeseen, unexpected. **2.** *n.m.* (*a*) unexpected character (of event); (*b*) unexpected, unforeseen, event; **sauf i., à moins d'i.,** barring accidents, unless something unforeseen happens; **en cas d'i.,** in (case of) an emergency.

imprimable [ɛ̃primabl̩] *a.* printable.

imprimatur [ɛ̃primatyr] *n.m.inv.* imprimatur.

imprimé [ɛ̃prime] **1.** *a.* printed. **2.** *n.m.* printed paper, book; **remplir un i.,** to fill in a form; *Post:* **imprimés,** printed matter; (*in library*) **département, catalogue, des imprimés,** department, catalogue, of printed books. **3.** *n.m. Tex:* print.

imprimer [ɛ̃prime] *v.tr.* **1.** to communicate (direction, etc.); **i. le mouvement à un corps,** to impart, transmit, motion to a body. **2.** (*a*) to (im)print, impress, stamp (sth. on sth.); (*b*) *Tex:* to print (material); **indienne imprimée,** printed cotton, cotton print; (*c*) *Elcs:* **circuit imprimé,** printed circuit. **3.** (*a*) *Typ:* to print; **presse à i.,** printing press; (*b*) to publish (book); **il aime à se voir imprimé,** he likes to see himself in print.

imprimerie [ɛ̃primri] *n.f.* **1.** (art of) printing; **caractères d'i.,** (i) type; (ii) block capitals. **2.** printing house, printing works, (printing) press; *U.S:* printery.

imprimeur [ɛ̃primœr] *n.m.* **1.** (*a*) (master) printer; **i.-libraire,** printer and publisher; (*b*) (working) printer. **2.** *Tex:* **i. d'indiennes,** calico printer.

improbabilité [ɛ̃prɔbabilite] *n.f.* improbability.

improbable [ɛ̃prɔbabl̩] *a.* improbable, unlikely.

improbité [ɛ̃prɔbite] *n.f. Lit:* dishonesty, lack of integrity.

improductif, -ive [ɛ̃prɔdyktif, -iv] *a.* unproductive.

improductivité [ɛ̃prɔdyktivite] *n.f.* unproductiveness.

impromptu [ɛ̃prɔ̃pty] **1.** *adv.* without preparation, impromptu. **2.** *a.* unpremeditated (departure, etc.); impromptu (meal, etc.); extempore, off the cuff (speech, etc.). **3.** *n.m. Th: Mus:* impromptu.

imprononçable [ɛ̃prɔnɔ̃sabl̩] *a.* unpronounceable.

impropre [ɛ̃prɔpr̩] *a.* (*a*) inappropriate, incorrect (term); (*b*) **i. à qch., à faire qch.,** unfit, unsuitable, for sth.; unfit to do sth.; **i. à la consommation,** unfit for human consumption.

improprement [ɛ̃prɔprəmɑ̃] *adv.* improperly, incorrectly.

impropriété [ɛ̃prɔprijete] *n.f.* impropriety; incorrectness (of word).

improuvable [ɛ̃pruvabl̩] *a.* unprovable.

improvisateur, -trice [ɛ̃prɔvizatœr, -tris] *n. Mus: etc:* improviser.

improvisation [ɛ̃prɔvizasjɔ̃] *n.f. Mus: etc:* improvisation.

improvisé [ɛ̃prɔvize] *a.* improvised, extempore, off the cuff (speech, etc.); impromptu (dance); *Sp:* scratch (team).

improviser [ɛ̃prɔvize] *v.tr.* to improvise; **i. (un discours),** to make an impromptu, extempore, speech; to speak off the cuff; *F:* to ad-lib; **i. à l'orgue,** to improvise on the organ.

improviste (à l') [alɛ̃prɔvist] *adv.phr.* unexpectedly, unawares, without any warning; **prendre qn à l'i.,** to take s.o. unawares, by surprise; **visite à l'i.,** surprise visit.

imprudemment [ɛ̃prydamɑ̃] *adv.* imprudently, rashly, recklessly, unwisely.

imprudence [ɛ̃prydɑ̃s] *n.f.* imprudence, foolhardiness, rashness, recklessness; **commettre une i.,** to act rashly, imprudently; *Jur:* **homicide par i.,** manslaughter (by negligence).

imprudent, -ente [ɛ̃prydɑ̃, -ɑ̃t] **1.** *a.* imprudent, foolhardy, rash, reckless; unwise. **2.** *n.* imprudent, rash, reckless, person.

impubère [ɛ̃pybɛr] *a. & n. Jur:* (person) under the age of puberty.
impubliable [ɛ̃pyblijabl̥] *a.* unpublishable.
impudemment [ɛ̃pydamɑ̃] *adv.* shamelessly; impudently; brazenly.
impudence [ɛ̃pydɑ̃s] *n.f.* **1.** impudence; (*a*) effrontery; (*b*) shamelessness. **2.** impudent action, remark.
impudent, -ente [ɛ̃pydɑ̃, -ɑ̃t] *a.* **1.** shameless, brazen. **2.** impudent, insolent.
impudeur [ɛ̃pydœr] *n.f.* shamelessness, immodesty.
impudicité [ɛ̃pydisite] *n.f.* shamelessness; lewdness.
impudique [ɛ̃pydik] *a.* shameless; lewd.
impudiquement [ɛ̃pydikmɑ̃] *adv.* shamelessly; lewdly.
impuissance [ɛ̃pɥisɑ̃s] *n.f.* **1.** impotence, powerlessness, helplessness; **i. à faire qch.,** powerlessness, inability, to do sth.; **je suis dans l'i. de le sauver,** it is beyond my power to save him. **2.** *Med:* impotence (of man).
impuissant [ɛ̃pɥisɑ̃] **1.** *a.* (*a*) impotent, powerless, helpless; **i. à faire qch.,** powerless, unable, to do sth.; (*b*) unavailing, ineffective (effort, etc.). **2.** *a. & n.m. Med:* impotent (man).
impulsif, -ive [ɛ̃pylsif, -iv] *a.* impulsive.
impulsion [ɛ̃pylsjɔ̃] *n.f.* **1.** (*a*) *Mec:* impulse; **force d'i.,** impulsive force; *El:* **i. de courant,** current impulse; **radar à impulsions,** pulse radar; (*b*) impulse, impetus; **donner de l'i. au commerce,** to give a stimulus to trade; **les affaires ont reçu une nouvelle i.,** business has received fresh impetus, shows renewed activity. **2.** impulse; **sous l'i. du moment,** on the spur of the moment.
impulsivité [ɛ̃pylsivite] *n.f.* impulsiveness.
impunément [ɛ̃pynemɑ̃] *adv.* with impunity.
impuni [ɛ̃pyni] *a.* unpunished.
impunité [ɛ̃pynite] *n.f.* impunity.
impur [ɛ̃pyr] *a.* (*a*) impure; foul, tainted; (*b*) *Rel:* unclean (flesh, etc.); (*c*) (morally) impure.
impurement [ɛ̃pyrmɑ̃] *adv.* impurely.
impureté [ɛ̃pyrte] *n.f.* **1.** (*a*) impurity, foulness (of water, etc.); (*b*) *Rel:* uncleanness; (*c*) (moral) impurity. **2.** *pl.* impurities (in water, etc.).
imputabilité [ɛ̃pytabilite] *n.f.* imputability.
imputable [ɛ̃pytabl̥] *a.* **1.** imputable, ascribable, attributable (**à,** to). **2. frais imputables sur un compte,** expenses chargeable to an account.
imputation [ɛ̃pytasjɔ̃] *n.f.* **1.** imputation, charge; **imputations calomnieuses,** slanderous charges. **2.** *Com:* charge, charging (of expenses, etc.); **i. d'une somme sur une quantité,** deduction of a sum from a quota.
imputer [ɛ̃pyte] *v.tr.* **1.** to impute, ascribe, attribute (crime, etc.) (**à,** to); **ils l'ont imputé à son ignorance,** they put it down to his ignorance. **2.** *Com:* **i. qch. sur qch.,** (i) to deduct sth. from sth., (ii) to charge sth. to sth.; **i. des frais sur un compte,** to charge expenses to an account.
imputrescible [ɛ̃pytrɛsibl̥] *a.* imputrescible, incorruptible.
inabordable [inabɔrdabl̥] *a.* (*a*) unapproachable, inaccessible; (*b*) prohibitive (price).
inabrogeable [inabrɔʒabl̥] *a.* unrepealable.
inaccentué [inaksɑ̃tɥe] *a.* **1.** unaccented (vowel). **2.** unstressed (syllable, etc.).
inacceptable [inaksɛptabl̥] *a.* unacceptable; objectionable.
inaccessibilité [inaksesibilite] *n.f.* inaccessibility.
inaccessible [inaksesibl̥] *a.* **1.** inaccessible; **dans une région i.,** in an out-of-the-way place, *F:* at the back of beyond. **2. i. à la pitié,** incapable of pity; **i. à la flatterie,** proof against, impervious to, flattery.
inaccompli [inakɔ̃pli] *a.* unaccomplished, unfulfilled.
inaccordable [inakɔrdabl̥] *a.* **1.** irreconcilable (facts). **2.** ungrantable, inadmissible (request, etc.).
inaccoutumé [inakutyme] *a.* unaccustomed. **1.** unused (**à,** to). **2.** unusual.
inachevé [inaʃve] *a.* unfinished, uncompleted.
inachèvement [inaʃɛvmɑ̃] *n.m.* incompletion.
inactif, -ive [inaktif, -iv] *a.* inactive; idle, not in action; *Com:* **marché i.,** dull market.
inaction [inaksjɔ̃] *n.f.* inaction, idleness.
inactivité [inaktivite] *n.f.* **1.** inactivity; *Com:* dullness (of market); **période d'i.,** period of inactivity; *Com:* dead period. **2.** *Adm: Mil:* **en i.,** (temporarily) unemployed; not on the active list.
inadaptation [inadaptasjɔ̃] *n.f.* maladjustment.
inadapté, -ée [inadapte] *a. & n.* maladjusted (person); **il est i.,** he's a (social) misfit; **les inadaptés,** the maladjusted, the social misfits; **vie inadaptée à ses besoins,** life unsuited to one's needs.
inadéquat [inadekwa] *a.* inadequate.
inadmissibilité [inadmisibilite] *n.f.* inadmissibility.
inadmissible [inadmisibl̥] *a.* inadmissible (request, etc.); **votre proposition est i.,** your proposal is out of the question.
inadvertance [inadvɛrtɑ̃s] *n.f.* **1.** inadvertence, inadvertency; **par i.,** inadvertently; by mistake. **2.** (*a*) oversight, mistake; (*b*) lapse of attention.
inaliénabilité [inaljenabilite] *n.f. Jur:* inalienability; indefeasibility (of right).
inaliénable [inaljenabl̥] *a. Jur:* inalienable, untransferable; indefeasible (right).
inalliable [inaljabl̥] *a. Metall:* that cannot be alloyed, non-alloyable.
inaltérabilité [inalterabilite] *n.f.* **1.** resistance to deterioration; permanence; fastness (of colour, *NAm:* color). **2.** (*a*) unalterableness (of planetary motion, etc.); (*b*) unfailingness (of good humour, *NAm:* humor, etc.).
inaltérable [inalterabl̥] *a.* **1.** that does not deteriorate; permanent; fast (colour, *NAm:* color); **i. à l'air, à l'eau,** unaffected by air, by water. **2.** (*a*) unalterable (course of the stars, etc.); (*b*) unfailing, unvarying (good humour, *NAm:* humor, etc.).
inaltéré [inaltere] *a.* unspoilt, unimpaired; (*of stone, etc.*) unweathered.
inamical, -aux [inamikal, -o] *a.* unfriendly.
inamovibilité [inamɔvibilite] *n.f. Adm:* fixity of tenure; irremovability (of judge, etc.).
inamovible [inamɔvibl̥] *a.* irremovable; (*a*) holding appointment for life; *F:* **il est vraiment i.,** he's a permanent fixture; (*b*) (post) held for life.
inanimé [inanime] *a.* (*a*) inanimate, lifeless; (*b*) senseless, unconscious; **tomber i.,** to fall down unconscious, to faint.
inanité [inanite] *n.f.* inanity, futility.
inanition [inanisjɔ̃] *n.f.* inanition; starvation; **mourir d'i.,** to die of starvation, to starve to death.
inapaisable [inapɛzabl̥] *a.* inappeasable (hunger, etc.); unquenchable (thirst); (grief) that nothing can assuage.
inapaisé [inapeze] *a.* unappeased (hunger, etc.); unquenched (thirst); unassuaged (grief, etc.).
inaperçu [inapɛrsy] *a.* unseen, unperceived; unobserved, unnoticed; **passer i.,** to escape notice, pass unnoticed.
inappétence [inapetɑ̃s] *n.f. Med:* lack of appetite.
inapplicable [inaplikabl̥] *a.* inapplicable.
inapplication [inaplikasjɔ̃] *n.f.* **1.** lack of application. **2. i. d'une loi,** failure to put a law into effect.
inappliqué [inaplike] *a.* **1.** (*of pers.*) lacking in application, careless. **2.** unapplied (method, etc.); (law) in abeyance.

inappréciable [inapresjabl̥] *a.* **1.** inappreciable (quantity, etc.); imperceptible (difference, etc.). **2.** inestimable, invaluable, priceless.
inapprécié [inapresje] *a.* unappreciated.
inapprivoisable [inaprivwazabl̥] *a.* untamable.
inapte [inapt] **1.** *a.* (*a*) inapt; unfit, unfitted (**à,** for); unsuited (**à,** to); **i. à faire qch.,** incapable of doing sth.; (*b*) *Mil:* unfit (for military service). **2.** *n.m.pl. esp. Mil:* **les inaptes,** the unfit; the incapacitated.
inaptitude [inaptityd] *n.f.* inaptitude; unfitness (**à,** for); incapacity (for work, military service, etc.).
inarticulé [inartikyle] *a.* (*a*) inarticulate (sound, etc.); (*b*) not jointed; *Z:* inarticulate(d).
inassimilable [inasimilabl̥] *a.* unassimilable.
inassouvi [inasuvi] *a.* unsatiated, unappeased, unsatisfied (hunger, etc.); unslaked, unquenched (thirst, etc.); unfulfilled (desire).
inassouvissable [inasuvisabl̥] *a.* insatiable.
inattaquable [inatakabl̥] *a.* unassailable (position, etc.); unquestionable (right, etc.); unimpeachable (evidence, etc.); *Ch: etc:* **i. par les acides,** acid-proof, acid-resisting.
inattendu [inatɑ̃dy] *a.* unexpected, unforeseen.
inattentif, -ive [inatɑ̃tif, -iv] *a.* inattentive (**à,** to); unobservant, heedless (**à,** of).
inattention [inatɑ̃sjɔ̃] *n.f.* inattention (**à,** to); carelessness; negligence, unobservance (**à,** of); **faute d'i.,** careless mistake; slip.
inaudible [inodibl̥] *a.* inaudible.
inaugural, -aux [inogyral, -o] *a.* inaugural; **voyage i.,** maiden voyage.
inauguration [inogyrasjɔ̃] *n.f.* inauguration; opening (of fête, etc.); unveiling (of statue); **discours d'i.,** inaugural address.
inaugurer [inogyre] *v.tr.* to inaugurate (building, etc.); to unveil (statue, etc.); to open (fête, etc.); to usher in (epoch).
inauthentique [inotɑ̃tik] *a.* unauthentic.
inavouable [inavwabl̥] *a.* unavowable; shameful.
inavoué [inavwe] *a.* unacknowledged; unconfessed, unavowed.
Inca [ɛ̃ka] *a.inv. & n. Hist:* Inca.
incalculable [ɛ̃kalkylabl̥] *a.* incalculable; **nombre i. de . . .,** countless number of . . ..
incandescence [ɛ̃kɑ̃desɑ̃s] *n.f.* incandescence; *El:* **lampe à i.,** incandescent lamp.
incandescent [ɛ̃kɑ̃desɑ̃] *a.* (*a*) incandescent; (*b*) glowing (imagination).
incantation [ɛ̃kɑ̃tasjɔ̃] *n.f.* incantation.
incantatoire [ɛ̃kɑ̃tatwar] *a.* magical, spell-binding; incantatory.
incapable [ɛ̃kapabl̥] **1.** *a. & n.* incapable, inefficient, incompetent (person); **c'est un i.,** he's useless, no use. **2.** *a.* **i. de faire qch.,** (i) incapable of doing sth.; (ii) unable to do sth.; (iii) unfit to do sth.
incapacité [ɛ̃kapasite] *n.f.* **1.** (*a*) incapacity, incapability, inefficiency, incompetence (of person); (*b*) **i. de faire qch.,** (i) incapability of doing sth., incapacity to do sth.; (ii) inability to do sth. **2.** disability; *Adm:* **i. permanente,** permanent disablement; **i. de travail,** industrial disablement.
incarcération [ɛ̃karserasjɔ̃] *n.f.* incarceration, imprisonment.
incarcérer [ɛ̃karsere] *v.tr.* **(j'incarcère; j'incarcérerai)** to incarcerate, imprison.
incarnat [ɛ̃karna] **1.** *a.* rosy pink; flesh-coloured. **2.** *n.m.* rosy tint (of dawn); rosiness (of complexion).
incarnation [ɛ̃karnasjɔ̃] *n.f.* **1.** incarnation; embodiment (of vice, etc.). **2.** *Med:* ingrowing (of the nails).
incarné [ɛ̃karne] *a.* **1.** (*a*) *Theol:* incarnate; (*b*) **la vertu incarnée,** virtue personified. **2.** *Med:* ingrowing (nail).
incarner [ɛ̃karne] **1.** *v.tr.* (*a*) to incarnate, embody, personify; (*b*) *Th: etc:* to play the part of (person). **2. s'i.** (*a*) to become incarnate; (*b*) *Med:* (*of nail*) to become ingrown.
incartade [ɛ̃kartad] *n.f.* **1.** prank; indiscretion. **2.** *Equit:* sudden swerve (of horse).
incassable [ɛ̃kasabl̥] *a.* unbreakable.
incendiaire [ɛ̃sɑ̃djɛr] **1.** *a.* incendiary (bomb); inflammatory (speech). **2.** *n.* (*pers.*) incendiary; arsonist, fire raiser; *Psy:* pyromaniac.
incendie [ɛ̃sɑ̃di] *n.m.* (*a*) (outbreak of) fire; conflagration; burning (of town, etc.); **i. de forêt,** forest fire; **échelle d'i.,** fire escape; **pompe à i.,** fire engine; **i. volontaire,** arson; **provoquer un i.,** (i) to start a fire; (ii) to commit arson; (*b*) *Lit:* **l'i. du soleil couchant,** the blaze of the setting sun.
incendié, -ée [ɛ̃sɑ̃dje] **1.** *a.* (*of house, etc.*) (i) on fire, burning; (ii) burnt down. **2.** *n.* victim of a fire.
incendier [ɛ̃sɑ̃dje] *v.tr.* (*a*) to set (house, etc.) on fire; to set fire to (sth.); to burn (sth.) down; (*b*) *Lit:* to set (sky, etc.) ablaze; to fire (imagination); (*c*) *P:* to tell (s.o.) off, tear (s.o.) off a strip.
incertain [ɛ̃sɛrtɛ̃] *a.* uncertain, doubtful; dubious (result, etc.); unsettled (weather); unreliable (memory); (*of pers.*) **i. de qch.,** (i) uncertain, unsure, of, about, sth.; (ii) undecided about sth.
incertitude [ɛ̃sɛrtityd] *n.f.* (*a*) uncertainty; doubt; dubiousness (of result, etc.); (*b*) indecision, perplexity (of mind); **être dans l'i.,** to be in a state of uncertainty.
incessamment [ɛ̃sesamɑ̃] *adv.* **1.** *A:* unceasingly, incessantly. **2.** immediately, without delay, at once, as soon as possible; **il arrivera i.,** he'll be arriving (at) any moment.
incessant [ɛ̃sesɑ̃] *a.* unceasing, incessant, ceaseless; unremitting.
incessibilité [ɛ̃sesibilite] *n.f. Jur:* inalienability.
incessible [ɛ̃sesibl̥] *a. Jur:* (*a*) inalienable (right); (*b*) not negotiable; untransferable.
inceste [ɛ̃sɛst] *n.m.* incest.
incestueux, -euse [ɛ̃sɛstɥø, -øz] *a. & n.* incestuous (person).
inchangé [ɛ̃ʃɑ̃ʒe] *a.* unchanged (price, etc.).
inchangeable [ɛ̃ʃɑ̃ʒabl̥] *a.* unchangeable.
inchantable [ɛ̃ʃɑ̃tabl̥] *a.* unsingable.
inchauffable [ɛ̃ʃofabl̥] *a.* (room, etc.) which cannot be heated.
inchavirable [ɛ̃ʃavirabl̥] *a.* uncapsizable, self-righting (boat).
incidemment [ɛ̃sidamɑ̃] *adv.* incidentally.
incidence [ɛ̃sidɑ̃s] *n.f.* **1.** *Tchn:* incidence; *Opt:* **angle d'i.,** angle of incidence. **2.** influence; repercussion; effect, impact. **3.** *Med:* incidence (of disease).
incident [ɛ̃sidɑ̃] **1.** *a.* (*a*) incidental (question, etc.); (*b*) *Opt:* incident (ray). **2.** *n.m.* (*a*) incident; occurrence, happening; (*b*) *Jur:* point of law; (*c*) difficulty, hitch; mishap; **i. technique,** technical hitch; **i. diplomatique,** diplomatic incident.
incinérateur [ɛ̃sineratœr] *n.m.* incinerator.
incinération [ɛ̃sinerasjɔ̃] *n.f.* (*a*) incineration; (*b*) cremation.
incinérer [ɛ̃sinere] *v.tr.* **(j'incinère; j'incinérerai)** (*a*) to incinerate; to burn to ashes; (*b*) to cremate.
incirconcis [ɛ̃sirkɔ̃si] *a.* uncircumcised.
incise [ɛ̃siz] *n.f. Gram:* interpolated clause, incidental clause.
inciser [ɛ̃size] *v.tr.* to incise, cut; to make an incision in (sth.); to lance (boil); to tap (tree) (for resin).
incisif, -ive [ɛ̃sizif, -iv] **1.** *a.* incisive, sharp, cutting (remark, etc.). **2.** *a. & n.f.* **(dent) incisive,** incisor (tooth).
incision [ɛ̃sizjɔ̃] *n.f.* incision. **1.** cutting; tapping (of

tree) (for resin); lancing (of boil). **2.** cut; **faire une i.,** to incise, make an incision.

incitateur, -trice [ɛ̃sitatœr, -tris] *n.* inciter (**à,** to); instigator.

incitation [ɛ̃sitasjɔ̃] *n.f.* incitement (**à,** to).

inciter [ɛ̃site] *v.tr.* to incite, urge (on); **i. qn à faire qch.,** to incite, prompt, s.o. to do sth.

incivil [ɛ̃sivil] *a.* uncivil, rude.

incivilisable [ɛ̃sivilizabl̥] *a.* which cannot be civilized.

incivilité [ɛ̃sivilite] *n.f.* **1.** incivility, rudeness. **2.** rude remark, action.

incivique [ɛ̃sivik] *a. O:* with no sense of civic duty.

inclassable [ɛ̃klasabl̥] *a.* unclass(ifi)able.

inclémence [ɛ̃klemɑ̃s] *n.f.* inclemency.

inclinaison [ɛ̃klinɛzɔ̃] *n.f.* (*a*) tilting, canting; (*b*) incline, gradient, slope (of hill, etc.); inclination (of line, etc.); pitch, slant, cant (of roof, etc.); tilt (of head, hat, etc.); heel, list (of ship); rake (of mast); dip (of magnetic needle); angle (of trajectory); **comble à forte, faible, i.,** high-pitched, low-pitched, roof; **degré d'i. d'une courbe,** steepness of a curve.

inclination [ɛ̃klinasjɔ̃] *n.f.* inclination. **1.** bending, bow(ing) (of body); nod (of head). **2.** (*a*) tendency; propensity; bent; **avoir de l'i. à faire qch.,** to be inclined to do sth.; **avoir de l'i. pour qch.,** to like, have a liking for, sth.; (*b*) **mariage d'i.,** love match.

incliné [ɛ̃kline] *a.* **1.** (*a*) **la tête inclinée,** with bowed head; (*b*) sloping, tilting, tilted; **plan i.,** inclined plane. **2. i. à qch., à faire qch.,** inclined, disposed, to sth., to do sth.

incliner [ɛ̃kline] **1.** *v.tr.* to incline; (*a*) to slant, slope, cant; (*b*) to tip up, tilt (plank, etc.); (*c*) to bend, bow, incline (the head, etc.); **i. la tête,** to nod (one's head); (*d*) **i. qn à faire qch.,** to predispose, influence, s.o. in favour, *NAm:* favor, of doing sth. **2.** *v.i.* (*a*) (*of wall, etc.*) to lean, slope; (*of ship*) to list; (*b*) **i. à la pitié,** to incline, be disposed, to pity; **i. à faire qch.,** to be, feel, inclined to do sth. **3. s'i.** (*a*) to slant, slope; (*of ship*) to heel (over); (*of aircraft*) to bank; (*b*) to bend over, down; (*c*) to bow (down) (**devant,** before); **s'i. devant les arguments de qn,** to bow, yield, to s.o.'s arguments; **j'ai dû m'i.,** I had to give in.

inclure [ɛ̃klyr] *v.tr.* (*conj. like* CONCLURE *except p.p.* **inclus,** *but little used except in p.p.*) **1.** to enclose (document in letter, etc.). **2.** *Jur:* to insert (clause in contract, etc.).

inclus [ɛ̃kly] *a.* (*a*) enclosed (in letter, etc.); (*b*) (amount) included; **jusqu'à la page 5 incluse,** up to and including page 5.

inclusif, -ive [ɛ̃klyzif, -iv] *a.* inclusive.

inclusion [ɛ̃klyzjɔ̃] *n.f.* (*a*) enclosing (of document in letter, etc.); (*b*) inclusion, insertion.

inclusivement [ɛ̃klyzivmɑ̃] *adv.* inclusively; **du vendredi au mardi i.,** from Friday to Tuesday inclusive, *NAm:* Friday through Tuesday.

incoercible [ɛ̃kɔɛrsibl̥] *a.* (*a*) *Ph: etc:* incoercible; (*b*) uncontrollable (cough); irrepressible (laughter).

incognito [ɛ̃kɔɲito] **1.** *adv.* incognito. **2.** *n.m.* **garder l'i.,** to preserve one's incognito, remain incognito.

incohérence [ɛ̃kɔerɑ̃s] *n.f.* (*a*) incoherence, incoherency; disjointedness (of speech, etc.); (*b*) inconsistency (in story, etc.).

incohérent [ɛ̃kɔerɑ̃] *a.* incoherent; inconsistent.

incollable [ɛ̃kɔlabl̥] *a. F:* (pers.) who cannot be caught out, stumped, floored.

incolore [ɛ̃kɔlɔr] *a.* colourless, *NAm:* colorless.

incomber [ɛ̃kɔ̃be] *v.i.* (*used only in third pers.*) **i. à qn,** to devolve, be incumbent, on s.o.; **les devoirs qui lui incombent,** the duties which fall on him; **la responsabilité incombe à l'auteur,** the responsibility lies, rests, with the author; it is the author's responsibility; **il m'incombe de pourvoir à ses besoins,** it is my duty to provide for his needs; **il incombe au gouvernement d'indemniser les sinistrés,** the onus lies on the government to compensate the victims.

incombustibilité [ɛ̃kɔ̃bystibilite] *n.f.* incombustibility.

incombustible [ɛ̃kɔ̃bystibl̥] *a.* incombustible, non-(in)flammable; fireproof.

incommensurable [ɛ̃kɔmɑ̃syrabl̥] *a.* **1.** *Mth:* incommensurable (**avec,** with); incommensurate; **racine i.,** irrational root. **2.** immeasurable, huge.

incommensurablement [ɛ̃kɔmɑ̃syrabləmɑ̃] *adv.* **1.** incommensurably. **2.** immeasurably.

incommodant [ɛ̃kɔmɔdɑ̃] *a.* unpleasant, disagreeable, annoying.

incommode [ɛ̃kɔmɔd] *a.* inconvenient; uncomfortable (chair, etc.); clumsy, awkward (tool, etc.).

incommodé [ɛ̃kɔmɔde] *a.* **1.** ill at ease; **être i. par la chaleur,** to feel the heat. **2.** *O:* unwell, off colour.

incommodément [ɛ̃kɔmɔdemɑ̃] *adv.* inconveniently; uncomfortably, awkwardly.

incommoder [ɛ̃kɔmɔde] *v.tr.* **1.** to inconvenience, incommode, disturb (s.o.); **la fumée ne vous incommode pas?** you don't mind my smoking? **2.** (*of food, etc.*) to disagree with (s.o.); to upset (s.o.).

incommodité [ɛ̃kɔmɔdite] *n.f.* (*a*) inconvenience; (*b*) discomfort; awkwardness (of situation).

incommunicable [ɛ̃kɔmynikabl̥] *a.* incommunicable.

incommutable [ɛ̃kɔmytabl̥] *a. Jur:* non-transferable (property); indefeasible (right).

incomparable [ɛ̃kɔ̃parabl̥] *a.* incomparable, unrivalled, matchless.

incomparablement [ɛ̃kɔ̃parabləmɑ̃] *adv.* incomparably, beyond compare.

incompatibilité [ɛ̃kɔ̃patibilite] *n.f.* incompatibility (of duties, etc.); **i. d'humeur,** incompatibility of temperament.

incompatible [ɛ̃kɔ̃patibl̥] *a.* incompatible, inconsistent, at variance (**avec,** with).

incompétence [ɛ̃kɔ̃petɑ̃s] *n.f.* (*a*) incompetence, incompetency (of person, tribunal); (*b*) **reconnaître ses incompétences,** to acknowledge one's ignorance, one's shortcomings.

incompétent [ɛ̃kɔ̃petɑ̃] *a.* incompetent; (*a*) inefficient; (*b*) *Jur:* not qualified, unqualified (to try case); (*c*) **i. en qch.,** ignorant about sth.

incomplet, -ète [ɛ̃kɔ̃plɛ, -ɛt] *a.* incomplete.

incomplètement [ɛ̃kɔ̃plɛtmɑ̃] *adv.* incompletely.

incomplétude [ɛ̃kɔ̃pletyd] *n.f. Psy:* (sense of) inadequacy, non-fulfilment.

incompréhensibilité [ɛ̃kɔ̃preɑ̃sibilite] *n.f.* incomprehensibility.

incompréhensible [ɛ̃kɔ̃preɑ̃sibl̥] *a.* incomprehensible.

incompréhensif, -ive [ɛ̃kɔ̃preɑ̃sif, -iv] *a.* uncomprehending; obtuse (mind, etc.); **père i.,** father who doesn't understand.

incompréhension [ɛ̃kɔ̃preɑ̃sjɔ̃] *n.f.* incomprehension; lack of understanding; obtuseness.

incompris [ɛ̃kɔ̃pri] *a.* misunderstood; unappreciated.

inconcevable [ɛ̃kɔ̃s(ə)vabl̥] *a.* inconceivable, unthinkable, unimaginable.

inconcevablement [ɛ̃kɔ̃s(ə)vabləmɑ̃] *adv.* inconceivably.

inconciliabilité [ɛ̃kɔ̃siljabilite] *n.f.* irreconcilability, incompatibility (of theories, etc.).

inconciliable [ɛ̃kɔ̃siljabl̥] *a.* irreconcilable, incompatible (**avec,** with).

inconditionné [ɛ̃kɔ̃disjɔne] *a. & n.m. Psy:* unconditional; unconditioned.

inconditionnel, -elle [ɛ̃kɔ̃disjɔnɛl] *a.* unconditional; unquestioning (obedience); absolute (liability, etc.); *Pol: etc:* unwavering (supporter).

inconditionnellement [ɛ̃kɔ̃disjɔnɛlmɑ̃] *adv.* unconditionally; unquestioningly.

inconduite [ɛ̃kɔ̃dɥit] *n.f.* loose living, laxity of conduct; *Jur:* misconduct.

inconfort [ɛ̃kɔ̃fɔr] *n.m.* discomfort.

inconfortable [ɛ̃kɔ̃fɔrtabl̥] *a.* uncomfortable.

inconfortablement [ɛ̃kɔ̃fɔrtabləmɑ̃] *adv.* uncomfortably.

incongru [ɛ̃kɔ̃gry] *a.* (*a*) incongruous (remark, etc.); out of place; (*b*) improper, unseemly (question, etc.).

incongruité [ɛ̃kɔ̃grɥite] *n.f.* **1.** (*a*) incongruity, absurdity; (*b*) impropriety (of behaviour). **2.** incongruity; improper remark, action.

incongrûment [ɛ̃kɔ̃grymɑ̃] *adv.* (*a*) incongruously; (*b*) improperly.

inconnaissable [ɛ̃kɔnɛsabl̥] *a.* & *n.m.* unknowable.

inconnu, -ue [ɛ̃kɔny] **1.** *a.* unknown (**de, à,** to); **il m'était i., il était i. de tout le monde,** I didn't know him, nobody knew him; **visages inconnus,** strange faces. **2.** *n.* (*a*) unknown person; (i) stranger; (ii) (mere) nobody; (*b*) *n.m.* **l'i.,** the unknown; **faire un saut dans l'i.,** to take a leap in the dark. **3.** *n.f. Mth: etc:* **inconnue,** unknown (quantity).

inconsciemment [ɛ̃kɔ̃sjamɑ̃] *adv.* unconsciously, unknowingly, unwittingly; unawares.

inconscience [ɛ̃kɔ̃sjɑ̃s] *n.f.* **1.** unconsciousness. **2.** unawareness, obliviousness (of sth.); **c'était de l'i. pure,** it was sheer thoughtlessness.

inconscient [ɛ̃kɔ̃sjɑ̃] **1.** *a.* (*a*) unconscious (act); automatic (movement, etc.); (*b*) **i. de ce qui se passe autour de lui,** oblivious, unaware, of what is going on around him. **2.** *n.m. Psy:* **l'i.,** the unconscious, the subconscious.

inconséquemment [ɛ̃kɔ̃sekamɑ̃] *adv.* inconsistently, inconsequently, inconsequentially.

inconséquence [ɛ̃kɔ̃sekɑ̃s] *n.f.* inconsistency, inconsequence.

inconséquent [ɛ̃kɔ̃sekɑ̃] *a.* (*a*) inconsistent, inconsequent(ial) (argument, person); rambling (speech); (*b*) irresponsible, rash (words).

inconsidéré [ɛ̃kɔ̃sidere] *a.* **1.** *O:* inconsiderate (person). **2.** unconsidered, ill considered, rash (act).

inconsidérément [ɛ̃kɔ̃sideremɑ̃] *adv.* inconsiderately, thoughtlessly, rashly.

inconsistance [ɛ̃kɔ̃sistɑ̃s] *n.f.* **1.** unsubstantiality; softness (of mud); looseness (of soil); weakness (of nature). **2.** inconsistency (of person, act).

inconsistant [ɛ̃kɔ̃sistɑ̃] *a.* **1.** unsubstantial; soft (mud); loose (soil); weak (nature). **2.** inconsistent (conduct, person).

inconsolable [ɛ̃kɔ̃sɔlabl̥] *a.* inconsolable; disconsolate (person).

inconsolé [ɛ̃kɔ̃sɔle] *a.* unconsoled.

inconsommable [ɛ̃kɔ̃sɔmabl̥] *a.* unfit for consumption.

inconstance [ɛ̃kɔ̃stɑ̃s] *n.f.* **1.** (*of pers.*) inconstancy, inconsistency; fickleness. **2.** *Lit:* (*of thg*) changeableness.

inconstant [ɛ̃kɔ̃stɑ̃] *a.* **1.** inconstant, inconsistent; fickle, flighty, erratic. **2.** *Lit:* (*of thg*) changeable.

inconstatable [ɛ̃kɔ̃statabl̥] *a.* unascertainable, unverifiable.

inconstitutionnalité [ɛ̃kɔ̃stitysjɔnalite] *n.f.* unconstitutionality.

inconstitutionnel, -elle [ɛ̃kɔ̃stitysjɔnɛl] *a.* unconstitutional.

inconstitutionnellement [ɛ̃kɔ̃stitysjɔnɛlmɑ̃] *adv.* unconstitutionally.

incontestabilité [ɛ̃kɔ̃tɛstabilite] *n.f.* incontestability.

incontestable [ɛ̃kɔ̃tɛstabl̥] *a.* incontestable, undeniable, indisputable; beyond all doubt.

incontestablement [ɛ̃kɔ̃tɛstabləmɑ̃] *adv.* incontestably, undeniably; beyond all doubt.

incontesté [ɛ̃kɔ̃tɛste] *a.* uncontested, undisputed.

incontinence [ɛ̃kɔ̃tinɑ̃s] *n.f.* (*a*) *A:* & *Lit:* incontinence; lack of restraint; (*b*) *Med:* incontinence; **i. nocturne,** bedwetting.

incontinent¹ [ɛ̃kɔ̃tinɑ̃] *a.* (*a*) *A:* & *Lit:* incontinent, unrestrained; (*b*) *Med:* incontinent.

incontinent² *adv. A:* & *Lit:* at once, forthwith.

incontrôlable [ɛ̃kɔ̃trolabl̥] *a.* difficult to verify, to check; unverifiable.

incontrôlé [ɛ̃kɔ̃trole] *a.* **1.** unchecked, unverified. **2.** uncontrolled.

inconvenance [ɛ̃kɔ̃vnɑ̃s] *n.f.* impropriety.

inconvenant [ɛ̃kɔ̃vnɑ̃] *a.* improper, indecorous; **il est vraiment i.,** he doesn't know how to behave, he has no manners.

inconvénient [ɛ̃kɔ̃venjɑ̃] *n.m.* disadvantage, drawback; difficulty; **les inconvénients qu'il y a à vivre si loin de la ville,** the inconvenience of living so far from town; **je n'y vois pas d'i.,** I can't see any objection(s) (to it); I've got nothing against it; **pouvez-vous sans i. me prêter ce livre?** would it be convenient for you to lend me this book? **nous pouvons sans i. modifier notre itinéraire,** we can easily change our route; **n'y a-t-il pas d'i. à laisser cet enfant jouer près de la rivière?** is there no risk, danger, in letting the child play near the river?

inconvertible [ɛ̃kɔ̃vɛrtibl̥], **inconvertissable** [ɛ̃kɔ̃vɛrtisabl̥] *a.* **1.** inconvertible (paper money, etc.). **2.** (*of pers.*) inconvertible; beyond hope of conversion.

incoordination [ɛ̃kɔɔrdinasjɔ̃] *n.f.* incoordination; (*a*) lack of coordination; (*b*) *Med:* ataxia.

incorporable [ɛ̃kɔrpɔrabl̥] *a.* incorporable.

incorporalité [ɛ̃kɔrpɔralite] *n.f.* incorporeality.

incorporation [ɛ̃kɔrpɔrasjɔ̃] *n.f.* (*a*) incorporation, blending (**de qch. dans qch.,** of sth. into, with, sth.); (*b*) *Mil:* conscription; **sursis d'i.,** deferment of call-up.

incorporéité [ɛ̃kɔrpɔreite] *n.f.* incorporeity.

incorporel, -elle [ɛ̃kɔrpɔrɛl] *a.* incorporeal; *Jur:* **biens incorporels,** intangible property.

incorporer [ɛ̃kɔrpɔre] *v.tr.* (*a*) **i. qch. à,** *occ.* **avec, qch.,** to blend, mix, incorporate, sth. into, with, sth.; (*b*) to incorporate (land) (**dans un domaine,** in(to) an estate); to insert (paragraph, etc.); (*c*) *Mil:* to draft (troops).

incorrect [ɛ̃kɔrɛkt] *a.* incorrect. **1.** (*a*) inaccurate, wrong; (*b*) defective, faulty. **2.** (*a*) contrary to etiquette; **tenue incorrecte,** (i) slovenly, (ii) unsuitable, clothes; (*b*) (*of pers.*) impolite, ill mannered, rude; **être i. avec qn,** to treat s.o. unfairly.

incorrectement [ɛ̃kɔrɛktəmɑ̃] *adv.* incorrectly. **1.** (*a*) inaccurately, wrongly; improperly; (*b*) defectively. **2.** (*a*) in a slovenly manner; unsuitably (dressed); (*b*) impolitely, rudely; **se conduire i. avec qn,** to treat s.o. (i) unfairly, (ii) impolitely, rudely.

incorrection [ɛ̃kɔrɛksjɔ̃] *n.f.* **1.** (*a*) incorrectness, inaccuracy; (*b*) incorrectness, slovenliness; unsuitability (of clothes); (*c*) impoliteness, lack of (good) manners, rudeness. **2.** (*a*) incorrect expression; (*b*) impolite, rude, remark, action.

incorrigibilité [ɛ̃kɔriʒibilite] *n.f.* incorrigibility.

incorrigible [ɛ̃kɔriʒibl̥] *a.* incorrigible (child, etc.); irreclaimable, hopeless (drunkard, etc.).

incorrigiblement [ɛ̃kɔriʒibləmɑ̃] *adv.* incorrigibly.

incorruptibilité [ɛ̃kɔryptibilite] *n.f.* incorruptibility.

incorruptible [ɛ̃kɔryptibl̥] *a.* incorruptible.

incorruptiblement [ɛ̃kɔryptibləmɑ̃] *adv.* incorruptibly.
incrédibilité [ɛ̃kredibilite] *n.f.* incredibility.
incrédule [ɛ̃kredyl] **1.** *a.* (*a*) incredulous; (*b*) *Theol:* unbelieving. **2.** *n.* unbeliever.
incrédulité [ɛ̃kredylite] *n.f.* **1.** incredulity; **avec i.,** incredulously. **2.** *Theol:* unbelief.
increvable [ɛ̃krəvabl̥] *a.* (*a*) unpuncturable, puncture-proof (tyre); (*b*) *P:* (*of pers.*) indefatigable, tireless.
incriminé [ɛ̃krimine] *a.* accused (person); offending (object).
incriminer [ɛ̃krimine] *v.tr.* to incriminate, accuse, indict (s.o.); to condemn (sth.).
incrochetable [ɛ̃krɔʃtabl̥] *a.* unpickable (lock); burglar-proof (safe).
incroyable [ɛ̃krwajabl̥] **1.** *a.* incredible, unbelievable; beyond belief; extraordinary; **il est d'une paresse i.,** he's incredibly lazy. **2.** *n. Hist: incroyable* (beau or belle of the French Directoire period).
incroyablement [ɛ̃krwajabləmɑ̃] *adv.* incredibly, unbelievably; beyond belief; extraordinarily.
incroyance [ɛ̃krwajɑ̃s] *n.f.* unbelief.
incroyant, -ante [ɛ̃krwajɑ̃, -ɑ̃t] **1.** *a.* unbelieving. **2.** *n.* unbeliever, non-believer.
incrustation [ɛ̃krystasjɔ̃] *n.f.* encrustation. **1.** (*a*) encrusting; *Join:* inlaying; (*b*) furring (up) (of boiler, etc.). **2.** (*a*) inlay; inlaid work; **avec incrustations de nacre,** inlaid with mother of pearl; (*b*) *Dressm:* insertion; **i. de dentelle,** lace inlay; (*c*) fur(ring), scale (in boiler, etc.).
incruster [ɛ̃kryste] **1.** *v.tr.* to encrust; (*a*) *Join:* to inlay (**de,** with); (*b*) to encrust, form a crust on (sth.); (*of water*) to scale, fur (up) (pipes, etc.). **2.** **s'i.** (*a*) to become encrusted; (*b*) (*of boiler, etc.*) to fur up; (*c*) **quand on l'invite, il s'incruste,** once you invite him you can't get rid of him.
incubateur, -trice [ɛ̃kybatœr, -tris] **1.** *a.* incubating (apparatus, etc.). **2.** *n.m.* (*a*) incubator; (*b*) *Pisc:* grille.
incubation [ɛ̃kybasjɔ̃] *n.f.* (*a*) incubation, hatching (of eggs); (*b*) sitting (of hens); (*c*) **période d'i.,** incubation period (of disease).
incube [ɛ̃kyb] *n.m.* incubus; nightmare.
incuber [ɛ̃kybe] *v.tr.* to incubate, hatch (out) (eggs).
inculcation [ɛkylkasjɔ̃] *n.f.* inculcating, inculcation.
inculpation [ɛ̃kylpasjɔ̃] *n.f.* indictment, charge.
inculpé, -ée [ɛ̃kylpe] *n. Jur:* **l'i.,** the accused; the defendant; the prisoner (in the widest sense).
inculper [ɛ̃kylpe] *v.tr.* to indict, charge (**de,** with).
inculquer [ɛ̃kylke] *v.tr.* to inculcate (**à,** in); to instil (**à,** into).
inculte [ɛ̃kylt] *a.* (*a*) uncultivated, wild (garden, etc.); waste (land); (*b*) unkempt (beard); (*c*) (*of pers.*) uneducated.
incultivable [ɛ̃kyltivabl̥] *a.* untillable, irreclaimable (land).
incultivé [ɛ̃kyltive] *a.* untilled, uncultivated (land).
inculture [ɛ̃kyltyr] *n.f.* lack of culture.
incunable [ɛ̃kynabl̥] *n.m.* early printed book; incunabulum, *pl.* incunabula.
incurable [ɛ̃kyrabl̥] *a.* & *n.* incurable.
incurablement [ɛ̃kyrabləmɑ̃] *adv.* incurably.
incurie [ɛ̃kyri] *n.f.* carelessness, negligence.
incursion [ɛ̃kyrsjɔ̃] *n.f.* inroad, foray, raid, incursion.
incurvation [ɛ̃kyrvasjɔ̃] *n.f.* bend; curve.
incurvé [ɛ̃kyrve] *a.* bent, curved.
incurver (s') [(s)ɛ̃kyrve] *v.tr.* & *pr.* to bend, curve.
indatable [ɛ̃databl̥] *a.* that cannot be dated.
Inde [ɛ̃d] *Pr.n.f. Geog:* (*a*) India; (*b*) **les Indes,** the Indies; (*c*) *Hist:* **les Indes occidentales,** the West Indies; **les Indes orientales,** the East Indies.
indébrouillable [ɛ̃debrujabl̥] *a.* inextricable, tangled (situation, etc.).
indécemment [ɛ̃desamɑ̃] *adv.* indecently.
indécence [ɛ̃desɑ̃s] *n.f.* indecency.
indécent [ɛ̃desɑ̃] *a.* indecent, improper.
indéchiffrable [ɛ̃deʃifrabl̥] *a.* (*a*) indecipherable (inscription); (*b*) illegible (writing); (*c*) unintelligible, incomprehensible; (*of pers.*) impenetrable, inscrutable.
indéchirable [ɛ̃deʃirabl̥] *a.* untearable, tearproof.
indécis [ɛ̃desi] *a.* **1.** undecided, unsettled (question, etc.); indecisive, doubtful (victory, etc.); vague, blurred (outline). **2.** (*of pers.*) (*a*) **être i. quant au parti à prendre,** to be undecided, in two minds, how to act; (*b*) indecisive, irresolute, hesitating; **c'est un i.,** he can never make his mind up.
indécision [ɛ̃desizjɔ̃] *n.f.* indecision, indecisiveness, irresolution; uncertainty.
indécollable [ɛ̃dekɔlabl̥] *a.* that cannot be unglued, unstuck.
indécomposable [ɛ̃dekɔ̃pozabl̥] *a.* irresolvable (element, etc.).
indécrottable [ɛ̃dekrɔtabl̥] *a.* **1.** uncleanable. **2.** *F:* incorrigible; hopeless (dunce, etc.).
indéfectibilité [ɛ̃defɛktibilite] *n.f. Theol:* indefectibility (of the church, etc.).
indéfectible [ɛ̃defɛktibl̥] *a.* (*a*) *Theol:* indefectible; (*b*) indestructible (friendship, etc.).
indéfendable [ɛ̃defɑ̃dabl̥] *a.* indefensible.
indéfini [ɛ̃defini] *a.* **1.** indefinite; *Gram:* **pronom i.,** indefinite pronoun. **2.** undefined.
indéfiniment [ɛ̃definimɑ̃] *adv.* indefinitely.
indéfinissable [ɛ̃definisabl̥] *a.* indefinable, undefinable (term, etc.); indeterminate (taste, etc.).
indéfrisable [ɛ̃defrizabl̥] *n.f. Hairdr: O:* permanent wave.
indélébile [ɛ̃delebil] *a.* indelible (ink, stain).
indélicat [ɛ̃delika] *a.* (*a*) indelicate, coarse (nature); tactless (action); (*b*) dishonest, unscrupulous.
indélicatement [ɛ̃delikatmɑ̃] *adv.* (*a*) indelicately; (*b*) unscrupulously.
indélicatesse [ɛ̃delikatɛs] *n.f.* **1.** (*a*) indelicacy; tactlessness; (*b*) unscrupulousness. **2.** (i) indelicate, tactless, (ii) unscrupulous, action.
indémaillable [ɛ̃demajabl̥] *a.* ladderproof, non-run (tights, etc.).
indemne [ɛ̃dɛmn] *a.* **1.** *Jur: A:* without loss. **2.** uninjured, unhurt, unharmed, unscathed.
indemnisable [ɛ̃dɛmnizabl̥] *a.* entitled to compensation.
indemnisation [ɛ̃dɛmnizasjɔ̃] *n.f.* indemnification; compensation; indemnity.
indemniser [ɛ̃dɛmnize] *v.tr.* to indemnify; **i. qn d'une perte,** to compensate s.o. for a loss; **i. qn en argent,** to pay s.o. compensation in cash.
indemnité [ɛ̃dɛmnite] *n.f.* (*a*) indemnity, indemnification, compensation (for loss sustained); **i. de guerre,** war indemnity; (*b*) compensation to other party, penalty (for delay, non-delivery, etc.); (*c*) *Adm:* allowance; grant; **i. de résidence,** living allowance; **i. de route, de déplacement,** travelling expenses; **i. parlementaire** = M.P.'s salary.
indémontrable [ɛ̃demɔ̃trabl̥] *a.* undemonstrable, unprovable.
indéniable [ɛ̃denjabl̥] *a.* undeniable.
indéniablement [ɛ̃denjabləmɑ̃] *adv.* undeniably.
indénouable [ɛ̃denwabl̥] *a.* that cannot be untied, unravelled.
indentation [ɛ̃dɑ̃tasjɔ̃] *n.f.* indentation.
indépassable [ɛ̃depasabl̥] *a.* (limit) which cannot be exceeded.

indépendamment [ɛ̃depɑ̃damɑ̃] *adv.* independently (**de,** of); **i. de l'ancienneté,** irrespective of seniority.
indépendance [ɛ̃depɑ̃dɑ̃s] *n.f.* independence.
indépendant [ɛ̃depɑ̃dɑ̃] *a.* (*a*) independent (**de,** of); **circonstances indépendantes de ma volonté,** circumstances beyond my control; **état i.,** free state; (*b*) self-reliant; (*c*) *Aut:* **roues (avant) indépendantes,** independent (front-wheel) suspension; (*d*) self-contained (flat, *NAm:* apartment, etc.).
indéracinable [ɛ̃derasinabl̥] *a.* ineradicable.
indéréglable [ɛ̃dereglabl̥] *a.* foolproof (mechanism).
indescriptible [ɛ̃dɛskriptibl̥] *a.* indescribable.
indésirable [ɛ̃dezirabl̥] *a. & n.* undesirable.
indestructibilité [ɛ̃dɛstryktibilite] *n.f.* indestructibility.
indestructible [ɛ̃dɛstryktibl̥] *a.* indestructible.
indéterminable [ɛ̃detɛrminabl̥] *a.* indeterminable.
indétermination [ɛ̃detɛrminasjɔ̃] *n.f.* indetermination. **1.** vagueness (of ideas). **2.** (*of pers.*) irresoluteness, irresolution.
indéterminé [ɛ̃detɛrmine] *a.* **1.** undetermined; indeterminate, indefinite, vague (ideas). **2.** (*of pers.*) irresolute, undecided.
index [ɛ̃dɛks] *n.m.* **1.** (*a*) forefinger, index finger; (*b*) pointer, needle (of balance, etc.); indicator. **2.** (*a*) index (of book); (*b*) *R.C.Ch:* **l'I.,** the Index; *Fig:* **mettre qn, qch., à l'i.,** to blacklist s.o., sth.
indexation [ɛ̃dɛksasjɔ̃] *n.f.* *Pol.Ec:* index linking, pegging (of prices, etc.).
indexé [ɛ̃dɛkse] *a.* (*of wages, etc.*) index-linked.
indexer [ɛ̃dɛkse] *v.tr.* *Pol.Ec:* to index-link, peg (prices, etc.); **salaires indexés sur l'indice du coût de la vie,** index-linked salaries.
indicateur, -trice [ɛ̃dikatœr, -tris] **1.** *a.* indicatory; **poteau i.,** signpost; **panneau i. (de route),** road sign. **2.** *n.* informer; (police) spy. **3.** *n.m.* (railway) timetable; guide; (street) directory. **4.** *n.m.* (*a*) indicator, pointer (of barometer, etc.); gauge (of boiler, etc.); *I.C.E:* **i. de niveau (de carburant),** (fuel) gauge; **i. de pression,** pressure gauge; *Mch: Veh:* **i. de vitesse,** speed indicator, tachometer; *Aut:* speedometer; *Av:* airspeed indicator; *Av:* **i. d'altitude,** altimeter; *W.Tel:* **i. de direction,** direction finder; (*b*) *Ch:* indicator.
indicatif, -ive [ɛ̃dikatif, -iv] **1.** *a.* indicative (**de,** of); indicatory. **2.** *a. & n.m.* *Gram:* **(mode) i.,** indicative (mood); **à l'i.,** in the indicative. **3.** *n.m.* (*a*) *Tp:* dialling code; (*b*) *W.Tel: etc:* **i. d'appel,** call sign; **i. du poste,** station signal; **i. (musical),** signature tune, theme tune (of programme).
indication [ɛ̃dikasjɔ̃] *n.f.* indication. **1.** indicating, pointing out. **2.** (*a*) (piece of) information; **fausse i. de revenu,** false declaration of income; **à titre d'i.,** for your, my, guidance; (*b*) sign, token (of guilt, etc.); clue; (*c*) notice; **indications topographiques,** survey marks, data. **3.** *esp. pl.* instruction(s); **indications du mode d'emploi,** directions for use; **sauf i. contraire,** unless otherwise stated; *Th:* **indications scéniques,** stage directions.
indice [ɛ̃dis] *n.m.* **1.** indication, sign; mark, token; evidence; rating (of popularity, etc.). **2.** *Mth: etc:* (i) index (number); (ii) factor; (iii) rating; **i. inférieur,** suffix; **i. d'octane,** octane rating (of petrol); *Pol.Ec:* **i. du coût de la vie,** cost of living index; **i. des prix de détail,** retail price index.
indicible [ɛ̃disibl̥] *a.* (*a*) inexpressible, unutterable; unspeakable (grief, rage); (*b*) indescribable.
indiciblement [ɛ̃disibləmɑ̃] *adv.* (*a*) inexpressibly, unutterably; unspeakably; (*b*) indescribably.
indien, -ienne [ɛ̃djɛ̃, -jɛn] **1.** (*a*) *a. & n.* Indian (of India, America); **l'océan i.,** the Indian Ocean; (*b*) *a.* **en, à la, file indienne,** in Indian, single, file. **2.** *n.f.* **indienne** (*a*) *Tex:* printed calico; cotton print; (*b*) *Swim:* **nage (à l')indienne,** overarm stroke.
indifféremment [ɛ̃diferamɑ̃] *adv.* (*a*) indifferently; (*b*) indiscriminately, equally.
indifférence [ɛ̃diferɑ̃s] *n.f.* **i. à, pour,** indifference to, lack of concern, of interest, in.
indifférenciation [ɛ̃diferɑ̃sjasjɔ̃] *n.f.* lack of differentiation.
indifférencié [ɛ̃diferɑ̃sje] *a.* undifferentiated.
indifférent [ɛ̃diferɑ̃] *a.* **1.** (*a*) indifferent (**à,** to); unaffected (**à,** by); unconcerned; **rester i. à tout,** to take no interest in anything; **il m'est i.,** I'm indifferent about him; (*b*) cold, insensible, emotionless (heart, etc.). **2.** immaterial, unimportant; **cela m'est i.,** it's all the same, quite immaterial, to me; I don't care either way; **il m'est i. de faire cela ou autre chose,** it doesn't matter to me, it's all the same to me, whether I do that or something else; **parler de choses indifférentes,** to chat (about nothing in particular).
indifférer [ɛ̃difere] *v.tr. def. used in 3rd pers. sing. & pl. with pronoun complement only* **(il indiffère, il indifférera)** *F:* **cela m'indiffère,** I'm indifferent, I couldn't care less, about it.
indigence [ɛ̃diʒɑ̃s] *n.f.* poverty; destitution; **tomber, être, dans l'i.,** be reduced to poverty; **i. d'idées,** penury, paucity, lack, of ideas.
indigène [ɛ̃diʒɛn] **1.** *a.* indigenous (**à,** to); native (population, etc.). **2.** *n.* native.
indigent, -ente [ɛ̃diʒɑ̃, -ɑ̃t] **1.** *a.* poor, needy, poverty-stricken; indigent. **2.** *n.* poor person; pauper; **les indigents,** the poor; the destitute.
indigeste [ɛ̃diʒɛst] *a.* **1.** indigestible; stodgy (food). **2.** undigested; confused, heavy (book, etc.).
indigestion [ɛ̃diʒɛstjɔ̃] *n.f.* indigestion; **avoir une i.,** to have an attack of indigestion; *F:* **j'en ai une i.,** I'm fed up with it.
indignation [ɛ̃diɲasjɔ̃] *n.f.* indignation.
indigne [ɛ̃diɲ] *a.* **1.** (*a*) unworthy; undeserving; **i. de notre confiance,** unworthy of our confidence; (*b*) **ce travail est i. de lui,** this work is not good enough for him, is far below his usual standard. **2.** shameful (action, conduct); **conduite i. d'une sœur, d'un père,** unsisterly, unfatherly, conduct.
indigné [ɛ̃diɲe] *a.* indignant (**de,** at); **d'un air, d'un ton, i.,** indignantly.
indignement [ɛ̃diɲmɑ̃] *adv.* **1.** unworthily. **2.** shamefully.
indigner [ɛ̃diɲe] **1.** *v.tr.* to rouse (s.o.) to indignation, make (s.o.) indignant. **2.** **s'i.,** to become, be, indignant; **s'i. de, contre, qch., qn,** to be indignant at sth., with s.o.; **s'i. que** + *sub.*, **de ce que** + *ind.*, to be indignant that . . .; **je m'indigne de voir ce crime impuni,** it makes me furious, annoys me, to see this crime go unpunished.
indignité [ɛ̃diɲite] *n.f.* **1.** (*a*) unworthiness; (*b*) baseness, vileness (of an action). **2.** shameful action; **souffrir des indignités,** to suffer indignities, humiliation.
indigo [ɛ̃digo] *n.m. & a.inv.* indigo(-blue).
indiquer [ɛ̃dike] *v.tr.* to indicate; (*a*) to point to, point (out); **i. qch. du doigt,** to point to sth., at sth., to point sth. out (with one's finger); **i. le chemin à qn,** to show s.o. the way, direct s.o.; (*b*) to mark, show, give (information); **le compteur indique cent,** the meter reads one hundred; **point indiqué sur la carte,** point shown, marked, on the map; **la maison indiquée sur le bordereau ci-joint,** the firm mentioned on the enclosed slip; (*c*) to show, tell; **indiquez-moi un bon médecin,** can you tell me of a good doctor? (*d*) to point to; **tout dans la maison indique un goût raffiné,** everything in the house indicates, shows, good taste; (*e*) to appoint, name (a day, etc.); **à l'heure indiquée,** at the appointed, scheduled, time;

(*f*) to draw up (procedure, etc.); to prescribe, lay down (line of action, etc.); **c'était indiqué,** it was the obvious thing to do; it was just the thing; **un sujet de plaisanterie tout indiqué,** an obvious subject for jokes; **nous nommerons X; il est tout à fait indiqué pour ce poste,** we shall appoint X; he's the very man, just the man, for the job; **ce n'est pas très indiqué,** it's not very advisable, suitable, appropriate; (*g*) to outline, sketch (features, plot, etc.).

indirect [ɛ̃dirɛkt] *a.* (*a*) indirect (route, *Gram:* object, etc.); roundabout (way); collateral (heirs); covert (attack); *Gram:* **discours i.,** indirect speech, reported speech; **éclairage i.,** concealed lighting; **contributions indirectes,** indirect taxation; excise revenue; (*b*) *Jur:* circumstantial (evidence).

indirectement [ɛ̃dirɛktəmɑ̃] *adv.* indirectly.

indiscernable [ɛ̃disɛrnabl̩] *a.* indistinguishable; indiscernible; scarcely perceptible.

indiscipline [ɛ̃disiplin] *n.f.* indiscipline, lack of discipline.

indiscipliné [ɛ̃disipline] *a.* undisciplined, unruly.

indiscret, -ète [ɛ̃diskrɛ, -ɛt] **1.** *a.* (*a*) *A:* indiscreet, imprudent, unguarded; (*b*) indiscreet, tactless (person); **à l'abri des regards indiscrets,** safe from prying eyes; **je me méfie des oreilles indiscrètes,** I'm on my guard against eavesdroppers. **2.** *n.* indiscreet, tactless, person; *F:* nosy parker.

indiscrètement [ɛ̃diskrɛtmɑ̃] *adv.* indiscreetly.

indiscrétion [ɛ̃diskresjɔ̃] *n.f.* indiscretion. **1.** indiscreetness; **peut-on vous demander sans i. . . .?** would it be indiscreet, rude, to ask . . .? **2.** indiscreet action, remark; **il lui échappe des indiscrétions,** he blurts out (i) tactless things, (ii) secrets.

indiscutable [ɛ̃diskytabl̩] *a.* indisputable, unquestionable.

indiscutablement [ɛ̃diskytabləmɑ̃] *adv.* indisputably, unquestionably.

indiscuté [ɛ̃diskyte] *a.* undisputed; unquestioned; beyond doubt.

indispensable [ɛ̃dispɑ̃sabl̩] *a.* indispensable (**à qn,** to s.o., **à, pour, qch.,** for sth., **pour faire qch.,** for doing sth.); essential (**à,** for, to); absolutely necessary; **il est i. que j'aie, il est i. d'avoir, votre autorisation écrite,** it is essential that I should have, it is essential to have, your authorization in writing; **il nous est i.,** we can't spare him, do without him; *n.m.* **ne prenez que l'i.,** don't take more than is strictly, absolutely, necessary.

indispensablement [ɛ̃dispɑ̃sabləmɑ̃] *adv.* indispensably.

indisponibilité [ɛ̃dispɔnibilite] *n.f.* **1.** *Jur:* inalienability. **2.** unavailability.

indisponible [ɛ̃dispɔnibl̩] *a.* **1.** *Jur:* inalienable (property); entailed (estate). **2.** (*of pers.*) not available (for duty, etc.); unavailable.

indisposé [ɛ̃dispoze] *a.* (*a*) indisposed, unwell, out of sorts; **se sentir vaguement i.,** to feel off colour, *NAm:* color; (*b*) (*of woman*) **être indisposée,** to have one's period, be unwell.

indisposer [ɛ̃dispoze] *v.tr.* **1.** to make (s.o.) unwell; (*of food, etc.*) to upset, disagree with (s.o.). **2.** to antagonize (s.o.); **i. qn contre qn,** to set s.o. against s.o.

indisposition [ɛ̃dispozisjɔ̃] *n.f.* (*a*) indisposition, (slight) illness, upset; (*b*) (*of woman*) (monthly) period.

indissociable [ɛ̃disɔsjabl̩] *a.* indissociable.

indissolubilité [ɛ̃disɔlybilite] *n.f.* indissolubility (of marriage, etc.).

indissoluble [ɛ̃disɔlybl̩] *a.* indissoluble (bond, friendship).

indissolublement [ɛ̃disɔlybləmɑ̃] *adv.* indissolubly.

indistinct [ɛ̃distɛ̃(kt)] *a.* indistinct; hazy, vague, blurred; faint (inscription).

indistinctement [ɛ̃distɛ̃ktəmɑ̃] *adv.* indistinctly; (*a*) indiscriminately; without distinction; (*b*) hazily, vaguely; faintly.

individu [ɛ̃dividy] *n.m.* **1.** *Nat.Hist: etc:* individual; *F:* **soigner son i.,** to look after number one. **2.** *usu. Pej:* individual, person, fellow; **i. louche,** shady customer, suspicious character.

individualisation [ɛ̃dividɥalizasjɔ̃] *n.f.* individualization.

individualiser [ɛ̃dividɥalize] *v.tr.* **1.** to individualize; to specify, particularize (case, etc.). **2. s'i.,** to take on individual characteristics.

individualisme [ɛ̃dividɥalism] *n.m.* individualism.

individualiste [ɛ̃dividɥalist] **1.** *a.* individualistic. **2.** *n.* individualist.

individualité [ɛ̃dividɥalite] *n.f.* individuality.

individuel, -elle [ɛ̃dividɥɛl] *a.* individual; personal (liberty, etc.); private (fortune, etc.).

individuellement [ɛ̃dividɥɛlmɑ̃] *adv.* individually, personally.

indivis [ɛ̃divi] *a.* *Jur:* **1.** undivided, joint (estate). **2.** joint (owners); **par i.,** jointly.

indivisément [ɛ̃divizemɑ̃] *adv.* *Jur:* jointly.

indivisibilité [ɛ̃divizibilite] *n.f.* indivisibility.

indivisible [ɛ̃divizibl̩] *a.* indivisible.

indivisiblement [ɛ̃divizibləmɑ̃] *adv.* indivisibly.

indivision [ɛ̃divizjɔ̃] *n.f.* *Jur:* joint possession.

Indochine [ɛ̃dɔʃin] *Pr.n.f.* *Geog: Hist:* Indochina.

indochinois, -oise [ɛ̃dɔʃinwa, -waz] *a.* & *n.* Indochinese.

indocile [ɛ̃dɔsil] *a.* intractable, disobedient.

indocilité [ɛ̃dɔsilite] *n.f.* intractability.

indo-européen, -enne [ɛ̃dɔørɔpeɛ̃, -ɛn] **1.** *a.* & *n.* *Ethn:* Indo-European; *pl.* *indo-européens, -ennes.* **2.** *n.m.* *Ling:* Indo-European.

indolemment [ɛ̃dɔlamɑ̃] *adv.* indolently.

indolence [ɛ̃dɔlɑ̃s] *n.f.* indolence, apathy, sloth.

indolent [ɛ̃dɔlɑ̃] *a.* (*a*) indolent, apathetic, slothful; (*b*) *Med:* painless, indolent (tumour, *NAm:* tumor).

indolore [ɛ̃dɔlɔr] *a.* painless.

indomptable [ɛ̃dɔ̃tabl̩] *a.* unconquerable (nation); untam(e)able (animal); unmanageable (horse); indomitable (pride); ungovernable, uncontrollable (passion).

indompté [ɛ̃dɔ̃te] *a.* unconquered (nation); untamed (animal); uncontrolled (passion); unbroken (spirit).

Indonésie [ɛ̃dɔnezi] *Pr.n.f.* *Geog:* Indonesia.

indonésien, -ienne [ɛ̃dɔnezjɛ̃, -jɛn] *a.* & *n.* *Geog:* Indonesian.

indou, -oue [ɛ̃du] *a.* & *n.* *Ethn: Rel:* Hindu.

in-douze [induz] *a.* & *n.m.inv.* *Typ:* duodecimo, (in) twelvemo.

indu [ɛ̃dy] *a.* undue (haste, etc.); unwarranted (remark, etc.); **à une heure indue,** at an ungodly hour; **il rentre à des heures indues,** he comes home at all hours of the night.

indubitable [ɛ̃dybitabl̩] *a.* beyond doubt, indubitable, undoubted; unquestionable.

indubitablement [ɛ̃dybitabləmɑ̃] *adv.* indubitably, undoubtedly, unquestionably.

inductance [ɛ̃dyktɑ̃s] *n.f.* *El:* inductance.

inducteur, -trice [ɛ̃dyktœr, -tris] *El:* **1.** *a.* inductive (capacity, etc.); inducing (current). **2.** *n.m.* inductor; field magnet (of dynamo).

inductif, -ive [ɛ̃dyktif, -iv] *a.* inductive.

induction [ɛ̃dyksjɔ̃] *n.f.* induction; *El:* **courant d'i.,** induced current; **bobine d'i.,** induction coil.

induire [ɛ̃dɥir] *v.tr.* (*pr.p.* **induisant;** *p.p.* **induit;** *pr.ind.* **j'induis, n. induisons, ils induisent;** *p.h.* **j'induisis;** *fu.* **j'induirai**) **1.** (*a*) *O:* to induce; **i. qn à faire qch.,** to lead, induce, tempt, s.o. to do sth.; (*b*) **i. qn**

en erreur, to lead s.o. astray, mislead s.o. **2.** *Log:* to infer, induce (conclusion).

induit [ɛ̃dɥi] *El:* **1.** *a.* induced, secondary (circuit). **2.** *n.m.* (*a*) induced circuit; **charge d'i.,** induced charge; (*b*) armature (of large dynamo, etc.).

indulgence [ɛ̃dylʒɑ̃s] *n.f.* **1.** indulgence, leniency; **avec i.,** indulgently, leniently; **avoir, montrer, de l'i. pour, envers, qn,** to be indulgent with s.o., make allowances for s.o. **2.** *Ecc:* indulgence.

indulgent [ɛ̃dylʒɑ̃] *a.* indulgent, lenient; (too) kind; long-suffering; **être i. pour, envers, qn,** to be indulgent, lenient, with s.o.

indûment [ɛ̃dymɑ̃] *adv.* unduly, improperly.

industrialisation [ɛ̃dystrijalizasjɔ̃] *n.f.* industrialization.

industrialiser [ɛ̃dystrijalize] **1.** *v.tr.* to industrialize. **2. s'i.,** to become industrialized.

industrialisme [ɛ̃dystrijalism] *n.m.* industrialism.

industrie [ɛ̃dystri] *n.f.* **1.** *A: & Lit:* (*a*) activity; industry (of bees, etc.); (*b*) ingenuity, cleverness, skill. **2.** industry; manufacturing; **l'i. lourde, légère,** heavy, light, industry; **i. de transformation,** processing industry; **l'i. automobile,** the motor industry; **l'i. du bâtiment,** the building trade; **l'i. de pointe,** advance technology industry; **l'i. du spectacle,** the entertainments industry, show business.

industriel, -elle [ɛ̃dystrijɛl] **1.** *a.* industrial (product, etc.). **2.** *n.m.* manufacturer; industrialist.

industriellement [ɛ̃dystrijɛlmɑ̃] *adv.* industrially; **vins produits i.,** mass-produced wines.

industrieux, -euse [ɛ̃dystrijø, -øz] *a. Lit:* industrious; skilful, ingenious.

inébranlable [inebrɑ̃labl̥] *a.* unshakeable; (*a*) immovable, solid, firm (wall, etc.); (*b*) steadfast (person); unswerving (purpose, etc.); unwavering (courage).

inébranlablement [inebrɑ̃labləmɑ̃] *adv.* unshakeably.

inéchangeable [ineʃɑ̃ʒabl̥] *a.* not exchangeable.

inécoutable [inekutabl̥] *a.* unbearable; impossible (to listen to).

inécouté [inekute] *a.* unheard; unheeded.

inédit [inedi] **1.** *a.* (*a*) unpublished (book, etc.); (*b*) unprecedented; new, original (show, plan). **2.** *n.m.* (*a*) unpublished work; (*b*) **l'i.,** the new, the original.

ineffable [inefabl̥] *a.* ineffable, unutterable.

ineffablement [inefabləmɑ̃] *adv.* ineffably.

ineffaçable [inefasabl̥] *a.* ineffaceable (mark, memory); indelible (stain).

ineffaçablement [inefasabləmɑ̃] *adv.* ineffaceably.

inefficace [inefikas] *a.* ineffective, ineffectual; inefficacious, useless (remedy); inefficient.

inefficacement [inefikasmɑ̃] *adv.* ineffectively.

inefficacité [inefikasite] *n.f.* ineffectiveness, ineffectualness; inefficacy (of remedy); inefficiency.

inégal, -aux [inegal, -o] *a.* **1.** unequal (parts, etc.). **2.** (*a*) uneven, rough (ground); (*b*) irregular (pulse, etc.); changeable (wind).

inégalable [inegalabl̥] *a.* matchless, incomparable.

inégalé [inegale] *a.* unequalled, unmatched.

inégalement [inegalmɑ̃] *adv.* (*a*) unequally, unevenly; (*b*) irregularly.

inégalité [inegalite] *n.f.* **1.** inequality, disparity (**de, entre,** between). **2.** (*a*) unevenness (of ground); **les inégalités du chemin,** the bumps in the road; (*b*) *Lit:* **i. d'humeur,** capriciousness. **3.** *Mth: etc:* inequality.

inélastique [inelastik] *a.* inelastic.

inélégamment [inelegamɑ̃] *adv.* inelegantly.

inélégance [inelegɑ̃s] *n.f.* inelegance.

inélégant [inelegɑ̃] *a.* inelegant.

inéligibilité [ineliʒibilite] *n.f.* ineligibility.

inéligible [ineliʒibl̥] *a.* ineligible.

inéluctable [inelyktabl̥] *a.* ineluctable; inescapable.

inéluctablement [inelyktabləmɑ̃] *adv.* ineluctably.

inemployable [inɑ̃plwajabl̥] *a.* unusable.

inemployé [inɑ̃plwaje] *a.* unemployed, unused.

inénarrable [inenarabl̥] *a.* comical, funny; **c'est dommage que vous ne l'ayez pas vu; c'était i.!** it was a shame you didn't see it; it was priceless!

inentamé [inɑ̃tame] *a.* intact; uncut (loaf, etc.).

inéprouvé [inepruve] *a.* **1.** untried, untested. **2.** not yet experienced, felt.

inepte [inɛpt] *a.* inept, foolish, idiotic (remark, etc.).

ineptie [inɛpsi] *n.f.* ineptitude. **1.** ineptness. **2. dire des inepties,** to talk nonsense, rubbish.

inépuisable [inepɥizabl̥] *a.* inexhaustible; unfailing.

inéquation [inekwasjɔ̃] *n.f. Mth:* inequation.

inéquitable [inekitabl̥] *a.* inequitable, unfair.

inerte [inɛrt] *a.* (*a*) inert (mass, etc.); sluggish (nature); dull (intelligence); (*b*) **résistance i.,** passive resistance.

inertie [inɛrsi] *n.f.* inertia; (*a*) *Mec: etc:* **force d'i.,** inertia, vis inertiae; **moment d'i.,** moment of inertia; (*b*) sluggishness, inertness (of mind, body); passivity.

inescomptable [inɛskɔ̃tabl̥] *a. Fin:* undiscountable.

inespéré [inɛspere] *a.* unhoped-for, unexpected.

inesthétique [inɛstetik] *a.* unaesthetic.

inestimable [inɛstimabl̥] *a.* inestimable, invaluable, priceless.

inévitable [inevitabl̥] *a.* unavoidable (accident, etc.); inevitable, inescapable (result); **c'est i.,** it's bound to happen.

inévitablement [inevitabləmɑ̃] *adv.* unavoidably, inevitably.

inexact [inɛgzakt] *a.* **1.** inexact, inaccurate, incorrect; wrong (amount, etc.). **2.** (*a*) unpunctual; (*b*) **i. (à remplir ses devoirs),** remiss, slack, lax (in one's duty).

inexactement [inɛgzaktəmɑ̃] *adv.* inexactly, inaccurately.

inexactitude [inɛgzaktityd] *n.f.* **1.** inaccuracy, inexactitude; (*a*) incorrectness; (*b*) mistake. **2.** (*a*) unpunctuality; (*b*) **i. (à remplir ses devoirs),** remissness, slackness, laxity (in one's duties).

inexaucé [inɛgzose] *a.* unanswered (prayer); unfulfilled (desire).

inexcusable [inɛkskyzabl̥] *a.* inexcusable; unwarrantable (action).

inexécutable [inɛgzekytabl̥] *a.* impracticable, impractical, unworkable (plan, etc.); (order) that cannot be carried out.

inexécuté [inɛgzekyte] *a.* unperformed; unfulfilled (promise); (order) not carried out.

inexécution [inɛgzekysjɔ̃] *n.f.* non-performance; non-fulfilment (of promise).

inexercé [inɛgzɛrse] *a.* **1.** unexercised, untrained. **2.** unpractised, unskilled; inexperienced (eye, etc.).

inexhaustible [inɛgzostibl̥] *a. Lit:* inexhaustible.

inexistant [inɛgzistɑ̃] *a.* non-existent.

inexistence [inɛgzistɑ̃s] *n.f.* non-existence.

inexorabilité [inɛgzɔrabilite] *n.f.* inexorability.

inexorable [inɛgzɔrabl̥] *a.* inexorable, unrelenting.

inexorablement [inɛgzɔrabləmɑ̃] *adv.* inexorably.

inexpérience [inɛksperjɑ̃s] *n.f.* inexperience.

inexpérimenté [inɛksperimɑ̃te] *a.* **1.** inexperienced; unpractised, unskilled (hand, etc.). **2.** untried, untested (process).

inexpert [inɛkspɛr] *a. Lit:* inexpert, unpractised.

inexpiable [inɛkspjabl̥] *a.* inexpiable, unatonable.

inexpié [inɛkspje] *a.* unatoned, unexpiated.

inexplicable [inɛksplikabl̥] *a.* inexplicable, unexplainable, unaccountable.

inexplicablement [inɛksplikabləmɑ̃] *adv.* inexplicably, unaccountably.
inexpliqué [inɛksplike] *a.* unexplained.
inexploitable [inɛksplwatabl̥] *a.* unworkable (mine).
inexploité [inɛksplwate] *a.* unworked (mine); undeveloped (land); **ressources inexploitées,** untapped resources.
inexplorable [inɛksplɔrabl̥] *a.* inexplorable.
inexploré [inɛksplɔre] *a.* unexplored.
inexplosible [inɛksplozibl̥] *a.* non-explosive.
inexpressif, -ive [inɛkspresif, -iv] *a.* inexpressive; expressionless (face).
inexprimable [inɛksprimabl̥] *a.* inexpressible; beyond words; unutterable.
inexprimé [inɛksprime] *a.* unexpressed.
inexpugnable [inɛkspygnabl̥] *a.* impregnable, inexpugnable; stormproof (fortress).
inextensible [inɛkstɑ̃sibl̥] *a.* inextensible.
inextinguible [inɛkstɛ̃g(ɥ)ibl̥] *a.* inextinguishable; unquenchable (fire, etc.); irrepressible, uncontrollable (laughter).
inextricable [inɛkstrikabl̥] *a.* inextricable.
inextricablement [inɛkstrikabləmɑ̃] *adv.* inextricably.
infaillibilité [ɛ̃fajibilite] *n.f.* infallibility.
infaillible [ɛ̃fajibl̥] *a.* infallible. **1.** unerring. **2.** certain, sure, unfailing (remedy, etc.).
infailliblement [ɛ̃fajibləmɑ̃] *adv.* infallibly.
infaisable [ɛ̃fəzabl̥] *a.* not feasible; impracticable.
infamant [ɛ̃famɑ̃] *a.* **1.** defamatory. **2.** ignominious; *Jur:* infamous; *Jur:* **peine infamante,** penalty involving loss of civil rights.
infâme [ɛ̃fɑm] *a.* infamous; foul (deed); unspeakable (crime, etc.); vile, squalid (slum).
infamie [ɛ̃fami] *n.f.* **1.** infamy. **2.** infamous action, statement; vile, foul, deed; **dire des infamies à qn, de qn,** to vilify, slander, s.o.
infant, -ante [ɛ̃fɑ̃, -ɑ̃t] *n. Spanish Hist:* infante, *f.* infanta.
infanterie [ɛ̃fɑ̃tri] *n.f.* infantry; **soldat d'i.,** infantryman, foot soldier; **i. aéroportée, de l'air,** airborne infantry; **i. de marine,** Marine Light Infantry.
infanticide[1] [ɛ̃fɑ̃tisid] **1.** *n.* infanticide; child murderer. **2.** *a.* infanticidal.
infanticide[2] *n.m.* infanticide; child murder.
infantile [ɛ̃fɑ̃til] *a.* infantile (disease, etc.); **mortalité i.,** infant mortality; **psychiatrie i.,** child psychiatry.
infantilisme [ɛ̃fɑ̃tilism] *n.m.* (*a*) *Med:* infantilism, retarded development; (*b*) **c'est de l'i.,** how infantile!
infarctus [ɛ̃farktys] *n.m. Med:* infarct, infarction; **i. du myocarde,** myocardial infarction; coronary thrombosis.
infatigable [ɛ̃fatigabl̥] *a.* indefatigable, untiring, tireless.
infatigablement [ɛ̃fatigabləmɑ̃] *adv.* indefatigably, untiringly, tirelessly.
infatuation [ɛ̃fatɥasjɔ̃] *n.f.* (*a*) *A:* infatuation; (*b*) self-conceit, self-importance.
infatué [ɛ̃fatɥe] *a.* (*a*) *A:* infatuated; (*b*) conceited; **i. (de soi-même),** full of one's own importance.
infatuer [ɛ̃fatɥe] **1.** *v.tr. A:* to infatuate. **2. s'i.** (*a*) *O:* **s'i. de qn, qch.,** to become infatuated with s.o., sth.; (*b*) **s'i. (de soi-même),** to become full of one's own importance, to become conceited.
infécond [ɛ̃fekɔ̃] *a.* barren, sterile; infertile.
infécondité [ɛ̃fekɔ̃dite] *n.f.* barrenness, sterility; infertility.
infect [ɛ̃fɛkt] *a.* (*a*) stinking (food); foul (air); noisome, putrid (smell); **odeur infecte,** stench; (*b*) **taudis i.,** filthy hovel; **repas i.,** rotten, revolting, meal; **temps i.,** filthy, foul, weather.
infectant [ɛ̃fɛktɑ̃] *a.* infectious (virus).
infecter [ɛ̃fɛkte] **1.** *v.tr.* (*a*) to infect; (*b*) to poison (the atmosphere); to contaminate, taint, pollute (water, etc.). **2. s'i.,** to turn, go, septic.
infectieux, -euse [ɛ̃fɛksjø, -øz] *a.* infectious.
infection [ɛ̃fɛksjɔ̃] *n.f.* **1.** infection; **i. virale,** viral infection. **2.** stench, stink.
inférence [ɛ̃ferɑ̃s] *n.f. Log:* inference.
inférer [ɛ̃fere] *v.tr.* **(j'infère; j'inférerai)** to infer, gather (**de,** from).
inférieur, -eure [ɛ̃ferjœr] *a.* inferior. **1.** lower; **partie inférieure (de qch.),** (i) lower part, bottom, (ii) under part (of sth.); **lèvre inférieure,** lower lip, bottom lip; **i. au niveau de la mer,** below sea level; (*of temperature, etc.*) **i. à la normale,** below normal. **2.** (*a*) **d'un rang i.,** of a lower rank, lower in rank; (*b*) poor (quality, goods, etc.); (*c*) **6 est i. à 8,** 6 is less than 8; **note inférieure à douze,** mark below twelve. **3.** *n.* inferior; **être l'i. de qn,** to be s.o.'s inferior.
inférieurement [ɛ̃ferjœrmɑ̃] *adv.* **1.** in a lower position; on the under side. **2.** in an inferior manner; less well.
infériorité [ɛ̃ferjɔrite] *n.f.* inferiority; (*a*) **i. numérique, en nombre,** numerical inferiority, inferiority in numbers; *Psy:* **complexe d'i.,** inferiority complex; (*b*) **i. de niveau,** difference, drop, in level.
infernal, -aux [ɛ̃fɛrnal, -o] *a.* infernal. **1. les puissances infernales,** the powers of hell. **2.** (*a*) devilish, diabolical (cunning, noise, etc.); (*b*) **machine infernale,** (i) *A:* infernal engine; (ii) booby trap. **3.** *F:* **cet enfant est i.,** this child's a little devil; **c'est i.!** it's hellish! it's sheer hell!
infertile [ɛ̃fɛrtil] *a.* infertile, unfruitful, barren.
infertilité [ɛ̃fɛrtilite] *n.f.* infertility.
infestation [ɛ̃fɛstasjɔ̃] *n.f. Med:* infestation.
infester [ɛ̃fɛste] *v.tr.* (*of vermin, etc.*) to infest, overrun; **infesté d'insectes,** infested, overrun, with insects; insect-ridden.
infidèle [ɛ̃fidɛl] **1.** *a.* (*a*) unfaithful, false, faithless, disloyal (**à,** to); untrue; **être i. à sa promesse,** to break one's promise; (*b*) incorrect; inaccurate; **mémoire i.,** untrustworthy memory. **2.** *a. & n. Rel:* infidel.
infidèlement [ɛ̃fidɛlmɑ̃] *adv.* **1.** unfaithfully. **2.** incorrectly, inaccurately.
infidélité [ɛ̃fidelite] *n.f.* (*a*) infidelity, unfaithfulness, faithlessness, disloyalty (**à,** to); (*b*) inaccuracy (in translation, etc.).
infiltration [ɛ̃filtrasjɔ̃] *n.f.* infiltration. **1.** percolation, seepage. **2.** filtering through (of traffic, etc.).
infiltrer (s') [sɛ̃filtre] *v.pr.* **1.** (*a*) (*of fluid*) to infiltrate, percolate, seep (**dans,** into; **à travers,** through); to soak, filter, in, through; (*b*) (*of idea, etc.*) to trickle in, filter in, soak in. **2.** (*of troops, etc.*) **s'i. dans un pays,** to infiltrate a country.
infime [ɛ̃fim] *a.* **1.** lowly, mean (rank, etc.). **2.** tiny, minute; infinitesimal (majority).
infini [ɛ̃fini] **1.** *a.* infinite; boundless, immeasurable (space, etc.); never-ending, eternal, endless (bliss, etc.); innumerable (arguments, etc.). **2.** *n.m.* **l'i.,** the infinite; *Phot:* **mettre au point sur l'i.,** to focus on infinity; **à l'i.,** to infinity, ad infinitum; boundlessly.
infiniment [ɛ̃finimɑ̃] *adv.* infinitely; extremely; **i. plus intelligent,** infinitely, much, more intelligent; **se donner i. de peine,** to give oneself an infinite amount, no end, of trouble; **je regrette i.,** I'm terribly sorry; **i. petit,** infinitesimally small.
infinité [ɛ̃finite] *n.f.* (*a*) *Mth: etc:* infinity; (*b*) **l'i. de l'espace,** the infinity, infinitude, boundlessness, of space; **une i. de raisons,** endless reasons.
infinitésimal, -aux [ɛ̃finitezimal, -o] *a. Mth: etc:* infinitesimal.
infinitif, -ive [ɛ̃finitif, -iv] *a. & n.m. Gram:* infinitive (mood); **à l'i.,** in the infinitive.

infirmation [ɛ̃firmasjɔ̃] *n.f. Jur:* invalidation; nullification; quashing.
infirme [ɛ̃firm] **1.** *a.* (*a*) infirm (old man, etc.); (*b*) disabled, crippled; **i. du bras gauche,** crippled in the left arm; (*c*) *A: & Lit:* weak. **2.** *n.* (*a*) invalid; (*b*) cripple; **les infirmes,** the disabled.
infirmer [ɛ̃firme] *v.tr.* **1.** (*a*) to show up the weakness of (proof, argument, etc.); (*b*) to weaken (s.o.'s authority); (*c*) to weaken, invalidate (evidence, claim). **2.** (*a*) *Jur:* to annul, quash (judgment); to set (verdict) aside; (*b*) to cancel (letter, etc.).
infirmerie [ɛ̃firməri] *n.f.* (*a*) infirmary; (*b*) (*in prison, etc.*) infirmary; (*in school, ship*) sick bay.
infirmier, -ière [ɛ̃firmje, -jɛr] **1.** *n.m.* (i) male nurse, *Mil:* medical orderly; (ii) ambulance man. **2.** *n.f.* **infirmière,** (hospital) nurse; **infirmière diplômée** = state-registered nurse; **infirmière en chef,** matron; **infirmière visiteuse,** district nurse.
infirmité [ɛ̃firmite] *n.f.* (*a*) infirmity; (*b*) physical disability; (*c*) *A: & Lit:* weakness, frailty.
inflammabilité [ɛ̃flamabilite] *n.f.* inflammability; *Tchn: & NAm:* flammability.
inflammable [ɛ̃flamabl̩] *a.* inflammable; *Tchn: & NAm:* flammable.
inflammation [ɛ̃flamasjɔ̃] *n.f. Med:* inflammation.
inflammatoire [ɛ̃flamatwar] *a. Med:* inflammatory.
inflation [ɛ̃flasjɔ̃] *n.f. Pol.Ec:* inflation; **politique d'i.,** inflationary policy.
inflationniste [ɛ̃flasjɔnist] (*a*) *n.* inflationist; (*b*) *a.* inflationary.
infléchi [ɛ̃fleʃi] *a.* **1.** inflected, bent (ray, etc.). **2.** *Gram:* inflected (vowel, etc.).
infléchir [ɛ̃fleʃir] **1.** *v.tr.* (*a*) to bend, inflect, curve (ray, etc.); (*b*) to change the direction, orientation, of (policy, etc.). **2. s'i.** (*a*) to bend, curve, deviate; *Opt:* (*of ray*) to be inflected; (*b*) (*of structure*) to cave in.
inflexibilité [ɛ̃flɛksibilite] *n.f.* inflexibility; rigidity.
inflexible [ɛ̃flɛksibl̩] *a.* inflexible, unbending; rigid; unyielding; **demeurer i. dans une résolution,** to stick to a resolution.
inflexiblement [ɛ̃flɛksibləmɑ̃] *adv.* inflexibly.
inflexion [ɛ̃flɛksjɔ̃] *n.f.* inflexion, inflection. **1.** (*a*) *Mth: Opt: etc:* bend(ing); change of direction (of curve, ray); (*b*) bend(ing) (of body); nod(ding) (of head); **légère i. du corps,** slight bow. **2.** modulation (of voice). **3.** *Ling: Gram:* inflection.
infliger [ɛ̃fliʒe] *v.tr.* **(j'infligeai(s), n. infligeons)** to inflict; **i. une peine à qn,** to impose a penalty on s.o.; **il nous a infligé sa présence,** he inflicted himself on us.
inflorescence [ɛ̃flɔresɑ̃s] *n.f. Bot:* inflorescence.
influençable [ɛ̃flyɑ̃sabl̩] *a.* susceptible to influence.
influence [ɛ̃flyɑ̃s] *n.f.* influence; **exercer une i. sur qch., sur qn,** to have an influence, an effect, on sth., on s.o.; **sous l'i. de qch.,** under the influence of sth.; **il a beaucoup d'i.,** he has a lot of influence, he's very influential; **sphère d'i.,** sphere of influence; **trafic d'i.,** corrupt practice.
influencer [ɛ̃flyɑ̃se] *v.tr.* **(j'influençai(s), n. influençons)** to influence, have an influence on (s.o., sth.); to sway (public opinion).
influent [ɛ̃flyɑ̃] *a.* influential.
influer [ɛ̃flye] *v.i.* **i. sur qn,** to influence s.o.; to exercise, have, (an) influence on, over, s.o.; **i. sur qch.,** to have an effect on sth.
influx [ɛ̃fly] *n.m.* **1.** *Lit:* influx. **2.** *Physiol:* **i. nerveux,** nerve impulse.
in-folio [infɔljo] *a.inv. & n.m.inv.* folio.
informateur, -trice [ɛ̃fɔrmatœr, -tris] *n.* informant.
informaticien, -ienne [ɛ̃fɔrmatisjɛ̃, -jɛn] *n.* computer scientist; data-processing expert.
informatif, -ive [ɛ̃fɔrmatif, -iv] *a.* informative.
information [ɛ̃fɔrmasjɔ̃] *n.f.* (*a*) inquiry; *Jur:* preliminary investigation (of a case); **ouvrir une i.,** to begin legal proceedings; (*b*) information; news (item); **je vous envoie pour votre i. . . .,** I'm sending you for your information . . .; *W.Tel: T.V: Journ:* **informations,** news (bulletin); *Journ:* **informations de la dernière heure,** latest intelligence; (*c*) *Cmptr:* data; **traitement de l'i., des informations,** data processing.
informatique [ɛ̃fɔrmatik] **1.** *n.f.* data processing; computer science; **cours d'i.,** computer course, data-processing course. **2.** *a.* **réseau i.,** computer network, information network.
informatisation [ɛ̃fɔrmatizasjɔ̃] *n.f.* computerization.
informatiser [ɛ̃fɔrmatize] *v.tr.* to computerize.
informe [ɛ̃fɔrm] *a.* (*a*) formless, unformed, shapeless (mass, etc.); crude (plan); (*b*) ill-formed, misshapen (monster, etc.).
informé [ɛ̃fɔrme] *n.m.* (*a*) *Jur:* result of inquiry; (*b*) **jusqu'à plus ample i.,** until we are better informed; until further notice.
informer [ɛ̃fɔrme] **1.** *v.tr.* **i. qn de qch.,** to inform s.o. of sth.; to tell s.o., let s.o. know, about sth.; to acquaint s.o. with (a fact); **veuillez m'en i.,** please let me know; **bien informé,** well informed; **mal informé,** misinformed. **2.** *v.i. Jur:* (*a*) **i. sur un crime,** to investigate, inquire into, a crime; (*b*) **i. contre qn,** to inform against s.o. **3. s'i.,** to make inquiries; **s'i. de qch.,** to inquire, ask, about sth.; **il cherche à s'i.,** he's trying to find out.
informulé [ɛ̃fɔrmyle] *a.* unformulated.
infortune [ɛ̃fɔrtyn] *n.f. esp. Lit:* misfortune; calamity; **compagnons d'i.,** companions in adversity, in distress; fellow sufferers; **tomber dans l'i.,** to meet with misfortune, fall on evil days.
infortuné [ɛ̃fɔrtyne] **1.** *a.* unfortunate, ill fated, unlucky, wretched. **2.** *n.* **les infortunés,** the unfortunate, the wretched.
infraction [ɛ̃fraksjɔ̃] *n.f.* infraction. **1.** infringement (of rights, etc.). **2.** offence; **i. à la loi,** breaking the law; **i. au devoir,** breach of duty; **i. à un ordre,** violation of an order; **être en i.,** to be committing an offence.
infranchissable [ɛ̃frɑ̃ʃisabl̩] *a.* impassable; insuperable, insurmountable (difficulty, etc.).
infrangible [ɛ̃frɑ̃ʒibl̩] *a.* infrangible.
infrarouge [ɛ̃fraruʒ] *a. & n.m.* infrared.
infrason [ɛ̃frasɔ̃] *n.m.* infrasonic vibration.
infra(-)sonore [ɛ̃frasɔnɔr] *a.* infrasonic; *pl. infra(-)sonores.*
infrastructure [ɛ̃frastryktyr] *n.f.* **1.** (*a*) *Civ.E:* substructure, understructure (of bridge, etc.); (*b*) *Pol.Ec:* infrastructure. **2.** *Tchn:* infrastructure, basic equipment (of railways, hospitals, etc.); ground environment (of radar system, etc.).
infréquentable [ɛ̃frekɑ̃tabl̩] *a.* **gens infréquentables,** people one doesn't want to know.
infroissable [ɛ̃frwasabl̩] *a. Tex: etc:* crease-resisting; uncrushable.
infructueux, -euse [ɛ̃fryktɥø, -øz] *a.* (*a*) unfruitful, barren (land, etc.); (*b*) fruitless, unavailing, unsuccessful (efforts); (*c*) unprofitable (investment).
infumable [ɛ̃fymabl̩] *a.* unsmokable (cigar, etc.).
infus [ɛ̃fy] *a.* inborn, innate (knowledge, etc.).
infuser [ɛ̃fyze] *v.* to infuse. **1.** *v.tr.* (*a*) to instil (**à,** into); (*b*) to steep, macerate (herbs, etc.). **2.** *v.i.* **faire i. le thé,** to infuse, brew, the tea; **laisser i. le thé,** to let the tea draw, brew.
infusible [ɛ̃fyzibl̩] *a.* infusible, non-fusible.

infusion [ɛ̃fyzjɔ̃] *n.f.* infusion; infusing (of herbs, tea); steeping (of herbs, etc.); **une i. de camomille,** an infusion of camomile; camomile tea.
ingambe [ɛ̃gɑ̃b] *a.* nimble, sprightly; alert.
ingénier (s') [sɛ̃ʒenje] *v.pr.* **s'i. à faire qch.,** to strain one's ingenuity in order to do sth.; to contrive, make an effort, to do sth.
ingénieur [ɛ̃ʒenjœr] *n.m.* (graduate, qualified) engineer; **i. (des travaux publics),** civil engineer; **i. des ponts et chaussées** = (government) civil engineer; **i. des mines,** mining engineer; **i. mécanicien,** mechanical engineer; **i. électronicien,** electronics engineer; **i. du son,** sound engineer; *Nau:* **i. des constructions navales,** naval constructor; **i. de l'artillerie navale,** naval ordnance officer; *Mil:* **Corps des Ingénieurs géographes** = Ordnance Survey.
ingénieusement [ɛ̃ʒenjøzmɑ̃] *adv.* ingeniously, cleverly.
ingénieux, -euse [ɛ̃ʒenjø, -øz] *a.* ingenious, clever.
ingéniosité [ɛ̃ʒenjozite] *n.f.* ingenuity, ingeniousness; cleverness (of person).
ingénu, -ue [ɛ̃ʒeny] **1.** *a. & n.* ingenuous, artless, simple, naïve, unsophisticated (person); **faire l'i.,** to affect simplicity. **2.** *n.f. Th:* ingénue.
ingénuité [ɛ̃ʒenɥite] *n.f.* ingenuousness, artlessness, simplicity, naïvety.
ingénument [ɛ̃ʒenymɑ̃] *adv.* ingenuously, artlessly, simply, naïvely.
ingérence [ɛ̃ʒerɑ̃s] *n.f.* (unwarrantable) interference, meddling.
ingérer [ɛ̃ʒere] **1.** *v.tr.* **(j'ingère; j'ingérerai)** *Physiol:* to ingest (food). **2. s'i. dans une affaire,** to interfere in, meddle with, a problem.
ingestion [ɛ̃ʒɛstjɔ̃] *n.f. Physiol:* ingestion.
ingouvernable [ɛ̃guvɛrnabl̥] *a.* **1.** ungovernable, unruly. **2.** unmanageable (ship, etc.).
ingrat, -ate [ɛ̃gra, -at] **1.** *a.* (*a*) ungrateful (**envers,** to, towards); (*b*) unproductive, unprofitable (soil, etc.); intractable (material); thankless (task); barren (subject); (*c*) disagreeable, repellent (work, etc.); (*d*) unattractive, unpleasant (appearance, etc.); **l'âge i.,** the awkward age. **2.** *n.* ungrateful, heartless, person.
ingratement [ɛ̃gratmɑ̃] *adv.* ungratefully.
ingratitude [ɛ̃gratityd] *n.f.* ingratitude, ungratefulness.
ingrédient [ɛ̃gredjɑ̃] *n.m.* ingredient, constituent.
inguérissable [ɛ̃gerisabl̥] *a.* (*a*) incurable; (*b*) inconsolable (grief).
ingurgitation [ɛ̃gyrʒitasjɔ̃] *n.f.* ingurgitation.
ingurgiter [ɛ̃gyrʒite] *v.tr.* to ingurgitate; to swallow, gulp down, knock back (drink, etc.).
inhabile [inabil] *a.* (*a*) *Jur:* **i. à tester,** incompetent to make a will; (*b*) unskilled (**à,** in); unskilful; clumsy, incompetent.
inhabilement [inabilmɑ̃] *adv.* unskilfully.
inhabileté [inabilte] *n.f.* lack of skill (**à faire qch.,** in doing sth.); clumsiness.
inhabilité [inabilite] *n.f. Jur:* incapacity, disability; **i. à succéder,** incompetency to succeed.
inhabitable [inabitabl̥] *a.* uninhabitable.
inhabité [inabite] *a.* uninhabited; unoccupied (house); **vol i.,** unmanned (space) flight.
inhabituel, -elle [inabitɥɛl] *a.* unusual.
inhalateur, -trice [inalatœr, -tris] **1.** *a.* inhaling (apparatus). **2.** *n.m.* inhaler.
inhalation [inalasjɔ̃] *n.f.* inhalation.
inhaler [inale] *v.tr.* to inhale.
inharmonieux, -ieuse [inarmɔnjø, -jøz] *a.* inharmonious, discordant; unmusical.
inhérence [inerɑ̃s] *n.f.* inherence, inherency.
inhérent [inerɑ̃] *a.* inherent (**à,** in).
inhiber [inibe] *v.tr.* to inhibit.
inhibiteur, -trice [inibitœr, -tris], **inhibitif, -ive** [inibitif, -iv] *a.* inhibitory (reflex, nerve, etc.).
inhibition [inibisjɔ̃] *n.f.* inhibition.
inhospitalier, -ière [inɔspitalje, -jɛr] *a.* inhospitable.
inhumain [inymɛ̃] *a.* inhuman; unfeeling.
inhumainement [inymɛnmɑ̃] *adv.* inhumanly.
inhumanité [inymanite] *n.f.* inhumanity.
inhumation [inymasjɔ̃] *n.f.* inhumation, burial, interment.
inhumer [inyme] *v.tr.* to inhume, bury, inter.
inimaginable [inimaʒinabl̥] *a.* unimaginable; inconceivable, unthinkable.
inimitable [inimitabl̥] *a.* inimitable; matchless.
inimitié [inimitje] *n.f.* enmity, hostility, ill feeling.
ininflammable [inɛ̃flamabl̥] *a.* non-(in)flammable; fireproof.
inintelligemment [inɛ̃teliʒamɑ̃] *adv.* unintelligently.
inintelligence [inɛ̃teliʒɑ̃s] *n.f.* lack of intelligence; unintelligence; obtuseness.
inintelligent [inɛ̃teliʒɑ̃] *a.* unintelligent; obtuse.
inintelligibilité [inɛ̃teliʒibilite] *n.f.* unintelligibility.
inintelligible [inɛ̃teliʒibl̥] *a.* unintelligible.
inintelligiblement [inɛ̃teliʒibləmɑ̃] *adv.* unintelligibly.
inintéressant [inɛ̃terɛsɑ̃] *a.* uninteresting.
ininterrompu [inɛ̃tɛrɔ̃py] *a.* uninterrupted, unremitting; unbroken (sleep, etc.); steady (progress).
inique [inik] *a.* iniquitous.
iniquement [inikmɑ̃] *adv.* iniquitously.
iniquité [inikite] *n.f.* iniquity.
initial, -ale, -aux [inisjal, -o] **1.** *a.* initial (letter, cost, etc.); starting (price); *Ball:* **vitesse initiale,** muzzle velocity. **2.** *n.f.* initial (letter).
initialement [inisjalmɑ̃] *adv.* initially.
initiateur, -trice [inisjatœr, -tris] **1.** *n.* initiator; originator, pioneer (of scheme, etc.). **2.** *a.* initiatory.
initiation [inisjasjɔ̃] *n.f.* initiation (**à,** to); **une i. à la musique,** an introduction to music.
initiatique [inisjatik] *a.* initiatory.
initiative [inisjativ] *n.f.* initiative; **sur l'i. de qn,** on s.o.'s initiative; **prendre l'i. d'une réforme,** to initiate a reform; **prendre l'i. de faire qch.,** to take the initiative in doing sth.; **faire qch. de sa propre i.,** to do sth. on one's own initiative; **il n'a aucune i.,** he's got no initiative; **syndicat d'i.,** tourist information bureau.
initié, -ée [inisje] *n.* (*a*) initiate; (*b*) person in the know.
initier [inisje] **1.** *v.tr.* to initiate (s.o.) (**à,** into); **c'est moi qui l'ai initié au grec,** it was me who introduced him to Greek. **2. s'i. à qch.,** to learn, be learning sth.; to get to know sth.
injectable [ɛ̃ʒɛktabl̥] *a.* injectable.
injecté [ɛ̃ʒɛkte] *a.* congested, inflamed; injected; **yeux injectés de sang,** bloodshot eyes.
injecter [ɛ̃ʒɛkte] **1.** *v.tr.* to inject. **2. s'i.,** (*of eyes, etc.*) to become bloodshot.
injecteur, -trice [ɛ̃ʒɛktœr, -tris] **1.** *a.* injecting (tube, etc.). **2.** *n.m.* injector; *Av: etc:* nozzle.
injection [ɛ̃ʒɛksjɔ̃] *n.f.* injection; *I.C.E:* **moteur à i.,** (fuel) injection engine.
injonction [ɛ̃ʒɔ̃ksjɔ̃] *n.f.* injunction; *Jur:* order.
injure [ɛ̃ʒyr] *n.f.* (*a*) insult; *pl.* abuse; (*b*) **faire i. à qn,** to insult s.o.; *Lit:* **l'i. des ans,** the ravages of time.
injurier [ɛ̃ʒyrje] *v.tr.* to abuse, insult (s.o.).
injurieux, -euse [ɛ̃ʒyrjø, -øz] *a.* insulting, abusive.
injuste [ɛ̃ʒyst] **1.** *a.* unjust; unfair (**envers, avec,** to). **2.** *n.m.* **le juste et l'i.,** right and wrong.
injustement [ɛ̃ʒystəmɑ̃] *adv.* unjustly.

injustice [ɛ̃ʒystis] *n.f.* **1.** injustice, unfairness (**envers,** to, towards). **2. faire une i. à qn,** to do s.o. an injustice; to wrong s.o.
injustifiable [ɛ̃ʒystifjabl̥] *a.* unjustifiable.
injustifié [ɛ̃ʒystifje] *a.* unjustified, unwarranted.
inlassable [ɛ̃lasabl̥] *a.* untiring, unflagging, unwearying (efforts, etc.); tireless (person).
inlassablement [ɛ̃lasabləmɑ̃] *adv.* untiringly, tirelessly.
inné [ine] *a.* innate, inborn.
innervation [inɛrvasjɔ̃] *n.f. Physiol:* innervation.
innerver [inɛrve] *v.tr. Physiol:* to innervate.
innocemment [inɔsamɑ̃] *adv.* innocently.
innocence [inɔsɑ̃s] *n.f.* innocence; (*a*) guiltlessness; (*b*) naïvety; (*c*) harmlessness (of joke).
innocent, -ente [inɔsɑ̃, -ɑ̃t] **1.** *a.* (*a*) innocent; not guilty; (*b*) innocent, pure; (*c*) naïve; (*d*) innocent, inoffensive (joke). **2.** *n.* (*a*) innocent person; (*b*) **les (saints) Innocents,** the Holy Innocents; (*c*) simpleton; **ne fais pas l'i.!** don't act so innocent! **l'i. du village,** the village idiot; *Prov:* **aux innocents les mains pleines,** (i) fortune favours, *NAm:* favors, fools; (ii) beginners have all the luck.
innocenter [inɔsɑ̃te] *v.tr.* **1. i. qn (d'une accusation),** to clear s.o. (of a charge); to declare s.o. not guilty. **2.** to excuse, justify (conduct).
innocuité [inɔkɥite] *n.f.* innocuousness, harmlessness.
innombrable [inɔ̃brabl̥] *a.* innumerable, numberless, countless.
innommable [inɔmabl̥] *a.* (*a*) unnamable; (*b*) unspeakable (behaviour, etc.).
innom(m)é [inɔme] *a.* unnamed, nameless.
innovateur, -trice [inɔvatœr, -tris] **1.** *a.* innovating; innovatory, innovative. **2.** *n.* innovator.
innovation [inɔvasjɔ̃] *n.f.* innovation.
innover [inɔve] **1.** *v.i.* to innovate; to introduce changes, innovations; to break new ground. **2.** *v.tr.* to introduce, invent (something new).
inobservable [inɔpsɛrvabl̥] *a.* **1.** that cannot be observed, that cannot be complied with. **2.** inobservable, hardly perceptible.
inobservance [inɔpsɛrvɑ̃s] *n.f.* non-observance, inobservance.
inobservation [inɔpsɛrvasjɔ̃] *n.f.* non-observance, disregard (of the law); inobservance; non-compliance (**de,** with).
inobservé [inɔpsɛrve] *a.* unobserved. **1.** (*of rule*) not kept, not complied with. **2.** unnoticed.
inoccupé, -ée [inɔkype] unoccupied. **1.** *a. & n.* idle (person). **2.** *a.* vacant (seat, house); uninhabited (house).
inoculation [inɔkylasjɔ̃] *n.f. Med:* inoculation.
inoculer [inɔkyle] *v.tr.* **1.** (*a*) **i. une maladie à qn,** to infect s.o. with a disease; **elle nous a inoculé sa gaieté,** we were swept away by her gaiety; (*b*) *Med:* **i. un virus à qn,** to inoculate s.o. with a virus. **2. i. qn (contre une maladie),** to inoculate s.o. (against a disease).
inodore [inɔdɔr] *a.* odourless, *NAm:* odorless; scentless.
inoffensif, -ive [inɔfɑ̃sif, -iv] *a.* inoffensive; harmless; innocuous.
inondable [inɔ̃dabl̥] *a.* (*of land*) liable to flooding.
inondation [inɔ̃dasjɔ̃] *n.f.* inundation; flood; flooding; deluge (of questions, etc.).
inondé, -ée [inɔ̃de] **1.** *a.* flooded; **visage i. de larmes,** face streaming with tears; **i. de lumière,** flooded with light; **i. d'invitations,** snowed under, swamped, with invitations. **2.** *n.* flood victim.
inonder [inɔ̃de] *v.tr.* (*a*) to inundate, flood (fields, etc.); to glut, swamp (the market); (*b*) to soak, drench; **nous avons été inondés par l'averse,** we were soaked by the shower.
inopérable [inɔperabl̥] *a. Surg:* inoperable.
inopérant [inɔperɑ̃] *a.* inoperative; ineffectual.
inopiné [inɔpine] *a.* sudden, unexpected.
inopinément [inɔpinemɑ̃] *adv.* unexpectedly.
inopportun [inɔpɔrtœ̃] *a.* inopportune; untimely, unseasonable, ill-timed.
inopportunément [inɔpɔrtynemɑ̃] *adv.* inopportunely.
inopportunité [inɔpɔrtynite] *n.f.* inopportuneness, inopportunity; unseasonableness, untimeliness.
inorganique [inɔrganik] *a.* inorganic.
inorganisé [inɔrganize] *a.* (*a*) disorganized; (*b*) unorganized; non-union (labour).
inoubliable [inublijabl̥] *a.* unforgettable.
inoublié [inublije] *a.* unforgotten.
inouï [inwi] *a.* unheard of; extraordinary; outrageous; **avec une violence inouïe,** with incredible, unprecedented, violence.
inox [inɔks] *a. & n.m. F:* **(acier) i.,** stainless steel.
inoxydable [inɔksidabl̥] *a.* rustproof; **acier i.,** *n.m.* **i.,** stainless steel.
inqualifiable [ɛ̃kalifjabl̥] *a.* unspeakable (behaviour).
inquiet, -ète [ɛ̃kjɛ, -ɛt] **1.** *a.* (*a*) restless; **sommeil i.,** troubled, broken, sleep; (*b*) anxious, apprehensive, uneasy; worried; **i. sur qch., de qn,** uneasy, worried, about sth., s.o. **2.** *n.* anxious person; worrier.
inquiétant [ɛ̃kjetɑ̃] *a.* disquieting, disturbing, upsetting, worrying.
inquiéter [ɛ̃kjete] **1.** *v.tr.* **(j'inquiète; j'inquiéterai)** (*a*) *Lit:* to disturb (s.o.'s peace, etc.); (*b*) to harass, worry (enemy, etc.); (*c*) to worry, trouble (s.o.); to make (s.o.) anxious; **sa santé m'inquiète,** I'm worried about his health. **2. s'i.,** to become anxious, get worried; **il n'y a pas de quoi s'i.,** there's nothing to get worried, upset, about; **ne vous inquiétez pas de cela,** don't worry, don't bother, about that.
inquiétude [ɛ̃kjetyd] *n.f.* **1.** *A: & Lit:* agitation; restlessness. **2.** anxiety; concern, misgivings, uneasiness; disquiet; **dissiper les inquiétudes de qn,** to set s.o.'s mind at rest; **état d'i.,** state of anxiety; anxious state of mind; **éprouver quelques inquiétudes,** to have a few qualms.
inquisiteur, -trice [ɛ̃kizitœr, -tris] **1.** *n.m.* inquisitor. **2.** *a.* inquisitive, prying (glance, etc.).
inquisition [ɛ̃kizisjɔ̃] *n.f.* inquisition.
inquisitorial, -aux [ɛ̃kizitɔrjal, -o] *a.* inquisitorial.
insaisissable [ɛ̃sezisabl̥] *a.* **1.** (*a*) that cannot be grasped; (*b*) difficult to catch; elusive; (*c*) imperceptible (sound, difference). **2.** *Jur:* (*of property*) not distrainable, not attachable.
insalissable [ɛ̃salisabl̥] *a.* dirtproof.
insalubre [ɛ̃salybr̥] *a.* insalubrious (climate); unhealthy (climate, occupation); insanitary (dwelling).
insalubrité [ɛ̃salybrite] *n.f.* insalubrity, unhealthiness.
insanité [ɛ̃sanite] *n.f.* insanity.
insatiabilité [ɛ̃sasjabilite] *n.f.* insatiability.
insatiable [ɛ̃sasjabl̥] *a.* insatiable; unquenchable.
insatiablement [ɛ̃sasjabləmɑ̃] *adv.* insatiably.
insatisfaction [ɛ̃satisfaksjɔ̃] *n.f.* dissatisfaction.
insatisfait [ɛ̃satisfɛ] *a.* (*a*) (*of pers.*) dissatisfied; (*b*) unsatisfied (desire).
inscription [ɛ̃skripsjɔ̃] *n.f.* **1.** (*a*) writing (down), inscribing; entering, recording (in diary, etc.); (*b*) registration, enrolment; **droit d'i.,** registration fee, entrance fee; **feuille d'i.,** entry form; **prendre son i.,** to enter one's name; *Jur:* **i. hypothécaire,** registry, registration, of mortgages; **i. de faux, en faux,** plea of forgery; **i. maritime,** seaboard conscription, re-

gistration, for the navy. **2.** (*a*) inscription (on tomb, etc.); entry (in account book, etc.); (*b*) directions (on signpost, etc.); notice.

inscrire [ɛ̃skrir] **1.** *v.tr.* (*pr.p.* **inscrivant;** *p.p.* **inscrit;** *pr.ind.* **j'inscris, il inscrit, n. inscrivons;** *p.h.* **j'inscrivis;** *fu.* **j'inscrirai)** (*a*) to inscribe, write down; to enter, take down, note (down) (details); **i. une question à l'ordre du jour,** to put, place, a question on the agenda; (*b*) to register (marriage, etc.); to enrol (s.o.); to enter (s.o.'s) name; **se faire i. à un cours,** to put one's name down, to enrol, register, for a course; (*c*) to inscribe, engrave (epitaph, etc.); (*d*) to inscribe (triangle, etc.) (**dans,** in). **2. s'i.** (*a*) to put one's name down, to register, enrol; (*b*) *Jur:* **s'i. en faux contre qch.,** to dispute the validity of sth., deny sth.; (*c*) **cette décision s'inscrit dans le cadre de la politique gouvernementale,** this decision is in keeping with the general pattern of the government's policy.

inscrit, -ite [ɛ̃skri, -it] **1.** *a.* (*a*) *Mth:* inscribed; (*b*) enrolled, registered (voter, etc.). **2.** (*a*) *n.* registered person, *esp.* voter; (*b*) *n.m. Navy:* **i. maritime,** seaman registered for service in the navy.

insécable [ɛ̃sekabl̥] *a.* indivisible.

insecte [ɛ̃sɛkt] *n.m.* insect.

insecticide [ɛ̃sɛktisid] **1.** *a.* insecticidal; **poudre i.,** insect powder. **2.** *n.m.* insecticide.

insectivore [ɛ̃sɛktivɔr] *Z:* **1.** *a.* insectivorous. **2.** *n.m.* insectivore; **insectivores,** Insectivora.

insécurité [ɛ̃sekyrite] *n.f.* insecurity.

insémination [ɛ̃seminasjɔ̃] *n.f.* insemination.

inséminer [ɛ̃semine] *v.tr.* to inseminate.

insensé, -ée [ɛ̃sɑ̃se] *a.* (*a*) mad, insane; *n.* madman, -woman; (*b*) senseless, foolish (action, etc.); (*c*) extravagant, wild, *F:* hare-brained (scheme, etc.).

insensibilisation [ɛ̃sɑ̃sibilizasjɔ̃] *n.f.* anaesthetization.

insensibiliser [ɛ̃sɑ̃sibilize] *v.tr.* to anaesthetize.

insensibilité [ɛ̃sɑ̃sibilite] *n.f.* insensitiveness, insensitivity; insensibility.

insensible [ɛ̃sɑ̃sibl̥] *a.* **1.** (*a*) insensitive (nerve, etc.); (*b*) insensitive, indifferent (**à,** to); insensible, unfeeling; **i. à la flatterie,** proof against flattery. **2.** imperceptible; hardly perceptible (difference, etc.).

insensiblement [ɛ̃sɑ̃sibləmɑ̃] *adv.* imperceptibly.

inséparable [ɛ̃separabl̥] **1.** *a.* inseparable. **2.** *n.m.pl. Orn:* lovebirds.

inséparablement [ɛ̃separabləmɑ̃] *adv.* inseparably.

insérable [ɛ̃serabl̥] *a.* insertable.

insérer [ɛ̃sere] **1.** *v.tr.* **(j'insère; j'insérerai)** to insert; **i. une annonce dans un journal,** to insert, put, an advertisement in a paper; **prière d'i.,** (i) for publication (in your columns); (ii) publisher's blurb. **2. s'i.** (*a*) to be attached (to); (*b*) to fit (**dans,** into).

insertion [ɛ̃sɛrsjɔ̃] *n.f.* insertion.

insidieusement [ɛ̃sidjøzmɑ̃] *adv.* insidiously.

insidieux, -euse [ɛ̃sidjø, -øz] *a.* insidious.

insigne¹ [ɛ̃siɲ] *a.* **1.** distinguished, remarkable; **faveur i.,** signal favour, *NAm:* favor. **2.** *Pej:* notorious; arrant (liar, etc.); **indiscrétion i.,** glaring indiscretion.

insigne² *n.m.* distinguishing mark; badge; **insignes de la royauté,** insignia of royalty; *Mil:* **i. de grade,** badge of rank.

insignifiance [ɛ̃siɲifjɑ̃s] *n.f.* insignificance, unimportance; triviality.

insignifiant [ɛ̃siɲifjɑ̃] *a.* insignificant, unimportant; trivial, trifling (loss, sum); nominal (payment).

insincère [ɛ̃sɛ̃sɛr] *a. Lit:* insincere.

insinuant [ɛ̃sinɥɑ̃] *a.* ingratiating.

insinuation [ɛ̃sinɥasjɔ̃] *n.f.* insinuation; innuendo.

insinuer [ɛ̃sinɥe] **1.** *v.tr.* to insinuate, suggest, hint at (sth.); **que voulez-vous i.?** what are you hinting at, getting at? **2. s'i.,** to penetrate; to creep, steal, in(to); **s'i. dans les bonnes grâces de qn,** to insinuate oneself, worm one's way, into s.o.'s good books; **s'i. entre les voitures,** to thread one's way through the traffic.

insipide [ɛ̃sipid] *a.* insipid; (*a*) tasteless (food); (*b*) dull, flat, uninteresting (conversation, etc.); tame, wishy-washy (story, ending).

insipidité [ɛ̃sipidite] *n.f.* insipidity, insipidness; (*a*) tastelessness (of food); (*b*) dullness, flatness (of conversation); tameness (of ending).

insistance [ɛ̃sistɑ̃s] *n.f.* insistence (**à faire qch.,** on doing sth.); **avec i.,** insistently, earnestly.

insistant [ɛ̃sistɑ̃] *a.* insistent; stubborn.

insister [ɛ̃siste] *v.i.* to insist; **i. sur un fait,** to dwell, lay stress, on a fact; to stress a fact; **i. sur ses demandes,** to stand out for, insist on, persist in, one's claims; **i. pour faire qch.,** to insist on doing sth.; **i. auprès de qn,** to take up a matter strongly with s.o.; **n'insistez pas trop,** (i) don't put too much emphasis on that; (ii) don't be too insistent; don't push the matter, your luck, too far.

insociable [ɛ̃sɔsjabl̥] *a.* unsociable.

insolation [ɛ̃sɔlasjɔ̃] *n.f.* (*a*) exposure (to the sun); (*b*) *Med:* insolation, sunstroke.

insolemment [ɛ̃sɔlamɑ̃] *adv.* insolently.

insolence [ɛ̃sɔlɑ̃s] *n.f.* **1.** insolence; impertinence; impudence; **répondre avec i.,** to answer insolently. **2.** insolent remark, action.

insolent [ɛ̃sɔlɑ̃] *a.* (*a*) insolent, impertinent, impudent, *F:* cheeky **(envers, avec,** to); (*b*) haughty, overbearing (in victory, etc.); (*c*) extraordinary (success, etc.); **luxe i.,** indecent, blatant, luxury.

insolite [ɛ̃sɔlit] *a.* unusual, unwonted; strange.

insolubilité [ɛ̃sɔlybilite] *n.f.* insolubility.

insoluble [ɛ̃sɔlybl̥] *a.* **1.** insoluble (substance). **2.** insoluble, insolvable (problem).

insolvabilité [ɛ̃sɔlvabilite] *n.f. Com:* insolvency.

insolvable [ɛ̃sɔlvabl̥] *a. Com:* insolvent.

insomniaque [ɛ̃sɔmnjak] *a. & n.* insomniac.

insomnie [ɛ̃sɔmni] *n.f.* insomnia, sleeplessness; **nuit d'i.,** sleepless night.

insondable [ɛ̃sɔ̃dabl̥] *a.* **1.** unfathomable, fathomless (ocean, etc.). **2.** unfathomable (mystery). **3.** immense, unbelievable (stupidity, etc.).

insonore [ɛ̃sɔnɔr] *a.* soundproof (studio, material).

insonorisation [ɛ̃sɔnɔrizasjɔ̃] *n.f.* insulation (of sound camera); soundproofing.

insonoriser [ɛ̃sɔnɔrize] *v.tr.* to insulate, soundproof.

insouciance [ɛ̃susjɑ̃s] *n.f.* (*a*) freedom from care; lack of concern; insouciance; (*b*) thoughtlessness.

insouciant [ɛ̃susjɑ̃] *a.* (*a*) carefree; unconcerned; (*b*) thoughtless, casual; happy-go-lucky.

insoucieux, -euse [ɛ̃susjø, -øz] *a.* heedless (**de,** of); **i. de l'avenir,** regardless of the future.

insoumis, -ise [ɛ̃sumi, -iz] **1.** *a.* unsubdued (people, etc.). **2.** *a. & n.* refractory, unruly, rebellious, insubordinate (person). **3.** *a. & n.m. Mil:* absentee (soldier).

insoumission [ɛ̃sumisjɔ̃] *n.f.* insubordination, rebelliousness; *Mil:* failure to (re)join one's unit.

insoupçonnable [ɛ̃supsɔnabl̥] *a.* beyond, above, suspicion.

insoupçonné [ɛ̃supsɔne] *a.* unsuspected (**de,** by).

insoutenable [ɛ̃sutnabl̥] *a.* **1.** untenable (opinion); unwarrantable (assertion); indefensible (position). **2.** unbearable, unendurable (agony).

inspecter [ɛ̃spɛkte] *v.tr.* to inspect (troops, school, etc.); to survey (field of battle); to examine (work).

inspecteur, -trice [ɛ̃spɛktœr, -tris] *n.* inspector; overseer (of works, etc.); surveyor (of mines, etc.); examiner (of business accounts, etc.); **i. de la sûreté,** detective inspector; **i. du travail,** factory inspector; **i. des contributions directes,** inspector of taxes; *Sch:* **i.**

d'Académie, school inspector = H.M.I.; **i. (de l'Enseignement) primaire,** primary school inspector.

inspection [ɛ̃spɛksjɔ̃] *n.f.* **1.** (*a*) inspection, inspecting; examination, examining; survey; **faire l'i. de,** to inspect, examine; *Mil: etc:* **passer l'i. (d'une compagnie, etc.),** to inspect (a company, etc.); (*b*) tour of inspection. **2.** inspectorship, inspectorate. **3.** body, board, of inspectors; inspectorate.

inspectorat [ɛ̃spɛktɔra] *n.m. Adm:* inspectorate, inspectorship.

inspirateur, -trice [ɛ̃spiratœr, -tris] **1.** *a.* (*a*) *Anat:* inspiratory (muscle, etc.); (*b*) inspiring (thought, etc.). **2.** *n.* inspirer; instigator (of plot).

inspiration [ɛ̃spirasjɔ̃] *n.f.* inspiration. **1.** *Physiol:* breathing in. **2.** prompting; **sous l'i. de qn,** at s.o.'s suggestion, instigation; **i. soudaine,** sudden inspiration, *F:* brainwave, *NAm:* brainstorm.

inspiré, -ée [ɛ̃spire] **1.** *a.* (*a*) inspired (writing, poet, etc.); (*b*) **bien, mal, i.,** well advised; ill advised. **2.** *n.* mystic; visionary.

inspirer [ɛ̃spire] **1.** *v.tr.* to inspire; (*a*) **i. qch. à qn,** to inspire s.o. with sth.; **i. le respect,** to inspire respect; **inspiré par la jalousie,** prompted, actuated, by jealousy; **contes inspirés de la vie des animaux,** tales drawn from, inspired by, animal life; (*b*) to breathe in (air, etc.). **2. s'i. de qn, qch.,** to take, draw, one's inspiration from s.o., sth.; to be inspired by s.o., sth.

instabilité [ɛ̃stabilite] *n.f.* instability; (*a*) shakiness, unsteadiness; *Nau:* crank (of ship); (*b*) inconstancy, fickleness, uncertainty (of fortune, etc.).

instable [ɛ̃stabl̩] *a.* unstable; (*a*) shaky, unsteady, *F:* wobbly; *Nau:* crank (ship); (*b*) unreliable, inconstant (person, nature, etc.); **population i.,** shifting population; (*c*) changeable (weather).

installateur [ɛ̃stalatœr] *n.m.* fitter.

installation [ɛ̃stalasjɔ̃] *n.f.* installation. **1.** installing; (*a*) induction (of clergyman); (*b*) setting up (of machine, house); fitting up, out, equipping (of workshop); fixing (of curtains, etc.). **2.** (*a*) arrangements, appointments (of house, etc.); fittings, equipment (of workshop, etc.); (*b*) *Ind:* plant; **i. de lavage,** washing bay; **i. (de) radio,** radio installation, set; (*at aerodrome*) **installations au sol,** ground installations, facilities.

installer [ɛ̃stale] **1.** *v.tr.* to install; (*a*) to induct (clergyman); (*b*) **i. qn dans un fauteuil,** to make s.o. comfortable in an armchair; (*c*) to set up (machine, etc.); to fit up, out, to equip (factory, etc.); to fix (curtains, etc.); **maison bien installée,** well appointed house; (*d*) to establish, settle (one's family, etc.); (*e*) *v.i. P:* **en i.,** to show off. **2. s'i.,** to install oneself; to settle (down); to make oneself at home; **s'i. à la campagne,** to settle in the country; **s'i. comme médecin,** to set (oneself) up as a doctor.

instamment [ɛ̃stamɑ̃] *adv.* insistently, earnestly; **on demande i. un médecin,** a doctor is urgently required.

instance [ɛ̃stɑ̃s] *n.f.* **1.** (*a*) (i) *A:* instancy, solicitation; (ii) **demander qch. à qn avec i.,** to beg, plead with, s.o. for sth.; **prier avec i.,** to pray earnestly; (*b*) *pl.* requests, entreaties; (*c*) *Jur:* process, suit; **introduire une i. (en justice),** to institute an action; **ils sont en i. de divorce,** their divorce proceedings are taking place; **tribunal d'i.** = magistrates' court; **tribunal de grande i.** = county court; **acquitté en seconde i.,** acquitted on appeal; (*d*) authority. **2. être en i. de départ,** to be on the point of departure, about to leave; **tout est encore en i.,** everything is still pending.

instant¹ [ɛ̃stɑ̃] *a. Lit:* pressing, urgent.

instant² *n.m.* moment, instant; **à chaque i., à tout i.,** continually; at every, any, moment; **par instants,** now and then; **un i. de délai,** a moment's delay; **pendant un i.,** for a moment; **un i.!** wait an instant, a moment! **à l'i.,** (i) a moment ago; (ii) immediately, instantly, at once; **pour l'i.,** for the moment; **dans un i.,** in a moment; **en un i.,** in no time; **un soin de tous les instants,** unremitting, ceaseless, care; **dès l'i. que** + *ind.*, (i) from the moment when . . .; (ii) since, seeing that . . . .

instantané [ɛ̃stɑ̃tane] **1.** *a.* instantaneous (death, etc.); sudden (fright). **2.** *n.m. Phot:* snapshot.

instantanément [ɛ̃stɑ̃tanemɑ̃] *adv.* instantaneously.

instar de (à l') [alɛ̃stardə] *prep.phr. Lit:* after the fashion, manner, of; like.

instaurateur, -trice [ɛ̃stɔratœr, -tris] *n. Lit:* founder, establisher.

instaurer [ɛ̃stɔre] *v.tr.* to found, establish (research centre, etc.); to set up (republic, etc.).

instigateur, -trice [ɛ̃stigatœr, -tris] *n.* instigator.

instigation [ɛ̃stigasjɔ̃] *n.f.* instigation, incitement (**à,** to); **agir à l'i. de qn,** to act at, on, s.o.'s instigation.

instillation [ɛ̃stilasjɔ̃] *n.f. Med:* instillation.

instiller [ɛ̃stile] *v.tr.* to instil; **i. le courage à qn,** to instil courage in(to) s.o.

instinct [ɛ̃stɛ̃] *n.m.* instinct; **l'i. de conservation,** instinct of self-preservation; **d'i.,** by instinct, instinctively.

instinctif, -ive [ɛ̃stɛ̃ktif, -iv] *a.* instinctive.

instinctivement [ɛ̃stɛ̃ktivmɑ̃] *adv.* instinctively.

instituer [ɛ̃stitɥe] *v.tr.* to institute; (*a*) to establish, set up, found (institution, etc.); to lay down (rule); (*b*) to appoint (official, *Jur:* heir).

institut [ɛ̃stity] *n.m.* **1.** institute, institution; **l'I. (de France),** the Institute (composed of the five Academies). **2.** (*a*) institute, institution, college; (*b*) **i. de beauté,** beauty salon, parlour, *NAm:* parlor.

instituteur, -trice [ɛ̃stitytœr, -tris] *n.* **1.** *A:* founder (of hospital, etc.). **2.** (*a*) (primary school) teacher; (*b*) *n.f.* **institutrice,** governess.

institution [ɛ̃stitysjɔ̃] *n.f.* **1.** *Jur:* appointing (of heir). **2.** (*a*) institution; (*b*) (educational, etc.) establishment; independent, private, school; college.

institutionnaliser [ɛ̃stitysjɔnalize] *v.tr.* to institutionalize.

institutionnel, -elle [ɛ̃stitysjɔnɛl] *a.* institutional.

instructeur [ɛ̃stryktœr] **1.** *n.m.* instructor; teacher; *Mil:* **sergent i.,** drill sergeant. **2.** *a. Jur:* **juge i.,** examining magistrate.

instructif, -ive [ɛ̃stryktif, -iv] *a.* instructive.

instruction [ɛ̃stryksjɔ̃] *n.f.* **1.** (*a*) *pl.* instructions, directions, orders; **conformément aux instructions,** as directed, as requested; (*b*) *Cmptr:* instruction. **2.** education, schooling; instruction; *Mil:* training (of troops); *Sch:* **i. primaire,** primary education; **i. professionnelle,** vocational training; **avoir de l'i.,** to be well educated; **sans i.,** uneducated. **3.** *Jur:* preliminary investigation (of case); **juge d'i.,** examining magistrate. **4.** (official) memo, circular.

instruire [ɛ̃strɥir] *v.tr.* (*pr.p.* **instruisant;** *p.p.* **instruit;** *pr.ind.* **j'instruis, il instruit, n. instruisons;** *p.h.* **j'instruisis**) **1.** (*a*) **i. qn de qch.,** to inform s.o. of sth.; (*b*) to teach, educate, instruct; **i. qn dans, en, qch., à faire qch.,** to instruct s.o. in sth., how to do sth.; (*c*) to train, drill (troops); (*d*) *Jur:* to examine, investigate (case). **2. s'i.** (*a*) to educate oneself; to improve one's mind; (*b*) **s'i. de qch.,** to find out, get information, about sth.

instruit [ɛ̃strɥi] *a.* **1.** (*a*) educated, learned; well-read; (*b*) trained (soldier, etc.). **2. i. de qch.,** acquainted with, aware of, sth.

instrument [ɛ̃strymɑ̃] *n.m.* (*a*) instrument; implement, tool; **i. de travail,** implement; **i. de navigation,** navigation(al) instrument; *Av:* **atterrissage aux instruments,** instrument landing; **servir d'i. à la ven-**

geance de qn, to serve as the instrument, the tool, of s.o.'s vengeance; (*b*) (musical) instrument; **i. à anche,** reed instrument; (*c*) (legal) instrument.

instrumentaire [ɛ̃strymɑ̃tɛr] *a. Jur:* **témoin i.**, witness to a deed.

instrumental, -aux [ɛ̃strymɑ̃tal, -o] *a.* instrumental (music, etc.).

instrumentation [ɛ̃strymɑ̃tasjɔ̃] *n.f. Mus:* scoring, instrumentation, orchestration.

instrumenter [ɛ̃strymɑ̃te] **1.** *v.i. Jur:* to draw up a document; **i. contre qn,** to order proceedings to be taken against s.o. **2.** *v.tr. Mus:* to score, instrument, orchestrate (opera, etc.).

instrumentiste [ɛ̃strymɑ̃tist] *n. Mus:* instrumentalist.

insu [ɛ̃sy] *n.m. used in the phr.* **à l'i. de,** without the knowledge of; **à l'i. de ses parents,** without his parents' knowing, knowledge; **à mon i.,** without my knowing.

insubmersible [ɛ̃sybmɛrsibl̥] *a.* unsinkable.

insubordination [ɛ̃sybɔrdinasjɔ̃] *n.f.* insubordination.

insubordonné [ɛ̃sybɔrdɔne] *a.* insubordinate.

insuccès [ɛ̃syksɛ] *n.m.* lack of success; failure.

insuffisamment [ɛ̃syfizamɑ̃] *adv.* insufficiently; inadequately.

insuffisance [ɛ̃syfizɑ̃s] *n.f.* **1.** insufficiency, deficiency; shortage (of staff); inadequacy (of means). **2.** incompetence, inefficiency.

insuffisant [ɛ̃syfizɑ̃] *a.* **1.** insufficient; inadequate (means, etc.); short (weight). **2.** incapable, incompetent.

insufflateur [ɛ̃syflatœr] *n.m. Med:* insufflator.

insufflation [ɛ̃syflasjɔ̃] *n.f. Med:* insufflation.

insuffler [ɛ̃syfle] *v.tr.* (*a*) to insufflate; to blow, breathe (air into sth.); **i. qch. à qn,** to inspire s.o. with sth.; (*b*) *Med:* to spray (throat, etc.).

insulaire [ɛ̃sylɛr] **1.** *a.* insular. **2.** *n.* islander.

insularité [ɛ̃sylarite] *n.f.* insularity.

insuline [ɛ̃sylin] *n.f. Med:* insulin.

insultant [ɛ̃syltɑ̃] *a.* insulting, offensive.

insulte [ɛ̃sylt] *n.f.* insult; *pl.* abuse; **faire une i. à qn,** to insult s.o.

insulté, -ée [ɛ̃sylte] **1.** *a.* insulted. **2.** *n.* injured party.

insulter [ɛ̃sylte] **1.** *v.tr.* to insult, affront (s.o.). **2.** *v.i.* **i. au malheur,** to jeer at misfortune; **i. au bon goût,** to insult good taste.

insulteur [ɛ̃syltœr] *n.m.* insulter.

insupportable [ɛ̃sypɔrtabl̥] *a.* unbearable, unendurable (pain); intolerable (conduct); insufferable (person); **il est i.,** he's infuriating; he's the limit!

insupportablement [ɛ̃sypɔrtabləmɑ̃] *adv.* unbearably; intolerably; insufferably.

insurgé, -ée [ɛ̃syrʒe] *a. & n.* insurgent, insurrectionist, rebel.

insurger (s') [sɛ̃syrʒe] *v.pr.* **(je m'insurgeai(s), n.n. insurgeons)** to rise (in rebellion); to revolt, rebel.

insurmontable [ɛ̃syrmɔ̃tabl̥] *a.* insurmountable, insuperable; unconquerable (aversion).

insurmontablement [ɛ̃syrmɔ̃tabləmɑ̃] *adv.* insurmountably.

insurpassable [ɛ̃syrpasabl̥] *a.* unsurpassable.

insurrection [ɛ̃syrɛksjɔ̃] *n.f.* insurrection, (up)-rising, rebellion; **en état d'i.,** insurgent.

insurrectionnel, -elle [ɛ̃syrɛksjɔnɛl] *a.* insurrectional, insurrectionary (troops, etc.).

intact [ɛ̃takt] *a.* intact; (*a*) untouched; undamaged, unbroken; (*b*) unsullied (reputation).

intaille [ɛ̃taj] *n.f. Lap:* intaglio (work, gem).

intangibilité [ɛ̃tɑ̃ʒibilite] *n.f.* intangibility.

intangible [ɛ̃tɑ̃ʒibl̥] *a.* intangible.

intarissable [ɛ̃tarisabl̥] *a.* inexhaustible (well, imagination, etc.); endless (chatter, etc.); unfailing.

intarissablement [ɛ̃tarisabləmɑ̃] *adv.* inexhaustibly.

intégrable [ɛ̃tegrabl̥] *a. Mth:* integrable.

intégral, -ale, -aux [ɛ̃tegral, -o] **1.** *a.* (*a*) entire, complete, whole, full-scale; **paiement i.,** payment in full; **texte i.,** full text; **édition intégrale,** (complete and) unabridged edition; (*b*) *Mth:* **calcul i.,** integral calculus. **2.** *n.f.* (*a*) *Mth:* integral; (*b*) **l'intégrale des symphonies de Beethoven,** (complete set of) all Beethoven's symphonies.

intégralement [ɛ̃tegralmɑ̃] *adv.* wholly, entirely, fully, in full.

intégralité [ɛ̃tegralite] *n.f.* **l'i.,** the whole; **dans son i.,** as a whole; in its entirety.

intégrant [ɛ̃tegrɑ̃] *a.* integral (part, etc.); **faire partie intégrante de,** to be an integral part of, part and parcel of.

intégration [ɛ̃tegrasjɔ̃] *n.f.* integration.

intègre [ɛ̃tɛgr̥] *a.* upright, honest.

intégrer [ɛ̃tegre] **1.** *v.tr.* **(j'intègre; j'intégrerai)** (*a*) to integrate (**à, dans,** into). **2. s'i.,** to become integrated (**à, dans,** into, with).

intégrité [ɛ̃tegrite] *n.f.* integrity. **1.** completeness, entirety. **2.** uprightness, honesty.

intellect [ɛ̃telɛkt] *n.m.* intellect.

intellectualisme [ɛ̃telɛktɥalism] *n.m.* intellectualism.

intellectualiste [ɛ̃telɛktɥalist] *a. & n.* intellectualist.

intellectualité [ɛ̃telɛktɥalite] *n.f. Lit:* intellectuality.

intellectuel, -elle [ɛ̃telɛktɥɛl] **1.** *a.* intellectual; mental (fatigue, etc.); *Pej:* highbrow. **2.** *n.* intellectual; *Pej:* highbrow.

intellectuellement [ɛ̃telɛktɥɛlmɑ̃] *adv.* intellectually.

intelligemment [ɛ̃teliʒamɑ̃] *adv.* intelligently.

intelligence [ɛ̃teliʒɑ̃s] *n.f.* **1.** understanding, comprehension; **avoir l'i. des affaires,** to have a good knowledge of, a good head for, business; **pour l'i. de ce qui va suivre,** in order to understand what follows. **2.** intelligence, intellect; brainpower; mind; **aiguiser l'i. de qn,** to sharpen s.o.'s wits. **3.** (*a*) **vivre en bonne, mauvaise, i. avec qn,** to be on good, bad, terms with s.o.; **être d'i. avec qn,** to have an understanding, be in collusion, with s.o.; (*b*) *pl.* **entretenir des intelligences avec qn,** to keep up a secret correspondence with s.o.; **avoir des intelligences avec l'ennemi,** to have (secret) dealings with the enemy.

intelligent [ɛ̃teliʒɑ̃] *a.* intelligent; bright, clever; *F:* brainy.

intelligibilité [ɛ̃teliʒibilite] *n.f.* intelligibility.

intelligible [ɛ̃teliʒibl̥] *a.* (*a*) intelligible, understandable; (*b*) clear, distinct.

intelligiblement [ɛ̃teliʒibləmɑ̃] *adv.* intelligibly.

intempérance [ɛ̃tɑ̃perɑ̃s] *n.f.* intemperance.

intempérant [ɛ̃tɑ̃perɑ̃] *a.* intemperate.

intempérie [ɛ̃tɑ̃peri] *n.f.* **1.** *A:* inclemency (of weather). **2.** *pl.* bad weather; **exposé aux intempéries,** exposed to the elements.

intempestif, -ive [ɛ̃tɑ̃pɛstif, -iv] *a.* untimely, ill-timed; unreasonable, inopportune (remark).

intemporel, -elle [ɛ̃tɑ̃pɔrɛl] *a.* (*a*) timeless; (*b*) immaterial.

intenable [ɛ̃t(ə)nabl̥] *a.* (*a*) untenable (position, etc.); (*b*) intolerable, unbearable (heat); *F:* **enfant i.,** uncontrollable child.

intendance [ɛ̃tɑ̃dɑ̃s] *n.f.* **1.** *A:* intendance; stewardship, managership (of estate). **2.** *Sch:* bursary. **3.** *Fr.Hist:* administration (of province). **4.** *Mil:* the Commissariat.

intendant [ɛ̃tɑ̃dɑ̃] *n.m.* **1.** *A:* intendant; steward, manager (of estate). **2.** *Sch:* bursar. **3.** *Fr.Hist:* administrator (of province). **4.** *Mil:* senior Commissariat officer. **5.** *n.f.* **intendante** (*a*) *A:* intendant's, steward's, wife; (*b*) *Sch:* (woman) bursar; (*c*) *Fr.Hist:* wife of the administrator (of province); (*d*) *Ecc:* Mother Superior (of certain convents).

intense [ɛ̃tɑ̃s] *a.* intense; severe (pain); heavy (gunfire); deep (blue); **temps d'un froid i.,** intensely cold weather; **circulation i.,** dense, heavy, traffic.

intensément [ɛ̃tɑ̃semɑ̃] *adv.* intensely.

intensif, -ive [ɛ̃tɑ̃sif, -iv] *a.* intensive.

intensifier [ɛ̃tɑ̃sifje] *v.tr.* to intensify.

intensité [ɛ̃tɑ̃site] *n.f.* **1.** intensity, intenseness; force (of wind); depth (of colour, *NAm:* color); severity (of cold); strength (of current); density (of magnetic field). **2.** *Ling:* **accent d'i.,** stress.

intensivement [ɛ̃tɑ̃sivmɑ̃] *adv.* intensively.

intenter [ɛ̃tɑ̃te] *v.tr. Jur:* **i. une action, un procès, à, contre, qn,** to bring an action, institute proceedings, against s.o.

intention [ɛ̃tɑ̃sjɔ̃] *n.f.* intention; (*a*) purpose, design; *Jur:* intent; **avec i. délictueuse,** with malicious intent; **sans mauvaise i.,** with no ill intent; **avoir l'i. de faire qch.,** to intend, mean, to do sth.; **je n'ai nullement l'i. d'accepter,** I have no intention of accepting; **il a de bonnes intentions,** he means well; **dans l'i. de faire qch.,** with a view to, with the intention of, doing sth.; (*b*) will, wish; *Prov:* **l'enfer est pavé de bonnes intentions,** the road to hell is paved with good intentions; **à l'i. de,** in honour, *NAm:* honor, of; for the sake of; in aid of; **voici une écharpe que j'ai achetée à votre i.,** here's a scarf I bought especially for you; **livres écrits à l'i. des enfants,** books for children.

intentionné [ɛ̃tɑ̃sjɔne] *a.* (*a*) **bien, mal, i.,** well, ill, disposed (**envers,** towards); **mieux i.,** better disposed; (*b*) **personne, démarche, bien intentionnée,** well intentioned person, step; well meaning person.

intentionnel, -elle [ɛ̃tɑ̃sjɔnɛl] *a.* intentional, wilful, deliberate.

intentionnellement [ɛ̃tɑ̃sjɔnɛlmɑ̃] *adv.* intentionally.

inter [ɛ̃tɛr] *n.m.* **1.** *Fb:* **i. droit, gauche,** inside right, left. **2.** *Tp:* trunk (line).

interaction [ɛ̃tɛraksjɔ̃] *n.f.* interaction.

interallié [ɛ̃tɛralje] *a.* interallied.

interarmes [ɛ̃tɛrarm] *a.inv. Mil:* combined (staff, operation, etc.).

interastral, -aux [ɛ̃tɛrastral, -o] *a.* interstellar.

intercalaire [ɛ̃tɛrkalɛr] *a.* **1.** intercalary (day, year, etc.). **2.** *Bookb:* **feuille i.,** interpolated sheet; **feuillet i.,** inset. **3. carte i.,** guide (card) (of card index, etc.).

intercalation [ɛ̃tɛrkalasjɔ̃] *n.f.* intercalation, interpolation, insertion; *El:* switching in (of resistance).

intercaler [ɛ̃tɛrkale] *v.tr.* to intercalate (day in year, etc.); to interpolate, insert; *El:* to cut in, switch in (resistance); **i. des citations dans un discours,** to intersperse, sprinkle, a speech with quotations.

intercéder [ɛ̃tɛrsede] *v.tr.* (*conj. like* CÉDER) to intercede (**auprès de,** with).

intercepter [ɛ̃tɛrsɛpte] *v.tr.* to intercept (letter, aircraft, etc.); to shut, cut, out, off.

intercepteur [ɛ̃tɛrsɛptœr] *n.m. Av:* interceptor.

interception [ɛ̃tɛrsɛpsjɔ̃] *n.f.* interception; cutting, shutting, out, off; *W.Tel:* **i. des émissions,** monitoring; **opérateur d'i.,** monitor; **avion d'i.,** interceptor (aircraft).

intercesseur [ɛ̃tɛrsesœr] *n.m.* intercessor; mediator.

intercession [ɛ̃tɛrsesjɔ̃] *n.f.* intercession.

interchangeable [ɛ̃tɛrʃɑ̃ʒabl̩] *a.* interchangeable.

interclasse [ɛ̃tɛrklas] *n.m. Sch:* (short) break (between classes).

intercommunication [ɛ̃tɛrkɔmynikasjɔ̃] *n.f.* intercommunication.

interconnexion [ɛ̃tɛrkɔnɛksjɔ̃] *n.f. El:* interconnection.

intercontinental, -aux [ɛ̃tɛrkɔ̃tinɑ̃tal, -o] *a.* intercontinental; **fusée intercontinentale,** intercontinental ballistic missile.

intercostal, -aux [ɛ̃tɛrkɔstal, -o] *a. & n.m. Anat:* intercostal (muscle).

interdépartemental, -aux [ɛ̃tɛrdepartəmɑ̃tal, -o] *a.* interdepartmental.

interdépendance [ɛ̃tɛrdepɑ̃dɑ̃s] *n.f.* interdependence.

interdépendant [ɛ̃tɛrdepɑ̃dɑ̃] *a.* interdependent.

interdiction [ɛ̃tɛrdiksjɔ̃] *n.f.* interdiction. **1.** prohibition, forbidding; **i. des essais atomiques,** atomic test ban. **2.** *Jur:* (*a*) state of minority declared by court; deprival of control over money; **i. d'un aliéné,** certifying of an insane person; (*b*) **i. légale,** suspension, (temporary) deprivation, of civil rights.

interdigital, -aux [ɛ̃tɛrdiʒital, -o] *a.* interdigital.

interdire [ɛ̃tɛrdir] **1.** *v.tr.* (*conj. like* DIRE, except *pr.ind.* **v. interdisez** and *imp.* **interdisez**) (*a*) to forbid, prohibit; to bar, ban; **i. qch. à qn,** to forbid s.o. sth.; **la passerelle est interdite aux voyageurs,** passengers are not allowed on the bridge; **il nous est interdit de révéler . . .,** we are not allowed to reveal . . .; **(il est) interdit de fumer,** no smoking; *P.N:* **entrée interdite (au public),** no admittance; *P.N:* **passage interdit,** no thoroughfare; **i. à qn de faire qch.,** to prohibit s.o. from doing sth., to forbid s.o. to do sth.; **i. à un pilote de voler,** to ground a pilot; (*b*) to suspend (s.o.) (from his post); *Jur:* **faire i. qn,** to have s.o. declared incapable of managing his own affairs. **2. s'i. qch.,** to give sth. up; to refrain from sth.; **il s'interdit d'y penser,** he doesn't let himself think about it.

interdit, -e [ɛ̃tɛrdi, -it] **1.** *a.* disconcerted, nonplussed, bewildered; taken aback. **2.** *n. Jur:* **(aliéné) i.,** certified person; **i. de séjour,** ex-convict prohibited from entering a certain area. **3.** *n.m. Ecc:* interdict; **frapper qn d'i.,** to lay s.o. under an interdict.

intéressant [ɛ̃teresɑ̃] *a.* interesting; **peu i.,** dull, uninteresting; **chercher à se rendre i.,** to try to make oneself interesting, to draw attention to oneself; **prix intéressants,** attractive, advantageous, prices.

intéressé [ɛ̃terese] *a.* **1. les parties intéressées,** *n.* **les intéressés,** the interested parties, the persons concerned, involved; **les premiers intéressés,** those most directly affected; **c'est vous le premier i.,** you are the most closely concerned. **2.** selfish, self-seeking; **amour i.,** cupboard love; **agir dans un but i.,** to have an axe to grind.

intéressement [ɛ̃terɛsmɑ̃] *n.m. Com: Ind:* profit(-)sharing (scheme).

intéresser [ɛ̃terese] **1.** *v.tr.* to interest; (*a*) **i. qn dans son commerce,** to give s.o. a financial interest, a partnership, in the business; **i. les employés (aux bénéfices),** to initiate a profit-sharing scheme; (*b*) to affect, concern; **question qui intéresse le monde entier,** question of worldwide interest; (*c*) to be interesting to (s.o.); **sujet qui m'intéresse beaucoup,** subject which interests me greatly; **ceci peut vous i.,** this may be of interest to you; (*d*) **i. qn à une cause,** to interest s.o. in a cause. **2. s'i.** (*a*) **s'i. dans une affaire,** to acquire a financial interest in, put money into, a business; (*b*) **s'i. à qn, à qch.,** to take an interest in s.o., sth.; to be interested in s.o., sth.

intérêt [ɛ̃terɛ] *n.m.* interest. **1.** share, stake (in business, etc.); **avoir un i. au jeu,** to have a stake in the game. **2.** advantage, benefit; **il y a i. à . . .,** it is desirable to . . .; **j'ai i. à le faire,** it's in my interest to do it; **agir dans son i.,** to act in, for, one's own interest; **i. personnel,** self interest; **il a fait un mariage d'i.,** he married for money; **il sait où se trouve son i.,** he knows where his advantage lies, *F:* which side his bread is buttered; **l'i. public,** public interest; *Rail:* **ligne d'i. local,** branch line, local line. **3.** (feeling of) interest; **ressentir de l'i. pour qn,** to feel interested in s.o.; **prendre de l'i. à qch.,** to take an interest in sth.; **livre sans i., dépourvu d'i.,** uninteresting book. **4.** *Fin:* **i. simple, composé,** simple, compound, interest; **placer son argent à 12% d'i.,** to invest one's money at 12% interest; **prêt à i.,** loan bearing interest; **intérêt(s) couru(s),** accrued interest; *St.Exch:* **i. de report,** contango.

interface [ɛ̃tɛrfas] *n.f. Cmptr: etc:* interface.

interférence [ɛ̃tɛrferɑ̃s] *n.f. Ph: W.Tel: etc:* interference.

interférent [ɛ̃tɛrferɑ̃] *a. Ph:* interfering (rays, etc.).

interférer [ɛ̃tɛrfere] *v.i.* **(il interfère; il interférait; il interférera) 1.** *Ph:* (*of light waves, etc.*) to interfere. **2.** (*of plans, etc.*) to interfere with each other.

interféron [ɛ̃tɛrferɔ̃] *n.m. Biol:* interferon.

interfolier [ɛ̃tɛrfɔlje] *v.tr.* to interleave, interpage.

intergouvernemental, -aux [ɛ̃tɛrguvɛrnəmɑ̃tal, -o] *a.* intergovernmental.

intérieur [ɛ̃terjœr] **1.** *a.* (*a*) interior, inner (room); inside (pocket); internal (part); inland (sea); **cour intérieure,** inner courtyard; (*b*) inward (feelings); **vie intérieure,** inner life; (*c*) domestic (administration); **commerce i.,** home trade, inland trade; **le Ministère de l'I.** = the Home Office; *Post:* **(tarif d')affranchissement en régime i.,** inland postage rate. **2.** *n.m.* (*a*) interior, inside; **à l'i.,** inside, on the inside; indoors; **à l'i. de la gare,** inside the station; **la porte était verrouillée à l'i.,** the door was bolted on, from, the inside; **une voix à l'i.,** a voice from (the) inside; **l'i. du pays,** the interior of the country; **dans l'i. du pays,** inland; (*b*) home, house; **vie d'i.,** home life, domestic life; **femme d'i.,** domesticated woman; **vêtements d'i.,** indoor clothes. **3.** *n.m. Fb:* **i. gauche, droit,** inside left, right.

intérieurement [ɛ̃terjœrmɑ̃] *adv.* inwardly, internally, inside, within; **rire i.,** to laugh to oneself.

interim [ɛ̃terim] *n.m.* interim; **dans l'i.,** in the interim, (in the) meanwhile; *Fin:* **dividende par i.,** interim dividend; **secrétaire par i.,** interim secretary; temporary secretary; **assurer l'i. (de qn),** to deputize, stand in (for s.o.); to act as locum (tenens).

intérimaire [ɛ̃terimɛr] **1.** *a.* temporary, provisional (duty, official, etc.); *Pol:* **cabinet i.,** caretaker cabinet; **directeur i.,** acting manager; **dividende, rapport, i.,** interim dividend, report. **2.** *n.* deputy; locum (tenens); *F:* temporary.

intériorisation [ɛ̃terjɔrizasjɔ̃] *n.f.* interiorization.

intérioriser [ɛ̃terjɔrize] *v.tr.* to interiorize.

interjectif, -ive [ɛ̃tɛrʒɛktif, -iv] *a.* interjectional.

interjection [ɛ̃tɛrʒɛksjɔ̃] *n.f.* **1.** *Gram:* interjection. **2.** *Jur:* lodging (of an appeal).

interjeter [ɛ̃tɛrʒəte] *v.tr.* (*conj. like* JETER) *Jur:* **i. appel (d'un jugement),** to lodge an appeal, give notice of appeal.

interlignage [ɛ̃tɛrliɲaʒ] *n.m. Typ:* leading out.

interligne [ɛ̃tɛrliɲ] **1.** *n.m.* space between two lines; *Typewr:* spacing; *Mus:* space (on the stave); **dans les interlignes,** between the lines; *Typewr:* **écrit à simple, double, i.,** typed in single, double, spacing. **2.** *n.f. Typ:* lead.

interligner [ɛ̃tɛrliɲe] *v.tr.* **1.** to write between the lines of (a text); to interline. **2.** *Typ:* to lead out.

interlinéaire [ɛ̃tɛrlineɛr] *a.* interlinear (notes, etc.).

interlocuteur, -trice [ɛ̃tɛrlɔkytœr, -tris] *n.* interlocutor, *f.* interlocutress; speaker (engaged in conversation).

interlocutoire [ɛ̃tɛrlɔkytwar] *Jur:* **1.** *a.* interlocutory. **2.** *n.m.* interlocutory judgement.

interlope [ɛ̃tɛrlɔp] *a.* (*a*) unauthorized, illegal (trade); (*b*) suspect, dubious, shady (house, etc.).

interloquer [ɛ̃tɛrlɔke] *v.tr.* to disconcert, nonplus (s.o.); to take (s.o.) aback.

interlude [ɛ̃tɛrlyd] *n.m. Mus: Th:* interlude.

intermède [ɛ̃tɛrmɛd] *n.m.* **1.** *Th:* interlude. **2.** interval; interruption; interlude.

intermédiaire [ɛ̃tɛrmedjɛr] **1.** *a.* intermediate, intermediary, intervening (state, time, etc.); *Mec.E:* **arbre i.,** countershaft. **2.** *n.* agent, intermediary, go-between; *Com:* middleman. **3.** *n.m.* intermediary, agency; **par l'i. de qn,** through, by means of, s.o.; **par l'i. de la presse,** through the medium of the press; **sans i.,** without transition, directly.

intermezzo [ɛ̃tɛrmɛdzo] *n.m. Mus:* intermezzo.

interminable [ɛ̃tɛrminabl̩] *a.* interminable; endless; never-ending.

interminablement [ɛ̃tɛrminabləmɑ̃] *adv.* interminably; endlessly.

interministériel, -ielle [ɛ̃tɛrministerjɛl] *a.* interministerial.

intermission [ɛ̃tɛrmisjɔ̃] *n.f. Med:* intermission.

intermittence [ɛ̃tɛrmitɑ̃s] *n.f.* (*a*) intermittency, intermittence; (*b*) *Med:* remission.

intermittent [ɛ̃tɛrmitɑ̃] *a.* intermittent; irregular (pulse); **travail i.,** casual work; *El:* **courant i.,** make-and-break current.

intermoléculaire [ɛ̃tɛrmɔlekylɛr] *a.* intermolecular.

internat [ɛ̃tɛrna] *n.m.* **1.** (*a*) living-in (system, period); *Sch:* boarding; (*b*) *Med:* resident medical studentship. **2.** boarding school. **3.** boarders.

international, -ale, -aux [ɛ̃tɛrnasjɔnal, -o] **1.** *a.* international. **2.** (*a*) *n. Sp:* international (player); (*b*) *n.f.* **l'Internationale,** the International(e) (society, hymn).

internationalement [ɛ̃tɛrnasjɔnalmɑ̃] *adv.* internationally.

internationalisation [ɛ̃tɛrnasjɔnalizasjɔ̃] *n.f.* internationalization.

internationaliser [ɛ̃tɛrnasjɔnalize] *v.tr.* to internationalize.

internationalisme [ɛ̃tɛrnasjɔnalism] *n.m.* internationalism.

internationaliste [ɛ̃tɛrnasjɔnalist] *a. & n.* internationalist.

internationalité [ɛ̃tɛrnasjɔnalite] *n.f.* internationality.

interne [ɛ̃tɛrn] **1.** *a.* (*a*) internal; inward (purity, etc.); inner (side); *Mth:* interior (angle); *Gram:* **accusatif i.,** cognate accusative; (*b*) *Sch:* **élève i.,** boarder. **2.** *n.* (*a*) *Sch:* boarder; (*b*) *Med:* house physician, houseman, *NAm:* intern.

interné, -ée [ɛ̃tɛrne] **1.** *a.* interned. **2.** *n.* internee.

internement [ɛ̃tɛrnəmɑ̃] *n.m.* internment (of alien); confinement (of the mentally ill).

interner [ɛ̃tɛrne] *v.tr.* to intern (alien, etc.); to shut up, confine (the mentally ill).

interocéanique [ɛ̃tɛrɔseanik] *a.* interoceanic.

interparlementaire [ɛ̃tɛrparləmɑ̃tɛr] *a. Pol:* interparliamentary; **commission i.,** joint committee.

interpellateur, -trice [ɛ̃tɛrpelatœr, -tris] *n.* interpellator; heckler.

interpellation [ɛ̃tɛrpelasjɔ̃] *n.f.* **1.** (*a*) question; (*b*) questioning; interpellation, interruption (at meeting, etc.); heckling. **2.** challenge (by sentry).

interpeller [ɛ̃tɛrpele] *v.tr.* **1.** to call upon (s.o.), challenge (s.o.); to heckle (s.o.); **les deux automobilistes s'interpellaient grossièrement,** the two drivers were exchanging insults. **2.** *Fr.Pol:* to put a question to (a minister, etc.); to interpellate.

interpénétration [ɛ̃tɛrpenetrasjɔ̃] *n.f. Pol.Ec: etc:* interpenetration.

interpénétrer (s') [sɛ̃tɛrpenetre] *v.pr.* to interpenetrate; **ces deux facteurs s'interpénètrent,** these two factors are interdependent.
interphone [ɛ̃tɛrfɔn] *n.m.* intercom.
interplanétaire [ɛ̃tɛrplanetɛr] *a.* interplanetary; **voyage i.,** space flight.
interpolateur, -trice [ɛ̃tɛrpɔlatœr, -tris] *n.* interpolater.
interpolation [ɛ̃tɛrpɔlasjɔ̃] *n.f.* interpolation.
interpoler [ɛ̃tɛrpɔle] *v.tr.* to interpolate.
interposer [ɛ̃tɛrpoze] **1.** *v.tr.* to interpose, place. **2. s'i.,** to interpose, intervene; to come between.
interposition [ɛ̃tɛrpozisjɔ̃] *n.f.* **1.** interposition. **2.** intervention.
interprétable [ɛ̃tɛrpretabl̩] *a.* interpretable.
interprétariat [ɛ̃tɛrpretarja] *n.m.* interpretership.
interprétatif, -ive [ɛ̃tɛrpretatif, -iv] *a.* interpretative, explanatory (note, etc.).
interprétation [ɛ̃tɛrpretasjɔ̃] *n.f.* **1.** interpreting (of speech, etc.). **2.** interpretation; (*a*) **fausse i.,** misinterpretation, misconstruction (of statement); **donner une fausse i. d'un passage,** to misinterpret a passage; (*b*) *Mus: Th:* rendering, rendition.
interprète [ɛ̃tɛrprɛt] *n.* **1.** interpreter; **servir d'i. à qn,** to act as interpreter to s.o. **2.** exponent (of text, etc.); interpreter, performer (of music, theatrical part, etc.); *Th:* **les interprètes,** the cast.
interpréter [ɛ̃tɛrprete] *v.tr.* **(j'interprète; j'interpréterai)** to interpret; (*a*) to act as interpreter; **i. un discours,** to interpret a speech; (*b*) to explain, expound (text, etc.); **mal i. les paroles de qn,** misinterpret s.o.'s words; **i. des signaux,** to read signals; **mal i. un signal,** to misread a signal; (*c*) *Mus: Th:* to render, perform (work, part).
interprofessionnel, -elle [ɛ̃tɛrprɔfɛsjɔnɛl] *a.* interprofessional.
interrègne [ɛ̃tɛrrɛɲ] *n.m.* interregnum.
interrogateur, -trice [ɛ̃tɛrɔgatœr, -tris] **1.** *a.* interrogatory, inquiring, questioning. **2.** *n.* questioner, interrogator; *Sch:* (oral) examiner.
interrogatif, -ive [ɛ̃tɛrɔgatif, -iv] **1.** *a.* inquiring, questioning (look, etc.); interrogative. **2.** *a. & n. Gram:* interrogative (pronoun, sentence, etc.).
interrogation [ɛ̃tɛrɔgasjɔ̃] *n.f.* interrogation. **1.** questioning; *Gram:* **point d'i.,** question mark. **2.** question, query; **i. orale, écrite,** oral, written, test.
interrogativement [ɛ̃tɛrɔgativmɑ̃] *adv.* interrogatively.
interrogatoire [ɛ̃tɛrɔgatwar] *n.m.* (*a*) *Jur:* interrogatory, (cross-)examination (of defendant, etc.); (*b*) interrogation, questioning (of prisoners, etc.).
interroger [ɛ̃tɛrɔʒe] **1.** *v.tr.* **(j'interrogeai(s); n. interrogeons)** (*a*) to (cross-)examine, interrogate, question (witness, etc.); to examine (candidate); **i. qn du regard,** to look at s.o. inquiringly, give s.o. a questioning look; (*b*) to consult (history, etc.); to sound (one's conscience). **2. s'i.,** to ask oneself, to wonder (**sur,** about; **si,** whether, if).
interrompre [ɛ̃tɛrɔ̃pr̩] (*conj. like* ROMPRE) **1.** *v.tr.* (*a*) to interrupt; to cut in; **veuillez bien ne pas nous i.,** please don't interrupt; **i. la conversation,** to break in on the conversation; (*b*) to intercept, interrupt (flow of river, etc.); (*c*) to stop, suspend (traffic, etc.); to cut short (s.o., conversation); to break off (negotiations); to break (journey); *El:* to break, switch off (current). **2. s'i.,** to break off; to stop (talking).
interrompu [ɛ̃tɛrɔ̃py] *a.* interrupted, broken off; **sommeil i.,** broken sleep.
interrupteur, -trice [ɛ̃tɛryptœr, -tris] **1.** *n.* interrupter. **2.** *n.m. El:* (*a*) switch; circuit breaker, contact breaker; **i. marche-arrêt,** on-off switch; **i. à bascule,** toggle switch; **i. à gradation de lumière,** dimmer (switch); **i. d'escalier,** two-way switch; (*b*) cut-out.
interruption [ɛ̃tɛrypsjɔ̃] *n.f.* (*a*) interruption; breaking in (on conversation); (*b*) stoppage, break; severance (of communication, etc.); breaking off (of negotiations); *El:* disconnection, switching off; breaking (of current); **sans i.,** unceasingly; without a break; uninterruptedly.
interscolaire [ɛ̃tɛrskɔlɛr] *a.* inter-school.
intersecté [ɛ̃tɛrsɛkte] *a.* **1.** *Arch:* intersecting, interlacing. **2.** *Mth:* intersected (line, etc.).
intersection [ɛ̃tɛrsɛksjɔ̃] *n.f.* intersection; **point d'i.,** point of intersection.
intersidéral, -aux [ɛ̃tɛrsideral, -o] *a.* intersidereal, interstellar; **course intersidérale,** space race.
interstellaire [ɛ̃tɛrstelɛr] *a. Astr:* interstellar.
interstice [ɛ̃tɛrstis] *n.m.* interstice; chink.
intertropical, -aux [ɛ̃tɛrtrɔpikal, -o] *a.* intertropical.
interurbain [ɛ̃tɛryrbɛ̃] **1.** *a.* interurban; *Tp:* **lignes interurbaines,** trunk lines. **2.** *n.m. Tp:* trunk (line).
intervalle [ɛ̃tɛrval] *n.m.* interval. **1.** distance, gap, space. **2.** period (of time); **visites à de longs intervalles,** visits at long intervals; **par intervalles,** at intervals; now and then; **dans l'i.,** in the meantime.
intervenant, -ante [ɛ̃tɛrvənɑ̃, -ɑ̃t] *Jur:* **1.** *a.* intervening. **2.** *n.* intervening party.
intervenir [ɛ̃tɛrvənir] *v.i.* (*conj. like* VENIR; *aux.* **être**) **1.** to intervene; (*a*) to interpose; to step in; **i. dans une conversation,** to break in on a conversation; to butt in; **faire i. la force armée,** to call out the military, bring in the army; (*b*) to interfere. **2.** to happen, take place; to occur, arise; **un accord est intervenu,** an agreement has been reached. **3.** *Med:* to operate.
intervention [ɛ̃tɛrvɑ̃sjɔ̃] *n.f.* **1.** intervening, intervention; **i. chirurgicale,** surgical operation; **offre d'i.,** offer of mediation; **i. parlementaire,** sponsoring of claims, of applications (by members of Parliament); *Mil.Av:* **i. aérienne,** air strike. **2.** interference.
interventionnisme [ɛ̃tɛrvɑ̃sjɔnism] *n.m. Pol: etc:* interventionism.
interversion [ɛ̃tɛrvɛrsjɔ̃] *n.f.* inversion, transposition, reversal (of order, dates, etc.).
intervertébral, -aux [ɛ̃tɛrvɛrtebral, -o] *a. Anat:* intervertebral; **disque i.,** (intervertebral) disc.
intervertir [ɛ̃tɛrvɛrtir] *v.tr.* to invert, transpose; to reverse (the order of sth.); **maintenant les rôles sont intervertis,** now the tables are turned.
interview [ɛ̃tɛrvju] *n.f.* interview.
interviewé, -ée [ɛ̃tɛrvjuve] *n.* interviewee.
interviewer [ɛ̃tɛrvjuve] *v.tr.* to interview.
interviewe(u)r [ɛ̃tɛrvjuvœr] *n.m.* interviewer.
intervocalique [ɛ̃tɛrvɔkalik] *a. Ling:* intervocalic.
intestat [ɛ̃tɛsta] *a.inv. Jur:* **mourir i.,** to die intestate.
intestin¹ [ɛ̃tɛstɛ̃] *a.* internal; domestic, civil (war, etc.).
intestin² *n.m. Anat:* **intestin(s),** intestine(s); **gros i.,** large intestine; **i. grêle,** small intestine.
intestinal, -aux [ɛ̃tɛstinal, -o] *a.* intestinal.
intimation [ɛ̃timasjɔ̃] *n.f. Jur:* notification (of an order); **i. de vider les lieux,** notice to quit.
intime [ɛ̃tim] **1.** *a.* intimate; (*a*) interior; inward, deep-seated (grief, etc.); **pensées intimes,** inmost, innermost, thoughts; **sens i. d'un passage,** inner meaning of a passage; (*b*) close (relations); cosy (room); **ami i.,** particular, intimate, close, friend; **dîner i.,** quiet dinner; dinner between old friends; (*c*) personal (hygiene); (*d*) private (secretary). **2.** *n.* intimate friend, close friend, bosom friend.
intimé, -ée [ɛ̃time] *n. Jur:* respondent, defendant.
intimement [ɛ̃timmɑ̃] *adv.* intimately.
intimer [ɛ̃time] *v.tr.* **1. i. qch. à qn,** to intimate sth. to s.o.; to notify s.o. of sth.; **i. à qn l'ordre de partir,** to give s.o. notice to go. **2.** *Jur:* **i. qn,** to summons s.o. to appear before the Court of Appeal.

intimidable [ɛ̃timidabl̥] *a.* easily intimidated.
intimidant [ɛ̃timidɑ̃] *a.* intimidating, awe-inspiring.
intimidateur, -trice [ɛ̃timidatœr, -tris] *a.* intimidating.
intimidation [ɛ̃timidasjɔ̃] *n.f.* intimidation; threatening; *esp. Jur:* undue influence.
intimider [ɛ̃timide] *v.tr.* (*a*) to intimidate, frighten; **nullement intimidé,** nothing daunted; (*b*) *esp. Jur:* to threaten; to exert undue influence on (s.o.).
intimisme [ɛ̃timism] *n.m. Lit: Art:* intimism.
intimiste [ɛ̃timist] *a. & n. Lit: Art:* intimist.
intimité [ɛ̃timite] *n.f.* **1.** in(ner)most parts, depths (of one's being, etc.); **dans l'i. de sa conscience,** in one's inner conscience. **2.** intimacy; (*a*) close connection (between actions, etc.); (*b*) closeness (of friendship); (*c*) **l'i. du chez-soi,** the privacy of one's home; **dans l'i.,** in private (life); **le mariage a été célébré dans la plus stricte i.,** it was a very quiet wedding.
intitulé [ɛ̃tityle] *n.m.* title (of document, book, etc.); heading (of chapter, etc.).
intituler [ɛ̃tityle] **1.** *v.tr.* to entitle, give a title to (book, etc.); **article intitulé . . .,** article headed . . .. **2. s'i.,** to be entitled; *often Pej:* to call oneself.
intolérable [ɛ̃tɔlerabl̥] *a.* intolerable, insufferable, unbearable; **vie i.,** life that is not worth living.
intolérablement [ɛ̃tɔlerabləmɑ̃] *adv.* intolerably.
intolérance [ɛ̃tɔlerɑ̃s] *n.f.* intolerance.
intolérant [ɛ̃tɔlerɑ̃] *a.* intolerant (**de,** of).
intonation [ɛ̃tɔnasjɔ̃] *n.f.* intonation.
intouchable [ɛ̃tuʃabl̥] *a. & n.* untouchable.
intoxicant [ɛ̃tɔksikɑ̃] *a. Med:* poisonous, toxic.
intoxication [ɛ̃tɔksikasjɔ̃] *n.f. Med:* intoxication, poisoning; **i. alimentaire,** food poisoning.
intoxiquer [ɛ̃tɔksike] **1.** *v.tr. Med:* to poison. **2. s'i.,** to poison oneself.
intradermique [ɛ̃tradɛrmik] *a. Anat:* intradermic, intradermal.
intrados [ɛ̃trado] *n.m.* (*a*) *Arch:* inner surface, soffit, intrados (of arch); (*b*) *Av:* under surface (of wing).
intraduisible [ɛ̃tradɥizibl̥] *a.* untranslatable.
intraitable [ɛ̃trɛtabl̥] *a.* intractable; obstinate, uncompromising; inflexible.
intramusculaire [ɛ̃tramyskylɛr] *a.* intramuscular.
intransigeance [ɛ̃trɑ̃ziʒɑ̃s] *n.f.* intransigence.
intransigeant, -ante [ɛ̃trɑ̃ziʒɑ̃, -ɑ̃t] **1.** *a.* intransigent; uncompromising, strict (moral code, etc.); peremptory (tone). **2.** *n. Pol:* intransigent.
intransitif, -ive [ɛ̃trɑ̃zitif, -iv] *a. & n.m. Gram:* intransitive.
intransitivement [ɛ̃trɑ̃zitivmɑ̃] *adv. Gram:* intransitively.
intransmissible [ɛ̃trɑ̃smisibl̥] *a.* intransmissible.
intransportable [ɛ̃trɑ̃spɔrtabl̥] *a.* (*a*) untransportable; (*b*) (*of injured person*) unfit to travel.
intra-utérin [ɛ̃trayterɛ̃] *a. Anat:* intra-uterine; *pl. intra-utérins, -ines.*
intraveineux, -euse [ɛ̃travɛnø, -øz] *a.* intravenous.
intrépide [ɛ̃trepid] *a.* intrepid, dauntless, undaunted, bold, fearless; **menteur i.,** barefaced liar.
intrépidement [ɛ̃trepidmɑ̃] *adv.* intrepidly.
intrépidité [ɛ̃trepidite] *n.f.* intrepidity, dauntlessness, fearlessness; **avec i.,** fearlessly.
intrigant, -ante [ɛ̃trigɑ̃, -ɑ̃t] **1.** *a.* scheming, designing. **2.** *n.* intriguer, schemer.
intrigue [ɛ̃trig] *n.f.* **1.** intrigue; (*a*) plot, scheme; (*b*) (love) affair. **2.** plot (of play, etc.).
intrigué [ɛ̃trige] *a.* intrigued, puzzled, curious, mystified.
intriguer [ɛ̃trige] **1.** *v.tr.* to intrigue, puzzle (s.o.). **2.** *v.i.* to scheme, plot, intrigue.
intrinsèque [ɛ̃trɛ̃sɛk] *a.* intrinsic; specific (value).
intrinsèquement [ɛ̃trɛ̃sɛkmɑ̃] *adv.* intrinsically.
introducteur, -trice [ɛ̃trɔdyktœr, -tris] *n.* (*a*) introducer; innovator (of fashion, etc.); (*b*) usher (at reception).
introductif, -ive [ɛ̃trɔdyktif, -iv] *a. Jur:* introductory.
introduction [ɛ̃trɔdyksjɔ̃] *n.f.* introduction. **1.** (*a*) insertion (of probe in wound, etc.); *Mch:* admission, induction (of steam, gas, etc.); (*b*) introducing, bringing in (of s.o. into s.o.'s presence, etc.); **lettre d'i.,** letter of introduction (**de la part de,** from; **auprès de,** to). **2.** introductory matter, chapter; **après quelques mots d'i.,** after a few introductory words.
introduire [ɛ̃trɔdɥir] **1.** *v.tr.* (*pr.p.* **introduisant;** *p.p.* **introduit;** *pr.ind.* **j'introduis, il introduit, n. introduisons;** *p.h.* **j'introduisis;** *fu.* **j'introduirai**) to introduce; (*a*) to insert, put (key in lock, etc.); (*b*) to bring in (goods, etc.); to admit, let in (steam, etc.); to launch (a fashion); (*c*) to usher in, show in (stranger, etc.); **introduisez ce monsieur,** show the gentleman in. **2. s'i.,** to get in, enter; **s'i. dans qch.,** to work, worm, one's way into sth.; **l'eau s'introduit partout,** the water is penetrating, creeping in, everywhere.
intromission [ɛ̃trɔmisjɔ̃] *n.f.* intromission.
intronisation [ɛ̃trɔnizasjɔ̃] *n.f.* **1.** enthroning, enthronement (*esp.* of bishop). **2.** establishment (of system, etc.).
introniser [ɛ̃trɔnize] *v.tr.* **1.** to enthrone (king, bishop). **2.** to set up, establish (new religion, etc.).
introspectif, -ive [ɛ̃trɔspɛktif, -iv] *a.* introspective.
introspection [ɛ̃trɔspɛksjɔ̃] *n.f.* introspection.
introuvable [ɛ̃truvabl̥] *a.* not to be found; unobtainable; untraceable; **l'assassin reste i.,** the murderer remains undiscovered.
introversion [ɛ̃trɔvɛrsjɔ̃] *n.f. Psy:* introversion.
introverti, -ie [ɛ̃trɔvɛrti] *Psy:* **1.** *a.* introverted. **2.** *n.* introvert.
intrus, -use [ɛ̃try, -yz] **1.** *a.* intruding. **2.** *n.* intruder; *F:* gatecrasher; *Jur:* trespasser.
intrusion [ɛ̃tryzjɔ̃] *n.f.* (*a*) intrusion; interference (in a matter); (*b*) *Geol:* **roches d'i.,** intrusive rocks.
intuitif, -ive [ɛ̃tɥitif, -iv] *a.* intuitive.
intuition [ɛ̃tɥisjɔ̃] *n.f.* intuition; **par i.,** intuitively.
intuitivement [ɛ̃tɥitivmɑ̃] *adv.* intuitively.
inusable [inyzabl̥] *a.* hard-wearing; everlasting.
inusité [inyzite] *a.* (*a*) unusual; (*b*) uncommon, not in common use.
inutile [inytil] *a.* (*a*) useless, unavailing, unprofitable; vain (effort); **je suis i. ici,** I'm (of) no use here; (*b*) needless, unnecessary; **c'est i.!** (i) it's no good! (ii) you needn't bother; **i. de dire que . . .,** needless to say . . .; **i. d'attendre,** it's no good waiting.
inutilement [inytilmɑ̃] *adv.* (*a*) uselessly; in vain; (*b*) needlessly, unnecessarily.
inutilisable [inytilizabl̥] *a.* unserviceable, unusable.
inutilisé [inytilize] *a.* unutilized, unused; untapped (resources).
inutilité [inytilite] *n.f.* (*a*) uselessness; (*b*) needlessness.
invaincu [ɛ̃vɛ̃ky] *a.* unconquered; unvanquished; unbeaten.
invalidation [ɛ̃validasjɔ̃] *n.f. Jur:* invalidation (of document, election, etc.); unseating (of elected member).
invalide [ɛ̃valid] **1.** *a.* invalid, infirm; disabled (soldier, etc.). **2.** *n.* disabled person; invalid.
invalider [ɛ̃valide] *v.tr. Jur:* to invalidate (will, election, etc.); to quash (election); to unseat (elected member).
invalidité [ɛ̃validite] *n.f.* (*a*) infirmity; disablement, disability; (*b*) chronic ill health.
invariabilité [ɛ̃varjabilite] *n.f.* invariability.

invariable [ɛ̃varjabl̥] *a.* invariable, unvarying.
invariablement [ɛ̃varjabləmɑ̃] *adv.* invariably.
invasion [ɛ̃vazjɔ̃] *n.f.* invasion; inroad; infestation (by vermin, etc.).
invective [ɛ̃vɛktiv] *n.f.* (*a*) invective; (*b*) *pl.* abuse.
invectiver [ɛ̃vɛktive] **1.** *v.i.* **i. contre qn,** to inveigh, rail, against s.o. **2.** *v.tr.* to hurl abuse at, abuse (s.o.).
invendable [ɛ̃vɑ̃dabl̥] *a.* unsaleable, unmarketable.
invendu [ɛ̃vɑ̃dy] **1.** *a.* unsold. **2.** *n.m.pl.* **invendus,** unsold goods; unsold copies (of newspapers, etc.).
inventaire [ɛ̃vɑ̃tɛr] *n.m.* inventory; (*a*) **faire, dresser, un i.,** to draw up, make, an inventory; **sous bénéfice d'i.,** conditionally; with reservations; **accepter une succession sous bénéfice d'i.,** to accept an estate without liability to debts beyond the assets descended; (*b*) *Com:* stocklist; **(établissement, levée, d')i.,** stocktaking; **faire, dresser, l'i.,** to take stock; (*c*) survey (of ancient monuments, paintings, etc.).
inventer [ɛ̃vɑ̃te] *v.tr.* to invent; (*a*) to find out, discover; **il n'a pas inventé la poudre,** he'll never set the Thames on fire; (*b*) to devise, contrive (machine, etc.); to dream up; to make up (story, etc.); to coin (phrase); **i. une histoire,** to spin a yarn; **i. de faire qch.,** to hit on the idea of doing sth.
inventeur, -trice [ɛ̃vɑ̃tœr, -tris] *n.* (*a*) inventor, discoverer (of process, etc.); (*b*) *Jur:* finder (of lost object, etc.).
inventif, -ive [ɛ̃vɑ̃tif, -iv] *a.* inventive.
invention [ɛ̃vɑ̃sjɔ̃] *n.f.* **1.** invention; (*a*) inventing; **nécessité est mère d'i.,** necessity is the mother of invention; (*b*) inventiveness, imagination. **2.** (*thg invented*) invention; (*a*) **brevet d'i.,** patent (for an invention); (*b*) fabrication, lie; **pure i. tout cela!** that's sheer invention, nothing but make-believe! **3.** *Jur:* **i. d'un trésor,** finding of treasure trove.
inventorier [ɛ̃vɑ̃tɔrje] *v.tr.* to make an inventory, a list, of (goods, etc.); to take stock.
invérifiable [ɛ̃verifjabl̥] *a.* unverifiable.
inverse [ɛ̃vɛrs] **1.** *a.* inverse, inverted, opposite, contrary; **en sens i. (de qch.),** in the opposite direction (to sth.); **dans l'ordre i.,** in (the) reverse order; *Mth:* **en raison i. de qch.,** in inverse ratio to sth. **2.** *n.m.* opposite, reverse; **faire l'i.,** to do the opposite; **à l'i. du bon sens,** unreasonably; against all reason. **3.** *n.f. Mth:* inverse, reciprocal (function, etc.).
inversement [ɛ̃vɛrsəmɑ̃] *adv.* inversely; conversely.
inverser [ɛ̃vɛrse] *v.tr.* to reverse (current, etc.); to invert (order); *I.C.E:* **carburateur inversé,** downdraught carburettor.
inverseur [ɛ̃vɛrsœr] *n.m.* reverser, reversing device; *El:* **i. du courant,** current reverser; change-over switch.
inversion [ɛ̃vɛrsjɔ̃] *n.f.* **1.** (*a*) *Gram: Mus: etc:* inversion; (*b*) transposition. **2.** reversal, reversing (of electric current, etc.); *Mch:* **i. de marche,** reverse gear.
invertébré [ɛ̃vɛrtebre] *a.* & *n.m.* invertebrate.
inverti, -ie [ɛ̃vɛrti] *n.* homosexual; invert.
investigateur, -trice [ɛ̃vɛstigatœr, -tris] **1.** *a.* investigative, investigating; inquiring, searching, scrutinizing (glance). **2.** *n.* investigator; inquirer.
investigation [ɛ̃vɛstigasjɔ̃] *n.f.* investigation, inquiry.
investir [ɛ̃vɛstir] *v.tr.* **1. i. qn d'une fonction,** to invest, vest, s.o. with an office; **i. qn d'une mission,** to entrust s.o. with a mission. **2.** *Mil: etc:* to besiege (town, etc.); to encircle (building). **3.** to invest (money).
investissement [ɛ̃vɛstismɑ̃] *n.m.* **1.** *Mil: etc:* besieging; encircling. **2.** *Fin:* investment; investing.
investiture [ɛ̃vɛstityr] *n.f.* investiture; induction (of bishop); *Pol:* nomination (of candidate).
invétéré [ɛ̃vetere] *a.* inveterate; deeply rooted (hatred, etc.); confirmed, irreclaimable (drunkard, criminal); intractable (disease).
invincibilité [ɛ̃vɛ̃sibilite] *n.f.* invincibility.
invincible [ɛ̃vɛ̃sibl̥] *a.* invincible, unconquerable; insuperable (difficulty).
invinciblement [ɛ̃vɛ̃sibləmɑ̃] *adv.* invincibly.
inviolabilité [ɛ̃vjɔlabilite] *n.f.* inviolability; sacredness (of office).
inviolable [ɛ̃vjɔlabl̥] *a.* inviolable; sacred.
inviolablement [ɛ̃vjɔlabləmɑ̃] *adv.* inviolably.
inviolé [ɛ̃vjɔle] *a.* inviolate; unbroken (vow).
invisibilité [ɛ̃vizibilite] *n.f.* invisibility.
invisible [ɛ̃vizibl̥] *a.* invisible; **il restait i.,** he was nowhere to be seen.
invisiblement [ɛ̃viziblәmɑ̃] *adv.* invisibly.
invitant [ɛ̃vitɑ̃] *a.* attractive, inviting.
invitation [ɛ̃vitasjɔ̃] *n.f.* invitation; **venir à, sur, l'i. de qn,** to come at s.o.'s invitation, at s.o.'s request; **venir sans i.,** to come uninvited.
invite [ɛ̃vit] *n.f.* (*a*) invitation; inducement; (*b*) **répondre à l'i. de qn,** to respond to s.o.'s advances.
invité, -ée [ɛ̃vite] *n.* guest; visitor.
inviter [ɛ̃vite] *v.tr.* to invite. **1. i. qn à dîner,** to invite, ask, s.o. to dinner; **être déjà invité,** to have a previous engagement; **i. qn à entrer,** to ask s.o. in. **2.** (*a*) **i. le désastre,** to court disaster; (*b*) **i. qn à faire qch.,** (i) to invite, request, (ii) to tempt, s.o. to do sth.
invivable [ɛ̃vivabl̥] *a.* unbearable, intolerable; (*a*) (life) not worth living; (*b*) *F:* (*of pers.*) impossible to live with.
invocation [ɛ̃vɔkasjɔ̃] *n.f.* invocation.
invocatoire [ɛ̃vɔkatwar] *a.* invocatory.
involontaire [ɛ̃vɔlɔ̃tɛr] *a.* involuntary, unintentional.
involontairement [ɛ̃vɔlɔ̃tɛrmɑ̃] *adv.* involuntarily, unintentionally.
involution [ɛ̃vɔlysjɔ̃] *n.f.* involution.
invoquer [ɛ̃vɔke] *v.tr.* **1.** (*a*) to call upon, invoke (the Deity, etc.); **i. l'aide de la justice,** to appeal to the law; (*b*) to invoke, call forth (a spirit). **2.** to call for, refer to (documents); to plead (forgetfulness, etc.); to put forward (reason, etc.).
invraisemblable [ɛ̃vrɛsɑ̃blabl̥] *a.* unlikely, improbable; implausible; hard to believe; **histoire i.,** tall story; **chapeau i.,** incredible hat; **ces gens-là sont invraisemblables,** those people are really extraordinary, fantastic, incredible.
invraisemblablement [ɛ̃vrɛsɑ̃blabləmɑ̃] *adv.* improbably; extraordinarily.
invraisemblance [ɛ̃vrɛsɑ̃blɑ̃s] *n.f.* **1.** unlikelihood, unlikeliness, improbability. **2.** implausible fact, statement.
invulnérabilité [ɛ̃vylnerabilite] *n.f.* invulnerability.
invulnérable [ɛ̃vylnerabl̥] *a.* invulnerable.
iode [jɔd] *n.m.* iodine; **teinture d'i.,** tincture of iodine; **lampe à i.,** tungsten lamp.
ioder [jɔde] *v.tr.* to iodize.
iodique [jɔdik] *a. Ch:* iodic.
iodler [jɔdle] *v.tr.* & *i.* to yodel.
iodoforme [jɔdɔfɔrm] *n.m.* iodoform.
iodure [jɔdyr] *n.m. Ch:* iodide.
ion [jɔ̃] *n.m.* ion.
ionien, -ienne [jɔnjɛ̃, -jɛn] **1.** *a.* & *n.* Ionian. **2.** *a.* Ionic (dialect, etc.).
ionique¹ [jɔnik] *a.* & *n.m. Arch:* Ionic (order).
ionique² *a. Ph: etc:* ionic; **accélération i.,** ion acceleration.
ionisant [jɔnizɑ̃] *a.* ionizing.
ionisation [jɔnizasjɔ̃] *n.f.* ionization.
ioniser [jɔnize] *v.tr. Ph: Ch:* to ionize.
ionosphère [jɔnɔsfɛr] *n.f.* ionosphere.

iota [jɔta] *n.m.* iota; **pas un i.,** not a bit, not one iota; not one jot.
iourte [jurt] *n.f.* yourt, yurt.
ipéca(cuana) [ipeka(kwana)] *n.m. Pharm:* ipecac(uanha).
Irak [irak] *Pr.n.m. Geog:* Iraq, Irak.
irakien, -ienne [irakjɛ̃, -jɛn] **1.** *a. & n. Geog:* Iraqi. **2.** *n.m. Ling:* Iraqi.
Iran [irɑ̃] *Pr.n.m. Geog:* Iran.
iranien, -ienne [iranjɛ̃, -jɛn] **1.** *a. & n. Geog:* Iranian. **2.** *n.m. Ling:* Iranian.
Iraq [irak] *Pr.n.m. Geog:* Iraq, Irak.
iraquien, -ienne [irakjɛ̃, -jɛn] *a. & n.* = IRAKIEN.
irascibilité [irasibilite] *n.f.* irascibility; testiness; quick temper.
irascible [irasibl̩] *a.* irascible, irritable, testy.
iridescent [iridesɑ̃] *a. Lit:* iridescent.
iridié [iridje] *a.* **platine i.,** iridioplatinum.
iridium [iridjɔm] *n.m. Ch:* iridium.
Iris [iris] **1.** *Pr.n.f. Myth:* Iris. **2.** *n.m.* (*a*) *Opt:* iris; (*b*) *Anat:* iris (of eye); *Phot:* **(diaphragme) i.,** iris diaphragm. **3.** *n.m. Bot:* iris, flag; **i. jaune, des marais,** yellow iris; **racine d'i.,** orris root.
irisation [irizasjɔ̃] *n.f.* iridescence, irisation.
irisé [irize] *a.* iridescent; rainbow-coloured.
iriser [irize] **1.** *v.tr.* to make iridescent. **2.** **s'i.,** to become iridescent.
irlandais, -aise [irlɑ̃dɛ, -ɛz] **1.** *a.* Irish. **2.** *n.* Irishman; Irishwoman; **les I.,** the Irish. **3.** *n.m. Ling:* Irish, Erse.
Irlande [irlɑ̃d] *Pr.n.f. Geog:* Ireland; **I. du Nord,** Northern Ireland.
ironie [irɔni] *n.f.* irony.
ironique [irɔnik] *a.* ironic(al).
ironiquement [irɔnikmɑ̃] *adv.* ironically.
ironiser [irɔnize] *v.i.* to speak ironically, be ironical (**sur,** about).
ironiste [irɔnist] *n.* ironist.
iroquois, -oise [irɔkwa, -waz] **1.** *a. & n. Ethn:* Iroquois, Iroquoian. **2.** *n.m. Ling:* Iroquoian.
irradiation [iradjasjɔ̃] *n.f. Ph: Med:* irradiation; radiation; *Phot:* halation.
irradier [iradje] **1.** *v.i.* to (ir)radiate; (*of pain, etc.*) to spread. **2.** *v.tr.* to irradiate, expose to (atomic) radiation.
irraisonné [irɛzɔne] *a.* unreasoned.
irrationalisme [irasjɔnalism] *n.m.* irrationalism.
irrationalité [irasjɔnalite] *n.f.* irrationality.
irrationnel, -elle [irasjɔnɛl] *a.* irrational.
irrationnellement [irasjɔnɛlmɑ̃] *adv.* irrationally.
irréalisable [irealizabl̩] *a.* unrealizable; impracticable, unfeasible.
irréalisé [irealize] *a.* unrealized.
irréalité [irealite] *n.f.* unreality.
irrecevabilité [irəsəvabilite] *n.f.* inadmissibility.
irrecevable [irəsəvabl̩] *a.* inadmissible (evidence); unacceptable (theory).
irréconciliable [irekɔ̃siljabl̩] *a.* irreconcilable.
irréconciliablement [irekɔ̃siljabləmɑ̃] *adv.* irreconcilably.
irrécouvrable [irekuvrabl̩] *a.* irrecoverable.
irrécupérable [irekyperabl̩] *a.* irreparable, irremediable (loss, etc.); irretrievable; irredeemable.
irrécusable [irekyzabl̩] *a.* unimpeachable, unexceptionable, irrecusable (evidence, etc.).
irréductibilité [iredyktibilite] *n.f.* irreducibility.
irréductible [iredyktibl̩] *a.* **1.** irreducible (equation, dislocation); *Mth:* **fraction i.,** fraction in its lowest terms. **2.** indomitable; unshakeable (attachment to s.o.); unyielding, relentless (opposition).
irréel, -elle [ireɛl] *a.* unreal.
irréfléchi [irefleʃi] *a.* **1.** unconsidered, thoughtless (action). **2.** hasty, rash, unthinking.
irréflexion [ireflɛksjɔ̃] *n.f.* thoughtlessness.
irréformable [irefɔrmabl̩] *a. Jur:* irrevocable, irreformable (decision, etc.).
irréfutable [irefytabl̩] *a.* irrefutable, indisputable.
irréfutablement [irefytabləmɑ̃] *adv.* irrefutably.
irréfuté [irefyte] *a.* unrefuted.
irrégularité [iregylarite] *n.f.* irregularity; variation; unevenness (of ground, pulse).
irrégulier, -ière [iregylje, -jɛr] **1.** *a.* irregular; uneven (ground); fitful, broken (sleep); unequal (braking); erratic (life, pulse). **2.** *n.m. esp.pl. Mil:* irregulars.
irrégulièrement [iregyljɛrmɑ̃] *adv.* irregularly.
irréligieux, -ieuse [ireliʒjø, -jøz] *a.* irreligious.
irréligion [ireliʒjɔ̃] *n.f.* irreligion.
irrémédiable [iremedjabl̩] *a.* irremediable (loss); incurable (disease); irreparable (injury).
irrémédiablement [iremedjabləmɑ̃] *adv.* irremediably; incurably; irreparably.
irrémissible [iremisibl̩] *a.* irremissible; unpardonable (crime).
irremplaçable [irɑ̃plasabl̩] *a.* irreplaceable.
irréparable [ireparabl̩] *a.* irreparable (wrong); irretrievable (loss, mistake); beyond repair.
irréparablement [ireparabləmɑ̃] *adv.* irreparably.
irrépréhensible [irepreɑ̃sibl̩] *a.* blameless.
irrépressible [irepresibl̩] *a.* irrepressible.
irréprochable [ireprɔʃabl̩] *a.* irreproachable; faultless.
irréprochablement [ireprɔʃabləmɑ̃] *adv.* irreproachably; faultlessly.
irrésistible [irezistibl̩] *a.* irresistible.
irrésistiblement [irezistibləmɑ̃] *adv.* irresistibly.
irrésolu [irezɔly] *a.* **1.** irresolute, indecisive (nature); faltering (steps). **2.** unsolved (problem).
irrésolument [irezɔlymɑ̃] *adv.* irresolutely.
irrésolution [irezɔlysjɔ̃] *n.f.* irresolution, irresoluteness, indecision.
irrespect [irɛspɛ] *n.m.* disrespect.
irrespectueusement [irɛspɛktɥøzmɑ̃] *adv.* disrespectfully.
irrespectueux, -euse [irɛspɛktɥø, -øz] *a.* disrespectful (**envers,** to, towards).
irrespirable [irɛspirabl̩] *a.* unbreathable.
irresponsabilité [irɛspɔ̃sabilite] *n.f.* irresponsibility.
irresponsable [irɛspɔ̃sabl̩] *a.* irresponsible.
irrétrécissable [iretresisabl̩] *a.* unshrinkable.
irrévérence [ireverɑ̃s] *n.f.* irreverence.
irrévérencieusement [ireverɑ̃sjøzmɑ̃] *adv.* irreverently, disrespectfully.
irrévérencieux, -euse [ireverɑ̃sjø, -øz] *a.* irreverent, disrespectful.
irréversible [ireversibl̩] *a.* irreversible.
irrévocabilité [irevɔkabilite] *n.f.* irrevocability.
irrévocable [irevɔkabl̩] *a.* irrevocable; binding (agreement); *Jur:* **décret i.,** decree absolute.
irrévocablement [irevɔkabləmɑ̃] *adv.* irrevocably.
irrigable [irigabl̩] *a.* irrigable.
irrigateur [irigatœr] *n.m.* (*a*) (garden) hose; (*b*) *Med:* irrigator (for wounds); (*c*) *Med:* enema; douche.
irrigation [irigasjɔ̃] *n.f.* **1.** *Agr:* (*a*) irrigation; (*b*) flooding. **2.** *Med:* irrigation; (*a*) spraying (of wound, etc.); (*b*) douching.
irriguer [irige] *v.tr.* **1.** *Agr:* (*a*) to irrigate; (*b*) to flood. **2.** *Med:* to irrigate; (*a*) to spray (wound); (*b*) to douche.
irritabilité [iritabilite] *n.f.* irritability.
irritable [iritabl̩] *a.* irritable.
irritant [iritɑ̃] **1.** *a.* irritating, exasperating. **2.** *a. & n.m. Med:* irritant.
irritation [iritasjɔ̃] *n.f.* irritation.

irrité [irite] *a.* irritated. **1.** angry (**contre,** with). **2.** *Med:* inflamed (wound).
irriter [irite] **1.** *v.tr.* (*a*) to irritate, annoy (s.o.); (*b*) to excite (passions, etc.); (*c*) *Med:* to irritate, inflame (wound, etc.). **2. s'i.** (*a*) **s'i. contre qn, de qch.,** to get angry, annoyed, with s.o., at sth.; (*b*) (*of sore, etc.*) to become irritated, inflamed.
irruption [irypsjɔ̃] *n.f.* (*a*) irruption; invasion, raid; **faire i. dans une salle,** to burst, rush, swarm, into a room; (*b*) overflow, flood (of river); inrush (of water); **i. de la mer,** tidal wave.
Isabelle [izabɛl] **1.** *Pr.n.f.* Isabel(la). **2.** *a.inv.* biscuit-coloured, *NAm:* -colored; cream-coloured. **3.** *a.inv.* & *n.m.* **(cheval) i.,** light-bay horse, light bay.
Isaïe [izai] *Pr.n.m. B.Hist:* Isaiah.
isard [izar] *n.m. Z:* izard, wild goat.
isba [izba] *n.f.* isba(h).
Islam [islam] *n.m. Rel:* Islam.
islamique [islamik] *a.* Islamic.
islamisation [islamizasjɔ̃] *n.f.* Islamization.
islamisme [islamism] *n.m.* Islamism.
islandais, -aise [islɑ̃dɛ, -ɛz] **1.** *Geog:* (*a*) *a.* Icelandic; (*b*) *n.* Icelander. **2.** *n.m. Ling:* Icelandic.
Islande [islɑ̃d] *Pr.n.f. Geog:* Iceland.
isobare [izɔbar] *Meteor:* **1.** *a.* isobaric. **2.** *n.f.* isobar.
isocèle [izɔsɛl] *a. Mth:* isosceles (triangle).
isochrone [izɔkrɔn], **isochronique** [izɔkrɔnik] *a. Mec:* isochronous, isochronal, isochronic.
isocline [izɔklin] *a.* & *n.f. Surv: etc:* isoclinal (line).
isolable [izɔlabl̩] *a. Ch: etc:* isolable.
isolant [izɔlɑ̃] **1.** *a.* (*a*) isolating (languages, etc.); (*b*) insulating; **bouteille isolante,** vacuum flask; **cabine isolante,** soundproof box; **ruban i.,** insulating tape. **2.** *n.m.* insulator; insulation material.
isolateur, -trice [izɔlatœr, -tris] *El:* **1.** *a.* insulating. **2.** *n.m.* insulator.
isolation [izɔlasjɔ̃] *n.f.* (*a*) *El:* insulation; (*b*) **i. acoustique, phonique,** soundproofing.
isolationnisme [izɔlasjɔnism] *n.m.* isolationism.
isolationniste [izɔlasjɔnist] *a.* & *n.* isolationist.
isolé [izɔle] *a.* **1.** isolated; lonely, remote (spot, etc.). **2.** *El:* insulated (cable, etc.).
isolement [izɔlmɑ̃] *n.m.* **1.** isolation; **hôpital d'i.,** isolation hospital. **2.** *El:* insulation.
isolément [izɔlemɑ̃] *adv.* separately, individually; solitarily; singly; in isolation.
isoler [izɔle] **1.** *v.tr.* (*a*) to isolate (**de,** from); **se trouver isolé,** to find oneself cut off; (*b*) *El:* to insulate; (*c*) to soundproof. **2. s'i.** (*a*) to become isolated, separated; (*b*) to live apart, hold aloof (from society).
isoloir [izɔlwar] *n.m.* polling booth.
isomère [izɔmɛr] **1.** *a. Ch: Bot:* isomeric. **2.** *n.m. Ch:* isomer.
isométrique [izɔmetrik] *a. Cryst: Mth:* isometric(al).
isomorphe [izɔmɔrf] *a. Cryst: Mth: etc:* isomorphous, isomorphic.
isomorphisme [izɔmɔrfism] *n.m. Cryst: Mth:* isomorphism.
Isorel [izɔrɛl] *n.m. R.t.m: Const:* hardboard.
isotherme [izɔtɛrm] *Meteor:* **1.** *a.* isothermal. **2.** *n.f.* isotherm.
isotope [izɔtɔp] *n.m. Ch:* isotope.
isotrope [izɔtrɔp] *a. Ch: Ph:* isotropic.
Israël [israɛl] *Pr.n.m. Geog:* Israel.
israélien, -ienne [israeljɛ̃, -jɛn] *a.* & *n. Geog:* Israeli.
Israélite [israelite] **1.** *a.* Jewish; *B.Hist:* Israelite. **2.** *n.* Jew, *f.* Jewess; *B.Hist:* Israelite.
issu [isy] *a.* descended (**de,** from); born (**de,** of); **être i. de,** to stem from.
issue [isy] *n.f.* **1.** exit, way out; outlet (of tunnel, etc.); **i. de secours,** emergency exit; **voie sans i.,** cul-de-sac, dead end; *P.N:* no through road; **se ménager une i.,** to find a loophole, a way out. **2.** issue, end, conclusion; outcome; **l'affaire a eu une i. heureuse,** the matter ended happily, had a happy ending; **la seule i. possible,** the only possible solution; **à l'i. de la réunion,** at the end, close, of the meeting. **3.** *pl.* (*a*) *Mill:* sharps, middlings; (*b*) offal.
Istamboul, Istanbul [istɑ̃bul] *Pr.n. Geog:* Istanbul.
isthme [ism] *n.m. Geog: Anat:* isthmus.
isthmique [ismik] *a.* isthmian (canal, games, etc.).
italianisant, -ante [italjanizɑ̃, -ɑ̃t] *n.* Italianist.
italianiser [italjanize] *v.tr.* to Italianize.
italianisme [italjanism] *n.m. Ling:* Italianism; Italian phrase, idiom.
Italie [itali] *Pr.n.f. Geog:* Italy.
italien, -ienne [italjɛ̃, -jɛn] **1.** *a.* & *n. Geog:* Italian. **2.** *n.m. Ling:* Italian.
italique [italik] **1.** (*a*) *a.* & *n.* Italic; (*b*) *n.m. Ling:* Italic. **2.** *a.* & *n.m. Typ:* italic (type); **en italique(s),** in italic(s).
item [itɛm] **1.** *adv.* item, likewise, also. **2.** *n.m.* item.
itératif, -ive [iteratif, -iv] *a.* **1.** *Jur:* reiterated, repeated (prohibition, etc.). **2.** *Gram:* iterative (verb).
Ithaque [itak] *Pr.n.f. Geog:* Ithaca.
itinéraire [itinerɛr] *n.m.* itinerary; (*a*) route, way; **tracer un i.,** to map out a route; (*b*) guide (book).
itinérant [itinerɑ̃] *a.* itinerant (preacher); **ambassadeur i.,** roving ambassador.
itou [itu] *adv. F: O:* also, too, likewise; **et moi i.!** (and) me too!
ivoire [ivwar] *n.m.* ivory. **1. i. vert,** raw ivory, live ivory; **crucifix d'i., en i.,** ivory crucifix; *Paint:* **noir d'i.,** ivory black; *Geog:* **la Côte d'I.,** the Ivory Coast; *Lit:* **tour d'i.,** ivory tower **2.** ivory (statuette, etc.).
ivoirien, -ienne [ivwarjɛ̃, -jɛn] *a.* & *n. Geog:* (inhabitant) of the Ivory Coast (Republic).
ivoirier [ivwarje] *n.m.* worker in ivory.
ivraie [ivrɛ] *n.f. Bot:* **1.** (*a*) darnel; (*b*) *B.Lit:* tares; **séparer l'i. d'avec le bon grain,** to separate the wheat from the tares. **2. i. vivace, fausse i.,** rye grass.
ivre [ivr̩] *a.* drunk, intoxicated; inebriated; **i. mort,** dead drunk; **i. de joie,** mad with joy.
ivresse [ivrɛs] *n.f.* (*a*) drunkenness, intoxication; inebriation, *Jur:* **en état d'i. publique** = drunk and disorderly; **conduite en état d'i.,** drunken driving; (*b*) *Lit:* rapture, ecstasy.
ivrogne [ivrɔɲ] **1.** *n.m.* drunkard; alcoholic. **2.** *a.* addicted to drink; drunken.
ivrognerie [ivrɔɲri] *n.f.* habitual drunkenness.
ivrognesse [ivrɔɲɛs] *n.f. F:* drunkard; alcoholic.

J

J, j [ʒi] *n.m.* the letter J, j; *Mil: etc:* **le jour J,** D day.
j' [ʒ] *pers.pron.* = JE; *used before a verb beginning with a vowel or h mute; also before* **en, y.**
jabot [ʒabo] *n.m.* **1.** crop (of bird); **enfler, gonfler, le j.,** (i) (*of pigeon*) to pout; (ii) *F:* (*of pers.*) to put on airs. **2.** *Cost:* frill, ruffle, jabot.
jacaranda [ʒakarɑ̃da] *n.m. Bot:* jacaranda.
jacassement [ʒakasmɑ̃] *n.m.* chatter(ing) (of magpie); *F:* (*of pers.*) jabber(ing).
jacasse [ʒakas] *n.f. Orn: F:* magpie.
jacasser [ʒakase] *v.i.* (*of magpie*) to chatter; *F:* (*of pers.*) to chatter, jabber, *U.S:* to yak.
jacasserie [ʒakas(ə)ri] *n.f. F:* chatter(ing); jabber(ing).
jachère [ʒaʃɛr] *n.f.* unploughed land, fallow; **champ en j.,** fallow field.
jacinthe [ʒasɛ̃t] *n.f.* **1.** *Bot:* hyacinth; **j. sauvage, des bois,** wild hyacinth, bluebell. **2.** *Miner:* jacinth.
jack [ʒak] *n.m. El: Tp: etc:* jack.
Jacob [ʒakɔb] *Pr.n.m.* Jacob; **l'échelle de J.,** Jacob's ladder; *F:* **bâton de J.,** (i) *Astr:* Orion's belt; (ii) *Bot:* yellow asphodel.
jacobin, -ine [ʒakɔbɛ̃, -in] *n.* **1.** *Ecc:* Dominican friar, nun. **2.** *Fr.Hist:* Jacobin.
jacobite [ʒakɔbit] *a. & n.m. Hist:* Jacobite.
jacquard [ʒakar] *n.m. Tex:* Jacquard loom.
Jacques [ʒak] *Pr.n.m.* (*a*) James; (*b*) **Maître J.,** factotum; (*c*) *Hist:* **J. (Bonhomme),** the French peasant; *F:* **faire le J.,** to act dumb.
jacquet [ʒakɛ] *n.m.* backgammon.
Jacquot [ʒako] **1.** *Pr.n.m. F:* = Jim, Jimmy. **2.** *n.m.* West African grey parrot; *F:* Poll (parrot), Polly.
jactance [ʒaktɑ̃s] *n.f.* **1.** boastfulness, boasting, bragging. **2.** *P:* talk; jabber(ing).
jacter [ʒakte] *v.i. P:* to talk, jabber, spout.
jade [ʒad] *n.m. Miner:* jade.
jadis [ʒadis] *adv. Lit:* formerly, once, of old; **les chevaliers de j.,** the knights of old; **le temps j.,** the olden days; **contes du temps j.,** tales of long ago.
jaguar [ʒagwar] *n.m. Z:* jaguar.
Jahvé [ʒave] *Pr.n.m. B.Lit:* Yahweh.
jaillir [ʒajir] *v.i.* to spring (up); to shoot (out); (*of water*) to gush (out), to spout up, out, to squirt (out); (*of blood*) to spurt; (*of sparks*) to fly; (*of light*) to flash.
jaillissant [ʒajisɑ̃] *a.* gushing, spouting, spurting; flying (sparks); **puits j.,** (mineral oil) gusher.
jaillissement [ʒajismɑ̃] *n.m.* gush(ing), spouting, spurt(ing), springing (out); **j. d'éloquence,** burst of eloquence; *El:* **j. d'étincelles,** sparking.
jaïnisme [ʒainism] *n.m. Rel:* Jainism.
jais [ʒɛ] *n.m. Miner:* jet.
jalon [ʒalɔ̃] *n.m.* (*a*) (surveyor's) staff; (range) pole; stake, rod; marker, sighting mark; *Fig:* **poser, planter, des jalons,** to show, to pave, the way; to blaze a trail; (*b*) landmark; milestone.
jalonnement [ʒalɔnmɑ̃] *n.m.* marking out, off.
jalonner [ʒalɔne] *v.tr. Surv:* to lay out, stake out, mark out (line, piece of ground, etc.); to peg (out) (claim); *Av:* to mark out, stake out (landing strip); *Mil:* to screen (enemy advance); **ils ont jalonné la route à ceux qui suivront,** they have shown the way to, blazed the trail for, their successors; **événements qui jalonnent la vie de qn,** events that stand out as landmarks, milestones, in s.o.'s life.
jalonneur [ʒalɔnœr] *n.m. Surv: Mil:* (*pers.*) marker.
jalousement [ʒaluzmɑ̃] *adv.* jealously.
jalouser [ʒaluze] *v.tr.* to envy, to be jealous of (s.o.).
jalousie [ʒaluzi] *n.f.* **1.** jealousy; envy. **2.** (*a*) (latticework) screen; (*b*) Venetian blind. **3.** *Bot:* sweet william; **j. des jardins,** rose campion.
jaloux, -ouse [ʒalu, -uz] *a.* (*a*) jealous; (*b*) zealous, careful; **j. de sa réputation,** careful of one's reputation.
jamaïquain, -aine [ʒamaikɛ̃, -ɛn] *a. & n. Geog:* Jamaican.
Jamaïque (la) [laʒamaik] *Pr.n.f. Geog:* Jamaica.
jamais [ʒamɛ] *adv.* **1.** ever; **plus cher que j.,** dearer than ever; **s'il revenait j., si j. il revenait,** if ever he came back; **avez-vous j. entendu chose pareille?** did you ever hear such a thing? **à j., pour j.,** for ever; **à tout j.,** for ever and ever, for evermore. **2.** (*with neg. expressed or understood*) never; **je ne l'ai j. vu,** I have never seen him; **j. homme ne fut plus admiré,** never was a man more admired; **sans j. y avoir pensé,** without ever having thought of it; **c'est le cas ou j.,** now or never; **on ne le voit presque j.,** one hardly ever sees him; **on ne le verra plus j., j. plus,** we shall never see him again; **avez-vous j. été à Rome?—j.,** have you ever been to Rome?—never; **j. de la vie!** never! out of the question! *F:* not on your life! no fear! *Prov:* **mieux vaut tard que j.,** better late than never. **3.** *n.m.* **j., au grand j., je n'admettrai cela,** I shall never, (repeat,) never, admit it.
jambage [ʒɑ̃baʒ] *n.m.* **1.** jamb (post), (side)post (of door, window, etc.); jamb, side, cheek (of fireplace). **2.** leg, standard (of crane, etc.). **3.** downstroke (of written letter).
jambe [ʒɑ̃b] *n.f.* **1.** leg; **jambes d'un pantalon,** trouser legs; **avoir de bonnes jambes,** to be a good walker; **aux longues jambes,** long-legged; *Hist:* **Édouard Longues-jambes,** Edward Longshanks; **il s'est sauvé à toutes jambes,** he ran off at full, at top, speed, as fast as his legs could carry him; *F:* **prendre ses jambes à son cou,** to take to one's heels, to show a clean pair of heels; **il se met dans vos jambes,** he gets under your feet, in your way; **travail fait par-dessous la j.,** botched, scamped, work; **c'est ça qui me fera une belle j.!** a (fat) lot of good that will do me! **avoir les jambes rompues,** to feel one's legs giving way under one; to be worn out; **couper, casser, bras et jambes à qn,** to cut the ground from under s.o.'s feet; to take the wind out of s.o.'s sails; **avoir dix kilomètres dans les jambes,** to have walked ten kilometres; **n'avoir plus de jambes,** to be tired out, exhausted; **je n'ai plus mes jambes de vingt ans,** I'm not as young as I was; *Box: Fb:* **jeu de jambes,** footwork. **2.** (*a*) stem (of a glass); leg (of compasses, etc.); **j. de force,** *Const:* strut, prop, brace; *Aut:* stay (rod), torque rod; (*b*) *Nau:* **j. de chien,** sheepshank.
jambier, -ière [ʒɑ̃bje, -jɛr] **1.** *a. & n.m. Anat:* **(muscle) j.,** leg muscle. **2.** *n.f.* **jambière** (*a*) *A.Arm:* greave; (*b*) elastic stocking; (*c*) *pl.* leggings; *Cr:* pads; *Fb:* shin guards.
jambon [ʒɑ̃bɔ̃] *n.m.* (*a*) ham; **j. de pays, de montagne,** smoked ham (for eating uncooked); (*b*) *P:* thigh.
jambonneau, -eaux [ʒɑ̃bɔno] *n.m.* **1.** knuckle of ham. **2.** foreleg ham; hand of pork.

jamboree [ʒɑ̃mbɔre] *n.m. Scout:* jamboree.
janissaire [ʒanisɛr] *n.m.* janissary, janizary.
jansénisme [ʒɑ̃senism] *n.m. Rel.H:* Jansenism.
janséniste [ʒɑ̃senist] *a. & n. Rel.H:* Jansenist.
jante [ʒɑ̃t] *n.f.* felloe, felly (of wheel); rim (of cycle or car wheel).
janvier [ʒɑ̃vje] *n.m.* January; **en j.,** in January; **au mois de j.,** in the month of January; **le premier, le sept, j.,** (on) January (the) first, (the) seventh.
Japon [ʒapɔ̃] **1.** *Pr.n.m.* Japan; **au J.,** in, to, Japan. **2.** *n.m.* (*a*) Japanese porcelain; (*b*) Japanese vellum.
japonais, -aise [ʒapɔnɛ, -ɛz] **1.** *a. & n.* Japanese. **2.** *n.m. Ling:* Japanese. **3.** *a.* **vernis j.,** japan.
japonaiserie [ʒapɔnɛzri] *n.f.*, **japonerie** [ʒapɔnri] *n.f.* article of Japanese art; Japanese curio.
japonisant, -ante [ʒapɔnizɑ̃, -ɑ̃t] *n.* specialist of Japanese (i) language, (ii) civilization, art.
jappement [ʒapmɑ̃] *n.m.* yelp(ing), yap(ping).
japper [ʒape] *v.i.* (*of dog*) to yelp, yap.
jappeur, -euse [ʒapœr, -øz] *a. & n.* yelping, yapping (dog, etc.).
jaquette [ʒakɛt] *n.f.* (*a*) (man's) morning coat, *NAm:* cutaway; (*b*) (woman's) jacket; (*c*) *Fr.C:* nightdress; (*d*) *Bookb:* dust jacket, cover.
jardin [ʒardɛ̃] *n.m.* garden; **j. potager,** kitchen garden; **j. d'agrément,** pleasure garden; **j. à l'anglaise,** landscape garden; **j. des plantes,** botanical garden; **j. d'hiver,** winter garden; **j. alpin,** rock garden; **j. japonais,** miniature Japanese garden; **jardins ouvriers,** allotments; *Sch:* **j. d'enfants,** kindergarten; *Th:* **côté j.,** prompt side; **cultiver son j.,** to lead a calm and peaceful life; **jeter des pierres dans le j. de qn,** to attack s.o. indirectly.
jardinage [ʒardinaʒ] *n.m.* **1.** gardening. **2.** flaw (in diamond).
jardiner [ʒardine] *v.i.* to garden.
jardinet [ʒardinɛ] *n.m.* small garden.
jardinier, -ière [ʒardinje, -jɛr] **1.** *a.* **plantes jardinières,** garden plants. **2.** *n.* gardener; **j. maraîcher,** market gardener. **3.** *n.f.* (*a*) (i) window box; (ii) jardinière; (*b*) *Cu:* **jardinière (de légumes),** mixed vegetables; (*c*) *Sch:* **jardinière d'enfants,** kindergarten mistress.
jargon [ʒargɔ̃] *n.m.* (*a*) jargon; **le j. du palais,** legal jargon; **j. journalistique,** journalese; (*b*) cant, slang; lingo; (*c*) gibberish.
jargonner [ʒargɔne] *v.i.* to talk jargon.
Jarnac [ʒarnak] *Pr.n.m. used in* **coup de J.,** treacherous stroke, stab in the back, low trick.
jarre [ʒar] *n.f.* (large glazed) earthenware jar.
jarret [ʒarɛ] *n.m.* **1.** bend of the knee; ham (in man); hock (of horse, etc.); **plier le j.,** to bend the knee; **avoir le j. solide,** to have a good pair of legs. **2.** *Cu:* knuckle (of veal); shin (of beef).
jarretelle [ʒartɛl] *n.f. Cost:* suspender, *U.S:* garter.
jarretière [ʒartjɛr] *n.f.* **1.** garter; **Ordre de la J.,** Order of the Garter. **2.** (*a*) picketing rope; (*b*) sling (for guns); (*c*) *Nau:* gasket.
jars [ʒar] *n.m.* gander.
jas [ʒa] *n.m. Nau:* stock (of anchor); **sans j.,** stockless.
jaser [ʒaze] *v.i.* (*a*) to chatter (**de,** about); to gossip; (*of child*) to prattle; **j. comme une pie (borgne),** to talk nineteen to the dozen; (*b*) to blab; to tell tales.
jaseur, -euse [ʒazœr, -øz] **1.** *a.* talkative. **2.** *n.* chatterbox; gossip. **3.** *n.m. Orn:* waxwing.
jasmin [ʒasmɛ̃] *n.m. Bot:* jasmine.
jaspe [ʒasp] *n.m. Miner:* jasper; **j. noir,** touch-stone; **j. sanguin,** bloodstone.
jasper [ʒaspe] *v.tr.* to marble, mottle (paper, etc.).
jaspure [ʒaspyr] *n.f.* marbling, mottling.
jatte [ʒat] *n.f.* bowl; (milk)pan; basin.
jattée [ʒate] *n.f.* bowlful; panful (of milk).
jauge [ʒoʒ] *n.f.* **1.** (*a*) gauge; (standard of) measure, capacity (of cask, etc.); (*b*) *Nau:* tonnage, burden (of ship). **2.** (*a*) *Tchn:* gauge; *Aut: etc:* **j. d'essence,** petrol gauge; **j. de niveau d'huile,** dipstick; (*b*) *Mec.E: etc:* gauge, templet; **j. micrométrique,** vernier cal(l)iper; (*c*) *Mch:* **j. de vapeur,** steam gauge; **robinet de j.,** gauge cock; (*d*) **bas de j. fine,** fine gauge stockings.
jaugeage [ʒoʒaʒ] *n.m.* gauging, measuring.
jauger [ʒoʒe] *v.tr.* (**je jaugeai(s); n. jaugeons**) **1.** (*a*) to gauge, measure, the capacity of (cask, etc.), the tonnage of (a ship); **j. un homme,** to size up a man; (*b*) to gauge, to measure, the output of (pump, well, etc.). **2.** (*of ship*) (*a*) **j. 300 tonneaux,** to be of 300 tons burden; **pétrolier qui jauge quarante mille tonneaux,** forty thousand ton tanker; (*b*) **j. deux mètres d'eau,** to draw two metres of water.
jaugeur [ʒoʒœr] *n.m.* **1.** (*pers.*) gauger. **2.** (*instrument*) gauge.
jaunâtre [ʒonɑtr̥] *a.* yellowish; sallow (complexion).
jaune [ʒon] **1.** (*a*) *a.* yellow; **j. comme un coing, comme un citron,** yellow as a guinea, a lemon; **chaussures jaunes,** brown shoes; **fièvre j.,** yellow fever; *Adm:* **livre j.** = Blue Book; *Aut:* **feu, lumière, j.,** amber light; (*b*) *a.inv.* **j. citron,** lemon yellow; **j. serin,** canary yellow; *adv.* **rire j.,** to give a sickly smile; to force a laugh. **2.** *n.m.* (*a*) yellow (colour, *NAm:* color); **j. d'ocre,** yellow ochre; **j. de chrome,** chrome yellow; (*b*) **j. d'œuf,** yolk (of egg); (*c*) *Ind: F:* strikebreaker, blackleg, scab.
jaunet, -ette [ʒonɛ, -ɛt] **1.** *a.* yellowish. **2.** *n.m. Bot:* **j. d'eau,** yellow water lily.
jauni, -ie [ʒoni] *a.* yellowed (by age, sun, etc.); faded; bleached (grass).
jaunir [ʒonir] *v.i. & tr.* to yellow, turn yellow; to become yellow; to fade.
jaunissant [ʒonisɑ̃] *a.* yellowing, turning yellow; **blés jaunissants,** ripening corn.
jaunisse [ʒonis] *n.f. Med:* jaundice; *F:* **il en ferait une j.,** he would be mad with jealousy, green with envy.
jaunissement [ʒonismɑ̃] *n.m.* yellowing; ripening (of wheat).
javanais, -aise [ʒavanɛ, -ɛz] *a. & n.* **1.** *Geog:* Javanese. **2.** *n.m.* (*a*) a form of cant popular under the Second Empire; (*b*) **c'est du j.,** it's double Dutch. **3.** *n.f. Danc:* Javanaise.
javel (eau de) [odʒavɛl] *n.f. Dom.Ec:* = bleach.
javelage [ʒavlaʒ] *n.m. Agr:* laying (of wheat) in swaths.
javeler [ʒavle] *v.* (**je javelle, n. javelons; je javellerai**) **1.** *v.tr. Agr:* to lay (cereals) in swaths. **2.** *v.i.* (*of reaped cereals*) to turn yellow.
javeline[1] [ʒavlin] *n.f.* javelin.
javeline[2] *n.f. Agr:* small swath (of wheat, etc.).
javelle [ʒavɛl] *n.f.* **1.** *Agr:* swath, loose sheaf. **2.** bundle (of hop poles, etc.).
javellisation [ʒavelizasjɔ̃] *n.f.* chlorination.
javelliser [ʒavelize] *v.tr.* to chlorinate.
javelot [ʒavlo] *n.m.* javelin.
jazz [dʒaz] *n.m.* jazz.
jazzman [dʒazman] *n.m. Mus:* jazz musician; *pl. jazzmen.*
je, *before a vowel sound* **j'** [ʒ(ə)] *pers.pron.nom.* I. **1.** (*unstressed*) **je vois,** I see; **j'ai,** I have; **j'en ai,** I have some; **que vois-je** [vwaʒ]? what do I see? **2.** (*stressed* [ʒə]) *Jur:* **je, soussigné,** I, the undersigned; *n.* **employer le je (dans un récit),** to write in the first person.
Jean[1] [ʒɑ̃] *Pr.n.m.* John; **(saint) J.-Baptiste** [batist], (St) John the Baptist; **la Saint-J.,** Midsummer Day.
jean[2] [dʒin] *n.m. Cost:* jeans.
jean-foutre [ʒɑ̃futr̥] *n.m.inv. P:* **c'est un j.-f.,** he's no good; you can't rely on him.

Jeanne [ʒan] *Pr.n.f.* Jane, Joan, Jean; **la Papesse J.,** Pope Joan; **J. d'Arc,** Joan of Arc; **cheveux à la J. d'Arc,** bobbed hair with a fringe.

Jeannette [ʒanɛt] **1.** *Pr.n.f.* Jenny, Janet. **2.** *n.f.* (*a*) small gold cross; (*b*) sleeveboard; (*c*) *Bot:* **j. jaune,** daffodil. **3.** *n.f. Scout:* Brownie.

Jeannot [ʒano] *Pr.n.m. F:* Johnny, Jack; **J. lapin,** bunny (rabbit).

jeep [(d)ʒip] *n.f. Aut:* jeep.

Jéhovah [ʒeɔva] *Pr.n.m.* Jehovah, Yahweh.

je-m'en-fichisme [ʒmɑ̃fiʃism], **je-m'en-foutisme** [ʒmɑ̃futism] *n.m. P:* couldn't-care-less attitude.

je-m'en-fichiste [ʒmɑ̃fiʃist], **je-m'en-foutiste** [ʒmɑ̃futist] *n. P:* person who doesn't care a damn about anything or anybody.

je(-)ne(-)sais(-)quoi [ʒənsɛkwa] *n.m.inv.* **un je-ne-s.-q.,** an indefinable something; **il y a un je-ne-s.-q. qui ne me plaît pas,** there's something about it I don't like.

jennérien, -ienne [ʒɛnerjɛ̃, -jɛn] *a. Med:* Jennerian.

jenny [ʒeni] *n.f. Tex:* spinning jenny.

jérémiade [ʒeremjad] *n.f.* jeremiad, lamentation; whining, complaining.

Jérémie [ʒeremi] *Pr.n.m.* Jeremiah; Jeremy.

jerez [kerɛs] *n.m.* **(vin de) j.,** sherry.

Jéricho [ʒeriko] *Pr.n.m. Geog:* Jericho.

Jéroboam [ʒerɔbɔam] **1.** *Pr.n.m.* Jeroboam. **2.** *n.m.* jeroboam (of champagne).

jerrican(e), jerrycan *n.m.* [(d)ʒerikan] jerrycan.

Jersey [ʒɛrzɛ] **1.** *Pr.n.m. Geog:* (Island of) Jersey. **2.** *n.m. Cost:* jersey. **3.** *n.m. Tex:* jersey; **j. de laine,** wool jersey; **j. de soie,** silk jersey; *Knit:* **point (de) j.,** stocking stitch.

jersiais, -aise [ʒɛrzjɛ, -ɛz] *a. & n.* (native, inhabitant) of Jersey; **(vache) jersiaise,** Jersey cow.

jésuite [ʒezɥit] *n.m. Ecc:* Jesuit.

jésuitique [ʒezɥitik] *a.* **1.** *Ecc:* jesuitic. **2.** *Pej:* jesuitic(al); plausible, specious.

jésuitisme [ʒezɥitism] *n.m.* (*a*) Jesuitism; (*b*) *Pej:* Jesuitry; hypocrisy.

Jésus [ʒezy] **1.** (*a*) *Pr.n.m.* Jesus; **J.-Christ,** Jesus Christ; **en l'an 44 avant J.-C., après J.-C.,** in the year 44 B.C., A.D.; (*b*) *n.m.* statue of the Christ Child; (*c*) *F:* **mon j.,** my little pet. **2.** *a.m. & n.m. Typ:* **(papier) j.** = super-royal, long royal (paper); **grand j.** = imperial.

jet¹ [ʒɛ] *n.m.* **1.** (*a*) throwing, casting; throw, cast (of net, dice, etc.); **à un j. de pierre de nous,** within a stone's throw of us; *Art: Lit:* **premier j.,** first sketch, rough outline; rough draft; **du premier j.,** at the first attempt; **force de j.,** impetus; **armes de j.,** missiles, projectiles; (*b*) *Metall:* cast, casting; **couler qch. d'un seul j.,** to cast sth. in one piece; *Fig:* **faire qch. d'un seul j.,** to do sth. at one go, at one sitting; (*c*) **j. (de marchandises) à la mer,** jettison(ing), throwing overboard (of cargo). **2.** (*a*) jet, gush, stream (of liquid); spurt (of blood); flash, ray (of light); **j. de vapeur,** jet of steam; **j. d'incendie,** jet of water from a fire hose; **j. d'eau,** (i) jet of water, fountain; (ii) nozzle (of hosepipe); (iii) *Const:* weatherboard; drip moulding (of windows); **j. de flamme,** (i) burst of flame; (ii) blowpipe flame; jetting; *Metalw: etc:* **j. de sable,** sand blast; (*b*) *Bot:* young shoot (of tree); **elle est tout d'un j.,** she is tall and slender. **3.** jet (of nozzle, etc.); spout (of pump, watering can, etc.); **j. de gaz,** gas jet.

jet² [dʒɛt] *n.m. Av: F:* jet (aircraft).

jeté [ʒ(ə)te] *n.m.* (*a*) *Danc:* jeté; (*b*) *Knit:* (wool) over, forward; **j. simple, j. double,** make one, make two; (*c*) *Sp:* (*weightlifting*) jerk; (*d*) **j. de table,** (table) runner; **j. de lit,** bedspread.

jetée [ʒ(ə)te] *n.f.* **1.** jetty, pier. **2.** breakwater.

jeter [ʒ(ə)te] *v.* **(je jette, n. jetons; je jetterai) 1.** *v.tr.* to throw, fling, cast; to throw away; **j. son argent par les fenêtres,** to throw one's money down the drain; **j. qch. à la tête de qn,** (i) to throw sth. at s.o.'s head; (ii) to blame, reproach, s.o.; to throw sth. in s.o.'s teeth; **j. des reproches à la tête de qn,** to hurl reproaches at s.o.; **j. un filet,** to cast a net; **j. bas qch., j. qch. à terre, par terre,** to throw sth. down; **j. ses armes,** to throw down one's arms; **à j.,** (i) to be thrown away; (ii) disposable (nappy, etc.); **j. un sort à qn,** to cast a spell on s.o.; **le sort en est jeté,** the die is cast; **j. un cri,** to utter a cry; **j. un soupir,** to heave a sigh; **j. un regard sur qn,** to glance at s.o.; **j. une ombre,** to cast a shadow; **j. qn dans l'embarras,** to throw, plunge, s.o. into confusion; **j. qn à la porte,** to throw s.o. out; **j. des racines,** to strike (root); **j. les fondements d'un édifice,** to lay the foundations of a building; **j. un pont sur une rivière,** to throw a bridge over a river; **navires jetés à la côte par la tempête,** ships driven ashore by the storm; *Metall:* **j. (une statue, etc.) en fonte,** to cast (a statue, etc.); *Nau:* **j. le plomb, la sonde,** to heave the lead; **j. l'ancre,** to cast anchor; **(faire) j. qch. à la mer, par-dessus bord,** to jettison sth.; **objets jetés à la mer,** jetsam; *Fig:* **j. l'éponge,** to throw in the sponge. **2. se j. par la fenêtre,** to throw oneself out of the window; **se j. aux pieds de qn,** to throw oneself at s.o.'s feet; **se j. sur qn,** to attack s.o.; **se j. (à corps perdu) dans une entreprise,** to fling oneself (body and soul) into an undertaking; **cours d'eau qui se jette dans la Seine,** stream that flows into the Seine.

jeton [ʒ(ə)tɔ̃] *n.m.* (*a*) *Cards: etc:* counter; chip; *Tp: etc:* token; *P:* **faux j.,** hypocrite; (*b*) **j. de présence,** tally, token (issued as voucher for attendance at meeting); director's fees; **toucher ses jetons,** to draw one's fees; (*c*) *P:* punch, blow; **avoir les jetons,** to have the jitters, the wind up.

jet-stream [dʒɛtstrim] *n.m. Meteor:* jet stream.

jeu, jeux [ʒø] *n.m.* **1.** (*a*) play; sport; **salle de jeux,** playroom; **j. de mots,** play on words, pun; **j. d'esprit,** witticism; **j. de main,** horseplay, rough and tumble; **jeux de la fortune,** tricks of fortune; **c'est un j. d'enfant,** it's child's play; **se faire (un) j. de (faire) qch.,** to make light of (doing) sth.; (*b*) (manner of) playing; acting (of actor); execution, playing (of musician); **j. muet,** dumb show; **jeux de scène,** stage business; **jeux de physionomie,** play of features. **2.** (*a*) **jeux d'adresse,** games of skill; **jeux olympiques,** Olympic games; **le j. de tennis,** (lawn) tennis; **jeux de société, petits jeux,** parlour, *NAm:* parlor, games; **jeux de hasard,** games of chance; **terrain de jeux,** sports ground; *F:* **ce n'est pas du j.,** that's not fair; **jouer beau j., jouer le j.,** to play the game, play fair; **où en est le j.?** what's the score? **on aurait beau j. de, à, répondre,** it would be quite easy to answer that; *Cards:* **avoir un beau j., avoir du j.,** to have a good hand; **vous avez beau j.,** now's your chance; **faire le j. de qn,** to play into s.o.'s hands; *Ten:* **j. et partie,** game and set; **en j.,** in play; **mettre la balle en j.,** to bring the ball into play; (*hockey*) to bully off; (*b*) (*place*) **j. de boules,** (*in Fr.*) bowling ground, (*in Eng.*) bowling green; **j. de quilles,** skittle alley. **3.** set; **j. d'échecs, de dominos,** chess set, set of dominoes; **j. de cartes,** pack, *NAm:* deck, of cards; **j. de fiches,** card index; *Mus:* **j. d'orgue,** (organ) stop; **j. d'outils,** set of tools. **4.** (*a*) gaming, gambling; **maison de j.,** gaming house; **perdre une fortune au j.,** to gamble away a fortune; **se ruiner au j.,** to ruin oneself gambling; **dettes de j.,** gambling, gaming, debts; **table de j.,** gaming table, card table; **jouer gros j.,** to play high, for high stakes; **les jeux sont faits,** (i) (*at roulette*) the stakes are down; (ii) *Fig:* the die is cast; the chips are down; **faites vos jeux!** place your stakes! **mettre qch. au j.,** to stake sth.; **mettre tout en j.,** to stake one's all; to risk everything; **être en j.,** to be at stake; **les intérêts en j.,** the interests at issue, at stake, involved; **le j. n'en vaut pas la chandelle,** the game isn't worth the candle; **cacher son j.,** to hide one's cards, play an underhand game; **montrer son j.,** to show one's hand, one's cards; (*b*) *St.Exch:* speculating. **5.** (*activity, action*) **les forces en j.,** the forces at work, involved; **mettre qch. en j.,** to set sth. in action, to bring, call, sth. into play, into action; **j. d'un piston,** length of stroke of a piston; **j. de lumière,** play of light; *Th:* **jeux de lumière,** lighting effects; **j. d'une serrure,** action of a lock; *Mec.E:* **en j.,** in gear. **6.** *Mec.E:* (*a*) **j. (utile),** clearance, play, free motion; **donner du j. à qch.,** to ease, slacken, sth.; (*b*) **j. (nuisible),** looseness, play, slack; (back)lash (of gear); **prendre du j.,** to work free, loose.

jeu-concours [ʒøkɔ̃kur] *n.m. W.Tel: T.V: etc:* quiz; competition; *pl. jeux-concours.*

jeudi [ʒødi] *n.m.* Thursday; **j. saint,** Maundy Thursday; *F:* **la semaine des quatre jeudis,** never; when pigs begin to fly.

jeun (à) [aʒœ̃] *adj.phr.* **1.** fasting; **boire à j.,** to drink on an empty stomach; *Med:* **à prendre à j.,** to be taken on an empty stomach. **2.** sober.

jeune [ʒœn] **1.** *a.* (*a*) young; youthful; **j. homme,** young man; *F:* **elle n'est plus très j.,** she's not so young as she was; *F:* **son j. homme,** her young man, her boy friend; **j. fille,** girl; young woman; **jeunes gens,** (i) young people; (ii) young men; **j. aveugle,** blind boy, girl; **un j. Français, un j. Anglais,** a French boy, an English boy; **une j. Indienne,** an Indian girl; **j. détenu,** juvenile offender; **dans son j. âge,** in his young(er) days; **j. d'esprit,** young in mind; (*b*) younger; **mon j. frère,** my younger brother; **le plus j. de mes frères,** my youngest brother; **je suis plus j. que lui de quatre ans,** I'm four years younger than him; **M. Martin J.,** Mr Martin junior; young Mr Martin; (*c*) **vin j.,** new wine. **2.** *n.* (*a*) **les jeunes,** young people; the younger generation; (*b*) young animal; *pl.* young.

jeûne [ʒøn] *n.m.* (*a*) fast; **rompre le j.,** to break one's fast; (*b*) fasting; **jour de j.,** day of fasting; fast day.

jeûner [ʒøne] *v.i.* to fast; to go without food.

jeunesse [ʒœnɛs] *n.f.* (*a*) youth; boyhood, girlhood; **je le connais de j.,** I have known him from my youth, since childhood, since I was young; **dans sa première j.,** in his, her, early youth; **ne pas être de la première j.,** not to be young any longer, to be getting on; **erreurs, péchés, de j.,** errors of youth, youthful indiscretions; (*b*) **avoir un air de j.,** to look young; (*c*) newness (of wine); (*d*) *coll.* **livres pour la j.,** children's books; **la j. du village,** the youth of the village.

jeunet, -ette [ʒœnɛ, -ɛt] *a. F:* youngish.

jeûneur, -euse [ʒønœr, -øz] *n.* (*pers.*) faster.

jeunot, -otte [ʒœno, -ɔt] *F:* **1.** *a.* young; youngish; on the young side. **2.** *n.* youngster.

jiu-jitsu [ʒyʒitsy] *n.m.inv. Sp:* jiu-jitsu.

joaillerie [ʒɔajri] *n.f.* **1.** jeweller's business, shop. **2.** jewellery, jewelry. **3.** jewellery trade.

joaillier, -ière [ʒɔaje, -jɛr] *n.* jeweller.

job¹ [ʒɔb] *n.m. F:* **monter le j. à qn,** to deceive s.o., pull s.o.'s leg.

Job² [ʒɔb] *Pr.n.m. B.Hist:* Job.

job³ [dʒɔb] *n.m. F:* job; task; work.

jobard, -arde [ʒɔbar, -ard] *F:* **1.** *a.* stupid; gullible; naïve. **2.** *n.* easy prey; easy mark; mug, sucker.

jobarderie [ʒɔbard(ə)ri] *n.f.,* **jobardise** [ʒɔbardiz] *n.f. F:* gullibility; **c'est de la j.,** it's a mug's game.

jockey [ʒɔkɛ] *n.m.* (*a*) jockey; (*b*) *A:* outrider.

Joconde (la) [laʒɔkɔ̃d] *Pr.n.f.* the Mona Lisa.

jodler [ʒɔdle] *v.i. & tr.* to yodel.

joie [ʒwa] *n.f.* **1.** joy; delight; gladness; **plein de j.,** full of joy; in high spirits; **sauter de j.,** to jump for joy; **à ma grande j.,** to my great delight; **accepter avec j.,** to accept with pleasure, gladly; **faire la j. de qn,** (i) to be s.o.'s joy; (ii) to make s.o. happy; **se faire une j. de faire qch.,** to delight, take a delight, in doing sth.; **feu de j.,** bonfire; **j. de vivre,** joy of living, joie de vivre; high spirits; **il se faisait une j. de vous voir,** he was looking forward (so much) to seeing you; **à cœur j.,** to one's heart's content. **2. fille de j.,** prostitute.

joindre [ʒwɛ̃dr] *v.* (*pr.p.* **joignant;** *p.p.* **joint;** *pr.ind.* **je joins, il joint, n. joignons, ils joignent;** *impf.* **je joignais;** *p.h.* **je joignis;** *fu.* **je joindrai) 1.** *v.tr.* to join; (*a*) to bring together; **j. les mains,** to clasp, join, fold, one's hands; **j. les deux bouts,** to make both ends meet; (*b*) to add (**à,** to); **le bon sens joint à l'intelligence,** common sense combined with intelligence; **j. le geste à la parole,** to suit the action to the word; **j. l'utile à l'agréable,** to combine business with pleasure; **j. sa voix aux protestations,** to join in the protests; *Com: etc:* **l'échantillon joint à votre lettre,** the sample attached to your letter; (*c*) to join (one's regiment, ship); (*d*) (= REJOINDRE) to meet, join (s.o.); **je vous joindrai à l'hôtel,** I shall meet, join, you at the hotel; **comment puis-je vous j.?** how can I get in touch with you? **2.** *v.i. & pr.* (*of boards, etc.*) to meet, fit; **fenêtre qui joint mal,** window that does not shut properly. **3. se j.,** to join, unite; **se j. à la conversation,** to join in the conversation; **voulez-vous vous j. à nous?** would you like to join us?

joint [ʒwɛ̃] **1.** *a.* joined, united; **pieds joints,** feet close together; **saut à pieds joints,** standing jump; **à mains jointes,** with clasped hands; **efforts joints,** combined efforts; *Corr:* **pièces jointes,** enclosures. **2.** *n.m.* (*a*) (*in wood, etc.*) joint, join; **trouver le j.,** to hit upon the right plan, to find a way; **j. abouté, en about, carré, plat,** butt joint; **j. biseauté,** scarf joint; **j. d'étanchéité,** gasket; seal; *Mec.E: etc:* **j. articulé, j. en charnière,** knuckle (joint); **j. universel, j. brisé, j. de cardan,** universal joint; cardan joint, coupling; **j. sphérique, à rotule,** ball(-and-socket) joint; **j. à brides,** flange joint; (*b*) *Mch:* packing (of piston, gland); **j. de presse-étoupe,** packing gasket, ring.

jointoiement [ʒwɛ̃twamɑ̃] *n.m. Const:* **1.** pointing, jointing (of wall, etc.). **2.** grouting.

jointoyer [ʒwɛ̃twaje] *v.tr.* (**je jointoie, n. jointoyons; je jointoierai**) *Const:* **1.** to point, joint (wall, etc.). **2.** to grout.

jointure [ʒwɛ̃tyr] *n.f. Anat: Tchn:* joint, join; (*of horse*) (i) fetlock (joint); (ii) pastern; **j. du genou,** knee joint; **les jointures des doigts,** the knuckles.

joker [ʒɔkɛr] *n.m. Cards:* joker.

joli [ʒɔli] *a.* pretty; good-looking (girl); **jolie comme un cœur, jolie à croquer,** pretty as a picture; **il a une jolie fortune,** he's pretty well off; *Iron: F:* **ce n'est pas j. j.,** that's a poor show; **le j. de l'affaire c'est que . . .,** the beauty of the thing, the best of it, is that . . ..

joliment [ʒɔlimɑ̃] *adv.* **1.** pleasantly; well; **j. habillé,** well, smartly, dressed; **c'est j. dit!** that's neatly put. **2.** (*intensive*) *F:* **j. amusant,** awfully, terribly, funny; **vous avez j. raison,** you're dead right; **on s'est j. amusé(s),** we had a marvellous time.

jonc [ʒɔ̃] *n.m.* **1.** (*a*) *Bot:* rush; **j. fleuri,** flowering rush; **j. des marais,** bulrush; (*b*) **j. d'Inde,** rattan; **(canne de) j.,** Malacca cane. **2.** keeper (ring).

joncher [ʒɔ̃ʃe] *v.tr.* to strew; **j. la terre de fleurs,** to strew the ground with flowers; **les débris de la statue jonchaient le pavé,** fragments of the statue lay strewn about the pavement; **plancher jonché de débris,** floor strewn, littered, with rubbish.

jonchets [ʒɔ̃ʃɛ] *n.m.pl. Games:* spillikins.

jonction [ʒɔ̃ksjɔ̃] *n.f.* junction, joining; **point de j.,** meeting point; **j. de deux routes,** junction of two roads; *Tchn:* **tuyau de j.,** joint pipe; *Rail:* **gare de j.,** junction (station); **voie de j.,** crossover; *Mil:* (*of troops*) **opérer une j.,** to join forces, come together.

jongler [ʒɔ̃gle] *v.i.* to juggle (**avec,** with).

jonglerie [ʒɔ̃gləri] *n.f.* juggling.

jongleur [ʒɔ̃glœr] *n.m.* **1.** *A:* jongleur; (medieval) minstrel. **2.** juggler.

jonque [ʒɔ̃k] *n.f.* (Chinese) junk.

jonquille [ʒɔ̃kij] **1.** *n.f. Bot:* (*a*) jonquil; (*b*) daffodil. **2.** *a.inv.* & *n.m.* bright yellow.

Jordanie [ʒɔrdani] *Pr.n.f. Geog:* Jordan.

jordanien, -ienne [ʒɔrdanjɛ̃, -jɛn] *a.* & *n. Geog:* Jordanian.

Joseph [ʒozɛf] **1.** *Pr.n.m.* Joseph. **2.** *a.m.* & *n.m.* **(papier) j.,** fine transparent filter paper.

Josué [ʒozɥe] *Pr.n.m. B.Hist:* Joshua.

jouable [ʒwabl̩] *a. Th: Mus: etc:* playable.

joual [ʒwal] *n.m. Fr.C:* French Canadian dialect.

joubarbe [ʒubarb] *n.f. Bot:* houseleek.

joue [ʒu] *n.f.* **1.** cheek (of person, horse); **danser j. contre j.,** to dance cheek to cheek; **tendre, présenter, l'autre j.,** to turn the other cheek; **mettre, coucher, qn en j.,** to aim (a gun) at s.o. **2.** side (of armchair, etc.); cheek (of bearing, mortise, etc.); flange (of wheel); web (of girder, etc.). **3.** *N.Arch: pl.* the bows.

jouée [ʒwe] *n.f. Arch:* reveal (of window).

jouer [ʒwe] *v.* to play. **I.** *v.i.* **1.** (*a*) **j. avec qn, avec qch.,** to play, trifle, with s.o., sth.; **j. avec ses lunettes,** to play, toy, fiddle, fidget, with one's glasses; **j. sur les mots,** to play on, with, words; (*b*) **j. à qch.,** to play at sth.; **j. aux soldats, aux Indiens,** to play (at) soldiers, Red Indians; **j. au cricket, aux cartes,** to play cricket, cards; **c'est à qui de j.?** whose turn, go, is it (to play)? (*at chess, etc.*) whose move is it? (*c*) **j. du piano, de la harpe,** to play the piano, the harp; **j. des coudes,** to elbow one's way (through a crowd). **2.** (*a*) to gamble; **j. aux courses,** to back horses; (*b*) *Fin:* to speculate; **j. à la hausse,** to gamble on a rise in prices; to bull the market; **j. à la baisse,** to gamble on a fall in prices; to bear the market. **3.** (*a*) to come into play; to work, act; **clef qui ne joue pas bien,** key that is hard to turn; **faire j. qch.,** to bring sth. into play, set sth. in motion; **faire j. un ressort,** to work, touch, release, a spring; (*b*) to be, become, operative; to operate; **l'augmentation des salaires joue depuis le 1er janvier,** the rise in salaries has been operative since January 1; (*c*) (*of wood*) to warp; (*d*) (*of part*) to fit loosely, have too much play. **II.** *v.tr.* **1.** (*a*) to stake; **j. cinq francs,** to stake five francs; **j. le jeu,** to play the game, to play ball; **j. sa tête,** to risk one's neck; (*b*) *Turf:* to back (horse); **j. un cheval gagnant et placé,** to back a horse each way. **2.** (*a*) to play (card, pawn); *Cards:* **j. trèfle,** (i) to play, (ii) to lead, clubs; **bien j. ses cartes,** to play one's cards well; *Chess: etc:* **j. une pièce,** to move a piece; (*b*) *Th:* to act, play, perform (role, etc.); *Mus:* **j. un air au piano, sur la flûte,** to play a tune on the piano, on the flute; **qu'est-ce qui se joue actuellement?** what are they playing, what's on, at the moment? **j. un rôle dans l'affaire,** to play a part in the affair; **j. la surprise,** to feign surprise, pretend to be surprised. **3.** to trick, fool, make a fool of (s.o.). **III. se jouer. 1. faire qch. (comme) en se jouant,** to do sth. easily, without any difficulty. **2. se j. de qn,** to trifle with, mock, make fun of, s.o.

jouet [ʒwɛ] *n.m.* (child's) toy, plaything; **être le j. d'une illusion,** to be the victim of an illusion.

jouette [ʒwɛt] *a. Belg:* **enfant j.,** child who loves playing.

joueur, -euse [ʒwœr, -øz] *n.* **1.** (*a*) player (of game); **j. de golf, de cricket, de football,** golfer, cricketer, footballer; **j. aux cartes,** card player; **être beau j., mauvais j.,** to be a good, bad, loser; *a.* **enfant j.,** playful child; (*b*) *Mus:* performer, player. **2.** (*a*) gambler; (*b*) *St.Exch:* speculator; **j. à la hausse,** bull; **j. à la baisse,** bear.

joufflu [ʒufly] *a.* chubby(-cheeked).

joug [ʒu] *n.m.* **1.** (*a*) yoke; **mettre les bœufs au j.,** to yoke the oxen; (*b*) **être sous le j. d'un tyran,** to be under the yoke of a tyrant; **secouer le j., s'affranchir du j.,** to throw off the yoke. **2.** beam (of balance).

jouir [ʒwir] *v.i.* (*a*) **j. de la vie, d'un bon dîner,** to enjoy life, a good dinner; (*b*) **j. de toutes ses facultés,** to be in full possession of all one's faculties; **j. d'une bonne réputation,** to have a good reputation; **j. d'une bonne santé,** to enjoy good health; (*c*) **gens qui ne pensent qu'à j.,** people who think only of enjoyment, pleasure; (*d*) to have an orgasm; to come.

jouissance [ʒwisɑ̃s] *n.f.* enjoyment; (*a*) **le travail est une j. pour lui,** work is a pleasure to him; (*b*) possession, tenure; **avoir la j. de certains droits,** to enjoy certain rights; **entrer en j. de ses biens,** to enter into possession of one's property; **maison à vendre avec j. immédiate,** house for sale with vacant possession; (*of accommodation*) **avec j. de la cuisine,** with use of kitchen; **j. de passage,** right of way.

jouisseur, -euse [ʒwisœr, -øz] *n.* sensualist.

joujou, -oux [ʒuʒu] *n.m. F:* toy, plaything; **faire j. avec une poupée,** to play with a doll.

joule [ʒul] *n.m. Ph: etc:* joule.

jour [ʒur] *n.m.* day. **1.** (day)light; (*a*) **avant le j.,** before dawn, before day(break); **en plein j.,** (i) in broad daylight; (ii) publicly; **il fait j.,** it's (getting) light; **il fait à peine j.,** it's hardly light; **le j. se faisait dans mon esprit,** I was beginning to understand, to see daylight; **voyager le j., de j.,** to travel by day, in the day(time); **travailler j. et nuit,** to work day and night; **bombardement de j.,** daylight bombing; *Min:* **travail au j.,** surface work; **ils sont le j. et la nuit,** they are as different as chalk and cheese; (*b*) **donner le j. à un enfant,** to give birth to a child; *Lit:* **j'ai vu le j. à Paris,** I was born in Paris; **mettre qch. au j.,** to bring sth. to light; to publish (a fact); (*c*) light(ing); **vous me cachez le j.,** you're in my light; **jeter le j. sur une affaire,** to throw light on a subject; **voir qch. sous un j. nouveau, sous son vrai j.,** to see sth. in a new light, in its true light; **présenter une affaire sous un j. favorable,** to present a matter in a favourable, *NAm:* favorable, light. **2.** (*a*) aperture, opening; **pratiquer un j. dans un mur,** to make, cut, an opening, a hole, in a wall; **il y a des jours entre les planches,** there are gaps, chinks, between the planks; **percer (qch.) à j.,** (i) to bore, go, right through (sth.); (ii) to see through (plan, etc.); to penetrate (a design); (*b*) *Needlew:* **à j.,** hemstitched; **à jours,** openwork (trimming, etc.); (*c*) (*of facts, etc.*) **se faire j.,** to come out, appear; **la vérité se fait j. dans son esprit,** the truth is dawning on him. **3.** (*a*) **huit jours,** a week; **quinze jours,** a fortnight; **c'est à un j. de voyage,** it's a day's journey (away); **quel j. (du mois) sommes-nous?** what's the date (today)? **quel j. (de la semaine) sommes-nous?** what day (of the week) is it (today)? *Prov:* **les jours se suivent et ne se ressemblent pas,** who knows what tomorrow holds? (*b*) *Com:* **intérêts à ce j.,** interest to date; **je l'ai vu l'autre j.,** I saw him the other day; **un j. ou l'autre,** one day, some time, or other; **d'un j. à l'autre, de j. en j.,** day by day, from day to day; **nous l'attendons d'un j. à l'autre,** we're expecting him any day (now); (*past*) **un j. (quand) je me promenais,** one day (when) I was out walking; (*future*) **un j. je vous le dirai,** one day, some day, I'll tell you; **tous les jours,** every day; **mes vêtements de tous les jours,** my everyday clothes; **il y a**

six ans j. pour j., six years ago to the (very) day; **vivre au j. le j.**, to live from day to day, from hand to mouth; **leur beauté n'est que d'un j.**, their beauty is ephemeral; **mettre, tenir (une liste, etc.) à j.**, to bring, keep (a list, etc.) up to date; **tenir qn à j.**, to keep s.o. up to date, posted; **un de ces jours**, one of these days: *F:* **à un de ces jours!** I'll be seeing you! see you soon! (*c*) *Mil: etc:* **service de j.**, day duty; **officier de j.**, duty officer; **être de j.**, to be on (day) duty; **j. de présence, d'absence**, day on duty, off duty; (*d*) **j. d'été**, summer's day; **prendre j. pour qch.**, to fix a day, make an appointment, for sth.; (*e*) **de nos jours**, these days, nowadays; **l'homme du j.**, the man of the moment; **le journal du j.**, today's paper; (*in restaurant*) **plat du j.**, dish of the day, *F:* today's special; **vieux jours**, old age; **je l'ai connue dans ses beaux jours**, I knew her in her prime; **mes beaux jours sont passés**, I've had my day.

Jourdain [ʒurdɛ̃] *Pr.n.m. Geog:* Jordan.

journal, -aux [ʒurnal, -o] *n.m.* journal. **1.** diary, record; *Book-k:* **(livre) j.**, account book; **tenir un j.**, to keep a diary; *Nau:* **j. de bord**, (ship's) log (book). **2.** (news)paper; **j. de mode**, fashion magazine; **les journaux**, the Press; **marchand de journaux**, (i) newsagent, *NAm:* news dealer; (ii) (news)paper seller; paperboy, *NAm:* newsboy; **j. parlé**, radio news.

journalier, -ière [ʒurnalje, -jɛr] **1.** *a.* daily (task, etc.); everyday (occurrence). **2.** *n.m.* day labourer, *NAm:* laborer.

journalisme [ʒurnalism] *n.m.* journalism; **l'influence du j.**, the influence of the press; **faire du j.**, to be a journalist.

journaliste [ʒurnalist] *n.* journalist; reporter; **j. politique**, political correspondent.

journalistique [ʒurnalistik] *a.* journalistic; **style j.**, journalese.

journée [ʒurne] *n.f.* **1.** day(time); **pendant la j.**, in the daytime; during the day; **toute la j.**, all day (long), the whole day; **je travaillais à longueur de j.**, I worked for days on end; **dans la j.**, in the course of the day; **j. de travail**, (i) day's work; (ii) working day; shift; **faire la j. continue**, (i) (*of shop, etc.*) to remain open at lunchtime; (ii) to work through lunch(time); **il ne fait rien de la j.**, he does nothing all day long. **2.** (*a*) day's work; **travailler à la j.**, to work by the day; **homme de j.**, (day) labourer, *NAm:* laborer; **femme de j.**, char(woman), daily help, *F:* daily; (*of charwoman*) **aller en j., faire des journées**, to do daily work (for s.o.); (*b*) day's wages; (*c*) day's march; (*d*) historic day; day of battle; **gagner la j.**, to win the day.

journellement [ʒurnɛlmɑ̃] *adv.* daily, every day.

joute [ʒut] *n.f.* **1.** *A.Sp:* joust, tilt, tilting. **2.** contest; *Fr.C:* game, match; **j. oratoire**, debate; contest in eloquence; **j. sur l'eau**, water tournament.

jouter [ʒute] *v.i.* **1.** *A.Sp:* to joust, tilt. **2.** to fight; **j. avec qn**, to argue, cross swords, with s.o.

jouvence [ʒuvɑ̃s] *n.f. Lit:* **Fontaine de J.**, Fountain of Youth.

jouvenceau, -elle, -eaux [ʒuvɑ̃so, -ɛl] *n. A:* stripling, youth, lad; *f.* maiden, girl.

jovial, -aux [ʒɔvjal, -o] *a.* jovial, jolly, merry; breezy.

jovialement [ʒɔvjalmɑ̃] *adv.* jovially.

jovialité [ʒɔvjalite] *n.f.* joviality; breeziness.

joyau, -aux [ʒwajo] *n.m.* jewel; gem; **les joyaux de la Couronne**, the Crown jewels, the regalia.

joyeusement [ʒwajøzmɑ̃] *adv.* joyously, joyfully.

joyeux, -euse [ʒwajø, -øz] *a.* happy, joyful; joyous; **j. Noël!** merry Christmas! **le j. mois de mai**, the merry month of May; **mine joyeuse**, cheerful expression.

jubé [ʒybe] *n.m. Arch:* rood loft, screen; jube.

jubilaire [ʒybilɛr] *a.* **année j.**, jubilee year.

jubilation [ʒybilasjɔ̃] *n.f.* jubilation.

jubilé [ʒybile] *n.m.* jubilee; golden wedding.

jubiler [ʒybile] *v.i. F:* to rejoice; to gloat.

jucher [ʒyʃe] **1.** *v.pr.* (*of birds, etc.*) to go to roost; to perch. **2.** *v.tr.* to perch.

juchoir [ʒyʃwar] *n.m.* perch (for fowl); roosting place; hen roost.

judaïque [ʒydaik] *a.* Judaic (law, etc.); Jewish.

judaïser [ʒydaize] *v.i.* to Judaize.

judaïsme [ʒydaism] *n.m.* Judaism.

Judas [ʒyda] **1.** *Pr.n.m. B.Hist:* Judas (Iscariot); **baiser de J.**, Judas kiss. **2.** *n.m.* (*a*) Judas; traitor, betrayer; (*b*) Judas (hole, trap); spy hole (in door).

Judée [ʒyde] *Pr.n.f. B.Hist:* Judaea; *Bot:* **arbre de J.**, Judas tree.

judéo-allemand [ʒydeɔalmɑ̃] *a. & n.m. Ling:* Yiddish; *pl. judéo-allemand(e)s.*

judiciaire [ʒydisjɛr] *a.* (*a*) judicial; legal (aid, etc.); **enquête j.**, judicial inquiry; **frais judiciaires**, legal charges; **erreur j.**, miscarriage of justice; **vente j.**, sale by order of the court; **poursuites judiciaires**, (i) proceedings; (ii) prosecution; (*b*) **le pouvoir j.**, (i) judicial power; (ii) = the Bench; **éloquence j.**, forensic eloquence.

judiciairement [ʒydisjɛrmɑ̃] *adv.* judicially.

judicieusement [ʒydisjøzmɑ̃] *adv.* judiciously.

judicieux, -euse [ʒydisjø, -øz] *a.* judicious, sensible; discerning; **peu j.**, injudicious, indiscreet.

judo [ʒydo] *n.m.* judo.

judoka [ʒydɔka] *n.* judoka.

juge [ʒyʒ] *n.m.* **1.** (*a*) *Jur:* judge; **j. d'instruction**, examining magistrate; **j. d'instance**, *A:* **j. de paix**, (i) conciliation magistrate (in commercial cases); (ii) police court magistrate = Justice of the Peace; **les juges** = the bench; *Games:* umpire; *Turf:* judge; **j. de touche**, *Fb:* linesman; *Rugby Fb:* touch judge. **2. être bon j. de qch.**, to be a good judge of sth.; **je vous en fais j.**, judge for yourself; I leave it to you to judge.

jugé [ʒyʒe] *n.m.* guesswork; **tirer au j.**, to fire blind.

jugement [ʒyʒmɑ̃] *n.m.* judg(e)ment. **1.** *Jur:* (*a*) trial (of case); **mettre, faire passer, qn en j.**, to bring s.o. to trial, up for trial; **mise en j.**, arraignment; **passer en j.**, to be brought up for trial, stand one's trial; **j. par défaut**, judgment by default; **le (jour du) j. dernier**, the Last Judgment, doomsday; (*b*) decision, award; (*in criminal cases*) sentence; **prononcer un j.**, to pass judgment, to adjudicate; **rendre un j. arbitral**, to make an award; **j. provisoire**, decree nisi; **j. déclaratif de faillite**, adjudication in bankruptcy. **2.** opinion, estimation; verdict; **au j. de bien des gens**, according to many (people); **porter un j. sur qch.**, to pass judgment, give an opinion, on sth. **3.** discernment, discrimination; **montrer du j.**, to show sound judgment, good sense; **erreur de j.**, error of judgment.

jugeote [ʒyʒɔt] *n.f. F:* common sense, gumption, nous; **avoir de la j.**, to know what's what.

juger[1] [ʒyʒe] *v.tr.* (**je jugeai(s), n. jugeons**) to judge. **1.** (*a*) *Jur:* to try, judge (a case); to sit in judgement, try (prisoner); to pass sentence, judgement, on (prisoner); to adjudicate, arbitrate (claim, etc.); (*b*) to appreciate (situation); to pass judgment on, criticize (book, etc.); **j. les gens sur la mine**, to judge people by, from, appearances; **un homme se juge par ses actions**, a man is judged by his actions. **2.** (*a*) to think, believe; to be of the opinion; **on le jugeait fou**, people thought him mad; **j. à propos, nécessaire, de faire qch.**, to think it advisable, necessary, to do sth.; (*b*) **j. de qch.**, to judge sth.; **j. de qn, de qch.**, to form an opinion of s.o., of sth.; **jugez de ma surprise**, imagine my surprise; **à en j. par . . .**, to judge by . . ., judging by . . .; **autant que je puisse en j.**, to the best of my judgment; **à vous d'en, de, j.,** it's up to you to draw your own conclusions.

juger² *n.m.* = JUGÉ.

jugulaire [ʒygylɛr] **1.** *a. & n.f. Anat:* jugular (vein). **2.** *n.f.* chin strap (of helmet).

juguler [ʒygyle] *v.tr.* (*a*) *A:* to jugulate; to throttle (s.o.); (*b*) to suppress, stifle, repress (revolt, etc.).

juif, juive [ʒɥif, ʒɥiv] **1.** *a.* Jewish. **2.** *n.* (*a*) Jew, *f.* Jewess; **le Juif errant,** the Wandering Jew; (*b*) *Anat: F:* **le petit j.,** the funnybone.

juillet [ʒɥijɛ] *n.m.* July; **en j.,** in July; **au mois de j.,** in the month of July; **le premier, le sept, j.,** (on) the first, the seventh, of July, (on) July (the) first, (the) seventh.

juin [ʒɥɛ̃] *n.m.* June; **en j.,** in June; **au mois de j.,** in the month of June; **le premier, le sept, j.,** (on) the first, the seventh, of June, (on) June (the) first, (the) seventh.

juiverie [ʒɥivri] *n.f.* (*a*) *A:* Jewry, ghetto; (*b*) *coll. Pej:* Jews, Jewry.

jujube [ʒyʒyb] *n.m. Pharm:* jujube (lozenge).

juke-box [(d)ʒykbɔks] *n.m.* jukebox; *pl. juke-boxes.*

julep [ʒylɛp] *n.m. Pharm:* julep.

Jules [ʒyl] **1.** *Pr.n.m.* Julius. **2.** *n.m. P:* chamber-pot, potty, jerry. **3.** *n.m. P:* man friend, boyfriend; **mon j.,** my husband, my old man.

Julien¹ [ʒyljɛ̃] *Pr.n.m.* Julian.

julien², -ienne¹ [ʒyljɛ̃, -jɛn] *a.* Julian; *Chr:* **année julienne,** Julian year.

Julienne² **1.** *Pr.n.f.* Juliana; Gillian. **2.** *n.f.* (*a*) *Bot:* rocket; (*b*) julienne (soup).

Juliette [ʒyljɛt] *Pr.n.f.* Juliet(te).

jumbo-jet [(d)jœmbod-ʒɛt] *n.m. F: Av:* jumbo (jet) *pl. jumbo-jets.*

jumeau, -elle, -eaux [ʒymo, -ɛl] **I. 1.** *a. & n.* (*a*) twin; **frères jumeaux, sœurs jumelles,** twin brothers, twin sisters; twins; **vrais jumeaux,** identical twins; **lits jumeaux,** twin beds; **maisons jumelles,** semidetached houses; (*b*) (*of fruit*) double. **2.** *n.m. Anat:* gemellus muscle. **II.** *n.f.pl.* **1.** *Opt:* binoculars; **jumelles de théâtre,** opera glasses; **jumelles de campagne,** field glass(es). **2.** (*a*) *Mec.E:* cheeks, side pieces; *Nau:* fishes (of mast); (*b*) *Veh:* (spring) shackles.

jumelage [ʒymlaʒ] *n.m.* **1.** coupling, pairing. **2.** twinning (of towns).

jumelé [ʒymle] *a.* arranged in pairs; coupled; **textes jumelés,** bilingual texts; **maison jumelée,** semi-detached house; **villes jumelées,** twinned towns; *Aut:* **pneus jumelés,** twin, dual, tyres.

jumeler [ʒymle] *v.tr.* (**je jumelle, n. jumelons; je jumellerai**) **1.** to pair; to arrange in pairs; to twin (towns). **2.** to fish (mast, beam, etc.).

jument [ʒymɑ̃] *n.f.* mare; **j. poulinière,** brood mare.

jumping [dʒœmpiŋ] *n.m. Equit:* (show)jumping.

jungle [ʒɔ̃gl, ʒœ̃gl] *n.f.* jungle.

junior [ʒynjɔr] *a. & n. Sp:* junior.

Junon [ʒynɔ̃] *Pr.n.f. Myth:* Juno.

junte [ʒœ̃t] *n.f. Pol:* junta.

jupe [ʒyp] *n.f. Cost:* skirt; *F:* **pendu aux jupes de sa mère,** tied to his mother's apron strings.

jupe-culotte [ʒypkylɔt] *n.f.* divided skirt; culotte(s); *pl. jupes-culottes.*

Jupiter [ʒypitɛr] *Pr.n.m. Myth:* Jupiter, Jove.

jupon [ʒypɔ̃] *n.m.* (*a*) waist petticoat, underskirt, slip; *F:* **il est toujours dans les jupons de sa mère,** he's always hanging on to his mother's apron strings; (*b*) *P:* woman, girl, (bit of) skirt; **courir le j.,** to run after women, to chase the girls.

Jura [ʒyra] *Pr.n.m. Geog:* **le J.,** the Jura (Mountains).

jurassien, -ienne [ʒyrasjɛ̃, -jɛn] *a. & n. Geog:* (native, inhabitant) of the Jura.

jurassique [ʒyrasik] *a. & n.m. Geol:* Jurassic.

juratoire [ʒyratwar] *a.* **caution j.,** guarantee given on oath.

juré, -ée [ʒyre] **1.** *a.* sworn; **ennemi j.,** sworn enemy; **expert j.,** sworn expert. **2.** *n.* juryman, juror; **les jurés,** the jury; **messieurs les jurés,** gentlemen of the jury.

jurer [ʒyre] *v.* to swear. **1.** *v.tr.* (*a*) **j. sa foi,** to pledge one's word; **j. sur la Bible,** to swear on the Bible; (*b*) (*to promise*) to vow; **j. la fidélité à qn,** to swear, pledge, fidelity to s.o.; **faire j. le secret à qn,** to swear s.o. to secrecy; **j. de faire qch.,** to swear to do sth.; **j. de se venger,** to swear revenge; (*c*) (*to assert*) **je vous jure que c'est vrai,** I swear that it is the truth; **j'en jurerais,** I would swear to it; *Prov:* **il ne faut j. de rien,** you never can tell. **2.** *v.i.* (*a*) to swear (profanely); to curse; *F:* **j. comme un charretier,** to swear like a trooper; (*b*) (*of colours, NAm: colors, etc.*) to clash, jar (**avec,** with).

juridiction [ʒyridiksjɔ̃] *n.f.* jurisdiction; **sous la j. de . . .,** within the jurisdiction of . . . .

juridictionnel, -elle [ʒyridiksjɔnɛl] *a.* jurisdictional.

juridique [ʒyridik] *a.* juridical, judicial; legal (tie, claim, etc.); **conseiller j.,** legal adviser.

juridiquement [ʒyridikmɑ̃] *adv.* juridically.

jurisconsulte [ʒyriskɔ̃sylt] *n.m.* jurisconsult; jurist; legal expert.

jurisprudence [ʒyrisprydɑ̃s] *n.f.* **1.** jurisprudence. **2.** statute law, case law. **3.** holding of the courts (on a question); the precedents (of a case).

juriste [ʒyrist] *n.m.* jurist; legal expert.

juron [ʒyrɔ̃] *n.m.* oath, curse; swearword.

jury [ʒyri] *n.m.* **1.** *Jur:* jury; **dresser la liste du j.,** to empanel the jury; **chef du j.,** foreman (of the jury); **membre du j.,** juror, juryman. **2.** selection committee, judges (for exhibition, etc.); **j. d'examen,** examining board, board of examiners.

jus [ʒy] *n.m.* **1.** juice; **j. de fruit,** fruit juice; **plein de j.,** juicy. **2.** *Cu:* juice (of meat); gravy; *F:* **cuire, mijoter, dans son j.,** to stew in one's own juice. **3.** *P:* (*a*) **il est tombé dans le j.,** he fell in (the water, the drink); (*b*) coffee; (*c*) (electric) current; juice; (*d*) **ça vaut le j.,** it's worth it.

jusant [ʒyzɑ̃] *n.m.* ebb (tide).

jusqu'au-boutisme [ʒyskobutism] *n.m.* hard-line attitude; going the whole hog.

jusqu'au-boutiste [ʒyskobutist] *n.* hard liner; whole-hogger; diehard.

jusque [ʒysk(ə)] *prep.* **1.** as far as, up to; **jusqu'ici,** up to here; thus far, so far; **venez jusqu'ici,** come over here; **j.-là** [ʒyskəla], thus far; up to there, that point; **jusqu'ici, j.-là, c'est très bien,** so far so good; **jusqu'où?** how far? **depuis Londres jusqu'à Paris,** all the way from London to Paris; **jusqu'au bout (de la rue, etc.),** as far as, (up) to, the end (of the street, etc.); **jusqu'à un certain point,** up to a certain point; **aller jusqu'à faire qch.,** to go so far as to do sth.; **j. chez lui,** up to his very door; **rougir jusqu'aux oreilles,** to blush right up to the ears; **compter jusqu'à dix,** to count up to ten; **jusqu'à concurrence de 5000 francs,** (up) to 5,000 francs; *Post:* **jusqu'à 250 gr.,** not over, not exceeding, 250 gr. **2.** (*a*) till, until; **attendez jusqu'après les vacances,** wait till after the holidays, the vacation; **jusqu'ici,** until, up to, now; to date, as yet; so far; **j.-là, jusqu'alors,** until then; **jusqu'à présent,** up to now; **jusqu'à hier, jusqu'à dix heures,** until, up to, yesterday, ten o'clock; **jusqu'à aujourd'hui,** until today; **jusqu'à fin mai,** until the end of May; **jusqu'à mon dernier jour,** to my dying day; **jusqu'au jour, jusqu'au moment où, que . . .,** (i) until (such time as) . . .; (ii) until the time when . . .; (*b*) **si nous remontons jusqu'en 1800,** if we go back as far as 1800. **3.** (*intensive*) (*a*) **il sait jusqu'à nos pensées,** he knows our very thoughts; **jusqu'à dix personnes l'ont vu,** as many as ten people saw it; **il a mangé l'oie jusqu'aux**

os, he ate the goose bones and all; (*b*) **il se montrait sévère jusqu'à mériter le reproche d'être cruel,** he was severe to the point of cruelty. **4.** *conj.phr.* **jusqu'à ce que** *usu.* + *sub.*, until, till; **jusqu'à ce que les portes soient fermées,** till the doors are shut.

jusques [ʒyskə] *prep.* (*a*) *A: & Lit:* = JUSQUE; (*b*) **j. et y compris** [ʒyskəzeikɔ̃pri] up to and including.

justaucorps [ʒystokɔr] *n.m. Cost:* **1.** *A:* jerkin. **2.** leotard.

juste [ʒyst] **1.** *a.* just, right, fair; (*a*) **esprit j.,** just, fair, mind; **traitement j.,** fair play; just treatment; **j. colère,** righteous, legitimate, anger; **rien de plus j.,** nothing could be fairer; (*b*) **être j. envers, pour, qn,** to give s.o. his due, be fair to s.o.; *n.* **les justes,** the just, the righteous; **j. ciel!** heavens above! **2.** *a.* right, exact, accurate; apt (word); (*a*) **quelle est l'heure j.?** what exactly is the time? **le mot j.,** the exact word, the right word; **raisonnement j.,** sound reasoning; **avoir l'oreille j.,** to have a good ear (for music); **ce piano n'est pas j.,** this piano is out of tune; **se faire une idée j. de la situation,** to form a true estimate of the situation; **j. milieu,** happy medium; **votre réponse n'est pas j.,** you have got the answer wrong; **balance j.,** accurate scales; **ma montre est j.,** my watch is right, on time; **arriver à l'heure j.,** to arrive right on time, on the dot; **c'est j.,** that's so! that's right! **rien de plus j.,** you're perfectly right; *Mus:* **quarte j.,** perfect fourth; (*b*) scanty, bare (allowance); tight (shoes); tightfitting, skimpy (garment); **c'est tout j., bien j.,** there's barely enough (food, etc.) to go round; **c'est tout j. s'il sait lire,** he can barely read; **il ne manque jamais son train, mais c'est tout j.,** he never misses his train, but he cuts it fine; *Com:* **au plus j. prix,** at rock bottom price. **3.** *adv.* (*a*) rightly; **parler j.,** to speak to the point; **frapper j.,** to strike home; to hit the nail on the head; **chanter j.,** to sing in tune; **sonner j.,** to ring true; **voir j.,** to take a right view of things; (*b*) exactly, precisely, just; **arriver à dix heures j.,** to arrive on the stroke of ten, at ten o'clock sharp; **j. au milieu,** right, plumb, in the centre; **j. à temps,** just in time, in the nick of time; **c'est j. l'homme qu'il nous faut,** he's exactly the man we want; **c'est j. ce qu'il faut,** it's the very thing; (*c*) barely, just; **n'avoir que j. le temps,** to have barely time, to have just (enough) time; **vous avez tout j. le temps,** you haven't a moment to spare; **il échappa tout j. à la mort,** he barely, narrowly, escaped death; (*d*) **je ne sais pas au j. si . . .,** I don't exactly know whether . . .; **comme de j.,** of course; as is only fair, only just.

justement [ʒystəmɑ̃] *adv.* **1.** justly, rightly, properly, deservedly. **2.** precisely, exactly, just; **voici j. la lettre que j'attendais,** here is the very letter I was waiting for.

justesse [ʒystɛs] *n.f.* **1.** exactness, correctness, precision, accuracy; **j. d'une vis,** exact fit of a screw; **j. d'une opinion,** soundness of an opinion; **j. d'une expression,** aptness, appropriateness, of an expression; **raisonner avec j.,** to argue soundly, rightly. **2. de j.,** just; by the skin of one's teeth.

justice [ʒystis] *n.f.* **1.** justice; **c'est j. que** + *sub.*, it is only right, fair, that . . .; **il est de toute j. de l'entendre,** it is only fair to give him a hearing; **en toute, bonne, j.,** in all fairness; by rights; **avec j.,** justly, deservedly; **faire, rendre, j. à qn,** (i) to do justice to s.o.; (ii) to deal with s.o. according to his deserts; **ce n'est que j.,** it's only just, fair; **se faire j. (à soi-même),** (i) to take the law into one's own hands; (ii) to commit suicide; **faire j. de qch.,** to refute, challenge, sth. **2.** law, legal proceedings; **gens de j.,** (i) officers of the law, of the court, (ii) lawyers; **action en j.,** action at law; **aller en j.,** to go to law; **poursuivre qn en j.,** to institute legal proceedings against s.o.; to take legal action against s.o.

justiciable [ʒystisjabl̥] **1.** *a.* **j. d'un tribunal,** justiciable to, in, amenable to, a court; *Med:* **cas j. d'un certain traitement,** case in which a certain treatment is indicated. **2.** *n.* the ordinary man (in the eyes of the law).

justicier, -ière [ʒystisje, -jɛr] *n.* (*a*) lover of justice; (*b*) administrator of justice, justiciary.

justifiable [ʒystifjabl̥] *a.* justifiable, warrantable.

justificateur, -trice [ʒystifikatœr, -tris] **1.** *a.* justificatory, justifying. **2.** *n.* justifier.

justificatif, -ive [ʒystifikatif, -iv] *a.* justificatory; **pièce justificative,** *n.m.* **j.,** (i) *Com:* voucher (copy); (ii) written proof; (iii) *Jur:* relevant document.

justification [ʒystifikasjɔ̃] *n.f.* **1.** justification; vindication. **2.** proof (of fact, identity). **3.** *Typ:* (*a*) justification (of lines); (*b*) type area.

justifié [ʒystifje] *a.* **1.** justified, justifiable (action); **peu j.,** hardly justifiable; unwarranted. **2.** *Jur:* **préjudice j.,** proved damages.

justifier [ʒystifje] *v.* (*impf. & pr.sub.* **n. justifiions, v. justifiiez**) **1.** *v.tr.* (*a*) to justify, vindicate (s.o.'s conduct, etc.); to bear out (statement, etc.); to warrant (action, expenditure); (*b*) to prove, give proof of, make good (assertion, etc.); (*c*) *Typ:* to justify, adjust (line of type, etc.). **2.** *v.ind.tr. Jur:* **j. de ses mouvements,** to account for one's movements; **j. de son identité,** to prove one's identity. **3. se j.,** to justify oneself; to clear oneself.

jute [ʒyt] *n.m. Tex:* jute; **toile de j.,** hessian.

juter [ʒyte] *v.i.* to be juicy, drip (with) juice.

juteux, -euse [ʒytø, -øz] **1.** *a.* juicy. **2.** *n.m. Mil: P:* warrant officer.

juvénile [ʒyvenil] *a.* juvenile; youthful.

juvénilité [ʒyvenilite] *n.f. Lit:* juvenility, youthfulness.

juxtalinéaire [ʒykstalineɛr] *a.* **traduction j.,** juxtalinear, line for line, translation.

juxtaposer [ʒykstapoze] *v.tr.* to juxtapose, place side by side.

juxtaposition [ʒykstapozisjɔ̃] *n.f.* juxtaposition.

K

K, k [ka] *n.m.* (the letter) K, k; *Ph:* **échelle K.** (= **Kelvin),** Kelvin, absolute, scale (of temperatures).
Kaboul [kabul] *Pr.n. Geog:* Kabul.
kabyle [kabil] **1.** *a. & n. Ethn:* Kabyle. **2.** *n.m. Ling:* Kabyle.
Kabylie [kabili] *Pr.n.f. Geog:* **(la Grande, Petite) K.,** (Great, Lesser) Kabylia.
Kairouan [kɛrwɑ̃] *Pr.n. Geog:* Kairwan.
kaiser [kajzɛr] *n.m.* kaiser.
kakatoès [kakatɔɛs] *n.m. Orn:* cockatoo.
kakémono [kakemɔno] *n.m. Art:* kakemono.
kaki[1] [kaki] *n.m. & a.inv. Tex:* khaki, *NAm:* olive-drab.
kaki[2] *n.m. Bot:* (Chinese) persimmon.
kaléidoscope [kaleidɔskɔp] *n.m.* kaleidoscope.
kaléidoscopique [kaleidɔskɔpik] *a.* kaleidoscopic.
kali [kali] *n.m.* (*a*) *Bot:* kali, glasswort, prickly saltwort; (*b*) *Ch:* kali, potash.
kalmouk, -ouke [kalmuk] **1.** *a. & n. Ethn:* Kalmuck. **2.** *n.m. Ling:* Kalmuck.
kamikaze [kamikaze] *n.m.* kamikaze.
Kamtchadale [kamtʃadal] *n. Geog:* (native, inhabitant) of Kamchatka.
Kamtchatka [kamtʃatka] *Pr.n. Geog:* Kamchatka.
kangourou [kɑ̃guru] *n.m. Z:* kangaroo; **k. de rochers,** wallaby; *Geog:* **île des Kangourous,** Kangaroo Island.
kantien, -ienne [kɑ̃tjɛ̃, -jɛn] *a. Phil:* Kantian.
kantisme [kɑ̃tism] *n.m. Phil:* Kantianism, Kantism.
kaolin [kaɔlɛ̃] *n.m.* kaolin.
kaolinisation [kaɔlinizasjɔ̃] *n.f.* kaolinization (of feldspar, etc.).
kapok [kapɔk] *n.m. Com:* kapok.
kapokier [kapɔkje] *n.m. Bot:* kapok tree.
karakul [karakyl] *n.m. Husb:* caracul, karakul (sheep).
karaté [karate] *n.m. Sp:* karate.
karbau [karbo] *n.m. Z:* carabao; water buffalo.
karité [karite] *n.m. Bot:* karite, shea(tree); **beurre de k.,** karite nut butter, shea butter.
karma [karma] *n.m. Buddhist Rel:* karma.
Karman [karmɑ̃] *n.m. Av:* **K. (de raccordement),** wing fillet, fin fillet.
Karpat(h)es [karpat] *Pr.n.m.pl. Geog:* the Carpathians.
karstique [karstik] *a. Geog:* karstic.
kart [kart] *n.m. Sp: Aut:* go-kart; cart, *NAm:* kart.
karting [kartiŋ] *n.m. Sp: Aut:* go-kart racing, *esp. NAm:* karting.
kasba(h) [kazba] *n.f.* casbah, kasbah.
kascher [kaʃɛr] *a.inv. Jew.Rel:* kosher.
Katanga [katɑ̃ga] *Pr.n.m. Geog:* Katanga.
katangais, -aise [katɑ̃gɛ, -ɛz] *a.* Katangan.
kava, kawa [kava] *n.f.* kava ((i) shrub, (ii) drink).
kayac, kayak [kajak] *n.m.* kayak.
Kelvin [kɛlvin] *Pr.n. Ph:* **échelle K.,** Kelvin, absolute, scale (of temperatures).
kénotron [kenɔtrɔ̃] *n.m. El:* kenotron.
képi [kepi] *Cost:* kepi.
kérabau [kerabo] *n.m. Z:* carabao, water buffalo.
kératectomie [keratɛktɔmi] *n.f. Surg:* keratectomy.
kératine [keratin] *n.f. Physiol: Ch:* keratin, ceratin.
kératinisation [keratinizasjɔ̃] *n.f.* keratinization.
kératite [keratit] *n.f. Med:* keratitis.
kératodermie [keratɔdɛrmi] *n.f. Med:* keratodermia, ceratodermia.
kératoïde [keratɔid] *a. Physiol:* keratoid, ceratoid.
kératoplastie [keratɔplasti] *n.f. Surg:* keratoplasty, corneal grafting.
kératoscope [keratɔskɔp] *n.m. Med:* keratoscope.
kératose [keratoz] *n.f. Med: Vet:* keratosis.
kératotomie [keratɔtɔmi] *n.f. Surg:* keratotomy.
kermès [kɛrmɛs] *n.m.* **1.** *Ent:* (al)kermes; **k. de la vigne,** vine scale. **2.** *Bot:* **chêne k.,** kermes oak. **3.** *Pharm: etc:* **k. minéral,** kermes mineral, amorphous sulphide of antimony, red antimony; kermesite.
kermesse [kɛrmɛs] *n.f.* (*a*) (Flemish) kermis; village fair; (*b*) (charity) fête.
kérosène [kerozɛn] *n.m.* paraffin (oil), *NAm:* kerosene; *Av:* **k. aviation,** kerosene; *Ch:* **k. chloré,** keryl.
ketch [kɛtʃ] *n.m. Nau:* ketch.
keynésien, -ienne [kenezjɛ̃, -jɛn] *a. & n. Pol.Ec:* Keynesian.
khalifat [kalifa] *n.m.* caliphate.
khalife [kalif] *n.m.* caliph.
khamsin [kamzin] *n.m. Meteor:* khamsin.
khan [kɑ̃] *n.m.* khan.
khédive [kediv] *n.m.* khedive.
khmer, khmère [kmɛr] **1.** *a. & n. Geog:* Khmer, Kmer. **2.** *n.m. Ling:* K(h)mer.
khôl [kol] *n.m. Toil:* kohl.
kibboutz [kibuts] *n.m. Pol.Ec:* kibbutz; *pl. kibboutsim, kibboutzim.*
kick(-starter) [kik(startɛr)] *n.m. Motor Cy:* kick starter.
kidnapper [kidnape] *v.tr.* to kidnap.
kidnappeur, -euse [kidnapœr, øz] *n.* kidnapper.
kidnapping [kidnapiŋ] *n.m.* kidnapping.
kieselguhr [kizɛlgur] *n.m. Miner:* kieselguhr.
kievien, -ienne [kjevjɛ̃, -jɛn] *a. & n.* Kievan; *Hist:* **Russie kievienne,** Kievan Russia.
kif-kif [kifkif] *a.inv. F:* same, likewise; **c'est k.-k. (bourricot),** *n.m. P:* **c'est du kif,** it's all the same, it's six of one and half a dozen of the other, it's as broad as it's long.
kiki [kiki] *n.m. P:* neck, throat; **serrer le k. à qn,** to throttle s.o.
kil [kil] *n.m. P:* litre, *NAm:* liter, of (red) wine; bottle of plonk.
kilo [kilo] *n.m. F:* (= KILOGRAMME) kilo.
kilocalorie [kilɔkalɔri] *n.f.* kilocalorie.
kilocycle [kilɔsikl̥] *n.m.* kilocycle.
kilogramme [kilɔgram] *n.m. Meas:* kilogram(me).
kilohertz [kilɔɛrts] *n.m.* kilocycle.
kilojoule [kilɔʒul] *n.m.* kilohertz.
kilolitre [kilolitr̥] *n.m.* kilolitre, *NAm:* kiloliter.
kilométrage [kilɔmetraʒ] *n.m.* **1.** (*a*) measuring (of road, etc.) in kilometres, *NAm:* kilometers; (*b*) = marking (of road) with milestones. **2.** length in kilometres; = mileage.
kilomètre [kilɔmɛtr̥] *n.m.* kilometre, *NAm:* kilometer; *Rail: Adm:* **voyageurs kilomètres,** passenger

kilometres; **tonnes-kilomètres marchandises,** ton kilometres.

kilomètre-passager [kilɔmɛtr̥pasaʒe] *n.m. Adm: Av:* passenger-kilometre, *NAm:* -kilometer; *pl. kilomètres-passagers.*

kilométrer [kilɔmetre] *v.tr.* (**je kilomètre, n. kilométrons; je kilométrerai**) (*a*) to measure (road, etc.) in kilometres, *NAm:* kilometers; (*b*) to mark off (road) with kilometre stones (= milestones).

kilomètre-voyageur [kilɔmɛtr̥vwajaʒœr] *n.m. Adm:* passenger-kilometre, *NAm:* -kilometer; *pl. kilomètres-voyageurs.*

kilométrique [kilɔmetrik] *a.* kilometric; **borne k.,** kilometre, *NAm:* kilometer, stone (= milestone); *Aut:* **indemnité k.** = mileage allowance.

kilotonne [kilɔtɔn] *n.f. Meas:* kiloton.

kilovolt [kilɔvɔlt] *n.m. A:* kilovolt.

kilowatt [kilɔwat] *n.m.* kilowatt.

kilowattheure [kilɔwatœr] *n.m. El:* kilowatt-hour.

kilt [kilt] *n.m. Cost:* kilt.

kimono [kimɔno] *n.m. Cost:* kimono; **manche k.,** kimono sleeve.

kinase [kinaz] *n.f. Bio-Ch:* kinase.

kinésimètre [kinezimɛtr̥] *n.m. Med:* kinesi(o)-meter.

kinésithérapeute [kineziterapøt] *n.* physio-therapist.

kinésithérapie [kineziterapi] *n.f. Med:* physio-therapy.

kinesthésie [kinɛstezi] *n.f.* kin(a)esthesia, kines-thesis.

king-charles [kiŋʃarl] *n.m.inv.* King Charles spa-niel.

kinkajou [kɛ̃kaʒu] *n.m. Z:* kinkajou, honey bear.

kiosque [kjɔsk] *n.m.* **1.** (*a*) kiosk; **k. de, à, musique,** bandstand; (*b*) **k. à journaux,** newspaper kiosk. **2.** *Nau:* (*a*) **k. de la barre,** wheelhouse; **k. de veille, de navigation,** pilot house, chart house, room; (*b*) conning tower (of submarine). **3.** *El:* **k. de transformation,** transformer box, tower.

kirghize, kirghise [kirgiz] *a. & n.m.inv. Ethn:* Kirghiz, Khirghiz.

kiwi [kiwi] *n.m. Orn:* kiwi.

klaxon, Klaxon [klaksɔn, -ɔ̃] *n.m. R.t.m: Aut:* horn, hooter.

klaxonner [klaksɔne] *v.i. Aut:* to hoot, sound one's horn.

klebs [klɛp(s)] *n.m. P:* dog, tyke, pooch.

kleptomane [klɛptɔman] *a. & n.* kleptomaniac.

kleptomanie [klɛptɔmani] *n.f.* kleptomania.

klystron [klistrɔ̃] *n.m. Elcs:* klystron.

knock-out [nɔkaut] *Box:* **1.** *a.inv.* **mettre (qn) k.-o.,** to knock (s.o.) out; **être k.-o.,** to be knocked out. **2.** *n.m.* knockout.

knout [knut] *n.m.* knout.

koala [kɔala] *n.m. Z:* koala (bear).

kobold [kɔbɔld] *n.m. Myth:* kobold.

kola [kɔla] *n.m. Bot:* cola, kola; **noix de k.,** kola nut.

kolatier [kɔlatje] *n.m. Bot:* cola, kola (tree).

kolkhoze [kɔlkoz] *n.m.* kolkhoz, collective farm.

kominform [kɔminfɔrm] *n.m. Pol.Hist:* cominform.

komintern [kɔmintɛrn] *n.m. Pol.Hist.* comintern.

kopeck [kɔpɛk] *n.m. Num:* kopeck.

Koran (le) [ləkɔrɑ̃] *Pr.n.m.* the Koran.

korrigan, -ane [kɔrigɑ̃, -an] *n.* (*in Brittany*) goblin.

koudou [kudu] *n.m. Z:* kudu; **grand k.,** greater kudu.

koukri [kukri] *n.m.* kukri, Gurkha knife.

koulak [kulak] *n.m.* kulak.

Kourile [kuril] *Geog:* **1.** *a.* **les îles Kouriles,** the Kuril(e) Islands. **2.** *n.* Kurile, Kurilian.

Kouro-sivo (le) [ləkurɔsivo] *Pr.n.m. Oc:* the Kur-osivo (current).

kraal [krɑl] *n.m.* kraal.

krach [krak] *n.m.* (financial) crash, smash; **il a perdu tout ce qu'il possédait dans le k. de sa banque,** he lost everything when his bank went smash.

kraft [kraft] *n.m. Paperm:* kraft.

kraken [krakɛn] *n.m. Myth:* kraken.

Kremlin (le) [ləkrɛmlɛ̃] *n.m.* the Kremlin.

kriss [kris] *n.m.* kris, Malay dagger.

krypton [kriptɔ̃] *n.m. Ch:* krypton.

ksar [ksar] *n.m.* (*in N. Africa*) fortress; fortified vil-lage; *pl. ksour* [ksur].

kumquat [kɔmkwat] *n.m. Bot:* kumquat, cumquat.

Kurde [kyrd] **1.** *n. Ethn:* Kurd. **2.** *a.* Kurdish. **3.** *n.m. Ling:* Kurdish.

Kurdistan [kyrdistɑ̃] *Pr.n.m. Geog:* Kurdistan.

kurtosis [kyrtozis] *n.m. Stat:* kurtosis.

kymographe [kimɔgraf] *n.m. Med: etc:* kymo-graph.

kymrique [kimrik] *a. & n.m. Ethn: Ling:* Cymric.

kyrie [kirje] *n.m. Ecc:* kyrie (eleison).

kyrielle [kirjɛl] *n.f.* **1.** *A:* litany. **2.** long string (of words, etc.).

kyste [kist] *n.m. Med:* cyst; **k. synovial,** ganglion.

kystique [kistik] *a. Med:* cystic.

kystitomie [kistitɔmi] *n.f. Surg:* cystotomy.

L

L, l [ɛl] *n.m. or f.* (the letter) L, l; *Phon: Ling:* **l. mouillé(e),** liquid l, palatal(ized) l.
l', la¹ [la] *def. article & pron. f. see* LE[1,2].
la² *n.m.inv. Mus:* **1.** (the note) A; **donner le la,** to give the, an, A; **les huit premières lignes donnent le la du livre,** the first eight lines set the tone of the book. **2.** lah (in tonic sol-fa).
là [la] *adv.* **1.** (*of place*) there; (*a*) **là où vous êtes,** where you are; **quand il n'est pas là,** when he isn't there, when he's away; **est-ce que le patron est là?** is the boss in? **les choses en sont là,** this is the state of things at the moment; **la question n'est pas là,** that's not the point; **de là au village il y a un kilomètre,** it's one kilometre, *NAm:* killometer, from there to the village; **à cinq pas de là se tenait l'agent de police,** five paces away stood the policeman; **de là à croire que tout est facile, il y a loin,** it's a long way to believing everything is easy; *F:* **ôtez-vous de là!** get out of there! **passez par là,** go that way; **là en bas,** down there; *F:* **elle a trente-cinq ans, par là,** she's about thirty-five; **il est là,** he's here; **viens là!** come here! (*b*) (*emphatic use*) **c'est là qu'il demeure,** that's where he lives; **c'est là où nous ne sommes plus d'accord,** that's where we disagree; **c'est là qu'elle fut interrompue,** it was at that moment that she was interrupted; **que dites-vous là?** what's that you're saying? what are you saying? **ces gens-là sont ennuyeux,** those people are boring; **il est bête à ce point-là?** is he (really) that stupid? *see also* CE[1] 1, CE[2] 5; **celui-là, celle-là,** *see* CELUI 4; (*c*) *F:* **il est un peu là,** he makes his presence felt; you can't miss him; **comme menteur il est un peu là!** he's a pretty good liar! **2.** (*of time*) then; **d'ici là,** between now and then; in the meantime; **à quelques jours de là,** some days after (that); a few days later. **3. qu'entendez-vous par là?** what do you mean by that? **de là on peut conclure que . . .,** from this, hence, one can conclude that . . . . **4.** *int.* (*a*) **hé là! doucement!** gently does it! **là, là! ne vous inquiétez pas,** there now, don't you worry; (*to child*) **là, là!** there, there; (*b*) **oh là là!** (i) oh dear! (ii) (*jeeringly*) look at him, her! (*c*) **alors là, ce n'est pas étonnant!** well, *that's* not surprising!
là-bas [labɑ] *adv.* over there; **le voilà là-b.,** there he is over there.
label [labɛl] *n.m. Com:* (*a*) trade-union mark, label (on manufactured article, on published work, etc.); (*b*) label, stamp; seal (of approval).
labeur [labœr] *n.m.* labour, *NAm:* labor; toil, hard work.
labial, -ale, -iaux [labjal, -jo] *a.* labial (muscle, etc.); *Ling:* **consonne labiale,** *n.f.* **labiale,** labial.
labié [labje] *a. Bot:* labiate, lipped.
labiodental, -ale, -aux [labjɔdɑ̃tal, -o] *Ling: a.* labiodental; *n.f.* **labiodentale,** labiodental.
labo [labo] *n.m. F:* lab.
laborantin, -ine [labɔrɑ̃tɛ̃, -in] *n.* laboratory assistant.
laboratoire [labɔratwar] *n.m.* laboratory; **l. de recherche, de langues,** research, language, laboratory; **l. d'analyses (médicales),** pathology laboratory.
laborieusement [labɔrjøzmɑ̃] *adv.* laboriously; **gagner l. sa vie,** to work hard for a living.
laborieux, -euse [labɔrjø, -øz] *a.* **1.** arduous, hard, painstaking (work, etc.); laboured, *NAm:* labored, laborious (style, etc.); *F:* **il n'a pas encore fini? c'est l.!** hasn't he finished yet? it's taking a long time! **2.** (*of pers.*) laborious, hard-working; **les masses laborieuses,** the toiling masses.
labour [labur] *n.m.* (*a*) ploughing, *NAm:* plowing; tilling; **l. à la bêche,** digging; **cheval de l.,** plough, *NAm:* plow, horse; (*b*) **(terre de) l.,** ploughed land.
labourable [laburabl̩] *a.* ploughable, *NAm:* plowable (land).
labourage [laburaʒ] *n.m.* ploughing, *NAm:* plowing; tilling; digging.
labourer [labure] *v.tr.* (*a*) to plough, *NAm:* to plow; to till (land); **l. à la bêche,** to dig; (*b*) *Nau:* **l. le fond,** (i) (*of ship*) to graze the bottom; (ii) (*of anchor*) to drag; (*c*) **se l. les mains,** to lacerate one's hands; **visage labouré de rides,** face furrowed with wrinkles.
laboureur [laburœr] *n.m. Agr:* ploughman, *NAm:* plowman.
labrador [labradɔr] *n.m.* Labrador (retriever).
labyrinthe [labirɛ̃t] *n.m.* **1.** labyrinth, maze. **2.** *Anat:* labyrinth (of the ear).
labyrinthique [labirɛ̃tik] *a.* labyrinthine.
lac [lak] *n.m.* **1.** *Geog:* lake; **l. de cirque,** tarn; **les lacs de l'Écosse,** the Scottish lochs; **le l. Léman, de Genève,** lake Geneva; *F:* (*of project, etc.*) **être, tomber, dans le l.,** to fizzle out; to fall through. **2.** pool (of blood, etc.).
laçage [lasaʒ] *n.m.* lacing (up) (of shoes, etc.).
lacement [lasmɑ̃] *n.m.* lacing (up) (of shoes, etc.).
lacer [lase] *v.tr.* **(je laçai(s); n. laçons)** to lace (up) (shoes, etc.); **ce corset se lace sur le côté,** this corset laces (up) at the side.
lacération [laserasjɔ̃] *n.f.* laceration. **1.** tearing, lacerating, slashing; ripping (up); defacing (of poster, etc.); mauling (by wild beast). **2.** tear, jagged wound.
lacérer [lasere] *v.tr.* **(je lacère, n. lacérons; je lacérerai)** to tear, lacerate, maul; to tear, rip, slash (sth.) to pieces; to deface (poster).
lacet [lasɛ] *n.m.* **1.** (*a*) (shoe)lace, bootlace; lace (of corset); *Nau:* lacing (of sail); **chaussures à lacets,** lace-up shoes, *F:* lace-ups; (*b*) (i) swaying, rocking (of vehicle); (ii) *Av:* yaw(ing); **axe de l.,** yaw axis; (*c*) *Needlw:* braid. **2.** (hairpin) bend, sharp bend (in road); **sentier en lacets,** winding, twisting, path; zigzag path; **la route monte en lacets,** the road winds steeply up. **3.** noose, springe, snare (for rabbits, etc.); **tendre un l.,** to set a snare.
lâchage [lɑʃaʒ] *n.m.* **1.** dropping (of parachutist, etc.). **2.** *F:* dropping, ditching (of friend); jilting (of lover).
lâche [lɑʃ] *a.* **1.** (*a*) loose, slack (spring, knot, etc.); loosely fitting (garment); lax (discipline); woolly, slipshod, careless (style); (*b*) *Lit:* weak, feeble (character, etc.). **2.** (*a*) cowardly; *n.* coward; (*b*) low, despicable.
lâché [lɑʃe] *a.* slovenly, slipshod (work, style).
lâchement [lɑʃmɑ̃] *adv.* **1.** loosely, slackly. **2.** like a coward.
lâcher¹ [lɑʃe] **1.** *v.tr.* to release; (*a*) to slacken, loosen (spring, etc.); **l. un coup de pied à qn,** to let fly at s.o. with one's foot; *Aut:* **l. le frein,** to release the brake; (*b*) to let go; to leave go of (sth.); to drop (sth.); *Av:* to release, drop (bomb, parachutist); **lâchez-moi!** let

me go! let go of me! (*of bird*) **l. sa proie,** to drop its prey; **il ne lâcha pas la corde,** he did not let go of the rope; **l. ses études,** to give up one's studies; **l. pied,** to give way; to give in; **l. prise,** (i) to let go; to lose one's hold; (ii) to give up; *F:* **l. qn,** to drop, ditch s.o.; to jilt (a lover); **il ne m'a pas lâché d'une semelle,** he stuck to me like a leech; *F:* **l. des sous,** *P:* **les l.,** to fork out; (*c*) to set free (prisoner, bird, etc.); to let (animal) loose; to let out (scream, etc.); **l. un chien,** to unleash a dog; to let a dog loose; *Ven:* to slip a dog; **l. le chien contre qn,** to set the dog on s.o.; *P:* **l. le paquet, le morceau,** to tell the truth, come clean. **2.** *v.i.* to get loose; (*of spring, etc.*) to slacken; (*of rope*) to slip; **mes freins ont lâché,** my brakes failed, gave out; **ses nerfs ont lâché,** she lost her nerve, she broke down.

lâcher² *n.m.* release (of pigeons, etc.).

lâcheté [lɑʃte] *n.f.* **1.** *Lit:* weakness; slackness. **2.** (*a*) cowardice, cowardliness; (*b*) act of cowardice. **3.** (*a*) despicableness; baseness; (*b*) low, despicable, action.

lâcheur, -euse [lɑʃœr, -øz] *n. F:* fickle, unreliable, person.

lacis [lasi] *n.m.* (*a*) network (of nerves, wire, etc.); **l. de ruelles,** maze of back streets; (*b*) *Lacem:* lacis.

laconique [lakɔnik] *a.* laconic.

laconiquement [lakɔnikmɑ̃] *adv.* laconically.

laconisme [lakɔnism] *n.m.* lacon(ic)ism, brevity.

lacrymal, -aux [lakrimal, -o] *a.* lachrymal (duct, etc.); **glande lacrymale,** tear gland.

lacrymogène [lakrimɔʒɛn] *a.* **gaz, grenade, l.,** tear gas, bomb.

lacs [lɑ] *n.m.* **1. l. d'amour,** love knot. **2.** *A: & Lit:* noose, snare, springe.

lactaire [laktɛr] **1.** *a.* lacteal. **2.** *n.m. Fung:* lactarius; **l. délicieux,** saffron milk cap.

lactation [laktasjɔ̃] *n.f.* **1.** *Physiol:* lactation. **2.** suckling, nursing.

lacté [lakte] *a.* lacteal, milky; **régime l.,** milk diet.

lactifère [laktifɛr] *a.* lactiferous; lacteal (duct).

lactique [laktik] *a. Ch:* lactic (acid).

lactose [laktoz] *n.f. Ch:* lactose.

lacunaire [lakynɛr] *a.* (*a*) lacunar(y), lacunal; (*b*) **documentation l.,** incomplete documentation.

lacune [lakyn] *n.f.* **1.** lacuna, gap, hiatus (in text, etc.); break (in succession, etc.); blank (in memory, etc.); **cette liste comporte plusieurs lacunes,** there are several items missing on this list. **2.** *Biol: Anat:* lacuna; *Bot:* air cell.

lacuneux, -euse [lakynø, -øz] *a.* = LACUNAIRE.

lacustre [lakystr̥] *a.* lacustrine, lacustrian (animal, dwelling); **habitation l.,** lake dwelling, pile dwelling.

lad [lad] *n.m.* stable lad, boy.

là-dedans [lad(ə)dɑ̃] *adv.* in there; inside, in it, in this; *F:* **debout là-d.!** rise and shine!

là-dessous [latsu] *adv.* under that, under there, underneath.

là-dessus [latsy] *adv.* on that, on it; **tout le monde est d'accord là-d.,** everybody is agreed about that; **là-d., il est sorti,** thereupon, with that, he went out; **nous reviendrons là-d.,** we shall come back to that.

ladre [ladr̥] **1.** *a.* (*a*) *A:* leprous; (*b*) *A:* niggardly, miserly, stingy; (*c*) *Vet:* measly, measled (pig). **2.** *n. A:* (*a*) leper; (*b*) *Lit:* niggard, miser, skinflint.

ladrerie [ladrəri] *n.f.* **1.** *A:* (*a*) leprosy; (*b*) lazar house. **2.** *A: & Lit:* meanness, stinginess. **3.** *Vet:* measles (of pigs).

lagon [lagɔ̃] *n.m.,* **lagune** [lagyn] *n.f. Geog:* lagoon.

lagopède [lagɔpɛd] *n.m. Orn:* lagopus; **l. des Alpes,** ptarmigan; **l. d'Écosse,** red grouse.

là-haut [lao] *adv.* up there; upstairs.

lai¹ [lɛ] *n.m. Lit: Pros:* lay.

lai² *a. Ecc:* **frère l., sœur laie,** lay brother, sister.

laïc [laik] *a.m. & n.m.* = LAÏQUE.

laîche [lɛʃ] *n.f. Bot:* sedge.

laïcisation [laisizasjɔ̃] *n.f.* laicization, secularization.

laïciser [laisize] *v.tr.* to laicize, secularize.

laïcisme [laisism] *n.m.* laicism.

laïcité [laisite] *n.f.* secularity (of schools, etc.); *Pol:* secularism.

laid [lɛ] **1.** *a.* (*a*) ugly; unsightly; unattractive; (*of face*) plain, *NAm:* homely; *F:* **l. comme un pou, à faire peur,** as ugly as sin; (*b*) mean, low (action, etc.); ugly (vice, etc.); (*to child*) **c'est l. de mentir,** it's very naughty to tell lies. **2.** *n.* (*a*) plain(-faced), *NAm:* homely, person; (*b*) *F:* **oh, le l.! la laide!** what a naughty boy, naughty girl! (*c*) **le l. et le beau,** the ugly and the beautiful.

laidement [lɛdmɑ̃] *adv.* **1.** in an ugly way. **2.** meanly, dishonestly.

laideron [lɛdrɔ̃] *n.m.* ugly, plain, *NAm:* homely, girl, woman; **un petit l.,** an ugly duckling; *a.* **une petite fille laideronne,** a plain little girl.

laideur [lɛdœr] *n.f.* **1.** ugliness, unsightliness, unattractiveness; plainness, *NAm:* homeliness (of features); **d'une l. épouvantable,** frighteningly ugly. **2.** (*a*) meanness, lowness (of conduct, etc.); (*b*) **les laideurs de la vie,** the ugly side of life.

laie¹ [lɛ] *n.f.* (wild) sow.

laie² *n.f.* forest track, ride.

laie³ *n.f. Tls: Stonew:* bush hammer.

lainage [lɛnaʒ] *n.m.* **1.** (*a*) fleece (of sheep); (*b*) woollen fabric, material; (*c*) woollen garment, article; *F:* woolly; *pl.* woollen goods, woollens. **2.** *Tex:* teaseling, napping.

laine [lɛn] *n.f.* **1.** wool; **bêtes à l.,** woolly-coated animals; **l. cardée,** carding wool; **pure l.,** pure wool; **l. peignée,** worsted; **l. à tricoter,** knitting wool; **l. perlée,** crochet wool; **jupe en, de, l.,** woollen skirt; **tapis de haute l.,** thick pile wool carpet; **se laisser manger, tondre, la l. sur le dos,** to (allow oneself to) be fleeced. **2. l. de bois,** wood fibre, *NAm:* fiber; **l. de verre,** glass wool; fibreglass, *NAm:* fiberglass.

lainer¹ [lene] *v.tr. Tex:* to teasel, nap (cloth).

lainer² *n.m. Tex:* nap (of cloth).

lainerie [lɛnri] *n.f.* (*a*) manufacture of woollens; (*b*) woollen mill; (*c*) woollen goods, woollens; (*d*) (wholesale) wool shop.

laineur, -euse¹ [lɛnœr, -øz] *n. Tex:* teaseler, napper.

laineux, -euse² [lɛnø, -øz] *a.* fleecy (cloth, etc.); woolly (sheep, hair, etc.).

lainier, -ière [lɛnje, -jɛr] **1.** *a.* woollen (trade, etc.); **industrie lainière,** wool industry. **2.** *n.* (*a*) wool merchant; (*b*) worker in a woollen mill; wool worker.

laïque [laik] **1.** *a.* laic; lay (dress, etc.); secular (education, etc.); **école, enseignement, l.** = (non-religious) state school, education. **2.** *n.* layman, *f.* laywoman; **les laïques,** the laity.

lais [lɛ] *n.m.* **1.** *For:* staddle. **2.** *Geog:* (*a*) **l. (de rivière),** alluvium; (*b*) foreshore.

laisse¹ [lɛs] *n.f.* leash, lead; *Ven:* slip; **tenir un chien en l.,** to keep a dog on a lead, on the leash; *F:* **mener, tenir, qn en l.,** to keep a tight rein on s.o.

laisse² *n.f.* **1.** *Pros:* laisse. **2.** *Geog:* foreshore; **l. de haute, basse, mer,** high-water, low-water, mark.

laissé-pour-compte [lesepurkɔ̃t] **1.** *a.* (*a*) *Com:* rejected, returned (article); unsold (goods); (*b*) rejected, unwanted (person). **2.** (*a*) *n.m. Com:* reject; unsold article; (*b*) *n.* unwanted person; misfit; *pl. laissé(e)s-pour-compte.*

laisser [lese] *v.tr.* **1.** to let, allow; **il le laissa partir,** he let him go, allowed him to go; **je les ai laissés dire,** I let them talk; **elle se laissa embrasser,** she allowed herself to be kissed, she let him (her) kiss her; **le toit laissait passer la pluie,** the roof let the rain in; **l. voir son mécontentement,** to show one's displeasure, disapproval; **l. tomber qch.,** to drop sth.; **se l. aller,** to let oneself go; **se l. décourager,** to let oneself be discouraged; *F:* **laissez-moi rire!** don't make me laugh! **ne vous laissez pas aller comme ça!** pull yourself together! *F:* **ce vin se laisse boire,** this wine is quite drinkable; **ce livre se laisse lire,** this book is easy to read; **se l. emporter par la colère,** to give way to anger; **l. sécher la peinture,** to allow the paint to dry; **laissez-les boire un verre de vin,** let them have a glass of wine; **laisse faire,** never mind; don't bother; **laissez-le faire!** leave it to him! let him get on with it; *F:* **l. courir,** to leave (things) alone; **il se laissa faire,** he offered no resistance; **allons, laisse-toi faire!** go on, be a devil! **vous n'allez pas me l. tout seul?** you aren't going to leave me all on my own? **2.** (*a*) to leave (s.o., sth., somewhere); **l. qn derrière soi,** (i) to leave s.o. behind; (ii) to be ahead of s.o. (in a subject, etc.); **allons, je vous laisse,** well, I'm going, I'm off; **il a laissé une veuve et trois enfants,** he left a widow and three children; **elle a laissé son mari,** she left, walked out on, her husband; **partir sans l. d'adresse,** to go away without leaving one's address; **l. qch. de côté,** to leave sth. out; to put sth. aside; **laissez-lui du gâteau,** save some cake for him; **l. là qn,** to leave s.o. in the lurch; **c'est à prendre ou à l.,** take it or leave it; (*b*) to leave, keep (s.o., sth., in a certain state); **l. la fenêtre ouverte,** to leave, keep, the window open; **je vous laisse libre d'agir,** I leave you free to act; **nous l'avions laissé pour mort,** we had left him for dead; **laissez-moi (tranquille)!** leave me alone! **laissons cela jusqu'à demain,** we will, let's, leave that until tomorrow; **laissez, c'est moi qui paie,** leave that, I'm paying; **vous pouvez nous l.,** you may leave us, you may go; (*c*) **laissez-lui son secret,** let him keep his secret; **cela nous laisse le temps de . . .,** that leaves us time to . . .; **l. à qn un héritage,** to leave s.o. a legacy; **laissez-moi vos clefs,** leave me, let me have, your keys; **je vous le laisserai pour 100 francs,** you can have it for 100 francs; (*d*) **je vous laisse à penser notre bonheur,** you can imagine how happy we are, were; **cela laisse (beaucoup) à désirer,** it leaves much to be desired; (*e*) *Lit:* **il ne laissera pas d'y aller,** he won't fail to go; **cela ne laisse pas de m'inquiéter,** I feel anxious all the same, nevertheless; I can't help worrying about it.

laisser-aller [leseale] *n.m.* **1.** casualness. **2.** carelessness, slovenliness (of appearance, etc.).

laisser-faire [lesefɛr] *n.m. Pol:* non-interference, laisser-faire, laissez-faire.

laissez-passer [lesepase] *n.m.inv.* pass, permit; *Dipl:* laissez-passer; *Cust:* transire; *Nau:* sea pass.

lait [lɛ] *n.m.* milk. **1. l. entier,** whole milk; **l. écrémé,** skimmed milk; **l. de beurre,** buttermilk; **petit l.,** whey; **l. condensé,** condensed milk; **l. concentré,** evaporated milk; **l. en poudre,** dried milk; **l. caillé,** curd, curdled milk; **café au l.,** white coffee; **chocolat au l.,** milk chocolate; *Cu:* **l. de poule,** egg flip, egg nog (without alcohol); **vache à l.,** (i) milch cow; (ii) *F:* (*pers.*) mug, sucker; **pot à l.,** milk jug; **dents de l.,** milk teeth; **l. maternel,** mother's milk; **frère, sœur, de l.,** foster brother, sister; **cochon de l.,** sucking pig. **2.** (*a*) **l. de coco,** coconut milk; (*b*) **l. de chaux,** limewater, whitewash; (*c*) *Pharm:* **l. d'amandes,** almond milk; *Toil:* **l. démaquillant,** cleansing milk.

laitage [lɛtaʒ] *n.m.* (*a*) milk; (*b*) dairy produce.

laitance [lɛtɑ̃s] *n.f.*, **laite** [lɛt] *n.f. Ich:* milt; *Cu:* soft roe.

laité [lete] *a.* soft-roed (fish).

laiterie [lɛtri] *n.f.* **1.** dairy. **2.** (*a*) dairying; (*b*) dairy farming.

laiteron [lɛtrɔ̃] *n.m. Bot:* sow thistle, milkweed, hogweed.

laiteux, -euse [lɛtø, -øz] *a.* **1.** *Med:* lacteal (disorder, etc.). **2.** milk-like; milky (light, etc.).

laitier[1], -ière [letje, lɛtjɛr] **1.** *a.* **l'industrie laitière,** the milk, dairy, industry; **produits laitiers,** dairy produce; **vache laitière,** *n.f.* **laitière,** milch cow. **2.** *n.* (*a*) milkman; milk woman; (*b*) dairyman; dairywoman.

laitier[2] *n.m. Metall: etc:* dross, slag.

laiton [lɛtɔ̃] *n.m.* brass; **(fil de) l.,** brass wire.

laitue [lety] *n.f.* (*a*) lettuce; **l. romaine,** cos lettuce; (*b*) green salad.

laïus [lajys] *n.m. F:* speech, lecture; talk, waffle; **faire un l.,** to make a speech, hold forth.

lama[1] [lama] *n.m.* (Buddhist) lama; **le Grand l., le dalaï l.,** the Dalai Lama.

lama[2] *n.m. Z: Tex:* llama.

lamanage [lamanaʒ] *n.m. Nau:* inshore pilotage.

lamaneur [lamanœr] *n.m. Nau:* inshore pilot.

lamantin [lamɑ̃tɛ̃] *n.m. Z:* manatee, seacow.

lamaserie [lamazri] *n.f.* lamasery.

lambeau, -eaux [lɑ̃bo] *n.m.* scrap, bit, shred (of cloth, paper, flesh, etc.); fragment (of music, conversation, etc.); **vêtements en lambeaux,** clothes in rags, in tatters; **mettre qch. en lambeaux,** to tear sth. up, to shreds.

lambin, -ine [lɑ̃bɛ̃, -in] *F:* **1.** *a.* dawdling, slow. **2.** *n.* dawdler, slowcoach.

lambiner [lɑ̃bine] *v.i. F:* to dawdle.

lambourde [lɑ̃burd] *n.f.* **1.** *Arb:* fruit shoot. **2.** *Const:* (*a*) wall plate, beam bearing; (*b*) bridging joist; bearing joist (of flooring).

lambrequin [lɑ̃brəkɛ̃] *n.m.* **1.** *Her:* mantling, lambrequin. **2.** *Furn:* valance, lambrequin, pelmet.

lambris [lɑ̃bri] *n.m. Const:* panelling; (*on wall*) wainscoting (in wood); casing, lining (in marble, etc.); **l. d'appui,** dado.

lambrissage [lɑ̃brisaʒ] *n.m. Const:* wainscoting, panelling (of room).

lambrisser [lɑ̃brise] *v.tr. Const:* **1.** to wainscot, panel (room, etc.); **plafond lambrissé,** panelled ceiling. **2.** to plaster (wall, ceiling).

lame [lam] *n.f.* **1.** (*a*) lamina, thin plate, strip, web (of metal, etc.); leaf (of spring); (microscope) slide; slat (of venetian blind); **l. de parquet,** floorboard; strip of parquet flooring; (*b*) blade (of sword, knife, etc.); **l. de rasoir,** razor blade; *Lit:* **une l.,** a sword; **c'est une fine l.,** he's a fine swordsman; **visage en l. de couteau,** hatchet face; (*c*) *Bot:* lamina; gill (of mushroom); *Anat:* lamina. **2.** wave; *Poet:* billow; **l. de fond,** ground swell; **l. de houle,** roller, surge.

lamé [lame] **1.** *a.* spangled, worked, with silver, gold; **robe lamée d'or,** gold lamé dress. **2.** *n.m.* **(robe en) l. (d')or, l. d'argent,** gold, silver, lamé (dress).

lamellaire [lamelɛr] *a. Miner: etc:* lamellar, lamellate, foliated.

lamelle [lamɛl] *n.f.* (*a*) lamella (of slate, etc.); thin sheet, plate (of iron, etc.); scale, flake (of mica, etc.); *Bot:* lamella, gill (of mushroom); **l. de jalousie,** blind slat; (*b*) (microscope) slide.

lamellé [lamele], **lamelleux, -euse** [lamelø, -øz] *a.* lamellate(d); foliated, fissile (slate, etc.).

lamentable [lamɑ̃tabl̩] *a.* **1.** lamentable, deplorable (accident, etc.); **sort l.,** terrible fate. **2.** mournful, woeful (voice, etc.). **3.** (*of result, etc.*) appalling, awful; **orateur l.,** pitiful speaker.

lamentablement [lamɑ̃tabləmɑ̃] *adv.* lamentably, miserably.

lamentation [lamɑ̃tasjɔ̃] *n.f.* lamentation. **1.** wailing. **2.** (*a*) lament; **cri de l.,** wail; **le mur des Lamentations,** the Wailing Wall (in Jerusalem); (*b*) moaning, complaining.

lamenter (se) [səlamɑ̃te] *v.pr.* **se l. sur son sort,** to bemoan, lament, one's fate; **se l. de son ignorance,** to deplore, regret, one's ignorance.

laminage [laminaʒ] *n.m.* laminating, lamination, rolling, flatt(en)ing (of metal, etc.).
laminaire [laminɛr] **1.** *a.* laminar. **2.** *n.f. Algae:* laminaria, sea tangle; oarweed.
laminé [lamine] **1.** *a.* laminate(d). **2.** *n.m.* rolled iron.
laminer [lamine] *v.tr.* **1.** to laminate, flat(ten), roll (metal). **2. ses revenus sont laminés par les impôts,** his income is eaten away by taxes.
lamineur [laminœr] **1.** *a* laminating; **cylindre l.,** roller. **2.** *n.m.* rolling mill operator; laminator.
laminoir [laminwar] *n.m.* **1.** *Metalw:* flatting mill, rolling mill; **l. de finissage,** finishing rolls; **faire passer qn au l.,** to put s.o. through the mill. **2.** *Paperm:* plate glazing calender.
lampadaire [lɑ̃padɛr] *n.m.* **1.** (*a*) standard lamp; (*b*) street lamp. **2.** candelabrum.
lampant [lɑ̃pɑ̃] *a.* illuminating, refined (oil).
lampe [lɑ̃p] *n.f.* lamp. **1.** (*a*) **l. à huile,** oil lamp, paraffin lamp; *Min:* **l. de mineur, de sécurité,** miner's (safety) lamp; **à (la lumière de) la l.,** by lamplight; *P:* **s'en mettre plein la l.,** to have a good blowout; (*b*) **l. à incandescence,** incandescent lamp; **l. à arc,** arc lamp; **l. au néon,** neon lamp; (*c*) **l. de bureau,** reading lamp; desk light, lamp; **l. de chevet,** bedside lamp; **l. de poche,** (electric) torch, *NAm:* flashlight; *Cin:* **l. à lueurs,** glowlamp; *Phot:* **l. éclair,** flashlight. **2.** *Elcs:* **l. (de radio),** (radio) valve; tube; **l. d'amplification,** amplifying tube. **3. l. à alcool,** spirit lamp; **l. à souder,** blowlamp, blowtorch.
lampée [lɑ̃pe] *n.f. F:* gulp, swig (of water, wine, etc.).
lamper [lɑ̃pe] *v.tr. F:* to swig, toss off, gulp down.
lampe-tempête [lɑ̃ptɑ̃pɛt] *n.f.* storm lantern; *pl. lampes-tempêtes.*
lampion [lɑ̃pjɔ̃] *n.m.* (*a*) fairylight (for illuminations); *F:* **crier sur l'air des lampions,** to chant (slogan, etc.); (*b*) Chinese lantern.
lampiste [lɑ̃pist] *n.m.* **1.** *A:* lamp maker; lamp seller. **2.** (*a*) light maintenance man; *Rail:* lampman; (*b*) *F:* underling, scapegoat, *NAm:* fall guy; **s'en prendre au l.,** to bully one's subordinate(s).
lampisterie [lɑ̃pistəri] *n.f.* **1.** *A:* lamp trade, works. **2.** *Rail: etc:* lamp room.
lamproie [lɑ̃prwa] *n.f. Ich:* lamprey.
lance [lɑ̃s] *n.f.* **1.** (*a*) spear; **percer un animal d'un coup de l.,** to spear an animal; **fer de l.,** spearhead; *Bot:* **en fer de l.,** lanceolate; (*b*) lance; **rompre une l., des lances, avec, contre, qn,** to cross swords with s.o.; **rompre des lances pour qn,** to take up s.o.'s defence, to defend s.o. **2. l. d'arrosage,** water-hose nozzle; **l. d'incendie,** fire-hose nozzle.
lancé [lɑ̃se] *a.* **train l. à toute vapeur,** train going at full speed; **le voilà l.,** (i) now he's got a start (in life, in his profession); (ii) *F:* now he's off on his pet subject; **jeune homme l.,** young man who has achieved (social) success, who has made his name, *F:* who has made it.
lance-bombes [lɑ̃sbɔ̃b] *n.m.inv. Av:* bomb thrower.
lancée [lɑ̃se] *n.f.* momentum, impetus; **continuer sur sa l.,** to keep going, to forge ahead.
lance-flammes [lɑ̃sflam] *n.m.inv. Mil:* flamethrower.
lance-fusées [lɑ̃sfyze] *n.m.inv. Mil: Ball:* rocket launcher.
lance-grenades [lɑ̃sgrənad] *n.m.inv. Mil:* grenade launcher.
lancement [lɑ̃smɑ̃] *n.m.* **1.** throwing, flinging; **l. du javelot, du disque,** throwing the javelin, the discus; **l. du poids,** putting the shot. **2.** (*a*) *Ball: etc:* launching (of missile, rocket); dropping, releasing (of bomb, etc.); throwing, launching (of grenade); sending up (of balloon); (*b*) *Nau:* launching (of ship); (*c*) *Mec.E:* starting (up) (of engine); (*d*) *Com:* floating (of company); launching (of new product, etc).
lancéolé [lɑ̃seɔle] *a. Bot:* lanceolate.
lance-pierre(s) [lɑ̃spjɛr] *n.m.inv.* catapult.
lancer[1] [lɑ̃se] *v.tr.* **(je lançai(s); n. lançons) 1.** (*a*) to throw, fling, cast, hurl; to shoot (an arrow); to send up (a rocket); **l. des pierres à qn,** to throw stones at s.o.; **l. des bombes,** to throw bombs; (*of aircraft*) to drop bombs; **l. de la fumée,** to puff out smoke; **l. des étincelles,** to shoot out sparks; *Fish:* **l. la ligne,** to cast the line; **l. qch. en l'air,** to toss sth. into the air; **l. un coup d'œil à qn,** to dart a glance at s.o.; **l. un mandat d'arrêt contre qn,** to issue a warrant for s.o.'s arrest; **l. un juron,** to let out a swearword; (*b*) *Sp:* to throw (a ball); (*at baseball*) to pitch; **l. le disque, le javelot,** to throw the discus, the javelin; **l. le poids,** to put the shot. **2.** to start, set (s.o., sth.) going; (*a*) **l. un cheval,** to start a horse off at full gallop; **l. un chien contre qn,** to set a dog on s.o.; **si vous le lancez sur ce sujet il ne s'arrêtera plus,** if you start him on this subject he will never stop; (*b*) to launch (ship, scheme, attack); to release (bomb, etc.); to send up (balloon); to float, promote (company); to bring out (actor, etc.); to initiate, launch, set (fashion); to start (up) (engine); **l. une marchandise,** to launch a (new) product; **l. une souscription,** to start a fund; **l. qn (dans les affaires, etc.),** to give s.o. a start, to set s.o. up (in business, etc.). **3. se l. en avant,** to rush, dash, shoot, forward; **se l. à la poursuite de qn,** to dash off in pursuit of s.o.; **se l. dans les affaires,** to launch out into business; **elle veut se l.,** she wants to make a name for herself.
lancer[2] *n.m.* (*a*) *Fish:* **(pêche au) l.,** casting; (*b*) *Sp:* throw; **l. du javelot, du disque,** throwing the javelin; discus throwing; **l. du poids,** putting the shot.
lance-roquettes [lɑ̃srɔkɛt] *n.m.inv. Mil:* rocket launcher.
lance-satellites [lɑ̃ssatelit] *n.m.inv.* satellite launcher.
lance-torpilles [lɑ̃stɔrpij] *n.m.inv. Navy:* **(tube) l.-t.,** torpedo tube.
lancette [lɑ̃sɛt] *n.f.* **1.** *Surg:* lancet. **2.** *Arch:* **(arc à) l.,** lancet arch.
lanceur, -euse [lɑ̃sœr, -øz] *n.* **1.** (*a*) thrower; *Cr:* bowler; (*at baseball*) pitcher; (*b*) *Ball: etc:* launcher (of satellite, spacecraft, etc.). **2.** promoter, floater (of company, etc.).
lancier [lɑ̃sje] *n.m.* **1.** *Mil:* lancer. **2.** *Danc:* **(quadrille des) lanciers,** lancers.
lancinant [lɑ̃sinɑ̃] *a.* shooting, throbbing (pain); haunting (memory); insistent, monotonous (tune).
lanciner [lɑ̃sine] **1.** *v.i.* (*of pain*) to shoot; (*of finger, etc.*) to throb. **2.** *v.tr.* to harass, trouble.
lançon [lɑ̃sɔ̃] *n.m. Ich:* launce, sand eel.
landais, -aise [lɑ̃dɛ, -ɛz] *a. & n. Geog:* (native, inhabitant) of the Landes.
landau [lɑ̃do] *n.m.* (*a*) *Veh:* landau; (*b*) baby carriage; pram.
lande [lɑ̃d] *n.f.* (sandy) moor; heath; waste; *NAm:* barren; **les Landes,** the Landes (region) (in southwest France).
landier [lɑ̃dje] *n.m.* andiron, fire dog.
langage [lɑ̃gaʒ] *n.m.* language; speech (of the individual, as opposed to the common language of a whole people); **tenir un l. grossier à qn,** to speak rudely to s.o.; **vous tenez là un drôle de l.,** that's a strange way to talk; **changer de l.,** to change one's tune; **en voilà un l.!** that's no way to talk! **surveillez votre l.!** watch your language! **l. argotique, populaire,** slang, popular speech; **le l. des fleurs, des animaux,** the language of flowers, of animals; **l. chiffré,** cipher, code.
langagier, -ière [lɑ̃gaʒje, -jɛr] *a.* linguistic.

lange [lɑ̃ʒ] *n.m. pl. A:* swaddling clothes; *Fig:* **être encore dans les langes,** to be still in (its) infancy.

langer [lɑ̃ʒe] *v.tr.* **(je langeai(s); n. langeons)** *A:* to wrap a baby in swaddling clothes.

langoureusement [lɑ̃gurøzmɑ̃] *adv.* languorously, languishingly.

langoureux, -euse [lɑ̃gurø, -øz] *a.* languorous; languishing.

langouste [lɑ̃gust] *n.f. Crust:* crayfish, crawfish.

langoustine [lɑ̃gustin] *n.f. Crust:* (*a*) Norway lobster; (*b*) Dublin Bay prawn; *Cu: pl.* scampi.

langue [lɑ̃g] *n.f.* **1.** (*a*) tongue; **tirer la l.,** (i) to put out, stick out, one's tongue **(à qn,** at s.o.); (ii) *F:* to be very thirsty; (iii) *F:* to have one's tongue hanging out (for sth.); **montrez-moi votre l.,** show me, put out, your tongue; **délier la l. à qn,** to loosen s.o.'s tongue; **avoir la l. bien pendue,** to have a ready tongue, *F:* the gift of the gab; **elle a la l. trop longue,** she can't keep her mouth shut, she talks too much; **il sait tenir sa l.,** he can keep a secret; **je l'avais sur le bout de la l.,** I had it on the tip of my tongue; **coup de l.,** (i) click (of the tongue); tonguing (on wind instrument); (ii) lick; (iii) cutting remark; (*with reference to riddle, etc.*) **je donne ma l. au chat,** I give up; I can't guess; **mauvaise l.,** backbiter, scandalmonger; **l. de vipère,** spiteful gossip; **se mordre la l. d'avoir parlé,** *F:* **s'en mordre la l.,** to regret bitterly having spoken; **prendre l. avec qn,** to establish, make, contact with s.o.; *F:* **avoir un cheveu sur la l.,** to lisp, have a (slight) lisp; (*b*) *Med:* **l. pâteuse,** coated tongue; (*c*) *Cu:* **l. de bœuf,** ox tongue. **2.** (*a*) **langues de feu,** tongues of flame; (*b*) **l. de terre,** strip, spit of land. **3.** language (of a people); **l. maternelle,** mother tongue; **langues étrangères,** foreign languages; **l. morte,** dead language; **professeur de langues vivantes,** modern language teacher; **avoir le don des langues,** to be a good linguist; **peuples, pays, de l. anglaise,** English-speaking people, countries; *Ling:* **l. de départ,** source language; **l. d'arrivée,** target language; **l. verte,** slang.

langue-de-bœuf [lɑ̃gdəbœf] *n.f.* **1.** *Fung:* beefsteak fungus. **2.** *Tls:* (heart-shaped) trowel; *pl. langues-de-bœuf.*

langue-de-cerf [lɑ̃gdəsɛr] *n.f. Bot:* hart's tongue; *pl. langues-de-cerf.*

langue-de-chat [lɑ̃gdəʃa] *n.f. Cu:* (flat) finger biscuit; langue-de-chat; *pl. langues-de-chat.*

languedocien, -ienne [lɑ̃gdɔsjɛ̃, -jɛn] *a. & n. Geog:* (native, inhabitant) of Languedoc.

languette [lɑ̃gɛt] *n.f.* small tongue (of wood, metal, land, etc.); tab; strip (of tinfoil, etc.); tongue (of shoe); thin slice (of bread); *Carp:* **assemblage à rainure et l.,** feather joint; *El:* **contact à l.,** snap contact.

langueur [lɑ̃gœr] *n.f.* **1.** languor, languidness; listlessness; *A:* **(maladie de) l.,** decline. **2.** languishment; **regard plein de l.,** languishing look.

languir [lɑ̃gir] **1.** *v.i.* to languish, pine; *Lit:* to waste away; (*of plant*) to wilt; **l. d'amour,** to be lovesick; **l. après qn, qch.,** to long, pine, yearn, for s.o., sth.; **ne nous faites pas l.,** don't keep us on tenterhooks, in suspense; **la conversation languit,** the conversation is flagging; *Dial:* **les affaires languissent,** business is slack. **2.** *Dial:* **se l.,** to be bored.

languissamment [lɑ̃gisamɑ̃] *adv. Lit:* languidly.

languissant [lɑ̃gisɑ̃] *a.* **1.** languid, listless; lagging, dragging (conversation). **2.** languishing (eyes, look).

lanière [lanjɛr] *n.f.* (thin) strip of material; *esp.* thin strap; thong; (leather) lace; lash (of whip); **découper qch. en lanières,** to cut sth. in strips.

lanifère [lanifɛr], **lanigère** [laniʒɛr] *a.* laniferous, wool-bearing.

lanoline [lanɔlin] *n.f.* lanoline.

lanterne [lɑ̃tɛrn] *n.f.* (*a*) lantern; **l. sourde,** dark lantern; **l. vénitienne,** Chinese lantern; **l. magique,** magic lantern; **l. de projection,** (slide) projector; (*b*) *Veh:* (side)light; *Aut:* **l. rouge,** (i) rear, tail, light (of convoy); (ii) *A:* red light (of brothel); *Sp:* **la l. rouge,** the last man in the race; (*c*) *A:* street lamp; *Fr.Hist:* (*during the Revolution*) **à la l.!** string them up!

lanterneau, -eaux [lɑ̃tɛrno] *n.m.* skylight (over staircase); lantern (light).

lanterner [lɑ̃tɛrne] *v.i.* to dawdle.

laotien, -ienne [laɔsjɛ̃, -jɛn] *a. & n. Geog:* Laotian.

La Palice [lapalis] *Pr.n.m. F:* **vérité de La P.,** truism, statement of the obvious.

lapalissade [lapalisad] *n.f.* = VERITÉ DE LA PALICE.

lapement [lapmɑ̃] *n.m.* lapping (up) (of milk, etc.).

laper [lape] *v.tr. & i.* (*of dog, cat, etc.*) to lap (up) (water, milk, etc.).

lapereau, -eaux [lapro] *n.m.* young rabbit.

lapidaire [lapidɛr] **1.** *a.* lapidary (inscription, style, etc.); concise (style). **2.** *n.m.* lapidary.

lapidation [lapidasjɔ̃] *n.f.* stoning.

lapider [lapide] *v.tr.* to lapidate; to stone (s.o.) to death; **l. un chien,** to throw stones at a dog.

lapin, -ine [lapɛ̃, -in] *n.* (buck) rabbit, *f.* doe; **l. de garenne,** wild rabbit; **l. domestique, de choux,** tame rabbit; *Com:* **peau de l.,** cony (skin); *P:* **poser un l. à qn,** to stand s.o. up; to fail to turn up; *F:* **un drôle de l.,** a queer customer; *F:* **un chaud l.,** a don Juan, a Casanova; *F:* **c'est un fameux l.,** he's quite a guy; **se sauver, courir, comme un l.,** to run like hell; **coup du l.,** (i) rabbit punch; (ii) *Med:* whiplash injury; **mon petit l.,** my darling, my lamb.

lapiner [lapine] *v.i.* (*of rabbit*) to litter.

lapinière [lapinjɛr] *n.f.* rabbit hutch.

lapis [lapis] *n.m.,* **lapis-lazuli** [lapislazyli] *n.m.inv. Miner:* lapis lazuli; *a.inv.* **ciel l.-l.,** bright blue sky.

lapon, -one [lapɔ̃, -ɔn] *Geog: Ethn:* **1.** *a.* Lappish, Lapp. **2.** *n.* Lapp, Laplander. **3.** *n.m. Ling:* Lappish, Lapp.

Laponie [lapɔni] *Pr.n.f. Geog:* Lapland.

laps[1] [laps] *n.m.* **un l. de temps,** a lapse, space, of time.

laps[2] *a. used only in Ecc:* **être l. et relaps,** to have abandoned the Catholic faith.

lapsus [lapsys] *n.m.* slip (of the tongue, pen); **l. de mémoire,** lapse of memory.

laquage [lakaʒ] *n.m.* lacquering.

laquais [lakɛ] *n.m.* lackey, footman; *Pej:* flunkey.

laque [lak] **1.** *n.f.* (*a*) lac; **l. en écailles,** shellac; **gomme l.,** gum lac; (*b*) *Paint:* lake; (*c*) (hair) lacquer, hair spray. **2.** *n.m.* (*a*) lacquer; **de l., en l.,** laquered; **l. (de Chine),** japan; (*b*) lacquer ware.

laqué [lake] *a.* japanned, lacquered (ware); lacquered (hair).

laquer [lake] *v.tr.* (*a*) to lacquer, to japan; (*b*) to enamel; **meubles laqués de blanc,** white-enamelled furniture.

laqueur [lakœr] *n.m.* lacquerer, japanner.

larbin [larbɛ̃] *n.m. F: usu. Pej:* flunkey.

larcin [larsɛ̃] *n.m.* (*a*) *Jur:* larceny; (petty) theft; (*b*) loot.

lard [lar] *n.m.* **1.** (*a*) fat, flare (*esp.* of pig); *F:* **(se) faire du l.,** to (sit around and) get fat; (*b*) bacon; **l. maigre,** streaky bacon; **l. gras,** fat bacon; **l. fumé,** smoked bacon; **omelette au l.,** bacon omelette; *P:* (*of pers.*) **gros l.,** big fat slob; **tête de l.,** pigheaded idiot; (*c*) (whale, etc.) blubber. **2. pierre de l.,** soapstone, steatite; tailor's chalk.

larder [larde] *v.tr.* to lard (piece of meat); **l. qn de coups de couteau,** to stab s.o. (all over) with a knife; **l. qn de ridicule,** to cover s.o. with ridicule; **l. un**

texte de citations, to (inter)lard, pepper, a text with quotations.

lardoire [lardwar] *n.f.* **1.** *Cu:* larding needle, pin. **2.** *F:* sword.

lardon [lardɔ̃] *n.m.* **1.** (*a*) *Cu:* piece of larding bacon, streaky bacon; lardon; (*b*) *O:* jibe, cutting remark. **2.** *P:* kid.

lare [lar] *n.m. Rom.Ant:* household god; lar; *esp. pl.* **dieux lares,** lares.

largable [largabl̩] *a. Av:* (*of container, equipment*) releasable.

largage [largaʒ] *n.m. Av:* dropping (of personnel, supplies, etc.); releasing (of bomb).

large [larʒ] **1.** *a.* (*a*) broad, wide; **l. d'épaules,** broad-shouldered; **route l. de dix mètres,** road ten metres, *NAm:* meters, wide; **vêtements larges,** loose-fitting clothes; **d'un geste l.,** with a broad, sweeping, gesture; **terme employé dans un sens l.,** term used in a broad sense; **avoir l'esprit l.,** to be broad-minded; *Art:* **style l.,** broad, bold, free, style; **mener une vie l.,** to spend freely; **il n'a pas été très l.,** he wasn't very generous; (*b*) large, big, ample; **de larges ressources,** ample resources. **2.** *n.m.* (*a*) room, space; **être au l.,** (i) to have plenty of room; (ii) to be well off; (*b*) *Nau:* open sea; **brise du l.,** sea breeze; *F:* **prendre le l.,** to decamp, to beat it; **gagner le l.,** to get an offing; **au l.!** (i) (*to small boat*) keep away! (ii) *F:* go on, beat it! **au l. de Cherbourg,** off Cherbourg; **trop au l.,** too far from the shore; (*c*) breadth; **route qui a dix mètres de l.,** road ten metres wide; **se promener de long en l.,** to walk up and down, to and fro; **il parcourut la pièce en long et en l.,** he walked up and down the room; *F:* **il examina la question en long et en l.,** he went into all aspects of the question. **3.** *adv.* **calculer l.,** to allow a wide margin for error; **cette robe habille l.,** this dress is loose fitting; **voir l.,** (i) to be broad-minded; (ii) to think big.

largement [larʒəmɑ̃] *adv.* (*a*) broadly, widely; **services l. rétribués,** highly paid services; **opinion l. répandue,** widely held opinion; *Art:* **peindre l.,** to paint in a free, broad, style; (*b*) amply; **avoir l. de quoi vivre,** to have ample means; **avoir l. le temps,** to have plenty of time; **elle a l. quarante ans,** she's at least forty (if not more); **il en a eu l. (assez),** he's had (more than) enough.

largesse [larʒɛs] *n.f.* **1.** liberality **(envers,** towards); **avec l.,** generously. **2.** *A:* bounty, largess(e); **faire l.,** to make handsome presents.

largeur [larʒœr] *n.f.* breadth, width; span (of arch); gauge (of railway track); breadth, beam (of ship); **avoir trois mètres de l.,** to be three metres, *NAm:* meters, wide; **en l., dans la l.,** widthwise, breadthwise; **distance en l.,** distance across; **l. de vues, d'esprit,** broadness of outlook, of mind; *F:* **dans les grandes largeurs,** in a big way, well and truly.

largue [larg] *a. Nau:* **1.** (*of rope, etc.*) loose, slack. **2.** (*of wind*) large, free; **naviguer vent l.,** *n.m.,* **avoir du l.,** to sail free, large; to sail off the wind; to run free.

larguer [large] *v.tr.* (*a*) *Nau:* to let go, loose (rope); **l. les amarres,** to cast off, slip, the mooring ropes; (*b*) *Av:* to drop (parachutist, etc.); (*c*) to let out, loose out, unfurl (sail); (*d*) *F:* to get rid of, drop, chuck (s.o.).

larme [larm] *n.f.* tear; **fondre en larmes,** to burst into tears; to break down; **verser des larmes de joie,** to shed tears of joy; **pleurer à chaudes larmes,** to weep bitterly; **avoir les larmes aux yeux,** to have tears in one's eyes; **elle était (tout) en larmes,** she was in tears; **avec des larmes dans la voix,** in a tearful voice; **au bord des larmes,** on the verge of tears; **avoir toujours la l. à l'œil,** to be easily moved to tears; **il a ri (jusqu')aux larmes,** he laughed till he cried; **larmes de crocodile,** crocodile tears; *F:* **une l. de rhum,** just a drop of rum.

larmier [larmje] *n.m.* **1.** *Anat:* (*a*) inner canthus; corner (of the eye); (*b*) tear bag (of deer); (*c*) temple (of horse). **2.** *Arch:* drip (stone); gutter overhang.

larmoiement [larmwamɑ̃] *n.m.* (*a*) *Med:* watering (of the eyes); (*b*) snivelling.

larmoyant [larmwajɑ̃] *a.* **1.** *Med:* **yeux larmoyants,** watering eyes. **2.** weepy, tearful, snivelling (voice, etc.); maudlin (story, etc.); soppy (sentimentality).

larmoyer [larmwaje] *v.i.* **(je larmoie, n. larmoyons; je larmoierai) 1.** (*of the eyes*) to water. **2.** to weep; to snivel.

larron [larɔ̃] *n.m.* **1.** *A:* robber, thief; *F:* **s'entendre comme larrons en foire,** to be as thick as thieves. **2.** (*a*) *Typ:* bite (in the paper); (*b*) *Bookb:* dog's ear.

larvaire [larvɛr] *a.* (*a*) larval; (*b*) rudimentary, embryonic (stage, etc.).

larve [larv] *n.f.* (*a*) larva; grub (of insect); (*b*) *Fig:* worm.

larvé [larve] *a.* (*a*) *Med:* larvate(d), masked (fever, etc.); (*b*) insidious, latent (war, etc.).

laryngé [larɛ̃ʒe] **laryngien, -ienne** [larɛ̃ʒjɛ̃, -jɛn] *a.* laryngeal (artery, etc.).

laryngectomie [larɛ̃ʒɛktɔmi] *n.f. Surg:* laryngectomy.

laryngite [larɛ̃ʒit] *n.f. Med:* laryngitis.

laryngologie [larɛ̃gɔlɔʒi] *n.f.* laryngology.

laryngologiste [larɛ̃gɔlɔʒist], **laryngologue** [larɛ̃gɔlɔg] *n. Med:* laryngologist.

laryngoscope [larɛ̃gɔskɔp] *n.m. Surg:* laryngoscope.

laryngotomie [larɛ̃gɔtɔmi] *n.f. Surg:* laryngotomy.

larynx [larɛ̃ks] *n.m. Anat:* larynx.

las[1] [lɑs] *int. A:* alack! alas!

las[2]**, lasse** [lɑ, lɑs] *a.* tired, weary; **être l. de qch.,** to be (sick and) tired of sth.; **de guerre lasse il consentit,** tired of resisting, he agreed.

lascar [laskar] *n.m. F:* (fine, clever, lazy, etc.) fellow, chap; smart character, rogue.

lascif, -ive [lasif, -iv] *a.* lascivious; lustful, sensual.

lascivement [lasivmɑ̃] *adv.* lasciviously, lustfully.

lasciveté [lasivte] *n.f.* lasciviousness, lust.

laser [lazɛr] *n.m. Ph:* laser.

lassant [lɑsɑ̃] *a.* wearisome, tedious.

lasser [lɑse] **1.** *v.tr.* to tire, weary; **l. la patience de qn,** to exhaust, tax, s.o.'s patience. **2. se l. de qn, de qch.,** to get tired of s.o., of sth.; **faire qch. sans se l.,** to do sth. without tiring; **on ne se lasse pas de l'écouter,** one is never tired of listening to him.

lassitude [lɑsityd] *n.f.* lassitude, weariness.

lasso [laso] *n.m.* lasso; **prendre au l.,** to lasso.

latence [latɑ̃s] *n.f.* latency.

latent [latɑ̃] *a.* latent (disease, heat, etc.); hidden, concealed; **état l.,** latency.

latéral, -aux [lateral, -o] *a.* lateral; **rue latérale,** side street; **entrée latérale,** side entrance; *a. & n.f. Ling:* **(consonne) latérale,** lateral (consonant).

latéralement [lateralmɑ̃] *adv.* laterally; on, at, the side.

latex [latɛks] *n.m. Bot: Ind:* latex.

latin, -ine [latɛ̃, -in] **1.** *a.* (*a*) Latin (people, etc.); *n.* **les Latins,** the Latin peoples; **le Quartier L.,** the Latin Quarter; **Amérique latine,** Latin America; (*b*) *Nau:* **voile latine,** lateen sail. **2.** *n.m. Ling:* Latin; **bas l.,** low Latin; **l. de cuisine,** dog Latin; **j'y perds mon l.,** I can't make head or tail of it.

latinisation [latinizasjɔ̃] *n.f.* Latinization.

latiniser [latinize] *v.tr. & i.* to Latinize.

latinisme [latinizm] *n.m.* Latinism, Latin idiom.

latiniste [latinist] *n.* Latinist, Latin scholar.

latino-américain, -aine [latinoamerikɛ̃, -ɛn] *a. & n. Geog:* Latin-American; *pl. latino-américain(e)s.*

latitude [latityd] *n.f.* latitude. **1.** scope, freedom;

avoir toute l. pour agir, to have free scope, full discretion, to act. **2.** *Geog:* (*a*) **à 30° de l. nord,** at latitude 30° North; (*b*) region; **sous toutes les latitudes,** in all climates, regions.
latitudinaire [latitydinɛr] *a. & n. Lit:* latitudinarian.
latrines [latrin] *n.f.pl.* latrines.
lattage [lataʒ] *n.m.* lathing (of ceiling, wall, etc.).
latte [lat] *n.f.* lath, batten, slat; **l. volige,** slate lath, roof batten; *Com:* **fer en lattes,** slat iron.
latter [late] *v.tr.* to lath; to batten.
lattis [lati] *n.m.* lathing, lathwork.
laudanum [lodanɔm] *n.m.* laudanum.
laudateur, -trice [lodatœr, -tris] *n.* laudator, lauder, praiser.
laudatif, -ive [lodatif, -iv] *a.* laudatory, lauding, praising.
lauréat, -ate [lɔrea, -at] **1.** *a.* prizewinning (pupil, etc.). **2.** *n.* laureate, prizewinner; **les lauréats du prix Nobel,** the Nobel prizewinners.
Laurent [lɔrɑ̃] *Pr.n.m.* Lawrence; Laurence; *Geog:* **le (fleuve) Saint L.,** the St Lawrence (River).
lauréole [lɔreɔl] *n.f. Bot:* daphne.
laurier [lɔrje] *n.m. Bot:* laurel; **l. commun,** bay laurel, sweet bay; *Cu:* **feuille de l.,** bay leaf; **couronne de lauriers,** laurel wreath; **se reposer, s'endormir, sur ses lauriers,** to rest on one's laurels.
laurier-rose [lɔrjeroz] *n.m. Bot:* common oleander, rose laurel; *pl. lauriers-roses.*
laurier-sauce [lɔrjesos] *n.m. Bot: Cu:* bay; *pl. lauriers-sauce.*
lavable [lavabl̩] *a.* washable.
lavabo [lavabo] *n.m.* **1.** *Ecc:* lavabo ((i) ritual, (ii) towel). **2.** washbasin. **3.** (*a*) (*place for washing*) washroom; (*b*) *pl.* toilets.
lavage [lavaʒ] *n.m.* washing; scrubbing (of gas); *Med:* (stomach) wash; **l. de cerveau,** brainwashing; **l. de tête,** dressing down.
lavallière [lavaljɛr] *n.f.* **(cravate) l.,** necktie with large bow.
lavande [lavɑ̃d] *n.f. Bot:* lavender; **(eau de) l.,** lavender water; **bleu l.,** lavender blue.
lavandière [lavɑ̃djɛr] *n.f.* **1.** washerwoman; laundress. **2.** *Orn:* wagtail.
lavaret [lavarɛ] *n.m. Ich:* lavaret, pollan.
lavasse [lavas] *n.f. F:* watery drink; hogwash, dishwater; slops.
lave [lav] *n.f. Geol:* lava.
lavé [lave] *a.* washed out; pale, faint, (wishy-)washy (colour, *NAm:* color); **dessin l.,** wash drawing.
lave-glace [lavglas] *n.m. Aut:* windscreen, *NAm:* windshield, washer; *pl. lave-glaces.*
lave-mains [lavmɛ̃] *n.m.inv.* (small) washbasin.
lavement [lavmɑ̃] *n.m. Med:* (rectal) injection; enema.
laver [lave] *v.tr.* to wash; (*a*) **l. qch. à l'eau froide,** to wash sth. in cold water; **l. à grande eau,** to swill down; **se l.,** to wash (oneself), to have a wash, *NAm:* to wash up; **se l. les dents,** to clean one's teeth; **se l. la tête,** to wash one's hair; *F:* **l. la tête à qn,** to tell s.o. off, haul s.o. over the coals; **se l. les mains,** to wash one's hands; **je m'en lave les mains,** I wash my hands of this affair; **l. à la brosse,** to scrub; **l. la vaisselle,** to wash up; to do the washing-up; to wash, do, the dishes; **ce tissu ne se lave pas,** this material won't wash, isn't washable; **machine à l.,** washing machine; **l. une tache,** to wash out a stain; **l. qn d'une accusation,** to clear s.o. from an accusation; **l. une plaie,** to bathe, cleanse, a wound; (*b*) to dilute (paint); **l. un dessin,** to wash a drawing.
laverie [lavri] *n.f.* (*a*) *Ind:* washing plant, washery; (*b*) **l. automatique,** launderette.
lavette [lavɛt] *n.f.* (*a*) (dish)mop; dishcloth; (*b*) *Sw.Fr:* facecloth; (*c*) *P:* spineless person; drip, wet.
laveur, -euse [lavœr, -øz] **1.** *n.* (*pers.*) washer; **laveuse (de linge),** washerwoman; **laveur, -euse, de vaisselle,** washer-up, *NAm:* dishwasher; **l. de vitres,** window cleaner. **2.** *n.m. Ind:* scrubber.
lave-vaisselle [lavvɛsɛl] *n.m.inv.* dishwasher; washing-up machine.
lavis [lavi] *n.m.* **1.** washing, tinting (of drawing). **2.** wash drawing.
lavoir [lavwar] *n.m.* **1.** (*a*) **l. (public),** (public) washhouse; (*b*) (cement) washtub. **2.** *Ind:* (*a*) washer; (*b*) washing plant.
lavure [lavyr] *n.f.* **1.** (*a*) dirty water; **l. (de vaisselle),** (kitchen) swill, dishwater; (*b*) insipid, watery, soup. **2.** *Ind:* (*a*) washing; (*b*) *pl.* metal turnings and filings.
laxatif, -ive [laksatif, -iv] *a. & n.m. Med:* laxative.
layer¹ [leje] *v.tr.* **(je laie, je laye, n. layons; je laierai, je layerai) 1.** to trace, open up, a path through (forest); to blaze a trail through (forest). **2.** to blaze (the trees to be left in a cutting).
layer² *v.tr. Stonew:* to tool (a stone).
layette [lɛjɛt] *n.f.* (set of) baby clothes; babywear; layette.
layon [lɛjɔ̃] *n.m.* forest track, trail; ride.
lazaret [lazarɛ] *n.m.* lazaret(to); lazar house.
lazulite [lazylit] *n.m. Miner:* lazulite, blue spar.
lazzi [lazi, ladzi] *n.m.* (*a*) piece of buffoonery; (*b*) jeers, hooting, cat calls; *pl. lazzi(s).*
le¹, la¹, les¹ [lə, la, le] *def.art.* **(le** *and* **la** *are elided to* **l'** *before a vowel or h mute;* **le** *and* **les** *contract with* **à, de,** *into* **au, aux; du, des)** the. **1.** (*particularizing the noun or pron.*) (*a*) **ouvrez la porte,** open the door; **il est venu la semaine dernière,** he came last week; **j'apprends le français,** I'm learning French; **la province a perdu le quart, le tiers, de ses habitants,** the province has lost a quarter, a third, of its inhabitants; **l'un . . . l'autre,** (the) one . . . the other; **mon livre et le tien,** my book and yours; **il est arrivé le lundi 12,** he arrived on Monday the 12th; **oh! le beau chat!** what a beautiful cat! **debout, les enfants!** time to get up, children! (*b*) **la France,** France; **l'Afrique,** Africa; **le Mont Blanc,** Mont Blanc; **les Alpes,** the Alps; (*c*) **l'empereur Guillaume,** the Emperor William; **le roi Édouard,** King Edward; **le cardinal Richelieu,** Cardinal Richelieu; *F:* **la Marie, le Pierre,** Mary, Peter; (*d*) (*with certain Italian names, certain actresses and female singers*) **le Dante,** Dante; **le Tasse,** Tasso; **la Callas,** Callas; (*e*) (*in front of proper noun*) **la Renault de mon père,** my father's Renault; (*f*) (*place names*) **Le Havre, La Rochelle; Le Caire,** Cairo; **je reviens du Havre,** I'm just back from le Havre; **je me rends au Caire,** I'm going to Cairo; (*g*) (*family names; always capital L*) **le peintre Le Brun,** the painter Le Brun; **les tableaux de Le Brun,** Le Brun's pictures; (*h*) (*with most feast days*) **la Toussaint,** All Saints' Day; *F:* **à la Noël,** at Christmas; (*i*) (*parts of the body*) **j'ai mal à la gorge,** I've got a sore throat; **elle a les yeux bleus,** she has blue eyes; **hausser les épaules,** to shrug one's shoulders; **elle ferma les yeux,** she closed her eyes; **il s'est pincé le doigt,** he pinched his finger; **le bras me fait mal,** my arm hurts. **2.** (*forming superlatives*) (*a*) **les jours les plus longs,** the longest days; **le meilleur vin de sa cave,** the best wine in his cellar; **mon amie la plus intime,** my most intimate friend; **c'est elle (qui est) la plus jolie,** she's the prettiest; (*b*) (*in the neuter*) (i) (*with adverbs*) **c'est elle qui travaille le mieux,** she's the one who works best; (ii) (*when there is an absolute superlative*) **c'est lorsqu'elle est seule qu'elle est le plus heureuse,** she's happiest when she's by herself. **3.** (*generalizing the noun*) **je préfère le café au thé,** I prefer coffee to tea. **4.** (*distributive*) **trois fois l'an,** three times a year; **cinq**

francs la livre, five francs a pound; **il vient le jeudi, les jeudis,** he comes on Thursdays, every Thursday. **5.** (*rendered by the indef. art. in Eng.*) (*a*) (*particularizing*) **j'ai le droit de vivre,** I have a right to live; **donner l'exemple,** to set an example; **demander le divorce,** to sue for a divorce; **la belle excuse!** a fine excuse! (*b*) (*generalizing*) **au petit trot,** at a slow trot; **il n'a pas le sou,** he hasn't (got) a penny. **6.** *partitive* **du, de la, des;** *see* DE III.

le², la², les² *pers.pron.* **1.** (*replacing n.*) him, her, it, them; (*a*) **je vous le, la, présenterai,** I'll introduce him, her, to you; **je ne le lui ai pas donné,** I didn't give it to him; **tu le sais aussi bien que moi,** you know it as well as I do; **êtes-vous les parents de cet enfant?—nous les sommes,** are you the parents of this child?—we are; **les voilà!** there they are! **ne l'abîmez pas!** don't spoil it! (*b*) (*following the vb*) **donnez-le-lui,** give it to him; **regardez-les,** look at them; **donne-le à ton frère,** give it to your brother. **2.** *neut. pron.* **le;** (*a*) (*replacing adj. or n. used as adj.*) **malheureux, je l'étais certainement,** unhappy, I certainly was; **son frère est médecin, il voudrait l'être aussi,** his brother is a doctor, he would like to be one too; (*referring to p.p. only implied*) **j'étais fatigué mais maintenant je ne le suis plus,** I was tired, but now I'm not; (*b*) (*replacing clause*) **il me l'a dit,** he told me so; **est-il parti?—je me le demande,** has he gone?—that's what I'm wondering; I wonder; **il est plus riche que vous (ne) le pensez,** he's richer than you think (he is); **vous le devriez,** you ought to.

lé [le] *n.m.* width, breadth (of cloth); strip (of wallpaper); *Dressm:* **jupe de quatre lés,** four-gore skirt.

leader [lidœr] *n.m.* (*a*) *Pol: Sp:* leader; (*b*) *Journ:* **(article) l.,** leader, editorial.

léchage [leʃaʒ] *n.m.* licking; *F:* **l. de bottes,** bootlicking; **l. de vitrines,** window shopping.

lèche [lɛʃ] *n.f. P:* bootlicking; **faire de la l. à qn,** to suck up to s.o.; to lick s.o.'s boots.

lèche-cul [lɛʃky] *n.m.inv. V:* arse-licker.

lèchefrite [lɛʃfrit] *n.f. Cu:* dripping pan.

lécher [leʃe] *v.tr.* **(je lèche, n. léchons; je lécherai) 1.** to lick; **le chat a léché tout le lait,** the cat lapped up all the milk; **l. le beurre d'une tartine,** to lick the butter off a slice of bread; **se l. les doigts,** to lick one's fingers; *F:* **il s'en léchait les doigts, les babines,** he licked his lips, his chops, over it; **l. les vitrines,** to go window shopping; **l. les bottes,** *V:* **le cul, de, à, qn,** to lick s.o.'s boots; to lick, kiss, s.o's arse. **2.** to over-polish, over-finish (work, style).

lécheur, -euse [leʃœr, -øz] *n. P:* bootlicker, toady.

lèche-vitrines [lɛʃvitrin] *n.m. F:* window shopping; **faire du l.-v.,** to go window shopping.

leçon [ləsɔ̃] *n.f.* **1.** (*a*) reading (of a manuscript, etc.); (*b*) *Ecc:* lesson. **2.** *Sch: etc:* (*a*) lesson, class; **l. de choses,** general science (in primary school); **leçons particulières,** private lessons, tuition; **leçons de chant,** singing lessons; **donner une l. à qn,** to teach s.o. a lesson; **espérons qu'il aura tiré la l.,** let's hope he's learnt his lesson; **que cela vous serve de l.,** let that be a lesson, a warning, to you; **faire la l. à qn,** (i) to give s.o. instructions, to coach s.o. (in what he has to say or do); (ii) to lecture s.o.; to give s.o. a lecture; (*b*) *Sch:* homework, prep; **réciter sa l.,** (i) to recite one's lesson; (ii) to repeat sth. parrot fashion.

lecteur, -trice [lɛktœr, -tris] *n.* **1.** (*a*) reader; (*b*) (publisher's) reader. **2.** (*a*) one who reads aloud; (*b*) foreign (language) assistant (in university). **3.** *n.m. Elcs: Cmptr:* reader; *Cin: etc:* **l. de son,** sound head, sound reader; **l. optique,** optical reader; visual scanner; **l. de cassettes,** cassette player.

lecture [lɛktyr] *n.f.* reading; (*a*) **enseigner la l. à qn,** to teach s.o. to read; **livre d'une l. agréable,** book that makes pleasant reading; **cabinet de l.,** reading room, news room (of library); **c'est un homme de grande l.,** he's very well read; **il m'a apporté de la l.,** he brought me something to read; *Mus:* **l. à vue,** sight reading; (*b*) **l. à haute voix,** reading aloud; **faire la l. à qn,** to read aloud to s.o.; *Pol:* **projet repoussé en deuxième l.,** bill rejected at the second reading; (*c*) *Cmptr:* read(ing); (*d*) *Cin:* **l. du son,** sound reproduction; *Rec:* **bras de l.,** pick-up arm; **tête de l.,** pick-up head; reading head; tape reader.

ledit, ladite, *pl.* **lesdits, lesdites** [lədi, ladit, ledi, ledit] *a.* (*with* **le** *and* **les** *the contractions are as shown under* LE¹; **audit, auxdit(e)s, dudit, desdit(e)s)** the aforesaid, the aforementioned, the said.

légal, -aux [legal, -o] *a.* legal; lawful; statutory; **fête légale,** statutory holiday; **avoir recours aux moyens légaux,** to institute legal proceedings, to take legal action; **par voies légales,** by legal process; **médecine légale,** forensic medicine; *Fin:* **taux l.,** official rate of interest; **monnaie légale,** legal tender.

légalement [legalmɑ̃] *adv.* legally, lawfully.

légalisation [legalizasjɔ̃] *n.f.* legalization; authentication (of signature, etc.).

légaliser [legalize] *v.tr.* **1.** to legalize (holiday, custom, etc.). **2.** to attest, certify, authenticate (signature, etc.).

légalité [legalite] *n.f.* legality, lawfulness; **rester dans la l.,** to keep within the law.

légat [lega] *n.m. Ecc: Rom.Ant:* legate; **l. du Pape,** Papal Legate.

légataire [legatɛr] *n. Jur:* legatee, heir; **l. universel,** sole legatee; **l. d'une propriété,** heir to an estate.

légation [legasjɔ̃] *n.f. Dipl:* legation.

lège [lɛʒ] *a.* (*of ship*) light.

légendaire [leʒɑ̃dɛr] *a.* (*a*) legendary (story, etc.); (*b*) epic (combat, etc.).

légende [leʒɑ̃d] *n.f.* **1.** legend; **entrer dans la l.,** to become a legend. **2.** (*a*) inscription, legend (on coin, etc.); (*b*) caption (of drawing, etc.); (*c*) list of references; key, legend (to diagram, map, etc.).

léger, -ère [leʒe, -ɛr] **1.** *a.* (*a*) light (weight, etc.); **l. comme une plume,** as light as a feather; **avoir le cœur l.,** to be light-hearted; **avoir le sommeil l.,** to be a light sleeper; **avoir la main légère,** to be (i) gentle, (ii) clever, with one's hands; (iii) to rule with a light hand; **conduite légère,** (i) flighty, (ii) fickle, conduct; **femme légère, de mœurs légères,** woman of easy virtue; **propos légers,** (i) frivolous, idle, talk; (ii) slightly improper talk; **repas l.,** light meal; (*b*) slight (pain, mistake, etc.); light, gentle (breeze); mild (tobacco); light (wine); weak (tea, coffee); faint (sound, tint, etc.); mild (injury); **il y a un l. mieux,** there is a slight improvement; he's a shade better; **perte légère,** trivial loss. **2.** *adv.phr.* **à la légère,** without due consideration; **parler à la légère,** to speak unthinkingly, thoughtlessly; **traiter une affaire à la légère,** to make light of a matter; not to take a matter seriously.

légèrement [leʒɛrmɑ̃] *adv.* **1.** (*a*) lightly (dressed, etc.); **manger l.,** to eat a light meal; (*b*) slightly (wounded, etc.); **il parut l. surpris,** he seemed a bit taken aback. **2. agir l.,** to act without due consideration; **traiter qch. l.,** to make light of sth.

légèreté [leʒɛrte] *n.f.* **1.** (*a*) lightness (of gas, etc.); nimbleness, agility (of dancer, etc.); **l. de main,** lightness of touch; (*b*) slightness (of injury, etc.); mildness (of tobacco, etc.); weakness (of tea, etc.). **2.** (*a*) levity; flightiness (of conduct); (*b*) fickleness.

légiférer [leʒifere] *v.i.* **(je légifère, n. légiférons; je légiférerai)** to legislate (**sur,** on).

légion [leʒjɔ̃] *n.f.* legion; **la L. (étrangère),** the Foreign Legion; **la L. d'honneur,** the Legion of Honour, *NAm:* Honor; **l. de moucherons,** host, swarm, of gnats; **ils sont l.,** they are legion; there are many of them.

légionnaire [leʒjɔnɛr] *n.m.* **1.** (*a*) *Hist:* legionary; (*b*) (*in Foreign Legion*) legionnaire. **2.** member of the Legion of Honour, *NAm:* Honor.

législateur, -trice [leʒislatœr, -tris] **1.** *n.* (*a*) legislator, lawgiver, lawmaker; (*b*) legislature. **2.** *a.* **puissance législatrice,** legislative power.

législatif, -ive [leʒislatif, -iv] *a.* legislative; (*a*) *Fr.Hist:* **l'Assemblée législative,** *n.* **la législative,** the Legislative Assembly; (*b*) **élection législative,** parliamentary election; **le pouvoir l.,** the legislature.

législation [leʒislasjɔ̃] *n.f.* (*a*) legislation; (*b*) (set of) laws; **l. criminelle,** criminal law.

législature [leʒislatyr] *n.f.* **1.** legislature, legislative body. **2.** term of office (of legislative body).

légiste [leʒist] *n.m.* legist, jurist; **médecin l.,** forensic pathologist.

légitimation [leʒitimasjɔ̃] *n.f.* **1.** legitimation, legitimization (of child). **2.** official recognition (of delegate, title, etc.). **3.** *Lit:* justification (of conduct).

légitime [leʒitim] *a.* **1.** legitimate, lawful (child, etc.); **propriétaire l.,** legal owner; **héritier l.,** rightful heir. **2.** rightful (claim); justifiable, justified (demand, etc.); legitimate (reasoning); well-founded (fears, etc.); just (reward); *Jur:* **l. défense,** self-defence. **3.** *P:* **ma l.,** the wife, the missus.

légitimement [leʒitimmɑ̃] *adv.* legitimately, lawfully, justifiably, rightfully.

légitimer [leʒitime] *v.tr.* **1.** to legitimate, legitim(at)ize (child, etc.). **2.** to justify (action, claim, etc.). **3.** to recognize (title, power).

légitimiste [leʒitimist] *a.* & *n.* *Hist:* legitimist.

légitimité [leʒitimite] *n.f.* legitimacy (of child, etc.).

legs [lɛ, lɛg] *n.m.* legacy, bequest; **faire un l. à qn,** to leave s.o. a legacy.

léguer [lege] *v.tr.* **(je lègue, n. léguons; je léguerai)** to bequeath, leave (personalty); to devise (realty) (**à qn,** to s.o.); to hand down, pass on (tradition, etc.).

légume [legym] **1.** *n.m.* (*a*) vegetable; *Cu:* **légumes verts,** greens; **légumes secs,** dried vegetables; (*b*) *Bot:* legume(n), pod. **2.** *n.f.* *P:* **grosse l.,** important person, bigwig, big shot.

légumier, -ière [legymje, -jɛr] **1.** *a.* of, pertaining to, vegetables; **jardin l.,** vegetable garden. **2.** *n.m.* vegetable dish. **3.** *n.* *Belg:* greengrocer.

légumineux, -euse [legyminø, -øz] *Bot:* **1.** *a.* leguminous. **2.** *n.f.* **légumineuse,** leguminous plant.

leitmotiv [laitmɔtiv] *n.m.* *Mus:* leitmotif, leitmotiv; *pl. leitmotive.*

Léman [lemɑ̃] *Pr.n.m.* *Geog:* **le lac L.,** Lake Geneva.

lemme [lɛm] *n.m.* *Mth:* lemma.

lemming [lemiŋ] *n.m.* *Z:* lemming.

lémur [lemyr] *n.m.* *Z:* lemur.

lendemain [lɑ̃dmɛ̃] *n.m.* next day; **le l. de la bataille,** the day after the battle; **le l. matin,** the next morning, the morning after; **il faut penser au l.,** one must think of the future; **il devint célèbre du jour au l.,** he became famous overnight; **au l. de son départ,** soon after, in the days following, his departure; **des succès sans l.,** short-lived successes; *F:* **le l. de cuite,** the morning after the night before.

lénifiant [lenifjɑ̃] *a.* *Med: etc:* assuaging, soothing.

lénifier [lenifje] *v.tr.* (*pr.sub.* &. *impf.* **n. lénifiions, v. lénifiiez)** *Med:* to assuage, soothe, alleviate.

léninisme [leninism] *n.m.* *Pol:* Leninism.

léniniste [leninist] *a.* & *n.* *Pol:* Leninist.

lénitif, ive [lenitif, -iv] *a.* & *n.m.* lenitive.

lent, lente[1] [lɑ̃, lɑ̃t] *a.* slow (movement, etc.); slow-acting (poison); **mort lente,** lingering death; **être l. à faire qch.,** to be slow to do sth.; **avoir l'esprit l.,** to be slow-witted, to be slow in understanding.

lente[2] *n.f.* nit; egg (of louse).

lentement [lɑ̃tmɑ̃] *adv.* slowly; **ruisseau qui coule l.,** slow-flowing stream; **l. mais sûrement,** slowly but surely.

lenteur [lɑ̃tœr] *n.f.* **1.** slowness; **mettre de la l. à faire qch.,** to be slow in doing sth.; **avec l.,** (i) slowly; (ii) with due deliberation. **2.** *pl.* slow progress; slowness.

lentille [lɑ̃tij] *n.f.* **1.** *Bot:* (*a*) *Cu:* lentil; (*b*) **l. d'eau,** lemna, duckweed. **2.** bob, ball (of pendulum). **3.** *Opt:* (*a*) lens; **l. cornéenne,** contact lens; (*b*) component (of photographic lens, etc.). **4.** freckle.

Léon [leɔ̃] *Pr.n.m.* Leo, Leon.

léonin [leɔnɛ̃] *a.* leonine; **partage l.,** lion's share.

Léonore [leɔnɔr] *Pr.n.f.* Leonora.

léopard [leɔpar] *n.m.* *Z:* leopard; **manteau de l.,** leopard skin coat.

lépidoptère [lepidɔptɛr] *Ent:* **1.** *a.* lepidopterous. **2.** *n.m.* lepidopteran; *pl.* Lepidoptera.

lèpre [lɛpr̥] *n.f.* (*a*) *Med:* leprosy; (*b*) **mur rongé d'une l.,** rotting wall; (*c*) *Lit:* evil.

lépreux, -euse [leprø, -øz] **1.** *a.* (*a*) *Med:* leprous; (*b*) peeling, scaly, dilapidated (wall). **2.** *n.* leper.

léproserie [leprozri] *n.f.* leper hospital.

lepte [lɛpt] *n.m.* *Arach:* leptus; **l. automnal,** harvest bug, harvest mite.

lequel, laquelle, lesquels, lesquelles [ləkɛl, lakɛl, lekɛl] *pron.* (*contracted with* **à** *and* **de** *to* **auquel, auxquel(le)s, duquel, desquel(le)s) 1.** *rel.pron.* who, whom; which; (*a*) (*of thgs after prep.*) **l'adresse à laquelle il devait m'écrire,** the address at which he was to write to me; **décision par laquelle . . .,** decision whereby . . .; (*b*) (*of pers.*) **ont comparu trois témoins, lesquels ont déclaré . . .,** three witnesses appeared, who averred . . .; **les deux officiers entre lesquels elle était assise,** the two officers between whom she was sitting; **la dame avec laquelle elle était sortie,** the lady with whom she had gone out; **il y avait beaucoup de gens, parmi lesquels mon cousin Paul,** there were a lot of people among whom was my cousin Paul; **la dame chez laquelle je l'ai rencontré,** the lady at whose house I met him; (*c*) (*of pers. or thg to avoid ambiguity*) **le père de cette jeune fille, lequel est très riche,** the girl's father, who is very rich; (*d*) (*adjectival*) **voici cent francs, laquelle somme vous était due par mon père,** here's a hundred francs, (which was) the sum my father owed you; **il écrira peut-être, auquel cas . . .,** perhaps he will write, in which case . . .. **2.** *interr.pron.* which (one)? **votre ami est venu—lequel?** your friend came—which one? **lequel (de ces chapeaux) préférez-vous?** which (of these hats) do you prefer? **lequel d'entre nous?** which one of us?

lerch(e) [lɛrʃ] *adv.* *P:* **pas l.,** not much.

lérot [lero] *n.m.* Z: lerot, garden dormouse.

lès [lɛ] *prep.* (*occurs only in place names*) near(by).

lesbien, -ienne [lɛsbjɛ̃, -jɛn] **1.** *a.* & *n.* *Geog:* Lesbian. **2.** *n.f.* **lesbienne,** lesbian.

lèse- [lɛz] *a.f.* injured; **crime de l.-société,** outrage against society.

lèse-majesté [lɛzmaʒɛste] *n.f.* *Jur:* high treason, lese-majesty.

léser [leze] *v.tr.* **(je lèse, n. lésons; je léserai)** (*a*) to wrong (s.o.); to wound, injure; *Jur:* **l. les droits de qn,** to encroach upon s.o.'s rights; **la partie lésée,** the injured party; (*b*) (*of action*) to endanger (s.o.'s interests, etc.); (*c*) *Med:* to injure (organ).

lésine [lezin] *n.f.* *O:* & *Lit:* stinginess.

lésiner [lezine] *v.i.* to be stingy; to skimp (**sur,** over).

lésinerie [lezinri] *n.f.* (*a*) stingy act; (*b*) stinginess.

lésineur, -euse [lezinœr, -øz] *n.* *O:* miser, niggard.

lésion [lezjɔ̃] *n.f.* *Med:* *Jur:* lesion; injury.

lessivable [lesivabl̥] *a.* washable (wallpaper, etc.).

lessivage [lesivaʒ] *n.m.* washing (of linen, wall, etc.); *Ch:* leaching.

lessive [lesiv] *n.f.* **1.** lye; detergent; washing powder. **2.** (household) washing; (*a*) wash; **faire la l.,** to do the washing; **jour de l.,** wash(ing) day; (*b*) soiled linen (going to the wash); (*c*) (clean) washing.

lessivé [lesive] *a. P:* (*of pers.*) exhausted, washed out.

lessiver [lesive] *v.tr.* **1.** (*a*) *O:* to wash, boil (linen, etc.); (*b*) to scrub, wash over (floor, etc.). **2.** *Ch:* to leach. **3.** *P:* to defeat, beat (s.o.); (*a*) (*at cards, etc.*) **se faire l.,** to be cleaned out; (*b*) to lick (s.o.).

lessiveuse [lesivøz] *n.f.* copper, boiler.

lest [lɛst] *n.m. no pl.* ballast (of ship, balloon, etc.); **faire son l.,** to take in ballast; **jeter du l.,** (i) to discharge ballast; (ii) to make sacrifices (in order to attain one's end).

lestage [lɛstaʒ] *n.m.* ballasting (of ship, etc.).

leste [lɛst] *a.* **1.** light; nimble, agile (person, animal); smart, brisk (motion); **avoir la main l.,** to be quick with one's hands. **2.** offhand (manner); risqué (jokes).

lestement [lɛstəmɑ̃] *adv.* lightly; nimbly; smartly.

lester [lɛste] *v.tr.* (*a*) to ballast (ship, balloon); (*b*) *F:* to fill, cram (pocket, wallet, etc.); **se l. (l'estomac),** to stuff oneself.

letchi [lɛtʃi] *n.m. Bot:* lychee, litchi.

léthargie [letarʒi] *n.f.* lethargy; (*a*) *Med:* coma; (*b*) inactivity.

léthargique [letarʒik] *a.* lethargic; *Med:* **sommeil l.,** comatose sleep.

Léthé [lete] *Pr.n.m. Myth:* (the river) Lethe.

lette [lɛt] *n.m.,* **lettique** [letik] *n.m. Ling:* Lettic, Lettish; Latvian.

letton, -onne [lɛtɔ̃, -ɔn] **1.** *a. & n.* (*a*) *Ethn:* Lett, Latvian; (*b*) *Geog:* Latvian. **2.** *n.m. Ling:* Lettic, Lettish, Latvian.

Lettonie [lɛtɔni] *Pr.n.f. Geog:* Latvia.

lettrage [lɛtraʒ] *n.m.* lettering.

lettre [lɛtr̥] *n.f.* **1.** letter (of the alphabet); **écrire qch. en toutes lettres,** to write sth. out in full; **c'est écrit en toutes lettres sur son visage,** it's written all over his face; **écrire une somme en (toutes) lettres,** to write an amount in words (not in figures); **c'est gravé en lettres d'or,** it will always be remembered. **2. selon la l. de la loi,** according to the letter of the law; **à la l., au pied de la l.,** to the letter, literally; **traduire à la l.,** to translate word for word; **il prend les choses à la l.,** he takes everything literally; **l. morte,** dead letter; **ce document est resté l. morte,** this document is now useless, worthless; *Engr:* **épreuve avant la l.,** proof before letter, proof engraving; **avant la l.,** before the final stage. **3.** (*a*) letter; **l. d'amour, d'affaires,** love, business, letter; **l. recommandée,** registered letter; **l. exprès, par avion,** express, airmail, letter; *Journ:* **l. ouverte,** open letter; *F:* **c'est pour moi lettres closes,** it's a mystery to me; *F:* **c'est passé comme une l. à la poste,** it went off without a hitch, smoothly; (*b*) **l. de grâce,** reprieve; *Hist:* **lettres patentes,** letters patent; **lettres de noblesse,** letters patent of nobility; *Bank: Com:* **l. de crédit,** letter of credit. **4.** *pl.* literature, letters; humanities; **homme, femme, de lettres,** man, woman, of letters; writer; **avoir des lettres,** to be well read; *Sch:* **faculté des lettres,** faculty of arts; **lettres classiques,** classics; *F:* **faire des lettres,** to study arts subjects, for an arts degree.

lettré [letre] **1.** *a.* well-read, cultured (person). **2.** *n.m.* scholar; well-read man.

lettrine [letrin] *n.f. Typ:* **1.** *O:* reference letter, superior letter. **2.** (*at beginning of chapters, etc.*) cocked up initial. **3.** (*in dictionary*) running head(line).

leu¹ [lø] *n.m. Num:* (Romanian) leu; *pl. lei.*

leu² *n.m. A:* wolf; *used only in the adv.phr.* **à la queue leu leu,** in single file, in Indian file.

leucémie [løsemi] *n.f. Med:* leuk(a)emia.

leucémique [løsemik] *Med:* (*a*) *a.* leuk(a)emic; (*b*) *n.* leuk(a)emia sufferer.

leucocyte [løkɔsit] *n.m. Physiol:* leucocyte.

leucoma, leucome [løkɔma, løkom] *n.m. Med:* leucoma, albugo.

leucorrhée [løkɔre] *n.f. Med:* leucorrh(o)ea.

leur¹ [lœr] **1.** *poss.a.* their; **leur oncle et leur tante,** their uncle and (their) aunt; **un(e) de leurs ami(e)s,** a friend of theirs, one of their friends; **leurs père et mère,** their father and mother. **2.** (*a*) *poss.pron.* **le leur, la leur, les leurs,** theirs; **j'ai écrit à mes amis et aux leurs,** I wrote to my friends and to theirs; **notre maison a plus de chambres que la leur,** our house has more rooms than theirs; *Lit:* **cette maison qui était l.,** this house of theirs, which was theirs; (*b*) *n.m.* **ils n'y mettent pas du leur,** they don't pull their weight, they don't do their share; **les leurs,** their own family, friends, etc.; **j'étais des leurs hier soir,** I was with them, I joined them, last night; **ils ont encore fait des leurs,** they've been up to their old tricks again.

leur², *see* LUI¹.

leurre [lœr] *n.m.* (*a*) lure (for hawks); (*b*) decoy (for birds); (artificial) bait, lure (for fish); (*c*) delusion, deception; illusion.

leurrer [lœre] *v.tr.* (*a*) to lure (hawk, etc.); (*b*) to deceive, delude (s.o.); **se l.,** to delude oneself; **il se laisse facilement l.,** he is easily taken in.

lev [lɛv] *n.m. Num:* (Bulgarian) lev; *pl. leva.*

levage [ləvaʒ] *n.m.* **1.** lifting (up), hoisting, raising; **câble de l.,** hoisting cable; **cric de l.,** lifting jack. **2.** rising (of dough, etc.).

levain [ləvɛ̃] *n.m.* leaven; **pain sans l.,** unleavened bread; **un l. de révolte,** a leaven of revolt.

levant [ləvɑ̃] **1.** *a.m.* **soleil l.,** rising sun; **il est parti au soleil l.,** he left at sunrise, *NAm:* at sunup. **2.** *n.m.* (*a*) **le l.,** the east, the orient; **du l. au couchant,** on the horizon; (*b*) *Geog:* **le L.,** the Levant.

levantin, -ine [ləvɑ̃tɛ̃, -in] *a. & n. Geog:* Levantine.

levé [ləve] **1.** *a.* (*a*) raised (hand, fist); **voter à mains levées,** to vote by a show of hands; **dessin à main levée,** freehand drawing; **pierre levée,** standing stone; (*b*) **pâte bien levée,** well risen dough; (*c*) (*of pers.*) up, out of bed; (*of sun, etc.*) up; **je suis l. de bonne heure,** I'm up early, I'm an early riser. **2.** *n.m.* (*a*) **voter par assis et l.,** to give one's vote by rising or remaining seated; (*b*) *Surv:* plan, survey (of a piece of land); **l. aérophotogrammétrique,** aerial survey; **faire le l. d'un terrain,** to survey a piece of land; (*c*) *Mus:* up beat.

levée [ləve] *n.f.* **1.** (*a*) raising, lifting; *Nau:* weighing (of anchor); (*b*) raising (of siege); lifting (of embargo, punishment, etc.); closing, adjourning (of meeting); (*c*) removal (of sth.); breaking (of seals); (*d*) collecting, gathering (of crops, etc.); levy(ing) (of troops, taxes); *Post:* (i) a collection (of letters); (ii) letters, mail, collected; **la l. est faite,** the post has been collected, *F:* has gone; *Mil:* **l. en masse,** levy en masse; *Fin:* **l. des actions,** taking (up) (of stock); (*e*) *Jur:* **l. d'un jugement,** transcript of a verdict. **2.** (*a*) rising (of court, etc.); (*b*) *Nau:* **l. de la mer,** rough sea, sea way; **l. de la lame,** surge, swell. **3.** (*a*) embankment, sea wall; dyke, levee; (*b*) *Cards:* trick; **faire une l.,** to take a trick.

lève-glace(s) [lɛvglas] *n.m.inv. Aut:* window winder, regulator.

lever¹ [ləve] *v.* **(je lève, n. levons; je lèverai)** to raise. **1.** *v.tr.* (*a*) to lift (up), to hold up; **l. la main sur qn,** to raise, lift, one's hand against s.o.; **l. les bras au ciel (dans un geste d'étonnement),** to throw up one's hands (in astonishment); **il ne veut pas l. le petit doigt,** he won't lift a finger, he won't do a thing; **l. la tête,** (i) to hold up one's head; (ii) to raise one's head, to look up; **l. un malade, un enfant,** to lift a patient; to help a child get up and dress; **l. les yeux (sur qn),** to look up (at s.o.); **l. la glace d'une voiture,** to close a car window; **l. son verre,** to raise one's glass (to s.o.); to drink a toast; **l. l'ancre,** (i) to weigh anchor; (ii) *F:* to leave, go; *Ven:* **l. un lièvre, une perdrix,** to start a hare, to flush a partridge; *P:* **l. une femme,** to pick up a woman; (*b*) to set upright; **l. une échelle,** to put up a ladder; **l. un étendard,** to raise a standard; (*c*) to raise (siege, etc.); to strike, break (camp); to lift (embargo, punishment, etc.); to close, adjourn (meeting); (*d*) *O:* to cut off length (from piece of material); (*e*) to remove (a difficulty, a doubt); **l. les scellés,** to break, remove, the seals. **2.** to raise, levy (troops); to levy (tax); *Post:* to collect (letters, mail); *Fin:* to take up (stock); *Cards:* **l. (les cartes),** to pick up a trick. **3.** to make, draw, get out (a plan). **4.** *v.i.* (*a*) (*of plants*) to shoot; (*b*) (*of dough*) to rise. **5. se l.,** to rise; to get up; (*a*) (*of hands, curtain, etc.*) to go up; (*b*) to stand up; **levez-vous,** stand up, get up; **se l. de table,** to leave the table; (*c*) to get up (from bed); **je me lève de bonne heure,** I'm an early riser, I get up early; **se l. du pied gauche,** to get out of bed on the wrong side; (*d*) **le jour se lève,** day is breaking, is dawning; **nous avons vu le soleil se l.,** we saw the sun rise; **le vent se lève,** the wind is rising, getting up; **le temps se lève,** the weather is clearing.

lever² *n.m.* **1.** (*a*) rising; getting up (from bed); (*b*) levee (of king, etc.); (*c*) **l. du soleil,** sunrise, *NAm:* sunup; **l. du jour,** daybreak. **2.** *Th:* rising, rise (of the curtain); **un l. de rideau,** a curtain raiser. **3.** = LEVÉ 2(*b*).

lève-tard [lɛvtar] *n.m.inv. F:* late riser.

lève-tôt [lɛvto] *n.m.inv. F:* early riser.

levier [ləvje] *n.m.* **1.** (*a*) *Ph: Mec:* lever; **bras de l.,** lever arm; **force de l.,** leverage; (*b*) *Tls:* crowbar, lever; **soulever, ouvrir, forcer, qch. avec un l.,** to prize, prise, lever, sth. up, open, out. **2.** lever, handle; *Mec.E:* **l. de commande,** control lever; **être aux leviers de commande,** to be in control, in command; **l. de frein,** brake lever; *Aut:* **l. (de changement) de vitesse,** gear lever, gear stick, *NAm:* gearshift.

lévitation [levitasjɔ̃] *n.f.* levitation.

lévite [levit] *n. Jew. Rel:* Levite.

levraut [ləvro] *n.m.* leveret; young hare.

lèvre [lɛvr̥] *n.f.* **1.** lip; **il avait un cigare aux lèvres,** he had a cigar between his lips; **j'ai le mot sur le bord des lèvres, sur les lèvres,** I have the word on the tip of my tongue; **manger du bout des lèvres,** to nibble, pick at, one's food; **il accepta, mais du bout des lèvres,** he grudgingly accepted; **rire du bout des lèvres,** to force a laugh; **il le dit des lèvres, mais le cœur n'y est pas,** he pays lip service; **pincer les lèvres,** to purse one's lips; **se mordre les lèvres (pour ne pas rire),** to bite one's lips (in order not to laugh). **2.** (*a*) rim (of crater); (*b*) lip (of wound); (*c*) *Bot:* lip, labium; (*d*) *pl. Anat:* lips, labia (of vulva).

levrette [ləvrɛt] *n.f.* **1.** greyhound bitch. **2. l. (d'Italie),** (small) Italian greyhound.

lévrier [levrije] *n.m.* greyhound; **l. irlandais, d'Irlande,** Irish wolf hound; **l. d'Italie,** Italian greyhound; **l. afghan,** Afghan hound; **l. russe,** borzoi; **courses de lévriers,** greyhound racing.

levure [ləvyr] *n.f.* yeast; **l. de bière,** brewer's yeast; **l. chimique** = baking powder.

lexème [lɛksɛm] *n.m. Ling:* lexeme.

lexical, -aux [lɛksikal, -o] *a.* lexical.

lexicographe [lɛksikɔgraf] *n.* lexicographer.

lexicographie [lɛksikɔgrafi] *n.f.* lexicography.

lexicographique [lɛksikɔgrafik] *a.* lexicographical.

lexicologie [lɛksikɔlɔʒi] *n.f.* lexicology.

lexicologique [lɛksikɔlɔʒik] *a.* lexicological.

lexicologue [lɛksikɔlɔg] *n.* lexicologist.

lexique [lɛksik] *n.m.* (*a*) lexicon; (*b*) small dictionary; glossary; vocabulary (at end of book, etc.).

lez [le] *prep.* (*occurs only in place names*) near(by).

lézard [lezar] *n.m.* (*a*) lizard; **l. gris, des murailles,** grey, wall, lizard; **l. vert,** green lizard; **faire le l.,** to bask, lounge, in the sun; (*b*) lizard skin.

lézarde [lezard] *n.f.* crevice, cranny, crack, chink.

lézardé [lezarde] *a.* (*of wall, plaster*) cracked, full of cracks; crannied.

lézarder [lezarde] **1.** *v.tr.* to crack, split (plaster, etc.); (*of wall*) **se l.,** to crack. **2.** *v.i. F:* to bask, lounge, in the sun.

liais [ljɛ] *n.m.* hard limestone.

liaison [ljɛzɔ̃] *n.f.* **1.** (*a*) joining, binding, connection; *Const:* (i) bonding (of bricks, etc.); (ii) mortar, cement; *Mus:* (i) slur; (ii) tie, ligature; (*b*) *Ch:* bond; (*c*) *Ling:* sounding of final consonant before initial vowel sound; liaison; *Gram:* **mot, terme, de l.,** link-word; (*d*) *Cu:* liaison, thickening (for sauce); (*e*) *Mil:* liaison, intercommunications; **être en l. avec . . .,** to be in touch with . . .; **se mettre en l. avec . . .,** to establish liaison, to liaise, to get in touch, with . . .; **établir une l. radio,** to establish radio contact; (*f*) **l. aérienne, maritime, ferrovière, routière,** air, sea, rail, road, link. **2.** (*a*) (close) contact, relationship; **l. d'affaires,** business connection; **travailler en l. (étroite) avec qn,** to work in (close) collaboration with s.o.; (*b*) **l. (amoureuse),** (love) affair; liaison.

liaisonner [ljɛzɔne] *v.tr. Const:* **1.** to bond (stones, etc.). **2.** to grout, point (stonework).

liane [ljan] *n.f. Bot:* liana; (tropical) creeper.

liant [ljɑ̃] **1.** *a.* sociable; friendly; **il est très l.,** he's quick to make friends; he's a good mixer. **2.** *n.m.* (*a*) engaging manner, sociable disposition; **avoir du l.,** to be sociable; (*b*) flexibility, pliability. **3.** *n.m.* binder; binding agent.

liard [ljar] *n.m. A:* half farthing; *F:* **il n'a pas un l.,** he hasn't (got) a farthing, a penny to his name.

lias [ljas] *n.m. Geol:* lias.

liasse [ljas] *n.f.* bundle, packet (of letters, etc.); wad (of banknotes); file (of papers); *Com: etc:* (i) multipart form; (ii) set of multipart forms.

libage [libaʒ] *n.m. Const:* bastard ashlar.

Liban [libɑ̃] *Pr.n.m. Geog:* Lebanon.

libanais, -aise [libanɛ, -ɛz] *a. & n. Geog:* Lebanese.

libation [libasjɔ̃] *n.f.* (*a*) *Ant:* libation; (*b*) **faire des libations,** to drink immoderately, like a fish.

libelle [libɛl] *n.m.* lampoon, scurrilous satire.

libellé [libele] *n.m.* wording, terms used (in document, etc.).

libeller [libele] *v.tr.* to draw up, word (document, etc.); **l. un chèque,** to make out, to write out, a cheque, *NAm:* check; **télégramme libellé comme suit . . .,** telegram worded as follows . . ., that reads as follows . . . .

libelliste [libelist] *n.m.* lampoonist.

libellule [libelyl] *n.f.* dragonfly.

libérable [liberabl̥] *a. & n.m. Mil:* (*pers.*) dischargeable; who can be demobbed; **congé, permission, l.,** demob leave.

libéral, -ale, -aux [liberal, -o] **1.** *a.* liberal; (*a*) **il exerce une profession libérale,** he's a professional man; (*b*) generous; open-handed; (*c*) broadminded. **2.** *a. & n. Pol:* liberal.

libéralement [liberalmɑ̃] *adv.* liberally.

libéralisation [liberalizasjɔ̃] *n.f.* liberalization, easing (of restriction, etc.).

libéraliser [liberalize] *v.tr.* to liberalize.

libéralisme [liberalism] *n.m.* liberalism.

libéralité [liberalite] *n.f.* liberality; (*a*) generosity; open-handedness; (*b*) (generous) gift; **faire des libéralités à qn,** to give liberally, freely, to s.o.

libérateur, -trice [liberatœr, -tris] **1.** *a.* liberating; **guerre libératrice,** war of liberation. **2.** *n.* liberator.

libération [liberasjɔ̃] *n.f.* (*a*) liberation, freeing, releasing; discharge, release (of prisoner); discharge (of soldier); **l. conditionnelle,** release (of prisoner) on parole; **mouvement de l. de la femme,** women's liberation movement, *F:* women's lib; (*b*) payment in full, discharge; (*c*) *Aer:* **vitesse de l.,** escape velocity, parabolic velocity.

libératoire [liberatwar] *a.* **paiement l.,** payment in full discharge from debt; (*of money*) **avoir force l.,** to be legal tender.

libéré [libere] **1.** *a.* liberated, free; *Fin:* (fully) paid-up (share). **2.** *n.m.* discharged soldier, prisoner.

libérer [libere] *v.tr.* **(je libère, n. libérons; je libérerai) 1.** (*a*) to liberate, release; to set (s.o.) free, to free (s.o.); to discharge (prisoner, soldier); *Med:* to unblock (passage); *Com:* to ease (restriction); **l. sa conscience,** to free one's conscience; (*b*) to free (s.o., an institution, etc., of debt, etc.); **titre de 1000 francs libéré de 750 francs,** 1000 franc share of which 750 francs are paid (up). **2. se l.,** to free oneself; **se l. (d'une dette),** to redeem, liquidate, a debt; **se l. pour deux jours,** to (arrange to) take two days off.

Libéria [liberja] *Pr.n.m. Geog:* Liberia.

libérien, -ienne [liberjɛ̃, -jɛn] *a. & n. Geog:* Liberian.

libertaire [libɛrtɛr] *a. & n.* libertarian.

liberté [libɛrte] *n.f.* liberty, freedom; **animaux en l.,** animals in the wild, running free; **mettre qn, un animal, en l.,** to set s.o., an animal, free; **être mis en l.,** to be allowed to go free; (*of accused*) to be discharged; **l'assassin est toujours en l.,** the murderer is still at large; **mise en l.,** (i) liberation, freeing, release (of prisoner); (ii) release (of gas); *Jur:* **(mise en) l. provisoire, sous caution,** (release on) bail; **l. conditionnelle,** parole; **avoir pleine l. d'action,** to have full freedom of action; to have a free hand; **l. de conscience, de la presse,** freedom of conscience, of the press; **l. d'expression, d'opinion,** freedom of expression, of speech; freedom of thought; **l. du culte,** freedom of worship; **parler avec l., en toute l.,** to speak freely, without restraint; **j'ai pris la l. de dire . . .,** I took the liberty of saying . . .; **si je puis prendre une telle l. . . .,** if I may be so bold . . .; **prendre des libertés avec qn,** to take liberties with s.o.; **jour de l.,** free day, day off; **avec tout ce travail je n'ai pas beaucoup de l.,** with all this work I haven't (got) much free time.

libertin, -ine [libɛrtɛ̃, -in] *a. & n.* libertine. **1.** *Hist:* (*a*) *a.* free-thinking; (*b*) *n.* free thinker. **2.** (*a*) *a.* licentious (book, etc.); dissolute (person); (*b*) *n.* dissolute person; *m.* rake.

libertinage [libɛrtinaʒ] *n.m.* libertinage; (*a*) *A:* free-thinking; (*b*) licentiousness, dissoluteness, debauchery.

libidineux, -euse [libidinø, -øz] *a.* libidinous, lustful.

libido [libido] *n.f. Psy:* libido.

libraire [librɛr] *n.* bookseller.

libraire-éditeur [librɛreditœr] *n.m.* publisher and bookseller; *pl. libraires-éditeurs.*

librairie [libreri] *n.f.* (*a*) book trade; bookselling; **ouvrages en l.,** published books; (*b*) bookshop; **l. d'art,** art bookshop; (*c*) publishing house (with own bookshops).

libre [libr̥] *a.* free. **1.** (*a*) **pays l.,** free country; **traduction l.,** free translation; **vers l.,** free verse; **je suis l. de onze heures à midi,** I'm free between eleven and twelve; (*to taxi driver*) *F:* **vous êtes l.?** are you free? **être l. de faire qch.,** to be free to do sth.; **laisser qn l. d'agir,** to leave s.o. a free hand, free to act; **vous êtes l. de le faire, l. à vous de le faire,** you are quite free, at liberty, to do it; **l. à vous d'essayer,** you're welcome to try; **l. arbitre,** free will; **l. parole,** free speech; **l. penseur, penseuse,** free thinker; **l. pensée,** free thinking, free thought; **l'homme est l.,** man is a free agent; **école l.,** independent (catholic) school; (*b*) (*of movement, etc.*) unrestrained; **robe qui laisse la taille l.,** dress which fits loosely round the waist; **elle a les cheveux libres,** she wears her hair loose; (*c*) **l. de préjugés,** free from prejudice; **l. de soucis,** free from care, carefree; (*d*) **être l. avec qn,** to be free with s.o., to treat s.o. in a familiar way; **allures, manières, libres,** free and easy manner. **2.** (*a*) clear, open (space, road, etc.); vacant, unoccupied (table, seat); **avoir du temps de l.,** to have some time free, some spare, free, time, some time to spare; **le lundi est mon jour l.,** Monday is my day off; **laisser le champ l.,** to leave the field clear; **je vous laisse le champ l.,** I'll leave you to it, you're free to do as you think best; **la voie est l.,** the coast is clear; *Rail:* **voie l.,** line clear; *Tp:* **la ligne n'est pas l.,** the line is engaged, busy; (*taxi sign*) **l.,** for hire; **à l'air l.,** in the open air; **l. possession,** vacant possession; (*b*) *Mec.E:* disengaged, running free, out of gear; *Cy: Aut:* **roue l.,** freewheel; **descendre une côte en roue l.,** to freewheel, coast, down a hill.

libre-échange [libreʃɑ̃ʒ] *n.m. Pol.Ec:* free trade.

libre-échangiste [libreʃɑ̃ʒist] *n.m.* free trader; *pl. libre-échangistes.*

librement [librəmɑ̃] *adv.* freely, unrestrainedly.

libre-réponse [librərepɔ̃s] *n.f. Post:* Freepost.

libre-service [librəsɛrvis] *n.m.* self-service; **(magasin, restaurant) l.-s.,** self-service shop, *NAm:* store, restaurant; *pl. libres-services.*

librettiste [libretist] *n.* librettist.

libretto [libreto] *n.m.* libretto; *pl. libretti, librettos.*

Libye [libi] *Pr.n.f. Geog:* Libya.

libyen, -enne [libjɛ̃, -jɛn] *a. & n. Geog:* Libyan.

lice [lis] *n.f. Hist:* lists; *Fig:* **entrer en l. contre qn,** to enter the lists against s.o.

licence [lisɑ̃s] *n.f.* licence. **1.** (*a*) leave, permission; *Adm:* **l. pour vendre qch.,** licence to sell sth.; **l. de débitant,** licence to sell beer, wines and spirits; *NAm:* liquor licence; **fabriqué sous l.,** made under licence; **l. d'importation, d'exportation,** import, export, licence; (*b*) *Sp:* permit (giving right of entry into competition); (*c*) *Sch:* bachelor's degree; **l. ès lettres, ès sciences, en droit,** bachelor's degree in arts, in science, in law; arts, science, law, degree; **passer sa l.,** to take one's degree (exams). **2.** (*a*) licence, abuse of liberty; **l. poétique,** poetic licence; **prendre des licences avec qn,** to take liberties with s.o.; (*b*) licentiousness.

licencié, -ée [lisɑ̃sje] **1.** *a.* **il est l.,** he's a graduate. **2.** *n.* (*a*) **l. ès lettres, l. ès sciences, de sciences, l. en droit,** bachelor of arts, of science, of law; arts, science, law, graduate; (*b*) *Sp:* permit holder.

licenciement [lisɑ̃simɑ̃] *n.m.* disbanding (of troops); redundancy (of workers); dismissal (of employee); sending home (of schoolchildren); **il y a eu beaucoup de licenciements,** many (people) were made redundant.

licencier [lisɑ̃sje] *v.tr.* (*pr.sub. & impf.* **n. licenciions, v. licenciiez)** to disband (troops); to make (workers) redundant; to dismiss (employee); to send home (schoolchildren).

licencieusement [lisɑ̃sjøzmɑ̃] *adv.* licentiously.

licencieux, -euse [lisɑ̃sjø, -øz] *a.* licentious.

lichen [likɛn] *n.m. Bot: Med:* lichen.

lichette [liʃɛt] *n.f. P:* small slice, nibble (of bread, cheese, etc.).

licite [licit] *a.* licit, lawful, permissible.

licitement [lisitmɑ̃] *adv.* licitly, lawfully.

licol [likɔl] *n.m. Harn:* halter.

licorne [likɔrn] *n.f.* **1.** *Myth: Her:* unicorn. **2.** *Z:* **l. de mer,** sea unicorn, narwhal.

licou [liku] *n.m. Harn:* halter.

licteur [liktœr] *n.m. Rom.Ant:* lictor.

lido [lido] *n.m.* (*a*) *Geog:* sand bar; (*b*) lido.

lie [li] *n.f.* dregs; **boire le calice jusqu'à la l.,** to drain the cup to the dregs; **l. (de vin),** lees, sediment, of wine; *a.inv.* **l.(-)de(-)vin,** purplish red, wine-coloured; **la l. de la société,** the scum, dregs, of society.

lié [lje] *a.* **1.** bound; **avoir les mains liées,** to have one's hands tied; **pieds et poings liés,** bound hand and foot; **avoir la langue liée,** to be bound to keep a secret. **2. être (très) l. avec qn,** to be (great) friends, intimately acquainted, with s.o. **avoir partie liée avec qn,** to be in league with s.o. **3.** *Mus:* **notes liées,** (i) tied, (ii) slurred, notes.

liège [ljɛʒ] *n.m.* (*a*) cork; **semelle de l.,** cork sole; **cigarette à bout de l.,** cork-tipped cigarette; (*b*) *Fish:* cork, float.

liégeois, -oise [ljeʒwa, -waz] *a. & n. Geog:* (native, inhabitant) of Liège; *Cu:* **café, chocolat, l.,** iced coffee, chocolate, topped with Chantilly cream.

lien [ljɛ̃] *n.m.* **1.** (*a*) tie, bond; **il s'est libéré de ses liens,** he freed himself from his bonds; **liens du sang,** blood ties; **l. de parenté,** family relationship; **mes liens de famille,** my family ties; **l. d'amitié,** bond of friendship; (*b*) link, connection; **il y a un l. entre ces événements,** there's a connection between these events. **2.** brace, tie, strap, band.

lier [lje] *v.* (*pr.sub. & impf.* **n. liions, v. liiez**) **1.** *v.tr.* (*a*) to bind, fasten, tie, tie up; **l. qch. avec une corde,** to bind sth. with a rope; **l. les pieds et les mains à qn,** to bind s.o. hand and foot; **on l'a lié à un arbre,** he was tied to a tree; **l. les lacets de ses souliers,** to tie, knot, one's shoelaces; **ce contrat vous lie,** you are bound by this agreement; **l'intérêt nous lie,** we have common interests; **l. les idées,** to connect, link, ideas; **l. deux mots,** to link two words (in pronunciation); to sound the liaison; *Mus:* **l. deux notes,** (i) to slur, (ii) to tie, two notes; (*b*) *Cu:* to thicken (sauce); (*c*) **l. amitié, conversation, avec qn,** to strike up a friendship with s.o.; to start a, enter into, conversation with s.o. **2. se l.** (*a*) **se l. avec qn,** to form, strike up, a friendship with s.o.; **il se lie facilement,** he makes friends easily; **je me suis lié d'amitié avec son père,** I have made friends with his father; (*b*) **le lait et le jaune d'œuf se lient facilement,** milk and yolk of egg blend easily.

lierre [ljɛr] *n.m. Bot:* **1.** ivy. **2. l. terrestre,** ground ivy.

liesse [ljɛs] *n.f. A:* jubilation, gaiety; *Lit:* **la foule était en l.,** the crowd was jubilant.

lieu, -eux [ljø] *n.m.* **1.** place; (*a*) locality, spot; **mettre qch. en l. sûr,** to put sth. in a safe place; **en tous lieux, en aucun l.,** everywhere, nowhere; **en haut l.,** in high circles, in high places; **le l. du crime,** the scene of the crime; **la police est sur les lieux de l'accident,** the police are at the scene of the accident; **j'étais sur les lieux,** I was on the spot; **mauvais l.,** disreputable house; **l. de rendez-vous,** meeting place, rendezvous; **l. public,** a public place; **l. de travail,** place of work; **en premier l.,** in the first place, first of all, firstly; **en troisième l.,** in the third place, thirdly; **en dernier l.,** last of all, lastly, finally; **en temps et l.,** at the proper time and place; **en son l.,** in due course; (*b*) *pl.* house, premises; **avant de quitter ces lieux,** before leaving this place, before leaving here; (*c*) *pl. O:* **lieux (d'aisances),** lavatory. **2.** (*a*) **avoir l.,** to take place; **la réunion aura l. à . . .,** the meeting will be held at . . .; (*b*) ground(s), cause; **il y a (tout) l., j'ai l., de supposer que** + *ind.*, there is, I have, (good) grounds, (every) reason, for supposing that . . .; **il y a l. d'attendre,** it would be advisable, as well, to wait; **je vous écrirai s'il y a l.,** I shall write to you if necessary; **donner l. à des désagréments,** to give rise to trouble; **tout donne l. de croire que . . .,** everything leads one, us, to believe that . . .; **son retour a donné l. à une réunion de famille,** his return was the occasion for a family gathering; (*c*) (*function*) **tenir l. de qch.,** to take the place of, stand instead of, sth.; **elle lui a tenu l. de mère,** she had been a mother to him; **au l. de,** instead of, in lieu of; **au l. d'être satisfait,** instead of being satisfied; **au l. que** + *ind.*, whereas; **au l. que** + *sub.*, instead of + *ger.* **3.** *Mth:* **l. géométrique,** locus. **4. l. commun,** commonplace.

lieu(-)dit [ljødi] *n.m.* (named) place; locality; *pl. lieux(-)dits.*

lieue [ljø] *n.f.* league (= 4 kilometres); **être à mille lieues de croire qch.,** to be far, miles, from believing sth.; **j'étais à cent lieues de penser que . . .,** I should never have dreamt that . . .; **il sent son docteur d'une l.,** you can tell he's a doctor a mile off.

lieur, -euse [ljœr, -øz] **1.** *n.* binder (of sheaves, etc.). **2.** *n.f. Agr:* **lieuse,** (mechanical) sheaf binder.

lieutenant [ljøtnɑ̃] *n.m.* (*a*) lieutenant; *Navy:* **l. de vaisseau,** lieutenant; *Av:* **l. (aviateur),** flying officer, *U.S:* first lieutenant; (*b*) (*Mercantile Marine*) mate; **premier l.,** second mate; (*c*) **l. de port,** deputy harbour, *NAm:* harbor, master.

lieutenant-colonel [ljøtnɑ̃kɔlɔnɛl] *n.m. Mil:* lieutenant-colonel; *Av:* wing commander; *pl. lieutenants-colonels.*

lièvre [ljɛvr̥] *n.m. Z:* hare; **c'est vous qui avez levé le l.,** you started it; **c'est là que gît le l.,** that's the crucial point, the crux of the matter; **courir deux lièvres à la fois,** to try to do two things at once; **mémoire de l.,** memory like a sieve.

liftier [liftje] *n.m.* lift attendant, *NAm:* elevator operator.

lifting [liftiŋ] *n.m. Surg:* face lift.

ligament [ligamɑ̃] *n.m.* ligament.

ligature [ligatyr] *n.f.* **1.** tying, binding. **2.** (*a*) *Mus:* tie; (*b*) *El: etc:* splice (in wire, cable); (*c*) *Surg: Typ:* ligature.

ligaturer [ligatyre] *v.tr.* to bind, splice; to tie (sth.) up; *Surg:* to ligature, ligate, tie (artery, etc.).

lige [liʒ] *a. Hist:* liege; **homme l.,** liegeman.

lignage¹ [liɲaʒ] *n.m. A:* lineage, descent.

lignage² *n.m. Typ:* linage (of a text, etc.).

ligne [liɲ] *n.f.* line. **1.** (*a*) cord; (fishing) line; **planter des arbres à la l.,** to plant trees straight by using a line, a cord; *Fish:* **l. de fond,** ledger line; (*b*) **l. droite,** straight line; **l. brisée,** broken line; **les lignes de la main,** the lines of the hand; *Mus:* **l. de portée,** stave line; **l. supplémentaire, additionnelle,** ledger line; *Fb:* **l. de touche,** touch line; *Ten:* **l. de fond, médiane,** base, centre, line; *T.V:* **définition de 625 lignes,** definition of 625 lines; *Aut:* **l. blanche,** white line, *U.S:* yellow line; (*c*) (out)line; **la l. du nez,** the line, contour, of the nose; **pureté des lignes,** purity of line (in picture); **l. élégante d'une voiture,** good lines of a car; **grandes lignes d'une œuvre,** broad, general, outline of a work; **garder sa l., soigner sa l.,** to keep, to watch, one's waistline; to keep one's figure; **avoir (de) la l.,** to have a good figure; (*d*) *Nau:* **l. de flottaison,** waterline (of ship); **l. de charge,** load line; *Ph:* **l. de force,** line of force; *Sm.a: Artil:* **l. de visée, de mire,** line of sight; **l. de tir,** line of fire; *Nau:* **la l. (équatoriale),** the line, the Equator; **passer la l.,** to cross the line; **suivre la l. du devoir,** to follow the path of duty; **descendre en l. directe, en droite l., de . . .,** to be directly descended from . . .; (*e*) **l. de maisons,** row of houses; **se mettre en l.,** to line up, to draw up in a line; **question qui vient en première l.,** question of primary importance; **hors l.,** out of the common; unrivalled, outstanding, incomparable (artist, etc.); **sur toute la l.,** completely; **il a raison sur toute la l.,** he's absolutely right; (*f*) line (of writing); **écris-moi deux lignes,** drop me a line; **lire entre**

les lignes, to read between the lines; **aller à la l.,** to begin a new line, a new paragraph; (*in dictating*) **à la l.,** new paragraph, new line. **2.** *Mil:* (*a*) **l. de front,** front line; **l. d'attaque,** line of attack; (*b*) **l. de bataille, de combat,** line of battle, fighting line; **(infanterie de) l.,** line infantry; *Navy: A:* **vaisseau de l.,** ship of the line. **3.** (*a*) *Rail:* line; **grandes lignes,** main lines; **l. maritime, aérienne,** shipping line, airline; **l. d'autobus,** bus (i) service, (ii) route; (*b*) *El:* (power) line; **l. de haute tension,** high tension wire, line; **l. télégraphique,** telegraph line; **l. téléphonique,** telephone line; **la l. est occupée,** the line is engaged, *NAm:* busy; **vous êtes en l.,** you're connected, you're through; *Tp: Pol:* **la l. rouge,** the hot line. **4.** *Can: Meas:* eighth of an inch (3.175 mm).

lignée [liɲe] *n.f.* (line of) descendants; line, lineage; **de bonne l. allemande,** of good German stock.

ligneux, -euse [liɲø, -øz] *a.* ligneous, woody.

lignite [liɲit] *n.m. Miner:* lignite, brown coal.

ligotage [ligɔtaʒ] *n.m.* binding, tying up (of s.o.).

ligoter [ligɔte] *v.tr.* to tie (s.o.) up; to bind (s.o.) hand and foot.

ligue [lig] *n.f.* league, confederacy.

liguer [lige] *v.tr.* **1.** to league, bond (nations, etc.) together; **être ligué avec qn,** to be in league with s.o. **2. se l.,** to league, to form a league **(avec, contre,** with, against); **ils se liguent contre moi,** they're conspiring against me.

ligueur, -euse [ligœr, -øz] *n.* member of a league.

lilas [lila] **1.** *n.m. Bot:* lilac. **2.** *a.inv.* lilac.

lilial, -iaux [liljal, -jo] *a. Lit:* lily-white.

lilliputien, -ienne [lilipysjɛ̃, -jɛn] *a. & n.* Lilliputian.

lillois, -oise [lilwa, -waz] *a. & n. Geog:* (native, inhabitant) of Lille.

limace [limas] *n.f.* **1.** *Moll:* slug; *P:* **c'est une vraie l.,** he's so slow, he's such a slowcoach. **2.** *P:* shirt.

limaçon [limasɔ̃] *n.m.* **1.** *O:* snail; **escalier en l.,** spiral staircase. **2.** *Anat:* cochlea (of the ear).

limage [limaʒ] *n.m.* filing (down, off).

limaille [limaj] *n.f.* filings; **l. de fer,** iron filings.

limande [limɑ̃d] *n.f.* **1.** *Ich:* dab; **l.-sole,** lemon sole; *F:* (*of woman*) **plate comme une l.,** as flat as a pancake. **2.** *Carp:* (*a*) graving piece; (*b*) straight edge.

limbe [lɛ̃b] *n.m.* **1.** *Astr: Mth:* limb; *Bot:* lamina, limb (of leaf). **2.** (*a*) *Theol:* **les Limbes,** limbo; (*b*) **le projet est dans les limbes,** the project is as yet undecided.

lime¹ [lim] *n.f.* **1.** *Tls:* file; **l. sourde,** dead-smooth file; **l. à ongles,** nail file; **l. émeri,** emery board; **aiguiser un outil à la l.,** to file up a tool; **donner un dernier coup de l. à un ouvrage,** to put the finishing touches to a piece of work. **2.** *Moll:* lima.

lime² *n.f. Bot:* lime.

limer [lime] *v.tr.* to file (up, off, down, through).

limeur, -euse [limœr, -øz] *n.* **1.** filer. **2.** *n.f.* **limeuse,** filing machine.

limier [limje] *n.m.* bloodhound; *Fig:* sleuth.

liminaire [liminɛr] *a.* **1.** *Typ:* **pièces, feuillets, liminaires,** preliminary pages, *F:* prelims. **2. épître l.,** introductory letter; foreword; introduction.

limitatif, -ive [limitatif, -iv] *a.* limiting, restrictive, restricting.

limitation [limitasjɔ̃] *n.f.* limitation, restriction; **l. des armements,** arms limitation; **l. des naissances,** birth control; family planning; **l. des salaires,** wage restraint; **l. de vitesse,** speed limit; **il n'y a pas de l. de temps,** there's no time limit.

limite [limit] *n.f.* **1.** (*a*) boundary (of country, field, etc.); limit (of s.o.'s power, etc.); **marquer les limites du terrain,** to mark out the ground; **l. d'âge,** age limit; **fixer, imposer, des limites à l'autorité de qn,** to set bounds to s.o.'s authority; **franchir, dépasser, les limites,** to go beyond the limits, to go too far; **mettre une l., des limites, à . . .,** to set a limit, limits, to . . .; **dans les limites du sujet,** within the limits of the subject; **dans une certaine l.,** up to a point; to a certain extent; **à la l. j'accepterais de le voir,** if pushed, if I have to, I'll (agree to) see him; **se battre jusqu'à la dernière l.,** to fight to the death; **il est à la l. de ses forces,** he's completely exhausted; **sans limites,** unbounded, limitless; **ma patience a des limites!** my patience is wearing thin! **son ambition ne connaît pas de limites,** his ambition knows no bounds; **limites d'un terrain de football,** boundary (lines) of a football pitch; (*b*) *Mec:* **l. d'élasticité,** elastic limit; **l. de rupture,** breaking point. **2. cas l.,** borderline case; **vitesse l.,** maximum speed; **charge l. d'un pont,** weight capacity of a bridge; **date l.,** closing date, deadline.

limité [limite] *a.* limited, restricted.

limiter [limite] *v.tr.* **1.** to bound, to mark the bounds of (countries, etc.). **2.** to limit, restrict; to set bounds, limits, to (s.o.'s power, rights, etc.); **se l. à . . .,** to limit, restrict oneself to . . . .

limitrophe [limitrɔf] *a.* adjacent **(de,** to); bordering **(de,** on); neighbouring; **être l. d'un autre pays,** to border on another country.

limogeage [limɔʒaʒ] *n.m. F:* (*a*) superseding (of general, etc.); (*b*) dismissal.

limoger [limɔʒe] *v.tr. F:* (*a*) to supersede (general, etc.); (*b*) to dismiss (s.o.).

limon¹ [limɔ̃] *n.m.* (*a*) silt, alluvium (on river banks, etc.); (*b*) *Geol:* limon.

limon² *n.m.* **1.** *Veh:* shaft, thill. **2.** *Const:* stringboard, stringer (of staircase).

limon³ *n.m. Bot: A:* lemon.

limonade [limɔnad] *n.f.* (*a*) (fizzy) lemonade; (*b*) *A:* lemon (and water) drink.

limonadier, -ière [limɔnadje, -jɛr] *n.* **1.** soft (fizzy) drinks manufacturer. **2.** keeper, owner, of a café.

limoneux, -euse [limɔnø, -øz] *a.* **1.** (*of water, etc.*) muddy, silty. **2.** *Geol:* alluvial.

limonier¹ [limɔnje] *n.m.* shaft horse.

limonier² *n.m. Bot: A:* lemon tree.

limousin, -ine [limuzɛ̃, -in] **1.** *a. & n. Geog:* (native, inhabitant) of the province of Limousin. **2.** *n.m. Ling:* Limousin dialect. **3.** *n.f.* **limousine** (*a*) (shepherd's) rough woollen cloak; (*b*) *Aut: A:* limousine.

limpide [lɛ̃pid] *a.* limpid, clear (quartz, water, etc.); clear (explanation).

limpidité [lɛ̃pidite] *n.f.* limpidity, clarity.

lin [lɛ̃] *n.m.* **1.** flax; **graine de l.,** linseed; **huile de l.,** linseed oil. **2.** *Tex:* **(tissu, toile, de) l.,** linen.

linceul [lɛ̃sœl] *n.m.* winding sheet, shroud.

linéaire [lineɛr] *a.* linear (equation, leaf, etc.); **dessin l.,** geometrical drawing; **récit l.,** direct, straightforward, narrative.

linéament [lineamɑ̃] *n.m.* lineament, feature (of face); line, outline (of shape, etc.).

linge [lɛ̃ʒ] *n.m.* **1.** (*a*) linen; **l. de table,** table linen; **l. de maison, gros l.,** household linen; **l. (de corps),** underwear; (*b*) washing; **corde à l.,** clothesline; *F:* **il faut laver son l. sale en famille,** don't wash your dirty linen in public. **2.** piece of linen; **essuyer qch. avec un l.,** to wipe sth. with a cloth.

lingère [lɛ̃ʒɛr] *n.f.* linen maid.

lingerie [lɛ̃ʒri] *n.f.* **1.** underwear, underclothing; **l. (de dame),** (women's) underwear, lingerie. **2.** linen room.

lingot [lɛ̃go] *n.m.* **1.** ingot; **l. d'or,** gold bar, ingot; *Fin:* **or, argent, en lingots,** bullion. **2.** *Typ:* slug.

lingual, -aux [lɛ̃gwal, -o] *a. Anat: Ling:* lingual.

linguiste [lɛ̃gɥist] *n.* linguist.

linguistique [lɛ̃gɥistik] **1.** *a.* linguistic. **2.** *n.f.* linguistics.

linguistiquement [lɛ̃gɥistikmɑ̃] *adv.* linguistically.
linier, -ière [linje, -jɛr] *a.* pertaining to linen, to flax; **industrie linière,** linen industry.
liniment [linimɑ̃] *n.m. Med:* liniment.
lino [lino] *n.m. F:* (= LINOLEUM) lino.
linoléum [linɔleɔm] *n.m.* linoleum.
linon [linɔ̃] *n.m. Tex:* lawn.
linotte [linɔt] *n.f. Orn:* linnet; *F:* **tête de l.,** scatterbrain.
Linotype [linɔtip] *n.f. R.t.m: Typ:* Linotype.
linotypie [linɔtipi] *n.f. Typ:* setting by Linotype.
linotypiste [linɔtipist] *n.* linotypist, Linotype operator.
linteau, -eaux [lɛ̃to] *n.m. Const:* lintel.
lion, -onne [ljɔ̃, -ɔn] *n.* **1.** (*a*) lion, *f.* lioness; **la part du l.,** the lion's share; *F:* **il a mangé,** *P:* **bouffé, du l.,** he's very (i) energetic, (ii) aggressive; (*b*) **l. de mer,** sea lion. **2.** (*a*) *A: & Lit:* celebrity, (literary) lion; (*b*) brave man. **3.** *Astr:* **le L.,** Leo.
lionceau, -eaux [ljɔ̃so] *n.m.* lion cub.
lipide [lipid] *n.m. Bio-Ch:* lipid.
lippe [lip] *n.f.* (thick) lower lip; **faire la l.,** to pout; to sulk.
lippu [lipy] *a.* (*a*) thick-lipped; (*b*) thick (lip).
liquéfaction [likefaksjɔ̃] *n.f.* liquefaction.
liquéfiable [likefjabl̩] *a.* liquefiable (gas).
liquéfiant [likefjɑ̃] *a.* liquefactive; liquefying.
liquéfier [likefje] *v.* (*pr.sub. & impf.* **n. liquéfiions, v. liquéfiiez**) **1.** *v.tr.* to liquefy. **2. se l.** (*a*) to liquefy; (*b*) (*of pers.*) to lose one's energy, one's moral strength.
liqueur [likœr] *n.f.* **1.** (*a*) (alcoholic) drink; liqueur; **vin de l.,** dessert, sweet, wine; (*b*) *Fr.C:* **l. (douce),** soft drink. **2.** (*a*) *A:* liquid; **l. séminale,** seminal fluid; (*b*) *Ch:* solution; **l. titrée,** standard solution.
liquidateur, -trice [likidatœr, -tris] *n. Jur:* liquidator.
liquidation [likidasjɔ̃] *n.f.* **1.** liquidation; (*a*) **l. forcée, volontaire,** compulsory, voluntary, liquidation; **entrer en l.,** to go into liquidation; (*b*) clearing (of accounts); *St.Exch:* settlement; **chambre de l.,** (bankers') clearing house. **2.** selling off (of stocks); clearance sale.
liquide [likid] **1.** *a.* liquid; **la soupe est trop l.,** the soup is too watery, too thin; **argent l.,** cash, ready money. **2.** *n.m.* (*a*) liquid, fluid; (*b*) (i) drink; (ii) liquid food; (*c*) ready cash; **je n'ai pas assez de l.,** I haven't (got) enough cash. **3.** *n.f. Ling:* **liquide,** liquid.
liquider [likide] *v.tr.* **1.** to liquidate; (*a*) to wind up (a business); (*b*) *v.i.* to go into liquidation; (*c*) to settle (account); (*d*) *F:* **l. qn,** to liquidate, eliminate, s.o.; **c'est liquidé,** it's (all) over. **2.** to sell off (stock).
liquidité [likidite] *n.f.* liquidity; *Fin: pl.* **liquidités,** liquid assets.
liquoreux, -euse [likɔrø, -øz] *a.* liqueur-like (wine, etc.); sweet.
lire[1] [lir] *v.tr.* (*pr.p.* **lisant;** *p.p.* **lu;** *pr.ind.* **je lis, il lit;** *impf.* **je lisais;** *p.h.* **je lus;** *fu.* **je lirai**) to read. **1. l. tout haut, à haute voix,** to read aloud; **l. une carte,** to map-read, to read a map; **l. qch. dans un livre,** to read sth. (i) in a book, (ii) (aloud) out of a book; **l. de la musique à première vue,** to sightread music; **ce livre se lit bien, se laisse l.,** it's a readable book; this book is very readable; **avoir beaucoup lu,** to be well read; **l. dans la pensée de qn,** to read s.o.'s thoughts; **l. dans le jeu de qn,** to know s.o.'s game; to know what s.o. is up to; **elle a voulu me l. les lignes de la main,** she wanted to read my hand; **cela se lit sur votre visage, dans vos yeux,** one can read it on your face, in your eyes; **la peur se lisait sur tous les visages,** fear was written on every face; *Corr:* **dans l'attente de vous l.,** hoping to hear from you. **2. l. une communication,** to read out, give out, a notice.
lire[2] *n.f. Num:* lira.
lis [lis] *n.m.* lily; **l. blanc,** white lily; **l. des vallées,** lily of the valley; **l. d'eau, l. d'étang,** water lily; **teint de l.,** lily-white complexion.
Lisbonne [lizbɔn], *Pr.n.f. Geog:* Lisbon.
lise [liz] *n.f.* quicksand.
liseré [lizre], **liséré** [lizere] *n.m. Needlew: etc:* border, edging; piping, binding (of skirt); strip (of different material, etc.).
liserer [lizre], **lisérer** [lizere] *v.tr.* (**je lisère, n. liserons** *or* **n. lisérons; je lisèrerai**) *Needlew:* (*a*) to border, edge; to sew an edging on (sth.); (*b*) to pipe; to trim (sth.) with piping.
liseron [lizrɔ̃] *n.m. Bot:* bindweed, convolvulus.
liseur, -euse [lizœr, -øz] **1.** *n.* reader. **2.** *n.f.* **liseuse** (*a*) bookmark(er) and paperknife combined; (*b*) book cover, (dust) cover, (dust) jacket; (*c*) (lady's) bed jacket.
lisibilité [lizibilite] *n.f.* legibility.
lisible [lizibl̩] *a.* **1.** legible (writing, etc.). **2.** readable; worth reading.
lisiblement [liziblәmɑ̃] *adv.* legibly.
lisière [lizjɛr] *n.f.* **1.** (*a*) selvage, selvedge; (*b*) **tenir qn en lisières,** to keep s.o. in leading strings. **2.** edge, border (of field, forest).
lissage [lisaʒ] *n.m.* smoothing, polishing (of stone, etc.); sleeking (of leather); glazing (of paper, etc.).
lisse[1] [lis] *n.f. N.Arch:* (*a*) ribband (of the hull); rail, strake; **lisses de l'avant,** harpings; (*b*) handrail (of the bulwarks).
lisse[2] *n.f. Tex:* = LICE[3].
lisse[3] **1.** *a.* smooth; polished; **cheveux lisses,** sleek hair. **2.** *n.f.* = LISSOIR.
lisser [lise] *v.tr.* to smooth, polish (stone, etc.); to smooth down (hair); to smooth out (crease); to sleek (leather); to glaze (paper, etc.); (*of bird*) **se l. les plumes,** to preen its feathers.
lisseur, -euse [lisœr, -øz] *n.* **1.** smoother, polisher. **2.** *n.f.* **lisseuse,** smoothing machine.
lissoir [liswar] *n.m. Tls:* smoother, polishing iron.
listage [listaʒ] *n.m. Cmptr:* listing.
liste [list] *n.f.* list; roll; *Mil:* roster; **l. officielle des taux,** schedule of charges; **l. électorale,** electoral roll; **l. civile,** Civil List; **l. noire,** blacklist; **l. d'envoi, des abonnés,** mailing list; **l. de mariage,** wedding list; **dresser, faire, une l.,** to draw up a list.
listel, -els, -eaux [listɛl, -o] *n.m.* **1.** *Arch: etc:* listel, fillet. **2.** *Num:* rim (of coin).
lister [liste] *v.tr. Cmptr:* to list.
lit [li] *n.m.* **1.** (*a*) **l. pour deux personnes, grand l.,** double bed; **lits jumeaux,** twin beds; **l. clos,** box bed; **l. de camp,** camp bed, *NAm:* cot; **l. pliant,** folding bed; **l. à colonnes,** four-poster (bed); **l. à baldaquin,** canopied four-poster; **lits superposés,** bunk beds, bunks; **l. d'enfant,** cot, *NAm:* crib; **l. de repos,** couch; **mettre un enfant au l.,** to put a child to bed; **au l. les enfants!** time for bed, bedtime, children! **aller au l.,** to go to bed; **se mettre au l.,** to get into bed; **rendre visite à qn au saut du l.,** to pay s.o. a visit in the early (hours of the) morning; **être au l., garder le l.,** to be, stay, in bed; **faire les lits,** to make the beds; **faire l. à part,** to sleep apart, in separate beds; **chambre à un l., à deux lits,** single-, twin-bedded room; **enfant du second l.,** child of the second marriage; **être sur son l. de mort,** to be on one's death bed; **mourir dans son l.,** to die of natural causes; **l. de douleur,** sick bed; bed of pain; (*b*) **bois de l.,** bedstead; **l. de fer,** iron bedstead; (*c*) bedding; **l. moelleux, dur,** soft, hard, bed, mattress; **l. de plume,**

feather bed. **2.** (*a*) bed, layer (of clay, stone, etc.); **l. de cendres,** bed of ashes; (*b*) bed (of river, etc.); **l. majeur (d'un fleuve),** flood plain; *Hyd:* **l. majeur, mineur,** high water, mean water, bed. **3.** set (of the tide, etc.); **être dans le l. de marée,** to be in the tideway; *Nau:* **dans le l. du vent,** in the wind's eye.

litanie [litani] *n.f.* (*a*) *pl.* litany; (*b*) (rambling) story; **c'est toujours la même l.,** it's the same old story.

lit-cage [likaʒ] *n.m.* folding bedstead; *pl. lits-cages.*

lit-canapé [likanape] *n.m.* sofa bed; *pl. lits-canapés.*

litchi [litʃi] *n.m. Bot:* lychee, litchi.

liteau[1], -eaux [lito] *n.m.* **1.** *Const:* batten, rail, ribband. **2.** *Tex:* band, stripe (on table linen, etc.).

liteau[2] *n.m.* haunt (of wolves during the day).

litée [lite] *n.f.* litter (of animals).

literie [litri] *n.f.* bedding; bed linen.

lithine [litin] *n.f. Ch:* lithia.

lithiné [litine] **1.** *a.* **eau lithinée,** lithia water. **2.** *n.m.pl.* **lithinés,** lithium salts.

lithium [litjɔm] *n.m. Ch:* lithium.

lithographe [litɔgraf] *n.* lithographer.

lithographie [litɔgrafi] *n.f.* **1.** lithography. **2.** lithograph.

lithographier [litɔgrafje] *v.tr.* (*pr.sub. & impf.* **n. lithographiions, v. lithographiiez**) to lithograph.

lithographique [litɔgrafik] *a.* lithographic.

lithosphère [litɔsfɛr] *n.f. Geol:* lithosphere.

Lithuanie [litɥani] *Pr.n.f. Geog:* Lithuania.

lithuanien, -ienne [litɥanjɛ̃, -jɛn] *a. & n.* = LITUANIEN, -IENNE.

litière [litjɛr] *n.f.* **1.** (stable) litter; **faire l. de qch.,** to throw sth. to the winds. **2.** litter, palanquin; **être porté en l.,** to be carried in a litter.

litige [litiʒ] *n.m.* litigation; dispute; lawsuit; **objet, point, en l.,** (i) subject of the action; (ii) bone of contention; **être en l.,** to be in dispute.

litigieux, -euse [litiʒjø, -øz] *a.* litigious; contentious.

litote [litɔt] *n.f. Rh:* litotes; understatement.

litre [litr̥] *n.m.* (*a*) *Meas:* litre, *U.S:* liter; (*b*) litre bottle.

litron [litrɔ̃] *n.m. P:* litre, *NAm:* liter, of wine.

littéraire [literɛr] **1.** *a.* (*a*) literary; (*b*) *Pej:* insincere, affected. **2.** *n.* (*a*) literary person; **c'est plutôt un l.,** his talents are literary; (*b*) arts student; (*c*) arts teacher; teacher of literature.

littérairement [literɛrmɑ̃] *adv.* literarily; in literary terms.

littéral, -aux [literal, -o] *a.* **1.** literal (translation, etc.); *Mth:* **coefficient l.,** literal coefficient. **2.** *Jur:* **preuve littérale,** documentary evidence.

littéralement [literalmɑ̃] *adv.* literally.

littéralité [literalite] *n.f.* literality, literalness.

littérateur [literatœr] *n.m.* literary man, man of letters; *Pej:* literary hack.

littérature [literatyr] *n.f.* literature; **faire carrière dans la l.,** to make a career in writing; **tout ça c'est de la l.,** all this is of trifling importance.

littoral, -aux [litɔral, -o] **1.** *a.* littoral, coastal (region, etc.). **2.** *n.m.* coastline, littoral.

Lituanie [litɥani] *Pr.n.f. Geog:* Lithuania.

lituanien, -ienne [litɥanjɛ̃, -jɛn] **1.** *a. Geog:* Lithuanian. **2.** (*a*) *n.m. Ling:* Lithuanian; (*b*) *n.* Lithuanian.

liturgie [lityrʒi] *n.f. Ecc:* liturgy.

liturgique [lityrʒik] *a.* liturgical.

liure [ljyr] *n.f.* lashing (of load on cart, etc.).

livarde [livard] *n.f. Nau:* sprit; **voile à l.,** spritsail.

livide [livid] *a.* (*a*) *Lit:* livid; (*b*) pallid, ghastly (pale) (complexion).

lividité [lividite] *n.f.* lividity, lividness.

living(-room) [liviŋ(rum)] *n.m.* living room.

livrable [livrabl̥] *a.* (*a*) *Fin:* deliverable; (*b*) *Com:* ready for delivery; **marchandises livrables à domicile,** goods delivered to your home.

livraison [livrɛzɔ̃] *n.f.* **1.** delivery (of goods, etc.); **l. franco,** free delivery, delivered free; **payable à la l.,** payable on delivery; **l. contre remboursement, paiement à la l.,** cash on delivery, *NAm:* collect on delivery; **faire l. de qch.,** to deliver sth.; **prendre l. de qch.,** to take delivery of sth.; **défaut de l.,** non-delivery; **voiture de l.,** delivery van; *P.N: Com:* **l. à domicile,** we deliver (anywhere); door-to-door delivery. **2.** part, instalment (of book published in parts).

livre[1] [livr̥] *n.f.* **1.** (*weight*) = pound; half a kilo; *Can:* pound (= 0.453 kg). **2.** (*money*) (*a*) **l. (sterling),** pound (sterling); (*b*) *A:* = franc.

livre[2] *n.m.* book; (*a*) **l'industrie du l., le l.,** the book trade; **l. relié,** bound book; **l. de classe,** school book; **l. de lecture,** reader, reading book; **l. de prix,** prize book; **l. d'images, d'enfant,** picture book, children's book; *Pol:* **l. blanc, bleu, jaune** = blue book; **l. de poche,** paperback; **l. d'heures,** book of hours; **parler comme un l.,** to talk like a book; **traduire un passage à l. ouvert,** to translate a passage at sight; (*b*) **l. de raison,** family record book; **l. d'or,** visitors' book; *Nau:* **l. de bord,** ship's book, register, log; (*c*) **livres de comptabilité, de commerce,** account books, the books; **l. de paie,** payroll; *Com:* **l. journal,** journal, day book; **tenir les livres,** to keep the accounts, the books; **tenue des livres,** book-keeping; (*d*) book (of Bible, etc.).

livrée [livre] *n.f.* **1.** livery; **valet en l.,** servant in livery, liveried servant; **porter la l. de qn,** to be in s.o.'s service. **2.** coat (of fox, etc.); plumage (of birds).

livrer [livre] *v.tr.* **I. 1.** (*a*) to deliver, surrender; to give (s.o., sth.) up; **l. qn à la justice,** to deliver, hand over, s.o. to justice; **l. qn à la mort,** to send s.o. to the scaffold, to his death; **livré à soi-même,** left to oneself; **l. un poste à l'ennemi,** to give up a post to the enemy; **l. un secret,** to betray a secret; **l. ses secrets à qn,** to confide one's secrets to s.o.; **l. passage à qn,** to let s.o. pass; (*b*) **l. un assaut à l'ennemi,** to deliver an attack on the enemy; **l. bataille,** to join battle (**à,** with); to give battle (**à,** to). **2.** to deliver (goods, etc.). **II. se l. 1. se l. à la justice,** to surrender to justice; to give oneself up; **se l. à qn, se l.,** to confide in s.o. **2.** (*a*) **se l. à un vice,** to indulge in, surrender to, a vice; **se l. à la boisson,** (i) to take to drink; (ii) to be a heavy drinker; **se l. au désespoir,** to give way to despair; (*b*) to be engaged in (an occupation); to hold, set up (an inquiry); **se l. à l'étude,** to devote oneself to study; **se l. à un sport,** to practise a sport; (*c*) (*of woman*) to surrender to a man.

livresque [livrɛsk] *a.* (*a*) acquired from books; **connaissances livresques,** book learning; (*b*) bookish (mind).

livret [livrɛ] *n.m.* **1.** small book, booklet; handbook; *Fin:* bank book; passbook; *Adm:* **l. de famille,** family record book for registration of births and deaths; **l. militaire individuel,** service record; **l. scolaire,** school report book. **2.** *Mus:* libretto, book (of opera).

livreur, -euse [livrœr, -øz] *n.* delivery man, boy, woman, girl.

lloyd [lɔjd] *n.m. M.Ins:* (any) association of marine brokers and underwriters.

lob [lɔb] *n.m. Ten:* lob.

lobe [lɔb] *n.m.* **1.** *Anat: Bot:* lobe; **l. de l'oreille,** ear lobe. **2.** *Arch:* foil.

lobé [lɔbe] *a.* (*a*) *Bot:* lobed, lobate; (*b*) *Arch:* foiled.

lobectomie [lɔbɛktɔmi] *n.f. Surg:* lobectomy.

lobélie [lɔbeli] *n.f. Bot:* lobelia.

lober [lɔbe] *v.tr. & i. Ten: Fb:* **1.** to lob (ball). **2.** to lob over (one's opponent).

lobotomie [lɔbɔtɔmi] *n.f. Surg:* lobotomy.
lobulaire [lɔbylɛr] *a.* lobular.
lobule [lɔbyl] *n.m. Anat:* lobule; *Bot:* lobelet.
local, -aux [lɔkal, -o] **1.** *a.* local (authority, etc.); *Med:* local, topical (disease, remedy); **anesthésie locale,** local anaesthetic, *U.S:* topical anesthetic; **couleur locale,** local colour, *NAm:* color. **2.** *n.m.* (*a*) premises; building; room; **l. d'habitation,** dwelling; **taxe sur les locaux loués meublés,** tax on rented, furnished, property; (*b*) *Nau:* **locaux affectés au personnel du bord,** crew's quarters; (*c*) *Fr.C: Tp:* extension.
localement [lɔkalmɑ̃] *adv.* locally.
localisation [lɔkalizasjɔ̃] *n.f.* localization.
localiser [lɔkalize] **1.** *v.tr.* (*a*) to localize, confine (epidemic, etc.); (*b*) to locate (noise, etc.). **2.** (*of disease, etc.*) **se l.,** to become localized.
localité [lɔkalite] *n.f.* locality, place, spot.
locataire [lɔkatɛr] *n.* **1.** tenant, occupier (of property); *Jur:* lessee, leaseholder. **2.** lodger, *NAm:* roomer.
locatif¹, -ive [lɔkatif, -iv] *a.* concerning the renting or letting of premises; **valeur locative,** rental (value); **réparations locatives,** repairs incumbent upon the tenant.
locatif², -ive *a. & n.m. Gram:* locative (case).
location [lɔkasjɔ̃] *n.f.* (*a*) hire, *U.S:* renting (of boat, etc.); (i) hiring; (ii) letting out on hire (of boat, etc.); **donner, prendre, qch. en l.,** to hire, *U.S:* to rent, sth. out, to hire, *U.S:* to rent, sth.; **l. de voitures (sans chauffeur),** (self-drive) car hire, car rental; **voiture de l.,** rented, hire, car; (*b*) (i) renting, tenancy; (ii) letting (of house, etc.); *Jur:* location; **prix de l.,** rent; (*c*) *Th: etc:* booking, reservation (of seats); **(bureau de) l.,** box office, booking office.
location-vente [lɔkasjɔ̃vɑ̃t] *n.f.* hire purchase (of property, equipment, etc.); *pl. locations-ventes.*
loch [lɔk] *n.m. Nau:* (ship's) log; **ligne de l.,** log line; **livre de l.,** log.
loche [lɔʃ] *n.f.* **1.** *Ich:* loach. **2.** *Moll:* grey slug.
lock-out [lɔkaut] *n.m.inv. Ind:* lockout.
lock(-)outer [lɔkaute] *v.tr. Ind:* to lock out (the personnel).
locomobile [lɔkɔmɔbil] *n.f.* (transportable) steam engine.
locomoteur, -trice [lɔkɔmɔtœr, -tris] **1.** *a.* locomotor(y) (organ, disorders, etc.). **2.** *n.f. Rail:* **locomotrice,** electric engine.
locomotif, -ive [lɔkɔmɔtif, -iv] **1.** *a.* locomotive. **2.** *n.f.* **locomotive** (*a*) *Rail:* locomotive, engine; **locomotive diesel (à transmission) électrique,** diesel-electric locomotive; (*b*) *Fig:* political leader; trendsetter.
locomotion [lɔkɔmosjɔ̃] *n.f.* locomotion; **moyens de l.,** means of transport.
locuteur, -trice [lɔkytœr, -tris] *n. Ling:* speaker.
locution [lɔkysjɔ̃] *n.f.* expression, phrase; **l. figée,** set phrase; **l. vicieuse,** incorrect expression; *Gram:* **l. adverbiale,** adverbial phrase.
lœss [løs] *n.m. Geol:* loess.
lof [lɔf] *n.m. Nau:* windward side (of ship); **venir, aller, au l.,** to sail into the wind; **virer l. pour l.,** to wear.
lofer [lɔfe] *v.i. Nau:* to luff.
logarithme [lɔgaritm] *n.m.* logarithm.
logarithmique [lɔgaritmik] *a.* logarithmic.
loge [lɔʒ] *n.f.* **1.** (*a*) *A:* hut, cabin; (*b*) (porter's, freemason's) lodge. **2.** *Th:* (*a*) box; **première l.,** first-tier box; **être aux premières loges,** to have a full view (of sth.); to have a ringside seat; (*b*) (artist's) dressing room. **3.** *Art: Mus:* individual exam room (for the *Prix de Rome*). **4.** *Arch:* loggia. **5.** *Bot:* cell.
logeable [lɔʒabl] *a.* (*of house*) habitable, fit for occupation.
logement [lɔʒmɑ̃] *n.m.* **1.** lodging, housing (of people); quartering, billeting (of troops); stabling (of horses, etc.); **crise du l.,** housing shortage. **2.** (*a*) accommodation; lodgings; **l. garni, meublé,** furnished rooms, flat; (*b*) *Mil:* quarters; (*in private house*) billet; *Nau:* berth. **3.** seating (of machine part); housing (of shaft).
loger [lɔʒe] *v.* **(je logeai(s); n. logeons) 1.** *v.i.* to lodge, live; (*of troops*) to be quartered, billeted; **l. à un hôtel,** to put up, stay, at a hotel; *Mil:* **l. chez l'habitant,** to be billeted (in private house); **être logé et nourri,** to have board and lodging, bed and board; **l. à la belle étoile,** to sleep in the open. **2.** *v.tr.* (*a*) to lodge, accommodate, house (s.o.); to quarter, billet (troops); to stable (horses); **l. un ami pour la nuit,** to put up a friend for the night; (*b*) to place, to put; **l. une balle dans qch.,** to lodge a bullet in sth. **3. se l.** (*a*) to find accommodation, a house; **nous avons trouvé à nous l.,** we've found somewhere to live; (*b*) **mon ballon s'est logé sur le toit,** my ball has got stuck on the roof; **la balle se logea dans le mur,** the bullet embedded itself in the wall; **le soupçon se logea dans son cœur,** suspicion became firmly fixed in his mind.
logeur, -euse [lɔʒœr, -øz] *n.* landlord, landlady (of furnished apartments).
loggia [lɔdʒja] *n.f. Arch:* loggia.
logiciel [lɔʒisjɛl] *n.m. Cmptr:* software.
logicien, -ienne [lɔʒisjɛ̃, -jɛn] *n.* logician
logique [lɔʒik] **1.** *a.* logical (reasoning, etc.); *Gram:* **analyse l.,** analysis (of sentence). **2.** *n.f.* logic; **vous manquez de l.,** you're not being very logical.
logiquement [lɔʒikmɑ̃] *adv.* logically.
logis [lɔʒi] *n.m.* (*a*) *O: & Lit:* home, house, dwelling; **quitter le l. familial,** to leave the family home; (*b*) inn; **corps de l.,** main (portion of) building.
logistique [lɔʒistik] **1.** *a.* logistic. **2.** *n.f. Mil: etc:* logistics.
logomachie [lɔgɔmaʃi] *n.f.* logomachy, battle of words.
loi [lwa] *n.f.* **1.** (*a*) law; **homme de l.,** lawyer, legal practitioner; **tomber sous le coup de la l.,** to come under the law; **c'est lui qui fait la l.,** he's the master, *F:* the boss; **ce qu'il dit fait l.,** his word is law; **c'est la l. et les prophètes,** it's the absolute, gospel, truth; **faire la l. à qn,** to lay down the law, to dictate, to s.o.; **se faire une l. de faire qch.,** to make a rule, a point, of doing sth.; **subir la l. de qn,** to be ruled by s.o., to be under s.o.'s thumb; **avoir la l. pour soi,** to have the law on one's side; **mettre qn hors la l.,** to outlaw s.o.; (*b*) law, enactment, statute; **projet de l. (émanant de l'initiative gouvernementale), proposition de l. (émanant de l'initiative parlementaire),** bill; **l. (votée),** act (of Parliament). **2.** law (of nature, etc.); *pl.* rules (of game, etc.); dictates (of fashion); **les lois de la politesse, de l'honneur,** the rules of etiquette, the code of honour, *NAm:* honor.
loi-cadre [lwakadr] *n.f.* outline law; *pl. lois-cadres.*
loi-programme [lwaprɔgram] *n.f. Fin: Pol:* law providing framework for long-term government programme; *pl. lois-programmes.*
loin [lwɛ̃] *adv.* far; **plus l.,** farther (on); further; **moins l.,** less far, not so far. **1.** (*of place*) (*a*) **est-ce l. d'ici?** is it far from here? **la poste est l.,** the post office is a long way off; **aller très l.,** to go far afield, far away; **ce jeune homme ira l.,** this young man will go far, will succeed; **l. derrière lui,** far, way, behind him; *Prov:* **l. des yeux, l. du cœur,** out of sight, out of mind; **il y a l. d'ici à Paris,** it's a long way to Paris; **de là à l'accuser de mensonge il n'y a pas l.,** that's not far from, it's close to, calling him a liar; *Prov:* **il y a l. de la coupe aux lèvres,** there's many a slip 'twixt (the) cup and (the) lip; **être l. de faire qch.,** to be far from doing sth.; **ne pas être l. d'une découverte,** to be on the brink of a discovery; **je ne suis pas**

fâché, (bien) l. de là! I am not angry, far from it, anything but! **vous allez trop l.,** you're going too far; (*b*) **de l.,** by far; **il est de l. plus intelligent que moi,** he is far more intelligent than I am; **c'est de l. son meilleur roman,** it's by far his best novel; **admirer qn de l.,** to admire s.o. at a distance, from afar; (*c*) **je l'ai reconnu de l.,** I recognized him from a distance, from a long way off; **ils sont parents, mais de l.,** they are only distantly related; *n.m.* **au l.,** in the distance; **apercevoir qn au l.,** to see s.o. a long way away, in the distance; **d'aussi l., du plus l., qu'il les voit, qu'il se souvienne,** as soon as he sees them, as far back as he can remember. **2.** (*of time*) (*a*) **la famille remonte bien l.,** the family goes back a long way; (*in text*) **voir plus l.,** see further on, see following pages; **il ne devait pas être l. de midi,** it must have been getting on for twelve (o'clock); **ce jour est encore l.,** that day is still distant, a long way off; (*b*) **voir l.,** (i) to be shrewd; (ii) to be far-sighted; (*c*) **de l. en l.,** at long intervals, now and then.

lointain [lwɛ̃tɛ̃] **1.** *a.* distant, remote, far-off, faraway (country, period, etc.); vague (resemblance); **mes souvenirs les plus lointains,** my earliest recollections; **dans un avenir l.,** in a distant, remote, future. **2.** *n.m.* distance; **dans le l.,** in the distance, in the background; **regard plongé dans le l.,** faraway look; *Art:* **les lointains,** the distances (of a picture).

loir [lwar] *n.m. Z:* dormouse; **dormir comme un l.,** to sleep like a log.

loisible [lwazibl̩] *a.* **il lui est l. de refuser,** it is open to him to refuse; he is free, he is entitled, to refuse.

loisir [lwazir] *n.m.* leisure; **les loisirs,** leisure, spare time (activities); **avoir des loisirs,** to have some spare time; **dans mes heures de l., pendant mes loisirs,** in my spare time; **donner, laisser, à qn le l. de faire qch.,** to give s.o. the opportunity, to allow s.o., to do sth.; **examiner qch. à l.,** to examine sth. at leisure; **je n'ai pas le l. d'un long entretien,** I have no time for a long conversation.

lokoum [lɔkum] *n.m. Comest:* Turkish delight.

lolo [lolo] *n.m. F:* (*child's word*) milk.

lombago [lɔ̃bago] *n.m. Med:* lumbago.

lombaire [lɔ̃bɛr] *a. & n.f. Anat:* lumbar; **ponction l.,** lumbar puncture.

lombard, -arde [lɔ̃bar, -ard] *a. & n. Geog: etc:* Lombard.

Lombardie [lɔ̃bardi] *Pr.n.f. Geog:* Lombardy.

lombes [lɔ̃b] *n.m.pl. Anat:* lumbar region; loins.

lombric [lɔ̃brik] *n.m. Ann:* lumbricus; earthworm.

londonien, -ienne [lɔ̃dɔnjɛ̃, -jɛn] **1.** *a.* of, pertaining to, London. **2.** *n.* Londoner.

Londres [lɔ̃dr̥] *Pr.n. Geog:* London.

londrès [lɔ̃drɛs] *n.m.* Havana cigar.

long, longue [lɔ̃, lɔ̃g] **1.** *a.* long; (*a*) (*of space*) **corde longue de 5 mètres,** rope 5 metres, *NAm:* meters, long, 5-metre rope; **prendre le chemin le plus l.,** to go the longest way (round); (*b*) (*of time; cf. also the note to* PROLONGÉ); **un l. hiver** [lɔ̃givɛr], a long, protracted, winter; **discours un peu l.,** somewhat lengthy speech; **longue histoire,** long drawn-out, lengthy, story; **il est l. comme un jour sans pain,** he's tall and lanky; **je trouve le temps l., les jours longs,** time seems to drag, I'm getting bored; **je ne serai pas l.,** I won't be long; **l. soupir,** long-drawn sigh; **c'est un travail l. à faire** [lɔ̃afɛr], it's slow work; this work takes a long time; **être l. à faire qch.,** to take a long time to do sth.; to be slow in doing sth.; **il s'en sortira, mais ce sera l.,** he'll recover but it'll take a long time; **projet à longue échéance,** long-term project; **bail à l. terme,** long lease; **à plus ou moins longue échéance, l. terme,** sooner or later; **disque (microsillon) de longue durée,** long-playing record; **à la longue,** in (the course of) time, in the long run, in the end; (*c*) *Cu:* **sauce longue,** thin sauce. **2.** *n.m.* length; (*a*) (*of space*) **table qui a 2 mètres de l.,** table 2 metres, *NAm:* meters, long, in length; **en l., de l.,** lengthwise; **de l. en large,** up and down, to and fro; **expliquer qch. en l. et en large,** to explain sth. in great detail, at great length; **racontez-moi cela tout au l., tout du l.,** tell me everything (from beginning to end); **étendu de tout son l.,** stretched out at full length; **tout le l. du rivage,** all along the shore; **tomber de tout son l.,** to fall flat on one's face; **le l. de,** along, alongside; **se faufiler, grimper, le l. du mur,** to creep along, to climb up, the wall; (*b*) (*of time*) **tout le l. du jour,** all day long, throughout the day. **3.** *adv.* (*a*) (*of amount*) **inutile d'en dire plus l.,** I need say no more; there's no need to say any more; **regard qui en dit l.,** meaningful, eloquent, look; **cette action en dit l. sur . . .,** this action speaks volumes for . . .; **en savoir l., plus l., trop l.,** to know a lot, more, too much; **il en sait l. sur votre compte,** he knows quite a lot about you; (*b*) **s'habiller l.,** to wear long clothes. **4.** *n.f.* **longue** (*a*) *Pros:* long syllable; (*b*) *Cards:* long suit; (*c*) *Mus:* long, longa.

longanimité [lɔ̃ganimite] *n.f.* long-suffering, forbearance.

long-courrier [lɔ̃kurje] *a. & n.m. Nau:* ocean-going (ship); ocean liner; *Av:* long-haul, long-range (aircraft); *pl. long-courriers.*

longe[1] [lɔ̃ʒ] *n.f. Harn:* (*a*) leading rein, halter, tether; (*b*) lunge, longe.

longe[2] *n.f. Cu:* loin (of veal, venison).

longer [lɔ̃ʒe] *v.tr.* **(je longeai(s); n. longeons)** to pass, go, along(side) (road, etc.); (*of path, etc.*) to border, run alongside; **la route longe un bois,** the road skirts a wood; **l. la côte,** to hug the coast.

longeron [lɔ̃ʒrɔ̃] *n.m.* **1.** *Civ.E:* stringer, longitudinal girder; beam, member (of bridge, etc.). **2.** (*a*) *Aut:* side member, side sill (of frame). **3.** *Av:* longeron; spar (of wing).

longévité [lɔ̃ʒevite] *n.f.* longevity, long life.

longitude [lɔ̃ʒityd] *n.f.* longitude; **par 10° (de) l. ouest,** at 10° longitude west.

longitudinal, -aux [lɔ̃ʒitydinal, -o] *a.* longitudinal, lengthwise, lengthways; *Nau:* fore-and-aft.

longitudinalement [lɔ̃ʒitydinalmɑ̃] *adv.* longitudinally, lengthwise, lengthways.

longrine [lɔ̃grin] *n.f.* (*a*) *Const:* longitudinal beam, girder, member; **l. de faîtage,** ridge bar; (*b*) *Rail:* longitudinal sleeper.

longtemps [lɔ̃tɑ̃] **1.** *adv.* long; a long time; **attendre l.,** to wait for a long time; **cela ne pouvait durer l.,** it couldn't last long; **ça ne va plus durer l. maintenant,** it won't be long now; **être l. à faire qch.,** to be a long time (i) doing sth., (ii) before one does sth.; **rester trop l.,** to stay too long. **2.** *n.m.* **il y a l.,** long ago, a long time ago; **il n'y a pas l.,** not long ago; **il y a l. qu'il est mort,** he has been dead (for) a long time; **il y a l. que je ne l'ai vu,** it's a long time since I saw him; **mettre l. à faire qch.,** to be a long time doing sth.; **cela existe depuis l.,** it has existed for a long time; **l. avant, après,** long before, after; **pendant l.,** for a long time; **avant l.,** before long; **cela ne se fera pas de l.,** it won't happen for a long time to come; **je n'en ai pas pour l.,** I shan't be long, it won't take me long; *F:* **il n'en a plus pour l.,** he hasn't much longer to live.

longuement [lɔ̃gmɑ̃] *adv.* **1.** for a long time. **2.** slowly, deliberately; **il la regarda l.,** he gazed earnestly at her. **3.** lengthily, at (great) length; **il faut entrer plus l. dans le détail,** you must go more fully into details; **parler l. avec qn,** to have a long talk with s.o.

longuet, -ette [lɔ̃gɛ, -ɛt] **1.** *a. F:* rather long, longish (book, time, etc.). **2.** *n.m.* bread stick.

longueur [lɔ̃gœr] *n.f.* length. **1. l. totale, l. hors tout,** length over all, overall length; **mesures de l.,** linear measures; **jardin qui a cent mètres de l., une l. de cent mètres,** garden a hundred metres, *NAm:* meters, long; **couper qch. en l., dans le sens de la l.,** to cut sth. lengthwise; (*of speech, etc.*) **traîner en l.,** to drag (on); **à l. de journée, de semaine, d'année,** throughout the day, week, year; all day, week, year, long; **à l. de journées,** for days on end. **2. les longueurs de la justice,** the law's delays; **roman plein de longueurs,** novel full of tedious passages. **3.** *Sp:* **mener, gagner, d'une l.,** to lead, win, by a length.

longue-vue [lɔ̃gvy] *n.f.* telescope, field glass; *pl. longues-vues.*

loofa [lufa] *n.m. Bot:* loofah.

looping [lupiŋ] *n.m. Av:* loop; **faire un l.,** to loop the loop.

lopin [lɔpɛ̃] *n.m.* **l. de terre,** piece, patch, plot, of ground; allotment.

loquace [lɔkwas, -kas] *a.* loquacious, talkative, garrulous.

loquacement [lɔkwasmɑ̃, -kasmɑ̃] *adv.* loquaciously, talkatively, garrulously.

loquacité [lɔkwasite, -kasite] *n.f.* loquacity, talkativeness, garrulity.

loque [lɔk] *n.f.* rag; **être en loques,** to be in rags, in tatters; **ses vêtements tombent en loques,** his clothes are falling to pieces; **je ne suis qu'une l.,** I'm worn out, I feel a wreck, like a wet rag.

loquet [lɔkɛ] *n.m.* **1.** latch (of door); **tirer le l.,** to open the door; **fermer la porte au l., pousser le l.,** to shut the door; to keep the door on the latch.

loqueteau, -eaux [lɔkto] *n.m.* small latch, catch (for shutter, etc.).

loqueteux, -euse [lɔktø, -øz] **1.** *a.* in rags, in tatters; ragged, tattered. **2.** *n.* ragamuffin.

lord [lɔr] *n.m.* lord; **la Chambre des lords,** the House of Lords.

lord-maire [lɔrmɛr] *n.m.* Lord Mayor (of London, etc.); *pl. lords-maires.*

lorgner [lɔrɲe] *v.tr.* to eye, peer at (sth.); **l. un poste,** to have one's eye on a post; **l. une femme,** to ogle, eye up, a woman; **l. qch. du coin de l'œil,** to cast a sidelong glance at sth.

lorgnette [lɔrɲɛt] *n.f.* (pair of) opera glasses; (small) field glasses; **regarder, voir, par le petit bout de la l.,** to exaggerate; to get things out of proportion.

lorgnon [lɔrɲɔ̃] *n.m.* (*a*) lorgnette; (*b*) pince-nez.

loriot [lɔrjo] *n.m. Orn:* **l. (jaune),** (golden) oriole.

lorrain, -aine [lɔrɛ̃, -ɛn] **1.** *a.* from, of, Lorraine. **2.** *n.* (*a*) inhabitant, native, of Lorraine; (*b*) *n.m. Ling:* Lorraine dialect. **3.** *Pr.n.f. Geog:* **la Lorraine,** Lorraine.

lorry [lɔri] *n.m. Rail:* (platelayer's) trolley, pushcar.

lors [lɔr] *adv. Lit:* (*a*) **depuis l.,** from that time, ever since then; (*b*) **l. . . . que,** (= LORSQUE) when; **l. même que nous serions heureux,** even if, even though, we were happy; **l. de sa naissance,** at the time of his birth, when he was born.

lorsque [lɔrsk(ə)] *conj.* (*becomes* **lorsqu'** *before* **il(s), elle(s), on, en, un(e)**) (at the time, moment) when; **l. je suis entré,** when I came in.

losange [lɔzɑ̃ʒ] *n.m.* **1.** (*a*) *Her:* lozenge; (*b*) **(forme de) l.,** diamond-shaped. **2.** *Mth:* rhomb(us).

losangé [lɔzɑ̃ʒe] *a.* diamond-shaped; with a diamond pattern; *Her:* lozengy.

lot [lo] *n.m.* **1.** (*a*) share (of estate); portion; **l. (de terre),** plot (of land); (*b*) lot, fate; (*c*) prize (at a lottery); **gros l.,** first prize; jackpot; *Fin:* **emprunt à lots,** lottery loan; **tirage à lots,** prize-drawing. **2.** batch (of goods, etc.); set (of towels, etc.); (*at auction*) lot.

loterie [lɔtri] *n.f.* (*a*) lottery; **l. nationale,** national lottery; sweepstake; **c'est une l.,** it's a matter of chance, the luck of the draw; (*b*) raffle, draw; **mettre une montre en l.,** to raffle a watch.

lotion [losjɔ̃] *n.f.* lotion; **l. capillaire,** hair lotion; **l. après rasage,** after-shave.

lotionner [losjɔne] *v.tr.* to apply lotion to (sth.).

lotir [lɔtir] *v.tr.* **1.** to divide (sth.) into lots, plots, batches. **2. l. qn de qch.,** to allot sth. to s.o.; **être bien, mal, loti,** to be well, badly, off.

lotissement [lɔtismɑ̃] *n.m.* **1.** (*a*) dividing (of goods, etc.) into lots; parcelling out (of land); (*b*) sale (by lots). **2.** (*a*) (building) plot; (*b*) housing estate; housing development.

loto [lɔto] *n.m. Games:* **1.** (*a*) lotto; (*b*) = bingo. **2.** lotto set.

lotte [lɔt] *n.f. Ich:* burbot; **l. de mer,** anglerfish.

lotus [lɔtys] *n.m.* **1.** *Bot:* (*a*) lotus; **l. sacré,** Indian lotus; (*b*) lotus tree. **2.** *Gr.Myth:* Lotus.

louable¹ [lwabl̥] *a.* laudable, praiseworthy, commendable.

louable² *a.* rentable; **appartement difficilement l.,** flat difficult to let.

louage [lwaʒ] *n.m.* **contrat de l.,** rental agreement, contract; **l. de services,** contract of employment; **voiture de l.,** rented, hire, car.

louange [lwɑ̃ʒ] *n.f.* praise; commendation; **chanter les louanges de qn,** to laud s.o. to the skies; to sing s.o.'s praises; **faire un discours à la l. de qn,** to make a speech in praise of s.o.; **c'est à sa l.,** it's to his credit.

louangeur, -euse [lwɑ̃ʒœr, -øz] *a.* adulatory, laudatory (poem, etc.).

loubar(d) [lubar] *n.m. F:* yob(bo); lout; *NAm:* hoodlum.

louche¹ [luʃ] *a.* **1.** *A:* cross-eyed, squint-eyed (person). **2.** (*a*) shady, suspicious (house, conduct, character, etc.); shifty (person); dubious, equivocal; **c'est l.,** it's odd, strange; **cela me paraît l.,** it looks suspicious, *F:* fishy, to me; *n.m.* **il y a du l. dans cette affaire,** this business is a bit shady; **il n'y a rien de l. là-dedans,** it is all fair and above board; (*b*) cloudy (wine, etc.); murky (light, etc.).

louche² *n.f.* (soup) ladle.

loucher [luʃe] *v.i.* to squint; to be cross-eyed; **l. de l'œil gauche,** to have a squint in the left eye; *F:* **l. vers, sur, qch.,** to cast longing eyes at, to ogle, sth.

loucherie [luʃri] *n.f.* squint(ing).

loucheur, -euse [luʃœr, -øz] *n.* cross-eyed, squint-eyed, person.

louchon, -onne [luʃɔ̃, -ɔn] *n. F:* cross-eyed person; squint-eyes.

louer¹ [lwe] *v.tr.* **1.** (*a*) to hire, rent, let, (out) (**à,** to); **maison à l.,** house to let; **l. une ferme à bail,** to lease out a farm; (*b*) (*of farmhand*) **se l. pour la saison,** to engage oneself for the season. **2.** to rent (house, etc.) (**à,** from); to reserve, book (seat, etc.); **l. une maison pour l'été,** to take a house for the summer; **cet appartement se loue très cher,** this flat is very expensive to rent.

louer² **1.** *v.tr.* to praise; to commend; **l. qn de, pour, qch.,** to praise s.o. for sth.; **louons le seigneur! Dieu soit loué!** thank God! **2. se l. de qch.,** to be pleased, well satisfied, with sth.; **se l. d'avoir fait qch.,** to congratulate oneself upon having done sth.; **je n'ai qu'à me l. de lui,** I have nothing but praise for him.

loueur¹, -euse [lwœr, -øz] *n.* hirer, letter, renter; **l. de bateaux,** boat keeper; **l. de chevaux,** jobmaster.

loufiat [lufja] *n.m. P:* waiter (in a café).

loufoque [lufɔk] *F:* (*a*) *a.* crazy, loony, barmy; (*b*) *n.* crackpot, nut, *NAm:* screwball.

loufoquerie [lufɔkri] *n.f. F:* (*a*) barminess, craziness; (*b*) crazy act.

lougre [lugr] *n.m. Nau:* lugger.

Louis [lwi] **1.** *Pr.n.m.* Lewis; Louis. **2.** *n.m. Num: A:* **l. (d'or),** twenty-franc piece.

Louise [lwiz] *Pr.n.f.* Louisa, Louise.

Louisiane [lwizjan] *Pr.n.f. Geog:* Louisiana.

loukoum [lukum] *n.m. Comest:* Turkish delight.

loulou [lulu] *n.m.* **1.** (*n.f.* **louloutte**) *F:* dear, darling. **2.** *F:* lout, yob(bo); *NAm:* hoodlum. **3.** spitz; **l. de Poméranie,** Pomeranian (dog), *F:* pom.

loup [lu] *n.m.* **1.** (*a*) wolf; **marcher à pas de l.,** to walk stealthily; to creep along, steal along; **avoir une faim de l.,** to be ravenously hungry; **il fait un froid de l.,** it's bitterly cold; **se jeter dans la gueule du l.,** to throw oneself into the lion's mouth; **il est connu comme le l. blanc,** everybody knows him; *Prov:* **quand on parle du l. on en voit la queue,** talk of the devil and he will appear; **les loups ne se mangent pas entre eux,** there is honour, *NAm:* honor, among thieves; dog doesn't eat dog; *F:* (*term of affection*) **mon petit l., mon gros l.,** my darling, my pet; (*b*) *Ich:* **l. (de mer),** sea perch, sea dace; *F:* **l. de mer,** (i) old salt, seadog, jack tar; (ii) striped tee-shirt. **2.** (*a*) flaw (in timber, etc.); *Ind:* defect; (*b*) *Th:* fluff, fluffed entrance. **3.** black velvet mask (worn at a masked ball).

loup-cervier [lusɛrvje] *n.m. Z:* lynx; *pl. loups-cerviers.*

loupe [lup] *n.f.* **1.** (*a*) *Med:* wen; (*b*) gnarl (on tree). **2.** lens, magnifying glass; **regarder qch. à la l.,** to put sth. under a microscope.

louper [lupe] *F:* **1.** *v.i.* **ça n'a pas loupé,** that's what happened, sure enough. **2.** *v.tr.* to botch, bungle (piece of work); to make a botch, a mess, of (piece of work); to miss (one's turn, opportunity, train); to fail, *NAm:* to flunk (exam); *Th:* to fluff (one's entrance); **la soirée est loupée,** the party's a flop; **il n'en loupe pas une!** he's always opening his big mouth!

loup-garou [lugaru] *n.m.* (*a*) *Myth:* wer(e)wolf; (*b*) bogeyman; *pl. loups-garous.*

loupiot, -iote[1] [lupjo, -jɔt] *n. F:* small child, brat, kid.

loupiote[2] *n.f. F:* small light, lamp.

lourd, -ourde [lur, -urd] **1.** *a.* (*a*) heavy (load, sleep, food, etc.); heavily-built, ungainly (person); **marcher d'un pas l.,** to tread heavily, walk with a heavy step; **yeux lourds de fatigue,** eyes heavy with tiredness; **avoir le sommeil l.,** to be a heavy sleeper; **j'ai la tête lourde,** my head feels heavy; **avoir l'estomac l.,** to feel bloated; **c'est l. à digérer,** it's difficult to digest, heavy on the stomach; **avoir la main lourde,** to be heavy-handed; **ce travail est trop l. pour elle,** this work is too much for her; *adv.* **peser l.,** to weigh heavy; (*b*) clumsy, awkward (action, etc.); heavy (movement, style); **avoir l'esprit l.,** to be slow-witted, dull-witted; (*c*) **lourde erreur,** serious mistake; **lourde perte,** heavy, severe, loss; (*d*) **incident l. de conséquences,** incident fraught with consequences; **silence l. de menaces,** ominous silence; **en avoir l. sur le cœur,** to feel very sad; (*e*) close, sultry, muggy (weather); drowsy (afternoon); (*f*) *F:* **il n'en reste pas l.,** there isn't much left, there aren't many left; **je n'en fais pas l.,** I don't exactly overwork. **2.** *n.f. P:* **lourde,** door.

lourdaud, -aude [lurdo, -od] **1.** *a.* awkward, clumsy, oafish (person). **2.** *n.* lout, oaf.

lourdement [lurdəmɑ̃] *adv.* (*a*) heavily, awkwardly, clumsily; **l. chargé,** heavily laden; (*b*) **se tromper l.,** to make a serious mistake.

lourdeur [lurdœr] *n.f.* heaviness (of burden, of style, etc.); massiveness (of building); clumsiness, unwieldiness, awkwardness, ungainliness; dullness (of intellect); severity (of a loss); weight (of a responsibility); sultriness, closeness (of the weather); **avoir des lourdeurs de tête,** to have fits of drowsiness, to feel headachy.

loustic [lustik] *n.m. F:* joker; **il fait le l.,** he's playing the fool, fooling around; **c'est un drôle de l.,** he's a strange bloke, guy; *NAm:* he's an oddball.

loutre [lutr̥] *n.f. Z:* (*a*) otter; **manteau de l.,** otter-skin coat; (*b*) **l. marine,** sea otter.

louve [luv] *n.f. Z:* she-wolf.

louveteau, -eaux [luvto] *n.m. Z:* wolf cub; *Scout:* cub (scout).

louvoiement [luvwamɑ̃] *n.m. Nau:* tacking; *Fig:* hedging, wavering.

louvoyer [luvwaje] *v.i.* **(je louvoie, n. louvoyons; je louvoierai)** *Nau:* to tack, to beat about; to beat to windward; **elle louvoyait, incapable de se décider,** she kept wavering, unable to make up her mind.

lover [lɔve] **1.** *v.tr.* to coil (rope). **2.** (*of snake, etc.*) **se l.** to coil up.

loxodromique [lɔksɔdrɔmik] *Nau:* loxodromic (curve, sailing); **navigation l.,** plane sailing.

loyal, -aux [lwajal, -o] *a.* **1.** honest, fair, upright, *F:* straight (person, answer, etc.); *F:* on the level; *NAm: F:* white; **être l. en affaires,** to be upright, straightforward, in business; **jeu l.,** fair play; *F:* **se battre à la loyale,** to fight cleanly. **2.** loyal, faithful (servant, heart); true, staunch (friend).

loyalement [lwajalmɑ̃] *adv.* **1.** honestly, fairly. **2.** loyally, faithfully.

loyalisme [lwajalism] *n.m.* **1.** loyalty (to the Crown, etc.). **2.** *Pol:* loyalism.

loyaliste [lwajalist] **1.** *a.* loyal. **2.** *n.* (*a*) loyal supporter; (*b*) *Pol:* loyalist.

loyauté [lwajote] *n.f.* **1.** honesty, uprightness, fairness; **manque de l.,** (i) dishonesty; (ii) unfairness. **2.** loyalty, fidelity (**envers,** to).

loyer [lwaje] *n.m.* **1.** rent, rental; **prendre une maison à l.,** to rent a house; **donner à l.,** to rent, let (out). **2.** *Fin:* **l. de l'argent,** interest rates, rates of interest.

lubie [lybi] *n.f.* whim, fad, craze; **c'est encore une de ses lubies!** it's another of his crazy ideas!

lubricité [lybrisite] *n.f.* lewdness, lust(fulness).

lubrifiant [lybrifjɑ̃] **1.** *a.* lubricating. **2.** *n.m.* lubricant.

lubrification [lybrifikasjɔ̃] *n.f.* lubrication, greasing.

lubrifier [lybrifje] *v.tr.* (*pr.sub. & impf.* **n. lubrifiions, v. lubrifiiez**) to lubricate; to grease, to oil.

lubrique [lybrik] *a.* libidinous, lustful, lewd.

lubriquement [lybrik(ə)mɑ̃] *adv.* libidinously, lustfully, lewdly.

Luc [lyk] *Pr.n.m.* Luke.

lucarne [lykarn] *n.f. Arch:* (*a*) dormer window, attic window; (*b*) skylight; (*c*) *Fb:* top corner (of net).

lucide [lysid] *a.* lucid, clear (mind, reasoning, etc.); clear-headed, clear-sighted (person).

lucidement [lysidmɑ̃] *adv.* lucidly, clearly.

lucidité [lysidite] *n.f.* lucidity, clearness; clear-mindedness, clear-headedness.

Lucie [lysi] *Pr.n.f.* Lucy.

Lucien [lysjɛ̃] *Pr.n.m.* Lucian.

Lucifer [lysifɛr] *Pr.n.m.* Lucifer.

luciole [lysjɔl] *n.f. Ent:* luciola, firefly.

lucratif, -ive [lykratif, -iv] *a.* lucrative, profitable, paying; **sans but l.,** non-profit-making.

lucrativement [lykrativmɑ̃] *adv.* lucratively.

lucre [lykr̥] *n.m. Pej:* lucre, profit.

ludion [lydjɔ̃] *n.m. Ph:* Cartesian diver.

luette [lyɛt] *n.f. Anat:* uvula.

lueur [lyœr] *n.f.* gleam, glimmer (of light, hope, etc.); **à la l. d'une bougie,** by candlelight; **les premières lueurs de l'aube,** the first light of dawn; **l. soudaine,** flash; **jeter une l.,** to flash.

luffa [lyfa] *n.m. Bot:* loofah.

luge [lyʒ] *n.f.* toboggan, sledge; sled.

luger [lyʒe] *v.i.* **(je lugeai(s); n. lugeons)** to toboggan, sledge; to sled.
lugeur, -euse [lyʒœr, -øz] *n. Sp:* tobogganer.
lugubre [lygybr̥] *a.* lugubrious, dismal, gloomy; doleful, mournful.
lugubrement [lygybrəmɑ̃] *adv.* lugubriously, dismally, dolefully.
lui¹, *pl.* **leur** [lɥi, lœr] *pers.pron. m. & f.* (to) him, her, it, them; (*a*) (*unstressed, attached to vb or its adjuncts*) **je le lui donne,** I give it (to) him, (to) her; **donnez-lui-en,** give him some; **cette maison leur appartient,** this house belongs to them; **je lui trouve mauvaise mine,** I think he, she, looks ill; **je lui ai serré la main,** I shook his, her, hand; **je lui ai entendu dire cela,** I heard him, her, say that; **il leur jeta une pierre,** he threw a stone at them; (*b*) (*stressed in imp.*) **donnez-le-lui,** give it (to) him; **montrez-le-leur,** show it to them.
lui², *pl.* **eux** [lɥi, ø] *stressed pers.pron. m.* (*a*) (*subject*) he, it, they; **c'est lui,** it's him; that's him; **ce sont eux,** *F:* **c'est eux,** it's them; **lui, il a raison; il a raison, lui; c'est lui qui a raison,** as for him, he's right; he's the one who is right; **qu'est-ce qu'il fait? –lui? rien,** what does he do? –him? nothing, he doesn't do anything; **c'est lui-même qui me l'a dit,** he told me so himself; **eux deux, eux tous,** the two of them, all of them; (*b*) (*object*) him, it, them; **j'accuse son frère et lui,** I accuse him and his brother; **lui, je le connais; je le connais, lui,** him, (yes) I know him; **elle est plus grande que lui,** she's taller than him; **elle m'a présenté à lui,** she introduced me to him; **ce livre est à lui, à eux,** this book is his, is theirs; **voilà une photo de lui,** here's a photo of him; **c'est pour lui,** it's for him; **j'ai confiance en lui,** I trust him; **c'est à lui de décider,** it's for him to decide; **c'est un ami à lui,** it's a friend of his; (*c*) (*refl.*) him(self), it(self), them(selves); **il les rassembla autour de lui,** he gathered them round him; **il ne pense qu'à lui,** he thinks only of himself; **chacun d'eux travaille pour lui-même,** each of them works for himself.
lui-même [lɥimɛm] *pers.pron.* himself, itself; *see* LUI² and MÊME 1 (*c*).
luire [lɥir] *v.i.* (*pr.p.* **luisant;** *p.p.* **lui** (*no f.*); *pr.ind.* **il luit, ils luisent;** *p.h.* **il luit, ils luirent,** *occ.* **il luisit;** *fu.* **il luira)** to shine, gleam, glow, glisten; (*of stars, etc.*) to glimmer; **l'espoir luit,** there's a glimmer of hope.
luisant [lɥizɑ̃] **1.** *a.* shining, bright (star, metal, etc.); shiny, glossy (surface, etc.); gleaming (eyes, etc.); glowing (embers, etc.); **front l. de sueur,** forehead glistening with perspiration; **manteau l. d'usure,** coat shiny with wear. **2.** *n.m.* shine, gloss, sheen.
lumbago [lɔ̃bago] *n.m. Med:* lumbago.
lumen [lymɛn] *n.m. Ph.Meas:* lumen.
lumière [lymjɛr] *n.f.* **1.** light; **l. (du jour), l. du soleil,** daylight, sunlight; **l. oxhydrique,** limelight; **l. électrique,** electric light; **donner de la l.,** to turn on the light, to switch, put, the light on; *Ph:* **l. blanche,** white light; **l. noire, de Wood,** black light; **à la l. de la lune,** by moonlight; **mettre qch. en l.,** to bring sth. to light; **jeter une l. nouvelle sur qch.,** to throw, shed, a new light on sth.; **faire (toute) la l. sur qch.,** to clarify sth., to make sth. (absolutely) clear; **les lumières de la raison,** the light of reason; (*of pers.*) **une des lumières de la science,** one of the leading lights in science; *F:* **ce n'est pas une l.,** he's not very bright; **avoir des lumières sur qch.,** to have some knowledge about sth.; **le siècle des lumières,** the Age of Enlightenment; *Astr:* **l. cendrée,** earthlight, earthshine. **2.** aperture (of sighting vane); *I.C.E:* slot (in piston wall); **l. d'admission, d'échappement,** inlet, exhaust, port.
lumignon [lymiɲɔ̃] *n.m.* **1.** (*a*) snuff (of candle); (*b*) candle end. **2.** dim light, lamp.
luminaire [lyminɛr] *n.m.* (*a*) light, candle (in church); (*b*) *coll.* lights, lighting (at party, etc.).
luminescence [lyminesɑ̃s] *n.f.* luminescence.
luminescent [lyminesɑ̃] *a.* luminescent.
lumineusement [lyminøzmɑ̃] *adv.* luminously; brightly; *Fig:* clearly.
lumineux, -euse [lyminø, -øz] *a.* luminous (body, dial, mind); **regard l.,** radiant look, expression; *F:* **c'est une idée lumineuse,** it's a brilliant idea, a brainwave, *NAm:* brainstorm; *Ph:* **onde lumineuse,** light wave.
luminosité [lyminozite] *n.f.* luminosity, brightness.
lunaire [lynɛr] **1.** *a.* lunar; moonlike. **2.** *n.f. Bot:* lunaria, *F:* honesty, moonwort.
lunaison [lynɛzɔ̃] *n.f. Astr:* lunation, lunar month.
lunatique [lynatik] *a.* whimsical, quirky, temperamental (person).
lunch [lœ̃ʃ] *n.m.* buffet lunch; *pl. lunches, lunchs.*
lundi [lœ̃di] *n.m.* Monday; **le l. de Pâques, de la Pentecôte,** Easter Monday, Whit Monday.
lune [lyn] *n.f.* **1.** (*a*) moon; **pleine l.,** full moon; **nouvelle l.,** new moon; **clair de l.,** moonlight; **nuit sans l.,** moonless night; **l. rousse,** April moon; **l. de miel,** honeymoon; **vieilles lunes,** (i) old times; the past; (ii) outdated notions; **demander la l.,** to ask for the moon; **promettre la l.,** to promise the moon; *F:* **être dans la l.,** to be starry-eyed, miles away, in the clouds; **être bête comme la l.,** to be completely stupid; (*b*) *A: & Poet:* month, moon. **2.** (*a*) **en forme de l.,** crescent-shaped; (*b*) (i) *F:* moonface; (ii) *P:* bum, backside. **3.** vagary, caprice, whim; **il est dans une bonne l., dans une mauvaise l.,** he is in one of his good moods, in one of his bad moods. **4.** (*a*) *Bot:* **l. d'eau,** white water-lily; (*b*) *Ich:* **l. de mer, poisson l.,** (ocean) sunfish; (*c*) *Lap:* **pierre de l.,** moonstone.
luné [lyne] *a.* **être bien, mal, l.,** to be in a good, bad, mood.
lunetier, -ière [lyntje, -jɛr] *n. & a.* **1.** *n.* spectacle manufacturer; optician. **2.** *a.* **industrie lunetière,** spectacle industry.
lunette [lynɛt] *n.f.* **1. l. d'approche,** (refracting) telescope, field glass; *Artil:* **l. de pointage,** sighting telescope; **l. astronomique,** astronomical telescope. **2.** *pl.* **(paire de) lunettes,** (pair of) glasses, spectacles, *F:* specs; **porter (des) lunettes,** to wear glasses, spectacles; **lunettes de protection,** goggles; **lunettes noires, de soleil,** sunglasses, dark glasses; **serpent à lunettes,** spectacled snake, Indian cobra. **3.** (*a*) *Arch: Fort:* lunette; (*b*) lunette (of guillotine). **4.** (*a*) seat (of w.c. pan); (*b*) *Rail:* cab window (of locomotive); *Aut:* **l. arrière,** rear window.
lunetterie [lynetri] *n.f.* spectacle trade.
lunettier, -ière [lynetje, -jɛr] *n.* = LUNETIER, -IÈRE.
lunule [lynyl] *n.f.* **1.** *Mth:* lune. **2.** *Anat:* lunula, (half-)moon (of finger nail).
lupanar [lypanar] *n.m.* brothel.
lupin [lypɛ̃] *n.m. Bot:* lupin.
lupus [lypys] *n.m. Med:* lupus.
lurette [lyrɛt] *n.f. F: used only in* **il y a belle l.,** a long time ago, ages ago.
luron, -onne [lyrɔ̃, -ɔn] *n. F:* **c'est un gai l., un joyeux l.,** he's a gay dog; he's quite a lad; **c'est une sacrée luronne,** she's quite a girl.
lusitanien, -ienne [lyzitanjɛ̃, -jɛn] *a. & n. A.Geog:* Lusitanian.
lustrage [lystraʒ] *n.m.* glossing, glazing, lustring (of cloth, etc.); polishing (of glass).
lustre¹ [lystr̥] *n.m.* **1.** (*a*) lustre, *NAm:* luster, polish, gloss, glaze (of silk, etc.); (*b*) *Lit:* renown; **ajouter un nouveau l. à sa gloire,** to add fresh lustre to one's glory. **2.** chandelier.

lustre² *n.m. Lit:* lustrum, lustre, *NAm:* luster; period of five years.
lustré [lystre] *a.* glazed; glossy; **étoffe lustrée par l'usure,** cloth shiny with wear.
lustrer [lystre] *v.tr.* to glaze, gloss, polish (up), lustre, *NAm:* luster (leather, etc.).
lustrerie [lystrəri] *n.f. Ind:* chandelier trade.
lustrine [lystrin] *n.f. Tex:* cotton lustre, *NAm:* luster.
lut [lyt] *n.m. Cer: Ind:* lute, luting, cement.
Lutèce [lytɛs] *Pr.n.f. A.Geog:* Lutetia.
lutécien, lutétien, -ienne [lytesjɛ̃, -jɛn] *a. & n.* Lutetian.
luter [lyte] *v.tr. Cer: Ind:* to lute; to seal with luting.
luth [lyt] *n.m. Mus:* lute.
luthéranisme [lyteranism] *n.m. Rel.H:* Lutheranism.
lutherie [lytri] *n.f. Mus:* (*a*) stringed instrument industry, trade; (*b*) *coll.* stringed instruments.
luthérien, -ienne [lyterjɛ̃, -jɛn] *a. & n. Rel.H:* Lutheran.
luthier [lytje] *n.m.* stringed instrument maker, violin maker.
luthiste [lytist] *n.m. Mus:* lutanist, lutenist, lute player.
lutin, -ine [lytɛ̃, -in] **1.** *n.m.* (*a*) mischievous sprite, imp, elf, goblin; (*b*) *F:* (*of child*) imp. **2.** *a.* mischievous, impish.
lutiner [lytine] *v.tr.* (*a*) to tease, plague, torment (s.o.); (*b*) to fondle, tickle (woman).
lutrin [lytrɛ̃] *n.m.* (*a*) *Ecc:* lectern; choir singing desk; (*b*) *Fr.C:* reading stand, music stand.
lutte [lyt] *n.f.* **1.** wrestling; **l. libre,** freestyle wrestling. **2.** (*a*) fight, struggle, tussle; conflict; **l. entre deux personnes,** contest between two people; **entrer, être, en l. avec qn,** to join battle with s.o.; to enter into, to be in, conflict with s.o.; **luttes parlementaires,** parliamentary clashes; **les partis en l.,** the opposing parties; **l. à mort,** life and death struggle; fight to the death; **l. contre l'alcoolisme,** campaign against alcoholism; **l. pour la vie,** (i) struggle for life; (ii) natural selection; **l. d'intérêts,** clash of interests; **gagner de haute,** *Lit:* **de vive, l.,** to win by sheer force, by force of arms; *Sp:* **l. de traction à la corde, l. à la jarretière,** tug-of-war; (*b*) strife; **la l. des classes,** the class struggle.
lutter [lyte] *v.i.* **1.** to wrestle (**avec, contre,** with). **2.** to struggle, contend, fight, compete; **l. contre la maladie,** to fight against, to combat, disease; **l. contre le vent,** to battle with the wind; **l. contre un incendie,** to fight a fire; **l. pour l'indépendance,** to fight for independence; **l. de vitesse avec qn,** to race s.o.
lutteur, -euse [lytœr, -øz] *n.* **1.** wrestler. **2.** fighter (for a cause, etc.).
lux [lyks] *n.m. Ph.Meas:* lux.
luxation [lyksasjɔ̃] *n.f. Med:* dislocation, luxation (of joint).
luxe [lyks] *n.m.* luxury; (*a*) luxuriousness, sumptuousness (of house, etc.); **vivre dans le l.,** to live in luxury; **étaler tout son l.,** to flaunt one's wealth; **c'est du l.,** that is quite unnecessary, a mere luxury; **je me suis payé le l. de le lui dire,** I gave myself the pleasure of telling him so; **se payer le l. d'un cigare,** to indulge in (the luxury of) a cigar; **articles de l.,** luxury articles; **édition de l.,** de luxe edition; **train de l.,** first-class and Pullman train; **taxe de l.,** luxury tax; (*b*) abundance, profusion (of food, etc.); **l. de précautions,** extravagant precautions.
Luxembourg [lyksɑ̃bur] *Pr.n.m. Geog:* (Grand Duchy of) Luxemburg.
luxembourgeois, -oise [lyksɑ̃burʒwa, -waz] *a. & n. Geog:* (native, inhabitant) of Luxemburg.
luxer [lykse] *v.tr.* to dislocate, luxate (joint, etc.); **se l. l'épaule,** to dislocate one's shoulder, to put one's shoulder out.
luxueusement [lyksɥøzmɑ̃] *adv.* luxuriously, sumptuously.
luxueux, -euse [lyksɥø, -øz] *a.* luxurious, sumptuous.
luxure [lyksyr] *n.f.* lewdness, lust.
luxuriance [lyksyrjɑ̃s] *n.f.* luxuriance.
luxuriant [lyksyrjɑ̃] *a.* luxuriant, lush (vegetation, etc.); fertile (imagination).
luxurieux, -euse [lyksyrjø, -øz] *a.* lascivious, lewd, lustful, sensual.
luzerne [lyzɛrn] *n.f. Bot:* lucern(e), alfalfa.
lycée [lise] *n.m.* **1.** *Gr.Ant:* **le L.,** the Lyceum. **2.** = grammar school, high school, secondary school; **l. technique,** technical high school.
lycéen, -éenne [liseɛ̃, -eɛn] *n.* = grammar school, high school, secondary school, pupil.
lydien, -ienne [lidjɛ̃, -jɛn] *a. & n. A.Geog:* Lydian; *Mus:* **(mode) l.,** lydian mode.
lymphatique [lɛ̃fatik] **1.** (*a*) *a. & n.* lymphatic (gland, etc.); (*b*) *n.m.* lymphatic (duct). **2.** *a.* lethargic, apathetic (person).
lymphe [lɛ̃f] *n.f.* lymph.
lymphocyte [lɛ̃fɔsit] *n.m.* lymphocyte.
lymphoïde [lɛ̃fɔid] *a. Anat:* lymphoid (cells, tissue).
lynchage [lɛ̃ʃaʒ] *n.m.* lynching.
lyncher [lɛ̃ʃe] *v.tr.* to lynch.
lynx [lɛ̃ks] *n.m.* lynx; **avoir des yeux de l.,** to be sharp-sighted.
Lyon [ljɔ̃] *Pr.n. Geog:* Lyons.
lyonnais, -aise [ljɔnɛ, -ɛz] *a. & n. Geog:* (native, inhabitant) of Lyons.
lyophilisation [ljɔfilizasjɔ̃] *n.f.* freeze-drying.
lyophiliser [ljɔfilize] *v.tr.* to freeze-dry (coffee, etc.).
lyre [lir] *n.f.* **1.** *Mus:* lyre; *Lit:* poetry; *F:* **toute la l.,** the whole lot (of them), the whole shoot. **2.** *Astr:* Lyra. **3.** *Orn:* **(oiseau-)l.,** lyre bird.
lyrique [lirik] **1.** (*a*) *a.* lyric(al) (poem, etc.); **poète l.,** lyric poet; **drame l.,** lyric drama, opera; **comédie l.,** comic opera, operetta; (*b*) **théâtre l.,** opera house. **2.** *n.m.* lyric poet.
lyrisme [lirism] *n.m.* **1.** lyricism. **2.** poetic enthusiasm. **3.** excessive enthusiasm.
lys [lis] *n.m. A:* = LIS.
lysergique [lizɛrʒik] *a.* lysergic; **acide l. (synthétique) diéthylamide,** lysergic acid diethylamide (L.S.D.).

M

M, m [ɛm] *n.m. or f.* (the letter) M, m.
m' **1.** *see* ME. **2.** *A: poss.a.f.* = **ma; m'amie,** my dear.
ma [ma] *see* MON.
maboul, -oule [mabul] *P:* **1.** *a.* mad, crazy, nuts, loony. **2.** *n.* loony.
maboulisme [mabulism] *n.m. P:* madness, craziness.
macabre [makɑbr̥] *a.* (*a*) **danse m.,** dance of Death; (*b*) macabre; gruesome (discovery); ghoulish, grim (humour, *NAm:* humor, etc.).
macache [makaʃ] *adv. P:* not likely! nothing doing! no fear!
macadam [makadam] *n.m.* **1.** macadam; **m. goudronné,** tarmac(adam). **2.** (macadamized) road.
macadamisage [makadamizaʒ] *n.m.* **macadamisation** [makadamizasjɔ] *n.f.* macadamization, macadamizing (of roads).
macadamiser [makadamize] *v.tr.* to macadamize, tarmac (road).
macaque [makak] *n.m.* **1.** *Z:* macaque; **m. rhésus,** bandar, rhesus (monkey). **2.** *F:* very ugly person.
macareux [makarø] *n.m. Orn:* puffin.
macaron [makarɔ̃] *n.m.* **1.** (*a*) *Cu:* macaroon; (*b*) *pl. Hairdr:* coils (over the ears), *F:* earphones. **2.** (*a*) *Cost:* (round) motif, ornamental button; badge; (*b*) *F:* rosette (of a decoration).
macaroni [makarɔni] *n.m.* **1.** *Cu:* macaroni. **2.** *P: Pej:* Italian, wop.
macaronique [makarɔnik] *a. Lit:* macaronic (verse).
Macchabée [makabe] **1.** *Pr.n.m. B.Hist:* Maccabaeus. **2.** *n.m. P:* corpse, stiff.
Macédoine [masedwan] **1.** *Pr.n.f. Geog:* Macedonia. **2.** *n.f.* (*a*) *Cu:* **m. de fruits,** fruit salad; **m. de légumes,** mixed vegetables, macedoine of vegetables; (*b*) medley, miscellany; *Pej:* hotchpotch.
macédonien, -ienne [masedɔnjɛ̃, -jɛn] *a. & n. Geog:* Macedonian.
macération [maserasjɔ̃] *n.f.* maceration.
macérer [masere] *v.tr.* **(je macère; je macérerai) 1.** to macerate; to steep, soak. **2.** to mortify (the flesh).
Mach [mak] *n.m. Aer:* **(nombre de) M.,** Mach (number).
mâche [mɑʃ] *n.f. Bot:* corn salad, lamb's lettuce.
mâchefer [mɑʃfɛr] *n.m.* clinker, slag.
mâchement [mɑʃmɑ̃] *n.m.* chewing, mastication.
mâcher [mɑʃe] *v.tr.* (*a*) to chew, masticate; to munch (biscuit, etc.); (*of animal*) to champ (fodder); (*of horse*) **m. le mors,** *F:* (*of pers.*) **m. son frein,** to champ at the bit; **je ne vais pas lui m. mes mots,** I won't mince my words with him; **m. les morceaux, la besogne, à qn,** to break the back of the work for s.o.; to spoonfeed s.o.; (*b*) (*of blunt tool, etc.*) **m. le bois,** to chew up the wood.
machette [maʃɛt] *n.f.* machete.
Machiavel [makjavɛl] *Pr.n.m.* Machiavelli.
machiavélique [makjavelik] *a.* Machiavellian.
machiavélisme [makjavelism] *n.m.* Machiavellism.
mâchicoulis [mɑʃikuli] *n.m. A.Fort:* machicolation; **à m.,** machicolated.
machin [maʃɛ̃] *n. F:* **1. monsieur M.,** Mr what's his name, what d'ye call him; Thingummy. **2.** *n.m.* thing(ummy), thingumajig, thingumabob; whatsit, what-not; what-d'ye-call-it; **passe-moi le m.(-chouette),** pass me the what's its name; **qu'est-ce que c'est que ce m.-là?** what's that gadget?
machinal, -aux [maʃinal, -o] *a.* mechanical, unconscious (action); automatic (reaction).
machinalement [maʃinalmɑ̃] *adv.* mechanically, unconsciously; instinctively; automatically.
machinateur, -trice [maʃinatœr, -tris] *n.* machinator, hatcher (of plot).
machination [maʃinasjɔ̃] *n.f.* machination, plot.
machine [maʃin] *n.f.* **1.** machine; (*a*) **m. à coudre,** sewing machine; **m. à laver,** washing machine; **m. à laver la vaisselle,** dishwasher; **m. à écrire,** typewriter; **écrire une lettre à la m.,** to type a letter; **écrit à la m.,** typed, typewritten; *F:* **trois pages de m.,** three typewritten pages; **m. à dicter,** dictating machine; **m. à calculer,** calculating machine, adding machine; **m. comptable,** accounting machine; **m. à sous,** (i) slot machine; (ii) fruit machine, one-armed bandit; *Ind:* **les machines,** the machinery; **les grosses machines,** the heavy plant; *Mec.E: etc:* **atelier des machines,** machine shop; **m. à aléser,** boring machine, fine borer; **m. à fraiser,** milling machine; **travailler le métal à la m.,** to machine metal; **fait à la m.,** machine-made; *Civ.E:* **m. à battre, à enfoncer, les pieux,** pile driver; *Typ:* **m. à composer,** typesetting machine; *Agr:* **m. à battre,** threshing machine; *Th:* **pièce à machines,** play with stage effects; **la m. administrative,** administrative machinery; (*b*) *F:* = (*vehicle, bicycle, motor cycle*) machine; **m. volante,** flying machine; (*c*) thing, gadget; contraption. **2.** engine; (*a*) **m. motrice,** prime mover; **m. thermique,** heat engine; **m. à combustion interne,** internal combustion engine; **m. à gaz,** gas engine; **m. à pétrole,** oil engine; **m. à vapeur,** steam engine; **m. à turbine,** turbine engine; **m. auxiliaire,** donkey engine; (*b*) *Rail:* locomotive; **m. de manœuvre,** shunting engine; **m. routière,** traction engine.
machine-outil [maʃinuti] *n.f.* machine tool; *pl. machines-outils.*
machiner [maʃine] *v.tr.* to scheme, plot, contrive; **affaire machinée d'avance,** put-up job.
machinerie [maʃinri] *n.f.* (*a*) machinery; *Ind:* plant; (*b*) *Ind:* machine shop, room; *Nau:* engine room.
machinisme [maʃinism] *n.m.* mechanization (of agriculture, etc.).
machiniste [maʃinist] *n.m.* **1.** driver (of bus, electric train, etc.). **2.** *Th:* scene shifter, stagehand.
machmètre [makmɛtr̥] *n.m. Aer:* machmeter.
mâchoire [mɑʃwar] *n.f.* **1.** jaw (of person, animal); **la m., les mâchoires,** the jaws; *P:* **jouer, travailler, des mâchoires,** to eat, nosh; *F:* **bâiller à se décrocher la m.,** to yawn one's head off. **2.** *Mec.E:* **mâchoires d'un étau,** jaws of a vice; **m. d'une poulie,** flange of a pulley; *Aut:* **mâchoires de frein,** brake shoes.
mâchonnement [mɑʃɔnmɑ̃] *n.m.* **1.** chewing. **2.** muttering, mumbling.
mâchonner [mɑʃɔne] *v.tr.* **1.** to chew (food, cigar); to munch; (*of horse*) to champ (the bit); **m. son crayon,** to chew (the end of) one's pencil. **2.** to mutter (threats, etc.); to mumble (prayer).
mâchouiller [mɑʃuje] *v.tr. F:* to chew away at (sth.).
mâchure [mɑʃyr] *n.f. Tex:* flaw (in velvet, etc.).

mâchurer[1] [mɑʃyre] *v.tr.* to soil, dirty; *Typ:* to smudge, mackle, blur (sheet).
mâchurer[2] *v.tr.* **1.** to bruise; *Mec.E:* to dent, bruise (metal part in the vice). **2.** to reduce (sth.) to pulp.
macis [masi] *n.m. Cu:* mace.
mackintosh [makintɔʃ] *n.m. Cost: A:* mackintosh.
macle[1] [makl] *n.f. Cryst:* macle, twin(ned) crystal.
macle[2] *n.f. Bot:* water chestnut.
maclé [makle] *a. Cryst:* twinned.
macler [makle] *v.tr. Glassm:* to mix, stir (glass).
maçon [masɔ̃] *n.m.* **1.** (*a*) (stone)mason; bricklayer; (*b*) (free)mason. **2.** *a.f. Ent:* **abeille maçonne** [masɔn], mason bee.
mâcon [mɑkɔ̃] *n.m.* (*also* **vin de M.**) Mâcon (wine).
maçonnage [masɔnaʒ] *n.m.* mason's work; bricklaying.
maçonner [masɔne] *v.tr.* (*a*) to build (wall, etc.); (*b*) to face (wall, etc.) with stone; (*c*) to wall up, brick up (door, etc.).
maçonnerie [masɔnri] *n.f.* **1.** masonry; stonework; brickwork. **2.** (free)masonry.
maçonnique [masɔnik] *a.* masonic (lodge, etc.).
macramé [makrame] *n.m.* macramé.
macre [makr] *n.f. Bot:* water chestnut.
macreuse [makrøz] *n.f.* **1.** *Orn:* scoter (duck). **2.** *Cu:* shoulder of beef.
macrobiotique [makrɔbjɔtik] *a.* macrobiotic.
macrocéphale [makrɔsefal] *a.* macrocephalic.
macrocosme [makrɔkɔsm] *n.m.* macrocosm.
macrophotographie [makrɔfɔtɔgrafi] *n.f.* macrophotography, photomacrography.
macropode [makrɔpɔd] **1.** *a. Nat.Hist:* macropodous. **2.** *n.m. Ich:* paradise fish.
macroscopique [makrɔskɔpik] *a.* macroscopic.
macule [makyl] *n.f.* **1.** (*a*) *A: & Lit:* stain, spot, blemish; (*b*) *Astr: Med:* macula. **2.** *Typ:* (*a*) mackle, blur; (*b*) waste sheet (used for packing, etc.).
maculer [makyle] **1.** *v.tr. Lit:* to stain, spot; *Typ:* to mackle, blur. **2.** *v.i.* (*of paper*) to mackle, blur; (*of engraving*) to fox.
Madagascar [madagaskar] *Pr.n.m. Geog:* Madagascar.
madame, *pl.* **mesdames** [madam, medam] *n.f.* **1.** (*a*) **M. Martin,** Mrs Martin; **Mesdames Martin,** the Mrs Martin; **M. Veuve X,** Mrs X, widow of (the late) (David) X; **m. la marquise, la comtesse, de X,** the Marchioness, the Countess, of X; Lady X; **je voudrais parler à m. la directrice,** I would like to speak to the manageress, to the headmistress; **comment va m. votre mère?** how is your mother? (*b*) (*used alone*) (*pl.* **ces dames**) (*said by servant*) her ladyship, the mistress; **voici le chapeau de m.,** here is your hat, madam; (*in shop*) **M. se plaint que . . .,** the lady, this lady, madam, is complaining that. . . . **2.** (*a*) (*in address*) madam, ma'am; (*to titled lady*) your ladyship; **non, m.,** no(,madam); **entrez, mesdames,** come in, ladies; **m. est servie,** dinner is served(,madam); (*b*) *Corr:* (*always written in full*) **Madame,** (Dear) Madam; **chère Madame,** Dear Mrs X. **3.** *F:* lady; **jouer à la m.,** to put on airs.
Madeleine [madlɛn] **1.** *Pr.n.f.* (*a*) *B.Hist:* Magdalen(e); *F:* **pleurer comme une M.,** to cry one's heart out; (*b*) Madeleine. **2.** *n.f. Cu:* madeleine.
mademoiselle, *pl.* **mesdemoiselles** [madmwazɛl, medmwazɛl] *n.f.* **1.** (*a*) Miss; **M. Martin,** Miss Martin; **Mesdemoiselles Martin,** the Misses Martin; (*b*) **m. la directrice,** the manageress, the headmistress; **comment va m. votre cousine?** how is your cousin? **2.** (*a*) (*in address*) **merci m.,** thank you, miss (X); (*b*) (*pl.* **ces demoiselles**) **m. est servie,** dinner is served(,madam); **ces demoiselles n'y sont pas,** the young ladies are not at home; (*in shop*) **M. se plaint que . . .,** the, this, young lady, is complaining that . . .; (*c*) *Corr:* (*always written in full*) **Mademoiselle,** (Dear) Madam; **Mesdemoiselles,** Mesdames; **chère Mademoiselle,** Dear Miss X.
Madère [madɛr] **1.** *Pr.n. Geog:* Madeira. **2.** *n.m.* (*also* **vin de M.**) Madeira (wine).
madone [madɔn] *n.f.* madonna.
Madras [madrɑs] **1.** *Pr.n. Geog:* Madras. **2.** *n.m. Tex:* (*a*) madras (cotton); Indian cotton; (*b*) (cotton) headscarf.
madré [madre] *a.* sly, crafty, wily; *n.* sly fox.
madrépore [madrepɔr] *n.m. Coel:* madrepore.
madrier [madrije] *n.m.* (piece of) timber; beam; thick board, plank.
madrigal, -aux [madrigal, -o] *n.m.* madrigal.
madrilène [madrilɛn] *a. & n. Geog:* of, from, Madrid.
maelstrom [malstrɔm] *n.m.* maelstrom.
maestria [maɛstrija] *n.f. Art:* mastery; **avec m.,** in a masterly manner; brilliantly.
maestro [maɛstro] *n.m. Mus:* maestro.
maf(f)ia [mafja] *n.f.* maf(f)ia.
mafflu [mafly] *a. A: & Lit:* heavy-jowled.
magasin [magazɛ̃] *n.m.* **1.** (*a*) shop, *NAm:* store; **grand m.,** department store; **m. à libre service,** self-service store; **m. à succursales multiples,** chain store; **employé(e) de m.,** shop assistant, *NAm:* salesclerk; **courir, faire, les magasins,** to go shopping; (*b*) store, warehouse; **garçon de m.,** warehouseman, storeman; **marchandises en m.,** stock in hand; **magasins généraux,** bonded warehouse(s); (*c*) *Mil:* **m. à poudre,** powder magazine; **m. d'armes,** armoury, *NAm:* armory. **2.** magazine (of rifle, projector).
magasinage [magazinaʒ] *n.m.* **1.** warehousing, storing (of goods). **2. (droits de) m.,** warehouse dues; storage (charges). **3.** *Fr.C:* **faire du m.,** to go shopping.
magasiner [magazine] *v.i. Fr.C:* to go shopping.
magasinier [magazinje] *n.m.* warehouseman, storekeeper, storeman.
magazine [magazin] *n.m.* magazine.
magdalénien, -ienne [magdalenjɛ̃, -jɛn] *a. & n.m. Prehist:* Magdalenian.
mage [maʒ] *n.m.* (*a*) magus; **les trois Mages,** (i) *B.Hist:* the Three Magi, the Three Wise Men; (ii) *Astr:* Orion's belt; (*b*) seer.
magicien, -ienne [maʒisjɛ̃, -jɛn] *n.* magician; wizard; sorcerer, *f.* sorceress.
magie [maʒi] *n.f.* magic, wizardry; **m. noire,** black magic; **comme par m.,** as if by magic.
magique [maʒik] *a.* magic(al); **baguette m.,** magic wand; **lanterne m.,** magic lantern.
magiquement [maʒikmɑ̃] *adv.* magically.
magister [maʒistɛr] *n.m.* **1.** *A:* pedagogue; (village) schoolmaster. **2.** *Pej:* pedant.
magistère [maʒistɛr] *n.m.* **1.** *Alch: R.C.Ch:* magisterium. **2. exercer un m.,** to exercise authoritative power.
magistral, -aux [maʒistral, -o] *a.* (*a*) magisterial, authoritative; masterful (manner); (*b*) masterly (work, etc.); *F:* colossal, sound (thrashing).
magistralement [maʒistralmɑ̃] *adv.* authoritatively.
magistrat [maʒistra] *n.m.* magistrate; justice; judge; **il est m.,** he sits on the Bench.
magistrature [maʒistratyr] *n.f.* magistrature; magistracy; **la m. assise,** the judges, the Bench; **la m. debout,** the (body of) public prosecutors; **entrer dans la m.,** to be appointed (i) judge, (ii) public prosecutor.
magma [magma] *n.m. Ch: Geol:* magma.
magnanerie [maɲanri] *n.f.* silkworm breeding; sericulture.
magnanier, -ière [maɲanje, -jɛr] *n.* silkworm breeder; sericulturist.

magnanime [maɲanim] *a.* magnanimous.
magnanimement [maɲanimmɑ̃] *adv.* magnanimously.
magnanimité [maɲanimite] *n.f.* magnanimity.
magnat [magna] *n.m.* **1.** *Hist:* magnate, grandee (of Poland, Hungary). **2.** *Com: Ind:* magnate, tycoon.
magner (se) [s(ə)maɲe] *v.pr. P:* to get a move on.
magnésie [maɲezi] *n.f.* **1.** *Ch: Pharm:* magnesia, magnesium oxide. **2.** *Pharm:* **sulfate de m.,** Epsom salts.
magnésite [maɲezit] *n.f. Miner:* **1.** magnesite. **2.** meerschaum.
magnésium [maɲezjɔm] *n.m. Ch:* magnesium; **éclair de m.,** magnesium light, flash.
magnétique [maɲetik] *a.* magnetic.
magnétisable [maɲetizabl̥] *a.* magnetizable.
magnétisation [maɲetizasjɔ̃] *n.f.* **1.** magnetization. **2.** mesmerizing.
magnétiser [maɲetize] *v.tr.* **1.** to magnetize (iron, etc.). **2.** to magnetize, mesmerize, hypnotize; **auditoire magnétisé,** spellbound audience.
magnétiseur, -euse [maɲetizœr, -øz] *n.* mesmerizer, hypnotizer.
magnétisme [maɲetism] *n.m.* **1.** *Ph:* magnetism; **m. rémanent,** residual magnetism. **2.** (*a*) mesmerism; (*b*) **m. personnel,** personal magnetism.
magnétite [maɲetit] *n.f. Miner:* magnetite, lodestone.
magnéto [maɲeto] *n.f. I.C.E:* magneto.
magnétophone [maɲetɔfɔn] *n.m.* tape recorder.
magnétoscope [maɲetɔskɔp] *n.m.* video tape recorder; magnetoscope.
magnificat [magnifikat] *n.m. Ecc:* magnificat.
magnificence [maɲifisɑ̃s] *n.f.* **1.** magnificence, splendour, *NAm:* splendor. **2.** *Lit:* munificence; lavishness.
magnifier [maɲifje] *v.tr.* (*pr.sub. & impf.* **n. magnifiions, v. magnifiiez**) to magnify, glorify.
magnifique [maɲifik] *a.* magnificent, splendid; grand, sumptuous; superb (view, etc.); glorious (weather, etc.); **situation m.,** wonderful job.
magnifiquement [maɲifikmɑ̃] *adv.* magnificently; wonderfully.
magnitude [magnityd] *n.f.* magnitude (of star).
magnolia [maɲɔlja], **magnolier** [maɲɔlje] *n.m. Bot:* magnolia (tree).
magnum [magnɔm] *n.m.* magnum (of champagne).
magot¹ [mago] *n.m. F:* hoard (of money); savings, pile.
magot² *n.m.* magot. **1.** *Z:* Barbary ape, pigmy ape; macaque. **2.** Chinese grotesque porcelain figure.
magyar, -are [magjar] *a. & n. Ethn:* Magyar.
maharajah [maaraʒa] *n.m.* maharaja(h).
maharani [maarani] *n.f.* maharanee.
mahatma [maatma] *n.m.* mahatma, saint.
ma(h)-jong [maʒɔ̃g] *n.m. Games:* mah-jong(g).
Mahomet [maɔmɛ] *Pr.n.m.* Mohammed, Mahomet.
mahométan, -ane [maɔmetɑ̃, -an] *a. & n. O:* Mohammedan, Mahometan, Moslem.
mahométisme [maɔmetism] *n.m. O:* Mohammedanism, Moslemism.
mai [mɛ] *n.m.* **1.** May; **en m.,** in May; **au mois de m.,** in the month of May; **le sept m.,** (on) the seventh of May; (on) May (the) seventh; **le premier m.,** May day. **2. (arbre de) m.,** maypole.
maigre [mɛgr̥] **1.** *a.* (*a*) thin, skinny, lean (person, animal); **m. comme un clou,** as thin as a lath, as a rake; **homme grand et m.,** *n.* **un grand m.,** a tall, thin man; *n.* **c'est une fausse m.,** she's not as thin as she looks; (*b*) lean (meat, etc.); meagre, *NAm:* meager (income, diet); scanty (vegetation, etc.); small (crop); infertile, poor (land, etc.); straggling (beard); **fromage m.,** skim milk cheese; **m. filet d'eau,** thin trickle of water; **m. repas,** scanty, frugal, meal; **repas m.,** meatless meal; **jour m.,** day of abstinence; **faire m.,** to abstain (from meat); **faire m. réception à qn,** to give s.o. a poor reception; *Typ:* **caractères maigres,** lightfaced type. **2.** *n.m.* (*a*) lean (part of meat); (*b*) *pl.* shallows (of river, etc.).
maigrelet, -ette [mɛgrəlɛ, -ɛt] *a.* thin, slight, skinny (person).
maigrement [mɛgrəmɑ̃] *adv.* meagrely, *NAm:* meagerly; poorly.
maigreur [mɛgrœr] *n.f.* **1.** (*a*) thinness, leanness, skinniness; (*b*) emaciation. **2.** poorness, meagreness, *NAm:* meagerness, scantiness (of a meal, etc.); baldness (of style).
maigrichon, -onne [megriʃɔ̃, -ɔn], **maigriot, -otte** [megrijo, -ɔt] *a.* thin, skinny.
maigrir [megrir] **1.** *v.i.* to get thin(ner), lose weight; **elle essaie de m.,** she's slimming; **j'ai maigri de dix kilos,** I've lost ten kilos; **régime pour m.,** reducing, slimming, diet. **2.** *v.tr.* (*a*) (*of illness*) to make (s.o.) thin(ner); (*b*) (*of garment*) to make (s.o.) look thin(ner); (*c*) to thin (piece of wood, etc.).
mail [maj] *n.m.* **1.** (*a*) *A:* mall (game, club, or alley); (*b*) avenue, promenade. **2.** sledgehammer.
maille¹ [mɑj] *n.f.* **1.** (*a*) stitch (in knitting, etc.); **m. à l'endroit,** plain (stitch); knit; **m. à l'envers,** purl (stitch); **m. qui file,** ladder, run (in stocking); (*b*) link (of chain); (*c*) *Arm:* (chain)mail; **cotte de mailles,** coat of mail. **2.** mesh (of net, etc.); **filet à larges mailles,** wide-mesh net.
maille² *n.f.* **il n'a ni sou ni m.,** he hasn't a penny to bless himself with; **avoir m. à partir avec qn,** to have a bone to pick with s.o.
maillechort [majʃɔr] *n.m.* nickel silver.
mailler [mɑje] *v.tr.* **1.** (*a*) to net (a purse, etc.); (*b*) to make (sth.) in lattice work. **2.** to shackle (two chains).
maillet [majɛ] *n.m.* (*a*) *Tls:* mallet, maul; beetle; (*b*) polo stick, mallet; (*c*) croquet mallet.
mailloche [majɔʃ] *n.f.* **1.** beetle; large mallet, maul. **2.** bass drumstick.
maillon [mɑjɔ̃] *n.m.* **1.** link (of a chain); **m. tournant,** swivel; (*of pers.*) **être le m. d'une chaîne,** to be a link in the chain. **2.** *Nau:* (*length of chain of 30 metres, NAm: meters*) shackle.
maillot [majo] *n.m.* **1.** *A:* swaddling clothes. **2.** (*a*) *Th: etc:* tights; leotard; (*b*) **m. de bain,** swimming costume, swimsuit; (*c*) (football) jersey; (running, rowing) vest, singlet; (*d*) **m. de corps,** (man's) vest, *NAm:* undervest, undershirt.
main [mɛ̃] *n.f.* **1.** hand; (*a*) **se laver les mains de qch.,** to wash one's hands of sth.; **soin des mains,** manicure; **donner la m. à qn,** (i) to take, hold, s.o.'s hand, lead s.o. by the hand; (ii) to shake hands with s.o.; **se donner la m.,** (i) to hold hands; (ii) to shake hands; **donner sa m. à qn,** (i) to shake hands with s.o.; (ii) (*of woman*) to give one's hand in marriage to s.o.; **je lui ai serré la m.,** I shook hands with him; **ils se tenaient la m.,** they were holding hands; **la m. dans la m.,** hand in hand; **faire qch. de la m. droite, de la m. gauche,** to do sth. righthanded, lefthanded, with one's right hand, left hand; **porter la m. à son chapeau,** to touch one's hat; **porter la m. sur qn,** to lay hands on s.o.; to strike s.o.; **je n'en mettrais pas la m. au feu,** I shouldn't like to swear to it; **sac à m.,** handbag; **en venir aux mains,** to come to blows; **ne pas y aller de m. morte,** (i) to put one's back into it; (ii) to exaggerate, lay it on; **homme de m.,** henchman; **faire m. basse sur qch.,** to help oneself to sth.; **faire m. basse sur une ville,** to pillage a town; **haut les mains!** hands up! **à bas les mains!** hands off! **sous la m.,** within reach; (near) at hand; to hand; **faire qch. (en) sous m.,** to do sth. in an underhand way; *Mil:*

coup de m., raid, surprise attack; **donner un coup de m., prêter la m., à qn,** to lend, give, s.o. a (helping) hand; *F:* **passer la m. dans le dos à qn,** to flatter s.o., butter s.o. up; *F:* **avoir le cœur sur la m.,** to be very generous, open-handed; *(b)* **prendre un plateau, son courage, à deux mains,** to take a tray, one's courage, in both hands; **épée à deux mains,** two-handed sword; **attaque à m. armée,** armed attack; **donner de l'argent à pleine(s) main(s),** to dish out money by the handful; **avoir une canne à la m.,** to have a stick in one's hand; **avoir, tenir, qch. dans la m.,** to have, hold, sth. in one's hand; **argent en main(s),** money in hand; **tenir le succès entre ses mains,** to have success within one's grasp; **passer aux mains de . . .,** to pass, fall, into the hands of . . .; **tomber aux mains, dans les mains, de l'ennemi,** to fall into enemy hands; **être en bonnes mains,** to be in good hands, in safe keeping; **prendre une affaire en m.,** to take a matter in hand; **mettre la m. sur qn,** to lay hands on s.o.; *F:* to collar, nab, s.o.; **mettre la m. sur qch.,** to lay hands on, take possession of, sth.; **je ne peux pas mettre la m. sur sa lettre,** I can't put my hand on his letter; **acheter qch. de première, seconde, m.,** to buy sth. (at) firsthand, secondhand; **article de seconde m.,** secondhand article; **renseignements de première m.,** firsthand information; **de m. en m.,** from hand to hand; **payer de la m. à la m.,** to hand over the money direct (without receipt or other formality); *(c)* **faire, fabriquer, qch. à la m.,** to do, make, sth. by hand; **fait à la m., fait m.,** handmade; **scie à m.,** handsaw; **dire adieu de la m. à qn,** to wave goodbye to s.o.; **écrire une lettre de sa propre m.,** to write a letter in one's own hand; **notes écrites à la m.,** handwritten notes; **de m. de maître,** by a master hand; **mettre la m. à la pâte,** to lend a hand, put one's hand to the plough; **mettre la dernière m. à qch.,** to put the finishing touches to sth.; **se faire la m.,** to get one's hand in, get the knack of sth.; **s'entretenir la m.,** to keep one's hand in; **il a perdu la m.,** he's out of practice, lost the knack; **dessin à m. levée,** freehand drawing; *(d)* **homme à toutes mains,** man ready to do anything; handyman; **il a sa voiture bien en m.,** he's got the feel of his car; **tenez-vous en m.,** control yourself; **avoir la haute m. dans une affaire,** to be in control, in charge, of a matter; **gagner haut la m.,** (i) *Turf:* to win in a canter; (ii) to win easily, hands down, with flying colours, *NAm:* colors; *(e)* **de longue m.,** for a long time (past); **ami de longue m.,** friend of long standing. **2.** *(a)* hand(writing); **avoir une belle m.,** to have a fine hand, to write well; *(b)* **m. courante,** (i) *Com:* rough book; (ii) handrail (on staircase). **3.** *Cards:* *(a)* hand; **avoir une m. longue,** to have a long suit in trumps; *(b)* **avoir la m.,** to have the deal; **passer la m.,** (i) to pass the deal; (ii) *Fig:* to stand aside, give someone else a chance; *(c)* **avoir la m.,** to have the lead. **4.** *(a)* (grocer's, etc.) scoop; *(b)* handle (of drawer, etc.). **5.** *Paperm:* **m. de papier (25 feuilles)** = approx. quire of paper (24 sheets).

mainate [mɛnat] *n.m. Orn:* myna(h) (bird).

main-d'œuvre [mɛ̃dœvr̥] *n.f.* **1.** labour, *NAm:* labor; manpower; **embaucher de la m.-d'œ.,** to take on hands. **2.** cost of labour; *pl. mains-d'œuvre.*

main-forte [mɛ̃fɔrt] *n.f.* **donner, prêter, m.-f. à qn,** to come to s.o.'s assistance, aid.

mainlevée [mɛ̃lve] *n.f. Jur:* **m. de saisie,** restoration of goods (taken in distraint); **m. d'opposition à mariage,** withdrawal of opposition to marriage; *Ecc:* **m. d'interdit,** removal of interdict.

mainmise [mɛ̃miz] *n.f.* **1.** *Hist:* manumission; freeing (of bondman). **2.** seizure **(sur,** of); distraint (upon property).

maint [mɛ̃] *a. Lit:* many (a . . .); **m. auteur,** many an author; **maintes et maintes fois, à maintes reprises, en mainte (et mainte) occasion,** time and (time) again.

maintenance [mɛ̃tnɑ̃s] *n.f.* **1.** *A:* maintaining (of law and order, etc.). **2.** *(a) Mil:* keeping up to strength (of unit and equipment); *(b) Ind: etc:* maintenance (service).

maintenant [mɛ̃tnɑ̃] *adv.* now; **vous devriez être prêt m.,** you ought to be ready by now; **à vous m.,** your turn next; **dès m., à partir de m.,** from now on(wards); henceforth; in future.

maintenir [mɛ̃tnir] *v.tr.* (*conj. like* TENIR) to maintain. **1.** *(a)* to keep, hold (sth.) in position; **colonnes qui maintiennent la voûte,** columns that keep up, support, the roof; **m. qn dans ses fonctions,** to maintain s.o. in office; **m. la foule,** to hold back the crowd; **m. son cheval,** to keep one's horse under control; *(b)* to uphold, keep (the law, discipline, etc.); to preserve (peace, etc.); to abide by (a decision); **m. sa position,** to hold one's own; **je maintiens que c'est faux,** I maintain that it is untrue. **2. se m.** *(a)* to remain, to last; *(b)* to hold on; **se m. dans les bonnes grâces de qn,** to keep in favour, *NAm:* favor, with s.o.; **se m. contre les attaques de l'ennemi,** to hold one's own, one's ground, against the enemy; **les prix se maintiennent,** prices are keeping up, remain steady; *F:* **comment ça va?—on se maintient,** how are you?—surviving; ticking over; *(c)* to be maintained, to continue; **cela ne peut pas se m. longtemps,** it cannot last long; **le temps se maintient,** the weather is holding.

maintien [mɛ̃tjɛ̃] *n.m.* **1.** maintenance, upholding, keeping (of order, etc.). **2.** bearing, carriage, deportment; **leçons de m.,** lessons in deportment.

maire [mɛr] *n.m.* mayor.

mairesse [mɛrɛs] *n.f. usu. Hum:* mayoress.

mairie [meri] *n.f.* town hall; municipal buildings; **c'est un employé de m.,** he works for the (local) council.

mais [mɛ] **1.** *adv.* *(a) A:* more; *(b) Lit:* **n'en pouvoir m.,** (i) to be exhausted, at the end of one's tether; (ii) to be too disconcerted to protest; *(c)* (*emphatic*) **m. oui!** oh yes! why, certainly! *NAm:* sure! **m. non!** oh no! not at all! **m. qu'avez-vous donc?** whatever's the matter? **m. c'est vrai!** but it's true! it really is true! **m. enfin!** well really! oh well! **2.** *conj.* but; **famille riche m. honnête,** rich but honest family; **non seulement . . ., m. aussi, m. encore . . .,** not only . . ., but also. . . . **3.** *n.m.* **il y a un m.,** there is one objection; **il n'y a pas de m.,** there's no but about it.

maïs [mais] *n.m.* maize, Indian corn, sweetcorn, *NAm:* corn; **farine de m.,** cornflour.

maison [mɛzɔ̃] *n.f.* **1.** *(a)* house; **m. de ville,** town house; **m. de campagne,** (i) house in the country; (ii) country cottage; **m. de chasse,** hunting lodge; **m. de rapport,** (block of) flats, apartment block; **m. d'habitation,** dwelling house; *(b)* home; **à la m.,** at home; **retournons à la m.,** let's go home; **dépenses de la m.,** household expenses; **tenir la m. de qn,** to keep house for s.o.; **il porte des pantoufles dans la m.,** he wears slippers indoors; *(c) Astrol:* house, mansion. **2.** *(a)* **m. centrale, m. de force,** prison; **m. d'arrêt, de justice,** prison, gaol (for prisoners awaiting trial); **m. de correction,** (i) prison (where short sentences are served); (ii) *A:* reformatory (school); **m. de santé,** (i) nursing home; (ii) mental home; **m. de repos, de convalescence,** rest home, convalescent home; **m. de retraite,** old people's home; **m. de la jeunesse,** youth centre, *NAm:* center; youth club; **m. religieuse,** convent; **m. de jeux,** gambling club, gaming club; **m. close, m. de tolérance, m. de passe,** brothel; *(b)* firm; *esp. Publ:* house; **m. de commerce,** business company; **la M. du**

Stylo, the Pen Shop; **m. mère,** (i) head office; (ii) *Ecc:* mother house. **3.** (*a*) family; **le fils de la m.,** the son of the house; **ami de la m.,** friend of the family; **être de la m.,** to be one of the family; (*b*) **la m. des Bourbons,** the House of Bourbon; (*c*) household, staff; **la m. du Roi,** the Royal Household; **gens de m.,** servants, (domestic) staff. **4.** *attrib.* (*a*) (*on menu*) **pâté m.,** home-made pâté; (*b*) *P:* extraordinarily good, fantastic; **ça, c'est m.!** that's excellent! *NAm:* swell!

maisonnée [mɛzɔne] *n.f.* household, family.

maisonnette [mɛzɔnɛt] *n.f.* small house; cottage.

maistrance [mɛstrɑ̃s] *n.f. Navy:* petty officers.

maître, -esse [mɛtr̥, mɛtrɛs] *n.* **1.** (*a*) master, *f.* mistress; **m., maîtresse, de maison,** master, mistress, of the house; **je veux être m. chez moi,** I insist on being master in my own house; **chauffeur de m.,** private chauffeur; **parler à qn en m.,** to speak authoritatively to s.o.; **être m. de la situation,** to be master of the situation; **être m. absolu de faire qch.,** to be entirely free to do sth.; **trouver son m.,** to meet one's match, master; **être m., maîtresse, de soi(-même),** to be self-possessed, have one's feelings under control; **être m. de sa voiture,** to be in control of one's car; **le conducteur n'était plus m. de sa voiture,** the driver lost control of the car; **navire qui n'est pas m. de sa manœuvre,** ship not under control; **se rendre m., maîtresse, de qch.,** (i) to take possession of sth.; (ii) to master, gain control of, sth.; (*b*) (school)teacher; (school)master, (school)mistress; **m., maîtresse, d'école,** primary, *NAm:* elementary, school teacher; **m. d'internat** = housemaster; **m. assistant** = assistant lecturer (at university); **m. de danse,** dancing master; **m. d'escrime, d'armes,** fencing master; **m. de chapelle,** choirmaster; **m. nageur,** swimming instructor; (*c*) **m. charpentier, m. maçon,** master carpenter, master mason; **m. queux,** chef; **main de m.,** master hand; **c'est fait de main de m.,** it's a masterpiece; **coup de m.,** master stroke; **être passé m. dans l'art de (faire) qch.,** to be a past master in sth., at doing sth.; **m. d'œuvre,** foreman; **m. clerc,** clerk (in barrister's chambers); *A:* **m. de forges,** ironmaster; *Navy:* **second m.,** petty officer; **premier m.,** chief petty officer; **m. d'équipage,** boatswain; **le m. du navire,** the master of the ship; **m. d'hôtel,** (i) butler; (ii) head waiter; (iii) *Nau:* chief steward; (*d*) (*title given to member of legal profession*) Maître. **2.** *attrib.* (*a*) **maîtresse femme,** capable, managing, woman; **m. sot,** utter fool; **m. filou,** arrant scoundrel; (*b*) chief, principal, main; **maîtresse poutre,** main girder, beam; **cheville maîtresse,** kingpin; **idée maîtresse d'un ouvrage,** governing idea of a work; *Games: Cmptr:* **carte maîtresse,** master card. **3.** *n.f.* **maîtresse,** mistress.

maître-autel [mɛtrotɛl] *n.m. Ecc:* high altar; *pl. maîtres-autels.*

maitrisable [metrizabl̥] *a.* controllable.

maîtrise [metriz] *n.f.* **1.** (*a*) *Sch:* = master's degree; (*b*) post of choirmaster (of cathedral); (*c*) choir school; (*d*) choir (of cathedral, etc.); (*e*) *Ind:* supervisory staff. **2.** mastery (of one's passions, an art, etc.); **m. de soi,** self-control, self-command; **m. des mers,** command, control, of the seas.

maîtriser [metrize] **1.** *v.tr.* to master (a horse, etc.); to subdue (a fire, etc.); to get (fire, etc.) under control; to curb, bridle (passion); to control (epidemic); to overpower (s.o.); to overcome (one's fears). **2. se m.,** to control oneself; **ne pas savoir se m.,** to have no self-control.

majesté [maʒɛste] *n.f.* majesty. **1. Sa M. le Roi, la Reine,** his Majesty the King, her Majesty the Queen; **Leurs Majestés,** their Majesties. **2.** (*a*) stateliness; dignity; (*b*) grandeur (of style, landscape).

majestueusement [maʒɛstɥøzmɑ̃] *adv.* majestically.

majestueux, -euse [maʒɛstɥø, -øz] *a.* majestic, stately (bearing, etc.); imposing (figure); **paysage m.,** magnificent landscape.

majeur, -eure [maʒœr] **1.** *a.* (*a*) major, greater; **la majeure partie de qch.,** the greater part, the bulk, the majority, of sth.; **la majeure partie du temps,** most of the time; **en majeure partie,** for the most part; *Log:* **prémisse majeure,** major premise; *Geog:* **le lac M.,** Lake Maggiore; *Ecc:* **les ordres majeurs,** the major sacred orders; (*b*) **affaire majeure,** matter of great importance; **raison majeure de qch.,** chief reason for sth.; **être absent pour raison majeure,** to be unavoidably absent; **cas de force majeure,** case of absolute necessity; (*c*) *Jur:* of age; **devenir m.,** to attain one's majority, come of age; (*d*) *Mus:* major (mode, etc.); **en sol bémol m.,** in G flat major; (*e*) *a. & n.f. Cards:* **(couleur) majeure,** major suit. **2.** (*a*) *n.* person who has reached the age of majority; major; (*b*) *n.m.* middle finger.

majolique [maʒɔlik] *n.f. Cer:* majolica.

major [maʒɔr] *n.m.* **1.** *Mil:* regimental adjutant (with administrative duties); **m. général,** chief of staff (of a commander-in-chief in the field); **m. du camp,** camp commandant. **2.** *Mil:* **(médecin) m.,** medical officer; M.O. **3.** *Sch:* **sortir m. (d'une grande école)** = to leave (a university, etc.) head of the list.

majoration [maʒɔrasjɔ̃] *n.f.* **1.** (*a*) overestimation, overvaluation (of assets, etc.); (*b*) additional charge (on bill); surcharge. **2.** (*a*) increase (in price); (*b*) increased allowance.

majordome [maʒɔrdɔm] *n.m.* major-domo; steward.

majorer [maʒɔre] *v.tr.* **1.** to overestimate, overvalue (assets, etc.). **2.** to make an additional charge on (bill); **m. une facture de 10%,** to put 10% a surcharge of 10%, on an invoice. **3.** to raise, put up, increase, the price of (sth.).

majorette [maʒɔrɛt] *n.f.* (drum-)majorette.

majoritaire [maʒɔritɛr] **1.** *Pol:* (*a*) *a.* of, pertaining to, a majority; **vote m., parti m.,** majority vote, party; (*b*) *n.* member of the majority (party). **2.** *a. & n. Fin:* majority (shareholder).

majorité [maʒɔrite] *n.f.* **1.** majority; **la m. silencieuse,** the silent majority; **les hommes en m.,** most men, the majority of men; **emporter la m.,** to secure a majority, carry a vote; **décision prise à la m. (des voix),** decision taken by a majority; **élu à la m. de dix,** elected by a majority of ten; **être en m., avoir la m.,** to be in a, in the, majority; **dans la m. des cas,** in most cases. **2.** *Jur:* majority, coming of age; **atteindre sa m.,** to attain one's majority, come of age. **3.** *Mil:* majority.

Majorque [maʒɔrk] *Pr.n.f. Geog:* Majorca.

majorquin, -ine [maʒɔrkɛ̃, -in] *a. & n. Geog:* Majorcan.

majuscule [maʒyskyl] **1.** *a.* capital (letter). **2.** *n.f.* capital letter; *Typ:* upper case letter; **majuscules d'imprimerie,** block capitals.

mal[1] [mal] *a.* (*a*) *A:* = MAUVAIS; (*b*) **bon an, m. an,** year in, year out; **bon gré, m. gré,** willy-nilly.

mal[2], maux [mal, mo] *n.m.* **1.** evil; (*a*) harm; hurt; **faire du m.,** to do harm; **faire du m. à qn,** to do s.o. harm, to injure, hurt, s.o.; **faire du m. à qch.,** to damage, harm, sth.; **il fait plus de bruit que de m.,** his bark is worse than his bite; **s'en tirer sans aucun m.,** to escape uninjured, unhurt, unscathed; **je ne lui veux pas de m.,** I mean him no harm; **cela fera plus de m. que de bien,** it will do more harm than good; **souffrir de grands maux,** to suffer great ills; **de deux maux il faut choisir le moindre,** one must choose the lesser of two evils; **il n'y a pas de m. à cela,** there's no harm in that; **il n'y a pas grand m.!** there's no great harm done! **m. lui en a pris,** he has had cause to regret it, to rue it; (*b*) **dire du m. de qn,** to speak ill of s.o.; **changement en m.,** change for the worse; **prendre qch. en m.,** to take sth. the wrong way; **tourner qch. en m.,** to put the worst interpretation on sth.; (*c*) wrong(doing); **le bien et le m.,** right and wrong, good and evil; **rendre le bien pour le m.,** to return good for evil; **penser à m.,** to have evil intentions; **il ne pense pas à m.,** he doesn't mean any harm; **mettre qn à m.,** to hurt s.o. badly. **2.** (*a*) disorder; disease, illness; ailment; sickness; pain, ache; **prendre (du) m.,** to be taken ill, to catch something; **m. de tête,** headache; **m. de dents,** toothache; **m. de gorge,** sore throat; **m. de cœur,** sickness, nausea; **avoir m. à l'estomac, aux dents, à la tête, à la gorge,** to have stomachache, toothache, a headache, a sore throat; **m. de mer,** seasickness; **avoir le m. de mer,** to be seasick; **m. de l'air, d'avion,** airsickness; **m. de la route,** carsickness; **m. des rayons,** radiation sickness; **m. du siècle,** worldweariness; **m. blanc,** whitlow; **où avez-vous m.?** where is the pain? where does it hurt? **vous me faites (du) m.,** you're hurting me; **mon genou me fait m.,** my knee's hurting; **spectacle qui fait m.,** painful sight; **être en m. de qch.,** to be badly in need of sth.; (*b*) **non sans m.,** not without trouble, without difficulty; **se donner du m. pour faire qch.,** to take pains to do sth.; **avoir du m. à faire qch.,** to have difficulty, trouble, in doing sth.

mal³ *adv.* **1.** (*a*) badly, ill; **se conduire m.,** to behave badly; **m. à l'aise,** ill at ease; **vous avez m. agi,** you did wrong, you acted badly; **biens m. acquis,** ill-gotten gains; **travail m. fait,** badly done work; **faire qch. tant bien que m.,** to do sth. after a fashion; **aller de m. en pis,** to go from bad to worse; **s'y m. prendre,** to go the wrong way about it; **m. choisir,** to choose wrongly; **m. comprendre,** to misunderstand; **m. interpréter,** to misinterpret, misconstrue, misread; **on voit m. d'ici,** you can't see well, properly, from here; **on voit m. comment . . .,** it's difficult, not easy, to see how . . .; **vous êtes m. informé,** you are ill-informed; **il a très m. pris la chose,** he took it very badly, the wrong way; **vous ne feriez peut-être pas m. de . . .,** it wouldn't be a bad thing (if you were) to . . .; (*b*) **aller, se porter, m.,** to be ill, in bad health; **comment allez-vous?—pas m.! pas trop m.!** how are you?—not so bad! pretty well! **être au plus m.,** to be dangerously ill, at death's door; **elle est, elle va, très m.,** she's in a very bad way; (*c*) **pas m. (de qch.),** a fair amount (of sth.); **il (n')y en a pas m.,** there are a good many, a good few, quite a lot; **cela m'a pris pas m. de temps,** it took me quite a time; **pas m. de gens,** a good many people. **2.** (*with adj. function*) (*a*) not right; **vous savez ce qui est bien et ce qui est m.,** you know the difference between right and wrong; **c'est très m. à lui,** (i) that's too bad of him; (ii) that's very unkind of him; (*b*) uncomfortable; badly off; **nous ne sommes pas m. ici,** we're quite comfortable, not at all badly off, here; (*c*) **il est, s'est mis, m. avec sa sœur,** he's on bad terms with his sister; (*d*) (*of health*) **se sentir m.,** to feel ill, sick, faint; **se trouver m.,** to faint; (*e*) **pas m.,** not bad, quite good; **ce n'était pas m. du tout,** it wasn't at all bad; **elle n'est pas m.,** she's quite good-looking.

malachite [malakit] *n.f. Miner:* malachite.

malade [malad] **1.** *a.* (*a*) (*of pers.*) ill, sick, poorly, unwell; (*of organ, etc.*) diseased; **être m.,** to be ill, poorly; **dent m.,** (i) aching tooth; (ii) decaying tooth; **jambe m.,** bad leg; **j'ai l'estomac m.,** I've got an upset stomach; **tomber m.,** to fall ill, be taken ill; **m. de la fièvre typhoïde,** ill with typhoid; **il a été m. comme un chien,** he was as sick as a dog; **être m. d'inquiétude,** to be sick with worry; *F:* **il en est m.,** he's really upset about it; **être m. du cœur,** to have heart trouble; **industrie m.,** industry in a bad way; **esprit m.,** disordered, unhealthy, mind; *Mil: etc:* **se faire porter m.,** to report, go, sick; (*b*) mad, crazy; *F:* **t'es pas m.?** are you off your rocker? **2.** *n.* sick person; invalid; *Med:* patient; case; **un grand m.,** a person who is very seriously ill; **les malades,** the sick; **faire le, la, m.,** to malinger.

maladie [maladi] *n.f.* (*a*) illness; sickness, disease, disorder, complaint; malady; **m. infantile,** child's complaint; **faire une m.,** to be ill; *F:* **il en fait une m.,** he's making a song and dance about it; **par suite de m.,** through illness; **m. de peau, cutanée,** skin disease; **m. de foie, de cœur,** liver, heart, complaint, disease; **m. bleue,** blue disease; **m. mentale,** mental illness; **m. du sommeil,** sleeping sickness; **congé de m.,** sick leave; **maladies des plantes,** diseases of plants; (*b*) *Vet:* **m. (des chiens),** distemper.

maladif, -ive [maladif, -iv] *a.* sickly; morbid, unhealthy.

maladivement [maladivmã] *adv.* morbidly.

maladresse [maladrɛs] *n.f.* **1.** (*a*) clumsiness, awkwardness; (*b*) tactlessness. **2.** blunder.

maladroit, -oite [maladrwa, -wat] **1.** *a.* (*a*) unskilful, clumsy, awkward (person); (*b*) blundering; tactless. **2.** *n.* (*a*) awkward, clumsy, person; (*b*) blunderer, tactless person.

maladroitement [maladrwatmã] *adv.* (*a*) clumsily; (*b*) tactlessly.

malais, -aise¹ [malɛ, -ɛz] **1.** *a. & n. Geog:* Malay(an). **2.** *n.m. Ling:* Malay(an).

malaise² [malɛz] *n.m.* **1.** uneasiness, discomfort; malaise; (political) unrest; **sentiment de m.,** (i) uneasy feeling; (ii) sick feeling. **2.** indisposition; (fit of) faintness; **avoir un m.,** to feel faint.

malaisé [maleze] *a.* difficult; **chose malaisée à faire,** difficult thing to do.

malaisément [malezemã] *adv.* with difficulty.

Malaisie [malɛzi] *Pr.n.f. Geog:* Malaya.

malappris, -ise [malapri, -iz] **1.** *a.* uncouth, ill-bred. **2.** *n.* ill-bred person; lout.

malard [malar] *n.m. Orn:* wild drake; mallard.

malaria [malarja] *n.f.* malaria.

malavisé, -ée [malavize] **1.** *a.* ill-advised; unwise, injudicious (person, etc.). **2.** *n. Lit:* tactless, foolish, person.

malaxage [malaksaʒ] *n.m.* **1.** kneading (of dough); working (of butter); mixing (of cement); pugging (of clay). **2.** massage, massaging (of legs, etc.).

malaxer [malakse] *v.tr.* **1.** to knead (dough); to work (butter); to mix (cement); to pug (clay). **2.** to massage (legs, etc.).

malaxeur [malaksœr] *n.m.* mixer, mixing machine. **1.** butter worker. **2.** cement mixer; **broyeur m.,** mixing mill. **3.** pug mill.

malchance [malʃɑ̃s] *n.f.* **1.** bad luck, ill luck; **par m.,** as ill luck would have it. **2.** mishap, misfortune.

malchanceux, -euse [malʃɑ̃sø, -øz] *a.* unfortunate, unlucky.

malcommode [malkɔmɔd] *a.* inconvenient; awkward; impractical.

maldonne [maldɔn] *n.f.* **1.** *Cards:* misdeal; **faire m.,** to misdeal. **2. il y a m.,** there's been a mistake, a misunderstanding.

mâle [mɑl] *a. & n.m.* **1.** male; cock (bird); buck (rabbit, antelope, etc.); dog (fox, wolf); bull (elephant, etc.); **un ours m.,** a he-bear; **héritier m.,** male heir; **un beau m.,** a fine specimen of manhood, *F:* a real he-man. **2.** manly (courage); virile (style).

malédiction [malediksjɔ̃] *n.f. Lit:* malediction, curse; **être sous le coup d'une m.,** to be under a curse.

maléfice [malefis] *n.m.* evil spell.

maléfique [malefik] *a.* maleficent; unlucky (star, etc.); evil (influence).

malencontreusement [malɑ̃kɔ̃trøzmɑ̃] *adv.* unfortunately.

malencontreux, -euse [malɑ̃kɔ̃trø, -øz] *a.* awkward, unfortunate, untoward (event, etc.).

mal-en-point [malɑ̃pwɛ̃] *adj.phr.* in a bad way.

malentendu [malɑ̃tɑ̃dy] *n.m.* misunderstanding; misapprehension.

malfaçon [malfasɔ̃] *n.f.* bad work(manship); defect.

malfaisance [malfəzɑ̃s] *n.f.* **1.** maleficence, evil-mindedness. **2.** *Jur:* malfeasance.

malfaisant [malfəzɑ̃] *a.* (*a*) maleficent; evil-minded (person); evil (influence); (*b*) *Jur:* malfeasant; (*c*) noxious, harmful (food, etc.).

malfaiteur, -trice [malfɛtœr, -tris] *n.* malefactor; criminal; wrongdoer.

malformation [malfɔrmasjɔ̃] *n.f.* malformation.

malfrat [malfra] *n.m. F:* shady character; tough.

malgache [malgaʃ] **1.** *a. & n. Geog:* Malagasy; Madagascan. **2.** *n.m. Ling:* Malagasy.

malgracieux, -ieuse [malgrasjø, -jøz] *a.* (*a*) ungracious, churlish, rude; (*b*) inelegant, clumsy.

malgré [malgre] **1.** *prep.* in spite of, despite, notwithstanding; **m. cela, m. tout,** for all that, nevertheless; yet; in spite of everything; **m. sa fortune,** for all his wealth; **je l'ai fait m. moi,** I did it in spite of myself. **2.** *conj.phr.* (*a*) **m. que vous en ayez,** in spite of all you may say, do; (*b*) **m. que je le déteste je l'aiderai,** although I hate him I'll help him.

malhabile [malabil] *a.* unskilful; clumsy, awkward; untutored.

malhabilement [malabilmɑ̃] *adv.* clumsily.

malheur [malœr] *n.m.* **1.** (*a*) misfortune; calamity; (serious) accident; **un m. n'arrive, ne vient, jamais seul,** misfortunes never come singly; **ils ont eu des malheurs,** they have been through difficult times; **quel m.!** what a tragedy! **le m. c'est que . . .,** the unfortunate thing is that . . .; *Prov:* **à quelque chose m. est bon,** it's an ill wind that blows nobody any good; (*b*) *F:* **faire un m.,** to do something desperate, do s.o. a mischief; **s'il entre ici je fais un m.!** if he comes in here I'll go mad. **2.** misfortune, unhappiness; **enfant qui fait le m. de ses parents,** child who brings sorrow to his parents; *Prov:* **le m. des uns fait le bonheur des autres,** one man's joy is another man's sorrow; **c'est dans le m. qu'on connaît ses vrais amis,** a friend in need is a friend indeed. **3.** (*a*) bad luck; **oiseau de m.,** bird of ill omen; **par m.,** unfortunately; **quel m. que je ne l'aie pas su,** what a pity I didn't know (about it); **je le connais pour mon m.,** unfortunately, unluckily, for me I know him; **porter m. à qn,** to bring s.o. bad luck; **ceux qui ont le m. de le connaître,** those who are unfortunate, unlucky, enough to know him; **jouer de m.,** to be unlucky, out of luck; *F:* **ces lettres de m.!** these blasted letters! (*b*) **m. à eux!** woe betide them! (*c*) *int.* hell!

malheureusement [malœrøzmɑ̃] *adv.* unfortunately, unhappily, unluckily.

malheureux, -euse [malœrø, -øz] *a.* (*a*) unfortunate, unhappy, wretched (person, business, etc.); poor, badly off (person); sad, miserable (expression, etc.); *n.* **les m.,** the unfortunate, the poor, the needy; **le m.! la malheureuse!** poor man! poor woman! poor wretch! **m. comme les pierres,** wretched, utterly miserable; (*b*) unlucky; **candidat m.,** unsuccessful candidate; **m. au jeu,** unlucky at gambling; **c'est bien m. pour vous!** it's hard lines on you! **il est bien m. que** + *sub.*, it's very unfortunate, a great pity, that . . .; **avoir la main malheureuse,** to be unlucky; *F:* **le voilà enfin, ce n'est pas m.!** here he comes at last, and a good job too! (*c*) *F:* paltry, wretched; **une malheureuse pièce de cinq francs,** a miserable five-franc piece.

malhonnête [malɔnɛt] *a.* (*a*) dishonest; crooked; (*b*) (*of pers.*) rude, impolite; (*c*) *A:* indecent (gesture); improper.

malhonnêtement [malɔnɛtmɑ̃] *adv.* (*a*) dishonestly; (*b*) rudely, impolitely.

malhonnêteté [malɔnɛtte] *n.f.* **1.** dishonesty. **2.** *O:* (*a*) rudeness, impoliteness; (*b*) rude remark.

malice [malis] *n.f.* **1.** (*a*) malice, spitefulness; **ne pas entendre m. à qch.,** (i) to see no harm in sth.; (ii) to mean no harm by sth.; (*b*) mischief, mischievousness, roguishness, naughtiness. **2.** (*a*) *O:* smart remark; dig (at s.o.); (*b*) *O:* trick, prank; (*c*) **sac à m.,** conjuror's deep pocket; bag of tricks; **boîte à m.,** box of tricks.

malicieusement [malisjøzmɑ̃] *adv.* mischievously.

malicieux, -ieuse [malisjø, -jøz] *a.* **1.** *A:* malicious, spiteful. **2.** (*a*) mischievous; naughty; impish; (*b*) mocking (smile); joking, bantering (remark).

malien, -ienne [maljɛ̃, -jɛn] *a. & n. Geog:* Mali.

malignement [maliɲmɑ̃] *adv.* maliciously.

malignité [maliɲite] *n.f.* (*a*) malignancy, spite(fulness); (*b*) *Med:* malignancy (of cancer).

malin, -igne [malɛ̃, -iɲ] *a.* **1.** (*a*) *A:* malignant, evil(-minded), wicked; (*b*) **l'esprit m.,** *n.* **le m.,** the Evil One, the Devil; (*c*) malicious (pleasure, etc.); (*d*) *Med:* malignant (cancer, etc.). **2.** (*a*) shrewd, cunning, sharp; knowing (look); **il est plus m. que ça,** he knows better; **m. comme un singe,** as artful as a cartload of monkeys; **elle n'est pas bien maligne,** she's not very clever, all that bright; **bien m. qui le trouvera!** it will take a smart one to find that! **ce n'était pas très m.,** that wasn't very bright, was it? (*b*) *n.* **c'est un m.,** he has his wits about him; *F:* he knows what's what; **un petit m.,** a crafty one; a smart Alec; **c'est une petite maligne,** she's a sly one, a little imp; **faire le m.,** to show off, try to be smart; (*c*) *F:* **c'est pas bien m.,** that's not very difficult! that's simple!

Malines [malin] **1.** *Pr.n.f. Geog:* Malines, Mechlin. **2.** *n.f.* Mechlin lace.

malingre [malɛ̃gr̥] *a.* sickly, puny.

malintentionné [malɛ̃tɑ̃sjɔne] *a.* (*of pers.*) ill-intentioned, spiteful.

mal-jugé [malʒyʒe] *n.m.inv. Jur:* miscarriage of justice.

malle [mal] *n.f.* **1.** (*a*) trunk; box; **faire sa m., ses malles,** (i) to pack (one's trunk); (ii) to get ready to leave; (*b*) *Aut:* boot, *NAm:* trunk. **2.** (*a*) *A:* mail coach; (*b*) *A:* mail boat; (*c*) *Fr.C:* **mettre une lettre à la m.,** to post, *NAm:* mail, a letter.

malléabilité [maleabilite] *n.f.* malleability.

malléable [maleab̥l] *a.* malleable.

malle-poste [malpɔst] *n.f. A.Veh:* mail (coach); *pl. malles-poste(s).*

mallette [malɛt] *n.f.* small (suit)case; overnight bag; attaché case.

malmener [malməne] *v.tr.* (*conj. like* MENER) (*a*) to maltreat, ill-treat, ill-use (s.o.); to mishandle, misuse (sth.); to manhandle (s.o.); to give (s.o.) a rough time; (*b*) to abuse, *F:* slate (s.o.).

malnutrition [malnytrisjɔ̃] *n.f.* malnutrition.

malodorant [malɔdɔrɑ̃] *a.* malodorous, smelly, stinking.

malotru, -ue [malɔtry] *n.* boor; uncouth, vulgar, person.

malouin, -ine [malwɛ̃, -in] *a. & n. Geog:* (native, inhabitant) of Saint-Malo.

malpoli [malpɔli] *a. F:* impolite.

malpropre [malprɔpr̥] *a.* (*a*) dirty, grubby (hands, etc.); slovenly, untidy (appearance etc.); (*b*) slovenly, slapdash (work); (*c*) smutty (story, etc.); unsavoury, *NAm:* unsavoury (business).

malproprement [malprɔprəmɑ̃] *adv.* in a slovenly manner.
malpropreté [malprɔprəte] *n.f.* **1.** (*a*) dirtiness, grubbiness, slovenliness; (*b*) smuttiness (of story); unsavouriness, *NAm:* unsavoriness (of business). **2.** (*a*) dirty trick; (*b*) **dire des malpropretés,** to talk smut.
malsain [malsɛ̃] *a.* **1.** (*a*) unhealthy (person, climate); (*b*) *Nau:* dangerous (coast). **2.** unwholesome (food); pernicious (literature, etc.).
malséance [malseɑ̃s] *n.f.* unseemliness.
malséant [malseɑ̃] *a.* unseemly; unbecoming.
malsonnant [malsɔnɑ̃] *a.* offensive (to the ear).
malt [malt] *n.m. Brew:* malt.
maltage [maltaʒ] *n.m. Brew:* malting.
maltais, -aise [maltɛ, -ɛz] **1.** *a. & n. Geog:* Maltese. **2.** *n.m. Ling:* Maltese.
Malte [malt] *Pr.n.f. Geog:* Malta; *Mec.E: etc:* **croix de M.,** Maltese cross.
malter [malte] *v.tr. Brew:* to malt.
malterie [malt(ə)ri] *n.f.* **1.** malthouse. **2.** malting.
malthusianisme [maltyzjanism] *n.m.* Malthusianism.
malthusien, -ienne [maltyzjɛ̃, -jɛn] *a. & n.* Malthusian.
maltose [maltoz] *n.m. Ch: Ind:* maltose.
maltraiter [maltrete] *v.tr.* to maltreat, ill-treat, ill-use; to treat (s.o.) badly, handle (s.o.) roughly; to manhandle (s.o.).
malveillance [malvɛjɑ̃s] *n.f.* (*a*) malevolence, ill will; **avec m.,** malevolently, spitefully; (*b*) foul play.
malveillant [malvɛjɑ̃] *a.* (*a*) malevolent, malicious; (*b*) spiteful (remark).
malvenu [malvəny] *a.* (*a*) ill-advised; unwarranted; (*b*) malformed (tree, etc.).
malversation [malvɛrsasjɔ̃] *n.f.* malversation, embezzlement, malpractice.
malvoisie [malvwazi] *n.m.* (*also* **vin de M.**) malmsey (wine).
maman [mamɑ̃] *n.f.* mum(my).
mamelle [mamɛl] *n.f.* (*a*) *Anat:* mamma; **enfant à la m.,** child at the breast; (*b*) udder; teat, dug (of animal.
mamelon [mamlɔ̃] *n.m.* **1.** *Anat:* mamilla; nipple, teat (of woman). **2.** *Geog:* hillock, knoll. **3.** *Mec.E:* boss.
mamelonné [mamlɔne] *a.* mamillate(d); **plaine mamelonnée de collines,** plain covered with rounded hillocks.
mamel(o)uk [mamluk] *n.m. Hist:* mameluke.
m'amie, mamie¹ [mami] *n.f. F: A:* my dear.
mamie² *n.f. F:* grandmother, gran(ny), nan.
mamillaire [mamilɛr] *a. Anat:* mamillary.
mammaire [mamɛr] *a. Anat:* mammary.
mammifère [mamifɛr] **1.** *a.* mammalian. **2.** *n.m.* mammal.
mammouth [mamut] *n.m.* mammoth.
mamours [mamur] *n.m.pl. F:* **faire des m. à qn,** to caress, fondle, s.o.
manade [manad] *n.f.* (*S. of Fr., esp. Camargue*) herd of cattle, horses.
management [manaʒmɛnt] *n.m. Com: etc:* management.
manager [manadʒɛr] *n.m. Ind: Cin: Sp: etc:* manager.
manant [manɑ̃] *n.m.* **1.** *Hist:* peasant, villager. **2.** (*a*) *A:* yokel; (*b*) *Lit:* churl, boor; lout.
manceau, -elle [mɑ̃so, -ɛl] *a. & n. Geog:* (native, inhabitant) of Le Mans.
manche¹ [mɑ̃ʃ] *n.f.* **1.** (*a*) sleeve; **être en manches de chemise,** to be in one's shirtsleeves; **manches à gigot,** leg-of-mutton sleeves; **robe sans manches,** sleeveless dress; **relever, retrousser, ses manches,** to roll up one's sleeves; **avoir qn dans sa m.,** to have s.o. in one's pocket; **se faire tirer par la m.,** to be dragged into doing sth.; *F:* **ça, c'est une autre paire de manches,** that's quite another matter; *F:* **faire la m.,** to have a collection, go round with the hat; (*b*) *Tchn:* **m. à eau, d'arrosage,** hose (pipe); **m. à incendie,** fire hose; **m. à air,** (i) *Nau:* (*also* **m. à vent**), windsail, ventilator; (ii) *Av:* wind sock; (*c*) *Aer:* neck (of balloon). **2.** *Sp: etc:* (i) heat; (ii) round; (iii) *Ten:* set; (iv) *Cards:* hand (played); (single) game; **nous sommes m. à m.,** we're even, neck and neck. **3.** *Geog:* **la M.,** the English Channel; **les Îles de la M.,** the Channel Islands.
manche² *n.m.* **1.** (*a*) handle (of hammer, saucepan, etc.); haft (of dagger, etc.); shaft (of golf club); stock (of whip); helve (of axe, etc.); neck (of violin, etc.); **m. de, à, balai,** broomstick; **couteau à m. d'ivoire,** ivory-handled knife; **m. à gigot,** leg-of-mutton holder (for carving); **m. d'un gigot,** knuckle (of a leg of lamb); **jeter le m. après la cognée,** to give up in despair, throw in one's hand; *F:* **être du côté du m.,** to be on the strongest, the winning, side; **branler dans le m.,** to be in a shaky, sticky, position; (*b*) *Av:* **m. (à balai),** control column, (joy)stick; (*c*) *F:* idiot, clot, nit; **s'y prendre comme un m.,** to go about things in an idiotic, a ham-handed, way. **2.** *Moll:* **m. de couteau,** razor (clam, shell).
Manche³ (la) *Pr.n.f. Geog:* La Mancha (Spain).
mancheron¹ [mɑ̃ʃrɔ̃] *n.m. Dressm:* (*a*) short sleeve; (*b*) upper part of sleeve.
mancheron² *n.m.* handle, stilt (of plough, *NAm:* plow).
manchette [mɑ̃ʃɛt] *n.f.* **1.** (*a*) cuff; wristband; **m. mousquetaire,** double cuff, turn-back cuff (of shirt); (*b*) gauntlet (of glove); (*c*) oversleeve, cuff protector; (*d*) *Wr:* forearm smash. **2.** headline (of newspaper).
manchon [mɑ̃ʃɔ̃] *n.m.* **1.** muff. **2.** *Tchn:* (*a*) sleeve (for axle, etc.); bush(ing) (of bearing, etc.); socket (for pivot, etc.); **m. d'accouplement,** coupling sleeve; (*b*) *Aut: etc:* **m. d'embrayage,** clutch; (*c*) casing; **m. de refroidissement,** cooling jacket (of machine gun, etc.); *Nau:* **m. d'écubier,** hawse pipe; (*d*) **m. à incandescence,** incandescent (gas) mantle.
manchot, -ote [mɑ̃ʃo, -ɔt] **1.** *a. & n.* one-armed, one-handed (person); *F:* **il n'est pas m.,** (i) he's clever with his hands; (ii) he's all there. **2.** *n.m. Orn:* penguin.
mandant [mɑ̃dɑ̃] *n.m.* **1.** *Jur:* principal (in transaction). **2.** *pl. Pol:* **le député et ses mandants,** the member and his constituents.
mandarin [mɑ̃darɛ̃] *n.m.* (*a*) *Chinese Hist:* mandarin; (*b*) mandarin; intellectual; *Pej:* pedant; (*c*) *Orn:* **(canard) m.,** mandarin duck.
mandarinat [mɑ̃darina] *n.m.* (*a*) *Chinese Hist:* mandarinate; (*b*) *Pej:* **le m.,** the intelligentsia, the pedants.
mandarine [mɑ̃darin] **1.** *n.f. Hort:* mandarin(e) (orange); tangerine. **2.** *a.inv.* tangerine(-coloured, *NAm:* -colored).
mandarinier [mɑ̃darinje] *n.m. Hort:* mandarin(e) (orange) tree; tangerine tree.
mandat [mɑ̃da] *n.m.* **1.** (*a*) mandate; commission; **territoires sous m.,** mandated territories; (*b*) **m. de député,** member's (electoral) mandate; **sans m.,** unauthorized; (*c*) *Jur:* power of attorney; proxy. **2.** warrant; (*a*) *Jur:* **m. de perquisition,** search warrant; **m. d'arrêt,** warrant for arrest; **m. de comparution,** summons (to appear); *esp. NAm:* subpoena; **décerner, lancer, un m.,** to issue a warrant; **m. de dépôt,** committal (of prisoner); (*b*) *Fin:* **m. du Trésor,** Treasury warrant. **3.** order (to pay); money order; draft; **m.(-poste), m. postal** = postal order; **m. international,** international money order.
mandataire [mɑ̃datɛr] *n.* **1.** mandatory (of electors,

etc.). **2.** proxy (at meeting); representative. **3.** *Jur:* authorized agent; attorney. **4.** trustee.
mandat-carte [mɑ̃dakart] *n.m. Post:* = postal order, money order (in postcard form); *pl. mandats-cartes.*
mandater [mɑ̃date] *v.tr.* **1.** to elect, send, commission (representative, etc.); to give a mandate to (a member of parliament). **2. m. des frais,** to pay expenses by money order, by draft.
mandat-lettre [mɑ̃dalɛtr̥] *n.m. Post:* = postal order, money order (in lettercard form); *pl. mandats-lettres.*
mandat-poste [mɑ̃dapɔst] *n.m. Post:* = postal order, money order; *pl. mandats-poste.*
mandchou, -oue [mɑ̃dʃu] **1.** *a. & n. Ethn:* Manchu, Manchurian. **2.** *n.m. Ling:* Manchu.
Mandchourie [mɑ̃tʃuri] *Pr.n.f. Geog:* Manchuria.
mandement [mɑ̃dmɑ̃] *n.m.* **1.** *A:* mandate, order. **2.** *Ecc:* pastoral (letter).
mander [mɑ̃de] *v.tr.* **1.** *A:* (*a*) **m. une nouvelle à qn,** to send news (by letter) to s.o.; (*b*) *Journ:* **on mande de . . .,** it is reported from . . .. **2.** *A:* **m. à qn de faire qch.,** to send word to s.o., instruct s.o., to do sth. **3.** *O: & Lit:* to summon (s.o. to attend); to send for (subordinate).
mandibule [mɑ̃dibyl] *n.f. Z:* mandible.
mandoline [mɑ̃dɔlin] *n.f. Mus: Dom.Ec:* mandolin(e).
mandragore [mɑ̃dragɔr] *n.f. Bot:* mandrake.
mandrill [mɑ̃dril] *n.m. Z:* mandrill.
mandrin [mɑ̃drɛ̃] *n.m.* **1.** *Mec.E:* (*a*) mandrel (of lathe); (*b*) chuck (of lathe); (*c*) pad (of brace). **2.** *Metalw:* (*a*) mandrel, swage; (*b*) punch; (*riveting*) drift.
manécanterie [manekɑ̃tri] *n.f.* choir school.
manège [manɛʒ] *n.m.* **1.** (*a*) horsemanship, riding; **maître de m.,** riding instructor, master; (*b*) training, breaking (in) (of a horse); (*c*) **(salle de) m.,** riding school; **m. découvert,** open-air riding school; (*d*) **m. (de chevaux de bois),** merry-go-round, roundabout. **2.** stratagem, trick; **j'observais leur m.,** I was watching their little game.
mânes [mɑn] *n.m.pl. Rom.Ant:* manes, shades, spirits (of the departed).
manette [manɛt] *n.f.* (*a*) handle, hand lever; *Aut:* **m. des gaz,** throttle lever; (*b*) switch; key; (*c*) *Nau:* spoke (of the wheel).
manganate [mɑ̃ganat] *n.m. Ch:* manganate.
manganèse [mɑ̃ganɛz] *n.m. Ch:* manganese.
manganite [mɑ̃ganit] *n.m. Ch:* manganite.
mangeable [mɑ̃ʒabl̥] *a.* edible, eatable.
mangeaille [mɑ̃ʒɑj] *n.f.* **1.** *A:* feed (for fowls, etc.). **2.** *F:* food, grub.
mangeoire [mɑ̃ʒwar] *n.f.* manger; (feeding) trough.
manger¹ [mɑ̃ʒe] *v.tr.* **(je mangeai(s); n. mangeons)** (*a*) to eat; **il a tout mangé,** he's eaten everything (up); **il mange de tout,** he'll eat anything; **mange ta soupe,** drink your soup (up); **m. dans une assiette,** to eat off a plate; **le fromage se mange avec du pain,** cheese is eaten with bread; **bon à m.,** good to eat; **salle à m.,** dining room; **m. au restaurant,** to eat out, go out for a meal; **donner à m. à qn,** to give s.o. sth. to eat; **donner à m. aux poules,** to feed the chickens; **m. comme quatre, comme un ogre,** to eat like a horse; **m. à sa faim,** to eat one's fill; **nous avons bien mangé,** we had a very good meal; **m. son pain blanc le premier,** to start with the easiest part of a job; **m. du curé,** to be violently anticlerical; **on ne vous mangera pas,** they won't eat you; (*b*) **la rouille mange l'acier,** rust eats into steel; **mangé par les, aux, mites,** motheaten; **chaudière qui mange beaucoup de charbon,** boiler that is very heavy on coal; **m. ses mots,** to mumble; *P:* **m. le morceau,** (i) to own up (to a crime); (ii) to let out a secret; (*c*) **m. son argent,** to squander, run through, one's money.
manger² *n.m.* food; (*of medicine*) **à prendre après m.,** to be taken after meals.
mange-tout [mɑ̃ʒtu] *a.inv. & n.m.inv. Hort:* (*a*) **(pois) m.-t.,** sugar pea; (*b*) **(haricot) m.-t.,** French bean, *NAm:* string bean.
mangeur, -euse [mɑ̃ʒœr, -øz] *n.* eater; **petit m.,** small eater; **gros m., grand m.,** hearty eater; **m. (d'argent),** spendthrift; **m. de livres,** bookworm.
manglier [mɑ̃glije] *n.m. Bot:* mangrove (tree).
mangouste [mɑ̃gust] *n.f. Z:* mongoose.
mangue [mɑ̃g] *n.f. Bot:* mango (fruit).
manguier [mɑ̃gje] *n.m. Bot:* mango (tree).
maniabilité [manjabilite] *n.f.* handiness (of tool, etc.); manoeuvrability, *NAm:* maneuverability (of aircraft, etc.); handling ability (of vehicle, etc.).
maniable [manjabl̥] *a.* manageable; easy to handle, to control; handy (tool); **caractère m.,** tractable nature; **peu m.,** awkward.
maniaque [manjak] *a. & n.* **1.** maniac; raving lunatic. **2.** finicky, faddy (person); *n.* fusspot, crank.
maniaquerie [manjakri] *n.f.* fussiness, faddiness.
manie [mani] *n.f.* (*a*) *Med: A:* mental derangement; (*b*) *Psy:* mania, obsession; **m. de la persécution,** persecution mania; (*c*) mania; craze; (inveterate) habit; idiosyncrasy; **avoir la m. de la propreté,** to be obsessed with cleanliness; **il a ses petites manies,** he has his little ways, his little fads.
maniement [manimɑ̃] *n.m.* handling (of tools, business, etc.); conduct (of affairs); **le m. des armes,** the handling of arms; *Mil:* **m. d'armes,** drill; arms' manual.
manier [manje] *v.tr.* (*impf. & pr.sub.* **n. maniions, v. maniiez) 1.** (*a*) *A:* to feel (cloth, etc.); (*b*) to handle (tool, rope, etc.). **2.** to handle, manage, control (horse, business, etc.); **m. les avirons,** to ply, pull, the oars; **savoir m. la parole,** to know how to handle words.
manière [manjɛr] *n.f.* **1.** (*a*) manner, way; **c'est sa m. d'être,** that's the way he is; **laissez-moi faire à ma m.,** let me do it my own way; **m. de voir, de penser,** way of looking at things; **s'y prendre de la bonne m.,** to set about it the right way; **de cette m.,** in this way; **tancer qn de la belle m.,** to give s.o. a good dressing down; **de m. ou d'autre, d'une m. ou d'une autre,** somehow or other, by some means or other; **en m. de consolation,** by way of consolation; **en quelque m.,** in a way; **d'une m. générale,** generally speaking; **en aucune m.,** under no circumstances; **de toute m.,** in any case; (*b*) *Art: Lit:* **tableau à la m. de Degas,** painting after the manner of Degas. **2.** *pl.* manners; **avoir de bonnes, de belles, manières,** to be well mannered; **avoir de mauvaises manières,** to be ill mannered; **faire des manières,** (i) to be affected; (ii) to pretend to be reluctant.
maniéré [manjere] *a.* **1.** affected (person, etc.). **2.** *Art: Lit:* mannered (style).
maniérisme [manjerism] *n.m.* **1.** *Art: Lit:* mannerism. **2.** affectation.
manieur, -euse [manjœr, -øz] *n.* handler, manager, controller (of men, business, etc.); **m. d'argent,** financier.
manif [manif] *n.f. F:* (= *manifestation*) demo.
manifestant, -ante [manifɛstɑ̃, -ɑ̃t] *n.* demonstrator.
manifestation [manifɛstasjɔ̃] *n.f.* (*a*) manifestation (of feeling, etc.); (*b*) (political) demonstration; (*c*) *Theol:* revelation; (*d*) **m. sportive,** sporting event.
manifeste¹ [manifɛst] *a.* **1.** manifest, evident, patent, obvious (truth, etc.); palpable (error). **2.** *Jur: O:* overt (act).

manifeste² *n.m.* **1.** manifesto, proclamation. **2.** *Nau: Av:* manifest.
manifestement [manifɛstəmɑ̃] *adv.* manifestly, obviously, patently; palpably.
manifester [manifɛste] **1.** *v.tr.* to reveal; to show, exhibit (confusion); **m. sa volonté,** make one's wishes clear. **2.** *v.i.* to demonstrate. **3. se m.,** to appear; **leur impatience se manifestait par de bruyantes interruptions,** their impatience showed itself in loud interruptions.
manifold [manifɔld] *n.m.* duplicate book.
manigance [manigɑ̃s] *n.f.* intrigue; *pl.* fiddling, wire-pulling; underhand practices.
manigancer [manigɑ̃se] *v.tr.* **(je manigançai(s); n. manigançons),** to scheme, to plot; **qu'est-ce qu'ils manigancent?** what's their (little) game?
Manille¹ [manij] **1.** *Pr.n. Geog:* Manilla. **2.** *n.m.* (*a*) Manil(l)a cheroot; (*b*) Manil(l)a straw hat.
manille² *n.f. Cards:* manille.
manille³ *n.f.* shackle (of prisoner, chain).
manillon [manijɔ̃] *n.m. Cards:* ace (at manille).
manioc [manjɔk] *n.m. Bot:* manioc, cassava.
manipulateur, -trice [manipylatœr, -tris] *n.* **1.** (*a*) manipulator; operator; handler (of money, goods, etc.); **m. de laboratoire,** laboratory technician, assistant; (*b*) conjuror. **2.** *n.m.* (*a*) **m. à distance,** remote (control) manipulator; (*b*) *Tg:* (sending) key.
manipulation [manipylasjɔ̃] *n.f.* **1.** (*a*) manipulation; handling; (*b*) *Med:* manipulation. **2.** *Sch: pl.* practical work (*esp.* in science). **3.** conjuring.
manipuler [manipyle] *v.tr.* **1.** to manipulate; to handle, operate (apparatus, etc.); *Tg:* to operate. **2.** to rig (election); to manoeuvre, *NAm:* maneuver (sth.).
manitou [manitu] *n.m.* **1.** manitou (of American Indians). **2.** *F:* **(grand) m.,** big boss, big shot.
manivelle [manivɛl] *n.f. Mec.E:* **1.** (*a*) crank; (*b*) pedal crank (of bicycle). **2.** crank (handle); *Aut:* starting handle.
manne¹ [man] *n.f.* **1.** *B:* manna. **2.** *Pharm:* **m. du frêne,** manna.
manne² *n.f.* basket, hamper; crate; (fishwife's) creel.
mannequin¹ [mankɛ̃] *n.m.* small hamper; wicker basket.
mannequin² *n.m.* **1.** (anatomical) manikin. **2.** *Dressm:* dummy, model; dress stand. **3.** (*pers*) mannequin; model.
manœuvrabilité [manœvrabilite] *n.f.* manoeuvrability, *NAm:* maneuverability.
manœuvrable [manœvrabl̩] *a.* manoeuvrable, *NAm:* maneuverable; manageable.
manœuvre [manœvr̩] **1.** *n.f.* (*a*) working, managing, driving (of machine, etc.); manoeuvring, *NAm:* maneuvering (of vehicle); **fausse m.,** false manoeuvre, *NAm:* maneuver; false move; (*b*) *Nau:* handling, manoeuvring (of ship); seamanship; **maître de m.,** boatswain; (*c*) *Mil: etc:* (i) drill, exercise; (ii) tactical exercise, manoeuvre; **grandes manœuvres,** army manoeuvres, exercises; **champ, terrain, de manœuvres,** drill ground, parade ground; (*d*) *Mil: etc:* movement, action; **m. d'encerclement,** encircling movement; **pivot de m.,** pivot of manoeuvre; (*e*) *Rail:* shunting, marshalling (of trains); **voie de m.,** shunting track, *NAm:* switching track; (*f*) scheme, manoeuvre, intrigue; **m. électorale,** vote-catching manoeuvre; (*g*) *pl.* scheming; **manœuvres frauduleuses,** swindling. **2.** *n.f. Nau:* rope; **manœuvres dormantes,** standing rigging; **manœuvres courantes,** running rigging. **3.** *n.m.* unskilled worker; **travail de m.,** manual labour, *NAm:* labor; unskilled work.
manœuvrer [manœvre] **1.** *v.tr.* (*a*) to work, operate (machine, etc.); **appareil facile à m.,** apparatus that works easily; (*b*) to manoeuvre, *NAm:* maneuver, handle (vehicle); (*c*) *Rail:* to shunt; to marshal (trucks); (*d*) *Fish:* to play (fish). **2.** *v.i.* (*a*) to manoeuvre; (*b*) to contrive, manoeuvre, scheme.
manœuvrier, -ière [manœvrije, -ijɛr] *n.* (*a*) expert (soldier, seaman, etc.); (*b*) clever politician; manoeuvrer, *NAm:* maneuverer.
manoir [manwar] *n.m.* (*a*) (feudal) manor; (*b*) manor house, country house.
manomètre [manɔmɛtr̩] *n.m.* manometer, pressure gauge.
manométrique [manɔmetrik] *a. Ph:* manometric(al); **hauteur m.,** head of water.
manquant, -ante [mɑ̃kɑ̃, -ɑ̃t] **1.** *a.* missing, absent. **2.** *n.* absentee, defaulter; **les manquants,** (i) those absent; (ii) the missing. **3.** *n.m. Com:* **les manquants,** (the) shortages; **éviter des manquants dans la marchandise,** to prevent short delivery.
manque [mɑ̃k] *n.m.* (*a*) lack; deficiency; shortage; shortfall; **m. d'oxygène,** lack of oxygen; **m. de cœur,** heartlessness; **m. de parole,** breach of faith; breaking one's word; **m. de crédit,** credibility gap; **m. de poids,** short weight; **dix kilos de m.,** ten kilos short; **par m. de,** through lack of (foresight, etc.); **m. de chance!** bad luck (for you, him)! *Med:* **(crise de) m.,** withdrawal symptoms; (*b*) *usu.pl.* shortcomings.
manqué [mɑ̃ke] *a.* **1.** missed (opportunity, etc.); unsuccessful, abortive (attempt, etc.); **coup m.,** (i) miss; (ii) failure; **vie manquée,** wasted life; **vêtement m.,** spoilt garment. **2. c'est un médecin m.,** he ought to have been a doctor; *F:* **c'est un garçon m.,** she's a real tomboy.
manquement [mɑ̃kmɑ̃] *n.m.* failure, shortcoming, omission, lapse; **m. à une règle,** violation of a rule; **m. à la discipline,** breach, infraction, of discipline; **m. au devoir,** breach, dereliction, of duty; **m. à l'appel,** failure to answer one's name; absence from rollcall.
manquer [mɑ̃ke] **I.** *v.i.* **1.** (*a*) **m. de qch.,** to lack, be short of, sth.; **m. de sucre,** to be out, to have run short, of sugar; **m. de politesse,** to be impolite; **m. de courage,** to lack courage; **ne m. de rien,** to have all that one needs; (*b*) **m. de faire qch.,** narrowly to miss doing sth.; **il a manqué de tomber,** he nearly, almost, fell; (*c*) *impers.* **il s'en manque de beaucoup,** far from it. **2.** (*a*) to be lacking, in short supply; **les vivres commencent à m.,** provisions are beginning to run short; **les chaussures qui manquent,** the missing shoes; **les mots me manquent pour exprimer . . .,** I'm at a loss for words to express . . .; **la place me manque,** I haven't any room (left); *impers.* **il ne manque pas de candidats,** there's no lack, no shortage, of candidates; **il ne manquait plus que cela!** that's all I, he, etc., needed; that's the last straw! **il manque quelques pages,** there are a few pages missing; **il lui manque un bras,** he has lost an arm; **il me manque dix francs,** I'm ten francs short; (*b*) to give way; **prenez garde que le pied ne vous manque,** be careful not to miss your footing; *Lit:* **le cœur lui manqua,** his heart failed him; (*c*) (*of pers.*) to be absent, missing; **m. à l'appel,** to be absent from rollcall; **m. à un rendez-vous,** fail to keep an appointment; **m. à qn,** to be missed by s.o.; **sa mère, sa maison, lui manque,** he's missing his mother, his house; (*d*) to fall short; **m. à son devoir,** to fail in one's duty; **m. à sa parole,** to break one's word; **m. à la consigne,** to disregard orders; **m. à une règle,** to violate a rule; **m. à qn,** (i) to fail in one's duty to s.o.; (ii) to be disrespectful to s.o.; **le projet, le coup, a manqué,** the plan, the attempt, failed; (*e*) **ne manquez pas de nous écrire,** don't forget to, be sure to, write to us; **personne ne peut m. d'avoir observé . . .,** no one can fail to have noticed . . .; **cela ne pouvait m. d'arriver,** it was bound to happen. **II.** *v.tr.* **1.** (*a*) to miss (target, train,

etc.); **j'ai manqué le train de trois minutes,** I missed the train by three minutes; **m. une occasion,** to lose, miss, an opportunity; **m. son coup,** (i) to miss one's aim, one's stroke, one's shot; (ii) to make an abortive attempt; to fail; **il l'a manqué belle,** he had a narrow escape, a close shave; *F:* **il n'en manque pas une,** he's always putting his foot in it; (*b*) to be absent from, fail to attend, miss (meeting, etc.). **2. m. sa vie,** to make a mess of one's life; **m. un tableau,** to spoil a picture.

mansarde [mɑ̃sard] *n.f. Arch:* **1. (toit, comble, en) m.,** mansard roof. **2.** attic.

mansardé [mɑ̃sarde] *a.* mansard-roofed; **chambre mansardée,** attic; room with sloping ceiling.

mante [mɑ̃t] *n.f. Ent:* mantis; **m. religieuse,** praying mantis.

manteau, -eaux [mɑ̃to] *n.m.* **1.** (*a*) (i) cloak; (ii) (woman's) coat; **m. de pluie,** raincoat; **m. du soir,** evening coat, cloak, wrap; **m. de neige,** mantle, blanket, of snow; **sous le m. de la nuit,** under (the) cover of darkness; **sous le m. de la religion,** under the cloak of religion; (*b*) mantle (of mollusc). **2.** (*a*) **m. (de cheminée),** mantel(piece); (*b*) *Th:* **m. d'Arlequin,** proscenium arch.

mantelé [mɑ̃tle] *a. Orn:* hooded (crow).

mantille [mɑ̃tij] *n.f. Cost:* mantilla.

manucure [manykyr] *n.* manicurist.

manucuré [manykyre] *a.* manicured.

manuel, -elle [manɥɛl] **1.** (*a*) *a.* manual (work, etc.); (*b*) *n.* manual worker. **2.** *n.m.* manual, handbook.

manufacture [manyfaktyr] *n.f.* **1.** *A:* manufacture. **2.** factory; **m. de porcelaine de Sèvres,** the Sèvres porcelain factory.

manufacturer [manyfaktyre] *v.tr.* to manufacture.

manufacturier, -ière [manyfaktyrje, -jɛr] *a.* manufacturing (town, etc.).

manuscrit [manyskri] *a.* & *n.m.* manuscript; **lettre manuscrite,** handwritten letter; **m. (dactylographié),** typescript.

manutention [manytɑ̃sjɔ̃] *n.f.* (*a*) handling (of goods); (*b*) storehouse; store(s).

manutentionnaire [manytɑ̃sjɔnɛr] *n.* warehouseman; storekeeper; packer.

manutentionner [manytɑ̃sjɔne] *v.tr.* to handle (goods).

maoïsme [maɔism] *n.m. Pol:* Maoism.

maoïste [maɔist] *a.* & *n. Pol:* Maoist.

maori, -ie [maɔri] **1.** *a.* & *n. Ethn:* Maori. **2.** *n.m. Ling:* Maori.

maous, maousse [maus] *a. P:* huge, enormous, tremendous; whacking great.

mappemonde [mapmɔ̃d] *n.f.* map of the world in two hemispheres; **m. céleste,** planisphere.

maquereau¹, -eaux [makro] *n.m. Ich:* mackerel.

maquereau², -elle, -eaux, -elles [makro, -ɛl] *n. P:* pimp, procurer; *f.* madam.

maquette [makɛt] *n.f.* (*a*) *Art:* model, (small) figure; (*b*) *Th:* model (of a stage setting); (*c*) *Publ:* (i) dummy (of book); (ii) paste-up (of page); (*d*) *Ind:* mock-up; (*e*) scale model; **m. (pour l'enseignement),** demonstration model.

maquettiste [maketist] *n.* model maker.

maquignon [makiɲɔ̃] *n.m.* **1.** horse trader, dealer. **2.** dishonest, crooked, dealer.

maquignonnage [makiɲɔnaʒ] *n.m.* **1.** horse trading, dealing. **2.** sharp practice.

maquignonner [makiɲɔne] *v.tr.* **1.** to fake up (horse). **2.** to conduct (business, etc.) dishonestly; **affaire maquignonnée,** put-up job.

maquillage [makijaʒ] *n.m.* **1.** (*a*) making up (of face); (*b*) disguising (of stolen car); (*c*) forging (of documents); faking (of pictures, etc.); fiddling (of accounts). **2.** *Toil:* makeup.

maquiller [makije] **1.** *v.tr.* (*a*) to make up (s.o., face); (*b*) to disguise (stolen car); (*c*) to forge (documents); to fake (pictures, etc.); to falsify, fiddle (accounts). **2. se m.,** to make (one's face) up.

maquilleur, -euse [makijœr, -øz] *n. Th: etc:* makeup assistant; makeup man, girl.

maquis [maki] *n.m.* (*a*) *Geog:* maquis; (*b*) (*1939–45 war*) maquis, underground forces; **prendre le m.,** to go underground, take to the maquis; (*c*) **le m. de la procédure,** the jungle of legal procedure.

maquisard [makizar] *n.m.* (*1939–45 war*) man of the maquis, maquisard.

marabout [marabu] *n.m.* **1.** marabout (priest, shrine). **2.** *A:* (round-bodied) jug. **3.** (*a*) *Orn:* marabou (stork); (*b*) marabou (feathers).

maraîchage [marɛʃaʒ] *n.m.* market gardening, *NAm:* truck farming.

maraîcher, -aîchère [marɛʃe, -ɛʃɛr] **1.** *a.* **industrie maraîchère,** market gardening, *NAm:* truck farming; **produits maraîchers,** market garden produce, *NAm:* truck. **2.** *n.* market gardener, *NAm:* truck farmer.

marais [marɛ] *n.m.* marsh(land); bog, fen; swamp; **m. tourbeux,** peat bog; **gaz des m.,** marsh gas; **m. salant,** saltmarsh.

marasme [marasm] *n.m.* (*a*) *Med:* marasmus; wasting; (*b*) stagnation, slackness, slump (in business).

marasquin [maraskɛ̃] *n.m.* maraschino (liqueur).

marathon [maratɔ̃] *n.m. Sp: etc:* marathon (race); **m. de danse,** dance marathon.

marâtre [marɑtr̥] *n.f.* (unnatural, cruel) stepmother, mother.

maraud, -aude¹ [maro, -od] *n. A:* villain, rascal, rogue; *f.* hussy.

maraudage [marodaʒ] *n.m.* = MARAUDE² (*a*), (*b*).

maraude² [marod] *n.f.* (*a*) marauding, plundering; (*b*) pilfering, petty thieving (from orchards, etc.); (*c*) **taxi en m.,** cruising taxi.

marauder [marode] *v.i.* (*a*) to maraud, plunder; (*b*) to thieve (from orchards, etc.); (*c*) (*of taxi*) to cruise (in search of fares).

maraudeur, -euse [marodœr, -øz] *n.* (*a*) marauder, plunderer; (*b*) petty thief; (*c*) *a.* **taxi m.,** cruising taxi; **loup m.,** prowling wolf.

marbre [marbr̥] *n.m.* **1.** (*a*) marble; **avoir un cœur de m.,** to have a heart of stone; (*b*) marble (statue, etc.); (*c*) marble top (of mantelpiece, etc.). **2.** *Bookb:* marbling. **3.** *Mec.E:* surface plate, face plate. **4.** *Typ:* (*a*) imposing stone; (*b*) bed (of press), press stone; **livre sur le m.,** book in type, at press.

marbré [marbre] *a.* marbled; mottled; veined.

marbrer [marbre] *v.tr. Bookb: etc:* to marble; to mottle, to vein; **le froid lui avait marbré la peau,** his skin was mottled, blotchy, from the cold.

marbrerie [marbrəri] *n.f.* **1.** (*a*) marble working, cutting; (*b*) marble work. **2.** marble mason's yard.

marbrier, -ière [marbrije, -ijɛr] **1.** *a.* marble (industry, etc.). **2.** *n.m.* monumental mason. **3.** *n.f.* **marbrière,** marble quarry.

marbrure [marbryr] *n.f.* **1.** marbling, veining. **2.** (*a*) mottling (of the skin); (*b*) mark, blotch (of bruise, etc.).

marc¹ [mar] *n.m.* (*a*) *A.Meas:* mark; (*b*) *Jur:* **au m. le franc,** pro rata.

marc² *n.m.* **1.** (*a*) marc (of grapes, olives, etc.); (*b*) **(eau de vie de) m.,** brandy (distilled from marc); marc (brandy). **2. m. de café, de thé,** coffee grounds, (used) tealeaves.

marcassin [markasɛ̃] *n.m. Z:* young wild boar.

marcassite [markasit] *n.f. Miner:* marcasite.

marchand, -ande [marʃɑ̃, -ɑ̃d] **1.** *n.* merchant; trader; shopkeeper; tradesman, tradeswoman; **m. au**

détail, retailer; **m. en gros,** wholesaler; **m. de chevaux, de tableaux,** horse dealer, picture dealer; **m. de légumes,** greengrocer; **m. de fromage,** cheesemonger; **m. de poisson,** fishmonger; **m. de tabac,** tobacconist; **m. ambulant,** hawker, travelling salesman; **m. des quatre saisons,** costermonger; barrow boy. **2.** *a.* (*a*) commercial; **denrées marchandes,** saleable, marketable, goods; **prix m.,** market price, trade price; (*b*) **marine marchande,** merchant navy.

marchandage [marʃɑ̃daʒ] *n.m.* bargaining, haggling.

marchander [marʃɑ̃de] *v.tr.* (*a*) **m. qch. avec qn,** to haggle, bargain, with s.o. over sth.; **il aime m.,** he loves haggling; (*b*) **ne pas m. sa peine,** to make every effort, spare no efforts (to do sth.).

marchandeur, -euse [marʃɑ̃dœr, -øz] *n.* haggler.

marchandise [marʃɑ̃diz] *n.f.* merchandise, goods, wares; commodity; *Nau:* cargo; **train de marchandises,** goods train, freight train; **vanter, étaler, faire valoir, sa m.,** (i) to boost one's wares; (ii) to make the most of oneself.

marchant [marʃɑ̃] *a.* **aile marchante,** (i) *Mil:* outer flank (of wheeling movement); (ii) (*of political group, etc.*) leading wing.

marche¹ [marʃ] *n.f.* march(es), border country.

marche² *n.f.* **1.** (*a*) (i) step, stair; (ii) tread (of step); **la m. du bas,** the bottom stair, step; **les marches du trône,** the steps of the throne; (*b*) treadle (of loom, etc.); pedal (of organ, etc.). **2.** (*a*) walk, walking; **aimer la m.,** to be fond of walking; **chaussures de m.,** walking shoes; **avoir une m. gracieuse,** to have a graceful walk; **ralentir sa m.,** to slacken one's pace; **continuer sa m.,** to walk on; **se mettre en m.,** to set out, start off, move off; **deux heures de m.,** two hours' walk(ing); (*b*) *Mil: etc:* march; **colonne en m.,** column on the march; **ordres de m.,** marching orders; **ouvrir la m.,** to lead the way; **fermer la m.,** to bring up the rear; **gagner une m. sur l'ennemi,** to steal a march on the enemy; (*c*) *Mus:* **m. nuptiale, funèbre,** wedding, funeral, march. **3.** (*a*) running (of trains, etc.); sailing (of ships); **mettre en m. un service,** to start, run, a service; (*b*) **en m.,** in motion, moving; **m. arrière,** (i) *Mec: Cin:* reverse motion; (ii) reversing, backing (of car, etc.); **entrer dans le garage en m. arrière,** to back, reverse, into the garage; **navire en m.,** ship under way. **4.** (*a*) running, working (of machine, etc.); **être en m.,** (i) (*of machine*) to be running; (ii) (*of furnace*) to be in blast; **(re)mettre une machine en m.,** to (re)start an engine; **en état de m.,** in working order; (*of machine*) **se mettre en m.,** to start; (*b*) course (of stars, events, etc.); march (of time); progress (of illness, etc.); **m. à suivre,** course to be followed; procedure; (*c*) *Mus:* **m. d'harmonie,** harmonic progression.

marché [marʃe] *n.m.* **1.** (*a*) dealing, buying; **m. noir,** black market; **faire son m.,** to do one's shopping; (*b*) deal, bargain, contract; **faire, conclure, un m.,** to strike a bargain; **m. de fourniture,** supply contract; **c'est m. fait,** it's a deal; *F:* done! **mettre à qn le m. en main,** to invite s.o. to take it or leave it; **par-dessus le m.,** into the bargain; *Fin:* **m. au comptant,** cash transaction; (*c*) **acheter, vendre, qch. (à) bon m.,** to buy, sell, sth. cheaply, cheap; **à meilleur m.,** more cheaply, cheaper; **articles bon m.,** low-priced, cheap, goods; bargains; **faire bon m. de qch.,** not to think much of sth.; **vous vous en êtes tiré à bon m.,** you got off lightly. **2.** market; (*a*) **jour de m.,** market day; **m. aux fleurs, à la volaille,** flower, poultry, market; **m. en plein vent,** openair market; **m. couvert,** covered market; **m. aux puces,** junk, flea, market; **lancer un article sur le m.,** to market an article; **article qui n'a pas de m.,** article for which there is no market, no sale; **étude de m.,** market research; *Pol.Ec:* **m. commun,** common market; (*b*) (state of the) market; **m. ferme,** steady, strong, firm, market.

marchepied [marʃəpje] *n.m.* (*a*) steps (of altar, etc.); step (of train, etc.); **sa position n'est qu'un m.,** his position is merely a stepping stone; (*b*) *Veh:* footboard; *Aut:* running board; (*c*) (pair of) steps; stepladder.

marcher [marʃe] *v.i.* **1.** to tread; **m. sur les pieds de qn,** to tread on s.o.'s toes; **ne marchez pas sur les pelouses,** keep off the grass; **m. sur les traces, sur les pas, de qn,** to follow in s.o.'s footsteps. **2.** (*a*) to walk, go; **l'enfant ne marche pas encore,** the child isn't walking yet; **il boite en marchant,** he's limping; he's got a limp; **façon de m.,** way of walking; **deux choses qui marchent toujours ensemble,** two things that always go together; **l'État marche à la ruine,** the State is heading for ruin; (*b*) *F:* to obey orders; **il marchera,** he'll do as he's told, as we want; **faire m. qn,** (i) to order s.o. about; (ii) to deceive, fool, s.o.; to pull s.o.'s leg; (*c*) *Mil: etc:* to march; **en avant, marche!** quick march! **m. à, contre, l'ennemi,** to advance, move, against the enemy. **3.** (*a*) (*of trains, etc.*) to move, travel, go; (*of ships*) to sail, steam; (*of plans, etc.*) to proceed, progress; (*of ship, etc.*) **m. à toute allure, à toute vitesse,** to proceed at full speed; **le temps marche,** time goes on; **les affaires marchent (bien),** business is brisk; **les affaires ne marchent plus,** business is at a standstill, is slack; **cela fait m. le commerce,** it's good for business; **est-ce que ça marche?** are you getting along all right? **ça ne marche pas si mal,** we're not doing too badly; **la répétition a bien, mal, marché,** the rehearsal went well, badly; (*b*) (*of machine*) to work, run, go; **ma montre ne marche plus,** my watch isn't working, won't go.

marcheur, -euse [marʃœr, -øz] **1.** *n.* (*a*) walker; **bon m.,** good walker; (*b*) *Pej: O:* **vieux m.,** old rake, old roué. **2.** *a.* (*a*) *Nat.Hist:* walking (animal); (*b*) **navire bon m.,** fast ship.

marcotte [markɔt] *n.f.* *Hort:* **1.** layer. **2.** runner, sucker.

marcotter [markɔte] *v.tr.* *Hort:* to layer.

mardi [mardi] *n.m.* Tuesday; **m. gras,** Shrove Tuesday.

mare [mar] *n.f.* (stagnant) pool; pond; **m. de sang,** pool of blood.

marécage [marekaʒ] *n.m.* marsh(land); fen, bog; swamp.

marécageux, -euse [marekaʒø, -øz] *a.* boggy, marshy, swampy.

maréchal, -aux [mareʃal, -o] *n.m.* **1.** = MARÉCHAL-FERRANT. **2.** marshal (of royal household, etc.). **3.** *Mil:* (*a*) **m. (de France)** = field marshal; (*b*) **m. des logis,** sergeant (in mounted arms).

maréchalat [mareʃala] *n.m.* marshalship.

maréchale [mareʃal] *n.f.* wife of field marshal.

maréchalerie [mareʃalri] *n.f.* (*a*) horse-shoeing, farriery; (*b*) smithy, forge.

maréchal-ferrant [mareʃalfɛrɑ̃] *n.m.* blacksmith; farrier; *pl. maréchaux-ferrants.*

maréchaussée [mareʃose] *n.f.* **1.** *Hist:* (*a*) = Marshalsea; (*b*) corps of mounted constabulary. **2.** *F:* **la m.,** the police.

marée [mare] *n.f.* **1.** tide; **m. haute,** high water, high tide; **m. basse,** low water, low tide; **m. montante,** flood tide; **m. descendante,** ebb tide; **grande m.,** spring tide; **fleuve à m.,** tidal river; **contre vents et marées,** (i) against wind and tide; (ii) in spite of all opposition; **port à m., de m.,** tidal harbour, *NAm:* harbor; **une m. humaine,** a flood of people; **m. noire,** oil slick. **2.** fresh (seawater) fish; **train de m.,** fish train; **arriver comme m. en carême,** to arrive just at the right moment, in the nick of time.

marelle [marɛl] *n.f.* *Games:* hopscotch.

marémoteur, -trice [maremɔtœr, -tris] *a.* tidal (power, etc.); **usine marémotrice,** tidal power station.

mareyage [marɛjaʒ] *n.m.* (the) fish trade.

mareyeur, -euse [marɛjœr, -øz] *n.* (wholesale) fishmonger.

margarine [margarin] *n.f.* margarine.

marge [marʒ] *n.f.* **1.** (*a*) border, edge (of ditch, road, etc.); **en m. de,** outside, apart from; **en m. de l'histoire,** a footnote to history; **vivre en m. (de la société),** (i) to lead a quiet life; (ii) to live on the fringe of society; (*b*) margin (of book); **écrire qch. en m.,** to write sth. in the margin; **note en m.,** marginal note; *Typ:* **illustrations à marges perdues,** bled-off illustrations. **2. m. de sécurité,** safety margin; **m. d'erreur,** margin of error; *Ind:* **m. de tolérance,** tolerance (margin); **accorder de la m. à qn,** to allow s.o. some latitude; **avoir de la m.,** to have plenty of (i) time, (ii) scope; *Com:* **m. bénéficiaire,** profit margin.

margelle [marʒɛl] *n.f.* coping, curb(stone) (of a well).

margeur [marʒœr] *n.m. Typewr:* margin stop.

marginal, -aux [marʒinal, -o] **1.** *a.* (*a*) marginal (note, etc.); (*b*) *Geog:* fringing (reef). **2.** *n.m.pl. Pol.Ec:* **les marginaux,** the fringe.

margoulin [margulɛ̃] *n.m.* dishonest businessman; rogue.

margrave [margrav] *Hist:* **1.** *n.m.* margrave. **2.** *n.f.* margravine.

Marguerite [margərit] **1.** *Pr.n.f.* Margaret. **2.** *n.f. Bot:* **(petite) m.,** daisy; **grande m.,** oxeye daisy, marguerite; **effeuiller la m.,** to play 'she loves me, she loves me not'.

marguillier [margije] *n.m. O:* churchwarden.

mari [mari] *n.m.* husband.

mariable [marjabḷ] *a.* marriageable.

mariage [marjaʒ] *n.m.* **1.** marriage; (*a*) wedlock, matrimony; (*b*) wedding; **m. d'amour, d'inclination,** love match; **faire un m. d'amour,** to marry for love; **m. de raison, de convenance,** marriage of convenience; **m. religieux,** church wedding; **m. civil,** civil marriage = register office wedding; **m. mixte,** mixed marriage; **acte de m.,** marriage certificate; **demande en m.,** proposal (of marriage); **liste de m.,** wedding list; **leur première année de m.,** the first year of their married life; **né hors du m.,** born out of wedlock; (*c*) combination, association (of wit and beauty, etc.); blend(ing) (of colours, *NAm:* colors, etc.). **2.** *Nau:* marrying (of two ropes).

Marianne [marjan] *Pr.n.f.* **1.** Marian(ne). **2.** *Fig:* the (French) Republic.

Marie [mari] *Pr.n.f.* Mary, Maria.

marié -ée [marje] *a. & n.* married (person); **nouveau m., nouvelle mariée,** (i) (*on wedding day*) (bride)-groom; *f.* bride; (ii) newly-married man, woman; **nouveaux mariés,** newly-married couple; newlyweds; **robe de mariée,** wedding dress; **oncle non m., tante non mariée,** unmarried uncle, aunt; bachelor uncle, maiden aunt.

marier [marje] (*pr.sub. & impf.* **n. mariions, v. mariiez**) **1.** *v.tr.* (*a*) (*of priest, etc.*) to marry (man and woman); (*b*) to marry (off) (daughter, etc.); **fille à m.,** marriageable daughter; (*c*) to join, unite; to blend (colours, *NAm:* colors, etc.); (*d*) *Nau:* to marry (ropes). **2. se m.,** to marry, get married; **se m. avec qn,** to marry s.o.; (*of colour, etc.*) **se m. avec qch.,** to blend, harmonize, with sth.

marie-salope [marisalɔp] *n.f.* **1.** *P:* slut. **2.** (*a*) (dredger's) mud barge; hopper (barge); (*b*) mud dredger; *pl. maries-salopes.*

marieur, -ieuse [marjœr, -jøz] *n.* matchmaker.

marigot [marigo] *n.m.* (*in tropical regions*) backwater (of river).

marihuana [marìɥana], **marijuana** [mariʒɥana] *n.f.* marihuana.

marin, -ine¹ [marɛ̃, -in] **1.** *a.* marine (plant, engine, etc.); **carte marine,** sea chart; **mille m.,** nautical mile; **costume m.,** sailor suit; **avoir le pied m.,** to be a good sailor. **2.** *n.m.* (*a*) seafaring man; mariner; seafarer; (*b*) sailor; seaman; **se faire m.,** to go to sea; **m. d'eau douce,** landlubber.

marina [marina] *n.f.* marina.

marinade [marinad] *n.f. Cu:* (*a*) pickle; brine, souse; (*b*) marinade; (*c*) *Fr.C:* **marinades,** pickles.

marinage [marinaʒ] *n.m. Cu:* (*a*) pickling, salting, sousing; (*b*) marinading, marinating.

marine² [marin] *n.f.* **1.** *Art:* seascape, seapiece. **2.** seamanship; **terme de m.,** nautical term. **3.** the sea service; **la m. marchande,** the merchant navy, the mercantile marine; **la m. de guerre,** the navy; **officier de m.,** naval officer. **4.** *a.inv.* navy (blue).

marine³ *n.m. Navy:* (*a*) (Royal) Marine; (*b*) *U.S:* marine.

mariné [marine] *a. Cu:* soused, pickled (herring, etc.).

mariner [marine] *Cu:* **1.** *v.tr.* to pickle, salt, souse. **2.** *v.tr. & i.* to marinade, marinate.

maringouin [marɛ̃gwɛ̃] *n.m. Ent:* (*in tropics, Canada*) mosquito.

marinier, -ière [marinje, -jɛr] **1.** *a.* (*a*) *A:* marine, naval; (*b*) **officier m.,** petty officer. **2.** *n.m.* waterman, bargee, *NAm:* bargeman. **3.** *n.f.* **marinière** (*a*) *Swim:* sidestroke; (*b*) *Cost:* (woman's) blouse.

mariol(l)e [marjɔl] *n.m. P:* **faire le m.,** to show off.

marionnette [marjɔnɛt] *n.f.* puppet; **m. à gaine,** glove puppet; **m. (à fil),** puppet, marionette; **(spectacle, théâtre, de) marionnettes,** puppet show, theatre, *NAm:* theater.

marionnettiste [marjɔnetist] *n.* puppeteer.

marital, -aux [marital, -o] *a.* marital.

maritalement [maritalmɑ̃] *adv.* maritally.

maritime [maritim] *a.* maritime (navigation, plant, etc.); **ville m.,** seaboard town; **commerce m.,** seaborne trade; **assurance m.,** marine insurance; **courtier m.,** shipbroker; **agent m.,** shipping agent; **arsenal m.,** naval dockyard; *Rail:* **gare m.,** harbour station, *NAm:* harbor station; *Geog:* **les (Provinces) Maritimes,** the Maritime Provinces.

maritorne [maritɔrn] *n.f.* sloven, slut.

marjolaine [marʒɔlɛn] *n.f. Bot:* (sweet) marjoram.

mark [mark] *n.m. Num:* (German) mark.

marketing [markətiŋ] *n.m.* marketing.

marlou [marlu] *n.m P:* procurer, pimp.

marmaille [marmɑj] *n.f. coll. F:* children; **rue pleine de m.,** street swarming with lads, with noisy little brats; **toute la m.,** the whole brood.

marmelade [marməlad] *n.f.* (*a*) compote (of fruit); **m. de pommes,** (i) stewed apples; (ii) apple purée; (*b*) **m. (d'oranges),** (orange) marmalade; (*c*) **viande en m.,** meat cooked to shreds; *F:* **mettre qch. en m.,** to pound sth. to a jelly, a pulp; (*d*) *F:* mess, hash, shambles.

marmite [marmit] *n.f.* **1.** (*a*) (i) (cooking) pot, (stew)-pan; (ii) potful, panful; **m. à conserves,** preserving pan; **m. autoclave,** pressure cooker; **faire bouillir la m.,** to keep the pot boiling; (*b*) *Mil:* dixy, camp kettle. **2.** *Mil: F: O:* heavy shell. **3.** *Geol:* **m. de géants,** pothole.

marmiter [marmite] *v.tr. O:* to bombard (place) with heavy shells; to shell (trenches, etc.).

marmiton [marmitɔ̃] *n.m.* kitchen boy.

marmonnement [marmɔnmɑ̃] *n.m.* mumbling, muttering.

marmonner [marmɔne] *v.tr.* to mumble, mutter.

marmoréen, -enne [marmɔreɛ̃, -ɛn] *a. Lit:* marmoreal, marmorean; **blancheur marmoréenne,** marble whiteness.

marmot [marmo] *n.m.* **1.** *F:* child, brat. **2.** (*a*) *A:* grotesque figure (*esp.* as door knocker); (*b*) *O:* **croquer le m.,** to be kept waiting; to cool one's heels.
marmotte [marmɔt] *n.f.* **1.** *Z:* marmot. **2.** *A.Cost:* headscarf, kerchief (tied over the forehead).
marmottement [marmɔtmɑ̃] *n.m.* mumbling, muttering.
marmotter [marmɔte] *v.tr.* to mumble, mutter.
marmotteur, -euse [marmɔtœr, -øz] *n.* mumbler, mutterer.
marnage¹ [marnaʒ] *n.m. Agr:* marling (of soil).
marnage² *n.m. Oc:* tidal range.
marne [marn] *n.f. Geol:* marl.
marner [marne] **1.** *v.tr. Agr:* to marl (soil). **2.** *v.i. P:* to work hard, to slog.
Maroc (le) [ləmarɔk] *Pr.n.m. Geog:* Morocco.
marocain, -aine [marɔkɛ̃, -ɛn] *a.* & *n. Geog:* Moroccan.
maronner [marɔne] *v.i. F:* to grouse, grumble.
maroquin [marɔkɛ̃] *n.m.* (*a*) morocco (leather); (*b*) minister's portfolio.
maroquinerie [marɔkinri] *n.f.* **1.** (*a*) morocco-leather tanning, leather working; (*b*) morocco-leather tannery. **2.** *Com:* (*a*) morocco-leather goods trade; (*b*) fancy leather work; (*c*) (fancy) leather shop.
maroquinier [marɔkinje] *n.m.* (*a*) morocco-leather tanner; leather worker; (*b*) dealer in fancy leather goods; (*c*) (fancy) leather shop.
marotte [marɔt] *n.f.* **1.** (*a*) (court fool's) bauble; cap and bells; (*b*) (milliner's, hairdresser's) dummy head. **2.** fad; hobby; **avoir une m.,** to have a bee in one's bonnet.
maroufle¹ [marufl̩] *n.m. A:* rogue, scoundrel.
maroufle² *n.f.* (strong) paste.
maroufler [marufle] *v.tr.* **1.** (*a*) to re-mount (picture) on a new foundation; (*b*) **m. une couture,** to tape a seam; **bande à m.,** taping, tape. **2.** to prime, size (canvas).
marquage [markaʒ] *n.m.* marking.
marquant [markɑ̃] *a.* **1.** prominent, outstanding (incident, person, etc.); *Lit:* **passages marquants,** purple passages. **2.** *Cards:* **carte marquante,** card that counts.
marque [mark] *n.f.* **1.** mark; badge, *pl.* insignia (of office, etc.); **m. d'identité,** identification mark; **marques distinctives des véhicules,** vehicle markings; **m. (de fabrique),** trademark; brand; **m. déposée,** registered trademark; **produits de m.,** branded goods; top quality goods; **m. courante,** standard make; **j'ai eu des voitures de trois marques,** I've had three makes of car; **vin de m.,** (i) wine from a well known vineyard; (ii) choice, vintage, wine; **personnage de m.,** person of distinction; distinguished, prominent, person; **m. à linge,** name tape, name tab; **m. de l'État,** government stamp; *Navy:* **la m. de l'amiral,** the admiral's flag; **m. au crayon,** pencil mark; **blessure qui laisse une m.,** wound that leaves a mark, a scar; **porter la m. du génie,** to bear the stamp, the hallmark, of genius; **marques d'amitié,** tokens of friendship; **m. du beau temps,** sign, indication, of good weather. **2.** marker; marking tool, branding iron. **3.** (*a*) *Com:* tally; (*b*) *Games:* scoreboard; marker; (*c*) *Games:* score; **tenir la m.,** to keep the score; (*d*) *Games:* counter; (*e*) *Sp:* **à vos marques! prêts? partez!** on your marks! get set! go!
marqué [marke] *a.* **1.** (*a*) marked (card, etc.); (*of pers.*) **être m.,** to have a lined, furrowed, face; (*b*) *Adm: Jur:* **papier m.,** stamped paper. **2.** marked, decided, unmistakable (difference, etc.); pronounced (features, etc.); distinct (inclination, etc.).
marquer [marke] **1.** *v.tr.* to mark; (*a*) to leave, put, a mark on (sth.); **m. du linge,** to mark linen; *Com:* **prix marqué,** (i) list price; (ii) price marked (in plain figures); **visage marqué par, de, la petite vérole,** pockmarked face; **m. un criminel,** to brand a criminal; **m. un arbre,** to blaze a tree; (*in train, etc.*) **m. sa place,** to leave one's hat, etc., on a seat (to show that it is taken); (*b*) to record, make a note of (sth.); *Games:* **m. un adversaire,** to mark a man; **m. un but,** to score a goal; **m. les points,** to keep the score; **m. trente points,** to score thirty; **ne m. aucun point,** to fail to score; (*c*) to indicate, show; **la pendule marque dix heures,** the clock says, points to, ten o'clock; **le thermomètre marque 25°,** the thermometer shows, registers, 25°; **m. la mesure,** to beat time; **m. le pas,** to mark time; **manteau qui marque bien la taille,** coat that shows off the figure; **il marque son âge,** he looks his age. **2.** *v.i.* (*a*) **crayon qui ne marque pas,** pencil that won't write; (*b*) to stand out; to leave, make, a mark; **notre famille n'a jamais marqué,** our family has never been outstanding, made its mark; *F:* (*of pers.*) **m. mal,** to make a bad impression.
marqueté [markəte] *a. Furn: etc:* inlaid.
marqueter [markəte] *v.tr.* **(je marquette; je marquetterai) 1.** to spot, speckle (fur, etc.). **2.** to inlay (table, etc.).
marqueterie [markətri] *n.f.* inlaid work, marquetry.
marqueteur [markətœr] *n.m.* worker in marquetry; inlayer.
marqueur, -euse [markœr, -øz] **1.** *n.* marker; (*a*) stamper, brander; stenciller (of boxes, etc.); (*b*) *Games:* scorekeeper, scorer; (*c*) *Fb: etc:* **m. (de but),** (goal) scorer. **2.** *n.m.* (felt-tip) marker (pen). **3.** *n.f. Ind:* **marqueuse,** stamp(er), stamping machine.
marquis [marki] *n.m.* marquis, marquess.
marquisat [markiza] *n.m.* marquisate.
marquise [markiz] *n.f.* **1.** marchioness. **2.** (*a*) awning (on pleasure boat, etc.); (*b*) (overhanging) shelter; canopy; glass porch.
Marquises [markiz] *Pr.n.f.pl. Geog:* **les (îles) M.,** the Marquesas (Islands).
marraine [marɛn] *n.f.* (*a*) godmother; sponsor (at baptism); (*b*) **m. de guerre,** self-constituted godmother, correspondent (of soldier at the front); (*c*) presenter (of débutante); (*d*) christener (of bell, ship, etc.).
marrant [marɑ̃] *a. P:* (*a*) (screamingly) funny; hilarious; (*b*) odd, strange, funny, queer; **vous êtes m., vous, alors!** you're the limit!
marre [mar] *adv. P:* **avoir m. de qch., de qn,** to be fed up with, have had enough of, sth., s.o.; **j'en ai m.!** I'm sick of it!
marrer (se) [səmare] *v.pr. P:* to laugh, kill oneself laughing.
marri [mari] *a. A:* & *Lit:* sad, sorry, grieved.
marron¹ [marɔ̃] *n.m.* **1.** (*a*) (large edible) chestnut; **tirer les marrons du feu pour qn,** to do whatever s.o. says; to be s.o.'s cat's paw; (*b*) **m. d'Inde,** horse chestnut; (*c*) *P:* blow, thump, wallop. **2.** *a.inv.* & *n.m.* chestnut(brown).
marron², -onne [marɔ̃, -ɔn] *a.* **1.** *Hist:* **nègre m.,** maroon, runaway negro slave. **2.** unlicensed (trader, etc.); unqualified (lawyer, etc.); quack (doctor).
marronnier [marɔnje] *n.m.* chestnut tree; **m. d'Inde,** horse-chestnut tree.
Mars [mars] **1.** *Pr.n.m. Myth: Astr:* Mars. **2.** *n.m.* March; **en m.,** in March; **au mois de m.,** in the month of March; **le premier, le sept, m.,** (on) the first, the seventh, of March; (on) March (the) first, (the) seventh; **blé de m.,** *pl.* **les m.,** spring wheat; **arriver comme m. en carême,** to come round as regularly as clockwork.

marseillais, -aise [marsɛjɛ, -ɛz] *a. & n. Geog:* Marseillais, -aise; **la Marseillaise,** the Marseillaise.
Marseille [marsɛj] *Pr.n. Geog:* Marseille(s).
marsouin [marswɛ̃] *n.m.* **1.** (*a*) *Z:* porpoise; (*b*) *Mil: F: A:* marine. **2.** *Nau:* forecastle awning.
marsupial, -iaux [marsypjal, -jo] *a. & n.m. Z:* marsupial.
marteau, -eaux [marto] **1.** *n.m.* (*a*) hammer; **m. à panne fendue,** claw hammer; **m. à deux mains,** sledge-hammer; **m. pneumatique,** pneumatic drill; **m. perforateur,** hammer drill; **coup de m.,** hammer stroke; **entre l'enclume et le m.,** between the devil and the deep blue sea; (*b*) (auctioneer's) hammer; gavel; **passer sous le m.,** to come under the hammer; (*c*) (door) knocker; striker (of gong, clock); **coup de m.,** knock (at the door); (*d*) *Ich:* **requin m.,** hammerhead (shark). **2.** *a. F:* **il est un peu m.,** he's crazy, he isn't all there, he's round the bend.
marteau-pilon [martopilɔ̃] *n.m. Metall:* power hammer; *pl. marteaux-pilons.*
marteau-piolet [martopjɔlɛ] *n.m. Mount:* piton hammer; *pl. marteaux-piolets.*
martel [martɛl] *n.m.* (*a*) *A:* hammer; (*b*) **se mettre m. en tête,** to be anxious; to worry.
martelage [martəlaʒ] *n.m.* hammering.
martelé [martəle] *a.* hammered; **argent m.,** beaten silver.
martèlement [martɛlmɑ̃] *n.m.* hammering; clanking, clanging (of boots, etc.).
marteler [martəle] *v.tr.* **(je martèle; je martèlerai)** to hammer; *Metalw:* **m. à froid,** to cold-hammer; **idée qui lui martelait la cervelle,** idea that kept hammering in his brain; **m. ses mots,** to hammer out one's words; **m. un air,** to pound out a tune.
martial, -aux [marsjal, -o] *a.* (*a*) martial; warlike; soldierly (bearing, etc.); (*b*) **loi martiale,** martial law; **code m.,** articles of war; **cour martiale,** court martial.
martialement [marsjalmɑ̃] *adv.* martially.
martien, -ienne [marsjɛ̃, -jɛn] *a. & n.* Martian.
Martin [martɛ̃] *Pr.n.m.* (*a*) Martin; (*b*) (*name given to a donkey*) = Neddy.
martinet[1] [martinɛ] *n.m.* **1.** *Metall:* tilt hammer, drop stamp. **2.** strap (for beating child).
martinet[2] *n.m. Orn:* swift.
martingale [martɛ̃gal] *n.f.* **1.** (*a*) *Harn:* martingale; (*b*) *Cost:* half belt (of greatcoat, etc.). **2.** *Gaming:* martingale.
martin-pêcheur [martɛ̃pɛʃœr] *n.m. Orn:* kingfisher; *pl. martins-pêcheurs.*
martre [martr̥] *n.f. Z:* martin; **m. zibeline,** sable; **m. du Canada,** mink.
martyr, -yre[1] [martir] *n.* martyr; *R.C.Ch:* **commun des martyrs,** common of martyrs; **un peuple m.,** a martyred people; **m. d'une cause,** martyr to a cause; **se donner des airs de m.,** to put on a martyred expression.
martyre[2] *n.m.* martyrdom; **souffrir le m.,** to suffer martyrdom, agonies; **mettre qn au m.,** to torture s.o.
martyriser [martirize] *v.tr.* **1.** to martyr (s.o. on account of his faith). **2.** to martyrize, torture; to make a martyr of (s.o.).
marxisme [marksism] *n.m.* Marxism.
marxiste [marksist] *a. & n.* Marxist.
mas [mɑ(s)] *n.m.* (*in S. of Fr.*) farm(house).
mascara [maskara] *n.m. Toil:* mascara.
mascarade [maskarad] *n.f.* masquerade.
mascaret [maskarɛ] *n.m.* bore, tidal wave (in estuary).
mascaron [maskarɔ̃] *n.m. Arch:* grotesque mask (on keystone of arch, etc.).
mascote [maskɔt] *n.f.* mascot; charm; *Sp: F:* **terrain m.,** lucky ground.
masculin [maskylɛ̃] **1.** *a.* (*a*) male (sex, voice, etc.); (*b*) masculine, mannish (woman). **2.** *a. & n.m. Gram:* masculine (gender); **ce mot est (du) m.,** this word is masculine; **au m.,** in the masculine.
masculinité [maskylinite] *n.f.* masculinity.
maskinongé [maskinɔ̃ʒe] *n.m. Ich: Fr.C:* maskinonge; *NAm:* muskellunge, *F:* muskie.
masochisme [mazɔʃism] *n.m. Psy:* masochism.
masochiste [mazɔʃist] *Psy:* **1.** *a.* masochistic. **2.** *n.* masochist.
masque [mask] *n.m.* **1.** (*a*) mask; **ôter, arracher, le m. à qn,** to unmask s.o.; **lever le m.,** to throw off the mask; **m. à gaz,** gas mask; **m. à oxygène,** oxygen mask; **m. sous-marin,** (skin diver's) mask; **m. mortuaire,** death mask; *Toil:* **m. (antirides, facial),** face pack; (*b*) (expression of the) face; features; **il a le m. mobile,** he has mobile features. **2.** (*a*) *A:* mask(er); (*b*) masquerader. **3.** protection, cover; *Artil:* shield, hood (of gun); *Civ.E:* **m. d'étanchéité,** cutoff.
masquer [maske] **1.** *v.tr.* (*a*) to put a mask on, mask (s.o.); **bal masqué,** masked ball; (*b*) to hide, screen, conceal (sth.); to shade (light); *Paint:* to mask, shield (surface); *Nau:* to darken (ship); **m. qch. à qn,** to conceal sth. from s.o.; **m. une odeur,** to disguise a smell; *Aut:* **virage masqué,** blind corner; *Mil:* **m. une batterie,** to conceal a battery; *Fig:* **m. ses batteries,** to conceal one's intentions; *Nau:* **naviguer à feux masqués,** to steam without lights; (*c*) *Nau:* to back (sail); **être masqué,** *v.i.* **m.,** to be caught aback, taken aback. **2. se m.,** to put a mask on.
massacrante [masakrɑ̃t] *a.f.* **être d'une humeur m.,** to be in a filthy, vile, temper.
massacre [masakr̥] *n.m.* (*a*) massacre, slaughter; butchery; (*b*) **jeu de m.** = Aunt Sally, *NAm:* straw man.
massacrer [masakre] *v.tr.* **1.** to massacre, butcher, slaughter. **2.** *F:* to bungle, spoil, make a hash of (work); to murder, massacre (music, etc.); to ruin (clothes); to hack up (piece of meat).
massacreur, -euse [masakrœr, -øz] *n.* **1.** slaughterer; butcher. **2.** *F:* bungler.
massage [masaʒ] *n.m.* massage.
masse[1] [mas] *n.f.* **1.** (*a*) mass; **tomber comme une m.,** to fall heavily, in a heap; **en m.,** (i) in a body; en masse; (ii) as a whole; **exécutions en m.,** mass executions; *F:* **avoir des livres en m.,** to have masses of books; **marchandises en m.,** goods in bulk; **se prendre en m.,** to solidify, coagulate; **taillé dans la m.,** carved from the block; (*b*) *Mil:* mass formation; (*c*) *Mec:* mass (of moving body); **m. spécifique,** density; *Atom.Ph:* **m. critique,** critical mass; (*d*) mass, crowd, body (of people); **les masses, la m.,** the masses; **la (grande) m. de,** the majority of; *F:* **il n'y en a pas des masses,** there aren't an awful lot. **2.** *Fin:* fund, stock; **la m. monétaire,** the (total amount of) money in circulation; *Jur:* **m. des biens (de la faillite),** (bankrupt's) total estate; **m. passive,** liabilities; **m. active,** assets. **3.** *El:* earth (constituted by frame of machine); **mettre le courant à la m.,** to earth, *NAm:* ground, the current.
masse[2] *n.f.* **1.** sledgehammer; **m. en bois,** beetle. **2.** (*a*) *A.Arms:* **m. (d'armes),** mace; (*b*) (ceremonial) mace.
massepain [maspɛ̃] *n.m.* marzipan.
masser[1] [mase] **1.** *v.tr.* (*a*) to mass (soldiers, etc.); (*b*) *Art:* to group (figures, etc.). **2. se m.,** to mass; to form a crowd.
masser[2] *v.tr.* to massage.
massette [masɛt] *n.f.* **1.** two-handed hammer. **2.** *Bot:* bulrush, reed mace, cat's tail.
masseur, -euse [masœr, -øz] *n.* masseur, *f.* masseuse.
massicot[1] [masiko] *n.m. Ch:* massicot, yellow lead.

massicot² *n.m. Bookb: etc:* guillotine, trimmer.
massicoter [masikɔte] *v.tr. Bookb: etc:* to guillotine.
massif, -ive [masif, -iv] **1.** *a.* (*a*) massive, bulky; heavy; *Lit:* gross, material (mind, etc.); (*b*) solid (silver, mahogany, etc.); (*c*) **action massive,** mass attack; **dose massive,** massive dose. **2.** *n.m.* (*a*) solid mass (of masonry, etc.); body (of a pier); (*b*) clump (of shrubs, etc.); (*c*) *Geog:* massif.
massique [masik] *a. Ph:* pertaining to the mass; *Mec.E:* **puissance m.,** power-to-weight ratio (of engine).
massue [masy] *n.f.* (*a*) club, bludgeon; **coup de m.,** (i) bludgeon stroke; (ii) staggering, crushing, blow; **argument m.,** sledgehammer argument; (*b*) Indian club.
mastic [mastic] **1.** *n.m.* (*a*) mastic (resin); (*b*) cement, mastic compound; (*for windows, etc.*) putty; (*for wood, etc.*) filler; stopping compound; (*c*) *Dent:* filling (compound). **2.** *a.inv.* putty-coloured; *NAm:* -colored.
masticage [mastikaʒ] *n.m.* cementing, puttying, filling.
masticateur, -trice [mastikatœr, -tris] **1.** *a.* masticatory (organ, etc.). **2.** *n.m.* masticator.
mastication [mastikasjɔ̃] *n.f.* mastication; chewing.
masticatoire [mastikatwar] *a. & n.m.* masticatory.
mastiquer¹ [mastike] *v.tr.* to cement; to fill (in) (cracks, etc.); to putty (window).
mastiquer² *v.tr.* to masticate, chew.
mastoc [mastɔk] *a.inv. F:* heavy, lumpish; clumsy (construction).
mastodonte [mastɔdɔ̃t] *n.m.* **1.** *Paleont:* mastodon. **2.** *F:* (*a*) **les mastodontes de la route,** huge lorries; juggernauts; (*b*) (*pers.*) colossus.
mastoïde [mastɔid] *a. Anat:* mastoid (bone, etc.).
mastroquet [mastrɔkɛ] *n.m. F:* (*a*) publican; (*b*) bar, pub.
masturbation [mastyrbasjɔ̃] *n.f.* masturbation.
masturber (se) [(sə)mastyrbe] *v.tr. & pr.* to masturbate.
m'as-tu-vu, -vue [matyvy] *n.inv. F:* show-off.
masure [mazyr] *n.f.* tumbledown cottage; hovel, shanty.
mat¹ [mat] *a.* mat(t), unpolished, dull (metal); flat (colour, *NAm:* color); **teint m.,** mat(t) complexion; **son m.,** dull sound; thud.
mat² [mat] *Chess:* **1.** *a.inv.* checkmated. **2.** *n.m.* (check)mate; **faire (échec et) m. en trois coups,** to mate in three.
mât [mɑ] *n.m.* mast; pole; (*a*) *Nau:* **grand m.,** mainmast; **m. d'artimon,** mizzenmast; **m. de misaine,** foremast; **m. de hune,** topmast; **m. de charge,** cargo boom; derrick; **navire à trois mâts,** three-masted ship; three-master; (*b*) **m. de tente,** tent pole; **m. de cocagne,** greasy pole.
matador [matadɔr] *n.m.* **1.** matador. **2.** *F: A:* bigwig, magnate.
matamore [matamɔr] *n.m.* braggart, boaster; **faire le m.,** to boast, brag.
match [matʃ] *n.m.* **1.** *Sp:* match; **m. d'aviron,** boat race; **m. prévu,** fixture; *Fb:* **m. de championnat (professionel),** league match; **faire m. nul,** to tie, draw. **2.** struggle; *pl. matchs, matches* [matʃ].
maté [mate] *n.m.* maté.
matelas [matla] *n.m.* (*a*) mattress; **m. pneumatique,** inflatable mattress, air bed; **toile à m.,** ticking; *Mch:* **m. de vapeur,** steam cushion; (*b*) *P:* wad of banknotes; bulging wallet.
matelassé [matlase], *a. & n.m. Tex:* quilted (material).
matelasser [matlase] *v.tr.* to pad, quilt, stuff, cushion (chair, etc.); **porte matelassée,** baize door.
matelassure [matlasyr] *n.f.* padding, stuffing, wadding (of mattress, saddle, etc.).
matelot [matlo] *n.m.* **1.** sailor, seaman; **m. (breveté) de première classe,** leading seaman; **m. de deuxième classe,** able seaman; **servir comme simple m.,** to sail before the mast. **2.** *Nau:* consort (ship); **m. d'avant, d'arrière,** next ship ahead, next astern.
matelotage [matlɔtaʒ] *n.m.* (*a*) seamanship; (*b*) sailor's pay.
matelote [matlɔt] *n.f.* **1. à la m.,** sailor-fashion. **2.** *Cu:* fish stew; matelote.
mater¹ [mate] *v.tr.* **1.** to mat(t), dull (metals, etc.). **2.** to caulk, hammer (boiler seams, etc.).
mater² *v.tr.* (*a*) *Chess:* to (check)mate; (*b*) to subdue, tame (s.o.); to bring (s.o.) to heel.
mâter [mɑte] *v.tr.* to mast (ship).
matérialisation [materjalizasjɔ̃] *n.f.* materialization, materializing.
matérialisé [materjalize] *a. Adm:* **voie matérialisée** = section of a road delimited by a white line.
matérialiser (se) [(sə)materjalize] *v.tr. & pr.* to materialize.
matérialisme [materjalism] *n.m.* materialism.
matérialiste [materjalist] **1.** *a.* materialistic. **2.** *n.* materialist.
matérialité [materjalite] *n.f.* materiality.
matériau [materjo] *n.m. Civ.E: Const:* (building, constructional) material.
matériaux [materjo] *n.m.pl.* material(s).
matériel, -elle [materjɛl] **1.** *a.* (*a*) material, physical (body); (*b*) materialistic, gross, sensual (pleasures, etc.); (*c*) **besoins matériels,** bodily needs; (*d*) *Jur:* **dommages matériels,** damage to property. **2.** *n.m.* (*a*) equipment; material; stock in trade; plant (of factory); **m. agricole,** farm equipment, machinery, implements; **m. d'école, m. scolaire,** school equipment; **m. de camping,** camping equipment, gear; *Rail:* **m. roulant,** rolling stock; *Mil:* **m. de guerre,** war equipment, material; **service du m.,** ordnance; (*b*) *Cmptr:* hardware.
matériellement [materjɛlmɑ̃] *adv.* (*a*) materially; **avoir de quoi vivre m.,** to have enough for one's material needs; **chose m. impossible,** physical impossibility; (*b*) materialistically; sensually.
maternel, -elle [matɛrnɛl] *a.* maternal. **1.** motherly (care, etc.); **école maternelle,** *n.f.* **maternelle,** nursery school. **2.** (*a*) **aïeul m.,** maternal grandfather; (*b*) **langue maternelle,** mother tongue, native tongue.
maternellement [matɛrnɛlmɑ̃] *adv.* maternally.
maternité [matɛrnite] *n.f.* **1.** (*a*) maternity, motherhood; (*b*) pregnancy. **2.** maternity hospital.
math(s) [mat] *n.f.pl. F:* maths, *NAm:* math; **m. élémentaires** = A Level maths class.
mathématicien, -ienne [matematisjɛ̃, -jɛn] *n.* mathematician.
mathématique [matematik] **1.** *a.* mathematical. **2.** *n.f.pl.* mathematics; **mathématiques pures, appliquées,** pure, applied, mathematics.
mathématiquement [matematikmɑ̃] *adv.* mathematically.
matheux, -euse [matø, -øz] *n. F:* (keen) mathematician.
matière [matjɛr] *n.f.* **1.** (*a*) matter; **m. inanimée,** inanimate matter; (*b*) *Phil: etc:* substance. **2.** matter, material, substance; **m. grise,** grey matter (of the brain); **matière(s) première(s),** raw material(s); **matière(s) plastique(s),** plastic(s); **matières grasses,** fats. **3.** subject (matter) (of speech, etc.); topic, theme (for discussion); (school) subject; **table des matières,** (table of) contents (of book); **entrer en m.,** to broach the subject; to begin (one's speech); **il n'y a pas m. à rire,** it's no laughing matter; **être bon juge en m. de musique,** to be a good judge of

music; **en m. de menuiserie,** as far as woodwork is concerned.

matin [matɛ̃] **1.** *n.m.* morning; **du m. au soir,** from morning till night; morning, noon and night; **quatre heures du m.,** four o'clock in the morning, 4 a.m.; **le jeudi deux au m.,** on the morning of Thursday the second; **c'est le m. que je travaille le mieux,** I work best in the morning(s); **demain m.,** tomorrow morning; **tous les lundis m.,** every Monday morning; **de grand, bon, m.; le m. de bonne heure,** early in the morning, in the early morning; **rentrer au petit m.,** to come home very early in the morning, *F:* with the milk; **un de ces (quatre) matins, un beau m.,** one of these (fine) days. **2.** *adv.* (early) in the morning; **se lever très m.,** to get up very early.

mâtin, -ine [matɛ̃, -in] **1.** *n.m.* large watchdog; mastiff. **2.** *n. F:* cunning person; sly dog, *f.* minx. **3.** *int. A:* **m.!** by Jove!

matinal, -aux [matinal, -o] *a.* **1.** morning (breeze, etc.); **à cette heure matinale,** at this early hour; **promenade matinale,** early morning walk. **2.** (*of pers.*) **comme tu es m. aujourd'hui!** you're up very early this morning! *n.* **c'est un m.,** he's an early riser.

mâtiné [mɑtine] *a.* mongrel, cross-bred.

matinée [matine] *n.f.* **1.** morning; **dans la m.,** in (the course of) the morning; **je ne l'ai pas vu de toute la m.,** I haven't seen him all morning; *F:* **faire la grasse m.,** to sleep late in the morning, to have a lie-in. **2.** *Th: etc:* matinée; afternoon performance.

matines [matin] *n.f.pl. Ecc:* matins.

matir [matir] *v.tr.* = MATER[1].

matité [matite] *n.f.* deadness, dullness (of sound, etc.).

matoir [matwar] *n.m.* **1.** matting tool. **2.** *Metalw:* caulking chisel. **3.** riveting hammer.

matois, -oise [matwa, -waz] **1.** *a.* sly, cunning, crafty. **2.** *n.* crafty person; **fin m.,** sly devil.

matou [matu] *n.m.* tom (cat).

matraquage [matrakaʒ] *n.m.* bludgeoning, *F:* coshing.

matraque [matrak] *n.f.* bludgeon, truncheon, *F:* cosh; *NAm:* blackjack; *F:* **coup de m.,** overcharging (in restaurant, etc.).

matraquer [matrake] *v.tr.* to bludgeon, *F:* cosh (s.o.).

matriarcal, -aux [matriarkal, -o] *a.* matriarchal.

matriarcat [matriarka] *n.m.* matriarchy.

matriçage [matrisaʒ] *n.m. Metalw:* die stamping.

matrice [matris] *n.f.* **1.** matrix; (*a*) *Anat:* uterus, womb; (*b*) *Metalw:* die; bolster; mould, *NAm:* mold; (*c*) *Typ:* type mould; (*d*) *Rec:* matrix. **2.** *Adm:* original (of register of taxes).

matricer [matrise] *v.tr.* to stamp (metal); **pièce matricée,** (i) stamping; (ii) drop forging.

matricide[1] [matrisid] **1.** *n.* (*pers.*) matricide. **2.** *a.* matricidal.

matricide[2] *n.m.* (*crime*) matricide.

matricule [matrikyl] **1.** *n.f.* (*a*) roll, register, list; *Mil:* regimental roll; (*b*) inscription, registration; enrolment, *NAm:* enrollment; (*c*) registration certificate. **2. numéro m.,** *n.m.* **m.,** (regimental, administrative) number.

matriculer [matrikyle] *v.tr.* **1.** to enter (s.o.'s) name on a register; to enrol (soldier, etc.). **2.** to mark, stamp (sth.) with a number.

matrimonial, -iaux [matrimɔnjal, -jo] *a.* matrimonial.

matrone [matrɔn] *n.f.* matron; *Pej:* **vieille m.,** (fat) old woman, old bag.

Matthieu [matjø] *Pr.n.m.* Matthew.

maturation [matyrasjɔ̃] *n.f.* maturation; ripening (of fruit); maturing (of tobacco, etc.).

mâture [mɑtyr] *n.f.* **1.** masts; masts and spars; **dans la m.,** aloft. **2.** mast crane, sheerlegs; **m. flottante,** sheer hulk.

maturité [matyrite] *n.f.* maturity; ripeness; **venir à m.,** to come to maturity.

maudire [modir] *v.tr.* (*pr.p.* **maudissant;** *p.p.* **maudit;** *pr.ind.* **je maudis, n. maudissons, v. maudissez, ils maudissent;** *pr.sub.* **je maudisse;** *p.h.* **je maudis;** *fu.* **je maudirai**) to curse (s.o., sth.).

maudit [modi] **1.** *a.* (*a*) (ac)cursed (crime, etc.); (*b*) **quel m. temps!** what filthy weather! **2.** *n.* **le M.,** the Devil; **les maudits,** the accursed, the damned.

maugréer [mogree] *v.i.* to curse, fume; to grumble, grouse (**contre,** about, at).

Maure [mɔr] *Ethn:* **1.** *n.m.* Moor. **2.** *a.m.* Moorish.

mauresque [mɔrɛsk] (*a*) *a.* & *n.f.* Moorish (woman); (*b*) *a.* Moorish (architecture, design).

Maurice [mɔris] *Pr.n.m.* Maurice; *Geog:* **l'île M.,** Mauritius.

mauricien, -ienne [mɔrisjɛ̃ -jɛn] *a.* & *n. Geog:* Mauritian.

Mauritanie [mɔritani] *Pr.n.f. Geog:* Mauritania.

mauritanien, -ienne [mɔritanjɛ̃, -jɛn] *a.* & *n. Geog:* Mauritanian.

mausolée [mozɔle] *n.m.* mausoleum.

maussade [mosad] *a.* (*a*) surly, sullen, glum; sulky; peevish; disgruntled; **d'un ton m.,** irritably; (*b*) **temps m.,** dull, gloomy, weather.

maussaderie [mosadri] *n.f.* sullenness, sulkiness, peevishness.

mauvais [mɔvɛ] *a.* (*a*) evil (thought); ill (omen); wicked (person); **mauvaise action,** wrong(doing); **de plus en plus m.,** worse and worse; **le plus m.,** the worst; **avoir l'air m.,** to look (i) wicked, (ii) fierce, vicious; **c'est un m. sujet, un m. garçon,** he's a bad lot; **m. ange,** evil influence; **né sous une mauvaise étoile,** born under an unlucky star; **le m. œil,** the evil eye; (*b*) ill-natured (**pour,** towards); **c'est une mauvaise langue,** she's got a vicious tongue; (*c*) nasty, unpleasant; bad (breath, dream); rough (sea); **m. temps,** bad weather; **prendre qch. en mauvaise part,** to take sth. in bad part; to take offence at sth.; *adv.* **sentir m.,** to smell (bad), to stink; **il fait m.,** the weather's bad; (*d*) **m. pour la santé, pour la digestion,** bad for the health, the digestion; (*e*) imperfect, poor, inadequate; **avoir m. air,** (i) to look ill; (ii) to have a poor appearance; **mauvaise santé,** bad, poor, health; **mauvaise vue,** poor eyesight; **il a fait une mauvaise bronchite,** he's had a bad attack of bronchitis; **faire de mauvaises affaires,** to be doing badly (in business); **m. frein,** defective brake; (*f*) wrong; **c'est la mauvaise clef,** it's the wrong key; **arriver au m. moment,** to come at an inconvenient time, at an awkward moment; **rire au m. endroit,** to laugh in the wrong place; **tenir qch. par le m. bout,** to hold sth. by the wrong end.

mauve [mov] **1.** *n.f. Bot:* mallow. **2.** *a.* & *n.m.* mauve.

mauviette [movjɛt] *n.f.* (*a*) *Cu: O:* lark (in season); (*b*) slight, frail, puny, person.

maxi [maksi] *n.m. or f. Cost: F:* maxi (coat, etc.).

maxillaire [maksilɛr] *a. Anat:* maxillary; *a.* & *n.m.* **(os) m.,** jawbone, maxilla.

maximal, -aux [maksimal, -o] *a.* **1.** maximum (effect, etc.). **2.** maximal.

maxime [maksim] *n.f.* maxim.

maximum [maksimɔm] maximum. **1.** *n.m.* **m. de rendement,** maximum efficiency; **porter la production au m.,** to raise production to a maximum; **m. de la peine,** maximum punishment; **thermomètre à maxima,** maximum thermometer; *pl. maximums, maxima.* **2.** *a. usu. inv.* **rendement m.,** maximum, peak, output; **pression m.,** maximum pressure.

Mayence [majɑ̃s] *Pr.n.f. Geog:* Mainz.

mayonnaise [majɔnɛz] *n.f. Cu:* mayonnaise.
mazout [mazut] *n.m.* (fuel) oil; **chauffage central au m.,** oil-fired central heating.
mazurka [mazyrka] *n.f.* mazurka.
me, *before a vowel sound* **m'** [m(ə)] *pers.pron.* (*a*) (*acc.*) me; **il m'aime,** he loves me; **me voici,** here I am; (*b*) (*dat.*) (to) me; **il m'a écrit,** he wrote to me; **il me l'a dit,** he told me so; **donnez-m'en,** give me some; (*c*) myself; **je m'amusais,** I was enjoying myself; **je me suis dit que . . .,** I said to myself that . . ..
mea-culpa [meakylpa] *n.m.inv.* **faire, dire, son m.-c.,** to confess one's sins.
méandre [meɑ̃dr̥] *n.m.* meander, loop (of river); winding, bend (of road).
mec [mɛk] *n.m. P:* chap, bloke, guy.
mécanicien, -ienne [mekanisjɛ̃, -jɛn] **1.** *n.* (*a*) (garage, motor) mechanic; **m. dentiste,** dental mechanic, technician; (*b*) *Nau:* engineer; *Navy:* engineroom artificer; *Av:* **m. de bord, m. navigant,** flight engineer; (*c*) **ingénieur m.,** mechanical engineer; (*d*) *Rail:* engine driver, *NAm:* engineer; (*e*) mechanician. **2.** *n.f.* **mécanicienne,** machinist (on sewing machine).
mécanique [mekanik] **1.** *a.* mechanical; (*a*) **métier m.,** power loom; **atelier(s) de constructions mécaniques,** engineering works; (*b*) machine-made (lace, tiles, etc.); (*c*) clockwork (railway, etc.). **2.** *n.f.* (*a*) (science of) mechanics; **m. quantique,** quantum mechanics; (*b*) engineering; (*c*) mechanism, piece of machinery; (*d*) mechanical, technical, skill; **la m. du piano,** piano technique.
mécaniquement [mekanikmɑ̃] *adv.* mechanically.
mécanisation [mekanizasjɔ̃] *n.f.* mechanization.
mécaniser [mekanize] *v.tr.* to mechanize.
mécanisme [mekanism] *n.m.* **1.** mechanism, machinery; works (of a watch, etc.); **m. du corps humain,** mechanics of the human body; **m. administratif,** administrative machinery. **2.** working; technique.
mécano [mekano] *n.m. F:* mechanic.
mécanographe [mekanɔgraf] *n.* accounting machine operator; *Cmptr:* punch(ed) card machine operator; junior programmer.
mécanographie [mekanɔgrafi] *n.f.* (*in offices*) (*a*) data processing; (*b*) data processing department.
mécanographique [mekanɔgrafik] *a.* **service m.,** data processing department; **fiche m.,** punch(ed) card.
Mécène [mesɛn] **1.** *Pr.n.m. Lt.Lit:* Maecenas. **2.** *n.m.* patron (of the arts).
méchamment [meʃamɑ̃] *adv.* (*a*) spitefully, maliciously; (*b*) mischievously.
méchanceté [meʃɑ̃ste] *n.f.* **1.** (*a*) spitefulness, maliciousness, unkindness; **faire qch. par m.,** to do sth. out of spite, out of malice; (*b*) wickedness; naughtiness, mischievousness. **2.** spiteful action, remark; **quelle m.!** what a spiteful, a nasty, an unkind, thing to do, say.
méchant, -ante [meʃɑ̃, -ɑ̃t] *a.* **1.** (*a*) *A:* miserable, wretched, poor, sorry (dwelling, etc.); **un m. billet de cent francs,** a paltry hundred-franc note; **méchante excuse,** lame excuse; (*b*) unpleasant, disagreeable (business, etc.); **être de méchante humeur,** to be in a (bad) temper. **2.** (*a*) spiteful, malicious, ill-natured, unkind (person); *F:* **pas m.,** harmless; (*b*) (*of pers., action*) wicked, evil; (*of child*) naughty, mischievous; *n.* **petit m.! petite méchante!** you naughty little boy, girl! **les méchants,** the wicked; (*c*) vicious, bad-tempered (animal); *P.N:* **chien m.** = beware of the dog.
mèche¹ [mɛʃ] *n.f.* **1** (*a*) wick (of candle, lamp); (*b*) match (for firing explosives); touch, fuse (of mine); *F:* **vendre la m.,** to give the game away, blow the gaff; **découvrir la m.,** to uncover the plot. **2.** lock (of hair); wisp, tuft (of wool, etc.); *Surg:* tent; *Hairdr:* **m. postiche,** hairpiece; (man's) toupee. **3.** (*a*) core, heart (of cable, etc.); *El:* **charbon à m.,** cored carbon; (*b*) *Nau:* mainpiece (of rudder); spindle (of capstan). **4.** *Tls:* (*a*) bit, drill; **m. anglaise, à trois pointes,** centre bit, *NAm:* center bit; **m. hélicoïdale,** twist bit, twist drill; auger bit; (*b*) *Carp:* auger, gimlet.
mèche² *n.inv.* (*a*) *P:* **il n'y a pas m.,** it's quite impossible; nothing doing; (*b*) *F:* **être de m. avec qn,** to be in collusion, in league, in cahoots, with s.o.
mécompte [mekɔ̃t] *n.m.* **1.** miscalculation, miscount; error. **2.** mistaken judgment; disappointment; **il a eu un grave m.,** he has been badly let down.
méconnaissable [mekɔnɛsabl̥] *a.* hardly recognizable; unrecognizable.
méconnaissance [mekɔnɛsɑ̃s] *n.f.* (*a*) failure to recognize, to appreciate (s.o.'s talent, etc.); misreading (of the facts); ignoring (one's obligations); (*b*) disavowal, repudiation (of an action, etc.).
méconnaître [mekɔnɛtr̥] *v.tr.* (*conj. like* CONNAÎTRE) (*a*) to fail to recognize, to fail to appreciate (s.o.'s talent, etc.); to belittle (plan, etc.); to disregard (duty); **m. les faits,** to ignore the facts; (*b*) to disown, repudiate (action, etc.).
méconnu [mekɔny] *a.* unrecognized, unappreciated (talent, etc.); misunderstood.
mécontent, -ente [mekɔ̃tɑ̃, -ɑ̃t] **1.** *a.* discontented, displeased, dissatisfied (**de,** with); **être m. que** + *sub.*, to be annoyed that . . .. **2.** *n.* grumbler; malcontent.
mécontentement [mekɔ̃tɑ̃tmɑ̃] *n.m.* dissatisfaction (**de,** with); displeasure (**de,** at); discontent; **marquer son m.,** to show, express, one's annoyance.
mécontenter [mekɔ̃tɑ̃te] *v.tr.* to dissatisfy, displease, annoy (s.o.).
Mecque (la) [lamɛk] *Pr.n.f. Geog:* Mecca.
mécréant, -ante [mekreɑ̃, -ɑ̃t] **1.** *a.* (*a*) *O:* misbelieving; (*b*) unbelieving. **2.** *n.* (*a*) *O:* misbeliever; (*b*) unbeliever, infidel; (*c*) *F: A:* miscreant, wretch.
médaille [medaj] *n.f.* **1.** medal; **le revers de la m.,** (i) the reverse of the medal; (ii) the other side of the picture. **2.** (official) badge.
médaillé, -ée [medaje] **1.** *a.* holding a medal; decorated. **2.** *n.* medal-holder; medallist.
médaillier [medaje] *n.m.* medal collection (in cabinet).
médaillon [medajɔ̃] *n.m.* **1.** (*a*) medallion; (*b*) pat (of butter). **2.** locket.
médecin [mɛdsɛ̃] *n.m.* doctor; physician; **femme m.,** woman doctor; **m. de médecine générale, m. généraliste,** general practitioner, G.P.; **m. consultant,** consulting physician, consultant; **m. légiste,** forensic pathologist; **m. militaire,** army medical officer, M.O.; **m. de bord,** ship's doctor; **qui est votre m. (traitant)?** who is your (regular) doctor?
médecine [mɛdsin] *n.f.* **1.** (art of) medicine; **docteur en m.,** doctor of medicine, M.D.; **étudiant en m.,** medical student; **école de m.,** medical school; **m. légale,** forensic medicine. **2.** *A:* (dose of) medicine.
médial, -ale, -aux [medjal, -o] **1.** *a. Ling:* medial (letter). **2.** *n.f. Stat:* median, mean.
médian, -iane [medjɑ̃, -jan] **1.** median (nerve, line, etc.); *Hairdr:* **raie médiane,** parting in the middle. **2.** *n.f.* (*a*) *Ling:* mid vowel; (*b*) *Stat:* median.
médiateur, -trice [medjatœr, -tris] **1.** *a.* mediating, mediatory. **2.** *n.* mediator; intermediary.
médiation [medjasjɔ̃] *n.f.* mediation.
médiator [medjatɔr] *n.m. Mus:* plectrum.
médical, -aux [medikal, -o] *a.* medical; **matière médicale,** materia medica; **examen m. (complet),** check-up; **certificat m.,** medical certificate.
médicalement [medikalmɑ̃] *adv.* medically.
médicament [medikamɑ̃] *n.m.* medicine; drug.

médicamenteux, -euse [medikamɑ̃tø, -øz] *a.* medicinal.
médication [medikasjɔ̃] *n.f.* medication, medical treatment.
médicinal, -aux [medisinal, -o] *a.* medicinal.
Medicis [medisis] *n.m.pl. Hist:* Medici (family).
médico-légal, -aux [medikɔlegal, -o] *a.* forensic.
médiéval, -aux [medjeval, -o] *a.* medi(a)eval.
médiéviste [medjevist] *n.* medi(a)evalist.
médiocre [medjɔkr̥] **1.** *a.* mediocre; indifferent (work); feeble (performance); second-rate; moderate (ability, etc.); **vin m.,** poor wine. **2.** *n.m.* mediocrity.
médiocrement [medjɔkrəmɑ̃] *adv.* indifferently, poorly; **m. riche,** not very rich.
médiocrité [medjɔkrite] *n.f.* (*a*) mediocrity; (*b*) **les médiocrités,** undistinguished people; second-raters.
médire [medir] *v.i.* (*conj. like* DIRE, *except pr.ind. and imp.* **médisez**) **m. de qn,** to speak ill of s.o.; to run s.o. down.
médisance [medizɑ̃s] *n.f.* **1.** slander, scandalmongering. **2.** (piece of) scandal, slander.
médisant, -ante [medizɑ̃, -ɑ̃t] **1.** *a.* slanderous, scandalmongering. **2.** *n.* slanderer, scandalmonger.
méditatif, -ive [meditatif, -iv] *a.* meditative; thoughtful.
méditation [meditasjɔ̃] *n.f.* meditation; musing; **plongé dans la m.,** lost in thought.
méditer [medite] **1.** *v.i.* to meditate, muse, ponder. **2.** *v.tr.* to contemplate, to meditate (on), ponder (over) (sth.); to have (sth.) in mind; **m. de faire qch.,** to be thinking of doing sth.
méditerrané [mediterane] *a.* (*a*) *A:* mediterranean, inland, landlocked (sea, etc.); (*b*) *Geog:* **la (mer) Méditerranée,** the Mediterranean (Sea).
méditerranéen, -enne [mediteraneɛ̃, -ɛn] *a. Geog:* Mediterranean.
médium [medjɔm] *n.m.* **1.** *Mus:* middle register (of the voice). **2.** *Psychics:* medium.
médius [medjys] *n.m.* middle finger.
médullaire [medylɛr] *a. Anat: Bot:* medullary.
Méduse [medyz] **1.** *Pr.n.f. Gr.Myth:* Medusa. **2.** *n.f. Coel:* medusa, jellyfish.
méduser [medyze] *v.tr. F:* to petrify, paralyse, stupefy.
meeting [mitiŋ] *n.m. Pol: Sp: etc:* meeting; **m. d'aviation,** air show.
méfait [mefɛ] *n.m.* misdeed; misdemeanour, *NAm:* misdemeanor; **méfaits d'un orage,** storm damage; **se déclarer l'auteur du m.,** to own up to the deed.
méfiance [mefjɑ̃s] *n.f.* distrust, mistrust; **avoir de la m. envers qn,** to distrust s.o.; **regarder qn avec m.,** to eye s.o. distrustfully, suspiciously.
méfiant [mefjɑ̃] *a.* distrustful, mistrustful, suspicious (**à l'égard de,** of).
méfier (se) [səmefje] *v.pr.* (*impf. & pr.sub.* **n.n. méfiions, v.v. méfiiez**) (*a*) **se m. de qn,** to distrust, mistrust, s.o.; **méfiez-vous des pickpockets,** beware of pickpockets; **se m. de qch.,** to be suspicious, wary, of sth., be on one's guard against sth.; (*b*) to be on one's guard.
méforme [mefɔrm] *n.f. Sp:* poor form, condition; **être en m.,** to be off form.
mégacycle [megasikl̥], **megahertz** [megaɛrts] *n.m. El.Meas:* megacycle.
mégalithe [megalit] *n.m.* megalith.
mégalithique [megalitik] *a.* megalithic.
mégalomane [megalɔman] *a. & n.* megalomaniac.
mégalomanie [megalɔmani] *n.f.* megalomania.
mégaphone [megafɔn] *n.m.* megaphone.
mégarde (par) [parmegard] *adv.phr.* inadvertently; accidentally.
mégatonne [megatɔn] *n.f.* megaton.
mégère [meʒɛr] *n.f.* shrew, termagant.
mégir [meʒir] *v.tr.*, **mégisser** [meʒise] *v.tr.* to taw, dress (light skins).
mégis [meʒi] *a.m.* **cuir m.,** tawed leather, white leather.
mégot [mego] *n.m. F:* cigarette end; fag end; stump, butt (of cigar); *NAm:* (cigarette) butt.
méhari [meari] *n.m.* fast dromedary, racing camel, mehari; *pl. méhara, méharis.*
méhariste [mearist] *n.m.* cameleer; meharist; *A: Mil:* member of camel corps, camelry (in Sahara).
meilleur, -eure [mɛjœr] *a.* **1.** (*comp. of* BON) better; **rendre qch. m.,** to improve sth.; **devenir m.,** to get better, improve; **je ne connais rien de m.,** I don't know anything better; **les choses prennent une meilleure tournure,** things are taking a turn for the better; **de meilleure heure,** earlier; **m. marché,** cheaper; *adv.* **il fait m.,** the weather's better; **il fait m. ici,** it's better here. **2.** (*sup. of* BON) **le m., la meilleure,** (i) the best (of several); (ii) the better (of two); (*a*) **m. ami,** best friend; **nous sommes les meilleurs amis du monde,** we're the best of friends; *Corr:* **meilleurs vœux,** with all good wishes, with best wishes; (*b*) *n.* **que le m. gagne,** may the best man win; **pour le m. et pour le pire,** for better (or) for worse; **donner le m. de soi-même,** to give of one's best; *Sp:* **prendre le m. sur son adversaire,** to get the better of one's opponent.
méjuger [meʒyʒe] (*conj. like* JUGER) **1.** *v.i. Lit:* **m. de qn, qch.,** to underestimate s.o., sth. **2.** *v.tr.* to misjudge. **3. se m.,** to underestimate oneself.
mélancolie [melɑ̃kɔli] *n.f.* **1.** melancholy; gloom. **2.** *Med:* melancholia.
mélancolique [melɑ̃kɔlik] *a.* **1.** melancholy, dejected, gloomy, mournful. **2.** *Med:* melancholic.
Mélanésie [melanezi] *Pr.n.f. Geog:* Melanesia.
mélange [melɑ̃ʒ] *n.m.* **1.** mixing; blending (of tea, etc.); crossing (of breeds); mingling. **2.** mixture; blend (of tea, etc.); intermixture, cross (of breeds, etc.); mix (of cement, etc.); miscellany (of objects); **sans m.,** unmixed, unadulterated; *I.C.E:* **m. explosif, détonant,** explosive mixture.
mélangé [melɑ̃ʒe] *a.* mixed (society, breed); motley (crowd).
mélanger [melɑ̃ʒe] **(je mélangeai(s); n. mélangeons) 1.** *v.tr.* to mix; to mingle; to blend (teas, etc.); to mix up (ideas, documents, etc.). **2. se m.,** to mix, mingle, blend.
mélangeur [melɑ̃ʒœr] *n.m.*, **mélangeuse** [melɑ̃ʒøz] *n.f.* mixer, mixing machine; *Elcs:* **mélangeur (de son),** mixer.
mélasse [melas] *n.f.* molasses, treacle; **m. raffinée,** golden syrup; *F:* **être dans la m.,** to be in a mess, in the soup.
mêlé [mele] *a.* **1.** mixed (feelings, company); mingled (tones). **2.** tangled (skein, hair, etc.); tousled (hair); involved (business).
mêlée [mele] *n.f.* (*a*) conflict; fray, mêlée; (*b*) *F:* scuffle, tussle, free-for-all; (*c*) scramble; (*d*) *Rugby Fb:* scrum(mage).
mêler [mele] **1.** *v.tr.* to mix, mingle, blend; (*a*) **m. qch. à, avec, qch.,** to mix, combine, sth. with sth.; **il est mêlé à tout,** he's got a finger in every pie; **m. son vin d'eau,** to mix water with one's wine; (*b*) to mix up, jumble up, muddle (up) (papers, etc.); to confuse, tangle (ideas, etc.); to shuffle (cards); *F:* **vous avez bien mêlé les cartes!** a nice mess you've made of it! (*c*) **m. qn à qch.,** to implicate s.o., involve s.o., in sth.; **m. qn à la conversation,** to bring s.o. into the conversation. **2. se m.,** to mix, mingle, blend; **se m. à la foule,** to mingle with, lose oneself in, the crowd; **se m. à la conversation,** to join in, take part in, the conversation; **mêlez-vous de ce qui vous regarde,** mind your own business; **ce n'est pas à moi de m'en m.,** it's not for me to interfere; **se m. de politique,** to dabble in politics.

mélèze [melɛz] *n.m.* larch (tree).

méli-mélo [melimelo] *n.m. F:* jumble (of facts, etc.); hotchpotch; medley (of people, etc.); clutter (of furniture, etc.); *pl. mélis-mélos.*

mélo [melo] *n.m. F:* melodrama.

mélodie [melɔdi] *n.f.* **1.** melody, tune. **2.** melodiousness (of verse, etc.).

mélodieusement [melɔdjøzmɑ̃] *adv.* melodiously; tunefully.

mélodieux, -ieuse [melɔdjø, -jøz] *a.* melodious, tuneful.

mélodique [melɔdik] *a. Mus:* melodic.

mélodiste [melɔdist] *n.* **1.** melody writer. **2.** melodist (as opposed to harmonist).

mélodramatique [melɔdramatik] *a.* melodramatic.

mélodrame [melɔdram] *n.m.* melodrama.

mélomane [melɔman] *n* music lover.

melon [məlɔ̃] *n.m.* **1.** *Bot:* melon; **m. d'eau,** water melon. **2. (chapeau) m.,** bowler (hat), *NAm:* derby.

melonnière [məlɔnjɛr] *n.f.* melon bed.

mélopée [melɔpe] *n.f. Mus:* **1.** art of recitative. **2.** chant, recitative.

membrane [mɑ̃bran] *n.f.* **1.** membrane; **m. poreuse,** porous membrane, diaphragm. **2.** (*in microphone, etc.*) diaphragm.

membraneux, -euse [mɑ̃branø, -øz] *a.* membranous.

membre [mɑ̃br̥] *n.m.* **1.** (*a*) limb; member; **m. viril,** penis; (*b*) member (of an association); *pl.* membership. **2.** (*constituent part*) (*a*) *Ling: Arch:* member; *Mth:* **premier m. d'une équation,** lefthand side of an equation; (*b*) rib, timber (of ship).

membrure [mɑ̃bryr] *n.f.* **1.** (*a*) *coll.* limbs; **homme à forte m.,** strong-limbed, powerfully built, man; (*b*) frame(work) (of building, etc.); (*c*) *coll.* ribs (of ship). **2.** *Civ.E:* flange (of web girder).

même [mɛm] **1.** *a.* (*a*) same; **une seule et m. chose,** one and the same thing; **ils sont du m. âge,** they're the same age; **ce m. jour,** the same day; **tous rassemblés en un m. lieu,** all gathered in the same place; **en m. temps,** at the same time; **elle est toujours la m.,** she's always the same; **cela revient au m.,** it comes, amounts, to the same thing; (*b*) (*following the noun*) very; **aujourd'hui m.,** this very day; **il habite ici m.,** he lives in this very place, in this very house; **les enfants mêmes le savaient,** even the children knew it; **c'est cela m.,** that's the very thing; **donner les chiffres mêmes,** to give the actual figures; **les deux concepts sont mêmes,** the two concepts are identical; (*c*) self; **elle est la bonté m.,** she's kindness itself; **moi-m.,** myself; **toi-m.,** yourself; **lui-m.,** himself, itself; **elle-m.,** herself, itself; **soi-m.,** oneself; **nous-mêmes,** ourselves; **vous-m.,** yourself; **vous-mêmes,** yourselves; **eux-mêmes, elles-mêmes,** themselves; **il l'a fait lui-m.,** he did it himself; **faire qch. de soi-m.,** to do sth. of one's own accord; **la chose n'est pas mauvaise en elle-m.,** the thing is not bad in itself, per se; **un autre lui-m.,** a second self. **2.** *adv.* even; **aimer m. ses ennemis,** to love even one's enemies; **je le pense et m. j'en suis sûr,** I think so; in fact I am sure of it; **je n'ai pas m., je n'ai m. pas, le prix de mon voyage,** I haven't even enough to pay my fare; **m. si je le savais,** even if I knew. **3. de m.,** in the same way; **faire de m.,** to do likewise; to do the same; **il en est de m. des autres,** it's the same, the same holds good, for the others; **de m. que,** (just) as, like; **tout de m.,** all the same; for all that; **mais tout de m.!** well really! **boire à m. la bouteille,** to drink (straight) out of the bottle; **des maisons bâties à m. le trottoir,** houses built flush with the pavement; **couché à m. le sable,** lying on the bare sand; **taillé à m. la pierre,** cut out of solid rock; **à m. la peau,** next to the skin; **être à m. de faire qch.,** to be able, in a position, to do sth.; **il n'est pas à m. de faire le voyage,** he's not up to making the journey; **cela me met à m. de le faire,** that enables me, puts me in a position, to do it.

mémé [meme] *n.f. F:* grandma, gran(ny), nan.

mémento [memɛ̃to] *n.m.* **1.** (*a*) memorandum, note; (*b*) memento, reminder. **2.** (*a*) notebook, memorandum book; (*b*) *Sch:* **m. de chimie,** revision notes in chemistry.

mémère [memɛr] *n.f. F:* **1.** grandma, gran(ny), nan. **2.** *F:* **le petit chien-chien à sa m.,** mummy's little doggie-woggie. **3.** *Pej:* (blousy) middle-aged woman; old girl.

mémoire¹ [memwar] *n.f.* memory; (*a*) **je n'ai pas la m. des noms,** I've no memory for names; **il n'a pas de m.,** he's got a bad memory; **si j'ai bonne m.,** if I remember rightly; (*b*) recollection, remembrance; **perdre la m. de qch.,** to forget sth.; **garder la m. de qch.,** to keep sth. in mind; **avoir m. de qch.,** to remember sth.; **rappeler qch. à la m. de qn,** to remind s.o. of sth.; **je vais lui rafraîchir la m.,** I'll send him a reminder; I'll jog his memory; **réciter qch. de m.,** to recite sth. from memory; **de m. d'homme,** within living memory; (*of monument, etc.*) **à la m. de qn,** in memory of s.o., to the memory of s.o.; (*c*) *Cmptr:* memory, store; storage.

mémoire² *n.m.* **1.** (*a*) memorandum; report; *Jur:* (written) statement (of case); (*b*) memoir, paper, dissertation, thesis. **2.** (contractor's) account; bill (of costs). **3.** *pl.* (*a*) (historical) memoirs; (*b*) transactions (of learned society, etc.).

mémorable [memɔrabl̥] *a.* memorable, noteworthy; eventful (year).

mémorandum [memɔrɑ̃dɔm] *n.m.* **1.** memorandum, note; *Adm: etc:* orders (in brief); *Navy:* **m. de combat,** battle orders. **2.** notebook.

mémorial, -iaux [memɔrjal, -jo] *n.m.* **1.** (*a*) (*monument*) memorial; (*b*) memoir. **2.** *Com:* daybook.

mémorisation [memɔrizasjɔ̃] *n.f.* memorization, memorizing.

mémoriser [memɔrize] *v.tr.* to memorize (sth.); to commit (sth.) to memory.

menaçant [mənasɑ̃] *a.* menacing, threatening; forbidding (look); lowering (sky).

menace [mənas] *n.f.* threat, menace; *pl. Jur:* intimidation; **menaces en l'air,** empty, idle, threats; **silence lourd de menaces,** ominous silence.

menacer [mənase] *v.tr.* **(je menaçai(s); n. menaçons)** to threaten, menace; (*a*) **m. qn du doigt, du poing,** to shake one's finger, one's fist, at s.o.; **m. qn d'un procès,** to threaten s.o. with legal proceedings; **m. de faire qch.,** to threaten to do sth.; (*b*) (*of building, etc.*) **m. ruine,** to be in danger of collapsing, of falling down; **la tempête menace,** a storm is brewing.

ménade [menad] *n.f. Gr.Myth:* maenad, bacchante.

ménage [menaʒ] *n.m.* **1.** (*a*) housekeeping; domestic arrangements; **jouer au m.,** to play at (keeping) house; **tenir le m. de qn,** to keep house for s.o.; **pain de m.,** large (homemade) loaf; (*b*) **faire le m.,** to do the housework; **les affaires du m., le m.,** household duties; *Fr.C:* **le grand m.,** spring cleaning; **faire des ménages,** to go out cleaning; **femme de m.,** cleaner, daily help, *F:* daily. **2.** (*a*) *A:* household goods; (*b*) **monter son m.,** to furnish one's house; **m. de poupée,** set of doll's furniture. **3.** household, family; **jeune m.,** young (married) couple; **m. à trois,** (matrimonial) triangle; **se mettre en m.,** to set up house; **faire bon, mauvais, m. (ensemble),** to get on well, badly, together. **4.** *A:* thrift.

ménagement [menaʒmɑ̃] *n.m.* care; caution, circumspection; consideration; **avec ménagement(s),** carefully, cautiously; considerately, tactfully; **parler sans ménagement(s),** to speak bluntly.

ménager¹ [menaʒe] **(je ménageai(s); n. ménageons)**

1. *v.tr.* (*a*) to save; to economize on (sth.); to use (sth.) sparingly, economically; **m. sa santé,** to take care of one's health; **m. son cheval,** to spare one's horse; **m. qn,** to treat s.o. tactfully, with consideration; **ne le ménagez pas,** don't spare him; **sans m. ses paroles,** without mincing one's words; (*b*) to contrive, arrange; **m. une réconciliation entre deux ennemis,** to bring about a reconciliation between two enemies; **m. une surprise à qn,** to prepare a surprise for s.o.; **m. une ouverture pour les fils,** to make an opening for the wires; **m. une sortie,** to provide an exit. **2. se m.,** to spare oneself, take care of oneself; *Pej:* to coddle oneself.

ménager², -ère [menaʒe, -ɛr] **1.** *a.* (*a*) household (equipment, etc.); **travaux ménagers,** housework; **arts ménagers,** domestic science; *Sch:* **enseignement m.,** domestic science; home economics; **eaux ménagères,** waste water; **Salon des Arts Ménagers** = Ideal Home Exhibition; (*b*) *A:* thrifty, sparing. **2.** *n.f.* **ménagère** (*a*) housewife; **elle est bonne ménagère,** she's a good housekeeper; (*b*) canteen of cutlery.

ménagerie [menaʒri] *n.f.* menagerie.

mendélien, -ienne [mɛ̃deljɛ̃, -jɛn] *a. Biol:* Mendelian.

mendélisme [mɛ̃delism] *n.m. Biol:* Mendelism.

mendiant, -ante [mɑ̃djɑ̃, -ɑ̃t] **1.** *a.* mendicant, begging (friar, order, etc.). **2.** *n.* mendicant; beggar(man, -woman); **les quatre mendiants,** (i) *Ecc.Hist:* the four mendicant orders; (ii) almonds, raisins, hazelnuts and figs (served as dessert).

mendicité [mɑ̃disite] *n.f.* mendicity; begging; **réduit à la m.,** reduced to beggary.

mendier [mɑ̃dje] (*impf. & pr.sub.* **n. mendiions, v. mendiiez**) **1.** *v.i.* to beg; **faire son chemin jusqu'à Paris en mendiant,** to beg one's way to Paris. **2.** *v.tr.* (*a*) to beg (for) (one's bread); (*b*) to canvass (votes).

mendigo(t), -ote [mɑ̃digo, -ɔt] *n. P:* beggar.

meneau, -eaux [məno] *n.m. Arch:* **m. vertical,** mullion; **m. horizontal,** transom.

menée [məne] *n.f.* underhand manoeuvre, *NAm:* maneuver; intrigue; *pl.* schemings (of political party, etc.); **déjouer les menées de qn,** to thwart, outwit, s.o.

mener [məne] *v.tr.* **(je mène; je mènerai) 1.** (*a*) to lead; to take (s.o. somewhere); **m. qn à sa chambre,** to take, show, s.o. to his room; **m. une ligne entre deux points,** to draw a line between two points; (*b*) to be, go, ahead (of); **m. la danse,** (i) to lead the dance; (ii) to give the orders, call the tune; **m. le deuil,** to be chief mourner; *Sp:* **la France mène (la Belgique) par 2 à 1,** France is leading (Belgium) by 2 to 1; (*c*) **chemin qui mène à la ville,** road that leads to the town; **cela ne mène à rien,** this is getting us nowhere; **cela nous mène à croire que . . .,** this leads us to believe that . . .; (*d*) to control, manage; **mari mené par sa femme,** henpecked husband; **m. son personnel au doigt et à l'œil,** to have one's staff well trained, under one's thumb. **2.** to drive (horse); to steer (boat); **m. de front plusieurs affaires,** to have several irons in the fire; *Mec.E:* **roue menée,** driven wheel. **3.** to manage, conduct (business, etc.); **m. qch. à bonne fin, à bien,** to bring sth. to a successful conclusion; to carry through, carry out, work out (plan); **m. une vie triste,** to lead a sad life; **ne pas en m. large,** to be in a tight corner.

ménestrel [menɛstrɛl] *n.m.* minstrel.

ménétrier [menetrije] *n.m.* (strolling) fiddler.

meneur, -euse [mənœr, -øz] *n.* (*a*) leader (of political party, etc.); **m. du jeu,** (i) moving spirit; (ii) *T.V: etc:* question master; quiz master; (*b*) ringleader (of revolt, etc.); agitator; (*c*) **m. de bœufs,** cattle drover; **m. d'ours,** bear leader.

menhir [menir] *n.m.* menhir.

méninge [menɛ̃ʒ] *n.f. Anat:* meninx; **les trois méninges,** the three meninges; *F:* **se creuser les méninges,** to rack one's brains; **il ne se fatigue pas les méninges,** he doesn't exactly overwork.

méningé [menɛ̃ʒe] *a. Anat:* meningeal.

méningite [menɛ̃ʒit] *n.f. Med:* meningitis.

ménopause [menɔpoz] *n.f. Physiol:* menopause.

ménorragie [menɔraʒi] *n.f. Med:* menorrhagia.

menotte [mənɔt] *n.f.* **1.** (*child's language*) little hand. **2.** (*a*) *pl.* handcuffs; manacles; (*b*) link, shackle (of shaft, spring, etc.).

mensonge [mɑ̃sɔ̃ʒ] *n.m.* (*a*) lie; **faire, dire, un m.,** to tell a lie; **petit m., m. innocent, pieux m.,** white lie; **gros m.,** downright lie; *F:* whopper; (*b*) lying; error, fallacy; delusion.

mensonger, -ère [mɑ̃sɔ̃ʒe, -ɛr] *a.* lying, untrue, mendacious (story); deceitful, false (look); vain, deceptive, illusory (hope).

menstruation [mɑ̃stryasjɔ̃] *n.f. Physiol:* menstruation.

menstruel, -elle [mɑ̃stryɛl] *a. Physiol:* menstrual.

menstrues [mɑ̃stry] *n.f.pl. Physiol:* menses.

mensualisation [mɑ̃sɥalizasjɔ̃] *n.f.* paying (of staff) by the month.

mensualiser [mɑ̃sɥalize] *v.tr.* to pay (staff) monthly.

mensualité [mɑ̃sɥalite] *n.f.* monthly payment; **payer par mensualités,** to pay monthly, by monthly instalments.

mensuel, -elle [mɑ̃sɥɛl] **1.** *a.* monthly. **2.** (*a*) *n.m.* monthly magazine; (*b*) *n.* employee paid monthly.

mensuellement [mɑ̃sɥɛlmɑ̃] *adv.* monthly.

mensuration [mɑ̃syrasjɔ̃] *n.f.* measurement; measuring; mensuration; *F:* (*of woman*) **mensurations,** vital statistics.

mental, -aux [mɑ̃tal, -o] *a.* mental (arithmetic, disease, etc.); **aliénation mentale,** mental alienation; insanity.

mentalement [mɑ̃talmɑ̃] *adv.* mentally.

mentalité [mɑ̃talite] *n.f.* mentality.

menteur, -euse [mɑ̃tœr, -øz] **1.** *a.* (*a*) lying, untruthful, mendacious (person); (*b*) false, deceptive (appearance). **2.** *n.* liar.

menthe [mɑ̃t] *n.f. Bot:* mint; **m. verte,** spearmint, garden mint; **m. anglaise, poivrée,** peppermint; **pastilles de m.,** (pepper)mints.

menthol [mɛ̃tɔl] *n.m. Ch: Pharm:* menthol.

mentholé [mɛ̃tɔle] *a. Pharm:* mentholated.

mention [mɑ̃sjɔ̃] *n.f.* (*a*) mention; **faire m. de qn, de qch.,** to refer to, mention, s.o., sth.; *Sch:* **reçu avec m.** = passed with distinction; (*b*) *Post:* endorsement (on envelope, etc.); **m.** *inconnu*, stamped *not known*; (*c*) reference (at head of letter).

mentionner [mɑ̃sjɔne] *v.tr.* to mention; **mentionné ci-dessus,** above-mentioned, aforesaid.

mentir [mɑ̃tir] *v.i.* (*pr.p.* **mentant;** *p.p.* **menti;** *pr.ind.* **je mens, il ment, n. mentons, ils mentent;** *p.h.* **je mentis;** *fu.* **je mentirai**) to lie, to tell lies; **sans m.!** honestly! **il en a menti!** that was a lie!

menton [mɑ̃tɔ̃] *n.m.* chin; **double m.,** double chin; **m. en galoche,** jutting chin; **m. fuyant,** receding chin; *F:* **s'en mettre jusqu'au m.,** to stuff oneself, have a good feed.

mentonnet [mɑ̃tɔnɛ] *n.m.* (*a*) catch (of latch, etc.); stop (on moving part of machine); (*b*) *Mec.E:* tappet, cam; (*c*) *Rail:* flange (of wheel); (*d*) lug; ear (of bomb).

mentonnier, -ière [mɑ̃tɔnje, -jɛr] **1.** *a. Anat:* of the chin. **2.** *n.f.* **mentonnière** (*a*) *Arm:* chinpiece (of helmet); (*b*) (bonnet) string; *Mil: etc:* chin strap; *Med:* chin bandage; (*c*) *Mus:* chin rest (of violin).

mentor [mɛ̃tɔr] *n.m. Lit:* mentor.

menu [məny] **1.** *a.* (*a*) small; fine (gravel, etc.); slender, slim, slight (figure); tiny (fragment); **m. plomb,** small shot, bird shot; **menue monnaie,** small change; (*b*) trifling, petty (incident, etc.); **menues réparations,** minor repairs; **menus détails,** small, minute, details; **menus frais,** minor expenses; **m. peuple,** humble people; **menus propos,** small talk. **2.** *adv.* small, fine; **hacher m.,** to chop (meat, etc.) up small; to mince (sth.); **il pleuvait dru et m.,** the rain came down in a steady drizzle; **écrire m.,** to write small. **3.** *n.m.* (*a*) *pl.* **menus,** small coal; slack; (*b*) **raconter qch. par le m.,** to relate sth. in detail; (*c*) menu, bill of fare.

menuet [mənɥɛ] *n.m. Danc: Mus:* minuet.

menuiser [mənɥize] *v.tr.* **1.** to cut down, plane down (wood to required size). **2.** to do joinery, woodwork.

menuiserie [mənɥizri] *n.f.* **1.** joinery, woodwork; carpentry. **2.** joiner's shop.

menuisier [mənɥizje] *n.m.* joiner; **m. en meubles,** cabinet maker; **m. en bâtiments,** carpenter.

méphistophélique [mefistɔfelik] *a.* Mephistophelian.

méphitique [mefitik] *a.* mephitic, foul, noxious.

méplat [mepla] **1.** *a.* flat; *Const:* (*of joist, etc.*) flat-laid; in planks. **2.** *n.m.* (*a*) flat part; flattening; ledge (of rock); (*b*) *Art:* **méplats du visage,** planes that build up the face.

méprendre (se) [səmeprɑ̃dr̥] *v.pr.* (*conj. like* PRENDRE) to be mistaken, make a mistake (**sur, quant à,** about); **se m. sur un motif,** to mistake, misjudge, misunderstand, a motive; **il n'y a pas à s'y m.,** there can be no mistake about it; **il imitait le maître à s'y m.,** he could give a lifelike imitation of the master.

mépris [mepri] *n.m.* contempt, scorn; **m. des richesses,** contempt for, scorn of, wealth; **avoir du m. pour qn,** to despise s.o.; **au m. de qch.,** in contempt, in defiance, of sth.; **avec m.,** scornfully, contemptuously; **sourire de m.,** contemptuous smile; *Prov:* **la familiarité engendre le m.,** familiarity breeds contempt.

méprisable [meprizabl̥] *a.* contemptible, despicable.

méprisant [meprizɑ̃] *a.* contemptuous, scornful.

méprise [mepriz] *n.f.* mistake, misapprehension; **par m.,** by mistake.

mépriser [meprize] *v.tr.* to despise, scorn; to hold (s.o., sth.) in contempt; **méprisé de, par, qn,** despised by s.o.; **m. les dangers,** to disregard, scoff at, make light of, dangers.

mer [mɛr] *n.f.* sea; (*a*) **la haute m., la grande m., la m. libre,** the open sea, the high seas; **en haute m., en pleine m.,** out at sea; **m. fermée,** inland sea, landlocked sea; *F:* **m. d'huile,** sea as smooth as a millpond; **d'une m. à l'autre,** from coast to coast; **au bord de la m.,** at the seaside; **homme, gens, de m.,** seaman, seamen; seafaring man, men; **grosse m.,** heavy sea; **il y a de la m.,** the sea is running high, there's a heavy sea; **essuyer un coup de m.,** to be struck by a heavy sea; **un homme à la m.!** man overboard! **servir sur m.,** to serve afloat, at sea; **voyage sur m.,** sea voyage; **prendre la m.,** to set sail, put (out) to sea; **mettre une embarcation à la m.,** to get out, lower, a boat; **tenir la m.,** (i) to keep the sea, remain at sea; (ii) to hold the seas, rule the waves; **navire qui tient bien la m.,** ship that behaves well in a seaway; *F:* **ce n'est pas la m. à boire,** it's quite easy; (*b*) tide; **m. haute, pleine m.,** high tide; **basse m.,** low tide; (*c*) **une m. de sable,** a vast expanse of sand; **une m. de sang,** a sea of blood.

mercanti [mɛrkɑ̃ti] *n.m.* **1.** (oriental) bazaar-keeper. **2.** *Pej:* profiteer; shark.

mercantile [mɛrkɑ̃til] *a.* **1.** *A:* mercantile (operation, etc.); commercial. **2.** *Pej:* **esprit m.,** grabbing, money-making, mentality.

mercantilisme [mɛrkɑ̃tilism] *n.m.* **1.** *Hist:* mercantilism. **2.** *Pej:* money-grabbing, profiteering.

mercenaire [mɛrsənɛr] **1.** *a.* mercenary. **2.** *n.m.* (*a*) *A:* hireling; (*b*) *Mil:* mercenary.

mercerie [mɛrsəri] *n.f.* **1.** drapery, haberdashery, *NAm:* notions. **2.** draper's, haberdasher's (shop).

merceriser [mɛrsərize] *v.tr. Tex:* to mercerize.

merci [mɛrsi] **1.** *n.f.* (*a*) **Dieu m.,** by the favour, *NAm:* favor, of God; thank God; (*b*) mercy; **être à la m. de qn,** to be at s.o.'s mercy; **crier m.,** to cry for mercy; to cry quarter; **sans m.,** merciless(ly), pitiless(ly), ruthless(ly). **2.** *adv.* (*a*) **m. (bien, beaucoup),** thank you (very much); **m. de, pour, votre offre,** thank you for your offer; *usu. Iron:* **grand m.!** (no) thank you! (*b*) no thank you; **prenez-vous du thé?—(non) m.!** will you have some tea?—no, thank you! no thanks! **3.** *n.m.* thank(-)you.

mercier, -ière [mɛrsje, -jɛr] *n.* haberdasher; draper.

mercredi [mɛrkrədi] *n.m.* Wednesday; **le m. des Cendres,** Ash Wednesday.

Mercure [mɛrkyr] **1.** *Pr.n.m. Myth: Astr:* Mercury. **2.** *n.m. Ch:* mercury.

mercuriale[1] [mɛrkyrjal] *n.f. Bot:* mercury.

mercuriale[2] *n.f.* reprimand, dressing down.

mercuriale[3] *n.f.* market price list, market prices (of cereals, etc.).

mercuriel, -ielle [mɛrkyrjɛl] *a. Pharm:* mercurial.

merde [mɛrd] *n.f. P:* **1.** excrement; shit; **il est dans la m.,** he's in a hell of a fix, he's in it up to his bloody neck. **2.** (*a*) (*pers.*) **il ne se croit pas de la m.,** he's got a bloody high opinion of himself; (*b*) (*thg*) shit, crap. **3.** *int.* shit! bloody hell! bugger (it)! Christ!

merdeux, -euse [mɛrdø, -øz] *P:* **1.** *a.* (*of linen, etc.*) soiled with faeces, *NAm:* feces; filthy, shitty; (*of pers.*) **c'est un bâton m.,** he's bloody impossible. **2.** *n.* (*pers.*) (dirty) swine, bugger; *f.* dirty bitch; **un petit m.,** a little squirt.

merdier [mɛrdje] *n.m. P:* **je suis dans un sacré m.,** I'm in a bloody mess, I'm really in the shit.

merdoyer [mɛrdwaje] *v.i.* (**je merdoie, n. merdoyons; je merdoierai**) *P:* to get all tangled up; to make a mess of (answer, etc.).

mère [mɛr] *n.f.* mother. **1.** (*a*) **elle est m. de famille,** she is the mother of a family; **sœur par la m.,** uterine sister, half-sister; **enfants sans m.,** motherless children; **m. nourrice,** wet nurse, fostermother; **m. célibataire,** unmarried mother; (*b*) *Z:* dam; **m. poule,** mother hen; (*c*) *F:* **la m. Martin,** old Mrs Martin; *P:* **et dites donc, la petite m.!** well, missus, duck; (*d*) *Ecc:* **m. abbesse,** abbess; **M. supérieure,** mother superior (of convent). **2.** (*source, origin*) (*a*) **m. de vinaigre,** mother of vinegar; **l'oisiveté est la m. de tous les vices,** idleness is the source, the root, of all evil; (*b*) *Art: Cer:* mould, *NAm:* mold, matrix (for plaster casts, etc.); *Mec.E:* die (of screw thread). **3.** (*a*) **la Reine M.,** the Queen Mother; (*b*) **langue m.,** mother tongue; *Biol:* **cellule m.,** mother cell; *Com:* **maison m.,** parent company.

mère-patrie [mɛrpatri] *n.f.* mother country; *pl. mères-patries.*

méridien, -ienne [meridjɛ̃, -jɛn] **1.** *a.* (*a*) meridian, meridional (line, etc.); (*b*) **chaleur méridienne,** midday heat; **ombre méridienne,** shadow at noon; **cercle m.,** transit (circle). **2.** *n.m.* meridian; **sous le m. de vingt degrés à l'ouest de Greenwich,** twenty degrees West of Greenwich. **3.** *n.f.* **méridienne** (*a*) (i) meridian line; (ii) meridian altitude; (*b*) midday siesta, nap.

méridional, -ale, -aux [meridjɔnal, -o] **1.** *a.* (*a*) meridional (distance, etc.); (*b*) south(ern). **2.** *n.* southerner (*esp.* of France).

meringue [mərɛ̃g] *n.f. Cu:* meringue.

meringuer [mərɛ̃ge] *v.tr. Cu:* **1.** to enclose (sweet, etc.) in meringue. **2. pommes meringuées,** apple snow.
mérinos [merinos] *n.m.* merino (sheep, cloth, etc.); *P:* **laisser pisser le m.,** to let things run their course.
merise [məriz] *n.f. Bot:* wild cherry; gean.
merisier [mərizje] *n.m. Bot:* wild cherry (tree); gean (tree).
méritant [meritɑ̃] *a.* meritorious, deserving; **peu m.,** undeserving.
mérite [merit] *n.m.* merit; (*a*) worth; **chose de peu de m.,** thing of little worth, value; **s'attribuer le m. de qch.,** to take the credit for sth.; **il faut dire à son m. que . . .,** it must be said to his credit that . . .; **par ordre de m.,** in order of merit; (*b*) excellence, talent; **homme de m.,** man of talent, of ability.
mériter [merite] *v.tr.* **1.** to deserve, merit; **il n'a que ce qu'il mérite,** he's got what he deserves; it serves him right; **bien m. de la patrie,** to deserve well of one's country; **livre qui mérite d'être lu,** book worth reading; **cela mérite réflexion,** it's worth thinking over; **cela mérite d'être vu, entendu,** it's worth seeing, hearing. **2. voilà ce qui lui a mérité cette renommée,** this is what earned him, entitled him to, this fame.
méritoire [meritwar] *a.* meritorious, deserving.
merlan [mɛrlɑ̃] *n.m. Ich:* whiting; *F:* **faire des yeux de m. frit,** to roll one's eyes.
merle [mɛrl] *n.m. Orn:* **1.** blackbird; **m. blanc,** (i) white blackbird; (ii) exceptional creature, thing; rare bird; (*b*) **vilain m.,** *Iron:* **beau m.,** unpleasant person; nasty piece of work. **2. m. d'eau,** water ouzel.
merlin[1] [mɛrlɛ̃] *n.m. Nau:* marline; small stuff.
merlin[2] *n.m.* axe, cleaver; felling axe; poleaxe.
merluche [mɛrlyʃ] *n.f.* **1.** *Ich:* hake. **2.** *Cu:* dried (unsalted) cod, stockfish.
mérou [meru] *n.m. Ich:* grouper.
mérovingien, -ienne [merɔvɛ̃ʒjɛ̃, -jɛn] *a. & n. Hist:* Merovingian.
merveille [mɛrvɛj] *n.f.* marvel, wonder; **les sept merveilles du monde,** the seven wonders of the world; **faire m., faire des merveilles,** to work, perform, wonders; **ce n'est pas m. qu'il soit parti,** it's not surprising he's left; **à m.,** excellently; **cette robe vous va à m.,** this dress suits you wonderfully, down to the ground; **se porter à m.,** to be in excellent health, in the best of health; **ce chèque tombe à m.,** this cheque's arrived at exactly the right moment.
merveilleusement [mɛrvɛjøzmɑ̃] *adv.* marvellously, wonderfully.
merveilleux, -euse [mɛrvɛjø, -øz] **1.** *a.* marvellous, wonderful. **2.** (*a*) *n.m.* **le m.,** the supernatural; (*b*) *n. Hist:* ultra-fashionable man, woman; *m.* fop.
mes [me] *see* MON.
mésalliance [mezaljɑ̃s] *n.f.* unsuitable alliance (*esp.* by marriage); misalliance; **faire une m.,** to marry beneath oneself.
mésallier (se) [səmezalje] *v.tr.* (*conj. like* ALLIER) to marry beneath oneself.
mésange [mezɑ̃ʒ] *n.f. Orn:* tit; **m. bleue,** bluetit; **m. charbonnière,** great tit; **m. noire,** coaltit.
mésaventure [mezavɑ̃tyr] *n.f.* misadventure, mishap, mischance.
mésentente [mezɑ̃tɑ̃t] *n.f.* misunderstanding; disagreement.
mésestimation [mezɛstimasjɔ̃] *n.f.* underestimation, underrating, undervaluing.
mésestime [mezɛstim] *n.f.* low esteem; **tenir qn en m.,** to have a poor, low, opinion of s.o.
mésestimer [mezɛstime] *v.tr.* **1.** to underestimate, undervalue, underrate. **2.** to have a poor, low, opinion of (s.o.).
mésintelligence [mezɛ̃teliʒɑ̃s] *n.f.* disagreement; **être en m. avec qn,** to be at variance, at loggerheads, with s.o.
mesmérisme [mɛsmerism] *n.m.* mesmerism.
méson [mezɔ̃] *n.m. Atom.Ph:* meson.
Mésopotamie [mezɔpɔtami] *Pr.n.f. Geog:* Mesopotamia.
mésopotamien, -ienne [mezɔpɔtamjɛ̃, -jɛn] *a. & n. Geog:* Mesopotamian.
mésozoïque [mezɔzɔik] *a. Geol:* mesozoic.
mesquin [mɛskɛ̃] *a.* (*a*) mean, shabby (appearance); paltry, petty (excuse, etc.); (*b*) (*of pers.*) mean, niggardly, stingy.
mesquinement [mɛskinmɑ̃] *adv.* meanly.
mesquinerie [mɛskinri] *n.f.* **1.** meanness; (*a*) pettiness, paltriness; (*b*) niggardliness. **2.** mean trick.
mess [mɛs] *n.m. Mil:* mess.
message [mesaʒ] *n.m.* message.
messager, -ère [mesaʒe, -ɛr] **1.** *n.* messenger; **m. de malheur,** bearer of bad news; *Lit:* **m. du printemps,** harbinger of spring. **2.** *n.m.* carrier (of parcels, cargo).
messagerie [mesaʒri] *n.f.* carrying trade; **service de messageries,** parcel delivery; **messageries maritimes,** (i) sea transport of goods; (ii) shipping line; **bureau de(s) messageries,** (i) *A:* stagecoach office; (ii) shipping office; (iii) *Rail:* parcel(s) office.
messe [mɛs] *n.f.* (*a*) *Ecc:* mass; low mass; **m. des morts,** requiem mass; **célébrer, dire, la m.,** to celebrate, say, mass; (*b*) **m. noire,** black mass.
messeoir [meswar] *v.ind.tr., def.* (*pr.p.* **messeyant;** *p.p. is lacking; pr.ind.* **il messied, ils messeyent;** *pr.sub.* **il messeye;** *impf.* **il messeyait;** *p.h. is lacking; fu.* **il messiéra)** *A: & Lit:* to be unbecoming, unseemly; to misbecome; **il lui messied de . . .,** it ill becomes him to . . . .
messianique [mesjanik] *a.* Messianic.
messianisme [mesjanism] *n.m.* Messianism.
messidor [mesidɔr] *n.m.* tenth month of the French Republican calendar (June-July).
Messie [mesi] *Pr.n.m.* Messiah.
messin, -ine [mesɛ̃, -in] *a. & n. Geog:* (native, inhabitant) of Metz.
messire [mesir] *n.m. A:* Sir; Master.
mesurable [məzyrabl̥] *a.* measurable, mensurable.
mesurage [məzyraʒ] *n.m.* measuring, measurement.
mesure [məzyr] *n.f.* measure. **1.** (*a*) (act of) measurement, measuring; **appareil de m.,** measuring apparatus; (*b*) **prendre les mesures de qn, qch.,** to take s.o.'s measurements; to measure s.o., sth.; **prendre la m. de qn,** to size s.o. up; **complet (fait) sur mesure(s),** made-to-measure, *NAm:* custom-made, suit; **donner sa m.,** to show what one is capable of; **être à la m. de qn, de qch.,** to measure up to s.o., to sth.; **dans une certaine m.,** in some degree; to a certain extent; **dans une large m.,** mainly; to a large extent; **dans la m. où,** insofar as; **je vous aiderai dans la m. de mes forces, du possible,** I'll help you to the best of my ability; **(au fur et) à m.,** in proportion; successively; one by one; **je vérifie les chiffres à m.,** I check the figures as I go along; **à m. que,** (in proportion) as; **à m. que je reculais, il s'avançait,** as (fast as) I retreated he advanced; (*c*) action, measure, step; **m. de sécurité,** safety precaution; **prendre des mesures,** to take action, adopt measures; **prendre des mesures pour faire qch.,** to take measures, steps, to do sth.; to make arrangements for doing sth.; **prendre des mesures contre qch.,** to make provision against sth.; **prendre ses mesures,** to make one's arrangements **(pour que,** in order that); **par m. d'économie,** as a measure of economy. **2.** (*a*) *Mth:* **commune m.,** common measure; (*b*) *Mth: Ph:* gauge, standard; **m. de longueur,** measure of length; **m. de surface, de superficie,** square measure; **m. de volume,** cubic measure; **poids et mesures,** weights and measures;

(*c*) (*quantity measured out*) **verser une m. de vin à qn,** to pour s.o. out a measure of wine; **faites-moi bonne m.,** give me good measure. **3.** (*a*) required size, amount; **pièces qui ne sont pas de m.,** pieces that are not the right size, that are not to size; **rester dans la juste m.,** to keep within bounds; **(dé)passer la m.,** to overstep the mark, overdo it; **ne garder aucune m., oublier toute m.,** to fling aside all restraint, lose all sense of moderation, proportion; **ambition sans m.,** unbounded ambition; (*b*) *Fenc:* measure, reach, distance; **être en m. de faire qch.,** to be in a position to do sth. **4.** (*a*) *Mus:* (i) bar; (ii) time; **m. à quatre temps,** four-four time, common time; **battre la m.,** to beat time; **en m.,** in (strict) time; **aller en m.,** to keep time; (*b*) *Pros:* metre, *NAm:* meter (of verse); measure.

mesuré [məzyre] *a.* measured (tread, etc.); temperate, moderate, restrained (language, etc.).

mesurément [məzyremɑ̃] *adv.* moderately; with, in, moderation.

mesurer [məzyre] **1.** *v.tr.* (*a*) to measure (dimensions); to measure out (corn, etc.); to measure up (wood, land); to measure off (cloth, etc.); **m. un client,** to take a customer's measurements; **m. qn des yeux,** to look s.o. up and down; (*b*) (*of pers.*) **m. deux mètres,** to be two metres, *NAm:* meters, tall; **la colonne mesure dix mètres,** the column measures ten metres, is ten metres high; (*c*) **m. la nourriture à qn,** to ration s.o.'s food; (*d*) to calculate; to weigh (one's words, etc.); to size (s.o., sth.) up; **m. sa dépense sur ses profits,** to cut one's coat according to one's cloth; **m. la distance à la vue,** to judge, estimate, gauge, distance by sight; **m. le châtiment à l'offense,** to make the punishment fit the crime. **2. se m. avec, à, qn,** to measure one's strength against s.o.; to measure, pit, oneself against s.o.; **vous n'êtes pas de force, de taille, à vous m. avec lui,** you're no match for him.

mesureur [məzyrœr] *n.m.* (*pers., device*) measurer; **m. de pression,** pressure gauge.

mésuser [mezyze] *v.ind.tr.* **m. de son bien,** to misuse one's wealth; **m. de son pouvoir,** to abuse one's power.

métabolique [metabɔlik] *a.* metabolic.

métabolisme [metabɔlism] *n.m.* metabolism.

métacarpe [metakarp] *n.m. Anat:* metacarpus.

métacarpien, -ienne [metakarpjɛ̃, -jɛn] *a. & n.m. Anat:* metacarpal.

métacentre [metasɑ̃tr̥] *n.m. Ph:* metacentre, *NAm:* metacenter.

métairie [meteri] *n.f.* small farm (held on *métayage* agreement).

métal, -aux [metal, -o] *n.m.* **1.** metal; **m. antifriction, m. blanc,** babbitt (metal), white metal; **m. (blanc) anglais,** Britannia metal. **2.** *Fin:* **m. en barres,** bullion.

métallifère [metalifɛr] *a.* metalliferous; metalbearing.

métallique [metalik] *a.* metallic; **câble m.,** wire rope; **plume m.,** steel nib; **rendre un son m.,** to clang, clank; *Fin:* **réserve m.,** metallic reserve, bullion reserve.

métallisation [metalizasjɔ̃] *n.f.* **1.** metallization; converting (of ore, etc.) into metal. **2.** plating (with metal). **3.** *Phot:* bronzing (of print).

métallisé [metalize] *a. esp. Aut:* metallic (paint, etc.).

métalliser [metalize] *v.tr.* **1.** to metallize. **2.** to cover with metal; to plate.

métallo [metalo] *n.m. F:* metalworker.

métallurgie [metalyrʒi] *n.f.* metallurgy.

métallurgique [metalyrʒik] *a.* metallurgic(al).

métallurgiste [metalyrʒist] *n.m.* (*a*) metallurgist; (*b*) metalworker.

métamorphique [metamɔrfik] *a. Geol:* metamorphic.

métamorphiser [metamɔrfize] *v.tr. Geol:* to metamorphose.

métamorphisme [metamɔrfism] *n.m. Geol:* metamorphism.

métamorphose [metamɔrfoz] *n.f.* metamorphosis, transformation.

métamorphoser [metamɔrfoze] **1.** *v.tr.* to metamorphose, transform. **2. se m.,** to change completely; to be transformed.

métaphore [metafɔr] *n.f.* metaphor; figure of speech; image; **m. disparate, incohérente,** mixed metaphor.

métaphorique [metafɔrik] *a.* metaphoric(al); figurative.

métaphoriquement [metafɔrikmɑ̃] *adv.* metaphorically; figuratively.

métaphysicien, -ienne [metafizisjɛ̃, -jɛn] *n.* metaphysician.

métaphysique [metafizik] **1.** *a.* metaphysical; abstract, abstruse. **2.** *n.f.* metaphysics.

métaphysiquement [metafizikmɑ̃] *adv.* metaphysically.

métapsychique [metapsiʃik] **1.** *a.* psychic (phenomenon). **2.** *n.f.* parapsychology.

métastase [metastɑz] *n.f.* metastasis.

métatarse [metatars] *n.m. Anat:* metatarsus.

métatarsien, -ienne [metatarsjɛ̃, -jɛn] *a. & n.m. Anat:* metatarsal.

métathèse [metatɛz] *n.f. Ling:* metathesis.

métayage [metɛjaʒ] *n.m. Agr:* sharecropping.

métayer, -ère [metɛje, -ɛr] *n. Agr:* sharecropper.

métazoaire [metazɔɛr] *n.m. Nat.Hist:* metazoan; *pl.* Metazoa.

métempsycose [metɑ̃psikoz] *n.f.* metempsychosis.

météo [meteo] *F:* **1.** *n.f.* (*a*) weather forecast, report; (*b*) (= **bureau central de météorologie**) meteorological office, met office. **2.** *n.m.* **Monsieur M.,** the weather man.

météore [meteɔr] *n.m.* meteor.

météorique [meteɔrik] *a.* meteoric.

météorite [meteɔrit] *n.m. or f.* meteorite.

météorologie [meteɔrɔlɔʒi] *n.f.* meteorology; **le bureau central de m.** = the meteorological office.

météorologique [meteɔrɔlɔʒik] *a.* meteorological; **bulletin m.,** weather report, weather forecast; **station m.,** meteorological station, weather station; **frégate, navire, m.,** weather ship.

météorologiste [meteɔrɔlɔʒist] *n.,* **météorologue** [meteɔrɔlɔg] *n.* meteorologist.

métèque [metɛk] *n.m.* (*a*) *Gr.Ant:* metic; (*b*) *F: Pej:* foreigner; dago; wog.

méthane [metan] *n.m. Ch:* methane.

méthanier [metanje] *n.m. Nau:* methane tanker.

méthode [metɔd] *n.f.* **1.** method, system; way; **m. pour faire qch.,** method of doing sth.; **elle a sa m.,** she has her own way of doing things; **il a beaucoup de m.,** he's very methodical; **avec m.,** methodical(ly), systematical(ly); **sans m.,** unmethodical(ly), unsystematical(ly). **2.** primer, grammar; **m. de piano,** piano tutor.

méthodique [metɔdik] *a.* methodical, systematic.

méthodiquement [metɔdikmɑ̃] *adv.* methodically, systematically.

méthodisme [metɔdism] *n.m. Rel:* Methodism.

méthodiste [metɔdist] *a. & n. Rel:* Methodist.

méthyle [metil] *n.m. Ch:* methyl.

méthylène [metilɛn] *n.m. Ch:* methylene.

méthylique [metilik] *a.* methyl(ic).

méticuleusement [metikyløzmɑ̃] *adv.* meticulously.

méticuleux, -euse [metikylø, -øz] *a.* meticulous,

punctilious (person, care, civility); scrupulous (care); **par trop m.,** over-scrupulous, over-particular.

méticulosité [metikylozite] *n.f.* meticulousness; over-carefulness; punctiliousness.

métier [metje] *n.m.* **1.** (*a*) trade, profession, craft, occupation, business; **quel est votre m.?** what do you do (for a living)? what's your job? **École des Arts et Métiers,** engineering college (of university level); **gens de m.,** experts; professionals; **terme de m.,** technical term; **armée de m.,** regular army; **exercer, faire, un m.,** to carry on a trade, a profession; **il est charpentier de son m.,** he's a carpenter by trade; **ils sont du m.,** they're in the trade; **ce n'est pas (de) mon m.,** that's not (in) my line; **tours de m.,** tricks of the trade; **parler m.,** to talk shop; *F:* **quel m.!** what a life! *Hist:* **corps de m.,** corporation; g(u)ild; trade association; **chacun son m.,** everyone to his trade; (*b*) craftsmanship; skill; **il a du m.,** he knows what he's doing; **il manque encore de m.,** he still lacks experience; **homme de m.,** craftsman. **2.** *Tex:* (*a*) **m. à tisser,** loom; **m. mécanique,** power loom; **avoir un ouvrage sur le m.,** to have a piece of work in hand; (*b*) **m. à filer,** spinning frame; (*c*) **m. à tapisserie,** tapestry frame; **m. à broder,** tambour frame, embroidery frame.

métis, -isse [meti, -is] **1.** *a.* (*of pers.*) halfcaste; *Pej:* halfbred; (*of animal*) crossbred; mongrel (dog); **plante métisse,** hybrid plant. **2.** *n.* (*pers.*) halfcaste; *Pej:* halfbreed; (*animal*) crossbreed; mongrel (dog, etc.). **3.** *a. & n.m. Tex:* **(tissu) m.,** linen-cotton mixture.

métissage [metisaʒ] *n.m.* crossbreeding.

métisser [metise] *v.tr.* to cross(breed).

métonymie [metɔnimi] *n.f. Ling:* metonymy.

métrage [metraʒ] *n.m.* **1.** (*a*) measuring, measure(ment); (*b*) *Civ.E:* quantity surveying. **2.** (*a*) (metric) length; *Cin:* footage, length (of film); **long m.,** full-length film; **court m.,** short; (*b*) metric area; (*c*) metric volume.

mètre[1] [mɛtr̥] *n.m. Pros:* metre, *NAm:* meter.

mètre[2] *n.m.* **1.** *Meas:* metre, *NAm:* meter; **m. carré, cube,** square, cubic, metre. **2.** (metre) rule; **m. pliant,** folding rule; **m. à ruban,** tape measure.

métré [metre] *n.m. Const:* (*a*) measurement(s) (of building land, etc.); quantity survey; (*b*) bill of quantities.

métrer [metre] *v.tr.* **(je mètre; je métrerai) 1.** to measure (by the metre, *NAm:* meter). **2.** *Civ.E:* to survey (for quantities).

métreur, -euse [metrœr, -øz] *n.* **m. (vérificateur),** quantity surveyor.

métrique[1] [metrik] **1.** *a. Pros:* metric(al). **2.** *n.f.* prosody, metrics.

métrique[2] *a.* metric.

métro (le) [ləmetro] *n.m. F:* the underground (railway), *NAm:* the subway; **le m. de Paris,** the Paris metro; **le m. de Londres,** the London underground (system); the tube.

métrologie [metrɔlɔʒi] *n.f.* metrology.

métrologique [metrɔlɔʒik] *a.* metrological.

métrologiste [metrɔlɔʒist] *n.* metrologist.

métronome [metrɔnɔm] *n.m. Mus:* metronome.

métropole [metrɔpɔl] *n.f.* (*a*) metropolis; capital; (*b*) mother country; (*c*) metropolis; see (of archbishop).

métropolitain [metrɔpɔlitɛ̃] **1.** (*a*) *a.* metropolitan; **armée métropolitaine,** home army; (*b*) *n.m. Adm:* underground (railway), *NAm:* subway. **2.** *Ecc:* (*a*) *a.* metropolitan (church, etc.); archiepiscopal; (*b*) *n.m.* metropolitan; archbishop.

mets [mɛ] *n.m.* dish (of food).

mettable [mɛtabl̥] *a.* (*of clothes, etc.*) wearable; **pas m.,** not fit to wear.

metteur, -euse [mɛtœr, -øz] *n.* **m. en œuvre,** mounter (of jewellery, etc.); *Rail:* **m. de rails,** platelayer, *NAm:* tracklayer; **m. en scène,** (i) *Th:* producer; (ii) *Cin:* director; *W.Tel:* **m. en ondes,** producer.

mettre [mɛtr̥] **I.** *v.tr.* (*pr.p.* **mettant;** *p.p.* **mis;** *pr.ind.* **je mets, il met, n. mettons, ils mettent;** *p.h.* **je mis;** *fu.* **je mettrai) 1.** (*a*) to put, lay, place, set; **mettez tout cela par terre,** put all that on the floor; **m. la table, le couvert,** to lay, set, the table; **m. la main sur qn,** to lay hands on s.o.; **m. un manche à un balai,** to fit a handle to a broom; **m. une annonce dans les journaux,** to put an advertisement in the (news)papers; **m. qn à la porte,** (i) to turn, throw, s.o. out; (ii) to dismiss, sack, s.o.; **je vais vous m. à votre porte,** I'll see, take, you home; **m. des enfants au collège,** to send children (away) to school; **m. qn à faire qch.,** to set s.o. to do sth.; **m. les volets,** to put up the shutters; *Gaming:* **m. un enjeu,** to lay a stake; **m. de l'argent sur un cheval,** to put, stake, money on a horse; to back a horse; **m. dans le blanc, dans le mille,** to get a bull's eye; to be successful, hit the nail on the head; **qu'est-ce qui vous a mis cela dans la tête?** what put that into your head? **j'y mettrai tous mes soins,** I'll give the matter my full attention; **m. le feu à qch.,** to set fire to sth., set sth. on fire; **m. du temps à faire qch.,** to take time over sth.; **j'ai mis deux ans à faire cela,** I took, it took me, two years to do that; **m. cinq cents francs à qch.,** to spend 500F. on sth., give 500F. for sth.; (*b*) to put on (clothes); **qu'est-ce que je vais m.?** what shall I wear? **mettez votre robe bleue,** put your blue dress on; **je n'ai rien à me m.,** I haven't got anything to wear; **ne plus m.,** to stop wearing, leave off (a garment); **j'ai du mal à m. mes souliers,** I find it difficult to get my shoes on; *P:* **il s'agit de les m.!** we'd better (i) scram, run for it, (ii) hurry up; (*c*) **m. sécher du linge, m. du linge à sécher,** to hang the washing up, out (to dry); **m. de l'eau à chauffer,** to put some water on to heat (up); **quand on le met à causer,** if once you start him, get him, talking. **2.** to set, put (in a condition); to put on, turn on, switch on (gas, television, etc.); **m. une machine en mouvement,** to set a machine going; **m. la radio plus fort,** to turn up the radio; **m. des vers en musique,** to set verse to music; **m. son argent en fonds de terre,** to invest one's money in real estate; **m. le réveil à cinq heures,** to set the alarm for five o'clock; **m. qn à la torture,** to put, subject, s.o. to torture; *Nau:* **m. une voile au vent,** to hoist, set, a sail; **m. à la voile,** to set sail. **3.** (*a*) to admit, grant; **mettons que vous avez, ayez, raison,** suppose you're right; **mettons cent francs,** (let's) call it a hundred francs; **mettons qu'il en soit ainsi,** let's assume that this is the case; (*b*) **mettez que je n'ai rien dit,** consider that unsaid. **II. se m. 1.** (*a*) to go, get; **se m. derrière un arbre,** to get behind a tree; **se m. au lit,** to get into bed; **se m. à table,** to sit down at (the) table; **se m. contre un mur,** to stand, lean, against a wall; **mettez-vous auprès du feu,** sit (down) by the fire; **je ne savais où me mettre,** I didn't know where to (i) go, stand, sit, (ii) put myself; **se m. au service de qn,** to enter s.o.'s service; **se m. d'une société,** to join a society; (*b*) to begin, start, set about (sth.); **se m. au travail,** to start work, set to work; **il est temps de s'y m.,** we'd better get down to it, get on with it; **il s'y est mis de bonne heure,** he started early, young; **se m. à la politique,** to go in for, take up, politics; **se m. à faire qch.,** to set about doing sth.; to begin to do sth.; **se m. à rire,** to begin, start, to laugh; to start laughing; **il s'est mis à boire,** he's taken to drink; **il s'est mis à pleuvoir,** it began to rain, came on to rain. **2.** to dress; **se m. à la mode, simplement,** to dress fashionably, simply; **se m. en smoking,** to put on a dinner jacket. **3. se m. en rage,** to get into a rage; **se m. en route,** to start off, set off, start on one's way; **se m. au pas,** (i) to fall into step; (ii) to subside into a walk (after running). **4. le temps se met au beau,** the weather's turning out fine; **le temps se met à la pluie,** it's turning to rain.

meublant [mœblɑ̃] *a.* **1.** furnishing (fabric, etc.). **2.** *Jur:* **meubles meublants,** moveables; (household) furniture.

meuble [mœbl̥] **1.** *a.* (*a*) movable; *a.* & *n.m.pl. Jur:* **(biens) meubles,** movables, personal estate, chattels, personalty; (*b*) *Agr:* **terre m.,** light, running, soil. **2.** *n.m.* piece of furniture; *pl.* furniture; **être dans ses meubles,** to have one's own furniture, a home of one's own.

meublé [mœble] **1.** *a.* furnished (room, etc.); **non m.,** unfurnished; **pièce pauvrement meublée,** barely, poorly, furnished room; **cave bien meublée,** well stocked cellar. **2.** *n.m.* furnished room, flat, apartment(s); **habiter en m.,** to live in a furnished flat, in lodgings.

meubler [mœble] **1.** *v.tr.* to furnish (room); to stock (farm, cellar, memory) **(de,** with); **m. sa tête de choses inutiles,** to fill one's head with useless things; **m. la conversation,** to stimulate the conversation. **2. se m.,** to furnish one's home.

meuglement [møgləmɑ̃] *n.m.* (*a*) lowing, mooing (of cow); (*b*) moaning (of siren, etc.).

meugler [møgle] *v.i.* (*of cow*) to low, moo.

meulage [mølaʒ] *n.m.* grinding (down).

meule [møl] *n.f.* **1.** (*a*) millstone; **m. courante,** runner; (*b*) **m. à aiguiser,** grindstone; **m. à polir,** buff(ing) wheel; (*c*) **m. de fromage,** round cheese. **2.** (*a*) stack, rick (of hay, etc.); (charcoal) stack, pile; clamp (of bricks); **mettre le foin en m.,** to stack, rick, the hay; **m. de foin,** haystack, hayrick; (*b*) *Hort:* hotbed; (*c*) manure heap.

meuler [møle] *v.tr.* to grind (chisel, etc.); to grind (down) (lens, etc.).

meulette [mølɛt] *n.f.* (*a*) small haystack; (*b*) shock, stook (of corn, etc.); **m. de foin,** haycock.

meulier, -ière [mølje, -jɛr] **1.** *a.* pertaining to millstones, grindstones; **pierre meulière,** *n.f.* **meulière,** millstone (grit). **2.** *n.m.* millstone maker, grindstone maker. **3.** *n.f.* **meulière,** millstone quarry.

meunerie [mønri] *n.f.* **1.** (flour) milling. **2.** milling trade.

meunier, -ière [mønje, -jɛr] **1.** *n.m.* miller; **garçon m.,** millhand. **2.** *n.f.* **meunière** (*a*) miller's wife; (*b*) *Orn:* (i) long-tailed tit; (ii) hooded crow, saddleback crow. **3.** *a.* (flour-)milling (plant, process, etc.).

meurt-de-faim [mœrdəfɛ̃] *n.inv. F:* down-and-out; starveling.

meurtre [mœrtr̥] *n.m.* (*a*) *Jur:* voluntary manslaughter; (*b*) murder; **au m.!** murder! **c'est un m. de retoucher ces tableaux,** it's a crime, downright vandalism, to touch up these pictures.

meurtri [mœrtri] *a.* bruised (arm, fruit, etc.); **visage m.,** (i) battered face; (ii) ravaged face; **être tout m.,** to be black and blue all over.

meurtrier, -ière [mœrtrije, -ijɛr] **1.** *a.* (*a*) murderous (war); deadly, lethal (weapon, etc.); **l'imprudence rend la route meurtrière,** rash driving turns roads into death traps; (*b*) *A:* (*of pers.*) murderous, guilty of murder. **2.** *n.* murderer, *f.* murderess. **3.** *n.f. Fort:* **meurtrière,** loophole.

meurtrir [mœrtrir] *v.tr.* to bruise (one's arm, fruit, etc.); **m. qn de coups,** to beat s.o. black and blue.

meurtrissure [mœrtrisyr] *n.f.* bruise.

Meuse [møz] *Pr.n.f. Geog:* (the river) Meuse, Maas.

meute [møt] *n.f.* (*a*) *Ven:* pack (of staghounds, etc.); (*b*) crowd, mob, pack (of people in pursuit).

mévente [mevɑ̃t] *n.f.* **1.** sale (of goods) at a loss. **2.** slump, stagnation (of business).

mexicain, -aine [mɛksikɛ̃, -ɛn] *a.* & *n. Geog:* Mexican.

Mexico [mɛksiko] *Pr.n. Geog:* Mexico City.

Mexique (le) [ləmɛksik] *Pr.n.m. Geog:* Mexico.

mezzanine [mɛdzanin] *n.f.* & *m.* **1.** mezzanine (floor). **2.** mezzanine window.

mezzo(-soprano) [mɛdzosɔprano] *Mus:* **1.** *n.m.* mezzo(-soprano) (voice). **2.** *n.f.* (*woman*) mezzo(-soprano); *pl. mezzo(-sopranos, -soprani).*

mezzo-tinto [mɛdzotinto] *n.m.inv. Engr:* mezzotint.

mi[1] [mi] *adv.* half, mid, semi-; **paupières mi-closes,** half-closed eyelids; **acier mi-doux,** semi-mild steel; **la mi-avril, -mai, etc.,** mid-April, -May, etc.; **à mi-hauteur,** halfway up, down; **faire qch. mi de gré mi de force,** to do sth. half willingly half under compulsion.

mi[2] *n.m.inv. Mus:* **1.** (*a*) (the note) E; **morceau en mi,** piece in E; (*b*) first string, E string (of violin). **2.** mi (in the Fixed Do system).

miaou [mjau] *n.m.* miaow, mew; (*of cat*) **faire m.,** to miaow, mew.

miasmatique [mjasmatik] *a.* miasmic, miasmatic, miasmal, noxious (exhalation, etc.).

miasme [mjasm] *n.m.* miasma.

miaulement [mjolmɑ̃] *n.m.* mewing, miaowing; caterwauling; whining.

miauler [mjole] *v.i.* to mew, miaow; to caterwaul; to whine.

miauleur, -euse [mjolœr, -øz] **1.** *a.* mewing, miaowing (cat); whining (person). **2.** *n.* whiner.

mi-bas [mibɑ] *n.m.inv.* knee(-length) sock; *Com:* half-hose.

mi-bois (à) [amibwa] *adv.phr. Carp:* **assemblage à mi-b.,** halved joint.

mica [mika] *n.m. Miner:* mica.

mi-carême [mikarɛm] *n.f.* mid-Lent; *pl. mi-carêmes.*

micaschiste [mikaʃist] *n.m. Miner:* mica schist.

miche [miʃ] *n.f.* (*a*) round loaf; cob (loaf); (*b*) *pl. P:* buttocks; bum, *NAm:* butt.

Michel [miʃɛl] *Pr.n.m.* Michael; **la Saint-M.,** Michaelmas.

Michel-Ange [mikɛlɑ̃ʒ] *Pr.n.m.* Michelangelo.

micheline [miʃlin] *n.f. Rail:* railcar (invented and equipped by the Michelin Tyre Company).

mi-chemin (à) [amiʃmɛ̃] *adv.phr.* halfway, midway.

mi-clos [miklo] *a.* half-closed, half-shut (eyes, etc.); *pl. mi-clos(es).*

micmac [mikmak] *n.m. F:* underhand intrigue; scheming; put-up job.

micocoulier [mikɔkulje] *n.m. Bot:* nettle tree.

mi-corps (à) [amikɔr] *adv.phr.* to the waist; **portrait à mi-c.,** half-length portrait; **saisi à mi-c.,** caught round the waist.

mi-côte (à) [amikot] *adv.phr.* halfway up, down, the hill.

mi-course (à) [amikurs] *adv.phr. Rac:* at the halfway mark, post.

micro [mikro] *n.m. F:* microphone, mike; **parler au m.,** to speak into the mike.

microanalyse [mikrɔanaliz] *n.f. Ch:* microanalysis.

microbalance [mikrɔbalɑ̃s] *n.f. Ph:* microbalance.

microbe [mikrɔb] *n.m.* microbe; germ; *F:* bug.

microbicide [mikrɔbisid] **1.** *a.* microbicidal, germ-killing. **2.** *n.m.* microbicide, germ-killer.

microbien, -ienne [mikrɔbjɛ̃, -jɛn] *a.* microbial, microbic (disease, etc.).

microbiologie [mikrɔbjɔlɔʒi] *n.f.* microbiology.

microbiologiste [mikrɔbjɔlɔʒist] *n.* microbiologist.

microcéphale [mikrɔsefal] **1.** *a.* microcephalous,

microcephalic. **2.** *n.* microcephalic.
microchirurgie [mikrɔʃiryrʒi] *n.f.* microsurgery.
microclimat [mikrɔklima] *n.m.* microclimate.
microcosme [mikrɔkɔsm] *n.m.* microcosm.
microfarad [mikrɔfarad] *n.m.* *El.Meas:* microfarad.
microfilm [mikrɔfilm] *n.m.* *Phot:* microfilm.
microfilmer [mikrɔfilme] *v.tr.* *Phot:* to microfilm.
micrographie [mikrɔgrafi] *n.f.* micrography.
micromètre [mikrɔmɛtr̥] *n.m.* micrometer.
micrométrique [mikrɔmetrik] *a.* micrometric(al); **vis m.,** micrometer screw.
micron [mikrɔ̃] *n.m.* micron.
micro-onde [mikrɔɔ̃d] *n.f.* micro-wave; *pl. micro-ondes.*
micro-organisme [mikrɔɔrganism] *n.m.* micro-organism; *pl. micro-organismes.*
microphone [mikrɔfɔn] *n.m.* microphone, *F:* mike; transmitter, mouthpiece (of telephone); **m. électrodynamique,** moving coil microphone; **m. caché,** *F:* bug.
microphotographie [mikrɔfɔtɔgrafi] *n.f.* **1.** microphotography; photomicrography. **2.** microphotograph; photomicrograph.
microphotographique [mikrɔfɔtɔgrafik] *a.* microphotographic; photomicrographic.
microplaquette [mikrɔplakɛt] *n.f.* *Elcs:* chip.
microscope [mikrɔskɔp] *n.m.* microscope; **m. électronique,** electron microscope; **m. optique,** light microscope; **visible au m.,** visible under the microscope.
microscopie [mikrɔskɔpi] *n.f.* microscopy.
microscopique [mikrɔskɔpik] *a.* microscopic.
microsillon [mikrɔsijɔ̃] *n.m.* *Rec:* **1.** microgroove. **2. (disque) m.,** long-playing record, L.P.
microthermie [mikrɔtɛrmi] *n.f.* *Ph.Meas:* microtherm.
microtome [mikrɔtɔm] *n.m.* microtome.
miction [miksjɔ̃] *n.f.* micturition; urination.
midi [midi] *n.m.* *no pl.* **1.** midday, noon, twelve o'clock; **il est m.,** it's twelve o'clock; **sur le m.,** *F:* **sur les m.,** about noon; **avant m.,** before noon; a.m.; **après m.,** after twelve (noon); p.m.; **m. et demi,** half-past twelve; **en plein m.,** (i) in broad daylight, (ii) in the full light of day; **repas de m.,** midday meal; **chercher m. à quatorze heures,** to look for difficulties where there are none; to complicate matters; **être au m. de la vie,** to be in the prime of life. **2.** (*a*) south; **chambre au m.,** room facing south; (*b*) southern part, south (of country); *esp.* **le M. (de la France),** the South of France.
midinette [midinɛt] *n.f.* office girl, shop girl; young dressmaker.
mi-distance (à) [amidistɑ̃s] *adv.phr.* halfway, midway.
midship(man) [mitʃip(man)] *n.m.* midshipman; *pl. midshipmen, midships.*
mie¹ [mi] *n.f.* **1.** crumb (of loaf, as opposed to crust); *P:* **à la m. de pain,** not worth a damn. **2.** *A:* **ne . . . m. (= ne . . . point),** not at all.
mie² *n.f.* *A: & Lit:* (= AMIE) **ma m., m'amie,** my pet, my love; darling, sweetheart.
miel [mjɛl] *n.m.* honey; **gâteau de m.,** honeycomb; **m. rosat,** rose honey; **elle était tout sucre et tout m.,** she was all sweet and sugary; **paroles de m.,** honeyed words; **lune de m.,** honeymoon.
miellé [mjele] *a.* *Lit:* honeyed.
mielleusement [mjɛløzmɑ̃] *adv.* blandly, smoothly.
mielleux, -euse [mjɛlø, -øz] *a.* **1.** *A:* tasting of honey. **2.** *Pej:* honeyed, sugary (speech, etc.); bland (smile); soapy, smooth(-tongued), unctuous (person).
mien, mienne [mjɛ̃, mjɛn] **1.** *poss. a.* *Lit:* mine; **un m. ami,** a friend of mine. **2. le m., la mienne, les miens, les miennes,** mine; (*a*) *poss. pron.* **j'ai pris ses mains dans les miennes,** I took her hands in mine; **il a donné des cadeaux à ses frères et aux miens,** he gave presents to his brothers and mine; (*b*) *n.m.* (i) my own (property, etc.); mine; **le m. et le tien,** mine and yours; **tels sont les faits, je n'y mets rien du m.,** these are the facts, I'm not adding anything of my own (invention); (ii) *n.m.pl.* **j'ai été renié par les miens,** I've been disowned by my own people; (*c*) *n.f.pl.* **on dit que j'ai encore fait des miennes,** they say I've been up to my old tricks again.
miette [mjɛt] *n.f.* (*a*) crumb (of broken bread); (*b*) morsel, scrap; **mettre qch. en miettes,** to smash sth. to pieces, to bits, to smithereens.
mieux [mjø] *adv.* **1.** *comp.* better; (*a*) **elle danse m. que moi,** she dances better than I do; **il faut m. les surveiller, les m. surveiller,** you must watch them more closely; **vous feriez m. de m'écouter,** you'd do better to, you'd better, listen to me; *Prov:* **m. vaut tard que jamais,** better late than never; **ça va m.,** things are improving; **pour m. dire,** to be more exact; **pour ne pas dire m., pour ne pas m. dire,** to say the least (of it); **de m. en m.,** better and better; **m. encore . . .,** better still . . .; **(faire qch.) à qui m. m.,** to vie with one another (in doing sth.); **ils criaient à qui m. m.,** it was a case of who could shout loudest; **tant m.!** so much the better! very good! **il va m.,** he's (feeling) better; (*b*) (*with adj. function*) (i) **c'est on ne peut m.,** it couldn't be better; **ce qui est m., qui m. est . . .,** what is better . . ., better still . . .; (ii) **vous serez m. dans ce fauteuil,** you'll be more comfortable in this armchair; (iii) **il est m.,** he's (feeling) better; (iv) **il est m. que son frère,** he's better-looking, more attractive, than his brother; (*c*) *n.m.* (i) **le m. est l'ennemi du bien,** leave well alone; **faute de m.,** for want of something better; **je ne demande pas m.!** I shall be delighted (to do so, etc.); **j'avais espéré m.,** I had hoped for better things; **vous ne trouverez pas m. comme hôtel,** you won't find a better hotel; (ii) *Med: etc:* **un m., du m.,** a change for the better, an improvement. **2.** *sup.* **le m.,** (the) best; (*a*) **la femme le m. habillée de Paris,** the best-dressed woman in Paris; **il s'en est acquitté le m. du monde,** nobody could have done it better; (*b*) (*with adj. function*) (i) **ce qu'il y a de m. à faire, c'est de . . .,** the best thing to do is to . . .; **ce que vous avez de m. à faire c'est de . . .,** the best thing you can do is to . . .; **c'est tout ce qu'il y a de m.,** there's absolutely nothing better; (ii) **être le m. du monde, être au m., avec qn,** to be on the best of terms with s.o.; (iii) **c'était la m. des trois sœurs,** she was the best-looking of the three sisters; (*c*) *n.m.* **faire, agir, pour le m.,** to act for the best; **le m. serait de . . .,** the best plan, thing, would be to . . .; **(en mettant les choses) au m.,** at best; **agir au m. des intérêts, de qn.,** to act in s.o.'s best interests; **faire qch. de son m.,** to do sth. to the best of one's ability; **faire de son m.,** to do one's best.
mieux-être [mjøzɛtr̥] *n.m.* *no pl.* improved condition; greater degree of comfort.
mièvre [mjɛvr̥] *a.* (insipidly) pretty; *Pej:* pretty-pretty.
mièvrerie [mjɛvrəri] *n.f.* (insipid) charm, prettiness.
mi-fin [mifɛ̃] *a.* *Com:* medium (grade, quality); *pl. mi-fins.*
mignard [miɲar] *a.* (*a*) *Pej:* affected; (*b*) dainty.
mignardise [miɲardiz] *n.f.* **1.** (*a*) *Lit:* daintiness; (*b*) affectedness. **2.** *Bot:* **(œillet) m.,** garden pink.
mignon, -onne [miɲɔ̃, -ɔn] **1.** *a.* dainty, delicate (person, etc.); **est-elle mignonne!** isn't she a darling! **son péché m.,** his particular weakness. **2.** *n.* (*a*) pet, darling, dear; (*b*) *A:* minion.
mignonnement [miɲɔnmɑ̃] *adv.* daintily.

mignonnette [miɲɔnɛt] *n.f.* **1.** *Bot:* (*a*) London pride; (*b*) wild succory; (*c*) clover. **2.** (*a*) mignonette lace; (*b*) coarse-ground pepper.
mignoter [miɲɔte] **1.** *v.tr. O:* to fondle, caress, pet (child). **2. se m.,** to titivate oneself.
migraine [migrɛn] *n.f.* migraine.
migrant, -ante [migrɑ̃, -ɑ̃t] *a. & n.* migrant.
migrateur, -trice [migratœr, -tris] *a.* migrating, migratory (bird, etc.); migrant (people).
migration [migrasjɔ̃] *n.f.* migration.
migratoire [migratwar] *a.* migratory.
mi-jambe(s) (à) [amiʒɑ̃b] *adv.phr.* halfway up, down, the leg(s).
mijaurée [miʒɔre] *n.f.* conceited, affected, woman.
mijoter [miʒɔte] **1.** *v.tr.* to simmer (sth.), let (sth.) simmer; to stew (sth.) slowly; **m. un projet,** to turn a scheme over in one's mind; **m. un complot,** to hatch a plot; **il se mijote quelque chose,** there's something in the wind, something's brewing. **2.** *v.i.* to simmer, stew.
mil¹ [mil] *n.m. Gym:* Indian club.
mil² [mil] *a.* (*used only in writing out dates A.D.*) thousand; **l'an m. neuf cent quatre-vingt-un,** the year nineteen hundred and eighty-one.
mil³ [mij] *n.m. Bot:* millet.
milady [miledi] *n.f.* **1.** (*title*) my Lady. **2.** titled (English) lady; *pl. miladys.*
Milan¹ [milɑ̃] *Pr.n. Geog:* Milan.
milan² *n.m. Orn:* kite.
mildiou [mildju] *n.m.* mildew; *Vit:* brown rot; **atteint de m.,** mildewed.
mildiousé [mildjuze] *a.* mildewed (vine, etc.).
miliaire [miljɛr] *Med:* **1.** *a.* miliary (gland, fever, etc.). **2.** *n.f.* miliary fever, prickly heat.
milice [milis] *n.f.* militia.
milicien, -ienne [milisjɛ̃, -jɛn] *n.* member of a militia; *m.* militiaman.
milieu, -ieux [miljø] *n.m.* **1.** middle; **au m. de,** in the middle of; *Lit:* amid(st), in the midst of; **au beau m. de la rue,** right in the middle of the street; **au m. du navire,** amidships; **au m. du courant,** in midstream; **le m. du jour,** midday; noon; **au m. de l'été, de l'hiver, de la nuit,** in the height of summer, in the depth of winter, at dead of night; **vers le m. du mois,** about the middle of the month; **la table du m.,** the middle table. **2.** (*a*) *Ph:* medium; (*b*) milieu, environment; surroundings; (social) sphere, circle; **je n'appartiens pas à leur m.,** I don't belong to their set, circle, class; **les milieux bien informés,** well informed people, quarters; (*c*) **le m., les gens du m.,** the underworld. **3.** middle course; mean; **il n'y a pas de m.,** there's no middle course; **le juste m.,** the happy medium, the golden mean; **tenir le m. entre . . . et . . .,** to steer a middle course between . . . and . . ..
militaire [militɛr] **1.** *a.* (*a*) military (discipline, service, etc.); **véhicule m.,** army vehicle, service vehicle; **à huit heures, heure m.,** at eight o'clock sharp; (*b*) **la marine m.,** the Navy; **port m.,** naval port. **2.** *n.m.* serviceman; soldier; **les militaires,** the military, the armed forces, the services.
militairement [militɛrmɑ̃] *adv.* militarily; **saluer m.,** to give a military salute; **occuper une ville m.,** to occupy a town by force of arms.
militant, -ante [militɑ̃, -ɑ̃t] *a. & n.* militant.
militantisme [militɑ̃tism] *n.m.* militancy.
militarisation [militarizasjɔ̃] *n.f.* militarization.
militariser [militarize] *v.tr.* to militarize.
militarisme [militarism] *n.m.* militarism.
militariste [militarist] *a. & n.* militarist.
militer [milite] *v.i.* to militate (**pour, en faveur de,** in favour, *NAm:* favor, of; **contre,** against); **cela milite en sa faveur,** that tells in his favour.
millage [milaʒ] *n.m. Fr.C:* mileage.
mille¹ [mil] **1.** *num.a.inv. & n.m.inv.* (*a*) thousand; **m. hommes,** a thousand men; one thousand men; **deux m.,** two thousand; **trois cent m. hommes,** three hundred thousand men; **ils sont morts par centaines de m.,** they died in hundreds of thousands; **m. un,** a thousand and one; one thousand and one; **Les M. et une Nuits,** the Arabian Nights; **l'an m.,** the year one thousand; **l'an m. neuf cent avant J.-C.,** the year nineteen hundred B.C.; (*b*) countless, many; **je vous l'ai dit m. fois,** I've told you a thousand times, time and time again; *F:* **il a des m. et des cents,** he's got pots of money. **2.** *n.m.* (*a*) *Com:* **un m. de briques,** a thousand bricks; (*b*) **mettre dans le m.,** (i) to hit, get, the bull's eye; (ii) to be successful, hit the nail on the head.
mille² *n.m.* (*a*) mile (= 1.609m.); (*b*) **m. (marin),** nautical mile.
mille(-)feuille [milfœj] **1.** *n.f. Bot:* milfoil, yarrow; *pl. mille-feuilles.* **2.** *n.m. Cu:* millefeuille, *NAm:* napoleon.
millénaire [milenɛr] **1.** *a.* millennial, millenary. **2.** *n.m.* thousand years; millenary, millennium.
millénium [milenjɔm] *n.m.* millenium.
mille-pattes [milpat] *n.m.inv.* centipede, millepede.
mille(-)pertuis [milpɛrtɥi] *n.m.inv. Bot:* St John's wort.
millésime [milezim] *n.m.* (*a*) date (on coin, etc.); (*b*) year of manufacture (of car, etc.); year, vintage (of wine).
millésimé [milezime] *a.* dated; vintage (wine).
millet [mijɛ] *n.m.* **1.** *Bot:* millet; wood millet grass; **m. long,** canary grass; **(grains de) m.,** birdseed, canary seed. **2.** *Med:* miliary eruption.
milliaire [miljɛr] *a. Rom.Ant:* **borne, pierre, m.,** milliary column.
milliampère [miliɑ̃pɛr] *n.m.* milliampere.
milliard [miljar] *n.m.* one thousand million(s), milliard, *NAm:* billion.
milliardaire [miljardɛr] *n.* multi-millionaire, *NAm:* billionaire.
milliardième [miljardjɛm] *num. a. & n.* one thousand millionth, *NAm*: billionth (part).
milliasse [miljas] *n.f. F:* enormous quantity, sum (of money); millions and millions.
millibar [milibar] *n.m. Meteor.Meas:* millibar.
millième [miljɛm] *num. a & n.* thousandth.
millier [milje] *n.m.* (about a) thousand; a thousand or so; **des milliers de personnes,** thousands of people; **par milliers,** in thousands.
milligramme [miligram] *n.m.* milligram(me).
millilitre [mililitr̥] *n.m.* millilitre, *NAm:* milliliter.
millimètre [milimɛtr̥] *n.m.* millimetre, *NAm:* millimeter.
millimétré [milimetre], **millimétrique** [milimetrik] *a.* **échelle m.,** millimetre, *NAm:* millimeter, scale; **papier m.,** graph paper.
million [miljɔ̃] *n.m.* million; **quatre millions d'hommes,** four million men; **riche à millions,** worth millions.
millionième [miljɔnjɛm] *num. a & n.* millionth.
millionnaire [miljɔnɛr] *n.* millionaire.
millithermie [militɛrmi] *n.f. Ph:* large calorie.
milord [milɔr] *n.m.* **1.** (*title*) my Lord. **2.** (*a*) (English) nobleman; (*b*) immensely wealthy man. **3.** *A.Veh:* victoria.
mi-lourd [milur] *a. & n.m. Box:* **(poids) mi-l.,** light heavyweight (boxer); *pl. mi-lourds.*
mime [mim] **1.** *n.m.* mime; (art of) miming. **2.** *n.* (*pers.*) (*a*) mime; (*b*) mimic.
mimer [mime] *v.tr.* **1.** to mime; **m. une scène,** to mime a scene, act a scene in dumb show. **2.** to mimic, ape.
mimétique [mimetik] *a.* mimetic.
mimétisme [mimetism] *n.m. Z:* mimesis; mimicry.

mimi [mimi] *n.m.* (*child's language*) pussy (cat); *F:* **mon petit m.,** darling; my pet.

mimique [mimik] **1.** *a.* mimic; **langage m.,** (i) sign language; (ii) mime, dumb show. **2.** *n.f.* (*a*) mimic art, mimicry; (*b*) mime, dumb show; sign language.

mimodrame [mimɔdram] *n.m.* *Th:* mimodrama, mime.

mimosa [mimoza] *n.m.* *Bot:* mimosa.

mi-moyen [mimwajɛ̃] *a.* & *n.m.* *Box:* **(poids) mi-m.,** welterweight (boxer); *pl. mi-moyens.*

minable [minabl̥] *a.* shabby, seedy(-looking) (person, etc.); pitiable (appearance, etc.); **salaire m.,** mere pittance (of a wage); pathetic salary.

minaret [minarɛ] *n.m.* minaret.

minauder [minode] *v.i.* to simper, mince.

minauderie [minodri] *n.f.* **1.** simpering, smirking. **2.** *pl.* simpering manner.

minaudier, -ière [minodje, -jɛr] *a.* & *n.* simpering, smirking, affected (person).

mince [mɛ̃s] **1.** *a.* thin (board, cloth, etc.); slender, slight, slim (person); **m. revenu,** slender, small, scanty, income; **minces arguments,** poor, feeble, arguments. **2.** *int.* *F:* **m. (alors)!** (i) well! just fancy that! (ii) blast (it)! **3.** *adv.* thinly.

minceur [mɛ̃sœr] *n.f.* (*a*) thinness; (*of pers.*) slenderness, slimness; (*b*) scantiness (of income).

mincir [mɛ̃sir] *v.i.* to get thinner, slimmer; to lose weight.

mine¹ [min] *n.f.* **1.** mine; **m. de houille, de charbon,** coalmine; colliery; pit; **m. d'or,** goldmine; **m. à ciel ouvert,** opencast mine; **exploitation des mines,** mining; **ingénieur des mines,** mining engineer; **une m. de renseignements, de faits,** a mine, storehouse, of information. **2. m. (de crayon),** (pencil) lead; **m. de plomb,** graphite, blacklead; **m. d'étain,** tinstone. **3.** *Mil: etc:* mine; (*a*) **coup de m.,** blast; **faire jouer une m.,** to fire a blast, a mine; *P.N:* **attention aux coups de m.!** danger, blasting; (*b*) **m. flottante,** floating mine; **poser, mouiller, une m.,** to lay a mine; **mouilleur de mines,** minelayer; **champ de mines,** minefield; **m. terrestre,** landmine.

mine² *n.f.* **1.** appearance, look; **juger les gens sur la m.,** to judge people by, on, appearances; **plat qui a bonne m.,** appetizing dish; dish that looks good; **ça ne paie pas de m.,** it isn't much to look at; **il ne paie pas de m.,** his appearance goes against him; **faire m. d'être fâché,** to pretend to be angry, look as though one is angry; **il a fait m. de me suivre,** he made as if to follow me; *F: Iron:* **nous avons bonne m. maintenant!** we *do* look silly! *P:* **m. de rien,** as if nothing had happened; casually. **2.** (*facial expression*) (*a*) **avoir bonne m., mauvaise m.,** to look well, ill; **vous avez meilleure m.,** you're looking better; **il en a une (sale) m.,** he *does* look ill; **m. boudeuse,** sulky expression; **avoir la m. longue,** to have a long face, a miserable expression; **faire triste m.,** to look disappointed; **faire bonne m. à qn,** to be pleasant to s.o., greet s.o. pleasantly, with a smile; **faire grise m. à qn,** to give s.o. a poor welcome; (*b*) *pl.* gestures, expressions (of a baby); *Pej:* **faire des mines,** to simper.

miner [mine] *v.tr.* **1.** to mine, undermine (fortress, etc.); **la mer mine les falaises,** the sea is undermining the cliffs, is eating the cliffs away; **la fièvre l'a miné,** fever has undermined, sapped, his strength; **miné par l'envie,** eaten up, consumed, with envy. **2.** to mine (road, etc.).

minerai [minrɛ] *n.m.* ore; **m. de fer,** iron ore.

minéral, -aux [mineral, -o] **1.** *a.* mineral; (*a*) **chimie minérale,** inorganic chemistry; (*b*) **eau minérale,** mineral water(s); **source minérale,** mineral spring; spa. **2.** *n.m.* mineral.

minéralier [mineralje] *n.m.* *Nau:* ore ship.

minéralisation [mineralizasjɔ̃] *n.f.* mineralization.

minéraliser [mineralize] *v.tr.* to mineralize.

minéralogie [mineralɔʒi] *n.f.* mineralogy.

minéralogique [mineralɔʒik] *a.* **1.** mineralogical. **2.** *Adm:* (*of vehicle*) **numéro m.,** registration number, *NAm:* license number; **plaque m.,** number plate, *NAm:* licence plate.

minéralogiste [mineralɔʒist] *n.* mineralogist.

Minerve [minɛrv] **1.** *Pr.n.f.* *Myth:* Minerva. **2.** *n.f.* *Med:* brace (for neck); (surgical) collar.

minet, -ette [minɛ, -ɛt] **1.** *n.* *F:* (*a*) pussy (cat); (*b*) **mon m., ma minette,** my darling, my pet; (*c*) fashionable young man, young woman. **2.** *n.f.* *Bot:* **minette,** black medic(k).

mineur¹ [minœr] *n.m.* (*a*) miner, *esp.* coalminer, collier; **m. de fond,** underground worker; (*b*) *Mil:* sapper.

mineur², -eure [minœr] **1.** *a.* (*a*) minor, lesser; **Asie Mineure,** Asia Minor; (*b*) *Jur:* under age; (*c*) *Mus:* minor (scale, etc.); **en ut m.,** in C minor. **2.** *n.* minor; *Jur:* infant. **3.** *n.m.* *Mus:* minor key.

mini [mini] *n.f.* *Cost:* *F:* mini(skirt).

miniature [minjatyr] *n.f.* miniature; **peintre de miniatures,** miniature painter, miniaturist; **en m.,** in miniature, on a small scale; **notre étang était un lac en m.,** our pond was a miniature lake; **golf m.,** miniature golf; **yacht m.,** model yacht.

miniaturisation [minjatyrizasjɔ̃] *n.f.* miniaturization.

miniaturiser [minjatyrize] *v.tr.* to miniaturize.

miniaturiste [minjatyrist] *n.* miniaturist, miniature painter.

minier, -ière [minje, -jɛr] **1.** *a.* mining (industry, district, etc.). **2.** *n.f.* **minière,** surface, opencast, mine.

mini(-)jupe [miniʒyp] *n.f.* miniskirt; *pl. mini(-)jupes.*

minimal, -aux [minimal, -o] *a.* minimal, minimum (effect).

minime [minim] **1.** *a.* minimal; small, tiny; trivial (loss); trifling (value). **2.** *n.m.* *Ecc.Hist:* Minim. **3.** *Sp:* junior (13–15 years of age).

minimiser [minimize] *v.tr.* to minimize; to reduce (sth.) to the minimum.

minimum [minimɔm] minimum. **1.** *n.m.* **réduire les frais au m.,** to reduce expenses to a minimum; **m. vital,** minimum living wage; **au m.,** as a minimum; at least; **thermomètre à minima,** minimum thermometer; *pl. minima, minimums.* **2.** *a.* **la largeur, les largeurs, minimum(s), minima,** the minimum width(s); **vitesse m.,** minimum speed; **prix m.,** reserve price (at auction); *El:* **charge m.,** base load (of a generator).

ministère [ministɛr] *n.m.* **1.** (*a*) *A: & Lit:* agency; **user du m. de qn,** to make use of s.o.'s services; (*b*) *Ecc:* **le saint m.,** the ministry. **2.** *Adm:* ministry; (*a*) office; **entrer au m.,** to take office; (*b*) **former un m.,** to form a government; (*c*) government department; **M. de l'Intérieur** = Home Office; **M. des Affaires étrangères** = Foreign (and Commonwealth) Office; *U.S:* State Department; *Can:* External Affairs Department; **M. de l'Éducation nationale** = Department of Education and Science; **M. de la Défense (nationale), de la Guerre** = Ministry of Defence; **M. des Travaux publics,** ministry of public works = Department of the Environment; **M. du Commerce** = Department of Trade; (*d*) *Jur:* **le M. public** = the (Department of the) Director of Public Prosecutions.

ministériel, -ielle [ministerjɛl] *a.* ministerial; **journal m.,** newspaper supporting the government; government organ; **crise ministérielle,** cabinet crisis; *Jur:* **officier m.,** law official (*i.e.* **avoué, huissier** *or* **notaire**).

ministrable [ministrabl̥] *Pol:* **1.** *a.* likely to become a minister. **2.** *n.* likely choice as minister.

ministre [ministr̥] *n.m.* **1.** (*a*) *A: & Lit:* servant, agent (of God, prince, etc.); (*b*) *Ecc:* (Protestant) minister; clergyman. **2.** *Adm:* minister; secretary (of State); **Premier m.,** Prime Minister; **M. de l'Intérieur** = Home Secretary; **M. des Affaires étrangères** = Foreign Secretary; *U.S:* Secretary of State; *Can:* Secretary of State for External Affairs; **M. de l'Éducation nationale** = Secretary of State for Education and Science; **M. de la Défense (nationale)** = Secretary of State for Defence; Minister of Defence; **M. des Travaux publics,** minister of public works = Secretary of State for the Environment; **M. des Finances** = Chancellor of the Exchequer; *U.S:* Secretary of the Treasury; *Can:* Minister of Finance; **M. de la Justice** = Lord Chancellor; *U.S:* Attorney General; *Can:* Minister of Justice and Attorney General; **M. du Commerce** = Secretary of State for Trade; **papier m.,** petition paper = official foolscap.

minois [minwa] *n.m.* (pretty) face (of child, young woman).

minoration [minɔrasjɔ̃] *n.f.* decrease.

minorer [minɔre] *v.tr.* **1.** to undervalue, underestimate. **2.** to decrease the importance of (sth.); to lower, reduce (figure, sum).

minoritaire [minɔritɛr] **1.** *a.* **parti m.,** minority party. **2.** *n.* member of a minority.

minorité [minɔrite] *n.f.* minority. **1.** *Jur:* nonage; infancy. **2. être en m.,** to be in the, in a, minority; **mettre en m.,** to defeat.

Minorque [minɔrk] *Pr.n.f. Geog:* Minorca.

minorquin, -ine [minɔrkɛ̃, -in] *a. & n. Geog:* Minorcan.

minoterie [minɔtri] *n.f.* **1.** (large) flour mill. **2.** flour-milling.

minotier [minɔtje] *n.m.* (flour) miller.

minou [minu] *n.m. F:* (*a*) pussy (cat); (*b*) **mon m.,** my darling, my pet.

minuit [minɥi] *n.m.* midnight; twelve o'clock (at night); **m. et demi,** half-past twelve at night; **sur le m.,** *F:* **sur les m.,** about midnight; **messe de m.,** midnight mass.

minuscule [minyskyl] *a.* (*a*) small, tiny, minute; minuscule; (*b*) **lettre m.,** *n.f.* **m.,** small letter; *Typ:* lower-case letter.

minus (habens) [minys(abɛ̃s)] *n.m.inv. F:* half-wit, moron, clot.

minutage [minytaʒ] *n.m.* **1.** *Mil: Th: etc:* timing. **2.** drafting (of document).

minute [minyt] *n.f.* **1.** minute (of hour, degree); **faire qch. à la m.,** to do sth. at a minute's notice, a moment's notice; **vous êtes à la m.,** you're punctual to the, a, minute; **réparations à la m.,** repairs while you wait; **la m. de vérité,** the moment of truth; *F:* **m. (papillon)!** just a minute! hold on! **2.** (*a*) minute, draft (of contract, etc.); **faire la m. d'un acte,** to draft an act; (*b*) record (of deed, of judgment).

minuter [minyte] *v.tr.* **1.** (*a*) to minute, draw up, draft (agreement, etc.); (*b*) to record, enter (deed, judgment). **2.** to time; **sa journée est soigneusement minutée,** every minute of his day is carefully planned; his day is run on a tight schedule.

minuterie [minytri] *n.f.* **1.** (*a*) *Clockm: etc:* motion-work, train of wheels; (*b*) **m. d'enregistrement,** counting mechanism (of meter). **2.** timer; (automatic) timeswitch.

minutie [minysi] *n.f.* **1.** (*a*) *O:* minute detail; (*b*) *pl.* trifles, petty details, minutiae. **2.** meticulousness; attention to detail.

minutieusement [minysjøzmɑ̃] *adv.* minutely; meticulously.

minutieux, -ieuse [minysjø, -jøz] *a.* scrupulously careful, meticulous (person); close, thorough, searching, minute, detailed (inspection, etc.).

miocène [mjɔsɛn] *a. & n.m. Geol:* Miocene.

mioche [mjɔʃ] *n. F:* child; kid(die), tot.

mi-parti [miparti] *a.* (*a*) equally divided (opinions, etc.); halved; (*b*) particoloured, *NAm:* particolored; *pl. mi-parti(e)s.*

mi-pente (à) [amipɑ̃t] *adv.phr.* halfway up, down, the hill.

mirabelle [mirabɛl] *n.f.* mirabelle plum.

mirabellier [mirabelje] *n.m.* mirabelle plum tree.

miracle [mirɑkl̥] *n.m.* **1.** miracle; **faire, opérer, un m.,** to perform, work, accomplish, a miracle; **cela tient du m.,** it's miraculous; **m. d'architecture,** marvel, miracle, of architecture; **fait à m.,** marvellously well done; **échapper comme par m.,** to have a miraculous escape, to escape by a hair's breadth; **par m.,** miraculously; **c'est (un) m. que** + *sub.*, it's a miracle, a wonder, that . . .; **crier (au) m.,** to go into raptures. **2.** *Lit.Hist:* miracle (play). **3.** *a.inv. F:* **produit m.,** miracle product, wonder product.

miraculé, -ée [mirakyle] *a. & n.* miraculously healed, saved (person).

miraculeusement [mirakyløzmɑ̃] *adv.* miraculously; by a miracle.

miraculeux, -euse [mirakylø, -øz] *a.* miraculous; wonderful; **remède m.,** miraculous, marvellous, cure; wonder drug.

mirador [miradɔr] *n.m.* **1.** mirador, belvedere. **2.** *Mil:* observation post (in tree, etc.). **3.** (traffic policeman's) raised platform. **4.** watchtower (of prison camp).

mirage [miraʒ] *n.m.* mirage.

mire [mir] *n.f.* **1.** (*a*) *A:* sighting, aiming (of firearm); (*b*) **ligne de m.,** line of sight; *Artil:* **angle de m.,** angle of sight; *Sm.a:* **point de m.,** aim; **point de m. de tous les yeux,** target for criticism; cynosure of every eye. **2.** (*a*) sighting mark; *T.V:* test card, pattern; (*b*) surveyor's pole; (levelling) staff, rod; (*c*) foresight (of rifle), bead.

mirer [mire] **1.** *v.tr.* (*a*) *O:* to aim at, take aim at (sth.); (*b*) *Lit:* to reflect, mirror; (*c*) to candle (eggs). **2.** *Lit:* **se m.,** to look at, admire, oneself (in mirror, etc.); **les arbres se mirent dans l'eau,** the trees are reflected in the water.

mirette [mirɛt] *n.f. P:* eye; *pl.* peepers.

mirifique [mirifik] *a. F:* wonderful, fabulous.

mirifiquement [mirifikmɑ̃] *adv. F:* wonderfully.

mirliflor(e) [mirliflɔr] *n.m. F:* dandy.

mirliton [mirlitɔ̃] *n.m.* **1.** toy flute, mirliton, kazoo; **vers de m.,** doggerel, trashy verse. **2.** *Cu:* cream horn.

mirmidon [mirmidɔ̃] *n.m. F:* whippersnapper, little runt.

mirobolant [mirɔbɔlɑ̃] *a. F:* wonderful, fabulous, astounding, staggering (news, etc.).

miroir [mirwar] *n.m.* **1.** (*a*) mirror; (looking) glass; **m. (pliant) à trois faces,** triple mirror; **m. à, aux, alouettes,** (i) *Ven:* lark mirror; twirl; (ii) *Fig:* snare, delusion; (*b*) *Bot:* **m. de Vénus,** Venus's looking glass. **2.** *Cu:* **œufs au m.,** fried eggs. **3.** speculum (on wing of bird); eye, ocellus (on peacock's feather).

miroitant [mirwatɑ̃] *a.* flashing; gleaming, glistening (silver, etc.); shimmering (lake, etc.); sparkling (jewel).

miroité [mirwate] *a.* dappled bay (horse).

miroitement [mirwatmɑ̃] *n.m.* flashing; gleam(ing), glistening (of silver, etc.); sheen, shimmer; sparkle, sparkling.

miroiter [mirwate] *v.i.* to flash; to gleam, glisten; (*of lake, etc.*) to shimmer; (*of jewel*) to sparkle; **faire m. l'avenir aux yeux de qn,** to lure s.o. with bright prospects.

miroton [mirɔtɔ̃] *n.m. Cu:* beef hash cooked with onions.

misaine [mizɛn] *n.f. Nau:* **(voile de) m.,** (square) foresail; **mât de m.,** foremast.
misanthrope [mizɑ̃trɔp] **1.** *n.m.* misanthropist, misanthrope. **2.** *a.* misanthropic.
misanthropie [mizɑ̃trɔpi] *n.f.* misanthropy.
misanthropique [mizɑ̃trɔpik] *a.* misanthropic.
miscellanées [miselane] *n.f.pl. Lit:* miscellany, miscellanea.
miscible [misibl̥] *a.* miscible.
mise [miz] *n.f.* **1.** (*a*) placing; putting (of sth. in a place); **m. à l'eau,** launching (of ship); **m. en bouteilles,** bottling (of wine, etc.); **m. à terre,** landing (of goods); (*of animal*) **m. bas,** dropping (of young); (*b*) **m. en pratique,** carrying out, practical application; putting into practice; **m. en jeu,** bringing into play; **m. en musique d'un poème,** setting of a poem to music; **m. à jour,** bringing (i) to light, (ii) up to date; **m. en garde,** warning, caution; **m. à mort,** killing, kill; **m. en eau (d'un barrage),** filling (of a reservoir); *Typ:* **m. en pages,** page-setting; **m. en marche,** starting (of engine, etc.); *W.Tel: etc:* **m. en ondes,** production; **m. en plis,** setting (of hair); **shampooing et m. en plis,** shampoo and set; **m. en liberté,** releasing, release; **m. en retraite,** pensioning (off); retiring (on a pension). **2.** dress, attire; **elle est simple dans sa m.,** she dresses simply. **3.** (*a*) *Gaming: Cards:* stake; (*b*) bid (at auction); **m. à prix,** reserve price; upset price; (*c*) *Com:* **m. de fonds,** putting up of money, of capital; outlay; **m. sociale,** working capital (of company); **m. d'un associé,** partner's holding (in a business).
miser [mize] *v.tr.* (*a*) to stake (**sur,** on); **m. sur un cheval,** to back a horse; **m. sur les deux tableaux,** to try to have it both ways; (*b*) *F:* to count, bank (**sur,** on).
misérable [mizerabl̥] **1.** *a.* (*a*) poor, wretched, miserable; **quartier m.,** poverty-stricken district; (*b*) wretched, miserable, worthless; **un m. salaire,** a mere pittance (of a wage); **pour un m. franc,** for a paltry, wretched, franc; (*c*) *O:* despicable, mean (action, etc.) **2.** *n.* (*a*) poor wretch; (*b*) *O:* scoundrel, wretch, villain.
misérablement [mizerabləmɑ̃] *adv.* miserably.
misère [mizɛr] *n.f.* **1.** misery; (*a*) *Lit:* **manger le pain de m.,** to eat the bread of affliction; **reprendre le collier de m.,** to go back to drudgery, to the treadmill; **lit de m.,** (i) bed of sickness; (ii) childbed; (*b*) trouble, misfortune; **misères domestiques,** domestic worries; **faire des misères à qn,** to tease s.o. unmercifully. **2.** extreme poverty, destitution; **dans la m.,** poverty-stricken; very badly off; **réduire qn à la m.,** to reduce s.o. to destitution; **dames réduites à la m.,** distressed gentlewomen; **crier m.,** to plead poverty; **vêtements qui crient m.,** shabby, threadbare, garments. **3.** trifle; **cent francs? une m.!** a hundred francs? a mere nothing! **4.** *Cards:* misère.
miserere, miséréré [mizerere] *n.m.inv. Ecc: Mus:* miserere.
miséreux, -euse [mizerø, -øz] *a. & n.* poverty-stricken, destitute (person).
miséricorde [mizerikɔrd] *n.f.* **1.** mercy, mercifulness; **crier m.,** to cry for mercy; **faire m. à qn,** to be merciful to s.o.; *Prov:* **à tout péché m.,** no sin but should find mercy; *Nau: A:* **ancre de m.,** sheet anchor. **2.** *int. O:* mercy on us! heaven help us!
miséricordieux, -ieuse [mizerikɔrdjø, -jøz] *a.* merciful (**envers,** to).
misogyne [mizɔʒin] **1.** *a.* misogynous. **2.** *n.* misogynist, woman-hater.
misogynie [mizɔʒini] *n.f.* misogyny.
miss [mis] *n.f.* (*a*) *A:* (English) governess; (*b*) beauty queen; **M. Monde,** Miss World; *pl. miss(es).*
missel [misɛl] *n.m. Ecc:* missal; (altar) mass book.
missile [misil] *n.m.* guided missile; **m. ballistique de moyenne portée,** intermediate range ballistic missile.
mission [misjɔ̃] *n.f.* mission. **1.** (*a*) **avoir m. de faire qch.,** to be commissioned to do sth.; **ministre en m. spéciale à Paris,** minister on (a) special mission to Paris; **partir en m. au pôle nord,** to go on an expedition to the North Pole; *Mil:* **en m.,** on detached service; **en m. de reconnaissance,** on reconnaissance duty; (*b*) *Ecc:* **missions étrangères,** foreign missions; (*c*) function, task, rôle, aim (of art, etc.). **2.** *Ecc:* mission station. **3.** delegation (of diplomats, etc.).
missionnaire [misjɔnɛr] *a. & n.* missionary.
missive [misiv] *n.f.* missive; letter.
mistigri [mistigri] *n.m. F:* (*name given to cat*) puss.
mistoufle [mistufl̥] *n.f.* **1.** *P:* **être dans la m.,** to be broke, hard up. **2.** *F:* **faire des mistoufles à qn,** to annoy, tease, plague, s.o.
mistral [mistral] *n.m. Meteor:* mistral.
mitaine [mitɛn] *n.f.* (*a*) *A: & Fr.C:* mitten; (*b*) *pl. Box: F:* gloves, mitts.
mite [mit] *n.f.* **1.** mite; **m. du fromage,** cheese mite. **2.** (*a*) moth worm; (*b*) clothes moth; **mangé des mites, aux mites, par les mites,** motheaten.
mité [mite] *a.* motheaten.
mi-temps [mitɑ̃] *n.f.inv.* **1.** *Fb: etc:* half-time; interval; **première, seconde, mi-t.,** first, second, half. **2.** **emploi à mi-t.,** part-time employment.
miter (se) [səmite] *v.pr.* to become motheaten.
miteux, -euse [mitø, -øz] **1.** *a.* shabby, tatty (clothes, etc.); seedy-looking (person). **2.** *n. F:* shabby, down-at-heel, person.
mitigation [mitigasjɔ̃] *n.f.* mitigation.
mitigé [mitiʒe] *a.* mitigated, modified; **morale mitigée,** lax morals; *Jur:* **peine mitigée,** reduced sentence.
mitiger [mitiʒe] *v.tr.* **(je mitigeai(s); n. mitigeons)** *O:* **1.** to mitigate (pain, penalty). **2.** to relax (rule, law).
mitonner [mitɔne] **1.** *v.tr.* (*a*) *Cu:* to simmer (soup, etc.); to let (soup) simmer; (*b*) to concoct, nurse (project, etc.); (*c*) to coddle, pamper (child, etc.). **2.** *v.i.* (*of soup, etc.*) to simmer.
mitoyen, -yenne [mitwajɛ̃, -jɛn] *a.* intermediate; **mur m.,** party wall; **cloison mitoyenne,** dividing wall (between two rooms).
mitoyenneté [mitwajɛnte] *n.f.* joint ownership (of party wall, hedge, etc.).
mitraillade [mitrɑjad] *n.f.* (volley of) shots, machine-gun fire.
mitraillage [mitrɑjaʒ] *n.m.* machine-gunning.
mitraille [mitrɑj] *n.f.* (*a*) *A.Mil:* caseshot, grapeshot; (*b*) hail of bullets.
mitrailler [mitrɑje] *v.tr.* (*a*) to machine-gun; (*b*) **m. qn de questions,** to fire questions at s.o.
mitraillette [mitrɑjɛt] *n.f.* submachine gun; tommy gun.
mitrailleur [mitrɑjœr] *n.m.* machine-gunner; *Mil.Av:* **m. arrière,** rear gunner; *a.* **fusil m.,** Bren gun.
mitrailleuse [mitrɑjøz] *n.f.* machine gun.
mitral, -aux [mitral, -o] *a.* mitral (valve of the heart).
mitre [mitr̥] *n.f.* **1.** mitre, *NAm:* miter (of bishop, etc.). **2.** (chimney) cowl.
mitré [mitre] *a.* mitred, *NAm:* mitered (abbot).
mitron [mitrɔ̃] *n.m.* baker's boy.
mi-vitesse (à) [amivitɛs] *adv.phr.* at half speed.
mi-voix (à) [amivwa] *adv.* in an undertone, under one's breath, in a subdued voice.
mixage [miksaʒ] *n.m. Cin: etc:* mixing (of sounds).
mixe(u)r [miksœr] *n.m. Dom.Ec:* **1.** mixer. **2.** liquidizer.
mixité [miksite] *n.f. Sch:* co-education.
mixte [mikst] *a.* **1.** mixed; **école m.,** co-educational school; **commission m.,** joint commission; *Ten:*

double m., mixed doubles. **2.** dual-purpose; **train m.**, composite train (goods and passengers); **billet m.**, combined rail and road ticket.
mixtion [mikstjɔ̃] *n.f.* **1.** compounding (of drugs, etc.). **2.** *Pharm:* mixture.
mixture [mikstyr] *n.f.* mixture (*esp.* of drugs).
mnémonique [mnemɔnik] *a.* & *n.f.* mnemonic.
mnémotechnie [mnemɔtɛkni] *n.f.* mnemonics.
mnémotechnique [mnemɔtɛknik] **1.** *a.* mnemotechnic. **2.** *n.f.* mnemonics.
mobile [mɔbil] **1.** *a.* (*a*) mobile, movable; **fête m.**, movable feast; (*b*) *O:* unstable, changeable, fickle (nature); restless, excitable (population); (*c*) detachable; **album à feuilles mobiles,** loose-leaf album; (*d*) moving (body, target, etc.); shifting, changing (expression, etc.); mobile (features); **organes mobiles,** sliding, working, parts; *Mil:* **colonne m.,** flying column; *Fr.Hist:* **garde m.,** militia (of 1848, of 1868–71); **La Garde M.,** the Mobile Guard = (State) security police. **2.** *n.m.* (*a*) *Ph: etc:* moving body; body in motion; (*b*) driving power; motive (of crime); (*c*) *Art:* mobile.
mobilier, -ière [mɔbilje, -jɛr] **1.** *a Jur:* movable, personal; **biens mobiliers,** personal estate, chattels, personalty; *Fin:* **valeurs mobilières,** stocks and shares; transferable securities. **2.** *n.m.* (*a*) furniture; (*b*) suite of furniture.
mobilisation [mɔbilizasjɔ̃] *n.f.* mobilization (of troops); liquidation, liberation (of capital).
mobilisé [mɔbilize] **1.** *a.* (*of troops*) mobilized, called up. **2.** *n.m.* serviceman.
mobiliser [mɔbilize] *v.tr.* to mobilize (troops); to call out, call up (reservist); *Fin:* to liberate (capital); **m. toute son énergie,** to summon up all one's strength.
mobilité [mɔbilite] *n.f.* **1.** mobility, moveableness. **2.** changeableness, instability (of character).
mobylette [mɔbilɛt] *n.f. R.t.m.* light motor cycle; moped.
mocassin [mɔkasɛ̃] *n.m.* mocassin.
moche [mɔʃ] *a. F:* rotten, lousy (treatment, etc.); poor; shoddy (work); ugly (individual); dowdy (woman).
modal, -aux [mɔdal, -o] *a.* modal.
modalité [mɔdalite] **1.** *Phil: Mus:* modality. **2.** mode (of application, etc.); *pl. Jur:* (restrictive) clauses; **modalités de paiement,** methods of payment; *Fin:* **modalités d'une émission,** terms and conditions of an issue.
mode¹ [mɔd] *n.f.* **1.** fashion; (*a*) *A:* **vivre à sa m.,** to live in one's own way; (*b*) **lancer la m. de qch., mettre qch. à la m.,** to bring sth. into fashion, set the fashion for sth.; **être à la m.,** to be in fashion, in vogue; to be all the rage; **revenir à la m.,** to come back into fashion; **passer de m.,** to go out of fashion; **à l'ancienne m.,** in the old style; **robe à la m.,** fashionable, stylish, dress; **coloris m.,** fashion shades, leading shades; *Com:* **la (haute) m.,** the fashion trade; **à la m. de . . .,** after the style, manner, of . . .. **2.** *pl. Com:* (*a*) (*clothes*) fashions; **gravures de modes,** fashion plates; (*b*) **(articles de) modes,** millinery; **magasin de modes,** milliner's shop.
mode² *n.m.* **1.** *Log:* mode, mood. **2.** *Gram:* mood, *NAm:* mode. **3.** *Mus:* (*a*) mode (in plainsong); (*b*) (major, minor) mode, *esp. U.S:* mood. **4.** method, mode (of education, etc.); **m. d'emploi,** directions for use; **m. de vie,** mode, way, of life.
modelage [mɔdlaʒ] *n.m.* **1.** modelling (in clay, etc.). **2.** model.
modèle [mɔdɛl] **1.** *n.m.* (*a*) model, pattern; **m. d'écriture,** handwriting copy; **machines toutes bâties sur le même m.,** machines all built to one pattern, on the same lines; **fabriqué sur trois modèles,** made in three styles; **voiture dernier m.,** car of the latest design; **m. déposé,** registered pattern; **m. réduit, à petite échelle,** scale model; **m. réduit de yacht,** model yacht; **prendre qn pour m.,** to take s.o. as one's model, as one's pattern; to model oneself on s.o.; **m. de vertu,** paragon of virtue; (*b*) *Metall:* pattern (of casting); *Cost:* model gown, hat; (*c*) (artist's) model; **dessiné d'après le m.,** drawn from the model; **servir de m. à un artiste,** to sit, model, for an artist. **2.** *a.* **époux m.,** model, exemplary, husband.
modelé [mɔdle] *n.m.* (*a*) *Art:* relief; (*b*) *Mapm:* hill shading.
modeler [mɔdle] **(je modèle; je modèlerai) 1.** *v.tr.* to model; to mould, *NAm:* mold (clay, etc.); **m. la destinée de qn,** to shape s.o.'s destiny. **2. se m. sur qn,** to take s.o. as one's model, as one's pattern; to model oneself on s.o.
modeleur, -euse [mɔdlœr, -øz] *n.* modeller, *NAm:* modeler; *Metall:* pattern maker.
modéliste [mɔdelist] *n.* (*a*) model maker; (*b*) dress designer.
modérateur, -trice [mɔderatœr, -tris] **1.** *a.* moderating, restraining. **2.** *n.* moderator, restrainer. **3.** *n.m.* regulator, governor (of engine, etc.); *El:* damper (of magnetic needle); *Atom.Ph:* moderator.
modération [mɔderasjɔ̃] *n.f.* **1.** moderation, restraint; temperateness; **avec m.,** temperately; in, with, moderation. **2.** reduction (in price); mitigation (of penalty); diminution (of taxes).
modéré, -ée [mɔdere] **1.** *a.* moderate; restrained, temperate (person); reasonable (price, etc.); subdued (cheers). **2.** *n. Pol:* moderate.
modérément [mɔueremɑ̃] *adv.* moderately, in moderation.
modérer [mɔdere] **1.** *v.tr.* **(je modère; je modérerai)** (*a*) to moderate, restrain, curb (passions, etc.); to reduce, slacken (speed); to regulate (machine); (*b*) to reduce (price); to mitigate (penalty). **2. se m.,** to control oneself, keep calm, calm down.
moderne [mɔdɛrn] **1.** *a.* modern; up-to-date. **2.** *n.m.* (*a*) **le m.,** modern things; (the) modern style; (*b*) (*pers.*) modern.
modernisation [mɔdɛrnizasjɔ̃] *n.f.* modernization.
moderniser [mɔdɛrnize] *v.tr.* to modernize; to bring up to date.
modernisme [mɔdɛrnism] *n.m.* modernism.
moderniste [mɔdɛrnist] *a.* & *n.* modernist.
modernité [mɔdɛrnite] *n.f.* modernity.
modern style [mɔdɛrnstil] *n.m.* & *a.* art nouveau.
modeste [mɔdɛst] *a.* modest (person, income); unassuming, self-effacing; simple, unpretentious; **avoir un train de vie m.,** to live quietly; **être d'une origine m.,** to be of humble origin; **un hôtel m.,** a small hotel; *n.* **ne faites pas le m.,** don't be (so) modest.
modestement [mɔdɛstəmɑ̃] *adv.* modestly.
modestie [mɔdɛsti] *n.f.* modesty (of person); unpretentiousness; **fausse m.,** false modesty.
modicité [mɔdisite] *n.f.* moderateness; slenderness (of means, etc.); lowness, reasonableness (of price).
modifiable [mɔdifjabl] *a.* modifiable.
modifiant [mɔdifjɑ̃] *a.* modifying (influence, etc.).
modificateur, -trice [mɔdifikatœr, -tris] **1.** *a.* modifying, modificatory. **2.** *n.* modifier. **3.** *n.m. Mch:* disengaging gear.
modificatif, -ive [mɔdifikatif, -iv] *a.* modifying.
modification [mɔdifikasjɔ̃] *n.f.* modification, alteration; **apporter, faire, une m. à qch.,** to make an alteration in sth.; to modify, amend (sth.).
modifier [mɔdifje] (*pr.sub.* & *impf.* **n. modifiions, v. modifiiez) 1.** *v.tr.* (*a*) to modify (statement); to alter, change (plan); *Nau:* **m. la route,** to alter course; (*b*) *Gram:* to qualify, modify (verb). **2. se m.,** to change, alter; to be modified, altered.

modique [mɔdik] *a.* moderate, reasonable (cost, charge, etc.); slender (income).
modiquement [mɔdikmɑ̃] *adv.* at a low price; **m. payé,** poorly paid.
modiste [mɔdist] *n.f.* milliner.
modulaire [mɔdylɛr] *a.* modular.
modulateur, -trice [mɔdylatœr, -tris] *W.Tel: etc:* **1.** *a.* modulating (valve, etc.). **2.** *n.m.* modulator.
modulation [mɔdylasjɔ̃] *n.f.* **1.** *Mus:* modulation, transition. **2.** modulation, inflexion (of the voice). **3.** *W.Tel: etc:* modulation; **m. d'amplitude,** amplitude modulation; **m. de fréquence,** frequency modulation.
module [mɔdyl] *n.m.* **1.** (*a*) *Arch: Hyd: etc:* module; (*b*) standard, unit (of length, etc.). **2.** *Mth: Mec:* modulus. **3.** *Space:* module; **m. de commande,** command module.
moduler [mɔdyle] **1.** *v.tr.* (*a*) to modulate (one's voice, *Ph: etc:* amplitude, etc.); to inflect (one's voice). **2.** *v.i. Mus:* to modulate.
moelle [mwal] *n.f.* **1.** marrow (of bone); *Anat:* medulla; **os à m.,** marrowbone; **anglais jusqu'à la m. (des os),** English to the backbone; **glacé jusqu'à la m. (des os),** frozen to the bone, to the marrow; **corrompu jusqu'à la m.,** rotten to the core; *Anat:* **m. épinière,** spinal cord. **2.** *Bot:* pith.
moelleusement [mwaløzmɑ̃] *adv.* softly, luxuriously.
moelleux, -euse [mwalø, -øz] **1.** *a.* (*a*) *A:* marrowy (bone); (*b*) *Bot:* pithy; (*c*) soft, velvety (to the touch); mellow (wine, voice); easy (motion); **couverture moelleuse,** luxurious, downy, blanket. **2.** *n.m.* softness (of colour); mellowness (of voice, etc.); ease (of motion).
moellon [mwalɔ̃] *n.m.* quarry stone; **m. brut,** rubble(stone); **m. d'appareil,** ashlar.
mœurs [mœr(s)] *n.f.pl.* (*a*) morals, manners (of people); customs, mores (of country, epoch, etc.); habits (of animals); **certificat de bonne vie et m.,** certificate of good character; **la police des m.,** *F:* **les M.** = the vice squad; **gens sans m.,** unprincipled people; **femme de m. faciles,** woman of easy virtue; (*b*) *A:* **bonnes m.,** morality; **avoir des m.,** to be of good moral character.
mofette [mɔfɛt] *n.f.* **1.** *Min: A:* choke damp. **2.** *Z:* skunk.
mohair [mɔɛr] *n.m. Tex:* mohair.
moi [mwa] **1.** *stressed pers.pron.* (*a*) (*subject*) I; **c'est m.,** it is I; it's me; **il est plus âgé que m.,** he is older than me, than I am; **elle est invitée et m. aussi,** she's invited and so am I; **m., je veux bien,** for my part, I'm willing; **je l'ai fait m.-même,** I did it myself; (*b*) (*object*) me; **il accuse mon frère et m.,** he accuses my brother and me; **vous me soupçonnez, m.!** do you suspect (even) me! **avec m.,** with me; **venez à m.,** come to me; **à m.!** help! **ce livre est à m.,** this book is mine, belongs to me; **un ami à m.,** a friend of mine; **ces vers ne sont pas de m.,** the verses are not mine; (*c*) (*after imp.*) (i) (*acc.*) **laissez-m. tranquille,** leave me alone; (ii) (*dat.*) **donnez-le-m.,** give it (to) me. **2.** *n.m.* ego, self; **culte du m.,** egoism.
moignon [mwaɲɔ̃] *n.m.* stump (of amputated limb, etc.).
moi-même [mwamɛm] *pers.pron.* myself; *see* MOI *and* MÊME 1 (*c*).
moindre [mwɛ̃dr̥] *a.* **1.** *comp.* less(er); lower (price); smaller (quantity); **question de m. importance,** question of less(er) importance, of minor importance; *n.* **de deux maux choisir le m.,** to choose the lesser of two evils. **2.** *sup.* **le, la, m.,** the least; **pas la m. chance,** not the slightest, remotest, faintest, chance; **c'est la m. des choses,** it's nothing; it's the least I can do; **je ne lui ai pas fait le m. reproche,** I didn't reproach him in the slightest, in the least; **le dernier, mais non le m.,** last but not least.
moindrement [mwɛ̃drəmɑ̃] *adv.* (*usu. with neg.*) less; **je ne suis pas m. atteint que vous,** I'm just as badly affected as you are; **sans être le m. intéressé,** without being in the least bit interested.
moine [mwan] *n.m.* **1.** monk, friar; *Prov:* **l'habit ne fait pas le m.,** it is not the cowl that makes the monk. **2.** *A:* bed warmer.
moineau, -eaux [mwano] *n.m. Orn:* sparrow; *F:* **c'est un vilain m.,** he's a bad lot, a nasty piece of work; *Com:* **têtes de m.,** nuts (of coal).
moinillon [mwanijɔ̃] *n.m. F:* young monk.
moins [mwɛ̃] **1.** *adv.* (*a*) *comp.* less; **je gagne m. que vous,** I earn less than you; **m. encore,** still less, even less; **elle est m. jolie que sa sœur,** she's not so, as, pretty as her sister; **beaucoup m. long,** much shorter; **m. d'argent,** less money, not so much money, not as much money; **m. d'hommes, d'occasions,** fewer, not so many, men, opportunities; **plus on le punit m. il travaille,** the more he's punished the less he works; **il travaille de m. en m.,** he's working less and less; **m. de dix francs,** less than ten francs; **il a m. de trente ans,** he's less than thirty, under thirty; **les m. de trente ans,** the under-thirties; **les jeunes et les m. jeunes,** the young and the not so young; **nous étions à m. d'un kilomètre de l'église,** we were within one kilometre, *NAm:* killometer, of the church; **en m. de dix minutes,** in less than ten minutes; **en m. de rien,** in less than no time; **en m. de deux,** in no time; **je ne peux pas vous le laisser à m.,** I can't let you have it for less; **dix francs de m.,** ten francs (i) less, (ii) short, too little; **il y a eu 20% de visiteurs de m., en m.,** there have been 20% fewer visitors; **à m. d'accidents,** barring accidents; **à m. d'avis contraire,** unless I hear to the contrary; **à m. de partir tout de suite,** unless I, you, etc., leave at once; **à m. que** + *sub.*, unless; **à m. que vous (ne) l'ordonniez,** unless you order it; **rien m. que,** (i) anything but; (ii) nothing less than; **ce n'est rien m. qu'un héros,** (i) he's nothing less than a hero; (ii) he's anything but a hero; **ce n'est rien (de) m. qu'un miracle,** it's nothing short of a miracle; **il mérite des éloges non m. que son frère,** he deserves praise quite as much as his brother; (*b*) *sup.* **le m.,** least; **les élèves les m. appliqués,** the least industrious pupils; **le m. de gens possible,** the smallest possible number of people; as few people as possible; **pas le m. du monde,** not in the least (degree); by no means; not in the slightest; *n.* **c'est (bien) le m. (qu'il puisse faire),** it's the least he can do; **du m.,** at least; that is to say; at all events; **au m.,** at least (= not less than); **gagner 100.000 francs par an (tout) au m., à tout le m., pour le m.,** to earn 100,000 francs a year at (the very) least, to say the least; *F:* **tu as fait ton travail, au m.?** you've done your work, I hope? **vous compterez cela en m.,** you may deduct that; **il est revenu avec un œil en m.,** he came back minus an eye. **2.** (*a*) *prep.* minus, less; **une heure m. cinq,** five (minutes) to one; **six m. quatre égale deux,** six minus four equals two; **il fait m. dix (degrés) (−10°),** it's minus ten (degrees); (*b*) *n.m. Mth:* minus (sign).
moins-value [mwɛ̃valy] *n.f.* depreciation; diminution, drop, in value; *pl. moins-values.*
moirage [mwaraʒ] *n.m.* watering (of silk, etc.).
moire [mwar] *n.f. Tex:* moire, moiré; watered material; **m. de soie,** watered silk.
moiré [mware] *Tex:* **1.** *a.* watered, moiré (silk, etc.). **2.** *n.m.* = MOIRURE.
moirer [mware] *v.tr.* to water (silk, etc.).
moirure [mwaryr] *n.f.* watered effect; moiré; *T.V:* shot-silk effect.
mois [mwa] *n.m.* (*a*) month; **au m. d'août,** in the month of August; **louer qch. au m.,** to hire sth. by

the month; **cent francs par m.,** a hundred francs a month; (*b*) month's wages, salary; monthly pay.

Moïse [mɔiz] **1.** *Pr.n.m. B.Hist:* Moses. **2.** *n.m.* (*a*) wicker cradle; Moses basket; bassinet; (*b*) carrycot.

moisi [mwazi] **1.** *a.* mouldy, *NAm:* moldy; mildewed, mildewy (bread, etc.); musty, fusty (taste, smell). **2.** *n.m.* mould, *NAm:* mold; mildew; **sentir le m.,** to smell musty, fusty.

moisir [mwazir] **1.** *v.tr.* to mildew; to make (sth.) mouldy, *NAm:* moldy. **2.** *v.i.* to mould, *NAm:* mold; to go mouldy.

moisissure [mwazisyr] *n.f.* **1.** mildew; mould, *NAm:* mold. **2.** mouldiness, *NAm:* moldiness; mustiness.

moisson [mwasɔ̃] *n.f.* **1.** (*a*) harvest(ing) (of cereals); **faire la m.,** to harvest; (*b*) harvest time. **2.** (cereal) crop; **rentrer la m.,** to gather in the crops, the harvest.

moissonnage [mwasɔnaʒ] *n.m.* harvesting; reaping.

moissonner [mwasɔne] *v.tr.* **1.** to reap (corn, field); to harvest, gather (cereal crops); *Lit:* **m. des lauriers,** to reap, win, laurels. **2.** *Lit:* **être moissonné dans la fleur de l'âge,** to be cut off in one's prime.

moissonneur, -euse [mwasɔnœr, -øz] **1.** *n.* (*pers.*) harvester, reaper. **2.** *n.f.* **moissonneuse,** reaping machine.

moissonneuse-batteuse [mwasɔnøzbatøz] *n.f.* combine (harvester); *pl. moissonneuses-batteuses.*

moissonneuse-lieuse [mwasɔnøzljøz] *n.f.* reaper-binder; *pl. moissonneuses-lieuses.*

moite [mwat] *a.* moist, sweaty (hands, etc.); muggy (weather); **(froid et) m.,** clammy.

moiteur [mwatœr] *n.f.* moistness, sweatiness (of hands, etc.); **m. froide,** clamminess.

moitié [mwatje] **1.** *n.f.* half; **perdre la m. de son argent,** to lose half one's money; **la m. du temps,** half the time; **la bouteille était à m. pleine, vide,** the bottle was half full, half empty; **couper qch. par m.,** to cut something in half; to halve sth.; **partagé en deux moitiés,** divided into two halves; halved; **vendre qch. à m. prix,** to sell sth. (at) half price; **s'arrêter à m. chemin,** to stop halfway; **m. plus,** half as much again; **plus grand de m.,** half as big again; **réduit de m.,** reduced by half; **m.-m.,** fifty-fifty; **se mettre de m., être de m., faire m., avec qn dans qch.,** to go halves with s.o. in sth.; to go fifty-fifty with s.o.; to share and share alike; *F:* **ma (chère) m.,** my better half; **à m.,** half; **à m. mort,** half-dead; **à m. cuit,** half-cooked; **faire les choses à m.,** to half-do things, do things by halves. **2.** *adv.* **m. riant, m. pleurant,** half laughing, half crying; **m. l'un, m. l'autre,** half and half.

moitir [mwatir] *v.tr. Tchn:* to moisten (paper, etc.).

Moka [mɔka] **1.** *Pr.n. Geog:* Mocha. **2.** *n.m.* (*a*) mocha (coffee); (*b*) *Cu:* mocha cake.

mol *see* MOU[1].

molaire [mɔlɛr] *n.f.* molar (tooth).

môle [mol] *n.m.* (*a*) mole; (harbour, *NAm:* harbor) breakwater; (*b*) pier.

moléculaire [mɔlekylɛr] *a.* molecular.

molécule [mɔlekyl] *n.f.* molecule.

molécule-gramme [mɔlekylgram] *n.f. Ph.Meas:* gram(me) molecule; *pl. molécules-grammes.*

molène [mɔlɛn] *n.f. Bot:* mullein.

moleskine [mɔlɛskin] *n.f.* imitation leather.

molestation [mɔlɛstasjɔ̃] *n.f.* molestation.

molester [mɔlɛste] *v.tr.* (*a*) *Lit:* to molest; (*b*) to treat (s.o.) roughly, manhandle (s.o.).

moletage [mɔltaʒ] *n.m.* milling, knurling.

moleter [mɔlte] *v.tr.* **(je molette; je moletterai)** to mill, knurl.

molette [mɔlɛt] *n.f.* **1.** *Pharm: A:* small pestle; muller. **2.** (*a*) serrated roller, wheel; knurl; rowel (of spur); **clef à m.,** adjustable spanner, *esp. NAm:* monkey wrench; (*b*) cutting wheel (for glass, etc.); *Phot:* trimmer (for prints); (*c*) *Hort:* grass edging iron.

mollah [mɔla] *n.m. MoslemRel:* mullah.

mollasse¹ [mɔlas] *a.* (*a*) soft, flabby; (*b*) (*of pers.*) slow, lazy; spineless (character); *n.* **grand(e) m.,** great lump (of a man, of a woman).

mol(l)asse² *n.f. Geol:* molasse; sandstone.

mollasson, -onne [mɔlasɔ̃, -ɔn] *F:* (*a*) *a.* (*of pers.*) slow, lazy; spineless, gormless; (*b*) *n.* great lump (of a man, of a woman).

molle *see* MOU[1].

mollement [mɔlmɑ̃] *adv.* (*a*) softly; (*b*) slackly, feebly; weakly, indolently.

mollesse [mɔlɛs] *n.f.* (*a*) softness (of cushion, etc.); flabbiness (of flesh, etc.); (*b*) weakness, lifelessness, spinelessness (of person); limpness, woolliness (of style); laxity (of government); **sans m.,** briskly, smartly.

mollet, -ette [mɔlɛ, -ɛt] **1.** *a.* softish; **pain m.,** (soft) bread roll; **œuf m.,** soft-boiled egg. **2.** *n.m.* calf (of leg).

molletière [mɔltjɛr] *a. & n.f. Cost:* **(bandes) molletières,** puttees.

molleton [mɔltɔ̃] *n.m.* (*a*) soft thick flannel, cotton; duffel; (*b*) swansdown, swanskin; fleece; (*c*) table felt.

molletonné [mɔltɔne] *a.* lined with fleece, with swansdown.

molletonner [mɔltɔne] *v.tr.* to line (gloves, etc.) with fleece, with swansdown.

mollir [mɔlir] **1.** *v.i.* (*a*) to soften, become soft; (*b*) (*of effort, etc.*) to slacken, slack off; (*of wind*) to die down, abate; (*of troops, etc.*) to give ground; **mes jambes mollissent,** my legs are giving way (beneath me). **2.** *v.tr. Nau:* to slacken, ease, slack off (rope); to ease (helm).

mollusque [mɔlysk] *n.m.* **1.** mollusc. **2.** *F:* (*pers.*) great lump; drip.

molosse [mɔlɔs] *n.m. Lit:* watchdog; mastiff.

molybdène [mɔlibdɛn] *n.m. Miner:* molybdenum.

môme [mom] **1.** *n. F:* child, kid, brat, youngster. **2.** *n.f. P:* (*a*) woman; bit of skirt; (*b*) mistress.

moment [mɔmɑ̃] *n.m.* **1.** (*a*) moment; **le m. venu,** when the time, has, had, come; **à ce m.-là,** at that moment, at that time; in those days, then; **à un m. donné,** at a given time; **au m. donné,** at the appointed time; **c'est le bon m. pour . . .,** now is the time to . . .; **un m.!** one moment! just a moment! **il est là en, à, ce m.,** he's there at the moment, (just) now, at present; **je suis à vous dans un m.,** I'll be with you in a moment; **il ne me faut rien pour le m.,** I don't need anything at the moment, for the moment, for the time being; **sur le m. je n'ai pas su que faire,** for a moment I was at a loss; **arriver au bon m.,** to arrive at just the right time, in the nick of time; **par moments,** at times, now and again; **d'un m. à l'autre,** at any moment; any time, any minute; **à tout m., à tous moments,** constantly; **dans un de ses bons moments,** in one of his good moods; **au m. de partir,** just as I, he, etc., was leaving, was about to leave; **au m. de sa naissance,** at the time of his birth; **jusqu'au m. où . . .,** until (such time as) . . .; **du m. que . . .,** (i) *O:* from the moment when . . .; (ii) seeing that . . .; (*b*) stage; **à quel m. de son développement?** at what stage of, point in, his development? **2.** *Mec:* moment (of force, inertia, etc.); **m. angulaire,** angular momentum.

momentané [mɔmɑ̃tane] *a.* momentary (effort, etc.); temporary (absence).

momentanément [mɔmɑ̃tanemɑ̃] *adv.* momentarily; temporarily; for a moment.

momerie [momri] *n.f. Lit:* mummery; insincerity.

momie [mɔmi] *n.f.* mummy.
momification [mɔmifikasjɔ̃] *n.f.* mummification.
momifier [mɔmifje] (*impf. & pr.sub.* **n. momifiions, v. momifiiez**) **1.** *v.tr.* to mummify. **2. se m.,** to become mummified; to fossilize.
mon, ma, mes [mɔ̃, ma, me] *poss.a.* (**mon** *is used instead of* **ma** *before f. words beginning with vowel or h mute*) my; **mon ami, mon amie,** my friend; **mon meilleur ami, ma meilleure amie,** my best friend; **c'est mon affaire à moi,** that's my (own) business; **un de mes amis,** a friend of mine; **mon père et ma mère,** *Lit:* **mes père et mère,** my father and mother; **non, mon colonel,** no, sir.
monacal, -aux [mɔnakal, -o] *a.* monac(h)al, monkish, monastic.
monachisme [mɔnaʃism] *n.m.* monachism, monasticism.
monade [mɔnad] *n.f. Phil: etc:* monad.
monandre [mɔnɑ̃dr̥] *a. Bot:* monandrous.
monarchie [mɔnarʃi] *n.f.* monarchy.
monarchique [mɔnarʃik] *a.* monarchic(al).
monarchisme [mɔnarʃism] *n.m.* monarchism.
monarchiste [mɔnarʃist] *a. & n.* monarchist.
monarque [mɔnark] *n.m.* monarch.
monastère [mɔnastɛr] *n.m.* monastery; convent.
monastique [mɔnastik] *a.* monastic.
monaural, -aux [mɔnɔral, -o] *a. Ac:* monaural.
monceau, -eaux [mɔ̃so] *n.m.* heap, pile.
mondain, -aine [mɔ̃dɛ̃, -ɛn] **1.** *a.* (*a*) mundane, worldly, earthly (pleasures, etc.); (*b*) fashionable (resort, etc.); **réunion mondaine,** society gathering; **carnet de la vie mondaine,** diary of social events; *Journ:* **chronique mondaine,** society news, gossip column; (*c*) **la police mondaine,** *F:* **la M.** = the vice squad. **2.** *n.* socialite; society man, woman; man about town.
mondanité [mɔ̃danite] *n.f.* **1.** worldliness. **2.** *pl.* social events; *Journ:* society news, gossip column.
monde [mɔ̃d] *n.m.* **1.** world; **le m. entier,** the whole world; **dans le m. entier,** all over the world; **le Nouveau M.,** the New World; **le tiers m.,** the third world; **que le m. est petit!** it's a small world! **mettre qn, qch., au m.,** to bring s.o., sth., into the world; to give birth to s.o., sth.; **être au m.,** to be in the land of the living; **être seul au m.,** to be alone in the world; **il est encore de ce m.,** he's still alive, still in the land of the living; **pour rien au m.,** not for the world, not on any account; **faire tout au m. pour obtenir qch.,** to do everything possible to get sth.; **personne au m.,** no man alive; **un des meilleurs hommes du m.,** one of the best men living, alive; **vieux comme le m.,** (as) old as the hills; **le bout du m.,** the ends of the earth, the world's end, the back of beyond; **ainsi va le m.,** it's the way of the world; **l'autre m.,** the next world. **2.** (*a*) **le (beau) m.,** (fashionable) society; **le grand m.,** high society; **aller (beaucoup) dans le m.,** to go out a great deal; to move in fashionable circles; **homme du m.,** society man; man of the world; (*b*) milieu; **le m. de la haute finance,** the financial world, financial circles; **je ne suis pas de leur m.,** I'm not in their set, crowd; **il faut de tout pour faire un m.,** it takes all sorts to make a world. **3.** people; (*a*) **peu de m., pas grand m.,** not many people, not a large crowd; **avoir du m. à dîner,** to have people to dinner; **il connaît son m.,** he knows the people he has to deal with; **tout le m.,** everybody, everyone; **comment va tout votre m.?** how are all your people, all your family? (*b*) *A:* servants, men, hands; staff.
mondial, -iaux [mɔ̃djal, -jo] *a.* worldwide (crisis, etc.); **la première, deuxième, guerre mondiale,** the First, Second, World War; World War One, Two; **guerre mondiale,** global warfare.
mondialement [mɔ̃djalmɑ̃] *adv.* throughout the world; universally.
monégasque [mɔnegask] *a. & n. Geog:* (native, inhabitant) of Monaco.
monétaire [mɔnetɛr] *a.* monetary; **unité m. d'un pays,** currency of a country; **questions monétaires,** questions of (i) currency, (ii) finance; **marché m.,** money market; **presse m.,** minting press.
monétiser [mɔnetize] *v.tr.* to monetize; to mint.
mongol, -ole [mɔ̃gɔl] **1.** *a. & n. Ethn:* Mongol, Mongolian. **2.** *n.m. Ling:* Mongolian.
Mongolie [mɔ̃gɔli] *Pr.n.f. Geog:* Mongolia.
mongolien, -ienne [mɔ̃gɔljɛ̃, -jɛn] *a. & n. Med:* mongol.
mongolique [mɔ̃gɔlik] *a. Ethn:* Mongol(ian).
mongolisme [mɔ̃gɔlism] *n.m. Med:* mongolism.
mongoloïde [mɔ̃gɔlɔid] *a. Med:* mongoloid.
moniteur, -trice [mɔnitœr, -tris] **1.** *n.* (*a*) instructor, *f.* instructress; *Sp:* coach; **m. d'auto-école,** driving instructor; (*b*) assistant (in holiday camp); *U.S:* (camp) counselor; (*c*) *W.Tel:* (foreign broadcast) monitor. **2.** *n.m.* (*device*) monitor.
monitoire [mɔnitwar] *a.* monitory.
monnaie [mɔnɛ] *n.f.* **1.** money; **pièce de m.,** coin; **m. légale,** legal tender; currency; **m. scripturale,** bank money, deposit money; **fausse m.,** counterfeit money, coinage; **frapper de la m., battre m.,** to coin, mint, money; **(l'hôtel de) la M.** = the Mint; **payer qn en m. de singe,** to fob s.o. off, let s.o. whistle for his money. **2.** change; **petite m.,** small change; **donner la m. de mille francs,** to give change for a thousand-franc note; **rendre à qn la m. de sa pièce,** to pay s.o. back in his own coin.
monnaie-du-pape [mɔnɛdypap] *n.f. Bot:* honesty; *pl. monnaies-du-pape.*
monnayage [mɔnɛjaʒ] *n.m.* minting, coining.
monnayer [mɔneje] *v.tr.* **(je monnaie; je monnaierai) 1.** to coin, mint (money). **2.** (*a*) to cash (a banknote); (*b*) to cash in on (one's influence, etc.).
monnayeur [mɔnɛjœr] *n.m.* coiner, minter; **faux m.,** counterfeiter.
mono [mɔno] *a.inv.* mono (record, etc.).
monoacide [mɔnɔasid] *a. Ch:* monoacid(ic).
monobloc [mɔnɔblɔk] *a.inv. I.C.E:* (*of cylinders, etc.*) made in one piece; cast solid.
monochrome [mɔnɔkrom] *a.* monochrome.
monocle [mɔnɔkl̥] *n.m.* monocle.
monocoque [mɔnɔkɔk] *a. Aut:* monoshell; **avion m.,** monocoque; (*of car*) **carrosserie m.,** integral all-steel welded body.
monocorde [mɔnɔkɔrd] **1.** *a.* (*a*) *Mus:* single-stringed (instrument); (*b*) monotonous (sound). **2.** *n.m.* monochord.
monocotylédone [mɔnɔkɔtiledɔn] *n.f. Bot:* monocotyledon.
monoculaire [mɔnɔkylɛr] *a.* monocular (field glass, vision, etc.); **cécité m.,** blindness in one eye.
monoculture [mɔnɔkyltyr] *n.f. Agr:* monoculture.
monocycle [mɔnɔsikl̥] *n.m. Cy:* monocycle.
monocylindrique [mɔnɔsilɛ̃drik] *a. Aut: etc:* single-cylinder (engine).
monogame [mɔnɔgam] *a.* monogamous.
monogamie [mɔnɔgami] *n.f.* monogamy.
monogamique [mɔnɔgamik] *a.* monogamic.
monogramme [mɔnɔgram] *n.m.* monogram.
monographie [mɔnɔgrafi] *n.f.* monograph.
monolingue [mɔnɔlɛ̃g] *a.* monolingual.
monolithe [mɔnɔlit] **1.** *a.* monolithic. **2.** *n.m.* monolith.
monolithique [mɔnɔlitik] *a.* monolithic.
monologue [mɔnɔlɔg] *n.m.* monologue, soliloquy.
monologuer [mɔnɔlɔge] *v.i.* to soliloquize; to talk to oneself.

monologueur [mɔnɔlɔgœr] *n.m.* soliloquist.

monomane [mɔnɔman], **monomaniaque** [mɔnɔmanjak] **1.** *a.* monomaniacal. **2.** *n.* monomaniac.

monomanie [mɔnɔmani] *n.f.* monomania.

monôme [mɔnom] *n.m.* **1.** *Mth:* monomial; single term. **2.** students' rag parade (through the streets in single file).

monomoteur [mɔnɔmɔtœr] **1.** *a.* single-engined. **2.** *n.m.* single-engined aircraft.

monophasé [mɔnɔfɑze] *El:* **1.** *a.* single-phase (current). **2.** *n.m.* **m. de traction,** single-phase traction current.

monoplace [mɔnɔplas] *a. & n.* single-seater (car, aircraft, etc.).

monoplan [mɔnɔplɑ̃] *n.m. Av:* monoplane.

monopole [mɔnɔpɔl] *n.m.* monopoly.

monopolisateur, -trice [mɔnɔpɔlizatœr, -tris] *n.* monopolizer; monopolist.

monopolisation [mɔnɔpɔlizasjɔ̃] *n.f.* monopolization.

monopoliser [mɔnɔpɔlize] *v.tr.* to monopolize; to have the monopoly of (sth.).

monorail [mɔnɔrɑj] *a.inv. & n.m.* monorail.

monosyllabe [mɔnɔsilab] **1.** *a.* monosyllabic. **2.** *n.m.* monosyllable.

monosyllabique [mɔnɔsilabik] *a.* monosyllabic.

monothéisme [mɔnɔteism] *n.m.* monotheism.

monothéiste [mɔnɔteist] **1.** *a.* monotheistic. **2.** *n.* monotheist.

monotone [mɔnɔtɔn] *a.* monotonous (speech, etc.); humdrum, dull (life).

monotonie [mɔnɔtɔni] *n.f.* monotony.

monotype [mɔnɔtip] *n.f. Typ: R.t.m:* Monotype (machine).

monovalent [mɔnɔvalɑ̃] *a. Ch:* monovalent; univalent.

monseigneur [mɔ̃sɛɲœr] *n.m.* **1.** (*a*) (*referring to prince*) His Royal Highness; (*to cardinal*) his Eminence; (*to duke, archbishop*) his Grace; (*to bishop*) his Lordship; **m., Mgr, l'évêque de . . .,** the Lord Bishop of . . .; *pl. nosseigneurs*; (*b*) (*when speaking to prince*) Your Royal Highness; (*to cardinal*) your Eminence; (*to duke, archbishop*) your Grace; (*to bishop*) my Lord (Bishop), your Lordship; *pl. messeigneurs.* **2. (pince) m.,** (burglar's) jemmy; *pl. monseigneurs.*

monsieur, *pl.* **messieurs** [m(ə)sjø, mesjø] *n.m.* **1.** (*a*) **M. Robert Martin,** Mr Robert Martin; **Messieurs Martin et Cie,** Messrs Martin and Co.; **m. le duc, le comte, de . . .,** the Duke, the Earl, of . . .; **m. le duc, m. le comte,** his, your, Grace, his, your, Lordship; (*b*) (*to or of small boy*) **M. Robert (Martin),** Master Robert (Martin); (*c*) (*used alone*) **voici le chapeau de m.,** (i) here's your hat, sir; (ii) here's the gentleman's hat; here's Mr X's hat; **m. n'est pas là,** Mr X is out. **2.** (*a*) (*when speaking to a man*) sir; (*to titled gentleman*) sir, your Grace, your Lordship, etc.; **bonsoir, messieurs,** goodnight, gentlemen; **m. a sonné?** did you ring, sir? **que prendront ces messieurs?** what will you have, gentlemen? **Mesdames, Messieurs,** ladies and gentlemen; *F:* (*usu. omitted in Eng.*) **bonjour, Messieurs-Dames!** good morning! (*b*) *Corr:* (*always written in full*) (i) (*to stranger*) **Monsieur,** (Dear) Sir; (ii) **Monsieur et cher Confrère, Monsieur et cher Collègue,** Dear Mr X; (iii) (*implying previous acquaintance*) **Cher Monsieur,** Dear Mr X; (*c*) (*on envelope*) **Monsieur T. Martin,** Mr T. Martin; T. Martin Esq. **3.** (gentle)man; **deux messieurs que je ne connais pas,** two men I don't know; **c'est un vilain m.,** he's a nasty piece of work.

monstre [mɔ̃stɽ] **1.** *n.m.* (*a*) monster, monstrosity; (*b*) *Myth: etc:* monster; **les monstres marins,** the monsters of the deep; (*of pers.*) **m. d'ingratitude,** monster of ingratitude; **ces monstres d'hommes,** those brutes of men; *F:* **cet enfant est un petit m.!** that child's a little devil, a little monster! **2.** *a. F:* huge; colossal; monster (demonstration).

monstrueusement [mɔ̃stryøzmɑ̃] *adv.* monstrously.

monstrueux, -euse [mɔ̃stryø, -øz] *a.* monstrous. **1.** unnatural; **ombre monstrueuse,** grisly shadow. **2.** huge, colossal. **3.** shocking, scandalous; dreadful.

monstruosité [mɔ̃stryozite] *n.f.* **1.** monstrousness (of crime, etc.). **2.** monstrosity.

mont [mɔ̃] *n.m.* mount, mountain; **le m. Sinaï,** Mount Sinai; **par monts et par vaux,** up hill and down dale; **être toujours par monts et par vaux,** to be always on the move; **promettre monts et merveilles à qn,** to promise s.o. the earth.

montage [mɔ̃taʒ] *n.m.* **1.** taking up, carrying up (of building materials, etc.). **2.** setting (of jewel, specimen, etc.); mounting (of photograph, fishhook, etc.); fitting (on) (of tyre, *NAm:* tire); fitting up, erecting, assembling, assembly (of apparatus); fitting out (of workshop, etc.); hanging (of door); *Cin:* editing; *Ind:* **chaîne de m.,** assembly line. **3.** *El:* connecting up; wiring (up).

montagnard, -arde [mɔ̃taɲar, -ard] **1.** *a.* mountain, highland (people, etc.). **2.** *n.* (*a*) mountain dweller; highlander; (*b*) *Fr.Hist:* member of the *Montagne.*

montagne [mɔ̃taɲ] *n.f.* **1.** (*a*) mountain; *B:* **le sermon sur la m.,** the Sermon on the Mount; *Pol.Ec: F:* **la m. de beurre,** the butter mountain; **une m. de choux,** a huge pile of cabbages; **se faire une m. de qch.,** to make mountains out of molehills; **c'est la m. qui accouche d'une souris,** what a lot of fuss for nothing; (*at fair*) **montagnes russes,** scenic railway, switchback, *esp. NAm:* roller coaster; (*b*) mountain region; highlands, uplands; **passer ses vacances à la m.,** to spend one's holiday in the mountains. **2.** *Fr.Hist:* (*during the Revolution*) **la M.,** the Mountain.

montagneux, -euse [mɔ̃taɲø, -øz] *a.* mountainous.

montant [mɔ̃tɑ̃] **1.** *a.* (*a*) rising, ascending; **chemin m.,** uphill road; **marée montante,** rising tide, flood tide; **col m.,** high, stand-up, collar; *Rail:* **train, quai, m.,** up train, platform; (*b*) *Mil:* **garde montante,** new guard, relieving guard. **2.** *n.m.* (*a*) upright (of ladder, etc.); leg (of trestle); column, pillar (in machine); pole (of tent); stile, jamb (of door, window); post (of gate); riser (of stair); *Harn:* cheek strap (of bridle); *Fb:* **les montants,** the goalposts; (*b*) (sum) total; total amount (of account); **j'ignore le m. de mes dettes,** I don't know what my debts amount to.

mont-de-piété [mɔ̃d(ə)pjete] *n.m. A:* (*now* **crédit municipal**) pawnshop; **mettre qch. au m.-de-p.,** to pawn sth.; *pl. monts-de-piété.*

monte [mɔ̃t] *n.f.* **1.** *Breed:* (*a*) covering (of mare); (*b*) breeding season, mating season (of domestic animals). **2.** *Turf:* (*a*) mounting (of horse); **jockey qui a eu trois montes dans la journée,** jockey who has ridden three times, who has had three mounts, during the day; (*b*) (method of) riding, horsemanship; **m. à l'obstacle,** jumping.

monté [mɔ̃te] *a.* **1.** mounted (soldier, etc.). **2. il était m., il avait la tête montée, contre qn,** he was worked up, set, against s.o. **3.** set (jewel); mounted (gun, etc.); equipped, fitted, appointed (ship, etc.); **photographies non montées,** unmounted photographs; **pièce mal montée,** badly produced play; **cave, boutique, bien montée,** well stocked cellar, shop; **coup m.,** plot, put-up job; frame-up.

monte-charge [mɔ̃tʃarʒ] *n.m.inv.* hoist, goods lift, *NAm:* goods elevator.

montée [mɔ̃te] *n.f.* **1.** rise; (*a*) rising; **mouvement de**

m., up motion; **pendant la m.,** as I, we, etc., were climbing, going, up; *Hyd.E: etc:* **tuyau de m.,** uptake pipe, riser; (*in reservoir*) **m. des eaux,** inflow; (*b*) uphill pull; climb; *Aut: Av:* **essai de m.,** climbing test; **vitesse en m.,** climbing speed, speed on a gradient. **2.** ascent, gradient, acclivity, slope (up); hill (in road).

monte-en-l'air [mɔ̃tɑ̃lɛr] *n.m.inv. F:* cat burglar.

monte-plats [mɔ̃tpla] *n.m.inv.* (*in restaurant*) service lift, *NAm:* elevator; hoist; dumb waiter.

monter [mɔ̃te] **I.** *v.i.* (*aux. usu.* **être,** *occ.* **avoir**) **1.** (*a*) to go up; to climb (up), mount, ascend; to go upstairs; (*of bird*) to soar; (*of aircraft*) to climb; **m. à, sur, un arbre, une échelle,** to climb (up) a tree, a ladder; **m. en haut d'une colline,** to climb, go up, (right) to the top of a hill; **m. en courant,** to run up; **m. se coucher,** to go (up) to bed; **faire m. qn,** to show s.o. up(stairs); **montez chez moi,** come up to my room; *Mil:* **m. en ligne,** to go to the front (line); **m. à l'assaut,** to go into the attack; *Ten:* **m. au filet,** to come, go, up to the net; *Nau:* **faire m. tous les hommes,** to order all hands on deck; (*b*) to climb, get, on, into (sth.); **m. sur une chaise,** to get onto, stand on, a chair; **m. en chaire,** to ascend the pulpit; **m. à cheval,** (i) to get on a horse; to mount (a horse); (ii) to ride; **montez-vous (à cheval)?** do you ride? *F:* **monter sur ses grands chevaux,** to get on one's high horse; **m. à bicyclette,** to ride a bicycle; **m. en voiture,** to get into a car; **m. à bord,** to go on board (ship); **faire m. qn (en voiture) avec soi,** to give s.o. a lift; **m. sur les planches,** to go on the stage. **2.** (*a*) (*of balloon, the sun, etc.*) to rise; (*of prices, barometer, etc.*) to rise, go up; (*of tide*) to rise, come in; **les frais montent,** the costs are mounting up; **la somme monte à cent francs,** the total amounts, comes, to a hundred francs; **faire m. les prix,** to raise prices; **empêcher les prix de m.,** to keep prices down; **le sang lui monta à la tête,** the blood rushed to his head; **faire m. les larmes aux yeux de qn,** to bring tears to s.o.'s eyes; **m. comme une soupe au lait,** to flare up, go off the deep end; **faire m. qn,** to get a rise out of s.o.; (*b*) (*of road, etc.*) to climb, slope up; **la rue va en montant,** the street climbs; (*c*) (*of pers., etc.*) **m. dans l'estime de qn,** to go up, rise, in s.o.'s estimation; **faire m. qn dans l'estime de qn,** to raise s.o. in s.o.'s estimation. **II.** *v.tr.* **1.** to mount; (*a*) to climb (up), go up, come up (hill, stairs, etc.); **m. la rue en courant,** to run up the street; **m. un fleuve,** to go, sail, steam, up a river; (*b*) *Mil:* **m. la garde,** (i) to mount guard; (ii) to go on guard; (*c*) to ride (horse). **2.** *Nau:* (*a*) to command (ship); (*b*) to man (boat). **3.** (*a*) to raise, carry up, take up, haul up; **m. du vin de la cave,** to fetch, bring up, wine from the cellar; **m. le gaz,** to turn up the gas; (*b*) **se m. la tête,** to get excited; **m. (la tête à) qn contre qn,** to set s.o. against s.o. **4.** (*a*) to set, mount (jewel); to mount (photo, fishhook, etc.); to fit (on) (tyre, *NAm:* tire); to set up, fit up, erect (apparatus, etc.); to hang (door); to fit out, equip (workshop, etc.); to assemble, erect (machine); *Th:* to set (scene); to stage, put on, produce (play); *Cin: etc:* to edit (film); *Dressm:* to make up (garment); **m. un magasin,** to set up, open, a shop; **m. un complot, un coup,** to hatch a plot; to plan a burglary, etc.; *F:* **m. le coup à qn,** to deceive s.o., take s.o. in; *Knit:* **m. les mailles,** to cast on (the stitches); (*b*) *El:* to connect up, wire (up). **III. se m.** (*a*) to amount; **à combien se monte tout cela?** how much does all this add up to, come to? (*b*) to equip oneself, fit oneself out (**en,** with); **se m. en vaisselle,** to set oneself up with crockery; (*c*) *F:* to lose one's temper, fly off the handle.

monteur, -euse [mɔ̃tœr, -øz] *n.* setter (of jewels); mounter (of pictures, etc.); *Cin:* editor; *Mec.E: etc:* fitter.

monticule [mɔ̃tikyl] *n.m.* hillock, mound; hummock.

mont(-)joie [mɔ̃ʒwa] *n.f.* cairn, heap of stones; *pl. monts-joie, montjoies.*

montoir [mɔ̃twar] *n.m.* mounting block, horse block; **côté (du) m.,** nearside (of horse); **côté hors (du) m.,** offside.

montrable [mɔ̃trabl̥] *a.* fit to be seen; presentable.

montre [mɔ̃tr̥] *n.f.* **1.** (*a*) show, display; **faire m. d'un grand courage,** to display great courage; *Lit:* **faire qch. pour la m.,** to do sth. merely for show; (*b*) (i) shop window, display window; (ii) showcase; **mettre qch. en m.,** to put sth. in the window, on show, on display. **2.** watch; **m. (de poignet),** (wrist)watch; **m. à recouvrement,** hunter; **m. à guichet,** half hunter; **m. marine,** ship's chronometer; **à ma m. il est midi,** by my watch it's midday; **cela lui a pris dix minutes m. en main,** it took him ten minutes by the clock; **course contre la m.,** race against time.

Montréal [mɔ̃real] *Pr.n. Geog:* Montreal.

montréalais, -aise [mɔ̃realɛ, -ɛz] *Geog:* **1.** *a.* of Montreal. **2.** *n.* Montrealer.

montre-bracelet [mɔ̃trəbraslɛ] *n.f.* wristwatch; *pl. montres-bracelets.*

montrer [mɔ̃tre] **1.** *v.tr.* to show; (*a*) to display, exhibit; **il a montré un grand courage,** he showed, displayed, great courage; **il n'y montre jamais le nez,** he never shows his face there; (*b*) to point out; **m. qn, qch., du doigt,** to point s.o., sth., out (with one's finger); **m. le chemin à qn,** to show s.o. the way; **m. la ville à qn,** to show s.o. round the town; (*c*) **montrer à qn à faire qch.,** to show s.o. how to do sth. **2. se m.** (*a*) to appear; to show oneself, one's face; (*b*) **des taches brunes se montrent sur la peau,** brown marks appear, can be seen, on the skin; (*c*) **il se montra prudent,** he showed prudence; **il s'est montré très gentil,** he proved, turned out, (to be) very friendly; **il s'est montré très courageux,** he displayed great courage.

montreur, -euse [mɔ̃trœr, -øz] *n.* showman, -woman (at fair, etc.); exhibitor (of wild beasts); **m. d'ours,** bear leader.

montueux, -euse [mɔ̃tɥø, -øz] *a.* hilly.

monture [mɔ̃tyr] *n.f.* **1.** (*horse, etc.*) mount; (saddle) horse. **2.** mounting (of photograph, etc.); mount (of picture, etc.); setting (of jewel); frame (of saw, umbrella, spectacles, etc.); stock (of gun, pistol); handle, guard (of sword); **lunettes sans m.,** rimless spectacles.

monument [mɔnymɑ̃] *n.m.* **1.** monument, memorial; **m. funéraire,** monument (over a tomb); **m. aux morts,** war memorial. **2.** public, historic, building. **3.** *F:* **cette armoire est un m.,** it's an enormous cupboard.

monumental, -aux [mɔnymɑ̃tal, -o] *a.* (*a*) monumental; (*b*) *F:* huge, colossal; **elle est d'une bêtise monumentale,** she's incredibly stupid.

moquer [mɔke] **1.** *v.tr. A:* to mock. **2. se m. de qn, de qch.,** to mock, make fun of, laugh at, poke fun at, s.o., sth.; **vous vous moquez,** you're joking, you're not serious; **se faire m. de soi,** to make a fool of oneself; **il se moque du tiers comme du quart,** he doesn't care, give, a damn about anybody or anything; **je m'en moque comme de l'an quarante, comme de ma première chemise,** I don't care two hoots, a tinker's cuss, a tinker's damn; **vous vous moquez, c'est se m., du monde!** it's the height of impertinence! what a cheek!

moquerie [mɔkri] *n.f.* mockery, jeering, scoffing; ridicule, derision.

moquette [mɔkɛt] *n.f.* (*a*) *Tex:* moquette; (*b*) (fitted) carpet(ing).

moqueur, -euse [mɔkœr, -øz] **1.** *a.* (*a*) mocking, jeering, scoffing; **rires moqueurs,** derisive laughter;

(*b*) given to mockery; facetious. **2.** *n.* mocker, scoffer. **3.** *n.m. Orn:* mockingbird.
moqueusement [mɔkøzmɑ̃] *adv.* mockingly.
moraillon [mɔrɑjɔ̃] *n.m.* hasp, clasp (of lock).
moraine [mɔrɛn] *n.f. Geol:* moraine.
moral, -aux [mɔral, -o] **1.** *a.* (*a*) moral; ethical (philosophy, etc.); **science morale,** moral science; ethics; (*b*) mental, intellectual, moral; **facultés morales,** faculties of the mind; **courage m.,** moral courage; **victoire morale,** moral victory; **certitude morale,** moral certainty. **2.** *n.m.* (*a*) (state of) mind; morale; **remonter le m. de, à, qn,** to raise s.o.'s spirits, cheer s.o. up; **son m. est bas,** his spirits are low; *F:* **avoir le m. à zéro,** to be down in the dumps; (*b*) *A: & Lit:* moral nature.
morale [mɔral] *n.f.* **1.** (*a*) morals; **contraire à la m.,** immoral; (*b*) ethics; moral science; **faire (de) la m. à qn,** to lecture s.o. **2.** moral (of story).
moralement [mɔralmɑ̃] *adv.* morally.
moralisateur, -trice [mɔralizatœr, -tris] **1.** *a.* (*a*) moralizing (person); (*b*) elevating, edifying (principles). **2.** *n.* moralizer.
moralisation [mɔralizasjɔ̃] *n.f. A:* moralization (of community, etc.).
moraliser [mɔralize] **1.** *v.i.* to moralize. **2.** *v.tr.* to lecture (s.o.).
moraliste [mɔralist] **1.** *a.* moralistic. **2.** *n.* moralist.
moralité [mɔralite] *n.f.* **1.** (*a*) morality; (good) moral conduct; **certificat de m.,** good conduct certificate; reference; (*b*) morals; honesty. **2.** moral lesson; moral (of story). **3.** *Lit.Hist:* morality (play).
morasse [mɔras] *n.f. Typ:* brush proof (of newspaper).
moratoire [mɔratwar] *Jur:* **1.** *a.* moratory (agreement, etc.); (payment) delayed by agreement; **intérêts moratoires,** interest on overdue payments. **2.** *n.m.* moratorium.
moratorium [mɔratɔrjɔm] *n.m. Jur:* moratorium.
morbide [mɔrbid] *a.* morbid.
morbidement [mɔrbidmɑ̃] *adv.* morbidly.
morbidité [mɔrbidite] *n.f.* morbidity, morbidness.
morbleu [mɔrblø] *int. A:* 'sdeath! zounds!
morceau, -eaux [mɔrso] *n.m.* **1.** piece, bit (of food); **m. de choix,** choice morsel; **bas morceaux,** cheap(er) cuts (of meat); **aimer les bons morceaux,** to like good things (to eat); *F:* **manger un m.,** to have a bite to eat, a snack; **emporter le m.,** (i) to be very cutting; (ii) to win (in deal, etc.); *F:* **lâcher le m.,** to give the game away, to split. **2.** piece (of soap, cloth, music, etc.); bit (of wood, etc.); scrap, fragment (of paper, etc.); lump (of sugar, etc.); patch (of land, etc.); length (of string); **sucre en morceaux,** lump sugar, cube sugar; **mettre qch. en morceaux,** to pull sth. to pieces, to bits; **tomber en morceaux,** to fall, be falling, to pieces; *Lit:* **morceaux choisis,** selected passages; extracts.
morceler [mɔrsəle] *v.tr.* **(je morcelle; je morcellerai)** to cut (sth.) up into small pieces; **m. une propriété,** (i) to break up, (ii) parcel out, an estate.
morcellement [mɔrsɛlmɑ̃] *n.m.* breaking up, parcelling out, cutting up, division (of estate, etc.).
mordache [mɔrdaʃ] *n.f. Tls:* clamp, claw (of vice); jaw, clip, grip, dog (of chuck).
mordacité [mɔrdasite] *n.f.* mordancy, mordacity (of critic, etc.).
mordant [mɔrdɑ̃] **1.** *a.* (*a*) mordant, biting, caustic, scathing (wit, speech, etc.); cutting (remark, etc.); (*b*) penetrating, piercing (sound); **froid m.,** biting cold. **2.** *n.m.* (*a*) bite (of file, etc.); (*b*) mordancy (of wit, etc.); keenness, dash, punch (of troops, etc.); (*c*) *Dy: etc:* mordant; (*d*) gold size; (*e*) *Mus:* mordent.
mordicus [mɔrdikys] *adv. F:* stoutly, doggedly.
mordieu [mɔrdjø] *int. A:* 'sdeath! zounds!
mordillage [mɔrdijaʒ] *n.m.* nibbling.
mordiller [mɔrdije] *v.tr. & i.* to nibble.
mordoré [mɔrdɔre] *a. & n.m.* bronze (colour, *NAm:* color).
mordorer [mɔrdɔre] *v.tr.* to bronze (leather, etc.).
mordorure [mɔrdɔryr] *n.f.* bronze finish (on leather, etc.).
mordre [mɔrdr̥] *v.tr. & ind.tr.* **1.** to bite; (*a*) **se m. la langue,** to bite one's tongue; **se m. la langue d'avoir parlé,** to regret bitterly having spoken; **se m. les lèvres,** to bite one's lips; **il s'en mord les lèvres,** he bitterly regrets it; **le froid lui mordait les doigts,** the cold nipped his fingers; **m. la poussière,** to bite the dust; (*b*) **lime, vis, qui mord,** file, screw, that bites, has a good bite; **l'ancre ne mord pas,** the anchor won't hold, grip; **acide qui mord (sur) les métaux,** acid that bites (into), eats away, acts on, metals; **m. à, dans, une pomme,** to bite into, take a bite out of, an apple; **m. sur qch.,** to encroach upon sth.; **m. à l'appât, à l'hameçon,** to rise to, swallow, the bait; *F:* **il mord au latin,** he's taking to Latin; *Fish:* **ça mord,** I've got a bite; (*c*) (*of cog wheels*) to catch, engage. **2.** *Engr:* **(faire) m. une planche,** to etch a plate.
mordu, -e [mɔrdy] **1.** *a.* (*a*) bitten; (*b*) *F:* madly in love. **2.** *n.* fan; **m. du bridge,** bridge fanatic, fiend.
more [mɔr] = MAURE.
morelle [mɔrɛl] *n.f. Bot:* nightshade.
moresque [mɔrɛsk] = MAURESQUE.
morfil [mɔrfil] *n.m.* wire edge (on tool).
morfondre [mɔrfɔ̃dr̥] **1.** *v.tr. A: & Lit:* (*of wind, etc.*) to chill (s.o.) to the bone. **2. se m.,** to be bored to death; to mope; **se m. à la porte de qn,** to stand waiting at s.o.'s door.
morfondu [mɔrfɔ̃dy] *a.* (*of pers.*) gloomy.
morganatique [mɔrganatik] *a.* morganatic.
morganatiquement [mɔrganatikmɑ̃] *a.* morganatically.
morgeline [mɔrʒəlin] *n.f. Bot:* **1.** scarlet pimpernel. **2.** chickweed.
morgue [mɔrg] *n.f.* **1.** pride, haughtiness, arrogance. **2.** mortuary, morgue.
moribond, -onde [mɔribɔ̃, -ɔ̃d] *a.* moribund, dying, at death's door; *n.* **les moribonds,** the dying.
moricaud, -aude [mɔriko, -od] *F:* **1.** *a.* dark-skinned, dusky, swarthy. **2.** *n.* black, *Pej:* nigger.
morigéner [mɔriʒene] *v.tr.* **(je morigène; je morigénerai)** to lecture (s.o.), take (s.o.) to task, give (s.o.) a good talking to.
morille [mɔrij] *n.f. Fung: Cu:* morel.
morillon [mɔrijɔ̃] *n.m.* **1.** *Orn:* tufted duck. **2.** *Lap:* rough emerald.
mormon, -one [mɔrmɔ̃, -ɔn] **1.** *n.* Mormon; Latter-Day Saint. **2.** *a.* Mormon (church, etc.).
mormonisme [mɔrmɔnism] *n.m.* Mormonism.
morne [mɔrn] *a.* dejected (person, etc.); gloomy (silence); dull (weather, etc.); bleak, dreary, dismal.
mornifle [mɔrnifl̥] *n.f. F:* slap, backhander.
morose [mɔroz] *a.* (*of pers.*) morose, moody, surly, sullen.
morosité [mɔrozite] *n.f.* moroseness, moodiness, surliness.
Morphée [mɔrfe] *Pr.n.m. Myth:* Morpheus; **dans les bras de M.,** in the arms of Morpheus.
morphine [mɔrfin] *n.f.* morphine; *occ.* morphia.
morphinisme [mɔrfinism] *n.m. Med:* morphinism.
morphinomane [mɔrfinɔman] **1.** *a.* addicted to morphine. **2.** *n.* morphine addict.
morphinomanie [mɔrfinɔmani] *n.f.* addiction to morphine.
morphologie [mɔrfɔlɔʒi] *n.f.* morphology.
morphologique [mɔrfɔlɔʒik] *a.* morphological.
morphologiquement [mɔrfɔlɔʒikmɑ̃] *adv.* morphologically.

morpion [mɔrpjɔ̃] *n.m.* **1.** *P:* crab (louse). **2.** *P:* child, kid, brat. **3.** *Games:* noughts and crosses, *NAm:* tick-tack-toe.

mors [mɔr] *n.m.* **1.** (*a*) *Tls:* jaw, chap, chop (of vice); (*b*) *Bookb:* joint. **2.** *Harn:* bit; **m. de bride,** curb bit, bridle bit; **m. de filet,** snaffle (bit); **prendre le m. aux dents,** (i) (*of horse*) to take the bit in its teeth; to bolt; (ii) (*of pers.*) to take the bit between one's teeth; to be carried away; to fly off the handle.

morse¹ [mɔrs] *n.m. Z:* walrus.

morse² *n.m. Tg:* Morse (code, etc.).

morsure [mɔrsyr] *n.f.* **1.** bite. **2.** *Engr:* biting.

mort¹, morte [mɔr, mɔrt] **1.** *a.* (*a*) dead (person, leaf, language, etc.); lifeless (expression, etc.); **m. et enterré,** dead and buried, dead and gone; **il est m.,** he's dead; **il est m. hier,** he died yesterday; *Prov:* **morte la bête, m. le venin,** dead men tell no tales; **m. de peur,** frightened to death; **plus m. que vif,** half-dead with fright; **un petit trou à moitié m.,** a dead(-and)-alive little hole (of a place); *Com:* **marché m.,** dead market; *Geog:* **la mer Morte,** the Dead Sea; (*b*) **temps m.,** (i) *Sp:* stoppage (in match); (ii) period of inactivity; *Mec.E:* **poids m.,** dead weight; *Civ.E:* dead load; *Mch:* **point m.,** (i) dead centre, *NAm:* center (of piston stroke); (ii) neutral position (of lever, etc.); *Aut:* neutral gear; *Aut:* **mettre le levier au point m.,** to put the (gear) lever into neutral; **arriver à un point m.,** to come to a standstill, to a deadlock; (*in car, etc.*) **angle m.,** blind spot; *N.Arch:* **œuvres mortes,** dead works; (*c*) **eau morte,** still, stagnant, water; *Art:* **nature morte,** still life; (*d*) **balle morte,** spent bullet. **2.** *n.* dead person; deceased; **les morts,** the dead, the departed; *Ecc:* **jour, fête, des Morts,** All Souls' day; **l'office des morts,** the burial service; **faire le m.,** (i) to pretend to be dead; (ii) to lie low; **tête de m.,** (i) death's head; skull; (ii) *F:* (round, redskinned) Dutch cheese. **3.** *n.m. Cards:* dummy; **faire le m.,** to be dummy.

mort² *n.f.* **1.** death; **pâle comme la m.,** as pale as death; **il n'y a pas eu m. d'homme,** there was no loss of life; **mettre qn à m.,** to put s.o. to death; **condamner qn à m.,** to condemn, *Jur:* sentence, s.o. to death; **sentence, arrêt, de m.,** death sentence, sentence of death; **à m. les traîtres!** death to the traitors! *P:* **m. aux vaches!** down with the cops! **blessé à m.,** mortally wounded; **lutte à la m.,** fight to the death; *F:* **freiner à m.,** to jam on the brakes; **se donner la m.,** to take one's (own) life; **vous allez attraper la m.!** you'll catch your death (of cold)! **mourir de sa belle m.,** to die a natural death; **être à la m., à l'article de la m.,** to be at death's door; **à la m. de son père,** on his father's death; **haïr qn à m.,** to hate s.o. like poison; **ennemis à m.,** deadly enemies; **silence de m.,** dead silence, deathlike hush; *Lit:* **il avait la m. dans l'âme,** he was sick at heart; **souffrir m. et passion,** to suffer agonies; **je m'en souviendrai jusqu'à la m.,** I'll remember it until my dying day; **à la vie, à la m.,** for ever, for life; **le monopole est la m. de l'industrie,** monopoly is the ruin, means the end, of industry. **2.** *Bot:* **m. aux loups,** wolfsbane; **m. aux poules,** henbane.

mortadelle [mɔrtadɛl] *n.f. Comest:* mortadella.

mortaise [mɔrtɛz] *n.f.* slot; (*a*) *Carp:* mortise; **assemblage à tenon et à m.,** mortise (and tenon) joint; (*b*) *Mec.E: etc:* **m. de clavette,** keyway.

mortaiser [mɔrteze] *v.tr.* to slot, mortise.

mortalité [mɔrtalite] *n.f.* mortality. **1.** *A:* mortal nature. **2.** death rate; *Ins:* **tables de m.,** mortality tables.

mort-aux-rats [mɔrora] *n.f.inv.* rat poison.

mort-bois [mɔrbwa] *n.m. For:* underwood, brushwood; *pl. morts-bois.*

morte-eau [mɔrto] *n.f.* neap tide(s); neaps; *pl. mortes-eaux.*

mortel, -elle [mɔrtɛl] *a.* mortal; (*a*) destined to die; *n.* **un m., une mortelle,** a mortal; (*b*) fatal (wound, etc.); **coup m.,** mortal blow, lethal blow, death blow; **rayon m.,** death ray; **il a fait une chute mortelle de 100 mètres,** he fell 100 metres, *NAm:* meters, to his death; (*c*) *F:* deadly dull, boring; **je l'ai attendu deux mortelles heures,** I waited two solid hours for him; (*d*) deadly (hatred, sin, etc.); **ennemi m.,** deadly enemy, mortal enemy; **d'une pâleur mortelle,** deathly pale; **poison m.,** deadly poison.

mortellement [mɔrtɛlmɑ̃] *adv.* mortally, fatally (wounded, etc.); **pécher m.,** to commit a mortal sin; **m. pâle,** deathly pale; **m. offensé,** mortally offended; *F:* **s'ennuyer m.,** to be bored to death; **m. ennuyeux,** deadly dull, boring.

morte-saison [mɔrt(ə)sɛzɔ̃] *n.f. Com: etc:* slack period, off season; *pl. mortes-saisons.*

mortier [mɔrtje] *n.m.* **1.** (*a*) *Cu: etc:* mortar; **pilon et m.,** pestle and mortar; (*b*) *Artil:* mortar; **obus de m.,** mortar shell. **2.** *Const:* **m. ordinaire,** lime mortar; **m. hydraulique,** hydraulic cement, hydraulic mortar; **m. liquide, clair,** grout(ing); **planche à m.,** mortarboard.

mortifiant [mɔrtifjɑ̃] *a.* mortifying.

mortification [mɔrtifikasjɔ̃] *n.f.* (*a*) mortification, chastening (of flesh, passions, etc.); (*b*) mortification, humiliation; chagrin; vexation; (*c*) *Cu:* hanging (of game, etc.); (*d*) *Med:* mortification, gangrene (of limb, etc.).

mortifié [mɔrtifje] *a.* (*a*) mortified, humiliated; chagrined; vexed; (*b*) *Med:* (*occ.*) gangrened.

mortifier [mɔrtifje] (*pr.sub. & impf.* **n. mortifiions, v. mortifiiez**) **1.** *v.tr.* (*a*) to mortify (flesh, passions, etc.); (*b*) to mortify (s.o.); to hurt (s.o.'s) feelings; (*c*) *Cu:* to hang (game, etc.); (*d*) *Med:* to gangrene; to cause (limb, etc.) to mortify. **2. se m.,** to mortify oneself.

mortinatalité [mɔrtinatalite] *n.f.* rate of stillbirths.

mort-né, -née [mɔrne] *a. & n.* stillborn (child, etc.); **projet m.-né,** abortive plan, plan destined to failure; *pl. mort-nés, -nées.*

mortuaire [mɔrtɥɛr] *a.* mortuary (urn, etc.); of death, of burial; **drap m.,** pall; **registre m.,** register of deaths; **avis m.,** announcement of death (in papers, etc.); **la maison m.,** the house of the deceased; **chambre m.,** death chamber; **dépôt m.,** mortuary.

morue [mɔry] *n.f. Ich:* cod; **huile de foie de m.,** cod-liver oil.

morutier, -ière [mɔrytje, -jɛr] **1.** *a.* cod-fishing (industry, etc.). **2.** *n.m.* (*a*) cod-fishing boat; banker; (*b*) cod-fisher(man).

morve [mɔrv] *n.f.* **1.** *Vet:* glanders. **2.** nasal mucus; *P:* snot.

morveux, -euse [mɔrvø, -øz] **1.** *a.* (*a*) *Vet:* glandered; (*b*) with a runny nose; *P:* snotty(-nosed); *Prov:* **qui se sent m. se mouche,** if the cap fits wear it. **2.** *n. F:* (*a*) child, kid, brat; (*b*) young upstart; pipsqueak.

mosaïque¹ [mɔzaik] *a. B.Hist:* Mosaic (law, etc.).

mosaïque² *n.f. Art: etc:* mosaic; **dallage en m.,** mosaic flooring; *T.V:* **m. photoélectrique,** photoelectric mosaic; **m. des plantes,** virus disease.

mosaïste [mɔzaist] *n. Art:* worker in mosaic.

Moscou [mɔsku] *Pr.n. Geog:* Moscow.

moscoutaire [mɔskutɛr] *a. & n. Pej:* Communist, *F:* Commie.

moscovite [mɔskɔvit] *a. & n. Geog:* Muscovite.

mosquée [mɔske] *n.f.* mosque.

mot [mo] *n.m.* word; **répéter qch. m. pour m.,** to repeat sth. word for word, verbatim; **traduire m. à m.** [motamo], **faire du m. à m.,** to translate word for word, literally; **prendre qn au m.,** to take s.o. at his word; **sans m. dire,** without (saying) a word; **qui ne**

dit m. consent, silence means consent; **ne pas souffler m. de qch.,** not to breathe a word about sth.; **dire un m., deux mots, à qn,** to have a word with s.o.; **dire un m. pour, en faveur de, qn,** to put in a good word for s.o.; **avoir des mots avec qn,** to have words, a quarrel, with s.o.; **vous avez dit le m.!** you've hit the nail on the head! you said it! **avoir le dernier m.,** to have the last word; **j'ignore le premier m., je ne sais pas un (traître) m., de la chimie,** I don't know the first thing about chemistry; **à ces mots . . .,** (i) with these words . . ., so saying . . .; (ii) at these words . . .; **en d'autres mots,** in other words; **en un m., en peu de mots, en quelques mots,** briefly, in a word; **en un m. comme en cent,** in a nutshell; **au bas m.,** at the lowest estimate; **gros m.,** coarse expression; swear word; **le m. de l'énigme,** the key to the enigma; **voilà le fin m. de l'affaire!** so that's what's at the bottom of it! **faire comprendre qch. à qn à mots couverts,** to give s.o. a hint of sth.; **m. de passe,** password; *Mil:* **m. de ralliement,** password; **m. d'ordre,** (i) *Mil:* password, countersign; (ii) shibboleth; keynote (of policy); watchword, slogan (of political party, etc.); **mots croisés,** crossword puzzle(s), crossword(s); **envoyer, écrire, un (petit) m. à qn,** to drop s.o. a line, write s.o. a note; **placer un m., avoir son m. à dire,** to have one's say; **il a toujours le m. pour rire,** he's always ready with a joke; **m. historique,** historic remark, memorable saying; **bon m.,** witty remark, witticism.

motard [mɔtar] *n.m. F:* (*a*) motorcyclist; (*b*) motorcycle policeman; speed cop; **m. d'escorte,** police outrider.

mot-clé [mokle] *n.m.* keyword; *pl. mots-clé(s).*

motel [mɔtɛl] *n.m.* motel.

motet [mɔtɛ] *n.m. Mus:* motet.

moteur, -trice [mɔtœr, -tris] **1.** *a.* (*a*) motive, propulsive, driving (power, etc.); **arbre m.,** driving shaft, main shaft; *Mec.E:* **unité motrice,** power unit; **force motrice,** driving force; *Cy:* **roue motrice,** back wheel; **voiture à roues avant motrices,** car with front-wheel drive; *I.C.E:* **temps m.,** power stroke; (*b*) *Anat:* motor (nerve, etc.). **2.** *n.m.* (*a*) (prime) mover; instigator (of a plot); (*b*) motor, engine; **m. à vapeur,** steam engine; **m. à combustion interne, m. à explosion,** internal combustion engine; **m. diesel,** diesel engine; **m. à gaz,** gas engine; **m. à pistons,** piston engine; **m. à deux, à quatre, temps,** two-stroke, four-stroke, engine; **m. à refroidissement par air,** air-cooled engine; **m. à réaction,** jet engine; **m. électrique,** electric motor; **commandé par m.,** motor(-driven), power(-driven); **à moteurs multiples, à plusieurs moteurs,** multi-engine(d) (aircraft, etc.); **m. d'avion,** aero-engine. **3.** *n.f. Rail:* **motrice,** motor coach, *NAm:* motor car.

motif [mɔtif] *n.m.* (*a*) motive, incentive, reason; **m. de mécontentement,** cause, grounds, for discontent; **avoir un m. pour faire qch.,** to have a motive in, for, doing sth.; *F:* **courtiser qn pour le bon m.,** to court s.o. with honourable, *NAm:* honorable, intentions; **soupçons sans m.,** groundless suspicions; **insulter qn sans m.,** to insult s.o. gratuitously; *Jur:* **motifs d'un jugement,** grounds upon which a judgment has been delivered; (*b*) *Mil: Jur:* charge; **porter le m.,** to put on a charge; (*c*) *Art:* motif; *Needlew:* design, pattern, motif (for embroidery, etc.); *Mus:* theme, motto, figure.

motilité [mɔtilite] *n.f.* motivity.

motion [mosjɔ̃] *n.f.* motion, proposal; **faire une m.,** to propose a motion, move a proposal; **la m. a été adoptée,** the motion was carried; **m. de censure,** motion of censure; **présenter une m.,** to table a motion.

motivation [mɔtivasjɔ̃] *n.f. Psy: etc:* motivation.

motivé [mɔtive] *a.* (*a*) motivated (person); (*b*) justified (action); **refus m.,** justifiable refusal; **opinion motivée,** considered opinion; **non m.,** unjustified, unwarranted; *Jur:* **sentence arbitrale motivée,** award stating the reasons on which it is based; **avis m.,** counsel's opinion.

motiver [mɔtive] *v.tr.* (*a*) to motivate (an action); (*b*) to justify, warrant, be the motive for (sth.); to state the reason for (refusal, etc.); **la situation motive des craintes,** the situation gives cause for apprehension.

moto [mɔto] *n.f. F:* motorbike.

motocross [mɔtɔkrɔs] *n.m. Sp:* motorcycle scramble; motocross.

motoculteur [mɔtɔkyltœr] *n.m. Agr:* motor cultivator.

motoculture [mɔtɔkyltyr] *n.f.* mechanized farming.

motocycle [mɔtɔsikl] *n.m. Adm:* motorcycle.

motocyclette [mɔtɔsiklɛt] *n.f.* motorcycle, *F:* motorbike.

motocycliste [mɔtɔsiklist] *n.m.* motorcyclist; *Mil:* dispatch rider.

motofaucheuse [mɔtɔfoʃøz] *n.f.* motor scythe.

motonautique [mɔtɔnotik] *a.* **sport m.,** motorboating.

motonautisme [mɔtɔnotism] *n.m.* motorboating.

motoneige [mɔtɔnɛʒ] *n.f.* snowmobile; *esp. Can:* skidoo.

motopompe [mɔtɔpɔ̃p] *n.f.* motor(-driven) pump.

motorisation [mɔtɔrizasjɔ̃] *n.f.* motorization; mechanization.

motorisé [mɔtɔrise] *a.* fitted with a motor, motorized; *F:* **vous êtes m.?** have you got a car? are you mobile?

motoriser [mɔtɔrize] *v.tr.* to motorize; to mechanize.

motoscie [mɔtɔsi] *n.f.* motor saw.

mot-outil [mouti] *n.m. Ling:* form word, link word; *pl. mots-outils.*

motrice *see* MOTEUR.

motricité [mɔtrisite] *n.f. Biol:* motivity; *Psy:* motor function.

motte [mɔt] *n.f.* **1.** *Archeol:* motte. **2.** clod, lump (of earth); *Hort:* ball (left on roots of tree); **m. de gazon,** sod, turf; **m. de tourbe,** (turf of) peat; **m. à brûler,** (i) sod of peat; (ii) briquette (of spent tan, etc.); **m. de beurre,** pat, block, of butter.

motteux [mɔtø] *n.m. Orn:* wheatear, stonechat.

motus [mɔtys] *int.* mum's the word!

mou[1], mol, *f.* **molle** [mu, mɔl] **1.** *a.* (*the masc. form* **mol** *is used before vowel or h mute*) soft; slack (rope); weak, lifeless, soft, languid, indolent, spineless (person); flabby, flaccid (flesh, hand); dull, flat (wine); woolly, limp (style); feeble (attempt); lax (government); close, muggy (weather); **rayons mous,** soft X-rays; **m., mol, au toucher,** soft to the touch; **un mol (et doux) oreiller,** a (soft and) downy pillow; **il est m. comme une chiffe, comme une chique,** *F:* **c'est un m.,** he's completely spineless. **2.** *n.m.* slack (of rope, etc.); **donner du m. à un cordage,** to slacken a rope; (*of rope*) **prendre du m.,** to slacken.

mou[2] *n.m.* lights, lungs (of slaughtered animal).

mouchage [muʃaʒ] *n.m.* **1.** wiping, blowing, s.o.'s nose, one's nose. **2.** snuffing (out) (of candles).

mouchard [muʃar] *n.m. F:* (*a*) informer; police spy; stool pigeon; *Sch:* sneak; (*b*) mechanical speed check (on trains and lorries); *F:* spy in the cab; (*c*) watchman's clock; (*d*) *Av:* observation plane.

mouchardage [muʃardaʒ] *n.m. F:* spying, sneaking.

moucharder [muʃarde] *v.tr. F:* to spy on, inform on (s.o.); to squeal.

mouche [muʃ] *n.f.* **1.** fly; **m. domestique,** housefly; **m.**

de la viande, m. bleue, blowfly, bluebottle; **m. à feu,** firefly; **m. à miel,** honey bee; **faire d'une m. un éléphant,** to make a mountain out of a molehill; **on aurait entendu voler une m.,** you could have heard a pin drop; **prendre la m.,** to fly into a temper; to take offence; **quelle m. vous pique?** what's the matter with you? what's bitten you? **c'est une fine m.,** he's a sharp customer; *Fish:* **m. mouillée,** wet fly; **m. à saumon,** salmon fly; **pêche à la m. sèche,** dry-fly fishing; *Box:* **poids m.,** flyweight. **2.** (*a*) *A:* spot, speck; stain (on garment, etc.); *Cost:* patch (on face); beauty spot; (*b*) tuft of hair (on lower lip); chin tuft; (*c*) bull's eye (of target); **faire m.,** to hit the bull's eye; to score a bull; (*d*) *Fenc:* covering of foil button; button (on sword).

moucher [muʃe] **1.** *v.tr.* (*a*) to wipe, blow (child's etc.) nose; (*b*) *F:* to put (s.o.) in his place; to snub (s.o.); to tell (s.o.) off; (*c*) to snuff (out) (candle). **2.** **se m.,** to wipe, blow, one's nose; *F:* **il ne se mouche pas du coude,** he thinks no small beer of himself.

moucheron¹ [muʃrɔ̃] *n.m.* gnat, midge.

moucheron² *n.m.* snuff (of candle).

moucheronner [muʃrɔne] *v.i.* (*of fish*) to leap at flies; to be on the rise.

moucheté [muʃte] *a.* (*a*) spotty, speckled, flecked; **cheval m.,** flea-bitten horse; **chat m.,** tabby cat; **blé m.,** smutty wheat; **mer mouchetée d'écume,** foam-flecked sea; (*b*) *Fenc:* buttoned (sword).

moucheter [muʃte] *v.tr.* **(je mouchette; je mouchetterai) 1.** to spot, speckle, fleck. **2.** *Fenc:* **m. un fleuret,** to cover the button of a foil; **m. une épée,** to put a button on a sword; to button a sword.

mouchette [muʃɛt] *n.f.* **1.** *pl.* (pair of) snuffers (for candles). **2.** *Arch:* outer fillet (of dripstone).

moucheture [muʃtyr] *n.f.* spot, speck, speckle, fleck.

mouchoir [muʃwar] *n.m.* handkerchief; **m. (de tête),** headscarf; **jardin grand comme un m. (de poche),** pocket handkerchief (of a) garden.

mouchure [muʃyr] *n.f.* **1.** nasal mucus. **2.** snuff (of candle).

moudre [mudr̥] *v.tr.* (*pr.p.* **moulant;** *p.p.* **moulu;** *pr.ind.* **je mouds, il moud, n. moulons, ils moulent;** *pr.sub.* **je moule;** *p.h.* **je moulus;** *fu.* **je moudrai**) (*a*) to grind, mill (corn, etc.); to grind (coffee, pepper); (*b*) to grind out (tune) (on barrel organ).

moue [mu] *n.f.* pout; **faire la m.,** to pout, purse one's lips, look sulky; **faire une vilaine m.,** (i) to pull a face; (ii) to scowl.

mouette [mwɛt] *n.f. Orn:* (sea)gull; seamew.

mouf(f)ette [mufɛt] *n.f. Z:* skunk.

moufle¹ [mufl̥] **1.** *n.f.* mitten; mitt. **2.** *n.m. or f.* (*a*) pulley block (with several sheaves); tackle block; (*b*) (=PALAN) (block and) tackle; purchase.

moufle² *n.m. Ch: Cer:* muffle; **(four à) m.,** muffle (furnace).

mouflet, -ette [muflɛ, -ɛt] *n. F:* child, kid, brat.

mouflon [muflɔ̃] *n.m. Z:* moufflon; wild sheep.

mouillage [mujaʒ] *n.m.* **1.** (*a*) moistening, damping; (*b*) (fraudulent) watering down (of wine). **2.** *Nau:* (*a*) casting anchor; anchoring; (*b*) laying, mooring (of mine); putting down (of buoy). **3.** anchorage, moorage, mooring ground; **être au m.,** to ride at anchor; **prendre son m.,** to anchor; **m. forain,** open berth.

mouillé [muje] *a.* **1.** moist, damp, wet; **m. jusqu'aux os,** wet through, soaked to the skin; *F:* (*pers.*) **poule mouillée,** softy, wet, drip. **2.** *Nau:* (*of ship*) (lying) at anchor; moored. **3.** *Ling:* palatalized (consonant).

mouillement [mujmɑ̃] *n.m.* **1.** moistening, damping. **2.** *Ling:* palatalization.

mouiller [muje] **1.** *v.tr.* (*a*) to wet, moisten, damp; *Cu:* to add liquid to (stew); **se m. les pieds,** to get one's feet wet; (*b*) to dilute, water down (wine, etc.); (*c*) *Nau:* to cast, drop (anchor); to anchor (ship), bring (ship) to anchor; **mouillez!** let go (the anchor)! (*d*) *Nau:* to lay (mine); to put down (buoy); (*e*) *Ling:* to palatalize (consonant). **2.** *v.i. Nau:* to anchor, lie at anchor. **3.** **se m.** (*a*) to become, get, wet; (*of eyes*) to fill with tears; (*b*) *F:* to get involved (in crime).

mouillette [mujɛt] *n.f.* finger (of bread, etc.).

mouilleur [mujœr] *n.m.* **1.** *Navy:* **m. de mines, de filets,** minelayer, net layer. **2.** (*a*) damper (for stamps, etc.); (*b*) *Nau:* timber (of anchor).

mouillure [mujyr] *n.f.* **1.** *Typ: etc:* damping, wetting. **2.** damp mark, stain. **3.** *Ling:* palatalization (of consonant).

mouise [mwiz] *n.f. P:* poverty; **être dans la m.,** to be hard up, in dire straits.

moujik [muʒik] *n.m.* moujik.

moujingue [muʒɛ̃g] *n. P:* child, kid, brat.

moulage¹ [mulaʒ] *n.m.* grinding, milling.

moulage² *n.m.* **1.** casting, moulding, *NAm:* molding; founding (of iron); **m. à cire perdue,** lost wax process. **2.** **m. au plâtre, en plâtre,** plaster cast.

moule¹ [mul] *n.m.* mould, *NAm:* mold; *Tchn:* matrix; **m. à gelée,** jelly mould; **m. à gâteaux,** cake tin; **m. à beurre,** butter print; **jeter qch. en, dans une, m.,** to cast sth.; **fait au m.,** exquisitely proportioned; shapely.

moule² *n.f.* **1.** *Moll:* mussel. **2.** *P:* (*pers.*) (*a*) drip, wet; (*b*) fool, idiot.

moulé [mule] *a.* cast, moulded, *NAm:* molded; **statue de plâtre m.,** plaster cast; **pain m.,** tin loaf; **écriture moulée,** copperplate handwriting; **lettres moulées,** (hand) printing.

mouler [mule] *v.tr.* (*a*) to cast (statue, etc.); to found (iron); (*b*) to mould, *NAm:* mold (statue, etc.); **robe qui moule la taille,** tightly fitting, figure-hugging, dress; dress that clings to the figure; **se m. sur qn,** to model oneself on s.o.

mouleur [mulœr] *n.m.* caster, moulder, *NAm:* molder.

moulière [muljɛr] *n.f.* mussel bed.

moulin [mulɛ̃] *n.m.* mill; (*a*) **m. à vent,** windmill; **se battre contre des moulins à vent,** to tilt at windmills (like Don Quixote); **m. à eau,** watermill; **roue de m.,** millwheel; **constructeur de moulins,** millwright; **faire venir de l'eau au m.,** to bring grist to the mill; **on y entre comme dans un m.,** anybody can go in; (*b*) **m. à minerai,** ore crusher; **m. à huile,** oil crusher; (*c*) **m. à poivre,** pepper mill; **m. à légumes,** food mill; **m. à café,** coffee grinder, coffee mill; **m. à prières,** prayer wheel; *F:* **m. à paroles,** chatterbox; windbag; (*d*) *F:* (car) engine.

mouliner [muline] *v.tr.* **1.** (*a*) *Tex:* to throw (silk); (*b*) *Fish:* to reel in (the line). **2.** *Cu: F:* to pass through a food mill.

moulinet [mulinɛ] *n.m.* **1.** (*a*) winch; (*b*) *Fish:* reel; **m. à cliquet,** click reel; (*c*) turnstile; (*d*) *Ind:* paddle. **2.** **faire des moulinets (avec sa canne),** to twirl one's stick.

Moulinette [mulinɛt] *n.f. Dom.Ec: R.t.m:* food mill.

moulu [muly] *a.* (*a*) ground, powdered (coffee, etc.); (*b*) very tired, dead-beat; **m. (de coups),** black and blue, aching all over.

moulure [mulyr] *n.f. Arch: Carp:* (ornamental) moulding, *NAm:* molding; profile; profiling.

moulurer [mulyre] *v.tr.* to cut a moulding, *NAm:* molding, on (sth.); **profils moulurés,** mouldings.

mourant, -ante [murɑ̃, -ɑ̃t] **1.** *a.* dying; faint (voice). **2.** *n.* dying man, woman; **les mourants,** the dying.

mourir [murir] (*pr.p.* **mourant;** *p.p.* **mort;** *pr.ind.* **je meurs, il meurt, n. mourons, ils meurent;** *pr.sub.* **je meure, nous mourions;** *p.h.* **il mourut;** *fu.* **je mourrai**

[murre]; *aux.* **être**) **1.** *v.i.* (*a*) (*of pers., animal, plant*) to die; **bien m.,** (i) to die in the faith; (ii) to meet death without flinching; **il est mort hier,** he died yesterday; **m. de faim,** (i) to die of starvation, starve to death; (ii) to be starving; **m. de mort naturelle,** to die a natural death; **elle l'aimait à en m.,** she was desperately in love with him; **m. avant l'âge,** to die before one's time; **m. à la peine,** to die in harness; **au moment de m.,** in the hour of death; **m. martyr d'une cause,** to die a martyr to a cause; **faire m. qn,** to put s.o. to death; *F:* **il me fera m.,** he'll be the death of me; **je mourais de peur,** I was frightened to death; **vous me faites m. d'impatience,** you're killing me with suspense; **faire m. qn à petit feu,** to keep s.o. on tenterhooks; **ennuyer qn à m.,** to bore s.o. to death; **m. d'envie de faire qch.,** to be dying to do sth.; **je mourais de rire,** I nearly died laughing; (*b*) (*of fire, etc.*) to die away, out; *Min:* (*of seam*) to peter out; (*of voice*) to trail off. **2.** *Lit:* **se m.,** to be dying; to die away, out; **je sens que je me meurs,** I feel that I am dying; **la lampe se mourait,** the lamp was fading, giving out.

mouron [murɔ̃] *n.m. Bot:* **m. rouge, des champs,** scarlet pimpernel; **m. blanc, des oiseaux,** chickweed; **m. d'eau,** water pimpernel, brookweed; *P:* **se faire du m.,** to worry oneself to death.

mousquet [muskɛ] *n.m.* musket.

mousquetaire [muskətɛr] *n.m.* musketeer; **gants (à la) m.,** gauntlet gloves.

mousqueterie [muskətri] *n.f.* musketry; **feu de m.,** rifle fire.

mousqueton [muskətɔ̃] *n.m.* **1.** *Artil:* (*a*) *A:* cavalry magazine rifle; (*b*) carbine. **2.** snap (hook).

moussaillon [musajɔ̃] *n.m. F:* young ship's boy.

moussant [musɑ̃] *a.* frothing, foaming.

mousse¹ [mus] *n.f.* **1.** moss; **couvert de m.,** moss-grown, mossy; *Prov:* **pierre qui roule n'amasse pas m.,** a rolling stone gathers no moss. **2.** (*a*) froth, foam (of sea, etc.); head (on glass of beer); lather (of soap); *F:* **se faire de la m.,** to fret, worry; (*b*) *Cu:* mousse. **3.** (*a*) *Ch:* **m. de platine,** platinum sponge; (*b*) **caoutchouc m.,** foam rubber; (*c*) *Knit:* **point m.,** moss stitch.

mousse² *n.m.* ship's boy.

mousse³ *a. Tchn:* blunt (blade, point, etc.).

mousseline [muslin] *n.f.* **1.** *Tex:* (*a*) muslin; **m. de soie,** chiffon; (*b*) *Bookb:* mull. **2.** (*a*) **verre m.,** muslin glass; (*b*) *Cu:* **pommes (de terre) m.,** creamed, mashed, potatoes.

mousser [muse] *v.i.* to froth, foam; (*of soapy water*) to lather; (*of wine, etc.*) to sparkle, effervesce; to fizz; *P:* **faire m. qn,** to make s.o. lose his temper, flare up.

mousseron [musrɔ̃] *n.m.* edible mushroom; *esp.* St George's agaric.

mousseux, -euse [musø, -øz] *a.* **1.** mossy. **2.** frothy, foaming. **3.** *a. & n.m.* sparkling (wine).

moussoir [muswar] *n.m. Dom.Ec:* whisk.

mousson [musɔ̃] *n.f.* monsoon.

moussu [musy] *a.* mossy; mossgrown.

moustache [mustaʃ] *n.f.* (*a*) **la m., les moustaches,** moustache; **m. à la gauloise,** walrus moustache; **m. en brosse,** toothbrush moustache; (*b*) whiskers (of cat, etc.).

moustachu [mustaʃy] *a.* with a large moustache.

moustiquaire [mustikɛr] *n.f.* mosquito net.

moustique [mustik] *n.m.* **1.** *Ent:* (*a*) mosquito; (*b*) *F:* gnat. **2.** *F:* child, little nipper.

moût [mu] *n.m.* must (of grapes); wort (of beer).

moutard [mutar] *n.m. P:* small boy, kid, nipper; *pl.* kids.

moutarde [mutard] *n.f.* mustard; **graine de m.,** mustard seed; **la m. lui est montée au nez,** he lost his temper, flared up; **gaz m.,** mustard gas; **(jaune) m.,** mustard (yellow).

moutardier [mutardje] *n.m.* **1.** mustard maker, seller; *F:* **il se croit le premier m. du pape,** he's too big for his boots. **2.** mustard pot.

moutier [mutje] *n.m. A:* monastery.

mouton [mutɔ̃] *n.m.* **1.** (*a*) sheep; **éleveur de moutons,** (i) sheep farmer; (ii) wool grower; **doux comme un m.,** as gentle as a lamb; **revenons à nos moutons,** let's get back to the subject; **c'est un m. à cinq pattes,** he's a rare bird; (*of horse*) **saut de m.,** buck; (*b*) *Cu:* mutton; **ragoût de m.,** mutton stew; (*c*) **(peau de) m.,** sheepskin; (*d*) *F:* (*in prisons*) (police) spy; (*e*) *pl.* white horses (on waves); (*f*) *pl.* fluff (under bed, etc.). **2.** *Civ.E: etc:* ram, monkey (of pile driver); head (of beetle, rammer); tup (of steam hammer); drop hammer. **3.** *a.* (*f.* **moutonne**) sheeplike.

moutonnant [mutɔnɑ̃] *a.* (*of sea*) covered with white horses; foam-flecked.

moutonné [mutɔne] *a.* fleecy (cloud, etc.); **tête moutonnée,** curly, frizzy, head of hair.

moutonnement [mutɔnmɑ̃] *n.m.* (*of sea*) breaking into white horses; frothing.

moutonner [mutɔne] **1.** *v.i.* (*of sea*) to break into white horses; to froth. **2.** (*of sky*) **se m.,** to become covered with fleecy clouds.

moutonneux, -euse [mutɔnø, -øz] *a.* **1.** (*of sea*) foam-flecked; covered with white horses. **2.** (*of sky*) covered with fleecy clouds.

moutonnier, -ière [mutɔnje, -jɛr] *a.* (*a*) *A:* ovine; (*b*) sheeplike (crowd, etc.); (*of pers.*) easily led.

mouture [mutyr] *n.f.* **1.** grinding, milling (of corn). **2.** milling dues; **tirer deux moutures d'un sac,** to get double profit out of sth. **3.** *Agr:* maslin. **4.** *Pej:* rehash (of article, etc.).

mouvant [muvɑ̃] *a.* moving; mobile; unstable, fickle, changeable; **sable m.,** driftsand; **sables mouvants,** shifting sands; quicksand.

mouvement [muvmɑ̃] *n.m.* **1.** movement; motion; gesture; **m. en arrière,** backward movement, motion; **rester sans m.,** to stand motionless, stockstill; **faire un m.,** to move; **il aime le m.,** he likes change; he can't stay still; **répondre d'un m. de tête,** to answer (i) with a shake of the head, (ii) with a nod; **mettre qch. en m., imprimer un m. à qch.,** to put, set, sth. in motion; to set sth. going; to start (engine); **se mettre en m.,** to start off, move off, get going; to stir; **se donner du m.,** (i) to bustle about, exert oneself; (ii) to take some exercise; **être toujours en m.,** to be always on the move; **le m. d'une grande ville,** the bustle, activity, of a large town; **petite ville sans m.,** lifeless, dull, little town; *Mus:* **presser, ralentir, le m.,** to quicken, slow, the tempo, the time; **symphonie à trois mouvements,** symphony in three movements; *Mec.E:* **m. acquis,** impressed motion; **m. perpétuel,** perpetual motion; **quantité de m.,** momentum, impulse; **pièces en m.,** moving parts (of machine); *Mil:* **m. de troupes,** troup movement; **guerre de m.,** mobile warfare, war of movement; **un m. audacieux leur a livré le village,** a daring move put them in possession of the village. **2.** (*a*) change, modification; *Geog:* fall, rise (in sea level); **m. de terrain,** undulation; **m. de personnel,** staff changes; **le m. des naissances,** the trend of the birthrate; *F:* **être dans le m.,** to be in the swim, abreast of the times, up to date; (*b*) **premier m.,** first impulse; **il a eu un m. d'éloquence,** he had a burst of eloquence; **m. d'humeur,** outburst of temper, of petulance; **de son propre m.,** of one's own accord; **avoir un bon m.,** to act on a kindly impulse; **m. de plaisir,** thrill, flutter, of pleasure; **dans un m. de colère,** in a fit of anger; (*c*) *Pol: etc:* movement; **m. insurrectionnel,** uprising; (*d*) line(s) (of drapery, etc.). **3.** traffic (on road, in port, etc.); *Rail:* **mouve-**

ments des trains, train arrivals and departures; **chef de m.,** traffic manager; *Journ:* **mouvements des navires,** shipping intelligence. **4.** works, action, movement (of clock, etc.); **m. d'horlogerie,** clockwork.

mouvementé [muvmɑ̃te] *a.* **1.** animated, lively (discussion, etc.); thrilling (voyage, etc.); full of incident; **une partie mouvementée,** an exciting game; **ville, rue, mouvementée,** busy town, street; **vie mouvementée,** eventful life. **2. terrain m.,** undulating ground.

mouvementer [muvmɑ̃te] *v.tr. Lit:* to enliven, animate (plot, etc.).

mouvoir [muvwar] (*pr.p.* **mouvant;** *p.p.* **mû, mue;** *pr.ind.* **je meus, il meut, n. mouvons, ils meuvent;** *pr.sub.* **je meuve, n. mouvions, ils meuvent;** *p.h.* **je mus** (*rare*); *fu.* **je mouvrai) 1.** *v.tr.* (*a*) (*rare*) to move; **m. qch. de sa place,** to move sth. from its place; (*b*) to drive, actuate (machine, etc.); to propel (ship, etc.); **mû à la vapeur,** propelled by steam; steam-driven; **mû par la colère, par l'intérêt,** moved by anger, prompted by interest. **2. se m.,** to move, stir.

moyen¹, -enne [mwajɛ̃, -ɛn] **1.** *a.* (*a*) middle; **les classes moyennes,** the middle class(es); **le m. âge** [mwajɛnɑʒ], the Middle Ages; **coutumes du m. âge,** medi(a)eval customs; **point m.,** midpoint; *Sch:* **cours m.,** intermediate class; (*b*) average, mean (pressure, speed, etc.); **le Français m.,** the average Frenchman; the man in the street; **temps m. de réaction,** mean reaction time; *Log:* **m. terme,** middle term; **prendre un m. terme,** to take a middle course; (*c*) medium (quality, etc.); average, moderate (price); **de taille, de grandeur, moyenne,** medium-sized, middle-sized. **2.** *n.f.* **moyenne** (*a*) *Mth:* mean; (*b*) average; **en m.,** on (an) average; *Aut:* **m. (horaire),** average (speed); (*c*) *Sch:* passmark; **travail au-dessus, au-dessous, de la m.,** work above, below, average, above, below, par.

moyen² *n.m.* means; (*a*) **le journal comme m. de réclame,** the newspaper as a vehicle, medium, for advertising; *Prov:* **la fin justifie les moyens,** the end justifies the means; **par tous les moyens,** by fair means or foul; **employer les grands moyens,** to take extreme measures; **au m., par (le) m., de qch.,** by means of, with the help of, sth.; **y a-t-il m. de le faire?** is it possible to do it? **il n'y a pas m.,** it can't be done; it's impossible; *F:* **pas m.!** no way! **le m. d'y aller?** how do we get there? **trouver (le) m. de faire qch.,** to find a means, a way, of doing sth.; **inventer un m. de s'échapper,** to invent a plan of escape; **faire qch. par ses propres moyens,** to do sth. on one's own; to draw upon one's own resources (to do sth.); **arriver par ses propres moyens,** to get there under one's own steam; **avec les moyens du bord,** with the means at one's disposal; **voies et moyens,** ways and means; **dans la (pleine) mesure de mes moyens,** to the best, to the utmost, of my ability; **enfant qui a des moyens,** bright, talented, child; **enlever les moyens à qn,** to upset, disconcert, s.o.; to cramp s.o.'s style; (*b*) **vivre au-dessus de ses moyens,** to live beyond one's means; **il a largement les moyens de faire construire,** he can well afford to build; **je n'en ai pas les moyens,** I can't afford it.

moyenâgeux, -euse [mwajɛnɑʒø, -øz] *a.* (*a*) medi(a)eval; (*b*) oldfashioned; outdated.

moyen-courrier [mwajɛ̃kurje] *a.* & *n.m. Av:* medium-range (aircraft); *pl. moyens-courriers.*

moyennant [mwajɛnɑ̃] *prep.* on (a certain) condition; **louer qch. m. cent francs par jour,** to hire sth. for, at (a charge of), a hundred francs a day; **faire qch. m. finance,** to do sth. for a consideration; **m. paiement de dix francs,** on payment of ten francs; **m. quoi,** in return for which, in consideration of which; *Lit:* **m. que . . .,** provided that . . . .

moyennement [mwajɛnmɑ̃] *adv.* moderately, fairly; **m. vite,** quite, fairly, fast; **travailler m.,** to work fairly well.

Moyen-Orient [mwajɛ̃nɔrjɑ̃] *Pr.n.m. Geog:* the Middle East.

moyette [mwajɛt] *n.f. Agr:* shock (of corn).

moyeu, -eux [mwajø] *n.m.* hub (of car wheel); nave (of cartwheel, etc.); boss (of propeller, etc.).

mozarabe [mɔzarab] *Hist:* **1.** *a.* Mozarabic. **2.** *n.* Mozarab.

mu [my] *n.m. Gr.Alph: Ph.Meas:* mu.

mû *see* MOUVOIR.

muance [mɥɑ̃s] *n.f. A:* **1.** *Mus:* mutation. **2.** breaking (of voice at puberty).

mucilage [mysilaʒ] *n.m.* mucilage; gum.

mucilagineux, -euse [mysilaʒinø, -øz] *a.* mucilaginous, viscous.

mucosité [mykozite] *n.f.* mucus, mucosity.

mucus [mykys] *n.m.* mucus.

mue [my] *n.f.* **1.** (*a*) moulting, *NAm:* molting (of birds); shedding, casting, of the coat, of the skin, of the antlers (of animals); sloughing (of reptiles); **serin en m.,** moulting canary; (*b*) moulting season; (*c*) feathers moulted, *NAm:* molted; antlers, etc., shed; slough (of snakes). **2.** breaking of the voice (at puberty). **3.** mew (for hawks); coop (for poultry).

muer [mɥe] **1.** *v.tr.* (*a*) *Lit:* to change (**en,** into); (*b*) (*of stag*) **m. sa tête,** to cast its antlers. **2.** *v.i.* (*a*) (*of bird*) to moult, *NAm:* molt; (*of animal*) to shed, cast, its coat, its antlers; (*of reptile*) to slough; to cast its skin; (*b*) (*of voice*) to break (at puberty). **3. se m. (en),** to be transformed, to change (oneself) (into).

muet, -ette [mɥɛ, -ɛt] **1.** *a.* (*a*) dumb; **m. de naissance,** born dumb; (*b*) **la stupeur m'a rendu m.,** I was struck dumb with astonishment; **j'écoutais, m. d'étonnement,** I listened in mute astonishment; **m. de colère,** speechless with anger; (*c*) dumb, mute; **rester m.,** to remain silent; **m. comme la tombe,** (as) silent as the grave; (*d*) silent (film, *Th:* part); **jeu m.,** dumb show; (*e*) blank (map, etc.); (*f*) *Ling:* silent (letter); **h muet(te),** mute h. **2.** (*a*) *n.* dumb person; mute; (*b*) *n.m.* **le m.,** silent films.

mufle [myfl̥] *n.m.* **1.** muffle; (hairless part of) muzzle (of ox, bison, etc.); nose, *F:* snout (of lion, etc.). **2.** *F:* lout, boor.

muflerie [myflәri] *n.f. F:* **1.** boorishness. **2.** low-down trick.

muflier [myflije] *n.m. Bot:* antirrhinum, snapdragon; **m. bâtard,** linaria.

mufti [myfti] *n.m. Moslem Rel:* mufti.

muge [myʒ] *n.m. Ich:* mullet.

mugir [myʒir] *v.i.* (*a*) (*of cow*) to low, moo; (*of bull*) to bellow; (*b*) (*of sea, wind*) to roar, boom, moan; (*of wind*) to howl.

mugissement [myʒismɑ̃] *n.m.* (*a*) lowing, mooing (of cow); bellowing (of bull); (*b*) roaring, booming, moaning (of sea, wind); howling (of wind).

muguet [mygɛ] *n.m.* **1.** *Bot:* lily of the valley. **2.** *Med:* thrush.

mulassier, -ière [mylasje, -jɛr] *a.* & *n.f.* **(jument) mulassière,** mule-breeding mare.

mulâtre [mylɑtr̥] **1.** *a.* mulatto, half-caste. **2.** *n.* (*f.* **mulâtre** *or* **mulâtresse** [mylɑtrɛs]) mulatto.

mule¹ [myl] *n.f.* (she-)mule.

mule² *n.f.* (*slipper*) mule; **la m. du Pape,** the Pope's slipper; **baiser la m. du Pape,** to kiss the Pope's toe.

mulet¹ [mylɛ] *n.m.* (he-)mule.

mulet² *n.m. Ich:* grey mullet.

muletier, -ière [myltje, -jɛr] **1.** *a.* **équipage m.,** mule train. **2.** *n.m.* mule driver, muleteer.

mulot [mylo] *n.m.* field mouse.

multicellulaire [myltiselylɛr] *a.* multicellular.

multicolore [myltikɔlɔr] *a.* multicoloured, *NAm:* multicolored.

multiflore [myltiflɔr] *a. Bot:* multiflorous.
multiforme [myltifɔrm] *a.* multiform.
multilatéral, -aux [myltilateral, -o] *a.* multilateral.
multimillionnaire [myltimiljɔnɛr] *a. & n.* multimillionaire.
multinational, -aux [myltinasjɔnal, -o] *a.* multinational.
multipare [myltipar] *a.* multiparous.
multiplace [myltiplas] *a. & n.m.* **(avion) m.** = passenger aircraft.
multiple [myltipl̩] **1.** *a.* multiple, manifold; multifarious (duties, etc.); **maison à succursales multiples,** multiple store, chain store; *Aut:* **klaxon à sons multiples,** multitone horn. **2.** *n.m. Mth:* multiple; **le plus petit commun m.,** the lowest common multiple.
multiplex [myltiplɛks] *a.inv. & n.m. W.Tel: etc:* multiplex.
multipliable [myltiplijabl̩] *a.* multipli(c)able.
multiplicande [myltiplikɑ̃d] *n.m. Mth:* multiplicand.
multiplicateur, -trice [myltiplikatœr, -tris] **1.** *a.* multiplying; **engrenage m.,** step-up gear. **2.** *n.m. Mth: El:* multiplier.
multiplicatif, -ive [myltiplikatif, -iv] *a.* multiplicative, multiplying.
multiplication [myltiplikasjɔ̃] *n.f.* **1.** *(a) Mth: etc:* multiplication; *(b)* **la m. des crimes,** the increase in crime; *(c) B:* **la m. des pains,** the miracle of the loaves and fishes. **2.** *Mec.E:* gear (ratio); step-up, stepdown (of gear); **grande, petite, m.,** high, low, gear; *Mec:* **m. du levier,** leverage.
multiplicité [myltiplisite] *n.f.* multiplicity; multifariousness (of duties, etc.).
multiplié [myltiplije] *a.* multiplied, multiple; manifold, multifarious.
multiplier [myltiplije] *(pr.sub. & impf.* **n. multipliions, v. multipliiez)** **1.** *v.tr. (a)* to multiply **(par,** by); *(b) Mec.E:* **m. la vitesse de révolution,** to gear up. **2. se m.** *(a)* to multiply; to increase; **les crimes se multiplient,** crime is on the increase; *(b)* to be in half a dozen places at once; **se m. pour aider qn,** to do one's utmost in order to help s.o.
multipolaire [myltipɔlɛr] *a. El: Biol:* multipolar.
multitude [myltityd] *n.f.* multitude **(de,** of); crowd; multiplicity (of books, etc.).
munichois, -oise [mynikwa, -waz] *a. & n. Geog:* (native, inhabitant) of Munich.
municipal, -aux [mynisipal, -o] *a.* municipal; **conseil m.,** town council; local council; **bibliothèque municipale,** public library; **loi municipale,** by-law; *A:* **la garde municipale,** the military police (of Paris).
municipalité [mynisipalite] *n.f.* **1.** municipality; *(a)* local administrative area; *(b)* corporation; local council. **2.** town hall.
munificence [mynifisɑ̃s] *n.f. Lit:* munificence.
munificent [mynifisɑ̃] *a. Lit:* munificent.
munir [mynir] **1.** *v.tr.* to supply, fit, equip, provide, furnish **(de,** with); **muni des sacrements de l'Église,** fortified with the rites of the Church. **2. se m.,** to provide oneself **(de,** with).
munition [mynisjɔ̃] *n.f.* **1.** *(a) A:* (i) munitioning, (ii) provisioning (of an army); **munitions de bouche,** provisions; *(b) Mil:* **pain de m.,** ration bread. **2.** *pl.* **munitions (de guerre),** ammunition; munitions.
munitionnaire [mynisjɔnɛr] *n.m. Mil: A:* commissary; supply officer.
muphti [myfti] *n.m. Moslem Rel:* mufti.
muqueux, -euse [mykø, -øz] **1.** *a.* mucous (membrane, etc.). **2.** *n.f.* **muqueuse,** mucous membrane.
mur [myr] *n.m.* wall; **m. de clôture,** enclosing wall; **m. d'appui,** low wall; **m. de refend,** partition (wall); **maison aux murs de briques,** brick(-built) house; **gros murs,** main walls; **ne laisser que les quatre murs,** to leave only the four walls (standing); **mettre qn au pied du m.,** to drive s.o. into a corner, have s.o. with his back to the wall; **se taper la tête contre les murs,** to hit one's head against a (brick) wall; **se heurter à un m. d'incompréhension,** to come up against a wall, a barrier, of incomprehension; **les murs ont des oreilles,** walls have ears; **le m. de Berlin,** the Berlin wall; *(of aircraft, etc.)* **franchir le m. du son,** to break the sound barrier.
mûr [myr] *a. (a)* ripe; mellow (wine, etc.); mature (age, mind, etc.); **après mûre réflexion,** after mature consideration; **m. pour qch.,** fit, ready, for sth.; *(b) P:* drunk, canned.
murage [myraʒ] *n.m.* walling (in); walling up, bricking up, blocking up (of doorway, etc.).
muraille [myrɑj] *n.f.* **1.** (high defensive) wall; **la Grande M. de Chine,** the Great Wall of China; **les murailles de la ville,** the town walls; **m. de glace,** ice barrier. **2.** side (of ship).
mural, -aux [myral, -o] *a.* mural; **peinture murale,** mural; wall painting; **pendule murale,** wall clock; **carte murale,** wall map; *Arch:* **console murale,** wall bracket.
mûre [myr] *n.f. Bot: (a)* mulberry; *(b)* **m. sauvage, de ronce,** blackberry.
mûrement [myrmɑ̃] *adv.* with mature consideration; **après avoir m. réfléchi,** after careful consideration.
murène [myrɛn] *n.f. Ich:* muraena; moray (eel).
murer [myre] **1.** *v.tr.* to wall in (town, etc.); to wall up, block up, brick up (doorway, etc.). **2. se m.,** to shut oneself away.
muret [myrɛ] *n.m.,* **murette** [myrɛt] *n.f.* low wall; dry stone wall.
mûrier [myrje] *n.m. Bot: (a)* mulberry (tree, bush); *(b)* **m. (sauvage),** bramble, blackberry bush.
mûrir [myrir] **1.** *v.tr.* to ripen, mature; to bring (abscess) to a head; **m. une question,** to give a question careful consideration. **2.** *v.i.* to ripen, mature; to come to maturity; *(of abscess)* to come to a head.
mûrissant [myrisɑ̃] *a.* ripening.
murmure [myrmyr] *n.m. (a)* murmur, murmuring; babbling (of stream); *(b) pl.* muttering; grumbling.
murmurer [myrmyre] *v.tr. & i.* to murmur; to grumble, complain; **m. entre ses dents,** to mutter.
mûron [myrɔ̃] *n.m.* **1.** blackberry. **2.** wild raspberry.
musaraigne [myzarɛɲ] *n.f.* shrew (mouse).
musard, -arde [myzar, -ard] *F:* **1.** *a.* dawdling, idling. **2.** *n.* dawdler, idler.
musarder [myzarde] *v.i.* to dawdle, idle.
musarderie [myzardəri], **musardise** [myzardiz] *n.f.* dawdling, idling.
musc [mysk] *n.m.* **1.** musk. **2.** *Z:* musk (deer).
muscade [myskad] *n.f.* **1. (noix) m.,** nutmeg; **fleur de m.,** mace. **2.** conjuror's vanishing ball, pea; **passez m.!** hey presto!
muscadier [myskadje] *n.m. Bot:* nutmeg (tree).
muscadin [myskadɛ̃] *n.m. A:* dandy, fop.
muscardin [myskardɛ̃] *n.m. Z:* dormouse.
muscat [myska] *a. & n.m. Vit:* muscat; **(raisin) m.,** muscat grape, muscatel (grape); **(vin) m.,** muscatel (wine).
muscle [myskl̩] *n.m.* muscle; *F:* **avoir du m.,** to have plenty of brawn.
musclé [myskle] *a.* muscular; sinewy; **il est bien m.,** he has well developed muscles.
musculaire [myskylɛr] *a.* muscular (system, tissue, strength); **fibre m.,** muscle fibre, *NAm:* fiber.
musculature [myskylatyr] *n.f.* musculature.
musculeux, -euse [myskylø, -øz] *a.* muscular (person, arm, etc.).
muse [myz] *n.f.* muse; **invoquer sa m.,** to call on one's muse.

museau, -eaux [myzo] *n.m.* (*a*) muzzle, snout (of animal); (*b*) *F:* face; **vilain m.,** ugly mug.
musée [myze] *n.m.* (*a*) museum; (*b*) **m. (de peinture, d'art),** art gallery.
museler [myzle] *v.tr.* **(je muselle; je musellerai) 1.** to muzzle (dog, the press, etc.). **2.** to gag (s.o.).
muselière [myzəljɛr] *n.f.* (*for animal*) muzzle; **mettre une m. à un chien,** to muzzle a dog.
musellement [myzɛlmɑ̃] *n.m.* muzzling (of animal, newspaper); gagging (of person).
muser [myze] *v.i. A: & Lit:* to idle, dawdle; to moon about.
muserolle [myzrɔl] *n.f. Harn:* noseband.
musette [myzɛt] *n.f.* **1.** (*a*) *A.Mus:* musette; (*b*) **orchestre m.,** band with accordions; **bal m.,** popular dance (hall) (with accordion band). **2.** (*a*) **m. (mangeoire),** (horse's) nosebag; (*b*) *A:* (schoolboy's) satchel; *Mil: etc:* haversack.
muséum [myzeɔm] *n.m.* natural history museum.
musical, -aux [myzikal, -o] *a.* musical (sound, evening, etc.); **l'art m.,** the art of music; **avoir l'oreille musicale,** to have an ear for music, a musical ear.
musicalement [myzikalmɑ̃] *adv.* musically.
musicalité [myzikalite] *n.f.* musicality; musical quality.
music-hall [myzikol] *n.m.* music hall; **numéros de m.-h.,** variety turns; *pl. music-halls.*
musicien, -ienne [myzisjɛ̃, -jɛn] *a. & n.* **1.** musician; **elle est bonne musicienne,** (i) she's very musical; (ii) she's a good musician. **2.** member of a band, an orchestra; *Mil: etc:* bandsman.
musicographe [myzikɔgraf] *n.* musicographer.
musicologue [mysikɔlɔg] *n.* musicologist.
musique [myzik] *n.f.* **1.** (*a*) music; **mettre des paroles en m.,** to set words to music; **instrument de m.,** musical instrument; **boîte à m.,** musical box; **m. de chambre,** chamber music; **m. d'ambiance, de fond,** background music; **faire de la m.,** (i) to make music; to play; (ii) to go in for music; (*b*) *F:* **il connaît la m.,** he knows what's what; he's up to all the tricks. **2.** band; **chef de m.,** bandmaster.
musoir [myzwar] *n.m.* pierhead, jetty head.
musqué [myske] *a.* **1.** (*a*) musky; scented with musk; **rose musquée, rosier m.,** musk rose; (*b*) *A:* affected (poet, style, etc.). **2. bœuf m.,** musk ox; **rat m.,** muskrat, musquash; **canard m.,** Muscovy duck, musk duck.
mussif [mysif] *n.m.* **or m.,** mosaic gold, disulphide of tin.
mustang [mystɑ̃g] *n.m.* mustang.
musulman, -ane [myzylmɑ̃, -an] *a. & n.* Moslem, Muslim.
mutabilité [mytabilite] *n.f.* **1.** mutability. **2.** *Jur:* alienability.
mutable [mytabl̩] *a.* **1.** changeable, mutable. **2.** *Jur:* alienable.
mutation [mytasjɔ̃] *n.f.* (*a*) change, alteration; *Mus: Biol:* mutation; (*b*) *Ling:* gradation (of vowel); shift (of consonant); (*c*) *Jur:* change of ownership; transfer (of property); (*d*) transfer (of personnel, *Fb:* of players).
muter [myte] *v.tr.* to transfer (personnel).
mutilateur, -trice [mytilatœr, -tris] *n.* mutilator; (*a*) maimer; (*b*) defacer.
mutilation [mytilasjɔ̃] *n.f.* (*a*) mutilation, maiming (of person); (*b*) defacement (of statue, etc.); mutilation (of book, statue, etc.).
mutilé, -ée [mytile] *a. & n.* mutilated, maimed (person); **mutilés de guerre,** disabled ex-servicemen; **les grands mutilés,** the severely disabled; **il est m. du bras,** he's lost an arm; **m. de la face,** disfigured.
mutiler [mytile] *v.tr.* (*a*) to mutilate, maim (s.o.); (*b*) to deface (book, statue, etc.).
mutin, -ine [mytɛ̃, -in] **1.** *a. & n.* (*a*) *A:* insubordinate; disobedient, unruly, unbiddable (child); (*b*) full of fun; cheeky (child). **2.** *n.m.* mutineer.
mutiné [mytine] **1.** *a.* rebellious; mutinous (troops). **2.** *n.m* mutineer.
mutiner (se) [səmytine] *v.pr.* to rise in revolt; to rebel; (*of troops*) to mutiny.
mutinerie [mytinri] *n.f.* **1.** *A:* roguishness. **2.** rebellion; mutiny (of troops).
mutisme [mytism] *n.m.* dumbness, muteness; mutism; **se renfermer dans le m.,** to maintain a stubborn silence.
mutité [mytite] *n.f. Med:* mutism.
mutualisme [mytɥalism] *n.m. Biol: Pol.Ec:* mutualism.
mutualiste [mytɥalist] **1.** *a.* mutualistic. **2.** *n.* (*a*) *Pol.Ec:* mutualist; (*b*) member of a mutual insurance company.
mutualité [mytɥalite] *n.f.* **1.** mutuality, reciprocity. **2.** mutual insurance; **société de m.,** friendly society.
mutuel, -elle [mytɥɛl] *a. & n.f.* mutual; **(société d'assurance) mutuelle,** mutual insurance company; friendly society.
mutuellement [mytɥɛlmɑ̃] *adv.* mutually.
mycologie [mikɔlɔʒi] *n.f. Bot:* mycology.
myéline [mjelin] *n.f. Anat:* myelin(e).
myélite [mjelit] *n.f. Med:* myelitis.
myélome [mjelom] *n.m. Med:* myeloma.
mygale [migal] *n.f. Arach:* trapdoor spider.
myocarde [mjɔkard] *n.m. Anat:* myocardium.
myocardite [mjɔkardit] *n.f. Med:* myocarditis.
myologie [mjɔlɔʒi] *n.f. Anat:* myology.
myope [mjɔp] **1.** *a.* myopic; shortsighted; **m. comme une taupe,** as blind as a bat. **2.** *n.* myope; shortsighted person.
myopie [mjɔpi] *n.f. Med:* myopia; shortsightedness.
myosotis [mjɔzɔtis] *n.m. Bot:* myosotis; forget-me-not.
myriade [mirjad] *n.f.* myriad.
myriapode [mirjapɔd] *n.m. Z:* myriapod; *pl.* Myriapoda.
myrmidon [mirmidɔ̃] *n.m. F:* whippersnapper, little runt.
myrrhe [mir] *n.f.* myrrh.
myrte [mirt] *n.m. Bot:* myrtle; **m. des marais,** sweet gale, bog myrtle.
myrtille [mirtij] *n.f. Bot:* bilberry, whinberry.
mystère [mistɛr] *n.m.* **1.** mystery; **on n'a jamais pénétré ce m.,** this mystery has never been fathomed (out); **je n'en fais pas m.,** I make no mystery, no secret, of it. **2.** *Lit.Hist:* mystery (play); **m. de la Passion,** Passion play.
mystérieusement [misterjøzmɑ̃] *adv.* mysteriously.
mystérieux, -euse [misterjø, -øz] *a.* mysterious; enigmatic; uncanny.
mysticisme [mistisism] *n.m.* mysticism.
mystifiable [mistifjabl̩] *a.* gullible.
mystificateur, -trice [mistifikatœr, -tris] **1.** *a.* mystifying. **2.** *n.* hoaxer.
mystification [mistifikasjɔ̃] *n.f.* (*a*) mystification; (*b*) hoax; practical joke.
mystifier [mistifje] *v.tr.* (*impf. & pr.sub.* **n. mystifiions, v. mystifiiez)** (*a*) to mystify; (*b*) to hoax, fool, bamboozle (s.o.); to play a practical joke on (s.o.); to pull (s.o.'s) leg.
mystique [mistik] **1.** *a.* mystic(al). **2.** *n.* mystic.
mystiquement [mistikmɑ̃] *adv.* mystically.
mythe [mit] *n.m.* myth, legend.
mythique [mitik] *a.* mythical.
mythologie [mitɔlɔʒi] *n.f.* mythology.

mythologique [mitɔlɔʒik] *a.* mythological.
mythologiquement [mitɔlɔʒikmɑ̃] *adv.* mythologically.
mythologue [mitɔlɔg] *n.* mythologist.
mythomane [mitɔman] *a. & n.* mythomaniac; pathological liar.
mythomanie [mitɔmani] *n.f.* mythomania.
myxœdème [mik· ˈɛm] *n.m. Med:* myxoedema, *NAm:* myxedema.
myxomatose [miksɔmatoz] *n.f.* myxomatosis.
myxomycètes [miksɔmisɛt] *n.m.pl. Fung:* myxomycetes.

N

N, n [ɛn] *n.m. & f.* (the letter) N, n; **à la $n^{ième}$ puissance,** to the nth (power); *F:* **pour la $n^{ième}$ fois,** for the nth, *F:* umpteenth, time.
na [na] *int. F:* so there!
nabab [nabab] *n.m.* nabob.
nabot, -ote [nabo, -ɔt] **1.** *n.* dwarf, midget. **2.** *a.* dwarfish, tiny (person).
Nabuchodonosor [nabykɔdɔnɔzɔr] *Pr.n.m. B. Hist:* Nebuchadnezzar.
nacelle [nasɛl] *n.f.* **1.** skiff, wherry. **2.** nacelle; basket (of balloon); gondola, car (of airship); pod (of aircraft engine).
nacre [nakr̥] *n.f.* mother of pearl.
nacré [nakre] *a.* pearly (lustre, *NAm:* luster, etc.).
nadir [nadir] *n.m. Astr:* nadir.
nævus [nevys] *n.m.* naevus, *NAm:* nevus; mole; *pl. nævi.*
nage [naʒ] *n.f.* **1.** rowing, sculling; **banc de n.,** thwart; **chef de n.,** stroke. **2.** (*a*) swimming; **se sauver à la n.,** to swim to safety; **traverser une rivière à la n.,** to swim across a river; *F:* **être (tout) en n.,** to be bathed in perspiration; (*b*) stroke (in swimming); **n. sur le dos,** backstroke; **n. libre,** freestyle.
nageoire [naʒwar] *n.f.* **1.** fin (of fish); flipper (of dolphin, etc.); **n. caudale,** tail flukes. **2.** float, water wings (to support swimmer); float (of seaplane).
nager [naʒe] *v.i.* **(je nageais; n. nageons) 1.** to row; **nagez partout!** pull away! **n. en arrière, à culer,** to back water; **n. plat,** to feather; **n. à, en, couple,** to (double) scull; **n. en pointe,** to row. **2.** (*a*) to swim; **n. vers la côte,** to swim for the shore; **n. la brasse,** to swim breaststroke; **n. à la chien,** to dogpaddle; **n. debout,** to tread water; (*b*) (*of wood, cork*) to float; **légumes qui nagent dans le beurre,** vegetables swimming in butter; **n. dans le sang,** to be bathed in blood; **n. dans l'abondance,** to be rolling in money; *F:* **je nage,** I'm all at sea.
nageur, -euse [naʒœr, -øz] **1.** *a.* swimming (animal). **2.** *n.* (*a*) swimmer; **n. de combat,** frogman; (*b*) oarsman, rower; **n. de l'arrière,** stroke; **n. de l'avant,** bow(oar).
naguère [nagɛr] *adv. Lit:* not long ago, a short time ago, lately.
naïade [najad] *n.f.* naiad, water nymph.
naïf, ïve [naif, -iv] *a.* **1.** naïve; ingenuous, innocent. **2.** simple-minded, credulous, unsophisticated, *F:* green; *n.* **vous me prenez pour un n.!** what sort of a fool do you take me for?
nain, naine [nɛ̃, nɛn] **1.** *n.* dwarf; midget; *Cards:* **N. jaune,** Pope Joan. **2.** *a.* dwarf(ish); **haricots nains,** dwarf beans.
naissain [nɛsɛ̃] *n.m.* (oyster, mussel) spawn; spat.
naissance [nɛsɑ̃s] *n.f.* **1.** birth; (*a*) **sourd de n.,** deaf from birth, born deaf; **jour de n.,** birthday; **lieu de n.,** birthplace; **donner n. à un enfant,** to give birth to a child; **acte de n.,** birth certificate; **extrait de n.** = (copy of) birth certificate; (*b*) descent; **français de n.,** French by birth; (*c*) **la n. du printemps,** the birth of spring; **la n. du jour,** dawn; the break of day; **donner n. à une rumeur,** to give rise to a rumour, *NAm:* rumor; **prendre n.,** to originate, start. **2.** root (of tongue, nail, etc.); source (of river); *Arch:* spring (of pillar, arch); **point de n.,** point of origin; **cicatrice à la n. des cheveux,** scar just where the hair begins.
naissant [nɛsɑ̃] *a.* newborn; dawning (day); nascent (beauty); **à l'aube naissante,** at break of day; **barbe naissante,** incipient beard; *Ch:* **à l'état n.,** nascent.
naître [nɛtr̥] *v.i.* (*pr.p.* **naissant;** *p.p.* **né;** *pr.ind.* **je nais, il naît, n. naissons, ils naissent;** *pr.sub.* **je naisse;** *p.h.* **je naquis;** *fu.* **je naîtrai;** *aux.* **être**) (*a*) to be born; **il naquit, est né, en 1880,** he was born in 1880; **enfant, poussin, qui vient de n.,** newly-born child, newly-hatched chick; **né de parents anglais,** of English parentage; **enfant à n.,** unborn child; **être né pour qch.,** to be cut out for sth.; **être né pour l'autre,** to be made for one another; **il est né poète,** he is a born poet; **je l'ai vu n.,** I have known him from birth, since he was a baby; **Christine Thomas, née Martin,** Christine Thomas, née Martin; **je ne suis pas né d'hier,** I wasn't born yesterday; (*b*) (*of hopes, fears, etc.*) to be born, to (a)rise, to spring up; **faire n.,** to give rise to, raise, breed (hope, anxiety, suspicion); to arouse (suspicion); to give rise to (doubt); to provoke (smile); (*c*) (*of plants*) to begin to grow, come up; to appear; (*of day*) to dawn; (*of project*) to originate.
naïvement [naivmɑ̃] *adv.* naïvely, ingenuously.
naïveté [naivte] *n.f.* **1.** naïvety; simplicity, ingenuousness. **2.** naïve, ingenuous, remark.
nanan [nanɑ̃, nɑ̃nɑ̃] *n.m. F:* something nice (to eat); **c'est du n.!** (i) yum-yum! (ii) it's a piece of cake!
nanisme [nanism] *n.m.* dwarfism.
Nankin [nɑ̃kɛ̃] **1.** *Pr.n. Geog:* Nanking. **2.** *n.m. & a. inv. Tex:* nankeen.
nansouk [nɑ̃zuk] *n.m. Tex:* nainsook.
nantir [nɑ̃tir] *v.tr.* (*a*) to give security to (creditor); (*b*) **n. qn de qch.,** to provide s.o. with sth.; **être bien nanti,** to be well off, well provided for; **se n. d'un parapluie,** to provide, arm, oneself with an umbrella.
nantissement [nɑ̃tismɑ̃] *n.m.* **1.** pledging, bailment. **2.** pledge, collateral security, cover; **déposer des titres en n.,** to lodge stock as security.
napalm [napalm] *n.m.* napalm; **bombe au n.,** napalm bomb.
naphtaline [naftalin] *n.f.*, **naphtalène** [naftalɛn] *n.m.* naphthalene; **n. blanche en boules,** white naphthalene in balls; *F:* mothballs.
naphte [naft] *n.m.* naphtha, mineral oil; **n. de goudron,** coal-tar naphtha.
Napoléon [napɔleɔ̃] **1.** *Pr.n.m.* Napoleon. **2.** *n.m. A:* twenty-franc piece (bearing the effigy of Napoleon).
napoléonien, -ienne [napɔleɔnjɛ̃, -jɛn] *a.* Napoleonic.
napolitain, -aine [napɔlitɛ̃, -ɛn] *a. & n. Geog:* Neapolitan; **tranche napolitaine,** Neapolitan ice (cream).
nappage [napaʒ] *n.m.* **1.** table linen. **2.** *Cu:* coating (with sauce).
nappe [nap] *n.f.* **1.** (*a*) tablecloth; **mettre, ôter, la n.,** to lay, remove, the cloth; (*b*) *Ecc:* **n. d'autel,** altar cloth. **2.** sheet (of ice, fire); **n. d'eau,** (i) sheet of water; (ii) underground water level; **n. de mazout,** oil slick; *Geol:* **n. éruptive,** lava flow; **n. pétrolifère,** oil layer; **n. aquifère,** water table.
napper [nape] *v.tr.* **1.** to cover with a cloth. **2.** *Cu:* to coat (with sauce).
napperon [naprɔ̃] *n.m.* (small linen) cloth, mat; **n. de plateau,** traycloth; **n. individuel,** place mat.

Narcisse [narsis] **1.** *Pr.n.m.* Narcissus. **2.** *n.m. Bot:* narcissus; **n. sauvage, des près,** daffodil; **n. des poètes,** pheasant's eye.
narcissisme [narsisism] *n.m. Psy:* narcissism.
narcomanie [narkɔmani] *n.f.* drug mania.
narcose [narkoz] *n.f. Med:* narcosis.
narcotique [narkɔtik] *a. & n.m. Med:* narcotic; *n.* opiate; **faire prendre un n. à qn,** to drug s.o.
nard [nar] *n.m. Bot: Pharm:* spikenard, nard.
narguer [narge] *v.tr.* to flout, scoff at (sth., s.o.).
narguilé, narghilé, narghileh [nargile] *n.m.* narghile, hookah.
narine [narin] *n.f.* nostril.
narquois, -oise [narkwa, -waz] *a.* mocking, bantering (tone, smile).
narquoisement [narkwazmɑ̃] *adv.* mockingly; in a mocking tone.
narrateur, -trice [naratœr, -tris] *n.* narrator; teller (of story); storyteller.
narratif, -ive [naratif, -iv] *a.* narrative.
narration [narasjɔ̃] *n.f.* **1.** narrating, narration; *Gram:* **présent de n.,** historic present. **2.** (*a*) narrative, account (of event); (*b*) *Sch:* narrative composition.
narrer [nare] *v.tr. Lit:* to narrate, relate.
narval [narval] *n.m.* narwhal, unicorn whale; *pl. narvals.*
nasal, -aux [nazal, -o] **1.** *a.* nasal (bone, sound). **2.** *n.f. Ling:* **nasale,** nasal.
nasaliser [nazalize] *v.tr.* to nasalize (sound).
nasarde [nazard] *n.f.* rap, flip, on the nose; **essuyer une n.,** to get a rebuff, a snub.
naseau, -eaux [nazo] *n.m.* nostril (of horse, ox); *F:* **les naseaux,** the nose.
nasillard [nazijar] *a.* nasal; **ton n.,** (nasal) twang; **parler d'une voix nasillarde,** to talk through one's nose.
nasillement [nazijmɑ̃] *n.m.* **1.** speaking through one's nose. **2.** (nasal) twang.
nasiller [nazije] *v.i.* to speak through one's nose, with a twang.
nasique [nazik] *n.m. Z:* proboscis monkey.
nasse [nas] *n.f.* eel pot, lobster pot; hoop net (for birds); trap (for rats); *F:* **tomber dans la n.,** to fall into a trap.
natal, -als [natal] *a.* (*rarely used in pl.*) native; **ville natale,** birthplace; **mon pays n.,** my native land; **ma maison natale,** the house where I was born.
natalité [natalite] *n.f.* birthrate; **forte n.,** high birthrate.
natation [natasjɔ̃] *n.f.* swimming; **école de n.,** swimming baths.
natatoire [natatwar] *a. Z:* natatory, natatorial (organ, membrane); *Ich:* **vessie n.,** swim(ming) bladder, air bladder; sound.
natif, -ive [natif, -iv] **1.** *a.* native; (*a*) **je suis n. de Londres,** I'm London born; (*b*) *Miner: etc:* native, virgin (gold, etc.); (*c*) natural, inborn; **bon sens n.,** mother wit. **2.** *n.* native.
nation [nasjɔ̃] *n.f.* nation; *Nau:* **pavillon de n.,** national flag; **l'Organisation des Nations Unies,** the United Nations Organization.
national, -ale, -aux [nasjɔnal, -o] **1.** *a.* national. **2.** *n.m.pl.* **nationaux,** nationals (of a country). **3.** *n.f.* **nationale,** main road = "A" road.
nationalement [nasjɔnalmɑ̃] *adv.* nationally.
nationalisation [nasjɔnalizasjɔ̃] *n.f.* nationalization.
nationaliser [nasjɔnalize] *v.tr.* to nationalize (industry).
nationalisme [nasjɔnalism] *n.m. Pol:* nationalism.
nationaliste [nasjɔnalist] **1.** *n. Pol:* nationalist. **2.** *a.* nationalist(ic); **la Chine n.,** Nationalist China.
nationalité [nasjɔnalite] *n.f.* nationality; **acte de n.,** (ship's) certificate of registry.
national-socialisme [nasjɔnalsɔsjalism] *n.m. Pol.Hist:* National Socialism.
nativement [nativmɑ̃] *adv.* innately, naturally.
nativité [nativite] *n.f. Ecc:* nativity.
natron [natrɔ̃], **natrum** [natrɔm] *n.m. Miner:* natron, native soda.
natte [nat] *n.f.* **1.** mat, matting (of rush, straw). **2.** plait, braid (of hair, gold thread, etc.); **porter des nattes, une n.,** to wear one's hair in plaits; to wear a pigtail.
natter [nate] *v.tr.* **1.** to cover (wall, etc.) with mats. **2.** to plait, braid (hair, straw, etc.).
naturalisation [natyralizasjɔ̃] *n.f.* **1.** *Adm:* naturalization. **2.** preservation, mounting (of botanical specimen, etc.); **n. d'animaux,** taxidermy. **3.** naturalizing, acclimatizing (of plant or animal).
naturalisé, -ée [natyralize] **1.** *a.* naturalized. **2.** *n.* naturalized subject, citizen.
naturaliser [natyralize] *v.tr.* **1.** *Adm:* to naturalize; **se faire n. français,** to become a naturalized Frenchman. **2.** to preserve, mount (botanical specimen); to mount, stuff (animal). **3.** to naturalize, acclimatize (plant, animal).
naturalisme [natyralism] *n.m.* naturalism.
naturaliste [natyralist] **1.** *n.* (*a*) naturalist; (*b*) taxidermist. **2.** *a.* naturalistic.
nature [natyr] *n.f.* **1.** nature; **les lois de la n.,** the laws of nature; **vice contre n.,** unnatural vice; **à l'état de n.,** in a state of nature; in the natural state; **plus grand que n.,** larger than life; **peindre d'après n.,** to paint from nature, from life; **n. morte,** still life (painting); *F:* **il s'est perdu, a disparu, dans la n.,** he's vanished into thin air; *Aut: F:* **partir dans la n.,** to run, smash, into a tree, bank, etc. **2.** nature; (*a*) kind, character; **n. du climat, du sol,** nature of the climate, of the soil; **faits de n. à nous étonner,** facts of an astonishing nature; astonishing facts; **ce n'est pas dans sa n.,** it's not in his nature; (*b*) character, disposition, temperament; **être d'une n. douce,** to be gentle; **il est timide de, par, n., il est d'une n. timide,** he's naturally shy, shy by nature; **il tient cela de sa n.,** it is in his nature, comes naturally to him; **c'est une bonne n.,** he's a kindly (sort of) man; **une n. violente,** a naturally violent person; *F:* **c'est une n.,** he's a real personality; *F:* **c'est une petite n.,** he's a weakly sort of person. **3.** kind; **payer en n.,** to pay in kind. **4.** *a.inv.* (*a*) *Cu: etc:* plain; **bœuf, pommes, n.,** (plain) boiled beef, potatoes; **café n.,** black coffee; (*b*) **grandeur n.,** full-scale, life-size(d).
naturel, -elle [natyrɛl] **1.** *a.* natural; (*a*) natural (history, law); **mort naturelle,** death from natural causes; **enfant n.,** natural, illegitimate, child; **de grandeur naturelle,** life-size(d); **c'est n. de le faire,** it's only natural, reasonable, to do so; **mais c'est tout n.,** it was a pleasure; *esp. NAm:* you're welcome; (*b*) native (wit); natural, innate (gift); natural, unaffected (person); simple, straightforward (answer); **il lui est n. de peindre,** it comes natural to him to paint; **alcool n.,** raw spirit; **vin n.,** unfortified wine; **soie naturelle,** pure, real, silk; (*c*) *Mus:* **note naturelle,** natural. **2.** *n.m.* (*a*) native (of country); (*b*) nature, character, disposition; **d'un bon n.,** of a kind disposition; *Prov:* **chassez le n., il revient au galop,** what's bred in the bone will come out in the flesh; (*c*) **voir les choses au n.,** to see things as they are; **peindre qch. au n.,** to paint sth. true to life, realistically.
naturellement [natyrɛlmɑ̃] *adv.* naturally; **n. timide,** naturally shy, shy by nature; **se conduire n.,** to behave naturally, without affectation; **vous vous en êtes fâché? n.!** you resented it? naturally! of course!

naturisme [natyrism] *n.m.* naturism.
naturiste [natyrist] **1.** *n.* naturist. **2.** *a.* naturist(ic).
naufrage [nofraʒ] *n.m.* (ship)wreck; **faire n.,** (*of ship*) to be wrecked; (*of sailor*) to be shipwrecked; **périr dans un n.,** to be lost at sea.
naufragé, -ée [nofraʒe] **1.** *a.* (*of ship*) wrecked; (*of sailor*) shipwrecked; castaway (crew). **2.** *n.* shipwrecked man, woman; castaway.
naufrageur, -euse [nofraʒœr, -øz] *n.* wrecker (of ships, plan).
nauséabond [nozeabɔ̃] *a.* nauseous, nauseating (smell, conduct); evil-smelling; stinking.
nausée [noze] *n.f.* (*a*) nausea; **avoir la n., des nausées,** to feel sick; **donner des nausées à qn,** to nauseate s.o.; (*b*) disgust; **l'hypocrisie me donne la n.,** hypocrisy makes me sick.
nauséeux, -euse [nozeø, -øz] *a.* (*a*) nauseating, nauseous; **odeur nauséeuse,** nauseating smell; (*b*) loathsome, nauseating (hypocrisy, etc.).
nautique [notik] *a.* nautical (term, instrument, etc.); **sports nautiques,** aquatic sports; **carte n.,** (sea) chart.
nautiquement [notikmɑ̃] *adv.* nautically.
nautisme [notism] *n.m. Sp:* sailing.
naval, -ale, -als [naval] *a.* naval; nautical; **termes navals,** nautical terms; **armée navale,** fleet, naval force; **architecture navale,** naval architecture; **construction navale,** shipbuilding; **chantier n.,** shipyard; **base navale,** naval base; **l'École navale,** *n.f.* **la Navale,** the Naval College.
navarin [navarɛ̃] *n.m. Cu:* lamb stew, casserole.
navet [navɛ] *n.m.* **1.** turnip; **n. de Suède,** swede. **2.** *F:* (*of book*) dud; (*of picture*) daub; (*of film, play*) tripe.
navette[1] [navɛt] *n.f.* **1.** incense boat; incense box. **2.** (*a*) shuttle; **faire la n. entre deux endroits,** (*of vehicle*) to ply between two places; (*of pers.*) to go to and fro; *Rail:* to commute; **navettes fréquentes entre la gare et la ville,** frequent (shuttle) service between station and town; **n. spatiale,** space shuttle; (*b*) netting needle.
navette[2] *n.f. Bot:* rape; **(huile de) n.,** rape (seed) oil, colza oil.
navicert [navisɛr] *n.m.* navicert.
naviculaire [navikylɛr] *a.* navicular (bone, etc.).
navigabilité [navigabilite] *n.f.* **1.** navigability (of river, etc.). **2. (état de) n.,** seaworthiness (of ship); airworthiness (of aircraft); **en (bon) état de n.,** seaworthy; airworthy.
navigable [navigabl̩] *a.* **1.** navigable (river). **2.** (*of ship*) seaworthy; (*of aircraft*) airworthy.
navigant [navigɑ̃] *a.* **personnel n.,** *n.m.pl.* **les navigants,** (i) seagoing personnel; (ii) flying personnel.
navigateur [navigatœr] **1.** *n.m.* (*a*) navigator (of ship, aircraft, etc.); (*b*) navigator, seafarer. **2.** *a.m.* **peuple n.,** seafaring people.
navigation [navigasjɔ̃] *n.f.* navigation; **n. sur arc de grand cercle,** great circle sailing, navigation; **n. à l'estime,** dead reckoning; **n. côtière,** coastal navigation; **n. au long cours, n. hauturière,** deep-sea, ocean, navigation; **n. intérieure, fluviale,** inland navigation; **n. à voile,** sailing; **n. de plaisance,** sailing, yachting; **école de n. (de la marine marchande),** nautical school; **compagnie de n.,** shipping company; **permis de n.,** ship's passport, sea letter; **journal de n.,** log(book); *Av:* **n. à vue, aux instruments,** visual, instrument flying; **n. spatiale,** space navigation; astronautics.
naviguer [navige] **1.** *v.i.* (*of ship, seaman*) to sail; **n. au commerce,** to be in the merchant service; **n. au long cours,** to be in the foreign trade; **navire qui navigue bien,** ship that behaves well at sea. **2.** *v.tr.* to navigate (ship, aircraft).
navire [navir] *n.m.* **1.** ship, vessel; **n. à voiles,** sailing ship; **n. à vapeur,** steamship, steamer; **n. école,** training ship; **n. frère, n. jumeau,** sister ship, twin ship; **n. de commerce, n. marchand,** merchantman, merchant ship; **n. de plaisance,** pleasure boat; yacht; **n. de pêche,** fishing boat; **n. au long cours,** ocean-going ship; **n. de guerre,** warship; **n. de combat,** battleship; **n. météo(rologique),** weather ship; *U.S:* ocean station vessel; **les navires dans le port,** the shipping in the harbour, *NAm:* harbor.
navire-citerne [navirsitɛrn] *n.m. Nau:* tanker; *pl. navires-citernes.*
navrant [navrɑ̃] *a.* heartrending, heartbreaking; **c'est n.,** it's very distressing.
navré [navre] *a.* heartbroken (person); woebegone (expression); **être n. de qch.,** to be (deeply) grieved at sth.; **je suis n. de l'apprendre,** I'm terribly sorry to hear it.
navrer [navre] *v.tr.* to grieve (s.o.) deeply; to break (s.o.'s) heart.
nazaréen, -enne [nazareɛ̃, -ɛn] *a.* & *n. B.Hist:* Nazarene.
nazi, -e [nazi] *a.* & *n. Hist: Pol:* Nazi.
nazisme [nazism] *n.m. Hist: Pol:* Nazism.
ne, n' [n(ə)] *neg.adv.* not. **1.** (*forming neg. vb with* **pas**) **je ne le connais pas,** I don't know him; **il ne m'avait pas vu,** he hadn't seen me; (*for the use of* **ne** *in conjunction with* **aucun, aucunement, goutte, guère, jamais, mie, mot, personne, plus, point, que (ne . . . que), rien,** *see these words*). **2.** (*used alone, chiefly in literary style with* **cesser, oser, pouvoir, savoir, importer,** *and often as an archaism with other verbs*) **il ne cesse de parler,** he is for ever talking; **je n'ose lui parler,** I dare not speak to him; **je ne puis vous le promettre,** I cannot promise you that; **je ne sais que faire,** I don't know what to do; **je ne saurais vous le dire,** I cannot tell you; *always used without* **pas** *in* **n'importe,** never mind, it doesn't matter. **3.** *in the following constructions* (*a*) **qui ne connaît cette œuvre célèbre?** who does not know this famous work? **que ne ferait-il pour vous?** what would he not do for you? (*b*) **je n'ai d'autre désir que celui de vous plaire,** I have no other desire than to please you; (*c*) **il n'est pas si stupide qu'il ne vous comprenne,** he is not so stupid that he cannot understand you; (*d*) **si je ne me trompe,** unless I am mistaken; (*e*) **voilà six mois que je ne l'ai vu,** it is now six months since I saw him; (*f*) **il n'y a personne à qui il ne se soit adressé,** there is no one to whom he did not apply; (*g*) **il n'eut garde d'y aller,** he took good care not to go; **qu'à cela ne tienne!** by all means! **je n'ai que faire de votre aide,** I don't need your help. **4.** (*used optionally in literary style with a vague negative connotation*) (*a*) (*expressions of fear*) **je crains qu'il (ne) prenne froid,** I am afraid he may catch cold; (*b*) **évitez, prenez garde, qu'on (ne) vous voie,** take care not to be seen; **peu s'en fallut qu'il (ne) tombât,** he nearly fell; **je ne nie pas que cela (ne) soit vrai,** I don't deny that it's true; (*c*) (*comparison*) **il est plus vigoureux qu'il (ne) paraît,** he is stronger than he looks; **il agit autrement qu'il ne parle,** his actions belie his words.
né [ne] *a.* born; **c'est un conteur né,** he's a born storyteller.
néanmoins [neɑ̃mwɛ̃] *adv.* nevertheless, nonetheless; for all that; yet.
néant [neɑ̃] *n.m.* **1.** (*a*) nothing; nought, naught; **sortir du n.,** to rise from nothing; **réduire qch. à n.,** to reduce sth. to nothing, to nought; (*b*) worthlessness, uselessness (of s.o., sth.); **le n. des grandeurs humaines,** the vanity of human greatness. **2.** (*on form, tax return, etc.*) none, nil.
nébuleux, -euse [nebylø, -øz] **1.** *a.* nebulous; (*a*) cloudy, hazy, misty (sky, view); (*b*) vague, hazy (ideas); obscure (writer, theory). **2.** *n.f. Astr:* **nébuleuse,** nebula.

nébulosité [nebylozite] *n.f.* nebulousness, cloudiness, haziness (of sky, idea, etc.); *Meteor:* **forte n.,** heavy cloud cover.

nécessaire [nesesɛr] **1.** *a.* necessary; indispensable; requisite; **n. à, pour, qch., qn,** necessary, indispensable, required, for sth., s.o.; **n. pour faire qch.,** necessary, indispensable, for doing sth.; **se rendre n. à qn,** to make oneself indispensable to s.o.; **avoir l'argent n.,** to have the necessary money; *n.* **faire le n.,** to play the busybody; **il n'est pas n. d'être impoli,** there is no need to be rude; **il est n. que vous teniez compte de cela,** you really must take notice of this; **peu n.,** needless, unnecessary. **2.** *n.m.* (*a*) necessities, necessaries; **le strict n.,** bare necessities; **se refuser le n.,** to deny oneself the necessities of life; **faire le n.,** to do what is necessary; (*b*) outfit, kit (of tools); **n. de réparation,** repair kit; **n. de toilette,** dressing case, toilet case; **n. de voyage,** overnight bag.

nécessairement [nesesɛrmɑ̃] *adv.* **1.** necessarily, of necessity. **2.** inevitably.

nécessité [nesesite] *n.f.* necessity. **1. de (toute) n.,** necessarily, of necessity; **il est de toute n. de faire qch.,** it is essential to do sth.; we simply must do sth.; **être dans la n. de faire qch.,** to be compelled to do sth.; **ce voyage est une n.,** this journey is essential; **quelle n. y avait-il de faire cela?** what need was there for doing that? **faire qch. par n.,** to do sth. out of necessity, to be compelled to do sth.; **faire de n. vertu,** to make a virtue of necessity. **2.** (*a*) need, want; **les nécessités de la vie,** the necessities of life; **objets de première n., de toute n.,** indispensable articles; **denrées de première n.,** essential foodstuffs; **selon les nécessités,** as circumstances require; **c'est une n.,** it's a must; (*b*) **être dans la n.,** to be in need, in straitened circumstances.

nécessiter [nesesite] *v.tr.* to require, demand, necessitate, entail (sth.).

nécessiteux, -euse [nesesitø, -øz] *a.* needy, in need; *n.pl.* **les n.,** the needy, poor, destitute.

nécrologe [nekrɔlɔʒ] *n.m.* necrology, obituary list, death roll.

nécrologie [nekrɔlɔʒi] *n.f.* necrology, obituary notice; *Journ:* deaths.

nécrologique [nekrɔlɔʒik] *a.* obituary (notice).

nécromancie [nekrɔmɑ̃si] *n.f.* necromancy.

nécromancien, -ienne [nekrɔmɑ̃sjɛ̃, -jɛn] *n.* necromancer.

nécrophore [nekrɔfɔr] *n.m. Ent:* carrion beetle, scavenger beetle.

nécropole [nekrɔpɔl] *n.f.* necropolis.

nécrose [nekroz] *n.f. Med:* necrosis.

nécroser [nekroze] *v.tr.* to cause necrosis in (bone).

nectaire [nɛktɛr] *n.m. Bot:* nectary.

nectar [nɛktar] *n.m.* nectar.

nectarine [nɛktarin] *n.f. Hort:* nectarine.

néerlandais, -aise [neɛrlɑ̃dɛ, -ɛz] *Geog:* **1.** *a.* of the Netherlands; Dutch; **le Gouvernement n.,** the Dutch Government. **2.** (*a*) *n.* Netherlander; Dutchman, Dutchwoman; (*b*) *n.m. Ling:* (*in the Netherlands*) Dutch; (*in Belgium*) Flemish.

nef [nɛf] *n.f.* **1.** nave (of church); **n. latérale,** aisle. **2.** *A: & Poet:* ship.

néfaste [nefast] *a.* luckless, ill-omened, inauspicious; **jour n.,** (i) *Rom.Ant: dies non;* (ii) ill-fated, evil, day; **influence n.,** disastrous influence.

nèfle [nɛfl̥] *n.f. Bot:* medlar (fruit); **n. du Japon,** loquat; *F:* **des nèfles!** no fear! nothing doing!

néflier [neflije] *n.m. Bot:* medlar (tree); **n. du Japon,** loquat (tree).

négateur, -trice [negatœr, -tris] **1.** *a.* denying. **2.** *n.* denier.

négatif, -ive [negatif, -iv] **1.** *a.* negative (answer, result, proposition, quantity, electricity); *Phot:* **épreuve négative,** *n.m.* **n.,** negative; **dessin n.,** blueprint. **2.** *n.f.* **négative,** negative; **je réponds par la négative,** my answer is no, is in the negative.

négation [negasjɔ̃] *n.f.* **1.** negation, denial. **2.** *Gram:* negative.

négativement [negativmɑ̃] *adv.* negatively; in the negative.

négligé [negliʒe] **1.** *a.* (*a*) neglected (opportunity, etc.); **épouse négligée,** neglected wife; (*b*) careless, slovenly (dress, appearance, style). **2.** *n.m.* (*a*) carelessness (in one's appearance); slovenliness; (*b*) **en n.,** not dressed; (*c*) *Cost:* négligé(e).

négligeable [negliʒabl̥] *a.* negligible; insignificant, inconsiderable.

négligemment [negliʒamɑ̃] *adv.* **1.** negligently, carelessly. **2.** casually, nonchalantly.

négligence [negliʒɑ̃s] *n.f.* negligence; neglect (of s.o., of duty); carelessness, lack of care; **n. à faire qch.,** (i) carelessness, (ii) remissness, in doing sth.; *Jur:* **n. coupable, criminelle,** criminal negligence; **négligences de style,** carelessness of style; **par n.,** through an oversight.

négligent [negliʒɑ̃] *a.* **1.** negligent; careless, neglectful (**de,** of); **être n. à faire qch.,** to be careless, remiss, in doing sth. **2.** indifferent, casual.

négliger [negliʒe] *v.tr.* **(je négligeai(s); n. négligeons)** to neglect. **1.** (*a*) to be neglectful of (one's health, duty, children); to be careless about (one's appearance, dress); **se n.,** to neglect oneself; *F:* to let oneself go; (*b*) **n. de faire qch.,** to neglect to do sth.; to leave sth. undone. **2.** to disregard (advice, etc.); to miss (opportunity); **ne rien n. pour obtenir qch.,** to leave no stone unturned (in order) to get sth.

négoce [negɔs] *n.m.* trade, trading, business; **le petit, le haut, n.,** small, big, business.

négociabilité [negɔsjabilite] *n.f.* negotiability.

négociable [negɔsjabl̥] *a.* negotiable, transferable (bond, bill, etc.).

négociant, -ante [negɔsjɑ̃, -ɑ̃t] *n.* (wholesale) merchant; dealer; **n. en gros,** wholesaler; **n. en vins,** wine merchant.

négociateur, -trice [negɔsjatœr, -tris] *n.* (*a*) negotiator (of treaty, deal, etc.); (*b*) intermediary.

négociation [negɔsjasjɔ̃] *n.f.* **1.** negotiation, negotiating (of treaty, bill); **en n.,** under negotiation; **entamer des négociations,** to enter into negotiations. **2.** negotiation, transaction.

négocier [negɔsje] *v.* (*impf. & pr.sub.* **n. négociions) 1.** *v.i.* (*a*) to negotiate; (*b*) *A:* to trade. **2.** *v.tr.* to negotiate (loan, bill, treaty, etc.).

nègre, négresse [nɛgr̥, negrɛs] **1.** *n.* (*a*) *Ethn: or Pej:* negro, *f.* negress; black; **la traite des nègres,** the slave trade; **parler petit n.,** to talk pidgin (French, etc.); (*b*) *F:* drudge; stooge; ghost (of literary man); devil (of barrister). **2.** *a.* (*f.* **nègre**) (*a*) negro (art, race); (*b*) *a.inv.* nigger(-brown); *F:* **propos n. blanc,** double talk.

négrier [negrije] **1.** *n.m.* (*a*) slave trader; *F:* owner of sweat shop; slave driver; (*b*) slave ship. **2.** *a.m.* **vaisseau n.,** slave ship.

négrillon, -onne [negrijɔ̃, -ɔn] *n. Pej:* (little) negro boy, girl.

négroïde [negrɔid] *a. Ethn:* negroid.

neige [nɛʒ] *n.f.* (*a*) snow; **la saison des neiges,** the snowy season; **neiges éternelles,** perpetual snow; **tempête de n.,** blizzard; **amas de n.,** snowdrift; **être bloqué par la n.,** to be snowed up, snowbound; **n. fondue,** (i) sleet; (ii) slush; **boule de n.,** snowball; **histoire qui fait boule de n.,** story that snowballs; **faire un bonhomme de n.,** to make a snowman; **train de n.,** winter sports train; **classe de n.,** class temporarily transferred to winter resort; **barbe de n.,** snowy beard; **blanc comme (la) n.,** snow-white; *Cu:* **blancs**

d'œufs battus en n., whites of eggs beaten stiff; œufs à la n., floating islands; *Ind:* n. carbonique, snow; dry ice; (*b*) *P:* cocaine, snow.

neiger [neʒe] *v.impers.* (il neigeait) to snow.

neigeux, -euse [nɛzø, -øz] *a.* **1.** snowy (peak, weather); snow-covered (roof, etc.). **2.** snow-white, snowy.

nématode [nematɔd] *n.m.* nematode threadworm.

nenni [nani] *adv. A:* nay!

nénuphar [nenyfar] *n.m. Bot:* nenuphar, water lily; **n. des étangs, n. jaune,** yellow pond lily.

néo-calédonien, -ienne [neɔkaledɔnjɛ̃, -jɛn] *a. & n. Geog:* New Caledonian; *pl. néo-calédoniens, -iennes.*

néo-classicisme [neɔklasisism] *n.m.* neoclassicism.

néo-colonialisme [neɔkɔlɔnjalism] *n.m.* neocolonialism.

néo-fascisme [neɔfasism, -ʃism] *n.m.* neofascism.

néo-gallois, -oise [neɔgalwa, -waz] *a. & n. Geog:* (native, inhabitant) of New South Wales; *pl. néo-gallois, -oises.*

néo-gothique [neɔgɔtik] *a. & n.m. Arch:* neo-gothic; *pl. néo-gothiques.*

néo-hébridais, -aise [neɔebridɛ, -ɛz] *a. & n. Geog:* (native, inhabitant) of the New Hebrides; *pl. néo-hébridais, -aises.*

néo-impressionnisme [neɔɛ̃prɛsjɔnism] *n.m. Art:* neo-impressionism.

néolithique [neɔlitik] *a. & n.m.* Neolithic (Age).

néologisme [neɔlɔʒism] *n.m.* neologism.

néon [neɔ̃] *n.m. Ch:* neon; **tube au n.,** neon tube.

néo-natal [neɔnatal] *a. Med:* neonatal; *pl. néo-natals.*

néophyte [neɔfit] *n.* (*a*) neophyte; (*b*) novice, tyro.

néo-zélandais, -aise [neɔzelɑ̃dɛ, -ɛz] **1.** *a. Geog:* New Zealand (government, butter). **2.** *n.* New Zealander; *pl. néo-zélandais, -aises.*

népérien, -ienne [neperjɛ̃, -jɛn] *a.* Napierian (logarithms).

néphrétique [nefretik] **1.** *a.* nephritic, renal (pain, colic). **2.** *n.* sufferer from nephritis; nephritic.

néphrite [nefrit] *n.f.* **1.** *Med:* nephritis; **n. chronique,** Bright's disease. **2.** *Miner:* nephrite, jade, greenstone.

népotisme [nepɔtism] *n.m.* nepotism.

néréide [nereid] *n.f.* nereid, sea nymph.

nerf [nɛr] *n.m.* **1.** (*a*) (optic, spinal) nerve; (*b*) **attaque de nerfs,** (fit of) hysterics; **il a les nerfs en pelote, à vif, en boule,** his nerves are on edge; **porter, donner, taper, sur les nerfs à qn,** to get, jar, on s.o.'s nerves; to exasperate s.o.; **je suis à bout de nerfs,** my nerves are frayed; **c'est un paquet de nerfs,** he, she, is a bundle of nerves; **être, vivre, sur les nerfs,** to live on one's nerves; **passer ses nerfs sur qn, qch.,** to work off one's irritation on s.o., sth. **2.** *F:* (*in sing. always* [nɛrf] *at the end of the word group*) sinew, tendon, ligament; *P:* **mets-y du n.!** put some energy, guts, into it! **caractère sans n.,** weak character; **avoir du n.,** to have stamina; **n. de bœuf,** life preserver; cosh; *NAm:* blackjack. **3.** *Bookb:* band, cord.

nerprun [nɛrprœ̃] *n.m. Bot:* buckthorn.

nervation [nɛrvasjɔ̃] *n.f. Bot: etc:* nervation, venation.

nervé [nɛrve] *a. Bot:* nervate, veined.

nerveusement [nɛrvøzmɑ̃] *adv.* **1.** energetically. **2.** impatiently, irritably; *F:* nervily; excitedly, hysterically; **rire n.,** to laugh excitedly, hysterically.

nerveux, -euse [nɛrvø, -øz] *a.* **1.** nervous (system, etc.); **centre n.,** nerve centre, *NAm:* center; **dépression nerveuse,** nervous breakdown. **2.** sinewy, wiry (arm, body); stringy (meat); vigorous, terse (style, etc.); **moteur n.,** responsive engine. **3.** excitable, highly-strung; *F:* nervy; **elle est nerveuse aujourd'hui,** she is on edge today; **rire n.,** hysterical laugh.

nervi [nɛrvi] *n.m.* henchman; thug.

nervosité [nɛrvozite] *n.f.* irritability, state of nerves, edginess.

nervure [nɛrvyr] *n.f.* (*a*) nervure, rib, vein (of leaf, insect wing); (*b*) flange, rib (on casting, etc.); gill (of radiator, etc.); *Av:* rib (of wing); *Bookb:* rib, raised band (on back of book); *Mec:* **n. de renfort,** stiffening rib; **n. de refroidissement,** cooling flange, fin; *Arch:* **voûte à nervures,** ribbed vault; **plafond à nervures,** filleted ceiling; *Dressm:* **nervures,** pin tucks.

nervuré [nɛrvyre] *a. Mec.E: Nat.Hist:* ribbed.

net, nette [nɛt] *a.* **1.** clean, spotless (plate, etc.); flawless (stone); clear, sound (conscience); *F:* **j'ai les mains nettes,** my hands are clean; I had nothing to do with it; **rente nette de tout impôt,** income free of tax; **cassure nette,** clean break; **faire place nette,** to clear out; to make a clean sweep; *Gaming:* **faire tapis n.,** to clear the board. **2.** (*a*) clear (sight, idea, style); distinct (print); sharp (outline); plain, straight (answer); **division nette,** clear-cut division; **écriture nette,** neat handwriting; *Phot:* **image nette,** sharp image; *n.m.* **mettre un devoir au n.,** to make a fair copy of an exercise; (*b*) net (weight, price); net, clear (profit). **3.** *adv.* (*a*) plainly, flatly, outright; **parler n.,** to speak plainly; **refuser qch. (tout) n.,** to refuse sth. point-blank, flatly; **s'arrêter n.,** to stop dead; **coupé n.,** cut clean through; (*b*) clearly, distinctly; (*c*) **cent francs n.,** a hundred francs net.

nettement [nɛtmɑ̃] *adv.* **1.** (*a*) cleanly; (*b*) clearly, distinctly; **profil n. découpé,** clear-cut, sharp-cut, profile; **partagé n. en deux classes,** sharply divided into two classes; **ce livre est n. pacifiste,** this book is definitely, markedly, pacifist. **2.** plainly, flatly; **parler n.,** to speak plainly, straight out.

netteté [nɛtte] *n.f.* **1.** cleanness (of break); **écrit avec n.,** neatly written. **2.** (*a*) clearness (of thought, style); distinctness (of vision, object); sharpness (of image); vividness (of memory); (*b*) flatness (of refusal).

nettoiement [nɛtwamɑ̃] *n.m.* cleaning (of streets); cleaning, clearing (of ground); **service du n.,** refuse collection.

nettoyage [nɛtwajaʒ] *n.m.* **1.** cleaning; **n. à sec,** dry cleaning; **n. par le vide,** vacuum cleaning; **faire le n.,** to clean up; **le grand n.,** spring cleaning; *Mil:* **opérations de n.,** mopping-up operations. **2.** cleaning out.

nettoyer [nɛtwaje] *v.tr.* **(je nettoie; je nettoierai)** (*a*) to clean (room, clothes, wound); to scour (pan, deck); to swab (deck); to wash out (bottle); to clean (corn); **n. à grande eau,** to swill (down); **n. une pièce à fond,** to turn out a room; **se n. les dents,** to clean one's teeth; **n. à sec,** to dry-clean; (*b*) *F:* (*of burglar*) to strip, clean out (a house); **se faire n. au jeu,** to get cleaned out gambling; (*c*) **n. un endroit de voleurs,** to rid a place of thieves; *Mil:* **n. les poches de résistance,** to mop up.

nettoyeur, -euse [nɛtwajœr, -øz] **1.** *a.* cleaning (apparatus, etc.). **2.** *n.* cleaner; *Ind:* scrubber; **n. de vitres,** window cleaner. **3.** *n.f.* **nettoyeuse,** cleaning machine, cleaner.

neuf[1] [nœf] *num.a.inv. & n.m.inv.* nine. **1.** *card. a.* (*at the end of the word group* [nœf]; *before* **ans** *and* **heures** [nœv], *otherwise before vowel sounds* [nœf]; *before a noun or adj. beginning with a consonant usu.* [nœ] often [nœf]) **j'en ai n.** [nœf], I have nine; **il a n. ans** [nœvɑ̃], he is nine years old; **n. et demi** [nœfedmi], nine and a half. **2.** *ordinal and other uses* (*always* [nœf]) **le n. mai,** the ninth of May; **Louis N.,** Louis the Ninth; **deux neufs,** two nines; **le n. de carreau,**

the nine of diamonds; *Mth: A:* **faire la preuve par n.,** to cast out the nines.

neuf², neuve [nœf, nœv] new. **1.** *a.* (*a*) (brand-)new (garment); new (thought, subject); **à l'état n.,** in new condition, as new; (*of postage stamp, book*) in mint condition, unused; **regarder qch. d'un œil n.,** to take a fresh view of sth.; (*b*) **herbe neuve,** new grass; **la curiosité neuve d'un enfant,** a child's newly awakened curiosity; **jeune homme bien n.,** a very raw, green, young man; **n. aux affaires,** new to business; (*c*) *F:* **qu'est-ce qu'il y a de n.?** what's the news? **il n'y a rien de n.,** there's nothing new. **2.** *n.m.* **habillé de n.,** wearing new clothes; **meublé de n.,** newly furnished; **trouver du n.,** to find sth. new; **il y a du n.,** I have news for you; *adv.phr.* anew; **refaire un mur à n.,** to rebuild a wall; **remettre qch. à n.,** to make sth. as good as new; to recondition, renovate, sth.; to do sth. up.

neurasthénie [nørasteni] *n.f. Med:* neurasthenia.

neurasthénique [nørastenik] *a. & n. Med:* neurasthenic.

neurochirurgie [nørɔʃiryrʒi] *n.f. Surg:* neurosurgery.

neurochirurgien, -ienne [nørɔʃiryrʒjɛ̃, -jɛn] *n. Surg:* neurosurgeon.

neurologie [nørɔlɔʒi] *n.f. Med:* neurology.

neurologiste [nørɔlɔʒist], **neurologue** [nørɔlɔg] *n.* nerve specialist, neurologist.

neurone [nørɔn] *n.m. Physiol:* neuron.

neuronique [nørɔnik] *a.* neuronic.

neuropsychiatrie [nørɔpsikiatri] *n.f.* neuropsychiatry.

neuropsychologie [nørɔpsikɔlɔʒi] *n.f.* neuropsychology.

neurotique [nørɔtik] *a. Med:* neurotic.

neutralisation [nøtralizasjɔ̃] *n.f.* neutralization, neutralizing (of country, acid, etc.).

neutraliser [nøtralize] *v.tr.* to neutralize (effort, country, acid, etc.).

neutralisme [nøtralism] *n.m. Pol:* neutralism, nonalignment.

neutraliste [nøtralist] *a. & n.* neutralist; **les pays neutralistes,** the non-aligned countries.

neutralité [nøtralite] *n.f.* neutrality; **garder la n.,** to remain neutral; **sortir de la n.,** to take sides.

neutre [nøtr̥] *a.* **1.** neuter; (*a*) **pronom n.,** neuter pronoun; *n.m.* **au n.,** in the neuter; (*b*) asexual; **abeille n.,** neuter, working, bee. **2.** neutral (nation, ship, *Ch:* salt; *El:* wire); *Mil:* **la zone n.,** no-man's land; **rester n.,** to remain neutral; **je resterai tout à fait n.,** I won't take sides. **3.** *n.m.* neutral.

neutron [nøtrɔ̃] *n.m. Atom.Ph:* neutron.

neuvaine [nœvɛn] *n.f. Ecc:* novena, neuvaine.

neuvième [nœvjɛm] **1.** *num. a. & n.* ninth. **2.** *n.m.* ninth (part). **3.** *n.f.* (*a*) *Mus:* ninth; (*b*) first form, *U.S:* grade (of junior school).

neuvièmement [nœvjɛmmɑ̃] *adv.* ninthly.

névé [neve] *n.m. Geol:* névé, granular ice.

neveu, -eux [nəvø] *n.m.* nephew; **n. à la mode de Bretagne,** first cousin once removed.

névralgie [nevralʒi] *n.f.* neuralgia.

névralgique [nevralʒik] *a.* neuralgic; *F:* **point n.,** sore point, sensitive subject.

névrite [nevrit] *n.f.* neuritis.

névritique [nevritik] *a.* neuritic.

névropathe [nevrɔpat] *n.* neuropath.

névrose [nevroz] *n.f. Med:* neurosis.

névrosé, -ée [nevroze] *a. & n.* neurotic, neurasthenic (patient).

névrotique [nevrɔtik] *a. Med:* neurotic (disorder, etc.).

newyorkais, -aise [njujɔrkɛ, -ɛz] **1.** *a.* of New York. **2.** *n.* New Yorker.

nez [ne] *n.m.* **1.** nose; (*a*) **parler, chanter, du n.,** to speak, sing, through one's nose; **mener, conduire, qn par le bout du n.,** to lead s.o. by the nose, to push s.o. around; **fourrer le n. dans les affaires d'autrui,** to pry, poke one's nose, into other people's business; **baisser le n.,** to look ashamed; **cela lui pend au n.,** it may well happen to him any day; **faire un pied de n. à qn,** to cock a snook at s.o.; *P:* **je l'ai dans le n.,** I can't stand him; **avoir un verre dans le n.,** to be a bit drunk, squiffy; *F:* **(en) faire un n.,** to pull a long face; **cela lui a passé sous le nez,** it slipped by, eluded, him; **il ne voit pas plus loin que le bout de son n.,** he can't see beyond the end of his nose; **se trouver n. à n. avec qn,** to find oneself face to face with s.o.; **regarder qn sous le n.,** to look defiantly at s.o.; **dire qch. au n. de qn,** to say sth. to s.o.'s face; **fermer la porte au n. de qn,** to shut the door in s.o.'s face; **jeter qch. au n. de qn,** (i) to throw sth. in s.o.'s face; (ii) to throw sth. in s.o.'s teeth; **à vue de n.,** at first sight; at a guess, at a rough estimate; **se casser le n.,** (i) to come a cropper; (ii) to find the door closed; (*b*) sense of smell; (*of dogs*) scent; **avoir bon n., le n. fin,** (i) to have a good nose, a keen sense of smell; (ii) *F:* to be shrewd, far-seeing. **2.** (*a*) nose, bow, head (of ship); nose (of aircraft); *Av:* **piquer du n.,** to nosedive; (*of cars*) **se rencontrer n. à n.,** to meet head on; (*b*) nosing (of step); nosepiece (of engine).

ni [ni] *conj.* (**ne** *is either expressed or implied*) nor, or; (*a*) **ni moi (non plus),** nor I (either); neither do, did, shall, I; **sans argent ni bagages,** without money or luggage; (*b*) **il ne mange ni ne boit,** he neither eats nor drinks; **il est parti sans manger ni boire,** he left without (either) eating or drinking; (*c*) **ni . . . ni,** neither . . . nor; **ni Pierre ni Henri ne sont** (*occ.* **n'est**) **là,** neither Peter nor Henry is there; **je n'ai ni femme ni enfant ni amis,** I have neither wife nor child nor friends; **ni l'un ni l'autre ne l'a vu,** neither (of them) saw it.

niais, -aise [njɛ, -ɛz] **1.** *a.* simple, foolish (person, answer, air); inane (smile); **je ne suis pas assez n. pour le lui dire,** I know better than to tell him. **2.** *n.* fool, simpleton; **petite niaise!** you little silly!

niaisement [njɛzmɑ̃] *adv.* foolishly; **rire n.,** to give a silly laugh.

niaiserie [njɛzri] *n.f.* **1.** silliness, foolishness. **2. dire des niaiseries,** to talk nonsense, make silly remarks.

Nicée [nise] *Pr.n.f. A.Geog:* Nicaea; **le symbole de N.,** the Nicene Creed.

niche¹ [niʃ] *n.f.* **1.** niche, nook, recess. **2. n. à chien,** dogkennel.

niche² *n.f. F:* trick, prank.

nichée [niʃe] *n.f.* nest(ful) (of birds); brood (of birds, children); litter (of mice, puppies).

nicher [niʃe] **1.** *v.i.* (*of birds*) to build a nest, to nest; *F:* (*of pers.*) to live; to hang out. **2.** (*of birds*) **se n.,** to (build a) nest; **maison nichée dans un bois,** cottage nestling, hidden away, in a wood; **niché dans un fauteuil,** curled up in an armchair.

nichet [niʃɛ] *n.m. Husb:* nest egg.

nichoir [niʃwar] *n.m.* breeding cage, coop, nesting box.

nichons [niʃɔ̃] *n.m.pl. P:* breasts; boobs; tits.

nickel [nikɛl] **1.** *n.m.* nickel. **2.** *a. F:* **c'est n.!** it's bang on! it's the goods!

nickelage [niklaʒ] *n.m.* nickelling, nickel plating.

nickelé [nikle] *a.* nickelled; nickel-plated; *F:* **avoir les pieds nickelés,** to sit tight, to refuse to budge.

nickeler [nikle] *v.tr.* **(je nickelle, n. nickelons; je nickellerai)** to nickel; to nickel-plate.

nickélifère [nikelifɛr] *a.* nickel-bearing.

niçois, -oise [niswa, -waz] *a. & n. Geog:* (native, inhabitant) of Nice.

nicotine [nikɔtin] *n.f. Ch:* nicotine.

nictation [niktasjɔ̃] *n.f.*, **nictitation** [niktitasjɔ̃] *n.f.* nictation, nictitation.
nictitant [niktitɑ̃] *a. Z:* nictitating (membrane).
nid [ni] *n.m.* **1.** nest (of bird, mouse, ant, etc.); **n. d'aigle,** eyrie; **trouver la pie au n.,** to have a lucky find; **mettre une poule au n.,** to set a hen; *Prov:* **petit à petit l'oiseau fait son n.,** little strokes fell great oaks; **n. de brigands,** robbers' den; **n. d'amoureux,** love nest; **n. à rats,** poky little place; **n. de poule,** pothole (in road); **n. à poussière,** dust trap. **2.** (*a*) **n. de mitrailleuses,** nest of machine guns; (*b*) *Nau:* **n. de corbeau, de pie,** crow's nest.
nièce [njɛs] *n.f.* niece; **n. à la mode de Bretagne,** first cousin once removed.
niellage [njɛlaʒ] *n.m.* inlaying with niello; niello work.
nielle[1] [njɛl] *n.f.* smut, blight (of wheat).
nielle[2] *n.f.* **n. des blés,** corn cockle.
nielle[3] *n.m. Metalw:* niello.
niellé [njele] *a.* **blé n.,** blighted wheat.
nieller [njele] *v.tr.* to inlay with niello.
nielleur [njɛlœr] *n.m.* niello worker.
niellure [njelyr] *n.f.* niello work.
nier [nje] *v.tr.* (*impf. & pr.sub.* **n. niions**) (*a*) to deny (a fact, God); **l'accusé nie,** the accused denies the charge; **je nie l'avoir vu,** I deny having seen him; **je nie qu'il m'ait vu,** I deny that he saw me; **il n'y a pas à le n.,** there is no denying it, no getting away from it; (*b*) **n. une dette,** to repudiate a debt.
nigaud, -aude [nigo, -od] (*a*) *n.* simpleton, *F:* clot, twit; (*b*) *a.* silly, simple, *F:* clottish.
nigelle [niʒɛl] *n.f. Bot:* nigella, love-in-a-mist.
nihilisme [niilism] *n.m.* nihilism.
nihiliste [niilist] **1.** *a.* nihilist(ic). **2.** *n.* nihilist.
Nil (le) [lənil] *Pr.n.m. Geog:* the (river) Nile; (*colour, NAm: color*) **vert (de) N.,** eau-de-nil.
nilgau(t) [nilgo] *n.m. Z:* nilgai.
nilotique [nilɔtik] *a. Geog:* Nilotic, of the Nile.
nimbe [nɛ̃b] *n.m.* nimbus, halo.
nimbé [nɛ̃be] *a.* haloed, nimbused.
nimbus [nɛ̃bys] *n.m. Meteor:* nimbus; raincloud.
ninas [ninas] *n.m.inv.* small cigar; whiff.
nippe [nip] *n.f. F:* **1.** *pl.* (shabby, old) clothes. **2.** *F:* garment; **je n'ai plus une n. à me mettre,** I haven't a rag to my back.
nipper [nipe] *v.tr. F:* to fit (s.o.) out; to rig (s.o.) out; **bien nippé,** well turned out.
nippon, -one [nipɔ̃, -ɔn] *a. & n.* Nipponese, Japanese.
nique [nik] *n.f. used only in F:* **faire la n. à qn,** to cock a snook at s.o.
nitouche [nituʃ] *n.f. F:* **sainte n.,** little hypocrite; **c'est une sainte n.,** butter wouldn't melt in her mouth.
nitrate [nitrat] *n.m. Ch:* nitrate.
nitre [nitr̥] *n.m.* nitre, saltpetre, *NAm:* niter, saltpeter.
nitré [nitre] *a.* nitrated; **composé n.,** nitro-compound.
nitreux, -euse [nitrø, -øz] *a.* nitrous.
nitrifier [nitrifje] *v.tr. Ch:* to nitrify.
nitrique [nitrik] *a. Ch:* nitric (acid).
nitrobenzine [nitrɔbɛ̃zin] *n.f. Ch:* nitrobenzine.
nitrocellulose [nitrɔselyloz] *n.f.* nitrocellulose.
nitroglycérine [nitrɔgliserin] *n.f.* nitroglycerine.
nitrure [nitryr] *n.m. Ch:* nitride.
niveau, -eaux [nivo] *n.m.* level. **1.** (*instrument*) (*a*) **n. à bulle d'air,** air, spirit, level; **n. de maçon, à plomb,** vertical level, plumb level; **n. à lunette,** surveyor's level; (*b*) gauge level; **n. d'eau, d'huile,** water, oil, gauge; **n. d'essence,** petrol gauge. **2.** (*a*) **n. de bruit,** noise level; *W.Tel:* **n. de transmission,** transmission level; (*b*) **le n. de l'eau, de la mer,** water, sea, level; **n. des basses, hautes, eaux,** low-water, high-water, mark; **jardin à trois niveaux,** garden on three levels; **immeuble à dix niveaux,** ten-storey, -floor, building; **être de n.,** to be level; **à franc n.,** (on a) dead level; **mettre qch. de n. à n.,** to level sth.; **navire de n.,** boat on an even keel; **passage à n.,** level crossing, *U.S:* grade crossing; **carburateur alimenté par différence de n.,** gravity-fed carburettor; (*c*) **n. de vie,** standard of living; **n. des études,** academic standard; **être au n. de qch., qn, être de n. avec qch., qn,** to be on a level, on a par, with sth., s.o.
nivelage [niv(ə)laʒ] *n.m.* levelling.
niveler [nivle] *v.tr.* **(je nivelle; je nivellerai) 1.** to take the level of, to survey (ground). **2.** to level, to even up (ground, fortunes); **n. au plus bas,** to level down.
niveleur, -euse [nivlœr, -øz] **1.** *a.* levelling. **2.** *n.* (*pers.*) leveller. **3.** *n.m.* small harrow.
nivellement [nivɛlmɑ̃] *n.m.* **1.** *Surv:* levelling; **repère de n.,** bench mark. **2.** levelling (of ground, social classes).
nivéole [niveɔl] *n.f. Bot:* snowflake.
nivôse [nivoz] *n.m. Fr.Hist:* fourth month of Republican calendar (Dec.-Jan.).
nobiliaire [nɔbiljɛr] *a.* nobiliary (rank, etc.); **almanach n.,** *n.m.* **n.,** peerage (list).
noble [nɔbl̥] **1.** *a.* (*a*) noble (family); (*b*) stately, lofty (air); *Th:* **père n.,** heavy father; (*c*) highminded. **2.** *n.* noble(man), noblewoman; **les nobles,** the nobility.
noblement [nɔbləmɑ̃] *adv.* nobly.
noblesse [nɔblɛs] *n.f.* **1.** nobility; (*a*) noble birth; **famille de n. récente,** family recently ennobled; (*b*) **la haute et la petite n.,** the nobility and gentry; **se marier dans la n.,** to marry a title. **2.** nobility, nobleness (of style, conduct).
noce [nɔs] *n.f.* **1.** (*a*) wedding; wedding festivities; **repas de n.,** wedding breakfast; (*b*) wedding party; (*c*) *pl. A:* marriage; (*still used in*) **nuit de noces,** wedding night; **voyage de noces,** honeymoon (trip); **robe de voyage de noces,** going-away dress; **noces d'argent, de vermeil, d'or, de diamant,** silver, ruby, golden, diamond, wedding; **il l'avait épousée en secondes noces,** she was his second wife. **2.** *F:* **faire la n.,** to go on a binge, to live it up; **usé par la n.,** worn out by dissipation; **je n'étais pas à la n.,** I was having a bad time.
noceur, -euse [nɔsœr, -øz] *n. F:* (*a*) reveller, roisterer; (*b*) fast liver; *m.* gay dog.
nocher [nɔʃe] *n.m. Poet:* pilot, boatman.
nocif, -ive [nɔsif, -iv] *a.* injurious, harmful, nocuous.
nocivité [nɔsivite] *n.f.* noxiousness; harmfulness.
noctambule [nɔktɑ̃byl] **1.** *a.* noctambulant. **2.** *n.* (*a*) somnambulist, sleepwalker; (*b*) *F:* night bird.
noctuelle [nɔktɥɛl] *n.f. Ent:* noctua, owlet moth.
nocturne [nɔktyrn] **1.** *a.* nocturnal (animal); night (attack, visit); *Bot:* night-flowering; **évasion n.,** escape by night. **2.** *n.m.* (*a*) *Ecc:* nocturn; (*b*) *Art: Mus:* nocturne; (*c*) *Sp:* **match (disputé) en n.,** evening game; (*d*) late evening opening (of shop, etc.). **3.** *n.m.pl. Orn:* night birds (of prey).
nodal, -aux [nɔdal, -o] *a.* nodal (point, line).
nodosité [nɔdozite] *n.f.* **1.** nodosity. **2.** *Bot: Med:* node, nodule.
nodule [nɔdyl] *n.m. Geol: Med: etc:* nodule.
Noé [noe] *Pr.n.m. B.Hist:* Noah.
Noël [nɔɛl] *n.m.* **1.** Christmas; yule(tide); **à la (fête de) N., à N.,** at Christmas (time); **le jour de N.,** Christmas day; **la nuit, la veillée, de N.,** Christmas Eve; **bûche de N.,** yule log; **le Père N.,** Father Christmas. **2.** (*a*) **un n.,** a Christmas carol; (*b*) **(petit) n.,** Christmas present.
Noémi [nɔemi] *Pr.n.f.* Naomi.
nœud [nø] *n.m.* **1.** (*a*) knot; *Nau:* hitch; bend; **n. coulant,** (i) slip knot; (ii) noose; **n. de grappin,** fisherman's bend; **n. droit, plat,** reef knot; **n. de vache,**

carrick bend; **n. de bois,** timber hitch; **corde à nœuds,** knotted rope; **faire, serrer, un n.,** to make, tie, a knot; **faire son n. de cravate,** to knot one's tie; **les nœuds de l'amitié,** the bonds, ties, of friendship; **trancher le n. gordien,** to cut the Gordian knot; (*b*) coil (of snake); (*c*) **le n. de la question,** the crux of the matter; (*d*) *Cost:* bow; **faire un n.,** to tie a bow; **n. papillon,** bow tie; **n. de diamants,** diamond cluster. **2.** node (of orbit, curve, oscillation). **3.** (*a*) knot, knur(l) (in timber); (*b*) node, joint, knot (in bamboo, etc.). **4. n. de voies ferrées,** railway junction. **5.** *Nau. Meas:* knot; **filer, faire, tant de nœuds,** to do so many knots.

noir, noire [nwar] **1.** *a.* black; (*a*) **robe noire,** black dress; **n. comme de l'ébène, comme de l'encre,** as black as ebony, ebony black, inky black, coal black; **n. comme (du) jais,** jet black; **n. comme poix,** pitch-black; **des yeux noirs,** dark eyes; **race noire,** negro race; **rendre qch. n.,** to blacken sth.; **la mer Noire,** the Black Sea; (*b*) dark, swarthy (skin, complexion); *F:* **être tout n. de coups,** to be black and blue; (*c*) dark (night, cell); gloomy (weather, thoughts); grim (irony); dire (poverty); **il faisait n., il faisait nuit noire,** it was pitch-dark; **avoir des idées noires,** to be down in the dumps, have the blues; **être d'une humeur noire,** to be depressed, in a black mood; **ma bête noire,** my pet aversion; *Th:* **four n.,** complete flop; *F:* **série noire,** chapter of accidents, run of bad luck; *adv.* **voir n.,** to see the gloomy side of everything; (*d*) dirty, grimy, black (hands, linen); (*e*) base (ingratitude); wicked (slander); heinous (crime); foul (deed); black (magic); **liste noire,** black list; **le (marché) n.,** the black market; **caisse noire,** bribery fund, slush fund; **il n'est pas aussi diable qu'il est n.,** he's not as black as he's painted; (*f*) *P:* dead drunk. **2.** *n.* black (man, woman); *A:* **traite des Noirs,** slave trade. **3.** *n.m.* black; (*a*) **d'un n. d'ébène,** as black as ebony; **c'était écrit n. sur blanc,** it was there in black and white; **voir tout en n.,** to look at the dark side of everything; **aller du blanc au n.,** to go from one extreme to the other; **ces tableaux ont poussé au n.,** these pictures have darkened (with time); (*b*) black (clothes); **être vêtu (tout) de n., être en n.,** to be dressed (all) in black; (*c*) bull's eye (of target); *F:* **mettre dans le n.,** to hit the mark; (*d*) **avoir des noirs,** to be bruised, black and blue; (*e*) **n. de Chine,** India(n) ink; (*f*) (cup of) black coffee; (*g*) **avoir peur du n., dans le n.,** to be afraid of the dark. **4.** *n.f. Mus:* **noire,** crotchet.

noirâtre [nwarɑtr̥] *a.* blackish, darkish.

noiraud, -aude [nwaro, -od] *a. & n.* swarthy (man, woman).

noirceur [nwarsœr] *n.f.* **1.** blackness (of ink, etc.); darkness, gloominess (of weather, etc.); heinousness, foulness (of crime). **2.** black spot; smudge; smut (on the face, etc.). **3.** base action; dirty trick.

noircir [nwarsir] **1.** *v.i.* to grow, become, turn, black, dark; to darken. **2.** *v.tr.* to blacken; to make (sth.) black; **se n. le visage,** to black one's face; *F:* **n. du papier,** to scribble; **n. la réputation de qn,** to blacken s.o.'s character; **n. la situation,** to paint things blacker than they are. **3. se n.,** to grow black, dark; (*of sky*) to darken, become overcast.

noircissement [nwarsismɑ̃] *n.m.* blackening.

noircissure [nwarsisyr] *n.f.* black spot, smudge.

noise [nwaz] *n.f. only in* **chercher n. à qn,** to try to pick a quarrel with s.o.

noisetier [nwaztje] *n.m.* hazel (tree, bush).

noisette [nwazɛt] *n.f.* **1.** hazel nut; **aller aux noisettes,** to go nutting; *Cu:* **n. de beurre,** knob, nut, of butter. **2. couleur (de) n.,** hazel, nut brown; *a.inv.* **yeux n.,** hazel eyes.

noix [nwa] *n.f.* **1.** walnut; *Cu:* **n. de beurre,** knob, nut, of butter. **2.** nut; (*a*) **n. d'Amérique, du Brésil,** Brazil nut; **n. d'acajou,** cashew nut; **n. vomique,** nux vomica; (*b*) *P:* head, nut; (*c*) *P:* **à la n.,** useless; **excuses à la n. (de coco),** trivial excuses; **travail à la n.,** shocking piece of work; (*d*) *P:* **quelle n.!** what a fool! what a nit! **3.** *Cu:* eye (of cutlet); pope's eye (of leg of mutton).

nom [nɔ̃] *n.m.* **1.** name; **un homme du n. de Pierre,** a man named Peter; **traiter qn de tous les noms,** to call s.o. names; **quelqu'un dont je tairai le n.,** someone who shall be nameless; **je le ferai ou j'y perdrai mon n.,** I'll do it or my name isn't (Jones); **n. de famille,** surname; **n. de baptême,** Christian name; forename; given name; **n. et prénoms,** full name; **n. de jeune fille,** maiden name; **n. de femme mariée, de mariage,** married name; **porter le n. de qn,** to be named, called, after s.o.; **n. de guerre,** assumed name; (journalist's) pen name; **n. de théâtre,** stage name; **voyager sous un faux n.,** to travel under an alias; **on le connaissait sous le n. de Leduc,** he went by the name of Leduc; **appeler les choses par leur n.,** to call a spade a spade; **impolitesse qui n'a pas de n.,** unspeakable rudeness; *F:* **n. de n.! n. d'une pipe! n. d'un chien!** hell! *Com:* **n. déposé,** registered (trade) name; **se faire un grand n.,** to win fame, make a name for oneself; **n'être maître que de n.,** to be master in name only; **ne connaître qn que de n.,** to know s.o. only by name; **au n. de la loi,** in the name of the law; **faire une proposition au n. de qn,** to make a proposal for s.o., on behalf of s.o.; **parler en son n.,** to speak for oneself. **2.** *Gram:* noun.

nomade [nɔmad] **1.** *a.* nomadic, wandering (life, tribe); migratory (game); roving (instinct). **2.** *n.m.pl.* **nomades** (*a*) nomads, wandering tribes; (*b*) gypsies.

nombre [nɔ̃br̥] *n.m.* number. **1.** (*a*) **n. entier,** whole number, integral number, integer; **n. atomique,** atomic number; (*b*) **(bon) n. de, un certain n. de, un assez grand n. de, gens,** a number of, a good many, people; **le plus grand n. est de cet avis,** the majority are of this opinion; **un grand, petit, n. d'entre nous,** many, (a) few, of us; **ils ont vaincu par le n.,** they conquered by force of numbers; **surpasser en n.,** to outnumber; **être en n.,** to have a quorum (at meeting); **sans n.,** countless, numberless; without number; **venez pour faire n.,** come and help make up the numbers; **en n. écrasant,** by an overwhelming majority; **ils sont au n. de huit,** they are eight in number; **être au n., du n., des élus,** to be one of, among, the elect; **mettre, compter, qn au n. de ses intimes,** to number s.o. among one's friends; *B:* **Le Livre des Nombres,** the Book of Numbers. **2.** *Gram:* number.

nombreux, -euse [nɔ̃brø, -øz] *a.* (*a*) numerous; large (family, army, group); **réunion peu nombreuse,** small party; **auditoire peu n.,** thin audience; (*b*) many (members, objects); **pendant de nombreuses générations,** for many generations; **nous sommes peu n.,** there are very few of us.

nombril [nɔ̃bri] *n.m.* (*a*) navel; *F:* **il se prend pour le n. du monde,** he thinks he's God's gift to mankind; (*b*) *Bot:* hilum.

nomenclature [nɔmɑ̃klatyr] *n.f.* **1.** nomenclature. **2.** list; catalogue, *NAm:* catalog; schedule.

nominal, -aux [nɔminal, -o] *a.* nominal; (*a*) **appel n.,** roll call, callover; (*b*) nominal (price, horsepower, authority); *Fin:* **valeur nominale,** face value; *El:* **courant n.,** rated current (of machine).

nominalement [nɔminalmɑ̃] *adv.* nominally.

nominalisme [nɔminalism] *n.m. Phil:* nominalism.

nominatif, -ive [nɔminatif, -iv] **1.** *a.* **état n.,** list of names; nominal roll; *Fin:* **titres nominatifs,** registered securities. **2.** *n.m. Gram:* nominative (case); **au n.,** in the nominative.

nomination [nɔminasjɔ̃] *n.f.* **1.** nomination (for an appointment); **poste à la n. du ministre,** post in the gift of the Minister. **2.** appointment; **recevoir sa n.,** to be appointed; **n. à un grade supérieur,** promotion. **3.** *Sch:* **il a eu deux nominations,** his name appears twice in the honours, *NAm:* honors, list.

nominativement [nɔminativmɑ̃] *adv.* by name.

nommément [nɔmemɑ̃] *adv.* **1.** (*a*) namely; (*b*) especially; in particular. **2. mentionner qn n.,** to mention s.o. by name.

nommer [nɔme] **1.** *v.tr.* (*a*) to name; to give a name to (s.o., sth.); **on le nomma Jean,** they named, called, him John; **on nomme aumôniers les prêtres attachés à un régiment,** priests attached to a regiment are called, styled, chaplains; (*b*) to name, to mention by name; **un homme que je ne nommerai pas,** a man who shall be nameless; **n. un jour,** to appoint a day; **à jour nommé,** on the appointed day; (*c*) to appoint, name (s.o. to an office); to commission (officer); **être nommé au grade supérieur,** to be promoted; **n. qn à un emploi,** to nominate s.o. for a job. **2. se n.** (*a*) to give one's name; (*b*) to be called, named; **comment vous nommez-vous?** what is your name?

non [nɔ̃] *adv.* (*no liaison with a following word*) no; not. **1.** (*a*) **fumez-vous?—n.,** do you smoke?—no(, I don't); **répondre par oui ou n.,** to answer yes or no; **c'est dégoûtant, n.?** isn't it disgusting? **il a commencé comme éboueur—n.!** he started as a dustman—really! **mais n.! dame n.! mon Dieu n.! que n.!** oh dear, no! no indeed! **n. pas!** not so! not at all! **n., je vous en prie,** please don't! **je pense que n.,** I don't think so; I think not; **je dis que n.,** I say no; **faire signe que n.,** to shake one's head; **il est respecté mais n. pas aimé,** he is respected but not loved; **qu'il vienne ou n.,** whether he comes or not; **n. (pas) que je le craigne,** not that I fear him; **n. que je ne vous plaigne,** not that I don't pity you; (*b*) *n.m.inv.* **répondre par un n.,** to answer in the negative; **les n. l'emportent,** the noes have it; **il se fâche pour un oui, pour un n.,** he flares up at the least thing. **2. n. loin de la ville,** not far from the town; **n. sans raison,** not without reason; **n. seulement . . ., mais encore . . .,** not only . . ., but also . . ..

non-activité [nɔnaktivite] *n.f.* non-activity; **mettre en n.-a.,** to suspend (employee); *Mil:* to put (officer) on half pay; **mise en n.-a.,** (i) suspension; (ii) *Mil:* placing (of officer) on halfpay.

nonagénaire [nɔnaʒenɛr] *a. & n.* nonagenarian.

non-agression [nɔnagresjɔ̃, nɔ̃-] *n.f.* non-aggression.

non-aligné [nɔnaliɲe] *a. Pol:* non-aligned, uncommitted; *pl. non-alignés.*

non-alignement [nɔ̃aliɲmɑ̃, nɔn-] *n.m. Pol:* non-alignment.

nonante [nɔnɑ̃t] *num.a. & n.m.inv. Belg: Sw.Fr:* ninety.

non-arrivée [nɔ̃arive, nɔn-] *n.f.* non-arrival.

non-belligérance [nɔ̃beliʒerɑ̃s] *n.f.* non-belligerency.

nonce [nɔ̃s] *n.m.* **n. du Pape,** Papal Nuncio.

nonchalamment [nɔ̃ʃalamɑ̃] *adv.* nonchalantly, unconcernedly, listlessly; **marcher n.,** to saunter along.

nonchalance [nɔ̃ʃalɑ̃s] *n.f.* nonchalance, unconcern, indifference.

nonchalant [nɔ̃ʃalɑ̃] *a.* nonchalant, unconcerned, indifferent.

nonciature [nɔ̃sjatyr] *n.f.* **1.** nunciature. **2.** nuncio's residence.

non-combattant [nɔ̃kɔ̃batɑ̃] *a. & n.m.* non-combatant; *pl. non-combattants.*

non-conformisme [nɔ̃kɔ̃fɔrmism] *n.m.* nonconformity.

non-conformiste [nɔ̃kɔ̃fɔrmist] **1.** *a.* (*a*) *Ecc:* nonconformist; (*b*) unconventional. **2.** *n.* nonconformist; *pl. non-conformistes.*

none [nɔn] *n.f.* **1.** *Rom.Ant:* (*a*) ninth hour (3 p.m.); (*b*) *pl.* nones. **2.** *Ecc:* nones.

non-être [nɔ̃ɛtr̥, nɔnɛtr̥] *n.m. Phil:* non-entity, non-existence.

non-exécution [nɔnɛgzekysjɔ̃] *n.f.* non-fulfilment (of agreement, etc.); non-performance.

non-existant [nɔnɛgzistɑ̃, nɔ̃-] *a.* non-existent; *pl. non-existants.*

non-existence [nɔnɛgzistɑ̃s, nɔ̃-] *n.f.* non-existence.

non-ferreux, -euse [nɔ̃fɛrø, -øz] *a.* non-ferrous; *pl. non-ferreux, -euses.*

non-inscrit [nɔnɛ̃skri] *n.m. Pol:* independent; *pl. non-inscrits.*

non-intervention [nɔnɛ̃tɛrvɑ̃sjɔ̃] *n.f.* non-intervention, non-interference.

non-interventionniste [nɔnɛ̃tɛrvɑ̃sjɔnist] *a. & n.* non-interventionist; *pl. non-interventionnistes.*

non-lieu [nɔ̃ljø] *n.m. Jur:* **ordonnance, arrêt, déclaration, de n.-l.,** nonsuit; *pl. non-lieux.*

non-livraison [nɔ̃livrɛzɔ̃] *n.f.* non-delivery (of goods).

nonne [nɔn] *n.f.* nun.

non-négociable [nɔ̃negɔsjabl̥] *a.* unnegotiable; *pl. non-négociables.*

nonnette [nɔnɛt] *n.f.* **1.** *F:* young nun. **2.** small cake of iced gingerbread. **3.** *Orn:* tit; tomtit.

nonobstant [nɔnɔpstɑ̃] *prep. & adv. A:* notwithstanding; **ce n.,** this notwithstanding.

non-paiement [nɔ̃pɛmɑ̃] *n.m.* non-payment.

nonpareil, -eille [nɔ̃parɛj] **1.** *a.* peerless, matchless (beauty); unparalleled (patience). **2.** *n.f. Typ:* six-point type, nonpareil.

non-pesanteur [nɔ̃pəzɑ̃tœr] *n.f.* weightlessness.

non-présentation [nɔ̃prezɑ̃tasjɔ̃] *n.f.* **n.-p. d'enfant,** concealment of birth.

non-recevoir [nɔ̃r(ə)səvwar] *n.m. Jur:* **opposer une fin de n.-r. à une réclamation,** to put in a plea in bar of a claim; to traverse a claim.

non-récupérable [nɔ̃rekyperabl̥] *a.* expendable, disposable; *pl. non-récupérables.*

non-retour [nɔ̃r(ə)tur] *n.m.* **point de n.-r.,** point of no return.

non-sens [nɔ̃sɑ̃s] *n.m.inv.* **c'est un n.-s.,** it's meaningless, (a) nonsense.

non-syndiqué, -ée [nɔ̃sɛ̃dike] **1.** *a.* non-union (employee). **2.** *n.* non-unionist; *pl. non-syndiqués, -ées.*

non-tarifé [nɔ̃tarife] *a.* duty-free; *pl. non-tarifés.*

non-usage [nɔnyzaʒ, nɔ̃-] *n.m.* disuse; *Jur:* non-user.

non-valable [nɔ̃valabl̥] *a.* **1.** *Jur:* invalid (clause, etc.). **2.** (*of ticket, etc.*) not valid; *pl. non-valables.*

non-valeur [nɔ̃valœr] *n.f.* **1.** (i) bad debt; (ii) unproductive asset; **pour nous c'est une n.-v.,** he's no use, *F:* a dead loss, to us. **2.** unproductiveness; **terres en n.-v.,** unproductive land; *pl. non-valeurs.*

non-violence [nɔ̃vjɔlɑ̃s] *n.f.* non-violence.

nopal, -als [nɔpal] *n.m. Bot:* nopal; cochineal cactus, cochineal fig.

nord [nɔr] *n.m. no pl.* **1.** north; **au n., dans le n.,** in the North; **au n. de Madrid,** (to the) north of Madrid; **borné au n. par la Belgique,** bounded on the north by Belgium; **maison exposée au n.,** house facing north; **voyager vers le n.,** to travel north-(ward(s)); **du n.,** of the north; from the north; northern (province); northerly, north (wind); **la mer du N.,** the North Sea; **l'Amérique du N.,** North America; **l'Irlande du N.,** Northern Ireland; **le grand N.,** the frozen North; *F:* **perdre le n.,** (i) to lose one's bearings; (ii) to lose one's head. **2.** *Nau:* **le n.,** the north wind. **3.** *a.inv.* north; **le Pôle N.,** the North Pole.

nord-africain, -aine [nɔrafrikɛ̃, -ɛn] *a. & n.* North African; *pl. nord-africains, -aines.*

nord-américain, -aine [nɔramerikɛ̃, -ɛn] *a. & n.* North American; *pl. nord-américains, -aines.*

nord-est [nɔr(d)ɛst] *n.m.* **1.** north-east. **2.** north-east wind, north-easter; *F:* nor'easter.

nordique [nɔrdik] **1.** *a.* Norse; Nordic. **2.** *n.m.* Norse (language).

nordir [nɔrdir] *v.i. Nau:* (*of the wind*) to veer north(ward).

nordiste [nɔrdist] **1.** *a. & n.m. U.S.Hist.* northerner. **2.** *a. Sp:* northern (club).

nord-nord-est [nɔrnɔr(d)ɛst] *n.m. & a.inv.* north-north-east.

nord-nord-ouest [nɔrnɔr(d)wɛst] *n.m. & a.inv.* north-north-west.

nord-ouest [nɔr(d)wɛst] *n.m.* **1.** north-west. **2.** north-west wind, north-wester; *F:* nor'wester.

noria [nɔrja] *n.f.* **1.** chainpump, bucketchain, noria. **2.** bucket conveyor.

normal, -aux [nɔrmal, -o] **1.** *a.* (*a*) normal (state, course, speed); **c'est tout à fait n. que la jeunesse se rebelle,** it's only natural for youth to rebel; **école normale,** college of education; **École normale supérieure,** *n.f. F:* **Normale,** college (of university level) preparing for the higher posts in teaching and other professions; (*b*) standard; **poids n.,** standard weight; **échantillon n.,** average sample; **aux cotes normales,** of normal dimensions; **vitesse normale,** rated speed. **2.** *n.f.* **la normale,** the normal; *Golf:* **la normale du parcours,** par for the course.

normalement [nɔrmalmɑ̃] *adv.* normally; in the ordinary course (of things).

normalien, -ienne [nɔrmaljɛ̃, -jɛn] *n.* student, former student, (i) of a college of education, (ii) of the *École normale supérieure*.

normaliser [nɔrmalize] *v.tr.* to normalize; to standardize.

normalité [nɔrmalite] *n.f.* normality.

normand, -ande [nɔrmɑ̃, -ɑ̃d] *a. & n.* **1.** Norman; of Normandy; *F:* **réponse normande,** non-committal, equivocal, evasive, answer; **c'est un fin N.,** he's shrewd; **à N. N. et demi,** set a thief to catch a thief. **2.** *Hist:* (*a*) **les Normands,** the Norsemen; (*b*) **la conquête normande,** the Norman conquest.

Normandie [nɔrmɑ̃di] *Pr.n.f. Geog:* Normandy.

norme [nɔrm] *n.f.* **1.** norm, standard; **n. de conduite,** rule of conduct; **qui échappe à la n.,** abnormal. **2.** *Ind: Com:* standard; (standard) specification.

norois, noroît [nɔrwa] *n.m.* north-west wind, north-wester, *F:* nor'wester.

Norvège [nɔrvɛʒ] *Pr.n.f. Geog:* Norway.

norvégien, -ienne [nɔrveʒjɛ̃, -jɛn] **1.** *a. & n.* Norwegian. **2.** *n.m. Ling:* Norwegian. **3.** *n.f.* **norvégienne,** round-stemmed rowing-boat.

nos [no] *see* NOTRE.

nostalgie [nɔstalʒi] *n.f.* nostalgia; homesickness; **avoir la n. du foyer,** to pine, long, yearn, for home; to be homesick.

nostalgique [nɔstalʒik] *a.* (*a*) nostalgic (memories, feelings); (*b*) homesick (person); (*c*) *n.* nostalgic person.

nostalgiquement [nɔstalʒikmɑ̃] *adv.* nostalgically.

nota [nɔta] *n.m.inv.* marginal note, footnote; **n. bene, N.B.** [nɔtabene], please note; nota bene.

notabilité [nɔtabilite] *n.f.* notability; person of distinction.

notable [nɔtabl̩] **1.** *a.* notable; worthy of note, considerable; **sans variation n.,** without appreciable change. **2.** *a. & n.* eminent, distinguished (person); person of distinction; **les notables de la ville,** the leading citizens.

notablement [nɔtabləmɑ̃] *adv.* notably; appreciably.

notaire [nɔtɛr] *n.m.* **1.** *Jur:* notary; *Scot:* notary public; **par-devant n.,** before a notary. **2.** *Ecc:* **n. apostolique,** apostolical notary.

notamment [nɔtamɑ̃] *adv.* notably; more particularly; especially, in particular.

notarié [nɔtarje] *a. Jur:* **acte n.,** deed executed by a notary.

notation [nɔtasjɔ̃] *n.f.* (*a*) notation; (*b*) *Sch:* marking (of work).

note [nɔt] *n.f.* **1.** (*a*) note; memorandum, memo, minute; **n. d'avis,** advice note; **prendre des notes,** to take (down) notes; **jeter quelques notes sur le papier,** to jot down a few notes; **s'aider de notes dans un discours,** to speak from notes; **prendre n. de qch., prendre qch. en n.,** to note sth.; to make a note of sth.; **prendre bonne n. de qch.,** to take due note of sth.; **n. diplomatique,** diplomatic note; *Const:* **n. de cubage,** statement of measurement; (*b*) annotation; **n. en, au, bas de la page,** footnote. **2.** *Sch: etc:* mark; **bonne, mauvaise, n.,** good, bad, mark; **notes trimestrielles,** (end-of-term) report. **3.** *Mus:* note; **fausse n.,** (i) wrong note; (ii) *Fig:* contretemps, jarring note; **donner la n.,** (i) to sound the keynote (to singers, etc.); (ii) *Fig:* to call the tune; **chanter sur une autre n., changer de n.,** to change one's tune; **forcer la n.,** (i) to exaggerate; (ii) to overdo it; **sa robe n'était pas dans la n.,** her dress didn't suit the occasion, struck the wrong note; **une n. d'originalité,** a touch, note, of originality. **4. un homme de n.,** a man of note. **5.** invoice; (*in hotel, etc.*) bill, *NAm:* check.

noté [nɔte] *a.* **homme mal n.,** man of bad reputation; (*of civil servant*) **être bien, mal, n.,** to have a good, bad, record.

noter [nɔte] *v.tr.* **1.** to note; to take notice of (sth.); **chose à n.,** thing worthy of notice; **notez bien cela,** take good note of this; **cela est à n.,** this is worth noting, remembering; **notez bien ce que je vous dis,** mark my words; **avez-vous noté l'heure?** did you note, notice, the time? **2.** (*a*) to put down, jot down (sth.); to take, make, a note of (sth.); **n. la consommation de combustible,** to keep track of the fuel consumption; (*b*) **n. un passage d'un trait,** to mark a passage; (*c*) *Sch:* to mark (work).

notice [nɔtis] *n.f.* **1.** notice, account. **2.** review (of book, etc.). **3.** book(let), handbook, manual; instructions, directions; **n. d'emploi,** directions for use; **n. publicitaire,** (i) advertising brochure; (ii) advertisement (in newspaper).

notification [nɔtifikasjɔ̃] *n.f. Jur:* notification, notice; **recevoir n. de qch.,** to be notified of sth.

notifier [nɔtifje] *v.tr.* (*impf. & pr.sub.* **n. notifiions**) **n. qch. à qn,** to notify s.o. of sth.; **n. son consentement,** to signify one's consent; **on lui notifia qu'il eût à déménager dans les vingt-quatre heures,** he received notice to quit within twenty-four hours.

notion [nosjɔ̃] *n.f.* notion, idea; **perdre la n. du temps, de la réalité,** to lose count of time, all sense of reality; **il a des notions de chimie,** he has a smattering of chemistry.

notoire [nɔtwar] *a.* well known (fact, public figure); notorious (criminal); **son avarice est n.,** his miserliness is notorious.

notoirement [nɔtwarmɑ̃] *adv.* (*a*) manifestly; (*b*) notoriously.

notoriété [nɔtɔrjete] *n.f.* **1.** notoriety (of fact); reputation (of person); **avoir de la n.,** to be well known, to have a (good or bad) reputation. **2.** *Jur:* **acte de n.,** attested affidavit.

notre, nos [nɔtr̥, no] *poss.a.* our; **nos père et mère,** our father and mother; **n. meilleur ami,** our best friend.

nôtre [notr̥] **1.** *poss.a.* ours; **sa maison est n.,** his house is ours. **2. le n., la n., les nôtres** (*a*) *poss.pron.* ours, our own; **il préfère vos tableaux aux nôtres,** he prefers your pictures to ours; (*b*) *n.m.* (i) **le n.,** our own, what is ours; **il faut y mettre du n.,** we shall have to make our own contribution; (ii) **les nôtres,** our own (friends, folk, etc.); **est-il des nôtres?** is he one of us? **vous serez des nôtres, n'est-ce pas?** you will join us, won't you?

Notre-Dame [nɔtrədam] *n.f. Ecc:* Our Lady; **la fête de N.-D.,** the feast of the Assumption.

nouba [nuba] *n.f.* **1.** Algerian military band. **2.** *P:* **faire la n.,** to paint the town red.

noue¹ [nu] *n.f.* marshy meadow, water meadow.

noue² *n.f. Const:* (*a*) valley (of roof); (*b*) gutter lead, flashing.

nouer [nwe] **1.** *v.tr.* (*a*) to tie, knot; **n. qch. serré,** to knot sth. tightly, to make a tight knot; **n. ses cheveux, se n. les cheveux,** to tie up one's hair; **n. qch. dans qch.,** to tie up, fasten, sth. in sth.; (*b*) *Needlew:* **point noué,** lock stitch (on machine); (*c*) **avoir la gorge nouée,** to have a lump in one's throat; (*d*) **n. conversation avec qn,** to enter into conversation with s.o.; **n. des relations avec qn,** to establish relations with s.o.; (*e*) **n. l'intrigue d'un roman,** to weave the plot of a novel; **pièce bien nouée,** well knit play. **2.** *v.i. Hort:* (*of blossom*) to set. **3. se n.** (*a*) (*of cord, thread*) to become knotted; to kink; (*b*) **se n. à qch.,** to fasten on, cling, to sth.; (*c*) *Hort:* (*of blossom*) to set.

noueux, -euse [nwø, -øz] *a.* knotty (string, wood); gnarled (stem, hands).

nougat [nuga] *n.m.* nougat.

nouille [nuj] *n.f.* **1.** *pl. Cu:* (ribbon) noodles. **2.** *F:* idiot; **c'est une n.,** he's a drip, a wet.

nounou [nunu] *n.f. F:* (*child's language*) nanny.

nounours [nunurs] *n.m.* (*child's language*) teddy (bear).

nourri [nuri] *a.* **1.** nourished, fed; **bien n.,** well fed; **mal n.,** undernourished, underfed. **2.** rich, copious (style); broad, firm (line in drawing); full (tone, sound); sustained (applause); **discussion nourrie,** heated debate, lively discussion; *Mil:* **feu n.,** brisk, well sustained, fire.

nourrice [nuris] *n.f.* **1.** (wet) nurse; **n. sèche,** dry nurse; **conte de n.,** nursery tale; **la mémoire est la n. du génie,** genius is fostered by memory. **2. mettre un enfant en n.,** to put out a child to nurse; **mise en n.,** fosterage; **enfant changé en n.,** changeling. **3.** *Tchn:* (*a*) auxiliary tank, service tank; (*b*) *Aut:* spare can (of petrol, *NAm:* gasoline).

nourricier, -ière [nurisje, -jɛr] **1.** *a.* nutritious, nutritive (juices, etc.). **2.** *n.m.* **(père) n.,** foster father; *n.f.* **(mère) nourricière,** foster mother.

nourrir [nurir] **1.** *v.tr.* to nourish; (*a*) to suckle, nurse (infant); **nourri au biberon,** bottle-fed; (*b*) to bring up, nurture, rear (children, etc.); **nourri dans la misère,** reared in poverty; (*c*) to feed (people, animals, the fire) **(de, avec,** with, on); **n. sa famille,** to maintain, keep, one's family; **n. des employés, des élèves,** to board workers, pupils; **travail qui nourrit son homme,** job that provides a living; **avoir tant par mois logé et nourri,** to get so much a month with board and lodging; **le lait nourrit,** milk is nourishing; **lectures qui nourrissent l'esprit,** reading that improves, feeds, the mind; (*d*) *Mus:* **n. le son,** to give fullness, body, to the tone; (*e*) to foster (hatred); to harbour, *NAm:* harbor (thoughts); to cherish, harbour, entertain (hope). **2. se n. de lait,** to live, subsist, on milk; **se n. de rien,** to eat next to nothing.

nourrissage [nurisaʒ] *n.m.* rearing, feeding (of cattle).

nourrissant [nurisɑ̃] *a.* nourishing, nutritive, nutritious; satisfying; substantial (food).

nourrisseur [nurisœr] *n.m.* **1.** (*a*) stockbreeder; (*b*) dairyman. **2.** feed roll (of various machines).

nourrisson [nurisɔ̃] *n.m.* **1.** baby at the breast; infant. **2.** nurs(e)ling.

nourriture [nurityr] *n.f.* **1.** *A:* feeding, suckling (of infant). **2.** food, nourishment; **priver qn de n.,** to starve s.o.; **n. de l'esprit,** food for the mind. **3.** board, keep; **il ne gagne pas sa n.,** he isn't worth his keep.

nous [nu] *pers.pron.* **1.** (*a*) (*subject*) we; (*b*) (*object*) us; to us; **il ne n. connaît pas,** he does not know us; **lisez-le-n.,** read it to us; **il n. en a parlé,** he spoke to us about it; (*c*) (*reflexive*) **n. n. chauffons,** we are warming ourselves; **n. n. sommes donné un bon dîner,** we gave ourselves a good dinner; **n. n. battions avec l'ennemi,** we were fighting the enemy; (*d*) (*reciprocal*) **n. n. connaissons,** we know each other. **2. n. deux, n. tous,** (i) we two, we all; both of us, all of us; (ii) us two, us all; all of us; **c'est n. qui sommes fautifs,** it is we who are to blame; **n. autres Anglais,** we English; **un ami à n.,** a friend of ours; **ce livre est à n.,** that book is ours, belongs to us; **c'est à n. de jouer,** it is our turn to play; **il était avec n.,** he was with us; **entre n. soit dit,** this is between ourselves. **3.** (*royal, editorial, we, with concords in the singular*) **n. sommes désolé de l'apprendre,** we are grieved to hear it.

nous-même(s) [numɛm] *pers.pron.* **1.** *pl.* **nous-mêmes,** ourselves; **nous l'avons fait nous-mêmes,** we did it ourselves. **2.** (*following royal, editorial, we*) **nous-même,** ourself; *see* MÊME 1 (*c*).

nouveau, -el, -elle¹, -eaux [nuvo, -ɛl] *a.* **(nouvel** *is used before m. sing. nouns beginning with a vowel or h mute*) new. **1.** (*a*) (*usu. follows noun*) **les voitures nouvelles,** new(-model) cars; **livres nouveaux,** new books, publications; **manteau n.,** coat of a new cut; **du vin n.,** new, young, wine; **l'herbe nouvelle,** young grass; **je suis n. aux affaires, dans ce métier,** I'm new to, inexperienced in, business, this trade; (*b*) **il n'y a rien de n.,** there's nothing new, no new developments; there's no news; *n.m.* **j'ai appris du n.,** I've heard something new; **c'est du n.,** that's news to me. **2.** (*usu. precedes noun*) fresh, another; **un n. chapitre,** a new, fresh, chapter; **une nouvelle raison,** a further, additional, reason; **jusqu'à nouvel ordre,** until further notice; **la nouvelle génération,** the new, rising, generation; **le nouvel an,** the new year; **la nouvelle lune,** the new moon; **vêtu à la nouvelle mode,** dressed in the latest fashion; **acheter une nouvelle voiture,** to buy a new, another, car; **il met tous les jours une nouvelle chemise,** he wears a different shirt every day; *n.m.pl.* **les nouveaux,** the newcomers; *Sch:* the new pupils, students. **3.** (*with adv. function*) **le nouvel arrivé, les nouveaux arrivés,** the newcomer(s); **les nouveaux pauvres,** the new poor; **les nouveaux convertis,** the new converts; **des œufs n. pondus,** new-laid eggs. **4. à n.,** (once) again; *Book-k:* **solde à n.,** balance brought forward; **de n.,** (over) again; afresh.

nouveau-né, -née [nuvone] *a.* & *n.* new-born (child); *pl. nouveau-nés, -nées.*

nouveauté [nuvote] *n.f.* **1.** newness, novelty. **2.** change, innovation; **voilà une n. de sa part!** that's a change, something new, for him! **3.** new invention, new publication, etc. **4.** *pl.* (*a*) fancy articles, fancy goods; **magasin de nouveautés,** draper's shop, *NAm:* dry goods store; (*b*) **les nouveautés de printemps,** the spring fashions.

nouvelle² [nuvɛl] *n.f.* **1.** (*a*) (piece of) news; **bonne, mauvaise, n.,** good, bad, news; **en voilà la première n.,** that's the first I've heard of it; **quelles nouvelles?** what is the news? *Journ:* **dernières nouvelles,** late news; **nouvelles de l'intérieur,** home news; (*b*) *pl.* news (of, about, s.o.); **demander, (aller) prendre, des nouvelles de (la santé de) qn,** to inquire, ask, about s.o.('s health); **envoyez-moi de vos nouvelles,** let me hear from you; **on n'eut plus jamais de ses nouvelles,** he was never heard of again; **goûtez cela, vous m'en direz des nouvelles,** taste this! I'm sure you'll like it; **vous aurez de mes nouvelles!** I'll give you something to think about! *Prov:* **pas de nouvelles, bonnes nouvelles,** no news is good news. **2.** *Lit:* short story.

Nouvelle-Angleterre [nuvɛlɑ̃glətɛr] *Pr.n.f. Geog:* New England.

Nouvelle-Calédonie [nuvɛlkaledɔni] *Pr.n.f. Geog:* New Caledonia.

Nouvelle-Écosse [nuvɛlekɔs] *Pr.n.f. Geog:* Nova Scotia.

Nouvelle-Galles du Sud [nuvɛlgaldysyd] *Pr.n.f. Geog:* New South Wales.

Nouvelles-Guinée [nuvɛlgine] *Pr.n.f. Geog:* New Guinea.

nouvellement [nuvɛlmɑ̃] *adv.* newly, lately, recently.

Nouvelle-Orléans [nuvɛlɔrleɑ̃] *Pr.n.f. Geog:* New Orleans.

Nouvelles-Hébrides [nuvɛlzebrid] *Pr.n.f. pl. Geog:* the New Hebrides.

Nouvelle-Zélande [nuvelzelɑ̃d] *Pr.n.f. Geog:* New Zealand.

nouvelliste [nuvelist] *n.* short-story writer.

nova [nɔva] *n.f. Astr:* nova; *pl. novæ.*

novateur, -trice [nɔvatœr, -tris] **1.** *a.* innovating. **2.** *n.* innovator.

novembre [nɔvɑ̃br̥] *n.f.* November; **en n.,** in November; **au mois de n.,** in the month of November; **le premier n.,** (on) the first of November, (on) November the first.

novice [nɔvis] **1.** *n.* novice (in convent); probationer (in profession); tiro, tyro; beginner; *Scout:* tenderfoot; *Nau:* **n. au commerce,** apprentice to the merchant service; ordinary seaman. **2.** *a.* **être n. à, dans, qch.,** to be new to sth., inexperienced in sth.

noviciat [nɔvisja] *n.m.* **1.** noviciate (of nun, monk). **2.** novices' quarters; noviciate.

noyade [nwajad] *n.f.* **1.** drowning (fatality). **2.** *Fr. Hist:* execution by drowning.

noyau, -aux [nwajo] *n.m.* **1.** stone (of fruit); kernel; **n. de cerise,** cherry stone, pit; **fruit à n.,** stone fruit; **enlever le n. d'un fruit,** to stone a fruit. **2.** nucleus (of atom, cell, comet, colony); core (of the earth); **n. de bombe nucléaire,** (nuclear) bomb core; *F:* **un petit n. de joueurs,** a small knot of players; *Pol:* **n. communiste,** communist cell; **le n. de la résistance,** the hard core of resistance. **3.** (*a*) newel (of stairs); **escalier à n. plein,** winding stair; (*b*) *El:* core (of armature); (*c*) *Metall:* core (of mould, *NAm:* mold); (*d*) **n. volcanique,** volcanic bomb.

noyautage [nwajotaʒ] *n.m. Pol:* infiltration.

noyauter [nwajote] *v.tr. Pol:* to infiltrate; to set up cells in (trade union, etc.).

noyé [nwaje] *a.* **1.** (i) drowned; (ii) drowning; *n.* **secours aux noyés,** first aid for the drowning. **2.** (*a*) **roche noyée,** sunken rock; (*b*) **yeux noyés,** swimming eyes.

noyer¹ [nwaje] *n.m.* walnut (tree, wood); **n. (blanc) d'Amérique,** hickory.

noyer² *v.* **(je noie, n. noyons; je noierai) 1.** *v.tr.* (*a*) to drown (s.o.); to swamp, inundate, deluge (the earth, etc.); **yeux noyés de larmes,** eyes brimming with tears; **noyé dans la foule,** lost in the crowd; **n. son chagrin dans le vin,** to drown one's sorrows in drink; **n. son vin, la sauce,** to put too much water into, to drown, one's wine; to make the sauce too thin; (*b*) to flood (bunker, carburettor); (*c*) to sink (sth.) in cement; (*d*) to countersink (screw); to drive (nail) in flush; (*e*) **n. le poisson,** (i) to play the fish; (ii) *F:* to tire out one's opponent. **2. se n.,** to drown oneself; (*as an accident*) to be drowned; **il se noierait dans un verre d'eau,** he makes a mountain out of a molehill; **se n. dans les détails,** to get bogged down in details; **se n. dans le vin,** to soak oneself in drink.

nu [ny] **1.** *a.* (*a*) naked (person); bare (shoulders, limbs, wire); *Art:* nude (figure); **mettez-vous torse nu,** strip to the waist; **elles se baignent toutes nues,** they bathe in the nude; **nu comme la main, comme un ver,** stark naked; in the buff; NOTE: **nu** *before the noun that it qualifies is invariable and is joined to the noun by a hyphen;* **aller tête nue, pieds nus, aller nu-tête, nu-pieds,** to go bareheaded, barefooted; **visible à l'œil nu,** visible to the naked eye; (*b*) uncovered, undisguised; naked (sword); **la vérité nue,** the plain, naked, truth; **châssis nu,** stripped chassis; *El:* **fil nu,** open wire; (*c*) bare (country, tree, room). **2.** *n.m. Art:* (the) nude; **des nus,** studies from the nude; nudes; **poser pour le nu,** to sit in the nude. **3. à nu,** bare, naked; **mettre à nu,** to lay bare, expose, uncover (sth.); to clear (land); to strip (tree, wire); to lay bare (one's heart); **monter un cheval à nu,** to ride a horse bareback.

nuage [nɥaʒ] *n.m.* (*a*) cloud; **n. en queue de vache,** cirrus, mare's tail; **nuages pommelés,** mackerel sky; **ciel couvert de nuages,** overcast sky; **sans nuages,** cloudless (sky); unclouded (life, future); **bonheur sans nuages,** perfect bliss; **n. de poussière, de fumée,** cloud of dust, of smoke; **n. artificiel,** smoke screen; (*b*) gloom, shadow; **un n. de tristesse assombrissait son front,** her face was clouded with sadness; (*c*) **se perdre dans les nuages,** to have one's head in the clouds; to daydream; (*d*) dash, tiny drop (of milk in a cup of tea).

nuageux, -euse [nɥaʒø, -øz] *a.* (*a*) cloudy (weather); overcast (sky); clouded over; (*b*) hazy (thought, ideas).

nuance [nɥɑ̃s] *n.f.* (*a*) shade (of colour, *NAm:* color); hue; *Mus:* **il joue sans nuances,** he plays without any light and shade; (*b*) gradation, slight difference, shade (in meaning, tone); **une n. d'amertume, de mépris,** a touch, tinge, suggestion, of bitterness, contempt; **je ne saisis pas la n.,** I don't quite see the difference.

nuancer [nɥɑ̃se] *v.tr.* **(je nuançai(s); n. nuançons) 1.** to blend, shade (colours, *NAm:* colors) **(de,** with). **2.** to vary (tone, etc.); to moderate (refusal); *Mus:* **n. son jeu,** to introduce light and shade into one's playing.

nuancier [nɥɑ̃sje] *n.m. Com:* sample card, chart (of colour, *NAm:* color, range).

nubile [nybil] *a.* marriageable, nubile; **âge n.,** age of consent.

nubilité [nybilite] *n.f.* nubility; marriageable age.

nucléaire [nykleɛr] *a. Biol: Ph:* nuclear.

nucléé [nyklee] *a. Biol: etc:* nucleate(d) (cell, etc.).

nucléique [nykleik] *a.* nucleic (acid).

nucléole [nykleɔl] *n.m. Biol:* nucleolus.

nucléon [nykleɔ̃] *n.m. Ph:* nucleon.

nucléonique [nykleɔnik] *Ph:* **1.** *a.* nucleonic. **2.** *n.f.* nucleonics.

nucléus [nykleys] *n.m.* nucleus.

nudisme [nydism] *n.m.* nudism.

nudiste [nydist] *n.* nudist.

nudité [nydite] *n.f.* **1.** (*a*) nudity, nakedness; (*b*) bareness (of rock, wall). **2.** *Art:* nude; nude figure.

nue [ny] *n.f.* (*a*) *A: & Lit:* high cloud(s); (*b*) *pl.* skies; *F:* **porter, élever, qn, qch., aux nues,** to laud, praise, s.o., sth., to the skies; **se perdre dans les nues,** to be lost in the clouds, in daydreams; **tomber des nues,** to be thunderstruck.

nuée [nɥe] *n.f.* (*a*) *Lit:* (large) cloud, storm cloud; (*b*) **n. ardente,** incandescent ash cloud (above volcano); (*c*) cloud (of insects); host (of enemies).

nuire [nɥir] *v.ind.tr.* (*pr.p.* **nuisant;** *p.p.* **nui;** *pr.ind.* **je nuis, n. nuisons;** *pr.sub.* **je nuise;** *p.h.* **je nuisis;** *fu.* **je nuirai) n. à qn, à qch.,** to be harmful, injurious, prejudicial, to s.o., to sth.; to harm s.o., sth.; **cela ne nuira en rien,** that will do no harm; **cela nuira à sa réputation,** it will injure his reputation; **n. aux intérêts de qn,** to prejudice s.o.'s interests; *Jur:* **dans l'intention de n.,** maliciously.

nuisance [nɥizɑ̃s] *n.f.* (cause of) nuisance, harm; harmful effect.

nuisibilité [nɥizibilite] *n.f.* harmfulness, injuriousness, noxiousness.

nuisible [nɥizibl̥] *a.* harmful, hurtful (**à,** to); **plantes nuisibles,** noxious plants; **animaux nuisibles,** vermin.

nuisiblement [nɥizibləmɑ̃] *adv.* harmfully, injuriously.

nuit [nɥi] *n.f.* (*a*) night; **la n. dernière,** last night; **cette n.,** (i) tonight; (ii) last night; **veiller jusqu'à une heure avancée de la n.,** to sit up far into the night; **passer la n. à faire qch.,** to sit up all night doing sth.; *F:* **on a passé la n. à faire la fête,** we made a night of it; **passer la n. chez des amis,** to stay overnight with friends; **bonne n.!** good night! **le bateau de n.,** the night boat; **vêtements de n.,** nightwear; *Com:* slumberwear; **oiseau de n.,** nightbird; *Art:* **effet de n.,** night effect, night piece; **voyager de n., la n.,** to travel by night, at night; **être de n.,** to be on night shift, night duty; **n. et jour** [nɥiteʒur], night and day; **je n'ai pas dormi de la n.,** I never slept a wink all night; (*b*) darkness; **il commence à faire n., il se fait n.,** night is falling; it is growing, getting, dark; **il fait déjà n.,** it is dark already; **à la n. tombante,** at nightfall, at dusk; **après la tombée de la n., à (la) n. close,** after dark; *Prov:* **la n. tous les chats sont gris,** by night all cats are grey; **la n. de l'ignorance,** the darkness of ignorance; **perdu dans la n. des temps,** lost in the mists of time.

nuitamment [nɥitamɑ̃] *adv.* by night.

nuitée [nɥite] *n.f.* overnight stay (in hotel, etc.).

nul, nulle [nyl] **1.** (*with* **ne** *expressed or understood*) (*a*) *indef. a.* no, not one; **n. espoir,** no hope; **il n'a nulle cause de se plaindre,** he has no reason to complain; **sans nulle vanité,** without any conceit; (*b*) *indef.pron.m.* no one, nobody; **n. que moi ne le sait,** none but I knows of it. **2.** *a.* (*following noun*) (*a*) worthless (argument, effort); empty (mind); **homme n.,** man of no account, nonentity; (*b*) *Jur:* **n. et de n. effet, n. et sans effet, n. et non avenu,** invalid, null and void; **bulletin (de vote) n.,** spoilt paper; *Sp:* **course, manche, nulle,** dead heat; **faire match n.,** to draw a game; **partie nulle,** drawn game, draw; (*c*) non-existent (funds, etc.); nil; **le solde est n.,** the balance is nil; *Mec:* **tension nulle,** zero tension.

nullard, -arde [nylar, -ard] *a. & n. P:* useless, hopeless (person); dud.

nullement [nylmɑ̃] *adv.* (*with* **ne** *expressed or understood*) not at all, by no means; **nous ne sommes n. surpris,** we are not in the least surprised; **il n'est n. sot,** he is by no means a fool.

nullification [nylifikasjɔ̃] *n.f.* nullification.

nullifier [nylifje] *v.tr.* (*impf. & pr.sub.* **n. nullifiions, v. nullifiiez)** to nullify, neutralize (effort, etc.).

nullité [nylite] *n.f.* **1.** nullity, invalidity (of deed, marriage, etc.); **frapper une clause de n.,** to render a clause void. **2.** incompetence; incapacity. **3.** nonentity; nobody.

nûment [nymɑ̃] *adv.* frankly, without embellishments.

numéraire [nymerɛr] **1.** *a.* (*of coins*) legal; **valeur n.,** legal-tender value. **2.** *n.m.* metallic currency, specie, current coin; **payer en n.,** to pay in cash.

numéral, -aux [nymeral, -o] *a. & n.m.* numeral.

numérateur [nymeratœr] *n.m. Mth:* numerator.

numération [nymerasjɔ̃] *n.f.* **1.** *Mth:* numeration; notation. **2. n. globulaire,** blood count.

numérique [nymerik] *a.* (*a*) numerical (value, superiority, etc.); (*b*) *Cmptr:* digital (computer, data).

numériquement [nymerikmɑ̃] *adv.* numerically.

numéro [nymero] *n.m.* number; (*a*) **n. d'ordre,** running number, serial number; **tirer un bon n.,** (i) to draw a lucky, winning, number; (ii) to have a stroke of luck; **j'habite au n. 10,** I live at number 10; **la chambre n. 20,** room number 20; *F:* **priorité n. un,** number one priority; **tenue n. un,** best clothes; **n. d'appel,** telephone number; (*b*) number, issue (of periodical); **n. du jour, de la semaine, du mois; dernier n.,** current issue, number; **ancien n., n. déjà paru,** back issue, number; **vente au n.,** single copies sold; (*c*) number (of sewing cotton, etc.); count (of yarn); size (in stock sizes); (*d*) *Th:* number, turn (on the programme); *F:* **il aime faire son petit n.,** he likes doing his little act; (*e*) (*of pers.*) **quel n.!** what a character!

numérotage [nymerɔtaʒ] *n.m.*, **numérotation** [nymerɔtasjɔ̃] *n.f.* numbering (of houses, etc.); paging (of book).

numéroter [nymerɔte] *v.tr.* to number (houses, etc.); to page, paginate (book); *Mil:* **numérotez-vous (à partir de la droite)!** (from the right) number!

numéroteur [nymerɔtœr] *n.m.* numbering machine, numbering stamp.

numismate [nymismat] *n.* numismatist.

numismatique [nymismatik] **1.** *a.* numismatic. **2.** *n.f.* numismatics, numismatology.

nummulaire [nymylɛr] *n.f. Bot:* moneywort.

nuptial, -iaux [nypsjal, -jo] *a.* nuptial; bridal; **anneau n.,** wedding ring; **vol n.,** nuptial flight (of bees).

nuptialité [nypsjalite] *n.f.* marriage rate.

nuque [nyk] *n.f.* nape of the neck; **saisir qn par la n.,** to catch hold of s.o. by the scruff of the neck.

nurse [nœrs] *n.f.* nanny, (children's) nurse.

nutation [nytasjɔ̃] *n.f.* nutation.

nutritif, -ive [nytritif, -iv] *a.* nutritive; nourishing (food); **valeur nutritive,** food value.

nutrition [nytrisjɔ̃] *n.f.* nutrition.

nutritionniste [nytrisjɔnist] *n.* nutritionist, dietician, dietitian.

nyctalope [niktalɔp] *a.* hemeralopic; day-blind; **oiseau n.,** bird that sees best in the dark.

nylon [nilɔ̃] *n.m. R.t.m:* nylon; **bas (de) n.,** nylon stockings, nylons.

nymphe [nɛ̃f] *n.f.* **1.** *Myth:* nymph. **2.** *Ent:* nymph, pupa, chrysalis.

nymphéa [nɛ̃fea] *n.m.* nymphea, white water lily.

nymphomane [nɛ̃fɔman] *n.f. Med:* nymphomaniac.

nymphomanie [nɛ̃fɔmani] *n.f. Med:* nymphomania.

O

O, o [o] *n.m.* (the letter) O, o.
ô [o] *int. Poet: etc:* O!
oasien, -ienne [ɔazjɛ̃, -jɛn] **1.** *a.* oasis (vegetation, etc.). **2.** *n.* oasis dweller.
oasis [ɔazis] *n.f. occ.m.* oasis.
obédience [ɔbedjɑ̃s] *n.f.* (*a*) *R.C.Ch:* obedience; (*b*) **musulman de stricte o.,** strict Moslem; **pays d'o. communiste,** countries of the Communist obedience.
obéir [ɔbeir] *v.ind.tr.* to obey; (*a*) **o. à qn,** to obey s.o.; to be obedient to s.o.; **o. à qn au doigt et à l'œil,** to be at s.o.'s beck and call; *v.tr.* **faire o. la loi,** to enforce obedience to the law; **il est obéi,** he is obeyed; (*b*) **o. à qch.,** to yield, submit, to sth.; **o. à un ordre,** to obey, comply with, an order; **o. à la force,** to yield to force; *Nau:* **o. à la barre,** to answer the helm; *Av:* **o. aux gouvernes,** to respond to the controls.
obéissance [ɔbeisɑ̃s] *n.f.* (*a*) obedience (**à,** to); **refus d'o.,** insubordination; (*b*) dutifulness (to parents); submission (to lawful authority); allegiance (to king); **devoir o. à qn,** to owe s.o. obedience, allegiance; **jurer o. au roi,** to swear allegiance to the king.
obéissant [ɔbeisɑ̃] *a.* obedient, dutiful (child); docile, biddable; submissive.
obèle [ɔbɛl] *n.m. Typ: Pal:* obelus, obelisk.
obélisque [ɔbelisk] *n.m. Arch:* obelisk; **l'o. de Cléopâtre,** Cleopatra's Needle.
obérer [ɔbere] *v.tr.* **(j'obère; j'obérerai)** to involve (s.o.) in debt; to burden with debt; **finances fort obérées,** heavily encumbered finances.
obèse [ɔbɛz] *a.* & *n.* obese, fat, corpulent (person).
obésité [ɔbezite] *n.f.* obesity, corpulence.
obier [ɔbje] *n.m. Bot:* guelder rose, snowball tree.
obituaire [ɔbitɥɛr] *a.* & *n.m. Ecc:* **(registre) o.,** obituary list; register of deaths.
objecter [ɔbʒɛkte] *v.tr.* to raise, interpose, (sth.) as an objection; **je n'ai rien à o. à la proposition,** I have no objection to raise, nothing to say, against the proposal; **o. qch. à qn,** to bring something up against s.o.; **on lui objecta sa jeunesse,** they took exception to his youth; his youth was against him.
objecteur [ɔbʒɛktœr] *n.m.* **o. de conscience,** conscientious objector.
objectif, -ive [ɔbʒɛktif, -iv] **1.** *a.* objective; unbiased. **2.** *n.m.* (*a*) aim, object(ive); end; **atteindre son o.,** to attain one's object; (*b*) *Mil: etc:* objective; (*c*) *Ball:* target. **3.** *n.m.* (*a*) object glass, objective (of microscope, etc.); (*b*) *Phot:* lens.
objection [ɔbʒɛksjɔ̃] *n.f.* objection; **faire, formuler, soulever, dresser, une o.,** to object (**à,** to); to make, raise, an objection; **o. de conscience,** conscientious objection.
objectivité [ɔbʒɛktivite] *n.f.* objectivity, objectiveness.
objet [ɔbʒɛ] *n.m.* **1.** article, thing; **o. de luxe,** luxury article; **o. d'art,** objet d'art. **2.** (*a*) *Gram:* object, complement; **o. direct,** direct object; (*b*) *Phil:* object; **quel o. affreux!** what a dreadful sight! **3.** (*a*) subject, (subject) matter; **l'o. de la conversation,** the subject of the conversation; **cela fera l'o. de ma conférence,** this will be dealt with in my lecture; **o. de pitié, de haine,** object of pity, hatred; (*b*) object, aim, purpose (of action); **remplir son o.,** to attain one's end; **sans o.,** aimless(ly), purposeless(ly); pointless(ly).
objurgation [ɔbʒyrgasjɔ̃] *n.f.* objurgation.
objurgatoire [ɔbʒyrgatwar] *a.* objurgatory (words, etc.).
oblat, -ate [ɔbla, -at] *n. Ecc:* oblate.
oblation [ɔblasjɔ̃] *n.f. Ecc:* oblation, offering.
obligataire [ɔbligatɛr] *n. Fin:* bondholder, debenture holder; holder of redeemable stock.
obligation [ɔbligasjɔ̃] *n.f.* **1.** (*a*) (moral) obligation; duty; **je me sens dans l'o. de vous avertir,** I feel compelled to warn you; **faire honneur, manquer, à ses obligations,** to meet, to fail to meet, one's obligations; **je me vois dans l'o. de me taire,** I find myself obliged to keep silent; *Ecc:* **fête d'o.,** day of obligation; (*b*) **o. du service militaire,** liability to military service. **2.** *Jur:* recognizance, bond; **o. alimentaire,** maintenance order; **contracter une o. irrévocable,** to enter into a binding agreement. **3.** *Fin:* bond, debenture, redeemable stock; **o. au porteur,** bearer bond. **4.** obligation, favour, *NAm:* favor; **avoir des obligations envers qn,** to be under an obligation to s.o.
obligatoire [ɔbligatwar] *a.* obligatory; mandatory; compulsory (military service); binding (agreement); **l'uniforme est o.,** uniform must be worn; *F:* **c'était o.,** it *had* to happen.
obligatoirement [ɔbligatwarmɑ̃] *adv.* compulsorily; **vous devez o. montrer votre passeport à la frontière,** you have to show your passport at the frontier.
obligé, -ée [ɔbliʒe] **1.** *a.* (*a*) obliged, bound, compelled (**de faire qch.,** to do sth.); (*b*) indispensable, necessary; (*c*) inevitable, sure to happen; **c'est o. qu'il rate son examen,** he's bound to fail his exam; (*d*) obliged, grateful (**de,** for); **bien o.!** many thanks! **2.** *n.* person under obligation; *Jur:* obligee.
obligeamment [ɔbliʒamɑ̃] *adv.* obligingly; courteously, kindly.
obligeance [ɔbliʒɑ̃s] *n.f.* obligingness; **ayez, veuillez avoir, l'o. de fermer la porte,** would you be good enough to, have the kindness to, close the door.
obligeant [ɔbliʒɑ̃] *a.* obliging, helpful; kind; civil; **c'est très o. de votre part,** it is very kind of you.
obliger [ɔbliʒe] *v.* **(j'obligeai(s); n. obligeons) 1.** *v.tr.* (*a*) to oblige, constrain, bind, compel; **ma signature m'y oblige,** my signature binds me, holds me, to it; **votre devoir vous y oblige,** you are in duty bound to do it; **o. qn à faire qch.,** to compel, force, s.o. to do sth.; to make s.o. do sth.; (*in the passive usu.* **de**) **être obligé de faire qch.,** to be obliged, compelled, to do sth.; to have to do sth.; (*b*) **o. qn,** to oblige s.o., to do s.o. a favour, *NAm:* favor; *Prov:* **qui oblige promptement oblige doublement,** he gives twice who gives quickly. **2. s'o. à faire qch.,** to bind oneself, to undertake, to do sth.; to make a point of doing sth.
oblique [ɔblik] **1.** *a.* (*a*) oblique (line, case, march, etc.); (*b*) slanting (stitch); skew (arch); **regard o.,** side glance; (*c*) *A:* indirect, crooked; underhand; devious. **2.** *n.m. Anat:* oblique muscle. **3.** *n.f.* oblique line; **pluie qui tombe en o.,** slanting rain; *Mil:* **o. à droite!** right incline!
obliquement [ɔblikmɑ̃] *adv.* (*a*) obliquely, slantwise, aslant, diagonally; on the skew; (*b*) indirectly.
obliquer [ɔblike] *v.i.* (*a*) to move in an oblique direction; to oblique; to edge; (*b*) to slant.
obliquité [ɔblikɥite] *n.f.* obliquity; obliqueness.

oblitérateur, -trice [ɔbliteratœr, -tris] **1.** *a.* obliterating. **2.** *n.m.* cancel (for stamps, etc.).
oblitération [ɔbliterasjɔ̃] *n.f.* obliteration; cancelling, cancellation (of stamps, etc.); **(cachet d')o.,** postmark.
oblitérer [ɔblitere] *v.tr.* **(j'oblitère, n. oblitérons; j'oblitérerai) 1.** to obliterate (marks, the past, etc.). **2.** to cancel, deface (stamp); **timbre oblitéré,** used stamp.
oblong, -ongue [ɔblɔ̃, -ɔ̃g] *a.* oblong.
obnubiler [ɔbnybile] *v.tr.* to obnubilate; to cloud (mind); to bemuse; to obsess (s.o.).
oboïste [ɔbɔist] *n. Mus:* oboist, oboe player.
obole [ɔbɔl] *n.f.* (*a*) *A.Num:* (Greek) obolus; (French) obole; (*b*) small offering; mite.
obscène [ɔpsɛn] *a.* obscene (language, book); lewd (gesture); smutty (talk, song).
obscénité [ɔpsenite] *n.f.* **1.** obscenity; lewdness; *F:* smuttiness. **2. faire circuler des obscénités,** to circulate obscene books, pictures, etc.
obscur [ɔpskyr] *a.* **1.** dark (night, room); gloomy (weather); sombre, *NAm:* somber (tint). **2.** obscure; (*a*) difficult to understand; abstruse (subject); recondite (writer); (*b*) indistinct, dim (horizon, etc.); vague, dim (forebodings); (*c*) unknown, lowly, humble (parentage); **un o. écrivain,** an unknown, obscure, writer.
obscurantisme [ɔpskyrɑ̃tism] *n.m.* obscurantism.
obscurcir [ɔpskyrsir] **1.** *v.tr.* to obscure; (*a*) to darken (room); cloud (sky); **yeux obscurcis par les larmes,** eyes dimmed with tears; (*b*) **o. un texte,** to make a text obscure, unintelligible. **2. s'o.,** to darken; to grow dark; (*of sky*) to cloud over; (*of sight, faculty*) to grow dim.
obscurcissement [ɔpskyrsismɑ̃] *n.m.* obscuring, obscuration (of light, meaning); darkening; dimming (of mind).
obscurément [ɔpskyremɑ̃] *adv.* obscurely, dimly.
obscurité [ɔpskyrite] *n.f.* obscurity; (*a*) darkness; (*b*) unintelligibility, abstruseness; (*c*) dimness (of a memory, etc.); **vivre dans l'o.,** to live in obscurity; **sortir de l'o.,** to become known.
obsédant [ɔpsedɑ̃] *a.* haunting (memory); obsessive (thought).
obsédé, -ée [ɔpsede] *n.* fanatic, maniac.
obséder [ɔpsede] *v.tr.* **(j'obsède; j'obséderai)** (*a*) *O:* to importune, worry, pester (s.o.); (*b*) (*of thought, memory*) to obsess (s.o.).
obsèques [ɔpsɛk] *n.f.pl.* obsequies; funeral.
obséquieusement [ɔpsekjøzmɑ̃] *adv.* obsequiously.
obséquieux, -euse [ɔpsekjø, -øz] *a.* obsequious.
observance [ɔpsɛrvɑ̃s] *n.f.* observance; (i) observing, keeping (of rule); (ii) rule observed.
observateur, -trice [ɔpsɛrvatœr, -tris] **1.** *n.* (*a*) observer (of events, phenomena, enemy's movements, etc.); *Mil: etc:* spotter; **o. des Nations Unies,** United Nations observer; (*b*) observer, keeper (of rules, laws). **2.** *a.* observant, observing.
observation [ɔpsɛrvasjɔ̃] *n.f.* **1.** observance, keeping (of laws, feasts). **2.** observation; observing; **être en o.,** to be on the lookout, on the watch; **tenir qn, qch., en o.,** to keep s.o., sth., under observation; to keep an eye on s.o., sth.; **malade en o.,** patient under observation; **poste d'o.,** observation post, station, lookout post; **avion d'o.,** observation aircraft. **3.** (*a*) observation, remark; **si je puis me permettre une o.,** if I may be allowed to say something; **il faisait toujours des observations à ses élèves,** he was always finding fault with his pupils; (*b*) **observations sur un auteur,** comments, notes, on an author.
observatoire [ɔpsɛrvatwar] *n.m.* **1.** *Astr:* observatory. **2.** *Mil:* observation post.
observer [ɔpsɛrve] **1.** *v.tr.* to observe; (*a*) to keep (to), to comply with, to adhere to (rules, laws, etc.); **o. une stricte économie,** to practise strict economy; **ne pas o. la loi, le dimanche,** to break the law, the sabbath; **o. le silence,** to keep silence; **o. les distances,** to keep one's distance; **o. une promesse,** to keep a promise; **faire o. la loi,** to enforce (obedience to) the law; (*b*) to watch (sth., s.o.); **on nous observe,** we are being watched; **observez votre langage,** keep a watch on your tongue; **je l'observais faire,** I watched him doing it; (*c*) to observe, study (the stars); to take, read (an angle); *Nau:* **o. le soleil,** to take the sun, to take a sight at the sun; (*d*) to note, notice; **faire o. qch. à qn,** to draw s.o.'s attention to sth.; to point sth. out to s.o. **2. s'o.,** to be circumspect, careful, cautious, wary.
obsession [ɔpsɛsjɔ̃] *n.f.* obsession (by evil spirit, idea, emotion).
obsidienne [ɔpsidjɛn] *n.f. Miner:* obsidian; *F:* volcanic glass.
obstacle [ɔpstakl̩] *n.m.* obstacle; impediment, hindrance; **sans o.,** unimpeded, without any obstacle; **dresser, susciter, des obstacles à qn,** to put obstacles in s.o.'s way; **faire o. à qch., à qn,** to stand in the way of sth., of s.o.; **je n'y vois pas d'o.,** I see no difficulty about it; **course d'obstacles,** (i) steeplechase; (ii) hurdle race; (iii) obstacle race.
obstétrical, -aux [ɔpstetrikal, -o] *a.* obstetric(al).
obstétrique [ɔpstetrik] *n.f.* obstetrics.
obstination [ɔpstinasjɔ̃] *n.f.* obstinacy, stubbornness; *F:* pigheadedness.
obstiné [ɔpstine] *a.* stubborn, headstrong, obstinate, *F:* pigheaded (person); stubborn, dogged (resistance); persistent (cough, fever).
obstinément [ɔpstinemɑ̃] *adv.* obstinately; stubbornly.
obstiner (s') [sɔpstine] *v.pr.* **s'o. à qch., à faire qch.,** to persist in sth., in doing sth.; to be bent on sth., on doing sth.; **s'o. au silence,** to remain stubbornly, obstinately, silent.
obstruction [ɔpstryksjɔ̃] *n.f.* obstruction; (*a*) blockage, blocking (of street, passage); clogging (of drain); choking (of outlet); *Med:* **o. intestinale,** stoppage of the bowels; (*b*) **faire de l'o.,** (i) *Pol:* to practise, use, obstruction; *NAm:* to filibuster; (ii) *Fb: etc:* to obstruct.
obstructionnisme [ɔpstryksjɔnism] *n.m. Pol:* obstruction(ism); *NAm:* filibustering.
obstructionniste [ɔpstryksjɔnist] *Pol:* **1.** *n.m.* obstructionist, *NAm:* filibusterer. **2.** *a.* obstructive, *NAm:* filibustering (tactics).
obstruer [ɔpstrye] *v.tr.* to obstruct, block (street, pipe); to choke (outlet).
obtempérer [ɔptɑ̃pere] *v.ind.tr.* **(j'obtempère, n. obtempérons; j'obtempérerai) o. à (qch.),** to obey (summons, order); to comply with (order); to accede to (demand).
obtenir [ɔptənir] *v.tr.* (*conj. like* TENIR) to obtain, get (goods, permission); to secure (promise); to gain (s.o.'s consent, etc.); to achieve (result); **où cela s'obtient-il?** where can you get it? **o. qch. de qn,** to obtain, get, sth. from s.o.; **j'ai obtenu de le voir,** I obtained, got, permission to see him; **j'ai obtenu qu'il revienne,** (i) I got him to come back; (ii) I arranged for him to come back.
obtention [ɔptɑ̃sjɔ̃] *n.f.* obtaining; **pour l'o. de qch.,** (in order) to obtain sth.
obturateur, -trice [ɔptyratœr, -tris] **1.** *a.* obturating, closing; *Anat:* obturator (vein, muscle); **aubage o.,** shutter vane (of turbine). **2.** *n.m.* (*a*) *Anat: Surg:* obturator (of aperture); (*b*) obturator, shutter; stopcock, stop valve; *I.C.E:* throttle; *Atom.Ph:* **o. à neutrons,** neutron shutter; (*c*) *Phot:* shutter; **o. de plaque,**

focal-plane shutter; **o. au diaphragme,** diaphragm shutter.

obturation [ɔptyrasjɔ̃] *n.f.* obturation; closing (of cavity); sealing (of pipe); filling, stopping (of tooth).

obturer [ɔptyre] *v.tr.* to stop, seal, obturate (pipe, aperture); to close (cavity); to fill, stop (tooth).

obtus [ɔpty] *a.* obtuse. **1.** blunt (point); rounded (leaf). **2.** dull (person). **3.** obtuse (angle).

obus [ɔby] *n.m. Artil:* shell; **o. armé,** live shell; **o. non explosé,** unexploded shell; **o. à balles, à mitraille,** shrapnel (shell).

obusier [ɔbyzjɛ] *n.m. Artil:* howitzer.

obvier [ɔbvje] *v.ind.tr.* (*impf. & pr.sub.* **n. obviions**) **o. à qch.,** to obviate, prevent, sth.; **o. à un accident,** to take precautions against an accident.

oc [ɔk] *adv. Hist. of Ling:* **la langue d'oc,** langue d'oc, southern French.

occasion [ɔkazjɔ̃] *n.f.* **1.** (*a*) opportunity, occasion, chance; **saisir une o.,** to take, seize, an opportunity; *F:* **sauter sur l'o.,** to jump at the chance; **l'o. fait le larron,** opportunity makes the thief; **avoir l'o. de faire qch.,** to have the opportunity of doing sth.; **si l'o. se présente, si vous en trouvez l'o.,** if the opportunity comes your way; if you get the chance; **attendre l'o.,** to bide one's time; **suivant l'o.,** as occasion arises; **à l'o.,** when the opportunity presents itself; **à la première o.,** at the first opportunity; (*b*) bargain; **vente d'o.,** (bargain) sale; **marchandises d'o.,** job lot; (*c*) **faire le neuf et l'o.,** to sell new and secondhand goods; **voitures, livres, meubles, d'o.,** secondhand cars, books, furniture. **2.** occasion, juncture; **à plusieurs occasions,** on several occasions; **pour l'o.,** for the occasion; in this particular case; **à l'o. de son mariage,** on the occasion of his marriage; **à l'o.,** in case of need; **par o.,** now and then, occasionally; **en pareille o.,** in similar circumstances; **en cette o.,** at this juncture; **dans les grandes occasions,** on great occasions; **connaissance d'o.,** chance acquaintance. **3.** motive, reason, cause, occasion; **o. d'une dispute,** cause of a dispute; **donner o. à la médisance,** to give rise to scandal.

occasionnel, -elle [ɔkazjɔnɛl] *a.* occasional; chance (meeting); casual (help); **cause occasionnelle d'une révolte,** event that led to a revolt.

occasionnellement [ɔkazjɔnɛlmɑ̃] *adv.* occasionally; accidentally.

occasionner [ɔkazjɔne] *v.tr.* to occasion, cause (dispute, delay); to give rise to, to bring about (unpleasantness).

occident [ɔksidɑ̃] *n.m.* west; occident; *Pol:* **l'O.,** the West.

occidental, -ale, -aux [ɔksidɑ̃tal, -o] **1.** *a.* west, western; **côte occidentale,** west coast; **l'Europe occidentale,** Western Europe; **les Indes occidentales,** the West Indies. **2.** *n.* Westerner; Occidental.

occidentaliser [ɔksidɑ̃talize] *v.tr.* to westernize.

occipital, -aux [ɔksipital, -o] *Anat:* **1.** *a.* occipital. **2.** *n.m.* occipital (bone).

occiput [ɔksipyt] *n.m. Anat:* occiput.

occire [ɔksir] *v.tr.* (*used only in inf. & p.p.* **occis**) *A: & Hum:* to slay, kill; *F:* **se faire o.,** to get bumped off.

occlusif, -ive [ɔklysif, -iv] *a.* occlusive.

occlusion [ɔklyzjɔ̃] *n.f.* occlusion; obstruction, stoppage (of bowel); cut-off (of steam).

occultation [ɔkyltasjɔ̃] *n.f. Astr:* occultation; **feu à occultations,** occulting, intermittent, light.

occulte [ɔkylt] *a.* occult (influence, science); secret (accounts); hidden (cause).

occultement [ɔkyltəmɑ̃] *adv.* occultly; secretly.

occulter [ɔkylte] *v.tr.* to occult (heavenly body, a light, a signal).

occultisme [ɔkyltism] *n.m.* occultism.

occupant, -ante [ɔkypɑ̃, -ɑ̃t] (*a*) *a.* occupying (tenant, forces); in possession (of property); (*b*) *n.* occupier; occupant; *Jur:* **premier o.,** occupant; *Mil:* **l'o.,** the occupying power.

occupation [ɔkypasjɔ̃] *n.f.* occupation. **1.** occupancy, occupation, possession (of house, etc.); occupation (of conquered country); **armée d'o.,** army of occupation; **l'O.,** the Occupation (1940–44); **grève avec o. des lieux,** sit-in strike. **2.** work, employment; **avoir de l'o.,** to be busy; **ne pas avoir d'o., être sans o.,** (i) to be unemployed, out of work, jobless; (ii) to have nothing to do; **cela me donne de l'o.,** I have my work cut out, my hands full; **vaquer à ses occupations,** to go about one's business.

occupé [ɔkype] *a.* **1.** busy; engaged; **o. aux, des, préparatifs du départ,** busy getting ready to leave; **c'est un homme fort o.,** he's a very busy man; **je suis o.,** (i) I'm busy; (ii) I'm engaged, not free. **2.** (*a*) **cette place est occupée,** this seat is taken; *Tp:* **ligne occupée,** line engaged, *esp. NAm:* busy; (*b*) **en territoire o.,** in occupied territory.

occuper [ɔkype] **1.** *v.tr.* to occupy; (*a*) to inhabit, reside in (house, etc.); (*b*) to hold, take possession of (town, building); (*c*) to fill, take up (time, space); **faire qch. pour o. le temps,** to do sth. to fill in (the) time; (*d*) to have, hold (an important job, etc.); (*e*) to give occupation to (s.o.); **o. vingt ouvriers,** to employ twenty workmen; **o. qn,** to give s.o. something to do, to think about. **2. s'o.** (*a*) to keep oneself busy; **s'o. à faire qch.,** to be engaged in, busy, doing sth.; **s'o. à la lecture,** to spend one's time reading; (*b*) **s'o. de qch.,** (i) to go in for, be interested in (photography, etc.); (ii) to apply oneself to, to attend to, sth.; **cette maison s'occupe surtout de l'argenterie,** this firm makes a speciality, *NAm:* specialty, of silverware; **je vais m'o. de l'affaire,** I shall deal with, go into, the matter; **il s'occupe de trop de choses,** he has too many irons in the fire; **nous allons maintenant nous o. du bilan,** we will now turn our attention to the balance sheet; **je m'en occuperai,** I'll see to it, see about it; **qui s'occupe de ce qu'il dit?** who cares (about) what he says? **occupe-toi de ce qui te regarde!** mind your own business! *P:* **t'occupe pas!** forget it! not to worry! **s'o. de qn,** to attend to s.o., to look after s.o.; *Com:* **est-ce qu'on s'occupe de vous?** are you being attended to, being served?

occurrence [ɔkyrɑ̃s] *n.f.* occurrence, event; emergency; **en l'o.,** in the circumstances, as it is, was.

océan [ɔseɑ̃] *n.m.* ocean; **d'un o. à l'autre,** from coast to coast; **les plages de l'O.,** the Atlantic resorts; **un o. de fleurs,** a sea of blossom.

Océanie (l') [lɔseani] *Pr.n.f. Geog:* Oceania.

océanien, -ienne [ɔseanjɛ̃, -jɛn] **1.** *a.* Oceanian. **2.** *n.* Oceanian; South Sea Islander.

océanique [ɔseanik] *a.* oceanic (current, etc.).

océanographie [ɔseanɔgrafi] *n.f.* oceanography.

océanographique [ɔseanɔgrafik] *a.* oceanographic(al).

ocelle [ɔsɛl] *n.m.* ocellus. **1.** simple eye (of insect). **2.** eye (on feather, insect's wing).

ocelot [ɔslo] *n.m.* ocelot.

ocre [ɔkr̥] *n.f. & a.inv.* ochre, *NAm:* ocher.

octaèdre [ɔktaɛdr̥] **1.** *a.* octahedral. **2.** *n.m.* octahedron.

octaédrique [ɔktaedrik] *a.* octahedral.

octane [ɔktan] *n.m. Ch:* octane; **essence à haut indice d'o.,** high-octane fuel, petrol, *NAm:* gasoline.

octant [ɔktɑ̃] *n.m.* octant.

octante [ɔktɑ̃t] *num.a. Sw.Fr:* eighty.

octave [ɔktav] *n.f. Mus: etc:* octave.

octobre [ɔktɔbr̥] *n.m.* October; **en o.,** in October; **au mois d'o.,** in the month of October; **le premier o.,** (on) October (the) first; (on) the first of October.

octogénaire [ɔktɔʒenɛr] *a. & n.* octogenarian.

octogonal, -aux [ɔktɔgɔnal, -o] *a.* octagonal.
octogone [ɔktɔgɔn] *n.m.* octagon.
octopode [ɔktɔpɔd] *a. & n.m. Moll:* octopod.
octosyllabe [ɔktɔsilab] **1.** *a.* octosyllabic. **2.** *n.m.* octosyllable.
octroi [ɔktrwa] *n.m.* **1.** concession, grant(ing) (of favour, *NAm:* favor). **2.** *Hist:* (*a*) town dues, city toll (on goods); (*b*) tollhouse.
octroyer [ɔktrwaje] *v.tr.* **(j'octroie, n. octroyons; j'octroierai) o. qch. à qn,** to grant, concede, allow s.o. sth., sth. to s.o.
octuor [ɔktyɔr] *n.m. Mus:* octet, octette.
octuple [ɔktypl̥] *a. & n.m.* octuple; eightfold (amount).
oculaire [ɔkylɛr] **1.** *a.* (*a*) ocular (demonstration, etc.); **témoin o.,** eyewitness; (*b*) **hygiène o.,** hygiene of the eye. **2.** *n.m. Opt:* eyepiece, ocular.
oculiste [ɔkylist] *n.* oculist; ophthalmologist.
ode [ɔd] *n.f. Lit:* ode.
odeur [odœr] *n.f.* odour, *NAm:* odor; smell; scent; **o. de brûlé,** smell of burning; **je sentais une o. de brûlé,** I could smell burning; **sans o.,** scentless; **bonne o.,** pleasant smell; **mauvaise o.,** bad smell; stench; **mourir en o. de sainteté,** to die in the odour of sanctity; *F:* **ne pas être en o. de sainteté auprès de qn,** to be in s.o.'s bad books.
odieusement [ɔdjøzmɑ̃] *adv.* odiously, hatefully.
odieux, -euse [ɔdjø, -øz] **1.** *a.* odious; hateful (person, vice); abominable (crime). **2.** *n.m.* odiousness, hatefulness (of an action); **il supporta tout l'o.,** he incurred all the odium.
odomètre [ɔdɔmɛtr̥] *n.m.* pedometer.
odontologie [ɔdɔ̃tɔlɔʒi] *n.f. Med:* odontology.
odorant [ɔdɔrɑ̃] *a.* (*a*) sweet-smelling, fragrant; (*b*) smelly, stinking.
odorat [ɔdɔra] *n.m.* (sense of) smell; **avoir l'o. fin,** to have a keen sense of smell.
odoriférant [ɔdɔriferɑ̃] *a.* odoriferous, sweet-smelling.
odyssée [ɔdise] *n.f.* (*a*) *Gr.Lit:* **l'O.,** the Odyssey; (*b*) odyssey, wanderings.
œcuménique [ekymenik] *a. Ecc:* (o)ecumenical.
œdème [edɛm] *n.m. Med:* oedema, *NAm:* edema.
Œdipe [edip] *Pr.n.m. Gr.Lit:* Oedipus; **complexe d'Œ.,** Oedipus complex.
œil, *pl.* **yeux** [œj, jø] *n.m.* **1.** eye; **il a les yeux bleus,** he has blue eyes; **hôpital pour les maladies des yeux,** ophthalmic, eye, hospital; **visible à l'o. nu,** visible to the naked eye; **fermer, ouvrir, les yeux,** to close, open, one's eyes; **je n'ai pas fermé l'o. de la nuit,** I didn't sleep a wink all night; **faire qch. les yeux fermés,** to do sth. with one's eyes shut; *P:* **mon o.!** my foot! **ouvrir de grands yeux,** to open one's eyes wide; to stare; **il avait les yeux hors de la tête,** his eyes were starting from his head; **faire les petits yeux,** to screw up one's eyes; **regarder qn entre (les) deux yeux, dans les yeux, dans le blanc des yeux,** to look s.o. full in the face, straight in the eye; **entre quatre yeux,** *F:* **entre quat'z'yeux** [katzjø], in private, between you and me (and the gatepost); **o. pour o., dent pour dent,** an eye for an eye, a tooth for a tooth; **épouser une femme pour ses beaux yeux,** to marry a woman for her (good) looks; **il ne travaille pour les beaux yeux de personne,** he doesn't do anything for love, for nothing; **chose qui saute aux yeux,** sth. obvious; **avoir du travail par-dessus les yeux,** to be up to one's eyes in work; *F:* **taper de l'o.,** to be sleepy, drowsy; **je m'en bats l'o.,** I don't care a hoot; I couldn't care less; **tourner de l'o.,** (i) *A:* to die; (ii) to faint; **mesurer qch. à l'o.,** to measure sth. by eye; *F:* **entrer à l'o.,** to get in free, gratis. **2.** sight; **avoir de bons, de mauvais, yeux,** to have good, bad, eyesight; **cela charme les yeux,** it delights the eye; **dès que j'eus jeté les yeux sur lui,** as soon as I had set eyes on him; **se consulter des yeux,** to exchange glances; **chercher qn des yeux,** to look about for s.o.; *F:* **est-ce que vous avez vos yeux dans votre poche?** where are your eyes? **aux yeux de la loi, de Dieu,** in the eyes of the law; in the sight of God; **à mes yeux,** in my opinion; **avoir qch. sous les yeux,** to have sth. before, in front of, one's eyes; *Ten: etc:* **avoir la balle dans l'o.,** to have one's eye in; **donner plus d'o. à un article,** to give an article a better appearance. **3.** attention, notice; **avoir l'o.,** to be observant, sharp-eyed; **avoir l'o. sur qn, avoir qn à l'o.,** to keep an eye on s.o.; **avoir l'o. à tout,** to see to everything; **avoir l'o. ouvert, les yeux ouverts,** to have one's eyes about one; **ouvrir l'o. (et le bon),** to keep one's eyes skinned; **avoir l'o. américain,** to be wide awake, alert; **fermer les yeux sur qch.,** to turn a blind eye to sth.; **j'accepte les yeux fermés ce que vous m'en dites,** I'll take your word for it; **coup d'o.,** (i) view; (ii) glance; **du, au, premier coup d'o.,** at first sight, at the outset; **jeter un coup d'o. sur qch.,** to run one's eye over sth.; to glance through, at, sth.; **avoir du coup d'o.,** to have good judgement; **voir, regarder, qn, qch., d'un mauvais o.,** to look unfavourably, *NAm:* unfavorably, disapprovingly, to frown, on s.o., sth.; **voir du même o. que qn,** to see eye to eye with s.o.; *F:* **faire de l'o. à qn,** to make eyes at s.o.; *F:* **taper dans l'o. de, à, qn,** to take s.o.'s fancy. **4.** (*a*) eye (of needle, etc.); hole (of hinge); eye (splice) (on rope); **piton à o.,** eye bolt; (*b*) hole (in bread, gruyère); speck of fat (on soup); *Hort:* eye (bud); (*c*) *Typ:* (*pl.* **œils**) face (of letter); **lettre d'un autre o.,** wrong fount. **5.** *Elcs: T.V:* **o. électrique,** electric eye; **o. magique, o. cathodique,** magic eye, cathode eye, electron ray tube. **6.** *Meteor:* eye (of cyclone).
œil-de-bœuf [œjdəbœf] *n.m. Arch:* œil-de-bœuf; bull's-eye (window); *pl. œils-de-bœuf.*
œil-de-chat [œjdəʃa] *n.m. Lap:* cat's eye; *œils-de-chat.*
œillade [œjad] *n.f.* glance; **lancer une o. à qn,** to glance meaningfully at s.o.; **lancer des œillades à qn,** to make eyes at s.o.
œillère [œjɛr] *n.f.* (*a*) (*on horse*) blinker, eye flap; *NAm:* blinder; (*of pers.*) **avoir des œillères,** to be narrow-minded; to go through life in blinkers; (*b*) eyebath, *esp. NAm:* eyecup.
œillet [œjɛ] *n.m.* **1.** eyelet (hole) (of boot, sail, etc.). **2.** *Bot:* pink; **o. des fleuristes,** clove pink, carnation; **o. de poète,** sweet william; **o. des prés,** ragged robbin; **o. d'Inde,** French marigold.
œilleton [œjtɔ̃] *n.m.* **1.** *Hort:* eye (bud). **2.** peephole; eyepiece (of viewfinder).
œillette [œjɛt] *n.f.* oil poppy, opium poppy; **huile d'o.,** poppy seed oil.
œnologie [enɔlɔʒi] *n.f.* oenology, *NAm:* enology.
œnométrie [enɔmetri] *n.f.* alcoholometry (of wines).
œsophage [ezɔfaʒ] *n.m. Anat:* oesophagus, *NAm:* esophagus; gullet.
œstre [ɛstr̥] *n.m. Ent: Vet:* oestrus, *NAm:* estrus; gadfly, warble (fly), bot(t) fly.
œstrogène [ɛstrɔʒɛn] *a. & n.m. Physiol:* (o)estrogen.
œuf, *pl.* **œufs** [œf, ø] *n.m.* **1.** (*a*) egg; **o. frais,** new-laid egg; **o. du jour,** (farm) fresh egg; **o. en poudre,** dried, dehydrated, egg; *Cu:* **o. à la coque,** boiled egg; **o. mollet,** soft-boiled egg; **o. dur,** hard-boiled egg; **œufs brouillés,** scrambled eggs; **o. sur le plat, au plat,** fried egg; **o. de Pâques,** Easter egg; **en o.,** egg-shaped; **mettre tous ses œufs dans le même panier,** to put all one's eggs in one basket; *F:* **marcher sur des œufs,** to tread on thin ice; **il tondrait un o.,** he would skin a flint; **faire d'un o. un bœuf,** to make a mountain out of a molehill; **donner un o. pour avoir un bœuf,** to

throw out a sprat to catch a mackerel; **tuer la poule aux œufs d'or,** to kill the goose that lays the golden egg(s); (*b*) *Biol:* ovum; egg (of insect); berry (of fish, lobster); *pl.* spawn (of frog, fish, etc.); hard roe (of fish); *F:* **étouffer qch. dans l'o.,** to nip sth. in the bud. **2. o. en faïence,** nest egg; **o. à repriser,** darning egg.

œufrier [œfrije] *n.m.* **1.** egg holder (for boiling eggs). **2.** egg stand, rack.

œuvé [œve] *a.* hard-roed (fish); berried (lobster).

œuvre [œvr̥] *n.f.* **1.** (*a*) work; working; **faire o. d'ami,** to behave, act, like a friend; **faire o. utile,** to do useful work; **leur rencontre était son o.,** it was thanks to him that they met; **mettre qn à l'o.,** to set s.o. to work; **se mettre à l'o.,** to get down to work; **mettre (qch.) en o.,** (i) to use, make use of (sth.); to bring (sth.) into operation; (ii) to put (a piece of work) in hand; (iii) to implement (a treaty); **mettre tout en o.,** to leave no stone unturned; **bois d'o.,** (constructional) timber; **faire de bonnes œuvres,** to do charitable, social, work; **quête au profit d'une o.,** collection in aid of a charity; *A:* **exécuteur des hautes œuvres,** executioner, hangman; (*b*) **o. de bienfaisance, de charité,** charitable society, institution; charity. **2.** (finished) work, production; **œuvres d'un peintre,** works of a painter; *Prov:* **à l'o. on connaît l'artisan,** a good carpenter is known by his chips. **3.** *Nau:* **œuvres vives,** quick works, vitals; **œuvres mortes,** dead works, upper works, topsides. **4.** *n.m.* (*a*) **gros o. (d'un bâtiment),** fabric (of a building); *Const:* **à pied d'o.,** on site; (*b*) **l'o. de Molière, de Mozart,** the works of Molière, of Mozart.

offensant [ɔfɑ̃sɑ̃] *a.* offensive, insulting.

offense [ɔfɑ̃s] *n.f.* **1.** offence, *NAm:* offense; **faire une o. à qn,** to offend s.o.; **soit dit sans o.,** with all due respect; *F:* **il n'y a pas d'o.,** no offence taken. **2.** *Theol:* transgression, sin, trespass; *Ecc:* **pardonne-nous nos offenses,** forgive us our trespasses. **3.** *Jur:* **o. à la Cour,** contempt of Court.

offensé, -ée [ɔfɑ̃se] *n.* offended, injured, party.

offenser [ɔfɑ̃se] **1.** *v.tr.* (*a*) **o. qn,** to offend s.o., to give offence, *NAm:* offense, to s.o.; (*b*) to offend against (grammar, good taste); **o. les regards,** to be an eyesore. **2. s'o.,** to take offence **(de,** at); to be offended **(de,** by).

offensif, -ive [ɔfɑ̃sif, -iv] **1.** *a.* offensive (war, weapon). **2.** *n.f.* **offensive** (*a*) offensive; **passer à l'o.,** to go over to the offensive; (*b*) **offensive de l'hiver, du froid,** onset of winter, sudden cold spell.

offensivement [ɔfɑ̃sivmɑ̃] *adv.* offensively.

offertoire [ɔfɛrtwar] *n.m. Ecc: Mus:* offertory.

office [ɔfis] **1.** *n.m.* (*a*) office, functions, duty; **remplir l'o. de chancelier,** to fill the office of chancellor; **faire o. de secrétaire,** to act as secretary; **la pilule a rempli son o.,** the pill did its job; **d'o.,** (i) officially; ex officio; (ii) automatically, as a matter of routine; **avocat nommé d'o.,** barrister appointed by the court; **il a gagné d'o.,** it was a walkover for him; (*b*) service, turn; **accepter les bons offices de qn,** to accept s.o.'s help; (*c*) *Ecc:* service; office (for the day, etc.); **l'o. des morts,** the burial service; the Office for the Dead; **livre d'o.,** prayer book; **aller à l'o.,** to go to church, chapel; (*d*) bureau, office; **o. de publicité,** advertising agency. **2.** *n.f.* (*a*) (butler's) pantry; (*b*) *O:* servants' hall.

officiant [ɔfisjɑ̃] *a.* & *n.m. Ecc:* officiating (priest); *n.* officiant.

officiel, -ielle [ɔfisjɛl] **1.** *a.* official (statement, language, visit, source); formal (call, etc.); **à titre o.,** officially, formally; **congé o.,** national holiday; **le Journal O.,** *n.m.* **l'O.** = the (official) Gazette; *Mil: Navy:* **être à l'O.,** to be gazetted. **2.** *n.* official.

officiellement [ɔfisjɛlmɑ̃] *adv.* officially.

officier¹ [ɔfisje] *v.i.* (*impf.* & *pr.sub.* **n. officiions)** to officiate.

officier² *n.m.* officer. **1. o. de l'état civil** = registrar (of births, marriages and deaths); **officiers ministériels,** (certain) law officials. **2.** *Mil:* (commissioned) officer; **o. supérieur,** field officer, *U.S:* senior officer; **o. général,** general officer; *Navy:* flag officer; **o. de marine,** naval officer; *Navy:* **o. de pont,** executive officer, deck officer; **o. de port,** harbour, *NAm:* harbor, master. **3. O. de la Légion d'honneur,** Officer of the Legion of Honour, *NAm:* Honor.

officieusement [ɔfisjøzmɑ̃] *adv.* unofficially, semi-officially.

officieux, -euse [ɔfisjø, -øz] **1.** *a.* (*a*) unofficial, semi-official; *Adm:* officious (information, etc.); *Journ:* **note d'origine officieuse,** inspired paragraph; **à titre o.,** unofficially; (*b*) *A:* officious; (over)obliging; (*c*) **mensonge o.,** white lie. **2.** *n. A:* busybody.

officinal, -aux [ɔfisinal, -o] *a. Pharm:* officinal (preparation); medicinal (plant).

officine [ɔfisin] *n.f.* **1.** *Pharm:* dispensary; *Adm:* pharmacy, chemist's shop. **2.** den (of shady business); thieves' kitchen; hotbed (of intrigue).

offrande [ɔfrɑ̃d] *n.f.* (*a*) offering, gift; (*b*) *Ecc:* offertory.

offrant [ɔfrɑ̃] *n.m.* **le plus o.,** the best offer; (*at auction*) the highest bidder.

offre [ɔfr̥] *n.f.* (*a*) offer, proposal; tender (for contract); (*at auction sale*) bid; **faire o. de qch.,** to offer sth.; **faire des offres de service à qn,** to offer to help s.o.; *Com:* to solicit orders; *Fin:* **o. publique d'achat,** takeover bid; (*b*) *Pol.Ec:* **l'o. et la demande,** supply and demand.

offrir [ɔfrir] *v.* (*pr.p.* **offrant;** *p.p.* **offert** [ɔfɛr]; *pr.ind.* **j'offre, n. offrons;** *p.h.* **j'offris;** *fu.* **j'offrirai) 1.** *v.tr.* (*a*) to give (present); to offer up (sacrifice); **c'est pour o.,** it's for a present; **o. un déjeuner à qn,** to invite s.o. to lunch; **s'o. un bon cigare,** to treat oneself to, to stand oneself, a good cigar; **ne pas pouvoir s'o. qch.,** to be unable to afford sth.; (*b*) **on lui a offert une place de mécanicien,** he was offered a job as a mechanic; **o. la main à qn,** to hold out one's hand to s.o.; **o. une résistance acharnée,** to put up a stiff resistance; **o. de faire qch.,** to offer to do sth.; **o. mille francs (de qch.),** (i) to offer, (ii) to bid, a thousand francs (for sth.); (*c*) **la campagne offre une vue splendide,** the countryside presents a magnificent view; **l'histoire en offre plusieurs exemples,** history affords several examples of it. **2. s'o.** (*a*) **s'o. comme guide,** to propose, offer, oneself as a guide; **s'o. au danger,** to court danger; **s'o. à faire qch.,** to offer, volunteer, to do sth.; (*b*) **quand l'occasion s'offrira,** when the opportunity occurs.

offusquer [ɔfyske] **1.** *v.tr.* to offend, shock (s.o.). **2. s'o. de qch.,** to take offence at sth.; **il s'offusque d'un rien,** he is easily shocked.

ogival, -aux [ɔʒival, -o] *a. Arch:* ogival; gothic (architecture).

ogive [ɔʒiv] *n.f.* **1.** *Arch:* (diagonal) rib (under a groin); **voûte d'ogives,** ribbed vault. **2.** *Ball: etc:* conical point, head (of shell); nose cone (of rocket); **o. atomique, nucléaire,** atomic, nuclear, warhead.

ogre, ogresse [ɔgr̥, ɔgrɛs] *n.* ogre, ogress; **manger comme un o.,** to eat like a horse.

oh [o] *int.* oh! **oh! hisse!** yo-heave-ho!

ohé [ɔe] *int.* hi! hullo! *Nau:* **o. du navire!** ship ahoy!

ohm [om] *n.m. El.Meas:* ohm.

ohmique [omik] *a.* ohmic.

ohmmètre [ommɛtr̥] *n.m. El:* ohmmeter.

oïdium [ɔidjɔm] *n.m.* oidium, (vine) mildew.

oie [wa] *n.f.* (*a*) goose; **conte de ma mère l'O.,** fairy tale; *F:* **ne faites pas l'o.,** don't be silly, don't be an idiot; *F:* **une o. blanche,** a naïve young girl; **pas de**

l'o., goose step; (*b*) **jeu de l'o.,** game of the snakes and ladders type.

oignon [ɔɲɔ̃] *n.m.* **1.** (*a*) onion; **petits oignons,** (i) spring onions; (ii) pickling onions; **aux petits oignons,** (i) *Cu:* stewed with spring onions; (ii) *F:* first-rate; **se mettre en rang d'oignons,** to form up in a row; *P:* **occupe-toi, mêle-toi, de tes oignons,** mind your own business; (*b*) *Bot:* bulb. **2.** *A:* watch, turnip. **3.** *Med:* bunion.

oïl [ɔil] *adv. Hist. of Ling:* **la langue d'o.,** langue d'oïl, northern French.

oindre [wɛ̃dr̥] *v.tr.* (*conj. like* CRAINDRE) **1.** *O:* to oil, to rub with oil. **2.** to anoint (king, etc.).

oint, ointe [wɛ̃, wɛ̃t] *a. & n.* anointed; **l'O. du Seigneur,** the Lord's anointed.

oiseau, -eaux [wazo] *n.m.* **1.** (*a*) bird; **oiseaux domestiques, de basse-cour,** poultry; **o. de proie,** bird of prey; **oiseaux de volière, d'appartement,** cage birds; **o. de passage,** bird of passage; **être comme l'o. sur la branche,** to be here today and gone tomorrow; **perspective à vue d'o.,** bird's eye view; *F:* **l'o. s'est envolé,** the bird's flown; there's nobody there; **à vol d'o.,** as the crow flies; (*b*) *F:* (*of pers.*) **drôle d'o.,** odd type, sort, customer; **c'est l'o. rare,** he's a rare bird; **mon petit o.,** my pet. **2.** (bricklayer's) hod.

oiseau-mouche [wazomuʃ] *n.m.* humming bird; *pl. oiseaux-mouches.*

oiseler [wazle] *v.* **(il oiselle, n. oiselons; il oisellera) 1.** *v.i.* to go bird-catching. **2.** *v.tr.* to fly (hawk).

oiselet [wazlɛ] *n.m. A: & Lit:* small bird.

oiseleur [wazlœr] *n.m.* fowler, bird catcher.

oiselier [wazəlje] *n.m.* bird seller, fancier.

oiselle [wazɛl] *n.f.* hen bird; *F:* naïve young girl.

oisellerie [wazɛlri] *n.f.* **1.** bird breeding; bird selling. **2.** aviary.

oiseusement [wazøzmɑ̃] *adv.* idly; unnecessarily.

oiseux, -euse [wazø, -øz] *a.* otiose; idle (talk); pointless (discussion); **explication oiseuse,** explanation that doesn't cut any ice, that gets you nowhere.

oisif, -ive [wazif, -iv] **1.** *a.* idle; unoccupied; **vie oisive,** idle life. **2.** *n.* (*a*) idler; (*b*) person of leisure.

oisillon [wazijɔ̃] *n.m.* fledgling; young bird; small bird.

oisivement [wazivmɑ̃] *adv.* idly.

oisiveté [wazivte] *n.f.* idleness; **l'o. est (la) mère de tous les vices,** idleness is the root of all evil.

oison [wazɔ̃] *n.m. Orn:* gosling; *F:* credulous person; mug.

okapi [ɔkapi] *n.m. Z:* okapi.

oléagineux, -euse [ɔleaʒinø, -øz] *a.* oleaginous. **1.** oily. **2.** oil-yielding; **graines oléagineuses,** *n.m.pl.* **o.,** oilseeds.

oléicole [ɔleikɔl] *a.* (*a*) olive-growing (land); (*b*) vegetable oil (industry).

oléiculteur [ɔleikyltœr] *n.m.* olive grower.

oléiculture [ɔleikyltyr] *n.f.* olive growing.

oléifère [ɔleifɛr] *a.* oil-producing, oleiferous.

oléique [ɔleik] *a. Ch:* oleic (acid).

oléoduc [ɔleɔdyk] *n.m.* (oil) pipeline.

olfactif, -ive [ɔlfaktif, -iv] *a.* olfactory (nerves, etc.).

olifant [ɔlifɑ̃] *n.m. Lit:* oliphant; ivory (hunting) horn.

oligarchie [ɔligarʃi] *n.f.* oligarchy.

oligarchique [ɔligarʃik] *a.* oligarchic(al).

oligarque [ɔligark] *n.m.* oligarch.

oligo-élément [ɔligɔelemɑ̃] *n.m. Biol:* trace element; *pl. oligo-éléments.*

olivacé [ɔlivase] *a.* olivaceous, olive-green.

olivaie [ɔlivɛ] *n.f.* olive plantation, grove.

olivaison [ɔlivɛzɔ̃] *n.f.* olive harvest.

olivâtre [ɔlivɑtr̥] *a.* olive(-coloured, *NAm:* -colored); sallow (complexion).

olive [ɔliv] *n.f.* **1.** (*a*) olive; **huile d'o.,** olive oil; (*b*) *a.inv. & n.m.* olive green. **2.** olive(-shaped button); toggle (of duffle coat); (olive-shaped) knob, handle, fishing lead, electric switch; *Arch:* olive moulding, *NAm:* molding.

oliveraie [ɔlivrɛ] *n.f.* olive plantation, grove.

oliverie [ɔlivri] *n.f.* (olive-)oil factory.

olivette [ɔlivɛt] *n.f.* **1.** olive plantation, grove. **2.** (*a*) olive-shaped grape; (*b*) plum tomato.

olivier[1] [ɔlivje] *n.m.* **1.** olive (tree); **le Mont des Oliviers,** the Mount of Olives; **se présenter un rameau d'o. à la main,** to hold out the olive branch. **2.** olive (wood).

Olivier[2] *Pr.n.m.* Oliver.

olographe [ɔlɔgraf] *a. Jur:* holograph, hand-written (will).

Olympe [ɔlɛ̃p] *Pr.n.m. Geog: Gr.Myth:* (Mount) Olympus; **les dieux de l'O.,** the Olympian gods.

olympiade [ɔlɛ̃pjad] *n.f.* olympiad.

olympien, -ienne [ɔlɛ̃pjɛ̃, -jɛn] *a. & n.* Olympian.

olympique [ɔlɛ̃pik] *a.* olympic (games, champion).

ombelle [ɔ̃bɛl] *n.f. Bot:* umbel; **en o.,** umbellate.

ombellifère [ɔ̃belifɛr] *Bot:* **1.** *a.* umbelliferous. **2.** *n.f.pl.* Umbelliferae, umbellifers.

ombilic [ɔ̃bilik] *n.m. Anat:* umbilicus, navel; *Bot:* hilum.

ombilical, -aux [ɔ̃bilikal, -o] *a.* umbilical; **cordon o.,** (i) umbilical cord, navel string; (ii) umbilical tether (of space suit).

omble [ɔ̃bl̥] *n.m. Ich:* **o. (chevalier),** char.

ombrage [ɔ̃braʒ] *n.m.* **1.** shade (of trees). **2. prendre o. de qch.,** (i) (*of horse*) to shy at sth.; (ii) (*of pers.*) to take offence, *NAm:* offense, umbrage, at sth.; **porter o. à qn,** to offend s.o.

ombragé [ɔ̃braʒe] *a.* shaded, shady.

ombrager [ɔ̃braʒe] *v.tr.* **(il ombrageait)** to shade; to protect (sth.) against the sun.

ombrageusement [ɔ̃braʒøzmɑ̃] *adv.* (*a*) (*of horse*) skittishly; (*b*) touchily.

ombrageux, -euse [ɔ̃braʒø, -øz] *a.* **1.** shy, skittish (horse). **2.** easily offended; touchy, quick to take offence, *NAm:* offense.

ombre[1] [ɔ̃br̥] *n.f.* **1.** shadow; *Astr:* umbra; **projeter une o.,** to cast a shadow; **suivre qn comme son o.,** to follow, stick to, s.o. like his shadow; **lâcher la proie pour l'o.,** to drop the substance for the shadow; **ombres chinoises,** shadow theatre, show. **2.** shade; **se reposer à l'o. d'un arbre,** to rest in, under, the shade of a tree; **quarante degrés à l'o.,** forty degrees in the shade; *P:* **mettre qn à l'o.,** to put s.o. in prison, in jug; **jeter une o. sur la fête,** to cast a gloom over the festivities; **vivre dans l'o. de qn,** to be (always) overshadowed by s.o.; **faire o. à qn,** to put s.o. in the shade. **3.** darkness; **à l'o. de la nuit,** under the cover of darkness. **4.** ghost; **n'être plus que l'o. de soi-même,** to be a mere shadow of one's former self. **5. vous n'avez pas l'o. d'une chance,** you haven't the ghost of a chance; **pas l'o. de bon sens,** not a grain, an atom, of common sense. **6.** *Art:* **l'o. et la lumière,** light and shade; *Fig:* **il y a une o. au tableau,** there's a fly in the ointment. **7.** *Toil:* **o. à paupières,** eye shadow.

ombre[2] *n.f.* **terre d'o.,** umber.

ombre[3] *n.m. Ich:* (*a*) **o. de rivière,** grayling; (*b*) **o. (chevalier),** char.

ombrelle [ɔ̃brɛl] *n.f.* **1.** sunshade, parasol. **2.** umbrella (of jellyfish).

ombrer [ɔ̃bre] *v.tr.* to shade (greenhouse, drawing).

ombreux, -euse [ɔ̃brø, -øz] *a.* shady (walk, grove).

Ombrie [ɔ̃bri] *Pr.n.f. Geog:* Umbria.

omelette [ɔmlɛt] *n.f.* omelet(te); **o. au jambon,** ham omelette; **on ne fait pas d'o. sans casser des œufs,** you can't make an omelette without breaking eggs.

omettre [ɔmɛtr̥] *v.tr.* (*conj. like* METTRE) to omit, miss out, pass over; to leave out (word); **o. de faire qch.,** to fail, omit, neglect, to do sth.

omission [ɔmisjɔ̃] *n.f.* omission; oversight; **péché, faute, d'o.,** sin of omission; *Typ:* **signe d'o.,** caret.

omnibus [ɔmnibys] **1.** *n.m.* (*a*) *A:* (horse) (omni)bus; (*b*) slow, stopping, *U.S:* accommodation, train. **2.** *a. inv.* (*a*) **train o.,** slow, stopping, train; (*b*) suitable for all cases; **règles o.,** blanket rules; *El:* **barre o.,** busbar.

omnipotence [ɔmnipɔtɑ̃s] *n.f.* omnipotence.

omnipotent [ɔmnipɔtɑ̃] *a.* omnipotent, all-powerful.

omnipraticien, -ienne [ɔmnipratisjɛ̃, -jɛn] *n. Med:* general practitioner.

omniprésence [ɔmniprezɑ̃s] *n.f.* omnipresence.

omniprésent [ɔmniprezɑ̃] *a.* omnipresent.

omniscience [ɔmnisjɑ̃s] *n.f.* omniscience.

omniscient [ɔmnisjɑ̃] *a.* omniscient.

omnium [ɔmnjɔm] *n.m.* **1.** *Pol.Ec:* combine; = holding company; *St. Exch:* **o. de valeurs** = investment trust. **2.** *Sp:* open race; *Turf:* open handicap; *Golf:* open championship; *Cy:* mixed race.

omnivore [ɔmnivɔr] **1.** *a.* omnivorous. **2.** *n.m. Z:* omnivore.

omoplate [ɔmɔplat] *n.f.* shoulder blade, scapula.

on [ɔ̃] *indef. pron. nom.* (*occ. becomes* **l'on,** *esp. after vowel sound*) one, people; we, they, etc. **1.** (*indeterminate*) **on ne sait jamais,** one never knows; you never can tell; **on n'en sait rien,** nobody knows anything about it; **on n'aime pas à être traité comme ça,** people don't like to be treated like that; **partout où l'on trouve de ces fossiles,** wherever these fossils are found; **on ne connaît jamais son bonheur,** one never knows one's own happiness; **quand on demande à une jeune fille d'être sa, votre, femme,** when a man asks a girl to be his wife; when you ask a girl to be your wife; **on était au sept mars,** it was the seventh of March; **on dit qu'elle était folle,** it's said, they say, that she was mad; she's said to have been mad; **on frappe à la porte,** someone's, somebody's, knocking; there's a knock at the door; **on a enfoncé la porte,** the door was burst open; **on demande une bonne cuisinière,** wanted, a good cook. **2.** (*specific pers. or people; a following adj., noun or p.p. is masc., fem. or pl. as the sense requires*) (*a*) **on parlait très peu au déjeuner,** we didn't talk much over lunch; **on ne s'était jamais séparés,** they had never been separated; **on n'est pas toujours jeune et belle,** women can't be young and beautiful for ever; **où va-t-on?** where are we going? **alors, on s'en va comme ça?** are you really going off like that? **nous, on est tous égaux,** we're all equal here.

onagre[1] [ɔnagr̥] *n.f. Bot:* evening primrose.

onagre[2] *n.m.* onager, wild ass.

once[1] [ɔ̃s] *n.f. Meas:* ounce.

once[2] *n.f. Z:* ounce, snow leopard.

oncial, -iaux [ɔ̃sjal, -jo] *a.* uncial (letter, MS.).

oncle [ɔ̃kl̥] *n.m.* uncle; **o. à la mode de Bretagne,** (i) first cousin once removed; (ii) distant relation.

oncques [ɔ̃k] *adv. A:* (*a*) ever; (*b*) (*with* **ne** *expressed or understood*) never.

onction [ɔ̃ksjɔ̃] *n.f. Ecc:* **l'extrême o.,** extreme unction.

onctueusement [ɔ̃ktɥøzmɑ̃] *adv.* unctuously.

onctueux, -euse [ɔ̃ktɥø, -øz] *a.* **1.** greasy, oily (substance). **2.** unctuous, oily (manner).

onctuosité [ɔ̃ktɥozite] *n.f.* oiliness.

onde [ɔ̃d] *n.f.* **1.** (*a*) *Lit:* wave, billow, water, tide; **sur la terre et sur l'o.,** on land and water; **les ondes de la foule,** the surging of the crowd; (*b*) wavy line; corrugation. **2.** *Ph:* (*a*) **o. calorifique, o. lumineuse, sonore,** heat, light, sound, wave; *Av:* **o. de choc,** shock wave; *W.Tel:* **ondes courtes,** short waves; **ondes moyennes, petites ondes,** medium waves; **grandes ondes,** long waves; *F:* **nous ne sommes pas sur la même longueur d'o.,** we're not on the same wavelength; (*b*) **les ondes,** the radio; **sur les ondes,** on the air, the radio.

ondé [ɔ̃de] *a.* waved, undulating, wavy (surface).

ondée [ɔ̃de] *n.f.* heavy shower; **temps à ondées,** showery weather.

ondemètre [ɔ̃dmɛtr̥] *n.m. W.Tel:* wavemeter.

ondin, -ine [ɔ̃dɛ̃, -in] *n. Myth:* water sprite; *f.* undine, nixie.

on-dit [ɔ̃di] *n.m.inv.* rumour, *NAm:* rumor; hearsay.

ondoiement [ɔ̃dwamɑ̃] *n.m.* **1.** undulation, wavy motion (of reeds, etc.). **2.** *Ecc:* private baptism (in emergency).

ondoyant [ɔ̃dwajɑ̃] *a.* **1.** undulating (ground); wavy; swaying (crowd, motion); waving (reeds). **2.** changeable (disposition).

ondoyer [ɔ̃dwaje] *v.* (**j'ondoie; j'ondoierai**) **1.** *v.i.* to undulate, wave, ripple; to float on the breeze; (*of flames, etc.*) to billow. **2.** *v.tr. Ecc:* to baptize privately (in emergency).

ondulant [ɔ̃dylɑ̃] *a.* undulating (landscape); waving (reeds); flowing (mane, drapery).

ondulation [ɔ̃dylasjɔ̃] *n.f.* **1.** (*a*) undulation (of water, etc.); wave motion; (*b*) rise (and fall), undulation (in the ground); **région à ondulations,** rolling country. **2.** *Hairdr:* wave (in hair).

ondulatoire [ɔ̃dylatwar] *a. Ph:* undulatory; **mouvement o.,** wave motion.

ondulé [ɔ̃dyle] *a.* undulating, rolling (ground); wavy, waved (hair); corrugated (iron, cardboard); **route ondulée,** switchback road.

onduler [ɔ̃dyle] **1.** *v.i.* to undulate, ripple. **2.** *v.tr.* to wave (the hair); to corrugate (iron, cardboard).

onduleux, -euse [ɔ̃dylø,-øz] *a.* undulating (plain); wavy (line).

onéreusement [ɔnerøzmɑ̃] *adv.* onerously.

onéreux, -euse [ɔnerø, -øz] *a.* onerous; burdensome (tax); heavy (expenditure); **à titre o.,** subject to certain liabilities, to payment.

ongle [ɔ̃gl̥] *n.m.* (finger)nail; claw (of animal); talon (of bird of prey); **ongles des orteils,** toenails; **coup d'o.,** scratch; **se faire les ongles,** to do, to cut, one's nails; **rogner les ongles à un animal,** *F:* **à qn,** to cut an animal's, *F:* s.o.'s, claws; **se ronger les ongles,** (i) to bite one's nails; (ii) to be restless, impatient; **avoir les ongles crochus,** to be mean, rapacious; **donner sur les ongles à qn,** to rap s.o. over the knuckles; **connaître, savoir, qch. sur le bout des ongles,** to know sth. perfectly; **il est français jusqu'au bout des ongles,** he's French to the finger tips, every inch a Frenchman.

onglée [ɔ̃gle] *n.f.* tingling, aching (of numbed finger tips); **j'ai l'o.,** my fingers are numb with cold.

onglet [ɔ̃glɛ] *n.m.* **1.** thumbnail groove (of penknife). **2.** *Bookb:* (*a*) guard; (*b*) tab (of thumb index); **dictionnaire à onglets,** thumb-indexed dictionary. **3.** *Bot:* unguis, claw (of petal). **4.** *Carp:* mitre, *NAm:* miter; **boîte à o.,** mitre box; **tailler à o.,** to mitre, *NAm:* miter. **5.** *Mth:* ungula.

onglier [ɔ̃glije] *n.m.* **1.** manicure set. **2.** *pl.* nail scissors.

onguent [ɔ̃gɑ̃] *n.m.* ointment, unguent, salve; **o. pour les yeux,** eyesalve.

onguiculé [ɔ̃gikyle] *a. Nat.Hist:* unguiculate.

ongulé [ɔ̃gyle] *a. & n.m. Z:* ungulate.

onirisme [ɔnirism] *n.m.* (state of) hallucination.

onirologie [ɔnirɔlɔʒi] *n.f.* oneirology.

onomatopée [ɔnɔmatɔpe] *n.f.* onomatopoeia.

ontogenèse [ɔ̃tɔʒənɛz] *n.f.* ontogenesis, ontogeny.

ontogénétique [ɔ̃tɔʒenetik] *a.* ontogenetic, ontogenic.

ontologie [ɔ̃tɔlɔʒi] *n.f. Phil:* ontology.

ontologique [ɔ̃tɔlɔʒik] *a. Phil:* ontological.

onyx [ɔniks] *n.m. Miner:* onyx; **marbre o.,** onyx marble.

onze [ɔ̃z] *num.a.inv. & n.m.inv.* (*the* **e** *of* **le, de,** *is not, as a rule, elided before* **onze** *and its derivatives*) (*a*) eleven; **nous n'étions que o. [kəɔ̃z], nous n'étions qu'o.,** there were only eleven of us; **le o. avril,** the eleventh of April; **Louis O.,** Louis the Eleventh; (*b*) *Fb: Cr:* **le o.,** the eleven.

onzième [ɔ̃zjɛm] **1.** *num.a. & n.* eleventh; **le o. jour,** the eleventh day. **2.** *n.m.* eleventh (part).

onzièmement [ɔ̃zjɛmmɑ̃] *adv.* eleventhly, in the eleventh place.

oolithe [ɔɔlit] *n.m.* oolite.

oolithique [ɔɔlitik] *a.* oolitic.

opacité [ɔpasite] *n.m.* **1.** opacity (of body); cloudiness (of liquid). **2.** darkness, denseness (of forest).

opale [ɔpal] **1.** *n.f.* opal. **2.** *a.inv.* opalescent; **verre o.,** opal glass; *El:* **ampoule o.,** pearl bulb.

opalescence [ɔpalesɑ̃s] *n.f.* opalescence.

opalescent [ɔpalesɑ̃] *a.* opalescent.

opalin, -ine [ɔpalɛ̃, -in] **1.** *a.* opaline (hue, reflection). **2.** *n.f.* **opaline,** opaline.

opaque [ɔpak] *a.* opaque.

opéra [ɔpera] *n.m.* **1.** opera; **grand o.,** grand opera; **o. bouffe,** opera bouffe, comic opera. **2.** opera house.

opérable [ɔperabl̥] *a. Surg:* operable (patient, tumour, *NAm:* tumor).

opéra-comique [ɔperakɔmik] *n.m.* opera comique, opera with spoken dialogue; *pl. opéras-comiques.*

opérateur, -trice [ɔperatœr, -tris] *n.* operator. **1.** (*a*) (machine) operator; *Typ:* machine setter; *Cin:* cameraman; **o. de radio,** radio operator; (*b*) operating surgeon. **2.** *n.m.* (*a*) *Mth:* operator; (*b*) working piece (of a machine).

opération [ɔperasjɔ̃] *n.f.* **1.** operation, working (of nature); process; **par l'o. du Saint-Esprit,** by the operation of the Holy Ghost; *F:* by magic. **2.** (*a*) **opérations militaires,** military operations; **o. publicité,** advertising campaign; (*b*) **o. (chirurgicale),** (surgical) operation; **subir une o.,** to undergo, have, an operation; **faire l'o. de l'appendicite,** to operate for appendicitis; **salle d'o.,** operating theatre, *U.S:* room; **o. à chaud,** emergency operation (for appendicitis, etc.). **3.** (commercial) transaction; deal; speculation; **opérations de Bourse,** Stock Exchange business, transactions.

opérationnel, -elle [ɔperasjɔnɛl] *a.* operational.

opératoire [ɔperatwar] *a. Surg:* operative (procedure, etc.); **médecine o.,** surgery.

opercule [ɔpɛrkyl] *n.m.* cover, lid, cap; *Nat.Hist:* operculum; gill cover (of fish); *Nau:* **o. de hublot,** deadlight.

operculé [ɔpɛrkyle] *a. Nat.Hist:* operculate(d).

opéré, -ée [ɔpere] *n.* patient (who has had an operation).

opérer [ɔpere] *v.* **(j'opère; j'opérerai)** to operate. **1.** *v.tr.* (*a*) to bring about, to work, to effect; **o. une réforme,** to carry out a reform; **o. une retraite,** to effect a retreat; **o. un sondage,** (i) to sink a borehole; (ii) to take an opinion poll; (*b*) to carry out, perform (multiplication, *Ch:* synthesis, etc.); (*c*) *Surg:* **o. un malade, un abcès,** to operate on a patient, an abscess; **être opéré de l'appendicite,** to be operated on for appendicitis; **se faire o.,** to undergo, have, an operation. **2.** *v.i.* **la façon dont les cambrioleurs ont opéré,** the way the burglars operated, went to work; **laisser o. la nature,** to leave it to nature; **son éloquence opéra sur la foule,** his eloquence swayed the crowd. **3. s'o.,** to come about, take place; **un changement complet s'est opéré dans sa vie,** a complete change has been brought about in his life.

opérette [ɔperɛt] *n.f.* operetta; musical comedy.

ophidien, -ienne [ɔfidjɛ̃, -jɛn] *a. & n.m.* ophidian.

ophite [ɔfit] *n.m. Miner:* ophite, serpentine.

ophrys [ɔfris] *n.f. Bot:* ophrys; **o. abeille,** bee orchid; **o. araignée,** spider orchid.

ophtalmie [ɔftalmi] *n.f.* ophthalmia; **o. des neiges,** snow blindness.

ophtalmique [ɔftalmik] *a.* ophthalmic.

ophtalmologie [ɔftalmɔlɔʒi] *n.f.* ophthalmology.

ophtalmologiste [ɔftalmɔlɔʒist], **ophtalmologue** [ɔftalmɔlɔg] *n.* ophthalmologist.

ophtalmoscope [ɔftalmɔskɔp] *n.m. Med:* ophthalmoscope.

opiacé [ɔpjase] *a.* containing opium; opiated.

opiacer [ɔpjase] *v.tr.* **(j'opiaçai(s); n. opiaçons)** to opiate; to mix with opium.

opiner [ɔpine] *v.i. O:* to opine; to be of the opinion (**que,** that); **o. pour, en faveur de, qch.,** to give an opinion in favour, *NAm:* favor of sth., to assent to, to vote for, in favour of, sth.; **o. de la tête, du bonnet,** to nod approval, signify assent.

opiniâtre [ɔpinjɑtr̥] *a.* obstinate; (*a*) headstrong; stubborn (mule, person); (*b*) persistent (cough); unyielding (opposition); stout, dogged (resistance).

opiniâtrement [ɔpinjɑtrəmɑ̃] *adv.* obstinately, stubbornly; stoutly; doggedly.

opiniâtrer (s') [sɔpinjɑtre] *v.pr. A:* **s'o. à qch., à faire qch.,** to persist in sth., in doing sth.

opiniâtreté [ɔpinjɑtrəte] *n.f.* (*a*) obstinacy, stubbornness; (*b*) perseverance, determination.

opinion [ɔpinjɔ̃] *n.f.* opinion (**de,** of; **sur,** about); view, judgment; **opinions politiques,** politicial opinions, views; **créer un mouvement d'o.,** to excite public opinion; **sondage d'o.,** opinion poll; **émettre une o.,** to express an opinion; **partager l'o. de qn,** to agree with s.o.; **amener qn à son o.,** to bring s.o. round to one's way of thinking; **avoir bonne, mauvaise, o. de qn,** to have a good, bad, opinion of s.o.; **donner bonne o. de soi,** to make a good impression.

opiomane [ɔpjɔman] *n.* opium addict.

opium [ɔpjɔm] *n.m.* opium.

opossum [ɔpɔsɔm] *n.m. Z:* opossum.

opportun, -une [ɔpɔrtœ̃, -yn] *a.* (*a*) opportune, timely, well timed, convenient; **arriver au moment o.,** to arrive opportunely, at the opportune, right, moment; (*b*) expedient, advisable.

opportunément [ɔpɔrtynemɑ̃] *adv.* opportunely, at the right moment.

opportunisme [ɔpɔrtynism] *n.m.* opportunism; timeserving.

opportuniste [ɔpɔrtynist] **1.** *a.* timeserving. **2.** *n.* opportunist; timeserver.

opportunité [ɔpɔrtynite] *n.f.* (*a*) opportuneness, timeliness; (*b*) expediency, advisability (of project, etc.).

opposant, -ante [ɔpozɑ̃, -ɑ̃t] **1.** *a.* opposing, adverse (party, etc.). **2.** *n.* opponent; *Pol:* member of the Opposition.

opposé [ɔpoze] **1.** *a.* (*a*) opposed, opposing (armies, characters, etc.); opposite (side, shore, direction); contrary (interests, advice); **angles opposés par le sommet,** vertically opposite angles; *Bot:* **feuilles opposées,** opposite leaves; **leurs opinions sont diamétralement opposées,** their views are poles apart; **tons opposés,** contrasting colours, *NAm:* colors; (*b*) **être o. à une mesure, à ce que qch. se fasse,** to be opposed to, against, a measure; to be opposed to, against, sth. being done. **2.** *n.m.* (*a*) **l'o.,** the contrary, reverse, opposite (of sth.); **à l'o.,** on the contrary; **à l'o. de l'attente,** contrary to expectation; (*b*) **la gare est à l'o.,** the station is (on the) opposite (side).

opposer [ɔpoze] **1.** *v.tr.* (*a*) to oppose; **o. qch. à qch.,** to set sth. against sth.; **o. une glace à une fenêtre,** to set a mirror opposite a window; **je n'ai rien à**

o. à ce raisonnement, I have nothing to urge against, no objection to, this argument; **o. une vigoureuse résistance,** to put up, offer, a vigorous resistance; to resist tooth and nail; **o. son veto,** to exercise one's veto; (*b*) to compare, to contrast (**à,** with); **o. le vice à la vertu,** to contrast vice with virtue. **2. s'o. à qch.,** to oppose sth.; to be opposed to sth.; **s'o. résolument à qch.,** to set one's face against sth.; **s'o. à un projet, à un mariage,** to set oneself against, to stand in the way of, a scheme, a marriage; **il n'y a pas de loi qui s'y oppose,** there is no law against it; **rien ne s'oppose à votre succès,** nothing stands between you and success.

opposite [ɔpozit] *n.m.* (*a*) *A:* opposite, contrary; (*b*) **maison à l'o. de l'église,** house opposite, facing, the church.

opposition [ɔpozisjɔ̃] *n.f.* **1.** (*a*) opposition; **mettre o. à qch.,** to oppose sth.; **agir en o. avec un droit,** to act in contravention of a right; **se mettre en o. avec qn,** to come into conflict with s.o.; *Pol:* **l'O.,** the Opposition; **frapper un chèque d'o.,** to stop payment of a cheque; (*b*) *Jur:* (i) **o. sur titre,** attachment against securities; (ii) **jugement susceptible d'o.,** judgment liable to stay of execution; (iii) caveat; **mettre o. à un mariage,** to enter a caveat to a marriage; to forbid the banns. **2.** contrast, antithesis; **par o. à qch.,** as opposed to sth.; **couleurs en o.,** contrasting colours, *NAm:* colors. **3.** *Astr:* opposition (of planets).

oppresser [ɔprese] *v.tr.* to oppress; (*a*) to cause (s.o.) difficulty in breathing; (*b*) to depress (s.o.); to weigh (s.o.) down.

oppresseur [ɔpresœr] **1.** *n.m.* oppressor. **2.** *a.m.* oppressive, tyrannical.

oppressif, -ive [ɔpresif, -iv] *a.* oppressive (government, etc.).

oppression [ɔpresjɔ̃] *n.f.* oppression. **1. o. de la poitrine,** tightness of the chest; difficulty in breathing. **2. o. d'un peuple,** oppression, crushing, of a nation.

oppressivement [ɔpresivmɑ̃] *adv.* oppressively, tyranically.

opprimé [ɔprime] *a.* oppressed, crushed, downtrodden; *n.pl.* **les opprimés,** the oppressed.

opprimer [ɔprime] *v.tr.* to oppress, crush (down) (a people, the weak); to suppress (freedom).

opprobre [ɔprɔbr̥] *n.m. Lit:* disgrace, shame, opprobrium, infamy; **il est l'o. du genre humain,** he is a disgrace to mankind.

optatif, -ive [ɔptatif, -iv] *a. & n.m.* optative (mood).

opter [ɔpte] *v.i.* to opt; **o. entre deux choses,** to choose between two things; **o. pour qch.,** to opt for sth.

opticien, -ienne [ɔptisjɛ̃, -jɛn] *n.* optician.

optimal, -aux [ɔptimal, -o] *a.* optimum, optimal.

optimisme [ɔptimism] *n.m.* optimism.

optimiste [ɔptimist] **1.** *a.* optimistic; sanguine (disposition). **2.** *n.* optimist.

optimum [ɔptimɔm] *a.inv. & n.m.inv.* optimum (conditions); **o. de population,** optimum population density; *pl. optimums, occ. optima.*

option [ɔpsjɔ̃] *n.f.* option, choice (**de, entre,** between); *St.Exch:* **o. d'achat, pour acheter,** call; **o. de vente,** put; **jour d'o.,** option day; **o. pour un sujet de film,** option on the film rights (of a book); *Sch:* **matières à o.,** optional subjects.

optique [ɔptik] **1.** *a.* optic (nerve); optic, visual (angle); optical (microscope); **télégraphie o.,** visual signalling; **verre o.,** optical glass. **2.** *n.f.* (*a*) optics; **instruments d'o.,** optical instruments; **o. électronique,** electron optics; *Tg:* **transmettre par o.,** to communicate by visual signals; (*b*) **o. du théâtre,** stage perspective; (*c*) point of view; way of looking at things. **3.** optical system (of projector, etc.).

optométriste [ɔptɔmetrist] *n.* optometrist.

opulence [ɔpylɑ̃s] *n.f.* opulence, affluence; **nager dans l'o.,** to be rolling in money.

opulent [ɔpylɑ̃] *a.* opulent, rich, monied, wealthy; affluent; abundant (harvest); buxom (figure).

opuscule [ɔpyskyl] *n.m.* opuscule; short treatise; tract.

or¹ [ɔr] *n.m.* **1.** gold; **la ruée vers l'or,** the gold rush; *F:* **or noir,** oil; **or en barres,** ingot gold; bullion; **c'est de l'or en barres,** it's as safe as the Bank of England; **poudre d'or,** gold dust; **montre d'or, en or,** gold watch; *F:* **j'ai une femme en or,** I've a wonderful wife; **or en feuille(s),** gold foil; **feuille d'or,** gold leaf; **payer qch. à prix d'or,** to pay a fortune for sth.; **affaire d'or,** excellent bargain, business; **il vaut son pesant d'or,** he's worth his weight in gold; **l'âge d'or,** the golden age; **cœur d'or,** heart of gold; **parler d'or,** to speak words of wisdom; **livre d'or,** (official) visitors' book; **faire un pont d'or à qn,** (i) to offer s.o. a very high salary (as an inducement); (ii) to give s.o. a golden handshake; **rouler sur l'or, être (tout) cousu d'or,** to be rolling in money. **2.** gold (colour, *NAm:* color); *Her:* or; **vieil or,** old gold; **chevelure d'or,** golden hair.

or² *conj.* now (then); well (then); **or, pour revenir à ce que nous disions,** now to come back to what we were saying; **or . . ., donc . . .,** now . . ., therefore . . .; **avant de le lire, je pensais que le livre était bon; or, il ne l'était pas,** before reading it, I thought the book was good; well, it wasn't.

oracle [ɔrɑkl̥] *n.m.* oracle; **parler d'un ton d'o.,** to speak with assurance.

orage [ɔraʒ] *n.m.* (thunder)storm; **le temps est à l'o.,** the weather's thundery; there's thunder in the air; **il va faire de l'o.,** there's a storm brewing; **o. magnétique,** magnetic storm; **o. politique,** political storm; **tenir tête à l'o.,** to face the music.

orageusement [ɔraʒøzmɑ̃] *adv.* stormily.

orageux, -euse [ɔraʒø, -øz] *a.* (*a*) thundery (weather, sky); lowering (clouds); (*b*) stormy (season, sea); (*c*) stormy (life, etc.); heated (discussion).

oraison [ɔrɛzɔ̃] *n.f.* **1. o. funèbre,** funeral oration. **2.** prayer; **faire ses oraisons,** to say one's prayers.

oral, -aux [ɔral, -o] **1.** *a.* (*a*) oral (tradition, teaching, examination); verbal (deposition); (*b*) *Anat:* oral (cavity); **par voie orale,** orally, by mouth. **2.** *n.m.* oral examination; viva voce examination; *F:* oral, viva.

oralement [ɔralmɑ̃] *adv.* orally; by word of mouth.

orange [ɔrɑ̃ʒ] **1.** *n.f.* orange; **o. amère,** bitter orange, Seville orange; **o. sanguine,** blood orange. **2.** *n.m.* orange (colour, *NAm:* color); *a.inv.* orange(-coloured, *NAm:* -colored); *Trans:* **carte o.,** monthly season (ticket).

orangé [ɔrɑ̃ʒe] *a. & n.m.* orange (colour, *NAm:* color); orange-coloured, *NAm:* -colored.

orangeade [ɔrɑ̃ʒad] *n.f.* orangeade.

oranger [ɔrɑ̃ʒe] *n.m.* orange tree; **fleurs d'o.,** orange blossom; **eau de fleur d'o.,** orange-flower water.

orangeraie [ɔrɑ̃ʒrɛ] *n.f.* orange grove.

orangerie [ɔrɑ̃ʒri] *n.f.* orangery.

orang-outan(g) [ɔrɑ̃utɑ̃] *n.m.* orang-outang, orang-utan; *pl. orangs-outan(g)s.*

orateur [ɔratœr] *n.m.* orator; (*at dinner, etc.*) speaker; **o. de carrefour,** soap-box orator.

oratoire¹ [ɔratwar] *a.* oratorical (talent, gesture); **l'art o.,** (the art of) oratory; public speaking.

oratoire² *n.m.* oratory. **1.** chapel for private prayer. **2. l'O.,** the Oratory.

oratorio [ɔratɔrjo] *n.m. Mus:* oratorio.

orbe¹ [ɔrb] *n.m.* orb.

orbe² *a.* **mur o.,** blind wall.

orbitaire [ɔrbitɛr] *a. Anat:* orbital (nerve, etc.).

orbital, -aux [ɔrbital, -o] *a.* orbital (motion).

orbite [ɔrbit] *n.f.* **1.** (*a*) orbit (of planet, spacecraft, electron); **en o., sur o.,** orbiting; in orbit; **mettre un satellite en o., sur o.,** to put a satellite in, into, orbit; (*b*) orbit, sphere of influence. **2.** *Anat:* socket, orbit (of the eye).

orbiter [ɔrbite] *v.i.* to orbit.

Orcades (les) [lezɔrkad] *Pr.n.f.pl. Geog:* the Orkneys, the Orkney Islands.

orchestral, -aux [ɔrkɛstral, -o] *a.* orchestral.

orchestration [ɔrkɛstrasjɔ̃] *n.f.* orchestration; (*a*) *Mus:* scoring; (*b*) organization (of campaign).

orchestre [ɔrkɛstr̥] *n.m.* **1.** *Th:* **fauteuil d'o.,** seat in the (orchestra) stalls. **2.** *Mus:* orchestra; **chef d'o.,** conductor.

orchestrer [ɔrkɛstre] *v.tr.* to orchestrate; (*a*) *Mus:* to score (opera, etc.); (*b*) to organize (campaign, etc.).

orchidée [ɔrkide] *n.f.* orchid.

orchis [ɔrkis] *n.m.* orchis, wild orchid; **o. militaire,** military orchid, soldier orchid; **o. à deux feuilles,** butterfly orchid.

ordalie [ɔrdali] *n.f. Hist:* ordeal; **o. de l'eau, de feu,** ordeal by water, by fire.

ordinaire [ɔrdinɛr] **1.** *a.* ordinary, usual, common; **vêtements ordinaires,** everyday clothes; **vin o.,** table wine; **il est o. de faire ses excuses,** it is usual, normal, to apologize; **peu, pas, o.,** unusual, uncommon, out of the ordinary; *F:* **celle-là n'est pas o.!** that's a bit much! *Mth:* **fractions ordinaires,** vulgar fractions; *Fin:* **actions ordinaires,** ordinary shares; **votre fournisseur o.,** your normal, regular, usual, supplier; **médecin o. du roi,** physician in ordinary to the king; **évêque o.,** diocesan bishop; **de taille o.,** ordinary-sized, average-sized; (*of pers.*) of average height; **vin très o.,** very indifferent wine. **2.** *n.m.* (*a*) custom, usual practice; **comme à, selon, son o.,** as he usually does; **contre mon o.,** contrary to my usual habit; **d'o., à l'o.,** usually, as a rule; **comme à l'o., comme d'o.,** as usual; (*b*) normal standard, usual state of things; **cela sort de l'o.,** it's unusual, out of the ordinary; **intelligence au-dessus de l'o.,** above-average intelligence; (*c*) standard menu (at inn, etc.); *Mil:* (company) mess; **auberge où l'o. est excellent,** inn where the fare, the food, is excellent; *Mil:* **fonds d'o.,** mess fund; (*d*) *R.C.Ch:* **l'o. de la messe,** the ordinary of the mass.

ordinairement [ɔrdinɛrmɑ̃] *adv.* as a rule, ordinarily, usually.

ordinal, -aux [ɔrdinal, -o] *a.* ordinal (adjective, etc.).

ordinand [ɔrdinɑ̃] *n.m. Ecc:* candidate for ordination; ordinand.

ordinateur [ɔrdinatœr] *n.m.* **1.** *Ecc:* ordainer, ordinant. **2.** computer.

ordination [ɔrdinasjɔ̃] *n.f. Ecc:* ordination.

ordonnance [ɔrdɔnɑ̃s] *n.f.* **1.** order, (general) arrangement (of building, etc.); disposition, grouping (of picture, etc.). **2.** (*a*) statute, enactment, ordinance, order; **o. d'amnistie,** amnesty ordinance; **o. de police,** police regulation; (*b*) order, ruling (of judge sitting alone); (*c*) **o. de paiement,** order, warrant, for payment. **3.** *Mil:* **habit d'o.,** uniform, regimentals; **bottes d'o.,** issue boots; **revolver d'o.,** service revolver; **officier d'o.,** aide-de-camp; *Navy:* flag lieutenant. **4.** *Mil: A:* orderly. **5.** *Med:* prescription; **délivré seulement sur o.,** available only on a doctor's prescription.

ordonnancement [ɔrdɔnɑ̃smɑ̃] *n.m.* (*a*) *Adm:* order to pay; (*b*) *Ind:* scheduling, organization (of production, processes).

ordonnancer [ɔrdɔnɑ̃se] *v.tr.* **(j'ordonnançai(s); n. ordonnançons)** *Adm:* to pass (account) for payment; to sanction (expenditure).

ordonnateur, -trice [ɔrdɔnatœr, -tris] *n.* **1.** director; organizer (of festivities), master of ceremonies. **2.** *Adm:* person authorized to pass accounts.

ordonné, -ée [ɔrdɔne] **1.** *a.* (*a*) orderly, well-ordered (life, arrangement); *Cmptr:* **traitement non o.,** random processing; (*b*) (person) of regular habits; tidy (person). **2.** *n.f. Mth:* **ordonnée,** ordinate; **axe des ordonnées,** Y-axis.

ordonner [ɔrdɔne] *v.tr.* **1.** to arrange (sth.); to set (sth.) to rights; *Mth:* to arrange (terms) in ascending, descending, order. **2.** to order, command, direct; **o. à qn de faire qch.,** to order s.o., to give s.o. orders, to do sth.; **o. à qn de se taire,** to tell s.o. to be quiet; **o. une grève,** to call a strike; **o. une enquête,** to order an enquiry; **o. un remède à qn,** to prescribe a remedy for s.o.

ordre [ɔrdr̥] *n.m.* order. **1.** methodical arrangement; **o. alphabétique,** alphabetical order; **par o. de date,** in date order; **numéro d'o.,** serial number; **c'est dans l'o. des choses,** it's in the nature of things; *Mil:* **o. serré, ouvert,** close, extended, order; **avec o.,** methodically; **sans o.,** untidy; untidily, unmethodical, unmethodically; *F:* higgledy-piggledy; **manque d'o.,** untidiness; **en bon o.,** (i) in (an) orderly manner; (ii) in good order; **en o. parfait,** in apple-pie order; all shipshape; **homme d'o.,** orderly, methodical, man; **il a de l'o.,** he is methodical, systematic, tidy; **(re)-mettre de l'o. dans qch.,** to set sth. in order, to rights; to tidy up (room); **mettre o. à ses affaires, mettre ses affaires en o.,** to put one's affairs in order, to settle one's affairs; to set one's house in order; (*of machine, etc.*) **en o. de marche,** in working order. **2.** orderliness, discipline; **assurer l'o.,** to preserve order; **maintenir l'o. dans une ville,** to maintain order in a town, to police a town; **le service d'o., les forces de l'o.,** the police (*esp.* at demonstration, etc.); **rappeler qn à l'o.,** to call s.o. to order; **o. public,** law and order; **délit contre l'o. public,** breach of the peace. **3. o. du jour,** (i) agenda (of meeting), business before the meeting; (ii) *Mil:* general orders, order of the day; *Mil:* **cité à l'o. du jour** = mentioned in despatches; **la guerre froide est à l'o. du jour,** the cold war is very much in the news. **4.** (*a*) order (of architecture, plants, animals, etc.); class, division, category; **les trois ordres (de l'État),** the three orders, classes (of the State); **de premier o.,** first-class, first-rate; **hôtel de troisième o.,** third-rate hotel; **tireur de premier o.,** crack shot; **renseignement d'o. général,** general information; **d'o. privé,** of a private nature; **de l'o. de dix tonnes,** in the order of, in the region of, about, ten tonnes; (*b*) **o. religieux,** monastic order; **o. de chevalerie,** order of knighthood; **o. de la Légion d'honneur,** Order of the Legion of Honour, *NAm:* Honor; **o. des avocats** = the Bar; (*c*) *pl. Ecc:* holy orders; **recevoir, entrer dans, les ordres,** to take holy orders. **5.** (*a*) command, warrant; **o. par écrit,** written order; **o. d'exécution,** death warrant; **o. d'écrou, de levée d'écrou,** order to confine, to release, prisoner; **donner o. à qn de faire qch.,** to order s.o. to do sth.; **donner des ordres à qn,** (i) to give s.o. orders; (ii) to order s.o. about; **par o., sur l'o., de qn,** by order of s.o.; **n'obéir qu'aux ordres de X,** to take orders only from X; **se mettre aux ordres de qn,** to put oneself at s.o.'s disposal; **être aux ordres de qn,** to be at s.o.'s beck and call; **jusqu'à nouvel o.,** until further orders, notice; for the time being; **à moins d'o., sauf o., contraire,** in the absence of orders to the contrary; unless otherwise directed; *Mil:* **o. d'appel (sous les drapeaux),** call-up papers; **o. de comparaître,** summons to attend; *Navy:* **ordres cachetés,** sealed orders; *Nau:* **l'o. d'appareiller,** sailing orders; (*b*) *Com:* **payez à l'o. de J. Martin,** pay to the order of J. Martin; **billet à o.,** bill of exchange payable to order.

ordure [ɔrdyr] *n.f.* **1.** (*a*) dirt, filth, muck; (*b*) excrement, dung, ordure; (*c*) filthiness, lewdness; (*in talk, writing*) smut. **2.** *pl.* rubbish, refuse; **ordures ménagères,** household rubbish, refuse, *NAm:* garbage; **boîte à ordures, aux ordures,** dustbin, refuse bin; *NAm:* trash can, garbage can.

ordurier, -ière [ɔrdyrje, -jɛr] *a.* obscene; smutty, filthy (book, song); filthy, foul (language); scurrilous (abuse).

oréade [ɔread] *n.f. Myth:* oread; mountain nymph.

orée [ɔre] *n.f.* **à l'o. de la forêt, du bois,** on the edge of the forest, wood.

oreillard [ɔrɛjar] *n.m.* **1.** *Z:* long-eared bat. **2.** wing (of armchair).

oreille [ɔrɛj] *n.f.* ear. **1. avoir mal à l'o., aux oreilles,** to have earache; **aux oreilles courtes,** short-eared; **à longues oreilles,** long-eared; **mettre, porter, son chapeau sur l'o.,** to cock, wear, one's hat on one side, over one ear; **baisser l'o., avoir l'o. basse,** to be crestfallen; **il partit l'o. basse,** he went off with his tail between his legs; (*of horse*) **coucher les oreilles,** to set, lay, its ears back; **tirer les oreilles à qn,** to pull, tweak, s.o.'s ears; *F:* **il s'est (bien) fait tirer l'o.,** he took a lot of coaxing; **il ne s'est pas fait tirer l'o.,** he didn't have to be asked twice; **montrer le bout de l'o.,** to show the cloven hoof; **être en dette jusqu'aux oreilles, par-dessus les oreilles,** to be up to the ears in debt; *F:* **(é)chauffer les oreilles à qn,** to annoy s.o., get on s.o.'s nerves; **ils se sont pris par les oreilles,** they had a set-to; **il a toujours l'o. déchirée,** he's always in the wars; *F:* **fendre l'o. à qn,** to retire (officer, official, etc.); **enseigner à qn que les enfants ne se font pas par l'o.,** to tell s.o. the facts of life. **2. n'écouter que d'une o.,** to listen with half an ear; **dire, souffler, qch. à l'o. de qn,** to whisper sth. in s.o.'s ear; **dresser, tendre, l'o.,** to prick up one's ears; **être tout oreilles,** to be all ears, all attention; **prêter l'o. à qn,** to lend an ear to s.o.; **fermer l'o. à la vérité,** to be deaf, to close one's ears, to the truth; **faire la sourde o.,** to turn a deaf ear; **il n'entend pas de cette o.-là,** he is deaf in that ear; *Fig:* **il ne l'entend pas de cette o.-là,** he won't hear of it; *F:* **casser les oreilles à qn,** to split s.o.'s eardrums, drive s.o. crazy (with questions, noise); **si cela parvient aux oreilles du principal,** if it should come to the headmaster's ears; **rebattre les oreilles à qn de qch.,** to din sth. in s.o.'s ears; **être dur d'o., avoir l'o. dure,** to be hard of hearing; **avoir l'o. juste, avoir de l'o.,** to have a good ear for music. **3.** ear, lug (of dish, bowl); handle (of vase); ear flap (of cap); lug, lobe, attachment, flange (of piece of machinery, etc.); palm (of anchor); **écrou à oreilles,** wing nut, butterfly nut; **bergère à oreilles,** wing chair; **faire une o. à une page,** to dog-ear a page. **4.** *Bot: F:* **o. d'ours,** auricula.

oreiller [ɔreje] *n.m.* pillow; *F:* **prendre conseil de son o.,** to sleep on it.

oreillette [ɔrɛjɛt] *n.f.* **1.** *Anat:* auricle (of the heart). **2. fauteuil à oreillettes,** wing chair; **casquette à oreillettes,** cap with ear flaps.

oreillons [ɔrɛjɔ̃] *n.m.pl. Med:* mumps.

Orénoque (l') [lɔrenɔk] *Pr.n.m. Geog:* the Orinoco (river).

ore(s) [ɔr] *adv. A:* now; *still used in* **d'o. et déjà,** now and henceforth, from now on, here and now.

orfèvre [ɔrfɛvr̥] *n.m.* goldsmith, gold- and silversmith; **être o. en la matière,** to be an expert in the matter.

orfèvrerie [ɔrfɛvrəri] *n.f.* **1.** (*a*) goldsmith's trade, craft, work; (*b*) goldsmith's shop. **2.** (*a*) (gold, silver) plate; (*b*) jewellery.

orfraie [ɔrfrɛ] *n.f. Orn:* sea eagle; *F:* **pousser des cris d'o.,** to shriek at the top of one's voice.

organdi [ɔrgɑ̃di] *n.m. Tex:* organdie; book muslin.

organe [ɔrgan] *n.m.* **1.** *Physiol:* organ. **2.** part, component (of machine); **organes de transmission,** transmission gear; *Cmptr:* **o. d'entrée,** input unit. **3.** organ; (*a*) voice; **o. mâle et sonore,** strong, manly, voice; (*b*) mouthpiece (of political party); spokesman; **certains organes,** a certain section of the press. **4.** instrument (of government, etc.); medium, agency; **o. de publicité,** advertising medium.

organeau, -eaux [ɔrgano] *n.m. Nau:* (*a*) mooring ring; (*b*) anchor ring.

organigramme [ɔrganigram] *n.m.* (*a*) administrative chart; organization chart; *Cmptr:* (data) flow chart.

organique [ɔrganik] *a.* organic (disease, chemistry, law).

organiquement [ɔrganikmɑ̃] *adv.* organically.

organisateur, -trice [ɔrganizatœr, -tris] **1.** *a.* organizing. **2.** *n.* organizer; promoter (of boxing match, etc.).

organisateur-conseil [ɔrganizatœrkɔ̃sɛj] *n.m.* time and motion consultant; *pl. organisateurs-conseils.*

organisation [ɔrganizasjɔ̃] *n.f.* **1.** organization, organizing, planning; **qualités d'o.,** organizing ability; *Cmptr:* **o. des données,** data organization; **o. scientifique du travail,** organization and methods. **2.** structure (of human body, etc.). **3.** (business, etc.) organization; **o. de voyage,** travel organization; **O. des Nations Unies,** United Nations Organization.

organisationnel, -elle [organizasjɔnɛl] *a.* organizational.

organisé [ɔrganize] *a.* **1.** organic (being, etc.). **2.** organized, constituted; **voyage o.,** conducted tour; **vol o.,** systematic robbery; (*of pers.*) **bien o.,** systematic; level-headed.

organiser [ɔrganize] **1.** *v.tr.* to organize; to arrange; to set up (business); to get up, arrange (entertainment, etc.); to plan (a journey, one's time). **2. s'o.,** to get down to work; to settle down; to get organized.

organisme [ɔrganism] *n.m.* **1.** *Biol:* organism; *Anat:* (the) system; **un o. de fer,** an iron constitution. **2.** *Adm:* organization; **un o. comme l'O.N.U.,** a body such as U.N.O.

organiste [ɔrganist] *n. Mus:* organist.

organothérapie [ɔrganɔterapi] *n.f. Med:* organotherapy.

orgasme [ɔrgasm] *n.m.* orgasm.

orge [ɔrʒ] *n.* barley. **1.** *n.f.* **sucre d'o.,** barley sugar. **2.** *n.m.* **o. mondé,** (i) hulled barley; (ii) barley water; **o. perlé,** pearl barley.

orgelet [ɔrʒəlɛ] *n.m.* stye (on the eye).

orgiaque [ɔrʒjak] *a.* orgiastic.

orgie [ɔrʒi] *n.f.* **1.** *pl. Ant:* (Bacchanalian) orgies. **2.** (*a*) orgy; drunken feasting; feast; (*b*) **une o. de couleurs,** a riot of colour, *NAm:* color.

orgue [ɔrg] *n.m.* **1.** (*also Ecc: n.f.pl.* **orgues**) *Mus:* (*a*) organ; **un bel o., de belles orgues,** a fine organ; **o. du chœur, d'accompagnement,** choir organ; **tenir l'o., les orgues,** to be, preside, at the organ; (*b*) **o. de salon,** harmonium; American organ. **2. o. de Barbarie,** barrel organ; **joueur d'o.,** organ grinder. **3.** *Geol:* **orgues de basalte,** basalt columns.

orgueil [ɔrgœj] *n.m.* pride, arrogance; **o. légitime,** just, legitimate, pride; **l'o. de la naissance,** pride of birth; **l'o. de la flotte,** the pride of the fleet; **mettre son o. à faire qch.,** to take a pride in doing sth.

orgueilleusement [ɔrgœjøzmɑ̃] *adv.* proudly; arrogantly.

orgueilleux, -euse [ɔrgœjø, -øz] *a.* proud, arrogant; haughty; **être o. de sa maison,** to be house-proud; *n.pl.* **les o.,** the proud.

oriel [ɔrjɛl] *n.m.* oriel window; bow window.

orient [ɔrjɑ̃] *n.m.* **1.** (*a*) east; (*b*) **l'O.,** the East, the Orient; **le proche, le moyen, l'extrême, O.,** the Near, Middle, Far, East; **en O.,** in the East; **peuples d'O.,** Eastern, Oriental, nations; **tapis d'O.,** oriental carpet; *Hist:* **l'Empire d'O.,** the Byzantine Empire. **2.** water, orient (of pearl).

orientable [ɔrjɑ̃tabl̩] *a.* adjustable; rotatable; swivelling; free to turn, directional.

oriental, -ale, -aux [ɔrjɑ̃tal, -o] **1.** *a.* eastern (people, coast); oriental (language); *Hist:* **les Indes orientales,** the East Indies. **2.** *n.* Oriental.

orientaliste [ɔrjɑ̃talist] *n.* orientalist.

orientation [ɔrjɑ̃tasjɔ̃] *n.f.* **1.** (*a*) orientation; **table d'o.,** orientation, panoramic, table; **sens de l'o.,** sense of direction; (*b*) *Sch:* **o. professionnelle,** careers advice, vocational guidance; **conseiller d'o. professionnelle,** careers adviser; (*c*) swivelling, steering (of crane, etc.); positioning (of aerial); **roue d'o.,** directing wheel (of windmill); **o. d'un canon,** training of a gun; **à o. libre,** free-moving; adjustable; rotatable. **2.** orientation, aspect (of house); **l'o. de la politique,** the trend of politics; **o. des voiles,** set, trim, of the sails.

orientement [ɔrjɑ̃tmɑ̃] *n.m.* **1.** (*a*) orient(at)ing (of building); (*b*) *Nau:* trimming (of sails). **2. prendre un o.,** to take a bearing.

orienter [ɔrjɑ̃te] **1.** *v.tr.* (*a*) to orient(ate) (building); **pièce orientée au sud,** room with a southerly aspect, facing south; (*b*) to slew, swing (crane, etc.); to train (gun); to point, direct (telescope); to trim (sail); (*c*) to direct, guide; **o. un élève vers la chimie,** to interest a pupil in chemistry; **o. une revue vers le goût féminin,** to slant a magazine for women readers; **ouvrage orienté politiquement,** work with a political bias; **o. la conversation vers d'autres sujets,** to turn the conversation into other channels; (*d*) to set (map) by the compass; to draw the North-South line on (sketch map). **2. s'o.** (*a*) to take, find, one's bearings; to orientate oneself; (*b*) to take a direction (**vers,** towards); **il s'oriente vers la carrière diplomatique,** he is preparing to enter the diplomatic service; **cette politique s'oriente vers le communisme,** this policy is tending, moving, towards Communism.

orienteur, -euse [ɔrjɑ̃tœr, -øz] **1.** *n.* careers master, mistress; vocational adviser. **2.** *n.m.* (*instrument*) orientator.

orifice [ɔrifis] *n.m.* aperture, opening, orifice; mouth (of shaft); *Mch:* **orifices d'admission,** intake ports.

oriflamme [ɔriflam] *n.f.* (*a*) *Hist:* oriflamme; (*b*) streamer, decorative banner.

origan [ɔrigɑ̃] *n.m. Bot:* oregano; marjoram.

originaire [ɔriʒinɛr] *a.* **1.** originating (**de,** from, in); native (**de,** of); **il est o. de la Russie, du Havre,** he comes, hails, from Russia, from Le Havre. **2.** original, foundation (member).

originairement [ɔriʒinɛrmɑ̃] *adv.* originally, at the beginning.

original, -ale, -aux [ɔriʒinal, -o] *a. & n.* **1.** original (text, manuscript); *Typewr:* top copy; **copier qch. sur l'o.,** to copy sth. from the original; **lire un auteur dans l'o.,** to read an author in the original (language); *Cin:* **copie originale (du film),** master print. **2.** (*a*) original (style, idea); inventive (genius); novel, fresh (idea); (*b*) odd, eccentric; **c'est un o.,** he's (quite) a character.

originalité [ɔriʒinalite] *n.f.* (*a*) originality; (*b*) eccentricity, oddity; (*c*) original, special, feature.

origine [ɔriʒin] *n.f.* origin. **1.** (*a*) beginning; **dès l'o.,** from the very beginning, from the outset; **à l'o., dans l'o.,** originally, in the beginning; (*b*) *Mth:* **(point) o.,** zero point. **2.** extraction, birth; **être d'o. illustre,** to be of noble descent; **la colonie devait son o. aux baleiniers,** the colony owed its birth to the whalers; **il est d'o. anglaise, il est anglais d'o.,** he is of English extraction, an Englishman by birth; *Breed:* **livre d'origines,** stud book. **3.** source; derivation (of word); origin (of custom); **tirer son o. de qch.,** to originate with, from, sth.; **bureau d'o.,** office of dispatch; **certificat d'o.,** certificate of origin; **vins d'o.,** vintage wines; **pneus d'o.,** original tyres.

originel, -elle [ɔriʒinɛl] *a.* original (sin, grace); primary (cause, meaning); **tache originelle,** inherited taint.

originellement [ɔriʒinɛlmɑ̃] *adv.* originally; from, at, the beginning.

orignal, -aux [ɔriɲal, -o] *n.m. Z:* moose; elk.

orillon [ɔrijɔ̃] *n.m.* ear, lug, handle (of bowl, etc.).

orin [ɔrɛ̃] *n.m. Nau:* buoy rope.

oripeau [ɔripo] *n.m.* **1.** tinsel, foil. **2.** *pl.* **oripeaux** (*a*) tawdry, cheap, finery; (*b*) rags, old clothes.

orléaniste [ɔrleanist] *a. & n. Fr.Hist:* Orleanist.

ormaie [ɔrmɛ] *n.f.* elm grove.

orme [ɔrm] *n.m.* elm (tree, wood); **o. blanc, o. de(s) montagne(s),** wych elm; **o. champêtre, à petites feuilles,** common elm, English elm; **maladie des ormes,** (Dutch) elm disease; *F:* **attendez-moi sous l'o.,** you'll have to wait until the cows come home.

ormeau, -eaux [ɔrmo] *n.m. Bot:* (young) elm.

orné [ɔrne] *a.* ornate, florid (style); **lettre ornée,** illuminated initial (letter).

ornement [ɔrnəmɑ̃] *n.m.* ornament; embellishment adornment; **sans o.,** plain, unadorned; *Ecc:* **ornements sacerdotaux,** vestments; *Mus:* **notes d'o.,** grace notes.

ornemental, -aux [ɔrnəmɑ̃tal, -o] *a.* ornamental, decorative.

ornementation [ɔrnəmɑ̃tasjɔ̃] *n.f.* ornamentation; decoration.

ornementer [ɔrnəmɑ̃te] *v.tr.* to ornament, decorate.

orner [ɔrne] *v.tr.* to ornament, decorate; **o. une robe de dentelles,** to trim a dress with lace.

ornière [ɔrnjɛr] *n.f.* rut; *F:* **sortir de l'o.,** (i) to get out of the rut; (ii) to get out of trouble, a fix.

ornithologie [ɔrnitɔlɔʒi] *n.f.* ornithology.

ornithologique [ɔrnitɔlɔʒik] *a.* ornithological.

ornithologiste [ɔrnitɔlɔʒist], **ornithologue** [ɔrnitɔlɔg] *n.* ornithologist.

ornithor(h)ynque [ɔrnitɔrɛ̃k] *n.m. Z:* ornithorhynchus, duck-billed platypus.

orobanche [ɔrɔbɑ̃ʃ] *n.f. Bot:* broomrape.

orogénèse [ɔrɔʒenɛz] *n.f. Geol:* orogenesis.

orographie [ɔrɔgrafi] *n.f.* orography.

oronge [ɔrɔ̃ʒ] *n.f. Fung:* royal agaric, Caesar's mushroom; **fausse o.,** fly agaric.

orpaillage [ɔrpajaʒ] *n.m.* gold washing, panning.

Orphée [ɔrfe] *Pr.n.m. Gr.Myth:* Orpheus.

orphelin, -ine [ɔrfəlɛ̃, -in] *n.* orphan; *a.* orphan(ed); **o. de père,** fatherless; **o. de mère,** motherless.

orphelinat [ɔrfəlina] *n.m.* orphanage, children's home.

orphéon [ɔrfeɔ̃] *n.m.* (*a*) *A:* choral society; (*b*) band.

orphéoniste [ɔrfeɔnist] *n.* member of a choral society, a band.

orphie [ɔrfi] *n.f. Ich:* garfish, sea pike.

orpiment [ɔrpimɑ̃] *n.m.* orpiment; yellow arsenic.

orpin [ɔrpɛ̃] *n.m.* **1.** orpiment. **2.** *Bot:* stonecrop.

orque [ɔrk] *n.f. Z:* orc, grampus.

Orsay [ɔrsɛ] *F:* **le Quai d'O.,** the French Foreign Office.

orseille [ɔrsɛj] *n.f. Bot: Dy:* orchil.

orteil [ɔrtɛj] *n.m.* toe; *esp.* **(gros) o.,** big toe.

orthochromatique [ɔrtɔkrɔmatik] *a. Phot:* orthochromatic.

orthodontie [ɔrtɔdɔ̃ti] *n.f. Dent:* orthodontics.

orthodoxe [ɔrtɔdɔks] *a.* orthodox (church, doctrine, opinion); **peu o.,** unorthodox; unconventional.
orthodoxie [ɔrtɔdɔksi] *n.f.* orthodoxy.
orthodromique [ɔrtɔdrɔmik] *a.* **navigation o.,** great circle sailing.
orthogénie [ɔrtɔʒeni] *n.f.* birth control, family planning.
orthogonal, -aux [ɔrtɔgɔnal, -o] *a.* orthogonal.
orthogonalement [ɔrtɔgɔnalmɑ̃] *adv.* orthogonally, at right angles.
orthographe [ɔrtɔgraf] *n.f.* orthography, spelling; **faute d'o.,** spelling mistake.
orthographier [ɔrtɔgrafje] *v.tr.* (*impf. & pr.sub.* **n. orthographiions**) to spell (word); **mal o.,** to spell (word) incorrectly.
orthographique [ɔrtɔgrafik] *a.* **1.** *Gram:* orthographic(al); **réforme o.,** spelling reform. **2.** *Mapm:* orthographic (projection, etc.).
orthopédie [ɔrtɔpedi] *n.f.* orthop(a)edics.
orthopédique [ɔrtɔpedik] *a.* orthop(a)edic.
orthopédiste [ɔrtɔpedist] *n.* **1.** orthop(a)edist. **2.** maker of orthop(a)edic apparatus.
orthophonie [ɔrtɔfɔni] *n.f.* speech therapy.
orthophoniste [ɔrtɔfɔnist] *n.* speech therapist.
ortie [ɔrti] *n.f.* nettle; **o. brûlante,** stinging nettle; **o. blanche,** dead nettle.
ortolan [ɔrtɔlɑ̃] *n.m. Orn:* ortolan (bunting).
orvet [ɔrvɛ] *n.m. Rept:* slow-worm, blindworm.
os [ɔs, *pl.* o] *n.m.* bone; (*a*) **à, aux, gros os,** big-boned; **n'avoir que la peau et les os, n'être qu'un paquet d'os,** to be nothing but skin and bone; to be just a bag of bones; **voir qn en chair et en os,** to see s.o. in the flesh; **mouillé, trempé, jusqu'aux os,** soaked to the skin, wet through; **casser, rompre, les os à qn,** to beat s.o. black and blue; **il ne fera pas de vieux os,** he won't make old bones; he's not long for this world; (*b*) **os à moelle,** marrow bone; **viande avec os,** meat on the bone; **viande sans os,** meat off the bone, boned meat; **cuiller en os.,** bone spoon; (*c*) *F:* snag, hitch; **tomber sur un os,** to run up against a difficulty, a snag; (*d*) **os de seiche,** cuttlebone.
oscillant [ɔsilɑ̃] *a.* **1.** oscillating (pendulum, *El:* discharge); rocking (shaft); jigging (sieve, etc.); *W.Tel:* **circuit o.,** oscillatory circuit. **2.** *Fin:* fluctuating (market).
oscillateur [ɔsilatœr] *n.m. W.Tel: Elcs:* oscillator; oscillating coil.
oscillation [ɔsilasjɔ̃] *n.f.* oscillation; (*a*) swing (of pendulum); *W.Tel: etc:* **oscillations amorties, entretenues,** damped, sustained, oscillations; (*b*) rocking (of boat); (*c*) *Mec.E:* vibration; (*d*) fluctuation (of the market, etc.); **oscillations d'un extrême à l'autre,** swings from one extreme to the other.
oscillatoire [ɔsilatwar] *a.* oscillatory (movement, circuit).
osciller [ɔsile] *v.i.* to oscillate; to sway. **1.** (*of pendulum*) to swing; (*of speedometer needle*) to flicker; (*of boat*) to rock. **2.** (*a*) **o. entre deux opinions,** to waver between two opinions; (*b*) *Fin:* (*of market*) to fluctuate.
oscillographe [ɔsilɔgraf] *n.m.* oscillograph; **o. cathodique,** cathode ray tube.
oscilloscope [ɔsilɔskɔp] *n.m.* oscilloscope.
osculateur, -trice [ɔskylatœr, -tris] *a.* osculatory, osculating (curve).
osculation [ɔskylasjɔ̃] *n.f.* osculation (of curves).
osé [oze] *a.* daring, audacious (person, etc.); risqué (joke); **être trop o.,** to go too far.
oseille [ozɛj] *n.f.* (*a*) *Bot:* sorrel; *P:* **la faire à l'o. à qn,** to trick s.o., put a fast one over on s.o.; (*b*) *P:* money, dough, lolly.
oser [oze] *v.tr.* **o. faire qch.,** *Lit:* **o. qch.,** to dare, venture, (to do) sth.; **je n'ose pas le faire,** I am afraid to do it; **je n'ose le faire,** I hesitate to do it; **vous n'oseriez (pas)!** you would not dare! **si j'ose (le) dire,** if I may venture to say so.
oseraie [ozrɛ] *n.f.* osier bed.
osier [ozje] *n.m.* **1.** *Bot:* osier. **2.** (*a*) **brin d'o.,** withy; (*b*) wicker(work); **panier d'o.,** wicker basket.
osmonde [ɔsmɔ̃d] *n.f. Bot:* **o. royale,** royal fern.
osmose [ɔsmoz] *n.f.* osmosis.
ossature [ɔsatyr] *n.f.* **1.** frame, skeleton (of man, animal); **d'une o. puissante,** powerfully built, of powerful build. **2.** frame(work) (of building, etc.); main girders (of bridge); **l'o. sociale,** the social structure.
osselet [ɔslɛ] *n.m.* **1.** knucklebone (of sheep); **jouer aux osselets,** to play at knucklebones. **2. les osselets de l'oreille,** the ossicles of the ear; the otic bones.
ossements [ɔsmɑ̃] *n.m.pl.* bones (of dead men, animals).
osseux, -euse [ɔsø, -øz] *a.* bony (face, hand); osseous (tissue); **système o.,** bone structure; **greffe osseuse,** bone graft.
ossification [ɔsifikasjɔ̃] *n.f. Med:* ossification.
ossifier [ɔsifje] **1.** *v.tr.* to ossify. **2. s'o.,** to become ossified, to ossify.
ossu [ɔsy] *a.* big-boned, raw-boned.
ossuaire [ɔsɥɛr] *n.m.* ossuary, charnel house.
ostensible [ɔstɑ̃sibl̩] *a.* open, patent, to all; visible.
ostensiblement [ɔstɑ̃sibləmɑ̃] *adv.* openly, publicly; obviously; markedly.
ostensoir [ɔstɑ̃swar] *n.m. Ecc:* monstrance.
ostentation [ɔstɑ̃tasjɔ̃] *n.f.* ostentation, show; display; **faire o. de sa misère,** to parade one's poverty; **agir par o.,** to do sth. out of, from motives of, ostentation, (in order) to show off.
ostentatoire [ɔstɑ̃tatwar] *a.* ostentatious.
ostentatoirement [ɔstɑ̃tatwarmɑ̃] *adv.* ostentatiously.
ostéo-arthrite [ɔsteɔartrit] *n.f. Med:* osteoarthritis.
ostéologie [ɔsteɔlɔʒi] *n.f.* osteology.
ostéomyélite [ɔsteɔmjelit] *n.f. Med:* osteomyelitis.
ostracisme [ɔstrasism] *n.m.* ostracism; **frapper qn d'o.,** to ostracize s.o.
ostréicole [ɔstreikɔl] *a.* **l'industrie o.,** the oyster industry.
ostréiculteur, -trice [ɔstreikyltœr, -tris] *n.* oyster farmer.
ostréiculture [ɔstreikyltyr] *n.f.* ostreiculture, oyster farming.
ostrogot(h), -ot(h)e [ɔstrɔgo, -ɔt] *n. Hist:* Ostrogoth.
otage [ɔtaʒ] *n.m.* hostage (**de,** for); **prendre qn pour o.,** to take s.o. (as) hostage.
otalgie [ɔtalʒi] *n.f. Med:* otalgia, earache.
otarie [ɔtari] *n.f. Z:* otary, sea lion, eared seal.
ôter [ote] **1.** *v.tr.* to remove, take away; to take off (garment); to take out (stain); **ô. le couvert,** to clear away; *Prov:* **en avril, n'ôtez pas un fil** = ne'er cast a clout till May be out; **ô. qch. à qn,** to take sth. away from s.o.; **cela n'ôte rien à sa valeur,** that detracts nothing from its value; **ô. qch. de qch.,** to take sth. away from sth.; **ôtez trois de cinq,** take away, deduct, three from five; **cela me l'a ôté tout à fait de l'esprit,** that drove, put, it entirely out of my head. **2. s'ô.,** to remove oneself, to move away; *F:* **ôtez-vous de là!** get out (of here)! **ôte-toi de là que je m'y mette!** get out and make room for me!
otique [ɔtik] *a. Anat:* otic (nerve, etc.).
otite [ɔtit] *n.f. Med:* otitis.
otologie [ɔtɔlɔʒi] *n.f.* otology.
oto-rhino-laryngologiste [ɔtɔrinɔlarɛ̃gɔlɔʒist], *F:* **oto-rhino** [ɔtɔrino] *n.* ear, nose and throat

specialist; *pl. oto-rhino-laryngologistes, F: oto-rhinos.*

otoscope [ɔtɔskɔp] *n.m. Med:* otoscope, ear speculum.

ottoman, -ane [ɔtɔmɑ̃, -an] **1.** *a. & n. Hist:* Ottoman. **2.** *n.f. Furn:* **ottomane,** divan, ottoman.

ou [u] *conj.* or; **voulez-vous du bœuf ou du jambon?** would you like beef or ham? **trois ou quatre fois par jour,** three or four times a day; **l'un ou l'autre,** one or the other; **entrez ou sortez,** either come in or go out; **vous ou moi, nous lui en parlerons,** (either) you or I will speak to him about it; **lui ou son frère va, vont, vous aider,** he or his brother will help you; **l'un ou l'autre devait forcément être le chef,** one or the other was bound to take the lead; **ou . . . ou (bien) . . .,** either . . . or (else) . . .; *Cmptr:* **circuit OU,** OR circuit.

où [u] *adv.* **1.** *interr.* where? **où habite-t-il?** where does he live? **où allez-vous?** where are you going? **où en êtes-vous?** how far have you got (with it); **par où est-il passé?** which way did he go? **jusqu'où les a-t-il suivis?** how far did he follow them? **mettez-le n'importe où,** put it down anywhere. **2.** *rel.* (*a*) where; **j'irai où vous voudrez,** I'll go where(ever) you wish; **partout où il va,** wherever he goes; **vous le trouverez là où vous l'avez laissé,** you will find it where you left it; **d'où on conclut qu'il est coupable,** from which one concludes that he is guilty; (*b*) when; **dans le temps où il était jeune,** in the days when he was young; (*c*) **(=dans lequel, auquel, etc.) la maison où il habite,** the house in which he lives, the house he lives in. **3.** (*concessive*) **où que vous soyez,** wherever you may be.

ouache [waʃ] *n.f. Fr.C:* bear's den.

ouaille [waj] *n.f. B.Lit:* sheep; **le pasteur et ses ouailles,** the minister and his flock.

ouais [wɛ] *int.* (*a*) *A:* (*of surprise*) what! my word! (*b*) yeah! *esp. NAm:* yep! (*sceptical*) oh yeah?

ouananiche [wananiʃ] *n.f. Fr.C: Ich:* freshwater salmon.

ouaouaron [wawarɔ̃] *n.m. Fr.C:* bullfrog.

ouate [wat] *n.f.* (*usu.* **la ouate,** *occ.* **l'ouate**) **1.** (*a*) wadding, padding; **doublé d'o.,** wadded, quilted; (*b*) cotton wool; **o. hydrophile,** (absorbent) cotton wool; (*c*) **o. de verre,** fibreglass, *NAm:* fiberglass.

ouaté [wate] *a.* **1.** wadded, padded; **robe de chambre ouatée,** quilted dressing gown. **2.** fleecy (cloud, snow); soft (footstep); woolly (outlines).

ouater [wate] *v.tr.* **1.** to wad; to pad; to line with wadding; to quilt; *F:* **o. qn,** to (molly)coddle s.o. **2.** **o. ses pas,** to tread softly, to deaden one's footsteps.

ouatine [watin] *n.f. Tex:* quilting (material).

ouatiné [watine] *a.* quilted (material); *F:* cosy (life).

oubli [ubli] *n.m.* **1.** (*a*) forgetting; neglect (of duty); **par o.,** inadvertently; by, through, an oversight; (*b*) forgetfulness; **l'o. de soi-même,** forgetfulness of self; (*c*) oblivion; **tomber dans l'o.,** to sink, fall, into oblivion; to be forgotten. **2.** omission, oversight; **réparer un o.,** to rectify an omission.

oubliable [ublijabl] *a.* forgettable.

oublier [ublije] *v.* (*impf. & pr.sub.* **n. oubliions**) **1.** *v.tr.* to forget; (*a*) **j'ai oublié son nom,** I have forgotten his name; his name has slipped my memory; **o. le passé,** to forget the past; to let bygones be bygones; **faire o. son passé,** to live down one's past; **o. de faire qch.,** to forget to do sth.; **on ne nous le laissera pas o.,** we shall never hear the last of it; **il mourut oublié de tous,** he died forgotten by all; (*b*) to overlook (an appointment); to neglect (duty); to leave (sth.) out, behind; **o. l'heure,** to lose count of time. **2.** **s'o.** (*a*) to forget one's manners, to forget oneself; **le chien s'est oublié sur le tapis,** the dog's made a mess on the carpet; (*b*) **s'o. à rêver,** to lose oneself in a daydream; *F:* **il ne s'oublie pas,** he's no altruist; he always thinks of number one.

oubliette [ublijɛt] *n.f. usu. pl.* oubliette, secret dungeon; *F:* **mettre qch. aux oubliettes,** to shelve sth. indefinitely.

oublieux, -euse [ublijø, -øz] *a.* forgetful; neglectful.

oued [wɛd] *n.m. Geog:* wadi.

Ouessant [wɛsɑ̃] *Pr.n.m. Geog:* Ushant.

ouest [wɛst] **1.** *n.m. no. pl.* west; **les provinces de l'O.,** the western provinces; **vent d'o.,** westerly wind; **le vent d'o.,** the west wind; **à l'o. de qch.,** (to the) west, (to the) westward, of sth.; **à l'o., dans l'o.,** in the west; **vers l'O.,** westward(s). **2.** *a.inv.* west (coast); westerly (wind); western (province).

ouest-allemand, -ande [wɛstalmɑ̃, -ɑ̃d] *a. & n. Geog:* West German; *pl. ouest-allemand(e)s.*

ouf [uf] *int.* **1.** ah! what a relief! **pousser un o. de soulagement,** to heave a sigh of relief. **2.** **o., on étouffe ici!** phew! it's stifling here; *F:* **il n'a pas dit o.!** he didn't say a word.

Ouganda [ugɑ̃da] *Pr.n.m. Geog:* Uganda.

oui [wi] yes. **1.** *adv.* (*a*) **vient-il?—o.,** is he coming?—yes (he is); **je crois que o.,** *F:* **qu'o.,** I think so; **faire signe que o., faire o. de la tête,** to nod in agreement; **mais o., bien sûr que o.,** (yes) of course; naturally; **o., o., allez toujours,** yes, get on with it; *Nau:* **o., commandant!** aye, aye, sir; (*b*) **ah, o.?** really? **tu viens, o.?** you're coming, aren't you? **2.** *n.m.inv.* **deux cents o. et trois cents non,** two hundred ayes and three hundred noes; **se quereller pour un o. pour un non,** to quarrel about nothing.

ouiche [wiʃ] *int. P:* pooh!

ouï-dire [widir] *n.m.inv.* hearsay; **je ne le sais que par o.-d.,** I know it only by, from, hearsay.

ouïe [wi] *n.f.* **1.** (sense of) hearing; **avoir l'o. fine,** to have keen, sharp, ears; to have excellent hearing; **avoir l'o. défectueuse,** to be hard of hearing; **à portée de l'o.,** within earshot, hearing distance; **être tout o.,** to be all ears, all attention. **2.** (*a*) *pl.* sound holes (of violin, etc.); (*b*) ear (of ventilator, etc.). **3.** *pl.* gills (of fish).

ouille [uj] *int.* ouch! ooh!

ouïr [wir] *v.tr.* (*only used in inf., p.p.* **(ouï),** *compound tenses, pr.p.* **oyant** *and imp.* **oyez;** *p.h.* **j'ouïs** *and fu.* **j'ouïrai** *occ. used*) *A:* to hear; **nous l'avons ouï dire à notre père,** we have heard our father say so; *Jur:* **o. les témoins,** to hear the witnesses.

ouistiti [wistiti] *n.m. Z:* marmoset.

ouragan [uragɑ̃] *n.m.* hurricane; **entrer en o. dans une pièce,** to burst into a room; **o. politique,** political storm.

Oural (l') [lural] *Pr.n.m. Geog:* (*a*) the Ural (river); (*b*) the Ural Mountains, the Urals.

ourdir [urdir] *v.tr.* **1.** (*a*) *Tex:* to warp (linen, cloth); (*b*) to plait (straw). **2.** to hatch, weave (plot).

ourdissage [urdisaʒ] *n.m. Tex:* warping.

ourdisseur, -euse [urdisœr, -øz] *n.* **1.** *Tex:* warper. **2.** plotter.

ourdou [urdu] *n.m. Ling:* Urdu.

ourler [urle] *v.tr.* **1.** to hem; **o. à jour,** to hemstitch. **2.** to edge, border (**de,** with). **3.** to lap-joint (metal sheets).

ourlet [urlɛ] *n.m.* **1.** hem; **o. à jour,** hemstitched hem; **faux o.,** false hem; **point d'o.,** hemming; hemstitch. **2.** edge (of crater); helix, rim (of ear). **3.** *Metalw:* lap joint, hem (of metal sheets).

ours, -e [urs] **1.** *n.* (*a*) *Z:* bear, *f.* she bear; **o. blanc, polaire,** polar bear; **o. brun,** brown bear; **o. gris d'Amérique,** grizzly bear; **Grand Lac de l'O.,** Great Bear Lake; **combats d'o.,** bear baiting; **o. en peluche,** teddy bear; *F:* **o. mal léché,** unlicked cub; **quel o.!** what a boor! *Prov:* **il ne faut pas vendre la peau de l'o. avant de l'avoir tué,** don't count your chickens before they are hatched; *Bot:* **raisin d'o.,** bearberry; (*b*) **o. marin,** sea bear, fur seal. **2.** *n.f. Astr:* **la Grande Ourse,** the Great Bear, the Big Dipper, Charles' Wain, the Plough; **la Petite Ourse,** the Little Bear, the Little Dipper.

oursin [ursɛ̃] *n.m. Echin:* sea urchin.

ourson [ursɔ̃] *n.m. Z:* bearcub.

oust(e) [ust] *int. P:* **allez o.!** (i) get a move on! (ii) hop it! scram!

outarde [utard] *n.f. Orn:* (*a*) bustard; (*b*) *Fr.C:* Canada goose.

outil [uti] *n.m.* tool; implement; **o. à main,** hand tool; **o. à moteur,** power tool; **o. coupant, o. de coupe, o. tranchant,** cutting tool, edge tool.

outillage [utijaʒ] *n.m.* (*a*) set of tools; *Aut: etc:* tool kit; (*b*) gear, plant, equipment (of factory).

outiller [utije] *v.tr.* to equip, fit out, supply (workman) with tools, (factory) with plant; **être bien outillé en livres,** to be well provided with books.

outrage [utraʒ] *n.m.* outrage; flagrant insult (to morals, good taste, etc.); **faire o. aux convenances,** to offend against propriety; *Jur:* **o.** (i) **(à agent),** insulting behaviour, *NAm:* behaviour; (ii) **(à magistrat)** = contempt of court; **o. aux bonnes mœurs, à la pudeur,** public indecency; *Lit:* **l'o. des ans,** the ravages of time.

outrageant [utraʒɑ̃] *a.* insulting (offer, refusal); offensive (joke); scurrilous (accusation).

outrager [utraʒe] *v.tr.* **(j'outrageai(s)) 1.** to insult; to attack scurrilously. **2.** to outrage, violate (woman, the truth).

outrageusement [utraʒøzmɑ̃] *adv.* (*a*) outrageously, insultingly; (*b*) excessively (stupid, etc.).

outrageux, -euse [utraʒø, -øz] *a. O:* insulting.

outrance [utrɑ̃s] *n.f.* excess; *used esp. in the adv.phr.* **à o.,** to the utmost; **combat à o.,** fight to the death; **attaque à o.,** all-out attack; **industrialisme à o.,** out and out industrialism; **travailler à o.,** to work excessively.

outrancier, -ière [utrɑ̃sje, -jɛr] *a.* extreme; out-and-out; extremist.

outre[1] [utr̥] *n.f.* goatskin bottle; wine skin.

outre[2] **1.** *prep.* (*a*) (*in a few set phrases*) beyond; **o. mesure,** beyond measure, inordinately, unduly, overmuch; **se fatiguer o. mesure,** to overtire oneself; (*b*) in addition to; **o. cette somme,** in addition to that sum; **o. cela,** in addition to that; besides; furthermore. **2.** *adv.* further, beyond; **passer o., aller o.,** to go on, proceed further; **passer o. à une interdiction,** to disregard, take no notice of, ignore, a prohibition; **passer o. à la loi,** to override the law; **en o.,** besides, moreover, further(more); also; again, over and above; **j'ai, en o., deux neveux,** I have, besides, two nephews; **en o. de sa paie il reçoit une indemnité pour débours,** in addition to, besides, over and above, his pay he gets his expenses; **o. (le fait) qu'il est riche,** apart from the fact that he's rich; apart from, besides, in addition to, being rich.

outré [utre] *a.* (*a*) exaggerated, extravagant, overdone (praise); overstated; **d'une activité outrée,** hyperactive; (*b*) indignant; **o. de colère,** beside oneself with anger.

outre-Atlantique [utratlɑ̃tik] *adv.phr.* on the other side of, across, the Atlantic; **d'o.-A.,** transatlantic.

outrecuidance [utrəkɥidɑ̃s] *n.f.* presumptuousness, effrontery.

outrecuidant [utrəkɥidɑ̃] *a.* (*a*) presumptuous; (*b*) impertinent.

outre-Manche [utrəmɑ̃ʃ] *adv.phr.* on the other side of, across, the Channel.

outremer [utrəmɛr] *n.m.* **1.** lapis lazuli. **2. (bleu d')o.,** ultramarine (blue).

outre-mer *adv.phr.* overseas; **commerce d'o.-m.,** oversea(s) trade; **nos collègues d'o.-m.,** our colleagues from abroad.

outre-monts [utrəmɔ̃] *adv.phr.* beyond the mountains.

outrepasser [utrəpase] *v.tr.* to go beyond (a limit, one's rights); to exceed (orders).

outrer [utre] *v.tr.* **1.** to carry (sth.) to excess, too far; to exaggerate; to overdo (a rôle). **2.** to infuriate.

outre-Rhin [utrərɛ̃] *adv.phr.* beyond the Rhine.

outre-tombe (d') [dutrətɔ̃b] *adv.phr.* from beyond the grave; posthumous.

ouvert [uvɛr] *a.* open; (*a*) **porte grande ouverte,** wide-open door; **plaie ouverte,** gaping wound; *Surg:* **à cœur o.,** open-heart (surgery); **accueillir qn à bras ouverts,** to welcome s.o. with open arms; *F:* **avoir la main ouverte,** to be open-handed; **faire qch. les yeux ouverts,** to do sth. with one's eyes open; **fleur ouverte,** flower in bloom; **voyelle ouverte,** open vowel; *Fb:* **jeu o.,** open, loose, game; (*b*) **ville ouverte,** open, unfortified, town; **bateau o.,** open boat; (*c*) **o. de 10 heures à 5 heures,** open from 10 to 5; **collection ouverte au public,** collection open to the public, on view; **o. à la navigation,** open to navigation; **compte o.,** open account, open credit; (*d*) **caractère o.,** frank, open, nature; **avoir l'esprit o.,** to be open-minded; **parler à cœur o.,** to speak freely; **guerre ouverte,** open warfare; (*e*) **le gaz est o.,** the gas is on.

ouvertement [uvɛrtəmɑ̃] *adv.* openly, frankly; overtly.

ouverture [uvɛrtyr] *n.f.* **1.** (*a*) opening (of door, book, session, shooting season, etc.); **o. d'hostilités,** outbreak of hostilities; **o. d'un compte, d'un crédit,** opening of an account, a credit; **conférence d'o.,** opening lecture; (*b*) **faire des ouvertures à qn,** to make overtures to s.o.; (*c*) *Mus:* overture (of opera, etc.); (*d*) **heures d'o.,** opening hours (of shop, etc.); visiting hours (of museum). **2.** (*a*) opening, aperture (in wall, etc.); mouth (of cave); gap, break (in hedge); **flacon à large o.,** wide-mouthed flask; **ouvertures d'une machine,** (steam) ports of an engine; (*b*) width, span (of arch, etc.); spread (of compass legs); *El:* **o. d'induit,** armature gap; (*c*) *Phot:* aperture. **3. o. de cœur,** frankness; **o. d'esprit,** open-mindedness.

ouvrable [uvrabl̥] *a.* **jour o.,** working day; **heures ouvrables,** business hours, working hours.

ouvrage [uvraʒ] *n.m.* work. **1.** (*a*) **il n'a pas d'o.,** he is out of work, out of a job; **se mettre à l'o.,** to set to work; **mettre qn à l'o.,** to set s.o. to work; **avoir du cœur à l'o.,** to work with a will; (*b*) workmanship. **2.** piece of work, product; book; **o. en prose,** prose work; **ouvrages de dames,** needlework, fancywork; **corbeille, boîte, à o.,** work basket, workbox; *n.f. F:* **c'est de la belle o.,** that's a nice bit of work.

ouvragé [uvraʒe] *a.* (*a*) = OUVRÉ; (*b*) elaborate.

ouvrager [uvraʒe] *v.tr.* **(j'ouvrageai(s))** to work (metal, jewel(le)ry); to figure (brocade).

ouvrant [uvrɑ̃] **1.** *a.* (*a*) opening (panel, etc.); *Aut:* sliding (roof). **2.** *n.m.* leaf (of door, shutter, etc.).

ouvré [uvre] *a.* (*a*) worked (timber); wrought (iron); (*b*) decorated; embroidered (tablecloth).

ouvre-boîte(s) [uvrəbwat] *n.m.* can opener, tin opener; *pl. ouvre-boîtes.*

ouvre-bouteille(s) [uvrəbutɛj] *n.m.* bottle opener; *pl. ouvre-bouteilles.*

ouvre-huître(s) [uvrɥitr̥] *n.m.* oyster knife; *pl. ouvre-huîtres.*

ouvre-lettres [uvrəlɛtr̥] *n.m.inv.* letter opener.

ouvrer [uvre] *v.tr.* to work (up) (wood, copper, etc.); to work, embroider (tablecloth, etc.).

ouvreur, -euse [uvrœr, -øz] *n.* **1.** (*a*) opener; *n.f. Th: Cin:* **ouvreuse,** usherette. **2.** *Cards:* player who opens the bidding.

ouvrier, -ère [uvrije, -ɛr] **1.** *n.* worker; workman; working man, woman; operative; **o. en bois, sur métaux,** woodworker, metalworker; **o. agricole,** agricultural labourer, *NAm:* laborer; farm worker; **o. qualifié,** skilled worker; craftsman; *Rail:* **o. de la voie,** platelayer, *NAm:* tracklayer; **ouvrière couturière,** seamstress; **il est l'o. de sa fortune,** he is a self-made man. **2.** *a.* (*a*) **la classe ouvrière, les classes ouvrières,** the working class(es); **agitation ouvrière,** industrial unrest; labour unrest, *NAm:* labor unrest; **contrôle o.,** workers' control; **syndicat o.,** trade union; **quartier o.,** working class district; (*b*) **abeille ouvrière,** worker bee; **fourmi ouvrière,** worker ant.

ouvriérisme [uvrijerism] *n.m.* control by the workers; trade unionism.

ouvrir [uvrir] *v.* (*pr.p.* **ouvrant;** *p.p.* **ouvert;** *pr.ind.* **j'ouvre;** *pr.sub.* **j'ouvre;** *p.h.* **j'ouvris**) **1.** *v.tr.* to open; (*a*) **o. une porte, une malle,** to open, unfasten **(avec une clef),** to unlock a door, a trunk; **o. à qn,** to answer the door to s.o., to let s.o. in; **o. la porte aux abus,** to open the door, the way, to abuses; **o. sa maison à qn,** to throw open one's house to s.o.; **il n'a pas ouvert la bouche,** *F:* **il ne l'a pas ouverte,** he didn't open his mouth; **o. le lit,** to turn down the bed(clothes); **o. un robinet, le gaz,** to turn on a tap, the gas; **o. l'électricité,** to switch on (the electricity); *F:* **o. le poste,** to switch on the radio, the television; *El:* **o. le circuit,** to break, switch off, the current; (*b*) **o. son cœur à qn,** to open one's heart, unburden oneself, to s.o.; **cela ouvre l'appétit,** it sharpens the appetite; (*c*) to cut through (wall, etc.); to open up (mine, etc.); to cut (canal); to cut open (box, etc.); *Med:* to open, lance (abscess); **s'o. un chemin à travers la foule,** to cut, push, one's way through the crowd; (*d*) to begin; to set going; **o. un débat,** to open, start, a debate; **o. le bal,** to open the ball; **o. une école, une boutique,** to open a school, a shop; **o. boutique,** to set up shop; **o. la marche,** to lead the way; **o. un compte chez qn,** to open an account with s.o. **2.** *v.i.* to open; (*a*) **la scène ouvre par un chœur,** the scene opens with a chorus; (*b*) **le salon ouvrait sur le jardin,** the drawing room opened on (to) the garden; (*c*) **les magasins n'ouvrent pas les jours de fête,** the shops do not open on public holidays. **3. s'o.** (*a*) (*of door, box, shop*) to open; **la porte s'ouvrit en coup de vent,** the door flew open; **un gouffre s'ouvrait sous mes pieds,** a chasm opened out, yawned, under my feet; **le bal s'ouvrit par une valse,** the ball opened, began, started, with a waltz; (*b*) (*of pers.*) **s'o. à qn,** to unburden oneself to s.o.; to confide in s.o.

ouvroir [uvrwar] *n.m.* (*a*) workroom, sewing room (in convent, etc.); (*b*) (ladies') work party; *NAm:* sewing bee.

ovaire [ɔvɛr] *n.m. Anat: Bot:* ovary.

ovale [ɔval] **1.** *a.* oval; egg-shaped; *Sp: F:* **ballon o.,** (i) rugger ball; (ii) rugger. **2.** *n.m.* oval; **en o.,** oval.

ovalisation [ɔvalizasjɔ̃] *n.f.* ovalization (of cylinders).

ovalisé [ɔvalize] *a.* ovalized (cylinder).

ovarien, -ienne [ɔvarjɛ̃, -jɛn] *a. Anat: Bot:* ovarian.

ovation [ɔvasjɔ̃] *n.f.* ovation; **faire une o. à qn,** to give s.o. an ovation.

ovationner [ɔvasjɔne] *v.tr.* to give (s.o.) an ovation.

ové [ɔve] *a.* egg-shaped, ovate (fruit, etc.).

oviducte [ɔvidykt] *n.m.* oviduct.

ovin [ɔvɛ̃] *Husb:* **1.** *a.* ovine (species, etc.). **2.** *n.m.pl.* **ovins,** sheep.

ovipare [ɔvipar] *a. Z:* oviparous.

ovoïde [ɔvɔid] *a.* ovoid, egg-shaped; *El:* **maillon o.,** egg insulator.

ovovivipare [ɔvɔvivipar] *a.* ovoviviparous.

ovulaire [ɔvylɛr] *a.* ovular.

ovulation [ɔvylasjɔ̃] *n.f.* ovulation.

ovule [ɔvyl] *n.m. Biol:* ovule.

oxalate [ɔksalat] *n.m. Ch:* oxalate.

oxalide [ɔksalid] *n.f.*, **oxalis** [ɔksalis] *n.m. Bot:* oxalis, wood sorrel.

oxhydrique [ɔksidrik] *a.* oxyhydrogen (burner).

oxyacétylénique [ɔksiasetilenik] *a.* oxyacetylene (gas, welding).

oxycoupage [ɔksikupaʒ] *n.m. Metalw:* oxygen cutting; oxyacetylene cutting out.

oxydable [ɔksidabl̩] *a.* (*a*) *Ch:* oxidizable; (*b*) liable to rust.

oxydant [ɔksidɑ̃] **1.** *a.* oxidizing. **2.** *n.m.* oxidizer, oxidizing agent.

oxydation [ɔksidasjɔ̃] *n.f. Ch:* oxidizing, oxidation.

oxyde [ɔksid] *n.m. Ch:* oxide; **o. de carbone,** carbon monoxide.

oxyder [ɔkside] **1.** *v.tr. Ch:* to oxidize. **2. s'o.** (i) to become oxidized; (ii) to rust.

oxygène [ɔksiʒɛn] *n.m. Ch:* oxygen; *Med:* **tente à o.,** oxygen tent.

oxygéné, -ée [ɔksiʒene] *a. Ch:* oxygenated; **eau oxygénée,** hydrogen peroxide; **cheveux oxygénés,** peroxide blonde, bleached, hair.

oxygéner [ɔksiʒene] *v.* **(il oxygène; il oxygénera) 1.** *v.tr.* to oxygenate, oxidize, oxygenize; *Hairdr:* to bleach (hair). **2.** *F:* **s'o.,** to take, get, a breath of fresh air.

oyat [ɔja] *n.m. Bot: F:* marram grass.

ozone [ɔzɔn] *n.f.* ozone.

ozonisation [ɔzɔnizasjɔ̃] *n.f.* ozonization.

ozoniser [ɔzɔnize] *v.tr.* to ozonize.

P

P, p [pe] *n.m.* (the letter) P, p.
pacage [pakaʒ] *n.m.* **1.** pasture(land). **2.** pasturing, grazing; *Jur:* **droit(s) de p.,** grazing rights, common of pasture.
pacager [pakaʒe] *v.tr.* **(je pacageai(s); n. pacageons)** to pasture, graze (beasts, field).
pacane [pakan] *n.f. Bot:* pecan (nut).
pacemaker [pɛsmɛkœr] *n.m. Sp: Med:* pacemaker.
pacha [paʃa] *n.m.* pasha; *F:* **mener une vie de p., faire le p.,** to lead an easy life.
pachyderme [paʃidɛrm] *Z:* **1.** *a.* pachydermatous, thick-skinned. **2.** *n.m.* pachyderm.
pacificateur, -trice [pasifikatœr, -tris] **1.** *a.* pacifying; pacificatory. **2.** *n.* pacifier; peacemaker.
pacification [pasifikasjɔ̃] *n.f.* pacification.
pacifier [pasifje] *v.tr.* (*impf. & pr.sub.* **n. pacifiions, v. pacifiiez**) to pacify (country); to appease, calm.
pacifique [pasifik] *a.* (*a*) pacific, conciliatory, peaceable; peace-loving; *n. B:* **bienheureux les pacifiques,** blessed are the peacemakers; (*b*) peaceful, quiet (reign, etc.); (*c*) **l'océan P., le P.,** the Pacific Ocean, the Pacific; (*d*) *Jur:* **possesseur p.,** uncontested owner.
pacifiquement [pasifikmɑ̃] *adv.* peaceably, quietly, peacefully.
pacifisme [pasifism] *n.m. Pol:* pacifism.
pacifiste [pasifist] *a. & n. Pol:* pacifist.
pack [pak] *n.m.* **1.** (ice)pack (of the polar seas). **2.** *Rugby Fb:* pack.
pacotille [pakɔtij] *n.f.* (*a*) *A:* private cargo; (*b*) **(marchandises de) p.,** shoddy goods; **bijoux de p.,** paste jewel(le)ry; (*c*) *A:* job lot (of various goods).
pacte [pakt] *n.m.* pact, agreement; covenant; **p. à quatre,** four-power pact; *Jur:* **p. de famille,** family settlement; **p. de préférence,** preference clause.
pactiser [paktize] *v.i.* **p. avec l'ennemi,** to come to terms, to treat, with the enemy; **p. avec sa conscience,** to compromise with one's conscience; **p. avec un crime,** to compound a felony.
paddock [padɔk] *n.m.* paddock; *P:* **se mettre au p.,** to go to bed, hit the sack.
Padoue [padu] *Pr.n.f. Geog:* Padua.
paf [paf] **1.** *int.* slap! bang! **2.** *a.inv. P:* **être p.,** to be drunk, tight.
pagaie [pagɛ] *n.f.* paddle (for canoe).
pagaïe, pagaille [pagaj] *n.f. F:* (*a*) disorder, clutter (of objects); **en p.,** in disorder; in a mess; at random; **tout ramasser en p.,** to bundle everything up; **quelle p.!** what a mess! what a shambles! (*b*) **il y en a en p.,** there's lots, loads, of it, of them.
paganisme [paganism] *n.m.* paganism.
pagayer [pageje] *v.tr. & i.* **(je pagaie, je pagaye)** to paddle.
pagayeur, -euse [pagɛjœr, -øz] *n.* paddler.
page¹ [paʒ] *n.f.* page (of book, etc.); chapter (of history); **p. blanche,** blank page; *Typ:* **mettre en pages,** to make up; **mise en pages,** making up; page setting; **pages de départ,** prelims; *F:* **être à la p.,** to be (i) up to date, (ii) in the know; **ne pas être à la p.,** to be behind the times.
page² *n.m.* page(boy).
page³, pageot [paʒo] *n.m. P:* bed, pit, sack.
pagination [paʒinasjɔ̃] *n.f.* paging, pagination.
paginer [paʒine] *v.tr.* to page, paginate.
pagne [paɲ] *n.m.* loincloth.
pagnoter (se) [sepaɲɔte] *v.pr. P:* to go to bed; to hit the sack.
pagode [pagɔd] **1.** *n.f.* (*a*) *Arch: A.Num:* pagoda; (*b*) *A:* (*nodding toy*) mandarin. **2.** *a.f. Cost:* **manches pagodes,** pagoda sleeves.
paie [pɛ] *n.f.* **1.** pay; wages; **feuille, bulletin, de p.,** pay (advice) slip. **2.** payment; **jour de p.,** pay day; **faire la p.,** to pay out the wages.
paiement [pɛmɑ̃] *n.m.* payment; discharge (of debt); **gros p.,** heavy disbursement; **p. d'avance,** payment in advance; prepayment; **p. contre livraison,** cash on delivery, C.O.D.; **p. à termes, par acomptes,** payment by instalments.
païen, -ïenne [pajɛ̃, -jɛn] *a. & n.* pagan, heathen.
paillage [pɑjaʒ] *n.m. Hort:* mulching.
paillard, -arde [pajar, -ard] **1.** *a.* ribald, lewd, lascivious; dirty (joke, etc.); **regard p.,** leer; **chanson paillarde,** bawdy song. **2.** *n. A:* debauchee; *m.* rake.
paillardise [pajardiz] *n.f.* **1.** lewdness; debauchery. **2.** crude, dirty, joke, story.
paillasse [pajas] **1.** *n.f.* (*a*) straw mattress, paillasse, palliasse, pallet; (*b*) *Dom.Ec:* draining board. **2.** *n.m.* clown, buffoon.
paillasson [pajasɔ̃] *n.m.* (*a*) (door)mat; **mettre la clef sous le p.,** to clear out, to flit; (*b*) servile person, *F:* doormat.
paille [pɑj] *n.f.* **1.** (*a*) straw; **botte de p.,** truss of straw; **p. de litière,** loose straw; **p. de riz, d'Italie,** rice straw; **chapeau de p.,** straw hat; **chaise de p.,** straw-bottomed chair; **homme de p.,** man of straw; dummy; *NAm:* straw man; **feu de p.,** flash in the pan; **être sur la p.,** to be destitute; **voir la p. dans l'œil du prochain,** to see the mote in one's brother's eye; **tirer à la courte p.,** to draw lots; (*b*) (drinking) straw; **boire qch. avec une p.,** to drink sth. through a straw; (*c*) *a.inv.* straw-coloured, *NAm:* -colored. **2. menue p., p. d'avoine,** chaff. **3. p. de fer,** steel wool. **4.** flaw (in gem, etc.).
paillé¹ [pɑje] *n.m. Husb:* stable litter.
paillé² *a.* **1.** flawy (metal, gem, etc.); scaly (metal). **2.** straw-coloured, *NAm:* -colored.
pailler¹ [pɑje] *n.m.* (*a*) farmyard, straw yard; (*b*) straw stack.
pailler² *v.tr.* **1.** *Hort:* to protect with straw; to mulch. **2.** to put a straw bottom in (a chair).
paillet [pajɛ] *n.m. Nau:* mat, fender; **p. d'abordage, p. makarov,** collision mat.
pailleté [pajte] *a.* spangled (**de,** with).
pailleter [pajte] *v.tr.* **(je paillette; je pailletterai)** to spangle.
paillette [pajɛt] *n.f.* **1.** spangle; sequin. **2.** (*a*) grain of gold dust (in stream); (*b*) flake (of mica, etc.); **savon en paillettes,** soap flakes. **3.** flaw (in gem).
pailleux, -euse [pɑjø, -øz] *a.* **1.** strawy (manure). **2.** flawy (iron, glass).
paillis [pɑji] *n.m. Hort:* mulch.
paillon [pɑjɔ̃] *n.m.* **1.** (large) spangle. **2.** (jeweller's) foil. **3.** *Tchn:* wisp of straw. **4.** straw case (for bottle).
paillote [pɑjɔt] *n.f.* straw hut.
pain [pɛ̃] *n.m.* **1.** (*a*) bread; **p. de seigle,** rye bread; **p. noir,** buckwheat bread, black rye bread; **p. bis,** brown bread; **p. complet,** wholemeal bread; **p. viennois,** wheaten bread; **p. frais, p. rassis,** fresh bread,

stale bread; **p. grillé,** toast; **p. perdu,** French toast; **p. d'épice** = gingerbread; **p. de Gênes,** Genoa cake; **mettre qn au p. et à l'eau, au p. sec,** to put s.o. on bread and water, on dry bread; **p. azyme,** unleavened bread; *Ecc:* **le p. et le vin,** the bread and wine; **bon comme bon p.,** good-hearted, good-natured; **acheter qch. pour une bouchée de p.,** to buy sth. for a mere song, for next to nothing; **il ne vaut pas le p. qu'il mange,** he isn't worth his salt; **manger son p. blanc le premier,** to have a good start (in life); **avoir du p. sur la planche,** (i) to have plenty of work on hand; (ii) to have a lot on one's plate; (*b*) **gagner son p.,** to earn one's living; **ôter à qn le p. de la bouche,** to take the bread out of s.o.'s mouth; **je ne mange pas de ce p.-là,** I'd rather starve (than get involved in this); (*c*) *Bot:* **arbre à p.,** breadfruit tree. **2.** (*a*) loaf; **p. de ménage,** (homemade) loaf; **p. de mie,** sandwich loaf; **p. de campagne, p. paysan,** farmhouse loaf; **petit p.,** (bread) roll; **p. au chocolat,** chocolate-filled roll; **ça se vend comme des petits pains,** it sells, it's selling, like hot cakes; *Cu:* **p. de poisson,** fish loaf; (*b*) bar (of wax); bar, cake (of soap); **p. de sucre,** sugar loaf; *Geog:* **(montagne en) p. de sucre,** sugar loaf (mountain). **3.** *A:* **p. à cacheter,** (sealing) wafer. **4.** *P:* blow, punch; **flanque-lui un p.,** sock him one.

pair [pɛr] **1.** *a.* even (number); *n.* **le p. et l'impair,** odd and even; **jours pairs,** even dates; **jouer p.,** to bet on the even numbers; *Rail:* **voie paire,** up line. **2.** *n.m.* (*a*) equal, peer; *Lit:* **être avec qn, traiter qn, de p. en compagnon,** to treat s.o. as an equal; **sans p.,** unequalled; peerless; **hors (de) p.,** unrivalled, beyond compare; (*b*) **de p. (avec),** (i) on a par, on an equal footing (with); (ii) at the same time (as), together (with); **le chômage va de p. avec les crises économiques,** unemployment and economic crises go hand in hand; (*c*) peer (of the realm). **3.** *n.m.* (state of) equality, par; (*a*) *Fin:* **p. du change,** par of exchange; **au-dessous, au-dessus, du p.,** below par, above par; (*b*) **travailler au p.,** to work in exchange for board and lodging; **(jeune fille) au p.,** au pair (girl).

paire [pɛr] *n.f.* pair (of shoes, spectacles, scissors, etc.); brace (of game birds, pistols); **p. de bœufs,** yoke of oxen; **ça, c'est une autre p. de manches,** that's another story; *F:* **les deux font la p.,** they're two of a kind; *P:* **se faire la p.,** to clear out, to beat it.

pairesse [pɛrɛs] *n.f.* peeress.

pairie [peri] *n.f.* peerage

paisible [pezibl̥] *a.* (*a*) peaceful, quiet (person); (*b*) peaceful, untroubled, quiet, calm; **silence p.,** undisturbed silence.

paisiblement [pezibləmɑ̃] *adv.* peaceably, peacefully, quietly, calmly.

paître [pɛtr̥] *v.* (*pr.p.* **paissant;** *pr.ind.* **je pais, il paît, n. paissons;** *pr.sub.* **je paisse;** *impf.* **je paissais;** *fu.* **je paîtrai;** *no p.h.; p.p.* **pu** *is used only in the phr. shown under* 2) **1.** *v.tr.* (*a*) *A: & Lit:* to feed, graze (cattle); (*b*) (*of animals*) to feed on (leaves, etc.); to crop (grass). **2.** *v.i.* (*of animals*) to feed; to graze, browse; to pasture; **faucon qui a pu,** hawk that has fed; *F:* **je l'ai envoyé p.,** I sent him packing.

paix [pɛ] *n.f.* peace; (*a*) **faire la p.,** to make peace; **faire la p. avec qn,** to make one's peace, to make it up, with s.o.; **demander la p.,** to sue for peace; **rester en p. avec un pays,** to remain at peace with a country; **en temps de p.,** in peacetime; (*b*) **observer, troubler, la p.,** to keep, to break, the peace; (*c*) peace, calm, quiet; **la p. du tombeau,** the quiet of the grave; **vivre en p.,** to live in peace (and quiet); **dormir en p.,** to sleep peacefully; **laissez-moi en p.,** leave me alone, in peace; *P:* **fiche-moi la p.!** don't bother me! shut up! **la p.!** hush! be quiet!

Pakistan [pakistɑ̃] *Pr.n.m. Geog:* Pakistan.

pakistanais, -aise [pakistanɛ, -ɛz] *a. & n.* Pakistani.

pal [pal] *n.m.* (*a*) pale, stake; *A:* **le (supplice du) p.,** impalement; (*b*) *Vit: etc:* planter, dibber.

palabre [palabr̥] *n.f. occ. m. usu. pl.* palaver; (interminable) discussion.

palabrer [palabre] *v.i.* to palaver, chatter; to talk, argue, interminably.

palace [palas] *n.m.* luxury hotel.

paladin [paladɛ̃] *n.m.* paladin; knight-errant.

palais¹ [palɛ] *n.m.* **1.** palace (of king, etc.); **le P. Bourbon,** the *Assemblée nationale.* **2. P. de Justice, le P.,** the law courts; **gens du, de, P., le P.,** lawyers; **terme de P.,** legal term.

palais² *n.m.* (*a*) *Anat:* palate; **voûte du p., p. dur,** hard palate; **voile du p., p. mou,** soft palate; **p. fendu,** cleft palate; (*b*) (sense of) taste; **avoir le p. fin,** to have a delicate palate.

palan [palɑ̃] *n.m.* hoist, hoisting gear; *Mec.E: Nau:* pulley block, purchase tackle, whip.

palanche [palɑ̃ʃ] *n.f.* yoke, shoulder piece (for carrying buckets, etc.).

palanque [palɑ̃k] *n.f. Fort:* (timber) stockade.

palanquer [palɑ̃ke] *v.i. Fort:* to stockade.

palanquin [palɑ̃kɛ̃] *n.m.* palanquin.

palastre [palastr̥] *n.m.* box (of lock); **serrure à p.,** rim lock.

palatal, -ale, -aux [palatal, -o] *a.* **1.** *Ling:* palatal; *n.f.* **palatale,** palatal; front consonant; **voyelle palatale,** front vowel. **2.** *Anat:* palatal (bones, etc.).

palatalisation [palatalizasjɔ̃] *n.f. Ling:* palatalization.

palataliser [palatalize] *v.tr. Ling:* to palatalize.

palatin, -ine [palatɛ̃, -in] **1.** *a. & n. Hist:* palatine; **Comte p.,** Count Palatine. **2.** *a.* **Le Mont P.,** the Palatine Hill (at Rome).

Palatinat (le) [ləpalatina] *Pr.n.m. Hist:* the Palatinate.

pale¹ [pal] *n.f.* **1.** blade (of oar, propeller); vane (of fan, etc.); **à trois, à quatre, pales,** three-, four-bladed propeller. **2.** sluice (gate); hatch (of mill).

pale² *n.f. Ecc:* pall(a), chalice cover.

pâle [pɑl] *a.* (*a*) pale; *Lit: Med:* pallid; **p. comme un linge, comme la mort,** as white as a sheet; deathly pale; **être p. de colère,** to be white, livid, with rage; *Mil: F:* **se faire porter p.,** to report sick; (*b*) pale (colour, *NAm:* color, sky); pale, faint (light); poor, pale (imitation); **un sourire p.,** a wan, faint, smile; *Lit:* **style p.,** colourless, *NAm:* colorless, style; *F:* **c'est un p. crétin,** he's a complete idiot, fool.

palefrenier [palfrənje] *n.m.* groom, stableman, stable boy, ostler.

palefroi [palfrwa] *n.m. Hist:* palfrey.

paléographe [paleɔgraf] *n.* pal(a)eographer.

paléographie [paleɔgrafi] *n.f.* pal(a)eography.

paléographique [paleɔgrafik] *a.* pal(a)eographic.

paléolithique [paleɔlitik] *a. & n.m.* Pal(a)eolithic (age).

paléontologie [paleɔ̃tɔlɔʒi] *n.f.* pal(a)eontology.

paléontologique [paleɔ̃tɔlɔʒik] *a.* pal(a)eontological.

paléontologiste [paleɔ̃tɔlɔʒist], **paléontologue** [paleɔ̃tɔlɔg] *n.* pal(a)eontologist.

paleron [palrɔ̃] *n.m.* shoulder blade, blade bone (of horse, ox, etc.); *Cu:* **p. de bœuf,** chuck.

Palestine [palɛstin] *Pr.n.f. Geog:* Palestine.

palestinien, -ienne [palɛstinjɛ̃, -jɛn] *a. & n.* Palestinian.

palet [palɛ] *n.m. Games:* **1.** quoit; **jouer au(x) palet(s),** to play at quoits. **2.** (metal, stone) disc (used for playing various games); (*for ice hockey*) puck.

paletot [palto] *n.m.* (*usu.* short) overcoat, jacket; *P:* **tomber sur le p. de qn,** to attack s.o., to jump on s.o.

palette [palɛt] *n.f.* **1.** (wooden) battledore. **2.** (*a*) paddle, float board (of paddle wheel); (*b*) pallet (of forklift truck, etc.); (*c*) *Cu:* shoulder (of mutton, pork). **3.** (painter's) palette.

palétuvier [paletyvje] *n.m. Bot:* mangrove.

pâleur [pɑlœr] *n.f.* pallor, paleness; **d'une p. mortelle,** deathly pale.

palier [palje] *n.m.* **1.** (*a*) *Arch:* landing (of stairs); **nous sommes voisins de p.,** we live on the same floor; (*b*) stage; level; **procéder par paliers,** to proceed in stages. **2.** (*a*) *Aut: Rail: etc:* level run, level stretch; **vitesse en p.,** speed on the level, on the flat; (*b*) *Av:* **voler en p.,** to fly level; (*c*) *Mth: etc:* plateau (of a graph); **le taux des naissances a atteint un p.,** the birthrate has levelled off. **3.** *Mch: Mec.E:* bearing; **p. d'arbre,** shaft bearing, spring bearing.

palière [paljɛr] *a.f.* **porte p.,** landing door, door opening onto the landing; **marche p.,** top step.

palindrome [palɛ̃drom] *n.m.* palindrome.

palinodie [palinɔdi] *n.f.* **1.** *Lit:* palinode. **2.** *pl.* recantations.

pâlir [pɑlir] **1.** *v.i.* to become pale, grow pale; (*of light, star, etc.*) to grow dim; (*of colour, NAm: color*) to fade; **p. d'horreur,** to turn pale, to go white, with horror; **ses joues ont pâli,** his cheeks have lost their colour; **faire p. qn,** to make s.o. green with envy. **2.** *v.tr.* to turn (s.o., sth.) pale.

palis [pali] *n.m.* paling. **1.** (*a*) fence, picket fence; (*b*) enclosure (within picket fence). **2.** pale, stake, picket.

palissade [palisad] *n.f.* (*a*) palisade, fence; picket fence; (*b*) *Agr:* hedgerow; (*c*) (street) hoarding, *NAm:* billboard.

palissader [palisade] *v.tr.* to palisade; to fence in, rail in; to enclose.

palissandre [palisɑ̃dr̥] *n.m. Bot:* Brazilian rosewood.

pâlissant [pɑlisɑ̃] *a.* (face) turning pale; fading, waning (light); fading (colour, *NAm:* color).

palladium¹ [paladjɔm] *n.m. Myth:* palladium; *Fig:* safeguard.

palladium² *n.m. Ch:* palladium.

palliatif, -ive [paljatif, -iv] **1.** *a.* palliative. **2.** *n.m. Med:* palliative; *Fig:* stopgap measure.

pallier [palje] (*impf. & pr.sub.* **n. palliions, v. palliiez**) **1.** *v.tr.* to palliate (pain, disease); to cover up, extenuate (offence, mistake). **2.** *v.i.* **p. aux conséquences d'une faute,** to mitigate the consequences of an error.

palmarès [palmarɛs] *n.m. Sch: etc:* prize list; honours list, *NAm:* honors list; *Sp:* (list of) medal winners; *W.Tel: etc:* **p. (de la chanson),** (the) charts; the top twenty, thirty, etc.

palme [palm] *n.f.* **1.** (*a*) *A:* palm (tree); (*b*) **huile, vin, de p.,** palm oil, wine. **2.** palm (branch); (*symbol*) palm; victory; **p. du martyre,** martyr's crown, crown of martyrdom; **palmes (académiques),** decoration given by the Ministry of Education; (*of decoration*) **avec p.** = with bar. **3.** flipper (of a frogman).

palmé [palme] *a.* **1.** *Bot:* palmate (leaf). **2.** *Orn:* webfooted; **pied p.,** webbed foot.

palmer [palmɛr] *n.m. Tchn:* micrometer.

palmeraie [palmərɛ] *n.f.* palm grove.

palmette [palmɛt] *n.f. Arch:* palm leaf (moulding, *NAm:* molding); palmette.

palmier [palmje] *n.m.* **1.** palm (tree); **cœur de p.,** palm tree heart. **2.** *Cu:* (sort of) biscuit in shape of palm leaf.

palmipède [palmipɛd] *a. & n.m. Orn:* palmiped(e); webfooted (bird).

palmiste [palmist] *n.m. Bot:* cabbage palm, cabbage tree; **chou p.,** palm tree heart.

palombe [palɔ̃b] *n.f.* ring dove, wood pigeon.

palonnier [palɔnje] *n.m.* (*a*) *Veh:* swingle bar, whipple tree; (*b*) *Av:* rudder bar; (*c*) *Aut:* **p. de freinage,** compensator.

pâlot, -otte [pɑlo, -ɔt] *a.* rather pale, peaky; sickly-looking (child).

palourde [palurd] *n.f. Moll:* clam; carpet shell.

palpable [palpabl̥] *a.* palpable. **1.** tangible. **2.** obvious, easily perceived, plain (truth, etc.); palpable (error).

palper [palpe] *v.tr.* to feel; to examine (sth.) by feeling; *Med:* to palpate; **p. un article,** to finger an article; *F:* **p. (de l'argent),** to receive, make, money; **qu'est-ce qu'il a dû p.!** he must have made a mint!

palpitant [palpitɑ̃] **1.** *a.* palpitating, fluttering; quivering (with emotion, etc.); **roman p. d'intérêt,** thrilling, exciting, novel. **2.** *n.m. P:* heart, ticker.

palpitation [palpitasjɔ̃] *n.f.* palpitation; (*a*) quivering (of limb); fluttering (of eyelid, pulse); (*b*) pounding (of heart); **avoir des palpitations,** to have palpitations.

palpiter [palpite] *v.i.* to palpitate; (*of pulse, eyelid*) to flutter; (*of limb*) to quiver; (*of heart*) to pound, to throb; (*of light, etc.*) to quiver; **il palpitait de peur,** he was quivering with fear.

paluche [palyʃ] *n.f. P:* hand, mitt, paw.

paludéen, -enne [palydeɛ̃, -ɛn] *a.* paludal; *Med:* malarial.

paludisme [palydism] *n.m. Med:* paludism, malaria.

palustre [palystr̥] *a.* paludal (plant, etc.); *Med:* malarial.

pâmer (se) [səpɑme] *v.pr.* (*a*) *A:* to swoon, to faint; (*b*) **se p. de rire,** to be convulsed, to split one's sides, with laughter; **se p. d'admiration,** to be in raptures, overcome with admiration (**sur,** over).

pâmoison [pɑmwazɔ̃] *n.f. A:* swoon; **tomber en p.,** to swoon; **tomber en p. devant qch.,** to go into raptures over sth.

pampa [pɑ̃pa] *n.f.* pampas (of S. America).

pamphlet [pɑ̃flɛ] *n.m.* satirical tract; lampoon.

pamphlétaire [pɑ̃fletɛr] *n.* lampooner.

pamplemousse [pɑ̃pləmus] *n.m.* (*a*) *Bot:* shaddock; (*b*) grapefruit.

pampre [pɑ̃pr̥] *n.m.* vine branch (with grapes).

pan¹ [pɑ̃] *n.m.* **1.** skirt, flap (of garment); tail (of shirt, coat); **se promener en p. de chemise,** to wander about in one's shirt tails. **2.** section, piece, surface; **p. de voûte,** severy; **p. de mur,** section of wall; **p. de bois,** timber framing; **p. de comble,** side, panel, of a roof; **p. de ciel,** patch of sky. **3.** face, side (of angular building, etc.); **tour à huit pans,** eight-sided, octagonal, tower; **p. coupé,** cant; **en p. coupé,** with the corner cut off.

Pan² *Pr.n.m. Myth:* Pan.

pan³ *int.* **1.** bang! crash! wham! **2.** *F:* (*to child*) **je vais te faire p. p.!** I'll smack you!

panacée [panase] *n.f.* panacea.

panachage [panaʃaʒ] *n.m.* **1.** mixing (of colours, *NAm:* colors, etc.). **2.** *Pol:* voting on the same "ticket" for candidates belonging to different parties; splitting of one's vote.

panache [panaʃ] *n.m.* **1.** (*a*) plume, panache; tuft (of feathers, etc.); **p. de fumée,** wreath, trail, of smoke; (*b*) *F:* **faire p.,** (*of rider*) to be pitched over the horse's head, to take a header; (*of cyclist*) to be pitched over the handlebars; (*c*) gallantry, dashing courage; (*d*) ostentation, panache; **il a du p.,** he has an air about him. **2.** *Arch:* panache (of pendentive).

panaché [panaʃe] *a.* variegated, multicoloured, *NAm:* multicolored (bird, flower); motley (crowd); *Cu:* **salade panachée,** mixed salad; **glace panachée,** mixed(-flavour, *NAm:* -flavor) ice cream; **bière panachée,** *n.m.* **p.,** shandy.

panacher [panaʃe] *v.tr.* (*a*) *Hort:* to variegate (with different colours, *NAm:* colors); (*b*) *Pol:* **p. une liste électorale,** to vote on the same "ticket" for candidates belonging to different parties; to split one's vote.

panachure [panaʃyr] *n.f.* variegation (on flowers, fruit, feathers).

panade [panad] *n.f. Cu:* bread soup; *F:* **être dans la p.,** (i) to be in the soup, in a fix; (ii) to be down and out.

panafricain [panafrikɛ̃] *a.* Pan-African.

panafricanisme [panafrikanism] *n.m.* Pan-Africanism.

panais [panɛ] *n.m.* parsnip.

Panama [panama] **1.** *Pr.n.m. Geog:* Panama. **2.** *n.m.* panama hat.

Paname [panam] *Pr.n.m. P:* Paris.

panaméricain [panamerikɛ̃] *a.* Pan-American.

panaméricanisme [panamerikanism] *n.m.* Pan-Americanism.

panarabisme [panarabism] *n.m.* Pan-Arabism.

panard [panar] **1.** *a.* (*of horse*) knock-kneed; cow-hocked. **2.** *n.m. P:* foot, hoof, *pl.* plates (of meat).

panaris [panari] *n.m. Med:* whitlow.

pancarte [pɑ̃kart] *n.f.* sign, notice; placard.

pancréas [pɑ̃kreas] *n.m. Anat:* pancreas.

pancréatique [pɑ̃kreatik] *a.* pancreatic.

panda [pɑ̃da] *n.m. Z:* panda.

pandit [pɑ̃di] *n.m.* (*Indian title*) pundit, pandit.

panégyrique [paneʒirik] *n.m.* panegyric; **faire le p. de qn,** to extol s.o.'s virtues, merits.

panégyriste [paneʒirist] *n.m.* panegyrist; eulogist.

paner [pane] *v.tr. Cu:* to cover, coat (meat, fish, etc.) with breadcrumbs; **escalope panée,** escalope coated with breadcrumbs; breaded veal.

paneterie [pantri] *n.f.* bread pantry; bread store (in barracks, schools, etc.).

panetière [pantjɛr] *n.f.* bread bin.

pangermanisme [pɑ̃ʒɛrmanism] *n.m.* Pan-Germanism.

panier [panje] *n.m.* **1.** (*a*) basket; **p. à anse(s),** hand basket; **mettre, jeter, qch. au p.,** to throw sth. into the wastepaper basket; to throw sth. away, out; **p. à provisions,** (i) shopping basket; (ii) picnic basket; **p. à salade,** (i) salad shaker; (ii) *F:* prison van, Black Maria; **p. à bouteilles,** bottle carrier; **mettre tous ses œufs dans le même p.,** to put all one's eggs in one basket; *F:* **p. percé,** spendthrift; (*b*) basket(ful) (of fruit, etc.); **le dessus du p.,** the pick of the bunch; **c'est un p. de crabes,** they're always fighting, at each other's throats; (*c*) *Fish:* lobster pot; (*d*) *Sp:* (*basketball*) basket; **réussir, marquer, un p.,** to score (a basket). **2.** *A.Cost:* pannier; hoop (petticoat). **3.** slide magazine (for projector).

panier-repas [panjerəpɑ] *n.m.* lunch(eon) basket; packed lunch; *pl. paniers-repas.*

panifiable [panifjabḷ] *a.* (cereals, etc.) suitable for making bread.

panifier [panifje] *v.tr.* (*impf. & pr.sub.* **n. panifiions, v. panifiiez**) to turn (flour) into bread.

panique [panik] **1.** *a.* panic (terror). **2.** *n.f.* panic, scare; **pris de p.,** panic-stricken; **pris de p. ils s'enfuirent,** they fled in a panic.

paniquer [panike] *F:* **1.** *v.tr.* to get (s.o.) into a panic. **2.** *v.i.* to (get into a) panic; to get panicky.

panislamisme [panislamism] *n.m.* Pan-Islamism.

panne¹ [pan] *n.f.* **1.** *Tex:* panne, plush. **2.** (hog's) fat; lard.

panne² *n.f.* **1.** *Nau:* **en p.,** hove to; **mettre un navire en p.,** to bring a ship to. **2.** (mechanical) breakdown; (electrical) failure, *U.S:* outage; **en p.,** out of order; **p. de courant, d'électricité,** power failure; power cut; blackout; *W.Tel: T.V:* **p. d'émission,** technical fault, hitch; **p. de moteur,** engine failure; **tomber en p. d'essence, en p. sèche,** to run out of petrol, *NAm:* of gas(oline); (*to motorist*) **vous êtes en p.?** have you broken down? *F:* (*of pers.*) **être en p.,** to be, get, stuck; **rester en p. devant une difficulté,** to stick at a difficulty; *F:* **laisser qn en p.,** to leave s.o. in the lurch, to let s.o. down; **je suis en p. d'allumettes,** I've run out of matches.

panne³ *n.f. Const:* purlin (of roof).

panne⁴ *n.f. Tchn:* pane, peen (of hammer).

panné [pane] *a. P:* (stony) broke; *n.* **c'est un p.,** he's penniless.

panneau, -eaux [pano] *n.m.* **1.** snare, net (for game); *Fig:* **tomber, donner, dans le p.,** to fall into the trap. **2.** panel; *pl.* panelling; **porte à panneaux,** panelled door; **p. vitré,** glass panel. **3.** *Nau: etc:* **p. d'écoutille, p. de cale,** hatch cover. **4.** board; **p. d'affichage,** (i) noticeboard; (ii) (advertisement) hoarding, *NAm:* billboard; *Aut:* **p. indicateur,** signpost; direction sign; **p. de signalisation (routière),** roadsign; **panneaux électoraux,** noticeboards for election posters.

panneau-réclame [panoreklam] *n.m.* (advertisement) hoarding, *NAm:* billboard; *pl. panneaux-réclame.*

panneton [pantɔ̃] *n.m.* **1.** web, bit (of key). **2.** window catch.

panonceau, -eaux [panɔ̃so] *n.m.* **1.** *A:* escutcheon. **2.** (*a*) escutcheon sign, plaque (of *notaire*, etc.); (*b*) sign; noticeboard.

panoplie [panɔpli] *n.f.* (*a*) panoply; full suit of plate armour, *NAm:* armor; (*b*) **p. de soldat,** soldier's outfit (for child); (*c*) set (of tools, etc.).

panorama [panɔrama] *n.m.* panorama.

panoramique [panɔramik] **1.** *a.* panoramic; **voiture avec carrosserie p.,** car with panoramic, wrap-round, windows. **2.** *n.m. Cin: T.V:* panning.

pansage [pɑ̃saʒ] *n.m.* grooming (of horse, etc.).

panse [pɑ̃s] *n.f.* **1.** (*a*) *F:* belly, paunch, pot; (*b*) first stomach, paunch, rumen (of ruminant). **2.** belly, bulge (of bottle, etc.); sound bow (of bell).

pansement [pɑ̃smɑ̃] *n.m. Med:* **1.** (action of) dressing (a wound); **faire un p.,** to dress a wound; to apply a dressing. **2.** dressing; bandage; **p. (adhésif),** (sticking) plaster; **il est couvert de pansements,** he's all bandaged up; **il faut mettre un p.,** you ought to put a bandage on it.

panser [pɑ̃se] *v.tr.* **1.** to groom, rub down (horse). **2.** to dress, to put a dressing on (a wound); to bandage (a limb); to put a plaster on (a finger).

panslavisme [pɑ̃slavism] *n.m.* Pan-Slavism.

pansu [pɑ̃sy] *a.* potbellied (person, bottle, etc.); paunchy (person).

pantagruélique [pɑ̃tagryelik] *a.* pantagruelian (meal, etc.).

pantalon [pɑ̃talɔ̃] **1.** *n.m. Cost:* (pair of) trousers, *NAm:* pants; (*for women*) slacks; **elle porte des pantalons,** she wears trousers. **2.** *Pr.n.m. Th:* **P.,** Pantaloon.

pantalonnade [pɑ̃talɔnad] *n.f.* (*a*) *Th.Hist:* burlesque farce; buffoonery; (*b*) piece of hypocrisy.

pantelant [pɑ̃tlɑ̃] *a.* (*a*) panting, gasping, heaving; (*b*) (*of dead animal, body*) quivering, twitching.

panteler [pɑ̃tle] *v.i.* **(je pantelle, n. pantelons; je pantellerai)** to pant; to gasp.

pantène, pantenne [pɑ̃tɛn] *n.f.* **1.** *Ven:* draw net. **2. en pantenne** (*a*) (*of ships, convoy*) in disorder; (*b*) **vergues en pantenne,** yard apeak, scandalized (as sign of mourning).

panthéisme [pɑ̃teism] *n.m.* pantheism.

panthéiste [pɑ̃teist] **1.** *a.* pantheistic(al). **2.** *n.* pantheist.

panthéon [pɑ̃teɔ̃] *n.m.* pantheon.

panthère [pɑ̃tɛr] *n.f.* **1.** *Z:* panther. **2.** *P:* **ma p.,** the wife, the missus.

pantin [pɑ̃tɛ̃] *n.m.* (*a*) *Toys:* jumping jack; (*b*) (*of pers.*) puppet, stooge.

pantographe [pɑ̃tɔgraf] *n.m. Draw: Rail:* pantograph.

pantois [pɑ̃twa] *a.* amazed, nonplussed, flabbergasted; **j'en suis tout p.,** I'm speechless.

pantomime [pɑ̃tɔmim] *n.f.* **1.** *Th:* (*a*) mime; (*b*) mime show. **2.** *Pej:* scene; **que signifie cette p.?** what on earth are you playing at?

pantouflard, -arde [pɑ̃tuflar, -ard] *a. & n. F:* stay-at-home.

pantoufle [pɑ̃tufl] *n.f.* slipper; **il était en pantoufles,** he was wearing, he was in, his slippers; **passer sa vie dans ses pantoufles,** to live a secluded life.

panure [panyr] *n.f. Cu:* breadcrumbs.

paon [pɑ̃] *n.m.* **1.** *Orn:* peacock; **pousser des cris de p.,** to screech like a peacock; **se parer des plumes du p.,** to take all the credit. **2.** *Ent:* peacock butterfly.

paonne [pan] *n.f. Orn:* peahen.

paonneau, -eaux [pano] *n.m.* peachick.

papa [papa] *n.m.* (*a*) dad(dy); pa, *NAm:* pop; (*b*) *F:* **faire qch. à la p.,** to do sth. in a leisurely fashion; **aller à la p.,** to dodder along; to potter along; (*c*) *F: Pej:* **de p.,** old-fashioned; behind the times; **c'est un film de p.,** this is an ancient film.

papal, -aux [papal, -o] *a.* papal.

papauté [papote] *n.f.* papacy.

papaye [papaj] *n.f. Bot:* pa(w)paw, papaya.

papayer [papaje] *n.m. Bot:* pa(w)paw, papaya (tree).

pape [pap] *n.m.* **1.** *Ecc:* pope. **2.** (undisputed) leader (of school, etc.); leading light.

papelard¹ [paplar] *a.* sanctimonious, smarmy (voice, etc.); **il a un air p.,** he looks as if butter wouldn't melt in his mouth.

papelard² *n.m. F:* (piece of) paper; (news)paper.

paperasse [papras] *n.f. Pej:* (*usu. pl.*) papers; forms; (*coll. sing.*) **c'est de la p.!** it's just a lot of (old) papers!

paperasserie [paprasri] *n.f. Pej:* **1.** (accumulation of) papers; forms; *F:* bumf. **2. la p. (administrative),** red tape; **il y a trop de p.,** there's too much paperwork.

paperassier, -ière [paprasje, -jɛr] *Pej:* **1.** *a.* (*a*) fond of paperwork; (*b*) cluttered up with red tape. **2.** *n.* (*a*) (i) scribbler, penpusher; (ii) amasser of (old) papers; (*b*) bureaucrat.

papeterie [papetri] *n.f.* **1.** (*a*) paper manufacturing; (*b*) paper mill, factory. **2.** (*a*) stationer's (shop); (*b*) stationery; (*c*) stationery trade.

papetier, -ière [paptje, -jɛr] *n.* (*a*) paper manufacturer; (*b*) stationer.

papetier-libraire [paptjelibrɛr] *n.m.* bookseller and stationer; *pl. papetiers-libraires.*

papier [papje] *n.m.* **1.** (*a*) paper; **pâte à p.,** pulp; **p. pelure,** India paper; **p. buvard,** blotting paper; **p. carbone,** carbon paper; **p. couché,** art paper; **p. glacé,** glazed paper; **p. émeri,** emery paper; **p. de verre,** glass paper, sandpaper; **p. gommé,** gummed paper; **p. gris,** brown paper; **p. kraft,** kraft (paper); **p. filtre,** filter paper; **p. journal,** newsprint; newspaper; **p. de soie,** tissue paper; **p. parcheminé,** greaseproof paper; **p. à cigarettes,** cigarette paper; *Phot:* **p. sensible,** sensitized paper; **p. calque,** tracing paper; **p. ministre,** official paper; **p. à lettres,** notepaper, writing paper; **p. à en-tête,** headed notepaper; **p. machine,** typing paper; **p. à dessin,** drawing paper; **p. réglé,** ruled, lined, paper; **p. à musique,** manuscript paper; **p. d'emballage,** wrapping paper; **p. hygiénique, p. toilette,** *P:* **p. cul,** toilet paper, *F:* loo paper, *P:* bog paper; **p. peint,** wallpaper; (*b*) **un p.,** a sheet, piece, of paper; **notez plutôt cela dans votre carnet que sur un p.,** put it down in your notebook rather than on a scrap of paper; (*c*) **sur le p.,** on paper, in theory; (*d*) **p. mâché,** papier mâché; **avoir une mine de p. mâché,** to look washed out. **2.** (*a*) paper, document; *Jur:* **papiers d'une affaire,** documents relating to a case; **vieux papiers,** old papers, waste paper; *F:* **être dans les petits papiers de qn,** to be in s.o.'s good books; *F:* **rayez cela de vos papiers,** don't count on it; (you can) forget it; (*b*) *Jur:* **p. timbré,** stamped paper (for official and legal documents); (*c*) *Fin:* bill(s); **p. de commerce,** commercial, trade, paper; **p. long, à long terme,** long(-dated) bill; (*d*) *pl. Adm:* **papiers (d'identité),** (identity) papers; **avoir ses papiers en règle,** to have one's papers in order; (*e*) *Journ:* article. **3. p. d'aluminium,** aluminium foil, tinfoil; **p. d'argent, d'étain,** silver foil, paper; tinfoil.

papier-monnaie [papjemɔnɛ] *n.m.* paper money; *pl. papiers-monnaie.*

papillaire [papilɛr] *a. Anat: etc:* papillary.

papille [papij, -il] *n.f. Anat: Bot:* papilla; **p. gustative,** taste bud.

papillon [papijɔ̃] *n.m.* **1.** *Ent:* butterfly; **p. de nuit,** moth; **c'est un p.,** she's flighty; *F:* **minute p.!** just a moment; hold on a minute! **nœud p.,** bow tie; *Swim:* **brasse p.,** butterfly stroke. **2.** (*a*) inset (in book); erratum slip; (*b*) handbill; (*c*) label; sticker; (*d*) *Aut:* (parking) ticket. **3.** *Tchn:* (*a*) butterfly (throttle); throttle valve; (*b*) thumb screw, butterfly nut, wing nut.

papillonnant [papijɔnɑ̃] *a.* (*a*) fluttering; flitting; (*b*) fickle; **esprit p.,** grasshopper mind.

papillonnement [papijɔnmɑ̃] *n.m.* fluttering; flitting (from place to place, person to person).

papillonner [papijɔne] *v.i.* to flit about (from person to person); to pass rapidly (from one subject to another).

papillotage [papijɔtaʒ] *n.m.* (*a*) **p. des yeux,** blinking (of the eyes); (*b*) *Typ:* mackling, slurring.

papillote [papijɔt] *n.f.* **1.** *A:* curl paper (for hair). **2.** twist of paper; frill (round knuckle of ham, etc.); sweet paper; **tu peux en faire des papillotes,** it's no good, you can throw it away. **3.** *Cu:* buttered paper (for cooking chops, etc.).

papillotement [papijɔtmɑ̃] *n.m.* twinkling; flickering; blinking.

papilloter [papijɔte] **1.** *v.i.* (*a*) (*of eyes*) to blink; (*of light*) to twinkle; *Cin: etc:* to flicker; (*b*) to dazzle, glitter; (*c*) *Typ:* to mackle, slur. **2.** *v.tr. A:* to put (hair) into curl papers.

papisme [papism] *n.m.* **1.** papism. **2.** *Pej:* popery.

papiste [papist] *n.* (*a*) papist; (*b*) *Pej:* Roman Catholic.

papoter [papɔte] *v.i. F:* to chatter; to have a natter.

papou, -oue [papu] *a. & n. Geog: Ling:* Papuan; *pl. papous, -oues.*

papouille [papuj] *n.f. F:* tickle; squeeze; *Pej:* **faire des papouilles à qn,** to paw s.o.

paprika [paprika] *n.m. Bot: Cu:* paprika.

papule [papyl] *n.f. Med:* papule; *F:* pimple; weal (of urticaria).

papyrus [papirys] *n.m.* papyrus.

pâque [pɑk] **1.** *n.f.* (Jewish) Passover. **2.** (*a*) *n.f.pl.* **Pâques,** Easter; **joyeuses Pâques,** happy Easter; **faire ses Pâques, ses pâques,** to take the sacrament at Easter; (*b*) *n.m.* (*contraction of* **jour de Pâques,** *used without article*) **Pâques,** Easter; **le lundi de Pâques,** Easter Monday; **œufs de Pâques,** Easter eggs; *F:* **remettre qch. à Pâques ou à la Trinité,** to put sth. off indefinitely.

paquebot [pakbo] *n.m. Nau:* liner; (steam)ship.

pâquerette [pɑkrɛt] *n.f. Bot:* daisy.

paquet [pakɛ] *n.m.* (*a*) parcel, packet; package; bundle; **p. de linge, de lettres,** bundle of linen, of letters; **faire un p.,** to make up, tie up, a parcel; **p. de**

café, bag of coffee; **p. de cigarettes,** packet, *NAm:* pack, of cigarettes; **il fume un p. par jour,** he smokes twenty a day; **faire son p., ses paquets,** to pack one's bags, to get ready to leave; *F:* **donner, lâcher, son p. à qn,** to give s.o. a piece of one's mind; **il a eu son p.,** I told him what I thought of him; *Fin:* **p. d'actions,** parcel of shares; **p. de billets,** wad of notes; *F:* **il a touché un joli p.,** he's made a nice sum, a nice packet; **mettre le p.,** to go all out; to pull out all the stops; *F:* **risquer le p.,** to risk, chance, the lot; **p. de neige,** heap of snow; snowdrift; **des paquets d'eau tombaient,** sheets of rain were coming down; **p. de mer,** big wave; heavy sea; **c'est un p. de nerfs, d'os,** he's a bundle of nerves; he's all skin and bone; (*b*) *Rugby Fb:* **p. (d'avants),** pack; (*c*) *Typ:* type matter; page.

paquetage [paktaʒ] *n.m. Mil: etc:* (soldier's) pack; **faire son p.,** to get one's kit ready.

par [par] *prep.* **1.** (*a*) (*in relations of place*) **on y arrive p. un escalier,** the place is reached by a flight of stairs; **jeter qch., regarder, p. la fenêtre,** to throw something, to look, out of the window; **il entra p. la fenêtre,** he came in through the window; **p. monts et p. vaux,** over hill and dale; **il court p. les rues,** he runs through the streets; **p. tout le pays,** throughout the country; **p. 10° de latitude nord,** at a latitude of 10° North; **passer p. Calais,** to travel by, via, Calais; **venez p. ici, allez p. là,** come this way, go that way; **c'est p. ici,** this is the way, it's this way; **p. où a-t-il passé?** which way did he go? (*b*) (*in relations of time*) **p. un jour d'hiver,** on a winter's day; **ne sortez pas p. cette chaleur,** don't go out in this heat; **p. le passé,** in the past; **je l'ai averti p. trois fois,** I warned him three times. **2.** (*a*) (*showing the agent*) (i) (*with a passive verb*) **il a été puni p. son père,** he was punished by his father; **accablé p. l'inquiétude,** overcome by, with, anxiety; (ii) (*with an active verb*) **faire qch. p. soi-même,** to do sth. unaided, on one's own initiative; **j'ai appris par les Martin que vous étiez malade,** I heard through, from, the Martins that you were ill; **faire faire qch. par qn,** to have sth. done by s.o.; (*b*) (*showing the means, instrument*) **il fut salué p. des acclamations,** he was hailed with cheers; **attacher qch. p. une chaîne,** to fasten sth. with a chain; **conduire, prendre, qn p. la main,** to lead, take, s.o. by the hand; **envoyer qch. p. la poste,** to send sth. by post, through the post; **je suis venu p. le train,** I came by train; **il a essayé p. tous les moyens,** he tried every possible means, he tried everything; **obtenir qch. p. la force,** to obtain sth. by force; **elle est remarquable p. sa beauté,** she is remarkable for her beauty; **appeler qn p. son nom,** to call s.o. by his name; (*c*) (*emphatic*) **vous êtes p. trop aimable,** you are far too kind; **examiner, juger, qch. p. soi-même,** to examine, judge, sth. (for) oneself. **3.** (*showing cause, motive*) **faire qch. p. habitude,** to do sth. out of habit; **j'ai fait cela p. amitié, p. respect, pour vous,** I did it out of friendship, out of respect, for you; **p. pitié!** for pity's sake! **p. hasard, p. erreur,** by chance, by mistake. **4.** (*distributive*) **p. ordre alphabétique,** in alphabetical order; **entrer deux p. deux,** to come in two by two, by twos, in twos; **trois fois p. jour,** three times a day; **10 000 francs p. an,** 10,000 francs a year, per annum; **il gagne 1 000 francs p. semaine,** he earns 1,000 francs a, per, week; **un guide p. groupe de six,** one guide per group of six, for each group of six. **5. p.** + *inf.* (*after verbs of beginning and ending*) **commencer, débuter, finir, achever, terminer, p. faire qch.,** to begin, end, by doing sth.; **commencez p. le commencement,** begin at the beginning; **il va finir p. m'agacer!** I've had enough of him! **6.** *adv.phr.* **p.-ci p.-là,** hither and thither; **c'est Charles p.-ci, Charles p.-là,** it's Charles here and Charles there. **7.** *prep.phr.* (*a*) **de p. le monde,** throughout the world; (*b*) (= *A:* **de part**) **de p. le Roi,** by order of the King, in the name of the King.

para [para] *n.m. F:* (= PARACHUTISTE) para.

parabole [parabɔl] *n.f.* **1.** parable. **2.** *Mth:* parabola.

parabolique [parabɔlik] *a.* parabolic; **radiateur p.,** *n.* **un p.,** electric fire (with parabolic reflector).

parachèvement [paraʃɛvmɑ̃] *n.m.* finishing, completion; perfecting, perfection.

parachever [paraʃve] *v.tr.* (*conj. like* ACHEVER) to complete; to finish (sth.) off; to perfect.

parachutage [paraʃytaʒ] *n.m.* parachute landing (of men, supplies); parachuting, dropping (by parachute); paradrop(ping).

parachute [paraʃyt] *n.m.* **1.** parachute; **p. dorsal, ventral,** back(-pack), lap-pack, parachute; **saut en p.,** parachute jump. **2. p. de mine,** safety device (of pit-shaft cage).

parachuter [paraʃyte] (*a*) *v.tr. & i.* to parachute, to drop by parachute, to paradrop; (*b*) *v.tr. F:* to pitchfork (s.o. into a job).

parachutisme [paraʃytism] *n.m.* parachuting.

parachutiste [paraʃytist] **1.** *n.* parachutist. **2.** *n.m.* paratrooper; *pl.* paratroops. **3.** *a.* parachute; **détachements parachutistes,** parachute detachments.

parade¹ [parad] *n.f.* **1.** *Equit:* stopping, pulling up (of horse). **2.** *Mil:* parade (for guard, etc.); guard mounting; **faire la p.,** to parade; *Navy:* **faire p.,** to dress ship. **3.** parade, show, ostentation; **faire p. de ses bijoux,** to display, show off, one's jewels; **faire p. de ses connaissances,** to boast about one's knowledge; **habits de p.,** full-dress, ceremonial, clothes.

parade² *n.f.* **1.** *Fenc:* parade, parry; *Box:* parry. **2.** answer, reply; riposte; repartee.

parader [parade] *v.i.* to make a display; to show off; to strut about.

paradigmatique [paradigmatik] *Ling:* **1.** *a.* paradigmatic. **2.** *n.f.* study of paradigmatic relationships.

paradigme [paradigm] *n.m. Ling:* paradigm.

paradis [paradi] *n.m.* paradise. **1. le P. terrestre,** the garden of Eden; **cette île est un P. terrestre,** this island is heaven on earth. **2. aller au, en, p.,** to go to heaven, to paradise; **il ne l'emportera pas au, en, p.,** he won't get away with it; *Th: F:* **le p.,** the gods; *Orn:* **oiseau de p.,** bird of paradise.

paradisiaque [paradizjak] *a.* paradisiac(al), paradisaic(al).

paradisier [paradizje] *n.m. Orn:* bird of paradise.

paradoxal, -aux [paradɔksal, -o] *a.* paradoxical.

paradoxalement [paradɔksalmɑ̃] *adv.* paradoxically.

paradoxe [paradɔks] *n.m.* paradox.

parafe [paraf] *n.m.* = PARAPHE.

parafer [parafe] *v.tr.* = PARAPHER.

paraffinage [parafinaʒ] *n.m.* paraffining.

paraffine [parafin] *n.f. Ch:* paraffin; *Com:* paraffin (wax); **huile de p.,** liquid paraffin.

paraffiner [parafine] *v.tr.* to paraffin.

parage¹ [paraʒ] *n.m. A:* birth, descent; **de haut p.,** of high lineage.

parage² *n.m.* (*a*) *Vit:* dressing of the ground (before the winter); (*b*) trimming (of joints of meat).

parage³ *n.m. usu. pl.* (*a*) *Nau:* sea area; waters; region(s); (*b*) *always pl.* **dans les parages de . . .,** in the vicinity of, near . . .; **que faites-vous dans ces parages?** what are you doing (around) here, in these parts?

paragraphe [paragraf] *n.m.* **1.** paragraph. **2.** *Typ:* section mark, paragraph.

Paraguay [paragwɛ] *Pr.n.m. Geog:* Paraguay.

paraguayen, paraguéen, -enne [parag(w)ɛjɛ̃, -ɛn] *a. & n. Geog:* Paraguayan.

paraître [parɛtr̥] *v.i.* (*pr.p.* **paraissant;** *p.p.* **paru;** *pr.ind.* **je parais, il paraît, n. paraissons;** *impf.* **je paraissais;** *p.h.* **je parus;** *fu.* **je paraîtrai**) to appear. **1.** (*a*) to make one's appearance; (*of star, moon, etc.*) to appear, come out; (*of actor*) to appear, come on; **le jour commençait à p.,** the day was dawning; **elle n'a pas paru de la journée,** she hasn't been seen, nobody's seen her, all day; (*b*) (*of book, etc.*) to be published, to come out; (*of periodical*) to appear, to come out; **faire p. un livre,** to publish a book; **vient de p.,** just out, just published. **2.** (*a*) to be visible, apparent; **cette tache paraît à peine,** the stain is hardly visible, hardly shows; **laisser p. ses sentiments,** to show, betray, one's feelings; **faire p. qch.,** to show, display, sth.; (*b*) **p. en public,** to appear in public; **elle aime un peu trop p.,** she likes to show off; (*c*) *impers.* **je suis très mal; —il n'y paraît pas,** I'm very ill; —you don't look it; **demain il n'y paraîtra plus,** there'll be no trace of it tomorrow; **sans qu'il y paraisse,** without its being apparent. **3.** to seem, to look; (*a*) **il paraît (avoir) trente ans,** (i) he looks about thirty, (ii) he looks no more than thirty; **elle a quarante ans, mais elle ne les paraît pas,** she is forty, but she doesn't look it; **elle paraît son âge,** she looks her age; **il paraissait furieux,** he sounded furious; **l'endroit lui parut familier,** the place seemed familiar to him; **il ne paraît pas remarquer leur présence,** he doesn't seem to notice their presence; (*b*) *impers.* **il paraît qu'elle s'en va,** it seems, appears, she's leaving; apparently, she's leaving; **il me paraît que . . .,** it seems to me, it strikes me, that . . .; **à ce qu'il paraît,** apparently, it would seem so; **il paraît que oui, que non,** so it appears; it appears not, it seems not; **elle va divorcer, paraît-il,** apparently she's getting a divorce; (*c*) *n.m.* **l'être et le p.,** being and seeming, reality and appearance.

parallaxe [paralaks] *n.f. Astr: etc:* parallax.

parallèle [paralɛl] **1.** *a.* (*a*) parallel (**à,** to, with); *Gym:* **barres parallèles,** parallel bars; **rue qui est p. à la rivière,** street that runs parallel to, with, the river; (*b*) similar; **mener une action p.,** to take a parallel, similar, action; to act along the same lines; (*c*) unofficial; *Pol.Ec:* **marché p.,** unofficial, illegal, market. **2.** *n.f.* (*a*) *Mth:* parallel (line); (*b*) *El:* **montage en p.,** parallel connection. **3.** *n.m.* (*a*) *Geog:* parallel (of latitude); (*b*) comparison, parallel; **mettre qn en p. avec qn,** to compare s.o. with s.o.; **établir un p. entre . . . et . . .,** to draw a parallel between . . . and . . ..

parallèlement [paralɛlmɑ̃] *adv.* parallel (**à,** to, with); concurrently; in the same way.

parallélépipède [paralelepipɛd] *n.m. Mth:* parallelepiped.

parallélisme [paralelism] *n.m.* parallelism; *Aut:* (wheel) alignment.

parallélogramme [paralelɔgram] *n.m.* parallelogram.

paralysant [paralizɑ̃] *a.* paralysing.

paralysé, -ée [paralize] **1.** *a.* paralysed, paralytic. **2.** *n.* paralytic.

paralyser [paralize] *v.tr.* (*a*) to paralyse; **paralysé des deux jambes,** paralysed in both legs; (*b*) to paralyse, incapacitate; to cripple (economy, etc.); **paralysé par la peur,** paralysed, helpless, with fear.

paralysie [paralizi] *n.f.* (*a*) *Med:* paralysis; **p. agitante,** Parkinson's disease; **p. générale (progressive),** creeping paralysis; (*b*) paralysis (of the mind, etc.).

paralytique [paralitik] *a. & n.* paralytic.

paramètre [paramɛtr̥] *n.m.* parameter.

paramilitaire [paramilitɛr] *a.* paramilitary.

parangon [parɑ̃gɔ̃] *n.m.* paragon.

paranoïa [paranɔja] *n.f.* paranoia.

paranoïaque [paranɔjak] *a. & n.* paranoiac.

paranoïde [paranɔid] *a.* paranoid.

parapet [parapɛ] *n.m.* parapet.

paraphe [paraf] *n.m.* (*a*) paraph; flourish (following signature); (*b*) initials (of one's name).

parapher [parafe] *v.tr.* to initial.

paraphrase [parafraz] *n.f.* paraphrase.

paraphraser [parafraze] *v.tr.* to paraphrase.

paraplégie [parapleʒi] *n.f. Med:* paraplegia.

paraplégique [parapleʒik] *a. & n. Med:* paraplegic.

parapluie [paraplɥi] *n.m.* umbrella.

parasitaire [parazitɛr] *a.* parasitic(al).

parasite [parazit] **1.** *n.m.* (*a*) *Biol:* parasite; (*b*) parasite, hanger-on, sponger; (*c*) *pl. W.Tel: T.V:* interference; atmospherics. **2.** *a.* (*a*) *Biol:* parasitic (insect, plant, etc.); (*b*) *W.Tel: T.V:* **bruits parasites,** interference.

parasitique [parazitik] *a.* parasitic(al).

parasitisme [parazitism] *n.m.* parasitism.

parasol [parasɔl] *n.m.* parasol, sunshade; beach umbrella; **pin p.,** parasol pine, umbrella pine.

paratonnerre [paratɔnɛr] *n.m.* lightning conductor.

paratyphoïde [paratifɔid] *a. & n.f. Med:* paratyphoid (fever).

paravent [paravɑ̃] *n.m.* (draught) screen; folding screen.

parbleu [parblø] *int.* good Lord, yes! of course!

parc [park] *n.m.* **1.** park; grounds (of castle, etc.); **p. naturel,** nature reserve. **2.** (*a*) enclosure (for special purposes); **p. de stationnement,** carpark, *NAm:* parking lot; **p. d'attractions,** amusement park, fun fair; **p. à bestiaux,** cattle pen; **p. à moutons,** sheepfold; **p. à huîtres,** oyster bed; **p. (pour enfants),** playpen; (*b*) *Mil:* **p. d'artillerie,** artillery park; **p. de munitions,** ammunition depot. **3.** fleet (of buses, cars, etc.); *Rail:* rolling stock; **p. automobile,** number of cars on the roads.

parcage [parkaʒ] *n.m.* parking (of car); enclosing, penning (of cattle); folding (of sheep).

parcellaire [parsɛlɛr] *a.* divided into small portions, into parcels (of land); **travail p.,** work divided into sections.

parcelle [parsɛl] *n.f.* (small) fragment; particle (of gold, etc.); parcel (of land); **il n'a pas la moindre p. de jugement,** he hasn't a scrap of common sense.

parcellisation [parsɛlizasjɔ̃] *n.f.* parcelling (of land); breakdown (of work, etc.) into sections.

parcelliser [parsɛlize] *v.tr.* to divide into small portions; to break down (work, etc.) into sections.

parce que [parskə] *conj.phr.* because; **je le dis p. q. c'est vrai,** I say so because it is true; **pourquoi ne viens-tu pas? p. q.,** why aren't you coming? just because (I'm not).

parchemin [parʃəmɛ̃] *n.m.* (*a*) parchment; *Bookb:* vellum; **papier p.,** vegetable parchment, parchment paper; (*b*) document; *pl.* titles of nobility; diploma.

parcheminé [parʃəmine] *a.* parchment-like; dried, wrinkled, wizened (skin, etc.).

parcheminer [parʃəmine] *v.tr.* to give a parchment finish to (paper); **se p.,** to shrivel up; (*of skin*) to become shrivelled.

parcimonie [parsimɔni] *n.f.* parsimony; **avec p.,** parsimoniously; sparingly.

parcimonieusement [parsimɔnjøzmɑ̃] *adv.* parsimoniously; sparingly.

parcimonieux, -euse [parsimɔnjø, -øz] *a.* parsimonious, mean, niggardly, stingy.

par-ci par-là [parsiparla] *adv.phr.* (*a*) here and there; (*b*) now and then; from time to time.

parcmètre, parcomètre [parkmɛtr̥, parkɔmɛtr̥] *n.m.* parking meter.

parcourir [parkurir] *v.tr.* (*conj. like* COURIR) **1.** to travel through, go over (a stretch of country); **p. les**

rues, to wander through the streets; **p. une distance de plusieurs kilomètres,** to cover a distance of several kilometres, *NAm:* kilometers; **p. les mers,** to sail the seas; **un frisson me parcourut,** a shiver went through me. **2.** to examine (cursorily); **p. qch. des yeux, du regard,** to glance at, over, sth.; **p. un livre,** to glance, skim, through a book.

parcours [parkur] *n.m.* **1.** (*a*) distance covered; **p. de 10 kilomètres,** run of 10 kilometres, *NAm:* kilometers; **le car fait le p. entre la ville et la côte,** the bus runs between the town and the coast; **payer le p.,** to pay the fare; (*b*) route (of procession, bus, etc.); course (of river); (*c*) *Sp:* circuit, course; *Golf:* course, links; *Mil:* **p. du combattant,** obstacle course.

par-delà [pardəla] *adv. & prep.* beyond.

par-dessous [pardəsu] *prep. & adv.* under, beneath, underneath; **je suis passé p.-d.,** I crept under.

pardessus [pardəsy] *n.m. Cost:* overcoat.

par-dessus [pardəsy] *prep. & adv.* over (the top of); **sauter p.-d. (la table),** to leap over (the table); **jeter qch. p.-d. bord,** to throw sth. overboard; **p.-d. le marché,** into the bargain; on top of it all; **j'en ai p.-d. la tête,** I can't stand it (any longer); I've had just about enough.

par-devant [pardəvɑ̃] *prep. & adv.* **1.** in front of; **passer p.-d. la maison,** to pass in front of the house. **2.** *Jur:* **acte signé p.-d. (le) notaire,** deed signed in the presence of a lawyer.

par-devers [pardəvɛr] *prep.* **1. p.-d. soi,** in one's possession. **2. p.-d. le juge,** before the judge.

pardi [pardi] *int. F:* of course! naturally!

pardon [pardɔ̃] *n.m.* pardon; (*a*) forgiveness (of an offence); *Jur:* (free) pardon; **demander p. à qn,** to apologize to s.o.; **(je vous demande) p.,** I beg your pardon; (I'm) sorry; excuse me; (*expressing contradiction*) **p., j'y suis allé,** I'm sorry, excuse *me,* I did go; (*in conversation*) **p.?** I beg your pardon? what did you say? (*b*) *Ecc:* (*in Brittany*) religious festival; (*c*) *Jewish Rel:* **Grand P., jour du P.,** Day of Atonement, Yom Kippur; (*d*) *P:* **le père était déjà costaud, mais alors le fils, p.!** the father was pretty beefy, but as for the son, he takes the cake!

pardonnable [pardɔnabl̩] *a.* pardonable, forgivable, excusable; **il s'est trompé mais c'est p.,** he made a mistake, but he can be forgiven.

pardonner [pardɔne] *v.tr.* to pardon, forgive, excuse; **p. (à) qn,** to forgive s.o.; **p. à qn d'avoir fait qch.,** to forgive s.o. for having done sth.; **pardonnez-moi si je vous contredis,** excuse me for contradicting you; **je ne me le pardonnerai jamais,** I'll never forgive myself; **c'est une erreur qui ne se pardonne pas,** it's an unforgivable mistake; **maladie, faute, qui ne pardonne pas,** fatal illness, mistake.

paré [pare] *a.* **1.** ready; **être p. contre le froid,** to be prepared for the cold (weather); **vous voilà p.!** you're all set! **2.** decorated, ornamented (**de,** with); (*of pers.*) dressed (up) (**de,** in); (*of lady*) wearing, covered in, jewels. **3.** (*of meat*) dressed.

pare-boue [parbu] *n.m.inv.* mudguard; mudflap (of car, bicycle).

pare-brise [parbriz] *n.m.inv. Aut: etc:* windscreen, *NAm:* windshield.

pare-chocs [parʃɔk] *n.m.inv. Aut:* bumper, *NAm:* fender.

pare-éclats [parekla] *n.m.inv. Mil:* splinter-proof shield (on trench parapet, etc.).

pare-étincelles [paretɛ̃sɛl] *n.m.inv.* fireguard.

pare-feu [parfø] *n.m.inv.* (*a*) firebreak (in forest); (*b*) fireguard.

parégorique [paregɔrik] *a. & n.m. Pharm:* paregoric.

pareil, -eille [parɛj] **1.** *a.* (*a*) like, alike, similar; **ce n'est pas p.,** it's not the same (thing); **en voici un tout p.,** here's one exactly like it; **p. que, à,** the same as, just like; **comment allez-vous? –toujours p.,** how are you? –same as ever; (*b*) (*of time*) same, indentical; **l'an dernier à pareille époque,** this time last year; (*c*) such; like that; **en p. cas,** in a case like this, in such cases; **comment a-t-il pu faire une chose pareille!** how could he do such a thing! **2.** *n.* (*a*) **mes pareils,** my equals; **lui et ses pareils,** he and people like him; (*b*) equal, fellow, match; **elle n'a pas sa pareille au monde,** there's no one like her; she's second to none; **il n'a pas son p. pour le travail,** there's no one to equal him for work; **sans p.,** peerless, matchless; unequalled; **méchanceté sans pareille,** unparalleled wickedness. **3.** *n.f.* **rendre la pareille à qn,** to retaliate, to give s.o. tit for tat, to pay s.o. back in his own coin; **si on me frappe je rends la pareille,** if any one hits me I hit back. **4.** *n.m. P:* **c'est du p. au même,** it's just the same; it comes to the same thing. **5.** *adv. P:* **faire p.,** to do the same; **ils s'habillent p.,** they dress the same.

pareillement [parɛjmɑ̃] *adv.* **1.** in a similar manner, in the same way. **2.** also; likewise; *F:* (*in answer to good wishes, to a toast*) the same to you! **et moi p.!** same here!

parement [parmɑ̃] *n.m.* (*a*) ornament; decoration, ornamentation; (*b*) cuff (of sleeve); (collar) facing; (*c*) **p. d'autel,** (altar) frontal; (*d*) *Const:* face, facing (of wall, etc.); (dressed) face (of stone, etc.).

parementer [parmɑ̃te] *v.tr. Const:* to face (wall, etc.).

parenchyme [parɑ̃ʃim] *n.m. Anat: Bot:* parenchyma.

parent, -ente [parɑ̃, -ɑ̃t] **1.** *n.m.pl.* (*a*) parents; father and mother; *F:* **venez ce soir, les parents seront absents,** come this evening, the parents will be out; **parents spirituels,** godparents; (*b*) *Lit:* forefathers, forbears. **2.** *n.* (*a*) (blood) relation, relative; **proche p., p. éloigné,** close, distant, relative; **être p. avec, de, qn,** to be related to s.o.; **nous sommes parents par alliance, par mon père,** we are related by marriage, on my father's side; (*b*) **traiter qn en p. pauvre,** to treat s.o. like a poor relation; (*c*) *n.m. Biol:* parent. **3.** *a.* related; similar; **intelligences parentes,** minds that think alike.

parental, -aux [parɑ̃tal, -o] *a.* parental (authority, etc.).

parenté [parɑ̃te] *n.f.* **1.** (*a*) relationship; kinship; **ils ont le même nom, mais il n'y a entre eux aucune p.,** they have the same name but they are not in any way related; (*b*) relationship, affinity (between two languages, etc.). **2.** *coll.* family; relations.

parenthèse [parɑ̃tɛz] *n.f.* **1.** (*a*) *Gram:* parenthesis; (*b*) parenthesis, digression. **2.** *Typ:* bracket; **mettre un mot entre parenthèses,** to put a word in brackets; **entre parenthèses,** incidentally, by the way.

paréo [pareo] *n.m. Cost:* **1.** pareo, grass skirt. **2.** beach skirt.

parer[1] [pare] **1.** *v.tr.* (*a*) to dress, trim (meat, leather); *Nau:* to clear (cable, anchor, etc.); (*b*) to deck out, adorn (s.o.) (**de,** with); **p. la mariée,** to dress the bride; (*c*) to decorate, to embellish; to arrange (room, etc.) with care, with taste; (*d*) **p. qn de toutes les qualités,** to attribute every quality to s.o. **2. se p.,** to dress oneself up; to deck oneself out, to adorn oneself (with jewels); **se p. d'un faux titre,** to assume a false title.

parer[2] **1.** *v.tr.* to avoid, ward off, stave off; (*a*) *Nau:* **p. un abordage,** to avoid, fend off, a collision; **p. un cap,** to clear, double, a headland; (*b*) *Box: Fenc:* to parry, ward off (blow, thrust). **2.** *v.i.* **p. à (qch.),** to provide, guard, against (sth.); to avert (accident); to obviate (difficulty); **p. à toute éventualité,** to be prepared for anything (to happen); **on ne peut pas p. à tout,** one cannot guard against everything; **p. au plus pressé,** to attend to the most urgent things first.

pare-soleil [parsɔlɛj] *n.m.inv. Aut: etc:* sun visor.

paresse [parɛs] *n.f.* (*a*) laziness, idleness; **par pure p.,** out of sheer laziness; (*b*) **p. d'esprit,** sluggishness of mind.

paresser [parese] *v.i.* to laze (about, around).

paresseusement [parɛsøzmɑ̃] *adv.* **1.** idly, lazily. **2.** sluggishly.

paresseux, -euse [parɛsø, -øz] **1.** *a.* (*a*) lazy; idle; indolent; **p. comme une couleuvre,** bone idle; **prendre la solution paresseuse,** to take the line of least resistance; **il est p. pour se lever,** you can't get him out of bed (in the morning); (*b*) sluggish (stomach, mind). **2.** *n.* lazy person, *F:* lazybones. **3.** *n.m. Z:* sloth.

parfaire [parfɛr] *v.tr.* (*conj. like* FAIRE; *used chiefly in inf. and p.p.*) to finish off, perfect, complete, round off (one's work, etc.); to make up (a sum).

parfait [parfɛ] **1.** *a.* (*a*) perfect; faultless; flawless; **beauté parfaite,** incomparable beauty; **en ordre p.,** in perfect order; **il est loin d'être p.,** he's no saint; **vous avez été p.,** you were wonderful, splendid; **(c'est, voilà qui est) p.!** (that's) splendid! fine! wonderful! *F:* great! (*b*) perfect, complete; thorough; **un p. orateur,** a finished speaker; *F:* **un p. imbécile,** an utter fool, a downright, complete, idiot; **en p. accord,** in full agreement; *Mus:* **accord p.,** perfect chord. **2.** *n.m.* (*a*) perfection; (*b*) *Gram:* perfect (tense); (*c*) *Cu:* parfait, ice cream; **p. au café,** coffee parfait.

parfaitement [parfɛtmɑ̃] *adv.* **1.** (*a*) perfectly; to perfection; **cela m'ira p.,** that will suit me beautifully; (*b*) completely, thoroughly; **je comprends p.,** I quite understand; **il est p. idiot,** he's utterly stupid; **il a p. le droit de le dire,** he has a perfect right to say it. **2.** (*emphatic answer*) certainly, exactly; **vous dites que vous l'avez vu?—p.,** you say you saw it?—I certainly did.

parfois [parfwa] *adv.* sometimes, at times; occasionally; (every) now and then; **p. elle lit, p. elle tricote,** sometimes she reads, other times she knits.

parfum [parfœ̃] *n.m.* **1.** perfume, fragrance, sweet smell, scent (of flower); bouquet, aroma (of wine); odour, *NAm:* odor (of praise); whiff (of scandal). **2.** *Toil:* scent, perfume. **3.** flavour, *NAm:* flavor (of ice cream). **4.** *P:* **être au p.,** to be in the know, to be wise to sth.

parfumé [parfyme] *a.* scented; fragrant (wine, air); **l'air p. du soir,** the balmy evening air; **elle est trop parfumée,** she wears too much scent.

parfumer [parfyme] *v.tr.* (*a*) to scent, to perfume; **elle se parfume trop,** she wears too much scent; (*b*) *Cu:* to flavour, *NAm:* flavor (**à,** with).

parfumerie [parfymri] *n.f.* (*a*) *Ind:* perfumery; (*b*) (*shop, department in store*) perfumery; (*c*) perfume shop; (*d*) (*product*) perfumery, perfumes.

parfumeur, -euse [parfymœr, -øz] *n.* perfumer.

pari [pari] *n.m.* **1.** bet, wager; **faire un p.,** to make, lay, a bet; **tenir un p.,** to take (up) a bet; **les paris sont ouverts,** its anyone's guess (how it will end). **2.** betting; **p. mutuel** = totalizator system, *F:* the tote; *NAm:* pari-mutuel.

paria [parja] *n.m.* (*a*) (*in India*) pariah; (*b*) pariah, (social) outcast.

parier [parje] *v.tr.* (*impf. & pr.sub.* **n. pariions, v. pariiez**) to bet, to wager; to lay, stake (money); **je parie une bouteille de vin qu'il ne viendra pas,** I bet a bottle of wine he won't come; **p. sur un cheval,** to back a horse; **p. avec qn,** to bet with s.o.; **il y a gros à p. que . . .,** it's virtually certain, the odds are, that . . .; **je te parie tout ce que tu veux . . .,** I bet you anything (you like) . . .; **je l'aurais parié,** I might have known (it).

pariétal, -aux [parjetal, -o] **1.** *a.* parietal (bone, etc.); **art p.,** cave painting. **2.** *n.m.* parietal bone.

parieur, -euse [parjœr, -øz] *n.* **1.** better, bettor, punter; *Sp: esp. Turf:* backer. **2.** betting man, woman; gambler.

parigot, -ote [parigo, -ɔt] *a. & n. P:* Parisian.

Paris [pari] *Pr.n.m. Geog:* Paris.

parisien, -ienne [parizjɛ̃, -jɛn] *a. & n.* Parisian; **le Bassin p., la banlieue parisienne,** the Paris Basin, suburbs.

paritaire [paritɛr] *a.* **commission p.,** equal representation; **réunion p.,** round table conference.

parité [parite] *n.f.* **1.** parity; equality (of rank, value); *Fin:* **p. de change,** equivalence of exchange. **2.** *Mth:* evenness (of number).

parjure [parʒyr] **1.** (*a*) *n.m.* perjury, *in the restricted senses of* (i) false swearing (as a moral offence); false oath; (ii) violation of one's oath; (*b*) *n.* perjurer (who has violated his oath). **2.** *a.* false (oath); faithless (person).

parjurer (se) [səparʒyre] *v.pr.* to forswear oneself, to perjure oneself; to be guilty of, commit, perjury.

parka [parka] *n.f. Cost:* parka.

parking [parkiŋ] *n.m.* (*a*) parking; (*b*) carpark, *NAm:* parking lot.

parlant [parlɑ̃] *a.* (*a*) speaking; talking; lifelike (portrait); eloquent, meaningful (gesture), vivid (description); *Tp:* **l'horloge parlante,** the speaking clock, *F:* Tim; (*b*) *F:* talkative, garrulous.

parlé [parle] **1.** *a.* spoken (language, word). **2.** *n.m.* spoken part (in opera).

parlement [parləmɑ̃] *n.m.* parliament; (*a*) *Fr. Hist:* high judicial court (in Paris and provinces); (*b*) legislative assembly.

parlementaire¹ [parləmɑ̃tɛr] **1.** *a. Pol:* parliamentary (government, etc.). **2.** *n.* (*a*) *Hist: Pol:* parliamentarian; (*b*) member of Parliament; *U.S:* congressman.

parlementaire² *n. Mil:* negotiator, mediator.

parlementarisme [parləmɑ̃tarism] *n.m.* parliamentary government.

parlementer [parləmɑ̃te] *v.i.* (*a*) to parley, to hold a parley (**avec,** with); to negotiate; (*b*) *F:* to talk, to argue, at length (**avec,** with).

parler¹ [parle] **1.** *v.i.* to speak, talk; (*a*) **son fils ne parle pas encore,** her son hasn't learnt to talk yet; **p. haut,** to talk loudly; **p. bas,** to speak in a low voice; **p. entre ses dents,** to mumble; **parlez plus haut, plus fort!** speak up! **p. du nez,** to talk through one's nose; **s'enrouer à force de p.,** to talk oneself hoarse; **p. par gestes,** to use sign language; (*b*) **parlez-vous sérieusement?** are you serious? do you really mean it? **laissez-le p.,** let him have his say; **p. pour ne rien dire,** (i) to talk for the sake of talking; (ii) to make small talk; **p. à tort et à travers,** to talk drivel; **généralement parlant,** generally speaking; **je ne peux pas le faire p.,** I can't get a word out of him; **on parlait très peu au petit déjeuner,** there was very little talking over breakfast; **c'est une façon de p.,** (i) it's a way of speaking; (ii) don't take it literally; *P:* **tu parles!** (i) you're telling me! you bet! (ii) you must be joking! no way! **tu parles si c'est utile!** a fat lot of use *that* is! (*c*) **p. à qn,** to talk to s.o.; **se p. à soi-même,** to talk to oneself; **n'en parlez à personne,** don't tell anyone about it; *F:* **ne m'en parlez pas!** you're telling me! *Fig:* **elle a trouvé à qui p.,** she has met her match; *F:* **c'est p. à un mur,** it's like talking to a brick wall; **nous ne nous parlons pas,** we are not on speaking terms; *Nau:* **p. à un navire,** to speak a ship; (*d*) **p. de qn, de qch.,** to mention, to refer to, speak of, s.o., sth.; **en avez-vous parlé aux autres?** have you spoken to the others about it? **il n'en parle jamais,** he never talks about it; **nous en parlerons après déjeuner,** we can talk it over after lunch; **n'en parlons plus,** let's drop the subject, let's say no more about it; **cela ne vaut pas la peine d'en p.,** it isn't worth talking about; **on parle d'organiser une fête,** there's some talk about (organizing) a party; **mal p. de qn,** to criticize s.o., run s.o. down; **j'entends beaucoup p. de lui,** I hear a good deal about him; **mon père ne veut pas en entendre p.,** my father won't hear of it; **je n'en ai jamais entendu p.,** I've never heard of it; **faire p. de soi,** to get talked about; **on ne parle que de cela,** everyone's talking about it, it's common gossip; **sans p. de lui,** to say nothing of him; let alone him; *P:* **tu parles d'une occasion!** that was a chance in a lifetime! **tu parles d'un idiot!** talk about an idiot! (*e*) **p. pour, contre, qn,** to speak for, against, s.o.; (*f*) **cette peinture parle à l'imagination,** this painting fires the imagination. **2.** *v.tr.* (*a*) **p. (le) français,** to talk, speak, French; **l'anglais se parle partout,** English is spoken everywhere; (*b*) **p. affaires, p. boutique,** to talk business, shop.

parler² *n.m.* (*a*) speech; **il a un p. rude,** he's got a coarse way of speaking; (*b*) dialect.

parleur, -euse [parlœr, -øz] *n.* talker, speaker; **beau p.,** fine speaker; glib talker.

parloir [parlwar] *n.m.* parlour, *NAm:* parlor, visiting room (of school, convent, etc.).

parlot(t)e [parlɔt] *n.f. F:* talk, gossip, chitchat, natter.

Parme [parm] *Pr.n.f. Geog:* Parma.

Parmentier [parmɑ̃tje] *Pr.n. Cu:* **hachis P.** = shepherd's, cottage, pie.

parmi [parmi] *prep.* among, amongst; **p. les arbres,** among the trees; **p. la foule,** among, in, the crowd; **nous souhaitons vous voir bientôt p. nous,** we hope that you'll soon be with us; **c'est une solution p. d'autres,** it's one of many solutions.

Parnasse (le) [ləparnas] *Pr.n.m.* (*a*) *A.Geog:* Parnassus; (*b*) *Fr.Lit.Hist:* the Parnassian School (of poetry, from 1860).

parnassien, -ienne [parnasjɛ̃, -jɛn] *a. & n.m. Fr.Lit.Hist:* Parnassian.

parodie [parɔdi] *n.f.* (*a*) parody; (*b*) mockery.

parodier [parɔdje] *v.tr.* (*impf. & pr.sub.* **n. parodiions, v. parodiiez**) (*a*) to parody; (*b*) to imitate (s.o.), take (s.o.) off; to make a mockery of (sth.).

parodique [parɔdik] *a. Lit:* parodic(al).

parodiste [parɔdist] *n.* parodist.

paroi [parwa] *n.f.* **1.** (*a*) partition (wall) (between rooms); (*b*) wall (of rock, tent, etc.); (inner) wall (of house); (rock) face; *Biol:* (cell) wall. **2.** inner side, surface (of vase, etc.); lining (of tunnel, stomach).

paroisse [parwas] *n.f.* (*a*) parish; **il n'est pas de la p.,** he's not from here; he's a foreigner; (*b*) parishioners.

paroissial, -aux [parwasjal, -o] *a.* parochial; **église paroissiale,** parish church; **salle paroissiale,** church hall.

paroissien, -ienne [parwasjɛ̃, -jɛn] **1.** *n.* parishioner. **2.** *n.m.* prayer book.

parole [parɔl] *n.f.* **1.** (spoken) word; *pl.* lyrics (of song); **ce sont ses propres paroles,** those are his very words; **romance sans paroles,** song without words; **la p. de Dieu,** the word of God; **p. blessante,** hurtful remark; *Iron:* **belles paroles,** fine words; **voilà une bonne p.!** well said! **2.** promise, word; **tenir (sa) p.,** to keep one's promise, one's word; **manquer à sa p.,** to break one's word; **il est (homme) de p., il a sa p., il n'a qu'une p.,** he's a man of his word; **(je vous donne ma) p.! p. d'honneur!** I give you my word (of honour, *NAm:* honor)! **je l'ai cru sur p.,** I took his word for it; **prisonnier sur p.,** prisoner on parole. **3.** (*a*) speech, speaking; delivery; **avoir la p. facile,** (i) to be a fluent speaker; (ii) to have the gift of the gab; **avoir le don de la p.,** to be a good speaker; **perdre la p.,** to lose the power of speech; **si les animaux avaient l'usage de la p.,** if animals could (only) speak; (*b*) (*action of speaking*) **adresser la p. à qn,** to speak to s.o.; **couper la p. à qn,** to cut s.o. short, to interrupt s.o.; **prendre la p.,** (to begin) to speak; **la p. est à M. X.,** Mr X will now speak; (*c*) *Cards:* **p.!** pass! no bid!

parolier, -ière [parɔlje, -jɛr] *n.* (*a*) *Th:* librettist; lyric writer; (*b*) song writer.

paronyme [parɔnim] *n.m.* paronym.

paronymie [parɔnimi] *n.f.* paronymy.

paroxysme [parɔksism] *n.m.* (*a*) *Med:* crisis (point) (of illness); (*b*) paroxysm (of anger, pain); **être au p. de la joie,** to be ecstatically happy; **atteindre son p.,** to reach its highest point.

parpaing [parpɛ̃] *n.m. Const:* parpen; bonder, bondstone; breezeblock.

Parque [park] *Pr.n.f. Myth:* Fate; *pl.* **les Parques,** the Parcae, the Fates.

parquer [parke] **1.** *v.tr.* to pen (cattle); to fold (sheep); to confine, pack in (people); to park (artillery, cars, etc.). **2.** *Aut:* **se p.,** to park.

parquet [parkɛ] *n.m.* **1.** (*a*) *Jur:* public prosecutor's room; **(membres du) p.,** public prosecutor and his deputies; **déposer une plainte au p.,** to lodge a complaint in court; (*b*) *St.Exch:* **le P.** = the Ring, the official market. **2.** (*a*) *Const:* (wooden, parquet) floor, flooring; **lame de p.,** floor plank; (*b*) (wooden) backing (of mirror); (*c*) *Nau:* **p. de chargement,** dunnage; **p. de chauffe,** stokehold platform.

parquetage [parkətaʒ] *n.m.* (*a*) making, laying, of (wooden, parquet) floors; (*b*) (wooden, parquet) flooring, floor.

parqueter [parkəte] *v.tr.* **(je parquette, n. parquetons; je parquetterai)** to lay a (wooden, parquet) floor in (room, etc.); to parquet.

parqueterie [parkətri] *n.f.* making, laying, of (wooden, parquet) floors.

parqueteur [parkətœr] *n.m.* parquet maker; parquet layer; = flooring contractor.

parrain [parɛ̃] *n.m.* (*a*) godfather; **être p.,** to stand godfather (**de,** to); (*b*) sponsor; proposer (of new member for club); namer (of ship); patron (of foundation).

parrainage [parɛnaʒ] *n.m.* **1.** sponsorship; proposing (for membership); naming (of ship); patronage. **2.** fostering (of child).

parrainer [parene] *v.tr.* **1.** to act as godfather to; to sponsor, propose; to name (ship); to patronize. **2.** to foster (child).

parricide¹ [parisid] **1.** *n.* parricide. **2.** *a.* parricidal.

parricide² *n.m.* (crime of) parricide.

parsec [parsɛk] *n.m. Astr.Meas:* parsec.

parsemé [parsəme] *a.* **ciel p. d'étoiles,** sky studded, spangled, with stars; **champ p. de pâquerettes,** field sprinkled, dotted, with daisies; **texte p. de coquilles,** text riddled with literals.

parsemer [parsəme] *v.tr.* (*conj. like* SEMER) to strew, sprinkle, scatter (**de,** with); **des feuilles parsemaient le chemin,** the path was scattered, covered, with leaves.

parsi, -ie [parsi] *a. & n. Rel:* Parsee.

part [par] *n.f.* **1.** share, part, portion; (*a*) **diviser un gâteau en parts,** to divide a cake into portions; **la p. du lion,** the lion's share; **faire la p. du feu,** to cut one's losses; **avoir, vouloir, sa p. du gâteau,** to have, to want, one's slice of the cake; *Fin:* **p. de fondateur,** founder's share(s); **avoir sa p. de qch.,** to come in for a share, one's share, of sth.; **ils viennent pour une bonne p. des environs de Lille,** they come very largely from the Lille area; (*b*) **pour ma p.,** as for me, as far as I am concerned; for my part; (speaking) for myself; (*c*) **prendre qch. en bonne p., en mauvaise p.,** to take sth. in good part, in bad part. **2.** share, participation; **avoir p. à qch.,** to have a hand, a share, in sth.; **avoir p. au gâteau,** to be involved in sth., have a finger in the pie; **prendre p. à qch.,** to take part in sth.; to join in sth.; to share in sth.; **prendre p. à la conversation,** to join in the conversation; **prendre p. à la joie de qn,** to share in s.o.'s joy; **je n'y ai pris aucune p.,** I had nothing to do with it; **faire p. de qch. à qn,** to inform s.o. of sth.; to tell s.o. about sth.; **lettre de faire-p.,** announcement (of wedding, death, etc.); **faire la p. de qch.,** to take sth. into account, into consideration; to make allowance(s) for sth. **3.** (*a*) **nulle p.,** nowhere; **autre p.,** elsewhere, somewhere else; **nulle p. ailleurs,** nowhere else; **de p. et d'autre,** here and there; **faire des concessions de p. et d'autre,** to make concessions on both sides; **de toute(s) part(s),** on all sides; **de p. en p.,** through and through, right through; **d'une p., d'autre p.,** on the one hand, on the other hand; (*b*) **je viens de la p. de . . .,** I represent . . .; I've come on behalf of . . .; *Tp:* **c'est de la p. de qui?** who's speaking, calling? **dites-lui de ma p. que . . .,** tell him from me that . . .; **ce serait bien aimable de votre p.,** it would be very kind of you; **cela m'étonne de sa p.,** that surprises me, coming from him. **4. à p.,** apart, separately; **prendre qn à p.,** to take s.o. aside; **mettre de l'argent à p.,** to put money by, aside; **plaisanterie à p.,** joking apart; **c'est une femme à p.,** she's an exceptional woman; she's in a class of her own; **un cas à p.,** a special case; **et à p. lui?** who besides him? **je me disais à p. moi que . . .,** I was saying to myself that . . ., **à p. quelques exceptions, quelques pages,** with a few exceptions; with the exception of a few pages; **à p. cela tout va bien,** apart from that all is well; *F:* **à p. que . . .,** apart from the fact that . . ..

partage [partaʒ] *n.m.* **1.** division; (*a*) dividing, sharing, distribution, apportionment; *Jur:* partition (of property); **faire le p. de qch.,** to divide, share out, sth.; (*b*) **il y a p. d'opinions,** opinions are divided; **p. des voix,** division of the votes; *Geog:* **ligne de p. des eaux,** watershed, *NAm:* divide. **2.** share, portion, lot; **donner, recevoir, qch. en p.,** to give, receive, sth. in a will; **la souffrance est le p. du genre humain,** suffering is the lot of mankind.

partagé [partaʒe] *a.* **1.** divided. **2.** shared; **amour p.,** mutual love.

partageable [partaʒabl̩] *a.* divisible, which can be divided.

partager [partaʒe] *v.tr.* **(je partageai(s); n. partageons) 1.** (*a*) to divide (into shares); to parcel out; to apportion (property, etc.); to share (out) (loot, etc.); **p. son temps entre deux occupations,** to divide one's time between two occupations; (*b*) to divide (into groups, sections, portions); **le fleuve partage le pays en deux,** the river divides, cuts, the country in two; **les avis sont partagés,** opinions are divided. **2.** to share; *v.i.* **elle n'aime pas p.,** she doesn't like sharing; **p. qch. avec qn,** to share sth. with s.o.; **p. la joie, l'avis, de qn,** to share s.o.'s joy, s.o.'s opinion; **p. le repas de qn,** to share s.o.'s meal, to share a meal with s.o. **3.** to endow; **être bien partagé,** to be well provided for. **4.** (*a*) **se p.,** to divide, to be divided; **le gâteau peut se p. en 4 morceaux,** the cake can be cut into 4 portions; (*b*) **ils se sont partagé les bénéfices,** they shared, divided, the profits between them.

partageur, -euse [partaʒœr, -øz] *a.* willing to share; **ce garçon n'est pas p.,** this boy doesn't like sharing.

partance [partɑ̃s] *n.f.* **en p.,** (*of train*) due to leave; (*of aircraft*) outward bound; **navire en p.,** ship about to sail, just sailing, outward bound; **en p. pour Bordeaux,** bound for Bordeaux; **train en p. pour Londres,** train for London, London train.

partant¹ [partɑ̃] *adv. Lit:* consequently, therefore.

partant² **1.** *a.* departing. **2.** *n.m.* (*a*) person leaving, departing traveller, etc.; **les arrivants et les partants,** the arrivals and departures; (*b*) *Turf: etc:* starter; runner; *F:* **je suis p.,** you can count me in.

partenaire [partənɛr] *n.* partner.

parterre [partɛr] *n.m.* **1.** *F:* floor. **2.** flower bed, border. **3.** *Th:* (*a*) (the) pit; (the) back of the stalls; (*b*) (the) audience (in the pit).

parthe [part] *a. & n. A.Ethn:* Parthian; **la flèche du P.,** the Parthian shot.

parthénogénèse [partenoʒenɛz] *n.f. Biol:* parthenogenesis.

parthénogénétique [partenoʒenetik] *a. Biol:* parthenogenetic.

Parthénon (le) [ləpartenɔ̃] *n.m. Gr.Ant:* the Parthenon.

parti¹ [parti] *n.m.* **1.** party; **le p. (communiste),** the Communist party, the Party; **prendre le p. de qn,** to stand up for s.o.; **prendre p. pour, contre, qn,** to side with, against, s.o.; **se mettre, se ranger, du p. de qn,** to side with s.o.; to take sides with s.o. **2.** (*marriageable person*) **un bon, beau, p.,** a good match. **3.** decision, choice, course; **prendre p.,** to come to a decision, to make up one's mind; **mon p. est pris,** my mind's made up; **en prendre son p.,** to resign oneself to the inevitable; to make the best of it; **prendre le p. de faire qch.,** to decide, resolve, to do sth.; **il ne savait quel p. prendre,** he did not know what course to take; **p. pris,** bias; prejudice; **de p. pris,** bias(s)ed, prejudiced; **sans p. pris,** unbias(s)ed. **4.** advantage, profit; **tirer p. de qch.,** to make use of sth.; to turn sth. to account; to take advantage of sth.; **tirer le meilleur p. possible de . . .,** to make the best possible use of . . .. **5. faire un mauvais p. à qn,** to ill-treat s.o., to handle s.o. roughly.

parti² *a. F:* drunk, tipsy, tight.

partial, -aux [parsjal, -o] *a.* partial, bias(s)ed; one-sided.

partialement [parsjalmɑ̃] *adv.* in a bias(s)ed way.

partialité [parsjalite] *n.f.* partiality (**envers,** for, to); bias (**contre,** against).

participant, -ante [partisipɑ̃, -ɑ̃t] **1.** *a.* participating. **2.** *n.* participant; member; competitor; **les participants à la manifestation,** those taking part in the demonstration.

participation [partisipasjɔ̃] *n.f.* **1.** participation (**à,** in); **cela s'est fait sans ma p.,** I didn't take part in it; I had no hand in it; **représentation avec la p. de plusieurs vedettes,** show with appearances by several stars; **p. aux frais,** (financial) contribution; cost. **2.** *Com:* share, interest (**à,** in); **p. aux bénéfices,** profit sharing; **p. majoritaire,** major shareholding; **p. ouvrière,** worker participation.

participe [partisip] *n.m. Gram:* participle.

participer [partisipe] *v.i.* **1. p. à** (*a*) to take part in (meeting, game, etc.); to participate in, take part in (discussion, etc.); (*of actor*) to appear in (show); to be involved in, be (a) party to (plot, etc.); **p. à la joie, au chagrin, de qn,** to share (in) s.o.'s joy, sadness; (*b*) to contribute (money) to (sth.); (*c*) to share in (profits, etc.). **2.** *Lit:* **p. de qch.,** to partake of, have some of the characteristics of, sth.

participial, -aux [partisipjal, -o] *a. Gram:* participial (phrase, etc.); *n.f.* **participiale,** participial clause.

particularisation [partikylarizasjɔ̃] *n.f.* particularization.

particulariser [partikylarize] (*a*) *v.tr.* to particularize; to give particulars, details, of (sth.); (*b*)

se p., to distinguish oneself from others; to be distinguished (**par,** by).

particularisme [partikylarism] *n.m. Pol: Theol: etc:* particularism.

particularité [partikylarite] *n.f.* **1.** *Lit:* detail; particular. **2.** (*a*) particularity; special nature (of sth.); (*b*) peculiarity; characteristic; (distinctive) feature.

particule [partikyl] *n.f.* **1.** particle; *Atom.Ph:* **p. alpha, p. bêta,** alpha, beta, particle. **2.** *Gram:* particle; **avoir un nom à p.,** to belong to the nobility, *F:* to have a handle to one's name.

particulier, -ière [partikylje, -jɛr] **1.** *a.* (*a*) particular, special; (*on passport*) **signes particuliers,** special peculiarities; (*b*) peculiar, characteristic; **attitude qui lui est particulière,** an attitude that is characteristic of him; **sa démarche bien particulière,** his own particular way of walking; (*c*) unusual, uncommon; exceptional; peculiar; **faire un travail avec un soin p.,** to carry out a piece of work with particular care; **mœurs particulières,** peculiar (sexual) tendencies; (*d*) private (room, life, etc.); personal (account); **secrétaire p., particulière,** private secretary; **leçons particulières,** private lessons, tuition; **j'ai des raisons particulières pour le désirer,** I have my own (private) reasons, reasons of my own, for wishing it; **à titre p.,** in a private capacity. **2.** *n.* private person, private individual; **simple p.,** ordinary person; *Pej:* **il y a un p. en bas qui désirerait vous parler,** there's a person downstairs who would like to speak to you; **que nous veut ce p.?** what does that character want? **3.** *n.m.* (*a*) **aller du p. au général,** to go from the specific to the general; (*b*) *adv.phr.* **en p.,** in particular; **notez en p. que . . .,** note particularly that . . .; **recevoir qn en p.,** to receive s.o. privately, in private; **prendre qn en p.,** to take s.o. aside.

particulièrement [partikyljɛrmɑ̃] *adv.* (*a*) particularly, (e)specially; **il aime tous les arts et p. la peinture,** he is fond of all the arts and especially painting; (*b*) particularly, outstandingly, exceptionally; **j'attire tout p. votre attention sur ce point,** I would particularly like to draw your attention to this point; (*c*) intimately; **je ne le connais pas p.,** I don't know him very well.

partie [parti] *n.f.* **1.** part (of a whole); (*a*) **la plus grande p. du chemin,** the best part of the way; **une bonne p. du papier est abîmée,** a good, great, deal of the paper is damaged; **les parties du corps,** the parts of the body; **les parties génitales,** *F:* **les parties,** the genitals, *F:* private parts, privates; *Gram:* **parties du discours,** parts of speech; **en p.,** partly, in part; **en grande, en majeure, p.,** largely, to a great extent, for the most part; **faire p. de qch.,** to be, form, part of sth.; **je ne fais plus p. de ce cercle,** I don't belong to this club any longer; **faire p. de la famille,** to be one of the family; (*b*) **comptabilité en p. simple, en p. double,** single entry, double entry, book-keeping; (*c*) line, particular branch (of a business, profession); field, subject; **ce n'est pas (de) ma p., je ne suis pas de la p.,** that's not (in) my line; (*d*) *Mus:* (*of voice, instrument*) part; **parties d'orchestre,** orchestral parts. **2.** (*a*) party; **p. de plaisir,** trip; outing; **ce n'est pas une p. de plaisir!** it's no picnic! it's not my idea of fun! **p. de chasse,** shooting party; **voulez-vous être de la p.?** will you join us? **p. fine,** pleasure party; (*b*) game; **faire une p. de cartes, d'échecs,** to have, to play, a game of cards, of chess; **p. nulle,** draw; **gagner la p.,** to win the game; **la p. se trouve égale,** it's a close, even, match; **se mettre, être, de la p.,** to join in; (*c*) duel; struggle; **p. inégale,** uneven struggle. **3.** *Jur:* (*a*) party (to dispute, in contract, etc.); **être juge et p.,** to be judge in one's own case; **entendre les avocats des deux parties,** to hear counsel on both sides; (*b*) opponent; **avoir affaire à forte p.,** to have a powerful opponent, *F:* a tough customer, to deal with; (*c*) **prendre qn à p. (de qch., d'avoir fait qch.),** to take s.o. to task, to call s.o. to account (for sth., for doing sth.); (*d*) **p. civile,** plaintiff claiming damages (in criminal case); (*e*) **les parties belligérantes,** the belligerent parties; the warring factions.

partiel, -elle [parsjɛl] *a.* partial; **paiement p.,** part payment; **travailler à temps p.,** to have a part-time job, to work part-time; *Pol:* **élection partielle,** by-election; *Sch:* **épreuve partielle,** *n.m.* **p.,** class exam.

partiellement [parsjɛlmɑ̃] *adv.* partially, partly, in part.

partir [partir] *v.i.* (*pr.p.* **partant;** *p.p.* **parti;** *pr.ind.* **je pars, il part, n. partons, ils partent;** *pr.sub.* **je parte;** *impf.* **je partais;** *p.h.* **je partis;** *fu.* **je partirai)** (*aux.* **être) 1.** (*a*) to depart, leave; to start, to set out; to set off, go off; to go away; to go off; (*of ship*) to sail; (*of pers.*) to walk off, away; (*of horseman*) to ride off; (*of motorist*) to drive off; (*of aircraft*) to take off; **je pars de la maison à huit heures,** I leave home at eight o'clock; **il est temps que je parte,** it's time I went, I left, I was off; **p. pour, à, Paris, pour le, au, Canada, pour la, en, France, pour la, à la, campagne,** to set out, leave, for Paris, Canada, France, the country; **p. en vacances,** to go on holiday; **p. chez qn,** to set out for s.o.'s house; **nous partons demain,** we're leaving tomorrow; **l'avion va p. dans une heure,** the plane will take off in an hour; **partez!** (i) get out! (ii) *Sp:* go! **p. de ce monde,** to die, to depart this life; **p. à toute vitesse, comme une flèche,** to set off at full speed; to be off like a shot; **cette affaire est bien, mal, partie,** this business has got off to a good, bad, start; *P:* **c'est parti, mon kiki!** off we go! here we go! **nous sommes partis pour une période de prospérité,** we are in for a period of prosperity; **p. de zéro,** to start from scratch; *Aut:* **le moteur est parti du premier coup,** the engine started (at the) first go; **le fusil est parti,** the gun went off; *F:* **être parti,** to be drunk, tipsy, tight; **p. à rire, p. d'un éclat de rire,** to burst out laughing; (*b*) to go, to give (way), to break; (*of pain*) to go; (*of button, etc.*) to come off; (*of paint, etc.*) to wear off, to peel; **la tache ne part pas,** the stain won't come off; (*c*) to emanate, spring, proceed (**de,** from); **mot qui part du cœur,** word which comes from the heart; **en partant du principe qu'il a raison,** assuming that he's right; **le chemin part du village,** the path starts at the village; (*d*) **à p. d'aujourd'hui,** from today (onwards); **à p. du 15,** on and after the 15th; **à p. de la route, il courut,** as soon as he got to the road he ran; *Com:* **robes à p. de 200 francs,** dresses from 200 francs (upwards); **c'est fait à p. de synthétiques,** it's made from synthetic materials. **2. faire p.,** to remove, get out (stain, etc.); to fire (gun); to let off (fireworks); to touch off (mine); to start (engine).

partisan, -ane [partizɑ̃, -an] **1.** *n.* partisan, follower; advocate, supporter (of custom, etc.). **2.** *n.m. Mil:* guer(r)illa (soldier), partisan; **guerre de partisans,** guer(r)illa warfare. **3.** *a.* (*a*) **querelles partisanes,** party, sectarian, quarrels; (*b*) **être p. de (faire) qch.,** to be in favour, *NAm:* favor, of (doing) sth.; **je suis p. de la réforme,** I'm all for reform.

partitif, -ive [partitif, -iv] *a. & n.m. Gram:* partitive (noun, article).

partition [partisjɔ̃] *n.f.* **1.** *Pol:* partition, division. **2.** *Mus:* score; **p. d'orchestre,** full score; **elle joue sans p.,** she plays without the music.

partouse, partouze [partuz] *n.f. P:* orgy.

partout [partu] *adv.* (*a*) everywhere; **chercher qch. p.,** to hunt for sth. high and low; **p. où,** wherever; **p. ailleurs,** anywhere else; **un peu p.,** all over the place; almost anywhere; **souffrir de p.,** to feel pain all over;

j'ai mal p., I ache all over; (*b*) all, all together; *Ten:* **30, 40, p.,** 30 all, deuce.

parturition [partyrisjɔ̃] *n.f.* parturition.

parure [paryr] *n.f.* **1.** (*action*) ornamenting, adorning. **2.** (*a*) costume, finery; (*b*) ornament; (*c*) set (of jewel(le)ry, lingerie, etc.); **p. de diamants,** set of diamonds; **p. de table,** table linen. **3.** *Tchn:* parings (of leather, etc.); trimmings (of meat).

parution [parysjɔ̃] *n.f.* *Publ:* appearance, publication, issue (of book, article, etc.).

parvenir [parvənir] *v.i.* (*conj. like* VENIR. *Aux.* **être**) **1.** (*a*) to arrive; **p. à un endroit,** to arrive at, to reach, a place; **votre lettre m'est parvenue,** I received your letter; **votre demande doit nous p. avant le 4,** your application must be in by the 4th; **faire p. qch. à qn,** to send, to forward, sth. to s.o.; (*b*) **écrits anciens qui sont parvenus jusqu'à nous,** ancient writings which have come down to us. **2.** (*a*) to attain, reach (a great age, etc.); to succeed; to achieve (one's purpose); **p. à faire qch.,** to manage to do sth.; to succeed in doing sth.; (*b*) *v.i.* to succeed, get on, in life.

parvenu, -ue [parvəny] *n.* parvenu, self-made person; upstart.

parvis [parvi] *n.m.* parvis, square (in front of a church).

pas¹ [pa] *n.m.* **1.** step, stride, pace; footstep; (*a*) **à chaque p.,** at every step; **p. à p.,** step by step, little by little; **allonger le p.,** to step out; **aller à p. comptés,** to walk with measured tread; **aller, avancer, marcher, à grands p.,** to stride along; **marcher à petits p.,** (i) (*of child, etc.*) to toddle (along); (ii) to walk with mincing steps; to mince along; **marcher d'un p. lourd,** to walk with a heavy tread; **faire un p.,** to take a step; **faire un p. en avant, en arrière,** to step forward, back; **faire les cent p.,** to pace up and down; **faux p.,** (i) slip, stumble; (ii) (social) blunder, faux pas; **il n'y a que le premier p. qui coûte,** only the beginning is difficult; **il a fait un grand p. en avant,** he has made great progress; **j'y vais de ce p.,** I'm going at once; **entendre des p., un bruit de p.,** to hear footsteps; **je l'ai reconnu à son p.,** I knew him by his step; **il habite à deux pas d'ici,** he lives a few yards away, within a stone's throw from here; **il était à deux p. de nous,** he was within a couple of paces of us; (*b*) pace; *Mil:* step; (*of horse*) walk; **au p.,** (i) at a walking pace; (ii) *P.N: Aut:* dead slow; **mettre son cheval au p.,** to walk one's horse; **marcher au p.,** to march in step, in time; **se mettre au p.,** to get in step; **marquer le p.,** to mark time; **changer le p.,** to change step; **hâter, presser, le p.,** to quicken (one's) pace; to hurry on; **ralentir le p.,** to slow down; **p. ordinaire,** marching step, normal step, pace; **p. redoublé,** double time; **marcher au p. cadencé,** to march in quick time; **p. de gymnastique,** double time; jog trot; **p. de l'oie,** goosestep; **p. de valse,** waltz step; (*c*) precedence; **avoir, prendre, le p. sur qn,** to have, take, precedence over s.o.; **céder le p. à qn,** (i) to give s.o. precedence; (ii) to allow s.o. to pass. **2.** footprint; **marcher sur les p. de qn,** (i) to follow in s.o.'s tracks; (ii) to imitate s.o.; **arriver sur les p. de qn,** to arrive just after s.o.; **revenir sur ses p.,** to retrace one's steps. **3.** (*a*) *A:* step (of stair); (*b*) **p. de la porte,** doorstep; **il est sur le p. de la porte,** he's standing in the doorway; **p. de porte,** key money. **4.** passage; (mountain) pass; strait; **le p. de Calais,** the Straits of Dover; **tirer qn d'un mauvais p.,** to get s.o. out of a hole, out of a fix; **sauter le p.,** to die. **5.** *Tchn:* pitch, thread (of screw); pitch (of propeller).

pas² *neg.adv.* **1.** (*a*) not; no; **je ne sais p.,** I don't know; **je ne l'ai p. encore vu,** I haven't seen him yet; **je n'en dis p. plus,** I won't say another word; **p. du tout, absolument p.,** not at all, by no means; *F:* not a bit of it; **pourquoi p.?** why not? **p. moi,** not I; I haven't, didn't, etc.; **qu'il vienne ou p. cela m'est égal,** it's all the same to me whether he comes or not; **tu es heureuse, p. vrai?** you're happy, aren't you? **tu m'écriras, p.?** you'll write, won't you? (*b*) *F:* (**ne** *omitted*) **c'est p. vrai!** you're kidding! no kidding! **connais p.!** I don't know him, her! **si c'est p. malheureux!** isn't that a shame! **p. possible!** no! incredible! (*c*) (*strengthening* **non**) **affaibli mais non p. découragé,** weakened but not discouraged; (*d*) **ce n'est p. qu'il soit beau,** he's not exactly handsome; (*e*) (*qualifying an adj.*) **des lilas p. fleuris,** lilac not yet in bloom. **2.** (*a*) **p. un mot ne fut dit,** not a word was spoken; (*b*) **fier comme p. un,** prouder than anyone; **il est menteur comme p. un,** he's a terrible liar.

pascal, -aux [paskal, -o] *a.* paschal (lamb); Easter (communion, etc.).

passable [pasabl̩] *a.* passable, tolerable; acceptable; *Sch:* **mention p.** = pass(mark); (*in degree exam*) = third class; **c'est p.,** it's not too bad.

passablement [pasabləmɑ̃] *adv.* (*a*) passably, tolerably; **dessiner p.,** to draw tolerably well; **c'est p. long,** it's rather, fairly, long; (*b*) **il a p. voyagé,** he has travelled a lot.

passade [pasad] *n.f.* **1.** (*a*) passing fancy, whim; (*b*) passing fancy, short liaison. **2.** *Equit:* passade.

passage [pasaʒ] *n.m.* passage. **1.** crossing (of sth.); passing over, through, across; going past (a place); (*a*) **la rivière est de p. facile,** the river is easy to cross; **elle guette le p. du facteur,** she's watching, on the lookout, for the postman; **j'attends le p. de l'autobus,** I'm waiting for the bus to come; **chacun sourit sur son p.,** every one smiles as he, she, goes by; **il y a toujours du p. ici,** there are always a lot of people (coming and going) here; **livrer p.,** to make way; *P.N:* **p. interdit (au public),** no entry; no thoroughfare; **oiseau de p.,** bird of passage; **droit de p.,** right of way; **être de p. dans une ville,** to be passing through, making only a short stay in, a town; **voyageur de p. à Paris,** traveller passing through Paris; **clientèle de p.,** *F:* **le p.,** casual trade; *Mus:* **note de p.,** passing note; **il m'a saisi au p.,** he caught me as I went past; *El:* **p. du courant,** flow of current; (*b*) *Nau:* passage; **payer son p.,** to pay for one's passage; (*c*) **p. du jour à la nuit,** transition, change, from day to night; **avec le p. du temps,** as the days passed, as time went on, by; **le p. du gaz à l'électricité,** the changeover from gas to electricity; (*d*) *F:* **p. à tabac,** beating up. **2.** (*a*) way, way through, thoroughfare; alley(way); passage(way); *Nau:* channel; **se frayer, se faire, un p.,** to force, elbow, one's way through; **barrer le p. à qn,** to stand in, to block, s.o.'s way; (*b*) (shopping) arcade, *NAm:* mall; (*c*) *Rail:* **p. à niveau,** level crossing, *NAm:* grade crossing; **p. souterrain,** subway, underpass, *NAm:* underground passage; **p. clouté,** pedestrian crossing; **p. pour piétons,** (i) pedestrian crossing; (ii) pedestrian subway; *Aut:* **p. protégé,** priority over secondary roads. **3.** passage (of book, etc.); piece (of music, etc.).

passager, -ère [pasaʒe, -ɛr] **1.** *a.* (*a*) **oiseau p.,** migratory bird; (*b*) fleeting, short-lived, transitory (beauty, etc.); momentary (pain, etc.); (*c*) **rue passagère,** busy street. **2.** *n.* passenger (by sea, air); **p. clandestin,** stowaway.

passagèrement [pasaʒɛrmɑ̃] *adv.* temporarily, for a short while.

passant, -ante [pasɑ̃, -ɑ̃t] **1.** *a.* (*of road, etc.*) busy; congested. **2.** *n.* passer-by. **3.** *n.m.* *Harn:* keeper, guide; **p. de courroie,** strap loop.

passation [pasasjɔ̃] *n.f.* drawing up, signing (of agreement); *Book-k:* entering (of items); **p. des pouvoirs,** transfer of power.

passavant [pasavɑ̃] *n.m.* **1.** *Nau:* (fore-and-aft) gangway, catwalk. **2.** *Cust:* transire.

passe¹ [pas] *n.f.* **1.** (*a*) **mot de p.,** password; (*b*) **passes magnétiques,** mesmeric, hypnotic, passes; (*c*) *Fb: etc:* pass; **p. en avant,** forward pass; (*d*) *Metalw:* cut (on lathe); (*e*) **maison de p.,** hotel used by prostitutes and their clients; (*f*) (*at roulette*) any number above 18. **2.** (*a*) *Fenc:* pass, thrust; (*b*) **p. d'armes,** passage at arms, heated exchange. **3.** *Nau:* pass, channel; **p. étroite,** narrows. **4. être en p. de faire qch.,** to be on the way to doing sth.; **il est en p. de faire fortune,** he looks as though he will make a fortune; **être dans une mauvaise p.,** to be in a tight corner, in a bad way. **5.** *Typ:* **(main de) p.,** overs, over sheets, overplus; *Publ:* **exemplaires de p.,** surplus copies (of book); over copies.

passe² *n.m. F:* pass key, skeleton key, master key.

passé [pase] **1.** *a.* (*a*) past, gone by; **la semaine passée,** last week; **il est quatre heures passées,** it's gone four; it's after four; **il a quarante ans passés,** he's over forty; (*b*) over; **l'orage est p.,** the storm is over; (*c*) faded (colour, *NAm:* color). **2.** *n.m.* **le p.** (*a*) the past; former times; **comme par le p.,** as in the past; **oublions le p.,** let bygones be bygones; (*b*) *Gram:* past (tense); **p. simple,** preterite, past historic; **p. composé,** perfect (tense). **3.** *prep.* beyond; **p. les arbres pas un abri,** beyond the trees there's no shelter; **p. cette date,** after this date.

passe-droit [pɑsdrwa] *n.m.* (undeserved) privilege, favour, *NAm:* favor; unfair promotion; **le fils du patron a eu un p.-d.,** the boss's son got preferential treatment; *pl. passe-droits.*

passéisme [paseism] *n.m. Pej:* addiction, attachment, to the past.

passéiste [paseist] *a. & n. Pej:* (person) addicted, attached, to the past.

passe-lacet [paslasɛ] *n.m.* bodkin; *pl. passe-lacets.*

passement [pasmɑ̃] *n.m.* (gold, silver, silk) braid(ing).

passementer [pasmɑ̃te] *v.tr.* to braid.

passementerie [pasmɑ̃tri] *n.f.* **1.** = haberdashery trade, *NAm:* notions trade. **2.** braid; trimmings.

passementier, -ière [pasmɑ̃tje, -jɛr] **1.** *a.* = haberdashery, *NAm:* notions (trade, etc.). **2.** *n.* = haberdasher, *NAm:* a dealer in notions.

passe-montagne [pasmɔ̃taɲ] *n.m.* balaclava (helmet); *pl. passe-montagnes.*

passe-partout [paspartu] *n.m.inv.* **1.** (*a*) master key, pass key; skeleton key; (*b*) general purpose, all-purpose, formula, etc. **2.** *Tls:* cross-cut saw. **3.** (photograph, etc.) frame (with removable back).

passe-passe [paspas] *n.m. no pl.* (*a*) legerdemain, sleight of hand, juggling; *esp.* **tour de p.-p.,** conjuring trick; (*b*) confidence trick, *F:* con trick.

passe-plats [paspla] *n.m.inv.* service hatch.

passepoil [paspwal] *n.m.* braid, piping (for garments).

passepoiler [paspwale] *v.tr.* to braid, to pipe (garment); **poche passepoilée,** welted pocket.

passeport [paspɔr] *n.m.* (*a*) *Adm:* passport; (*b*) *Nau:* sea pass, sea letter.

passer [pase] **I.** *v.i.* **1.** (*the aux. is* **avoir** *or* **être**) to pass; to go (on, by, along); to proceed; (*a*) **p. sur un pont,** to cross (over) a bridge; **il est passé, a passé, devant le magasin,** he went by, passed (by), the shop; **p. par-dessus, par-dessous, qch.,** to get over, under, sth.; **la voiture lui a passé sur les jambes,** the car ran over his legs; **la bouteille a passé de main en main,** the bottle was passed round; **faire p. les gâteaux,** to hand round, pass round, the cakes; **par où est-il, a-t-il, passé?** which way did he go? **je ne peux pas p.,** I can't get by, past; **je regardais p. la procession,** I was watching the procession; *P.N:* **on ne passe pas,** no thoroughfare; **défense de p.,** no entry; **laisser p.,** to let in (light, air, etc.); to let through (pers., etc.); **laisser p. une erreur,** to overlook a mistake; **p. à l'ennemi,** to go over to the enemy; to defect; **passons à la salle à manger,** let's go into the dining room; *Sch:* **p. dans la classe supérieure,** to be moved up (a form); **p. sur une difficulté,** to pass over a difficulty; **passons!** well, let's leave it at that! **en passant,** by the way; **dire qch. en passant,** to mention sth. in passing; **soit dit en passant,** by the way, incidentally; (*b*) **passons à autre chose,** (i) let's pass on to other matters; (ii) let's change the subject; *Aut:* **p. en seconde,** to go, change, into second (gear); (*c*) **p. à la postérité,** to go down to posterity; **l'héritage est passé à sa fille,** the inheritance went to his daughter; **le mot est passé dans l'usage,** the word is in common use; (*d*) **la route passe par le village,** the road runs through the village; **il est passé par l'université,** he did a university course; **il dit tout ce qui lui passe par la tête,** he says anything, the first thing, that comes into his head; **mon dîner ne passe pas,** my dinner won't go down; (*e*) to go through; **passez par la fenêtre,** go through the window; **faire p. un tuyau à travers le mur,** to run a pipe through the wall; **sa chemise passait,** his shirt was hanging out; **il faut que le café passe très lentement,** coffee must filter very slowly; *Fr.C:* **j'ai passé tout droit,** I overslept; (*f*) *with cogn. acc.* **p. son chemin,** to go one's way; (*g*) *W.Tel:* **cette chanson n'a pas passé à la radio,** this song hasn't been played on the radio; *Cin:* **ce film a passé la semaine dernière,** this film was on, shown, last week; (*h*) **le chiffre d'affaires a passé de deux à trois millions,** our turnover has gone up from two to three million. **2.** (*aux.* **être**) **p. chez qn,** to call on s.o.; **je passerai chez vous ce soir,** I'll come round this evening; **en passant, je suis entré dire bonjour,** I just looked in, dropped in, on my way by; **je ne fais que p. pour demander de vos nouvelles,** I just called to see how you were; **est-ce que le facteur est passé?** has the postman been? has the post come? **3.** (*aux.* **avoir**) to undergo, pass through; **il a passé par des difficultés,** he had a difficult, bad, time; **j'ai passé par là,** I've been through it; **tout le monde y passe,** it happens to us all; *F:* **il a failli y p.,** he nearly died, passed on; **toute sa fortune y a passé,** she spent her whole fortune on it. **4.** (*aux. usu.* **avoir**) (*a*) to disappear, to cease; **la douleur a passé,** the pain has gone; **le vert est passé de mode,** green is out of fashion; **le plus dur est passé,** the worst is over; **ça lui passera (avec l'âge),** he'll grow out of it; **couleurs qui passent,** colours, *NAm:* colors, that fade; **il faut laisser p. l'orage,** we must let the storm blow over; **cela a fait p. mon mal de tête,** it has cured my headache; **laisser p. sa dernière chance,** to miss one's last chance; (*b*) (*of time*) to elapse, to go by; **des années ont passé depuis . . .,** years have passed, it's been years, since . . .; **à mesure que les années passent,** as the years go by; **comme le temps passe (vite)!** how time flies! **faire p. le temps,** to pass the time. **5.** (*a*) (*aux.* **avoir** *or* **être**) to become; **p. capitaine,** to be promoted (to) captain; **ce mot est passé en proverbe,** this saying has become a proverb; (*b*) (*aux.* **avoir**) to be considered, to pass for; **p. pour riche,** to be considered rich; **p. pour avoir fait qch.,** to be credited with having done sth.; **ceci passe pour vrai,** everyone believes this is true; **se faire p. pour . . .,** to pass oneself off, to pose, as . . .. **6.** (*aux.* **avoir**) to be accepted; **la loi a passé,** the bill has been carried, has gone through; **qu'il revienne demain, passe encore,** if he returns tomorrow, I have nothing to say against it, well and good; **cela peut p., cela ne passe pas,** it will, won't, do; *F:* **cette histoire-là ne passe pas,** that story won't wash. **7.** (*aux.* **avoir**) *Jur:* (*of lawsuit*) **p. en jugement,** to come up for judgment; **l'affaire passera en janvier, demain,** the case will be heard in January, comes on tomorrow. **II.** *v.tr.* **1.** to pass, cross, go over (bridge, river, sea); to go through, pass through (a doorway, a gate); to go through, clear (customs); to cross (a frontier); **vous avez passé la maison,** you've gone past the house. **2.** (*a*) to convey, carry, across; to ferry (goods, passengers) over; **p. des marchandises en fraude,** to smuggle goods; (*b*) **p. qch. à qn,** to hand sth. to s.o.; **voulez-vous me p. l'eau, s'il vous plaît,** please pass me the water; **p. un message,** to give (s.o.) a message; **il m'a passé son rhume,** I caught his cold; **p. une commande,** to place an order (**de qch. à qn,** for sth. with s.o.); *Sp:* **p. le ballon,** to pass the ball; *Tp:* **passez-moi M. X,** give me, put me through to, Mr X; **passez-moi un coup de fil demain,** call me tomorrow; **p. sa colère sur qn,** to vent one's anger on s.o.; (*c*) **p. une éponge sur le tableau,** to wipe the blackboard; *Fig:* **passons l'éponge là-dessus,** let's say no more about it; **se p. la main dans les cheveux,** to run one's fingers through one's hair; **p. sa tête par la fenêtre,** to put one's head out of the window; **je lui ai passé mon bras autour de la taille,** I slipped my arm round her waist; **p. une chemise, une robe,** to slip on a shirt, a dress; *Aut:* **p. la seconde, la troisième,** to go, change, into second, third (gear); *Nau:* **p. une manœuvre,** to reeve a rope; *P:* **qu'est-ce que je vais lui p.!** I shan't half tell him off! he won't half catch it! (*d*) (*to put sth. through a process*) **p. un couteau à la meule,** to sharpen a knife; **p. un parquet à la cire,** to polish a (parquet) floor; **p. des troupes en revue,** to inspect, review, troops; (*e*) *Cin:* to show (film); **salle qui passe** *Hamlet*, cinema showing *Hamlet*; **p. un disque,** to put on, play, a record, disc. **3.** to pass, spend (time, one's life); **pour p. le temps,** in order to pass, while away, the time. **4.** to pass, go beyond, exceed, surpass; **il a passé la soixantaine,** he's in his sixties; **cela passe les limites, les bornes,** that's going too far; **le vieux ne passera pas l'hiver,** the old man won't last through the winter. **5.** (*a*) to pass over; to excuse (fault, etc.); **on ne lui passe rien,** he doesn't get away with anything; **passez-moi l'expression,** (if you'll) pardon the expression; **se p. une fantaisie,** to indulge a whim; (*b*) to omit, leave out; **p. qch. sous silence,** to make no mention of sth.; to keep quiet about sth.; **il est beau, intelligent, instruit, et j'en passe,** he's handsome, intelligent, cultured, and that's not all; (*c*) *Cards:* **passe!** pass! no bid! **6.** (*a*) *Jur:* to reach (an agreement); to enter into, sign (a contract); *Book-k:* **p. un article en compte,** to post an entry; (*b*) **p. une loi,** to pass a law; (*c*) **p. un examen,** to sit for, to take, an exam(ination). **7.** to strain (liquid); to sift (flour); **p. le café,** to filter the coffee. **III. se passer 1.** to happen; to take place; **cela s'est passé il y a dix ans,** it happened ten years ago; **que se passe-t-il? qu'est-ce qui se passe?** what's going on? what's happening? **tout s'est bien passé,** everything went (off) smoothly; **mon histoire se passe en France,** my story is set in France; *F:* **ça ne se passera pas comme ça,** I won't stand for it. **2.** to pass away, to cease; (*of time*) to elapse, go by, to be spent; **mon mal de tête se passe,** my headache is going. **3. se p. de qn, de qch.,** to do without, to dispense with, s.o., sth.; **je m'en passerai,** I'll do without it; I shall manage without it; **ces faits se passent de commentaires,** these facts need no comment.

passereau, -eaux [pasro] *n.m. Orn:* **1.** *A:* sparrow. **2.** *pl.* **passereaux,** passerines, passeriformes.

passerelle [pasrɛl] *n.f.* **1.** footbridge. **2.** *Nau:* **p. (de commandement),** bridge; **p. de navigation,** navigation bridge; **p. de débarquement, d'embarquement,** (i) *Nau:* gangway, gangplank; (ii) *Av:* (passenger) steps, passenger bridge.

passe-temps [pastɑ̃] *n.m.inv.* pastime; hobby.

passe-thé [paste] *n.m.inv.* tea strainer.

passeur, -euse [pasœr, -øz] *n.* (*a*) ferryman, ferrywoman; (*b*) *Pol:* **p. (de frontière),** frontier runner; escape agent.

passible [pasibl̩] *a.* liable (**de,** to, for); **p. d'une amende,** liable to a fine; (*of pers.*) **p. de l'impôt,** liable for tax.

passif, -ive [pasif, -iv] **1.** *a.* (*a*) passive (obedience, etc.); *Gram:* **forme passive,** passive; (*b*) *Com:* **dettes passives,** liabilities. **2.** *n.m.* (*a*) *Gram:* passive; (*b*) *Com:* liabilities, debt.

passion [pasjɔ̃] *n.f.* **1. la P.,** the Passion (of Christ); **semaine de la P.,** Passion Week; *Mus:* **la P. selon saint Jean,** the St John Passion. **2.** passion; **p. pour la musique,** passion for music; **aimer qn à la, avec, p.,** to be passionately in love with s.o.; **il a la p. des voitures,** he has a passion for cars; **la moto est sa p.,** he's mad about motorbikes; **parler avec p., sans p.,** to speak passionately, dispassionately.

passionnant [pasjɔnɑ̃] *a.* exciting, fascinating, gripping, thrilling (story, etc.).

passionné [pasjɔne] (*a*) *a.* passionate, impassioned; **p. de, pour, qn, qch.,** passionately fond of s.o., sth.; (*b*) *n.* enthusiast; **c'est un p. de motos,** he's a motorbike fanatic.

passionnel, -elle [pasjɔnɛl] *a.* pertaining to the passions; **crime p.,** crime of passion.

passionnément [pasjɔnemɑ̃] *adv.* passionately.

passionner [pasjɔne] **1.** *v.tr.* to impassion; to interest passionately, to intrigue; **le sport le passionne,** he is passionately fond of, keen on, sport; sport is his passion; **livre qui passionne,** fascinating book. **2. se p. de, pour, qch.,** to become passionately fond of, (madly) enthusiastic about, sth., to conceive a passion for sth.

passivement [pasivmɑ̃] *adv.* passively.

passivité [pasivite] *n.f.* passivity, passiveness.

passoire [paswar] *n.f. Cu:* strainer; **p. à légumes,** colander; **sa mémoire est une p.,** he's got a head, a memory, like a sieve.

pastel [pastɛl] *n.m.* **1.** *Bot:* woad. **2.** *Art:* (*a*) pastel; **tableau au p.,** picture in pastel; **bleu p.,** pastel blue; (*b*) pastel drawing.

pastelliste [pastelist] *n.* pastellist.

pastèque [pastɛk] *n.f.* water melon.

pasteur [pastœr] *n.m.* **1.** *Lit:* shepherd; *Ecc:* **le bon P.,** the Good Shepherd. **2.** *Ecc:* pastor, *esp.* (Protestant) minister.

pasteurisation [pastœrizasjɔ̃] *n.f.* pasteurization.

pasteuriser [pastœrize] *v.tr.* to pasteurize.

pastiche [pastiʃ] *n.m.* pastiche.

pasticher [pastiʃe] *v.tr.* to do a pastiche of.

pastille [pastij] *n.f.* pastille; lozenge; **p. contre la toux,** cough drop, sweet; throat pastille; **p. de menthe,** (pepper)mint.

pastis [pastis] *n.m.* (*a*) aniseed aperitif; pastis; (*b*) *F:* fix, trouble; **quel p.!** what a mess!

pastoral, -aux [pastɔral, -o] **1.** *a.* pastoral. **2.** *n.f.* **pastorale** (*a*) *Lit:* pastoral (play, poem); (*b*) *Mus:* pastoral(e).

pastorat [pastɔra] *n.m.* pastorate.

pastoureau, -eaux, -elle [pasturo, -ɛl] **1.** *n. A: & Poet:* shepherd lad, lass. **2.** *n.f.* **pastourelle** (*a*) *Mus:* pastourelle; (*b*) *Danc:* fourth figure of the quadrille.

pat [pat] *n.m.inv. Chess:* stalemate; *a.inv.* **faire p.,** to stalemate.

patachon [pataʃɔ̃] *n.m. P:* **mener une vie de p.,** to lead a wild, disorderly, life.

Patagonie [patagɔni] *Pr.n.f. Geog:* Patagonia.

patapouf [patapuf] **1.** *int.* flop! **2.** *n.m. F:* **gros p.,** fat lump of a man, of a child.

pataquès [patakɛs] *n.m. F:* (*a*) faulty liaison; (*b*) serious mistake (in pronunciation, etc.).

patata [patata] *see* PATATI.
patate [patat] *n.f.* **1.** *Bot:* sweet potato. **2.** (*a*) *F:* potato, spud; (*b*) *P:* idiot, clot.
patati [patati] *F:* **et p. et patata,** and so on and so forth.
patatras [patatra] *int. F:* crash!
pataud, -aude [pato, -od] **1.** (*a*) *n.m.* puppy with big paws; (*b*) *n. O:* chubby child; lumpish person. **2.** *a. F:* heavy, clumsy (person).
patauger [patoʒe] *v.i.* **(je pataugeai(s); n. pataugeons)** (*a*) to splash, wade, squelch, in the mud; to paddle (in the water); (*b*) to become embarrassed, to get in a muddle, to flounder (in speech, etc.).
patchouli [patʃuli] *n.m. Bot: etc:* patchouli.
pâte [pɑt] *n.f.* **1.** (*a*) *Cu:* pastry; (cake) mixture; **p. à pain,** dough; **p. brisée,** short (crust) pastry; **p. à choux,** choux pastry; **p. feuilletée,** flaky, puff, pastry; **p. à frire,** batter; **p. à crêpes,** pancake batter; **pâtes (alimentaires),** pasta, noodles; **être de la p. dont on fait les héros,** to be of the stuff that heroes are made of; **c'est une bonne p.,** he's a good sort; **une p. molle,** a spineless person; **mettre la main à la p.,** (i) to lend a hand; (ii) to get down to it; **être comme un coq en p.,** to be in clover; (*b*) **fromage à p. dure, molle,** hard, soft, cheese; **p. de fruits,** fruit jelly; **p. d'amandes,** almond paste; (*c*) **p. à papier,** pulp; **p. dentifrice,** toothpaste; **p. à modeler,** modelling clay; (*d*) *Art:* paint, colours, *NAm:* colors, paste. **2.** (printer's) pie.
pâté [pɑte] *n.m.* **1.** *Cu:* (*a*) **p. en croûte,** meat (etc.) pie; (*b*) pâté; **p. de foie,** liver pâté; (*c*) **p. (de sable),** sand castle; mud pie. **2.** block (of houses). **3.** *F:* blot, blob (of ink).
pâtée [pɑte] *n.f.* **1.** mash (for poultry, pigs); dogs' food, cats' food. **2.** *P:* thrashing, good hiding.
patelin [patlɛ̃] *n.m. F:* village, small place; **quel sale p.!** what a dump! what a hole!
patelle [patɛl] *n.f.* **1.** *Rom.Ant:* patella. **2.** *Moll:* limpet.
patène [patɛn] *n.f. Ecc:* paten.
patenôtre [patnotr̥] *n.f.* (*a*) *A:* paternoster; (*b*) *F:* prayer; (*c*) *F:* gibberish.
patent [patɑ̃] *a.* (*a*) **lettres patentes,** letters patent; (*b*) obvious, evident; **il est p. que . . .,** it is patently obvious that . . ..
patentable [patɑ̃tabl̥] *a.* (trade, etc.) subject to a licence, requiring a licence.
patente [patɑ̃t] *n.f.* **1.** (*a*) licence (to exercise a trade or profession); (*b*) tax (paid by merchants and professional men); **payer p.,** to be duly licensed. **2.** *Nau:* **p. (de santé),** bill of health.
patenté [patɑ̃te] *a.* (*a*) licensed; (*b*) *F:* established; **imbécile p.,** out-and-out fool.
patenter [patɑ̃te] *v.tr.* to license.
pater [patɛr] *n.m.inv.* **1.** *Ecc:* (*a*) the Lord's prayer; paternoster; (*b*) great bead of a rosary; paternoster (bead). **2.** *F:* pater, the old man, *NAm:* pop.
patère [patɛr] *n.f.* (*a*) hat peg, coat peg; (*b*) curtain holder, hook.
paternalisme [patɛrnalism] *n.m.* paternalism.
paternaliste [patɛrnalist] *a.* paternalistic.
paterne [patɛrn] *a.* benevolent; soft-spoken.
paternel, -elle [patɛrnɛl] *a.* paternal; (*a*) **du côté p.,** on the father's side; **le domicile p.,** (the family) home; *n.m. F:* **le p.,** father, the old man, *NAm:* pop; (*b*) fatherly, kindly (tone, advice); fatherly (care).
paternellement [patɛrnɛlmɑ̃] *adv.* paternally, in a fatherly way.
paternité [patɛrnite] *n.f.* paternity, fatherhood; *Jur:* **recherche de la p.,** affiliation; **revendiquer, désavouer, la p. d'un livre,** to claim, to repudiate, the authorship of a book.
pâteux, -euse [pɑtø, -øz] *a.* (*a*) pasty; doughy (bread); **langue pâteuse,** coated, furred, tongue; **bouche pâteuse,** dry mouth; (*b*) thick, dull (voice); muddy (ink); **style p.,** woolly style.
pathétique [patetik] *Lit:* **1.** *a.* (*a*) pathetic, touching, moving (story, situation, tone); (*b*) *Anat:* pathetic (muscle). **2.** *n.m.* pathos.
pathétiquement [patetikmɑ̃] *adv.* pathetically, movingly.
pathétisme [patetism] *n.m.* pathos.
pathogène [patɔʒɛn] *a. Med:* pathogenic.
pathologie [patɔlɔʒi] *n.f.* pathology.
pathologique [patɔlɔʒik] *a.* pathological.
pathologiquement [patɔlɔʒikmɑ̃] *a.* pathologically.
pathologiste [patɔlɔʒist] *n.* pathologist.
pathos [patos] *n.m.* affected pathos; bathos.
patibulaire [patibylɛr] *a.* relating to the gallows; **fourches patibulaires,** gibbet; **avoir une mine p.,** to have a sinister look.
patiemment [pasjamɑ̃] *adv.* patiently.
patience¹ [pasjɑ̃s] *n.f.* patience, long-suffering; (*a*) **avoir de la p., prendre p.,** to have patience, to be patient; **montrer de la p. envers qn,** to be patient with s.o.; **attendre avec p.,** to wait patiently; **ma p. est à bout, je suis à bout de p.,** my patience is exhausted, is at an end; **(prenez) p.!** (have) patience! *F:* hang on (a moment)! **perdre p.,** to lose patience; **jeu de p.,** (jigsaw) puzzle; (*b*) *Cards:* patience; **faire des patiences,** to play patience.
patience² *n.f. Bot:* patience (dock); spinach dock.
patient, -ente [pasjɑ̃, -ɑ̃t] **1.** *a.* patient; (*a*) enduring; (*b*) forbearing, long-suffering. **2.** *n. Med:* patient.
patienter [pasjɑ̃te] *v.i.* to exercise patience; **patientez encore un peu,** have a little more patience.
patin [patɛ̃] *n.m.* **1.** (*a*) *A.Cost:* patten; (*b*) cloth pad (used as a mat on parquet floors). **2.** (*a*) skate; **patins à glace, à roulettes,** ice skates, roller skates; **faire du p.,** to go skating; to skate; (*b*) runner (of sledge, etc.). **3.** (*a*) slipper, (drag) shoe, skid (pan) (of wheel); (*b*) **p. (de frein),** brake block. **4.** base (of rails). **5.** *P:* French kiss.
patinage¹ [patinaʒ] *n.m.* **1.** skating; **p. artistique,** figure skating; **p. de vitesse,** speed skating. **2.** (*of wheel*) skidding; slipping; spinning.
patinage² *n.m.* patination (of bronze, etc.).
patine [patin] *n.f.* patina.
patiner¹ [patine] *v.i.* **1.** to skate. **2.** (*of wheel*) to skid, slip; to spin; (*of belt, clutch*) to slip.
patiner² *v.tr.* to give a patina to, to patinate (bronze, etc.).
patinette [patinɛt] *n.f.* (child's) scooter.
patineur, -euse [patinœr, -øz] *n.* skater.
patinoire [patinwar] *n.f.* skating rink, ice rink.
patio [patjo] *n.m. Arch:* patio.
pâtir [pɑtir] *v.i. A:* to suffer (**de,** because of, on account of).
pâtis [pɑti] *n.m.* grazing ground, pasture.
pâtisserie [pɑtisri] *n.f.* **1.** pastry; (small) cake; *coll.* pastries; *Com:* confectionery; **elle fait de la bonne p.,** she's a good pastrycook. **2.** pastry making. **3.** cake shop; confectioner's.
pâtissier, -ière [pɑtisje, -jɛr] **1.** *n.* pastrycook; confectioner. **2.** *a.* **crème pâtissière,** confectioner's custard.
patois [patwa] **1.** *n.m.* patois, provincial dialect. **2.** *a.* patois (word, etc.).
patouiller [patuje] *F:* **1.** *v.i.* to splash, flounder (in the mud). **2.** *v.tr.* to paw (s.o., sth.).
patraque [patrak] *F:* **1.** *n.f. A:* watch, ticker. **2.** *a.* (*of pers.*) out of sorts, under the weather.
pâtre [pɑtr̥] *n.m. Lit:* herdsman; shepherd.
patriarcal, -aux [patriarkal, -o] *a.* patriarchal.

patriarcat [patriarka] *n.m.* **1.** *Ecc:* patriarchate. **2.** *Anthr:* patriarchy.
patriarche [patriarʃ] *n.m.* patriarch.
patricien, -ienne [patrisjɛ̃, -jɛn] *a. & n.* patrician.
patrie [patri] *n.f.* native country; homeland, fatherland; birthplace; **mère p.,** mother country; **mourir pour la p.,** to die for one's country.
patrimoine [patrimwan] *n.m.* patrimony; heritage; *Biol:* **p. héréditaire,** genotype.
patrimonial, -aux [patrimɔnjal, -o] *a.* patrimonial.
patriotard [patrijɔtar] **1.** *a.* jingoistic. **2.** *n.m.* jingoist.
patriote [patrijɔt] **1.** *a.* patriotic (person). **2.** *n.* patriot.
patriotique [patrijɔtik] *a.* patriotic.
patriotiquement [patrijɔtikmɑ̃] *adv.* patriotically.
patriotisme [patrijɔtism] *n.m.* patriotism.
patron, -onne [patrɔ̃, -ɔn] **1.** *n.* (*a*) patron, patroness; protector, protectress; (*b*) patron saint. **2.** (*a*) master, mistress (of house); employer (of workforce); chief, head, owner, *F:* boss (of firm, business); proprietor, proprietress (of hotel); *Sch:* **p. de thèse,** supervisor of postgraduate student; (*b*) = senior consultant (of teaching hospital); (*c*) *Nau:* skipper, master (of small vessel); shipmaster; coxswain (of boat). **3.** *n.m.* (*a*) (sewing, knitting) pattern; (*b*) **p. (ajouré),** stencil (plate).
patronage [patrɔnaʒ] *n.m.* **1.** patronage; *Com:* custom. **2.** (*a*) (church) youth club; (*b*) meeting place, headquarters, of youth club.
patronal, -aux [patrɔnal, -o] *a.* **1.** of, pertaining to, the patron saint; **fête patronale,** patronal festival. **2.** of, pertaining to, employers; **syndicat p.,** employers' association.
patronat [patrɔna] *n.m.* (body of) employers.
patronner [patrɔne] *v.tr.* to patronize, protect, support (person, hospital, charity, etc.); to sponsor (s.o.).
patronnesse [patrɔnɛs] *a. & n.f. usu. Iron:* **(dame) p.,** patroness.
patronyme [patrɔnim] *n.m.* patronymic.
patronymique [patrɔnimik] *a.* patronymic.
patrouille [patruj] *n.f. Mil: etc:* patrol; **aller en p., être de p.,** to go, be, on patrol.
patrouiller [patruje] *v.i.* to patrol, to be on patrol.
patrouilleur [patrujœr] *n.m.* (*a*) *Mil:* member of a patrol; soldier on patrol; (*b*) *Av:* patrol aircraft; (*c*) *Navy:* patrol boat, ship.
patte [pat] *n.f.* **1.** paw (of cat, dog, etc.); foot (of bird); leg (of insect); *F:* (*of pers.*) (i) hand, paw; (ii) foot; (iii) leg; *F:* **pattes de mouche(s),** cramped, spidery handwriting; **pattes (de lapin),** sideboards, sideburns; **marcher à quatre pattes,** to go on all fours; **pattes de devant,** forelegs, forefeet; **pattes de derrière,** hind legs, hind feet; **bas, court, sur pattes,** short-legged; **faire p. de velours,** (i) (*of cat*) to draw in its claws; (ii) *Fig:* to show the velvet glove; **coup de p.,** (i) scratch, claw; (ii) cutting remark; *F:* dig; (*of painter*) **avoir le coup de p.,** to have talent; **tenir qn sous sa p.,** to have s.o. at one's mercy, under one's thumb; **tomber dans les pattes de qn,** to fall into s.o.'s clutches; *F:* **bas les pattes!** hands off! *F:* **graisser la p. à qn,** to bribe s.o., oil s.o.'s palm; **pantalon à pattes d'éléphant,** bell-bottomed, flared, trousers. **2.** flap (of pocket, envelope), tongue (of wallet, shoe). **3.** (*a*) clamp, clip, fastening; (*b*) *Nau:* fluke, palm (of anchor); claw (of grapnel). **4.** *Dressm: etc:* strap (on garment); **pattes d'épaule,** shoulder straps.
patte-d'oie [patdwa] *n.f.* **1.** crossroads. **2.** (*wrinkle*) crow's foot. **3.** *Bot:* goose foot; *pl. pattes-d'oie.*
pattemouille [patmuj] *n.f.* damping cloth (for ironing).
pattu [paty] *a.* **1.** large-pawed (dog, etc.). **2.** feather-legged (pigeon).
pâturage [pɑtyraʒ] *n.m.* **1.** grazing; *Jur:* grazing rights. **2.** (*a*) pasture, grazing ground; (*b*) *pl.* pasture land.
pâture [pɑtyr] *n.f.* **1.** food, feed, fodder (of animals); **p. intellectuelle,** food for the mind. **2.** pasture; *Jur:* **vaine p.,** (right of) common.
pâturer [pɑtyre] **1.** *v.i.* (*of cattle, etc.*) to graze, to feed. **2.** *v.tr.* (*of cattle, etc.*) to graze (on) (meadow).
pâturin [pɑtyrɛ̃] *n.m. Bot:* meadow grass.
paturon [patyrɔ̃] *n.m.* pastern (of horse).
paume [pom] *n.f.* **1.** palm (of hand). **2.** *Games:* **(jeu de) p.,** (i) real tennis; (ii) real tennis court.
paumé, -ée [pome] **1.** *a.* (*a*) *P:* broke, hard up; (*b*) *F:* lost; **il est complètement p.,** he doesn't know where he is. **2.** *n. P:* (*pers.*) wreck; bum.
paumelle [pomɛl] *n.f.* **1.** *Nau: etc:* (sailmaker's) palm; hand leather. **2.** (*a*) plate (of door hinge); (*b*) door hinge.
paumer [pome] *P:* **1.** *v.tr.* (*a*) **se faire p.,** to get nabbed, copped; (*b*) to lose. **2. se p.,** to get lost.
paupérisme [poperism] *n.m.* pauperism.
paupière [popjɛr] *n.f.* eyelid.
paupiette [popjɛt] *n.f. Cu:* (meat) olive.
pause [poz] *n.f.* **1.** pause; *Fb: etc:* half time; *Ind: etc:* meal break; **p. café,** coffee break, (=) tea break; **faire une p.,** to pause, to have a break. **2.** *Mus:* semibreve rest.
pauser [poze] *v.i. Mus:* to pause.
pauvre [povr̥] **1.** *a.* (*a*) poor; **p. comme Job,** as poor as a church mouse; **p. d'esprit,** half-witted; **minerai p. en métal,** ore with a low metal content; *Aut:* **mélange p.,** weak mixture; (*b*) poor, unfortunate; **le p. homme!** poor chap! **p. de moi!** poor me! (*c*) shabby (dress, furniture, etc.); paltry (excuse); pathetic, weak (argument, etc.); bad (speaker); *F:* (*pers.*) **c'est un p. type,** he's pathetic, a poor sod; **p. idiot!** silly fool! *n.* **le p., il n'a pas de chance!** poor chap, he hasn't much luck! **mon, ma, p.,** my dear (friend). **2.** *n.* poor man, poor woman; **les pauvres et les riches,** the poor and the rich; **p. d'esprit,** half-wit.
pauvrement [povrəmɑ̃] *adv.* poorly; **p. vêtu,** poorly, shabbily, dressed.
pauvresse [povrɛs] *n.f.* poor woman.
pauvret, -ette [povrɛ, -ɛt] (*a*) *a. A: & Lit:* poor; (*b*) *n. F: O:* **le p., la pauvrette,** the poor little thing.
pauvreté [povrəte] *n.f.* (*a*) poverty; *Ecc:* **vœu de p.,** vow of poverty; **p. du sol,** poorness of the soil; (*b*) poorness (of language); baldness (of style, etc.).
pavage [pavaʒ] *n.m.* **1.** (*action*) paving; cobbling. **2.** paving; cobblestones.
pavane [pavan] *n.f. Danc: Mus:* pavan.
pavaner (se) [səpavane] *v.pr.* to strut about.
pavé [pave] *n.m.* **1.** (*a*) paving stone, paving block; cobblestone; **un p. dans la mare,** a (nice) bit of scandal; **avoir un p. sur l'estomac,** to feel a weight on one's stomach; (*b*) **p. de viande,** thick piece of meat; (*c*) *F:* (i) prominent article (in newspaper); (ii) long and tedious article. **2.** (*a*) pavement, paving; (*b*) paved road; **brûler le p.,** to run very fast; (*in car*) to race along; **tenir le haut du p.,** (i) to belong to the upper class; (ii) to be the leader, the boss; (*c*) the street, the streets; **battre le p.,** to loaf about the streets; **être sur le p.,** (i) to be homeless; (ii) to be out of work.
pavement [pavmɑ̃] *n.m.* (ornate) paving, pavement.
paver [pave] *v.tr.* to pave, cobble (street, etc.); **cour pavée,** paved yard.
paveur [pavœr] *n.m.* paver, paviour, *NAm:* pavior.
pavillon [pavijɔ̃] *n.m.* **1.** (*a*) *Mil: A:* tent, pavilion; (*b*) detached house; **p. de banlieue,** suburban house; **p. d'entrée (d'une propriété),** (gate) lodge; **p. de jardin,**

summerhouse, pavilion; **p. de chasse,** shooting lodge; (*c*) (*isolated building in hospital, university, etc.*) pavilion, block, wing. **2.** (*a*) horn (of hooter, loudspeaker, siren); bell (of brass instrument); mouth (of funnel); *Tp:* **p. d'écouteur,** earpiece; (*b*) *Anat:* **p. de l'oreille,** pavilion, auricle, external ear. **3.** *Nau:* flag, colours, *NAm:* colors; **p. de départ, de partance,** Blue Peter; **p. noir,** Jolly Roger; **p. de quarantaine,** yellow flag; **p. de détresse,** flag of distress; **hisser, arborer, son p.,** to hoist one's colours; **battre un p.,** to fly a flag; **amener, baisser, le p.,** (i) *Navy:* to strike one's flag, to surrender; (ii) to admit defeat.

pavois [pavwa] *n.m.* **1.** *A.Arm:* (body) shield; pavis(e). **2.** *Nau:* (*a*) bulwark; (*b*) *coll.* flags (for dressing ship); dressing; **mettre, hisser, le grand p.,** to dress over all.

pavoiser [pavwaze] **1.** *v.tr.* (*a*) *Nau:* to dress (ship); (*b*) to deck (house, etc.) with flags; to put out bunting. **2.** *v.i.* (*a*) *Nau:* to dress ship; (*b*) to put out the flags; (*c*) *F:* to rejoice.

pavot [pavo] *n.m. Bot:* poppy; **p. sommifère,** opium poppy; **tête de p.,** poppyhead; **graine(s) de p.,** poppy seed.

payable [pɛjabl̩] *a.* payable; *Com:* **p. à la livraison,** payable on delivery.

payant [pɛjɑ̃] *a.* (*a*) paying (guest, etc.); **spectateur p.,** spectator who pays (for admission); **élèves payants,** paying pupils; (*b*) charged for; **spectacle p.,** show with charge for admission; **toutes les places sont payantes,** no free seats; (*c*) **affaire payante,** business that pays, profitable business.

payer [peje] *v.* **(je paye, je paie; je payerai, je paierai) 1.** *v.tr.* (*a*) **p. qn,** to pay s.o.; **combien vous a-t-il fait p.?** how much did he charge you? **p. qn de ses services,** to pay s.o. for his services; **trop payé, trop peu payé,** overpaid, underpaid; **p. qn de paroles, de mots,** to put s.o. off with fine words; (*b*) to pay, discharge, settle (debt, etc.); **p. la note,** to pay, to foot, the bill; *Com:* **p. un effet,** to honour, *NAm:* honor, a bill; **congés payés,** holidays with pay; paid leave; (*c*) **p. qch.,** to pay for sth.; **la viande a été payée,** the meat's (been) paid for; **p. qch. à qn,** to pay s.o. for sth.; **je le lui ai payé cent francs,** I paid him a hundred francs for it; **p. le dîner à qn,** to treat s.o. to dinner; **c'est moi qui paie (la tournée),** it's my round; **port payé,** carriage paid; post paid; *Tg:* **réponse payée,** answer prepaid; (*d*) **il a payé sa témérité de sa vie,** he paid for his rashness with his life; **faire p. ses méfaits à qn,** to bring s.o. to account; **vous me le paierez!** you'll pay for this! *F:* **je suis payé pour le savoir,** I've learnt it the hard way; **il l'a payé cher,** (i) he paid a lot for it; (ii) *Fig:* he paid dearly for it. **2.** *v.i.* (*a*) **p. rubis sur l'ongle,** to pay on the nail; (*b*) **p. de sa personne,** (i) to risk one's own skin; (ii) to bear the brunt (of the work, etc.); **p. d'audace,** (i) to take the risk; (ii) to face the music; (iii) (*also* **p. d'effronterie**) to brazen it out, to put a bold face on it; (*c*) (*of crime, business, etc.*) to pay. **3. se p.** (*a*) (*when offering large note in payment*) **voilà monsieur, payez-vous,** here you are, take it out of that; (*b*) **je me suis payé une glace,** I treated myself to an icecream; **se p. la tête de qn,** to make fun of s.o.; *F:* **s'en p. une tranche,** to have a good time; (*c*) **cela ne se paie pas,** it's something money can't buy.

payeur, -euse [pɛjœr, -øz] *n.* **1.** payer. **2.** *Adm: etc:* disbursements officer; pay clerk; *Mil: etc:* paymaster.

pays¹ [pei] *n.m.* country; (*a*) land; **visiter des p. étrangers,** to visit foreign countries, lands; **il a vu du p.,** he has seen the world, travelled around a lot; **p. du rêve,** dreamland; (*b*) region, district, locality; **vous n'êtes donc pas de ce p.?** so you don't belong to these parts? **p. perdu,** out-of-the-way place; **être en p. de connaissance,** to be among friends; **denrées du p.,** home(grown) produce; **vin de p., du p.,** local wine; (*c*) **p. de montagne(s),** hill country; *pl.* **p. bas,** lowlands; (*d*) native land, home; **avoir le mal du p.,** to be homesick.

pays², payse [pei, peiz] *n. F:* fellow-countryman, -woman; **nous sommes p.,** we're from the same area, the same place.

paysage [peizaʒ] *n.m.* **1.** landscape; scenery. **2.** *Art:* landscape (painting); *F:* **cela fait bien dans le p.,** that looks good there.

paysagiste [peizaʒist] *n.m.* (*a*) landscape painter; (*b*) **(jardinier) p.,** landscape gardener.

paysan, -anne [peizɑ̃, -an] *n. & a.* peasant; rustic; country(-man, -woman); **les paysans,** (i) *esp. Hist:* the peasants, the peasantry; (ii) country people; **p. (propriétaire),** farmer.

paysannerie [peizanri] *n.f.* **1.** (*a*) *esp. Hist:* peasantry; (*b*) country people. **2.** *Lit:* story of peasant life.

Pays-Bas (les) [lepeibɑ] *Pr.n.m.pl. Geog:* the Netherlands.

péage [peaʒ] *n.m.* **1.** toll; **barrière de p.,** turnpike; **pont à p.,** toll bridge. **2.** toll house.

péager, -ère [peaʒe, -ɛr] *n. A:* toll collector.

péan [peɑ̃] *n.m. Gr.Ant:* paean; song of triumph.

peau, -eaux [po] *n.f.* **1.** skin; **beauté à fleur de p.,** skin-deep beauty; **prendre qn par la p. du cou,** to take s.o. by the scruff of the neck; **faire p. neuve,** to turn over a new leaf; **il n'a que la p. et les os,** he's nothing but skin and bone; **je ne voudrais pas être dans sa p.,** I wouldn't like to be in his shoes; **risquer sa p.,** to risk one's neck; **sauver sa p.,** to save one's skin, bacon; **craindre pour sa p.,** to fear for one's life; *F:* **avoir qn dans sa p.,** to be crazy about s.o.; *F:* **se sentir mal dans sa p.,** to feel uncomfortable; *Th:* **entrer dans la p. d'un personnage,** to identify oneself with a character; to get right inside a part; *P:* **se faire crever la p.,** to get killed, bumped off; *P:* **j'aurai sa p.!** I'll get him! *P:* **la p.! p. de balle, de zébi!** nothing doing! no way! *P: O:* **vieille p.,** old hag; old bag. **2.** (*a*) hide, pelt, fell, fur (of animals); **p. de lapin,** rabbit skin; cony(skin); (*b*) prepared hide, leather; **p. de mouton,** sheepskin; **p. de chevreau,** kid; **p. de daim,** buckskin; **p. de veau,** calfskin, box calf; **p. de requin,** shagreen; **p. de serpent,** snakeskin; *F:* **p. d'âne,** diploma; *P:* **c'est une p. de vache,** he's a bastard; she's a cow; (*c*) **p. de tambour,** (i) drum parchment; (ii) drumhead. **3.** peel, skin (of fruit). **4.** film, skin (of milk).

peaucier [posje] *a. & n.m. Anat:* **(muscle) p.,** platysma.

Peau-Rouge [poruʒ] *n. & a.* Red Indian, redskin; *pl. Peaux-Rouges.*

peausserie [posri] *n.f.* **1.** (*a*) skin dressing; (*b*) skin trade. **2.** leatherwear, leather goods.

peaussier [posje] *n.m.* (*a*) skinner, skin dresser; (*b*) fellmonger.

pébroc, pébroque [pebrɔk] *n.m. P:* umbrella, brolly.

pécari [pekari] *n.m. Z:* peccary; Mexican hog.

peccadille [pekadij] *n.f.* peccadillo.

pechblende [pɛʃblɛ̃d] *n.f. Miner:* pitchblende.

pêche¹ [pɛʃ] *n.f.* (*a*) peach; **p.-abricot,** yellow peach; **p. Melba,** peach Melba; (*b*) *P:* blow, clout.

pêche² *n.f.* **1.** fishing; **p. à la truite,** trout fishing; **p. (à la ligne),** angling; **p. à la mouche,** fly fishing; **aller à la p.,** to go fishing. **2.** catch; **faire une heureuse p.,** to get a good haul; *B:* **la p. miraculeuse,** the miraculous draught of fishes. **3.** fishery; **grande p.,** high-sea fishery; **p. à la baleine,** whaling.

péché [peʃe] *n.m.* sin; transgression; **p. mortel,** mortal sin; **les sept péchés capitaux,** the seven deadly sins;

vivre dans le p., (i) to lead a sinful life; (ii) (*unmarried*) to live in sin; **son p. mignon,** his besetting sin, his weakness; **à tout p. miséricorde,** there is mercy for everything; **péchés de jeunesse,** youthful indiscretions.

pécher [peʃe] *v.i.* **(je pèche, n. péchons; je pécherai)** to sin; to transgress; **p. par orgueil,** to commit the sin of pride; **il pèche par trop de timidité,** his failing is his excessive shyness; **p. par excès, par défaut,** to exceed, fall short of, what is required.

pêcher[1] [peʃe] *n.m.* peach tree.

pêcher[2] *v.tr.* **1.** to fish for (trout, etc.); **p. à la ligne,** to angle (with rod and line); **p. à la mouche,** to fly fish; **p. en mer,** to go sea fishing; **p. le corail,** to dive for coral; **p. la baleine,** to hunt whales; **p. en eau trouble,** to fish in troubled waters. **2.** *F:* **où avez-vous pêché cela?** where did you pick that up? where did you get hold of that?

pêcherie [pɛʃri] *n.f.* fishery, fishing ground.

pécheur, pécheresse [peʃœr, peʃrɛs] **1.** *n.* sinner, transgressor. **2.** *a.* sinning; sinful.

pêcheur, -euse [pɛʃœr, -øz] *n.* fisher, fisherman, -woman; **p. à la ligne,** angler; **p. de baleines,** whaler; **p. de perles,** pearl diver; *a.* **bateau p.,** fishing smack.

pécore [pekɔr] **1.** *n.f. F:* silly, stuck-up, girl, woman; silly goose. **2.** *n. P:* country bumpkin.

pectine [pɛktin] *n.f.* pectin.

pectique [pɛktik] *a.* pectic (acid).

pectoral, -aux [pɛktɔral, -o] **1.** *a.* pectoral (muscle, fin, etc.); **sirop p.,** expectorant; **pastille de pâte pectorale,** cough lozenge. **2.** *n.m.* pectoral muscle.

pécule [pekyl] *n.m.* (*a*) savings; nest egg; (*b*) earnings of convict (paid on discharge); (*c*) *Mil: Navy:* gratuity (on discharge).

pécuniaire [pekynjɛr] *a.* pecuniary; financial (position); **être dans un embarras p.,** to be short of money.

pécuniairement [pekynjɛrmɑ̃] *adv.* financially.

pédagogie [pedagɔʒi] *n.f.* pedagogy, pedagogics.

pédagogique [pedagɔʒik] *a.* pedagogic(al), educational; teaching (methods).

pédagogiquement [pedagɔʒikmɑ̃] *adv.* pedagogically.

pédagogue [pedagɔg] *n.* pedagogue; educationalist.

pédale [pedal] *n.f.* **1.** pedal (of cycle, car, piano, etc.); *Mec.E:* pedal, treadle (of lathe, etc.); **p. d'embrayage,** clutch pedal; *F:* **perdre les pédales,** to lose one's head; to get all mixed up. **2.** *Mus:* **(note de) p.,** pedal (note). **3.** *P:* (*a*) homo(sexual), queer, poof(ter), gay; (*b*) **il est de la p.,** he's gay.

pédaler [pedale] *v.i.* **1.** (*a*) to pedal; (*b*) to cycle. **2.** *P:* to hurry, to rush along.

pédaleur, -euse [pedalœr, -øz] *n.* cyclist.

pédalier [pedalje] *n.m.* **1.** crank gear (of cycle, etc.). **2.** pedal board (of organ).

pédalo [pedalo] *n.m.* pedal boat, pedalo.

pédant, -ante [pedɑ̃, -ɑ̃t] **1.** *n.* pedant. **2.** *a.* pedantic.

pédanterie [pedɑ̃tri] *n.f.* pedantry.

pédantesque [pedɑ̃tɛsk] *a.* pedantic.

pédantisme [pedɑ̃tism] *n.m.* pedantry.

pédé [pede] *n.m. P:* homo(sexual), queer, poof(ter), gay.

pédéraste [pederast] *n.m.* p(a)ederast, homosexual.

pédérastie [pederasti] *n.f.* p(a)ederasty, homosexuality.

pédestre [pedɛstr̥] *a.* pedestrian; (journey) on foot.

pédiatre [pedjatr̥] *n. Med:* paediatrician, *NAm:* pediatrician.

pédiatrie [pedjatri] *n.f. Med:* paediatrics, *NAm:* pediatrics.

pédicelle [pedisɛl] *n.m. Nat.Hist:* pedicel, pedicle.

pédiculaire [pedikylɛr] **1.** *a.* pedicular, lousy; *Med:* **maladie p.,** phthiriasis, pediculosis. **2.** *n.f. Bot:* lousewort.

pédicule [pedikyl] *n.m. Biol: Anat:* pedicle, peduncle.

pédicure [pedikyr] *n.* chiropodist.

pedigree [pedigri] *n.m.* pedigree.

pédomètre [pedɔmɛtr̥] *n.m.* pedometer.

pédoncule [pedɔ̃kyl] *n.m. Nat.Hist:* peduncle.

pedzouille [pɛdzuj] *n.m. P:* peasant, country bumpkin.

pègre [pɛgr̥] *n.f.* the underworld.

peignage [pɛɲaʒ] *n.m. Tex:* combing, carding (of wool, etc.).

peigne [pɛɲ] *n.m.* **1.** comb; **p. fin, (**fine) toothcomb; **passer qch. au p. fin,** to go through sth. with a fine toothcomb; **se donner un coup de p.,** to run a comb through one's hair. **2.** *Tex:* (i) card (for wool); hackle (for hemp); (ii) **p. de métier à tisser,** reed. **3.** *Moll:* pecten; comb(shell); scallop.

peigné [peɲe] *a.* **1.** combed; **bien p.,** well groomed (person); **mal p.,** unkempt; tousled (hair). **2.** *Tex:* (*a*) worsted (yarn); (*b*) *n.m.* worsted (yarn).

peigne-cul [pɛɲky] *n.m. P:* (*pers.*) (*a*) creep; (*b*) yob(bo); *pl. peigne-culs.*

peignée [peɲe] *n.f.* **1.** *Tex:* cardful (of wool, flax, hemp). **2.** *F:* thrashing, good hiding.

peigner [peɲe] **1.** *v.tr.* (*a*) to comb (out) (hair, etc.); **p. un enfant,** to comb a child's hair; *F:* **p. la girafe,** to waste one's time; (*b*) *Tex:* to card, comb (wool); to hackle (hemp). **2. se p.,** to comb one's hair.

peignoir [pɛɲwar] *n.m.* (*a*) *Hairdr:* cape, overall (to protect customer's clothes); (*b*) dressing gown; housecoat; (*c*) bath robe.

peinard [pɛnar] *a. P:* cushy; **rester p.,** to take things easy; **tiens-toi p.,** keep quiet, keep your nose clean.

peindre [pɛ̃dr̥] *v.tr.* (*pr.p.* **peignant;** *p.p.* **peint;** *pr.ind.* **je peins, il peint, n. peignons;** *impf.* **je peignais;** *p.h.* **je peignis;** *fu.* **je peindrai) 1.** to paint; **p. qch. en vert,** to paint sth. green; **papier peint,** wallpaper; **p. qch. à la chaux,** to whitewash sth. **2.** to paint, portray, depict, represent (in colours, *NAm:* colors); **p. un coucher de soleil,** to paint a sunset; **p. à l'huile, à l'aquarelle,** to paint in oils, in water colours; **p. tout en rose,** to paint everything in rosy colours; **l'innocence se peint sur son visage,** innocence is written on his face.

peine [pɛn] *n.f.* **1.** punishment, penalty; **p. capitale,** capital punishment; **la p. de mort,** the death penalty; **défense d'entrer sous p. d'amende,** trespassers will be prosecuted; **errer comme une âme en p.,** to wander about like a lost soul. **2.** (*a*) sorrow, sadness; **j'ai beaucoup de p.,** I feel very sad; **faire de la p. à qn,** to grieve, distress, s.o.; **je m'en suis séparé avec beaucoup de p.,** I was very sorry to part with it; **cela fait p. à voir,** it's painful to see; (*b*) **être dans la p.,** to be in trouble, in distress. **3.** pains, trouble; **se donner de la p. pour faire qch.,** to take trouble, pains, to do sth.; **se donner beaucoup de p.,** to take great pains; *O:* **donnez-vous, prenez, la p. de vous asseoir,** please take a seat; **en vous donnant un peu de p. vous y arriverez,** with a little effort you'll manage it; **c'est p. perdue,** it is a waste of time; **en être pour sa p.,** to have all one's trouble for nothing; **il lui a donné 100 francs pour sa p.,** he gave him 100 francs for his trouble; **cela vaut la p. d'essayer,** it's worth trying; **cela ne vaut pas la p.,** it's not worth the trouble; **ce n'est pas la p. de changer de robe,** you needn't bother to change your dress; *Iron:* **c'était bien la p. de venir!** we might just as well have stayed at home! **4.** difficulty; **j'ai eu toutes les peines du monde à le trouver,** I had the utmost difficulty in finding it; **j'ai p. à croire que** + *sub.,* I find it hard to believe that . . .; **avoir p. à retenir ses larmes,** to be on the brink of tears; **ne jamais être en p. de trouver une excuse,** never to be at a loss for an excuse; **avec p., à grand-p.,** with (great) difficulty; **sans p.,** (i) easily; (ii) willingly. **5.** *adv.phr.* **à p.,** hardly, barely, scarcely; **c'est à p. si je le connais,** I hardly know him; **il est à p. 3 heures,** it's barely 3 o'clock; **à p. étions-nous sortis qu'il se mit à pleuvoir,** we had only just gone out when it began to rain.

peiner [pene] **1.** *v.tr.* to pain, grieve, upset, distress (s.o.); **cette nouvelle m'a beaucoup peiné,** I was very sad at the news; **d'un ton peiné,** in an aggrieved tone. **2.** *v.i.* to toil, labour, *NAm:* labor, drudge; **il peinait sur son travail,** he was struggling over his work; *Aut:* **le moteur peine,** the engine is labouring.

peintre [pɛ̃tr̥] *n.m.* painter. **1. (artiste) p.,** artist; **une femme p.,** a woman artist; **p. de portraits,** portrait painter, portraitist. **2. p. en bâtiment(s), p. décorateur,** (house) painter; painter and decorator; *Th:* **p. de décors,** scene painter.

peinture [pɛ̃tyr] *n.f.* **1.** (art of) painting; (*a*) **faire de la p.,** to paint; **p. à l'huile, à l'aquarelle, à l'eau,** oil painting, watercolour, *NAm:* watercolor (painting); (*b*) **p. en bâtiments,** (house) painting; **p. au pistolet,** spray painting. **2.** picture, painting; **p. des mœurs de l'époque,** portrayal, description, of the customs of the period. **3.** paint; *P.N:* **attention p. fraîche! attention à la p.!** wet paint; **p. à la colle, en détrempe,** size paint, distemper; **p. mate,** matt emulsion (paint); **p. brillante, laquée,** gloss paint.

peinturer [pɛ̃tyre] *v.tr.* to daub (with paint).

peinturlurer [pɛ̃tyrlyre] *v.tr. F:* to paint (building, etc.) in all the colours, *NAm:* colors, of the rainbow; to daub (with paint).

péjoratif, -ive [peʒɔratif, -iv] *a. & n.m.* pejorative; disparaging (sense, etc.).

péjorativement [peʒɔrativmɑ̃] *adv.* pejoratively.

Pékin [pekɛ̃] **1.** *Pr.n.m. Geog:* Peking. **2.** *n.m.* (*a*) *Tex:* Pekin (fabric); (*b*) *Mil: F:* civilian; **être en p.,** to be in civvies.

pékinois, -oise [pekinwa, -waz] (*a*) *a. & n. Geog:* Pekin(g)ese; (*b*) *n.m.* (*dog*) pekin(g)ese, *F:* peke.

pelade [pəlad] *n.f. Med:* alopecia.

pelage [pəlaʒ] *n.m.* coat, wool, fur (of animal).

pélagique [pelaʒik] *a. Oc:* pelagic, pelagian (fauna, etc.).

pélargonium [pelargɔnjɔm] *n.m. Bot:* pelargonium ((i) stork's bill; (ii) *Hort: F:* geranium).

pelé [pəle] (*a*) *a.* bald; hairless (skin); bare (countryside); threadbare (material); (*b*) *n.* bald-headed man, *F:* baldie; *F:* **il n'y avait que trois pelés et un tondu,** there was hardly anyone there.

pêle-mêle [pɛlmɛl] **1.** *adv.* pell-mell; higgledy-piggledy; **mettre tout p.-m.,** to jumble everything up; **tout est entassé p.-m.,** everything is piled any old how. **2.** *n.m.inv.* jumble; muddle.

peler [pəle] **1.** *v.tr.* to peel, skin (vegetables, fruit); **la pêche se pèle facilement,** peaches peel easily, are easy to peel. **2.** *v.i.* (*of skin, etc.*) to peel.

pèlerin, -ine [pɛlrɛ̃, -in] **1.** *n.* pilgrim. **2.** *n.m.* (*a*) *Ich:* basking shark; (*b*) *Orn:* peregrine falcon. **3.** *n.f.* **pèlerine** (*a*) cape, cloak; (*b*) hooded cape.

pèlerinage [pɛlrinaʒ] *n.m.* **1.** pilgrimage. **2.** place of pilgrimage.

pélican [pelikɑ̃] *n.m. Orn:* pelican.

pelisse [pəlis] *n.f.* fur-lined coat; pelisse.

pellagre [pelagr̥] *n.f. Med:* pellagra.

pelle [pɛl] *n.f.* **1.** shovel, scoop; (*a*) **p. à charbon,** coal shovel; **p. à tarte,** tart slice; **p. à ordures,** dustpan; **ramasser qch. à la p.,** to shovel sth. up; **remuer, ramasser, l'argent à la p.,** to be rolling in money, raking it in; *F:* **ramasser une p.,** to fall flat on one's face; (*b*) *Civ.E: etc:* **p. mécanique,** (i) mechanical shovel; (ii) shovel dredger. **2.** (child's, gardener's) spade.

pelleter [pɛlte] *v.tr.* (**je pellette** [pɛlt], **n. pelletons; je pelletterai** [pɛltre]) to shovel (up).

pelleterie [pɛltri] *n.f.* **1.** (*a*) *coll.* fur skins, peltry; (*b*) pelt. **2.** (*a*) fur making; (*b*) fur trade, furriery.

pelleteuse [pɛltøz] *n.f. Civ.E:* mechanical shovel.

pelletier, -ière [pɛltje, -jɛr] *n.* furrier.

pellicule [pelikyl] *n.f.* **1.** (*a*) pellicle; thin skin; thin layer; film; (*b*) grape skin; (*c*) *Phot:* film. **2.** *pl.* **pellicules,** dandruff.

Pélopon(n)èse (le) [ləpelɔpɔnɛz] *Pr.n.m. Geog:* (the) Peloponnese.

pelotage [p(ə)lɔtaʒ] *n.m. P:* petting, necking.

pelotari [p(ə)lɔtari] *n.m.* pelota player.

pelote [p(ə)lɔt] *n.f.* **1.** ball (of wool, string); **p. (à épingles),** pincushion; *F:* **faire sa p.,** to make one's pile; to feather one's nest; **avoir les nerfs en p.,** to be on edge, nervy. **2.** *Games:* **p. (basque),** pelota.

peloter [p(ə)lɔte] *v.tr.* (*a*) *A:* to wind (wool, string, etc.) into a ball; (*b*) *P:* to pet, paw (a woman); (*c*) to flatter, suck up to (s.o.).

peloteur, -euse [p(ə)lɔtœr, -øz] **1.** *a. F:* **mains peloteuses,** wandering hands. **2.** *n.* (*a*) *Tex:* (*pers.*) ball winder; (*b*) *F:* (i) flatterer, fawner; (ii) cuddler. **3.** *n.f.* **peloteuse,** balling machine.

peloton [p(ə)lɔtɔ̃] *n.m.* **1.** ball (of wool, string, etc.). **2.** group (of people); cluster (of bees, caterpillars); *Rac:* **le p.,** the main body (of runners); the bunch. **3.** *Mil:* (*a*) troop (of cavalry), platoon (of tanks, etc.); (*b*) class, party; **p. d'instruction,** training unit; **p. de discipline, de punition,** punishment squad; **p. d'exécution,** firing squad.

pelotonner [p(ə)lɔtɔne] **1.** *v.tr.* to wind (wool, string, etc.) into a ball. **2. se p.,** to curl up (into a ball); to coil, roll, oneself up; to huddle up; **se p. entre les bras de qn,** to snuggle into s.o.'s arms.

pelouse [p(ə)luz] *n.f.* lawn; *Turf:* **la P.,** the public enclosures, the ground within the track.

peluche [p(ə)lyʃ] *n.f.* (*a*) *Tex:* plush; **jouet en p.,** soft toy; teddy bear; (*b*) (piece of) fluff.

peluché [p(ə)lyʃe] *a.* fluffy, shaggy, nappy (material).

pelucher [p(ə)lyʃe] *v.i.* (*of worn material*) to become fluffy, nappy.

pelucheux, -euse [p(ə)lyʃø, -øz] *a.* fluffy; downy.

pelure [p(ə)lyr] *n.f.* (*a*) peel, skin (of apple, onion, etc.), peeling (of vegetables); **p. d'oignon,** dark rosé wine; *Com:* **(papier) p.,** copying paper; (*b*) *F:* outdoor clothes; coat.

pelvien, -ienne [pɛlvjɛ̃, -jɛn] *a. Anat:* pelvic.

pelvis [pɛlvis] *n.m. Anat:* false pelvis.

pénal, -aux [penal, -o] *a.* penal (code); **clause pénale,** penalty clause (in contract).

pénalisation [penalizasjɔ̃] *n.f. Sp:* penalization, penalizing.

pénaliser [penalize] *v.tr. Sp:* to penalize.

pénalité [penalite] *n.f.* **1.** penal system. **2.** *Jur: Sp: etc:* penalty; *Fb:* **coup de pied de p.,** penalty kick.

penalty [penalti] *n.m. Fb:* penalty; *pl. penalties.*

pénates [penat] *n.m.pl.* (*a*) *Rom.Ant:* penates; (*b*) **regagner ses p.,** to return home.

penaud [pəno] *a.* sheepish; **d'un air p.,** sheepishly.

penchant [pɑ̃ʃɑ̃] **1.** *a.* sloping, inclined, leaning (wall, tower). **2.** *n.m.* (*a*) *A: & Lit:* slope; **p. de la colline,** hillside; (*b*) propensity, tendency; leaning (towards sth.); **p. à faire qch.,** inclination to do sth.; **un p. à la boisson,** a fondness, partiality, for drink; **il a un p. pour, à, la paresse,** he tends to be lazy; (*c*) **avoir un p. pour qn,** to be rather fond of s.o.

penché [pɑ̃ʃe] *a.* **1.** leaning; sloping, slanting (handwriting). **2.** stooping; **p. sur le berceau,** bending over the cradle.

pencher [pɑ̃ʃe] **1.** *v.tr.* to bend, lean; **p. une assiette,** to tilt a plate; **p. la tête en avant,** to bend, lean, forward; **p. les épaules,** to stoop. **2.** *v.i.* (*a*) to lean (over); **le navire penche sur le côté,** the ship is listing; **faire p. la balance,** to tip the scales; **le tableau penche vers la droite,** the picture is tilting to the right; (*b*) **p. vers, pour, qch.,** to incline, lean, towards sth.; **p. pour cette solution,** to prefer, favour, *NAm:* favor, this solution. **3. se p.** (*a*) to bend, stoop, lean; **se p. en avant,** to bend forward; **se p. (en, au) dehors,** to lean out; **se p. à, par, la fenêtre,** to lean out of the window; (*b*) **se p. sur un problème,** to look into a problem; **se p. sur qn,** to take care of s.o.

pendable [pɑ̃dabl̩] *a.* (*a*) *A:* (crime) for which the penalty is hanging; (*b*) **cas p.,** reprehensible action; **le cas n'est pas p.,** it's nothing serious; (*c*) outrageous, abominable (trick, etc.).

pendaison [pɑ̃dɛzɔ̃] *n.f.* (*a*) hanging; (*b*) **p. de la crémaillère,** housewarming (party).

pendant[1] [pɑ̃dɑ̃] *a.* **1.** hanging, pendent; dangling (legs); drooping (moustache); **oreilles pendantes,** flap ears, lop ears. **2.** pending, undecided, outstanding (lawsuit, question, etc.); in abeyance.

pendant[2] *n.m.* **1.** pendant; **p. (d'oreille),** drop earring; *Mil:* **p. de ceinturon,** sword-belt sling, frog. **2.** counterpart, match (of picture, etc.); **ces deux tableaux (se) font p.,** these two pictures make a pair.

pendant[3] **1.** *prep.* during; **p. l'été,** during the summer; in summer; **restez là p. quelques minutes,** stay there for a few minutes; **route bordée d'arbres p. un kilomètre,** road lined with trees for a kilometre, *NAm:* killometer. **2.** *conj.phr.* **p. que,** while; whilst; **p. que j'y pense,** while I think of it; **p. que vous y êtes,** while you're about it. **3.** *adv.* **avant la guerre et p.,** before and during the war.

pendard, -arde [pɑ̃dar, -ard] *n. F: A:* rogue; scoundrel.

pendeloque [pɑ̃dlɔk] *n.f.* (*a*) drop earring; (*b*) pendant, crystal (of chandelier).

pendentif [pɑ̃dɑ̃tif] *n.m.* **1.** *Arch:* pendentive. **2.** *Jewel:* pendant.

penderie [pɑ̃dri] *n.f.* wardrobe, (hanging) cupboard; *NAm:* closet.

pendiller [pɑ̃dije] *v.i.* to dangle.

pendoir [pɑ̃dwar] *n.m.* hook (for hanging meat).

pendouiller [pɑ̃duje] *v.i. F:* to hang loosely, untidily; to dangle.

pendre [pɑ̃dr̩] **1.** *v.tr.* (*a*) to hang (sth.) (up); **p. du linge pour le faire sécher,** to hang the washing out to dry; **p. la crémaillère,** to give a housewarming party; *F:* **il est toujours pendu à mes jambes,** he follows me about like a dog; (*b*) to hang (on the gallows); *F:* **qu'il aille se faire p. ailleurs,** let him go hang, go to hell; **je veux être pendu si . . .,** I'll be hanged if . . .. **2.** *v.i.* (*a*) to hang; (*of hair, etc.*) to hang down; **les voiles pendaient le long des mâts,** the sails were flapping idly against the masts; (*b*) **jupe qui pend par derrière,** skirt hanging down, dipping, at the back; (*c*) **cela lui pend sur la tête,** it's hanging over him, threatening him; *F:* **ça lui pend au nez,** he's got it coming to him. **3. se p.** (*a*) to hang oneself; (*b*) **se p. à qch.,** to hang on, cling, to sth.; **se p. au cou de qn,** to hang round s.o.'s neck; to hug s.o.

pendu [pɑ̃dy] **1.** *a.* hanged; hung, hanging; **p. aux jupes de sa mère,** clinging to his mother's skirts; **avoir la langue bien pendue,** to be a great talker; to be very talkative. **2.** *n.* hanged man, woman.

pendulaire [pɑ̃dylɛr] *a.* swinging, pendulous, pendular (motion).

pendule [pɑ̃dyl] **1.** *n.m.* pendulum. **2.** *n.f.* clock; **p. à coucou,** cuckoo clock.

pendulette [pɑ̃dylɛt] *n.f.* small clock; travelling clock.

pêne [pɛn] *n.m.* bolt (of lock); latch.

pénéplaine [peneplɛn] *n.f. Geol:* peneplain.

pénétrabilité [penetrabilite] *n.f.* penetrability.

pénétrable [penetrabl̩] *a.* (*a*) penetrable; (*b*) understandable.

pénétrant [penetrɑ̃] *a.* penetrating; sharp (object); piercing (wind, cold); drenching (rain); pervasive, obtrusive, strong (smell); subtle (poison, scent); searching, keen (glance); acute, discerning (person); shrewd (mind); **plaie pénétrante,** perforating wound.

pénétration [penetrasjɔ̃] *n.f.* (*a*) penetration (of chemical, bullet, etc.); (*b*) penetration, insight; acuteness (of mind); acumen, shrewdness.

pénétré [penetre] *a.* penetrated, impressed, imbued (**de,** with); **il est p. de son importance,** he's filled with, full of, his own importance; **d'un ton p.,** in a voice full of conviction; **d'un air p.,** with an earnest air.

pénétrer [penetre] *v.* **(je pénètre, n. pénétrons; je pénétrerai)** to penetrate. **1.** *v.i.* to enter; **la baïonnette pénétra jusqu'au poumon,** the bayonet penetrated to the lung; **un cambrioleur a pénétré dans la maison,** a burglar broke into the house; **l'eau avait pénétré partout,** the water had got in everywhere; **p. dans les détails,** to go into details. **2.** *v.tr.* (*a*) **la balle pénétra l'os,** the bullet penetrated, pierced, the bone; **p. un secret,** to fathom a secret; **p. la pensée, les intentions, de qn,** to see through s.o.; (*b*) **être pénétré d'un sentiment, d'une idée,** to be imbued with a feeling, an idea. **3. se p.** (*a*) (*of substances*) to combine; (*b*) to become impregnated (**de,** with); to absorb; (*c*) to become imbued (**de,** with); **se p. d'une idée,** to let an idea sink in.

pénible [penibl̩] *a.* **1.** laborious, arduous, hard (task, etc.); laboured, *NAm:* labored, heavy (breathing, style); rough (road); **vie p.,** hard, difficult (life). **2.** painful, distressing (spectacle, news, etc.); **l'idée m'est trop p.,** I can't bear the idea of it; **p. à voir,** painful to see. **3.** *F:* (*of pers.*) difficult; **ce qu'elle est p.!** she's impossible!

péniblement [penibləmɑ̃] *adv.* laboriously, arduously, painfully; with difficulty; **avancer, aller, marcher, p.,** to plod, trudge, along; **respirer p.,** to breathe heavily.

péniche [peniʃ] *n.f. Nau:* pinnace; canal boat, barge; coal barge; lighter; *Mil:* **p. de débarquement,** landing craft.

pénicilline [penisilin] *n.f.* penicillin.

péninsulaire [penɛ̃sylɛr] *a.* peninsular.

péninsule [penɛ̃syl] *n.f.* peninsula; **P. Ibérique,** Iberian Peninsula.

pénis [penis] *n.m. Anat:* penis.

pénitence [penitɑ̃s] *n.f.* **1.** penitence, repentance. **2.** (*a*) penance; **faire p.,** to do penance (**de,** for); (*b*) punishment; **mettre un enfant en p.,** to punish a child, *esp.* to put a child in the corner; **il est en p.,** he's in disgrace; (*c*) *Games:* forfeit.

pénitencier [penitɑ̃sje] *n.m.* **1.** (*R.C.Ch:* penitentiary (priest). **2.** (*a*) penitentiary, reformatory prison; (*b*) convict station.

pénitent, -ente [penitɑ̃, -ɑ̃t] *a. & n.* penitent.

pénitentiaire [penitɑ̃sjɛr] *a.* penitentiary (system).

pénitentiel, -ielle [penitɑ̃sjɛl] **1.** *a.* penitential. **2.** *n.m.* **p.,** penitential (book).

penne [pɛn] *n.f.* (*a*) quill (feather); (*b*) feather (of arrow).

Pennsylvanie [pɑ̃silvani, pɛ̃-] *Pr.n.f. Geog:* Pennsylvania.

pénombre [penɔ̃br̩] *n.f.* (*a*) penumbra; (*b*) half light, semi-darkness, shadowy light; **rester dans la p.,** to remain inconspicuous, in the background.

pensant [pɑ̃sɑ̃] *a.* thinking (man, woman); **bien p.,** orthodox, right thinking; **mal p.,** unorthodox.

pense-bête [pɑ̃sbɛt] *n.m. F:* memory jogger; *pl.* *pense-bêtes.*

pensée[1] [pɑ̃se] *n.f. Bot:* pansy.

pensée[2] *n.f.* **1.** thought; **absorbé, perdu, dans ses pensées,** lost in thought; **se représenter clairement**

qch. par la p., to have a clear conception, a clear idea, of sth.; **il me vint dans la p. que . . .**, the thought occurred to me that . . .; **entrer dans la p. de qn**, to understand what is in s.o.'s mind; **je l'ai fait dans la p., avec la p., que . . .**, I did it with the idea that . . .; **dire sa p.**, to speak one's mind; **saisir la p. de qn**, to grasp s.o.'s meaning; **il partage ma p.**, he shares my opinion; **libre p.**, free thought, free thinking. **2.** thinking; **la p. marxiste**, marxist thought.

penser^1 [pɑ̃se] *v.* to think. **1.** *v.ind.tr.* (*a*) **p. à qn, à qch.**, to think of s.o., sth.; **il pense à elle**, he's thinking of her; **à quoi pensez-vous?** (i) what are you thinking of, about? (ii) how could you (think of such a thing)? **p. tout haut**, to think aloud; **je l'ai fait sans y p.**, I did it without thinking; **pensez-vous!** what an idea! don't you believe it! **est-ce qu'il a donné un bon pourboire?—pensez-vous!—tu penses!** did he give a good tip?—you're joking! no fear! **vous n'y pensez pas!** you don't mean it! **n'y pensez plus**, forget about it; **ah, j'y pense!** by the way! **rien que d'y p., ça me donne des frissons**, I shiver at the mere thought (of it); **p. à faire qch.**, (i) to think of doing sth.; (ii) to remember to do sth.; (*b*) **il me fait p. à mon frère**, he reminds me of my brother. **2.** *v.i.* **manière de p.**, attitude of mind; **il pense par lui-même**, he thinks for himself; **je pense comme vous**, I agree with you; **voilà ma façon de p.**, that's my way of thinking; that's the way I see it; **pensez donc!** just fancy! **3.** *v.i. with cogn.acc.* (*a*) **p. vacances**, to think about holidays; (*b*) **il faut p. européen**, we must think European. **4.** *v.tr.* (*a*) **p. qch.**, (i) to think, believe, sth.; (ii) to imagine, picture, sth.; **je le pensais bien**, I thought as much, I thought so; **je pense que oui, que non**, I think so, I think not; **pensez si j'étais furieux**, you can imagine how angry I was; **je ne savais plus que p.**, I no longer knew what to think; (*b*) **je le pense fou**, I think he's mad; (*c*) **p. qch. de qn, de qch.**, to think sth. of s.o., of sth.; **j'en pense le plus grand bien**, I have a very high opinion of him, her, it; **p. du mal de qn**, to have a poor opinion of s.o.; **je lui ai dit carrément ce que j'en pensais, ce que je pensais, ma façon de p.**, I told him straight what I thought; I gave him a piece of my mind; (*d*) **p. faire qch.** (i) to expect to do sth.; **je pense le voir demain**, I hope to see him tomorrow; (ii) (= FAILLIR) **j'ai pensé mourir de rire**, I nearly died with laughter; (*e*) **p. qch.**, to think sth. out; **les plans ont été mal pensés**, the plans were badly conceived.

penser^2 *n.m. A: & Lit:* thought.

penseur, -euse [pɑ̃sœr, -øz] *n.* thinker; **libre p.**, freethinker.

pensif, -ive [pɑ̃sif, -iv] *a.* thoughtful, pensive.

pension [pɑ̃sjɔ̃] *n.f.* **1.** pension, allowance; **p. de retraite**, retirement, old age, pension; **p. viagère**, life annuity; **p. alimentaire**, (i) living allowance; (ii) maintenance allowance; alimony. **2.** (*a*) (*payment for board (and lodging)*) **être en p. chez qn**, to board with s.o.; **p. entière**, full board; **chambre et p.**, board and lodging; (*b*) **p. de famille**, residential hotel, pension; boarding house. **3.** (private) boarding school.

pensionnaire [pɑ̃sjɔnɛr] *n.* boarder (i) in boarding house, (ii) in boarding school; resident (in hotel); paying guest, lodger (in private house); *F:* patient, inmate (of hospital).

pensionnat [pɑ̃sjɔna] *n.m.* **1.** boarding school. **2.** (school) boarders.

pensionné, -ée [pɑ̃sjɔne] **1.** *a.* pensioned (soldier, employee). **2.** *n.* pensioner.

pensionner [pɑ̃sjɔne] *v.tr.* to pension.

pensivement [pɑ̃sivmɑ̃] *adv.* pensively, thoughtfully.

pensum [pɛ̃sɔm] *n.m. Sch: O:* imposition; lines.

pentagonal, -aux [pɛ̃tagɔnal, -o] *a. Mth:* pentagonal.

pentagone [pɛ̃tagɔn] **1.** *Mth:* (*a*) *a.* pentagonal; (*b*) *n.m.* pentagon. **2.** *Pr.n.m. U.S: Mil:* **le P.**, the Pentagon.

pentamètre [pɛ̃tamɛtr̥] *a. & n.m. Pros:* pentameter.

Pentateuque (le) [ləpɛ̃tatøk] *n.m. B:* the Pentateuch.

pentathlon [pɛ̃tatlɔ̃] *n.m. Sp:* pentathlon.

pente [pɑ̃t] *n.f.* (*a*) slope; incline; gradient, *NAm:* grade; **p. ascendante**, uphill slope, slope up, *NAm:* upslope; rising gradient, *NAm:* upgrade; **p. descendante**, downhill slope, slope down, *NAm:* downslope; falling gradient, *NAm:* downgrade; **à faible, à forte, p.**, gently, steeply, sloping; **colline à vingt-cinq pour cent de p.**, hill with a gradient of one in four; *P.N: Aut:* **p. 10%**, slope of 10%; hill 1 in 10; **en p.**, sloping; shelving; **rue en p.**, steep street; **p. d'une rivière**, fall of a river; *P:* **avoir la dalle en p.**, to be a bit of a boozer; *F:* **être sur une mauvaise p.**, to be on a downward path, a slippery slope, to be going downhill; *Fig:* **remonter la p.**, to get back on one's feet; (*b*) camber (of road); pitch (of roof); *Mth:* slope (of a curve); *Surv: etc:* **angle de p.**, angle of slope; (*c*) *Av:* slope (of flight path).

Pentecôte [pɑ̃tkot] *n.f.* Pentecost; Whitsun(tide); **dimanche de la P.**, Whit Sunday.

penture [pɑ̃tyr] *n.f.* strap hinge (of door, etc.); **p. et gond**, hook and hinge; *pl. Nau:* **pentures du gouvernail**, rudder braces.

pénultième [penyltjɛm] *a. & n.f.* penultimate.

pénurie [penyri] *n.f.* scarcity, dearth, shortage (of money, etc.).

pépé [pepe] *n.m. F:* grandfather; grandad, grandpa, *U.S:* gramp(s).

pépée [pepe] *n.f. P:* girl, bird, chick, *NAm:* broad.

pépère [pepɛr] *F:* **1.** *n.m.* (*a*) **c'est un gros p.**, (i) he's an old fatty; (ii) (*of child*) he's a chubby little chap; (*b*) grandfather; grandad, grandpa, *U.S:* gramp(s). **2.** *a.* (*a*) **un gueuleton p.**, a really good meal, blowout; (*b*) **un petit coin p.**, a nice quiet little spot; **un travail p.**, a cushy little job, number. **3.** *adv. Aut:* **rouler p.**, to potter along.

pépettes, pépètes [pepɛt] *n.f.pl. P:* money, lolly, dough.

pépie [pepi] *n.f.* (*disease of birds*) pip; *F:* **avoir la p.**, to have a terrible thirst, to be parched.

pépiement [pepimɑ̃] *n.m.* cheep(ing), chirp(ing), peep(ing) (of birds).

pépier [pepje] *v.i.* (*of birds*) to cheep, chirp, peep.

pépin^1 [pepɛ̃] *n.m.* **1.** pip (of apple, grape, etc.); **sans pépins**, seedless. **2.** *F:* hitch; **avoir un p.**, to be in trouble, in difficulties.

pépin^2 *n.m. F:* umbrella, brolly.

pépinière [pepinjɛr] *n.f.* **1.** *Hort:* seed bed; nursery (of young trees). **2.** nest, breeding ground.

pépiniériste [pepinjerist] *n.* nurseryman, nursery gardener.

pépite [pepit] *n.f.* nugget (of gold).

pepsine [pɛpsin] *n.f. Bio-Ch:* pepsin.

peptique [pɛptik] *a.* peptic.

peptone [pɛptɔn] *n.f. Physiol: Ch:* peptone.

péquenaud, -aude [pekno, -od] *n. P:* peasant, country bumpkin, yokel.

péquenot [pekno] *n.m. P:* = PÉQUENAUD.

péquiste [pekist] *Fr.C. Pol:* **1.** *a.* pertaining to, of, the *Parti Québécois*. **2.** *n.* member of the *Parti Québécois*.

perçage [pɛrsaʒ] *n.m.* piercing, boring, drilling.

percale [pɛrkal] *n.f. Tex:* percale.

percaline [pɛrkalin] *n.f. Tex:* percaline; *Dressm: etc:* glazed lining; calico.

perçant [pɛrsɑ̃] *a.* piercing, penetrating (eyes,

shriek); shrill (voice); keen, sharp (wits); **vent p.,** biting wind.

perce [pɛrs] *n.f.* **1.** *Tls:* borer, drill, punch. **2.** hole (of wind instrument). **3. mettre en p.,** to broach, to tap (wine, etc.).

percé [pɛrse] *a.* (*a*) pierced, bored (hole, etc.); **p. de vers,** wormeaten (fruit, wood); (*b*) (*of garments, etc.*) in holes; **pantalon p.,** trousers with a hole in the seat; **complot p. à jour,** plot brought to light.

percée [pɛrse] *n.f.* opening. **1.** (*a*) cutting (in a forest); break (in hedge, etc.); glade; vista; **faire une p. dans un bois,** to make an opening in, cut a passage through, a wood; (*b*) breach, gap (in wall). **2.** *Mil: Sp:* breakthrough; **faire une p.,** to break through; **p. technologique,** technological breakthrough. **3.** *Metall:* **p. (de coulée),** (i) tapping (of blast furnace), (ii) tap hole.

percement [pɛrs(ə)mɑ̃] *n.m.* boring (of hole, passage); opening (of street); cutting (of canal); driving (of tunnel).

perce-muraille [pɛrs(ə)myraj] *n.f. Bot:* wall pellitory; *pl. perce-murailles.*

perce-neige [pɛrs(ə)nɛʒ] *n.m. or f.inv. Bot:* snowdrop.

perce-oreille [pɛrsɔrɛj] *n.m. Ent:* earwig; *pl. perce-oreilles.*

perce-pierre [pɛrs(ə)pjɛr] *n.f. Bot:* **1.** samphire, sea fennel. **2.** (white, meadow) saxifrage; *pl. perce-pierres.*

percepteur, -trice [pɛrsɛptœr, -tris] **1.** *a.* perceiving, discerning. **2.** *n.m. Adm:* tax inspector, collector; *F:* tax man.

perceptibilité [pɛrsɛptibilite] *n.f.* perceptibility.

perceptible [pɛrsɛptibl̥] *a.* **1.** perceptible (**à,** by, to); discernible; **p. à l'oreille,** audible. **2.** collectable (tax).

perceptiblement [pɛrsɛptibləmɑ̃] *adv.* perceptibly; audibly.

perceptif, -ive [pɛrsɛptif, -iv] *a.* perceptive.

perception [pɛrsɛpsjɔ̃] *n.f.* **1.** perception (through the senses). **2.** *Adm:* collection, receipt (of taxes, duties, rent); levying (of taxes); **(bureau de) p.,** tax inspector's office, revenue office.

percer [pɛrse] *v.* **(je perçai(s); n. perçons) 1.** *v.tr.* (*a*) to pierce, to go through (sth.); **vous me percez les oreilles,** you're deafening me; **p. un abcès,** to lance an abscess; **p. qn d'un coup de couteau,** to stab s.o.; **le soleil perce les nuages,** the sun is breaking through the clouds; **p. le cœur à qn,** to cut s.o. to the heart; **p. l'avenir,** to foresee the future; **p. un complot,** to uncover a plot; **p. qch. à jour,** to find sth. out; **p. la foule,** to make, elbow, one's way through a crowd; (*b*) to perforate; to make a hole, an opening, in (sth.); to drill, bore (hole); to drive (tunnel); to open (street); to cut (canal); **p. un mur,** to make a hole in a wall; **p. un tonneau,** to broach, tap, a cask; **p. une porte dans un mur,** to make, open, a door in a wall; **se faire p. les oreilles,** to have one's ears pierced. **2.** *v.i.* to pierce; to come, break, through; **le soleil commence à p.,** the sun is coming out; **ses dents percent,** he is cutting his teeth; **l'abcès a percé,** the abscess has burst; **rien n'a percé de leur entretien,** nothing came out of their meeting; **auteur qui commence à p.,** author who is beginning to make a name; **laisser p. ses sentiments,** to show one's feelings.

perceur, -euse [pɛrsœr, -øz] **1.** *n.* (*pers.*) driller; drilling machine operator; puncher (of sheet metal, etc.). **2.** *n.f.* **perceuse,** boring, drilling, machine; drill. **3.** *n.m.* **p. de coffres-forts,** safe breaker.

percevable [pɛrsəvabl̥] *a.* **1.** perceivable. **2.** collectable, leviable (tax).

percevoir [pɛrsəvwar] *v.tr.* (*pr.p.* **percevant;** *p.p.* **perçu;** *pr.ind.* **je perçois, n. percevons, ils perçoivent;** *pr.sub.* **je perçoive, n. percevions, ils perçoivent;** *impf.* **je percevais;** *p.h.* **je perçus;** *fu.* **je percevrai) 1.** to perceive, discern (with the senses, the intellect); **p. un bruit,** to hear, catch, a sound. **2.** to collect (taxes, rents, etc.); to levy (taxes). **3.** to receive, be paid (interest, etc.).

perche[1] [pɛrʃ] *n.f.* (*a*) (thin) pole; **p. à houblon,** hop pole; *Sp:* **saut à la p.,** pole vaulting; *Cin: T.V:* **p. (à son),** boom; **conduire un bateau à la p.,** to punt a boat; **tendre la p. à qn,** to give s.o. a helping hand, a broad hint; (*b*) *F:* tall, lanky, person; beanpole; (*c*) *Rail:* coupling pole.

perche[2] *n.f. Ich:* perch.

percher [pɛrʃe] **1.** *v.i.* (*of birds*) to perch, roost; *F:* **il perche au quatrième,** he lives up on the fourth floor; **où perchez-vous?** where do you hang out? **2.** *v.tr. F:* **p. un vase sur une armoire,** to put, stick, a vase on top of a wardrobe. **3.** (*of bird*) **se p. sur une branche,** to perch on a branch; *F:* **il s'est perché sur le mur pour voir mieux,** he perched himself on the wall to see better.

percheur, -euse [pɛrʃœr, -øz] *a.* perching, roosting (bird).

perchiste [pɛrʃist] *n.* (*a*) pole vaulter; (*b*) *Cin: T.V:* boom operator.

perchlorate [pɛrklɔrat] *n.m. Ch:* perchlorate.

perchlorique [pɛrklɔrik] *a. Ch:* perchloric.

perchoir [pɛrʃwar] *n.m.* (bird's) perch, roost.

perclus [pɛrkly] (*f.* **percluse** [pɛrklyz], *F:* **perclue**) *a.* (*a*) (partly) paralysed, *esp. NAm:* paralyzed; stiff (leg, etc.); **il est p. de sa jambe gauche,** he has lost the use of his left leg; **p. de rhumatismes,** crippled with rheumatism; (*b*) paralysed (with fright, etc.).

perçoir [pɛrswar] *n.m. Tls:* (*a*) punch; drill, borer, broach; (*b*) awl, gimlet.

percolateur [pɛrkɔlatœr] *n.m.* (coffee) percolator.

percussion [pɛrkysjɔ̃] *n.f.* (*a*) percussion; impact; (*b*) *Med:* sounding (by percussion); percussion; (*c*) *Mus:* **instruments à p.,** percussion instruments.

percussionniste [pɛrkysjɔnist] *n. Mus:* percussionist.

percutant [pɛrkytɑ̃] *a.* (*a*) percussive; *Artil:* **obus p.,** *n.m.* **p.,** percussion fuse shell; (*b*) forceful (speech); incisive (style).

percuter [pɛrkyte] **1.** *v.tr.* (*a*) to strike (sth.) sharply; *Sm.a:* **p. l'amorce,** to strike the primer; **l'avion percuta une colline,** the plane crashed into a hillside; (*b*) *Med:* to sound (chest) by percussion; to percuss. **2.** *v.i.* **l'avion percuta contre le sol,** the plane crashed to the ground; **la voiture est allée p. contre un arbre,** the car crashed into a tree.

percuteur [pɛrkytœr] *n.m.* striker, hammer (of gun, fuse); needle (of rifle); firing pin (of machine gun).

percuti-réaction [perkytireaksjɔ̃] *n.f. Med:* percutaneous reaction; *pl. percuti-réactions.*

perdant, -ante [pɛrdɑ̃, -ɑ̃t] **1.** *a.* losing; **billet p.,** blank (ticket, at lottery). **2.** *n.* loser.

perdition [pɛrdisjɔ̃] *n.f.* **1.** *Rel:* perdition; **lieu de p.,** den of vice, of iniquity. **2.** *Nau:* **navire en p.,** ship (i) in distress, (ii) sinking.

perdre [pɛrdr̥] **I.** *v.tr.* **1.** to ruin, destroy; **l'ambition l'a perdu,** ambition was his undoing, his downfall. **2.** to lose; (*a*) **p. son père,** to lose one's father; **p. la partie,** to lose the game; **il perd son pantalon,** his trousers are falling down; **p. la raison, la tête,** *F:* **le nord, la boule,** to go mad; to go round the bend, *NAm:* to go bananas; **p. le fil,** to lose the thread (of the conversation); **p. haleine,** to get out of breath; **faire p. une habitude à qn,** to break s.o. of a habit; **cela se perd facilement,** it's easily lost; **vous ne perdrez rien pour attendre,** you will lose nothing by waiting; **tu ne perds rien pour attendre!** just you wait! **n'avoir rien à p.,** to have nothing to lose; **p. son chemin,** to lose one's way; **perdre son temps,** to waste (one's) time; **faire qch. sans p. de temps,** to do sth. without losing any time; to lose no time in doing sth.; **il n'y a pas de temps, un instant, à p.,** there is no time to lose; **p. du terrain,** to lose ground; **p. pied,** (*of swimmer, etc.*) to get out of one's depth; (*of climber*) to lose one's footing; **p. qn, qch., de vue,** to lose sight of s.o., sth.; **p. une occasion,** to miss (i) an opportunity, (ii) a bargain; (*b*) *Obst:* **elle a perdu les eaux,** her waters have broken. **II.** *v.i* (*a*) **vous n'y perdez rien,** you haven't missed, lost, anything (by it); (*b*) **la marée perd,** the tide is ebbing; (*c*) **fût qui perd,** leaking cask; (*d*) *Nau:* to fall, to drop, astern. **III. se perdre. 1.** to be lost; (*a*) **le navire se perdit corps et biens,** the ship was lost with all hands; (*b*) **se p. dans la foule,** to disappear, lose oneself, in the crowd; **cet usage se perd,** this custom is dying out; **se p. dans ses pensées,** to be lost in thought; (*c*) (*of mechanical power, etc.*) to be wasted, to run to waste; (*of food*) to go bad. **2.** to lose one's way; **il s'est perdu dans le bois,** he got lost in the wood; *F:* **je m'y perds,** I can't make head or tail of it; **il y a des fessées qui se perdent,** he, she, needs a good spanking.

perdreau, -eaux [pɛrdro] *n.m.* young partridge.

perdrix [pɛrdri] *n.f.* partridge; **p. des neiges,** ptarmigan.

perdu [pɛrdy] *a.* **1.** ruined; **ma robe est perdue,** my dress is ruined; **âme perdue,** lost soul; *n.* **crier comme un p.,** to shout like a madman. **2.** lost; **à mes moments perdus, à mes heures perdues,** in my spare time; **il habite un trou p.,** he lives at the back of beyond; **p. dans ses pensées,** lost in thought; **je suis p.,** (i) I'm lost; (ii) I'm totally confused; **ma tête est perdue,** I'm going mad; **c'est peine perdue,** it's a waste of time, of effort; *Com:* **emballage p.,** non-returnable packing. **3.** *adv.phr.* **à corps p.,** without restraint, recklessly; **se jeter à corps p. dans la mêlée,** to hurl oneself into the fray.

père [pɛr] *n.m.* **1.** (*a*) father; **de p. en fils,** from father to son, from generation to generation; *Prov:* **tel p. tel fils,** like father like son; **M. Martin p.,** Mr Martin senior; **p. de famille,** father; family man; **en bon p. de famille,** wisely; *Th:* **p. noble,** heavy father; **nos pères,** our forefathers, our ancestors; *F:* **petit p.,** old chap, *NAm:* old buddy; **le p. Jean,** old John; (*b*) **p. nourricier,** foster father; (*c*) founder, creator. **2.** *Ecc:* father; (*a*) **le Saint-P.,** the Holy Father, the Pope; **p. spirituel,** (i) *Ecc:* father confessor; (ii) spiritual father; **le (Révérend) P. X,** Father X; **mon p.,** father; (*b*) **notre P. qui es aux cieux,** our Father who art in heaven. **3.** *Theol:* **le P., le Fils et le Saint-Esprit,** the Father, the Son, and the Holy Spirit. **4.** *Breed:* sire.

pérégrination [peregrinasjɔ̃] *n.f.* peregrination.

péremption [perɑ̃psjɔ̃] *n.f. Jur:* time limitation (in a suit); lapsing.

péremptoire [perɑ̃ptwar] *a.* **1.** (*a*) peremptory (tone); (*b*) **argument p.,** unanswerable argument. **2.** *Jur:* **délai p.,** strict time limit.

péremptoirement [perɑ̃ptwarmɑ̃] *adv.* peremptorily.

pérenniser [perɛnize] *v.tr.* to perpetuate.

pérennité [perenite] *n.f.* perenniality, everlastingness, perpetuity.

péréquation [perekwasjɔ̃] *n.f. Adm:* equalization (of taxes, salaries); *Rail:* standardizing (of freight charges, tariffs).

perfectibilité [pɛrfɛktibilite] *n.f.* perfectibility.

perfectible [pɛrfɛktibl̩] *a.* perfectible.

perfectif, -ive [pɛrfɛktif, -iv] *a. & n.m. Gram:* perfective.

perfection [pɛrfɛksjɔ̃] *n.f.* (*a*) perfection; **à la p.,** to perfection, perfectly; (*b*) *F:* **notre femme de ménage est une p.,** our daily help's an absolute godsend.

perfectionnement [pɛrfɛksjɔnmɑ̃] *n.m.* **1.** perfecting (of machine, method); improving; further training; **brevet de p.,** patent relating to improvements; *Sch:* **cours de p.,** refresher course. **2.** improvement.

perfectionner [pɛrfɛksjɔne] **1.** *v.tr.* (*a*) to perfect; to bring (sth.) to perfection; (*b*) to improve (machine, method, one's style). **2. se p.,** to improve; to increase one's knowledge; **se p. en allemand,** to improve one's German.

perfectionnisme [pɛrfɛksjɔnism] *n.m.* perfectionism.

perfectionniste [pɛrfɛksjɔnist] *a. & n.* perfectionist.

perfide [pɛrfid] **1.** *a.* treacherous (**envers,** to); perfidious; falsehearted (friend, etc.); false, deceitful (promises, etc.). **2.** *n. A. & Lit:* traitor, deceiver.

perfidement [pɛrfidmɑ̃] *adv.* perfidiously, treacherously, falsely.

perfidie [pɛrfidi] *n.f. Lit:* (*a*) treachery, perfidy, perfidiousness; (*b*) treacherous act.

perforage [pɛrfɔraʒ] *n.m.* punching; perforation; boring.

perforant [pɛrfɔrɑ̃] *a.* perforating, perforative; **obus p.,** armour-piercing shell.

perforateur, -trice [pɛrfɔratœr, -tris] **1.** *a.* perforating, perforative. **2.** (*a*) *n.m.* perforator; punch; *Cmptr:* card punch; (key) punch; **p. de bande,** tape perforator, tape punch; (*b*) *n.* punch card operator. **3.** *n.m. Surg:* perforator. **4.** *n.f.* **perforatrice** (*a*) *Civ.E:* rock drill, driller, borer; drilling machine; (*b*) **(pince) p.,** ticket punch.

perforation [pɛrfɔrasjɔ̃] *n.f.* **1.** (*a*) perforation, perforating; (*b*) *Cmptr:* punching, perforation. **2.** perforation; *Cmptr:* punch (hole).

perforer [pɛrfɔre] *v.tr.* (*a*) to perforate; to bore (through), to drill (material); to punch (leather, etc.); (*b*) *Cmptr:* (i) (*of machine*) to perforate (tape, etc.); to punch hole in (card); (ii) (*of pers.*) to key punch; **carte perforée,** punch card; **bande perforée,** punched card.

perforeuse [pɛrfɔrøz] *n.f.* perforator; card punch.

performance [pɛrfɔrmɑ̃s] *n.f. Sp: etc:* performance.

perfusion [pɛrfyzjɔ̃] *n.f. Med:* perfusion.

pergola [pɛrgɔla] *n.f.* pergola.

péri [peri] *n.* (oriental) peri; genius; fairy.

péricarde [perikard] *n.m. Anat:* pericardium.

péricliter [periklite] *v.i.* (*of business, undertaking*) to be in danger, in jeopardy; **ses affaires périclitent,** his business is about to collapse.

péridot [perido] *n.m. Lap:* peridot, chrysolite.

périgée [periʒe] *n.m. Astr:* perigee.

périglaciaire [periglasjɛr] *a. Geog:* periglacial.

périhélie [perieli] *n.m. Astr:* perihelion.

péril [peril] *n.m.* peril, danger; risk, hazard; **au p. de sa vie,** at the risk of one's life; **en p.,** in danger, in peril; **mettre qch. en p.,** to imperil, endanger, jeopardize, sth.; **à ses risques et périls,** at one's own risk.

périlleusement [perijøzmɑ̃] *adv.* perilously.

périlleux, -euse [perijø, -øz] *a.* perilous, hazardous, dangerous; **saut p.,** somersault.

périmé [perime] *a.* **1.** *Jur:* barred by limitation. **2.** out-of-date (coupon, etc.); expired (bill); (ticket) no longer valid; lapsed (money order, ticket, etc.).

périmer [perime] **1.** *v.i.* (*a*) *Jur:* to lapse, to become out of date; (*b*) **laisser p. un passeport,** to let a passport expire. **2. se p.** (*a*) *Jur:* to lapse; (*b*) (*of passport, ticket*) to expire.

périmètre [perimɛtr̩] *n.m.* (*a*) *Mth:* perimeter, periphery; (*b*) area.

périnée [perine] *n.m. Anat:* perineum.

période [perjɔd] **1.** *n.f.* period (of recurring phenomenon, of cycle); **nombre de périodes par seconde,** frequency (of sound wave, etc.); *Mth:* **p. d'une fraction décimale,** repetend of a (recurring) decimal. **2.** *n.f.* period of time; age, era; **première p. de l'existence,** early stages of life; **longue p. de beau temps,** long spell of fine weather; *Mil:* **p. (d'instruction),** (completion of) training. **3.** *n.f.* (*a*) *Gram: Rh:* period, complete sentence; (*b*) **p. (musicale),** phrase. **4.** *n.m. Lit:* **le plus haut p. (de la gloire, etc.),** the highest point, pitch, degree, the height (of glory, etc.).

périodicité [perjɔdisite] *n.f.* periodicity.

périodique [perjɔdik] **1.** *a.* periodic; periodical, recurrent, recurring (at regular intervals); intermittent; recurrent (fever); **fraction p.,** recurring decimal. **2.** *n.m.* periodical.

périodiquement [perjɔdikmɑ̃] *adv.* periodically; at regular intervals.

périoste [perjɔst] *n.m. Anat:* periosteum.

péripatéticien, -ienne [peripatetisjɛ̃, -jɛn] (*a*) *a.* & *n. Phil:* peripatetic; (*b*) *n.f. F:* **péripatéticienne,** prostitute, street walker.

péripétie [peripesi] *n.f.* **1.** *Lit:* peripet(e)ia; sudden change of fortune (in novel, in life). **2.** *pl.* vicissitudes, ups and downs (of life); mishaps, adventures.

périphérie [periferi] *n.f.* **1.** *Mth:* periphery; circumference. **2.** outskirts (of town).

périphérique [periferik] *a.* peripheral; **boulevard p.,** *n.m.* **p.,** ring road.

périphrase [perifraz] *n.f. Gram:* periphrasis, periphrase, circumlocution.

périphrastique [perifrastik] *a. Gram:* periphrastic; circumlocutory.

périple [peripl̥] *n.m.* (*a*) sea voyage; (*b*) (long) tour; journey.

périr [perir] *v.i.* (*aux.* **avoir**) to perish, to die (unnaturally); to be destroyed; (*of ship*) to be wrecked, lost; (*of empire*) to fall into ruin; **p. noyé,** to drown, be drowned; **faire p. qn,** to kill s.o.; **p. d'ennui, s'ennuyer à p.,** to die of boredom; **son nom ne périra pas,** his name will live (on); **p. victime d'un accident,** to die as a result of an accident.

périscope [periskɔp] *n.m.* periscope.

périscopique [periskɔpik] *a.* periscopic.

périssable [perisabl̥] *a.* perishable.

périssoire [periswar] *n.f.* (single-seater river) canoe.

péristaltique [peristaltik] *a. Physiol:* peristaltic (motion).

péristaltisme [peristaltism] *n.m. Physiol:* peristalsis.

péristyle [peristil] *n.m. Arch:* peristyle.

péritoine [peritwan] *n.m. Anat:* peritoneum.

péritonite [peritonit] *n.f. Med:* peritonitis.

perle [pɛrl] *n.f.* **1.** (*a*) pearl; **p. fine,** real pearl; **p. de culture,** cultured pearl; **fil de perles,** string of pearls; **nacre de p.,** mother-of-pearl; **jeter des perles aux pourceaux,** to cast pearls before swine; **ma bonne est une p.,** my maid is a gem, a treasure; (*b*) *Sch:* mistake, howler. **2.** (*a*) bead (of glass, metal, etc.); (*b*) **p. de rosée,** dewdrop.

perlé [pɛrle] *a.* **1.** (*a*) resembling pearls; pearly (teeth, etc.); **riz p.,** husked, polished, rice; **orge p.,** pearl barley; (*b*) set with pearls, pearled; (*c*) beaded; (*d*) **rire p.,** rippling laughter. **2.** (*of needlework, musical execution, etc.*) tastefully, exquisitely, done.

perler [pɛrle] **1.** *v.tr.* to execute (piece of embroidery, of music) to perfection. **2.** *v.i.* (*of tears, sweat, etc.*) to form in beads; **la sueur perlait sur son front,** beads of perspiration stood out on his forehead.

perlier, -ière [pɛrlje, -jɛr] *a.* containing, producing, pearls; pearl-bearing; **huître perlière,** pearl oyster.

perlimpinpin [pɛrlɛ̃pɛ̃pɛ̃] *n.m.* **poudre de p.,** quack powder, wonder(-working) powder.

permanence [pɛrmanɑ̃s] *n.f.* **1.** permanence; **assemblée en p.,** permanent assembly; **en p.,** permanently; continuously. **2. p. électorale,** (parliamentary candidate's) committee rooms; **p. de police,** police station open night and day; **la p. est assurée le dimanche,** there is someone on duty on Sundays; **être de p.,** to be on duty, on call. **3.** *Sch:* = prep. room.

permanent [pɛrmanɑ̃] **1.** *a.* permanent (court, etc.); standing (order, committee); continuous (performance); *Cin:* **p. de 2 heures à 11 heures,** continuous showings from 2 o'clock till 11 o'clock. **2.** *n.f. Hairdr:* **permanente,** permanent wave, *F:* perm. **3.** *n.m. Pol:* official, permanent representative.

permanganate [pɛrmɑ̃ganat] *n.m. Ch:* permanganate.

perme [pɛrm] *n.f.* (= PERMISSION) *Mil: F:* leave.

perméabilité [pɛrmeabilite] *n.f.* permeability, perviousness; susceptibility (to influence, etc.).

perméable [pɛrmeabl̥] *a.* **1.** permeable, pervious (**à,** to). **2.** sensitive, susceptible (**à,** to).

permettre [pɛrmɛtr̥] *v.* (*conj. like* METTRE) **1.** *v.tr.* to permit, allow; **p. qch. à qn,** to allow s.o. sth.; **p. à qn de faire qch.,** to allow s.o. to do sth.; to let s.o. do sth.; to give s.o. permission to do sth.; **mes moyens ne me le permettent pas,** I can't afford it; **est-il permis d'entrer?** may I come in? **s'il est permis de s'exprimer ainsi,** if I, we, may say so; **autant qu'il est permis d'en juger,** as far as one can tell; **il se croit tout permis,** he thinks he can do anything he likes; **il n'est pas permis à tout le monde de . . .,** not everyone can, is able to . . .; not everyone is capable of . . .; **permettez-moi de vous dire . . .,** may I be allowed to say that . . .; excuse me, but . . .; **permettez!** excuse me! not so fast! if you don't mind! **vous permettez?** may I? do you mind? **si le temps le permet,** weather permitting. **2. se p.** (*a*) **se p. de faire qch.,** to take the liberty of doing sth.; to venture to do sth.; **je me permets d'attirer votre attention sur . . .,** I venture to draw, take the liberty of drawing, your attention to . . .; (*b*) **se p. qch.,** to allow oneself, to indulge in, sth., **il se permet bien des choses,** he takes a lot of liberties.

permis [pɛrmi] **1.** *a.* allowed, permitted; lawful; allowable, permissible. **2.** *n.m. Adm:* permit; licence; **p. de chasse,** shooting licence; game licence; **p. de séjour (pour des étrangers),** residence permit; **p. d'inhumer,** burial certificate; **p. de construire,** planning permission; building licence; *Aut:* **p. (de conduire),** driving (i) licence, (ii) test.

permissif, -ive [pɛrmisif, -iv] *a.* (*a*) *Rail:* **bloc p.,** permissive block; (*b*) permissive (attitude, etc.).

permission [pɛrmisjɔ̃] *n.f.* (*a*) permission, leave; **demander, donner, la p. de faire qch.,** to ask, give, permission to do sth.; **il n'a pas même demandé la p.,** he didn't even ask permission; **avec votre p.,** if I may say so; I'm sorry, excuse me, but . . .; (*b*) *Mil: etc:* leave (of absence); short leave; (*certificate*) pass; **en p.,** on leave; **il s'est marié pendant sa p.,** he got married while on leave.

permissionnaire [pɛrmisjɔnɛr] *n.m.* **1.** person possessing a permit; licence holder. **2.** *Mil: etc:* man on leave; *Navy:* liberty man; *a.* **officier p.,** officer on leave.

permutabilité [pɛrmytabilite] *n.f.* permutability, interchangeability.

permutable [pɛrmytabl̥] *a.* permutable, interchangeable.

permutation [pɛrmytasjɔ̃] *n.f.* **1.** exchange of posts; *Mil:* transfer. **2.** *Mth: etc:* permutation; transposition (of figures, letters). **3.** *Ling:* metathesis.

permuter [pɛrmyte] **1.** *v.tr.* (*a*) *O:* to exchange (post) (**avec qn,** with s.o.); (*b*) *Mth: etc:* to permute. **2.** *v.i.* to exchange posts (with colleague).

pernicieusement [pɛrnisjøzmɑ̃] *adv.* perniciously.

pernicieux, -ieuse [pɛrnisjø, -jøz] *a.* pernicious, injurious, harmful.

péroné [perɔne] *n.m. Anat:* fibula.

péroraison [perɔrɛzɔ̃] *n.f.* peroration.

pérorer [perɔre] *v.i.* to hold forth; to speechify, spout.

Pérou (le) [ləperu] *Pr.n.m. Geog:* Peru; *Fig:* **gagner le P.,** to make a big fortune; **ce n'est pas le P.,** it's no great catch, it's not highly paid.

peroxyde [pɛrɔksid] *n.m. Ch:* peroxide.

perpendiculaire [pɛrpɑ̃dikylɛr] **1.** *a. Mth: etc:* perpendicular (**à, sur,** to); plumb, upright. **2.** *n.f.* **tirer une p.,** to drop, draw, a perpendicular (**à, sur,** to).

perpendiculairement [pɛrpɑ̃dikylɛrmɑ̃] *adv.* perpendicularly; **p. à,** perpendicular to.

perpète, perpette (à) [apɛrpɛt] *adv.phr. P:* for ever; **condamné à p.,** sentenced for life; **jusqu'à p.,** till the cows come home.

perpétration [pɛrpetrasjɔ̃] *n.f.* perpetration.

perpétrer [pɛrpetre] *v.tr.* (**je perpètre; je perpétrerai**) to perpetrate (crime, etc.).

perpétuation [pɛrpetɥasjɔ̃] *n.f.* perpetuation.

perpétuel, -elle [pɛrpetɥɛl] *a.* (*a*) perpetual; everlasting; permanent (secretary, etc.); **rente perpétuelle,** rent in perpetuity; perpetuity; **mouvement p.,** perpetual motion; (*b*) constant, endless (strife, chatter); **commentaire p.,** running commentary.

perpétuellement [pɛrpetɥɛlmɑ̃] *adv.* (*a*) perpetually, everlastingly; (*b*) constantly.

perpétuer [pɛrpetɥe] **1.** *v.tr.* to perpetuate; to carry on (name, etc.); **p. le souvenir de qn,** to keep s.o.'s memory alive. **2. se p.,** to remain, survive; to become established; **se p. dans son œuvre,** to live on in one's work.

perpétuité [pɛrpetɥite] *n.f.* perpetuity; endlessness; **à p.,** in perpetuity, for ever; (penal servitude) for life.

perplexe [pɛrplɛks] *a.* **1.** perplexed, puzzled, confused.

perplexité [pɛrplɛksite] *n.f.* perplexity; **être dans la plus complète p.,** to be completely baffled, utterly perplexed.

perquisition [pɛrkizisjɔ̃] *n.f. Jur:* thorough search or inquiry; **mandat de p.,** search warrant; **faire une p. chez qn,** to search s.o.'s premises.

perquisitionner [pɛrkizisjɔne] *v.i. Jur:* to make, conduct, carry out, a search (of premises, etc.); **p. au domicile de qn,** to search s.o.'s house.

perré [pere] *n.m. Civ.E:* stone pitching, facing (of road, embankment).

perron [pɛrɔ̃] *n.m. Arch:* (flight of) steps (leading to building); perron; *NAm:* stoop.

perroquet [pɛrɔkɛ] *n.m.* **1.** (*a*) *Orn:* parrot; **répéter qch. comme un p.,** to repeat sth. parrot fashion, like a parrot; (*b*) (i) absinthe; (ii) pastis with mint. **2.** *Nau:* topgallant (sail).

perruche [pɛryʃ] *n.f.* **1.** *Orn:* (*a*) parakeet, small (long-tailed) parrot; (*b*) hen parrot; (*c*) **p. (ondulée),** budgerigar. **2.** *Nau:* mizzen topgallant sail.

perruque [pɛryk] *n.f.* (*a*) wig; *Hist:* periwig, peruke; (*b*) *Fish:* tangled line; *F:* bird's nest.

perruquier, -ière [pɛrykje, -jɛr] *n.* wig maker.

pers [pɛr] *a.* sea-green, grey, greenish-blue, blue-green.

persan, -ane [pɛrsɑ̃, -an] **1.** *a. & n. Geog:* Persian. **2.** *n.m. Ling:* Persian. **3.** *a. Z:* **chat p.,** Persian cat.

Perse [pɛrs] **1.** *Pr.n.f. Geog:* Persia; **tapis de P.,** Persian rug, carpet. **2.** *a. & n. A.Geog:* (native, inhabitant) of ancient Persia; Persian. **3.** *n.m. Ling: A:* Persian. **4.** *n.f. Tex:* chintz.

persécuté, -ée [pɛrsekyte] **1.** *a. & n.* persecuted (person). **2.** *n.* sufferer from persecution mania.

persécuter [pɛrsekyte] *v.tr.* (*a*) to persecute; (*b*) to importune, harass, pester.

persécuteur, -trice [pɛrsekytœr, -tris] **1.** *n.* persecutor. **2.** *a.* persecuting.

persécution [pɛrsekysjɔ̃] *n.f.* (*a*) persecution; *Med:* **manie, folie, délire, de p.,** persecution mania; (*b*) *occ.* importunity.

persévérance [pɛrseverɑ̃s] *n.f.* perseverance.

persévérant [pɛrseverɑ̃] *a.* persevering.

persévérer [pɛrsevere] *v.i.* (**je persévère, n. persévérons; je persévérerai**) to persevere (**dans,** in); **il n'a guère persévéré,** he didn't show much perseverance.

persicaire [pɛrsikɛr] *n.f. Bot:* persicaria, lady's thumb.

persienne [pɛrsjɛn] *n.f.* (slatted) shutter.

persiflage [pɛrsiflaʒ] *n.m.* banter; mockery, mocking.

persifler [pɛrsifle] *v.tr.* to ridicule (s.o.); to make fun of (s.o.).

persifleur, -euse [pɛrsiflœr, -øz] **1.** *n.* banterer; mocker. **2.** *a.* derisive, mocking (tone, etc.).

persil [pɛrsi] *n.m. Bot:* parsley.

persillade [pɛrsijad] *n.f. Cu:* (*a*) beef salad (seasoned with chopped parsley, etc); (*b*) sauce seasoned with parsley, garlic, etc.

persillé [pɛrsije] *a.* **1.** veined (cheese); **fromage à pâte persillée,** blue cheese. **2.** (*of meat*) marbled. **3.** sprinkled with chopped parsley.

persique [pɛrsik] *a.* (ancient) Persian; *Geog:* **le Golfe P.,** the Persian Gulf.

persistance [pɛrsistɑ̃s] *n.f.* **1.** persistence, persistency (**à faire qch.,** in doing sth.); **avec p.,** persistently; **p. dans le mensonge,** persistent lying. **2.** persistence, continuance (of fever, etc.).

persistant [pɛrsistɑ̃] *a.* **1.** persistent (efforts, etc.). **2.** lasting, enduring (perfume, etc.); *Bot:* (*of leaves*) persistent, indeciduous.

persister [pɛrsiste] *v.i.* to persist. **1. il faut p.,** you must persevere, keep going, keep it up; **p. à faire qch.,** to persist in doing sth.; **il y persiste,** he persists in it; he sticks to it. **2. la fièvre persiste,** the fever continues.

personnage [pɛrsɔnaʒ] *n.m.* (*a*) personage; person of rank, of distinction; **p. connu,** celebrity; **un grand p.,** a great figure; **les personnages de l'histoire,** the great names in history; **il est devenu un p.,** he's become quite an important person, *F:* quite a big shot; (*b*) *Pej:* person, individual; **c'est un triste p.,** he's a poor specimen; (*c*) (public) image (of politician, etc.); (*d*) character (in play, novel); **personnages,** dramatis personae; (*e*) figure (in a painting).

personnalisation [pɛrsɔnalizasjɔ̃] *n.f.* personalization.

personnaliser [pɛrsɔnalize] *v.tr.* to personalize; to give a personal touch to (a room, etc.).

personnalité [pɛrsɔnalite] *n.f.* personality. **1.** individuality, individual characteristics. **2.** person, personage, personality; **c'est une p.,** he's an important man, *F:* he's somebody.

personne [pɛrsɔn] **1.** *n.f.* person; (*a*) (*individual*) **la p. dont je parlais,** the person of whom I was speaking; **une assemblée de trois cents personnes,** an assembly of three hundred people; **une tierce p.,** a third party; **cela coûte 3 francs par p.,** it costs 3 francs per head; **une p. âgée,** an elderly person; **grande p.,** adult, grown-up; *Jur:* **personnes physiques ou morales,** individual and legal entities; **erreur sur la p.,** mistaken identity; **personnes à la charge,** dependants; **la p. et l'œuvre,** the man and his work; (*b*) (*one's own self*) **être satisfait, faire grand cas, de sa**

(petite) p., to be self-satisfied, to think no small beer of oneself; **en p.,** in person, personally; **le roi est venu en p.,** the king came in person; **il est la bonté en p.,** he is kindness itself, kindness personified; (*c*) **elle est bien de sa p.,** she's very attractive, good-looking; **exposer sa p.,** to expose oneself to danger; to risk death; (*d*) *Gram:* **écrire à la troisième p. du singulier,** to write in the third person singular. **2.** *pron.indef. m.inv.* (*a*) anyone, anybody; **il le sait aussi bien, mieux, que p.,** nobody knows it better than he does; **je ne dois rien à p.,** I don't owe anything to anyone; I don't owe anyone a penny; (*b*) (*with* **ne** *expressed or understood*) no one, nobody; **p. n'est venu,** nobody has come; **qui est là?—p.,** who's there?—nobody; **que p. ne sorte,** nobody is to leave; **il n'y a p. de blessé,** nobody has been injured; there were no casualties; **p. d'autre n'était à bord,** there was no one else on board; **dans cette maison p. ne se connaissait,** in this house no one knew anyone else; (*c*) **sans nommer p.,** without naming anybody, naming no names.

personnel, -elle [pɛrsɔnɛl] **1.** *a.* (*a*) personal (letter, business, interest, *Gram:* pronoun); not transferable (ticket, pass); confidential (letter, etc.); **objets personnels,** personal belongings; **fortune personnelle,** private means, income; (*b*) **intérêt p.,** self-interest; (*c*) selfish. **2.** *n.m.* (*a*) personnel, staff (of institution, school, firm); workforce; employees; **p. de bureau,** clerical staff, office staff, secretarial staff; **p. réduit,** reduced staff, skeleton staff; **faire partie du p. de . . .,** to be on the staff of . . .; **manquer de p.,** to be understaffed; (*b*) *Mil: etc:* personnel, manpower; *Navy:* complement; *Av:* **p. au sol,** *F:* **p. rampant,** ground personnel, staff; ground crew.

personnellement [pɛrsɔnɛlmɑ̃] *adv.* personally.

personification [pɛrsɔnifikasjɔ̃] *n.f.* personification; embodiment.

personnifier [pɛrsɔnifje] *v.tr.* (*impf. & pr.sub.* **n. personnifiions, v. personnifiiez**) to personify (inanimate object, virtue, vice, etc.); to impersonate; **elle personnifie toute la bonté humaine,** she is the embodiment, personification, of all human kindness; **il personnifie son pays,** he typifies his country.

perspectif, -ive [pɛrspɛktif, -iv] **1.** *a.* perspective (plan). **2.** *n.f.* **perspective** (*a*) *Art: etc:* (linear) perspective; **perspective à vol d'oiseau,** bird's-eye view (of country, etc.); **dessin en perspective,** drawing in perspective; (*b*) outlook, view, prospect; **en perspective,** in the future; **avoir qch. en perspective,** to have sth. in view; **j'envisage avec plaisir la perspective de le revoir,** I am looking forward to seeing him again; **perspectives d'avenir,** future prospects; (*c*) viewpoint; **dans une p. marxiste,** from the marxist point of view.

perspicace [pɛrspikas] *a.* perspicacious, shrewd.

perspicacité [pɛrspikasite] *n.f.* perspicacity, insight, acumen, shrewdness.

persuadé [pɛrsɥade] *a.* persuaded, convinced, sure (**de,** of; **que,** that).

persuader [pɛrsɥade] *v.tr. & pr.* **1.** (*a*) *Lit:* **p. qch. à qn,** to persuade s.o. of sth., to make s.o. believe sth.; (*b*) **ils se sont persuadé que . . .,** they are convinced that . . .. **2. p. qn,** to persuade, convince, s.o.; **p. qn de qch., de faire qch.,** to persuade, convince, s.o. of sth.; to persuade s.o. to do sth.; **j'ai fini par les p.,** in the end I convinced them, persuaded them, talked them round. **3. p. à qn de faire qch.,** to persuade, induce, s.o. to do sth.

persuasif, -ive [pɛrsɥazif, -iv] *a.* persuasive (manner); convincing (language).

persuasion [pɛrsɥazjɔ̃] *n.f.* **1.** persuasion. **2.** conviction, belief.

perte [pɛrt] *n.f.* **1.** ruin, destruction; **il court à sa p.,** he is heading for disaster; *Nau:* **p. corps et biens,** loss of vessel with all hands. **2.** loss (of money, relative, lawsuit, sight, reason, etc.); **pertes et profits,** profit and loss; **vendre qch. à p.,** to sell sth. at a loss; **être en p.,** to be out of pocket; **p. sèche,** dead loss; **à p. de vue,** as far as the eye can see; **p. de temps,** waste of time; **dépense en pure p.,** wasteful expenditure. **3.** (*a*) loss, leakage; **p. de chaleur,** loss of heat; *El:* **p. de charge,** drop in voltage; **p. à la terre,** earth leakage; (*b*) *Med:* **pertes (de sang),** flooding; **pertes blanches,** vaginal discharge, leucorrhoea.

pertinemment [pɛrtinamɑ̃] *adv.* **1.** pertinently, to the point. **2. savoir qch. p.,** to know sth. for a fact.

pertinence [pɛrtinɑ̃s] *n.f.* pertinence, pertinency, appositeness, relevance.

pertinent [pɛrtinɑ̃] *a.* pertinent, apposite, relevant (**à,** to).

pertuis [pɛrtɥi] *n.m.* **1.** sluice. **2.** *Geog:* (*a*) narrows (of a river); (*b*) strait(s), (narrow) channel.

perturbateur, -trice [pɛrtyrbatœr, -tris] **1.** *a.* disturbing, upsetting. **2.** *n.* disturber; troublemaker.

perturbation [pɛrtyrbasjɔ̃] *n.f.* perturbation; disruption; disturbance; **p. (atmosphérique),** (atmospheric) disturbance; *Ind: etc:* **p. dans le service,** breakdown; technical hitch.

perturber [pɛrtyrbe] *v.tr.* to disrupt (public services, etc.); to disturb; *Astr:* to perturb.

péruvien, -ienne [peryvjɛ̃, -jɛn] *a. & n. Geog:* Peruvian.

pervenche [pɛrvɑ̃ʃ] *n.f.* **1.** *Bot:* periwinkle; *inv.* **(bleu) p.,** periwinkle blue. **2.** *F:* (woman) traffic warden.

pervers, -erse [pɛrvɛr, -ɛrs] **1.** *a.* perverse; perverted; depraved; **goûts p.,** depraved tastes; **conseils p.,** evil advice. **2.** *n.* depraved person; pervert.

perversion [pɛrvɛrsjɔ̃] *n.f.* (*a*) perversion (of taste, morals); (*b*) warping (of the mind); (*c*) **p. sexuelle,** sexual perversion.

perversité [pɛrvɛrsite] *n.f.* perversity, depravity.

perverti, -ie [pɛrvɛrti] *a. & n.* perverted, depraved (person); pervert.

pervertir [pɛrvɛrtir] **1.** *v.tr.* to pervert (person, taste, meaning); to deprave; to corrupt. **2. se p.,** to become perverted, depraved, corrupted.

pesage [pəzaʒ] *n.m.* **1.** weighing. **2.** *Turf:* (*a*) weigh-in; (*b*) weighing room; (*c*) enclosure.

pesamment [pəzamɑ̃] *adv.* heavily; **marcher p.,** to walk with a heavy tread.

pesant [pəzɑ̃] **1.** *a.* heavy, weighty; ponderous, clumsy (style, writer); sluggish (mind); deep (sleep); **marcher à pas pesants,** to walk heavily. **2.** *n.m.* **cela vaut son p. d'or,** it is worth its weight in gold.

pesanteur [pəzɑ̃tœr] *n.f.* **1.** weight; *Ph:* gravity; **p. spécifique,** specific gravity. **2.** (*a*) heaviness; **j'ai une p. d'estomac,**there is something lying heavy on my stomach; (*b*) inelegance, unwieldiness (of movement, walk); (*c*) slowness, sluggishness (of mind).

pèse-alcool [pɛzalkɔl] *n.m.* alcoholometer; *pl. pèse-alcools.*

pèse-bébé [pɛzbebe] *n.m.* baby scales; *pl. pèse-bébés.*

pesée [pəze] *n.f.* **1.** (*a*) weighing; *Box: Turf:* weigh-in; **faire la p. de qch.,** to weigh sth.; (*b*) amount weighed at one time. **2.** force, leverage, effort; **exercer une p. sur une porte,** to try to force a door.

pèse-lait [pɛzlɛ] *n.m.inv.* lactometer.

pèse-lettre(s) [pɛzlɛtr̥] *n.m.* letter scales; *pl. pèse-lettres.*

pèse-personne [pɛzpɛrsɔn] *n.m.* (bathroom) scales; *pl. pèse-personnes.*

peser [pəze] *v.* **(je pèse, n. pesons; je pèserai) 1.** *v.tr.* to weigh (parcel, etc.); **p. ses paroles,** to weigh one's words; to think before one speaks; **réponse bien pesée,** considered, careful, answer; **se p.,** *Sp:* **se faire**

p., to weigh oneself; to weigh in. **2.** *v.i.* (*a*) to weigh; to have weight; to be heavy; **il ne pèse pas lourd,** (i) he doesn't weigh much; (ii) *Fig:* he doesn't count for much; **paquet qui pèse deux kilos,** parcel weighing two kilos; **aliment qui pèse sur l'estomac,** food that lies heavy on the stomach; **un silence pesait sur l'assemblée,** a heavy silence hung over the meeting; **le temps lui pèse,** time hangs heavy on his hands; **une lourde responsabilité pèse sur lui,** he is weighed down by a heavy responsibility; **ça lui pèse sur la conscience,** it lies heavy on his conscience; (*b*) (*of argument, etc.*) to carry weight; (*c*) **p. sur, contre, qch.**, to bear on, press on, against, sth.; **p. sur un mot,** to lay stress on, to stress, a word.

pèse-vin [pɛzvɛ̃] *n.m.* oenometer; *pl. pèse-vins.*

peson [pəzɔ̃] *n.m.* balance.

pessaire [pesɛr] *n.m. Med:* pessary.

pesse [pɛs] *n.f.*, **pessereau** [pɛsro] *n.m. Bot:* horse tail, equisetum.

pessimisme [pesimism] *n.m.* pessimism.

pessimiste [pesimist] **1.** *a.* pessimistic. **2.** *n.* pessimist.

peste [pɛst] *n.f.* (*a*) plague, pestilence; **p. bubonique, noire,** bubonic plague, *Hist:* the Black Death; *F:* **fuir qch., qn, comme la p.,** to avoid sth., s.o., like the plague; *Lit:* **p.!** good gracious! heavens! *A: & Lit:* **p. soit du vieux fou!** a plague on the old fool! (*b*) (*of child*) pest, nuisance; **petite p.,** little devil, pest.

pester [pɛste] *v.i.* **p. contre qn, qch.,** to storm, curse, rave, at s.o., sth.; **il pestait,** he was cursing.

pesticide [pɛstisid] **1.** *a.* pesticidal. **2.** *n.m.* pesticide.

pestiféré, -ée [pɛstifere] *a. & n.* plague-stricken (person); plague victim; **fuir qn comme un p.,** to avoid s.o. like the plague.

pestilence [pɛstilɑ̃s] *n.f.* stench, stink.

pestilentiel, -elle [pɛstilɑ̃sjɛl] *a.* stinking, f(o)etid.

pet [pɛ] *n.m. P:* (*a*) breaking of wind; fart; **faire un p.,** to break wind; to fart; *F:* **ça ne vaut pas un p. (de lapin),** it isn't worth a damn; (*b*) **il va y avoir du p.,** there's going to be trouble, a nice bit of scandal; **p.! le voilà!** look out! he's coming! **faire le p.,** to be on the watch, on the lookout; (*c*) [pɛt] **ta voiture a pris un p.,** your car's taken a bash.

pétainiste [petenist] *a. & n. Hist:* follower of Pétain, Pétainist.

pétale [petal] *n.m. Bot:* petal.

pétanque [petɑ̃k] *n.f.* (*in the Midi*) game of bowls.

pétant [petɑ̃] *a. P:* **à neuf heures pétantes,** on the stroke, dot, of nine.

pétarade [petarad] *n.f.* (*a*) (*of horse*) (succession of) farts; (*b*) crackling (of fireworks, firearms); (*c*) *I.C.E:* backfiring, backfire.

pétarader [petarade] *v.i.* (*a*) (*of horse*) to let off a succession of farts; (*b*) (*of fireworks, firearms*) to crackle; (*c*) *I.C.E:* to backfire.

pétard [petar] *n.m.* **1.** (*a*) *Mil:* petard, explosive charge; (*b*) *Min:* shot, blast; (*c*) *Rail:* detonator, fog signal; (*d*) (*firework*) cracker, banger; **faire partir un p.,** to let off a banger; (*e*) *P:* revolver, gat. **2.** *F:* (*a*) noise, din, racket; **il va y avoir du p.,** there's going to be a hell of a row; **faire du p.,** to raise a stink; (*b*) **être en p.,** to be in a flaming temper. **3.** *P:* backside, bum; *NAm:* ass, fanny.

pétaudière [petodjɛr] *n.f.* disorderly meeting; bedlam; bear garden.

pet-de-nonne [pɛd(ə)nɔn] *n.m. Cu:* (type of) fritter; *pl. pets-de-nonne.*

péter [pete] *v.* **(je pète, n. pétons; je péterai) 1.** *v.i.* (*a*) *P:* to break wind, to fart; **il l'a envoyé p.,** he told him to go to hell; **p. plus haut que le cul, plus haut que son derrière,** (i) to show off, swank; to be above oneself; (ii) to try to bite off more than one can chew; (*b*) (*of burning wood, etc.*) to crack, crackle; (*of cork, etc.*) to pop; (*of string, etc.*) to break, bust; **tous les boutons étaient prêts à p.,** all the buttons were about to burst off. **2.** *v.tr.* (*a*) *F:* **p. du feu, des flammes,** to be bursting with energy, with vitality; **ça va p. des flammes,** there's going to be a hell of a row; (*b*) *P:* to break, bust (sth.); **il s'est pété la gueule,** he had an accident.

pète(-)sec [pɛtsɛk] *n.m.inv. F:* martinet; disciplinarian.

péteux, -euse [petø, -øz] *n. P:* coward; yellow-belly.

pétillant [petijɑ̃] *a.* crackling (fire); semi-sparkling (wine); bubbly, fizzy (water); sparkling (eyes, wit); sprightly (wit).

pétillement [petijmɑ̃] *n.m.* crackling (of burning wood); sparkling, fizzing, bubbling (of champagne); sparkling (of the eyes).

pétiller [petije] *v.i.* (*of burning wood*) to crackle; (*of drink*) to sparkle, fizz, bubble; (*of eyes*) to sparkle; **p. de joie,** to bubble over with joy; **p. d'esprit,** to sparkle with wit.

pétiole [pesjɔl] *n.m. Bot:* petiole, leaf stalk.

petiot, -ote [pətjo, -ɔt] *a. & n. F:* tiny, wee (child); **ma petiote,** my little girl; **viens ici, p.,** come here, little chap.

petit, -ite [p(ə)ti, -it] *a. & n.* **1.** *a.* (*a*) small; little; **un p. homme,** a little man; **c'est un homme p.,** he's small, short; **une toute petite maison,** a tiny little house; **p. bois,** kindling wood; **petite distance,** short distance; **mes chaussures sont trop petites,** my shoes are too small (for me); **en p.,** on a small scale, in miniature; **p. à p.,** little by little, bit by bit; gradually; **se faire tout p.,** (i) to make oneself as small, as inconspicuous, as possible; (ii) to cower (**devant,** before, in front of); **le monde est p.,** it's a small world; *F:* **le p. coin,** the toilet, the loo, *U.S:* the john; (*b*) **un p. coup de rouge,** a nice drop of red wine; **p. misérable!** little wretch! **mais ma petite Louise . . .,** but my dear Louise . . .; **p. ami, petite amie,** boyfriend, girlfriend; (*c*) lesser, minor; **les petits talents,** the lesser talents; *Sch:* **les petites classes,** the lower forms; **la petite industrie,** light industry; *Com:* **petite caisse,** petty cash; *Comest:* **petits fours,** petits fours; **petits pois,** (garden) peas; **p. salé** = streaky bacon. **2.** *a.* (*a*) small, insignificant, unimportant, petty; minor; **p. commerçant,** small shopkeeper; **les petits propriétaires,** the small landowners; **petites routes,** minor roads; **ce n'est pas une petite affaire,** that's no small matter; **p. accident,** minor accident; **j'ai un p. rhume,** I've a slight cold, a bit of a cold; **les petites gens,** people in humble circumstances; **mon p. frère,** my little brother; **p. cousin, petite cousine,** second cousin; (*b*) feeble, poor, delicate; **il a une petite santé,** he's never really well. **3.** *a.* mean, petty; ungenerous; **c'est un p. esprit,** he's got a small mind. **4.** (*a*) *a.* **p. enfant,** little child; **petite fille,** little girl; **un p. Anglais,** an English boy; **les petits Thomas,** the Thomas children; (*b*) *n.* little boy; little girl; **pauvre petit(e),** poor little thing; *Sch:* **les petits,** the juniors; *F:* (*term of affection*) (*to woman*) **bonjour, mon p.,** good morning, my dear; (*c*) *n.m.* young (of animal); **petits du chien, du chat,** (dog's) puppies, (cat's) kittens; **faire des petits,** to have young; (*of bitch*) to pup, to whelp; (*of lion, etc.*) to whelp; (*of sow*) to farrow; (*of cat*) to kitten; (*of wolf*) to cub; *F:* (*of money*) to increase, multiply.

petit-bourgeois, petite-bourgeoise [p(ə)tiburʒwa, p(ə)titburʒwaz] **1.** *a.* (*a*) lower middle class; petit-bourgeois; (*b*) *Pej:* narrow-minded. **2.** *n.* member of the lower middle class; *pl. petit(e)s-bourgeois(es).*

petite-fille [p(ə)titfij] *n.f.* grand-daughter; *pl. petites-filles.*

petitement [pətitmɑ̃] *adv.* poorly, meanly, pettily; **elle est logée p.,** she lives in cramped accommodation.

petite-nièce [p(ə)titnjɛs] *n.f.* great-niece; *pl. petites-nièces.*

petitesse [p(ə)titɛs] *n.f.* **1.** (*a*) smallness, small size (of any object); slenderness (of figure); (*b*) meanness, pettiness; paltriness; **p. d'esprit,** narrow-mindedness. **2. faire des petitesses,** to do mean, shabby, things.

petit-fils [p(ə)tifis] *n.m.* grandson; *pl. petits-fils.*

petit-gris [p(ə)tigri] *n.m.* **1.** (*a*) *Z:* Siberian squirrel; (*b*) squirrel (fur). **2.** *Comest:* edible brown snail; *pl. petits-gris.*

pétition [petisjɔ̃] *n.f.* (*a*) petition; **adresser une p. à qn,** to petition s.o.; **faire signer une p.,** to set up a petition; (*b*) *Log:* **p. de principe,** petitio principii; begging the question.

pétitionnaire [petisjɔnɛr] *n.* petitioner.

petit-lait [p(ə)tilɛ] *n.m.* whey; *pl. petits-laits.*

petit-maître [p(ə)timɛtr̥] *n.m. A:* fop, dandy; *pl. petits-maîtres.*

petit-nègre [pətinɛgr̥] *n.m. Ling: F:* (*a*) pidgin French; (*b*) ungrammatical, bad, French.

petit-neveu [p(ə)tinvø] *n.m.* great-nephew; *pl. petits-neveux.*

petits-enfants [p(ə)tizɑ̃fɑ̃] *n.m.pl.* grandchildren.

pétoche [petɔʃ] *n.f. P:* fear, (blue) funk; **avoir la p.,** to be scared, in a blue funk.

pétoire [petwar] *n.f.* **1.** (child's) peashooter. **2.** *F:* poor sort of gun, popgun.

peton [pətɔ̃] *n.m. F:* (*in nursery speech*) tiny foot, tootsy-wootsy; *pl.* tootsies.

pétoncle [petɔ̃kl̥] *n.m. Moll:* scallop.

Pétrarque [petrark] *Pr.n.m.* Petrarch.

pétrel [petrɛl] *n.m. Orn:* petrel; **p. tempête,** storm petrel.

pétri [petri] *a.* kneaded, moulded, *NAm:* molded (**de,** out of); **un homme p. d'orgueil,** a man eaten up with pride; **p. d'ignorance,** steeped in ignorance.

pétrifiant [petrifjɑ̃] *a.* petrifying, petrifactive.

pétrification [petrifikasjɔ̃] *n.f.* petrification, petrifaction.

pétrifier [petrifje] *v.* (*impf. & pr.sub.* **n. pétrifiions, v. pétrifiiez) 1.** *v.tr.* (*a*) to petrify; **pétrifié de peur,** petrified; paralysed, *NAm:* paralyzed, with fear; (*b*) to encrust with lime. **2. se p.,** to petrify, become petrified; **son sourire se pétrifia,** his smile became fixed.

pétrin [petrɛ̃] *n.m.* kneading trough; **p. mécanique,** kneading machine; **se mettre dans le p.,** to get into trouble, into a mess, into a fix; **être dans le p., dans un beau p.,** to be in a jam, in a tight corner, in a mess.

pétrir [petrir] *v.tr.* (*a*) to knead (dough, bread); to knead, shape, mould, *NAm:* mold (clay); (*b*) **p. l'esprit de qn,** to mould, shape, a person's character; (*c*) *Med:* **p. un muscle,** to knead a muscle.

pétrissage [petrisaʒ] *n.m.* kneading.

pétrisseur, -euse [petrisœr, -øz] **1.** *n.* kneader. **2.** *n.f.* **pétrisseuse,** kneading machine.

pétrochimie [petrɔʃimi] *n.f.* petrochemistry.

pétrochimique [petrɔʃimik] *a.* petrochemical.

pétrochimiste [petrɔʃimist] *n.* petrochemist.

pétrodollar [petrodɔlar] *n.m. Fin:* petrodollar.

pétrographie [petrɔgrafi] *n.f. Geol:* petrography.

pétrole [petrɔl] *n.m.* petroleum, (mineral) oil; **p. brut,** crude (oil); **p. lampant,** paraffin (oil), *NAm:* kerosene; **gisement de p.,** oil deposit; oilfield; **puits de p.,** oil well.

pétrolette [petrɔlɛt] *n.f. F:* moped.

pétroleuse [petrɔløz] *n.f. Hist:* (1871) incendiary, pétroleuse.

pétrolier, -ière [petrɔlje, -jɛr] **1.** *a.* **l'industrie pétrolière,** the petroleum, oil, industry; **pays p.,** oil-producing country. **2.** *a. & n.m.* **(navire) p.,** (oil) tanker. **3.** *n.m.* (*a*) oil magnate; oilman; (*b*) petroleum engineer.

pétrolifère [petrɔlifɛr] *a.* petroliferous, oil-bearing; **gisement p.,** oilfield.

pétulance [petylɑ̃s] *n.f.* liveliness, exuberance.

pétulant [petylɑ̃] *a.* lively, exuberant, irrepressible.

pétunia [petynja] *n.m. Bot:* petunia.

peu [pø] **1.** *adv.* (*a*) little; **p. ou point,** little or none; **manger p. (ou point),** to eat little (or nothing); **p. de viande,** not much meat, very little meat; **pour p. qu'il pleuve, je resterai à la maison,** even if it only rains a little I'll stay at home; **ce n'est pas p. dire,** that's saying a good deal; **quelque p.,** to a slight extent; **je suis quelque p. surpris,** I am somewhat surprised; **tant soit p.,** somewhat; **p. de chose,** (very) little, not much; **pour si p. de chose,** for so small a matter; (*b*) few; **p. de gens,** few people; **en p. de mots,** in a few words; **p. d'entre eux avaient voyagé,** few of them had travelled; (*c*) not very; un-; **p. utile,** not very useful; **p. intelligent,** unintelligent, not over-intelligent; **p. honnête,** dishonest; **p. profond,** shallow. **2.** *n.m.* (*a*) little, bit; **le p. qu'il y a est à votre disposition,** you are welcome to the little there is; **son p. d'éducation,** (i) what little education he has had; (ii) his lack of education; **il a p. fait pour nous,** he has done (very) little for us; **il a un p. moins, un p. plus, de quarante ans,** he's a little under, a little over, forty; **un p. de vin,** a little wine; **un tout petit p.,** a tiny bit, drop; **encore un p.,** a little more, a few more; **il sait un p. d'anglais,** he knows a little English, has a smattering of English; **vous êtes allé un p. loin!** you went a bit far! **je suis un p. en retard,** I'm a bit late; *F:* **ça, c'est un p. fort!** that's a bit much! **un p. plus et il tombait dans l'eau,** he very nearly fell in the water; **pour un p. je l'aurais jeté dehors,** I all but, nearly, threw him out; **écoutez un p.,** just listen; *F:* **je vous demande un p.!** I ask you! *F:* **très p. pour moi!** not for me! I'm not having any! *F:* **tu ferais ça? – un p.!** you'd do that? – you bet! **p. à p.,** gradually; little by little; **fort p.,** very little; (*b*) (*of time*) **restez encore un p.,** stay a bit, a little (while), longer; **p. après,** shortly after(wards); not long after; **sous p., dans p., avant p., d'ici p.,** soon, before long; **depuis p.,** lately; recently; **j'ai manqué le train de p.,** I just missed the train; **il y a p.,** not (very) long ago; recently.

peuchère [pøʃɛr] *int. Dial:* (*S. of Fr.*) strewth! heavens!

peuh [pø] *int.* pooh! bah!

peuplade [pœplad] *n.f.* small tribe (of primitive peoples).

peuple [pœpl̥] *n.m.* **1.** people, nation; **le p. français,** the French people; **le p. élu,** the chosen race. **2.** (*a*) people (considered as a political entity); **le roi et son p.,** the king and his subjects; (*b*) **le p.,** the people, the masses; **les gens du p., le bas, petit, p.,** the lower, the working, classes; (*c*) *Lit:* crowd (of people); *a.inv. Pej:* **ça fait p.,** that's vulgar, common.

peuplé [pœple] *a.* inhabited; **très, peu, p.,** densely, sparsely, populated.

peuplement [pœpləmɑ̃] *n.m.* peopling, populating (of a region); stocking (of fish pond, game preserve, etc.); planting (with trees); **régions à faible p.,** sparsely populated areas.

peupler [pœple] **1.** *v.tr.* to people, populate (country); to stock (fish pond, etc.); to plant (with trees); **rue peuplée de gens,** crowded street; **ville peuplée de souvenirs,** town full of memories. **2. se p.,** to become populated; **la rue s'est peuplée peu à peu,** the street gradually filled (up) with people.

peupleraie [pøplərɛ] *n.f.* poplar plantation.

peuplier [pøplije] *n.m.* poplar; **p. tremble,** aspen.

peur [pœr] *n.f.* **1.** fear, fright; dread; **avoir p.,** to be, feel, frightened; **avoir p. du chien,** to be afraid of the dog; **j'ai p. pour lui,** I'm afraid for him; **j'avais p. de vous gêner,** I was afraid I might be in your way; **n'ayez pas p.!** don't be afraid! **j'en ai bien p.,** I'm afraid so; **j'ai p. qu'il (ne) soit en retard,** (i) I'm worried in case he should be late; (ii) I'm afraid he may be late; *F:* **vous n'avez pas p.!** (i) you're not easily put off! (ii) you've got a nerve! **prendre p.,** to take fright; *F:* **avoir une p. bleue,** to be in a blue funk, to be scared to death; **en être quitte pour la p.,** to get off with a fright; **il a eu plus de p. que de mal,** he is, was, more frightened than hurt; **faire p. à qn,** to frighten s.o.; to give s.o. a fright; *F:* **il m'a fait une de ces peurs!** (i) he gave me such a fright! (ii) I was terrified for him! **être laid à faire p.,** to be frightfully ugly; **sans p.,** fearless, fearlessly. **2.** (*a*) *prep.phr.* **de p. de,** for fear of (sth.); (*b*) *conj.phr.* **de p. que . . . (ne)** + *subj.,* for fear that; in case.

peureusement [pœrøzmɑ̃] *adv.* fearfully; timidly, nervously.

peureux, -euse [pœrø, -øz] **1.** *a.* fearful, timorous (person, glance); easily frightened; nervous; timid (nature). **2.** *n.* fearful, timid, nervous, person.

peut-être [pøtɛtr̥] *adv.* (*a*) perhaps, maybe, possibly; **il est p.-ê. rentré chez lui,** he may have gone home; **p.-ê. bien qu'il viendra,** he will very likely, possibly, come; (*b*) *Iron:* **tu le sais mieux que moi, p.-ê.?** you think you know better, do you? **je ne sais pas faire la cuisine, p.-ê.?** you think I can't cook!

pèze [pɛz] *n.m. P:* money, dough, lolly.

pff [pf], **pfft** [pft], **pffut** [pfyt] *int.* pooh!

phacochère [fakɔʃɛr] *n.m. Z:* warthog.

phaéton [faetɔ̃] *n.m. A.Veh:* phaeton.

phagocyte [fagɔsit] *n.m. Biol:* phagocyte.

phalange [falɑ̃ʒ] *n.f.* **1.** (*a*) *Gr.Ant: Mil:* phalanx; (*b*) *Spanish Pol:* **la P.,** the Falange, Falangist party; (*c*) *Lit:* host, army. **2.** *Anat:* phalanx.

phalangette [falɑ̃ʒɛt] *n.f. Anat:* ungual phalanx, top joint (of finger, toe).

phalangien, -ienne [falɑ̃ʒjɛ̃, -jɛn] *a. Anat:* phalangeal.

phalangiste [falɑ̃ʒist] *n. Spanish Pol:* Falangist.

phalanstère [falɑ̃stɛr] *n.m. Hist. of Pol.Ec:* phalanstery.

phalène [falɛn] *n.f.* (*occ. n.m. in poetry*) *Ent:* geometrid (moth).

phallique [falik] *a.* phallic.

phallocrate [falɔkrat] *n.m.* chauvinist; *F:* male chauvinist pig.

phalloïde [falɔid] *a. Nat.Hist:* phalloid; *Fung:* **amanite p.,** amanita phalloides, death cap.

phallus [falys] *n.m.* phallus.

phantasme [fɑ̃tasm] *n.m.* phantasm.

pharamineux, -euse [faraminø, -øz] *a. F:* staggering, fantastic; colossal.

pharaon [faraɔ̃] *n.m.* **1.** *Hist:* Pharaoh. **2.** *Cards:* faro.

phare [far] *n.m.* **1.** lighthouse; **p. à éclats,** flashing light; **p. à feu fixe, à feu tournant,** fixed, revolving, light. **2.** *Av:* beacon; **p. d'atterrissage,** landing light. **3.** *Aut: etc:* headlight; **mettre les phares en code, en veilleuse,** to dip the headlights; **p. code,** dipped headlight; **rouler pleins phares,** to drive on full beam, full headlights, *NAm:* high beams; **p. anti-brouillard,** foglamp; **p. de recul,** reversing light.

pharisaïque [farizaik] *a.* Pharisaic; pharisaic(al).

pharisien, -ienne [farizjɛ̃, -jɛn] *n.* (*a*) *Rel.H:* Pharisee; (*b*) pharisee; hypocrite.

pharmaceutique [farmasøtik] *a.* pharmaceutic(al).

pharmacie [farmasi] *n.f.* **1.** pharmacy; dispensing. **2.** (*a*) pharmacy; chemist's (shop); *NAm:* drugstore; (*b*) dispensary. **3.** (*a*) pharmaceuticals; medicines; (*b*) **(armoire à) p.,** medicine chest, cabinet; **p. portative,** first-aid kit.

pharmacien, -ienne [farmasjɛ̃, -jɛn] *n.* pharmacist, (dispensing) chemist; *NAm:* druggist.

pharmacologie [farmakɔlɔʒi] *n.f.* pharmacology.

pharmacologique [farmakɔlɔʒik] *a.* pharmacological.

pharmacopée [farmakɔpe] *n.f.* pharmacopoeia.

pharyngé [farɛ̃ʒe], **pharyngien, -ienne** [farɛ̃ʒjɛ̃, -jɛn] *a. Anat:* pharyng(e)al.

pharyngite [farɛ̃ʒit] *n.f. Med:* pharyngitis.

pharynx [farɛ̃ks] *n.m. Anat:* pharynx.

phascolome [faskɔlɔm] *n.m. Z:* wombat.

phase [fɑz] *n.f.* **1.** *Astr:* phase, phasis (of moon, etc.). **2.** (*a*) phase, stage (of an illness, etc.); (*b*) *El:* **en p.,** in phase, in step; **décalage de p.,** difference of phase, phase displacement.

Phebus [febys] *Pr.n.m. Myth:* Phoebus.

Phèdre [fɛdr̥] *Pr.n.f. Myth:* Phaedra.

Phénicie [fenisi] *Pr.n.f. A.Geog:* Phoenicia.

phénicien, -ienne [fenisjɛ̃, -jɛn] *Hist:* **1.** *a. & n. Geog:* Phoenician. **2.** *n.m. Ling:* Phoenician.

phénix [feniks] *n.m.* (*a*) *Myth:* phoenix; (*b*) paragon.

phénol [fenɔl] *n.m.* (*a*) *Ch:* phenol; (*b*) *Com:* carbolic acid.

phénoménal, -aux [fenɔmenal, -o] *a.* phenomenal; prodigious, amazing.

phénoménalement [fenɔmenalmɑ̃] *adv.* phenomenally, amazingly.

phénomène [fenɔmɛn] *n.m.* (*a*) phenomenon; (*b*) (*pers.*) (i) phenomenon, marvel; (ii) freak, outlandish character; (*c*) (*in fairs, etc.*) freak (of nature).

philanthrope [filɑ̃trɔp] *n.* philanthropist.

philanthropie [filɑ̃trɔpi] *n.f.* philanthropy.

philanthropique [filɑ̃trɔpik] *a.* philanthropic(al).

philatélie [filateli] *n.f.*, **philatélisme** [filatelism] *n.m.* philately, stamp collecting.

philatélique [filatelik] *a.* philatelic.

philatéliste [filatelist] *n.* philatelist, stamp collector.

philharmonie [filarmɔni] *n.f.* philharmonic society.

philharmonique [filarmɔnik] *a.* philharmonic (society, etc.).

philhellène [filelɛn] **1.** *n.m.* Philhellene. **2.** *a.* philhellenic.

philhellénisme [filelenism] *n.m.* philhellenism.

Philippe [filip] *Pr.n.m.* Philip.

philippin, -ine [filipɛ̃, -in] *a. & n. Geog:* Filipino.

Phillipines (les) [lefilipin] *Pr.n.f.pl. Geog:* the Philippines.

philistin, -ine [filistɛ̃, -in] *a. & n.* (*a*) *A.Geog: B.Lit:* Philistine; (*b*) philistine.

philo [filo] *n.f. Sch: F:* philosophy.

philologie [filɔlɔʒi] *n.f.* philology.

philologique [filɔlɔʒik] *a.* philological.

philologiquement [filɔlɔʒikmɑ̃] *adv.* philologically.

philologue [filɔlɔg] *n.* philologist.

philosophale [filɔzɔfal] *a.f.* **la pierre p.,** the philosophers' stone.

philosophe [filɔzɔf] **1.** *n.* philosopher. **2.** *a.* philosophical.

philosopher [filɔzɔfe] *v.i.* to philosophize.

philosophie [filɔzɔfi] *n.f.* (*a*) philosophy; (*b*) *Sch:* = art subjects; **(classe de) p.,** philosophy class (= upper VIth, arts).

philosophique [filɔzɔfik] *a.* philosophical.

philosophiquement [filɔzɔfikmɑ̃] *adv.* philosophically.

philtre [filtr̥] *n.m.* philtre, *NAm:* philter; love potion.

phlébite [flebit] *n.f. Med:* phlebitis.

phlébotomie [flebɔtɔmi] *n.f. Med:* phlebotomy.
phlegmon [flɛgmɔ̃] *n.m. Med:* phlegmon.
phlox [flɔks] *n.m. Bot:* phlox.
phobie [fɔbi] *n.f Med:* phobia; morbid fear.
phobique [fɔbik] *a. Med:* phobic.
phonation [fɔnasjɔ̃] *n.f. Physiol: Ling:* phonation.
phonatoire [fɔnatwar] *a.* phonatory.
phone [fɔn] *n.m. Ac.Meas:* phon.
phonème [fɔnɛm] *n.m. Ling:* phoneme.
phonémique [fɔnemik] *a. Ling:* phonemic.
phonéticien, -ienne [fɔnetisjɛ̃, -jɛn] *n.* phonetician.
phonétique [fɔnetik] **1.** *a.* phonetic. **2.** *n.f.* phonetics.
phonétiquement [fɔnetikmɑ̃] *adv.* phonetically.
phoniatre [fɔnjatr̥] *n. Med:* speech therapist.
phoniatrie [fɔnjatri] *n.f. Med:* speech therapy.
phonie [fɔni] *n.f.* wireless telegraphy, radiotelegraphy.
phonique [fɔnik] *a.* phonic; acoustic.
phono [fɔno] *n.m. F:* = PHONOGRAPHE.
phonographe [fɔnɔgraf] *n.m.* (*a*) *A:* phonograph; (*b*) gramophone, *NAm:* phonograph; record player.
phonographique [fɔnɔgrafik] *a.* phonographic.
phonologie [fɔnɔlɔʒi] *n.f. Ling:* phonology.
phonologique [fɔnɔlɔʒik] *a.* phonologic(al).
phonologue [fɔnɔlɔg] *n. Ling:* phonologist.
phonothèque [fɔnɔtɛk] *n.f.* sound archives.
phoque [fɔk] *n.m.* (*a*) *Z:* seal; **souffler comme un p.,** to (puff and) blow like a grampus; (*b*) *Com:* sealskin.
phosgène [fɔsʒɛn] *n.m. Ch:* phosgene (gas).
phosphate [fɔsfat] *n.m. Ch:* phosphate.
phosphaté [fɔsfate] *a. Ch:* phosphatic, phosphated.
phosphater [fɔsfate] *v.tr.* to treat with phosphates, to phosphate.
phosphène [fɔsfɛn] *n.m. Physiol:* phosphene.
phosphore [fɔsfɔr] *n.m. Ch:* phosphorus; **p. blanc,** yellow phosphorus.
phosphoré [fɔsfɔre] *a.* phosphorated; phosphorus.
phosphorescence [fɔsfɔresɑ̃s] *n.f.* phosphorescence.
phosphorescent [fɔsfɔresɑ̃] *a.* phosphorescent.
phosphoreux, -euse [fɔsfɔrø, -øz] *a. Ch:* phosphorous.
phosphorique [fɔsfɔrik] *a. Ch:* phosphoric.
phosphure [fɔsfyr] *n.m. Ch:* phosphide.
photo [foto] *n.f.* photograph, photo; **prendre qn en p.,** to take a photograph of s.o.
photocalque [fɔtɔkalk] *n.m. Ind:* phototype (from tracing); blueprint.
photochimie [fɔtɔʃimi] *n.f.* photochemistry.
photochimique [fɔtɔʃimik] *a.* photochemical.
photocopie [fɔtɔkɔpi] *n.f.* photocopy.
photocopier [fɔtɔkɔpje] *v.tr.* (*conj. like* COPIER) to photocopy; to photostat.
photocopieur [fɔtɔkɔpjœr] *n.m.*, **photocopieuse** [fɔtɔkɔpjøz] *n.f.* photocopier.
photo(-)électricité [fɔtɔelɛktrisite] *n.f.* photoelectricity.
photo(-)électrique [fɔtɔelɛktrik] *a.* photoelectric (cell, effect).
photo-finish [fɔtɔfiniʃ] *n.f.inv. Sp:* (*a*) photo finish; (*b*) photo-finish camera.
photogénique [fɔtɔʒenik] *a. Phot:* photogenic.
photographe [fɔtɔgraf] *n.* (*a*) photographer; **reporter p.,** press photographer; (*b*) camera dealer, photographer.
photographie [fɔtɔgrafi] *n.f.* **1.** photography; **faire de la p.,** to be an amateur photographer; to take photographs. **2.** photograph; **p. aérienne,** aerial photograph; **prendre une p. de qn,** to take s.o.'s photograph.
photographier [fɔtɔgrafje] *v.tr.* (*impf. & pr.sub.* **n. photographiions, v. photographiiez**) to photograph; to take a photograph of (sth.); **se faire p.,** to have one's photograph taken.
photographique [fɔtɔgrafik] *a.* photographic (reproduction, description, etc.); **appareil p.,** camera.
photographiquement [fɔtɔgrafikmɑ̃] *adv.* photographically.
photograveur [fɔtɔgravœr] *n.m.* photoengraver.
photogravure [fɔtɔgravyr] *n.f.* photoengraving; photogravure (process or print).
photolithographie [fɔtɔlitɔgrafi] *n.f.* photolithography.
photomécanique [fɔtɔmekanik] *a.* photomechanical (process, etc.).
photomètre [fɔtɔmɛtr̥] *n.m.* photometer.
photométrie [fɔtɔmetri] *n.f.* photometry.
photométrique [fɔtɔmetrik] *a.* photometric(al).
photomontage [fɔtɔmɔ̃taʒ] *n.m.* photomontage.
photon [fɔtɔ̃] *n.m. Opt.Meas:* photon.
photophobie [fɔtɔfɔbi] *n.f. Med:* photophobia.
photo-robot [fɔtɔrɔbo] *n.m.* identikit (picture); *pl. photos-robots.*
photosensible [fɔtɔsɑ̃sibl̥] *a.* photosensitive.
photosphère [fɔtɔsfɛr] *n.f. Astr:* photosphere.
photostat [fɔtɔsta] *n.m.* photostat.
photosynthèse [fɔtɔsɛ̃tɛz] *n.f. Biol:* photosynthesis.
photothèque [fɔtɔtɛk] *n.f.* photographic library.
photothérapie [fɔtɔterapi] *n.f.* phototherapy.
phragmite [fragmit] *n.m.* **1.** *Bot:* reed. **2.** *Orn:* sedge warbler.
phrase [fraz] *n.f.* **1.** sentence; **p. toute faite,** stock phrase; **faire des phrases,** to speak in flowery language; **sans phrases,** straight out, without mincing matters; *Gram:* **membre de p.,** phrase. **2.** *Mus:* phrase.
phrasé [fraze] *n.m. Mus:* phrasing.
phraséologie [frazeɔlɔʒi] *n.f.* (*a*) phraseology; (*b*) flowery, high-flown, language.
phraser [fraze] **1.** *v.tr. Mus:* to phrase. **2.** *v.i.* to use high-flown language.
phréatique [freatik] *a. Geol:* phreatic; **nappe p.,** ground water.
phrénologie [frenɔlɔʒi] *n.f.* phrenology.
phrénologique [frenɔlɔʒik] *a.* phrenological.
phrénologiste [frenɔlɔʒist] *n.m.* phrenologist.
phrygane [frigan] *n.f. Ent:* phryganea, *esp.* caddis fly, may fly; **larve de p.,** caddis worm.
Phrygie [friʒi] *Pr.n.f. A.Geog:* Phrygia.
phrygien, -ienne [friʒjɛ̃, -jɛn] *a. & n. A.Geog:* Phrygian; *Hist:* **bonnet p.,** Phrygian cap (as emblem of liberty).
phtisie [ftizi] *n.f. Med: A:* phthisis; consumption; **p. galopante,** galloping consumption.
phylactère [filaktɛr] *n.m. Jew.Rel:* phylactery.
phylloxéra, phylloxera [filɔksera] *n.m. Ent:* phylloxera.
physicien, -ienne [fizisjɛ̃, -jɛn] *n.* physicist; **p. de l'atome,** nuclear physicist.
physico-chimie [fizikɔʃimi] *n.f. no pl.* physicochemistry.
physico-chimique [fizikɔʃimik] *a.* physico-chemical; *pl. physico-chimiques.*
physiocrate [fizjɔkrat] *n.m. Pol.Ec:* physiocrat.
physiologie [fizjɔlɔʒi] *n.f.* physiology.
physiologique [fizjɔlɔʒik] *a.* physiological.
physiologiquement [fizjɔlɔʒikmɑ̃] *adv.* physiologically.
physiologiste [fizjɔlɔʒist] *n.* physiologist.
physionomie [fizjɔnɔmi] *n.f.* physiognomy; face, countenance; (*of thg*) appearance, aspect; **il manque de p.,** his face lacks character; **jeux de p.,** mimicry.

physionomiste [fizjɔnɔmist] *n.* physiognomist; good judge of faces; **je ne suis pas p.,** I've no memory for faces.
physique [fizik] **1.** *a.* physical; **douleur p.,** bodily pain; **culture p.,** physical culture, training; **force p.,** physical force, strength. **2.** *n.f.* (*a*) physics; **p. nucléaire,** nuclear physics; **p. du globe,** geophysics; (*b*) *Sch:* physics textbook. **3.** *n.m.* physique (of person); external appearance; **au p.,** physically; to look at (him, her, etc.); **il a le p. de l'emploi,** he looks the part.
physiquement [fizikmɑ̃] *adv.* physically.
pi [pi] *n.m. Gr.Alph:* pi; *Mth:* π.
piaf [pjaf] *n.m. P:* sparrow.
piaffement [pjafmɑ̃] *n.m. Equit:* pawing (the ground).
piaffer [pjafe] *v.i.* (*a*) (*of horse*) to paw the ground; (*b*) to stamp one's feet; (*c*) **p. d'impatience,** to fidget.
piaillard, -arde [pjɑjar, -ard] *a. & n. F:* = PIAILLEUR, -EUSE.
piaillement [pjajmɑ̃] *n.m. F:* cheeping (of bird); squalling, squawking (of child).
piailler [pjaje] *v.i. F:* (*of small birds*) to cheep; (*of children, etc.*) to squall, squeal; to squawk.
piaillerie [pjajri] *n.f. F:* = PIAILLEMENT.
piailleur, -euse [pjajœr, -øz] *F:* **1.** *a.* cheeping (bird); squalling, squawking (child). **2.** *n.* (*bird*) cheeper; (*pers.*) squaller, squealer, squawker.
piane-piane [pjanpjan] *adv. F:* very slowly, very softly, very gently.
pianiste [pjanist] *n.* pianist.
piano¹ [pjano] *n.m.* piano; **p. à queue,** grand piano; **p. demi-queue,** baby grand; **p. droit,** upright piano; **p. mécanique,** player piano; **jouer du p.,** to play the piano.
piano² *adv. & n.m. Mus:* piano, softly; *F:* **allez-y p.,** gently does it; go easy.
pianotage [pjanɔtaʒ] *n.m. F:* strumming, tinkling away (on piano); drumming (of fingers).
pianoter [pjanɔte] *v.i. F:* to strum, tinkle away (on piano); **ses doigts pianotent sur la nappe,** his fingers are drumming, tapping out a tune, on the tablecloth.
piastre [pjastr̥] *n.f. Num:* piastre; *Fr.C: P:* dollar.
piaule [pjol] *n.f. P:* room, pad; digs.
piaulement [pjolmɑ̃] *n.m.* cheep(ing) (of chicks); whimpering, whining (of children).
piauler [pjole] *v.i.* (*of chicks*) to cheep; (*of children*) to whine, whimper.
pic¹ [pik] *n.m.* **1.** pick, pickaxe, *U.S:* pickax; **p. pneumatique,** pneumatic pick, drill; **p. de mineur,** miner's pick. **2.** (mountain) peak; *adv.phr.* **à p.,** perpendicular(ly), sheer, abrupt; **sentier à p.,** precipitous path; **promontoire à p.,** sheer headland; bluff; (*of ship, etc.*) **couler à p.,** to sink straight to the bottom; to sink like a stone; *F:* **tomber à p.,** to happen at the right moment; *F:* **il est arrivé à p.,** he turned up in the nick of time.
pic² *n.m. Orn:* woodpecker.
picaillons [pikajɔ̃] *n.m.pl. P:* money; dough.
picard, -arde [pikar, -ard] *a. & n. Geog:* (native, inhabitant) of Picardy; *Cu:* **ficelle picarde** = ham and cheese pancake.
Picardie [pikardi] *Pr.n.f. Geog:* Picardy.
picaresque [pikarɛsk] *a.* picaresque (novel).
pic(c)olo [pikɔlo] *n.m. Mus:* piccolo.
pichenette [piʃnɛt] *n.f.* flip, flick (of the finger).
pichet [piʃɛ] *n.m.* (small) jug; pitcher.
pickpocket [pikpɔkɛt] *n.m.* pickpocket.
pick-up [pikœp] *n.m. Rec:* (*a*) pick-up (arm); (*b*) record player.
picoler [pikɔle] *v.i. P:* to tipple, to booze.
picorer [pikɔre] (*of bird, etc.*) **1.** *v.i.* to pick, scratch, about, for food; to peck; to feed. **2.** *v.tr.* to peck at (food).
picot [piko] *n.m.* **1.** splinter (of wood). **2.** pick hammer. **3.** *Needlew: Lacem:* picot.
picotement [pikɔtmɑ̃] *n.m.* pricking, tingling, smarting (sensation).
picoter [pikɔte] **1.** *v.tr.* (*a*) to prick tiny holes in (sth.); (*b*) (*of bird*) to peck, peck at (fruit, etc.); (*c*) to produce a tingling sensation in (sth.); to tickle (throat); to prickle (skin); **la fumée me picotait les yeux,** the smoke made my eyes sting, smart. **2.** *v.i.* (*of eyes, etc.*) to smart, sting; (*of throat*) to tickle; (*of skin*) to prickle.
picotin [pikɔtɛ̃] *n.m. Husb:* (*a*) peck (of oats); (*b*) feed, ration (of oats).
picrate [pikrat] *n.m.* **1.** *Ch:* picrate. **2.** *P:* cheap wine, plonk.
Pictes [pikt] *n.m.pl. Ethn: Hist:* Picts.
pictographie [piktɔgrafi] *n.f.* pictography, picture writing.
pictographique [piktɔgrafik] *a.* pictographic.
pictural, -aux [piktyral, -o] *a.* pictorial.
pic(-)vert [pikvɛr] *n.m. Orn:* green woodpecker; *pl. pics(-)verts.*
pie [pi] **1.** *n.f.* (*a*) *Orn:* magpie; *F:* **bavarder comme une p.,** to chatter like a magpie; (*b*) *F:* chatterbox. **2.** *a.inv.* **cheval p., jument p.,** piebald horse, mare; **vache p.,** black and white cow; **voiture p. (de la police)** = Panda car.
pie² *a.f. A:* pious, charitable; *still used in* **œuvre(s) pie(s),** charitable, good, deed(s), work(s).
Pie³ *Pr.n.m.* Pius.
pièce [pjɛs] *n.f.* **1.** piece (as a whole); (*a*) **p. de musée,** museum piece; **p. de bétail, de gibier,** head of cattle, of game; **p. de blé,** wheatfield; **p. d'eau,** ornamental lake, pond; **p. de vin,** barrel, cask, of wine; **p. (de monnaie),** coin; **p. de dix francs,** ten-franc piece; **donner la p. à qn,** to give s.o. a tip; to tip s.o.; **p. d'étoffe,** roll of material; *Cu:* **p. montée,** ornamental cake; **p. de résistance,** pièce de résistance, main dish; **ils coûtent dix francs (la) p.,** they cost ten francs each, apiece; **ils se vendent à la p.,** they are sold singly, separately; **marchandises à la p.,** piece goods; **travailler aux pièces,** to do piece work; *F:* **on n'est pas aux pièces,** we're not in a hurry; (*b*) *Artil:* **p. (d'artillerie),** piece of ordnance; **p. de campagne,** field gun; **chef de p.,** number one, squad leader, *U.S:* chief of (piece) section; (*c*) **p. (de théâtre),** play; **monter une p.,** to put on a play; (*d*) *Mus: Lit:* piece; (*e*) *Jur: Adm: etc:* document, paper; **p. justificative,** document in proof; **p. à conviction,** exhibit (in criminal case); **p. à l'appui,** supporting document; **p. jointe,** enclosure; (*f*) *adj. & adv.phr.* **tout d'une p.,** all of a piece; **être tout d'une p.,** to be (i) blunt, (ii) narrow-minded. **2.** piece (as part of a whole); (*a*) **p. de bœuf,** joint of beef; **histoire inventée de toutes pièces,** made-up story; (*b*) *Mec.E:* part (of machine, clock, etc.); component part; **p. rapportée,** patch; insert; **pièces de rechange, pièces détachées,** replacement parts, spare parts, spares; (*c*) patch; **mettre, poser, une p. à un vêtement,** to patch a garment; (*d*) room (of house); **un appartement de trois pièces, un trois pièces,** a three-roomed flat, *NAm:* apartment; (*e*) *Games:* (chess) piece; draughts(man), *NAm:* checker; (*f*) *Her:* piece, ordinary, charge; **p. honorable,** honourable ordinary, *NAm:* honorable ordinary. **3.** fragment, bit; **vêtements en pièces,** tattered garments; **mettre qch. en pièces,** to break, smash, sth. to bits, to pieces; to pull sth. to pieces; to tear (garment, etc.) to pieces; **tailler l'ennemi en pièces,** to cut the enemy to pieces; *adv.phr.* **p. à p.,** bit by bit, piece by piece.
piécette [pjesɛt] *n.f.* small coin.
pied [pje] *n.m.* **1.** (*a*) foot (of man, of hoofed animal);

p. bot, p. plat, club foot, flat foot; *F:* **avoir les pieds nickelés,** (i) to sit tight, to refuse to budge; (ii) to be lazy; *F:* **être bête comme ses pieds,** to be unbelievably stupid; **il n'avait pas de chaussures aux pieds,** he had no shoes to his feet; he was barefoot; **se jeter aux pieds de qn,** to throw oneself at s.o.'s feet; **avoir bon p. bon œil,** to be hale and hearty; **se lever du p. gauche,** to get out of bed on the wrong side; **il ne peut pas mettre un p. devant l'autre,** (he's so weak) he can hardly put one foot in front of the other; **de la tête aux pieds, de p. en cap** [dəpjetɑ̃kap], from head to foot, from top to toe; **faire des pieds et des mains pour . . .,** to do one's utmost, to move heaven and earth, (in order) to . . .; *F:* **faire du p. à qn,** (i) to give s.o. a kick (as a warning); (ii) to play footsie with s.o.; *F:* **ça lui fera les pieds!** that'll serve him right! *P:* **il me casse les pieds,** he's a frightful bore; he gets on my nerves; **mettre p. à terre** [pjetatɛr], to get out (of car, etc.); to dismount (from horse); **je ne remettrai jamais les pieds chez lui,** I'll never set foot in his house again; **je n'ai pas mis le p. dehors de toute la journée,** I haven't set foot outside all day; *F:* **mettre les pieds dans le plat,** to put one's foot in it; *F:* **ne pas savoir sur quel p. danser,** not to know which way to turn; **marcher sur les pieds de qn,** to tread on s.o.'s toes; *F:* **lever le p.,** to make off (with the money); **faire qch. au p. levé,** to do sth. straight off, at a moment's notice; **frapper du p.,** to stamp (one's foot); **pousser qch. du p.,** to kick sth.; (*b*) **coup de p.,** kick; **donner, envoyer, un coup de p. à qn,** to kick s.o.; **chasser qn à coups de p.,** to kick s.o. out; **enfoncer une porte à coups de p.,** to kick a door in; (*c*) **à p.,** on foot; **aller à p.,** to walk; **faire deux kilomètres à p.,** to walk two kilometres, *NAm:* killometers; **vous en avez pour vingt minutes à p.,** it will take you twenty minutes to walk (it), twenty minutes on foot; **course à p.,** foot race; **mettre qn à p.,** to suspend s.o.; (*d*) **sur p.,** standing; on one's feet; **il est sur p. de bonne heure,** he's up early; **mettre une affaire sur p.,** to set up, start, a business; **il est de nouveau sur p.,** he's up and about, getting about, again; (*e*) **portrait en p.,** full-length portrait; (*f*) *Cu:* **p. de veau,** calf's foot; **p. de cochon,** pig's trotter; (*g*) *P:* fool, idiot; **quel p.!** what a twit! **jouer comme un p.,** to play very badly; **il conduit comme un p.,** he's a lousy driver. **2.** (*a*) footing; foothold; **avoir le p. marin,** to be a good sailor; (*of swimmer*) **avoir p.,** to be within one's depth; **perdre p.,** (i) to get out of one's depth; (ii) to be confused, at a loss; **prendre p.,** (i) to get a foothold, a footing; (ii) *Fig:* to take root; **lâcher p.,** (i) to give in (to opponent); (ii) to give up; *P:* **prendre son p.,** to get a kick (out of sth.); *P:* **c'est le p.!** it's fantastic! great! **être sur le même p. avec qn,** to be on an equal footing with s.o.; **sur un p. d'égalité,** as an equal; **vivre sur un grand p.,** to live on a grand scale; (*b*) footprint, track (of animal). **3.** (*a*) foot (of stocking, tree, staircase, bed); foot, base (of column, wall); foot (of mountain); *Mth:* foot (of a perpendicular); *Civ.E: etc:* **à p. d'œuvre,** on site; (*b*) leg (of chair, table, etc.); stem, foot (of glass); **p. de lampe, de lampadaire,** lampstand; (*c*) stalk (of plant); stock (of vine); **p. de céleri, d'asperges, de salade,** head of celery, of asparagus, of lettuce; (*d*) stand, rest (for telescope, etc.); *Phot:* foot; **p. (à trois branches),** tripod; (*e*) *Nau:* step, heel (of mast); (*f*) *Bookb:* tail (of book). **4.** (*a*) *Meas:* foot; **p. carré,** square foot; **p. cube,** cubic foot; **au petit p.,** (in) miniature; **p. à p.** [pjeapje], foot by foot, step by step; (*b*) foot rule; **p. à coulisse,** calliper square. **5.** *Pros:* (metrical) foot.

pied-à-terre [pjetatɛr] *n.m.inv.* pied-à-terre; small flat, *NAm:* apartment (in town).

pied-bot [pjebo] *n.m.* club-footed person; *pl. pieds-bots.*

pied-d'alouette [pjedalwɛt] *n.m. Bot:* larkspur; delphinium; *pl. pieds-d'alouette.*

pied-de-biche [pjedbiʃ] *n.m.* **1.** bell pull. **2.** (*a*) nail extractor, nail claw; (*b*) presser foot (of sewing machine). **3.** cabriole leg (of chair, table, etc.); *pl. pieds-de-biche.*

pied-de-poule [pjedpul] *a. & n.m. Tex:* broken check, houndstooth (material); *pl. pieds-de-poule.*

pied-de-roi [pjedrwa] *n.m. Fr.C:* folding rule.

pied-droit [pjedrwa] *n.m.* **1.** *Civ.E:* pier (of arch, of bridge). **2.** *Arch:* engaged pier; *pl. pieds-droits.*

piédestal, -aux [pjedɛstal, -o] *n.m.* pedestal.

pied-noir [pjenwar] *n. F:* Algerian-born Frenchman, Frenchwoman; *pl. pieds-noirs.*

piédouche [pjeduʃ] *n.m.* small pedestal.

piédroit [pjedrwa] *n.m.* = PIED-DROIT.

piège [pjɛʒ] *n.m.* trap, snare; **p. à loups,** mantrap; **dresser, tendre, un p.,** to set a trap (**à,** for); **prendre un animal au p.,** to trap an animal; **attirer l'ennemi dans un p.,** to ambush the enemy; **donner, tomber, dans le p.,** to walk, fall, into the trap; **être pris à son propre p.,** to be caught in one's own trap; **dictée pleine de pièges,** dictation full of pitfalls.

piégeage [pjeʒaʒ] *n.m.* trapping (of animals).

piéger [pjeʒe] *v.tr.* (**je piège, n. piégeons; je piégeai(s); je piégerai**) **1.** to trap (animal, s.o.). **2.** (*a*) to set a trap in (sth.); (*b*) to booby-trap.

piégeur [pjeʒœr] *n.m.* trapper.

pie-grièche [pigriɛʃ] *n.f.* **1.** *Orn:* shrike. **2.** *F:* (*woman*) shrew; *pl. pies-grièches.*

pie-mère [pimɛr] *n.f. Anat:* pia mater; *pl. pies-mères.*

Piémont [pjemɔ̃] *Pr.n.m. Geog:* Piedmont.

piémontais, -aise [pjemɔ̃tɛ, -ɛz] **1.** *a. & n.* Piedmontese. **2.** *n.m. Ling:* Piedmont.

piéride [pjerid] *n.f. Ent:* pierid; **p. du chou,** cabbage white butterfly.

pierraille [pjɛraj] *n.f.* broken stones, loose stones, rubble; ballast.

pierre[1] [pjɛr] *n.f.* stone; (*a*) *Miner:* **p. de touche,** touchstone; **p. ponce,** pumice (stone); (*b*) **pierres de gué,** stepping stones; **p. d'achoppement,** stumbling block; *Prov:* **p. qui roule n'amasse pas mousse,** a rolling stone gathers no moss; **avoir un cœur de p.,** to have a heart of stone; **assaillir qn à coups de pierres,** to pelt s.o. with stones; **jeter la p. à qn,** to cast a stone at s.o.; to accuse s.o.; **c'est une p. dans votre jardin,** that's a dig at you; **faire d'une p. deux coups,** to kill two birds with one stone; **malheureux comme les pierres,** bitterly unhappy; (*c*) *Prehist:* **âge de la p.,** stone age; **outils en p.,** flint implements; (*d*) *Const:* **p. à bâtir,** building stone; **p. de taille,** ashlar, freestone; **p. angulaire,** corner stone; **poser la première p.,** to lay the foundation stone; **mur de p.,** stone wall; **mur en pierres sèches,** drystone wall; **p. à p.,** stone by stone; **ils n'ont pas laissé p. sur p.,** they didn't leave a stone standing; (*e*) gem; **p. précieuse,** precious stone; gem; **p. fine,** semi-precious stone; (*f*) *Tchn:* **p. à affûter, à aiguiser,** whetstone, grindstone; **p. à briquet,** (lighter) flint; **p. à fusil,** gun flint.

Pierre[2] *Pr.n.m.* Peter.

pierreries [pjɛr(ə)ri] *n.f.pl.* precious stones, jewels, gems.

pierreux, -euse [pjɛrø, -øz] *a.* (*a*) stony (ground, road, etc.); gravelly (bed of river); gritty (pear); (*b*) *Med:* calculous (formation).

Pierrot [pjɛro] *n.m.* (*a*) *Th:* Pierrot; clown; (*b*) *Orn: F:* sparrow.

piétaille [pjetaj] *n.f. F:* (*a*) *Mil:* rank and file, infantrymen; (*b*) pedestrians.

piété [pjete] *n.f.* (*a*) piety; **articles de p.,** devotional objects; (*b*) **p. filiale,** filial piety, devotion.

piétinement [pjetinmɑ̃] *n.m.* **1.** stamping, trampling (with the feet). **2.** lack of progress; **à cause du p. de l'enquête,** because the enquiry is at a standstill.

piétiner [pjetine] **1.** *v.tr.* (*a*) to trample, stamp, on (sth.); to trample (sth.) down; to tread (sth.) underfoot; **p. un cadavre,** to speak ill of the dead; (*b*) to have no respect for (s.o.'s convictions, etc.). **2.** *v.i.* **p. d'impatience,** to stamp (one's feet) with impatience, impatiently; **p. sur place,** to mark time; **l'instruction piétine,** the judge's investigation is making no headway.

piétisme [pjetism] *n.m. Rel.H:* Pietism.

piéton, -onne [pjetɔ̃, -ɔn] *n.* pedestrian; **sentier pour piétons,** *a.* **sentier p.,** footpath.

piètre [pjɛtr̥] *a.* wretched, poor; lame, paltry (excuse); **faire p. figure,** to cut a poor figure; **p. consolation,** cold comfort.

piètrement [pjɛtrəmɑ̃] *adv.* wretchedly, poorly.

pieu¹, -ieux [pjø] *n.m.* **1.** stake, post. **2.** *Civ.E: etc:* pile; **p. creux,** tubular pile; **enfoncer, battre, un p.,** to drive (in) a pile.

pieu² *n.m. P:* bed; pit; **se mettre au p.,** to hit the hay, the sack.

pieusement [pjøzmɑ̃] *adv.* (*a*) piously, reverently; (*b*) dutifully.

pieuter (se) [səpjøte] *v.pr. P:* to go to bed; to hit the hay, the sack.

pieuvre [pjœvr̥] *n.f.* (*a*) *Moll:* octopus; (*b*) (*of pers.*) leech.

pieux, -euse [pjø, -øz] *a.* (*a*) pious; **p. mensonge,** white lie; (*b*) dutiful, (respectfully) devoted.

pif¹ [pif] *int.* bang! crack! smack!

pif² *n.m. P:* **1.** large nose; conk. **2. faire qch. au p.,** to do sth. by guess(work).

pif(f)er [pife] *v.tr. P:* **j'peux pas le p.,** I can't stand (the sight of) him, I can't stomach him.

pifomètre [pifɔmɛtr̥] *n.m. F:* **au p.,** at a rough guess.

pige [piʒ] *n.f.* **1.** measuring rod. **2.** *Typ:* take; amount of copy to be set up in a given time; *Journ:* **être payé à la p.,** to be paid by the line. **3.** *P:* year; **il a 45 piges,** he's 45; **à 60 piges,** at 60.

pigeon, -onne [piʒɔ̃, -ɔn] **1.** *n.* (*a*) *Orn:* pigeon; **p. mâle, femelle,** cock pigeon, hen pigeon; **p. voyageur,** carrier pigeon, homing pigeon; **p. colombin, p. bleu,** stock dove; **p. ramier,** ring dove, wood pigeon; **p. paon,** fantail; **p. d'argile,** clay pigeon; **p. vole,** children's game with forfeits; = Simon says; (*b*) *F:* (*pers.*) sucker; mug. **2.** *n.m. Const:* (*a*) builder's plaster; (*b*) hard lump, nodule (in lime).

pigeonnant [piʒɔnɑ̃] *a. F:* (*of bust*) high; **soutien-gorge p.,** uplift bra.

pigeonneau, -eaux [piʒɔno] *n.m.* young pigeon; squab.

pigeonner [piʒɔne] *v.tr. F:* to swindle, to cheat; to dupe; **je me suis laissé, fait, p.,** I've been had.

pigeonnier [piʒɔnje] *n.m.* **1.** pigeon house, dovecot(e). **2.** *F:* garret, attic.

piger [piʒe] *v.tr.* **(je pigeai(s); n. pigeons) 1.** *Dial:* to measure. **2.** *P:* (*a*) **pige-moi ça!** take a look at that! take a dekko at that! (*b*) to understand; **tu piges la combine?** d'you get what they're, we're, up to? *v.i.* **tu piges?** get it? **il a pigé,** he's twigged, the penny's dropped.

pigiste [piʒist] *n. Journ:* journalist paid at space rates; freelance journalist.

pigment [pigmɑ̃] *n.m.* pigment.

pigmentaire [pigmɑ̃tɛr] *a.* pigmentary.

pigmentation [pigmɑ̃tasjɔ̃] *n.f.* pigmentation.

pigmenter [pigmɑ̃te] *v.tr.* to pigment.

pigne [piɲ] *n.f. Bot:* pine cone, fir cone.

pignocher [piɲɔʃe] *v.i.* to pick at one's food.

pignon¹ [piɲɔ̃] *n.m. Const:* gable (end); **avoir p. sur rue,** to have well situated premises; to run a prosperous business.

pignon² *n.m. Mec.E:* pinion; gear; **p. de chaîne,** sprocket wheel, chain sprocket (of motor cycle, etc.); **grand p.,** front chain wheel (of bicycle).

pignon³ *n.m. Bot:* pine kernel.

pignouf [piɲuf] *n.m. P:* boor, lout; yob(bo).

pilaf [pilaf] *n.m. Cu:* pilaf, pilaw, pilau.

pilage [pilaʒ] *n.m.* pounding, crushing, grinding.

pilaire [pilɛr] *a.* relating to the hair; hairy.

pilastre [pilastr̥] *n.m. Arch:* pilaster; newel (at bottom of handrail).

Pilate [pilat] *Pr.n.m. Hist:* **Ponce P.,** Pontius Pilate.

pile¹ [pil] *n.f.* **1.** pile; heap, stack (of books, etc.); **mettre en p.,** to heap, to stack, to pile up. **2.** pier (of bridge). **3.** (*a*) *El:* battery; cell; **p. sèche,** dry cell; **p. de rechange,** spare battery (for torch, etc.); (*b*) *Atom.Ph:* **p. atomique,** atomic pile, nuclear reactor.

pile² *n.f. F:* belting, beating, thrashing; **flanquer, donner, une p. à qn,** to give s.o. a thrashing; to lick s.o.; **recevoir une p.,** to have a crushing defeat; to take a hammering, to be beaten hollow.

pile³ **1.** *n.f.* reverse (of coin); **p. ou face,** heads or tails; **jouer à p. ou face,** to toss (up) for it. **2.** *adv.* **s'arrêter p.,** to stop short; to come to a dead stop; to stop dead; **vous tombez p.,** you've come just at the right moment, in the nick of time; that's just what was wanted now; **à six heures p.,** on the dot of six.

piler [pile] *v.tr.* (*a*) to pound; to crush, grind (in mortar, mill, etc.); to powder, pestle (drug); to grind (almonds); **poivre pilé,** ground pepper; (*b*) *F:* to thrash (s.o.); **notre équipe s'est fait p.,** our team was badly beaten, got a good thrashing.

pilet [pilɛ] *n.m. Orn:* **(canard) p.,** pintail (duck).

pileux, -euse [pilø, -øz] *a.* pilose, hairy; **système p.,** hair.

pilier [pilje] *n.m.* (*a*) pillar, column; post; shaft (of column); (*b*) *Rugby Fb:* prop forward; (*c*) support, mainstay; (*of pers.*) **p. d'église,** staunch supporter, pillar, of the church; *F: Pej:* **c'est un p. de cabaret, de bistrot,** he's always propping up the bar.

pillage [pijaʒ] *n.m.* (*a*) pillage, looting, plunder(ing) (by soldiers, etc.); **mettre une ville au p.,** to sack a town; (*b*) (i) pilfering, filching; (ii) waste(fulness); (*c*) plagiarism.

pillard, -arde [pijar, -ard] **1.** *a.* (*a*) pillaging; looting; (*b*) thieving, pilfering. **2.** *n.* pillager, looter, plunderer.

piller [pije] *v.tr.* **1.** (*a*) to pillage, plunder, loot, sack, ransack (town, etc.); (*b*) to rob (s.o.); (*c*) **p. un auteur,** to plagiarize, steal from, an author.

pilleur, -euse [pijœr, -øz] **1.** *a.* pillaging, plundering, looting. **2.** *n.* pillager, plunderer; looter; *Nau:* **p. d'épaves,** wrecker.

pilon [pilɔ̃] *n.m.* **1.** (*a*) *Pharm: etc:* pestle; (*b*) (earth) rammer, punner; (*c*) **p. mécanique,** power hammer; **mettre un livre au p.,** to pulp a book. **2.** (*a*) drumstick (of chicken, etc.); (*b*) wooden leg.

pilonnage [pilɔnaʒ] *n.m.* pounding, ramming, punning; *Mil:* heavy bombing; shelling.

pilonner [pilɔne] *v.tr.* to pound (drugs, etc.); to pulp (paper, etc.); to ram, beat, pun (earth, concrete, etc.); *Mil:* to shell, to bombard.

pilori [pilɔri] *n.m.* pillory; **clouer, mettre, qn au p.,** to pillory s.o.

pilosité [pilozite] *n.f.* pilosity; hairiness.

pilot [pilo] *n.m. Civ.E:* pile; **p. de pont,** bridge pile.

pilotage [pilɔtaʒ] *n.m.* **1.** *Nau:* pilotage, piloting; **(droits, frais, de) p.,** pilotage (dues). **2.** *Av:* pilotage, piloting, flying; **poste de p.,** cockpit; (*in larger aircraft*) flight deck; **p. automatique,** automatic piloting; **école de p.,** flying school.

pilote [pilɔt] *n.m.* **1.** (*a*) *Nau:* pilot; (*b*) *Av:* pilot; **p. d'essai,** test pilot; **p. de ligne,** airline pilot; **p. breveté,** licensed pilot; *Mil.Av:* certified pilot; **p. automatique,** automatic pilot, *F:* George; (*c*) driver, pilot (of racing car, etc.); (*d*) **bateau p.,** pilot boat, cutter; **usine, installation, p.,** pilot factory, pilot plant. **2.** *Ich:* pilot fish.
piloter [pilɔte] *v.tr.* (*a*) *Nau:* to pilot (ship); (*b*) *Av:* to pilot, fly (aircraft); (*c*) to drive, pilot (racing car, etc.); (*d*) *F:* **p. qn dans Londres,** to guide, show, s.o. round London.
pilotis [pilɔti] *n.m. Civ.E:* piling; **bâti sur p.,** built on piles.
pilou [pilu] *n.m. Tex:* flannelette, cotton flannel.
pilule [pilyl] *n.f. Pharm:* pill; (*contraceptive*) **la p.,** the pill; **elle prend la p.,** she's on the pill; *F:* **prendre une, la, p.,** to have a crushing defeat; to take a hammering; to be beaten hollow; *Fig:* **avaler la p.,** to swallow the pill, to submit to the humiliation.
pimbêche [pɛ̃bɛʃ] *a. & n.f.* affected, *F:* stuck-up (girl, woman).
piment [pimɑ̃] *n.m.* (*a*) *Bot:* pimento, capsicum; *Cu:* **p. rouge,** (i) red pepper; (ii) chilli; pimento; (*b*) **donner du p. à une histoire,** to add piquancy, spice to a story.
pimenté [pimɑ̃te] *a.* (*a*) *Cu:* highly spiced; hot; (*b*) spicy (story).
pimenter [pimɑ̃te] *v.tr. Cu:* to season (sth.) with pimento, with red pepper; **p. son récit,** to give piquancy, spice, to one's story.
pimpant [pɛ̃pɑ̃] *a.* smart, spruce, trim (dress, person); chic and attractive (woman).
pimprenelle [pɛ̃prənɛl] *n.f. Bot:* burnet, bloodwort.
pin [pɛ̃] *n.m.* (*a*) pine (tree); **p. maritime,** maritime pine; **p. d'Écosse,** Scotch pine, Scotch fir; **p. sylvestre,** Norway pine; **p. pignon, p. parasol,** parasol pine, umbrella pine; **p. de montagne,** silver pine, white pine; **p. de Virginie,** scrub pine; **pomme de p.,** pine, fir, cone; (*b*) pine(wood).
pinacle [pinakl̩] *n.m.* pinnacle; **porter qn au p.,** to praise s.o. to the skies; **être au p.,** to be at the top (of the tree).
pinacothèque [pinakɔtɛk] *n.f.* picture gallery, art gallery.
pinailler [pinaje] *v.i. P:* to quibble, split hairs; to be finicky.
pinailleur, -euse [pinajœr, -øz] *P:* **1.** *a.* quibbling, nitpicking. **2.** *n.* quibbler, nitpicker.
pinard [pinar] *n.m. P:* wine, plonk.
pinasse [pinas] *n.f. Nau:* pinnace, shallop.
pinçage [pɛ̃saʒ] *n.m. Hort:* (*a*) pinching off, nipping off (of buds); (*b*) topping.
pince [pɛ̃s] *n.f.* **1.** (*a*) *Tls:* pincers; pliers; *Metalw:* tongs; *Surg:* forceps; *Toil:* **p. à épiler,** tweezers; **pince(s) coupante(s),** cutting pliers, wire cutters; **p. universelle,** (universal) pliers; *Dom.Ec: etc:* **p. à sucre,** sugar tongs; *Toil:* **p. à ongles,** nail clippers; (*b*) clip; **p. à cravate,** tie clip; **p. de cycliste,** bicycle clip; **p. à papier,** paper clip; **p. à linge,** clothes peg, *NAm:* clothes pin; *Surg:* **p. hémostatique,** artery clip; *El:* **p. de raccordement,** connecting clamp, connector; **p. pour fil terminal,** terminal clamp; (*c*) crowbar, lifting bar; pinch bar. **2.** (*a*) claw, nipper (of crab, etc.); *P:* hand, paw, mitt; (*b*) incisor (of herbivorous animal); (*c*) toe, point (of horse's hoof or shoe); *P:* (*of pers.*) **aller à pinces,** to foot it. **3.** *Dressm:* dart; pleat.
pincé [pɛ̃se] *a.* affected, supercilious; prim (person, style, etc.); glum (face); **sourire p.,** tight-lipped smile; **répondre d'un ton p.,** to answer stiffly, starchily.
pinceau, -eaux [pɛ̃so] *n.m.* **1.** (*a*) (paint)brush; **coup de p.,** stroke of the brush; (*b*) brushwork; (*c*) *P:* foot. **2.** *Opt:* **p. de lumière,** pencil of light.
pince-fesses [pɛ̃sfɛs] *n.m.inv. P:* rowdy party, dance, *NAm:* shindig.
pincée [pɛ̃se] *n.f.* pinch (of salt, snuff, etc.).
pincement [pɛ̃smɑ̃] *n.m.* **1.** (*a*) pinching, nipping; (*b*) pang, twinge (of regret, etc.); **il a eu un p. au cœur,** his heart missed a beat. **2.** *Mus:* plucking (of strings of guitar, etc.). **3.** *Hort:* pinching off, nipping off (of buds).
pince-monseigneur [pɛ̃smɔ̃sɛɲœr] *n.f.* (burglar's) jemmy; *pl. pinces-monseigneur.*
pince-nez [pɛ̃sne] *n.m.inv.* pince-nez.
pincer [pɛ̃se] *v.tr.* **(je pinçai(s); n. pinçons) 1.** to pinch, nip; (*a*) **se p. le doigt dans la porte,** to catch one's finger in the door; **son grand-père lui pinça la joue,** her grandfather pinched her cheek; **p. les lèvres,** to purse one's lips; **se p. le nez,** to hold one's nose; *F:* **ça pince dur ce matin!** it's pretty nippy this morning; (*b*) *Hort:* (i) to nip off (buds); (ii) to top (plant); (*c*) *Mus:* to pluck (strings of harp, etc.); *Dressm:* to put darts in (a garment). **2.** to grip, hold fast; *F:* **p. un voleur,** to catch a thief; **se faire p.,** to get caught, nicked, copped; *F:* **en p. pour qn,** to be keen on, crazy about, s.o.
pince-sans-rire [pɛ̃ssɑ̃rir] *n.m.inv.* person of dry (and ironical) humour, *NAm:* humor; *a.* **répondre d'un air p.-s.-r.,** to answer drily, with dry sarcasm.
pincette [pɛ̃sɛt] *n.f.* (*a*) tweezers; (*b*) *pl.* (fire) tongs; pair of tongs; *F:* **il n'est pas à prendre avec des pincettes,** (i) he's filthy (dirty); (ii) he's like a bear with a sore head.
pinçon [pɛ̃sɔ̃] *n.m.* pinch mark (on the skin); blood blister.
pindarique [pɛ̃darik] *a.* Pindaric (ode).
pinéal, -aux [pineal, -o] *a. Anat:* pineal.
pinède [pinɛd] *n.f.* (*in S. of Fr.*) pine forest.
pineraie [pinrɛ] *n.f.* pine plantation, pinewood.
pingouin [pɛ̃gwɛ̃] *n.m. Orn:* (*a*) auk; (*b*) penguin; **p. royal,** king penguin.
ping-pong [piŋpɔ̃g] *n.m. no pl. R.t.m.* ping pong (*R.t.m.*), table tennis.
pingre [pɛ̃gr̩] *F:* **1.** *a.* miserly, mean, stingy. **2.** *n.* miser, skinflint, *NAm:* tightwad.
pingrerie [pɛ̃grəri] *n.f. F:* stinginess, niggardliness.
pinson, -onne [pɛ̃sɔ̃, -ɔn] *n. Orn:* finch; chaffinch; **être gai comme un p.,** to be as happy as a lark.
pintade [pɛ̃tad] *n.f. Orn:* guinea fowl; **p. mâle,** guinea cock; **p. femelle,** guinea hen.
pintadeau, -eaux [pɛ̃tado] *n.m. Orn:* young guinea fowl; guinea poult.
pinte [pɛ̃t] *n.f.* (*a*) *Meas:* (i) *A:* (*in Fr.*) pint (*about* 0·9 litres, *NAm:* liters); (ii) (*Eng: U.S:*) pint; (iii) *Fr.C:* quart; (*b*) *F: O:* **se payer une p. de bon sang,** to have a good time, a good laugh.
pinter [pɛ̃te] *v.i. & tr. P:* to swill (beer, wine); to booze; **il est pinté,** he's tight, sozzled.
pin up [pinœp] *n.f.inv. P:* pinup (girl).
pioche [pjɔʃ] *n.f.* **1.** pickaxe, *NAm:* pickax, pick, mattock. **2.** (*dominoes*) stock.
piocher [pjɔʃe] **1.** *v.tr.* (*a*) to dig (with a pick); to pick; (*b*) *F:* to grind at, swot up (sth.); **p. son allemand,** to swot up, mug up, one's German. **2.** *v.i.* (*a*) to dig; to delve (**dans,** into); (*b*) (*dominoes*) to draw from the stock; (*c*) to slog, to sweat.
piocheur, -euse [pjɔʃœr, -øz] **1.** *a. F:* hardworking. **2.** *n. Sch: F:* swot, swotter; slogger. **3.** *n.f. Civ.E:* **piocheuse,** digger, mechanical excavator.
piolet [pjɔlɛ] *n.m.* (mountaineer's) ice axe.
pion [pjɔ̃] *n.m.* **1.** *Sch: F:* = prefect (paid to supervise pupils). **2.** (*a*) *Chess:* pawn; (*b*) *Games:* piece, draughts(man), *NAm:* checker.

pioncer [pjɔ̃se] *v.i.* **(je pionçai(s); n. pionçons)** *P:* to sleep; to have a kip, a snooze.

pionne [pjɔn] *n.f. Sch: F:* = prefect (paid to supervise pupils).

pionnier [pjɔnje] *n.m. Mil: etc:* pioneer.

pipe [pip] *n.f.* **1.** pipe, tube (for liquid, gas). **2.** pipe, large cask (for wine, spirits, etc.). **3.** (*a*) (tobacco) pipe; **p. de bruyère, en terre,** briar, clay, pipe; *P:* **casser sa p.,** to die, to kick the bucket; *F:* **nom d'une p.!** heavens above! *P:* **20 francs par tête de p.,** 20 francs a head; *P:* **se fendre la p.,** to split one's sides laughing, to laugh one's head off; (*b*) pipeful of tobacco; (*c*) *P:* cigarette, fag.

pipeau, -eaux [pipo] *n.m.* **1.** *Mus:* (reed) pipe; shepherd's pipe; **p. de chasse,** bird call. **2.** *pl.* limed twigs (to snare birds).

pipée [pipe] *n.f.* bird snaring, bird catching (with bird calls and limed twigs).

pipelet, -ette [piplɛ, -ɛt] *n. F:* concierge, porter, *NAm:* janitor.

pipe(-)line [piplin] *n.m.* pipeline; *pl. pipe(-)lines.*

piper [pipe] **1.** *v.i. F:* **ne pas p.,** not to say a word; to keep silent. **2.** *v.tr.* (*a*) to lure (birds by means of bird calls); (*b*) to load (dice); to mark (cards).

pipette [pipɛt] *n.f. Ch: etc:* pipette.

pipi¹ [pipi] *n.m. F:* pee; (*child's language*) wee-wee; **faire p.,** to piddle, to pee; (*child's language*) to wee-wee; **aller faire p.,** to go to the loo, to go for a pee; **il y a du p. de chien sur le tapis,** the dog's made a puddle on the carpet; *P:* **c'est du p. de chat,** it's dish-water, cat's piss.

pipi² *n.m.*, **pipit** [pipit] *n.m. Orn:* pipit; **p. des prés,** meadow pipit, meadow titlark.

pipistrelle [pipistrɛl] *n.f. Z:* (small) bat, pipistrelle.

piquage [pikaʒ] *n.m.* (machine) stitching.

piquant [pikɑ̃] **1.** *a.* (*a*) prickling; pointed; prickly, thorny (plant); stinging (nettle); (*b*) bristly, prickly (beard); biting (wind); piquant (taste); *Cu:* **sauce piquante,** piquant sauce; *F:* **eau piquante,** fizzy water; (*c*) mordant; **remarques piquantes,** cutting remarks; (*d*) piquant, striking, stimulating (beauty); stimulating, interesting (remarks). **2.** *n.m.* (*a*) prickle, thorn (of plant); quill, spine (of porcupine); bristle (of hedgehog); spike, barb (of barbed wire, etc.); (*b*) piquancy; pungency (of style); **le changement donne du p. à la vie,** variety is the spice of life.

pique¹ [pik] **1.** *n.f.* (*a*) *A.Arms:* pike; (*b*) (*of picador*) lance. **2.** *n.m. Cards:* spade(s).

pique² *n.f.* **1.** *O:* pique, ill-feeling. **2.** taunt, spiteful remark, *F:* dig; **envoyer, lancer, des piques à qn,** to get at s.o.

piqué, -ée [pike] *a.* **1.** (*a*) quilted (coverlet, garment); **p. à la machine,** machine-quilted; machine-stitched; (*b*) *n.m.* quilting; piqué. **2.** (*a*) wormeaten (wood, book); (damp-, dust-, mould-, *NAm:* mold-) spotted (mirror, etc.); foxed (page, engraving); pitted (metal); **p. des mouches,** fly-spotted; **ciel p. d'étoiles,** sky studded with stars; (*b*) *F:* batty, barmy, loony; *n.* **c'est une vieille piquée,** she's a nutter. **3.** sour, tart (wine). **4.** *Mus:* staccato (notes). **5.** *n.m. Av:* **descente en p.,** vertical dive, nose dive; **bombardement en p.,** dive bombing.

pique-assiette [pikasjɛt] *n.m. & f.inv. F:* scrounger, sponger; *NAm:* freeloader.

pique-bœuf [pikbœf] *n.m. Orn:* beefeater, ox-pecker; *pl. pique-bœufs* [pikbø].

pique-feu [pikfø] *n.m.inv.* poker; fire rake.

pique-fleurs [pikflœr] *n.m.inv.* (glass) flower holder.

pique-nique [piknik] *n.m.* picnic; **faire un p.-n.,** to go for a picnic; to picnic; *pl. pique-niques.*

pique-niquer [piknike] *v.i.* to (have a) picnic.

pique-niqueur, -euse [piknikœr, -øz] *n.* picnicker; *pl. pique-niqueurs, -euses.*

piquer [pike] **I.** *v.tr.* **1.** (*a*) to prick, sting; (*of flea*) to bite; **être piqué par une guêpe,** to be stung by a wasp; *F:* **quelle mouche vous pique?** what's biting you? **p. un cheval de l'éperon,** to prick, spur, a horse; **p. des deux,** (i) to spur on one's horse, to gallop off; (ii) to rush, dash, off; **p. les bœufs,** to goad the oxen; **moutarde qui pique,** hot mustard; *F:* **eau qui pique,** fizzy water; **vent qui pique,** keen, biting, wind; **ça pique,** it pricks, stings; (*to unshaven man*) you're all bristly; (*b*) *Med:* to give (s.o.) an injection; **se faire p. contre qch.,** to be vaccinated against sth.; *F:* **p. un chien,** to put a dog down; (*c*) to pique, offend (s.o.); **p. qn au vif,** to cut s.o. to the quick; (*d*) **p. la curiosité de qn,** to arouse, excite, s.o.'s curiosity. **2.** (*a*) **p. une surface,** to eat into, to pit, a surface; (*of worms*) to eat into (wood); (*b*) to spot, to mark; **mains piquées de tâches de rousseur,** freckled hands; (*c*) *P:* **se p. le nez,** to tipple; to hit the bottle. **3.** *Nau:* **p. l'heure,** to strike the hour. **4.** (*a*) to prick, puncture (sth.); to (back)stitch; to quilt (counterpane, etc.); **p. du cuir,** to stitch leather; **p. (à la machine),** to machine (stitch); *Cu:* **p. de la viande,** to lard meat; **rôti piqué d'ail,** joint stuck with garlic; **p. des petits pois,** to stab peas; (*b*) *Mus:* **p. une note,** to play a note staccato; (*c*) *F:* to pinch, swipe **(qch. à qn,** sth. from s.o.). **5.** to stick, insert (sth. into sth.); **p. une photo au mur,** to pin a photograph on the wall. **6.** (*a*) **p. une tête,** to take a header, to dive; (*b*) *v.i. Av:* to nosedive; *Nau:* **p. de l'avant,** to go down by the bows. **7.** *F:* **p. un cent mètres,** to sprint (off), to go into a sprint; **p. un plongeon,** to dive; **p. un roupillon,** to have forty winks; **p. une crise,** to throw a fit; **p. une crise de larmes,** to burst into tears; **p. un soleil, un fard,** to go bright red, to blush. **II. se piquer 1.** (*a*) to prick oneself; to get stung; (*b*) (i) to give oneself an injection; (ii) to take drugs; to give oneself a shot; **il se pique,** he's a drug addict. **2.** to take offence, to get irritated. **3. se p. de faire qch.,** to pride oneself on doing sth.; **se p. de littérature,** to pride oneself on one's knowledge of literature. **4. se p. au jeu,** to get excited, to warm up, over a game; to be stimulated by opposition; **je m'étais piqué au jeu,** I was on my mettle. **5.** to become spotted (with rust, mould, *NAm:* mold, etc.); (*of metals*) to pit; (*of wood*) to become wormeaten; (*of clothes, etc.*) to become motheaten. **6.** (*of wine*) to turn acid, sour.

piquet¹ [pikɛ] *n.m.* **1.** peg, stake, post; **mettre, attacher, les chevaux au p.,** to tether the horses; **p. de tente,** tent peg; **droit comme un p.,** as straight as a ramrod; **raide comme un p.,** as stiff as a post. **2.** *Mil: etc:* picket; **p. d'incendie,** fire picket; **piquets de grève,** strike pickets; *Sch:* **être au p.** = to stand in the corner.

piquet² *n.m. Cards:* piquet; **faire un p.,** to play a hand at piquet.

piquetage [piktaʒ] *n.m.* staking (out).

piqueter [pikte] *v.tr.* **(je piquette, n. piquetons; je piquetterai) 1.** to stake out, mark out (road, ground, etc.). **2.** to picket (factory, etc.). **3.** to spot, dot; **piqueté de noir,** dotted with black.

piquette [pikɛt] *n.f.* **1.** (*a*) *marc* diluted with water; (*b*) acid, vinegary, wine; plonk; *F:* **ça n'était pas de la p.,** that was no small matter. **2.** *P:* **prendre une p.,** to get a good thrashing; to get a hammering.

piqueur, -euse [pikœr, -øz] **1.** *n.m.* (*a*) *Ven:* whipper-in; huntsman; (*b*) *Equit:* groom. **2.** *n. Ind:* (*a*) (leather) stitcher; (*b*) *esp. f.* sewer; stitcher. **3.** *n.m. Min: etc:* hewer, pickman; *Mch:* **p. de chaudières,** scurfer. **4.** *n.m. Rail:* foreman platelayer, *NAm:* tracklayer.

piquoir [pikwar] *n.m. Art:* (draughtsman's) needle; pricker.

piqûre [pikyr] *n.f.* **1.** (*a*) prick, sting, bite (of insect); **p. d'épingle,** pin prick; (*b*) (subcutaneous, hypodermic) injection; *F:* shot, jab; **faire une p. à qn,** to give s.o. an injection. **2.** puncture, small hole; pit (in metal, etc.); (*a*) **p. de vers,** wormhole (in wood, book); moth-hole (in garment); **p. d'aiguille,** pinhole (in leather, etc.); (*b*) (back)stitching (of material, leather); quilting; **(point de) p.,** lockstitch (of sewing machine). **3.** spot, speck (of rust, dust, mould, *NAm:* mold); foxing (of paper); pitting (in metal); **p. de mouches,** fly speck.

piranha [piraɲa] *n.m. Ich:* piranha, piraña.

pirate [pirat] *n.m.* (*a*) pirate; **p. de l'air,** hijacker, skyjacker; (*b*) pirate, shark; plagiarist; (*c*) *a.* clandestine; *W.Tel:* **station p.,** pirate station.

pirater [pirate] *v.tr.* to pirate, plagiarize.

piraterie [piratri] *n.f.* **1.** (*a*) piracy; *Av:* **p. aérienne,** hijacking, skyjacking; (*b*) plagiarism, piracy. **2.** act of piracy.

pire [pir] **1.** *comp.a.* worse; (*a*) **cela est bien p.,** that's much worse; **le remède est p. que le mal,** the cure is worse than the complaint; *Prov:* **il n'est p. eau que l'eau qui dort,** still waters run deep; (*b*) (*with neuter or indef.pron.*) **rien n'est p. que . . .,** nothing is worse than . . .; **ce qui est p.,** what is worse. **2.** *sup.* **le p., la p., les pires,** the worst; (*a*) *a.* **un voyou de la p. espèce,** the worst kind of scoundrel; **nos pires erreurs,** our worst mistakes; (*b*) *n.* **le p. de l'histoire, c'est que . . .,** the worst of the story is that . . .; **pour le meilleur et pour le p.,** for better, for worse; **s'attendre au p.,** to expect the worst.

Pirée (le) [ləpire] *Pr.n.m. Geog:* Piraeus.

piriforme [pirifɔrm] *a.* pear-shaped, pyriform.

pirogue [pirɔg] *n.f.* **1.** pirogue; (dugout) canoe. **2.** canoe.

piroguier [pirɔgje] *n.m.* boatman (in a pirogue).

pirouette [pirwɛt] *n.f.* (*a*) *Danc: Equit:* pirouette; *F:* **répondre par des pirouettes,** to reply (to sth. serious) with a joke; (*b*) reversal, change, of opinion; about-turn.

pirouetter [pirwete] *v.i.* to pirouette.

pis¹ [pi] *n.m.* udder (of cow, etc.).

pis² *adv., a. & n.m.* **1.** *comp.* worse; (*a*) *adv.* **p. que tout cela,** worse than all that; **il y a p.,** there is, are, worse; **de p. en p.,** worse and worse; **aller de mal en p.,** to go from bad to worse; **tant p.!** it can't be helped! never mind! (*b*) (*with adj. function*) **cela serait encore p.,** that would be worse still; **et qui p. est,** and what is worse; **le malade est p. que jamais,** the patient is worse; (*c*) *n.neut.* **pour ne pas dire p.,** to say no more; **il a fait tout cela et p.,** he did all that and (something even) worse. **2.** *sup.* **le p.,** the worst; (*a*) (*with adj. function*) **ce qu'il y a de p.,** (i) what is worst; (ii) the worst there is; (*b*) *n.neut.* **faire p.,** to do the worst; **en mettant les choses au p.,** if the worst comes to the worst; **au p. aller** [opizale], at the very worst.

pis(-)aller [pizale] *n.m.inv.* last resort; makeshift; stopgap.

piscicole [pisikɔl] *a.* piscicultural.

pisciculteur [pisikyltœr] *n.m.* pisciculturist, fish breeder.

pisciculture [pisikyltyr] *n.f.* pisciculture; fish breeding.

pisciforme [pisifɔrm] *a.* fish-shaped, pisciform.

piscine [pisin] *n.f.* **1.** swimming pool; **p. publique,** swimming baths. **2.** *Ecc:* piscina.

piscivore [pisivɔr] *a.* piscivorous.

Pise [piz] *Pr.n.f. Geog:* Pisa.

pisé [pize] *n.m. Const:* pisé, rammed earth; cob.

pissaladière [pisaladjɛr] *n.f. Cu: Dial:* (open) onion and tomato tart, garnished with anchovies or sardines and olives.

pissat [pisa] *n.m.* urine (of horse, donkey, etc.).

pisse [pis] *n.f. P:* (*not used in polite company*) piss, pee.

pisse-froid [pisfrwa] *n.m.inv. F:* (*pers.*) cold fish; wet blanket.

pissenlit [pisɑ̃li] *n.m. Bot:* dandelion; *F:* **manger les pissenlits par la racine,** to be dead, to be pushing up the daisies.

pisser [pise] *v.i. P:* (*a*) (*not used in polite company*) to (have a) piss, to (have a) pee; **il a pissé dans sa culotte,** he's wet his pants; **c'est comme si je pissais dans un violon,** it's like water off a duck's back; **laisse p. (le mérinos)!** leave it! forget it! (*b*) to leak, gush out; **tonneau qui pisse,** leaky barrel; (*c*) (*with cog-n.acc.*) **p. du sang,** (i) to pass blood with the urine; (ii) to bleed like a stuck pig; (*d*) *impers.* (*of rain*) **ça pisse dur,** it's pissing down.

pissette [pisɛt] *n.f. Ch:* washing bottle, wash bottle.

pisseur, -euse¹ [pisœr, -øz] *n. P:* (*a*) (*not used in polite company*) **c'est un p.,** he's always going for a piss, pee; (*b*) *Journ:* **p. de copie,** writer who churns out rubbish; (*c*) *n.f.* **pisseuse,** little girl; brat.

pisseux, -euse² [pisø, -øz] *a. F:* (*a*) smelling of urine; (*b*) stained with urine; (*c*) (*of colour, NAm:* color) faded, washed out, yellowy.

pissoir [piswar] *n.m. F:* urinal.

pissotière [pisɔtjɛr] *n.f. F:* (public) urinal.

pistache [pistaʃ] **1.** *n.f. Bot:* pistachio (nut). **2.** *a.inv.* pistachio (green).

pistachier [pistaʃje] *n.m. Bot:* pistachio tree.

pistage [pistaʒ] *n.m.* tracking; trailing; tailing.

pistard [pistar] *n.m. Cy:* track racer.

piste [pist] *n.f.* **1.** *Ven:* track, trail, scent; **suivre la p.,** to follow (i) the track, (ii) the footprints; **être sur la p. de qn, de qch.,** (i) to be on the track of s.o., sth.; (ii) to be in search of s.o., sth.; **la police a plusieurs pistes,** the police have several leads; **suivre une fausse p.,** to be on the wrong track. **2.** *Sp: etc:* (*a*) racecourse; (*b*) running track; racetrack, racing track; **p. cendrée,** cinder track; **tour de p.,** lap; (*c*) *Aut: etc:* **p. de vitesse,** racing track; **p. d'essai,** test track; (*d*) **p. (de circus),** (circus) ring; **p. de patinage,** skating rink; **p. de ski,** ski piste, run; **p. de danse,** dance floor; (*e*) *Av:* runway; **p. d'envol,** take-off strip; **p. d'atterrissage,** landing strip; (*f*) (*path*) track, trail; **p. pour cavaliers, p. cavalière,** bridle path. **3.** *Rec:* track (of tape recorder); *Cin:* **p. sonore,** soundtrack.

pister [piste] *v.tr.* to track, trail; **p. qn,** to follow, tail, shadow, s.o.; **attention, on nous piste!** look out, there's someone on our track!

pisteur [pistœr] *n.m.* ski run attendant, supervisor.

pistil [pistil] *n.m. Bot:* pistil.

pistole [pistɔl] *n.f. A.Num:* pistole.

pistolet [pistɔlɛ] *n.m.* **1.** (*a*) pistol; gun; *Hist:* **p. d'arçon,** horse pistol; **p. à air comprimé,** air pistol; *Sp:* **p. de starter,** starting pistol; *Toys:* **p. à bouchon,** popgun; **p. à eau,** water pistol; *F:* **c'est un drôle de p.,** he's a queer customer, fish, *NAm:* duck; (*b*) *Artil: etc:* **p. de tir,** firing pistol; (*c*) *Tchn:* **p. (à peinture), p. (vaporisateur),** paint gun, spray gun; **peinture au p.,** spray painting, spraying. **2.** *Cu:* (milk) roll. **3.** *Draw:* French curve. **4.** bed urinal, bottle.

pistolet-mitrailleur [pistɔlɛmitrajœr] *n.m.* submachine gun, sten gun, tommy gun; *pl. pistolets-mitrailleurs.*

piston [pistɔ̃] *n.m.* **1.** (*a*) *Mec.E:* piston (of machine, pump, jack, etc.); **p. à air, à eau,** air, water, piston; **tête de p.,** piston head; (*b*) *Hyd.E:* **p. plongeur,** plunger (of force pump, etc.); ram (of hydraulic press); (*c*) string-pulling; **avoir du p.,** to have friends in the right places, *esp. U.S:* to have clout; **il a eu une place par p.,** someone pulled strings to get him the job. **2.** *Mus:* (*a*) valve (of cornet, etc.); (*b*) **cornet à pistons, p.,** cornet.

pistonner [pistɔne] *v.tr.* to use one's influence, *esp. U.S:* one's clout, to help (s.o.); to pull strings, wires, for (s.o.); **il s'est fait p.,** he got s.o. to pull strings for him.

pistou [pistu] *n.m. Cu:* **soupe de, au, p.,** vegetable soup flavoured with basil.

pitance [pitɑ̃s] *n.f.* **1.** *A:* (*in convent, etc.*) allowance (of food). **2.** *Pej: O:* sustenance, food; **se faire une maigre p.,** to eke out a living.

pitchpin [pitʃpɛ̃] *n.m. Bot:* pitchpine.

piteusement [pitøzmɑ̃] *adv.* piteously; miserably.

piteux, -euse [pitø, -øz] *a.* piteous, woeful, pitiable, miserable; **faire piteuse mine,** to look crestfallen; **p. résultat,** poor, miserable, result; **être dans un p. état,** to be in a poor way.

pithécanthrope [pitekɑ̃trɔp] *n.m. Anthr:* pithecanthrope.

pitié [pitje] *n.f.* pity, compassion; **avoir p. de qn,** to pity s.o.; to take, have, pity on s.o.; to have mercy on s.o.; **prendre p. de qn, prendre qn en p.,** to take pity on s.o.; **sans p.,** pitiless(ly), merciless(ly), ruthless(ly); **par p.,** for pity's sake; out of pity; **p.!** (have) mercy! for pity's sake! **faire p.,** to arouse pity, compassion; **il me faisait p.,** I felt sorry for him; **cela faisait p. à voir,** it was pitiable to see (it); **c'est p. qu'il soit resté seul,** it's sad that he should have been left alone; **c'est à faire p.!** it's lamentable! it's pitiful!

piton [pitɔ̃] *n.m.* **1.** *Tchn:* (metal) eye, eye bolt; **p. (d'alpiniste),** piton, peg; **p. à vis,** screw eye; screw ring; **p. à boucle,** ring bolt. **2.** peak (of mountain).

pitoyable [pitwajab̥l̥] *a.* (*a*) pitiable, pitiful, piteous, lamentable (tale, condition, etc.); (*b*) paltry, despicable, wretched (excuse, etc.).

pitoyablement [pitwajabləmɑ̃] *adv.* pitifully.

pitre [pitr̥] *n.m.* **1.** (circus) clown. **2.** clown, buffoon; **faire le p.,** to clown, play the fool.

pitrerie [pitrəri] *n.f. F:* piece of clowning; foolery, buffoonery.

pittoresque [pitɔrɛsk] **1.** *a.* picturesque; colourful, *NAm:* colorful, graphic (description, style). **2.** *n.m.* picturesqueness; vividness (of style, etc.).

pituitaire [pitɥitɛr] *a. Anat:* pituitary.

pivert [pivɛr] *n.m. Orn:* green woodpecker.

pivoine [pivwan] *n.f. Bot:* peony; **rouge comme une p.,** red as a beetroot.

pivot [pivo] *n.m.* **1.** pivot; (*a*) *Mec.E:* pin, axis; swivel (of gun, etc.); *Mec:* fulcrum (of lever); **p. à rotule,** ball pivot; **p. de compas, de boussole,** centre pin of a compass; **à p., monté sur p.,** pivoted, swivelling; **canon à p.,** swivel gun; (*b*) *Dent:* pivot, post; (*c*) *Mil:* pivot (man); (*d*) central figure (of drama, etc.); key man (of industry, etc.); mainspring. **2.** *Bot:* tap root. **3.** *Games:* (*basketball*) pivot.

pivotant [pivɔtɑ̃] *a.* **1.** pivoting; swivelling, revolving (base, etc.); slewing (crane, etc.); **fauteuil p.,** swivel chair. **2.** *Bot:* tap-rooted (tree, plant); **racine pivotante,** tap root.

pivoter [pivɔte] *v.i.* **1.** (*a*) to pivot; to swivel, revolve; to turn, hinge (**sur,** upon); **faire p. qch.,** to turn, swivel, sth. round; **p. sur ses talons,** to swing round on one's heels; (*b*) *Mil: etc:* (*of troops*) to wheel; to change direction. **2.** *Bot:* (*of plant*) to form a tap root.

placage [plakaʒ] *n.m.* **1.** veneering (of wood); facing (of stone); **bois de p.,** veneer. **2.** plating (of metal); **p. au chrome,** chromium plating. **3.** *Rugby Fb:* tackle.

placard [plakar] *n.m.* **1.** (wall) cupboard. **2.** poster, bill, placard; notice; *Journ:* **p. de publicité, publicitaire,** advertisement (in newspaper). **3.** *Typ:* **(épreuve en) p.,** slip proof, galley proof. **4.** (*a*) *Nau:* patch (on sail); (*b*) panel (of door); (*c*) *F:* thick layer, coating.

placarder [plakarde] *v.tr.* **1.** (*a*) **p. une affiche,** to stick a bill, poster, on a wall; (*b*) **p. un mur,** to stick bills, posters, on a wall, to placard a wall with posters. **2.** *Typ:* to pull (text) in slips.

placardeur [plakardœr] *n.m.* billsticker, billposter.

place [plas] *n.f.* place. **1.** (*a*) position; **changer sa chaise de p.,** to shift one's chair; **mettre qch. en p.,** to put sth. in its place, in position; **mise en p.,** putting into place, into position; setting, fitting, mounting; **tout est à sa p.,** everything's in its place; **remettez vos livres à leur p.,** put your books away; **ils y sont à leur p.,** they are not out of place there; **remettre qn à sa p.,** to put s.o. in his place; **à vos places!** take your seats; **voulez-vous prendre ma p.?** would you like to change places with me? **il ne peut pas rester en p.,** he can't keep still; **il ne tient pas en p. aujourd'hui,** he is very fidgety today; **son nom a pris p. dans l'histoire,** his name has found a place in history; (*b*) stead; **je viens à la p. de mon père,** I've come instead of my father, in my father's place; **à votre p. je . . .,** in your place, if I were you, I . . .; (*c*) **faire p. à qch.,** to give place to sth.; (*d*) room; **occuper beaucoup de p.,** to take up a great deal of room; **nous n'avons pas de p. pour mettre un piano,** we have no room for a piano; **faire p. à qn,** to make room, make way, for s.o.; **(faites) p.!** stand aside! **faites-lui un peu de p.,** make room for him; **céder, laisser, la p. à qn,** to give way to s.o. **2.** (*a*) seat; *Th: etc:* **restez à votre p.,** keep your seat; **louer deux places au théâtre,** to book two seats at the theatre, *NAm:* theater; **il n'y avait pas une p.,** there wasn't a seat to be found, to be had; **p. avant, arrière,** front, back, seat (in car); **voiture à deux, à quatre, places,** two-seater, four-seater (car); *Aut:* **une deux places,** a two-seater; **prix des places,** (i) fares; (ii) prices of admission; **payer p. entière,** to pay (i) full fare, (ii) full price; (*b*) situation, office, post; **quitter, perdre, sa p.,** to leave, to lose, one's job; **une personne en p.,** a person in high office. **3.** locality, spot; (*a*) square; **p. du marché,** market place; **p. d'armes,** drill ground, parade ground; **sur p.,** on the spot; on site; **faire du sur p.,** to mark time; **il lut la lettre sur p.,** he read the letter then and there; **personnel engagé sur p.,** staff engaged locally; **rester sur p.,** to stay put; (*b*) **achats sur p.,** local purchases; **prix sur p.,** loco price; **avoir du crédit sur la p.,** to have credit (facilities) locally; *Bank: Fin:* **affaires sur la p. de Paris,** business on the Paris market; (*c*) *Mil:* **p. (forte, de guerre),** fortress, fortified town; fortified place.

placé [plase] *a. & n.m. Turf:* placed (horse); **arriver p.,** to be placed.

placement [plasmɑ̃] *n.m.* **1.** placing; seating; investing (of money); **bureau, agence, de placement(s),** employment (i) bureau, agency, (ii) exchange; job centre, *NAm:* center. **2.** investment; **faire des placements,** to invest (money), to make investments; **p. avantageux,** good investment; *F:* **p. de père de famille,** gilt-edged investment; blue chip.

placenta [plasɛ̃ta] *n.m. Bot: Obst:* placenta.

placentaire [plasɛ̃tɛr] *a. Anat: Obst: Bot:* placental; placentary.

placer [plase] *v.* **(je plaçai(s); n. plaçons)** to place. **1.** *v.tr.* (*a*) to put, set (in a certain place), to find a place, places, for (spectators, guests, etc.); *Th: etc:* **p. qn,** to show s.o. to his seat; **vous êtes mieux placé que moi pour en juger,** you're better placed than I am to judge; **vous êtes bien placé pour le savoir,** you're in a position to, you ought to, know; **je n'ai pas pu p. un mot,** I couldn't get a word in edgeways; **p. une sentinelle,** to post a (soldier on) sentry (duty); **maison bien placée,** well situated house; **confiance mal placée,** misplaced confidence; (*b*) to place (s.o.); to find a post, a job, for (s.o.); **p. un apprenti chez qn,** to apprentice s.o. to s.o.; **ils n'arrivent pas à p. leur fille,** they haven't been able to marry off their daughter; (*c*) to invest (money); to place (shares); (*d*) to sell, dispose of (goods); **valeurs difficiles à p.,** bills difficult to negotiate; **marchandises qui se placent facilement,** goods that sell readily. **2. se p.** (*a*) to take one's seat, one's place (at dinner party, etc.); to take up one's position, one's stand; **dites-moi où me p.,** tell me where to sit; (*b*) to obtain, find, a job; **se p. comme vendeuse,** to get a job as a salesgirl.

placet [plasɛ] *n.m. A:* petition, address.

placeur, -euse [plasœr, -øz] *n.* **1.** employment agent, consultant. **2.** (*a*) steward (at public meetings); (*b*) *Th:* usher, *f.* usherette.

placide [plasid] *a.* placid, calm.

placidement [plasidmɑ̃] *adv.* placidly, calmly.

placidité [plasidite] *n.f.* placidity, placidness, calmness.

placier [plasje] *n.m. Com:* travelling salesman, traveller.

plafond [plafɔ̃] *n.m.* **1.** (*a*) ceiling; **p. à caissons,** coffered ceiling; **chambre haute, basse, de p.,** high-, low-ceilinged room; (*b*) roof (of car, of cave); (*c*) *Meteor:* **p. (nuageux),** ceiling (of clouds). **2.** (*maximum attainable or permissible*) (*a*) **prix p.,** maximum price; ceiling (price); **fixer un p. à un budget,** to fix a ceiling to a budget; (*b*) *Av:* ceiling, flying height (of aircraft); *Aut:* top, maximum, speed.

plafonnage [plafɔnaʒ] *n.m. Const:* ceiling work.

plafonnement [plafɔnmɑ̃] *n.m.* **la production automobile est en plein p.,** car production has reached its ceiling, has peaked.

plafonner [plafɔne] **1.** *v.tr.* to put a ceiling in (room). **2.** *v.i.* (*a*) *Av:* to fly at the ceiling; *Aut:* to go at maximum speed; (*b*) (*of price, etc.*) to reach a ceiling, a maximum; to peak.

plafonneur [plafɔnœr] *n.m.* plasterer of ceilings.

plafonnier [plafɔnje] *n.m.* ceiling light, (electric) ceiling fitting; *Aut:* courtesy, interior, light.

plage [plaʒ] *n.f.* **1.** (*a*) beach; **p. de sable, de galets,** sandy, pebble, beach; (*b*) seaside resort. **2.** *Navy:* freeboard deck (of battleship); **p. arrière,** (i) *Navy:* quarter deck; (ii) *Aut:* window shelf. **3.** (*a*) area; *Opt:* **p. lumineuse,** light area, high light; (*b*) *W. Tel: T.V:* (time) segment (of broadcast); (*c*) range; *W.Tel:* **p. d'écoute (d'un appareil),** tuning range; *Com:* **p. de prix,** price range; (*d*) track, band (of gramophone record).

plagiaire [plaʒjɛr] *n.* plagiarist.

plagiat [plaʒja] *n.m.* plagiarism, plagiary.

plagier [plaʒje] *v.tr.* (*impf. & pr.sub.* **n. plagiions, v. plagiiez**) to plagiarize.

plagiste [plaʒist] *n.* beach attendant, manager.

plaid [plɛd] *n.m.* travelling rug.

plaidant [plɛdɑ̃] *a. Jur:* pleading (counsel); **les parties plaidantes,** the litigants.

plaider [plede] **1.** *v.tr.* to plead (a cause); **la cause s'est plaidée hier,** the case was heard yesterday; **son défenseur va p. la folie,** his counsel will plead insanity, will put forward a plea of insanity; **p. le faux pour savoir le vrai,** to make a false allegation in order to get at the truth; **p. coupable, non coupable,** to plead guilty, not guilty. **2.** *v.i.* to plead (**pour,** for, **contre,** against); to go to court, to litigate; **p. contre qn,** to take s.o. to court, to take proceedings against s.o.; *Fig:* **p. pour, en faveur de, qn,** to speak for s.o., to defend s.o.

plaideur, -euse [plɛdœr, -øz] *n.* litigant.

plaidoirie [plɛdwari] *n.f.* counsel's speech.

plaidoyer [plɛdwaje] *n.m.* (*a*) *Jur:* address to the Court (*usu.* by counsel, *esp.* for the defence); speech for the defence; (*b*) defence, plea (for s.o., sth.).

plaie [plɛ] *n.f.* **1.** wound, sore; cut; **p. profonde,** deep wound; **rouvrir d'anciennes plaies,** to open old wounds; **retourner, remuer, le couteau, le fer, dans la p.,** to turn the knife in the wound; **mettre le doigt sur la p.,** to put one's finger on the source of the trouble. **2.** (*a*) affliction, evil; scourge; **les dix plaies d'Égypte,** the ten plagues of Egypt; (*b*) *F:* (*of pers.*) pest, menace; **quelle p.!** what a pest!

plaignant, -ante [plɛɲɑ̃, -ɑ̃t] *a. & n. Jur:* plaintiff; **partie plaignante,** plaintiff, complainant.

plain-chant [plɛ̃ʃɑ̃] *n.m. Mus:* plainsong, plain chant; *pl. plains-chants.*

plaindre [plɛ̃dr̥] *v.* (*pr.p.* **plaignant;** *p.p.* **plaint;** *pr.ind.* **je plains, il plaint, n. plaignons, ils plaignent;** *pr.sub.* **je plaigne;** *impf.* **je plaignais;** *p.h.* **je plaignis;** *fu.* **je plaindrai**) **1.** *v.tr.* (*a*) to pity; **il est fort à p.,** he is greatly to be pitied; **elle n'est pas à p.,** (i) she hasn't anything to worry about; (ii) she doesn't deserve any sympathy; (*b*) *A: & Dial:* to grudge, begrudge; **on n'a pas plaint l'argent,** there was no stint of money; **il ne plaint pas sa peine,** he spares himself no trouble. **2. se p.,** to complain; (*a*) to moan, groan; (*b*) **se p. de qn, de qch.,** to complain of, about, to find fault with, s.o., sth.; **il n'y a pas de quoi vous p., vous n'avez pas à vous p.,** you have nothing to complain about; you needn't grumble; **se p. que** + *ind. or sub.*; **on se plaint que vous vous conduisez mal,** people complain that you behave badly.

plaine [plɛn] *n.f. Geog:* plain.

plain-pied [plɛ̃pje] *adv.phr.* **de p.-p.,** on one floor, on a level; **salon de p.-p. avec le jardin,** drawing room on a level with the garden; **de p.-p. avec,** (i) flush with; (ii) on an equal footing with.

plainte [plɛ̃t] *n.f.* **1.** moan, groan. **2.** (*a*) complaint; (*b*) *Jur:* indictment, complaint; **porter p., déposer une p., contre qn,** to lodge a complaint against s.o. **(auprès de,** with); to bring an action against s.o.; to sue s.o.; **p. en diffamation,** action for libel.

plaintif, -ive [plɛ̃tif, -iv] *a.* plaintive (tone).

plaintivement [plɛ̃tivmɑ̃] *adv.* plaintively.

plaire [plɛr] *v.* (*pr.p* **plaisant;** *p.p.* **plu;** *pr.ind.* **je plais, il plaît, n. plaisons, ils plaisent;** *pr.sub.* **je plaise;** *impf.* **je plaisais;** *p.h.* **je plus;** *fu.* **je plairai**). **1.** *v.ind.tr.* **p. à qn,** to please s.o.; **cet homme me plaît,** I like this man; **ce livre m'a plu,** I liked, enjoyed, this book; **la nouvelle robe lui plaît beaucoup,** she's very pleased with the new dress; **cette offre devrait lui p.,** this offer should appeal to him; **chercher à p. à qn,** to try to please s.o.; **elle ne lui plaît pas,** he's not attracted to her; he doesn't care for her; **je le ferai si cela me plaît,** I'll do it if I want to, if I feel like it; *impers.* **s'il vous plaît,** (if you) please; **vous plairait-il de nous accompagner?** would you like to come with us? **plaît-il?** I beg your pardon? what did you say? **comme il vous plaira,** (just) as you like; **plaise à Dieu qu'il vienne!** God grant, please God, that he may come! **à Dieu ne plaise (que . . .),** God forbid (that . . .); **plût au ciel que . . .!** would to heaven that . . .! **2. se p. à faire qch.,** to enjoy doing sth.; **je me plais beaucoup à Paris,** I enjoy, I love, being in Paris; **il ne se plaît pas ici,** he doesn't like it, he's unhappy, here; **la vigne se plaît sur les coteaux,** the vine thrives, does well, on hillsides.

plaisamment [plɛzamɑ̃] *adv.* (*a*) pleasantly; (*b*) funnily, amusingly; (*c*) ridiculously.

plaisance [plɛzɑ̃s] *n.f.* (*a*) *A:* pleasure; (*b*) **bateau de p.,** pleasure boat; **maison de p.,** country house; **navigation de p., la p.,** yachting.

plaisancier [plɛzɑ̃sje] *n.m.* yachtsman

plaisant [plɛzɑ̃] **1.** *pr.p. of* PLAIRE. **2.** *a.* (*a*) pleasant, agreeable; **p. à l'œil,** pleasing to the eye; (*b*) funny, amusing; droll; *n.m.* **le (plus) p. de l'affaire c'est que . . .,** the funniest thing about it is that . . .; (*c*) *O:* (*always before the noun*) ridiculous, absurd, ludicrous (person, answer). **3.** *n.m.* (*a*) *A:* wag, joker; (*b*) **mauvais p.,** practical joker.

plaisanter [plɛzɑ̃te] **1.** *v.i.* to joke; to jest; **je ne plaisante pas,** I'm serious; I'm not joking; **dire qch. en plaisantant,** to say sth. as a joke, in jest; **vous plaisantez!** you're joking! you don't mean it! **c'est un homme avec qui on ne plaisante pas,** he is not a man to be trifled with; **il ne plaisante pas là-dessus,** he takes such matters seriously. **2.** *v.tr.* to tease s.o. (**sur qch.,** about sth.); to poke fun at, make fun of (s.o.).

plaisanterie [plɛzɑ̃tri] *n.f.* joke; jest; joking; jesting; **faire des plaisanteries,** to tell, crack, jokes; **faire des plaisanteries à qn,** to play tricks, (practical) jokes, on s.o.; **une mauvaise p.,** (i) a silly joke; (ii) a spiteful trick; **tourner une chose en p.,** to laugh something off; **entendre la p.,** to know how to take a joke; **par p.,** for fun, for a joke.

plaisantin [plɛzɑ̃tɛ̃] *n.m.* practical, malicious, joker.

plaisir [plezir] *n.m.* pleasure. **1.** delight; **j'apprends avec p. que vous êtes de mon avis,** I'm delighted, so glad, to hear you agree with me; **faire p. à qn,** to please s.o.; **cela m'a fait p. de le revoir,** it gave me great pleasure to see him again; **cela me fait grand p. de vous voir,** I'm delighted to see you; **cela fait p. à voir,** it's a pleasure to see; **faire à qn le p. de . . .,** to do s.o. the favour, *NAm:* favor, of . . .; **voulez-vous me faire le p. de vous taire!** will you *please* be quiet! **ils vous prient de leur faire le p. de dîner avec eux,** they request the pleasure of your company to dinner; **j'ai le p. de vous apprendre que . . .,** I have pleasure in informing you, I'm pleased to be able to tell you, that . . .; **au p. de vous revoir,** goodbye; I hope we'll meet again; *P:* **au p.!** goodbye; see you (again)! **prendre p. à qch.,** to enjoy sth.; **prendre p., avoir du p., à faire qch.,** to enjoy doing sth.; **avec p.!** with pleasure! **à p.,** (i) wantonly, without cause; (ii) ad lib; **se tourmenter à P.,** to worry for the sake of worrying; **c'est par p. que vous faites cela?** are you doing that because you like it, for the fun of the thing? **parler pour le p. de parler,** to talk for talking's sake. **2.** (*a*) amusement, enjoyment; **menus plaisirs,** amusement(s); pastimes; entertainment; **jouer (aux cartes, etc.) pour le p., pour son p.,** to play (cards, etc.) for pleasure, for enjoyment, for love; **partie de p.,** outing, trip, picnic; (*b*) *Lit:* **le p., les plaisirs,** dissipation; **lieu de p.,** place of amusement; night haunt.

plan¹ [plɑ̃] **1.** *a.* even, level, flat (ground, surface); plane (surface). **2.** *n.m.* (*a*) *Mth: etc:* plane; **p. incliné,** inclined plane; *Surv:* **p. de référence,** datum plane, level; *Opt:* **p. focal,** focal plane; **p. d'eau,** stretch of water; reach (of a river); (*b*) *Art: etc:* **premier p.,** foreground; **second p.,** middle ground; **au second p.,** in the middle distance; **cette question occupe le premier p.,** this question is very much to the fore; **reléguer qn au second p.,** to push s.o. into the background, out of the limelight; **un artiste de premier p.,** an artist of the first rank; a first-rate artist; **sur le même p.,** at, on, the same level; **sur le p. politique,** (i) in the political field, sphere; (ii) from the political point of view; (*c*) *Cin:* shot; **p. rapproché,** close shot, close-up; (*d*) *Av:* plane, surface, wing; aerofoil, *NAm:* airfoil; **p. fixe horizontal,** tail plane; **p. supérieur,** upper wing, plane (of biplane); (*e*) *Dom.Ec:* **p. de travail,** work(ing) surface, worktop (of kitchen unit).

plan² *n.m.* **1.** (*a*) plan, drawing; draft, draught (of construction); blueprint; **p. géométral,** ground plan; **tracer un p.,** to draw a plan; (*b*) plan, map (of town, etc.); *Surv:* **p. cadastral,** cadastral map, survey; **lever le p. d'une région,** to survey, map out, an area. **2.** plan, scheme, project, design; **faire, arrêter, le p. de qch.,** to plan sth.; **sans p. arrêté,** without any set plan; **p. de travail,** plan, schedule, of work; **p. d'études,** study plan, programme; curriculum; **p. de campagne,** plan of campaign; *Av:* **p. de vol,** flight plan.

plan³ *n.m. F:* **laisser qn en p.,** to leave s.o. in the lurch; to leave s.o. stranded.

planage [planaʒ] *n.m. Tchn:* smoothing; planing (of wood); planishing (of metal).

planche [plɑ̃ʃ] *n.f.* **1.** (*a*) board; plank; *Const:* (flooring) batten; shelf (in cupboard, etc.); *F:* ski; **p. à dessin,** drawing board; *Fig:* **c'est ma p. de salut,** it's my sheet anchor, my last hope; *Swim:* **faire la p.,** to float on one's back; (*b*) **p. à pain,** breadboard; **p. à découper, à hacher,** chopping board; **p. à laver,** washboard; **p. à pâtisserie,** pastry board; **p. à fromage,** cheeseboard; **p. à repasser,** ironing board; *Fig:* **avoir du pain sur la p.,** to have plenty of work to do; to have enough on one's plate; *F:* **c'est une p. à pain, à repasser,** she's flat-chested, as flat as a board; (*c*) *Nau:* **p. (de débarquement),** gangplank; **jour de p.,** lay day; *A:* **passer à la p.,** to walk the plank; (*d*) *Th:* **monter sur les planches,** to go on the stage; **être sur les planches,** to be on the stage; *F:* to tread the boards. **2.** *Art: Engr:* (i) (metal) plate, block (for printing, etching, etc.); (ii) (printed) plate, (wood)-cut, engraving; **planches en couleurs,** colour, *NAm:* color, plates. **3.** *Hort:* (rectangular) (flower) bed.

planchéiage [plɑ̃ʃejaʒ] *n.m.* (*a*) boarding, planking (of partition, of deck); (*b*) flooring (of room, etc.).

planchéier [plɑ̃ʃeje] *v.tr.* (*impf. & pr.sub.* **n. planchéiions**) (*a*) to board (partition, etc.); to board over, plank over (deck); to batten (floor); (*b*) to floor (room, etc.).

plancher¹ [plɑ̃ʃe] *v.i. Sch: F:* to be called up to the blackboard (for questioning, etc.).

plancher² *n.m.* (*a*) floor; *F:* **le p. des vaches,** dry land, terra firma; **prix p.,** bottom price; (*b*) planking (of deck); floorplates (of engine room); flooring (of trench); (*c*) *Hyd.E:* bottom (of lock); (*d*) *Anat:* floor (of cavity).

planchette [plɑ̃ʃɛt] *n.f.* **1.** small board, plank; (small) shelf; *Phot:* **p. d'objectif,** lens panel. **2.** *Surv:* plane table.

plançon [plɑ̃sɔ̃] *n.m. Hort:* (*a*) sapling; (*b*) set, slip (for planting).

plan-concave [plɑ̃kɔ̃kav] *a. Opt:* plano-concave (lens); *pl. plan-concaves.*

plan-convexe [plɑ̃kɔ̃vɛks] *a. Opt:* plano-convex (lens); *pl. plan-convexes.*

plancton [plɑ̃ktɔ̃] *n.m. Biol:* plankton.

plane [plan] *n.f. Tls:* (*a*) drawing knife; (*b*) turning chisel, planisher.

plané [plane] *a. & n.m. Av:* **(vol) p.,** gliding; **descendre en vol p.,** to glide down; *F:* **faire un vol p.,** to fall (heavily).

planéité [planeite] *n.f.* evenness, flatness.

planer¹ [plane] *v.tr. Tchn:* to smooth; to plane (wood); to planish (metal).

planer² *v.i.* **1.** (*a*) (*of bird*) to soar; to hover; (*of balloon*) to float; (*b*) *Av:* to glide. **2.** (*a*) (*of mist, etc.*) to hover; **p. sur qch., qn,** to hang over sth., s.o.; (*b*) *Lit:* to look down (from the air, from on high) (**sur,** upon).

planétaire [planetɛr] **1.** *a.* (*a*) *Astr:* planetary (system, etc.); (*b*) *Mec.E:* **engrenage p.,** planet gear. **2.** *n.m.* planetarium, orrery.

planétarium [planetarjɔm] *n.m. Astr:* planetarium.

planète [planɛt] *n.f. Astr:* planet.

planétoïde [planetɔid] *n.m. Astr:* planetoid.

planeur¹ [planœr] *n.m. Metalw:* planisher.

planeur² *n.m. Av:* glider.

planeuse [planøz] *n.f. Tls:* planing machine; planishing machine.

planificateur, -trice [planifikatœr, -tris] *esp. Pol.Ec:* **1.** *a.* planning (authority, etc.). **2.** *n.* planner.

planification [planifikasjɔ̃] *n.f. Pol.Ec:* planning.

planifier [planifje] *v.i.* (*impf. & pr.sub.* **n. planifiions**) *Pol.Ec:* to plan.

planisme [planism] *n.m. Pol.Ec:* planning.

planisphère [planisfɛr] *n.m.* planisphere.

planning [planiŋ] *n.m.* (*a*) *Ind:* planning; (*b*) *Ind:* work schedule; (*c*) **p. familial,** family planning.

planque [plɑ̃k] *n.f. P:* (*a*) hiding place, hideout; (*b*) easy job; cushy number.

planquer [plɑ̃ke] *P:* **1.** *v.tr.* to hide, stash (sth.) (away). **2. se p.,** to hide, take cover, shelter.

plant [plɑ̃] *n.m. Hort:* **1.** (*a*) (nursery) plantation (of trees, bushes); (*b*) **p. de choux,** cabbage patch. **2.** sapling, set, slip; **jeunes plants,** seedlings.

plantain [plɑ̃tɛ̃] *n.m. Bot:* plantain.

plantard [plɑ̃tar] *n.m. Hort:* (*a*) sapling; (*b*) set, slip (for planting).

plantation [plɑ̃tasjɔ̃] *n.f.* **1.** (*a*) planting (of trees, seeds); (*b*) *Th:* erection (of scenery). **2.** (sugar, tea) plantation; **p. d'oranges,** orange grove.

plante[1] [plɑ̃t] *n.f.* sole (of the foot).

plante[2] *n.f.* plant; **p. potagère,** herb; vegetable; **p. marine,** seaweed; **p. à fleurs,** flowering plant; **plantes vertes, à feuilles persistantes,** evergreens; **p. d'appartement,** (indoor) pot plant, house plant; **p. de serre,** hothouse plant; **Jardin des Plantes,** Botanical Gardens.

planté [plɑ̃te] *a.* **1.** planted; **colline plantée d'arbres,** hill planted with trees. **2.** situated, placed; **maison bien plantée,** pleasantly situated house; **enfant bien p.,** sturdy, healthy, child; *F:* **ne la laissez pas plantée là,** don't leave her standing there.

planter [plɑ̃te] **1.** *v.tr.* (*a*) to plant, set (seeds, flowers); (*b*) to fix, set (up); **p. un pieu dans le sol,** to drive, stick, a stake in the ground; to set a stake; **p. une échelle contre le mur,** to stand, fix, set, a ladder against the wall; **p. sa tente,** to put up, pitch, one's tent; *F:* **p. son chapeau sur la tête,** to put, stick, one's hat on one's head; **p. un baiser sur la joue de qn,** to plant a kiss on s.o.'s cheek; *F:* **p. là qn,** to leave s.o. in the lurch; to desert, jilt, s.o. **2. se p.,** to stand, take one's stand (firmly); **se p. devant qn,** to plant oneself, stand squarely, in front of s.o.

planteur [plɑ̃tœr] *n.m.* (*a*) planter, grower (of vegetables, etc.); (*b*) planter, settler (in new colony).

planteuse [plɑ̃tøz] *n.f. Agr:* potato planting machine.

plantigrade [plɑ̃tigrad] *a. & n.m. Z:* plantigrade.

plantoir [plɑ̃twar] *n.m. Hort:* dibber, dibble.

planton [plɑ̃tɔ̃] *n.m. Mil:* orderly; **être de p.,** to be on orderly duty; *F:* **faire le p.,** to kick one's heels, hang around.

plantureusement [plɑ̃tyrøzmɑ̃] *adv.* copiously.

plantureux, -euse [plɑ̃tyrø, -øz] *a.* **1.** copious, abundant; lavish (meal); (*of woman*) buxom. **2.** fertile (countryside); luxuriant (vegetation).

plaquage [plakaʒ] *n.m.* **1.** *Rugby Fb:* tackle. **2.** *P:* abandoning, chucking, jilting (*esp.* of lover).

plaque [plak] *n.f.* **1.** (*a*) plate, sheet (of metal); slab (of marble, etc.); block (of chocolate); patch (of ice, etc.); layer (of snow); **p. de blindage,** armour plate, *NAm:* armor plate; **p. de cheminée,** fireback; **p. de propreté,** fingerplate (of door); **p. chauffante,** hotplate; **p. de four,** baking sheet, tray; *NAm:* cookie sheet; **p. de trou d'homme, p. d'égout,** manhole cover; (*b*) **p. d'assise,** (i) *Const:* wall plate; (ii) *Mch:* base plate; *Metall:* **p. de fond,** base plate; *Rail:* **p. tournante,** turntable; **c'est la p. tournante du projet,** the plan hinges on it; (*c*) *El:* **p. d'accumulateur,** accumulator plate; **p. à grille,** grid plate; **p. empâtée,** pasted plate; (*in telephone*) **p. vibrante,** vibrating diaphragm; (*d*) *W.Tel:* plate, anode; **tension de p.,** plate voltage, anode voltage; (*e*) **p. photographique,** photographic plate; **p. stéréoscopique,** stereo slide. **2.** (*a*) (ornamental) plaque; **p. commémorative,** commemorative tablet; **p. funéraire, mortuaire, en cuivre,** church brass; (*b*) **p. de porte,** door plate; name plate; **p. indicatrice de rue,** name plate (of street); (*c*) **p. d'identité,** (soldier's) identification plate, identity disc; *esp. NAm:* dog tag; **p. d'identification,** name plate, number plate (of machine); *Aut: etc:* **p. d'immatriculation, de police, p. minéralogique,** number plate, *NAm:* license plate; (*d*) badge (of office); star (of an order). **3.** (*a*) *Med:* plaque, patch (on skin); (*b*) **p. sanguine,** red blood disc; (*c*) *Dent:* plaque.

plaqué [plake] *a. & n.m.* **1. (métal) p.,** plated metal, plated goods; (electro)plate. **2. (bois) p.,** veneered wood.

plaquemine [plakmin] *n.f. Bot:* persimmon.

plaqueminier [plakminje] *n.m. Bot:* persimmon (tree).

plaquer [plake] **1.** *v.tr.* (*a*) to veneer (wood); to plate (metal); to flash (glass); to lay on (plaster); to plaster down (hair); **le vent lui plaquait son manteau sur les jambes,** the wind blew his coat against his legs; **il avait les épaules plaquées au mur,** he stood with his shoulders (pinned, pressed) to the wall; (*b*) *Rugby Fb:* to tackle, bring down (opponent); (*c*) *Mus:* **p. un accord,** to strike (and hold) a chord; (*d*) *P:* abandon, desert, ditch, chuck, jilt (s.o.); **tout p.,** to chuck everything up. **2. se p. au sol, contre un mur,** to lie flat on the ground, flatten oneself against a wall.

plaquette [plakɛt] *n.f.* **1.** small plate, block (of metal, etc.); small plaque. **2.** booklet; slim volume. **3. plaquettes sanguines,** blood platelets.

plaqueur [plakœr] *n.m.* (*a*) plater (of metal); (*b*) veneerer.

plasma [plasma] *n.m.* plasma.

plastic [plastik] *n.m.* plastic explosive.

plasticage [plastikaʒ] *n.m.* plastic bomb attack.

plasticité [plastisite] *n.f.* plasticity.

plastifiant [plastifjɑ̃] *n.m.* plasticizer.

plastifier [plastifje] *v.tr.* (*impf. & pr.sub.* **n. plastifiions**) to plasticize; *Bookb:* to laminate; **jaquette plastifiée,** laminated jacket.

plastiquage [plastikaʒ] *n.m.* = PLASTICAGE.

plastique [plastik] **1.** *a.* plasticmalleable (nature); **aux formes plastiques,** with a fine figure. **2.** *n.f.* (*a*) *Sculp: etc:* plastic art, art of modelling; (*b*) figure, physique (of actress, dancer). **3.** *a. & n.m.* **(matière) p.,** plastic.

plastiquer [plastike] *v.tr.* to attack, destroy (sth.) with plastic explosive.

plastiqueur, -euse [plastikœr, -øz] *n.* person responsible for a plastic bomb explosion.

plastron [plastrɔ̃] *n.m.* **1.** breastplate (of cuirass). **2.** (fencer's) plastron, pad. **3.** *Cost:* front (of dress, etc.); (man's) shirt front; dick(e)y.

plastronner [plastrɔne] **1.** *v.tr.* to put a plastron on (s.o.). **2.** *v.i.* to throw out one's chest; to strut, swagger.

plat [pla] **1.** *a.* (*a*) flat, level; **chaussure plate,** low-heeled, flat, shoe; **avoir la poitrine plate, les pieds plats,** to be flat-chested, flat-footed; **cheveux plats,** straight hair; **mer plate,** smooth sea; **calme p.,** dead calm; **vis à tête plate,** screw with countersunk head; **vaisselle plate,** (i) flatware; (ii) (solid) plate; (*b*) flat, dull, insipid, tame; **style p.,** commonplace style; **vin p.,** dull, flat, wine; **être p. devant qn,** to grovel to s.o.; (*c*) **à p.,** flat; **couché à p. sur le sol,** lying flat on the ground; (*of play, etc.*) **tomber à p.,** to fall flat, be a flop; **tomber à p. ventre,** to fall flat on one's face; **se mettre à p. ventre devant qn,** to grovel to s.o.; **pneu à p.,** flat tyre, *NAm:* tire; **accu à p.,** flat battery; *F:* **être à p.,** (i) to be exhausted, all in, run down; (ii) *Aut:* to have a flat tyre; **cette maladie l'a mis à p.,** this illness has taken it out of him. **2.** *n.m.* (*a*) flat (part) (of hand, etc.); blade (of oar); face (of hammer); *Bookb:* **plats,** boards, sides; **plats toile,** cloth boards; *Cu:* **p. de côtes,** top ribs (of beef); *Sp:* **le p.,** flat racing; *Swim:* **faire un p.,** to do a bellyflop; *F:* **faire du p. à qn,** (i) to flatter s.o., grovel to s.o.; (ii) to make advances to s.o.; (*b*) *Cu:* (*container or contents*) dish; **mettre les petits plats dans les grands,** to put on a great spread; **mettre les pieds dans le p.,** to put one's foot in it; *F:* **en faire tout un p.,** to make a great fuss about sth.; to pile on the agony; *Mil: etc:* **faire p. avec qn,** to mess with s.o.; *Navy:* **camarade de p.,** messmate; (*c*) *Cu:* course (at dinner, etc.); **p. de résistance,** main course, main dish; **p. cuisiné,** ready-cooked dish, takeaway dish; (*d*) (*in church*) **p. de quête,** collection plate.

platane [platan] *n.m. Bot:* plane tree.

plat-bord [plabɔr] *n.m. Nau:* gunwale, gunnel; **hauteur au-dessus du p.-b.,** height above the hull; *pl. plats-bords.*

plate [plat] *n.f. Nau:* (*a*) punt; (*b*) flat-bottomed fishing boat.

plateau, -eaux [plato] *n.m.* **1.** (*a*) tray; **p. d'argent,** silver salver; **p. à, de, fromages,** cheeseboard; (*b*) pan, scale (of balance); (*c*) shelf (of oven, etc.); top (of table). **2.** *Geog:* (*a*) plateau, tableland; **p. continental,** continental shelf; (*b*) *Med:* dead level (of a disease). **3.** platform; (*a*) *Artil:* **p. de chargement,** loading tray; (*b*) *Th:* floor (of the stage); *Cin:* set; **p. tournant,** revolving stage; (*c*) *Rail: etc:* flat truck, open truck, *NAm:* flatcar. **4.** (*a*) *Mec.E: etc:* plate, disc, *NAm:* disk; face plate, chuck (plate), table (of lathe, etc.); *Cy:* chain wheel; **p. de pédalier,** front chain wheel; *I.C.E:* **raccordement à plateaux,** flange assembly; *Mch:* **accouplement à plateaux,** plate coupling; **p. d'excentrique,** (eccentric) sheave; *Aut: etc:* **p. d'embrayage,** clutch plate; (*b*) turntable (of record deck).

plate-bande [platbɑ̃d] *n.f.* flower bed; *F:* **ne marchez pas sur mes plates-bandes,** mind your own business.

plate-forme [platfɔrm] *n.f.* (*a*) platform (of bus, etc.); flat roof (of house); footplate (of locomotive); *Geog:* **p.-f. continentale,** continental shelf; (*b*) *Rail: etc:* flat truck, open truck, *NAm:* flatcar; (*c*) *Artil:* **p.-f. de tir,** gun platform; **p.-f. tournante,** turntable; (*d*) *Pol:* platform; *pl. plates-formes.*

plate-longe [platlɔ̃ʒ] *n.f. Harn:* (*a*) kicking strap; (*b*) leading rein; *pl. plates-longes.*

platement [platmɑ̃] *adv.* flatly; dully, prosaically.

platinage [platinaʒ] *n.m.* platinum plating.

platine¹ [platin] *n.f.* plate (of lock, watch, etc.); lock (plate) (of rifle); platen (of printing press, typewriter); stage (of microscope); turntable (of record deck).

platine² **1.** *n.m.* platinum; **éponge, mousse, de p.,** platinum sponge. **2.** *a.inv.* platinum; **cheveux (blonds) p.,** platinum blond hair.

platiné [platine] *a.* **1.** (*a*) platinum-plated, platinized; (*b*) **cheveux platinés,** platinum blond hair. **2.** platinum-tipped (screw); *Aut:* **vis platinées,** points.

platiner [platine] *v.tr.* to plate with platinum, platinize.

platitude [platityd] *n.f.* **1.** flatness, dullness (of character, etc.); vapidity (of style). **2.** (*a*) commonplace remark; platitude; **débiter des platitudes,** to platitudinize; (*b*) *A:* **faire des platitudes à qn,** to grovel to s.o.

Platon [platɔ̃] *Pr.n.m.* Plato.

platonicien, -ienne [platɔnisjɛ̃, -jɛn] **1.** *a.* Platonic (school, philosopher). **2.** *n.* Platonist.

platonique [platɔnik] *a.* **1.** platonic (love, etc.). **2.** useless; futile (attempt, etc.).

platonisme [platɔnism] *n.m.* Platonism.

plâtrage [plɑtraʒ] *n.m.* plastering (of wall, etc.); *Const:* plasterwork.

plâtras [plɑtra] *n.m.* debris of plasterwork; rubble.

plâtre [plɑtr̥] *n.m.* **1.** (*a*) plaster; **p. de moulage,** plaster of Paris; **pierre à p.,** gypsum; **enduire qch. de p.,** to plaster over sth.; (*b*) *pl.* plasterwork (on house, etc.); *F:* **essuyer les plâtres,** to be the first occupant of a house. **2.** plaster cast.

plâtrer [plɑtre] *v.tr.* **1.** (*a*) to plaster (wall, ceiling); to plaster up (hole, crack); *F:* **se p. (le visage),** to plaster one's face with make-up; (*b*) *Med:* to put (leg, etc.) in plaster. **2.** *Agr:* to dress (soil) with sulphate, *NAm:* sulfate, of lime.

plâtrerie [plɑtrəri] *n.f.* (*a*) (*factory*) plasterworks; (*b*) **travaux de p.,** plasterwork, plastering.

plâtreux, -euse [plɑtrø, -øz] *a.* (wall, etc.) covered with plaster; chalky (water, cheese).

plâtrier [plɑtrije] *n.m.* plasterer.

plâtrière [plɑtrijɛr] *n.f.* **1.** gypsum quarry. **2.** plaster kiln, gypsum kiln.

plausibilité [plozibilite] *n.f.* plausibility.

plausible [plozibl̥] *a.* plausible (statement).

plausiblement [plozibləmɑ̃] *adv.* plausibly.

plèbe [plɛb] *n.f. Hist:* **la p.,** the plebs; the lower orders, the common people.

plébéien, -ienne [plebejɛ̃, -jɛn] *a. & n.* plebeian.

plébiscite [plebisit] *n.m.* plebiscite.

plébisciter [plebisite] *v.tr.* (*a*) to vote for (s.o., sth.) by plebiscite; (*b*) to elect (s.o.) by a large majority.

plectre [plɛktr̥] *n.m. Mus:* plectrum.

pléiade [plejad] *n.f. Astr: Lit:* pleiad.

plein [plɛ̃] **1.** *a.* full (**de,** of); (*a*) filled, replete (**de,** with); **bouteille pleine,** full bottle; **pleine bouteille,** bottleful; **joues pleines,** full, plump, cheeks; **p. comme un œuf,** chock-full; **l'autobus est p.,** the bus is full; *F:* **être p.,** to be drunk, have had a skinful; **salle pleine à craquer,** room full to bursting point; **avoir le ventre p.,** to be full (up); to have eaten one's fill; **ne parle pas la bouche pleine,** don't speak with your mouth full; **entreprise pleine de dangers,** enterprise fraught with dangers; **il a les doigts pleins d'encre,** his fingers are covered with ink; (*b*) (*of animal*) pregnant; **jument, brebis, chèvre, pleine,** mare in foal, ewe with lamb, goat in kid; (*c*) complete, entire, whole; **pleine lune,** full moon; **p. sud,** due south; **pleine mer,** (i) high tide; (ii) the open sea; **reliure pleine peau,** full leather binding; **p. pouvoir,** full power; *Jur:* power of attorney; **de son p. gré,** of one's own free will; (*d*) solid (tyre, *NAm:* tire, axle, etc.); continuous (line); **table en acajou p.,** solid mahogany table; (*e*) **en p. visage,** full, right, in the face; **en p. hiver,** in the depth, the middle, of winter; **en p. air,** in the open (air); **restaurant en p. air,** open air restaurant; **marché en p. vent,** open air market; **en p. jour,** (i) in broad daylight; (ii) publicly; **s'arrêter en p. milieu de la place,** to stop right in the middle of the square; **en pleine nuit,** in the middle of the night, at dead of night; **en pleine saison,** at the height of the season; **semer en pleine terre,** to sow in the open ground; **en pleine mer,** out at sea, in the open sea; **en p. tribunal,** in open court; **être en p. travail,** to be (i) hard at work, (ii) (*of factory, etc.*) in full production; (*f*) **respirer à pleine poitrine, à pleins poumons,** to breathe deeply; **boire à p. verre,** to drink deeply; **crier à pleine gorge,** to shout at the top of one's voice; **apporter des fleurs à pleins bras,** to bring armfuls of flowers; **à pleines voiles,** with all sails set, under full sail. **2.** *adv.* **il avait des larmes p. les yeux,** his eyes were full of tears; **il a des livres p. ses poches,** his pockets are stuffed with books; **avoir de l'argent p. les poches,** to have plenty of money; *F:* **tout p.,** very, very much, very many; **elle est mignonne tout p.,** she's awfully sweet; *F:* **il y avait p. de gens,** there were lots of people; *Nau:* **porter p.,** to keep her full; **près et p.,** full and by; by and large. **3.** *n.m.* (*a*) **faire le p. d'un réservoir,** to fill (up) a tank; *Aut:* **faire le p. (d'essence),** to fill up (with petrol); **faites le p., s'il vous plaît,** fill her up, please! (*of ship*) **avoir son p.,** to be fully laden; (*b*) full (extent, height, etc.); **le p. de la lune,** the full moon; **le p. (de la mer),** high tide; (*of the tide*) **battre son p.,** to be at the full; **la saison bat son p., c'est le p. de la saison,** the season is at its height, is in full swing; (*c*) **en p. dans le centre,** full, right, in the middle; (*d*) downstroke (in writing); *Typ:* thick stroke.

pleinement [plɛnmɑ̃] *adv.* fully, entirely; to the full.

plein-emploi [plɛnɑ̃plwa] *n.m.inv. Pol.Ec:* full employment.

pléistocène [pleistɔsɛn] *a. & n.m. Geol:* pleistocene.

plénier, -ière [plenje, -jɛr] *a.* (*a*) *A:* full, complete; absolute; (*b*) plenary (court, indulgence).

plénipotentiaire [plenipɔtɑ̃sjɛr] (*a*) *a. & n.m.* plenipotentiary; (*b*) *n.m.* authorized agent.

plénitude [plenityd] *n.f.* plenitude, fullness (of time, power, etc.); completeness (of victory, etc.).

pléonasme [pleɔnasm] *n.m.* pleonasm; **par p.,** pleonastically.

pléonastique [pleɔnastik] *a.* pleonastic.

plésiosaure [plezjɔzɔr] *n.m. Paleont:* plesiosaurus.

pléthore [pletɔr] *n.f.* plethora.

pléthorique [pletɔrik] *a.* (*a*) *Med:* full-blooded, plethoric; (*b*) superabundant; over-crowded (class, etc.).

pleur [plœr] *n.m. Lit: usu. pl.* tear; **verser des pleurs,** to shed tears; **fondre en pleurs,** to dissolve into tears; **cessez vos pleurs,** dry your tears; **être tout en pleurs,** to be bathed in tears.

pleural, -aux [plœral, -o] *a. Anat:* pleural.

pleurant, -ante [plœrɑ̃, -ɑ̃t] **1.** *a. A:* crying, weeping. **2.** *n.m. Sculp:* weeper, mourner (on a tomb).

pleurard, -arde [plœrar, -ard] **1.** *a.* whimpering, fractious (child); whining, tearful (voice). **2.** *n.* whimperer; *F:* crybaby.

pleurer [plœre] **1.** *v.tr.* to weep for, mourn (for) (s.o., sth.); to lament (s.o., sth.); to bewail, bemoan; **mourir sans être pleuré,** to die unmourned, unwept; **p. toutes les larmes de ses yeux,** to cry one's eyes out; **p. misère,** (i) to complain; (ii) to plead poverty. **2.** *v.i.* (*a*) to cry, weep, shed tears (**sur,** over; **pour,** for); **p. de joie,** to weep for joy; **p. à chaudes larmes,** to cry bitterly; to sob, cry, one's heart out; **s'endormir en pleurant,** to cry oneself to sleep; **faire p. qn,** to make s.o. cry; **c'est à faire p.,** it's enough to make you weep, cry; (*b*) (*of the eyes*) to water, to run.

pleurésie [plœrezi] *n.f. Med:* pleurisy.

pleurétique [plœretik] *Med:* **1.** *a.* pleuritic (pain). **2.** *n.* pleurisy patient.

pleureur, -euse [plœrœr, -øz] **1.** (*a*) *n. O:* one who weeps easily; (*b*) *n.f.* **pleureuse,** hired mourner. **2.** *a.* crying, weeping, whimpering, tearful; **saule p.,** weeping willow.

pleurite [plœrit] *n.f. Med:* dry pleurisy.

pleurnichement [plœrniʃmɑ̃] *n.m.* = PLEURNICHERIE.

pleurnicher [plœrniʃe] *v.i.* to whimper, whine, snivel, grizzle.

pleurnicherie [plœrniʃri] *n.f.* whimpering, whining, snivelling, grizzling.

pleurnicheur, -euse [plœrniʃœr, -øz] **1.** *n.* whiner, sniveller; crybaby. **2.** *a.* whimpering, whining, snivelling, grizzling.

pleutre [pløtr̥] *Lit:* (*a*) *a.* cowardly; (*b*) *n.m.* coward.

pleuvasser [pløvase], **pleuviner** [pløvine] *v. impers.* to drizzle.

pleuvoir [pløvwar] *v.* (*pr.p.* **pleuvant;** *p.p.* **plu;** *pr.ind.* **il pleut, ils pleuvent;** *impf.* **il pleuvait;** *p.h.* **il plut;** *fu.* **il pleuvra**) to rain. **1.** *v.impers.* **il pleut à verse, à seaux,** it's raining hard; it's pouring (with rain); **il pleut à petites gouttes,** it's drizzling; **les jours où il pleut,** wet, rainy, days; **il pleuvait des coups,** blows fell thick and fast. **2.** *v.i. & tr.* **faire p. des coups sur qn,** to rain, shower, blows (down) on s.o.; **les invitations pleuvent sur lui,** invitations are pouring in on him.

pleuvoter [pløvɔte] *v.impers.* to drizzle.

plèvre [plɛvr̥] *n.f. Anat:* pleura.

plexus [plɛksys] *n.m. Anat:* plexus; **p. solaire,** solar plexus.

pleyon [plɛjɔ̃] *n.m. Agr:* withe, osier tie.

pli [pli] *n.m.* **1.** (*a*) pleat; fold (in curtains, etc.); *Dressm:* **p. creux, rentré, inverti, double p.,** box pleat, inverted pleat; **p. couché,** knife pleat; **petit p.,** tuck; **jupe à plis,** pleated skirt; **faire des plis à une robe,** to pleat a dress; *Hairdr:* **mise en plis,** set; **faire une mise en plis à qn,** to set s.o.'s hair; (*b*) wrinkle, pucker; *Geol:* fold; **p. de terrain,** undulation; (*of garment*) **faire des plis,** to pucker, wrinkle; (*c*) crease (in trousers, etc.); **(faux) p.,** (unintentional) crease; (*d*) habit, custom; **prendre le p. de faire qch.,** to get into the habit of doing sth. **2.** bend (of the arm, leg); **p. du jarret,** hollow of the knee. **3.** (*a*) cover, envelope (of letter); **sous p. séparé,** under separate cover; **nous vous envoyons sous ce p. . . .,** we send you herewith . . ., please find enclosed . . .; (*b*) letter, note; *Navy:* **p. cacheté,** sealed orders; *Nau: etc:* **plis consulaires,** consular packages. **4.** *Cards:* **faire un p.,** to take a trick.

pliable [plijabl̥] *a.* foldable; pliable, flexible; **canot p.,** folding boat.

pliage [plijaʒ] *n.m.* folding; bending.

pliant [plijɑ̃] **1.** *a.* folding (chair, etc.); collapsible (table, etc.); **pied p.,** folding tripod. **2.** *n.m.* folding chair, stool; campstool.

plie [pli] *n.f. Ich:* plaice.

pliement [plimɑ̃] *n.m.* folding; bending.

plier [plije] *v.* (*impf. & pr.sub.* **n. pliions**) **1.** *v.tr.* (*a*) to fold (up); to turn down (page); to furl (sail); (*b*) to bend (bough, knee, etc.); (*of pers.*) **plié en deux,** bent double, doubled up; (*c*) **p. la tête,** to bow one's head; to submit; **p. qn à la discipline,** to bring s.o. under discipline; (*d*) to adapt (s.o.) (to circumstances, etc.). **2.** *v.i.* (*a*) to bend (over); **poutre qui plie sous le poids,** beam that bends, gives, sags, under the weight; (*b*) to submit, yield; (*of troops in battle*) to give in, give way; **tout plie devant lui,** he carries all before him. **3. se p.,** to fold (up); to bend; **se p. aux circonstances, à la discipline,** to yield, bow, submit, to circumstances; to conform to discipline; **se p. aux lois,** to obey the law.

plieur, -euse [plijœr, -øz] **1.** *n.* (*pers.*) folder. **2.** *n.f.* **plieuse,** folding machine.

Pline [plin] *Pr.n.m. Lt.Lit:* Pliny.

plinthe [plɛ̃t] *n.f.* **1.** *Arch:* plinth (of column). **2.** skirting(board).

pliocène [plijɔsɛn] *a. & n.m. Geol:* Pliocene.

plioir [plijwar] *n.m.* **1.** *Bookb:* folder; paper knife. **2.** winder (for fishing line).

plissage [plisaʒ] *n.m.* pleating (of material).

plissé [plise] **1.** *a.* (*a*) pleated (dress, etc.); (*b*) **lèvres plissées,** puckered lips; **front p.,** wrinkled brow. **2.** *n.m.* pleat(ing), pleats; tucks.

plissement [plismɑ̃] *n.m.* **1.** pleating (of material); folding (of paper, etc.); corrugation (of metal, paper). **2.** creasing, crumpling (of material); puckering (of the skin); crinkling (of paper); *Geol:* fold.

plisser [plise] **1.** *v.tr.* (*a*) to pleat (skirt, etc.); to fold (paper, etc.); (*b*) to crease, crumple; to crinkle (paper); to corrugate (metal, paper); **un sourire plissait sa figure, ses lèvres,** a smile wrinkled his face, puckered his lips; **p. les yeux,** to screw up one's eyes. **2.** *v.i. & pr.* (*of garment, etc.*) to crease, crumple; to pucker, wrinkle.

plisseur, -euse [plisœr, -øz] **1.** *n.* (*pers.*) pleater, folder. **2.** *n.f.* **plisseuse,** pleating machine.

plissure [plisyr] *n.f.* pleats.

pliure [plijyr] *n.f.* **1.** *Bookb:* folding (of paper, etc.). **2.** fold (in material, etc.).

ploc [plɔk] *int.* splosh! plop! splat!

ploiement [plwamɑ̃] *n.m.* bending; *Mil: A:* ployment (of front from line to column).

plomb [plɔ̃] *n.m.* **1.** lead; (*a*) **p. laminé, en feuilles,** sheet lead; **tuyau de p.,** lead pipe; **blanc de p.,** white lead; **sommeil de p.,** deep, heavy, sleep; **ciel de p.,** leaden, grey, sky; **soleil de p.,** blazing (hot) sun; **n'avoir pas de p. dans la tête,** to be scatterbrained; (*b*) *Arch:* **plombs,** leadwork, leads (of window); **mise en p.,** leading; (*c*) *Typ:* type; metal. **2.** *Ven:* shot; **petit, menu, p.,** small shot; **gros p.,** buckshot. **3.** *pl. A:* (housemaid's) sink. **4.** (*a*) lead (weight); *Fish:* sinker; *Nau:* **jeter, lancer, le p. (de sonde),** to heave the lead; (*b*) **fil à p.,** plumb line; **à p.,** upright, vertical(ly); **le soleil donnait à p. sur nous,** the sun was beating straight down on our heads. **5.** lead seal (on meter, etc.). **6.** *El:* **p. (fusible),** fuse; **faire sauter les plombs,** to blow the fuses.

plombage [plɔ̃baʒ] *n.m.* **1.** (*a*) covering (sth.) with lead; (*b*) weighting (sth.) with lead; (*c*) *Cer:* lead glazing; (*d*) *Dent:* filling, stopping (of tooth); (*e*) sealing (of parcel, etc.) (with lead). **2.** *Dent:* filling.

plombagine [plɔ̃baʒin] *n.f. Miner:* black lead, graphite; plumbago.

plombe [plɔ̃b] *n.f. P:* hour (struck); **voilà quatre plombes,** it's striking four.

plombé [plɔ̃be] *a.* (*a*) leaded (window, etc.); lead (-covered) (roof, etc.); (*b*) leaden, livid (complexion, sky); (*c*) (lead-)sealed (parcel, etc.).

plomber [plɔ̃be] **1.** *v.tr.* (*a*) to cover (sth.) with lead; (*b*) to weight (sth.) with lead; (*c*) *Cer:* to glaze; (*d*) to give a leaden, livid, hue to (complexion, sky); (*e*) *Dent:* to fill, stop (tooth); (*f*) *Const:* to plumb (wall); (*g*) to seal (parcel, meter, etc.) (with lead). **2.** (*of complexion, sky*) **se p.,** to become leaden, livid.

plomberie [plɔ̃bri] *n.f.* **1.** plumbing. **2.** (*a*) leadworks; (*b*) plumber's shop.

plombeur [plɔ̃bœr] *n.m.* affixer of seals (to parcels, etc.).

plombier [plɔ̃bje] *n.m.* plumber.

plonge [plɔ̃ʒ] *n.f.* washing up (in restaurant).

plongeant [plɔ̃ʒɑ̃] *a.* plunging (fire, neckline, etc.); **vue plongeante,** view from above, bird's eye view.

plongée [plɔ̃ʒe] *n.f.* **1.** (*a*) plunge, dive; **p. sous-marine,** skin diving; (*b*) (*of submarine*) submergence, submersion; **effectuer sa p.,** to dive, submerge; **vitesse en p.,** speed submerged; **p. raide,** crash-dive. **2.** dip, slope, incline (of ground). **3.** *Cin: T.V:* high angle shot; bird's eye view.

plongement [plɔ̃ʒmɑ̃] *n.m.* plunging; immersion.

plongeoir [plɔ̃ʒwar] *n.m.* diving board.

plongeon [plɔ̃ʒɔ̃] *n.m.* **1.** *Orn:* diver; loon. **2.** plunge, dive; **p. de haut vol,** high dive; **faire le p.,** (i) to dive; (ii) *F:* to suffer a heavy loss (in business).

plonger [plɔ̃ʒe] *v.* **(je plongeai(s); n. plongeons) 1.** *v.i.* to plunge; (*a*) to dive; **p. dans sa poche pour y prendre de la monnaie,** to dive into one's pocket for change; (*b*) to become immersed; (*of submarine*) to submerge; **p. raide,** to crash-dive; (*of angler's float*) to bob under; (*c*) **les murs plongent dans le fossé,** the walls plunge, run, steeply down into the moat; (*d*) *Nau:* (*of ship*) **p. du nez,** to pitch; (*e*) (*of road, etc.*) to dip. **2.** *v.tr.* to plunge, immerse (s.o., sth., in sth.); to quench (steel, etc.); **p. la main dans sa poche,** to thrust one's hand, to dive, into one's pocket; **être plongé dans ses pensées,** to be immersed, lost, deep, in thought. **3. se p.,** to immerse oneself (**dans,** in); **se p. dans l'étude,** to bury oneself in one's studies; **se p. dans le vice, dans le sang,** to be steeped, to wallow, in vice, in blood.

plongeur, -euse [plɔ̃ʒœr, -øz] **1.** *a.* diving (bird, etc.). **2.** *n.m.* (*a*) diver; **cloche à plongeurs,** diving bell; **p. sous-marin,** skin diver; (*b*) washer-up, bottle-washer (in restaurant); (*c*) *Orn:* diver, diving bird; (*d*) plunger (of pump).

plosive [ploziv] *n.f. Ling:* plosive (consonant).

plot [plo] *n.m. El:* contact (stud).

plouf [pluf] *int.* plop! splosh!

ploutocrate [plutɔkrat] *n.m.* plutocrat.

ploutocratie [plutɔkrasi] *n.f.* plutocracy.

ploutocratique [plutɔkratik] *a.* plutocratic.

ployable [plwajabl̥] *a.* pliable, flexible.

ployage [plwajaʒ] *n.m.* bending (of branch, etc.).

ployer [plwaje] *v.* **(je ploie, n. ployons; je ploierai) 1.** *v.tr. A: & Lit:* to bend (branch, knee). **2.** *v.i.* (*a*) to bend; to sag; to give (way); to bow (under yoke, burden); (*b*) *Lit:* to submit, yield; (*of troops in battle*) to give in, give way.

pluches [plyʃ] *n.f.pl. Mil: F:* cookhouse fatigue.

pluie [plɥi] *n.f.* (*a*) rain; shower; **p. battante, torrentielle,** pouring, pelting, rain; downpour; **p. fine,** drizzle; **goutte de p.,** raindrop; **le temps est à la p.,** it looks like rain; **temps de p.,** rainy, wet, weather; **jour sans p.,** dry day; **sous la p.,** in the rain; (*on package*) **craint la p.,** to be kept dry; **parler de la p. et du beau temps,** to talk about the weather, about nothing in particular; *F:* **il n'est pas tombé de la dernière p.,** he's no fool; there are no flies on him; *Prov:* **après la p. le beau temps,** every cloud has a silver lining; *F:* **faire la p. et le beau temps,** to be the boss, rule the roost; (*b*) shower (of blows, etc.); hail (of bullets, etc.); **p. d'or,** (i) shower of gold; (ii) *Pyr:* golden rain.

plumage [plymaʒ] *n.m.* plumage; feathers.

plumard [plymar] *n.m. P:* bed; pit.

plum-cake [plumkɛk] *n.m. O:* fruit cake; *pl. plum-cakes.*

plume¹ [plym] *n.f.* **1.** feather; **oiseau sans plumes,** callow, unfledged, bird; **gibier à plumes,** game birds; *F:* **il y a laissé des plumes,** he didn't get away unscathed; **léger comme une p.,** as light as a feather; *Prov:* **la belle p. fait le bel oiseau,** fine feathers make fine birds; **lit de plume(s),** feather bed; *Box:* **poids p.,** featherweight. **2.** (*a*) **p. (d'oie),** quill (pen); (*b*) (pen) nib; **p. à dessin,** drawing pen; **dessin à la p.,** pen (and ink) drawing; **trait de p.,** stroke of the pen; **prendre la p. (en main),** to put pen to paper; **vivre de sa p.,** to make one's living by writing, live by one's pen.

plume² *n.m. P:* bed; pit.

plumeau, -eaux [plymo] *n.m.* feather duster.

plumer [plyme] **1.** *v.tr.* to pluck (poultry); to scrape (asparagus); *F:* to rob, fleece (s.o.). **2.** *v.i. Row:* to feather.

plumet [plymɛ] *n.m.* (*a*) plume (of helmet, etc.); (*b*) ostrich feather (as ornament).

plumetis [plymti] *n.m. Needlew:* **1.** (raised) satin stitch. **2.** Swiss muslin.

plumeux, -euse [plymø, -øz] *a.* feathery.

plumier [plymje] *n.m.* (*a*) pen tray; (*b*) pencil box, case.

plum(-pudding) [plum(pudiŋ)] *n.m.* plum pudding, Christmas pudding; *pl. plum-puddings.*

plupart (la) [laplypar] *n.f.* most, the greatest part; the greater part, number; **la p. des hommes,** most (of the) men, the majority of (the) men; **la p. d'entre eux,** most of them; **la p. du temps,** most of the time;

in most cases, generally; **pour la p.,** for the most part, mostly.

plural, -aux [plyral, -o] *a.* plural (vote, etc.).

pluralité [plyralite] *n.f.* (*a*) plurality, multiplicity; *Ecc:* **p. des bénéfices,** pluralism; (*b*) *A:* **élu à la p. des voix,** elected by a majority.

pluriel, -elle [plyrjɛl] *a. & n.m.* plural; **au p.,** in the plural.

plus [ply] (*often* [plys] *at the end of a word group;* [plyz] *before a vowel:* **plus on est de fous, plus on rit** [plyzɔ̃nɛdfuplyzɔ̃ri]) **1.** *adv.* (*a*) more; **soyez p. réaliste!** be more realistic! **ils sont p. nombreux, beaucoup p. nombreux,** there are more of them, far more of them; **il est p. grand que moi,** he's taller than I (am), than me; **je ne suis pas p. grand que lui,** I'm no taller than he (is), than him; **elle écoute p. attentivement,** she listens more attentively; **une fenêtre p. haute que large,** a window higher than it is wide; **il a p. de patience que moi,** he has more patience than I (have), than me; **deux fois p. grand,** twice as big; **je gagne p. que vous,** I earn more than you; **p. qu'à moitié** (*often* [plyskamwatje]), more than half (done, etc.); **p. d'une fois,** more than once; **p. de dix hommes,** more than ten men; **il a p. de vingt ans,** he's over twenty; **pendant p. d'une heure,** for over, for more than, an hour; **la maladie pas p. que les obstacles, non p. que les obstacles, ne put le vaincre,** neither disease nor difficulties could vanquish him; **p. loin,** farther on; **p. tôt,** sooner; **p. . . . (et) p. . . .,** the more . . ., the more . . .; **p. on est de fous p. on rit,** the more the merrier; **p. je lis, moins je retiens,** the more I read the less I remember; **et qui p. est** [plyzɛ], and what is more; moreover; **j'en ai trois fois p. qu'il ne m'en faut,** I've (got) three times as much as I need; **il y en a tant et p.,** there's an awful lot (of it, them); (*b*) **(le) p.,** (the) most; **la p. longue rue, la rue la p. longue, de la ville,** the longest street in the town; **la p. belle femme que j'aie jamais vue,** the most beautiful woman I've ever seen; **c'est vous qui avez fait le p. de fautes,** you've made (the) most mistakes; **c'est à trente ans qu'elle a été le p. belle,** she was at her best at thirty; **ce que je désire le p.,** what I most desire; **crier le p. fort,** to shout (the) loudest; **faites le p. que vous pourrez,** do the most you can; **(tout) au p.,** at the (very) most, at the (very) outside, at best; **c'est tout au p. s'il est midi,** it's twelve o'clock at the latest; **c'est tout ce qu'il y a de p. simple,** nothing could be simpler; (*c*) **ne . . . p.,** no more, no longer, not again; **je ne veux p. de cela,** I don't want any more of that; **je ne la verrai p. (jamais),** I'll never see her again; **il n'est p.,** he's dead; **je n'ai p. d'argent,** I haven't any money left; **sans p. attendre,** without waiting any longer; **p. de doute,** there is no more doubt about it; **p. de potage, merci,** no more soup, thank you; **il n'y en a p.,** there's no more, there's none left; **il n'y a p. rien,** there's nothing left, nothing more; **p. que dix minutes!** only ten minutes left! (*d*) **non p.,** (not) either; **je n'en ai pas non p.,** I haven't (got) any either; **ni moi non p.,** neither do I, neither did I, etc.; I don't, didn't, etc., either; **jamais non p. je n'avais songé à . . .,** nor had I ever thought of . . .; **vous n'en avez guère non p.,** you haven't much either; (*e*) [plys] plus, also, besides, in addition; **sept p. neuf p. un,** seven plus nine plus one; **il fait p. 20 (degrés),** its plus 20 (degrees); **500 francs d'amende, p. les frais,** 500 francs fine and costs; *Golf:* **p. quatre** [plyskatr̥], plus four; (*f*) **de p.,** more; **une journée de p.,** one day more, one more day; **il a trois ans de p. que moi,** he's three years older than I (am), than me; **rien de p., merci,** nothing more, nothing else, thank you; **de p. en p.,** more and more; **de p. en p. froid,** colder and colder; **en p.,** in addition ((i) into the bargain; (ii) extra); **le vin est en p.,** wine is extra; **il y en a trois en p. de lui,** there are three more besides him; **en p. de ce qu'il me doit,** over and above what he owes me; **p. ou moins** [plyzumwɛ̃], more or less; **ni p. ni moins,** neither more (n)or less. **2.** *n.m.* (*a*) more; **qui peut le p. peut le moins,** he who can do more can do less; **sans p.,** (just that and) nothing more; **sans p. il les mit à la porte,** without further, more, ado he turned them out; (*b*) *Mth:* plus (sign); (*c*) *Golf:* **le p.** [ləplys], the odd.

plusieurs [plyzjœr] *a. & pron. pl.* several; **p. personnes l'ont remarqué,** a number of people noticed it; **de p. manières,** in more ways than one; **j'en ai p.,** I have several; **un ou p.,** one or more.

plus-que-parfait [plyskəparfɛ] *n.m. Gram:* pluperfect (tense); *pl. plus-que-parfaits.*

plus-value [plyvaly] *n.f.* **1.** (*a*) *Pol.Ec: etc:* increase in value; increment value; appreciation (of land, etc.); surplus, excess yield (of tax, etc.); **les recettes présentent une p.-v. de . . .,** the receipts show an increase of . . .; (*b*) *Fin:* appreciated surplus, betterment; **impôt sur les plus-values,** capital gains tax. **2.** extra payment.

plutonium [plytɔnjɔm] *n.m. Ch:* plutonium.

plutôt [plyto] *adv.* (*a*) rather, sooner; **p. la mort que l'esclavage,** sooner death than slavery; **p. souffrir que mentir,** it is better to suffer than to lie; **il récite p. qu'il ne chante,** he recites rather than sings; **p. que de partir,** rather than leave; instead of leaving; **demande p. à ta mère,** (you'd) better ask your mother; **ne pleurez pas, riez p.,** don't cry, laugh instead; (*b*) rather, on the whole; **il faisait p. froid (que chaud),** the weather was cold if anything; **son discours était p. long,** his speech was somewhat long.

pluvial, -iaux [plyvjal, -jo] *a.* pluvial; rainy (season, etc.); **eau pluviale,** rainwater.

pluvier [plyvje] *n.m. Orn:* plover.

pluvieux, -ieuse [plyvjø, -jøz] *a.* rainy (season); wet (weather).

pluviner [plyvine] *v.i.* to drizzle.

pluviomètre [plyvjɔmɛtr̥] *n.m. Meteor:* rain gauge; pluviometer.

pluviôse [plyvjoz] *n.m. Fr.Hist:* fifth month of the Fr. Republican calendar (Jan.-Feb.).

pluviosité [plyvjozite] *n.f. Meteor:* rainfall.

pneu [pnø] *n.m.* tyre, *NAm:* tire; **p. à carcasse radiale,** radial tyre; **p. à carcasse croisée,** cross-ply tyre.

pneumatique [pnømatik] **1.** *a.* pneumatic; air (pump, etc.); inflatable (raft, etc.); **canot p.,** rubber dinghy. **2.** *n.m.* (*a*) = PNEU; (*b*) *A:* (*in Paris*) express letter (transmitted by pneumatic tube).

pneumocoque [pnømɔkɔk] *n.m. Bac:* pneumococcus.

pneumologie [pnømɔlɔʒi] *n.f. Med:* pneumology.

pneumologue [pnømɔlɔg] *n. Med:* chest specialist.

pneumonie [pnømɔni] *n.f. Med:* pneumonia.

pneumothorax [pnømɔtɔraks] *n.m. Med:* pneumothorax.

Pô (le) [ləpo] *Pr.n.m. Geog:* the (river) Po.

pochade [pɔʃad] *n.f.* rapid sketch.

pochard, -arde [pɔʃar, -ard] *n. F:* drunkard, boozer.

poche[1] [pɔʃ] *n.f.* **1.** pocket; **p. de poitrine,** breast pocket; **p. intérieure,** inside (breast) pocket; **p. revolver,** hip pocket; **p. carnier,** poacher pocket; *F:* **faire les poches à qn,** to go through s.o.'s pockets; **calculateur de p.,** pocket calculator; **carnet de p.,** pocket book; **livre de p.,** paperback; **argent de p.,** pocket money; **avoir la p. vide,** to have empty pockets; to be penniless; **avoir toujours la main à la p.,** to be always paying out; **j'en suis de ma p.,** I'm out of pocket by it; **payer de sa p.,** to pay out of one's own money; **j'ai cent francs en p.,** I've (got) a hundred francs on me; **mettre qch. dans sa p.,** to put sth. in one's pocket; to pocket sth.; *F:* **mettez ça dans votre p. (et votre mouchoir dessus),** put that in your pipe and smoke it; **connaître qch. comme sa p.,** to know sth. inside out, like the back of one's hand; **il n'a pas sa langue dans sa p.,** he's (got) plenty to say for himself; *F:* **c'est dans la p.,** it's in the bag. **2.** (*a*) bag, pouch, sack; **p. à cartes,** map case; *Fig:* **acheter chat en p.,** to buy a pig in a poke; **p. d'air,** (i) *Av:* air pocket; (ii) *Hyd.E:* airlock; (*b*) *Biol: Med:* sac; (*c*) *Z:* pouch (of kangaroo, etc.). **3.** (*a*) **pantalon qui fait des poches aux genoux,** trousers that are baggy at the knees; (*b*) **poches sous les yeux,** bags under the eyes.

poche² *n.f. Metall:* **p. à couler, de coulée,** casting ladle.

poche³ *n.m. F:* paperback.

pocher¹ [pɔʃe] **1.** *v.tr. Cu:* to poach (eggs); *F:* **p. l'œil à qn,** to give s.o. a black eye; **œil poché,** black eye; *P:* **la ferme, ou je te poche un œil!** shut up, or I'll give you a sock in the eye! **2.** *v.i.* (*of clothes*) to get baggy.

pocher² *v.tr.* to dash off (sketch, etc.).

pochette [pɔʃɛt] *n.f.* (*a*) pouch; envelope (for papers, etc.); case (for instruments, etc.); **p. d'allumettes,** book of matches; (*b*) *Rec:* sleeve (of record).

pocheuse [pɔʃøz] *n.f. Dom.Ec:* (egg) poacher.

pochoir [pɔʃwar] *n.m.* stencil (plate); **passer qch. au p.,** to stencil sth.

podagre [pɔdagr̥] *A:* **1.** *n.f.* gout (in the feet). **2.** *a.* & *n.* gouty (person).

podium [pɔdjɔm] *n.m.* podium; *Sp:* rostrum.

podomètre [pɔdɔmɛtr̥] *n.m.* pedometer.

poêle¹ [pwal] *n.f.* frying pan, *NAm:* skillet.

poêle² *n.m.* **1.** *A:* (marriage) canopy. **2.** (funeral) pall; **porteurs des cordons du p.,** pall bearers.

poêle³ *n.m.* stove; **p. à feu continu,** slow-burning, slow-combustion, stove; **p. à bois, à mazout,** wood(-burning) stove, oil stove.

poêlée [pwale] *n.f.* panful.

poêler [pwale] *v.tr.* to cook in a frying pan; to fry.

poêlon [pwalɔ̃] *n.m.* small saucepan; casserole.

poème [pɔɛm] *n.m.* poem; *F:* **c'est tout un p.,** it's priceless.

poésie [pɔezi] *n.f.* **1.** poetry. **2.** poem; piece of poetry.

poète [pɔɛt] **1.** *n.m.* poet. **2.** *a.* **femme p.,** woman poet; poetess.

poétesse [pɔetɛs] *n.f.* poetess.

poétique [pɔetik] **1.** *a.* poetic (inspiration, licence, etc.); **l'art p.,** the art of poetry. **2.** *n.f.* poetics.

poétiquement [pɔetikmɑ̃] *adv.* poetically.

poétiser [pɔetize] *v.tr.* to poet(ic)ize.

pogne [pɔɲ] *n.f. P:* hand, paw, mitt.

pognon [pɔɲɔ̃] *n.m. P:* money, lolly, dough.

pogrom [pɔgrɔm] *n.m.* pogrom.

poids [pwa] *n.m* weight. **1.** (*a*) heaviness; **de tout son p.,** with all, with the whole of, one's weight; **perdre du p.,** to lose weight; **vendre au p.,** to sell by weight; **vendre qch. au p. de l'or,** to sell sth. for its weight in gold; **faire bon p.,** to give good weight; **ajouter qch. pour faire le p.,** to throw sth. in as a makeweight; *F:* **il ne fait pas le p.,** he's not up to the job, up to scratch; **p. atomique,** atomic weight; **p. spécifique,** *Ph:* specific weight; *Ch:* specific gravity; *Box:* **p. coq,** bantamweight; **p. lourd,** heavyweight; **p. moyen,** middleweight; **p. mouche,** flyweight; *Box: Wr:* **p. à volonté,** catchweight; (*b*) importance; **donner du p. à qch.,** to give weight to sth.; **son opinion a du p.,** his opinion carries weight. **2.** weight (in clock, etc.); **poids et mesures,** weights and measures; *Sp:* **lancer le p.,** to put the shot. **3.** load, burden; *Lit:* **le p. des ans,** the weight of years; *Trans:* **p. utile,** live weight; useful load; *Av:* payload; **p. mort,** dead weight; dead load; **p. brut,** gross weight; **p. net,** net weight; **p. en charge,** laden weight; *Aut:* **p. lourd,** heavy goods vehicle; heavy lorry, *esp. NAm:* truck; **le p. des impôts,** the burden of taxation.

poignant [pwaɲɑ̃] *a.* poignant; harrowing (experience, etc.); **spectacle p.,** (i) agonizing, (ii) moving, sight.

poignard [pwaɲar] *n.m.* dagger; **coup de p.,** stab; **donner un coup de p. à qn,** to stab s.o.

poignarder [pwaɲarde] *v.tr.* to stab (s.o.); to knife (s.o.).

poigne [pwaɲ] *n.f.* grip, grasp; **homme à p., qui a de la p.,** strong, forceful, firm, man.

poignée [pwaɲe] *n.f.* **1.** (*a*) handful; fistful; **à poignées,** in handfuls; by the handful; **p. d'hommes,** handful of men; (*b*) **p. de main,** handshake; **donner une p. de main à qn,** to shake hands with s.o. **2.** handle (of door, etc.); grasp (of oar); grip (of pistol); hilt (of sword); haft (of tool); pull (of bell, etc.). **3.** hank (of thread, etc.).

poignet [pwaɲɛ] *n.m.* **1.** wrist; **faire qch. à la force du p.,** to do sth. by sheer strength, by sheer hard work. **2.** (*of garment*) cuff; wristband.

poil [pwal] *n.m.* **1.** (*a*) (*of animal*) hair, fur; **p. de chameau,** camel hair; **à p. long,** long-haired, shaggy; **tomber sur le p. à qn,** to attack, go for, s.o.; *A:* **monter un cheval à p.,** to ride a horse bareback; (*b*) coat (of animals); **cheval d'un beau p.,** sleek horse; **chien au p. rude, à p. dur,** wire-haired, rough-coated, dog; (*c*) nap (of cloth); pile (of velvet); (*d*) bristle (of brush). **2.** hair (on the body); **poils follets,** down; *F:* **à p.,** naked; **se mettre à p.,** to strip to the skin, to the buff; *F:* **avoir un p. dans la main,** to be workshy, bone idle. **3.** *F:* **être de bon, de mauvais, p.,** to be in a good, bad, mood. **4.** *F:* **(fait) au quart de p.,** perfectly (done); **à un p. près,** as near as dammit; **un p. plus vite,** a fraction faster; *int.* **au p.!** wonderful! super!

poilant [pwalɑ̃] *a. P:* hilarious; screamingly funny.

poiler (se) [sәpwale] *v.pr. P:* to kill oneself laughing.

poilu [pwaly] **1.** *a.* (*a*) hairy, shaggy; (*b*) *Nat.Hist:* pilose. **2.** *n.m. F:* French soldier (1914–1918).

poinçon [pwɛ̃sɔ̃] *n.m.* **1.** (*a*) (engraver's) point; chasing chisel; (*b*) awl, bradawl; *Needlw:* bodkin; (embroiderer's) stiletto; (sailmaker's) stabber; *Dom.Ec:* **p. à glace,** ice pick. **2.** (*a*) (perforating) punch; **(coup de) p. sur un billet,** punch hole in a ticket; (*b*) die, stamp; **p. à chiffrer,** number punch; (*c*) stamped mark; **p. de contrôle,** hallmark (stamp). **3.** *Rec:* stamper. **4.** *Const:* kingpost, crown post.

poinçonnage [pwɛ̃sɔnaʒ] *n.m.* **1.** *Ind:* pricking, boring, punching. **2.** (*a*) punching (of ticket, etc.); (*b*) stamping, hallmarking.

poinçonner [pwɛ̃sɔne] *v.tr.* **1.** *Ind:* to prick, bore, punch. **2.** (*a*) to punch, clip (ticket, etc.); (*b*) to stamp, hallmark.

poinçonneur, -euse [pwɛ̃sɔnœr, -øz] **1.** *n.* (*pers.*) (*a*) *Ind:* puncher; (*b*) *Trans:* ticket collector. **2.** *n.f.* **poinçonneuse** stamping, punching, machine; punch; ticket punch.

poindre [pwɛ̃dr̥] *v.i.* (*pr.p.* **poignant;** *p.p.* **point;** *pr.ind.* **il point, ils poignent;** *impf.* **il poignait;** *p.h.* **il poignit;** *fu.* **il poindra;** *used esp. in 3rd pers. and in inf.*) (*of daylight*) to dawn, break; (*of plants, etc.*) to come up, sprout, come out; (*of ship*) **p. à l'horizon,** to heave in sight.

poing [pwɛ̃] *n.m.* fist; **poings nus,** bare knuckles; **sabre, revolver, au p.,** sword, revolver, in hand; **serrer les poings,** to clench one's fists; **menacer qn du p., montrer le p. à qn,** to shake one's fist at s.o.; **dormir à poings fermés,** to sleep soundly, like a log; **coup de p.,** punch; **donner un coup de p. à qn,** to punch s.o.;

il est tombé sur eux à coups de p., he went for them with his fists.

point¹ [pwɛ̃] *n.m.* **1.** (*a*) *Needlew:* stitch; **p. devant, glissé, coulé,** running stitch; **p. arrière,** backstitch; **p. de chausson,** herringbone stitch; **p. noué,** knot stitch; **p. de chaînette,** chainstitch; **p. roulé,** whipping; **p. croisé,** cross-stitch; **p. de languette, de feston,** blanket stitch, buttonhole stitch; **p. perdu,** blind stitch, slip stitch; **coudre qch. à points perdus,** to blindstitch, slipstitch, sth.; **faire un p. à un vêtement,** to put a few stitches in a garment; *Knit:* **p. de riz,** moss stitch; **p. mousse,** plain knitting, garter stitch; *Lacem:* **p. de Bruxelles,** Brussels lace; (*b*) **p. de côté,** stitch (in the side); **avoir un p. au dos,** to have a stabbing pain in one's back. **2.** point; (*a*) (*in time*) **le p. du jour,** daybreak; **être sur le p. de faire qch.,** to be on the point of doing sth.; to be about to do sth.; **sur le p. de mourir,** at, on, the point of death; **arriver à p. nommé, juste à p.,** to arrive in the nick of time, just at the right moment; **tout vient à p. à qui sait attendre,** everything comes to him who waits; (*b*) (*in space*) **p. de départ,** starting point, place; *Mil: etc:* **p. de dispersion,** dispersal point (of column, etc.); **p. d'eau,** (i) waterhole (in desert); (ii) tap (in campsite); **p. de vue,** (i) (*panorama*) viewpoint, view; (ii) point of view, viewpoint, standpoint; **à tous les points de vue,** in all respects, in every respect; **au, du, p. de vue international,** from an international angle; **du, au, p. de vue caractère,** as far as (his, etc.) character is concerned; (*in war, etc.*) **p. chaud,** hot spot; *Tchn:* **p. critique,** critical point; *Av:* **essai au p. fixe,** ground run; **p. d'appui,** (i) *Mil: etc:* base of operations; strong point; *Navy:* outlying station; (ii) *Mec:* fulcrum (of lever); purchase; **p. mort,** neutral (gear); *Mec.E:* **p. de graissage,** lubricating point; *Com:* **p. de vente,** stockist; *Nau: Av: etc:* **p. estimé,** dead reckoning (position); **faire le p.,** to take bearings, find one's position on a map; **faire le p. (d'une question),** to take stock (of a question); **au p.,** (i) *Opt:* in focus; (ii) *I.C.E:* tuned up; **mettre au p.,** to focus (lens, etc.); to perfect (design, etc.); to tune (engine); to adjust (sth.); to finalize (arrangements); **cette question reste à mettre au p.,** this question remains to be settled; **mise au p.,** focusing (of lens); perfecting (of technique, etc.); tuning (of engine); adjusting; finalizing (of arrangements); restatement (of question); **recherche et mise au p.,** research and development; (*c*) *Nau:* **p. de voile,** clew, corner, of a sail. **3.** (*a*) point, dot; pip (on dice, etc.); punctuation mark; **mettre les points sur les i,** (i) to dot one's i's; (ii) to make one's meaning perfectly plain; **p. (final),** full stop, *NAm:* period; **deux points,** colon; **p. d'interrogation,** question mark; **p. d'exclamation,** exclamation mark, *NAm:* exclamation point; *F:* **un p., c'est tout!** and that's that! *Tg:* **points et traits,** dots and dashes (of Morse alphabet); (*b*) *Mus:* **p. d'orgue,** pause, fermata; (*c*) *Games:* point, score; **marquer les points,** to keep the score; **il a marqué 10 points,** he scored 10 points; *Box:* **gagner aux points,** to win on points; **rendre des points à qn,** to give s.o. points; to be more than a match for s.o.; (*d*) *Sch:* mark; **mauvais p.,** bad mark; (*e*) *Typ:* point; **caractères de huit points,** eight-point type; (*f*) speck, spot, dot; **le navire n'est qu'un p. à l'horizon,** the ship is a mere speck on the horizon; **p. noir,** (i) (*on skin*) blackhead; (ii) problem; cloud on the horizon; (iii) *Aut:* (accident) black spot. **4.** (*a*) point, stage, degree; extent; **p. d'ébullition,** boiling point; **p. d'éclair,** flash point; **p. de fusion, de congélation,** melting point, freezing point; **jusqu'à un certain p.,** to a certain extent, up to a certain point; **au p. où en sont les choses,** as matters stand; **à ce p. que, à tel p. que, au p. que . . .,** to such a point, stage, that . . .; so much so that . . .; **vous n'êtes pas malade à ce p.-là,** you're not as ill as all that; **au dernier p.,** to, in, the last degree; (*b*) **mal en p.,** in a bad way; ill; *A:* **en bon p.,** in good condition; (*c*) **à p.,** in the right condition; *Cu:* done to a turn; (*of steak*) medium. **5.** point, particular; **p. de droit,** point of law; **le p. capital,** the main point; **mettre son p. d'honneur à ne pas céder,** to make it a point of honour, *NAm:* honor, not to yield; **n'ayez aucune** crainte sur ce p., don't worry on that score, on that count; **en tous points,** in every way; in all respects; **exécuter un ordre de p. en p.,** to carry out an order exactly, to the letter.

point² *adv. A: Lit: Dial:* = PAS²; **peu ou p.,** little or not at all; **le connaissez-vous?—p.!** do you know him?—not at all.

pointage [pwɛ̃taʒ] *n.m.* (*a*) checking, ticking off (of names on list, etc.); scrutiny (of votes, etc.); *Nau:* pricking (of chart); plotting (of position on map); (*b*) *Ind:* clocking in, out; timekeeping; (*c*) *Mus:* dotting (of note); (*d*) pointing, levelling, training (of telescope, etc.); aiming, laying (of gun, etc.).

pointe [pwɛ̃t] *n.f.* **1.** (*a*) point (of pin, knife, etc.); tip, head (of arrow, lance); nose (of bullet); toe (of shoe); top (of spire); peak (of roof); **p. d'aiguille,** (i) needlepoint; (ii) *Rail:* point of a switchblade; **p. d'une épigramme,** point, sting, of an epigram; **coup de p.,** thrust; **à la p. de l'épée,** at the point of the sword; by force; **p. d'asperge,** asparagus tip; **en p.,** pointed; tapering; **aller en p.,** to taper; **tailler en p.,** to sharpen (pencil, etc.); **barbe en p.,** pointed beard; **p. de lance,** spearhead; **marcher, se tenir, sur la p. des pieds,** to walk, stand, on tiptoe; **entrer sur la p. des pieds,** to tiptoe in; *Danc:* **faire des pointes,** to dance on point(s); (*b*) peak (*Mth:* of curve, *El:* of load, *Med:* of fever); **heures, période, de p.,** peak period, rush hour(s); (*c*) *Mil:* point (of advanced guard); **faire une p.,** to push a small force far in advance of main army; **pousser une p. sur . . .,** to launch a spearhead against . . .; **nous avons poussé une p. jusqu'à Paris,** we pressed on to Paris; *Navy:* **tir en p.,** firing ahead; **être à la p. de qch.,** to set the pace, lead, in sth.; to be in the forefront of sth.; **industrie de p.,** advance technology industry; (*d*) *Row:* **huit de p.,** eight(-oared boat); (*e*) **p. du jour,** daybreak; **p. de douleur,** twinge of pain; pang; **parler avec une p. d'accent étranger,** to speak with a hint of a foreign accent; **p. d'ironie,** touch of irony; **p. d'ail, de vanille,** touch of garlic, dash of vanilla; *Sp: etc:* **p. de vitesse,** spurt, sprint; **vitesse de p.,** highest speed; (*f*) witty phrase; quip; (*g*) *Nau:* **p. de canot,** canvas. **2.** *Geog:* **p. (de terre),** foreland, head(land); cape; spit, tongue (of land). **3.** *Tls:* (stonemason's) point; *Carp:* **p. carrée,** bradawl; **p. à tracer,** scribe; *Engr:* **p. (sèche),** (dry) point; etching needle; **la p. sèche,** dry-point etching. **4.** (*a*) nail, tack; (*b*) *Sp:* spike (on shoe); **chaussures à pointes,** spiked shoes; spikes. **5.** *Med:* **pointes de feu,** ignipuncture. **6.** (*a*) (triangular) (baby's) nappy, *NAm:* diaper; (*b*) (triangular) scarf; (*c*) *Nau:* gore (of sail).

pointeau, -eaux [pwɛ̃to] *n.m.* **1.** *Mec.E:* centre punch, *NAm:* center punch. **2.** *I.C.E:* (float) needle, float spindle (of carburettor). **3.** (*pers.*) checker; timekeeper.

pointer¹ [pwɛ̃te] **1.** *v.tr.* (*a*) to check, tick off (names on list, etc.); to scrutinize (votes, etc.); *Nau: etc:* to prick (the chart); to plot (position) (on the map); (*b*) *Mus:* to dot (a note); **note pointée,** dotted note; (*c*) to point, level, train (telescope, etc.); to aim, lay (gun); to train (searchlight) (**sur,** on). **2.** *v.i. & pr.* (*a*) *Ind:* **(se) p. (à l'arrivée, à la sortie),** to clock in, out; (*b*) *F:* **se p.,** to turn up, show up.

pointer² [pwɛ̃te] **1.** *v.tr.* (*a*) to thrust, stab (with sword, etc.); to prick (with needle, etc.); (*b*) to point (needle); to sharpen (pencil); (*c*) (*of horse, etc.*) **p. les oreilles,** to prick up its ears. **2.** *v.i.* to appear; (*of plant*) to sprout, come up; (*of bird*) to soar; (*of horse*) to rear.

pointer³ [pwɛ̃tœr] *n.m. Z:* pointer.

pointeur, -euse [pwɛ̃tœr, -øz] *n.* **1.** checker; *Ind:* timekeeper; *Sp: etc:* marker, scorer. **2.** *Artil:* gun layer.

pointillage [pwɛ̃tijaʒ] *n.m. Art: etc:* dotting; stippling.

pointillé [pwɛ̃tije] **1.** *a.* dotted (line); stippled (engraving); *Tex:* pinhead (cloth). **2.** *n.m.* (*a*) dotted line; perforations; **détacher suivant le p.,** tear along the dotted line; (*b*) stippling; stipple; **dessin en p.,** stippled design.

pointiller¹ [pwɛ̃tije] *v.tr.* **1.** to dot; **roue à p.,** dotting wheel. **2.** *Art:* to stipple.

pointiller² *v.i. A:* to cavil, bicker (over trifles); to split hairs.

pointilleux, -euse [pwɛ̃tijø, -øz] *a.* **1.** captious (person); carping (critic). **2.** particular (**sur,** about); fastidious; finicky, pernickety.

pointillisme [pwɛ̃tijism] *n.m. Art:* pointillism.

pointilliste [pwɛ̃tijist] *Art:* (*a*) *n.* pointillist; (*b*) *a.* pointillistic.

pointu [pwɛ̃ty] **1.** *a.* (*a*) (sharp-)pointed (knife, etc.); (*b*) touchy (disposition); shrill (voice). **2.** *adv. F:* (*in S. of Fr.*) **parler p.,** to speak with a Parisian accent.

pointure [pwɛ̃tyr] *n.f.* size (in shoes, gloves, etc.); **quelle est votre p. (de gants)?** what size (gloves) do you take?

point-virgule [pwɛ̃virgyl] *n.m.* semicolon; *pl. points-virgules.*

poire [pwar] *n.f.* **1.** pear; **entre la p. et le fromage** = at the end of the meal; *Fig:* **garder une p. pour la soif,** to put something by for a rainy day; **couper la p. en deux,** to compromise, split the difference. **2.** (pear-shaped) bulb (of camera shutter, etc.); (pear-shaped) switch (of electric light). **3.** *P:* (*a*) face, mug; **il a une bonne p.,** (i) he looks a decent sort; (ii) he looks a bit of a mug; (*b*) (*pers.*) mug, sucker.

poiré [pware] *n.m.* perry.

poireau, -eaux [pwaro] *n.m.* **1.** (*a*) leek; (*b*) *F:* **faire le p.,** to be kept waiting; to kick, cool, one's heels.

poireauter [pwarote] *v.i. F:* to be kept waiting; to kick, cool, one's heels.

poirée [pware] *n.f. Bot:* white beet.

poirier [pwarje] *n.m.* (*a*) pear tree; *Gym:* **faire le p.,** to do a headstand; (*b*) pear-tree wood.

pois [pwa] *n.m.* **1.** *Bot:* pea; **p. chiche,** chickpea; **p. carré,** marrowfat pea; **p. de senteur,** sweet pea; *F:* **la fleur des p.,** the pick of the bunch. **2.** *Cu:* **petits p.,** garden peas; **p. cassés,** split peas; **purée de p.,** (i) thick pea soup; (ii) pease pudding; (iii) *F:* peasouper (fog). **3. cravate bleue à p. blancs,** blue tie with white spots; blue polka dot tie; **tissu à p.,** spotted, polka dot, material.

poison [pwazɔ̃] **1.** *n.m.* poison. **2.** *F:* (*a*) *n.m. & f.* (*pers.*) pest; horror; (*b*) *n.m.* (*thg*) **quel p.!** how boring! what a bind!

poissard, -arde [pwasar, -ard] **1.** *a.* vulgar, low. **2.** *n.f.* **poissarde** (*a*) *A:* fishwife; (*b*) vulgar, foul-mouthed, woman.

poisse [pwas] *n.f. F:* bad luck; **c'est la p.!** just my luck!

poisser [pwase] **1.** *v.tr.* (*a*) to pitch; **fil poissé,** waxed thread; (*b*) to make (hands, etc.) sticky (with jam, etc.); (*c*) *P:* to catch, nab (s.o.). **2.** *v.i.* (*of substance*) to be sticky.

poisseux, -euse [pwasø, -øz] *a.* sticky.

poisson [pwasɔ̃] *n.m.* **1.** fish; **p. d'eau douce, de mer,** freshwater, saltwater, fish; **p. chat,** catfish; **p. lune,** sunfish, moonfish; **p. pilote,** pilot fish; **p. plat,** flat fish; **p. rouge,** goldfish; **p. volant,** flying fish; **p. d'avril!** April fool! **être (heureux) comme un p. dans l'eau,** to be as happy as a sandboy; to be in one's element; **être comme un p. hors de l'eau,** to be like a fish out of water; *F:* **engueuler qn comme du p. pourri,** to tell s.o. off, give s.o. a good slanging; *Astr:* **les Poissons,** Pisces. **2.** *Ent:* **p. d'argent,** silver fish.

poissonnerie [pwasɔnri] *n.f.* fish market; fish shop; fishmonger's.

poissonneux, -euse [pwasɔnø, -øz] *a.* (*of lake, etc.*) full of fish.

poissonier, -ière [pwasɔnje, -jɛr] **1.** *n.* fishmonger; *f.* fishwife. **2.** *n.f.* **poissonnière,** fish kettle.

poitrail [pwatraj] *n.m.* **1.** *Const:* breastsummer. **2.** (*a*) breast (of horse); (*b*) *Harn: A:* breast strap, breastplate.

poitrinaire [pwatrinɛr] *a. & n. A:* consumptive.

poitrine [pwatrin] *n.f.* **1.** chest; **rhume de p.,** cold on the chest; **chanter à pleine p.,** to sing at the top of one's voice; *Mus:* **voix de p.,** chest voice; *A:* **s'en aller de la p.,** to be dying of consumption. **2.** (*a*) chest; (*of woman, Lit: of man*) breast; bosom; **tour de p.,** (i) (*of man, child*) chest measurement; (ii) (*of woman*) bust measurement; **avoir la p. plate,** to be flat-chested; (*b*) *Cu:* breast (of veal); brisket (of beef); belly (of pork).

poivrade [pwavrad] *n.f.* (*a*) highly peppered salad dressing; (*b*) **manger des artichauts à la p.,** to eat artichokes (raw) with salt and pepper.

poivre [pwavr̥] *n.m.* pepper; **p. blanc, noir,** white, black, pepper; **p. de Cayenne,** Cayenne pepper, red pepper; **grain de p.,** peppercorn; **p. et sel,** pepper-and-salt (colour, *NAm:* color); iron-grey (hair).

poivré [pwavre] *a.* peppery (food); pungent (smell); spicy (story); exorbitant (price).

poivrer [pwavre] **1.** *v.tr.* to pepper; to season with pepper. **2.** *F:* **se p.,** to get drunk, tipsy, canned.

poivrier [pwavrije] *n.m.* **1.** *Bot:* pepper plant. **2.** pepper pot.

poivrière [pwavrijɛr] *n.f.* **1.** pepper plantation. **2.** (*a*) pepper pot; (*b*) *Arch:* pepperbox (turret).

poivron [pwavrɔ̃] *n.m.* sweet pepper; capsicum; **p. vert, rouge,** green, red, pepper.

poivrot, -ote [pwavro, -ɔt] *n. P:* drunkard, boozer.

poix [pwa] *n.f.* (*a*) pitch; **p. sèche,** resin; **noir comme p.,** pitch black; (*b*) **p. liquide,** tar.

poker [pɔkɛr] *n.m. Cards:* poker; **p. d'as,** poker dice.

polaire [pɔlɛr] **1.** *a.* polar; **l'étoile p.,** *n.f.* **la p.,** the pole star; **froid p.,** intense, Arctic, cold. **2.** *n.f. Mth:* polar.

polarimètre [pɔlarimɛtr̥] *n.m. Ph:* polarimeter.

polarisant [pɔlarizɑ̃] *a.* polarizing.

polarisation [pɔlarizasjɔ̃] *n.f. Ph:* polarization, polarizing (of light, electrodes); *Elcs:* **p. de grille,** grid bias; **résistance de p. de grille,** bias resistor.

polariscope [pɔlariskɔp] *n.m. Opt:* polariscope.

polariser [pɔlarize] *v.tr.* to polarize.

polariseur [pɔlarizœr] *n.m. Opt:* polarizer.

polarité [pɔlarite] *n.f.* polarity.

polatouche [pɔlatuʃ] *n.m. Z:* flying squirrel.

polder [pɔldɛr] *n.m. Geog:* polder.

pôle [pol] *n.m.* (*a*) pole; *Geog:* **p. nord, sud,** north, south, pole; *Magn:* **pôles semblables,** like poles; **pôles contraires,** opposite poles; (*b*) centre, *NAm:* center (of attention); focus (of interest).

polémique [pɔlemik] **1.** *a.* polemic(al). **2.** *n.f.* polemic, controversy.

polémiquer [pɔlemike] *v.i.* to polemize.

polémiste [pɔlemist] *n.* polemi(ci)st.

poli [pɔli] **1.** *a.* (*a*) polished; burnished, bright (steel, etc.); buffed; glossy, sleek (coat of animal); (*b*) polished, elegant (style, writer); polite, courteous (person, manners); polite, civil (answer); **être très p.**

avec qn, to be very polite, very courteous, to s.o.; **peu p.,** rude, discourteous. **2.** *n.m.* polish, gloss.

police¹ [pɔlis] *n.f.* **1.** maintenance of law and order; policing; **exercer, faire, la p.,** to maintain law and order; to keep order; **p. du roulage, de la circulation,** traffic regulations; **numéro de p. d'un véhicule,** registration number, *NAm:* license number, of a vehicle; *Jur:* **tribunal de (simple) p.,** magistrate's court; *Mil:* **salle de p.,** guardroom. **2. la p.,** the police (force); **p. de la circulation,** traffic police; **p. judiciaire (P.J.)** = Criminal Investigation Department (C.I.D.); **p. mondaine, des mœurs** = vice squad; **appeler p. secours** = to dial 999 (for the police); **être de, dans, la p.,** to be a member of the police force, in the police; **agent de p.,** police constable, policeman; police officer; **inspecteur de p.** = police inspector; **commissaire de p.** = police superintendent; **préfet de p.,** chief commissioner of the Paris police; **remettre qn entre les mains de la p.,** to give s.o. in charge; **la p. est à vos trousses,** the police are after you.

police² *n.f.* (insurance) policy; **p. d'assurance (sur la) vie, (contre l')incendie,** life insurance, fire insurance, policy; **prendre une p.,** to take out a policy.

policer [pɔlise] *v.tr.* **(je poliçai(s); n. poliçons) 1.** *A:* to bring (country) under orderly government. **2.** *A: & Lit:* to civilize.

polichinelle [pɔliʃinɛl] *n.m.* **1.** Punch; Punchinello; **théâtre de p.** = Punch and Judy show; **secret de p.,** open secret. **2.** buffoon; figure of fun; **faire le p.,** to act the fool.

policier, -ière [pɔlisje, -jɛr] **1.** *a.* police (enquiry, state, dog, etc.); detective (novel). **2.** *n.m.* (*a*) policeman; police officer; detective; (*b*) *F:* detective novel.

poliment [pɔlimɑ̃] *adv.* politely, courteously.

polio [pɔljo] *n.f. Med: F:* polio.

poliomyélite [pɔljɔmjelit] *n.f. Med:* poliomyelitis.

polir [pɔlir] *v.tr.* **1.** to polish; to burnish, buff (metal, etc.); **poli par l'usage,** shiny with use; **se p. les ongles,** to polish, buff, one's nails. **2.** to polish (up) (style); to refine (manners).

polissage [pɔlisaʒ] *n.m.* polishing; burnishing (of metal); buffing (of metal, fingernails).

polisseur, -euse [pɔlisœr, -øz] **1.** *n.* (*pers.*) polisher; (gem) cutter. **2.** *n.f.* **polisseuse,** polishing machine.

polissoir [pɔliswar] *n.m. Tls:* polisher; burnisher; buffing wheel; *Toil:* nail buffer.

polissoire [pɔliswar] *n.f.* **1.** polishing brush (for shoes). **2.** *Ind:* polishing shop.

polisson, -onne [pɔlisɔ̃, -ɔn] **1.** *n.* (*a*) *O:* street urchin; (*b*) naughty child; rascal; scamp. **2.** *a.* (*a*) naughty, mischievous (child); (*b*) dirty (story); smutty (joke); **regard p.,** leer.

polissonner [pɔlisɔne] *v.i.* (*of child*) to be mischievous, naughty.

polissonnerie [pɔlisɔnri] *n.f.* **1.** (child's) mischievous trick. **2.** dirty remark; smutty joke.

politesse [pɔlitɛs] *n.f.* (*a*) politeness; good manners; courtesy; **brûler la p. à qn,** to leave s.o. abruptly, without saying goodbye; (*b*) **faire des politesses à qn,** to treat s.o. courteously, politely; **faire échange de politesses,** to exchange compliments.

politicaillerie [pɔlitikajri] *n.f. F:* political manoeuvring, *NAm:* maneuvering, *U.S:* peanut politics.

politicard [pɔlitikar] *n.m. F:* political manoeuvrer, *NAm:* maneuverer.

politicien, -ienne [pɔlitisjɛ̃, -jɛn] *n. often Pej:* politician.

politique [pɔlitik] **1.** *a.* (*a*) political; **(homme) p.,** politician; **le corps p.,** the body politic; **économie p.,** economics; (*b*) *A: & Lit:* politic, prudent, shrewd; diplomatic (answer, conduct). **2.** *n.f.* (*a*) policy; **p. intérieure, extérieure,** home policy, foreign policy; (*b*) politics; **se lancer dans la p.,** to go into politics.

politiquement [pɔlitikmɑ̃] *adv.* (*a*) politically; from a political angle; (*b*) *Lit:* prudently, diplomatically.

politiquer [pɔlitike] *v.i. F: A:* **2.** to talk politics.

politiser [pɔlitize] *v.tr.* to politicize; to bring politics into (sth.).

polka [pɔlka] *n.f. Danc: Mus:* polka.

pollen [pɔlɛn] *n.m. Bot:* pollen; **taux du p.,** pollen count.

pollinisation [pɔlinizasjɔ̃] *n.f. Bot:* pollination.

polluant [pɔlɥɑ̃] **1.** *a.* polluting. **2.** *n.m.* pollutant; **polluants atmosphériques,** air pollution.

polluer [pɔlɥe] *v.tr.* (*a*) *A: & Lit:* to pollute, defile, (holy place); (*b*) to pollute (atmosphere, etc.).

pollution [pɔlysjɔ̃] *n.f.* (*a*) *A: & Lit:* pollution, defilement (of holy place); (*b*) pollution (of the air, etc,); (*c*) *Med:* **pollutions nocturnes,** wet dreams.

polo [polo] *n.m.* **1.** *Sp:* polo. **2.** *Cost:* sweatshirt.

polochon [pɔlɔʃɔ̃] *n.m. P:* bolster; **combat à coups de polochons,** pillow fight.

Pologne [pɔlɔɲ] *Pr.n.f. Geog:* Poland.

polonais, -aise [pɔlɔnɛ, -ɛz] **1.** *Geog:* (*a*) *a.* Polish; (*b*) *n.* Pole; *F:* **soûl comme un P.,** as drunk as a lord. **2.** *n.m. Ling:* Polish. **3.** *n.f. Danc: Mus:* **polonaise,** polonaise.

poltron, -onne [pɔltrɔ̃, -ɔn] **1.** *a.* easily frightened; cowardly; timid. **2.** *n.* coward.

poltronnerie [pɔltrɔnri] *n.f.* cowardice; timidity.

polyamide [pɔljamid] *n.m. Ch:* polyamide.

polyandre [pɔljɑ̃dr̥] *a. Anthr: Bot:* polyandrous.

polyandrie [pɔljɑ̃dri] *n.f. Anthr:* polyandry.

polychrome [pɔlikrom] *a.* polychrome, polychrom(at)ic.

polychromie [pɔlikrɔmi] *n.f.* polychromy.

polyclinique [pɔliklinik] *n.f. Med:* polyclinic.

polycopie [pɔlikɔpi] *n.f.* stencilling, duplicating, process.

polycopier [pɔlikɔpje] *v.tr.* to duplicate, stencil; to cyclostyle; *Sch:* **(cours) polycopié,** duplicated lecture notes.

polyculture [pɔlikyltyr] *n.f.* polyculture, mixed farming.

polyèdre [pɔliɛdr̥] *Mth:* **1.** *a.* polyhedral. **2.** *n.m.* polyhedron.

polyédrique [pɔliedrik] *a. Mth:* polyhedral, polyhedric.

polyester [pɔliɛstɛr] *n.m. Ch:* polyester.

polyéthylène [pɔlietilɛn] *n.m. Ch:* polyethylene, polythene.

polygame [pɔligam] **1.** *a.* polygamous. **2.** *n.* polygamist.

polygamie [pɔligami] *n.f.* polygamy.

polyglotte [pɔliglɔt] *a. & n.* polyglot.

polygonal, -aux [pɔligɔnal, -o] *a.* polygonal.

polygone [pɔligɔn] *n.m.* (*a*) *Mth:* polygon; (*b*) *Artil:* experimental range, shooting range.

polymère [pɔlimɛr] *Ch:* **1.** *a.* polymeric. **2.** *n.m.* polymer.

polymérisation [pɔlimerizasjɔ̃] *n.f. Ch:* polymerization.

polymorphe [pɔlimɔrf] *a. Biol: Ch:* polymorphous, polymorphic.

polymorphie [pɔlimɔrfi] *n.f.*, **polymorphisme** [pɔlimɔrfism] *n.m. Biol: Ch:* polymorphism.

Polynésie [pɔlinezi] *Pr.n.f. Geog:* Polynesia.

polynésien, -ienne [pɔlinezjɛ̃, -jɛn] *a. & n. Geog:* Polynesian.

polynôme [pɔlinom] *n.m. Mth:* polynomial.

polype [pɔlip] *n.m.* **1.** *Coel:* polyp. **2.** *Med:* polyp(us).

polypétale [pɔlipetal] *a. Bot:* polypetalous.

polypeux, -euse [pɔlipø, -øz] *a. Med:* polypous.

polyphasé [pɔlifaze] *a. El:* polyphase, multiphase (system).
polyphonie [pɔlifɔni] *n.f. Mus:* polyphony.
polysoc [pɔlisɔk] *n.m. Agr:* multiple plough, *NAm:* plow.
polystyrène [pɔlistirɛn] *n.m. Ch:* polystyrene.
polysyllabe [pɔlisilab] **1.** *a.* polysyllabic (word). **2.** *n.m.* polysyllable.
polysyllabique [pɔlisilabik] *a.* polysyllabic.
polytechnicien, -ienne [pɔlitɛknisjɛ̃, -jɛn] *n.* (i) student at, (ii) graduate of, the *École polytechnique.*
polytechnique [pɔlitɛknik] *a. A:* polytechnic.
polythéisme [pɔliteism] *n.m.* polytheism.
polythéiste [pɔliteist] *a. & n.* polytheist.
polythène [pɔlitɛn] *n.m.* polythene.
polyuréthane [pɔliyretan] *n.m. Ch:* polyurethane.
polyvalence [pɔlivalɑ̃s] *n.f. Ch:* polyvalence, polyvalency; multivalence.
polyvalent [pɔlivalɑ̃] **1.** *a.* (*a*) *Ch:* polyvalent; multivalent; (*b*) multiple-purpose (building, etc.); versatile, general-purpose (tool, etc.). **2.** *n.m. Adm:* tax inspector.
polyvinyle [pɔlivinil] *n.m. Ch:* polyvinyl.
pomiculteur [pɔmikyltœr] *n.m.* fruit grower.
pommade [pɔmad] *n.f.* (*a*) *A:* pomade (for the hair, etc.); (*b*) ointment (for skin troubles); **p. pour les lèvres,** lip salve; (*c*) **passer de la p. à qn,** to flatter s.o., butter s.o. up.
pommader [pɔmade] *v.tr. A:* to pomade.
pomme [pɔm] *n.f.* **1.** (*a*) apple; **p. à cuire,** cooking apple, cooker; **p. à couteau,** eating apple; **p. à cidre,** cider apple; **p. sauvage,** crab apple; **compote de pommes,** (i) stewed apples, apple purée; (ii) apple sauce; **p. de discorde,** bone of contention; apple of discord; *F:* (*of child*) **haut comme trois pommes,** knee-high to a grasshopper; *Anat:* **p. d'Adam,** Adam's apple; (*b*) **p. de terre,** potato; *Cu:* **pommes (à la) vapeur, à l'anglaise,** steamed, boiled, potatoes; **pommes chips,** potato crisps; **bifteck aux pommes,** steak and chips; *F:* **tomber dans les pommes,** to pass out, faint; (*c*) **p. épineuse,** thorn apple; **p. de chêne,** oak apple; **p. de pin,** pine cone, fir cone. **2.** heart (of lettuce, cabbage). **3.** (*a*) knob (of bedstead, walking stick, etc.); head (of cabbage, lettuce, etc.); rose (of watering can, etc.); **canne à p. d'or,** gold-headed stick; (*b*) *Nau:* truck (of mast).
pommé [pɔme] *a.* (*a*) (*of cabbage, etc.*) well rounded, round; **laitue pommée,** cabbage lettuce; **choux bien pommés,** fine heads of cabbage; (*b*) *F:* complete, utter, absolute, downright (fool, blunder, etc.).
pommeau, -eaux [pɔmo] *n.m.* pommel (of sword, saddle); butt (of fishing rod); knob (of walking stick).
pommelé [pɔmle] *a.* dappled, mottled; **gris p.,** dapple-grey (horse); **ciel p.,** mackerel sky.
pommeler (se) [səpɔmle] *v.pr.* **(il se pommelle; il se pommellera) 1.** (*of sky*) to become, covered, dappled with small fleecy clouds. **2.** = POMMER.
pommelle [pɔmɛl] *n.f.* grating, strainer (over drainpipe, etc.).
pommer [pɔme] *v.i.* (*of cabbage, etc.*) to form a head, heart; to heart (up).
pommeraie [pɔmrɛ] *n.f.* apple orchard.
pommette [pɔmɛt] *n.f.* **1.** knob; ball ornament. **2.** cheekbone.
pommier [pɔmje] *n.m.* apple tree; **p. sauvage,** crab (apple) tree.
pompage [pɔ̃paʒ] *n.m.* pumping (up, out).
pompe¹ [pɔ̃p] *n.f.* pomp, ceremony, display; *Lit:* **renoncer aux pompes du siècle,** to renounce the pomps and vanities of this wicked world; **ordonnateur, entrepreneur, de pompes funèbres,** undertaker, funeral director, *esp. U.S:* mortician.
pompe² *n.f.* **1.** (*a*) pump; **p. aspirante,** suction pump, lift pump; **p. (re)foulante,** force pump; **p. aspirante et foulante,** lift-and-force pump; **p. à incendie,** fire engine; *Mch:* **p. d'alimentation, alimentaire,** feed pump, donkey pump; **épuiser l'eau à la p.,** to pump out the water; **eau de p.,** pump water; *F:* **Château-la-P.** = Adam's ale, tap water; *F:* **avoir le coup de p.,** to be exhausted, worn out, fagged out; *F:* **à toutes pompes,** as quickly as possible, at top speed; *F:* **faire des pompes,** to do push-ups, press-ups; (*b*) **p. à air, p. pneumatique,** air pump, pneumatic pump; **p. à vide,** vacuum pump; **p. de bicyclette,** bicycle pump; (*c*) **p. à graisse,** grease gun; **p. à essence,** (i) petrol pump; *NAm:* gas pump; (ii) petrol station; *NAm:* gas station. **2.** *Mus:* **p. d'accord,** (tuning) slide (of wind instrument). **3. serrure à p.,** Bramah lock. **4.** *P:* **pompes,** shoes.
Pompée [pɔ̃pe] *Pr.n.m. Rom.Hist:* Pompey.
Pompéi [pɔ̃pei] *Pr.n.f. Geog:* Pompeii.
pomper [pɔ̃pe] *v.tr. & i.* (*a*) to pump (water, air); to suck up, suck in (liquid); *F:* **tu me pompes l'air,** you're exhausting me, wearing me out; (*b*) *Sch: P:* to copy (sth.) (**sur qn,** from s.o.); (*c*) *P:* to drink; to knock back (a drink); (*d*) to exhaust (s.o.), wear (s.o.) out; **être pompé,** to be worn out, fagged out.
pompette [pɔ̃pɛt] *a. F:* drunk, tight, tipsy.
pompeusement [pɔ̃pøzmɑ̃] *adv.* pompously.
pompeux, -euse [pɔ̃pø, -øz] *a.* pompous.
pompier [pɔ̃pje] **1.** *n.m.* fireman; *pl.* fire brigade. **2.** *a. & n.m. Art: Lit:* conventional, traditional (artist).
pompiste [pɔ̃pist] *n. Aut:* (petrol, *NAm:* gas) pump attendant; forecourt attendant.
pompon [pɔ̃pɔ̃] *n.m.* pompom; *F:* bobble; *F:* **ça, c'est le p.!** that's the limit! *F: O:* **avoir son p.,** to be drunk.
pomponner (se) [səpɔ̃pɔne] *v.pr.* to doll oneself up.
ponçage [pɔ̃saʒ] *n.m.* **1.** pumicing; sandpapering; rubbing down, sanding down (of paint). **2.** *Draw:* pouncing.
ponce [pɔ̃s] *n.f.* **1. (pierre) p.,** pumice (stone). **2.** *Draw:* pouncing bag.
ponceau¹, -eaux [pɔ̃so] *n.m.* culvert.
ponceau², -eaux *n.m.* **1.** *Bot:* (corn) poppy. **2.** *n.m. & a.inv.* poppy-red, flame.
Ponce Pilate [pɔ̃spilat] *Pr.n.m. B.Hist:* Pontius Pilate.
poncer [pɔ̃se] *v.tr.* **(je ponçai(s); n. ponçons) 1.** to pumice; to sandpaper; to rub down, sand down (paint). **2.** *Draw:* to pounce.
ponceuse [pɔ̃søz] *n.f. Tls:* sanding machine; sander.
poncho [pɔ̃tʃo] *n.m. Cost:* poncho.
poncif [pɔ̃sif] *n.m.* **1.** *Draw:* pouncing pattern. **2.** *Art: Lit: F:* banality, commonplace.
ponction [pɔ̃ksjɔ̃] *n.f. Med:* puncture; tapping (of lung, etc.); pricking (of blister).
ponctionner [pɔ̃ksjɔne] *v.tr. Med:* to puncture; to tap (lung, patient); to prick (blister).
ponctualité [pɔ̃ktɥalite] *n.f.* punctuality.
ponctuation [pɔ̃ktɥasjɔ̃] *n.f.* punctuation.
ponctuel, -elle [pɔ̃ktɥɛl] *a.* **1.** punctual. **2.** *Ph:* **source ponctuelle de chaleur,** pinpoint flame.
ponctuellement [pɔ̃ktɥɛlmɑ̃] *adv.* punctually.
ponctuer [pɔ̃ktɥe] *v.tr.* to punctuate (sentence); to emphasize, accentuate (one's words in speaking).
pondaison [pɔ̃dɛzɔ̃] *n.f.* egg-laying time.
pondérable [pɔ̃derabl̩] *a. Tchn:* weighable.
pondérateur, -trice [pɔ̃deratœr, -tris] *a.* balancing; stabilizing.
pondération [pɔ̃derasjɔ̃] *n.f.* (*a*) balance; equilibrium; (*b*) (*of pers.*) levelheadedness; coolness; poise; (*c*) *Pol.Ec:* weighting (of index).
pondéré [pɔ̃dere] *a.* (*a*) well balanced (mind); cool,

levelheaded, poised (person); (*b*) *Pol.Ec:* **indice p.,** weighted index.
pondérer [pɔ̃dere] *v.tr.* **(je pondère; je pondérerai)** (*a*) to balance (powers, etc.); (*b*) *Pol.Ec:* to weight (index).
pondéreux, -euse [pɔ̃derø, -øz] *a. Tchn:* heavy (goods, etc.).
pondeur, -euse [pɔ̃dœr, -øz] *a. & n.* (egg-)laying; **(poule) pondeuse,** laying hen; (good) layer; *Pej:* **p. de prose,** prolific author.
pondoir [pɔ̃dwar] *n.m.* laying place (for hens); nest box.
pondre [pɔ̃dr̥] *v.tr.* (*a*) (*of birds, etc.*) to lay (eggs); **œuf frais pondu,** new laid egg; (*b*) *F:* (*of writer, etc.*) to produce, bring out (novel, etc.).
poney [pɔnɛ] *n.m.* pony.
pongiste [pɔ̃ʒist] *n.* table tennis player.
pont¹ [pɔ̃] *n.m.* **1.** (*a*) bridge; **p. pour piétons,** footbridge; **p. volant,** flying bridge; **p. tubulaire,** box (girder) bridge; **p. suspendu,** suspension bridge; **p. cantilever, à consoles, en encorbellement,** cantilever bridge; **p. basculant, à bascule,** drawbridge, bascule bridge; **p. tournant, pivotant,** swing bridge; **p. de bateaux,** floating bridge, pontoon bridge; *Adm:* **les Ponts et Chaussées** = the department of civil engineering, the Highways Department; *F:* **faire le p.,** to take the intervening working day(s) off; to make a long weekend of it; *F:* **faire un p. d'or à qn,** to offer s.o. a lot of money to take on a new job; to make it worth s.o.'s while; **vivre sous les ponts,** to be a tramp; **p. aux ânes** [pɔ̃tozan], *pons asinorum*; common knowledge; (*b*) *Ind: etc:* platform, stage, bridge; **p. de décharge, à chariots culbuteurs,** tipping stage; *Aut:* (*in garage*) **p. élévateur,** (repair) ramp; (*c*) *Ind:* **p. roulant,** overhead crane, travelling crane; gantry; (*d*) *El:* **p. de Wheatstone,** Wheatstone's bridge; (*e*) *Av:* **p. aérien,** airlift. **2.** *Nau:* deck (of ship); **p. avant,** foredeck; **p. arrière,** after deck; **p. principal,** main deck; **p. supérieur, p. des gaillards,** upper deck; **p. inférieur,** lower deck; **navire à un p.,** single-decker, single-deck, ship; **navire à deux, à trois, ponts,** two-, three-decker; **homme, matelot, de p.,** deck hand, *Navy:* upper-deck rating; **monter sur le p.,** to go, come, on deck; **être sur le p.,** to be on deck; **tout le monde sur le p.!** *Nau:* all hands on deck! *Navy:* clear lower deck! *Nau:* **commander tout le monde sur le p.,** to pipe up all hands; **passage, voyage, sur le p.,** deck passage; *Com:* **sur p.,** free on board, f.o.b; **faux p.,** orlop deck; **p. des embarcations,** boat deck; **p. des emménagements, p. des premières,** saloon deck; **p. promenade,** promenade deck, sun deck, hurricane deck (on liner); **p. de manœuvre,** hurricane deck; *Navy:* **p. d'envol,** flight deck (of aircraft carrier, etc.). **3.** *Mec.E:* live axle; *Aut:* **p. arrière,** rear axle, back axle. **4.** *Cost: A:* **culotte à p.,** full-fall trousers. **5.** *Cards:* bridge (in a card).
Pont² (le) *Pr.n.m. A.Geog:* **1.** the (Kingdom of) Pontus. **2. le P.-Euxin,** the Euxine, the Black Sea.
pontage [pɔ̃taʒ] *n.m.* **1.** bridge building; bridging. **2.** *Nau:* decking.
pont-bascule [pɔ̃baskyl] *n.m.* (*a*) drawbridge, bascule bridge; (*b*) weighbridge; *pl. ponts-bascules.*
ponte¹ [pɔ̃t] *n.f.* (*a*) laying (of eggs); (*b*) eggs (laid).
ponte² *n.m.* (*a*) *Gaming:* punter; (*b*) *F:* important person; big shot.
ponté [pɔ̃te] *a.* decked (boat); **non p.,** open (boat).
pontée [pɔ̃te] *n.f. Nau:* deck load; deck cargo.
ponter¹ [pɔ̃te] *v.tr.* **1.** *Nau:* to lay the decks of, to deck (vessel). **2.** to bridge (river, etc., *esp.* with pontoon bridge).
ponter² *v.i. Gaming:* to punt.
pontier [pɔ̃tje] *n.m.* keeper of swing bridge.
pontife [pɔ̃tif] *n.m.* (*a*) pontiff; **le souverain P.,** the sovereign pontiff, the Pope; (*b*) *F:* pundit.
pontifiant [pɔ̃tifjɑ̃] *a. F:* pontificating.
pontifical, -aux [pɔ̃tifikal, -o] **1.** *a.* pontifical, papal. **2.** *n.m.* pontifical.
pontificat [pɔ̃tifika] *n.m.* pontificate.
pontifier [pɔ̃tifje] *v.i.* (*impf. & pr.sub.* **n. pontifiions; v. pontifiiez)** to pontificate; (*a*) to officiate as pontiff; (*b*) *F:* to lay down the law.
pont-levis [pɔ̃l(ə)vi] *n.m.* drawbridge (of castle, etc.); **p.-l. à fléau, à balancier,** lever drawbridge; *pl. ponts-levis.*
Pont-Neuf [pɔ̃nœf] *Pr.n.m.* **être solide comme le P.-N.,** to be as strong as a horse, as fit as a fiddle.
ponton [pɔ̃tɔ̃] *n.m.* **1.** hulk; prison ship. **2.** *Mil:* pontoon. **3.** (*a*) *Nau:* **p. à mâture,** sheer hulk; (*b*) **p. d'incendie,** fire float. **4.** (floating) landing stage.
pontonnier [pɔ̃tɔnje] *n.m.* **1.** *Mil:* pontoneer, pontonier. **2.** (bridge, ferry) toll collector. **3.** landing stage attendant. **4.** keeper of swing bridge.
pool [pul] *n.m.* **1.** *Pol.Ec: etc:* pool; common stock, fund; combine; syndicate. **2.** *Com:* **p. de dactylos,** typing pool.
pop [pɔp] *a.inv. & n.m.* **(musique) p.,** pop (music).
pope [pɔp] *n.m. Ecc:* pope (of the Orthodox church).
popeline [pɔplin] *n.f. Tex:* poplin.
popote [pɔpɔt] **1.** *n.f.* (*a*) *F:* (child's word for) soup; **faire la p.,** to do the cooking; (*b*) *Mil: etc:* canteen; officers' mess. **2.** *a.inv. F:* stay-at-home (person).
popotin [pɔpɔtɛ̃] *n.m. P:* buttocks, backside, *NAm:* ass; **se manier le p.,** to hurry, get a move on.
populace [pɔpylas] *n.f. Pej:* populace, rabble, riffraff.
populacier, -ière [pɔpylasje, -jɛr] *a.* of the rabble; common, vulgar, low.
populage [pɔpylaʒ] *n.m. Bot:* marsh marigold.
populaire [pɔpylɛr] *a.* popular; (*a*) *Pol: etc:* of the people; **démocratie p.,** people's democracy; **manifestation p.,** mass demonstration; (*b*) **chanson p.,** (i) folk song; (ii) popular song; **expression p.,** slang expression; **les classes populaires,** the working classes; **quartier p.,** working class district; (*c*) *Th: etc:* **places populaires,** cheap seats; (*d*) **se rendre p.,** to make oneself popular.
populariser [pɔpylarize] *v.tr.* to popularize.
popularité [pɔpylarite] *n.f.* popularity.
population [pɔpylasjɔ̃] *n.f.* population.
populeux, -euse [pɔpylø, -øz] *a.* populous; densely populated.
populo [pɔpylo] *n.m. F:* (*a*) **le p.,** the (common) people; *Pej:* the rabble; (*b*) crowd; people.
poquet [pɔkɛ] *n.m. Agr:* seed hole.
porc [pɔr] *n.m.* **1.** (*a*) pig, *NAm:* hog; **gardeur de porcs,** pig keeper; pigman; *A:* swineherd; (*b*) **(peau de) p.,** pigskin; (*c*) *F:* (*pers.*) pig, swine. **2.** *Cu:* pork; **côtelette de p.,** pork chop.
porcelaine [pɔrsəlɛn] *n.f.* **1.** *Moll:* cowrie, porcelain shell. **2.** *Cer:* porcelain; china(ware); **p. de Chine,** china; **p. de Saxe,** Dresden china; **p. tendre (anglaise),** bone china.
porcelainier, -ière [pɔrsəlenje, -jɛr] **1.** *a.* **industrie porcelainière,** porcelain, china, industry. **2.** *n.m.* porcelain manufacturer.
porcelet [pɔrsəlɛ] *n.m.* young pig; piglet.
porc-épic [pɔrkepik] *n.m.* (*a*) *Z:* porcupine; (*b*) *F:* (*pers.*) prickly customer; *pl. porcs-épics* [pɔrkepik].
porche [pɔrʃ] *n.m.* porch.
porcher, -ère [pɔrʃe, -ɛr] *n.* pig keeper; pigman; *A:* swineherd.
porcherie [pɔrʃəri] *n.f.* pigsty; piggery.
porcin [pɔrsɛ̃] **1.** *a.* porcine; **élevage p.,** pig breeding; **peste porcine,** swine fever; *NAm:* hog cholera. **2.** *n.m.pl.* **porcins,** pigs; swine; *NAm:* hogs.

pore [pɔr] *n.m.* pore (of skin, plant, stone).
poreux, -euse [pɔrø, -øz] *a.* porous.
porion [pɔrjɔ̃] *n.m.* overseer, foreman (in coalmine).
pornographe [pɔrnɔgraf] *n.* pornographer.
pornographie [pɔrnɔgrafi] *n.f.* pornography.
pornographique [pɔrnɔgrafik] *a.* pornographic.
porosité [pɔrozite] *n.f.* porosity, porousness.
porphyre [pɔrfir] *n.m.* *Miner:* porphyry.
port¹ [pɔr] *n.m.* **1.** harbour, *NAm:* harbor; port; **p. naturel,** natural harbour; **p. à, de, marée,** tidal harbour; **p. de toute marée, p. en eau profonde,** deep-water harbour; **capitaine de p.,** harbour master; **droits de p.,** harbour dues; port charges; **p. artificiel,** artificial port; **entrer dans le p.,** to enter harbour; **entrer au p.,** to come into port; **quitter le p.,** to leave port, clear the harbour; **arriver à bon p.,** to come safe into port; *F:* **le p. des navires perdus** = Davy Jones' locker. **2.** (*town*) port; **p. de mer, p. maritime,** seaport; **p. fluvial,** river port; **p. militaire, de guerre,** naval port, naval base; **p. de pêche,** fishing port; *Nau: Navy:* **les ports de la métropole,** the home ports; **p. d'armement,** port of registry, *U.S:* port of documentation; **p. d'attache,** home port, port of commissioning; *Cust:* **p. d'entrée,** port of entry; *Com:* **p. franc,** free port.
port² *n.m.* **1.** (*a*) (act of) carrying; **permis de p. d'armes,** permit for carrying firearms; *Mil:* **se mettre au p. d'armes,** to shoulder arms; (*b*) wearing (of uniform, etc.); manner of carrying (sword, etc.). **2.** cost of transport; porterage, carriage (of goods); postage (of parcel, letter); delivery charge (of telegram); *Com:* **ports de lettres, frais de p.,** postage, postal charges; **franc de p., p. payé, perçu,** carriage paid, post paid; **en p. dû,** carriage forward. **3.** bearing, gait, carriage (of person); *Bot:* habit (of plant). **4.** *Nau:* burden, tonnage (of ship). **5.** *Mus:* **p. de voix,** glide, portamento.
port³ *n.m.* pass (in the Pyrenees).
portable [pɔrtabl̩] *a.* **1.** portable (typewriter, etc.). **2.** wearable, presentable (garment, etc.).
portage [pɔrtaʒ] *n.m.* (*a*) porterage, conveyance, transport (of goods); **frais de p.,** porterage; (*b*) portage; conveying of a boat across land between navigable waters.
portail [pɔrtaj] *n.m.* portal (of church, etc.).
portance [pɔrtɑ̃s] *n.f.* *Aer:* lift (per unit area).
portant [pɔrtɑ̃] **1.** *a.* (*a*) bearing, carrying (part of machine, etc.); **à bout p.,** point-blank; *Av:* **surface portante,** aerofoil; *NAm:* airfoil; *Nau:* **vent p.,** fair wind; (*b*) **être bien p.,** to be in good health; **être mal p.,** to be in poor health, to be unwell. **2.** *n.m.* (*a*) *Tchn:* upright; supporter, stay, strut; (*b*) (lifting) handle (of trunk, etc.); (*c*) armature, keeper (of magnet); (*d*) tread (of wheel).
portatif, -ive [pɔrtatif, -iv] *a.* portable (typewriter, etc.); **armes portatives,** small arms; **glaces portatives,** ice cream to take away.
porte [pɔrt] *n.f.* **1.** (*a*) gateway, doorway, entrance; **portes d'une ville,** gates of a town; *Pol.Ec:* **politique de la porte ouverte,** open-door policy; **p. cochère, charretière,** carriage entrance, gateway; **les portes de l'enfer,** the gates of hell; **être aux portes de la mort,** to be at death's door; *Hist:* **la (Sublime-)P., la P. ottomane,** the (Sublime) Porte, the Turkish government; (*b*) *Ind:* **p. de visite,** inspection door; manhole door, cover; *Min: etc:* **p. d'aérage,** air gate, trap (door); *Hyd.E:* **p. d'écluse,** (lock) gate; (*c*) *Ski:* gate, pair of flags. **2.** door (of house, cupboard, etc.); **p. d'entrée,** entrance door, front door; **p. de sortie,** (i) way out, exit; (ii) *Fig:* way out, means of escape; **p. de derrière, de service,** back door; tradesmen's entrance; **à ma p.,** on my doorstep; *F:* **entrer dans une profession par la petite p.,** to get into a profession by the back door; **p. à deux battants,** double door; **p. battante,** swing door; **p. tournante,** revolving door; **p. roulante, p. coulissante,** sliding door; **p. vitrée,** glass door; **aller ouvrir la p.,** to answer the door; **gagner, prendre, la p.,** to make for the door, make off; *F:* **je lui ai parlé entre deux portes,** I spoke to him for a brief moment; **trouver p. close,** (i) to find nobody at home; (ii) to be refused entrance; **mettre qn à la p.,** (i) to throw, kick, s.o. out; (ii) to fire, sack, s.o.; **refuser, fermer, défendre, sa p. à qn,** to refuse s.o. admission, close one's door to s.o.; **habiter p. à p.,** to be next-door neighbours, *NAm;* neighbors; *n.m.* **faire du p. à p.,** to go from door to door (selling, canvassing, etc.); **écouter aux portes,** to eavesdrop. **3.** eye (of hook and eye). **4.** *usu.pl.* gorge; defile, pass.
porté [pɔrte] *a.* inclined, disposed; **être p. à l'indulgence,** to be inclined to be indulgent; **être p. à la colère,** to be quick-tempered; **p. à faire qch.,** inclined to do sth., given to doing sth.; **être p. à oublier,** to be apt to forget; **p. sur qn, qch.,** fond of s.o., of sth.
porte(-)à(-)faux [pɔrtafo] *n.m.inv.* overhang; cantilever; **en p. à f.,** overhanging, overhung; **situation en p. à f.,** uncertain, unstable, position.
porte-affiche(s) [pɔrtafiʃ] *n.m.* noticeboard; *pl. porte-affiches.*
porte-aiguille [pɔrteguij] *n.m.* *Surg:* needle holder; *pl. porte-aiguille(s).*
porte-aiguilles [pɔrteguij] *n.m.inv.* *Needlew:* needle case.
porte-allumettes [pɔrtalymɛt] *n.m.inv.* match holder.
porte-amarre [pɔrtamar] *n.m.inv.* *Nau:* line-throwing apparatus; **flèche p.-a.,** line-throwing rocket; *pl. porte-amarre(s).*
porte-avions [pɔrtavjɔ̃] *n.m.inv.* *Navy:* aircraft carrier.
porte-bagages [pɔrtbagaʒ] *n.m.inv.* (*a*) luggage rack; (*b*) *Aut: etc:* (luggage) carrier; (*on car*) roof rack.
porte-baïonnette [pɔrtbajɔnɛt] *n.m.* bayonet frog; *pl. porte-baïonnette(s).*
porte-balais [pɔrtbalɛ] *n.m.inv.* *El:* brush holder (of dynamo, etc.).
porte-bébé(s) [pɔrtbebe] *n.m.inv.* **1.** baby carrier (on bicycle). **2.** carry cot.
porte-billets [pɔrtbijɛ] *n.m.inv.* notecase, *NAm:* billfold.
porte-bombes [pɔrtbɔ̃b] *n.m.inv.* *Mil.Av:* bomb rack.
porte-bonheur [pɔrtbɔnœr] *n.m.inv.* (lucky) charm; amulet, mascot; **petit cochon p.-b.,** lucky pig.
porte-bouteilles [pɔrtbutɛj] *n.m.inv.* bottle rack, wine rack.
porte-brosses [pɔrtbrɔs] *n.m.inv.* **p.-b. (à dents),** toothbrush holder.
porte-carte(s) [pɔrtəkart] *n.m.inv.* (*a*) card holder, wallet; (*b*) map case, holder.
porte-chapeaux [pɔrtʃapo] *n.m.inv.* hat stand.
porte-chars [pɔrtʃar] *n.m.inv.* *Mil:* tank transporter.
porte-cigares [pɔrtsigar] *n.m.inv.* cigar case.
porte-cigarettes [pɔrtsigarɛt] *n.m.inv.* cigarette case.
porte-clefs [pɔrtkle] *n.m.inv.* **1.** *A:* turnkey, prison warder. **2.** key ring.
porte-copie [pɔrtkɔpi] *n.m.* *Typewr:* copy holder; *pl. porte-copie(s).*
porte-couteau [pɔrtkuto] *n.m.* knife rest; *pl. porte-couteau(x).*
porte-croix [pɔrtəkrwa] *n.m.inv.* *Ecc:* cross bearer.
porte-documents [pɔrtdɔkymɑ̃] *n.m.inv.* document case; briefcase.

porte-drapeau [pɔrtdrapo] *n.m. Mil:* colour bearer, *NAm:* color bearer; *Fig:* standard bearer; *pl. porte-drapeau(x)*.

portée [pɔrte] *n.f.* **1.** (*a*) *Const:* bearing (of beam); span (of roof, bridge); (*b*) *Nau:* **p. en lourd, en poids,** deadweight (capacity). **2.** (*a*) litter, brood (of animals); farrow (of pigs); (*b*) *Mec.E:* bearing surface; **portées d'un arbre,** (main) journals; (*c*) *Mec.E: etc:* boss (on shaft, etc.); (*d*) *Mus:* stave; staff. **3.** (*a*) reach (of arm, etc.); radius (of crane jib, etc.); range (of gun, radio station, etc.); scope (of treaty, etc.); compass (of voice, etc.); **à p. (de tir, etc.),** within range; **à p. de fusil,** within rifle range, within gunshot; **à p. de canon,** within gun range; **(à) courte p., (à) petite p.,** (at) short range; **(à) grande p., (à) longue p.,** (at) long range; **canon à longue p.,** long-range gun; **à p. de (la) voix,** within call; **à p. d'oreille,** within hearing, within earshot; **hors de p. de voix,** out of earshot; **à p. de (la) vue,** within sight; **à ma p.,** within my reach; **hors de ma p.,** (i) beyond my reach; (ii) beyond the compass of my voice; (iii) beyond my understanding; (iv) beyond my means; **hors de p.,** out of reach, range; beyond reach; **à p. de la main,** (i) within reach; to hand; (ii) within striking distance; **livre à la p. de tout le monde,** (i) book available to everybody; (ii) book that anyone can understand; (*b*) bearing, (full) significance (of a statement); implication, import (of words); **conséquences d'une p. incalculable,** far-reaching consequences.

porte-étendard [pɔrtetɑ̃dar] *n.m.inv. A:* standard bearer (in cavalry).

portefaix [pɔrtəfɛ] *n.m. A:* porter, *esp.* (i) street porter, (ii) dock hand.

porte-fenêtre [pɔrtfənɛtr̥] *n.f.* French window; *pl. portes-fenêtres*.

portefeuille [pɔrtəfœj] *n.m.* (*a*) portfolio (for drawings, etc.); **ministre sans p.,** minister without portfolio; *Com:* **p. d'assurances,** portfolio (of insurance broker); (*b*) wallet, *NAm:* billfold; **avoir un p. bien garni,** to be rich; **lit en p.,** apple pie bed; **jupe p.,** wrapover, *U.S:* wraparound, skirt; (*c*) *Fin:* **effets en p.,** bills in hand, holdings; **p. (titres),** investments, securities.

porte-greffe(s) [pɔrtəgrɛf] *n.m.inv. Hort:* stock; *pl. porte-greffe(s)*.

porte-hélicoptères [pɔrtelikɔptɛr] *n.m.inv. Nau:* helicopter carrier.

porte-jarretelles [pɔrtʒartɛl] *n.m.inv. Cost:* suspender belt.

porte-journaux [pɔrtʒurno] *n.m.inv.* newspaper rack.

porte-jupe [pɔrtəʒyp] *n.m.* skirt hanger; *pl. porte-jupe(s)*.

porte-malheur [pɔrtmalœr] *n.m.inv.* bringer of bad luck; Jonah.

portemanteau, -eaux [pɔrtmɑ̃to] *n.m.* **1.** *A:* portmanteau. **2.** coat(-and-hat) rack, stand; hallstand.

portement [pɔrtəmɑ̃] *n.m.* **p. de croix,** (Christ's) bearing of the Cross.

porte-menu [pɔrtməny] *n.m.inv.* menu holder.

porte(-)mine [pɔrt(ə)min] *n.m.* propelling pencil; *pl. porte-mine(s)*.

porte-monnaie [pɔrtmɔnɛ] *n.m.inv.* purse.

porte-musique [pɔrtmyzik] *n.m.inv.* music case; music folio.

porte-objet [pɔrtɔbʒɛ] *n.m.* (i) (object) slide, (ii) stage (of microscope); *pl. porte-objet(s)*.

porte-outil [pɔrtuti] *n.m.* tool holder (of machine tool); brace chuck; slide rest (of lathe); *pl. porte-outil(s)*.

porte-papier [pɔrtpapje] *n.m.inv.* **p.-p. (hygiénique),** toilet roll holder.

porte-parapluies [pɔrtparaplɥi] *n.m.inv.* umbrella stand.

porte-parole [pɔrtparɔl] *n.m.inv.* spokesman; *f.* spokeswoman; mouthpiece (of deputation, etc.); organ (of political party, etc.).

porte-pipes [pɔrtəpip] *n.m.inv.* pipe rack.

porte-plat [pɔrtəpla] *n.m.* (dish) stand; *pl. porte-plat(s)*.

porte-plume [pɔrtəplym] *n.m.inv.* penholder.

porter [pɔrte] **1.** *v.tr.* (*a*) to carry; to bear, support (burden, etc.); **p. qn en triomphe,** to carry s.o. shoulder high; **la lettre porte la date du 2 juin,** the letter is dated June 2nd; *v.i.* **croyez-vous que la glace porte,** do you think the ice will hold, bear? **ces abus portent en eux leur propre châtiment,** these abuses carry their own punishment; **elle porte bien son âge,** she's wearing well; **elle porte, ne porte pas, son âge,** she looks, doesn't look, her age; **p. qn dans son cœur,** to have a great affection for s.o.; *v.i.* **les juments portent onze mois,** the gestation period of a mare is eleven months; (*b*) to produce; **p. des fruits,** to bear fruit; **terres qui portent du blé,** wheat-producing lands; **argent qui porte intérêt,** money that bears, brings in, interest; **cela vous portera bonheur,** that will bring you luck; *Prov:* **la nuit porte conseil,** sleep on it; (*c*) to carry (sth.) habitually; to wear (garment, etc.); **le chameau porte deux bosses,** the camel has two humps; **p. des lunettes, une bague, du noir, une moustache,** to wear spectacles, a ring, black, a moustache; **le bleu se porte beaucoup cette année,** blue is being worn a lot, is very fashionable, this year; **p. des cicatrices,** to bear scars; **p. la tête haute,** to hold, carry, one's head high; **il porte le nom de son oncle,** he's called after his uncle; *Mil:* **portez armes!** shoulder arms! *Nau:* (*of ship*) **p. tout dessus,** to have all sails set; (*d*) to carry, convey, take (sth. somewhere); **p. qch. dans la maison, p. qch. dehors,** to carry, bring, sth. in, out; **p. une lettre à la poste,** to take a letter to the post; **p. le lait à domicile,** to deliver milk to the door; **il porta le verre à ses lèvres,** he raised, lifted, set, the glass to his lips; **p. qn en terre,** to carry s.o. to his grave; **courant qui porte au sud,** current that sets to the south; (*e*) **p. un coup à qn, p. la main sur qn,** to strike s.o., to deal, aim, strike, a blow at s.o.; **il porta la main à sa casquette,** he touched his cap; **p. ses regards sur qn,** to look at s.o.; **p. son attention sur qch.,** to give sth. one's attention; **p. un différend devant un tribunal,** to bring a dispute before a court; **p. une accusation contre qn,** to bring, lay, a charge against s.o.; **p. qch. à la connaissance de qn,** to bring sth. to s.o.'s knowledge, let s.o. know sth.; (*f*) to inscribe, enter; **p. une position sur une carte,** to mark, show, a position on a map; **p. une somme au crédit de qn, d'un compte,** to credit a sum to s.o., to an account; **p. une somme au débit de qn,** to debit s.o. with a sum; **se faire p. malade,** to report sick; *Mil: etc:* **p. qn manquant à l'appel,** to report s.o. absent from roll call; **p. qn déserteur,** to declare s.o. a deserter; *Nau:* **p. un homme au rôle de l'équipage,** to enter a seaman on the ship's books; (*g*) to induce, incline, prompt; **p. qn à qch.,** to incite s.o. to sth.; **tout me porte à croire que . . .,** everything leads, inclines, me to believe that . . .; (*h*) to raise, carry; **p. la température à 100°,** to raise the temperature to 100°; **p. la production au maximum,** to raise, increase, production to a maximum; (*i*) to show, entertain (interest, affection, for s.o., sth.); **par la tendresse que je vous porte,** by the love I bear you; (*j*) to declare, state; **le rapport ne porte rien de tout cela,** nothing of the kind is mentioned in the report; **la loi porte que . . .,** the law provides that . . .; *Mil: etc:* **la décision porte que . . .,** it is stated in orders that . . .; **p. témoignage,** to bear witness. **2.** *v.i.* (*a*) to rest, bear; **tout le poids porte sur cette poutre,** all the weight bears on this beam; **la discussion porte toujours sur le même sujet,** the discussion always turns on the same subject; **faire p. son attention sur qch.,** to bring one's mind to bear on sth.; **la perte a porté sur nous,** we had to stand the loss; (*b*) to hit, reach (target, mark); **aucun des coups n'a porté,** none of the blows took effect; **chaque coup, chaque mot, a porté,** every shot, every word, told, went home; **coup qui porte, qui a porté,** telling blow; **son discours a porté sur ses auditeurs,** his speech made an impact on his audience; **sa voix porte bien,** his voice carries well; *F:* **ce bruit me porte sur les nerfs,** that noise gets on my nerves; **sa tête a porté sur le trottoir,** his head hit, struck, knocked against, the pavement; (*c*) *Nau:* (*of sail*) to fill, draw; **portez plein!** keep her full! (*d*) *Nau:* **laisser p.,** to bear away; **laisser p. sur un navire,** to bear down upon, run down, a ship. **3. se p.** (*a*) to go, proceed (to a place); **se p. au secours de qn,** to go to s.o.'s help; **la foule s'est portée vers la gare,** the crowd made for the station; **se p. à des voies de fait, à des extrémités,** to commit acts of violence, go to extremes; **son regard se portait vers son frère,** he looked, his eyes turned, towards his brother; *Mil:* **se p. en avant,** to advance; **la conversation s'est portée sur l'Extrême-Orient,** the conversation turned to the Far East; (*b*) **se p. bien, à merveille,** to be well, in good health; to enjoy the best of health; **comment vous portez-vous?** how are you? **je ne m'en porte pas plus mal,** I'm none the worse for it; (*c*) **se p. candidat, caution,** to offer oneself, stand, as candidate, as surety.

porte-revues [pɔrtrəvy] *n.m.inv.* newspaper, magazine, rack.

porterie [pɔrtəri] *n.f.* gatehouse (of convent, etc.).

porte-savon [pɔrtsavɔ̃] *n.m.* soapdish; *pl. porte-savon(s).*

porte-serviettes [pɔrtsɛrvjɛt] *n.m.inv.* towel rail.

porte-toasts [pɔrtətost] *n.m.inv.* toast rack.

porteur, -euse [pɔrtœr, -øz] **1.** *n.* (*a*) bearer, carrier (of message, etc.); **p. de nouvelles,** bearer, bringer, of news; **j'arrivais p. d'heureuses nouvelles,** I arrived bringing good news; **par p.,** by messenger; (*b*) (railway, etc.) porter; **p. d'eau,** water carrier; **chaise à porteurs,** sedan chair; *Med:* **p. de germes,** (germ) carrier; (*c*) *Fin:* bearer, endorsee, payee (of a cheque); **p. de titres,** holder of stock, stockholder; **p. d'actions,** shareholder; **payable au p.,** payable to bearer; **effets au p.,** bearer stock(s). **2.** *a.* (*a*) *Mch:* **essieu p.,** bearing axle, carrying axle; **câble p.,** suspension cable; (*b*) *El:* **fréquence porteuse,** carrier frequency; **onde porteuse,** carrier wave.

porte-vent [pɔrtəvɑ̃] *n.m.inv.* **1.** air duct; wind chest (of organ). **2.** *Metall:* blast pipe.

porte-voix [pɔrtəvwa] *n.m.inv.* loudhailer; megaphone.

portier, -ière[1] [pɔrtje, -jɛr] *n.* (*a*) porter, doorman; doorkeeper; commissionaire; janitor, caretaker; (*b*) *Lit:* gatekeeper; (*c*) *Ecc:* **(frère) p.,** porter; **(sœur) portière,** portress.

portière[2] [pɔrtjɛr] *n.f.* **1.** door (of car, railway carriage, *NAm:* railroad coach). **2.** door curtain. **3.** raft, cut (of pontoon bridge).

portillon [pɔrtijɔ̃] *n.m.* (*a*) wicket (gate); *Rail:* side gate (at level crossing, *NAm:* grade crossing); (*b*) gate, barrier (at station); *F:* **cela se bouscule au p.,** he can't get his words out.

portion [pɔrsjɔ̃] *n.f.* portion; share; part; section; **p. de viande,** portion, helping, of meat.

portique [pɔrtik] *n.m.* **1.** (*a*) portico, porch; (*b*) *Gym:* crossbeam (for hanging apparatus); (*c*) *Rail:* **p. à signaux,** signal gantry. **2. grue à p.,** travelling gantry crane.

portland [pɔrtlɑ̃d] *n.m.* Portland cement.

Porto [pɔrto] **1.** *Pr.n.m. Geog:* Oporto. **2.** *n.m.* (*wine*) port.

portoricain, -aine [pɔrtɔrikɛ̃, -ɛn] *a. & n. Geog:* Puerto Rican.

Porto Rico [pɔrtɔriko] *Pr.n.m. Geog:* Puerto Rico.

portrait [pɔrtrɛ] *n.m.* **1.** (*a*) portrait; likeness; **p. en pied, en buste,** full-length, half-length, portrait; **faire le p. de qn,** to make, paint, draw, a portrait of s.o.; **c'est le p. vivant de son père,** he's the living image of his father; **p. en prose,** portrait in prose; word portrait; **p. littéraire,** character sketch; (*b*) *P:* face; **il s'est fait abîmer le p.,** his face is a real mess. **2. l'art du p.,** the art of portraiture.

portraitiste [pɔrtretist] *n.* portrait painter.

portraiturer [pɔrtretyre] *v.tr.* to portray.

portuaire [pɔrtɥɛr] *a.* **installations portuaires,** harbour, *NAm:* harbor, installations; port installations.

portugais, -aise [pɔrtygɛ, -ɛz] **1.** *a. & n.* Portuguese. **2.** *n.m. Ling:* Portuguese. **3.** *n.f.* **portugaise,** Portuguese oyster.

Portugal [pɔrtygal] *Pr.n.m. Geog:* Portugal.

pose [poz] *n.f.* **1.** placing; putting up, hanging (of curtain, etc.); hanging (of picture, etc.); laying (of bricks, carpet, etc.); setting (of stones, etc.); fitting (of watchglass, etc.); installation (of electricity, etc.); **p. de câbles,** cable laying. **2.** (*a*) pose, posture; attitude; **prendre une p.,** to assume, strike, a pose; (*b*) posing, affectation, posturing; **sans p.,** unaffected(ly); (*c*) *Golf:* lie (of a ball). **3.** *Phot:* (*a*) exposure; **temps de p.,** exposure time; **p. instantanée,** instantaneous exposure; (*b*) time exposure.

posé [poze] *a.* **1.** *Ven:* sitting (bird). **2.** staid, serious, calm, grave, sedate (person); steady (bearing, etc.); sober (appearance); **écrire à main posée,** to write slowly, carefully; *Mus:* **voix bien posée,** even, steady, voice.

posément [pozemɑ̃] *adv.* sedately, calmly; steadily, deliberately.

posemètre [pozmɛtr̥] *n.m. Phot:* exposure meter.

poser [poze] **1.** *v.i.* (*a*) (*of beam, etc.*) to rest, lie (on sth.); (*b*) to pose (as artist's model); to sit (for one's portrait); (*c*) to show off; to pose, strike an attitude; **p. pour la galerie,** to play to the gallery; (*d*) *F:* **je ne pose pas à l'ange,** I don't pretend to be an angel. **2.** *v.tr.* (*a*) to put, place, lay, set, (down) (sth. somewhere); **pose-le sur la table,** put it (down), stand it, on the table; **p. les armes,** to lay down one's arms; **p. un avion,** to land an aircraft; **p. sa candidature,** to stand (as a candidate) (**aux élections,** for the elections); to apply (**à un poste,** for a job); **p. une question à qn,** to put a question to s.o., ask s.o. a question; **p. la question de confiance,** to table a motion of confidence; **p. un problème,** to pose a problem; **p. un problème à qn,** to set s.o. a problem; **p. une règle de conduite,** to lay down a rule of conduct; *Mth:* **p. un chiffre,** to put down, set down, a number; **je pose deux et je retiens un,** put down two, two down, (and) carry one; (*b*) to put up, hang (curtain, etc.); to hang (picture, etc.); to lay (bricks, carpet, foundation stone, rails, etc.); to set (stones, rivets, boiler); to fit (watchglass, etc.); **p. une vitre,** to put in a pane of glass; **p. l'électricité,** to install electricity; (*c*) **p. qn,** to establish s.o.'s reputation (as an author, etc.); (*d*) to suppose, admit, grant; **posons le cas que cela soit,** supposing, let's suppose, that that is the case; **cela posé,** assuming this to be true; (*e*) *Art:* to pose (model); (*f*) *Mus:* **bien p. la voix,** to pitch (one's voice) correctly. **3. se p.** (*a*) (*of bird, etc.*) to settle, alight (**sur,** on); (*of aircraft, etc.*) to land; (*b*) **un nouveau problème se pose,** we are faced with a new problem; (*c*) **se p. comme prêtre,** to pretend to be, pose as, a priest; **se p. en réformateur,** to set oneself up as, claim to be, a reformer.

poseur, -euse [pozœr, -øz] **1.** *n. Tchn:* layer (of cables, etc.); **p. d'affiches,** billsticker, billposter; *Rail:* **p. de rails, de voie,** platelayer, *NAm:* tracklayer; *Navy:* **p. de mines,** minelayer. **2.** *a. & n.* (person) who poses; show-off, swank; poseur; **il est p.,** he's always striking attitudes; he's rather affected.

positif, -ive [pozitif, -iv] **1.** *a.* (*a*) positive, actual, real (fact, etc.); **c'est p.,** it's a positive fact; (*b*) *Mth: El: etc:* positive (number, pole, etc.); (*c*) practical, unsentimental, matter-of-fact (person); **esprit p.,** practical mind. **2.** *n.m.* (*a*) *Mus:* choir organ (of full organ); (*b*) *Phot:* positive (print).

position [pozisjɔ̃] *n.f.* position. **1.** (*a*) position (of ship, aircraft, etc.); *Golf:* lie (of the ball); *Aut:* **feux de p.,** sidelights; **prendre p. (sur une question),** to take, adopt, a definite position on a matter; (*b*) *Mil: etc:* **p. clef,** key position; **p. masquée,** position behind cover; **p. défensive, de défense,** defensive position; **p. de repli, de recueil,** position to fall back on. **2.** posture, attitude (of the body, etc.); stance; *Danc:* position (of the feet); **p. debout,** standing position; (*of aircraft*) **p. d'atterrissage,** landing attitude. **3.** (*a*) condition, circumstances; **p. sociale,** social standing, position, status; **p. gênante,** embarrassing situation; **il est dans une meilleure p. au point où il en est,** he's better off where he is; **voici ma p.,** this is how I stand, how I'm situated; **être en p. de faire qch.,** to be in a position to do sth.; (*b*) *Fin:* account; **demander sa p.** = to ask for one's balance.

positivement [pozitivmɑ̃] *adv.* positively; **je ne le sais pas p.,** I don't know it for certain.

positivisme [pozitivism] *n.m.* (*a*) *Phil:* positivism; (*b*) materialism.

positiviste [pozitivist] *a. & n. Phil:* positivist.

positivité [pozitivite] *n.f. El: Phil:* positivity.

positon [pozitɔ̃] *n.m. Atom.Ph:* positon.

posologie [pozɔlɔʒi] *n.f. Med: etc:* posology; dosage (of drug).

possédant, -ante [pɔsedɑ̃, -ɑ̃t] *a. & n.* **les possédants, les classes possédantes,** the propertied, moneyed, classes; the wealthy.

possédé, -ée [pɔsede] **1.** *a.* possessed (**de,** by, of); dominated (by passion, etc.); **p. du diable,** possessed by the devil. **2.** *n.* person possessed; madman, madwoman; maniac.

posséder [pɔsede] *v.* **(je possède; je posséderai) 1.** *v.tr.* to be in possession of (sth.); (*a*) to possess, own; to have (property, etc.); **p. un titre,** to hold a title; **p. un million,** to be worth a million; (*b*) to have a thorough knowledge of, be master of (subject, etc.); (*c*) *A: & Lit:* to curb, control (one's tongue, etc.); **p. son âme en paix,** to possess one's soul in peace; (*d*) (*of demon, etc.*) to possess (s.o.); **ils étaient tous possédés de la même illusion,** they all laboured, *NAm:* labored, under the same delusion; (*e*) *F:* to fool (s.o.); **je me suis fait p.,** I've been had. **2. se p.,** to control oneself, one's temper; **il ne se possédait plus de joie,** he was beside himself with joy.

possesseur [pɔsesœr] *n.m.* possessor, owner.

possessif, -ive [pɔsesif, -iv] *a. & n.m. Gram: etc:* possessive.

possession [pɔsesjɔ̃] *n.f.* **1.** possession; ownership; **être en p. de qch.,** to be in possession of sth., to own sth.; *Jur:* to be possessed of sth.; *Com:* **nous sommes en p. de votre lettre du 4 mars,** we are in receipt of, have received, your letter of 4th March; **avoir qch. en sa p.,** to have sth. in one's possession; **entrer en p. d'un héritage,** to enter into possession of an inheritance; **entrée en p. d'un patrimoine,** accession to an estate; **prendre p. (de qch.),** to take possession (of sth.); to take over (authority), assume (power); **rentrer en p. de qch.,** to regain possession of sth., recover sth.; **p. vaut titre,** possession is nine points of the law. **2.** possession; *esp.* property, estate. **3.** possession (by evil spirit). **4. p. de soi-même,** self-control.

possessoire [pɔseswar] *Jur:* **1.** *a.* **intenter une action p.,** to undertake an action for possession (of land). **2.** *n.m.* right of possession (of property).

possibilité [pɔsibilite] *n.f.* (*a*) possibility; feasibility; **voir la p. de faire qch.,** to consider it possible to do sth.; **si j'ai la p. de lui écrire,** if it's possible for me, if I can manage, to write to him; (*b*) *pl.* (*of pers.*) capacity, capabilities; **chacun doit payer selon ses possibilités,** each should pay according to his means.

possible [pɔsibl̩] **1.** *a.* possible; feasible; **c'est (bien) p.,** it's (quite) possible; it's quite likely; (very) possibly; very likely; **est-ce p.? ce n'est pas p.!** *F:* **pas p.!** it's not possible! impossible! you can't mean it! **si (c'est) p.,** if possible; **est-il p. de faire des fautes pareilles?** how can people make such mistakes? **il ne m'est pas p. de le faire,** I can't possibly do it; **il ne m'est guère p. de le faire,** I can't very well do it; **il est p. qu'il soit mort,** it's possible that he's dead; he may, might, be dead; **il n'est pas p. que j'y aille,** it's impossible for me to go (there); there's no possibility of my going there; **aussitôt que p., dès que p.,** as soon as possible; **le moins souvent p.,** as infrequently as possible; **le moins de détails possible(s),** as few details as possible; **tous les détails possibles,** every possible detail; **la boîte la plus grande p.,** the largest box possible, the largest possible box; **dans la plus large mesure p.,** as far as possible; *Corr: Com:* **le plus tôt qu'il vous sera p.,** at your earliest convenience; **danger p.,** possible, potential, danger. **2.** *n.m.* what is possible; **dans la mesure du p.,** as far as possible; **faire tout son p. pour . . .,** to do all one (possibly) can (do), do one's utmost, do one's best, make every endeavour, *NAm:* endeavor, try one's hardest, to . . .; **il s'est montré aimable au p.,** he was extremely pleasant; he couldn't have been kinder, nicer.

postal, -aux [pɔstal, -o] *a.* postal (service, etc.); **sac p.,** mailbag; **carte postale,** postcard.

postcombustion [pɔstkɔ̃bystjɔ̃] *n.f.* afterburning, reheat (of rocket, turbojet); **dispositif de p.,** afterburner.

postcommunion [pɔstkɔmynjɔ̃] *n.f. Ecc:* postcommunion.

postdater [pɔstdate] *v.tr.* to postdate (letter, etc.).

poste¹ [pɔst] *n.f.* **1.** *A:* post, relay (of horses); **chevaux de p.,** posthorses; **maître de p.,** postmaster; **aller en p.,** to travel post; **courir la p.,** to go posthaste. **2.** (*a*) post, *NAm:* mail; **les Postes et Télécommunications,** the postal services = the Post Office; **par la p.,** by post; **par p. aérienne,** by airmail; **mettre une lettre à la p.,** to post, *NAm:* mail, a letter; (*b*) **(bureau de) p.,** post office; **grande p.,** head, general, post office (in a town); **receveur, -euse, des postes,** postmaster, postmistress.

poste² *n.m.* **1.** (*a*) post, station (of soldier, etc.); **être à son p.,** to be at one's post; *Mil:* **p. avancé,** advanced, outlying, post; **p. d'écoute,** listening station; **p. d'observation,** observation post; *Mil: Navy:* **chef de p.,** guard commander; **à vos postes!** take post! to your post! stand by! **p. de commandement,** *Mil:* headquarters, *U.S:* command post; *Navy:* control room; *Navy:* **postes de combat,** action stations; *Nau:* **p. de mouillage,** anchoring berth; **p. d'amarrage,** mooring berth, mooring(s); **mettre les ancres à p.,** to stow the anchors; **être solide au p.,** to be still going strong; (*b*) *Nau: Navy:* **p. d'équipage,** crew's quarters; (*in merchant service*) forecastle; *Navy:* **p. des maîtres,** warrant officers' wardroom; **p.**

des aspirants, gunroom; (*c*) **p. de police,** (i) police station; (ii) *Mil:* (*also* **p. de garde**) guardroom; **p. de la Croix-Rouge,** Red Cross station; **p. de secours,** first aid post; **p. d'incendie,** (i) fire station; (ii) fire equipment; **p. frontière,** frontier post; **p. d'essence,** petrol station, filling station, *NAm:* gas station; *Trans: etc:* **p. de contrôle,** checkpoint; *Av:* **p. de pilotage,** cockpit, flight deck; *Rail:* **p. d'aiguillage,** signal box; **p. de signaux,** signal tower; (*d*) *W.Tel:* **p. émetteur,** broadcasting station; transmitter; (*e*) *W.Tel: etc:* **p. (de) radio,** radio set; **p. de télévision,** television set; **p. récepteur,** receiver, receiving set; **ouvrir, fermer, le p.,** to switch the radio, the television, on, off; (*f*) *Tp:* telephone; **p. 35,** extension 35. **2.** (*a*) post, appointment, job; **occuper un p. de confiance,** to have a position of trust; (*b*) *Ind:* **p. de jour, de nuit,** day, night, shift. **3.** *Book-k:* entry, item.

poster¹ [pɔste] **1.** *v.tr.* to post (sentry, etc.); to station (men). **2. se p.,** to take up a position; to take one's stand.

poster² [pɔste] *v.tr.* to post, *NAm:* mail (letter, etc.).

poster³ [pɔstɛr] *n.m.* poster.

postérieur [pɔsterjœr] **1.** *a.* posterior; (*a*) (*of time*) subsequent (**à,** to); later; **p. à son décès,** after his death; (*b*) (*of place*) hind, back; **partie postérieure de la tête,** back part of the head. **2.** *n.m. F:* buttocks, bottom, backside, posterior, *NAm:* fanny.

postérieurement [pɔsterjœrmɑ̃] *adv.* subsequently (**à,** to); at a later date.

postériorité [pɔsterjɔrite] *n.f.* posteriority.

postérité [pɔsterite] *n.f.* posterity; (*a*) descendants; **mourir sans (laisser de) p.,** to die without issue; (*b*) **la p.,** generations yet unborn.

postface [pɔstfas] *n.f.* postscript, postface.

posthume [pɔstym] *a.* posthumous.

postiche [pɔstiʃ] **1.** *a.* false (hair, eyelashes, etc.). **2.** *n.m.* hairpiece.

postier, -ière [pɔstje, -jɛr] *n.* post office employee.

postillon [pɔstijɔ̃] *n.m.* **1.** *A:* postilion. **2. envoyer des postillons,** to splutter, sputter (in speaking).

postillonner [pɔstijɔne] *v.i.* to splutter, sputter (in speaking).

postnatal, -als [pɔstnatal] *a.* postnatal.

postopératoire [pɔstɔperatwar] *a. Med:* post-operative (care, etc.).

postscolaire [pɔstskɔlɛr] *a.* continuation (classes, etc.); **enseignement p.,** further education.

post-scriptum [pɔstskriptɔm] *n.m.inv.* postscript; P.S.

postsynchronisation [pɔstsɛ̃krɔnizasjɔ̃] *n.f. Cin:* postsynchronization; dubbing.

postsynchroniser [pɔstsɛ̃krɔnize] *v.tr. Cin:* to postsynchronize; to dub.

postulant, -ante [pɔstylɑ̃, -ɑ̃t] *n.* (*a*) candidate, applicant (for post); (*b*) *Ecc:* postulant.

postulat [pɔstyla] *n.m. Log:* postulate, assumption.

postuler [pɔstyle] **1.** *v.tr.* (*a*) to apply for (post, etc.); (*b*) *Log:* to postulate. **2.** *v.i.* (*of lawyer*) **p. pour un client,** to act on behalf of a client.

posture [pɔstyr] *n.f.* **1.** posture, attitude (of the body, etc.). **2.** position (in society, etc.); **être en p. de faire qch.,** to be in a position, in a situation, to do sth.; **être en bonne, en mauvaise, p.,** to be well placed, badly placed, in a good, bad, position.

pot [po] *n.m.* **1.** pot, jug, can, jar; **p. de terre,** earthenware pot; **p. d'étain,** pewter tankard; **p. de confiture,** pot, jar, of jam; **p. de chambre,** chamber pot; *F:* (*for child*) **petit p.,** potty; **p. de fleurs,** (i) pot plant; (ii) pot, vase, of flowers; **p. à fleurs,** flowerpot, plant pot; **p. de colle,** (i) pot of glue; (ii) *F:* (*pers.*) pain in the neck; **p. à bière,** beer mug; **pot(s) à eau** [pɔtao], water jug(s); **p. à lait** [potalɛ], **p. au lait** [pɔtolɛ], milk jug, milk can; **mettre en p.,** to pot (plant, meat, etc.); *Nau:* **le p. au noir,** the doldrums; *F:* **allons prendre un p.,** let's go and have a drink; *F:* **avoir du p., un coup de p.,** to be lucky; **manque de p.,** hard luck; *F:* **payer les pots cassés,** to carry the can; **manger à la fortune du p.,** to take pot luck; *F:* **c'est le p. de terre contre le p. de fer,** he's met more than his match; **en trois coups de cuiller à p.,** in a twinkling; **sourd comme un p.,** as deaf as a post. **2.** *I.C.E:* **p. d'échappement,** exhaust (pipe, system); silencer, *NAm:* muffler.

potable [pɔtabl̥] *a.* **1.** drinkable, fit to drink; **eau p.,** drinking water. **2.** *F:* fair; good enough; **travail p.,** tolerably good work.

potache [pɔtaʃ] *n.m. Sch: F:* schoolboy (attending *collège* or *lycée*).

potage [pɔtaʒ] *n.m.* (*a*) soup; (*b*) *A: & Lit:* **pour tout p.,** all told, (all) in all.

potager, -ère [pɔtaʒe, -ɛr] **1.** *a.* **herbes potagères,** pot herbs; **plante potagère,** vegetable. **2.** *a. & n.m.* **(jardin) p.,** kitchen garden.

potasse [pɔtas] *n.f. Ch:* potash; **chlorate de p.,** potassium chlorate.

potassique [pɔtasik] *a. Ch:* (of, containing) potassium; potassic (salt).

potassium [pɔtasjɔm] *n.m. Ch:* potassium.

pot-au-feu [pɔtofø] **1.** *n.m.inv.* boiled beef with vegetables. **2.** *a.inv. F:* stay-at-home (person).

pot-de-vin [podvɛ̃] *n.m.* **1.** gratuity, tip. **2.** (*a*) bribe; (*b*) hush money; *pl. pots-de-vin.*

pote [pɔt] *n.m. P:* friend, pal.

poteau, -eaux [pɔto] *n.m.* **1.** (*a*) post, pole, stake; *Min:* pit prop; *Sp:* goalpost; **p. indicateur,** signpost; **p. télégraphique,** telegraph pole; *Sp:* **p. de départ,** starting post; **p. d'arrivée,** finishing post, winning post; (*of horse*) **rester au p.,** to be left at the post; (*b*) **p. (d'exécution),** execution post (for s.o. about to be shot); **mettre qn au p.,** to put s.o. against the wall; **le général au p.!** down with the general! **2.** *P: O:* friend, pal.

potée [pɔte] *n.f.* (*a*) *O:* potful, jugful; (*b*) *Cu:* stew (*esp.* cabbage and carrots with pork, etc.); (*c*) *F: O:* swarm (of children, etc.); **j'en ai une p.,** I've (got) lots, loads, of them.

potelé [pɔtle] *a.* plump and dimpled (arm, etc.); chubby (cheek, child).

potence [pɔtɑ̃s] *n.f.* **1.** gallows, gibbet; **mettre qn à la p.,** to hang s.o. on the gallows; **échapper à la p.,** to cheat the gallows; **gibier de p.,** gallows bird. **2.** (*a*) support, arm, crosspiece, bracket; jib (of crane); *Cy:* stem (of handlebar); **en p.,** T-shaped; (*b*) *Nau: Artil:* davit.

potentat [pɔtɑ̃ta] *n.m.* potentate.

potentialité [pɔtɑ̃sjalite] *n.f.* potentiality.

potentiel, -elle [pɔtɑ̃sjɛl] **1.** *a.* potential. **2.** *n.m.* (*a*) potential; potentialities (of a country, etc.); (*b*) *El:* potential; *W.Tel:* **p. de grille,** grid potential; (*c*) *Gram:* potential (mood).

potentiellement [pɔtɑ̃sjɛlmɑ̃] *adv.* potentially.

potentille [pɔtɑ̃tij] *n.f. Bot:* **p. (rampante),** cinquefoil.

potentiomètre [pɔtɑ̃sjɔmɛtr̥] *n.m. Elcs:* potentiometer; *Cin:* fader (of sound).

poterie [pɔtri] *n.f.* **1.** (*a*) pottery (works); (*b*) potter's workshop, studio; (*c*) potter's art. **2.** (piece of) pottery; **p. (de terre),** earthenware; **p. de grès,** stoneware. **3.** *Tchn:* **p. d'étain,** pewter(ware).

poterne [pɔtɛrn] *n.f.* postern (gate).

potiche [pɔtiʃ] *n.f.* **1.** (large) vase (*esp.* of Chinese or Japanese porcelain). **2.** (*pers.*) figurehead.

potier [pɔtje] *n.m.* potter.

potin [pɔtɛ̃] *n.m. F:* **1.** *pl.* gossip, tittle-tattle. **2.** noise, row, rumpus; **faire du p.,** to make a din, kick up a row.

potion [posjɔ̃] *n.f. Med: etc:* potion, draught, *esp. US:* draft; concoction.
potiron [pɔtirɔ̃] *n.m.* pumpkin.
pot-pourri [popuri] *n.m. Mus: etc:* pot pourri, medley; *pl. pots-pourris.*
potron-minet [pɔtrɔ̃minɛ] *n.m. F:* **dès p.-m.,** at daybreak, at crack of dawn.
pou, poux [pu] *n.m.* **1.** (*a*) louse, *pl.* lice; **œuf de p.,** nit; *F:* **laid comme un p.,** as ugly as sin; *F:* **chercher des poux dans la tête de qn,** to pick a quarrel with s.o. (about nothing); (*b*) **p. de mouton,** sheep tick. **2.** *Crust:* **p. de mer,** sea louse.
pouah [pwa] *int.* ugh!
poubelle [pubɛl] *n.f.* dustbin; (refuse) bin, *NAm:* garbage can, trash can; **p. à pédale,** pedal bin; **jeter qch. à la p.,** (i) to put sth. in the dustbin, throw sth. away; (ii) *F:* to reject sth. as rubbish.
pouce [pus] *n.m.* **1.** (*a*) thumb; *F:* **donner un coup de p. à qn, qch.,** (i) to pull strings for s.o.; (ii) to deflect the course of (justice, etc.); **donner le coup de p. à qch.,** to put the finishing touches to sth.; *F:* **manger sur le p.,** to have a (quick) snack; **se tourner les pouces,** to twiddle one's thumbs; **mettre les pouces,** to give in, knuckle under; *P:* **et le p.,** and a bit more besides; and the rest; *Sch: P:* **p.!** pax! (*b*) *occ:* big toe. **2.** (*a*) *Fr.C.Meas:* inch; (*b*) **ne pas bouger d'un p.,** not to move an inch.
Poucet [pusɛ] *Pr.n.m.* **le Petit P.,** Tom Thumb.
poucettes [pusɛt] *n.f.pl. A:* thumbscrew(s).
poucier [pusje] *n.m.* **1.** thumbstall. **2.** thumb piece (of door latch).
pouding [pudiŋ] *n.m. Cu:* (plum, etc.) pudding.
poudingue [pudɛ̃g] *n.m. Miner:* conglomerate, puddingstone.
poudrage [pudraʒ] *n.m. Tchn:* powdering.
poudre [pudr] *n.f.* **1.** (*a*) *A:* dust; (*b*) **jeter de la p. aux yeux de qn,** to try to dazzle, impress, s.o. **2.** (*a*) powder; **réduire qch. en p.,** to reduce sth. to powder; to powder, pulverize, sth.; **p. d'or,** gold dust; **p. dentifrice,** tooth powder; **p. à récurer,** scouring powder; **café en p.,** instant coffee; **sucre en p.,** caster sugar; (*b*) **p. (de riz),** (face) powder. **3.** (explosive) powder; **p. de chasse,** sporting powder; **p. à canon,** gunpowder; (*of pers.*) **être vif comme la p.,** to be fiery-tempered, very excitable; **la nouvelle s'est répandue comme une traînée de p.,** the news spread like wildfire; **il n'a pas inventé la p.** = he won't set the Thames on fire.
poudrer [pudre] **1.** *v.tr.* to powder; to sprinkle with powder. **2.** *v.i. Fr.C:* **il poudre,** it's snowing slightly. **3. se p.,** to powder one's face, etc.
poudrerie [pudrəri] *n.f.* **1.** (gun)powder factory. **2.** *Fr.C:* flurry of snow.
poudreux, -euse [pudrø, -øz] **1.** *a.* dusty; powdery. **2.** *a. & n.f.* **(neige) poudreuse,** powdered, powdery, snow. **3.** *n.f.* sugar sprinkler, sugar castor.
poudrier [pudrije] *n.m. Toil:* powder box; (powder) compact.
poudrière [pudrijɛr] *n.f.* **1.** *A:* powder flask, powder horn. **2.** powder magazine.
poudrin [pudrɛ̃] *n.m.* spindrift.
poudroiement [pudrwamɑ̃] *n.m.* clouds of dust (on road, etc.); dust haze.
poudroyer [pudrwaje] *v.i.* **(il poudroie; il poudroiera)** to form clouds of dust; **la route poudroie,** the dust whirls up from the road.
pouf [puf] **1.** *int.* wallop! bump! **2.** *n.m.* (*a*) *Furn:* pouf(fe); (*b*) *A.Cost:* bustle.
pouffer [pufe] *v.i.* **p. (de rire),** to burst out laughing; to guffaw.
pouffiasse [pufjas] *n.f. P:* prostitute, tart; **une grande p.,** a great fat cow.
pouillerie [pujri] *n.f.* **1.** abject poverty; squalor. **2.** filthy place, lousy hole.
pouilleux, -euse [pujø, -øz] **1.** *a.* (*a*) lousy, verminous; (*b*) wretched, miserable; abjectly poor; **quartier p.,** slum. **2.** *n.* tramp, beggar.
pouillot [pujo] *n.m. Orn:* warbler.
poulailler [pulaje] *n.m.* (*a*) hen house, hen roost; (*b*) *Th: F:* **le p.,** the (top) gallery; the gods.
poulain [pulɛ̃] *n.m.* **1.** (*a*) colt, foal; (*b*) *Sp: etc:* trainee; protégé. **2.** *Tchn:* skid (for unloading barrels, etc.).
poulaine [pulɛn] *n.f. Nau:* (*a*) (ship's) head; (*b*) **les poulaines,** the latrines (for crew); *F:* the heads.
poularde [pulard] *n.f. Cu:* fattened pullet.
poulbot [pulbo] *n.m.* street urchin (of Montmartre).
poule [pul] *n.f.* **1.** (*a*) hen; *Cu:* (boiling) fowl; **p. au pot,** boiled chicken; **ma (petite) p.!** my dear, my pet! **la p. aux œufs d'or,** the goose that laid the golden eggs; **lait de p.,** (non-alcoholic) egg flip, egg nog; **quand les poules auront des dents,** when pigs can fly; (*b*) **p. d'eau,** moorhen; **p. faisane,** hen pheasant; **petite p. de bruyère,** grey hen; (*c*) *P:* (fast young) woman; bird; tart; *NAm:* broad. **2.** (*a*) *Games:* (*stakes*) pool; (*b*) *Fenc: etc:* pool; tournament.
poulet [pulɛ] *n.m.* **1.** (*a*) chicken; **p. fermier,** free-range chicken; (*b*) **mon p.,** my darling, my pet; (*c*) *F:* policeman, cop. **2.** *A:* (witty, amorous) letter.
poulette [pulɛt] *n.f.* **1.** *O:* young hen, pullet. **2.** *F:* girl, lass; **ma p.,** my darling, my pet.
pouliche [puliʃ] *n.f.* filly.
poulie [puli] *n.f.* **1.** pulley (i) sheave, (ii) block; **p. simple, double,** single block, double block; **p. fixe,** fixed pulley, standing block. **2.** (belt) pulley; driving wheel; **p. folle,** loose pulley.
pouliner [puline] *v.i.* (*of mare*) to foal.
poulinière [pulinjɛr] *a.f. & n.f.* **(jument) p.,** brood mare.
pouliot¹ [puljo] *n.m. Bot:* pennyroyal.
pouliot² *n.m.* windlass (on dray, etc.).
poulot, -otte [pulo, -ɔt] *n. F:* (*in addressing children*) (my) pet, darling.
poulpe [pulp] *n.m. Moll:* octopus.
pouls [pu] *n.m.* pulse; **tâter le p. de qn,** (i) to feel s.o.'s pulse; (ii) to sound s.o. (out); **prendre le p. à qn,** to take s.o.'s pulse.
poumon [pumɔ̃] *n.m.* lung; **p. d'acier,** iron lung; **respirer à pleins poumons,** to take a deep breath; **crier à pleins poumons,** to shout at the top of one's voice.
poupard [pupar] **1.** *n.m.* (*a*) chubby baby; (*b*) *O:* baby doll. **2.** *a.* chubby(-cheeked); **physionomie pouparde,** baby face.
poupart [pupar] *n.m. Crust:* edible crab.
poupe [pup] *n.f. Nau:* stern, poop; **avoir le vent en p.,** (i) to have the wind aft; (ii) *Fig:* to be in luck, favoured, *NAm:* favored, by fortune.
poupée [pupe] *n.f.* **1.** (*a*) doll; dolly; **maison de p.,** doll's house; **jouer à la p.,** to play with dolls; (*b*) *F:* girl, bird, doll, chick. **2.** dummy; (milliner's) block. **3.** finger bandage; bandaged finger. **4.** headstock, poppet (head) (of lathe); *Nau:* **p. de cabestan,** capstan head. **5.** *Nau:* **p. d'amarrage,** bollard; belaying pin.
poupin, -ine [pupɛ̃, -in] *a.* chubby(-cheeked); **visage p.,** baby face.
poupon [pupɔ̃] *n.m.* (tiny) baby.
pouponner [pupɔne] *v.i.* to play the doting (little) mother.
pouponnière [pupɔnjɛr] *n.f.* day nursery, crèche.
pour¹ [pur] *prep.* for. **1.** (*a*) **allez-y p. moi,** go for me, instead of me, in my stead; **mot p. mot,** word for word; **jour p. jour,** to the (very) day; **agir p. qn,** to act on s.o.'s behalf; (*b*) **il la veut p. femme,** he wants her for, as, his wife; **tenir qn p. fou,** to regard s.o. as

a madman; **prendre qn p. un autre,** to take s.o. for someone else; **laisser qn p. mort,** to leave s.o. for dead; *F:* **c'est p. de bon, p. de vrai,** I mean it, I'm serious; really; (*c*) (*direction*) **je pars p. la France,** I'm off to, starting for, France; **le train p. Paris,** the Paris train; (*d*) (*time*) **je vais en Suisse p. quinze jours,** I'm going to Switzerland for a fortnight; **p. dans trois jours,** in three days, in three days' time; **p. toujours,** for ever; **p. le moment,** for the time being; **il sera ici p. quatre heures,** he'll be here (i) for four hours, (ii) by four o'clock; **j'en ai p. une heure,** it'll take me an hour; I'll be an hour; **donnez-moi p. 100 francs d'essence,** give me 100 francs' worth of petrol, *NAm:* gas; **j'en ai p. mon argent,** I've got my money's worth; **être p. beaucoup, p. peu, dans une affaire,** to count for much, for little, in a business; (*e*) (*purpose*) **je suis ici p. affaires,** I'm here on business; **vêtements p. hommes,** clothes for men; **j'épargne p. quand je serai vieux,** I'm saving for my old age; **je viens p. le compteur,** I've come about the (gas, etc.) meter; **c'est p. cela qu'il est venu,** that's why he came; (*f*) because of, for the sake of; **p. l'amour de Dieu,** for God's sake, heaven's sake; **faites-le p. moi,** do it for my sake; **j'avais peur p. lui,** I was nervous on his account; **mourir p. sa patrie,** to die for one's country; **l'art p. l'art,** art for art's sake; **p. la forme,** for form's sake; **beaucoup de bruit p. rien,** a lot of fuss, *Lit:* much ado, about nothing; (*g*) **parler p. qn,** to speak in favour, *NAm:* favor, of s.o.; **je suis p. la libération de la femme,** I'm all for women's liberation; *adv. F:* **moi, je suis p.,** I'm in favour of it, all for it; **le vote est p.,** the voting is for it, the ayes have it; **parler p. et contre,** to speak for and against; (*h*) **p. mon compte,** for my part, as far as I'm concerned; **il est grand p. son âge,** he's tall for his age; **p. ce qui est de . . .,** as regards . . ., with regard to . . .; **p. (ce qui est de) moi,** as for me, for my part, as far as I'm concerned; **p. moi c'est absurde,** in my opinion it's ridiculous; **p. moi, je veux bien,** personally, I'm willing; **p. cela,** for all that; *F:* **p. de la chance, c'est de la chance,** you're in luck and no mistake; (*i*) **dix p. cent,** ten per cent; (*j*) **être bon p. les animaux,** to be kind to animals. **2. p.** + *inf.* (*a*) (in order) to; **il faut manger p. vivre,** one must eat to live; **p. ainsi dire,** so to speak; **il s'en va p. ne jamais revenir,** he's going away for good; **nous nous sommes dépêchés p. ne pas être en retard,** we hurried so as not to be late; (*b*) (*after* **assez, trop**) **être trop faible p. marcher,** to be too weak to walk; (*c*) considering; **il est bien ignorant p. avoir étudié si longtemps,** he's very ignorant considering how long he's studied; (*d*) although; **p. être petit, il n'en est pas moins brave,** though small, he is none the less brave; (*e*) **être puni p. avoir désobéi,** to be punished for having disobeyed, for disobeying; **je le sais p. l'avoir vu,** I know from having seen it; **il est mort p. avoir trop travaillé,** he died of overwork; (*f*) of a nature to; **cela n'est pas p. me surprendre,** that does not come as a surprise to me; **cette amitié n'était pas p. lui plaire,** this friendship was not to his liking; (*g*) *F:* **être p. partir,** to be about to start, on the point of departure; (*h*) **mourir p. mourir,** if we must die. **3.** (*a*) **p. que** + *sub.*, in order that; **je vous dis cela p. que vous soyez sur vos gardes,** I'm telling you this in order to put you on your guard; **il est trop tard p. qu'elle sorte,** it is too late for her to go out; **mettez-le là, p. qu'on ne l'oublie pas,** put it there so that it won't be forgotten; (*b*) *Lit:* (*concessive*) **p.** (+ *adj.* or *n.*) **que** + *sub.*, however; although; **p. court qu'il soit, le livre est très intéressant,** (as) short as it is, short though it may be, the book is very interesting; (*c*) **p. peu que** + *sub.*, if only, if ever; **p. peu que vous hésitiez vous êtes fichu,** if you hesitate for a moment, hesitate at all, you've had it.

pour² *n.m.* **peser le p. et le contre,** to weigh the pros and cons; **entendre le p. et le contre,** to hear both sides.

pourboire [purbwar] *n.m.* tip, gratuity; **donner un p. au porteur,** to tip the porter.

pourceau, -eaux [purso] *n.m.* hog, pig, swine; **jeter des perles aux pourceaux,** to cast pearls before swine.

pourcentage [pursɑ̃taʒ] *n.m.* (*a*) percentage; amount per cent; rate (of interest); commission; (*b*) *Civ.E:* **rampe à fort p.,** steep gradient.

pourchasser [purʃase] *v.tr.* to pursue; to dun, harry (debtor); to hunt (down) (criminal); **pourchassé de rue en rue,** hounded from street to street.

pourchasseur, -euse [purʃasœr, -øz] *n.* pursuer.

pourlécher [purleʃe] *v.* **(je pourlèche; je pourlécherai) 1.** *v.tr.* (*a*) *A:* to lick (sth.) (all) over; **se p. les babines,** to lick one's lips; (*b*) *O:* to polish up (verses, etc.). **2. se p.,** to lick one's lips.

pourparler [purparle] *n.m. usu. pl.* (*a*) *Mil:* parley; (*b*) talks; **entrer en pourparlers,** to begin, enter into, negotiations (**avec,** with).

pourpier [purpje] *n.m. Bot:* purslane.

pourpoint [purpwɛ̃] *n.m. A.Cost:* pourpoint, doublet.

pourpre [purpr̥] **1.** *n.f.* (*a*) purple (dye) (of the ancients); (*b*) royal, imperial, dignity; **né dans la p.,** born in the purple. **2.** (*a*) *n.m.* crimson; rich red (colour, *NAm:* color); **le p. lui monta au visage,** he turned crimson; *Physiol:* **p. rétinien,** red pigment, visual purple; (*b*) *a.* crimson; (*of pers.*) purple (with rage).

pourpré [purpre] *a. Lit:* purple, crimson.

pourquoi [purkwa] **1.** *adv. & conj.* why; **p. faire?** what for? **p. cela?** why? **p. êtes-vous venu?** what have you come for? **dis-moi p.,** tell me why; **mais p. donc?** what on earth for? **voilà p.,** that's (the reason) why; **c'est p. . . .,** and that's why . . ., and so . . .; **p. pas? p. non?** why (ever) not? **2.** *n.m.inv.* **je ne sais pas le p.,** I don't know the reason why; **les p. et les comment,** the whys and wherefores.

pourri [puri] **1.** *a.* rotten (fruit, wood); rotted, decayed (wood); putrid (flesh); addle(d) (egg); bad (meat); damp (climate); wet (weather); **il est p. de vices,** he's rotten to the core; **p. d'orgueil,** eaten up with conceit; **gouvernement p.,** corrupt government. **2.** *n.m.* (*a*) rotten, bad, decayed, part (of an apple, etc.); **sentir le p.,** to smell rotten; (*b*) *P:* (*pers.*) swine, stinker.

pourrir [purir] **1.** *v.i. & pr.* to rot, decay; to putrefy, decompose; to go rotten, bad; (*of egg*) to addle; **p. en prison,** to rot in prison; **faire p.,** to rot (wood, etc.); **laisser p. la situation,** to allow the situation to deteriorate. **2.** *v.tr.* to rot.

pourrissement [purismɑ̃] *n.m.* deterioration (of a situation).

pourrissoir [puriswar] *n.m.* **1.** *Lit:* muck heap. **2.** *Paperm:* steeping vats.

pourriture [purityr] *n.f.* **1.** rotting, rot, decay; **p. sèche (du bois),** dry rot; **en p.,** rotting, putrescent. **2.** rottenness. **3.** *F:* (*pers.*) swine, stinker.

poursuite [pursɥit] *n.f.* **1.** (*a*) pursuit; chase (of enemy ship); hunt(ing), tracking (of criminal); **être à la p. de qch.,** to be in pursuit of sth.; **se mettre, se lancer, à la p. de qn,** to set off in pursuit of s.o.; to chase after s.o.; **p. d'un travail,** carrying out of a piece of work; *Com:* **p. du client,** follow-up system; (*b*) *Elcs:* tracking (of aircraft, missile, etc.); **radar de p.,** tracking radar. **2.** *usu. pl. Jur:* lawsuit, action; prosecution; suing (of debtor); **engager, entamer, intenter, des poursuites (judiciaires) contre qn,** to take, institute (legal) proceedings, take (legal) action, against s.o.

poursuiteur [pursɥitœr] *n.m. Cy:* pursuit cyclist.

poursuivant, -ante [pursɥivɑ̃, -ɑ̃t] **1.** *a. Jur:* prosecuting (party). **2.** *n.* (*a*) *Jur:* plaintiff, prosecutor; (*b*) pursuer.

poursuivre [pursɥivr̥] *v.* (*conj. like* SUIVRE) **1.** *v.tr.* (*a*) to pursue; to go after, chase, hunt (s.o., an animal); to seek for, after (sth.); to hound (s.o.); to harry (enemy); **ce songe me poursuit,** that dream haunts me; **poursuivi par la guigne,** dogged by bad luck; (*b*) *Jur:* **p. qn (en justice),** to prosecute, sue, s.o.; to take proceedings against s.o.; (*c*) to pursue, continue, proceed with, go on with (story, etc.); **p. un travail,** to carry on (with) a piece of work; **p. un avantage,** to follow up, press, an advantage; **p. un but,** to work towards an end. **2.** *v.i.* **poursuivez,** go on, continue (your story). **3. les préparatifs se poursuivent,** preparations are continuing, going on.

pourtant [purtɑ̃] *adv.* nevertheless, however, still, (and) yet; **vous n'allez p. pas nous quitter?** you're surely not going to leave us? you're not going to leave us though, are you?

pourtour [purtur] *n.m.* periphery, circumference, compass (of building, etc.); precincts (of a cathedral); **mur de p.,** enclosure wall (of prison, town, etc.).

pourvoi [purvwa] *n.m. Jur:* (*a*) appeal; (*b*) **p. en grâce,** petition for mercy.

pourvoir [purvwar] *v.* (*pr.p.* **pourvoyant;** *p.p.* **pourvu;** *pr.ind.* **je pourvois, n. pourvoyons;** *pr.sub.* **je pourvoie;** *impf.* **je pourvoyais;** *p.h.* **je pourvus;** *fu.* **je pourvoirai**) to provide. **1.** *v.ind.tr.* **p. aux besoins de qn,** to provide for, attend to, see to, cater for, supply, s.o.'s needs; **p. aux frais d'un voyage,** to defray the cost of a journey; **p. à un emploi,** to fill a job; **on n'y a pas pourvu,** no provision has been made for it. **2.** *v.tr.* (*a*) **p. qn de qch.,** to supply, provide, furnish, equip, s.o. with sth.; **p. qn d'une charge,** to invest s.o. with, appoint s.o. to, an office; (*b*) to equip, fit (**de,** with). **3. se p.** (*a*) to provide oneself (**de,** with); (*b*) *Jur:* to appeal, lodge an appeal; **se p. en grâce,** to petition for mercy.

pourvoyeur, -euse [purvwajœr, -øz] *n.* purveyor, supplier; provider; contractor; caterer.

pourvu que [purvykə] *conj.phr.* + *sub.* provided (that); so long as; **p. qu'il ne fasse pas de gaffes!** I only hope he won't make any blunders!

poussa(h) [pusa] *n.m.* (*a*) (toy) tumbler; (*b*) potbellied man.

pousse [pus] *n.f.* **1.** growth (of leaves, hair, feathers); cutting (of teeth). **2.** (young) shoot, sprout.

poussé [puse] *a.* elaborate (ornamentation, etc.); deep, searching (study); **il aboutit à un scepticisme assez p.,** he carries scepticism to some lengths, pretty far; **faire des études très poussées,** to pursue one's studies to a very advanced level; *Phot:* **cliché trop p.,** over-developed negative; *Aut:* **moteur p.,** hotted-up, souped-up, engine.

pousse-café [puskafe] *n.m.inv. F:* (glass of) liqueur (after coffee).

poussée [puse] *n.f.* **1.** (*a*) thrust; **p. latérale d'une voûte,** lateral thrust of an arch; (*b*) **p. du vent,** wind pressure; **centre de p.,** aerodynamic centre, *NAm:* center; centre of pressure; *Ph:* **axe de p.,** aerodynamic axis; (*c*) buoyancy (of liquid); **force de p.,** upward thrust; **centre de p.,** centre of buoyancy. **2.** pushing, pressure (of crowd, etc.). **3.** (*a*) thrust; push, shove; **écarter qch. d'une p.,** to push, shove, sth. aside; **p. vitale,** vital impetus; (*b*) heave (of the sea). **4.** (*a*) growth; (*b*) *Med:* eruption, outbreak (of pimples, etc.); **p. de fièvre,** sudden rise of temperature; (*c*) upsurge (of passion, etc.); bulge (in profits, etc.); **forte p. en hausse,** strong upward tendency (of the market, etc.).

pousse-pousse [puspus] *n.m.inv.* rickshaw.

pousser [puse] **1.** *v.tr.* (*a*) to push, shove, thrust; to drive (cattle); to wheel (bicycle); (*of wind*) to blow, drive (boat, etc.); to shoot (bolt); **ne poussez pas!** don't push! **p. qn du coude, du genou,** to nudge s.o.; **p. la porte,** to push the door (i) to, (ii) open; (*boating*) **p. du fond,** to punt; (*b*) to drive (on), impel, urge; **p. qn à faire qch.,** to push s.o. into doing sth.; to induce s.o., lead s.o., egg s.o. on, to do sth.; **poussé par la pitié,** prompted by pity; (*c*) to push on, urge forward (piece of work); to pursue, extend (studies); to elaborate (ornamentation, etc.); to urge on (horse); to push (pupil); **p. une attaque à fond,** to push, thrust, drive, an attack home; **p. une promenade jusqu'à la ville,** to walk on as far as the town; **p. trop loin une plaisanterie,** to take, carry, a joke too far; **p. la guerre jusqu'au bout,** to carry the war to its conclusion; **p. la vente de qch.,** to push the sale of sth.; *Mch:* **p. les feux,** to raise steam, stoke up; (*d*) (*of trees, etc.*) to put out, shoot (out), grow (leaves, roots); (*of child*) to cut (teeth); (*e*) to utter (cry); to heave (sigh); to give (cheer); **p. un cri,** to shout; (*f*) *F:* **il nous en a poussé une,** he gave us a song. **2.** *v.i.* (*a*) to push; **p. à la roue,** to put one's shoulder to the wheel; (*b*) to push on, push forward, make one's way (to a place); (*c*) (*of plants, etc.*) to grow, shoot, sprout, spring up; (*of hair, nails*) to grow; (*of teeth*) to come through; **laisser p. sa barbe,** to grow a beard; **ses dents commencent à p.,** he's beginning to cut his teeth; **tous ces enfants poussent,** these children are all shooting up. **3. se p.** (*a*) to push oneself forward; to make one's way (in society, etc.); to shove, elbow, one's way to the front; (*b*) to move up (to make room).

poussette [pusɛt] *n.f.* (*a*) (child's) pushchair; (*b*) shopping trolley.

poussier [pusje] *n.m.* coal dust, screenings; slack.

poussière [pusjɛr] *n.f.* (*a*) dust; **p. d'or,** gold dust; **enlever la p. des meubles,** to dust the furniture; **couvert de p.,** dusty; **s'en aller en p.,** to crumble into dust; **réduire qch. en p.,** (i) to reduce sth. to dust; (ii) to smash sth. to atoms; **mordre la p.,** to bite the dust; (*b*) speck of dust; *F:* **10 francs et des poussières,** ten francs plus (a bit).

poussiéreux, -euse [pusjerø, -øz] *a.* **1.** dust-like. **2.** dusty.

poussif, -ive [pusif, -iv] *a.* (*a*) broken-winded (horse); (*b*) wheezy, short-winded (person); puffing (engine).

poussin [pusɛ̃] *n.m.* **1.** (*a*) chick; (*b*) *Cu:* spring chicken; (*c*) *F:* **mon p.,** pet.

poussinière [pusinjɛr] *n.f.* chicken (i) coop, (ii) incubator.

poussivement [pusivmɑ̃] *adv.* breathlessly.

poussoir [puswar] *n.m.* push button (of electric bell, etc.); thumb piece; *Mec.E:* push rod (of a valve, etc.); **p. à ressort,** trigger.

poutrage [putraʒ] *n.m.* framework of beams; joist framing.

poutre [putr̥] *n.f.* **1.** (wooden) beam; **grosse p.,** ba(u)lk; **p. de faîte,** ridge piece, roof tree; **p. de plancher,** ceiling joist; **poutres apparentes,** exposed beams. **2.** (metal) girder; **p. à âme pleine,** plate girder; **p. à caisson,** box girder.

poutrelle [putrɛl] *n.f.* small beam, girder.

pouvoir[1] [puvwar] *v.tr.* (*pr.p.* **pouvant;** *p.p.* **pu;** *pr.ind.* **je peux, je puis** (*always* **puis-je** [pɥiʒ]), **tu peux, il peut, n. pouvons, ils peuvent;** *pr.sub.* **je puisse, n. puissions;** *impf.* **je pouvais;** *p.h.* **je pus;** *fu.* **je pourrai** [pure]) **1.** to be able; can; **je ne peux (pas) le faire,** I cannot, can't, do it; I'm unable to do it; **cela ne peut (pas) se faire,** it cannot, can't, be done; **comment a-t-il pu dire cela?** how could he say that? **il aurait pu le faire s'il avait voulu,** he could have done it if he had wanted to; **si vous aviez pu le voir,** if you'd been able to see him; if you could have seen him; **il ne pouvait pas l'accompagner,** he couldn't go with her; he wasn't able, he was unable, to go with her; **faire tout ce qu'on peut,** to do one's (level) best, the best one can, all one can; **j'ai fait toutes les démarches que j'ai pu,** I took every step that I possibly could; **j'ai pu le revoir,** I managed, was able, to see him again; **je n'y peux rien,** I can't help it; **on n'y peut rien,** (i) it can't be helped; (ii) there's nothing that can be done about it; **il a été on ne peut plus grossier,** he was as rude as could be; he was most rude; **il travaille on ne peut mieux,** he couldn't work better; **il n'en peut plus (de fatigue),** he's quite exhausted, worn out, tired out; **sauve qui peut,** every man for himself; **on ne peut pas ne pas l'admirer,** one cannot help admiring him; one has to admire him; **je viendrai aussitôt que je pourrai,** I'll come as soon as I can; **qu'est-ce qu'il peut bien me vouloir?** whatever can he want? **où pouvait-il bien être à cette heure?** wherever could he be at this time? **la loi ne peut rien contre lui,** the law can't touch him. **2.** may; (*a*) to be allowed; **vous pouvez partir,** you may go; **elle ne peut pas sortir seule,** she can't go out alone; she isn't allowed out alone; **puis-je entrer?** may I, shall I, come in? **quand pourrai-je emménager?** when can I move in? (*b*) *Lit:* **puisse-t-il défendre nos lois!** may he defend our laws! **3.** to be possible, probable; *v.pr.* **cela se peut (bien),** it may be; it could well be; it's quite possible; maybe! possibly! **cela ne se peut pas,** it can't be done; that's impossible; **la porte a pu se fermer toute seule,** the door may have, could have, closed on its own; **nous pourrions le trouver si nous nous dépêchions,** we might find him if we hurried; **il pouvait avoir dix ans,** he may, might, have been ten; **advienne que pourra,** come what may; **tout de même vous auriez (bien) pu faire moins de bruit,** all the same you could have, might have, made less noise; **il peut se faire, il peut arriver, que . . .** + *sub.*, it may be, may happen, that . . .; **il se peut qu'il ne soit pas coupable,** he may not, might not, be guilty; **il se peut qu'il vienne,** he may come, could well come.

pouvoir² *n.m.* **1.** (*a*) power, force, means; capacity; **il n'est pas en mon p. de . . .,** it is not within, it is beyond, my power to . . .; **je ferai tout ce qui est en mon p.,** I'll do everything in my power; **avoir le p. de faire qch.,** to have the power, the ability, to do sth.; (*b*) *Ch: Ph: etc:* **p. calorifique,** calorific value; **p. rayonnant,** radiating capacity; *Pol.Ec:* **p. d'achat,** purchasing power. **2.** influence; power; **avoir un p. absolu sur qn,** to have complete power over s.o.; **tomber au p. de l'ennemi,** to fall into enemy hands; **elle est en son p.,** she's in his power. **3.** authority; (*a*) **p. paternel,** paternal authority; (*b*) competence, power; **abuser de son p., de ses pouvoirs,** to abuse one's authority; (*c*) **p. politique,** political power; **ambitionner le p.,** to aim at power; **prendre le p.,** (i) to assume power; (ii) to take, come into, office; **le parti au p.,** the party in power; **quand les Libéraux sont au p.,** when the Liberals are in (power); **les pouvoirs publics,** the administration, the authorities; **p. exécutif,** executive power; **p. législatif,** legislative power; **p. judiciaire,** judicial power; the judiciary. **4.** *Jur:* power of attorney; **avoir, recevoir, plein(s) pouvoir(s) pour agir,** to have full powers, be (fully) empowered, authorized, to act; **se présenter sans pouvoirs réguliers,** to come without full credentials.

pragmatique [pragmatik] *a.* pragmatic.

pragmatisme [pragmatism] *n.m.* pragmatism.

pragmatiste [pragmatist] *a. & n.* pragmatist.

praire [prɛr] *n.f. Moll:* clam.

prairial [prɛrjal] *n.m. Fr.Hist:* ninth month of Fr. Republican Calendar (May-June).

prairie [preri] *n.f.* **1.** (*a*) meadow; (*b*) grassland; *NAm:* prairie. **2.** *Geog:* **la P.,** the Prairies.

praline [pralin] *n.f. Cu:* praline; burnt almond.

praliné [praline] *a. Cu:* containing ground praline; **amandes pralinées,** burnt almonds.

praliner [praline] *v.tr. Cu:* to brown (almonds, etc.) in sugar.

praticable [pratikabl̩] *a.* practicable; (*a*) feasible (plan, idea, etc.); (*b*) passable, negotiable (road, etc.); (*c*) *Th:* practicable (door, window).

praticien, -ienne [pratisjɛ̃, -jɛn] *n.* (*a*) (legal, medical) practitioner; (*b*) practician, expert; (*c*) sculptor's assistant.

pratiquant [pratikɑ̃] *a.* practising (religious observances); *a. & n.* **(catholique) p.,** practising Catholic; **les pratiquants,** (regular) churchgoers.

pratique¹ [pratik] *a.* practical, useful (method, article, etc.); handy (gadget, etc.); convenient (time, etc.); **avoir l'esprit p.,** to have a practical turn of mind; **sens p.,** practical common sense.

pratique² *n.f.* **1.** practice; application (of theory); **mettre qch. en p.,** to put sth. into practice; to apply (system, etc.); **c'est une p. courante,** it's common practice; it's quite usual; **en p.,** in practice. **2.** (*a*) practice, experience; *Lit:* practising (of virtue); **p. du théâtre,** theatrical experience; **la p. d'un sport,** the practice of a sport; **perdre la p. de qch.,** to lose the knack of sth.; to get out of practice; **avoir une longue p. de qch.,** to have a long practical experience of sth.; (*b*) *Jur:* practice (of the law); **terme de p.,** legal term; (*c*) *esp. pl. A:* dealings (with the enemy, etc.); **il avait vécu dans la p. des hauts fonctionnaires,** he had associated with high-ranking civil servants. **3. pratiques religieuses,** religious practices, observances; **pratiques clandestines,** underhand practices. **4.** *A:* practice (of lawyer, doctor); custom, business (of tradesman). **5.** *A:* (lawyer's) client; (doctor's) patient; (tradesman's) customer. **6.** *Jur:* **libre p.,** free exercise (of one's religion, etc.); *Nau:* **avoir libre p.,** to be out of quarantine.

pratiquement [pratikmɑ̃] *adv.* **1.** in practice. **2.** (*a*) in actual fact; (*b*) practically, virtually.

pratiquer [pratike] *v.tr.* **1.** to practise (rules, virtues, etc.); to put into practice; to employ, use; **il pratique le football,** he plays football; **elle pratique la natation,** she's a (keen) swimmer; **voilà comment cela se pratique ici,** that's how it's usually done here; **p. les conseils de qn,** to put s.o.'s advice into practice; *Med:* **p. une intervention,** to operate, carry out an operation; **il ne pratique pas (sa religion),** he doesn't practise his religion; **médecin qui pratique dans cette ville,** doctor who practises in this town; **il ne pratique plus,** he's no longer in practice; *Com:* **les cours pratiqués,** the ruling prices. **2. p. un escalier dans l'épaisseur d'un mur,** to cut a stair in, fit a stair into, the thickness of a wall; **p. une ouverture dans un mur,** to make an opening in a wall; **p. un sentier,** to make, open up, a path. **3.** (*a*) *A:* to frequent, associate with (s.o.); (*b*) to study (book).

pré [pre] *n.m.* meadow; *A:* **aller sur le p.,** to fight a duel.

préalable [prealabl̩] **1.** *a.* (*a*) previous, prior (**à,** to); **formalités préalables au débat,** formalities that precede the debate; (*b*) preliminary (agreement, etc.); **à titre de mesure p.,** as a preliminary. **2.** *n.m.* (*a*) prerequisite, condition; **au p.,** to begin with, first (of all), beforehand; (*b*) *A:* preliminary.

préalablement [prealabləmɑ̃] *adv.* beforehand, first (of all); **p. à . . .,** prior to . . . .

préambule [preɑ̃byl] *n.m.* preamble (**de,** to); prelude.

préamplificateur [preɑ̃plifikatœr] *n.m. Elcs:* preamplifier.

préau, -aux [preo] *n.m.* (*a*) (court)yard (*esp.* of prison); open space (of cloister); (*b*) covered (part of) playground.

préavis [preavi] *n.m.* (previous, advance) notice; **sans p.,** without notice, warning; **exiger un p. de trois mois,** to require three months' notice.

prébende [prebɑ̃d] *n.f.* **1.** *Ecc:* prebend. **2.** *Lit:* sinecure.

prébendé [prebɑ̃de] *a. Ecc:* prebendal.

prébendier [prebɑ̃dje] *n.m. Ecc:* prebendary.

précaire [prekɛr] *a.* precarious (tenure, state of health, etc.); delicate (health).

précairement [prekɛrmɑ̃] *adv.* precariously.

précarité [prekarite] *n.f.* precariousness.

précaution [prekosjɔ̃] *n.f.* **1.** precaution; **prendre des précautions,** to take precautions (**pour,** for); **mesures de p.,** precautionary measures; **par (mesure de) p.,** as a precaution. **2.** caution, wariness; care; **avec p.,** cautiously, warily; carefully.

précautionner [prekosjɔne] **1.** *v.tr. A:* to warn, caution (**contre,** against). **2. se p. contre qch.,** to take precautions, to guard, against sth.

précautionneusement [prekosjɔnøzmɑ̃] *adv.* cautiously, warily; carefully.

précautionneux, -euse [prekosjɔnø, -øz] *a.* cautious, wary; careful.

précédemment [presedamɑ̃] *adv.* previously, already, before.

précédent [presedɑ̃] **1.** *a.* preceding, previous, former; **le jour p.,** the day before, the previous day. **2.** *n.m.* precedent; **créer un p.,** to create, set, a precedent; **sans p.,** unprecedented.

précéder [presede] *v.tr.* (*conj. like* CÉDER) **1.** to precede; to go, come, before; **la musique précède les troupes,** the band marches in front of the troops; **l'antichambre qui précède le salon,** the antechamber leading to the drawing room; **la page qui précède,** the preceding page, the page before; **ce qui précède,** the foregoing. **2. p. qn (en dignité),** to have precedence of, over, s.o.

précepte [presɛpt] *n.m.* precept.

précepteur, -trice [presɛptœr, -tris] *n.* (private) tutor, teacher; *f.* governess.

préceptoral, -aux [presɛptɔral, -o] *a.* tutorial.

préceptorat [presɛptɔra] *n.m.* tutorship.

précession [presesjɔ̃] *n.f. Astr: etc:* precession.

préchambre [preʃɑ̃br̥] *n.f.* precombustion chamber (of diesel engine).

prêche [prɛʃ] *n.m.* sermon.

prêcher [preʃe] **1.** *v.tr. & i.* to preach (the Gospel, etc.) (**à,** to); *Pej:* to preachify, sermonize; **p. l'économie,** to preach economy; **p. d'exemple,** to practise what one preaches. **2.** *v.tr.* to preach to (s.o.); to lecture (s.o.), tell (s.o.) off; *F:* **p. un converti,** to preach to the converted.

prêcheur, -euse [prɛʃœr, -øz] **1.** *a.* (*a*) *Ecc:* preaching (friar); (*b*) sermonizing (person). **2.** *n. Fig:* sermonizer, preacher.

prêchi-prêcha [preʃipreʃa] *n.m.inv. F:* preaching; preachifying, sermonizing.

précieusement [presjøzmɑ̃] *adv.* **1.** very carefully; **garder qch. p.,** to treasure sth. **2.** *Lit:* with preciosity, preciously, affectedly.

précieux, -euse [presjø, -øz] **1.** *a.* precious; (*a*) valuable (advice, time, etc.) (**à,** to); (*b*) *Lit:* affected, mannered (style). **2.** *n.f. Fr.Lit.Hist:* précieuse.

préciosité [presjozite] *n.f.* (*a*) *Lit:* preciosity; (*b*) affectation, affectedness; preciousness.

précipice [presipis] *n.m.* chasm; abyss; precipice.

précipitamment [presipitamɑ̃] *adv.* precipitately; hurriedly, hastily; **entrer, sortir, p.,** to rush, hurry, dash, in, out; **agir trop p.,** to be too precipitate.

précipitation [presipitasjɔ̃] *n.f.* **1.** precipitation; violent hurry, great haste; **sortir avec p.,** to hurry, rush, dash, out. **2.** (*a*) *Ch: Ph:* precipitation; (*b*) *Meteor: esp. pl.* precipitation.

précipité [presipite] **1.** *a.* precipitate; hasty; hurried, headlong (flight, etc.); abrupt (departure); racing (pulse); **s'avancer à pas précipités,** to rush forward, along; **un bruit de pas précipités,** quick footsteps. **2.** *n.m. Ch: etc:* precipitate.

précipiter [presipite] **1.** *v.tr.* (*a*) to throw down, hurl down; **p. qn dans le désespoir,** to plunge s.o. into despair; **p. un peuple dans la guerre,** to precipitate a nation into war; (*b*) to hurry, hasten, rush; to precipitate (events); **il ne faut rien p.,** we mustn't rush things; we mustn't be over hasty; (*c*) *Ch:* to precipitate (substance). **2.** *v.i. Ch:* (*of substance*) to precipitate. **3. se p.** (*a*) to dash, rush (headlong), make a rush (**sur,** at, upon); (*b*) *Ch:* to precipitate.

précis [presi] **1.** *a.* precise, exact, accurate, definite; unambiguous; **exiger d'une façon précise que . . .,** to call definitely for . . .; **à deux heures précises,** at two o'clock precisely; at two o'clock sharp; **je suis parti sans raison précise,** I left for no definite reason, for no particular reason; **en termes p.,** in distinct terms; distinctly. **2.** *n.m.* abstract, summary, précis (of document, etc.); epitome; **p. d'histoire de France,** short history of France.

précisément [presizemɑ̃] *adv.* **1.** (*a*) precisely, exactly; accurately; definitely; (*b*) **c'est p. l'homme que je cherche,** he's just the man I'm looking for. **2.** as it happens, as it happened; as a matter of fact.

préciser [presize] **1.** *v.tr.* (*a*) to specify; to state (sth.) precisely, specifically; **il faut p. vos affirmations,** you must be more explicit in your statements; **p. les détails,** to go into more detail; **je tiens à p. que . . .,** I wish to make it clear that . . .; **p. la date de . . .,** to give the exact date of . . . . **2.** *v.i.* to be precise, explicit. **3.** (*of ideas*) **se p.,** to become clear(er), (more) explicit; to take shape.

précision [presizjɔ̃] *n.f.* **1.** precision, preciseness; exactness, accuracy; **avec p.,** precisely, accurately; **p. de tir,** accuracy of fire; **instruments de p.,** precision instruments. **2. donner, apporter, des précisions sur qch.,** to give precise details about sth.; **demander des précisions sur qch.,** to ask for more information, for full particulars, about sth.

précité [presite] *a.* aforesaid, aforementioned; above(-mentioned).

précoce [prekɔs] *a.* precocious; early, forward (fruit, etc.); premature (senility, etc.); **enfant p. pour son âge,** child who is advanced for his age.

précocement [prekɔsmɑ̃] *adv.* precociously.

précocité [prekɔsite] *n.f.* precocity; precociousness; earliness, forwardness (of fruit, season, etc.).

précombustion [prekɔ̃bystjɔ̃] *n.f.* precombustion.

précompte [prekɔ̃t] *n.m.* deduction (from an account, salary).

précompter [prekɔ̃te] *v.tr.* to deduct (income tax, etc.) (from s.o.'s salary, etc.).

préconception [prekɔ̃sɛpsjɔ̃] *n.f.* preconception; prejudice.

préconçu [prekɔ̃sy] *a.* preconceived.

préconiser [prekɔnize] *v.tr.* to (re)commend, advocate.

précontraint [prekɔ̃trɛ̃] *a. & n.m.* **(béton) p.,** prestressed concrete.

précurseur [prekyrsœr] **1.** *n.m.* precursor, forerunner; *Lit:* harbinger (of spring, etc.). **2.** *a.m.* precursory; premonitory (sign).

prédateur, -trice [predatœr, -tris] **1.** *a.* predatory; **oiseau p.,** bird of prey. **2.** *n.m.* predator; bird, beast, of prey.

prédécéder [predesede] *v.tr.* (*conj. like* DÉCÉDER) to predecease.

prédécesseur [predesesœr] *n.m.* predecessor.
prédestination [predɛstinasjɔ̃] *n.f.* predestination.
prédestiné [predɛstine] *a.* predestined; fated (**à,** to).
prédestiner [predɛstine] *v.tr.* to predestine (**à,** to).
prédétermination [predetɛrminasjɔ̃] *n.f.* predetermination.
prédéterminer [predetɛrmine] *v.tr.* to predetermine.
prédicant [predikɑ̃] *n.m. Ecc:* predicant.
prédicat [predika] *n.m. Gram:* predicate.
prédicateur, -trice [predikatœr, -tris] *n.* preacher.
prédicatif, -ive [predikatif, -iv] *a. Gram:* predicative.
prédication [predikasjɔ̃] *n.f.* **1.** preaching. **2.** sermon.
prédiction [prediksjɔ̃] *n.f.* prediction. **1.** predicting, foretelling. **2.** forecast.
prédigéré [prediʒere] *a.* predigested.
prédilection [predilɛksjɔ̃] *n.f.* predilection; partiality, fondness; **auteur de p.,** favourite, *NAm:* favorite, author.
prédire [predir] *v.tr.* (*conj. like* DIRE *except pr.ind. & imp.* **(v.) prédisez**) to predict, prophesy, foretell.
prédisposer [predispoze] *v.tr.* to predispose; **être prédisposé aux accidents,** to be accident prone.
prédisposition [predispozisjɔ̃] *n.f.* predisposition (**à,** to); **p. au vice,** propensity to vice.
prédominance [predɔminɑ̃s] *n.f.* predominance, prevalence.
prédominant [predɔminɑ̃] *a.* predominant; prevailing, prevalent.
prédominer [predɔmine] *v.i.* to predominate, prevail; to have the upper hand (**sur,** over); to be uppermost.
prééminence [preeminɑ̃s] *n.f.* pre-eminence.
prééminent [preeminɑ̃] *a.* pre-eminent.
préemption [preɑ̃psjɔ̃] *n.f.* pre-emption.
préétablir [preetablir] *v.tr.* to pre-establish.
préexistant [preɛgzistɑ̃] *a.* pre-existent.
préexistence [preɛgzistɑ̃s] *n.f.* pre-existence.
préexister [preɛgziste] *v.i.* to pre-exist; to be pre-existent (**à,** to).
préfabrication [prefabrikasjɔ̃] *n.f.* prefabrication.
préfabriqué [prefabrike] **1.** *a.* prefabricated. **2.** *n.m.* prefabricated house, *F:* prefab.
préface [prefas] *n.f.* **1.** preface, foreword (**à, de,** to). **2.** *Ecc:* preface.
préfacer [prefase] *v.tr.* to write a preface to, for (a book); to preface.
préfacier [prefasje] *n.m.* writer of a preface.
préfectoral, -aux [prefɛktɔral, -o] *a.* prefector(i)al; of the prefect.
préfecture [prefɛktyr] *n.f.* **1.** *Rom.Ant: Fr.Adm:* prefecture. **2. la P. de police,** the headquarters of the Paris police. **3. p. maritime,** (i) area under command of a port admiral; (ii) naval superintendent's office, port admiral's office.
préférable [preferabl̩] *a.* preferable (**à,** to); more advisable; **il serait p. de le revoir, qu'on le revoie,** it would be better to see him again.
préférablement [preferabləmɑ̃] *adv.* preferably.
préféré, -ée [prefere] *a. & n.* favourite, *NAm:* favorite.
préférence [preferɑ̃s] *n.f.* preference; **de p.,** preferably; **de p. à . . .,** in preference to . . .; **donner, accorder, la p. à qn,** to give s.o. preference (**sur,** over); *Jur:* **droits de p.,** priority rights; *Fin:* **actions de p.,** preference shares, preferred shares.
préférentiel, -elle [preferɑ̃sjɛl] *a.* preferential.
préférer [prefere] *v.tr.* **(je préfère; je préférerai)** to prefer (**à,** to); to like better; **je préfère du thé,** I'd rather have tea; **je préférerais que vous veniez,** I would rather you came; **il préféra mourir plutôt que de se rendre,** he preferred death to surrender.
préfet [prefɛ] *n.m.* **1.** *Rom.Ant: Fr.Adm:* prefect. **2. p. de police,** prefect = chief commissioner, of the Paris police. **3.** *Navy:* **p. maritime,** port admiral; commander-in-chief of the port.
préfète [prefɛt] *n.f.* prefect's wife.
préfiguration [prefigyrasjɔ̃] *n.f.* prefiguration; foreshadowing.
préfigurer [prefigyre] *v.tr.* to prefigure, foreshadow.
préfixe [prefiks] *n.m. Gram: etc:* prefix.
préfixer [prefikse] *v.tr.* to prefix.
préformation [prefɔrmasjɔ̃] *n.f.* preformation.
préglaciaire [preglasjɛr] *a. Geol:* pre-glacial.
préhenseur [preɑ̃sœr] *a.m.* prehensile.
préhensile [preɑ̃sil] *a.* prehensile.
préhension [preɑ̃sjɔ̃] *n.f.* gripping.
préhistoire [preistwar] *n.f.* prehistory.
préhistorique [preistɔrik] *a.* prehistoric.
préjudice [preʒydis] *n.m.* prejudice, detriment; (moral) injury; wrong, damage; *Jur:* tort; **porter p. à qn,** to inflict injury, loss, on s.o.; (*of action*) to be prejudicial to s.o.'s interests; **au p. de qn,** to the prejudice, detriment, of s.o.; **sans p. de . . .,** without prejudice to . . ..
préjudiciable [preʒydisjabl̩] *a.* prejudicial, injurious, detrimental, harmful (**à,** to).
préjudiciel, -elle [preʒydisjɛl] *a. Jur:* interlocutory (question, etc.); prejudicial (action).
préjudicier [preʒydisje] *v.i.* (*pr.sub. & impf.* **n. préjudiciions**) *A: & Lit:* to be detrimental, prejudicial (**à,** to).
préjugé [preʒyʒe] *n.m.* **1.** *Jur:* precedent (in law). **2.** prejudice; preconception; **avoir un p. pour, vers, qch.,** to be prejudiced, have a prejudice, in favour, *NAm:* favor, of sth.; **gens sans préjugés,** unprejudiced people; **p. favorable,** preconceived favourable, *NAm:* favorable, opinion.
préjuger [preʒyʒe] *v.ind.tr. & tr.* (*conj. like* JUGER) **p. de qch.,** *A: & Lit:* **p. qch.,** to prejudge sth.; **autant qu'on peut p.,** as far as one can judge beforehand.
prélart [prelar] *n.m. Nau: etc:* tarpaulin.
prélasser (se) [səprelase] *v.pr.* to lounge, loll (in an armchair, etc.); to bask (in the sun).
prélat [prela] *n.m.* prelate.
prélature [prelatyr] *n.f.* prelacy.
prêle, prèle [prɛl] *n.f. Bot:* horsetail.
prélèvement [prelɛvmɑ̃] *n.m.* **1.** deduction in advance; setting apart (of a portion); **p. d'échantillons,** sampling; *Med:* **p. de sang,** taking of blood (for a test); **p. sur le capital, sur la fortune,** capital levy. **2.** (*a*) sample; *Med:* swab; (*b*) amount deducted; *Bank:* = standing order.
prélever [prelve] *v.tr.* (*conj. like* LEVER) to deduct, set apart (portion) in advance; to levy (tax); **p. une commission de deux pour cent,** to deduct, charge, a commission of two per cent; **p. un échantillon,** to take, cut off, a sample.
préliminaire [preliminɛr] **1.** *a.* preliminary; **vue p.,** preview. **2.** *n.m.pl.* preliminaries.
préliminairement [preliminɛrmɑ̃] *adv.* preliminarily.
prélude [prelyd] *n.m.* prelude (**de, à,** to).
préluder [prelyde] *v.i.* **1.** *Mus:* to play a prelude. **2. p. à qch.,** to serve as (a) prelude to sth.
prématuré, -ée [prematyre] **1.** *a.* premature; untimely. **2.** *n.* premature baby.
prématurément [prematyremɑ̃] *adv.* prematurely.
prématurité [prematyrite] *n.f.* prematureness, prematurity.
préméditation [premeditasjɔ̃] *n.f.* premeditation; **avec p.,** deliberately; *Jur:* with malice aforethought.

préméditer [premedite] *v.tr.* to premeditate; **insulte préméditée,** deliberate insult, studied insult; **elle n'avait pas prémédité de lui demander de rester,** she hadn't planned, intended, to ask him to stay.

prémices [premis] *n.f.pl. A: & Lit:* (*a*) first fruits; (*b*) early beginnings.

premier, -ière [prəmje, -jɛr] *a. & n.* first. **1.** (*a*) **le p. jour du mois,** the first day of the month; **le p. janvier,** the first of January; January (the) first; **le p. de l'an,** New Year's day; **les trois premières années,** the first three years; **les premières heures après minuit,** the (wee) small hours; **première éducation,** early education; **premières difficultés,** initial difficulties; **dans les premiers temps,** in early times, in former times, in the earliest times; **les premiers temps elle n'osait pas parler,** at first she didn't dare speak; **en p. (lieu),** in the first place, first, firstly; **dès le p. jour,** from the first day, the beginning, the outset; **du, au, p. coup,** at the first attempt; **arriver le p., en p.,** to arrive first; **nous sommes arrivés les premiers,** we were the first to arrive; **arriver bon p.,** to come in an easy first; **être le p. à faire qch.,** to be (the) first to do sth.; **les premiers venus,** the first to arrive; **le p. venu vous dira cela,** anybody will tell you that; **ce n'est pas le p. venu,** he isn't just anybody, anyone; **au p. jour,** at the first opportunity; (*at hairdresser's, etc.*) **au p. de ces messieurs,** next gentleman, please; **il n'a pas le p. sou,** he hasn't (got) two halfpennies to rub together; **p. voyage,** maiden voyage; *Fin:* **p. cours,** opening price; *Aut:* **première (vitesse),** first (gear); *Typ:* **première (épreuve),** first proof; (*b*) **sens p. d'un mot,** original meaning of a word; **cause première d'un malheur,** prime, primary, cause of a misfortune; **vérité première,** basic truth; *Ind:* **matières premières,** raw materials. **2. habiter au p. (étage),** to live on the first, *NAm:* the second, floor; **p. plan,** foreground; *Fig:* forefront; **première marche,** bottom stair; *Th:* **premières loges,** first tier boxes; *Fig:* **être aux premières loges,** to have a front seat; *Mount:* **p. de cordée,** leader. **3. au p. rang,** in the first rank; **au tout p. rang,** in the forefront; **le tout p.,** the foremost; *Sp: etc:* **prendre la première place,** to take the lead; **le p. chirurgien de Paris,** the leading surgeon in Paris; **p. ministre,** Prime Minister, Premier; **p. commis,** principal clerk; head clerk; *Navy:* **p. maître,** chief petty officer; **capitaine en p.,** senior captain; **p. choix,** best quality; **travail de première urgence,** work of immediate urgency; **de première importance,** of the highest importance, of prime importance; **de première nécessité,** essential; *Rail: etc:* **billet de première (classe),** first-class ticket; **voyager en première,** to travel first class; *Mth:* **nombres premiers,** prime numbers; *Th: etc:* **p. rôle,** leading part, lead; **jeune p.,** juvenile lead; **première danseuse,** leading dancer; *Sch:* **(classe de) première** = lower sixth (form); **il est le p. de sa classe,** he's (the) top of his form; *P:* **de première,** first-rate, first-class. **4.** *n.f.* **première** (*a*) *Dressm: etc:* forewoman; (*b*) *Th: etc:* first performance, first night; première; (*c*) *Mount:* first ascent; (*d*) *Fin:* **p. de change,** first of exchange; (*e*) *Bootm:* inner sole, insole.

premièrement [prəmjɛrmɑ̃] *adv.* first, firstly, in the first place.

premier-né, première-née [prəmjene, prəmjɛrne] *a. & n.* firstborn; *pl. premiers-nés, premières-nées.*

prémilitaire [premilitɛr] *a.* premilitary.

prémisse [premis] *n.f. Log:* premise, premiss.

prémolaire [premɔlɛr] *n.f.* premolar (tooth).

prémonition [premɔnisjɔ̃] *n.f.* premonition.

prémonitoire [premɔnitwar] *a.* premonitory.

prémunir [premynir] **1.** *v.tr.* **p. qn contre qch.,** to caution, forewarn, s.o., to put s.o. on his guard, against sth. **2. se p. contre qch.,** to provide, be on one's guard, against sth.

prenable [prənabl̩] *a.* (town, fort) that can be taken, seized.

prenant [prənɑ̃] *a.* (*a*) *Fin:* **partie prenante,** payee; recipient; (*b*) prehensile (tail); (*c*) engaging (voice, etc.); fascinating (book, etc.).

prénatal, -als [prenatal] *a.* antenatal, *esp. NAm:* prenatal.

prendre [prɑ̃dr̩] *v.* (*pr.p.* **prenant;** *p.p.* **pris;** *pr.ind.* **je prends, il prend, n. prenons, ils prennent;** *pr.sub.* **je prenne, n. prenions;** *impf.* **je prenais, n. prenions;** *p.h.* **je pris, n. prîmes;** *fu.* **je prendrai**) to take. **I.** *v.tr.* **1.** (*a*) to take (up), take hold of (sth.); **p. les armes,** to take up arms; **p. brusquement qch.,** to snatch (up), seize, sth.; **p. qn par les cheveux,** to grasp, grab, s.o. by the hair; **je suis allé p. mon parapluie,** I went to get my umbrella; **p. qch. avec des pincettes,** to pick sth. up with a pair of tongs; **je sais comment le p.,** I know how to (i) handle him, (ii) get round him; **p. qch. dans un tiroir,** to take, get, sth. out of a drawer; **p. qch. sur la table,** to take sth. from, off, the table; **je l'ai prise dans mes bras,** I took her in my arms; **p. qn dans un coin,** to take s.o. into a corner; **où avez-vous pris cela?** where did you get (i) that, (ii) that idea (from)? (*b*) to take (in) (lodgers, etc.); **p. qch. sur soi,** to take responsibility for sth.; **p. sur soi de faire qch.,** to take it upon oneself to do sth.; **vous avez mal pris mes paroles,** you've misunderstood me; **il a très mal pris la chose,** he took it very badly; (*c*) **p. qch. à qn,** to take sth. from s.o.; to steal sth. from s.o.; to rob, deprive, s.o. of sth.; **cela me prend tout mon temps,** it takes (up) all my time; **mon temps est entièrement pris,** I haven't a free minute; **c'est autant de pris,** so far so good; **j'ai dû p. sur mes économies,** I had to draw on my savings; (*d*) **prenez ce que je vous offre,** take what I'm offering you; **dites-moi ce que vous prenez pour cela,** tell me what you charge for that; *F:* **il prend cher,** he charges a lot; he's expensive; **c'est à p. ou à laisser,** take it or leave it; **j'en prends et j'en laisse,** I'm taking that with a pinch of salt; **à tout p.,** on the whole, all in all; **à bien p. les choses,** rightly speaking; **prenons qu'il en soit ainsi,** let's take it that this is the case. **2.** to take, seize, catch, capture; (*a*) **p. une ville d'assaut,** to take a town by assault; **p. un poisson, un voleur,** to catch a fish, a thief; *Prov:* **tel est pris qui croyait p.,** it's a case of the biter bit; **se faire p.,** to be, get, caught; **se laisser p.,** to let oneself be caught, taken in; **il s'y est laissé p.,** he fell into the trap; **p. qn à voler,** to catch s.o. stealing; **être pris à faire qch.,** to be caught doing sth.; **p. qn sur le fait,** to catch s.o. in the act; **que je vous y prenne!** let me catch you (at it)! **on ne m'y prendra plus,** I won't be caught, taken in, had, again; I'll know better in future; **être pris par le brouillard,** to be caught in the fog; **il s'est pris le pied contre une racine,** he caught his foot on a root; **être pris, rester pris,** to get, be, stuck; **elle a été prise d'une crise de larmes,** she burst into tears; (*b*) **le vin lui, le, prend à la tête,** wine goes to his head; **l'envie lui a pris de partir,** he was seized with a desire to leave; **si jamais l'envie vous en prenait,** if ever you should feel so inclined; **qu'est-ce qui lui prend?** what's come over him? what's up with him? **bien lui en a pris,** it was lucky for him that he did. **3.** (*a*) to call for, collect, fetch (s.o.); (*of taxi, etc.*) to pick (s.o.) up; **prends ton frère avec toi,** take your brother with you; (*of boat*) **p. des marchandises,** to take in cargo; *Nau:* **p. de l'eau douce,** to fill up with fresh water; (*b*) to buy, take, book (tickets, etc.); **p. un billet direct pour Londres,** to book (straight) through to London; (*in hotel*) **p. une chambre,** to book, take, a room; **il n'a pas pris de vacances l'année dernière,** he didn't take, have, a holiday last year; **p. des renseignements,** to make inquiries; **p. des notes, quelques notes,** to take notes, take down a few notes; (*c*) to engage, take on (staff); **p. qn comme exemple,** to take s.o. as an example; (*d*) **p. qn, qch., pour . . .,** to mistake, take, s.o., sth., for . . .; **il se faisait p. pour un colonel,** he passed himself off as a colonel; (*e*) to take, eat, have (food); to take (medicine); **qu'est-ce que vous pren(dr)ez?** what will you have (to drink)? *F:* **qu'est-ce que tu vas p.!** you're for it! you'll catch it! (*f*) to catch (illness); to acquire (accent, habits); **p. froid,** to catch cold; (*g*) to take on, assume (appearance); to strike (attitude); **p. un ton sévère,** to put on a severe manner; **p. du poids,** to put on, gain, weight; **p. de l'âge,** to be getting old, on; (*h*) *Med:* **p. du sang,** to draw off blood. **4.** to take, go by (train, bus, etc.); **prenez une chaise,** (i) take a chair; (ii) have a seat; sit down; **p. le chemin de, pour, Paris,** to take the road to Paris; **p. à travers champs,** to strike across the fields; *Aut:* **p. un virage,** to take a bend; *Nau:* **p. le large,** to take to the open sea; (*of horse*) **p. le trot,** to break into a trot. **II.** *v.i.* **1.** (*a*) (*of mortar, jelly, etc.*) to set; (*of milk*) to curdle; (*b*) (*of river, etc.*) to freeze; (*c*) (*of engine, etc.*) to seize, jam; (*d*) *Cu:* (*of milk, etc.*) to catch (in the pan). **2.** (*a*) (*of plant, etc.*) to take (root); (*b*) (*of fire*) to take, catch; (*of match*) to strike, light; **le feu a pris à sa robe,** her dress caught fire; (*c*) **le vaccin a pris,** the vaccine has taken (effect); **cette mode ne prendra pas,** this fashion won't catch on; *F:* **ce truc-là prend toujours,** this trick is always successful; **cela ne prend pas avec moi!** you can't fool me! it won't wash with me! (*d*) **p. à gauche,** to bear (to the) left, fork left. **III. se prendre 1.** (*a*) to catch, be caught; **son manteau s'est pris dans la porte, à un clou,** her coat (got) caught in the door, on a nail; (*b*) (*of jelly, etc.*) to set; (*of river, etc.*) to freeze; (*c*) **médicament qui se prend le soir,** medicine to be taken in the evening; (*d*) **il se prend pour un héros,** he thinks he's a hero; (*e*) **se p. d'amitié pour qn,** to take a liking to s.o., form a friendship with s.o. **2.** *Lit:* **se p. à faire qch.,** to begin to do sth., begin, start, doing sth. **3. s'en p. à qn,** to attack, blame, s.o.; to put, lay, the blame on s.o.; **ne vous en prenez pas à moi,** don't take it out on me; **ne t'en prends qu'à toi-même,** you've only (got) yourself to blame. **4. il sait comment s'y p.,** he knows how to go, set, about it, how to manage it; **je sais comment m'y p. avec lui,** I know how to deal with him, handle him; **vous vous y prenez mal,** you're going the wrong way about it; **il s'y prend bien,** he sets, goes, about it in the right way; he tackles the job well; **s'y p. à deux fois,** to make two attempts, have two goes (at sth.).

preneur, -euse [prənœr, -øz] *n.* taker; (*a*) *Com: Fin:* buyer, purchaser; payee (of cheque); **je suis p.,** I'll take it; (*b*) *Jur:* lessee, leaseholder; (*c*) *Turf:* **les preneurs,** the takers of odds.

prénom [prenɔ̃] *n.m.* Christian name; first name, *NAm:* given name.

prénommé [prenɔme] **1.** *a.* called, named; **le p. Victor,** the man called Victor. **2.** *a.* & *n. Jur:* **(le) p.,** (the) abovenamed, (the) aforesaid.

prénommer [prenɔme] **1.** *v.tr.* to give (a child) a (Christian) name. **2. il se prénomme Adam,** his first name, Christian name, *NAm:* given name, is Adam.

prénuptial, -aux [prenypsjal, -o] *a.* premarital; antenuptial.

préoccupant [preɔkypɑ̃] *a.* worrying.

préoccupation [preɔkypasjɔ̃] *n.f.* (*a*) preoccupation (**de,** with); concern; **ma seule p. a été d'assurer . . .,** my only concern has been to ensure . . .; (*b*) anxiety, worry; **préoccupations matérielles,** material cares.

préoccupé [preɔkype] *a.* preoccupied (**de,** with); absentminded; **d'un ton p.,** (i) absentmindedly; (ii) in a worried tone.

préoccuper [preɔkype] **1.** *v.tr.* to preoccupy, engross (s.o.); **elle a quelque chose qui la préoccupe,** she's got something on her mind, she's preoccupied; **sa santé me préoccupe,** I'm anxious about his health. **2. se p. de qch.,** to give one's attention, to attend, see, to sth.; to care about sth.; **il se préoccupe de la disparition de son chien,** he's worried about the disappearance of his dog.

préparateur, -trice [preparatœr, -tris] *n.* **1.** *A:* preparer. **2.** assistant (in laboratory); demonstrator; **p. en pharmacie,** (dispensing) chemist's assistant.

préparatifs [preparatif] *n.m.pl.* preparations (**de,** for); **faire ses p. de départ,** to prepare for departure.

préparation [preparasjɔ̃] *n.f.* **1.** (*a*) preparation, preparing, getting ready (**à,** for); making, cooking, *NAm:* fixing (of meal, etc.); **parler sans p.,** to speak extempore; **annoncer une nouvelle sans p.,** to blurt out a piece of news; (*b*) *Ind:* dressing (of raw material); (*c*) *Sch:* preparation (of an exercise, etc.). **2.** *Pharm: etc:* preparation; *Cu:* **p. pour gâteau,** cake mix.

préparatoire [preparatwar] *a.* preparatory; preliminary; *Sch:* **cours p.** = first year infants' class.

préparer [prepare] **1.** *v.tr.* (*a*) to prepare; to get ready; to make preparations for, arrange (meeting, etc.); to make (up) (bed); *Pharm:* to make up (prescription); **elle prépare le déjeuner,** she's getting (the) lunch ready; she's cooking, *NAm:* fixing (the) lunch; (*b*) *Ind:* to dress (raw materials); (*c*) **p. qn à qch.,** (i) to prepare, (ii) to train, coach, fit, s.o. for sth.; (*d*) to prepare, study, for (exam). **2. se p.** (*a*) **un orage se prépare,** a storm is brewing; **il se prépare quelque chose,** there's something afoot, in the air; (*b*) **se p. à qch., à faire qch.,** to prepare (oneself), get ready, for sth., to do sth., **se p. à, pour, un voyage,** to get ready for a journey; *Mil: etc:* **se p. au combat,** to prepare for action.

prépayé [prepeje] *a.* prepaid.

prépondérance [prepɔ̃derɑ̃s] *n.f.* preponderance (**sur,** over).

prépondérant [prepɔ̃derɑ̃] *a.* preponderant; **voix prépondérante,** casting vote.

préposé, -ée [prepoze] *n.* **1.** employee; *Adm:* official; attendant; **p. (des postes),** postman, *NAm:* mailman; **p. des douanes,** customs officer. **2.** *Jur:* **commettant et p.,** principal and agent.

préposer [prepoze] *v.tr.* **p. qn à une fonction,** to appoint s.o. to an office; to put s.o. in charge of a job.

prépositif, -ive [prepozitif, -iv] *a. Gram:* prepositional (phrase).

préposition [prepozisjɔ̃] *n.f. Gram:* preposition.

prépositionnel, -elle [prepozisjɔnɛl] *a. Gram:* prepositional.

prépuce [prepys] *n.m. Anat:* prepuce, foreskin.

préraphaélite [prerafaelit] *a.* & *n.m. Hist. of Art:* Pre-Raphaelite.

préretraite [prerətrɛt] *n.f.* early retirement.

prérogative [prerɔgativ] *n.f.* prerogative; **p. parlementaire,** parliamentary privilege.

près [prɛ] **1.** *adv.* near; **il habite tout p.,** he lives nearby, close by, near here, close at hand; **vous êtes trop p.,** you're too close; **plus p.,** nearer. **2.** *adv.phr.* **à cela p.,** except on that point, with that one exception; **à ce détail p.,** except for this detail; **à cela p. que . . .,** except that . . .; **à peu d'exceptions p.,** with (a) few exceptions; **à cinq centimètres p.,** to within five centimetres, *NAm:* centimeters; **il devinerait votre poids à un milligramme p.,** he would guess your weight to the nearest milligram; **nous n'en sommes pas à un ou deux jours p.,** a day or two more or less doesn't matter; **je ne suis pas à cela p.,** I haven't come to that (yet); **je l'ai raté à deux minutes p.,** I missed him by two minutes; **un chef-d'œuvre à peu de chose p.,** little short of a masterpiece; **à peu p.,** nearly, about, approximately; **le travail est à peu p. achevé,** the work is almost, just about, more or less, completed; **il était à peu p. certain que . . .,** it was fairly, tolerably, certain that . . .; **le mieux équipé à beaucoup p.,** by far the best equipped; **ce n'est pas à beaucoup p. la somme qu'il me faut,** that's nothing like, nowhere near, the amount I need; *Nau:* **courir au plus p.,** to sail on a wind, close to the wind, on a bowline; **de p.,** close, near, (from) close to; **tirer de p.,** to fire at close range; **examiner qch. de p.,** to examine sth. closely; **suivre qn de p.,** to follow s.o. closely; to follow hard, close, on s.o.; **quand je l'ai vu de p.,** when I saw him at close quarters. **3.** *pre-p.phr.* **p. de qn, de qch.,** near (to), close to, s.o., sth.; **p. de là,** nearby; **p. de chez eux,** near (to) them; *Adm:* **ambassadeur p. le gouvernement français,** ambassador to the French government; *Nau:* **courir p. du vent,** to sail close to the wind; **il est p. de midi,** it's nearly, almost, twelve (o'clock); **elle était p. d'éclater en sanglots,** she was on the brink, the verge, of tears; **il y a p. de dix ans,** nearly, close on, ten years ago; **p. de partir,** on the point of leaving, about to leave; **nous ne sommes pas p. de le revoir,** it will be a long time before we see him again; **est-il p. d'avoir fini?** is he anywhere near finished? *adv.phr. F:* **être (très) p. de ses sous,** to be mean, tight-fisted.

présage [prezaʒ] *n.m.* presage, portent, foreboding; **mauvais p.,** bad omen; **oiseau de mauvais p.,** bird of ill omen.

présager [prezaʒe] *v.tr.* **(je présageai(s); n. présageons)** to presage. **1.** to (fore)bode, portend, betoken; **cela ne présage rien de bon,** it bodes no good; that's very ominous. **2.** to predict, to augur.

présalaire [presalɛr] *n.m.* = student's grant.

pré-salé [presale] *n.m.* (*a*) salt-meadow sheep; (*b*) (*meat*) salt-meadow lamb; *pl. prés-salés.*

présanctifié [presɑ̃ktifje] *a. Ecc:* presanctified.

presbyte [prɛzbit] *a.* presbyopic, long-sighted.

presbytère [prɛzbitɛr] *n.m. R.C.Ch:* presbytery.

presbytérianisme [prɛzbiterjanism] *n.m.* Presbyterianism.

presbytérien, -ienne [prɛzbiterjɛ̃, -jɛn] *a. & n.* Presbyterian.

presbytie [prɛsbisi] *n.f.* presbyopia, long-sightedness.

prescience [presjɑ̃s] *n.f.* prescience, foreknowledge.

prescient [presjɑ̃] *a.* prescient.

préscolaire [preskɔlɛr] *a.* preschool.

prescription [prɛskripsjɔ̃] *n.f.* **1.** *Jur:* prescription; **invoquer la p.,** to raise a defence under the statute of limitations. **2.** (*a*) *Med:* direction(s) (for treatment); (*b*) regulation(s); instructions.

prescrire [prɛskrir] *v.* (*conj. like* ÉCRIRE) **1.** *v.tr.* (*a*) to prescribe, ordain, lay down (time, etc.); to stipulate (quality, etc.); to prescribe (remedy); **à la date prescrite,** on the date fixed; (*b*) *Jur:* to prescribe; to bar by the statute of limitations. **2.** *Jur:* **se p.,** to become void by prescription; to be statute-barred; **ces dettes se prescrivent par cinq ans,** these debts are barred at the end of five years.

préséance [preseɑ̃s] *n.f.* precedence (**sur,** over, of); priority (**sur,** over); **avoir la p. sur qn,** to take precedence over s.o.

présélection [preselɛksjɔ̃] *n.f.* **1.** (*a*) preselection, preselecting (for specialized training, etc.); (*b*) short-listing (for a job). **2.** *Aut:* **boîte de vitesses à p.,** preselector gearbox.

présélectionner [preselɛksjɔne] *v.tr. Tchn:* preselect.

présence [prezɑ̃s] *n.f.* **1. avoir de la p.,** to have great presence, a forceful personality. **2.** presence, attendance; **je désire sa p.,** I wish him to come, be, here; **il ignore votre p.,** he doesn't know you're here; **faire acte de p.,** to put in an appearance; to show up; *Sch:* **régularité de p.,** regular attendance; **feuille de p.,** attendance register; *Ind:* time card; **en p.,** face to face, facing one another; **mettre les deux parties en p.,** to bring the two parties together; **en p. de la mort,** in the presence of death; **en p. de ces faits,** in view of these facts, faced with these facts; **cela s'est fait en ma p.,** it was done in my presence; **cela s'est dit en ma p.,** it was said in my hearing; *Theol:* **p. réelle,** real presence; **p. d'esprit,** presence of mind.

présent¹ [prezɑ̃] *a. & n.* present; (*a*) **les personnes présentes, les présents,** those present; **être p. à un spectacle,** to be present at a performance; **cela m'est toujours p. à l'esprit,** it's always present in my mind; I always keep it in mind; **il n'est pas p. à ce que je dis,** he's not attending to what I'm saying; **la présente convention,** this convention; *Jur:* **par la présente (lettre),** hereby; by these presents; **le (temps) p.,** the present (time); *Gram:* the present (tense); **à p.,** at present, (just) now; *esp. NAm:* presently; **jusqu'à p.,** up to the present (time); until now, as yet; **dès à p.,** from now on; *Lit:* henceforth; **à p. que . . .,** now that . . .; (*b*) **esprit p.,** alert, quick, mind; ready wit.

présent² *n.m. Lit:* present, gift; **faire p. de qch. à qn,** to make a present of sth. to s.o.; to present s.o. with sth.

présentable [prezɑ̃tabl̩] *a.* presentable; **je ne suis pas p.,** I'm not fit to be seen.

présentateur, -trice [prezɑ̃tatœr, -tris] *n.* presenter; (*a*) introducer (of pers.); (*b*) *Ecc:* patron (of a living); (*c*) *W.Tel: T.V:* announcer.

présentation [prezɑ̃tasjɔ̃] *n.f.* **1.** (*a*) presentation (of play, facts, etc.); *Bank:* **p. à l'encaissement d'un chèque,** clearance of a cheque, *NAm:* check; *Com:* **payable à p.,** payable on demand, on presentation, at sight; (*b*) appearance, presentation; *Cmptr: etc:* display; **livre de bonne p.,** well produced book; (*c*) *Obst:* presentation. **2.** (*a*) introduction (**à qn,** to s.o.); presentation (at court); **lettre de p.,** letter of introduction; *Ecc:* **la P. de la Vierge,** (Feast of) the Presentation (of the Blessed Virgin Mary); *Mil:* **p. du drapeau,** trooping the colour, *NAm:* color; *Com:* **p. de collections,** fashion show, parade; (*b*) *Cin:* trailer, *U.S:* preview. **3.** *Av:* **p. trop courte,** undershoot; **p. trop longue,** overshoot.

présenter [prezɑ̃te] **1.** *v.tr.* to present, offer; (*a*) to put in (witness, claim); **p. qch. à qn,** to present s.o. with sth.; to present sth. to s.o.; **p. sa main à qn,** to hold out one's hand to s.o.; **p. une excuse à qn,** to offer an apology to s.o.; **p. ses hommages à qn,** to pay one's respects to s.o.; **p. ses pièces d'identité,** to submit proof of identity; **p. son passeport,** to produce, show, one's passport; *Sch:* **p. le français (à un examen),** to take French (at an examination); *Mil:* **p. les armes,** to present arms; **présentez armes!** present arms! (*b*) to table (motion); to put (resolution); *T.V: etc:* to compere, *NAm:* emcee (show); **il m'a présenté tous les faits,** he put, laid, set out, before me all the facts of the case; **p. des conclusions,** to bring up, submit, conclusions (at a meeting); **p. un projet de loi,** to bring in, introduce, a bill; **son travail est bien présenté,** his work is well set out; (*c*) **p. qn à qn,** to introduce, present, s.o. to s.o.; **p. qn comme candidat,** to put s.o. up as a candidate. **2.** *v.i. F:* **il présente bien,** he's a man of good appearance. **3. se p.** (*a*) **une occasion se présente (de faire qch.),** an opportunity presents itself, occurs (for doing sth.); **un beau spectacle s'est présenté à mes yeux,** a fine sight met my eyes; **si le cas se présente,** if the case arises, occurs; **attendre que quelque chose se présente,** to wait for something to turn up, crop up; **la chose se présente bien,** the matter looks promising; **l'affaire se présente sous un jour nouveau,** the matter appears in a new light; (*b*) to present oneself; *Mil: etc:* to report (oneself); **se p. à un examen,** to go in for, sit (for), enter for, take, an examination; **se p. chez qn,** to call on s.o.; **se p. à qn,** to introduce oneself to s.o.; **se p. aux élections,** to stand (as a candidate) at the elections; **se p. comme candidat,** to come forward as a candidate; **il se présente bien,** he makes a good impression; (*c*) *Obst:* to present; **l'enfant se présente mal,** the child presents badly.

présentoir [prezɑ̃twar] *n.m. Com:* display unit.

préservateur, -trice [prezɛrvatœr, -tris] **1.** *a. A:* preservative; preventive. **2.** *n.m.* preservative (in food, etc.).

préservatif, -ive [prezɛrvatif, -iv] **1.** *a. & n.m.* preservative; preventive (**contre,** of); protective. **2.** *n.m. Hyg:* (contraceptive) sheath; protective.

préservation [prezɛrvasjɔ̃] *n.f.* preservation, protection (of crops, etc.).

préserver [prezɛrve] *v.tr.* to preserve, protect (**de,** from); **le ciel m'en préserve!** heaven forbid! **à p. de l'humidité,** to be kept dry.

présidence [prezidɑ̃s] *n.f.* **1.** (*a*) presidency; (*b*) chairmanship; (*at meeting*) **prendre la p.,** to take the chair. **2.** president's house.

président, -ente [prezidɑ̃, -ɑ̃t] *n.* **1.** (*a*) president (of legal tribunal, etc.); presiding judge; (*b*) president (of republic, etc.); **la Présidente,** the President's wife; *U.S:* the First Lady. **2.** (*a*) chairman; *F:* chairperson, chairwoman (of meeting, etc.); **être élu p.,** to be voted into the chair; **Monsieur le p., Madame la présidente, permettez-moi de . . .,** Mr Chairman, Madam Chairman, allow me to . . .; (*b*) *Pol.Hist:* **p. du Conseil** = Prime Minister; (*c*) **p. du jury,** (i) *Jur:* foreman of the jury; (ii) *Sch:* chief examiner; (iii) (*for a competition*) chairman of the adjudicating committee; (*d*) *Ind: Com:* **p. directeur général,** chairman and managing director.

présidentiel, -elle [prezidɑ̃sjɛl] **1.** *a.* presidential. **2.** *n.f.pl.* **présidentielles,** presidential elections.

présider [prezide] *v.tr. & i.* (*a*) to preside over (council); to chair (meeting); (*b*) to preside, be in the chair, take the chair; **p. (à) une réunion,** to preside at, over, a meeting; (*c*) **p. aux destinées de . . .,** to preside over the destinies of . . ..

présomptif, -ive [prezɔ̃ptif, -iv] *a.* **héritier p.,** heir presumptive, *esp.* heir apparent.

présomption [prezɔ̃psjɔ̃] *n.f.* **1.** presumption; presumptive evidence; *Ins:* **il y a p. de perte,** the ship is a presumptive loss; *Jur:* **preuve par p.,** circumstantial evidence. **2.** presumption, presumptuousness.

présomptueusement [prezɔ̃ptɥøzmɑ̃] *adv.* presumptuously.

présomptueux, -euse [prezɔ̃ptɥø, -øz] *a.* presumptuous, presuming; *n.* **un jeune p.,** a presumptuous young man.

presque [prɛsk(ə)] *adv.* **1.** (*a*) almost, nearly; **c'est p. impossible,** it's almost, next to, all but, well nigh, impossible; **je les ai p. tous,** I have nearly all of them; **c'est p. de la folie,** it's little short of madness; (*b*) *Lit:* **j'en ai la p. certitude,** I am almost, practically, certain of it. **2.** (*with negative*) scarcely, hardly; **p. jamais,** hardly ever, almost never; **p. rien,** scarcely anything, next to nothing; **p. personne,** hardly anyone.

presqu'île [prɛskil] *n.f.* peninsula.

pressage [prɛsaʒ] *n.m.* pressing (of grapes, laundry, gramophone records, etc.).

pressant [prɛsɑ̃] *a.* pressing, urgent (need, etc.); insistent (creditor, etc.); **en termes pressants,** in pressing terms; **cas p.,** urgent case.

presse [prɛs] *n.f.* **1.** press, pressing machine; squeezer; (*a*) **p. hydraulique à estamper,** drop forging press; **p. mécanique,** power press; **p. à vis,** screw press; **travailler du métal à la p.,** to stamp metal; **p. à copier,** letter press, copying press; (*b*) **p. à imprimer, d'imprimerie,** printing press; **p. à bras,** hand press; **p. rotative,** rotary press; **livre sous p.,** book in the press; **prêt à mettre sous p.,** ready for press; (*c*) *Bookb: etc:* **p. à rogner,** guillotine. **2.** press; newspapers; magazines; **photographe de p.,** press photographer; **avoir bonne, mauvaise, p.,** to have a good, bad, press; **service de p.,** publicity (department); **exemplaire de service de p.,** press copy, review copy. **3.** (*a*) *A: & Lit:* press, crowd, throng; **fendre la p.,** to force one's way through the crowd; (*b*) *A.Nau: etc:* press (gang). **4.** (*a*) haste, urgency; **il n'y a pas de p.,** there's no hurry; (*b*) **moments de p.,** busy periods.

pressé [prese] *a.* **1.** (*a*) pressed; compressed; **citron p.,** fresh lemon juice; **p. à froid,** cold-pressed; (*b*) crowded, close together; **pressés les uns contre les autres,** crowded together, packed together; pressed together, squashed together. **2.** (*a*) hurried; in a hurry; **je suis très p.,** I'm in a great hurry; I'm very pressed for time; **p. de partir,** in a hurry to go; **avoir un air p.,** to look as though one is in a hurry; (*b*) urgent, pressing (work, etc.); **ce n'est pas p.,** it's not urgent, there's no hurry; *n.m.* **aller au plus p.,** to attend to the most urgent thing(s) first.

presse-bouton [prɛsbutɔ̃] *a.inv.* push-button (war, etc.).

presse-citrons [prɛssitrɔ̃] *n.m.inv.* lemon squeezer.

presse-étoupe [prɛsetup] *n.m.inv. Mch:* stuffing box, packing box (and gland).

presse-fruits [prɛsfrɥi] *n.m.inv.* juice extractor, *U.S:* juicer.

presse-livres [prɛslivr̥] *n.m.inv.* book ends.

pressentiment [presɑ̃timɑ̃] *n.m.* presentiment, forewarning; foreboding; premonition; **j'ai comme un p. que . . .,** I have a feeling that . . ..

pressentir [presɑ̃tir] *v.tr.* (*conj. like* SENTIR) **1.** to sense (sth.); to have a presentiment, a foreboding, of (sth.); to have a feeling that sth. is going to happen; **faire, laisser, p. qch.,** to forebode, foreshadow, portend, sth.; **faire p. qch. à qn,** to give s.o. an inkling, a hint, of sth. **2. p. qn (sur qch.),** (i) to sound s.o. out (on sth.); (ii) to approach s.o. (about sth.).

presse-papier(s) [prɛspapje] *n.m.inv.* paperweight.

presse-purée [prɛspyre] *n.m.inv.* potato masher.

presser [prese] **1.** *v.tr.* (*a*) to press, squeeze (lemon, sponge, etc.); *Rec:* to press (record); **p. à froid,** to cold-press; **p. du raisin, des pommes,** to press grapes, apples; **p. un vêtement,** to steam-press a garment; **p. qn contre son cœur,** to clasp s.o. in one's arms; **il m'entraînait en me pressant le bras,** he dragged me off clutching me by the arm; (*b*) to press, push (switch, button); (*c*) **pressé par ses créanciers,** hard pressed, dunned, by his creditors; **p. l'ennemi,** to press hard upon the enemy; **p. qn de questions,** to ply s.o. with questions, question s.o. closely; **p. qn de faire qch.,** to press, urge, s.o. to do sth.; (*d*) to hurry (s.o.) (up, on); to accelerate, speed up (work, movement); **p. le pas,** to quicken one's pace; **p. le départ de qn,** to hasten s.o.'s departure; **qu'est-ce qui vous presse?** why are you in such a hurry? what's the hurry? **le temps presse,** time presses; **l'affaire presse,** the matter is urgent; **il n'y a rien qui presse, rien ne presse,** *F:* **ça ne presse pas,** there's no hurry, no rush. **2. se p.** (*a*) to press, crowd, throng; to squash up, crush; **on s'y presse toujours à six heures,** there's always a crowd there at six o'clock; (*b*) **elle s'est pressée contre lui,** she pressed (herself), snuggled (up), against him; (*c*) to hurry (up); **pressez-vous!** hurry up! **répondre sans se p.,** to answer deliberately, leisurely; **se p. de monter, de descendre,** to hurry up, down.

presse-raquette [prɛsrakɛt] *n.m.inv.* racket press.

pressing [presiŋ] *n.m. Com:* (*a*) steam pressing; dry cleaning; (*b*) dry cleaner's.

pression [prɛsjɔ̃] *n.f.* **1.** pressure; (*a*) **p. atmosphérique,** atmospheric pressure; **p. artérielle,** blood pressure; **p. en colonne d'eau,** hydraulic head; **bière (à la) p.,** draught beer; (*in café*) **un demi p.** = a half of (draught) beer, *esp. U.S:* draft beer; *Aut: etc:* **jauge de p.,** pressure gauge (for tyres, *NAm:* tires, etc.); *Mch:* **machine à haute, basse, p.,** high-pressure, low-pressure, engine; **mettre sous p.,** to pressurize; **mettre (la chaudière) sous p.,** to get up steam; **graissage sous p.,** pressure greasing; (*of aircraft, etc.*) **cabine sous p.,** pressurized cabin; (*b*) *Mch:* tension (of steam); (*c*) **vis de p.,** binding screw; (*d*) **exercer une p. sur qn,** to bring pressure to bear, put pressure, on s.o.; **faire p. sur qn,** to pressurize, influence, s.o.; **groupe de p.,** pressure group; (*of pers.*) **être sous p.,** to be under pressure; to be pent up. **2. un bouton (à) p., un, une, p.,** a press stud, snap fastener, *F:* popper.

pressoir [prɛswar] *n.m.* (*a*) wine press; cider press; oil press; (*b*) press house, room.

pressurage [presyraʒ] *n.m.* pressing (of fruit, etc.).

pressurer [presyre] *v.tr.* **1.** to press (fruit, etc.). **2.** to squeeze, grind down, extort money from (s.o.).

pressurisation [presyrizasjɔ̃] *n.f.* pressurization.

pressuriser [presyrize] *v.tr.* to pressurize.

prestance [prɛstɑ̃s] *n.f.* fine presence; imposing bearing, appearance.

prestant [prɛstɑ̃] *n.m. Mus:* diapason (stop) (of organ).

prestataire [prɛstatɛr] *n.m. Adm:* person receiving benefits, allowances.

prestation [prɛstasjɔ̃] *n.f.* **1.** furnishing, loan(ing) (of money). **2.** *Jur:* **p. de serment,** taking the oath; *Hist:* **p. de foi,** oath of fealty. **3.** *Mil: pl.* allowances. **4.** *Ins:* benefit; *Adm:* allowance; benefit; **prestations familiales** = family allowances; **prestations sociales,** national insurance benefits. **5.** (*of sportsman, etc.*) performance.

preste [prɛst] *a.* quick, sharp, nimble; alert; **avoir la main p.,** to be skilful with one's hands.

prestement [prɛstəmɑ̃] *adv.* quickly; promptly.

prestidigitateur, -trice [prɛstidiʒitatœr, -tris] *n.* conjurer.

prestidigitation [prɛstidiʒitasjɔ̃] *n.f.* conjuring; legerdemain, sleight of hand; **tour de p.,** conjuring trick.

prestige [prɛstiʒ] *n.m.* **1.** *A:* marvel. **2.** prestige; glamour, *NAm:* glamor; **sans p.,** undistinguished; **publicité de p.,** prestige advertising.

prestigieux, -euse [prɛstiʒjø, -øz] *a.* (*a*) *Lit:* marvellous, wonderful, amazing; (*b*) prestigious; **un nom p.,** a great name.

presto [prɛsto] *adv.* **1.** *Mus:* presto. **2.** *F:* quickly, straight away.

présumable [prezymabl̩] *a.* presumable.

présumer [prezyme] *v.tr.* to presume. **1. p. qn innocent,** to presume, assume, s.o. (to be) innocent; **le coupable présumé, le présumé coupable,** the supposed culprit; **le voleur présumé,** the alleged thief; **il est à p., on présume, qu'il est mort,** he is assumed to be dead. **2.** (*a*) **p. de faire qch.,** to presume to do sth.; (*b*) **trop p. de soi,** to presume too much, be overconfident; **trop p. de ses forces,** to overestimate, overrate, one's strength.

présupposé [presypoze] (*a*) *a.* presupposed; (*b*) *n.m.* presupposition.

présupposer [presypoze] *v.tr.* to presuppose; to take (sth.) for granted.

présupposition [presypozisjɔ̃] *n.f.* presupposition.

présure [prezyr] *n.f.* rennet.

prêt[1] [prɛ] *a.* ready; prepared; **p. à l'emploi, à servir,** ready for use; **se tenir p.,** to be ready; **être p. à tout,** (i) to be ready, game, for anything; (ii) to be prepared to do anything (to achieve one's purpose); **p. à partir,** ready to start; **être p. à commencer,** to be all set (to begin); **p. à rendre service,** willing to help.

prêt[2] *n.m.* **1.** lending; loan; **p. de 1000 francs,** loan of 1,000 francs; **p. à terme,** loan at notice; **p. à court terme,** short loan; **p. d'honneur,** loan on trust; **p. hypothécaire,** mortgage loan; **p. sur titres,** loan on securities; **p. sur gage(s),** pawnbroking; **à titre de p.,** as a loan, on loan. **2.** (*a*) *Mil:* pay; (*b*) advance (on wages).

prêt-à-porter [prɛtapɔrte] *n.m. coll.* ready-made, ready-to-wear, clothes; **en p.-à-p.,** off the peg.

prêté [prete] *n.m.* **c'est un p. pour un rendu,** it's tit for tat.

prétendant, -ante [pretɑ̃dɑ̃, -ɑ̃t] **1.** *n.* applicant, candidate (**à,** for); claimant; pretender (to a throne). **2.** *n.m.* suitor.

prétendre [pretɑ̃dr̥] *v.tr.* **1.** to claim (as a right); to require; (*a*) *A: & Lit:* **que prétendez-vous de moi?** what do you require, want, of me? (*b*) **je prétends être obéi,** I expect to be obeyed; **prétendez-vous me faire la loi?** do you think you have the right to dictate to me? **2.** *A:* to mean, intend. **3.** to maintain, assert; to claim; **je prétends que ce n'est pas vrai,** I maintain that it is not true; **on prétend que . . .,** people say that . . .; it is said that . . .; **à ce qu'il prétend,** according to him; **ils prétendent être de nos amis,** they claim to be friends of ours; **on le prétend fou,** they say he's mad; **il ne prétend pas être artiste,** he doesn't pretend to be artistic. **4.** *v.ind.tr.* **p. à qch.,** to lay claim to sth.; **p. aux honneurs,** to aspire to honours, *NAm:* honors; *Lit:* **p. à la main de qn,** to aspire to marry s.o.

prétendu, -ue [pretɑ̃dy] **1.** *a.* alleged; would-be; **p. voleur,** alleged thief; **un p. baron,** a self-styled, bogus, baron; **prétendus progrès,** so-called progress. **2.** *n. A: & Dial:* **mon p., ma prétendue,** my fiancé, fiancée.

prête-nom [prɛtnɔ̃] *n.m. Fig:* figurehead; man of straw; *pl. prête-noms.*

prétentieusement [pretɑ̃sjøzmɑ̃] *adv.* pretentiously.

prétentieux, -euse [pretɑ̃sjø, -øz] **1.** *a.* pretentious; showy. **2.** *n.* pretentious person; **un jeune p.,** a conceited young idiot.

prétention [pretɑ̃sjɔ̃] *n.f.* (*a*) pretension, claim (**à,** to); **renoncer à ses prétentions,** to renounce one's claims; **avoir des prétentions à la sagesse,** to have some claim to wisdom; **il n'a aucune p. à l'esprit,** he makes no pretence, no pretension, to wit; **je n'ai pas la p. de remporter le prix,** I don't for a moment suppose I shall get the prize; **je n'ai pas la p. de vous être supérieur,** I don't pretend, claim, to be better than you are; (*b*) pretentiousness, pretension; **homme sans prétention(s),** unassuming, unpretentious, man; **écrire avec p.,** to write pretentiously, in a pretentious style; (*c*) (*in advertisement for a job*) **envoyer curriculum vitae et prétentions,** send curriculum vitae and state salary required.

prêter [prete] **1.** *v.tr.* (*a*) to lend, *esp. NAm:* to loan; **p. qch. à qn,** to lend sth. to s.o.; **p. sur gage(s),** to lend against security; (*b*) **p. son appui, son concours, à qn,** to give, lend, s.o. one's support; **p. la main à qn,** to lend s.o. a hand; **p. l'oreille,** to listen; **p. attention,** to pay attention; **p. serment,** to take an oath, to be sworn; **p. le flanc à la critique,** to expose oneself, lay oneself open, to criticism; **p. son nom,** to lend one's name, allow one's name to be used; (*c*) to attribute, ascribe (**à,** to); **on me prête des discours que je n'ai jamais faits,** I am credited with speeches which I never made; (*d*) *v.i.* **p. à qch.,** to give rise to sth.; **privilège qui prête aux abus,** privilege that lends itself to, that is open to, that invites, abuse. **2.** *v.i.* (*of gloves, material, etc.*) to give, stretch. **3. se p.** (*a*) to lend oneself, be a party (**à,** to); **se p. à un accommodement,** to consent to, fall in with, an arrangement; (*b*) **sujet qui se prête à des développements variés,** subject that lends itself to a varied treatment.

prétérit [preterit] *n.m. Gram:* preterite (tense).

préteur [pretœr] *n.m. Rom.Hist:* praetor.

prêteur, -euse [prɛtœr, -øz] **1.** *n.* lender; **p. sur gages,** pawnbroker. **2.** *a.* ready, willing, to lend; **je ne suis pas p.,** I don't believe in lending.

prétexte [pretɛkst] *n.m.* pretext, excuse; plea; **prendre p. de qch. pour faire qch.,** to make a pretext of sth. for doing sth.; **sous p. de . . .,** on, under, (the) pretext, on a plea, of . . .; ostensibly to . . .; **sous p. d'amitié,** under the pretext of friendship; **sous aucun p.,** on no account, under no circumstances.

prétexter [pretɛkste] *v.tr.* to allege as a pretext; **p. la fatigue,** to plead fatigue, give fatigue as an excuse.

prétoire [pretwar] *n.m.* (*a*) *Rom.Ant:* praetorium; (*b*) *Jur:* (floor of the) court.

prétorien, -ienne [pretɔrjɛ̃, -jɛn] *a. & n.m. Rom.Ant:* praetorian.

prêtre [prɛtr̥] *n.m.* priest; **grand p.,** high priest.

prêtre-ouvrier [prɛtruvrije] *n.m.* worker priest; *pl. prêtres-ouvriers.*

prêtresse [prɛtrɛs] *n.f.* priestess.

prêtrise [pretriz] *n.f.* priesthood; **recevoir la p.,** to take (holy) orders.

preuve [prœv] *n.f.* (*a*) proof, evidence; token; **faire la p. de qch.,** to prove sth.; **faire p. d'intelligence,** to give proof of, to show, intelligence; **faire ses preuves,** to prove oneself; to show one's mettle; **cette méthode a fait ses preuves,** this method has stood the test of time; **fournir la p. contraire,** to produce proof to the contrary; **comme p.,** by way of proof; *F:* **le directeur est incapable, à p. le déficit de la maison,** the manager is incompetent, witness the firm's deficit; **à p. que . . .,** witness the fact that . . .; (*b*) *Jur:* **le soin, l'obligation, de faire la p.,** the onus, burden, of proof; **p. directe,** direct evidence; **p. indirecte,** circumstantial evidence; **preuves testimoniales,** (witnesses') evidence.

preux [prø] *A: & Lit:* **1.** *a.m.* gallant, valiant, doughty. **2.** *n.m.* valiant knight; champion.

prévaloir [prevalwar] *v.* (*conj. like* VALOIR, *except pr.sub.* **je prévale**) **1.** *v.i.* to prevail (**sur, contre,** over, against); **faire p. son droit,** to make good one's right; **faire p. son opinion,** to win acceptance for one's opinion. **2. se p. (de qch.),** to avail oneself, take advantage, of (sth.); to exercise (a right); to presume on (one's birth, wealth).

prévaricateur, -trice [prevarikatœr, -tris] **1.** *a.* unjust, dishonest (judge, etc.). **2.** *n.* unjust judge; betrayer of trust.

prévarication [prevarikasjɔ̃] *n.f.* breach of trust; maladministration.

prévariquer [prevarike] *v.i.* (*of judge, etc.*) to depart from justice; to betray one's trust.

prévenance [prɛvnɑ̃s] *n.f.* **1.** attention, kindness, consideration; thoughtfulness. **2. avoir des prévenances pour qn,** to be attentive to s.o.

prévenant [prɛvnɑ̃] *a.* **1.** kind, attentive, considerate (**envers,** to); thoughtful. **2.** pleasing, prepossessing (manner, appearance).

prévenir [prɛvnir] *v.tr.* (*conj. like* VENIR *but with aux.* AVOIR) **1.** (*a*) to forestall, anticipate (s.o., s.o.'s desires, etc.); (*b*) to prevent, ward off, stave off (illness, danger); to avert (accident); *Prov:* **mieux vaut p. que guérir,** prevention is better than cure. **2.** to predispose, bias; **p. qn en faveur de qn,** to predispose s.o. in favour, *NAm:* favor, of s.o.; **p. qn contre qn,** to prejudice s.o. against s.o.; **son visage prévient en sa faveur,** he has a prepossessing face. **3.** to inform, forewarn; **p. qn de qch.,** to give s.o. notice of sth.; **je vais le p. que vous êtes ici,** I'll let him know you're here; **on m'avait prévenu que la police était à mes trousses,** I had been warned that the police were after me; **vous auriez dû m'en p.,** you should have told me about it beforehand.

préventif, -ive [prevɑ̃tif, -iv] *a.* **1.** preventive (medicine, etc.); **à titre p.,** as a preventive; **exercer un effet p.,** to act as a deterrent; *Cards:* **ouverture préventive,** pre-emptive bid. **2.** *Jur:* **détention préventive,** detention awaiting trial, committal for trial; **être en détention préventive,** to be in custody.

prévention [prevɑ̃sjɔ̃] *n.f.* **1.** predisposition (**en faveur de,** in favour, *NAm:* favor, of); prejudice, bias (**contre,** against); **observateur sans p.,** unprejudiced, unbias(s)ed, observer. **2.** *Jur:* **être en état de p.,** to be in custody, committed for trial; **mise en p.,** committal for trial. **3.** prevention (of disease, etc.); **p. routière,** road safety (measures).

préventivement [prevɑ̃tivmɑ̃] *adv.* (*a*) *Jur:* **arrêter qn p.,** to arrest s.o. on suspicion; **détenu p.,** committed for trial; (*b*) as a preventive.

préventorium [prevɑ̃tɔrjɔm] *n.m.* observation sanatorium.

prévenu, -ue [prɛvny] **1.** *a.* prejudiced, predisposed, bias(s)ed. **2.** *Jur:* (*a*) *a.* **p. de vol,** accused of, charged with, theft; (*b*) *n.* **le p., la prévenue,** the prisoner, the accused.

prévisible [previzibl̥] *a.* foreseeable.

prévision [previzjɔ̃] *n.f.* anticipation, expectation; prevision; **en p. de qch.,** in the expectation, in anticipation, of sth.; **selon toute p.,** in all likelihood; **contre toute p.,** contrary to all expectations; **dépasser les prévisions,** to exceed all expectation; **p. du temps,** weather forecasting; **prévisions météorologiques,** weather forecast; *Fin:* **prévisions budgétaires,** budget estimates.

prévisionnel, -elle [previzjɔnɛl] *a.* estimated.

prévoir [prevwar] *v.tr.* (*conj. like* VOIR *except in fu. and condit.* **je prévoirai, je prévoirais**) **1.** to foresee, forecast, anticipate (events, etc.); **tout laisse prévoir . . .,** all signs point to . . .; **rien ne fait p. un changement de temps,** there appears to be no prospect of a change in the weather. **2.** to take measures beforehand; to provide for (sth.); **dépenses prévues au budget,** expenses provided for in the budget; **la loi n'a pas prévu un cas semblable,** the law makes no provision for a case of this kind; **la réunion est prévue pour demain,** the meeting is arranged, planned, scheduled, for tomorrow; **le personnel prévu dans le contrat,** the personnel laid down in the agreement; **on ne peut pas tout p.,** one cannot think of, provide for, everything; **p. des rectifications,** to allow for readjustments; **comme prévu,** as (was) planned; (*of ship*) **vitesse prévue,** designed speed; (*of lorry, etc.*) **charge prévue,** specified load.

prévôt [prevo] *n.m.* (*a*) *Hist: & Jur:* provost; (*b*) *Mil:* assistant provost marshal; **grand p.,** provost marshal; (*c*) *Fenc:* **p. de salle,** assistant fencing master.

prévoyance [prevwajɑ̃s] *n.f.* foresight, forethought; precaution; **fonds de p.,** contingency fund; reserve fund; **société de p.,** provident society.

prévoyant [prevwajɑ̃] *a.* provident; foreseeing; far-sighted (administration, etc.).

prie-Dieu [pridjø] *n.m.inv.* prie-dieu, prayer stool.

prier [prije] *v.* (*impf. & pr.sub.* **n. priions, v. priiez**) **1.** *v.tr.* (*a*) to pray to (God, etc.); **je prie Dieu qu'il en soit ainsi,** I pray (to) God that it may be so; (*b*) to beg, beseech, entreat; **elle a accepté l'invitation après s'être fait un peu p.,** she accepted the invitation after a little persuasion; **se faire p.,** to require a great deal of persuasion; **sans se faire p.,** readily, willingly; (*c*) to ask, request; **p. qn de faire qch.,** to ask s.o. to do sth.; **puis-je vous p. de vouloir bien fermer la porte?** would you be so kind as to close the door? **p. qn d'entrer,** to ask s.o. in; **p. qn de sortir,** (i) to ask s.o. to leave; (ii) to ask s.o. to come out; **dites-moi, je vous prie,** would you please tell me; **je vous en prie,** (i) please do! of course! (ii) please don't! (iii) (*when thanked for sth.*) it's, it was, a pleasure; *F:* that's all right! *NAm:* you're welcome! *Corr:* **je vous prie de bien vouloir recevoir l'assurance de mes sentiments les meilleurs,** yours sincerely; (*d*) *A: & Lit:* to invite (s.o.) (**à dîner,** to dinner); (*e*) (*formal invitation*) **Monsieur et Madame Hugo prient Monsieur et Madame Adam de leur faire l'honneur d'assister à . . .,** Mr and Mrs Hugo request the pleasure of Mr and Mrs Adam's company at . . .. **2.** *v.i.* to pray (**pour,** for).

prière [prijɛr] *n.f.* **1.** prayer; **faire, dire, ses prières,** to say one's prayers; **faire la p.,** to offer prayer; to pray (in common); **être en prières,** to be praying, at prayer; **p. avant le repas,** grace. **2.** request, entreaty; **être accessible aux prières,** to be open to requests; **à la p. de qn,** at s.o.'s request; **p. de ne pas fumer,** please do not smoke; **p. de fermer la porte,** please close the door.

prieur, -eure [prijœr] *n. Ecc:* prior, *f.* prioress.

prieuré [prijœre] *n.m.* **1.** priory. **2.** priorship.

primage [primaʒ] *n.m. Mch:* priming.

primaire [primɛr] **1.** *a.* (*a*) primary (school, etc.); *Jur:* **délinquant p.,** first offender; (*b*) *Pej:* (*of pers.*) of limited outlook. **2.** *n.m.* (*a*) *Sch:* primary education; (*b*) *Geol:* primary era; (*c*) *El:* primary (winding); (*d*) man of limited outlook.

primat [prima] *n.m. Ecc:* primate.

primate [primat] *n.m. Z:* primate.

primauté [primote] *n.f.* **1.** *Ecc: etc:* primacy. **2.** (*a*) priority; (*b*) lead (at cards, etc.).

prime¹ [prim] **1.** *a.* (*a*) *A: & Lit:* first; (*b*) **de p. abord,** to begin with; at first. **2.** *n.f.* (*a*) *Ecc:* prime; **chanter p.,** to sing the prime; (*b*) *Fenc:* prime.

prime² *n.f.* **1.** (*a*) *Fin: Ins:* premium; **faire p.,** to be at a premium; (*b*) *St.Exch:* **marché à p.,** (i) option (bargain); (ii) option market. **2.** (*a*) *Com: Adm: etc:* subsidy; grant; bonus; bounty; **p. de déménagement, de vie chère,** removal, cost-of-living, allowance; *Ind:* **p. de rendement,** productivity bonus; *Mil:* **p. de démobilisation,** demobilization gratuity; (*b*) *Com:* free gift.

primer¹ [prime] *v.tr. & i.* to excel, surpass; to take precedence over, of (s.o., sth.); to take the lead; **considération qui prime toutes les autres,** consideration of the first importance.

primer² *v.tr.* **1.** to award a prize to (cattle at show, etc.); **taureau primé,** prize bull; **roman primé,** prize-winning novel. **2.** to give, award, a bonus to (s.o., sth.); **industrie primée,** subsidized industry.

primerose [primroz] *n.f. Bot:* hollyhock.

primesautier, -ière [primsotje, -jɛr] *a.* impulsive, spontaneous; ready, quick.

primeur [primœr] *n.f.* **1.** (*a*) *A: & Lit:* newness, freshness; (*b*) **avoir la p. d'une nouvelle,** to be the first to hear a piece of news. **2. cultiver des primeurs,** to grow early produce, early vegetables (and, or, fruit).

primevère [primvɛr] *n.f. Bot:* primula; **p. à grandes fleurs,** primrose; **p. officinale,** mountain primrose; **p. commune,** cowslip; **p. des jardins,** polyanthus.

primitif, -ive [primitif, -iv] *a.* **1.** (*a*) primitive, primeval, original, earliest; **couleurs primitives,** primary colours, *NAm:* colors; *Gram:* **temps primitifs,** primary tenses; *n.m. Art:* **les primitifs,** the primitives; the early masters; (*b*) first, original; **la question primitive,** the original question. **2.** primitive, crude (methods, customs, etc.).

primitivement [primitivmɑ̃] *adv.* originally.

primo [primo] *adv.* firstly, in the first place.

primogéniture [primɔʒenityr] *n.f.* primogeniture.

primordial, -aux [primɔrdjal, -o] *a.* (*a*) primordial; primeval; (*b*) **d'une nécessité primordiale,** of prime necessity.

prince [prɛ̃s] *n.m.* prince; **p. héritier, royal, impérial,** crown prince; **p. consort,** prince consort; **le p. des ténèbres,** the prince of darkness; **être bon p.,** to be generous, openhanded.

princeps [prɛ̃sɛps] *a.inv.* **édition p.,** first edition.

princesse [prɛ̃sɛs] *n.f.* princess; **p. royale,** princess royal; *F:* **aux frais de la p.,** at government, the firm's, expense; on the house.

princier, -ière [prɛ̃sje, -jɛr] *a.* princely.

princièrement [prɛ̃sjɛrmɑ̃] *adv.* like a prince, in princely fashion; royally.

principal, -aux [prɛ̃sipal, -o] **1.** *a.* principal, chief, leading (person, thing); **associé p.,** senior partner; **agent p.,** head agent; **but p.,** main object; **un des principaux actionnaires,** a major shareholder; *Gram:* **proposition principale,** main clause; **chaudière principale,** main boiler (of ship, etc.); *El:* **câble p.,** main cable. **2.** *n.m.* (*a*) principal, chief; headmaster, head (of college, etc.); senior partner (of a business); (lawyer's) head clerk; (*b*) principal thing, main thing, main point; **le p. est de réussir,** the great thing is to succeed; (*c*) *Com:* principal; capital sum.

principalement [prɛ̃sipalmɑ̃] *adv.* principally.

principauté [prɛ̃sipote] *n.f.* principality.

principe [prɛ̃sip] *n.m.* principle. **1. aboutir à un accord de p.,** to reach an agreement in principle; **p. de nos actions,** mainspring of our actions. **2. les principes de la géométrie,** the principles of geometry; **poser qch. en p.,** to lay sth. down as a principle. **3.** *Ch:* element, constituent (of a substance); **p. actif,** active principle, constituent. **4.** rule of conduct; **par p.,** on principle; **en p.,** in principle; theoretically, in theory; **avoir des principes,** to have (high) principles; **avoir pour p. de . . .,** to make it a matter of principle to . . .; **sans principes,** unprincipled.

printanier, -ière [prɛ̃tanje, -jɛr] *a.* spring (flowers, etc.); spring-like (temperature, etc.).

printemps [prɛ̃tɑ̃] *n.m.* spring; springtime; **au p.,** in (the) spring; *Fr.C: F:* **avoir la fièvre du p.,** to have spring fever.

prioritaire [priɔritɛr] (*a*) *n.* priority holder; **être p.,** to have priority; (*b*) *a.* **droits prioritaires,** priority rights; *Fin:* **action p.,** preference share; **le véhicule venant de la droite est p.,** the vehicle coming from the right has (the) right of way, has priority.

priorité [priɔrite] *n.f.* priority; **droits de p.,** priority rights; *Fin:* **actions de p.,** preference shares; **réclamer la p.,** to claim the right to speak first; **avoir la p. sur,** to take priority, precedence, over; *Aut:* **p. (de passage),** right of way; priority; **route à p.,** major road; *P.N:* **p. à droite** = give way (to vehicles coming from the right).

pris [pri] *a.* **1.** (*a*) (*of seat, etc.*) occupied, taken; **tout est p.,** everything is booked; **avoir les mains prises,** to have one's hands full; (*b*) (*of pers.*) engaged; occupied; busy; **je suis très p. ce matin,** I'm very busy this morning. **2.** (*a*) **p. de peur,** panic-stricken; seized with fear; **p. de remords,** smitten with remorse; **p. de**

colère, in a rage; **p. de boisson,** under the influence of alcohol; the worse for drink; (*b*) **avoir le nez p.,** to have a blocked nose; **avoir la gorge prise,** to have a sore throat. **3.** (*of pers., figure*) well proportioned, shapely; (*of pers.*) well built. **4.** (*of jelly, etc.*) set; (*of river, etc.*) frozen (over).

prise [priz] *n.f.* **1.** hold, grasp, grip; (*a*) **trouver (une) p. à, sur, qch.,** to get a grip, a hold, on sth.; to gain a purchase on sth.; **avoir p. sur qn,** to have a hold on, over, s.o.; **lâcher p.,** to lose one's hold, let go; **donner p. aux reproches,** to lay oneself open to reproaches; **je n'avais pas de p. (pour me hisser, etc.),** I had no purchase (with which to pull myself up, etc.); (*b*) *Wr: etc:* hold; (*c*) **être, en venir, aux prises avec qn, qch.,** to come to grips, grapple, with s.o., sth.; **mettre aux prises des intérêts,** to bring interests into conflict; (*d*) *Mec.E:* engagement, mesh(ing); **en p.,** in gear, engaged; **mettre en p.,** to engage, put into gear; *Aut:* **en p. (directe),** in top (gear); **p. directe,** direct drive; *Fig:* **en p. (directe) sur, avec, qch.,** in touch, in contact, with sth.; **hors de p.,** out of gear. **2.** solidification, congealing, setting; **ciment à p. rapide,** quick-setting cement; (*of cement*) **faire p.,** to set. **3.** (*a*) taking (up); capture, seizure (of town, prisoners, etc.); *Mil: etc:* **p. d'armes,** parade under arms; *Jur:* **p. de corps,** arrest; **la p. de la Bastille,** the fall of the Bastille; **p. de colis à domicile,** collection of parcels; **p. de vues,** taking of photographs; *Cin: T.V:* shooting; *Cin: T.V:* **p. de vue,** shot; take; *T.V:* **p. de vues en direct,** live broadcast; *Cin: T.V:* **p. de son,** sound recording; (*b*) *Nau:* prize; **être de bonne p.,** to be (a) lawful prize; **part de p.,** prize money; **cour des prises,** prize court; **équipage de p.,** prize crew. **4.** (*thg taken*) catch (of fish); dose (of medicine); pinch (of snuff); sample (of ore, etc.); *Med:* **faire une p. de sang,** to take a blood sample. **5.** *Mch: etc:* **p. d'air,** (i) ventilation aperture; (ii) *I.C.E:* air intake, inlet; (iii) *Aer:* air scoop; **p. de vapeur,** steamcock, steam valve, injection cock; **p. d'eau,** (i) intake of water; (ii) cock, tap, valve; (fire) hydrant; (iii) water catchment; (iv) offtake (of canal, from river, etc.); *El:* **p. de courant,** (i) plug; (ii) socket, plug; (power) point; (iii) current collector (of trolley); **p. de bobine,** coil tap; **p. de terre,** earth, *NAm:* ground (connection); **faire une p. à une rivière,** *El:* **sur un câble,** to tap a river, *El:* a cable.

prisée [prize] *n.f. Jur:* valuation (of goods).

priser¹ [prize] *v.tr. & i.* to snuff (sth.) up (through the nose); to take snuff; **tabac à p.,** snuff.

priser² *v.tr.* (*a*) *A:* to appraise, value (goods); (*b*) *Lit:* to set a (high) value on sth.; to prize, value.

priseur¹, -euse [prizœr, -øz] *n.* snuff taker.

priseur² *n.m.* (official) valuer; auctioneer.

prismatique [prismatik] *a.* prismatic.

prisme [prism] *n.m.* prism; **jumelles à p.,** prism(atic) binoculars.

prison [prizɔ̃] *n.f.* **1.** prison, gaol, jail; **être, aller, en p.,** to be in, to go to, prison, jail; **s'échapper de p.,** to break prison; **tenir qn en p.,** to keep s.o. imprisoned; *A:* **p. pour dettes,** debtors' prison. **2.** imprisonment; **faire de la p.,** to be in prison; to serve a prison sentence; **cinq ans de p.,** five years' imprisonment; *Mil:* **trois jours de p.,** three days' cells, *F:* three days in the glasshouse.

prisonnier, -ière [prizɔnje, -jɛr] **1.** *n.* prisoner; **p. de guerre,** prisoner of war; **camp de prisonniers (de guerre),** prison camp; prisoner-of-war camp; **faire qn p.,** to take s.o. prisoner; **se constituer p.,** to give oneself up; **il a été emmené p.,** he was remanded in custody. **2.** *a.* imprisoned, in prison; captive.

privatif, -ive [privatif, -iv] *Gram:* (*a*) *a.* privative; (*b*) *n.m.* privative prefix.

privation [privasjɔ̃] *n.f.* **1.** deprivation, deprival; loss; **p. de la vue,** loss of sight. **2.** privation, hardship; **s'imposer des privations,** to deprive oneself.

privautés [privote] *n.f.pl.* (undue) familiarity; **prendre des p. avec qn,** to take liberties, be overfamiliar, with s.o.

privé [prive] **1.** *a.* private (individual, enterprise, etc.); **se réunir en séance privée,** to sit in private; **renseignements privés,** inside information; **visite privée,** unofficial visit; *Hist:* **le Conseil p.,** the Privy Council. **2.** *n.m.* private life; *Ind:* **le p.,** the private sector; **parler à qn en p.,** to speak to s.o. in private; **connaître qn dans le p.,** to know s.o. in private life.

priver [prive] **1.** *v.tr.* **p. qn de qch.,** to deprive s.o. of sth.; (*to child*) **tu seras privé de dessert,** you'll have to go without your pudding; **je ne vous en prive pas?** can you spare it? **2. se p. de qch.,** to do, to go, without sth.; to go short of sth.; to deprive oneself of sth.; to deny oneself sth.

privilège [privilɛʒ] *n.m.* **1.** privilege; (*a*) **c'est là un p. de la vieillesse,** that is a prerogative of old age; **jouir du p., avoir le p., de faire qch.,** to be privileged to do sth., enjoy the privilege of doing sth.; *Iron:* **il a le p. de me déplaire,** I have a particular dislike for him; (*b*) licence, grant; charter (of bank). **2.** *Jur:* preferential claim.

privilégié, -ée [privileʒje] **1.** *a.* (*a*) privileged; (*b*) licensed; **banque privilégiée,** chartered bank; (*c*) **créancier p.,** preferential creditor; **action privilégiée,** preference share. **2.** *n.* privileged person; **quelques privilégiés l'ont vu,** a privileged few have seen it.

privilégier [privileʒje] *v.tr.* (*pr.sub. & impf.* **n. privilégiions, v. privilégiiez**) to privilege.

prix [pri] *n.m.* **1.** (*a*) value, worth, cost; **à tout p.,** at all costs; at any price; **faire qch. à p. d'argent,** to do sth. for money; (*of goods*) **se vendre à p. d'or,** to fetch huge prices; **à aucun p.,** not on any terms, not at any price; **au p. de,** (i) at the price of; (ii) in comparison with; **au p. de sa vie,** at the cost, expense, of his life; **attacher beaucoup de p., un grand p., à qch.,** to set a high value on sth.; to set great store by sth.; to prize sth. highly; (*b*) price; **acheter qch. à bas p., à juste p.,** to buy sth. at a low price, a fair price; **p. de vente,** selling price; **p. au comptant,** cash price; **p. courant,** current price, market price; **p. initial,** prime cost; **à, au, p. coûtant, au p. de revient,** at cost price; **p. de gros,** wholesale price; **p. de détail,** retail price; **vous pouvez l'acheter si vous y mettez le p.,** you can buy it at a price; **faire un p. à qn,** to quote s.o. a price; **je vous ferai un p. (d'ami),** I'll let you have it cheap; **une voiture dans mes p.,** a car I can afford, within my means; **c'est plutôt dans mes p.,** that's more in my line; *St.Exch:* **actions cotées au p. de . . .,** shares quoted at the rate of . . .; (*in restaurant*) **(repas à) p. fixe,** set (price) meal; **articles de p.,** expensive goods; **coûter un p. fou,** to cost the earth; **c'est hors de p.,** the price is prohibitive; **ne pas avoir de p.,** to be priceless; **mettre à p. la tête de qn,** to put a price on s.o.'s head; **mise à p. d'une propriété,** upset price of an estate; (*at auction*) **mise à p.,** reserve price (of article); (*c*) charge; **p. d'un voyage,** fare. **2.** (*a*) prize; reward; **avoir, remporter, le p.,** to win, carry off, the prize; **le p. Nobel,** the Nobel Prize; **distribution des p.,** prizegiving; *Sch:* speech day; **livre de p.,** prize book; (*b*) **un p. Nobel,** a Nobel prizewinner; (*c*) prizewinning work, *usu.* book; (*d*) *Sp:* race.

prix-courant [prikurɑ̃] *n.m. Com:* price list; catalogue; *pl. prix-courants.*

pro [pro] *n.m.inv. Sp: etc: F:* professional, pro.

probabilité [prɔbabilite] *n.f.* probability, likelihood; **selon toute p.,** in all likelihood, most probably.

probable [prɔbabl̩] *a.* probable, likely; **il est p. qu'elle viendra,** she'll probably come; **peu p.,** improbable, unlikely; **il est peu p., il n'est pas p., qu'elle vienne,** she's not likely, she's unlikely, to come; **c'est très p.,** (it's) very likely; **c'est plus que p.,** it's more than likely.

probablement [prɔbabləmɑ̃] *adv.* probably.

probant [prɔbɑ̃] *a.* probative, convincing, conclusive (evidence, etc.); **peu p.,** unconvincing.

probation [prɔbasjɔ̃] *n.f. Ecc:* probation.

probatoire [prɔbatwar] *a.* probative; *Sch:* **examen p.,** grading examination.

probe [prɔb] *a. Lit:* honest, upright.

probité [prɔbite] *n.f.* probity, integrity.

problématique [prɔblematik] *a.* problematic(al); questionable (morals, etc.).

problématiquement [prɔblematikmɑ̃] *adv.* problematically.

problème [prɔblɛm] *n.m.* problem; *Sch:* **faire des problèmes,** to do sums; *F:* **il n'y a pas de p.,** (i) that's easy, simple; (ii) naturally! of course! certainly!

procédé [prɔsede] *n.m.* **1.** proceeding, dealing, conduct; **procédés honnêtes,** (i) courteous behaviour, *NAm:* behavior; (ii) square dealing; **échange de bons procédés,** exchange (i) of courtesies, of civilities, (ii) of friendly services; **c'est un échange de bons procédés,** one good turn deserves another. **2.** process; method (of working); **p. de travail,** operating procedure; **p. de fabrication,** manufacturing process. **3.** tip (of billiard cue).

procéder [prɔsede] *v.* (*conj. like* CÉDER) **1.** *v.i.* (*a*) to proceed (**de,** from); to originate (**de,** in); **sa maladie procède de l'intempérie du climat,** his illness arises from the bad climate; (*b*) to proceed, act; **p. avec méthode,** to proceed methodically. **2.** *v.ind.tr.* **p. à une enquête,** to institute, initiate, an enquiry.

procédure [prɔsedyr] *n.f.* **1.** *Jur: etc:* procedure; **terme de p.,** law, legal, term. **2.** *Jur:* proceedings.

procédurier, -ière [prɔsedyrje, -jɛr] **1.** *a.* pettifogging (lawyer, etc.); quibbling. **2.** *n.* pettifogger; quibbler.

procès [prɔsɛ] *n.m.* **1.** (legal) proceedings; action at law; cause, case; **p. civil,** lawsuit; **p. criminel,** (criminal) trial; **engager un p.,** to engage in a lawsuit; **faire, intenter, un p. à qn,** (i) to bring an action against s.o.; to institute proceedings against s.o.; to sue s.o.; (ii) to prosecute s.o.; **être en p. avec qn,** to be at law with s.o.; **intenter un p. en divorce à qn,** to institute divorce proceedings against s.o.; **gagner, perdre, son p.,** to win, lose, one's case; **faire le p. de qn, qch.,** to criticize s.o., sth.; **sans autre forme de p.,** without (any) further ceremony; without further ado; out of hand. **2.** *Anat:* process.

procession [prɔsesjɔ̃] *n.f.* procession; **aller en p.,** to go, walk, in procession.

processionnaire [prɔsesjɔnɛr] *a. & n.f. Ent:* **(chenille) p.,** processionary caterpillar.

processionnel, -elle [prɔsesjɔnɛl] *a.* processional (hymn, march).

processionnellement [prɔsesjɔnɛlmɑ̃] *adv.* in procession.

processus [prɔsesys] *n.m.* **1.** *Anat:* process. **2.** (*a*) progress, course, process; (*b*) method, process; **le p. est toujours le même,** the method of operation, the process, is always the same.

procès-verbal [prɔsɛvɛrbal] *n.m.* **1.** (official) report; proceedings, minute(s) (of meeting); record (of evidence, etc.); **registre des p.-verbaux,** minute book. **2.** policeman's report (about an offence); (*of policeman*) **dresser le p.-v. d'une contravention, dresser (un) p.-v., à, contre, qn** = to report, *F:* book, s.o.; *pl. procès-verbaux.*

prochain [prɔʃɛ̃] **1.** *a.* (*a*) nearest (village, etc.); **cause prochaine,** proximate cause, immediate cause; (*b*) next; **dimanche p.,** next Sunday; **la semaine prochaine,** next week; **le p. numéro,** the next number (of magazine); (*c*) near at hand; **une auberge prochaine,** a neighbouring, *NAm:* neighboring, inn; **son p. départ, son départ p.,** his approaching, impending, departure; **dans un avenir p.,** in the near future, before long. **2.** *n.m.* neighbour, *NAm:* neighbor; fellow being.

prochainement [prɔʃɛnmɑ̃] *adv.* shortly, soon.

proche [prɔʃ] **1.** *adv.* **tout p.,** close at hand; nearby, close by; **de p. en p.,** step by step, by degrees; **p. de mourir,** near(ing) death; **p. de la ruine,** on the verge of ruin. **2.** *a.* near (**de,** to); neighbouring, *NAm:* neighboring; **la ville la plus p.,** the nearest town; **l'italien est p. du français,** Italian is close to French; **l'heure est p.,** the hour is at hand; **ses proches (parents),** his close, near, relations; his next of kin; **ils sont proches parents,** they are closely related.

Proche-Orient (le) [ləprɔʃɔrjɑ̃] *Pr.n.m. Geog:* the Near East.

proclamateur, -trice [prɔklamatœr, -tris] *n.* proclaimer.

proclamation [prɔklamasjɔ̃] *n.f.* proclamation.

proclamer [prɔklame] *v.tr.* to proclaim, declare, publish; **p. le résultat du scrutin,** to declare the poll; **on proclama que . . .,** it was given out that . . .; **p. qn roi,** to proclaim s.o. king.

proclitique [prɔklitik] *a. & n.m. Ling:* proclitic.

proconsul [prɔkɔ̃syl] *n.m. Hist:* proconsul.

proconsulaire [prɔkɔ̃sylɛr] *a.* proconsular.

proconsulat [prɔkɔ̃syla] *n.m. Hist:* proconsulate.

procréateur, -trice [prɔkreatœr, -tris] **1.** *a.* procreative. **2.** *n.* procreator.

procréation [prɔkreasjɔ̃] *n.f.* procreation, begetting.

procréer [prɔkree] *v.tr.* to procreate, beget.

procurateur [prɔkyratœr] *n.m. Hist:* procurator.

procuration [prɔkyrasjɔ̃] *n.f. Com: Fin: Jur:* procuration, proxy, power of attorney; **par p.,** by proxy; per pro(curationem); **voter par p.,** to vote by proxy; **donner (la) p. à qn,** to confer powers of attorney on s.o.

procurer [prɔkyre] *v.tr. & pr.* **p. qch. à qn,** to procure, obtain, get, sth. for s.o.; **se p. de l'argent,** to raise, obtain, find, money; **où peut-on se p. ce livre?** where can one get this book? **impossible à se p.,** unobtainable.

procureur, procuratrice [prɔkyrœr, prɔkyratris] **1.** *n. Jur:* procurator, proxy. **2.** *n.m. Jur:* (*a*) *A:* attorney (at law); (*b*) **p. de la République** = public prosecutor, *U.S:* district attorney; **p. général** = Attorney General.

prodigalement [prɔdigalmɑ̃] *adv.* prodigally; lavishly.

prodigalité [prɔdigalite] *n.f.* prodigality, lavishness; wealth (of detail); extravagance.

prodige [prɔdiʒ] *n.m.* prodigy, wonder, marvel; **faire des prodiges,** to do, work, wonders; **tenir du p.,** to be extraordinary, inexplicable; **c'est un p.,** (i) he's a prodigy; (ii) it's prodigious; *a.* **enfant p.,** child prodigy.

prodigieusement [prɔdiʒjøzmɑ̃] *adv.* prodigiously.

prodigieux, -euse [prɔdiʒjø, -øz] *a.* prodigious, extraordinary; phenomenal, stupendous.

prodigue [prɔdig] *a. & n.* prodigal. **1.** *a.* (*a*) lavish, unsparing (**de,** of); **p. d'excuses,** profuse in apologies; **être p. de son argent,** to spend lavishly; to be free with one's money; (*b*) wasteful, spendthrift; *B:* **l'enfant p.,** the prodigal son. **2.** *n.* spendthrift, squanderer.

prodiguer [prɔdige] **1.** *v.tr.* (*a*) to be prodigal, lavish, of (sth.); **p. qch. à qn,** to lavish sth. on s.o.; **p. sa santé,** to be unsparing of one's health; (*b*) to waste, squander. **2. se p.** (*a*) to lay oneself out to please; (*b*) **se p. en éloges,** to be lavish of praise; (*c*) **le médecin se prodigue pour ses malades,** the doctor does not spare himself to help his patients.

prodrome [prɔdrom] *n.m.* premonitory symptom (of disease); preamble (to a treatise).

producteur, -trice [prɔdyktœr, -tris] **1.** *a.* productive (**de,** of); producing; **pays p. de blé,** wheat-growing country. **2.** (*a*) *n.* producer; (*b*) *n.m. Cin:* producer; backer.

productible [prɔdyktibḷ] *a.* producible.

productif, -ive [prɔdyktif, -iv] *a.* productive.

production [prɔdyksjɔ̃] *n.f.* **1.** production; (*a*) *Jur: etc:* exhibiting; **p. des pièces,** exhibition of documents; (*b*) producing; generation (of electricity, etc.); **augmenter la p.,** to increase production, output; *Cin:* **directeur de p.,** producer. **2.** (*a*) product; *pl.* produce; **p. littéraire,** literary output; **p. du génie,** work of genius; (*b*) yield (of mine, etc.); output (of factory).

productivité [prɔdyktivite] *n.f.* productivity, productiveness; productive capacity.

produire [prɔdɥir] *v.* (*pr.p.* **produisant;** *p.p.* **produit;** *pr.ind.* **je produis, n. produisons;** *impf.* **je produisais;** *p.h.* **je produisis;** *fu.* **je produirai**) **1.** *v.tr.* (*a*) *Jur: etc:* to produce, bring forward, adduce (evidence, etc.); (*b*) to produce, yield; to bring forth, bear (offspring, etc.); to generate (heat, etc.); **argent qui produit de l'intérêt,** money that yields interest; **p. cent voitures par jour,** to produce, turn out, a hundred cars a day; (*c*) to produce, bring about (result, effect); **p. une impression favorable,** to produce, create, make, a favourable, *NAm:* favorable, impression; (*d*) *Cin: etc:* to produce (film, etc.). **2. se p.** (*a*) to occur, happen, arise; to take place; to come into being; **il pourrait se p. des incidents,** there might be trouble; (*b*) (*of actor, etc.*) to appear.

produit [prɔdɥi] *n.m.* **1.** (*a*) product; produce; **produits agricoles,** agricultural produce; **produits de marque,** branded goods; **p. manufacturé,** manufactured article; **produits chimiques,** chemicals; **produits de beauté,** beauty preparations; cosmetics; *Pol.Ec:* **p. national brut,** gross national product; (*b*) yield; **p. d'une vente,** proceeds of a sale; *Com:* **le p. de la journée,** the day's takings, receipts; **le p. de dix années de travail,** the product, result, of ten years' work. **2.** *Mth:* product (of multiplication).

proéminence [prɔeminɑ̃s] *n.f.* **1.** prominence. **2.** protuberance.

proéminent [prɔeminɑ̃] *a.* prominent, projecting, protuberant.

prof [prɔf] *n. F:* (= PROFESSEUR) (school)teacher; (university) (i) professor, prof, (ii) lecturer.

profanateur, -trice [prɔfanatœr, -tris] *n.* profaner; desecrator.

profanation [prɔfanasjɔ̃] *n.f.* profanation; desecration; violation (of grave, etc.).

profane [prɔfan] **1.** *a.* profane; secular (music, etc.); unhallowed. **2.** *n.* uninitiated person; layman.

profaner [prɔfane] *v.tr.* **1.** to profane; to desecrate (church, etc.); to violate (grave, etc.). **2.** to misuse, degrade (one's talent, etc.).

proférer [prɔfere] *v.tr.* (**je profère; je proférerai**) to utter; **sans p. une (seule) parole,** without a word.

profès, -esse [prɔfɛ, -ɛs] *a. & n. Ecc:* professed (monk, nun).

professer [prɔfese] *v.tr.* **1.** to profess (religion, opinion); to hold (views). **2.** to teach; **il professe la physique au lycée,** he teaches physics at the *lycée*; **il professe à la Sorbonne,** he's (i) a professor, (ii) a lecturer, at the Sorbonne.

professeur [prɔfɛsœr] *n.m.* (school)teacher; (school)-master, *f.* (school)mistress; (*at university*) (i) professor; (ii) lecturer; don; **elle est p. de piano,** she teaches the piano; **p. principal, de classe,** form teacher, master, mistress; **p. de chant,** singing teacher, master, mistress; **p. de natation,** swimming instructor.

profession [prɔfɛsjɔ̃] *n.f.* **1. p. de foi,** profession of faith; *Ecc:* **faire sa p. (dans un ordre),** to make one's profession (in an order); **faire p. de qch.,** to profess sth. **2.** profession, occupation; calling; business, trade; **p. libérale,** (liberal) profession; **médecin de (sa) p.,** doctor by profession; **menuisier de p.,** carpenter by trade; **ballerine de p.,** professional ballet dancer; *Adm:* **femme sans p.** = housewife.

professionnalisme [prɔfɛsjɔnalism] *n.m.* professionalism.

professionnel, -elle [prɔfɛsjɔnɛl] **1.** *a.* (*a*) professional; vocational (training, etc.); **maladies professionnelles,** occupational diseases; **syndicat p.,** trade association; (*b*) professional (footballer, etc.); **écrivain p.,** writer by profession. **2.** *n.* (*a*) *esp. Sp:* professional; (*b*) *Ind: etc:* skilled worker.

professionnellement [prɔfɛsjɔnɛlmɑ̃] *adv.* professionally.

professoral, -aux [prɔfɛsɔral, -o] *a.* professorial.

professorat [prɔfɛsɔra] *n.m.* **1.** teaching post; (*at university*) professorship. **2.** *coll.* professoriate; teaching profession; **choisir le p.,** to chose teaching as one's profession.

profil [prɔfil] *n.m.* **1.** profile; **dessiner qn de p.,** to draw s.o. in profile; **vue de p.,** side view. **2.** profile, contour, outline, section; **p. en travers,** cross section; **p. de l'horizon,** skyline.

profilage [prɔfilaʒ] *n.m.* (*a*) profiling; (*b*) *Metalw:* shaping; (*c*) streamlining (of car body, etc.).

profilé [prɔfile] **1.** *a.* (*a*) streamlined (car, etc.); (*b*) *Metalw: etc:* **pièce profilée,** shaped piece; **fers profilés,** sectional irons, iron sections. **2.** *n.m. Metalw:* extrusion; **profilés en acier,** steel sections; sectional steel.

profiler [prɔfile] **1.** *v.tr.* (*a*) to profile; to draw (sth.) in section; (*b*) to shape (a piece); (*c*) to streamline (car, etc.). **2. se p.,** to stand out in profile, to be outlined, to be silhouetted (**à, sur, contre,** on, against).

profit [prɔfi] *n.m.* profit, benefit; **profits et pertes,** profit and loss; **faire (son) p. de qch.,** to profit by sth.; **vendre à p.,** to sell at a profit; **mettre qch. à p.,** to turn sth. to (good) account; **tirer p. de qch.,** (i) to take advantage of, derive benefit from, sth.; (ii) to make use of sth.; **j'en ai eu peu de p.,** I gained little advantage from it; **travail sans p.,** unprofitable, profitless, work; **au p. de qn,** on behalf of, for the benefit of, s.o.; **au p. des pauvres,** in aid of the poor; **les socialistes perdront au p. des communistes,** votes will swing from the Socialists to the Communists.

profitable [prɔfitabḷ] *a.* profitable; advantageous; beneficial.

profitablement [prɔfitabləmɑ̃] *adv.* profitably.

profiter [prɔfite] *v.i.* **1.** (*a*) **p. de qch.,** to take advantage of sth.; to turn sth. to (good) account; to (derive) benefit from sth.; **p. de l'occasion,** to seize the opportunity; **il a profité de ce que tout le monde dormait encore pour s'esquiver,** he took advantage of the fact that everyone was still asleep to slip away; (*b*) **p. sur une vente,** to make a profit on a sale. **2. p. à qn,** to be profitable to s.o.; to benefit s.o.; to be, turn out, to s.o.'s advantage; to be of benefit to s.o. **3.** *F:* (*of child, plant, etc.*) to thrive, grow.

profiterole [prɔfitrɔl] *n.f. Cu:* profiterole.

profiteur, -euse [prɔfitœr, -øz] *n.* profiteer.

profond [prɔfɔ̃] **1.** *a.* (*a*) deep; **puits p. de six mètres,** well six metres, *NAm:* meters, deep; **révérence profonde,** low, deep, bow; **voix profonde,** deep voice; **peu p.,** shallow; (*b*) deep-seated; underlying (cause, etc.); (*c*) profound (wisdom, scholarship, etc.); thorough (knowledge, etc.); deep, sound (sleep); **p. soupir,** heavy sigh; **p. dégoût,** deep disgust. **2.** *adv.* **creuser p.,** to dig deep. **3.** *n.m.* **au plus p. de mon cœur,** in the depths of my heart, in my heart of hearts; **au plus p. de la nuit,** at dead of night.

profondément [prɔfɔ̃demɑ̃] *adv.* profoundly, deeply; **dormir p.,** to sleep soundly; **p. endormi,** sound, fast, asleep; **s'incliner p.,** to make a deep, low, bow.

profondeur [prɔfɔ̃dœr] *n.f.* **1.** depth (of water, etc.); deepness (of voice, etc.); **avoir dix mètres de p.,** to be ten metres, *NAm:* meters, deep, ten metres in depth; **en p.,** in depth; **peu de p.,** shallowness. **2.** profoundness, profundity (of knowledge, etc.); depth (of feeling).

profus [prɔfy] *a. Lit:* profuse.

profusément [prɔfyzemɑ̃] *adv. Lit:* profusely.

profusion [prɔfyzjɔ̃] *n.f.* (*a*) profusion, profuseness; abundance; wealth (of detail, etc.); **à p.,** in profusion; **des bouteilles à p.,** bottles galore; (*b*) lavishness.

progéniture [prɔʒenityr] *n.f.* progeny, progeniture, offspring.

prognathe [prɔgnat] *a. Anthr:* prognathous, prognathic; underhung, undershot (jaw).

programmateur, -trice [prɔgramatœr, -tris] *n.* (*pers.*) programme planner.

programmation [prɔgramasjɔ̃] *n.f.* (*a*) *T.V: etc:* programme planning; (*b*) *Cmptr:* programming.

programme [prɔgram] *n.m.* (*a*) programme, *NAm:* program (of concert, etc.); **hors p.,** not on, in, the programme; (*b*) *Sch:* **p. (d'études),** curriculum; syllabus; **les auteurs au, du, p.,** the set books; (*c*) programme, platform (of political party); (*d*) *Cmptr:* program(me).

programmer [prɔgrame] *v.tr. Cmptr: T.V: etc:* to program(me).

programmeur, -euse [prɔgramœr, -øz] *n. Cmptr:* (*pers.*) programmer.

progrès [prɔgrɛ] *n.m.* progress; (*a*) advance (of army, etc.); spread(ing) (of epidemic, etc.); **la maladie fait du p.,** the disease is making progress, is making headway; (*b*) advancement, improvement; (*of pupil, etc.*) **faire des p.,** to make progress, improve, get on well; **le malade fait des p. satisfaisants,** the patient is progressing satisfactorily; **la science a fait de grands p.,** science has made great strides forward; **suivre les p. d'une science,** to keep abreast of a science; **suivre les p. d'une affaire,** to keep track of a matter; *Pol:* **parti du p.,** progressive party.

progresser [prɔgrese] *v.i.* (*a*) to progress, advance; to make (head)way; to gain ground; (*b*) to improve.

progressif, -ive [prɔgresif, -iv] *a.* progressive; gradual (growth, etc.); **impôt p.,** graduated tax.

progression [prɔgrɛsjɔ̃] *n.f.* **1.** progress(ion); moving forward; advance(ment). **2.** *Mth:* **p. arithmétique,** arithmetical progression; *Mus:* **p. harmonique,** harmonic progression.

progressiste [prɔgresist] *a. & n.* progressive.

progressivement [prɔgresivmɑ̃] *adv.* progressively.

progressivité [prɔgresivite] *n.f.* progressiveness.

prohiber [prɔibe] *v.tr.* to prohibit, forbid; **p. à qn de faire qch.,** to prohibit s.o. from doing sth.; **p. le tabac à qn,** to forbid s.o. tobacco; **marchandises prohibées,** prohibited goods; **temps prohibé,** close season (for hunting, etc.).

prohibitif, -ive [prɔibitif, -iv] *a.* **1.** prohibitory (law, etc.). **2.** prohibitive (price, etc.).

prohibition [prɔibisjɔ̃] *n.f.* prohibition.

prohibitionnisme [prɔibisjɔnism] *n.m. Pol.Ec: etc:* prohibition(ism).

prohibitionniste [prɔibisjɔnist] *a. & n. Pol.Ec: etc:* prohibitionist.

proie [prwa] *n.f.* prey; *Ven:* quarry; **oiseau de p.,** bird of prey; (*of animal*) **faire sa p. de qch.,** to prey on sth.; **être la p. de qn, de qch.,** to be the prey, the victim, of s.o., sth.; **être en p. aux remords,** to be (a) prey to remorse; to be tormented by remorse; **tomber en p. à la tentation,** to fall prey to temptation.

projecteur [prɔʒɛktœr] *n.m.* (*a*) (slide, film) projector; (*b*) searchlight; floodlight (on building, etc.); *Th:* spotlight; **illuminé par des projecteurs,** floodlit.

projectif, -ive [prɔʒɛktif, -iv] *a.* projective.

projectile [prɔʒɛktil] *n.m.* projectile; missile.

projection [prɔʒɛksjɔ̃] *n.f.* **1.** (*a*) projection; throwing forward, up, out (of heavy body, etc.); sp(l)atter(ing), splash(ing) (of liquid); *Geol:* **projections volcaniques,** (volcanic) ejecta; (*b*) *Cin: etc:* projection; **appareil de p.,** (slide, film) projector; **cabine de p.,** projection room; **p. par transparence,** rear projection; **conférence avec projections,** lecture (illustrated) with slides; (*c*) beam (of light). **2.** *Mth: Arch: etc:* projection, plan; **p. horizontale,** ground plan.

projectionniste [prɔʒɛksjɔnist] *n. Cin:* projectionist.

projet [prɔʒɛ] *n.m.* (*a*) plan, project; scheme; **faire des projets,** to make plans; **faire, former, un p.,** to make, devise, a plan; to concoct a scheme; **former le p. de faire qch.,** to plan to do sth.; (*b*) plan (of building, etc.); blueprint; rough sketch, preliminary design; draft (of novel, etc.); **p. de contrat,** draft agreement; **p. de loi,** (draft) bill; **à l'état de p.,** at the planning stage.

projeter [prɔʒte] *v.* (*conj. like* JETER) **1.** *v.tr.* (*a*) to project; to throw, cast (shadow); (*b*) (*of volcano*) to eject (ash); **l'explosion les a projetés au loin,** the explosion flung, hurled, them far away; (*c*) to show, screen (film); (*d*) to plan, contemplate (journey, etc.); **je projette de partir demain,** I'm thinking of leaving, planning to leave, tomorrow. **2. se p.,** to project, stand out; to jut out; **une ombre s'est projetée sur le mur,** a shadow fell, was cast, on the wall.

prolapsus [prɔlapsys] *n.m. Med:* prolapse.

prolétaire [prɔletɛr] *a. & n.m.* proletarian.

prolétariat [prɔletarja] *n.m.* proletariat.

prolétarien, -ienne [prɔletarjɛ̃, -jɛn] *a.* proletarian.

prolétarisation [prɔletarizasjɔ̃] *n.f.* proletarianization.

prolétariser [prɔletarize] *v.tr.* to proletarianize.

prolifération [prɔliferasjɔ̃] *n.f.* proliferation.

prolifère [prɔlifɛr] *a. Nat.Hist:* proliferous.

proliférer [prɔlifere] *v.i.* **(il prolifère; il proliférera)** to proliferate.

prolifique [prɔlifik] *a.* prolific.

prolixe [prɔliks] *a.* prolix, verbose; wordy.

prolixement [prɔliksəmɑ̃] *adv.* at great length.

prolixité [prɔliksite] *n.f.* prolixity; verbosity.

prologue [prɔlɔg] *n.m.* prologue (**de,** to).

prolongation [prɔlɔ̃gasjɔ̃] *n.f.* prolongation (in time); protraction; lengthening (of stay); extension (of leave); *Fb:* **jouer les prolongations,** to play extra time.

prolonge [prɔlɔ̃ʒ] *n.f.* **1.** *Rail: etc:* lashing rope. **2.** *Artil:* ammunition wagon; **p. d'artillerie,** gun carriage (at military funeral).

prolongé [prɔlɔ̃ʒe] *a.* **1.** long(-continued); prolonged (absence, etc.); **soupir p.,** long-drawn(-out) sigh; **applaudissements prolongés,** sustained applause. **2.** *Mth:* prolate (ellipsoid).

prolongement [prɔlɔ̃ʒmɑ̃] *n.m.* (*a*) prolongation (in space); continuation (of street, etc.); lengthening, extension (of wall, railway, etc.); (*b*) *pl.* developments, consequences (of an action, etc.).

prolonger [prɔlɔ̃ʒe] *v.* **je prolongeai(s); n. prolon-**

geons) 1. *v.tr.* to prolong, extend; to protract, draw out, spin out (argument, etc.); **visite très prolongée,** protracted call; *Rail:* **p. un billet,** to extend a ticket; *Mth:* **p. une droite,** to continue, produce, a line. **2. se p.,** to be prolonged; to continue, extend; **la guerre s'est prolongée jusqu'à l'année suivante,** the war went on, (was) carried on, until the following year.

promenade [prɔmnad] *n.f.* **1.** (*a*) (*as exercise*) walking; (*b*) walk; stroll; outing, trip (in car, etc.); **faire une p. (à pied),** to go for a walk; **faire une p. en voiture,** to go for a drive; **faire une p. à bicyclette,** to go for a bicycle ride; **faire une p. à cheval,** to go (horse)riding, for a ride; **p. en bateau,** row; sail; **être en p.,** to be out walking; to be out for a walk, drive, etc.; **faire faire une p. à qn,** to take s.o. (out) for a walk; **p. militaire,** route march. **2.** (*place for walking*) promenade; (public) walk; parade.

promener [prɔmne] *v.* **(je promène; je promènerai) 1.** *v.tr.* (*a*) to take (s.o.) (out) for a walk, drive, etc.; (*b*) to take, lead (s.o.) about; to take (dog) for a walk; to exercise (horse); **cela vous promènera un peu,** that will get you out a bit; **p. des amis à travers Paris,** to show, take, friends round Paris; (*c*) **p. sa main sur qch.,** to pass, run, one's hand over sth.; **p. ses yeux sur qch.,** to run one's eye(s) over sth. **2. se p.** (*a*) to walk; to go (out) for a walk, stroll, drive, etc.; **se p. dans sa chambre,** to pace up and down in one's room; **mener p. les enfants,** to take the children (out) for a walk; *F:* **envoyer p. qn,** to send s.o. packing; **va te p.!** get out! buzz off! (*b*) (*of eyes, thoughts, etc.*) to wander; *F:* **il laisse p. ses affaires partout,** he leaves his things lying around all over the place.

promeneur, -euse [prɔmnœr, -øz] **1.** *n.* walker; stroller; rambler. **2.** *n.f.* **promeneuse d'enfants,** mother's help (who takes children for a walk).

promenoir [prɔm(ə)nwar] *n.m.* promenade; (covered) walk; lobby (of law courts, etc.).

promesse [prɔmɛs] *n.f.* **1.** (*a*) promise, assurance; **faire une p.,** to make a promise; **tenir sa p.,** to keep one's promise; **manquer à sa p.,** to break one's promise; (*b*) **entreprise pleine de promesses,** promising undertaking. **2.** *Com: etc:* undertaking to pay.

prometteur, -euse [prɔmɛtœr -øz] *a.* promising; attractive (invitation); full of promise.

promettre [prɔmɛtr̥] *v.* (*conj. like* METTRE) **1.** *v.tr.* to promise; (*a*) **p. qch. à qn,** to promise s.o. sth.; to promise sth. to s.o.; **p. à qn de faire qch.,** to promise s.o. to do sth.; **il m'a promis qu'il le ferait,** he promised me he'd do it; *F:* **je vous promets qu'on s'est amusé,** we had a really great time; (*b*) **le temps promet de la chaleur,** it promises to be hot; it looks as though it will be hot; **il promet d'éclipser tous ses rivaux,** he bids fair to eclipse all his rivals; (*c*) *v.i.* **les vignes promettent,** the vines look promising; **enfant qui promet,** promising child; child who shows promise; **c'est un projet qui promet,** the plan has possibilities; *F:* **ça promet!** that looks promising! it's looking good! **2. se p. qch.,** to promise oneself sth.; **se p. des plaisirs nouveaux,** to anticipate new pleasures; **se p. de travailler,** to make up one's mind, resolve, to work.

promis, -ise [prɔmi, -iz] **1.** *a.* (*a*) promised; **la Terre promise,** the Promised Land; (*b*) **p. à,** destined for. **2.** *n. A: & Dial:* fiancé(e), betrothed.

promiscuité [prɔmiskɥite] *n.f.* promiscuity.

promontoire [prɔmɔ̃twar] *n.m.* promontory; headland, cape.

promoteur, -trice [prɔmɔtœr, -tris] *n.* (*a*) promoter, originator **(de,** of); (*b*) *Sp: etc:* promoter, organizer; (*c*) **p. (de construction),** property developer.

promotion [prɔmosjɔ̃] *n.f.* **1.** promotion (to a higher post); *esp. Ecc:* preferment; **p. à l'ancienneté,** promotion by seniority. **2.** *coll. Sch:* (students of the same) year; *NAm:* = class; **camarade de p.,** fellow student; **le premier de sa p.,** the first in his year. **3.** *Com:* **p. des ventes,** sales promotion.

promotionnel, -elle [prɔmosjɔnɛl] *a. Com:* **vente promotionelle** =special offer.

promouvoir [prɔmuvwar] *v.tr.* (*conj. like* MOUVOIR) to promote; **il a été promu chef du personnel,** he's been promoted to personnel manager.

prompt [prɔ̃] *a.* prompt, quick, ready; swift; hasty; **esprit p.,** quick mind; ready wit; **être d'humeur prompte,** to be quick-tempered; **il est p. à la colère, à se fâcher,** he loses his temper, flares up, easily; **p. à agir,** quick to act; **p. à la riposte,** prompt, quick, in repartee; **prompte vengeance,** speedy revenge.

promptement [prɔ̃tmɑ̃] *adv.* promptly, quickly.

promptitude [prɔ̃tityd] *n.f.* promptitude, promptness; quickness, swiftness; alertness; **avec toute la p. possible,** with all possible dispatch.

promu, -ue [prɔmy] *a. & n.* (person) who has been promoted; *Sch:* **les nouveaux promus** = this year's graduates (of a *grande école*).

promulgation [prɔmylgasjɔ̃] *n.f.* promulgation.

promulguer [prɔmylge] *v.tr.* to promulgate (law); to publish, issue (decree).

prône [pron] *n.m. Ecc:* sermon; homily.

prôner [prone] *v.tr.* (*a*) to praise, extol; (*b*) to recommend (sth.).

pronom [prɔnɔ̃] *n.m. Gram:* pronoun.

pronominal, -aux [prɔnɔminal, -o] *a. Gram:* pronominal.

pronominalement [prɔnɔminalmɑ̃] *adv.* pronominally.

prononçable [prɔnɔ̃sabl̥] *a.* pronounceable.

prononcé [prɔnɔ̃se] **1.** *a.* pronounced, decided, (well-)marked (taste, feature, etc.); **courbe prononcée,** sharp curve; **accent étranger très p.,** strong, marked, foreign accent; **peu p.,** faint. **2.** *n.m. Jur:* decision; **p. du jugement,** verdict.

prononcer [prɔnɔ̃se] *v.* **(je prononçai(s); n. prononçons) 1.** *v.tr.* (*a*) to utter, say (word); **sans p. un mot,** without (uttering) a word; **il a prononcé quelques mots entre ses dents,** he muttered a few words; **il ne faut jamais p. son nom,** you must never mention him, his name; (*b*) to deliver, make (speech); *Jur:* **p. une sentence,** to pass, pronounce, sentence; (*c*) to pronounce (word); **mal p. un mot,** to mispronounce a word; **cette lettre ne se prononce pas,** this letter is not pronounced. **2.** *v.i.* to pronounce (**sur qch.,** on sth.); **p. en faveur de qn,** to decide, declare, in favour, *NAm:* favor, of s.o.; **p. sur une question,** to adjudge, adjudicate, a question. **3. se p.,** to declare, pronounce, express, one's opinion, decision; to make, come to, a decision; **le médecin ne s'est pas encore prononcé,** the doctor has not yet given his verdict.

prononciation [prɔnɔ̃sjasjɔ̃] *n.f.* **1.** delivery (of speech); passing (of sentence). **2.** pronunciation; **défaut de p.,** speech defect; **faute de p.,** mispronunciation.

pronostic [prɔnɔstik] *n.m.* **1.** prognostic(ation); *Sp: etc:* forecast. **2.** *Med:* prognosis.

pronostiquer [prɔnɔstike] *v.tr.* to forecast; to prognosticate; *Med:* **p. au plus grave,** to give a very serious prognosis.

propagande [prɔpagɑ̃d] *n.f.* propaganda; publicity; *Com:* **faire de la p.,** to advertise.

propagandiste [prɔpagɑ̃dist] *n.* propagandist.

propagateur, -trice [prɔpagatœr, -tris] *n.* propagator, spreader (of news, disease, etc.); disseminator (of ideas).

propagation [prɔpagasjɔ̃] *n.f.* (*a*) spread(ing); propagation; dissemination (of news); (*b*) **p. d'une espèce,** propagation of a species.

propager [prɔpaʒe] *v.* **(je propageai(s); n. propageons) 1.** *v.tr.* to propagate; to spread (abroad); to disseminate (news). **2. se p.** (*a*) (*of disease, etc.*) to spread; (*b*) (*of light, sound*) to be propagated; (*c*) *Nat.Hist:* (*of plant, etc.*) to propagate, reproduce.

propane [prɔpan] *n.m. Ch:* propane.

propédeutique [prɔpedøtik] *n.f.* (*a*) propaedeutics; (*b*) first year of university course.

propension [prɔpɑ̃sjɔ̃] *n.f.* propensity, tendency, inclination (**à,** to).

propergol [prɔpɛrgɔl] *n.m.* (rocket) propellant.

prophète, prophétesse [prɔfɛt, prɔfetɛs] *n.* prophet; seer; *f.* prophetess; **p. de malheur,** prophet of doom, of evil; Jeremiah.

prophétie [prɔfesi] *n.f.* prophecy.

prophétique [prɔfetik] *a.* prophetic(al).

prophétiquement [prɔfetikmɑ̃] *adv.* prophetically.

prophétiser [prɔfetize] *v.tr.* to prophesy; to foretell.

prophylactique [prɔfilaktik] *a. Med:* prophylactic.

prophylaxie [prɔfilaksi] *n.f.* prophylaxis.

propice [prɔpis] *a.* propitious (**à,** to); auspicious; favourable, *NAm:* favorable; **né sous une étoile p.,** born under a lucky star; **peu p.,** (i) unpropitious; (ii) inauspicious (moment, etc.); **si la fortune nous est p.,** if all goes well with us.

propitiation [prɔpisjasjɔ̃] *n.f.* propitiation.

propitiatoire [prɔpisjatwar] *a.* propitiatory.

proportion [prɔpɔrsjɔ̃] *n.f.* **1.** proportion; ratio; **varier en p. directe, en p. inverse,** to vary in direct ratio, in inverse ratio; **p. d'alcool dans un vin,** percentage of alcohol in a wine; **à p., en p. (de),** in proportion (to); proportional (to); proportionally, proportionately (to); **à p. que** + *ind.,* (in proportion) as; **hors de (toute) p. avec,** out of (all) proportion to; **défaut de p.,** disproportion (**entre,** between); **toute(s) proportion(s) gardée(s),** all things considered, making all due allowance. **2.** *pl.* size; **salle de vastes proportions,** hall of vast dimensions; **dans de plus vastes proportions,** on a greater, wider, scale; **si les commandes diminuent dans de sérieuses proportions,** if orders should decrease to any great extent.

proportionné [prɔpɔrsjɔne] *a.* **1. bien p.,** well proportioned (body, etc.). **2.** proportionate, proportional, suited (**à,** to); commensurate (**à,** with).

proportionnel, -elle [prɔpɔrsjɔnɛl] **1.** *a.* proportional (**à,** to); **inversement p.,** inversely proportional, in inverse ratio (**à,** to). **2.** *n.f. Mth:* **proportionnelle,** proportional.

proportionnellement [prɔpɔrsjɔnɛlmɑ̃] *adv.* proportionally, proportionately, in proportion (**à,** to).

proportionner [prɔpɔrsjɔne] *v.tr.* to proportion, adjust, adapt (**à,** to).

propos [prɔpo] *n.m.* **1.** *Lit:* purpose, resolution; intention; **avoir le ferme p. de faire qch.,** to have the firm intention of doing sth.; **de p. délibéré,** deliberately, on purpose; with set purpose. **2.** subject, matter; **à ce p., à p.,** talking of that, in connection with that, while we're on the subject; **à p., avez-vous lu ce livre?** by the way, that reminds me, have you read this book? **à tout p.,** at every turn; at any time; **dire qch. à p.,** to say sth. to the point; to say sth. suitable, appropriate; **mot jeté à p.,** timely word; **remarque faite à p.,** apt, relevant, pertinent, apposite, remark; **faire qch. à p.,** to do sth. at the right moment; **arriver fort à p.,** to arrive at just the right moment, in the nick of time; **juger à p. de . . .,** to consider it advisable, to see fit, to . . .; **mal à p.,** at the wrong time, moment; inopportunely; **hors de p.,** ill-timed, irrelevant (remark); **c'était hors de p.,** it was out of place; **à p. de,** in connection with, with regard to, on the subject of, apropos of; **à p. de rien,** for nothing at all, for no reason whatever; **à p. de quoi? à quel p.?** in what connection? about what? what about? **3.** remark; *pl.* talk; **p. méchants,** malicious gossip; **des p. de table,** table talk; **changer de p.,** to change the subject.

proposer [prɔpoze] **1.** *v.tr.* to propose (plan); to propound (theory); to move, put forward (amendment); **p. une définition pour un mot,** to suggest a definition for a word; **p. qn comme modèle,** to hold, set, s.o. up as a model; **p. de l'argent à qn,** to offer s.o. money; **être proposé pour un emploi,** to be suggested, proposed, recommended, for a job; **p. un candidat,** to put forward, put up, propose, a candidate; **p. que l'on fasse qch.,** to propose, suggest, that sth. should be done; **je lui ai proposé de le faire,** I proposed, suggested, that he should do it; **l'homme propose et Dieu dispose,** man proposes, God disposes. **2. se p.** (*a*) to propose oneself, come forward, offer one's services; **se p. comme secrétaire,** to offer to act as secretary; (*b*) **se p. qch.,** to have sth. in view; to be considering sth.; **se p. de faire qch.,** to mean, intend, to do sth.

proposition [prɔpozisjɔ̃] *n.f.* **1.** proposal, proposition; offer; **faire une p.,** to make a proposal; (*in an assembly*) to put, propose, a motion; **mettre une p. aux voix,** to put a motion to the vote; **propositions de paix,** peace proposals. **2.** (*a*) *Log: Mth: etc:* proposition; (*b*) *Gram:* clause.

propre [prɔpr̥] **1.** *a.* (*a*) proper; **signification p. d'un mot,** proper meaning of a word; **ce sont là ses propres paroles,** these are his very words; (*b*) peculiar, proper (**à,** to); **une façon de marcher à lui p.,** his own particular, characteristic, way of walking; (*c*) *Ph:* **fréquence p.,** natural frequency; (*d*) own; **mon p. argent,** my own money; **ses idées lui sont propres,** his ideas are his own; **voir avec ses propres yeux,** to see with one's own eyes; **je le lui ai remis en main(s) propre(s),** I delivered it to him personally; **à remettre en main p.,** to be delivered to the addressee in person; (*e*) appropriate, suitable, proper, fit(ting); **p. à qch.,** adapted, fitted, suited, to sth.; **l'endroit le plus p. au camping,** the likeliest place for camping; **exercice p. à aiguiser l'intelligence,** exercise calculated to sharpen the wits; **p. à tout,** fit for anything; **p. à rien,** good for nothing; (*f*) clean; neat; **chambre p. et nette,** clean and tidy room; **p. comme un sou neuf,** as clean as a new pin; spick and span; *F:* **nous voilà propres!** we're in a nice mess! **c'est du p.!** what a mess! *n.m. Sch:* **recopier au p.,** to make a fair copy; (*g*) **le chat est très p.,** the cat is a very clean animal; **mon bébé était p. à treize mois,** my baby was dry at thirteen months. **2.** *n.m.* (*a*) property, attribute, nature, characteristic (of nation, pers., etc.); (*b*) **employer un mot au p.,** to use a word in its literal sense, literally; (*c*) **avoir qch. en p.,** to possess sth. in one's own right; **la maison m'appartient en p.,** the house is my own; **il a un exemplaire en p.,** he has a copy of his own.

propre(-)à(-)rien [prɔprarjɛ̃] *n.* good-for-nothing; dead loss; ne'er-do-well; *pl. propres*(-)*à*(-)*rien.*

proprement [prɔprəmɑ̃] *adv.* **1.** properly; in fact; appropriately; perfectly, absolutely, simply; literally; *F:* well and truly; **à p. parler,** strictly speaking; **pas à p. parler,** not exactly; **p. dit,** actual; **pierres précieuses p. dites,** precious stones proper. **2.** (*a*) cleanly; neatly; tidily; (*b*) *F:* well; efficiently; **assez p.,** tolerably well.

propret, -ette [prɔprɛ, -ɛt] *a.* neat, tidy.

propreté [prɔprəte] *n.f.* cleanliness; cleanness; neatness, tidiness; *Navy:* **postes de p.,** cleaning stations.

propriétaire [prɔprietɛr] *n.* **1.** proprietor, *f.* proprietress; owner; **se rendre p. de qch.,** to acquire sth.; **p. (de maison),** householder; **qui est le p. de cette terre?** who owns this land? **p. foncier,** (i) ground landlord; (ii) landowner; **être p.,** (i) to be a man of property, a landowner; (ii) to have a house of one's own. **2.** landlord, *f.* landlady.

propriété [prɔpriete] *n.f.* **1.** (*a*) proprietorship, ownership; property; **p. privée, publique,** private, public, property; **p. foncière (perpétuelle et) libre,** freehold; **titres de p.,** title deeds; **p. littéraire,** literary property; copyright; **p. industrielle,** patent rights; (*b*) property, estate; holding; **p. foncière,** landed property, landed estate; **propriétés immobilières,** real estate, realty. **2.** property, characteristic, peculiar quality (of metal, plant, etc.). **3.** propriety, correctness (of language, etc.).

proprio [prɔprio] *n.m. P:* landlord.

propulser [prɔpylse] *v.tr.* to propel.

propulseur [prɔpylsœr] **1.** *a.* propellant, propellent, propulsive, propelling. **2.** *n.m.* (*a*) propellant, propellent; (*b*) propeller.

propulsif, -ive [prɔpylsif, -iv] *a.* = PROPULSEUR 1.

propulsion [prɔpylsjɔ̃] *n.f.* propulsion, propelling; impulsion, impelling; drive, driving; **réacteur de p.,** propulsion jet; **sous-marin à p. nucléaire,** nuclear-powered submarine; **véhicule à p. électrique,** electrically propelled, powered, vehicle.

pro rata [prɔrata] *n.m.inv.* proportional part; proportion; **paiement au p.,** payment pro rata; **au p. de qch.,** in proportion to sth.

prorogatif, -ive [prɔrɔgatif, -iv] *a.* proroguing.

prorogation [prɔrɔgasjɔ̃] *n.f.* **1.** prorogation (of parliament). **2.** *esp. Jur:* extension of time.

proroger [prɔrɔʒe] *v.tr.* **(je prorogeai(s); n. prorogeons) 1.** to prorogue, adjourn (parliament). **2.** to extend (time limit).

prosaïque [prozaik] *a.* prosaic; commonplace; pedestrian.

prosaïquement [prozaikmɑ̃] *adv.* prosaically.

prosaïsme [prozaism] *n.m.* prosaicness.

prosateur [prozatœr] *n.m.* prose writer.

proscenium [prɔsenjɔm] *n.m. Th:* (*a*) *Ant:* proscenium (arch); (*b*) proscenium, apron.

proscription [prɔskripsjɔ̃] *n.f.* (*a*) proscription; banishment, outlawing; (*b*) condemning, forbidding (of sth.).

proscrire [prɔskrir] *v.tr.* (*conj. like* ÉCRIRE) (*a*) to proscribe, outlaw, banish; **p. qn de la société,** to proscribe, ostracize, s.o. from society; (*b*) to condemn, forbid (sth.).

proscrit, -ite [prɔskri, -it] **1.** *a.* proscribed. **2.** *n.* outlaw.

prose [proz] *n.f.* prose; **en p.,** in prose; **poème en p.,** prose poem.

prosélyte [prɔzelit] *n.* proselyte.

prosélytisme [prɔzelitism] *n.m.* proselytism.

prosodie [prɔzɔdi] *n.f.* prosody.

prosodique [prɔzɔdik] *a.* prosodic.

prospecter [prɔspɛkte] *v.tr.* **1.** *Min:* to prospect. **2.** *Com:* to canvass.

prospecteur, -trice [prɔspɛktœr, -tris] **1.** *esp. Min:* prospector. **2.** *Com:* canvasser.

prospectif, -ive [prɔspɛktif, -iv] *a.* prospective.

prospection [prɔspɛksjɔ̃] *n.f.* **1.** *Min:* prospecting. **2.** canvassing.

prospectus [prɔspɛktys] *n.m.* **1.** prospectus. **2.** handbill, leaflet; brochure.

prospère [prɔspɛr] *a.* prosperous, thriving, flourishing.

prospérer [prɔspere] *v.i.* **(je prospère; je prospérerai)** to prosper, thrive, flourish; to do well.

prospérité [prɔsperite] *n.f.* prosperity, prosperousness; *Com:* **vague de p.,** boom.

prostate [prɔstat] *n.f. Anat:* prostate (gland).

prostatique [prɔstatik] *a. Anat:* prostatic.

prostatite [prɔstatit] *n.f. Med:* prostatitis.

prosternation [prɔstɛrnasjɔ̃] *n.f. Lit:* (*a*) prostration; (*b*) grovelling, kowtowing.

prosterné [prɔstɛrne] *a.* prostrate.

prosternement [prɔstɛrnəmɑ̃] *n.m.* (*a*) prostration; prostrate attitude; (*b*) *Lit:* humiliation.

prosterner [prɔstɛrne] **1.** *v.tr. Lit:* to bend, bow (head, etc.). **2. se p.** (*a*) to prostrate oneself **(devant,** before); to bow down **(devant,** to, before); (*b*) to grovel, kowtow **(devant,** to).

prostituée [prɔstitɥe] *n.f.* prostitute.

prostituer [prɔstitɥe] **1.** *v.tr.* to prostitute (person, talent, etc.). **2. se p.,** to prostitute oneself.

prostitution [prɔstitysjɔ̃] *n.f.* prostitution.

prostration [prɔstrasjɔ̃] *n.f.* prostration; (*a*) lying prone; (*b*) *Med:* (nervous) exhaustion.

prostré [prɔstre] *a.* prostrate(d); exhausted.

protagoniste [prɔtagɔnist] *n.m.* protagonist.

prote [prɔt] *n.m. Typ:* foreman, overseer.

protecteur, -trice [prɔtɛktœr, -tris] **1.** *n.* (*pers.*) (*a*) protector, *f.* protectress; (*b*) patron, *f.* patroness (of the arts, etc.). **2.** *n.m.* protector, shield; guard (for machine tool, etc.). **3.** *a.* (*a*) protecting; **société protectrice des animaux** = society for the prevention of cruelty to animals; (*b*) patronizing (tone, etc.); (*c*) protective (device, tariff, etc.).

protection [prɔtɛksjɔ̃] *n.f.* **1.** protection **(contre,** from, against); conservation (of the environment, etc.); **p. civile,** civil defence; **p. de l'enfance,** child welfare; **sous la p. de la police,** under police protection; **dispositif de p.,** safety device, protective device. **2.** patronage; influence; **prendre qn sous sa p.,** to take s.o. under one's wing; *Pej:* **par p.,** through influence.

protectionnisme [prɔtɛksjɔnism] *n.m. Pol.Ec:* protection(ism).

protectionniste [prɔtɛksjɔnist] *a. & n. Pol.Ec:* protectionist.

protectorat [prɔtɛktɔra] *n.m.* protectorate.

protégé, -ée [prɔteʒe] **1.** *a.* protected; *P.N: Aut:* **passage p.,** priority (over vehicles entering from minor road ahead). **2.** *n.* favourite, *NAm:* favorite; protégé, *f.* protégée.

protège-cahier [prɔtɛʒkaje] *n.m.* exercise-book cover; *pl. protège-cahiers.*

protège-dents [prɔtɛʒdɑ̃] *n.m.inv. Box:* gum shield.

protéger [prɔteʒe] *v.tr.* **(je protège, n. protégeons; je protégeai(s); je protégerai) 1.** (*a*) to protect; to shelter, shield, guard **(contre,** against, from); **se p. de qch.,** to protect oneself from sth.; to guard against sth.; (*b*) *Pol.Ec:* to protect (industry, etc.). **2.** (*a*) to patronize; to be a patron of (the arts, etc.); (*b*) to give (s.o.) one's support.

protège-tibia [prɔtɛʒtibja] *n.m. Sp:* shin guard; *pl. protège-tibias.*

protège-tympan [prɔtɛʒtɛ̃pɑ̃] *n.m.inv.* earplug(s).

protéine [prɔtein] *n.f.* protein.

protéique [prɔteik] *a. Ch.* protein(ic).

protestable [prɔtɛstabl̥] *a. Jur:* which may be protested.

protestant, -ante [prɔtɛstɑ̃, -ɑ̃t] *a. & n.* Protestant.

protestantisme [prɔtɛstɑ̃tism] *n.m.* Protestantism.

protestataire [prɔtɛstatɛr] **1.** *a.* (letter, etc.) of protest. **2.** *n.* protester, protestor; objector.

protestation [prɔtɛstasjɔ̃] *n.f.* **1.** protestation; declaration, affirmation; **faire une p., des protestations, de son innocence,** to protest, declare, one's innocence. **2.** protest; **faire une p. contre qch.,** to make a protest against sth.; **élever des protestations énergiques,** to raise a strong protest; **réunion de p.,** protest meeting.

protester [prɔtɛste] **1.** *v.tr.* (*a*) to protest, declare; (*b*) *Com:* to protest (bill). **2.** *v.i.* **p. de son innocence,** to protest one's innocence; **p. contre qch.,** to protest, make a protest, against sth.; to challenge sth.

protêt [prɔtɛ] *n.m. Com: Jur:* protest; **dresser un p.,** to make a protest.

prothèse [prɔtɛz] *n.f.* (*a*) *Surg:* prosthesis, prosthetics; (*b*) **(appareil de) p.,** prosthesis; artificial limb, etc.; **p. dentaire,** dental prosthesis; false teeth; denture(s).

protocolaire [prɔtɔkɔlɛr] *a.* formal; pertaining to protocol, etiquette; **clauses protocolaires d'accord,** formal provisions of agreement.

protocole [prɔtɔkɔl] *n.m.* protocol; (*a*) ceremonial procedure; (*b*) etiquette; formalities, social conventions.

protohistoire [prɔtɔistwar] *n.f.* protohistory.

proton [prɔtɔ̃] *n.m. Atom.Ph:* proton.

protoplasma [prɔtɔplasma] *n.m.*, **protoplasme** [prɔtɔplasm] *n.m. Biol:* protoplasm.

prototype [prɔtɔtip] *n.m.* prototype.

protoxyde [prɔtɔksid] *n.m. Ch:* monoxide; **p. d'azote,** nitrous oxide.

protozoaire [prɔtɔzɔɛr] *n.m. Z:* protozoan, protozoon; **les protozoaires,** the Protozoa.

protrusion [prɔtryzjɔ̃] *n.f.* protrusion.

protubérance [prɔtyberɑ̃s] *n.f.* protuberance; *Astr:* (solar) prominence; *Anat:* bump (on the skull); knob (on stick, etc.).

protubérant [prɔtyberɑ̃] *a.* protuberant.

prou [pru] *adv.* (*a*) *A:* much; many; (*b*) *Lit:* **peu ou p.,** more or less; not much; not many; **ni peu ni p.,** not at all; none at all.

proue [pru] *n.f.* prow, stem, bow(s) (of ship).

prouesse [pruɛs] *n.f.* **1.** *Lit:* prowess, valour, *NAm:* valor. **2.** feat; achievement (in sport, etc.).

prouver [pruve] *v.tr.* **1.** to prove (fact); **p. le bien-fondé d'une réclamation,** to substantiate a claim; to make good one's claim. **2. p. sa capacité,** to give proof, show proof, of (one's) capacity.

provenance [prɔvnɑ̃s] *n.f.* source, origin; **de p. anglaise,** of English origin; **pays de p.,** country of origin; **train en p. de Bordeaux,** train from Bordeaux.

provençal, -ale, -aux [prɔvɑ̃sal, -o] **1.** *a. & n. Geog:* Provençal; of Provence. **2.** *n.m. Ling:* Provençal.

provende [prɔvɑ̃d] *n.f. Husb:* provender, fodder.

provenir [prɔvnir] *v.i.* (*conj. like* VENIR) to proceed, result, arise, come, derive, be derived (**de,** from); to originate (**de,** in); *Jur:* **les enfants provenant, provenus, de ce mariage,** the children issuing from this marriage.

proverbe [prɔvɛrb] *n.m.* proverb; **passer en p.,** to become a proverb; to become proverbial.

proverbial, -aux [prɔvɛrbjal, -o] *a.* proverbial.

proverbialement [prɔvɛrbjalmɑ̃] *adv.* proverbially.

providence [prɔvidɑ̃s] *n.f.* providence; **être la p. de qn,** to be s.o.'s guardian angel; **l'État P.,** the Welfare State.

providentiel, -elle [prɔvidɑ̃sjɛl] *a.* providential.

providentiellement [prɔvidɑ̃sjɛlmɑ̃] *adv.* providentially.

provignage [prɔviɲaʒ] *n.m.*, **provignement** [prɔviɲmɑ̃] *n.m.* layering (of vine).

provigner [prɔviɲe] *v.tr.* to layer (vine).

provin [prɔvɛ̃] *n.m. Vit:* layered branch, stock.

province [prɔvɛ̃s] *n.f.* **1.** province; region (of country); **les Provinces Maritimes,** the Maritime Provinces. **2. la p.,** the provinces, the country; **vivre en p.,** to live in the provinces; **vie de p.,** provincial life; **mentalité de p.,** small-town mentality; **cousin de p.,** country cousin; **aller en p.** = to leave town.

provincial, -ale, -aux [prɔvɛ̃sjal, -o] **1.** *a.* provincial; *Pej:* countrified (manners, etc.); parochial; **manières provinciales,** small-town, provincial, ways. **2.** (*a*) *n.* provincial; (*b*) *n.m. Ecc:* provincial.

provincialisme [prɔvɛ̃sjalism] *n.m.* provincialism; provincial, regional (i) word, expression, (ii) pronunciation.

proviseur [prɔvizœr] *n.m. Sch:* headmaster (of a *lycée*).

provision [prɔvizjɔ̃] *n.f.* **1.** provision, store, stock, supply; **faire p. de charbon,** to lay in a stock of coal; **provisions de bouche,** food; **provisions de guerre,** munitions; **faire ses provisions,** to go shopping; **sac à provisions,** shopping bag. **2.** (*a*) *Com:* funds, cover, reserve, margin; **verser une p., des provisions,** to pay a deposit; **faire p. pour une lettre de change,** to provide for a bill; **insuffisance de p.,** insufficient funds (to meet cheque, *NAm:* check, etc.); **chèque sans p.,** bad, *F:* dud, cheque; cheque that bounced; (*b*) retaining fee (paid to lawyer); (*c*) **par p.,** provisional(ly).

provisionnel, -elle [prɔvizjɔnɛl] *a. Jur:* provisional (division of estate, etc.).

provisoire [prɔvizwar] **1.** *a.* provisional; provisory; acting (manager, etc.); temporary; **nommé à titre p.,** appointed provisionally; **dividende p.,** interim dividend; **habitation p.,** emergency, temporary, accommodation. **2.** *n.m.* sth. temporary; **s'installer dans le p.,** to treat sth. temporary as permanent.

provisoirement [prɔvizwarmɑ̃] *adv.* provisionally, temporarily.

provocant [prɔvɔkɑ̃] *a.* provocative. **1.** aggressive (language, etc.). **2.** tantalizing, alluring (smile, etc.).

provocateur, -trice [prɔvɔkatœr, -tris] **1.** *a.* provocative; **agent p.,** agent provocateur. **2.** *n.* (*a*) aggressor; (*b*) instigator (of disturbance, etc.).

provocation [prɔvɔkasjɔ̃] *n.f.* **1.** provocation; **lancer des provocations à qn,** to hurl defiance at s.o.; **p. en duel,** challenge to a duel. **2.** instigation; **p. au crime,** incitement to crime.

provoquer [prɔvɔke] *v.tr.* **1.** to provoke; **p. qn en duel,** to challenge s.o. to a duel. **2.** to induce, instigate; **p. qn au crime,** to incite s.o. to crime. **3.** to cause, bring about (desired result, etc.); to give rise to (comment, etc.); to produce (response); **p. un courant d'air,** to create a draught, *NAm:* draft; **p. le sommeil, la sueur,** to induce sleep, perspiration; **p. la curiosité,** to arouse curiosity; **p. la gaieté,** to cause, provoke, cheerfulness; **p. un sourire,** to raise a smile.

proxénète [prɔksenɛt] *n.* procurer, *f.* procuress; *m.* pimp, pander.

proxénétisme [prɔksenetism] *n.m.* procuring.

proximité [prɔksimite] *n.f.* **1.** proximity; nearness, closeness; imminence (of event); **à p.,** near at hand, close by; **à p. de qch.,** close to sth., in the vicinity of sth. **2. p. de parenté,** near relationship.

proyer [prwaje] *n.m. Orn:* **(bruant) p.,** bunting.

prude [pryd] **1.** *a.* prudish. **2.** *n.f.* prude.

prudemment [prydamɑ̃] *adv.* prudently; carefully, cautiously.

prudence [prydɑ̃s] *n.f.* prudence; carefulness, cautiousness, caution; wisdom; **agir avec p.,** to act prudently; *Prov:* **p. est mère de sûreté,** discretion is the better part of valour, *NAm:* valor.

prudent [prydɑ̃] *a.* prudent; careful, cautious (pers., etc.); wise, well advised (decision, etc.); advisable; **il faut être très p. en . . .,** the greatest care must be taken in . . ..

pruderie [prydri] *n.f.* prudery, prudishness.

prud'homme [prydɔm] *n.m.* **conseil des prud'hommes,** conciliation board (in industrial disputes).
prudhommerie [prydɔmri] *n.f.* pomposity, sententiousness.
pruine [prɥin] *n.f.* bloom (on fruit).
prune [pryn] *n.f.* **1.** plum; **p. de Damas,** damson; **verre de p.,** a glass of plum brandy; *P:* **pour des prunes,** for nothing; **des prunes!** no fear! not (bloody) likely! **2.** *a.inv.* plum(-coloured, *NAm:* -colored).
pruneau, -eaux [pryno] *n.m.* **1.** prune. **2.** *P:* (rifle) bullet.
prunelle [prynɛl] *n.f.* **1.** *Bot:* sloe; **(liqueur de) p.,** sloe gin. **2.** pupil (of the eye); **comme la p. de ses yeux,** like the apple of one's eye; *F:* **jouer de la p.,** to make eyes (at s.o.).
prunellier [prynelje] *n.m.* blackthorn; sloe (bush).
prunier [prynje] *n.m.* plum tree; *F:* **secouer qn comme un p.,** to give s.o. a good (i) shaking, (ii) telling off.
Prusse [prys] *Pr.n.f. Geog: Hist:* Prussia; **bleu de P.,** Prussian blue; *F:* **travailler pour le roi de P.,** to work for nothing, for peanuts.
prussiate [prysjat] *n.m. Ch:* cyanide.
prussien, -ienne [prysjɛ̃, -jɛn] *a. & n. Geog: Hist:* Prussian.
prytanée [pritane] *n.m.* military school (for sons of officers).
psallette [psalɛt] *n.f.* choir school.
psalmiste [psalmist] *n.m.* psalmist.
psalmodie [psalmɔdi] *n.f.* (*a*) *Ecc:* psalmody; intoning (of psalms); (*b*) droning.
psalmodier [psalmɔdje] *v.* (*pr.sub. & impf.* **n. psalmodiions, v. psalmodiiez**) **1.** *v.tr.* (*a*) *Ecc:* to intone, chant (office, etc.); (*b*) to drone out (sth.), recite (sth.) monotonously. **2.** *v.i.* (*a*) *Ecc:* to intone, chant; to psalmodize; (*b*) to drone (on, away).
psaltérion [psalterjɔ̃] *n.m. Mus:* psaltery.
psaume [psom] *n.m.* psalm.
psautier [psotje] *n.m.* psalter, psalm book.
pseudo-membrane [psødɔmɑ̃bran] *n.f. Med:* pseudomembrane, false membrane; *pl. pseudo-membranes.*
pseudonyme [psødɔnim] *n.m.* pseudonym; assumed name; pen name; nom de plume.
pseudo-rubis [psødɔrybi] *n.m.inv. Miner:* rose quartz.
pseudo-saphir [psødɔsafir] *n.m. Miner:* blue quartz; *pl. pseudo-saphirs.*
psitt [psit] *int.* psst!
psittacose [psitakoz] *n.f. Med: Vet:* psittacosis.
pst [pst] *int.* psst!
psychanalyse [psikanaliz] *n.f.* psychoanalysis.
psychanalyser [psikanalize] *v.tr.* to psychoanalyse.
psychanalyste [psikanalist] *n.* psychoanalyst.
psychanalytique [psikanalitik] *a.* psychoanalytic(al).
Psyché [psiʃe] **1.** *Pr.n.f. Gr.Myth:* Psyche. **2.** *n.f.* (*a*) *Phil:* psyche; (*b*) cheval glass, swing mirror.
psychédélique [psikedelik] *a.* psychedelic.
psychiatre [psikjatr̥] *n.* psychiatrist.
psychiatrie [psikjatri] *n.f.* psychiatry.
psychiatrique [psikjatrik] *a.* psychiatric; mental (hospital, etc.).
psychique [psiʃik] *a.* psychic(al).
psychologie [psikɔlɔʒi] *n.f.* psychology.
psychologique [psikɔlɔʒik] *a.* psychological; **le moment p.,** the psychological moment.
psychologiquement [psikɔlɔʒikmɑ̃] *adv.* psychologically.
psychologue [psikɔlɔg] *n.* psychologist.
psychonévrose [psikɔnevroz] *n.f.* psychoneurosis.
psychopathe [psikɔpat] *n.* psychopath.
psychopathie [psikɔpati] *n.f.* psychopathy.
psychopathologie [psikɔpatɔlɔʒi] *a.* psychopathology.
psychopédagogie [psikɔpedagɔʒi] *n.f.* application of experimental psychology to education.
psychophysiologie [psikɔfizjɔlɔʒi] *n.f.* psychophysiology.
psychose [psikoz] *n.f.* **1.** *Med:* psychosis; **p. traumatique,** shellshock. **2.** obsession; **p. de guerre,** fear of war.
psychosomatique [psikɔsɔmatik] *a. Med:* psychosomatic.
psychotechnique [psikɔtɛknik] **1.** *a.* psychotechnical. **2.** *n.f.* psychotechnology, psychotechnics.
psychothérapeute [psikɔterapøt] *n.* psychotherapist.
psychothérapie [psikɔterapi] *n.f.* psychotherapy.
psychothérapique [psikɔterapik] *a.* psychotherapeutic; **intervention p.,** psychotherapeutic treatment.
psychotique [psikɔtik] *a. & n. Med:* psychotic.
psychromètre [psikrɔmɛtr̥] *n.m. Meteor:* psychrometer.
ptérodactyle [pterɔdaktil] *n.m. Paleont:* pterodactyl.
ptérosaurien [pterɔsɔrjɛ̃] *n.m. Paleont:* pterosaur.
Ptolémée [ptɔleme] *Pr.n.m. A.Hist:* Ptolemy; *Astr:* **système de P.,** Ptolemaic system.
ptomaïne [ptɔmain] *n.f. Bio-Ch:* ptomaine.
puant [pɥɑ̃] *a.* (*a*) stinking, foul-smelling; fetid; *Ch: F:* **gaz p.,** hydrogen sulphide; **boule puante,** stink bomb; (*b*) (*of pers.*) (offensively) pretentious; conceited.
puanteur [pɥɑ̃tœr] *n.f.* stink, stench.
pubère [pybɛr] *a.* pubescent.
puberté [pybɛrte] *n.f.* puberty.
pubescent [pybesɑ̃] *a. Bot:* pubescent, downy.
pubien, -ienne [pybjɛ̃, -jɛn] *a. Anat:* pubic.
pubis [pybis] *n.m. Anat:* pubis, pubes; pubic bone.
publiable [pybliabl̥] *a.* fit for publication.
public, -ique [pyblik] **1.** *a.* public; open (meeting); **la chose publique,** (i) the public welfare, service; (ii) state, government, commonwealth; **service p.,** public utility (service); **travailler pour le bien p.,** to work for the common good; **force publique,** (civil) police; **la dette publique,** the national debt; *Adm:* **ministère p.** = public prosecutor. **2.** *n.m.* **le p.,** the public, the people; **le grand p.,** the general public; **un p. cultivé,** (i) a cultured, an educated, audience; (ii) cultured, discerning, readers; **en p.,** in public, publicly.
publicain [pyblikɛ̃] *n.m. Rom.Hist:* tax gatherer; *B:* publican.
publication [pyblikasjɔ̃] *n.f.* publication. **1.** publishing; (*a*) issue (of an order); **p. de vente aux enchères,** notice of sale by auction; (*b*) bringing out (of book). **2.** published work; **p. périodique,** periodical.
publiciste [pyblisist] *n.* publicist; publicity agent.
publicitaire [pyblisitɛr] **1.** *a.* concerned with publicity, advertising; **campagne p.,** advertising, publicity, campaign; **agence p.,** advertising agency; **vente p.,** promotional sale. **2.** *n.* publicity agent, man, *F:* adman.
publicité [pyblisite] *n.f.* (*a*) publicity; advertising; **faire de la p.,** to advertise; **agence de p.,** advertising agency; **exemplaires de p.,** press copies; (*b*) (*in newspaper, etc.*) advertisement, *F:* ad(vert); (*on T.V., radio*) commercial.
publier [pyblije] *v.tr.* (*pr.sub. & impf.* **n. publiions, v. publiiez**) to publish. **1.** to make public, make known; to proclaim; to issue (an order); **p. la nouvelle que . . .,** to release the news that . . .. **2.** to bring out (book); **ce journal est publié sur seize pages,** this paper runs to sixteen pages.

publiquement [pyblikmɑ̃] *adv.* publicly; in public; openly.

puce [pys] **1.** *n.f.* flea; **piqûre de p.,** fleabite; **marché aux puces, les puces,** flea market; **mettre la p. à l'oreille à qn,** to arouse s.o.'s suspicions; *F:* **secouer les puces à qn,** to give s.o. a good telling off; **jeu de p.,** tiddlywinks; *Bot:* **herbe aux puces,** fleawort. **2.** *a.inv.* puce(-coloured, *NAm:* -colored).

puceau, -elle [pyso, -ɛl] **1.** *a.m. & n.m. F:* virgin. **2.** *a.f. & n.f. A: & Hum:* virgin; maid(en); *Hist:* **la Pucelle d'Orléans,** the Maid of Orleans.

puceron [pysrɔ̃] *n.m.* plant louse, greenfly, aphid.

pucier [pysje] *n.m. P:* bed, pit.

pudding [pudiŋ] *n.m. Cu:* (plum) pudding, Christmas pudding.

puddlage [pydlaʒ] *n.m. Metall:* puddling.

puddler [pydle] *v.tr. Metall:* to puddle.

pudeur [pydœr] *n.f.* modesty; sense of decency; **sans p.,** unblushing(ly), shameless(ly); **rougir de p.,** to blush for shame.

pudibond [pydibɔ̃] *a.* easily shocked; prudish.

pudibonderie [pydibɔ̃dri] *n.f.* prudishness.

pudicité [pydisite] *n.f. Lit:* chastity; modesty; sense of decency.

pudique [pydik] *a.* modest; chaste.

pudiquement [pydikmɑ̃] *adv.* modestly.

puer [pɥe] *v.i. & tr.* to stink; **p. l'ail,** to smell, stink, of garlic; **il puait le vin,** he reeked of wine.

puéricultrice [pɥerikyltris] *n.f.* nursery nurse.

puériculture [pɥerikyltyr] *n.f.* child care, infant welfare.

puéril [pɥeril] *a.* puerile, childish.

puérilement [pɥerilmɑ̃] *adv.* childishly.

puérilité [pɥerilite] *n.f.* puerility; childishness.

puerpéral, -aux [pɥɛrperal, -o] *a. Obst:* puerperal.

puffin [pyfɛ̃] *n.m. Orn:* shearwater.

pugilat [pyʒila] *n.m.* (*a*) pugilism, boxing; (*b*) fight, brawl, *F:* set-to.

pugiliste [pyʒilist] *n.m.* pugilist, boxer.

pugnace [pygnas] *a. Lit:* pugnacious.

pugnacité [pygnasite] *n.f.* pugnacity, pugnaciousness.

puîné, -ée [pɥine] *a. & n. O:* younger, youngest (brother, sister).

puis [pɥi] *adv.* then, afterwards, next; **et p. c'est tout,** and that's all (there is to it); **et p.,** and then; moreover; (and) besides; **et p.? et p. quoi? et p. après?** (i) what then? what next? (ii) *F:* so what?

puisage [pɥizaʒ] *n.m.* drawing (up) (of water).

puisard [pɥizar] *n.m.* sunk draining trap; cesspool, sink; *Min: Mch: etc:* sump, well.

puisatier [pɥizatje] *n.m.* (*a*) well maker, well sinker; (*b*) *Min:* shaft sinker.

puisement [pɥizmɑ̃] *n.m.* = PUISAGE.

puiser [pɥize] *v.tr.* (*a*) to draw (water) (**à, dans,** from); **p. dans son sac,** to dip into one's bag; (*b*) **p. une idée chez un auteur,** to take, get, draw, derive, an idea from an author; **p. aux sources,** to draw on the original authorities; to go to the source, the fountainhead.

puisque [pɥisk(ə)] *conj.* since, as, seeing that; **je le ferai, puisqu'il le faut,** I shall do it, since I must; **p. je te dis que je l'ai vu!** but I'm telling you I *did* see it!

puissamment [pɥisamɑ̃] *adv.* powerfully; **p. riche,** exceedingly rich.

puissance [pɥisɑ̃s] *n.f.* power. **1.** force (of habit); strength (of wind, etc.); **p. d'une machine,** power of an engine; *Mil:* **p. de, du, feu,** fire power; *Mec:* **p. en chevaux,** horsepower; **p. au frein,** brake horsepower; *Adm:* **p. fiscale d'une voiture,** treasury rating of a car; *W.Tel:* **p. d'antenne,** aerial capacity; **poste émetteur de haute p.,** high-power radio transmitter. **2.** *Mth:* **élever un nombre à la nième p.,** to raise a number to the nth power; **dix (à la) p. quatre (10^4),** ten to the fourth, to the power of four. **3. avoir qn en sa p.,** to have s.o. in one's power; **être en p. de mari,** to be under a husband's control, authority; **p. paternelle,** paternal authority. **4.** (*a*) *Pol:* **les grandes puissances,** the great powers; (*b*) **les puissances célestes,** the powers above; **les puissances des ténèbres,** the powers of darkness. **5. en p.,** potential(ly).

puissant [pɥisɑ̃] **1.** *a.* (*a*) powerful; strong (man, wind, etc.); (*b*) potent (remedy, etc.); **en p. relief,** in bold relief; **une des plus puissantes maisons du pays,** one of the leading firms in the country. **2.** *n.m.pl.* **les puissants,** the powerful, the mighty (ones).

puits [pɥi] *n.m.* **1.** well; hole; **p. de sondage,** boring; **p. artésien,** artesian well; **p. à ciel ouvert,** open well; **p. absorbant, p. perdu,** cesspool; **c'est un p. de science,** he's a mine of information, a fount of knowledge. **2.** (*a*) shaft, pit (of mine); **p. d'aération, d'aérage,** air shaft, ventilation shaft; **p. d'extraction,** winding shaft; (*b*) *Ind:* **p. de montage,** erecting pit. **3.** *Ball:* **p. de lancement,** launching silo.

pull [pul] *n.m. Cost: F:* pullover.

pullman [pulman] *n.m. Rail:* Pullman (car).

pull-over [pulɔvœr] *n.m. Cost:* pullover; *pl. pull-overs.*

pullulation [pylylasjɔ̃] *n.f.*, **pullulement** [pylylmɑ̃] *n.m.* (*a*) pullulation, rapid multiplication (of animals, etc.); (*b*) swarm(ing) (of children, etc.).

pulluler [pylyle] *v.i.* to pullulate; (*a*) to multiply rapidly; (*b*) to be found in profusion; to swarm.

pulmonaire [pylmɔnɛr] **1.** *a.* pulmonary; **congestion p.,** congestion of the lungs. **2.** *n.f. Bot:* lungwort.

pulpe [pylp] *n.f.* **1.** pulp; **réduire qch. en p.,** to reduce sth. to a pulp; to pulp sth. **2.** pad (of finger or toe); *Dent:* pulp.

pulpeux, -euse [pylpø, -øz] *a.* pulpy.

pulsation [pylsasjɔ̃] *n.f.* pulsation; (*a*) throbbing; beating (of the heart, etc.); (*b*) throb; (heart)beat.

pulsative [pylsativ] *a.f. Med:* **douleur p.,** throbbing pain; pulsatory pain.

pulsion [pylsjɔ̃] *n.f. Psy:* impulse; **p. sexuelle,** sex drive; **p. de mort,** death wish.

pulsomètre [pylsɔmɛtr̥] *n.m. Ind:* pulsometer; (steam-condensing) vacuum pump.

pulsoréacteur [pylsɔreaktœr] *n.m. Av:* pulse jet.

pulvérisable [pylverizabl̥] *a.* (*a*) pulverizable; (*b*) (liquid) that can be sprayed.

pulvérisateur [pylverizatœr] *n.m.* (*a*) pulverizer (of hard substances); (*b*) spray(er); vaporizer; atomizer.

pulvérisation [pylverizasjɔ̃] *n.f.* (*a*) pulverization, pulverizing, crushing (of hard substances); (*b*) spray(ing), atomization, atomizing, vaporization (of liquids).

pulvériser [pylverize] *v.tr.* (*a*) to pulverize; to grind, reduce (substance) to powder; (*b*) to spray, atomize, vaporize (liquid); (*c*) *Fig:* to pulverize (s.o.); to knock (s.o.) into a cocked hat; *Sp: F:* to smash (record).

pulvériseur [pylverizœr] *n.m. Agr:* disc harrow, *NAm:* disk harrow.

pulvérulence [pylverylɑ̃s] *n.f.* powderiness, dustiness.

pulvérulent [pylverylɑ̃] *a.* pulverulent; powdery, dusty.

puma [pyma] *n.m. Z:* puma; cougar; mountain lion.

punaise [pynɛz] *n.f.* **1.** (*a*) *Ent:* bug; **p. des lits,** bed bug, house bug; **p. des bois,** stinkbug; *F:* **p. de sacristie,** bigoted churchwoman; (*b*) *int. F: & Dial:* good heavens! **2.** drawing pin, *NAm:* thumbtack.

punch[1] [pɔ̃ʃ] *n.m. Cu:* punch; **bol à p.,** punchbowl.

punch[2] [pœnʃ] *n.m. Box: & F:* punch.

punching-ball [pœnʃiŋbol] *n.m. Box:* punchball; *pl. punching-balls.*
punique [pynik] *a. Hist:* Punic (wars, etc.); *Lit:* **foi p.,** Punic faith; treachery.
punir [pynir] *v.tr.* to punish; to avenge (crime); **p. qn de mort, de prison,** to punish s.o. with death, with imprisonment; **p. qn d'un crime, pour un mensonge,** to punish s.o. for a crime, for a lie; **être puni par où l'on a péché,** to reap what one has sown; **être puni de ses crimes,** to pay the penalty for one's crimes; *Mil:* **homme puni,** defaulter.
punissable [pynisabl̥] *a.* punishable.
punitif, -ive [pynitif, -iv] *a.* punitive.
punition [pynisjɔ̃] *n.f.* **1.** punishing; punishment; **proportionner la p. à l'offense,** to make the punishment fit the crime; **en p. de qch.,** as a punishment for sth.; **par, pour, p.,** for, by way of, punishment; as a punishment. **2.** *Games:* forfeit.
pupe [pup] *n.f. Ent:* **1.** pupa case. **2.** pupa, chrysalis.
pupillaire¹ [pypilɛr] *a. Jur:* pupil(l)ary, pertaining to a ward.
pupillaire² *a. Anat:* pupil(l)ary (membrane, etc.).
pupillarité [pypilarite] *n.f. Jur:* pupil(l)age.
pupille¹ [pypil] *n.* (*a*) *Jur:* ward; (*b*) **pupilles de la Nation,** war orphans; **p. de l'État,** child in (state) care.
pupille² *n.f. Anat:* pupil (of the eye).
pupitre [pypitr̥] *n.m.* **1.** desk; **p. à musique,** music stand. **2.** *Mus:* group (of instruments); **chef de p.,** leader (of a group).
pur [pyr] *a.* pure. **1. or p.,** pure gold; **vin p.,** neat, unmixed, undiluted, wine; **liquide p. de tout mélange,** liquid free from all admixture; **p. hasard,** pure chance, mere chance; **la pure vérité,** the simple, plain, honest, unvarnished, truth; **la vérité pure et simple,** the pure and simple truth; **l'invitation est de pure forme,** the invitation is merely a formality; **par pure malice,** out of pure, sheer, malice; **travailler en pure perte,** to work for nothing, to no purpose; **cheval p. sang,** thoroughbred horse. **2. air p.,** pure air; **ciel p.,** clear sky; **conscience pure,** clear conscience; **p. d'esprit,** pure-minded; *n. Pol: etc:* **un p.,** an uncompromising member of a party; a die-hard.
purée [pyre] *n.f.* (*a*) *Cu:* purée; **p. (de pommes de terre),** potato purée; mashed, creamed, potato(es); *F:* mash; **p. de pois,** (i) pease pudding; (ii) (*fog*) pea-souper; *F:* **être dans la p.,** to be down on one's luck; to be in the soup; (*b*) *int. P:* **p.!** hell! blast (it)!
purement [pyrmɑ̃] *adv.* purely.
pureté [pyrte] *n.f.* purity; pureness; clearness (of the sky).
purgatif, -ive [pyrgatif, -iv] *Med:* **1.** *a.* purgative. **2.** *n.m.* purgative; purge.
purgation [pyrgasjɔ̃] *n.f.* purging; purgation.
purgatoire [pyrgatwar] *n.m. Theol:* purgatory.
purge [pyrʒ] *n.f.* **1.** (*a*) *Med:* purge; purgative; (*b*) *Tex:* cleaning (of yarn); (*c*) *Pol:* purge. **2.** *Mch:* draining (of liquid); **robinet de p.,** drain cock; **vis de p.,** bleed screw. **3.** *Jur:* redemption, paying off (of mortgage).
purgeoir [pyrʒwar] *n.m.* purifying tank, filtering tank (of water supply, etc.).
purger [pyrʒe] *v.* **(je purgeai(s); n. purgeons) 1.** *v.tr.* (*a*) to purge, clean, cleanse, clear; **p. un malade,** to purge a patient; **p. les intestins,** to clear out the bowels; **p. un pays de voleurs,** to rid a country of bandits; **p. ses terres de dettes,** to clear, disencumber, one's estate of debt; *Nau:* **p. la quarantaine,** to clear one's quarantine; (*b*) *Jur:* to redeem, pay off (mortgage); (*c*) *Mch:* to blow off (steam); to blow out, drain (cylinder, etc.); *Mec.E:* to bleed. **2. se p.** (*a*) *Med:* to take a purgative, a laxative; (*b*) **se p. d'une accusation,** to clear oneself of an accusation.
purgeur [pyrʒœr] *n.m. Mch:* drain cock, bleeding cock; **p. de vapeur,** blow-off cock; steam trap.
purifiant [pyrifjɑ̃] *a.* purifying, cleansing.
purificateur, -trice [pyrifikatœr, -tris] **1.** *a.* purifying, cleansing. **2.** *n.* purifier, cleanser.
purification [pyrifikasjɔ̃] *n.f.* purification; purifying (of metals, etc.); cleansing, purging (of the blood, etc.).
purifier [pyrifje] *v.* (*pr.sub. & impf.* **n. purifiions, v. purifiiez) 1.** *v.tr.* to purify, cleanse; to refine (metal); to purge (blood, etc.). **2. se p.,** to become pure; to be purified.
purin [pyrɛ̃] *n.m. Agr:* liquid manure; **fosse à p.,** manure pit, sump.
purisme [pyrism] *n.m.* purism (of language, etc.).
puriste [pyrist] *n.* purist.
puritain, -aine [pyritɛ̃, -ɛn] **1.** *n.* puritan. **2.** *a.* puritan(ical).
puritanisme [pyritanism] *n.m.* puritanism.
purotin [pyrɔtɛ̃] *n.m. P:* man who is always hard up; down-and-out; loser.
purpurin, -ine [pyrpyrɛ̃, -in] *a. Lit:* (*a*) crimson; (*b*) purplish.
pur-sang [pyrsɑ̃] *n.m.inv.* thoroughbred (horse).
purulence [pyrylɑ̃s] *n.f. Med:* purulence.
purulent [pyrylɑ̃] *a. Med:* purulent; **foyer p.,** abscess.
pus [py] *n.m. Med:* pus, matter.
pusillanime [pyzilanim] *a. Lit:* pusillanimous; faint-hearted.
pusillanimité [pyzilanimite] *n.f. Lit:* pusillanimity; faint-heartedness.
pustule [pystyl] *n.f.* pustule.
pustuleux, -euse [pystylø, -øz] *a.* pustulous.
putain [pytɛ̃] *n.f. P:* (*a*) prostitute, whore; tart; (*b*) **cette p. de guerre,** this bloody war; (*c*) *int.* bloody hell!
putatif, -ive [pytatif, -iv] *a.* putative, supposed, presumed.
pute [pyt] *n.f. P:* = PUTAIN.
putois [pytwa] *n.m.* polecat; **p. (d'Amérique),** skunk; **crier comme un p.,** to squeal like a pig.
putréfaction [pytrefaksjɔ̃] *n.f.* putrefaction; **matière en p.,** putrefying matter.
putréfier [pytrefje] **1.** *v.tr.* to putrefy, rot. **2. se p.,** to putrefy; to become putrid.
putrescence [pytresɑ̃s] *n.f.* putrescence.
putrescent [pytresɑ̃] *a.* putrescent.
putrescible [pytresibl̥] *a.* liable to putrefy.
putride [pytrid] *a.* putrid, tainted; **fermentation p.,** putrefactive fermentation.
putridité [pytridite] *n.f.* putridity, putridness.
puy [pɥi] *n.m. Geol:* puy.
puzzle [pœzl̥] *n.m.* (jigsaw) puzzle.
pyélite [pjelit] *n.f. Med:* pyelitis.
pygmée [pigme] *n.m.* pygmy, pigmy.
pyjama [piʒama] *n.m.* pyjamas, *NAm:* pajamas; **un p.,** a pair of pyjamas.
pylône [pilon] *n.m.* **1.** *A.Arch:* pylon (of Egyptian temple). **2.** pylon; *El:* tower; lattice mast (supporting telegraph wires, etc.); **grue à p.,** tower crane.
pylore [pilɔr] *n.m. Anat:* pylorus.
pyorrhée [pjɔre] *n.f. Med:* pyorrhoea, *NAm:* pyorrhea.
pyramidal, -aux [piramidal, -o] *a.* pyramidal; *F: A:* **succès p.,** tremendous, colossal, success.
pyramide [piramid] *n.f.* pyramid.
pyrénéen, -enne [pireneɛ̃, -ɛn] *a. & n. Geog:* Pyrenean.
Pyrénées (les) [lepirene] *Pr.n.f.pl. Geog:* the Pyrenees.
pyrèthre [pirɛtr̥] *n.m. Bot:* (*a*) feverfew, pyrethrum;

poudre de p., pyrethrum (powder), insect powder; (*b*) pellitory of Spain.
Pyrex [pirɛks] *n.m. Glassm: R.t.m:* Pyrex.
pyrexie [pirɛksi] *n.f. Med:* pyrexia, fever.
pyrite [pirit] *n.f. Miner:* (iron) pyrites; **p. de cuivre,** copper pyrites.
pyrogallique [pirɔgalik] *a. Ch:* pyrogallic.
pyrogallol [pirɔgalɔl] *n.m. Ch:* pyrogallol.
pyrogravure [pirɔgravyr] *n.f.* poker work.
pyromane [pirɔman] *n.* pyromaniac.
pyromanie [pirɔmani] *n.f.* pyromania.
pyromètre [pirɔmɛtr̥] *n.m. Ph:* pyrometer.
pyrosis [pirɔzis] *n.m. Med:* pyrosis, heartburn.
pyrotechnie [pirɔtɛkni] *n.f.* pyrotechnics.
pyrotechnique [pirɔtɛknik] *a.* pyrotechnic(al).
Pythagore [pitagɔr] *Pr.n.m.* Pythagoras; **théorème de P.,** Pythagoras' theorem.
python [pitɔ̃] *n.m.* python.
pyxide [piksid] *n.f.* **1.** *Bot:* pixidium, pyxis. **2.** *Ecc:* pyxis.

Q

Q, q [ky] *n.m.* (the letter) Q, q.
quadragénaire [kwadraʒenɛr] *a. & n.* quadragenarian.
Quadragésime [kwadraʒezim] *n.f. Ecc:* **(le dimanche de) la Q.,** Quadragesima (Sunday).
quadrangulaire [kwadrɑ̃gylɛr] *a.* quadrangular, four-angled; four-cornered (building).
quadrant [k(w)adrɑ̃] *n.m. Mth:* quadrant.
quadratique [kwadratik] *a.* **1.** *Mth:* quadratic. **2.** *Cryst:* quadratic, tetragonal.
quadrature [kwadratyr] *n.f.* **1.** *Mth:* quadrature, squaring (*esp.* of the circle); *Fig:* **chercher la q. du cercle,** to try to square the circle. **2.** *Astr: Ph:* quadrature; **marées de q.,** neap tides, neaps.
quadrichromie [kwadrikrɔmi] *n.f.* four-colour, *NAm:* -color, printing.
quadriennal, -aux [kwadrijenal, -o] *a.* quadrennial. **1.** lasting for four years; four-year (plan, term). **2.** occurring every four years; four-yearly (festival).
quadrifolié [kwadrifɔlje] *a.* quadrifoliate; four-leaved.
quadrijumeaux [kwadriʒymo] *n.m.pl.* quadruplets.
quadrilatère [k(w)adrilatɛr] *n.m. Mth: Mil: etc:* quadrilateral.
quadrillage [kadrijaʒ] *n.m.* **1.** (*a*) cross ruling, squaring (of paper, map); (*b*) *Mil: etc:* partitioning (of zone in search operations). **2.** (pattern of) checks, squares; chequer work, *esp. NAm:* checker work; *Mapm:* grid, graticule.
quadrille [kadrij] *n.m. Danc:* quadrille; **q. des lanciers,** lancers.
quadrillé [kadrije] *a.* squared, cross-ruled (paper); checked; **carte quadrillée,** grid map; *Aut:* **zone quadrillée,** box junction.
quadriller [kadrije] *v.tr.* (*a*) to rule in squares, to cross-rule (paper); (*b*) to comb (district for criminals, etc.).
quadrimoteur, -trice [k(w)adrimɔtœr, -tris] *a. & n.m.* four-engined (aircraft).
quadriparti [kwadriparti], **quadripartite** [kwadripartit] *a.* quadripartite (corolla, treaty); four-party, four-power (conference).
quadriréacteur [k(w)adrireaktœr] *n.m.* four-engined jet aircraft.
quadrisyllabe [kwadrisilab] *n.m.* quadrisyllable.
quadrisyllabique [kwadrisilabik] *a.* quadrisyllabic.
quadrumane [k(w)adryman] **1.** *a.* quadrumanous, four-handed (animal). **2.** *n.m.* quadrumane.
quadrupède [k(w)adrypɛd] **1.** *a.* quadruped, four-footed (animal). **2.** *n.m.* quadruped.
quadruple [k(w)adrypl̩] *a. & n.m.* quadruple, fourfold; **être payé au q.,** to be repaid fourfold; **payer le q. du prix,** to pay four times the price.
quadrupler [k(w)adryple] *v.tr. & i.* to quadruple; to increase fourfold.
quadruplés -ées [k(w)adryple] *n.pl.* quadruplets, *F:* quads.
quai [ke] *n.m.* (*a*) *Nau:* quay; wharf; pier; **amener un navire à q.,** to bring a ship alongside, to berth a ship; **q. des pétroliers,** oil wharf; **droits de q.,** wharfage; pier dues; *Com:* (*of goods*) **livrable à q.,** ex-quay, ex-wharf; (*b*) embankment (along river); *F:* **le Q. d'Orsay,** the French Foreign Office; (*c*) *Rail:* platform; *P.N:* **accès aux quais** = to the trains; **q. d'arrivée, de départ,** arrival, departure, platform; **le train est à q.,** the train is in; (*d*) *Rail: etc:* **q. de chargement,** loading platform, bay.
quaker, -eresse [kwɛkœr, -(ə)rɛs; kwa-] *n.* Quaker, Quakeress; Friend.
quakerisme [kwɛkrism, kwak(ə)rism] *n.m.* Quakerism.
qualifiable [kalifjabl̩] *a.* **1.** definable; **conduite peu q.,** indescribable conduct. **2.** qualifiable.
qualificatif, -ive [kalifikatif, -iv] *Gram:* **1.** *a.* qualifying (adjective, etc.). **2.** *n.m.* qualifier, epithet.
qualification [kalifikasjɔ̃] *n.f.* **1.** (*a*) *Gram:* qualifying (of noun, etc.); (*b*) *Jur:* legal definition (of crime, etc.). **2.** designation, name, title; **s'attribuer la q. de colonel,** to call oneself colonel. **3.** qualification; **q. professionnelle,** professional qualifications; *Sp:* **obtenir sa q.,** to qualify.
qualifié [kalifje] **1.** *a.* (*a*) **q. pour faire qch.,** qualified to do sth.; **ouvrier q., non q.,** skilled, unskilled, worker; **le ministre q.,** the competent minister; **je suis certainement q. pour en parler,** I am surely entitled, qualified, to speak about it; (*b*) *Jur:* aggravated (offence). **2.** *a. & n. Sp:* **(cheval, coureur) q.,** qualifier; **équipe qualifiée,** qualifying team.
qualifier [kalifje] *v.* (*impf. & pr.sub.* **n. qualifiions)** **1.** *v.tr.* (*a*) to style, call, term, qualify; **acte qualifié (de) crime,** action termed a crime; **q. qn de son titre, de son grade,** to address, designate, s.o. by his correct title; **q. qn de charlatan,** to call s.o. a quack; **conduite qu'on ne saurait q.,** unspeakable conduct; (*b*) *Gram:* to qualify; (*c*) **q. qn à faire qch.,** to qualify s.o. to do sth. **2. se q.** (*a*) **se q. colonel,** to call, style, oneself colonel; (*b*) **se q. pour une fonction,** to qualify for an office; *Sp:* **il s'est qualifié pour la finale,** he qualified for the finals.
qualitatif, -ive [kalitatif, -iv] *a.* qualitative; *Ch:* **analyse qualitative,** qualitative analysis.
qualité [kalite] *n.f.* **1.** quality; (*a*) **bonne, mauvaise, q.,** high, poor, quality; **de première q.,** high-grade, first-rate; **blé de première q.,** prime wheat; **vin de première q.,** choice wine; **minerai de q. inférieure,** low-grade ore; (*b*) (good) quality; **vin qui a de la q.,** wine that has quality; **homme qui a beaucoup de qualités,** man who has many good qualities, points. **2.** quality, property (of sth.); **qualités fébrifuges,** antifebrile properties. **3.** qualification, capacity; profession, occupation; **décliner ses titres et qualités,** to enumerate one's titles and qualifications; to give an account of oneself; to introduce oneself; *Adm:* **nom, prénom et q.,** surname, forename and occupation or description; **il nous révéla sa q. de prêtre,** he disclosed the fact that he was a priest; **agir en q. de tuteur,** to act (in one's capacity) as guardian; **ès qualités,** ex officio; **avoir q. pour agir,** to have authority to act; **avoir les qualités requises pour un emploi,** to have the necessary qualifications, to be qualified, for a job. **4.** *O:* **gens de q.,** people of quality; gentlefolk.
quand [kɑ̃] when. **1.** *conj.* (*a*) **je lui en parlerai q. je le verrai,** I'll mention it to him when I see him; *F:* **q. je vous le disais!** didn't I tell you so! (*b*) **q. (même),** even if, even though, although; **q. il** [kɑ̃til] **me**

l'affirmerait je n'en croirais rien, even if he assured me of it I wouldn't believe it; **je n'en voudrais pas q. (bien) même on me le donnerait,** I wouldn't have it as a gift; **je le ferai q. même,** I'll do it all the same, in spite of everything. **2.** *adv.* **q. viendra-t-il?** when will he come? **dites-moi q. il viendra,** tell me when he will come; **n'importe q.,** no matter when, at any time; **jusqu'à q. serez-vous à Paris?** until when, how long, will you be in Paris? **depuis q. êtes-vous à Paris?** how long, since when, have you been in Paris? **à q. le mariage?** when will the wedding be? **de q. est ce journal?** what is the date of this paper? **pour q. est la réunion,** when is the meeting?

quant à [kɑ̃ta] *prep.phr.* as for; **q. à moi,** as for me, for my part; as far as I am concerned; **q. à cela,** as to that, for that matter; **q. à l'avenir,** as for the future; **q. à le demander, je n'y aurais pas songé,** as for asking for it, I wouldn't have dreamt of it.

quant-à-moi [kɑ̃tamwa], **quant-à-soi** [kɑ̃taswa] *n.m.inv.* dignity, reserve; **rester sur, tenir, son q.-à-s.,** to stand on one's dignity; to keep oneself to oneself.

quantième [kɑ̃tjɛm] *n.m.* day of the month; **quel q. (du mois) sommes-nous?** what's the date?

quantique [kwɑ̃tik] *a. Ph: etc:* quantum (theory, mechanics, number, etc.).

quantitatif, -ive [kɑ̃titatif, -iv] *a.* quantitative (analysis, etc.)

quantité [kɑ̃tite] *n.f.* **1.** quantity; *Mth:* **q. variable,** variable quantity; *Ph:* **q. de mouvement,** momentum, impulse. **2.** (*a*) quantity, amount; **en grande, petite, q.,** in large, small, quantities, amounts; **dans la q. prescrite,** in the prescribed dose; (*b*) **en q.,** in quantity, in bulk; **q., des quantités, de gens,** a lot, a great number, of people.

quantum, *pl.* **-a** [kwɑ̃tɔm, -a] *n.m.* **1.** *Ph:* quantum; **théorie des quanta,** quantum theory. **2.** amount, proportion, ratio; **fixer le q. des dommages-intérêts,** to fix the amount of damages, to assess the damages.

quarantaine [karɑ̃tɛn] *n.f.* **1.** (about) forty, some forty; **approcher de la q.,** to be getting on for forty. **2.** quarantine; **mettre un navire en q.,** to quarantine a ship; **pavillon de q.,** quarantine flag; **purger la q.,** to clear one's quarantine; *F:* **mettre qn en q.,** to send s.o. to Coventry.

quarante [karɑ̃t] *num.a.inv. & n.m.inv.* forty; **page q.,** page forty; **habiter au (numéro) q.,** to live at number forty; **les Q.,** the Forty, the French Academy; *F:* **je m'en fiche comme de l'an q.,** I don't care a damn; *Ten:* **q. partout,** deuce; **les années q.,** the (nineteen) forties.

quarantenaire [karɑ̃tnɛr] *a.* (*a*) *Jur:* lasting for forty years; (*b*) quarantine (regulations, etc.).

quarantième [karɑ̃tjɛm] *num.a. & n.* fortieth.

quart¹ [kar] *n.m.* fourth person, party; **le tiers et le q.,** everybody; anybody; *F:* **il se fiche du q. comme du tiers,** he doesn't give a damn for anybody.

quart² *n.m.* **1.** quarter, fourth part; (*a*) **donner un q. de tour à une vis,** to give a screw a quarter turn; *Com:* **remise du q.,** discount of 25%; **q. d'heure,** quarter of an hour; **dans un petit q. d'heure,** in ten minutes or so; **pour le q. d'heure,** for the time being, for the moment; *F:* **passer un mauvais q. d'heure,** to have a bad time, a trying moment; **trois quarts,** three quarters; **les trois quarts du temps,** most of the time; *F:* **être aux trois quarts ivre, mort,** to be three parts drunk, all but dead; **il est deux heures et q., deux heures un q.,** it's (a) quarter past two; **six heures moins le q., cinq heures trois quarts,** (a) quarter to six; **q. de cercle,** quadrant; *Mus:* **q. de soupir,** semi-quaver rest; *Sp:* **q. de finale,** quarter final; (*b*) **un q. de beurre,** a quarter of a kilo of butter; (*c*) quarter litre, *NAm:* liter, bottle; *Mil:* quarter litre mug. **2.** *Nau:* **q. (de vent),** point of the compass; **nord-est q. est,** north-east by east. **3.** (*a*) *Nau:* watch; **q. en bas,** watch below; **q. en haut,** watch on deck; **petit q.,** dog watch; **officier de q.,** officer of the watch; **homme de q.,** watch keeper; **être de q.,** to be on watch; **faire le q.,** to keep watch; *F:* (*of prostitute*) to walk her beat; (*of policeman*) **battre son q.,** to be on one's beat; (*b*) *Ind:* shift; (*c*) *P:* police station.

quarte [kart] *n.f.* **1.** *Mus:* fourth. **2.** *Fenc:* quart, quarte, carte; **parer en q.,** to parry in carte.

quarteron, -onne [kart(ə)rɔ̃, -ɔn] *a. & n.* quadroon.

quartier [kartje] *n.m.* **1.** quarter, fourth part; **bois de q.,** quartered logs; **la lune est au premier q.,** the moon is in the first quarter; *Cu:* **q. d'agneau, de bœuf,** quarter of lamb, of beef; **cinquième q.,** offal; *Her:* **quartiers de l'écusson,** quarters, quarterings, of the shield. **2.** part, piece; portion (of cake); segment, quarter (of orange); plot (of land); **mettre qch. en quartiers,** to tear sth. to pieces; **q. de lard,** gammon of bacon; **q. de chevreuil,** haunch of venison. **3.** (*a*) district, neighbourhood, *NAm:* neighborhood; *Adm:* ward (of town); **q. des spectacles,** theatreland, *NAm:* theaterland; **q. réservé,** red-light district; **je ne suis pas du q.,** I don't belong to this district; **médecin, cinéma, de q.,** local practitioner, cinema; (*b*) *Mil:* quarters; **rentrer au q.,** to return to quarters, to barracks; **avoir q. libre,** to be off duty; **quartiers d'hiver,** winter quarters; **Q. général,** headquarters; **Grand Q. général,** General Headquarters. **4. faire q. à qn,** to give s.o. quarter; **demander q.,** to ask for quarter; **il ne fait de q. à personne,** he spares nobody.

quartier-maître [kartjemɛtr̥] *n.m. Navy:* leading seaman; *pl. quartier(s)-maîtres.*

quartile [kwartil] *n.m. Stat:* quartile.

quartz [kwarts] *n.m.* (*a*) quartz, rock crystal; (*b*) *Elcs:* quartz crystal; **piloté par q.,** crystal-controlled; **horloge à q.,** quartz clock.

quartzeux, -euse [kwartsø, -øz] *a.* **sable q.,** quartz sand.

quartzite [kwartsit] *n.f.* quartzite, quartz rock.

quasar [kwazar, ka-] *n.m. Astr:* quasar.

quasi¹ [kazi] *n.m. Cu:* chump end (of loin of veal, beef).

quasi² *adv.* quasi, almost; **q. aveugle,** almost blind; **je n'ai q. rien senti,** I felt scarcely anything; **j'en ai la q.-certitude,** I am practically certain of it; *Jur:* **q.-contrat,** implied contract; **q.-délit,** technical offence.

quasiment [kazimɑ̃] *adv. F:* almost, as it were, as one might say; to all intents and purposes; **q. guéri,** as good as cured.

Quasimodo [kazimɔdo] *n.f.* First Sunday after Easter, Low Sunday; **le lundi de (la) Q.,** Low Monday.

quassia [kwasja] *n.m.* **1.** *Bot:* quassia (tree). **2.** *Pharm:* quassia; **q. en copeaux,** quassia chips.

quaternaire [kwatɛrnɛr] *a. Ch: Geol: etc:* quaternary.

quatorze [katɔrz] *num.a.inv. & n.m.inv.* fourteen; **page q.,** page fourteen; **Louis Q.,** Louis the Fourteenth.

quatorzième [katɔrzjɛm] **1.** *num.a. & n.* fourteenth. **2.** *n.m.* fourteenth (part).

quatorzièmement [katɔrzjɛmmɑ̃] *adv.* in the fourteenth place.

quatrain [katrɛ̃] *n.m. Pros:* quatrain.

quatre [katr̥] *num.a.inv. & n.m.inv.* four; **Henri Q.,** Henry the Fourth; **il est arrivé q. ou cinquième,** he arrived fourth or fifth; **le q. août,** the fourth of August; August (the) fourth; **habiter au (numéro) q.,** to live at number four; **pain de q. livres,** quartern loaf; *Row:* **q. barré,** a coxed four; **par q.,** in fours; **se mettre par q.,** to form fours; **clair comme deux et**

deux font q., as clear as daylight; **monter l'escalier q. à q.**, to go upstairs four at a time; to rush upstairs; **avoir la tête en q.**, to have a splitting headache; **se mettre en q. pour faire qch.**, to do one's utmost to accomplish sth.; **il se couperait, se mettrait, en q. pour vous**, he would do anything for you; **se mettre en q. pour plaire à qn**, to bend over backwards to please s.o.; **je me tenais à q. pour ne pas rire**, it was all I could do not to laugh.

Quatre-Cantons [katr(ə)kɑ̃tɔ̃] *n.m.pl. Geog:* **lac des Q.-C.**, Lake Lucerne.

quatre-mâts [katrəmɑ] *n.m.inv.* four-masted ship; four master.

quatre-saisons [katrəsɛzɔ̃] *n.f.inv.* **1.** *Hort:* perpetual-fruiting strawberry; **laitue des q.-s.**, all-the-year-round lettuce. **2. marchand des q.-s.**, costermonger, barrow boy.

Quatre-Temps [katrətɑ̃] *n.m.pl. Ecc:* Ember days.

quatre-vingt-dix [katrəvɛ̃dis] *num.a. & n.m.* ninety.

quatre-vingt-dixième [katrəvɛ̃dizjɛm] *num.a. & n.* ninetieth.

quatre-vingtième [katrəvɛ̃tjɛm] *num.a. & n.* eightieth.

quatre-vingts [katrəvɛ̃] *num.a. & n.m.* (*omits the final* s *when followed by another num.a. or when used as an ordinal*) eighty; **ils étaient q.-vingts**, there were eighty of them; **page q.-vingt**, page eighty; **q.-vingt-un**, eighty-one; **q.-vingt-onze**, ninety-one.

quatrième [katrijɛm] **1.** *num.a. & n.* fourth; **habiter au q. (étage)**, to live on the fourth, *NAm:* the fifth, floor. **2.** *n.f.* (*a*) sequence of four (in card games); (*b*) *Sch:* **(classe de) q.** = *approx.* third form (of secondary school).

quatrièmement [katrijɛm(ə)mɑ̃] *adv.* fourthly; in the fourth place.

quatuor [kwatɥɔr] *n.m. Mus:* quartet(te).

quayage [kejaʒ] *n.m.* quayage, wharfage.

que¹ [k(ə)] *rel.pron.* (*of pers.*) that, whom; (*of thg*) that, which; (*neut.*) which, what; (*in Eng. often omitted*) **1.** (*subject*) *in the phrs.* **advienne q. pourra**, come what may; **coûte q. coûte**, cost what it may. **2.** (*attrib.*) **il mourut en brave soldat qu'il était**, he died like the gallant soldier he was; **idiot q. je suis**, fool that I am; **menteur q. tu es!** you liar! **couvert qu'il était de poussière**, covered with dust as he was; **purs mensonges q. tout cela!** that's all a pack of lies! **c'est une belle maison q. la vôtre**, yours is a beautiful house. **3.** (*object*) **l'homme q. vous voyez**, the man (whom, that) you see; **montrez-moi les livres q. vous avez achetés**, show me the books you have bought; **c'est le meilleur q. nous ayons**, it is the very best we have; **il n'est venu personne q. je sache**, no one has come as far as I know; **4.** (*adv. use*) **les jours qu'il fait chaud**, on hot days; **un jour q. j'étais de service**, one day when I was on duty; **du temps q. les automobiles n'existaient pas**, before cars existed; **depuis trois mois q. j'habite Paris**, for the three months I have been living in Paris; **les trois ans q. j'ai habité à Paris**, the three years (during which) I lived in Paris.

que² *interr.pron.neut.* what? **1.** (*object*) **q. voulez-vous?** what do you want? **q. dit Jean?** what does John say? **qu'y a-t-il à voir dans cette ville?** what is there to be seen in this town? **q. faire?** what can I, we, one, do? what's to be done? **q. dire?** what could I say? **il ne savait q. penser**, he didn't know what to think; **je n'ai q. faire de vos souhaits**, I don't want your good wishes; **q. prendrez-vous, du lait ou de la crème?** which will you take, milk or cream? **2.** (*a*) (*logical subject*) **qu'est-il arrivé? q. s'est-il passé?** what has happened? (*b*) **qu'êtes-vous?** what are you? **qu'est-ce?** what is it? **q. devenir?** what's to become of us, him, etc.? **3.** (*adv. use*) (*a*) (*interr.*) **q. ne le disiez-vous?** why didn't you say so? (*b*) (*exclamatory*) (i) **qu'il est beau!** how handsome he is! **q. c'est bien vrai!** how true! (ii) **q. de déceptions!** how many, what a lot of, disappointments!

que³ *conj.* **1.** that (*often omitted in Eng.*); **je vois qu'il me trompe**, I see (that) he's deceiving me; **je ne doute pas qu'il (ne) consente**, I have no doubt he will consent; **je désire qu'il vienne**, I want him to come; **j'ai peur qu'il ne vienne**, I'm afraid he will come; **je pense q. non**, I think not. **2.** (*a*) (*imp. or optative*) **qu'elle entre!** let her come in! **q. Dieu lui pardonne!** may God forgive him! **q. je vous y reprenne!** just let me catch you at it again! (*b*) (*hypothetical*) **q. la machine chauffe, et il y aura un accident**, let the machine run hot and there will be an accident; (*c*) **(soit) qu'il pleuve ou qu'il fasse du vent**, whether it rains or blows; **q. tu le veuilles ou non**, whether you wish it or not. **3.** (*a*) (*linking up two verbs in the condit.*) **il l'affirmerait q. je ne le croirais pas**, even if he said it was true, I would not believe it; (*b*) **il ne se passe jamais une année qu'il ne nous écrive**, a year never goes by without his writing to us. **4.** (*a*) (*equivalent to*) **afin que, alors que, avant que, depuis que, puisque, sans que, tant que, etc.; approchez qu'on vous entende**, come nearer so that we can hear you; **à peine étais-je rentré q. le téléphone a sonné**, I'd scarcely come in when the telephone rang; **je ne le quitterai pas q. l'affaire ne soit terminée**, I will not leave him till the matter has been settled; **il y a trois jours q. je ne l'ai vu**, it is three days since I saw him; **ne partez pas q. je ne vous aie parlé**, don't go before I have had a talk with you; (*b*) (*to avoid repetition of another conj.*) **quand il entrera et qu'il vous trouvera ici**, when he comes in and finds you here; **quoiqu'il pleuve et qu'il fasse froid**, although it is rainy and cold; **si on vient et qu'on veuille me consulter**, if anyone comes and wants to consult me. **5.** (*in comparison*) **aussi grand q. moi**, as tall as I (am); **tout autre q. moi**, anyone but me; **un autre parapluie q. celui-là**, another umbrella besides that one; **vous écrivez plus correctement q. vous (ne) parlez**, you write more correctly than you speak; **il habite la même maison q. moi**, he lives in the same house as I do, as me. **6.** (*a*) **ne . . . q.**, only; **il n'est q. blessé**, he is only wounded; **il n'a qu'une jambe**, he has only one leg; **il n'a fait qu'entrer et sortir**, he just slipped in and out again; **il ne fait q. de sortir**, he has only just gone out; **je n'en ai q. trop**, I have all too many; **il n'y a pas q. lui qui le sache**, he is not the only one who knows it; **l'homme ne vit pas q. de pain**, man does not live by bread alone; **il ne me reste plus q. vingt francs**, I have only twenty francs left; **je ne bois jamais q. de l'eau**, I never drink anything but water; (*b*) *A: & Lit:* **q. si vous savez la vérité, il est de votre devoir de la révéler**, if you know the truth, it is your duty to reveal it. **7.** *F:* (*a*) **ah! q. non! q. si! q. oui!** ah! surely not! yes indeed! (*b*) **il va au cercle—qu'il dit!** he goes to the club—so he says! (*c*) **ton manteau est dans un état, q. c'est une horreur!** your coat is in a terrible state!

Québec [kebɛk] *Pr.n.m. Geog:* Quebec.

québecois, -oise [kebɛkwa, -waz] *a. & n. Geog:* Quebecer; (native, inhabitant) of Quebec.

quel, quelle [kɛl] *a. & pron.* what, which. **1.** (*correlative*) (*a*) **q. que soit le résultat**, whatever the result may be; **quelle que soit mon affection pour vous**, however great my affection for you, much as I love you; **quels que soient ces hommes**, whoever these men may be; **q. que soit l'endroit où**, wherever, no matter where; (*b*) **à quelle époque que ce soit**, at whatever time; (*c*) **mettez-moi à n'importe quelle table**, put me at any table you like. **2.** (*interr.*) (*a*) **quelle réponse a-**

t-il faite? what was his reply? **quelle heure est-il?** what is the time? **dites-moi quelle heure il est,** tell me the time, what time it is; **q. livre avez-vous pris?** what, which, whose, book did you take? **q. homme?** which man? **q. genre d'homme est-ce?** what sort of a man is he? **je ne sais q. auteur l'a dit,** some author or other has said it; (*b*) **quels sont ces messieurs?** who are these gentlemen? **de ces deux projets q. est le plus sûr?** which is the safer of these two plans? **3.** (*exclamatory*) **q. homme!** what a man! **quelle bonté!** how kind!

quelconque [kɛlkɔ̃k] *a.* **1.** any (whatever); **décrire un cercle passant par trois points quelconques,** to describe a circle passing through any three points; **entrer par l'une q. des portes,** to enter by one or other of the doors. **2. un q. général X,** some general X or other; **répondre d'une façon q.,** to make some sort of reply; **parler de choses quelconques,** to talk about one thing and another. **3.** ordinary, commonplace; **on ne peut pas lui donner un emploi q.,** we can't give him an ordinary job, *F:* any old job; **son travail est q.,** his work isn't up to much.

quelque [kɛlk(ə)] **1.** *a.* (*a*) some, any; **il arrivera q. jour,** he will arrive some day; **adressez-vous à q. autre,** apply to someone else; **avez-vous q. ami qui puisse vous aider?** have you any, some, friend who can help you? (*b*) some, some little, a few; **pendant q. temps,** for some time; **il y a quelques jours,** a few days ago; **je ressentais q. inquiétude,** I felt some slight uneasiness; **cent et quelques mètres,** a hundred metres, *NAm:* meters, plus; **nous étions quarante et quelques,** there were rather more than forty of us; we were forty odd; (*c*) (*correlative to* **qui, que** + *sub.*) **q. ambition qui l'agite,** whatever ambition moves him; **quelques fautes qu'il ait commises,** whatever faults he has committed; **sous q. prétexte que ce soit,** under any pretext whatever; **tout traité de q. nature qu'il soit,** every treaty of whatsoever character; **de q. côté que vous regardiez,** whichever way you look. **2.** *adv.* (*a*) some, about; **q. dix ans,** some, about, ten years; **les q. mille francs qu'il m'a prêtés,** the thousand francs or so, or thereabouts, that he lent me; (*b*) (*correlative to* **que** + *sub.*) **q. grandes que soient ses fautes,** however great his faults may be; **q. méchant qu'il fût,** wicked as he was.

quelque chose [kɛlkəʃoz] *indef.pron.m.inv.* something, anything; **q. c. me dit qu'il viendra,** something tells me he will come; **avez-vous q. c. à dire?** have you anything to say? **q. c. de nouveau, d'autre,** something new, something else; *F:* **il a q. c.,** there's something the matter with him; **il y a q. c.,** there's something up, afoot; **il y est pour q. c.,** he has something to do with it; **cela m'a fait q. c.,** I felt it a good deal; **ça te ferait vraiment q. c. si je m'en allais?** would it really matter to you if I went away? **c'est déjà q. c.,** anyhow that's something; *F:* **q. c. comme deux ans,** something like, about, two years.

quelquefois [kɛlkəfwa] *adv.* sometimes, now and then.

quelque part [kɛlkəpar] *adv.* **1.** somewhere; **cela doit bien venir de q. p.,** it must come from somewhere. **2.** (*correlative to* **que** + *sub.*) **q. p. qu'il fouillât,** wherever he searched.

quelqu'un, quelqu'une [kɛlkœ̃, kɛlkyn], *pl.* **quelques-uns, -unes** [kɛlkəzœ̃, -yn] *indef. pron.* **1.** *m. & f.* (*a*) *sg. A:* **quelqu'une de ces dames va s'en occuper,** one of the ladies will see to it; (*b*) *pl.* **quelques-uns des magasins,** some of the shops; **j'ai lu quelques-unes des lettres,** I have read a few of the letters; **quelques-un(e)s d'entre nous,** a few of us. **2.** *m.* someone, somebody; anyone, anybody; **q. me l'a dit,** someone told me; **si q. vient,** if anybody, somebody, comes; **q. de plus,** someone extra; **q. de trop,** one too many; **y a-t-il eu q. de blessé?** was anyone wounded, injured? **il faudra q. d'assez fort,** it will need someone fairly strong; *F:* **est-il q.?** is he anybody? **ils sont q. dans leur village,** they are somebodies in their own village.

quémander [kemɑ̃de] **1.** *v.i. A:* to beg (from door to door). **2.** *v.tr.* **q. qch. à qn,** to beg for, solicit, sth. from s.o.

quémandeur, -euse [kemɑ̃dœr, -øz] *n. Lit:* beggar; cadger.

qu'en-dira-t-on (le) [ləkɑ̃diratɔ̃] *n.m.inv.* gossip, tittle-tattle; **se moquer du q.,** not to care what people say.

quenelle [kənɛl] *n.f. Cu:* quenelle.

quenotte [kənɔt] *n.f. F:* (*child's language*) tooth.

quenouille [kənuj] *n.f.* **1.** distaff; **succession qui tombe en q.,** succession that falls to the distaff side. **2.** bedpost (of four-poster bed).

querelle [kərɛl] *n.f.* quarrel, dispute; row; **chercher q. à qn,** to try to pick a quarrel with s.o.; **avoir une q. avec qn,** to have a quarrel, a row, with s.o.; **q. d'Allemand,** trumped-up quarrel; **querelles de famille,** family squabbles; **q. d'amoureux,** lovers' tiff; **q. d'ivrognes,** drunken brawl; **familles en q. ouverte,** families in open feud; **épouser la q. de qn,** to take up s.o.'s cause.

quereller [kərele] *v.* **1.** *v.tr.* to quarrel with (s.o.); to nag, scold (s.o.). **2. se q.,** to quarrel, wrangle; to fall out (**avec,** with); to have a tiff.

querelleur, -euse [kərɛlœr, -øz] **1.** *n.* quarreller; *f.* scold. **2.** *a.* quarrelsome.

quérir [kerir] *v.tr.* (*used only in the infin. after the verbs* **aller, venir, envoyer**) **aller q. qn, qch.,** to go and fetch s.o., sth.; to go for s.o., sth.

qu'est-ce que [kɛskə] *interr.pron.* what? (*a*) (*object*) **q. q. vous voulez?** what do you want? (*b*) **q. q. la grammaire?** what is grammar? **q. q. c'est que ça?** what's that? (*c*) *F:* **qu'est-ce qu'il fait beau!** how fine it is! **qu'est-ce qu'on rigole!** what a laugh! (*d*) **q. q. tu avais besoin d'aller lui dire ça?** why did you have to go and tell him that?

qu'est-ce qui [kɛski] *interr.pron.* (*subject*) **1.** what? **q. q. est arrivé?** what has happened? **2.** *F:* who? **q. q. est là?** who's there? **je ne savais pas q. q. était là,** I didn't know who was there.

question [kɛstjɔ̃] *n.f.* **1.** (*a*) question; query; **faire, poser, adresser, une q. à qn,** to ask s.o. a question; **sa fidélité ne fait pas q.,** there is no doubt, no question, of his loyalty; **mettre qch. en q.,** to question sth.; to challenge (statement, s.o.'s loyalty); **voici un point qui fait q.,** this is a debatable point; **il n'y a pas de q.,** there is no doubt about it; (*b*) question, matter, point, issue; **je voudrais vous consulter sur une q. d'affaires,** I would like to consult you on a matter of business; **questions d'actualité,** topics of the day; **ce n'est qu'une q. d'argent,** it is simply a question of money; **il ne saurait être q. de les inviter,** we couldn't think of inviting them; **la personne en q.,** the person in question; *F:* **la q. alcoolisme,** the problem of alcoholism; **ce n'est pas là la q.,** that is not the point; **sortir de la q.,** to wander from the point; **rappeler qn à la q.,** to call s.o. to order; **de quoi est-il q.?** what is it all about? **qu'il n'en soit plus q.,** let us say no more about it; let the subject be dropped; **il est q. de lui élever une statue,** there is some talk of putting up a statue to him; (*c*) *Jur:* (point at) issue; **q. de fait, de droit,** issue of fact, of law. **2.** *Hist:* question; (judicial) torture; **appliquer la q. à qn, mettre qn à la q.,** to put s.o. to the question; to torture s.o.

questionnaire [kɛstjɔnɛr] *n.m.* questionnaire.

questionner [kɛstjɔne] *v.tr.* to question (s.o.); to ask (s.o.) questions.

questionneur, -euse [kɛstjɔnœr, -øz] *a. & n.* inquisitive (person).

quête [kɛt] *n.f.* **1.** (*a*) quest, search; **se mettre en q. de qch., aller à la q. de qch.,** to set out, go, in search of sth.; **gens en q. de plaisirs,** pleasure seekers; (*b*) *Ven:* beating (for the game); tracking, scenting. **2.** collection; **faire la q.,** (i) *Ecc:* to take the collection; (ii) to make a collection (for a fund); *F:* to pass the hat round.

quêter [kete] *v.tr. & i.* (*a*) to collect (alms, etc.); to raise funds (for charity); (*b*) to seek (approval, praise); to fish, angle (for compliments); (*c*) (*of hounds*) to seek (game); to quarter.

quêteur, -euse [kɛtœr, -øz] *n.* alms collector; *Ecc:* taker of the collection.

quêteux [kɛtø] *n.m. Fr.C:* beggar.

queue [kø] *n.f.* **1.** tail; **couper la q. à un cheval,** to dock a horse, a horse's tail; **cheval à longue q.,** long-tailed horse; **cheval à q. écourtée,** bobtail (horse); **q. de renard,** fox's brush; **q. de rat,** rat tail; *Hairdr:* **q. de cheval,** pony tail; **q. de poisson,** (i) fish tail; (ii) *Aut: F:* tail wobble; *F:* (*of play, novel, etc.*) **finir en q. de poisson,** to tail off, fizzle out; **sans q.,** tailless; **à la q. gît le venin,** the sting is in the tail; **il s'en retourna la q. entre les jambes,** he went off with his tail between his legs; *F:* **pas la q. d'un, d'une,** not a blessed one. **2.** tail (of comet, kite, letter); trail (of meteor); stem (of crotchet, quaver); handle (of pan); stalk (of fruit, flower); shank (of button); pin (of brooch); tailpiece (of violin); train (of dress); pigtail, queue (of hair); fang, tang, shank (of tool); rod, stem (of valve); **avion sans q.,** tailless aircraft; **bouton à q.,** shanked button; **habit à q.,** tail coat; **piano à q.,** grand piano; *Typ:* **lettre à q. inférieure,** descending letter. **3.** (tail) end (of a procession, book, winter, piece of material, etc.); tailings (of ore, grain, etc.); **venir en q. (du cortège),** to bring up the rear; *Turf:* **arriver en q.,** to come in at the tail end; **être à la q. de la classe,** to be at the bottom of the class; **une histoire sans q. ni tête,** a story one cannot make head or tail of; **voiture en q. de train, du train,** carriage, *NAm:* coach, in the rear of the train; **wagon de, en, q.,** end carriage; rear portion; **attaquer une armée en q.,** to attack an army in the rear. **4.** queue, file (of people); **faire (la) q.,** to form a queue; to queue up, *NAm:* stand in line; **faire une heure de q.,** to queue, stand in a queue, for an hour. **5.** *Bill:* cue; **faire fausse q.,** to miscue.

queue-d'aronde [kødarɔ̃d] *n.f. Carp:* dovetail, fantail; **assemblage à q.-d'a.,** dovetail(ed) joint; *pl. queues-d'aronde.*

queue-de-chat [kødʃa] *n.f.* **1.** cat-o'-nine-tails. **2.** mare's tail (cloud); *pl. queues-de-chat.*

queue-de-cochon [kødkɔʃɔ̃] *n.f. Tls:* auger bit, gimlet; *pl. queues-de-cochon.*

queue-de-morue [kødmɔry] *n.f.* **1. (habit à) q.-de-m.,** tail coat, *F:* tails. **2.** (painter's) flat brush; *pl. queues-de-morue.*

queue-de-pie [kødpi] *n.f.* = QUEUE-DE-MORUE 1; *pl. queues-de-pie.*

queue-de-rat [kødra] *n.f. Tls:* (*a*) rat tail, rat-tailed file; (*b*) reamer; *pl. queues-de-rat.*

qui¹ [ki] *rel.pron.m. & f. sg. & pl.* **1.** (*subject*) who, that; (*of thg*) which, that; **homme, femme, q. parle français,** man, woman, who speaks French; **phrases q. ne sont pas françaises,** sentences that are not French; **vous q. êtes libres,** you who are free; **c'est la plus âgée q. a répondu,** it was the eldest who answered; **il y a peu de gens q. sachent cela,** there are few people who know that; **il n'y a personne q. ne comprenne cela,** there is no one who does not understand that; **dans ce match, q. était son premier, l'équipe a fait preuve de résistance,** in this their first match, the team showed staying power; **je le vois q. vient,** I see him coming; **c'est un homme charmant, et q. a du talent,** he is a charming man, and talented. **2.** (*a*) (=**celui qui**) **q. vivra verra,** he who lives will see; **tout vient à point à q. sait attendre,** all things come to him who waits; **sauve q. peut,** every man for himself; **adressez-vous à q. vous voudrez,** apply to anyone you like; *F:* **comme q. dirait,** so to speak; in a way; (*b*) (= **ce qui**) **q. plus est,** what is more; **q. pis est,** what is worse; **voilà q. me plaît,** this is what I like; (*c*) **ce q.** *see* CE¹ 3. **3.** (*after prep.*) whom, *occ.* which; (*in Eng. may be omitted*) **voilà l'homme à q. je pensais,** there is the man of whom I was thinking, the man I was thinking about; **il cherche quelqu'un avec q. jouer,** he is looking for someone to play with. **4.** *indef.* some; **on se dispersa, q. d'un côté, q. d'un autre,** we scattered, some going one way, some another. **5. q. que,** who(so)ever, whom(so)ever; **q. que ce soit q. sonne, ne laissez pas entrer,** whoever rings, no matter who rings, don't admit him; **q. que ce soit,** anyone (whatever); **je défie q. que ce soit de le prouver,** I challenge anyone to prove it; **je n'ai trouvé q. que ce soit,** I found no one whatever.

qui² *interr.pron.m.sg.* who? whom? **q. a dit cela?** who said that? **savez-vous q. a dit cela?** do you know who said that? **q. désirez-vous voir?** who(m) do you wish to see? **q. vient à la réunion?** who is coming to the meeting? **devinez q. est arrivé le premier,** guess who was here first; **de q. parlez-vous?** of whom are you speaking? who are you talking about? **à q. est ce canif?** whose knife is this? **de q. êtes-vous fils?** whose son are you? **q. d'autre?** who(m) else? **c'est à q. entrera le premier,** it's a question of who comes in first; **c'était à q. l'aiderait,** they vied with, outdid, each other in helping him; *F:* **il est là,—q. ça? q. donc?** he's there,—who? **q. de vous me suivra?** which of you will follow me?

quia (à) [akɥia] *adv.phr.* **être à q.,** to be in a quandary; **réduire, mettre, qn à q.,** to nonplus, floor, stump, s.o.

Quichotte, Don [dɔ̃kiʃɔt] *Pr.n.m.* Don Quixote; **agir en D. Q.,** to act quixotically.

quiconque [kikɔ̃k] *indef.pron.m.sg.* **1.** who(so)ever; anyone who, anybody who; **q. désobéira sera puni,** whoever disobeys, anyone who disobeys, will be punished. **2.** (= **qui que ce soit**) anyone (else), anybody (else); **q. de mes amis,** any of my friends.

quidam [k(ɥ)idam] *n.m.* (*a*) *Jur:* person (unnamed); (*b*) someone, somebody, an individual.

qui est-ce que [kiɛskə] *interr.pron.m.sg.* whom? **qui est-ce que vous désirez voir?** who(m) do you wish to see?

qui est-ce qui [kiɛski] *interr.pron.m.sg.* who?

quiet, -ète [kjɛ, -ɛt] *a. A:* calm.

quiétisme [kɥietism, kje-] *n.m. Rel.H:* quietism.

quiétiste [kɥietist, kje-] *a. & n. Rel.H:* quietist.

quiétude [kɥietyd, kje-] *n.f.* quietude; peace(fulness); **en toute q.,** with an easy mind.

quignon [kiɲɔ̃] *n.m.* chunk, hunk (of bread).

quille¹ [kij] *n.f.* (*a*) ninepin, skittle; **jeu de quilles,** (i) set of skittles; (ii) skittle alley; **être reçu comme un chien dans un jeu de quilles,** to be treated as an intruder; **se tenir droit comme une q.,** to hold oneself as straight as a ramrod; (*b*) *P:* leg, pin; **il ne tient pas sur ses quilles,** he's shaky on his pins.

quille² *n.f. N.Arch:* keel; **fausse q.,** false keel, outer keel; **q. de roulis, q. latérale,** bilge keel; **poser la q. d'un navire,** to lay down a ship.

quilleur, euse [kijœr, -øz] *n. Fr.C:* skittle player.

quillier [kije] *n.m.* set of skittles.

quincaillerie [kɛ̃kajri] *n.f.* **1.** hardware, ironmongery. **2.** hardware business; ironmonger's.

quincaillier, -ière [kɛ̃kaje, -jɛr] *n.* hardware merchant; ironmonger.

quinconce [kɛ̃kɔ̃s] *n.m.* quincunx; **rivetage en q.,** staggered, zigzag, riveting.

quinine [kinin] *n.f.* quinine; sulphate of quinine.

quinquagénaire [k(ɥ)ɛ̃k(w)aʒenɛr] *a. & n.* quinquagenarian.

Quinquagésime [k(ɥ)ɛ̃kwaʒezim] *n.f. Ecc:* Quinquagesima (Sunday).

quinquennal, -aux [kɛ̃kenal, -o] *a.* quinquennial; five-year (plan); five-yearly (festival).

quinquennat [kɛ̃kena] *n.m.* five-year period, quinquennium.

quinquina [kɛ̃kina] *n.m.* (*a*) *Pharm:* cinchona, quinquina (bark, tree); Peruvian bark; (*b*) **(vin de) q.,** (aperitif) tonic wine.

quint [kɛ̃] *a. A:* fifth; *Hist:* **Charles-Q.,** Charles the Fifth (Holy Roman Emperor).

quintal, -aux [kɛ̃tal, -o] *n.m. Meas:* quintal (= 100 kg).

quinte [kɛ̃t] *n.f.* **1.** *Mus:* fifth, quint; **q. juste,** perfect fifth. **2.** *Cards:* quint. **3.** *Fenc:* quinte. **4.** (*a*) **q. de toux,** fit of coughing; (*b*) fit of bad temper.

quintefeuille [kɛ̃tfœj] (*a*) *n.f. Her: Bot:* cinquefoil; (*b*) *n.m. Arch:* cinquefoil.

quintessence [kɛ̃tesɑ̃s] *n.f.* quintessence.

quintessencié [kɛ̃tesɑ̃sje], **quintessenciel, -elle** [kɛ̃tesɑ̃sjɛl] *a.* quintessential.

quintette [k(ɥ)ɛ̃tɛt] *n.m. Mus:* quintet(te).

quinteux, -euse [kɛ̃tø, -øz] *a.* capricious, crotchety (person); restive (horse).

quintuple [kɛ̃typl̥] *a. & n.m.* quintuple; fivefold; **être payé au q.,** to be repaid fivefold; **trente est (le) q. de six,** thirty is five times as much as six.

quintuplé, -ée [kɛ̃typle] *n.* quintuplet, *F:* quin.

quintupler [kɛ̃typle] *v.tr. & i.* to quintuple; to increase fivefold; to multiply by five.

quinzaine [kɛ̃zɛn] *n.f.* **1.** (about) fifteen, some fifteen; **une q. de francs,** fifteen francs or so. **2.** (*a*) fortnight; **remettre une cause à q.,** to adjourn a case for a fortnight; (*b*) fortnight's pay, wages.

quinze [kɛ̃z] *num.a.inv. & n.m.inv.* **1.** fifteen; **Louis Q.,** Louis the Fifteenth; **le q. mai,** (on) the fifteenth of May; (on) May (the) fifteenth; **demeurer au (numéro) q.,** to live at number fifteen; *Ten:* **q. partout,** fifteen all; *Rugby Fb:* **le q. de France,** the French fifteen. **2. q. jours,** a fortnight; **demain en q.,** a fortnight (from) tomorrow, tomorrow fortnight; **tous les q. jours,** every fortnight, once a fortnight, fortnightly; every other week.

quinzième [kɛ̃zjɛm] **1.** *num. a. & n.* fifteenth. **2.** *n.m.* fifteenth (part).

quinzièmement [kɛ̃zjɛmmɑ̃] *adv.* fifteenthly; in the fifteenth place.

quiproquo [kiprɔko] *n.m.* (*taking of one person, thing, for another*) mistake; misunderstanding.

quittance [kitɑ̃s] *n.f.* receipt, discharge; **q. de loyer,** rent receipt; **q. pour solde,** receipt in full.

quittancer [kitɑ̃se] *v.tr.* **(je quittançai(s))** to receipt (bill).

quitte [kit] *a.* **1.** free, quit, rid **(de,** of); discharged **(de,** from); **être q. de dettes,** to be out of debt; **je suis q. envers vous,** I am no longer in your debt; **nous sommes quittes,** we are quits, square; **tenir qn q. de qch.,** to release s.o. from, let s.o. off, sth.; **je vous tiens q. du reste,** never mind the rest; **il en a été q. pour la peur,** he got off, escaped, with a fright; **ils en ont été quittes à bon compte,** they came off, got off, lightly; **jouer (à) q. ou double,** to play double or quits; *n.m.* (*quiz competition*) **un q. ou double,** double or quits. **2.** *inv.* **q. à,** even if it entails; **je le ferai, q. à être grondé,** I'll do it even if I'm scolded; I'll do it and chance the scolding; **il abandonne ce travail, q. à le reprendre plus tard,** he's giving up this work (i) but may resume it later, (ii) only to resume it later.

quitter [kite] *v.tr.* **1. q. la partie,** to give up; to throw up the sponge. **2.** to leave, quit (place, person); to vacate (office); **q. la grande route,** to turn off the main road; (*of train*) **q. les rails,** to jump the rails; *Nau:* **q. la jetée, le quai,** to cast off; **q. le service,** to leave, quit, the service; **q. le théâtre,** to give up the stage; **q. les affaires,** to retire from business; **q. ses mauvaises habitudes,** to leave off, give up, one's bad habits; **q. la vie,** to depart this life; **quel plaisir de tout q.!** how nice to get away from it all! **il ne l'a pas quittée des yeux,** he never took his eyes off her; **ne le quittez pas des yeux,** keep your eye on him; don't let him out of your sight; **ils se sont quittés bons amis,** they parted good friends; *Tp:* **ne quittez pas (l'écoute)!** hold on! hold the line!

quitus [k(ɥ)itys] *n.m.* receipt in full; *Jur:* quietus, final discharge (from debt, liability, etc.).

qui-vive [kiviv] *n.m.inv.* **être, se tenir, sur le q.-v.,** to be on the quivive, on the alert.

quoi¹ [kwa] *rel.pron.neut.* what. **1. ce sur q. l'on discute,** what is being discussed; **ce à q. je m'oppose,** what I object to; **c'est en q. vous vous trompez,** that is where you are wrong; **après q.,** after which; **travaille, sans q. tu ne mangeras pas,** work, otherwise you won't eat. **2. il a bien autre chose à q. penser!** he has something else to think about! **un autre fait, à q. vous n'avez pas pris garde,** another fact, which you have left out of consideration; **il a de q. vivre,** he has enough to live on; *F:* **il a de q.,** he's well off, comfortably off; **il y a de q. vous faire enrager,** it's enough to drive you mad; **il n'y a pas de q. être fier,** there's nothing to be proud of; (*when receiving thanks, apologies*) **il n'y a pas de q.,** don't mention it; not at all; *NAm:* you're welcome! **avez-vous de q. écrire?** have you anything to write with? **il faut trouver de q. allumer le feu,** we must find something to light the fire with. **3. voilà comme q. je me suis trouvé là,** that's how I happened to be there. **4.** (*correlative to* **qui, que** + *sub.*) (*a*) **q. qui survienne, restez calme,** whatever comes of it, keep calm; **q. qu'il en soit,** however that may be; **q. qu'on fasse, il n'est jamais content,** no matter what you do, whatever you do, he's never satisfied; (*b*) **q. que ce soit,** anything (whatever); **puis-je vous être utile en q. que ce soit?** can I be of use to you in any way? **avez-vous dit q. que ce soit?** did you say anything (at all)? **q. que ce soit qui l'en empêche,** whatever may be preventing him.

quoi² *interr.pron.neut.* what? **1. qui ou q. vous a donné cette idée?** who or what gave you the idea? **q. d'autre?** what else? **q. de nouveau?** what news? **q. de plus simple?** what could be simpler, easier? **eh bien! q.?** well, what about it? **vous désirez q.?** what is it you want? **les journaux ne savent (pas) q. ébruiter,** the papers don't know what to disclose; **de q. parlez-vous?** what are you talking about? **à q. pensez-vous?** what are you thinking of? **en q. puis-je vous être utile?** can I help you? **à q. bon (faire qch.)?** what's the use, the good (of doing sth.)? **en q. est-ce? c'est en q.?** what is it made of? **on te demande—q.?** you are wanted—what (did you say)? **2.** *int.* **(mais) q.! q. donc!** what! what's that? **q., c'est vous!** what, is it you?

quoique [kwak(ə)] *conj. usu.* + *sub.* (al)though; (*a*) **quoiqu'il soit pauvre il est généreux,** although he is poor he is generous; (*b*) (*with ellipsis of verb*) **je suis heureux q. garçon,** I am happy though a bachelor; *F:* **nous recevons souvent des coups, q., vous savez, nous en donnons aussi,** we often receive blows, but then, of course, we hit back.

quolibet [kɔlibɛ] *n.m.* gibe; **poursuivre qn de quolibets,** to gibe, jeer, at s.o.

quorum [k(w)ɔrɔm] *n.m.* quorum.
quota [k(w)ɔta] *n.m.* quota.
quote-part [kɔtpar] *n.f.* share, quota, portion; *pl. quotes-parts.*
quotidien, -ienne [kɔtidjɛ̃, -jɛn] **1.** *a.* daily, everyday; **la vie quotidienne,** everyday life. **2.** *n.m.* **les quotidiens,** the daily papers, the dailies.
quotidiennement [kɔtidjɛnmɑ̃] *adv.* daily, every day.
quotient [kɔsjɑ̃] *n.m.* **1.** *Mth: etc:* quotient. **2. q. électoral,** electoral quota; **q. intellectuel,** intelligence quotient, I.Q.
quotité [kɔtite] *n.f.* quota, share, proportion; *Jur:* **q. disponible,** disposable portion of estate.

R

R, r [ɛr] *n.m.* (the letter) R, r; **rouler les r,** to roll one's r's.
rabâchage [rabɑʃaʒ] *n.m.* (tedious) repetition.
rabâcher [rabɑʃe] **1.** *v.i.* to say the same thing over and over again. **2.** *v.tr.* **ils rabâchent toujours la même chose,** they're always harping on the same string; **r. une leçon,** to learn a lesson by going over it again and again.
rabâcheur, -euse [rabɑʃœr, -øz] *n. & a.* repetitive (person); **il est très r.,** he's always repeating himself, always harping on the same thing.
rabais [rabɛ] *n.m.* reduction (in price); allowance, rebate, discount; **r. en cas de paiement comptant,** discount for cash; **faire un r. sur qch.,** to make a reduction, an allowance, on sth.; **vendre qch. au r.,** to sell sth. at a discount, at a reduced price.
rabaissement [rabɛsmɑ̃] *n.m.* **1.** lowering (of blind, price). **2.** disparagement.
rabaisser [rabese] **1.** *v.tr.* (*a*) to lower (sth.); to reduce (price); (*b*) to depreciate, disparage, belittle (s.o., talent, etc.). **2. se r.,** to humble, lower, oneself.
rabat [raba] *n.m.* **1.** bands, cravat (of official costume); turned-down piece; flap (of handbag, etc.). **2.** *Ven:* beating (for game).
rabat-joie [rabaʒwa] *n.m. inv.* killjoy, spoilsport; wet blanket.
rabattable [rabatabl̥] *a.* that can be folded back; *Aut:* **capote r.,** drophead.
rabattage [rabataʒ] *n.m.* beating (for game), driving (of game); heading off (of fugitives).
rabatteur, -euse [rabatœr, -øz] *n.* **1.** *Ven:* beater. **2.** tout; *esp.* hotel tout.
rabattre [rabatr̥] (*conj. like* BATTRE) **1.** *v.tr.* (*a*) to fold (sth.) back; to shut down (lid); to lower, pull down (blind); to turn down (collar); to tilt back (seat); **r. une couture,** (i) to fell a seam; (ii) to press down, flatten, a seam; **r. le bord d'une tôle,** to flange a plate; **porte rabattue contre la paroi,** door folded back to the wall; **le vent rabat la fumée,** the wind is driving down the smoke; (*b*) to reduce, lessen, diminish; to cut back (tree, branch); **r. tant du prix,** to take, *F:* knock, so much off the price; **je n'en rabattrai pas un sou,** I won't take a penny less for it; **r. l'orgueil de qn,** to humble s.o.'s pride; **r. de ses prétentions, en r.,** to climb down, to draw in one's horns; *Knit:* **r. les mailles,** to cast off; (*c*) to drive, head off (game, fugitives); (*d*) *v.i.* **il faut r. à droite,** you must turn off, bear, to the right. **2. se r.** (*a*) **table qui se rabat,** folding, drop leaf, table; (*b*) **l'armée se rabattit sur la ville,** the army fell back on the town; (*c*) **ayant épuisé ce sujet, il se rabattit sur la politique,** having exhausted this subject, he fell back on politics; (*d*) *Rac: Aut:* to cut in (after overtaking).
rabattu [rabaty] *a.* turned down; **col r.,** turn(ed)-down collar; **chapeau r.,** slouch hat; **couture rabattue,** run and fell seam.
rabbin [rabɛ̃] *n.m.* rabbi; **grand r.,** Chief Rabbi.
rabbinique [rabinik] *a.* rabbinical.
rabbinisme [rabinism] *n.m.* rabbinism.
rabbiniste [rabinist] *n.m. & f.* rabbinist.
rabdomancie [rabdɔmɑ̃si] *n.f.* rhabdomancy, water divining.
rabelaisien, -ienne [rablɛzjɛ̃, -jɛn] *a.* Rabelaisian.
rabiot [rabjo] *n.m. P:* **1.** *Mil:* extra ration; buckshee. **2.** (*a*) extra work; overtime; (*b*) *Mil:* extra period of service.
rabioter [rabjɔte] *v.i. P:* **1.** (*a*) to appropriate, scrounge, surplus food, etc.; (*b*) *v.tr.* to wangle (sth.). **2.** to make illicit profits; to make a bit on the side.
rabique [rabik] *a.* rabic, rabid (virus).
râble[1] [rɑbl̥] *n.m.* back (of hare, rabbit); *Cu:* **r. de lièvre,** saddle of hare; *F:* **il m'a sauté sur le r.,** he jumped on me.
râble[2] *n.m.* fire rake.
râblé [rable] *a.* broad-backed, strong-backed, strapping (fellow).
rabot [rabo] *n.m. Join:* plane; **r. à languette,** grooving plane, tongue plane.
rabotage [rabɔtaʒ] *n.m. Join:* planing.
raboter [rabɔte] *v.tr.* (*a*) to plane (wood); (*b*) to scrape, rub, graze (surface); **r. son style,** to polish one's style.
raboteur [rabɔtœr] *n.m. Join:* planer.
raboteuse[1] [rabɔtøz] *n.f. Join:* planing machine, planer.
raboteux, -euse[2] [rabɔtø, -øz] *a.* **1.** rough, uneven (surface); knotty (wood); bumpy (road). **2.** unpolished, rugged (style).
rabougri [rabugri] *a.* stunted (plant, person).
rabougrir [rabugrir] **1.** *v.tr.* to stunt the growth of (sth.). **2.** *v.i. & pr.* to become stunted, shrunken.
rabouter [rabute] *v.tr.* to join end to end.
rabrouer [rabrue] *v.tr.* to snub (s.o.); to brush (s.o.) off.
racaille [rakaj] *n.f.* rabble, riff-raff.
raccommodable [rakɔmɔdabl̥] *a.* mendable, repairable.
raccommodage [rakɔmɔdaʒ] *n.m.* **1.** mending, repairing (of garments, etc.); darning. **2.** mend, repair; darn.
raccommodement [rakɔmɔdmɑ̃] *n.m.* reconciliation.
raccommoder [rakɔmɔde] *v.tr.* **1.** to mend, repair (dress, watch, etc.); to darn (stocking). **2.** to reconcile (two persons); **ils se sont raccommodés,** they made it up, became friends again.
raccommodeur, -euse [rakɔmɔdœr, -øz] *n.* mender, repairer.
raccompagner [rakɔ̃paɲe] *v.tr.* to accompany (s.o.) back; **je vais vous r.,** I'll take you back, see you home, go back with you.
raccord [rakɔr] *n.m.* **1.** linking up. **2.** join (in a building, picture, etc.); **papier sans raccords,** (wall)-paper with no pattern repeat; **faire des raccords (de peinture),** to touch up (the paintwork); *Rec:* **faire un r. à une bande magnétique,** to splice a tape; *F:* **faire un r.,** to touch up one's make-up. **3.** connection, coupling; joint; nipple, union (of pipes); **bouchon de r.,** adapter plug; *El:* **r. mâle et femelle,** plug and socket connection; **r. de lampe,** lamp adapter, connector; **r. de graissage,** grease nipple.
raccordement [rakɔrdəmɑ̃] *n.m.* **1.** adjusting; *Rail: Civ.E:* **rayon de r. d'une courbe,** transition radius of a curve. **2.** joining; linking up; connecting; **pièces de r.,** making-up lengths (of piping, etc.); *Rail:* **voie de r.,** (i) junction line, loop line; (ii) factory siding; *El:* **boîte de r.,** connecting box (for cables, etc.).
raccorder [rakɔrde] **1.** *v.tr.* (*a*) to join (up), connect,

unite, couple; to link up (buildings, roads); *El:* **r. à la masse, à la terre,** to earth; *NAm:* to ground; (*b*) to bring (parts) into line; to make (parts) flush; (*c*) *Rec:* to splice (a tape). **2. se r.,** to fit together, to link up.

raccourci [rakursi] *n.m.* (*a*) abridgment, abbreviation; (*b*) **en r.,** briefly, in brief; **voici l'histoire en r.,** this, in brief, is the story; these are the outlines of the story; **la famille est la société en r.,** the family is society in miniature; (*c*) *Art:* foreshortening; **bras en r.,** foreshortened arm; (*d*) short cut (to a place); **prendre (par) un r.,** to take a short cut.

raccourcir [rakursir] **1.** *v.tr.* (*a*) to shorten; to take up (sleeve, etc.); to reduce the length of (sth.); **r. ses pas,** to take shorter steps; **r. son bras,** to draw up one's arm; **tomber à bras raccourcis sur qn,** to pitch into s.o.; to go for s.o. tooth and nail; **r. son chemin,** to take a short cut; (*b*) to abridge, curtail; to cut (speech, etc.) short; (*c*) *Art:* to foreshorten. **2.** *v.i. & pr.* to grow shorter; to shorten; **les jours (se) raccourcissent,** the days are growing shorter, drawing in.

raccourcissement [rakursismɑ̃] *n.m.* shortening. **1.** (*a*) reducing (in length); (*b*) abridging, abridgment; (*c*) *Art:* foreshortening. **2.** growing shorter; shrinking (of cloth); drawing in (of days).

raccroc [rakro] *n.m.* fluke, lucky stroke; **par r.,** by a fluke.

raccrochage [rakrɔʃaʒ] *n.m.* accosting; soliciting; touting.

raccrocher [rakrɔʃe] **1.** *v.tr.* (*a*) to hook up, hang up, (sth.) again; *Tp:* **r. (l'appareil),** to put down the receiver; to ring off; to hang up; **ce boxeur devrait r.,** it's time this boxer retired; (*b*) *F:* to recover (sth.); to get hold of (s.o., sth.) again; (*c*) to stop (s.o., in the street, etc.); (*of prostitute*) to accost (passer-by). **2. se r.** (*a*) **se r. à qch.,** to catch hold of sth.; to catch on to sth.; **se r. à une espérance,** to cling to a hope; **se r. à tout,** to clutch at every straw; (*b*) *F:* to recoup one's losses.

raccrocheuse [rakrɔʃøz] *n.f.* street walker.

race [ras] *n.f.* race. **1.** ancestry, descent; **de r. noble,** of noble blood. **2.** stock, breed; **la r. blanche,** the white race; **la r. chevaline,** the horse species; **améliorer, croiser, les races,** to improve, to cross, breeds; **chien, taureau, de r., qui a de la r.,** pure-bred dog, bull; pedigree dog, bull; **cheval de r.,** thoroughbred horse; *Prov:* **bon chien chasse de r.,** what's bred in the bone comes out in the flesh; **il chasse de r.,** he's a chip off the old block; **elle a de la r.,** she's distinguished, aristocratic; *F:* **quelle (sale) r.!** what a brood! what a set!

racé [rase] *a.* (*of animal*) thoroughbred, pure bred; true to stock; (*of pers.*) aristocratic; distinguished; **Basque r.,** pure Basque; *F:* **profil r.,** clean, elegant, lines (of car, yacht).

racème [rasɛm] *n.m. Bot:* raceme.

rachat [raʃa] *n.m.* (*a*) repurchase, buying back; **pacte de r.,** covenant of redemption; **avec faculté de r.,** with option of repurchase, of redemption; **r. des captifs,** ransom of the prisoners; (*b*) *Ins:* surrender (of policy); **valeur de r.,** surrender value; (*c*) **r. d'un péché,** atonement for a sin.

rachetable [raʃtabl̥] *a.* redeemable (stock); atonable (sin).

racheter [raʃte] *v.tr.* (*conj. like* ACHETER) **1.** (*a*) to repurchase; to buy (sth.) back; (*at auction*) to buy (sth.) in; (*b*) to redeem (debt, pledge); to make up, compensate, for (a fault); to ransom (prisoner); **Jésus-Christ est mort pour r. les hommes,** Christ died to redeem mankind; **r. ses péchés,** to atone for one's sins; **r. son honneur,** to retrieve one's honour; (*c*) *Ins:* to surrender (policy); to redeem (annuity). **2.** to make a further purchase of (sth.), to buy some more of (sth).

rachidien, -ienne [raʃidjɛ̃, -jɛn] *a. Anat:* rachidian (bulb, canal).

rachis [raʃis] *n.m. Anat: Bot:* rachis.

rachitique [raʃitik] *a. & n. Med:* rachitic; rickety.

rachitisme [raʃitism] *n.m. Med:* rachitis; rickets.

racial, -aux [rasjal, -o] *a.* racial.

racine [rasin] *n.f.* (*a*) root (of plant, hair, nail, tooth, etc.); *Bot:* **r. pivotante,** tap root; **r. de gingembre,** ginger race; **cultiver des racines,** to grow root vegetables; **jeter, pousser, des racines,** to throw out roots, to strike (root); **prendre r.,** to take root; (*of pers.*) to stay put; **couper le mal dans sa r.,** to strike at the root of the evil; (*b*) *Mth:* **r. carrée, cubique,** square, cube, root; (*c*) *Ling:* **r. d'un mot,** root of a word.

raciner [rasine] *v.tr. Bookb:* to marble (the covers).

racisme [rasism] *n.m.* rac(ial)ism.

raciste [rasist] rac(ial)ist.

racket [rakɛt] *n.m. F:* racket.

racketteur [rakɛtœr] *n.m. F:* racketeer.

raclage [raklaʒ] *n.m.* scraping.

raclée [rakle] *n.f. F:* hiding, licking; **flanquer, administrer, une r. à qn,** to give s.o. a thrashing, a licking.

raclement [rakləmɑ̃] *n.m.* scraping (noise).

racler [rakle] *v.tr.* **1.** to scrape (skin, carrot, etc.); **r. une allée,** to rake a drive; *F:* **r. les fonds de tiroirs,** to scrape the barrel; **r. du, le, violon,** to scrape, saw, on the fiddle; **se r. la gorge,** to clear one's throat.

raclette [raklɛt] *n.f. Tls:* (*a*) scraper; (*b*) *Phot: etc:* squeegee; (*c*) *Hort:* hoe; (*d*) (baby's) pusher.

racleur, -euse [raklœr, -øz] **1.** *n.* scraper. **2.** *n.m. I.C.E:* **(segment) r. d'huile,** scraper ring.

racloir [raklwar] *n.m. Tls:* (*a*) scraper; (*b*) spokeshave; (*c*) squeegee.

racolage [rakɔlaʒ] *n.m.* **1.** (*a*) *Hist:* crimping; impressing (into army, navy); (*b*) **r. de partisans,** enlisting of supporters. **2.** *Jur:* soliciting, accosting.

racoler [rakɔle] *v.tr.* **1.** (*a*) *Hist:* to crimp, impress (men into army, navy); (*b*) **r. des partisans,** to enlist, tout for, supporters. **2.** *Jur:* to solicit, accost.

racoleur, -euse [rakɔlœr, -øz] *n.* **1.** (*a*) *Hist:* crimp; (*b*) propagandist; tout. **2.** *n.f.* **racoleuse,** street walker.

racontable [rakɔ̃tabl̥] *a.* relatable, tellable.

racontar [rakɔ̃tar] *n.m. F:* story, piece of gossip; **ce n'est que des racontars,** it's just tittle-tattle.

raconter [rakɔ̃te] *v.tr.* to tell, relate, narrate, recount; **r. de longues histoires,** to spin long yarns; **il en a raconté de belles,** he told some fine, tall, stories; **qu'est-ce qu'il raconte là?** what ever is he talking about? **allez, racontez!** out with it!

raconteur, -euse [rakɔ̃tœr, -øz] *n.* (story)teller, narrator.

racoon [rakun] *n.m. Z:* rac(c)oon.

racornir [rakɔrnir] **1.** *v.tr.* (*a*) to make (sth.) hard, tough (as horn); (*b*) to shrivel (sth.) (up). **2. se r.** (*a*) to grow horny, hard, tough; to harden; (*b*) to shrivel up.

racornissement [rakɔrnismɑ̃] *n.m.* (*a*) hardening; toughening; (*b*) shrivelling.

racquitter (se) [sərakite] *v.pr.* to recoup oneself; to retrieve one's losses.

radar [radar] *n.m.* radar; **r. à ondes entretenues,** continuous-wave radar; **balayage r.,** radar scan; **écho r.,** radar echo; **r. d'autoguidage,** homing radar.

radariste [radarist] *n.m. & f.* radar operator.

rade [rad] *n.f. Nau:* roadstead, roads; **r. foraine, ouverte,** open roadstead; **r. fermée,** sheltered roadstead; **navire en r.,** ship in the roads; **mettre un navire en r.,** to lay up a ship; **mettre qn, un projet, en r.,** to leave s.o. in the lurch; to shelve a project.

radeau, -eaux [rado] *n.m.* raft; (*a*) **r. de sauvetage,** life raft; (*b*) raft (of floating logs).

radial, -ale, -aux [radjal, -o] *a. & n.* radial. **1.** (*a*) *a.* **pneumatique à carcasse radiale,** radial-ply tyre; (*b*) *n.f.* **radiale,** radial road. **2.** *a. & n.m. Anat:* radial (muscle, nerve).

radian [radjɑ̃] *n.m. Mth:* radian.

radiance [radjɑ̃s] *n.f.* radiance.

radiant [radjɑ̃] **1.** *a.* radiant (heat, etc.); **pouvoir r.,** radiating capacity. **2.** *n.m. Astr:* radiant (point).

radiateur [radjatœr] *n.m.* radiator; (*a*) **r. à eau chaude,** hot-water radiator; **r. électrique,** electric fire, radiator; **r. soufflant,** fan heater; (*b*) *Aut: etc:* **r. à nid d'abeilles,** honeycomb radiator.

radiation[1] [radjasjɔ̃] *n.f.* (*a*) erasure, striking out, crossing out; cancellation (of debt); (*b*) striking off the roll; disbarment (of barrister); striking off (of solicitor).

radiation[2] *n.f. Ph:* radiation; **r. cosmique,** cosmic radiation; *Elcs:* **r. (de) haute fréquence,** high-frequency radiation; *Atom.Ph:* **r. alpha, bêta,** alpha, beta, radiation; alpha-ray, beta-ray, emission.

radical, -ale, -aux [radikal, -o] **1.** *a.* (*a*) *Mth: Bot: Pol:* radical; **signe r.,** radical, root, sign; (*b*) radical, complete; **réformes radicales,** radical, sweeping, reforms. **2.** *n. Pol:* radical. **3.** *n.m. Ling:* root, radical; *Mth:* radical, root sign; *Ch:* radical; group.

radicalement [radikalmɑ̃] *adv.* radically.

radicalisme [radikalism] *n.m. Pol:* radicalism.

radical-socialisme [radikalsɔsjalism] *n.m. Pol:* radical socialism.

radical-socialiste [radikalsɔsjalist] *a. & n.m. & f. Pol:* radical socialist; *pl. radicaux-socialistes.*

radicelle [radisɛl] *n.f. Bot:* radicel, rootlet.

radicule [radikyl] *n.f. Bot:* radicle.

radier[1] [radje] *n.m. Civ.E:* frame, floor, bed; sill (of lock gate); apron (of dock); **r. de fondation,** foundation raft.

radier[2] *v.tr.* (*impf. & pr.sub.* **n. radiions**) to erase; to strike (sth.) out; to strike (sth., s.o.) off, cross (sth., s.o.) off (a list, etc.).

radiesthésie [radjɛstezi] *n.f.* radiesthesia; dowsing.

radiesthésiste [radjɛstezist] *n.m. & f.* radiesthesist; dowser.

radieux, -euse [radjø, -øz] *a.* radiant (sun, eyes); dazzling; beaming (with joy).

radin [radɛ̃] *a. & n.m. P:* mean, stingy (person).

radiner [radine] *v.i. P:* to come (back); to turn up.

radio [radjo] *F:* **1.** *n.m.* (*a*) radio(gram); (*b*) radio operator. **2.** *n.f.* (*a*) radio, wireless; (i) **à la r.,** on the radio; **passer à la r.,** to broadcast, go on the air, the radio; (ii) radio (set); (*b*) radiotelegraphy; (*c*) radiotelephony; (*d*) (i) X-ray photograph; (ii) **passer à la r., passer une r.,** to be X-rayed.

radioactif, -ive [radjɔaktif, -iv] *a.* radioactive.

radioactivité [radjɔaktivite] *n.f.* radioactivity.

radioalignement [radjɔaliɲ(ə)mɑ̃] *n.m. Av: Nau:* radio-beacon route; **voler par r.,** to fly airways.

radioastronomie [radjɔastrɔnɔmi] *n.f.* radio astronomy.

radiobalisage [radjɔbalizaʒ] *n.m.* radio-beacon navigation; *Av:* airways navigation.

radiobalise [radjɔbaliz] *n.f.* radio beacon; marker beacon.

radiocommunication [radjɔkɔmynikasjɔ̃] *n.f.* radiocommunication.

radiocompas [radjɔkɔ̃pɑ] *n.m. Av:* radio compass.

radioconducteur [radjɔkɔ̃dyktœr] *n.m.* radio conductor; coherer.

radiodermite [radjɔdɛrmit] *n.f. Med:* radiodermatitis; X-ray dermatitis.

radiodiagnostic [radjɔdjagnɔstik] *n.m. Med:* X-raydiagnosis.

radiodiffuser [radjɔdifyze] *v.tr. W.Tel:* to broadcast.

radiodiffusion [radjɔdifysjɔ̃] *n.f. W.Tel:* broadcasting.

radioélectricien, -ienne [radjɔelɛktrisjɛ̃, -jɛn] *n.* radio (and television) technician.

radiogénique [radjɔʒenik] *a. F:* **il a une voix r.,** he has a good broadcasting voice.

radiogoniomètre [radjɔgɔnjɔmɛtr̥] *n.m.* radiogoniometer, direction finder.

radiogoniométrie [radjɔgɔnjɔmetri] *n.f.* radiogoniometry; direction finding.

radiogramme [radjɔgram] *n.m.* radiogram. **1.** radiograph, X-ray photograph. **2.** radio telegram.

radiographe [radjɔgraf] *n.m. & f.* radiographer.

radiographie [radjɔgrafi] *n.f.* (*a*) radiography, X-ray photography; (*b*) X-ray photograph, radiograph.

radiographier [radjɔgrafje] (*impf. & pr.sub.* **n. radiographiions**) *v.tr.* to radiograph; to X-ray.

radiographique [radjɔgrafik] *a.* radiographic; **examen r.,** X-ray examination.

radioguidage [radjɔgidaʒ] *n.m. Av: Nau:* radio control; radio direction; radio guidance; *Ball:* homing; *W.Tel:* traffic information (for motorists).

radioguidé [radjɔgide] *a.* radio-controlled; guided (missile).

radio(-)journal [radjɔʒurnal] *n.m. W.Tel:* (broadcast) news, news bulletin.

radiologie [radjɔlɔʒi] *n.f.* radiology.

radiologique [radjɔlɔʒik] *a.* radiological; **examen r.,** X-ray examination.

radiologue [radjɔlɔg], **radiologiste** [radjɔlɔʒist] *n.* radiologist.

radiomètre [radjɔmɛtr̥] *n.m. Ph:* radiometer.

radionavigant [radjɔnavigɑ̃] *n.m. Nau: Av:* radio officer.

radionavigation [radjɔnavigasjɔ̃] *n.f.* navigation by radar.

radiophare [radjɔfar] *n.m. Nau: Av:* radio beacon.

radiophonie [radjɔfɔni] *n.f.* radiophony; wireless telephony.

radiorepérage [radjɔrəperaʒ] *n.m.* radiolocation.

radioreportage [radjɔrəpɔrtaʒ] *n.m. W.Tel:* broadcasting (of news); running commentary.

radioreporter [radjɔrəpɔrtɛr] *n.m. W.Tel:* reporter, commentator.

radioscopie [radjɔskɔpi] *n.f.* radioscopy; X-ray examination.

radioscopique [radjɔskɔpik] *a.* **examen r.,** X-ray examination.

radiosonde [radjɔsɔ̃d] *n.f.* **1.** *Meteor:* radiosonde. **2.** *Av:* radio altimeter.

radiotechnique [radjɔtɛknik] *n.f.* radiotechnology.

radiotélégramme [radjɔtelegram] *n.m.* radio telegram.

radiotélégraphie [radjɔtelegrafi] *n.f.* radio telegraphy, wireless telegraphy.

radiotélégraphier [radjɔtelegrafje] *v.tr.* (*conj. like* TÉLÉGRAPHIER) to radio (a telegram).

radiotélégraphique [radjɔtelegrafik] *a.* radiotelegraphic, wireless.

radiotéléphonie [radjɔtelefɔni] *n.f.* radiotelephony, wireless telephony.

radiotélescope [radjɔtelɛskɔp] *n.m.* radio telescope.

radiotélévisé [radjɔtelevize] *a.* broadcast on both radio and television.

radiothérapie [radjɔterapi] *n.f.* radiotherapy; X-ray treatment.

radis [radi] *n.m.* radish; *F:* **ne pas avoir un r.,** to be (stony) broke; **je ne dépense pas un r. de plus,** I'm not spending a penny more.

radium [radjɔm] *n.m.* radium.

radius [radjys] *n.m. Anat:* radius.

radotage [radɔtaʒ] *n.m.* rambling talk (of old person); twaddle.

radoter [radɔte] *v.i.* (*a*) to ramble on (incoherently); **il commence à r.,** he's getting a bit gaga; (*b*) to keep on repeating oneself.

radoteur, -euse [radɔtœr, -øz] *n.* dotard.

radoub [radu] *n.m. Nau:* graving (of ship); **navire en r.,** ship under repair, in dry dock; **bassin de r.,** graving dock, dry dock.

radouber [radube] *v.tr.* (*a*) to repair the hull of (ship); to dock (ship in dry dock); (*b*) to mend, repair (net); *F:* to patch (sth.) up.

radoucir [radusir] **1.** *v.tr.* to calm, soften; to calm, smooth (s.o.) down; to mollify (s.o.); **la pluie a radouci le temps,** the rain has brought milder weather. **2. se r.,** to calm down; (*of weather*) to become milder.

radoucissement [radusismɑ̃] *n.m.* (*a*) softening (of voice, etc.); calming down; (*b*) *Meteor:* milder spell; change for the better.

rafale [rafal] *n.f.* (*a*) squall; strong gust, blast (of wind); **vent à rafales,** blustering wind; gusty wind; **temps à rafales,** squally weather; (*b*) burst (of gunfire).

raffermir [rafɛrmir] **1.** *v.tr.* (*a*) to harden (once more); to make (sth.) firm(er); (*b*) to confirm, strengthen (authority, resolution); to fortify, reinforce, restore (courage, spirit); to steady (prices, nerves). **2. se r.** (*a*) (*of ground, muscle, etc.*) to harden; (*of health*) to improve; **ses jambes se raffermissent,** his legs are growing stronger again; (*b*) (*of prices*) to steady, harden; **son autorité, son crédit, se raffermit,** he is recovering his authority, his credit; **il se raffermit dans sa résolution,** he is more determined than ever.

raffermissement [rafɛrmismɑ̃] *n.m.* **1.** hardening (again); making firm(er). **2.** strengthening, confirmation (of authority, power); improvement, building up (of health); hardening, steadying (of prices).

raffinage [rafinaʒ] *n.m.* (oil, sugar, etc.) refining.

raffiné [rafine] *a.* **1.** refined (sugar, etc.). **2.** subtle (mind); delicate (taste, etc.); refined, polished (manners, style); nice (appreciation); **friandises raffinées,** choice dainties.

raffinement [rafinmɑ̃] *n.m.* refinement (of language, manners); affectation; subtlety (of thought, policy); refinement (of luxury, cruelty).

raffiner [rafine] *v.tr.* **1.** to refine (sugar, oil, etc.). **2. r. sur la propreté,** to carry cleanliness to extremes; **vous raffinez!** you're being too subtle!

raffinerie [rafinri] *n.f.* (oil, sugar) refinery.

raffineur, -euse [rafinœr, -øz] *n.* (oil, sugar) refiner.

raffolement [rafɔlmɑ̃] *n.m. F:* infatuation (**de,** for).

raffoler [rafɔle] *v.i. F:* **r. de qn, de qch.,** to be infatuated with, dote on, s.o.; to adore, to be mad on (s.o., sth.).

raffut [rafy] *n.m. F:* noise, row, shindy.

raffûter [rafyte] *v.tr.* to (re)sharpen, (re)set (tool).

rafiau, rafiot [rafjo] *n.m. Nau:* (*a*) skiff (with lateen sail); (*b*) **vieux r.,** old tub.

rafistolage [rafistɔlaʒ] *n.m. F:* patching up.

rafistoler [rafistɔle] *v.tr. F:* to patch up.

rafle [rafl] *n.f.* (*a*) looting; *F:* clean sweep (by burglars, etc.); **r. d'étalage avec bris de devanture,** smash-and-grab raid; (*b*) round-up, raid (by the police).

rafler [rafle] *v.tr.* to carry off (contents of house, etc.).

rafraîchir [rafrɛʃir] **1.** *v.tr.* (*a*) to cool, refresh (sth.); to air (room); (*b*) to freshen up, revive (colour); to do up, renovate (picture); to touch up (edged tool); **r. les cheveux à qn,** to trim, clip, s.o.'s hair; **r. la mémoire à qn,** to refresh s.o.'s memory. **2.** *v.i.* **mettre le vin à r. à la cave,** to put the wine to cool in the cellar. **3. se r.** (*a*) (*of the weather*) to grow, turn, cooler; (*b*) (i) to freshen oneself up; (ii) *F:* to have a drink.

rafraîchissant [rafrɛʃisɑ̃] *a.* refreshing (breeze, drink); cooling; **simplicité rafraîchissante,** refreshing simplicity.

rafraîchissement [rafrɛʃismɑ̃] *n.m.* **1.** (*a*) cooling (of temperature, liquid, etc.); (*b*) freshening up, reviving (of colour). **2.** (*a*) cold drink; (*b*) *pl.* (cold) refreshments.

ragaillardir [ragajardir] *v.tr.* (*a*) to revive (s.o.), to make (s.o.) feel better; (*b*) to cheer (s.o.) up; **se r.,** to cheer up, *F:* buck up.

rage [raʒ] *n.f.* **1.** rabies, hydrophobia. **2.** (*a*) rage, fury, frenzy; **la tempête fait r.,** the storm is raging; **l'incendie faisait r.,** the fire was blazing furiously; (*b*) passion, mania (for sth.); **avoir la r. du jeu, d'écrire,** to have a passion for gambling, for writing; *F:* **c'est pas de l'amour, c'est de la r.,** that's not love, it's madness; (*c*) acute pain; **r. de dents,** raging toothache.

rageant [raʒɑ̃] *a. F:* infuriating.

rager [raʒe] *v.i.* (**je rageai(s); n. rageons)** *F:* to rage; to be in a rage; to fume; **ça me fait r. de voir ça!** it makes me wild, mad, to see it!

rageur, -euse [raʒœr, -øz] *a.* violent-tempered, infuriated (tone).

rageusement [raʒøzmɑ̃] *adv.* furiously.

raglan [raglɑ̃] *n.m.* raglan coat; *a.inv.* **manches r.,** raglan sleeves.

ragondin [ragɔ̃dɛ̃] *n.m. Z:* coypu; *Com:* nutria (fur).

ragot, -ote [rago, -ɔt] **1.** *n.m. Ven:* boar in its third year. **2.** *a. & n.* dumpy, squat, stocky (person).

ragoter [ragɔte] *v.i. F:* to gossip.

ragots [rago] *n.m.pl. F:* (*usu.* ill natured) gossip, tittle-tattle.

ragoût [ragu] *n.m. Cu:* stew, ragout; **r. de mouton,** stewed mutton; **(faire) cuire qch. en r.,** to stew sth.

ragoûtant [ragutɑ̃] *a. usu. with neg.* tempting, appetizing; **peu r.,** unpleasant; disgusting; uninviting.

ragréer [ragree] *v.tr.* (*a*) to finish off (stonework, woodwork); to clean up, trim up (joint, etc.); (*b*) to clean (façade of building).

rahat-lokoum [raatlokum], **rahat-loukoum** [raatlukum] *n.m.* Turkish delight.

raid [rɛd] *n.m.* **1.** *Mil:* raid. **2.** *Sp:* long-distance rally, flight; endurance test.

raide [rɛd] **1.** *a.* (*a*) stiff (limb, joints, drapery); taut (rope); **corde r.,** tightrope; **mettre un câble au r.,** to take up the slack in a cable; **cheveux raides,** straight hair; **assis r. sur sa chaise,** sitting bolt upright on his chair; *F:* **r. (comme un passe-lacet),** (stony) broke; (*b*) stiff (manner); inflexible, unbending, unyielding (character, etc.); **réponse r.,** brusque reply; stinging retort; (*c*) steep (stair, slope); (*d*) *F:* **histoire r.,** (i) tall story; (ii) risqué story; **ça c'est un peu r.!** that's a bit thick! **il en a vu de raides,** he's had some queer experiences; (*e*) *P:* **boire du r.,** to drink raw spirits. **2.** *adv.* (*a*) (to strike) hard; (to drive) fast; (*b*) (to climb) steeply; (*c*) **tuer qn r.,** to kill s.o. outright; **tomber r. mort,** to drop dead.

raidement [rɛdmɑ̃] *adv.* stiffly; tensely.

raideur [rɛdœr] *n.f.* **1.** stiffness (of limb, joints, movement); tightness (of rope); **donner plus de r. à qch.,** to stiffen sth. **2.** stiffness, starchiness (of manner); inflexibility (of character); severity. **3.** steepness, abruptness (of slope).

raidillon [rɛdijɔ̃] *n.m.* (short and steep) rise (in a road); steep path.

raidir [redir] **1.** *v.tr.* (*a*) to stiffen; to tighten, tauten (rope, etc.); to make (sth.) stiff, hard; to brace (one's arms); (*b*) to harden, stiffen (resistance, etc.). **2. se r.** (*a*) (*of limbs, joints*) to stiffen, to grow stiff; (*of cable*) to tauten; **il se raidit,** he grew tense, rigid;

(*b*) **se r. contre le malheur,** to steel, brace, oneself against misfortune.

raidissement [rɛdismɑ̃] *n.m.* stiffening; tautening.

raidisseur [rɛdisœr] *n.m. Tchn:* wire stretcher, stiffener.

raie[1] [rɛ] *n.f.* **1.** line, stroke (on paper, etc.). **2.** (*a*) streak, stripe; **chaussettes à raies,** striped socks; (*b*) *Opt:* **raies du spectre, raies spectrales,** spectrum lines. **3.** parting, *U.S:* part (in the hair). **4.** *Agr:* (i) furrow; (ii) ridge (between furrows).

raie[2] *n.f. Ich:* ray, skate; **r. bouclée,** thornback.

raifort [rɛfɔr] *n.m.* horseradish.

rail [rɑj] *n.m.* (*a*) rail; **r. noyé,** sunken rail; **r. conducteur,** conductor rail, live rail (of electrified railway); (*of train*) **quitter les rails, sortir des rails,** to jump the metals; to be derailed; **remettre l'économie sur les rails,** to put the economy on its feet again; (*b*) railways; *NAm:* railroads; **travailleurs du r.,** railwaymen; *NAm:* railroaders.

railler [rɑje] **1.** *v.tr.* to laugh at, make fun of (s.o.); *v.i.* **je ne raille pas,** I'm not joking. **2. se r. de qch.,** to scoff at s.o., sth.

raillerie [rɑjri] *n.f.* **1.** joking; banter; **il n'entend pas r. là-dessus,** he is very touchy on that point; **sans r.,** joking apart; seriously. **2. recueillir des railleries,** to be scoffed at, made fun of.

railleur, -euse [rɑjœr, -øz] **1.** *a.* mocking, bantering. **2.** *n.* scoffer; banterer.

railleusement [rɑjøzmɑ̃] *adv.* mockingly.

rainer [rene] *v.tr.* to groove, flute; to slot (nut).

rainette [rɛnɛt] *n.f.* **1.** tree frog. **2.** *Hort:* pippin (apple); **r. grise,** russet.

rainure [renyr] *n.f.* **1.** groove, channel, furrow, rabbet; slot; **r. de clavette,** keyway, key slot; **à rainure(s),** grooved, channelled, slotted, fluted; *El.* **induit à rainures,** slotted armature. **2.** *Astr:* rille (on the moon).

raiponce [rɛpɔ̃s] *n.f. Bot:* rampion.

raisin [rɛzɛ̃] *n.m.* **1. (grain de) r.,** grape; **grappe de r.,** bunch of grapes; **raisin(s) de table,** dessert grapes; **manger du r.,** to eat grapes; **raisins secs,** raisins; **raisins de Corinthe,** (dried) currants; **raisins de Smyrne,** sultanas. **2.** *Bot:* **r. de renard,** herb Paris; *Moll:* **r. de mer,** sea grapes, cuttle-fish eggs. **3.** *Paperm:* **grand r.** *approx.* = royal.

raisiné [rɛzine] *n.m.* fruit preserved in grape jelly.

raison [rɛzɔ̃] *n.f.* **1.** reason, motive, ground (**de,** for); **ce n'est pas une r.,** that doesn't follow; **pour des raisons de convenance,** on grounds of expediency; **pour quelle r.?** why? what for? **sans r.,** without reason, needlessly; **en, pour, r. de qch.,** by reason of, on account of, sth.; **en r. de son âge,** because of his age; **en r. d'un deuil récent,** owing to a recent bereavement; **à plus forte r.,** with greater reason, all the more; **r. de plus,** all the more reason; **r. d'être de qch.,** raison d'être, object, justification, of sth.; **la r. pour laquelle il est venu,** the reason why he came. **2.** (faculty of) reason; **il n'a pas toute sa r.,** he is not quite sane, in his right mind; **revenir, se mettre, à la r.,** to come to one's senses, see reason; **vous perdez la r.!** have you taken leave of your senses? **entendre r.,** to listen to reason; **rendre r. de qch.,** to give an explanation of sth., to account for sth.; **l'âge de r.,** years of discretion; **mariage de r.,** marriage of convenience. **3. avoir r.,** to be right; **avoir r. de faire qch.,** to be justified, right, in doing sth.; **donner r. à qn,** to admit that s.o. is right; **l'événement lui donna r.,** he was justified in the event; **ce n'est pas r. d'agir ainsi,** there is no justification for such an action; **se faire une r.,** to accept the inevitable, to make the best of a bad job; to resign oneself; **avec r.,** rightly; **boire plus que de r.,** to drink too much; **comme de r.,** as a matter of course, as one might expect. **4.** satisfaction, reparation; **demander r. d'un affront,** to demand satisfaction for an insult; **se faire r. à soi-même,** to take the law into one's own hands; **avoir r. de qn, de qch.,** to get the better of s.o., sth. **5.** *Com:* **r. sociale,** style, trade name (of a firm). **6.** *Mth:* **r. géométrique, arithmétique,** geometrical, arithmetical, ratio; **r. directe, inverse,** direct, inverse, ratio; **le poids est en r. directe du volume,** the weight is directly proportional to the volume; **travail payé à r. de cinquante francs l'heure,** work paid at the rate of fifty francs an hour; **à r. de deux par minute,** at the rate of two per, a, minute; **à r. de huit mots par ligne,** on the basis of eight words to a line.

raisonnable [rɛzɔnabl̥] *a.* reasonable. **1. être r.,** rational being; **soyez r.,** be sensible, do listen to reason; **à son âge il devrait être plus r.,** he is old enough to know better. **2.** (*a*) according to reason; **interprétation r.,** reasonable interpretation; (*b*) **prix r.,** reasonable, moderate, fair, price; **d'une grandeur r.,** reasonably large, decent-sized.

raisonnablement [rɛzɔnabləmɑ̃] *adv.* **1.** reasonably; rationally; **tout ce qu'on pouvait r. demander,** all that one could reasonably ask for. **2.** (*a*) reasonably, fairly (large, etc.); (to eat, etc.) moderately, in moderation; (*b*) *F:* (to work, etc.) fairly well, reasonably well.

raisonné [rɛzɔne] *a.* reasoned (argument); rational, analytical (grammar); *Com:* **catalogue r.,** descriptive catalogue.

raisonnement [rɛzɔnmɑ̃] *n.m.* (*a*) reasoning; **homme de r. juste,** man of sense; (*b*) **pas de raisonnements!** don't argue!

raisonner [rɛzɔne] **1.** *v.i.* (*a*) to reason (**sur,** about, upon); to argue (**sur,** about); (*b*) **ne raisonnez pas tant,** don't be so argumentative. **2.** *v.tr.* (*a*) **r. ses actions,** to consider, study, one's actions; (*b*) to reason with (s.o.).

raisonneur, -euse [rɛzɔnœr, -øz] **1.** *a.* (*a*) reasoning, rational; (*b*) argumentative. **2.** *n.* reasoner; arguer.

raja(h) [raʒa] *n.m.* raja(h).

rajeunir [raʒœnir] **1.** *v.tr.* (*a*) to rejuvenate (s.o.); **ce chapeau la rajeunit de dix ans,** this hat makes her look ten years younger; **ça me rajeunit,** it makes me feel much younger; **le comité a besoin d'être rajeuni,** the committee needs new blood; (*b*) to renovate, do up (clothes, etc.); to revive (expression, etc.). **2.** *v.i.* to grow young again; to get younger. **3. se r.** (*a*) to make oneself look younger; (*b*) to make oneself out younger than one is.

rajeunissement [raʒœnismɑ̃] *n.m.* rejuvenation.

rajouter [raʒute] *v.tr.* to add (sth.); to add more of (sth.).

rajustement [raʒystəmɑ̃] *n.m.* readjustment.

rajuster [raʒyste] *v.tr.* (*a*) to readjust (sth.); to put (sth.) straight; **se r.,** to tidy oneself (up); (*b*) **r. les salaires,** to bring wages into line with the cost of living.

râle[1] [rɑl] *n.m. Orn:* **r. d'eau,** water rail; **r. de genêts,** corncrake.

râle[2] *n.m.*, **râlement** [rɑlmɑ̃] *n.m.* rattle (in the throat); **le r. (de la mort),** the death rattle.

ralenti [ralɑ̃ti] **1.** *a.* slow(er); **au trot r.,** at a slow trot. **2.** *n.m.* (*a*) slow motion; *Aut:* **prendre un virage au grand r.,** to take a corner dead slow; *Cin:* **scène au, en, r.,** scene in slow motion; *Ind:* **travail au r.,** go-slow (strike); (*b*) *I.C.E: Mch:* idling, slow running; (*of engine*) **tourner au r.,** to idle, to tick over.

ralentir [ralɑ̃tir] **1.** *v.tr. & i.* to slow down; to slacken (speed); *P.N:* **r.!** slow! **r. la marche,** to reduce speed; **r. ses efforts,** to ease up. **2. se r.,** (*of movements*) to slow down; (*of enthusiasm*) to abate, flag.

ralentissement [ralɑ̃tismɑ̃] *n.m.* slowing up, slowing down; abatement, flagging (of zeal); **périodes de r. dans les affaires,** slack times in business.

ralentisseur [ralɑ̃tisœr] *n.m.* **1.** *Mec.E:* retarder. **2.** *Atom.Ph:* moderator.

râler [rɑle] *v.i.* **1.** to be at one's last gasp. **2.** (*of tiger*) to growl *F:* (*of pers.*) to grouse, growl; **r. en silence,** to fume.
râleur, -euse [rɑlœr, -øz] *n. F:* grumbler, grouser.
ralingue [ralɛ̃g] *n.f. Nau:* (*a*) bolt rope (of sail); (*b*) **tenir les voiles en r.,** to keep the sails shivering.
ralinguer [ralɛ̃ge] *Nau:* **1.** *v.tr.* to rope (a sail). **2.** *v.i.* (*of sails*) to shiver.
ralliement [ralimɑ̃] *n.m.* (*a*) rally(ing), assembly (of troops, ships); **mot de r.,** password; **point de r.,** rallying point; (*b*) homing (of aircraft); (*c*) winning over (of adherents).
rallier [ralje] (*impf. & pr.sub.* **n. ralliions**) **1.** *v.tr.* (*a*) to rally, assemble (troops, ships, etc.); (*b*) *Mil: etc.* to rejoin (unit); to make one's way back to (base); **r. le bord,** to rejoin one's ship; *Nau:* **r. la terre,** to stand in for land; (*c*) to win (s.o.) over, to bring (s.o.) round (to a party, opinion). **2. se r.** (*a*) (*of troops, etc.*) to rally; (*b*) **se r. à un parti,** to join a party; **se r. à une opinion,** to come round to an opinion.
rallonge [ralɔ̃ʒ] *n.f.* (*a*) extension piece (of lifting jack, etc.); lengthening piece; extension leaf (of table); **table à rallonge(s),** extending table; *F:* **nom à r.,** double-barrelled name; **mettre une r. à une jupe,** to lengthen a skirt; (*b*) *F:* additional payment.
rallongement [ralɔ̃ʒmɑ̃] *n.m.* lengthening, extension.
rallonger [ralɔ̃ʒe] **(je rallongeai(s); n. rallongeons)** (*a*) *v.tr.* to lengthen; to make (sth.) longer; (*b*) *v.i. F:* **les jours rallongent,** the days are lengthening, drawing out.
rallumer [ralyme] **1.** *v.tr.* to relight (lamp, fire); to rekindle (fire); to revive (anger, hope, etc.). **2. se r.,** to rekindle; to light up, blaze up, again; (*of anger*) to revive.
rallye [rali] *n.m. Sp:* (car) rally.
ramage [ramaʒ] *n.m.* **1.** floral design. **2.** song, twittering, chirping (of birds).
ramas [ramɑ] *n.m. F:* = RAMASSIS.
ramassage [ramasaʒ] *n.m.* gathering, collecting, picking up; **r. à la pelle,** shovelling up; **lait de grand r.,** milk collected over a wide area; **r. scolaire,** school bus service.
ramassé [ramase] *a.* **1.** thick-set, stocky. **2.** compact (machine, style).
ramasse-miettes [ramasmjɛt] *n.m.inv.* crumb tray, scoop.
ramasse-poussière [ramaspusjɛr] *n.m.inv.* dustpan.
ramasser [ramase] **1.** *v.tr.* (*a*) to gather (sth.) together (in a mass); **village ramassé autour de son église,** village clustering round its church; **le tigre ramasse son corps avant de bondir,** the tiger crouches, gathers itself, before springing; **r. toutes ses forces,** to gather, muster, all one's strength; (*b*) to collect, gather (several things); **r. les cartes,** to gather up the cards; **r. ses affaires,** to collect one's belongings together; **r. de l'argent,** to collect money; *F:* to make one's pile; **r. des bribes de connaissances,** to pick up scraps of knowledge; *P:* **se faire r.,** to be run in, picked up (by the police); *Aut: F:* **r. un procès-verbal,** to get a ticket; (*c*) to pick up, take up; **r. son mouchoir,** to pick up one's handkerchief; **r. à la pelle,** to shovel up; **r. qn,** to help s.o. up, to his feet; *F:* **r. une bûche, une pelle,** to come a cropper. **2. se r.** (*a*) to gather oneself (for an effort); (*of tiger*) to crouch (for a spring); (*b*) to pick oneself up (after a fall).
ramassette [ramasɛt] *n.f. esp. Belg:* dustpan.
ramasseur, -euse [ramasœr, -øz] *n.* collector, gatherer; **r. de lait,** collector of milk (from farms).
ramassis [ramasi] *n.m. Pej:* heap, pile (of thgs); bunch (of people).
rambarde [rɑ̃bard] *n.f. Nau: etc:* (guard) rail.
rame¹ [ram] *n.f. Hort:* stick, prop (for peas, etc.); **haricots à rames,** stick beans.
rame² *n.f.* oar, scull; **aller à la r.,** to row; **faire force de rames,** to row hard; **faire fausse r.,** to catch a crab.
rame³ *n.f.* **1.** ream (of paper). **2.** string, tow (of barges); *Rail:* **r. (de wagons),** made-up train; **la r. directe pour Tours,** the through coach(es) for Tours; **r. (de Métro),** underground train.
rameau, -eaux [ramo] *n.m.* **1.** (*a*) (small) branch, bough; twig; *Ecc:* **le dimanche des Rameaux, les Rameaux,** Palm Sunday. **2.** branch, (of family, language). **3.** *Anat:* ramification.
ramée [rame] *n.f.* **1.** green boughs; arbour. **2.** cut branches.
ramener [ramne] (*conj. like* MENER) **1.** *v.tr.* (*a*) to bring (s.o., sth.) back (again); **r. qn chez lui en voiture,** to drive s.o. home; **r. un malade à la vie,** to bring a patient round; **r. la conversation sur un sujet,** to lead the conversation back to a subject; **r. le compteur à zéro,** to reset the speedometer at zero; *P:* **r. sa gueule, sa fraise, la r.,** to have a big mouth, to lay down the law; (*b*) **r. tout à un seul principe,** to reduce everything to a single principle; **r. une fraction à sa plus simple expression,** to reduce a fraction to its simplest terms; (*c*) **r. son chapeau sur ses yeux,** to pull down one's hat over one's eyes; (*d*) **r. la paix,** to restore peace. **2. se r.** (*a*) *F:* (*of pers.*) to come, arrive; *F:* to roll up; (*b*) **voici à quoi se ramène son raisonnement,** this is what his argument amounts to, *F:* boils down to.
ramequin [ramkɛ̃] *n.m. Cu:* ramekin, ramequin.
ramer¹ [rame] *v.tr.* to stick, prop, stake (peas, etc.).
ramer² *v.i.* to row; to pull (at the oar); **r. en couple,** to scull; **r. à rebours,** to back water.
rameur, -euse¹ [ramœr, -øz] *n.* rower; oarsman, -woman; **r. de couple,** sculler.
rameux, -euse² [ramø, -øz] *a.* ramose; branching.
rami [rami] *n.m. Cards:* rummy.
ramie [rami] *n.f. Bot:* ramie; **(toile de) r.,** grass cloth.
ramier [ramje] *a.m. & n.m.* **(pigeon) r.,** ring dove, wood pigeon.
ramification [ramifikasjɔ̃] *n.f.* ramification; (*a*) branching; (*b*) branch.
ramifier (se) [səramifje] *v.pr.* to ramify, branch out.
ramille [ramij] *n.f.* **1.** branchlet, twig. **2.** small wood; kindling.
ramolli, -ie [ramɔli] *F:* **1.** *a.* soft(witted), soft-headed. **2.** *n.* dodderer.
ramollir [ramɔlir] **1.** *v.tr.* to soften. **2. se r.,** to soften; to grow soft; **son cerveau se ramollit,** he has softening of the brain.
ramollissement [ramɔlismɑ̃] *n.m.* softening.
ramollo(t) [ramɔlo] *n.m. F:* **un vieux r.,** an old dodderer.
ramonage [ramɔnaʒ] *n.m.* chimney sweeping; cleaning (of boiler tubes).
ramoner [ramɔne] **1.** *v.tr.* to sweep (chimney); to take out (flue); *Mch:* to clean (fire tubes). **2.** *v.i. Mount:* to climb a chimney.
ramoneur [ramɔnœr] *n.m.* (chimney) sweep.
rampant [rɑ̃pɑ̃] *a.* **1.** (*a*) *Her:* **lion r.,** lion rampant; (*b*) **arche, voûte, rampante,** rampant arch, vault. **2.** (*a*) creeping (plant); crawling (animal); *Av: F:* **personnel r.,** ground staff; (*b*) grovelling, cringing (person, character); pedestrian (style).
rampe [rɑ̃p] *n.f.* **1.** slope, incline, rise; gradient (of road); *Aut:* **vitesse en r.,** speed when (hill) climbing. **2.** (*a*) **r. d'accès,** access, ramp (of bridge); (*b*) ramp, gangway; **r. mobile,** portable ramp, movable gangway; *Ball:* **r. de lancement,** launching ramp. **3.** (*a*)

bank (of projectors, etc.); *Av:* **r. (lumineuse) d'atterrissage,** illuminated landing strip; *Mch:* **r. de graissage,** lubricating rack; oil distributor; (*b*) *Th:* footlights, float(s); **être sous les feux de la r.,** to be in the limelight; **pièce qui ne passe pas la r.,** play that fails to get across. **4.** banisters, hand rail (of stair); *P:* **lâcher la r.,** to die; *F:* **tenir bon la r.,** to be still going strong.

rampement [rɑ̃pmɑ̃] *n.m.* creeping, crawling.

ramper [rɑ̃pe] *v.i.* to creep; to crawl: (*of plant*) to creep, trail; **entrer, sortir, en rampant,** to crawl in, out; **r. à quatre pattes,** to creep, crawl, on all fours; **r. devant les chefs,** to truckle to, to grovel before, the bosses; **style qui rampe,** uninspired, prosy, style.

ramure [ramyr] *n.f.* **1.** branches, boughs, foliage. **2.** antlers (of stag).

rancard [rɑ̃kar] *n.m. P:* **1.** information, tip, gen. **2.** date, rendezvous.

rancart [rɑ̃kar] *n.m.* **mettre qch. au r.,** to discard sth.; to shelve (project).

rance [rɑ̃s] *a.* rancid, rank; *n.m.* **sentir le r.,** to smell rancid.

ranch [rɑ̃ʃ] *n.m.* ranch; **exploiter un r.,** to ranch.

rancidité [rɑ̃sidite] *n.f.* rancidness.

rancir [rɑ̃sir] *v.i.* to become, grow, rancid.

rancissement [rɑ̃sismɑ̃] *n.m.* growing, becoming, rancid; souring.

rancœur [rɑ̃kœr] *n.f.* rancour; bitterness; resentment; **j'ai gardé de cette déception une r.,** this disappointment still rankles.

rançon [rɑ̃sɔ̃] *n.f.* ransom; **mettre qn à r.,** to hold s.o. to ransom; **payer la r. de qn,** to ransom s.o.; **la r. du progrès,** the price paid for progress.

rançonner [rɑ̃sɔne] *v.tr.* to hold (s.o.) to ransom; to hold up (and rob) (traveller); *F:* to fleece (customer, etc.).

rancune [rɑ̃kyn] *n.f.* rancour, spite, malice; **garder r. à qn, avoir de la r. contre qn,** to harbour resentment against s.o., to have a grudge against s.o., to bear s.o. malice; **par r.,** out of spite; **sans r.!** no ill feelings! **il y a de vieilles rancunes entre eux,** there is bad blood between them.

rancunier, -ière [rɑ̃kynje, -jɛr] *a. & n.* vindictive, spiteful (person).

randonnée [rɑ̃dɔne] *n.f.* outing, run, trip, excursion; *Aut: Cy:* long run; **r. à pied,** hike.

rang [rɑ̃] *n.m.* **1.** (*a*) row, line (of trees, columns, etc.); row (of onions, seats, knitting); bank (of oars); **machine à quatre rangs de touches,** four-bank typewriter; **r. de perles,** string, rope, of pearls; **cinq jours de r.,** five days in a row; (*b*) *Mil:* rank; **sur deux rangs,** in two ranks; two deep; **par rangs de trois,** three abreast; **formez vos rangs!** fall in! **serrer les rangs,** to close ranks, close up; **en rangs serrés,** in close order; **rompre les rangs,** to break ranks; to fall out; **sortir des rangs,** to fall out (of line), to break rank; **homme du r.,** private; **officier sorti du r.,** officer promoted from the ranks; **sortir du r.,** to rise from the ranks; (*c*) **se mettre sur les rangs,** to enter the lists; to come forward (as a candidate), to put in for the job; **il y avait déjà quelqu'un sur les rangs,** there was already someone in the field; (*d*) *Fr.C:* (i) line, concession road; (ii) concession, rural district. **2.** rank, place; station (in life); **avoir r. de colonel,** to hold the rank of colonel; **r. élevé,** high rank; **dame de haut r.,** lady of rank; **r. social,** social status; **il faut tenir notre r.,** we have to keep up our position; **de premier r.,** first-class, first-rate; **arriver au premier r.,** to come to the front; **il est au premier r. de sa profession,** he is at the top of the tree in his profession; **venir au, en, troisième r.,** to rank third; **par r. d'âge,** according to age; **être mis sur le même r.,** to be placed on the same footing; **occuper un r. supérieur à qn,** to rank above s.o.; **prendre r., avoir r., avant, après, qn,** to rank before, after, s.o.; **il a pris r. parmi les grands poètes,** he has taken his place, is counted, among the great poets; **prendre r. dans un parti,** to join a party.

rangé [rɑ̃ʒe] *a.* **1. bataille rangée,** pitched battle. **2.** tidy, orderly; well-ordered, regular (life), steady (person); **fille rangée,** dutiful daughter.

rangée [rɑ̃ʒe] *n.f.* row, line (of persons, trees); row (of buttons, seats); tier (of seats on a slope).

rangement [rɑ̃ʒmɑ̃] *n.m.* (*a*) tidying, putting in order; *esp. Cmptr:* storage; **la manie du r.,** mania for tidiness; **volume de r.,** storage space; **(meuble de) r.,** storage unit; **r. de cuisine,** kitchen cabinet; (*b*) arrangement; **r. rationnel,** logical arrangement.

ranger [rɑ̃ʒe] **(je rangeai(s); n. rangeons) 1.** *v.tr.* (*a*) to arrange; to draw up, marshal (troops, etc.); (*b*) to put (sth.) away; to put (sth.) back in its place; to stow away, tidy away (objects); to stow (goods); *Cmptr:* **r. en mémoire,** to store; *Aut:* **r. une voiture,** to pull in to the side; *F:* **être rangé (du côté) des voitures,** to be a reformed character; (*c*) to arrange, tidy (room, etc.); to set (things) to rights; (*d*) **r. qn parmi les grands écrivains,** to rank, count, s.o. amongst the great writers; *Nau:* **r. la côte,** to run along the shore, to hug the coast. **2. se r.** (*a*) (*of troops, etc.*) to draw up, line up; *Nau:* **se r. à quai,** to berth; (*b*) **se r. du côté de qn,** to take sides, to side, with s.o.; **se r. à l'opinion de qn,** to fall in with, come round to, s.o.'s opinion; (*c*) **se r. (de côté),** to get out of the way; to draw to one side; to stand aside; **on se rangea pour nous laisser passer,** they stood aside, made way, for us; (*d*) **il s'est rangé,** he has steadied down, settled down.

rani [rani] *n.f.* ranee.

ranimation [ranimasjɔ̃] *n.f.* resuscitation; reanimation.

ranimer [ranime] **1.** *v.tr.* to revive; to put new life into (s.o., sth.); to bring (s.o.) back to life; to bring (fainting person) round; to revive (plant, colour); to stir up (the fire); to reawaken, rekindle (anger, hope); to liven up (the conversation); to cheer (s.o.) up again; to hearten (s.o.). **2. se r.,** to revive; (*of fire*) to burn up; **elle ne fut pas longtemps à se r.,** she soon came round.

Raoul [raul] *Pr.n.m.* Ralph; Rollo.

rapace [rapas] *a.* **1.** predatory; **oiseau r.,** *n.m.* **r.,** bird of prey. **2.** rapacious, grasping (person).

rapacité [rapasite] *n.f.* rapacity; **avec r.,** rapaciously.

râpage [rɑpaʒ] *n.m.* rasping; grating (of nutmeg); grinding (of wood).

rapatrié, -iée [rapatrije] *n.* repatriate.

rapatriement [rapatrimɑ̃] *n.m.* repatriation.

rapatrier [rapatrije] *v.tr.* **1.** to repatriate; to send (s.o.) home (from abroad). **2.** to reconcile.

râpe [rɑp] *n.f.* (*a*) grater; **r. à muscade,** nutmeg grater; (*b*) rasp, rough file.

râpé [rɑpe] **1.** *a.* (*a*) grated (cheese, etc.); (*b*) worn out, threadbare (garment). **2.** *n.m.* (*a*) rape wine; (*b*) grated cheese.

râper [rɑpe] *v.tr.* to rasp (wood); to grate (carrot, nutmeg); to grind (snuff).

rapetassage [raptasaʒ] *n.m. F:* patching up; cobbling.

rapetasser [raptase] *v.tr. F:* to patch up, do up (garment); to cobble.

rapetissement [raptismɑ̃] *n.m.* reducing, diminishing.

rapetisser [raptise] **1.** *v.tr.* to make (sth.) smaller; to reduce; to shorten, take in (garment); to shrink (material); **la distance rapetisse les objets,** distance makes things look smaller. **2.** *v.i. & pr.* to shorten; to become smaller, shorter; to shrink.

râpeux, -euse [rɑpø, -øz] *a.* raspy (tongue); harsh (wine); grating (noise).
raphia [rafja] *n.m.* raphia (palm); *Com:* raffia.
rapiat, -ate [rapja, -at] *F:* **1.** *a.* stingy, miserly. **2.** *n.* miser, skinflint.
rapide [rapid] **1.** *a.* (*a*) rapid, swift, fast (current, etc.); speedy (recovery); fast (runner, film); **r. comme une flèche,** as swift as an arrow; **faire des progrès rapides,** to make rapid progress; **fusil à tir r.,** quick-firing rifle; *Sp:* **piste r.,** fast track; (*b*) steep (slope). **2.** *n.m.* (*a*) rapid (in river); (*b*) express (train); inter-city train.
rapidement [rapidmɑ̃] *adv.* (*a*) rapidly, swiftly; **le temps passe r.,** time flies; (*b*) steeply.
rapidité [rapidite] *n.f.* (*a*) rapidity, swiftness; (*b*) steepness (of slope).
rapiéçage [rapjesaʒ], **rapiècement** [rapjɛsmɑ̃] *n.m.* patching (of garment).
rapiécer [rapjese] *v.tr.* **(je rapièce, n. rapiéçons; je rapiécerai)** to patch (garment).
rapière [rapjɛr] *n.f.* rapier; **traîneur de r.,** swash-buckler.
rapin [rapɛ̃] *n.m. Art: F:* dauber.
rapine [rapin] *n.f.* rapine, pillage, depradation; **habitudes de r.,** predatory habits.
raplapla [raplapla] *a.inv. F:* (*of pers.*) dead beat; washed out.
rappareiller [rapareje] *v.tr.* to match, complete (set of china, etc.).
rapparier [raparje] *v.tr.* (*impf. & pr.sub.* **n. rappariions**) to match, complete (pair); to pair (two things).
rappel [rapɛl] *n.m.* **1.** (*a*) recall (of general, ambassador); **lettres de r.,** letters of recall; (*b*) *Com:* calling in (of sum advanced); (*c*) **r. à l'ordre,** call(ing) to order; (*d*) calling to mind, recalling (of incident, etc.); (*e*) *Mil:* **r. sous les drapeaux,** recall to the colours (of reservists); (*f*) *Th:* curtain call. **2.** (*a*) reminder; **lettre de r.,** (letter of) reminder; (*b*) **r. de traitement, de solde,** back pay. **3.** (*a*) readjustment; **vis de r.,** adjusting screw; **r. de l'usure,** taking up of the wear; (*b*) back motion; return; **ressort de r.,** return spring, drawback spring; *Typewr:* **r. de chariot,** return of carriage; **r. arrière,** (i) back spacing; (ii) back space key; (*c*) **fil de r.,** bracing wire, straining wire; **tige de r.,** stay rod. **4.** *Mil:* **battre le r.,** to call, beat, to arms; *F:* **battre le r. de ses amis,** to drum up one's friends. **5.** *Mount:* **faire une descente en r.,** to rope down. **6.** *Med:* **injection de r.,** booster injection.
rappeler [raple] (*conj. like* APPELER) **1.** *v.tr.* (*a*) to call (s.o.) again, afresh; *Tp:* to ring, call, again; (*b*) to recall (ambassador); to call, summon (s.o.) back; *Th:* **être rappelé trois fois,** to take three curtain calls; **r. son chien,** to call off one's dog; **r. qn à l'ordre,** to call s.o. to order; **r. qn à la vie,** to restore s.o. to life; to resuscitate s.o.; to bring s.o. round; (*c*) **r. son courage,** to summon up one's courage (again); (*d*) to call (back) to mind, to recall (sth.); **rappelez-moi votre nom,** what was your name again? **r. qch. à qn,** to remind s.o. of sth.; **vous me rappelez mon oncle,** you put me in mind of my uncle; **cela me rappelle mon enfance,** it brings back my childhood to me; **rappelez-moi à son bon souvenir,** remember me (kindly) to him; **choses qu'il vaut autant ne pas r.,** things best forgotten; *Com:* **prière de r. ce numéro,** in reply please quote this number; (*e*) to draw back (machine part, etc.); *Typewr:* **r. le chariot,** (i) to return the carriage; (ii) to backspace; (*f*) (*of guy rope*) to brace back; (*of tie rod*) to tie, stay; (*g*) *Mount:* **r. (la corde),** to rope down. **2. se r. qch.,** to recall, recollect, remember, sth.; to call sth. to mind; **se r. (d')avoir promis qch.,** to remember having promised sth.; **rappelez-vous que ce n'est qu'une enfant,** remember, bear in mind, that she is only a child.
rappliquer [raplike] *v.i. P:* to come back; to turn up; **r. à la maison,** to roll back home.
rapport [rapɔr] *n.m.* **I. 1.** yield, return, profit; **capital en r.,** interest-bearing, productive, capital; **fruitier en plein r.,** fruit tree in full yield); **maison de r.,** block of flats (for letting); **d'un bon r.,** profitable; that brings in a good return; that pays well; productive (land). **2.** (*a*) account, report, statement; *F:* **faire des rapports,** to tell tales (out of school); **au r. de notre représentant,** according to our representative; (*b*) (official) report; return (of expenses, etc.); **faire, rédiger, un r. sur qch.,** to make, draw up, a report on sth.; **r. de gestion,** annual report (of company); **r. financier,** treasurer's report; *Nau:* **r. de mer,** (ship's) protest; (*c*) *Mil:* daily parade for issue of orders; **salle des rapports,** orderly room. **3. terres de r.,** made ground, artificial soil; **pièces de r.,** built-up parts (of machinery). **II. 1.** relation, connection (**avec,** with); **sans r. avec le sujet,** without any bearing on, unconnected with, irrelevant to, the subject; **avoir r. à qch.,** to relate, refer, to sth.; **question qui a un r. très étroit avec une autre,** question that is closely connected with another; **rôle en r. avec votre dignité,** role in keeping with your dignity; **par r. à qch.,** (i) with regard, respect, to sth.; in relation to sth.; (ii) in comparison with, compared with, sth.; **sous ce r.,** in this respect; **sous tous les rapports,** in all respects, in every respect. **2.** ratio, proportion; **le résultat n'est pas en r. avec l'effort fourni,** the result is not proportional to the effort expended; *Mth:* **r. arithmétique, géométrique,** arithmetical, geometrical, ratio; **dans le r. de un à trois,** in the ratio of one to three; **le r. maître-élèves est de 1 pour 20,** the staff-student ratio is 1 to 20; *Mec.E:* **r. des engrenages,** gear ratio. **3.** relations (between people); **mettre qn en r. avec qn,** to bring s.o. into contact, put s.o. in touch, with s.o.; **avoir des rapports avec qn,** (i) to have dealings, relations, with s.o.; (ii) to be in touch with s.o.; (iii) to have sexual intercourse with s.o.; **avoir de bons rapports avec qn,** to be on good terms with s.o.; **cesser tout r. avec qn,** to break off all relations with s.o.
rapportable [rapɔrtabl̩] *a.* **1. pièces rapportables,** pieces that fit together. **2.** referable, attributable (**à,** to).
rapportage [rapɔrtaʒ] *n.m. Sch: F:* taletelling, sneaking.
rapporté [rapɔrte] *a.* **1. terre rapportée,** made ground. **2.** (*a*) built-up (machine); compound (girder); (*b*) **étau à mâchoires rapportées,** vice with detachable jaws, inserted jaws; *Dressm:* **manche rapportée,** set-in sleeve; **poches rapportées,** patch pockets; *Bootm:* **bout r.,** toecap.
rapporter [rapɔrte] **1.** *v.tr.* (*a*) to bring back, carry back; to return (borrowed article); (*of dog*) to retrieve (game); **rapportez-moi un kilo de sucre,** bring me back a kilo of sugar; **il n'en a rapporté que la honte,** all he got out of it was disgrace; (*b*) to add, join, put in, insert (pieces to build up a machine); to sew on (a binding); **r. des terres,** to carry in earth (to build up terrace); (*c*) to bring in, bear, yield, produce; **placement qui rapporte dix pour cent,** investment that brings in, returns, ten per cent; **arbres qui rapportent beaucoup,** trees that yield well; **cela ne rapporte rien,** it doesn't pay; *v.i.* **la publicité rapporte,** it pays to advertise; **affaire qui rapporte,** paying business; (*d*) (i) to report, give an account of (sth.); *v.i.* **r. sur un projet,** to report on a plan; (ii) *v.i.* to tell tales; to sneak; **r. sur le compte de qn,** to tell on s.o.; **vous n'auriez pas dû le r.,** you shouldn't have

repeated it; (*e*) **r. qch. à une cause,** to attribute, ascribe, sth. to a cause; **r. un événement à une époque,** to assign, refer, an event to a period; **r. tout à soi, à ses intérêts,** to view everything in terms of self; (*f*) *Book-k:* to post (item); (*g*) to rescind, revoke (decree); to withdraw, cancel, (order); **r. un ordre de grève,** to call off a strike; (*h*) *Surv: etc:* to plot, set off, lay off (angle). **2. se r.** (*a*) to agree, tally (**avec,** with); **couleurs qui se rapportent bien,** colours that go well together; (*b*) (*of part*) to fit (**avec,** with); (*c*) to refer, relate (**à,** to); to have reference (to); **les documents qui se rapportent à l'affaire,** the relevant documents; (*d*) **s'en r. à qn, au témoignage de qn,** to refer to, to rely on, to put one's faith in, s.o., s.o.'s evidence; **je m'en rapporte à vous,** (i) I take your word for it; (ii) I leave it to you.

rapporteur, -euse [rapɔrtœr, -øz] *n.* **1.** tale-bearer, telltale, sneak. **2.** *n.m.* reporter, recorder; (*a*) *Pol:* **r. d'une commission,** chairman of a committee; **r. d'une conférence,** rapporteur of a conference; (*b*) *Mil:* judge advocate (at court martial). **3.** *n.m. Mth:* protractor; **r. à limbe complet,** circular protractor.

rapprendre [raprɑ̃dr̥] *v.tr.* (*conj. like* PRENDRE) **1.** to learn (sth.) (over) again. **2.** to teach (sth.) again.

rapproché [raprɔʃe] *a.* near (in space, time); **maisons très rapprochées,** houses very close, near, to one another; **yeux rapprochés,** close-set eyes; **espèces rapprochées,** closely related species.

rapprochement [raprɔʃmɑ̃] *n.m.* **1.** (*a*) bringing, placing, together (of two things); bringing together, reconciling (of two persons); (*b*) setting side by side, putting together, comparing (of facts, ideas). **2.** nearness, proximity, closeness (of two objects). **3.** (*a*) coming together; (*b*) reconciliation; rapprochement.

rapprocher [raprɔʃe] **1.** *v.tr.* (*a*) to bring (sth.) near (again); (*b*) to bring (objects) nearer, closer, together; **r. les lèvres d'une plaie,** to draw together, join, the lips of a wound; **r. une chaise du feu,** to draw up a chair to the fire; **une lunette rapproche les objets,** a field-glass makes objects look nearer; **chaque jour les rapproche de la fin,** each day brings them nearer the end; (*c*) to bring (two people) together; **un intérêt commun les rapproche,** a common interest brings, draws, them together; (*d*) to put together, to compare (facts, ideas). **2. se r.** (*a*) **se r. de qch.,** to draw near(er) to sth.; (*b*) **son costume se rapprochait d'un uniforme,** his clothes looked almost like, came near to being, a uniform; **se r. de la vérité,** to approximate to the truth; (*c*) **se r. de qn,** to become reconciled, to make it up, with s.o.; **la France et l'Espagne s'étaient rapprochées,** a rapprochement had taken place between France and Spain.

rapsodie [rapsɔdi] *n.f.* rhapsody.

rapt [rapt] *n.m.* abduction; kidnapping.

râpure [rɑpyr] *n.f.* raspings; gratings; filings.

raquer [rake] *v.tr. P:* to fork out; to cough up.

raquette [rakɛt] *n.f.* **1.** (tennis) racket, racquet; bat (for table tennis); battledore; *Aut: F:* **coups de r.,** jolts. **2.** regulating lever (of watch). **3.** snowshoe. **4.** *Bot: F:* prickly pear.

rare [rar] *a.* **1.** rare (book, insect); **visites rares et éloignées,** visits few and far between; **je suis un des rares à aimer la pluie,** I am one of the few who like rain; **se faire r.,** to be seldom seen; **vous devenez r. comme les beaux jours,** you are quite a stranger; **la main-d'œuvre, l'argent, était r.,** there was a shortage of labour; money was scarce, tight; *F:* **ça n'aurait rien de r.,** that wouldn't be anything out of the ordinary. **2.** rare, uncommon, exceptional (merit, beauty); **r. courage,** rare, singular, courage. **3.** thin, sparse, scanty (hair, etc.). **4.** *Ph:* rare (atmosphere).

raréfaction [rarefaksjɔ̃] *n.f.* (*a*) rarefaction (of gas, air); (*b*) depletion (of supplies); growing scarcity (of product, money).

raréfier [rarefje] **1.** *v.tr.* (*a*) *Ph:* to rarefy; (*b*) to deplete; to make (sth.) scarce. **2. se r.** (*a*) to become rarefied, to rarefy; to get thinner; (*b*) to become scarce, infrequent.

rarement [rarmɑ̃] *adv.* rarely, seldom, infrequently, not often.

rareté [rarte] *n.f.* **1.** (*a*) rarity, tenuity (of gas, etc.); (*b*) scarceness, scarcity, dearth (of objects); infrequency (of visits); (*c*) novelty, singularity, unusualness (of phenomenon). **2.** (*a*) **cabinet plein de raretés,** cabinet full of rare objects, of rarities, of curiosities; (*b*) rare occurrence.

ras [rɑ] **1.** *a.* (*a*) close-cropped (hair, head); close-shaven (beard, chin); short-napped (velvet); short-pile (carpet); **couper r. les cheveux,** to crop the hair short, close; **chien à poil r.,** short-haired dog; (*b*) bare, blank; **en rase campagne,** in the open country; **faire table rase de qch.,** to make a clean sweep of sth.; **sa mémoire est une table rase,** his memory is a complete blank; (*c*) **mesure rase,** full (level) measure; **verser du vin à qn à r. bord,** to fill s.o.'s glass to the brim. **2.** *prep.phr.* **à, au, r. de,** (on a) level with, flush with; **vaisseau chargé au r. de l'eau,** vessel laden to the water line; **voler au r. du sol,** to fly close to the ground; to skim (along) the ground.

rasade [razad] *n.f.* brim-full glass (of wine); bumper.

rasage [razaʒ] *n.m.* shaving; shave; **lotion après-r.,** after-shave lotion.

rasant [razɑ̃] *a.* **1. tir r.,** grazing fire; **trajectoire rasante,** flat trajectory; **vol r.,** flight that skims the ground; **lumière rasante,** oblique, (almost) horizontal, light. **2.** *F:* boring (person, speech).

rascasse [raskas] *n.f.* scorpion fish; hog fish.

rasé [raze] *a.* shaven; **r. de près,** close-shaven; **entièrement r.,** clean-shaven.

rase-mottes [razmɔt] *n.m.inv. Av:* **vol en r.-m.,** *F:* hedge hopping; **faire du, voler en, r.-m.,** to skim the ground, *F:* to hedge hop.

raser [raze] **1.** *v.tr.* (*a*) to shave (head, beard); to shave off (moustache); to shear (cloth); **raser qn,** to shave s.o., to give s.o. a shave; (*b*) *F:* to bore (s.o.); (*c*) to raze (building) (to the ground); to pull down (house); to level (house, etc.) with the ground; *Nau:* to dismast, *A:* to razee (ship); (*d*) to graze, brush, skim (over); **l'hirondelle rase le sol,** the swallow skims the ground; **r. la côte, le mur,** to hug the shore, the wall. **2. se r.** (*a*) to shave; (*b*) *F:* to be bored.

raseur, -euse [razœr, -øz] *n.* **1.** *Tex:* shearer. **2.** *F:* bore.

rasibus [razibys] *adv. F:* **couper r.,** to cut quite close.

rasoir [razwar] *n.m.* **1.** razor; **r. de sûreté,** safety razor; **r. électrique,** electric razor, shaver; **pierre à r.,** hone; **cuir à r.,** strop. **2.** *F:* (*pers.*) bore; *a.* boring.

rassasié [rasazje] *a.* **1.** satisfied; *F:* full. **2.** surfeited, sated (**de,** with).

rassasiement [rasazimɑ̃] *n.m.* **1.** satisfying (of hunger). **2.** satiety, surfeit.

rassasier [rasazje] **1.** *v.tr.* (*a*) **1.** to satisfy (hunger, curiosity, passion); **r. qn,** to satisfy s.o.'s hunger; **les fruits ne rassasient pas,** fruit does not fill one's stomach; **r. son regard à contempler qch.,** to feast one's eyes on sth.; (*b*) to sate, satiate, surfeit, cloy (**de,** with). **2. se r.,** to eat one's fill; **se r. d'un mets, de plaisirs,** to take one's fill of a dish, pleasures; to gorge oneself on a dish.

rassemblement [rasɑ̃bləmɑ̃] *n.m.* **1.** assembling, collecting, gathering (of documents, troops, tools); *Mil:* fall in; parade; **sonner le r.,** to sound the assembly; **r.!** fall in! form up! **2.** crowd, gathering; **provoquer un r.,** to draw a crowd.

rassembler [rasɑ̃ble] **1.** *v.tr.* (*a*) to reassemble (persons, pieces of machinery); to bring together again; (*b*) to assemble, muster (troops); to collect, to gather together, get together (persons, things); **r. ses idées,** to collect one's thoughts; **r. toutes les pièces d'un procès,** to bring together all the documents of a case; **r. toutes ses forces,** to muster, summon up, all one's strength; *Equit:* **r. un cheval,** to gather a horse. **2. se r.** (*a*) to re-assemble; (*b*) to assemble, to come together, to get together, to gather; *Mil:* to fall in, to muster.

rasseoir [raswar] (*conj. like* ASSEOIR) **1.** *v.tr.* to seat (s.o.) again; **r. une statue sur sa base,** to replace a statue on its base. **2. se r.** (*a*) to sit down again; **faire r. qn,** to make s.o. sit down again; (*b*) (*of liquid*) to settle; **laisser r. le vin,** to let the wine settle.

rasséréner [raserene] **(je rassérène, n. rassérénons; je rassérénerai) 1.** *v.tr.* to calm (s.o.); to restore (s.o.'s) equanimity, peace of mind. **2. se r.** (*a*) (*of sky*) to clear (up); (*b*) (*of pers.*) to recover one's serenity.

rassir [rasir] *v.i.* to get stale; **je laisse r. mon pain,** I let my bread go stale; **se r.,** to get stale.

rassis [rasi] *a.* (*a*) **pain r.,** stale bread; (*b*) settled, calm, sober (disposition); **faire qch. de sens r.,** to do sth. coolly.

rassortir [rasɔrtir] *v.tr.* = RÉASSORTIR.

rassurant [rasyrɑ̃] *a.* reassuring, heartening; **peu rassurant,** disquieting.

rassurer [rasyre] **1.** *v.tr.* to reassure, cheer, hearten; **je suis assez peu rassuré,** I have my misgivings. **2. se r.,** to feel reassured; **rassurez-vous là-dessus,** make yourself easy, set your mind at rest, on that point.

rat [ra] *n.m.* **1.** (*a*) rat; **r. surmulot,** brown, Norway, rat; **r. noir,** black rat; **mort aux rats,** rat poison; **chasse aux rats,** rat catching; **preneur de rats,** rat-catcher; *Adm:* rodent operator; *F:* **c'est un r.,** he's stingy, a miser; **être fait comme un r.,** to be caught out; (*b*) **r. des champs,** field mouse; **r. d'eau,** water vole; **r. musqué,** musk rat, musquash; **r. géant (des Indes),** bandicoot; **r. d'Égypte, de Pharaon,** ichneumon, mongoose; **r. d'Amérique,** (i) guinea pig; (ii) coypu. **2. r. de cave,** (i) *A:* exciseman; (ii) wax taper; **r. d'église,** constant churchgoer; **pauvre comme un r. d'église,** as poor as a church mouse; **r. d'hôtel,** hotel thief; *F:* **petit r. (d'Opéra),** young ballet pupil; *F:* **mon petit r.,** darling.

rata [rata] *n.m. Mil: P:* (= RATATOUILLE) stew.

ratage [rataʒ] *n.m. F:* failure; misfire.

rataplan [rataplɑ̃] *n.m.* rub-a-dub (of a drum).

ratatiné [ratatine] *a.* (*a*) shrivelled, shrunken (apple, face); **petite vieille ratatinée,** wizened little old woman; (*b*) *F:* smashed-up (car).

ratatinement [ratatinmɑ̃] *n.m.* shrivelling up; crinkling.

ratatiner [ratatine] *v.tr. & pr.* **1.** to shrivel (up); to shrink; (*of parchment*) to crinkle up. **2.** *P:* (*a*) to bump (s.o.) off; (*b*) to beat (s.o.) up.

ratatouille [ratatuj] *n.f. Cu:* (*a*) *P:* stew; (*b*) ratatouille.

rate[1] [rat] *n.f.* spleen; *F:* **se dilater la r.,** to have a good laugh; **ne pas se fouler la r.,** to take things pretty easy.

rate[2] *n.f.* female rat.

raté, -ée [rate] *n.* **1.** (*pers.*) failure. **2.** *n.m.* misfire (of gun, engine); **le moteur avait des ratés,** the engine was misfiring.

râteau, -eaux [rɑto] *n.m.* **1.** (*a*) rake; **r. mécanique,** raker; **r. faneur,** tedder; (*b*) *Nau:* **r. de pont,** squeegee; (*c*) (croupier's) rake; (*d*) *F:* comb. **2.** wards (of a lock).

râtelage [rɑtlaʒ] *n.m.* raking.

râteler [rɑtle] *v.tr.* **(je râtelle, n. râtelons; je râtellerai)** to rake up (hay, etc.).

râtelier [rɑtəlje] *n.m.* **1.** rack (in stable); *F:* **quand il n'y a plus de foin dans le r.,** when we're broke; **manger au r. de qn,** to live at s.o.'s expense; **il mange à tous les râteliers,** all's grist that comes to his mill. **2. r. d'armes, à outils, à pipes, à seaux,** arm rack, tool rack, pipe rack, bucket rack. **3.** *F:* set of false teeth; denture.

rater [rate] **1.** *v.i.* (*of gun*) to misfire; to fail to go off; (*of motor engine*) to misfire; (*of enterprise*) to fail; to miscarry, misfire. **2.** *v.tr.* (*a*) **r. son coup,** to miss one's shot, to miss the mark; *Golf:* to foozle (one's shot); **coup raté,** miss; *F:* fluff; *Av:* **atterrissage raté,** bad landing; **r. un lièvre,** to miss a hare; (*b*) *F:* **r. un coup,** to fail in an attempt; not to bring it off; **r. son train,** to miss one's train; **r. son bac,** to fail in one's *baccalauréat;* **j'ai raté l'occasion,** I missed, lost, the chance.

ratiboiser [ratibwaze] *v.tr. P:* **1. r. qch. à qn,** to do s.o. out of sth.. **2.** to rook (s.o.), to clean (s.o.) out.

raticide [ratisid] *n.m.* rat poison, raticide.

ratier [ratje] *a. & n.m.* **(chien) r.,** ratter.

ratière [ratjɛr] *n.f.* rat trap.

ratification [ratifikasjɔ̃] *n.f.* ratification.

ratifier [ratifje] *v.tr.* to ratify (treaty, act); to confirm (decision).

ratiociner [rasjɔsine] *v.i.* to split hairs.

ration [rasjɔ̃] *n.f.* ration(s); (horse's) feed; **r. de combat,** iron rations; **rations imposées en temps de guerre,** wartime rations; **r. calorique,** caloric intake.

rationalisation [rasjɔnalizasjɔ̃] *n.f.* rationalization; rationalizing (of industry).

rationaliser [rasjɔnalize] *v.tr.* to rationalize.

rationalisme [rasjɔnalism] *n.m.* rationalism.

rationaliste [rasjɔnalist] *a. & n.m. & f.* rationalist.

rationalité [rasjɔnalite] *n.f.* rationality.

rationnel, -elle [rasjɔnɛl] *a.* (*a*) rational (system, quantity); theoretical (mechanics); (*b*) rational, reasonable, sensible.

rationnellement [rasjɔnɛlmɑ̃] *adv.* rationally; sensibly.

rationnement [rasjɔnmɑ̃] *n.m.* rationing.

rationner [rasjɔne] *v.tr.* to ration (population, patient, supplies).

ratissage [ratisaʒ] *n.m.* **1.** (*a*) raking; (*b*) (*at casino*) raking in (of the stakes). **2.** *F:* combing, thorough search (of district, by police, etc.).

ratisser [ratise] *v.tr.* **1.** (*a*) to rake (path); (*b*) to rake (up) leaves; (*c*) (*at casino*) **r. les mises,** to rake in the stakes. **2.** *F:* to rook, fleece (s.o.); to ruin (s.o.). **3.** *F:* to search, comb (a district).

ratissoire [ratiswar] *n.f.* hoe, scuffle.

raton [ratɔ̃] *n.m.* **1.** young rat. **2. r. laveur,** raccoon.

rattachement [rataʃmɑ̃] *n.m.* (*a*) fastening, tying up (again); (*b*) re-attachment; **le r. de l'Alsace à la France,** the return of Alsace to France.

rattacher [rataʃe] **1.** *v.tr.* (*a*) to fasten, tie (up), (sth.) again; to refasten; **rattachez le chien,** tie up the dog (again); (*b*) **les liens qui vous rattachent à la famille,** the ties that bind one to the family; (*c*) **r. qch. à qch.,** to link up, connect, sth. with sth.; (*d*) *Mil:* **unité rattachée,** attached unit. **2. se r. à qch,** (i) to be fastened to sth.; (ii) to be connected with sth.

rattrapage [ratrapaʒ] *n.m.* **1.** *Mec.E:* **r. du jeu,** taking up of play; compensation for play. **2.** *Sch:* **cours de r.,** special course, for backward pupils.

rattrape-jeu [ratrapʒø] *n.m.inv. Mec.E:* **(dispositif) r.-j.,** device for taking up play.

rattraper [ratrape] **1.** *v.tr.* (*a*) to recapture; to catch (s.o., sth.) again; *F:* **on ne m'y rattrapera pas!** you won't catch me doing that again! (*b*) to overtake; to catch (s.o.) up; to come up with (s.o.); **r.**

l'arriéré de besogne, to catch up with arrears of work; (*c*) **r. son argent, sa santé,** to recover one's money, one's health; **r. le temps perdu,** to make up for lost time; (*d*) *Mec.E:* **r. le jeu, l'usure,** to take up the play, the wear; (*e*) to correct, retrieve (mistake, etc.); *Cu:* **r. une mayonnaise,** to retrieve a (curdled) mayonnaise. **2. se r.** (*a*) **se r. à une branche,** to save oneself by catching hold of a branch; (*b*) **se r. de ses pertes,** to make good one's losses; to recoup oneself; (*c*) to catch up; (*d*) to stop oneself (before making a mistake); (*e*) **se r. auprès de qn,** to get back into favour with s.o.

rature [ratyr] *n.f.* erasure; **faire une r.,** to scratch out, cross out, a word.

raturer [ratyre] *v.tr.* **1.** to erase, scratch out, cross out (word). **2.** to scrape.

raucité [rosite] *n.f.* raucousness; hoarseness.

raugmenter [rogmɑ̃te] *v.i. P:* (*of price*) to rise, go up again.

rauque [rok] *a.* hoarse, raucous, rough, harsh, (voice, etc.).

ravage [ravaʒ] *n.m. usu. pl.* havoc, devastation; ravages (of war, disease); **faire des ravages,** to work havoc.

ravagé [ravaʒe] *a.* (*a*) **visage r.,** ravaged, haggard, face; (*b*) *F:* mad, cracked.

ravager [ravaʒe] *v.tr.* **(je ravageai(s); n. ravageons)** to ravage, devastate; to lay waste; to play havoc with (sth.); **visage ravagé par la petite vérole,** face pitted with smallpox.

ravageur, -euse [ravaʒœr, -øz] **1.** *a.* ravaging; devastating (storm); destructive (birds). **2.** *n.* ravager; destroyer.

ravalement [ravalmɑ̃] *n.m.* (*a*) *Const:* (i) repointing, scraping, re-dressing (of stonework); (ii) roughcasting; (iii) (coat of) roughcast; (*b*) cutting back (of tree); (*c*) disparagement, depreciation (of s.o.).

ravaler [ravale] **1.** *v.tr.* (*a*) to swallow (sth.) again, to swallow (sth.) down; **r. un sanglot, sa colère,** to choke down a sob; to suppress one's anger; **je lui ferai r. ses paroles,** I'll make him eat his words; (*b*) (i) to degrade, lower (s.o.); **r. sa femme au rôle de servante,** to treat one's wife like a servant; (ii) to disparage, depreciate, to take (s.o.) down; to slight (s.o.); (*c*) to cut back (tree); (*d*) *Const:* (i) to re-dress, to resurface and repoint (stonework); (ii) to roughcast (wall). **2. se r.,** to degrade, lower, debase, oneself; **vous ne vous ravaleriez pas jusque-là,** you would not stoop to that.

ravaleur [ravalœr] *n.m.* roughcaster, plasterer.

ravaudage [ravodaʒ] *n.m.* **1.** (*a*) mending, darning; (*b*) botching, bungling. **2.** (*a*) mend; darn; (*b*) botch.

ravauder [ravode] *v.tr.* (*a*) to mend (clothes); to darn; (*b*) *F:* to botch, bungle (work).

ravaudeur, -euse [ravodœr, -øz] *n.* (*a*) mender; darner; (*b*) *F:* botcher, bungler.

rave [rav] *n.f.* (i) radish; (ii) turnip; **céleri r.,** celeriac.

ravi [ravi] *a.* delighted (**de,** with); **r. de joie,** overjoyed; **je suis r. de vous voir,** I'm delighted to see you; **d'un air r.,** delightedly.

ravier [ravje] *n.m.* radish dish; hors-d'œuvres dish.

ravigoter [ravigɔte] *v.tr. F:* to cheer (s.o.) up, buck (s.o.) up.

ravin [ravɛ̃] *n.m.* ravine, gully.

ravine [ravin] *n.f.* (*a*) *A:* (mountain) torrent; (*b*) gully.

ravinement [ravinmɑ̃] *n.m.* gullying, channelling (by running water).

raviner [ravine] *v.tr.* (*of storm torrents*) to gully, channel (the ground); to furrow, cut up (road).

ravir [ravir] *v.tr.* **1.** to ravish, carry off (s.o.); **r. qch. à qn,** to rob s.o. of sth.; to steal sth. from s.o. **2.** to delight; **belle à r.,** ravishingly beautiful; **elle chante à r.,** she sings charmingly.

raviser (se) [səravize] *v.pr.* to change one's mind; to think better of it; to think again.

ravissant [ravisɑ̃] *a.* **1.** *A:* ravening (wolf, etc.). **2.** entrancing, ravishing, delightful.

ravissement [ravismɑ̃] *n.m.* **1.** carrying off, ravishment. **2.** rapture, ecstasy, delight; **être dans le r.,** to be in a transport of delight, in raptures.

ravisseur, -euse [ravisœr, -øz] **1.** *a.* predatory, *A:* ravening (wolf, etc.). **2.** *n.* ravisher; abductor; kidnapper.

ravitaillement [ravitajmɑ̃] *n.m.* **1.** *Mil: etc:* supply(ing), revictualling, provisioning (**en,** with); **r. (en carburant),** refuelling; **r. en munitions,** ammunition supply; **distribution du r.,** issue of supplies; **convoi de r.,** supply column; **r. à la mer,** replenishment, refuelling, at sea; **r. en vol,** in-flight refuelling; **le r. des grandes villes est un des problèmes de la guerre,** maintaining supplies in large cities is one of the problems of war; *F:* **aller au r.,** to go shopping. **2.** supplies (of food, fuel, etc.).

ravitailler [ravitaje] **1.** *v.tr.* to supply, provision, revictual (**en,** with); to feed (people); **r. un avion en vol,** to refuel an aircraft in flight. **2. se r.,** to take in (fresh) supplies; to revictual (**en,** with); **se r. (en carburant),** to refuel; *F:* **se r. dans le voisinage,** to shop, stock up, locally.

ravitailleur [ravitajœr] *n.m. Mil: etc:* supply truck, ship, aircraft; tender; *a.* **navire r.,** supply ship.

ravivage [ravivaʒ] *n.m.* reviving, brightening up (of colour); cleaning (of metal surfaces).

raviver [ravive] **1.** *v.tr.* (*a*) to revive (fire, memory, pain); (*b*) to brighten up, to touch up (colour); to clean (surfaces to be soldered); **r. une plaie,** (i) *Med:* to trim a wound; (ii) to re-open an old sore. **2. se r.,** to revive.

ravoir [ravwar] *v.tr.* (*only in inf.*) **1.** (*a*) to have (sth.) (once) again; (*b*) to get (sth.) back again; to recover (sth.). **2.** *F:* (*in neg.*) to clean (up); **je n'arrive pas à r. cette casserole,** I can't get this pan properly clean.

rayage [rɛjaʒ] *n.m.* **1.** (*a*) scratching, scoring (of glass, etc.); (*b*) ruling (of paper, etc.); (*c*) striping (of fabric); (*d*) rifling (of gun). **2.** striking out (of word, etc.); striking off (of name from list).

rayé [reje] *a.* **1.** striped; **pantalon r.,** striped trousers; **tablier r. rouge et bleu,** red and blue striped apron; **chat orange r.,** orange tabby cat. **2.** lined, ruled (paper). **3.** rifled, grooved (gun); **âme rayée,** rifle(d) bore.

rayer [reje] *v.tr.* **(je raie, je raye, n. rayons; je raierai, je rayerai) 1.** (*a*) to scratch (glass, etc.); to score (surface); (*b*) to rule, line (paper); (*c*) to stripe (fabric); (*d*) to rifle (gun); to groove (cylinder). **2.** to strike out, delete; **on vous a rayé, on a rayé votre nom, de la liste,** you have, your name has been struck off the list; *Mil:* **r. qn des contrôles,** to strike s.o. off the strength.

rayon¹ [rɛjɔ̃] *n.m.* **1.** ray (of light, hope); beam (of light); **un faible r. de lumière,** a faint gleam of light; **r. de soleil,** sunbeam; **r. visuel,** (i) visual ray, beam; (ii) line of sight; **rayons cosmiques,** cosmic rays; **rayons X,** X-rays; *Med:* **mal des rayons,** radiation sickness; **r. électronique,** electron beam. **2.** (*a*) radius (of circle); *Veh:* **r. de braquage,** radius of turning circle; (*b*) range; **dans un r. de deux kilomètres,** within a radius of two kilometres; **r. d'action,** range of action, of operation (of aircraft, etc.); **avion à grand r. d'action,** long-range aircraft; **r. d'action d'une campagne publicitaire,** coverage, range, of an advertising campaign; **cette entreprise a étendu son r. d'action,** this firm has extended its scope. **3.** (*a*) spoke (of wheel); (*b*) **étoile à cinq rayons,** five-point star; (*c*) *Bot:* ray.

rayon² *n.m.* **1. r. de miel,** honeycomb. **2.** (*a*) shelf (of cupboard, etc.); *pl.* set of shelves; (*b*) (*in shop*) (i) department; (ii) counter; **magasin à rayons multiples,** department store; **r. des soldes,** bargain counter; **chef de r.,** head, buyer, of department; **ce n'est pas mon r.,** (i) that's nothing to do with me, not my business; (ii) that's not in my line; **c'est son r.,** that's right up his street.

rayon³ *n.m. Hort:* drill; **r. d'oignons,** row of onions.

rayonnage [rɛjɔnaʒ] *n.m.* (*a*) shelving; (set of) shelves; (*b*) shelf space.

rayonnant [rɛjɔnɑ̃] *a.* **1.** (*a*) radiant (heat, sun); (*b*) radiant, beaming (face); **r. de santé,** glowing with health. **2.** (*a*) *Bot:* radiating; (*b*) *Arch:* rayonnant.

rayonne [rɛjɔn] *n.f. Tex:* rayon.

rayonnement [rɛjɔnmɑ̃] *n.m.* (*a*) *Ph:* radiation; **protection contre le r.,** glow screen; (*b*) radiance (of sun, etc.); (*c*) influence.

rayonner¹ [rɛjɔne] *v.i.* (*a*) *Ph:* to radiate; *W.Tel:* **r. dans l'antenne,** to howl; (*b*) to beam, shine; **il rayonnait de joie,** he was radiant, beaming, with joy; (*c*) to radiate (from a centre); **r. autour d'Avignon,** to make Avignon the centre (for excursions).

rayonner² *v.tr.* to fit with shelves; to shelve (room, etc.).

rayure [rejyr] *n.f.* (*a*) stripe, streak; **tissu à rayures,** striped material; (*b*) scratch, score; (*c*) *Sm.a:* groove (of rifling).

raz [ra] *n.m.* **r. (de courant),** strong current (in estuary); race; **r. de marée,** (i) tidal wave; (ii) *F:* upheaval; *Pol:* landslide.

razzia [razja] *n.f.* (*a*) incursion, raid, razzia; (*b*) *F:* **faire (une) r. sur les soldes,** to make a clean sweep of, to snap up, the bargains.

ré [re] *n.m.inv. Mus:* **1.** (the note) D. **2.** re (in the Fixed Do system).

réa [rea] *n.m.* sheave; pulley wheel.

réabonnement [reabɔnmɑ̃] *n.m.* renewal of subscription.

réabonner (se) [səreabɔne] *v.tr. & pr.* to renew (s.o.'s, one's) subscription (**à,** to).

réabsorber [reapsɔrbe] *v.tr.* to reabsorb.

réabsorption [reapsɔrpsjɔ̃] *n.f.* reabsorption.

réaccoutumer [reakutyme] *v.tr.* to re-accustom (**à,** to).

réactance [reaktɑ̃s] *n.f. El:* reactance.

réacteur, -trice [reaktœr, -tris] **1.** *n. A:* reactionary. **2.** *n.m.* (*a*) jet engine, reaction engine; (*b*) jet aircraft. **3.** *n.m. Atom.Ph:* (atomic, nuclear) reactor; atomic, nuclear, pile; **r. propulseur de navire,** ship-propulsion reactor.

réactif, -ive [reaktif, -iv] **1.** *a.* reactive; **non r.,** non-reactive; *Ch:* **papier r.,** reagent paper, test paper; *El:* **courant r.,** reactive current; **couplage r.,** feedback coupling. **2.** *n.m. Ch:* reagent; **r. à base de mercure,** mercury reagent.

réaction [reaksjɔ̃] *n.f.* **1.** (*a*) *Ch: Ph:* reaction; **faire la r. des alcaloïdes,** to test for alkaloids; **r. en chaîne,** chain reaction; (*b*) *El:* reaction, feedback; *W.Tel:* **amplificateur, récepteur, à r.,** regenerative receiver; **r. dans l'antenne,** howling; (*c*) *Mec:* reaction; kick (of rifle); **r. réciproque,** interaction; **tube de r.,** torque tube; **moteur à r.,** jet engine; reaction engine, motor; **propulsion par r.,** jet propulsion, reaction propulsion; **avion à r.,** jet (-propelled) aircraft, jet plane, *F:* jet. **2.** *Physiol:* reaction, response (of organ, etc.); **r. cutanée,** cutaneous, skin, reaction; *Med:* skin test; **r. à une situation nouvelle,** reaction to a new situation; **avoir des réactions lentes,** to be slow to react; **psychologie de r.,** behaviourism. **3.** *Pol:* **la r.,** (i) reactionary attitude; (ii) reactionaries.

réactionnaire [reaksjɔnɛr] *a. & n.m. & f. Pol:* reactionary.

réactiver [reaktive] *v.tr.* **1.** to revive; to regenerate; **r. le feu,** to revive, poke (up), the fire. **2.** to reactivate (catalyst, serum).

réactivité [reaktivite] *n.f.* reactivity.

réadaptation [readaptasjɔ̃] *n.f.* **1.** rehabilitation (of invalid, prisoner). **2.** readjustment.

réadapter [readapte] *v.tr.* **1.** to rehabilitate. **2.** to readjust.

réadmettre [readmɛtr̥] *v.tr.* (*conj. like* METTRE) to readmit.

réadmission [readmisjɔ̃] *n.f.* readmission.

réaffecter [reafɛkte] *v.tr.* **r. qn à son premier emploi,** to reinstate s.o. in his former job; **r. une subvention à sa destination première,** to reallocate funds to their original use.

réaffirmer [reafirme] *v.tr.* to reaffirm.

réagir [reaʒir] *v.i.* to react (**sur,** on; **contre,** against; **à,** towards); **r. réciproquement,** to interact.

réajuster [reaʒyste] *v.tr.* = RAJUSTER.

réal, -aux [real, -o] *n.m. Num:* real.

réalisable [realizabl̥] *a.* **1.** realizable, feasible (plan). **2.** realizable (assets).

réalisateur, -trice [realizatœr, -tris] **1.** *a.* **il a l'esprit r.,** he can work things out, get results. **2.** *n. Cin: W.Tel:* producer.

réalisation [realizasjɔ̃] *n.f.* **1.** (*a*) realization, carrying out, accomplishment (of plan, etc.); creation (of work of art); (*b*) *Cin: T.V:* production. **2.** *Fin:* realization.

réaliser [realize] **1.** *v.tr.* to realize; (*a*) to achieve (an ambition, success); to carry out, implement (plan); to effect (cure); to create (work of art); *Cin: etc:* to produce (film, programme); (*b*) to convert (asset) into cash; to make (profit); (*c*) *F:* to understand (mistake, situation). **2.** **se r.** (*a*) (*of projects, etc.*); to materialize; (*of prediction, etc.*) to come true; (*b*) to fulfil oneself.

réalisme [realism] *n.m.* realism.

réaliste [realist] **1.** *a.* realistic. **2.** *n.* realist.

réalité [realite] *n.f.* reality; actuality, fact; **en r.,** in reality; really; actually, as a matter of fact.

réanimation [reanimasjɔ̃] *n.f.* resuscitation.

réanimer [reanime] *v.tr.* to resuscitate (drowned person, etc.).

réapparaître [reaparɛtr̥] *v.i.* (*conj. like* APPARAÎTRE; *aux. usu.* **être**) to reappear.

réapparition [reaparisjɔ̃] *n.f.* reappearance.

réapprovisionnement [reaprɔvizjɔnmɑ̃] *n.m.* replenishing of supplies; revictualling; *Com:* restocking.

réapprovisionner [reaprɔvizjɔne] *v.tr. & pr.* to replenish (s.o.'s, one's) supplies (**en,** of); to restock (shop) (**en,** with).

réargenter [rearʒɑ̃te] *v.tr.* to resilver, replate.

réarmement [rearməmɑ̃] *n.m.* **1.** rearming, rearmament; *Pol:* **r. moral,** moral rearmament. **2.** *Nau:* refitting, recommissioning.

réarmer [rearme] *v.tr.* **1.** (*a*) to rearm; (*b*) to recock (gun); to reset (camera shutter, etc.). **2.** *Nau:* to refit, recommission.

réassortiment [reasɔrtimɑ̃] *n.m.* **1.** (*a*) (re)matching (of colours, etc.); (*b*) *Com:* restocking. **2.** *Com:* new stock.

réassortir [reasɔrtir] *v.tr.* (*conj. like* ASSORTIR) **1.** to obtain a match for (sth., a set). **2.** to restock (shop); **se r.,** to restock.

réassurance [reasyrɑ̃s] *n.f.* reinsurance, reassurance (of a risk).

réassurer [reasyre] *v.tr.* to reinsure.

réassureur [reasyrœr] *n.m.* reinsurer.

rebaisser [rəbese] *v.i.* (*of price*) to come down again.

rebaptiser [rəbatize] *v.tr.* to rename (street, etc.).

rébarbatif, -ive [rebarbatif, -iv] *a.* grim, forbidding, unprepossessing, repugnant; surly (expression).

rebâtir [rəbɑtir] *v.tr.* to rebuild (house); **r. par le pied,** to underpin.

rebattre [rəbatr̥] *v.tr.* (*conj. like* BATTRE) (*a*) to beat (sth.) again; (*b*) to reshuffle (the cards); (*c*) *F:* **r. les oreilles à qn de qch.,** to din sth. into s.o.'s ears.

rebattu [rəbaty] *a.* hackneyed, trite (story).

rebelle [rəbɛl] **1.** *a.* rebellious (person, spirit, etc.); stubborn, obstinate (fever); intractable, unworkable (material); **r. à toute discipline,** unamenable to discipline. **2.** *n.* rebel.

rebeller (se) [sərəbele] *v.pr.* (*a*) to rebel, to revolt (**contre,** against); (*b*) to protest.

rébellion [rebeljɔ̃] *n.f.* rebellion, rising, revolt; **en état de r.,** insurgent.

rebiffer (se) [sərəbife] *v.pr. F:* to get one's back up.

reboire [rəbwar] *v.tr.* (*conj. like* BOIRE) to drink again; **jamais je ne reboirai de ce vin,** I shall never touch that wine again.

reboisement [rəbwazmɑ̃] *n.m.* (re)afforestation.

reboiser [rəbwaze] *v.tr.* to (re)afforest.

rebond [rəbɔ̃] *n.m.* rebound, bounce (of ball).

rebondi [rəbɔ̃di] *a.* rounded, chubby (cheeks); plump (person); **ventre r.,** corporation.

rebondir [rəbɔ̃dir] *v.i.* (*a*) to rebound; (*of ball*) to bounce; (*b*) *Fig:* to start off, up, again.

rebondissement [rəbɔ̃dismɑ̃] *n.m.* (*a*) rebound(ing); bounce; (*b*) new development (in a case, etc.).

rebord [rəbɔr] *n.m.* **1.** edge, border, rim; hem (of garment); lip (of cup); **r. d'une fenêtre,** window sill, ledge. **2.** raised edge; flange.

reborder [rəbɔrde] *v.tr.* **1.** to put a new edging, border, hem, to (sth.). **2. r. qn dans son lit,** to tuck s.o. up (in bed) again.

reboucher [rəbuʃe] *v.tr.* **1.** to stop, block, (sth.) up again; to recork (bottle). **2.** to stop out (woodwork) (with putty).

rebours [rəbur] *n.m.* wrong way (of the grain, nap); contrary, reverse; **à r.,** against the grain, the wrong way, backwards; **caresser un chat à r.,** to stroke a cat the wrong way; **prendre à r. une rue à sens unique,** to enter a one-way street at the wrong end; **prendre tout à r.,** to take everything the wrong way, to misconstrue everything; **compter à r.,** to count backwards; *Ball:* **compte à r.,** count down; **compliment à r.,** backhanded compliment.

rebouter [rəbute] *v.tr.* to set (broken limb); to reduce (dislocation).

rebouteur, -euse, rebouteux, -euse [rəbutœr, rəbutø, -øz] *n.* bonesetter.

reboutonner [rəbutɔne] *v.tr.* to rebutton; to button up again.

rebrousse-poil (à) [arəbruspwal] *adv.phr.* **brosser un chapeau à r.-p.,** to brush a hat against the nap, the wrong way; **caresser le chat à r.-p.,** to stroke the cat the wrong way, against the fur; *F:* **prendre qn à r.-p.,** to rub s.o. up the wrong way.

rebrousser [rəbruse] *v.tr.* **1.** to turn up, brush up (hair, nap). **2. r. chemin,** to retrace one's steps, to turn back.

rebuffade [rəbyfad] *n.f.* rebuff; snub.

rébus [rebys] *n.m.* rebus; *Fig:* enigma, puzzle.

rebut [rəby] *n.m.* **(article de) r.,** reject; rubbish; **papier de r.,** waste paper; **habits de r.,** cast-off clothing; *Ind:* **pièces de r.,** rejects; throw-outs; **marchandises de r.,** rubbishy goods, trash; **mettre qch. au r.,** to throw sth. away; to scrap sth.; *Post:* **bureau des rebuts,** dead-letter office; **le r. de la population,** the dregs of the population.

rebutant [rəbytɑ̃] *a.* **1.** tiresome, irksome; disheartening (work). **2.** disagreeable (manner), unprepossessing (person).

rebuter [rəbyte] **1.** *v.tr.* (*a*) to rebuff, repulse (s.o.); (*b*) to reject, discard (sth.); (*c*) to dishearten, discourage; (*d*) to shock, disgust. **2. se r.,** to lose heart; to give up the attempt.

recalage [rəkalaʒ] *n.m. F:* failure (in an exam).

recalcifier [rəkalsifje] *v.tr.* to (re)calcify.

récalcitrance [rekalsitrɑ̃s] *n.f.* recalcitrance, refractoriness.

récalcitrant, -ante [rekalsitrɑ̃, -ɑ̃t] **1.** *a.* recalcitrant, refractory, obstinate (person, horse). **2.** *n.* recalcitrant; rebel.

recaler [rəkale] *v.tr. F:* to fail, plough (s.o. in exam); **être recalé,** to fail.

récapitulatif, -ive [rekapitylatif, -iv] *a.* recapitulatory, recapitulative; *Cmptr:* **carte récapitulative,** summary card.

récapitulation [rekapitylasjɔ̃] *n.f.* (*a*) recapitulation; summing up; (*b*) summary, résumé.

récapituler [rekapityle] *v.tr.* to recapitulate; to sum up (proceedings); *Sch:* to revise.

recaser [rəkɑze] *v.tr. F:* (*a*) to find another job for (s.o.); (*b*) to rehouse (s.o.).

recel [rəsɛl] *n.m. Jur:* receiving (and concealing) (of stolen goods); harbouring (of criminal).

receler [rəs(ə)le] *v.tr.* **(je recèle, n. recelons; je recèlerai); recéler** [rəsele] *v.tr.* **(je recèle, n. recélons; je recélerai)** (*a*) *Jur:* to receive (stolen goods); to harbour (criminal); to conceal (child); (*b*) **la terre recèle de grands trésors,** great treasures lie hidden in the earth.

receleur, -euse [rəs(ə)lœr, -øz] *n. Jur:* receiver (of stolen goods); *F:* fence.

récemment [resamɑ̃] *adv.* recently, lately, of late.

recensement [rəsɑ̃smɑ̃] *n.m.* (*a*) census; return (of population, horses, resources); counting (of votes); *Mil:* registration; **faire un r.,** to take a census; **agent chargé du r.,** recording official; (*b*) *Com:* new inventory.

recenser [rəsɑ̃se] *v.tr.* (*a*) to take the census of (town, etc.); to record; *Mil:* to register; to count (votes); (*b*) to check off (goods).

recenseur, -euse [rəsɑ̃sœr, -øz] *n.* census taker; enumerator; teller (of votes).

récent [resɑ̃] *a.* recent.

recéper [rəsepe] *v.tr.* **(je recèpe, n. recépons; je recéperai)** to cut back (tree, vine stock, to the stump).

récépissé [resepise] *n.m.* (*a*) (acknowledgement of) receipt; **r. d'entrepôt,** warehouse receipt; (*b*) acknowledgement (of complaint, etc.).

réceptacle [resɛptakl̥] *n.m.* **1.** receptacle; repository. **2.** *Bot:* receptacle.

récepteur, -trice [resɛptœr, -tris] **1.** *a.* receiving (apparatus, set). **2.** *n.m.* (*a*) *Physiol:* receptor (of stimulus); (*b*) *Mec.E:* driven part (of machine); (*c*) *Tp:* receiver; **décrocher le r.,** to lift the receiver; *Tg:* **r. Morse,** Morse receiver, tape machine; (*d*) (*radio, T.V., radar*) receiver, (receiving) set; *Cmptr:* **r. de données,** data receiver.

réceptif, -ive [resɛptif, -iv] *a.* receptive.

réception [resɛpsjɔ̃] *n.f.* **1.** (*a*) receipt (of letter, order, goods); **accuser r. de qch.,** to acknowledge receipt of sth.; (*b*) taking delivery (of goods); acceptance (after inspection); taking over (of equipment); **de r.,** acceptance test. **2.** reception (of candidate by learned body, etc.); admission (to membership). **3.** (*a*) welcome; **faire une bonne r. à qn,** to welcome s.o. warmly; to give s.o. a good reception; (*b*) (official, court) reception; party; **salle de r.,** reception room; **frais de r.,** entertainment expenses; **jour de r.,** at-home day; (*c*) (hotel) reception desk, office; enquiry office. **4.** *Tp: Tg: W.Tel: T.V: Elcs:* receiving, reception; **appareil, poste, de r.,** receiving set.

réceptionnaire [resɛpsjɔnɛr] *n.* **1.** *Com: Ind:* receiving agent, clerk; **ingénieur r.,** acceptance-test engineer. **2.** receiver, consignee (of goods).

réceptionner [resɛpsjɔne] *v.tr.* to check and sign for (goods on delivery).

réceptionniste [resɛpsjɔnist] *n.m. & f.* receptionist.

réceptivité [resɛptivite] *n.f.* receptivity; susceptibility (to infection).

récessif, -ive [resesif, -iv] *a. Biol:* recessive.

récession [resesjɔ̃] *n.f. Pol.Ec:* recession.

recette [rəsɛt] *n.f.* **1.** receipts, returns, takings, *Sp:* gate money; **dépenses et recettes,** expenses and receipts; outgoings and incomings; (*of play, film*) **faire r.,** to be a (box-office) success. **2.** (*a*) collection (of moneys due); **garçon de r.,** bank messenger; (*b*) receiving; receipt (of stores); acceptance (from contract); **prendre qch. en r.,** to accept (delivery of) sth. **3.** *Adm:* (*a*) receivership, collectorship (of rates and taxes, etc.); (*b*) receiver's office, collector's office. **4.** *Cu:* recipe; *Pharm:* formula; **recettes de métier,** tricks of the trade.

recevable [rəsəvabl̩] *a.* **1.** admissible, acceptable (excuse); (goods) fit for acceptance; *Jur:* admissible (evidence). **2. être r. dans une demande,** to be entitled to proceed with a claim.

receveur, -euse [rəsəvœr, -øz] *n.* **1.** receiver; recipient (of letter, blood transfusion); *Med:* **r. universel,** universal recipient. **2.** (*a*) collector (of taxes, excise, customs); **r., receveuse, des Postes,** postmaster, postmistress; **r. buraliste,** tobacconist; (*b*) (bus) conductor, conductress.

recevoir [rəsəvwar] *v.tr.* (*pr.p.* **recevant;** *p.p.* **reçu;** *pr.ind.* **je reçois, il reçoit, n. recevons, ils reçoivent;** *pr.sub.* **je reçoive, n. recevions;** *impf.* **je recevais;** *p.h.* **je reçus;** *fu.* **je recevrai**) **1.** (*a*) to receive, get (letter, present); **r. qch. de qn,** to receive sth. from s.o.; **r. un conseil,** to receive, be given, advice; **r. la communion, l'absolution,** to receive communion, absolution; *Com:* **nous avons bien reçu votre lettre,** we are in receipt of your letter; (*b*) to receive (punishment, wound); to incur (blame). **2.** (*a*) to receive, welcome (s.o.); **être mal reçu,** to meet with a poor reception; (*b*) to entertain (friends); to receive (clients); **r. des amis à dîner,** to have friends to dinner; **ils reçoivent très peu,** they don't do much entertaining; **le médecin reçoit à 6 heures,** the doctor's surgery is at 6 o'clock; (*c*) to receive, admit; *Sch:* **élèves reçus en première,** pupils admitted, promoted, to the top form; **elle reçoit des pensionnaires,** she takes boarders, lodgers; (*d*) **être reçu à un examen,** to pass an exam(ination); **être reçu premier,** to be, come out, first, top; **être reçu médecin,** to qualify as a doctor; *Nau:* **être reçu capitaine,** to get one's captain's certificate; (*e*) to receive, take; **r. de l'eau dans un vase,** to catch water in a vessel; (*f*) *W.Tel:* to receive (transmission). **3.** to accept, admit (opinion, excuse); **coutumes reçues,** accepted customs. **4.** *Sp:* **se r.,** to land (after jump).

rechange [rəʃɑ̃ʒ] *n.m.* replacement; **linge de r.,** change of linen; **r. de vêtements,** spare set of clothes; **trousse de r.,** duplicate set (of tools, etc.); *Aut: etc:* **pièces de r., rechanges,** spare parts, spares; **pile de r.,** refill (for torch).

rechanger [rəʃɑ̃ʒe] *v.tr.* (*conj. like* CHANGER) to change, to exchange, (sth.) again.

rechanter [rəʃɑ̃te] *v.tr.* to sing again; to repeat.

rechapage [rəʃapaʒ] *n.m.* retreading (of tyre).

rechaper [rəʃape] *v.tr.* to retread (tyre); **pneu rechapé,** retread.

réchappé, -ée [reʃape] *n.* survivor (of disaster, wreck); **r. de potence,** gallow's bird.

réchapper [reʃape] *v.i.* (*aux.* **avoir** *or* **être**) to escape (**de,** from); **il a réchappé du naufrage,** he survived the wreck; **il n'en réchappera pas,** it is all up with him; **r. à une crise,** to come through a crisis.

recharge [rəʃarʒ] *n.f.* (*a*) refill (for ball-point pen, etc.); (*b*) recharging (of battery); **mettre l'accumulateur en r.,** to put the battery on charge.

rechargement [rəʃarʒəmɑ̃] *n.m.* **1.** recharging (of accumulator); reloading (of vehicle, gun, ship). **2.** remetalling (of road); reballasting.

recharger [rəʃarʒe] *v.tr.* (*conj. like* CHARGER) **1.** (*a*) to recharge (accumulator); (*b*) to reload (lorry, gun, camera); to refill (pen); to make up (the fire). **2.** to remetal (road); to reballast (railway track).

rechasser [rəʃase] *v.tr.* to chase, (s.o.) out again; to drive back (ball).

réchaud [reʃo] *n.m.* (*a*) stove; **r. à gaz,** gas ring; **r. à alcool,** spirit lamp; (*b*) hot plate; plate warmer.

réchauffage [reʃofaʒ] *n.m.* reheating; warming up.

réchauffé [reʃofe] *n.m.* (*a*) warmed-up food; (*b*) *F:* rehash; stale news, joke.

réchauffement [reʃofmɑ̃] *n.m.* warming up (of atmosphere, etc.).

réchauffer [reʃofe] **1.** *v.tr.* (*a*) to reheat; to warm (sth.) again, to warm up (s.o., food); **r. une vieille histoire,** to revive an old story; (*b*) **r. le courage de qn,** to rekindle, stir up, s.o.'s courage; **r. le cœur à qn,** to put new heart into s.o.; **cela me réchauffe le cœur,** it does my heart good; (*c*) **r. une couche,** to put fresh manure on a hot bed. **2. se r.,** to get warm (again).

réchauffeur [reʃofœr] *n.m.* heating, warming, device; *Mch:* (re)heater; **r. d'eau d'alimentation,** feed-water heater; **serpentin r.,** heating coil.

réchauffoir [reʃofwar] *n.m.* plate warmer (in stove).

rechausser [rəʃose] **1.** *v.tr.* (*a*) to put (s.o.'s) shoes, boots, on again (for him); to fit (s.o.) with new boots; (*b*) **r. une voiture,** to fit a car with new tyres; (*c*) to underpin (structure); to bank up the foot of (tree, etc.). **2. se r.,** to put one's shoes (and stockings) on again.

rêche [rɛʃ] *a.* harsh, rough (surface, wine); prickly, crossgrained (person).

recherche [rəʃɛrʃ] *n.f.* **1.** (*a*) search, quest, pursuit; **la r. de la vérité,** the search for, after, truth; **r. des plaisirs,** pleasure seeking; **r. de débouchés,** market research; marketing; **r. de filons,** prospecting; **r. pétrolifère,** oil prospecting; *El:* **r. de dérangements,** locating of faults; **être à la r. de qn, de qch.,** to be looking for, in search of, s.o., sth.; **j'ai couru à la r. d'un médecin,** I ran for, to find, a doctor; (*b*) **r. scientifique, médicale,** scientific, medical, research; **faire de la r.,** to be a research worker; **faire des recherches sur qch.,** (i) to do research on sth.; (ii) to enquire into sth.; (*c*) searching; *Cust:* **droit de r.,** right of search (at sea). **2.** effort, affectation, studied elegance; meticulous care; **style sans r.,** straightforward, unaffected, style.

recherché [rəʃɛrʃe] *a.* **1.** sought after; in demand. **2.** (*a*) choice, elaborate (dress, etc.); studied (speech); **d'un travail r.,** of exquisite workmanship; (*b*) strained, affected (style).

rechercher [rəʃɛrʃe] *v.tr.* (*a*) to search for, seek (s.o., sth.); to search, inquire, into (causes, etc.); *Tp: etc:* **r. un dérangement,** to try to locate a fault; **homme recherché par la police,** man wanted by the police; **r. un mot dans le dictionnaire,** to look up a word in the dictionary; (*b*) to seek (after), try to obtain (favours, etc.); to court (praise).

rechigné [rəʃiɲe] *a.* sour-tempered, sullen.

rechigner [rəʃiɲe] *v.i. F:* to grimace, look sour; **faire qch. en rechignant,** to do sth. with a bad grace; **r. à la besogne,** to jib, ba(u)lk, at work; **r. à faire qch.,** to jib, boggle, at doing sth.

rechute [rəʃyt] *n.f.* **1.** *Med:* relapse, setback. **2. r. dans le vice,** relapse into vice.
rechuter [rəʃyte] *v.i. Med:* to have a relapse.
récidive [residiv] *n.f.* **1.** repetition of an offence; relapse (into crime). **2.** recurrence (of a disease).
récidiver [residive] *v.i.* **1.** to repeat an offence. **2.** (*of disease*) to recur.
récidiviste [residivist] *n.m. & f.* recidivist, habitual criminal; hardened offender.
récif [resif] *n.m.* reef; **r. (en) barrière,** barrier reef; **r. de corail, corallien,** coral reef.
récipient [resipjɑ̃] *n.m.* container, vessel, receptacle; (storage) bin; tank; receiver (of air pump, retort, etc.); **r. cylindrique,** drum.
réciprocité [resiprɔsite] *n.f.* reciprocity.
réciproque [resiprɔk] **1.** *a.* (*a*) reciprocal, mutual (benefits, love, etc.); (*b*) *Gram: Mth: Log:* reciprocal inverse (ratio); *Mth:* converse (propositions); *Mec:* reversible (motion). **2.** *n.f.* (*a*) **rendre la r. à qn,** to pay s.o. back in his own coin, be even with s.o.; (*b*) *Log: Mth:* converse; *Mth:* reciprocal.
réciproquement [resiprɔkmɑ̃] *adv.* reciprocally. **1.** mutually; **ils s'aident r.,** they help one another. **2.** conversely; vice versa.
récit [resi] *n.m.* **1.** narration, narrative; account; recital, relation (of events); **il nous fit le r. de ses aventures,** he gave us an account of his adventures. **2.** *Mus:* solo (in concerted piece); **jeux de r., clavier de r.,** solo organ, swell organ.
récital [resital] *n.m.* recital; *pl. récitals.*
récitant, -ante [resitɑ̃, -ɑ̃t] *a. & n.* (*a*) solo (voice, instrument); (*b*) narrator.
récitatif [resitatif] *n.m. Mus:* recitative.
récitation [resitasjɔ̃] *n.f.* (*a*) recitation, reciting; (*b*) *Sch:* **apprendre une r.,** to learn a text by heart.
réciter [resite] *v.tr.* to recite (poem, etc.); *F:* **r. la même leçon,** to tell the same story.
réclamant, -ante [reklamɑ̃, -ɑ̃t] *n.* claimant.
réclamation [reklamasjɔ̃] *n.f.* (*a*) complaint; objection, protest; (*b*) claim; **faire, déposer, une r.,** to make, put forward, a claim; **prouver le bien-fondé d'une r.,** to substantiate a claim; **r. d'indemnité,** claim for compensation.
réclame [reklam] *n.f.* (*a*) advertising; **faire de la r.,** to advertise; **faire de la r. pour qn,** to boost s.o.; **article (en) r.,** special offer; **vente r.,** bargain sale; (*b*) advertisement; **r. lumineuse,** illuminated sign.
réclamer [reklame] **1.** *v.i.* to complain; **r. contre qch.,** to protest against sth.; to object to sth.; to appeal against (decision). **2.** *v.tr.* (*a*) to lay claim to (sth.), to claim (a right); to (re)claim (lost property); **r. son argent,** to ask for one's money back; **r. de l'argent à qn,** to dun s.o.; (*b*) to call for (s.o., sth.); **r. qch., qn, à grands cris,** to clamour for sth., s.o.; (*c*) **plante qui réclame des soins continuels,** plant that requires continual care. **3. se r. de qn, de qch.,** to appeal to s.o., call s.o., to witness; to quote s.o., sth., as one's authority.
reclassement [rəklasmɑ̃] *n.m.* **1.** (*a*) reclassifying; reclassification; (*b*) regrading (of staff). **2.** rehabilitation.
reclasser [rəklase] *v.tr.* **1.** (*a*) to reclassify; to regroup, rearrange; (*b*) to regrade (staff). **2.** to rehabilitate.
reclouer [rəklue] *v.tr.* to nail (sth.) (up) again.
reclus, -use [rəkly, -yz] **1.** *a.* secluded; cloistered. **2.** *n.* (*a*) (i) hermit, recluse; (ii) cloistered monk, nun; (*b*) recluse; **vivre en r.,** to live like a hermit.
réclusion [reklyzjɔ̃] *n.f.* **1.** reclusion, seclusion, **2.** *Jur:* imprisonment; **r. à perpétuité,** life sentence.
réclusionnaire [reklyzjɔnɛr] *n.m. & f. Jur:* prisoner (serving term).
récognition [rekɔgnisjɔ̃] *n.f. Phil:* recognition, identification.
recoiffer [rəkwafe] *v.tr.* **1. r. qn,** to do s.o.'s hair again; **se r. avant de sortir,** to do, comb, one's hair before going out. **2. se r.,** to put on one's hat again.
recoin [rəkwɛ̃] *n.m.* nook, recess; **coins et recoins,** nooks and crannies.
recollage [rəkɔlaʒ] *n.m.* gluing up (again), sticking together (again).
récollection [rekɔlɛksjɔ̃] *n.f. Rel:* recollection; meditation.
recoller [rəkɔle] **1.** *v.tr.* to paste, glue (sth.) together again; to repaste, restick. **2.** *v.i. Rac:* to catch up. **3.** (*of broken bone*) **se r.,** to knit; *P:* **ils se sont recollés,** they are living together again.
récoltable [rekɔltabl̥] *a.* ready for harvesting, for picking.
récolte [rekɔlt] *n.f.* **1.** (*a*) harvesting, gathering (of crops); vintaging (of grapes); **faire une r.,** to produce a crop; **faire la r. du blé,** to harvest the wheat; (*b*) collecting, gathering (of specimens, etc.). **2.** (*a*) harvest, crop(s); vintage; **rentrer la r.,** to get in, gather in, the harvest, the crops; (*b*) collection (of objects).
récolter [rekɔlte] *v.tr.* to harvest, gather in, get in (crop); **ces fraises se récoltent en juin,** these strawberries are ready for picking in June; *Prov:* **qui sème le vent récolte la tempête,** he who sows the wind shall reap the whirlwind; *F:* **je n'en ai récolté que des injures,** all I got out of it was insults.
recommandable [rəkɔmɑ̃dabl̥] *a.* **1.** commendable; **peu r.,** undesirable; poor (hotel). **2.** advisable, recommendable.
recommandation [rəkɔmɑ̃dasjɔ̃] *n.f.* **1.** recommendation, recommending; **(lettre de) r.,** (i) letter of recommendation, of introduction; (ii) testimonial. **2.** recommendation, injunction, advice. **3.** *Post:* registration (of letter).
recommandé [rəkɔmɑ̃de] *a. Post:* registered; *n.m.* **envoi en r.,** *F:* **un r.,** registered letter, parcel.
recommander [rəkɔmɑ̃de] **1.** *v.tr.* (*a*) to recommend (hotel, product); **r. qn à un employeur,** to recommend s.o. to an employer; **r. son âme à Dieu,** to commend one's soul to God; (*b*) **r. la prudence à qn,** to advise s.o. to be prudent; **je vous recommende de rester,** I advise you to stay; (*c*) *Post:* to register (letter, parcel). **2. se r.** (*a*) **se r. à Dieu,** to commend oneself to God; (*b*) **se r. de qn,** to give s.o. as a reference; (*c*) to merit consideration **(de qch.,** for sth.).
recommencement [rəkɔmɑ̃smɑ̃] *n.m.* beginning, starting, again.
recommencer [rəkɔmɑ̃se] **(je recommençai(s); n. recommençons) 1.** *v.tr.* to recommence; to begin, start, (sth.) (over) again; **r. sa vie,** to start life afresh; **r. à faire qch.,** to begin to do, doing, sth. again; **tout est à r.,** we shall have to start all over again. **2.** *v.i.* (*a*) to do it again; to begin again; to start afresh; **ne recommencez pas!** don't (you) do it again! **le voilà qui recommence!** he's at it again!
récompense [rekɔ̃pɑ̃s] *n.f.* (*a*) recompense, reward; **mille francs de r.,** a thousand francs reward; **en r. de vos services,** as a reward for your services; in return for your services; **la juste r. de ses crimes,** just retribution for his crimes; (*b*) **distribution des récompenses,** giving out of the awards, prizes.
récompenser [rekɔ̃pɑ̃se] *v.tr.* to reward, recompense; **r. qn de qch.,** to reward s.o. for sth.
recomposer [rəkɔ̃poze] *v.tr.* **1.** *Ch:* to recompose, recombine (elements). **2.** *Typ:* to reset (matter).
recomposition [rəkɔ̃pozisjɔ̃] *n.f.* **1.** *Ch:* recombining. **2.** *Typ:* resetting.
recompter [rəkɔ̃te] *v.tr.* to recount, to count again.
réconciliateur, -trice [rekɔ̃siljatœr, -tris] *n.* reconciler.
réconciliation [rekɔ̃siljasjɔ̃] *n.f.* reconciliation;

amener une r. entre deux personnes, to bring about a reconciliation, to heal the breach, between two people.

réconcilier [rekɔ̃silje] *v.tr.* to reconcile (persons, inconsistencies); **se r. avec qn,** to make it up, be friends again, with s.o.; **se r. avec Dieu,** to make one's peace with God.

reconduction [rəkɔ̃dyksjɔ̃] *n.f.* (*a*) *Jur:* renewal (of lease); **tacite r.,** renewal by tacit agreement; (*b*) continuation (of budget, measures).

reconduire [rəkɔ̃dɥir] *v.tr.* (*conj. like* CONDUIRE) (*a*) to see, escort, take, (s.o.) home; to accompany, take, bring (s.o.) back; (*b*) to see, show, (s.o.) out, to the door; (*c*) to renew (lease, etc.); *Adm:* to continue (temporary measure).

réconfort [rekɔ̃fɔr] *n.m.* comfort, consolation; **paroles de r.,** comforting words; *F:* **une petite goutte de r.,** a little drop of comfort.

réconfortant [rekɔ̃fɔrtɑ̃] **1.** *a.* (*a*) strengthening, stimulating; tonic (medicine); (*b*) comforting, cheering (words). **2.** *n.m.* tonic, stimulant.

réconforter [rekɔ̃fɔrte] *v.tr.* **1.** to strengthen, fortify, refresh (s.o.); **il est l'heure de se r.,** it's time to take a little refreshment. **2.** to comfort; to cheer (s.o.) up.

reconnaissable [rəkɔnɛsabl̥] *a.* recognizable (**à,** by, from, through); **il n'est plus r.,** you wouldn't know him again.

reconnaissance [rəkɔnɛsɑ̃s] *n.f.* **1.** recognition (of s.o., sth.); *Mil:* **signal de r.,** recognition signal. **2.** (*a*) acknowledgement (of promise, debt); recognition (of government); admission (of a lapse); (*b*) *Com:* note of hand; acknowledgement of indebtedness (in writing); **donner une r. à qn,** to give s.o. an i.o.u.; **r. (de dépôt de gage),** pawn ticket. **3.** (*a*) *Mil:* reconnaissance, reconnoitring; *F:* recce; **détachement, avion, de r.,** reconnaissance, party, aircraft; **être en r.,** to be reconnoitring, on (a) reconnaissance; (*b*) inspection, exploration, examination (of ground, site); *Min:* prospecting; *Surv:* reconnaissance, surveying, charting; **levé de r.,** exploratory survey. **4.** (*a*) gratitude; **témoigner de la r. à qn,** to show gratitude to s.o.; **avec r.,** gratefully; (*b*) **r. de, pour, qch.,** thankfulness for sth.; **avec r.,** thankfully.

reconnaissant [rəkɔnɛsɑ̃] *a.* (*a*) grateful; **être r. à qn de qch.,** to be grateful to s.o. for sth.; (*b*) thankful (**de,** for).

reconnaître [rəkɔnɛtr̥] *v.tr.* (*conj. like* CONNAÎTRE) **1.** (*a*) to recognize; to know (s.o., sth.) again; to identify (aircraft, a body); **r. qn à sa démarche,** to recognize, know, tell, s.o. by his walk; **comment m'avez-vous reconnu comme Américain?** how did you know I was an American? **gaz qui se reconnaît à son odeur,** gas recognizable by its smell; **je vous reconnais bien là!** that's just like you! that's you all over! **ils se ressemblent tant qu'on ne peut les r.,** they are so alike that one cannot tell them apart; **c'est à ne pas s'y r.,** it's all very confusing; (*b*) *Nau:* **r. la terre,** to sight land. **2.** (*a*) to recognize, acknowledge (truth, right, government); to acknowledge, admit (mistake); **r. qn pour chef,** to acknowledge s.o. as leader; **r. qch. pour vrai,** to acknowledge sth. to be true, to admit the truth of sth.; **reconnu pour, comme, incorrect,** admittedly incorrect; **r. qu'on s'est trompé,** to admit, own, that one was mistaken; (*b*) **r. un enfant** to acknowledge, own, a child. **3.** (*a*) to reconnoitre, make a reconnaissance of (a position, etc.); to explore (the ground); (*b*) *Min:* to prospect.

reconquérir [rəkɔ̃kerir] *v.tr.* (*conj. like* CONQUÉRIR) to regain, recover, reconquer (province); to regain (esteem).

reconquête [rəkɔ̃kɛt] *n.f.* reconquest.

reconsidérer [rəkɔ̃sidere] *v.tr.* (*conj. like* CONSIDÉRER) to reconsider.

reconsolider [rəkɔ̃sɔlide] *v.tr.* to reconsolidate.

reconstituant [rəkɔ̃stitɥɑ̃] *a. & n.m. Med:* tonic.

reconstituer [rəkɔ̃stitɥe] *v.tr.* (*a*) to reconstitute; to reconstruct (a crime); to restore (damaged building); to reconstruct (a system); (*b*) to restore (health).

reconstitution [rəkɔ̃stitysjɔ̃] *n.f.* reconstitution, reconstruction (of government, company); restoration (of building, etc.); **r. d'un crime,** reconstruction of a crime.

reconstruction [rəkɔ̃stryksjɔ̃] *n.f.* reconstruction, rebuilding.

reconstruire [rəkɔ̃strɥir] *v.tr.* (*conj. like* CONSTRUIRE) to reconstruct, rebuild.

reconventionnel, -elle [rəkɔ̃vɑ̃sjɔnɛl] *a. Jur:* **demande reconventionelle,** counter claim.

reconversion [rəkɔ̃vɛrsjɔ̃] *n.f. Pol.Ec:* (*a*) reconversion (of factory, etc.); (*b*) to redeploy (staff); (*c*) redeployment (of workers).

reconvertir [rəkɔ̃vɛrtir] *v.tr. Pol.Ec:* (*a*) to reconvert (factory, etc.); (*b*) to redeploy (staff); (*c*) **se r.,** to change one's occupation.

recopier [rəkɔpje] *v.tr.* (*conj. like* COPIER) (*a*) to recopy; to take another copy of (sth.); (*b*) to make a fair copy of (draft).

recoquillé [rəkɔkije] *a.* cockled, curled up; dog-eared (page).

record [rəkɔr] *n.m. Sp: etc:* record; **battre le r.,** to break, beat, the record; **détenir le r.,** to hold the record; **vitesse r.,** record speed; **dans, en, un temps r.,** in record time; **attirer une affluence r.,** to draw record crowds; **chiffre r. d'accidents,** record accident figure.

recorder [rəkɔrde] *v.tr.* **1.** to rope up (bale) again; to retie (packet). **2.** to restring (racket).

recordman [rəkɔr(d)man] *n.m.* record holder; *pl. recordmen.*

recordwoman [rəkɔr(d)woman] *n.f.* woman record holder; *pl. recordwomen.*

recors [rəkɔr] *n.m. Jur: A: F:* bailiff's man; **les r. de la justice,** the minions of the law.

recoucher [rəkuʃe] **1.** *v.tr.* (*a*) to put (s.o.) to bed again; (*b*) to lay (person, object) down again. **2. se r.,** to go to bed again; to go back to bed.

recoudre [rəkudr̥] *v.tr.* (*conj. like* COUDRE) to sew up (tear, wound); to sew (button) on again.

recoupement [rəkupmɑ̃] *n.m.* **1.** *Const:* batter (of wall). **2.** cross checking (of information).

recouper [rəkupe] *v.tr.* **1.** (*a*) to cut again; (*b*) *Const:* to step (wall). **2.** to (re)blend (wines, etc.). **3.** to confirm, support; **les deux témoignages se recoupent,** the two statements tally.

recourbé [rəkurbe] *a.* bent, curved; bent back; reflexed; **poignée recourbée,** crook handle.

recourber [rəkurbe] *v.tr.* to bend (down, back, round).

recourir [rəkurir] *v.i.* (*conj. like* COURIR) **1.** (*a*) to run again; (*b*) **r. jusque chez soi,** to run back home (for sth.). **2.** (*a*) **r. à qn, à l'aide de qn,** to call on s.o. for help; to turn to s.o.; **r. à qch.,** to have recourse to sth.; to resort to (violence, etc.); **r. à la justice,** to take legal proceedings; (*b*) *Jur:* **r. en cassation,** to appeal.

recours [rəkur] *n.m.* (*a*) recourse, resort, resource; **en dernier r.,** as a last resort; **avoir r. à qn, à qch.,** to have recourse to s.o., to sth.; to resort to sth.; (*b*) *Jur:* **r. en cassation,** appeal; **r. en grâce,** petition for reprieve; **n'avoir aucun r. contre qn,** (i) to have no claim whatever on s.o.; (ii) to have no remedy at law; *Ins:* **s'assurer contre le r. des tiers,** to insure against a third party claim.

recouvrement[1] [rəkuvrəmɑ̃] *n.m.* (*a*) recovery (of health, etc.); (*b*) recovery, collection (of debts, bill);

collection (of tax); **r. par la poste,** payment by cash on delivery.

recouvrement[2] *n.m.* **1.** re-covering. **2.** (*a*) covering; **tôle de r.,** covering plate; (*b*) (over)lapping; lap (of slates); overlap (of map sheets, strata); **à r.,** lapped; lap-jointed; **en r.,** overlapping; **planches à r.,** weather-boarding; *Geol:* **lambeau de r.,** outlier; (*c*) cover; *Mch:* lap, cover (of slide valve).

recouvrer [rəkuvre] *v.tr.* **1.** to recover, retrieve, get back (one's property); to regain (strength, freedom). **2.** to recover, collect, get in (debts, taxes); **créances à r.,** outstanding debts.

recouvrir [rəkuvrir] (*conj. like* COUVRIR) **1.** *v.tr.* (*a*) to re-cover (umbrella, roof); (*b*) to cover (over), overlay, cap (**de,** with); **fauteuil recouvert de velours,** armchair covered in velvet; (*c*) to cover up, hide (faults); (*d*) to (over)lap (slates, etc.). **2. se r.,** (*of sky*) to cloud over (again).

recracher [rəkraʃe] **1.** *v.tr.* to spit (sth.) out (again). **2.** *v.i.* to spit again.

récréatif, -ive [rekreatif, -iv] *a.* entertaining, amusing (occupation); recreative; **lecture récréative,** light reading; **séance récréative,** entertainment.

récréation [rekreasjɔ̃] *n.f.* **1.** recreation, amusement; relaxation. **2.** *Sch:* recreation, break, playtime, *U.S:* recess; **cour de r.,** playground.

recréer [rəkree] *v.tr.* to recreate; to create, establish (sth.) again.

recrépir [rəkrepir] *v.tr.* to roughcast again; to renew the roughcast of, to replaster, to repoint (wall).

recrépissage [rəkrepisaʒ] *n.m.* replastering.

recreuser [rəkrøze] *v.tr.* (*a*) to hollow (sth.) out again; (*b*) to dig, go deeper into (ground, question, etc.).

récrier (se) [sərekrije] *v.pr.* (*conj. like* CRIER) **1.** to exclaim, cry out. **2. se r. contre, sur, qch.,** to cry out, expostulate, protest, against sth. **3.** (*of hounds*) to be in full cry.

récriminateur, -trice [rekriminatœr, -tris] *a.* recriminative.

récrimination [rekriminasjɔ̃] *n.f.* recrimination.

récriminer [rekrimine] *v.i.* to recriminate (**contre qn,** against s.o.).

récrire [rekrir] *v.* (*conj. like* ÉCRIRE) **1.** *v.tr.* to rewrite; to write (sth.) over again. **2.** *v.i.* to write (to s.o.) again.

recroquevillé [rəkrɔkvije] *a.* (*a*) shrivelled, curled up, cockled (leaf, etc.); (*b*) knotted (fingers); (*c*) **r. dans un fauteuil,** curled up, huddled (up), in an armchair.

recroqueviller (se) [sərəkrɔkvije] *v.pr.* (*a*) to shrivel (up); to curl up; to cockle; to crumple up; (*of flower*) to wilt; (*b*) (*of pers., animal*) to curl up, huddle (up).

recru [rəkry] *a.* **r. (de fatigue),** tired out, worn out; dead tired.

recrudescence [rəkrydesɑ̃s] *n.f.* recrudescence; renewed, fresh, outbreak (of fire, disease).

recrudescent [rəkrydesɑ̃] *a.* recrudescent.

recrue [rəkry] *n.f.* recruit; new member (of party, team); *Mil:* recruit; **jeune r.,** raw recruit.

recrutement [rəkrytmɑ̃] *n.m.* recruiting, recruitment (of soldiers, staff, etc.); *Pol:* **campagne de r.,** membership drive.

recruter [rəkryte] *v.tr.* to recruit (regiment, men, supporters).

recruteur [rəkrytœr] *a.* recruiting (officer).

recta [rɛkta] *adv.* punctually; **payer, arriver, r.,** to pay on the nail; to arrive on the dot.

rectal, -aux [rɛktal, -o] *a. Anat:* rectal.

rectangle [rɛktɑ̃gl̩] **1.** *a.* right-angled. **2.** *n.m.* rectangle; *T.V:* **r. blanc,** "for adults only" sign.

rectangulaire [rɛktɑ̃gylɛr] *a.* rectangular; *Mth:* right-angled (co-ordinates).

recteur, -trice [rɛktœr, -tris] **1.** *n.m.* (*a*) *Sch:* (*in Fr.*) rector of educational district; (*b*) *Ecc: A:* rector (of Jesuit college). **2.** *a.* & *n.f. Orn:* **(penne) rectrice,** tail feather.

rectificateur [rɛktifikatœr] *n.m.* (*a*) *Dist: etc:* rectifier; (*b*) *El:* (current) rectifier.

rectificatif, -ive [rɛktifikatif, -iv] **1.** *a.* rectifying; correcting; **facture rectificative,** amended invoice. **2.** *n.m.* corrigendum; correction.

rectification [rɛktifikasjɔ̃] *n.f.* rectification. **1.** (*a*) amendment, correction (of document, text); rectification, correction (of calculation, mistake); adjustment (of account); (*b*) adjustment (of instrument); (*c*) rectification (of curve, boundary); straightening (of alignment). **2.** tru(e)ing (of work on lathe). **3.** rectifying, redistilling (of alcohol, petroleum). **4.** *El:* rectification (of current).

rectifier [rɛktifje] *v.tr.* **1.** (*a*) to amend, correct (document, text); to rectify, correct (calculation, mistake); to put (mistake) right; to adjust (account, prices); to amend (account); (*b*) to adjust (instrument); (*c*) to rectify (boundary, curve); to straighten (alignment); *Mil:* **r. l'alignement,** to dress the ranks. **2.** *Mec.E:* to true; to grind (true). **3.** *Ch:* to rectify, re-distil (alcohol, petroleum). **4.** *El:* to rectify (current). **5.** *P:* to kill (s.o.), to bump (s.o.) off.

rectiligne [rɛktiliɲ] *a.* rectilinear; in a straight line.

rectilinéaire [rɛktilineɛr] *a. Phot:* rectilinear (lens).

rectitude [rɛktityd] *n.f.* **1.** straightness (of line). **2.** rectitude; (*a*) correctness, soundness (of judgment); (*b*) uprightness, integrity.

recto [rɛkto] *n.m.* recto, right-hand side (of page); view side, front (of picture postcard).

rectorat [rɛktɔra] *n.m.* rectorship, rectorate.

rectum [rɛktɔm] *n.m. Anat:* rectum.

reçu [rəsy] **1.** *a.* received, accepted, recognised (opinion, custom). **2.** *n.m.* receipt, voucher (for goods, money).

recueil [rəkœj] *n.m.* collection, compilation (of poems, etc.); miscellany; compendium (of laws); **r. de morceaux choisis,** selection, anthology.

recueillement [rəkœjmɑ̃] *n.m.* self-communion, meditation, contemplation; **r. d'esprit,** composure.

recueilli [rəkœji] *a.* collected, meditative, contemplative, rapt.

recueillir [rəkœjir] (*conj. like* CUEILLIR) **1.** *v.tr.* (*a*) to collect, gather (anecdotes, curios); to make a collection of (author's works); **r. l'eau de pluie,** to catch the rainwater; **r. des renseignements,** to obtain, pick up, information; **r. ses forces,** to collect, gather, all one's strength; **r. ses idées,** to collect one's thoughts; (*b*) to get in, gather (crops); to recover (by-products); to win (votes, praise); **r. le fruit de ses travaux,** to reap the fruit of one's labours; **r. un héritage,** to inherit; (*c*) to take in, to shelter (s.o.); to give (s.o.) a home. **2. se r.,** to collect oneself, one's thoughts; to be in deep meditation.

recuire [rəkɥir] *v.tr.* (*conj. like* CUIRE) **1.** to cook, bake, (sth.) again; *Cer:* to rekiln. **2.** to anneal, temper (steel); to anneal (glass).

recuisson [rəkɥisɔ̃] *n.f.* **1.** recooking; rebaking. **2.** reheating; tempering (of steel); annealing (of glass).

recuit [rəkɥi] *n.m.* reheating; tempering (of steel); annealing (of steel, glass); **r. blanc,** bright annealing.

recul [rəkyl] *n.m.* **1.** receding, recession (of sea, etc.); retreat (of glacier, army); backing (of horse); backward movement; return (of control lever); **il eut un brusque mouvement de r.,** he started back; *Aut:* **phare de r.,** reversing light. **2.** (*a*) *Ball:* recoil (of cannon); kick (of rifle); (*b*) *Nau:* slip (of propeller). **3.** room to move back; **manquer de r.,** to be too close for a proper view.

reculade [rəkylad] *n.f.* retreat; (*a*) backward movement; (*b*) *F:* climb(ing) down.
reculé [rəkyle] *a.* distant, remote (time, place); early (times).
reculement [rəkylmɑ̃] *n.m.* **1.** backing (of carriage, etc.). **2.** *Harn:* breech band.
reculer [rəkyle] **1.** *v.i.* to move back, step back, draw back, recede; to fall back, retreat, lose ground; (*of horse, car*); to back; (*of gun*) to recoil; (*of rifle*) to kick; **r. contre qch.,** to back into sth.; **faire r. un cheval,** to back a horse; **ses affaires ont reculé,** his business has fallen off; **r. devant qch.,** to draw back, shrink, from sth.; to recoil, flinch, before sth.; *F:* to jib at sth.; **il ne recule à rien,** he is ready for anything; *F:* **r. pour mieux sauter,** to put off the evil day. **2.** *v.tr.* (*a*) to move back (chair); to back (horse); **r. les frontières,** to push forward, extend, the frontiers; (*b*) to postpone, defer, put off (payment, decision). **3.** **se r.,** to draw back; to stand, step, move, back.
reculons (à) [ar(ə)kylɔ̃] *adv.phr.* **marcher à r.,** (i) to walk backwards; (ii) to lose ground; **sortir à r.,** to back out.
récupérable [rekyperabl̥] *a.* recoverable; **ferraille r.,** scrap metal.
récupérateur [rekyperatœr] *n.m.* *Ind:* regenerator, recuperator; *Artil:* recuperator; *Mch:* **r. d'huile,** oil extractor.
récupération [rekyperasjɔ̃] *n.f.* recuperation. **1.** (*a*) recovery (of debt); *Ind:* recovery, salvage (of waste products); **four à r.,** regenerative furnace; (*b*) recovery (of spacecraft). **2.** recovery (from illness).
récupérer [rekypere] *v.tr.* **(je récupère, n. récupérons; je récupérerai) 1.** (*a*) to recover (debt); to get back (book, etc.); to collect, pick up (s.o.); to recover (spacecraft); **r. ses forces,** *v.i.* **r.,** to recuperate; to recover (one's strength). **2.** (*a*) to recover (waste products); to salvage; **r. de la ferraille,** to collect scrap; (*b*) to rehabilitate, find alternative employment for (s.o.); (*c*) *F:* to exploit (s.o.); to make capital out of (sth.). **3.** to retrieve, recoup (a loss); to make up (lost time).
récurage [rekyraʒ] *n.m.* scouring.
récurer [rekyre] *v.tr.* to scour, clean (pots and pans).
récureur, -euse [rekyrœr, -øz] **1.** *n.* (*pers.*) scourer. **2.** *n.m.* scourer, scouring agent.
récurrence [rekyrɑ̃s] *n.f.* recurrence.
récurrent [rekyrɑ̃] *a.* **1.** *Anat:* recurrent (nerve, vein). **2.** recurrent, recurring; **fièvre récurrente,** recurrent fever; *Mth:* **série récurrente,** recurrent series; *Cmptr:* **processus r.,** recursive process.
récusable [rekyzabl̥] *a.* *Jur:* challengeable (juryman); impugnable (evidence).
récusation [rekyzasjɔ̃] *n.f.* *Jur:* **r. de juré, d'arbitre,** challenge of, exception to, objection to, a juryman, an arbitrator; **r. de témoignage,** impugnment of evidence.
récuser [rekyze] **1.** *v.tr.* to challenge, take exception to, object to (witness, etc.); to impugn (evidence); to reject (authority). **2.** **se r.,** *Jur:* to decline to give an opinion; to disclaim competence.
recyclage [rəsiklaʒ] *n.m.* **1.** *Sch:* reorientation (of student); *Ind:* retraining (of staff); readaptation (to new techniques, etc.); refresher course(s). **2.** reprocessing; recycling.
recycler [rəsikle] *v.tr.* **1.** *Sch:* to reorientate (pupil's studies); *Ind:* to retrain (staff). **2.** to reprocess, recycle.
rédacteur, -trice [redaktœr, -tris] *n.* (*a*) writer, drafter (of deed, communiqué); (*b*) *Journ:* member of editorial staff; **r. en chef,** editor; **r. aux actualités,** news editor; **r. politique,** political correspondent.
rédaction [redaksjɔ̃] *n.f.* **1.** (*a*) drafting, drawing up, writing (of deed, etc.); (*b*) *Journ:* editing; editorship. **2.** *Journ:* (*a*) editorial staff; (*b*) (newspaper) office(s). **3.** *Sch:* essay, composition.
reddition [redisjɔ̃, rɛddi-] *n.f.* **1.** surrender (of town, army) **2.** rendering (of account).
redécouvrir [rədekuvrir] *v.tr.* (*conj. like* COUVRIR) to rediscover.
redemander [rədmɑ̃de] *v.tr.* **1.** to ask for (sth.) again; to ask for more, a second helping, of (sth.). **2.** to ask for (sth.) back (again).
rédempteur, -trice [redɑ̃ptœr, -tris] **1.** *a.* redeeming. **2.** *n.* redeemer.
rédemption [redɑ̃psjɔ̃] *n.f.* redemption, redeeming.
redescendre [rədesɑ̃dr̥, -dɛ-] **1.** *v.i.* to come, go, down again; *Nau:* (*of the wind*) to back. **2.** *v.tr.* (*a*) to take, bring, let, (sth.) down again; (*b*) to come, go, down (stairs, river) again.
redevable [rəd(ə)vabl̥] *a.* **être r. de qch. à qn,** to be indebted to s.o. for sth.; **je vous suis r. de cent francs,** I still owe you a hundred francs.
redevance [rəd(ə)vɑ̃s] *n.f.* (*a*) rent; *Tp: etc:* rental; (*b*) dues; (*c*) **redevances d'auteur,** author's royalties; **r. pétrolière,** oil royalty; (*d*) (television, etc.) licence fee.
redevenir [rədəvnir] *v.i.* (*conj. like* DEVENIR) **r. jeune,** to become, grow, young again; **r. malade,** to fall ill again.
redevoir [rəd(ə)vwar] *v.tr.* (*conj. like* DEVOIR) to owe a balance of (a sum); **il me redoit dix francs,** he still owes me ten francs.
rédhibitoire [redibitwar] *a.* (*a*) *Jur:* **vice r.,** redhibitory defect; (*b*) **être étranger ici est r.,** being a foreigner here rules you out.
rediffusion [rədifyzjɔ̃] *n.f.* *W.Tel:* *T.V:* repeat broadcast, showing.
rédiger [rediʒe] *v.tr.* **(je rédigeai(s); n. rédigeons) 1.** to draw up, to draft, to write (out) (agreement, letter, etc.); to write (article). **2.** to edit (periodical).
redingote [rədɛ̃gɔt] *n.f.* (*a*) frock coat; (*b*) (woman's) fitting coat.
redire [rədir] *v.tr.* (*conj. like* DIRE) **1.** to tell, say, (sth.) again; to repeat (sth.). **2.** **trouver à r. à qch.,** to take exception to sth.; to find fault with, *F:* pick holes in, sth.; **il n'y a rien à r. à cela,** there's nothing to be said against that.
redistribuer [rədistribɥe] *v.tr.* to redistribute; to reallocate; to redeal (cards).
redistribution [rədistribysjɔ̃] *n.f.* redistribution; re-allocation.
redite [rədit] *n.f.* (useless) repetition.
redondance [rədɔ̃dɑ̃s] *n.f.* redundance, redundancy.
redondant [rədɔ̃dɑ̃] *a.* redundant (word, style, *Cmptr:* code).
redonner [rədɔne] **1.** *v.tr.* (*a*) to give (sth.) again; *Cards:* to redeal; **on redonne "Hamlet,"** "Hamlet" is on again; (*b*) to give more of (sth.); (*c*) to give (sth.) back; to restore, return. **2.** *v.i.* **r. dans des excès,** to fall into excesses again; **r. dans l'exagération,** to go on exaggerating.
redormir [rədɔrmir] *v.i.* (*conj. like* DORMIR) to sleep, go to sleep, again.
redoublant, -ante [rədublɑ̃, -ɑ̃t] *n. Sch:* pupil who remains a second year in the same class.
redoublé [rəduble] *a.* **rime redoublée,** double rhyme; **battre qn à coups redoublés,** to thrash s.o. soundly.
redoublement [rədubləmɑ̃] *n.m.* **1.** redoubling (of joy, etc.); **avec un r. de zèle,** with redoubled zeal. **2.** *Ling:* reduplication.
redoubler [rəduble] **1.** *v.tr.* (*a*) to redouble, increase (dose, efforts, etc.); **r. le chagrin de qn,** to add to s.o.'s grief; **r. ses cris,** to redouble one's cries; to

shout louder than ever; (*b*) *Sch:* **r. une classe,** to stay in a class for a second year, to stay down; (*c*) to reline (garment). **2.** *v.i.* to redouble; **la pluie redoubla,** the rain came on worse than ever; **r. d'efforts,** to strive harder than ever, to redouble one's efforts.

redoutable [rədutabl̩] *a.* redoubtable, formidable, dangerous (enemy).

redoute [rədut] *n.f.* **1.** *Fort:* redoubt. **2.** *A:* gala evening (at dance hall).

redouter [rədute] *v.tr.* to fear, dread; to be in awe of (s.o.); **r. d'apprendre qch.,** to dread, be in fear of, hearing sth.; **je redoute surtout de devenir aveugle,** the thing I fear most is to go blind.

redoux [rədu] *n.m. Meteor:* rise in temperature.

redresse [rədrɛs] *n.f.* (*a*) *Nau:* **palans de r.,** righting tackle; (*b*) *P:* **c'est un type à la r.,** he's got his wits about him.

redressement [rədrɛsmɑ̃] *n.m.* **1.** (*a*) re-erecting; setting up again (of fallen object); (*b*) righting (of boat); (*c*) *Opt:* erecting (of inverted image). **2.** (*a*) straightening; tru(e)ing (of a surface); **r. économique,** economic recovery; **maison de r.** = *Hist:* approved school, reformatory; (*b*) *El:* rectification (of alternating current); **valve de r.,** rectifying valve; (*c*) rectification, correction (of account, mistake).

redresser [rədrɛse] **1.** *v.tr.* (*a*) to re-erect (fallen statue); to set upright again; (*b*) to right (boat); to straighten up, lift the nose of (aircraft); (*c*) *Opt:* to erect (inverted image); (*d*) to straighten (out) (bent wood, warped metal); to true (surface); (*e*) **r. la tête,** to hold up one's head; to look up; (*f*) *El:* to rectify (current); (*g*) to redress, right (wrong, grievance); to rectify (mistake); to adjust (account). **2. se r.** (*a*) to stand up (straight) again; **se r. sur son séant,** to sit up straight (again); (*b*) (*of economy, etc.*) to recover, return to normal; (*c*) to draw oneself up, to hold one's head high; (*d*) to mend one's ways.

redresseur, -euse [rədrɛsœr, -øz] **1.** *n.* righter (of wrongs); **r. de torts,** knight errant. **2.** *n.m. El:* rectifier (of current). **3.** *a.* (*a*) *El:* rectifying (device); (*b*) *Opt:* erecting (prism); **viseur r.,** reversal finder.

redû [rədy] *n.m.* balance due.

réducteur, -trice [redyktœr, -tris] **1.** *a.* reducing; *Ch:* **agent r.,** reducing agent; *Mec.E:* **ensemble r.,** reduction gear assembly. **2.** *n.m.* (*a*) reducer; *Ch:* reducing agent; *Mec.E:* reduction gear, unit; *Th:* **r. d'éclairage,** dimmer; (*b*) *Anthr:* **r. de têtes,** head shrinker.

réductible [redyktibl̩] *a.* reducible.

réduction [redyksjɔ̃] *n.f.* **1.** (*a*) reduction, reducing; cutting down (of expenditure); mitigation (of penalty); writing down (of capital); setting (of fracture); gearing down (of machinery); stepping down (of voltage); (*b*) capture, reduction (of town). **2.** (*a*) **réductions de salaires,** wage cuts; **grandes réductions de prix,** great reductions (in price); (*b*) *Mus:* **r. pour piano,** short score (of opera, etc.); (*c*) reduced copy, reduction; **bateau en r.,** scaled-down model of a ship.

réduire [redɥir] (*pr.p.* **réduisant;** *p.p.* **réduit;** *pr.ind.* **je réduis, il réduit, n. réduisons;** *impf.* **je réduisais;** *p.h.* **je réduisis;** *fu.* **je réduirai**) to reduce. **1.** *v.tr.* (*a*) (i) to reduce (pressure, amount; speed); to lower, bring down, cut (price); to lower (interest rate); to curtail, cut down (expenses); to restrict (freedom); to write down (capital); to step down (voltage); **billet à prix réduit,** cheap ticket; **édition réduite,** abridged edition; **modèle réduit,** scaled down model; (ii) **r. un homme à un grade inférieur,** *Mil:* to reduce, *Navy:* to disrate, a man; (iii) **r. du bois en cendres,** to reduce wood to ashes; **r. qch. en miettes,** to crumble sth. up; **r. des francs en centimes,** to reduce francs to centimes; (iv) *Ch:* to reduce (oxide); *Cu:* **r. une sauce,** to reduce a sauce; (v) *Mth:* to reduce (fractions); (vi) *Mus:* **r. une partition,** to arrange a score for the piano; (*b*) **r. qn à la misère, au désespoir,** to reduce s.o. to poverty; to drive s.o. to despair; **r. qn à demander pardon,** to compel s.o. to ask for forgiveness; **r. qn par la famine,** to starve s.o. into submission; (*c*) to reduce (fracture, dislocation). **2. se r.** (*a*) **se r. au strict nécessaire,** to confine oneself to what is strictly necessary; (*b*) **les frais se réduisent à peu de chose,** the expenses come to very little; **à quoi se réduit tout cela?** what does all that amount, boil down, to? **se r. en poussière,** to crumble into dust; **la sauce s'est réduite,** the sauce has boiled down; **faire r. un sirop,** to reduce, boil down, a syrup.

réduit [redɥi] *n.m.* **1.** (*a*) small, poor, room, quarters; hovel; (*b*) alcove; nook. **2.** *Fort:* keep, redoubt.

réduplication [redyplikasjɔ̃] *n.f.* reduplication.

réédification [reedifikasjɔ̃] *n.f.* rebuilding, re-erection.

réédifier [reedifje] *v.tr.* (*conj. like* ÉDIFIER) to rebuild; to re-erect.

rééditer [reedite] *v.tr.* (*a*) to republish, re-issue (book); (*b*) to rake up (old story).

réédition [reedisjɔ̃] *n.f.* (*a*) re-issue (of book, etc.), republication; (*b*) *F:* repetition; **c'est une r. du match France-Écosse,** it's the France-Scotland match all over again.

rééducatif, -ive [reedykatif, -iv] *a.* **thérapie rééducative,** occupational therapy.

rééducation [reedykasjɔ̃] *n.f.* (*a*) *Med:* re-education (of nerve-centres after paralysis, etc.); rehabilitation; **r. de la parole,** speech therapy; **centre de r. (professionnelle),** rehabilitation centre; (*b*) re-education (of delinquents).

rééduquer [reedyke] *v.tr. Med:* to re-educate; to rehabilitate (the disabled).

réel, -elle [reɛl] **1.** *a.* (*a*) real, actual (fact, person); *Mth:* real (number); *Opt:* true (image); **salaire nominal et salaire r.,** nominal wage rate and net earnings; **offre réelle,** cash offer; (*b*) (*before noun*) real, great (pleasure, etc.). **2.** *n.m.* **le r.,** the real; reality.

réélection [reelɛksjɔ̃] *n.f.* re-election.

rééligible [reeliʒibl̩] *a.* re-eligible.

réélire [reelir] *v.tr.* (*conj. like* ÉLIRE) to re-elect.

réellement [reɛlmɑ̃] *adv.* really; in reality; actually.

réembarquer [reɑ̃barke] *v.tr. & i.* to re-embark.

réémetteur [reemɛtœr] *n.m. T.V: W.Tel:* relay transmitter.

réemploi [reɑ̃plwa] *n.m.* re-employment.

réemployer [reɑ̃plwaje] *v.tr.* to re-employ.

réensemencer [reɑ̃s(ə)mɑ̃se] *v.tr.* to resow (field).

réescompter [reɛskɔ̃te] *v.tr. Fin:* to rediscount (bill).

réévaluation [reevalɥasjɔ̃] *n.f.* revaluation.

réévaluer [reevalɥe] *v.tr.* to revalue.

réexpédier [reɛkspedje] *v.tr.* (*conj. like* EXPÉDIER) **1.** to send on, to forward (letters, goods). **2.** to send back.

réexpédition [reɛkspedisjɔ̃] *n.f.* **1.** sending on, forwarding; redirection (of parcel). **2.** sending back, return(ing) (to sender).

réexportation [reɛkspɔrtasjɔ̃] *n.f.* re-exportation.

réexporter [reɛkspɔrte] *v.tr.* to re-export.

refaçonner [rəfasɔne] *v.tr.* to remake, refashion.

réfaction [refaksjɔ̃] *n.f.* allowance, rebate (on damaged, substandard, goods).

refaire [rəfɛr] (*conj. like* FAIRE) **1.** *v.tr.* (*a*) to remake; to do again; to make (journey) again; **r. sa malle,** to pack one's trunk again; **c'est à r.,** it will have to be done again; (*b*) to repair, mend; to recover (one's strength); to do up, renovate; *F:* **elle se refait une beauté,** she's doing her face again; (*c*) *F:* to do, diddle (s.o.); to take (s.o.) in; **on vous a refait,**

you've been had. **2. se r.** (*a*) to recover (one's health); to recuperate; to pick up again; (*b*) to change one's ways; (*c*) to retrieve one's losses; to recoup oneself.

réfection [refɛksjɔ̃] *n.f.* **1.** remaking; rebuilding; repairing, restoration; doing up; **route en r.,** road under repair. **2.** (*in convent*) meal.

réfectoire [refɛktwar] *n.m.* refectory, dining hall.

refend [rəfɑ̃] *n.m.* **1. bois de r.,** wood in planks. **2. pierre de r.,** corner stone; **mur de r.,** partition (wall).

refendre [rəfɑ̃dr̥] *v.tr.* to split, cleave (slates); to slit (leather); to rip (timber).

référé [refere] *n.m. Jur:* summary procedure; **(ordonnance de) r.,** provisional order; injunction.

référence [referɑ̃s] *n.f.* reference; referring; (*a*) **livre de r.,** reference book; **faire r. à un ouvrage,** to refer to a work, a book; **références au bas des pages,** footnotes; *Surv:* **r. topographique,** map reference; **plan de r.,** datum plane, plane of reference; (*b*) reference (on letter, document); **r. à rappeler,** in replying please quote; (*c*) *pl.* (employee's) reference, testimonial.

référencé [referɑ̃se] *a. Com: F:* bearing a reference number.

referendum, référendum [referɛ̃dɔm] *n.m.* referendum.

référer [refere] **(je réfère, n. référons; je référerai) 1.** *v.i.* **r. à qn d'une question,** to refer a matter to s.o.; **en r. à la cour,** to report, to submit the case, to the court. **2. se r.** (*a*) **se r. à qch.,** to refer to sth.; (*b*) **se r., s'en r., à qn d'une question,** to refer a matter to s.o.

refermer [rəfɛrme] **1.** *v.tr.* to shut, close (up) again; **il referma la porte sur lui,** he closed the door after him. **2. se r.,** to close (again); (*of wound*) to close up, to heal.

refiler [rəfile] *v.tr. P:* **r. qch. à qn,** to palm off sth. on s.o.; to foist, unload, sth. on s.o.

réfléchi [refleʃi] *a.* **1.** reflective, thoughtful (person); deliberate, considered (action, opinion); **tout bien r.,** everything considered, after due consideration. **2.** reflexive (verb, pronoun).

réfléchir [refleʃir] **1.** *v.tr.* to reflect, to throw back (image, light, sound); to bend back (light). **2.** *v.i.* (*a*) **r. à, sur, qch.,** to reflect on sth., to ponder, consider, weigh, sth.; to turn sth. over in one's mind; **réfléchissez-y,** think it over; **donner à r. à qn,** to give s.o. food for thought; to make s.o. think twice; **parler sans r.,** to speak without thinking, hastily; (*b*) *v.tr.* **il réfléchit que son argent ne suffirait pas,** it occurred to him that his money would not be enough. **3.** (*of light, heat, sound, etc.*) **se r.,** to be reflected, thrown back; to reverberate.

réfléchissement [refleʃismɑ̃] *n.m.* reflection, reflecting (of light, etc.).

réflecteur, -trice [reflɛktœr, -tris] **1.** *a.* reflecting (mirror, panel). **2.** *n.m.* reflector; reflecting panel, mirror, telescope.

réflectif, -ive [reflɛktif, -iv] *a.* (*a*) reflective; (*b*) *Physiol:* reflex.

reflet [rəflɛ] *n.m.* reflection; reflected light, image; sheen (of silk, etc.); **r. des eaux,** gleam on the waters; **les reflets de la lune sur le lac,** the reflection of the moon on the lake; **chevelure à reflets d'or,** hair with glints of gold; **r. des glaces,** ice blink; **reflets changeants,** play of colours; **être le r. de qch.,** to reflect, be an indication of, sth.

refléter [rəflete] *v.tr.* **(je reflète, n. reflétons; je refléterai)** to reflect (scattered light); **le Louvre se reflète dans la Seine,** the Louvre is mirrored, reflected, in the Seine.

refleurir [rəflœrir] *v.i.* **1.** to flower, blossom, again. **2.** (*of art, literature*) to flourish again; to revive.

reflex [rəflɛks] *a. & n.m.* **(appareil) r.,** reflex camera.

réflexe [reflɛks] **1.** *a. Ph: Physiol:* reflex. **2.** *n.m.* (*a*) *Physiol:* reflex; **r. rotulien,** knee reflex, jerk; (*b*) reflex, reaction; **avoir de bons réflexes,** to react quickly.

réflexif, -ive [reflɛksif, -iv] *a. Phil: Mth:* reflexive.

réflexion [reflɛksjɔ̃] *n.f.* **1.** reflection, reflexion (of image, light, sound); **angle de r.,** angle of reflection. **2.** reflection, thought; **agir sans r.,** to act hastily, without thinking; **(toute) r. faite, à la r.,** everything considered; on further consideration, on second thoughts; **à la r. vous changerez d'avis,** on reflection, when you think it over, you will change your mind. **3.** remark; **une r. désobligeante,** an unpleasant remark.

refluer [rəflye] *v.i.* to flow back; (*of tide*) to ebb; **le sang lui reflua au visage,** the blood surged to her cheeks; **la foule a reflué vers la ville,** the crowd swept back towards the town.

reflux [rəfly] *n.m.* (*a*) reflux, flowing back; ebb(ing) (of tide); ebb tide; **le flux et le r.,** the ebb and flow; (*b*) surging back.

refondre [rəfɔ̃dr̥] *v.tr.* **1.** to recast (metal, a bell); to recoin, remint (money). **2.** to recast, remodel (poem).

refonte [rəfɔ̃t] *n.f.* **1.** recasting (of metals); recoinage (of money). **2.** recasting (play); remodelling, reorganization (of factory); reconstruction.

réformateur, -trice [refɔrmatœr, -tris] **1.** *a.* reforming. **2.** *n.* reformer.

réformation [refɔrmasjɔ̃] *n.f.* reformation, reform; *Rel.H:* **la R.,** the Reformation.

réformatoire [refɔrmatwar] *a.* reformatory, reformative.

réforme [refɔrm] *n.f.* **1.** reform (of abuses, calendar); *Rel.H:* **la R.,** the Reformation. **2.** *Mil:* discharge (for physical unfitness); invaliding out; rejection (of recruit); **r. temporaire,** deferment (of military service); **commission de r.,** special medical board; **mettre à la r.,** to discharge (man, officer) from the service, to cast (horse); *Ind:* **matériel en r.,** scrapped plant.

réformé, -ée [refɔrme] *a. & n.* **1.** Protestant; *a.* reformed (church). **2.** (serviceman, -woman) discharged for unfitness; rejected (recruit); **r. temporaire,** deferred recruit.

reformer [rəfɔrme] *v.tr.* to form again, to reform; **r. les rangs,** to fall into line again; **l'opposition se reformait,** the opposition was getting together again.

réformer [refɔrme] *v.tr.* **1.** to reform (abuse, law); *Jur:* to reverse (decision). **2.** (*a*) *Mil: Navy:* (i) to discharge as unfit; to invalid out of the service; to reject (recruit); (*b*) to condemn, scrap (equipment).

refoulé, -ée [rəfule] *a. & n. Psy:* repressed; inhibited (person).

refoulement [rəfulmɑ̃] *n.m.* (*a*) pressing, driving, forcing, back; driving in or out (of pin, bolt); backing (of train); upsetting (of metal); tamping (of earth); (*b*) delivery, discharge, output (of pipe); **soupape de r.,** delivery valve (of pump); **tuyau de r.,** exhaust pipe; (*c*) *Psy:* (unconscious) repression; inhibition.

refouler [rəfule] *v.tr.* **1.** to drive back, force back, press back; *Adm:* to expel, to turn back (an alien); to drive, force, in or out (bolt, pin); (*of ship*) to stem (the tide); to back (train); to upset (metal); to tamp (earth); to deliver, discharge (water); **pompe refoulante,** force pump. **2.** to repress, suppress, contain, (one's feelings); to force back (tears); *Psy:* to repress (an instinct). **3.** *v.i. Mec.E:* (*of pin*) to go the wrong way; to refuse.

refouloir [rəfulwar] *n.m.* (*a*) tamping tool; *Artil: A:* rammer; (*b*) door spring.

réfractaire [refraktɛr] **1.** *a.* (*a*) refractory, rebellious, insubordinate; **r. à la loi,** unwilling to accept the law; *Fr.Hist:* **prêtre r.,** non-juring priest; (*b*) refractory (ore); fireproof, fire (brick, clay); (*c*) resistant; **r. aux acides,** acid-proof; **le coton est r. à la teinture,** cotton does not take dyes well. **2.** *n.* rebel; conscientious objector; defaulter.

réfracter [refrakte] *v.tr.* to refract, bend (rays, etc.).

réfracteur [refraktœr] **1.** *a.m.* refracting. **2.** *n.m.* refractor.

réfraction [refraksjɔ̃] *n.f.* refraction, bending (of ray); **indice de r.,** index of refraction, refractive index; *Cin:* **film à r.,** three-D(imensional) film.

refrain [rəfrɛ̃] *n.m.* **1.** refrain, burden (of song); **chanter de vieux refrains,** to sing old songs, old ditties; *F:* **c'est toujours le même r.,** it's always the same old story. **2. r. en chœur,** chorus.

réfrangible [refrɑ̃ʒibl̩] *a. Ph:* refrangible.

refréner [rəfrene] *v.tr.* **(je refrène, n. refrénons; je refrénerai)** to curb, bridle, restrain, control (feelings).

réfrigérant [refriʒerɑ̃] **1.** *a.* (*a*) refrigerating, cooling (action, apparatus); freezing (mixture); (*b*) chilling (reception). **2.** *n.m.* (*a*) refrigerator, condenser (of still); **r. à cheminée,** cooling tower.

réfrigérateur [refriʒeratœr] *n.m.* refrigerator; *F:* frig, fridge; **mettre un projet au r.,** to shelve a plan; to put a plan on ice.

réfrigération [refriʒerasjɔ̃] *n.f.* refrigeration; chilling (of meat).

réfrigérer [refriʒere] *v.tr.* **(je réfrigère, n. réfrigérons; je réfrigérerai)** to refrigerate; **viande réfrigérée,** chilled meat; **camion réfrigéré,** refrigerated van.

réfringence [refrɛ̃ʒɑ̃s] *n.f. Ph:* refringency.

réfringent [refrɛ̃ʒɑ̃] *a.* refringent.

refroidir [rəfrwadir] **1.** *v.tr.* (*a*) to cool, chill (water, temperature); (*b*) to cool (engine, fluid); *Metall:* to quench (metal); **refroidi par (l')air,** air-cooled; (*c*) to cool, chill (friendship, etc.); to damp (sympathy); to cool (off), dash (enthusiasm); (*d*) *P:* to kill (s.o.); *F:* to do (s.o.) in; *F:* **un refroidi,** a corpse, a stiff. **2.** *v.i. & pr.* (*a*) to grow cold; to cool down, off; **laisser r. son thé,** to let one's tea get cold; **le temps a refroidi, s'est refroidi,** it has grown colder; (*b*) *Med:* **se r.,** to catch a chill.

refroidissement [rəfrwadismɑ̃] *n.m.* **1.** (*a*) cooling; **r. du temps,** fall in temperature; (*b*) cooling (of engine); *Metall:* quenching (of metal); **agent de r.,** cooling agent, coolant. **2. attraper un r.,** to catch a chill. **3.** cooling off (of friendship).

refroidisseur [rəfrwadisœr] *n.m.* (*a*) cooler; refrigerator unit; **système r.,** cooling system; (*b*) *Atom.Ph:* cooler, coolant.

refuge [rəfyʒ] *n.m.* **1.** refuge; shelter; **(lieu de) r.,** place of refuge. **2.** (*a*) (climbers') hut, refuge; (*b*) (bird) sanctuary; (*c*) traffic island. **3. Dieu est mon r.,** God is my refuge.

réfugié, -ée [refyʒje] *n.* refugee.

réfugier (se) [sərefyʒje] *v.pr.* to take refuge; to find shelter; to shelter; **se r. dans les mensonges,** to have recourse to, fall back on, lies.

refus [rəfy] *n.m.* refusal; denial; **essuyer un r.,** to meet with a refusal; **r. d'obéissance,** insubordination; *Jur:* contempt of court; *F:* **ce n'est pas de r.,** I can't say no; I accept gladly; **je n'admettrai pas de r.,** I won't take no for answer; **visser, serrer, un boulon à r.,** to screw a bolt home, tight.

refusé, -ée [refyze] *n.* (*a*) *Art:* **salon des refusés,** exhibition of rejected work; (*b*) *Sch:* failed candidate.

refuser [rəfyze] **1.** *v.tr.* (*a*) to refuse, decline (sth.); to turn down (offer); **r. tout net,** to refuse point blank; **r. mille francs d'un tableau,** to refuse a thousand francs for a picture; **r. qch. à qn,** to refuse, deny, s.o. sth.; **il ne se refuse rien,** he doesn't stint himself; **r. toute qualité à qn,** to refuse to see any good in s.o.; **r. la porte à qn,** to deny s.o. admittance; (*of horse*) **r. (l'obstacle),** to refuse, to ba(u)lk; *Mil:* **r. le combat,** to decline battle; **r. de faire qch.,** to refuse to do sth.; (*of ship*) **r. de virer,** not to obey the helm; (*b*) to reject (a man) for military service; to turn (s.o.) down; *Sch:* to fail (candidate); **être refusé,** to fail; **r. du monde,** to turn people away. **2.** *v.i. Nau:* (*of wind*) to veer forward. **3. se r. à qch.,** to set one's face against, to resist, sth.; to shut one's eyes to (a fact); **se r. à faire qch.,** to refuse, decline, to do sth.

réfutation [refytasjɔ̃] *n.f.* refutation, rebuttal.

réfuter [refyte] *v.tr.* to refute, confute; to disprove.

regagner [rəgɑɲe] *v.tr.* **1.** to regain, recover, win back (confidence, etc.); to win (s.o.) back; to recover, win back, get back (money, etc.); **r. le temps perdu,** to make up for lost time. **2.** to get back to (a place); to reach (a place) again; **r. son foyer,** to get back home.

regain [rəgɛ̃] *n.m.* **1.** *Agr:* aftermath. **2.** renewal (of youth); revival (of activity); **r. de vie,** new lease of life.

régal [regal] *n.m.* (*a*) feast, banquet; (*b*) delicious dish; treat; **c'est un vrai r. de l'écouter,** it is a treat, a pleasure, to listen to him; *pl. régals.*

régalade [regalad] *n.f. F:* **boire à la r.,** to pour a drink down one's throat without touching the bottle with one's lips.

régale [regal] *a.f. Ch:* **eau r.,** aqua regia.

régaler¹ [regale] *v.tr.* to level (ground).

régaler² **1.** *v.tr. F:* to entertain, feast (friends); **r. qn de qch.,** to regale s.o. with sth.; to treat s.o. to sth.; **c'est moi qui régale,** I'm standing treat. **2.** *F:* **se r.,** to feast **(de,** on); to treat oneself **(de,** to); **on s'est bien régalé,** we had a slap-up meal.

regard [rəgar] *n.m.* **1.** (*a*) look, glance, gaze; **r. de côté,** sidelong glance; **r. vitreux,** glassy stare; **jeter un r. à qn,** to glance at s.o.; **jeter un r. sur qch.,** to cast a glance, to glance, at, over, sth.; **chercher qn du r.,** to look round for s.o.; **interroger qn du r., lancer à qn un r. interrogateur,** to give s.o. a questioning look; to look at s.o. inquiringly; **lancer un r. furieux à qn,** to glare at s.o.; **détourner le r.,** to look away, to avert one's eyes; **exposé aux regards,** exposed to view; **caché aux regards,** out of sight; **attirer le(s) regard(s),** to attract attention, to be conspicuous; (*b*) **en r. de qch.,** (i) opposite, facing, sth.; (ii) compared with sth.; **texte avec illustration en r.,** text with illustration (on the) opposite (page); **au r. de qch.,** with regard to sth., compared with sth. **2.** (*a*) **r. (d'accès, de visite),** manhole (of sewer); inspection hole; (*b*) peephole (of oven); draught hole (of furnace); observation aperture. **3.** control; *Jur:* **droit de r.,** right of inspection.

regardant, -ante [rəgardɑ̃, -ɑ̃t] *a.* close(-fisted), stingy (person).

regarder [rəgarde] *v.tr.* **1.** (*a*) to regard, consider (s.o., sth.); **r. qch. comme un crime,** to regard, look on, sth. as a crime; (*b*) **ne r. que ses intérêts,** to consider only one's own interests; (*c*) *v.i.* **r. à qch.,** to pay attention to sth.; **sans r. à la dépense,** regardless of expense; **je ne regarde pas à vingt francs,** I am not particular, worried, about twenty francs more or less; **à y bien r.,** on thinking it over; **y bien r., y r. à deux fois, avant de faire qch.,** to think twice before doing sth.; **je n'y regarde pas de si près,** I'm not as particular, fussy, as all that; (*d*) to concern (s.o.); **cela ne vous regarde pas,** that's no concern of yours; that's none of your business; **en ce qui me regarde,** as far as I am concerned. 2. (*a*) to look at (sth., s.o.); to watch (game, etc.); **r. qn dans les yeux,** to look s.o. in the eyes; **r. qn fixement,** to stare at s.o.; **r. qn de travers,** to look askance at s.o.; **r. qn avec méfiance,** to eye s.o. suspiciously; **ils se regardaient**

en chiens de faïence, they were glaring at each other; **se faire r.,** to attract attention; to make oneself conspicuous; **r. qn faire qch.,** to watch s.o. doing sth.; *F:* **non, mais tu ne m'as pas regardé!** what d'you take me for? (*b*) *v.i.* **r. à la fenêtre,** to look in at the window; **r. par la fenêtre,** to look out of the window; **r. à sa montre,** to look at one's watch, at the time; **puis-je r.?** may I have a look? **r. par le trou de la serrure,** to peep through the keyhole. **3.** to look on to, to face (sth.); **nos deux maisons se regardent,** our houses are opposite each other; **fenêtre qui regarde sur le jardin,** window that looks on to the garden.

regarnir [rəgarnir] *v.tr.* to regarnish; to refill (one's purse); to re-stock (larder); to retrim (dress).

régate [regat] *n.f.* **1.** regatta; **r. à voiles,** yacht races; **r. à l'aviron,** boat races. **2.** (narrow) sailor-knot tie.

regazonner [rəgazɔne] *v.tr.* to returf.

regel [rəʒɛl] *n.m.* renewed frost.

regeler [rəʒle] *v.tr. & i.* (**il regèle; il regèlera**) to freeze again.

régence [reʒɑ̃s] *n.f.* regency; *Fr.Hist:* **la R.,** the Regency (1715–1723); *a.inv.* **style R.,** Régence style.

régénérateur, -trice [reʒeneratœr, -tris] **1.** *a.* regenerating, regenerative; *Ecc:* **eau régénératrice,** baptismal water; *Atom.Ph:* **pile régénératrice,** breeder reactor. **2.** *n.m. Ind:* regenerator; regenerating plant, furnace.

régénération [reʒenerasjɔ̃] *n.f.* **1.** regeneration. **2.** *Ind:* recuperation; reconditioning; *Atom.Ph:* breeding; regeneration.

régénérer [reʒenere] *v.tr.* (**je régénère, n. régénérons; je régénérerai**) **1.** to regenerate. **2.** to reactivate (catalyst).

régent, -ente [reʒɑ̃, -ɑ̃t] *n.* **1.** regent. **2.** *Fin:* director. **3.** *Belg:* (secondary) schoolmaster. **4. le R.,** the Regent diamond. **5.** *a.* **reine régente, prince r.,** Queen Regent, Prince Regent.

régenter [reʒɑ̃te] *v.tr.* to domineer over, dictate to (s.o.); **il veut tout r.,** he wants to run everything, to the show.

régicide[1] [reʒisid] **1.** *n.m. & f.* (*pers.*) regicide. **2.** *a.* regicidal.

régicide[2] *n.m.* (*crime*) regicide.

régie [reʒi] *n.f.* **1.** (*a*) administration, stewardship (of property); management, control; **en r.,** (i) in the hands of trustees; (ii) under state supervision; **r. du dépôt légal,** copyright department; (*b*) public corporation; state-owned company. **2.** (*a*) **r. des impôts indirects,** excise (administration); (*b*) Customs and Excise; **employé de la r.,** exciseman. **3.** *Th:* management; *Cin:* production; *T.V:* central control room.

regimbement [rəʒɛ̃b(ə)mɑ̃] *n.m.* refractoriness.

regimber [rəʒɛ̃be] *v.i.* (*of horse*) to kick (**contre,** at, against); (*of pers.*) to jib, to ba(u)lk (**contre,** at); **il est toujours à (se) r.,** he's always jibbing at sth.

regimbeur, -euse [rəʒɛ̃bœr, -øz] *a.* refractory; recalcitrant.

régime [reʒim] *n.m.* **1.** form of government, of administration; regime; **r. des hôpitaux,** hospital regulations, rules; **le r. du travail,** the organization of labour; **le r. féodal,** the feudal system; *Fr.Hist:* **l'ancien r.,** the old regime (before 1789); **r. parlementaire,** parliamentary regime, system; **le r. actuel,** the present order of things. **2.** (*a*) **r. (nominal),** rating (of engine, motor, generator); **r. de marche normal,** normal working, operating, conditions; **charge de r.,** rated load; **puissance de r.,** normal power; *Av: Nau: Aut:* **r. de croisière,** cruising speed; *Aut:* **r. de ville,** town conditions; **gardez ce r.,** keep to this speed; (*b*) *El.E:* **r. de charge (d'un accumulateur),** charging rate; **variations de r.,** load variations; (*c*) *Geog:* (rate of) flow (of river, etc.); **r. climatérique,** climatic conditions; **r. thermique,** temperature pattern. **3.** diet; **r. lacté,** milk diet; **être au r.,** to be on a diet; **se mettre au r.,** to diet; *Sp:* **r. d'entraînement,** training. **4.** *Gram:* object; **cas r.,** objective case; **r. direct, indirect,** direct, indirect, object. **5.** bunch, stem (of bananas, dates).

régiment [reʒimɑ̃] *n.m. Mil:* regiment; *F:* **aller au r.,** to join the army; **quand j'étais au r.,** when I was in the army, was doing my military service; **un r. d'admirateurs,** a host, swarm, of admirers.

régimentaire [reʒimɑ̃tɛr] *a.* regimental.

région [reʒjɔ̃] *n.f.* region; area; **r. militaire,** military distric, = (northern, etc.) command; **les régions polaires,** the polar regions; **r. du coton,** cotton-growing area; cotton belt; *Anat:* **la r. lombaire,** the lumbar region.

régional, -ale, -aux [reʒjɔnal, -o] **1.** *a.* regional (expressions, cooking); local (committee). **2.** *n.m.* *Tp:* area telephone system.

régionalisme [reʒjɔnalism] *n.m.* regionalism.

régionaliste [reʒjɔnalist] **1.** *a.* (*a*) regional (novel, etc.); (*b*) regionalistic (policy). **2.** *n.* (*a*) regional writer; (*b*) *Pol: etc:* regionalist.

régir [reʒir] *v.tr.* (*a*) to govern, rule; to manage (estate); (*b*) *Gram:* to govern (case, noun).

régisseur [reʒisœr] *n.m.* manager; agent, steward; (farm) bailiff; *Th:* stage manager; *Cin:* assistant director.

registre [rəʒistr̥] *n.m.* **1.** register, record; account book; minute book; **rapporter un article sur un r.,** to post, enter, an item in a register; **les registres de l'état civil,** the registers of births, marriages, and deaths; *Breed:* **r. des chevaux,** stud book; **r. d'une machine,** log book of a machine. **2.** *Mus:* register; (i) compass, (ii) tone quality. **3.** *Typ:* register (of page with page). **4.** (*a*) **r. d'aérage,** ventilation flap; **r. de cheminée,** register, damper (of furnace or chimney); (*b*) *Mch:* regulator lever, throttle (valve); (*c*) draw stop (of organ). **5.** *Cmptr:* register.

réglable [reglabl̥] *a.* adjustable.

réglage [reglaʒ] *n.m.* **1.** ruling (of paper). **2.** (*a*) regulating, adjusting, adjustment, setting (of apparatus); rating (of chronometer); **r. automatique,** automatic control; **à r. automatique,** self-adjusting; **vis de r.,** set screw; **r. de la vitesse,** speed control; *Artil:* **r. du tir,** ranging; (*b*) *W.Tel: etc:* adjustment; control; tuning; **réglages,** dial readings; **r. de la luminosité,** brightness control.

règle [rɛgl̥] *n.f.* **1.** (*a*) rule, ruler; **r. à araser,** straight edge; **r. divisée,** scale; **r. à calcul,** slide rule; (*b*) *Surv:* measuring rod. **2.** rule (of conduct, art, grammar, etc.); **les règles de l'honneur,** the code of honour; *Ecc:* **r. d'un ordre,** rule of an order; *Nau:* **règles de route,** rule of the road (at sea); **les règles du jeu,** the rules of the game; *Com:* **pour la bonne r.,** for order's sake; **se faire une r. de se coucher de bonne heure,** to make it a rule to go to bed early; **mettre qch. en r.,** to put sth. in order, to rights; **tout est en r.,** everything is in order, correct; **votre passeport est-il en r.?** is your passport in order? **reçu en r.,** formal receipt; **bataille en r.,** battle according to the rules; *F:* regular set-to; **en r. générale,** as a general rule; **agir dans les règles,** to act according to rule; **jouer selon les règles,** to play according to rule; to play the game; **comme c'est la r., comme de r.,** as is the rule; **r. d'or,** golden rule; *Mth: O:* **r. de trois,** rule of three. **3. prendre qn pour r.,** to take s.o. as a guide, an example. **4.** *Physiol:* **avoir ses règles,** to have one's period.

réglé [regle] *a.* **1.** ruled (paper); **papier non r.,** plain paper. **2.** regular, well-ordered; fixed; steady; **vie réglée,** well-ordered life; **à des heures réglées,** at set, stated, hours; *F:* **r. comme du papier à musique,** as regular as clockwork.

règlement [rɛgləmɑ̃] *n.m.* **1.** settlement, adjustment (of difficulty, account); payment; **r. judiciaire,** rule of Court; **r. à l'amiable,** amicable settlement; **faire un r. par chèque,** to pay by cheque; **pour r. de tout compte,** in full settlement; **faire un r. de compte(s) (avec qn),** to take the law into one's own hands. **2.** regulation(s); statutes (of university); rules (of a society); **règlements de police,** by(e)-laws; **les règlements militaires,** army regulations.

réglementaire [rɛgləmɑ̃tɛr] *a.* regular, statutory, prescribed; **tenue r.,** regulation uniform; **ce n'est pas r.,** it's against the rules.

réglementairement [rɛgləmɑ̃tɛrmɑ̃] *adv.* in the regular, prescribed, manner; according to the rules.

réglementation [rɛgləmɑ̃tasjɔ̃] *n.f.* **1.** regulating, regulation; **r. du trafic des changes,** exchange control. **2.** *coll.* regulations; rules.

réglementer [rɛgləmɑ̃te] *v.tr.* to regulate; to make rules for (sth.); to bring (sth.) under regulation; **r. le droit de grève,** to control the right to strike.

régler [regle] *v.tr.* **(je règle, n. réglons; je réglerai) 1.** to rule (paper). **2.** (*a*) to regulate, order (one's life, conduct, etc.); **r. sa journée,** to plan one's day; **r. ses dépenses sur son revenu,** to cut one's coat according to one's cloth; *Sp:* **r. l'allure,** to set the pace; *Artil:* **r. le tir,** to range; (*b*) to regulate, adjust, set (mechanism); to adjust (compass); to rate (chronometer); **r. une montre,** (i) to regulate a watch; (ii) to set a watch right; **la pendule est bien réglée,** the clock keeps good time; *I.C.E:* **r. l'allumage, le moteur,** to time the ignition; to tune the engine. **3.** (*a*) to settle (question, quarrel); **r. ses affaires,** to put one's business in order; **l'affaire s'est réglée à l'amiable,** the business was settled on a friendly basis; (*b*) to settle (account); to pay (bill); **r. les livres,** to balance, make up, the books; **r. son compte, ses comptes, avec qn,** (i) to settle one's account(s), one's bill(s), with s.o.; (ii) to settle accounts with s.o., to have one's own back on s.o.; **r. de vieux comptes,** to pay off old scores; **r. le boulanger,** to pay the baker; **c'est moi qui règle,** I'm paying; *F:* this is on me.

régleur, -euse [reglœr, -øz] *n.* **1.** (*pers.*) regulator, adjuster (of mechanism). **2.** *n.f.* **régleuse,** ruling machine (for paper).

réglisse [reglis] **1.** *n.f. Bot:* liquorice. **2.** *n.m.* **bâton de r.,** stick of liquorice.

réglure [reglyr] *n.f.* ruling (of, on, paper).

règne [rɛɲ] *n.m.* **1.** (vegetable, animal) kingdom. **2.** reign (of king); sway (of fashion); **sous le r. de Louis XIV,** in the reign of Louis XIV.

régner [reɲe] *v.i.* **(je règne, n. régnons; je régnerai) 1.** (*of monarch*) to reign, rule; (*of conditions, opinion*) to prevail, to be prevalent; to obtain; **r. sur l'opinion,** to dominate opinion. **2. une galerie règne le long du bâtiment,** a gallery runs, extends, along the building.

regonfler [rəgɔ̃fle] **1.** *v.tr.* (*a*) to reinflate (balloon); to blow up, pump up (tyre); (*b*) *F:* to put new life into (s.o.). **2.** *v.i.* (*of river*) to swell, rise (again).

regorger [rəgɔrʒe] **(je regorgeai(s); n. regorgeons) 1.** *v.i.* (*a*) to overflow, run over; to brim over; (*b*) to abound **(de,** in); to be glutted **(de,** with); **les trains regorgent de gens,** the trains are packed (with people); **les rues regorgeaient de monde,** the streets were teeming, swarming, with people; **sa maison regorge de livres,** his house is cram full of books; **il regorge de santé,** he is bursting with health. **2.** *v.tr.* to bring up, regurgitate (food); *F:* **faire r. à qn ce qu'il a volé,** to make s.o. cough up what he has stolen.

regratter [rəgrate] *v.tr. Const:* to scrape, rub down (wall).

regreffer [rəgrefe] *v.tr. Hort:* to regraft.

régresser [regrese] *v.i.* to regress; to diminish (in intensity).

régressif, -ive [regresif, -iv] *a.* regressive; *Biol:* **forme régressive,** throwback; *Geol:* **érosion régressive,** headwater erosion.

régression [regresjɔ̃] *n.f.* **1.** regression; **r. marine,** recession of sea (from the coast); *Mth:* **coefficient de r.,** regression coefficient. **2.** *Biol:* (*a*) retrogression; (*b*) throwback; regression; (*c*) *Psy:* regression. **3.** decline (in business); drop (in sales); **épidémie en r.,** epidemic on the decline.

regret [rəgrɛ] *n.m.* **1.** regret **(de,** for); (*a*) **exprimer le r. de ne pouvoir être présent,** to express regret at not being able to be present; **avoir du r.,** to feel regret; to be sorry; **avoir r. de qch., d'avoir fait qch.,** to regret sth., having done sth.; **j'ai r. à vous quitter,** I am sorry to leave you; **j'ai le r., je suis au r., de vous annoncer que . . .,** I am sorry to inform you that . . .; **j'en suis au r.,** I am sorry; **faire qch. à r.,** to do sth. with regret, regretfully, reluctantly; **à mon (grand) r.,** (much) to my regret; *F:* **tous mes regrets!** sorry! apologies! (*b*) **le r. de la patrie,** homesickness; **mourir sans laisser de regrets,** to die unlamented.

regrettable [rəgrɛtabl̩] *a.* regrettable; unfortunate (mistake, etc.).

regrettablement [rəgrɛtabləmɑ̃] *adv.* regrettably.

regretter [rəgrete] *v.tr.* **1.** to regret (s.o., sth.); **mourir regretté de tous,** to die regretted by all; **r. d'avoir fait qch.,** to regret, be sorry for, having done sth.; **je regrette qu'il soit parti si tôt,** I am sorry that he left so early; I wish he hadn't left so early; **vous le regretterez,** you'll be sorry for it; **je regrette!** (I'm) sorry! **2.** (*a*) **r. un absent,** to miss an absent friend; (*b*) **r. son argent,** to wish one had one's money back.

regrimper [rəgrɛ̃pe] *v.tr. & i.* to climb (up) again; **r. l'escalier, r. à l'arbre,** to climb the stairs, the tree, again.

regrossir [rəgrosir] *v.i.* to put on weight again.

regroupement [rəgrupmɑ̃] *n.m.* regrouping; amalgamation; **r. parcellaire,** consolidation (of land holdings).

regrouper [rəgrupe] *v.tr. & pr.* (*a*) to regroup; (*b*) to rally; (*c*) to amalgamate.

régularisation [regylarizasjɔ̃] *n.f.* (*a*) regularization, regularizing; making (sth.) regular; putting in order; (*b*) regulation, regulating (of river, mechanism); **r. de la circulation,** traffic control.

régulariser [regylarize] *v.tr.* (*a*) to regularize; to make regular; to put (document) into proper form; to put in order; **r. la pente d'une route,** to grade a road; (*b*) to regulate, steady (the running of a machine); **r. un fleuve,** to regulate the flow of a river; **r. la circulation,** to regulate, control, the traffic.

régularité [regylarite] *n.f.* (*a*) regularity (of features, shape, habits); (*b*) steadiness, evenness, regularity (of motion); **épreuve de r.,** reliability trial; (*c*) equability; (*d*) punctuality.

régulateur, -trice [regylatœr, -tris] **1.** *a.* regulating, regulative (force); regulating (mechanism); **soupape régulatrice,** governor valve. **2.** *n.m. Tchn:* regulator; (*a*) *Clockm:* regulator, governor, balance wheel; (*b*) regulator, governor (of steam engine, turbine); throttle valve (of steam engine); *Nau:* governor (of log); *Typewr:* **r. de marge,** margin stop; *Th:* **r. d'éclairage de scène,** stage dimmer. **3.** *n.m.* (*a*) *Rail:* controller; *NAm:* dispatcher; (*b*) *Navy:* guide (of the fleet).

régulation [regylasjɔ̃] *n.f.* **1.** regulation, readjustment (of compass). **2.** control, regulation; **r. des naissances,** birth control; **r. de la circulation,** traffic control; *Mec.E:* **dispositif, système, de r. (du carburant, de la pression, etc.),** (fuel, pressure, etc.) control system; *El:* **r. de la tension,** voltage regulation.

régulier, -ière [regylje, -jɛr] **1.** *a.* (*a*) regular (features, polygon); valid (passport); **quittance ré-**

gulière, receipt in due form; proper receipt; *Gram:* **verbe r.,** regular verb; **ce n'est pas r.,** that's not according to the rules; (*b*) steady (pulse, increase); even (motion); regular (bus service); steady, ordered (life); steady (work, worker); **être r. dans ses habitudes,** to be regular in one's habits; **humeur régulière,** even temper. **2.** *a. & n.m.* regular (priest, soldier); **troupes régulières,** regular troops; regulars.
régulièrement [regyljɛrmɑ̃] *adv.* regularly; (*a*) in accordance with the regulations; **membres r. désignés,** properly elected members; (*b*) steadily, evenly; at regular intervals.
régurgitation [regyrʒitasjɔ̃] *n.f.* regurgitation.
régurgiter [regyrʒite] *v.tr.* to regurgitate (food).
réhabilitation [reabilitasjɔ̃] *n.f.* **1.** rehabilitation; recovery of civil rights; discharge (of bankrupt); re-establishment (of reputation). **2.** rehabilitation (of slum district).
réhabilité, -ée [reabilite] *n.* discharged bankrupt.
réhabiliter [reabilite] *v.tr.* **1.** to rehabilitate (s.o.); to clear (s.o., s.o.'s good name); to discharge (bankrupt); **r. qn dans ses droits,** to reinstate s.o. in his rights; **se r.,** to re-establish one's good name. **2.** to renovate (old building); to rehabilitate (slum district).
réhabituer [reabitɥe] *v.tr.* to reaccustom (**à,** to); **se r. à faire qch.,** to get used, accustomed, to doing sth. again.
rehaussement [rəosmɑ̃] *n.m.* **1.** raising, heightening (of wall, of picture on wall, etc.). **2.** heightening, enhancing (of colour, beauty); touching up (of colour).
rehausser [rəose] *v.tr.* **1.** to raise, heighten (wall, etc.); to make (sth.) higher. **2.** to heighten, enhance, set off (colour, complexion); to touch up (a colour); **r. un détail,** to accentuate a detail.
rehaut [rəo] *n.m. Art:* touch-up (to a picture); **les rehauts,** the highlights.
réimperméabiliser [reɛ̃pɛrmeabilize] *v.tr.* to reproof (raincoat).
réimportation [reɛ̃pɔrtasjɔ̃] *n.f.* **1.** reimportation. **2.** reimport.
réimporter [reɛ̃pɔrte] *v.tr.* to reimport.
réimposer [reɛ̃poze] *v.tr.* **1.** to tax (s.o.) again; to reimpose (tax). **2.** *Typ:* to reimpose.
réimposition [reɛ̃pozisjɔ̃] *n.f.* **1.** further taxation; reimposition (of tax). **2.** *Typ:* reimposition.
réimpression [reɛ̃presjɔ̃] *n.f.* **1.** reprinting. **2.** reprint.
réimprimer [reɛ̃prime] *v.tr.* to reprint.
Reims [rɛ̃s] *Pr.n.m. Geog:* Rheims.
rein [rɛ̃] *n.m.* **1.** *Anat:* kidney; **r. artificiel,** kidney machine. **2.** *pl.* loins, back; **la chute, le creux, des reins,** the small of the back; **douleur, mal, aux reins,** backache; **casser les reins à qn,** to ruin s.o.; **il a les reins solides,** (i) he has a strong back; he is sturdily built; (ii) he is a man of substance.
réincarnation [reɛ̃karnasjɔ̃] *n.f.* reincarnation.
réincarner (se) [səreɛ̃karne] *v.pr.* to be reincarnated.
réincorporer [reɛ̃kɔrpɔre] *v.tr.* to reincorporate.
reine [rɛn] *n.f.* **1.** (*a*) queen; **la r. Anne,** Queen Anne; **r. mère,** queen mother; (*b*) queen (bee); (*c*) *Chess:* queen. **2. r. de beauté,** beauty queen; **la r. du bal,** the belle of the ball.
reine-claude [rɛnklod] *n.f.* greengage; *pl. reines-claudes.*
reine-des-prés [rɛndepre] *n.f. Bot:* meadowsweet; *pl. reines-des-prés.*
reine-marguerite [rɛnmargərit] *n.f. Bot:* China aster; *pl. reines-marguerites.*
reinette [rɛnɛt] *n.f.* pippin (apple); **r. grise,** russet.
réinhumation [reinymasjɔ̃] *n.f.* reinterment.
réinhumer [reinyme] *v.tr.* to reinter.
réinscrire [reɛ̃skrir] *v.tr.* (*conj. like* INSCRIRE) (*a*) to inscribe again; (*b*) to re-register.
réinstaller [reɛ̃stale] *v.tr.* to reinstall, reinstate; **il s'est réinstallé,** he has (i) settled down again, (ii) set himself up again.
réintégration [reɛ̃tegrasjɔ̃] *n.f.* **1.** (*a*) reinstatement (of official, etc.); restoration; (*b*) **r. des démobilisés dans la vie civile,** rehabilitation of ex-servicemen. **2. r. de domicile,** resumption of residence; *Jur:* **r. du domicile conjugal,** restitution of conjugal rights.
réintégrer [reɛ̃tegre] *v.tr.* (*conj. like* INTÉGRER) **1. r. qn (dans ses fonctions),** to reinstate s.o.; to restore s.o. to his position, his office; **r. des employés,** to take employees on again. **2. r. son domicile,** to resume possession of one's domicile; to return to one's home.
réintroduction [reɛ̃trɔdyksjɔ̃] *n.f.* reintroduction.
réintroduire [reɛ̃trɔdɥir] *v.tr.* (*conj. like* INTRODUIRE) to reintroduce.
réitératif, -ive [reiteratif, -iv] *a.* reiterative.
réitération [reiterasjɔ̃] *n.f.* reiteration.
réitérer [reitere] *v.tr.* (**je réitère, n. réitérons; je réitérerai**) to reiterate, repeat.
reître [rɛtr̥] *n.m.* ruffianly soldier.
rejaillir [rəʒajir] *v.i.* (*a*) to spurt back, to gush out; to spurt, splash, up, out; to spout; (*b*) **sa honte a rejailli sur nous,** we were involved in his disgrace; **tout ceci rejaillit sur moi,** all this is a reflection on me.
rejaillissement [rəʒajismɑ̃] *n.m.* (*a*) springing (up), gushing (out), spurting (back, up, out), spouting (of liquid); (*b*) reflection (of glory).
rejet [rəʒɛ] *n.m.* **1.** (*a*) throwing out, throwing up; casting up; (*b*) material thrown out; spoil (earth); (*c*) *Geol:* throw (of fault); **r. horizontal,** heave. **2.** rejection (of proposal, *Med:* of transplant); setting aside (of claim); dismissal (of an appeal). **3.** *Hort:* shoot. **4.** *Pros:* enjambment.
rejeter [rəʒte] (*conj. like* JETER) **1.** *v.tr.* (*a*) to throw again; (*b*) (i) to throw, fling, back; to return (ball); **r. son chapeau en arrière,** to tilt one's hat back; (ii) to throw up, cast up; (*c*) to transfer; **r. le blâme sur d'autres,** to shift, lay, the blame on others; (*d*) to reject, set aside; to refuse to acknowledge (s.o.); to reject, dismiss, turn down (an offer); to disallow (an expense); **r. un projet de loi,** to reject, throw out, a bill; *Jur:* **r. un pourvoi,** to dismiss an appeal; (*e*) *Knit:* **r. les mailles,** to cast off. **2. se r.** (*a*) to fall back (**sur,** on); **se r. sur les circonstances,** to lay the blame on circumstances; (*b*) **se r. en arrière,** to leap, spring, back(wards); to dodge; (*of horse*) to shy.
rejeton [rəʒtɔ̃] *n.m.* **1.** *Hort:* shoot, sucker. **2.** descendant, offspring (of family).
rejoindre [rəʒwɛ̃dr̥] (*conj. like* JOINDRE) **1.** *v.tr.* (*a*) to rejoin, reunite; to join (together) again; to connect (streets, rivers, etc.); **sa pensée rejoint la mienne,** his ideas are akin to mine; (*b*) **r. qn,** to rejoin s.o.; to overtake s.o.; to catch s.o. up (again); **r. son régiment,** to (re)join one's regiment; **il a évité de r. la grande route,** he avoided joining the main road. **2. se r.** (*a*) to meet; (*b*) to meet again.
rejointoyer [rəʒwɛ̃twaje] *v.tr.* (*conj. like* JOINTOYER) *Const:* to (re)joint, (re)point (walls).
rejouer [rəʒwe] *v.tr.* to replay (match); to play (piece of music) again.
réjoui [reʒwi] *a.* jolly, cheerful, merry.
réjouir [reʒwir] **1.** *v.tr.* (*a*) to delight, gladden, cheer (s.o.); **cela me réjouit le cœur de l'entendre,** it makes my heart glad, it does my heart good, to hear it; **r. l'œil,** to delight the eye; (*b*) to amuse, divert, entertain. **2. se r.** (*a*) to rejoice (**de,** at, in); to be glad (**de,** of); to be delighted (**de,** at); **je me réjouis de le revoir,**

I am delighted to see him again; (*b*) to enjoy oneself.

réjouissance [reʒwisɑ̃s] *n.f.* rejoicing; **réjouissances publiques,** public festivities.

réjouissant [reʒwisɑ̃] *a.* **1.** cheering, heartening. **2.** amusing, diverting.

réjuvénescence [reʒyvenesɑ̃s] *n.f.* rejuvenescence.

relâche [rəlɑʃ] **1.** *n.m.* (*a*) slackening, loosening (of rope); (*b*) relaxation, respite, rest; **travailler sans r.,** to work without respite, without a break; **prendre un peu de r., se donner r.,** to have a rest; (*c*) *Th:* **il y a r. ce soir,** there is no performance this evening; (*of theatre*) **faire r.,** to be closed; *P.N:* **r.,** closed. **2.** *n.f. Nau:* (*a*) call; **faire r. dans un port,** to call at, put into, a port; (*b*) port of call.

relâché [rəlɑʃe] *a.* relaxed; (*a*) slack (rope); (*b*) loose, lax (morals, conduct).

relâchement [rəlɑʃmɑ̃] *n.m.* (*a*) relaxing, slackening (of muscle, cord); (*b*) relaxation, falling off (of discipline); abatement (of weather); looseness, laxity (of morals); (*c*) relaxation (from work).

relâcher [rəlɑʃe] **1.** *v.tr.* (*a*) to loosen, slacken, ease, release (cord, etc.); to relax (muscle); to loosen (the bowels); to relax (discipline, morals); **se r. l'esprit,** to rest one's mind; (*b*) to release, let go (prisoner, caged bird). **2.** *v.i. Nau:* to put into port. **3. se r.** (*a*) (*of rope*) to slacken; (*of shoelace*) to come loose; (*of fever*) to abate; (*of pers.*) to become slack; (*of zeal*) to flag, to fall off; (*of morals*) to grow lax; (*b*) (*of pers.*) to relax, take a rest.

relais¹ [rəlɛ] *n.m.* sandbank (along river); sand flats (along shore); silt, warp.

relais² *n.m.* **1.** (*a*) relay (of post horses, runners, hounds); shift (of workmen); **chevaux de r.,** post horses; **ouvriers de r.,** shift workers; **travail sans r.,** unrelieved (spell of) work; *Sp:* **course de r.,** relay race; **prendre le r.,** to take over (**de qn,** from s.o.); (*b*) coaching inn; post house; **r. gastronomique,** restaurant with a reputation for good food; *Aut:* **r. routier,** service station (with café). **2.** *Mec.E: etc:* relay (unit); *El:* relay; *W.Tel:* **r. de radio-diffusion,** relay broadcasting station.

relance [rəlɑ̃s] *n.f.* (*a*) *Cards:* raise; **poker sans maximum de r.,** roofless poker; (*b*) boost; fresh start; revival (of economy, etc.); (*c*) *Com:* following up (of customer); **lettre de r.,** follow-up letter.

relancement [rəlɑ̃smɑ̃] *n.m.* **1.** throwing back; throwing again. **2.** restarting (of machine, etc.); boosting (production, etc.).

relancer [rəlɑ̃se] *v.tr.* (*conj. like* LANCER) **1.** to throw (sth.) again; to throw (sth.) back; *Ten:* to return (the ball). **2.** (*a*) to restart (engine); *Ven:* to start (quarry) again; (*b*) to boost (trade); (*c*) (i) to give (s.o.) a reminder; *F:* to wake (s.o.) up; (ii) to badger (s.o.); to harass (debtor). **3.** *v.i. Cards: etc:* to increase the stake; to raise the bid.

relanceur, -euse [rəlɑ̃sœr, -øz] *n. Ten:* striker (out); **avantage au r.,** advantage striker.

relaps, -e [rəlaps] *a. & n.* relapsed (heretic).

rélargir [relarʒir] *v.tr.* to widen; to make (sth.) wider.

relater [rəlate] *v.tr.* to relate, state (facts).

relatif, -ive [rəlatif, -iv] *a.* (*a*) relative (position, value; *Gram:* pronoun, clause); *Mus:* **tons relatifs,** related keys; (*b*) **questions relatives à un sujet,** questions related to, connected with, a subject; (*c*) comparative; limited; **vivre dans un luxe r.,** to live in comparative luxury.

relation [rəlasjɔ̃] *n.f.* relation. **1.** connection; (*a*) **les relations humaines,** human relations, intercourse; **nos relations avec la Hollande,** our relations with Holland; **entamer des relations, se mettre, entrer, en relations, avec qn,** to enter into relations, get into touch, with s.o.; **avoir, entretenir, des relations avec qn,** to be in touch, to have dealings, with s.o.; **être en r. avec qn,** to be in communication, in touch, with s.o.; **être en relations d'amitié avec qn,** to be on friendly terms with s.o.; **relations d'affaires,** business connection; **il a de belles relations,** (i) he is well connected; (ii) he has influential friends; **faire jouer ses relations,** to pull strings; **cesser ses relations avec qn,** to drop s.o.'s acquaintance; *F:* to drop s.o.; **relations avec le public, relations publiques,** public relations; (*b*) **r. entre la cause et l'effet, r. de cause à effet,** relation, connection, between cause and effect; **r. étroite entre deux faits,** close connection between two facts; *Rail:* **r. entre Paris et Lille,** service between Paris and Lille; *Anat:* **relations de deux organes,** relative positions of two organs. **2.** account, report, narrative, statement; **faire la r. de qch.,** to give an account of sth.

relativement [rəlativmɑ̃] *adv.* relatively; (*a*) in relation (**à,** to); (*b*) comparatively.

relativité [rəlativite] *n.f.* relativity.

relaver [rəlave] *v.tr.* to wash (sth.) again.

relaxation [rəlaksasjɔ̃] *n.f.* relaxation.

relaxe¹ [rəlaks] *n.f.* **1.** release, discharge (of accused person). **2.** relaxation.

relaxe² *a.* relaxing; **fauteuil r.,** reclining chair.

relaxer [rəlakse] **1.** *v.tr.* (*a*) to relax; (*b*) *Jur:* to release, discharge (prisoner). **2. se r.,** to relax.

relayer [rəleje] (**je relaie, je relaye, n. relayons; je relaierai, je relayerai**) **1.** *v.i. A:* to relay; to change horses. **2.** *v.tr.* (*a*) to relay, relieve, take turns with, change with (s.o.); to take over from (s.o.); (*b*) to relay (broadcast).

relégation [rəlegasjɔ̃] *n.f. Jur:* relegation (to a penal colony); transportation.

reléguer [rəlege] *v.tr.* (*conj. like* LÉGUER) to relegate; (*a*) to transport (convict); (*b*) **r. un tableau au grenier,** to relegate, consign, a picture to the attic; **se trouver relégué au deuxième rang,** to find oneself pushed into the background.

relent [rəlɑ̃] *n.m.* musty smell, taste; unpleasant, stale, smell.

relevable [rəlvabl̥] *a.* adjustable (for height); hinged (counter flap, etc.); *Av:* **train d'atterrissage r.,** retractable undercarriage.

relevage [rəlvaʒ] *n.m.* raising, lifting; salving (of submarine); **dispositif de r.,** luffing gear (of crane).

relevailles [rəlvaj] *n.f. pl.* churching (of woman after childbirth); **faire ses r.,** to be churched.

relève [rəlɛv] *n.f.* **1.** *Mil:* relief (of troops, sentry); changing (of the guard, *Ind:* of shift); **troupes de r., la r.,** relieving troops; **prendre la r. de qn,** to relieve s.o., take over from s.o. **2.** relief; relieving sentry, etc.

relevé [rəlve] **1.** *a.* (*a*) raised, erect (head, etc.); turned up (collar, sleeve); **chapeau r.,** off-the-face hat; **pantalon à bords relevés,** turn-up trousers; turn-ups; (*b*) exalted, high (position); noble (sentiment); lofty (style); (*c*) highly-seasoned (sauce). **2.** *n.m.* (*a*) abstract, summary, account, statement; **r. de consommation (du gaz),** meter reading; **r. des naissances,** table, summary, of births; **r. de compte,** statement (of account); (*b*) survey; **faire le r. d'un terrain,** to plot a piece of land.

relèvement [rəlɛvmɑ̃] *n.m.* **1.** (*a*) raising up, setting up again (of fallen object); (*b*) raising, heightening (of picture, wall); recovery, revival (of business); increase (in wages); raising (of tariff, tax). **2.** *Com:* statement. **3.** *Nau: Surv:* bearing (by compass); position; **r. radio(goniométrique),** radio bearing, *F:* fix; **faire, prendre, un r.,** to take a bearing, bearings.

relever [rəlve] (*conj. like* LEVER) **1.** *v.tr.* (*a*) (i) to raise, lift, set, up again; to set (s.o.) on his feet again;

to rebuild (wall); to right (a ship); (ii) to pick up (from the ground); **r. le gant,** to pick up, take up, the gauntlet; to accept the challenge; *Sch:* **r. les compositions,** to take in, collect, the essays; (iii) (to raise (higher); to heighten (sth.); to turn up (one's collar, etc.); to tuck up, roll up (one's sleeves); to take up, pick up (stitch); to raise, refloat (sunken ship); **r. ses cheveux,** to put one's hair up; **r. la tête,** to hold up one's head (again); to look up; **r. les salaires, les prix,** to raise, increase, wages, prices; **r. les espérances,** to raise, revive, hopes; **r. la fortune de qn,** to restore s.o.'s fortune; (*b*) to call attention to (sth.); to note, notice; to point out (defects); to pick up (mistake); to challenge (statement); (*c*) to bring into relief; to enhance, heighten, set off (colour, etc.); to season, to add condiments to (sauce); to enliven (story); (*d*) to relieve (troops, a sentry); **r. qn,** to take s.o.'s place (on duty); to take over; (*e*) **r. qn d'un vœu,** to release s.o. from a vow; **r. qn de ses fonctions,** to relieve s.o. of his office; to dismiss s.o.; (*f*) to note; to take down (statement, etc.); to record (temperature); to make out (account); to read (meter); **r. des empreintes digitales,** to take fingerprints; (*g*) *Nau:* to take the bearings of (a place); to sight (land); *Surv:* to survey, plot (piece of land); *Mth:* to plot (graph). **2.** *v.i.* (*a*) **r. de maladie,** to be recovering from an illness; (*b*) **r. de qn, de qch.,** to be dependent on, answerable to, responsible to, s.o., sth.; **r. de l'article 7,** to come under article 7. **3. se r.** (*a*) to rise to one's feet (again); to get up from one's knees; to pick oneself up; (*of ship*) to right itself; (*b*) (*of trade, courage*) to revive, recover; (*c*) **se r. de qch.,** to recover from sth.; **il ne s'en relèvera pas,** he will never get over it.

releveur, -euse [rəlvœr, -øz] **1.** *a.* & *n.m.* *Anat:* **(muscle) r.,** levator (muscle). **2.** *n.* meter reader.

relief [rəljɛf] *n.m.* **1.** *Art:* relief; relievo; *Geog:* relief; **carte en r.,** relief, raised, map; **télévision en r.,** stereoscopic television; **mettre qch. en r., donner du r. à qch.,** to throw sth. into relief; to bring out (contrast); to set off (beauty); **position très en r.,** prominent position. **2.** *pl.* remains (of meal); scraps.

relier [rəlje] *v.tr.* (*impf.* & *pr.sub.* **n. reliions**) **1.** to bind, tie, again; to refasten. **2.** (*a*) to connect, link, bind, join (things, persons); **r. les bords d'une brèche,** to bridge a gap; (*b*) to bind (book); **r. un livre de nouveau,** to rebind a book; **relié en veau,** bound in calf; (*c*) to hoop (cask).

relieur, -euse [rəljœr, -øz] *n.* (book)binder.

religieusement [rəliʒjøzmɑ̃] *adv.* religiously; (*a*) piously; (*b*) scrupulously.

religieux, -euse [rəliʒjø, -øz] **1.** *a.* religious; sacred (music); devotional (books); **mariage r.,** church wedding; **soin r.,** religious, scrupulous, care. **2.** *n.* religious; *m.* monk, friar; *f.* nun. **3.** *n.f.* *Cu:* **religieuse,** cream éclair.

religion [rəliʒjɔ̃] *n.f.* (*a*) religion; **avoir de la r.,** to be religious; **mourir en r.,** to die in the faith; **entrer en r.,** to enter into religion, to take the vows; **minorités de r.,** religious minorities; (*b*) **se faire une r. de qch.,** to make a religion of sth.; to make sth. a point of conscience; **la r. du serment,** the sanctity of the oath.

religiosité [rəliʒjozite] *n.f.* religiosity.

reliquaire [rəlikɛr] *n.m.* reliquary; shrine.

reliquat [rəlika] *n.m.* (*a*) remainder, residue; unexpended balance; (*b*) balance (of an account); (*c*) after effects (of an illness).

relique [rəlik] *n.f.* relic (of saint); **garder qch. comme une r.,** to treasure sth.

relire [rəlir] (*conj. like* LIRE) **1.** *v.tr.* to re-read; to read (over) again. **2. se r.,** to read over what one has written.

reliure [rəljyr] *n.f.* **1.** bookbinding; **atelier de r.,** bindery. **2. r. anglaise, en toile,** cloth binding; **r. pleine,** full leather binding.

relogement [rəlɔʒmɑ̃] *n.m.* rehousing.

reloger [rəlɔʒe] *v.tr.* (*conj. like* LOGER) to rehouse.

relouer [rəlue] *v.tr.* **1.** to relet (house, etc.). **2.** to rent again.

reluire [rəlɥir] *v.i.* (*conj. like* LUIRE) to shine (by reflected light); to glitter, glisten, gleam; **faire r. qch.,** to polish sth. up; *Prov:* **tout ce qui reluit n'est pas or,** all that glitters is not gold.

reluisant [rəlɥizɑ̃] *a.* shining, gleaming, glossy; **visage r. de propreté,** scrubbed and shining face; *F:* **cela n'est pas très r.,** it's not all that wonderful.

reluquer [rəlyke] *v.tr.* *F:* to eye, ogle (s.o.).

remâchement [rəmɑʃmɑ̃] *n.m.* chewing over; turning over in one's mind.

remâcher [rəmɑʃe] *v.tr.* (*a*) to chew again; (*b*) to ruminate on, over (sth.); to turn (sth.) over in one's mind; to brood over (sth.).

remailler [rəmaje] *v.tr.* to mend the meshes of, to re-mesh (net); to mend a ladder in (stocking).

remake [rimek] *n.m.* *Cin:* *Rec:* remake.

rémanence [remanɑ̃s] *n.f.* remanence, residual magnetism; *Opt:* **r. des images visuelles,** persistence of vision.

rémanent [remanɑ̃] *a.* *El:* *Magn:* residual, remanent; *Opt:* persistent (image).

remanger [rəmɑ̃ʒe] *v.tr.* (*conj. like* MANGER) to eat again; **j'en ai remangé,** I had some more.

remaniement [rəmanimɑ̃] *n.m.* **1.** rehandling; altering; reshaping. **2.** alteration, modification, change; **apporter des remaniements à un travail,** to alter, recast, a work; *Pol:* **r. ministériel,** Cabinet reshuffle.

remanier [rəmanje] *v.tr.* (*impf.* & *pr.sub.* **n. remaniions**), to recast, reshape, alter, adapt (literary work, etc.); to make changes in (team); to reshuffle (Cabinet).

remariage [rəmarjaʒ] *n.m.* remarriage.

remarier [rəmarje] **1.** *v.tr.* to marry (one's daughter) again. **2. se r.,** to remarry; to marry again.

remarquable [rəmarkabl̩] *a.* (*a*) remarkable, noteworthy (**par,** for); distinguished (**par,** by); **faits remarquables de la semaine,** outstanding events, highlights, of the week; **orateur r.,** remarkable, outstanding, speaker; (*b*) strange, astonishing; **il est r. qu'il n'ait rien entendu,** it's a wonder that he heard nothing.

remarquablement [rəmarkabləmɑ̃] *adv.* remarkably.

remarque [rəmark] *n.f.* **1.** remark; **faire une r.,** (i) to make, pass, a remark; (ii) to make a critical observation, remark; **faire la r. de qch.,** to remark on sth.; **digne de r.,** noteworthy. **2.** inset engraving.

remarquer [rəmarke] *v.tr.* **1.** to mark (linen) again. **2.** (*a*) to remark, observe, notice; **je n'ai pas remarqué son absence,** I didn't notice his absence; **cette tache ne se remarque pas,** this stain isn't noticeable, doesn't show; **faire r. qch. à qn,** to point sth. out to s.o., to call s.o.'s attention to sth.; **r. qn dans la foule,** to notice s.o. in the crowd; **se faire r.,** to attract attention; to make oneself conspicuous; (*b*) to remark, observe, say.

remballage [rɑ̃balaʒ] *n.m.* repacking, re-baling.

remballer [rɑ̃bale] *v.tr.* **1.** to repack; to pack (goods) (up) again; to rebale (goods). **2.** *P:* to send (s.o.) packing.

rembarquement [rɑ̃barkəmɑ̃] *n.m.* re-embarking, re-embarkation; reshipping, reshipment (of goods).

rembarquer [rɑ̃barke] **1.** *v.tr.* to re-embark; to reship (goods); to hoist in (boat). **2.** *v.i.* & *pr.* to re-embark; to go on board again.

rembarrer [rɑ̃bare] *v.tr.* *F:* to rebuff, snub (s.o.); to put (s.o.) in his place; to sit on (s.o.); to go for (s.o.); to tell (s.o.) off.

remblai [rɑ̃blɛ] *n.m. Civ.E:* **1.** (*a*) filling up, filling in (with earth, etc.); (*b*) embanking; banking (up). **2.** filling (material); earth. **3.** embankment, bank; **route en r.,** embanked road.

remblayage [rɑ̃blɛjaʒ] *n.m.* = REMBLAI 1.

remblayer [rɑ̃bleje] *v.tr.* **(je remblaie, je remblaye, n. remblayons; je remblaierai, je remblayerai)** *Civ.E:* (*a*) to fill (up), pack (sunk part of ground); (*b*) to embank, to bank (up) (road, railway line).

rembobinage [rɑ̃bɔbinaʒ] *n.m. Cin: Typewr:* re-winding.

rembobiner [rɑ̃bɔbine] *v.tr.* to rewind (film, type-writer ribbon).

remboîtage [rɑ̃bwataʒ] *n.m.* re-casing (of book).

remboîtement [rɑ̃bwatmɑ̃] *n.m.* **1.** re-casing (of book). **2.** *Surg:* setting (of dislocated bone).

remboîter [rɑ̃bwate] *v.tr.* **1.** to re-case (book). **2.** (*a*) to reassemble; to fit (pieces) together again; (*b*) *Surg:* to set (dislocated bone).

rembourrage [rɑ̃buraʒ] *n.m.* **1.** stuffing, padding, upholstering. **2.** stuffing (material); padding, up-holstery.

rembourrer [rɑ̃bure] *v.tr.* to stuff, pad, upholster (chair, mattress, etc.); *Tail:* to pad (shoulders); *F:* (*of pers.*) **bien rembourré,** plump, well padded.

remboursable [rɑ̃bursabl̥] *a.* repayable, reimburs-able, refundable; redeemable (annuity, etc.).

remboursement [rɑ̃bursəmɑ̃] *n.m.* repayment, refunding (of expenses); redeeming, redemption (of annuity, etc.); **emprunt de r.,** refunding loan; **livraison contre r.,** payment, cash, on delivery; C.O.D.

rembourser [rɑ̃burse] *v.tr.* **1.** to repay, refund (expenses); to redeem, pay off (annuity, bond); to return (loan). **2. r. qn de qch.,** to reimburse, repay, s.o. for sth.; **on m'a remboursé,** I got my money back.

rembrayer [rɑ̃breje] *v.i. Aut:* to let the clutch in again; *F:* to start work again.

rembrunir [rɑ̃brynir] **1.** *v.tr.* (*a*) to make (sth.) dark(er); to darken (sth.); (*b*) to cast a gloom over (the company). **2. se r.,** (*of the sky*) to cloud over, to grow dark; (*of pers.*) to become gloomy.

rembucher [rɑ̃byʃe] *v.tr. Ven:* to drive (quarry) to covert.

remède [rəmɛd] *n.m.* remedy, cure **(à, pour, contre,** for); **r. de bonne femme,** old wives' remedy; **le r. est pire que le mal,** the cure is worse than the disease; **r. héroïque,** heroic remedy, kill-or-cure remedy; *Prov:* **aux grands maux les grands remèdes,** desperate ills call for desperate remedies; **c'est sans r.,** it is past, beyond, remedy; there's no help for it.

remédier [rəmedje] *v.ind.tr.* (*impf. & pr.sub.* **n. re-médiions) r. à qch.,** to remedy, cure, sth.; to put sth. right; **r. à l'usure,** to make good the wear and tear.

remembrement [rəmɑ̃brəmɑ̃] *n.m. Adm:* re-allo-cation, regrouping (of land).

remembrer [rəmɑ̃bre] *v.tr. Adm:* to re-allocate, regroup (land).

remémorer [rəmemɔre] *v.tr.* **r. qch. à qn,** to remind s.o. of sth.; **se r. qch.,** to remember sth., to call sth. to mind.

remerciement [rəmɛrsimɑ̃] *n.m.* thanks, acknow-ledgement; **lettre de r.,** letter of thanks; **faire ses remerciements à qn pour qch.,** to thank s.o. for sth.

remercier [rəmɛrsje] *v.tr.* (*impf. & pr.sub.* **n. re-merciions) 1.** to thank **(de, pour,** for); **je vous remercie de m'avoir aidé,** thank you for helping me; **remerciez-les bien de ma part,** give them my sincere thanks; **il me remercia d'un sourire,** he smiled his thanks; **voulez-vous du café?—je vous remercie,** will you have some coffee?—no, thank you. **2.** to dismiss, dis-charge (employee).

remetteur, -euse [rəmɛtœr, -øz] **1.** *a.* remitting (bank, etc.). **2.** *n.* remitter.

remettre [rəmɛtr̥] (*conj. like* METTRE) **1.** *v.tr.* to put back (again); (*a*) **r. son chapeau, son manteau,** to put one's hat, one's coat, on again; **r. qch. à sa place,** to replace sth.; to put sth. back in its place; *F:* **r. qn à sa place,** to put s.o. in his place; to snub s.o.; **r. qn sur le trône,** to restore s.o. to the throne; *Fb:* **r. le ballon en jeu,** to throw the ball in; *Ten:* **(balle) à r.,** let (ball); **r. un os,** to set a bone; **r. qn dans son chemin,** to set s.o. on his way again; **r. qch. en usage,** to bring sth. into use again; **r. un manche à un balai,** to put a new handle on a broom; **r. une doublure à un habit,** to reline a coat; **r. en état,** to repair, to overhaul; **r. en marche,** to restart (engine); **r. une pièce au théâtre,** to put on a play again; to revive a play; **r. à la voile,** to put to sea again, to set sail again; (*b*) **r. l'esprit de qn,** to calm, compose, s.o.'s mind; **r. qn (sur pied),** to restore s.o. to health; to put s.o. on his feet again; (*c*) **(se) remettre qch., qn,** to recall, recollect, sth., s.o.; **je ne vous remets pas,** I don't remember you; I can't place you; (*d*) **r. bien ensemble des personnes brouillées,** to bring together, to reconcile, people who have quarrelled; **se r. bien ensemble,** to make it up again; (*e*) to hand over, deliver (letter, etc.); to send in (application); **r. qn à la justice, entre les mains de la police,** to hand, turn, (s.o.) over to justice, the police; **r. son âme à Dieu,** to commit one's soul to God; **r. une charge à qn,** to hand over one's duties to s.o.; (*f*) (i) to remit (penalty); to pardon, forgive (offence); (ii) to allow (discount); (*g*) to postpone; **r. une affaire au lendemain,** to put off, postpone, defer, a matter till the next day; **r. une cause à huitaine,** to adjourn, remand, case for a week; **r. à plus tard,** to put off (doing sth.); *Chess: etc.* **partie remise,** drawn game; **c'est partie remise,** it's only a pleasure deferred; (*h*) *F:* (i) **remettons ça!** let's begin again! let's have another drink; (ii) **en r.,** to lay it on thick. **2. se r.** (*a*) **se r. au lit,** to go back to bed; **se r. en route,** to start off on one's way again; **le temps se remet (au beau),** the weather is clearing up (again); (*b*) **se r. au travail, à travailler,** to start, to set to, work again; **se r. au français,** to take up French again; (*c*) **se r. d'une maladie, d'une alerte,** to recover from, get over, an illness, an alarm; **voyons, remettez-vous!** come on, pull yourself together! (*d*) **s'en r. à qn de qch.,** to rely on s.o. for sth.; to leave it to s.o.

remeubler [rəmœble] *v.tr.* to refurnish (house).

rémige [remiʒ] *n.f. Orn:* wing quill.

réminiscence [reminisɑ̃s] *n.f.* **1.** *Phil: Psy:* re-miniscence. **2.** vague recollection.

remisage [rəmizaʒ] *n.m.* putting (of vehicle, engine) into a shed; garaging (of car).

remise [rəmiz] *n.f.* **1.** (*a*) putting back (of sth. in its place); *Fb:* **r. en jeu,** throw-in; (*b*) **r. en état,** repairing; overhauling; **r. en ordre,** putting in order; **r. en marche,** restarting. **2.** (*a*) delivery (of letter, etc.); **payable contre r. du coupon,** payable on presentation of the coupon; **r. des clefs,** handing over of the keys (of flat, etc.); (*b*) remission (of penalty, tax); **faire r. d'une dette,** to remit, cancel, a debt. **3.** (*a*) remit-tance; **faire une r. (de fonds) à qn,** to send s.o. a remittance; (*b*) discount, rebate, allowance; **r. sur marchandises,** trade discount; **faire une r. sur un article,** to allow a discount, make a reduction, on an article. **4.** *A:* postponement; *still used in* **je partirai demain sans r.,** I shall start tomorrow without fail. **5.** shed, outhouse; *Rail:* engine shed; *A:* coachhouse; **voiture de (grande) r.,** hired car (with chauffeur); *A:* **(voiture de) r.,** hired, livery, carriage.

remiser [rəmize] *v.tr.* **1.** (*a*) *A:* to put (carriage) in the coachhouse; (*b*) to garage (car); to put (engine) in the shed; **r. sa valise,** to put one's case away. **2.** *P:* to take (s.o.) down a peg or two; to snub (s.o.).

remisier [rəmizje] *n.m. St.Exch:* half-commission man.

rémissible [remisibl̥] *a.* remissible.

rémission [remisjɔ̃] *n.f.* **1.** remission (of sin, of debt); **sans r.,** (i) unremitting(ly); without a break; (ii) relentless(ly); (iii) (to pay, etc.) without delay; **tous sans r.,** all without exception. **2.** *Med:* remission, abatement (of fever).

rémittent [remitɑ̃] *a. Med:* remittent.

remmaillage [rɑ̃majaʒ] *n.m.* mending the meshes (of net); invisible mending (of stocking).

remmailler [rɑ̃maje] *v.tr.* to mend the meshes of (net); to mend a ladder in (stocking).

remmancher [rɑ̃mɑ̃ʃe] *v.tr.* to put a new handle on (sth.).

remmener [rɑ̃mne] *v.tr.* (*conj. like* MENER) to lead away (again); **il fut remmené en prison,** he was taken back to prison.

remodelage [rəmɔdlaʒ] *n.m.* remodelling.

remodeler [rəmɔdle] *v.tr.* (*conj. like* MODELER) (*a*) to remodel; (*b*) to restructure; to reorganize.

remontage [rəmɔ̃taʒ] *n.m.* **1.** going up; going upstream. **2.** winding up (of clock). **3.** putting together, (re)assembling (of parts of machinery, etc.); vamping (of shoes).

remontant [rəmɔ̃tɑ̃] **1.** *a.* (*a*) stimulating, strengthening, tonic (drink, etc.); (*b*) *Hort:* remontant (rose). **2.** *n.m.* stimulant, tonic; *F:* pick-me-up.

remonte [rəmɔ̃t] *n.f.* **1.** run (of fish to spawn). **2.** *Mil:* remounting (of cavalry); **cheval de r.,** remount.

remontée [rəmɔ̃te] *n.f.* **1.** climb (after descent); *Sp:* **une belle r.,** a good recovery. **2. r. mécanique,** ski lift. **3.** *Min:* raising (to the surface).

remonte-pente [rəmɔ̃tpɑ̃t] *n.m.* ski lift; *pl. remonte-pentes.*

remonter [rəmɔ̃te] **1.** *v.i.* (*the aux. is usu.* **être,** *occ.* **avoir**) (*a*) to go up again; **je suis remonté lui parler,** I went upstairs again to speak to him; **r. sur son cheval,** to remount one's horse; **r. en voiture,** to get into one's car again; **r. vers la source de la rivière,** to proceed, sail up, row up, towards the source of the river; **r. sur l'eau,** to come (up) to the surface again; **le baromètre remonte,** the glass is rising; **le soleil remonte,** the sun is getting higher; **les actions pétrolières ont remonté,** oil shares have gone up again; *F:* **ses actions remontent,** things are looking up for him; **votre cravate remonte par derrière,** your tie is riding up; (*b*) to go back (in time); **r. à l'origine de qch.,** to go back to the origin of sth.; **il fait r. sa famille aux Croisades,** he can trace back his family to the Crusades; **cette dette remonte à plusieurs années,** this debt dates back several years; (*c*) (*of the tide*) to flow; (*d*) *Nau:* **r. au, dans le, vent,** to beat up to windward. **2.** *v.tr.* (*a*) to go up, climb up (hill, stairs) again; **r. la rue,** to go, walk, drive, ride, up the street; **r. la rivière,** (i) to go, row, sail, swim, upstream; (ii) (*of fish*) to run up; (*b*) to take, carry, raise, up (again); *Min:* to raise (miners, coal); **r. ses chaussettes,** to pull up one's socks; **r. son pantalon,** to hitch up one's trousers; **r. un mur,** to heighten a wall; (*c*) to remount, provide remounts for (cavalry); (*d*) **r. une horloge,** to wind (up) a clock; **r. (les forces de) qn,** to put new life into s.o.; **un verre de vin vous remontera,** a glass of wine will do you good; (*e*) **r. un vin en alcool,** to fortify a wine; (*f*) to refit; to reassemble (mechanism); to vamp (shoes); (*g*) to restock (shop); to replenish (one's wardrobe); (*h*) *Th:* to put (a play) on again. **3. se r.,** to recover one's strength, one's spirits; **prendre qch. pour se r.,** to take a tonic.

remontoir [rəmɔ̃twar] *n.m.* winder, button (of watch).

remontrance [rəmɔ̃trɑ̃s] *n.f.* remonstrance; **faire des remontrances à qn,** to remonstrate with s.o., to admonish s.o.

remontrer [rəmɔ̃tre] *v.tr.* **1.** to show, demonstrate (sth.) again. **2.** (*a*) to point out (error); (*b*) **(en) r. à qn,** to give advice to s.o.; to put s.o. right; **il en remontrerait au diable,** he could teach the devil a trick or two.

remordre [rəmɔrdr̥] **1.** *v.tr.* to bite again. **2.** *v.i.* **r. à qch.,** to bite at sth. again; to have another bite, another go, at sth.; *F:* **r. à l'hameçon,** to be taken in again by the same trick.

remords [rəmɔr] *n.m.* remorse, self reproach, compunction; **un r.,** a twinge of remorse; **r. de conscience,** twinges of conscience; **atteint de r.,** conscience-stricken.

remorquage [rəmɔrkaʒ] *n.m.* towage, haulage; towing; **barre de r.,** tow bar (of glider).

remorque [rəmɔrk] *n.f.* **1.** towing; **prendre un navire, une voiture, en, à la, r.,** to take a ship, a car, in tow; to tow a ship, etc.; **croc de r.,** tow hook; *Veh:* **timon de r.,** tow bar; **être à la r.,** to be in, on, tow; **sortir du port à la r.,** to be towed out of harbour; **se mettre, être, à la r. de qn,** to follow in s.o.'s wake; to follow s.o.'s lead; **politique à la r.,** follow-my-leader policy. **2. (câble de) r.,** tow line, tow rope; *Nau:* **donner la r.,** to give, pass, a tow line. **3.** (*a*) tow; vessel towed; (*b*) *Veh:* trailer; **r. de plaisance, r. (de) camping,** caravan, *NAm:* camping trailer; (*c*) *Rail:* **rame r.,** slip portion; **voiture r.,** slip coach.

remorquer [rəmɔrke] *v.tr.* to tow (ship, car); to haul, tug (ship); to haul (trailer); to pull, draw (train).

remorqueur, -euse [rəmɔrkœr, -øz] **1.** *a.* towing (boat, etc.); *Rail:* relief (engine). **2.** (*a*) *n.m.* tug; tow boat; (*b*) *n.m. or f.* traction engine; tractor.

remoudre [rəmudr̥] *v.tr.* (*conj. like* MOUDRE) to regrind; to grind (corn, coffee) again.

remouiller [rəmuje] *v.tr.* **1.** to wet, moisten (sth.) again. **2.** *Nau:* **r. (l'ancre),** to cast anchor again.

rémoulade [remulad] *n.f. Cu:* remoulade sauce.

remoulage[1] [rəmulaʒ] *n.m.* remoulding.

remoulage[2] *n.m.* **1.** regrinding, remilling (of cereals). **2.** bran.

remouler [rəmule] *v.tr.* to remould; to mould (sth.) anew.

rémouleur [remulœr] *n.m.* knife grinder.

remous [rəmu] *n.m.* (*a*) eddy; wash (of ship); swirl (of the tide); backwash; **r. d'eau,** whirlpool; *Av:* **r. d'air,** (i) slip stream; (ii) eddy (current); (*b*) disturbance; **ce livre va provoquer des r.,** this book is going to cause a stir.

rempaillage [rɑ̃pajaʒ] *n.m.* re-seating, re-bottoming (of rush-bottomed chairs).

rempailler [rɑ̃paje] *v.tr.* to re-seat, re-bottom (rush-bottomed chair).

rempailleur, -euse [rɑ̃pajœr, -øz] *n.* upholsterer, chair bottomer.

rempaqueter [rɑ̃pakte] *v.tr.* (*conj. like* PAQUETER) to pack, wrap, up again.

rempart [rɑ̃par] *n.m.* rampart; **le r. de nos libertés,** the bulwark of our liberties.

rempiéter [rɑ̃pjete] *v.tr.* **(je rempiète, n. rempiétons; je rempiéterai) 1.** *Const:* to underpin (wall). **2.** to refoot (socks).

rempiler [rɑ̃pile] **1.** *v.tr.* to stack, pile up, again. **2.** *v.i. Mil: F:* to re-enlist.

remplaçable [rɑ̃plasabl̥] *a.* replaceable.

remplaçant, -ante [rɑ̃plasɑ̃, -ɑ̃t] *n.* (*pers.*) substitute, replacement (for duty); *Sp:* reserve (for team); locum (tenens) (of doctor, clergyman); *Sch:* supply teacher.

remplacement [rɑ̃plasmɑ̃] *n.m.* (*a*) replacing, replacement; substitution; **en r. de qch.,** in place of sth.; in lieu of sth.; as a replacement for sth.; **faire un r.,** to act as replacement, to stand in (for s.o.); **dactylo qui fait des remplacements,** temporary, supply, typist; *F:* temp.; (*b*) **de r.,** spare (tyre); substitute (food); alternative (facilities); **pile de r.,** (torch) refill; *Ins:* **valeur de r.,** replacement value.

remplacer [rɑ̃plase] *v.tr.* (*conj. like* PLACER) **1.** to take, fill, the place of, to serve as a substitute for, to take, do, duty for (s.o., sth.); to deputize for (s.o.). **2.** (*a*) to replace (broken pane, etc.); **r. qch. par qch.,** to put sth. in place of sth.; (*b*) to supersede, appoint a successor to (official).

remplage [rɑ̃plaʒ] *n.m. Arch:* (window) tracery.

rempli [rɑ̃pli] **1.** *a.* full (**de,** of). **2.** *n.m. Dressm:* tuck.

remplir [rɑ̃plir] *v.tr.* **1.** to fill up, refill (glass) (**de,** with); to fill in (gap, space); **une vague remplit d'eau notre embarcation,** a wave swamped our boat; **cela a rempli mon temps,** it occupied, took up, all my time. **2.** to fill; **les étrangers remplissaient la ville,** the town was filled with strangers; **r. l'air de ses cris,** to fill the air with one's cries. **3.** to fill up, fill in, complete (form, etc.). **4.** to fulfil (promise, order); to carry out (instructions); to perform (one's duty); **r. le but,** to serve, answer, the purpose; *Th:* **r. un rôle,** to fill, sustain, a part.

remplissage [rɑ̃plisaʒ] *n.m.* **1.** filling (up) (of cask, reservoir). **2.** (*a*) filling (in) (of hole, gap); (*b*) padding (of literary work).

remplisseur, -euse [rɑ̃plisœr, -øz] **1.** *n.* filler (in). **2.** *n.f. Ind:* **remplisseuse,** bottle-filling machine.

remploi [rɑ̃plwa] *n.m.* **1.** (*a*) re-employment; (*b*) re-use. **2.** *Jur:* re-investment.

remployer [rɑ̃plwaje] *v.tr.* (*conj. like* EMPLOYER) **1.** (*a*) to employ (s.o.) again; (*b*) to make use of (sth.) again. **2.** to re-invest (money).

remplumer (se) [sərɑ̃plyme] *v.pr.* **1.** (*of bird*) to get new feathers, new plumage. **2.** *F:* (*of pers.*) (*a*) to be in funds again; (*b*) to put on weight again.

rempocher [rɑ̃pɔʃe] *v.tr.* to put (sth.) back in one's pocket.

remporter [rɑ̃pɔrte] *v.tr.* **1.** to carry, take, (sth.) back; to carry, take, (sth.) away. **2.** to win, carry off (prize); to achieve (success); to win, reap, gain (victory, advantage) (**sur,** over); **r. la première place,** to obtain first place.

rempotage [rɑ̃pɔtaʒ] *n.m.* repotting.

rempoter [rɑ̃pɔte] *v.tr.* to repot (plant).

remprunter [rɑ̃prœ̃te] *v.tr.* to borrow again.

remuant [rəmɥɑ̃] *a.* restless, bustling; active (person).

remue-ménage [rəmymenaʒ] *n.m.inv.* stir, bustle, confusion, hubbub.

remuement [rəmymɑ̃] *n.m.* **1.** moving, stirring (of chairs, feet). **2.** stir, disturbance.

remuer [rəmɥe] *v.* **1.** *v.tr.* (*a*) to move (one's head); to move, shift (furniture); (*b*) to stir (sauce, coffee); to turn up, turn over, disturb (the ground); to stir up, rouse (s.o.); **r. ciel et terre,** to move heaven and earth, to leave no stone unturned; **r. qn, le cœur de qn,** to stir, move, s.o., s.o.'s heart. **2.** *v.i.* to move, stir, *F:* budge; **ne remue pas tout le temps!** don't fidget! **dent qui remue,** loose tooth. **3. se r.,** to move, stir; to bustle about; to be active; **remuez-vous un peu!** get a move on!

rémunérateur, -trice [remyneratœr, -tris] **1.** *a.* remunerative (work, etc.); paying, profitable. **2.** *n.* remunerator, rewarder.

rémunération [remynerasjɔ̃] *n.f.* remuneration, payment (**de,** for); consideration (for services rendered).

rémunératoire [remyneratwar] *a.* (sum) granted as a recompense.

rémunérer [remynere] *v.tr.* (**je rémunère, n. rémunérons; je rémunérerai**) to remunerate. **1.** to reward (s.o.); to pay (helpers). **2.** to pay for (services).

renâcler [rənɑkle] *v.i.* (*a*) (*of horse*) to snort; (*of pers.*) to sniff, snort; (*b*) to show reluctance; to hang back; **r. à la besogne,** to jib at one's work; to be workshy; **il a accepté en renâclant,** he accepted grudgingly.

renaissance [rənɛsɑ̃s] *n.f.* **1.** (*a*) rebirth; (*b*) renewal; revival (of letters); **r. du printemps,** reappearance of spring. **2.** *Art: Lit:* **la R.,** the Renaissance; *a.inv.* **châteaux R.,** Renaissance châteaux.

renaissant [rənɛsɑ̃] *a.* **1.** renascent; reviving; (vegetation) that springs up again; constantly recurring (problem, etc.). **2.** *F:* (of the) Renaissance.

renaître [rənɛtr̥] *v.i.* (*conj. like* NAÎTRE, *but p.p.* **rené** *and compound tenses not in use, and p.h.* **je renaquis** *rare*) **1.** to be born again; **ville qui renaît de ses cendres,** town that is rising again from its ashes; **r. à la vie,** to take on a new lease of life. **2.** to return, reappear; (*of plants*) to grow again, to spring up again; (*of nature, the arts*) to revive; **faire r. les espérances de qn,** to revive s.o.'s hopes.

rénal, -aux [renal, -o] *a.* renal; **calcul r.,** kidney stone.

renard [rənar] *n.m.* **1.** (*a*) fox; **r. argenté,** silver fox; **la chasse au r.,** (fox) hunting; **c'est un fin r.,** he's as sly as a fox; (*b*) fox (fur). **2.** leak, fissure (in boiler, dam, etc.).

renarde [rənard] *n.f.* vixen.

renardeau, -eaux [rənardo] *n.m.* fox cub.

renardière [rənardjɛr] *n.f.* (*a*) fox's hole, earth; (*b*) fox farm.

renauder [rənode] *v.i. P:* to grumble, complain, *F:* beef.

rencaissage [rɑ̃kɛsaʒ] *n.m.* **rencaissement** [rɑ̃kɛsmɑ̃] *n.m.* **1.** putting (of plants) in boxes, tubs, again. **2.** receiving back (of money).

rencaisser [rɑ̃kese] *v.tr.* **1.** to put (plants) in boxes, tubs, again; to re-box (orange trees, etc.). **2.** to receive back (money); to have (money) refunded.

rencard, rencart [rɑ̃kar] *n.m. P:* (*a*) date, rendezvous; (*b*) dope, gen, information.

renchéri, -ie [rɑ̃ʃeri] *a. & n.* particular, fastidious, fussy (person).

renchérir [rɑ̃ʃerir] **1.** *v.tr.* to make (sth.) dearer; to raise the price of (sth.). **2.** *v.i.* (*a*) (*of goods*) to get dearer; to increase, rise, go up, in price; (*b*) **r. sur qn,** to outdo s.o.; to go one better than s.o.; **r. sur une histoire,** to improve on a story; **r. sur une citation,** to cap a quotation.

renchérissement [rɑ̃ʃerismɑ̃] *n.m.* rise, increase, in price.

rencogner [rɑ̃kɔɲe] *v.tr.* to push, drive (s.o.) into a corner; **il s'est rencogné contre sa mère,** he huddled up against his mother.

rencontre [rɑ̃kɔ̃tr̥] *n.f.* **1.** (*a*) meeting, encounter (of persons); meeting (of streams); junction (of roads); collision (between two cars); **faire la r. de qn, faire une r.,** to meet s.o.; **aller à la r. de qn,** to go to meet s.o.; **faire une mauvaise r.,** to come up against something unpleasant; **connaissance de r.,** chance acquaintance; (*b*) *Clockm:* **roue de r.,** balance wheel; (*c*) **r. de pétrole,** strike, striking, of oil. **2.** encounter (of opponents); duel; skirmish; *Sp:* match, meeting; *Box:* fight; **une r. avec l'ennemi,** a brush with the enemy. **3.** *A: & Lit:* **par r.,** by chance.

rencontrer [rɑ̃kɔ̃tre] **1.** *v.tr.* to meet; (*a*) to come upon (sth.); to encounter, meet with (opposition, difficulty); **r. qn sur son chemin,** to run, come, across s.o.; **r. l'ennemi,** to encounter the enemy; **r. les yeux de qn,** to meet s.o.'s glance; **la voiture a rencontré un autobus,** the car collided with, ran into, a bus; **r. un**

indice, to hit upon a clue; **r. le bonheur auprès de qn,** to find happiness with s.o.; (*b*) **je vais le r. ce matin,** I shall be meeting him this morning; *Sp:* **r. une autre équipe,** to meet, play against, another team. **2. se r.** (*a*) to meet; **leurs yeux se rencontrèrent,** their eyes met; **je dois me r. avec lui à six heures,** I am to meet him at six o'clock; (*b*) to collide, to run into each other; (*c*) to occur, to be found; **comme cela se rencontre!** how lucky! (*d*) (*of ideas*) to agree, tally.

rendement [rɑ̃dmɑ̃] *n.m.* **1.** (*a*) produce, yield (of land, mine, tax); return, profit (on investment); **actions à gros r.,** shares that yield high interest; (*b*) output (of workers); output, production (of works); throughput (of computer); **r. individuel,** output per man; **travailler à plein r.,** (*of works*) to work to full capacity; (*of machine*) to work at full load; (*c*) efficiency, performance (of machine, etc.); **machine à grand r.,** heavy-duty machine. **2.** *Rac:* **r. de temps,** time handicap.

rendez-vous [rɑ̃devu] *n.m.inv.* **1.** rendezvous; appointment; **donner (un) r.-v., fixer un r.-v., à qn, prendre r.-v. avec qn.,** to make, fix, an appointment with s.o., to arrange to meet s.o.; *F:* to make a date with s.o.; **se rencontrer sur r.-v.,** to meet by appointment; **r.-v. d'affaires,** business appointment; **r.-v. spatial,** docking in space. **2.** meeting place; rendezvous; resort, haunt (of group); **r.-v. de chasse,** venue of the meet.

rendormir [rɑ̃dɔrmir] (*conj. like* DORMIR) **1.** *v.tr.* to send, lull (s.o.) to sleep again. **2. se r.,** to fall asleep again; to go, drop off, to sleep again.

rendre [rɑ̃dr̥] **1.** *v.tr.* (*a*) to give back, return, restore; to repay, pay back (money); to take back, return (a purchase); **r. son salut à qn,** to return s.o.'s greeting; **r. qn à la santé,** to restore s.o. to health; **r. la monnaie d'un billet de cent francs,** to give change for a hundred franc note; **r. le bien pour le mal,** to return good for evil; *F:* **je le lui rendrai!** I'll get even with him! (*b*) **r. hommage à qn,** to render, do, pay, homage to s.o.; **r. grâce à qn,** to give, render, thanks to s.o.; **r. service à qn,** to render, do, s.o. a service; **r. la justice,** to dispense, administer, justice; (*c*) to yield (produce, etc.); (*of land, taxes*) to give, produce, yield; **placement qui rend 10%,** investment that brings in 10%; **terre qui ne rend rien,** unproductive land; **le moteur rend bien,** the engine runs, performs, well; (*d*) to convey, deliver; **r. des marchansises à destination,** to deliver goods, (to their destination); **prix rendu,** delivery price; (*e*) to bring up, throw up (food, etc.); *v.i.* to vomit, to be sick; **r. l'âme, la vie,** to breathe one's last, to give up the ghost; (*f*) to give up, surrender (one's arms, a fortress); (*g*) to issue, pronounce (decree); to deliver (judgment); to bring in, return (verdict); (*h*) to reproduce, render, express; **r. le sens de l'auteur,** to render, convey, the author's meaning; **elle rend très bien Chopin,** she plays Chopin very well; (*i*) **le homard me rend malade,** lobster makes me ill; **il se rend ridicule,** he is making himself ridiculous; **vous me rendez fou!** you're driving me mad! **2. se r.** (*a*) **se r. dans un lieu,** to go, make one's way, to a place; **se r. en toute hâte à un endroit,** to hurry to a place; **se r. chez qn,** to call on s.o.; (*b*) to surrender; to give in, to yield; **se r. prisonnier,** to give oneself up; **rendez-vous!** hands up! (*c*) **se r. à la raison,** to yield to reason.

rendu [rɑ̃dy] **1.** *a.* **r. (de fatigue),** exhausted, all in, done in, dead beat. **2.** *n.m.* (*a*) *Art:* rendering (of subject); **r. exact des couleurs,** exact reproduction of colour; (*b*) *Com:* returned article; return.

rendurcir [rɑ̃dyrsir] *v.tr.* to harden, make harder.

rendurcissement [rɑ̃dyrsismɑ̃] *n.m.* hardening.

rêne [rɛn] *n.f. usu. pl.* rein; **fausses rênes,** bearing rein, check rein; **rênes de bride,** bit reins; **rênes de mors,** curb reins; **à bout de rênes,** with reins slack; **lâcher les rênes,** to loosen the reins; to give a horse his head; **tenir les rênes du gouvernement,** to hold the reins of government.

renégat, -ate [rənega, -at] *n.* renegade, turncoat.

renfaîtage [rɑ̃fɛtaʒ] *n.m.* new-ridging (of roof).

renfaîter [rɑ̃fete] *v.tr.* to new-ridge (roof).

renfermé [rɑ̃fɛrme] **1.** *a.* uncommunicative, close (person). **2.** *n.m.* **odeur de r.,** close, fusty, smell; **sentir le r.,** to smell stuffy, musty.

renfermer [rɑ̃fɛrme] **1.** *v.tr.* (*a*) to shut up, lock up, (s.o., sth.) again; (*b*) to shut, lock, up; *El:* **fusible renfermé,** enclosed fuse; (*c*) to contain, comprise, include, enclose; **livre qui renferme des idées nouvelles,** book that contains new ideas; **le genre renferme l'espèce,** the genus includes the species. **2. se r.** (*a*) **se r. en soi-même, dans le silence,** to withdraw into oneself, into silence; (*b*) **se r. dans ses instructions,** to limit, confine, oneself to one's instructions.

renfiler [rɑ̃file] *v.tr.* to rethread, restring, (beads, etc.); *F:* **r. qch. à sa place,** to slip sth. back into place.

renflé [rɑ̃fle] *a.* swollen; *Nau:* bluff-bowed (ship).

renflement [rɑ̃fləmɑ̃] *n.m.* bulge, swell (of pillar, etc.).

renfler [rɑ̃fle] *v.tr. & i.* to swell (out); to enlarge, to (re)inflate; to expand.

renflouage [rɑ̃fluaʒ] *n.m.*, **renflouement** [rɑ̃flumɑ̃] *n.m.* floating off, refloating (of stranded ship).

renflouer [rɑ̃flue] *v.tr.* to float off, refloat (stranded ship); **r. une entreprise,** to set a business on its feet again; **r. qn,** to keep s.o. afloat (financially).

renfoncement [rɑ̃fɔ̃smɑ̃] *n.m.* (*a*) hollow, recess, cavity, dent; **r. d'une porte,** doorway; (*b*) *Geol:* downcast fault; (*c*) *Typ:* indentation (of line).

renfoncer [rɑ̃fɔ̃se] (*conj. like* ENFONCER) **1.** *v.tr.* (*a*) to knock in, drive in; to drive further in; to pull down (one's hat); **r. ses larmes,** to choke back one's tears; (*b*) to recess, set back (façade, etc.); *Typ:* to indent (line). **2. se r.,** to sink in; *Art:* (*of background*) to recede.

renforçage [rɑ̃fɔrsaʒ] *n.m.* **1.** strengthening, reinforcing. **2.** *Phot:* intensification.

renforcement [rɑ̃fɔrsəmɑ̃] *n.m.* (*a*) strengthening, reinforcement, stiffening, bracing, trussing (of beam, etc.); (*b*) intensifying, reinforcing (of sound); *Phot:* intensification.

renforcer [rɑ̃fɔrse] (*conj. like* FORCER) **1.** *v.tr.* (*a*) to reinforce (garrison); to strengthen, reinforce, stiffen, brace (wall, beam); to truss (girder); to back (wall, map); to strengthen (a law); to back up (statement); (*b*) to reinforce, magnify (sound); to intensify (colour, negative). **2.** *v.i.* (*of wind*) to grow stronger. **3. se r.,** to grow stronger, more vigorous; to gather strength.

renfort [rɑ̃fɔr] *n.m.* **1.** reinforcement(s); fresh supply (of troops); **envoyé en r.,** sent up to reinforce; **cheval de r.,** extra horse, trace horse; **à grand r. d'épingles,** using, with (the help of), lots of pins. **2.** reinforcement; strengthening piece; stiffener, backing, lining (of sail); *Join:* tusk (of tenon); **plaque, tôle, de r.,** stiffening plate.

renfrogné [rɑ̃frɔɲe] *a.* frowning (brow, face); sullen, scowling (person); glum (look).

renfrogner (se) [sərɑ̃frɔɲe] *v.pr.* to frown, scowl; to look glum.

rengagé [rɑ̃gaʒe] *a. & n.m. Mil:* re-enlisted (man, N.C.O.).

rengagement [rɑ̃gaʒmɑ̃] *n.m.* re-engagement, rejoining; *Mil:* re-enlistment.

rengager [rɑ̃gaʒe] (*conj. like* ENGAGER) **1.** *v.tr.* to re-engage; to engage (s.o.) again; to renew (combat). **2.** *v.i. & pr. Mil:* **(se) r.,** to re-enlist. **3.** *v.i.* to begin again.

rengaine [rɑ̃gɛn] *n.f.* catchword; catchy tune; **vieille r.,** old refrain; **c'est toujours la même r.,** it's always the same old story.

rengainer [rɑ̃gene] *v.tr.* to sheathe, put up (one's sword); *F:* **r. son compliment,** to shut up, to say no more.

rengorger (se) [sərɑ̃gɔrʒe] *v.pr.* (*conj. like* ENGORGER) (*of bird*) to strut; (*of pers.*) to strut, swagger, throw out one's chest.

rengraisser [rɑ̃grɛse] *v.i.* to grow fat again; to put on weight.

reniement [rənimɑ̃] *n.m.* **1.** disowning (of friend); denial (of Christ); disavowal (of action). **2.** repudiation (of opinions); abjuration (of faith).

renier [rənje] *v.tr.* (*conj. like* NIER) **1.** to disown, renounce (friend); to deny (Christ); to disavow (action). **2.** to repudiate (opinion); to abjure (one's faith).

reniflement [rəniflәmɑ̃] *n.m.* **1.** sniffling, snuffling, snorting. **2.** sniff, snort.

renifler [rənifle] **1.** *v.i.* to sniff, snort, snuffle; **r. sur qch.,** to sniff at, turn up one's nose at, sth.; (*of horse*) **r. sur l'avoine,** to be off his feed. **2.** *v.tr.* to sniff (up) (snuff, etc.); to sniff, smell (flower, etc.); **il sait r. une bonne affaire,** he's got a (good) nose for a bargain.

renifleur, -euse [rəniflœr, -øz] **1.** *n.* sniffler; *a.* **des enfants renifleurs,** sniffing children. **2.** *n.m. I.C.E:* breather (pipe).

renne [rɛn] *n.m.* reindeer.

renom [rənɔ̃] *n.m.* renown, fame; **en r.,** famous, celebrated, well known; **médecin en grand r.,** doctor with a great reputation; **aïeux de grand r.,** famous ancestors.

renommé [rənɔme] *a.* renowned, famous, well-known (**pour,** for).

renommée [rənɔme] *n.f.* **1.** (*a*) renown, fame; good name; reputation; (*b*) reputation; **connaître qn de r.,** to know s.o. by repute. **2.** report; *Jur:* **(preuve par) commune r.,** hearsay evidence.

renommer [rənɔme] *v.tr.* to re-elect, re-appoint.

renonce [rənɔ̃s] *n.f. Cards:* **1.** renounce; inability to follow suit; **avoir une r. à cœur,** to be short of hearts. **2. fausse r.,** revoke; **faire une fausse r.,** to revoke.

renoncement [rənɔ̃smɑ̃] *n.m.* **1.** renouncing, renouncement (**à,** of). **2.** self denial; **vie de r.,** a life of renunciation.

renoncer [rənɔ̃se] (**je renonçai(s); n. renonçons**) **1.** *v.ind.tr.* (*a*) **r. à qch.,** to renounce sth.; **r. à qn,** to drop s.o.; **r. à faire qch.,** (i) to give up, forgo, doing sth.; (ii) to give up, drop, the idea of doing sth., **r. à un droit,** to waive a right; **r. à une réclamation,** to renounce, withdraw, a claim; **r. à la lutte,** to give up the struggle, *F:* to throw up the sponge; **y r.,** to give up; **deux des coureurs ont renoncé,** two of the runners dropped out; (*b*) **r. à sa religion,** to abnegate one's religion; (*c*) *v.i. Cards:* (i) to renounce, to fail to follow suit; (ii) to revoke. **2.** *v.tr.* to renounce, disown, repudiate (s.o.); **r. sa foi,** to renounce, abnegate, one's faith.

renonciation [rənɔ̃sjasjɔ̃] *n.f.* **1.** *Jur:* **r. à un droit,** renunciation, disclaimer, waiver, of a right. **2.** renunciation, abnegation.

renoncule [rənɔ̃kyl] *n.f. Bot:* ranunculus; (wild) buttercup; **r. flottante,** water crowfoot; **fausse r.,** lesser celandine.

renouée [rənwe] *n.f.* polygonum, knot grass.

renouer [rənwe] *v.tr.* (*a*) to tie (up). knot (sth.) again; (*b*) to renew, resume (conversation, etc.); **r. (amitié) avec qn,** to renew one's friendship with s.o.

renouveau [rənuvo] *n.m.* (*a*) springtide; spring (of the year); (*b*) **r. de vie,** new lease of life; **r. religieux, r. des arts,** religious, artistic, revival.

renouveler [rənuvle] (**je renouvelle, n. renouvelons; je renouvellerai**) **1.** *v.tr.* (*a*) to renew, renovate (one's wardrobe, etc.); **r. ses pneus,** to get a new set of tyres; **r. l'air d'une salle,** to air a room; (*b*) to change (method, team, staff) completely; **r. la face du pays,** to alter the whole appearance of the country; to transform the country. **2.** *v.tr.* to renew (promise, alliance, lease, passport); to revive (custom); to renew (acquaintance, a quarrel); **r. le souvenir de qch.,** to refresh one's memory about sth.; *Com:* **r. une commande,** to repeat an order. **3.** *v.i.* (*a*) **la lune vient de r.,** the moon is new; (*b*) **r. de zèle,** to act with renewed zeal. **4. se r.** (*a*) to be renewed; (*b*) to recur, to happen again; **que cela ne se renouvelle pas!** don't let it happen again! (*c*) to change; **il ne se renouvelle pas,** it's always the same with him.

renouvellement [rənuvɛlmɑ̃] *n.m.* **1.** replacement (of stock, equipment); **r. échelonné du matériel,** phasing out of equipment. **2.** reform (of system); improvement. **3.** renewing, renewal (of treaty, lease); increase (of zeal, etc.).

rénovateur, -trice [renɔvatœr, -tris] **1.** *a.* renovating. **2.** *n.* renovator, restorer.

rénovation [renɔvasjɔ̃] *n.f.* **1.** renovation, restoring, restoration (of building). **2.** revival (of religion).

rénover [renɔve] *v.tr.* (*a*) to renovate (building); (*b*) to revive (literary genre).

renseigné [rɑ̃seɲe] *a.* well informed; knowledgeable.

renseignement [rɑ̃sɛɲmɑ̃] *n.m.* (*a*) (piece of) information, intelligence; indication; *Tp: etc:* **renseignements,** inquiries; **donner des renseignements sur qch.,** to give information, particulars, about sth.; **prendre des renseignements sur qch.,** to make inquiries, to inquire, about sth.; **bons renseignements sur qn,** favourable report on s.o.; **embaucher qn sans renseignements,** to engage s.o. without references; **bureau de renseignements,** information bureau, inquiry office; (*b*) **renseignements (techniques),** data; (*c*) *Mil: etc:* **service de r.,** intelligence branch, service, department; **organes de renseignements et de sécurité,** security; **agent de, du, r.,** (intelligence) agent; **exploitation du r.,** processing of information.

renseigner [rɑ̃seɲe] **1.** *v.tr.* **r. qn sur qch.,** to inform s.o., give s.o. information about sth.; **on vous a mal renseigné,** you have been misinformed; **être bien renseigné sur qch.,** to be well informed about sth.; **je vais vous r. sur lui,** I'll tell you something about him. **2. se r. sur qch.,** to get information, find out, about sth.; to inquire, ask, make inquiries, about sth.

rentabiliser [rɑ̃tabilize] *v.tr.* to make (an enterprise) profitable.

rentabilité [rɑ̃tabilite] *n.f.* profitability; economy of operation; **taux de r.,** rate of profitability.

rentable [rɑ̃tabl̥] *a.* profitable; profit-earning; paying; **ce n'est pas r.,** it doesn't pay; **loyer r., peu r.,** economic, uneconomic, rent.

rente [rɑ̃t] *n.f.* **1.** *Pol.Ec:* revenue, rent; **r. foncière,** ground rent. **2.** *usu. pl.* (unearned) income; **vivre de ses rentes,** to live on one's private income. **3.** annuity, pension, allowance; **r. viagère,** life annuity; **faire une r. à qn,** to make an (annual) allowance to s.o.; **on lui a fait une r.,** he has been pensioned off. **4. rentes (sur l'État),** (government) stocks, funds, bonds.

rentier, -ière [rɑ̃tje, -jɛr] *n.* person of independent means, who lives on his (unearned) income; **petit r.,** small investor.

rentoiler [rɑ̃twale] *v.tr.* to remount (map); to put a new canvas to (a painting).

rentrant, -ante [rɑ̃trɑ̃, -ɑ̃t] **1.** *a.* (*a*) *Mth:* **angle r.,** reflex angle; *Phot:* **monture rentrante,** sunk mount; (*b*) *Av:* **train d'atterrissage r.,** retractable undercarriage. **2.** *n. Games:* new player; *Cards:* cutter in.

rentré [rɑ̃tre] **1.** *a.* (*a*) hollow, sunken (cheeks); (*b*) repressed (feelings); suppressed (laughter, rage).

rentrée [rɑ̃tre] *n.f.* **1.** (*a*) return, return home, homecoming; *Space:* **r. atmosphérique,** re-entry into the atmosphere; *Mus:* **r. d'un motif, d'un instrument,** re-entry of a theme, an instrument; (*b*) re-opening (of schools, law courts, theatres); re-assembly (of Parliament); *Sch:* **la r. (des classes),** the beginning of term; *Publ:* **la r. littéraire,** this autumn's new books. **2.** (*a*) taking in, receipt, encashment (of money); **faire des rentrées d'argent,** to get some money in; (*b*) getting in (of crops). **3.** *Fb:* **r. en touche,** throw-in.

rentrer [rɑ̃tre] **I.** *v.i.* (*the aux. is* **être**) **1.** (*a*) to re-enter; to come, go, in again; to return; (*of spacecraft*) to re-enter (the atmosphere); **r. dans sa chambre,** to go back into one's room; **lorsqu'il rentra en France, à Paris,** when he returned to France, to Paris; **r. au port,** to return, put back, to port; **r. dans l'armée,** to rejoin the army; **r. dans les bonnes grâces de qn,** to regain favour with s.o.; **r. dans ses droits,** to recover one's rights; **r. dans ses frais,** to be reimbursed (for one's expenses); **r. en correspondance avec qn,** to resume correspondence with s.o.; **r. dans son bon sens,** to recover one's senses; **r. dans le bon chemin,** to mend one's ways, to turn over a new leaf; (*of actor*) **r. en scène,** to come on again; (*b*) to return home, come home; **il est l'heure de r.,** it's time we went home; **r. dîner,** to go home to dinner, for dinner; **elle rentre de Paris,** she is just home from Paris; (*c*) (*of school, law courts, etc.*) to re-open, to resume; (*of Parliament*) to re-assemble; (*of schoolboy*) to go back to school; (*of actor*) to return to the stage, to make a re-appearance; (*of official*) **r. en fonction(s),** to resume duty; (*d*) (*of thgs*) to go back, go in; **faire r. qch. dans sa boîte,** to put sth. back into its box; (*e*) (*of money, etc.*) to come in; **faire r. ses fonds,** to call in one's money. **2.** (*intensive form of* **entrer**) (*a*) to enter, go in; *Cards:* to cut in; **r. en soi-même,** to retire into oneself, to examine one's conscience; **ils se sont rentrés en plein dedans,** they ran slap (bang) into each other; (*b*) **tubes qui rentrent les uns dans les autres,** tubes that fit into one another; *F:* **les jambes me rentrent dans le corps,** I'm too tired to stand; (*c*) **cela ne rentre pas dans mes fonctions,** that doesn't come within my province, that's not part of my job; **r. dans une catégorie,** to fall into a category; (*d*) *Typ:* **faire r. une ligne,** to indent a line. **II.** *v.tr.* (*aux.* **avoir**) **1.** to take in, bring in, get in, draw in, pull in (sth.); to heave in, haul in (rope); to haul down, strike (the colours); to ship (the oars); to take (anchor) aboard; to haul up (boat); *Av:* to retract, raise (landing gear); **r. la récolte,** to get, gather, in the harvest; **qui va rentrer les chaises?** who's going to carry in the chairs, to take the chairs in? **r. sa chemise,** to tuck in one's shirt; **r. un désir,** to repress a desire. **2.** to take (s.o., sth.) home.

renversant [rɑ̃vɛrsɑ̃] *a. F:* astounding, staggering.

renverse [rɑ̃vɛrs] *n.f.* **1.** shift, turn (of tide, current); change round (of the wind). **2.** *adv. phr.* **tomber à la r.,** (i) to fall backwards, on one's back, head over heels; (ii) to be staggered, bowled over.

renversé [rɑ̃vɛrse] *a.* **1.** inverted, reversed (image, etc.); inverted (arch); **écriture renversée,** backhanded writing; *Cu:* **crème renversée,** custard mould; *F:* **c'est le monde r.!** it's preposterous! what's the world coming to! **2.** overturned, upset; *F:* **il avait le visage r.,** he looked terribly upset.

renversement [rɑ̃vɛrsəmɑ̃] *n.m.* **1.** (*a*) reversal; inversion (of image, proposition, *Mus:* of interval, chord); **r. des valeurs,** inversion of values; **r. de situation,** reversal of a situation; (*b*) turn(ing) (of the tide); shift(ing), backing (of the wind); **r. de la vapeur,** reversing (of engine). **2.** (*a*) turning upside down; overturning, upsetting; **charrette à r.,** tip-up cart; *Mec:* **couple de r.,** torque (reaction); (*b*) overthrow (of regime, etc.).

renverser [rɑ̃vɛrse] **1.** *v.tr.* (*a*) to reverse, invert (image, proposition, *Mus:* interval, chord); **r. les fusils,** to reverse arms; *Navy:* **r. la ligne,** to turn the line; **r. un levier,** to throw over a lever; **r. la marche,** *Mch:* to reverse (the engine); *Aut:* to go into reverse; **r. la vapeur,** (i) to reverse steam; (ii) to go back on one's decision; **r. les rôles,** to turn the tables on s.o.; (*b*) to turn upside down; **ne pas r.,** this side up; (*c*) to knock, throw, (s.o., sth.) over, down; to overturn, upset (pail); to capsize (boat); to spill (liquid); **r. qn d'un coup de poing,** to strike s.o. down; **il fut renversé par une auto,** he was knocked down by a car; *F:* **cela me renverse,** it staggers me; (*d*) to overthrow (regime, etc.). **2.** *v.i.* (*of vehicle*) to overturn, upset; (*of boat*) to capsize; (*of liquid*) to spill; (*of tide*) to turn. **3. se r.,** to fall over, fall down; to upset, overturn; to capsize; **se r. sur sa chaise,** (i) to lean back, loll back, in one's chair; (ii) to tilt one's chair back.

renvoi [rɑ̃vwa] *n.m.* **1.** sending back, return(ing) (of goods, etc.); throwing back (of ball); *Ten:* return; *Cmptr:* feedback. **2.** dismissal (of employee); discharge (of troops); expulsion (of pupil). **3.** putting off, postponement; adjournment. **4.** referring, reference (to committee, etc.); transfer (of case to another court). **5.** *Typ:* reference (mark); cross reference; **r. en marge,** marginal alteration. **6.** *Mec.E:* **r. de mouvement,** counter gear(ing), motion; reverse motion; **r. de commande,** shafting; **levier de r.,** reversing lever; **engrenage de r.,** reversing gear; **poulie de r.,** return pulley. **7. r. de courant,** cross current. **8.** burp, belch; (*of food*) **donner des renvois,** to repeat.

renvoyer [rɑ̃vwaje] *v.tr.* (*conj. like* ENVOYER) **1.** to send (s.o., sth.) back; to return (gift, ball); to throw back, re-echo (sound); to reflect (heat, light); *Cards:* to return (suit). **2.** (*a*) to send, turn, (s.o.) away; *Jur:* to discharge (defendant); **r. des troupes dans leurs foyers,** to dismiss troops; *F:* **r. qn bien loin,** to send s.o. packing; (*b*) to dismiss, *F:* sack (employee); to send down (university student); to expel (pupil from school). **3.** to put off, postpone, defer, adjourn (a matter, debate); *Jur:* **r. le prévenu à une autre audience,** to remand the accused. **4.** to refer (s.o., a matter, to an authority); *Pol:* **r. un projet à une commission,** to send a bill to a committee; **les numéros renvoient (le lecteur) aux notes,** the numbers refer to the notes.

réoccupation [reɔkypasjɔ̃] *n.f.* reoccupation, reoccupying (of territory, etc.).

réoccuper [reɔkype] *v.tr.* to re-occupy; to resume (an office).

réorganisateur, -trice [reɔrganizatœr, -tris] *n.* reorganizer.

réorganisation [reɔrganizasjɔ̃] *n.f.* reorganization; reorganizing; re-arrangement; **r. foncière,** consolidation.

réorganiser [reɔrganize] *v.tr.* to reorganize.

réorienter [reɔrjɑ̃te] *v.tr.* to reorient(ate).

réouverture [reuvɛrtyr] *n.f.* reopening (of theatre); resumption (of proceedings).

repaire [rəpɛr] *n.m.* den (of lions, thieves); lair; nest (of pirates); haunt (of criminals).

repairer [rəpere] *v.tr.* (*of game*) to have gone to earth; to be in cover(t).

repaître [rəpɛtr̥] (*pr.p.* **repaissant;** *p.p.* **repu;** *pr.ind.* **je repais, n. repaissons;** *pr.sub.* **je repaisse**) **1.** *v.tr.* (*a*) to feed (animals); (*b*) **r. ses yeux de qch.,** to feast one's eyes on sth. **2. se r.** (*a*) (*of animal*) to eat it's fill; (*b*) **se r. de sang,** to wallow in blood; **se r. de chimères,** to indulge in vain imaginings.

répandre [repɑ̃dr̥] **1.** *v.tr.* (*a*) to pour out; to spill (salt, wine); to drop; to shed (tears, blood); (*b*) to spread, diffuse, scatter; to shed (light); to give off, give out (heat, scent); to strew (flowers); to sprinkle (sand); **r. du sable sur le plancher,** to sprinkle the floor with sand; **r. la terreur,** to spread terror; **cette nouvelle répandit la tristesse dans la ville,** this news cast a gloom over the town; **r. une nouvelle,** to spread, circulate, broadcast, a piece of news; (*c*) to lavish (benefits, etc.). **2. se r.** (*a*) **se r. dans le monde,** to lead a social life; **il faut vous r.,** you should go about more; **se r. en explications,** to launch forth into explanations; **se r. en excuses,** to apologize profusely; to be full of apologies; **se r. sur un sujet,** to spread oneself on a subject; (*b*) (*of liquid*) to spill; to run out; to run over; (*of smell, panic, rumour*) to spread; **les touristes se répandent dans la ville,** tourists are invading, overrunning, the town; **cette opinion se répand,** this opinion is gaining ground, is spreading; **la nouvelle s'est répandue peu à peu,** the news spread gradually; **l'usage de cet article s'est répandu,** this article is now widely used.

répandu [repɑ̃dy] *a.* **1.** widespread, prevalent, in general use; widely-read (magazine); widely-held (opinion). **2.** (*of pers.*) widely known, much in evidence; **il est très r. dans les milieux politiques,** he is well known in political circles.

réparable [reparabl̥] *a.* (*a*) repairable, mendable; (*b*) reparable (mistake, loss).

reparaître [rəparɛtr̥] *v.i.* (*conj. like* PARAÎTRE; *aux. usu.* **avoir**) to reappear; (*of disease*) to recur.

réparateur, -trice [reparatœr, -tris] **1.** *a.* repairing, restoring; refreshing (sleep). **2.** *a.* repairer, mender.

réparation [reparasjɔ̃] *n.f.* **1.** repair(ing) (of house, machine); mending (of clothes); restoring, restoration (of one's strength); **réparations d'entretien,** maintenance; **être en r.,** to be under repair; **route en r.,** road up for repairs; **faire des réparations,** to make repairs. **2.** reparation, amends, redress; *A:* satisfaction (by duel); **en r. d'un tort,** in reparation of, in atonement for, a wrong; **réparations de guerre,** war reparations; *Jur:* **r. légale,** legal redress; **r. civile,** compensation; *Fb:* **coup de pied de r.,** penalty kick.

réparer [repare] *v.tr.* **1.** to repair, mend (shoe, machine); to overhaul (machine); to refit (ship); **r. ses forces,** to restore one's strength; **r. le désordre,** to put things in order; **r. ses pertes,** to retrieve, make good, one's losses; **la maison a besoin d'être réparée,** the house is in need of repair. **2.** to make atonement, amends, for (misdeed); to rectify (mistake), to put (mistake) right; to make good, rectify (omission); to redress (wrong); to make good (damage).

reparler [rəparle] *v.i.* **r. de qch.,** to speak about sth. again; **il ne faut plus en r.,** it must not be mentioned again; **r. à qn,** to speak to s.o. again; to be on speaking terms with s.o. again.

repartager [rəpartaʒe] *v.tr.* (*conj. like* PARTAGER) to share out, divide, again.

repartie [rəparti] *n.f.* repartee; retort, rejoinder; **avoir l'esprit de r., avoir la r. prompte,** to be quick at repartee.

repartir [rəpartir] *v.i.* (*conj. like* PARTIR) **1.** (*aux.* **être**) to set out, start off, again; **je repars pour Paris,** I'm off to Paris again; **r. à zéro,** to start from scratch again; to go back to square one; **r. à rire,** to burst out laughing again. **2.** (*aux.* **avoir**) to retort, reply.

répartir [repartir] *v.tr.* **(je répartis, n. répartissons) 1.** to distribute, divide, share out (**entre,** among); **r. un dividende,** to distribute a dividend; **versements répartis sur plusieurs années,** payments spread over several years; **charge uniformément répartie,** evenly distributed load; *Dressm:* **r. le surplus du col,** to ease the collar (on to the neckband). **2.** to apportion; to assess (taxes), to allot, allocate (shares); *M.Ins:* **r. une avarie,** to adjust an average.

répartiteur [repartitœr] *n.m.* distributer, divider, apportioner; *M.Ins:* adjuster (of average); **(commissaire) r.,** assessor of taxes.

répartition [repartisjɔ̃] *n.f.* **1.** (manner of) distribution; **r. de la population par groupes d'âge,** breakdown of the population by age groups. **2.** (*a*) distribution; dividing up, sharing out **(entre plusieurs personnes,** between several people); apportionment, allocation (of expenses, liabilities, etc.); assessment (of taxes); *M.Ins:* **r. d'avarie,** adjustment of average; (*b*) (i) allotment (of shares); **(lettre d')avis de r.,** letter of allotment; (ii) dividend, distribution; **première et unique r.,** first and final dividend; **dernière r.,** final dividend.

repas [rəpɑ] *n.m.* meal; feed, feeding (of animal); **r. de noce** = wedding breakfast; **faire un r.,** to have a meal; **léger r., petit r.,** light meal; snack; quick lunch; **aux heures de r.,** at meal times; **prendre ses r. chez qn,** to board with s.o.

repassage [rəpasaʒ] *n.m.* **1.** sharpening, whetting, grinding; stropping (of razor). **2.** ironing (of clothes); **n'exigeant aucun r.,** non-iron.

repasser [rəpase] **1.** *v.i.* (*aux. usu.* **être**) (*a*) to repass; to pass (by) again, go by again, come by again; **r. chez qn,** to call on s.o. again; **une idée me repasse dans l'esprit,** an idea keeps running through my mind; *F:* **vous repasserez!** you've got another think coming! (*b*) *Cmptr:* to rerun; *Rec:* **faites r. la dernière phrase,** play back the last sentence. **2.** *v.tr.* (*a*) to repass; to pass by, pass over, cross (over), again; **r. la mer,** to cross the sea again; (*b*) to go over, look over, say over (again); to replay, play back (tape, record); **r. qch. dans son esprit,** to go over sth. in one's mind; **r. une leçon, un rôle,** to look over, go over, a lesson, a part; (*c*) to take, convey, pass, over again; **le batelier nous repassera,** the boatman will ferry us back; **r. un plat à qn,** to pass s.o. a dish again; **r. une fausse pièce à qn,** to palm off, foist, unload, a dud coin on s.o.; (*d*) to sharpen, whet, grind (knife, tool); to set (razor); **r. un rasoir sur le cuir,** to strop a razor; (*e*) to iron (clothes); **fer à r.,** (flat, laundry) iron; **planche à r.,** ironing board.

repasseur, -euse [rəpasœr, -øz] *n.* **1.** *n.m.* (knife) grinder. **2.** *n.f.* **repasseuse,** (i) ironer; (ii) ironing machine.

repavage [rəpavaʒ] *n.m.*, **repavement** [rəpavmɑ̃] *n.m.* repaving.

repaver [rəpave] *v.tr.* to repave.

repayer [rəpeje] *v.tr.* (*conj. like* PAYER) to pay again.

repêchage [rəpɛʃaʒ] *n.m.* (*a*) fishing up (again), fishing out (again); picking up (of torpedo, etc.); (*b*) helping, rescuing (s.o. in difficulties); **épreuve de r.,** (i) *Sch:* supplementary examination (for candidates who have failed); (ii) *Sp:* repêchage; extra heat (for runners-up).

repêcher [rəpeʃe] *v.tr.* (*a*) to fish (sth.) up, out, (again); (*b*) to rescue; to help out (s.o. in difficulties); **r. un noyé,** to save a drowning man; *Sch:* **r. un candidat à l'oral,** to let a candidate scrape through at the oral; **ceux qui ont échoué au mois de juillet peuvent se r. en octobre,** those who failed in July may sit the exam again in October.

repeindre [rəpɛ̃dr̥] *v.tr.* (*conj. like* PEINDRE) **1.** to repaint; to paint again. **2. se r. un événement passé,** to recall to mind, to revisualize, a past event.

repeint [rəpɛ̃] *n.m. Art:* touching-up.

repenser [rəpɑ̃se] **1.** *v.i.* to think again (**à,** of, about); **j'y repenserai,** I shall think it over; **je n'y ai pas re-**

pensé, I did not give it another thought. **2.** *v.tr.* to reconsider (a problem).

repentant [rəpɑ̃tɑ̃] *a.* repentant.

repenti, -ie [rəpɑ̃ti] *a. & n.* repentant; **(fille) repentie,** reformed prostitute.

repentir[1] **(se)** [sərəpɑ̃tir] *v.pr.* (*pr.p.* **se repentant;** *p.p.* **repenti;** *pr.ind.* **je me repens, il se repent;** *pr.sub.* **je me repente;** *p.h.* **je me repentis**) **se r. de qch., d'avoir fait qch.,** to repent, be sorry for, sth., having done sth.

repentir[2] *n.m.* repentance; remorse.

repérage [rəperaʒ] *n.m.* **1.** (*a*) marking with guide marks, reference marks; **numéros de r.,** key numbers (on a squared map); (*b*) adjusting, fixing, setting (of instrument) by guide marks; lining up; *Typ:* **bon r.,** good lay, register. **2.** (*a*) locating (of fault, target, etc.); *F:* spotting (of enemy aircraft, etc.); **r. radio,** radio location, radio fix; (*b*) *Artil:* ranging, registration.

repercer [rəpɛrse] *v.tr.* (*conj. like* PERCER) to pierce (metal).

répercussion [repɛrkysjɔ̃] *n.f.* (*a*) repercussion; backlash (of an explosion); reverberation (of sound); (*b*) impact; consequential effects (of an action).

répercuter [repɛrkyte] **1.** *v.tr.* (*a*) to reverberate, reflect back (sound); to reflect (light, heat); (*b*) to pass on (an order, a price increase). **2. se r.,** to have repercussions, to react (**sur,** on).

reperdre [rəpɛrdr̥] *v.tr.* to lose again.

repère [rəpɛr] *n.m.* (*a*) reference (to datum line); *Surv:* **ligne de r.,** datum line; (*b*) reference mark, guide mark (on instrument); marker; *Surv:* bench mark; *Mec.E:* **r. de montage, d'ajustage,** assembly mark, line-up mark; (*c*) **point de r.,** landmark; **les points de r. dans la vie,** the landmarks in one's life.

repérer [rəpere] **(je repère, n. repérons; je repérerai) 1.** *v.tr.* (*a*) to mark (instrument) with guide marks, reference marks; (*b*) to adjust, fix, set, (instrument) by guide marks; *Typ:* to register (impression); (*c*) to locate (fault, target, etc.); to identify, *F:* spot (aircraft); **r. qn dans la foule,** to spot s.o., pick s.o. out, in the crowd; *Turf:* **r. les gagnants,** to pick the winners; **se faire r.,** to attract attention. **2. se r.,** to get one's bearings; to find one's way about (in a town); **je n'arrive pas à me r. dans ce problème,** I can't make head or tail of this problem.

répertoire [repɛrtwar] *n.m.* **1.** index, table, list, catalogue; **r. à onglets,** thumb index; **r. d'adresses,** (i) directory; (ii) address book. **2.** repertory, repository (of information, etc.). **3.** *Th:* repertoire, repertory; **pièce de, du, r.,** stock piece; **il a un r. de trois discours,** he has three stock speeches.

répertorier [repɛrtɔrje] *v.tr.* (*impf. & pr.sub.* **n. répertoriions**), to index, list (item).

repeser [rəpəze] *v.tr.* (*conj. like* PESER) to reweigh.

répéter [repete] **(je répète, n. répétons; je répéterai) 1.** *v.tr.* (*a*) to repeat (words, secret); to say or do (sth.) (over) again; **des assauts répétés,** charge after charge; **je ne me le ferai pas r.,** I shall not need to be told twice; (*b*) to rehearse (play); to learn (part, lesson). **2. se r.,** (*of pers.*) to repeat oneself; (*of event, etc.*) to recur, to happen again.

répétiteur, -trice [repetitœr, -tris] *a. & n.* **1.** (*a*) *Sch: A:* assistant in charge of preparation, etc.; (*b*) private tutor, coach. **2.** *n.m.* (*a*) *Navy:* (signal) repeater; (*b*) *Nau: Av:* indicator.

répétitif, -ive [repetitif, -iv] *a.* repetitive.

répétition [repetisjɔ̃] *n.f.* **1.** repetition; **fusil à r.,** repeating rifle; **montre à r.,** repeater (watch). **2.** *Sch:* private lesson. **3.** (band, choir) practice; rehearsal (of play); **r. générale, en costume,** dress rehearsal; **mettre une pièce en r.,** to put a play into rehearsal.

repeuplement [rəpœpləmɑ̃] *n.m.* repeopling, repopulation (of country); restocking (of pond); *For:* replanting.

repeupler [rəpœple] *v.tr.* to repeople, repopulate (country); to restock (pond); to replant (forest); **la ville se repeuple,** the population of the town is increasing again.

repincer [rəpɛ̃se] *v.tr.* (*conj. like* PINCER) *F:* **on ne m'y repincera pas,** you won't catch me at it again.

repiquage [rəpikaʒ] *n.m.* **1.** pricking, piercing, again. **2.** mending, repairing (of road). **3.** pricking out, planting out (of seedlings). **4.** *Bac:* sub(-)culture. **5.** *Rec:* (re)recording.

repiquer [rəpike] **1.** *v.tr.* (*a*) to prick, pierce, (sth.) again; (*b*) to mend, repair (road); (*c*) *Needlew:* to restitch; (*d*) to prick out, plant out (seedlings); **plant à r.,** bedding plant; (*e*) to dress (millstone); (*f*) *Bac:* to sub(-)culture; (*g*) *Rec:* to re-record. **2.** *v.i. F:* **r. au plat,** to have a second helping; **r. au truc,** to begin again, to start (all over) again.

répit [repi] *n.m.* respite; breathing space; **jours de r.,** days of grace; **laisser un moment de r. à qn,** to give s.o. a breather; **prendre un moment de r.,** to break off from work; **travailler sans r.,** to work without a break; **souffrir sans r.,** to have no respite from pain.

replacement [rəplasmɑ̃] *n.m.* **1.** (*a*) replacement, replacing; putting back (of sth.) in its proper place; (*b*) reinvestment (of funds). **2. r. de qn,** finding a new job for s.o.

replacer [rəplase] *v.tr.* (*conj. like* PLACER) **1.** (*a*) to replace; to put (sth.) back in its place; (*b*) to reinvest (funds). **2.** to find fresh employment for (s.o.); **se r.,** to find a new job.

replanter [rəplɑ̃te] *v.tr.* to replant.

replat [rəpla] *n.m. Mount:* shelf.

replâtrage [rəplɑtraʒ] *n.m.* **1.** (*a*) replastering; (*b*) patching up. **2.** (*a*) superficial repair; (*b*) patched-up peace.

replâtrer [rəplɑtre] *v.tr.* **1.** to replaster (wall). **2.** to patch up, tinker up (sth. unsound); to patch up (quarrel).

replet, -ète [rəplɛ, -ɛt] *a.* stoutish, podgy, dumpy (person).

réplétion [replesjɔ̃] *n.f.* (*a*) repletion; (*b*) surfeit (of food).

repli [rəpli] *n.m.* **1.** fold, crease, turn (in cloth); **replis du terrain,** folds in the ground; **les plis et les replis du cœur,** the innermost recesses of the heart. **2.** winding, bend, meander (of river); coil (of rope, snake). **3.** *Mil:* falling back, withdrawal.

repliable [rəplijabl̥] *a.* that may be folded (up, back); *Av:* folding (wings).

repliement [rəplimɑ̃] *n.f.* **1.** folding up, back. **2.** *Mil:* falling back, withdrawal. **3.** (*of pers.*) withdrawal; withdrawing (into one's shell).

replier [rəplije] (*conj. like* PLIER) **1.** *v.tr.* (*a*) to fold, turn, up (again); to coil up; to bend back; to turn in, tuck in (edge); (*of bird*) to fold (wings); (*of cat*) to draw in (claws); (*b*) to withdraw, pull back (troops). **2. se r.,** (*a*) (*of thg*) to fold up, back; (*of snake*) to coil up; (*b*) (*of stream, path*) to wind, turn, twist, bend; (*of stream*) to meander; (*c*) **se r. sur soi-même,** to retire within oneself; (*d*) (*of troops*) to fall back, retire, withdraw.

réplique [replik] *n.f.* **1.** (*a*) retort, rejoinder; **avoir la r. prompte,** to be ready with an answer; **preuve qui ne souffre aucune r.,** incontrovertible proof; **argument sans r.,** unanswerable argument; **obéir sans r.,** to obey without a word; *F:* **et pas de r.!** don't answer (me) back! (*b*) *Th:* cue; **manquer sa r.,** to miss one's cue; **donner la r. à un acteur,** (i) to give an actor his cue; (ii) to play opposite an actor. **2.** replica; counterpart.

répliquer [replike] **1.** *v.tr.* **r. qch. à qn,** to say sth. in answer to s.o.; **"pas de danger!" répliqua-t-il,** "not likely!" he retorted. **2.** *v.i.* to retort; **r. à qn,** to answer s.o. back.

replissage [rəplisaʒ] *n.m.* re-pleating.

replisser [rəplise] *v.tr.* to re-pleat (skirt).

replonger [rəplɔ̃ʒe] (*conj. like* PLONGER) **1.** *v.tr.* to plunge, dip, immerse (sth.) again; **se r. dans l'étude,** to become immersed again in study. **2.** *v.i.* to dive (in) again.

repolir [rəpɔlir] *v.tr.* to repolish; to reburnish (metal); to rub up (spoon); *Fig:* to polish up (one's style).

répondant [repɔ̃dɑ̃] *n.m.* **1.** server (at mass). **2.** surety, security, referee, reference, guarantor.

répondeur, -euse [repɔ̃dœr, -øz] **1.** *a.* given to answering back; cheeky (child). **2.** *n.m.* (*a*) **r. téléphonique,** answering service; **r. enregistreur,** automatic message recorder; (*b*) *Telecom:* responder.

répondre [repɔ̃dr̥] **1.** *v.tr.* to answer, reply, respond; (*a*) **r. la messe,** to make the responses at Mass; (*b*) **r. qch.,** to say sth. in reply; **je n'ai rien répondu,** I made no reply, gave no answer; **il répondit n'en rien savoir,** he answered that he knew nothing about it. **2.** *v.ind.tr.* (*a*) **r. à qn, qch.,** to answer, reply to, s.o., sth.; to return, acknowledge (greeting); to answer (accusation); to comply with, fall in with (request); **r. à une lettre,** to answer a letter; **r. par écrit,** to reply in writing, to write back; **r. à l'appel,** to answer the roll, to one's name; **r. à un coup de sonnette,** to answer the bell; **r. à l'amour de qn,** to respond to, return, s.o.'s love; **le moteur n'a pas répondu,** there was no response from the engine; (*b*) **r. à qch.,** to answer, meet (requirements, purpose); to come up to (standard, expectations); to comply, agree, with (formula); **ne pas r. à l'attente,** to fall short of expectation. **3.** *v.i.* **r. de qn, qch.,** to answer for s.o., sth.; to be answerable, accountable, responsible, for s.o., sth.; **il va revenir, je vous en réponds,** he will come back, I assure you, take my word for it; **j'en répondrais,** I'd take my oath on it.

réponse [repɔ̃s] *n.f.* **1.** (*a*) answer, reply; **avoir, trouver, r. à tout,** to have, find, an answer for everything; never to be at a loss for an answer; **rendre r. à qn,** to return s.o. an answer, to reply to s.o.; **argument sans r.,** unanswerable argument; **pour toute r., elle éclata en sanglots,** her only answer was to break into sobs; **en r. à votre lettre,** in answer, reply, to your letter; **lettre restée sans r.,** letter left unanswered; *Post:* **r. payée,** reply paid; *Jur:* **droit de r.,** right to reply (in the press); (*b*) response (to an appeal). **2.** (*a*) *Physiol:* responsiveness, response (to stimulus); (*b*) response (of engine, etc.); (*c*) *Cmptr:* answering; **r. automatique,** unattended answering.

repopulation [rəpɔpylasjɔ̃] *n.f.* repopulation, repopulating; restocking (of river, etc.).

report [rəpɔr] *n.m.* **1.** *Book-k:* (*a*) carrying forward, bringing forward; (*b*) amount carried forward; carry forward, carry over; (*c*) posting (of journal entries). **2.** *St.Exch:* contango(ing), continuation; **prendre des actions en r.,** to take in stock; **(taux de) r.,** contango (rate), continuation rate. **3.** *Phot: Lith:* transfer; **papier (à) r.,** transfer paper. **4.** *Typ:* lines carried over. **5.** *Rad:* plot(ting); **table de r.,** plotting board. **6.** *Cmptr:* carry. **7.** *Turf:* (*betting*) double.

reportage [rəpɔrtaʒ] *n.m. Journ:* **1.** reporting. **2.** (newspaper) report; **r. en exclusivité,** scoop. **3.** set of articles (on a topical subject). **4.** *W.Tel:* running commentary (on a match, etc.).

reporter¹ [rəpɔrte] **1.** *v.tr.* (*a*) to carry back; to take (sth.) back; **r. un livre à qn,** to take a book back to s.o.; (*b*) to take, carry, (s.o.) back (in thought, time); to trace back (origins); (*c*) **r. qch. à plus tard,** to postpone, defer, sth. until later, to a later date; (*d*) *Book-k:* (i) to carry forward, bring forward, carry over (total); (ii) to post (journal entry); **à r.,** carried forward; (*e*) *St.Exch:* to contango; to carry over; **(faire) r. des titres,** to take in, borrow, carry, stock; (*f*) *Lith: Phot:* to transfer. **2.** **se r.** (*a*) **se r. à un document,** to refer, turn, to a document; **se r. à . . .,** the reader is referred to . . .; see . . .; (*b*) **se r. au passé,** to look back to the past.

reporter² [rəpɔrtɛr] *n.m. Journ:* reporter; **r. photographe,** press photographer.

repos [rəpo] *n.m.* **1.** (*a*) rest, repose; **au r., en r.,** at rest; in repose; **se tenir au r., en r.,** to keep quiet, still; **se donner, prendre, du r.,** to take a rest; **le r. éternel,** eternal rest, the last sleep; **terre au r.,** fallow land; *Mil:* **repos!** stand at ease! (*b*) *Tchn:* **au r.,** (*rifle*) at halfcock; (*mechanism*) in neutral position; (*machine*) out of gear; *Tp:* **contact r.-travail,** make-and-break contact; (*c*) pause, rest (in a verse). **2.** peace, tranquillity (of mind); **être en r. au sujet de qn,** to feel easy in one's mind about s.o.; **laisser qn en r.,** to leave s.o. alone, in peace; **de tout r.,** absolutely safe, reliable; **valeur de tout r.,** safe investment, gilt-edged security.

reposant [rəpozɑ̃] *a.* restful; refreshing (sleep).

reposé [rəpoze] *a.* **1.** rested, refreshed; **s'éveiller bien r.,** to awake refreshed. **2.** sedate, quiet, calm; **à tête reposée,** deliberately, coolly; **laissez-moi y réfléchir à tête reposée,** give me time to think it over.

repose-fer [rəpozfɛr] *n.m.* iron(ing) stand; *pl. repose-fers.*

repose-pied [rəpozpje] *n.m.inv.* foot rest (of motor cycle, chair).

reposer [rəpoze] **1.** *v.tr.* (*a*) to put, place, lay, set (sth.) back (in its place); to replace (sth.); *Mil:* **reposez arme!** order arms! (*b*) to re-lay (railway line); (*c*) to rest; **r. sa tête sur un coussin,** to rest one's head on a cushion; **r. l'esprit,** to rest, refresh, the mind; **couleur qui repose les yeux,** colour that is restful to the eyes; (*d*) to restate (problem), to ask (question) again. **2.** *v.i.* to lie, rest; (*a*) **le corps reposait sur son lit de parade,** the body was lying in state; **ici repose . . .,** here lies (buried) . . .; (*b*) to be built (on rock, etc.); **le commerce repose sur le crédit,** commerce is based on credit. **3.** **se r.** (*a*) to rest, to take a rest; to relax; **faire r. ses chevaux,** to rest one's horses; **laisser r. la terre,** to let the ground rest, lie fallow; (*b*) **se r. sur qn, qch.,** to rely upon, put one's trust in, s.o., sth.; **se r. sur qn du soin de qch.,** to rely upon s.o. to look after sth.; (*c*) (*of liquid*) to settle.

repose-tête [rəpoztɛt] *n.m.inv. Aut:* headrest.

reposoir [rəpozwar] *n.m.* wayside altar; temporary altar.

repoussage [rəpusaʒ] *n.m.* chasing, embossing, repoussé work.

repoussant [rəpusɑ̃] *a.* repulsive, repellent (appearance); offensive (smell).

repousse [rəpus] *n.f.* **1.** growing again. **2.** fresh growth.

repoussé [rəpuse] **1.** *a.* chased, embossed, repoussé; **cuivre r.,** spun copper. **2.** *n.m.* chasing, embossing, repoussé.

repoussement [rəpusmɑ̃] *n.m.* recoil, kick (of firearm).

repousser [rəpuse] **1.** *v.tr.* (*a*) to push back, push away, drive off, thrust aside; to repel, beat off (attack); to reject, turn down (offer, proposal); **repoussé de tout le monde,** spurned by all; **r. un projet de loi,** to throw out a bill; (*b*) to postpone (event); (*c*) to be repellent to (s.o.); to repel; (*d*) to emboss (leather); to chase (metal); to work (metal) in repoussé. **2.** *v.i.* (*of tree, plant*) to shoot (up) again, spring (up) again, sprout again; (*of hair*) to grow again.

repoussoir [rəpuswar] *n.m.* **1.** (*a*) *Tls:* drift (bolt); (*b*) embossing punch; (*c*) *Toil:* cuticle pen. **2.** (*a*) *Art:* strong piece of foreground; (*b*) **servir de r. à la beauté de qn,** to set off, serve as a foil to, s.o.'s beauty.

répréhensible [repreɑ̃sibl̥] *a.* reprehensible.

répréhensiblement [repreɑ̃sibləmɑ̃] *adv.* reprehensibly.

répréhensif, -ive [repreɑ̃sif, -iv] *a.* reprehensive.

répréhension [repreɑ̃sjɔ̃] *n.f.* reprehension.

reprendre [rəprɑ̃dr̥] (*conj. like* PRENDRE) **1.** *v.tr.* (*a*) to retake, recapture (town, escaped prisoner); (*b*) **r. du pain,** to take, have, some more bread; (*c*) to take, get, pick up, (sth.) again; **je suis allé r. mon parapluie,** I went to recover my umbrella; **r. sa place,** to resume one's seat; **r. connaissance,** to recover consciousness; to come to; **je vous reprendrai en passant,** I'll pick you up again as I go by; (*d*) **la fièvre l'a repris,** he has had another bout of fever; **sa timidité l'a repris,** his shyness got the better of him again; *F:* **on ne m'y reprendra plus,** I shan't be had, caught, another time; **que je ne vous y reprenne plus!** don't let me catch you at it again! (*e*) to take back (gift, unsold goods); to re-engage (employee); to retract (promise); to go back on (one's word); (*f*) to resume, take up again (conversation, habits, work); **reprenons les faits,** let us recapitulate (the facts); **r. l'affaire à son origine,** to go back to the beginning; **r. du goût pour qch.,** to recover one's taste for sth.; **r. la route,** to take the road again; **r. une pièce,** to revive a play; **r. des forces,** to regain strength; **r. courage,** to take courage again; **r. la parole,** to resume, go on; **oui, reprit-il,** yes, he replied; (*g*) to repair, mend; **r. un mur en sous-œuvre,** to underpin a wall; (*h*) to reprove, reprimand (**de,** for); to find fault with (s.o., sth.); **r. qn aigrement,** to take s.o. up sharply. **2.** *v.i.* (*a*) to recommence; (*of fashion*) to return, be revived; (*of patient, business*) to recover, pick up again; **le froid a repris,** the cold weather has set in again; (*b*) (*of plant*) to take root again; to strike (root). **3. se r.** (*a*) to recover, to pull oneself together; **donnez-moi le temps de me r.,** give me time to collect myself, my thoughts; (*b*) to correct oneself (in speaking); (*c*) **se r. à espérer,** to begin to hope again; **se r. à la vie,** to take a new lease of life; (*d*) **s'y r. à plusieurs fois pour faire qch.,** to make several attempts, have several goes at sth. (before succeeding).

représailles [rəprezaj] *n.f.pl.* reprisals, retaliation; **en r. pour, de, qch.,** as a reprisal for sth.; **expédition de r.,** punitive expedition.

représentant, -ante [rəprezɑ̃tɑ̃, -ɑ̃t] *n.* (*a*) representative; *U.S:* **la Chambre des représentants,** the House of Representatives; (*b*) *Com:* (i) agent; (ii) representative, *F:* rep; (*c*) *Jur:* representative (heir).

représentatif, -ive [rəprezɑ̃tatif, -iv] *a.* (*a*) representative; (*b*) *F:* (*of pers.*) dignified, impressive.

représentation [rəprezɑ̃tasjɔ̃] *n.f.* **1.** (*a*) *Pol: Jur: etc:* representation; *Pol:* **r. proportionnelle,** proportional representation; (*b*) agency; **r. exclusive d'une maison,** sole agency for a firm; (*c*) *Psy:* **faculté de la r. spatiale,** space perception. **2.** *Jur:* production (of documents, etc.). **3.** *Th:* performance (of a play); **troupe en r.,** company on tour; **droits de r.,** performing rights. **4.** dignity (of state official); **frais de r.,** entertainment allowance; *F:* **être en r.,** to be trying to impress. **5. faire des représentations à qn,** to remonstrate with s.o.

représenter [rəprezɑ̃te] *v.tr.* **1.** to present (sth.) again. **2.** *Jur:* to produce (documents). **3.** to represent; (*a*) **tableau représentant un moulin,** picture representing a mill; **représentez-vous mon étonnement,** just imagine my astonishment; **r. qn comme un imposteur,** to represent s.o. as an impostor; **se r. comme officier,** to describe oneself as an officer; **il me représente son père,** he puts me in mind of his father; (*b*) to stand for, act for (s.o.); **se faire r.,** to appoint, send, a representative; **r. une circonscription,** to represent, sit for, a constituency; **r. une maison de commerce,** to represent, be the agent(s) for, a firm; **r. qn en justice,** to appear for s.o.; (*c*) to correspond to, account for, represent (an amount); **ceci représente de nombreuses heures de travail,** this represents many working hours; **cela ne représente pas une grosse somme, beaucoup, pour lui,** this does not mean much to him. **4.** *Th:* (*a*) to perform, act, produce, give (a play); to put on (a play); (*b*) to act (part); to take the part of (Hamlet). **5. r. qch. à qn,** to represent, point out, sth. to s.o. **6.** *v.i.* (*a*) to have a good presence; **il ne représente pas au physique,** he's not very impressive physically; (*b*) to live up to one's official position; to make a show. **7. se r.** (*a*) **se r. à un examen,** to resit an exam; (*b*) (*of opportunity*) to occur again, to recur.

répressif, -ive [represif, -iv] *a.* repressive (law).

répression [represjɔ̃] *n.f.* repression.

réprimandable [reprimɑ̃dabl̥] *a.* deserving reproof, censure; blameworthy.

réprimande [reprimɑ̃d] *n.f.* reprimand, reproof; **faire une r. à qn,** to reprimand s.o., *F:* to tell s.o. off.

réprimander [reprimɑ̃de] *v.tr.* to reprimand, reprove; to take (s.o.) to task, *F:* to tell (s.o.) off.

réprimer [reprime] *v.tr.* to suppress, repress; (*a*) to check, curb (desire, etc.); to strangle (sneeze); (*b*) to quell, put down (revolt).

repris [rəpri] *n.m.* **r. de justice,** habitual criminal, old offender.

reprisage [rəprizaʒ] *n.m.* darning; mending.

reprise [rəpriz] *n.f.* **1.** (*a*) retaking, recapture, recovery (of position, etc.); (*b*) **r. des invendus,** taking back of unsold goods; *Jur:* **droit de r.,** right to recover possession; (*c*) taking over (of fittings, etc. with house); (*d*) trade-in (allowance). **2.** (*a*) resumption (of work); renewal (of negotiations); return (of fashion); *Th:* revival (of play); *Cin:* rerun (of film); *T.V:* repeat; *Cmptr:* rerun; (*b*) renewal (of activity); new spell (of cold weather); fresh bout (of fever); **r. des affaires,** recovery, revival, of business; **mouvement de r.,** upward movement; (*c*) *I.C.E:* **r. (de vitesse),** pick-up, acceleration (of engine); (*d*) *Box:* round; *Fenc:* bout; *Fb:* second half (of game); (*e*) **faire qch. à plusieurs reprises,** to do sth. several times, repeatedly, on several occasions; **à trois reprises,** three times (over, running); (*f*) *Mus:* (i) repeat; (ii) re-entry (of theme). **3.** (*a*) *Needlew:* (i) darning; mending; (ii) darn; **r. perdue,** invisible mend; (*b*) *Const:* **r. en sous-œuvre,** underpinning.

repriser [rəprize] *v.tr.* to mend, darn; **boule, œuf, à r.,** darning ball, egg; mushroom.

réprobateur, -trice [reprɔbatœr, -tris] *a.* reproachful; reproving.

réprobation [reprɔbasjɔ̃] *n.f.* reprobation; (severe) disapproval.

reproche [rəprɔʃ] *n.m.* **1.** reproach; **faire des reproches à qn,** to reproach, censure, upbraid, s.o.; **je ne vous fais pas de reproches,** I am not blaming you; **ton de r.,** reproachful, reproving, tone; **vie sans r.,** blameless life. **2.** *Jur:* **r. de témoin,** objection to witness.

reprocher [rəprɔʃe] *v.tr.* **1.** to reproach; **r. ses fautes à qn,** to reproach s.o. for his faults; **on lui reproche la moindre peccadille,** he is taken to task for the merest trifle; **r. qn d'avoir fait qch.,** to reproach, blame, s.o. for doing sth.; **qu'est-ce que vous reprochez à ce livre?** what do you find wrong with this book? **2. r. son aide à qn,** to help s.o. grudgingly. **3.** *Jur:* to object to (witness, evidence).

reproducteur, -trice [rəprɔdyktœr, -tris] **1.** *a.* (*a*) reproductive (organ, etc.); (*b*) (animal) kept for breeding; stud (horse). **2.** *n.m.* animal kept for breeding; *pl.* breeding stock; **r. d'élite,** pedigree sire.

reproductif, -ive [rəprɔdyktif, -iv] *a.* reproductive.

reproduction [rəprɔdyksjɔ̃] *n.f.* **1.** (*a*) reproduction; **les organes de la r.,** the reproductive organs; **animaux élevés en vue de la r.,** breeding stock; **r. sexuée, asexuée,** sexual, asexual, reproduction; (*b*) reproduction, reproducing; duplicating (of documents, etc.); *Publ:* **droits de r.,** reproduction rights; **droits de r. en feuilleton,** serial rights. **2.** copy, reproduction.

reproductivité [rəprɔdyktivite] *n.f.* reproductiveness.

reproduire [rəprɔdɥir] (*conj. like* PRODUIRE) **1.** *v.tr.* to reproduce (sound, etc.); to copy, make a copy of (picture, etc.); *Journ:* to reprint (article). **2.** **se r.** (*a*) to reproduce, breed, multiply; (*b*) (*of events*) to recur, happen again.

reprographie [rəprɔgrafi] *n.f.* duplicating (of documents).

réprouvé, -ée [repruve] *n.* outcast; reprobate.

réprouver [repruve] *v.tr.* **1.** to condemn (crime); to disapprove of (s.o., sth.). **2.** *Theol:* to damn.

reps [rɛps] *n.m. Tex:* rep(p).

reptile [rɛptil] *a. & n.m.* reptile.

repu [rəpy] *a.* satiated, full; **être r. de qch.,** to have had one's fill of sth.

républicain, -aine [repyblikɛ̃, -ɛn] *a. & n.* republican.

républicanisme [repyblikanism] *n.m.* republicanism.

république [repyblik] *n.f.* (*a*) republic; *F:* **on est en r.,** it's a free country; (*b*) commonwealth, community; **la r. des lettres,** the world of letters.

répudiation [repydjasjɔ̃] *n.f.* **1.** repudiation (of wife, doctrine, debt). **2.** *Jur:* renunciation (of succession); relinquishment.

répudier [repydje] *v.tr.* (*impf. & pr.sub.* **n. répudiions**) **1.** to repudiate (wife, opinion). **2.** *Jur:* to renounce, relinquish (succession).

répugnance [repyɲɑ̃s] *n.f.* **1.** repugnance; (*a*) dislike (**pour, à,** of, for); aversion (**pour, à,** to, from, for); (*b*) loathing (**pour, à,** of, for). **2.** **r. à faire qch.,** reluctance to do sth.; **avec r.,** reluctantly, unwillingly.

répugnant [repyɲɑ̃] *a.* repugnant, loathsome, offensive; disgusting.

répugner [repyɲe] *v.i.* **1.** **r. à qch., à faire qch.,** to feel repugnance to, to revolt at, sth., doing sth.; to be lo(a)th to do sth. **2.** **r. à qn,** to be repugnant, distasteful, to s.o.; *impers.* **il me répugne de le faire,** I am reluctant, lo(a)th, to do it; I loathe doing it.

répulsif, -ive [repylsif, -iv] *a.* repulsive.

répulsion [repylsjɔ̃] *n.f.* (*a*) *Ph:* repulsion; (*b*) **éprouver de la r. pour qn,** to feel repulsion, an aversion, for s.o.; to be repelled by s.o.

réputation [repytasjɔ̃] *n.f.* reputation; good or bad name; character; **jouir d'une bonne r.,** to have a good reputation, name; to be well spoken of; **cela a fait sa r.,** it made his name; **sa r. de chirurgien,** his reputation as a surgeon; **connaître qn de r.,** to know s.o. by reputation, by repute; **il a (une) mauvaise r.,** he has a bad reputation, a bad character; **maison de mauvaise r.,** disreputable house.

réputé [repyte] *a.* well-known, famous (expert, inn); highly esteemed (wine); **r. pour qch.,** well known, with a good reputation, for sth.

réputer [repyte] *v.tr.* to consider, think, deem; **il est réputé ne rien ignorer de cette science,** he is reputed to know everything about this science.

requérant, -ante [rəkerɑ̃, -ɑ̃t] *Jur:* **1.** *a.* **partie requérante,** applicant, claimant. **2.** *n.* plaintiff, petitioner, applicant.

requérir [rəkerir] *v.tr.* (*conj. like* ACQUÉRIR) **1.** to solicit, seek (favour); to request (s.o.'s presence). **2.** (*a*) to demand, claim (assistance); **opération qui requiert des mains habiles,** operation that requires, calls for, skilled hands; (*b*) to conscript (civilians); (*c*) *Jur:* (*of prosecution*) to demand, call for (sentence).

requête [rəkɛt] *n.f.* request, suit, petition; **adresser une r. à qn,** to petition s.o.; **à, sur, la r. de qn,** at s.o.'s request; *Jur:* **r. en cassation,** appeal.

requiem [rekɥi(j)ɛm] *n.m.* requiem; **messe de r.,** requiem (mass).

requin [rəkɛ̃] *n.m.* **1.** *Ich:* shark; **peau de r.,** shagreen. **2.** *F:* shark, swindler.

requinquer [rəkɛ̃ke] *v.tr. F:* **1.** to buck (s.o.) up. **2.** **se r.,** to recover, pick up, perk up.

requis [rəki] **1.** *a.* required, requisite, necessary. **2.** *n.m.* labour conscript.

réquisition [rekizisjɔ̃] *n.f.* **1.** (*a*) requisitioning; commandeering; **r. civile,** conscription for a public service; **mettre en r.,** to requisition, to levy; (*b*) requisition, demand; **agir sur, à, la r. de qn,** to act on s.o.'s requisition. **2.** *Jur:* prosecution address.

réquisitionner [rekizisjɔne] *v.tr.* to requisition; to commandeer (provisions, etc.); to conscript (manpower).

réquisitoire [rekizitwar] *n.m. Jur:* (Public Prosecutor's) charge, indictment.

rescapé, -ée [rɛskape] *a. & n.* (person) rescued; survivor (of disaster, shipwreck, etc.).

rescinder [resɛ̃de] *v.tr.* to rescind, annul.

rescision [resizjɔ̃] *n.f. Jur:* rescission, annulment.

rescousse [rɛskus] *n.f.* **aller, venir, à la r. de qn,** to go, come, to the rescue of s.o.

rescrit [rɛskri] *n.m.* rescript.

réseau, -eaux [rezo] *n.m.* **1.** (*a*) netting, network (for lace); *Arch:* tracery; *Anat:* plexus (of nerves); *Biol:* (nuclear) meshwork; *Opt:* diffraction grating; *Atom. Ph:* lattice (of reactor); *Mil:* **r. de barbelés,** barbed wire entanglement. **2.** (*a*) network, system (of roads, railways, rivers, etc.); *W.Tel: T.V:* network; *El:* **r. national,** national grid system; **r. de distribution urbain,** town mains; *Tp:* **r. urbain,** local area, network; **r. interurbain,** trunk circuit; (*b*) **r. d'espionnage,** spy ring, network; **r. de résistance,** resistance network.

réséda [rezeda] *n.m.* (*a*) *Bot:* **r. odorant,** mignonette; (*b*) reseda (green).

réservation [rezɛrvasjɔ̃] *n.f.* (*a*) reservation, reserving; **r. faite de tous mes droits,** without prejudice to my rights; (*b*) (hotel, etc.) reservation.

réserve [rezɛrv] *n.f.* **1.** (*a*) reserve, reservation; **faire des réserves,** to make reserves, reservations; **apporter une r. à un contrat,** to enter a reservation in respect of an agreement; **à la réserve de . . .,** except for . . .; **sous (la) r. de qch.,** subject to, contingent on, sth.; *Jur:* **sous r.,** without prejudice; **sous toutes réserves,** without committing oneself; **sans r.,** without reservation; unreservedly; **éloges sans r.,** unqualified praise; receipt; (*b*) reserve; reticence; caution; **se tenir, demeurer, sur la r.,** to refuse to commit oneself; **être sur la r.,** to be on one's guard; **quand il sort de sa r.,** when he breaks through his reserve. **2.** (*a*) reserve (of provisions, troops, equipment); **réserves mondiales,** world reserves (of oil, etc.); **réserves bancaires,** bank reserves; **puiser dans les réserves,** to draw on the reserves; (*b*) **r. de l'armée active,** reserve of the regular army; **officier de r.,** officer of the Reserve; (*c*) *Jur:* **r. légale,** legal share (of inheritance); **en r.,** in reserve; **mettre qch. en r.,** to reserve sth.; to put sth. by; **tenir qch. en r.,** to keep sth. in reserve, in store; **fonds de r.,** reserve fund; **vivres de r.,** reserve, emergency, rations; iron rations; **pièces de r.,** spare parts; **machine de r.,** standby engine. **3.** (*a*) (forest, nature) reserve; (game) preserve; *NAm:* **réserves (indiennes),** (Indian) reservation; (*b*) store(-house, -room); (*library, etc.*) stack room, storeroom, reserve. **4.** *Engr: Dy:* resist.

réservé [rezɛrve] *a.* reserved; (*a*) guarded, cautious; (*b*) shy; reticent.

réserver [rezɛrve] *v.tr.* (*a*) to reserve; to set (sth.) aside; to put, lay, (sth.) by; to save (sth.) up; to keep (sth.) back; to keep (sth.) in store; **r. une place à qn,** to keep, save, a seat for s.o.; **r. des places,** to book seats; **place réservée,** reserved seat; **r. du bois pour l'hiver,** to store wood for the winter; **se r. un droit,** to reserve oneself a right; **tous droits réservés,** all rights reserved; **je me réserve,** I shall wait and see; I'll bide my time; *R.C.Ch:* **cas réservé,** reserved sin; *Jur:* **biens réservés de la femme mariée,** married woman's separate estate; *P.N:* **pêche réservée,** private fishing; *Adm:* **quartier réservé,** red-light district; (*b*) to set apart, put aside, earmark (money for a purpose).

réserviste [rezɛrvist] *n.m. Mil:* reservist.

réservoir [rezɛrvwar] *n.m.* **1.** (*a*) reservoir; **r. de barrage,** storage basin; (*b*) fish pond, tank. **2.** (*a*) tank, holder, container; **r. à gaz,** gas holder, gasometer; **r. à minerai,** ore bin, bunker; **r. à mazout,** fuel-oil tank; (*b*) *Mec.E:* tank, reservoir, drum; cistern, well (of pump); **r. à graisse,** grease box; *I.C.E:* **r. d'essence,** petrol tank.

résidant [rezidɑ̃] *a.* resident.

résidence [rezidɑ̃s] *n.f.* residence; (*a*) residing; **lieu de r.,** place of residence; **en r. surveillée,** under house arrest; (*b*) home; **r. secondaire,** second(ary) home, weekend cottage; **changer de r.,** to change one's residence; to move; (*c*) block of luxury flats.

résident, -ente [rezidɑ̃, -ɑ̃t] *n.* **1.** *Dipl:* resident; **ministre r.,** minister resident. **2.** (*alien*) resident.

résidentiel, -elle [rezidɑ̃sjɛl] *a.* residential.

résider [rezide] *v.i.* **1.** to reside, live (**à, dans,** at, in); **les chanoines ne résidaient pas,** the canons were non-resident. **2. toute la difficulté réside en ceci,** all the difficulty rests, lies, consists, in this.

résidu [rezidy] *n.m.* **1.** residue, residuum; **résidus urbains,** town refuse; **résidus de fission,** radioactive waste. **2.** *Mth:* residue (of a function).

résiduaire [rezidɥɛr] *a.* waste; *Ind:* **eaux résiduaires,** waste water, process water.

résiduel, -elle [rezidɥɛl] *a.* residual; *Physiol:* **air r.,** supplemental air (in the lungs).

résignation [reziɲasjɔ̃] *n.f.* resignation. **1.** submissiveness; **avec r.,** resignedly. **2.** giving up (of an office).

résigné, -ée [reziɲe] *a.* resigned (**à,** to); submissive.

résigner [reziɲe] **1.** *v.tr.* to resign, give up (position, possessions); **r. sa charge, ses fonctions,** to give up, relinquish, one's appointment; to resign; **r. le pouvoir,** to lay down office. **2. se r. à qch.,** to resign oneself, to submit, to sth.

résiliable [reziljabl̥] *a.* annullable, cancellable.

résiliation [reziljasjɔ̃] *n.f.* cancellation, annulment, termination (of contract).

résilience [reziljɑ̃s] *n.f. Mec:* resilience, impact strength.

résilient [reziljɑ̃] *a.* resilient.

résilier [rezilje] *v.tr.* to annul, cancel, terminate (agreement).

résille [rezij] *n.f.* **1.** hairnet. **2.** cames, lattice (of window).

résine [rezin] *n.f.* resin.

résiné [rezine] *a. & n.m.* **(vin) r.,** retsina.

résiner [rezine] *v.tr.* **1.** to resin, dip in resin. **2.** to tap (tree) for resin.

résineux, -euse [rezinø, -øz] *a.* resinous; **forêt résineuse,** coniferous forest.

résistance [rezistɑ̃s] *n.f.* resistance. **1.** (*a*) opposition (**à,** to); **n'offrir aucune r.,** to offer, make, no resistance; *Hist:* **la Résistance,** the Resistance (movement); (*b*) **r. à la maladie, à la contagion,** resistance to disease, to contagion; (*c*) **r. de l'air,** resistance of the air; air friction; **r. à l'avancement,** drag; (*d*) *El:* **unité de r.,** unit of resistance; ohm; **boîte de résistances,** resistance box; **r. à curseur,** rheostat. **2.** (*a*) strength, toughness (of materials); **r. à la flexion,** bending strength; **r. à la traction,** tensile strength; **r. au choc,** impact resistance; **limite de la r.,** yield point; **acier à haute r.,** high-resistance, high-tensile, steel; **tissu qui n'a pas de r.,** flimsy material; (*b*) resistance, staying power, stamina, endurance; (*c*) **pièce de r.,** (i) *Cu:* main course, dish; (ii) principal feature, item (of entertainment, etc.).

résistant, -ante [rezistɑ̃, -ɑ̃t] **1.** *a.* (*a*) resistant (medium); strong, stout (material); tough (wood); fast (colour); **r. à l'acide,** acid-proof; **r. à la chaleur,** heatproof; **r. au choc,** shockproof; **r. (à l'usure),** strong, hard-wearing; *Hort:* **r. au froid,** frost-hardy; (*b*) (*of pers.*) strong, tough; (*c*) *Pol: etc:* rebellious. **2.** *n.* (*a*) *Pol: etc:* rebel; (*b*) *Hist:* member of the Resistance movement.

résister [reziste] *v.ind.tr.* to resist; (*a*) **r. à qn, à la justice,** to resist, offer resistance to, s.o., the law; **r. à faire qch.,** to show resistance to do sth.; (*b*) **r. à (qch.),** to resist (temptation); to hold out against (attack); to bear (up against), to withstand (pain); to stand up to (ill treatment, etc.); (*c*) **ces couleurs ne résistent pas,** these colours are not fast.

résolu [rezɔly] *a.* resolute, determined (person).

résoluble [rezɔlybl̥] *a.* **1.** solvable, resoluble (problem). **2.** *Jur:* annullable, terminable (contract).

résolument [rezɔlymɑ̃] *adv.* resolutely, determinedly.

résolution [rezɔlysjɔ̃] *n.f.* **1.** (*a*) resolution (of substance, dissonance); solution (of problem); (*b*) *Jur:* termination (of agreement); cancelling, cancellation (of sale). **2.** resolution; (*a*) resolve; **prendre la r. de faire qch.,** to resolve, determine, to do sth.; (*b*) resoluteness, determination, strength of will; (*c*) **prendre une r.,** to pass a resolution.

résonance [rezɔnɑ̃s] *n.f.* (*a*) resonance; *Mus:* **caisse de r.,** sound box; (*b*) *Fig:* response, echo; (*c*) repercussion.

résonateur [rezɔnatœr] *n.m. Ac: El:* resonator.

résonnant [rezɔnɑ̃] *a.* resounding, resonant, sonorous.

résonner [rezɔne] *v.i.* to resound, re-echo, resonate, reverberate; (*of metal*) to ring, clang, clank; (*of bell*) to ring; (*of string*) to twang; **l'air résonnait de leurs cris,** the air rang with their cries.

résorber [rezɔrbe] *v.tr.* to resorb, reabsorb; to absorb, reduce (surplus); **r. la crise économique,** to solve the economic crisis from within.

résorption [rezɔrpsjɔ̃] *n.f.* absorption; reduction (of surplus); *Med:* resorption.

résoudre [rezudr̥] (*pr.p.* **résolvant;** *p.p.* **résolu,** *occ.* **résous, -oute;** *pr.ind.* **je résous, il résout, n. résolvons;** *impf.* **je résolvais;** *p.h.* **je résolus;** *fu.* **je résoudrai**) **1.** *v.tr.* (*a*) **r. qch. en qch.,** to resolve, break up, sth. into sth.; (*b*) to annul, cancel, terminate, rescind (contract, etc.); (*c*) to resolve, clear up (difficulty); to solve (equation, problem); to work out (problem); to settle (question); *Mus:* **r. une dissonance,** to resolve a discord; (*d*) **r. qn à faire qch.,** to induce, persuade, prevail upon, s.o. to do sth.; (*e*) **r. qch.,** to decide on, determine on, sth.; **r. de partir,** to decide to go. **2.** (*a*) **se r. en qch.,** to resolve, dissolve, into sth.; (*b*) **se r. à faire qch.,** to resolve, make up one's mind, to do sth.

respect [rɛspɛ] *n.m.* respect, regard; **avoir le r. des lois,** to respect, have regard for, the law; **parler avec r.,** to speak respectfully; **r. de soi,** self-respect; **r. humain** [rɛspɛkymɛ̃], deference to public opinion; common decency; **faire qch. par r. pour qn,** to do sth. out of respect for s.o.; **manquer de r. envers qn,** to be disrespectful to s.o.; **tenir qn en r.,** (i) to keep s.o. at a respectful distance; (ii) to keep s.o. in awe; **sauf le r. que je vous dois, sauf votre r.,** with all due respect, with all due deference (to you); **rendre ses respects à qn,** to pay one's respects to s.o.

respectabilité [rɛspɛktabilite] *n.f.* respectability.

respectable [rɛspɛktabl̩] *a.* **1.** respectable, worthy of respect. **2.** respectable, fairly large; **un nombre r. de spectateurs,** a respectable, fair, number of spectators.

respectablement [rɛspɛktabləmɑ̃] *adv.* respectably.

respecter [rɛspɛkte] *v.tr.* to respect, have regard for (sth., s.o.); **r. la loi,** to abide by the law; **faire r. la loi,** to enforce the law; **se faire r.,** to command respect; **le feu ne respecta rien,** the fire spared nothing; **un homme qui se respecte,** any self-respecting man; **il se respecte trop pour faire cela,** he's above doing that.

respectif, -ive [rɛspɛktif, -iv] *a.* respective.

respectivement [rɛspɛktivmɑ̃] *adv.* respectively.

respectueusement [rɛspɛktɥøzmɑ̃] *adv.* respectfully.

respectueux, -euse [rɛspɛktɥø, -øz] *a.* respectful; **r. des lois,** respectful of the law; law-abiding; **être r. des opinions d'autrui,** to show respect for the opinions of others; **se tenir à distance respectueuse,** to keep at a safe, respectful, distance; *Corr:* **veuillez agréer mes sentiments r.,** yours sincerely.

respirateur [respiratœr] *n.m.* respirator.

respiration [respirasjɔ̃] *n.f.* respiration, breathing; **r. artificielle,** artificial respiration; **couper la r. à qn,** (i) to wind s.o.; to hit, catch, s.o. in the wind; (ii) to take s.o.'s breath away, to flabbergast s.o.

respiratoire [rɛspiratwar] *a.* respiratory (organ, etc.); breathing (apparatus, exercise); **casque r.,** (fireman's) smoke helmet.

respirer [rɛspire] **1.** *v.i.* to breathe; **r. longuement,** to draw a long breath; **laissez-moi r.,** let me get my breath; **je n'ai pas respiré de la journée,** I haven't had time to breathe all day. **2.** *v.tr.* (*a*) to breathe in, inhale; **aller r. un peu d'air,** to go for a breather; (*b*) **r. la vengeance,** to breathe (out, forth) vengeance; **ici tout respire la paix,** here everything breathes peace.

resplendir [rɛsplɑ̃dir] *v.i.* to be resplendent, to shine, to glitter.

resplendissant [rɛsplɑ̃disɑ̃] *a.* resplendent, shining; glittering; **visage r. de santé,** face glowing, aglow, with health.

responsabilité [rɛspɔ̃sabilite] *n.f.* responsibility; accountability, liability (**de,** for); **r. de l'employeur,** employer's liability; **accepter une r.,** to assume, accept, a responsibility; **j'ai la r. de l'entretien de la maison,** I am responsible for the upkeep of the house; **faire qch. sous sa (propre) r.,** to do sth. on one's own responsibility; **r. civile,** civil liability.

responsable [rɛspɔ̃sabl̩] **1.** *a.* responsible, accountable, answerable (**de qch.,** for sth.); **r. pour ses enfants,** answerable for one's children; **le ministre est r. devant, envers, les Chambres,** the Minister is responsible to Parliament; **rendre qn r. d'un malheur,** to blame s.o. for a misfortune; **être r. du dommage,** to be liable for the damage. **2.** *n.* (*a*) person responsible (**de,** for); culprit; (*b*) person in charge.

resquillage [rɛskijaʒ] *n.m.*, **resquille** [rɛskij] *n.f.* *F:* sneaking in (to theatre, etc.) without paying.

resquiller [rɛskije] **1.** *v.tr.* *F:* to get (seat at theatre) without paying. **2.** *v.i.* to avoid paying for (sth.).

resquilleur, -euse [rɛskijœr, -øz] *n.* *F:* (*a*) cheat (who has not paid for ticket, etc.); (*b*) queue jumper.

ressac [rəsak] *n.m.* **1.** undertow. **2.** surf.

ressaisir [rəsezir] **1.** *v.tr.* to recapture (sth.); to recover possession of (sth.); **la peur l'a ressaisi,** fear gripped him again. **2. se r.** (*a*) to regain one's self-control; to pull oneself together; (*b*) to recover one's balance (after stumbling).

ressasser [rəsɑse] *v.tr.* to turn (sth.) over in one's mind; **r. la même histoire,** to hark back to the same old story; **plaisanterie ressassée,** chestnut.

ressaut [rəso] *n.m.* **1.** (*a*) *Arch:* projection; *Mec.E:* swell, lug; *Geol:* rock step; **faire r.,** to project; (*b*) sharp rise, bump (in the ground) **2.** (*a*) *Equit:* rise (in the saddle); (*b*) bounce (of vehicle); **les sauts et ressauts de la conversation,** sudden changes in conversation.

ressauter [rəsote] **1.** *v.i.* (*a*) to start, jump (with fear, etc.); (*b*) to jump back. **2.** *v.tr.* to jump (over) again.

ressemblance [rəsɑ̃blɑ̃s] *n.f.* resemblance, likeness; **avoir, offrir, de la r. avec qn, à, avec, qch.,** to bear, show, a resemblance to s.o., to sth; to be like sth.

ressemblant [rəsɑ̃blɑ̃] *a.* like, alike; **portrait bien r.,** good likeness; **peu r.,** unlike.

ressembler [rəsɑ̃ble] **1.** *v.ind.tr.* **r. à qn, à qch.,** to resemble, to be like, to look like, sound like, s.o., sth.; *F:* **cela ne ressemble à rien,** (i) it's like nothing on earth; (ii) it just doesn't make sense; **cela ne lui ressemble pas de se plaindre,** it's not like him to complain. **2. se r.,** to be (a)like; **ils se ressemblent comme deux gouttes d'eau,** they are as like as two peas (in a pod).

ressemeler [rəsəmle] *v.tr.* (*conj. like* SEMELER) to resole (shoes).

ressentiment [rəsɑ̃timɑ̃] *n.m.* resentment (**de,** at; **contre,** against); **avec r.,** resentfully.

ressentir [rəsɑ̃tir] (*conj. like* SENTIR) **1.** *v.tr.* (*a*) to feel (pain, emotion); **r. de l'affection pour qn,** to be fond of s.o.; **r. vivement la perte de qn,** to feel deeply, to be deeply affected by, the loss of s.o.; (*b*) to resent (an injury); (*c*) to feel, experience (shock, etc.). **2. se r. d'un accident,** to feel the effects of an accident; *F:* **s'en r. pour qch.,** to feel fit for, up to, sth.

resserre [rəsɛr] *n.f.* (*a*) tool shed; (*b*) store room; (*c*) **r. à légumes,** vegetable rack.

resserré [rəsere] *a.* narrow, confined, cramped, shut in.

resserrement [rəsɛrmɑ̃] *n.m.* **1.** contraction, tightening, narrowing; constriction. **2.** tightness, scarceness (of money); **r. du crédit,** credit squeeze.

resserrer [rəsere] **1.** *v.tr.* (*a*) to contract, restrain, confine, narrow, constrict, pinch; **r. un récit,** to condense, compress, a story; (*b*) to tie (up) again; to draw (sth.) tighter, closer; to tighten. **2. se r.** (*a*) to contract, shrink; to become closer, narrower, tighter; (*b*) to draw closer together.

resservir [rəsɛrvir] (*conj. like* SERVIR) **1.** *v.tr.* to serve again; **r. un plat,** to serve up a dish again; **resservez-vous,** have some more, another helping. **2.** *v.i.* to be used again.

ressort [rəsɔr] *n.m.* **1.** (*a*) elasticity, springiness; **faire r.,** to be elastic, springy; to spring back, fly back; **avoir du r.,** to be resilient, buoyant; (*b*) spring; **r. de sommier,** bed spring; **r. de montre,** watch spring; **r. à boudin, en spirale,** coil spring, spiral spring; **r. à feuilles, à lames,** leaf, laminated, spring; **r. moteur, grand r.,** mainspring; **actionné, mû, par r.,** spring-driven, -loaded; **commutateur à r.,** snap switch; **verrou à r.,** spring bolt; **suspendu à ressort(s),** sprung (cart, etc.); **sans ressort(s),** unsprung; *F:* **faire jouer**

tous les ressorts, to pull all the strings; **l'intérêt est un puissant r.,** self-interest is a powerful motive. **2.** *Jur:* (*a*) province, scope, competence; (extent of) jurisdiction; **être du r. de la cour,** to be within the competence of the court; **cela n'est pas de son r.,** that does not fall within his province; that's not in his line; (*b*) **en dernier r.,** without appeal; *F:* in the last resort.

ressortir [rəsɔrtir] *v.i.* (*conj. like* SORTIR, *except in* **3**) **1.** (*aux.* **être**) to come, go, out again. **2.** (*aux. usu.* **être**) (*a*) to stand out (in relief); to be evident; **faire r. des couleurs,** to bring out, set off, colours, **faire r. un fait,** to dwell on, emphasize, accentuate, lay stress on, a fact; **faire r. le sens de qch.,** to bring out the meaning of sth.; (*b*) to result, follow, appear, be deduced (**de,** from); **le prix moyen ressort à vingt francs,** the average price works out at twenty francs. **3.** (*aux.* **avoir**) (*pr.p.* **ressortissant;** *pr.ind.* **il ressortit;** *impf.* **il ressortissait**) (*a*) **r. à qn, à qch.,** to be under the jurisdiction of s.o., sth., **ces affaires ressortissent au tribunal d'instance,** these cases belong to, come before, a magistrate's court; (*b*) **concepts qui ressortissent à la géométrie,** concepts that come under the heading of geometry.

ressortissant, -ante [rəsɔrtisɑ̃, -ɑ̃t] **1.** *a.* under the jurisdiction (**à,** of). **2.** *n.* **les ressortissants d'un pays,** the nationals of a country.

ressouder [rəsude] **1.** *v.tr.* to resolder; to reweld. **2.** (*of bone*) **se r.,** to knit again, join again.

ressource [rəsurs] *n.f.* resource. **1.** (*a*) resourcefulness; **personne de r.,** resourceful person; (*b*) **ruiné sans r.,** irretrievably, irremediably, ruined; **sans r. et sans espoir,** helpless and hopeless. **2.** expedient, shift; **avoir mille ressources,** to be very resourceful; **il me reste encore une r.,** I have still one string to my bow; **je n'avais d'autre r. que la fuite,** there was no course open to me but flight; **en dernière r.,** in the last resort. **3.** *pl.* resources, means; **être à bout de ressources,** to be at the end of one's resources; **ressources personnelles,** private means. **4.** *Av:* flattening out, pull-out (from dive).

ressouvenir (se) [sərəsuvnir] *v.pr.* (*conj. like* VENIR) **se r. de qch.,** to remember sth. (from long ago); to recollect sth.; **faire r., qn de qch.,** to remind s.o. of sth.

ressusciter [resysite] **1.** *v.tr.* (*a*) to resuscitate; to restore to life; to raise (the dead); **ce vin me ressuscite,** this wine is putting new life into me; (*b*) to revive (quarrel, fashion). **2.** *v.i.* to resuscitate, revive, come to life again; **ressuscité d'entre les morts,** risen from the dead.

restant, -ante [rɛstɑ̃, -ɑ̃t] **1.** *a.* (*a*) remaining, left; (*b*) **poste restante,** poste restante, *U.S:* general delivery. **2.** *n.* remaining person, person left behind; **il est le seul r. de sa famille,** he is the only one of his family left. **3.** *n.m.* remainder, rest; remains (of meal); *Com:* **r. d'un compte,** balance of an account.

restaurant [rɛstɔrɑ̃] *n.m.* restaurant; **manger au r.,** to eat out; **r. libre-service,** cafeteria; **r. universitaire,** university canteen; **r. routier** = transport café.

restaurateur, -trice [rɛstɔratœr, -tris] *n.* **1.** restorer (of buildings, pictures). **2.** restaurateur; proprietor, manager, of a restaurant.

restauration [rɛstɔrasjɔ̃] *n.f.* **1.** restoration (of building, statue, dynasty); restoring, re-establishment (of discipline, etc.). **2.** (*a*) catering; (*b*) *Sw.Fr:* restaurant.

restaurer [rɛstɔre] **1.** *v.tr.* (*a*) to restore (building, dynasty, health); **r. la discipline, l'autorité,** to re-establish discipline, authority; (*b*) to refresh (s.o.) **2.** **se r.** (*a*) to take some refreshment; (*b*) to build oneself up (after illness).

reste [rɛst] *n.m.* **1.** rest, remainder, remains; *Mth:* remainder; **le r. de la vie,** the rest, remainder, of one's life; **avoir un r. d'espoir,** to have still some hope left; **elle a de beaux restes,** she still has traces of beauty; **jouir de son r.,** to make the most of what is left, of one's remaining time; **ne pas demander son r.,** to have had enough of it; **je ferai le r.,** I shall do the rest; **et le r.,** and everything else; and so on; and so forth; **payer le r. par acomptes,** to pay the balance in instalments; **être en r.,** (i) to be indebted, in arrears; (ii) to be backward, behindhand; **de r.,** (to) spare; left (over); over and above; **quand j'ai du temps de r.,** when I have some spare time, time to spare; **avoir de l'argent de r.,** to have more than enough money; **du r., au r.,** besides, moreover. **2.** *pl.* (*a*) remnants, remains, leavings, scraps (of a meal, etc.); leftovers; (*b*) **restes mortels,** mortal remains; (*c*) remnant (of an army).

rester [rɛste] *v.i.* (*aux.* **être**) **1.** to remain, to be left; **les cinq francs qui restent,** the remaining five francs; **il me reste cinq francs,** I have five francs left; **il ne me reste qu'à vous remercier,** it only remains for me to thank you; **(il) reste à savoir s'il a raison,** it remains to be seen whether he's right; **dix-neuf divisé par cinq, je pose 3, reste 4,** nineteen divided by five makes 3, and 4 over. **2.** (*a*) to remain; to stay; **il est resté à travailler,** he stayed behind to work; **les mots lui restèrent dans la gorge,** the words stuck in his throat; **il restait là à me regarder,** he remained, sat, stood, there looking at me; **restez où vous êtes,** keep, stay, where you are; **r. assis,** to remain sitting; **r. (à) dîner,** to stay to dinner; **r. en route,** to stop on the way; *F:* to get stuck; to come to a full stop; **r. sur place,** to stay where one is, *F:* to stay put; *F:* **j'y suis, j'y reste,** here I am and here I stay; **y r.,** to peg out, to die; **en r. là,** to proceed no further; **où en sommes-nous restés (de notre lecture, etc.)?** where did we leave off? **la chose en resta là,** there the matter rested, remained; **que cela reste entre nous,** this is strictly between ourselves; (*b*) **r. tranquille, calme,** to stay still; to remain calm; **r. en bonne santé,** to remain, keep, in good health; **r. bien avec qn,** to remain, keep, on good terms with s.o.; (*c*) to last, endure; **cela restera,** it will last; it's here to stay. **3.** to stay (in hotel, etc.).

restituable [rɛstitɥabl̩] *a.* returnable, repayable.

restituer [rɛstitɥe] *v.tr.* **1.** to restore (inscription, text). **2.** to restore, to make restitution of (sth.); to hand (sth.) back; to return, refund (money). **3.** to release (energy); to reproduce (sound).

restitution [rɛstitysjɔ̃] *n.f.* **1.** restoration (of text, ancient monument). **2.** restitution.

restreindre [rɛstrɛ̃dr̩] **1.** *v.tr.* (*pr.p.* **restreignant;** *p.p.* **restreint;** *pr.ind.* **je restreins, il restreint, n. restreignons;** *p.h.* **je restreignis;** *fu.* **je restreindrai**) to restrict, to curb; to cut down (production); to limit (authority); **r. les dépenses,** to restrict, curtail, expenses; **offre restreinte aux abonnés,** offer limited to subscribers. **2.** **se r.,** to cut down expenses.

restreint [rɛstrɛ̃] *a.* restricted; confined (space); narrow (limits); **dans un sens r.,** in a restricted, limited, qualified, sense; **édition à tirage r.,** limited edition.

restrictif, -ive [rɛstriktif, -iv] *a.* restrictive (term, clause).

restriction [rɛstriksjɔ̃] *n.f.* restriction; limitation; **r. mentale,** mental reservation; **apporter des restrictions à la consommation,** to place restrictions on consumption; **sans r.,** unreservedly.

restructurer [rəstryktyre] *v.tr.* to restructure.

résultant, -ante [rezyltɑ̃, -ɑ̃t] **1.** *a.* resultant; resulting (**de,** from). **2.** *n.f.* **résultante,** consequence, result; resultant.

résultat [rezylta] *n.m.* result (of calculation); result, outcome (of action, investigation, etc.); result, effect (of disease, treatment); *pl.* **résultats,** results (of examination, contest); **sans r.,** without result; inconclusive (experiment); ineffective (remedy); **résultats de l'exercice, de l'exploitation,** trading results; **ces révélations eurent pour r. la chute du Ministère,** these revelations led to, resulted in, the fall of the Government; **donner des résultats,** to yield results.

résulter [rezylte] *v.i.* (*used only in the third pers. & pr.p.; aux. usu.* **être**) to result, follow, arise (**de,** from); **qu'en est-il résulté?** what was the result of it? what came of it? what was the outcome?

résumé [rezyme] *n.m.* summary, abstract, résumé, abridgement; *Jur:* **r. des débats,** summing up; **au r., en r.,** in short, to sum up, in brief.

résumer [rezyme] *v.tr.* to summarize; to give a summary of (sth.); to sum up (an argument); *Jur:* **r. les débats,** to sum up; **pour r. les faits, pour me r.,** to sum up; **voilà toute l'affaire résumée en un mot,** that's the whole thing in a nutshell; **voilà à quoi tout cela se résume,** that's what it all amounts to, *F:* boils down to.

resurgir [rəsyrʒir] *v.i.* to re-appear; to rise up again (above the water).

resurrection [rezyrɛksjɔ̃] *n.f.* **1.** resurrection. **2.** revival (of the arts, etc.).

retable [rətabl̥], **rétable** [retabl̥] *n.m.* retable, reredos, altar piece.

rétablir [retablir] **1.** *v.tr.* to re-establish, restore, set up again; (*a*) to restore (order, communications); to retrieve (one's reputation); **r. sa santé,** to recover one's health; **r. un malade,** to restore a patient to health; (*b*) **r. les faits,** to set the facts in their true light; (*c*) to reinstate (official); **r. un officier dans son commandement,** to restore an officer to his command. **2. se r.** (*a*) to recover; to get well again; to pick up again; (*b*) **l'ordre se rétablit,** order is being restored; (*c*) **se r. dans les bonnes grâces de qn,** to re-establish oneself in s.o.'s good graces.

rétablissement [retablismɑ̃] *n.m.* **1.** re-establishment; restoration (of order, a dynasty); reinstatement (of official); retrieval (of fortune); **r. d'un édifice,** repair, restoration, of a building; **r. de la religion,** religious revival. **2.** recovery (after illness). **3.** *Gym:* pull-up; **faire un r.,** to heave oneself up.

retailler [rətaje] *v.tr.* to cut (sth.) again; to prune again; to re-sharpen pencil.

rétamer [retame] *v.tr.* **1.** to re-tin (pan). **2.** to re-silver (mirror). **3.** *F:* **être rétamé,** (i) to be drunk, tight; (ii) to be fagged out; (iii) to be broke.

rétameur [retamœr] *n.m.* **1.** tinsmith. **2.** silverer.

retapage [rətapaʒ] *n.m.* doing up; retouching; re-casting (of speech, play).

retape [rətap] *n.f. F:* **faire la r.,** to solicit.

retaper [rətape] **1.** *v.tr.* (*a*) *F:* **1.** to patch up, do up; to smooth (bedclothes); to touch up (speech); **se r. le moral,** to buck up; **ça vous retapera,** that will buck you up; **se r. les cheveux,** to tidy one's hair; (*b*) to type (letter) again. **2. se r.,** to recover (one's health); to pick up.

retapisser [rətapise] *v.tr.* to repaper (room).

retard [rətar] *n.m.* **1.** (*a*) delay; **une heure de r.,** an hour's delay; **agir sans r.,** to act without delay; **le train a du r.,** the train is (running) late; **le train a dix minutes de r., est en r. de dix minutes,** the train is ten minutes late; **ma montre prend du r.,** my watch is slow; **apporter du r. à (faire) qch.,** to be slow in doing sth.; **mettre qn en r.,** to make s.o. late; to delay s.o.; **arriver en r.,** to arrive late; **être en r.,** (i) to be late; (ii) to be behindhand, in arrears; (iii) (*of clock*) to be slow; **compte en r.,** account outstanding, overdue; (*b*) **élève, pays, en r. sur les autres,** backward pupil, country; **en r. sur son siècle,** behind the times; **mesures en r. sur les événements,** out-of-date measures; **être en r. pour, dans, qch.,** to be, lag, behind in sth. **2.** lag (of tides, etc.); *Mch:* **r. à l'admission,** retarded, late, admission; admission lag; *El:* **r. d'aimantation,** magnetic lag.

retardataire [rətardatɛr] **1.** *a.* (*a*) late, behind time; behindhand, in arrears; (*b*) backward (pupil, race). **2.** *n.* (*a*) latecomer; (*b*) loiterer; laggard.

retardateur, -trice [rətardatœr, -tris] *a.* retarding; delaying (tactics).

retardé [rətarde] *a.* delayed (departure); backward, retarded (child).

retardement [rətardəmɑ̃] *n.m.* **1.** retardment, retarding. **2.** delay; *Mil:* **action de r.,** delaying action; **bombe à r.,** time bomb.

retarder [rətarde] **1.** *v.tr.* (*a*) to retard, delay, hold up (s.o., sth.); to make (s.o.) late; (*b*) to delay, put off (event); to defer (payment). **2.** *v.i.* (*a*) to be late, slow, behindhand; **l'horloge retarde,** the clock (i) loses (time), (ii) is slow; **ma montre retarde,** *F:* **je retarde, de dix minutes,** my watch is ten minutes slow; **pendule qui retarde de dix minutes par jour,** clock that loses ten minutes a day; **il retarde sur son siècle,** he is behind the times; **vous retardez,** you're not up to date; (*b*) *Tchn:* to lag.

retâter [rətɑte] **1.** *v.tr.* (*a*) to touch, feel (sth.) again; (*b*) *F:* to sound (s.o.) again. **2.** *v.i.* **r. de qch.,** to have another taste of sth.; *F:* **r. de la prison,** to do another stretch.

reteindre [rətɛ̃dr̥] *v.tr.* (*conj. like* TEINDRE) to redye.

retéléphoner [rətelefɔne] *v.tr.* to ring (s.o.) up, call (s.o.), again.

retendre [rətɑ̃dr̥] *v.tr.* **1.** to stretch (sth.) again; to tighten (strings) again; to reset (trap). **2.** to hold out (one's hand) again.

retenir [rətnir] (*conj. like* TENIR) **1.** *v.tr.* (*a*) to hold (s.o., sth.) back; to detain, delay (s.o.); **r. l'attention,** to hold, arrest, the attention; **r. qn au lit,** to keep s.o. in bed; to confine s.o. to bed; **r. qn à dîner,** to keep s.o. for dinner; **r. la foule,** to keep back, hold back, the crowd; **r. qn prisonnier,** to keep s.o. prisoner; **je ne vous retiens pas,** I mustn't keep you; **qu'est-ce qui vous retient?** what prevents, hinders you? what's keeping you? *Nau:* **retenu par les glaces,** ice-bound; (*b*) to hold in position; to secure; to hold up, keep from falling; **r. l'eau,** to hold water, be watertight; (*c*) to retain; **r. une somme sur le salaire de qn,** to keep back, deduct, so much from s.o.'s wages; (*d*) to remember; **retenez ce numéro,** don't forget the number; (*e*) to reserve, book (seat, room, table); to engage (staff); (*f*) *Mth:* **je pose 2 et je retiens 5,** put down 2 and carry 5; (*g*) to restrain, curb, check (one's anger); to keep back, hold back (one's tears); to stifle (a cry); **r. son souffle,** to hold one's breath; **r. qn de faire qch.,** to restrain s.o., hold s.o. back, from doing sth. **2. se r.** (*a*) **se r. à qch.,** to catch hold of, cling to, clutch at, sth.; (*b*) to restrain, control, contain, oneself; to hold oneself in; **se r. de faire qch.,** to stop oneself, refrain, from doing sth.

rétenteur, -trice [retɑ̃tœr, -tris] *a.* retaining (force); *Anat:* **muscle r.,** retentor (muscle).

rétention [retɑ̃sjɔ̃] *n.f.* holding back. **1.** *Med:* retention (of water, etc.). **2.** *Jur:* **droit de r. ,** lien (**de,** on).

retentir [rətɑ̃tir] *v.i.* (*a*) to (re)sound, echo, ring, reverberate; (of horn) to sound; **le champ retentit de leurs cris,** the field resounded with their shouts; (*b*) (*of action*) to have repercussions.

retentissant [rətɑ̃tisɑ̃] *a.* resounding, ringing, loud (voice, noise); resounding (success); dismal (failure); **discours r.,** speech that arouses world-wide interest.

retentissement [rətɑ̃tismɑ̃] *n.m.* resounding, echoing sound, noise; reverberation; repercussions (of event, etc.); **procès qui a eu un grand r.,** lawsuit that aroused wide interest, that made a great stir.

retenu [rət(ə)ny] *a.* prudent, circumspect, cautious.

retenue [rət(ə)ny] *n.f.* **1.** (*a*) deduction, docking (of pay, etc.); **faire une r. de 5% sur les salaires,** to stop, deduct, 5% from the wages; (*b*) sum kept back, stoppage (from wages, etc.); (*c*) *Mth:* carry over. **2.** *Sch:* detention, keeping in; **mettre un élève en r.,** to keep a pupil in; to give a boy detention. **3.** reserve, discretion; restraint; **manger avec r.,** to eat sparingly; **s'exprimer sans r.,** to express oneself unreservedly. **4.** (*a*) holding back; damming (of water); **clapet de r.,** back-pressure, non-return, valve; (*b*) holding up, down; staying; (*c*) holding (of goods by Customs). **5.** (*a*) dam, reservoir; (*b*) water (retained in reservoir). **6.** stay, guy.

réticence [retisɑ̃s] *n.f.* reticence, reserve; *Jur:* **sans r.,** unreservedly.

réticent [retisɑ̃] *a.* (*a*) reticent; (*b*) unwilling.

réticulaire [retikylɛr] *a.* reticular.

réticule [retikyl] *n.m.* **1.** (small) ladies' handbag; reticule. **2.** *Opt:* reticle, cross wires.

réticulé [retikyle] *a.* reticulate(d).

rétif, -ive [retif, -iv] *a.* restive, stubborn (animal, person).

rétine [retin] *n.f.* retina.

rétinien, -ienne [retinjɛ̃, -jɛn] *a.* retinal.

retirable [rətirabl̥] *a.* withdrawable.

retiré [rətire] *a.* retired, secluded, remote (place); solitary (life); **vivre r.,** to live in seclusion.

retirer [rətire] **1.** *v.tr.* (*a*) to pull, draw, take, (sth., s.o.) out, to withdraw (sth.); **r. un enfant du collège,** to remove a child, take a child away, from school; **r. de l'argent d'une banque,** to withdraw money from a bank; **r. des marchandises de la douane,** to take goods out of bond; to clear goods; **r. des bagages,** to take out, check out, luggage; **r. son manteau,** to take off one's coat; **r. un bouchon,** to draw a cork; **r. ses mains de ses poches,** to take one's hands out of one's pockets; (*b*) **r. un profit de qch.,** to derive, draw, get, a profit from sth.; **combien en avez-vous retiré?** how much did you get out of it? (*c*) to extract (oil from shale, etc.); (*d*) **r. qch. à qn,** to withdraw sth. from s.o.; to take, snatch, sth. back from s.o.; **r. le permis de conduire à qn,** to take away s.o.'s driving licence; to disqualify, ban, s.o. from driving; (*e*) to withdraw, take back (remark, promise); **r. sa candidature,** to withdraw one's candidature; to stand down; *Jur:* **r. une plainte,** to withdraw an action; (*f*) (i) to fire (gun) again; (ii) *Typ:* to reprint (book). **2. se r.** (*a*) to retire, withdraw; **se r. dans sa chambre,** to retire to one's bedroom; **vous pouvez vous r.,** you may go; **se r. à la campagne,** to retreat to the country; **se r. de la lutte,** to retire from the field; to beat a retreat; (*of candidate*) **se r. en faveur de qn,** to stand down in favour of s.o.; (*b*) **se r. des affaires,** to retire (from business); (*c*) (*of cloth*) to shrink; (*d*) (*of floods*) to subside; (*of sea*) to recede; (*of tide*) to ebb.

retombant [rətɔ̃bɑ̃] *a.* drooping; hanging.

retombée [rətɔ̃be] *n.f.* **1.** *Arch:* spring(ing) (of arch). **2.** *pl.* (*a*) **retombées radioactives,** radioactive fallout; (*b*) **la grève aura des retombées sur les prix,** the strike will have repercussions on prices.

retombement [rətɔ̃bmɑ̃] *n.m.* falling down (again); collapse; falling back; relapse.

retomber [rətɔ̃be] *v.i.* (*aux. usu.* **être**) **1.** (*a*) to fall (down) again; (*b*) to land (after a jump, etc.); **il retombe toujours sur ses pieds,** he always falls, lands, on his feet; (*c*) **r. dans le vice,** to relapse into vice; **r. malade,** to fall, become, ill again. **2. r. dans son fauteuil,** to fall back, sink back, into one's armchair; **faire r. un store,** to let down, pull down, a blind; **laisser r. ses bras,** to drop one's arms; **le blâme retombera sur lui,** the blame will fall on him; **faire r. le blâme sur qn,** to lay the blame on s.o.; **la responsabilité retombe sur moi,** the responsibility falls on me; *F:* **tout ça retombera sur moi,** it'll all come back on me. **3.** (*of hair, draperies*) to hang down.

retordre [rətɔrdr̥] *v.tr.* **1.** to wring out (washing) again. **2.** *Tex:* to twist (thread, yarn); **machine à r.,** twisting machine; twister; *F:* **il vous donnera du fil à r.,** he will give you trouble; **vous avez là du fil à r.,** you've got your work cut out.

rétorquer [retɔrke] *v.tr.* (*a*) to retort; (*b*) to cast back, hurl back (accusation); **r. un argument contre qn,** to turn s.o.'s argument against himself.

retors, -orse [rətɔr, -ɔrs] *a.* **1.** (*a*) *Tex:* twisted (thread, cord); (*b*) curved (beak). **2.** crafty, wily, intriguing, devious (person).

rétorsion [retɔrsjɔ̃] *n.f.* (*a*) retorting; throwing back (of an argument); (*b*) *Jur:* retortion; **mesures de r.,** retaliatory measures.

retouche [rətuʃ] *n.f.* slight alteration, touching up, touch up; *Art:* retouch (to painting, etc.); *Phot:* retouching; **faire des retouches à un vêtement,** to make alterations to a garment.

retoucher [rətuʃe] **1.** *v.tr.* to retouch, touch up (picture, photograph, etc.); to alter, make alterations to (garment). **2.** *v.ind.tr.* **votre article est bien, n'y retouchez pas,** your article is a good one, don't alter a word of it, leave it alone.

retoucheur, -euse [rətuʃœr, -øz] *n.* **1.** *Art: Phot:* retoucher. **2.** *n.f. Tail:* alteration hand.

retour [rətur] *n.m.* **1.** (*a*) turn, bend, angle (of wall); **tours et retours,** twists and turns; **en r. d'équerre,** at right angles; (*b*) turn, vicissitude, reversal (of fortune, opinion); revulsion of feeling; swing back; **r. de conscience,** qualms of conscience; **faire un r. sur le passé,** to look back on the past. **2.** return, going back, coming back; (*a*) **être de r.,** to be back again; **un journaliste (de) r. de Paris,** a reporter just back from Paris; **de r. chez moi, je lui écrivis,** on my return home I wrote to him; **être sur son r.,** to be about to return, on the point of returning; **à mon r.,** on my return; **partir sans r.,** to depart for ever; **être perdu sans r.,** to be irretrievably lost, past praying for; **point de non-r.,** point of no return; *F:* **cheval de r.,** old offender, old lag; **voyage de r.,** return journey; return trip; **billet de r., d'aller et r.,** return ticket; **coupon de r.,** return half; **par r. (du courrier),** by return of post; **le r. de l'hiver, d'une maladie,** the return of winter, recurrence of a disease; *Mil:* **r. offensif,** counter attack, counter stroke; *Row:* **le r. sur l'avant,** the recover, the swing forward; *Cin:* **r. en arrière,** flashback; *Biol:* **r. à un type,** reversion to (a) type; **être sur le r.,** to be past middle age, past one's prime; **beauté sur le r.,** beauty on the wane; **le r. d'âge,** the change of life. **3.** (*a*) backlash (of mechanism); return (of machine part).; **course de r.,** back stroke (of piston); *I.C.E:* **r. de carburateur,** backfire; **avoir des retours,** to backfire; **r. de manivelle,** backfire kick; *Typewr:* **r. de chariot,** carriage return; **r. arrière,** backspace; **r. automatique de ruban,** automatic ribbon reverse; *Cmptr:* **r. d'information,** feedback; (*b*) *El:* **conducteur de r.,** return conductor; **r. à la terre, à la masse,** earth connection, earthing, *NAm:* grounding. **4.** (*a*) return (of goods, letter); **marchandises de r.,** *F:* **retours,** returnable goods, returns; **vendu avec faculté de r.,** on sale or return; (*b*) dishonoured bill; (*c*) *Jur:* reversion; **faire r. à un ascendant,** to revert to an ascendant. **5. payer qn de r.,** to requite s.o.; **payer de r. l'affection de qn,** to return s.o.'s affection; **aimer qn en r.,** to return s.o.'s love; **à beau jeu beau r.,** one good turn deserves another; *Sp:* **match r.,** return match.

retournement [rəturnəmɑ̃] *n.m.* turning; turning

round; turning over; turning inside out; reversal.

retourner [rəturne] **1.** *v.tr.* (*a*) to turn (a skin, an umbrella) inside out; *Tail:* to turn (garment); **retournez vos poches,** turn out your pockets; (*b*) to turn over; to turn up, down, back; to turn over, up (the soil); to turn (hay, omelette); to turn up (card); **on avait retourné la pièce pour trouver la lettre,** they had ransacked the room, turned the room upside down, to find the letter; **r. une idée,** to turn over an idea; **tourner et r. qch.,** to turn sth. over and over (again); **r. une question dans tous les sens,** to thrash out a question; *F:* **votre récit m'a tout retourné,** your story upset me, gave me quite a turn; (*c*) to turn (sth.) round; **r. la tête,** to turn one's head; to look round; **r. un argument contre qn,** to turn an argument against s.o.; **r. une situation,** to reverse, upset, a situation; to turn the tables; **r. qn,** to make s.o. alter his views; (*d*) **r. qch. à qn,** to return sth. to s.o., to give, send, sth. back to s.o.; **r. le compliment,** to return the compliment; **r. un effet impayé,** to return a bill dishonoured. **2.** *v.i.* (*aux. usu.* **être**) (*a*) to return; to go back; to drive, fly, ride, sail, walk, back; **sa fortune retourne à sa famille,** his fortune reverts to his family; **r. déjeuner chez soi,** to go home to lunch; **r. sur le passé,** to go back, revert, to the past; *Biol:* **r. à un type,** to revert to a type; (*of a crime, mistake*) **r. sur qn,** to return, come back, recoil, on s.o.; to come home to roost; (*b*) *impers.* **de quoi retourne-t-il?** (i) *Cards:* what are trumps? (ii) *F:* what's it all about? what's up? **3. se r.** (*a*) to turn (round); to turn over (in bed, etc.); **avoir le temps de se r.,** to have time to look round; (*b*) to turn round, look round, look back; to veer (in one's opinion); **se r. contre qn,** to turn against s.o.; to round on s.o.; (*c*) **s'en r. à un endroit,** to return, go back to a place; to make one's way back; **il s'en retourna sans dire un mot,** he went off without saying a word.

retracer [rətrase] *v.tr.* (*conj. like* TRACER) **1.** to retrace (a line); to mark out (path) again. **2.** to recall, recount (event).

rétractation [retraktasjɔ̃] *n.f.* retraction, recantation; *Jur:* rescinding (of sentence).

rétracter¹ [retrakte] **1.** *v.tr.* to retract, to draw in (claws, etc.). **2. se r.,** to shorten; (*of materials*) to shrink; (*of muscle*) to retract.

rétracter² **1.** *v.tr.* to retract; to withdraw, to go back on (opinion); **r. un arrêt,** to rescind, retract, a decree. **2. se r.** (*a*) to retract, recant; *F:* to eat one's words; (*b*) to withdraw a charge.

rétracteur [retraktœr] *a. & n.m.* (**muscle**) **r.,** retractor (muscle).

rétractile [retraktil] *a.* retractile.

rétraction [retraksjɔ̃] *n.f.* contraction, shortening; retraction (of muscle).

retraduire [rətradɥir] *v.tr.* (*conj. like* TRADUIRE) to retranslate.

retrait [rətrɛ] *n.m.* **1.** (*a*) shrinkage, shrinking (of wood, cement, etc.); **caler une frette à r.,** to shrink on a ring; (*b*) subsiding (of flood); retreat (of glacier). **2.** withdrawal (of order, candidature, troops, etc.); cancelling (of licence); scratching (of horse in race); **r. de fonds,** withdrawal of money invested; **r. d'un ordre de grève,** calling off a strike. **3.** recess (in wall, etc.); **en r.,** recessed (shelves, etc.); sunk (panel); **maison en r.,** house standing back, set back (from the road); (*of pers.*) **rester en r.,** to be, stay, in the background; *Typ:* **ligne en r.,** indented line.

retraite [rətrɛt] *n.f.* **1.** *Mil: etc:* retreat, withdrawal; **battre en r.,** to beat a retreat; to retire; **battre, sonner, la r.,** to beat, to sound, the retreat; *Navy:* **tirer en r.,** to fire astern; **en ordre de r.,** in retiring order; (*in argument*) **faire r.,** to withdraw. **2.** tattoo; **battre, sonner, la r.,** to beat, sound, the tattoo; *Navy:* **coup de canon de r.,** evening gun; **r. aux flambeaux,** torchlight tattoo, procession. **3.** (*a*) retirement (from active life); **caisse de r.,** superannuation fund, pension fund; **être à la, en, r.,** to be retired, (*of army officer*) on the retired list; **militaire en r.,** army pensioner; **mettre qn à la r.,** to retire s.o., pension off s.o.; (*b*) retirement pension; **jouir d'une petite r.,** to have a small pension. **4.** (*a*) **vivre dans la r.,** to live in retirement; **maison de r.** (**pour vieillards**), old people's home; (*b*) *Ecc:* retreat; **faire une r.,** to go into retreat. **5.** (*a*) retreat, place of retirement; (*b*) (place of) shelter; refuge; lair, haunt (of wild beasts); (thieves') hideout. **6.** shrinking. **7.** *Arch:* offset (of wall, between storeys); recess (in wall).

retraité, -ée [rətrete] **1.** *a.* retired; pensioned; (*of officer*) on the retired list; **soldat r.,** army pensioner. **2.** *n.* pensioner.

retraiter¹ [rətrete] *v.tr.* to pension (off); to retire, superannuate.

retraiter² *v.tr.* to reprocess.

retranchement [rətrɑ̃ʃmɑ̃] *n.m.* **1.** cutting off; stopping (of ration, etc.); docking (of pension); excision (of word); **r. des abus,** suppression of abuses. **2.** *Mil:* entrenchment; *Fig:* **forcer qn dans ses (derniers) retranchements,** to drive s.o. to the wall.

retrancher [rətrɑ̃ʃe] **1.** *v.tr.* (*a*) **r. qch. de qch.,** to cut off sth. from sth.; **r. un passage d'un livre,** to cut, strike, a passage out of a book; **r. un nombre d'un autre,** to subtract a number from another; **r. qch. sur une somme,** to deduct sth. from a sum of money; (*b*) **r. qch. à qn,** to dock s.o. of sth.; **r. le superflu,** to cut out everything superfluous; (*c*) *Mil:* to entrench (post). **2. se r.** (*a*) to entrench oneself; to dig in; (*b*) **se r. dans le silence,** to take refuge in silence.

retransmetteur [rətrɑ̃smɛtœr] *n.m. W.Tel:* retransmitter.

retransmettre [rətrɑ̃smɛtr̥] *v.tr.* (*conj. like* TRANSMETTRE) to retransmit.

retransmission [rətrɑ̃smisjɔ̃] *n.f.* retransmission.

retravailler [rətravaje] **1.** *v.tr.* to work (sth.) over again; to touch (sth.) up. **2.** *v.i.* to get to work again.

retraverser [rətravɛrse] *v.tr.* to recross.

rétréci [retresi] *a.* narrow, contracted, restricted; **esprit r.,** narrow mind.

rétrécir [retresir] **1.** *v.tr.* (*a*) to narrow (street, the mind); to take in (garment); (*b*) to shrink (garment). **2.** *v.i. & pr.* (*a*) to contract; to narrow, to get narrower; (*b*) (*of cloth*) to shrink.

rétrécissement [retresismɑ̃] *n.m.* **1.** (*a*) narrowing, contracting; *Med:* stricture; *Aut:* **r. du cadre,** insweeping of the frame; (*b*) shrinking (of cloth). **2.** narrow part, neck (of tube, etc.).

retrempe [rətrɑ̃p] *n.f.* retempering (of steel).

retremper [rətrɑ̃pe] **1.** *v.tr.* (*a*) to soak, steep, (linen, etc.) again; (*b*) to retemper (steel); (*c*) to tone, brace, (s.o.) up; to reinvigorate (s.o.). **2. se r.** (*a*) to bathe again; (*b*) **se r. dans un milieu sympathique,** to get new strength from a congenial atmosphere.

rétribuer [retribɥe] *v.tr.* to remunerate, pay (employee, service); **travail rétribué,** paid work.

rétribution [retribysjɔ̃] *n.f.* **1.** remuneration, reward, payment (for services); salary; **fonctions sans r.,** honorary duties. **2.** recompense.

retrier [rətrije] *v.tr.* to re-sort.

rétro [retro] **1.** *n.m.* (*a*) *Bill:* pull-back, screwback (stroke); (*b*) = RÉTROVISEUR. **2.** *a. inv.* going back to the past (*esp.* this century); period (play, etc.).

rétroactif, -ive [retrɔaktif, -iv] *a.* retroactive, retrospective (law, etc.); **augmentation avec effet r. au 1ᵉʳ juillet,** increase backdated to July 1st.

rétroaction [retrɔaksjɔ̃] *n.f.* **1.** retroaction, retrospective effect. **2.** *Elcs: W.Tel:* feedback.

rétroactivement [retrɔaktivmɑ̃] *adv.* retroactively, retrospectively.
rétroactivité [retrɔaktivite] *n.f.* retroactivity, retrospective effect.
rétrocéder [retrɔsede] (*conj. like* CÉDER) **1.** *v.tr.* to retrocede (right, etc.) to resell. **2.** *v.i. Med:* to retrocede.
rétrocessif, -ive [retrɔsesif, -iv] *a.* retrocessive.
rétrocession [retrɔsesjɔ̃] *n.f.* retrocession.
rétrofusée [retrɔfyze] *n.f.* retro rocket.
rétrogradation [retrɔgradasjɔ̃] *n.f.* **1.** (*a*) *Astr:* retrogradation, retrogression; (*b*) slipping back; **r. morale,** moral lapse. **2.** reduction (of N.C.O.) to lower rank, (of official) to lower grade.
rétrograde [retrɔgrad] **1.** *a.* retrograde, backward, reversed (motion); *Bill:* **effet r.,** pull back, screw back; **amnésie r.,** retrograde amnesia; **phrase r.,** palindrome. **2.** *a. & n.* reactionary.
rétrograder [retrɔgrade] **1.** *v.i.* to retrogress; to move backwards; (*of planet, glacier*) to retrograde; *Mil:* to fall back, to retreat; *Aut: F:* to change down. **2.** *v.tr.* to reduce (N.C.O.) to lower rank, (official) to lower grade.
rétrogression [retrɔgresjɔ̃] *n.f.* retrogression.
rétropédalage [retrɔpedalaʒ] *n.m. Cy:* back pedalling.
rétropédaler [retrɔpedale] *v.i.* to back-pedal.
rétropropulsion [retrɔprɔpylsjɔ̃] *n.f. Av: etc:* reverse thrust.
rétrospectif, -ive [retrɔspɛktif, -iv] (*a*) *a.* retrospective; in retrospect; (*b*) *n.f. Art:* **rétrospective,** retrospective (exhibition); *Cin:* **r. René Clair,** René Clair season; (*c*) *n.m. Cin:* flashback.
rétrospection [retrɔspɛksjɔ̃] *n.f.* retrospection.
rétrospectivement [retrɔspɛktivmɑ̃] *adv.* retrospectively; in retrospect.
retroussement [rətrusmɑ̃] *n.m.* turning up, tucking up; curling (of the lips).
retroussé [rətruse] *a.* **nez r.,** snub nose; turned-up nose.
retrousser [rətruse] *v.tr.* to turn up, roll up (one's sleeves, trousers); to tuck up, pull up, bunch up (one's skirt); to curl (up) (one's lip); **se r. pour monter l'escalier,** to hold up one's skirt to go upstairs.
retroussis [rətrusi] *n.m.* **1.** turned-back facings; **bottes à r.,** topboots. **2.** curling up (of hair, lips).
retrouvable [rətruvabl̥] *a.* recoverable; retrievable; easily found.
retrouvaille [rətruvɑj] *n.f.* (*a*) finding again; (*b*) *pl.* meeting again.
retrouver [rətruve] **1.** *v.tr.* (*a*) to find (again); to meet (again); to rediscover; **r. son chemin,** to find one's way again; **la clef a été retrouvée,** the key has been found; **r. la parole, sa santé,** to recover one's speech, one's health; **on ne retrouve plus cet auteur dans son dernier roman,** we don't recognize this author in his last novel; this author's last novel is uncharacteristic; (*b*) **aller r. qn,** to go and join s.o.; **je vous retrouverai ce soir,** I shall see you again this evening. **2. se r.** (*a*) **se r. dans la même position,** to find oneself, to be, in the same position again; **se r. à Paris,** to be back in Paris; (*b*) to find one's bearings; **je ne puis m'y r.!** I can't make it out! *F:* **s'y r.,** to cover one's expenses, to break even; (*c*) to meet again; **comme on se retrouve!** fancy meeting you! it's a small world!
rétroviseur [retrɔvizœr] *n.m. Aut:* driving mirror, rearview mirror.
rets [rɛ] *n.m.* (hunting) net; *Lit:* **prendre qn dans ses r.,** to catch s.o. in one's toils.
réuni [reyni] *a.* united; (joined) together; *Com:* amalgamated, united (dairies, etc.).
réunification [reynifikasjɔ̃] *n.f. Pol:* reunification.
réunion [reynjɔ̃] *n.f.* reunion. **1.** bringing together, reuniting; joining up again; connection; connecting; *Surg:* (re)union; **r. d'une province à la France,** union of a province with France. **2.** (*a*) coming together; **droit de r.,** right of assembly; **salle de r.,** assembly room; (*b*) assembly, gathering, meeting; session, sitting (of a commission); **r. publique,** public meeting; (*c*) social gathering, party; function.
Réunion (La) [lareynjɔ̃] *Pr.n.f. Geog:* Reunion.
réunir [reynir] **1.** *v.tr.* to unite; to join, put (things) together; to bring (people) together; **r. qch. à qch.,** to join sth. to, with, sth.; to unite sth. with sth.; **r. une somme,** to collect, get together, a sum of money; **r. une armée,** to raise an army; **r. un comité,** to convene a committee; to call a committee together. **2. se r.** (*a*) to meet, to gather together; (*b*) (*of banks, etc.*) to amalgamate; (*of churches, etc.*) to unite; (*c*) to join forces, to join together; **tout se réunissait contre nous,** everything combined against us.
réussi [reysi] *a.* successful, successfully done, well performed; **mal r.,** unsuccessful, badly done; spoilt.
réussir [reysir] **1.** *v.i.* (*a*) to turn out (well or badly); **le projet avait mal réussi,** the plan had proved a failure; *F:* **le homard ne me réussit pas,** lobster doesn't agree with me; (*b*) to succeed; **r. dans qch.,** to succeed, be successful, at, in, sth.; **r. à un examen,** to pass an examination; **r. à faire qch.,** to succeed in doing sth.; to manage to do sth.; **c'est un garçon qui réussira,** he's a boy who will do well; **ne pas r. à faire qch.,** to fail to do sth.; (*c*) (*of play*) to be a success; (*of business*) to prosper; (*of plant*) to thrive; **tout lui réussit,** he's successful in everything; **ce truc-là ne réussira pas,** that trick won't work, won't come off. **2.** *v.tr.* to make a success of (sth.); to be successful with (sth.); **elle réussit bien les omelettes,** she makes very good omelettes; *Cards:* **r. son contrat,** to make one's contract; *F:* **r. le coup,** to do the trick, bring it off.
réussite [reysit] *n.f.* **1.** issue, result, upshot; outcome. **2.** success, successful result. **3.** *Cards:* patience.
revacciner [rəvaksine] *v.tr.* to revaccinate.
revaloir [rəvalwar] *v.tr.* (*conj. like* VALOIR; *used chiefly in the fu.*) to return, pay back, (*esp.* evil) in kind; **je vous revaudrai cela!** (i) I'll pay you back for that! (ii) I'll do the same for you another time.
revaloriser [rəvalɔrize] *v.tr.* **1.** (*a*) to revalue (currency); (*b*) to give a new value to (idea, etc.); to bring into favour, currency, again. **2.** to reassess (pensions, prices) at a higher level.
revanchard, -arde [rəvɑ̃ʃar, -ard] *a. & n. Pol: Pej:* revanchist.
revanche [rəvɑ̃ʃ] *n.f.* **1.** (*a*) revenge; **prendre sa r. sur qn,** to get one's own back on s.o., to get even with s.o.; **je prendrai ma r. un jour,** it will be my turn one day; (*b*) **jouer la r.,** to play the return match, game. **2.** return service; **en r.,** in return, in compensation; to make up for it; **faible en mathématiques, mais en r. très bon latiniste,** weak in mathematics, but on the other hand very good at Latin; **à charge de r.,** on condition that I do the same for you.
revancher (se) [sərəvɑ̃ʃe] *v.pr.* to revenge oneself, to be revenged, get one's own back.
rêvasser [rɛvase] *v.i.* to daydream, let one's ideas wander; to muse.
rêvasserie [rɛvasri] *n.f.* **1.** musing, daydreaming. **2.** *pl.* daydreams.
rêvasseur, -euse [rɛvasœr, -øz] *n.* (day) dreamer.
rêve [rɛv] *n.m.* **1.** dream; **faire un r.,** to (have a) dream; **voir qch. en r.,** to see sth. in a dream, in one's dreams; **la psychologie du r.,** the psychology of dreams, of dreaming. **2.** daydream; **rêves de gloire,** dreams of glory; **la maison de nos rêves,** our dream

house, our ideal house; **c'est le r.!** it's all you could wish for; it's ideal.

revêche [rəvɛʃ] *a.* **1.** bad-tempered, cantankerous; sour. **2.** harsh, rough (cloth, etc.).

réveil [revɛj] *n.m.* **1.** (*a*) waking, awakening; **à mon r.,** on waking; **le r. de la nature,** the awakening of Nature; **avoir un fâcheux r.,** to have a rude awakening; (*b*) *Mil:* reveille; **sonner le r.,** to sound reveille. **2.** alarm (clock).

réveille-matin [revɛjmatɛ̃] *n.m.inv.* alarm clock.

réveiller [reveje] **1.** *v.tr.* (*a*) to (a)wake, (a)waken (s.o.); to wake (s.o.) up; to rouse (s.o.); **réveillez-moi à sept heures,** wake me up, call me, knock me up, at seven o'clock; **ne réveillez pas le chat qui dort,** let sleeping dogs lie; (*b*) to stir up, rouse (s.o.); to awaken (memories); to revive (memory, courage). **2. se r.** (*a*) to awake; to wake (up); **se r. d'un sommeil agité,** to wake out of, from, a troubled sleep; (*b*) (*of feelings*) to be awakened, roused, stirred up; to revive; (*c*) (*of nature, vegetation*) to revive.

réveillon [revɛjɔ̃] *n.m.* midnight supper (*esp.* after midnight mass on Christmas Eve, New Year's Eve); **faire r.** = RÉVEILLONNER.

réveillonner [revɛjɔne] *v.i.* to have a midnight supper; to see Christmas, the New Year, in.

révélateur, -trice [revelatœr, -tris] **1.** *a.* revealing, tell-tale (sign); *Ch:* tracer (substance). **2.** *n.* revealer, discoverer, discloser (of plot, etc.). **3.** *n.m.* (*a*) *Phot:* developer; (*b*) detector (of leakages, etc.).

révélation [revelasjɔ̃] *n.f.* **1.** (*a*) revelation, disclosure (of secret, etc.); (*b*) **ce fut une r.!** that was an eye-opener! **la dernière r. du ballet français,** the latest discovery, find, in French ballet. **2.** *Theol:* revelation; **la r. divine,** the revealed religion.

révéler [revele] **(je révèle, n. révélons; je révélerai) 1.** *v.tr.* (*a*) to reveal, disclose; **il révéla maladroitement la vérité,** he blurted, let, out the truth; **somme dont le montant n'a pas été révélé,** undisclosed amount; (*b*) to show (talent); to reveal (kindness, good humour); to betray, reveal (faults); (*c*) *Phot:* to develop. **2. se r.** (*a*) to reveal oneself, one's character; **se r. difficile,** to prove, show oneself, difficult; (*b*) (*of mystery*) to be revealed; (*of fact*) to come to light.

revenant [rəvnɑ̃] **1.** *a. O:* pleasing, prepossessing. **2.** *n.m.* ghost; **histoire de revenants,** ghost story; *F:* **quel r. vous faites!** you're quite a stranger!

revendeur, -euse [rəvɑ̃dœr, -øz] *n.* (*a*) retailer, middleman; (*b*) secondhand dealer.

revendicateur, -trice [rəvɑ̃dikatœr, -tris] **1.** *a.* demanding, claiming (of rights). **2.** *n.* claimant, claimer.

revendicatif, -ive [rəvɑ̃dikatif, -iv] *a.* demanding, claiming; **mouvements revendicatifs,** protest movements.

revendication [rəvɑ̃dikasjɔ̃] *n.f.* **1.** claiming. **2.** claim, demand **(sur,** on); **les revendications ouvrières,** the demands of labour; *Jur:* **(action en) r.,** action for recovery of property.

revendiquer [rəvɑ̃dike] *v.tr.* (*a*) to claim, demand; to assert, insist on (one's rights); to lay claim to (territory); (*b*) to assume (responsibility).

revendre [rəvɑ̃dr] *v.tr.* to resell; to sell again; *F:* **avoir de qch. à r.,** to have enough and to spare of sth.

revenez-y [rəvnezi] *n.m.inv. F:* **1.** going back, return (to the past); **un r.-y de tendresse,** a return, renewal, of affection. **2. ce gâteau a un goût de r.-y,** this cake tempts you to take more, *F:* is very more-ish.

revenir [rəvnir] *v.i.* (*conj. like* VENIR, *aux.* **être) 1.** (*a*) to return; to come back, come again; to walk, ride, drive, sail, fly, back; **r. à la hâte,** to hurry back; **je l'ai rencontré en revenant de l'église,** I met him on my way back, home, from church; **r. sur ses pas,** to retrace one's steps, to turn back; **le temps passé ne revient plus,** time that is past will never come again; **l'herbe reviendra,** the grass will come, grow, again; **fête qui revient tous les dix ans,** festival that occurs, recurs, comes round, every ten years; **esprit qui revient,** ghost that walks; **je suis revenu au régime lacté,** I have gone back to a milk diet; **r. sur ses aveux, une promesse,** to retract one's confession; to go back on a promise; **r. sur son opinion,** to reconsider one's opinion; **r. sur un sujet,** to hark back to, bring up, a subject again; **r. sur le passé,** to rake up the past; **il n'y a pas à y r.,** there is no going back on it; (*b*) **aliments qui reviennent,** food that repeats. **2.** (*a*) to return, come back (**à qn,** to s.o.); **la mémoire me revient,** my memory is coming back; **il me revient encore 100 francs,** I have still 100 francs to get; **honneur qui me revient,** honour that falls to me by right; **à chacun ce qui lui revient,** to each his due; (*b*) **cela me revient à la mémoire,** I am beginning to recall it; it's coming back to me; **votre nom ne me revient pas,** your name has slipped from my memory; I can't think of your name; (*c*) **son visage ne me revient pas,** I don't like, don't fancy, his looks; (*d*) *impers.* **il me revient que vous dites du mal de moi,** I hear, I have been told, that you are speaking ill of me. **3.** (*a*) **r. de sa surprise, d'une maladie,** to recover from, get over, one's surprise, an illness; **r. d'une théorie,** to abandon a theory; **r. d'une erreur,** to realize one's mistake; **je suis revenu de toutes mes illusions,** I have lost all my illusions; **je n'en reviens pas!** it's amazing! I can't get over it! **r. à la santé,** to recover one's health; **il revient de loin,** he has been at death's door; **r. à soi,** to recover consciousness; *F:* to come round, to come to; (*b*) *Cu:* **faire r.,** to brown. **4. en r. à qch., y r.,** to revert, hark back, to sth.; **pour en r. à la question,** to come back to our subject. **5.** (*a*) to cost; **sa maison lui revient à une forte somme,** his house has cost him a lot of money; (*b*) **cela revient au même,** it amounts, comes, to the same thing. **6.** *F:* **s'en r.,** to return, make one's way back.

revente [rəvɑ̃t] *n.f.* resale; **objet de r.,** secondhand article.

revenu [rəv(ə)ny] *n.m.* **1.** (*a*) income (of pers.); revenue (of the State); **impôt sur le r.,** income tax; **dépenser tout son r.,** to live up to one's income; (*b*) yield (of investment); interest on capital; *pl.* incomings (of enterprise). **2.** *Metall:* tempering (of steel).

rêver [reve] **1.** *v.i.* to dream; (*a*) **r. de qch.,** to dream (in one's sleep) about sth.; (*b*) **r. à, sur, de, qch.,** to muse on, ponder over, sth.; **r. creux,** to daydream; **r. de voyager,** to dream of travel; (*c*) **vous rêvez!** you're dreaming! **on croirait r.,** you'd think you were dreaming; it can't be real. **2.** *v.tr.* to dream of (sth.); **r. la gloire,** to dream of glory; **c'était pour elle le mari rêvé,** he was the husband of her dreams; **vous l'avez rêvé!** you must have dreamt it!

réverbération [revɛrberasjɔ̃] *n.f.* reverberation, reflection (of light, heat); re-echoing (of sound).

réverbère [revɛrbɛr] *n.m.* **1.** street lamp. **2.** (heat) reflector.

réverbérer [revɛrbere] *v.tr.* **(il réverbère; il réverbérera)** to reverberate; to reflect, throw back (heat, light); to re-echo (sound); to make (sth.) reverberate.

reverdir [rəvɛrdir] **1.** *v.i.* to grow, turn, green again; **2.** *v.tr.* to paint or make (sth.) green again.

révérence [reverɑ̃s] *n.f.* **1.** (*a*) reverence **(envers, pour,** for); **r. parler,** with all due respect; (*b*) **Votre R.,** your Reverence. **2.** bow; curtsey; **faire la r. à qn,** to curtsey to s.o.; **tirer sa r. à la compagnie,** to bow oneself out; **je vous tire ma r.,** I must go.

révérenciel, -ielle [reverɑ̃sjɛl] *a.* reverential; **il**

m'inspire une crainte révérencielle, I live in holy fear of him.

révérencieusement [reverɑ̃sjøzmɑ̃] *adv.* with much ceremony; ceremoniously.

révérencieux, -euse [reverɑ̃sjø, -øz] *a.* over-polite, ceremonious.

révérend, -ende [reverɑ̃, -ɑ̃d] *a. Ecc:* reverend; **le r. père Martin,** Reverend Father Martin; **la révérende mère supérieure,** the Reverend Mother Superior.

révérer [revere] *v.tr.* **(je révère, n. révérons; je révérerai)** to revere; to reverence.

rêverie [rɛvri] *n.f.* reverie; dreaming, musing; **plongé dans de vagues rêveries,** in a brown study.

revernir [rəvɛrnir] *v.tr.* to revarnish.

revers [rəvɛr] *n.m.* **1.** (*a*) reverse (side) (of coin, etc.); wrong side (of material); other side (of page); **r. de la main,** back of the hand; **donner un r. de main à qn,** to deal s.o. a backhanded blow; **(coup de) r.,** *Ten:* backhand stroke; *Fenc:* reverse; **prendre une position à r.,** to capture a position in the rear; (*b*) facing, lapel, revers (of coat); turnover (of sock); boot top; **r. de pantalon,** trouser turn-up; **habit à r. de velours,** coat faced with velvet; **bottes à r.,** top boots. **2.** reverse (of fortune); setback; **les succès et les r. de la vie,** the ups and downs of life.

reverser [rəvɛrse] *v.tr.* **1.** (*a*) to pour (sth.) out again; (*b*) to pour (sth.) back. **2.** to shift (blame); *Book-k:* to transfer (entry).

réversible [revɛrsibl̥] *a.* **1.** reversible (process, garment, etc.); **l'histoire n'est pas r.,** you can't put the clock back. **2.** *Jur:* revertible (succession).

réversion [revɛrsjɔ̃] *n.f. Jur: Biol:* reversion.

revêtement [rəvɛtmɑ̃] *n.m.* **1.** coating, covering (for protection); (*with metal*) plating; (*on inside*) lining; **matière de r.,** coating compound. **2.** (*a*) coat(ing); (*with metal*) cladding, plating, sheath(ing); (*interior*) lining; *Av:* skin (of fuselage); *Join:* veneer; **câble à r. en caoutchouc,** rubber covered cable; **r. calorifuge,** lagging (of boiler, etc.); (*b*) facing (of wall); revetment (of embankment); surface (material) (of road).

revêtir [rəvetir] (*conj. like* VÊTIR) **1.** *v.tr.* (*a*) to clothe, dress; **r. qn de qch.,** to dress s.o. in sth.; **r. qn d'une dignité,** to invest s.o. with a dignity; **pièce revêtue de votre signature,** document bearing your signature; *Lit:* **revêtu de verdure,** verdure-clad; (*b*) to face, coat, cover, case, line, sheathe; to lag (boiler); *Fort:* to revet; **murs revêtus de boiseries,** panelled walls; **route non revêtue,** unsealed road; (*c*) **r. un uniforme,** to put on a uniform; **r. la forme humaine,** to assume, put on, human shape; **fait qui revêt de l'importance,** fact that takes on importance. **2. se r. de qch.,** to put on, dress oneself in (uniform, robes); to put on (appearance); to assume (dignity).

rêveur, -euse [rɛvœr, -øz] **1.** *a.* dreaming, dreamy, musing. **2.** *n.* dreamer, muser.

rêveusement [rɛvøzmɑ̃] *adv.* dreamily.

revient [rəvjɛ̃] *n.m.* **1. (prix de) r.,** cost price, prime cost. **2.** *Metalw:* tempering.

revigorer [rəvigɔre] *v.tr.* to reinvigorate.

revirement [rəvirmɑ̃] *n.m.* **1.** *Nau:* tacking about, going about. **2.** sudden change (of fortune); revulsion, reversal (of feeling).

révisable [revizabl̥] *a.* reviewable (case); **prix r.,** price subject to modification, open to offer.

réviser [revize] *v.tr.* **1.** (*a*) to revise (text, etc.); to audit (accounts); *Jur:* to review, reconsider (case). **2.** (*a*) *Sch:* to revise; (*b*) to service (car, etc.).

réviseur [revizœr] *n.m.* reviser; examiner; *Typ:* proof reader; **r. (comptable),** auditor.

révision [revizjɔ̃] *n.f.* **1.** (*a*) revision, examination; *Typ:* proof reading; (*b*) auditing (of accounts); (*c*) *Sch:* revision; (*d*) review, reconsideration (of legal case); revision (of dictionary, etc.); **r. déchirante,** agonizing re-appraisal. **2.** (*a*) inspection, testing (of boilers, etc.); (*b*) overhaul(ing) (of car, etc.); (*c*) *Mil:* medical examination (of recruits); **conseil de r.,** medical board (for recruits).

révisionniste [revizjɔnist] **1.** *a.* revisory; revisionist (party). **2.** *n.m. & f.* revisionist.

revivifier [rəvivifje] *v.tr.* (*impf. & pr.sub.* **n. revivifiions, v. revivifiiez**) to revivify, revive.

revivre [rəvivr̥] (*conj. like* VIVRE) (*a*) *v.i.* to live again, to come to life again; **se sentir r.,** to feel oneself restored to life; **faire r. qn,** to bring s.o. to life again; to revive s.o.; **faire r. une coutume,** to revive a custom; (*b*) *v.tr.* to relive (the past); to live through (sth.) again.

révocabilité [revɔkabilite] *n.f.* revocability.

révocable [revɔkabl̥] *a.* **1.** revocable, subject to repeal. **2.** removable (official); subject to dismissal.

révocation [revɔkasjɔ̃] *n.f.* **1.** revocation (of testament, edict, etc.); rescinding, countermanding (of order). **2.** removal, dismissal (of official).

révocatoire [revɔkatwar] *a.* revocatory.

revoici [rəvwasi] *prep. F:* **me r.!** here I am again!

revoilà [rəvwala] *prep. F:* **le r.!** there he is again!

revoir [rəvwar] *v.tr.* (*conj. like* VOIR) **1.** to see (s.o., sth.) again; to meet (s.o.) again; **on se reverra!** we shall meet again! *n.m.inv.* **au r.,** goodbye (for the present); **des au r. sans fin,** endless goodbyes. **2.** to revise (text, lesson); to re-examine, to look over (accounts, manuscript) again; to read (proofs).

révoltant [revɔltɑ̃] *a.* revolting, sickening, shocking (sight); outrageous (behaviour).

révolte [revɔlt] *n.f.* **1.** revolt, rebellion. **2.** mutiny.

révolté, -ée [revɔlte] *n.* rebel, insurgent; *Mil:* mutineer.

révolter [revɔlte] **1.** *v.tr.* (*a*) to induce (s.o.) to revolt; (*b*) to revolt, disgust, shock. **2. se r.** (*a*) to revolt, rebel (**contre,** against); *Mil:* to mutiny; (*b*) **le bon sens se révolte contre une telle supposition,** common sense revolts against such a supposition.

révolu [revɔly] *a.* (*of time*) completed; **avoir quarante ans révolus,** to have completed one's fortieth year; **quand le temps sera révolu,** in the fullness of time; **une époque révolue,** an age that has gone.

révolution [revɔlysjɔ̃] *n.f.* **1.** revolution (of the earth, a wheel). **2.** (industrial, political) revolution; upheaval; **toute la ville est en r.,** the whole town is in revolt, up in arms; *Hist:* **la R.,** the French Revolution (1789).

révolutionnaire [revɔlysjɔnɛr] *a. & n.* revolutionary.

révolutionner [revɔlysjɔne] *v.tr.* to revolutionize (industry, etc.).

revolver [revɔlvɛr] *n.m.* **1.** revolver, *F:* gun; **r. à six coups,** six-shooter. **2.** (*a*) **(porte-outils) r.,** revolving tool holder; **tour (à) r.,** turret lathe, capstan lathe; (*b*) revolving nose piece (of microscope).

révoquer [revɔke] *v.tr.* **1.** to dismiss; to remove from office; to recall (ambassador). **2.** (*a*) to revoke, repeal, rescind (decree); to countermand (an order); (*b*) **r. qch. en doute,** to call sth. in question.

revouloir [rəvulwar] *v.tr.* (*conj. like* VOULOIR) to want (sth.) again; **en reveux-tu?** would you like some more?

revue [rəvy] *n.f.* **1.** review, survey, inspection; *Mil:* review; muster (of troops); inspection (of barracks); **r. de santé,** medical inspection; **faire la r. des troupes,** to review, inspect, the troops; **passer en r.,** to be reviewed, inspected; *F:* **je suis encore de la r.,** I've had all this trouble for nothing. **2.** (*a*) *Publ:* review, magazine; journal; **r. scientifique,** scientific journal; (*b*) *Th:* revue. **3.** *F:* **nous sommes de r., des gens de r.,** we shall meet again.

révulser [revylse] *v.tr.* **1.** *Med:* to counter-irritate. **2.**

son regard se révulsa, he showed the whites of his eyes.

révulsif, -ive [revylsif, -iv] *a. & n.m. Med:* revulsive; counter-irritant.

révulsion [revylsjɔ̃] *n.f. Med:* revulsion; counter-irritation.

rez-de-chaussée [redʃose] *n.m.inv.* (*a*) ground level, street level; (*b*) ground floor, *NAm:* first floor; **au r.-de-c.,** on the ground floor; (*c*) ground floor flat, *NAm:* first floor apartment.

rhabillage [rabijaʒ] *n.m.* **1.** repairing, overhaul. **2.** getting dressed again.

rhabiller [rabije] **1.** *v.tr.* (*a*) to repair, overhaul (watch, etc.); (*b*) to dress (s.o.) again; to put (child's) clothes on again; (*c*) to give a new look to (building, old idea). **2. se r.** (*a*) to put on one's clothes again; to get dressed again; *F:* **il peut aller se r.,** he'd better give up! **va te r.!** get lost! (*b*) to buy a new outfit.

rhabilleur [rabijœr] *n.m.* **1.** repairer (of clocks, etc.). **2.** *F:* bonesetter.

rhapsode [rapsɔd] *n.m.* rhapsode, rhapsodist.

rhapsodie [rapsɔdi] *n.f.* rhapsody.

rhapsodique [rapsɔdik] *a.* rhapsodic.

rhénan, -ane [renɑ̃, -an] *Geog:* **1.** *a.* Rhenish, (of the) Rhine. **2.** *n.* Rhinelander.

Rhénanie (la) [larenani] *Pr.n.f. Geog:* the Rhineland.

rhéostat [reɔsta] *n.m. El:* rheostat; variable resistance; **r. de démarrage,** rheostatic starter (of electric motor).

rhésus [rezys] *n.m.* **1.** *Z:* rhesus (monkey). **2.** *Physiol:* **facteur r.,** rhesus factor.

rhéteur [retœr] *n.m.* (*a*) *A:* rhetor; (*b*) rhetorician.

rhétoricien, -ienne [retɔrisjɛ, -jɛn] *n.* rhetorician.

rhétorique [retɔrik] *n.f.* (*a*) rhetoric; **figure de r.,** figure of speech; (*b*) *Sch: A:* **(classe de) r.** = sixth form.

rhéto-roman, -ane [retɔrɔmɑ̃, -an] *a. & n. Ling:* Rhaeto-Romanic.

Rhin (le) [lərɛ̃] *Pr.n.m.* the (river) Rhine.

rhingrave [rɛ̃grav] *n.m. Hist:* Rhinegrave.

rhinite [rinit] *n.f. Med:* rhinitis, coryza; nasal catarrh.

rhinocéros [rinɔserɔs] *n.m. Z:* rhinoceros.

rhinologie [rinɔlɔʒi] *n.f. Med:* rhinology.

rhinoscopie [rinɔskɔpi] *n.f. Med:* rhinoscopy.

rhizome [rizom] *n.m. Bot:* rhizome.

rhodanien, -ienne [rɔdanjɛ̃, -jɛn] *a. Geog:* of the Rhone.

Rhodésie [rɔdezi] *Pr.n.f. Hist:* Rhodesia.

rhododendron [rɔdɔdɛ̃drɔ̃] *n.m. Bot:* rhododendron.

Rhône (le) [ləron] *Pr.n.m.* the (river) Rhone.

rhum [rɔm] *n.m.* rum.

rhumatisant, -ante [rymatizɑ̃, -ɑ̃t] *a. & n. Med:* rheumatic (patient).

rhumatismal, -aux [rymatismal, -o] *a. Med:* rheumatic (pain, fever).

rhumatisme [rymatism] *n.m. Med:* rheumatism; **r. articulaire,** rheumatoid arthritis; *F:* **être perclus de rhumatismes,** to be crippled with rheumatism.

rhumatoïde [rymatɔid] *a. Med:* rheumatoid.

rhumatologie [rymatɔlɔʒi] *n.m. Med:* rheumatology.

rhumatologue [rymatɔlɔg] *n* rheumatologist.

rhume [rym] *n.m. Med:* cold; **gros r.,** heavy cold; **r. de cerveau,** cold in the head; **r. des foins,** hay fever; **prendre, attraper, un r.,** to catch (a) cold.

rhumerie [rɔmri] *n.f.* rum distillery.

ria [rija] *n.f. Geog:* ria; **côte à rias,** ria coast.

riant [rijɑ̃] *a.* **1.** smiling (face). **2.** cheerful, agreeable, pleasant (prospect); **les riantes campagnes,** the smiling countryside.

ribambelle [ribɑ̃bɛl] *n.f. F:* long string (of animals, insults); **r. d'enfants,** swarm, whole lot, of children.

ribaud, -aude [ribo, -od] *a. & n.* dissolute, bawdy (person).

riboflavine [ribɔflavin] *n.f. Ch:* riboflavin, vitamin B_2.

ribonucléique [ribɔnykleik] *a.* ribonucleic (acid).

ribote [ribɔt] *n.f. F:* drunken bout; binge; **être en r.,** to be tipsy, tight.

ribouldingue [ribuldɛ̃g] *n.f. P:* spree; binge.

ricain, -aine [rikɛ̃, -ɛn] *a. & n. F:* American, Yank.

ricanement [rikanmɑ̃] *n.m.* contemptuous, sneering, derisive, laugh.

ricaner [rikane] *v.i.* to laugh contemptuously, derisively; to sneer.

ricaneur, -euse [rikanœr, -øz] **1.** *a.* derisive, sneering. **2.** *n.* sneerer.

richard, -arde [riʃar, -ard] *n. F:* rich person; moneybags.

riche [riʃ] *a.* **1.** rich, wealthy; well off; **être r. à millions,** to be worth millions; **r. d'espérances,** rich in hope; **musée r. en tableaux,** museum rich in paintings; **r. en protéine,** with high protein content; **langue r.,** rich language; *Pros:* **rime r.,** rich rhyme; **végétation r.,** rich, exuberant, vegetation. **2.** valuable, handsome (gift); rich (ore); rich, abundant (harvest); **faire un r. mariage,** to marry into a wealthy family; *F:* to marry money; *Com:* **article r.,** superior article; *I.C.E:* **mélange r.,** rich mixture. **3.** *F:* **une r. idée,** a splendid idea; **ce n'est pas r.,** it's not up to much. **4.** *n.* rich person; **les riches,** the rich, the wealthy; **nouveau r.,** nouveau riche.

richelieu [riʃəljø] *n.m.* lace-up shoe, Oxford (shoe).

richement [riʃmɑ̃] *adv.* richly; (*a*) abundantly; **pourvoir r. ses enfants,** to make abundant provision for one's children; (*b*) sumptuously.

richesse [riʃɛs] *n.f.* **1.** wealth; (*a*) **la r. publique,** public wealth; **r. en matières premières,** resources in raw materials; (*b*) *pl.* riches. **2. musée plein de richesses,** gallery full of valuable objects, of treasures. **3.** richness; fertility (of soil); exuberance (of vegetation); sumptuousness (of furniture).

richissime [riʃisim] *a. F:* extremely rich, rolling in wealth.

ricin [risɛ̃] *n.m.* castor-oil plant; **huile de r.,** castor oil.

ricocher [rikɔʃe] *v.i.* (*a*) to rebound; to glance off; (*b*) (*bullet*) to ricochet.

ricochet [rikɔʃɛ] *n.m.* (*a*) rebound; **faire des ricochets (sur l'eau),** to make ducks and drakes; (*b*) ricochet; *F:* **apprendre qch. par r.,** to hear of sth. indirectly.

ric-rac [rikrak] *adv. F:* **payer r.-r.,** to pay to the very last farthing.

rictus [riktys] *n.m.* **1.** rictus. **2.** grin, grimace.

ride [rid] *n.f.* **1.** wrinkle (on the face); **front creusé de rides profondes,** deeply lined brow. **2.** ripple (on water, sand); ridge (of sand); (*on beach*) ripple mark; *Nau:* (shroud) lanyard.

ridé [ride] *a.* **1.** wrinkled; **pomme ridée,** shrivelled apple. **2.** ribbed, corrugated.

rideau, -eaux [rido] *n.m.* **1.** screen, curtain (of trees, etc.); *Mil:* **r. de troupes,** screen of troops; **r. de feu,** fire curtain; **r. de fumée,** smoke screen. **2.** (*a*) curtain, *NAm:* drape; **rideaux de fenêtre,** window curtains; **lit garni de rideaux,** curtained bed; **rideaux de lit,** bed hangings; **tirer les rideaux,** to draw the curtains; *F:* **tirer le r. sur qch.,** to draw a veil over sth.; (*b*) *Th:* (drop) curtain; **r. d'entr'acte,** act drop; **r. à huit heures précises,** the curtain rises at eight sharp; *P:* **r.!** let's call it a day! (*c*) **r. de fer,** (i) *Th:* safety curtain; (ii) metal shutter (of shop); (iii) *Pol:* Iron Curtain; (*d*) register, blower (of fireplace); roll top (of desk); **classeur à r.,** roll-shutter cabinet.

ridelle [ridɛl] *n.f.* rack, rail (of cart, lorry); **fausses ridelles,** floating raves.

rider [ride] **1.** *v.tr.* (*a*) to wrinkle, line (forehead); to shrivel (skin); (*b*) to ripple, ruffle (the water, etc.); (*c*) *Nau:* to set up, tighten (the shrouds). **2. se r.** (*a*) to wrinkle; (*of forehead*) to become lined; (*of apple*) to shrivel up; (*b*) (*of water*) to ripple.

ridicule [ridikyl] **1.** *a.* ridiculous, laughable, ludicrous, absurd; **se rendre r.,** to make a fool of oneself. **2.** *n.m.* (*a*) ridiculousness, absurdity; **c'est d'un r. achevé,** it is perfectly ridiculous, the height of absurdity; **tomber dans le r.,** to make oneself ridiculous; **se couvrir de r.,** to make a fool of oneself; (*b*) ridicule; **craindre le r.,** to fear ridicule; **tourner qn en r.,** to hold s.o. up to ridicule; to poke fun at s.o.; (*c*) ridiculous habit; **les ridicules de notre époque,** the absurdities of our time.

ridiculement [ridikylmɑ̃] *adv.* ridiculously, absurdly, laughably, ludicrously.

ridiculiser [ridikylize] *v.tr.* to ridicule; to make ridiculous; to hold up to ridicule; **se r.,** to make oneself ridiculous, to make a fool of oneself.

rien [rjɛ̃] **I.** *pron.indef.m.* **1.** anything; (*in questions* **rien** *is preferred to* **quelque chose** *when a negative answer is expected*) **y a-t-il r. de plus triste?** is there anything more depressing? **2.** nothing, not anything; (*a*) (*with* **ne** *expressed*) **r. ne l'intéresse,** nothing interests him; **je n'ai r. vu,** I saw nothing; **je n'ai r. à faire,** I have nothing to do; **il n'y a r. à faire,** there is nothing to be done; it can't be helped; **il ne faut r. lui dire,** he must not be told anything; **personne n'osa r. lui dire,** nobody ventured to say anything to him; **n'en dites r.,** say nothing about it; **il n'est r. de tel que de se bien porter,** there is nothing like health; **je n'ai r. de nouveau à vous dire,** I have nothing new to tell you; **il ne vous faut r. d'autre?** do you require anything else? **cela ne fait r.,** that doesn't matter, it makes no difference, *F:* no odds; **cela ne fait r. à l'affaire,** that is nothing to do with it; **si cela ne vous fait r.,** if you don't mind; **comme si de r. n'était,** as if nothing had happened; **il n'en est r.!** nothing of the kind! **je n'en ferai r.,** I shall do nothing of the sort; **sa fille n'a r. de lui,** his daughter doesn't take after him in any way; **il n'était pour r. dans l'affaire,** he had nothing to do with, had no hand in, the matter; *F:* **il ne sait r. de r.,** he knows nothing at all, nothing about anything; (*b*) (*with* **ne** *understood*) **que faites-vous?—r., presque r.,** what do you do?—nothing, hardly anything; **r. du tout,** nothing at all; **c'est tout ou r.,** it's all or nothing; **avoir qch. pour r.,** to get sth. for (next to) nothing; **parler pour r.,** to waste one's breath; **pourquoi demandez-vous cela?—oh, pour r.!** why do you ask that?—oh, I just wondered; **se fâcher de r.,** to get angry about nothing; **merci, monsieur—de r., monsieur,** thank you (very much) – it was a pleasure; (please) don't mention it; **en moins de r.,** in less than no time, in no time; **une affaire de r. (du tout),** an insignificant matter; **une petite pièce de r. du tout,** a wretched little room; **un homme de r. du tout,** a man of no account, a nobody; **un, une, r.(-)du(-)tout,** a (mere) nobody; **pour trois fois r.,** for next to nothing; **faire qch. comme (un) r.,** to do sth. easily, make nothing of sth.; *Ten:* **quinze à r.,** fifteen love; (*c*) (*the negation is expressed or implied elsewhere in the sentence*) **il est inutile de r. dire,** you needn't say anything; **sans r. faire,** without doing anything; (*d*) **r. que,** nothing but; only, merely; **je frémis r. que d'y songer,** the mere thought (of it) makes me shudder; **r. que pour aller à un bal,** for the sake of going, just to go, to a dance; **il m'a confié le secret, r. qu'à moi,** he told the secret just to me, to me alone; **r. que cela!** is that all? (*e*) (*with* **ne . . . pas) on ne peut pas vivre de r.,** you can't live on nothing; **ce n'est pas r.!** that's something! **3.** *P:* **elle est r. chic!** she isn't half smart! **II.** *n.m.* **1.** trifle, mere nothing; **se piquer d'un r.,** to take offence at the slightest thing; **perdre son temps à des riens,** to trifle away one's time; **dire des riens,** to indulge in small talk. **2.** just a little; **un r. d'ail, de fromage,** a touch of garlic, a taste of cheese; **en un r. de temps,** in no time (at all); **un r. de femme,** a tiny little woman. **3. il est un r. pédant,** he is a trifle pedantic.

rieur, -euse [rijœr, -øz] **1.** *a.* laughing; fond of laughter; merry. **2.** *n.* laugher; **avoir les rieurs de son côté,** to have the laugh on one's side.

rififi [rififi] *n.m. P:* brawl, free-for-all.

riflard¹ [riflar] *n.m. Tls:* **1.** coarse file (for metals). **2.** paring chisel. **3.** jackplane.

riflard² *n.m. F:* umbrella, *F:* brolly.

rifler [rifle] *v.tr.* (*a*) to plane; (*b*) to pare; (*c*) to file.

rigide [riʒid] *a.* rigid; tense (muscle); inflexible (system); fixed (axle).

rigidement [riʒidmɑ̃] *adv.* rigidly; tensely.

rigidité [riʒidite] *n.f.* rigidity, stiffness; tenseness (of muscles); inflexibility (of system); **r. cadavérique,** rigor mortis.

rigolade [rigɔlad] *n.f. F:* fun; lark, joke.

rigolard [rigɔlar] *a. F:* fond of a lark, a joke.

rigole [rigɔl] *n.f.* (*a*) (furrow) drain; trench, gutter, channel, ditch; (*b*) rivulet (of water).

rigoler [rigɔle] *v.i. F:* (*a*) to laugh; (*b*) to have some fun, to enjoy oneself.

rigoleur, -euse [rigɔlœr, -øz] **1.** *a.* fond of fun; jolly. **2.** *n.* wag, joker.

rigolo, -ote [rigɔlo, -ɔt] *F:* **1.** *a.* (*a*) comic, laughable, funny; **ce n'est pas r.,** it's no joke; (*b*) surprising, queer, odd. **2.** *n.m.* wag, joker. **3.** *n.m.* revolver.

rigorisme [rigɔrism] *n.m.* rigorism, strictness.

rigoriste [rigɔrist] **1.** *a.* rigorous; strict. **2.** *n.* rigorist; rigid moralist.

rigoureusement [rigurøzmɑ̃] *adv.* **1.** rigorously. **2.** strictly; **à parler r., ce n'est pas vrai,** strictly speaking, it is not true; **r. exact,** absolutely correct.

rigoureux, -euse [rigurø, -øz] *a.* rigorous. **1.** severe, harsh; hard (winter). **2.** strict; **observer une neutralité rigoureuse,** to observe strict neutrality; **au sens r. du mot,** in the strict sense of the word.

rigueur [rigœr] *n.f.* **1.** rigour, harshness, severity; **prendre des mesures de r.,** to take rigorous, severe, measures; **r. du temps,** severity of the weather; **avant les rigueurs de l'hiver,** before the severe part of the winter sets in; **user de r. avec qn,** to be severe with, hard on, s.o.; **tenir r. à qn,** not to forgive s.o. **2.** strictness (of rules, etc.); **la r. d'un raisonnement,** the closeness, exactness, of an argument; **style qui manque de r.,** sloppy style; **être de r.,** to be compulsory, obligatory; **délai de r.,** deadline; **l'habit n'est pas de r.,** evening dress is optional; **à la r.,** if need be, if really necessary; **à la r. on peut se servir d'un succédané,** at a pinch one may use a substitute.

rillettes [rijɛt] *n.f.pl. Cu:* potted mince (of pork, etc.).

rime [rim] *n.f.* rhyme; **rimes croisées, alternées,** alternate rhymes; **dictionnaire de rimes,** rhyming dictionary; *F:* **sans r. ni raison,** without rhyme or reason.

rimer [rime] **1.** *v.tr.* to versify, to put (tale, etc.) into rhyme; **poésie rimée,** rhyming verse. **2.** *v.i.* (*a*) to rhyme (**avec,** with); *F:* **à quoi cela rime-t-il?** what sense, what meaning, is there in that? **cela ne rime à rien,** there's no sense, neither rhyme nor reason, in it; (*b*) to write verses, poetry.

rimeur [rimœr] *n.m.* rhymer, rhymester.

rinçage [rɛ̃saʒ] *n.m.* rinsing; *Hairdr:* (colour) rinse.

rinceau, -eaux [rɛ̃so] *n.m. Arch:* foliated scroll.

rince-bouteilles [rɛ̃sbutɛj] *n.m.inv.* bottle-washing machine.

rince-doigts [rɛ̃sdwa] *n.m.inv.* finger bowl.

rincée [rɛ̃se] *n.f.* **1.** *P:* thrashing. **2.** downpour.
rincer [rɛ̃se] *v.tr.* **(je rinçai(s); n. rinçons) 1.** to rinse (clothes); to rinse (out) (glass); **se r. la bouche,** to rinse one's mouth; *P:* **se r. le gosier, la dalle,** to wet one's whistle; **se r. l'œil,** to get an eyeful. **2.** *P:* **se faire r.,** to be cleaned out (gambling).
rincette [rɛ̃sɛt] *n.f. P:* nip (of brandy after coffee).
rinceur, -euse [rɛ̃sœr, -øz] **1.** *n.* (*pers.*) rinser. **2.** *n.f.* (*machine*) (*a*) rinser; (*b*) bottle-washing machine.
rinçure [rɛ̃syr] *n.f.* (*a*) rinsings, slops; (*b*) *F:* poor wine; dishwater.
ring [riŋ] *n.m. Box:* ring.
ringard [rɛ̃gar] *n.m.* (furnace) fire iron, poker, clinker bar.
ripage [ripaʒ] *n.m.* **1.** (*a*) scraping, polishing (of stones); (*b*) sliding along, shifting (of load). **2.** skidding; slipping; shifting.
ripaille [ripaj] *n.f. F:* feast; *F:* blow-out.
ripailler [ripaje] *v.i. F:* to feast; to have a good blow-out.
riper [ripe] **1.** *v.tr.* (*a*) to scrape, polish (stone); (*b*) to slide along, shift (load); *Rail:* to shift (the track). **2.** *v.i.* (*a*) (*of hawser*) to slip (on the capstan); (*of wheels*) to skid; (*of cargo*) to shift; (*b*) *P:* to clear off.
riposte [ripɔst] *n.f.* riposte. **1.** counter stroke; *Box: Fenc:* return, counter. **2.** retort; pat answer.
riposter [ripɔste] *v.i.* **1.** *Box: Fenc:* to riposte, counter; **je riposterai,** I'll give as good as I get. **2.** to retort; to answer pat.
riquiqui [rikiki] *a. inv. F:* mean; wretched (little); **ça fait r.,** it looks a bit stingy, shabby, tatty.
rire¹ [rir] *v.i.* (*pr.p.* **riant;** *p.p.* **ri;** *pr.ind.* **je ris, n. rions, ils rient;** *pr.sub.* **je rie;** *p.h.* **je ris;** *fu.* **je rirai**) **1.** to laugh; **se tenir les côtes de r., r. comme un bossu,** to be doubled up, convulsed, with laughter; **r. bruyamment,** to guffaw; **r. en soi-même, r. tout bas,** to laugh to oneself; to chuckle; **r. en dedans,** to laugh up one's sleeve; **r. faux, pointu,** to give a forced laugh; **r. bêtement,** to giggle, titter; **dire qch. en riant,** to say sth. (i) laughingly, with a laugh, (ii) by way of a joke; **il a ri (jusqu')aux larmes,** he laughed till he cried; **c'était à mourir,** *F:* **à crever, de r.,** it was killingly funny; we nearly died with laughter; **ne pas avoir le cœur à r.,** not to be in a laughing mood; **il n'y a pas de quoi r.,** it's no laughing matter; **cela nous a souvent fait r.,** we have had many a laugh over it; **il nous faisait tordre, mourir, de r.,** he made us split our sides laughing; **r. de qn,** to laugh at s.o.; **ne riez pas de lui,** don't make fun of him; **r. d'une histoire,** to laugh over a story; **il rit de vos menaces,** he laughs at your threats; **il prête à r.,** he makes himself a laughing stock; **vous me faites r.!** nonsense! you must be joking! **laissez-moi r.! ne me faites pas r.!** don't make me laugh! **2.** to jest, joke; **nous allons r.,** we'll have some fun; **vous voulez r.!** are you joking? do you really mean it? **prendre qch. en riant,** to laugh sth. off; **pour r.,** for fun, for a joke; *F:* **c'était pour de r.,** it was only for fun; **roi pour r.,** sham king; **soldats pour r.,** make-believe soldiers; **je l'ai fait, histoire de r.,** I did it for a joke, for fun. **3.** (*of eyes, landscape*) to smile; **la fortune lui rit,** fortune smiles on him. **4. se r. de qn,** to laugh at, make fun of, s.o.; **se r. de qch.,** to laugh at, make light of, sth.
rire² *n.m.* (*a*) laughter, laughing; **éclat de r.,** burst of laughter; **avoir un accès de fou r.,** to laugh uncontrollably; (*b*) **un r.,** a laugh; **provoquer, exciter, les rires,** to cause laughter; **r. moqueur,** sneer; **il eut un r. d'incrédulité,** he laughed incredulously; **un gros r. bruyant,** a horse laugh; a guffaw.
ris¹ [ri] *n.m.* laugh, laughter.
ris² *n.m. Nau:* reef (in sail); **prendre un r.,** to take in a reef; **larguer un r.,** to shake out a reef.
ris³ *n.m. Cu:* **r. (de veau),** (calf's) sweetbread.
risée [rize] *n.f.* **1.** (*a*) mockery, derision; **s'exposer à la r. publique,** to expose oneself to public scorn, derision; (*b*) laughing stock, butt. **2.** *Nau:* light squall; flurry (of wind).
risette [rizɛt] *n.f.* (child's) laugh, smile; **fais (la) r. à papa!** now smile for daddy!
risible [riziblˌ] *a.* laughable (mistake).
risotto [rizɔto] *n.m. Cu:* risotto.
risque [risk] *n.m.* risk; (*a*) **courir un r.,** to run a risk; **à tout r.,** at all hazards; **prendre un r., des risques,** to take a risk, risks; **vous le faites à vos risques et périls,** you do it at your own risk; **au r. de sa vie,** at the risk, peril, of his life; **au r. de manquer le train,** at the risk of missing the train; **risques du métier,** occupational hazards; (*b*) *Ins:* **police tous risques,** comprehensive, all-risks, policy; **r. d'incendie,** fire risk; **souscrire un r.,** to underwrite a risk.
risqué [riske] *a.* (*a*) risky, hazardous (business); (*b*) risqué, *F:* near the knuckle.
risquer [riske] **1.** *v.tr.* to risk, venture, chance; **r. sa vie,** to risk, venture, one's life; **il faut r. le combat,** we must risk a battle; **je ne veux rien r.,** I am not taking any risks, any chances; **r. gros,** to play for heavy stakes; *Prov:* **qui ne risque rien n'a rien,** nothing venture, nothing gain; **r. le coup,** to chance it; **il risquait de tout perdre,** he risked, ran the risk of, losing everything; **la grève risque de durer longtemps,** the strike may (well) go on for a long time; *F:* **il risque de gagner,** he has a good chance of winning; **r. un œil,** to peep out. **2. se r.,** to take a risk; to take risks; **se r. à faire qch.,** to venture to do sth.
risque-tout [riskətu] *n.m.inv.* daredevil.
rissole [risɔl] *n.f. Cu:* (meat, etc.) patty.
rissoler [risɔle] *v.tr. & i. Cu:* to brown.
ristourne [risturn] *n.f.* (*a*) refund; rebate; (*b*) *Com:* discount; commission.
ristourner [risturne] *v.tr.* to refund, return (amount overpaid); to give a rebate (of so much).
rite [rit] *n.m.* rite; **les rites de la vie quotidienne,** the ritual of everyday life.
ritournelle [riturnɛl] *n.f. Mus:* ritornelle; *F:* **c'est toujours la même r.,** it's always the same old story.
ritualisme [ritɥalism] *n.f. Ecc:* ritualism.
ritualiste [ritɥalist] **1.** *a.* ritualistic. **2.** *n.m. & f.* ritualist.
rituel, -elle [ritɥɛl] **1.** *a.* ritual (service, etc.). **2.** *n.m.* (*a*) ritual; (*b*) ritual (book).
rivage [rivaʒ] *n.m.* beach (of sea, lake); bank (of river); strand; shore.
rival, -ale, -aux [rival, -o] *a. & n.* rival: **sans r.,** unrivalled.
rivaliser [rivalize] *v.i.* **r. avec qn,** to rival s.o.; to compete, vie, with s.o.; to hold one's own with s.o.; **r. d'adresse avec qn,** to vie in skill with s.o.
rivalité [rivalite] *n.f.* rivalry, competition.
rive [riv] *n.f.* **1.** bank (of river); shore (of lake, sea); waterside; verge (of road); **la Rive gauche,** the left bank (of the Seine). **2.** *Tchn:* edge, edging; lip (of oven).
river [rive] *v.tr.* (*a*) to rivet; **être rivé à un emploi,** to be stuck, fixed, in a job; (*b*) to clinch (nail); *F:* **r. son clou à qn,** to give s.o. a clincher; to leave s.o. speechless.
riverain, -aine [rivrɛ̃, -ɛn] **1.** *a.* (*a*) riparian, riverside, waterside, riverain (owner, property, etc.); (*b*) bordering on a road; wayside (property, etc.). **2.** *n.* (*a*) riverside resident; riverain; (*b*) resident; **les riverains de cette rue,** the people who live along this street; *P.N:* **route interdite sauf aux riverains,** access only.
rivet [rivɛ] *n.m.* (*a*) rivet; (*b*) clinch.

rivetage [rivtaʒ] *n.m.* (*a*) riveting; (*b*) clinching.
riveter [rivte] *v.tr.* (**je rivette, n. rivetons**) to rivet.
riveteuse [rivtøz] *n.f.* riveting machine.
rivière [rivjɛr] *n.f.* **1.** (*a*) river; stream; (*b*) *Sp:* water jump. **2. r. de diamants,** diamond rivière.
rivoir [rivwar] *n.m.* **1.** riveting hammer. **2.** riveting machine; riveter.
rivure [rivyr] *n.f.* **1.** riveting. **2.** (*a*) rivet(ed) joint; (*b*) rivet head. **3.** (*a*) pin joint; (*b*) hinge pin.
rixe [riks] *n.f.* brawl, scuffle; row.
riz [ri] *n.m.* rice; **r. en paille,** paddy; **r. décortiqué,** husked rice; **eau de r.,** rice water; *Cu:* **r. au lait,** rice pudding.
riziculteur [rizikyltœr] *n.m.* rice grower.
riziculture [rizikyltyr] *n.f.* rice growing.
rizière [rizjɛr] *n.f.* rice field(s), paddy field(s).
riz-pain-sel [ripɛ̃sɛl] *n.m.inv.* *Mil:* the commissariat.
rô [ro] *n.m.* *Gr.Alph:* rho.
robe [rɔb] *n.f.* **1.** (*a*) (lady's) dress; gown; **r. du soir,** evening dress; (*b*) **r. d'intérieur,** housecoat; **r. de chambre,** dressing gown; *NAm:* robe; *Cu:* **pommes de terre en r. de chambre, en r. des champs,** jacket potatoes; (*c*) (long) robe, gown (of lawyer, etc.); **les gens de r., la r.,** the legal profession. **2.** (*a*) skin (of onion, sausage); husk (of bean); wrapper (leaf) (of cigar); (*b*) coat (of horse, etc.).
robin [rɔbɛ̃] *n.m.* *Pej:* lawyer.
robine [rɔbin] *n.f.* *Fr.C:* *P:* surgical spirit; methylated spirits.
robinet [rɔbinɛ] *n.m.* tap, cock, *NAm:* faucet; **r. d'eau froide,** cold-water tap; **r. d'arrêt, de fermeture,** stopcock, shut-off (valve); **r. de vidange, de purge,** drain cock; **à flotteur,** ballcock; *Nau:* **r. de prise d'eau à la mer,** sea cock; **ouvrir, fermer, le r.,** to turn on, turn off, the tap; **r. d'arrivée d'essence,** petrol tap.
robinetterie [rɔbinɛtri] *n.f.* taps, cocks and fittings; valves and fittings.
robineux [rɔbinø] *n.m.* *Fr.C:* *P:* methylated spirits drinker.
robinier [rɔbinje] *n.m.* *Bot:* robinia; false acacia.
robot [rɔbo] *n.m.* robot; **avion r.,** pilotless plane; **photo-r., portrait-r.,** photo-fit identikit (picture).
robre [rɔbr̥] *n.m.* *Cards:* rubber.
robuste [rɔbyst] *a.* robust (person, health); sturdy (child); stout (faith); hardy (plant); strongly built (bicycle).
robustesse [rɔbystɛs] *n.f.* robustness, sturdiness, hardiness.
roc [rɔk] *n.m.* rock; **bâti sur le r.,** built on rock; **ferme comme un r.,** as firm as a rock.
rocade [rɔkad] *n.f.* lateral, parallel, road; bypass.
rocaille [rɔkaj] *n.f.* (*a*) rock work; **jardin de r.,** rockery; rock garden; (*b*) rubble.
rocailleux, -euse [rɔkajø, -øz] *a.* (*a*) rocky, pebbly, stony; (*b*) rugged, harsh (style, etc.).
rocambole [rɔkɑ̃bɔl] *n.f.* **1.** *Bot:* Spanish garlic. **2.** traveller's tale, cock-and-bull story.
rocambolesque [rɔkɑ̃bɔlɛsk] *a.* fantastic, incredible (adventures.)
rochassier, -ière [rɔʃasje, -jɛr] *n.* *Mount:* rock climber.
roche [rɔʃ] *n.f.* (*a*) rock; boulder; (*b*) *Geol:* **roches ignées, sédimentaires, metamorphiques,** igneous, sedimentary, metamorphic, rocks; **r. de fond,** bedrock; **eau de r.,** clear spring water; **clair comme de l'eau de r.,** as clear as crystal; **avoir un cœur de r.,** to have a heart of stone; **homme de la vieille r.,** one of the old school.
rocher [rɔʃe] *n.m.* (*a*) rock; crag; **r. branlant,** rocking stone, logan stone; **côte hérissée de rochers,** rock-bound coast; **le R. de Gibraltar,** the Rock of Gibraltar; *F:* the Rock; (*b*) **r. artificiel,** rockery.
rochet[1] [rɔʃɛ] *n.m.* **1.** ratchet; **roue à r.,** ratchet wheel. **2.** *Tex:* (large) bobbin.
rochet[2] *n.m.* *Ecc.Cost:* rochet.
rocheux, -euse [rɔʃø, -øz] *a.* rocky; **masse rocheuse,** rock mass; **les (montagnes) Rocheuses,** the Rocky Mountains, the Rockies.
rocking(chair) [rɔkiŋ(tʃɛr)] *n.m.* rocking chair; *pl. rocking-chairs.*
rococo [rokoko] *n.m. & a. inv.* *Art:* rococo; *F:* old-fashioned (dress, etc.).
rodage [rɔdaʒ] *n.m.* grinding. **1.** lapping, polishing (of gem); grinding in (of glass stopper, valve); running in (of engine); *Aut:* **en r.,** running in. **2.** wearing (of parts).
rodeo, rodéo [rɔdeo] *n.m.* rodeo.
roder [rɔde] *v.tr.* to grind; (*a*) to lap, polish (gem); to grind in (glass stopper, valve); *El:* to bed (brushes); **poudre à r.,** abradant; (*b*) *Aut:* to run in (new car); **être rodé,** (*of theatrical production*) to have got into its stride; (*of pers.*) to have been broken in (to a job); (*c*) to wear (down) (surface).
rôder [rode] *v.i.* **1.** to prowl, be on the prowl; **r. les rues,** to prowl about, hang about, the streets. **2.** (*of ship*) **r. sur son ancre,** to veer at anchor.
rôdeur, -euse [rodœr, -øz] **1.** *a.* prowling. **2.** *n.* prowler.
rodoir [rɔdwar] *n.m.* grinding tool; lap, polisher, hone.
Rodolphe [rɔdɔlf] *Pr.n.m.* Rudolph, Ralph.
Rodrigue [rɔdrig] *Pr.n.m.* Roderigo, Roderick.
Rogations [rɔgasjɔ̃] *n.f.pl.* *Ecc:* rogations.
rogatoire [rɔgatwar] *a.* *Jur:* rogatory.
rogaton [rɔgatɔ̃] *n.m.* scrap (of food), leftover.
rognage [rɔɲaʒ] *n.m.,* **rognement** [rɔɲmɑ̃] *n.m.* clipping, trimming, paring.
rogne [rɔɲ] *n.f.* *F:* bad temper; **être en r.,** to be cross, in a temper; to be ratty; **se ficher en r.,** to see red.
rogner [rɔɲe] *v.tr.* to clip, trim, pare, cut, cut down; to clip (coin); **r. les tranches,** to cut, trim, the edges (of a book); **r. la pension de qn,** to whittle down s.o.'s allowance; **r. (sur) les dépenses,** to cut down, curtail, reduce, expenses.
rognoir [rɔɲwar] *n.m.* paring tool, parer, clipper, trimmer, scraper.
rognon [rɔɲɔ̃] *n.m.* *esp. Cu:* kidney.
rognonner [rɔɲɔne] *v.i.* *F:* to grumble, growl, grouse.
rognures [rɔɲyr] *n.f.pl.* clippings, parings, trimmings, scraps.
rogomme [rɔgɔm] *n.m.* *F:* **voix de r.,** (drunkard's) husky voice.
rogue [rɔg] *a.* arrogant, haughty.
roi [rwa] *n.m.* (*a*) king; **le r. Louis XIII,** King Louis XIII (the thirteenth); *B:* **les rois (mages),** the three kings, the Magi; **jour, fête, des Rois,** Twelfth Day; Epiphany; (*b*) *attrib.inv.* **bleu r.,** royal blue; (*c*) **r. des resquilleurs,** champion gatecrasher; (*d*) *Cards:* *Chess:* king.
roide [rwad], **roideur** [rwadœr], **roidir** [rwadir] = RAIDE, RAIDEUR, RAIDIR.
roitelet [rwatlɛ] *n.m.* **1.** petty king. **2.** *Orn:* wren; **r. huppé,** goldcrest.
rôle [rol] *n.m.* **1.** list; register; roster; *Jur:* roll (of court); **à tour de r.,** in turn, by turns, in rotation; **faire qch. à tour de r.,** to take turns in doing sth.; **les rôles de l'armée active,** the active list; *Nau:* **r. de l'équipage,** list of the crew; muster roll; *Adm:* **r. des impôts, d'impôt,** assessment book. **2.** *Th:* part, role; **premier r.,** lead; leading man; leading lady; **second r.,** supporting part, role; **Mme X dans le r. de la Tosca,** Mme X as Tosca; **assigner un r. à qn,** to cast s.o. for a part; **distribution des rôles,** cast(ing); **jouer le r. de Macbeth,** to play (the part of) Macbeth; *F:*

jouer un r. secondaire, to play second fiddle; **sortir de son r.,** (i) to go beyond one's part; (ii) to take too much upon oneself.

rollier [rɔlje] *n.m. Orn:* roller.

romain, -aine¹ [rɔmɛ̃, -ɛn] *a. & n.* Roman; **l'Empire r.,** the Roman Empire; **l'Église romaine,** the Church of Rome; **chiffres romains,** Roman figures, numerals; *Typ:* **(caractère) r.,** roman type.

romaine² *n.f.* steelyard.

romaïque [rɔmaik] *a. & n.m. Ling:* Romaic; modern Greek.

roman¹ [rɔmɑ̃] *n.m.* **1.** (*a*) novel; **r. policier,** detective novel; **r. noir,** thriller; **r.-cycle, r.-fleuve,** saga (novel); **r.-photo,** story told in photographs; **r.-feuilleton,** serial (story); **votre histoire, c'est du r.,** your story is just a fairy tale; (*b*) **l'histoire de notre rencontre est tout un r.,** the story of our meeting is quite a romance; (*c*) **le r., les romans,** fiction. **2.** *Lit:* romance; **le R. de la Rose,** the Romaunt of the Rose.

roman², -ane [rɔmɑ̃, -an] *a. & n.m.* **1.** *Ling:* Romance, Romanic. **2.** *Arch:* romanesque; (*in Eng.*) Norman.

romance [rɔmɑ̃s] *n.f. Mus:* (sentimental) song, drawing-room ballad.

romancer [rɔmɑ̃se] *v.tr.* to fictionalize.

romancier, -ière [rɔmɑ̃sje, -jɛr] *n.* novelist; fiction writer.

romand [rɔmɑ̃] *a. Geog:* **la Suisse romande,** French(-speaking) Switzerland.

romanesque [rɔmanɛsk] *a.* romantic.

romanesquement [rɔmanɛskəmɑ̃] *adv.* romantically.

romanichel, -elle [rɔmaniʃɛl] *n.* (*a*) gipsy, romany; (*b*) vagrant.

romaniste [rɔmanist] *n.m.* **1.** *Ecc:* Romanist. **2.** *Ling:* Romanist; student of the Romance languages.

romantique [rɔmɑ̃tik] **1.** *a.* romantic; *Lit.Hist:* belonging to the romantic school of literature. **2.** *n. Lit.Hist:* romanticist.

romantiquement [rɔmɑ̃tikmɑ̃] *adv.* romantically.

romantisme [rɔmɑ̃tism] *n.m. Lit.Hist:* romanticism.

romarin [rɔmarɛ̃] *n.m. Bot:* rosemary.

rombière [rɔ̃bjɛr] *n.f. P:* tiresome woman; **vieille r.,** old bag.

Rome [rɔm] *Pr.n.f. Geog:* Rome; *Prov:* **tous les chemins mènent à R.,** all roads lead to Rome.

rompre [rɔ̃pr̥] (*pr.ind.* **je romps, il rompt, ils rompent**) **1.** *v.tr.* to break; (*a*) to break in two); to snap (stick); **r. le pain,** to break bread; **se r. le cou,** to break one's neck; (*b*) (*of stream*) **r. ses digues,** to burst its banks; **se r. une artère,** to burst an artery; *Th:* **applaudir à tout r.,** to bring down the house; *Mil:* **r. les rangs,** to disperse, to dismiss; (*c*) **r. le silence,** to break the silence; **r. une promesse,** to break a promise; (*d*) **r. un choc,** to deaden a shock; (*e*) to interrupt; to break off (conversation engagement, diplomatic relations); to call off (deal); to break (a spell); **r. un tête-à-tête,** to interrupt, break in on, a private conversation; *El:* **r. un circuit,** to break, disconnect, open, a circuit; (*f*) **r. l'équilibre,** to upset the balance; **r. les chiens,** (i) to call off the hounds; (ii) to change the subject; (*g*) **r. un cheval,** to break in a horse; **r. qn à la discipline, à la fatigue,** to break s.o. in to discipline; to inure s.o. to fatigue. **2.** *v.i.* (*a*) to break (off, up, in two); **r. avec qn,** to break with s.o.; **r. avec une habitude,** to break (oneself of) a habit; **r. avec sa vie passée,** to break away from one's past life; (*b*) (*of troops*) **r. devant l'ennemi,** to break before the enemy; (*c*) *Box: Fenc:* to break. **3. se r.** (*a*) to break (in two); (*of branch*) to snap, break off; (*of ice*) to break (up); **son cœur battait à se r.,** his heart was throbbing violently; (*b*) **se r. à qch.,** to break oneself in, to accustom oneself, to sth.; to inure oneself to (fatigue).

rompu [rɔ̃py] *a.* (*a*) broken; **chemin r.,** road full of potholes; **être r. de fatigue,** to be worn out, done up; **couleur rompue,** colour with a shot effect; (*b*) broken-in; **être r. aux affaires,** to be experienced in business.

ronce [rɔ̃s] *n.f.* **1.** *Bot:* bramble; blackberry bush. **2. ronce(s) artificielle(s),** barbed wire. **3.** curl (in grain of wood); **r. de noyer,** bur walnut.

ronce-framboise [rɔ̃sfrɑ̃bwaz] *n.f. Hort:* loganberry; *pl. ronces-framboises.*

ronceraie [rɔ̃srɛ] *n.f.* bramble patch.

ronchonnement [rɔ̃ʃɔnmɑ̃] *n.m. F:* grumbling, grousing.

ronchonner [rɔ̃ʃɔne] *v.i. F:* to grumble, grouse.

ronchonneur, -euse [rɔ̃ʃɔnœr, -øz] *n. F:* grumbler, grouser; *f.* scold.

roncier [rɔ̃sje] *n.m.,* **roncière** [rɔ̃sjɛr] *n.f.* thick bramble bush.

rond, ronde [rɔ̃, rɔ̃d] **1.** *a.* (*a*) round (ball, table); rounded (arm); plump (person, figure); **écriture ronde,** round hand; (*b*) **voix ronde,** full voice; **vent r.,** brisk wind; **en chiffres ronds,** in round figures; **compte r.,** round sum; *F:* **homme tout r.,** straightforward man; (*c*) *P:* tipsy, drunk. **2.** *adv.* **tourner r.,** (*of wheel*) to run true; (*of engine, factory*) to run smoothly; *F:* **cela ne tourne pas r.,** it's not working properly; things are not going well. **3.** *n.m.* (*a*) round, circle; **le chat se met en r.,** the cat coils itself up; **danser en r.,** to dance in a ring; **tourner en r.,** (i) to go round in a circle; (ii) to get nowhere, to go round in circles; *Danc:* **r. de jambe,** sweep of the leg; *F:* **faire les ronds de jambe,** to bow and scrape; **r. de serviette,** napkin ring; (*b*) disc, slice, round (of sausage); pat (of butter); **r. de cuir,** (round leather) chair cushion; *P:* **il n'a pas un r.,** he hasn't a brass farthing; (*c*) rounded moulding; **quart de r.,** quarter-round. **4.** *n.f.* **ronde** (*a*) round (dance); *Mus:* round, roundelay; (*b*) *Mil: etc:* round(s); (*of policeman*) beat; **faire la ronde,** to go the rounds; *A:* **la ronde de nuit,** (i) the watch patrol; (ii) the watch; *Fort:* **chemin de ronde,** parapet walk, rampart walk; (*c*) round hand (writing); (*d*) *Mus:* semibreve; (*e*) *adv.phr.* **à la ronde,** around; **à dix lieues à la ronde,** for thirty miles round; **(faire) passer le vin à la ronde,** to pass the wine round, to hand round the bottle; **boire à la ronde,** to drink in turn.

rond-de-cuir [rɔ̃dkɥir] *n.m. F:* (*a*) clerk (*esp.* in government service); pen-pusher; (*b*) bureaucrat; *pl. ronds-de-cuir.*

rondeau, -eaux [rɔ̃do] *n.m.* **1.** *Fr.Lit:* rondeau. **2.** *Mus:* rondo.

rondelet, -ette [rɔ̃dlɛ, -ɛt] *a.* roundish, plump (person); podgy (fingers); **somme rondelette,** good round sum; tidy sum.

rondelle [rɔ̃dɛl] *n.f.* **1.** small round; disc (of cardboard, etc.); slice (of gherkin); *Fr.C:* **r. (de hockey),** puck; **r. fusible,** fusible plug (of boiler). **2.** (*a*) ring (of umbrella, etc.); (*b*) washer; **r. de robinet,** tap washer.

rondement [rɔ̃dmɑ̃] *adv.* (*a*) roundly, briskly, promptly, smartly; **mener r. les choses,** to hustle things on; to make short work of it; (*b*) **il nous a dit r. qu'il n'était pas d'accord,** he told us straight, bluntly, that he didn't agree.

rondeur [rɔ̃dœr] *n.f.* **1.** (*a*) roundness, rotundity; (*b*) fullness (of shape); *pl.* rounded forms, lines; (*of woman*) curves. **2.** frankness, straightforwardness, plain dealing.

rondin [rɔ̃dɛ̃] *n.m.* (*a*) (round) billet; log; **chemin de rondins,** corduroy road; (*b*) thick stick; cudgel.

rondouillard [rɔ̃dujar] *a.* plump, fat.

rond-point [rɔ̃pwɛ̃] *n.m.* (*a*) circus (where several roads meet); (*b*) **r.-p. (à sens giratoire),** roundabout, *N.Am:* traffic circle; *pl. ronds-points.*

ronflant [rɔ̃flɑ̃] *a.* **1.** *Med:* **râle r.,** rhonchus. **2.** (*a*) roaring, rumbling, booming, humming, whirring, throbbing (noise, etc.); (*b*) high-sounding, sonorous (title); bombastic (speech).

ronflement [rɔ̃fləmɑ̃] *n.m.* **1.** (*a*) snoring; (*b*) snore. **2.** roaring, rumbling, booming, humming, whirring; *W.Tel:* buzzing; hum (in loudspeaker).

ronfler [rɔ̃fle] *v.i.* **1.** to snore. **2.** (*of wind, fire*) to roar; (*of organ*) to boom; (*of top*) to hum; (*of engine*) to whirr.

ronflette [rɔ̃flɛt] *n.f. P:* sleep, snooze.

ronfleur, -euse [rɔ̃flœr, -øz] *n.* **1.** snorer. **2.** *n.m. Tp:* buzzer;

rongeant [rɔ̃ʒɑ̃] *a.* (*a*) corroding (acid, etc.); rodent (ulcer); (*b*) gnawing (anxiety).

ronger [rɔ̃ʒe] **(je rongeai(s); n. rongeons) 1.** *v.tr.* (*a*) to gnaw, nibble; **r. un os,** (*of dog*) to gnaw a bone; (*of pers.*) to pick a bone; **rongé par les vers,** worm-eaten; **se r. le cœur, les sangs,** to eat one's heart out; (*b*) (*of acid, rust*) to corrode; to eat away (metal); (*of the sea*) to erode (cliffs); **être rongé de chagrin,** to be consumed, tormented, with grief. **2. se r.,** to worry, fret; **se r. de chagrin,** to eat one's heart out.

rongeur, -euse [rɔ̃ʒœr, -øz] **1.** *a.* rodent, gnawing (animal); gnawing (anxiety). **2.** *n.m.* rodent.

ronron [rɔ̃rɔ̃] *n.m.* purr(ing); **faire r.,** to purr; to hum, whirr, drone.

ronronnement [rɔ̃rɔnmɑ̃] *n.m.* (*a*) purring; (*b*) *Mch: W.Tel:* humming; *Av:* drone (of engine).

ronronner [rɔ̃rɔne] *v.i.* (*a*) to purr; (*b*) *Mch: W.Tel:* to hum.

roque [rɔk] *n.m. Chess:* castling.

roquer [rɔke] *v.i.* **1.** *Chess:* to castle. **2.** *Games:* to (loose-)croquet (the ball).

roquet [rɔkɛ] *n.m.* pug (dog).

roquette¹ [rɔkɛt] *n.f. Bot:* rocket; **r. des jardins,** winter cress.

roquette² *n.f. Ball:* rocket.

rorqual [rɔrkwal] *n.m. Z:* rorqual; fin-back (whale).

rosace [rozas] *n.f. Arch:* (*a*) rose (window); (*b*) **r. de plafond,** ceiling rose; rosette.

rosacé [rozase] *Bot:* **1.** *a.* rosaceous, rose-like. **2.** *n.f.pl.* **rosacées,** Rosaceae, rosaceous plants.

rosaire [rozɛr] *n.m. Ecc:* rosary; **dire le r.,** to tell one's beads.

rosâtre [rozɑtr̥] *a.* pinkish; dirty pink.

rosbif [rɔzbif] *n.m.* roast beef.

rose [roz] **1.** *n.f. Bot:* rose; (*a*) **r. incarnate,** damask rose; **r. mousseuse,** moss rose; **r.-thé,** tea rose; **r. sauvage,** wild rose, dog rose; **eau de r.,** rosewater; *F:* **roman à l'eau de r.,** sugary, sentimental, novel; **essence de roses,** attar, otto, of roses; **lèvres de r.,** rosy lips; **tout n'est pas r. dans ce monde,** life is not a bed of roses; **(il n'est) pas de r. sans épines,** no rose without a thorn; *F:* **découvrir le pot aux roses** [pɔtoroz], to find out the secret; **envoyer qn sur les roses,** to send s.o. packing; (*b*) **bois de r.,** rosewood. **2.** (*a*) *a.* pink (dress); rosy (complexion); (*inv. in compounds*) **des rubans rose pivoine,** peony-red ribbons, *F:* **ce n'est pas bien r., cette histoire-là,** it's a pretty grim story; (*b*) *n.m.* rose (colour); pink; **voir tout en r.,** to see everything through rose-coloured spectacles. **3.** *n.f.* (*a*) *Arch:* rose (window); (*b*) *Nau:* **r. des vents,** compass card; **dire la r.,** to box the compass; **r. mobile,** floating dial; (*c*) rose (diamond), rose-cut diamond.

rosé [roze] *a.* rosy, rose-pink; **(vin) r.,** rosé (wine).

roseau, -eaux [rozo] *n.m.* reed; **r. aromatique,** sweet flag, sweet rush; **s'appuyer sur un r.,** to lean on a broken reed.

rose-croix [rozkrwa] *n.m.inv.* Rosicrucian.

rosée [roze] *n.f.* dew; **goutte de r.,** dewdrop; **couvert, humecté, de r.,** dewy; *Ph:* **point de r.,** dew point.

roselet [rozlɛ] *n.m. Com:* ermine.

roselier, -ière [rozəlje, -jɛr] **1.** *a.* reed-bearing, (marsh). **2.** *n.f.* **roselière,** reed bed.

roséole [rozeɔl] *n.f. Med:* roseola, rose rash.

roser [roze] *v.tr.* to make (sth.) pink, rosy.

roseraie [rozrɛ] *n.f.* rosery; rose garden.

rosette¹ [rozɛt] *n.f.* (*a*) bow (of ribbon); (*b*) rosette (*esp.* of the Legion of Honour); **recevoir la r.,** to be awarded the Legion of Honour.

Rosette² *Pr.n.* **la pierre de R.,** the Rosetta stone.

rosier [rozje] *n.m.* rose tree, rose bush; **r. sur tige,** standard rose; **r. sauvage,** briar.

rosiériste [rozjerist] *n.m. & f.* rose grower.

rosir [rozir] **1.** *v.tr.* to turn (s.o., sth.) rosy, pink. **2.** *v.i.* (*a*) to become, turn, rosy; (*b*) to blush.

rosse [rɔs] **1.** *n.f.* (*a*) *F:* (*horse*) nag, screw; (*b*) *P:* objectionable, ill-natured, person; *F:* beast, swine; **c'est une petite r.,** she's a little bitch. **2.** *a. P:* objectionable, ill natured; nasty (person); low-down (trick).

rossée [rɔse] *n.f. F:* beating, thrashing, hiding.

rosser [rɔse] *v.tr. F:* to beat, thrash (s.o.).

rosserie [rɔsri] *n.f. F:* **1.** nastiness, unpleasantness (of conduct). **2.** (*a*) nasty, dirty, low, trick; **faire une r. à qn,** to do the dirty on s.o.; (*b*) spiteful remark.

rossignol [rɔsiɲɔl] *n.m.,* **1.** *Orn:* nightingale; *n.f.* **rossignole,** hen nightingale. **2.** picklock, skeleton key. **3.** *F:* old unsaleable article; white elephant; **vieux rossignols,** old stock.

rossinante [rɔsinɑ̃t] *n.f. F:* old wornout hack.

rot [ro] *n.m. P:* belch; burp.

rôt [ro] *n.m. A:* roast (meat).

rotarien [rɔtarjɛ̃] *n.m.* rotarian, member of a rotary club.

rotatif, -ive [rɔtatif, -iv] **1.** *a.* rotary (pump, etc.). **2.** *n.f.* **rotative,** rotary printing press.

rotation [rɔtasjɔ̃] *n.f.* **1.** *Mec: Ph:* rotation; spin (of projectile); revolution; **mouvement de r.,** rotational motion; **corps en r.,** rotating body; **pièce à r.,** revolving part; **axe de r.,** axis of rotation; *Mth:* **faire faire une r. de 90° à une droite,** to rotate a line through an angle of 90°. **2.** (*a*) **r. des cultures,** rotation of crops; (*b*) turnround (of ship, buses, etc.); turn-over (of stocks, capital, staff).

rotatoire [rɔtatwar] *a.* **1.** rotatory (movement); rotational (force). **2.** rotary (polarization).

roter [rɔte] *v.i. P:* to belch, burp.

rôti [roti] *n.m.* roast (meat); **r. de porc,** (joint of) roast pork; *F:* **ne vous endormez pas sur le r.,** don't dawdle.

rôtie [roti] *n.f.* round of toast.

rotin¹ [rɔtɛ̃] *n.m.* **1.** *Bot:* rattan; **sièges en r.,** cane chairs. **2.** rattan walking stick.

rotin² *n.m.* **rien! pas un r.!** not a penny, a cent!

rôtir [rotir] **1.** *v.tr.* (*a*) to roast (meat, chestnut); to toast (bread); (*b*) *F:* (*of the sun*) to scorch, dry up (grass, etc.); **se r. au soleil,** to roast in the sun. **2.** *v.i.* to roast; to toast; to scorch; **on rôtit ici,** it's scorching hot here.

rôtisserie [rotisri] *n.f.* (*a*) *A:* cook-shop; eating-house; (*b*) grill room.

rôtisseur, -euse [rotisœr, -øz] *n.* grill-room proprietor.

rôtissoire [rotiswar] *n.f.* spit roaster; *NAm:* broiler.

rotogravure [rɔtɔgravyr] *n.f. Typ:* rotogravure.

rotonde [rɔtɔ̃d] *n.f.* (*a*) rotunda, circular hall; (*b*) *Rail:* (circular) engine shed; roundhouse.

rotondité [rɔtɔ̃dite] *n.f.* rotundity. **1.** (*a*) roundness; (*b*) plumpness, stoutness. **2.** rounded part, curve.

rotor [rɔtɔr] *n.m. El:* rotor (of dynamo, turbine); *Av:* rotor (of helicopter).

rotule [rɔtyl] *n.f.* **1.** *Anat:* kneecap, patella; *F:* **être sur les rotules,** to be fagged out, on one's last legs. **2.** *Mec.E:* knee joint; ball(-and-socket) joint; *Aut:* **r. de direction,** steering knuckle.

rotulien, -ienne [rɔtyljɛ̃, -jɛn] *a. Anat:* patellar.

roture [rɔtyr] *n.f. Hist:* **1. terre en r.,** land held by a commoner. **2.** *coll.* commonalty, commons.

roturier, -ière [rɔtyrje, -jɛr] **1.** *a.* common, of the common people. **2.** *n.* commoner.

rouage [rwaʒ] *n.m.* **1.** wheels, wheelwork, gear work; **rouage(s) d'une montre,** works, train of wheels, of a watch; **r. d'horloge,** clockwork; **les rouages de l'administration,** the wheels of government. **2.** (toothed) wheel, cog wheel.

rouan, -anne [rwɑ̃, -an] *a.* roan (horse).

roublard, -arde [rublar, -ard] *a. & n. F:* foxy, wily, crafty (person); **un fin r.,** an old fox.

roublardise [rublardiz] *n.f. F:* **1.** cunning, craftiness. **2.** crafty trick.

rouble [rubl̥] *n.m. Num:* rouble.

roucoulement [rukulmɑ̃] *n.m.* cooing.

roucouler [rukule] *v.i. & tr.* to coo; **r. une chanson,** to warble a song.

roue [ru] *n.f.* wheel; (*a*) **véhicule à quatre roues,** four-wheeled vehicle; **r. de secours,** spare wheel; **rouler en r. libre,** to coast; *Fig:* to do as one likes; *F:* **la cinquième r. du carosse,** an entirely useless person, thing; **pousser à la r.,** to put one's shoulder to the wheel, to lend a helping hand; **sans roues,** wheelless; *Nau:* **la r. du gouvernail,** the wheel; **faire la r.,** (i) (*of peacock*) to spread its tail; (ii) to strut, to swagger; (iii) to turn cartwheels (*b*) **r. à corde,** cable pulley; (*c*) **r. à aile, r. volante,** flywheel; **r. dentée, r. d'engrenage,** toothed wheel, cogwheel, rack wheel, gear (wheel); **r. de commande, de transmission, r. motrice,** driving wheel, pinion; **r. de turbine,** turbine wheel, impeller; (*d*) **r. à eau, r. hydraulique,** water wheel, hydraulic wheel; **r. en dessous,** undershot (water)-wheel; **r. en dessus,** overshot (water)wheel; **r. de moulin,** mill wheel; *Nau:* **bateau à roues,** paddle boat; (*e*) **la r. de la fortune,** the wheel of fortune; (*f*) *Pyr:* **r. à feu,** Catherine wheel; (*g*) *A:* **condamner un criminel à la r.,** to condemn a criminal to the wheel.

roué, -ée [rwe] **1.** *n.m.* rake, profligate; roué. **2.** *a. & n.* cunning, sly (person).

rouelle [rwɛl] *n.f.* round slice (of lemon, etc.); **r. de veau,** fillet of veal.

rouennerie [rwanri] *n.f. Tex:* printed cotton goods.

rouer [rwe] *v.tr.* (*a*) *A:* to break (s.o.) on the wheel; (*b*) *F:* **r. qn de coups,** to beat s.o. black and blue.

rouet [rwɛ] *n.m.* **1.** spinning wheel. **2.** (*a*) sheave (of pulley); pulley wheel; **r. de pompe,** pump impeller; (*b*) *Nau:* gin. **3.** scutcheon (of lock).

rouf [ruf] *n.m. Nau:* deck house.

rouge [ruʒ] **1.** *a.* red; (*a*) **fer r.,** red-hot iron; **être r. de honte,** to be red, to blush, with shame; (*of pers.*) **r. comme une tomate, une écrevisse,** as red as a beetroot; **le chapeau r.,** the cardinal's (red) hat; *Pol:* **le drapeau r.,** the red flag; **porto r.,** ruby port; *adv.* **se fâcher tout r.,** to lose one's temper completely; **voir r.,** to see red; (*b*) (*inv. in compounds*) **des rubans rouge cerise,** cherry-red ribbons; **r. sang,** blood-red; **r. drapeau,** pillar-box red. **2.** *n.m.* (*a*) red (colour); **porter le fer au r.,** to make the iron red-hot; **r. blanc,** white heat; *Pol:* **c'est un r.,** he's a Red, a Communist; *Prov:* **r. le soir, espoir,** red sky at night (is the) shepherd's delight; (*b*) *Toil:* rouge; **r. à lèvres, bâton de r.,** lipstick; (*c*) **r. d'Angleterre, de Prusse,** (jewellers') rouge; (*d*) red wine; **gros r.,** coarse red wine.

rougeâtre [ruʒɑtr̥] *a.* reddish.

rougeaud, -eaude [ruʒo, -od] **1.** *a. & n.* red-faced (person).

rouge-gorge [ruʒgɔrʒ] *n.m. Orn:* robin; redbreast; *pl. rouges-gorges.*

rougeole [ruʒɔl] *n.f. Med:* measles.

rougeoyant [ruʒwajɑ̃] *a.* glowing; lurid (flame, etc.).

rougeoyer [ruʒwaje] *v.i.* **(il rougeoie; il rougeoiera)** (*of thgs*) (*a*) to turn red; (*b*) to glow red.

rouge-queue [ruʒkø] *n.m. Orn:* redstart; *pl. rouges-queues.*

rouget [ruʒɛ] *n.m. Ich:* red mullet; **r. grondin,** gurnard.

rougeur [ruʒœr] *n.f.* **1.** blush; flush; **faire monter la r. au visage de qn,** to make s.o. flush, blush. **2.** red spot, blotch (on skin).

rougir [ruʒir] **1.** *v.tr.* (*a*) to redden; to turn (sth.) red; **eau rougie,** water with a little red wine; (*b*) **fer rougi au feu,** iron heated red-hot; **r. le fer au blanc,** to make iron white-hot; (*c*) to flush (the face). **2.** *v.i.* (*a*) to redden, to turn red; **faire r. un métal,** to heat a metal red-hot; (*b*) (*of pers.*) to turn, go, red; to colour; to blush; to flush (up); **faire r. qn,** to make s.o. blush; **r. jusqu'aux oreilles,** to blush to the roots of one's hair; **r. d'un faux pas,** to be ashamed of an indiscretion; **r. de qn,** to blush for s.o.; **r. de colère,** to flush with anger.

rougissant [ruʒisɑ̃] *a.* (*a*) reddening, turning red; (*b*) blushing.

rougissement [ruʒismɑ̃] *n.m.* (*a*) reddening, turning red; (*b*) blushing, going red.

rouille [ruj] *n.f.* **1.** rust; **tache de r.,** iron stain, iron mould (on cloth). **2.** *Agr:* rust, mildew, blight. **3.** *a.inv.* rust(-coloured).

rouillé [ruje] *a.* **1.** rusty; (*a*) rusted (metal, etc.); (*b*) rust-coloured; (*c*) out of practice. **2.** mildewed (plant).

rouiller[1] [ruje] **1.** *v.tr.* (*a*) to rust; to make (iron, etc.) rusty; (*b*) to mildew, blight (plant). **2. se r.** (*a*) to rust (up); to get rusty; (*b*) **je me rouille,** I am getting rusty, out of practice; (*c*) (*of plant*) to become mildewed.

rouillure [rujyr] *n.f.* **1.** rustiness. **2.** rust, blight (of plants).

rouir [rwir] **1.** *v.tr.* to steep, ret (flax, etc.). **2.** *v.i.* to steep, ret.

rouissage [rwisaʒ] *n.m.* steeping, retting (of flax).

roulade [rulad] *n.f.* **1.** roll (in the dust, downhill). **2.** *Mus:* roulade, vocal flourish. **3.** *Cu:* beef, etc. olive.

roulage [rulaʒ] *n.m.* **1.** (*a*) rolling (of ploughed land, of metal, etc.); (*b*) easy running (of vehicle). **2.** carriage, cartage (of goods); haulage; **entrepreneur de r.,** carrier; haulage contractor; **cheval de r.,** cart horse, draught horse. **3.** road traffic.

roulant, -ante [rulɑ̃, -ɑ̃t] **1.** *a.* (*a*) rolling; sliding (door); moving (staircase); travelling (crane); **allure roulante,** rolling gait; **voiture bien roulante,** smooth-running car; *Rail:* **matériel r.,** rolling stock; **personnel r.,** train, lorry, bus, etc. crews; (*b*) smooth; **chemin bien r.,** good road, easy(-running) road. **2.** *a. Com:* **affaire roulante,** going concern; **fonds r.,** working capital. **3.** *a. F:* side-splitting (joke). **4.** *n.f. F: Mil:* **roulante,** field kitchen.

roulé [rule] **1.** *a.* rolled; **col r.,** roll collar; polo neck; turtle neck. **2.** *n.m.* (*a*) *Cu:* rolled joint; (*b*) **r. à la confiture,** Swiss roll.

rouleau, -eaux [rulo] *n.m.* **1.** roller; (*a*) **roulements à rouleaux,** roller bearings; (*b*) **r. compresseur,** road roller; **r. à vapeur,** steam roller; **r. pour gazon,** garden roller; **passer le gazon au r.,** to roll the grass; **r. à pâtisserie,** rolling pin; (*c*) **r. porte-serviettes,** towel roller; *Typewr:* **r. porte-papier,** impression roller; **r. à mise en plis,** (hair) roller; **(store sur) r.,** roller blind; (*d*) *Typ:* (ink) roller; *Phot:* roller (squeegee); **r. à peinture,** paint roller. **2.** roll (of paper, etc.); roll, spool (of film); coil (of rope); twist (of tobacco); scroll (of parchment); **être au bout de son r.,** (i) to be at the end of one's tether; (ii) to be near one's end. **3.** *Oc:* billow, roller. **4.** *Sp:* (*high jump*) roll; **r. ventral,** straddle.

roulée [rule] *n.f. P:* thrashing, licking.

roulement [rulmɑ̃] *n.m.* **1.** (*a*) rolling (of ball, etc.); **r. d'yeux,** rolling of the eyes; (*b*) rolling (of vehicle); *Av:* taxying; **bande de r.,** tread (of tyre); **train de r.,** bogie; **galet de r.,** bogie wheel; (*c*) running, working (of a machine); **r. silencieux,** smooth running. **2.** rumbling (of waggon, thunder); rattle (of vehicle on stones); rolling (of drum). **3.** *Mec.E:* bearing; **r. à billes,** ball bearing; **r. à galets, à rouleaux,** roller bearing. **4.** (*a*) *Com:* **r. de fonds,** circulation of capital; (*b*) alternation, taking turns (in duties, etc.); rotation; **par r.,** in rotation.

rouler [rule] **1.** *v.tr.* (*a*) to roll (stone, cask, etc.) (along, about); to cast (dice); *Min:* to haul (coal); **r. les yeux,** to roll one's eyes; **r. un projet dans sa tête,** to turn over a plan in one's mind; **r. de mauvaises pensées,** to think evil thoughts; **se r. les pouces,** to twiddle one's thumbs; *P:* **se les r.,** to have a cushy time; (*b*) *F:* **r. qn,** to take s.o. in; **il m'a roulé de deux mille francs,** he has done me out of two thousand francs; (*c*) to roll up (map, one's sleeves); to roll (meat, fish); to roll (cigarette); to roll up, furl, (umbrella); to roll out (pastry); (*d*) **r. un champ, un tennis,** to roll a field, a tennis court; (*e*) **r. les r,** to roll one's r's; (*f*) **r. qn dans une couverture,** to roll, wrap, s.o. up in a blanket. **2.** *v.i.* (*a*) to roll (over, along, about); **r. sur une pente,** to roll down a slope; **r. (en voiture),** to drive; **nous avons roulé toute la nuit,** we travelled all night; **cette voiture a peu roulé,** this car has a low mileage; *Av:* **r. sur le sol,** to taxi; *F:* **ça roule,** everything's fine; **je ne roule pas sur l'or,** I'm not rolling in money; *Fin:* **l'argent roule,** money is circulating freely; **la conversation roulait sur le sport,** the talk ran, turned, on sport; **r. dans tous les pays,** to knock about the world; *Prov:* **pierre qui roule n'amasse pas mousse,** a rolling stone gathers no moss; (*b*) (*of thunder, etc.*) to roll, rumble; (*c*) *Nau:* (*of ship*) to roll; (*d*) to rotate, to take turns; **r. ensemble,** to take it in turns. **3. se r.** (*a*) to roll, to turn over and over; (*b*) **le hérisson se roule en boule,** the hedgehog rolls up into a ball; (*c*) *F:* **se r. (par terre),** to be convulsed with laughter.

roulette [rulɛt] *n.f.* **1.** (*a*) caster; roller; small wheel; **chaise à roulettes,** chair on casters; **patins à roulettes,** roller skates; **ça marche, va, comme sur des roulettes,** things are going like clockwork; *Av:* **r. de nez, de queue,** nose wheel, tail wheel; (*b*) (bookbinder's) fillet; (shoemaker's) pricking wheel; *Dressm:* tracing wheel, tracer; *Cu:* pastry wheel; (*c*) (spring) tape measure; (*d*) *F:* dentist's drill. **2.** (game of) roulette; **r. russe,** Russian roulette.

rouleur, -euse [rulœr, -øz] **1.** *n.m.* (*a*) roller, haulage man; (*b*) *F:* **c'est un r.,** he's a man who always gets the best of the bargain; (*c*) rolling stone; *F:* **r. de cabarets,** pub crawler; (*d*) *Cy:* **un bon r.,** a steady, fast, performer on the flat. **2.** *n.m. Nau:* ship that rolls heavily. **3.** *n.f. Ent:* **rouleuse,** leaf roller, leaf crumpler.

roulis [ruli] *n.m. Nau: Av:* roll(ing); **coup de r.,** roll, lurch; **quille de r.,** rolling chock, bilge keel; **table à r.,** fiddle.

roulotte [rulɔt] *n.f.* (gipsies', touring) caravan; trailer.

roulotté [rulɔte] *a. & n.m. Needlew:* **(ourlet) r.,** rolled hem.

roumain, -aine [rumɛ̃, -ɛn] *a. & n. Geog: Ling:* Rumanian, Ro(u)manian.

Roumanie [rumani] *Pr.n.f. Geog:* Rumania, Ro(u)mania.

round [rawnd, rund] *n.m. Box:* round.

roupie¹ [rupi] *n.f. Num:* rupee.

roupie² *n.f. F:* **avoir la r.,** to have a drippy nose; **c'est de la r. de sansonnet,** it's worthless rubbish.

roupiller [rupije] *v.i. F:* to sleep; to snooze, take a nap.

roupilleur, -euse [rupijœr, -øz] *n. F:* snoozer.

roupillon [rupijɔ̃] *n.m. F:* nap, snooze; **piquer un r.,** to take a nap.

rouquin, -ine [rukɛ̃, -in] **1.** *a. & n. F:* red-haired, ginger-haired (person); *n.* redhead. **2.** *n.m. P:* rough red wine.

rouspétance [ruspetɑ̃s] *n.f. F:* grousing, bellyaching.

rouspéter [ruspete] *v.i.* **(je rouspète; je rouspéterai)** *F:* to grouse, bellyache, protest; **r. contre tout le monde,** to be up against everybody.

rouspéteur, -euse [ruspetœr, -øz] *F:* **1.** *a.* grumbling, grouchy. **2.** *n.* grumbler, grouser.

roussâtre [rusatr̥] *a.* reddish (hair).

rousserolle [rusrɔl] *n.f. Orn:* (i) reed warbler; (ii) sedge warbler.

roussette [rusɛt] *n.f.* **1.** *Ich:* spotted dogfish. **2.** *Z:* flying fox. **3.** russet pear.

rousseur [rusœr] *n.f.* redness (of hair, etc.); **tache de r.,** freckle; **couvert de taches de r.,** freckled.

roussi [rusi] **1.** *a.* browned; scorched. **2.** *n.m.* **ça sent le r.,** (i) there's a smell of something burning; (ii) there's trouble ahead.

roussin [rusɛ̃] *n.m.* (*horse*) cob.

roussir [rusir] **1.** *v.tr.* (*a*) to turn (sth.) russet, brown; to redden; to brown (meat); (*b*) to scorch, singe (linen). **2.** *v.i.* (*a*) to turn brown, russet; to redden; (*b*) *Cu:* **faire r. du beurre,** to brown butter; (*c*) to scorch, singe; to get scorched.

routage [rutaʒ] *n.m. Post:* sorting and routing (of printed papers).

route [rut] *n.f.* **1.** road; **r. nationale, grande r.,** main road, major road, *NAm:* highway; = A road; **r. départementale,** secondary road; **prendre la r. de Paris,** to take the road for, to, Paris; **r. à double voie,** dual carriageway; **par la r.,** by road; **code de la r.,** highway code; **chanson de r.,** marching song; **l'état des routes,** road conditions. **2.** route, way; (*a*) **se mettre en r.,** to start on one's way, to set out; (*of ship*) to get under way; to be on one's way, on the way; **navire en r. pour l'étranger,** ship outward bound; **en r.!** (i) let's go! (ii) off you go! **faire r. ensemble,** to travel together; **marchandises avariées en cours de r.,** goods damaged in transit; **frais de r.,** travel(ling) expenses; **barrer la r. à qn,** to bar s.o.'s way; **montrer la r. à qn,** to show s.o. the way; **r. de mer,** sea route; **r. de navigation,** (shipping) lane, ocean lane; **r. terrestre,** (over)land route; **r. commerciale,** trade route; (*b*) *Nau:* **r. (à suivre),** course; **r. (suivie),** track; **suivre une r.,** to steer a course; **faire r. sur Calais,** to steer, make, for Calais; (*c*) **mettre le moteur en r.,** to start up the engine; **mettre des travaux en r.,** to start operations.

router [rute] *v.tr. Post:* to sort and route (printed papers).

routier¹, -ière [rutje, -jɛr] *a. & n.* **1.** *Nau: Av:* **(livre) r.,** track chart. **2. carte routière,** road map; **police routière,** traffic police; **pont r.,** road bridge; **bicyclette routière,** *n.m.* **r.,** roadster; **locomotive routière,** traction engine; **transports routiers,** road transport, haulage; **gare routière,** (i) bus, coach, station; (ii) road haulage depot. **3.** *n.m.* **gros r.,** heavy (goods) lorry; *NAm:* heavy truck. **4.** (*pers.*) (*a*) long-distance lorry driver; *NAm:* teamster, truck driver; (*b*) *Cy:* road racer. **5.** *n.f. Aut:* **routière,** tourer.

routier² *n.m.* (*a*) *Mil: A:* mercenary; (*b*) *F:* **vieux r.,** old campaigner; old hand; (*c*) *Scout:* rover.

routine [rutin] *n.f.* (*a*) routine; **examen de r.,** routine examination; (*b*) routinism; **faire qch. par r.,** (i) to do sth. by rule of thumb; (ii) to do sth. out of sheer habit.

routinier, -ière [rutinje, -jɛr] **1.** *a.* (*a*) routine (duties, etc.); (*b*) (person) who sticks to routine, is stuck in a rut. **2.** *n.* slave to routine; **un parfait r.,** a regular stick-in-the-mud.

rouvrir [ruvrir] *v.tr., i. & pr.* (*conj. like* OUVRIR) to reopen.

roux, rousse [ru, rus] **1.** (*a*) (russet-)red, (reddish)-brown; (*of hair*) red; *inv. in compounds*; **chevelure blond r.,** sandy hair; *Cu:* **beurre r.,** brown butter; (*b*) *n.* red-haired, sandy-haired, person; redhead. **2.** *n.m.* (*a*) russet, reddish-brown (colour); (*b*) *Cu:* roux.

royal, -aux [rwajal, -o] *a.* royal; regal, kingly; **prince r.,** crown prince.

royalement [rwajalmɑ̃] *adv.* royally, regally; *F:* **s'amuser r.,** to enjoy oneself immensely, hugely; **je m'en fiche r.,** I couldn't care less about it.

royaliste [rwajalist] *a. & n.* royalist; **être plus r. que le roi,** to out-Herod Herod.

royaume [rwajom] *n.m.* kingdom, realm; **le r. des cieux,** the kingdom of heaven.

Royaume-Uni (le) [lərwajomyni] *Pr.n.m.* the United Kingdom.

royauté [rwajote] *n.f.* royalty; kingship.

ruade [rɥad] *n.f.* lashing out, fling out, buck, kick (of horse); **allonger, décocher, lancer, une r.,** to lash out (**à,** at).

ruban [rybɑ̃] *n.m.* **1.** (*a*) ribbon, band; **r. de chapeau,** hatband; **le r. rouge,** the red ribbon (of the Legion of Honour); (*b*) **r. de fil,** tape; **mètre à r., en r.,** measuring tape; **r. adhésif,** adhesive tape; **r. magnétique,** magnetic, recording, tape; *Typwr:* **r. encreur,** inking ribbon; *El:* **r. isolant,** insulating tape. **2. r. d'acier,** steel band; **fer à r.,** hoop iron; **scie à r.,** band saw, belt saw. **3. r. roulant, transporteur,** belt conveyor.

rubané [rybane] *a.* **1.** *Nat.Hist:* striped; *Miner:* **agate rubanée,** ribbon agate, banded agate. **2. canon r.,** strip-wound gun barrel.

rubaner [rybane] *v.tr.* **1.** (*a*) to trim (sth.) with ribbon; (*b*) *El:* to tape (wire). **2.** to cut (sth.) into ribbons, strips.

rubanerie [rybanri] *n.f.* **1.** ribbon manufacture, trade. **2.** ribbon factory.

rubéole [rybeɔl] *n.f. Med:* rubella; German measles.

rubican [rybikɑ̃] *a.* roan (horse).

rubicond [rybikɔ̃] *a.* rubicond, florid (complexion).

rubis [rybi] *n.m.* ruby; **r. balais,** balas ruby; **r. spinelle,** spinel ruby; **r. de Bohème,** rose quartz; **montre montée sur r.,** jewelled watch; *F:* **faire r. sur l'ongle,** to drink to the last drop; **payer r. sur l'ongle,** to pay cash on the nail.

rubrique [rybrik] *n.f.* (*a*) *Ecc: Jur:* rubric; (*b*) imprint (of book); (*c*) *Journ:* heading; item; **il tient la r. de la mode au Figaro,** he writes the fashion columns in the *Figaro*; **sous la même r.,** under the same heading.

ruche [ryʃ] *n.f.* **1.** (bee)hive; **r. en paille,** bee-skep; *F:* **r. d'industrie,** regular hive of industry. **2.** *Needlew:* ruche, ruching.

ruchée [ryʃe] *n.f.* hive(ful).

rucher¹ [ryʃe] *n.m.* apiary.

rucher² *v.tr. Needlew:* to ruche.

rude [ryd] *a.* **1.** (*a*) uncouth, unpolished, primitive (people, manners); (*b*) rough (skin, cloth, wine); stiff, hard (brush); harsh, grating (voice); rugged (path). **2.** (*a*) hard, severe (winter); stiff, arduous (task); heavy, severe (blow); rude (shock); stiff, steep (climb); **il a été à r. école,** he had a strict upbringing; (*b*) gruff, ungracious, brusque; hard (master). **3.** *F:* (*intensive*) **r. appétit,** hearty appetite; **faire une r. gaffe,** to put one's foot in it in no uncertain manner.

rudement [rydmɑ̃] *adv.* **1.** (*a*) roughly, harshly, severely; **être r. éprouvé,** to be severely tried; **travailler r.,** to work hard; (*b*) roughly, coarsely. **2.** *F:* (*intensive*) **je suis r. fatigué,** I'm awfully, terribly, tired.

rudesse [rydɛs] *n.f.* **1.** uncouthness, primitiveness. **2.** roughness, ruggedness (of a surface, style); coarseness (of material); roughness (of wine); harshness (of voice). **3.** (*a*) severity (of winter, task); (*b*) ungraciousness; brusqueness, abruptness; bluntness; gruffness; **traiter qn avec r.,** to browbeat s.o.

rudiment [rydimɑ̃] *n.m.* **1.** rudiment (of organ, etc.). **2.** *pl.* rudiments, smattering (of knowledge); beginnings (of scheme).

rudimentaire [rydimɑ̃tɛr] *a.* rudimentary.

rudoyer [rydwaje] *v.tr.* (**je rudoie; je rudoierai**) to treat (s.o.) roughly; (i) to browbeat, bully (s.o.); (ii) to knock (s.o.) about.

rue¹ [ry] *n.f.* **1.** street, thoroughfare; **r. principale,** main thoroughfare; **la grande r.,** the high street, the main street; **petite r. écartée,** back street; **le peuple descendit dans la r.,** people were out on the streets (to protest, fight); **être à la r.,** to find oneself out on the street; **courir les rues,** (i) to run about the streets; (ii) (*of news, etc.*) to be common talk, to be in everyone's mouth; (*of rumour*) to be rife; **l'homme de la r.,** the man in the street. **2.** *pl. Th:* slips.

rue² *n.f. Bot:* (*a*) rue; (*b*) **r. des murailles,** wall rue.

ruée [rɥe] *n.f.* rush, onrush; **la r. sur, vers, les plages,** the rush for the seaside; **la r. vers l'or,** the gold rush.

ruelle [rɥɛl] *n.f.* **1.** lane; alley. **2.** *A:* (*a*) space between the bedside and the wall; (*b*) literary clique, coterie.

ruer [rɥe] **1.** *v.i.* (*of animal*) to kick, fling out, lash out. **2. se r. sur qn, qch.,** to hurl, fling, oneself at s.o., sth.; **se r. à l'attaque,** to throw oneself into the attack; **se r. à la porte,** to rush, make a rush, for the door.

rugby [rygbi] *n.m.* rugby (football), *F:* rugger.

rugbyman, *pl.* **-men** [rygbiman, -mɛn] *n.m.* rugby player.

rugir [ryʒir] *v.i.* to roar; (*of wind*) to howl; **r. de colère,** to roar with rage.

rugissement [ryʒismɑ̃] *n.m.* **1.** roaring (of lion); howling (of storm). **2.** roar, bellow.

rugosité [rygozite] *n.f.* ruggedness, roughness.

rugueux, -euse [rygø, øz] *a.* rugose; rugged, rough; gnarled (tree, bark).

ruine [rɥin] *n.f.* ruin. **1.** (*a*) downfall; decay (of building, etc.); **tomber en r.,** to fall in(to) ruin(s); **maisons qui tombent en r.,** tumbledown houses; **tout tombe en r.,** everything is going to (w)rack and ruin; (*b*) downfall (of pers., society); **aller, courir, à la r.,** to be on the road to ruin; **ce sera sa r.,** it will be the ruin, the ruination, of him. **2.** (*usu. pl.*) **les ruines de Troie,** the ruins of Troy; **leur château est une vieille r.,** their castle is an old ruin.

ruiner [rɥine] *v.tr.* to ruin, destroy; **r. qn,** to bankrupt s.o.; **se r. la santé,** to ruin one's health; **un homme ruiné,** a broken man.

ruineusement [rɥinøzmɑ̃] *adv.* ruinously.

ruineux, -euse [rɥinø, -øz] *a.* ruinous. **1.** falling into ruin. **2.** (*a*) disastrous (war); (*b*) expensive; **ce n'est pas r.,** it won't ruin us, break us (to buy it).

ruisseau, -eaux [rɥiso] *n.m.* **1.** (*a*) brook, (small) stream, rivulet; (*b*) stream (of blood, lava); flood (of tears). **2.** (street) gutter; **calomnie ramassée dans le r.,** slander picked up in the gutter.

ruisselant [rɥislɑ̃] *a.* streaming; dripping (wet); **eaux ruisselantes,** (i) running waters; (ii) trickling water.

ruisseler [rɥisle] *v.i.* (**il ruisselle; il ruissellera**) **1.** (*of liquid*) (*a*) to stream, run; **l'eau ruisselait par la porte,** the water was streaming, pouring, in (or out) at the door; (*b*) to trickle. **2.** (*of surface*) to run, to drip; **le parquet ruisselait,** the floor was running with water; **front ruisselant de sueur,** forehead dripping with sweat.

ruisselet [rɥislɛ] *n.m.* brooklet, rivulet, rill.

ruissellement [rɥisɛlmɑ̃] *n.m.* **1.** (*a*) streaming, running (of water, etc.); *Hyd.E: Geog:* runoff; (*b*) trickling, dripping. **2.** shimmer (of jewellery, etc).

rumba [rumba] *n.f. Danc:* rumba.

rumen [rymɛn] *n.m. no pl.* rumen (of ruminant).

rumeur [rymœr] *n.f.* **1.** (*a*) confused, distant, murmur; hum (of traffic); (*b*) din, clamour, uproar; **tout est en r.,** everything is in an uproar. **2.** rumour; **r. publique,** common report; **la r. court qu'il est ruiné,** it is rumoured that he's ruined.

ruminant [ryminɑ̃] *a. & n.m. Z:* ruminant.

rumination [ryminasjɔ̃] *n.f.* rumination, ruminating.

ruminer [rymine] **1.** *v.i.* (*of animal*) to ruminate; to chew the cud. **2.** *v.tr.* **r. une idée,** to ruminate on, over, an idea.

rumsteck [rɔmstɛk] *n.m.* rumpsteak.

runabout [rynabu] *n.m. Nau:* runabout; speedboat.

rune [ryn] *n.f.* rune.

runique [rynik] *a.* runic.

rupestre [rypɛstr̥] *a.* **dessins rupestres,** rock drawings; **peintures rupestres,** cave paintings.

rupin, -ine [rypɛ̃, -in] *a. & n. P:* rich (person); (person) rolling in money; **les rupins,** the rich.

rupiner [rypine] *v.i. P:* **r. à un examen,** to do well in an examination.

rupteur [ryptœr] *n.m. El:* contact breaker, circuit breaker; *Aut:* **r. (d'allumage),** make-and-break.

rupture [ryptyr] *n.f.* breaking, rupture; (*a*) breaking down (of beam, etc.); bursting (of dam, etc.); **point de r.,** breaking-down point; (*b*) breaking (in two); rupture (of blood vessel, ligament); fracture (of bone); parting (of hawser); (*c*) breaking up (of surface, etc.); *Artil:* **obus de r.,** armour-piercing shell; (*d*) breaking off (of battle, negotiations); calling off (of a deal); breach (of contract, of promise of marriage); **r. de fiançailles,** breaking off of an engagement; **magasin en r. de stock,** shop that is out of stock; **il y a eu r. entre eux,** they've quarrelled; there's been a split between them; *El:* **r. du circuit,** breaking of, break in, the circuit.

rural, -aux [ryral, -o] **1.** *a.* rural; **vie rurale, chemin r.,** country life, lane. **2.** *n.m.* countryman, rustic; **les ruraux,** country people.

ruse [ryz] *n.f.* ruse, trick, wile, dodge; **r. de guerre,** stratagem (of war); **obtenir qch. par r.,** to obtain sth. by cunning.

rusé [ryze] *a. & n.* artful, crafty, sly, cunning, wily; **c'est une petite rusée,** she's an artful, a sly, little thing.

ruser [ryze] *v.i.* to use craft, trickery.

rush [rœʃ] *n.m.* **1.** *Sp:* sprint, spurt (at end of race). **2.** *F:* rush (of people).

russe [rys] *a. & n.* Russian.

Russie [rysi] *Pr.n.f. Geog:* Russia.

russifier [rysifje] *v.tr.* (*pr.sub. & impf.* **n. russifiions**), to Russianize.

russule [rysyl] *n.f. Fung:* russula.

rustaud, -aude [rysto, -od] **1.** *a.* boorish, uncouth. **2.** *n.* boor; bumpkin; *NAm:* hick.

rusticité [rystisite] *n.f.* **1.** rusticity. **2.** hardiness (of plant).

rustique [rystik] *a.* (*a*) rustic; **danse r.,** country dance; **mobilier r.,** rustic, cottage, furniture; **petit pont de bois r.,** little rustic bridge; (*b*) *Const:* **ouvrage r.,** rustic (stone)work; (*c*) hardy (plant).

rustiquement [rystikmɑ̃] *adv.* rustically.

rustre [rystr̥] **1.** *a.* boorish, loutish. **2.** *n.m.* boor, lout; bumpkin; *NAm:* hick.

rut [ryt] *n.m.* (*of animals*) rut(ting).

rutabaga [rytabaga] *n.m.* swede; *NAm:* rutabaga.

rutilance [rytilɑ̃s] *n.f.* glow(ing) (of colour).

rutilant [rytilɑ̃] *a.* glowing red, gleaming.

rutilement [rytilmɑ̃] *n.m.* glow(ing), gleam(ing).

rutiler [rytile] *v.i.* to glow; to gleam red.

rythme [ritm] *n.m.* rhythm; **r. respiratoire,** breathing rate; **le r. de la vie moderne,** the tempo of modern life; *Com:* **r. des livraisons,** delivery rate.

rythmé [ritme] *a.* rhythmic(al).

rythmer [ritme] *v.tr.* to put rhythm into (movement, sentence); to mark the rhythm of (tune).

rythmique [ritmik] **1.** *a.* rhythmic(al). **2.** *n.f.* rhythmics.

S

S, s [ɛs] *n.m.* (the letter) S, s; **faire des s,** to zigzag; **en S,** S-shaped; **sentier en s,** winding path.
Saba [saba] *Pr.n.f. Geog:* Sheba.
sabaye [sabɛj] *n.f. Nau:* (*a*) mooring rope; (*b*) towline.
sabayon [sabajɔ̃] *n.m. Cu:* zabaglione.
sabbat [saba] *n.m.* **1.** (Jewish) Sabbath; **jour du s.,** Sabbath day; **observer, violer, le s.,** to keep, break, the Sabbath. **2.** (witches') midnight revels, sabbath; *F:* **faire un s. de tous les diables,** to make a hell of a row; **s. de chats,** caterwauling.
sabbatique [sabatik] *a.* sabbatic(al) (year, etc.).
sabin, -ine [sabɛ̃, -in] *a. & n. A.Hist:* Sabine; **l'enlèvement des Sabines,** the rape of the Sabine women.
sabir [sabir] *n.m. Ling:* lingua franca.
sablage [sablaʒ] *n.m.* **1.** *Ind:* sandblasting (of casting). **2.** sanding (of icy road).
sable[1] [sabl̥] *n.m.* **1.** sand; **sables mouvants,** quicksands; **tempête de s.,** sandstorm; *Const:* **s. liant, s. mordant,** sharp sand; *Nau:* **fond de s.,** sandy bottom; *F:* **être sur le s.,** (i) to be left high and dry; (ii) to be down and out; **avoir du s. dans les yeux,** to be sleepy; **le marchand de s. passe,** the sandman is coming. **2. s. de fer,** fine iron filings.
sable[2] *n.m. Her: etc:* sable.
sablé [sable] **1.** *a.* sanded, gravelled (path, etc.) **2.** *n.m. Cu:* (sort of) shortbread.
sabler [sable] *v.tr.* **1.** to sand, gravel (path, etc.); to sand, grit (icy road). **2.** (*a*) to cast (medal, etc.) in a sand mould, *NAm:* mold; (*b*) *F:* **s. le champagne,** to swig, celebrate with, champagne. **3.** to sandblast (casting).
sableur, -euse[1] [sablœr, -øz] **1.** *n.* sand moulder, *NAm:* molder. **2.** *n.f. Mch:* **sableuse,** sandblast, sand jet.
sableux, -euse[2] [sablø, -øz] *a.* sandy.
sablier [sablije] *n.m.* hourglass; *Cu:* egg timer.
sablière[1] [sablijɛr] *n.f.* **1.** sandpit. **2.** sand box (of locomotive).
sablière[2] *n.f. Const: etc:* (lengthwise) beam, stringer, templet.
sablon [sablɔ̃] *n.m.* scouring sand; welding sand.
sablonner [sablɔne] *v.tr.* to sand.
sablonneux, -euse [sablɔnø, -øz] *a.* sandy.
sablonnière [sablɔnjɛr] *n.f.* sandpit.
sabord [sabɔr] *n.m. Nau:* port(hole); **s. d'aération,** air port; **s. de charge,** cargo door; **faux s.,** deadlight; *P: O:* **mille sabords!** shiver my timbers!
sabordage [sabɔrdaʒ] *n.m.,* **sabordement** [sabɔrdəmɑ̃] *n.m. Nau:* scuttling.
saborder [sabɔrde] *v.tr.* **1.** to scuttle (ship, plan, etc.). **2.** to ruin, destroy.
sabot [sabo] *n.m.* **1.** (*a*) wooden shoe, clog, sabot; *Fig:* **je vous entends, vois, venir avec vos gros sabots,** I can see what you're after; (*b*) *P:* old, useless, article; old tub (of a ship); old crock; (*c*) *F:* **jouer, chanter, comme un s.,** to play, sing, like an old boot. **2.** hoof (of horse, etc.). **3.** *Tchn:* shoe, sabot (of pile, etc.); caster socket (of furniture); **s. d'enrayage,** drag, skid, shoe, trig (of wheel); **s. d'arrêt,** scotch; **s. de frein,** brake block, brake shoe; **s. de pompe,** pump piston, bucket; *Aut:* **s. (de pare-chocs),** overrider. **4.** whipping top. **5.** *Bot:* **s. de Vénus,** lady's slipper. **6.** *Conch:* turban shell.
sabotage [sabɔtaʒ] *n.m.* **1.** sabot making. **2.** *Rail:* chairing (of sleepers). **3.** *F:* (*a*) scamping, botching (of work); (*b*) botched (up) job. **4.** (act of) sabotage; *Typ:* intentional garbling (of copy).
saboter [sabɔte] *v.tr.* (*a*) *Tchn:* to shoe (a pile, etc.); (*b*) *Rail:* to chair (sleeper); (*c*) *F:* to botch, make a mess of (a job); to murder (song, etc.); (*d*) to sabotage (sth.).
saboteur, -euse [sabɔtœr, -øz] *n.* **1.** bungler, botcher. **2.** saboteur.
sabre [sabr̥] *n.m.* sabre, *NAm:* saber; broadsword; **traîner, faire sonner, son s.,** to rattle one's sabre; **s. d'abordage,** cutlass; **s. au clair,** (with) drawn sword; **s. de bois,** (i) (Harlequin's) lath; (ii) hell!
sabrer [sabre] *v.tr.* **1.** (*a*) to cut down (s.o.) with the sword; (*b*) *F:* to make drastic cuts in (a MS., a play); (*c*) *F:* to criticize, slate (s.o., a play); (*d*) *F:* to dismiss, sack (employee). **2.** *F:* to botch (a job).
sabreur [sabrœr] *n.m.* **1.** (dashing) swordsman. **2.** *F:* **s. de besogne,** slapdash worker.
sac[1] [sak] *n.m.* **1.** (*a*) sack, bag, pouch; **s. de, en, papier,** paper bag; **s. à blé,** grain sack; **s. à main,** handbag, *NAm:* purse; **s. à, en, bandoulière,** shoulder bag; **s. à ouvrage,** workbag; **s. à outils,** tool bag; **s. de voyage, de nuit,** travel bag, overnight bag; **s. à dos, de campeur,** rucksack; **s. alpin (de scout),** knapsack; **course en s.,** sack race; *Mil:* **s. de fantassin, de soldat,** pack, knapsack; **s. à munitions,** cartridge pouch; **s. de couchage,** *F:* **s. à viande,** sleeping bag; **s. de sable, de terre,** sandbag; *Nau:* **s. (de) marin,** kitbag; *F:* **s. d'os,** bag of bones; *F:* **donner à qn le s.,** to dismiss, sack, s.o.; *F:* **un s. (de nœuds),** a muddle; *Box: F:* **travailler le s.,** to practise with the punchball; **s. à fourrages,** nosebag; **s. à poussières,** dustbag (for vacuum cleaner, etc.); **s. de sauvetage,** canvas escape chute; *F:* **s. percé,** spendthrift; **s. à vin,** boozer; *P:* **il en a plein son s.,** he's drunk, got a skinful, he's tight; **homme de s. et de corde,** out-and-out scoundrel, gallowsbird; *P:* **ils ont le s., il y a le s.,** they've got (pots of) money; **faire, gagner, son s.,** to make one's pile; **épouser le (gros) s.,** to marry money; *F:* **prendre qn la main dans le s.,** to catch s.o. red-handed; *F:* **vider son s.,** (i) to clear one's bowels; (ii) to get it off one's chest; to come clean; *P:* **remplir son s.,** to fill one's belly; *F:* **mettez ça dans votre s.,** put that in your pipe and smoke it! *F:* **l'affaire est dans le s.,** it's in the bag; (*of sail, etc.*) **faire s.,** to bag, to belly; *int. A:* **s. à papier!** damn it! (*b*) *F:* a hundred francs; (*c*) *Anat: Bot:* sac; (*d*) pouch (of marsupial); (*e*) *Fish:* poke net; (*f*) *Av:* **s. à vent,** wind cone; (*g*) **s. de minerai,** pocket of ore. **2.** sackcloth; **sous le s. et la cendre,** in sackcloth and ashes.
sac[2] *n.m.* sacking, pillage; **mettre à s. une ville,** to sack, plunder, a town; **faire le s. d'une maison,** to ransack a house.
saccade [sakad] *n.f.* jerk, jolt; violent pull; *Mec.E:* backlash; **s. de bride,** sharp jerk of the bridle; **par saccades,** in jerks; in, by, fits and starts.
saccadé [sakade] *a.* jerky, abrupt (movement, style); **d'une voix saccadée,** in a jerky, staccato, voice; **style s.,** jerky style; **respiration saccadée,** irregular breathing; gasping.
saccader [sakade] *v.tr.* to jerk (a horse's rein).
saccage [sakaʒ] *n.m.* havoc.

saccager [sakaʒe] *v.tr.* **(je saccageai(s); n. saccageons)** (*a*) to sack, pillage (town); to ransack (house, etc.); (*b*) **ils ont tout saccagé,** they turned everything upside down.
saccageur, -euse [sakaʒœr, -øz] *n.* plunderer.
saccharifier [sakarifje] *v.tr.* (*pr.sub. & impf.* **n. saccharifiions, v. saccharifiiez)** *Ch:* to saccharify.
saccharimètre [sakarimɛtr̥] *n.m.* **1.** *Ch:* saccharimeter. **2.** *Brew:* saccharometer.
saccharin [sakarɛ̃] *a.* saccharine.
saccharine [sakarin] *n.f. Ch: etc:* saccharin(e).
saccharomètre [sakarɔmɛtr̥] *n.m.* saccharometer.
saccharose [sakaroz] *n.m. Ch:* saccharose.
sacerdoce [sasɛrdɔs] *n.m.* priesthood; ministry (of the Church); **pour lui, c'est un s.,** he is dedicated; **le s. de la médecine,** dedication to medicine.
sacerdotal, -aux [sasɛrdɔtal, -o] *a.* priestly.
sachem [saʃɛm] *n.m.* (*N. American Indian chief*) sachem.
sachet [saʃɛ] *n.m.* sachet, (small) bag; packet; **s. de thé,** teabag; **s. de lavande,** lavender bag, sachet.
sacoche [sakɔʃ] *n.f.* **1.** satchel; money bag. **2.** (*a*) saddlebag; (*b*) tool bag; (*c*) *Belg:* handbag.
sacquer [sake] *v.tr. F:* to dismiss, sack (s.o.).
sacral, -aux [sakral, -o] *a.* sacral.
sacraliser [sakralize] *v.tr.* to make, consider (sth., s.o.) sacred.
sacramentel, -elle [sakramɑ̃tɛl] *a.* (*a*) *Ecc:* sacramental; (*b*) solemn, binding; ritual.
sacre [sakr̥] *n.m.* anointing (of king); consecration (of bishop); rite.
sacré[1] [sakre] *a.* **1.** holy (scripture, etc.); sacred, consecrated (vessel, place, etc.); **art s.,** sacred art; **les ordres sacrés,** holy orders; **pour lui rien n'est s.,** to him nothing is sacred; **il a le feu s.,** he is truly inspired; **il n'a pas le feu s.,** his heart isn't in it. **2.** sacred (duty, etc.); inviolable (trust, law, etc.). **3.** *P:* damn(ed), bloody; **votre s. chien,** your damn, bloody, dog; **s. imbécile,** bloody fool; **il a une sacrée chance,** he's damn lucky; **s. nom de Dieu, d'un chien!** damn and blast it!
sacré[2] *a. Anat:* sacral.
Sacré-Cœur [sakrekœr] *n.m. Ecc:* Sacred Heart (of Jesus).
sacredieu [sakrədjø], **sacredié** [sakrədje] *int. Dial:* good God!
sacrement [sakrəmɑ̃] *n.m. Ecc:* (*a*) sacrament; **les sacrements,** the sacraments; the means of grace; **le saint S.,** the Blessed Sacrament; **fréquenter les sacrements,** to be a regular communicant; (*b*) the marriage tie.
sacrément [sakremɑ̃] *adv. P:* damn(ed); **il fait s. chaud,** it's damn hot, bloody hot.
sacrer [sakre] **1.** *v.tr.* (*a*) to anoint (a king); to consecrate (a bishop); (*b*) **s. qn roi,** to anoint, crown, s.o. king. **2.** *v.i. F:* to curse and swear.
sacret [sakrɛ] *n.m. Orn:* sakeret.
sacrifiable [sakrifjabl̥] *a.* expendable.
sacrificateur, -trice [sakrifikatœr, -tris] *n.* sacrificer; **grand s.,** (Jewish) High Priest.
sacrifice [sakrifis] *n.m.* sacrifice; **offrir qch. en s.,** to offer up sth. as a sacrifice; **faire à qn le s. de sa vie,** to sacrifice one's life for s.o.; **faire des sacrifices,** to make sacrifices; to go without; *Ecc:* **le saint s.,** mass.
sacrifier [sakrifje] *v.tr.* (*impf. & pr.sub.* **n. sacrifiions, v. sacrifiiez)** (*a*) to sacrifice (victim); *v.i.* **s. aux idoles,** to sacrifice to idols; **s. à la mode,** to conform to fashion; *Com:* **s. des marchandises,** to sell goods at a loss; (*b*) to sacrifice, give up, devote (time, money, comfort, etc.) **(à,** to); **il a réussi en sacrifiant sa santé,** he succeeded at the cost of his health; **elle s'est sacrifiée pour vous,** she sacrificed herself for you; **s. sa vie pour son pays,** to lay down one's life for one's country; **s. sa vie à une cause,** to devote one's (entire) life to a cause.
sacrilège[1] [sakrilɛʒ] *n.m.* sacrilege; **ce serait un s. que de . . .,** it would be sacrilege to . . ..
sacrilège[2] **1.** *a.* sacrilegious (action, thought, etc.). **2.** *n.* sacrilegious person.
sacristain [sakristɛ̃] *n.m.* **1.** *Ecc:* sacristan; sexton. **2.** *Cu:* (kind of) small flaky pastry.
sacristi [sakristi] *int. A:* **1.** the devil! **2.** good Lord!
sacristie [sakristi] *n.f. Ecc:* sacristy, vestry.
sacro-saint [sakrɔsɛ̃] *a.* sacrosanct; *Iron:* precious.
sacrum [sakrɔm] *n.m. Anat:* sacrum.
sadique [sadik] **1.** *a.* sadistic. **2.** *n.* sadist.
sadisme [sadism] *n.m.* sadism.
sadomasochisme [sadɔmazɔʃism] *n.m. Psy:* sadomasochism.
sadomasochiste [sadɔmazɔʃist] *Psy:* **1.** *a.* sadomasochistic. **2.** *n.* sadomasochist.
saducéen, -enne [sadyseɛ̃, -ɛn] *n.* Sadducee.
safari [safari] *n.m.* safari; **en s.,** on safari.
safran[1] [safrɑ̃] *n.m.* **1.** *Bot:* saffron, crocus. **2.** (*a*) *Cu: Dy: etc:* saffron; **riz au s.,** saffron rice; (*b*) *a.inv.* saffron (yellow).
safran[2] *n.m. Nau:* rudder blade.
safrané [safrane] *a.* saffron(-coloured, -flavoured, *NAm:* -colored, -flavored).
safraner [safrane] *v.tr. Cu:* to flavour, *NAm:* flavor, with saffron.
saga [saga] *n.m. Lit:* saga.
sagace [sagas] *a.* sagacious, acute, shrewd.
sagacement [sagasmɑ̃] *adv.* sagaciously, shrewdly.
sagacité [sagasite] *n.f.* sagacity, shrewdness; **avec s.,** sagaciously.
sagaie [sagɛ] *n.f.* assegai.
sage [saʒ] *a.* **1.** wise; *n.m.* sage; wise man. **2.** prudent, wise (policy, etc.); sensible (person); **politique peu s.,** unwise policy. **3.** well behaved, good (child); quiet, docile (animal); steady (horse); modest, sober (dress, conduct); **sois s.!** be good! **s. comme une image,** as good as gold. **4.** moderate.
sage-femme [saʒfam] *n.f.* midwife; *pl. sages-femmes.*
sagement [saʒmɑ̃] *adv.* **1.** wisely, sensibly. **2.** properly; quietly.
sagesse [saʒɛs] *n.f.* **1.** (*a*) wisdom; (*b*) prudence, discretion; **agir avec s.,** to act wisely; **dent de s.,** wisdom tooth. **2.** (*a*) good behaviour, *NAm:* behavior; (*b*) modesty, chastity (of a woman). **3.** moderation.
sagittaire [saʒitɛr] *n.m. Astr: Her:* Sagittarius.
sagou [sagu] *n.m. Comest:* sago.
sagouin [sagwɛ̃] *n.m.* **1.** *Z:* squirrel monkey. **2.** *F:* slovenly, dirty, fellow; **vieux s.,** revolting old man.
Sahara (le) [ləsaara] *Pr.n.m. Geog:* the Sahara (Desert).
saharien, -ienne [saarjɛ̃, -jɛn] (*a*) *a.* Saharan; desert (troops); (*b*) *n.f.* **sahariennne,** bush jacket, shirt.
sahib [saib] *n.m.* sahib.
saïga [saiga] *n.m. Z:* saiga antelope.
saignant [sɛɲɑ̃] *a.* **1.** bleeding, raw (wound, etc.). **2.** *Cu:* rare (meat).
saignée [seɲe] *n.f.* **1.** (*a*) *Med:* blood-letting; *Med: Fig:* **faire une s. à qn,** to bleed s.o.; **faire une s. dans un arbre,** to tap a tree (for gum, etc.); (*b*) drain (on one's resources). **2.** bend of the arm, the knee. **3.** (*a*) (drainage) trench, ditch; (*b*) *Mec.E:* groove (for oil, etc.); (*c*) *Const:* hole (in a wall, for pipe, cable, etc.).
saignement [sɛɲmɑ̃] *n.m.* bleeding; **s. de nez,** nosebleed.
saigner [seɲe] **1.** *v.i.* (*of pers., wound, etc.*) to bleed; **je saigne du nez,** my nose is bleeding; *Fig:* **le cœur m'en saigne,** it makes my heart bleed; **c'est une plaie qui**

saigne encore, the wound still rankles. **2.** *v.tr.* (*a*) *Med: Fig:* to bleed (s.o.); **s. un porc, un poulet,** to bleed, stick, a pig; to bleed a chicken; **s. à blanc,** to bleed (an animal, *Fig:* s.o.) white; **se s. aux quatre membres, aux quatre veines,** to sacrifice oneself, to bleed oneself white; (*b*) **s. un arbre,** to tap a (gum) tree; **s. un fossé,** to drain a ditch; **s. une rivière,** to divert water from a river.

saigneur [sɛɲœr] *n.m.* (*a*) slaughterman; (*b*) collector of rubber (in plantation).

saigneux, -euse [sɛɲø, -øz] *a.* bloody; **bout s.,** scrag end (of mutton, etc.).

saillant [sajɑ̃] **1.** *a.* (*a*) projecting, jutting out (roof, cornice, etc.); prominent, high (cheekbones); protruding (teeth); bulging (muscles); *Fort: etc:* salient (angle); (*b*) salient, striking, outstanding (feature, etc.). **2.** *n.m. Mil:* salient.

saillie [saji] *n.f.* **1.** (*a*) *A:* spurt, bound; (*b*) *Breed:* covering (by male); (*c*) *Lit:* (i) sally, flash of wit; (ii) outburst (of passion, etc.). **2.** protrusion; *Arch: Const:* projection, ledge, set-off; **en s.,** projecting, jutting out; **s. du mollet,** swell of the calf; **faire s.,** to project, jut out; (*of pockets*) to bulge; (*of knees of trousers*) to bag; **menton qui fait s.,** protruding chin.

saillir [sajir] **1.** *v.tr.* (*pr.p.* **saillissant;** *p.p.* **sailli;** *pr.ind.* **je saillis, n. saillissons;** *fu.* **je saillirai**) *Breed:* (*of male*) to cover (female). **2.** *v.i.* (*used only in pr.p.* **saillant;** *p.p.* **sailli;** *pr.ind.* **il saille, ils saillent;** *fu.* **il saillera**) to jut out **(sur,** over), to stand out; **la poutre saille de 25 cm.,** the beam projects 25 cm.

sain, saine [sɛ̃, sɛn] *a.* (*a*) healthy (person); sound (horse, fruit, timber, etc.); sound, clear (judgement); wholesome (food); **climat, exercice, s.,** healthy climate, exercise; **s. et sauf,** safe and sound; **s. de corps et d'esprit,** sound in body and mind; (*b*) *Nau:* clear, safe (coast, anchorage).

sainbois [sɛ̃bwa] *n.m. Bot:* spurge flax.

saindoux [sɛ̃du] *n.m. Cu:* lard.

sainement [sɛnmɑ̃] *adv.* **1.** healthily. **2.** sanely.

sainfoin [sɛ̃fwɛ̃] *n.m. Bot: Agr:* sainfoin.

saint, sainte [sɛ̃, sɛ̃t] **1.** *a.* holy; (*a*) *Ecc:* **la Sainte Église,** the Holy Church; **guerre sainte,** holy war; **semaine sainte,** Holy Week; **le Vendredi s.,** Good Friday; (*b*) saintly, godly (person, life); (*c*) sanctified, consecrated; **lieu s.,** holy place; *F:* **toute la sainte journée,** the whole blessed day; (*d*) saint; **s. Pierre, sainte Catherine,** St Peter, St Catherine; **l'église S.-Pierre,** St Peter's (church); **la S. Georges,** St George's day. **2.** *n.* saint; **s. d'une ville,** patron saint of a town; **c'est un petit s. (de bois),** he's a little prig; **il lasserait la patience d'un s.,** he would try the patience of a saint; **il prêche pour son s.,** he has his own axe to grind; **ne savoir plus à quel s. se vouer,** to be at one's wits' end; *Rel:* **les Saints du dernier jour,** the Latter-day Saints. **3.** *n.m.* **le S. des Saints,** the Holy of Holies.

saint-bernard [sɛ̃bɛrnar] *n.m.inv.* St Bernard (dog); *F:* **c'est un vrai s.-b.,** he's a good Samaritan.

Saint-Cyr [sɛ̃sir] *Pr.n.m.* Saint-Cyr military academy.

Saint-Cyrien [sɛ̃sirjɛ̃] *n.m.* cadet training at Saint-Cyr; *pl. Saint-Cyriens.*

Saint-Domingue [sɛ̃dɔmɛ̃g] *Pr.n.m. Geog:* Santo Domingo.

Sainte-Croix [sɛ̃tkrwa] *Pr.n. Geog:* **l'île S.-C.,** Santa Cruz island.

Sainte-Hélène [sɛ̃telɛn] *Pr.n. Geog:* St Helena.

Saint-Elme [sɛ̃tɛlm] *Pr.n.m.* **feu S.-E.,** St Elmo's fire.

Sainte-Lucie [sɛ̃tlysi] *Pr.n. Geog:* St Lucia.

saintement [sɛ̃tmɑ̃] *adv.* righteously; **mourir s.,** to die a godly death.

Saint-Esprit [sɛ̃tɛspri] *Pr.n.m.* **le S.-E.,** the Holy Ghost, Holy Spirit.

sainteté [sɛ̃tte] *n.f.* holiness, saintliness (of pers.); sanctity (of the law, of a vow); *Ecc:* **sa S.,** His Holiness (the Pope).

Sainte-Touche [sɛ̃ttuʃ] *n.f. F:* pay day.

saint-frusquin [sɛ̃fryskɛ̃] *n.m. no pl. P:* **tout le s.-f.,** the whole caboodle; the whole damn lot.

Saint-Glinglin [sɛ̃glɛ̃glɛ̃] *used in F:* **jusqu'à la S.-G.,** till the cows come home; till doomsday.

Saint-Graal (le) [ləsɛ̃grɑl] *n.m. Lit:* the (holy) Grail.

saint-honoré [sɛ̃tɔnɔre] *n.m.* (type of) cream tart.

Saint-Jean (la) [lasɛ̃ʒɑ̃] *n.f.* Midsummer Day.

Saint-Laurent (le) [ləsɛ̃lɔrɑ̃] *Pr.n.m. Geog:* the Saint Lawrence (river).

Saint-Lundi [sɛ̃lœ̃di] *used in F:* **faire la S.-L.,** to take Monday off.

Saint-Marin [sɛ̃marɛ̃] *Pr.n. Geog:* (the Republic of) San Marino.

Saint-Martin (la) [lasɛ̃martɛ̃] *n.f.* St Martin's day; Martinmas; **été de la S.-M.,** Indian summer.

Saint-Michel (la) [lasɛ̃miʃɛl] *n.f.* Michaelmas.

Saint-Office [sɛ̃tɔfis] *n.m.* **1.** *R.C.Ch:* the Holy Office. **2.** *Ecc.Hist:* the Inquisition.

Saint-Père (le) [ləsɛ̃pɛr] *n.m. Ecc:* the Holy Father, the Pope.

saint-pierre [sɛ̃pjɛr] *n.m.inv. Ich:* John Dory.

Saint-Siège (le) [ləsɛ̃sjɛʒ] *n.m. Ecc:* the Holy See.

Saint-Simonisme [sɛ̃simɔnism] *n.m. Pol.Ec:* Saint-Simonianism; Saint-Simonism.

Saint-Sylvestre (la) [lasɛ̃silvɛstr̥] *n.f.* New Year's Eve; **faire la veillée de la S.-S.,** to see the new year in.

saisi [sezi] *n.m. Jur:* distrainee.

saisie [sezi] *n.f.* (*a*) seizure (of contraband goods, etc.); (*b*) *Jur:* distraint, execution; foreclosure, foreclosing (of a mortgage); *Nau:* embargo; (*c*) *Cmptr:* **s. de données,** data acquisition.

saisie-arrêt [seziarɛ] *n.f. Jur:* attachment, garnishment; *Scot:* arrestment; *pl. saisies-arrêts.*

saisir [sezir] *v.tr.* **1.** to seize; (*a*) to grasp; to take hold, catch hold, of (s.o., sth.); **s. qn par le bras, au collet,** to seize, catch, s.o. by the arm, by the collar; **s. un trône, une ville,** to seize, take possession of, a throne, a town; **s. l'occasion (de faire qch.),** to seize the opportunity (to do sth.); **être saisi (d'étonnement),** to be startled, staggered; (*b*) *Jur:* to seize, attach (real estate, a ship); to distrain upon (goods); **s. une hypothèque,** to foreclose a mortgage; (*c*) *Nau:* to stow, secure (the anchors, the boats); (*d*) to perceive, grasp (the truth, s.o.'s meaning); **je ne saisis pas (bien),** I don't (quite) get the idea; **je n'ai pas saisi son nom,** I didn't catch his name; **mal s. qch.,** to misunderstand sth.; **l'artiste a bien saisi la ressemblance,** the artist has caught the likeness; **il saisit vite,** he's quick (on the uptake). **2.** *Jur:* **s. un tribunal d'une affaire,** to refer a matter to a court, to lay a matter before a court; **nous sommes saisis de deux questions,** we have two questions before us; **s. la chambre d'un projet de loi,** to table a bill. **3.** *Cu:* to seal (meat.). **4. se s. de qn, de qch.,** to seize on s.o., sth.

saisissable [sezisabl̥] *a.* **1.** perceptible, distinguishable. **2.** *Jur:* distrainable, attachable.

saisissant, -ante [sezisɑ̃, -ɑ̃t] *a.* **1.** *Jur:* (*a*) distraining (party); (*b*) *n.* distrainer. **2.** (*a*) biting (cold); (*b*) striking (resemblance); gripping (words); thrilling (spectacle).

saisissement [sezismɑ̃] *n.m.* (*a*) sudden chill; (*b*) access (of joy); (*c*) shock.

saison [sɛzɔ̃] *n.f.* season; (*a*) **en cette s.,** at this time of year; **en toute(s) saison(s),** all the year round; **très tôt en s.,** very early in the season; **la s. nouvelle,**

spring (time); **la mauvaise, la belle, s.,** the winter, summer, months; (*b*) (*in the tropics*) (rainy, dry) season; (*c*) time (of year, etc.); **la s. des semailles,** sowing time; **la haute s.,** the tourist season; **la s. bat son plein,** it is the height of the season; **la s. de grand travail, le fort de la s.,** the busy season; **la s. creuse,** the slack season; the off season; **de s.,** (i) in season, seasonable; (ii) timely; **hors de s.,** (i) (*of vegetables, etc.*) out of season; (ii) unseasonable (weather); (iii) ill-timed, inopportune (remark, etc.); (*d*) **faire une s.,** to take a cure (at a spa); *F:* **faire les saisons,** to do seasonal work (in resorts).

saisonnier, -ière [sɛzɔnje, -jɛr] (*a*) *a.* seasonal; (*b*) *n.* seasonal worker.

sajou [saʒu] *n.m. Z:* capuchin monkey.

sake [sake] *n.m.*, **saki**[1] [saki] *n.m. Dist:* saké, saki.

saki[2] *n.m. Z:* saki (monkey).

salade[1] [salad] *n.f.* **1.** (*a*) salad; **panier à s.,** (i) salad shaker; (ii) *F:* = Black Maria; (*b*) **s. de fruits,** fruit salad; **s. de homard,** lobster salad; **s. russe,** Russian salad; *F:* **mettre tout en s.,** to throw everything into confusion; **quelle s.!** what a shambles! (*c*) *pl. P:* (i) lies; (ii) nonsense. **2.** *Hort: Cu:* salad vegetable; lettuce, etc.; green salad.

salade[2] *n.f. Arm:* sallet, salade.

saladier [saladje] *n.m.* salad bowl.

salage [salaʒ] *n.m.* salting.

salaire [salɛr] *n.m.* **1.** wage(s); pay; **s. à la tâche, aux pièces,** piece wage(s); **s. à forfait,** job wages; **s. au rendement,** efficiency wages, *U.S:* incentive wages; **s. indexé,** index-linked wages; **s. de base,** basic wage; **s. légal,** legal rate of pay; **s. minimum interprofessionnel de croissance (S.M.I.C.)** = guaranteed minimum wage; **s. indirect,** fringe benefits; *Prov:* **toute peine mérite s.,** the labourer, *NAm:* laborer, is worthy of his hire. **2.** reward, recompense, retribution; **le s. du péché,** the wages of sin.

salaison [salɛzɔ̃] *n.f.* (*a*) salting; (*b*) (degree of) salinity.

salamalec [salamalɛk] *n.m. F:* **faire des salamalecs à qn,** to bow and scrape to s.o.

salamandre [salamɑ̃dr̥] *n.f.* **1.** *Amph:* (*a*) salamander; (*b*) **s. aquatique,** newt. **2.** salamander stove; slow-burning, slow-combustion, stove.

salami [salami] *n.m. Comest:* salami (sausage).

salant [salɑ̃] *a.* salt (marsh, etc.).

salarial, -aux [salarjal, -o] *a.* **politique salariale,** wages policy.

salariat [salarja] *n.m.* **1.** wage-earning. **2.** *coll.* the wage earners.

salarié, -ée [salarje] **1.** *a.* (*a*) wage-earning; (*b*) paid (work). **2.** *n.* (*a*) wage earner; (*b*) *Pej:* hireling.

salaud [salo] *n.m. P:* bastard, bugger, sod; louse; **tour de s.,** dirty trick.

sale [sal] *a.* **1.** (*a*) dirty; filthy; *P:* (*in neg.*) **c'était pas s.!** it was pretty good! it was quite something! (*b*) offensive, filthy, coarse (word, story). **2.** *F:* (*always before the noun*) nasty; **s. individu, s. type,** louse; **s. fasciste!** filthy Fascist! **s. coup,** (i) nasty blow; (ii) dirty trick; **s. temps,** foul weather. **3.** *n.m. F:* **mettre du linge au s.,** to put dirty clothes in the wash.

salé [sale] *a.* **1.** salt (fish, etc.); salted (butter, nuts); **eau salée,** (i) salt water; (ii) brine; *Geog:* **le Grand Lac S.,** the Great Salt Lake; **le potage est trop s.,** the soup is too salt(y); *Husb:* **pain s.,** lick, *NAm:* salt lick; *Husb:* **prés salés,** saltings, salt meadows; *n.m.* **du s.,** salt pork; **petit s.** = streaky bacon; *P:* **un (petit) s., un morceau de s.,** a (newborn) child, baby, brat. **2.** (*a*) *A:* witty; (*b*) spicy, risqué (tale, joke); (*c*) *F:* stiff (price, sentence).

salement [salmɑ̃] *adv.* **1.** dirtily; in a disgusting manner. **2.** *P:* (very) badly; **s. difficile,** bloody difficult.

saler [sale] *v.tr.* to salt. **1.** (*a*) to season (sth.) with salt; (*b*) *F:* to overcharge; to fleece (customers); **s. la note,** to bump up the bill; **on nous a salés,** we were stung; **on l'a salé,** he got a tough sentence. **2.** to salt, cure (bacon, etc.).

saleté [salte] *n.f.* **1.** (*a*) dirtiness, filthiness (of person, street, clothes, etc.); (*b*) dirt, filth; mess; (*c*) trashy goods, rubbish, junk. **2.** (*a*) nastiness, obscenity; coarseness; (*b*) nasty, coarse, remark, joke; (*c*) mean, dirty, trick.

saleur, -euse [salœr, -øz] *n.* salter.

salicoque [salikɔk] *n.f. Crust:* prawn.

salicorne [salikɔrn] *n.f. Bot:* glasswort; saltwort.

salicylate [salisilat] *n.m. Ch:* salicylate.

salicylique [salisilik] *a.m. Ch:* salicylic (acid).

salière [saljɛr] *n.f.* **1.** (*a*) salt cellar; (*b*) (kitchen) salt box. **2.** (*a*) eye socket (of horse); (*b*) *F:* (*hollow above collar bone*) salt cellar.

salifier [salifje] *v.tr.* (*impf. & pr.sub.* **n. salifiions, v. salifiiez)** *Ch:* to salify.

saligaud, -aude [saligo, -od] *n. P:* (*a*) dirty beast; *f.* slut; (*b*) bastard, bugger, swine; *f.* bitch.

salin, -ine [salɛ̃, -in] **1.** *a.* saline; salty (taste). **2.** *n.m.* (*a*) salt marsh; (*b*) *Ch: Ind:* salin(e). **3.** *n.f.* **saline** (*a*) salt works; (*b*) salt marsh.

salinage [salinaʒ] *n.m.* **1.** salt works. **2.** (*a*) concentrating of the brine; (*b*) saturated solution of salt.

salingue [salɛ̃g] *P:* **1.** *a.* filthy. **2.** *n.* filthy, disgusting, person.

salinier, -ière [salinje, -jɛr] **1.** *a.* salt (industry, etc). **2.** *n.m.* (*a*) salt-mine owner; (*b*) salt merchant; salter.

salinité [salinite] *n.f.* saltness, salinity (of sea water, etc.).

salique [salik] *a. Hist:* Salic (law).

salir [salir] **1.** *v.tr.* to dirty, soil (one's hands, linen, etc.); to make (ship's bottom, etc.) foul; to corrupt (the imagination); **s. le plancher,** (i) to make the floor dirty; (ii) (*of animal*) to make a mess on the floor; **s. sa réputation,** to tarnish one's reputation. **2. se s.,** to get dirty, soiled; to soil, dirty, one's clothes.

salissant [salisɑ̃] *a.* **1.** soiling, that dirties; **travail s.,** dirty, messy, work. **2.** easily soiled (material, etc.); **c'est peu s.,** it doesn't show the dirt.

salissure [salisyr] *n.f.* stain, dirty mark.

salivaire [salivɛr] *a.* salivary (gland, etc.).

salivation [salivasjɔ̃] *n.f.* salivation.

salive [saliv] *n.f.* saliva; *F:* **perdre sa s.,** to waste one's breath.

saliver [salive] *v.i.* to salivate.

salle [sal] *n.f.* **1.** hall; (*usu.* large) room; (*a*) **s. de séjour,** living room; **s. à manger,** (i) dining room; (ii) *Furn:* dining room suite; *Fr.C:* **s. à dîner,** dining room; **s. de bain(s),** (i) bathroom; (ii) bathroom suite; **s. d'eau,** shower room; *Sch:* **s. de classe,** classroom; **s. de cours, de conférences,** lecture room; **s. des professeurs,** staff room; (*b*) **s. des fêtes** = (community) hall; village hall; **s. de récréation,** recreation room; *Sp:* **partie en s.,** indoor game; **les salles du Louvre,** the galleries of the Louvre; (*c*) **s. d'attente,** waiting room; **s. du conseil,** council room, chamber; *Ind: etc:* boardroom; **s. des dactylo(graphe)s,** typing pool; *Com: etc:* **s. d'exposition,** showroom; **s. de ventes,** saleroom; *Ind:* **s. de dessin,** drawing office; **s. des chaudières,** boiler room; **s. des machines,** engine room; plant room; **s. d'exploitation radar,** radar operations room; (*of spacecraft*) **s. de contrôle,** control room; *Cin: T.V:* **s. de régie,** control room; *Cin:* **s. de projection, de vision,** viewing room; **s. des pas perdus,** waiting hall (of law courts, railway station, etc.); lobby (of Houses of Parliament); **s. d'hôpital,** (hospital) ward; **s. d'opérations,** (operating) theatre, *NAm:* theater; *Mil:* **s. de garde,** guardroom; **s. de police,** (i) prisoners' room; (ii) guardroom; **s. de service,** orderly room; **s. des opérations,** operations room. **2.** *Th: etc:* auditorium, house; **s. pleine,** full house; **toute la s. applaudit,** the whole house, audience, applauded.

salmigondis [salmigɔ̃di] *n.m.* hotchpotch.

salmis [salmi] *n.m. Cu:* salmi; ragout (of roasted game).

salmonellose [salmɔneloz] *n.f. Med: Vet:* salmonellosis.

saloir [salwar] *n.m.* **1.** salting tub. **2.** *Dom.Ec:* salt sprinkler.

Salomon [salɔmɔ̃] *Pr.n.m.* Solomon; *Geog:* **les îles S.,** the Solomon Islands.

salon [salɔ̃] *n.m.* (*a*) drawing room; sitting room; lounge; **petit s.,** (i) morning room; (ii) *Furn:* three-, five-piece suite; (*in hotel, etc.*) **s. réservé,** private room; **jeux de s.,** parlour, *NAm:* parlor, games; (*b*) saloon, cabin (in ship, etc.); saloon car (in train); (*c*) **s. de thé,** tea room(s); **s. de coiffure,** hairdressing salon; (*d*) (art, etc.) exhibition; (motor, boat, trade) show; (*e*) *Fr.Lit.Hist:* salon.

salop, -ope [salo, -ɔp] *n. P:* (*a*) bastard; *f.* bitch; (*b*) *n.f.* prostitute, tart.

salopard [salɔpar] *n.m. P:* **1.** bastard. **2.** *Hist:* rebel fighter.

saloper [salɔpe] *v.tr. P:* to botch (a piece of work).

saloperie [salɔpri] *n.f. P:* **1.** (*a*) filth, mess; (*b*) trashy goods; rubbish. **2.** (*a*) dirty trick; (*b*) **dire des saloperies,** to talk smut.

salopette [salɔpɛt] *n.f.* dungarees; overalls, *NAm:* coverall(s).

salpêtrage [salpɛtraʒ] *n.m.* (*a*) manufacture, formation, of saltpetre, *NAm:* saltpeter; (*b*) treatment with saltpetre.

salpêtre [salpɛtr̥] *n.m.* (*a*) saltpetre, *NAm:* saltpeter; (*b*) saltpetre rot.

salpêtrer [salpetre] *v.tr.* **1.** to cover, treat (ground) with saltpetre, *NAm:* saltpeter. **2.** to rot (walls).

salpicon [salpikɔ̃] *n.m. Cu:* filling for vol-au-vent, etc.

salse [sals] *n.f. Geol:* salse, mud volcano.

salsepareille [salsəparɛj] *n.f. Bot: Pharm:* sarsaparilla.

salsifis [salsifi] *n.m. Bot: Cu:* salsify.

saltatoire [saltatwar] *a. Ent: Med:* saltatory.

saltimbanque [saltɛ̃bɑ̃k] *n.* acrobat.

salubre [salybr̥] *a.* healthy (climate, diet).

salubrité [salybrite] *n.f.* healthiness (of climate, etc.); **s. publique,** public health.

saluer [salɥe] *v.tr.* **1.** (*a*) to salute; to bow to (s.o.); to greet (s.o.); *Av:* to dip; **s. qn d'un coup de chapeau,** to raise one's hat to s.o.; **s. qn de la main,** (i) to wave, (ii) to touch one's hat, to s.o.; **passer qn sans le s.,** to cut s.o. (dead); *Bill:* **s. la bille,** to miss; *Mil: etc:* **s. du drapeau,** to lower the colour, *U.S:* to droop the color; *Nau:* **s. (du pavillon),** to dip (the flag); **s. de vingt coups,** to fire a twenty gun salute; **s. qn par un vivat,** to cheer s.o.; (*b*) to greet, hail (s.o.); **saluez-le de ma part,** give him my regards; **je vous salue, Marie,** hail, Mary. **2.** *Nau:* **s. un grain,** to reduce sail for a squall.

salure [salyr] *n.f.* saltness.

salut [saly] *n.m.* **1.** (*a*) safety; **chercher son s. dans la fuite,** to fly for one's life; **port de s.,** haven of refuge; (*b*) salvation; **faire son s.,** to find salvation; **travailler à son s.,** to work out one's own salvation; **l'Armée du S.,** the Salvation Army; (*c*) saving (of lives, souls). **2.** (*a*) bow, salutation, greeting; **adresser un s. à qn,** (i) to bow, (ii) to raise one's hat, to s.o.; *F:* **s. (à tous)!** (i) hullo, hello, hi(, everybody)! (ii) (*on leaving*) so long (everybody)! *F:* **bonjour, s.!** hullo, how are you? (*b*) *Mil: etc:* salute; **faire un s.,** to give a salute; **faire le s. militaire,** to salute; **s. du drapeau,** lowering of the colour, *U.S:* drooping of the color; *Nau:* **s. du pavillon,** dipping of the flag. **3.** *R.C.Ch:* Benediction (of the Holy Sacrament).

salutaire [salytɛr] *a.* salutary; beneficial.

salutation [salytasjɔ̃] *n.f.* salutation, greeting; *Corr:* **agréez mes meilleures salutations,** yours sincerely.

salutiste [salytist] *n.* Salvationist; member of the Salvation Army.

salvateur, -trice [salvatœr, -tris] *a. Lit:* saving.

salve [salv] *n.f. Artil: Sm.a:* salvo, volley; **tirer une s. (d'honneur),** to fire a salute; **s. d'applaudissements,** burst of applause.

samare [samar] *n.f. Bot:* (sycamore, etc.) key.

samaritain, -aine [samaritɛ̃, -ɛn] *a. & n.* Samaritan; *B:* **le bon S.,** the good Samaritan.

samedi [samdi] *n.m.* Saturday; **le S. saint,** (the) Saturday before Easter, Holy Saturday.

samouraï, samurai [samuraj] *n.m. Japanese Hist:* samurai.

samovar [samɔvar] *n.m.* samovar.

sampan(g) [sɑ̃pɑ̃] *n.m.* sampan.

sana [sana] *n.m. F:* sanatorium.

sanatorium [sanatɔrjɔm] *n.m.* sanatorium.

sanctificateur, -trice [sɑ̃ktifikatœr, -tris] **1.** *a.* sanctifying. **2.** *n.* sanctifier; **le S.,** the Holy Ghost, the Sanctifier.

sanctification [sɑ̃ktifikasjɔ̃] *n.f.* sanctification.

sanctifier [sɑ̃ktifje] *v.tr.* (*impf. & pr.sub.* **n. sanctifiions, v. sanctifiiez)** to sanctify; to make holy; to hallow; **que Ton nom soit sanctifié,** hallowed be Thy Name.

sanction [sɑ̃ksjɔ̃] *n.f.* sanction. **1.** approbation, assent. **2.** (*a*) **s. (pénale),** penalty; punishment; (*b*) *Pol:* **prendre des sanctions contre un pays, contre des grévistes,** to impose sanctions on a country; to take action against strikers; (*c*) **la s. de la paresse,** the price, the consequence, of laziness.

sanctionner [sɑ̃ksjɔne] *v.tr.* to sanction. **1.** to approve, ratify, countenance; **sanctionné par l'usage,** sanctioned by custom. **2.** (*a*) to attach a penalty to (decree); (*b*) to penalize (offence, person).

sanctuaire [sɑ̃ktɥɛr] *n.m.* sanctuary.

sanctus [sɑ̃ktys] *n.m. Ecc: Mus:* sanctus.

sandale [sɑ̃dal] *n.f.* sandal.

sandalette [sɑ̃dalɛt] *n.f.* light sandal.

sandow [sɑ̃do] *n.m. R.t.m:* **1.** *Gym:* chest expander. **2.** *Mec.E: Av: etc:* rubber extensible spring.

sandwich [sɑ̃dwi(t)ʃ] *n.m.* sandwich; **homme(-)s.,** sandwich man; **verre s.,** laminated glass; *F:* **pris en s.,** stuck, sandwiched **(entre,** between); *pl. sandwich(e)s.*

sang [sɑ̃] *n.m.* **1.** blood; **animaux à s. chaud, froid,** warm-blooded, cold-blooded, animals; **coup de s.,** stroke; **yeux injectés de s.,** bloodshot eyes; **répandre, verser, le s.,** to shed blood; **il y a du s. versé entre eux,** there's a blood feud between them; **victoire sans effusion de s.,** bloodless victory; **le prix du sang,** blood money; **écoulement de s.,** bleeding, haemorrhage, *NAm:* hemorrhage; **je n'arrive pas à arrêter le s.,** I can't stop the bleeding; **il était tout en s.,** he was covered with blood; **taché de s.,** bloodstained; *Fig:* **avoir le s. chaud,** to be quick-tempered; **le s. lui monta au visage,** the blood rushed to his face; **cela fait bouillir le s.,** it makes one's blood boil; **cela me glace le s.,** it makes my blood run cold; **il n'a pas de s. dans les veines,** he's gutless; **se faire du mauvais s., se manger les sangs,** to worry; **se faire du bon s.,** (i) to laugh heartily; (ii) to enjoy oneself, to enjoy life; **se faire un s. d'encre,** to worry oneself sick; **suer s. et eau** [sɑ̃keo], to sweat blood; **conte à tourner les sangs,** bloodcurdling tale; **tout mon s. n'a fait qu'un tour,** my heart missed a beat; *Ind: etc:* **apport en s.**

frais, (i) new blood; (ii) fresh, additional, capital; *P:* **bon s. (de bon s.)! bon s. de bon Dieu!** damn and blast it! *P:* **bon s. d'imbécile!** (you) bloody fool! **2.** (*a*) blood, race, lineage; **Indiens pur s.,** full-blooded Indians; **(homme de) s. mêlé,** half-caste; (*of horse*) **avoir du s.,** to be blooded; **cheval de s.,** blood horse; **cheval pur s.,** full bred horse; thoroughbred; **c'est dans le s.,** it's in his, our, blood; **s. bleu,** blue blood; (*b*) blood, kinship, relationship; **son propre s.,** one's own flesh and blood; **droit du s.,** birthright.

sang-froid [sɑ̃frwa] *n.m. no pl.* coolness, composure, sang-froid; **garder, conserver, son s.-f.,** to keep (i) (one's) cool, (ii) one's temper; **perdre son s.-f.,** to lose (i) one's self-control, (ii) one's temper; *adv.phr.* **de s.-f.,** deliberately; in cold blood.

sanglant [sɑ̃glɑ̃] *a.* **1.** (*a*) bloody (wound, battle, tale); bloodstained (handkerchief, etc.); (*b*) blood-red. **2.** (*a*) cruel (reproach, etc.); **larmes sanglantes,** bitter tears, tears of blood; **critique sanglante,** scathing criticism; (*b*) **affront s.,** deadly insult.

sangle [sɑ̃gl] *n.f.* strap; *Harn:* girth; *Furn:* webbing; **lit de s.,** camp bed.

sangler [sɑ̃gle] *v.tr.* (*a*) to girth (horse); (*b*) **sanglé dans son uniforme,** buttoned up tight in his uniform.

sanglier [sɑ̃glije] *n.m. Z:* (wild) boar.

sanglot [sɑ̃glo] *n.m.* sob; **pousser un s.,** to give a sob; **elle pleurait à gros sanglots,** she was sobbing her heart out.

sangloter [sɑ̃glɔte] *v.i.* to sob.

sang-mêlé [sɑ̃mele] *n.m.inv.* person of mixed blood; half-caste; (*S. Africa*) coloured, *NAm:* colored, person.

sangsue [sɑ̃sy] *n.f.* leech.

sanguin, -ine [sɑ̃gɛ̃, -in] **1.** *a.* (*a*) *Anat:* of blood; **groupe s.,** blood group; **transfusion sanguine,** blood transfusion; (*b*) sanguine, fiery (temperament); ruddy (complexion). **2.** *n.m.* dogwood. **3.** *n.f.* **sanguine,** (*a*) red chalk; (*b*) bloodstone; (*c*) blood orange.

sanguinaire [sɑ̃ginɛr] *a.* bloodthirsty (man); bloody (fight).

sanguinelle [sɑ̃ginɛl] *n.f. Bot:* dogwood

sanguinolent [sɑ̃ginɔlɑ̃] *a.* **1.** tinged with blood. **2.** *Nat.Hist:* blood-red.

sanie [sani] *n.f. Med:* sanies, pus.

sanitaire [sanitɛr] **1.** *a.* (*a*) medical (staff, equipment); health (measures); *Mil: etc:* **voiture s.,** ambulance; (*b*) *Plumb:* sanitary (equipment, engineering); **système s.,** sanitation. **2.** *n.m.* **le s.,** *F:* **les sanitaires,** sanitary installations; (the) plumbing. **3.** *n.f. Mil: etc:* ambulance.

sans [sɑ̃] *prep.* **1.** (*a*) without; **partez s. moi,** go without me; **il est revenu s. argent, s. un sou, s. le sou,** he came back without any money, without a penny; **il arriva s. argent ni bagages,** he arrived without either money or luggage; **s. faute,** without fail; **suffisant, s. plus,** adequate but no more (than that); **s. parler,** without speaking; **cela va s. dire,** it goes without saying; (it's a matter) of course; **vous n'êtes pas s. le connaître,** you must know him; **ces questions n'étaient pas s. m'embarrasser,** these questions were naturally somewhat embarrassing; **non s. difficulté,** not without difficulty; *F:* **que ferais-tu s.?** how would you manage without? *conj.phr.* **s. que** + *sub.,* without + *ger.;* **s. que nous le sachions,** without our knowing; **il ne parlait jamais s. qu'on lui parlât,** he never spoke unless he was spoken to; (*b*) -less, -lessly, -free; un-; **plaintes s. fin,** endless complaints; **se plaindre s. fin,** to complain endlessly; **être s. le sou,** to be broke, penniless; **s. enfants,** childless; **s. sel,** salt-free (diet); **baignade s. danger,** safe bathing; **s. cesse,** unceasingly; **s. hésiter,** unhesitatingly. **2. s. vous je ne l'aurais jamais fait,** but for you, if it hadn't been for you, I should never have done it; **s. cela, s. quoi,** otherwise.

sans-abri [sɑ̃zabri] *n.inv.* homeless person.

sans-cœur [sɑ̃kœr] *n.inv. F:* heartless person.

sanscrit [sɑ̃skri] *a. & n.m. Ling:* Sanskrit.

sans-culotte [sɑ̃kylɔt] *n.m. Hist:* (*Fr. Revolution*) sansculotte; extreme republican; *pl. sans-culottes.*

sans-façon [sɑ̃fasɔ̃] **1.** *n.m.* (*a*) bluntness (of speech, etc.); (*b*) informality; (*c*) offhand manner. **2.** *a. & n.inv.* (*a*) informal (person); (*b*) offhand (person).

sans-fil [sɑ̃fil] *n.inv. O:* **1.** *n.f.* wireless **2.** *n.m.* radio, wireless, message.

sans-gêne [sɑ̃ʒɛn] **1.** *n.m.* (offensive) offhandedness, over-familiarity; *F:* cheek. **2.** *a.inv.* offhand (person).

sanskrit [sɑ̃skri] *a. & n.m. Ling:* Sanskrit.

sans-logis [sɑ̃lɔʒi] *n.inv.* homeless person.

sansonnet [sɑ̃sɔnɛ] *n.m. Orn:* starling; *F:* **c'est de la roupie de s.,** it's rubbish.

sans-parti [sɑ̃parti] *n.inv. Pol:* non-Party member.

sans-patrie [sɑ̃patri] *n.inv.* stateless person.

sans-soin [sɑ̃swɛ̃] *n.inv. F:* careless person.

sans-souci [sɑ̃susi] *a.inv.* happy-go-lucky.

sans-travail [sɑ̃travaj] *n.inv.* unemployed person.

santal [sɑ̃tal] *n.m.* sandalwood.

santé [sɑ̃te] *n.f.* (*a*) health; wellbeing; **être en bonne s.,** to be well, in good health; **s. de fer,** iron constitution; **ne pas avoir de s., avoir une s. fragile, une s. délicate,** *F:* **une petite s.,** to have poor health, to be delicate; **respirer la s.,** to look the picture of health; **absent pour raison de s.,** absent on medical grounds; **maison de s.,** (private) nursing home, clinic; **boire à la s. de qn,** to drink s.o.'s health; **à votre s.!** your health! *F:* cheers! *Sw.Fr: F:* (*when s.o. sneezes*) **s.!** (God) bless you! (*b*) *Adm:* **Ministère de la S. et de la Sécurité sociale,** Department of Health and Social Security; **médecin de la s.,** medical officer of health; *Nau:* **agent de (la) s.,** quarantine officer.

santon [sɑ̃tɔ̃] *n.m.* (*in Provence*) clay, carved wood, figure (in Christmas crib).

saoul [su], **saoulard** [sular], **saouler** [sule] = SOÛL, SOÛLARD, SOÛLER.

sapajou [sapaʒu] *n.m. Z:* sapajou.

sape [sap] *n.f.* **1.** (*a*) undermining (of wall, tower, etc.); *Mil:* sapping; (*b*) sap, trench. **2.** mattock. **3.** *pl. P:* **sapes,** clothes, togs.

saper [sape] *v.tr.* **1.** *Mil: etc. & Fig:* to undermine. **2.** *P:* to dress; **être bien sapé,** to be well dressed.

saperlipopette [sapɛrlipɔpɛt], **saperlotte** [sapɛrlɔt] *int. A:* gad!

sapeur [sapœr] *n.m. Mil:* sapper; *F:* **fumer comme un s.,** to smoke like a chimney.

sapeur-pompier [sapœrpɔ̃pje] *n.m. Adm:* fireman; **les sapeurs-pompiers,** the fire brigade.

saphique [safik] *a.* **1.** *Pros:* sapphic. **2.** lesbian.

saphir [safir] *n.m.* sapphire.

saphisme [safism] *n.m.* sapphism; lesbianism.

sapin [sapɛ̃] *n.m.* **1.** (*a*) *Bot:* fir (tree); (*b*) *Com:* **(bois de) s.,** deal. **2.** *F:* coffin; **sentir le s.,** to have one foot in the grave; **toux qui sent le s.,** churchyard cough.

sapine [sapin] *n.f.* (*a*) fir plank; deal board; (*b*) *Const:* crane tower; (*c*) *Vit:* deal tub.

sapinière [sapinjɛr] *n.f.* fir plantation.

saponacé [sapɔnase] *a.* saponaceous, soapy.

saponaire [sapɔnɛr] *n.f. Bot:* soapwort.

saponifiant [sapɔnifjɑ̃] *Ch:* **1.** *a.* saponifying. **2.** *n.m.* saponifier, saponifying agent.

saponification [sapɔnifikasjɔ̃] *n.f.* saponification.

saponifier [sapɔnifje] *v.tr.* (*impf. & pr.sub.* **n. saponifiions, v. saponifiiez)** to saponify.

saponite [sapɔnit] *n.f. Miner:* saponite.

sapristi [sapristi] *int. F:* good heavens!

saprophage [saprɔfaʒ] *a. Ent:* saprophagous.

saprophyte [saprɔfit] *n.m. Biol:* saprophyte.
saquebute [sakbyt] *n.f. Mus: A:* sackbut.
saquer[1] [sake] *v.tr. Nau:* to jerk (heavy body) along.
saquer[2] *v.tr. F:* to dismiss, sack (s.o.).
sarabande [sarabɑ̃d] *n.f.* (*a*) *Danc: Mus:* saraband; (*b*) *F:* uproar, bedlam.
sarbacane [sarbakan] *n.f.* blowpipe; (*toy*) peashooter.
sarcasme [sarkasm] *n.m.* (piece of) sarcasm.
sarcastique [sarkastik] *a.* sarcastic.
sarcelle [sarsɛl] *n.f. Orn:* teal.
sarclage [sarklaʒ] *n.m.* weeding.
sarcler [sarkle] *v.tr.* **1.** to clean (a field); to weed (garden, etc); to hoe, spud (crop). **2.** to hoe up, out (weeds).
sarclet [sarklɛ] *n.m.*, **sarclette** [sarklɛt] *n.f.* (weeding) hoe.
sarcloir [sarklwar] *n.m.* (weeding) hoe; spud.
sarcome [sarkom] *n.m. Med:* sarcoma.
sarcophage [sarkɔfaʒ] **1.** *n.m.* sarcophagus. **2.** *n.f. Ent:* bluebottle.
sarcoplasme [sarkɔplasm] *n.m. Anat:* sarcoplasm(a).
sarcopte [sarkɔpt] *n.m. Arach:* sarcoptid; mite.
Sardaigne [sardɛɲ] *Pr.n.f. Geog:* Sardinia.
sarde [sard] **1.** *a. & n. Geog:* Sardinian. **2.** *n.m. Lap: A:* sard. **3.** *n.f. Ich:* bonito.
sardine [sardin] *n.f.* **1.** sardine; *F:* **serrés comme des sardines,** packed like sardines. **2.** *Mil: F:* N.C.O.'s stripe.
sardinerie [sardinri] *n.f.* sardine cannery.
sardinier, -ière [sardinje, -jɛr] **1.** *n.* (*a*) sardine fisher; (*b*) sardine packer. **2.** *n.m.* (*a*) sardine net; (*b*) sardine boat.
sardonique [sardɔnik] *a.* sardonic.
sardonyx [sardɔniks] *n.f. Miner:* sardonyx.
sargasse [sargas] *n.f.* sargasso, gulf weed; *Geog:* **la mer des Sargasses,** the Sargasso Sea.
sari [sari] *n.m. Cost:* sari.
sariette [sarjɛt] *n.f. Bot: Cu:* savory.
sarigue [sarig] *n.m. & f. Z:* opossum.
sarment [sarmɑ̃] *n.m.* (*a*) vine shoot; (*b*) (any) woody climbing stem; bine.
sarmenteux, -euse [sarmɑ̃tø, -øz] *a.* climbing (plant).
sarong [sarɔ̃] *n.m. Cost:* sarong.
sarrasin, -ine [sarazɛ̃, -in] **1.** *a. & n. Hist:* Saracen. **2.** *n.m. Agr:* buckwheat. **3.** *n.f.* **sarrasine,** portcullis.
sarrau [saro] *n.m. Cost:* overall, smock.
Sarre (la) [lasar] *Pr.n.f. Geog:* the Saar.
sarriette [sarjɛt] *n.f. Bot: Cu:* savory.
sas[1] [sɑ] *n.m.* sieve; **passer qch. au s.,** to sift sth.
sas[2] *n.m.* (*a*) *Hyd.E:* lock chamber; coffer; (*b*) *Civ.E: Nau: Space:* airlock.
sassafras [sasafrɑ] *n.m. Bot:* sassafras.
sassage[1] [sasaʒ] *n.m.* sifting.
sassage[2] *n.m.* passing (of a boat) through a lock.
sassement[1,2] [sasmɑ̃] *n.m.* = SASSAGE[1,2].
sasser[1] [sase] *v.tr.* to sift, bolt, screen (flour, plaster); to winnow (grain); *Min:* to jig (ore).
sasser[2] *v.tr.* to pass (a boat) through a lock.
sasseur, -euse [sasœr, -øz] *n.* sifter.
satané [satane] *a. F:* confounded; **s. temps!** filthy weather!
satanique [satanik] *a.* satanic; fiendish (cruelty); diabolical (idea, grin, etc.).
satanisme [satanism] *n.m.* satanism.
satellisation [satelizasjɔ̃] *n.f.* (*a*) putting into orbit, orbiting (of satellite, spacecraft); **programme de s.,** space programme; (*b*) *Pol:* (*of country*) becoming a satellite (state).
satelliser [satelize] *v.tr.* (*a*) to put (satellite, spacecraft, man, etc.) into orbit; (*b*) *Pol:* to make (a country) into a satellite (state).
satellite [satelit] **1.** *n.m.* (*a*) *Astr:* satellite, secondary planet; **s. artificiel,** artificial satellite; **s. terrestre, lunaire,** earth-orbiting, moon-orbiting, satellite; **s. de télécommunications,** (tele)communications satellite; comsat; **s. météorologique,** weather, meteorological, satellite; metsat; (*b*) *a. & n.m. Pol:* **(pays) s.,** satellite (state); (*c*) *Tchn:* planet wheel, bevel gear; **engrenage à satellites,** (sun-and-)planet gear. **2.** *a.* (*a*) *Anat:* **veines satellites,** companion veins; (*b*) **agglomération s.,** satellite town.
satiété [sasjete] *n.f.* satiety; surfeit; **à s.,** more than enough.
satin [satɛ̃] *n.m.* **1.** *Tex:* satin. **2.** (*a*) **bois de s.,** satinwood; (*b*) *Bot:* **s. blanc,** honesty.
satinage [satinaʒ] *n.m.* (*a*) satining (of ribbon, cloth); glazing (of leather); hot pressing (of paper, linen); surfacing (of paper); (*b*) *Phot:* burnishing, enamelling (of print).
satiné [satine] **1.** *a.* satiny, satin-like; glazed (leather, paper). **2.** *n.m.* (*a*) gloss; (*b*) smoothness.
satiner [satine] *v.tr.* to give a glossy surface to (material, etc.); to glaze (leather).
satinette [satinɛt] *n.f. Tex:* sateen, satinet(te).
satire [satir] *n.f.* satire (**contre,** on); **trait de s.,** epigram; **faire la s. de son époque,** to satirize one's times.
satirique [satirik] **1.** *a.* satiric(al). **2.** *n.* satirist.
satiriquement [satirikmɑ̃] *adv.* satirically.
satiriser [satirize] *v.tr.* to satirize.
satisfaction [satisfaksjɔ̃] *n.f.* **1.** satisfaction, contentment; gratification; **donner de la s. à qn,** to give s.o. cause for satisfaction; **donner s. aux vœux de qn,** to satisfy s.o.'s desires; **avoir la s. de faire qch.,** to have the satisfaction of doing sth. **2.** reparation, amends **(pour, de,** for); *Theol:* atonement.
satisfaire [satisfɛr] (*conj. like* FAIRE) **1.** *v.tr.* (*a*) to satisfy, please (s.o.); to gratify (one's curiosity, etc.); **s. le désir de qn,** (i) to meet, grant, (ii) to carry out, (iii) to gratify, s.o.'s wish; **s. l'attente de qn,** to come up to s.o.'s expectations; **de manière à vous s.,** to your satisfaction; (*b*) to make amends to (s.o.); *Theol:* to make atonement; (*c*) **se s. de peu,** to be content with very little; (*d*) **se s.,** to relieve oneself. **2.** *v.ind.tr.* (*a*) *A:* **s. à qn,** to give s.o. satisfaction; to meet s.o.'s challenge; (*b*) **s. (à qch.),** to meet (demands, condition, objection); to fulfil, carry out (an undertaking, one's desires); to comply with (regulation, etc.); **s. à un examen,** to satisfy the examiners.
satisfaisant [satisfəzɑ̃] *a.* satisfactory (reply, work); satisfying (meal).
satisfait, -aite [satisfɛ, -ɛt] (*a*) *a.* satisfied, contented; pleased; *Iron:* **vous voilà s.!** well, you asked for it! **je n'en suis pas s.,** I'm not pleased with it, not happy about it; *Com:* **j'espère que vous en serez entièrement s.,** I hope it will give you complete satisfaction; **mal s.,** dissatisfied (**de,** with); (*b*) *n.* satisfied, contented, person.
satsuma [satsyma] **1.** *n.m. Cer:* Satsuma ware. **2.** *n.f.* satsuma (orange).
saturable [satyrabl̩] *a.* saturable.
saturant [satyrɑ̃] *a.* saturating, saturant; **vapeur saturante,** saturated vapour, *NAm:* vapor.
saturateur [satyratœr] *n.m.* (*a*) *Ch: Ind:* saturator; (*b*) humidifier.
saturation [satyrasjɔ̃] *n.f.* (*a*) saturation; (*b*) (*in advertising*) **campagne de s.,** all-out (publicity) campaign.
saturé [satyre] *a.* saturated (solution, compound); *Com:* **le marché est s.,** the market has reached saturation point; **ville saturée,** overcrowded city; **j'en suis s.,** I'm sick of it, them.
saturer [satyre] *v.tr.* to saturate **(de,** with).

saturnales [satyrnal] *n.f.pl. Rom.Ant: & Fig:* saturnalia.
Saturne [satyrn] *Pr.n.m. Myth: Astr:* Saturn.
saturnie [satyrni] *n.f. Ent:* emperor moth.
saturnien, -ienne [satyrnjɛ̃, -jɛn] *a.* saturnine.
saturnin [satyrnɛ̃] *a.* **intoxication saturnine,** lead poisoning.
saturnisme [satyrnism] *n.m. Med:* lead poisoning.
satyre [satir] *n.m.* **1.** *Myth: Ent:* satyr. **2.** *F:* sex maniac.
satyrique [satirik] *a. Gr.Ant:* satyric.
sauce [sos] *n.f.* **1.** sauce; **s. aux champignons,** mushroom sauce; **rallonger la s.,** (i) to water down the sauce; (ii) *F:* to pad out a book; to spin out a story; *F:* **accommoder un même sujet à toutes les sauces,** to dish up the same subject in every shape; **à quelle s. sera-t-il mangé?** how shall we deal with it, him? *F:* **être dans la s.,** to be in the soup. **2.** *Draw:* soft black crayon, black chalk, lamp black. **3.** *F:* (rain) shower.
saucée [sose] *n.f. F:* (*a*) downpour; (*b*) **recevoir une s.,** to get a wetting, a soaking.
saucer [sose] *v.tr.* **(je sauçai(s); n. sauçons)** (*a*) to mop up the sauce from (one's plate); (*b*) *F:* **se faire s.,** to get soaked, wet through.
saucier [sosje] *n.m.* sauce cook.
saucière [sosjɛr] *n.f. Dom.Ec:* sauceboat.
sauciflard [sosiflar] *n.m. P:* sausage, banger.
saucisse [sosis] *n.f.* **1.** (*a*) sausage; *F:* **il n'attache pas ses chiens avec des saucisses,** he's careful with his money; (*b*) *P:* idiot, nit. **2.** *Mil: F:* barrage balloon.
saucisson [sosisɔ̃] *n.m.* **1.** (*a*) (cooked, dried) sausage; cold sausage; **s. à l'ail,** garlic sausage; (*b*) *P:* idiot, nit; (*c*) cylindrical loaf. **2.** *Exp:* powder hose.
saucissonner [sosisɔne] *F:* **1.** *v.tr.* to tie up like a sausage. **2.** *v.i.* to picnic, to eat a snack.
saucissonneur, -euse [sosisɔnœr, -øz] *n. F:* picnicker.
sauf¹, sauve [sof, sov] *a.* safe, unscathed, unhurt; **sain et s.,** safe and sound; **s'en tirer la vie sauve,** to get off with one's life.
sauf² *prep.* save, but, except; **il est indemne s. une écorchure au bras,** he is unhurt except for a grazed arm; **il n'a rien s. son salaire,** he has nothing except his wages; **s. correction,** subject to correction; **s. avis contraire,** unless you, I, hear to the contrary; **s. indication contraire,** unless otherwise stated, specified; s. de rares exceptions, with very few exceptions; **s. accidents, s. imprévu,** barring accidents, unless anything unforeseen occurs; **s. erreur ou omission,** errors and omissions excepted; **je consens, s. à revenir sur ma décision,** I consent, but I reserve the right to reconsider my decision; **s. s'il pleut,** unless it rains, if it doesn't rain; **je n'ai rien fait, s. d'écrire des lettres,** I haven't done anything, except for, apart from, writing some letters; *conj.phr. F:* **s. que** + *ind.,* except that; **tout se passa bien s. que la mariée arriva en retard,** everything went off well, apart from the fact that the bride was late.
sauf-conduit [sofkɔ̃dɥi] *n.m.* safe conduct, pass; *pl. sauf-conduits.*
sauge [soʒ] *n.f.* (*a*) *Bot: Cu:* sage; (*b*) *Bot:* salvia.
saugrenu [sogrəny] *a.* absurd, preposterous.
saule [sol] *n.m. Bot:* willow; **s. pleureur,** weeping willow.
saumâtre [somɑtr̥] *a.* **1.** brackish, briny (taste, water). **2.** *F:* (*a*) (*of pers.*) bitter, sour; (*b*) **je la trouve s.,** I think it's a bit thick, a bit much.
saumon [somɔ̃] *n.m.* **1.** *Ich:* salmon; *a.inv.* **rubans s.** salmon-pink ribbons. **2.** *Metall:* ingot (of tin, etc.); pig (of lead, etc.).
saumoné [somɔne] *a.* **truite saumonée,** sea trout, salmon trout.
saumure [somyr] *n.f.* (pickling) brine.
saumuré [somyre] *a.* pickled (in brine).
saumurer [somyre] *v.tr.* to pickle.
sauna [sona] *n.m.* sauna.
saupiquet [sopikɛ] *n.m. Cu:* (spiced sauce for) stew.
saupoudrage [sopudraʒ] *n.m.* sprinkling, dredging.
saupoudrer [sopudre] *v.tr.* **1.** *A:* to sprinkle (sth.) with salt. **2.** to sprinkle, dust, dredge (**de,** with).
saupoudreuse [sopudrøz] *n.f.*, **saupoudroir** [sopudrwar] *n.m.* dredger; castor; sifter.
saur [sɔr] *a.m.* **hareng s.,** red herring; kipper.
saurer [sɔre] *v.tr.* to kipper (herrings); to smoke (fish, bacon).
saurien [sɔrjɛ̃] *a. & n.m. Rept:* saurian.
saut [so] *n.m.* **1.** (*a*) jump; leap; vault; *Sp:* **s. en longueur, en hauteur,** long, *NAm:* broad, jump; high jump; **s. en, à, skis,** ski jump(ing); **s. en parachute,** parachute drop; **faire un s.,** to take a leap; **se lever d'un s.,** to leap up; **au s. du lit,** on getting out of bed; **de plein s.,** at one bound; **faire le s.,** to take a decision, the plunge; **la voiture a fait un s. de 50m. dans la mer,** the car plunged 50m. into the sea; **s. périlleux,** somersault; **par sauts et par bonds,** jerkily; in fits and starts; **faire un s. à Paris, chez le boulanger,** to pop over to Paris, round to the baker's; **il n'y a qu'un s. d'ici là,** it's only a stone's throw (away); (*b*) **s. de température,** sudden rise, jump, in temperature; (*c*) *Mus:* skip; disjunct interval; (*d*) *Cmptr:* jump, skip (instruction); (*e*) *Breed:* covering. **2.** waterfall.
saut-de-lit [sodli] *n.m.* (light) dressing gown; *pl. sauts-de-lit.*
saut-de-loup [sodlu] *n.m.* ha-ha, sunk fence; *pl. sauts-de-loup.*
saut-de-mouton [sodmutɔ̃] *n.m. Civ.E:* flyover, *NAm:* overpass; *pl. sauts-de-mouton.*
saute [sot] *n.f.* (sudden) change (of wind, mood); jump (in temperature, price).
sauté [sote] *a. & n.m. Cu:* sauté.
saute-mouton [sotmutɔ̃] *n.m. no pl.* leapfrog.
sauter [sote] **1.** *v.i.* (*the aux. is* **avoir**) (*a*) to jump; to leap; **s. à la perche,** to pole-vault; **s. à la corde,** to skip, *NAm:* to skip rope; **s. du lit, à cheval,** to leap out of bed, on to one's horse; **s. à terre,** to jump down; **s. du coq à l'âne,** to skip from one subject to another; **s. à la gorge de qn,** to fly at s.o., at s.o.'s throat; **cela saute aux yeux,** it's obvious; *F:* **et que ça saute!** and make it snappy! step on it! **s. au cou de qn,** to fling one's arms round s.o.'s neck; *Fig:* **s. au plafond,** (i) to jump out of one's skin; (ii) to be overjoyed; (iii) to hit the roof; **s. sur qn,** to fly, fling oneself, at s.o.; **s. sur une offre,** to jump at an offer; (*b*) to explode; to blow up; (*of business, government, etc.*) to collapse; (*of button, etc.*) to come off, fly off; (*of rivet*) to start; *El:* (*of fuse*) to blow, *F:* to go; (*c*) **faire s.,** to blast (rock); to blow up (bridge, etc.); to explode (mine); to burst (boiler); to wreck (plan, etc.); to bring down (government, etc.); to sack, fire (official); to dandle (child); *Cu:* to sauté (potatoes); to toss (pancake); **faire s. une serrure,** to burst a lock (open); **faire s. un piège,** to spring a trap; **faire s. le bouchon,** to pop the cork (of a bottle); **se faire s. la cervelle,** to blow one's brains out; *Gaming:* **faire s. la banque,** to break the bank; *El:* **faire s. les plombs,** to blow the fuses. **2.** *v.tr.* (*a*) to jump (over), leap over, clear (ditch, fence, etc.); **s. le pas,** to take the plunge; (*b*) to skip (page); to leave out (line in copying, etc.); to drop (a stitch); *Sch:* **s. une classe,** to skip a form; *Typ:* **s. un mot,** to make an out; *F:* **je la saute,** (i) I've got to skip the meal; (ii) I'm ravenous; (*c*) (*of stallion*) to cover (mare); *P:* to lay (a girl).

sauterelle [sotrɛl] *n.f. Ent:* grasshopper; **grande s. d'Orient,** locust.
sauterie [sotri] *n.f.* party, *F:* hop.
saute-ruisseau [sotrɥiso] *n.m.inv. F: A:* errand boy.
sauteur, -euse [sotœr, -øz] **1.** *a.* leaping, jumping (insect, etc.). **2.** *n.* (*a*) leaper, jumper; (*b*) *F:* weathercock; unreliable person. **3.** *n.f.* **sauteuse** (*a*) frying pan; (*b*) *P:* prostitute, tart.
sautillant [sotijɑ̃] *a.* hopping (bird); skipping (child); **style s.,** jerky style.
sautillement [sotijmɑ̃] *n.m.* hop(ping).
sautiller [sotije] *v.i.* (*a*) to hop (about); (*b*) *Pej:* to skip from one subject to another.
sautoir [sotwar] *n.m.* **1.** (*a*) St Andrew's cross; *Her:* saltire; **porté en s.,** worn (i) crosswise, over the shoulder, (ii) on a chain, ribbon, round the neck; (*b*) chain. **2.** *Sp:* jumping area.
sauvage [sovaʒ] **1.** *a.* (*a*) wild (plant, animal); savage, brutal (person); **chat s.,** (i) wildcat; (ii) *Fr.C:* raccoon; **lieu s.,** wild, uninhabited, spot; (*b*) *O:* primitive (people); (*c*) unsociable; shy, retiring; (*d*) unauthorized; **grève s.,** wildcat strike; (*e*) **soldes sauvages,** slashed prices. **2.** *n.* (*f. occ.* **sauvagesse**) (*a*) *O:* savage; *Fr.C:* (American) Indian; (*b*) unsociable, retiring, person.
sauvagement [sovaʒmɑ̃] *adv.* wildly; savagely.
sauvageon, -onne [sovaʒɔ̃, -ɔn] **1.** *n.m. Arb:* wild stock (for grafting). **2.** *n.* little savage.
sauvagerie [sovaʒri] *n.f.* **1.** savagery, brutality, barbarity. **2.** unsociability; shyness.
sauvagin, -ine [sovaʒɛ̃, -in] **1.** *a.* (taste, smell) of wildfowl. **2.** *n.f.* **chasse à la sauvagine,** wildfowling.
sauvegarde [sovgard] *n.f.* **1.** safeguard (**contre,** against); safe keeping; safety; **sous la s. de qn,** under s.o.'s protection; **clause de s.,** saving clause. **2.** *Nau:* (*a*) lifeline; (*b*) oar lanyard; (*c*) rudder chain.
sauvegarder [sovgarde] *v.tr.* to safeguard.
sauve-qui-peut [sovkipø] *n.m.inv.* stampede, headlong flight.
sauver [sove] **1.** *v.tr.* (*a*) to save, rescue (s.o.) (**de,** from); *Ecc:* to save (s.o., s.o.'s soul); **s. la vie à, de, qn,** to save s.o.'s life; **Dieu sauve le roi!** God save the King! (*b*) to salvage (ship, goods); *F:* **s. les meubles,** to save something from the wreck; *F:* **s. sa peau, sa tête,** to save one's skin. **2. se s.** (*a*) to escape (**de,** from); **sauve qui peut!** every man for himself! (*b*) to run away, to be off; **il se fait tard, je me sauve,** it's getting late, I'm off, I must fly; (*c*) (*of milk, etc.*) to boil over.
sauvetage [sovtaʒ] *n.m.* (*a*) life saving; rescue; **s. aérien en mer,** air-sea rescue; **il a fait plusieurs sauvetages en mer,** he has saved several lives at sea; **appareil de s.,** life-saving, rescue, apparatus; **ceinture, gilet, de s.,** lifebelt; **bouée de s.,** lifebuoy; **ligne de s.,** lifeline; **canot, embarcation, de s.,** lifeboat; **échelle de s.,** fire escape; (*b*) salvage (of ship, goods).
sauveteur [sovtœr] **1.** *n.m.* rescuer. **2.** *a.m.* **bateau s.,** (i) (coastal) lifeboat; (ii) salvage vessel.
sauvette (à la) [alasovɛt] *adv.phr.* (i) in a hurry; (ii) furtively; **marchand à la s.,** illicit street vendor.
sauveur, salvatrice [sovœr, salvatris] **1.** *n.* saviour, *NAm:* savior. **2.** *a.* saving.
savamment [savamɑ̃] *adv.* (*a*) learnedly; (*b*) knowingly; **j'en parle s.,** I know what I'm talking about.
savane [savan] *n.f.* **1.** *Geog:* savanna(h). **2.** *Fr.C:* swamp.
savant, -ante [savɑ̃, -ɑ̃t] **1.** *a.* (*a*) learned (**en,** in); erudite, scholarly; well informed, knowledgeable (**en,** about); (*b*) skilful, clever, able; **chien s.,** performing dog. **2.** *n.* scientist; scholar.
savarin [savarɛ̃] *n.m. Cu:* savarin.
savate [savat] *n.f.* **1.** old, worn-out, shoe; *F:* **traîner la s.,** to be down at heel. **2.** *Tchn:* sole (plate). **3.** foot boxing; French boxing. **4.** *F:* clumsy oaf; **comme une s.,** abominably, very badly.
saveur [savœr] *n.f.* **1.** taste, flavour, *NAm:* flavor; **sans s.,** tasteless, insipid. **2.** *Fig:* spice, pungency.
Savoie [savwa] *Pr.n.f. Geog:* Savoy; *Cu:* **biscuit de S.** = sponge cake.
savoir[1] [savwar] *v.tr.* (*pr.p.* **sachant;** *p.p.* **su;** *pr.ind.* **je sais, il sait, n. savons, ils savent;** *pr.sub.* **je sache, n. sachions, ils sachent;** *imp.* **sache, sachons, sachez;** *impf.* **je savais;** *p.h.* **je sus;** *fu.* **je saurai)** to know. **1. s. qch. par cœur,** to know sth. by heart; **s. une langue, le chemin,** to know a language, the way; **il en sait des choses, plus d'une,** he knows a thing or two. **2.** to be aware of (sth.); (*a*) **je ne savais pas cela,** I did not know, was not aware of, that; **je (le) sais bien!** I know! **elle est jolie, et elle le sait bien,** she's pretty, and doesn't she know it! **ce n'est pas bien, tu sais!** it isn't right, you know! **je n'en sais rien,** I know nothing about it; I don't know; **en s. trop,** to know too much; **je n'en sais trop rien, je ne sais trop,** I'm not (very) sure; **comment le saurais-je? qu'est-ce j'en sais?** how should I know? **peut-on s.?** what's it (all) about? can you tell me sth. about it? **je ne veux pas s.,** I don't want any explanations, to know anything about it; *F:* **je ne veux pas le s.,** that's nothing to do with me; *F:* **est-ce que je sais (,moi)?** I haven't a clue! don't ask me! **des stylos, des crayons, est-ce que je sais, moi?** pens, pencils—anything you like, —what have you; *Lit:* **je ne sais,** I do not know; **sans le s.,** unconsciously; without being aware of it; **pas que je sache,** not to my knowledge; **(à ce) que je sache,** so far as I know; **(pour) autant que je sache,** (i) as far as I know; (ii) for all I know; **la question est de s. si elle viendra,** the question is whether she will come; **on ne sait pas,** there is no saying, knowing; **on ne sait jamais,** one never knows; you never can tell; **si jeunesse savait!** if youth but knew! **si j'avais su,** had I known; (*b*) to know of (s.o.); **je sais un bon horloger,** I know (of) a good watchmaker; (*c*) *Lit:* (*in first pers. only*) **je ne sache pas qu'on vous ait invité,** I am not aware that you have been invited; (*d*) **je me savais très malade,** I knew I was very ill; **des parents que je sais venir de Londres,** relatives who I know come from London. **3.** to understand; **il sait ce qu'il veut,** he knows what he wants; he knows his own mind; **je ne sais (pas) où le trouver,** I don't know where to find him; **ne s. que faire, que dire,** not to know, to be at a loss, what to do, to say; **je ne sais que penser,** I don't know what to think; **sachez que . . .,** I would have you know that . . . . **4.** to be well informed of (sth.); (*a*) **c'est à s.,** that remains to be seen; **reste à s. si . . .,** it remains to be seen whether . . ., if . . .; **je crois s. qu'il est ici,** I understand he is here; **je voudrais bien s. pourquoi,** I wonder why; **il n'a rien voulu s.,** he wouldn't listen to us; (*b*) **faire s. qch. à qn,** to inform s.o. of sth.; to tell s.o. sth.; **vous auriez dû le lui faire s.,** you should have let him, her, know; (*c*) *conj.phr.* **(à) s.,** to wit, namely, viz., that is to say. **5.** (*a*) to know how, to be able (to do sth.); **savez-vous nager?** can you swim? **je sais y aller,** I know how to go, get, there; **je crois que je saurai le faire,** I think I can manage it; **s. vivre,** to know how to behave; (*b*) **je ne saurais guère vous le dire,** I'm afraid I can't tell you. **6.** (*a*) *pron.phr.* **je ne sais qui,** somebody or other; **je ne sais qui de ses amis,** some friend or other of his; **un je ne sais quoi de déplaisant,** something vaguely unpleasant; **c'est je ne sais quoi qu'elle a mangé,** its something she's eaten; **un je sais tout,** a know-all, *NAm:* a know-it-all; (*b*) *adj.phr.* **je ne sais quelle maladie,** some illness or other; (*c*) *adv.phr.* **je suis tout je ne sais comment,** I feel very odd; **il y a je ne sais combien de temps,** ages ago, heaven knows how long ago; (*d*) **des robes, des chapeaux, des gants,**

que sais-je? dresses, hats, gloves, what have you, whatever, and goodness knows what else; **il a des amis, Dieu sait,** God knows, he has plenty of friends! **Dieu sait comment,** heaven knows how.

savoir[2] *n.m.* knowledge, learning.

savoir-faire [savwarfɛr] *n.m.inv.* savoir-faire; ability; know-how.

savoir-vivre [savwarvivr̥] *n.m.inv.* savoir-vivre; good manners; tact.

savon [savɔ̃] *n.m.* soap; **(pain de) s.,** bar, tablet, cake, of soap; **s. à barbe,** shaving soap, stick; **s. de Marseille** = household soap; **eau de s.,** soap suds; *F:* **donner, flanquer, passer, un s. à qn,** to give s.o. a good talking to; *Miner:* **s. blanc, minéral, de montagne,** mountain soap, rock soap; **s. naturel, des soldats,** smectic clay; **pierre de s.,** soapstone; talc; steatite.

savonnage [savɔnaʒ] *n.m.* soaping, washing (of clothes, etc.).

savonner [savɔne] *v.tr.* (*a*) to (wash with) soap; to lather (chin before shaving); *Aut:* **piste savonnée,** skidpan; (*b*) *Tchn:* to rub, grind (glass with glass soap).

savonnerie [savɔnri] *n.f.* soap factory.

savonnette [savɔnɛt] *n.f.* bar, cake, tablet, of (toilet) soap.

savonneux, -euse [savɔnø, -øz] *a.* soapy.

savourer [savure] *v.tr.* to relish, enjoy.

savoureusement [savurøzmɑ̃] *adv.* with relish.

savoureux, -euse [savurø, -øz] *a.* tasty (dish); full-flavoured, *NAm:* -flavored (wine); spicy (story).

Saxe [saks] *Pr.n.f. Geog:* Saxony; **porcelaine de S.,** *n.m.* **s.,** Dresden china.

saxhorn [saksɔrn] *n.m. Mus:* saxhorn; **s. basse,** euphonium.

saxifrage [saksifraʒ] *n.f. Bot:* saxifrage.

saxo [sakso] *n.m. F:* saxophone, sax.

saxon, -onne [saksɔ̃, -ɔn] **1.** *a. & n. Hist: Geog:* Saxon. **2.** *a. & n.m. Ling:* Saxon.

saxophone [saksɔfɔn] *n.m. Mus:* saxophone.

saxophoniste [saksɔfɔnist] *n. Mus:* saxophonist.

saynète [sɛnɛt] *n.f. Th:* playlet, short comedy.

sbire [sbir] *n.m. F: Pej:* (i) (officious) policeman, pig; (ii) thug.

scabieux, -ieuse [skabjø, -jøz] **1.** *a.* scabby. **2.** *n.f. Bot:* **scabieuse,** scabious.

scabreux, -euse [skabrø, -øz] *a.* **1.** *Lit:* difficult, tricky. **2.** indecent, shocking.

scalaire[1] [skalɛr] *n.f. Ich:* angel fish.

scalaire[2] *a. & n.m. Mth:* scalar.

scalène [skalɛn] *a. Mth: Anat:* scalene.

scalp(e) [skalp] *n.m.* scalp(ing).

scalpel [skalpɛl] *n.m. Surg:* scalpel.

scalper [skalpe] *v.tr.* to scalp.

scandale [skɑ̃dal] *n.m.* scandal; (cause of) shame; **faire (un) s., causer du s.,** to create a scandal; **au grand s. de ses parents,** to the great indignation, disgust, of his parents.

scandaleusement [skɑ̃daløzmɑ̃] *adv.* scandalously; disgracefully; disgustingly; dreadfully.

scandaleux, -euse [skɑ̃dalø, -øz] *a.* scandalous; disgraceful; shocking.

scandaliser [skɑ̃dalize] *v.tr.* to scandalize, shock; **il ne se scandalise de rien,** nothing shocks him.

scander [skɑ̃de] *v.tr. Pros:* to scan (verse); *Mus:* to mark, stress (a phrase); **s. un slogan,** to chant a slogan.

scandinave [skɑ̃dinav] *a. & n. Geog:* Scandinavian.

Scandinavie [skɑ̃dinavi] *Pr.n.f. Geog:* Scandinavia.

scandium [skɑ̃djɔm] *n.m. Ch:* scandium.

scansion [skɑ̃sjɔ̃] *n.f.* scansion, scanning.

scaphandre [skafɑ̃dr̥] *n.m.* (*a*) diving suit; **s. autonome,** aqualung, scuba; (*b*) space suit.

scaphandrier [skafɑ̃drije] *n.m.* diver (in diving suit).

scaphoïde [skafɔid] *a. & n.m. Anat: Nat.Hist:* scaphoid.

scapulaire [skapylɛr] *a. & n.m.* scapular.

scarabée [skarabe] *n.m.* beetle; scarab.

scare [skar] *n.m. Ich:* parrot fish, scar.

scarificateur [skarifikatœr] *n.m.* (*a*) *Agr:* harrow, scarifier; (*b*) *Surg:* scarificator.

scarifier [skarifje] *v.tr.* (*impf. & pr.sub.* **n. scarifiions, v. scarifiiez)** *Agr: Surg:* to scarify; *Biol:* to abrade.

scarlatine [skarlatin] *n.f. Med:* scarlatina, scarlet fever.

scarlatineux, -euse [skarlatinø, -øz] *a. & n.* (patient) suffering from scarlatina, scarlet fever.

scarole [skarɔl] *n.f. Bot:* endive.

scatologie [skatɔlɔʒi] *n.f.* scatological humour, *NAm:* humor, literature.

scatologique [skatɔlɔʒik] *a.* scatological (literature).

scatophage [skatɔfaʒ] **1.** *a.* scatophagous (fish, insect). **2.** *n.m. Ent:* scatophage; dung fly.

scatophagie [skatɔfaʒi] *n.f.* scatophagy.

sceau, *pl.* **sceaux** [so] *n.m.* seal; **S. de l'État,** State seal; **mettre, apposer, son s. à un document,** to set one's seal to a document; **mettre le s. à la réputation de qn,** to set the seal on s.o.'s reputation; **s. du génie,** mark, stamp, of genius; *Bot:* **s. de Salomon,** Solomon's seal.

scélérat, -ate [selera, -at] *A: & Lit:* **1.** *a.* wicked. **2.** *n.* scoundrel.

scellé [sele] **1.** *a.* sealed; under seal. **2.** *n.m. Jur:* (imprint of official) seal.

scellement [sɛlmɑ̃] *n.m. Const:* (*a*) sealing, setting; fixing, bedding (of a post in stone, in concrete); (*b*) socket; (wall) plug; (*c*) end (of post, etc., fitting in socket).

sceller [sele] *v.tr.* **1.** (*a*) to seal; (*b*) to ratify, confirm. **2.** *Const:* to bed, fasten, fix in.

scénario [senarjo] *n.m.* (*a*) scenario; (*b*) film script.

scénariste [senarist] *n.* scenario writer; script writer.

scène [sɛn] *n.f. Th:* **1.** (*a*) stage; **entrer en s.,** (i) *Th:* to appear, come on; (ii) to appear on the scene; (*of actor*) **être en s.,** to be on; **en s. pour le un!** beginners please! **mise en s.,** (i) staging, production; (ii) setting (of a play); **metteur en s.,** producer; **mettre qch. en s.,** to stage sth.; **porter qch. à la s.,** to adapt sth. for the theatre, *NAm:* theater; **elle a la folie de la s.,** she's stagestruck; **quitter la s.,** to retire from the stage, from acting; (*b*) theatre, drama; dramatic art; (*c*) **la s. politique,** the political scene. **2.** scene; (*a*) **changement de s.,** change of scene; **la s. se passe au moyen âge,** the action takes place in the middle ages; **revoir les scènes de sa jeunesse,** to revisit the scenes of one's youth; (*b*) **troisième s. du second acte,** act two scene three; (*c*) **ce fut une s. pénible,** it was a painful scene; **scènes de la vie des camps,** scenes of camp life; (*d*) *F:* scene, row; **faire une s.,** to make a scene; **s. de ménage,** domestic squabble.

scénique [senik] *a.* theatrical; (of the) stage; **éclairage s.,** stage lighting; **indications scéniques,** stage directions.

scéniquement [senikmɑ̃] *adv.* from the theatrical point of view; theatrically speaking.

scénographe [senɔgraf] *n.* scenographer.

scénographie [senɔgrafi] *n.f.* **1.** *Art: etc:* scenography. **2.** *Th:* scenography; scenecraft.

scepticisme [sɛptisism] *n.m.* scepticism, *NAm:* skepticism.

sceptique [sɛptik] **1.** *a.* sceptical, *NAm:* skeptical. **2.** *n.* sceptic, *NAm:* skeptic.

sceptiquement [sɛptikmɑ̃] *adv.* sceptically, *NAm:* skeptically.
sceptre [sɛptr̥] *n.m.* sceptre, *NAm:* scepter; *Fig:* **s. de fer,** rod of iron.
schako [ʃako] *n.m. Mil.Cost:* shako.
scheik [ʃɛk] *n.m.* sheik.
schelem [ʃlɛm] *n.m. Cards:* slam; **petit, grand, s.,** little, grand, slam.
schéma [ʃema] *n.m.* (*a*) diagram; (sketch) plan; (*b*) project, plan (for a book, etc.); scheme, arrangement.
schématique [ʃematik] *a.* (*a*) diagrammatic; schematic; (*b*) *Pej:* oversimplified.
schématiquement [ʃematikmɑ̃] *adv.* (*a*) schematically, diagrammatically; (*b*) in outline; in a simplified manner.
schématisation [ʃematizasjɔ̃] *n.f.* schematization; reduction to essentials.
schématiser [ʃematize] *v.tr.* to schematize; to make a diagram of; to simplify.
schématisme [ʃematism] *n.m.* (*a*) *Phil:* schematism; (*b*) *often Pej:* simplification.
schème [ʃɛm] *n.m.* (*a*) *Phil: Psy:* schema; (*b*) *Art: etc:* design.
scherzando [skɛrtsando, skɛrdz-] *adv. Mus:* scherzando.
scherzo [skɛrtso, -dzo] *Mus:* **1.** *n.m.* scherzo. **2.** *adv.* scherzando.
schibboleth [ʃibɔlɛt] *n.m.* shibboleth.
schilling [ʃiliŋ] *n.m. Num:* (Austrian) schilling.
schismatique [ʃismatik] *a. & n.* schismatic.
schisme [ʃism] *n.m.* schism.
schiste [ʃist] *n.m. Geol:* schist, shale.
schisteux, -euse [ʃistø, -øz] *a. Geol:* schistose.
schistoïde [ʃistɔid] *a.* schistoid.
schistosomiase [ʃistɔzomjaz] *n.f. Med:* schistosomiasis.
schizogamie [skizɔgami] *n.f. Biol:* schizogamy.
schizoïde [skizɔid] *a. & n. Psy:* schizoid.
schizoïdie [skizɔidi] *n.f. Psy:* schizoidism; schizothymia.
schizoïdique [skizɔidik] *a. Psy:* schizoid.
schizophasie [skizɔfazi] *n.f. Psy:* schizophasia.
schizophrène [skizɔfrɛn] *a. & n. Psy:* schizophrenic.
schizophrénie [skizɔfreni] *n.f. Psy:* schizophrenia.
schizophrénique [skizɔfrenik] *a. & n. Psy:* schizophrenic.
schizothymie [skizɔtimi] *n.f. Psy:* schizothymia.
schizothymique [skizɔtimik] *a. Psy:* schizothymic.
schlass [ʃlas] *a. P:* drunk, tight, sozzled.
schlinguer [ʃlɛ̃ge] *v.i. P:* to stink, to pong.
schlittage [ʃlitaʒ] *n.m.* transporting on a *schlitte.*
schlitte [ʃlit] *n.f.* (timber) sledge (for transporting lumber); *U.S:* dray.
schlitter [ʃlite] *v.tr.* to transport (lumber) on a *schlitte.*
schnaps [ʃnaps] *n.m.* schnapps.
schnau(t)zer [ʃnawzɛr] *n.m.* (*dog*) schnauzer.
schnock, schnoque [ʃnɔk] *P:* **1.** *a.* (*of pers.*) mad, batty, crazy, daft. **2.** *n.* idiot, nit.
schnorchel, schnorkel [ʃnɔrkɛl] *n.m.* snorkel.
schnouff [ʃnuf] *n.f. P:* (*narcotic*) dope, junk.
schofar [ʃɔfar] *n.m. Jew.Rel: Mus:* shophar.
schooner [skunœr, ʃunɛr] *n.m. Nau:* schooner.
schorre [ʃɔr] *n.m.* salt meadow.
schuss [ʃus] *n.m. Ski:* schuss.
sciage [sjaʒ] *n.m.* sawing.
sciant [sjɑ̃] *a. P:* boring; **il est s.,** (i) he's a damn nuisance; (ii) he bores me stiff.
sciaphile [sjafil] *a. Biol:* shade-loving.
sciatique [sjatik] **1.** (*a*) *a. Anat:* sciatic (nerve, artery, etc.); (*b*) *n.m.* sciatic nerve. **2.** *n.f. Med:* sciatica.
scie [si] *n.f.* **1.** saw; (*a*) *Tls:* **s. à bois,** wood saw; **s. à métaux,** hacksaw; **s. mécanique,** power saw; **s. circulaire,** circular saw, *NAm:* buzz saw; **s. articulée, s. à chaîne(tte),** chain saw; **s. à chantourner,** (i) (*handsaw*) bow saw, turning saw; (ii) (*machine*) jigsaw, scroll saw; **s. à découper, s. anglaise,** (i) (*handsaw*) fretsaw; (ii) (*machine*) jig saw; **en dents de s.,** serrate(d); (*b*) *Games:* **jeu de la s.,** cat's cradle; (*c*) *Med:* **bruit de s.,** rasping murmur. **2.** *Ich:* **(poisson) s.,** sawfish; *Ent:* **mouche à s.,** sawfly. **3.** *F:* (*a*) bore, nuisance; (*b*) catch phrase; (*c*) hit tune.
sciemment [sjamɑ̃] *adv.* knowingly; on purpose.
science [sjɑ̃s] *n.f.* **1.** knowledge, learning; skill; ability; *Theol:* **s. infuse,** intuition; mystical vision. **2.** (*a*) science; **la s. n'a pas de patrie,** science knows no frontiers; **homme de s.,** scientist; (*b*) *pl.* **doué pour les sciences,** good at science; **préparer une licence ès sciences,** to study for a degree in science; **les sciences exactes,** the exact sciences; **sciences physiques, naturelles, appliquées,** physical, natural, applied, science; **sciences humaines,** humanities; **sciences sociales,** social science(s); **les sciences occultes,** the occult sciences.
science-fiction [sjɑ̃sfiksjɔ̃] *n.f.* science fiction.
scientifique [sjɑ̃tifik] **1.** *a.* scientific. **2.** *n.* scientist.
scientifiquement [sjɑ̃tifikmɑ̃] *adv.* scientifically.
scientisme [sjɑ̃tism] *n.m.* (*a*) scientism; (*b*) (doctrines of) Christian Science.
scientiste [sjɑ̃tist] **1.** *a.* scientistic. **2.** *n.* (*a*) (*adept of scientism*) scientist; (*b*) **s. chrétien(ne),** Christian Scientist.
scier¹ [sje] *v.tr.* (*pr.sub. & impf.* **n. sciions, v. sciiez) 1.** to saw; *F:* **s. qn,** (i) *A:* to bore s.o. stiff; (ii) to amaze s.o. **2.** to saw off (branch, etc.).
scier² *v.i. Row:* to back water, to back the oars.
scierie [siri] *n.f.* sawmill.
scieur [sjœr] *n.m.* sawyer; **s. de long,** (pit) sawyer.
scieuse [sjøz] *n.f.* mechanical saw.
scille [sil] *n.f.* (*a*) *Bot:* scilla, squill; **s. maritime,** sea onion; (*b*) *Pharm:* squills.
scinder [sɛ̃de] **1.** *v.tr.* to divide, split up. **2. se s.,** to split up.
scinque [sɛ̃k] *n.m. Rept:* skink.
scintillant [sɛ̃tijɑ̃] **1.** *a.* scintillating, twinkling; sparkling (wit). **2.** *n.m.* tinsel decoration(s).
scintillation [sɛ̃tijasjɔ̃] *n.f.*, **scintillement** [sɛ̃tijmɑ̃] *n.m.* (*a*) scintillation (of star, etc.); (*b*) *Cin: T.V:* flicker(ing); (*c*) **scintillement,** sparkling, twinkling (of eyes, stars, jewellery, etc.).
scintiller [sɛ̃tije] *v.i.* to scintillate; to sparkle; (*of star*) to twinkle; *Elcs: T.V: Cin:* to flicker; **esprit qui scintille,** sparkling wit.
scion [sjɔ̃] *n.m.* **1.** *Hort:* scion, shoot. **2.** tip (of fishing rod).
scirpe [sirp] *n.m. Bot:* club rush, bulrush.
scissile [sisil] *a. Atom.Ph:* fissionable (material).
scission [sisjɔ̃] *n.f.* (*a*) *Pol: etc:* split, division; (*b*) secession; **faire s.,** to secede; (*c*) *Ch:* scission, cleavage; *Atom.Ph:* fission, splitting; **s. nucléaire,** nuclear fission.
scissionniste [sisjɔnist] *a. & n.* secessionist.
scissipare [sisipar] *a. Biol:* fissiparous.
scissiparité [sisiparite] *n.f. Biol:* schizogenesis, fissiparity.
scissure [sisyr] *n.f. Anat: etc:* fissure, cleavage, cleft.
sciure [sjyr] *n.f.* **s. (de bois),** sawdust; **s. de marbre,** marble dust.
scléral, -aux [skleral, -o] *a. Anat:* scleral, sclerotic.
sclérenchyme [sklerɑ̃ʃim] *n.m. Nat.Hist:* sclerenchyma.

scléreux, -euse [sklerø, -øz] *a. Med:* sclerous, sclerosed, hard (tissue).
sclérifié [sklerifje] *a. Nat.Hist:* sclerosed, hardened (tegument, etc.).
sclérodermé [sklerɔdɛrme] *a. Z:* sclerodermatous, sclerodermic.
sclérodermie [sklerɔdɛrmi] *n.f. Med:* scleroderma.
sclérogène [sklerɔʒɛn] *a. Med:* sclerogenic.
sclérome [sklerom] *n.m. Med:* scleroma.
scléromètre [sklerɔmɛtr̥] *n.m. Ph:* sclerometer.
sclérophylle [sklerɔfil] *Bot:* (*a*) *a.* sclerophyllous; (*b*) *n.m.* sclerophyll.
scléroprotéine [sklerɔprɔtein] *n.f. Bio-Ch:* scleroprotein.
sclérose [skleroz] *n.f. Med:* sclerosis; *Fig:* ossification, mental sclerosis; **s. vasculaire, des artères,** arterio-sclerosis; **s. en plaques,** multiple sclerosis.
sclérosé [skleroze] *a. Med:* sclerosed; *Fig:* rigid, hidebound; ossified.
scléroser [skleroze] *v.tr. Med:* to sclerose, harden; *Fig:* **se s.,** to become hidebound, too rigid.
sclérotique [sklerɔtik] *Anat:* **1.** *a.* sclerotic. **2.** *n.f.* sclerotic, sclera (of the eye).
scolaire [skɔlɛr] *a.* (*a*) scholastic; academic (success); educational (reform, organisation, insurance); **vie s.,** school life; **année s.,** school, academic, year; **enfant d'âge s.,** child of school age; **frais scolaires,** school fees; **livres scolaires,** school books; text books; (*b*) *Pej:* bookish; pedestrian; laboured, *NAm:* labored.
scolarisation [skɔlarizasjɔ̃] *n.f.* **1.** school attendance. **2.** education; schooling.
scolariser [skɔlarize] *v.tr.* to provide education for (children); to equip, provide (an area) with schools.
scolarité [skɔlarite] *n.f. Sch:* **s. obligatoire,** compulsory school attendance; **prolongation de la s.,** raising of the school-leaving age; **s. à temps partiel** = day release classes; **frais de s.,** school fees.
scolasticat [skɔlastika] *n.m.* theological college; theological training.
scolastique [skɔlastik] **1.** *a.* scholastic (philosophy, etc.). **2.** *n.m.* schoolman, scholastic. **3.** *n.f.* scholasticism, school theology.
scolex [skɔlɛks] *n.m.inv. Z:* scolex, head (of tapeworm).
scoliaste [skɔljast] *n.m.* scholiast.
scoliose [skɔljoz] *n.f. Med:* scoliosis, lateral curvature of the spine.
scolopendre¹ [skɔlɔpɑ̃dr̥] *n.f. Myr:* scolopendra, centipede.
scolopendre² *n.f. Bot:* hart's tongue, scolopendrium.
scombéroïde [skɔ̃berɔid] *n.m. Ich:* scombroid.
scombre [skɔ̃br̥] *n.m. Ich:* scombrid; *esp.* mackerel.
sconse [skɔ̃s] *n.m. Z:* skunk; *Com:* skunk (fur).
scooter [skutɛr] *n.m.* (motor) scooter.
scootériste [skuterist] *n.* scooter rider, scooterist.
scopie [skɔpi] *n.f. F:* radioscopy.
scopolamine [skɔpɔlamin] *n.f. Ch: Pharm:* scopolamine; hyoscine.
scops [skɔps] *n.m. Orn:* scops owl.
scorbut [skɔrbyt] *n.m. Med:* scurvy, scorbutus.
scorbutigène [skɔrbytiʒɛn] *a. Med:* scurvy-producing (diet).
scorbutique [skɔrbytik] *a. & n. Med:* scorbutic.
score [skɔr] *n.m. Psy: Sp:* score.
scoriacé [skɔrjase] *a. Metall: Geol: etc:* slaggy.
scorie [skɔri] *n.f. usu.pl.* **1.** *Metall:* slag, cinders, scoria; (iron) dross; clinker. **2.** *Geol:* **scories (volcaniques),** scoria; volcanic slag. **3.** mediocre, inferior, part (of sth.).
scorpène [skɔrpɛn] *n.f. Ich:* scorpion fish.
scorpioïde [skɔrpjɔid] *a. Bot:* scorpioid.
scorpion [skɔrpjɔ̃] *n.m.* **1.** (*a*) *Arach:* scorpion; (*b*) *Astr:* **le S.,** Scorpio. **2.** (*a*) *Ent:* **s. aquatique, d'eau,** water scorpion; (*b*) *Ich:* **s. de mer,** scorpion fish.
scorsonère [skɔrsɔnɛr], **scorzonère** [skɔrzɔnɛr] *n.f. Bot:* scorzonera, black salsify.
scotch [skɔtʃ] *n.m.* **1.** scotch (whisky); **un double s.,** a double scotch; *pl. scotches.* **2.** *R.t.m:* **Scotch,** self-adhesive (cellulose) tape; *R.t.m:* Sellotape, *NAm:* Scotch(tape).
scotch-terrier [skɔtʃtɛrje] *n.m. Z:* Scottish, Scotch, terrier; *pl. scotch-terriers.*
scotie [skɔti] *n.f. Arch:* scotia (of pillar).
scotome [skɔtom] *n.m. Med:* scotoma.
scotopique [skɔtɔpik] *a. Med:* scotopic.
scottish-terrier [skɔtiʃtɛrje] *n.m. Z:* Scottish, Scotch, terrier; *pl. scottish-terriers.*
scout [skut] *n.m.* (boy) scout.
scoutisme [skutism] *n.m.* scouting.
scratch [skratʃ] *n.m. Sp:* scratch; **partir s.,** to start (at) scratch; **(course) s.,** scratch race; **(joueur) s.,** scratch player.
scratcher [skratʃe] *v.tr. Turf: etc:* to scratch (horse, competitor).
scribe [skrib] *n.m.* (*a*) *Ant:* scribe; (*b*) *Pej:* copyist, pen-pusher.
scribouillard, -arde [skribujar, -ard] *n. F: Pej:* clerk, pen-pusher.
script¹ [skript] *n.m. Fin:* scrip.
script² **1.** *n.m.* (*a*) (*handwriting*) script; **écriture s.,** script printing; (*b*) *F:* film script. **2.** *n.f. Cin: F:* continuity girl.
script-girl [skriptgœrl] *n.f. Cin:* continuity girl; *pl. script-girls.*
scriptural, -aux [skriptyral, -o] *a.* (*a*) scriptural; (*b*) *Bank:* **monnaie scripturale,** bank or other forms of financial credit.
scrofulaire [skrɔfylɛr] *n.f. Bot:* figwort.
scrofule [skrɔfyl] *n.f. Med:* scrofula; *A.Med:* **les scrofules,** scrofula; the king's evil.
scrofuleux, -euse [skrɔfylø, -øz] *a. & n. Med:* scrofulous (person).
scrotum [skrɔtɔm] *n.m. Anat:* scrotum.
scrupule [skrypyl] *n.m.* **1.** *A.Meas:* scruple. **2.** scruple, (conscientious) doubt **(sur,** about); **sans scrupules,** unscrupulous(ly); **se faire (un) s. de faire qch., avoir des scrupules à faire qch.,** to have scruples, qualms, about doing sth.; **il ne se fait pas s. d'emprunter à la caisse,** he has no scruples about borrowing from the till; **exact jusqu'au s.,** scrupulously exact.
scrupuleusement [skrypyløzmɑ̃] *adv.* scrupulously.
scrupuleux, -euse [skrypylø, -øz] *a.* scrupulous **(sur,** about, over, as to; **à faire qch.,** in doing sth.); **peu s.,** unscrupulous.
scrutateur, -trice [skrytatœr, -tris] **1.** *a. Lit:* searching (mind, look). **2.** *n.* (*a*) scrutinizer; (*b*) teller, scrutineer (of a ballot, poll).
scruter [skryte] *v.tr.* to scrutinize; to scan; to examine closely.
scrutin [skrytɛ̃] *n.m.* **1.** poll; **s. d'arrondissement** = constituency poll; **s. secret,** secret vote; **s. découvert,** open vote; **dépouiller le s.,** to count the votes. **2.** **tour de s.,** ballot; **voter au s.,** to ballot; **élire qn au s.,** to ballot for s.o. **3.** voting (in an assembly); (parliamentary) division; **procéder au s.,** to take the vote; (*in Eng. Parliament*) to divide; **demander le s.,** to ask for a count; **projet adopté sans s.,** bill passed without a division.
scrutiner [skrytine] *v.i.* (*a*) to poll, vote; to go to the poll; (*b*) to ballot.
scull [skyl, skœl] *n.m. Sp: Nau:* (*a*) scull, skiff; (*b*) sculling.

sculpter [skylte] *v.tr.* to sculpture, sculpt; to carve (**dans,** in, out of); **bois sculpté,** carved wood.

sculpteur [skyltœr] *n.m.* sculptor; **femme s.,** woman sculptor, sculptress; **s. sur bois,** woodcarver.

sculptural, -aux [skyltyral, -o] *a.* sculptural (art); statuesque (figure).

sculpture [skyltyr] *n.f.* sculpture; **s. sur bois,** woodcarving.

scutellaire [skytelɛr] **1.** *a. Ent:* scutellar. **2.** *n.f. Bot:* scutellaria, skull cap.

scutum [skytɔm] *n.m. Rom.Ant: Nat.Hist:* scutum.

scyphoméduse [sifɔmedyz] *n.f. Coel:* scyphomedusan; *pl.* **scyphoméduses,** Scyphomedusae.

se *before a vowel sound* **s'** [s(ə)] *pers. pron. acc. & dat. unstressed, attached to the verb or its adjuncts.* **1.** (*a*) (*reflexive*) oneself; himself, herself, itself, themselves; **se flatter,** to flatter oneself; **il se rase,** he is shaving; **elle s'est coupée au doigt, s'est coupé le doigt,** she has cut her finger; **il se parle (à lui-même),** he's talking to himself; **ils se sont fait mal,** they hurt themselves; (*b*) (*reciprocal*) each other, one another; **se nuire (l'un à l'autre),** to hurt one another; **il est dur de se quitter,** it is hard to part. **2.** (*giving passive meaning to active vbs*) **la clef s'est retrouvée,** the key has been found; **cet article se vend partout,** this article is on sale everywhere; **la porte s'est ouverte,** the door opened, came open. **3.** (*in purely pronom. conjugation*) *See* S'EN ALLER, SE BATTRE, SE DÉPÊCHER, SE FÂCHER, *etc.* NOTE: **se** *is usu. omitted before an infinitive dependent on* **faire, laisser, mener, envoyer, voir;** *e.g:* **se taire: faire taire les enfants.**

séance [seɑ̃s] *n.f.* **1.** *A:* seat (at a council table, etc.). **2.** sitting, session, meeting; (*of parliament*) **être en s.,** to be sitting, in session; **la s. s'ouvrira, sera levée, à huit heures,** the meeting will open, adjourn, at eight; **en s. publique,** at an open meeting; *Jur:* in open court; **s. d'information,** briefing. **3.** (cinema, etc.) performance; show; **s. de spiritisme,** seance. **4.** (*a*) sitting (for one's portrait, etc.); **faire une longue s. à table,** to sit a long time over one's meal; *Med:* **traitement de trois séances,** course of three treatments; (*b*) period; **s. de travail, d'entraînement,** working, training, period, session.

séant [seɑ̃] **1.** *a.* (*a*) sitting, in session; (*b*) *A: & Lit:* becoming (**à,** to); fitting. **2.** *n.m.* **se mettre sur son s.,** to sit up (in bed); **être sur son s.,** to be in a sitting position; **tomber sur son s.,** to sit down with a bump.

seau, *pl.* **seaux** [so] *n.m.* pail, bucket; **s. à glace, à rafraîchir,** ice bucket; **s. à incendie,** fire bucket; **s. à charbon,** coal scuttle; **s. à biscuits,** biscuit barrel; **apporter un s. d'eau,** to bring a bucket(ful), pail(ful), of water; *F:* **il pleut à seaux,** it's pouring down, bucketing down.

sébacé [sebase] *a.* sebaceous (gland).

sébifère [sebifɛr] *a. Anat: Bot:* sebiferous.

sébile [sebil] *n.f.* wooden bowl.

séborrhée [sebɔre] *n.f. Med:* seborrh(o)ea.

séborrhéique [sebɔreik] *a. Med:* seborrh(o)eic.

sébum [sebɔm] *n.m. Anat:* sebum.

sec, sèche [sɛk, sɛʃ] **1.** *a.* (*a*) dry (weather, linen, ground, throat); **regarder d'un œil s.,** to look on dry-eyed; **mettre qn au pain s. et à l'eau,** to put s.o. on bread and water; **mur de pierres sèches,** drystone wall; *Aut:* **être en panne sèche,** to (have) run out of petrol, *NAm:* gas; **traverser un torrent à pied s.,** to cross a torrent dryshod; **s. comme une allumette,** bone dry; *Adm:* **le régime s.,** the dry regime; prohibition; **pays secs,** prohibitionist countries; dry countries; (*b*) dried (cod, fruit, etc.); seasoned, matured (wood, cigar); dry (wine); (*c*) **perte sèche,** dead loss; **en cinq s.,** in no time. **2.** *a.* (*a*) spare, gaunt (person); lean (figure, horse); **s. et nerveux,** wiry; **s. comme un coup de trique,** as thin as a rake; *n.* **un vieux s.,** a wizened old man; (*b*) sharp, dry, curt (remark, answer); incisive (tone); sharp (blow); **casser qch. d'un coup s.,** to snap sth. off; **faire un accueil très s. à qn,** to give s.o. a very cool reception; **mine sèche,** sour face; (*c*) unsympathetic, unfeeling (heart, etc.); (*d*) dry, bald (narrative, style). **3.** *adv.* (*a*) **boire s.,** (i) to drink one's spirits neat, straight; (ii) to drink hard; (*b*) hard; sharply; **la voiture a viré très s.,** the car swung round sharply; (*of coin*) **sonner s.,** to chink; **fermer s. le couvercle,** to slam down the lid; (*c*) **rire s.,** to give a harsh, dry, laugh. **4.** *adv.phr.* (*a*) **à s.,** (i) dry; (ii) dried up; (iii) *F:* hard up, broke; *F:* **au bout de cinq minutes il était à s.,** at the end of five minutes he had nothing to say, he had dried up; (*b*) **nettoyage à s.,** dry cleaning; **maçonnerie à s.,** dry masonry; (*c*) **navire à s., au s.,** ship aground, high and dry; (*d*) (*of ship*) **filer, courir, fuir, à s. (de toile),** to run under bare poles; (*e*) **tout s.,** only, merely; *P:* **aussi s.,** at once, straight away; right away. **5.** *n.m.* (*a*) dryness; drought; (*b*) **tenir au s.,** keep in a dry place. **6.** *n.f. P:* **sèche,** cigarette, fag.

sécable [sekabl̩] *a.* divisible.

secam [sekam] *a. & n.m. T.V:* secam.

sécant, -ante [sekɑ̃, -ɑ̃t] *Mth:* **1.** *a.* secant, cutting (line, surface). **2.** *n.f.* **sécante,** secant.

sécateur [sekatœr] *n.m.* secateur(s); pruning shears.

sécession [sesesjɔ̃] *n.f.* secession; **faire s.,** to secede (**de,** from).

sécessionniste [sesesjɔnist] *a. & n.* secessionist.

séchage [seʃaʒ] *n.m.* drying (of hay, clothes, etc.); seasoning (of wood).

sèche-cheveux [sɛʃʃəvø] *n.m.inv.* hair drier.

sèche-linge [sɛʃlɛ̃ʒ] *a.inv. Dom.Ec:* **armoire s.-l.,** drying cupboard.

sèchement [sɛʃmɑ̃] *adv.* **1.** curtly; tartly. **2. écrire s.,** to write in a bald style; **traiter un sujet s.,** to treat a subject baldly.

sécher [seʃe] **(je sèche, n. séchons; je sécherai) 1.** *v.tr.* (*a*) to dry (clothes, etc.); to dry up; **s. ses larmes,** to dry one's tears; (*b*) *F:* **s. un verre,** to drain a glass; (*c*) *F: Sch: etc:* **s. un cours,** to skip, cut, a lecture. **2.** *v.i.* (*a*) to (become) dry; **faire s. du bois,** (i) to dry, (ii) to season, wood; **faire s. du linge,** to dry the linen; (*b*) **s. d'impatience,** to be consumed with impatience; (*of plant, Fig: of pers.*) **s. sur pied,** to wilt; (*c*) *F:* not to know what to say, to dry up; *Sch:* to be stumped (by an examiner).

sécheresse [seʃrɛs, sɛ-] *n.f.* **1.** (*a*) dryness (of the air, ground, throat, etc.); (*b*) drought. **2.** (*a*) curtness (of manner, etc.); (*b*) coldness, unfeelingness (of heart, etc.); (*c*) baldness (of style).

sécherie [seʃri, sɛ-] *n.f.* **1.** drying room, ground, yard, floor. **2.** drying machine, drier.

sécheur [seʃœr] *n.m. Tchn:* drying apparatus, chamber; drier.

séchoir [seʃwar] *n.m. Tchn:* **1.** drying room, loft, ground; **s. à houblon,** oasthouse. **2.** (*a*) drier, drying apparatus; desiccator; **s. (à cheveux),** (hairdresser's) hair drier; *Ind:* **s. à vapeur,** steam drier; (*b*) clothes horse, towel rail.

second, -onde [səgɔ̃, -ɔ̃d] **1.** *a.* second; (*a*) **une seconde fois,** a second time; twice; **en s. lieu,** in the second place; **seconde nature,** second nature (**chez qn,** with s.o.); *a. & n.m.* **au s. (étage),** on the second, *NAm:* third, floor; **votre ami est un s. Sherlock Holmes,** your friend is another, a second, Sherlock Holmes; *Mus:* **les seconds violons,** the second violins; *Gram:* **la seconde personne du singulier,** the second person singular; **de seconde main,** secondhand; **au s. plan,** in the background; **le don de seconde vue,** the gift of second sight; (*b*) (*taking second place; inferior*) *Com:* junior (partner); *Th:* supporting (role); **de s.**

ordre, de s. choix, secondrate; *Sp:* **finir bon s.,** to come in a good second; (*c*) *Phil: etc:* **causes secondes,** second causes; (*d*) **état s.,** (i) *Med:* semi-conscious state (of a sleepwalker); (ii) trance, daze. **2.** *n.m.* (*a*) principal assistant; second (in command); *Nau:* first mate; *Navy:* **commandant, officier, en s.,** *F:* **le s.,** executive officer; **commander en s.,** to be second in command; *Jur:* (*of notary*) **signer en s.,** to countersign (deed); (*b*) second (in a duel, of boxer). **3.** *n.f.* **seconde** (*a*) *Typ:* second proof; revise; *Aut:* second (gear); *Rail: etc:* **voyager en seconde,** to travel second (class); *Sch:* **(classe de) seconde** = fifth form; **élève de seconde** = fifth-former; *Mus:* **seconde majeure, mineure,** major, minor, second; (*b*) second (of time, arc, angle); **aiguille des secondes,** second hand (of a watch); **(attendez) une seconde!** just a second! just a moment! **en un quart, une fraction, de seconde,** in a split second, in no time.

secondaire [səgɔ̃dɛr] *a.* **1.** secondary; **établissement d'enseignement s.,** secondary school; **centre d'études secondaires** = comprehensive school. **2.** subordinate, of minor importance; *Rail:* **voie s.,** side track; *Ling:* **accent s.,** secondary accent, secondary stress; *Mus:* **temps s.,** weak beat; *Th: Lit:* **intrigue s.,** subplot. **3.** (*a*) *n.m. El:* secondary winding; *W.Tel:* secondary (of transformer); (*b*) *a. & n.m. Geol:* **l'ère s., le s.,** the secondary (era); (*c*) *a. & n.m. Pol.Ec:* secondary (activities).

secondement [səgɔ̃dmɑ̃] *adv.* secondly, in the second place.

seconder [səgɔ̃de] *v.tr.* **1.** to second, back up, support (s.o.). **2.** to forward, further, promote (s.o.'s interests, plans, etc.).

secouage [səkwaʒ] *n.m.*, **secouement** [səkumɑ̃] *n.m.* **1.** shaking; shake (of the head). **2.** shaking; jolt.

secouer [səkwe] *v.tr.* **1.** (*a*) to shake (tree, one's head, etc.); to plump up, shake up (a pillow); (*of shock, illness*) to shake, affect (s.o.); (*of wind*) to buffet (boat); *v.i.* **voiture qui secoue,** bumpy, jolting, car; **nous avons été secoués pendant la traversée,** we had a rough crossing; (*b*) **il est impossible de s. son indifférence,** it is impossible to shake him out of his indifference; *F:* **secouez-vous!** pull yourself together! get down to it! get a move on! snap out of it! *F:* **s. (les puces à) qn,** (i) to tell s.o. off; (ii) to rouse s.o. to action. **2.** to shake down (fruit, etc.); to shake off (the yoke, the dust).

secourable [səkurabḷ] *a.* helpful, willing to help; **main s.,** helping hand; **peu s.,** unhelpful.

secourir [səkurir] *v.tr.* (*conj. like* COURIR) to help, aid.

secourisme [səkurism] *n.m. Med:* first aid.

secouriste [səkurist] *n.* first-aid worker.

secours [səkur] *n.m.* help, relief, aid, assistance; **crier au s.,** to call for help; **appel au s.,** call for help; **au s.!** help! **porter, prêter, (du) s. à qn,** to help s.o.; *Med:* **premiers s.,** first aid; **boîte, trousse, de s.,** first-aid kit, box, outfit; **s. en montagne,** mountain rescue (work, service); **demander (du) s.,** to ask for help; **aller, se porter, au s. de qn,** to go to s.o.'s aid; *Mil:* **se porter au s. d'un bataillon,** to go in support of a battalion; **cela m'a rendu grand s., cela m'a été d'un grand s.,** it has been a great help; **puis-je vous être d'aucun s.?** can I be of help? **le s. aux enfants,** child welfare work; **caisse de s.,** relief fund; **société de s. mutuels,** benefit society, friendly society; **sortie, porte, de s.,** emergency exit; *Aut:* **roue de s.,** spare wheel; **éclairage de s.,** emergency lighting system; *Mil:* **troupes de s.,** *n.m.pl.* **s.,** relief troops, relieving force; *Rail:* **convoi, corvée, de s.,** breakdown train, gang; **locomotive, train, de s.,** relief engine, train.

secousse [səkus] *n.f.* shake, shaking; jolt, jerk; shock; **s. sismique,** earth tremor; **les secousses de la route, de la voiture,** the jolts, bumps, of the road, the jolting of the car; **se dégager d'une s.,** to jerk, wrench, shake, oneself free; **sans s.,** smoothly; **par secousses,** (i) (to move) jerkily; (ii) (to work) in fits and starts; (iii) (to breathe) in gasps; **s. politique,** political upheaval; **se remettre d'une s.,** to recover from a shock.

secret¹, -ète¹ [səkrɛ, -ɛt] *a.* (*a*) secret (orders, signal, treaty, etc.); hidden (feelings); occult (science); *Adm:* **très s., ultra-s.,** top secret; **la police secrète,** *n.* **la secrète** = the Criminal Investigation Department, the C.I.D.; **fonds secrets,** secret service funds; (*b*) reticent (person).

secret² *n.m.* **1.** secret; **garder un s.,** to keep a secret; **mettre qn dans le s.,** to let s.o. into the secret; **être du s., dans le s.,** to be in the secret, *F:* in the know; **n'avoir point de s. pour qn,** to have no secrets from s.o.; **trahir un s.,** to betray a secret; **le s. du bonheur,** the secret of happiness; **trouver le s. de faire qch.,** to find the knack of doing sth.; **bureau à s.,** desk with a secret compartment. **2.** secrecy, privacy; **dire qch. à qn sous le sceau du s.,** to tell s.o. sth. under pledge of secrecy; **en s.,** in secret, privately; **abuser du, trahir le, s. professionnel,** to commit a breach of confidence; *Ecc:* **le s. de la confession,** the seal of confession. **3. mettre qn au s.,** to put s.o. in solitary confinement.

secrétaire [səkretɛr] **1.** *n.m. or f.* secretary; **s. particulier,** private secretary; **s. médicale,** (i) doctor's, (ii) dentist's, secretary; **s. d'État,** Secretary of State; *Dipl:* **s. d'ambassade,** (first, second, third) secretary; *Journ:* **s. de la rédaction,** sub-editor; **s. général,** Secretary General; *Adm:* **s. de direction,** executive secretary; principal assistant; **s. d'administration** = assistant principal; **s. de mairie** = town clerk; (*in village*) mayor's secretarial assistant. **2.** *n.m. Orn:* secretary bird. **3.** *n.m.* secretaire, writing desk.

secrétariat [səkretarja] *n.m.* **1.** secretaryship. **2.** secretary's office; secretariat.

secrète² [səkrɛt] *n.f. Ecc:* secret.

secrètement [səkrɛtmɑ̃] *adv.* secretly, in secret.

sécréter [sekrete] *v.tr.* **(il sécrète; il sécrétera)** (*of gland, etc.*) to secrete.

sécréteur, -trice, *occ.* **-euse** [sekretœr, -tris, -øz] *a.* secreting, secretary (gland, etc.).

sécrétion [sekresjɔ̃] *n.f. Physiol:* secretion; **glande à s. externe, interne,** exocrine, endocrine, gland.

sécrétoire [sekretwar] *a. Physiol:* secretory.

sectaire [sɛktɛr] *a. & n.* sectarian.

sectarisme [sɛktarism] *n.m.* sectarianism.

secte [sɛkt] *n.f.* sect.

secteur [sɛktœr] *n.m.* **1.** (*a*) *Astr: Mth:* sector; *Draw:* **graphique à secteurs,** pie chart; (*b*) *Mec.E: Mch:* sector, quadrant, arc; *Aut: etc:* **s. de direction,** steering sector; **s. de frein,** quadrant, ratchet, of the handbrake; *I.C.E:* **s. de commande (de gaz),** (control) quadrant; *Nau:* **s. dangereux,** dangerous quadrant (of storm). **2.** area, district; (*a*) *Com:* **s. de vente,** sales area; (*b*) *Mil:* sector, area (of responsibility, of attack, etc.); (*c*) **s. de surveillance,** (i) *Rad: etc:* surveillance sector, area; (ii) (policeman's) beat; (*d*) *El:* **secteur (de distribution électrique),** mains. **3.** (*a*) *Pol.Ec: etc:* field (of activity); **le s. privé,** the private sector, private enterprise; **le s. public,** the public sector, state enterprise; *F:* **ce n'est pas mon s.,** that's not my line; (*b*) *Cmptr:* **le s.,** the field.

section [sɛksjɔ̃] *n.f.* **1.** section, cutting; *Vet:* docking (of tail); **s. des tendons,** cutting of the tendons. **2.** (*a*) section (of chapter, building, etc.); (*b*) *Nat.Hist:* section (of a genus); (*c*) *Adm:* branch (of a department, polictical party, etc.); (electoral) division; ward; **s. de vote,** polling station; (*d*) *Mil:* platoon (of infantry); section (of artillery); **chef de s.,** platoon commander; *Mil. Av:* flight commander; (*e*) *Navy:* sub-division (of fleet); (*f*) *Mil.Av:* **s. de bombardiers,** bomber flight. **3.** (*a*) *Mth:* (i) section; (ii) intersection; **point de s.,** point of intersection; (*b*) *Arch:* section, profile; (*c*) *El:* **s. morte,** idle coil; (*d*) *Cmptr:* bay, section; (*e*) *Atom.Ph:* **s. efficace,** cross section; (*f*) *Hyd.E:* **s. mouillée,** wetted section. **4.** (*a*) stage (on bus route, etc.); **changement de s.,** fare stage; (*b*) *Rail:* **s. de block,** block section.

sectionnement [sɛksjɔnmɑ̃] *n.m.* **1.** division into sections. **2.** cutting, severing.

sectionner [sɛksjɔne] *v.tr.* **1.** to divide (district, etc.) into sections. **2.** (*a*) to cut (off), sever; (*b*) to cut into pieces; to dissect.

sectionneur [sɛksjɔnœr] *n.m.* *El:* disconnecting switch, isolating switch.

séculaire [sekylɛr] *a.* **1.** (*a*) centennial (event); secular (trend); (*b*) **année s.,** last year of a century; (*c*) *Astr:* secular. **2.** century-old, centuries-old; age-old.

sécularisation [sekylarizasjɔ̃] *n.f.* secularization.

séculariser [sekylarize] *v.tr.* to secularize; to deconsecrate (church).

séculier, -ière [sekylje, -jɛr] **1.** *a.* (*a*) secular (clergy, jurisdiction); **le bras s.,** the secular arm; (*b*) lay, laic. **2.** *n.* layman; **les séculiers,** the laity.

secundo [səgɔ̃do, sek-] *Lt.adv.* secondly, in the second place.

sécurité [sekyrite] *n.f.* **1.** (*a*) security, secureness; reliability; **en s. contre,** safe from; **s. de l'emploi,** security of employment; *Adm:* **S. sociale** = National Health (Service); Social Security; (*b*) (feeling of) security, confidence. **2.** (*a*) safety; **s. de la route,** road safety; *Adm:* **s. publique,** public safety; **services de s.,** (i) *Mil:* security forces; (ii) stewards (at demonstration, etc.); security police (in firm, etc.); *Nau:* **officier de s.,** officer in charge of fire precautions; (*b*) *Mec.E: Civ.E: Ind:* **marge de s.,** security margin; **règles de s.,** safety rules, code; **dispositif de s.,** safety device; **verre de s.,** safety glass, splinterproof glass; *El:* **éclairage de s.,** emergency lighting.

sédatif, -ive [sedatif, -iv] *a & n.m. Med:* sedative.

sédation [sedasjɔ̃] *n.f. Med:* sedation.

sédentaire [sedɑ̃tɛr] *a.* **1.** sedentary (occupation, life). **2.** fixed, stationary, settled; garrison(ed) (troops); non-migrant (bird).

sédentairement [sedɑ̃tɛrmɑ̃] *adv.* sedentarily.

sédiment [sedimɑ̃] *n.m.* sediment, deposit.

sédimentaire [sedimɑ̃tɛr] *a.* *Geol: etc:* sedimentary.

sédimentation [sedimɑ̃tasjɔ̃] *n.f.* sedimentation.

séditieux, -euse [sedisjø, -øz] **1.** *a.* (*a*) seditious (speech, assembly); **tenir des propos s.,** to talk treason; (*b*) mutinous, rebellious. **2.** *n.m.* rebel, mutineer.

sédition [sedisjɔ̃] *n.f.* sedition; mutiny.

séducteur, -trice [sedyktœr, -tris] **1.** *n.* seducer, *f.* seductress. **2.** *a.* fascinating, beguiling.

séduction [sedyksjɔ̃] *n.f.* **1.** seduction. **2.** charm, attraction; **séductions physiques,** physical attraction; **la s. des richesses,** the lure of wealth.

séduire [sedɥir] *v.tr.* (*conj. like* CONDUIRE) **1.** to seduce (s.o.); *A:* to bribe, suborn (witnesses). **2.** to fascinate, captivate, charm; to attract s.o.; to appeal to (s.o., the imagination); **cela m'a séduit du premier coup,** it took my fancy at once.

séduisant [sedɥizɑ̃] *a.* attractive (person, face, manner); appealing, tempting (idea).

segment [sɛgmɑ̃] *n.m.* **1.** *Mth: Anat: etc:* segment. **2.** *I.C.E: Mch: etc:* **s. de piston,** piston ring, packing ring; **s. de frein,** brake shoe; **frein à segments,** segmented brake.

segmentation [sɛgmɑ̃tasjɔ̃] *n.f.* segmentation.

segmenter [sɛgmɑ̃te] *v.tr.* to segment; to divide into segments; *Cmptr:* to partition, section, segment.

ségrégation [segregasjɔ̃] *n.f.* segregation; setting apart; isolation.

ségrégationnisme [segregasjɔnism] *n.m.* *Pol:* (policy of) racial segregation.

ségrégationniste [segregasjɔnist] *a.* & *n.* *Pol:* segregationist.

seiche[1] [sɛʃ] *n.f.* *Moll:* cuttlefish; **os de s.,** cuttlebone.

seiche[2] *n.f.* seiche, tidal wave.

seigle [sɛgl] *n.m.* rye.

seigneur [sɛɲœr] *n.m.* **1.** (*a*) lord; **mon s. et maître,** my lord and master; (*b*) lord of the manor; = squire; **le s. de Sercq,** the seigneur, *f.* the dame, of Sark; (*c*) nobleman, noble; *Hist:* **les seigneurs,** the nobility; **mener une vie de grand s.,** to live like a lord; **ne faites pas le grand s.,** don't try and lord it over us; **en grand s.,** in grand style. **2. le S.,** God; the Lord; **Notre-S.,** our Lord; **le jour du S.,** the Lord's day; *F:* **S.! S. Dieu!** good Lord! **3.** *Ich:* lumpfish.

seigneurial, -aux [sɛɲœrjal, -o] *a.* (*a*) *A:* seigniorial; (*b*) stately, lordly.

seigneurie [sɛɲœri] *n.f.* (*a*) *Hist:* seigniory; (*b*) (*as a title*) **votre s.,** your Lordship; *Iron:* **sa s.** his lordship, *P:* his nibs.

sein [sɛ̃] *n.m.* **1.** (*a*) (woman's, *Lit:* man's) breast, bosom; **donner le s. à un enfant,** to suckle, breastfeed, a child; (*b*) **au s. de la famille,** in the bosom of the family; **au s. du luxe,** in the lap of luxury; **au s. de la commission,** within the committee; *Lit:* **enfant que j'ai porté dans mon s.,** child that I carried in my womb; **le s. de la terre,** the bowels of the earth.

seine [sɛn] *n.f.* *Fish:* seine, draw net.

seing [sɛ̃] *n.m.* *Jur:* **acte sous s. privé,** private agreement.

séisme [seism] *n.m.* (*a*) earthquake; (*b*) *Lit:* upheaval.

séismique [seismik] *a.* seismic.

séismo- [seismɔ-] *comb.fm. see* SISMO-

seize [sɛz] *num.a.inv.* & *n.m.inv.* sixteen; **Louis S.,** Louis the Sixteenth; **le s. mai,** (on) the sixteenth of May; (on) May (the) sixteenth; **demeurer au numéro s.,** to live at number sixteen.

seizième [sɛzjɛm] **1.** *num.a.* & *n.* sixteenth. **2.** *n.m.* sixteenth (part).

séjour [seʒur] *n.m.* **1.** (*a*) stay; **s. de quinze jours,** fortnight's stay; (*b*) **(salle de) s.,** living room. **2.** *Lit:* abode.

séjourner [seʒurne] *v.i.* (*of pers.*) to stay; (*of snow, etc.*) to lie.

sel [sɛl] *n.m.* **1.** salt; (*a*) **s. de cuisine,** cooking salt; **s. fin,** fine salt; **gros s.,** coarse salt; **régime sans s.,** salt-free diet; *F:* **mettre son grain de s.,** to butt in; (*b*) *Pharm:* **s. d'Angleterre, d'Epsom,** Epsom salts; *Toil:* **s. pour bains,** bath salts; (*c*) *pl.* **sels (volatils) anglais,** smelling salts; (*d*) *Ch:* **s. double,** double salt. **2.** piquancy, wit.

select *a.inv.*, **sélect** *a.* [selɛkt] *F: O:* select (gathering); **le monde s.,** high society.

sélecteur, -trice [selɛktœr, -tris] **1.** *a.* selecting; *El:* **commutateur s.,** selector switch. **2.** *n.m.* selector; switch; *Aut: etc:* selector, automatic gear-shift lever.

sélectif, -ive [selɛktif, -iv] *a.* selective.

sélection [selɛksjɔ̃] *n.f.* **1.** selection, choice; **faire, opérer, une s. parmi,** to make a selection from among; **s. professionnelle,** professional aptitude test; *Sp:* **match de s.,** trial game; *Nat.Hist:* **s. naturelle,** natural selection. **2.** *Mus:* selection **(sur,** from).

sélectionné [selɛksjɔne] *a.* & *n.* selected (player, etc.); *Cmptr:* **élément s.,** selected cell.

sélectionner [selɛksjɔne] *v.tr.* to choose, select; *Cmptr:* (i) to dial; (ii) to pick, to select.

sélectionneur, -euse [selɛksjɔnœr, -øz] *n.* selector.
sélectivité [selɛktivite] *n.f.* selectivity.
sélénieux [selenjø] *a.m. Ch:* selenious (acid).
sélénique¹ [selenik] *a. Ch:* selenic (acid).
sélénique² *a. Astr:* selenic, selenian.
sélénite¹ [selenit] *n.m. Ch:* selenite.
sélénite² *n.* selenite, inhabitant of the moon.
sélénite³ *n.f. Miner:* selenite; crystalline, foliated, gypsum.
sélénium [selenjɔm] *n.m. Ch:* selenium.
sélénographie [selenɔgrafi] *n.f.* selenography.
sélénographique [selenɔgrafik] *a.* selenographic(al) (map, etc.).
self [sɛlf] *n.f. El:* **(bobine de) s.(-induction),** inductance coil.
self-inductance [sɛlfɛ̃dyktɑ̃s] *n.f. El:* self-induction; inductance.
self-induction [sɛlfɛ̃dyksjɔ̃] *n.f. El:* self-induction; inductance.
selle [sɛl] *n.f.* **1.** (*a*) *A:* seat, stool; (*b*) *Physiol:* motion of the bowels; stool; **aller à la s.,** to have a motion. **2.** (*a*) saddle; **se mettre en s.,** to mount; **être bien en s.,** (i) to have a good seat; (ii) *Fig:* to be firmly established; **aider qn à monter en s.,** (i) to help s.o. into the saddle; (ii) *F:* to give s.o. a leg up, a helping hand; **monter sans s.,** to ride bareback; (*b*) (bicycle) saddle. **3.** *Cu:* **s. de mouton,** saddle of mutton; **s. de bœuf,** baron of beef. **4.** (sculptor's) turntable.
seller [sele] *v.tr.* to saddle (horse).
sellerie [sɛlri] *n.f.* **1.** saddlery. **2.** harness room, tack room.
sellette [sɛlɛt] *n.f.* **1.** (*a*) *F:* **mettre qn, être, sur la s.,** to have s.o., to be, on the carpet; (*b*) (small) seat, stool; *esp.* painter's cradle; bosun's chair; (*c*) (sculptor's) turntable. **2.** saddle (of draught horse).
sellier [selje] *n.m.* saddler, harness maker.
selon [s(ə)lɔ̃] *prep.* (*a*) according to; **s. moi,** in my opinion, as I see it; **s. lui,** according to him; *F:* **c'est s.,** it all depends; (*b*) *conj.phr.* **s. que** + *ind.*, depending on whether.
seltz [sɛls] *n.m.* **eau de s.,** soda water.
semailles [səmaj] *n.f.pl.* **1.** sowing; **le temps des s.,** sowing time, seedtime. **2.** *coll.* seeds.
semaine [s(ə)mɛn] *n.f.* (*a*) week; **deux fois par s.,** twice a week; **une s. de vacances,** a week's holiday; **fin de s.,** weekend; **jour de s.,** weekday; **la s. seulement,** weekdays only; **il est toujours à Paris en s.,** he is always in Paris during the week; *Sch:* **pensionnaire à la s.,** weekly boarder; *F:* **politique à la petite s.,** shortsighted policy; *F:* **la s. des quatre jeudis,** never (in a month of Sundays); (*b*) working week; **faire la s. anglaise,** to work a five-day week; (*c*) *Mil: etc:* week's duty; **officier de s.,** duty officer for the week; (*d*) week's pay, wages; (*e*) set of seven (objects).
semainier, -ière [s(ə)menje, -jɛr] **1.** *n.* person on duty, duty officer, for the week. **2.** *n.m.* (*a*) *Furn:* semainier; (*b*) desk diary. **3.** *a.* weekly, week's (output, issue, etc.).
sémantème [semɑ̃tɛm] *n.m. Ling:* semanteme.
sémanticien, -ienne [semɑ̃tisjɛ̃, -jɛn] *n.* semanticist.
sémantique [semɑ̃tik] *Ling:* **1.** *a.* semantic. **2.** *n.f.* semantics.
sémaphore [semafɔr] *n.m.* semaphore; *Rail:* semaphore signal; *Nau:* signal station (on land).
semblable [sɑ̃blabl̩] **1.** *a.* (*a*) alike; similar (**à,** to); like; **deux cas tout à fait semblables,** two cases absolutely alike; **s. à son père,** like his father; **triangles semblables,** similar triangles; (*b*) such; **de semblables projets,** such plans; **des choses semblables,** things like that; **je n'ai rien dit de s.,** I said nothing of the sort, no such thing. **2.** *n.* fellow; (*a*) like, equal, counterpart; **vous et vos semblables,** you and people like you; (*b*) **nos semblables,** our fellow men, fellow creatures.
semblant [sɑ̃blɑ̃] *n.m.* semblance, appearance; (outward) show; **faux s.,** pretence, sham; **elle portait un s. de jupe,** she was wearing an apology for a skirt; **faire un s. de résistance,** to make a show of resistance; **faire s. de faire qch.,** to pretend to be doing sth.; **sans faire s. de rien,** without seeming to take any notice, as if nothing had happened.
sembler [sɑ̃ble] *v.i.* (*the aux. is* **avoir**) (*a*) to seem, to appear; **elle semblait malade,** she seemed (to be) ill; (*b*) *impers.* **il me semblait rêver,** it seemed to me, I thought, (that) I was dreaming; **il me semble l'entendre encore,** I can hear him still; **il me semble avoir entendu son nom,** I seem to have heard his name; **à ce qu'il me semble,** it strikes me (that . . .); I think; **faites comme bon vous semble(ra),** do as you think best; **il semble que** + *ind. or sub*, it seems that . . . , it looks as if . . .; **il me semble que** + *ind.*, it seems to me that . . . .
sème [sɛm] *n.m. Ling:* sememe.
semé [s(ə)me] *a.* strewn; sprinkled (with quotations); dotted (with daisies).
séméio- [semejɔ-] *comb.fm. see* SÉMIO-.
semelle [s(ə)mɛl] *n.f.* **1.** (*a*) sole (of shoe); foot (of stocking); **s. intérieure,** insole, inner sole; **chaussures à semelles de caoutchouc,** rubber-soled shoes; **s. compensée,** wedge heel; **remettre une s. à une chaussure,** to re-sole a shoe; (*b*) foot's length; **ne pas avancer d'une s.,** to make no progress; **il ne reculera pas d'une s.,** he won't give (way) an inch; **il ne me quitte pas d'une s.,** he's always at my heels. **2.** (*a*) *Const: Min: etc:* ground sill, sole piece; sleeper; footing (of an upright); (*b*) **s. de poutre,** girder flange; **s. de coussinet de rail,** chair foot; (*c*) bed plate (of machine, lathe); (*d*) shoe (of anchor, sledge). **3.** *Nau:* **s. de dérive,** leeboard.
semence [s(ə)mɑ̃s] *n.f.* **1.** (*a*) seed; **blé de s.,** seed corn; **semences de discorde,** seeds of discord; (*b*) *Physiol:* semen. **2.** (*a*) **s. de perles,** seed pearls; **s. de diamants,** diamond sparks; (*b*) (*flat-headed nail*) (tin)tack.
semer [s(ə)me] *v.tr.* **(je sème, n. semons; je sèmerai) 1.** to sow (seeds, a field). **2.** to strew, scatter (flowers, etc.); to spread (news, discord); **s. de l'argent,** to spend money recklessly, to throw money about. **3.** *F:* (*a*) to shake off, get rid of (s.o.); (*b*) to lose, *F:* shed (sth.).
semestre [s(ə)mɛstr̩] *n.m.* **1.** half-year. **2.** six-monthly payment. **3.** *Sch:* semester.
semestriel, -elle [səmɛstrijɛl] *a.* half-yearly, six-monthly.
semestriellement [səmɛstrijɛlmɑ̃] *adv.* half-yearly, every six months.
semeur, -euse [s(ə)mœr, -øz] *n.* **1.** *Agr:* sower; *Fig:* spreader, disseminator (of news, etc.). **2.** *n.f. Agr:* **semeuse,** drill (for sowing).
semi- [səmi] *pref.* semi-; NOTE: *in the plural of compound words prefixed by* **semi-, semi-** *remains invariable and the following noun or adj. takes the pl. form.*
semi-automatique [səmiɔtɔmatik] *a.* semi(-)automatic.
semi-chenillé [səmiʃənije] *a. & n.m.* half-track (vehicle).
semi-circulaire [səmisirkylɛr] *a.* semicircular.
semi-conducteur [səmikɔ̃dyktœr] *n.m. El:* semi(-)conductor.
semi-conserve [səmikɔ̃sɛrv] *n.f.* semi-preserved food; **semi-conserves,** semi-preserved goods.
semi-consonne [səmikɔ̃sɔn] *n.f.* semivowel, semiconsonant.
semi-fixe [səmifiks] *a.* semi-fixed; semi-portable.
semi-historique [səmiistɔrik] *a.* semi-historical.
semi-illettré [səmiiletre] *a.* semi-literate.

sémillant [semijɑ̃] *a.* lively, bright (child, wit); bright, engaging (glance).
semi-lunaire [səmilynɛr] *a.* semilunar; half-moon-shaped.
semi-mensuel, -elle [səmimɑ̃sɥɛl] *a.* fortnightly, bi-monthly (periodical, etc.).
séminaire [seminɛr] *n.m.* (*a*) **(grand) s.,** (Roman Catholic) seminary; training college (for the priesthood); **petit s.,** secondary school (staffed by priests); (*b*) *Sch:* seminar; (*c*) conference.
séminal, -aux [seminal, -o] *a. Biol:* seminal.
séminariste [seminarist] *n.m.* seminarist.
semi-officiel, -ielle [səmiɔfisjɛl] *a.* semi(-)official.
sémiologie [semjɔlɔʒi] *n.f. Med: Ling:* sem(e)iology.
sémiologique [semjɔlɔʒik] *a. Med: Ling:* sem(e)iological.
semiologue [semjɔlɔg] *n. Med: Ling:* sem(e)iologist.
sémiotique [semjɔtik] *Mth: Log:* **1.** *a.* semiotic. **2.** *n.f.* semiotics.
semi-perméable [səmipɛrmeabl̩] *a.* semipermeable, partially permeable.
semi-portique [səmipɔrtik] *n.m.* semi-portal bridge crane.
semi-précieux, -ieuse [səmipresjø, -jøz] *a.* semi-precious (stone).
semi-public, -ique [səmipyblik] *a.* semi(-)public.
sémique [semik] *a. Ling:* semic.
semi-remorque [səmir(ə)mɔrk] *n.f. Veh:* (*a*) trailer; (*b*) articulated vehicle; semitrailer.
semi-rigide [səmiriʒid] *a.* semi-rigid (airship).
semis [s(e)mi] *n.m. Agr: Hort:* **1.** sowing. **2.** seed bed. **3.** seedlings.
Sémite [semit] **1.** *n.* Semite. **2.** *a.* Semitic.
sémitique [semitik] *a.* Semitic.
sémitisant, -ante [semitizɑ̃, -ɑ̃t] *n.*, **sémitiste** [semitist] *n.* Semitic scholar, Semitist.
sémitisme [semitism] *n.m.* Semitism.
semi-ton [səmitɔ̃] *n.m. Mus:* semitone.
semi-voyelle [səmivwajɛl] *n.f. Ling:* semivowel.
semoir [s(ə)mwar] *n.m. Agr:* **1.** seed bag. **2.** sowing machine, seeder.
semonce [səmɔ̃s] *n.f.* **1.** *Navy:* **coup de s.,** warning shot. **2.** reprimand, scolding, lecture.
semoule [səmul] *n.f.* semolina; **sucre s.,** caster sugar.
sempiternel, -elle [sɛ̃pitɛrnɛl] *a.* sempiternal, never-ending.
sempiternellement [sɛ̃pitɛrnɛlmɑ̃] *adv.* sempiternally; endlessly.
sénat [sena] *n.m.* **1.** senate. **2.** senate house.
sénateur [senatœr] *n.m.* senator.
sénatorial, -aux [senatɔrjal, -o] *a.* senatorial.
séné [sene] *n.m. Bot: Pharm:* senna.
sénéchal, -aux [seneʃal, -o] *n.m. Hist:* seneschal.
sénéchaussée [seneʃose] *n.f. Hist:* (*a*) seneschalsy, seneschal's jurisdiction; (*b*) seneschal's court.
séneçon [sɛnsɔ̃] *n.m. Bot:* groundsel.
Sénégal [senegal] *Pr.n.m. Geog:* Senegal.
sénégalais, -aise [senegalɛ, -ɛz] *a. & n. Geog:* Senegalese.
Sénégambie [senegɑ̃bi] *Pr.n.f. Geog:* Senegambia.
Sénèque [senɛk] *Pr.n.m. Lt.Lit:* Seneca.
sénescence [senesɑ̃s] *n.f. Biol:* senescence.
sénescent [senesɑ̃] *a. Biol:* senescent.
sénevé [senve] *n.m.* **1.** *Bot:* mustard. **2.** mustard seed.
sénile [senil] *a.* senile.
sénilité [senilite] *n.f.* senility; senile decay.
senior [senjɔr] *a. & n. Sp:* (*usu. = over 20*) senior.
senne [sɛn] *n.f. Fish:* seine, draw net.
senorita [senjɔrita] *n.m.* small cigar, whiff.
sens [sɑ̃s] *n.m.* **1.** (*a*) sense (of touch, sight, beauty, time, etc.); **le sixième s.,** the sixth sense; **perdre, reprendre, ses s.,** to lose, regain, consciousness; **s. moral,** moral sense; conscience; **avoir le s. des affaires,** to have a good business sense, head; (*b*) **plaisir des s.,** sensual pleasures; **éveiller les s.,** to excite the senses. **2.** sense, judgement; **s. commun, bon s.,** common sense, good sense; **un homme de bon s.,** a sensible man; **gros, robuste, bon s.,** elementary common sense; **cela n'a pas de s. commun, de bon s.,** there's no sense in it; **agir, faire qch., en dépit du bon s.,** to do something stupid; **vous avez perdu le s. commun,** you've taken leave of your senses; **rentrer dans son bon s.,** to come to one's senses again; **le bon s. veut que . . .,** it stands to reason that . . .; **s. pratique,** practical (common) sense; **il n'a aucun s. pratique,** he's completely unpractical; **à mon s.,** in my opinion; **j'abonde dans votre s.,** I entirely agree with you. **3.** sense, meaning (of a word, etc.); **s. propre,** literal, basic, meaning; **au s. ordinaire du mot,** in the ordinary meaning of the word; **mot à double s.,** word with a double meaning; **faire un faux s.,** to misinterpret, to misunderstand (a passage, a word); **ces paroles n'ont pas de s. pour moi,** these words mean, convey, nothing to me; **en ce s. que . . .,** in that . . .. **4.** direction, way; **dans le bon s.,** in the right direction; the right way (round, up); **dans le mauvais s.,** in the wrong direction; the wrong way (round, up); **en s. inverse,** in the opposite direction; **dans le s. du courant,** with the current, with the stream; **dans le s. de la longueur,** lengthwise; **dans le s. de la largeur,** breadthwise; across; **dans les deux s.,** both ways; **tailler dans le s. du bois,** to cut wood with the grain; **dans le s. inverse du grain,** against, across, the grain; **dans le s. (inverse) des aiguilles d'une montre,** (anti-, *NAm:* counter)clockwise; **courir dans tous les s.,** to run in all directions; **s. de la circulation,** direction of the traffic; **rue à double s.,** street with two-way traffic; *P.N:* **s. unique,** one-way street; *P.N:* **s. interdit,** no entry; *Rail:* **voyager dans le s. de la marche,** to travel facing the engine; *Mth:* **s. direct,** positive direction; **s. rétrograde,** negative direction; *Cmptr:* **s. de déroulement,** flow direction; *adv.phr.* **s. dessus dessous** [sɑ̃tsytsu], (i) upside down; the wrong way round, up; (ii) in a mess, in a muddle; in a state of confusion; **s. devant derrière,** back to front.
sensas(s) [sɑ̃sas] *a. F:* smashing, great, superb.
sensation [sɑ̃sasjɔ̃] *n.f.* sensation. **1.** feeling (of warmth, of cold); **cela donne la s. de . . .,** it feels like . . .. **2.** excitement; **roman, nouvelles, à s.,** sensational novel, news; **faire s.,** to create, make, a sensation; **la pièce a fait s.,** the play was a hit.
sensationnel, -elle [sɑ̃sasjɔnɛl] *a.* (*a*) sensational (news, novel, etc.); (*b*) *F:* superb; fantastic.
sensé [sɑ̃se] *a.* sensible (person, action).
senseur [sɑ̃sœr] *n.m. Elcs:* sensor, sensing device.
sensibilisateur, -trice [sɑ̃sibilizatœr, -tris] **1.** *Phot: etc:* (*a*) *a.* sensitizing; (*b*) *n.m.* sensitizer, sensitizing bath. **2.** *n.f. Biol:* **sensibilisatrice,** sensitizer.
sensibilisation [sɑ̃sibilizasjɔ̃] *n.f. Phot: Med:* sensitization; growing public awareness (**à,** of).
sensibiliser [sɑ̃sibilize] *v.tr. Phot: Med: etc:* to sensitize; to make (s.o.) sensitive to, aware of (sth.).
sensibilité [sɑ̃sibilite] *n.f.* (*a*) sensitiveness, sensitivity (of a person); **enfant d'une grande s.,** extremely sensitive child; (*b*) compassion, feeling; **avoir de la s.,** to be soft-hearted; (*c*) sensitiveness (of skin, balance, film, etc.); sensitivity (of an instrument).
sensible [sɑ̃sibl̩] *a.* **1.** (= SENTANT) sentient. **2.** (*a*) sensitive (**à,** to; **sur,** about); susceptible (to pain, influence); aware (of danger); **peu s.,** insensitive, *F:* thick-skinned; **avoir l'oreille s.,** to have a sensitive

ear, a keen sense of hearing; **avoir la peau s.,** (i) to have a sensitive skin; (ii) *F:* to be thin-skinned; **ouïe peu s.,** dull hearing; **être s. au froid,** to feel the cold; *Hort:* to be frost tender; **être s. au ridicule,** to be sensitive to ridicule; **être s. aux bontés de qn,** to appreciate s.o.'s kindness; **être s. à la musique,** to have a feeling for music; *Mus:* **la note s.,** *n.f.* **la s.,** the leading note; **toucher la note, la corde, s.,** to appeal to the emotions, to touch a chord; (*b*) sympathetic; **cœur s.,** tender heart; **peu s.,** callous; impervious (**à,** to); (*c*) sensitive (plate, balance, thermometer, etc.); (*d*) painful, sore (when touched); sensitive, tender (tooth, etc.); **s. au toucher,** tender to the touch; **toucher qn à un endroit s.,** to touch s.o. on a tender spot, on the raw; *Fig:* **blesser qn à l'endroit s.,** to tread on s.o.'s corns. **3.** sensible; perceptible, appreciable, considerable (difference, progress, etc.); **le monde s.,** the tangible world; **d'une manière s.,** perceptibly, appreciably; **dommages sensibles,** serious damage; **un vide s.,** a noticeable gap; **éprouver un plaisir s.,** to feel a keen pleasure.

sensiblement [sɑ̃sibləmɑ̃] *adv.* **1.** appreciably, perceptibly; obviously. **2.** approximately, roughly, more or less.

sensiblerie [sɑ̃sibləri] *n.f.* sentimentality.

sensitif, -ive [sɑ̃sitif, -iv] **1.** *a.* (*a*) *Lit:* over-sensitive; (*b*) *Physiol:* sensory. **2.** *n.f. Bot:* **sensitive,** sensitive plant, mimosa pudica.

sensoriel, -ielle [sɑ̃sɔrjɛl] *a.* sensorial, sensory.

sensorimoteur, -trice [sɑ̃sɔrimɔtœr, -tris] *a. Med:* sensorimotor.

sensualisme [sɑ̃sɥalism] *n.m.* **1.** sensualism. **2.** *Phil:* sensationalism.

sensualiste [sɑ̃sɥalist] **1.** *n.* sensualist. **2.** *a.* sensual(ist) (philosopy, etc.).

sensualité [sɑ̃sɥalite] *n.f.* (*a*) sensuality; (*b*) voluptuousness.

sensuel, -elle [sɑ̃sɥɛl] **1.** *a.* sensual; sensuous. **2.** *n.* (*a*) sensualist; (*b*) voluptuary.

sentant [sɑ̃tɑ̃] *a.* sentient.

sentence [sɑ̃tɑ̃s] *n.f.* **1.** maxim. **2.** (*a*) sentence, judgment; (*b*) decision, award.

sentencieusement [sɑ̃tɑ̃sjøzmɑ̃] *adv.* sententiously.

sentencieux, -ieuse [sɑ̃tɑ̃sjø, -jøz] *a.* sententious.

senteur [sɑ̃tœr] *n.f.* **1.** *Ven: Lit:* scent. **2.** *Bot:* **pois de s.,** sweet pea.

senti [sɑ̃ti] **1.** *a.* heartfelt (words); **quelques mots bien sentis,** a few well chosen words. **2.** *n.m. Psy:* sense datum; that which is felt.

sentier [sɑ̃tje] *n.m.* (foot)path; **s. pour cavaliers,** bridle path; **s. battu,** beaten track.

sentiment [sɑ̃timɑ̃] *n.m.* **1.** (*a*) sensation, feeling (of joy, relief, hunger, etc.); **contenir ses sentiments,** to repress one's feelings, to keep one's feelings under control; (*b*) sense (of beauty, duty); consciousness; **avoir le s. que . . .,** to have a feeling that . . ., to be conscious that . . .; **privé de s.,** devoid of feeling; numb (limb, etc.); **juger par s.,** to judge by one's impressions; (*c*) **faire appel aux bons sentiments de qn,** to appeal to s.o.'s finer feelings. **2.** (*a*) sentiment, sensibility, feeling; **le s. de la nature,** a feeling for nature; **ses sentiments vis-à-vis de moi,** his feelings towards me; **jouer avec s.,** to play (the piano, etc.) with feeling; **faire du s.,** to sentimentalize; **je ne fais pas de s. en affaires,** I don't let sentiment interfere with business; *F:* **le faire au s.,** to appeal to the emotions; (*b*) **avoir du s. pour qn,** to be drawn to s.o., to feel attracted to s.o.; (*c*) *Corr:* **veuillez agréer (l'expression de) mes sentiments distingués,** yours faithfully; **veuillez bien recevoir l'expression de mes sentiments les meilleurs,** yours sincerely. **3.** *Lit:* opinion.

sentimental, -ale, -aux [sɑ̃timɑ̃tal, -o] *a.* (*a*) **intrigue sentimentale,** love affair; (*b*) sentimental; *n.* **c'est un s., une sentimentale,** he, she, is very sentimental.

sentimentalement [sɑ̃timɑ̃talmɑ̃] *adv.* sentimentally.

sentimentalisme [sɑ̃timɑ̃talism] *n.m.* sentimentality.

sentimentaliste [sɑtimɑ̃talist] *a. & n.* sentimentalist.

sentimentalité [sɑ̃timɑ̃talite] *n.f.* sentimentality.

sentine [sɑ̃tin] *n.f. Nau:* bilge (of ship); *Lit:* **s. de tous les vices,** sink of iniquity.

sentinelle [sɑ̃tinɛl] *n.f. Mil:* **1.** sentry. **2.** guard(ing), watch; **en s.,** on guard, on sentry duty.

sentir [sɑ̃tir] (*pr.p.* **sentant;** *p.p.* **senti;** *pr.ind.* **je sens, il sent, n. sentons, ils sentent;** *pr.sub.* **je sente;** *impf.* **je sentais;** *p.h.* **je sentis;** *fu.* **je sentirai) 1.** *v.tr.* (*a*) to feel (pain, hunger, cold, joy, sorrow, etc.); **je sentais trembler le plancher,** I could feel the floor trembling; **je sens l'hiver qui vient,** I can feel winter coming; **s. qch. pour qn,** to feel affection for s.o., to feel drawn to s.o.; **je ne sens rien pour lui,** I have no particular feelings for him; *F:* **s. ses bras, ses jambes,** to feel pains in one's arms, one's legs; **je ne sens plus mes jambes, mes pieds,** I can hardly feel my feet; (*b*) to be conscious of, to feel (insult, one's strength, etc.); to be aware of, conscious of (danger); **s. grandir son influence,** to feel one's influence growing; **je sens que vous avez raison,** I have a feeling that you are right; (*of ship*) **s. la barre,** to answer to the helm; **il m'a fait s. que . . .,** he gave me to understand that . . .; **faire s. son autorité,** to make one's authority felt; **l'effet se fera s.,** the effect will be felt; (*c*) to smell (odour, *NAm:* odor, flower); **je ne sens rien,** I can't smell anything; *F:* **je ne peux pas le s.,** I can't bear him, can't stand (the sight of) him; *Fig:* **s. le cadavre,** to scent disaster, to smell ruin; **s. qch. de loin,** to feel sth. coming; **s. qn de loin,** (i) to have a feeling that s.o. is coming; (ii) to see through s.o. **2.** *v.i.* (*a*) (*with cogn.acc.*) to taste of, smell of (sth.); **cela sent le brûlé,** there's a smell of burning; **vin qui sent le bouchon,** corked wine; **la pièce sent l'humidité,** the room smells, feels, damp; **la salle sentait le tabac à plein nez,** the room was reeking of tobacco; **il sentait l'acteur à plein nez,** he had actor written all over him; *Fig:* **il sent le cadavre,** he looks as if he were not long for this world; (*b*) **s. bon, mauvais,** to smell good, bad; **ça sent bon le pain frais,** there's a delicious smell of fresh bread; **fleurs qui sentent bon,** sweet-smelling flowers; (*c*) *F:* to smell bad, to stink; **il sent des pieds,** his feet smell. **3. se s.** (*a*) **cela se sent,** it is something one can feel, that needs no explanation; (*b*) **se s. bien, fatigué,** to feel well, tired; **se s. dix ans de moins,** to feel ten years younger; **elle se sentait mourir,** she felt she was dying; **se s. du courage,** to feel brave, full of courage; **je ne m'en sens pas le courage,** I don't feel equal to it; (*c*) **il ne se sent pas de joie,** he is beside himself with joy; *F:* **tu ne te sens plus?** have you taken leave of your senses?

seoir [swar] *v.i.* (*used only in pr.p.* **seyant, séant;** *pr.ind.* **il sied, ils siéent;** *pr.sub.* **il siée, ils siéent;** *impf.* **il seyait, ils seyaient;** *fu.* **il siéra, ils siéront**) to suit, become; **cette robe vous sied bien,** that dress suits you, is very becoming, attractive; **il lui sied mal de . . .,** it ill becomes him to . . .; **comme il sied,** as is fitting.

sépale [sepal] *n.m. Bot:* sepal.

séparable [separabl̥] *a.* separable (**de,** from); **deux théories difficilement séparables,** two theories which it is difficult to separate.

séparateur, -trice [separatœr, -tris] **1.** *a.* separating, separative; *Opt:* resolving (power). **2.** *n.m. Tchn:* separator.

séparation [separasjɔ̃] *n.f.* (*a*) separation; **s. d'avec qn,** (i) separation from s.o.; (ii) parting with s.o.; **la s. de l'erreur et de la vérité,** discrimination between error and truth; **s. de la tête du corps,** severance of the head from the body; **s. de corps,** legal separation (of husband and wife); **s. de fait, s. amiable,** *de facto* separation; *Jur:* **s. de biens,** marriage settlement under which husband and wife administer their separate properties; **s. de l'Église et de l'État,** disestablishment (of the church); (*b*) partition, division; boundary; **mur de s.,** dividing wall.

séparatisme [separatism] *n.m. Pol:* separatism.

séparatiste [separatist] **1.** *n.* separatist, seceder, secessionist. **2.** *a.* separatist, seceding.

séparé [separe] *a.* **1.** separate, different, distinct. **2.** separated, apart.

séparément [separemɑ̃] *adv.* separately.

séparer [separe] **1.** *v.tr.* (*a*) to separate (**de,** from); **s. les bons d'avec les mauvais,** to separate the good from the bad; **s. une chambre en trois,** to divide a room into three; **s. deux combattants,** to part, separate, two fighters; *Box:* **séparez!** break! **personne ne peut nous s.,** no one can come between us; *Petr:* **s. l'huile de l'eau,** to knock down oil; (*b*) *Cmptr:* to unpack; (*c*) to divide, keep apart; to distinguish (sth. from sth.); **mur qui sépare deux champs,** wall dividing two fields. **2. se s.** (*b*) to separate, part (**de,** from); to part company; **nous ne nous séparerons jamais,** we shall never part; **se s. de sa femme, d'avec sa femme,** to separate from one's wife; **l'armée se sépara,** the army disbanded; (*b*) (*of river, road, etc.*) to divide, branch off; **ici je me sépare entièrement de vous,** here I disagree, part company, with you; *Ch:* (*of salt*) **se s. à l'état cristallin,** to crystallize out; (*c*) (*of crowd, assembly, etc.*) to break up, disperse.

sépia [sepja] *n.f.* sepia.

sept [sɛt] *num.a.inv. & n.m.inv.* seven; **le s. mai,** (on) the seventh of May; (on) May (the) seventh; **Édouard S.,** Edward the Seventh; *Cards:* **le s. de cœur,** the seven of hearts.

septain [sɛtɛ̃] *n.m. Pros:* seven-line stanza.

septante [sɛptɑ̃t] *num.a.inv. & n.m.inv.* (*a*) *Belg: Sw.Fr:* seventy; (*b*) **la version des S.,** the Septuagint (version of the Bible).

septembre [sɛptɑ̃bʀ̥] *n.m.* September; **en s.,** in September; **le premier, le sept, s.,** (on) the first of September, (on) September (the) first.

septennal, -aux [sɛptɛnal, -o] *a.* septennial, seven-year (period, parliament).

septennat [sɛptɛna] *n.m.* seven-year term.

septentrion [sɛptɑ̃trijɔ̃] *n.m. Lit:* north.

septentrional, -aux [sɛptɑ̃trijɔnal, -o] **1.** *a.* northern. **2.** *n.m.pl.* **septentrionaux,** northerners.

septicémie [sɛptisemi] *n.f. Med:* septicaemia, *NAm:* septicemia; blood poisoning.

septicémique [sɛptisemik] *a. Med:* septicaemic, *NAm:* septicemic.

septième [sɛtjɛm] **1.** *num.a & n.* seventh; **être au s. ciel,** to be in (the) seventh heaven; **s. (étage),** seventh, *NAm:* eighth, floor. **2.** *n.m.* seventh (part); **trois septièmes,** three sevenths. **3.** *n.f.* (*a*) *Mus:* seventh; (*b*) = top form of primary school.

septièmement [sɛtjɛmmɑ̃] *adv.* in the seventh place.

septique [sɛptik] *a. Med:* septic; *Hyg:* **fosse s.,** septic tank.

septuagénaire [sɛptɥaʒenɛr] *a. & n.* septuagenarian.

septuagésime [ˈsɛptɥaʒezim] *n.f.* Septuagesima.

septum [sɛptɔm] *n.m. Anat: Bot:* septum.

septuor [sɛptɥɔr] *n.m. Mus:* septet(te).

septuple [sɛptypl̥] *a. & n.m.* septuple, sevenfold; **au s.,** sevenfold; **le s. de deux,** seven times two.

septupler [sɛptyple] *v.tr. & i.* to increase sevenfold.

sépulcral, -aux [sepylkral, -o] *a.* sepulchral.

sépulcre [sepylkʀ̥] *n.m.* sepulchre; **le saint s.,** the Holy Sepulchre.

sépulture [sepyltyr] *n.f.* **1.** burial, sepulture; **refuser la s. à qn,** to refuse Christian burial to s.o. **2.** burial place; **sépultures militaires,** war cemeteries.

séquelles [sekɛl] *n.f.pl.* aftermath, after effects.

séquence [sekɑ̃s] *n.f.* sequence; *Cards:* run.

séquentiel, -ielle [sekɑ̃sjɛl] *a.* sequential.

séquestration [sekɛstrasjɔ̃] *n.f.* **1.** *Jur:* sequestration (of goods). **2.** confinement (of s.o.).

séquestre[1] [sekɛstʀ̥] *n.m. Jur:* sequestration; embargo (on ship); **mettre en, sous, s. les biens de qn,** to sequester, sequestrate, s.o.'s property.

séquestre[2] *n.m. Jur:* receiver, depositary, trustee, administrator (of sequestrated property).

séquestrer [sekɛstre] **1.** (*a*) *v.tr.* to sequester, sequestrate (property); *Nau:* to lay an embargo upon (ship); (*b*) to keep (s.o.) locked up; *Jur:* to confine (s.o.) illegally. **2. se s.,** to cut oneself off from the world.

sequoia [sekɔja] *n.m. Bot:* sequoia.

sérac [serak] *n.m. Geol:* serac.

sérail [seraj] *n.m.* seraglio; *pl. sérails.*

séraphin [serafɛ̃] *n.m.* seraph.

séraphique [serafik] *a.* seraphic, angelic.

serbe [sɛrb] *a. & n. Geog:* Serb, Serbian.

Serbie [sɛrbi] *Pr.n.f. Geog:* Serbia.

serbo-croate [sɛrbɔkrɔat] **1.** *a. & n. Geog:* Serbo-Croat(ian). **2.** *n.m. Ling:* Serbo-Croat.

Sercq [sɛrk] *Pr.n.m. Geog:* (the island of) Sark.

serein[1] [sərɛ̃] *a.* serene, calm.

serein[2] *n.m.* evening dew.

sereinement [sərɛnmɑ̃] *adv,* serenely, calmly.

sérénade [serenad] *n.f.* serenade; **donner une s. à qn,** to serenade s.o.

sérénité [serenite] *n.f.* serenity, calmness; equanimity.

séreux, -euse [serø, -øz] *a. Anat: Med:* serous.

serf, serve [sɛrf, sɛrv] **1.** *n. Hist:* serf. **2.** *a.* (*a*) *Hist:* **condition serve,** serfdom; (*b*) (*of land*) in bondage, in villein tenure; (*c*) servile (outlook, etc.).

serfouette [sɛrfwɛt] *n.f. Hort:* combined hoe and fork.

serge [sɛrʒ] *n.f. Tex:* (woollen) serge.

sergent[1] [sɛrʒɑ̃] *n.m.* sergeant; **s. fourrier, s. comptable,** quartermaster sergeant; **s. instructeur,** drill sergeant; *A:* **s. de ville,** policeman.

sergent[2] *n.m. Tchn:* cramp; clamp.

sergent-chef [sɛrʒɑ̃ʃɛf] *n.m. Mil:* quartermaster-sergeant; *pl. sergents-chefs.*

séricicole [serisikɔl] *a.* seri(ci)cultural.

sériciculteur [serisikyltœr] *n.m.* seri(ci)culturist, silkworm breeder.

séri(ci)culture [seri(si)kyltyr] *n.f.* seri(ci)culture, silkworm breeding.

séricole [serikɔl] *a.* seri(ci)cultural.

série [seri] *n.f.* **1.** (*a*) series, succession (of events, etc.); **s. de catastrophes, s. noire,** series, chapter, of accidents; run of bad luck; **s. de jours chauds,** spell of hot weather; **s. de conférences,** series, course, of lectures; *W.Tel: T.V:* **s. (d'émissions),** (radio, television) series; (*b*) *Bill: etc:* break; *Bill:* run (of cannons); (*c*) *Sp:* heat; **s. éliminatoire,** qualifying heat. **2.** (*a*) series (of press articles, postage stamps, etc.); set (of documents, tools, etc.); range (of sizes, samples, etc.); **en, par, série(s),** in series, serially; (*b*) *Ind: Com:* range, line (of goods, etc.); **fabrication, production, en (grande(s)) série(s),** mass production;

chaîne de fabrication en s., production line; *Adm: etc:* **prix de s.,** contract price (for public works, etc.); *Com:* **fins de séries,** ends of lines, oddments, remnants; *Publ:* remainders; **article hors s.,** custom-made, custom-built, article; *Fig:* **c'est tout à fait hors s.,** it's quite exceptional; (*c*) *Mth: Ch: Atom.Ph: etc:* series; (*d*) *El:* **en s.,** in series; (*e*) group, category; *Sp:* rating; *Box:* **s. poids plumes,** featherweight rating; *Cin:* **film de s. B,** B-category film; *Pej:* **film de s. Z,** nth grade film.

sériel, -ielle [serjɛl] *a.* serial; *Mus:* twelve-tone, serial, dodecaphonic.

sérier [serje] *v.tr.* (*impf. & pr.sub.* **n. sériions, v. sériiez**) to arrange in series; **s. les questions,** to take the questions one by one.

sérieusement [serjøzmɑ̃] *adv.* (*a*) seriously, solemnly; (*b*) seriously, in earnest, genuinely; **parlez-vous s.?** are you serious? do you really mean it? (*c*) seriously, gravely (ill, wounded).

sérieux, -euse [serjø, -øz] **1.** *a.* (*a*) serious, grave, sober; *F:* **sérieux comme un pape,** as solemn as a judge; (*b*) serious-minded (person); (*c*) serious, earnest, genuine; responsible, reliable (person); **êtes-vous s.?** are you serious, in earnest? do you mean it? **d'un ton, d'un air, s.,** seriously; **offre sérieuse,** bona fide offer; **acheteur s.,** genuine purchaser; **peu s.,** irresponsible (person); (*d*) important (matter, etc.); serious (illness); *Com:* **client s.,** good customer. **2.** *n.m.* seriousness, gravity; **garder son s.,** to keep a straight face; **se prendre au s.,** to take oneself seriously; **je vous ai pris au s.,** I thought you were serious; I thought you meant it; **manque de s.,** (i) levity; (ii) irresponsibility.

sérigraphie [serigrafi] *n.f.* silk screen printing.

serin, -ine [sərɛ̃, -in] **1.** (*a*) *n.m. Orn:* canary; (*b*) *a.inv.* **jaune s.,** canary-yellow. **2.** *a. & n. F:* silly, stupid, idiotic (person); *n.* idiot, nit.

seriner [sərine] *v.tr.* (*a*) **s. un air à un oiseau,** to teach a bird to sing by means of the bird organ; (*b*) **s. (qch. à) qn,** to teach s.o. sth. (by constant repetition), to drum sth. into s.o.

seringa(t) [sərɛ̃ga] *n.m. Bot:* seringa.

seringue [sərɛ̃g] *n.f.* syringe; **s. de jardin,** garden syringe; *Med:* **s. à injections,** hypodermic syringe; *Aut:* **s. à graisse,** grease gun.

seringuer [sərɛ̃ge] *v.tr. Med:* to syringe; to inject; *Hort:* to spray.

serment [sɛrmɑ̃] *n.m.* (solemn) oath; **prêter s. (entre les mains de qn),** to take an oath, to be sworn (before s.o.); (*of jury, etc.*) to be sworn in; **faire prêter s. à qn,** to administer the oath to s.o.; **déclarer sous s.,** to state, declare, under oath; *Pol:* **s. politique,** *U.S:* oath of office; *Adm:* **s. professionnel,** swearing in (of magistrates, lawyers, police, etc.); **violer un s.,** to break an oath; **être sous la foi du s.,** to be on oath; **faire s. de faire qch.,** to swear to do sth.; **certifier qch. sous s.,** to declare sth. on oath; **déclaration sous s.,** sworn statement; **faire un faux s.,** to commit perjury.

sermon [sɛrmɔ̃] *n.m.* (*a*) sermon (**sur,** on); (*b*) *F:* talking-to, sermon, lecture.

sermonner [sɛrmɔne] *v.tr. F:* to lecture (s.o.); to give (s.o.) a good talking to.

sermonneur, -euse [sɛrmɔnœr, -øz] *F:* **1.** *a.* sermonizing; fault-finding. **2.** *n.* sermonizer.

serpe [sɛrp] *n.f.* billhook.

serpent [sɛrpɑ̃] *n.m.* **1.** (*a*) snake; **s. femelle,** female snake; **s. d'eau,** grass snake; **s. de verre,** slow-worm; **s. à coiffe, à lunettes,** (Indian) cobra; **s. à sonnettes,** rattlesnake; **s. à sonnettes cornu,** horned rattlesnake; *U.S: F:* sidewinder; **s. de mer,** (i) *Myth:* sea serpent; (ii) *Ich:* pipe fish; (iii) *Journ:* stock article; *B:* **le s.,** the Serpent; (*b*) snake-like object; (*c*) *Fin:* (monetary) snake. **2.** *Mus: A:* serpent.

serpentaire[1] [sɛrpɑ̃tɛr] *n.f. Bot:* serpentaria; **s. de Virginie,** snakeroot.

serpentaire[2] *n.m. Orn:* serpent eater, secretary bird.

serpentant [sɛrpɑ̃tɑ̃] *a.* winding, snaky (road); meandering (stream).

serpenteau, -eaux [sɛrpɑ̃to] *n.m.* **1.** young snake. **2.** *Pyr:* serpent, squib.

serpenter [sɛrpɑ̃te] *v.i.* (*of river, road, etc.*) to wind, curve, meander; **le chemin monte, descend, en serpentant,** the road winds up, down, the hill.

serpentin, -ine [sɛrpɑ̃tɛ̃, -in] **1.** *a.* (*a*) serpentine; (*b*) **marbre s.,** serpentine (marble), ophite. **2.** *n.m.* (*a*) coil (of tubing, etc.); (*b*) paper streamer (as used at fêtes). **3.** *n.f. Miner:* serpentine, ophite.

serpette [sɛrpɛt] *n.f. Hort:* pruning knife.

serpillière [sɛrpijɛr] *n.f. Dom.Ec:* floorcloth.

serpolet [sɛrpɔlɛ] *n.m. Bot:* wild thyme.

serrage [sɛraʒ] *n.m. Tchn:* securing; tightening (of screw, etc.); screwing tight (of nut, etc.); clamping (of joint, etc.); **s. des freins,** application of the brakes; braking; **vis de s.,** set screw, locking screw.

serre [sɛr] *n.f.* **1.** greenhouse; conservatory; glass-house; **s. chaude,** hothouse; **s. de palmiers,** palm house; **plante de s. chaude,** hothouse plant; **plantes sous s.,** plants under glass. **2.** pressing, squeezing (of grapes, etc.). **3.** *pl.* claws, talons (of bird of prey).

serré [sere] **1.** *a.* tight (boots, clothes, knot, screw, etc.); close (texture); compact, serried (ranks); dense (formation); narrow (defile, pass); **pluie serrée,** teeming rain; **deux pages d'une écriture serrée,** two closely written pages; **les dents serrées, les lèvres serrées,** with clenched teeth; **maisons serrées,** houses huddled together; **serrés comme des harengs, des sardines,** packed like sardines; **avoir le cœur s.,** to be sad at heart, to have a heavy heart; **surveillance serrée,** close supervision; **étude serrée,** intensive study (of a text); **style s.,** concise style; *Rac: etc:* **arrivée serrée,** close finish. **2.** *adv.* **jouer s.,** to play a cautious game; to take no chances.

serre-frein(s) [sɛrfrɛ̃] *n.m.inv. Rail:* brakeman.

serre-joint(s) [sɛrjwɛ̃] *n.m.inv. Tls:* clamp.

serre-livres [sɛrlivr̥] *n.m.inv.* book ends.

serrement [sɛrmɑ̃] *n.m.* **1.** squeezing, pressure; **s. de main,** handshake; **s. de cœur,** pang. **2.** *Min:* dam, partition (to keep out water).

serrer [sɛre] **1.** *v.tr.* (*a*) to press, squeeze, clasp; **s. la main à, de, qn,** to shake hands with s.o.; **tenir qch. sans s.,** to hold sth. loosely; **s. qn entre ses bras,** to clasp s.o. in one's arms; to hug s.o.; **s. le cou à qn,** to strangle s.o.; **s. qch. dans sa main,** to grip, grasp, sth.; **cela me serre le cœur,** it wrings my heart; *Equit:* **s. un cheval,** to keep a horse well in hand; (*b*) to tighten (knot, joint, screw, belt, etc.); to furl, take in (sails); to screw up, tighten (nut); to screw down (packing); to clench (one's fists, teeth); to knit (one's brows); **s. les freins,** to apply the brakes; *Mus:* **en serrant,** stringendo; (*c*) to close up, press close together; *Mil:* to close (ranks); **s. son style,** to condense one's style; **s. son jeu,** to play a close game; *Typ:* **s. une ligne,** to reduce the spaces in a line; (*d*) to keep close to (s.o., sth.); to hug (*Nau:* the shore, *Aut:* the kerb); *Sp:* to jostle (a competitor); **s. qn de près,** to follow s.o. closely; **s. une question de près,** to go closely into a question; *P.N:* **serrez à droite!** = keep to nearside (lane)! *F:* **se s. les coudes,** to back one another up. **2. se s.** (*a*) to stand, sit, close together; to crowd; **serrez-vous!** close up! sit closer! **se s. les uns contre les autres,** to huddle together; **se s. contre qn,** to snuggle up to s.o.; to cling close to s.o; (*b*) to tighten, to become tighter; **mon cœur se serra,** my heart sank; (*c*) *Fig:* to tighten one's belt.

serre-tête [sɛrtɛt] *n.m.inv.* **1.** headband; hairband; *Sp:* ear protector; scrum cap. **2.** leather helmet.
serrure [seryr] *n.f.* lock; **s. de sûreté,** safety lock; **trou de la s.,** keyhole.
serrurerie [seryrri] *n.f.* **1.** (*a*) locksmithing; locksmith's trade; (*b*) locksmith's (shop). **2.** iron work, metal work; **s. d'art,** (i) art metal work; (ii) art metal trade; **grosse s.,** heavy ironwork.
serrurier [seryrje] *n.m.* **1.** locksmith. **2.** ironsmith.
sertir [sɛrtir] *v.tr.* (*a*) to set (precious stone) in a bezel; (*b*) *Metalw:* to crimp.
sertissage [sɛrtisaʒ] *n.m.* (*a*) setting (of jewels); (*b*) crimping (of cartridge, tin, etc.).
sertisseur, -euse [sɛrtisœr, -øz] **1.** *n.m.* (*a*) setter (of jewels); (*b*) crimping tool; (*c*) (*pers.*) crimper. **2.** *n.f. Ind:* **sertisseuse,** sealer, crimper (for tins, etc.).
sertissure [sɛrtisyr] *n.f.* setting (of precious stone); bezel.
sérum [serɔm] *n.m.* (*a*) *Physiol: Med:* serum; **s. sanguin,** blood serum; **s. de vérité,** truth serum, *F:* truth drug; (*b*) **s. (lactique),** whey.
servage [sɛrvaʒ] *n.m.* serfdom, bondage.
serval [sɛrval] *n.m. Z:* serval; *pl. servals.*
servant, -ante [sɛrvɑ̃, -ɑ̃t] **1.** *a.* serving; **frère s.,** lay brother; **gentilhomme s.,** gentleman-in-waiting. **2.** *n.m.* (*a*) *Artil:* gunner; (*b*) *Ten:* server; (*c*) **s. (de messe),** server. **3.** *n.f.* **servante,** (*a*) (maid)servant, servant (girl); (*b*) *Furn:* dinner waggon, *NAm:* wagon; (tea) trolley; (*c*) *Tchn:* (adjustable) support.
serveur, -euse [sɛrvœr, -øz] *n.* **1.** (*a*) barman, *f.* barmaid; (*b*) (*in restaurant*) waiter, *f.* waitress. **2.** *Cards:* dealer. **3.** *Ten:* server.
serviabilité [sɛrvjabilite] *n.f.* obligingness; helpfulness.
serviable [sɛrvjabl̩] *a.* obliging; helpful.
service [sɛrvis] *n.m.* **1.** (*a*) (domestic, etc.) service; **entrer en s. (chez qn),** to go into (s.o.'s) service; **gens de s.,** domestic staff; **être au s. de qn,** to be in s.o.'s service, in attendance on s.o.; to attend s.o. **(en qualité de,** as); to be under s.o.; **mourir au s. du roi,** to die in the king's service; **escalier de s.,** back stairs; **porte de s.,** tradesmen's entrance; back door; (*b*) service (in hotel, restaurant, etc.); **s. (non) compris,** service (not) included; **libre s.,** self-service (in shop, etc.); *Com:* **s. après vente,** after-sales service; (*c*) *Adm:* **s. contractuel,** contract service; **indications de s.,** service instructions; *Adm: Mil:* **états de s.,** service record; *Tp:* **communication, conversation, de s.,** service call; *Mil: etc:* **s. militaire (obligatoire),** (compulsory) military service; **en s. actif, en activité de s.,** on the active list; **service(s) de guerre,** active service; **en s. aux armées,** on active service; **(in)apte au s.,** (un)fit for service; **être libéré du s.,** to be discharged; **libération du s.,** discharge; (*d*) *Fin:* **s. des intérêts,** interest charges; (*e*) *Sp:* (i) *Cr:* bowling; (ii) *Ten:* service; **au s., Martin,** Martin to serve. **2.** duty; **s. de jour,** day duty; **s. de nuit,** night duty, *Navy:* orders for the night; **être de s., ne pas être de s.,** to be on, off, duty; **tableau de s.,** duty chart, list, roster; **à quelle heure prenez-vous, quittez-vous, votre s.?** at what time do you go on duty, off duty? *Mil: etc:* **mort en s. commandé,** killed on active service; **s. de corvée,** *Mil:* fatigue duty; *Navy:* duty; **s. de garde,** guard duty; **planton de s.,** duty orderly; **officier, sous-officier, de s.,** duty officer, non-commissioned officer; *F:* **être s. s.,** to be a stickler for rules and regulations. **3.** branch, department, service; (*a*) *Adm:* **chef de s.,** head of department, *U.S:* executive; **s. central,** headquarters; **s. de renseignements,** enquiry office, department, *Tp:* directory enquiries; **les services publics,** public utilities, *U.S:* utilities; **s. des eaux,** water supply; **s. des postes, s. postal,** postal service, mail service; **s. gouvernemental,** government agency; **correspondance de s.,** official correspondence; (*b*) *Mil:* corps, service, department; **s. des renseignements,** intelligence (service); (*c*) (health, social, dental, etc.) service; **s. des contagieux,** isolation ward; (*d*) *Com:* (accounts, dispatch, purchasing, etc.) department (of firm); **s. technique,** technical branch; engineering department; *Journ:* **s. des informations (d'un journal),** information service (of a newspaper). **4.** (*a*) running (of machine, etc.) **s. à bras, s. manuel,** hand, manual, operation; (*b*) use (of machine, etc.); **en s.,** in service, in use, in operation; (*of aircraft, ship*) in commission; **aptitude au s.,** serviceability; **en (bon) état de s., propre au s.,** in (good) working order, serviceable; **hors (de) s.,** (*of thg*) out of use, out of service, unserviceable; (*of machine, mechanism*) not working; (*of gun, etc.*) out of action; disabled (ship, etc.); **mettre en s.,** to bring, put, introduce, into service, (*of aircraft, ship*) into commission; **retirer du s.,** to withdraw from service, from use; **retirer graduellement du s.,** to phase out; (*c*) *Trans:* service (of train, liner, aircraft, etc.); **assurer, faire, le s. entre . . . et . . .,** to run between . . . and . . .; **s. de voyageurs,** passenger service; **s. assuré toute l'année,** all the year round service; **s. de marchandises,** goods, freight, service. **5. rendre (un) s. à qn,** to do s.o. a service, a favour, *NAm:* a favor, a good turn; **rendre un bon, un mauvais, s. à qn,** to do s.o. a good, a bad, turn; **les services qu'il a rendus à l'enseignement,** his services to education; **à votre s.,** at your service; **qu'y a-t-il pour votre s.?** what can I do for you? **ce manteau m'a fait un bon s.,** this coat has worn well; **ce livre m'a rendu grand s.,** this book was very useful to me. **6.** *Breed:* service (of stallion). **7.** (*a*) course (of a meal); (*b*) *Rail: etc:* **dernier s. à deux heures,** last sitting (for lunch) at two o'clock. **8.** set (of utensils, etc.); **s. de table,** dinner service; **s. à découper,** set of carvers; **s. américain,** set of table mats.
serviette [sɛrvjɛt] *n.f.* **1.** (*a*) (table) napkin; serviette; **s. d'enfant,** feeder, bib; (*b*) **s. (de toilette),** (hand) towel; **s. sans fin,** roller towel; **s. hygiénique,** sanitary towel, *U.S:* sanitary napkin. **2.** briefcase.
serviette-éponge [sɛrvjetepɔ̃ʒ] *n.f.* (terry, Turkish) towel; *pl. serviettes-éponges.*
servile [sɛrvil] *a.* (*a*) servile (pers., *A:* condition); (*b*) slavish (imitation).
servilement [sɛrvilmɑ̃] *adv.* servilely; slavishly.
servilité [sɛrvilite] *n.f.* servility; slavishness.
servir [sɛrvir] *v.* (*pr.p.* **servant;** *p.p.* **servi;** *pr.ind.* **je sers, il sert, n. servons;** *pr.sub.* **je serve;** *impf.* **je servais;** *p.h.* **je servis;** *fu.* **je servirai)** to serve. **1.** *v.i.* (*a*) to be useful **(à qn,** to s.o.); to be in use; **la machine peut encore s.,** the machine is still fit for use; **cela peut s. un de ces jours,** it may come in handy one day; **toujours prêt à s.,** always ready for use; (*b*) **s. à qch., à faire qch.,** to be useful, used, for sth., for doing sth.; **ne s. à rien,** to be (of) no use, useless; **à quoi cela sert-il?** what is the good, the use, of that? *F:* **à quoi sert ce truc-là?** what's that gadget for? **ça ne servira pas à grand-chose,** that won't be much good, much use; **cela ne sert qu'à l'irriter,** it only irritates him; **je ne vois pas à quoi sert d'y aller,** I do not see the good of going; (*c*) **s. de,** to serve as, be used as (s.o., sth.); (*of pers.*) to act as; **les pupitres servent de tables,** the desks are used as tables; **s. de prétexte,** to serve as a pretext; **elle lui a servi de mère,** she has been a mother to him; (*d*) *impers.* **il ne sert à rien de pleurer,** it's no good, use, crying; **à quoi sert qu'on l'attende?** what's the use of waiting for him? **2.** *v.tr.* (*a*) to be a servant to (s.o.); to serve (s.o.); **s. Dieu,** to serve God; **s. sa patrie, une cause,** to serve one's country, a cause; **nous sommes très bien servis,** we have very good (domestic) help; **ce cours d'eau sert le moulin,** this stream drives the mill;

(*b*) *v.i.* to serve (in army, etc.) (**sous,** under); **en âge de s.,** of military age; (*c*) to serve, attend to (customer, etc.); to wait on (diner); **est-ce qu'on vous sert?** are you being attended to? **madame est servie,** dinner is served, madam; **s. à table,** to wait at table; *F:* **en fait de pluie, nous sommes servis,** as far as rain goes, we get more than our share; (*d*) (*of tradesman*) to supply (s.o. with goods); **s. une rente à qn,** to pay an annuity to s.o.; (*in bus*) **tout le monde est servi?** any more fares please? (*e*) to serve, bring in (dinner, the cheese, etc.); **s. qch. chaud,** to serve sth. hot; (*f*) to serve (the fish, etc.); **s. à qn d'un plat,** to help s.o. to a dish; **s. à boire à qn,** to fill s.o.'s glass; (*g*) to help, assist, be of service to (s.o.); to further (s.o.'s interests); **en quoi puis-je vous s.?** what can I do for you? **sa mémoire l'a mal servi,** his memory played him a false trick; (*h*) to serve (gun); to work, operate (gun, pump); (*i*) *Ecc:* **s. la messe,** to serve at mass; (*j*) *Ten:* to serve; *Cr:* **s. la balle,** to bowl; *Cards:* **à vous de s.,** (it's) your deal; (*k*) (*of stallion*) to serve, cover (mare); (*l*) *Ven:* to dispatch (an animal). **3. se s.** (*a*) **se s. d'un plat,** to help oneself to a dish; **servez-vous!** help yourself! go ahead! (*b*) **se s. chez Martin,** to shop at Martin's; (*c*) **se s. de qch., de qn,** to use sth., s.o.; to make use of sth., of s.o.

serviteur [sɛrvitœr] *n.m.* servant; **s. de l'État,** civil servant; *Corr: A:* **votre s.,** your obedient servant; **personne ne le sait mieux que votre s.,** no one knows it better than your humble servant, than yours truly.

servitude [sɛrvityd] *n.f.* **1.** (*a*) servitude; (*b*) constraint; **la s. de la mode,** the tyranny of fashion. **2.** *Jur:* easement, charge (on real estate); **s. de passage,** right of way.

servocommande [sɛrvɔkɔmɑ̃d] *n.f. Av: Aut: etc:* servo(-control).

servofrein [sɛrvɔfrɛ̃] *n.m. Aut: etc:* servobrake.

servograisseur [sɛrvɔgrɛsœr] *n.m. Aut: etc:* pressure oiler.

servomécanisme [sɛrvɔmekanism] *n.m. Tchn:* servomechanism; servo system.

servomoteur [sɛrvɔmɔtœr] *n.m. Mch:* servomotor.

sésame [sezam] *n.m. Bot:* sesame; **s., ouvre-toi!** open, sesame!

sessile [sɛsil] *a. Nat.Hist:* sessile (leaf, horn, etc.).

session [sesjɔ̃] *n.f.* **1.** session, sitting (of parliament, etc.). **2.** *Jur: Sch:* session, term.

sesterce [sɛstɛrs] *n.m. Rom.Ant:* sestertius, sesterce; **grand s.,** sestertium.

set [sɛt] *n.m.* **1.** *Ten:* set. **2.** *Cin:* set. **3.** *Dom.Ec: F:* **s. (de table),** set of table mats.

sétacé [setase] *a Nat. Hist:* setaceous, bristly.

séton [setɔ̃] *n.m. Surg: Vet:* seton.

setter [setɛr] *n.m. Z:* (*dog*) setter.

seuil [sœj] *n.m.* **1.** threshold; doorstep; *Fig:* brink (of death, etc.); **franchir le s.,** to cross the threshold; **sur le s., au s.,** on the threshold; **être au s. de la célébrité,** to stand on the threshold of fame; *Pol.Ec:* **s. de rentabilité,** break-even point; *Physiol:* **s. de sensibilité,** threshold of sensitivity, of response; **s. de la conscience,** limen. **2.** *Geog:* **s. continental,** continental shelf. **3.** *Hyd.E:* sill (of dry dock, lock).

seul [sœl] *a.* **1.** (*preceding the n.*) (*a*) only, sole, single; **un s. homme,** one man only, only one man; one single man; **le gouvernement d'un s.,** absolute rule, monarchy; **son s. exécuteur testamentaire,** his sole executor; **son s. souci,** his one, only, sole, care; **il ne suffit pas d'un s. exemple,** a single example will not suffice; **mon s. et unique stylo,** my one and only pen; **un s. mot, et je te quitte,** one word from you and I'll go; **pas un s.,** not (a single) one, none whatever; not a single person; **vous êtes le s. qui puissiez m'aider,** you alone can help me; **il était le s. à nous encourager,** he was the only one who encouraged us, he alone encouraged us; (*b*) **la seule pensée m'effraie,** the mere, very, thought frightens me. **2.** (*following the n. or used predicatively*) alone, by oneself; on one's own; **un homme s.,** a man alone, by himself; **se sentir très s.,** to feel very lonely; (*of bachelor*) **être garçon s.,** to be unattached; **il peut marcher tout s. maintenant,** he can walk by himself now; **parler s. à s. à qn,** to speak to s.o. tête à tête; to have a private conversation with s.o.; **s. (à s.) avec soi-même,** alone with one's, thoughts; **l'œuvre seule de . . .,** the exclusive work of . . .; **j'ai une cachette que moi s. connais,** I have a hiding place which I alone know; **je l'ai fait tout s., à moi s.,** I did it (by) myself, alone, singlehanded; **cela va tout s.,** it's plain sailing; **cela ne va pas tout s.,** it isn't easy; it isn't all plain sailing; **parler, chanter, etc., tout s.,** to talk, sing, etc., to oneself; *Mus:* **passage pour violin s.,** passage for an unaccompanied violin. **3.** (*following the n. or preceding the article or poss. adj.*) alone (*after noun*); only; **la violence seule, seule la violence, le contraindrait,** only violence, violence alone, nothing short of violence, would compel him; **seule la chasse les fait vivre,** hunting is their only source of food; **s. un expert pourrait nous conseiller,** only an expert could advise us; **nous sommes seuls à le savoir,** we are the only people who know of it.

seulement [sœlmɑ̃] *adv.* **1.** (*a*) only; **nous sommes s. deux,** there are only two of us; **venir s. de faire qch.,** to have only just done sth.; **non s. . . ., mais aussi . . ., mais encore . . .,** not only . . ., but also . . .; (*b*) solely, merely; **il y va s. pour vous faire plaisir,** he is going merely to please you; (*c*) *F:* **entrez s.,** do come in. **2.** even; **sans s. me regarder,** without even looking at me; **il ne m'a pas s. regardé,** he didn't even, so much as, look at me; **si s. . . .!** if only . . .! **3.** (*with conj. force*) **je viendrais bien, s. . . .,** I should like to come, but . . ., only . . ..

sève [sɛv] *n.f.* (*a*) *Bot:* sap (of plant); (*b*) vigour, *NAm:* vigor; go; **plein de s.,** full of vitality.

sévère [sevɛr] *a.* severe. **1.** stern, hard, harsh (judge, etc.); severe (look, beauty); **climat s.,** hard climate; **être s. envers qn, pour qn, avec qn, pour les fautes de qn,** to be hard on s.o., on s.o.'s failings; **mener un train s.,** to set a gruelling pace. **2.** strict, rigid (discipline, morals); **architecture, style, s.,** severe architecture, style; **morale peu s.,** lax morals.

sévèrement [sevɛrmɑ̃] *adv.* **1.** severely, sternly, harshly. **2.** strictly, rigidly.

sévérité [severite] *n.f.* (*a*) severity (of punishment); sternness (of face, look); strictness (of discipline); **avec s.,** severely; (*b*) severity (of style, etc.).

sévices [sevis] *n.m.pl.* brutality, cruelty.

sévir [sevir] *v.i.* **1. s. contre qn, qch.,** to deal severely with s.o., sth. **2.** (*of epidemic, war*) to rage; **la crise qui sévit actuellement,** the present acute crisis.

sevrage [səvraʒ] *n.m.* **1.** weaning; *Med:* **symptômes de s.,** withdrawal symptoms. **2.** *Hort:* separating (of layer, scion, from plant).

sevrer [səvre] *v.tr.* **(je sèvre, n. sevrons; je sèvrerai) 1.** to wean (child, lamb); *Lit:* to deprive s.o. (of his rights, of amusements). **2.** *Hort:* to separate (layer, scion, from plant).

sexage [sɛksaʒ] *n.m.* sexing (of poultry).

sexagénaire [sɛgzaʒenɛr] *a. & n.* sexagenarian.

Sexagésime [sɛgzaʒezim] *n.f.* Sexagesima (Sunday).

sex-appeal [sɛksapil] *n.m. F:* sex appeal.

sexe [sɛks] *n.m.* **1.** sex; **le s. fort,** the stronger sex, the male sex; **le (beau) s., le s. faible,** the fair sex; the weaker sex. **2.** genitals.

sexisme [sɛksism] *n.m.* sexism.

sexiste [sɛksist] *a. & n.* sexist.

sexologie [sɛksɔlɔʒi] *n.f.* sexology.
sexologique [sɛksɔlɔʒik] *a.* sexological.
sexologue [sɛksɔlɔg] *n.* sexologist.
sextant [sɛkstɑ̃] *n.m. Mth: Nau:* sextant.
sextuor [sekstɥɔr] *n.m. Mus:* sextet(te).
sextuple [sɛkstypl̩] *a. & n.m.* sextuple; sixfold; six times.
sextuplé, -ée [sɛkstyple] *n.* sextuplet.
sextupler [sɛkstyple] **1.** *v.tr.* to sextuple (a number). **2.** *v.tr. & i.* to increase sixfold.
sexualiser [sɛksɥalize] *v.tr.* to sexualize.
sexualité [sɛksɥalite] *n.f.* sexuality.
sexué [sɛksɥe] *a.* sexed (plant, etc.); sexual (reproduction).
sexuel, -elle [sɛksɥɛl] *a.* sexual.
sexy [sɛksi] *a.inv. P:* sexy.
seyant [sejɑ̃] *a.* becoming (garment, etc.).
shah [ʃa] *n.m.* shah.
shake-hand [ʃɛkɑ̃d] *n.m.inv. A: & Hum:* handshake.
shaker [ʃɛkœr] *n.m.* cocktail shaker.
shak(e)spearien, -ienne [ʃɛkspirjɛ̃, -jɛn] *a.* Shakespearian.
shako [ʃako] *n.m. Mil. Cost:* shako.
shampooing [ʃɑ̃pwɛ̃] *n.m.* **1.** (*action*) shampoo; **faire, donner, un s. à qn,** to shampoo s.o.'s hair. **2.** (*product*) shampoo; **s. sec,** dry shampoo.
sheik [ʃɛk] *n.m.* sheik.
shérif [ʃerif] *n.m.* sheriff.
sherpa [ʃɛrpa] *n. Ethn:* Sherpa.
Shetland [ʃɛtlɑ̃d] *Pr.n.m.* **1.** *Geog:* **les (îles) S.,** the Shetland Islands, the Shetlands. **2.** *n.m. Tex:* Shetland wool.
shibboleth [ʃibɔlɛt] *n.m.* shibboleth.
shift [ʃift] *n.m. Ind:* shift.
shilling [ʃiliŋ] *n.m.* shilling.
shimmy [ʃimi] *n.m. Aut:* shimmy.
shinto [ʃɛ̃to] *n.m.* Shintoism.
shogoun [ʃɔgun] *n.m. Japanese Hist:* shogun.
shoot [ʃut] *n.m. Fb:* shot.
shooter [ʃute] *v.i. Fb:* to shoot.
shopping [ʃɔpiŋ] *n.m.* shopping; **faire du s.,** to go shopping.
short [ʃɔrt] *n.m. Cost:* shorts.
shunt [ʃœt] *n.m. El: Surg:* shunt.
si¹ [si] *conj.* (*by elision* **s'** *before* **il, ils**) **1.** if; (*a*) **je ne sortirai pas s'il pleut,** I shall not go out if it rains; **si on ne le surveille pas, il s'échappera,** unless he is watched he will escape; **s'il n'avait pas plu, nous serions partis,** if it hadn't rained we should have started; **s'il vient, vous m'avertirez,** if he comes, let me know; **j'aurais été soldat, si je n'étais poète,** I would have been a soldier if I were not a poet; **si j'avais su,** if I'd known; *Lit:* had I but known; **si ce n'est toi, c'est donc ton frère,** if it is not you, then it is your brother; **qui le fera si ce n'est moi?** who will do it unless I do? **si ce n'était que je l'ai vu moi-même,** if I hadn't seen it myself; **si ce n'était mon rhumatisme, je vous accompagnerais,** if it weren't for my rheumatism I would go with you; **s'il fait beau et si je suis libre je sortirai,** if it's fine and (if) I am free, I shall go out; **si je ne me trompe,** if I am not mistaken; **si seulement j'étais à Paris!** if only I were in Paris! *Lit:* **si tant est que +** *sub.*, if so it be, provided, that . . .; (*b*) (*concessive*) **s'il fut sévère, il fut juste,** if he was severe, he was just; **si je me plains, c'est que j'en ai sujet,** if I complain, I have good cause; **s'il est malheureux et s'il a des ennuis, c'est bien de sa faute,** if he is unhappy and in trouble, it is entirely his own fault; **ce fut à peine s'il put distinguer l'heure à sa montre,** he could scarcely see the hands of his watch; **c'est tout au plus si l'on peut compter jusqu'à vingt femmes dans la salle,** at the most there are only about twenty women in the hall; **le père Martin, (un) brave homme s'il en fut,** old Martin, a worthy man if ever there was one. **2.** whether, if; **je me demande si c'est vrai, s'il viendra,** I wonder whether, if, it is true, whether, if, he will come; **je lui ai demandé s'il était marié et s'il avait des enfants,** I asked him whether he was married, and if he had a family; *F:* **vous connaissez Paris?—si je connais Paris!** you know Paris?—of course, I know Paris! *F:* **si c'est pas malheureux de voir ça!** isn't it dreadful to see that! **3.** how, how much; **pensez si j'étais furieux!** you can imagine how angry I was! **4.** what if, suppose; **et si elle l'apprend,** and what if she hears of it? **si nous changions de sujet?** suppose we change the subject? **si on faisait une partie de bridge?** what about a game of bridge? **5.** *n.m.* **tes si et tes mais,** your ifs and buts; *Prov:* **avec des si on mettrait Paris dans une bouteille,** if ifs and ands were pots and pans there'd be no need for tinkers.
si² *adv.* **1.** so, so much; (*a*) **ne courez pas si vite,** don't run so fast; **il est si faible que . . .,** he is so weak that . . .; **un si bon dîner,** such a good dinner; **de si bons dîners,** such good dinners; **il n'est pas si à plaindre que cela,** he is not so much to be pitied as all that; **ce n'est pas si facile,** it's not so easy; (*b*) (= AUSSI *in neg. clause*) **il n'est pas si beau que vous,** he is not as handsome, not so handsome, as you; (*c*) **donnez-m'en si peu que vous voudrez, si peu que rien,** give me just a (very) little; (*d*) **si bien que . . .,** with the result that . . .; **il dépensa sans regarder, si bien qu'en fin de compte il fut ruiné,** he spent recklessly so that in the end he was ruined. **2.** (*concessive*) **si . . . que +** *sub.*, however; **si jeune qu'il soit,** however young he may be; young as he is; **aucun médecin, si habile soit-il,** no doctor, however capable he is; **si peu que ce soit,** however little it may be; **votre méthode, si parfaite soit-elle . . .,** your method, however perfect in itself . . .; **si bien qu'il s'y prenne,** however skilfully he sets about it. **3.** (*a*) (*in answer to a neg. question*) yes; **si fait,** yes indeed; **ça ne fait rien;—si, ça fait quelque chose,** it doesn't matter;—it *does* matter! **il n'est pas parti?—si, je crois que si,** he hasn't gone?—yes, he has; yes, I think he has; **mais si, je l'ai vu,** yes I *did* see him; **il ne s'en remettra pas—que si!** he won't get over it—of course, he will! yes, he will! (*b*) *F:* **tu t'en souviens, je pense?—mais si, bien sûr . . .,** you remember it, I think?—yes, of course; (*to stress affirmative after a negation*) **vous en voulez?—merci—mais si,** do have some?—no, thank you—oh, do.
si³ *n.m.inv. Mus:* **1.** (the note) B; **morceau en si,** piece in B; **en si bémol,** in B flat. **2.** si (in the fixed do system).
Siam [sjam] *Pr.n.m. Geog:* Siam.
siamois, -oise [sjamwa, -waz] **1.** *a. & n. Geog:* Siamese; **(chat) s.,** Siamese cat; **frères s., sœurs siamoises,** Siamese twins. **2.** *n.m. Ling:* **le s.,** Siamese.
Sibérie [siberi] *Pr.n.f. Geog:* Siberia; **chien de S.,** Siberian dog.
sibérien, -ienne [siberjɛ̃, -jɛn] *a. & n. Geog:* Siberian.
sibilant [sibilɑ̃] *a. esp. Med:* sibilant, hissing.
sibylle [sibil] *n.f.* sibyl.
sibyllin [sibilɛ̃] *a.* (*a*) sibylline (books, etc.); (*b*) cryptic, enigmatic.
sic [sik] *adv.* (*a*) sic; (*b*) *F:* **la sincérité-s., le socialisme-s.,** so-called sincerity, socialism.
siccatif, -ive [sikatif, -iv] *a & n.m.* siccative.
Sicile [sisil] *Pr.n.f. Geog:* Sicily.
sicilien, -ienne [sisiljɛ̃, -jɛn] **1.** *a. & n. Geog:* Sicilian. **2.** *n.f. Mus: Danc:* **sicilienne,** Siciliana.
sicle [sikl̩] *n.m. A.Num:* shekel.
side(-)car [sidkar] *n.m.* (motor-cycle and) sidecar.

sidéral, -aux [sideral, -o] *a.* sidereal.
sidérant [siderɑ̃] *a. F:* staggering (news).
sidéré¹ [sidere] *a. Miner:* siderous.
sidéré² *a.* (*a*) *O:* struck dead (by lightning, apoplexy); (*b*) *F:* flabbergasted, staggered.
sidérer [sidere] *v.tr.* **(il sidère; il sidérera) 1.** *O:* (*of lightning, apoplexy, etc.*) to strike (s.o.) dead, to strike (s.o.) down. **2.** *F:* to flabbergast, stagger (s.o.).
sidérose [sideroz] *n.f.* **1.** *Miner:* siderite. **2.** *Med:* siderosis.
sidérostat [siderɔsta] *n.m. Astr:* siderostat.
sidérurgie [sideryrʒi] *n.f.* the metallurgy of iron and steel.
sidérurgique [sideryrʒik] *a.* **industrie s.,** iron and steel industry; **usine s.,** iron and steel works.
sidérurgiste [sideryrʒist] *n.* iron and steel metallurgist.
sidi [sidi] *n.m. P:* Arab (*esp.* living in France); wog.
siècle [sjɛkl̥] *n.m.* **1.** century; **au vingtième s.,** in the twentieth century; **lit vieux d'un bon s.,** bed at least a hundred, a good hundred, years old. **2.** age, period (of time); **le s. de Louis XIV, le grand s.,** the age of Louis XIV; **notre s.,** the age we live in, the present time; **c'est un homme de son s., d'un autre s.,** he's a man of his times, he belongs to another age, another century; **jusqu'à la fin des siècles,** to the end of (all) time; *Ecc:* **pour les siècles des siècles,** world without end; *F:* **il y a un s. que je ne vous ai vu,** I haven't seen you for ages. **3.** the world; worldly life.
siège [sjɛʒ] *n.m.* **1.** (*a*) seat, centre, *NAm* center (of learning, of government, of activity, etc.); *Min:* workings; **s. social,** head office, registered office (of a company); **chef de s.,** engineer in charge (of mine, etc.); (*b*) *Ecc:* **s. épiscopal,** see. **2.** *Mil:* siege; **mettre le s. devant une ville, faire le s. d'une ville,** to lay siege to a town; **lever le s.,** (i) to raise the siege; (ii) *F:* to get up and go. **3.** seat, chair; (coachman's) box; **s. à la Chambre,** seat in Parliament; **le s. du juge,** the judge's bench; *Veh:* **s. avant, arrière,** front, back, seat; **prenez un s.,** take a seat; (do) sit down; **il occupe un s. important,** he holds an important position. **4.** (*a*) seat (of chair, etc.); *Av:* **s. éjectable,** ejection, ejector, seat; (*b*) (*in certain expressions*) seat (of pers.); **bain de s.,** sitz bath; hip bath; *Obst:* **accouchement par le s.,** *F:* **un s.,** breech delivery; (*c*) *Hyg:* (lavatory) seat; (*d*) seating (of valve, etc.).
siège-baquet [sjɛʒbakɛ] *n.m. Aut:* bucket seat; *pl. sièges-baquets.*
siéger [sjeʒe] *v.i.* **(je siège, n. siégeons; je siégeai(s); je siégerai) 1.** (*of company, etc.*) to have its head office, headquarters; (*of bishop*) **après avoir siégé à Bayeux pendant dix ans,** having held the see of Bayeux for ten years; *Med:* **c'est là que siège le mal,** that is the seat of the trouble. **2.** (*of court of law, judge, assembly, etc.*) to sit. **3.** (*a*) **s. à la Chambre,** to have a seat, to sit, in Parliament; (*b*) *Jur:* **s. au tribunal,** to be on the bench.
sien, sienne¹ [sjɛ̃, sjɛn] his, hers, its, one's. **1.** *poss.a.* **adopter qch. comme s.,** to adopt sth. as one's own; **faire s.,** to accept as one's own. **2. le s., la sienne, les siens, les siennes** (*a*) *poss. pron.* **ma sœur est plus jolie que la sienne,** my sister is prettier than his, than hers; **il prit mes mains dans les deux siennes,** he took my hands in both of his; (*b*) *n.m.* (i) one's own, his own (property, etc.); **à chacun le s.,** to each his own; **y mettre du s.,** to contribute (to an undertaking); **ajouter du s. à un récit,** to improve upon a tale; (ii) *pl.* his own, her own, one's own (family, friends, etc.); (iii) **faire des siennes,** to be up to one's tricks.
Sienne² [sjɛn] *Pr.n.f. Geog:* Sienna; *Com:* **terre de S. naturelle, brûlée,** raw, burnt, sienna.
sierra [sjɛra] *n.f. Geog:* sierra.
sieste [sjɛst] *n.f.* siesta, nap; **faire la s.,** to take a siesta; to take a nap (after lunch).
sieur [sjœr] *n.m. A: & Jur:* Mr; *Pej:* **un s. Martin,** one Mr Martin.
sifflant, -ante [siflɑ̃, -ɑ̃t] **1.** *a.* hissing (sound); whistling (note); wheezing, wheezy (breath); sibilant (consonant). **2.** *n.f. Ling:* **sifflante,** sibilant.
sifflement [sifləmɑ̃] *n.m.* **1.** whistling, whistle (of s.o., the wind, etc.); hiss(ing) (of snake, goose, steam); swish(ing) (of whip); whizz (of bullet, arrow); wheezing (of asthmatic person); singing, hissing, sizzling (of food in the frying pan, of arc lamp). **2.** whistling, hissing, booing.
siffler [sifle] **1.** *v.i.* (*a*) (*of pers., bird, engine, ship, the wind*) to whistle; (*of serpent, goose, etc.*) to hiss; (*of asthmatic pers.*) to wheeze; (*of food frying, of arc lamp*) to sizzle; *Navy:* to pipe; (*b*) to blow a, the, whistle. **2.** *v.tr.* (*a*) to whistle (a tune); *Nau:* to pipe (a command); *Sp:* **s. une faute, la mi-temps,** to blow the whistle for a foul, for half time; (*b*) to whistle for, whistle up (a taxi, etc.); to whistle for, after (a dog, etc.); *Aut: F:* **je me suis fait s. (par la police),** I've been pulled up (by the police); *F:* **s. une fille,** to wolf-whistle; (*c*) *Th: etc:* to hiss, boo, hoot; *F:* to give the bird to (actor, etc.); **être sifflé,** to be hissed (off the stage, etc.), to get the bird; *P:* **sifflé!** rubbish! boo! (*d*) *P:* to swig (a glass of beer, etc.).
sifflet [siflɛ] *n.m.* **1.** (*instrument*) whistle; *Navy:* (boatswain's) pipe; **coup de s.,** blast of the whistle; *Mil:* call; *Navy:* pipe; *Sp:* **coup de s. final,** final whistle; *Mch:* **s. à vapeur,** steam whistle; *Nau:* **s. de brume,** fog whistle; *P:* **serrer le s. à qn,** to strangle s.o.; *Row:* **attaquer en s.,** to catch a crab. **2.** (*sound*) whistle; *Th: etc:* catcall, boo, hiss.
siffleur, -euse [siflœr, -øz] **1.** *n.* whistler; *Th:* hisser, booer. **2.** *n.m.* (*a*) *Orn:* widgeon; (*b*) *Z:* whistler, Canadian marmot. **3.** *a.* whistling (bird, duck); hissing (snake); wheezy (horse, etc.); *Orn:* **canard s.,** baldpate.
siffleux [siflø] *n.m. Fr.C: Z:* ground hog, whistler, woodchuck.
sifflotement [siflɔtmɑ̃] *n.m.* whistling (softly, to oneself).
siffloter [siflɔte] *v.tr. & i.* to whistle (a tune) to oneself, under one's breath.
sigillaire [siʒilɛr] *a.* **anneau s.,** signet ring.
sigillé [siʒile] *a. Bot: Cer: etc:* sigillate(d).
sigle [sigl̥] *n.m.* set of initials; abbreviation; acronym; **langage des sigles,** *F:* initialese.
sigma [sigma] *n.m. Gr.Alph:* sigma.
signal, -aux [siɲal, -o] *n.m.* (*a*) signal; **faire des signaux,** to make signals, to signal; **envoyer, lancer, un s.,** to send a signal; *Fig:* **donner le s. de qch.,** to be the signal for sth., to signal the start of sth.; **s. de départ,** starting signal (of train, race, etc.); **au s. donné, tous se levèrent,** on a gesture of command, they all stood up; **s. à vue, s. optique,** visible signal, visual signal; **s. à bras,** hand signal, semaphore signal; *Mil:* **s. par fanions,** *Nau:* **s. à pavillons,** flag signal; **s. lumineux,** light signal; *Adm:* **signaux lumineux,** traffic lights; **s. avertisseur, s. d'avertissement, s. d'alerte,** warning signal; **s. d'alerte aérienne,** air-raid warning (signal); **s. de fin d'alerte (aérienne, etc.),** all-clear (signal); **s. d'alarme,** alarm signal; **s. d'incendie,** fire alarm; *Nau:* **s. de brume,** fog signal; **s. de détresse,** distress, S.O.S., signal; *Nau: W.Tel:* **s. horaire,** time signal; *Rail:* **s. à distance, s. avancé,** distant (block) signal; **s. rapproché, s. d'entrée,** home signal; **s. d'arrêt,** danger signal; **s. à l'arrêt,** signal at danger; **s. d'arrêt absolu,** stop signal; *Aut:* **signaux routiers,** road signs; (*b*) *Elcs: W.Tel:* signal; *Rad:* trace, signal; *T.V: etc:* **s. d'image, s. vidéo,** picture signal, video signal; **signaux parasites,** clutter;

Tp: **s. d'appel,** calling signal; *Cmptr:* **s. d'invitation à transmettre,** proceed-to-send signal, *U.S:* start dialling signal; **s. de (sortie) lecture,** sense signal; (*c*) *Surv:* target (over a bench mark).

signalé [siɲale] *a.* **1.** *Trans: etc:* indicated by a warning sign. **2.** *Lit:* signal, outstanding (service).

signalement [siɲalmɑ̃] *n.m.* description; particulars.

signaler [siɲale] **1.** *v.tr.* (*a*) *O:* to make (sth.) conspicuous; (*b*) to point out (**qch. à qn,** sth. to s.o.); to call, draw, attention to (sth.); to signal (s.o., sth.) out; to refer to (a fact); **s. un livre à qn,** to recommend a book to s.o.; (*c*) to notify; to report; **rien à s.,** nothing to report; *Nau:* **date à laquelle un navire a été signalé pour la dernière fois,** date when a ship was last spoken; (*d*) to signal (train, ship, etc.); *Av:* to indicate the position of (a runway); (*e*) *Cmptr:* to post. **2. se s.,** to distinguish oneself (**par,** by); to have a reputation (for); **se s. dans les sciences,** to have reputation as a scientist; **se s. à l'attention de qn,** to catch s.o.'s eye.

signalétique [siɲaletik] *a. Adm:* descriptive (of a person); **fiche s.,** description (in police records).

signaleur [siɲalœr] *n.m. Mil: etc:* signaller; *Rail:* signalman.

signalisation [siɲalizasjɔ̃] *n.f.* **1.** signalling. **2.** (*a*) (road, etc.) signs; signposting; **s. routière internationale,** international (system of) road signs; **panneau de s.,** direction indicator; **feux de s.,** traffic lights; (*b*) *Av:* beaconing (of runway).

signaliser [siɲalize] *v.tr.* to signpost (road).

signataire [siɲatɛr] *n.* signer, signatory.

signature [siɲatyr] *n.f.* **1.** signing; **pour s.,** for signature. **2.** signature; **apposer sa s. à un acte,** to sign a document; *Com:* **la s. sociale,** the signature of the firm; **avoir la s.,** to be authorized to sign (on behalf of the firm, etc.); **livre de signatures,** autograph book. **3.** *Typ:* signature.

signe [siɲ] *n.m.* **1.** sign; indication (of rain, etc.); symptom (of illness); mark, token (of friendship, etc.); **ne donner aucun s. de vie, ne pas donner s. de vie,** to show no sign of life; **un s. des temps,** a sign of the times; **la réunion a eu lieu sous le s. de la cordialité,** cordiality was the keynote of the proceedings; **c'est bon s., mauvais s.,** it's a good, bad, sign. **2.** sign, symbol, mark; insignia (of rank); **s. algébrique,** algebraical sign; **les signes de (la) ponctuation,** the punctuation marks; *Typ:* **signes de correction,** proof correction marks; *Mus:* **signes constitutifs,** key signature; **s. du zodiaque,** sign of the zodiac; **s. de chance,** lucky sign; *Cmptr:* **chiffre de s.,** sign digit. **3.** (distinctive) mark (on the body); *Adm:* **signes particuliers,** special peculiarities (of pers.). **4.** sign, gesture, motion; **parler par signes,** to talk by signs; **s. d'adieu,** farewell wave (of the hand); **s. de l'œil,** wink; **faire s. à qn,** (i) to make a sign to s.o.; (ii) to get in touch with s.o.; **faire s. à qn de faire qch.,** to signal to s.o. to do sth.; **je lui ai fait s. de venir,** I beckoned to him to come; **il fit s. de se taire,** he gave a signal for silence; **faire s. à qn de la main de reculer, de s'écarter, de partir,** to wave s.o. back, aside, off, away; **faire s. que oui,** to nod (in agreement); **faire s. que non,** to shake one's head (in dissent).

signer [siɲe] **1.** *v.tr.* to sign (a document); *v.ind.tr.* **s. à un document,** to witness a document; **s. (à) un contrat,** to become a party to an agreement; *Com:* **s. à l'arrivée,** to check in; to sign for (goods); *Nau:* **s. l'engagement,** to sign on; *F:* **c'est signé,** it's easy to guess who did that; **c'est signé Paul,** that's just like Paul, it's typical of Paul; (*b*) **2.** *Tchn:* to hallmark (jewellery). **2.** *Ecc:* **se s.,** to cross oneself.

signet [siɲɛ] *n.m. Bookb:* bookmark(er).

signifiant [siɲifjɑ̃] **1.** *a.* (*a*) *Lit:* meaningful, expressive; (*b*) *Theol:* significant (signs of grace). **2.** *n.m. Ling:* significans.

significatif, -ive [siɲifikatif, -iv] *a.* significant.

signification [siɲifikasjɔ̃] *n.f.* **1.** meaning, significance, sense, acceptation (of a word, symbol). **2.** *Jur:* notification; serving (of writ).

signifié [siɲifje] *n.m. Ling:* signification.

signifier [siɲifje] *v.tr.* (*impf. & pr.sub.* **n. signifiions, v. signifiiez**) **1.** (*a*) to mean, signify; **que signifie ce mot, cette cérémonie?** what is the meaning of this word, the significance of this ceremony? **cela ne signifie rien,** (i) it doesn't mean anything; (ii) it's of no importance; **des remarques qui ne signifient rien,** meaningless remarks; (*b*) *F:* (*denoting indignation*) **qu'est-ce que cela signifie?** what's the meaning of this? (*c*) **liberté ne signifie pas nécessairement anarchie,** liberty need not mean anarchy; **la moindre imprudence signifierait la mort pour eux,** the slightest imprudence would mean death for them. **2.** to notify (**qch. à qn,** s.o. of sth.); (*of landlord, employer*) **s. son congé à qn,** to give s.o. notice.

sikh, -e [sik] *a. & n. Indian Rel: Ethn:* Sikh.

silence [silɑ̃s] *n.m.* **1.** silence; *Rec:* pause; **il se fit un s. subit,** there was a sudden silence, a sudden pause (in the conversation), a sudden hush; **un s. de mort,** a deathly hush; **s. ému, anxieux,** breathless silence; **réduire qn au s.,** to reduce s.o. to silence; to silence s.o.; **rompre le s.,** to break (the) silence; **garder, observer, le s.,** to keep silent (**sur,** about); **(du) s.!** silence! hush! be quiet! **souffrir en s.,** to suffer in silence; **passer qch. sous s.,** to hush sth. up; to keep sth. secret; **écrire à qn après un s. de deux ans,** to write to s.o. after a break, a silence, of two years; **préparer qch. dans le s.,** to prepare sth. in secrecy; **faire jurer le s. à qn,** to swear s.o. to secrecy; *Aer:* **cône de s.,** cone of silence; *Elcs:* **zone de s.,** silent zone. **2.** *Mus:* rest.

silencieusement [silɑ̃sjøzmɑ̃] *adv.* silently.

silencieux, -ieuse [silɑ̃sjø, -jøz] **1.** *a.* silent (person, footsteps); peaceful (evening); quiet (engine). **2.** *n.m.* (*a*) *I.C.E:* silencer, *NAm:* muffler; (*b*) *Sm.a:* silencer; (*c*) *W.Tel:* squelch.

Silène [silɛn] **1.** *Pr.n.m. Myth:* Silenus. **2.** *n.m.* (*a*) *Bot:* catchfly; campion; (*b*) *Z:* Silenus ape.

Silésie [silezi] *Pr.n.f. Geog:* Silesia.

silex [silɛks] *n.m.inv.* flint; **des s.,** flint implements.

silhouette [silwɛt] *n.f.* (*a*) silhouette; **en s.,** silhouetted; (*b*) (*of pers.*) figure; (*of building, etc.*) outline; (*c*) *Mil:* figure target.

silhouetter [silwete] **1.** *v.tr.* (*a*) to outline; (*b*) *Phot:* to block out. **2. se s.,** to be silhouetted, to stand out, show up (against the horizon, etc.).

silicate [silikat] *n.m. Ch:* silicate; **s. de potasse,** waterglass.

silice [silis] *n.f. Ch:* silica; silicon dioxide.

siliceux, -euse [silisø, -øz] *a.* siliceous.

silicium [silisjɔm] *n.m. Ch:* silicon.

silicone [silikɔn] *n.f. Ch:* silicone.

silicose [silikoz] *n.f. Med:* silicosis.

silique [silik] *n.f. Bot:* siliqua, silique; pod.

sillage [sijaʒ] *n.m.* (*a*) wake, track, furrow (of ship); **marcher dans le s. de qn,** to follow in s.o.'s wake; (*b*) *Av: etc:* slipstream; **s. aérodynamique,** aerodynamic drag.

sillet [sijɛ] *n.m.* nut (of stringed instrument).

sillon [sijɔ̃] *n.m.* **1.** (*a*) *Agr:* furrow; (small) drill; (*b*) *pl. Lit:* fields, country; (*c*) furrow, line (on the forehead, etc.). **2.** track, trail (of wheel); wake (of ship); path (of projectile); **s. de lumière, de feu,** streak of light, of fire (of rocket, etc.). **3.** *Anat: Rec:* groove.

sillonner [sijɔne] *v.tr.* (*a*) to furrow; to plough, *NAm:* plow (the seas); **flanc de montagne sillonné par les torrents,** mountainside grooved, scored, by torrents; **forêt sillonnée de nombreux sentiers,** forest crossed by many paths; **front sillonné de rides,** furrowed brow; (*b*) (*of light, lightning, etc.*) to streak (the sky).

silo [silo] *n.m.* (*a*) *Agr:* silo; clamp; **mettre en s.,** to silo, to bury; (*b*) silo, elevator; **s. à blé,** grain elevator; (*c*) **s. à ciment,** cement bin; (*d*) *Ball:* **s. de lancement,** launching silo.

silotage [silɔtaʒ] *n.m. Agr: etc:* ensilage.

silure [silyr] *n.m. Ich:* catfish, sheatfish.

silurien, -ienne [silyrjɛ̃, -jɛn] *a. & n.m. Geol:* Silurian; **s. inférieur,** Ordovician.

simagrée [simagre] *n.f.* (*a*) pretence; (*b*) *usu. pl.* affected airs; grimaces; affectation; **ne fais pas tant de simagrées,** don't make so much fuss.

simien, -ienne [simjɛ̃, -jɛn] *Z:* **1.** *a.* simian. **2.** *n.m.pl.* **simiens,** Simiidae, the simians.

simiesque [simjɛsk] *a.* simiesque; monkey-like, apelike, apish (face, grimace).

similaire [similɛr] **1.** *a.* similar (**à** to); like; of the same kind. **2.** *n.m. Nau:* sister ship.

similairement [similɛrmɑ̃] *adv.* similarly.

similarité [similarite] *n.f.* similarity, likeness.

simili [simili] **1.** *pref.* imitation; artificial. **2.** *n.m. F: O:* imitation; *Tex:* silk-finished cotton; *Phot:* halftone; **bijoux en s.,** imitation, costume, jewel(le)ry. **3.** *n.f. F:* = SIMILIGRAVURE.

similicuir [similikɥir] *n.m.* artificial leather, imitation leather; leatherette.

similigravure [similigravyr] *n.f.* process engraving; half-tone (engraving, block).

similisage [similizaʒ] *n.m. Tex:* silk finishing (of cottons).

similiser [similize] *v.tr. Tex:* to silk-finish, schreiner (cotton).

similitude [similityd] *n.f.* resemblance, likeness (of two people, things); similarity (of ideas, expressions).

simoniaque [simɔnjak] *Ecc:* **1.** *a.* simoniac(al). **2.** *n.m.* simoniac, simonist.

simonie [simɔni] *n.f. Ecc:* simony.

simoun [simun] *n.m. Meteor:* simoom, simoon.

simple [sɛ̃pl̥] *a.* simple. **1.** (*a*) single (flower, ticket, etc.); *n.m. Ten:* **jouer un s.,** to play a singles match; **s. messieurs, dames,** men's, ladies', singles; (*b*) (*not compound*) *Turf:* **faire un pari s.,** to back a horse to win; *Gram:* **passé s.,** past historic (tense); *Ch:* **corps s.,** element; *Mth:* **équation s.,** simple equation. **2.** (*a*) ordinary, common; **un s. particulier,** a private citizen; **s. soldat,** private (soldier); **s. matelot,** ordinary seaman; (*b*) **condamner qn sur un s. soupçon,** to condemn s.o. on a mere, bare, suspicion; **c'est une s. question de temps,** it is simply a matter of time; **c'est de la folie pure et s.,** it's sheer madness; **croire qn sur sa s. parole,** to believe s.o. on his word alone; **la s. prudence veut que . . .,** ordinary, elementary, prudence demands that . . .; (*c*) plain, simple, unaffected (pers.); simple (dress, food, truth); **modestie s.,** unaffected, natural, modesty; (*d*) easy, straightforward (method); **c'est s. comme bonjour,** it's as easy as pie, as falling off a log. **3.** (*a*) simple-minded; *n.m.* **c'est un s. (d'esprit),** he's a moron, a halfwit; (*b*) ingenuous; credulous; *F:* green. **4.** *n.m. usu.pl.* **simples,** medicinal herbs.

simplement [sɛ̃pləmɑ̃] *adv.* simply. **1.** plainly (dressed, etc.); **vivre s.,** to live simply. **2.** naturally, unaffectedly; **le plus s. du monde,** without any fuss. **3.** ingenuously. **4.** just, merely; **purement et s.,** purely and simply.

simplet, -ette [sɛ̃plɛ, -ɛt] *a.* simple, artless, ingenuous.

simplex [sɛ̃plɛks] *n.m. Cmptr:* simplex.

simplicité [sɛ̃plisite] *n.f.* **1.** (*a*) simplicity (of dress, manners, etc.); **en toute s.,** without affectation; simply; naturally; **venez en toute s.,** (i) come as you are; (ii) come and take pot luck; (*b*) elementary nature (of atoms, etc.). **2.** artlessness, simpleness; simplemindedness.

simplifiable [sɛ̃plifjabl̥] *a.* that can be simplified, capable of simplification.

simplificateur, -trice [sɛ̃plifikatœr, -tris] **1.** *a.* simplifying (method). **2.** *n.m.* simplifier.

simplification [sɛ̃plifikasjɔ̃] *n.f.* simplification; *Mth:* cancelling (out); *Ind: etc:* **s. du travail,** time and motion study.

simplifier [sɛ̃plifje] *v.tr.* (*impf. & pr.sub.* **n. simplifiions, v. simplifiiez**) to simplify; **s. une fraction,** to reduce a fraction to its lowest terms; **trop s.,** to oversimplify.

simplisme [sɛ̃plism] *n.m.* over-simplification.

simpliste [sɛ̃plist] *a.* simplistic, over-simple (theory, explanation); superficial (mind).

simulacre [simylakr̥] *n.m.* (*a*) simulacrum, image; (*b*) semblance, show; pretence; *Mil:* dummy (grenade, tank, etc.); **s. de résistance,** show of resistance; *Mil:* **s. de combat,** sham fight; **son procès ne fut qu'un s.,** his trial was a mere mockery.

simulateur, -trice [simylatœr, -tris] (*a*) *n.* pretender; malingerer; (*b*) *n.m. Tchn:* simulator; *Av:* **s. de vol,** flight simulator.

simulation [simylasjɔ̃] *n.f.* (*a*) simulation; pretence; malingering; (*b*) *Av: Elcs: Cmptr: etc:* simulation.

simulé [simyle] *a.* feigned (illness); sham (fight); bogus (sale); simulated (ivory, etc.).

simuler [simyle] *v.tr.* to simulate; to feign, sham; **s. une maladie,** to pretend to be ill; to malinger.

simultané [simyltane] *a.* simultaneous.

simultanéité [simyltaneite] *n.f.* simultaneousness, simultaneity.

simultanément [simyltanemɑ̃] *adv.* simultaneously.

sinapisé [sinapize] *a.* **bain s.,** mustard bath.

sinapisme [sinapism] *n.m. Med:* (*a*) mustard plaster; sinapism; (*b*) mustard poultice.

sincère [sɛ̃sɛr] *a.* **1.** sincere, frank, candid (person); candid (opinion). **2.** (*a*) sincere, genuine, honest (person); (*b*) genuine, sincere (joy, sorrow, etc.); sincere, earnest (effort, etc.); **vœux, remerciements, sincères,** heartfelt wishes, thanks; **agréez mes sincères salutations,** yours sincerely; (*c*) (*of document, etc.*) authentic.

sincèrement [sɛ̃sɛrmɑ̃] *adv.* sincerely. **1.** frankly, candidly. **2.** genuinely (glad, etc.).

sincérité [sɛ̃serite] *n.f.* (*a*) sincerity, frankness, candour, *NAm:* candor; (*b*) genuineness (of regret, etc.).

sinécure [sinekyr] *n.f.* sinecure; *F:* **ce n'est pas une s.,** it's not exactly a rest cure.

sine die [sinedje] *adv.phr.* sine die.

sine qua non [sinekwanɔn] *adj.phr.* sine qua non.

Singapour [sɛ̃gapur] *Pr.n.m. Geog:* Singapore.

singe [sɛ̃ʒ] *n.m.* **1.** (*a*) monkey; ape; **laid comme un s.,** as ugly as sin; *Prov:* **on n'apprend pas à un vieux s. à faire des grimaces,** don't teach your grandmother to suck eggs; (*b*) *F:* ape, imitator; (*c*) *F:* ugly person; fright; scarecrow. **2.** *Cu: P:* **du s.,** bully beef. **3.** *P:* **le s.,** the boss.

singer [sɛ̃ʒe] *v.tr.* **(je singeai(s); n. singeons)** to ape, mimic (s.o.); to take (s.o.) off.

singerie [sɛ̃ʒri] *n.f.* **1.** (*a*) grimace, monkey trick; (*b*) (grotesque) imitation. **2.** monkey house; apery.

single [siŋgl̥] *n.m.* **1.** *Ten:* singles (game). **2.** single-berth compartment (in wagon-lit, *esp. NAm:* sleeping car).

singulariser [sɛ̃gylarize] **1.** *v.tr.* to make (s.o.) conspicuous. **2. se s.,** to attract attention, make oneself conspicuous.

singularité [sɛ̃gylarite] *n.f.* singularity. **1.** (*a*) peculiarity; (*b*) **la s. de ces faits,** the unusualness of these facts. **2.** oddness, eccentricity (of conduct, etc.); **esprit de s.,** desire to be different. **3.** *Gram:* singular connotation (of an ending, etc.).

singulier, -ière [sɛ̃gylje, -jɛr] *a.* singular. **1.** (*a*) (*referring to one*) **combat s.,** single combat; *n. Gram:* **au s.,** in the singular; (*b*) peculiar (**à,** to). **2.** (*a*) peculiar, remarkable; (*b*) odd, curious, strange, queer (person, method, custom, fact); **il est s. qu'il ne soit pas encore arrivé,** it is strange that he has not arrived yet; (*c*) conspicuous; different (from other people).

singulièrement [sɛ̃gyljɛrmɑ̃] *adv.* **1.** (*a*) singularly; in a peculiar manner; (*b*) oddly, strangely, queerly; (*c*) conspicuously. **2.** specially, in particular, particularly, mainly.

sinistre [sinistr̥] **1.** *a.* (*a*) sinister; ominous; **événement s.,** fatal occurrence; **sourire s.,** sinister smile; (*b*) **un s. menteur,** an awful, a terrible, liar. **2.** *n.m.* (*a*) disaster, catastrophe (*esp.* fire, earthquake, shipwreck); (*b*) loss, damage (through disaster); *Ins:* **bonification pour non-s.,** no-claims bonus.

sinistré, -ée [sinistre] **1.** *a.* **bâtiment s.,** damaged, bombed, burnt-out, building; **zone sinistrée,** disaster area. **2.** *n.* victim of a disaster.

sinistrement [sinistrəmɑ̃] *adv.* sinisterly.

sinologue [sinɔlɔg] *n.* sinologue, sinologist; Chinese scholar.

sinon [sinɔ̃] *conj.* **1.** otherwise, (or) else, if not. **2.** except, unless; **il ne fait rien s. manger et boire,** he does nothing except eat and drink; **s. que,** except that.

sinoque [sinɔk] *a. P:* mad, crackers, crazy, nuts.

sinueux, -euse [sinɥø, -øz] *a.* sinuous; circuitous, winding (path); meandering (stream); tortuous (reasoning).

sinuosité [sinɥozite] *n.f.* **1.** (*a*) winding; meandering; (*b*) deviousness; tortuousness. **2.** bend, loop (of river, etc.).

sinus[1] [sinys] *n.m. Anat:* sinus.

sinus[2] *n.m. Mth:* sine.

sinusite [sinyzit] *n.f. Med:* sinusitis.

sinusoïdal, -aux [sinyzɔidal, -o] *a. Mth:* sinusoidal.

sinusoïde [sinyzɔid] *n.f. Mth:* sinusoid, sine curve.

sionisme [sjɔnism] *n.m.* Zionism.

sioniste [sjɔnist] *a. & n.* Zionist.

sioux [sju] *a. & n.inv. Ethn:* Sioux; **s'avancer avec des ruses de S.,** to proceed stealthily.

siphon [sifɔ̃] *n.m.* **1.** (*a*) *Ph: etc:* siphon; (*b*) (soda water) siphon; (*c*) *Const: etc:* trap (of sink pipe, drain, etc.); (*d*) *Geol:* siphon. **2.** *Z:* siphon, siphuncule.

siphonné [sifɔne] *a. F:* mad, crackers, crazy, nuts.

siphonner [sifɔne] *v.tr.* to siphon.

sire [sir] *n.m.* **1.** (*a*) *A:* lord, sir; **beau s.,** fair sir; (*b*) *Pej:* **un triste s.,** a sad specimen (of humanity). **2.** (*to emperor or king*) Sire.

sirène [sirɛn] *n.f.* **1.** (*a*) *Myth:* siren, mermaid; **chant de s.,** siren song; (*b*) *Fig:* (*woman*) siren. **2.** *Nau: Ind:* (*a*) siren, hooter, buzzer; (*b*) foghorn. **3.** *Rept:* siren.

siroc(c)o [sirɔko] *n.m. Meteor:* sirocco (wind).

sirop [siro] *n.m.* syrup; (fruit) cordial; *Med:* linctus; **s. de sucre,** golden syrup; **s. contre la toux,** cough mixture.

siroter [sirɔte] *v.tr. F:* to sip (one's wine, etc.).

sirupeux, -euse [sirypø, -øz] *a.* (*a*) syrupy; (*b*) sentimental.

sis [si] *a. Jur: & Lit:* located; **maison sise rue Saint-Honoré,** house situate(d) in the Rue Saint-Honoré.

sisal [sizal] *n.m. Bot:* sisal.

sismal, -aux [sismal, -o] *a.* seismal.

sismicité [sismisite] *n.f.* seismicity.

sismique [sismik] *a.* seismic (movement).

sismogramme [sismɔgram] *n.m.* seismogram.

sismographe [sismɔgraf] *n.m.* seismograph.

sismographie [sismɔgrafi] *n.f.* seismography.

sismologie [sismɔlɔʒi] *n.f.* seismology.

sismomètre [sismɔmɛtr̥] *n.m.* seismometer.

site [sit] *n.m.* **1.** (*a*) (picturesque) site; beauty spot; (*b*) (building, archaeological) site. **2.** (*a*) *Civ.E: Mil:* lie of the ground; (*b*) *Artil: Surv: etc:* **ligne de s.,** line of sight.

sitôt [sito] *adv.* (*a*) (= AUSSITÔT) as soon, so soon; **s. le soleil couché,** as soon as the sun was set; **s. dit s. fait,** no sooner said than done; *conj.phr.* **s. que** + *ind.*, as soon as . . .; *Lit:* **s. après,** immediately after; (*b*) (*with neg.*) **vous ne le reverrez pas de s.,** it will be some time, a good while, before you see him again.

situation [sitɥasjɔ̃] *n.f.* **1.** (*a*) situation, position, site (of a town, etc.); (*b*) *Nau:* bearing. **2.** (*a*) state, condition; (social, financial, etc.) position, standing; **être en s. de faire qch.,** to be in a position to do sth.; **je lui ai exposé ma s.,** I explained to him how I was placed, how I stood; *F:* **elle est dans une s. intéressante,** she is pregnant, in an interesting condition; **l'homme de la s.,** the right man in the right place; *adv.phr.* **en s.,** appropriate; (*b*) *Adm: Mil: etc:* report, return; **s. de la banque,** bank return, bank statement. **3. il a une belle s.,** he has a good job; **se faire une belle s.,** to work one's way up into a good position; *Journ:* **situations vacantes,** appointments, situations, vacant.

situé [sitɥe] *a.* (*of town, house, etc.*) situated (**à,** at).

situer [sitɥe] *v.tr.* to place, situate, locate (a house, etc.); to place (sth. in its context); *F:* **s. qn,** to make s.o. out, size s.o. up; *Th: etc:* **l'action se situe à Rome en 1516,** the action takes place in Rome in 1516.

six *num.a.inv. & n.m.* (*before noun beginning with consonant* [si]; *before noun beginning with vowel sound* [siz]; *otherwise* [sis]) six; **le s. mai,** the sixth of May, May (the) sixth; **Charles S.,** Charles the Sixth; **le s. de cœur,** the six of hearts.

sixain [sizɛ̃] *n.m.* = SIZAIN.

six-huit [sisɥit] *n.m. Mus:* six-eight time.

sixième [sizjɛm] **1.** *num.a. & n.* sixth; **au s. (étage),** on the sixth floor, *NAm:* seventh floor. **2.** *n.m.* sixth (part); **cinq sixièmes,** five sixths. **3.** *n.f. Sch:* = first form (of secondary school).

sixièmement [sizjɛmmɑ̃] *adv.* in the sixth place.

six-quatre-deux (à la) [alasiskatdø] *adv.phr. F:* **faire qch. à la s.-q.-d.,** to do sth. in a slapdash manner; to dash sth. off.

sixte [sikst] *n.f.* **1.** *Mus:* sixth. **2.** *Fenc:* sixte.

Sixtine [sikstin] *a.f.* Sistine (Chapel).

sizain [sizɛ̃] *n.m.* **1.** set of six packs, *NAm:* decks, of playing cards. **2.** *Pros:* sextain, six-line stanza.

sizaine [sizɛn] *n.f. Scout:* (cub, brownie) six.

sketch [skɛtʃ] *n.m. Th:* sketch; *pl. sketches.*

ski [ski] *n.m.* **1.** ski; **descendre à, en, skis,** to ski down; **saut en, à, ski(s),** ski jump(ing). **2.** skiing; **faire du s.,** to ski; **il aime faire du s.,** he's fond of skiing; **chaussures de s.,** ski boots; **saut de s.,** (i) ski jump; (ii) *Civ.E:* ski jump, spillway. **3. s. nautique,** water skiing; **faire du s. nautique,** to water-ski.

skiable [skjabl̥] *a.* fit for skiing.

skier [skje] *v.i.* to ski.

skieur, -euse [skjœr, -øz] *n.* skier; *Mil:* **éclaireurs skieurs,** ski troops.

skiff [skif] *n.m. Nau:* skiff.

skip [skip] *n.m. Ind:* skip.

slalom [slalɔm] *n.m. Ski:* slalom; *F:* **faire du s. entre les voitures,** to dodge in and out among the cars.

slave [slav] **1.** *a.* Slav(onic). **2.** *n.* Slav. **3.** *n.m. Ling:* Slavonic.

slavisant, -ante [slavizɑ̃, -ɑ̃t] *n.*, **slaviste** [slavist] *n.* Slavist.
sleeping [slipiŋ] *n.m. Rail: F: O:* (*a*) sleeping car; (*b*) berth.
slip [slip] *n.m.* **1.** *Cost:* briefs; (woman's) pants, panties, knickers; (men's) underpants, *NAm:* shorts; **s. de bain,** swimming trunks; **s. de soutien (pour sportifs),** athletic support, *F:* jockstrap. **2.** *Nau:* slipway.
slogan [slɔgɑ̃] *n.m. Com: Pol:* slogan.
sloop [slup] *n.m. Nau:* sloop; **s. à tape-cul,** yawl.
sloughi [slugi] *n.m.* (*dog*) saluki.
slovaque [slɔvak] *a. & n. Geog: Ling:* Slovak.
slovène [slɔvɛn] **1.** *a. & n. Ethn:* Slovene, Slovenian. **2.** *n.m. Ling:* **le s.,** Slovenian.
slow [slo] *n.m.* slow music, dance, foxtrot.
smala [smala] *n.f.* (*a*) (Arab chief's) retinue; (*b*) *F:* (*family, etc.*) **toute la s.,** the whole tribe.
smash [smaʃ] *n.m. Ten: etc:* smash.
smasher [smaʃe] *v.tr. & i. Ten: etc:* to smash (the ball).
smectique [smɛktik] *a.* **argile s.,** fuller's earth.
smicard, -arde [smikar, -ard] *n. F:* worker on minimum basic wage.
smocks [smɔk] *n.m.pl. Needlew:* smocking.
smoking [smɔkiŋ] *n.m.* dinner jacket, *NAm:* tuxedo.
snack(-bar) [snak(bar)] *n.m. F:* snack bar; *pl. snack-bars, snacks.*
snob [snɔb] **1.** snob. **2.** *a.* (*a*) snobbish, snobby; (*b*) pretentious; posh, smart (restaurant, etc.).
snober [snɔbe] *v.tr. Pej:* to look down on (s.o.); to snub (s.o.).
snobinard, -arde [snɔbinar, -ard] *a. & n. F: Pej:* **il est, c'est un, s.,** he's a bit of a snob.
snobisme [snɔbism] *n.m.* snobbery; **s. à rebours,** inverted snobbery.
sobre [sɔbr̥] *a.* **1.** temperate; abstemious (person); moderate (meal). **2.** sparing (of words, praise). **3.** restrained (drawing, style).
sobrement [sɔbrəmɑ̃] *adv.* soberly. **1.** moderately, frugally. **2.** quietly (dressed).
sobriété [sɔbrijete] *n.f.* temperateness, abstemiousness (in food and drink); moderation (in speech, etc.); restraint (in style); **manger et boire avec s.,** to eat and drink in moderation.
sobriquet [sɔbrikɛ] *n.m.* nickname.
soc [sɔk] *n.m.* ploughshare, *NAm:* plowshare.
sociabilité [sɔsjabilite] *n.f.* sociability, sociableness.
sociable [sɔsjabl̥] *a.* sociable; **peu s.,** unsociable.
social, -ale, -aux [sɔsjal, -o] *a.* (*a*) social; **l'ordre s.,** the social order; **science sociale,** social science, sociology; **œuvres sociales,** welfare activities; **guerre sociale,** class war; **l'échelle sociale,** the social ladder; *Z:* **animal s.,** social animal; (*b*) *Com:* **nom s., raison sociale,** name, style, of the firm; **siège s.,** head office.
social-démocrate [sɔsjaldemɔkrat] *a. & n. Pol:* social democrat; *pl. sociaux-démocrates.*
social-démocratie [sɔsjaldemɔkrasi] *n.f. Pol:* social democracy.
socialement [sɔsjalmɑ̃] *adv.* socially.
socialisant, -ante [sɔsjalizɑ̃, -ɑ̃t] *a. & n. Pol:* (person) with socialist tendencies.
socialisation [sɔsjalizasjɔ̃] *n.f. Pol.Ec:* socialization, collectivization (of capital, industries).
socialiser [sɔsjalize] *v.tr. Pol.Ec:* to socialize, collectivize (property, etc.).
socialisme [sɔsjalism] *n.m.* socialism; **s. d'État,** State socialism; **s. chrétien,** Christian socialism.
socialiste [sɔsjalist] *a. & n.* socialist.
sociétaire [sɔsjetɛr] *n.* (*a*) member; (*b*) shareholder.
société [sɔsjete] *n.f.* **1.** (*a*) society; community; **devoirs envers la s.,** duty to society, to the community; (*b*) company, gathering; group, circle; **ça ne se fait pas dans la bonne s.,** that is not done in the best society; (*c*) **animaux qui vivent en s.,** social animals. **2.** (*a*) society, association; *Sp:* club; *Hist:* **la S. des Nations,** the League of Nations; **s. de secours aux blessés,** first-aid association; (*b*) *Com: Ind:* company, firm; partnership; **s. par actions,** joint-stock company, *U.S:* incorporated company; **s. anonyme,** public company; **s. à responsabilité limitée** = limited (liability) company; **s. d'utilité publique,** public utility company, *U.S:* utility; **s. de crédit mutuel,** friendly society; *Fin:* **s. à portefeuille,** holding company; **s. de placement,** investment trust. **3.** (*a*) company, companionship; **il aime la s.,** he likes company; (*b*) (fashionable) society; **femmes de s.,** society women; (*c*) **jeux de s.,** parlour, *NAm:* parlor, games.
socio-culturel, -elle [sɔsjɔkyltyrɛl] *a.* sociocultural; *pl. socio-culturel, -elles.*
sociodrame [sɔsjɔdram] *n.m. Psy:* sociodrama.
socio-économique [sɔsjɔekɔnɔmik] *a.* socio-economic; *pl. socio-économiques.*
sociogramme [sɔsjɔgram] *n.m. Psy:* sociogram.
sociologie [sɔsjɔlɔʒi] *n.f.* sociology.
sociologique [sɔsjɔlɔʒik] *a.* sociological.
sociologisme [sɔsjɔlɔʒism] *n.m.* sociologism.
sociologue [sɔsjɔlɔg] *n.* sociologist.
sociométrie [sɔsjɔmetri] *n.f.* sociometry.
socle [sɔkl̥] *n.m.* base, pedestal, plinth (for statue, column); stand (for apparatus); base, socket (for mast, etc.); bed plate (of engine); *Geol:* insular shelf; base; *Const:* **s. de lambris,** skirting board.
socque [sɔk] *n.m.* clog; patten.
socquette [sɔkɛt] *n.f.* ankle sock, *NAm:* bobby sock.
Socrate [sɔkrat] *Pr.n.m.* Socrates.
socratique [sɔkratik] *a.* Socratic.
soda [sɔda] *n.m.* **s. à l'orange,** orangeade.
sodique [sɔdik] *a. Ch:* (of) sodium.
sodium [sɔdjɔm] *n.m. Ch:* sodium.
sodomie [sɔdɔmi] *n.f.* sodomy.
sodomite [sɔdɔmit] *n.m.* sodomite.
sœur [sœr] *n.f.* **1.** sister; **baiser de s.,** sisterly kiss; *P:* **et ta s.!** tell that to the marines! **2.** *Ecc:* sister, nun; **entrez, ma s.,** come in, sister.
sofa [sɔfa] *n.m.* sofa, settee.
soffite [sɔfit] *n.m. Arch:* soffit.
software [sɔftwɛr] *n.m. Cmptr:* software.
soi [swa] *pers.pron.* (*stressed, usu., but not always, referring to an indef. subject*) oneself; himself, herself, itself, etc. **1.** (*reflexive or reciprocal*) **parler de s.,** to talk about oneself; **chacun pour s.,** everyone for himself; **en s.,** in itself, per se; **il va de s. que . . .,** it goes without saying that . . .; **avoir la loi pour s.,** to have the law on one's side; **il n'est plus maître de s.,** he is no longer master of himself; **se parler à s.-même,** to talk to oneself; **petits services qu'on se rend entre s.,** small mutual services. **2.** (*emphatic*) **pour s'assurer qu'une chose sera bien faite, il faut la faire s.-même,** if you want a thing well done, you must do it yourself.
soi-disant [swadizɑ̃] **1.** *a.inv.* (*a*) self-styled, would-be; **une s.-d. comtesse,** a self-styled countess; (*b*) so-called; **les arts s.-d. libéraux,** the so-called liberal arts. **2.** *adv.* supposedly, ostensibly; **il est parti s.-d. pour réfléchir,** he went away, ostensibly to think it over.
soie[1] [swa] *n.f.* **1.** bristle (of wild boar, caterpillar, etc.); **couvert de soies,** bristly. **2.** (*a*) silk; **robe de s.,** silk dress; **papier de s.,** tissue paper; (*b*) **s. de verre,** fibreglass, *NAm:* fiberglass.
soie[2] *n.f. Tchn:* tang (of file, blade, etc.).
soierie [swari] *n.f.* silk goods; silk trade.
soif [swaf] *n.f.* thirst; (*a*) **avoir s.,** to be thirsty, dry; **boire à sa s.,** *F:* **boire jusqu'à plus s.,** to drink one's

fill; **cela me donne s.,** it makes me thirsty; **rester sur sa s.,** to remain unsatisfied; (*b*) thirst, craving (for wealth, power, etc.); **avoir s. de sang,** to be bloodthirsty.

soiffard, -arde [swafar, -ard] *a. & n. P:* boozy (person); *n.* boozer.

soigné [swaɲe] *a.* (*a*) well finished, carefully done; neat; trim; carefully prepared (meal); polished (style); groomed (appearance, horse); well-kept (hands); **elle est très soignée de sa personne,** she is very careful, particular, about her appearance; **peu s.,** slovenly; (*b*) *P:* **une raclée soignée,** a sound thrashing; **un rhume s.,** a hell, a stinker, of a cold.

soigner [swaɲe] *v.tr.* to look after, take care of (s.o., sth.); to attend to (sth.); (*a*) to nurse, look after; (*of doctor*) to attend (a patient); **s. une maladie,** to treat an illness; **se s.,** (i) to take care of, look after, oneself; (ii) *F:* to coddle oneself; (iii) *F:* to do oneself well; **cette maladie ne se soigne pas bien,** this disease is very difficult to treat; **il faut te faire s.,** (i) you should have treatment, see a doctor; (ii) *F:* you need your head examining! (*b*) to keep (sth.) in good order; to take care over (sth.); **s. sa popularité,** to nurse one's public; **s. sa ligne,** to watch one's figure.

soigneur [swaɲœr] *n.m. Cy: Rac: etc:* second; trainer.

soigneusement [swaɲøzmɑ̃] *adv.* carefully.

soigneux, -euse [swaɲø, -øz] *a.* careful; tidy (person, work).

soi-même [swamɛm] *pers.pron.* oneself; *see* SOI *and* MÊME 1 (*c*).

soin [swɛ̃] *n.m.* (*a*) care; **le s. des enfants,** the care of children; looking after children; **avoir, prendre, s. de qn, de qch.,** to look after, take care of, s.o., sth.; **confier qch. aux soins de qn,** to place sth. in s.o.'s care; to entrust s.o. with sth.; (*on letters, etc.*) **aux (bons) soins de . . .,** care of . . ., c/o; **par les soins de . . .,** by courtesy of . . .; thanks to . . .; **les soins du ménage,** housekeeping; **il prend peu de s. de sa personne,** he is very careless, slovenly, about his appearance; (*b*) care, trouble; attention; **avoir s., grand s., bien s., de faire qch.,** to take (particular) care, to be careful, to do sth.; to make a point of doing sth.; **avoir s. que** + *sub.*, to see that (sth. is done, etc.); to make a point of (sth. being done, etc.); **mettre tous ses soins à faire qch., à ce que qch. soit fait,** to put oneself to great trouble, take great pains, to do sth., to see that sth. is done; **je vous laisse le s. de décider,** I leave it to you to decide; (*c*) **avoir beaucoup de s.,** to be very tidy, orderly; **avec s.,** carefully; with care; **avec (beaucoup de) s.,** with (great) care; **sans s.,** careless(ly); untid(il)y; **manque de s.,** carelessness; (*d*) *pl.* care, attention; **soins médicaux,** medical care, aid; **premiers soins,** first aid; **les soins dont il entoure sa femme, son jardin,** the care he lavishes on his wife, his garden; **être aux petits soins pour, avec, qn,** to fuss over s.o.; to wait hand and foot on s.o.; (*e*) *A:* anxiety, worry.

soir [swar] *n.m.* evening; **ce s.,** this evening, tonight; **à ce s.!** see you tonight, this evening! **il fait frais le s.,** it's cool in the evening; **que faites-vous le s.?** what do you do in the evening? **à dix heures du s.,** at ten (o'clock) in the evening; **lundi, demain, hier, (au) s.,** Monday, tomorrow, yesterday, evening; **tous les lundis s.,** every Monday evening; **le lendemain s.,** the next evening; **la veille au s.,** the evening before, on the previous evening; **travailler du matin au s.,** to work from morning until night.

soirée [sware] *n.f.* **1.** (duration of) evening; **passer la s. chez un ami,** to spend the evening at a friend's house; **les longues soirées d'hiver,** the long winter evenings; **bonne s.!** have a good evening (out)! enjoy your evening! **2.** (*a*) (evening) party; **s. dansante,** dance; **s. musicale,** musical evening; **tenue de s.,** evening dress; **en fin de s.,** (i) late in the evening; (ii) last thing in the evening; (*b*) *Th: etc:* **représentation de s., donnée en s.,** evening performance.

soissons [swasɔ̃] *n.m.* (variety of) haricot bean.

soit [swa; *before a vowel or as int:* swat] (*third pers. of pr.sub. of* **être**) **1.** (*a*) *int.* all right! O.K.! agreed! **s., allez,** all right then, go; (*b*) suppose; if for instance; **s. trois multiplié par six,** if three is multiplied by six; **s.** *ABC* **un triangle,** let *ABC* be a triangle; given a triangle *ABC*; (*c*) **trois objets à dix francs, s. trente francs,** three articles at ten francs, that is to say thirty francs. **2.** (*a*) *conj.* **s. . . . s. . . .; s. . . . ou . . .,** either . . . or . . .; whether . . . or . . .; **s. l'un s. l'autre,** either one or the other; **s. maintenant ou demain, cela arrivera sûrement,** whether it happens today or tomorrow, it is bound to happen; **s. modestie, s. paresse, il n'a jamais rien écrit,** whether from modesty or through laziness, he has never written anything; (*b*) *conj.phr.* **s. qu'il vienne, s., ou, qu'il ne vienne pas,** whether he comes or not.

soixantaine [swasɑ̃tɛn] *n.f.* (approximately) sixty, about sixty; **elle approche de la s.,** she's getting on for sixty; **avoir passé la s.,** to be in one's sixties.

soixante [swasɑ̃t] *num.a.inv. & n.m.inv.* sixty; **page s.,** page sixty; **s. et un,** sixty-one; **s. et onze,** seventy-one; **s. et onzième,** seventy-first.

soixante-dix [swasɑ̃tdis] *num.a.inv. & n.m.inv.* seventy.

soixante-dixième [swasɑ̃tdizjɛm] **1.** *num.a. & n.* seventieth. **2.** *n.m.* seventieth (part).

soixantième [swasɑ̃tjɛm] **1.** *num.a. & n.* sixtieth. **2.** *n.m.* sixtieth (part).

soja [sɔja] *n.m. Bot:* soya bean, soy.

sol¹ [sɔl] *n.m.* (*a*) ground, earth; **le s. natal,** one's native soil; **au s.,** at ground level; *El:* **relier un fil au s.,** to earth, *NAm:* ground, a wire; **conducteur au s.,** earthed, *NAm:* grounded, conductor; **cloué au s.,** (i) *Av:* grounded; (ii) *Fig:* rooted to the spot; **position s.,** ground position; *Aer:* **personnel au s.,** ground staff; (*b*) *Geol: Agr:* soil; (*c*) floor.

sol² *n.m.inv. Mus:* **1.** (the note) G; **morceau en s.,** piece in G. **2.** sol, soh (in the fixed do system).

sol-air [sɔlɛr] *a.inv. Ball:* ground-to-air (missile).

solaire [sɔlɛr] *a.* solar; **cadran s.,** sundial; **lunettes solaires,** sunglasses; **crème s.,** sun lotion; *Med:* **traitement s.,** sunray treatment; *Astr:* **taches solaires,** sunspots; *Anat:* **plexus s.,** solar plexus.

solarium [sɔlarjɔm] *n.m.* (*a*) *Med:* solarium (for sunbathing); (*b*) suntrap; sun terrace.

soldat, -ate [sɔlda, -at] **1.** *n.m.* soldier; serviceman; **s. du génie,** engineer; **s. de marine,** marine; **s. de 2e classe, simple s.,** private; **les simples soldats,** the rank and file; **le S. inconnu,** the Unknown Warrior; **se faire s.,** to go into the army; **s. de fortune,** soldier of fortune; **vieux s.,** old campaigner; (*b*) *n.m. Av:* **s. de 2e classe, de première classe,** aircraftman second-class, first-class; (*c*) *n.f.* **soldate,** servicewoman; (*d*) *adv.phr.* **à la soldate,** in a soldierly, soldier-like, way, fashion; (*e*) *n.m. Toys:* **s. de plomb,** tin soldier. **2.** *n.m.* (*a*) *Ent:* **s. des bois,** soldier (ant); (*b*) *Crust:* **s. marin,** soldier (crab).

soldatesque [sɔldatɛsk] *Pej:* **1.** *a.* barrackroom (language, manners). **2.** *n.f.* army rabble.

solde¹ [sɔld] *n.f. Mil: etc:* pay; *Mil: Ind:* **feuille de s.,** payroll; **soldes et indemnités,** ordinary pay and allowances; **officier en demi-s.,** officer on half pay; **cahier de s.,** ledger; *Pej:* **être à la s. de qn,** to be in s.o.'s pay.

solde² *n.m. Com:* **1.** balance; **s. de compte,** balance of account; balance due; **s. débiteur, s. déficitaire,** debit balance; **s. créditeur,** credit balance, balance in hand; **paiement pour s.,** payment of balance, final instalment; **pour s. (de tout compte),** in (full) settlement; to close the account. **2.** (*a*) surplus stock, job lot, remnant; (*b*) **(vente de) soldes,** (i) (clearance) sale; (ii) bargain counter; **courir les soldes,** to go round the sales; *Publ:* **s. d'édition,** remainder(s); **(en) s.,** to clear; **je l'ai eu en s.,** I got it in a sale, the sales; **prix de s.,** bargain prices.

solder [sɔlde] *v.tr.* **1.** (*a*) *Com:* to balance (an account); **les comptes se soldent par un bénéfice net de . . .,** the accounts show a net profit of . . .; (*b*) *Com:* to settle, discharge, pay (off) (an account); **s. l'arriéré,** to make up back payments; (*c*) **se s. par,** to end in (failure, etc.). **2.** to sell off, clear (surplus stock); *Publ:* to remainder (book).

soldeur, -euse [sɔldœr, -øz] *n. Com:* buyer of clearance lines.

sole[1] [sɔl] *n.f.* sole (of animal's hoof).

sole[2] *n.f.* **1.** *Mec.E: Metall:* bed plate; *Min: Const:* sill. **2.** *Nau:* flat bottom (of vessel).

sole[3] *n.f. Ich:* sole.

sole[4] *n.f. Agr:* field (under crop rotation).

solécisme [sɔlesism] *n.m.* solecism.

soleil [sɔlɛj] *n.m.* **1.** (*a*) sun; **s. de minuit,** midnight sun; **s. d'eau,** watery sun; **il n'y a rien de nouveau sous le s.,** there is nothing new under the sun; *Fr.Hist:* **le Roi S.,** the Sun King, Louis XIV; *Cost:* **plissé s.,** sunray pleats; (*b*) **faux s.,** parhelion, mock sun, sun dog. **2.** sunshine; **il fait du s.,** the sun is shining; it's sunny; **dans le s.,** against the sun; **au (grand) s.,** in the sunshine, full in the sun; **avoir sa place au s.,** to have one's place in the sun; **prendre des bains de s.,** to sunbathe; **jour de s.,** sunny day; **sans s.,** sunless; **coup de s.,** (i) sunburn; (ii) touch of sunstroke; *F:* **piquer un s.,** to blush; **ôte-toi de mon s.!** get out of my light! **3.** *Bot:* sunflower. **4.** *Gym:* **grand s.,** grand circle. **5.** *Pyr:* Catherine wheel, *NAm:* pinwheel.

solennel, -elle [sɔlanɛl] *a.* **1.** solemn; formal, official (occasion, etc.). **2.** grave, solemn (tone); impressive (silence).

solennellement [sɔlanɛlmɑ̃] *adv.* solemnly. **1.** with ceremony; in state. **2.** impressively.

solenniser [sɔlanize] *v.tr.* to solemnize; to celebrate.

solennité [sɔlanite] *n.f.* **1.** (*a*) solemnity; (*b*) solemn ceremony. **2. avec s.,** impressively, solemnly.

solenoïde [sɔlenɔid] *n.m. El:* solenoid.

soleret [sɔlrɛ] *n.m. A.Arm:* solleret.

solfatare [sɔlfatar] *n.f. Geol:* solfatara, sulphur spring.

solfège [sɔlfɛʒ] *n.m. Mus:* solfa; **apprendre le s.,** to learn the rudiments of music.

solidaire [sɔlidɛr] *a.* **1.** *Jur:* joint and several; jointly liable, responsible **(de,** for); **obligation s.,** obligation binding on all parties. **2.** interdependent; **nous sommes tous solidaires,** we are interdependent; we all stand together; **ses intérêts sont solidaires des nôtres,** his interests are bound up with ours; **être s. d'un mouvement,** to associate oneself with a movement; *Tchn:* **roue s. d'une autre,** wheel integral with another.

solidairement [sɔlidɛrmɑ̃] *adv.* jointly.

solidariser [sɔlidarize] *v.tr.* **1.** (*a*) to render jointly liable, jointly responsible; (*b*) **se s.,** to make common cause, to show solidarity **(avec,** with). **2.** *Tchn:* **mécanisme à action solidarisée,** interlocking gear.

solidarisme [sɔlidarism] *n.m. Pol.Ec:* solidarism.

solidarité [sɔlidarite] *n.f.* **1.** *Jur:* joint responsibility. **2.** (*a*) interdependence (of parts); (*b*) fellowship, solidarity; community of interests; **grève de s.,** sympathetic strike; **débrayer par s. (avec),** to come out (on strike) in sympathy (with).

solide [sɔlid] **1.** *a.* (*a*) solid (body, food, earth); *Mth:* **angle s.,** solid angle; (*b*) solid, strong (wall, cloth); solid, secure (foundation); solid, sturdy (pers.); hearty (meal, appetite); sound (argument, education); fast (colour, *NAm:* color); *Com:* sound, solvent (pers.); well established (position, business); **peu s.,** weak; flimsy; **un coup de poing s.,** a vigorous blow; **qualités solides,** sterling qualities; **garantie s.,** reliable guarantee; **ami s.,** staunch, reliable, trusty, friend; **avoir la tête s.,** to have a good head for drink; (*c*) strong, strapping, hefty (man); **être encore s. (comme un chêne),** to be still hale and hearty. **2.** *n.m.* solid (body); *Mth:* **s. de révolution,** solid of revolution.

solidement [sɔlidmɑ̃] *adv.* solidly, firmly, securely, soundly.

solidification [sɔlidifikasjɔ̃] *n.f.* solidification.

solidifier [sɔlidifje] *v.tr. & pr.* (*impf. & pr.sub.* **n. solidifiions, v. solidifiiez**) to solidify.

solidité [sɔlidite] *n.f.* solidity; strength (of building, material); soundness (of a company, of judgment); strength, stability (of friendship); fastness (of colour, *NAm:* color); **c'est d'une s. à toute épreuve,** it stands up to anything.

soliloque [sɔlilɔk] *n.m.* soliloquy.

soliloquer [sɔlilɔke] *v.i.* to soliloquize.

solin [sɔlɛ̃] *n.m. Const:* (*a*) (i) space, (ii) plaster filling (between joists); (*b*) **bande de s.,** flashing.

solipède [sɔlipɛd] *Z: a. & n.m.* solidungulate.

soliste [sɔlist] *n.* soloist.

solitaire [sɔlitɛr] **1.** *a.* (*a*) solitary, lonely, lonesome; deserted (spot); **pin s.,** lone, isolated, pine; **ver s.,** tapeworm; (*b*) **avoir l'humeur s.,** to be fond of solitude. **2.** *n.m.* (*a*) (*pers.*) (i) hermit, recluse; (ii) lone wolf; **en s.,** alone, solo; (*b*) solitaire (game); (*c*) solitaire (diamond); (*d*) *Ven:* old boar.

solitairement [sɔlitɛrmɑ̃] *adv.* solitarily; alone.

solitude [sɔlityd] *n.f.* **1.** solitude, loneliness; **j'aime la s.,** I like being, living, alone. **2.** *Lit:* (*usu. pl.*) lonely spot; wilderness; solitude.

solive [sɔliv] *n.f. Const:* joist.

sollicitation [sɔlisitasjɔ̃] *n.f.* **1.** entreaty, request. **2. les sollicitations de la faim, de l'ambition,** the call of hunger, of ambition.

solliciter [sɔlisite] *v.tr.* **1.** to request, beg for (interview, etc.); **s. un emploi (de qn),** to apply (to s.o.) for a job; **s. des voix,** to canvass for votes; **s. qn de faire qch.,** to appeal to s.o. to do sth.; **il est sollicité de toutes parts,** he is very much in demand. **2.** to attract (attention); to appeal to (curiosity).

solliciteur, -euse [sɔlisitœr, -øz] *n.* petitioner; applicant **(de,** for).

sollicitude [sɔlisityd] *n.f.* (*a*) solicitude; (tender) care; (*b*) anxiety, concern **(pour,** for).

solo [sɔlo] **1.** *n.m.* solo; *Mus:* **s. de violon,** violin solo; **jouer en s.,** to play solo. **2.** *a.inv.* **violon s.,** solo violin.

sol-sol [sɔlsɔl] *a.inv. Ball:* ground-to-ground (missile).

solstice [sɔlstis] *n.m.* (summer, winter) solstice.

solubiliser [sɔlybilize] *v.tr.* to render (sth.) soluble.

solubilité [sɔlybilite] *n.f.* **1.** solubility (of a body). **2.** solvability (of a problem).

soluble [sɔlybl̩] *a.* **1.** soluble (substance); **café s.,** instant coffee. **2.** solvable (problem).

soluté [sɔlyte] *n.m. Pharm:* aqueous solution.

solution [sɔlysjɔ̃] *n.f.* **1. s. de continuité,** (i) solution of continuity; gap; break; (ii) *El: etc:* break of continuity; fault. **2.** *Ch: Ph: etc:* solution (of solid in liquid); **sel en s. (dans l'eau),** salt in solution (in water); **s. détergente,** cleaning solution. **3.** solution, answer (to question, problem, equation); **s. de paresse, de facilité,** easy way out; **brusquer la s. d'une crise,** to find a quick way to end a crisis.

solutionner [sɔlysjɔne] *v.tr.* to solve (problem, difficulty).
solvabilité [sɔlvabilite] *n.f.* solvency.
solvable [sɔlvabl̥] *a.* (financially) solvent.
solvant [sɔlvɑ̃] *n.m. Ch:* solvent.
soma [sɔma] *n.m. Biol:* soma.
somali, -ie [sɔmali] **1.** *a. & n. Geog:* Somali; **les Somalis,** the Somali; **Côte française des Somalis,** French Somaliland. **2.** *n.m. Ling:* **le s.,** Somali.
Somalie [sɔmali] *Pr.n.f.* **1.** *Hist:* **S. britannique, S. italienne,** British, Italian, Somaliland. **2.** *Geog:* **(République démocratique de) S.,** Somalia.
somatique [sɔmatik] *a.* somatic.
somatotrope [sɔmatɔtrɔp] *a.* somatotropic.
sombre [sɔ̃br̥] *a.* sombre, *NAm:* somber; dark, gloomy; (*a*) *inv.* **des robes bleu s.,** dark blue dresses; (*b*) dim (forest, room, light, etc.); dull, overcast (sky); **il fait s.,** it is dark, dull, weather; **il faisait très s. dans la pièce,** it was very dark in the room; (*c*) dismal, melancholy (face, thoughts, character); dark (despair); **une s. histoire de s. assassinat,** a sinister tale of foul murder; *F:* **un s. imbécile,** a first-class imbecile, idiot.
sombrement [sɔ̃brəmɑ̃] *adv.* gloomily, sombrely, *NAm:* somberly.
sombrer [sɔ̃bre] *v.i. Nau:* (*of ship*) to sink; (*of empire*) to founder; (*of business*) to come to grief; (*of pers.*) to sink (into sleep, despair); **il vit s. sa fortune,** he saw his fortune swallowed up; **il vit s. ses espérances,** he saw his hopes dashed; **sa raison sombra,** his mind, his reason, gave way.
sommaire [sɔmɛr] **1.** *a.* (*a*) summary, succinct, concise (account); **tenue s.,** scant attire; (*b*) hasty, improvised; (*c*) *Jur:* summary (proceedings). **2.** *n.m.* summary, synopsis.
sommairement [sɔmɛrmɑ̃] *adv.* **1.** summarily; **vêtu s.,** scantily dressed. **2. s. organisé,** hastily improvised.
sommation¹ [sɔmasjɔ̃] *n.f.* **1.** *Jur:* summons (**de faire qch.,** to do sth.); request, demand; notice (to perform contract); **faire les trois sommations légales,** to read the riot act. **2.** (sentry's) challenge.
sommation² *n.f. Mth:* summation (of a series).
somme¹ [sɔm] *n.f.* **bête de s.,** (i) beast of burden; (ii) drudge.
somme² *n.f.* **1.** sum; total; amount; (*a*) **faire la s. de dix nombres,** to add (up) ten numbers; **s. générale, s. totale,** general total, total sum; **la s. des trois angles d'un triangle vaut deux angles droits,** the sum of the three angles of a triangle is two right angles, 180°; (*b*) number (of thgs); amount (of sth.); **en s.,** on the whole; all things considered; in short; **s. toute,** altogether; when all is said and done; (*c*) sum (of money); **payer une s. de 200 francs,** to pay (a sum of) 200 francs; **dépenser des sommes folles,** to spend vast sums, a mint, of money; **être mis à l'amende pour la s. de 500 francs,** to be fined (a total of) 500 francs; **un million! c'est une s.!** a million! that's a lot of money! **2.** epitome; outline.
somme³ *n.m.* nap; short sleep; **faire un (petit) s.,** to take a nap, to have forty winks; **ne faire qu'un s., dormir d'un s.,** to sleep the night through.
sommeil [sɔmɛj] *n.m.* **1.** sleep; slumber; **s. de mort, de plomb,** heavy sleep; **dormir d'un s. de plomb,** to sleep like a log; **avoir le s. léger, profond,** to be a light, a heavy, sleeper; **avoir le s. dur,** to be hard to wake; **chercher le s.,** to try to sleep; **j'en perds le s.,** I lose sleep over it; (*of plants, etc.*) **en s.,** (lying) dormant; **s. hibernal (des animaux),** winter sleep. **2.** sleepiness, drowsiness; **avoir s.,** to feel sleepy, drowsy; **le s. me gagne,** I'm beginning to fall asleep; **je tombe, je meurs, de s.,** I can't keep awake; I'm ready to drop with sleep; *Med:* **maladie du s.,** sleeping sickness.
sommeiller [sɔmeje] *v.i.* **1.** to sleep lightly; to doze; to take a nap. **2.** *Fig:* to lie dormant (within s.o.).
sommelier [sɔməlje] *n.m.* wine waiter.
sommellerie [sɔmɛlri] *n.f.* **1.** wine waiter's job. **2.** wine cellar.
sommer¹ [sɔme] *v.tr. Mth:* to sum.
sommer² *v.tr.* to summon; **s. qn de faire qch.,** to call on s.o. to do sth.
sommet [sɔmɛ] *n.m.* top, summit (of roof, hill); vertex (of angle, curve, trajectory, cone); crest (of wave); crown (of arch, of the head); pinnacle (of power, fame); **être au s. de l'échelle,** to be at the top of the ladder; *Pol:* **conférence, réunion, rencontre, au s.,** summit meeting, conference; *F:* summit.
sommier¹ [sɔmje] *n.m.* (*a*) *Furn:* base, springing (of bed); (*b*) wind chest (of organ); string plate (of piano); (*c*) (*part under load, under strain*) springer (of arch); lintel (of door, etc.); cross beam (of floor); stringer (of bridge); beam (of balance); *Mec.E:* bed (of machine); (*d*) *Rail: Veh:* bolster.
sommier² *n.m.* **1.** *Adm: etc:* register; *Jur:* **sommiers judiciaires,** criminal records; **il n'y a rien sur lui au s.,** he's got a clean record. **2.** *Com:* cash book.
sommier-divan [sɔmjedivɑ̃] *n.m. Furn:* divan (bed); *pl. sommiers-divans.*
sommité [sɔmite] *n.f. Bot:* head; *Fig:* **sommités de l'art,** leading lights in the art world.
somnambule [sɔmnɑ̃byl] **1.** *a.* somnambulistic, somnambulant. **2.** *n.* somnambulist, sleepwalker; **il est s.,** he walks in his sleep.
somnambulisme [sɔmnɑ̃bylism] *n.m.* **1.** somnambulism, sleepwalking. **2. s. provoqué,** hypnotic state; artificial somnambulism.
somnifère [sɔmnifɛr] *a. & n.m. Med:* soporific; **(comprimé) s.,** sleeping tablet, sleeping pill.
somnolence [sɔmnɔlɑ̃s] *n.f.* somnolence; sleepiness, drowsiness.
somnolent [sɔmnɔlɑ̃] *a.* somnolent; sleepy, drowsy.
somnoler [sɔmnɔle] *v.i.* to drowse, doze.
somptuaire [sɔ̃ptɥɛr] *a.* (*a*) *A.Jur:* sumptuary (law); (*b*) *Fin:* **taxes somptuaires,** tax on luxury articles; **dépenses somptuaires,** expenditure on luxuries.
somptueusement [sɔ̃ptɥøzmɑ̃] *adv.* sumptuously.
somptueux, -euse [sɔ̃ptɥø, -øz] *a.* sumptuous.
somptuosité [sɔ̃ptɥozite] *n.f.* sumptuousness.
son¹, sa, ses [sɔ̃, sa, se] *poss.a.* (**son** *is used instead of* **sa** *before fem. nouns beginning with a vowel or* **h** *mute*) his, her, its, one's; **son père, sa mère, et ses enfants,** his, her, father, mother, and children; **tirer son épée,** to draw one's sword; **il tira son épée,** he drew his sword; **un de ses amis,** a friend of his, of hers; **un militaire de ses amis,** a soldier friend of his, hers; **ses père et mère,** his, her, father and mother; **à sa pensée,** the thought of him, her.
son² *n.m.* (*a*) sound (of voice, instrument, etc.); ringing, tinkle (of a bell); clang (of a big bell); **le s. profond de la cloche,** the deep tone of the bell; **s. du tambour, de la trompette,** beat of the drum, blare of the trumpet; **annoncer une nouvelle à s. de trompe,** to blare out a piece of news; *Nau:* **s. de sirène, de sifflet,** blast of the siren; (*b*) *Ac: Ph: Mus:* sound, tone; low-pitched sound, tone; deep tone; **s. différentiel,** difference tone; **s. pur,** clean tone; **niveau du s.,** sound level; **vitesse du s.,** sound velocity; *Av:* **mur du s.,** sonic wall, sound barrier; *Cin: Rec:* **enregistrement du s.,** sound recording; **prise de s.,** sound pick-up; **la prise de s. est bonne,** the recording is good; *Cin: etc:* **ingénieur du s.,** sound engineer; **(spectacle) s. et lumière,** son et lumière.
son³ *n.m.* bran; *Husb:* **s. mouillé,** bran mash; **tache de s.,** freckle.
sonar [sɔnar] *n.m. Nau: Navy:* sonar.
sonate [sɔnat] *n.f. Mus:* sonata.

sonatine [sɔnatin] *n.f.* sonatina.

sondage [sɔ̃daʒ] *n.m.* **1.** (*a*) *Nau: Av: etc:* sounding; probe; **faire des sondages,** to take soundings; **ballon de s.,** pilot balloon, sounding balloon; (*b*) *Min:* boring; **appareil de s.,** drilling rig; (*c*) *Metall:* **essai de s.,** probe test; (*d*) *Med:* probing (of wound); (*e*) **s. Gallup, s. d'opinion,** Gallup poll, public opinion poll; **s. aléatoire,** random sampling; **sondages de paix,** peace feelers. **2.** *Min:* borehole, drill hole.

sonde [sɔ̃d] *n.f.* **1.** (*a*) *Nau:* (sounding) lead, sounding line, plummet; **naviguer à la s.,** to navigate by soundings; **être sur la s.,** to be in soundings; to have struck soundings; (*b*) sounding rod (for pump, well, etc.); (*c*) (*of whale*) **faire la s.,** to sound; (*d*) *Meteor: Av:* **s. aérienne,** sounding balloon; **s. spatiale,** space probe; *Av:* **s. de réservoir,** tank probe; **s. à fil chaud,** hot-wire anemometer. **2.** *Med:* probe; **s. (creuse),** catheter; **nourri à la s.,** tube-fed. **3.** (*a*) taster (for cheese, etc.); (*b*) (grain) sampler. **4.** *Min:* borer; drill.

sonder [sɔ̃de] *v.tr.* **1.** (*a*) *Nau:* to sound; to fathom (a mystery); (*b*) *v.i.* (*of whale*) to sound; (*c*) **s. l'atmosphère,** to make soundings in the atmosphere; (*d*) *Min:* **s. un terrain,** *v.i.* **s.,** to make borings. **2.** to sound, probe, examine, investigate, test; (*a*) to probe, taste (a cheese); to examine (a beam); to scan (the horizon); to go into (the statements of a witness); (*b*) to sound (s.o.) (out); **je l'ai sondé là-dessus,** I sounded him on the matter; **s. l'opinion,** to sound public opinion; to make a survey of public opinion; **s. le terrain,** to feel one's way, to see how the land lies. **3.** *Med:* to sound, probe (a wound); to sound (a patient).

sondeur, -euse [sɔ̃dœr, -øz] **1.** *n.m.* (*a*) *Nau:* leadsman; (*b*) *Min:* borer, driller. **2.** *n.m. Nau:* sounder. **3.** *n.f. Min: etc:* **sondeuse,** borer, drill.

songe [sɔ̃ʒ] *n.m.* dream; **faire un s.,** to dream; to have a dream; **en s.,** in a dream.

songe-creux [sɔ̃ʒkrø] *n.m.inv. Lit:* dreamer.

songer [sɔ̃ʒe] *v.i.* (**je songeai(s); n. songeons**) **1.** (*a*) *A:* to dream (**de,** of); (*b*) to muse (**à,** on); to (day)dream; to think, dream (**à faire qch.,** of doing sth.); **je ne songeais guère que . . .,** little did I dream that . . .. **2.** (*a*) **s. à qch.,** to think of sth.; to consider, think over, sth.; **il ne faut pas y s.,** that's quite out of the question; **sans s. à mal,** without meaning any harm; **s. à faire qch.,** to think of doing sth.; **il ne songe qu'à gagner de l'argent,** he can't think of anything but making money; **s. à l'avenir,** to plan for the future; **sans y s.,** without thinking; **songez à ce que vous faites!** think what you're doing! (*b*) to imagine; **songez si j'étais furieux,** you can imagine how angry I was; **songez donc!** just think! just imagine! (*c*) to remember; **songez à lui,** keep, bear, him in mind; **je ne songeais pas que . . .,** I had forgotten that . . ..

songerie [sɔ̃ʒri] *n.f.* (day) dreaming; reverie.

songeur, -euse [sɔ̃ʒœr, -øz] *a.* (*a*) dreamy (person, nature); (*b*) pensive, thoughtful.

sonique [sɔnik] *a.* sonic (boom); sound (barrier); supersonic (aircraft).

sonnaille [sɔnaj] *n.f.* cattle bell.

sonnant [sɔnɑ̃] *a.* **1.** striking (clock); **à dix heures sonnant(es),** on the stroke of ten. **2.** sounding, resounding; **monnaie sonnante,** hard cash.

sonné [sɔne] *a.* **1. il est dix heures sonnées,** it is past ten, it's gone ten; **elle a quarante ans (bien) sonnés,** she's on the wrong side of forty. **2.** *F:* (*a*) *Box: etc:* groggy; punch-drunk; (*b*) crazy, cracked.

sonner [sɔne] **1.** *v.i.* to sound; (*of clocks*) to strike; (*of bells*) to ring; to toll; **s. creux,** to sound hollow; **sa réponse a sonné faux,** his answer did not ring true; **l'italien sonne bien à l'oreille,** Italian is a pleasant-sounding language; **cela sonne bien,** it sounds well, good; **adresse qui sonne bien,** good address; **l'r sonne dans "mer",** the r is sounded in "*mer*"; **faire s. les r.,** to roll one's r's; **faire s. un mot,** to emphasize a word; **faire s. son argent, ses clefs,** to jingle one's money, one's keys; **six heures sonnèrent,** the clock struck six; **midi vient de s.,** it has just struck twelve; **les vêpres sonnent,** the bells are ringing for vespers; **son heure a sonné,** his (last) hour has come; **la trompette sonne,** the trumpet is sounding; **les oreilles lui sonnaient,** his ears were buzzing. **2.** *v.tr.* (*a*) to sound; to cause (sth.) to sound; **s. la cloche,** to ring the bell; *v.i.* **on sonne,** the bell is ringing, there's a ring at the door; **horloge qui sonne les heures,** clock that strikes the hours; **ne (pas) s. mot,** not to utter a word; **s. la messe, l'office,** to ring for mass, for church; **s. pour les morts,** to toll for the dead; **s. le dîner,** to ring the dinner bell; *v.ind.tr.* **s. du clairon,** to sound the bugle; *Th:* **s. pour faire lever le rideau, pour faire baisser le rideau,** to ring up, ring down, the curtain; *Mil:* **s. la charge, la retraite,** to sound the charge, the retreat; *F:* **il va se faire s. (les cloches)!** he'll catch it! (*b*) to ring for (s.o.); *P:* **on ne vous a pas sonné!** mind your own business! (*c*) *P:* **s. qn,** to knock s.o. down, out; to beat s.o. up; (*d*) *Tchn:* to sound (metal for cracks); to ring, test (coin); (*e*) **s. le creux,** to have a hollow ring.

sonnerie [sɔnri] *n.f.* **1.** (*a*) ringing (of bells); (*b*) (set of) bells, chimes. **2.** (*a*) striking mechanism (of clock); **pendule à s.,** striking clock; (*b*) (electric, telephone, alarm) bell; **bouton de s.,** bell push; **fil à s.,** bell wire. **3.** *Mil:* (trumpet, bugle) call.

sonnet [sɔnɛ] *n.m.* sonnet.

sonnette [sɔnɛt] *n.f.* **1.** (*a*) small bell; (*b*) handbell; (*c*) (house) bell; **cordon de s.,** bell pull; **s. d'alarme,** alarm bell; **coup de s.,** ring (at the door, etc.); **personne ne répondit à mon coup de s.,** no one answered the bell; **poseur de sonnettes,** bellhanger. **2.** *Civ.E:* pile driver. **3. serpent à sonnettes,** rattlesnake.

sonneur, -euse [sɔnœr, -øz] **1.** *n.* bellringer; *F:* **dormir comme un s.,** to sleep like a log. **2.** *n.m. Civ.E:* pile-driver operator.

sono [sɔno] *n.f. F:* P.A. (system), sound system.

sonore [sɔnɔr] *a.* (*a*) resonant; echoing (vault, etc.); (*b*) ringing (voice, etc.); clear-toned (bell, etc.); resounding (laughter, etc.); *Pej:* high-sounding (phrases); **niveau (d'intensité) s.,** sound (intensity) level; (*c*) *Ling:* **consonne s.,** *n.f.* **s.,** voiced consonant; (*d*) acoustic(al); **église s.,** church with good acoustics; **vibrations sonores,** acoustic resonance; **onde s.,** soundwave; *Cin:* **film s.,** sound film; **effets sonores,** sound effects; **bande, piste, s.,** sound track.

sonorisation [sɔnɔrizasjɔ̃] *n.f.* (*a*) *Ling:* voicing (of consonant); (*b*) *Cin:* (i) scoring; (ii) providing of sound effects; (*c*) wiring (of room) for sound.

sonoriser [sɔnɔrize] *v.tr.* (*a*) *Ling:* to voice; (*b*) **s. un film,** (i) to score a film; (ii) to add the sound effects to a film; (*c*) **s. une salle,** to wire a hall for sound.

sonorité [sɔnɔrite] *n.f.* (*a*) (good, pleasing) tone; (*b*) resonance; (*c*) acoustics (of a room, etc.).

sophisme [sɔfism] *n.m.* sophism; *Log:* fallacy.

sophiste [sɔfist] **1.** *a.* sophistical. **2.** *n.* sophist.

sophistication [sɔfistikasjɔ̃] *n.f.* **1.** *O:* adulteration (of wine, etc.). **2.** sophistication, use of sophistry. **3.** (*of pers.*) (over-)sophistication, artificiality, affectation.

sophistique [sɔfistik] **1.** *a.* sophistic(al). **2.** *n.f.* sophistry.

sophistiqué [sɔfistike] *a.* **1.** *O:* adulterated (wine, etc.). **2.** (*a*) *Pej:* sophisticated, affected; (*b*) sophisticated, advanced (equipment, etc.).

Sophocle [sɔfɔkl̩] *Pr.n.m. Gr.Lit:* Sophocles.

soporifique [sɔpɔrifik] *a.* & *n.m.* (*a*) soporific; sleep-inducing (drug); (*b*) *F:* boring (speech, book).

sopraniste [sɔpranist] *n.m. Mus:* sopranist, male soprano singer.

soprano [sɔprano] *Mus:* (*a*) *n.m.* soprano voice; (*b*) *n.* (*pers.*) soprano; (*c*) *a.* **saxophone s.,** soprano saxophone.

sorbe [sɔrb] *n.f. Bot:* sorb apple, service apple.

sorbet [sɔrbɛ] *n.m. Cu:* sorbet, water ice.

sorbetière [sɔrbətjɛr] *n.f.* ice-cream freezer.

sorbier [sɔrbje] *n.m. Bot:* (i) service tree; (ii) rowan (tree), mountain ash.

sorbique [sɔrbik] *a. Ch:* sorbic (acid).

sorbonnard, -arde [sɔrbɔnar, -ard] *F: Pej:* (*a*) *n.* (i) student, (ii) lecturer, at the Sorbonne; (*b*) *a.* pedantic.

sorcellerie [sɔrsɛlri] *n.f.* magic, witchcraft.

sorcier, -ière [sɔrsje, -jɛr] *n.* sorcerer, *f.* sorceress; wizard, *f.* witch; **s. guérisseur,** witch doctor, medicine man; **chasse aux sorcières,** witch hunt; *F:* **vieille sorcière,** old hag, old witch; *a. F:* **ce n'est pas bien s.,** there's no magic about that; you couldn't call that difficult; **cercle, rond, de sorcières,** fairy ring.

sordide [sɔrdid] *a.* **1.** sordid, filthy (clothes); squalid (room). **2.** sordid (crime).

sordidement [sɔrdidmɑ̃] *adv.* sordidly; **vivre s.,** to live in squalor.

sorg(h)o [sɔrgo] *n.m. Bot:* sorghum.

Sorlingues (les) [lesɔrlɛ̃g] *Pr.n.f.pl. Geog:* the Scilly Isles.

sornette [sɔrnɛt] *n.f. usu. pl.* nonsense; rubbish.

sororité [sɔrɔrite] *n.f. Sch: NAm:* sorority.

sort [sɔr] *n.m.* **1.** (*a*) lot; condition in life; **assurer le s. de ses enfants,** to provide for one's children; *F:* **faire un s. à qch., à qn,** to dispose of (sth., s.o.); to polish off (the bottle, a whole chicken); (*b*) **il fait un s. à chaque phrase,** he emphasizes each sentence. **2.** destiny, fate; **notre s. est décidé,** our fate is sealed; **l'artillerie fit le s. de la bataille,** the artillery decided the battle; **coup, ironie, du s.,** stroke, irony, of fate. **3.** chance, fortune, lot; **tirer au s.,** (i) to draw lots; (ii) to toss, to spin, a coin; **tirer une place, etc., au s.,** to ballot for a place, etc.; **tirage au s.,** (i) drawing of lots; balloting; (ii) *Fb: etc:* toss; **le s. en est jeté,** the die is cast. **4.** spell, charm; **jeter un s. à qn,** to cast a spell on, over, s.o.

sortable [sɔrtabl̥] *a.* (*a*) *A:* eligible (young man); (*b*) *F:* presentable.

sortant, -ante [sɔrtɑ̃, -ɑ̃t] *a.* coming out; winning (number in lottery); outgoing, retiring (members of committee); **élèves sortants,** pupils in their last term; cadets passing out; **foule sortante,** outgoing crowd; *n.pl.* **les sortants,** those coming out.

sorte [sɔrt] *n.f.* **1.** manner, way; **ne parlez pas de la s.,** don't talk like that, in that way, in that fashion; *adv.phr.* **en quelque s.,** as it were, in a way; *conj.phr.* **il est sorti sans pardessus, de s. qu'il a attrapé un rhume,** he went out without his overcoat, so that, with the result that, he caught cold; **parlez de (telle) s. qu'on vous comprenne,** speak so as to be understood; **faites en s. que tout soit prêt à temps,** see to it that everything is ready in time. **2.** sort, kind; **toute(s) sorte(s) de choses, des choses de toute(s) sorte(s),** all sorts, kinds, of things; **un homme de la s.,** a man of that sort, of that kind; **une s. de ragoût,** a sort, some sort, of stew; **je n'ai rien dit, rien fait, de la s.,** I said, did, no such thing, nothing of the kind; **j'ai une s. d'impression qu'il viendra,** I have a sort of feeling he'll come.

sortie [sɔrti] *n.f.* **1.** (*a*) going out; coming out; departure; *Th:* exit; **faire une s. pour prendre l'air,** to go out to get a breath of (fresh) air; **c'était ma première s. depuis mon accident,** it was my first time out, my first outing, after my accident; **à la s. du théâtre,** at the end of the performance; **à la s. des classes,** when the children come, came, out of school; after school; **on a annoncé la s. d'un nouveau modèle,** a new model has been put on the market; (*b*) leaving (for good); retirement (of official, etc.); **à ma s. d'école,** when I left school; **à la s. de l'hiver,** when winter is over; (*c*) flowing out (of liquid); *Hyd.E: Mec.E:* outlet (of fluid); **tuyaux de s.,** outgoing pipes; (*d*) *El: Elcs:* output; (*e*) *Cmptr:* (i) exit; (ii) output; (*f*) *Tchn:* delivery (of sheets from printing press, etc.); **table de s.,** delivery table; (*g*) *Com:* export (of goods); **sorties de fonds,** outgoings, expenses; (*h*) *Fin:* **les sorties or,** the gold withdrawals; **s. de devises, de capitaux,** currency, capital, outflow; (*i*) *Adm:* issue (of stores). **2.** (*a*) trip, excursion; outing; leave; **faire une s. en mer,** to go for a short sea trip; **jour de s.,** day out, holiday; **avoir un jour de s. par semaine,** to have one free day a week; *Navy:* **s. à terre,** shore leave; (*b*) **l'année dernière les canots de sauvetage ont fait cinquante sorties,** last year the lifeboats went out fifty times. **3.** (*a*) *Mil:* sally, sortie; *Fb:* run out (by goalkeeper); (*b*) *F:* outburst, tirade; **faire une s. à, contre, qn,** to lash out at s.o.; **elle est capable de n'importe quelle s. devant les gens,** she is capable of saying anything in front of people. **4.** (*a*) exit, way out; **s. de secours,** emergency exit; **il y a une s. sur la ruelle,** there is a way out into the lane; **à la s. de la gare,** at the station exit; **par ici la s.,** this way out; (*b*) (water, steam) outlet. **5. s. de bain,** bathwrap; *O:* **s. de bal,** evening wrap, opera cloak.

sortilège [sɔrtilɛʒ] *n.m.* spell, charm.

sortir¹ [sɔrtir] *v.* (*pr.p.* **sortant;** *p.p.* **sorti;** *pr.ind.* **je sors, il sort, n. sortons, ils sortent;** *pr.sub.* **je sorte;** *impf.* **je sortais;** *p.h.* **je sortis;** *fu.* **je sortirai) I.** *v.i.* (*aux.* **être**) **1.** (*a*) to go, come, out; to leave the room, the house, etc.; **s. de la salle,** to go, walk, out of the room; **faire s. qn,** (i) to take s.o., out (for a walk); (ii) to rout s.o. out; (iii) to order s.o. out of the room, out of the house; **il ne sort pas de chez moi,** he practically lives at my place; **entrer par une porte et s. par l'autre,** to go, in at one door and out at the other; **s. de son lit,** (i) to get out of bed; (ii) to leave one's bed (after illness); (iii) (*of river*) to overflow its banks; *Th:* **Macbeth sort,** exit Macbeth; *F:* **d'où sortez-vous?** where have you been all this time (that you don't know that)? (*of ship*) **s. du port,** to leave harbour, *NAm:* harbor; **s. d'un emploi,** to leave a job; **s. de la vie,** to depart this life; **cela m'est sorti de la mémoire, de la tête,** it has slipped my memory, gone out of my head; **il ne sortira pas grand-chose de tout cela,** not much will come of all this; *Ind:* **s. de la chaîne de fabrication,** to come off the production line; **le premier numéro de cette revue sortira le 8 mars,** the first number of this review will come out on the 8th of March; *Sch: F:* **est-ce que je peux s.?** may I be excused? *Fin:* (*of bonds*) **s. au tirage,** to be drawn; *Cards:* **le dix de carreau est sorti,** the ten of diamonds turned up; (*b*) (*of horseman*) to ride out; (*of driver or vehicle*) to drive out; (*of captain or ship*) to sail out; (*c*) **s. en courant, en dansant,** to run, dance, out; **s. précipitamment, à la hâte, en toute hâte,** to hurry out; **s. furtivement, à pas de loup,** to steal, creep, out; **parvenir à s.,** to (manage to) get out; (*d*) (*of flowers, etc.*) to come out, up; to spring up; *Sch:* **cette question est sortie (à l'examen),** this question was set (in the examination); (*e*) to have just come out; **je sors du collège, de table,** I have just left school, (the) table; **s. de l'enfance,** to emerge from childhood; **je sors d'une typhoïde,** I am just recovering from typhoid; **on sortait de l'hiver,** winter was just over; **il sort d'ici,** he has just left; (*f*) *A: & F:* **s. de faire qch.,** to have just done sth.; *P:* **merci bien! je sors d'en prendre,** no thank you! once is enough; (*g*) to swerve, deviate (from one's duty, etc.); **s. de son sujet,** to depart, wander, from one's subject; **cela sort de ma compétence,** that doesn't come within my scope; it's quite beyond me; **s. des bornes de la bienséance,** to overstep the bounds of decency; **s. d'une règle,** (i) to ignore, depart from, a rule; (ii) to transgress a rule; (*of train*) **s. des rails,** to jump the rails; **il ne sort pas de là, il n'en sort pas,** he sticks to his point; that is his firm conviction; *Danc: etc:* **s. de cadence,** to get out of step; *Mus:* **s. de mesure,** to be, get, out of time; **s. du ton,** to get out of tune. **2.** to go out; **Madame X est sortie; elle est sortie à trois heures,** Mrs X is out; she went out at three o'clock; **s. à cheval, à pied,** to go out riding, walking. **3.** to get out of, extricate oneself from (a difficulty, danger); **aider qn à s. d'une difficulté,** to help s.o. out; **il n'y a pas à s. de là,** there is no way out; **soyez plus précis ou nous n'en sortirons pas,** be more precise or we shall never get to the end of it; *F:* **j'ai trop à faire, je n'en sors pas,** I've too much to do, I shall never get through it. **4.** to come (from a good family, etc.); **ce livre sort de ma plume,** the book is one of mine; **s. de l'université,** to graduate (from university); **cheval sorti d'un bon haras,** horse (that comes) from a good stud, stable. **5.** (*a*) to stand out, stick out, protrude, project; to emerge (from the fog, from obscurity); **pierre qui sort du mur,** stone that projects from the wall; **yeux qui sortent de la tête,** protruding eyes; **les yeux lui sortaient de la tête,** his eyes were starting out of his head; (*b*) (*of figure in picture, of thought, characteristic*) to stand out, to be prominent; **faire s. un trait de caractère, un rôle,** to emphasize a characteristic, a part. **II.** *v.tr.* (*aux.* **avoir**) (*a*) to take out, bring out, pull out; to take out (a child, a dog); to throw out (an intruder); **s. la voiture,** to get out the car; **cela nous sortira de l'ordinaire,** that will make a change; **sortez-moi de cette affaire, de ce mauvais pas,** get me out of this business, out of this fix; **le malade s'en sortira,** the patient will pull through; **s. les mains de ses poches,** to take one's hands out of one's pockets; **il sortit sa pipe,** he brought out, took out, got out, his pipe; **s. un revolver,** to produce a revolver; **l'escargot sort ses cornes,** the snail puts out its horns; *Publ:* **s. un ouvrage,** to publish, bring out, a book; **s. un livre de la bibliothèque,** to take a book out of the library; *F:* **il nous en a sorti une bien bonne,** he came out with a good one; *Typ:* **s. une ligne,** to run out a line (into the margin); (*b*) *Cmptr:* to output.

sortir² *n.m.* **au s. du cinéma,** on coming out of the cinema; **au s. de l'école,** (i) when school ends, ended; when they, we, come, came, out of school; (ii) on leaving school (for good); **au s. de la table,** at the end of the meal; when we, they, got up from table; **au s. de l'hiver, de la réunion,** at the end of the winter, meeting.

sortir³ *v.tr.* (*conj. like* FINIR; *used only in third pers.*) *Jur:* to obtain, have (effect); **cette sentence sortira son plein (et entier) effet,** this decision shall have full effect.

sosie [sɔzi] *n.m.* (s.o.'s) double.

sot, sotte [so, sɔt] **1.** *a.* (*a*) silly, stupid, foolish (person, answer, plan); (*b*) embarrassed, disconcerted. **2.** *n.* fool, idiot, ass.

sot-l'y-laisse [solilɛs] *n.m.inv. Cu:* oyster, oyster piece (of poultry).

sottement [sɔtmɑ̃] *adv.* stupidly, foolishly.

sottise [sɔtiz] *n.f.* **1.** stupidity, silliness, foolishness. **2.** (*a*) foolish act; stupid remark; **faire, dire, des sottises,** to do, say, silly things; to talk nonsense; **ai-je dit une s.?** have I said something stupid? (*b*) offensive remark, insult; **dire des sottises à qn,** to abuse, slang, s.o.

sottisier [sɔtizje] *n.m.* collection of howlers.

sou [su] *n.m.* (*still used, esp. colloquially, though there is no longer a coin of that name*) (*a*) sou (= 5 centimes); *F: A:* **pièce de cent sous,** five-franc piece; (*b*) **des gens à gros sous,** (very) rich people; **être près de ses sous,** to count every penny; **amasser une fortune s. par s.,** to scrape a fortune together; **payer s. à s.,** to pay in small instalments; **ne pas avoir le s.,** to be penniless; **appareil, machine, à sous,** slot machine; one-armed bandit; **cela vaut cent mille francs comme un s.,** it's worth a hundred thousand francs if it's worth a penny; **affaire de quatre sous,** twopenny-halfpenny business; **pas ambitieux pour deux sous, pour un s.,** not in the least ambitious; **il n'a pas pour deux sous de courage,** he hasn't a scrap of courage; (*c*) *Fr.C:* cent.

souahéli [swaheli], **souahili** [swahili] **1.** *a. & n. Ethn:* Swahili. **2.** *n.m. Ling:* **le s.,** Swahili.

souazi [swazi] *a. & n. Geog:* Swazi.

Souaziland (le) [ləswazilɑ̃d] *Pr.n.m. Geog:* Swaziland.

soubassement [subɑsmɑ̃] *n.m.* **1.** (*a*) *Arch:* sub-foundation; base, basement (of building); **le s. social,** the social substructure; (*b*) base (plate) (of machine tool, etc.); (*c*) *Geol:* bedrock. **2.** *Aut:* sub-frame; **s. de châssis,** underframe.

soubresaut [subrəso] *n.m.* (*a*) sudden start; jolt (of vehicle); (*b*) **cette nouvelle m'a donné un s.,** the news made me gasp, gave me a start.

soubrette [subrɛt] *n.f. Th:* soubrette, maidservant.

souche [suʃ] *n.f.* **1.** (*a*) stump, stub (of tree, etc.); root stock (of iris, etc.); vine stock; *F:* **rester (là) comme une s.,** to stand stock still; **dormir comme une s.,** to sleep like a log; (*b*) *F:* idiot, nit. **2.** (*a*) head, founder (of family); **faire s.,** to found a family; **il vient de bonne s.,** he comes of sound stock; **famille de vieille s.,** an old family; (*b*) strain (of virus, etc.). **3.** *Com:* counterfoil, stub (of cheque, *NAm:* check, ticket, etc.). **4.** shaft, stack (of chimney).

souci¹ [susi] *n.m. Bot:* marigold; **s. d'eau,** marsh marigold.

souci² *n.m.* **1.** care; solicitude; preoccupation; concern (**de,** for); regard (**de,** for); **avoir le s. de plaire,** to be anxious to please; **avoir le s. de la vérité, de l'exactitude,** to be meticulously truthful, accurate; **ne prendre nul s. des conseils de qn,** to take no notice of s.o.'s advice; **il ne prend s. de rien,** he doesn't care about anything; **c'est le moindre, le dernier, le cadet, de mes soucis,** that's the least of my worries. **2.** (*a*) anxiety, worry; **se faire du s.,** to worry; **sans s., libre de soucis,** carefree; free from anxiety; (*b*) **cet enfant est un perpétuel s.,** this child is a perpetual (source of) worry; **soucis d'argent, soucis financiers,** money troubles, financial worries.

soucier [susje] *v.* (*impf. & pr.sub.* **n. souciions, v. souciiez**) **1.** *v.tr. A:* (*of thg*) to trouble, disturb (s.o.). **2. se s. de qn, de qch., de faire qch.,** to worry, be concerned, about s.o., sth.; **il se soucie toujours des autres,** he is always worrying about other people; **ne se s. de rien,** not to worry, bother, about anything; *F:* **je m'en soucie comme de l'an quarante, de ma première chemise,** I don't care a damn about that.

soucieux, -ieuse [susjø, -jøz] *a.* (*a*) anxious, concerned (**de,** about); **être s. de faire qch.,** to be anxious to do sth.; **peu s.,** unconcerned (**de,** about); **peu s. de se rencontrer avec elle,** not very anxious to meet her; (*b*) anxious, worried, bothered; **avoir un air s.,** to look anxious, worried.

soucoupe [sukup] *n.f.* (*a*) saucer; (*b*) *F:* **s. volante,** flying saucer.

soudage [sudaʒ] *n.m.* **1. s. (hétérogène),** soldering. **2. s. (autogène),** (autogenous) welding (of metals).

soudain [sudɛ̃] **1.** *a.* sudden, unexpected. **2.** *adv.* suddenly, all of a sudden.

soudainement [sudɛnmɑ̃] *adv.* suddenly.
soudaineté [sudɛnte] *n.f.* suddenness.
Soudan (le) [ləsudɑ̃] *Pr.n.m. Geog:* the Sudan.
soudant [sudɑ̃] *a. Metalw:* **blanc s.,** welding heat.
soudard [sudar] *n.m. usu. Pej:* **(vieux) s.,** (hardened) old soldier, old trooper.
soude [sud] *n.f.* **1.** *Bot:* saltwort, (prickly) glasswort. **2.** *Ch: Ind:* soda; **(carbonate de) s.,** *F:* **cristaux de s., s. ordinaire,** washing soda, common soda; **bicarbonate de s.,** bicarbonate of soda; **s. caustique,** caustic soda.
souder [sude] **1.** *v.tr.* (*a*) to solder; **s. au cuivre, au laiton,** to braze, to hard solder; **s. à l'étain,** to soft solder; (*b*) to weld; **s. à l'arc (électrique),** to arc weld; **machine à s.,** welding machine, welder; **s. par points,** to spot weld; (*c*) to join, unite (fractured bone, etc.). **2. se s.** (*a*) to join together; to weld, fuse, together; (*b*) (*of bones*) (i) to knit (together); (ii) to become anchylosed; (*c*) (*of group*) to unite.
soudeur, -euse [sudœr, -øz] **1.** *n.* (*pers.*) (*a*) solderer; (*b*) welder; **s. par points,** spot welder; **s. au chalumeau,** lamp, torch, welder. **2.** *n.f.* **soudeuse,** welder, welding machine; **s. par points,** spot welder.
soudoir [sudwar] *n.m. Tls:* soldering iron.
soudoyer [sudwaje] *v.tr.* **(je soudoie, n. soudoyons; je soudoierai) 1.** *A:* to pay (mercenaries). **2.** (*a*) to hire (assassin, etc.); (*b*) *Pej:* to bribe, buy (s.o.).
soudure [sudyr] *n.f.* **1.** (*a*) soldering; **s. au cuivre, au laiton,** brazing, hard soldering; **s. à l'étain,** sweating, soft soldering; (*b*) soldered joint; **s. à nœud,** wipe(d) joint; (*c*) (*metal alloy for soldering*) solder. **2.** (*a*) welding; (*b*) (welded, brazed) seam; weld; **sans soudure(s),** seamless, weldless. **3.** (*a*) union, join (of bones, etc.); (*b*) *Hyd.E:* bonding; (*c*) *Pol.Ec:* **faire la s.,** to bridge the gap; to tide over.
soufflage [suflaʒ] *n.m.* **1.** glass blowing. **2.** sheathing (of ship's bottom). **3.** blowing, blow, blast (of furnace).
soufflant, -ante [suflɑ̃, -ɑ̃t] **1.** *a.* (*a*) blowing; **machine soufflante,** blowing engine, blast engine; (*b*) *Ling:* fricative (consonant); (*c*) *F:* breathtaking. **2.** *n.f. Mec.E:* **soufflante,** blower, fan; **soufflante de sustentation,** lift fan (of hovercraft); *I.C.E: etc:* **soufflante de suralimentation,** supercharger.
soufflard [suflar] *n.m. Geol:* fumarole.
souffle [sufl̥] *n.m.* breath. **1.** (*a*) puff, blast, breath (of air, wind); **pas un s. de vent,** not a breath of air; (*b*) blast (of exploding shell); muzzle blast (of gun); (*c*) *Av:* slipstream, wash (of propeller); (*d*) **le s. poétique,** poetic inspiration. **2.** (*a*) respiration, breathing; **retenir son s.,** to hold one's breath; **éteindre une chandelle avec son s.,** to blow out a candle; **couper le s. à qn,** to take s.o.'s breath away; **le s. vital, de la vie,** the breath of life; **exhaler son dernier s.,** to breathe one's last; **n'avoir plus que le s.,** to be at one's last gasp; **sa vie ne tient qu'à un s.,** his life hangs by a thread; *F:* **c'est à vous couper le s.,** it's breathtaking; *F:* **il ne manque pas de s.!** he's got a cheek, a nerve! (*b*) *Med:* **(bruit de) s.,** murmur; (*c*) breath, wind (of runner, etc.); **être à bout de s.,** to be winded, out of breath, *F:* puffed; **manquer de s.,** to be short of breath, short-winded; **reprendre son s.,** to get one's second wind.
soufflé [sufle] *a.* (*a*) puffed up; soufflé (omelette, potatoes); (*b*) *F:* flabbergasted, taken aback. **2.** *n.m. Cu:* soufflé; **moule à soufflés,** soufflé dish.
soufflement [sufləmɑ̃] *n.m.* blowing.
souffler [sufle] **1.** *v.i.* (*a*) to blow; (*of cat, etc.*) to spit; **s. dans ses doigts,** to blow on one's fingers; *F:* **tu peux s. dessus,** you can whistle for it! *F:* **s. aux oreilles de qn,** to have a quiet, private, word with s.o.; (*b*) to get one's breath back; **laisser s. un cheval,** to let a horse get its wind; to give a horse a breather; (*c*) to pant; to puff; **suant et soufflant,** puffing and blowing; (*d*) (*of the wind, etc.*) to blow; **regarder, voir, d'où, de quel côté, souffle le vent,** to see which way the wind is blowing; **un vent de révolte soufflait,** there was a spirit of revolt in the air; (*e*) (*of buffalo*) to snort. **2.** *v.tr.* (*a*) to blow (glass); to blow up (balloon, etc.); (*b*) to blow (the organ); to blow up (the fire); to blow off (dust); to blow out (a candle); **s. la discorde,** to stir up discord; (*c*) to breathe, utter (a sound); to whisper; (*d*) **s. (son rôle à) un acteur,** to prompt an actor; (*e*) *Games:* (*at draughts*) to huff (a man, an opponent); *F:* **s. qch. à qn,** to pinch sth. from s.o.; (*f*) *Nau:* to sheathe (ship's bottom); (*g*) (*of explosion*) to blast (building, etc.); *F:* (*of event, etc.*) to take (s.o.) aback; *F:* **son culot nous a soufflés,** his cheek took our breath away.
soufflerie [sufləri] *n.f.* **1.** bellows (of organ, forge). **2.** (*a*) *Ind:* blower; (*b*) wind tunnel.
soufflet [suflɛ] *n.m.* **1.** (*a*) (pair of) bellows; (*b*) *Ind: etc:* fan, fanner. **2.** (*a*) **valise à soufflets,** expanding suitcase; (*b*) *Rail:* concertina vestibule (joining coaches); (*c*) *Dressm:* gusset; (*d*) *Mus:* swell (of organ). **3.** slap in the face.
souffleter [sufləte] *v.tr.* **(je soufflette, n. souffletons; je souffletterai)** (*a*) *A:* to slap s.o.'s face; (*b*) *Lit:* to insult s.o.
souffleur, -euse [suflœr, -øz] *n.* **1. s. de verre,** glass blower. **2.** *Th:* prompter. **3.** *n.f.* **souffleuse** (*a*) snow-blower; (*b*) *Agr:* blower container (for seeds, etc.).
soufflure [suflyr] *n.f.* blister, bubble, flaw (in paint, glass, metal); bulge (in tyre, *NAm:* tire).
souffrance [sufrɑ̃s] *n.f.* **1. en s.,** (work) awaiting attention, pending; (candidates) on the waiting list; (bills) overdue, outstanding; (parcels) held up in transit or awaiting delivery. **2.** suffering, pain.
souffrant [sufrɑ̃] *a.* (*a*) *Lit:* suffering; (*b*) unwell, poorly, indisposed; **il a l'air s.,** he doesn't look well.
souffre-douleur [sufrədulœr] *n.m.inv.* butt (of one's jokes, etc.); scapegoat.
souffreteux, -euse [sufrətø, -øz] *a.* sickly (child, etc.).
souffrir [sufrir] (*pr.p.* **souffrant;** *p.p.* **souffert;** *pr.ind.* **je souffre, il souffre, n. souffrons, ils souffrent;** *impf.* **je souffrais;** *p.h.* **je souffris;** *fu.* **je souffrirai**) to suffer. **1.** *v.tr.* (*a*) to endure, undergo, bear, put up with (pain, fatigue, cold, loss, insult, etc.); *F:* **ils ne peuvent pas se s.,** they can't stand each other; **je ne peux pas s. qu'on vienne me déranger,** I cannot bear to be disturbed; (*b*) to permit, allow; **je ne saurais s. cela,** I cannot allow that; **souffrez que je vous dise la vérité,** allow me to tell you the truth; **situation qui ne souffre aucun retard,** situation that admits of no delay; *Breed:* (*of mare*) **s. l'étalon,** to take the stallion. **2.** *v.i.* (*a*) to feel pain; to suffer (from rheumatism, headaches, thirst); **souffre-t-il?** is he in pain? **mon bras me fait s.,** my arm is hurting (me); **je souffre de le voir si changé,** it pains, grieves, me, I am very sorry, to see him so changed; **nous avons beaucoup souffert de la guerre,** we were hard hit by the war; **je souffre à marcher,** I find walking painful; **avoir cessé de s.,** to be out of pain; (*b*) to suffer injury; (*of thgs*) to be damaged; **les vignes ont souffert de la gelée,** the vines have suffered from the frost; (*c*) (*of crops, trade, etc.*) to be in a bad way.
soufrage [sufraʒ] *n.f.* sulphuring, *NAm:* sulfuring (of matches, plants, etc.).
soufre [sufr̥] *n.m.* **1.** sulphur, *NAm:* sulfur. **2. s. végétal,** vegetable sulphur; lycopodium.
soufré [sufre] *n.m. Ent:* sulphur, brimstone (butterfly).
soufrer [sufre] *v.tr.* to sulphur, *NAm:* sulfur; to treat (sth.) with sulphur.
souhait [swɛ] *n.m.* wish; desire; **présenter ses souhaits**

à qn, to offer s.o. one's good wishes; *adv.phr.* **à s.,** to one's liking; **avoir tout à s.,** to have everything one could wish for; **réussir à s.,** to succeed to perfection; *F:* (*when s.o. sneezes*) **à vos souhaits!** (God) bless you!

souhaitable [swɛtabl̥] *a.* desirable, to be wished for; **il est s. que** + *sub.*, it is to be hoped that . . .; **ce n'est guère s.,** one can hardly wish for that.

souhaiter [swete] *v.tr.* (*a*) to wish; **s. les richesses,** to wish for wealth, to want to be rich; **je souhaite que vous réussissiez, je vous souhaite de réussir,** I hope you will succeed; (*b*) **je vous souhaite une bonne année,** here's wishing you a happy new year; **s. bon voyage à qn,** to wish s.o. a good journey; *F: Iron:* **je vous en souhaite!** you'll be lucky!

souiller [suje] *v.tr.* **1.** to soil, dirty (garments, etc.) (**de,** with); **vêtements souillés de boue,** mudstained clothes. **2.** to pollute; to contaminate; to taint; **s. ses mains de sang,** to stain one's hands with blood. **3.** to tarnish, dishonour, *NAm:* dishonor (memory, etc.).

souillon [sujɔ̃] **1.** *n. A:* slut. **2.** *n.f.* slovenly maid.

souillure [sujyr] *n.f.* spot (of dirt); stain (on garment, etc.); *Lit:* blot, blemish (on one's reputation).

souk [suk] *n.m.* (*a*) (*in Middle East and N. Africa*) souk, market; (*b*) *P:* (*of place*) shambles.

soûl [su] **1.** *a.* (*a*) *A:* gorged (with food, drink, etc.); *Lit:* **être s. de plaisir, de musique,** to have had a surfeit of pleasure, of music; (*b*) *F:* drunk; **s. comme un Polonais, comme un cochon, comme une bourrique,** drunk as a lord; **s. perdu,** blind drunk. **2.** *n.m. F:* **boire, manger, rire, chanter, tout son s.,** to drink, eat, laugh, sing, to one's heart's content; to drink, eat, one's fill.

soulagement [sulaʒmɑ̃] *n.m.* relief.

soulager [sulaʒe] *v.* **(je soulageai(s); n. soulageons) 1.** *v.tr.* to ease (pressure); to relieve, alleviate (pain, grief); to soothe, comfort (s.o.'s mind, sorrow); **on soulage ses maux à les raconter,** it is a relief, a comfort, to speak of one's troubles; **s. une poutre,** to ease the strain on a beam; **s. les soupapes,** to blow off steam; **cela me soulage l'esprit d'un grand poids,** that's a great weight off my mind; *F:* **s. qn de son portefeuille,** to relieve s.o. of his wallet. **2. se s.** (*a*) to ease up, to take things more easily; (*b*) to relieve one's feelings, one's mind; (*c*) *F:* to relieve oneself.

soûlard, -arde [sular, -ard], **soûlaud, -aude** [sulo, -od] *n. P:* drunkard, boozer, soak.

soûler [sule] *v.tr.* **1.** *O:* to surfeit (s.o.), to fill (s.o.) to repletion (**de,** with). **2.** *F:* to get, make (s.o.) drunk; **se s. de paroles,** to get drunk with the sound of one's own voice.

soûlerie [sulri] *n.f. P:* (*a*) drinking bout, booze-up; binge; (*b*) drunkenness.

soulèvement [sulɛvmɑ̃] *n.m.* (*a*) rising, heaving (of the ground, stomach); **s. de cœur,** nausea; (*b*) *Geol:* upheaval, upthrust; (*c*) revolt, uprising (of a people).

soulever [sulve] **(je soulève, n. soulevons; je soulèverai) 1.** *v.tr.* (*a*) to raise (*usu.* with effort); to lift (up) (a weight); **s. un malade, un charge,** to lift a patient, a load; **la marée soulèvera le bateau,** the tide will float the boat off; **s. le porte-monnaie de qn,** to steal, *F:* lift, s.o.'s purse; (*b*) to raise (sth.) slightly; (*c*) to raise (doubts, a question, an objection); (*d*) to rouse, stir up (people to revolt); (*e*) to excite, provoke, rouse (passion, indignation). **2. se s.** (*a*) to rise; (*of sea, stomach, etc.*) to heave; (*b*) to raise oneself up; (*c*) to revolt; to rise (in rebellion).

soulier [sulje] *n.m.* shoe; **souliers de marche,** walking shoes; *F:* **être dans ses petits souliers,** to be in an awkward situation.

soulignage [suliɲaʒ] *n.m.*, **soulignement** [suliɲmɑ̃] *n.m.* underlining.

souligner [suliɲe] *v.tr.* (*a*) to underline (word, passage); (*b*) to emphasize (word, fact).

soumettre [sumɛtr̥] *v.tr.* (*conj. like* METTRE) **1.** to subdue (people, passions). **2.** to refer, submit (a question, a request, to s.o.); **s. ses projets à qn,** to lay, put, one's plans before s.o. **3.** to subject (sth. to an examination); **s. qn à une épreuve,** to put s.o. through a test; **être soumis à des règles strictes,** to be bound by strict rules. **4. se s.,** to submit (to authority); to comply (with s.o.'s wishes); to abide by (s.o.'s decision).

soumis [sumi] *a.* **1.** submissive, obedient. **2.** subject (to law, authority, delay, etc.); liable, subject (to tax); **non s.,** unconquered; *A:* **fille soumise,** registered prostitute.

soumission [sumisjɔ̃] *n.f.* **1.** (*a*) submission; **faire (sa) s.,** to surrender, yield; (*b*) obedience, submissiveness (**à,** to). **2.** *Com:* tender; **faire une s. pour un travail,** to tender for a job.

soumissionnaire [sumisjɔnɛr] *n.m.* tenderer.

soumissionner [sumisjɔne] *v.tr.* to tender for (a job).

soupape [supap] *n.f. Tchn:* valve; *Tchn: Fig:* **s. de sûreté,** safety valve; **s. d'admission, d'arrivée,** inlet valve, induction valve; **s. d'échappement, s. de décharge,** outlet valve, exhaust valve, escape valve; **s. à flotteur,** ballcock; *I.C.E:* **soupapes en tête, en chandelle,** overhead valves; **soupapes latérales, en chapelle,** side valves.

soupçon [supsɔ̃] *n.m.* **1.** suspicion; distrust; **s'exposer aux soupçons,** to lay oneself open to suspicion; **devenir l'objet des soupçons,** to fall under suspicion; **éveiller, endormir, les soupçons,** to arouse, allay, suspicion; **avoir des soupçons à l'endroit de qn,** to feel suspicious about s.o.; **j'en avais le s.!** I thought so! I suspected as much! **il est au-dessus de tout s.,** he is above suspicion; **arrêter qn sur un s.,** to arrest s.o. on suspicion. **2.** suspicion, surmise, conjecture; **je n'en avais pas le moindre s.,** I never suspected it for a moment. **3.** *F:* dash, hint, soupçon (of vinegar, garlic, etc.); touch (of fever, rouge, irony, etc.); drop (of wine).

soupçonnable [supsɔnabl̥] *a.* open to suspicion.

soupçonner [supsɔne] *v.tr.* **1.** to suspect; **s. qn de qch., d'avoir fait qch.,** to suspect s.o. of sth., of having done sth. **2.** to surmise, suspect, conjecture; **je ne soupçonnais pas que . . .,** I had no suspicion, no idea, that . . ..

soupçonneux, -euse [supsɔnø, -øz] *a.* suspicious.

soupe [sup] *n.f.* **1.** (*a*) *A:* sop; soaked slice of bread; (*b*) **s. au lait,** bread and milk; *F:* **il monte comme une s. au lait, il est très s. au lait,** he flares up very easily, he's always flying off the handle. **2.** (*a*) soup; **s. aux pois, à l'oignon,** pea soup, onion soup; *F:* **il mange la s. à la grimace,** his wife isn't speaking to him; *P:* **par ici la bonne s.!** that's the way to make money! (*b*) meal; *F:* **à la s.!** grub's up! (*c*) *Ski: F:* soft snow.

soupente [supɑ̃t] *n.f.* closet; cupboard (*esp.* under the stairs).

souper¹ [supe] *v.i.* (*a*) *A: & Dial:* to have supper, dinner, the evening meal; (*b*) to have a late supper; *F:* **j'en ai soupé,** I've had enough of it, I'm fed up with it.

souper² *n.m.* (*a*) *A: & Dial:* supper, dinner, evening meal; (*b*) (late) supper.

soupeser [supəze] *v.tr.* **(je soupèse, n. soupesons; je soupèserai)** to try the weight of (sth.); to weigh (sth.) in the hand; *esp. NAm:* to heft (sth).; to weigh up (a problem).

soupière [supjɛr] *n.f.* soup tureen.

soupir [supir] *n.m.* **1.** sigh; **pousser un s.,** to (heave a) sigh; **s. de soulagement,** sigh of relief; **un gros s.,** a heavy sigh; **rendre le dernier s.,** to breathe one's last;

s. du vent, sighing of the wind. **2.** *Mus:* crotchet rest; **(demi-)quart de s.,** (demi)semiquaver rest.

soupirail, -aux [supiraj, -o] *n.m.* (*a*) (cellar) ventilator; (*b*) (small) basement window.

soupirant [supirɑ̃] *n.m. A: & Hum:* suitor, admirer.

soupirer [supire] *v.i.* (*a*) to sigh; **en soupirant,** with a sigh; (*b*) **s. après, pour, à, vers, qch.,** to long, yearn, sigh, for sth.

souple [supl̥] *a.* supple; (*a*) flexible (branch, etc.); lithe (body, figure); limp (binding); soft (leather, hair); **esprit s.,** adaptable, versatile, mind; *I.C.E:* **moteur s.,** flexible engine; (*b*) (*of pers.*) docile, tractable; accommodating.

souplesse [suplɛs] *n.f.* **1.** suppleness; flexibility; litheness (of body, movement, etc.); adaptability (of mind); versatility; ease (of style). **2. il a beaucoup de s.,** he knows how to be diplomatic.

souquenille [suknij] *n.f. O:* smock.

souquer [suke] *Nau:* **1.** *v.tr.* to haul (rope) taut. **2.** *v.i.* **s. sur les avirons,** to pull (hard) at the oars.

source [surs] *n.f.* **1.** (*a*) spring; source (of a river); **eau de s.,** spring water; **s. d'eau minérale,** mineral spring; **s. thermale,** hot spring; *F:* **ça coule de s.,** it's (i) obvious, (ii) inevitable, natural; (*b*) **s. de pétrole,** oil spring; **s. jaillissante,** gusher; **s. boueuse,** mud geyser, mud volcano; (*c*) *Opt:* **s. lumineuse,** light source; *El:* **s. d'énergie, s. d'alimentation,** power supply; *Cmptr:* **s. de données,** data source; **code s.,** source code. **2.** origin (of evil, wealth, news, etc.); *Fin:* **imposé à la s.,** taxed at source; **aller à la s. du mal,** to get to the root of the evil; **informations de s. américaine,** information from an American source; **je le tiens de bonne s.,** I have it on good authority.

sourcier, -ière [sursje, -jɛr] *n.* water diviner; dowser; **baguette de s.,** divining rod, dowsing rod.

sourcil [sursi] *n.m.* eyebrow; **aux sourcils épais,** beetle-browed, with shaggy eyebrows.

sourcilier, -ière [sursilje, -jɛr] *a. Anat:* superciliary.

sourciller [sursije] *v.i.* to frown; **sans s.,** without batting an eyelid, without turning a hair.

sourcilleux, -euse [sursijø, -øz] *a.* **1.** *Lit:* haughty. **2.** fussy, finicky.

sourd, sourde [sur, surd] **1.** (*a*) *a.* deaf; **s. d'une oreille,** deaf in one ear; *F:* **s. comme un pot,** deaf as a post; **rester s. aux prières,** to turn a deaf ear, to be deaf, to entreaties; (*b*) *n.* deaf person; **crier comme un s.,** to yell; **frapper, taper, comme un s.,** to hit out wildly; **autant vaut parler à un s.,** you might as well talk to a brick wall; **un dialogue de sourds,** a dialogue of the deaf. **2.** *a.* dull (tint, pain); dull, muffled (noise); muted (string); hollow (voice); secret (desire); veiled (hostility); underhand (agitation); *Ling:* **(consonne) sourde,** voiceless consonant.

sourdement [surdəmɑ̃] *adv.* (*a*) dully, with a dull, hollow, sound; (*b*) secretly.

sourdine [surdin] *n.f.* (*a*) *Mus:* mute; **en s.,** (i) softly, quietly; (ii) under one's breath; (iii) in secret, on the sly; **violons en s.,** muted violins; **mettre une s. à ses plaintes,** to tone down one's complaints; (*b*) *W.Tel: etc:* damper.

sourdingue [surdɛ̃g] *a. & n. P:* deaf (person).

sourd-muet, sourde-muette [surmɥɛ, surdmɥɛt] **1.** *a.* deaf-and-dumb. **2.** *n.* deaf mute; *pl. sourds-muets, sourdes-muettes.*

sourdre [surdr̥] *v.i.* (*used only in 3rd pers.* **il sourd, ils sourdent,** *and in inf.; the past tenses are rare*) *A: & Lit:* (*of water*) to spring, rise (up); (*of emotion*) to well up.

souriant [surjɑ̃] *a.* smiling; pleasant (climate, surroundings).

souriceau, -eaux [suriso] *n.m.* young mouse.

souricier [surisje] *n.m.* (*cat, etc.*) mouser.

souricière [surisjɛr] *n.f.* (*a*) mousetrap; (*b*) trap, *esp.* police trap.

sourire[1] [surir] *v.i.* (*conj. like* RIRE) **1.** to smile (**à,** at); **faire s.,** to provoke a smile. **2.** (*a*) (*of thgs*) to please; to appeal (**à qn,** to s.o.); (*b*) **tout lui sourit,** he, she, makes a success of everything.

sourire[2] *n.m.* smile; **large s.,** broad smile; grin; **le s. aux lèvres,** with a smile on his lips; **adresser un s. à qn,** to give s.o. a smile; **garder le s.,** to keep smiling.

souris [suri] *n.f.* **1.** (*a*) mouse; **s. de terre,** field mouse; **s. d'eau,** water shrew; **s. sauteuse, s. de montagne,** jerboa, jumping mouse; **s. blanche,** white mouse; **on aurait entendu trotter une s.,** you could have heard a pin drop; *a.inv.* **(couleur) gris (de) s.,** mouse colour, *NAm:* color; (*b*) *P:* bird, dame; **s. d'hôtel,** (female) hotel thief. **2.** knuckle end (of leg of mutton).

sournois, -oise [surnwa, -waz] *a.* sly, crafty (person); cunning, shifty (look); underhand (person, dealings).

sournoisement [surnwazmɑ̃] *adv.* slyly.

sournoiserie [surnwazri] *n.f.* **1.** slyness; craftiness. **2.** underhand trick.

sous [su] *prep.* **1.** under(neath), beneath, below; (*a*) **s'asseoir s. un arbre,** to sit down under a tree; **s. terre,** underground, below ground; **s. clef,** under lock and key; **s. le sceau du secret,** under pledge of secrecy; **s. nos propres yeux,** before our very eyes; **chercher un mot s. la lettre S,** to look up a word under (the letter) S; **connu s. le nom de . . .,** known as, by the name of . . .; **s. la pluie,** in the rain; *Mil:* **s. les armes,** under arms; fighting; *Nau:* **s. pavillon anglais,** flying the English flag; **s. le vent,** under the lee; (*b*) **s. les tropiques,** in the tropics; **s. l'équateur,** at the equator; (*c*) **s. Louis XIV,** under, in the reign of, Louis XIV; **s. peine de mort,** on, under, pain of death; **s. un prétexte,** under a pretext. **2.** within; **s. trois jours,** within three days; **s. peu,** before long.

sous- [su] *before vowel sound* [suz] *comb.fm.* sub-; under-; assistant. NOTE: *in the plural of hyphenated words of which the first element is* **sous-, sous-** *remains invariable and the second element takes the pl. form.*

sous-affréter [suzafrete] *v.tr.* (*conj. like* FRÉTER) to sub-charter (ship, etc.).

sous-aide [suzɛd] *n.* junior assistant.

sous-alimentation [suzalimɑ̃tasjɔ̃] *n.f.* malnutrition; undernourishment; underfeeding.

sous-alimenté, -ée [suzalimɑ̃te] *a. & n.* underfed, undernourished (person).

sous-arrondissement [suzarɔ̃dismɑ̃] *n.m.* subdistrict (of naval administration).

sous-bail [subaj] *n.m.* sublease; *pl. sous-baux.*

sous-bibliothécaire [subiblijɔtekɛr] *n.* sub-librarian, assistant librarian.

sous-bois [subwa] *n.m.inv.* **1.** undergrowth; underwood. **2.** *Art:* picture of a forest interior.

sous-brigadier [subrigadje] *n.m.* lance-corporal (of excise officers, of police).

sous-calibré [sukalibre] *a. Artil:* subcalibre (projectile).

sous-centre [susɑ̃tr̥] *n.m. Cmptr:* subcentre, *NAm:* subcenter.

sous-chef [suʃɛf] *n.m.* **1.** deputy chief clerk. **2.** assistant manager; **s.-c. de gare,** deputy stationmaster. **3.** *Mus:* deputy conductor.

sous-classe [suklas] *n.f. Nat.Hist:* subclass.

sous-commission [sukɔmisjɔ̃] *n.f.* **1.** subcommittee. **2.** subcommission.

sous-consommation [sukɔ̃sɔmasjɔ̃] *n.f.inv. Pol. Ec:* underconsumption.

sous-continent [sukɔ̃tinɑ̃] *n.m. Geog:* subcontinent.

sous-couche [sukuʃ] *n.f.* substratum.

souscripteur, -trice [suskriptœr, -tris] *n.* subscriber.
souscription [suskripsjɔ̃] *n.f.* **1.** *Fin: etc:* subscription, application (**à des actions,** for shares). **2.** subscription, contribution (of sum of money); **lancer une s.,** to start a fund.
souscrire [suskrir] (*conj. like* ÉCRIRE) **1.** *v.tr.* (*a*) to sign; (*b*) to subscribe (money to a charity); to take out (a subscription, *Ins:* a policy); to subscribe, apply, for (shares). **2.** *v.i.* (*a*) **s. à une nouvelle édition,** to subscribe for a new edition; *Fin:* **s. à une émission,** to apply for, subscribe to, an issue; **s. à des actions,** to take up shares; (*b*) **s. pour (la somme de) mille francs,** to subscribe a thousand francs; **s. pour une œuvre de bienfaisance,** to subscribe to a charity; (*c*) to subscribe to, to endorse (an opinion).
sous-critique [sukritik] *a. Atom.Ph: etc:* subcritical.
sous-cutané [sukytane] *a.* subcutaneous.
sous-développé, -ée [sudevlɔpe] *a.* (*a*) *Pol.Ec:* underdeveloped (country, etc.); (*b*) underequipped, undermechanized (factory, etc.).
sous-développement [sudevlɔpmɑ̃] *n.m. Pol.Ec:* underdevelopment.
sous-diacre [sudjakr̥] *n.m.* subdeacon.
sous-directeur, -trice [sudirɛktœr, -tris] *n.* **1.** assistant manager(ess). **2.** *Sch:* deputy head(master, -mistress).
sous-diviser [sudivize] *v.tr.* to subdivide.
sous-division [sudivizjɔ̃] *n.f.* subdivision.
sous-dominante [sudɔminɑ̃t] *n.f. Mus:* subdominant; fa (of movable do system).
sous-économe [suzekɔnɔm] *n.* assistant treasurer, assistant bursar.
sous-embranchement [suzɑ̃brɑ̃ʃmɑ̃] *n.f. Nat. Hist:* subphylum.
sous-emploi [suzɑ̃plwa] *n.m.inv. Pol.Ec:* underemployment.
sous-ensemble [suzɑ̃sɑ̃bl̥] *n.m. Mec.E: Mth: Cmptr:* subassembly; subset.
sous-entendre [suzɑ̃tɑ̃dr̥] *v.tr.* to understand; to imply; *Gram:* **on sous-entend "pendant",** "*pendant*" is understood.
sous-entendu [suzɑ̃tɑ̃dy] *n.m.* (*a*) thing understood; (*b*) implication; *Pej:* insinuation.
sous-entrepreneur [suzɑ̃trəprənœr] *n.m. Const:* subcontractor.
sous-équipé [suzekipe] *a. Pol.Ec:* underequipped.
sous-espace [suzɛspas] *n.m. Mth:* subspace.
sous-espèce [suzɛspɛs] *n.f.* subspecies.
sous-estimation [suzɛstimasjɔ̃] *n.f.*, **sous-évaluation** [suzevalɥasjɔ̃] *n.f.* undervaluation.
sous-estimer [suzɛstime], **sous-évaluer** [suzevalɥe] *v.tr.* to underestimate, undervalue, underrate.
sous-exposer [suzɛkspoze] *v.tr. Phot:* to underexpose.
sous-exposition [suzɛkspozisjɔ̃] *n.f. Phot:* underexposure.
sous-famille [sufamij] *n.f. Nat.Hist:* subfamily.
sous-fifre [sufifr̥] *n.m. F:* second fiddle; dogsbody.
sous(-)garde [sugard] *n.f. Sm.a:* trigger guard.
sous-genre [suʒɑ̃r] *n.m. Nat.Hist:* subgenus.
sous-gouverneur [suguvɛrnœr] *n.m.* deputy governor, vice-governor.
sous-groupe [sugrup] *n.m. Nat.Hist: Mth:* subgroup.
sous-ingénieur [suzɛ̃ʒenjœr] *n.m. Ind: etc:* assistant engineer.
sous-inspecteur, -trice [suzɛ̃spɛktœr, -tris] *n.* assistant inspector, inspectress.
sous-jacent [suʒasɑ̃] *a.* underlying.
Sous-le-vent [sulvɑ̃] *Pr.n. Geog:* **les îles S.-le-v.,** the Leeward Islands.
sous-lieutenant [suljøtnɑ̃] *n.m. Mil:* second lieutenant; *Navy:* sub-lieutenant; *Av:* **s.-l. (aviateur),** pilot officer.
sous-locataire [sulɔkatɛr] *n.* subtenant, sublessee.
sous-location [sulɔkasjɔ̃] *n.f.* **1.** (*a*) subletting; (*b*) subrenting. **2.** subtenancy; sublease.
sous-louer [sulwe] *v.tr.* **1.** to sublet (house). **2.** to rent (house) from a tenant.
sous-main [sumɛ̃] *n.m.inv.* blotting pad; *F:* **en s.-m.,** secretly; behind the scenes.
sous-maître, -maîtresse [sumɛtr̥, -mɛtrɛs] *A:* **1.** *n. Sch:* teacher's assistant. **2.** *n.f.* assistant to brothel keeper.
sous-marin [sumarɛ̃] **1.** *a.* (*a*) submarine (vessel, volcano, etc.); submerged (reef); (*b*) underwater; **chasse s.-marine,** underwater fishing; **masque s.-m.,** frogman's mask. **2.** *n.m.* submarine; **s.-m. nucléaire,** nuclear-powered submarine; **s.-m. de poche,** pocket submarine.
sous-marinier [sumarinje] *n.m.* submariner.
sous-maxillaire [sumaksilɛr] *a. Anat:* submaxillary (glands, etc.).
sous-médiante [sumedjɑ̃t] *n.f. Mus:* supertonic; re (of Movable Do system).
sous-ministre [suministr̥] *n.m. Fr.C: Adm:* deputy minister.
sous-multiple [sumyltipl̥] *a. & n.m. Mth:* submultiple (**de,** of).
sous-nappe [sunap] *n.f.* underlay (for tablecloth).
sous-œuvre [suzœvr̥] *n.m. Const: Civ.E:* **(reprise en) s.-o.,** underpinning.
sous-off [suzɔf] *n.m. Mil: F:* N.C.O., non-com.
sous-officier [suzɔfisje] *n.m.* **1.** *Mil:* non-commissioned officer; warrant officer. **2.** *Navy:* petty officer.
sous-ordre [suzɔrdr̥] *n.m.* **1.** *Pej:* subordinate, underling. **2.** *Nat.Hist:* suborder.
sous-palan (en) [ɑ̃supalɑ̃] *adv.phr. Com: Nau:* **livraison en s.-p.,** delivery (of goods) ready for shipping.
sous-payer [supeje] *v.tr.* (*conj. like* PAYER) to underpay.
sous-préfectoral, -aux [suprefɛktɔral, -o] *a.* subprefectorial.
sous-préfecture [suprefɛktyr] *n.f.* subprefecture.
sous-préfet [suprefɛ] *n.m. Adm:* sub-prefect.
sous-principal, -aux [suprɛ̃sipal, -o] *n.m. Sch:* vice-principal.
sous-production [suprɔdyksjɔ̃] *n.f. Pol.Ec:* underproduction.
sous-produit [suprɔdɥi] *n.m. Ind: etc:* by-product; secondary product.
sous-programme [suprɔgram] *n.m. Cmptr:* subroutine, subprogram(me).
sous-race [suras] *n.f. Z:* subrace.
sous-refroidissement [surəfrwadismɑ̃] *n.m. Ph:* supercooling.
sous-secrétaire [susəkretɛr] *n.* undersecretary.
sous-secrétariat [susəkretarja] *n.m.* undersecretaryship.
sous-seing [susɛ̃] *n.m.* private agreement, contract.
soussigné, -ée [susiɲe] *a. & n.* undersigned.
sous-sol [susɔl] *n.m.* **1.** *Geol:* subsoil, substratum. **2.** *Const:* basement.
sous-station [sustasjɔ̃] *n.f. El:* substation.
sous-tasse [sutas] *n.f.* saucer.
sous-tendre [sutɑ̃dr̥] *v.tr.* **1.** *Mth:* to subtend. **2.** *Fig:* to underlie.
sous-tension [sutɑ̃sjɔ̃] *n.f. El:* undervoltage.
sous-titrage [sutitraʒ] *n.m.; Cin:* subtitling.
sous-titre [sutitr̥] *n.m.* subtitle.

sous-titrer [sutitre] *v.tr. Cin:* to subtitle; **film sous-titré en anglais,** film with English subtitles.

soustractif, -ive [sustraktif, -iv] *a. Mth: Phot:* subtractive.

soustraction [sustraksjɔ̃] *n.f.* (*a*) removal; (*b*) *Mth: Elcs:* subtraction.

soustraire [sustrɛr] (*conj. like* TRAIRE) **1.** *v.tr.* (*a*) to take away, remove; (*b*) to protect, shield (s.o. from sth.); (*c*) *Mth: etc:* to subtract (**de,** from). **2. se s. à qch.,** to avoid, elude, sth.; **se s. à une obligation,** to back out of an obligation.

sous-traitance [sutrɛtɑ̃s] *n.f.* subcontracting.

sous-traitant [sutrɛtɑ̃] *n.m.* subcontractor.

sous-traité [sutrete] *n.m.* subcontract.

sous-traiter [sutrete] *v.tr.* **1.** to subcontract. **2.** to sublet (a contract).

sous-variété [suvarjete] *n.m.* subvariety.

sous-ventrière [suvɑ̃trijɛr] *n.f. Harn:* (*a*) belly-band; (*b*) saddlegirth.

sous-verre [suvɛr] *n.m.inv.* glass, passe-partout, mount(ing).

sous-vêtement [suvɛtmɑ̃] *n.m.* undergarment; **sous-vêtements,** underwear.

sous-virer [suvire] *v.i. Aut:* to understeer.

soutache [sutaʃ] *n.f. Cost:* braid.

soutacher [sutaʃe] *v.tr. Cost:* to braid.

soutane [sutan] *n.f.* cassock, soutane; **prendre la s.,** to take (holy) orders; **la s.,** the cloth.

soute [sut] *n.f. Nau:* store room; (sail, rope) locker; (water, oil) tank; **s. à charbon,** coal bunker; **s. à munitions,** magazine; **s. aux bagages,** (i) *Nau:* luggage room, baggage room; (ii) *Av:* luggage, *NAm:* baggage, compartment; **s. à valeurs,** strongroom; *Av:* **s. à essence,** refuelling point; *Mil.Av:* **s. à bombes,** bomb bay.

soutenable [sutnabḷ] *a.* (*a*) *A:* bearable, supportable (burden, existence, etc.); (*b*) tenable (opinion); arguable (theory); **peu s.,** untenable.

soutenance [sutnɑ̃s] *n.f. Sch:* defence (of a thesis).

soutènement [sutɛnmɑ̃] *n.m.* support; *Arch: Civ.E:* **mur de s.,** retaining, supporting, sustaining, wall.

souteneur, -euse [sutnœr, -øz] **1.** *n.* upholder (of system, etc.). **2.** *n.m.* pimp, ponce.

soutenir [sutnir] (*conj. like* TENIR) **1.** *v.tr.* (*a*) to support (s.o., sth.); to hold (s.o., sth.) up; to sustain (s.o.), to keep (s.o.) going; (*b*) to keep, maintain (parents, family); (*c*) to back (up), support (undertaking, cause, person); to back (s.o. financially); (*in games*) to back up (one's partner); *Mil:* to support (troops); (*d*) to maintain, uphold (opinion, one's character); to assert, affirm (fact); *Sch:* to defend (a thesis); (*e*) to keep up, maintain (conversation, speed, a struggle, one's rank, a part, one's credit); **il ne soutient pas la boisson,** he can't take his drink; (*f*) to bear (slight, reproach, comparison); to hold out against (siege, attack). **2. se s.** (*a*) **se s. sur ses pieds,** to stand on one's feet; **je ne me soutiens plus,** I'm ready to drop; (*b*) *Fig:* to keep one's head; (*c*) (*of fashion, friendship, etc.*) to last, continue; **l'intérêt se soutient,** the interest is kept up, does not flag.

soutenu [sutny] *a.* **1.** sustained (attention, effort); unflagging, constant (interest); steady (trot, market). **2.** sustained (style of writing, etc.). **3.** firm (outline); solid, strong (colour, *NAm:* color).

souterrain [sutɛrɛ̃] **1.** *a.* (*a*) underground, subterranean (water, passage); **passage s.,** subway; **chemin de fer s.,** underground railway, *NAm:* subway; (*b*) *Fig:* underhand (methods). **2.** *n.m.* underground passage; tunnel.

soutien [sutjɛ̃] *n.m.* **1.** *Pol: Mil: etc:* support; **en s.,** in support; *Mil:* **unité de s.,** support unit. **2.** (*a*) support, prop; **il est sans s.,** he has nobody behind him; (*b*) supporter; mainstay; *Adm:* **s. de famille,** breadwinner.

soutien-gorge [sutjɛ̃gɔrʒ] *n.m. Cost:* brassière, *F:* bra; *pl. soutiens-gorge.*

soutirage [sutiraʒ] *n.m.* drawing off, racking, clarifying (of wine, etc.).

soutirer [sutire] *v.tr.* to draw off, rack (wine, etc.); to extract (money, etc., from s.o.).

souvenance [suvnɑ̃s] *n.f. A: & Lit:* recollection.

souvenir[1] [suvnir] (*conj. like* VENIR; *aux.* **être**) **1.** *v.impers. Lit:* **il me souvient de . . .,** I remember . . .. **2. se s. de qch., de qn,** to remember, recall, sth., s.o.; **nous nous souviendrons de lui,** we shall remember him; **autant que je m'en souviens, que je m'en souvienne,** to the best of my memory, recollection; **faire s. qn de qch.,** to remind s.o. of sth.

souvenir[2] *n.m.* **1.** recollection, memory; **avoir gardé un bon s. de qch.,** to have a pleasant recollection of sth.; **je n'en ai pas s.,** I have no recollection of it; **si mes souvenirs sont exacts,** if my memory serves me (well); **souvenirs de ma jeunesse,** memories of my youth; **pays riche en souvenirs historiques,** country rich in historical associations; **veuillez me rappeler à son bon s.,** please remember me to him; **ma mère vous envoie son affectueux s.,** mother sends her love; **en s. de qn,** in remembrance of s.o.; **en s. du passé,** for old times' sake. **2.** (*token of remembrance*) (*a*) keepsake, souvenir, memento (of pers., place); (*b*) **offrir un s. à qn,** to make a presentation to s.o. (on retirement, etc.).

souvent [suvɑ̃] *adv.* often; **peu s.,** not often; seldom, infrequently; **il ne vient pas s. nous voir,** he doesn't often come and see us; **il est malade plus s. qu'à son tour,** he has more than his share of illness; **le plus s.,** usually; as often as not; more often than not; *P:* **plus s.!** no fear! not likely!

souventefois, souventes fois [suvɑ̃tfwa] *adv. A:* oft(-times).

souverain, -aine [suvrɛ̃, -ɛn] **1.** *a.* sovereign (power, prince, state, beauty, remedy, etc.); supreme (happiness, contempt, *Jur:* court). **2.** (*a*) *n.* sovereign; (*b*) *n.m. Num: A:* sovereign.

souverainement [suvrɛnmɑ̃] *adv.* **1.** supremely; intensely. **2.** *Jur:* **juger s.,** to judge without appeal.

souveraineté [suvrɛnte] *n.f.* sovereignty, supreme authority (over s.o.); supremacy (of law, right).

soviet [sɔvjɛt] *n.m.* soviet.

soviétique [sɔvjetik] *a. & n.* Soviet (citizen).

soviétiser [sɔvjetize] *v.tr.* to sovietize.

soya [sɔja] *n.m. Bot:* soya (bean).

soyeux, -euse [swajø, -øz] **1.** *a.* silky. **2.** *n.m.* silk merchant.

spacieux, -euse [spasjø, -øz] *a.* spacious (room); roomy (car).

spadassin [spadasɛ̃] *n.m.* (*a*) *A:* swordsman; (*b*) hired assassin.

spadice [spadis] *n.m. Bot:* spadix.

spaghetti [spageti] *n.m.pl. Cu:* spaghetti.

spahi [spai] *n.m. Mil:* spahi.

spalax [spalaks] *n.m. Z:* spalax; mole rat.

spallation [spalasjɔ̃] *n.f. Atom.Ph:* spallation.

sparadrap [sparadra] *n.m.* (adhesive, sticking) plaster.

spart [spart] *n.m. Bot:* esparto (grass).

sparte[1] [spart] *n.m. Bot:* esparto (grass).

Sparte[2] *Pr.n.f. Geog:* Sparta.

spartiate [sparsjat] **1.** *a. & n. Geog: & Fig:* Spartan. **2.** *n.f.* leather sandal.

spasme [spasm] *n.m.* spasm.

spasmodique [spasmɔdik] *a. Med:* spasmodic; spastic.

spasmodiquement [spasmɔdikmɑ̃] *adv.* spasmodically.

spath [spat] *n.m. Miner:* spar.
spathique [spatik] *a. Miner:* spathic, sparry.
spatial, -aux [spasjal, -o] *a.* spatial, relating to space; **engin s.,** spacecraft; **voyage s.,** space flight; **combinaison spatiale,** spacesuit; **guerre spatiale,** space warfare; *Elcs:* **charge spatiale,** space charge.
spatialisation [spasjalizasjɔ̃] *n.f.* spatialization.
spatialiser [spasjalize] *v.tr.* **1.** to spatialize. **2.** to send, project, into space; to put into orbit.
spatio-temporel, -elle [spasjɔtɑ̃pɔrɛl] *a.* space-time; *pl. spatio-temporel(le)s.*
spatule [spatyl] *n.f.* **1.** (*a*) spatula; **en s.,** spatulate; (*b*) ski tip. **2.** *Orn:* spoonbill.
spatulé [spatyle] *a.* spatulate.
speaker [spikœr] *n.m. W.Tel: T.V:* announcer.
speakerine [spikrin] *n.f. W.Tel: T.V:* (woman) announcer.
spécial, -aux [spesjal, -o] *a.* special; particular; specialized (knowledge); **privilège s. aux militaires,** privilege reserved for, restricted to, military men; *Journ:* **envoyé s.,** special correspondent; *F:* **c'est un peu s.,** it's rather odd, peculiar; **mœurs spéciales** = homosexuality.
spécialement [spesjalmɑ̃] *adv.* (e)specially, particularly.
spécialisation [spesjalizasjɔ̃] *n.f.* specialization, specializing.
spécialisé [spesjalize] *a.* specialized, special (work, materials, etc.); **ouvrier s.,** semi-skilled worker.
spécialiser [spesjalize] (*a*) *v.tr. A:* to specify; (*b*) **se s. dans qch.,** to specialize, be a specialist, in sth.
spécialiste [spesjalist] *n.* specialist (**en,** in); expert (**en,** on); *Med:* **s. du cœur,** heart specialist; **s. du vol à voile,** gliding expert; *Iron: F:* **elle est s. de ce genre de gaffes,** she specializes in that sort of blunder.
spécialité [spesjalite] *n.f.* **1.** speciality, *NAm:* specialty; special feature, function, class of goods, line of business; particular branch (of a service); **faire sa s. de qch.,** to specialize in, make a special study of, sth.; **il a la s. de me taper sur les nerfs,** he has a knack of getting on my nerves. **2. spécialités pharmaceutiques,** patent medicines.
spécieusement [spesjøzmɑ̃] *adv.* speciously.
spécieux, -euse [spesjø, -øz] *a.* specious; plausible (pretext, etc.).
spécification [spesifikasjɔ̃] *n.f.* specification.
spécificité [spesifisite] *n.f. Med: etc:* specificity.
spécifier [spesifje] *v.tr.* (*impf. & pr. sub.* **n. spécifiions, v. spécifiiez**) to specify; to state definitely; **compte spécifié,** detailed account, itemized account.
spécifique [spesifik] **1.** *a.* specific; *Cmptr:* **équipement terminal s.,** job-oriented terminal. **2.** *n.m. Med:* specific (remedy) (**contre,** for).
spécifiquement [spesifikmɑ̃] *adv.* specifically.
spécimen [spesimɛn] *n.m.* specimen; *Publ:* inspection copy; **page s.,** specimen page.
spectacle [spɛktakl̥] *n.m.* **1.** spectacle, sight, scene; **se donner en s.,** to make an exhibition of oneself. **2.** *Th:* play, entertainment, show; **aller au s.,** to go to the theatre, *NAm:* theater; **salle de s.,** (concert, etc.) hall; theatre; *Th:* **pièce à grand s.,** spectacular play, lavish production; *Cin:* **film à grand s.,** epic.
spectaculaire [spɛktakylɛr] *a.* (*a*) spectacular; (*b*) dramatic.
spectateur, -trice [spɛktatœr, -tris] *n.* spectator, onlooker; witness (of accident, etc.); *pl. Th:* audience.
spectral, -aux [spɛktral, -o] *a.* spectral. **1.** ghostly. **2.** *Opt:* of the spectrum.
spectre [spɛktr̥] *n.m.* **1.** ghost, apparition; spectre, *NAm:* specter (of war, etc.). **2.** *Ph: etc:* spectrum.
spectrogramme [spɛktrɔgram] *n.m.* spectrogram(me).
spectrographe [spɛktrɔgraf] *n.m.* spectrograph.
spectroscope [spɛktrɔskɔp] *n.m. Opt:* spectroscope.
spectroscopie [spɛktrɔskɔpi] *n.f.* spectroscopy.
spéculaire [spekylɛr] *a.* (*a*) specular (mineral); (*b*) *Med:* **écriture s.,** mirror writing.
spéculateur, -trice [spekylatœr, -tris] *n. Fin:* speculator.
spéculatif, -ive [spekylatif, -iv] *a. Phil: Fin:* speculative.
spéculation [spekylasjɔ̃] *n.f.* **1.** speculation (**sur,** on); theory, hypothesis. **2.** *Fin:* speculation.
spéculer [spekyle] *v.i.* **1.** to speculate, cogitate (**sur,** on, about); to ponder (**sur,** over). **2.** *Fin:* to speculate (**sur,** in; **à,** for); *Fig:* **s. sur qch.,** to count, bank, on sth.
speculum, spéculum [spekylɔm] *n.m. Med:* speculum.
spéléologie [speleɔlɔʒi] *n.f.* spel(a)eology; caving; potholing, *NAm:* spelunking.
spéléologique [speleɔlɔʒik] *a.* spel(a)eological.
spéléologue [speleɔlɔg] *n.* spel(a)eologist; potholer, *NAm:* spelunker.
spencer [spɛ̃sɛr] *n.m. Cost:* **1.** *Nau:* monkey jacket; *Mil: etc:* mess jacket. **2.** (woman's) (i) short jacket, (ii) *A:* spencer.
spermaceti [spɛrmaseti] *n.m.* spermaceti.
spermatique [spɛrmatik] *a. Anat:* spermatic.
spermatogénèse [spɛrmatɔʒenɛz] *n.f. Biol:* spermatogenesis.
spermatozoaire [spɛrmatɔzɔɛr] *n.m.,* **spermatozoïde** [spɛrmatɔzɔid] *n.m. Biol:* spermatozoon, *pl.* spermatazoa.
sperme [spɛrm] *n.m.* **1.** *Physiol:* sperm, semen. **2. s. de baleine,** spermaceti.
spermicide [spɛrmisid] *a. Med:* **1.** *a.* spermicidal. **2.** *n.m.* spermicide.
spermophile [spɛrmɔfil] *n.m. Z:* spermophile, gopher.
sphaigne [sfɛɲ] *n.f. Bot:* sphagnum, peat moss.
sphénoïde [sfenɔid] *a. & n.m. Anat:* sphenoid.
sphère [sfɛr] *n.f.* **1.** sphere; *Geog:* **s. terrestre,** globe. **2.** sphere (of activity, influence, etc.).
sphéricité [sferisite] *n.f.* sphericity.
sphérique [sferik] *a.* spherical.
sphéroïde [sferɔid] *n.m.* spheroid.
sphéromètre [sferɔmɛtr̥] *n.m.* spherometer.
sphincter [sfɛ̃ktɛr] *n.m. Anat:* sphincter.
sphinx [sfɛ̃ks] *n.m.* **1.** *Myth:* sphinx; **sourire de s.,** sphinx-like smile. **2.** *Ent:* hawkmoth.
sphygmomanomètre [sfigmɔmanɔmɛtr̥] *n.m. Med:* sphygmomanometer.
spic [spik] *n.m. Bot:* spike lavender.
spicule [spikyl] *n.m. Spong: Astr: etc:* spicule.
spin [spin] *n.m. Atom.Ph:* spin.
spina-bifida [spinabifida] *n.m. Med:* spina bifida.
spinal, -aux [spinal, -o] *a. Anat:* spinal.
spinelle[1] [spinɛl] *a. & n.m. Miner:* spinel.
spinelle[2] *n.f. Nat.Hist:* spinule.
spinnaker [spinakɛr] *n.m. Nau:* spinnaker.
spinule [spinyl] *n.f. Nat.Hist:* spinule.
spiracle [spirakl̥] *n.m. Amph:* spiracle (of a tadpole).
spiral, -aux [spiral, -o] **1.** *a.* spiral. **2.** *n.m.* hairspring (of watch). **3.** *n.f.* **spirale,** spiral, helix; **en spirale,** (i) *adv.* in a spiral, spirally; (ii) *adj.* spiral; **descendre, monter, en spirale,** to spiral down, up.
spirant, -ante [spirɑ̃, -ɑ̃t] *Ling:* **1.** *a.* spirant. **2.** *n.f.* **spirante,** spirant.
spire [spir] *n.f.* (single) turn (of spiral, *El:* of coil); whorl.
spirée [spire] *n.f. Bot:* spiraea, *NAm:* spirea.
spirille [spirij] *n.m. Bac:* spirillum.

spirite [spirit] *Psychics:* **1.** *a.* spiritualistic. **2.** *n.* spiritualist.
spiritisme [spiritism] *n.m. Psychics:* spirit(ual)ism.
spiritualiser [spiritɥalize] *v.tr.* to spiritualize.
spiritualisme [spiritɥalism] *n.m. Phil:* spiritualism.
spiritualiste [spiritɥalist] *Phil:* **1.** *a.* spiritualistic (philosophy). **2.** *n.* spiritualist.
spiritualité [spiritɥalite] *n.f. Phil:* spirituality.
spirituel, -elle [spiritɥɛl] **1.** (*a*) *a.* spiritual (being, power, life, etc.); sacred (music); **père s.,** spiritual father; (*b*) *n.m.* **le s.,** (i) things spiritual; (ii) spiritual power. **2.** *a.* witty (person, answer, etc.).
spirituellement [spiritɥɛlmɑ̃] *adv.* **1.** spiritually. **2.** wittily.
spiritueux, -euse [spiritɥø, -øz] **1.** *a.* spirituous (liquor). **2.** *n.m. Adm:* spirituous liquor; **les s.,** spirits.
spiroïdal, -aux [spirɔidal, -o] *a.* spiroid(al).
splanchnique [splɑ̃knik] *a. Anat:* splanchnic.
spleen [splin] *n.m. Lit:* spleen.
spleenétique [splinetik] *a.* splenetic.
splendeur [splɑ̃dœr] *n.f.* splendour, *NAm:* splendor; (*a*) *Lit:* radiance, brightness; (*b*) grandeur, glory.
splendide [splɑ̃did] *a.* splendid. **1.** brilliant (sun). **2.** magnificent (palace, victory, meal); glorious (sunset).
splendidement [splɑ̃didmɑ̃] *adv.* splendidly.
splénectomie [splenɛktɔmi] *n.f. Surg:* splenectomy.
splénétique [splenetik] *a.* splenetic.
splénique [splenik] *a. Anat:* splenic (artery, disease).
spoliateur, -trice [spɔljatœr, -tris] **1.** *n.* despoiler. **2.** *a.* spoliatory (law, etc.).
spoliation [spɔljasjɔ̃] *n.f.* despoiling, robbing (of s.o.); plundering, rifling (of tomb, house, etc.).
spolier [spɔlje] *v.tr.* (*impf. & pr.sub.* **n. spoliions, v. spoliiez**) to despoil, rob (s.o.) (**de,** of); to plunder, rifle (tomb, house, etc.).
spondée [spɔ̃de] *n.m. Pros:* spondee.
spondylarthrite [spɔ̃dilartrit] *n.f. Med:* spondylarthritis; **s. ankylosante,** ankylosing spondylitis.
spondylite [spɔ̃dilit] *n.f. Med:* spondylitis; **s. tuberculeuse,** Pott's disease.
spondylose [spɔ̃diloz] *n.f. Med:* spondylosis.
spongieux, -ieuse [spɔ̃ʒjø, -jøz] *a.* spongy.
spontané [spɔ̃tane] *a.* spontaneous (action, combustion, *Biol:* generation).
spontanéité [spɔ̃taneite] *n.f.* spontaneity.
spontanément [spɔ̃tanemɑ̃] *adv.* spontaneously.
sporadique [spɔradik] *a.* sporadic.
sporadiquement [spɔradikmɑ̃] *adv.* sporadically.
sporange [spɔrɑ̃ʒ] *n.m. Bot:* sporangium, spore case.
spore [spɔr] *n.f.* spore.
sporozoaire [spɔrɔzɔɛr] *n.m. Prot:* sporozoan.
sport [spɔr] **1.** *n.m.* sport; games; **sports d'hiver,** winter sports; **chaussures de s.,** sports shoes; *F:* **vous allez voir du s.,** now you're going to see some excitement. **2.** *a. inv.* (*a*) **vêtements s., costume s.,** casual clothes; **voiture s.,** sports car; (*b*) (*of pers.*) sporting.
sportif, -ive [spɔrtif, -iv] **1.** *a.* (*a*) sporting; (of) sport; devoted to sport, athletic; **édition sportive,** sports edition (of newspaper); **réunion sportive,** athletic meeting; **esprit s.,** sporting spirit; **être très s.,** to be (i) fond of sport, (ii) a good loser; (*b*) *Biol:* **variation sportive,** sport, *F:* freak (of nature). **2.** *n.* sportsman, -woman; games player; athlete.
sportivement [spɔrtivmɑ̃] *adv.* in a sporting spirit.
sportivité [spɔrtivite] *n.f.* sportsmanship; **il eut la s. de . . .,** he was sporting enough to . . ..
sporuler [spɔryle] *v.i. Biol:* to sporulate.
spot [spɔt] *n.m.* **1.** *T.V: Elcs: etc:* spot; *Rad:* blip. **2.** *Th:* spot(light).
spoutnik [sputnik] *n.m.* sputnik, artificial satellite.
sprat [sprat] *n.m. Ich:* sprat.
spray [sprɛ] *n.m.* spray, aerosol.
springbok [spriŋbɔk] *n.m. Z:* springbok.
springer [spriŋœr] *n.m. Z:* springer (spaniel).
sprint [sprint] *n.m. Sp:* sprint.
sprinter[1] [sprintœr] *n.m. Sp:* sprinter.
sprinter[2] [sprinte] *v.i. Sp:* to sprint.
sprue [spry] *n.f. Med:* sprue; psilosis.
squale [skwal] *n.m. Ich:* dogfish; shark.
squame [skwam] *n.f. Med: etc:* squama; scale.
squameux, -euse [skwamø, -øz] *a.* squamous, scaly.
square [skwar] *n.m.* (public) square (with garden).
squatter [skwatɛr] *n.m.* squatter.
squaw [skwo] *n.f.* (Indian) squaw.
squelette [skəlɛt] *n.m.* (*a*) skeleton; **c'est un vrai s.,** he's a living skeleton; (*b*) skeleton, framework (of ship, novel, etc.).
squelettique [skəletik] *a.* skeletal.
squille [skij] *n.f. Bot: Crust:* squill.
squirr(h)e [skir] *n.m. Med:* scirrhus.
stabilisant [stabilizɑ̃] *n.m. Ch:* stabilizing agent.
stabilisateur, -trice [stabilizatœr, -tris] **1.** *a.* stabilizing; **appareil s.,** stabilizing device, stabilizer gear. **2.** *n.m.* (*a*) *Aer: Nau: Mec.E: etc:* stabilizer; *Av:* tailplane; *El:* (frequency) monitor; (*b*) *Ch:* stabilizer.
stabilisation [stabilizasjɔ̃] *n.f.* stabilization.
stabilisé [stabilize] *a. Mec: Ch: Pol.Ec: etc:* stabilized; *Biol:* balanced.
stabiliser [stabilize] *v.tr.* to stabilize.
stabilité [stabilite] *n.f.* stability.
stable [stabl̥] *a.* stable (substance, equilibrium, character); lasting (peace).
stabulation [stabylasjɔ̃] *n.f.* (*a*) keeping (of cattle) in sheds; stabling (of horses); (*b*) *Pisc:* storing in tanks.
staccato [stakato] *adv. & n.m. Mus:* staccato.
stade [stad] *n.m.* **1.** stadium; sports ground. **2.** (*a*) stage (of evolution, development, disease, etc.); (*b*) *Ent:* instar (of caterpillars, etc.).
staff [staf] *n.m. Const:* (*building material*) staff.
stage [staʒ] *n.m.* period of probation, instruction, training; training course; (*of teacher*) teaching practice; (*of nurse*) probationary period.
stagiaire [staʒjɛr] **1.** *a.* training (period); (period) of instruction, probation; **interprète s.,** trainee interpreter. **2.** *n.* trainee; probationer.
stagnant [stagnɑ̃] *a.* stagnant (water, etc.).
stagnation [stagnasjɔ̃] *n.f.* stagnation; stagnancy (of water, etc.); *Fig:* **en s.,** at a standstill, stagnant.
stagner [stagne] *v.i.* (*of water, trade*) to stagnate.
stakhanovisme [stakanɔvism] *n.m.* stakhanovism.
stalactite [stalaktit] *n.f. Geol:* stalactite.
stalagmite [stalagmit] *n.f. Geol:* stalagmite.
stalinien, -ienne [stalinjɛ̃, -jɛn] *a. & n.* Stalinist.
stalinism [stalinism] *n.m.* Stalinism.
stalle [stal] *n.f.* **1.** stall (in cathedral). **2.** stall, box (in stable).
stance [stɑ̃s] *n.f. Pros:* stanza.
stand [stɑ̃d] *n.m.* **1.** stand (on racecourse, at exhibition, etc.); stall (at fete); *Rac: Aut:* **les stands de ravitaillement,** the pits. **2. s. (de tir),** rifle range. **3.** stand, rest (for typewriter, etc.).
standard [stɑ̃dar] **1.** *n.m.* (*a*) standard; (*b*) **s. de vie,** standard of living; (*c*) *Tp:* switchboard. **2.** *a.inv.* standard.
standardisation [stɑ̃dardizasjɔ̃] *n.f.* standardization.
standardiser [stɑ̃dardize] *v.tr.* to standardize.
standardiste [stɑ̃dardist] *n. Tp:* switchboard operator.
standing [stɑ̃diŋ] *n.m. F:* status, standing; **apparte-**

ment de grand s., luxury, flat, apartment; **quartier de grand s.,** select district.
stanneux, -euse [stanø, -øz] *a.* (*a*) *Ch:* stannous (oxide); (*b*) tinny (smell).
stannique [stanik] *a. Ch:* stannic (acid).
staphylin [stafilɛ̃] *n.m. Ent:* staphylinid, rove beetle, *F:* devil's coach horse.
staphylocoque [stafilɔkɔk] *n.m. Bac:* staphylococcus.
star [star] *n.f. Cin:* (*actress*) star.
starlette [starlɛt] *n.f. Cin:* (*young actress*) starlet.
starter [startɛr] *n.m.* **1.** *Rac:* starter (who gives the signal). **2.** *Aut:* choke.
stase [staz] *n.f. Med:* stasis.
statice [statis] *n.m. Bot:* statice, sea lavender.
station [stasjɔ̃] *n.f.* **1.** position; **s. debout,** standing position; **cela me fatigue de faire des stations debout,** standing tires me; **mise en s.,** setting up (of instrument, etc.). **2.** (*a*) break (in journey); halt, stop; **faire une s. à . . .,** to halt, stop, at . . .; (*b*) *Ecc:* station (of the Cross). **3.** (*a*) (bus) stop; *Rail:* halt; (underground, *NAm:* subway) station; (taxi) rank; *Aut:* **s. de lavage,** washing bay; (*b*) (ski, health, etc.) resort; (*c*) (research, etc.) establishment; (*d*) **s. radio,** radio station; **s. de télévision,** television broadcast station; (*e*) *El:* **s. centrale,** power station; *Hyd.E:* **s. pompage,** pumping station; (*f*) *Mil: etc:* post, station.
stationnaire [stasjɔnɛr] **1.** *a.* stationary; steady (barometer). **2.** *n.m. Navy:* guardship, station ship.
stationnement [stasjɔnmɑ̃] *n.m.* **1.** stopping, parking (of cars, etc.); **s. interdit,** no parking; no waiting. **2.** (*a*) (taxi, cab) rank; (*b*) car park, *NAm:* parking lot; (*c*) *Av:* **aire de s.,** apron.
stationner [stasjɔne] *v.i.* to stop; (*of car, etc.*) to park (in street, etc.); *P.N:* **défense de s.,** no parking; no waiting.
station-service [stasjɔ̃sɛrvis] *n.f. Aut:* service station; filling station; petrol, *NAm:* gas, station; *pl. stations-service.*
statique [statik] **1.** *a.* static (electricity, etc.). **2.** *n.f.* statics.
statiquement [statikmɑ̃] *adv.* statically.
statisticien, -ienne [statistisjɛ̃, -jɛn] *n.* statistician.
statistique [statistik] **1.** *a.* statistical. **2.** *n.f.* (*a*) statistics; (*b*) *pl.* statistical tables; statistics, figures.
statistiquement [statistikmɑ̃] *adv.* statistically.
statoréacteur [statɔreaktœr] *n.m. Av:* ramjet.
statuaire [statɥɛr] **1.** *a.* statuary (art, marble, etc.). **2.** *n.* sculptor, *f.* sculptress. **3.** *n.f.* (art of) statuary.
statue [staty] *n.f.* statue; image; **immobile comme une s.,** stock-still.
statuer [statɥe] *v.i.* to give a decision, a ruling (**sur,** on).
statuette [statɥɛt] *n.f.* statuette.
statufier [statyfje] *v.tr.* (*impf. & pr.sub.* **n. statufiions, v. statufiiez**) *F:* to erect a statue to (s.o.).
statu quo [statykwo] *n.m.* status quo.
stature [statyr] *n.f.* stature; height; **de haute s.,** (i) very tall; (ii) *Fig:* of (great) stature.
statut [staty] *n.m.* **1.** statute, regulation; by(e)-law. **2.** *Dipl: etc:* status.
statutaire [statytɛr] *a.* statutory.
statutairement [statytɛrmɑ̃] *adv. Fin: etc:* in accordance with the articles.
stayer [stɛjœr] *n.m. Sp:* long-distance runner, cyclist; *Turf:* stayer.
steak [stɛk] *n.m. Cu:* steak; **s. frites,** steak and chips.
stéarine [stearin] *n.f. Ch:* stearin.
stéarique [stearik] *a. Ch:* stearic (acid).
stéatite [steatit] *n.f. Miner:* steatite, soapstone.
stéatose [steatoz] *n.f. Med:* steatosis.
steeple(chase) [stipl̩, stiplətʃɛs] *n.m. Rac:* steeplechase; *pl. steeple-chases.*
stèle [stɛl] *n.f.* stele.
stellaire [stelɛr] **1.** *a.* stellar (light, etc.). **2.** *n.f. Bot:* stellaria; starwort.
stem(m) [stɛm] *n.m. Ski:* stem turn.
stencil [stɛnsil] *n.m.* stencil.
sténo [steno] *F:* **1.** *n.f.* stenography; shorthand. **2.** *n.* stenographer; shorthand reporter.
sténodactylo [stenɔdaktilo] *n.* shorthand typist.
sténodactylo(graphie) [stenɔdaktilɔ(grafi)] *n.f.* shorthand typing.
sténographe [stenɔgraf] *n.* stenographer.
sténographie [stenɔgrafi] *n.f.* stenography; shorthand.
sténographier [stenɔgrafje] *v.tr.* (*pr.sub. & impf.* **n. sténographiions, v. sténographiiez**) to take (sth.) down in shorthand.
sténographique [stenɔgrafik] *a.* shorthand (writing, etc.).
sténotyper [stenɔtipe] *v.tr.* to stenotype.
sténotypiste [stenɔtipist] *n.* stenotypist.
Stentor [stɑ̃tɔr] **1.** *Pr.n.m. Gr.Lit:* Stentor; **voix de S.,** stentorian voice. **2.** *n.m. Prot:* stentor.
stéphanois, -oise [stefanwa, -waz] *a. & n. Geog:* (native, inhabitant) of Saint-Étienne.
steppe [stɛp] *n.f. Geog:* steppe.
stercoraire [stɛrkɔrɛr] **1.** *a. Med:* stercoraceous. **2.** *n.m.* (*a*) *Ent:* dung beetle; dor; (*b*) *Orn:* skua.
stère [stɛr] *n.m. Meas:* stere.
stéréo [stereo] *a.inv. & n.f. F:* stereo.
stéréogramme [stereɔgram] *n.m. Opt: Phot:* stereogram; stereograph.
stéréographie [stereɔgrafi] *n.f. Opt:* stereography.
stéréophonie [stereɔfɔni] *n.f.* stereophony.
stéréophonique [stereɔfɔnik] *a.* stereophonic.
stéréoscope [stereɔskɔp] *n.m. Opt:* stereoscope.
stéréoscopique [stereɔskɔpik] *a.* stereoscopic.
stéréotype [stereɔtip] *n.m.* cliché.
stéréotypé [stereɔtipe] *a.* stereotyped; **expression stéréotypée,** hackneyed phrase; cliché.
stéréotypie [stereɔtipi] *n.f. Typ: Psy:* stereotypy.
stérile [steril] *a.* sterile; barren (**en,** of); childless (marriage); unproductive (land); fruitless (efforts); unprofitable (work); *Med: etc:* **instruments stériles,** sterile, sterilized, instruments.
stérilet [sterilɛ] *n.m. Hyg:* coil, loop, I.U.D.
stérilisant [sterilizɑ̃] *a. & n.m.* sterilizing (agent).
stérilisateur [sterilizatœr] *n.m.* sterilizer.
stérilisation [sterilizasjɔ̃] *n.f.* sterilization.
stériliser [sterilize] *v.tr.* to sterilize.
stérilité [sterilite] *n.f.* sterility (of pers.); barrenness (of land); *Fig:* unfruitfulness, unproductiveness.
sterling [stɛrliŋ] *a.inv.* sterling; **dix livres s.,** ten pounds sterling.
sterne [stɛrn] *n.f. Orn:* tern.
sternum [stɛrnɔm] *n.m. Anat:* sternum, breastbone.
stéroïde [sterɔid] *n.m. Biol: Med:* steroid.
stérol [sterɔl] *n.m. Ch: Physiol:* sterol.
stertoreux, -euse [stɛrtɔrø, -øz] *a. Med:* stertorous (breathing).
stéthoscope [stetɔskɔp] *n.m. Med:* stethoscope.
steward [stiwart] *n.m. Nau: Av:* steward.
stick [stik] *n.m. Mil: Sp: Av: etc:* stick; riding whip.
stigmate [stigmat] *n.m.* **1.** (*a*) scar; *Fig:* mark (of vice, etc.); (*b*) *Med:* stigma; (*c*) *pl. Rel.H:* stigmata. **2.** *Bot: Ent:* stigma.
stigmatisation [stigmatizasjɔ̃] *n.f.* stigmatization.
stigmatisé, -ée [stigmatize] **1.** *a.* stigmatized. **2.** *n. Rel.H:* stigmatist; stigmatic.
stigmatiser [stigmatize] *v.tr.* **1.** to stigmatize, condemn (s.o.); to brand (**de,** with). **2.** to pockmark (s.o.).
stillation [stilasjɔ̃] *n.f.* dripping; oozing.

stimulant [stimylɑ̃] **1.** *a.* stimulating. **2.** *n.m.* (*a*) *Med: etc:* stimulant; (*b*) stimulus, spur, incentive, inducement.
stimulateur [stimylatœr] *n.m. Med:* **s. cardiaque,** pacemaker.
stimulation [stimylasjɔ̃] *n.f.* stimulation.
stimuler [stimyle] *v.tr.* to stimulate. **1.** to incite; to spur (s.o.) on. **2.** to stimulate (enthusiasm, the digestion); to whet (the appetite); to encourage (friendship, trade).
stimulus [stimylys] *n.m.* stimulus.
stipendiaire [stipɑ̃djɛr], **stipendié** [stipɑ̃dje] *a. & n.m. usu. Pej:* hired; mercenary (soldier); hireling.
stipendier [stipɑ̃dje] *v.tr.* (*pr.sub. & impf.* **n. stipendiions, v. stipendiiez**) *Pej:* to keep (criminals, politicians, etc.) in one's pay.
stipulation [stipylasjɔ̃] *n.f.* stipulation; condition.
stipuler [stipyle] *v.tr.* to stipulate.
stock [stɔk] *n.m. Com:* stock (of goods), *NAm:* inventory; *F:* **tout un s., un vrai s.,** a whole stock, plenty (of sth.).
stockage [stɔkaʒ] *n.m.* **1.** stocking (of goods); *Ind: Cmptr: etc:* storage. **2.** building up of stocks.
stock-car [stɔkkar] *n.m. Aut:* stock car; *pl. stock-cars.*
stocker [stɔke] *v.tr.* (*a*) to stock (goods); (*b*) to stockpile; (*c*) *Cmptr:* to store (data).
stockiste [stɔkist] *n.m. Com:* stockist, *NAm:* dealer; *Aut: etc:* agent.
stoïcien, -ienne [stɔisjɛ̃, -jɛn] **1.** *a.* stoical, stoic. **2.** *n.* stoic.
stoïcisme [stɔisism] *n.m.* stoicism.
stoïque [stɔik] **1.** *a.* stoic, stoical. **2.** *n.* stoic.
stoïquement [stɔikmɑ̃] *adv.* stoically.
stolon [stɔlɔ̃] *n.m. Bot:* stolon, runner.
stomatite [stɔmatit] *n.f. Med:* stomatitis.
stomatologie [stɔmatɔlɔʒi] *n.f.* stomatology.
stop [stɔp] **1.** *int.* stop! **2.** *n.m. Aut:* (*a*) brake light (on car); (*b*) stop sign; red light. **3.** *n.m. F:* **faire du s.,** to hitchhike; **aller à Paris en s.,** to hitchhike to Paris.
stoppage[1] [stɔpaʒ] *n.m.* stoppage, stopping.
stoppage[2] *n.m.* invisible mending (of garment).
stopper[1] [stɔpe] *v.tr. & i.* to stop.
stopper[2] *v.tr.* to repair by invisible mending.
stoppeur, -euse[1] [stɔpœr, -øz] *n. F:* hitchhiker.
store [stɔr] *n.m.* (roller, Venetian, etc.) blind; shade; (*outside*) awning.
strabisme [strabism] *n.m.* strabism(us); squinting.
stramonium [stramɔnjɔm] *n.m. Bot:* stramonium.
strangulation [strɑ̃gylasjɔ̃] *n.f.* strangulation.
strapontin [strapɔ̃tɛ̃] *n.m.* (*a*) *Aut: Th: etc:* folding seat; tip-up seat; (*b*) *F:* minor job.
stras(s) [stras] *n.m.* paste (jewel).
stratagème [strataʒɛm] *n.m.* stratagem.
strate [strat] *n.f. Geol:* stratum, layer.
stratège [stratɛʒ] *n.m.* strategist.
stratégie [strateʒi] *n.f.* strategy.
stratégique [strateʒik] *a.* strategic.
stratégiquement [strateʒikmɑ̃] *adv.* strategically.
stratification [stratifikasjɔ̃] *n.f.* stratification.
stratifié [stratifje] **1.** *a.* stratified. **2.** *n.m.* laminated wood, plastic, glass.
stratifier [stratifje] *v.tr.* to stratify.
strato-cumulus [stratɔkymylys] *n.m.inv. Meteor:* stratocumulus.
stratosphère [stratɔsfɛr] *n.f. Meteor:* stratosphere.
stratosphérique [stratɔsferik] *a.* stratospheric.
stratus [stratys] *n.m. Meteor:* stratus (cloud).
streptocoque [strɛptɔkɔk] *n.m. Bac:* streptococcus.
streptomycine [strɛptɔmisin] *n.f. Med:* streptomycin.
stress [strɛs] *n.m. Med:* stress.
striation [strijasjɔ̃] *n.f.* striation.
strict [strikt] *a.* (*a*) strict (obligation); bare (essentials, minimum); (*b*) exact, strict (person) (**sur,** about); (*c*) severe (suit, hairstyle).
strictement [striktəmɑ̃] *adv.* (*a*) strictly; (*b*) in a severe manner.
striction [striksjɔ̃] *n.f.* **1.** *Mth:* striction. **2.** *Metalw:* contraction of cross section; reduction of area. **3.** *Med:* constriction.
strident [stridɑ̃] *a.* strident, shrill, harsh, grating.
stridulation [stridylasjɔ̃] *n.f.* stridulation.
strie [stri] *n.f.* **1.** score, scratch; *Anat: Bot: Geol:* stria. **2.** (*a*) ridge; (*b*) streak (of colour, *NAm:* color).
strié [strije] *a.* **1.** scored, scratched; striped; *Bot: Geol: Anat:* striated. **2.** (*a*) fluted, grooved (column); ridged; (*b*) streaked (marble).
strier [strije] *v.tr.* (*impf. & pr.sub.* **n. striions, v. striiez**) **1.** to striate, score, scratch. **2.** (*a*) to groove, corrugate; (*b*) to streak.
strioscopie [strijɔskɔpi] *n.f. Opt:* strioscopy, streak photography, Schlieren photography.
stripper [stripɛr] *n.m. Surg:* (*instrument*) stripper.
strip-teaseuse [striptizøz] *n.f.* stripper, striptease artiste.
stripping [stripiŋ] *n.m. Atom.Ph: Petr: Surg:* stripping.
striptease [striptiz] *n.m.* striptease.
striure [strijyr] *n.f.* striation.
stroboscope [strɔbɔskɔp] *n.m. Opt:* stroboscope.
strontium [strɔ̃sjɔm] *n.m. Ch:* strontium.
strophe [strɔf] *n.f. Pros:* stanza.
structural, -aux [stryktyral, -o] *a.* structural.
structuralement [stryktyralmɑ̃] *adv.* structurally.
structuralisme [stryktyralism] *n.m.* structuralism.
structuraliste [stryktyralist] *a. & n.* structuralist.
structuration [stryktyrasjɔ̃] *n.f.* structuration; structuring.
structure [stryktyr] *n.f.* structure.
structurel, -elle [stryktyrɛl] *a.* structural.
structurellement [stryktyrɛlmɑ̃] *adv.* structurally.
structurer [stryktyre] *v.tr.* to structure.
strume [strym] *n.f. Med:* **1.** *A:* scrofula. **2.** goitre.
strychnine [striknin] *n.f. Ch: Pharm:* strychnine.
stuc [styk] *n.m. Const:* stucco.
stucage [stykaʒ] *n.m. Const:* stucco work; **enduire de s.,** to stucco.
stucateur [stykatœr] *n.m.* stucco worker.
studieusement [stydjøzmɑ̃] *adv.* studiously.
studieux, -ieuse [stydjø, -jøz] *a.* studious.
studio [stydjo] *n.m.* **1.** (artist's, film, broadcasting, recording, etc.) studio. **2.** one-roomed flat, studio apartment.
stupéfaction [stypefaksjɔ̃] *n.f.* stupefaction, amazement.
stupéfait [stypefɛ] *a.* stupefied, stunned, amazed.
stupéfiant [stypefjɑ̃] **1.** *a.* (*a*) *Med:* stupefying, stupefacient (drug); (*b*) astounding (news). **2.** *n.m. Med:* narcotic, stupefacient; drug.
stupéfier [stypefje] *v.tr.* (*impf. & pr.sub.* **n. stupéfiions, v. stupéfiiez**) to stupefy, stun, amaze.
stupeur [stypœr] *n.f.* stupor. **1.** dazed state. **2.** amazement; **muet de s.,** dumbfounded.
stupide [stypid] *a.* (*a*) *Lit:* stunned with surprise; (*b*) stupid, silly, foolish.
stupidement [stypidmɑ̃] *adv.* stupidly.
stupidité [stypidite] *n.f.* **1.** stupidity; foolishness. **2.** stupid thing to say, do; **répondre par une s.,** to give a silly answer.
stuquer [styke] *v.tr. Const:* to stucco.
stygien, -ienne [stiʒjɛ̃, -jɛn] *a.* Stygian (darkness).
style [stil] *n.m.* **1.** (*a*) *Ant:* stylus, style (as writing implement); (*b*) stylus, graver, etching needle; *Rec:*

record cutter; (*c*) style, pin, gnomon (of sundial); hand (of barometer); (*d*) *Bot:* style. **2.** *Lit: Arch: etc:* style; **dans le s. de,** in the style of; **meubles, robe, de s.,** period furniture, dress; *Chr:* **vieux s., nouveau s.,** Old Style, New Style (of calendar).
stylé¹ [stile] *a. Nat.Hist:* stylate.
stylé² *a.* trained, schooled (**à,** in).
styler [stile] *v.tr.* to train, form; *F:* to put a polish on (s.o.).
stylet [stilɛ] *n.m.* **1.** stiletto. **2.** *Surg:* stylet, probe. **3.** *Z:* stylet. **4.** *Cmptr:* **s. lumineux,** light pen, gun.
stylisation [stilizasjɔ̃] *n.f.* stylization.
styliser [stilize] *v.tr. Art:* to stylize.
stylisme [stilism] *n.m. Lit: Cost: Com:* stylism.
styliste [stilist] *n. Lit: Cost: Com:* stylist.
stylisticien, -ienne [stilistisjɛ̃, -jɛn] *n.* expert in stylistics.
stylistique [stilistik] **1.** *a.* stylistic. **2.** *n.f.* stylistics.
stylite [stilit] *a. & n.m. Rel.H:* stylite.
stylo [stilo] *n.m.* (fountain, ballpoint) pen.
stylographe [stilɔgraf] *n.m. A:* fountain pen.
styptique [stiptik] *a. & n.m. Med:* styptic.
styrax [stiraks] *n.m. Bot:* styrax.
styrène [stirɛn] *n.m. Ch:* styrene.
su [sy] *n.m.* knowledge; **à mon (vu et) su,** to my (certain) knowledge.
suage¹ [sɥaʒ] *n.m.* sweating, oozing (of timber, etc.).
suage² *n.m. Metalw:* fillet (border) (of candlestick, of silver plate).
suaire [sɥɛr] *n.m.* **1.** winding sheet; shroud. **2.** *Ecc:* sudarium, veronica.
suant [sɥɑ̃] *a.* (*a*) sweating; sweaty; (*b*) *P:* boring.
suave [sɥav] *a.* (*a*) sweet, pleasant (music, scent, etc.); soft (shade); mild (cigar); (*b*) suave, smooth (tone, manner).
suavement [sɥavmɑ̃] *adv.* (*a*) pleasantly; (*b*) suavely.
suavité [sɥavite] *n.f.* (*a*) sweetness (of perfume, melody); (*b*) suavity (of manner).
subaigu, -uë [sybegy] *a. Med:* subacute.
subalpin [sybalpɛ̃] *a.* subalpine.
subalterne [sybaltɛrn] **1.** *a.* subordinate, minor (official, position, part); inferior (mind); junior (employee). **2.** *n.m.* (*a*) underling; (*b*) *Mil:* subaltern (officer), captain.
subaquatique [sybakwatik] *a.* subaquatic; underwater.
subatomique [sybatɔmik] *a.* subatomic.
subconscient [sybkɔ̃sjɑ̃] *a. & n.m.* subconscious.
subdiviser [sybdivize] *v.tr.* to subdivide.
subdivision [sybdivizjɔ̃] *n.f.* subdivision.
subéquatorial, -aux [sybekwatɔrjal, -o] *a. Geog:* subequatorial.
subéreux, -euse [syberø, -øz] *a. Bot:* suberose; corky.
subir [sybir] *v.tr.* to undergo (trial, examination, operation, torture, change); to suffer (death); to serve (one's sentence); to come, be, under (an influence); to suffer, sustain (defeat, casualties, loss); to submit to, suffer, put up with (punishment, one's fate); **faire s. qch. à qn,** to subject s.o. to sth, to inflict sth. on s.o.
subit [sybi] *a.* sudden, unexpected (death, change).
subitement [sybitmɑ̃] *adv.* suddenly; all of a sudden.
subito [sybito] *adv. F: O:* (*a*) all of a sudden; (*b*) at once.
subjectif, -ive [sybʒɛktif, -iv] *a. Phil: Gram:* subjective; *Gram:* **cas s.,** nominative case.
subjectivement [sybʒɛktivmɑ̃] *adv.* subjectively.
subjectivisme [sybʒɛktivism] *n.m. Phil:* subjectivism.
subjectivité [sybʒɛktivite] *n.f.* subjectivity.
subjonctif, -ive [sybʒɔ̃ktif, -iv] *a. & n.m. Gram:* subjunctive (mood); **au s.,** in the subjunctive.
subjugation [sybʒygasjɔ̃] *n.f.* subjugation.
subjuguer [sybʒyge] *v.tr.* to subjugate, subdue (people, nation); to subdue, master (a horse); to captivate (hearts).
sublimation [syblimasjɔ̃] *n.f. Ch: Psy:* sublimation.
sublime [syblim] *a.* **1.** sublime; lofty, exalted; *n.* **le s.,** the sublime. **2.** *Anat:* sublime (muscle).
sublimé [syblime] **1.** *a.* sublimated. **2.** *n.m. Ch:* sublimate.
sublimer [syblime] *v.tr. Ch: Psy:* to sublimate.
subliminal, -aux [sybliminal, -o] *a.*, **subliminaire** [sybliminɛr] *a.* subliminal.
sublimité [syblimite] *n.f. Lit:* sublimeness.
sublingual, -aux [syblɛ̃gwal, -o] *a. Anat:* sublingual (gland, etc.); *Pharm:* **comprimé s.,** pill to be placed under the tongue.
submerger [sybmɛrʒe] *v.tr.* **(je submergeai(s); n. submergeons) 1.** to submerge; to flood (meadow); to swamp (boat); to immerse (object). **2.** to overwhelm; **submergé de travail,** snowed under with work.
submersible [sybmɛrsibl̥] **1.** *a.* (*a*) submersible (boat); (*b*) *Bot:* submerged (plant); (*c*) (ground) liable to flooding. **2.** *n.m. Navy:* submarine.
submersion [sybmɛrsjɔ̃] *n.f.* submersion; flooding; **mort par s.,** death by drowning.
subodorer [sybɔdɔre] *v.tr.* to suspect, scent (danger, etc.); *F:* **il a subodoré quelque chose,** he smelt a rat.
subordination [sybɔrdinasjɔ̃] *n.f.* subordination.
subordonnant [sybɔrdɔnɑ̃] *a. Gram:* subordinating (conjunction, etc.).
subordonné, -ée [sybɔrdɔne] **1.** *a. Gram:* subordinate (clause). **2.** (*a*) *n.* subordinate; (*b*) *n.f. Gram:* subordinate clause. **3.** *a. Cmptr:* **s. au temps d'entrée,** input limited.
subordonner [sybɔrdɔne] **1.** *v.tr.* to subordinate (**à,** to); **s. ses dépenses à son revenu,** to cut one's coat according to one's cloth; **le service est subordonné au nombre des voyageurs,** the service depends on the number of travellers. **2. se s.,** to submit to authority.
subornation [sybɔrnasjɔ̃] *n.f. Jur:* subornation.
suborner [sybɔrne] *v.tr. Jur:* to suborn, to tamper with.
suborneur, -euse [sybɔrnœr, -øz] **1.** *n. Jur:* suborner, briber (of witnesses, etc.). **2.** *n.m. Lit:* seducer.
subreptice [sybrɛptis] *a.* surreptitious.
subrepticement [sybrɛptismɑ̃] *adv.* surreptitiously.
subrogation [sybrɔgasjɔ̃] *n.f. Jur:* **1.** subrogation, substitution. **2.** delegation (of powers, rights).
subrogé, -ée [sybrɔʒe] **1.** *a.* subrogated; deputy, surrogate (guardian). **2.** *n. Ecc: Jur:* surrogate, deputy.
subroger [sybrɔʒe] *v.tr.* **(je subrogeai(s); n. subrogeons)** *Jur:* to subrogate; to substitute.
subséquent [sypsekɑ̃] *a.* subsequent. **1.** ensuing. **2.** later (testament, etc.). **3.** *Geog:* subsequent (stream).
subside [sypsid] *n.m.* subsidy; allowance.
subsidence [sypsidɑ̃s, sybz-] *n.f.* subsidence.
subsidiaire [sypsidjɛr, sybz-] *a.* subsidiary.
subsidiairement [sypsidjɛrmɑ̃, sybz-] *adv.* subsidiarily, in addition (**à,** to).
subsistance [sybzistɑ̃s] *n.f.* **1.** subsistence; livelihood; maintenance; (one's) keep. **2.** *pl.* provisions; *Mil:* supplies.
subsistant [sybzistɑ̃] *a.* subsisting, existing, still extant.
subsister [sybziste] *v.i.* to subsist. **1.** to (continue to) exist; to remain. **2.** to live (**de,** on); **moyens de s.,** means of subsistence.
subsonique [sypsɔnik] *a. Av:* subsonic.
substance [sypstɑ̃s] *n.f.* substance. **1.** gist (of an

article); **sans s.**, insubstantial (arguments); **en s.**, in substance. **2.** matter, material, stuff; **s. étrangère,** extraneous substance.
substantialité [sypstɑ̃sjalite] *n.f.* substantiality.
substantiel, -ielle [sypstɑ̃sjɛl] *a.* substantial.
substantiellement [sypstɑ̃sjɛlmɑ̃] *adv.* substantially; in substance.
substantif, -ive [sypstɑ̃tif, -iv] **1.** *a.* substantive. **2.** *n.m. Gram:* substantive, noun.
substantiver [sypstɑ̃tive] *v.tr. Gram:* to use (word, phrase) as a noun.
substituer [sypstitɥe] **1.** *v.tr.* (*a*) to substitute (**à** for); (*b*) *Jur:* **s. un héritier,** to appoint an heir in succession to another, failing another; **s. un héritage,** to entail an estate. **2. se s. à qn, à qch.**, to substitute for s.o.; to take the place of s.o., sth.
substitut [sypstity] *n.m.* substitute; *Jur:* deputy public prosecutor.
substitution [sypstitysjɔ̃] *n.f.* **1.** (*a*) substitution (**à**, for). **2.** *Jur:* entail (to grandchildren, etc.).
substrat [sypstra] *n.m. Geol: Ling: Phil:* substratum; *Phot: Biol: Cmptr:* substrate.
subterfuge [syptɛrfyʒ] *n.m.* subterfuge.
subtil [syptil] *a.* subtle. **1.** (*a*) *A:* tenuous, thin; fine (dust); (*b*) pervasive (poison, scent, etc.). **2.** (*a*) discerning, shrewd (mind, leader); *A:* acute, keen (senses); (*b*) delicate, fine (distinction, etc.); (*c*) ingenious (argument).
subtilement [syptilmɑ̃] *adv.* (*a*) subtly; (*b*) craftily.
subtiliser [syptilize] *v.tr.* **1.** (*a*) *A:* to refine (a substance); (*b*) to make (an argument, an answer) too subtle; *v.i.* to split hairs. **2.** *F:* to steal, sneak (s.o.'s watch, etc.); to pinch (s.o.'s money).
subtilité [syptilite] *n.f.* **1.** (*a*) shrewdness (of mind); (*b*) subtlety, fineness (of distinction); (*c*) subtlety (of argument); (*d*) artfulness, craftiness. **2.** subtle argument, distinction.
subtropical, -aux [syptrɔpikal, -o] *a.* subtropical.
suburbain [sybyrbɛ̃] *a.* suburban.
subvenir [sybvənir] *v.ind.tr.* (*conj. like* VENIR) (*aux.* **avoir**) **s. à,** to come to the aid of (s.o.), to provide for (s.o.'s needs); to meet (expenses); to relieve (distress).
subvention [sybvɑ̃sjɔ̃] *n.f.* subsidy, grant (of money).
subventionner [sybvɑ̃sjɔne] *v.tr.* to subsidize; to grant financial aid to (undertaking, institution, etc.); **subventionné,** subsidized (industry), maintained (school), grant-aided (student).
subversif, -ive [sybvɛrsif, -iv] *a.* subversive.
subversion [sybvɛrsjɔ̃] *n.f.* subversion.
subversivement [sybvɛrsivmɑ̃] *adv.* subversively.
subvertir [sybvɛrtir] *v.tr.* to subvert.
suc [syk] *n.m.* (*a*) (fruit, meat, etc.) juice; *Bot:* sap; *Physiol:* (gastric, etc.) juice; (*b*) *Fig:* essence, pith.
succédané [syksedane] *a. & n.m.* substitute (**de,** for).
succéder [syksede] *v.ind.tr.* **(je succède, n. succédons; je succéderai) 1. s. à qn, à qch.**, to succeed, follow after, s.o., sth.; **un sentiment de pitié succéda à sa rage,** his anger gave way to a feeling of pity; **s. au trône,** to succeed to the throne; **s. à une fortune,** to inherit a fortune; **les révolutions se succédèrent,** revolution followed revolution; there was a succession of revolutions. **2.** *A:* (*a*) (*of activity*) to be successful; (*b*) to happen, occur.
succès [syksɛ] *n.m.* **1.** *A:* result. **2.** success; **avoir du s.**, (*of undertaking*) to turn out a success; *Com:* (*of product*) to be a success, to catch on; **remporter de grands s.**, to achieve great triumphs; **sans s.**, unsuccessful(ly); **une seconde tentative n'eut pas plus de s.**, a second attempt met with no better success; **livre à s.**, bestseller; **auteur à s.**, bestselling author, *F:* bestseller; **avoir grand s.**, to be a great, a huge, success; **s. fou,** great success, *Th:* smash hit; **pièce à s.**, hit.
successeur [syksesœr] *n.m.* successor (**de,** to, of).
successif, -ive [syksesif, -iv] *a.* successive.
succession [syksesjɔ̃] *n.f.* **1.** (*a*) succession; series, sequence (of ideas, sounds, days, etc.); (*b*) succession (to the crown, to the presidency); **prendre la s. d'une maison de commerce,** to take over a business. **2.** *Jur:* inheritance.
successivement [syksesivmɑ̃] *adv.* successively.
succinct [syksɛ̃, syksɛ̃kt] *a.* **1.** succinct, brief, concise; *F:* **repas s.**, scanty meal. **2.** *Cmptr:* **résumé s.**, compendium.
succinctement [syksɛ̃tmɑ̃, -ɛ̃ktəmɑ̃] *adv.* succinctly, briefly; *F:* (to eat) frugally.
succion [syksjɔ̃] *n.f.* suction; sucking.
succomber [sykɔ̃be] *v.i.* to succumb. **1.** to sink (under the weight); **je succombe au sommeil,** I can't stay awake. **2.** (*a*) to be overpowered **(sous le nombre,** by numbers); (*b*) to yield (to grief, temptation, etc.); to be overcome (by emotion); **ne nous laissez pas s. à la tentation,** lead us not into temptation; (*c*) to die; to succumb (to an illness).
succube [sykyb] *n.m.* succubus, succuba.
succulence [sykylɑ̃s] *n.f. Lit:* succulence.
succulent [sykylɑ̃] *a.* succulent (food); tasty (morsel); *Bot:* fleshy (leaf); **plante succulente,** succulent.
succursale [sykyrsal] *n.f. Com:* branch.
sucer [syse] *v.tr.* **(je suçai(s); n. suçons)** to suck (milk, orange, bone, etc.); **se s. les doigts,** to suck one's fingers; *F:* **s. qn jusqu'au dernier sou, jusqu'à la moelle des os,** to suck s.o. dry; to bleed s.o. white; *P:* **s. la poire à qn,** to kiss s.o.
sucette [sysɛt] *n.f.* (*a*) (baby's) dummy, *NAm:* pacifier; (*b*) lollipop, *F:* lolly; **s. glacée,** ice lolly, *NAm:* popsicle.
suceur, -euse [sysœr, -øz] **1.** *n.* (*a*) sucker; (*b*) *n.m. Ich:* sucker, sucking fish. **2.** (*a*) *n.m.* nozzle (of vacuum cleaner); (*b*) *n.f.* **suceuse,** suction dredger.
suçon [sysɔ̃] *n.m. F:* love bite.
suçoter [sysɔte] *v.tr. F:* to suck (away) at (sth.).
sucrage [sykraʒ] *n.m. Wine-m:* sugaring.
sucrase [sykraz] *n.f. Ch:* invert sugar.
sucre [sykr̥] *n.m.* sugar; (*a*) **s. de canne,** cane sugar; **s. de betterave,** beet sugar; **s. en pains,** loaf sugar; **montagne en pain de s.**, sugar-loaf mountain; **s. en poudre, s. semoule,** caster sugar; **s. cristallisé,** granulated sugar; **s. farine, s. glace, s. à glacer,** icing sugar; **s. en morceaux,** lump sugar; **s. brut,** crude sugar; **s. d'orge,** barley sugar; *F:* **s. noir,** liquorice; *F:* **il a été tout s. tout miel,** he was all honey; *P:* **c'est un vrai s.**, he's a honey; *Fr.C:* **partie de s.**, sugaring party; (*b*) *Ch:* **s. de lait,** lactose; **s. de fruit,** fructose.
sucré [sykre] *a.* **1.** sugared, sweetened (coffee, etc.); sweet (fruits, etc.); **mon thé est trop s.**, my tea is too sweet; **eau sucrée,** sugar and water. **2.** sugary (words, manner, smile); **elle fait la sucrée,** butter wouldn't melt in her mouth.
sucrer [sykre] *v.tr.* to sugar; to sweeten; *F:* **sucrez-vous,** help yourself to sugar; *P:* **se s.**, to get rich, line one's own pockets; *F:* **s. les fraises,** (i) to shake; (ii) to be an old dodderer.
sucrerie [sykrəri] *n.f.* **1.** sugar refinery. **2.** *pl.* sweets, confectionery, *NAm:* candy; **aimer les sucreries,** to have a sweet tooth. **3.** *Fr.C:* maple tree grove.
sucrier, -ère [sykrije, -ɛr] **1.** *a.* (of) sugar; **industrie sucrière,** sugar industry. **2.** *n.* sugar manufacturer. **3.** *n.m.* sugar bowl, basin.
sud [syd] **1.** *n.m. no pl.* (*a*) south; **un vent du s.**, a southerly wind; **le vent du s.**, the south wind; **maison exposée au s.**, house that faces south; **dans le s. de l'Angleterre,** in the south of England; **au s.**, in the

south; **au s. de Paris,** (to the) south of Paris; **l'Amérique du S.,** South America; **vers le s.,** southward; (*b*) *Nau:* **le s.,** the south wind. **2.** *a.inv.* south, southerly (wind); southern (part, latitude); **le pôle s.,** the south pole; **le côté s.,** the south side (of house, wall, etc.).

sud-africain, -aine [sydafrikɛ̃ -ɛn] *a. & n. Geog:* South African; **la République sud-africaine,** the Republic of South Africa; *pl. sud-africain(e)s.*

sud-américain, -aine [sydamerikɛ̃, -ɛn] *a. & n. Geog:* South American; *pl. sud-américain(e)s.*

sudation [sydasjɔ̃] *n.f. Med: etc:* sudation, sweating.

sud-est [sydɛst] **1.** *n.m. no pl.* southeast; **vers le s.-e.,** southeastward. **2.** *a.inv.* southeast, south-easterly (wind); southeastern (region).

sudiste [sydist] *n.m.* (*in the American Civil War*) Southerner; *a.* Southern (army, troops).

sudorifère [sydɔrifɛr] *a.* = SUDORIPARE.

sudorifique [sydɔrifik] *a. & n.m. Pharm:* sudorific.

sudoripare [sydɔripar] *a. Anat:* sudoriferous; **glande s.,** sweat gland.

sud-ouest [sydwɛst] **1.** *n.m. no pl.* (*a*) southwest; **vers le s.-o.,** southwestward; (*b*) southwest wind, southwester. **2.** *a.inv.* south-westerly (wind); southwestern (region).

Sud-Ouest Africain (le) [ləsydwɛstafrikɛ̃] *Pr.n.m. Geog:* South West Africa.

sud-vietnamien, -ienne [sydvjɛtnamjɛ̃, -jɛn] *a. & n. Geog:* South Vietnamese; *pl. sud-vietnamiens, -iennes.*

Suède [sɥɛd] *Pr.n.f. Geog:* Sweden; **gants de s.,** suede gloves.

suédé [sɥede] *n.m. Tex:* imitation suede.

suédine [sɥedin] *n.f. Tex:* suedette, suede cloth.

suédois, -oise [sɥedwa, -waz] **1.** *a.* Swedish; *Gym:* **la gymnastique suédoise,** *n.f.* **la suédoise,** Swedish gymnastics, exercises. **2.** *n.* Swede. **3.** *n.m. Ling:* Swedish.

suée [sɥe] *n.f.* **1.** sweating, sweat; **une bonne s.,** a good sweat. **2.** *P:* (*a*) cold sweat; (*b*) hard job; sweat.

suer [sɥe] **1.** *v.i.* (*a*) to perspire, sweat; *F:* **s. comme un phoque,** to sweat like a pig; **faire s. qn,** (i) to make s.o. sweat; (ii) *F:* to annoy, sicken, s.o.; **tu me fais s.!** you make me sick! (*b*) (*of walls, etc.*) to ooze; (*c*) to labour, *NAm:* labor, sweat. **2.** *v.tr.* to sweat (blood); to ooze (piety); **maison qui sue le crime,** house that reeks of crime.

sueur [sɥœr] *n.f.* sweat, perspiration; **être en s.,** to be sweating, in a sweat; **avoir des sueurs froides,** to be in a cold sweat; **à la s. de son front,** by the sweat of one's brow; **le fruit de mes sueurs,** the fruits of my labour, *NAm:* labor.

Suez [sɥɛz] *Pr.n. Geog:* Suez; **le canal de S.,** the Suez Canal.

suffire [syfir] *v.i.* (*pr.p.* **suffisant;** *p.p.* **suffi;** *pr.ind.* **je suffis, n. suffisons, ils suffisent;** *pr.sub.* **je suffise;** *impf.* **je suffisais;** *p.h.* **je suffis;** *fu.* **je suffirai**) (*a*) to suffice; to be enough; **cela ne me suffit pas (pour vivre),** that is not enough for me (to live on); *Prov:* **à chaque jour suffit sa peine,** sufficient unto the day is the evil thereof; *impers.* **il a suffi de quelques mots pour le persuader,** a few words were enough to persuade him; **il suffit de l'écouter pour . . .,** one only has to, one need only, listen to him to . . .; **il suffit qu'il le dise,** (it is) enough for him to say so; *F:* **(il) suffit! ça suffit!** that's enough! that'll do! **il suffit d'une heure pour . . .,** it only takes an hour to . . .; (*b*) **s. à qch., à faire qch.,** to be equal to sth., to doing sth.; **cela suffit à mes besoins,** that's enough for my needs; **je n'y suffis plus,** it's too much for me; *F:* I can't cope; **il s'est toujours suffi,** he has always supported himself, earned his own living; **pays qui se suffisent à eux-mêmes,** self-supporting countries.

suffisamment [syfizamɑ̃] *adv.* sufficiently, enough, adequately; **agir sans avoir s. réfléchi,** to act without sufficient thought.

suffisance [syfizɑ̃s] *n.f.* **1.** (*a*) sufficiency; adequacy; **avoir s. de qch.,** to have enough of sth.; **manger à sa s.,** to eat one's fill; **avoir de qch. à s., en s.,** to have plenty of sth.; (*b*) *A:* competence; **homme de s.,** competent man. **2.** complacency; self-importance; conceit; **il est d'une s. insupportable,** he is unbearably conceited.

suffisant [syfizɑ̃] *a.* **1.** sufficient, adequate, enough; **c'est plus que s.,** that is more than enough. **2.** self-satisfied, self-important, conceited (air, tone); **faire le s.,** to give oneself airs.

suffixe [syfiks] *n.m. Gram:* suffix.

suffixer [syfikse] *v.tr. Gram:* to add a suffix to.

suffocant [syfɔkɑ̃] *a.* (*a*) suffocating, stifling; (*b*) stunning, overwhelming (news).

suffocation [syfɔkasjɔ̃] *n.f.* suffocation; (fit of) choking.

suffoquer [syfɔke] **1.** *v.tr.* (*a*) *A:* to suffocate (s.o.); (*b*) (*of smell, etc.*) to suffocate, stifle; (*of news, etc.*) to stagger (s.o.), to take (s.o.'s) breath away; **les sanglots la suffoquaient,** she was choking with sobs. **2.** *v.i.* to suffocate, choke.

suffragant [syfragɑ̃] *a. & n.m. Ecc:* suffragan (bishop).

suffrage [syfraʒ] *n.m. Pol:* suffrage, vote; **dix mille suffrages,** ten thousand votes; **s. universel,** universal franchise, suffrage; **s. universel pur et simple,** one-man-one-vote suffrage.

suffragette [syfraʒɛt] *n.f. Pol:* suffragette.

suffusion [syfyzjɔ̃] *n.f. Med:* suffusion (*esp.* of blood); flush.

suggérer [sygʒere] *v.tr.* (**je suggère, n. suggérons; je suggérerai**) to suggest (**à,** to); **s. de faire qch.,** to suggest doing sth.; **s. à qn de faire qch.,** to suggest to s.o. that he should do sth.

suggestibilité [sygʒɛstibilite] *n.f.* suggestibility.

suggestible [sygʒɛstibḷ] *a.* suggestible.

suggestif, -ive [sygʒɛstif, -iv] *a.* (*a*) evocative; (*b*) suggestive (joke, gesture, etc.).

suggestion [sygʒɛstjɔ̃] *n.f.* suggestion; (*a*) (evil) suggestion, incitement; (*b*) **suggestions en vue d'une amélioration,** suggestions for improvement; **pas la moindre s. de . . .,** not the slightest hint of . . .; (*c*) (hypnotic) suggestion.

suggestionner [sygʒɛstjɔne] *v.tr.* to put an idea, ideas, into (s.o.'s) head; **se laisser s.,** to succumb to suggestion.

suicidaire [sɥisidɛr] **1.** *a.* suicidal (tendencies, etc.). **2.** *n.* suicidal person.

suicide [sɥisid] *n.m.* suicide; **faux s.,** attempted suicide; *a. Hist:* **avion-s.,** suicide plane.

suicidé, -ée [sɥiside] (*a*) *a.* (pers.) who has committed suicide; (*b*) *n.* (*pers.*) suicide.

suicider (se) [səsɥiside] *v.pr.* to commit suicide; **se s. politiquement,** to commit political suicide.

suie [sɥi] *n.f.* soot.

suif [sɥif] *n.m.* (*a*) tallow; **s. de mouton,** mutton fat; **chandelle de s.,** tallow candle; (*b*) *P: A:* **recevoir un s.,** to get a dressing down; *P:* **faire du s.,** to kick up a row; *P:* **chercher du s.,** to be out for a fight.

suifer [sɥife] *v.tr.* to tallow (leather, etc.); to grease (a hinge).

suint [sɥɛ̃] *n.m.* (natural) grease (of wool).

suintant [sɥɛ̃tɑ̃] *a.* oozing, dripping (wall, etc.).

suintement [sɥɛ̃tmɑ̃] *n.m.* oozing, dripping; sweating (of water, of rock, wall); running, weeping (of wound).

suinter [sɥɛ̃te] **1.** *v.i.* (*a*) to ooze, drip; (*b*) (*of vessel*) to leak; (*of wound*) to run, to weep. **2.** *v.tr.* to exude, to ooze (hatred, etc.).

Suisse¹ [sɥis] *Pr.n.f. Geog:* Switzerland; **la S. alémanique, romande, italienne,** German-, French-, Italian-speaking, Switzerland.
suisse² **1.** *a.* Swiss. **2.** *n.m.* (*a*) **un S.,** a Swiss (man); **les Suisses,** the Swiss; (*b*) *Hist:* (i) Swiss mercenary; (ii) Swiss guard (at the Vatican); *F:* **boire en s.,** to drink on one's own; (*c*) *Ecc:* verger (in full regalia); (*d*) **petit s.** = small cream cheese; petit suisse; (*e*) *Fr.C: Z:* **s. (rayé),** chipmunk.
Suissesse [sɥisɛs] *n.f. often Pej:* Swiss (woman).
suite [sɥit] *n.f.* **1.** (act of) following, pursuit; **être à la s. de qn,** to be in pursuit of s.o., *F:* after s.o. **2.** (*a*) continuation; what follows; (*in restaurant*) the next course; **j'oublie la s. de l'air,** I forget how the tune goes on; **faire s. à qch.,** to be a continuation of sth.; (*of room*) to lead out of (another room); *Corr:* **comme s. à notre lettre d'hier,** further to our letter of yesterday; **à la s. de votre demande,** with reference to your request; *Com:* **donner s. à,** to deal with, carry out (an order); to give effect to (a decision); **pour s. à donner,** (passed to you) for action; (*of article*) **sans s.,** cannot be repeated; **prendre la s. des affaires d'une maison,** to succeed to, take over, a business; **à la s. les uns des autres,** one after another; **les historiens venus à sa s.,** the historians who came after him; **les maux que la guerre traîne à sa s.,** the evils that war brings in its wake, train; **se mettre à la s.,** to join (the back of) the queue, *NAm:* the line; *adv.phr.* **de s.,** (i) in succession; (ii) consecutively; **dix camions de s.,** ten lorries, trucks, in a row; **dix heures de s.,** ten hours on end; **dix jours de s.,** ten days running; **pendant plusieurs semaines de s.,** for several weeks at a time; **et ainsi de s.,** and so on; *adv.phr.* **tout de s.,** *F:* **de s.,** at once, immediately; **dans la s.,** subsequently; **par la s.,** later on, afterwards, eventually; (*b*) sequel (of book, film, etc.); *Journ:* **s. à la page 30,** continued on page 30; **s. et fin,** concluded; (*c*) coherence, consistency (in reasoning); **sans s.,** (i) incoherent, disconnected (words, thoughts); (ii) disconnectedly, incoherently; **s. dans les idées,** singleness of mind; **manquer (d'esprit) de s.,** to lack (i) application, perseverance, (ii) method. **3.** suite, retinue, train, attendants (of monarch, etc.). **4.** (*a*) series, sequence, succession (of events, etc.); line (of ancestors); set (of prints); *Hyd.E:* flight (of locks); **s. de malheurs,** run of misfortunes, chapter of accidents; **dans la s. des siècles,** in the course of time, of centuries; (*b*) *Mth:* series; (*c*) *Mus:* (orchestral) suite. **5.** consequence, result, issue; aftereffects (of illness, etc.); **mourir des suites d'une blessure,** to die (as the result) of a wound; *adv.phr.* **par s.,** consequently; *prep.phr.* **par s. de, en s. de, s. à,** in consequence of, through, on account of; **par s. de maladie,** owing to illness; **par s. d'une erreur,** by, through, an error; **par s. de sa blessure,** as a result of his wound.
suivant¹ [sɥivɑ̃] *prep.* **1.** in the direction of; along (a line). **2.** according to, in accordance with (one's means, instructions); **s. lui,** in his opinion, according to him; *conj.phr.* **s. que** + *ind.,* depending on whether, according to whether.
suivant², -ante [sɥivɑ̃, -ɑ̃t] **1.** *a.* (*a*) next, following (page, day, etc.); **voir page 6 et suivantes,** see page 6 *et seq*; **les trois jours suivants,** the next three days; **pas dimanche prochain mais le dimanche s.,** not this Sunday but the next one, the one after; **notre méthode est la suivante,** our method is as follows; **au s.!** next (person) please! (*b*) *Cmptr:* **caractère de mise en début de ligne suivante,** new line character. **2.** *n.m.* (*a*) follower, attendant; (*b*) *A:* descendant. **3.** *n.f. Th:* **suivante,** waiting maid; attendant.
suiveur, -euse [sɥivœr, -øz] (*a*) *n.m.* follower (**de,** of); (*b*) *a.* **voiture suiveuse,** car following a cycle race, etc.
suivi [sɥivi] **1.** *a.* connected (speech); sustained, coherent (reasoning); regular (correspondence); consistent (work, effort, quality); steadfast, unwavering (policy); *Com:* steady, persistent (demand). **2.** *a.* well attended, popular (course of lectures, etc.). **3.** *n.m.* follow-up; **faire le s. de qch.,** to keep track of sth., follow sth. up.
suivre [sɥivr̥] *v.tr.* (*pr.p.* **suivant;** *p.p.* **suivi;** *pr.ind.* **je suis, il suit, n. suivons, ils suivent;** *pr.sub.* **je suive;** *impf.* **je suivais;** *p.h.* **je suivis;** *fu.* **je suivrai)** to follow. **1.** (*a*) to go after, behind (s.o., sth.); **s. qn de près,** to follow close on s.o.'s heels; **partez, je vous suis,** you go on, I'm just coming, I'll follow on; **elle le suivit des yeux,** (i) her eyes never left him; (ii) she watched him go; **faire s. une lettre,** to forward, to redirect, a letter; (*on letter*) **(prière de) faire s.,** please forward; *Typ:* **(faire) s.,** run on; (*in serial stories*) **à s.,** to be continued; **arguments qui se suivent bien,** arguments that are connected, coherent; *Com:* **s. une affaire,** to follow up business; *Com:* **nous n'avons pas suivi cet article,** we have discontinued this line; *Ten: etc:* **s. la balle,** to follow through; (*b*) to understand; **je ne vous suis pas,** (i) I don't follow you; (ii) I don't agree with you; (*c*) to escort, attend, accompany (s.o.); (*d*) to pursue (animal, enemy); (*e*) to be attentive to (sth.); **il parle si vite que je ne peux pas le s.,** he talks so quickly that I cannot follow him; **suivez attentivement,** pay great attention; (*f*) to watch, observe (s.o.'s progress, course of events, etc.); (*g*) to follow up (a clue). **2.** (*a*) to succeed; to come, happen, after (sth.); **le printemps suit l'hiver,** spring follows winter; winter is succeeded by spring; **ces deux mots se suivent,** these two words are consecutive; **événements qui se suivent de près,** events that follow each other in quick succession; **conditions ainsi qu'il suit,** terms as follows; **les personnes dont les noms suivent,** the following persons; (*b*) to result from, be the consequence of (sth.); *impers.* **il suit de là que . . .,** it follows (from this) that . . .; **que s'en est-il suivi?** what came of it? what was the consequence? **3.** (*a*) to go along, follow (road, train of thought, etc.); **s. son chemin,** to go on one's way; **suivez le bord de la rivière,** keep along the river; **la rivière suit son cours,** the river follows its course; **la justice suivra son cours,** justice will take its course; (*b*) to obey, conform to (fashion, law, etc.); to follow, act upon (advice); to pursue (line of conduct); **s. son penchant,** to follow one's bent. **4.** (*a*) to attend (series of concerts, lectures, etc.) (regularly); *Med:* to follow (a course of treatment); **s. un cours,** to take a course (of study); (*b*) to practise, exercise (profession, calling); (*c*) to be a disciple of (s.o.); (*d*) **s. son temps,** to keep abreast of the times.
sujet¹, -ette [syʒɛ, -ɛt] **1.** *a.* subject; (*a*) *A:* dependent; (*b*) liable, prone, exposed (**à,** to); **s. à la mort,** mortal; **s. à oublier, à mentir,** apt to forget, given to lying; (*c*) liable, subject (to tax, duty). **2.** *n.* subject (of a state).
sujet² *n.m.* **1.** subject; (*a*) cause, reason, ground (for complaint, anxiety); cause, subject (of quarrel); reason, grounds (for doing sth.); **un s. de pitié,** an object of pity; **le Déluge avait été le s. de ses études,** the Flood had been the object of his studies; **si je me plains c'est que j'en ai s.,** if I complain I have good cause; **agir avec s.,** to act with good reason; *prep.phr.* **au s. de qn, de qch.,** relating to, concerning, about, s.o., sth.; **au s. de votre lettre,** with reference to your letter; **éprouver des craintes au s. de qch.,** to have fears about sth.; (*b*) subject (matter), theme (of speech, book, play, picture, discussion, etc.); topic (of conversation); *Mus:* subject (of fugue, etc.); **un beau s. de roman,** a fine subject for a novel; (*c*) *Gram:* **s. du verbe,** subject of the

verb; (*d*) *Psy: Med: etc:* subject (of an experiment); *F:* guinea pig. **2.** work of art; piece (of china, etc.). **3.** individual, fellow; **mauvais s.,** (i) bad lot, ne'er do well; (ii) *Sch:* poor student; **bon s.,** (i) steady, reliable, person; (ii) *Sch:* good student. **4.** *Hort:* stock.

sujétion [syʒesjɔ̃] *n.f.* **1.** subjection **(à,** to); servitude; **s. aux lois,** subservience to the laws; **une habitude devient vite une s.,** we soon become slaves to a habit. **2.** constraint, obligation; **emploi d'une grande s.,** job that keeps one tied down.

sulf(o)- [sylf(ɔ)-] *pref. Ch:* sulph(o)-, sulf(o)-; NOTE: *the spelling* **sulf(o)-,** *now largely American, may gradually replace* **sulph(o)-** *in international scientific use.*

sulfamide [sylfamid] *n.m. Ch:* sulphamide, sulfamide; sulpha, sulfa, drug.

sulfatage [sylfataʒ] *n.m.* **1.** *Ch: Ind:* sulphating, sulfating; *El:* corrosion (on battery terminals). **2.** *Vit:* treating (of vines) with copper sulphate, sulfate.

sulfate [sylfat] *n.m. Ch:* sulphate, sulfate.

sulfaté [sylfate] *a.* sulphated, sulfated (lime, etc.).

sulfater [sylfate] *v.tr. Ch: Ind:* to sulphate, sulfate.

sulfateuse [sylfatøz] *n.f.* (*a*) *Vit:* sulphate, sulfate, sprayer; (*b*) *P:* submachine-gun.

sulfhydrique [sylfidrik] *a. Ch:* **acide s.,** hydrogen sulphide, sulfide; sulphuretted, sulfuretted, hydrogen.

sulfitage [sylfitaʒ] *n.m.* sulphiting, sulfiting.

sulfite [sylfit] *n.m. Ch:* sulphite, sulfite.

sulfurage [sylfyraʒ] *n.m. Agr: Vit:* sulphiding, sulfiding.

sulfuration [sylfyrasjɔ̃] *n.f. Ch:* sulphur(iz)ation, sulfurization.

sulfure [sylfyr] *n.m. Ch:* sulphide, sulfide; **s. de fer,** iron pyrites.

sulfuré [sylfyre] *a. Ch:* sulphuretted, sulfuretted; **hydrogène s.,** hydrogen sulphide, sulfide; sulphuretted hydrogen; *Miner:* **fer s.,** iron pyrites.

sulfurer [sylfyre] *v.tr.* to sulphurize, sulfurize; sulphurate.

sulfureux, -euse [sylfyrø, -øz] *a. Ch:* sulphurous, sulfurous; sulphur, sulfur (water, spring).

sulfurique [sylfyrik] *a. Ch:* sulphuric, sulfuric.

sulfurisé [sylfyrize] *a.* sulphurized, sulfurized; **papier s.,** greaseproof paper.

sultan [syltɑ̃] *n.m.* sultan.

sultanat [syltana] *n.m.* sultanate.

sultane [syltan] *n.f.* sultana, sultaness.

sumac [symak] *n.m. Bot:* sumac(h).

sumérien, -ienne [symerjɛ̃, -jɛn] **1.** *a. & n. A.Geog: Ethn:* Sumerian. **2.** *n.m. Ling:* Sumerian.

summum [sɔmɔm] *n.m.* acme, summit.

sunlight [sœnlait] *n.m. Cin:* sunlight lamp.

super[1] [sypɛr] *F:* **1.** *a.* super, great, terrific. **2.** *n.m. Aut:* = four-, five-star, petrol; premium-grade petrol, *NAm:* gas.

super[2] [sype] **1.** *v.tr. Nau:* (*of pump*) to suck. **2.** *v.i.* (*a*) (*of pipe, etc.*) to get blocked; (*b*) **navire supé,** vessel stuck in the mud.

superbe [sypɛrb] **1.** *a.* (*a*) *A: & Lit:* proud, haughty; (*b*) superb; stately (building); (*c*) magnificent (horse); splendid, marvellous (weather, show); **il fait des affaires superbes,** he is doing splendid business; **étalage s.,** magnificent display. **2.** *n.f. A: & Lit:* pride, haughtiness.

superbement [sypɛrbəmɑ̃] *adv.* **1.** *A:* haughtily. **2.** superbly, magnificently.

supercarburant [sypɛrkarbyrɑ̃] *n.m.* high-grade, premium-grade, petrol, *NAm:* gasoline.

supercherie [sypɛrʃəri] *n.f.* swindle; hoax.

superciment [sypɛrsimɑ̃] *n.m. Const:* rapid-hardening (Portland) cement.

supérette [sypeʀɛt] *n.f. Com:* small supermarket.

superfétation [sypɛrfetasjɔ̃] *n.f. Lit:* superfluity (of words, etc.).

superfétatoire [sypɛrfetatwar] *a.* superfluous.

superficialité [sypɛrfisjalite] *n.f.* superficiality.

superficie [sypɛrfisi] *n.f.* (*a*) surface; (*b*) (surface) area (of field, triangle); (*c*) **tout en s.,** all on the surface, entirely superficial.

superficiel, -elle [sypɛrfisjɛl] *a.* superficial (area, wound, knowledge, observer); skin-deep (wound, beauty); shallow (mind); *Geog:* **eau superficielle,** surface water; *Ph:* **tension superficielle,** surface tension.

superficiellement [sypɛrfisjɛlmɑ̃] *adv.* (*a*) superficially; (*b*) in area.

superfin [sypɛrfɛ̃] *a. Com:* superfine.

superflu [sypɛrfly] **1.** *a.* (*a*) superfluous, unnecessary; (*b*) vain, useless (regrets); (*c*) *Cmptr:* redundant. **2.** *n.m.* superfluity; surplus.

supérieur, -eure [syperjœr] **1.** *a.* (*a*) upper (storey, limb, province); (*b*) superior **(à,** to); **s. à la moyenne,** above, better than, average; **lutter, combattre, contre des forces supérieures,** to fight against odds; **se montrer s. aux événements,** to rise above events; **nommer qn à un emploi s.,** to appoint s.o. to a higher post; (*c*) higher, upper; *Sch:* advanced (course); *Mil: etc:* **un commandement s.,** a senior command; **classes supérieures,** (i) upper classes (of society); (ii) upper forms (in school); **enseignement s.,** higher, university, education; **offre supérieure,** higher bid; **les animaux supérieurs,** the higher animals; *Jur:* **cour supérieure,** higher court; (*d*) *Com:* of superior quality; (*e*) superior, condescending (manner). **2.** *n.* (*a*) **il est votre s.,** (i) he is your superior; (ii) he is a better man than you; **il est mon s. hiérarchique,** he is above me in rank; (*b*) head of a convent, etc.; **la Mère supérieure, la Supérieure,** the Mother Superior.

supériorité [syperjɔrite] *n.f.* superiority **(de,** in); **s. d'âge,** seniority; **un air de s.,** a superior air; **s. sur les marchés mondiaux,** command of the world markets; **lutter contre une s. écrasante,** to fight against crushing odds.

superlatif, -ive [sypɛrlatif, -iv] *a. & n.m.* superlative; **laid au s.,** superlatively ugly.

superlativement [sypɛrlativmɑ̃] *adv. F:* superlatively.

supermarché [sypɛrmarʃe] *n.m. Com:* supermarket.

supernova [sypɛrnɔva] *n.f. Astr:* supernova.

superphosphate [sypɛrfɔsfat] *n.m. Agr:* superphosphate.

superposable [sypɛrpozabl̩] *a.* super(im)posable; *Furn:* **chaise s.,** stacking chair.

superposé [sypɛrpoze] *a.* superimposed (images); *El: Elcs:* superposed.

superposer [sypɛrpoze] *v.tr.* to superpose, pile **(à,** (up)on); to superimpose (images).

superposition [sypɛrpozisjɔ̃] *n.f.* superposition (of triangles, geological strata, etc.); *Phot: Cin:* superimposition.

superproduction [sypɛrprɔdyksjɔ̃] *n.f. Cin: Th:* spectacular.

supersonique [sypɛrsɔnik] *a.* supersonic.

superstitieusement [sypɛrstisjøzmɑ̃] *adv.* superstitiously.

superstitieux, -euse [sypɛrstisjø, -øz] *a.* superstitious.

superstition [sypɛrstisjɔ̃] *n.f.* **1.** superstition. **2.** **avoir la s. du passé,** to be foolishly attached to the past.

superstrat [sypɛrstra] *n.m. Ling:* superstratum.

superstructure [sypɛrstryktyr] *n.f.* superstructure.

superviser [sypɛrvize] *v.tr.* to supervise; *Cmptr:* to control.

superviseur [sypɛrvizœr] *Cmptr:* **1.** *a.* supervisory. **2.** *n.m.* supervisor.

supin [sypɛ̃] *n.m. Gram:* supine.

supplanter [syplɑ̃te] *v.tr.* to supplant, supersede.

suppléance [sypleɑ̃s] *n.f.* temporary, supply, post; **remplir une s.,** to deputize, stand in, supply, for someone.

suppléant, -ante [sypleɑ̃, -ɑ̃t] **1.** *n.* (*pers.*) substitute (**de,** for); supply teacher; (doctor's) locum; *Th:* understudy. **2.** *a.* (*a*) acting, temporary (official, etc.); surrogate (judge); **professeur s.,** (i) (assistant) lecturer; (ii) supply teacher; (*b*) *Gram:* substitute (verb, etc.).

suppléer [syplee] **1.** *v.tr. A: & Lit:* (*a*) to supply, make up (for) (what is lacking); (*b*) to take the place of, deputize for (s.o.); **se faire s.,** to find a substitute, a deputy. **2.** *v.i.* **s. à qch.,** to make up, compensate, for sth.; **s. au vin par le cidre,** to eke out the wine with cider; **s. à un poste vacant,** to fill a vacant post.

supplément [syplemɑ̃] *n.m.* (*a*) supplement, addition; **en s.,** additional; extra; supplementary; (*b*) extra, additional, payment; *Rail:* excess fare, extra fare; **s. de prix,** extra charge; **s. de solde,** extra pay; **s. d'imposition,** additional tax; (*c*) supplement (to book, magazine, etc.); (*d*) (*in restaurant*) extra (dish); extra charge (for special dish); (*e*) *Mth:* supplement (of an angle).

supplémentaire [syplemɑ̃tɛr] *a.* supplementary, additional, extra, further; *Ind:* **une heure s.,** an hour's overtime; *Rail:* **train s.,** relief train; *Mth:* **angles supplémentaires,** supplementary angles; *Mus:* **lignes supplémentaires,** ledger lines, added lines.

supplémenter [syplemɑ̃te] *v.tr.* **s. un billet,** to issue a supplementary ticket for an excess fare.

supplétif, -ive [sypletif, -iv] *a. & n.m. Mil:* auxiliary (troops).

suppliant, -ante [syplijɑ̃, -ɑ̃t] **1.** *a.* imploring, pleading (look, etc.); **d'un air s.,** imploringly. **2.** *n.* suppliant, supplicant.

supplication [syplikasjɔ̃] *n.f.* supplication, entreaty.

supplice [syplis] *n.m.* (*a*) (severe corporal) punishment; torture; **le s. du fouet,** the penalty of the lash; **le dernier s.,** capital punishment, the extreme penalty; (*b*) torment, anguish, agony; **la goutte est un s.,** gout is a real torture; **être au s.,** to be in agonies (of suspense, embarrassment, etc.).

supplicié, -ée [syplisje] *n.* (i) criminal facing execution; (ii) tortured prisoner, etc.

supplicier [syplisje] *v.tr.* (*impf. & pr.sub.* **n. suppliciions, v. suppliciiez**) to torture (s.o.).

supplier [syplije] *v.tr.* (*impf. & pr.sub.* **n. suppliions, v. suppliiez**) to beseech; to beg, implore; **s. qn pour obtenir qch.,** to beg s.o. for sth.; **s. qn de faire qch.,** to implore, entreat, beg, s.o. to do sth.; **taisez-vous, je vous en supplie,** be quiet, I beg you.

supplique [syplik] *n.f.* petition.

support [sypɔr] *n.m.* **1.** support, prop, stay; *Carp:* strut; *Sp:* (athletic) support. **2.** *Her:* supporter (of shield). **3.** *Tchn:* (*a*) rest (for tools, etc.); stand (for lamp, test tube, etc.); holder (for memo block, etc.); mount (of photograph); *Arch: Const:* support (of structure, arch, etc.); **s. de bicyclette,** bicycle stand; **s. pour bicyclettes,** bicycle rack; *Bootm:* **s. plantaire,** arch support; (*b*) *Mec.E:* bearer, bracket, support (of machine part); (*c*) *Nau:* bracket, crutch (of spar, appliances); (*d*) *El:* (electrode) support. **4.** *Phot: Cin:* backing (of emulsion); *Com:* **s. publicitaire,** publicity, advertising, medium. **5.** *Cmptr:* **s. (d'information),** medium.

supportable [sypɔrtabl̩] *a.* **1.** supportable, bearable, endurable; **pas s.,** intolerable; unbearable. **2.** tolerably good, fair.

supportablement [sypɔrtabləmɑ̃] *adv.* fairly well; tolerably well.

supporter¹ [sypɔrte] *v.tr.* **1.** to support, prop, hold up, sustain, bear, carry (ceiling, arch); to support, back up (person, theory); to bear (cost of sth.); *Sp: F:* to support (team). **2.** (*a*) to endure, bear; to withstand (heat, misfortune, etc.); to be equal to (a test); to stand up to (investigation); to take, carry (one's drink); *Nau:* to weather (a storm); **il ne supporte plus de se coucher tard,** he is no longer equal to staying up late; (*b*) to tolerate, put up with, stand (rudeness, etc.); **cela ne peut pas se s.,** that is intolerable; **je ne peux pas le s.,** I can't stand him; **ne pouvoir s. que qn fasse qch.,** to be unable to stand s.o. doing sth.

supporter² [sypɔrtɛr] *n.m. Sp:* supporter.

supposé [sypoze] *a.* (*a*) supposed, alleged (thief, etc.); (*b*) assumed, false, fictitious (name, etc.); forged (will).

supposer [sypoze] *v.tr.* **1.** to suppose, assume, imagine; **l'auteur suppose tout et ne prouve rien,** the author assumes everything and proves nothing; **s. vrai ce qui est en question,** to beg the question; **en supposant que** + *sub.*, **à s. que** + *sub.*, **supposons que** + *sub.*, suppose that . . .; **on suppose que** + *ind.*, it is thought, inferred, that . . .; **elle lui supposait une grande fortune,** she credited him with a large fortune; *v.i..* **vous avez supposé juste,** you guessed right; **on le suppose à Paris, on suppose qu'il est à Paris,** he is supposed to be in Paris; **supposez-vous à Paris,** imagine yourself in Paris. **2.** to presuppose, imply; **cela lui suppose du courage,** it implies courage on his part. **3.** *Jur:* to put forward (an impostor); to present (a forged will).

supposition [sypozisjɔ̃] *n.f.* supposition, conjecture, assumption; **si par s. il revenait,** supposing (that) he came back.

suppositoire [sypozitwar] *n.m. Med:* suppository.

suppôt [sypo] *n.m.* (*pers.*) tool (of another); henchman; **s. de Satan,** hellhound, fiend.

suppression [sypresjɔ̃] *n.f.* **1.** (*a*) suppression (of law, tax, journal, etc.); discontinuance (of a service, etc.); removal (of difficulty); **la Commission pour la s. du bruit,** the Noise Abatement Commission; (*b*) *Jur:* concealment. **2.** *Typ:* cancel matter. **3.** *Cmptr:* delete, suppression.

supprimable [syprimabl̩] *a.* suppressible.

supprimer [syprime] *v.tr.* **1.** (*a*) to suppress (newspaper, document, etc.); to abolish, do away with (law, tax, etc.); to put an end to; to withdraw (credit); to omit, leave out (word, sentence); to cancel (train, etc.); to remove (difficulty); to dispose of (objections); to quell (revolt); *Cmptr:* to delete; *F:* **s. qn,** to kill s.o., to bump s.o. off; *F:* **se s.,** to commit suicide; *Typ:* **à s.,** delete; (*b*) *Jur:* to conceal (document, fact); to suppress, withhold, burke (fact). **2. s. qch. à qn,** to deprive s.o. of sth.

suppurant [sypyrɑ̃] *a. Med:* suppurating.

suppuration [sypyrasjɔ̃] *n.f.* suppuration.

suppurer [sypyre] *v.i.* (*of wound, sore*) to suppurate.

supputation [sypytasjɔ̃] *n.f.* computation, calculation.

supputer [sypyte] *v.tr.* to compute, calculate.

supraconductivité [syprakɔ̃dyktivite] *n.f. Ph: El:* supraconductivity.

supranational, -aux [sypranasjɔnal, -o] *a.* supranational.

supraterrestre [sypratɛrɛstr̥] *a.* superterrestrial.

suprématie [sypremasi] *n.f.* supremacy.

suprême [syprɛm] **1.** *a.* (*a*) supreme; highest (degree); **le pouvoir s.,** sovereignty; (*b*) last (requests, moments). **2.** *n.m. Cu:* suprême (of chicken).

suprêmement [syprɛmmɑ̃] *adv.* supremely.

sur¹ [syr] *prep.* **1.** (*a*) on, upon; **assis s. une chaise,**

sitting on a chair; *P.N:* **virages s. 2 kilomètres,** bends for 2 kilometres, *NAm:* killometers; **ville s. la Seine,** town on the Seine; **se promener s. l'avenue,** to walk in the avenue; **je suis venu s. le bateau,** I came by boat; *F:* **la clef est s. la porte,** the key is in the door; **je n'ai pas d'argent s. moi,** I have no money on me; **fenêtre qui donne s. le jardin,** window which looks on to the garden; **page s. page,** page after page; **juger qn s. la mine,** to judge s.o. by appearances; **s. sa bonne réputation,** on the strength of his, her, good reputation; **s. un ton de reproche,** in a reproachful tone; **chanter qch. s. un certain air,** to sing sth. to a certain tune; **vente s. catalogue,** mail order (business); **s. une fausse accusation,** on a false accusation; (*b*) **marcher, fonctionner, s.,** to work, operate, on, off; (*c*) towards; **avancer s. qn,** to advance on, against, s.o.; **les trains s. Orléans,** the trains for Orleans; (*d*) over, above; **les astres s. nos têtes,** the stars above our heads; **dormir s. son travail,** to go to sleep over one's work; **être s. un travail,** to be engaged in, on, a piece of work; **avoir autorité s. qn,** to have authority over s.o.; **s. toute(s) chose(s),** above all (things); **un pont s. une rivière,** a bridge across a river; (*e*) about, concerning. **2.** (*of time*) (*a*) about (midday); towards (evening); **s. mes dix-huit ans,** when I was about eighteen; (*b*) **s. ce, s. quoi,** whereupon; **s. ce, je vous quitte,** and now I must leave you; **il est s. son départ,** he is about to leave. **3.** (*a*) out of; in; **une fois s. deux,** every other time; **on paie les pompiers s. les fonds de la ville,** the firemen are paid out of the town funds; (*b*) (*in measurements*) by; **huit mètres s. six,** eight metres, *NAm:* meters, by six.

sur² *a.* sour (fruit, etc.); tart.

sûr [syr] *a.* sure. **1.** (*a*) safe, secure (locality, shelter, beach); **peu s.,** insecure; unsafe; **jouer au plus s.,** to play for safety; **le plus s. serait de . . .,** the safest course would be to . . .; **pour le plus s.,** to be on the safe side; (*b*) trustworthy, reliable (person, memory); trusty, true, staunch (friend); reliable (memory, information, firm); **temps s.,** settled weather; **avoir le coup d'œil s.,** to have an accurate eye; **goût s.,** discerning taste; **avoir la main sûre, le pied s.,** to have a steady hand, to be surefooted; **frapper un coup s., à coup s.,** to strike an unerring blow; **mettre son argent en mains sûres,** to put one's money into safe hands. **2.** certain; infallible (remedy); **c'est une affaire sûre,** it's a certainty, a sure thing, *F:* a dead cert; **être s. de réussir,** to be sure of success; **être s. de qch.,** to be sure, certain, of sth.; **je suis s. de lui,** I can depend on him; **s. de soi,** self-assured; **parier à coup s.,** to bet on a certainty; **à coup s.,** for certain; without fail; *F:* **bien s.! pour s.!** of course! *NAm:* sure! *F:* **bien s.?** you really mean it? **bien s. que non!** of course not! **3.** *adv. F:* surely; **pas s.!** perhaps not!

surabondance [syrabɔ̃dɑ̃s] *n.f.* superabundance; *Com:* glut.

surabondant [syrabɔ̃dɑ̃] *a.* superabundant, overabundant; superfluous.

surabonder [syrabɔ̃de] *v.i.* to superabound; **s. de, en, qch.,** to have an excess, an abundance, of sth.

suractivité [syraktivite] *n.f. Physiol:* overactivity.

suraigu, -uë [syregy] *a.* highpitched.

suralimentation [syralimɑ̃tasjɔ̃] *n.f.* **1.** *Med:* feeding (up). **2.** overfeeding. **3.** *I.C.E:* supercharging.

suralimenter [syralimɑ̃te] *v.tr.* **1.** *Med:* to feed up, overfeed (a person). **2.** *I.C.E:* to supercharge (engine).

suranné [syrane] *a.* out of date. **1.** *A:* expired (passport, etc.). **2.** old-fashioned; **beauté surannée,** faded beauty.

surbaissé [syrbese] *a.* **1.** *Arch:* depressed, flattened (arch, vault). **2.** *Aut: etc:* dropped (axle, frame, etc.); (extra-)low, underslung (chassis).

surbaissement [syrbɛsmɑ̃] *n.m. Arch:* surbasement.

surbaisser [syrbese] *v.tr.* **1.** *Arch:* to surbase, flatten, depress (arch, vault). **2.** *Aut: etc:* to drop, undersling (frame, etc.).

surboum [syrbum] *n.f. F: A:* party.

surcapacité [syrkapasite] *n.f. Ind: etc:* surplus production capacity.

surcapitalisation [syrkapitalizasjɔ̃] *a.* overcapitalization.

surcharge [syrʃarʒ] *n.f.* **1.** overloading. **2.** (*a*) overload, *El:* overcharge (of accumulator); (*b*) excess weight (of luggage); (*c*) weight handicap (of racehorse). **3.** (*a*) overtax, overcharge; (*b*) additional charge (on account rendered); *Typ: etc:* extras. **4.** *Typ:* interlineation. **5.** surcharge (on postage stamp).

surcharger [syrʃarʒe] *v.tr.* (**je surchargeai(s); n. surchargeons**) **1.** (*a*) to overburden, overload (vehicle, horse, one's stomach, etc.); *El:* to overcharge (accumulator); **s. ses employés de travail,** to overwork one's employees; *Fin:* **s. le marché,** to overload, glut, the market; (*b*) to overtax, overcharge. **2.** (*a*) *Typ:* to write over (other words); (*b*) to surcharge, overprint (postage stamp).

surchauffe [syrʃof] *n.f.* **1.** overheating (of oven). **2.** superheating (of steam). **3.** superheat (in steam). **4.** *Pol.E:* **s. (économique),** inflation.

surchauffer [syrʃofe] *v.tr.* **1.** to overheat (oven, etc.). **2.** to superheat (steam).

surchoix [syrʃwa] *n.m.* finest quality.

surclasser [syrklase] *v.tr.* to outclass.

surcompensation [syrkɔ̃pɑ̃sasjɔ̃] *n.f. Psy:* overcompensation.

surcompression [syrkɔ̃presjɔ̃] *n.f. I.C.E:* supercharging.

surcomprimer [syrkɔ̃prime] *v.tr. I.C.E:* to pressurize; to supercharge.

surconsommation [syrkɔ̃sɔmasjɔ̃] *n.f. Pol.Ec:* overconsumption.

surcontrer [syrkɔ̃tre] *v.tr. Cards:* to redouble.

surcouper [syrkupe] *v.tr. Cards:* to overtrump.

surcroît [syrkrwa] *n.m.* addition, increase; **avoir un grand s. de travail,** to have a great deal of extra work; **un s. d'effort,** an extra effort; **pour donner un s. d'effet à . . .,** to give an added effect to . . .; **par s.,** in addition; **par s. de besogne,** to add to my work; **pour s. de malheur,** to make matters worse.

surdéveloppé [syrdevlɔpe] *a. Pol.Ec:* (*a*) highly developed; (*b*) overdeveloped.

surdi-mutité [syrdimytite] *n.f.* deaf-muteness.

surdité [syrdite] *n.f.* deafness; **s. musicale,** tone deafness.

surdosage [syrdozaʒ] *n.m.* overdosage.

surdoué [syrdwe] *a.* exceptionally gifted (child).

sureau, -eaux [syro] *n.m.* elder (tree); **baie de s.,** elderberry.

surélévation [syrelevasjɔ̃] *n.f.* raising.

surélevé [syrɛlve] *a.* **1.** elevated (railway). **2.** *Arch:* raised (arch, etc.).

surélever [syrɛlve] *v.tr.* (*conj. like* ÉLEVER) **1.** *Const: etc:* to heighten, to raise. **2.** (*a*) to raise (prices, tariff, etc.); to force up (prices, etc.); (*b*) *El:* to boost (potential).

sûrement [syrmɑ̃] *adv.* **1.** steadily, unhesitatingly, confidently. **2.** surely, certainly; **il va s. y avoir des changements,** there are sure to be (some) changes. **3.** (*a*) surely, securely, safely; reliably; (*b*) **frapper s.,** to strike an unerring blow.

suremploi [syrɑ̃plwa] *n.m.* overemployment.

surenchère [syrɑ̃ʃɛr] *n.f.* (*a*) higher bid, further bid; outbidding; **faire une s. sur qn,** to outbid s.o.; (*b*)

une s. de violence, ever-increasing violence; **faire de la s. électorale,** to make more extravagant promises to catch the votes; (*c*) *F:* one-upmanship.

surenchérir [syrɑ̃ʃerir] *v.i.* (*a*) to overbid; **s. (sur qn),** to bid higher (than s.o.); to outbid s.o.; *F:* to go one better than s.o.; (*b*) to rise higher in price.

surencombré [syrɑ̃kɔ̃bre] *a.* appallingly congested (street, etc.).

surencombrement [syrɑ̃kɔ̃brəmɑ̃] *n.m.* severe congestion.

surentraînement [syrɑ̃trɛnmɑ̃] *n.m. Sp:* overtraining.

surentraîner [syrɑ̃trɛne] *v.tr. Sp:* to overtrain.

suréquipement [syrekipmɑ̃] *n.m. Pol.Ec:* overequipment.

suréquiper [syrekipe] *v.tr. Pol.Ec:* to overequip.

surestimation [syrɛstimasjɔ̃] *n.f.* overestimate, overvaluation.

surestimer [syrɛstime] *v.tr.* to overestimate, overvalue (price, cost); **s. qn,** to overrate s.o.

suret, -ette [syrɛ, -ɛt] *a.* sour(ish); tart.

sûreté [syrte] *n.f.* **1.** (*a*) safety, security, safe-keeping; **lieu de s.,** place of safety; **être en s.,** to be safe, in a safe place, out of harm's way; **mettre qn en (lieu de) s.,** to put s.o. (i) in prison, (ii) in safe keeping, out of harm's way; **pour plus de s.,** for greater safety; **rasoir, serrure, de s.,** safety razor, lock; (*b*) security, protection; (*Police*) **la S.** = Scotland Yard; **agent de la s.,** detective. **2.** sureness (of hand, foot); soundness (of vision, taste, judgment); unerringness (of blow, stroke); **s. de soi,** self-confidence, self-assurance. **3.** *Com:* surety, security, guarantee.

surévaluer [syrevalɥe] *v.tr.* to overestimate.

surexcitable [syrɛksitabl̥] *a.* easily excited.

surexcitation [syrɛksitasjɔ̃] *n.f.* **1.** (over)excitement. **2.** *Med: etc:* overstimulation.

surexciter [syrɛksite] *v.tr.* to (over)excite.

surexposer [syrɛkspoze] *v.tr. Phot:* to overexpose.

surexposition [syrɛkspozisjɔ̃] *n.f. Phot:* overexposure.

surf [sœrf] *n.m. Sp:* surfing.

surface [syrfas] *n.f.* surface; (*a*) **eau de s.,** surface water; *Ph:* **tension de s.,** surface tension (of liquid); *Rec:* **bruit de s.,** surface noise; (*of submarine*) **vitesse en s.,** surface speed; **faire s., revenir en s.,** (i) (*of submarine*) to (break) surface; (ii) *F:* (*of pers.*) to come to; to surface; **en s.,** superficially; **tout en s.,** superficial; (*b*) *Mth:* **s. de révolution, de rotation,** surface of revolution; (*c*) area; **s. d'appui, s. de portée, s. portante,** bearing area, surface; **s. utile,** useful, working, surface; *Const:* **s. couverte,** floor area; **s. de voilure,** sail area; *F:* **il présente une s. financière suffisante,** his financial standing is satisfactory.

surfaceur, -euse [syrfasœr, -øz] *Tchn:* **1.** *n.* (*pers.*) polisher. **2.** *n.f.* surfacer, planing machine.

surfaire [syrfɛr] *v.tr.* (*conj. like* FAIRE) *Lit:* (*a*) to overcharge; to ask too much for (sth.); (*b*) to overestimate, overrate (person, talent, etc.); to overpraise.

surfait [syrfɛ] *a.* excessive (prices); overrated (reputation).

surfilage [syrfilaʒ] *n.m. Dressm: Needlew:* overcasting.

surfiler [syrfile] *v.tr.* **1.** *Dressm: Needlew:* to overcast, to oversew. **2.** *Tex:* to give an extra twist to (the thread).

surfin [syrfɛ̃] *a. Com:* superfine, of highest quality.

surgélateur [syrʒelatœr] *n.m.* freezer.

surgélation [syrʒelasjɔ̃] *n.f.* deep freezing; *NAm:* quick freezing.

surgelé [syrʒəle] *a. & n.m.* deep-frozen, *NAm:* quick-frozen; **(produits) surgelés,** deep-frozen foods.

surgeler [syrʒəle] *v.tr.* (*conj. like* GELER) to deep-freeze, *NAm:* to quick-freeze.

surgénérateur, -trice [syrʒeneratœr, -tris] *a. Atom.Ph:* **réacteur s.,** breeder reactor.

surgeon [syrʒɔ̃] *n.m. Hort:* sucker.

surgir [syrʒir] *v.i.* (*aux.* **avoir,** *occ.* **être**) to rise; to come into view; to loom (up); **s. brusquement,** to appear suddenly; (*of plant*) to spring up; (*of difficulty*) to crop up.

surhaussé [syrose] *a. Arch: etc:* raised.

surhaussement [syrosmɑ̃] *n.m. Arch: etc:* superelevation, raising; *Civ.E:* banking (of one side of a road).

surhausser [syrose] *v.tr.* to raise (wall, price, etc.).

surhomme [syrɔm] *n.m.* superman.

surhumain [syrymɛ̃] *a.* superhuman.

surimposer [syrɛ̃poze] *v.tr.* to increase the tax on (sth.); to overtax.

surimposition [syrɛ̃pozisjɔ̃] *n.f.* **1.** increase of taxation; overtaxation. **2.** *Geol:* pseudomorphism; superimposition.

surimpression [syrɛ̃presjɔ̃] *n.f. Phot: Cin:* superimposition.

suriner [syrine] *v.tr. P: O:* to knife (s.o.).

surinfection [syrɛ̃fɛksjɔ̃] *n.f. Med:* secondary infection.

surintendance [syrɛ̃tɑ̃dɑ̃s] *n.f.* superintendence.

surintendant [syrɛ̃tɑ̃dɑ̃] *n.m. Hist:* superintendent (*esp.* of finance).

surir [syrir] *v.i.* (*of wine, soup, etc.*) to turn sour.

surjet [syrʒɛ] *n.m. Needlew:* overcasting, whipping (of seams).

surjeter [syrʒəte] *v.tr.* (*conj. like* JETER) *Needlew:* to overcast, whip (seam).

sur-le-champ [syrləʃɑ̃] *adv.* at once; on the spot, immediately.

surlendemain [syrlɑ̃dmɛ̃] *n.m.* **le s.,** the day after the next; two days later.

surmenage [syrmənaʒ] *n.m.* overwork; **s. intellectuel,** mental fatigue.

surmenant [syrmənɑ̃] *a.* exhausting (work, etc.).

surmené [syrməne] *a.* overworked; exhausted.

surmener [syrməne] *v.tr.* (*conj. like* MENER) to overwork; to exhaust; to work (employees) too hard; **se s.,** to overwork; to work too hard; to overdo it.

sur-moi [syrmwa] *n.m. no pl. Psy:* **le s.,** the superego.

surmontable [syrmɔ̃tabl̥] *a.* surmountable.

surmonter [syrmɔ̃te] **1.** *v.tr.* (*a*) to surmount; **colonne surmontée d'une croix,** column surmounted, topped, by a cross; (*b*) to overcome, surmount (obstacle, difficulty); to master, get the better of (one's anger, grief); *Lit:* to overcome (one's enemies). **2. se s.,** to master, control, one's feelings, one's passions.

surmultiplication [syrmyltiplikasjɔ̃] *n.f. Aut:* overdrive (system).

surmultiplié [syrmyltiplije] *a. & n.f. Aut:* **(vitesse) surmultipliée,** overdrive.

surnager [syrnaʒe] *v.i.* **(je surnageai(s); n. surnageons)** (*a*) to float on the surface; (*b*) to survive, remain.

surnatalité [syrnatalite] *n.f.* excessively high birthrate.

surnaturel, -elle [syrnatyrɛl] *a.* (*a*) supernatural; *n.* **le s.,** the supernatural; (*b*) inexplicable; uncanny.

surnom [syrnɔ̃] *n.m.* appellation; nickname.

surnombre [syrnɔ̃br̥] *n.m.* **en s.,** too many; spare; (*of workers*) redundant; **exemplaires en s.,** excess, spare, copies.

surnommer [syrnɔme] *v.tr.* **s. qn, qch.,** to (nick)name s.o., sth.

surnuméraire [syrnymerɛr] *a. & n.* supernumerary.

suroffre [syrɔfr̥] *n.f.* better offer, better bid.
suroît [syrwa] *n.m. Nau:* **1.** southwest. **2.** sou'wester (wind or hat).
suroxygéner [syrɔksiʒene] *v.tr.* **(je suroxygène, n. suroxygénons; je suroxygénerai)** *Ch:* to superoxygenate.
surpaie [syrpɛj, -pɛ] *n.f.* overpaying, overpayment.
surpasser [syrpɑse] *v.tr.* to surpass; to exceed (one's hopes); to outdo (a rival); to transcend (s.o.); **dépense qui surpasse mes moyens,** expense beyond my means; **s. qn en éclat,** to outshine s.o.; **s. une armée en nombre,** to outnumber an army; *F:* **cela me surpasse,** that beats me; **il s'est surpassé,** he has surpassed himself.
surpatte [syrpat] *n.f. F:* surprise party.
surpaye [syrpɛj, -pɛ] *n.f.* overpaying, overpayment.
surpayer [syrpeje] *v.tr.* (*conj. like* PAYER) to overpay (s.o.); to pay too much for (sth.).
surpeuplé [syrpœple] *a.* overpopulated; overcrowded.
surpeuplement [syrpœpləmɑ̃] *n.m.* overpopulation; overcrowding.
sur(-)place [syrplas] *n.m.* balance (of cyclist before starting a race); *Aut: F:* **faire du s.,** to crawl.
surplis [syrpli] *n.m. Ecc:* surplice.
surplomb [syrplɔ̃] *n.m.* overhang; **en s.,** overhanging.
surplomber [syrplɔ̃be] *v.i. & tr.* to overhang.
surplus [syrply] *n.m.* surplus, excess; **le s.,** the rest, what is over; **payer le s.,** to pay the difference; **au s.,** besides, what is more; **de s.,** over and above; **les s. du gouvernement,** government surplus (stock).
surpopulation [syrpɔpylasjɔ̃] *n.f.* overpopulation.
surprenant [syrprənɑ̃] (*a*) *a.* surprising, astonishing; **chose surprenante,** strange to say; **rien de s. si . . .,** I shouldn't be surprised if . . .; **il est s. que vous le sachiez,** it is surprising that you should know of it; (*b*) *n.m.* **le s.,** (i) the astonishing (thing); (ii) the unexpected.
surprendre [syrprɑ̃dr̥] *v.tr.* (*conj. like* PRENDRE) to surprise. **1.** (*a*) to come upon (s.o., sth.) unexpectedly; to catch (s.o.) unawares; **aller s. un ami chez lui,** to drop in unexpectedly on a friend; **la nuit nous surprit,** night overtook us; **être surpris par la pluie,** to be caught in the rain; **s. qn à faire qch.,** to catch s.o. (in the act of) doing sth.; **je me surpris à pleurer,** I found myself crying; (*b*) to intercept (letter, glance); to overhear (conversation, etc.); **s. le secret de qn,** to detect s.o.'s secret. **2.** to astonish; **ce qui me surprend c'est que . . .,** what surprises me is that . . .; **cela me surprendrait qu'il revienne, s'il revenait,** I should be surprised if he came back; **ça a l'air de vous s.,** you seem surprised; **ce n'est pas pour me s.,** it doesn't surprise me in the least.
surpression [syrpresjɔ̃] *n.f.* overpressure; excessive pressure.
surprime [syrprim] *n.f. Ins:* extra premium.
surpris [syrpri] *a.* surprised; **je m'arrêtai, s.,** I paused in surprise; **s., je les regardais,** I watched them in surprise; **s. que** + *sub.*, **si** + *ind.*, surprised that, if; **je ne serais pas s. qu'il revienne, s'il revenait,** I should not, wouldn't, be surprised if he came back.
surprise [syrpriz] *n.f.* **1.** surprise; **à sa grande s.,** to his great surprise, much to his surprise; **s'emparer d'une ville par s., par un coup de s.,** to capture a town by surprise; **il m'a fait sa demande par s.,** he sprang his request on me; **craindre une s.,** to fear a sudden attack; **quelle bonne s.!** what a pleasant surprise! **attendez-vous à une drôle de s.,** be prepared for a shock; *Toys:* **boîte à s.,** Jack-in-the-box. **2. pochette s.,** lucky dip; surprise packet.
surprise-partie [syrprizparti] *n.f.* (*a*) *A:* surprise party; (*b*) (dancing) party; *pl. surprises-parties.*
surproduction [syrprɔdyksjɔ̃] *n.f.* overproduction.
surproduire [syrprɔdɥir] *v.tr. & i.* to overproduce.
surréalisme [syrealism] *n.m.* surrealism.
surréaliste [syrealist] *a. & n.* surrealist.
surréel, -elle [syreɛl] **1.** *a.* surreal(istic). **2.** *n.m.* the surreal.
surrégénérateur, -trice [syreʒeneratœr, -tris] *a. Atom.Ph:* **réacteur s.,** breeder reactor.
surrénal, -aux [syrenal, -o] *a. Anat:* surrenal (artery, ganglion); adrenal (gland).
sursalaire [syrsalɛr] *n.m.* bonus.
sursaut [syrso] *n.m.* (involuntary) start, jump; **faire un s.,** to start, to (give a) jump; **en s.,** with a start; **se lever en s.,** to start up; **dans un s. d'énergie,** with a (final) burst of energy; **un s. de terrorisme,** a new outburst of terrorism.
sursauter [syrsote] *v.i.* to start (involuntarily); to (give a) jump; **faire s. qn,** to startle s.o.; **s. d'indignation,** to leap up in indignation.
surseoir [syrswar] *v.ind.tr.* (*pr.p.* **sursoyant;** *p.p.* **sursis;** *pr.ind.* **je sursois, n. sursoyons;** *pr.sub.* **je sursoie;** *impf.* **je sursoyais;** *p.h.* **je sursis;** *fu.* **je surseoirai)** *Jur:* **s. à un jugement,** to suspend a judgment; **s. à l'exécution d'un condamné,** to reprieve a condemned man; **ordonnance de s. (à un jugement),** stay of execution.
sursis [syrsi] *n.m. Jur:* delay; stay of proceedings; respite; reprieve (from execution); **condamné à un an de prison avec s.,** given a suspended prison sentence of one year; *Mil:* **s. d'appel,** deferment (of call-up).
sursitaire [syrsitɛr] *n.m. Mil:* conscript provisionally exempted.
surtaux [syrto] *n.m.* overassessment.
surtaxe [syrtaks] *n.f.* **1.** supertax; surtax, extra tax. **2.** excessive tax.
surtaxer [syrtakse] *v.tr.* (*a*) *Adm:* to surtax, overtax; (*b*) to surcharge (letter, etc.).
surtension [syrtɑ̃sjɔ̃] *n.f. El:* overvoltage, surge (of voltage).
surtout¹ [syrtu] *adv.* particularly, especially; above all; **ayez s. soin de . . .,** be specially careful to . . .; **s. n'oubliez pas de . . .,** above all, do not forget to . . .; *conj.phr. F:* **s. que . . .,** especially as . . . .
surtout² *n.m.* **1.** *Cost: A:* overcoat. **2.** centrepiece, *NAm:* centerpiece (on dinner table).
surveillance [syrvɛjɑ̃s] *n.f.* supervision, watching, superintendence, surveillance; *Mil:* observation; *Sch:* invigilation; *Elcs:* monitoring; **exercer une s. discrète sur qn, sur qch.,** to keep a discreet watch on s.o., on sth.; **être sous la s. de la police,** to be under police supervision, *esp. NAm:* surveillance.
surveillant, -ante [syrvɛjɑ̃, -ɑ̃t] *n.* **1.** supervisor, superintendent, overseer; shopwalker; *Rail:* inspector. **2.** keeper, guardian, watchman; sentry (at palace gates, etc.). **3.** *n.f. Med:* **surveillante,** (ward) sister.
surveiller [syrveje] **1.** *v.tr.* (*a*) to supervise (work, workers); to tend (machine); (*b*) to watch (over), observe, look after (s.o.); *Sch:* to invigilate; **s. les enfants,** to look after, keep an eye on, the children; **s. la situation de près,** to keep a close eye on the situation; **il a besoin qu'on le surveille,** he needs looking after; *Jur:* **en liberté surveillée,** on probation; **le français parlé surveillé,** careful French speech; (*c*) *W.Tel:* to monitor. **2. se s.,** to keep a watch on oneself; to be on one's best behaviour, *NAm:* behavior.
survenir [syrvənir] *v.i.* (*conj. like* VENIR; *aux.* **être)** (*of events*) to happen, occur; *F:* to crop up; (*of difficulty*) to arise; (*of pers.*) to arrive unexpectedly; *impers.* **s'il ne survient pas de complications,** if no complications arise, occur.

survenue [syrvəny] *n.f.* unexpected arrival, supervention, supervening.
survêtement [syrvɛtmɑ̃] *n.m.* tracksuit.
survie [syrvi] *n.f. Jur: Ins: etc:* survival; *Rel:* afterlife; *Space: etc:* **équipement de s.,** life support equipment.
survirer [syrvire] *v.i. Aut:* to oversteer.
survivance [syrvivɑ̃s] *n.f.* **1.** (*a*) survival (*Biol:* of the fittest); (*b*) *Rel:* afterlife. **2.** survival, relic (of times past).
survivant, -ante [syrvivɑ̃, -ɑ̃t] **1.** *a.* surviving. **2.** *n.* survivor.
survivre [syrvivr̥] *v.ind.tr.* (*conj. like* VIVRE; *aux.* **avoir**); **s. à qn, à qch.,** to survive, outlive, s.o., to survive sth.; **va-t-il s.?** will he live? **se s.,** (i) to live on (in one's works, etc.); (ii) to outlive one's day.
survol [syrvɔl] *n.m.* (*a*) *Av:* flight over (place, etc.); (*b*) cursory glance (at a problem).
survoler [syrvɔle] *v.tr.* (*a*) *Av:* to fly over (mountain, locality); (*b*) **s. une question,** to get a general view of a problem.
survoltage [syrvɔltaʒ] *n.m. El:* boosting.
survolté [syrvɔlte] *a.* **1.** *El:* boosted. **2.** *F:* excited, worked up.
survolteur, -trice [syrvɔltœr, -tris] *a.* & *n.m. El:* booster.
sus [sy(s)] **1.** *adv.* **courir s. à son adversaire,** to rush upon, at, one's opponent; to charge one's opponent; *prep.phr.* **en s. de,** in addition to, over and above. **2.** *int.* **s. à l'ennemi!** at them!
susceptibilité [sysɛptibilite] *n.f.* **1.** susceptibility, sensitiveness; **blesser les susceptibilités de qn,** to wound s.o.'s feelings. **2.** *Magn:* susceptibility.
susceptible [sysɛptibl̥] *a.* **1. s. de,** susceptible of (proof); open to (improvement); **s. de faire qch.,** capable of doing sth.; liable, likely, to do sth. **2.** susceptible, touchy, thin-skinned, easily offended.
susciter [sysite] *v.tr.* to give rise to (difficulties); to cause (astonishment); to arouse (hostility).
suscription [syskripsjɔ̃] *n.f.* address (on letter).
susdit, -ite [sysdi, -it] *a.* & *n. Jur:* aforesaid, abovementioned.
sus-dominante [sysdɔminɑ̃t] *n.f. Mus:* submediant; la (of movable do system); *pl. sus-dominantes.*
susmentionné [sysmɑ̃sjɔne] *a.* & *n. Jur:* abovementioned, aforesaid.
susnommé [sysnɔme] *a.* & *n. Jur:* above-named.
suspect, -ecte [syspɛ(kt), -ɛkt] **1.** *a.* suspicious, doubtful, questionable, suspect; **s. de,** suspected of, under suspicion of; **cela m'est s.,** I don't like the look of it; **tenir qn pour s.,** to be suspicious of s.o.; **devenir s. (à qn),** to arouse (s.o.'s) suspicion. **2.** *n.* suspect.
suspecter [syspɛkte] *v.tr.* to suspect (s.o.) (of sth., of doing sth.); to question, doubt (sth.); to cast suspicion on (s.o.'s good faith, etc.).
suspendre [syspɑ̃dr̥] **1.** *v.tr.* to suspend; (*a*) to hang up (clothes, lamp); to sling (a hammock); (*b*) to defer, postpone; to suspend, stop (payment, work); **s. son jugement,** to suspend judgment; **la séance est suspendue,** we will now adjourn; **les abonnements sont suspendus pour ce soir,** season tickets are not valid tonight; *Aut:* **s. un permis de conduire,** to suspend a driving licence; (*c*) to suspend (an official, etc.). **2.** **se s.,** to hang (**à,** from; **par,** by).
suspendu [syspɑ̃dy] *a.* suspended, hanging; (*a*) **les jardins suspendus de Babylone,** the hanging gardens of Babylon; **pont s.,** suspension bridge; *Aut:* **voiture bien suspendue,** car with good suspension; (*b*) clinging (to sth.); poised (on sth.); **lampe suspendue au plafond,** lamp hanging from the ceiling; **être s. aux lèvres de qn,** to be hanging on s.o.'s words, lips.
suspens [syspɑ̃] *n.m.* **1. en s.,** in suspense; (i) (*of pers.*) in doubt, in uncertainty; (ii) (*of thg*) in abeyance; (problem) that has been shelved, has still to be solved; **tenir qn en s.,** to keep s.o. in suspense. **2.** *Lit:* suspense.
suspense [syspɛns] *n.m. Cin: etc:* suspense.
suspensif, -ive [syspɑ̃sif, -iv] *a. Jur:* suspensive (veto, etc.).
suspension [syspɑ̃sjɔ̃] *n.f.* suspension. **1.** (*a*) hanging (up); (*b*) *Ch:* **en s.,** in suspension, suspended. **2.** (*a*) (temporary) discontinuance, interruption (of work, etc.); suspension (of hostilities, payment); stoppage (of traffic); abeyance (of law); *Gram:* **points de s.,** points of suspension; dots; *Aut:* **s. pour un an du permis de conduire,** a year's driving ban; *Jur:* **arrêt de s.,** injunction; (*b*) suspension (of an official). **3.** (*a*) light pendant; ceiling lamp; (*b*) *Furn: Aut: etc:* suspension, springing, springs.
suspicieux, -euse [syspisjø, -øz] *a.* suspicious.
suspicion [syspisjɔ̃] *n.f. esp. Jur:* suspicion.
sustentateur, -trice [systɑ̃tatœr, -tris] *Aer:* **1.** *a.* lifting (force, etc.); **effort s.,** lift; **surface sustentatrice,** aerofoil, *NAm:* airfoil. **2.** *n.m.* **s. rotatif,** rotor (of helicopter).
sustentation [systɑ̃tasjɔ̃] *n.f.* (*a*) support; **base, trapèze, de s.,** basis of support, of equilibrium; (*b*) *Aer:* lift.
sustenter [systɑ̃te] **1.** *v.tr. A:* to sustain, nourish. **2.** *F:* **se s.,** to take nourishment, keep up one's strength.
sus-tonique [systɔnik] *n.f. Mus:* supertonic; re (of movable do system); *pl. sus-toniques.*
susurrement [sysyrmɑ̃] *n.m. Lit:* susurration, murmuring.
susurrer [sysyre] *v.i. Lit:* to susurrate; to murmur; *with cogn.acc.* to whisper (sth.).
suture [sytyr] *n.f. Anat: Surg:* suture; **(point de) s.,** stitch.
suturer [sytyre] *v.tr. Surg:* to stitch, suture.
suzerain, -aine [syzrɛ̃, -ɛn] *a.* & *n.* suzerain.
suzeraineté [syzrɛnte] *n.f.* suzerainty; lordship.
svastika [svastika] *n.m.* swastika.
svelte [svɛlt] *a.* slender, svelte; willowy.
sveltesse [svɛltɛs] *n.f.* slenderness, slimness.
sweater [switœr] *n.m. Cost:* sweater.
sweepstake [swipstɛk] *n.m. Turf:* sweepstake.
swing [swiŋ] *n.m.* (*a*) *Box: Golf:* swing; (*b*) *Mus: F:* swing.
sybarite [sibarit] *a.* & *n.* sybarite; voluptuary.
sybaritique [sibaritik] *a.* sybaritic.
sybaritisme [sibaritism] *n.m.* sybaritism.
sycomore [sikɔmɔr] *n.m. Bot:* sycamore.
sycophante [sikɔfɑ̃t] *n.m.* informer.
syllabe [silab] *n.f.* syllable; **pas une s.,** not a word.
syllabique [silabik] *a.* syllabic.
syllogisme [silɔʒism] *n.m.* syllogism.
syllogistique [silɔʒistik] *a.* syllogistic.
sylphe [silf] *n.m.*, **sylphide** [silfid] *n.f.* sylph; **taille de sylphide,** sylphlike waist.
sylvestre [silvɛstr̥] *a. Bot:* woodland (tree, etc.).
sylviculteur [silvikyltœr] *n.m.* sylviculturist.
sylviculture [silvikyltyr] *n.f.* sylviculture, forestry.
symbiose [sɛ̃bjoz] *n.f. Biol:* symbiosis.
symbole [sɛ̃bɔl] *n.m.* **1.** symbol. **2.** *Ecc:* creed.
symbolique [sɛ̃bɔlik] **1.** *a.* (*a*) symbolic, token (payment); (*b*) *Cmptr:* symbolic. **2.** *n.f.* (*a*) symbolics; (*b*) system of symbols; (*c*) **la s. des rêves,** the interpretation of dreams.
symboliquement [sɛ̃bɔlikmɑ̃] *adv.* symbolically.
symboliser [sɛ̃bɔlize] *v.tr.* to symbolize.
symbolisme [sɛ̃bɔlism] *n.m.* symbolism.
symboliste [sɛ̃bɔlist] **1.** *a.* symbolistic. **2.** *n.* symbolist.
symétrie [simetri] *n.f.* symmetry.
symétrique [simetrik] *a.* symmetrical (**par rapport à,** about); *Elcs:* balanced (circuit).

symétriquement [simetrikmɑ̃] *adv.* symmetrically.
sympa [sɛ̃pa] *a. F:* likeable, attractive; nice.
sympathicectomie [sɛ̃patisɛktɔmi] *n.f.*, **sympathectomie** [sɛ̃patɛktɔmi] *n.f. Surg:* sympathectomy.
sympathie [sɛ̃pati] *n.f.* sympathy; (*a*) instinctive attraction, liking; **avoir de la s. pour qn,** to feel drawn to s.o.; to like s.o.; **concevoir de la s., se prendre de s., pour qn,** to take (a liking) to s.o.; **sympathies et antipathies,** likes and dislikes; (*b*) **idées qui ne sont pas en s.,** conflicting ideas.
sympathique [sɛ̃patik] *a.* **1.** sympathetic; in sympathy (with s.o.'s ideas). **2.** likeable, attractive, nice (personality); congenial (surroundings); **personnalité peu s.,** unattractive personality; **il m'a été tout de suite s.,** I took to him at once; **il m'est devenu s.,** I came to like him; **Paul est fort s. à ma mère,** my mother is very fond of Paul. **3. encre s.,** invisible ink. **4.** *Anat: Physiol: etc:* sympathetic (nerve, etc.); *n.m. Anat:* sympathetic nervous system.
sympathiquement [sɛ̃patikmɑ̃] *adv.* kindly; in a friendly way; warmly.
sympathisant, -ante [sɛ̃patizɑ̃, -ɑ̃t] **1.** *a.* sympathizing. **2.** *n. Pol: etc:* sympathizer.
sympathiser [sɛ̃patize] *v.i.* to get on well (together, with s.o.); to be friendly.
symphonie [sɛ̃fɔni] *n.f. Mus: Fig:* symphony.
symphonique [sɛ̃fɔnik] *a. Mus:* symphonic (form, etc.); symphony (orchestra).
symphoniste [sɛ̃fɔnist] *n.* **1.** symphonist. **2.** orchestral player.
symphyse [sɛ̃fiz] *n.f. Anat:* symphysis.
symposium [sɛ̃pozjɔm] *n.m.* symposium.
symptomatique [sɛ̃ptɔmatik] *a.* symptomatic.
symptomatiquement [sɛ̃ptɔmatikmɑ̃] *adv.* symptomatically.
symptôme [sɛ̃ptom] *n.m.* (*a*) symptom; (*b*) sign, indication.
synagogue [sinagɔg] *n.f.* synagogue.
synapse [sinaps] *n.f.* **1.** *Anat:* synapse. **2.** *Biol:* synapsis.
synchrone [sɛ̃kron] *a.* synchronous (**de,** with).
synchronie [sɛ̃krɔni] *n.f. Ling: etc:* synchrony.
synchronisation [sɛ̃krɔnizasjɔ̃] *n.f.* synchronization.
synchronisé [sɛ̃krɔnize] *a.* synchronized; linked (traffic signals).
synchroniser [sɛ̃krɔnize] *v.tr.* to synchronize (**qch. avec qch.,** sth. with sth.).
synchroniseur, -euse [sɛ̃krɔnizœr, -øz] **1.** *n.m.* (*a*) *El: etc:* synchronizer; (*b*) *Aut:* synchromesh device. **2.** *n.f. Cin:* **synchroniseuse,** film synchronizer.
synchronisme [sɛ̃krɔnism] *n.m.* synchronism; **en s.,** in synchronism; in time; **hors de s.,** out of synchronism, *Cin: F:* out of sync(h).
synchrotron [sɛ̃krɔtrɔ̃] *n.m. Atom.Ph:* synchrotron.
synclinal, -aux [sɛ̃klinal, -o] *a. Geog:* synclinal.
syncope [sɛ̃kɔp] *n.f.* **1.** *Med:* syncope; fainting fit; **tomber en s.,** to faint. **2.** *Gram:* syncope. **3.** *Mus:* (*a*) syncopation; (*b*) syncopated note.
syncopé [sɛ̃kɔpe] *a.* syncopated.
syncrétisme [sɛ̃kretism] *n.m. Phil:* syncretism.
syndic [sɛ̃dik] *n.m.* syndic; **s. de faillite** = official receiver.
syndical, -aux [sɛ̃dikal, -o] *a.* **1.** syndical. **2. mouvement s.,** trade-union movement.
syndicalisme [sɛ̃dikalism] *n.m.* trade unionism.
syndicaliste [sɛ̃dikalist] (*a*) *a.* syndicalist(ic); trade-union (doctrine, etc.); (*b*) *n.* syndicalist; *esp.* trade unionist.
syndicat [sɛ̃dika] *n.m.* **1.** trusteeship (in bankruptcy). **2.** syndicate; (*a*) (trade, tenants', producers') association; (employers') federation; (financial) syndicate; **s. d'initiative,** tourist (information) office, bureau; (*b*) **s. (ouvrier),** trade union.
syndicataire [sɛ̃dikatɛr] **1.** *a.* of a syndicate. **2.** *n.* member of a syndicate.
syndiqué, -ée [sɛ̃dike] **1.** *a.* (*a*) belonging to a syndicate; (*b*) **ouvriers syndiqués,** trade unionists; **ouvriers non syndiqués,** non-union men. **2.** *n.* union member.
syndiquer [sɛ̃dike] **1.** *v.tr.* to form (workers, etc.) into a trade union, to unionize (an industry, etc.). **2. se s.,** to form a union; to join a union.
syndrome [sɛ̃drom] *n.m. Med:* syndrome.
synérèse [sinerɛz] *n.f. Ph: Ling:* synaeresis, *NAm:* syneresis.
synergie [sinɛrʒi] *n.f.* synergy.
synesthésie [sinɛstezi] *n.f. Psy:* syn(a)esthesia.
syngnathe [sɛ̃gnat] *n.m. Ich:* pipefish.
synode [sinɔd] *n.m. Ecc:* synod.
synodique [sinɔdik] *a.* **1.** *Astr:* synodic(al). **2.** *Ecc:* synodal.
synonyme [sinɔnim] **1.** *a.* synonymous (**de,** with). **2.** *n.m.* synonym.
synonymie [sinɔnimi] *n.f.* synonymy, synonymity.
synopse [sinɔps] *n.f.* synoptic table of the Gospels.
synopsis [sinɔpsis] *n.f.* synopsis.
synoptique [sinɔptik] *a.* synoptic; **les Évangiles synoptiques,** the Synoptic Gospels; **tableau s.,** conspectus (of a science, etc.).
synovial, -iaux [sinɔvjal, -jo] *a. Anat:* synovial.
synovie [sinɔvi] *n.f. Anat: Physiol:* synovia; *Med:* **épanchement de s.,** water on the knee, housemaid's knee.
synovite [sinɔvit] *n.f. Med:* synovitis.
syntacticien, -ienne [sɛ̃taktisjɛ̃, -jɛn] *n. Gram:* syntactician.
syntactique [sɛ̃taktik] *a. Gram:* syntactic(al).
syntaxe [sɛ̃taks] *n.f. Gram: etc:* syntax.
syntaxique [sɛ̃taksik] *a. Gram:* syntactic(al).
synthèse [sɛ̃tɛz] *n.f.* synthesis; **de s.,** synthetic.
synthétique [sɛ̃tetik] *a.* synthetic.
synthétiquement [sɛ̃tetikmɑ̃] *adv.* synthetically.
synthétiser [sɛ̃tetize] *v.tr.* to synthesize.
synthétiseur [sɛ̃tetizœr] *n.m. Elcs:* synthesizer.
syntonie [sɛ̃tɔni] *n.f. Psy: W.Tel:* syntony.
syphilis [sifilis] *n.f. Med:* syphilis.
syphilitique [sifilitik] *a. & n. Med:* syphilitic.
Syrie [siri] *Pr.n.f. Geog:* Syria.
syringe [sirɛ̃ʒ] *n.f.* syrinx.
systématique [sistematik] **1.** *a.* (*a*) sytematic; (*b*) *F:* hide-bound (opinions, person). **2.** *n.f.* systematics.
systématiquement [sistematikmɑ̃] *adv.* systematically.
systématisation [sistematizasjɔ̃] *n.f.* system(at)ization.
systématiser [sistematize] *v.tr.* to system(at)ize.
système [sistɛm] *n.m.* **1.** (*a*) system; method, scheme, plan; (*b*) **agir par s.,** to stick to a system; **avoir l'esprit de s.,** to refuse to deviate from the (established) system; **le s. D,** resourcefulness, wangling; (*c*) set (of wheels, of valves, etc.); network (of roads); *Physiol:* (lymphatic, nervous) system; *F:* **il me tape sur le s.,** he gets on my nerves. **2. fusils de divers systèmes,** rifles of various makes, types; **cravate s.,** clip-on tie.
systémiques [sistemik] *n.m.pl.* pesticides; systemic insecticides.
systole [sistɔl] *n.f. Physiol:* systole.
syzygie [siziʒi] *n.f. Astr:* syzygy; **marées de s.,** spring tides.

T

T, t [te] *n.m.* (the letter) T, t; (*a*) **t euphonique** *forms a link between verbal endings* **-a, -e** *and the pronouns* **il, elle, on; va-t-il? ira-t-elle? donne-t-on?** (*b*) **en T,** T-shaped.

ta [ta] *see* TON[1].

tabac[1] [taba] *n.m.* **1.** *Bot:* tobacco (plant). **2.** (*a*) **t. à chiquer, à mâcher, à fumer,** chewing, smoking, tobacco; **(débit, bureau, de) t.,** tobacconist's (shop); *F:* **c'est du même t.,** it's the same thing; (*b*) **t. à priser, t. râpé,** snuff; **prendre du t.,** to take snuff. **3. les Tabacs,** the Tobacco Department. **4.** *a.inv.* tobacco-coloured, snuff-coloured, *NAm:* -colored.

tabac[2] *n.m. F:* (*esp. of the police*) **passer qn à t.,** to handle s.o. roughly; to put s.o. through it; **il y a du t.,** we're up against it; *F:* we're for it.

tabagie [tabaʒi] *n.f.* **1.** *F:* place reeking of stale tobacco smoke. **2.** *Fr.C:* tobacconist's (shop).

tabar(d) [tabar] *n.m. Cost:* (herald's) tabard.

tabassée [tabase] *n.f. F:* beating, (good) thrashing.

tabasser [tabase] *v.tr. F:* to beat up.

tabatière [tabatjɛr] *n.f.* (*a*) snuffbox; (*b*) *Const:* hinged skylight.

tabellion [tabeljɔ̃] *n.m. F: Hum:* lawyer.

tabernacle [tabɛrnakl̥] *n.m.* tabernacle.

tabes, tabès [tabɛs] *n.m. Med:* tabes.

table [tabl̥] *n.f.* table. **1.** (*a*) **t. de salle à manger, de jeu, de billard,** dining, card, billiard, table; **t. (à thé) roulante,** tea trolley; **t. de toilette,** dressing table; **t. à dessiner,** draughtsman's, *NAm:* draftsman's, table, board; **t. d'opération,** operating table; *Lit:* **la T. ronde,** the Round Table; *Pol: Ind:* **t. ronde,** round-table conference; *Psychics:* **tables frappantes,** table rapping; (*b*) board; **t. d'honneur,** high table (at a college); head table (at a banquet, etc.); **mettre la t.,** to lay, set, the table; **aimer la t.,** to be fond of good food; **la t. est bonne,** the food is good; **se mettre à t.,** (i) to sit down to table, to dinner, etc.; (ii) *P:* to confess, to come clean; **à t.!** dinner, lunch, is ready! **être à t.,** to be at table, at dinner, etc.; **(service de) petites tables,** separate tables (at a restaurant); *Mil:* **t. d'officiers,** officers' mess; *F:* **sous la t.,** secretly; *Ecc:* **la Sainte T.,** the Communion table. **2.** (*flat surface*) (*a*) *Dom.Ec:* **t. de cuisson,** hob (unit), boiling ring unit; **t. de travail,** work(ing) surface, top; (*b*) *Lap:* table (of gem); (*c*) *Mus:* sound board, belly (of instrument); (*d*) *Her:* **t. d'attente,** field; (*e*) face (of hammer, valve, etc.); flange (of girder); *Rail:* **t. de roulement,** tread (of rail); (*f*) *Tp:* switchboard; **t. interurbaine,** trunk switchboard; (*g*) *Elcs:* table, board. **3.** (*a*) slab (of stone, etc.); tablet; *Prehist:* cap stone (of a dolmen); *B.Hist:* **les tables de la loi,** the Tables of the Law; (*b*) list, catalogue; (multiplication, conversion, etc.) table; **t. des matières,** (table of) contents; *Mil: etc:* **t. de tir,** firing table, range table.

tableau, -eaux [tablo] *n.m.* **1.** (*a*) board; **t. d'annonces,** notice board; **t. d'affichage,** (i) poster frame; (ii) *Sp: etc:* scoring board; (iii) (*in clubs, etc.*) notice board, *NAm:* bulletin board; *Sch:* **t. (noir),** (black)-board; *El: Tp:* **t. de distribution, t. commutateur,** switchboard; distribution board, panel; **t. de contrôle,** (i) *Mec.E:* control panel; (ii) *Tp:* monitoring board; *El: etc:* **t. d'éclairage,** lighting panel; **t. de manœuvre,** instrument board, panel; **t. de bord,** (i) *Aut:* dashboard; (ii) *Av:* instrument panel; *Cmptr:* **t. de connexions,** plugboard; (*b*) (*in hotel*) key rack, board. **2.** (*a*) picture; painting; **de la colline se découvre un magnifique t.,** there is a beautiful view from the hill; *F:* **vieux t.,** (painted) old hag; (*b*) *Th:* (i) tableau (at end of act, etc.); (ii) scene. **3.** (*a*) list, table; chart; **t. par doit et avoir,** balance sheet; *Adm: etc:* (promotion, duty, etc.) roster; *Ind: etc:* schedule; *Rail:* (service) timetable; *Nau:* list of sailings; *Navy:* sailing list, order; *Med:* **t. clinique,** clinical picture; **mettre sous forme de t.,** to tabulate; *F:* **gagner sur tous les, sur les deux, tableaux,** to win all along the line, on all counts; (*b*) *Jur:* roll (of lawyers); panel (of jurymen, doctors, etc.); **être rayé du t.,** to be struck off the rolls; **se faire inscrire au t.,** to be called to the bar; (*c*) *Sch:* **t. d'honneur,** honours, *NAm:* honors, board; (*d*) *Typ:* (i) table; (ii) table work. **4.** *Ven:* bag.

tabler [table] *v.i.* **t. sur qch.,** to count, bank, on sth.

tablette [tablɛt] *n.f.* **1.** (*a*) shelf (of bookcase, etc.); **t. à coulisse,** pull-out flap (of desk); (*b*) flat top (of piece of furniture, etc.); **t. de fenêtre,** window sill; **t. de piano,** music rest; *El:* **t. à bornes,** terminal plate. **2.** *pl. A:* writing tablets; *Fig:* **mettre qch. sur ses tablettes,** to make a note of sth. **3.** bar (of chocolate); *Cu:* (stock) cube; *Pharm:* tablet.

tablier [tablije] *n.m.* **1.** apron; pinafore; **t. blouse,** (woman's) overall; *F:* (*of servant*) **rendre son t.,** to give notice. **2.** (*a*) *Veh: Artil:* footboard (of limber); *Aut:* dashboard; foot rest (of scooter); (*b*) hood (of fireplace). **3.** (steel) shutter. **4.** deck, road(way) (of bridge); *Mch:* footplate (of locomotive). **5.** *Metall:* (*a*) table (of rolling mill); apron (of lathe); *Ind:* **t. sans fin,** apron feed; (*b*) hearth (of forge). **6.** *Anat:* (Hottentot) apron.

tabloïde [tablɔid] *n.m.* **1.** *Pharm:* tablet. **2.** tabloid (newspaper).

tabou [tabu] *a.* (*often inv.*) *& n.m.* taboo.

tabou(is)er [tabw(iz)e] *v.tr.* to declare (sth.) taboo.

tabouret [taburɛ] *n.m.* stool; footstool.

tabulaire [tabylɛr] *a.* tabular.

tabulateur [tabylatœr] *n.m. Typewr:* tabulator.

tabulatrice [tabylatris] *n.f.* tabulator (in punched-card system, etc.)

tac [tak] *n.m.* click (of steel); **t. t. t.,** rattle (of machine gun); **riposter, répondre, du t. au t.,** to give tit for tat, to make a lightning retort.

tacet [tasɛt] *n.m. Mus:* tacet.

tachant [taʃɑ̃] *a.* staining.

tache [taʃ] *n.f.* (*a*) stain, spot (of grease, mud, etc.); blob, splash (of paint); flaw, blemish (in precious stone, work of art, fruit); blot (of ink); *Fig:* blot, stain (on reputation, etc.); **t. de suie,** fleck of soot; smut; **t. solaire, t. du soleil,** sunspot; **t. de lumière,** *Th: Cin:* hot spot; *T.V:* shading; **sans t.,** spotless; without blemish; **sa réputation était sans t.,** he had a blameless reputation; (*b*) (*on human body*) **t. de rousseur,** freckle; **t. de vin,** strawberry mark; **chien blanc à taches feu,** white dog with reddish markings, patches, spots; *Anat:* **t. jaune (de la rétine),** yellow spot; **t. de Mariotte,** blind spot (of the eye).

tâche [tɑʃ] *n.f.* task; job; **travail à la t.,** (i) *Ind:* piece-work; (ii) jobbing (work); **ouvrier à la t.,** (i) *Ind:* piece worker; (ii) jobbing workman; **prendre à t. de**

faire qch., to undertake to do sth.; to make a point of doing sth.
taché [taʃe] *a.* **1.** *Nat.Hist:* spotted. **2.** bruised (fruit).
tachéomètre [takeɔmɛtr̥] *n.m. Surv:* tachymeter.
tachéométrie [takeɔmetri] *n.f. Surv:* tachymetry.
tacher [taʃe] **1.** *v.tr.* to stain, spot (garment, etc.); to sully, tarnish (reputation, etc.); **taché d'encre,** ink-stained. **2. se t.**, to get dirty; (i) to soil one's clothes; (ii) to stain.
tâcher [tɑʃe] *v.i.* to try, endeavour, *NAm:* endeavor; **t. de faire qch.**, to try, attempt, to do sth.; **tâchez de ne pas oublier,** try not to forget.
tâcheron [tɑʃrɔ̃] *n.m.* **1.** pieceworker (on land). **2.** *Pej:* plodder. **3.** *Const: etc:* subcontractor, jobber.
tacheté [taʃte] *a.* spotted, speckled, mottled; brindle(d); tabby (cat).
tachisme [taʃism] *n.m. Art:* tachism.
tachiste [taʃist] *a. & n. Art:* tachist.
tachycardie [takikardi] *n.f. Med:* tachycardia.
tachygraphe [takigraf] *n.m. Mec.E:* tachograph.
tachymètre [takimɛtr̥] *n.m. Mec.E: etc:* tachometer, speedometer.
tachymétrie [takimetri] *n.f. Mec.E:* tachometry.
tachyon [takjɔ̃] *n.m. Atom.Ph:* tachyon.
tacite [tasit] *a.* tacit (consent, etc.); implied.
tacitement [tasitmɑ̃] *adv.* tacitly.
taciturne [tasityrn] *a.* taciturn, silent.
tacot [tako] *n.m. Veh: F:* rattletrap, jalopy.
tact [takt] *n.m.* **1.** (sense of) touch. **2.** tact; **avoir du t., être plein de t.,** to be tactful; **manquer de t.,** to be tactless; **(agir) avec t., sans t.,** (to do sth.) tactfully, tactlessly.
tacticien, -ienne [taktisjɛ̃, -jɛn] *n.* tactician.
tactile [taktil] *a.* tactile.
tactilité [taktilite] *n.f.* tactility.
tactique [taktik] **1.** *a.* tactical. **2.** *n.f.* tactics; **une t. nouvelle,** new tactics.
tadorne [tadɔrn] *n.m. Orn:* sheldrake, shelduck.
tænia [tenja] *n.m. Med:* t(a)enia, tapeworm.
taffetas [tafta] *n.m.* (*a*) *Tex:* taffeta; (*b*) *Med:* **t. anglais, gommé,** sticking plaster.
Tahiti [taiti] *Pr.n. Geog:* Tahiti.
tahitien, -ienne [taisjɛ̃, -jɛn] *a. & n.* Tahitian.
taïaut [tajo] *int. Ven:* tally-ho!
taie [tɛ] *n.f.* **1. t. d'oreiller,** pillowcase, pillowslip. **2.** *Med:* leucoma; white speck on the eye.
taïga [taiga] *n.f. Geog:* taiga.
taillade [tajad] *n.f.* slash; gash.
taillader [tajade] *v.tr.* to slash, gash; *Cost:* **tailladé,** slashed.
taillandier [tajɑ̃dje] *n.m.* maker of edge tools.
taille [taj] *n.f.* **1.** (*a*) cutting (of stone, gems, garments, hair, etc.); pruning, trimming (of shrubs); clipping (of hedge); *Mount:* step cutting; *Mec.E:* (gear) milling, cutting; **une t. de cheveux,** a haircut; (*b*) *Surg:* lithotomy. **2.** (*method of cutting*) cut; *Tls:* **à t. double,** double-cut (file); **grosse t.,** rough cut; **t. douce,** smooth cut; *Stonew:* **t. brute, plane,** rough, smooth, dressing. **3.** (*a*) edge (of sword, etc.); (*b*) *For:* **une jeune t.,** a coppice; (*c*) *Min:* (i) working face; (ii) stall. **4.** (*a*) stature, height (of pers.); dimensions (of monument, etc.); **t. debout,** full height (of s.o.); **de grande t., de t. moyenne,** very tall, of medium height; **de petite t.,** small; *Com:* **quelle est votre t.?** what size do you take? **pour les tailles exceptionnelles, pour les grandes tailles,** (for) outsize(s); **il est de t. à vous battre,** he is big enough, strong enough, to beat you; **il n'est pas de t. à être chef,** he is not cut out to be a leader; **il n'est pas de t. à lutter contre vous,** he is no match for you; he stands no chance against you; **le mensonge est de t.,** it's a thumping lie; (*b*) waist; **tour de t.,** waist measurement; **avoir la t. bien prise,** to have a slim waist; **prendre qn par la t.,** (i) to seize s.o. round the waist; (ii) to put an arm round s.o.'s waist; *Dressm:* **t. normale,** natural waistline; **pardessus à t.,** fitted overcoat; **en t.,** with no (over)coat on. **5.** *Hist:* tallage, tax, toll.
taillé [taje] *a.* **bien t.,** well built; **t. pour commander,** cut out to be a leader.
taille-crayon(s) [tajkrɛjɔ̃] *n.m.inv.* pencil sharpener.
taille-douce [tajdus] *n.f. Engr:* copper-plate engraving; *pl tailles-douces.*
tailler [taje] **1.** *v.tr.* (*a*) to cut (stone, diamond, grass, hair); to mill (gearwheels); to prune (tree); to trim, clip (hedge, beard, etc.); to dress (vine); to sharpen (pencil); to cut, slice (bread); **t. une armée en pièces,** to cut an army to pieces; **se t. un chemin à travers . . .,** to carve one's way through . . .; **lion taillé dans le roc,** lion carved in the stone; (*b*) **t. un vêtement,** to cut out a garment; **bien taillé,** well cut; *Prov:* **il faut t. la robe selon le corps,** you must cut your coat according to your cloth. **2.** *v.i.* (*a*) *Surg:* to make an incision; (*b*) *Mount:* to cut steps. **3.** *P:* **se t.**, to leave, buzz off.
tailleur, -euse [tajœr, -øz] **1.** *n.* (*a*) cutter (of stone, gems, trees, files, etc.); (*b*) tailor; **s'asseoir en t.,** to sit cross-legged. **2.** *n.m.* (woman's tailored) suit.
tailleur-pantalon [tajœrpɑ̃talɔ̃] *n.m. Cost:* (woman's) trouser suit; *pl. tailleurs-pantalons.*
taillis [taji] *n.m.* **dans les t.,** in the woods, in the bush; *a.* **bois t.,** copsewood, brushwood.
tain [tɛ̃] *n.m.* **1.** silvering (for mirrors); **glace sans t.,** plate glass; **miroir sans t.,** two-way mirror. **2.** *Ind:* tin bath (for tinning iron).
taire [tɛr] *v.* (*pr.p.* **taisant;** *p.p.* **tu;** *pr.ind.* **je tais, il tait, n. taisons, ils taisent;** *pr.sub.* **je taise;** *impf.* **je taisais;** *p.h.* **je tus;** *fu.* **je tairai**) **1.** *v.tr.* to say nothing about (sth.), not to mention (sth.), to suppress (sth.), to hush (sth.) up; **une dame dont je tairai le nom,** a lady who shall be nameless; **t. qch. à qn,** to keep, hide, conceal, sth. from s.o. **2. se t.**, to hold one's tongue, to be(come) silent; to keep quiet (**sur,** about); (*of sound*) to cease; **tais-toi!** hold your tongue! be quiet! *F:* shut up! dry up! **faire t. (qn),** to silence (s.o.); to hush (a child); to keep (a child) quiet; *F:* to shut (s.o.) up; **faire t. sa douleur,** to stifle one's grief.
talc [talk] *n.m. Miner:* talc; *Toil:* talc(um powder).
talent [talɑ̃] *n.m.* **1.** *Gr.Ant:* talent. **2.** talent, aptitude, faculty, gift; high mental capacity; **avoir du t.,** to be talented; **homme de t.,** talented man; **avoir le t. des langues,** to have a gift for languages; **son t. de pianiste,** his talent as a pianist; **il a le t. de se faire des amis, des ennemis,** he has a gift for making friends, enemies; **faire appel à tous les talents,** to call in the best brains, all the available talent.
talentueux, -euse [talɑ̃tɥø, -øz] *a.* talented.
taler [tale] *v.tr.* **1.** to bruise (fruit, etc.). **2.** *Dial:* to annoy.
taleth [talɛt] *n.m. Jew.Rel:* tallith.
talion [taljɔ̃] *n.m.* retaliation; **la loi du t.,** the law of retaliation; tit for tat.
talisman [talismɑ̃] *n.m.* talisman.
talitre [talitr̥] *n.m. Crust:* sand flea, sand hopper.
talle [tal] *n.f. Agr: Hort:* (*a*) sucker; (*b*) tiller.
Talmud [talmyd] *Pr.n.m. Jew.Rel:* **le T.,** the Talmud.
talmudique [talmydik] *a.* Talmudic(al).
talmudiste [talmydist] *n.m.* Talmudist.
taloche [talɔʃ] *n.f. F:* blow, cuff; clout on the head.
talocher [talɔʃe] *v.tr. F:* to hit, clout (s.o.); to box (s.o.'s) ears.
talon [talɔ̃] *n.m.* **1.** heel (of foot or shoe); **marcher sur**

les talons de qn, to follow close on s.o.'s heels; **être toujours sur les talons de qn,** to dog s.o.'s footsteps; **donner du t. à son cheval,** to give one's horse the spur; **montrer, tourner, les talons, jouer des talons,** to take to one's heels; **t. d'Achille,** Achilles' heel. **2.** *Tchn:* heel (of tool, mast, golf club, rifle butt, keel); heel, nut (of violin, bow); butt (of billiard cue); shoulder (of sword blade, bayonet, pulley block, axle). **3.** (*a*) (*at cards, etc.*) stock; reserve; talon; (*b*) fag end (of bread, cheese); heel (of loaf); (*c*) counterfoil, stub (of cheque, *NAm:* check, etc.). **4.** *Arch:* ogee moulding, *NAm:* molding; talon.

talonner [talɔne] **1.** *v.tr.* (*a*) to follow (s.o.) closely; to dog (s.o.'s) footsteps; *F:* to breathe down s.o.'s neck; to pursue (s.o.) vigorously; (*b*) to spur on (horse, *Fig:* pupil); (*c*) *Rugby Fb:* to heel (out). **2.** *v.i. Nau:* (*of ship, boat*) to touch, to bump; to strike.

talonnette [talɔnɛt] *n.f.* **1.** heel piece (of shoe). **2.** (rubber) elevator, *NAm:* lift (inside shoe). **3.** binding (inside trouser bottoms).

talonneur [talɔnœr] *n.m. Rugby Fb:* hooker.

talquer [talke] *v.tr.* to sprinkle with talc.

talqueux, -euse [talkø, -øz] *a. Miner:* talcose.

talure [talyr] *n.f.* bruise (on fruit).

talus [taly] *n.m.* **1.** slope; **en t.,** sloping. **2.** (*a*) embankment, slope, ramp; (*b*) *Geol:* talus; scree (slope).

talweg [talvɛg] *n.m. Geog:* t(h)alweg.

tamanoir [tamanwar] *n.m. Z:* great anteater, ant bear.

tamarin¹ [tamarɛ̃] *n.m. Bot:* tamarind.

tamarin² *n.m. Z:* silky marmoset; tamarin.

tamarinier [tamarinje] *n.m. Bot:* tamarind tree.

tamaris [tamaris] *n.m. Bot:* tamarisk.

tambouille [tɑ̃buj] *n.f. Mil: P:* (*a*) cooking; (*b*) food, grub.

tambour [tɑ̃bur] *n.m.* **1.** drum; **battre du t.,** to play the drum; to drum; **bruit de t.,** drumming; **chasser un soldat au son du t.,** to drum a soldier out; **peau de t.,** drum-head; **t. de basque,** tambourine; **coup de t.,** beat, roll, on the drum; **sans t. ni trompette,** quietly, without fuss. **2.** drummer; **t. de ville,** town crier. **3.** *Tchn:* (*a*) (*cylindrical container*) barrel, cylinder, drum; (*b*) vestibule (of church, etc.); revolving door (of vestibule); *N.Arch:* (engine, etc.) casing; (*c*) (*case*) *Mec.E:* drum (of compressor, turbine, etc.); brake drum; *N.Arch:* paddle box; (*d*) (*cylinder*) drum (of measuring or recording instrument); *Arch:* drum (of column, etc.); *Cmptr:* **t. (de) programme,** program(me) drum; (*e*) *Civ.E: El: Nau:* (*reel*) drum (of capstan, etc.); *El:* cylinder (of coil); **t. de câble,** cable drum; (*f*) (embroidery) frame.

tambourin [tɑ̃burɛ̃] *n.m.* (*a*) long, narrow drum (of Provence); tambourin; (*b*) tambourine.

tambourinage [tɑ̃burinaʒ] *n.m.* drumming.

tambourinaire [tɑ̃burinɛr] *n.m.* (*in S. of Fr.*) (*a*) tambourin player; pipe and tabor player; (*b*) town crier.

tambourinement [tɑ̃burinmɑ̃] *n.m.* = TAMBOURINAGE.

tambouriner [tɑ̃burine] **1.** *v.i.* to drum (with the fingers); **la pluie tambourine sur le toit,** the rain is drumming on the roof. **2.** *v.tr.* (*a*) to drum (out) (rhythm); (*b*) *A:* to announce (a piece of news).

tambour-major [tɑ̃burmaʒɔr] *n.m. Mil:* drum major; *pl tambours-majors.*

tamil [tamil] *a. & n.m. Ethn: Ling:* Tamil.

tamis [tami] *n.m.* sieve, sifter; (*for liquids*) strainer; *Ind:* riddle, screen; **passer qch. au t.,** (i) to sift, strain, sth.; (ii) to sift, examine (evidence, etc.) thoroughly.

tamisage [tamizaʒ] *n.m.* sifting (of sand, etc.); filtering, straining (of liquid); filtering (of air).

Tamise (la) [latamiz] *Pr.n.f. Geog:* the (river) Thames.

tamiser [tamize] **1.** *v.tr.* to sift, screen (gravel, etc.); to bolt (flour); to strain, filter (liquids); to filter (air); **rideaux qui tamisent la lumière,** curtains that filter, soften, the light. **2.** *v.i.* (*of dust, light, etc.*) to filter through.

tamoul [tamul] *a. & n.m. Ethn: Ling:* Tamil.

tampon [tɑ̃pɔ̃] *n.m.* **1.** (*a*) plug, stopper; waste plug (of bath, etc.); bung (of cask); (*b*) *Const:* wall plug. **2.** (*a*) (i) *Surg:* pad, plug, tampon; (ii) *Hyg:* **t. hygiénique, périodique,** tampon; (*b*) pad (of flute key, etc.); (*c*) *Engr: Typ: etc:* (inking) pad; (*d*) rubber stamp; *Post:* postmark; (*e*) **t. buvard,** blotter; (*f*) (French polisher's) pad. **3. t. de choc,** buffer; *Dipl:* **état t.,** buffer state; *F:* **servir de t. (entre deux personnes),** to act as a buffer (between two people).

tamponnage [tɑ̃pɔnaʒ] *n.m.,* **tamponnement** [tɑ̃pɔnmɑ̃] *n.m.* **1.** plugging (of wound, etc.); stopping up. **2.** dabbing (with pad). **3.** *Rail:* (*a*) (end-on) collision; (*b*) collision with a buffer. **4.** *Ch:* **tamponnage,** neutralizing.

tamponner [tɑ̃pɔne] *v.tr.* **1.** (*a*) to plug; to stop up; *Med:* (i) to put a wad over, (ii) to plug (wound); (*b*) *Const:* to plug (wall). **2.** (*a*) to dab (with pad); to ink up (type, metal plate); to rubberstamp; **se t. les yeux,** to dab one's eyes; *P:* **s'en t. (le coquillard),** not to give a damn; **se t. le front,** to mop one's brow; (*b*) to French-polish (furniture); (*c*) *Metall:* to dust (mould, *NAm:* mold); (*d*) *Ch:* to neutralize. **3.** to run into, collide with (another car or train).

tamponneur, -euse [tɑ̃pɔnœr, -øz] **1.** *a.* **train t.,** train that ran into another; **autos tamponneuses,** dodgems, bumper cars. **2.** *n.* official (who stamps documents, etc.).

tam-tam [tamtam] *n.m.* **1.** (*a*) tom-tom; (*b*) *F:* fuss, ballyhoo (**autour de,** about). **2.** (Chinese) gong; *pl. tam-tams.*

tan [tɑ̃] *n.m.* tan, (tanner's) bark.

tanaisie [tanezi] *n.f. Bot:* tansy.

tancer [tɑ̃se] *v.tr.* **(je tançai(s); n. tançons)** *Lit:* to berate, scold.

tanche [tɑ̃ʃ] *n.f. Ich:* tench.

tandem [tɑ̃dɛm] *n.m.* (*a*) **chevaux attelés en t.,** horses driven tandem; (*b*) *Cy:* tandem (bicycle); (*c*) *esp. Sp:* twosome; *F:* pair (of criminals); (*d*) *Mch:* **cylindres en t.,** tandem cylinders; (*e*) *Cmptr:* **central t.,** tandem exchange, tandem central office.

tandis [tɑ̃di(s)] *conj.phr.* **t. que** [tɑ̃di(s)kə] + *ind.* (*a*) *A:* so long as; (*b*) whereas, while; **lui s'amuse, t. que nous, nous travaillons,** he plays, whereas, while, we have to work; (*c*) (= **pendant que**) while, whilst; **il s'amuse t. que nous travaillons,** he plays while we work.

tangage [tɑ̃gaʒ] *n.m. Nau: Av: etc:* pitching.

tangara [tɑ̃gara] *n.m. Orn:* tanager.

tangelo [tɑ̃ʒlo] *n.m. Hort:* tangelo, ugli.

tangence [tɑ̃ʒɑ̃s] *n.f. Mth:* tangency; **point de t.,** point of contact.

tangent, -ente [tɑ̃ʒɑ̃, -ɑ̃t] **1.** *a. Mth:* tangential, tangent (**à,** to); *P:* **c'est t.,** (i) it's as near as dammit; (ii) it's touch and go. **2.** *n. F:* (*in examination*) borderline case. **3.** *n.f. Mth:* tangent; *F:* **s'échapper par la tangente, prendre la tangente,** (i) to dodge the question; (ii) to slip away.

tangentiel, -ielle [tɑ̃ʒɑ̃sjɛl] *a. Mth:* tangential.

Tanger [tɑ̃ʒe] *Pr.n. Geog:* Tangier(s).

tangible [tɑ̃ʒibl] *a.* tangible.

tangiblement [tɑ̃ʒibləmɑ̃] *adv.* tangibly.

tango [tɑ̃go] *n.m. Danc:* tango.

tangon [tɑ̃gɔ̃] *n.m. Nau:* ((i) swinging, (ii) (spinnaker) boom.

tanguer [tɑ̃ge] *v.i.* (*a*) *Av: Nau:* to pitch; (*b*) to reel, sway.

tanière [tanjɛr] *n.f.* (*a*) den, lair (of wild animal); (*b*) hovel; (*c*) retreat.

tanin [tanɛ̃] *n.m. Ch: Ind:* tannin.

tank [tɑ̃k] *n.m.* **1.** *Mil:* tank. **2.** *Nau:* tank (of oil tanker).

tanker [tɑ̃kɛr] *n.m. Nau:* tanker.

tannage [tanaʒ] *n.m.* tanning (of hides).

tannant [tanɑ̃] *a. P:* boring; annoying; **il est t.!** he's a drag!

tanne [tan] *n.f.* **1.** spot (on leather). **2.** blackhead (on face).

tanné [tane] **1.** *a.* tanned. **2.** *n.m.* (*a*) tan (colour); (*b*) **gants en t.,** tan(ned) leather gloves.

tanner [tane] *v.tr.* **1.** to tan (hides). **2.** *P:* (*a*) to pester (s.o.); (*b*) **t. (le cuir à) qn,** to thrash s.o.; to tan s.o.'s hide.

tannerie [tanri] *n.f.* **1.** tannery. **2.** tanning (of hides).

tanneur [tanœr] *n.m.* tanner (of hides).

tannin [tanɛ̃] *n.m. Ch: Ind:* tannin.

tannique [tanik] *a. Ch:* tannic (acid).

tanrec [tɑ̃rɛk] *n.m. Z:* tanrec, tenrec.

tan-sad [tɑ̃sad] *n.m.* pillion(-seat); *pl. tan-sads.*

tant [tɑ̃] *adv.* **1.** (*a*) so much; **t. de bonté,** so much, such, kindness; **il a t. bu que . . .,** he has drunk so much that . . .; **ce n'est pas la peine de t. vous presser,** you needn't be in such a hurry; **pour t. faire, à t. faire,** *F:* **t. qu'à faire, j'aimerais autant . . .,** while I'm at it, about it, I would just as soon . . .; **t. pour cent,** so much per cent; **être t. à t.,** to be even (at play); **onze cent et t.,** eleven hundred and something; **votre lettre du t.,** your letter of such and such a date; **il a t. et plus d'argent,** he has any amount of money; **ils tiraient t. et plus,** they were pulling for all they were worth; **je me suis ennuyé t. et plus,** I was bored to tears, to death; **faire t. (et si bien) que . . .,** to work to such good purpose that . . .; **j'ai crié t. et t. qu'il est parti,** I shouted so much that he went; **t. s'en faut,** far from it; **t. soit peu,** a little; somewhat; **il y a une école dans tout village t. soit peu considérable,** there is a school in every village of any importance; **ils sont t. soit peu cousins,** they are more or less cousins; **il est t. soit peu avare,** he's a bit of a miser; *Lit:* **si t. est qu'il soit mort,** if he really is dead; **il y en a peu, si t. est qu'il y en ait du tout,** there is little, there are few, if any; (*b*) so many; as many; **t. de fois,** so many times, so often; **t. d'amis,** so many friends; **il a t. et plus d'amis,** he has plenty of friends; (*c*) **t. que** = **autant que;** (*d*) so, to such a degree; **il ne peut pas se lever, t. il est malade,** he cannot get up, he is so ill; **t. était grande sa discrétion que . . .,** so great was his discretion that . . .; **t. il est vrai que . . .,** so true is it that . . .; **elle est t. aimée,** she is so greatly, much, loved; **elle n'est pas t. sotte!** she is not so stupid! **n'aimer rien t. que . . .,** to like nothing so much as . . .; **en t. que,** in so far as; **je suis Russe en t. que je suis né en Russie,** I am a Russian in so far as I was born in Russia; **l'homme en t. qu'il diffère des animaux,** man, as distinct from animals; **en t. que vieil ami de votre père,** as a very old friend of your father('s); (*e*) (*concessive* = QUELQUE) **t. aimable qu'il soit,** however pleasant he may be; (*f*) *adv. phr.* **t. mieux,** so much the better; that's all to the good! good! **t. pis!** too bad! it can't be helped! what a pity! never mind! **2.** (*a*) as much, as well (as); **j'ai couru t. que j'ai pu,** I ran as hard as I could; *F:* **il pleut t. qu'il peut,** it's raining like anything; **t. aux Indes qu'ailleurs,** both in India and elsewhere; **t. pour vous que pour moi,** as much for your sake as mine; **t. avec la maison qu'avec le bureau,** what with the house and the office; **t. bien que mal,** somehow or other, after a fashion; (*b*) as long, as far (as); **t. que je vivrai,** as long as I live; **t. que la vue s'étend,** as far as the eye can see; **t. que vous y êtes,** while you're at it; (*c*) so long (as); **il n'y a rien à faire t. qu'il ne sera pas là,** there is nothing to be done so long as he isn't there. **3.** *P:* **t. qu'à** = **quant à.**

Tantale¹ [tɑ̃tal] *Pr.n.m. Myth:* Tantalus.

tantale² *n.m. Ch:* tantalum.

tante [tɑ̃t] *n.f.* **1.** aunt; **t. à la mode de Bretagne,** (i) first cousin once removed; (ii) very distant relative; *P:* **chez ma t.,** at my uncle's; at the pawnbroker's; in hock. **2.** *P:* (male) homosexual, poof, queer.

tantième [tɑ̃tjɛm] *n.m. Com:* percentage, quota (of profits, etc.).

tantine [tɑ̃tin] *n.f. F:* auntie, aunty.

tantinet [tɑ̃tinɛ] *n.m. F:* tiny bit, least bit; **un t. plus long,** a shade, a fraction, longer.

tantôt [tɑ̃to] *adv.* **1** (*a*) *A:* soon, presently; (*b*) this afternoon; **il pleuvra, il a plu, t.,** it will rain, it rained, this afternoon. **2.** *A:* just now, a little while ago. **3.** **t. triste, t. gai,** now sad, now gay; **t. je suis à Paris, t. à Londres,** sometimes I am in Paris, sometimes in London.

tantouse [tɑ̃tuz] *n.f. P:* (male) homosexual, pansy.

Tanzanie [tɑ̃zani] *Pr.n.f. Geog:* Tanzania.

taôiste [taɔist] *a. & n. Rel.H:* Taoist.

taon [tɑ̃] *n.m.* gadfly, horsefly, cleg.

tapage [tapaʒ] *n.m.* (*a*) din; uproar; *F:* racket, row; (*b*) fuss, scandal; controversy.

tapageur, -euse [tapaʒœr, -øz] **1.** *a.* (*a*) noisy (child, etc.); rowdy, uproarious (party, etc.); (*b*) loud, flashy (clothes, etc.). **2.** *n.* (*a*) rowdy; (*b*) **petit t., petite tapageuse,** noisy little brat.

tapant [tapɑ̃] *a.* **à sept heures tapant(es),** on the stroke of seven, at seven, on the dot.

tape [tap] *n.f.* tap; pat; slap; **il m'a donné une t. sur l'épaule, une petite t. sur la joue,** he slapped me on the shoulder; he patted my cheek.

tapé [tape] *a.* **1.** (*of fruit*) (*a*) dried; (*b*) damaged. **2.** *P:* **réponse tapée,** smart answer. **3.** *F:* nuts, cracked.

tape-à-l'œil [tapalœj] **1.** *a.inv.* loud, gaudy, flashy. **2.** *n.m.* gimcrack goods, flashy rubbish.

tape(-)cul [tapky] *n.m.* **1.** seesaw. **2.** counterpoise barrier. **3.** *Nau:* jigger (sail). **4.** *Veh:* rattletrap, boneshaker; *pl. tape(-)culs.*

tapée [tape] *n.f. F:* masses, lots, heaps, loads.

taper¹ [tape] **1.** *v.tr.* to tap, smack, slap, hit; (*a*) **t. du tambour,** to beat the drum; **t. la porte,** to slam the door; **se t. les cheveux,** to pat one's hair; **t. une lettre (à la machine),** to type a letter; *v.i.* **savoir t.,** to be able to type; **t. un air (au piano),** to thump out a tune (on the piano); *F:* **t. la carte,** to play cards; *P:* **se t. qch.,** (i) to treat oneself to sth.; (ii) to let oneself in for sth.; **se t. le derrière par terre,** to split one's sides laughing; *F:* **se t. de qn,** to make fun of s.o.; (*b*) *F:* **t. qn de mille francs,** to touch s.o. for a thousand francs; *P:* **tu peux te t.!** you'll be lucky! nothing doing! **2.** *v.i.* (*a*) to tap, rap, bang (**sur,** on); to strum (on piano); **se t. sur la cuisse,** to slap one's thigh; *F:* **t. sur le ventre à qn,** to give s.o. a dig in the ribs (as a mark of familiarity); **le soleil nous tapait sur la tête,** the sun was beating down on us; *F:* **ça tape,** it's pretty hot; **t. au toucher,** to touch-type; **t. sur qn,** to abuse, slate, slang, s.o.; **on lui a tapé dessus,** they had a go at him; **t. dans,** to help oneself to, to have a go at (food, etc.); **t. du pied,** to stamp one's foot; **je les regardais se t.,** I watched them knocking each other about; *Mil:* *F:* **t. sur un objectif,** to strafe a target; **t. à côté,** to miss the target; (*of wine*) **t. à la tête,** to go to the head; (*b*) *P:* to stink; **ça tape ici!** what a stink!

taper² *v.tr.* to plug, stop up (hole, etc.).

tapette [tapɛt] *n.f.* **1.** (*a*) mallet; (*b*) carpet beater; (*c*) (engraver's) pad; (*d*) fly swatter; (*e*) *P:* tongue, clapper; **il a une fière t.,** he *can* talk! **2.** gentle tap. **3.** *P:* (male) homosexual, fairy.

tapeur, -euse [tapœr, -øz] *n. F:* cadger.

tapin [tapɛ̃] *n.m.* (*a*) *F: A:* drummer; (*b*) *P:* **faire le t.,** to solicit, to walk the streets.

tapinois (en) [ɑ̃tapinwa] *adv.phr.* **en t.,** stealthily, on the sly.

tapioca [tapjɔka] *n.m.* (*a*) tapioca; (*b*) tapioca soup.

tapir[1] [tapir] *n.m.* **1.** *Z:* tapir. **2.** *Sch: F:* pupil who takes private lessons.

tapir[2] (se) [sətapir] *v.pr.* to crouch, cower, hide; **maison tapie dans un bois,** house nestling in a wood.

tapis [tapi] *n.m.* **1.** cloth, cover; **t. de sol,** groundsheet; **t. de selle,** saddlecloth; **t. de billard,** billiard cloth; **t. vert,** (i) gaming table; (ii) conference table; **le t. brûle!** put down your stakes! **mettre qch. sur le t.,** to bring sth. up for consideration, for discussion. **2.** (*a*) carpet; **t. de haute laine, de laine rase,** long-pile carpet, short-pile carpet; **t. à prière,** prayer mat; **recouvrir le plancher d'un t.,** to carpet the floor; **t. de pied,** rug; **terrain recouvert d'un t. de gazon,** ground carpeted with turf; (*b*) carpeting. **3. t. roulant,** *Ind: etc:* conveyor belt; *Trans:* moving walkway. **4.** *Box: Wr:* canvas; *Wr:* mat; **aller au t.,** to be knocked down.

tapis-brosse [tapibrɔs] *n.m.* doormat; *pl. tapis-brosses.*

tapisser [tapise] *v.tr.* (*a*) to hang (wall, etc.) with tapestry; (*b*) to (wall)paper (room); **les murs sont tapissés de jaune,** the walls are papered in yellow; **mur tapissé d'affiches,** wall plastered, covered, with posters; **une membrane tapisse l'estomac,** the stomach is lined with a membrane; **mur tapissé de lierre,** wall covered with ivy; ivy-clad wall.

tapisserie [tapisri] *n.f.* **1.** (*a*) tapestry making, weaving; (*b*) tapestry works. **2.** tapestry, hangings; **chaise en t.,** chair upholstered with tapestry; (*at a ball*) **faire t.,** to be a wallflower. **3. t. (au, sur, canevas),** tapestry work, crewel work; **pantoufles en t.,** carpet slippers. **4.** wallpaper.

tapissier, -ière [tapisje, -jɛr] *n.* **1.** (*a*) tapestry maker; (*b*) crewel worker. **2.** (*a*) (interior) decorator; (*b*) upholsterer.

tapon [tapɔ̃] *n.m.* plug; stopper; **en t.,** (i) (*of clothes, etc.*) bundled up; (ii) (*of hair*) screwed up into a ball, a bun.

tapotement [tapɔtmɑ̃] *n.m.* tapping; strumming.

tapoter [tapɔte] *v.tr.* to pat (child's cheek, etc.); to drum on (the table, etc.); **t. un air (au piano),** to strum a tune (on the piano).

taquet [takɛ] *n.m.* **1.** (*a*) *Carp: etc:* angle block; (*b*) flange; lug. **2.** *Mec.E: etc:* stop(per), block; **t. de sûreté,** safety stop; **t. d'arrêt,** (i) *Veh:* scotch; (ii) *Rail:* stop block; (iii) *Mec.E:* retaining lug; *Typewr:* **poser un t. (de tabulateur),** to set a tab(ulator stop). **3.** *Agr: Surv:* small picket, peg. **4.** *Nau:* **t. (de tournage),** (belaying) cleat.

taquin, -ine [takɛ̃, -in] **1.** *a.* (given to) teasing. **2.** *n.* (*pers.*) tease.

taquiner [takine] *v.tr.* (*a*) to tease (s.o.); to fiddle with (sth.); *F:* **t. le goujon,** to go fishing; (*b*) (*of thg*) to bother, worry (s.o.).

taquinerie [takinri] *n.f.* teasing.

tarabiscoté [tarabiskɔte] *a.* **1.** grooved (panel, etc.). **2.** over-elaborate (style, etc.).

tarabuster [tarabyste] *v.tr.* (*a*) (*of pers.*) to pester (s.o.); (*b*) (*of thg*) to bother, worry (s.o.).

tarage [taraʒ] *n.m. Com:* allowance for tare.

taratata [taratata] *int.* rubbish!

taraud [taro] *n.m. Tls:* (screw) tap.

taraudage [tarodaʒ] *n.m.* screw cutting; tapping.

tarauder [tarode] *v.tr.* (*a*) *Tchn:* to tap, cut, screw, thread (rod, nut, etc.); (*b*) (*of insect*) to bore into (wood).

taraudeuse [tarodøz] *n.f. Tls:* tapper; thread cutter.

tarbouch(e) [tarbuʃ] *n.m. Cost:* tarboosh.

tard [tar] (*a*) *adv.* late; **plus t.,** later; later on; **au plus t.,** at the latest; **tôt ou t.,** sooner or later; *impers.* **il est t., il se fait t.,** it's (getting) late; **je ne pensais pas qu'il fût si t.,** I did not think it was so late; **je me suis couché t.,** I went to bed late; I was late in going to bed; **il se maria t.,** he married late in life; **deux minutes plus t. et je manquais le bateau,** another two minutes and I should have missed the boat; *Prov:* **mieux vaut t. que jamais,** better late than never; **il est t. dans la nuit,** it is late (at night); **je le ferai et pas plus t. que ce soir,** I'll do it this very evening; **pas plus t. qu'hier,** only yesterday; (*b*) *n.m.* **sur le t.,** (i) *A:* late in the day; (ii) late in life.

tarder [tarde] *v.i.* **1.** (*a*) to delay; **pourquoi tarde-t-il?** why is he so long? **il ne tardera pas maintenant,** he won't be long now; **t. en chemin,** to loiter on the way; **t. à faire qch.,** (i) to put off doing sth., (ii) to be a long time (starting, coming, etc.); to be slow in (paying, etc.); (*b*) **nous ne tarderons pas à le voir venir,** it won't be long before he appears. **2.** *impers.* **il lui tarde de partir, qu'elle revienne,** he is longing to get away, for her to return.

tardif, -ive [tardif, -iv] *a.* belated (regrets, etc.); late (hour, fruit).

tardivement [tardivmɑ̃] *adv.* belatedly.

tare [tar] *n.f.* **1.** (*a*) *Com:* loss in value (owing to damage or waste); (*b*) (physical, moral) defect. **2.** *Com:* tare; **faire la t.,** to ascertain, allow for, the tare.

taré [tare] *a.* **1.** spoilt (fruit, etc.); damaged (goods). **2.** (*a*) depraved, corrupt; (*b*) degenerate.

tarentelle [tarɑ̃tɛl] *n.f. Danc: Mus:* tarantella.

tarentule [tarɑ̃tyl] *n.f. Arach:* tarantula.

tarer [tare] *v.tr. Com:* to weigh (packing case, etc.).

taret [tarɛ] *n.m. Moll:* teredo; shipworm.

targette [tarʒɛt] *n.f.* flat door bolt.

targuer (se) [sətarge] *v.pr.* **se t. de qch., de faire qch.,** to pride oneself on sth., on doing sth.

targui, *pl.* **touareg** [targi, twarɛg] *a. & n. Ethn:* Touareg.

tarière [tarjɛr] *n.f.* **1.** *Tls:* (*a*) auger; (*b*) drill; *Min:* borer. **2.** *Ent:* terebra.

tarif [tarif] *n.m.* (*a*) tariff, price list; (*b*) tariff, rate; scale; schedule of charges; **t. douanier,** customs tariff; *Post:* **tarifs postaux,** postal, postage, rates; **t. (des) lettres,** letter rate; **t. intérieur,** inland rate; **t. d'urgence** = first-class rate; *Rail: etc:* **plein t.,** (i) full fare, adult fare (for passengers); (ii) full tariff (for goods, etc.); (iii) *F:* maximum penalty (for crime, etc.); **billet (à) plein t.,** full-fare ticket.

tarifaire [tarifɛr] *a.* **lois tarifaires,** tariff laws.

tarifer [tarife] *v.tr.* to tariff; to fix the rate of (duties, price of goods, etc.).

tarin [tarɛ̃] *n.m.* **1.** *Orn:* siskin. **2.** *P:* nose, beak, conk.

tarir [tarir] **1.** *v.tr.* to dry up (spring, river, tears); (*of river, milk, etc.*) **se t.,** to dry up. **2.** *v.i.* (*a*) (*of waters*) to dry up, run dry; **la source a tari,** the spring has dried up; **la source est tarie,** the spring is dry; (*b*) (*of conversation, flow of tears, etc.*) to cease, stop, be exhausted; to dry up; **ne pas t. d'éloges sur qch.,** to be for ever praising sth.; **une fois sur ce sujet il ne tarit pas,** once he is on this subject he never stops.

tarissement [tarismɑ̃] *n.m.* running dry (of waters); exhausting (of resources, etc.).

tarmacadam [tarmakadam] *n.m. Civ.E: A:* tarmacadam.

tarot [taro] *n.m. Cards:* **(jeu de) tarot(s),** tarot (pack).

tarsal, -aux [tarsal, -o] *a. Anat: Z:* tarsal.

tarse [tars] *n.m. Anat: Z:* tarsus.

tarsien, -ienne [tarsjɛ̃, -jɛn] *a. Anat:* tarsal (bone).
tarsier [tarsje] *n.m. Z:* tarsier.
tartan [tartɑ̃] *n.m.* tartan (cloth, plaid).
tartane [tartan] *n.f. Nau:* tartan (of the Mediterranean).
tartare [tartar] **1.** *a. & n. Ethn:* Tartar. **2.** *a. & n.m. Cu:* **sauce t.,** tartar(e) sauce; **un (steak) t.,** steak tartare.
tarte [tart] **1.** *n.f. Cu:* (open) tart; flan; **t. aux pommes,** apple tart; **t. à la crème,** custard tart; *Cin: F:* custard pie (thrown at s.o.); *F:* **c'est de la t.,** it's easy, a piece of cake. **2.** *n.f. P:* slap. **3.** *a. F:* (*a*) (*of pers.*) stupid, ridiculous; (*b*) (*of thg*) ugly; lousy.
tartelette [tartəlɛt] *n.f. Cu:* tartlet.
tartine [tartin] *n.f.* **1.** slice of bread and butter, etc.; **t. de confiture,** bread and jam. **2.** *F:* long-winded speech; rambling article, rigmarole.
tartiner [tartine] *v.tr.* to spread (bread) with butter, etc.; to butter; **fromage à t.,** cheese spread.
tartre [tartr̥] *n.m.* tartar (on teeth, etc.); fur, scale (in boiler, kettle).
tartrique [tartrik] *a. Ch:* tartaric (acid).
tartuf(f)e [tartyf] *n.m.* tartuf(f)e; (sanctimonious) hypocrite.
tas [ta] *n.m.* **1.** (*a*) heap, pile (of stones, mud, wood, etc.); stook, shock (of corn); **t. de fumier,** manure heap; **mettre des objets en t.,** to heap up, pile up, things; *Min:* **t. de déblais,** dump; (*b*) mass (of things, people); **un t. de mensonges,** a pack of lies; *F:* **il y en a des t. (et des t.),** there are heaps of them; **des t. de fois,** lots of times; *Pej: F:* **tout un t. de gens,** a whole gang (of people); **t. d'imbéciles!** bunch of idiots! (*c*) **tirer dans le t.,** to fire into the crowd. **2.** *Metalw:* stake (anvil). **3.** building under construction; building site; **être sur le t.,** to be at work, on the job; *Ind: etc:* **formation sur le t.,** on-the-job training; **grève sur le t.,** sit-down strike. **4.** *Arch: Civ.E:* **t. de charge,** tas-de-charge, springing stones (on pier).
tassage [tasaʒ] *n.m. Sp:* crowding (of opponent).
tasse [tas] *n.f.* (*a*) cup; **t. à café,** coffee cup; **t. de café,** cup of coffee; **t. en métal,** tin mug; **boire dans une t.,** to drink out of a cup; *F:* **la grande t.,** the sea, the drink; **boire à la grande t.,** to get drowned (at sea); (*b*) cupful; **boire une, la, t.,** to get a mouthful (when swimming).
tassé [tase] *a.* **1.** huddled up; **t. par l'âge,** shrunk with age. **2.** *F:* (*a*) full, complete; **1500 pages bien tassées,** a good 1500 pages; **un verre bien t.,** a good glassful; (*b*) **bien t.,** stiff (whisky); strong (coffee).
tasseau[1], -eaux [taso] *n.m.* batten (supporting shelf, etc.).
tasseau[2] *n.m. Metalw:* stake (anvil).
tassement [tasmɑ̃] *n.m.* **1.** cramming, compressing (of objects) together; packing (of earth, etc.). **2.** (*a*) (i) settling, consolidation, (ii) sinking, subsidence (of foundations, etc.); (*b*) *Fin: St.Exch:* setback.
tasser [tase] **1.** *v.tr.* (*a*) to cram, squeeze, (objects) together; to ram, pack, tamp (earth, etc.); to cram, pack (passengers into a vehicle); to firm (the soil); (*b*) *Sp:* to crowd (an opponent). **2.** *v.i.* (*of plants*) to grow thick(ly). **3. se t.** (*a*) (*of foundations, etc.*) (i) to settle, set; (ii) to sink, subside; **les opinions se sont tassées,** opinions have consolidated; *F:* **ça se tassera,** things will settle down; **il commence à se t.,** he is beginning to shrink (with age); (*b*) to crowd (up) together; **tassez-vous un peu,** squeeze up a bit.
taste-vin [tastəvɛ̃] *n.m.inv.* (*pers. or thg*) wine taster.
tata [tata] *n.f.* **1.** *F:* (*child's word*) auntie, aunty. **2.** *P:* (male) homosexual, fairy.
tatar, -are [tatar] **1.** *a. & n. Ethn: O:* Ta(r)tar. **2.** *n.m. Ling:* **le t.,** Ta(r)tar.
tâter [tɑte] **1.** *v.tr.* to feel, touch; to try, test (s.o.'s courage, etc.); **t. le pouls à qn,** (i) to feel s.o.'s pulse; (ii) to sound s.o. (on a matter); **t. le terrain,** to throw out a feeler; to see how the land lies; **avancer en tâtant,** to grope one's way forward; **t. la porte pour trouver la poignée,** to feel for the door handle. **2.** *v.ind.tr.* (*a*) *Lit:* **t. d'un mets,** to taste a dish; (*b*) **t. d'un métier,** to try one's hand at a trade; *F:* **il a tâté de la prison,** he's done time. **3. se t.** (*a*) to feel oneself (for injuries); (*b*) to think it over.
tâte-vin [tɑtvɛ̃] *n.m.inv.* (*pers. or thg*) wine taster.
tatillon, -onne [tatijɔ̃, -ɔn] *a. & n.* finicky, fussy (person).
tâtonnement [tɑtɔnmɑ̃] *n.m.* **procéder par tâtonnements,** to proceed by trial and error.
tâtonner [tɑtɔne] *v.i.* **1.** to grope (in the dark); **se diriger en tâtonnant vers . . .,** to grope, feel, one's way towards . . .. **2.** to proceed cautiously, tentatively.
tâtons (à) [atɑtɔ̃] *adv.phr.* **avancer, entrer, sortir, à t.,** to grope, feel, one's way along, in, out; **chercher qch. à t.,** to grope, feel, for sth.
tatou [tatu] *n.m. Z:* armadillo.
tatouage [tatwaʒ] *n.m.* **1.** tattooing. **2.** tattoo.
tatouer [tatwe] *v.tr.* to tattoo.
tatoueur [tatwœr] *n.m.* tattooist.
taud [to] *n.m. Nau:* rain awning; boat cover.
taudis [todi] *n.m.* slum.
taulard, -arde [tolar, -ard] *n. P:* prisoner, convict; old lag.
taule [tol] *n.f. P:* (*a*) room; (*b*) prison; *Mil: F:* glasshouse; **faire de la t.,** to do a stretch.
taulier, -ière [tolje, -jɛr] *n. P:* owner, keeper (of lodging house, etc.).
taupe [top] *n.f.* **1.** *Z:* mole; *Ich:* **t. de mer,** porbeagle; **myope comme une t.,** blind as a bat; **noir comme une t.,** black as pitch. **2.** moleskin. **3.** *Sch: F:* special maths class. **4.** *P:* **vieille t.,** old crone, old hag.
taupier [topje] *n.m.* mole catcher.
taupin [topɛ̃] *n.m.* **1.** *Mil: A:* sapper. **2.** *Sch: F:* student in special maths class. **3.** *Ent:* click beetle.
taupinière [topinjɛr] *n.f., A:* **taupinée** [topine] *n.f.* molehill; mole cast.
taureau, -eaux [tɔro] *n.m.* **1.** bull; **au cou de t.,** bull-necked; **course, combat, de taureaux,** bullfight; *F:* **prendre le t. par les cornes,** to take the bull by the horns. **2.** *Astr:* **le T.,** Taurus.
taurillon [tɔrijɔ̃] *n.m.* bull calf.
tauromachie [tɔrɔmaʃi] *n.f.* tauromachy; bullfighting.
tauromachique [tɔrɔmaʃik] *a.* of bullfighting.
tautologie [tɔtɔlɔʒi] *n.f.* tautology.
tautologique [tɔtɔlɔʒik] *a.* tautological.
taux [to] *n.m.* (*a*) rate (of wages, of exchange); (established standard) price (of commodities, shares, etc.); *Adm:* **t. de pension,** pension scale; *Fin:* **t. du change,** rate of exchange; (*b*) proportion, ratio; *Mil:* scale (of rations); *Mec.E: Ind:* **t. de rendement,** coefficient of efficiency, utilization factor; *I.C.E:* **t. de compression,** compression ratio; (*c*) percentage; rate; **t. d'intérêt,** rate of interest; **t. des naissances,** birth rate; *Mil:* **t. de pertes,** casualty rate; *Med:* **t. d'invalidité,** degree of disablement; *Rail: etc:* **t. de pente,** rate of grade, gradient; (*d*) *Cmptr:* ratio; rate.
tavelé [tavle] *a.* speckled.
taveler [tavle] *v.tr.* **(il tavelle; il tavellera)** to spot, speckle; (*of fruit*) **se t.,** to become marked, speckled.
tavelure [tavlyr] *n.f.* spots, speckles; *Hort:* scab.
taverne [tavɛrn] *n.f.* **1.** *A:* tavern. **2.** (*a*) café-restaurant; (*b*) *Fr.C:* beer parlo(u)r.
tavernier, -ière [tavɛrnje, -jɛr] *n. A:* innkeeper; landlord, landlady.
taxable [taksabl̥] *a. Cmptr:* chargeable.
taxateur [taksatœr] **1.** *n.m.* taxer, assessor. **2.** *a.m.* taxing (official).

taxation [taksasjɔ̃] *n.f.* **1.** fixing of prices, wages, etc.; *Jur:* taxing (of costs). **2.** *Adm:* (*a*) taxation; (*b*) assessment. **3.** *Tp:* **zone de t.,** charging area; *Cmptr:* **période de t.,** charging period.

taxe [taks] *n.f.* **1.** (*a*) fixed price, official price; fixed rate (of wages); (*b*) charge (for service); rate; **t. postale, des lettres,** postage. **2.** (*a*) tax, duty, rate; **t. à la production, à l'achat, de consommation,** purchase tax; **t. à la valeur ajoutée,** value added tax, *U.S:* processing tax; **t. sur les chiens,** dog tax; **t. de séjour,** visitors' tax; **t. d'habitation,** inhabited house duty; **t. officielle,** assessment; *Th: etc:* **t. sur les spectacles,** entertainment tax; (*b*) **t. de port,** harbour, *NAm:* harbor, dues. **3.** *Jur:* taxing, taxation (of costs).

taxer [takse] *v.tr.* **1.** (*a*) to regulate the price of (bread, etc.), the rate of (wages, postage); (*b*) to surcharge (letter); (*c*) *Tp:* to charge for (call). **2.** to tax, impose a tax on (s.o., sth.). **3.** (*a*) *Jur:* to tax (costs); (*b*) *Com:* to bill. **4.** to tax (**de,** with); to accuse (**de,** of); to denounce (**de,** as).

taxi [taksi] *n.m.* (*a*) taxi (cab); **conducteur de t., chauffeur de t.,** taxi driver; (*b*) *F:* taxi driver.

taxidermie [taksidɛrmi] *n.f.* taxidermy.

taximètre [taksimɛtr̥] *n.m.* taximeter.

taxinomie [taksinɔmi] *n.f. Nat.Hist:* taxonomy.

taxiphone [taksifɔn] *n.m. Tp:* public call box.

taxonomie [taksɔnɔmi] *n.f. Nat.Hist:* taxonomy.

tchécoslovaque [tʃekɔslɔvak] *a. & n. Geog:* Czech, Czechoslovak, Czechoslovakian.

Tchécoslovaquie [tʃekɔslɔvaki] *Pr.n.f. Geog:* Czechoslovakia.

tchèque [tʃɛk] **1.** *a. & n.* Czech. **2.** *n.m. Ling:* Czech.

te, *before a vowel sound* **t'** [t(ə)] *pers.pron., unstressed, attached to the verb or its adjuncts;* (*for the use of* **te** *cf.* TU) **1.** (*a*) (*acc.*) you; **il t'adore,** he adores you; **te voilà,** there you are; (*b*) (*dat.*) (to) you; **il t'a écrit,** he wrote to you; **il te l'a dit,** he told you so; (*c*) (*with pr.vbs*) yourself (*or not rendered into English*); **tu te fatigues,** you are tiring yourself; **tu vas te faire mal,** you will hurt yourself; **à quelle heure t'es-tu levé(e)?** (at) what time did you get up? **va-t'en,** go away. **2.** *A: & Lit:* thee, thyself; (*a*) (*in addressing the Deity*) Thee; You; (*b*) *Dial: etc:* **va-t'en,** get thee gone.

té [te] *n.m.* **1.** (the letter) T, tee; **en té,** T-shaped. **2.** **(équerre en) té,** T-square.

technicien, -ienne [tɛknisjɛ̃, -jɛn] *n.* technician; expert.

technicité [tɛknisite] *n.f.* technical nature.

technique [tɛknik] **1.** *a.* technical. **2.** *n.f.* (*a*) technology; **t. de l'ingénieur,** engineering; **t. électrique,** electrical engineering; **t. des ultrasons,** ultrasonics; (*b*) technique (of artist, specialist, etc.).

techniquement [tɛknikmɑ̃] *adv.* technically.

technocrate [tɛknɔkrat] *a. & n.* technocrat.

technocratie [tɛknɔkrasi] *n.f. Pol.Ec:* technocracy.

technologie [tɛknɔlɔʒi] *n.f.* technology.

technologique [tɛknɔlɔʒik] *a.* technological.

technologiste [tɛknɔlɔʒist] *n.,* **technologue** [tɛknɔlɔg] *n.* technologist.

teck [tɛk] *n.m. Bot: Com:* teak.

teckel [tɛkɛl] *n.m.* dachshund.

tectonique [tɛktɔnik] **1.** *a.* tectonic. **2.** *n.f.* tectonics.

tee [ti] *n.m. Golf:* tee.

tee(-)shirt [tiʃœrt] *n.m. Cost:* teeshirt; *pl. tee(-)shirts.*

tégument [tegymɑ̃] *n.m. Nat.Hist:* (in)tegument.

teigne [tɛɲ] *n.f.* **1.** (*a*) moth; **t. des draps,** clothes moth; (*b*) *P:* unpleasant character, stinker. **2.** *Med:* tinea; ringworm.

teigneux, -euse [tɛɲø, -øz] **1.** *a. & n. Med:* (person) suffering from tinea, from ringworm. **2.** *n.m. P:* unpleasant character, stinker.

teindre [tɛ̃dr̥] *v.* (*pr.p.* **teignant;** *p.p.* **teint;** *pr.ind.* **je teins, il teint, n. teignons;** *pr.sub.* **je teigne;** *impf.* **je teignais;** *p.h.* **je teignis;** *fu.* **je teindrai) 1.** *v.tr.* (*a*) to dye; **t. qch. en rouge,** to dye sth. red; **faire t. une robe,** to have a dress dyed; (*b*) to stain (hands, etc.). **2. se t.** (*a*) to dye one's hair; (*b*) *Lit:* to be tinged (**de,** with).

teint [tɛ̃] *n.m.* **1.** dye, colour, *NAm:* color; **bon t., grand t.,** fast colour; **bon t.,** (i) lasting; (ii) genuine; authentic; (iii) staunch. **2.** complexion, colour; **au t. frais,** fresh-complexioned; **au t. jaune,** sallow.

teinte [tɛ̃t] *n.f.* (*a*) tint, shade; (*b*) touch, tinge (of irony, melancholy); hint (of pedantry).

teinter [tɛ̃te] *v.tr.* (*a*) to tint; (*b*) **t. (légèrement),** to tinge.

teinture [tɛ̃tyr] *n.f.* **1.** (*a*) dyeing (of cloth, hair, etc.); (*b*) tinting (of a drawing, etc.). **2.** (*a*) dye; **tissu qui prend bien la t.,** material that dyes well; **couvertures sans t.,** undyed blankets; (*b*) colour, *NAm:* color; hue, tinge. **3.** *Pharm:* tincture.

teinturerie [tɛ̃tyr(ə)ri] *n.f.* **1.** dyeing. **2.** dry cleaner's.

teinturier, -ière [tɛ̃tyrje, -jɛr] *n.* **1.** dyer. **2.** dry cleaner.

tek [tɛk] *n.m.* teak.

tel, telle [tɛl] *a.* **1.** such; (*a*) **un t. homme,** such a man; **de telles choses,** such things; (*b*) this; **en t. lieu,** in such and such a place; **dans telle et telle rue,** in such and such a street; **inutile de demander si t. ouvrage remplit son but mieux que t. autre,** it is useless to ask whether one book achieves its aim better than another; **dans telles circonstances qu'on le jugera convenable,** under such conditions as may be deemed suitable; **vous amènerez telle personne que vous voudrez,** you may bring any person you like; (*c*) **sa bonté est telle que . . .,** so great is her kindness that . . .; **t. charlatan qu'il puisse être,** no matter how much of a quack he may be; **à t. point,** to such an extent, to such a pitch; **de telle sorte que,** (i) + *ind.* (*result*), (ii) + *sub.* (*purpose*), in such a way that; **il parle de telle sorte que je ne le comprends pas,** he speaks in such a way that I don't understand him; **je m'arrangerai de telle sorte qu'elle puisse partir dimanche,** I will arrange things so that she can leave on Sunday. **2.** (*a*) like; as; **t. père, t. fils,** like father like son; **t. font les parents, t. feront les enfants,** as the parents do so will the children; (*b*) **t. que,** such as, like; **un homme t. que lui,** a man like him; **une lassitude telle qu'on en éprouve par un jour orageux,** a tiredness such as one feels on a stormy day; **la clause telle qu'elle est,** the clause as it stands; **voir les hommes tels qu'ils sont,** to see men as they are; *F:* **t. que,** straight out; (*c*) **rien de t. qu'un bon cigare,** there's nothing like, you can't beat, a good cigar; **il n'est rien de t. que d'être jeune,** there's nothing like being young; (*d*) *Lit:* **il allait et venait, telle une bête en cage,** he paced to and fro like a caged animal; (*e*) **t. quel,** *P:* **t. que,** just as it is; just as he is; **je vous achète la maison telle quelle,** I'll buy the house from you (just) as it stands; **j'ai retrouvé la maison telle quelle,** I found the house just as I left it. **3.** *pron.* (*a*) such a one; **t. l'en blâmait, t. l'en excusait,** one would blame him, another would excuse him; **t. admire le père qui blâme le fils,** some who blame the son admire the father; *Prov:* **t. qui rit vendredi, dimanche pleurera,** laugh today, cry tomorrow; (*b*) **t. fut son langage,** such were his words; **il n'est pas beau mais il se prend pour t.,** he is not handsome but he thinks himself so; *n.* **un t., une telle,** so-and-so; **Monsieur un t., un T.,** Mr So-and-so; **t. ou t. vous dira que . . .,** some people will tell you that . . .; **je serais incapable d'attribuer l'article à t. ou t.,** I

cannot attribute the article to any particular person.
télé [tele] *n.f. F:* telly; the box.
télébenne [telebɛn] *n.f.*, **télécabine** [telekabin] *n.f.* telpher carrier, car; cable car.
télécinéma [telesinema] *n.m.* telecine, telecinema.
télécommande [telekɔmɑ̃d] *n.f.* remote control; radio control.
télécommander [telekɔmɑ̃de] *v.tr.* to operate by remote control; to radio-control; **télécommandé,** remote-controlled.
télécommunication [telekɔmynikasjɔ̃] *n.f.* telecommunication.
télécran [telekrɑ̃] *n.m.* large-sized telescreen, television screen (for an auditorium).
télédiffusé [teledifyze] *a.* televised (programme).
téléférique [teleferik] **1.** *a.* telpher (cable, etc.). **2.** *n.m.* (*a*) telpher (line, railway); (*b*) telpher car, carrier; cable car.
télégénique [teleʒenik] *a.* telegenic, who televises well.
télégestion [teleʒɛstjɔ̃] *n.f. Cmptr:* teleprocessing, remote processing.
télégramme [telegram] *n.m.* telegram.
télégraphe [telegraf] *n.m.* telegraph.
télégraphie [telegrafi] *n.f.* telegraphy; *O:* **t. sans fil,** wireless (telegraphy).
télégraphier [telegrafje] *v.tr. & i.* (*impf. & pr.sub.* **n. télégraphiions, v. télégraphiiez**) to telegraph, to wire.
télégraphique [telegrafik] *a.* telegraphic; **dépêche t.,** telegram; **style t.,** telegraphic style, *F:* telegraphese.
télégraphiste [telegrafist] *n.* telegraphist; telegraph operator; **petit t.,** telegraph boy.
téléguidage [telegidaʒ] *n.m.* radio control; remote control.
téléguidé [telegide] *a.* (radio-)guided; remote-controlled; **engin t.,** guided missile.
téléguider [telegide] *v.tr.* to radio-control; to guide (aircraft, missile, etc.); to operate by remote control.
téléimprimeur [teleɛ̃primœr] *n.m.* teleprinter, telewriter; (*R.t.m.*) Teletype, *NAm:* teletypewriter.
téléjournal, -aux [teleʒurnal, -o] *n.m.* (television) news.
télékinésie [telekinezi] *n.f. Psychics:* telekinesis.
télémanipulateur [telemanipylatœr] *n.m. Atom. Ph:* remote manipulator.
télémark [telemark] *n.m. Ski:* telemark.
télémesure [teleməzyr] *n.f. Surv: Elcs:* telemetering, telemetry.
télémètre [telemɛtr] *n.m.* telemeter; *Mil: etc:* rangefinder.
télémétrie [telemetri] *n.f.* telemetry; *Mil: etc:* range finding.
téléobjectif [teleɔbʒɛktif] *n.m. Phot:* telephoto lens; **photographie au t.,** telephotography.
téléologie [teleɔlɔʒi] *n.f. Phil:* teleology.
téléostéen [teleɔsteɛ̃] *n.m. Ich:* teleost.
télépathe [telepat] *Psychics:* **1.** *a.* telepathic. **2.** *n.* telepath.
télépathie [telepati] *n.f. Psychics:* telepathy.
télépathique [telepatik] *a.* telepathic.
téléphérage [teleferaʒ] *n.m. Ind:* telpherage; overhead cable transport.
téléphérique [teleferik] *a. & n.m.* = TÉLÉFÉRIQUE.
téléphonage [telefɔnaʒ] *n.m.* telephoning (of telegram).
téléphone [telefɔn] *n.m.* telephone, *F:* phone; **t. bâtiment-terre,** ship to shore telephone; *Pol:* **t. rouge,** hot line; **t. vert,** hot line (Élysée to Kremlin); *F:* **t. arabe,** bush telephone, grapevine; **être abonné au t., avoir le t.,** to be on the phone; **coup de t.,** telephone call; **appeler qn au t., donner un coup de t. à qn,** to ring s.o. (up), to phone s.o.; *esp. NAm:* to call s.o. (up); **parler à qn au t., par t.,** to speak to s.o. on the phone; **demander qch. par t.,** to phone for sth.
téléphoner [telefɔne] *v.tr. & i.* **1.** to telephone (a piece of news, etc.); to give (a piece of news, etc.) on the telephone, by (tele)phone. **2. t. à qn,** to ring s.o. (up), to phone s.o., *esp.NAm:* to call s.o. (up); to give s.o. a call; **t. à qn de venir,** to telephone for s.o. **3.** *Sp:* **t. ses coups,** to telegraph one's strokes, one's punches; *Pol: etc:* **une manœuvre téléphonée,** an obvious manœuvre, *NAm:* maneuver.
téléphonie [telefɔni] *n.f.* telephony; **t. sans fil,** wireless telephony, radio telephony.
téléphonique [telefɔnik] *a.* telephonic; telephone (booth, call); **commande t.,** order by telephone.
téléphoniste [telefɔnist] *n.* telephonist; telephone operator.
téléphotographie [telefɔtɔgrafi] *n.f.* **1.** *Tg:* phototelegraphy. **2.** *Phot:* (*a*) telephotography; (*b*) telephotograph.
téléreportage [telerəpɔrtaʒ] *n.m.* television newscasting, commentary.
téléroman [telerɔmɑ̃] *n.m.* television serial.
télescopage [telɛskɔpaʒ] *n.m.* telescoping (of parts, trains, etc.); *Aut:* **t. en série,** pile-up.
télescope [telɛskɔp] *n.m.* telescope.
télescoper [telɛskɔpe] **1.** *v.tr.* (*a*) (*of railway coaches, etc.*) to telescope; to crumple up; (*b*) *Ling:* to telescope (words). **2. se t.,** to crumple up, to concertina.
télescopique [telɛskɔpik] *a.* telescopic.
téléscripteur [teleskriptœr] *n.m.* teleprinter, telewriter; (*R.t.m.*) Teletype, *NAm:* teletypewriter.
télésiège [telesjɛʒ] *n.m.* chair lift; ski lift.
téléski [teleski] *n.m.* drag lift; ski lift, tow.
téléspectateur, -trice [telespɛktatœr, -tris] *n.* (tele)viewer.
télétype [teletip] *n.m.* teleprinter, telewriter; (*R.t.m.*) Teletype, *NAm:* teletypewriter.
téléviser [televize] *v.tr.* to televise; **journal télévisé,** television news.
téléviseur [televizœr] *n.m.* television set.
télévision [televizjɔ̃] *n.f.* (*a*) television; **t. en couleur(s),** colour, *NAm:* color, television; **t. en circuit fermé,** closed-circuit television; **t. scolaire,** television for schools; **à la t.,** on television; (*b*) *F:* television (set).
télévisuel, -elle [televizɥɛl] *a.* televisual; television (version of play, etc.).
télex [telɛks] *n.m.* (*R.t.m.*) telex (machine).
tellement [tɛlmɑ̃] *adv.* **1.** *A:* so; in such a way. **2.** to such a degree, so; **c'est t. facile,** it's so (very) easy; **il est t. sourd qu'il faut crier,** he is so deaf that one has to shout; *F:* **t. de,** so much, so many; *F:* **ce n'est pas t. beau,** it's not all that beautiful.
tellurique¹ [telyrik] *a. Ch:* telluric (acid).
tellurique² *a.* telluric (fever, currents); **secousse t.,** earth tremor.
téméraire [temerɛr] *a.* (*a*) rash, reckless; daring (pers.); (*b*) rash (judgment, statement).
témérairement [temerɛrmɑ̃] *adv.* rashly, recklessly.
témérité [temerite] *n.f.* **1.** temerity, rashness. **2.** reckless action; bold, daring, speech.
témoignage [temwaɲaʒ] *n.m.* **1.** (*a*) testimony, evidence; **recueillir des témoignages,** to collect evidence; **porter t.,** to certify, bear witness, give evidence; **rendre t. de qch.,** (i) to give evidence about sth.; (ii) to bear testimony to sth.; **rendre t. à qn.,** to testify in s.o.'s favour, *NAm:* favor; **appeler qn en t.,** to call s.o. as witness; **invoquer le t. de qn,** to call s.o. to witness; **faux t.,** false witness, false evidence; perjury; (*b*) evidence; statement; **d'après son t.,** according to his statement; **t. des sens,** evidence of the senses. **2.**

Jur: hearing (of witnesses). **3.** token (of friendship, etc.).

témoigner [temwaɲe] **1.** *v.i.* to testify (in s.o.'s favour, *NAm:* favor, against s.o.); to give evidence. **2.** *v.tr. or ind.tr.* **t. (de),** to show, prove, give evidence of (gratitude, good will); **t. d'un goût pour . . .,** to show, display, a taste for . . .; **t. de l'intérêt à qn,** to show an interest in s.o.; **t. du dédain à qn,** to show contempt for s.o.; **t. que . . .,** to show that . . ..

témoin [temwɛ̃] *n.m.* **1.** (*a*) witness; **être t. de qch.,** to witness sth., to see sth. happen; **t. à un acte, d'un mariage,** witness to a signature, at a marriage; **parler à qn sans témoins,** to speak to s.o. in private; **mes yeux en sont témoins,** I saw it with my own eyes; (*b*) *Jur:* **t. à charge, à décharge,** witness for the prosecution, for the defence; **barre des témoins,** witness box; **t. oculaire,** eyewitness; **citer qn comme t.,** to call s.o. as witness; **je vous prends tous à t. que . . .,** I take you to witness that . . .; **Dieu m'est t. que . . .,** God is my witness that . . .; **t. les coups que j'ai reçus,** witness the blows which I received; (*c*) second (in duel). **2.** (= TÉMOIGNAGE) proof, evidence. **3.** (*a*) boundary mark; (*b*) sample; *Ch:* reference solution; *Phot:* **plaque t., épreuve t.,** pilot print; (*c*) *El: Ind: etc:* **lampe t.,** telltale lamp, pilot light, warning light; (*d*) *Bookb:* dog's ear (showing size before trimming); (*e*) *Sp:* baton, etc. (in relay race); (*f*) **denrée t.,** basic commodity; (*g*) **appartement t.,** show flat.

tempe [tɑ̃p] *n.f. Anat:* temple.

tempera (a) [atɑ̃pera] *Art:* (*a*) *adj.phr.* **peinture a t.,** tempera painting; (*b*) *adv.phr.* **peindre a t.,** to paint in tempera.

tempérament [tɑ̃peramɑ̃] *n.m.* **1.** (*a*) (physical) constitution, temperament; **t. de fer,** iron constitution; **se tuer le t.,** to ruin one's health; (*b*) (moral) temperament; disposition; (*c*) **avoir du t.,** to have character; (*d*) *A:* (amorous) temperament. **2.** (*a*) *A:* moderation; restraint; (*b*) *Mus:* temperament. **3.** *Com:* **à t.,** by instalments; **vente à t.,** hire purchase.

tempéramental, -aux [tɑ̃peramɑ̃tal, -o] *a.* temperamental; constitutional.

tempérance [tɑ̃perɑ̃s] *n.f.* (*a*) temperance, moderation; (*b*) temperance; teetotalism.

tempérant [tɑ̃perɑ̃] *a.* temperate.

température [tɑ̃peratyr] *n.f.* temperature; **t. du corps humain,** temperature of the human body; blood heat; *Med: F:* **avoir, faire, de la t.,** to have a (high) temperature; *Ph:* **t. d'ébullition,** boiling point; *Fig:* **prendre la t. de l'auditoire,** to gauge the temperature of the audience.

tempéré [tɑ̃pere] *a.* **1.** temperate, moderate (climate, speech); restrained, sober (style); constitutional (monarchy). **2.** *Mus:* tempered.

tempérer [tɑ̃pere] *v.tr.* **(je tempère, n. tempérons; je tempérerai)** to temper, moderate (heat, passions, etc.).

tempête [tɑ̃pɛt] *n.f.* storm (of wind); *Nau:* hurricane; (*on barometer*) **t.,** stormy; **t. de neige,** blizzard, snowstorm; **il faisait une t.,** a storm was raging; **une t. dans un verre d'eau,** a storm in a teacup; **t. d'injures, d'applaudissements,** storm of abuse, of applause.

tempêter [tɑ̃pete] *v.i.* (*of pers.*) to storm; to rage.

tempétueux, -euse [tɑ̃petɥø, -øz] *a.* tempestuous; stormy (wind, sea, etc.); boisterous (welcome); turbulent (life).

temple [tɑ̃pl̩] *n.m.* temple; (protestant) church, chapel; *Hist:* **les chevaliers du T.,** the Knights Templars.

templier [tɑ̃plije] *n.m. Hist:* (Knight) Templar.

tempo [tɛ̃po, tɛmpo] *n.m. Mus: Fig:* tempo.

temporaire [tɑ̃pɔrɛr] *a.* **1.** temporary; provisional. **2.** *Mus:* **valeur t. d'une note,** time value of a note.

temporairement [tɑ̃pɔrɛrmɑ̃] *adv.* temporarily.

temporal, -ale, -aux [tɑ̃pɔral, -o] *Anat:* **1.** *a.* temporal (bone, artery). **2.** *n.m.* (*a*) temporal bone; (*b*) temporal muscle, temporalis. **3.** *n.f.* **temporale,** temporal (artery).

temporalité [tɑ̃pɔralite] *n.f. Ecc: Phil: Gram:* temporality.

temporel, -elle [tɑ̃pɔrɛl] *a.* (*a*) temporal; worldly; (*b*) *Gram:* temporal (clause, etc.).

temporellement [tɑ̃pɔrɛlmɑ̃] *adv.* temporally.

temporisateur, -trice [tɑ̃pɔrizatœr, -tris] **1.** *n.* temporizer; procrastinator. **2.** *a.* temporizing. **3.** *n.m. El:* (automatic) time switch.

temporisation [tɑ̃pɔrizasjɔ̃] *n.f.* temporizing; calculated delay.

temporiser [tɑ̃pɔrize] *v.i.* to temporize; to play for time.

temps [tɑ̃] *n.m.* **1.** (*a*) time; **mettre beaucoup de t. à faire qch.,** to take a long time doing sth., over (doing) sth.; **tuer le t.,** to kill time; **vous avez bien le t., vous avez tout le t.,** you have plenty of time; **cela prend du t.,** it takes, requires, time; **prendre (tout) son t.,** to take one's time; **(donnez-moi) le t. de signer, que je signe, et je suis à vous,** just give me time, a minute, to sign my letters and I'll be with you; **nous n'avons pas le t. à présent,** there's no time now; **nous n'avons que le t. de . . .,** we have only just time to . . .; **combien de t. faut-il pour . . .?** how long does it take to . . .? **gagner du t.,** (i) to gain time; (ii) to temporize, to play for time; **perdre du t.,** to waste time; **dans le cours du t., dans la suite du t., avec le t.,** in (the process of) time, with time; in the long run; **de t. en t.,** now and then; from time to time; **en d'autres t.,** at any other time; **en tout t.,** at all times; **en même t.,** at the same time; **travailler à plein t.,** to work full time; **prendre, se donner, du bon t.,** to have a good time, to enjoy oneself; *Prov:* **le t., c'est de l'argent,** time is money; *Myth: etc:* **le T.,** (Father) Time; (*b*) time, period; **un (certain) t., quelque t.,** for a while, for a time; **cela ne durera qu'un t.,** it will only last for a while; it won't last for ever; **tout n'a qu'un t.,** there is an end to everything; **chaque chose a son t.,** everything has its day; **le t. de la moisson,** harvest time; **le t. des cerises,** the cherry season; **T. de l'Ascension,** Ascensiontide; **il y a peu de t.,** a little while ago; not long ago; **peu de t. après,** not long after; **d'ici quelque t.,** for some time to come; **au bout de très peu de t.,** in a very short space of time; **entre t.,** meanwhile; **il est beau t. qu'il est parti,** he left a long time ago; **faire un t. de galop,** to have a short gallop, to gallop for a time; **t. d'arrêt,** pause, halt; **marquer un t.,** to pause; (*c*) term (of service, etc.); **faire son t.,** to serve one's time; (*of convict*) to serve one's sentence, to do one's time; **cette théorie a fait son t.,** this theory is out of date, out-dated; (*d*) *Mec.E:* **t. à vide,** off-load period (of machine, etc.); **t. de fonctionnement,** running time (of machine); **t. mort,** idle time, period (of machine, etc.); dead time; interruption; *Av:* **t. mort au sol,** turnround time; *Ind:* **étude des t. et ordonnancements,** time and motion study; *El: Elcs:* **t. d'ouverture,** on period; *Cmptr:* **utilisation (d'un ordinateur) en t. partagé,** time sharing; **t. machine,** computer time; **en t. réel,** real time; **base de t.,** time base; clock; (*e*) age, days, time(s); **les t. préhistoriques,** prehistoric times; **les hauts t.,** remote antiquity; **le bon vieux t.,** the good old days; **l'Angleterre des t. passés,** the England of the past; **dans le t., au t. jadis,** in times past, in the old days; **dans la suite des t.,** in the course of time; **en d'autres t.,** (i) formerly, in other times; (ii) in time to come; **dans ce t.-là,** at that time; **ces t.-ci,** these days; **ce fut un grand homme dans son t.,** he was a great man in his day; **elle a eu son t. de beauté,** she was a beauty in her day; **du t., au t., de Napoléon,**

in Napoleon's time; **du t. de ma jeunesse, du t. où j'étais jeune,** when I was young; in my youth; **les t. sont durs,** times are hard; **il fut un t. où . . .,** there was a time when . . .; **signe des t.,** sign of the times; **par le t. qui court, par les t. qui courent,** as things are at present; **être de son t., marcher, vivre, avec son t.,** to move with the times; to be up to date; **vous n'êtes pas de votre t.,** you're behind the times; **de notre t.,** in our days; **il n'en était pas ainsi de mon t.,** it wasn't so in my day; **cela est arrivé de mon t.,** it happened in my time; **de tout t., en tout t.,** at all times; always; (*f*) time; hour; **arriver à t.,** to arrive in (good) time; **arriver juste à t.,** to arrive just in time, in the nick of time; **je ne suis pas arrivé à t.,** I was (too) late; **en t. voulu, utile,** in due time; **je serai de retour en t. voulu,** I shall be back in, on, time; **il est (grand) t. qu'elle descende,** it is (high) time she came down; **il est grand t. que . . .,** it's high time, about time, that . . .; **il serait t.!** it's about time! **il n'est plus t.,** it is too late; **il n'était que t.,** it was only just in time; **il n'est que t. de faire cela,** it's high time to do this; **il était t.!** it was a narrow escape! (*of event*) **venir en son t.,** to be timely; (*g*) *Astr:* **t. apparent,** apparent time; **t. vrai,** true time; **t. moyen local,** local mean time; **t. astronomique,** astronomical time; (*h*) time, occasion, opportunity; **il y a t. pour tout,** there is a time for everything; **chaque chose en son t.,** everything in good time; **en t. et lieu,** in the proper time and place; **prendre son t.,** to choose one's time; **je le ferai à mon t.,** I shall do it in my own time, when it suits me. **2.** weather; **par tous les t.,** in all weathers; **vous sortez par un pareil t., par le t. qu'il fait!** you're going out in such weather, in weather like this, in this weather! **quel t. fait-il?** what's the weather like? **quelque t. qu'il fasse,** whatever the weather (is like); **si le t. le permet,** weather permitting; **beau t.,** fine weather; *F:* **il fera beau t. quand je ferai cela,** it'll be a long time before I do that; *Nau:* **gros t.,** heavy weather; **le t. est à la pluie,** it looks like rain; we're going to have rain; **prévision du t.,** weather forecast; **une robe couleur du t.,** a sky-blue dress. **3.** *Gram:* (*a*) tense; **t. primitifs,** principal parts (of a verb); (*b*) **adverbes de t.,** adverbs of time. **4.** (*a*) *Mus:* measure, beat; **mesure à trois t.,** three-four time; (*b*) *Mil: etc:* **exercice en trois t.,** exercise in three motions; **au t.!** as you were! **au t. pour moi,** my mistake! *Fenc:* **coup de t.,** time thrust, feint; (*c*) *I.C.E:* **moteur à deux, à quatre, t.,** two-stroke, four-stroke, engine; (*d*) *Surg: etc:* stage (of operation, of labour, *NAm:* labor).

tenable [tənabl̩] *a.* (*usu. with negation*) **1.** *Mil: etc:* tenable, defensible (position). **2.** bearable (state of affairs); **par cette chaleur, le bureau n'est pas t.,** in this heat the office is unbearable.

tenace [tənas] *a.* tenacious; obstinate (pers.); clinging (perfume); fast (colour, *NAm:* color); dogged, stubborn (will, purpose); retentive (memory); persistent (prejudice, illness); **espoir t.,** fond hope; **les vieilles habitudes sont tenaces,** old habits die hard.

tenacement [tənasmɑ̃] *adv.* stubbornly.

ténacité [tenasite] *n.f.* tenacity; stubbornness; persistence.

tenaille [tənaj] *n.f. Tls:* (*a*) tongs; **t. à vis,** hand vice; **t. de cordonnier,** shoemaker's nippers; (*b*) *pl.* **tenailles,** pincers (for drawing nails); *Mil:* **manœuvre en tenailles,** pincer movement.

tenailler [tənaje] *v.tr.* to torture; **tenaillé par la faim, par le remords,** gnawed by hunger, remorse.

tenancier, -ière [tənɑ̃sje, -jɛr] *n.* **1.** *A:* holder (of land). **2.** tenant farmer. **3.** manager (of hotel, etc.); keeper (of brothel, gambling house).

tenant, -ante [tənɑ̃, -ɑ̃t] **1.** *a.* (*a*) **séance tenante,** (i) during the sitting; (ii) then and there, on the spot; (*b*) *Cost:* **chemise col t.,** shirt with collar attached. **2.** *n.* (*a*) champion, defender (of s.o., of an opinion); (*b*) *Sp:* holder (of title); (*c*) *n.m. Her:* supporter (of shield). **3.** *n.m.* (*of landed property*) **tout d'un (seul) t.,** continuous; all in one block; lying together; **tenants et aboutissants,** (i) adjacent parts (of estate); (ii) ins and outs, full details (of an affair); **les tenants et aboutissants de l'affaire,** the ins and outs of the case.

tendance [tɑ̃dɑ̃s] *n.f.* tendency, inclination; propensity; trend (of opinion); **tendances vers le communisme,** communist leanings; **avoir (une) t. à qch., à faire qch.,** to be inclined to sth., to do sth.; to have a tendency to sth., to do sth.; to be apt, liable, to do sth.

tendancieusement [tɑ̃dɑ̃sjøzmɑ̃] *adv.* tendentiously.

tendancieux, -ieuse [tɑ̃dɑ̃sjø, -jøz] *a.* tendentious; *Jur:* leading (question).

tender [tɑ̃dɛr] *n.m. Rail: Nau:* tender.

tendeur, -euse [tɑ̃dœr, -øz] **1.** *n.* (*a*) layer (of carpets); hanger (of tapestries); (*b*) setter, layer (of traps, snares). **2.** *n.m.* (*a*) *Tchn:* stretcher, tightener, tension rod; (wire) strainer; runner (of guy rope); *Cy:* **t. de chaîne,** chain adjuster, tightener; **t. à vis,** turnbuckle; (*b*) tension (device) (of sewing machine); (*c*) **t. pour chaussures,** shoe tree.

tendineux, -euse [tɑ̃dinø, -øz] *a. Anat:* tendinous; **viande tendineuse,** stringy meat.

tendinite [tɑ̃dinit] *n.f. Med:* tendinitis.

tendon [tɑ̃dɔ̃] *n.m. Anat:* tendon, sinew; **t. d'Achille,** Achilles tendon; **t. du jarret,** hamstring.

tendre¹ [tɑ̃dr̥] **1.** *a.* tender; (*a*) soft (stone, porcelain, wood, metal, grass, pencil, etc.); delicate (colour, *NAm:* color, etc.); new (bread); **viande t.,** tender meat; **peau t.,** sensitive, tender, skin; **avoir la peau t.,** to be thin-skinned, touchy; *Equit:* **cheval t. à l'éperon,** horse tender to the spur; (*b*) early (age, childhood); **dès ma plus t. enfance,** from my earliest youth; (*c*) fond, affectionate, loving; tender (heart); **ne pas être t.,** to be hard, severe; **il a le vin t.,** drink makes him sentimental. **2.** *n.m. F:* **avoir un t. pour qn,** to have a soft spot for s.o. **3.** *n.m. Cu:* **t. de tranche,** topside (of beef).

tendre² **1.** *v.tr.* (*a*) to stretch, tighten (a belt); to tighten (a violin string); to bend, draw (a bow); to set (a spring, a trap); (*b*) to fix up (tent, net, ropes, etc.); to spread (sail, net, etc.); to lay (carpet); to hang (wallpaper, tapestry); to pitch (tent); (*c*) to stretch out, hold out; **t. la main,** (i) to hold out one's hand; (ii) to beg; **t. le cou,** to crane one's neck; (*d*) to (over)strain; to stretch. **2.** *v.i.* to tend, lead (**à,** to); **vos paroles ne tendent qu'à le fâcher,** your words only tend to annoy him; **où tendent ces questions?** where are these questions leading? **nez tendant à l'aquilin,** nose inclined to be aquiline; (*of thg*) **t. à sa fin,** to be near its end; **les voyelles faibles tendent à disparaître,** there is a tendency for weak vowels to disappear. **3.** **se t.,** to become taut; (*of relations*) to become strained; (*of prices, etc.*) to harden, stiffen.

tendrement [tɑ̃drəmɑ̃] *adv.* tenderly, fondly, affectionately.

tendresse [tɑ̃drɛs] *n.f.* (*a*) tenderness; fondness, love; **avec t.,** fondly, lovingly; (*b*) *pl.* tokens of affection, caresses; (*c*) **tendresses royalistes,** royalist sympathies.

tendreté [tɑ̃drəte] *n.f.* tenderness (of food).

tendron [tɑ̃drɔ̃] *n.m.* **1.** *Bot:* tender shoot. **2.** *Cu:* tendron, gristle (of veal). **3.** *F:* very young, innocent girl.

tendu [tɑ̃dy] *a.* (*a*) stretched, taut, tight; *Ball: etc:* flat (trajectory); strained (relations); tense (situation); distended (stomach); **corde tendue,** (i) taut rope; (ii) *Gym:* tightrope; **chaîne mal tendue,** slack chain; **avoir les nerfs tendus,** to be tense, strung-up; **style t.,** strained, stilted, style; *St.Exch:* **prix tendus,** stiff, hard, firm, prices; (*b*) *Ling:* strong (sound); voiceless (consonant); (*c*) **main tendue,** outstretched hand; **politique de la main tendue,** policy of making friendly overtures.

ténèbres [tenɛbr̥] *n.f.pl.* darkness, gloom; **les t. de la nuit,** the shades of night; **le Prince des T.,** the Prince of Darkness; **t. de l'ignorance,** darkness of ignorance.

ténébreux, -euse [tenebrø, -øz] *a.* **1.** gloomy, dark, sombre (wood, prison, etc.). **2.** mysterious, sinister; obscure (style, period of history).

teneur¹, -euse [tənœr, -øz] *n.* **1.** *Typ:* **t. de copie,** copy holder. **2. t. de livres,** book-keeper.

teneur² *n.f.* **1.** (*a*) tenor, terms (of document, etc.); (*b*) tenor (of life). **2.** *Tchn:* amount, content, percentage; (*a*) *Ind: etc:* content; **t. en eau,** water content, moisture content; (*b*) *Miner: etc:* grade, tenor (of ore, metal, etc.); **minerai, acier, de haute t.,** high-grade ore, steel; (*c*) *Ch:* (standard) strength, titration (standard) (of solution); (*d*) *Atom.Ph:* **t. isotopique,** isotopic abundance.

ténia [tenja] *n.m. Med:* t(a)enia, tapeworm.

tenir [tənir] *v.* (*pr.p.* **tenant;** *p.p.* **tenu;** *pr.ind.* **je tiens, il tient, n. tenons, v. tenez, ils tiennent;** *pr.sub.* **je tienne, n. tenions;** *impf.* **je tenais;** *p.h.* **je tins, n. tînmes, v. tîntes, ils tinrent;** *p.sub.* **je tinsse, il tînt, n. tinssions;** *fu.* **je tiendrai) I.** *v.tr.* **1.** to hold; (*a*) to have hold of (s.o., sth.); **t. qch. à la main, sur ses genoux,** to hold sth. in one's hand, on one's lap; **ils se tenaient par la main,** they were holding hands; **se t. les côtes de rire,** to hold one's sides laughing; *F:* **t. un bon rhume,** to have a stinking cold; *v.i. P:* **qu'est-ce qu'il tient!** (i) he's completely sozzled! (ii) what an idiot! **je tiens mon homme,** I've got my man; **t. tout dans un coup d'œil,** to take in everything at a glance; **t. qn de près,** to keep s.o. under strict control; *Aut:* **t. bien la route,** to hold the road well; *Prov:* **un "tiens" vaut mieux que deux "tu l'auras"; mieux vaut t. que courir,** a bird in the hand is worth two in the bush; **tiens! tenez!** look! look here! **tenez, mon chien à moi . . .,** now, that dog of mine . . .; **tenez! (ceci est pour vous),** here you are! **tenez, ôtez-moi cela,** here, take this away; (*b*) to hold, contain, have capacity for (a certain quantity); **voiture qui tient six personnes,** *v.i.* **voiture où l'on tient à six,** car that takes, holds, six; *v.i.* **on tient douze à cette table,** this table seats twelve; **tous ces livres tiendront dans cette caisse,** all these books will easily fit, go, into this box; **tout ça tient en deux mots,** all that can be said in a couple of words; (*c*) to retain; **baril qui tient l'eau,** barrel that holds water, that is watertight; (*d*) **t. de,** to have, get, derive, (sth.) from; **j'en suis sûr; je le tiens de mon député,** I am sure of it; I have it from my M.P.; **il tient sa timidité de sa mère,** he gets his shy nature from his mother; (*e*) to keep, stock (groceries, etc.); (*f*) (*of partridge, etc.*) **elle en tient** (*i.e.* **du plomb**), she's winged; *F:* (*of pers.*) **il en tient,** he's had a nasty blow; *P:* **en t. une,** to be gloriously drunk. **2.** to keep, run (a shop, a school); to have charge of (the cash); **chambre bien tenue,** well kept, tidy, room; **Mlle X tenait le piano,** Miss X was at the piano; **le marché se tient le samedi,** the market is held on Saturdays. **3.** (*a*) to hold, maintain (opinion, certain line of conduct); to keep (one's word, promise); (*b*) to deliver (speech, etc.); (*c*) **t. qn en mépris, en grand respect,** to hold s.o. in contempt, in great esteem. **4.** to hold back, restrain (one's tongue, one's impatience); to control (children, a horse). **5.** (*a*) to hold, keep (in a certain position); **cette poutre tient le plafond,** that beam holds up the ceiling; **mon rhume me tient à la maison,** my cold is keeping me indoors; **il nous a tenus debout pendant deux heures,** he kept us standing for two hours; **t. qch. en état, en bon état,** to keep sth. in good order; **t. (qn) à l'œil,** to keep an eye on (s.o.); **cette visite m'a tenu longtemps,** this visit kept, delayed, me a long time; **tenez votre gauche, votre droite,** keep to the left, to the right; (*b*) to be confined to (one's room, one's bed); (*c*) **t. la mer,** (i) (*of ship*) to keep the sea; to hold on (in heavy weather); (ii) (*of country*) to be master, mistress, of the seas; *Aut:* **t. la route,** to hold the road; **capable, incapable, de t. la mer,** seaworthy, unseaworthy (ship). **6.** to occupy, take up (space); **vous tenez trop de place,** you are taking up too much room; **la table tient la moitié de la pièce,** the table occupies half the floor space; (*of car*) **t. toute la route,** to hog the road. **7. t. les yeux fermés,** to keep one's eyes shut; **t. qn captif,** to keep, hold, s.o. prisoner; **t. qn pour habile,** to think, consider, s.o. clever; **t. qch. comme établi,** to assume sth.; **tenez cela pour fait,** consider it done; **il se le tint pour dit,** he took the lesson to heart. **II.** *v.i.* **1.** (*a*) to hold; to adhere, hold on firmly; **clou qui tient bien,** nail that holds well; **la porte tient,** the door won't open; **vêtements qui ne tiennent plus (ensemble),** garments that won't hold together, that are falling to pieces; *F:* **cela tient comme poix,** it sticks like pitch; *F:* **ses pieds ne tiennent pas à terre,** he is never still for a minute; (*b*) to border on; to adjoin; **sa terre tient à la mienne,** his estate borders on mine; (*c*) to remain; **il ne tient plus sur ses jambes,** he is ready to drop (with fatigue); **elle ne pouvait t. en place,** she couldn't keep still. **2.** (*a*) **t. (bon, ferme),** to hold out, to stand fast; to resist; to hold on; to hold one's own; (*of cable, etc.*) to stand the strain, to hold; **tenez bon!** hold on! **votre argument ne tient guère,** your argument hardly stands up; **tenez bon, ferme!** (i) hold tight! *Nau:* (a)vast! (ii) never say die! **je n'y tiens plus,** I can't stand it any longer; (*b*) to last, endure; **ma mise en plis n'a pas tenu deux jours,** my set didn't last, stay in, two days; **le vent va t.,** the wind will last; **son commerce ne tiendra pas,** his business won't last; **couleur qui tient bien,** fast colour, *NAm:* color; **mon offre, le pari, tient toujours,** my offer, the bet, stands; (*c*) to sit, be held, take place; **le marché tient tous les samedis,** the market is held on Saturdays. **3. t. pour,** to hold for, be in favour, *NAm:* favor, of, stand up for (s.o., sth.); **je tiens pour la liberté,** I am all for liberty; **en t. pour qn,** to be fond of s.o.; to be in love with s.o.; **en t. pour son idée,** to stick to one's idea. **4. t. à qch.,** (*a*) to value, prize, sth.; **t. à la vie,** to value one's life; to cling to life; **t. à faire qch.,** to be bent on doing sth.; **je n'y tiens pas,** (i) I don't care for it; (ii) I would rather not; *F:* **je n'y tiens pas plus que cela,** I'm not keen on it; **je tiens à vous le dire,** I am anxious to tell you, I am making a point of telling you; **t. à ce qu'on fasse qch.,** to be anxious, insistent, that sth. should be done; **je tiens beaucoup à ce qu'il vienne,** I am very anxious that he should come, for him to come; **puisque vous y tenez,** since you are set on it; (*b*) to depend on, result from, sth.; to be due to sth.; **cela tient à son éducation,** that's the result, the fault, of his education; **à quoi cela tient-il?** what's the reason for it? what is it due to? **cela tient à ce que vous êtes Écossais,** that comes of your being Scottish; *impers.* **il ne tient qu'à vous de le faire,** it rests, lies, entirely with you to do it; **il ne tient qu'à vous que cela se fasse,** it depends entirely on you whether it is done; **qu'à cela ne tienne,** never mind that, that need be no obstacle; **s'il ne tient qu'à cela,** if that is all (the difficulty); **il n'a tenu à rien qu'il ne se noyât,** he was as near as could be to getting drowned. **5. t. de qn,** to take after s.o. (*cp.* I.1); **cela tient du miracle,** there is something miraculous about it; it sounds like a miracle; **cela tient de (la) famille,** it runs in the family; **avoir de qui t.,** to be of good stock; **il a de qui t.,** (i) blood will tell; (ii) *often Pej:* what's bred in the bone will come out in the flesh. **III. se tenir 1.** (*a*) to keep, be, remain, stand, sit; **se t. chez soi,** to stay, remain, at home; **tenez-vous là!** stand there! stay where you are! don't move! **tenez-vous droit,** (i) sit up, sit straight; (ii) stand (up) straight; **se t. tranquille,** to keep quiet; **se bien, mal, t. à cheval,** to sit a horse well, badly, to have a good, a poor, seat; **tiens-toi,** (i) be on your best behaviour, *NAm:* behavior; (ii) behave yourself; *F:* **on sait se t. avec les femmes,** I, we, know how to behave in the presence of ladies; **tenez-vous bien! vous n'avez qu'à vous bien t.!** you'd better watch your step; **tenez-vous bien, la voiture a disparu,** prepare yourself for a shock; the car has disappeared; (*b*) **se t. à qch.,** to hold on to sth.; (*on bus, etc.*) **tenez-vous bien!** hold tight! (*c*) **la boisson, la misère, le crime, tout cela se tient,** drink, poverty, crime, all these go together; **ses arguments se tiennent (bien),** his arguments hold together. **2.** to contain oneself; **il ne se tient pas de joie,** he cannot contain himself for joy; **je ne pouvais me t. de rire,** I couldn't help laughing; **je ne pus me t. de l'embrasser,** I couldn't resist giving her a kiss. **3. se, s'en, t. à (qch.),** to keep to (sth); to adhere to, abide by (a decision, a treaty); **se t. à ce qu'on a décidé,** to stick to, abide by, what was decided; **s'en t. à qch.,** to confine oneself to sth.; to be satisfied, contented, with sth.; **il ne s'en tint pas là,** he did not stop at that; **tenons-nous-en là,** let it go at that; **je ne sais pas à quoi m'en t.,** I don't know what to believe; I don't know how I stand.

tennis [tenis] *n.m.* **1.** (lawn) tennis; **t. de table,** table tennis. **2. (court de) t.,** (lawn) tennis court.

tennisman, *pl.* **tennismen** [tenisman, tenismɛn] *n.m. F:* tennis player.

tenon [tənɔ̃] *n.m.* **1.** *Carp:* tenon. **2.** *Mec.E:* lug. **3.** nut (of anchor). **4.** *Dent:* pivot (of crowned tooth).

ténor [tenɔr] *n.m.* (*a*) *Mus:* tenor; (*b*) *F: Pol: Sp: etc:* star performer.

tenrec [tɑ̃rɛk] *n.m. Z:* tenrec, tanrec.

tenseur [tɑ̃sœr] *a. & n.m.* **1.** (*a*) *Anat:* **(muscle) t.,** tensor; (*b*) *n.m. Mth:* tensor. **2.** *Tchn:* = TENDEUR 2.

tensioactif, -ive [tɑ̃sjɔaktif, -iv] *a. & n.m. Ch:* (*a*) surface-active (agent); (*b*) wetting (agent).

tension [tɑ̃sjɔ̃] *n.f.* **1.** (*a*) tension; stretching (of muscles, etc.); tightening (of guyrope, etc.); **écrou à t.,** tightening nut; (*b*) *Mec:* **t. de rupture,** breaking strain, stress; *Metall:* **t. de cisaillement,** shear stress. **2.** (*a*) tightness (of rope, etc.); tenseness (of relations, etc.); *Ph:* **t. superficielle,** surface tension; *Mec.E:* **t. de courroie,** belt tension; **acier à haute t.,** high-tensile steel; **période de t. internationale,** period of international tension; **t. des esprits,** tenseness of attitude; (*b*) *St.Exch:* hardness, stiffness, firmness (of prices). **3.** (*a*) pressure (of steam, etc.); *Med:* **t. artérielle, t. du sang,** blood pressure; *F:* **avoir, faire, de la t.,** to suffer from high blood pressure; (*b*) *El: Elcs:* voltage; tension; **basse, haute, t.,** low, high, voltage; **t. nulle,** zero voltage; zero potential; **sans t.,** dead; **mettre sous t.,** to apply the voltage to, to switch on (circuit, etc.); **fil sous t.,** live, charged, wire; **montage des piles en t.,** connection of batteries in series.

tensoriel, -ielle [tɑ̃sɔrjɛl] *a. Mth:* tensorial.

tentaculaire [tɑ̃takylɛr] *a. Z:* tentacular; **villes tentaculaires,** sprawling towns.

tentacule [tɑ̃takyl] *n.m. Z: Bot:* tentacle.

tentant [tɑ̃tɑ̃] *a.* tempting, alluring, enticing; attractive (offer).

tentateur, -trice [tɑ̃tatœr, -tris] **1.** *n.* tempter, *f.* temptress; **le T.,** the Tempter. **2.** *a.* tempting.

tentatif, -ive [tɑ̃tatif, -iv] **1.** *a.* tentative. **2.** *n.f.* **tentative,** attempt, endeavour, *NAm:* endeavor; bid; **t. d'évasion,** attempt to escape; escape bid; **t. d'assassinat,** attempted murder; **t. de résistance,** attempt to resist.

tentation [tɑ̃tasjɔ̃] *n.f.* temptation **(de faire qch.,** to do sth.); **je n'ai pas pu résister à la t. de lui faire la grimace,** I couldn't resist making a face at him.

tente[1] [tɑ̃t] *n.f.* (*a*) tent; **t. conique,** bell tent; *Med:* **t. à oxygène,** oxygen tent; **coucher sous la t.,** to sleep under canvas; **se retirer dans, sous, sa t.,** to sulk in one's tent (like Achilles); (*b*) booth (at fair, market); (*c*) *Nau:* awning.

tente[2] *n.f. Surg: A:* tent, (linen) probe.

tenter [tɑ̃te] *v.tr.* **1.** (*a*) *A: & B:* to tempt, prove, try; to put (s.o.) to the test; (*b*) **t. la chance, la fortune,** to try one's luck; **t. la Providence,** to tempt Providence. **2.** to tempt (s.o.); **se laisser t.,** to allow oneself to be tempted; to yield to temptation; **je fus tenté d'essayer,** I was tempted to try. **3.** to attempt, try; **t. d'inutiles efforts pour . . .,** to make useless attempts to . . .; **t. une expérience,** to try an experiment; **t. de,** *occ.* **à, faire qch.,** to try, endeavour, *NAm:* endeavor, to do sth.

tenture [tɑ̃tyr] *n.f.* **1.** hanging (of tapestry, etc.). **2.** (*a*) hangings, tapestry; (*b*) **(papier-)t.,** wallpaper; (*c*) *Fr.C:* curtain, *NAm:* drape.

tenu [təny] **1.** *a. & p.p.* (*a*) kept; **bien t.,** well kept, tidy (house, etc.); neat, trim (garden, etc.); **mal t.,** badly kept, ill-kept, neglected, uncared for (child, garden, etc.); untidy (house, etc.); (*b*) **être t. de, à, faire qch.,** to be bound, obliged, to do sth.; **les passants sont tenus de marcher sur le trottoir,** pedestrians must walk on the pavement; **le médecin est t. au secret professionnel,** the doctor is bound by professional secrecy; (*c*) *St.Exch:* firm, hard (prices); (*d*) (*of a bet*) **t.!** done! you're on! **2.** *n.m. Box:* hold; *Sp:* holding (of the ball).

ténu [teny] *a.* tenuous, thin; slender; fine (thread, etc.); light (mist); thin (voice); subtle, fine (distinction); thin, watery (fluid, etc.).

tenue [təny] *n.f.* **1.** (*a*) keeping, holding (of position etc.); (*b*) sitting, session (of an assembly, etc.); (*c*) keeping, managing, running (of shop, house, etc.); **t. des livres,** book-keeping; *Bank:* (*Giro account*) **t. de compte,** service charge; *Mch:* **t. des chaudières,** care of the boilers. **2.** (*a*) bearing, behaviour, *NAm:* behavior; carriage; **Paul, de la t.!** Paul, behave yourself! **un peu de t.!** mind your manners! **la haute t. de ce périodique,** the high standard maintained by this periodical; *Equit:* **bonne, mauvaise, t.,** good, poor, seat; (*b*) *Aer:* **t. en l'air, t. aéronautique,** behaviour in the air; airworthiness; *Av:* **t. en vol,** attitude of flight; *Aut:* **t. en côte,** climbing ability; **t. de route,** road-holding qualities. **3.** dress; clothes; **t. de soirée,** evening dress; *Mil: etc:* mess dress; **t. de ville,** (i) (woman's) town clothes; (ii) (man's) lounge suit; **elle était en t. de ville,** she was dressed for going out; **t. de loisirs, de tous les jours,** casuals; *F:* **je vais me mettre en t.,** I'm going to change; *Mil: etc:* **en t.,** in uniform; **t. de combat,** battledress; **t. civile, bourgeoise,** plain clothes, civilian clothes, *F:* civvies, mufti. **4.** *Mus:* holding note, sustained note. **5.** steadiness, firmness (of prices); tone (of the market).

ténuité [tenɥite] *n.f.* tenuity, tenuousness; thinness; slenderness; fineness (of sand, of distinction, etc.); wateriness (of liquid).

tenure [tənyr] *n.f.* **1.** tenure. **2.** holding, estate.

ter [tɛr] *Lt.adv.* (*a*) *Mus:* ter; (*b*) (*in an address*) **numéro 5 t.,** No. 5b, *occ.* 5c.

tératogène [teratɔʒɛn] *a. Med:* teratogen(et)ic.

tératologie [teratɔlɔʒi] *n.f.* teratology.

tercet [tɛrsɛ] *n.m. Pros:* tercet, triplet.

térébelle [terebɛl] *n.f.*, **terebellum¹** [terebɛlɔm] *n.m. Ann:* terebella.
terebellum² [terebɛlɔm] *n.m. Moll:* terebellum.
térébenthine [terebɑ̃tin] *n.f.* turpentine.
térébinthe [terebɛ̃t] *n.m. Bot:* terebinth; turpentine tree.
térébrant [terebrɑ̃] *a.* (*a*) terebrant, boring (insect, etc.); (*b*) *Med:* probing, boring (pain); deep (ulceration).
tergal¹, -aux [tɛrgal, -o] *a. Z:* tergal.
tergal² *n.m. R.t.m: Tex:* Terylene.
tergiversation [tɛrʒivɛrsasjɔ̃] *n.f.* tergiversation, shuffling; beating about the bush; evasiveness.
tergiverser [tɛrʒivɛrse] *v.i.* to equivocate; to beat about the bush.
terme¹ [tɛrm] *n.m.* **1.** *Rom.Ant: Sculp:* terminus. **2.** term, end, limit (of life, journey, race, etc.); **toucher à son t.,** to be near one's end; **t. d'un mandat,** date of completion of a mandate; **mettre un t. à qch.,** to put a term, an end, a stop, to sth.; **il y a t. à tout,** there is an end to everything; **mener qch. à bon t.,** to bring sth. to a successful conclusion; to carry sth. through. **3.** (*a*) (appointed) time; (*of pregnant woman*) **être à t.,** to have reached her time; **avant t.,** prematurely; **accouchement avant t.,** premature birth; *Mil: etc:* **engagement à long t.,** long service; **dans le t. de trois mois,** within three months; **t. de rigueur,** latest time, latest date; **marché à t.,** (i) *Com:* terminal market; *St.Exch:* settlement market; (ii) transactions on credit; *Com:* forward, terminal, transaction; *St.Exch:* settlement bargain; **avance à long t.,** long-term advance; (*of bills*) **à court t., à long t.,** short-dated, long-dated; **argent à court t.,** money at short notice, at call; *St.Exch:* **le t.,** the settlement; **valeurs à t.,** securities dealt in for the account; **acheter à t.,** (i) *Com:* to buy on credit; (ii) *St.Exch:* to buy for the settlement, for the account; *Ind: etc:* **prévisions à court t., à long t.,** short-range, long-range, forecasts; (*b*) delay (for payment); **demander un t. de grâce,** to ask for time to pay; (*c*) instalment; **payable à deux termes,** payable in two instalments. **4.** (*a*) quarter (of rent); term; (*b*) quarter's rent; *F:* **je suis un t. en retard,** I owe a quarter's rent; (*c*) quarter day.
terme² *n.m.* **1.** term, expression; **t. de métier,** technical term; **t. de médecine, de droit,** medical term, legal term; **employer les termes propres,** to use the appropriate terms; **il m'a dit en termes propres, en termes exprès, que . . .,** he told me in so many words that . . .; **en d'autres termes,** in other words; **il n'a pas ménagé ses termes,** he didn't mince his words; **il m'a parlé de vous en très bons termes,** he spoke very well, favourably, *NAm:* favorably, of you; **termes contradictoires,** contradiction in terms; *Mth:* **t. d'une progression,** term of a progression; **termes d'une équation,** terms of an equation. **2.** *pl.* wording (of clause, etc.); terms, conditions; **termes d'un contrat,** terms of a contract. **3.** *pl.* terms, footing; **être en bons termes avec qn,** to be on good terms, on friendly terms, with s.o.
terminaison [tɛrminɛzɔ̃] *n.f.* termination; *Anat:* (nerve) ending; *Gram:* **t. masculine,** masculine termination, ending.
terminal, -ale, -aux [tɛrminal, -o] **1.** *a.* terminal; final; *Sch:* **les classes terminales** = the sixth forms; *Cmptr:* **marque terminale,** end mark. **2.** *n.f. Sch: F:* **terminale** = upper sixth (form). **3.** *n.m. Cmptr:* terminal (unit). **4.** *n.m. Petr:* pipeline terminal.
terminer [tɛrmine] *v.* to terminate. **1.** *v.tr.* to end, finish, to bring (war, speech, etc.) to an end, to a close; to settle, conclude (bargain, etc.); to complete (piece of work); to wind up (meeting, etc.) (**par,** with); to end (one's days); **il faut en t.,** we must make an end; **nous en avons terminé avec ça,** we have finally finished with it; **t. court,** to come to an abrupt ending; *W.Tel:* **terminé!** out! **2. se t.,** to end, to come to an end; to turn out (well, badly); **la guerre venait de se t.,** the war was just over; **mot qui se termine par une voyelle,** word that ends in a vowel.
terminologie [tɛrminɔlɔʒi] *n.f.* terminology.
terminus [tɛrminys] **1.** *n.m.* (railway, coach, etc.) terminus. **2.** *a.inv.* **gare t.,** terminus.
termite [tɛrmit] *n.m. Ent:* termite, white ant.
termitière [tɛrmitjɛr] *n.f. Ent:* termitarium.
ternaire [tɛrnɛr] *a. Mth: Ch:* ternary; *Mus:* triple (time).
terne [tɛrn] *a.* dull, lustreless, *NAm:* lusterless (metal); drab (clothes, existence); dull, lifeless (eyes); flat (voice); dull, flat (style).
ternir [tɛrnir] *v.tr.* to tarnish (metal); to dull, deaden; to damage, tarnish (a reputation); **l'argenterie se ternit,** the silver is getting tarnished.
ternissure [tɛrnisyr] *n.f.* (*a*) tarnished appearance; dull spot (on metal, etc.); (*b*) blemish, stain (on reputation, etc.).
terrafungine [tɛrafɔ̃ʒin] *n.f. Pharm:* oxytetracycline; *R.t.m:* Terramycin.
terrain [tɛrɛ̃] *n.m.* **1.** (*a*) (piece of) ground, plot of land; **terrains à bâtir,** development site; building land; **terrains vagues,** waste ground; (*b*) *Geog: etc:* country, ground; **relief du t.,** relief; (*c*) soil, ground; **t. gras,** rich soil; (*d*) (cricket, football) field; (golf) course, links; **t. de jeux,** (i) playground; (ii) playing field; *Av:* **t. d'atterrissage,** landing strip, airstrip; **t. de manœuvres,** drill ground, parade ground; **aller sur le t.,** to fight a duel; **rester sur le t.,** (i) to be killed (in a duel); (ii) to be defeated; *Mil: etc:* **gagner du t.,** to gain ground; **perdre, céder, du t.,** to lose ground; **sonder, tâter, le t.,** to see how the land lies; **être sur son t.,** to be on familiar ground; **je ne suis plus sur mon t.,** I'm out of my depth; **préparer le t.,** to pave the way; *Cin:* **t. (de studio),** (studio) lot; *Ind: etc:* **sur le t.,** in the field; **travaux sur le t.,** fieldwork. **2.** *Geol:* (rock) formation.
terrarium [tɛrarjɔm] *n.m.* terrarium.
terrasse [tɛras] *n.f.* (*a*) terrace; bank; **jardin en t.,** terraced garden; *Geog:* **cultures en terrasses,** terrace cultivation; (*b*) **nous étions assis à la t.,** we were sitting outside (the café); (*c*) *Const:* veranda, terrace, balcony; **nous étions assis sur la t.,** we were sitting on the terrace, the balcony; **(toit en) t.,** flat roof.
terrassement [tɛrasmɑ̃] *n.m.* **1.** banking, digging (of earth). **2.** earthwork, embankment.
terrasser [tɛrase] *v.tr.* **1.** to work the soil of (vineyard, etc.). **2.** (*a*) to lay (s.o.) low; *F:* to down (s.o.); **t. un adversaire,** to bring down, *Wr:* to throw, an opponent; (*b*) to overwhelm, dismay, crush; **terrassé par le chagrin,** prostrated with grief.
terrassier [tɛrasje] *n.m.* navvy, labourer, *NAm:* laborer.
terre [tɛr] *n.f.* **1.** earth; (*a*) the world; **être encore sur t.,** to be still in the land of the living; **revenir sur t.,** to come down to earth; **qui a les pieds sur t.,** down-to-earth; (*b*) ground, land; **t. ferme,** continent, mainland; **armée, forces, de t.,** land forces; **pénétrer dans les terres,** to go inland; **basses terres,** lowlands; **hautes terres,** highlands; **tremblement de t.,** earthquake; **à t., par t.,** on the ground, to the ground; **frapper qn à t.,** to strike s.o. when he is down; **tomber par t.,** to fall down (from standing position); **tomber à t.,** to fall down (from height); **être assis, couché, par t.,** to sit, lie, on the ground; **mettre pied à t.,** to set foot to ground; to dismount (from horse); **attaquer une ville par t. et par mer,** to attack a town by land and sea; **tactique, politique, de la t. brûlée,** scorched earth policy; **appuyer son oreille contre t.,** to put

one's ear to the ground; **sous t.,** underground; **être sous t., en t.,** to be in one's grave; (*c*) *El:* **mettre, relier, raccorder, à la t.,** to earth, *NAm:* to ground; *Nau:* (*of ship*) **être à t.,** to be aground, ashore; **mettre qn à t.,** to land s.o.; to put s.o. ashore; **descendre à t., prendre t.,** to land, go ashore; **perdre t.,** to lose sight of land; **t. (en vue)!** land ho! *adj.phr.* **t. à t.,** matter-of-fact, down-to-earth. **2.** soil, land; **cultiver la t.,** to cultivate the soil; **t. grasse,** rich soil. **3.** (*a*) estate, property; **il a une t. en Normandie,** he has an estate in Normandy; (*b*) territory; **terres étrangères,** foreign countries, lands; **la T. Sainte,** the Holy Land; **La T. de Feu,** Tierra del Fuego. **4.** (*a*) loam, clay; **t. végétale, franche, naturelle,** mould, *NAm:* mold; loam; **sol en t. battue,** mud floor; **t. à potier,** potter's clay; **t. de pipe,** pipeclay; **pipe en t.,** clay pipe; **t. cuite,** (i) baked clay; (ii) terracotta; *Art:* **une t. cuite,** a terracotta; **cruche de, en, t.,** earthenware jar; **t. de Chine, à porcelaine,** kaolin; **t. à poêle,** fireclay; (*b*) *Ch:* **terres rares,** rare earths.

terreau, -eaux [tɛro] *n.m. Hort:* compost.

Terre-Neuve [tɛrnœv] **1.** *Pr.n.f. Geog:* Newfoundland. **2.** *n.m.inv.* **un t.-n.,** a Newfoundland (dog).

terre-neuvien, -ienne [tɛrnœvjɛ̃, -jɛn] *Geog:* (*a*) *a.* Newfoundland; (*b*) *n.* Newfoundlander; *F:* Newfie; *pl. terre-neuviens, -iennes.*

terre-neuvier, -ière [tɛrnœvje, -jɛr] **1.** *a.* Newfoundland (fisherman, etc.). **2.** *n.m.* (*a*) Newfoundland fisherman; (*b*) Newfoundland fishing vessel, banker; Newfoundlander; *pl. terre-neuviers.*

terre-plein [tɛrplɛ̃] *n.m.* earth platform; terrace; raised strip of ground (with trees, etc.); *NAm:* boulevard (running along a street, etc.); (*on road*) **t.-p. de stationnement,** layby; **t.-p. central,** central reservation; *NAm:* median strip, *U.S:* mall; **t.-p. circulaire,** central island (of roundabout); *pl. terre-pleins.*

terrer [tɛre] **1.** *v.tr.* (*a*) *Hort:* to earth up (tree, plant); (*b*) to spread earth over (ground); (*c*) *Tex:* to full (cloth). **2. se t.,** *Ven: & Fig:* to go to earth; *Mil:* to entrench oneself.

terrestre [tɛrɛstr̥] *a.* (*a*) ground (plant); land (animal); earthly, worldly (thoughts, etc.); (*b*) **rotation t.,** rotation of the earth; (*c*) **paradis t.,** earthly paradise; *Mil:* **effectifs terrestres,** land forces.

terreur [tɛrœr] *n.f.* **1.** (*a*) terror; dread; **fou de t.,** wild with fear; **être dans la t.,** to be in terror; **t. du noir,** fear of the dark; (*b*) **gouverner par la t.,** to rule by terror; *Fr.Hist:* **la T.,** the (Reign of) Terror (1793). **2.** (*a*) (*pers.*) terror (of the town, etc.); **il est la t. de ses ennemis,** he is an object of dread to his enemies; (*b*) *F:* gangster, thug.

terreux, -euse [tɛrø, -øz] *a.* (*a*) earthy (matter, taste, smell); (*b*) grubby (hands); muddy (complexion, etc.); sickly (face); gritty (lettuce).

terrible [tɛribl̥] *a.* (*a*) terrible, terrifying; appalling (catastrophe); (*b*) dreadful (cold); terrific (thunderstorm); awful (weather, temper); **enfant t.,** enfant terrible; (*c*) *F:* **c'est un type t.,** he's terrific, great, incredible.

terriblement [tɛribləmɑ̃] *adv.* terribly, dreadfully; frightfully.

terrien, -ienne [tɛrjɛ̃, -jɛn] **1.** *a.* (*a*) possessing land; landed (proprietor); (*b*) inland; terrestrial; (*c*) country; rural; (*d*) of the earth. **2.** *n.* (*a*) landowner; landed proprietor; (*b*) *Nau:* landsman; (*c*) countryman, countrywoman; (*d*) earthman, earthwoman.

terrier¹ [tɛrje] *n.m.* burrow, hole (of rabbit, etc.); earth (of fox); set (of badger).

terrier², -ière [tɛrje, -jɛr] *a. & n.* **(chien) t., (chienne) terrière,** terrier (dog, bitch).

terrifiant [tɛrifjɑ̃] *a.* terrifying.

terrifier [tɛrifje] *v.tr.* (*impf. & pr.sub.* **n. terrifiions, v. terrifiiez**) to terrify.

terrine [tɛrin] *n.f.* (*a*) earthenware vessel, pan (for milk, etc.); (*b*) (*pot or pâté*) terrine.

terrir [tɛrir] *v.i.* **1.** (*of turtles*) to go ashore (to lay eggs). **2.** *Fish:* **poissons qui terrissent,** fish living in coastal waters.

territoire [tɛritwar] *n.m.* territory (of state, *Nat. Hist:* of bird, animal); district, area, or region under jurisdiction.

territorial, -aux [tɛritɔrjal, -o] **1.** *a.* territorial (tax, army, waters). **2.** *Mil.Hist:* *F:* (*a*) *n.m.* territorial (soldier); (*b*) *n.f.* **la territoriale,** the territorial army.

territorialité [tɛritɔrjalite] *n.f.* territoriality.

terroir [tɛrwar] *n.m. Agr:* soil; (*of wine, etc.*) **goût de t.,** tang of the soil, native tang; **accent du t.,** local brogue.

terroriser [tɛrɔrize] *v.tr.* to terrorize.

terrorisme [tɛrɔrism] *n.m.* (*a*) terrorism; (*b*) terrorist régime.

terroriste [tɛrɔrist] *a. & n.* terrorist.

tertiaire [tɛrsjɛr] **1.** *a.* tertiary; *Pol.Ec:* **secteur t.,** tertiary industries. **2.** *n.m. Geol:* the Tertiary. **3.** *n. R.C.Ch:* tertiary.

tertio [tɛrsjo] *adv.* thirdly.

tertre [tɛrtr̥] *n.m.* hillock, mound; knoll; *Archeol:* **t. funéraire,** barrow, tumulus.

tes [te] *poss.a.pl. see* TON¹.

tesson [tesɔ̃] *n.m.* potsherd, fragment.

test¹ [tɛst] *n.m. Z:* test (of echinoderm, etc.).

test² *n.m. Med: etc:* test, trial; **t. professionnel,** vocational, trade, occupational, test.

testament¹ [tɛstamɑ̃] *n.m.* (*a*) will, testament; **absence de t.,** intestacy; **ceci est mon t.,** this is my last will and testament; **mourir sans t.,** to die intestate; *F:* **il peut faire son t.,** he may as well make his will; (*b*) *Fig:* artist's, statesman's, testament.

testament² *n.m. B:* (Old, New) Testament.

testamentaire [tɛstamɑ̃tɛr] *a.* **disposition t.,** clause (of a will); **exécuteur, -trice, t.,** executor, executrix.

testateur, -trice [tɛstatœr, -tris] *n.* testator, testatrix; *Jur:* devisor.

tester¹ [tɛste] *v.i.* to make one's will.

tester² *v.tr.* to test.

testiculaire [tɛstikylɛr] *a. Anat:* testicular.

testicule [tɛstikyl] *n.m. Anat:* testicle; testis.

testimonial, -aux [tɛstimɔnjal, -o] *a. Jur:* (proof) by witnesses, oral (evidence).

testostérone [tɛstɔsterɔn] *n.f. Biol: Physiol:* testosterone.

têt [tɛ] *n.m.* **1.** *A:* potsherd. **2.** *Ch:* (*a*) **t. à gaz,** beehive shelf; (*b*) **t. à rôtir,** roasting crucible.

tétanie [tetani] *n.f. Med:* tetany.

tétanique [tetanik] *Med:* **1.** *a.* tetanic. **2.** *n.* (*pers.*) tetanus subject.

tétaniser [tetanize] *v.tr. Med:* to tetanize (s.o.).

tétanos [tetanos, -ɔs] *n.m. Med:* tetanus, lockjaw.

têtard [tɛtar] *n.m.* **1.** (*a*) tadpole; (*b*) *P:* child, son. **2.** *Arb:* pollard.

tête [tɛt] *n.f.* head. **1.** (*a*) **de la t. aux pieds,** from head to foot, from top to toe; **dépasser qn de la t.,** to stand head and shoulders above s.o.; **t. nue,** bareheaded; **vieillard à t. grise,** grey-headed old man; *F:* **une grosse t.,** an intellectual, a highbrow; **monstre à deux têtes,** two-headed monster; **corps sans t.,** headless body; *F:* **faire la t.,** to sulk; *F:* **faire sa t.,** to give oneself airs; *Ven:* **faire t.,** to stand at bay; **faire, tenir, t. à qn,** to stand up to s.o.; to oppose s.o.; **faire, tenir, t. au malheur,** to bear up against misfortune; **tenir t. à l'orage,** to confront the storm; *F:* to face the music; **les nuages qui flottent sur nos têtes,** the clouds overhead; **endetté par-dessus la t.,** up to the eyes in debt; **j'en ai par-dessus la t.,** I can't stand it any longer; **la t. en bas,** head downwards; (*of thg*) upside down; **la t. la première,** head foremost; head first; **tomber sur la t.,** (i) to fall on one's face; (ii) *P:* to go mad, crackers; **ne (pas) savoir où donner de la t.,** not to know which way to turn; **t. couronnée,** crowned head; **payer tant par t.,** *F:* **par t. de pipe,** to pay so much a head; **dîner t. à t.,** to dine tête-à-tête; **mettre tous ses biens sur la t. de sa femme,** to settle all one's property on one's wife; **il y va de votre t.,** your life is at stake; **ça va lui en coûter la t.,** it is going to cost him his life; **j'en donnerais ma t. à couper que . . .,** I'll bet, stake, anything you like that . . .; **signe de t.,** nod (of the head); **mal de t.,** headache; **avoir mal à la t.,** to have a headache; **t. chauve,** bald head; **t. ronde,** (i) bullet head; *Hist:* Roundhead; **à t. ronde,** bullet-headed; *Fb:* **faire une t.,** to head the ball; *Swim:* **piquer une t.,** to take a header, to dive; *Gym: Mil:* **t. (à) droite!** eyes right! *Num:* **t. d'une médaille,** obverse of a medal; *A:* **t. ou pile?** heads or tails? (*b*) head of hair; **se laver la t.,** to wash one's hair; (*c*) face, appearance; *Th:* **se faire la t. d'un rôle,** to make up for a part; *F:* **faire une t.,** to pull a long face, to look glum; **je ne sais pas quelle t. il fera,** I don't know how he will take it; **faire la t. à qn,** (i) to frown at s.o.; (ii) to be sulky with s.o.; **faire une t. de circonstance,** to put on an expression to suit the occasion; **je connais cette t.-là,** I know that face; *P:* **t. d'imbécile!** you idiot! you clot! (*d*) head (of animal, fish, bird, etc.); jowl (of fish); *Vet:* **t. noire,** blackhead; (*e*) *Nau:* (*of ship*) **faire t. sur son ancre,** to be brought up by her anchor; (*f*) *Art: Sculp:* **t. plate,** beakhead; (*g*) fancy headdress. **2.** headpiece, brains, mind; **une pareille idée ne me serait jamais passée par la t.,** such an idea would never have entered my head; **se creuser la t.,** to rack one's brains; **avoir de la t.,** to have a good head on one's shoulders; **c'est une femme de t.,** she's a capable woman; **avoir la t. légère,** to be irresponsible, featherbrained; **avoir la t. dure,** to be (i) stupid, thickheaded, (ii) pigheaded; **c'est une t. de mule,** *F:* **de pioche, de cochon,** *P:* **de lard,** he's, she's, pigheaded, as stubborn as a mule; *F:* **c'est une t. à gifles, à claques,** he just asks for it; **il s'est mis dans la t. d'écrire un roman,** he has set his mind on writing a novel; **avoir qch. dans la t.,** to have sth. on the brain; **je l'ai en t.,** I'm bearing it in mind; **ça m'est sorti de la t.,** I've forgotten, it's gone out of my head; **il a quelque chose en t.,** he's planning something, *F:* he's up to something; **forte t.,** strong-minded person; **mauvaise t.,** rebellious person; unruly boy, etc.; **faire la mauvaise t.,** to be a rebel; **t. chaude,** hothead; **c'est une t. brûlée,** he has a bit of the devil in him; **travail de t.,** brainwork; **calculer de t.,** to reckon in one's head; **calcul de t.,** mental arithmetic; **en faire à sa t.,** to go one's own way; **il n'en fait qu'à sa t.,** he does exactly what he pleases; **avoir sa petite t. à soi,** to have a mind of one's own; **idée de derrière la t.,** idea at the back of one's mind; **où ai-je la t.!** what am I thinking about! **conserver sa t.,** to keep one's head; to remain calm; **est-ce que vous perdez la t.?** have you taken leave of your senses? **ne perdez pas la t.,** don't get flurried, excited; **faire perdre la t. à un candidat,** to fluster a candidate; **c'était à perdre la t.,** it was bewildering; **avoir toute sa t.,** to have one's wits about one; **il a encore toute sa t.,** his faculties are unimpaired; **il n'avait plus sa t. à lui,** he was no longer in his right mind; **il a la t. montée,** his blood is up; **à t. reposée,** at one's leisure; **il faut ne rien faire qu'à t. reposée,** we must do nothing without thinking it out carefully. **3.** (*a*) leader (of society, establishment); (*b*) summit, crown, top (of volcano, tree, etc.); head, top (of book); *Nau: Oc:* **t. de roche,** rock summit; *I.C.E:* **soupapes en t.,** overhead valves; *Bookb:* **doré en t.,** gilt-topped; *Typ:* **blanc de t.,** margin at the head of a book; **ligne de t.,** headline; **t. de chapitre,** chapter heading; (*c*) loaf, head (of cabbage); (*d*) *Anat:* apophysis (of the femur); head (of the humerus); **t. du condyle,** condyle head; (*e*) *Tchn:* head (of violin, mast, nail, pin, rivet, screw, etc.); butt (of a plank); *Furn:* **t. de lit,** bed head; **t. (de rivet) ronde, cylindrique, plate,** cheese-head (of rivet); **t. (de rivet) hémisphérique,** cup head (of rivet); *Tls: Mec.E:* **t. d'un marteau,** (i) head, (ii) face, of a hammer; **t. de hache,** axe head; **t. de benne,** grab head; **t. de cabestan,** drum head; **t. de flèche,** jib head (of crane); *Mch.Tls:* **t. porte-outil,** tool head; **t. porte-foret, t. de perçage,** drill(ing) head; **t. porte-fraise, t. de fraisage,** cutter head, milling head; **t. porte-segments,** grinding attachment (of grinding machine); **t. filière,** die head (of threading machine); *Min:* **t. de sonde,** casing head; *Petr:* **t. d'injection,** swivel; **t. inclinable,** tilting head (of machine tool, of camera or instrument stand); *Sm.a:* **t. mobile,** bolt head (of rifle); (*f*) **t. d'électrode,** electrode tip; **t. de câble,** cable terminal; *Elcs:* **t. d'effacement,** erasing head (of tape recorder, etc.); **t. d'enregistrement, t. enregistreuse,** record(ing) head (of computer, tape recorder, record player); **t. de lecture,** (i) *Cin:* sound head; (ii) reading, read, play-back, head (of computer); (iii) *Rec:* tape reader; **t. magnétique,** magnetic head; **t. sonore,** sound head; *Cmptr:* **t. d'écriture,** writing, write, head; (*g*) *Ball:* **t. (de fusée),** warhead; **t. nucléaire,** nuclear warhead; **t. chercheuse,** homing device, head (of missile, etc.); (*h*) front place; head (of line); **colonne de t.,** leading column; **taxi en t. de file,** taxi at the head of the rank; *Rail:* **voiture de t.,** front carriage; **en t. du train,** at the front of the train; **à la t. du régiment,** at the head of the regiment; **marcher en t.,** to lead the way, to lead the van; **marcher à la t., en t., du cortège,** to head the procession; **venir tout en t.,** to come foremost; **venir en t. du scrutin,** to head the poll; **s'inscrire en t. de la liste,** to head the list; **être à la t. de la classe,** to be at the top of the form; *Ten:* **têtes de série,** seeded players, *F:* seeds; *Rac: etc:* **prendre la t.,** to take the lead; *Mil:* **t. de pont,** (i) bridgehead; (ii) beach head; *Rail: etc:* **t. de ligne,** (i) starting point; terminus; (ii) railhead.

tête-à-queue [tɛtakø] *n.m.inv.* **faire (un) t.-à-q.,** (i) *Aut:* to spin, slew, round; (ii) (*of horse*) to whip round.

tête-à-tête [tɛtatɛt] *n.m.inv.* **1.** private interview, tête-à-tête; **en t.-à-t.,** in private; **en t.-à-t. avec,** alone with. **2.** (*a*) sofa, settee (for two); tête-à-tête; (*b*) tea, coffee, breakfast, set for two.

tête-bêche [tɛtbɛʃ] *adv.* (*of two pers. or thgs*) head to foot (alongside one another); head to tail; top to bottom.

tête-de-loup [tɛtdəlu] *n.f.* ceiling brush; *pl. têtes-de-loup.*

tête(-)de(-)maure [tɛtdəmɔr] *n.f.* Dutch cheese; *pl. têtes-de-maure.*

tête-de-mort [tɛtdəmɔr] *n.f.* **1.** death's-head; **pavillon à t.-de-m.,** skull-and-crossbones flag, Jolly Roger. **2.** *Ent:* death's-head moth. **3.** Dutch cheese; *pl. têtes-de-mort.*

tête-de-nègre [tɛtdənɛgr̥] *a. & n.m.inv.* dark brown, *not NAm:* nigger-brown.

tétée [tete] *n.f.* **1.** milk taken by a baby at one feed. **2.** (action of) suckling by baby.

téter [tete] *v.tr.* **(il tète; il tètera)** (*a*) (*of infant or young*) to suck; **donner à t. à un enfant,** to feed a child (at the breast); to suckle a child; **enfant qui tète son pouce,** child sucking its thumb; (*b*) *F:* to suck (on) (cigar, pipe, etc.).

têtière [tɛtjɛr] *n.f.* **1.** *Harn:* headstall. **2.** antimacassar, chair back.

tétin [tetɛ̃] *n.m. O.* (*of pers.*) nipple; (*of cow, etc.*) dug.

tétine [tetin] *n.f.* **1.** dug (of animal); (*a*) udder; (*b*) teat. **2.** (rubber) nipple, teat (of feeding bottle); **t. (sur anneau),** baby's comforter; dummy; *NAm:* pacifier.
téton [tetɔ̃] *n.m. F:* (woman's) breast, boob.
tétrachlorure [tetraklɔryr] *n.m. Ch:* tetrachloride; **t. de carbone,** carbon tetrachloride.
tétracorde [tetrakɔrd] *n.m. A.Mus:* tetrachord.
tétraèdre [tetraɛdr̥] *Mth:* **1.** *a.* tetrahedral. **2.** *n.m.* tetrahedron.
tétraédrique [tetraedrik] *a. Mth:* tetrahedral.
tétralogie [tetralɔʒi] *n.f. Lit: Th:* tetralogy; *Mus:* **la T. (de Wagner),** The Ring, Wagner's Ring.
tétramètre [tetramɛtr̥] *n.m. Pros:* tetrameter.
tétrapode [tetrapɔd] *a. & n.m.* tetrapod.
tétrarque [tetrark] *n.m.* tetrarch.
tétras [tetrɑ] *n.m. Orn:* grouse.
tétrasyllabe [tetrasilab], **tétrasyllabique** [tetrasilabik] *a. Gram:* tetrasyllabic; **mot t.,** tetrasyllable.
têtu [tety] *a.* stubborn, obstinate; *F:* pigheaded; *F:* **t. comme un mulet, comme une mule,** as stubborn, obstinate, as a mule.
teuton, -onne [tøtɔ̃, -ɔn] **1.** *a.* Teuton(ic). **2.** *n.* Teuton. **3.** *n.m. Ling:* **le t.,** Germanic, Teutonic.
teutonique [tøtɔnik] *a.* Teutonic.
texan, -ane [tɛksɑ̃, -an] *a. & n. Geog:* Texan.
texte [tɛkst] *n.m.* (*a*) text (of author, book, etc.); (actor's) lines; **erreur de t.,** textual error; **critique des textes,** textual criticism; **revenons à notre t.,** let us return to our subject; *Bookb:* **gravure hors t.,** plate; full-page engraving; (*b*) letterpress (to illustration); (*c*) *Cmptr:* text.
textile [tɛkstil] **1.** *a.* textile. **2.** *n.m.* (*a*) textile; **textiles artificiels,** synthetic textiles; (*b*) **le t.,** the textile industries.
textuel, -elle [tɛkstɥɛl] *a.* textual; word-for-word, literal (quotation).
textuellement [tɛkstɥɛlmɑ̃] *adv.* textually; word for word; literally; verbatim.
texture [tɛkstyr] *n.f.* (*a*) texture; consistency; (*b*) texture (of play, novel, etc.).
thaï [tai] **1.** *a.* Thai. **2.** *n.m. Ling:* (*a*) Thai; (*b*) Thai group.
thaïlandais, -aise [tailɑ̃dɛ, -ɛz] *a. & n. Geog:* Thai.
Thaïlande [tailɑ̃d] *Pr.n.f. Geog:* Thailand.
thalamus [talamys] *n.m. Anat: Bot:* thalamus.
thalidomide [talidɔmid] *n.f. Pharm:* thalidomide.
thalle [tal] *n.m. Bot:* thallus.
thallium [taljɔm] *n.m. Ch:* thallium.
thalweg [talvɛg] *n.m. Geol:* t(h)alweg.
thaumaturge [tomatyrʒ] **1.** *a.* thaumaturgic; miracle-working. **2.** *n.m.* thaumaturge, thaumaturgist, miracle worker.
thé [te] *n.m.* **1.** (*a*) tea; **t. de Ceylan,** Ceylon tea; **t. indien, de l'Inde,** Indian tea; **t. de Chine,** China tea; **t. nature, au lait, au citron,** tea without milk, with milk; lemon tea; **négociant en t.,** tea merchant; **c'est l'heure du t.,** it's teatime; *a.inv.* **rose t.,** tea rose; (*b*) **t. de bœuf,** beef tea. **2.** (*a*) tea party; (*b*) **salon de t.,** teashop, tearoom(s).
théâtral, -aux [teɑtral, -o] *a.* theatrical; dramatic (effect); stage (performance); *Pej:* stagy.
théâtralement [teɑtralmɑ̃] *adv.* theatrically.
théâtraliser [teɑtralize] *v.tr. Th:* to dramatize (a novel, etc.).
théâtralité [teɑtralite] *n.f.* theatricalness.
théâtre [teɑtr̥] *n.m.* **1.** (*a*) theatre, *NAm:* theater; playhouse; **t. de verdure,** open-air theatre; **t. en rond,** arena theatre; (*b*) *Mil:* theatre (of war); scene (of accident). **2.** stage, scene; **mettre une pièce au t.,** to stage, put on, a play; **se retirer du t.,** to give up the stage. **3.** (*a*) dramatic art; **pièce de t.,** play; **costumier de t.,** theatrical costumier; **faire du t.,** to be an actor, be on the stage; **coup de t.,** dramatic, sensational, turn (to events); (*b*) plays, dramatic works (of s.o.); **le t. anglais,** English drama.
théâtreuse [teɑtrøz] *n.f. F: Pej:* actress (of sorts); showgirl.
thébaïsme [tebaism] *n.m. Med:* thebaism, opium poisoning.
théier, -ière [teje, -jɛr] **1.** *a.* tea (industry, etc.). **2.** *n.m. Bot:* tea (plant). **3.** *n.f.* **théière,** teapot.
théine [tein] *n.f. Ch:* theine.
théisme[1] [teism] *n.m. Med:* theism; tea poisoning.
théisme[2] *n.m. Theol:* theism.
théiste [teist] **1.** *a.* theistic. **2.** *n.* theist.
thématique [tematik] *a.* thematic.
thème [tɛm] *n.m.* **1.** (*a*) theme, topic; subject (of discourse, musical composition, etc.); (*b*) *Mus:* antecedent, subject (of fugue); (*c*) *Sch:* prose; **t. latin,** Latin prose (composition); *F:* **fort en t.,** good and hard-working pupil. **2.** *Gram:* stem, theme (of verb, noun).
théocratie [teɔkrasi] *n.f.* theocracy.
théocratique [teɔkratik] *a.* theocratic.
théodicée [teɔdise] *n.f. Phil:* theodicy.
théodolite [teɔdɔlit] *n.m. Surv:* theodolite.
théologal, -aux [teɔlɔgal, -o] *a.* **les trois vertus théologales,** the three theological virtues.
théologie [teɔlɔʒi] *n.f.* theology; **docteur en t.,** doctor of divinity, D.D.
théologien [teɔlɔʒjɛ̃] *n.m.* theologian.
théologique [teɔlɔʒik] *a.* theological.
théologiquement [teɔlɔʒikmɑ̃] *adv.* theologically.
théophylline [teɔfilin] *n.f. Ch:* theophylline.
théorbe [teɔrb] *n.m. A.Mus:* theorbo.
théorème [teɔrɛm] *n.m.* theorem; **le t. de Newton,** the binomial theorem.
théorétique [teɔretik] *Phil:* **1.** *a.* theoretic(al). **2.** *n.f.* theoretics.
théoricien, -ienne [teɔrisjɛ̃, -jɛn] *n.* theor(et)ician, theorist.
théorie[1] [teɔri] *n.f.* **1.** theory; **en t.,** in theory; *Mth: Cmptr:* **t. des probabilités,** theory of probability. **2.** *Mil:* (*a*) theoretical instruction; (*b*) training manual; **conforme à la t.,** (strictly) according to the book.
théorie[2] *n.f.* **1.** *Gr.Ant:* theory, theoria. **2.** *Lit:* procession.
théorique [teɔrik] *a.* theoretic(al).
théoriquement [teɔrikmɑ̃] *adv.* theoretically.
théoriser [teɔrize] *v.tr. & i.* to theorize.
théosophe [teɔzɔf] *n.* theosophist.
théosophie [teɔzɔfi] *n.f.* theosophy.
thèque [tɛk] *n.f. Anat: Bot:* theca.
thérapeute [terapøt] *n.* **1.** *Rel.H:* therapeutic monk, nun. **2.** *Med:* therapist.
thérapeutique [terapøtik] **1.** *a.* therapeutic. **2.** *n.f.* therapeutics, therapy.
thérapie [terapi] *n.f. Med:* therapy.
thermal, -aux [tɛrmal, -o] *a.* thermal; **eaux thermales,** thermal springs, hot springs; **établissement t.,** hydropathic establishment; **station thermale,** spa.
thermalisme [tɛrmalism] *n.m.* (*a*) organization of spas; (*b*) hydrotherapy; (*c*) balneology.
thermes [tɛrm] *n.m.pl.* **1.** *Gr. & Rom.Ant:* thermae, public baths. **2.** thermal baths.
thermicien, -ienne [tɛrmisjɛ̃, -jɛn] *n.* heat engineer.
thermidor [tɛrmidɔr] *n.m. Fr.Hist:* Thermidor; eleventh month of Fr. Republican calendar (July–August).
thermie [tɛrmi] *n.f. Ph:* thermal unit (= 1000 great calories).
thermique [tɛrmik] **1.** *a. Ph:* thermic, thermal; heat (engine, screen, treatment); *El:* **centrale t.,** thermal

power station; *Aer:* **courant t.,** thermal (current); *Elcs:* **relais t.,** thermorelay; *Ch:* **analyse t.,** thermoanalysis; *Geog:* **régime t.,** temperature regime, pattern; *Physiol:* **sensibilité t.,** temperature sense. **2.** *n.m. Aer:* thermal. **3.** *n.f.* science of heat.

thermisteur [tɛrmistœr] *n.m.,* **thermistor** [tɛrmistɔr] *n.m. El:* thermistor.

thermocautère [tɛrmɔkotɛr] *n.m. Surg:* thermocautery.

thermochimie [tɛrmɔʃimi] *n.f.* thermochemistry.

thermocollage [tɛrmɔkɔlaʒ] *n.m.* heat sealing.

thermocouple [tɛrmɔkupl̥] *n.m. El:* thermocouple.

thermodynamique [tɛrmɔdinamik] **1.** *a.* thermodynamic. **2.** *n.f.* thermodynamics.

thermoélectricité [tɛrmɔelɛktrisite] *n.f.* thermoelectricity.

thermoélectrique [tɛrmɔelɛktrik] *a. Ph:* thermoelectric(al); **pince t.,** thermocouple; **couple t.,** thermoelectric couple; **pile t.,** thermopile.

thermoélectronique [tɛrmɔelɛktrɔnik] *a. Ph:* thermoelectronic.

thermogène [tɛrmɔʒɛn] *a. Physiol:* thermogenic; heat-producing.

thermogénie [tɛrmɔʒeni] *n.f. Ph: Ch:* thermogenesis.

thermographe [tɛrmɔgraf] *n.m. Ph:* thermograph.

thermomagnétisme [tɛrmɔmaɲetism] *n.m. Ph:* thermomagnetism.

thermomètre [tɛrmɔmɛtr̥] *n.m.* thermometer; **t. médical, de clinique,** clinical thermometer; **t. à maxima et minima,** maximum and minimum thermometer.

thermométrie [tɛrmɔmetri] *n.f. Ph:* thermometry.

thermométrique [tɛrmɔmetrik] *a.* thermometric(al).

thermonucléaire [tɛrmɔnykleɛr] *a. Atom.Ph:* thermonuclear.

thermopile [tɛrmɔpil] *n.f. El:* thermopile.

thermoplastique [tɛrmɔplastik] *a. & n.m.* thermoplastic.

thermoplongeur [tɛrmɔplɔ̃ʒœr] *n.m.* immersion heater.

thermopompe [tɛrmɔpɔ̃p] *n.f.* heat pump.

thermopropulsion [tɛrmɔprɔpylsjɔ̃] *n.f. Av:* thermopropulsion.

thermorégulateur [tɛrmɔregylatœr] *n.m.* thermoregulator, thermostat.

thermorégulation [tɛrmɔregylasjɔ̃] *n.f.* thermoregulation.

thermorésistant [tɛrmɔrezistɑ̃] *a.* heat-resisting.

Thermos [tɛrmɔs] *n.m. or f. trademark applied to vacuum flasks and other articles manufactured by Thermos (1925) Limited;* **(bouteille) T.,** Thermos flask, *NAm:* bottle.

thermoscope [tɛrmɔskɔp] *n.m. Ph:* thermoscope.

thermostable [tɛrmɔstabl̥] *a. Ch: Med:* thermostable.

thermostat [tɛrmɔsta] *n.m.* thermostat; **réglage par t.,** thermostatic control.

thermothérapie [tɛrmɔterapi] *n.f.* heat treatment, thermotherapy.

thésard, -arde [tezar, -ard] *n. Sch: F:* student preparing a thesis.

thésaurisation [tezɔrizasjɔ̃] *n.f.* hoarding of money; building up of capital.

thésauriser [tezɔrize] *v.tr. & i.* to hoard (money).

thésauriseur, -euse [tezɔrizœr, -øz] *n. Lit:* hoarder of treasure, of money.

thesaurus [tezɔrys] *n.m.* thesaurus.

thèse [tɛz] *n.f.* **1.** thesis, proposition, argument; **pièce à t.,** (i) propaganda play; (ii) problem play, drama of ideas. **2.** *Sch:* thesis (submitted for degree).

Thésée [teze] *Pr.n.m. Myth:* Theseus.

thêta [tɛta] *n.m. Gr.Alph:* theta.

thiamine [tjamin] *n.f. Bio-Ch:* thiamin(e), aneurin(e).

thibaude [tibod] *n.f.* carpet felt, felt underlay.

thioalcool [tjɔalkɔl] *n.m. Ch:* thioalcohol.

thionate [tjɔnat] *n.m. Ch:* thionate.

thionine [tjɔnin] *n.f. Ch:* thionine.

thionique [tjɔnik] *a. Ch:* thionic.

thiosulfate [tjɔsylfat] *n.m. Ch:* thiosulphate, *NAm:* thiosulfate.

thiosulfurique [tjɔsylfyrik] *a. Ch:* thiosulphuric, *NAm:* thiosulfuric.

thio(-)urée [tjɔyre] *n.f. Ch:* thiourea.

thixotropique [tiksɔtrɔpik] *a. Ch: Ph:* thixotropic.

thixotropie [tiksɔtrɔpi] *n.f. Ch: Ph:* thixotropy.

tholos [tɔlɔs] *n.f. Archeol:* tholos.

Thomas [tɔmɑ] **1.** *Pr.n.m.* Thomas; **Saint T. d'Aquin,** St Thomas Aquinas. **2.** *n.m. P: O:* chamberpot, jerry.

thomisme [tɔmism] *n.m. Theol:* Thomism.

thomiste [tɔmist] *a. & n. Theol:* Thomist.

thon [tɔ̃] *n.m. Ich:* tunny(fish), tuna(fish).

thonaire [tɔnɛr] *n.f. Fish:* tunny net.

thonier [tɔnje] *n.m.* tunny boat.

thoracique [tɔrasik] *a. Anat:* thoracic; **cage t.,** rib cage.

thoracoplastie [tɔrakɔplasti] *n.f. Surg:* thoracoplasty.

thorax [tɔraks] *n.m.* thorax.

thorium [tɔrjɔm] *n.m. Ch:* thorium.

thoron [tɔrɔ̃] *n.m. Atom.Ph:* thoron.

thrène [trɛn] *n.m. Gr.Ant:* threnody.

thrips [trips] *n.m. Ent:* thrips, thysanopter.

thrombine [trɔ̃bin] *n.f. Bio-Ch:* thrombin.

thrombocyte [trɔ̃bɔsit] *n.m. Physiol:* thrombocyte.

thrombophlébite [trɔ̃bɔflebit] *n.f. Med:* thrombophlebitis.

thrombose [trɔ̃boz] *n.f. Med:* thrombosis.

thrombus [trɔ̃bys] *n.m. Med:* thrombus.

thulium [tyljɔm] *n.m. Ch:* thulium.

thune [tyn] *n.f. P:* (*a*) *A:* five-franc piece; (*b*) **sans une t.,** without a penny.

thuriféraire [tyriferɛr] *n.m.* (*a*) *Ecc:* thurifer, incense bearer; (*b*) *F:* flatterer (of s.o.); fawner (on s.o.).

thuya [tyja] *n.m. Bot:* thuja, thuya, arbor vitae.

thylacine [tilasin] *n.m. Z:* thylacine; Tasmanian wolf.

thym [tɛ̃] *n.m. Bot:* thyme; **t. bâtard,** wild thyme.

thymique¹ [timik] *a. Anat: Med:* thymic (asthma, etc.).

thymique² *a. Ch:* thymic.

thymol [timɔl] *n.m. Pharm:* thymol.

thymus [timys] *n.m. Anat:* thymus, thymus gland.

thyroglobuline [tirɔglɔbylin] *n.f. Bio-Ch:* thyroglobulin.

thyroïde [tirɔid] *a. & n.f. Anat:* thyroid (gland).

thyroïdectomie [tirɔidɛktɔmi] *n.f. Surg:* thyroidectomy.

thyroïdien, -ienne [tirɔidjɛ̃, -jɛn] *Anat:* **1.** *a.* thyroid (hormone). **2.** *n.f.* **thyroïdienne,** thyroid artery; thyroid vein.

thyroïdisme [tirɔidism] *n.m. Med:* thyroidism.

thyroïdite [tirɔidit] *n.f. Med:* thyroiditis.

thyrse [tirs] *n.m. Gr.Ant: Bot:* thyrse, thyrsus.

tiare [tjar] *n.f.* (*esp.* papal) tiara.

Tibet [tibɛ] *Pr.n.m. Geog:* Tibet; *Z:* **dogue du T.,** Tibetan mastiff; **griffon du T.,** Tibetan terrier, chrysanthemum dog.

tibia [tibja] *n.m.* (*a*) *Anat:* tibia; **s'érafler le t.,** to bark one's shin; (*b*) *Ent:* tibia.

tibial, -iaux [tibjal, -jo] *a. Anat:* tibial.

tic [tik] *n.m.* (*a*) *Med:* tic; twitching; **il a un t.,** he has a twitch, a tic; his face twitches; **t. douloureux,** facial neuralgia; (*b*) vicious habit (of horse, etc.); (*c*) *F:* (unconscious) habit; mannerism.

ticket [tikɛ] *n.m.* (*a*) ticket; numbered slip, check (at restaurant, cloakroom, etc.); *Rail:* **t. de quai,** platform ticket; *War Adm: A:* **t. de pain,** bread coupon; *Ins:* **t. modérateur,** quota, portion, of the cost of treatment paid by the insured (in Fr.); (*b*) *Cmptr:* tag; (*c*) *P:* 1,000 (old) franc note; (*d*) *P:* **avoir un t. avec qn,** to be popular, to click, with s.o.

ticket-repas [tikɛrəpɑ] *n.m.*, **ticket-restaurant** [tikɛrɛstɔrɑ̃] *n.m.* = luncheon voucher; *pl. tickets-repas, -restaurant.*

tic(-)tac [tiktak] *n.m.* tick-tock; tick, ticking (of clock); **faire t.-t.,** to tick.

tictaquer [tiktake] *v.i.* (*of clock*) to tick; (*of heart*) to go pit-a-pat.

tiédasse [tjedas] *a. F:* lukewarm, tepid.

tiède [tjɛd] *a.* tepid; lukewarm (bath, friendship); (*of air*) mild; *adv.* **je bois toujours t.,** I always take the chill off my drink.

tièdement [tjɛdmɑ̃] *adv.* lukewarmly, half-heartedly.

tiédeur [tjedœr] *n.f.* tepidness; lukewarmness (of water, friendship, etc.); *F:* **avec t.,** halfheartedly.

tiédir [tjedir] **1.** *v.i.* to become tepid, lukewarm; (*of friendship, etc.*) to cool off. **2.** *v.tr.* to make tepid, lukewarm; to take the chill off, to warm (water, etc.).

tiédissement [tjedismɑ̃] *n.m.* **1.** cooling (off). **2.** warming (up).

tien, tienne [tjɛ̃, tjɛn] yours; thine; (*for the use of* **tien** *as opp. to* **vôtre,** *cf.* TU; *in Eng. "thine" is used only in prayers, occ. in Quaker speech, in dialect, and in literature*) **1.** *occ. poss. a.* **mes intérêts sont tiens,** my interests are yours. **2. le t., la tienne, les tiens, les tiennes** (*a*) *poss.pron.* **ses enfants ressemblent aux tiens,** his children are like yours; (*b*) *n.m.* (i) your own (property, etc.); yours; thine; **si tu veux du mien, donne-moi du t.,** if you want to have some of mine, give me some of yours; **le t. et le mien,** questions, arguments, about property; **y mettre du t.,** to contribute your share; to make concessions; to add to (a story); (ii) *pl.* your own (friends, etc.); **les tiens t'ont renié,** your own (people) have disowned you; (iii) *F:* **tu as encore fait des tiennes,** you've been up to your old tricks again.

tiens [tjɛ̃] *int. see* TENIR. **1.** hello! hullo! **2.** look! hey! here! **3. t., t.!** indeed? well, well! you don't say! *NAm:* my! **t., t.! c'est curieux,** hullo! that's curious.

tierce[1] [tjɛrs] **1.** *see* TIERS. **2.** *n.f.* (*a*) *Astr: Mth:* third (= sixtieth part of a second); (*b*) *Fenc:* tierce; (*c*) *Ecc:* terce, tierce; (*d*) *Mus:* third; (*e*) *Typ:* final revise, press proof; (*f*) *Cards:* tierce.

tiercé [tjɛrse] *a.* **1.** *Agr:* ploughed, *NAm:* plowed, for the third time. **2.** *Her:* tierced, tiercé. **3.** *Pros:* **rimes tiercées,** terza rima. **4.** *Turf:* **pari t.,** *n.m.,* **le t.,** forecast of the first three horses; **un beau t.,** a good win on the *tiercé.*

tiercelet [tjɛrs(ə)lɛ] *n.m. Ven:* tercel, male falcon.

tiercer [tjɛrse] *v.tr.* **(je tierçai(s); n. tierçons)** *Agr:* to plough, *NAm:* plow (land) for the third time.

tierceron [tjɛrs(ə)rɔ̃] *n.m. Arch:* tierceron (rib).

tiers, tierce[2] [tjɛr, tjɛrs] **1.** *a. A:* third (person, power, etc.); *Hist:* **le t. état,** the third estate, the commonalty; *Ecc:* **t. ordre,** Third Order; *Jur:* **en main tierce,** in the hands of a third party; **t. porteur,** second endorser (of bill). **2.** *n.m.* (*a*) third (part); **remise d'un t. (du prix),** discount of a third; *F:* a third off; **perdre le t., les deux t., de son argent,** to lose a third, two thirds, of one's money; (*b*) third person, third party; **être en t.,** to be present as a third party, to make a third; *F: A:* **le t. et le quart,** everybody, anybody; **prendre le parapluie d'un t.,** to take a perfect stranger's umbrella; *Ins:* **assurance au t.,** third party insurance.

tiers-arbitre [tjɛrarbitr̥] *n.m.* referee, arbitrator; *pl. tiers-arbitres.*

tiers-monde [tjɛrmɔ̃d] *n.m. Pol:* **le t.-m.,** the uncommitted countries; the third world.

tiers-point [tjɛrpwɛ̃] *n.m.* **1.** *Arch:* **arc en t.-p.,** pointed equilateral arch. **2.** *Tls:* triangular file; *pl. tiers-points.*

tifs, tiffes [tif] *n.m.pl. P:* hair, thatch.

tige [tiʒ] *n.f.* **1.** (*a*) stem, stalk (of plant); scape (of feather); (*b*) trunk, bole (of tree); **(arbre à) haute t.,** tall standard; (*c*) stock (of family); *Lit:* **faire t.,** to found a line. **2.** (*a*) shaft (of column); stem (of valve, candlestick, etc.); shank (of rivet, key, anchor, *Typ:* of letter); body (of penholder); stick (of violin bow); matchstick; leg (of pedestal table); *Typewr:* **t. à caractères,** type bar; (*b*) *Mec.E:* rod (of pump, piston, etc.); *Petr:* **t. de forage,** drill(ing) pipe; *I.C.E: etc:* **t. de jauge,** dipstick; **t. de paratonnerre,** lightning rod; *Cy:* **t. de selle,** saddle pin; saddle pillar; *Veh:* **t. de frein,** brake rod; **t. à vis du frein,** brake screw; (*c*) leg (of stocking); leg, upper (of boot); **bottes à tiges,** top boots; (*d*) *P:* cigarette.

tiglon [tiglɔ̃] *n.m. Z:* tigon.

tignasse [tiɲas] *n.f.* mop (of tousled hair).

tigre[1], **tigresse** [tigr̥, tigrɛs] *n. Z:* tiger, tigress; **jaloux comme un t., jalouse comme une tigresse,** as jealous as hell; *F:* **c'est une vraie tigresse,** she's a jealous cat.

Tigre[2] **(le)** *Pr.n.m. Geog:* the (river) Tigris.

tigré [tigre] *a.* striped (fur); spotted (skin); tabby (cat); **lis t.,** tiger lily.

tigron [tigrɔ̃] *n.m. Z:* tigon.

tilbury [tilbyri] *n.m. A.Veh:* tilbury, gig.

tilde [tild] *n.m. Typ: etc:* tilde.

tillac [tijak] *n.m. Nau: A:* upper deck.

tilleul [tijœl] *n.m.* **1.** *Bot:* lime (tree). **2. (infusion de) t.,** lime-blossom tea.

timbale [tɛ̃bal] *n.f.* **1.** *Mus:* kettle drum; (*in orchestra*) **les timbales,** the timpani. **2.** metal drinking cup, mug. **3.** *Cu:* (*a*) timbale mould, *NAm:* mold; (*b*) **t. de langouste,** lobster timbale.

timbalier [tɛ̃balje] *n.m. Mus:* timpanist.

timbrage [tɛ̃braʒ] *n.m.* stamping (of passport, letter, etc.).

timbre [tɛ̃br̥] *n.m.* **1.** (*a*) (fixed) bell (with striking hammer); **t. électrique,** electric bell; **presser le t.,** to press, ring, the (electric) bell; *F: A:* **avoir le t. fêlé,** to be mad, cracked, daft; to have a screw loose; (*b*) *Mus:* snare (of drum); (*c*) timbre, quality in tone (of voice, instrument); **voix sans t.,** toneless voice. **2.** (*a*) stamp (on document, etc.); **t. sec,** embossed stamp; **t. de la poste,** postmark; (*b*) **t.(-poste),** (postage) stamp; (*c*) stamp(ing instrument); **t. sec,** embossing press; **t. humide,** rubber stamp; **t. à date, t. dateur,** date stamp; **t. à encrage automatique,** self-inking stamp; (*d*) stamp duty; (*e*) **le T.,** the Stamp Office.

timbré [tɛ̃bre] *a.* **1.** sonorous (voice). **2.** *F:* mad; cracked (brain), crack-brained (person). **3.** stamped (paper, document).

timbre-épargne [tɛ̃breparɲ] *n.m.* savings-bank stamp; *pl. timbres-épargne.*

timbre-poste [tɛ̃br(ə)pɔst] *n.m.* postage stamp; *pl. timbres-poste.*

timbre-prime [tɛ̃br(ə)prim] *n.m. Com:* trading stamp; *pl. timbres-prime.*

timbre-quittance [tɛ̃br(ə)kitɑ̃s] *n.m.* receipt stamp; *pl. timbres-quittance.*

timbrer [tɛ̃bre] *v.tr.* (*a*) to stamp (passport, etc.); to postmark (letter); **lettre timbrée de Paris,** letter with a Paris postmark; (*b*) **papier timbré au chiffre de qn,**

paper stamped with s.o.'s arms; (*c*) **t. une lettre,** to (stick a) stamp (on) a letter.
timbre-taxe [tɛ̃br(ə)taks] *n.m.* postage-due stamp; *pl. timbres-taxe.*
timide [timid] *a.* timid; (*a*) timorous, apprehensive; (*b*) shy (person, smile); diffident (**envers,** with); (*c*) *n.* **c'est un grand t.,** he's very shy.
timidement [timidmɑ̃] *adv.* timidly; (*a*) timorously, apprehensively; (*b*) shyly, diffidently.
timidité [timidite] *n.f.* timidity; (*a*) timorousness; (*b*) shyness, bashfulness, diffidence.
timon [timɔ̃] *n.m.* **1.** (*a*) pole (of vehicle); beam (of plough, *NAm:* plow); (*b*) *occ. pl.* shafts (of vehicle). **2.** *Nau: A:* tiller; *Fig:* helm.
timonerie [timɔnri] *n.f.* **1.** *Nau:* (*a*) steering (of ship); **(kiosque de) t.,** wheelhouse, pilot house; (*b*) (naval) signalling. **2.** *Aut:* (*a*) steering gear; (*b*) brake gear.
timonier [timɔnje] *n.m.* **1.** *Nau:* (*a*) helmsman, man at the wheel; (*b*) quartermaster; (*c*) *Navy:* signalman. **2.** *Veh:* wheelhorse; wheeler.
timoré [timɔre] *a.* timorous, fearful; **conscience timorée,** overscrupulous conscience.
tin [tɛ̃] *n.m.* block; (boat) chock; *pl. N.Arch:* keel blocks (in dry dock); stocks (on slip).
tinctorial, -iaux [tɛ̃ktɔrjal, -jo] *a.* tinctorial, dyeing (plant, process).
tinette [tinɛt] *n.f.* **1.** tub. **2.** *Hyg:* (sanitary) soil tub.
tintamarre [tɛ̃tamar] *n.m. F:* (*a*) din, racket, noise; (*b*) *O:* mock serenade; (*c*) publicity, ballyhoo.
tintement [tɛ̃t(ə)mɑ̃] *n.m.* **1.** ringing (of bell); **t. funèbre,** tolling. **2.** tinkling, tinkle (of small bells, glasses, etc.); jingling, jingle (of sleigh bells, keys); chink(ing) (of coins, glasses). **3.** buzzing, singing (in the ears); *Med:* tinnitus.
tinter [tɛ̃te] **1.** *v.tr.* to ring, toll (bell); **t. la messe,** to ring for mass. **2.** *v.i.* (*a*) (*of bell*) to ring; to toll; (*of small bells, etc.*) to tinkle; (*of coins*) to chink; (*of sleigh bells, keys*) to jingle; (*of glasses*) to clink; **faire t. les verres,** to clink glasses; (*b*) (*of the ears*) to buzz; **les oreilles me tintaient,** my ears were ringing, buzzing; **les oreilles ont dû vous t. hier soir,** your ears must have been burning last night (*i.e.* you were talked about).
tintin [tɛ̃tɛ̃] **1.** *n.m.* tinkle, chink, clink (of glasses, etc.). **2.** *int. F:* no go! nothing doing!
tintinnabuler [tɛ̃tinabyle] *v.i. Lit:* (*of bells*) to tintinnabulate, tinkle.
tintouin [tɛ̃twɛ̃] *n.m.* (*a*) din, racket; (*b*) trouble, worry.
tipule [tipyl] *n.f. Ent:* tipula; cranefly.
tique [tik] *n.f. Arach:* tick.
tiquer [tike] *v.i.* **1.** *F:* to wince; to show a slight sign of emotion, interest; **il n'a pas tiqué,** he didn't turn a hair; **ça m'a fait t.,** it gave me a jolt. **2.** *Vet:* (*of horse*) to have a stable vice; to suck wind, crib(-bite).
tiqueté [tikte] *a.* speckled, mottled, variegated.
tir [tir] *n.m.* **1.** (*a*) shooting; *Artil:* gunnery; **t. aux pigeons,** pigeon shooting; (*b*) shooting match, competition. **2.** (*a*) fire, firing; **champ de t.,** range; **t. au but,** precision firing; **t. au fusil,** rifle shooting; **habileté au t.,** marksmanship; *Artil: etc:* **champ de t. (d'une arme),** field of fire (of weapon); **cadence, régime, vitesse, du t.,** rate of fire; **directeur du t.,** fire-control officer; **allonger, raccourcir, le t.,** to increase, reduce, the range; **t. d'artillerie,** artillery fire; **t. de batterie,** battery fire; *Navy:* **t. en chasse,** bow fire; **t. en retraite,** stern fire; (*b*) *Min:* blasting; (*c*) *Fb:* **t. au but,** shot (at goal). **3.** (*a*) rifle range; (*b*) **(jeu de) t.,** shooting gallery.
tirade [tirad] *n.f.* tirade.
tirage [tiraʒ] *n.m.* **1.** (*a*) pulling, hauling (of carriages, etc.); **cheval de t.,** draught, *NAm:* draft, horse; *El:* **interrupteur à t.,** pull-and-push switch; (*b*) *F:* trouble, difficulty; **il y a du t. entre eux,** there's friction between them; they don't get on together; (*c*) (i) towing (of barges); (ii) towpath; (*d*) *Metalw:* wire drawing; (*e*) quarrying, extraction (of stone); **t. à la poudre,** blasting. **2.** *Phot:* extension, *A:* focal length (of camera). **3.** draught (of flue); **t. renversé, inverti,** back draught; *I.C.E:* **carburateur à t. en bas,** down-draught carburettor. **4.** drawing (of lottery, bonds). **5.** *Typ: Phot: etc:* (*a*) printing (off); (*b*) number printed, printing, edition (of book, engraving, etc.); edition (of recording); **un mille de t.,** run, printing, of a thousand; **journal à gros t.,** paper with a wide circulation; **édition à t. limité,** limited edition; (*c*) *Typ:* **t. héliographique,** arc print; *Cin:* **t. en surimpression,** overprint. **6.** *Bank: etc:* drawing, emission (of cheque, *NAm:* check, bill of exchange); **t. en blanc, en l'air,** emission of a dud cheque, etc.
tiraillement [tirajmɑ̃] *n.m.* **1.** tugging (on rope, etc.). **2. t. d'estomac,** gnawing at, of, the stomach; pangs of hunger. **3.** *F:* disagreement, wrangling, friction.
tirailler [tiraje] **1.** *v.tr.* to pull (s.o., sth.) about; to tug at (s.o.); *F:* **tiraillé entre deux émotions,** torn between two opposing feelings. **2.** *v.i.* (*a*) to shoot wildly, aimlessly; (*b*) *A:* to fire in skirmishing order. **3. se t.,** to get on badly (with s.o.).
tiraillerie [tirajri] *n.f.* **1.** (*a*) wrangling, friction; (*b*) pestering. **2.** wild firing; aimless firing.
tirailleur [tirajœr] *n.m.* **1.** *Mil:* skirmisher, sharpshooter; *A:* **tirailleurs algériens, sénégalais,** native Algerian, Senegalese, infantry; **en tirailleurs,** in skirmishing order. **2.** *F:* freelance journalist.
tirant [tirɑ̃] *n.m.* **1.** drawstring. **2.** (*a*) boot strap; (*b*) boot tag. **3.** (*a*) *Const:* tie beam (of roof); (*b*) *Tchn:* stay, brace; **t. de frein,** brake rod. **4.** *Nau:* **t. d'eau,** (ship's) draught, *NAm:* draft; **avoir dix pieds de t. d'eau,** to draw ten feet of water; **navire à faible t. d'eau,** shallow-draught ship; **échelle de t. d'eau,** draught marks, numbers; *Civ.E: etc:* **t. d'air,** head room.
tirasse [tiras] *n.m.* **1.** *Ven:* draw net. **2.** *Mus:* pedal coupler (of organ).
tire [tir] *n.f.* **1.** *A:* pull(ing); *still used in the phr.* **voleur à la t.,** pickpocket; **(vol à) la t.,** pickpocketing. **2.** *Fr.C:* molasses toffee, *NAm:* molasses candy, taffy; *U.S:* taffy pull; **t. d'érable,** maple taffy. **3.** *P:* car.
tiré, -ée [tire] **1.** *a.* (*a*) drawn, worn-out, peaked, haggard (features); pinched (with hunger); **il avait les traits tirés,** his face was drawn; **aux cheveux tirés,** with her hair scraped back; (*b*) *Fig:* **t. par les cheveux,** far-fetched; (*c*) *Golf:* **coup t.,** pulled shot; pull; (*d*) **broderie à fils tirés,** drawn-thread work. **2.** *n. Com:* drawee. **3.** *n.m. Ven:* shoot. **4.** *n.m. Typ:* **t. à part,** offprint. **5.** *n.f.* **tirée** (*a*) *F:* long distance, drag; **il y a encore toute une tirée,** there's still a long haul ahead; (*b*) *F:* **une tirée de qch.,** loads of sth.
tire-au-cul [tiroky] *n.m.inv. P:,* **tire-au-flanc** [tiroflɑ̃] *n.m.inv. F: Mil: etc:* malingerer; skiver; lazy sod, bastard.
tire-bouchon [tirbuʃɔ̃] *n.m.* **1.** corkscrew; **en t.-b.,** in a spiral, in corkscrews. **2.** *Hairdr:* corkscrew curl; *pl. tire-bouchons.*
tire(-)bouchonné [tirbuʃɔne] *a.* twisted; crumpled; *pl. tire(-)bouchonné(e)s.*
tire-bouton [tirbutɔ̃] *n.m.* buttonhook; *pl. tire-boutons.*
tire-clous [tirklu] *n.m.inv.* nail puller; nail wrench.
tire-d'aile (à) [atirdɛl] *adv.phr.* **s'envoler à t.-d'a.,** to fly swiftly away.
tire-fesses [tirfɛs] *n.m.inv. F:* drag lift, ski tow.
tire-filet [tirfilɛ] *n.m. Tls:* screw-cutting, thread-cutting, tool; threader; *pl. tire-filets.*

tire-fond [tirfɔ̃] *n.m.inv.* **1.** long bolt, screw spike; *Rail:* sleeper screw. **2.** eye bolt.
tire-jus [tirʒy] *n.m.inv. P:* nosewipe, snot rag.
tire-lait [tirlɛ] *n.m.inv.* breast pump.
tire-larigot (à) [atirlarigo] *adv.phr. F:* **boire à t.-l.,** to drink to one's heart's content, like a fish.
tire-ligne [tirliɲ] *n.m.* drawing pen; *pl. tire-lignes.*
tirelire [tirlir] *n.f.* **1.** money box. **2.** *P:* (*a*) face, mug; (*b*) head, nut; (*c*) belly.
tire-pognon [tirpɔɲɔ̃] *n.m. F:* one-arm(ed) bandit, fruit machine; *pl. tire-pognons.*
tirer [tire] **I.** *v.tr.* **1.** (*a*) to pull out, lengthen (out), stretch; to draw (wire); to pull up (socks); **t. une affaire en longueur,** to spin out a piece of business; *F:* **encore une heure à t. d'ici le déjeuner!** still another hour to get through before lunch! *P:* **t. cinq ans,** to get five years, a five-year stretch; *v.i. F:* **t. à la ligne,** to pad out an article; (*b*) *Dial:* to milk (a cow, etc.). **2.** to pull, tug, draw, drag, haul; **t. qn par la manche,** to tug at s.o.'s sleeve; **t. les cheveux à qn,** to pull s.o.'s hair; **t. la jambe,** *F:* **t. la patte,** (i) to limp; (ii) to lag behind; **t. les rideaux,** to draw the curtains, *NAm:* the drapes; *F:* **t. la couverture à soi,** to want more than one's share; *F:* **ça tire!** this is tough going! **tableau qui tire l'œil,** arresting picture; *A:* **t. un criminel à quatre (chevaux),** to (hang,) draw and quarter a criminal; *Mus:* (*violin*) **tire!** down bow! **3. t. son chapeau à qn,** to raise, lift, one's hat to s.o. **4.** to pull out, draw out, take out, extract; to draw (water, etc.); **t. un journal de sa poche,** to pull a paper out of one's pocket; **t. une dent à qn,** to pull out, draw, s.o.'s tooth; **t. les cartes,** to tell fortunes with cards; *Cards:* **t. pour la donne,** to cut for deal; **t. plaisir de qch.,** to derive pleasure from sth.; **t. de l'argent de qn,** to get money out of s.o.; to extract money from s.o.; **t. de l'huile des olives,** to extract oil from olives; **mot tiré du latin,** word derived from Latin; **t. la racine carrée d'un nombre,** to extract the square root of a number; **t. qn d'un mauvais pas,** to get s.o. out of a difficulty; **t. qn de son lit,** to drag s.o. out of bed; **t. qn du sommeil,** to drag s.o. from his sleep. **5.** (*a*) to draw (line); (*b*) to pull, print (off), strike off (engraving, proof); **donner le bon à t. d'un volume,** to pass a book for press; **t. une épreuve d'un cliché,** to take a print from a negative; (*c*) *Com:* to draw (bill of exchange); **t. un chèque sur une banque,** to draw a cheque, *NAm:* check, on a bank. **6.** (*a*) to fire (shot); to shoot (arrow); to let off (fireworks); **t. un coup de revolver sur qn,** to fire, shoot, at s.o. with a revolver; **t. un lièvre,** to shoot a hare; (*b*) *v.i.* to shoot; (*of firearm*) to go off; **t. au hasard,** to fire at random; **t. à couvert,** to fire from behind cover; **t. sur qn, sur qch.,** to shoot, fire, at s.o., at sth. **7.** *Nau:* **navire qui tire vingt pieds,** ship that draws twenty feet (of water). **II.** *v.i.* **1.** to pull (on cable, bridle, etc.); **t. sur sa pipe,** to have a pull at one's pipe. **2.** (*a*) to tend (to), incline (to); to verge (on); **bleu tirant sur le vert,** blue verging on green; **le jour tire à sa fin,** the day is drawing to its close; **le bonhomme tire à sa fin,** the old man's life is drawing to a close; **nos provisions tirent à leur fin,** our stores are running low, are giving out; **t. sur la soixantaine,** to be getting on for sixty; (*b*) **t. sur la gauche,** to pull to the left; **t. au large,** (i) *Nau:* to stand out to sea; (ii) *F:* to leave, scram, beat it. **3.** (*of chimney, etc.*) to draw. **III. se tirer 1.** (*a*) **se t. d'un mauvais pas,** to extricate oneself from a difficulty; to get out of a fix; **vous ne vous en tirerez pas avec cette excuse-là,** you won't get away with that excuse; **s'en t. sans aucun mal,** to escape uninjured; **s'en t. tout juste,** to escape by the skin of one's teeth; **on s'en tire, voilà tout!** we just manage to make both ends meet; we just get by; (*b*) *F:* to come to an end; **ça se tire,** it'll soon be done now; **ça s'est bien tiré?** I hope it went well! **2.** *F:* (*of pers.*) to be off, to make tracks, to beat it.
tiret [tirɛ] *n.m. Typ:* (*a*) hyphen; (*b*) dash, rule; (*c*) **ligne de tirets,** broken line.
tirette [tirɛt] *n.f.* **1.** writing slide (of desk); leaf (of table). **2.** *Mec.E:* pull handle, pull knob; flue damper (of furnace, etc.); *Aut: etc:* (pull-out) knob.
tireur, -euse [tirœr, -øz] *n.* **1.** (*a*) *Com:* drawer (of bill of exchange, etc.); (*b*) **t. de cartes,** fortune teller; (*c*) *Mil: etc: P:* **t. au flanc,** malingerer, shirker, lazy bastard. **2.** *Phot:* (*a*) printer; (*b*) *n.f.* **tireuse,** printing box, printer. **3.** (*a*) shooter; firer; marksman; **c'est un bon t., un t. d'élite,** he's a good shot; **mauvais t.,** bad shot; **t. d'élite** marksman; sharpshooter; **t. embusqué,** sniper; (*b*) **t. d'armes,** fencer; (*c*) pickpocket. **4.** *n.f. Winem:* **tireuse,** bottle filler, bottle-filling machine.
tiroir [tirwar] *n.m.* **1.** drawer (of table, etc.); *Lit:* **roman, comédie, à tiroir(s),** episodic novel, play. **2.** *Mec.E:* slide, slide valve (of steam engine); *Hyd.E:* **t. de soutirage,** weirbox.
tiroir-caisse [tirwarkɛs] *n.m. Com:* till; *pl. tiroirs-caisses.*
tisane [tizan] *n.f.* **1.** infusion, decoction; (herb, etc.) tea; **t. de camomille,** camomile tea; **t. d'orge,** barley water. **2.** *Winem:* **t. de champagne,** light champagne. **3.** *P:* thrashing, hiding.
tison [tizɔ̃] *n.f.* **1.** (fire)brand; half-burned log; **garder les tisons,** to stay by the fire. **2.** fusee (match).
tisonné [tizɔne] *a.* (*of horse's coat*) with black spots.
tisonner [tizɔne] *v.tr.* to poke (the fire).
tisonnier [tizɔnje] *n.m.* poker.
tissage [tisaʒ] *n.m. Tex:* **1.** weaving; **t. à la main, à bras,** handloom weaving; **t. mécanique,** power-loom weaving. **2.** cloth mill, works.
tisser [tise] *v.tr.* (*a*) to weave; (*b*) *F:* to concoct a string of, to fabricate (lies, etc.).
tisserand, -ande [tisrɑ̃, -ɑ̃d] **1.** *n.* weaver. **2.** *n.m. Orn:* weaver(bird).
tisserin [tisrɛ̃] *n.m. Orn:* weaver(bird).
tisseur, -euse [tisœr, -øz] *n.* weaver.
tissu [tisy] *n.m.* (*a*) texture; weave; (*b*) fabric, tissue, textile; **t. métallique,** wire gauze; **t. de mensonges, d'absurdités,** string, tissue, of lies, of absurdities; (*c*) *Biol:* (organic, cellular) tissue.
tissu-éponge [tisyepɔ̃ʒ] *n.m. Tex:* (terry) towelling; *pl. tissus-éponges.*
tissulaire [tisylɛr] *a. Biol:* of tissue.
Titan [titɑ̃] *Pr.n.m. Myth: Astr:* Titan; **travail de T.,** titanic work; gigantic work; *Ind:* **grue T.,** giant crane, Titan crane.
titane [titan] *n.m. Ch:* titanium.
titanesque [titanɛsk] *a.* titanesque, titanic.
titi¹ [titi] *n.m. P:* street arab, cheeky urchin.
titi² *n.m. Z:* titi (monkey), teetee.
titianesque [tisjanɛsk] *a. Art:* Titianesque.
titillation [titilasjɔ̃] *n.f.* titillation; tickling.
titiller [titile] *v.tr.* to titillate; to tickle.
titisme [titism] *n.m. Pol:* Titoism.
titiste [titist] *a. & n. Pol:* Titoist.
titrage [titraʒ] *n.m.* **1.** *Ch: Ind:* titration, titrating; standardizing (of a solution); assaying (of ore, etc.); determination of the strength (of alcohol, wine, etc.). **2.** *Cin:* titling.
titre [titr̥] *n.m.* **1.** (*a*) title (of nobility, etc.); official title; **porter le t. de duc,** to bear the title of duke; **se donner le t. de . . .,** to style oneself . . .; (*b*) **sans t. officiel,** without any official status; *adj.phr.* **en t.,** titular; on the regular staff; *F:* **la maîtresse en t. du roi,** the King's acknowledged mistress; *Jur:* **propriétaire en t.,** legal owner; (*c*) *pl.* qualifications (of an official for an appointment); (*d*) *Sp:* title; *Box:* **combat comptant, ne comptant pas, pour le t.,** title,

non-title, fight. **2.** (*a*) *Sch: etc:* diploma, certificate; **pourvu de tous ses titres,** fully qualified; (*b*) voucher; *Rail:* **t. de transport,** ticket; *Mil:* **t. de permission,** pass (for leave); (*c*) *Jur:* title deed; (*d*) *Fin: Com:* warrant, bond, certificate; *pl.* stocks and shares, securities; **t. au porteur,** bearer bond, negotiable instrument. **3.** title, claim, right; **t. juridique à qch.,** legal claim to sth.; **à t. de,** by way of, as a, by right of, by virtue of; **à t. d'office,** ex officio; **à t. de précaution,** just in case; **à t. d'ami,** as a friend; **à t. d'essai,** as a trial measure, experimentally; **à t. de faveur,** as a favour, *NAm:* favor; **à bon t., à juste t.,** fairly, rightly; **à quel t.?** by what right? upon what grounds? **au même t.,** for the same reason; **à t. gratuit,** free of charge. **4.** (*a*) title (of book, song, etc.); **(page du) t.,** title page; (*b*) heading (of chapter, page); *Typ:* **t. courant,** running headline; **les gros titres,** the large headlines; (*c*) part, section (of regulations, etc.). **5.** (*a*) title, titre, *NAm:* titer (of solution, gold); grade, content (of ore); fineness (of coinage); **t. d'eau,** degree of humidity; (*b*) size, number (of cotton, wire).

titré [titre] *a.* **1.** titled. **2.** *Sch:* qualified (teacher). **3.** *Ch:* titrated, standard (solution).

titrer [titre] *v.tr.* **1.** to give a title to (s.o., sth.); *Cin:* to insert the titles in (a film); *v.i.* **la presse titrait en énormes manchettes,** the press printed enormous headlines. **2.** *Tchn:* (*a*) *Ch: Ind:* to titrate; to standardize (solution); to assay (ore, etc.); to determine the strength of (alcohol, wine, etc.); (*b*) to size, number (cotton, wire, etc.); to determine the blend of (textile material). **3.** (*of ore, etc.*) **t. tant % de métal,** to assay so much % of metal.

titreuse [titrøz] *n.f. Cin:* (*device*) titler.

titubant [titybɑ̃] *a.* reeling, lurching, staggering.

tituber [titybe] *v.i.* to reel (about); to lurch; to stagger, totter; **marcher, entrer, sortir, en titubant,** to stagger, lurch, along, in, out.

titulaire [titylɛr] **1.** *a.* titular (bishop, professor, etc.). **2.** *n.* holder, titular (of right, title, certificate, etc.); bearer (of passport); occupant (of office); *Ecc:* incumbent (of parish).

titularisation [titylarizasjɔ̃] *n.f. Adm:* establishment (of civil servants, etc.).

titulariser [titylarize] *v.tr. Adm: etc:* to confirm (s.o.) in his post, appointment; to establish (s.o.).

toast [tost] *n.m.* toast. **1. porter un t. à qn,** to drink s.o.'s health, to toast s.o. **2. t. beurré,** buttered toast.

toboggan [tɔbɔgɑ̃] *n.m.* **1.** (*a*) toboggan; **piste de t.,** toboggan run; (*b*) chute (in swimming bath); (fairground) slide; (*c*) *Com: etc:* parcels, goods, chute. **2.** *Civ.E:* overpass.

toc [tɔk] **1.** (*a*) *int.* tap, tap! (*b*) *n.m.* tap, rap (on door, etc.). **2.** *F:* (*a*) *n.m.* sham gold; **bijoux, articles, en t.,** imitation jewellery; (*b*) *a.inv.* **être un peu t.,** to be a bit crazy, dotty, touched.

tocante [tɔkɑ̃t] *n.f. F:* watch, ticker.

tocard, -arde [tɔkar, -ard] *P:* **1.** *a.* (i) worthless, trashy, of poor quality; (ii) ugly. **2.** (*a*) *n.m. Rac:* (rank) outsider; (*b*) *n.* (*pers.*) hopeless case, dead loss.

toccata [tɔkata] *n.f. Mus:* toccata.

tocsin [tɔksɛ̃] *n.m.* tocsin (alarm (i) signal, (ii) bell).

toc-toc [tɔktɔk] *a.inv. F:* crazy, daft, dotty.

toge [tɔʒ] *n.f.* (*a*) *Rom.Ant:* toga; (*b*) *Jur: Sch:* gown.

tohu-bohu [tɔybɔy] *n.m.* chaos; confusion, hubbub.

toi [twa] *stressed pers.pron.* (*for the use of* **toi,** *cf.* TU) (*a*) you (*subject or object*); **c'est t.,** it's you; **t. et moi nous irons ensemble,** you and I will go together; **il est plus âgé que t.,** he is older than you; **il n'aime que t.,** he loves only you; **tu as raison, t.,** you are right; **avec t.,** with you; **ce livre est à t.,** this book is yours, belongs to you; **tu le vois par t.-même,** you can see for yourself; **moi, je reste, et t., tu pars,** I'll stay and you go; (*after the imp.*) **tais-t.!** hold your tongue, be quiet, *F:* shut up! (*b*) (*to the Deity, in dialect and literature*) thou, thee; you; **connais-t. t.-même,** know thyself.

toile [twal] *n.f.* **1.** (*a*) linen, linen cloth; **t. à matelas,** tick, ticking; **drap de t.,** linen sheet; *F:* **se mettre dans les toiles,** to go to bed; **pantalon de t.,** duck trousers; **marchand de t.,** linen draper; (*b*) cloth; **t. de crin,** horsehair cloth; **t. de coton,** calico; **t. peinte,** print; **t. cirée,** (i) American cloth, oilcloth; (ii) *Nau:* oilskin; **t. vernie,** oilskin; **t. à voiles,** canvas, sailcloth; **t. à bâches,** tarpaulin; **reliure en t.,** cloth binding; **t. de sauvetage,** jumping sheet, life net; (*c*) canvas; **t. de tailleur,** tailor's canvas; *F:* **coucher sous la t.,** to sleep under canvas; **seau en t.,** canvas bucket; **collé sur t.,** mounted on canvas; **papier collé sur t.,** linen-backed paper; (*d*) **t. métallique,** wire gauze; **t. (d')émeri,** emery cloth; **t. d'amiante,** asbestos; (*e*) **t. d'araignée,** cobweb; spider's web. **2.** (*a*) oil painting (on canvas); canvas; (*b*) *Th:* curtain; **t. de fond,** backdrop, backcloth; **derrière la t.,** behind, off. **3.** (*a*) *Nau:* sail; **à sec de t.,** under bare poles; (*b*) *pl.* sails (of windmill).

toilerie [twalri] *n.f.* cotton, linen and hemp industry, trade.

toilettage [twalɛtaʒ] *n.m.* grooming and trimming (of pets, etc.).

toilette [twalɛt] *n.f.* **1.** (*a*) washstand; (*b*) dressing table. **2.** (*a*) washing (and dressing); *Lit:* toilet; **faire sa t.,** to wash and dress; **faire un bout, un brin, de t.,** to have a wash and brush up; to freshen up; **le chat fait sa t.,** the cat is washing; **faire la t. d'une voiture,** to clean a car; **cabinet de t.,** washroom; bathroom; *NAm:* lavatory; *U.S:* toilet; **trousse, sac, de t.,** (i) sponge bag, toilet case, bag; (ii) (*larger*) (woman's) vanity case; **gant de t.** = facecloth, (face) flannel; **savon de t.,** toilet soap; (*b*) *P.N:* **toilettes,** toilets; public conveniences, lavatory. **3.** (woman's) dress, clothes; **être en (grande) t.,** to be in formal dress; **t. de bal,** ball dress.

toiletter [twalete] *v.tr.* to trim and groom (a pet).

toi-même [twamɛm] *pers.pron.* yourself; *A: & Lit:* thyself; *see* TOI *and* MÊME 1. (*c*).

toise [twaz] *n.f.* measuring apparatus; **passer sous la t.,** to be measured (for height); **je mesure 1 m. 78 à, sous, la t.,** my official height is 1 m. 78.

toisé [twaze] *n.m.* measuring (up); measurement.

toiser [twaze] *v.tr.* to eye (s.o.) from head to foot (*esp.* contemptuously).

toison [twazɔ̃] *n.f.* (*a*) fleece; *Myth:* **la T. d'or,** the Golden Fleece; (*b*) *F:* mop (of hair).

toit [twa] *n.m.* **1.** roof; **t. d'ardoises, de tuiles, de chaume,** slate roof, tiled roof, thatched roof; *Art:* **paysage de toits,** roofscape; **des ruines sans toits,** roofless ruins; **habiter sous les toits,** to live in a garret; **publier, crier, qch. sur les toits,** to proclaim sth. from the housetops; *Aut:* **t. ouvrant,** sunshine roof; (*of tent*) **double t.,** flysheet; **le t. paternel,** the home, the paternal roof. **2.** *Min:* top, roof (of mine); hanging wall (of lode).

toiture [twatyr] *n.f.* roofing, roof.

tokai, tokay [tɔkɛ] *n.m.* tokay (wine).

tôle[1] [tol] *n.f.* **1.** sheet metal; (*a*) sheet iron; **t. d'acier,** sheet steel; **t. ondulée,** corrugated iron; **malle de t.,** tin trunk; (*b*) **t. de cuivre,** copper sheets. **2.** *N.Arch: etc:* (steel, iron) plate; boiler plate.

tôle[2] *n.f. P:* = TAULE.

tôlé [tole] *a.* (*a*) built of, covered with, sheet metal; **panneau t.,** metal panel; (*b*) *Mount: Ski:* **neige tôlée,** *n.f.* **tôlée,** crusted snow.

tolérable [tɔlerabl̩] *a.* bearable, tolerable; permissible.

tolérance [tɔlerɑ̃s] *n.f.* tolerance. **1.** toleration (in religious matters, etc.); **par t.,** on sufferance; *A:* **maison de t.,** licensed brothel. **2.** (*a*) *Mec.E:* margin, limits, tolerance; **t. nulle,** zero allowance; **t. sur l'épaisseur, sur la longueur,** thickness margin, length margin; **t. de fonctionnement,** operational tolerance; *Elcs:* **t. de fréquence,** frequency tolerance; (*b*) *Cust:* **t. (permise),** tolerance, allowance; **il y a une t. d'un demi-litre,** you are allowed to bring in half a litre, *NAm:* liter, free of duty; (*c*) concession. **3.** *Med:* (*of patient*) tolerance (of a drug, etc.); *Bot:* (*of plant*) tolerance (of parasites).

tolérant, -ante [tɔlerɑ̃, -ɑ̃t] *a.* tolerant.

tolérantisme [tɔlerɑ̃tism] *n.m.* (religious) toleration.

tolérer [tɔlere] *v.tr.* **(je tolère, n. tolérons; je tolérerai)** (*a*) to tolerate (opinions, religions, etc.); *F:* to put up with (s.o., sth.); **t. qu'on fasse qch.,** to allow sth. to be done; (*b*) to allow tacitly, wink at (abuses, etc.); (*c*) *Med:* to tolerate (drug).

tôlerie [tolri] *n.f.* sheet-iron and steel-plate trade, works, goods.

tolet [tɔlɛ] *n.m.* *Nau:* thole pin.

tôlier[1] [tolje] *n.m.* **1.** sheet-iron merchant. **2.** sheet-metal worker; *Aut:* panel beater.

tôlier[2] *n.m.* *P:* = TAULIER.

tollé [tole] *n.m.* outcry (of indignation).

toluène [tɔlɥɛn] *n.m.* *Ch:* toluene, methyl benzene.

tomahawk [tɔmaok] *n.m.* tomahawk.

tomaison [tɔmɛzɔ̃] *n.f.* *Typ:* volume number(ing).

tomate [tɔmat] *n.f.* (*a*) *Bot:* tomato; **sauce t.,** tomato sauce; *F:* **être (rouge) comme une t.,** to be as red as a beetroot; (*b*) *P:* pastis (or absinthe) with grenadine.

tombal, -aux [tɔ̃bal, -o] *a.* **pierre tombale,** tombstone, gravestone.

tombant [tɔ̃bɑ̃] *a.* (*a*) falling; **à la nuit tombante,** at nightfall; (*b*) flowing (hair, lines of dress); drooping (branch, moustache); **épaules tombantes,** sloping shoulders.

tombe [tɔ̃b] *n.f.* (*a*) tomb, grave; **t. collective,** mass grave; **être dans la t.,** to be dead; **avoir un pied dans la t.,** to have one foot in the grave; (*b*) tombstone.

tombé [tɔ̃be] *a.* fallen; **roi t.,** fallen king; *Rugby Fb:* **coup de pied t.,** drop kick.

tombeau, -eaux [tɔ̃bo] *n.m.* tomb; monument (over grave or vault); **t. de famille,** family vault; **être aux portes du t.,** to have one foot in the grave; **mise au t.,** entombment; *F:* **il me mettra, conduira, au t.,** (i) he will outlive me; (ii) he'll be the death of me.

tombée [tɔ̃be] *n.f.* fall (of rain, night, etc.); **t. du jour, de la nuit,** nightfall.

tomber[1] [tɔ̃be] **I.** *v.i.* (*aux.* **être**) **1.** to fall (down); (*of aircraft*) to crash; **le plafond est tombé,** the ceiling has come down; **tout tombe en poussière,** everything is crumbling to dust; **la neige tombe,** snow is falling; *impers.* **il tombe de la pluie, de la grêle,** it is raining, hailing; **t. à bas d'une échelle,** to fall off a ladder; **t. de cheval,** to fall off a horse; **t. la tête la première,** to fall head first; **t. sur ses pieds,** to fall on one's feet; *F:* **t. dans les pommes,** to pass out, to faint; **je tombe de fatigue, de sommeil,** I'm ready to drop; **faire t. (qn, qch.),** (i) to knock, push (s.o., sth.) over; (ii) to bring down (the government, etc.); **laisser t. qch.,** to drop sth.; *F:* **laisser t. qn,** (i) to drop s.o.; (ii) to let s.o. down; **se laisser t. dans un fauteuil,** to drop, sink, *F:* flop, into an armchair; **mes cheveux commencent à t.,** I'm beginning to lose my hair; **t. à l'eau,** to fall in (the water); *Journ:* **le journal est tombé,** the paper has gone to bed; *F:* **les bras m'en tombent,** I can't believe it; **fruits tombés,** windfalls; **les feuilles tombent,** the leaves are falling. **2.** (*of wind, anger, fever, etc.*) to drop, abate, subside, die down; (*of conversation*) to flag; **laisser t. sa voix,** to drop one's voice; **la nuit, le jour, tombe,** night is falling; **une fois la nuit tombée,** after dark; **le vent, la conversation, tomba,** there was a lull in the wind, in the conversation; **le vent tombe,** the wind is dropping. **3. t. entre les mains, aux mains, sous la main, de qn,** to fall into s.o.'s hands, s.o.'s clutches; **t. dans un piège,** to fall into a trap; **t. en disgrâce,** to fall into disgrace; *Nau:* **t. sous le vent,** to fall off; to fall to leeward. **4. t. sur l'ennemi,** to attack, fall on, the enemy; *F:* **t. sur qn,** to pitch into s.o. **5. t. sur qn, sur qch.,** to come across, upon, s.o., sth.; **ce livre m'est tombé sous la main,** I came across this book; **il va nous t. sur le dos d'un moment à l'autre,** he'll be bursting in on us any moment; **Noël tombe un jeudi cette année,** Christmas falls, is, on a Thursday this year; **vous tombez bien,** (i) you've come at the right moment, in the nick of time; (ii) you've guessed right; **comme ça tombe!** what a coincidence! **t. juste,** (i) (*of thg*) to happen at the right time; (ii) (*of pers.*) to come at the right moment; (iii) *Mth:* to come out exactly; **cet argent lui tombe du ciel,** this money is a godsend to him. **6.** to fail; *Th:* **la pièce est tombée (à plat),** the play flopped, was a failure. **7.** (*of hair, drapery, etc.*) to fall, hang down; **ses cheveux lui tombent dans le dos,** her hair hangs down her back; **jupe qui tombe bien,** skirt that hangs well. **8. t. amoureux de qn,** to fall in love with s.o.; **t. malade,** to fall ill; **t. mort,** to drop dead. **II.** *v.tr.* (*aux.* **avoir**) (*a*) *Wr:* **t. un adversaire,** to throw, give a fall to, an opponent; *P:* **t. une femme,** to have, lay, a woman; (*b*) *Metalw:* to flange; (*c*) *F:* **t. la veste,** to take off one's jacket.

tomber[2] *n.m.* **1. au t. du jour,** at nightfall. **2.** *Wr:* fall.

tombereau, -eaux [tɔ̃bro] *n.m.* tip-cart; **t. à ordures,** dustcart, *NAm:* garbage truck; **un t. de fumier,** a cartload of manure.

tombeur [tɔ̃bœr] *n.m.* **t. (de femmes),** ladykiller.

tombola [tɔ̃bɔla] *n.f.* tombola, raffle.

Tombouctou [tɔ̃buktu] *Pr.n.* *Geog:* Timbuctoo.

tome [tɔm] *n.m.* volume; tome; part (of book).

tomer [tɔme] *v.tr.* *Typ:* to divide into volumes, parts.

tomme [tɔm] *n.f.* cheese (made in Savoie and Dauphiné).

tom-pouce [tɔmpus] *n.m.* **1.** *F:* dwarf; midget. **2.** stumpy umbrella, Tom Thumb umbrella; *pl. tom-pouces.*

ton[1], **ta, tes** [tɔ̃, ta, te] *poss.a.* (**ton** *is used instead of* **ta** *before fem. words beginning with a vowel or* **h** *mute; for the use of* **ton** *as opp. to* **votre**, *cf.* TU) **1.** your; **t. ami, t. amie,** your friend; **un de tes amis,** a friend of yours; **ta propre fille,** your own daughter; **c'est t. affaire à toi,** that's your business; *Lit:* **tes père et mère,** your father and mother. **2.** (*in Biblical style; in addressing the Deity; in dialect and literature*) thy; **que ta volonté soit faite,** Thy will be done.

ton[2] *n.m.* **1.** (*a*) tone, intonation; **parler d'un t. doux, sur un t. amical,** to speak gently, in a gentle tone, in a friendly tone; **hausser le t.,** to raise (the tone of) one's voice; **forcer le t.,** to speak more loudly and more urgently; **entre deux tons,** in an undertone; **les employés prennent le t. du chef,** the employees take their tone from the boss; **changer de t.,** to change one's tone; *F:* **faire baisser le t. à qn,** to take s.o. down a peg (or two); **écrire sur un t. de plaisanterie,** to write in a humorous tone, style; **elle le prend sur ce t.?** is that how she speaks to you? (*b*) tone, manners, breeding; **le bon t.,** good form; **c'est de mauvais t.,** it is bad form, bad manners, vulgar; (*c*) *Mus:* tone (of instrument). **2.** *Mus:* (*a*) **(hauteur du) t.,** pitch; **donner le t.,** (i) to give (an orchestra) the tuning A; (ii) *F:* to set, lead, the fashion; **sortir du t.,** to be out of tune; **se mettre dans le t.,** to tune up; (*b*) key; **le t. d'ut,** the key of C; **t. d'église,** church mode; *F:* **chanter sur un autre t.,** to change one's tune; **parler d'un t. bas,** to speak in a low key; (*of voice*) **monter de t.,** to rise in pitch; (*c*) **tons et demi-tons,** tones and semitones; **t. entier,** whole tone. **3.** *Ling:*

pitch, accent. **4.** *Art: Phot:* tone, tint, colour, *NAm:* color; shade; **tons chauds,** warm tints; **tapis dans le t. des rideaux,** carpet toning with the curtains; **peinture, voiture, deux tons,** two-tone paint, car. **5.** *Med: A:* tone. **6.** *Ven:* **t. de chasse,** hunting call (to hounds).

tonal, -als [tɔnal] *a. Mus:* tonal.

tonalité [tɔnalite] *n.f. Art: Phot: Mus:* tonality; **paysage d'une t. claire,** landscape in a light key; *Tp:* **t. (continue),** dialling tone; **t. d'appel,** ringing tone.

tondeur, -euse [tɔ̃dœr, -øz] **1.** *n.* shearer (of cloth, sheep). **2.** *n.f.* **tondeuse** (*a*) *Husb: Tex:* shearing machine; shears (for cloth, sheep); clippers (for human hair, for animal's coat); (*b*) **tondeuse (à gazon),** lawn mower.

tondre [tɔ̃dr̥] *v.tr.* to shear (cloth, sheep); to crop (cloth); to clip (hair, horse, hedge); to mow (the lawn); *F:* to fleece (s.o.).

tondu [tɔ̃dy] **1.** *a.* mown (grass); clipped (hedge); shorn (sheep); *F:* (*of pers.*) shorn. **2.** *n.m. Ecc:* monk; *Hist: F:* **le petit t.,** Napoleon (Bonaparte).

tonicardiaque [tɔnikardjak] *a. & n.m.* cardiotonic; heart stimulant.

tonicité [tɔnisite] *n.f. Med:* tonicity, elasticity (of the muscles, etc.); tonus.

tonifiant [tɔnifjɑ̃] *a.* bracing, tonic.

tonification [tɔnifikasjɔ̃] *n.f.* toning up.

tonifier [tɔnifje] *v.tr.* (*impf. & pr.sub.* **n. tonifiions, v. tonifiiez**) to tone up (the nervous system, a patient, etc.); to give tone to (the skin, etc.); to invigorate.

tonique [tɔnik] *a.* **1.** *Med:* (*a*) **convulsion t.,** tonic spasm, tonus; (*b*) **médicament t.,** *n.m.* **t.,** tonic (medicine); (*c*) *n.m. F:* tonic water; (*d*) stimulating, revivifying. **2.** *Ling:* tonic (accent); accented, stressed (syllable); **l'accent t. tombe sur . . .,** the stress falls on . . .. **3.** *Mus:* **note t.,** *n.f.* **t.,** tonic, keynote; do (of movable do system).

tonitruant [tɔnitryɑ̃] *a.* like thunder, thundering, resounding (voice).

tonitruer [tɔnitrye] *v.i.* to thunder, resound.

tonka [tɔ̃ka] *n.m. Bot:* tonka bean (plant); **fève t.,** *n.f.* **t.,** tonka bean.

tonnage [tɔnaʒ] *n.m. Nau:* **1.** tonnage (of ship); **t. brut,** gross tonnage; **t. net,** register tonnage; *N. Arch:* displacement (of warship). **2.** tonnage (of a port). **3. (droit de) t.,** (duty based on) tonnage.

tonnant [tɔnɑ̃] *a.* thundering; **voix tonnante,** voice of thunder.

tonne [tɔn] *n.f.* **1.** tun; (large) cask. **2.** (*a*) *Meas:* (metric) ton (= 1000 kilogrammes); tonne; **t. courte,** short ton (= 907.185 kg); **t. forte,** long ton, gross ton (= 1016.06 kg); **t. kilométrique,** ton kilometre, *NAm:* kilometer; *F:* **des tonnes de,** tons of; (*b*) *Nau:* **t. de déplacement,** ton of displacement; **t. de jauge,** gross ton, register ton.

tonneau, -eaux [tɔno] *n.m.* **1.** (*a*) cask, tun, barrel; **un t. de vin,** a barrel, a cask, of wine; **bière au t.,** beer from the wood; draught, *NAm:* draft, beer; **du même t.,** of the same kind; alike; **petit t.,** keg; (*b*) **t. à mortier,** mortar mixer; (mixing, steaming, tumbling) drum; *Hist:* **le t. de Diogène,** Diogenes' tub; (*c*) **t. d'arrosage,** water cart. **2.** *Nau:* **navire de 500 tonneaux,** 500-tonner, ship of 500 tons burden. **3.** *A.Veh:* governess cart. **4.** (*a*) *Av:* roll; (*b*) **faire un t.,** to flip, roll, over; **la voiture a fait trois tonneaux,** the car turned over three times.

tonnelet [tɔnlɛ] *n.m.* small cask; keg.

tonnelier [tɔnəlje] *n.m.* (wet) cooper.

tonnelle [tɔnɛl] *n.f.* **1.** (*a*) arbour, *NAm:* arbor; bower; (*b*) *Arch:* semicircular arch, perfect arch. **2.** *Ven: A:* tunnel net (for catching partridges).

tonnellerie [tɔnɛlri] *n.f.* cooperage.

tonner [tɔne] *v.i.* **1.** to thunder; *impers.* **il tonne,** it is thundering. **2.** (*of cannon, etc.*) to boom; *F:* **t. contre qn, qch.,** to thunder against s.o., sth.

tonnerre [tɔnɛr] *n.m.* (*a*) thunder; **coup de t.,** (i) clap, peal, of thunder; thunderclap; (ii) *Fig:* bombshell; **roulement de t.,** roll of thunder; **t. d'applaudissements,** thunderous applause; **(voix de) t.,** voice of, like, thunder; (*b*) thunderbolt; lightning; **le t. est tombé sur une maison,** a house was struck by lightning; (*c*) *int.* **t. (de Dieu, de Brest)!** heavens above! *attrib. F:* **du t.,** wonderful, terrific; **il fera un marin du t. (de Dieu),** he'll make a thundering good, a hell of a good, sailor; **un dîner du t. de Dieu,** a stupendous dinner.

tonométrie [tɔnɔmetri] *n.f.* tonometry.

tonsure [tɔ̃syr] *n.f.* (*a*) tonsure; (*b*) *F:* bald patch.

tonsurer [tɔ̃syre] *v.tr.* to tonsure (a cleric); **tête tonsurée,** shaven head; *n.m.* **un tonsuré,** a cleric; a priest.

tonte [tɔ̃t] *n.f.* **1.** *Husb:* (*a*) sheep shearing; (*b*) clip; (*c*) shearing time. **2.** *Hort:* mowing (of lawn).

tontine¹ [tɔ̃tin] *n.f. Ins:* tontine.

tontine² *n.f.* protective sacking (round roots of trees to be transplanted).

tonton [tɔ̃tɔ̃] *n.m. F:* uncle.

tonus [tɔnys] *n.m.* (*a*) *Med:* tonicity (of muscle); tonus, tone; (*b*) (*of pers.*) energy, dynamism.

top [tɔp] *n.m. W.Tel: T.V:* time signal; **les tops,** the pips; *Elcs:* **t. d'écho,** blip, *U.S:* pip; **t. de synchronisation,** synchronizing signal; *int.* **un, deux, trois, t.!** one, two, three, now!

topaze [tɔpaz] *n.f.* topaz.

toper [tɔpe] *v.i. F:* to agree (**à qch.,** to sth.); **tope (là)!** done! agreed!

tophus [tɔfys] *n.m. Med:* tophus.

topinambour [tɔpinɑ̃bur] *n.m. Bot: Cu:* Jerusalem artichoke.

topique [tɔpik] **1.** *a. Med:* topical, local; **remède t.,** *n.m.* **t.,** topical remedy. **2.** *Phil:* (*a*) *a.* **lieu t.,** commonplace; (*b*) *n.f.* **la t.,** topics.

topo [tɔpo] *n.m. F:* (*a*) *Journ:* article; (*b*) lecture; **c'est toujours le même t.,** it's always the same old story.

topographe [tɔpɔgraf] *n.* topographer.

topographie [tɔpɔgrafi] *n.f.* **1.** topography. **2.** map, plan.

topographique [tɔpɔgrafik] *a.* topographic(al); surveying (instruments).

topologie [tɔpɔlɔʒi] *n.f.* topology.

topologique [tɔpɔlɔʒik] *a.* topologic(al).

toponyme [tɔpɔnim] *n.m.* toponym, place name.

toponymie [tɔpɔnimi] *n.f.* toponymy.

toponymiste [tɔpɔnimist] *n.* toponymist.

toquade [tɔkad] *n.f. F:* craze (for sth.); infatuation (with s.o.).

toquante [tɔkɑ̃t] *n.f. F:* watch, ticker.

toquard [tɔkar] = TOCARD.

toque [tɔk] *n.f. Cost:* cap.

toqué [tɔke] *a. F:* **1.** crazy, nuts. **2.** infatuated, madly in love (**de,** with).

toquer [tɔke] **1.** *v.tr. Dial: & F:* to knock, rap (at door, etc.). **2.** *F:* **se t. de qn,** to fall for s.o., to go crazy over s.o.

torche [tɔrʃ] *n.f.* torch; **t. électrique,** electric torch; *NAm:* flashlight.

torché [tɔrʃe] *a. F:* (*a*) **bien t.,** well done, (pretty) good; (*b*) botched, scamped (work, etc.).

torche-cul [tɔrʃky] *n.m.inv. P:* (*a*) loo paper, bog roll; (*b*) trashy book, article.

torchée [tɔrʃe] *n.f. P:* good thrashing.

torcher [tɔrʃe] *v.tr.* **1.** *F:* to wipe (sth.) clean; *P:* **je m'en torche,** I don't care a damn; *P:* **tu peux te t.!** you've had it! **2.** *F:* to do (sth.) in a hurry; to botch, scamp (sth.).

torchère [tɔrʃɛr] *n.f.* candelabra.

torchis [tɔrʃi] *n.m. Const:* cob, daub.

torchon [tɔrʃɔ̃] **1.** *n.m.* (*a*) (kitchen) cloth; floorcloth; dishcloth; tea towel; duster; *F:* **le t. brûle chez eux,** they lead a cat and dog life; **il ne faut pas mélanger les torchons et les serviettes,** we mustn't get our values mixed; (*b*) *F:* badly written article; (*newspaper*) rag. **2.** *a.inv. Art:* **papier t.,** torchon paper.
torchonner [tɔrʃɔne] *v.tr. F:* to scamp, botch (piece of work).
torcol [tɔrkɔl] *n.m. Orn:* **t. (fourmilier),** wryneck.
tordant [tɔrdɑ̃] *a. F:* screamingly funny.
tord-boyaux [tɔrbwajo] *n.m. P:* (*poor quality brandy*) rotgut.
tordeur, -euse [tɔrdœr, -øz] **1.** *n. Tex:* twister. **2.** *n.f.* **tordeuse** (*a*) cable-twisting machine; (*b*) *Ent:* leaf roller.
tordre [tɔrdr̥] **1.** *v.tr.* to twist (wool, wire, etc.); to wring (clothes, etc.); to twist (one's hair into a bun); **t. le cou à un poulet,** *F:* **à qn,** to wring a chicken's, s.o.'s, neck; **t. la bouche,** to pull a face; **se t. le pied,** to twist one's ankle. **2. se t.,** to writhe, twist (with pain, etc.); *F:* **se t. (de rire), rire à se t.,** to split one's sides laughing; **il y a de quoi se t.,** it's enough to make a cat laugh.
tordu, -ue [tɔrdy] *a.* **1.** twisted, distorted (limbs, features); bent, buckled (chassis, etc.); *P:* **avoir la gueule tordue,** to be as ugly as sin. **2.** (*a*) warped (mind); (*b*) *F:* mad, cracked, round the bend; *n.* **c'est un t., une tordue,** he's, she's, (quite) mad.
tore [tɔr] *n.m. Arch: Bot: Mth:* torus; *Cmptr:* (magnetic) core.
toréador [tɔreadɔr] *n.m.* toreador, bullfighter.
toréer [tɔree] *v.i.* to fight (in the bullring).
torgnole [tɔrɲɔl] *n.f. P:* blow, slap, clout.
toril [tɔril] *n.m.* bull pen.
torique [tɔrik] *a. Mth: Opt: etc:* toric.
tormentille [tɔrmɑ̃tij] *n.f. Bot:* tormentil.
tornade [tɔrnad] *n.f.* tornado; hurricane (of abuse, etc.); **entrer comme une t.,** to come in like a whirlwind.
toron [tɔrɔ̃] *n.m.* strand (of rope).
torpédo [tɔrpedo] *n.f. Aut: A:* open tourer.
torpeur [tɔrpœr] *n.f.* torpor; **je voulus le faire sortir de sa t.,** I tried to rouse him.
torpide [tɔrpid] *a.* torpid.
torpillage [tɔrpijaʒ] *n.m.* torpedoing.
torpille [tɔrpij] *n.f.* **1.** *Ich:* torpedo (ray), electric ray. **2.** *Navy: etc:* (*a*) torpedo; **t. d'avion,** aerial torpedo; (*b*) *occ.* mine.
torpiller [tɔrpije] *v.tr.* to torpedo (ship, oil well, *Fig:* project).
torpillerie [tɔrpijri] *n.f.* torpedo store, gear.
torpilleur [tɔrpijœr] *n.m. Navy: A:* torpedo boat.
torque [tɔrk] **1.** *n.m. A.Cost:* torque. **2.** *n.f.* coil of wire.
torréfacteur [tɔrefaktœr] *n.m.* roaster (for coffee, etc.).
torréfaction [tɔrefaksjɔ̃] *n.f.* torrefaction.
torréfiant [tɔrefjɑ̃] *a.* roasting.
torréfier [tɔrefje] *v.tr.* (*impf. & pr.sub.* **n. torréfiions, v. torréfiiez)** to roast (coffee, maize, etc.).
torrent [tɔrɑ̃] *n.m.* torrent, mountain stream; **il pleut à torrents,** it's raining in torrents; **t. de larmes, de lumière,** flood of tears, of light; **t. d'injures,** torrent of abuse.
torrentiel, -ielle [tɔrɑ̃sjɛl] *a.* torrential.
torrentueux, -euse [tɔrɑ̃tɥø, -øz] *a. Lit:* torrent-like (river, etc.); stormy, tempestuous (life, etc.).
torride [tɔrid] *a.* torrid (zone, etc.); scorching (heat, etc.).
tors, torse, *occ.* **torte** [tɔr, tɔrs, tɔrt] **1.** *a.* twisted. **2.** *n.m.* twist (of rope, etc.).
torsade [tɔrsad] *n.f.* **1.** twisted fringe, cord; **t. de cheveux,** twist, coil, of hair; *Knit:* **(point) t.,** cable stitch. **2.** *Arch:* rope moulding, cable moulding, *NAm:* molding.
torsadé [tɔrsade] *a. El: Tp:* **paire torsadée,** twisted pair; **raccord t.,** twist joint.
torsader [tɔrsade] *v.tr.* **1.** to twist (rope, wire, etc.); to coil (hair). **2.** to twist (wires, etc.) together.
torse [tɔrs] *n.m.* torso, trunk; **le t. nu,** stripped to the waist; **bomber le t.,** (i) to stick out one's chest; (ii) *Fig:* to be swollen with pride.
torseur [tɔrsœr] *n.m. Mec:* torque.
torsion [tɔrsjɔ̃] *n.f.* torsion; twisting.
tort [tɔr] *n.m.* wrong. **1.** error, fault; **avoir t., être dans son t.,** to be wrong, in the wrong; **il a eu le t. de ne pas demander de reçu,** he made the mistake of not asking for a receipt; **donner t. à qn,** to lay the blame on s.o.; **avoir des torts envers qn,** to have treated s.o. badly; **il a tous les torts,** he is entirely to blame; *adv. phr.* **à t.,** wrongly; **à t. ou à raison,** rightly or wrongly; **à t. et à travers,** at random, without rhyme or reason. **2.** injury, harm, detriment, hurt; **la grêle a fait beaucoup de t.,** the hail has done a great deal of damage; **faire du t. à qn,** (i) to wrong s.o.; to do s.o. an injustice; (ii) to damage s.o.'s cause, business, reputation; **quel t. cela peut-il vous faire?** what harm can it do you?
torticolis [tɔrtikɔli] *n.m. Med:* stiff neck; torticollis.
tortillard [tɔrtijar] *n.m.* local train (on a narrow gauge line).
tortillement [tɔrtijmɑ̃] *n.m.* twisting, twist; wiggling (of hips).
tortiller [tɔrtije] **1.** *v.tr.* (*a*) to twist (up) (paper, ribbon, hair, etc.); (*b*) *P:* to wolf down, make short work of (food). **2.** *v.i.* (*a*) **t. des hanches,** to swing, wiggle, the hips; (*b*) *F:* to quibble. **3. se t.,** to wriggle; *Fig:* to bend over backwards (to do sth.).
tortillon [tɔrtijɔ̃] *n.m.* **1.** twist (of paper, etc.); sweet wrapper. **2.** pad (on head, for carrying loads).
tortillonner [tɔrtijɔne] *v.i. & tr.* (*a*) to twist and turn; (*b*) to quibble; to hedge.
tortionnaire [tɔrsjɔnɛr] *n.m.* torturer.
tortu [tɔrty] *a. Lit:* crooked.
tortue [tɔrty] *n.f.* **1.** tortoise; **t. de mer,** turtle; **à pas de t.,** at a snail's pace; *F:* **c'est une vraie t.,** he's a real slowcoach. **2.** *Rom.Ant:* testudo, tortoise. **3.** *Ent:* tortoiseshell (butterfly).
tortueusement [tɔrtɥøzmɑ̃] *adv.* tortuously.
tortueux, -euse [tɔrtɥø, -øz] *a.* tortuous, winding, meandering (river, street); devious (conduct, person).
torturant [tɔrtyrɑ̃] *a.* tormenting (thoughts, etc.).
torture [tɔrtyr] *n.f.* torture; **mettre qn à la t.,** to torture s.o.
torturer [tɔrtyre] *v.tr.* **1.** to torture (prisoner, etc.); **la jalousie le torturait,** he was tortured by jealousy; **se t. l'esprit,** to rack one's brains. **2.** to strain, distort.
torve [tɔrv] *a.* grim; menacing.
toscan, -ane[1] [tɔskɑ̃, -an] *a. & n. Geog: Arch:* Tuscan.
Toscane[2] *Pr.n.f. Geog:* Tuscany.
tôt [to] *adv.* (*a*) soon; **le plus t. possible,** as soon as possible; **mardi au plus t.,** (on) Tuesday at the earliest; **le plus t. sera le mieux,** the sooner the better; **t. après,** soon after; **t. ou tard,** sooner or later; **nous n'étions pas plus t. rentrés que . . .,** we had no sooner returned than . . .; **revenez au plus t.,** come back as soon as possible; (*b*) early; **se lever t.,** to get up early; **t. dans l'après-midi,** early in the afternoon; **vous auriez dû me le dire plus t.,** you should have told me so sooner, earlier, before; *a.* **il est trop t. pour manger,** it's too early to have a meal; *P:* **c'est pas trop t.!** and about time too!
total, -aux [tɔtal, -o] **1.** *a.* total (sum, eclipse, war,

destruction); complete, whole. **2.** *n.m.* whole, total; **faire le t. de,** to add up; **au t.,** all in all; *F:* **et t., on l'a sacqué,** and, to cut a long story short, he got the sack.

totalement [tɔtalmɑ̃] *adv.* totally, completely.

totalisateur, -trice [tɔtalizatœr, -tris] **1.** *a.* adding (machine, etc.). **2.** *n.m.* adding machine; *Turf:* totalizer, totalizator, *F:* tote.

totalisation [tɔtalizasjɔ̃] *n.f.* totalling, adding up.

totaliser [tɔtalize] *v.tr.* **1.** to total, add up. **2.** to total, add up to.

totalitaire [tɔtalitɛr] *a.* totalitarian.

totalitarisme [tɔtalitarism] *n.m.* totalitarianism.

totalité [tɔtalite] *n.f.* totality, whole; **la (presque) t. de,** (almost) all of; **en t.,** wholly; **pris dans sa t.,** taken as a whole.

totem [tɔtɛm] *n.m.* totem.

toto [tɔto] *n.m.* *P:* (body) louse; cootie.

toton [tɔtɔ̃] *n.m.* teetotum.

touage [twaʒ] *n.m.* *Nau:* towing.

Touareg [twarɛg] **1.** *a. & n.inv.* *Ethn:* T(o)uareg. **2.** *n.m.* *Ling:* T(o)uareg.

toubib [tubib] *n.m.* *F:* doctor, quack.

toucan [tukɑ̃] *n.m.* *Orn:* toucan.

touchant [tuʃɑ̃] **1.** *a.* touching, moving (sight, speech). **2.** *prep.* *Lit:* touching, concerning, about.

touche [tuʃ] *n.f.* **1.** (*a*) touch, touching; **pierre de t.,** touchstone; (*b*) *Art:* (brush)stroke; **comme t. finale,** as a finishing touch; (*c*) touch, manner (of painter); style (of writer); (*d*) *Bill:* *Fenc:* *Lit:* hit; (*e*) *Fish:* bite, nibble; *F:* **avoir, faire, une t. avec qn,** to make a hit with s.o.; (*f*) *Sp:* (*hockey*) roll-in; *Fb:* (i) touch(line); (ii) throw-in; **rester sur la t.,** to stay on the sidelines; (*g*) *P:* appearance, look(s); **drôle de t.,** weird-looking guy; (*h*) *P:* shot, jab (of narcotic, etc.). **2.** (*a*) key (of piano, typewriter, computer, etc.); (*b*) finger board (of violin); *pl.* frets, stops (of guitar, etc.).

touche-à-tout [tuʃatu] *F:* **1.** *a.inv.* meddling, meddlesome. **2.** *n.inv.* (*a*) meddler, busybody; (*b*) Jack-of-all-trades.

toucher[1] [tuʃe] **1.** *v.tr.* (*a*) to touch (s.o. on the shoulder, etc.); *Fb:* to handle (the ball); to hit (*Bill:* a ball, *Fenc:* one's opponent, *Artil:* the mark); *F:* **touche du bois!** touch wood; *v.ind.tr.* **t. du piano,** to play the piano; *F:* (*to child*) **pas touche!** don't touch! **ils se sont touché dans la main,** they shook hands on it; **t. ses appointements,** *v.i.* **t.,** to draw, receive, one's salary; to be paid; **t. un chèque,** to cash a cheque, *NAm:* check; *Rugby Fb:* **t. dans les buts,** to touch down; (*b*) to move, touch (s.o.); **t. qn jusqu'aux larmes,** to move s.o. to tears; (*c*) to concern, affect; **en ce qui vous touche,** as far as you are concerned; (*d*) *Nau:* to touch (land); *v.i.* (*of ship*) **t. à un port,** to touch, call, at a port; (*e*) *Min:* **t. le pétrole,** to strike oil; (*f*) *Nau:* **t. (le fond),** (i) to strike, touch (bottom); (ii) to be aground; (*g*) to get hold of (s.o.); (*of letter*) to reach (s.o.); (*h*) to touch on, deal with (fact, subject); **je lui en toucherai un mot, deux mots,** I'll mention it to him. **2.** *v.ind.tr.* to meddle, interfere (**à,** with); to touch, to tamper with (sth.); **n'y touchez pas!** (keep your) hands off! **on ne touche pas!** hands off! **il n'avait pas touché à la nourriture,** he had left the food untouched; **avoir l'air de ne pas y t., n'avoir pas l'air d'y t.,** to look as if butter wouldn't melt in one's mouth. **3.** *v.i.* (*a*) **t. à qch.,** to be in touch, in contact, with sth.; to be near, close, to sth.; to border on (a country); to adjoin (house, garden); **économie qui touche à l'avarice,** thrift that borders on avarice; **l'année touche à sa fin,** the year is drawing to a close; **t. à la quarantaine,** to be nearing forty; (*b*) **t. à,** to concern; to affect; (*c*) **palmes qui touchent au plafond,** palms that touch, reach, the ceiling; **t. à terre,** to touch the ground.

toucher[2] *n.m.* **1.** (*a*) touch, feel; **reconnaître qch. au t.,** to know sth. by the touch, by the feel of it; **le mur était chaud au t.,** the wall was hot to the touch, felt hot; (*b*) *Med:* examination. **2.** (pianist's) touch.

touchette [tuʃɛt] *n.f.* fret (of mandolin, guitar).

toucheur, -euse [tuʃœr, -øz] *n.* (cattle) drover.

touée [twe] *n.f.* *Nau:* **1.** (*a*) warping; (*b*) kedging; **ancre de t.,** kedge. **2.** scope (of towline, etc.). **3.** warp(ing rope), cable.

touer [twe] *v.tr.* *Nau:* (*a*) to warp; (*b*) to kedge.

toueur [twœr] *n.m.* *Nau:* tug.

touffe [tuf] *n.f.* tuft (of hair, grass, etc.); clump (of trees).

touffeur [tufœr] *n.f.* *A:* suffocating heat (of a room).

touffu [tufy] *a.* bushy (beard, etc.); thick (wood); solid, abstruse (book).

touillage [tujaʒ] *n.m.* *F:* mixing, stirring.

touiller [tuje] *v.tr.* *F:* to stir (up); to mix, toss (salad, etc.); to shuffle (cards).

toujours [tuʒur] *adv.* **1.** always; ever; **un ami de t.,** a lifelong friend; **pour t., à t.,** for ever. **2.** still; **il fait t. aussi chaud,** it is as hot as ever; **cherchez t.,** go on looking; **allez t.!** go ahead! go on! **3.** nevertheless, all the same, anyhow, always; but; **je peux t. essayer,** I can always, at least, try; **entrez t.,** come in anyhow; **t. est-il que . . .,** the fact remains that . . .; anyhow . . .; **c'est t. ça,** it's better than nothing at any rate; it's always something.

toundra [tundra] *n.f.* *Geog:* tundra.

toupet [tupɛ] *n.m.* **1.** (*a*) tuft of hair, quiff; (*b*) forelock; *Hairdr:* **(faux) t.,** toupee, toupet. **2.** *F:* **quel t.!** what a cheek, a nerve! **il a eu le t. de . . .,** he had the cheek, the nerve, to . . ..

toupie [tupi] *n.f.* **1.** (*toy*) top. **2.** (*a*) *Carp: etc:* moulding, *NAm:* molding, machine; (*b*) *Furn:* moulded, *NAm:* molded, foot (Louis XVI style). **3.** *F:* **vieille t.,** old frump; old trout.

toupillon [tupijɔ̃] *n.m.* small tuft of hair, of branches.

tour[1] [tur] *n.f.* **1.** (*a*) tower; **(immeuble) t.,** tower block; **t. de moulin à vent,** tower of windmill; **t. d'observation,** watchtower, observation tower; conning tower; **la T. Eiffel,** the Eiffel Tower; (*b*) *Av:* **t. de contrôle,** control tower; *Ball:* **t. de remplissage,** umbilical tower (for rocket fuelling); (*c*) *Ind:* *Ch:* **t. de fractionnement,** fractionating tower; **t. de réfrigération,** cooling tower; **t. de sondage, de forage,** derrick; rig; (*d*) *F:* massively built person. **2.** *Chess:* castle, rook.

tour[2] *n.m.* **1.** (*a*) (turning) lathe; **fait au t.,** (i) machine-turned; (ii) *F:* shapely (leg, etc.); **atelier des tours,** turning shop; (*b*) (potter's) wheel. **2.** (*a*) circumference, circuit; **ville qui a dix kilomètres de t.,** town ten kilometres, *NAm:* kilometers, in circumference; **faire le t. du monde,** to go round the world; **faire un t. d'horizon,** to make a general survey of the situation; *Sp:* **t. de piste, de circuit,** lap; **T. de France (cycliste),** Tour de France (cycle race); **faire le t. du cadran,** to sleep the clock round; **faire le grand t.,** to take the longest way round; **avoir 75 cm. de t. de taille,** to have a waist measurement of 75 cm.; **arbre qui a deux mètres de t.,** tree with a girth of two metres, *NAm:* meters; (*b*) **t. de lit,** bed valence; (*c*) *Nau: etc:* turn (round the bitt); **prendre un t.,** to take a turn; **avoir des tours,** to have a foul hawse; (*d*) **tours et retours d'un chemin,** twists and turns of a road; (*e*) turn (of phrase); shape, contour (of face, etc.); course, direction (of business affair); **l'affaire prend un mauvais t.,** the matter is taking a bad turn; **donner un autre t. à la conversation,** to turn the conversation; **t. d'esprit,** turn of mind; (*f*) **se donner un t. de reins,** to strain, (w)rick, one's back. **3.** (*a*) round, revolution, turn (of wheel, engine); **donner un t. de clef à la porte,** to turn the key in, to lock, the door; **frapper à t. de bras,** to strike with all one's might; *F:* **le sang ne m'a fait qu'un t.,** my heart seemed to stop beating; (*b*) stroll; **faire un t. de jardin,** to have, take, a turn, a stroll, round the garden; *F:* **faire un petit t.,** to go and spend a penny; (*c*) trip, tour; **faire un t.,** to go for a tour; (*d*) row (of crochet, knitting). **4.** (*a*) rotation, turn; **à qui le t.?** whose turn is it? **t. de service,** spell of duty; **chacun à son t.,** each one in his turn; **t. à t.,** in turn; by turns; turn and turn about; **s'emporter et se calmer t. à t.,** to flare up one moment and calm down the next; (*b*) *Cards:* round; *Th: etc:* turn; number; **t. de chant,** vocal number. **5.** trick, feat; **faire, jouer, un mauvais t. à qn,** to play s.o. a nasty trick; **un t. de main,** a flick of the wrist; *F:* **il peut faire ça en un t. de main,** he can do it standing on his head; **je n'ai pas le t. de main,** I haven't the knack of it; **t. de force,** feat of strength; *F:* **avoir plus d'un t. dans son sac,** to have more than one trick up one's sleeve.

tourbe [turb] *n.f.* peat; turf.

tourbeux, -euse [turbø, -øz] *a.* peaty, boggy (soil, etc.).

tourbière [turbjɛr] *n.f.* peat bog; peatery.

tourbillon [turbijɔ̃] *n.m.* **1.** whirlwind; (*of dust*) **monter en tourbillons,** to swirl up; **t. de neige,** flurry of snow. **2.** (*a*) whirlpool; (*b*) eddy (of water, wind); (*c*) *Ph: etc:* vortex; (*d*) whirl (of life, business, pleasures, etc.). **3.** *Astr: Phil:* vortex.

tourbillonnaire [turbijɔnɛr] *a.* vortical; swirling.

tourbillonnant [turbijɔnɑ̃] *a.* whirling (wheels, senses, etc.).

tourbillonnement [turbijɔnmɑ̃] *n.m.* whirl(ing).

tourbillonner [turbijɔne] *v.i.* to whirl (round); to eddy, swirl.

tourelle [turɛl] *n.f.* (*a*) *Arch:* turret; (*b*) *Fort: Mil: Navy:* (gun) turret; (*c*) *Opt: Phot:* **t. à objectifs,** lens turret; (*d*) *Mec.E:* capstan (head), turret (head) (of lathe).

tourillon [turijɔ̃] *n.m.* **1.** (*a*) pivot (pin); (*b*) link pin; (*c*) (wheel) spindle. **2.** (*a*) journal (of shaft, axle); (*b*) trunnion (of gun, etc.).

tourisme [turism] *n.m.* tourism; touring; tourist trade; **agence, bureau, de t.,** travel agency, tourist agency; **centre, ville, de t.,** tourist centre, *NAm:* center.

touriste [turist] *n.* tourist; (holiday) visitor; *Pej:* tripper; *Nau: Av:* **classe t.,** tourist class.

touristique [turistik] *a.* tourist (guide, information).

tourmaline [turmalin] *n.f. Miner:* tourmaline.

tourment [turmɑ̃] *n.m.* (*a*) *A: & Lit:* torture (of prisoner, etc.); (*b*) torture, anguish; *pl.* pangs (of hunger, jealousy); torment (of uncertainty); (*c*) (*of pers.*) cause of great anxiety; bane (of s.o.'s life).

tourmente [turmɑ̃t] *n.f.* (*a*) *Lit:* gale, tempest; **t. de neige,** blizzard; (*b*) (political, etc.) upheaval.

tourmenté [turmɑ̃te] *a.* (*a*) distorted, contorted; jagged (coastline); wild (landscape); (*b*) tortured (conscience, face); (*c*) turbulent (sea, life, mind); (*d*) *Art: Arch: etc:* unnatural, exaggerated; overelaborate.

tourmenter [turmɑ̃te] **1.** *v.tr.* *A:* to torture (prisoner, etc.); (*b*) to torture, harass (s.o.); **l'ambition tourmente l'homme,** man is tormented by ambition; **il est tourmenté par la goutte,** he is racked, tortured, with gout; (*c*) to harry, pester, plague (s.o.). **2. se t.,** to be anxious, uneasy; to worry; **ne vous tourmentez pas!** don't worry!

tourmentin [turmɑ̃tɛ̃] *n.m.* **1.** *Nau:* storm jib. **2.** *Orn:* petrel.

tournage [turnaʒ] *n.m.* **1.** (*a*) turning (on the lathe); lathe work; (*b*) *Cer:* turning; shaping (on the wheel). **2.** *Nau:* belaying. **3.** *Cin:* shooting.

tournailler [turnaje] *F:* *v.i.* to keep wandering round and round; to prowl (about).

tournant, -ante [turnɑ̃, -ɑ̃t] **1.** *a.* (*a*) turning; revolving (bookcase, etc.); live (axle); **fauteuil t., siège t.,** swivel chair, seat; **pont t.,** swing bridge; *Rail: etc:* **plaque tournante,** turntable; **plateau t.,** turntable (of record player); (*b*) winding (road, etc.); spiral (staircase). **2.** *n.m.* (*a*) turning; bend (in road, river); (street) corner; *F:* **savoir prendre le t.,** to know how to adapt oneself to a situation; *F:* **je l'aurai au t.!** I'll get him yet! (*b*) turning point (**de,** in).

tourne [turn] *n.f.* **1.** (*a*) turning, going sour (of milk); (*b*) souring (of wine). **2.** *Journ:* continuation (of article on another page).

tourné [turne] *a.* **1.** turned (on a lathe); shaped, made; **bien t.,** well made; **une petite brune bien tournée,** a little brunette with a lovely figure; **phrase bien tournée,** neatly turned sentence; **mal t.,** (i) badly made; (ii) ugly; unattractive; **avoir l'esprit mal t.,** to have an unpleasant turn of mind. **2.** sour (milk, etc.); spoilt, sour (wine). **3.** *prep.* **t. le coin c'est la deuxième maison,** when you have turned the corner it's the second house.

tourne-à-gauche [turnagoʃ] *n.m.inv.* *Tls:* wrench.

tournebouler [turnəbule] *v.tr.* *F:* to upset (s.o.).

tournebroche [turnəbrɔʃ] *n.m.* *Cu:* **1.** roasting jack. **2.** *A:* turnspit (dog or boy).

tourne-disque(s) [turnədisk] *n.m.* record player; *pl. tourne-disques.*

tournedos [turnədo] *n.m.* *Cu:* tournedos; fillet steak.

tournée [turne] *n.f.* **1.** (official's, doctor's, postman's) round; *Th:* **en t.,** on tour; **faire la t. des musées,** to go round, *F:* to do, the art galleries; **faire une t. en France,** to go on a trip through France; **faire une t. électorale,** to canvass a constituency; **t. de golf,** round of golf. **2.** (*a*) *F:* **payer une t.,** to stand a round (of drinks), to pay for, stand, drinks all round; (*b*) *P:* **flanquer une t. à qn,** to thrash s.o.

tournemain [turnəmɛ̃] *n.m.* *used in the phr.* **en un t.,** in an instant, in the twinkling of an eye.

tourner [turne] *v.* to turn. **1.** *v.tr.* (*a*) to fashion, shape, turn (sth.) on lathe; to turn (a phrase); *Cer:* to throw (a pot); (*b*) to revolve, turn round, rotate (wheel, etc.); to turn (key in lock); *F:* **t. qn. à son gré,** to twist s.o. round one's little finger; **t. qch. autour de qch.,** to wind sth. round sth.; *Nau:* **tournez au taquet!** take a turn round the cleat! **t. la tête, les yeux, vers qn,** to turn one's head, one's eyes, towards s.o.; **t. le dos à qn, à qch.,** (i) to turn one's back on s.o., on sth.; to turn away from s.o.; (ii) to have one's back turned to s.o., to sth.; to face the other way; **t. le dos à ses assaillants,** to turn tail; **t. les pieds en dedans, en dehors,** to turn in, turn out, one's toes; *Cin:* **t. un film,** to make a film; **t. une scène, un roman,** to film a scene, a novel; *Cu:* **t. une crème,** to stir a custard; (*c*) to change, convert; to translate (**en,** into); **t. tout en bien, en mal,** to put a good, a bad, interpretation on everything; **t. qch. en plaisanterie,** to turn sth. into a joke; to laugh sth. off; (*d*) to turn over (page, etc.); to turn up (card); **t. et retourner qch.,** to turn sth. over and over; **t. une affaire en tous sens,** to turn a matter over and over (in one's mind); (*e*) to get round (corner, obstacle, etc.); (i) to outflank, (ii) to circumvent (enemy); to evade, get round (difficulty, the law); **vous trouverez l'épicerie en tournant le coin,** you will find the grocer round the corner; *Nau:* **t. un promontoire,** to weather a headland; (*f*) *F:* **t. le lait,** to turn the milk sour; **il lui a tourné la tête,** she has become infatuated with him; **les honneurs ne lui ont pas tourné la tête,** success hasn't gone to his head; **cela m'a tourné l'estomac,** it turned my stomach. **2.** *v.i.* (*a*) to revolve; to go round; (*of machine*) to run; (*of top*) to spin; **t. autour de qn, de qch.,** to move, turn, hang, hover, round s.o., sth.; *F:* **t. autour du pot,** to beat about the bush; **tout tourne autour de lui, la tête lui tourne,** he feels giddy; his head is swimming, spinning; **le sentier tourne autour de la pelouse,** the path winds round the lawn; **faire t. la machine,** to set the machinery going; **faire t. la clef dans la serrure,** to turn the key in the lock; **faire t. une pièce de monnaie,** to spin a coin; **le pied lui a tourné,** he twisted his ankle; (*b*) to change direction; **tournez à gauche,** turn left; **t. court,** (i) to turn short, sharply; (ii) *F:* to make off; (iii) to end suddenly; **ne savoir de quel côté t.,** not to know which way to turn; to be at one's wits' end; **le vent a tourné à l'ouest,** the wind has changed, shifted, to the west; **le temps tourne au froid,** it is turning cold; **sa chance a tourné,** his luck has turned; **il a tourné contre moi,** he has turned against me; **son amour a tourné en haine,** his love has turned, changed, to hatred; (*c*) (*of fruit, etc.*) to colour, *NAm:* color; to ripen; (*d*) to turn out, result; **les choses tournent bien, mal,** things are turning out well, badly; (*of pers.*) **mal t.,** to turn out badly, go to the bad; **cela tournait mal,** things were taking a bad turn; **cela tournera mal,** no good will come of it; (*e*) to tend (**à,** to); to turn; **portraits qui tournent à la caricature,** portraits that are almost caricatures; **l'affaire tournait au tragique,** the matter was taking a tragic turn, was turning to tragedy; (*of wine*) **t. au vinaigre,** to turn acid; **lait qui tourne à l'aigre,** *v.i.* **qui tourne,** milk that is turning (sour); (*f*) *Cin:* **t. dans un film,** to act in a film; to play in a film. **3.** *impers. Cards:* **il tourne carreau,** the turn-up is diamonds. **4. se t.** (*a*) **se t. vers qn,** to turn towards s.o.; **ses yeux se tournèrent vers la porte,** his eyes turned to the door; (*b*) **se t. contre qn,** to turn against s.o.; **c'est sa femme qui l'a fait t. contre vous,** it was his wife who turned him against you; (*c*) **se t. du côté du peuple,** to side with the people; (*d*) to turn round; (*e*) **son amour se tourna en haine,** his love turned to hate; (*of wine*) **se t. en vinaigre,** to turn into vinegar.

tournesol [turnəsɔl] *n.m.* **1.** *Bot:* sunflower. **2.** *Dy: Ch:* **papier (de) t.,** litmus paper.

tournette [turnɛt] *n.f.* **1.** reel; wool winder. **2.** washer cutter; circular glass cutter; *Phot:* circular print trimmer.

tourneur [turnœr] **1.** *a.m.* dancing, whirling (dervish). **2.** *n.m.* turner; *Cer:* thrower; **t. de vis,** screw-cutter.

tournevis [turnəvis] *n.m. Tls:* screwdriver.

tournicoter [turnikɔte] *v.i.*, **tourniquer** [turnike] *v.i. F:* to wander round and round; to hover (round).

tourniquet [turnikɛ] *n.m.* **1.** (*a*) **t.(-compteur),** turnstile; *Mil: P:* **passer au t.,** to be court-martialled; (*b*) revolving display stand. **2.** (*a*) roller (for ropes, etc., to pass over); (*b*) swivel; (*c*) button, turnbuckle (on shutter, etc.). **3.** (*a*) *Toys:* whirligig; (*b*) *Pyr:* Catherine wheel; (*c*) *Hort:* sprinkler. **4.** *Med:* tourniquet.

tournis [turni] *n.m.* (*a*) *Vet:* staggers, gid; (*b*) **donner le t. à qn,** to make s.o. giddy.

tournoi [turnwa] *n.m. Hist: Sp: Cards: etc:* tournament; **t. d'éloquence,** contest of eloquence.

tournoiement [turnwamɑ̃] *n.m.* **1.** whirling; spinning (of suspended object); wheeling (of birds); eddying, swirling (of water). **2.** (*a*) giddiness, dizziness; (*b*) *Vet:* staggers, gid.

tournoyant [turnwajɑ̃] *a.* turning, whirling; wheeling (birds); eddying, swirling (water).

tournoyer [turnwaje] *v.i.* **(je tournoie, n. tournoyons; je tournoierai)** to turn round and round; (*of suspended object*) to spin; (*of birds*) to wheel; (*of water*) to eddy, swirl; **descendre en tournoyant,** to come whirling down; **faire t. qch.,** to twirl, whirl, sth.

tournure [turnyr] *n.f.* **1.** turn, direction, course; **les affaires prennent (une) meilleure, une mauvaise, t.,** things are taking a turn for the better, the worse; **donner une t. agréable à la conversation,** to give a pleasant turn to the conversation. **2.** shape, form, figure, appearance (of pers., etc.); **t. d'esprit,** turn of mind; **t. de phrase,** turn of phrase; **prendre t.,** to take shape.

tourte [turt] *n.f.* (*a*) *Cu:* (covered) tart; **t. aux pommes,** apple pie, apple tart; (*b*) *F:* idiot, clot; *a.* thick.

tourteau, -eaux [turto] *n.m.* **1.** *Husb:* cattle cake. **2.** *Crust:* **t. (dormeur),** edible crab.

tourtereau, -eaux [turtəro] *n.m.* (*a*) *Orn:* young turtledove; (*b*) *Fig:* lovebird.

tourterelle [turtərɛl] *n.f. Orn:* turtledove.

tourtière [turtjɛr] *n.f.* **1.** tart plate. **2.** *Fr.C:* (minced) pork pie.

tous [tu(s)] *see* TOUT.

touselle [tuzɛl] *n.f. Bot:* beardless wheat.

toussailler [tusaje] *v.i.* to have a nervous little cough.

Toussaint (la) [latusɛ̃] *Pr.n.f.* All Saints' day; All Hallows; **la veille de la T.,** Hallowe'en.

tousser [tuse] *v.i.* (*a*) (i) to cough; (ii) to clear one's throat; **il toussa pour m'avertir,** he gave a cough to warn me; (*b*) **moteur qui tousse,** spluttering engine.

toussotement [tusɔtmɑ̃] *n.m.* slight cough.

toussoter [tusɔte] *v.i.* (*a*) to clear one's throat; to cough slightly; (*b*) to have a slight cough.

tous-temps [tutɑ̃] *a.* all-weather.

tout, toute, *pl.* **tous, toutes** [tu, tut, tu, tut] (*when* **tous** *is a pron. it is pronounced* [tus]) all. **I.** *a.* **1.** any, every, all; **t. travail lui est interdit,** he is forbidden to do any work; **pour toute arme il avait une canne,** his only weapon was a walking stick; **pour toute réponse il éclata de rire,** his only answer was to burst out laughing; **t. autre que vous,** anybody but you; **toute liberté d'agir,** full liberty to act; **j'ai toute raison de croire que . . .,** I have every reason to believe that . . .; **repas à toute heure,** meals served at any time. **2.** (*intensive*) **dans sa toute jeunesse,** when he was quite a child, in his early youth; **à la toute dernière minute,** at the very last minute; **des arbres de toute beauté,** most beautiful trees; **à toute vitesse,** at full speed; **t., toute, à vous,** entirely yours; **de toute importance,** of the first importance, all-important; **il est de toute importance que** + *sub.*, it is of the utmost importance that . . .; *Nau:* **la barre toute!** hard over! **3.** the whole, all; **t. le monde,** everybody, everyone; **toute la famille,** the whole family, all the family; **t. mon argent,** all my money; **t. le jour, toute la journée,** the whole day, all day long; **pendant t. l'hiver,** throughout the winter; all through the winter; **répéter t. le temps la même chose,** to keep on saying the same thing; **au milieu de t. ça . . .,** in the midst of it all . . .; **t. Paris est en danger,** the whole of Paris is in danger; **t. La Haye se trouvait dans les rues,** the whole population of the Hague was in the streets; **t. mars se passa sans nouvelles,** the whole of March went by without news. **4.** all, every; (*a*) **tous les invités,** all the guests; **tous ces livres,** all these books; **tous les jours,** every day; **tous les quarts d'heure,** every quarter of an hour; **toutes les fois que . . .,** whenever . . .; each time that . . .; (*b*) **au-dessus de toutes choses,** above all; **de tous (les) côtés, de toutes parts,** on all sides; (from) everywhere; **de toutes (les) couleurs,** of every (possible) colour, *NAm:* color;

toutes proportions gardées, making due allowance. **5.** (*with numerals*) **tous (les) deux,** both; **tous (les) trois, (les) dix,** all three, all ten; **tous les deux jours,** every other day; **tous les trois jours,** every third day. **6.** (*with* **un**) **t. un quartier de la ville,** a whole district of the town; **c'est toute une histoire,** (i) it's a long story; (ii) it's quite a job. **II.** *pron.* **1.** *sg.neut.* all, everything; **l'argent n'est pas t.,** money isn't everything; **il faut t. lui montrer,** we must show him everything; **je crois que c'est t.,** I think that's (about) all; *F:* **et t. et t.,** and all the rest of it; **t. est bien qui finit bien,** all's well that ends well; **voilà t. ce que je sais,** that's all I know; **j'aime t. ce qui est français,** I love anything, everything, French; **t. ce qui vous plaira,** whatever you like; anything you like; **c'est t. ce qu'il y a de plus beau, de plus drôle,** it is most beautiful; nothing could be funnier; **il a t. mangé,** he has eaten everything, the whole lot; **il mange de tout,** he eats anything (and everything); **on trouve de t. à Paris,** you find all sorts of things in Paris; **depuis lors j'ai fait de t.,** since then I've done a bit of everything; **il est capable de t.,** he is capable of anything; *F:* **il a t. du fonctionnaire,** he's the typical, complete, civil servant; **c'est t. dire,** I needn't say more; **c'est t. un,** it's all one; **homme à t. faire,** (i) all-rounder; (ii) Jack-of-all-trades; (iii) odd-job man; **à t. prendre . . .,** on the whole; taking it all in all; *F:* **drôle comme t.,** awfully funny; **rire comme t.,** to laugh like anything. **2.** *pl.* **une (bonne) fois pour toutes,** once (and) for all; **venez tous** [tus]! come along all of you! **ils sont tous là** [tusla], they are all there; **il faut tous faire votre devoir,** all of you must do your duty; **le meilleur de tous,** the best of them all; **il est impossible de les nommer tous,** it is impossible to name them all; **on nous en offrit un verre à tous,** we were all offered a glass; **leur bonheur à tous,** the happiness of all of them; **tous à la fois,** all together; *F:* **on l'aimait bien tous,** we were all very fond of him; **nous tous, vous tous, eux tous,** all of us, of you, of them; **combien d'argent ont-ils à eux tous?** how much money have they between them? **III.** *n.m.* **1. le t.,** the whole, the lot; **le t. est de réussir,** the main thing is to succeed; **jouer le t. pour le t.,** to stake everything; **son fils est son t.,** her son is everything to her; *F:* **ce n'est pas le t., ça!** that's not getting us very far! *adv.phr.* **du t. au t.,** entirely; **en t.,** in all; wholly; **(pas) du t.,** not at all; **pardon, madame!—du t., monsieur!** I beg your pardon! —that's quite all right! please . . .! **2.** *Mth:* (*pl.* **touts**) total; (*in riddles*) **mon t.,** my all, my whole. **IV.** *adv.* (*intensive*) (*before a fem.adj. beginning with a consonant or* **h** *aspirate* **tout** *becomes* **toute**) **1.** quite, entirely, completely, very; **t. nouveau(x), toute(s) nouvelle(s),** quite new; **ils sont t. seuls, elles sont toutes seules,** they are (quite) alone; **elle était encore toute jeune,** she was still quite young; **hommes t. bon(s) ou t. mauvais,** men entirely good or entirely bad; **toute vêtue de noir,** dressed all in black; **elle était toute honteuse,** she was utterly ashamed; **des lutteurs de t. premier ordre,** wrestlers of the very first order; **une t. autre personne,** an entirely different person; **t. droit,** bolt upright; **t. neuf,** brand new; **t. nu,** stark naked; **t. éveillé,** wide awake; **vêtement t. fait,** ready-made garment; **viande toute cuite,** ready-cooked meat; **t. au bout,** right at the end, at the very end; **t. là-bas,** right over there, away in the distance; **t. contre le mur,** right against the wall; **mains t. en sang,** hands all covered with blood; **c'est t. comme chez nous!** it's just like home; **il est t. à son commerce,** he is entirely absorbed in his business; **t. doux!** gently! *adv.phr.* **t. à fait,** quite, entirely, altogether; thoroughly; **cela me va t. à fait,** it suits me perfectly, down to the ground; **il lui ressemble t. à fait,** he is just like him; **t. au plus,** at the very most; **t. au moins, t. le moins,** at the very least; *Corr:* **t. à vous,** yours ever. **2. t. en parlant,** while speaking. **3. t. ignorant qu'il soit, qu'il est,** however ignorant he is; ignorant though, as, he is; ignorant though he may be; **t. père, toute mère, que je suis,** although I am a father, a mother. **4. être t. oreilles,** to be all ears; **il était toute crainte et toute haine,** he was all fear and hate; **elle était t. attention,** she was all attention; **elle est t. le portrait de sa mère,** she is the living image of her mother.

tout-à-l'égout [tutalegu] *n.m.inv.* main(s) drainage.

toute-épice [tutepis] *n.f. Bot:* allspice; *pl. toutes-épices.*

toutefois [tutfwa] *adv.* yet, nevertheless, however, still.

toute-puissance [tutpɥisɑ̃s] *n.f.* (*a*) *Theol:* omnipotence; (*b*) *Pol: etc:* absolute power.

tout-fou [tufu] *F:* (*a*) *a.m.* crazy; (*b*) *n.m.* idiot, nut; *pl. tout-fous.*

toutou [tutu] *n.m.* (*esp. child's word*) doggie; **filer comme un t.,** to let oneself be led; *pl. toutous.*

tout-puissant, *f.* **toute-puissante** [tupɥisɑ̃, tutpɥisɑ̃t] *a.* almighty, omnipotent; overwhelming (desire); *n.m.* **le T.-P.,** the Almighty; *pl. tout-puissants, toutes-puissantes.*

tout-terrain [tutɛrɛ̃] *a.* (*a*) cross-country; (*b*) **véhicule t.-t.,** all-purpose vehicle; jeep; *pl. tous-terrains.*

tout-venant [tuvnɑ̃] *n.m. Com:* ungraded product, *esp.* unsorted coal; *Fig:* **le t.-v.,** the ragtag and bobtail.

toux [tu] *n.f.* cough; **accès de t.,** fit of coughing; **t. sèche, grasse,** dry, loose, cough.

toxémie [tɔksemi] *n.f. Med:* tox(a)emia, blood-poisoning.

toxicité [tɔksisite] *n.f.* toxicity.

toxicologie [tɔksikɔlɔʒi] *n.f.* toxicology.

toxicologique [tɔksikɔlɔʒik] *a.* toxicological.

toxicologue [tɔksikɔlɔg] *n.* toxicologist.

toxicomane [tɔksikɔman] *n.* drug addict.

toxicomanie [tɔksikɔmani] *n.f.* drug addiction.

toxine [tɔksin] *n.f. Physiol:* toxin.

toxique [tɔksik] **1.** *a.* toxic; **gaz t.,** poison gas. **2.** *n.m.* poison.

trac¹ [trak] *n.m. F:* fright, funk; **il a le t.,** he's got the wind up; *Th:* he's got stage fright.

trac² *n.m.* **tout à t.,** thoughtlessly; out of the blue.

traçage [trasaʒ] *n.m.* tracing (of diagrams, etc.); laying out (of roads, gardens, etc.).

traçant [trasɑ̃] (*a*) *a. Bot:* running, creeping (root); (*b*) *a. & n.* **(obus) t.,** tracer shell; **(balle) traçante,** tracer bullet.

tracas [traka] *n.m.* worry, trouble, bother.

tracasser [trakase] **1.** *v.tr.* to worry, bother, plague (s.o.). **2. se t.,** to worry.

tracasserie [trakasri] *n.f.* pestering, worrying (of s.o.); *pl.* interference; harassment.

tracassier, -ière [trakasje, -jɛr] *a.* pestering, interfering (person).

trace [tras] *n.f.* trace. **1.** (*a*) trail, track, spoor (of beast); footprint(s), trail (of person); (wheel) track (of vehicle); **t. de lumière,** trail of light; *Mount: Ski: etc:* **faire la t.,** to break trail; *Ski:* **t. directe,** direct descent; **être sur la t. de qn, qch.,** to be on s.o.'s tracks; to be on the track of sth.; **retrouver la t.,** to pick up the scent, the trail; **il suit les traces de son père,** he's following in his father's footsteps; **laisser une t. profonde,** to leave a deep impression behind; **retrouver t. de qn, de qch.,** to find a trace of s.o., sth.; *F:* to get on s.o.'s track again; **on n'a plus retrouvé t. des explorateurs,** no trace was ever found of the explorers; *Elcs:* **t. du spot,** trace (in cathode ray tube); (*b*) scar, mark (of wound, burn, etc.);

marks (of suffering); (*c*) (slight) trace (of poison, regret, foreign blood). **2.** *Mth:* trace (of line).

tracé [trase] *n.m.* **1.** (*a*) tracing, sketching; plotting (of curve, etc.); laying out (of road, etc.); **faire le t. de,** to trace, sketch (figure); to set out, plot (curve); to lay out (road); (*b*) layout (of town, etc.); lie, alignment (of road, etc.). **2.** (*a*) outline, sketch, diagram, drawing; (*b*) graph (of curve, etc.); *Rad:* plot.

tracer [trase] *v.* **(je traçai(s); n. traçons) 1.** *v.tr.* to trace; (*a*) to lay out (road, railway); to plot (curve, graph, etc.); to map out (route, policy); (*b*) to draw (a line); to sketch, draw, outline (plan, pattern, etc.). **2.** *v.i.* (*a*) *Hort:* (*of roots*) to run out; to creep; (*b*) *Dial: & P:* to move quickly, get a move on.

traceret [trasrɛ] *n.m. Tls:* scriber; tracing awl.

traceur, -euse [trasœr, -øz] (*a*) *n. Ind: etc:* tracer; (*b*) *n.m.* **t. (radioactif),** tracer; (*c*) *n.m. Cmptr:* **t. (de courbes),** plotter; (*d*) *a.* tracer (shell, bullet).

trachéal, -aux [trakeal, -o] *a. Anat:* tracheal.

trachée [traʃe] *n.f.* (*a*) *Anat: Z:* trachea; (*b*) *Bot:* trachea, vessel, duct.

trachéite [trakeit] *n.f. Med:* tracheitis.

trachéo-bronchite [trakeɔbrɔ̃ʃit] *n.f. Med:* tracheobronchitis.

trachéotomie [trakeɔtɔmi] *n.f.* tracheotomy.

trachome [trakom] *n.m. Med:* trachoma.

trachyte [trakit] *n.m. Miner:* trachyte.

traçoir [traswar] *n.m. Tls:* scriber; tracing awl.

tract [trakt] *n.m.* **1.** tract. **2.** leaflet.

tractable [traktabl̩] *a.* towable.

tractation [traktasjɔ̃] *n.f. often Pej:* deal; *pl.* dealings; bargaining.

tracté [trakte] *a.* tractor-drawn.

tracter [trakte] *v.tr.* to draw by tractor.

tracteur, -trice [traktœr, -tris] **1.** *n.m.* (*a*) tractor; **t. et semi-remorque,** articulated vehicle; (*b*) traction engine. **2.** *a.* (*a*) towing; (*b*) *Geog:* **force tractrice,** transport capacity (of a current).

traction [traksjɔ̃] *n.f.* (*a*) traction; pulling; **effort de t.,** tractive effort, pull; **t. magnétique,** magnetic pull; *Mec:* **résistance à la t.,** tensile strength; *Gym:* **faire une t.,** (i) to chin the bar; (ii) to do push-ups, press-ups; (*b*) traction, draught, *NAm:* draft; haulage; *Aut:* **t. avant,** front-wheel drive.

tractoriste [traktɔrist] *n.* tractor driver.

tractus [traktys] *n.m. Anat:* tract; system.

tradescantia [tradɛskɑ̃sja] *n.m. Bot:* tradescantia.

tradition [tradisjɔ̃] *n.f.* **1.** tradition; **de t.,** traditional. **2.** *Jur:* delivery, handing over (of property, etc.).

traditionalisme [tradisjɔnalism] *n.m.* traditionalism.

traditionaliste [tradisjɔnalist] *n.* traditionalist.

traditionnel, -elle [tradisjɔnɛl] *a.* traditional; usual, habitual; standard (excuse, equipment, etc.); standing (joke).

traditionnellement [tradisjɔnɛlmɑ̃] *adv.* traditionally.

traducteur, -trice [tradyktœr, -tris] *n.* translator.

traduction [tradyksjɔ̃] *n.f.* **1.** translating; *Cmptr:* **t. des informations,** data reduction. **2.** translation; **t. simultanée,** simultaneous translation.

traduire [tradɥir] *v.tr.* (*pr.p.* **traduisant;** *p.p.* **traduit;** *pr.ind.* **je traduis, il traduit, n. traduisons, ils traduisent;** *impf.* **je traduisais;** *p.h.* **je traduisis;** *fu.* **je traduirai) 1.** *Jur:* **t. qn en justice,** to sue, prosecute, indict, s.o. **2.** (*a*) to translate (**de,** from; **en,** into); (*b*) **t. un câblogramme,** to decode a cable; (*c*) *Cmptr:* **t. (une carte),** to interpret (a card); (*d*) to represent; to express (feeling, idea, etc.); **vous traduisez mal ma pensée,** you're misinterpreting me, my thoughts; **sa douleur se traduisit par des larmes,** his grief found expression in tears; *Com:* **les comptes se traduisent par une perte de *x* francs,** the accounts show a loss of *x* francs.

traduisible [tradɥizibl̩] *a.* **1.** *Jur:* **t. en justice,** liable to prosecution. **2.** translatable; **ce jeu de mots n'est pas t.,** this play on words is untranslatable.

Trafalgar [trafalgar] *Pr.n.m.* Trafalgar; **coup de T.,** underhand trick.

trafic [trafik] *n.m.* **1.** (*a*) *O:* trading, trade; (*b*) *Pej:* traffic, illicit trading; **t. des stupéfiants,** drug traffic; **t. des armes,** traffic in arms; *F:* **faire t. de ses charmes,** to be a prostitute; *F:* **un drôle de t.,** a queer sort of business. **2.** *Trans: Elcs:* traffic.

traficoter [trafikɔte] *v.i. Pej: F:* to traffic (in).

trafiquant, -ante [trafikɑ̃, -ɑ̃t] *n. Pej:* trafficker; **t. de, en, stupéfiants,** drug trafficker; dope peddler, pedlar; **t. du marché noir,** black marketeer.

trafiquer [trafike] **1.** *v.i. Pej:* **t. de, en, qch.,** to traffic in sth.; to make (illicit) profit out of sth.; **t. de sa conscience,** to sell one's conscience. **2.** *v.tr.* (*a*) to negotiate (a bill, etc.); (*b*) *F:* to doctor (wine, car engine, etc.).

trafiqueur, -euse [trafikœr, -øz] *n. Pej:* trafficker (**de, en,** in).

tragédie [traʒedi] *n.f.* tragedy; *F:* **jouer la t.,** to put on a tragic act.

tragédien, -ienne [traʒedjɛ̃, -jɛn] *n.* tragic actor, actress; tragedian.

tragi-comédie [traʒikɔmedi] *n.f.* tragi-comedy; *pl. tragi-comédies.*

tragi-comique [traʒikɔmik] *a.* tragi-comic; *pl. tragi-comiques.*

tragique [traʒik] **1.** (*a*) *a.* tragic (writer, play, role, event); (*b*) *n.m.* tragic side (of an event); **cela tourne au t.,** the thing is becoming tragic, serious; **prendre qch. au t.,** to make a tragedy of sth.; **ne le prenez pas si au t.,** don't take it so much to heart. **2.** *n.* writer of tragedies. **3.** *n.m. Th:* **le t.,** tragedy.

tragiquement [traʒikmɑ̃] *adv.* tragically.

trahir [trair] *v.tr.* **1.** (*a*) *A:* **t. qch., qn, à qn,** to betray sth., s.o., to s.o.; (*b*) to reveal, give away (secret); **je fus trahi par les aboiements d'un chien,** I was betrayed by a dog barking; **t. sa pensée, se t.,** to give oneself away. **2.** to betray (s.o.'s confidence, s.o.'s interests); to play (s.o.) false; to deceive (s.o.); *F:* to let (s.o.) down; **t. ses serments,** to go back on one's word; **au premier pas ses jambes le trahirent,** at the first step his legs failed him.

trahison [traizɔ̃] *n.f.* **1.** (*a*) treachery; (*b*) *Jur:* treason; **haute t.,** high treason. **2.** betrayal, betraying.

traille [traj] *n.f.* **1.** ferry cable. **2.** ferry.

train [trɛ̃] *n.m.* **1.** (*a*) train, string, line (of pack animals, vehicles, etc.); series; set (of wheels, etc.); **t. de bois,** timber raft, float; *Aut:* **t. avant,** front axle (assembly); **t. de pensées,** train of thought; (*b*) *Metall:* train, rolls, mill; (*c*) *Rail:* train; **t. de voyageurs,** passenger train; **t. de marchandises,** goods train, *NAm:* freight train; **t. supplémentaire,** relief train; **t. de neige,** winter sports train; **t. militaire,** troop train; **voyager en t., par le t.,** to travel by train; **comme une vache qui regarde passer un t.,** passively; phlegmatically; (*d*) *Mil:* train (of transport); **le t.,** *approx.* = transport branch of Army Service Corps; *U.S:* transportation company; (*e*) *A:* suite, attendants; train (of servants, etc.); (*f*) (i) quarters (of horse); **t. de derrière, de devant,** hindquarters, forequarters; (ii) *P:* backside, rear (of pers.); **se manier le t.,** to get a move on; (*g*) **t. de roulement,** undercarriage (of wheeled vehicle); suspension and tracks (of tracked vehicle); *Av:* **t. (d'atterissage),** landing gear, undercarriage; **t. avant,** nose gear, nose wheel; (*h*) *Typ:* (press) carriage. **2.** movement; (*a*) pace, rate; action, gait (of horse); **aller bon t.,** to go at a good pace; **aller son petit t.,** to jog along; **à fond de**

t., at full, top, speed; at full tilt; all out; **au t. où il va, à ce t.-là,** at the rate he's going, at that rate; **tout d'un t.**, without stopping; *Sp:* **meneur de t.**, pacemaker; **mener le t.**, to set the pace; **mise en t.**, warming-up; **faire tout le t.**, to make all the running; **gagner au t.**, to win at a steady pace; (*b*) **il y a qch. en t.**, there's sth. afoot, in the wind; **mettre qch. en t.**, to start sth.; to set sth. going; to get (negotiations, etc.) under way; *Typ:* **mettre en t.**, to make ready; *F:* **mettre qn en t.**, to get s.o. going; **c'est lui qui met tout en t.**, he's the life and soul of the party; *F:* **il était un peu en t.**, he'd had a drop (too much); **l'affaire est mal en t.**, the business is hanging fire, has had a bad start; **être en bon t.**, to make good progress; **être en t. de faire qch.**, to be busy, in the act of, doing sth.; (*usu. translated simply by the present or past continuous*) **il est en t. d'écrire,** he is writing; **il était en t. de travailler,** he was (busy) working; **le t. ordinaire des jours,** the daily routine; **les choses vont leur t.**, things are proceeding, going along, as usual; **dans le t.**, up to date, abreast of the times; (*c*) **t. de vie,** way of life; **t. de maison,** style of living; **mener grand t.**, to live on a grand scale; **mener un t. d'enfer,** to live it up; (*d*) *F:* noise, row; clatter; **faire du t., faire un t. de tous les diables,** to kick up (a hell of) a row. **3.** mood; **être en t.**, to be in good spirits, in good form; **il n'était pas en t. ce jour-là,** he wasn't at his best that day; **être mal en t.**, to be out of sorts; to feel unwell; **je ne suis pas en t. pour travailler,** I'm not in a working mood.

traînage [trɛnaʒ] *n.m.* (*a*) hauling; *esp.* sledging; (*b*) *Min:* haulage (of trains); **câble de t.**, haulage rope; (*c*) sleigh transport.

traînailler [trɛnaje] *F:* = TRAÎNASSER.

traînant [trɛnɑ̃] *a.* **1.** dragging, trailing (on the ground). **2.** languid, listless (life); drawling (voice); dawdling (walk).

traînard, -arde [trɛnar, -ard] *n.* straggler; dawdler, *F:* slowcoach.

traînasser [trɛnase] **1.** *v.tr. A:* to drag out (one's existence, etc.). **2.** *v.i.* to loaf, loiter, trail, about.

traîne [trɛn] *n.f.* **1.** *Nau:* **à la t.**, (small boat) in tow; *F:* **être à la t.**, to lag behind. **2.** train (of dress). **3.** *Fish:* seine (net), drag net. **4.** *Fr.C:* **t. sauvage,** toboggan.

traîneau, -eaux [trɛno] *n.m.* **1.** sledge, sleigh; **faire une promenade en t.**, to go sledging; **chien de t.**, sledge dog; husky. **2.** *Fish:* = TRAÎNE 3.

traîne-bûches [trɛnbyʃ] *n.m.inv. Fish: F:* caddis worm, bait.

traîne-buisson [trɛnbɥisɔ̃] *n.m. Orn:* dunnock, hedge warbler; *pl. traîne-buissons.*

traînée [trene] *n.f.* **1.** (*a*) trail (of smoke, blood, light; of a snail, etc.); train (of gunpowder); *Av:* contrail; vapour, *NAm:* vapor, trail; **semer une t. de persil,** to sow a row of parsley; **se répandre comme une t. de poudre,** to spread like wildfire; (*b*) *Av: etc:* drag. **2.** *P:* prostitute, tart.

traîne-misère [trɛnmizɛr] *n.m.inv. F:* miserable wretch.

traînement [trɛnmɑ̃] *n.m.* dragging, trailing; drawling (of voice).

traîner [trene] **1.** *v.tr.* to drag, trail (s.o., sth.) along; to pull, haul (*Rail:* coaches); to draw (coach); to tow (barges); to drag on, drag out (one's existence); to spin out, drag out (speech, business, etc.); to drawl (one's words); **elle traînait cinq enfants après elle,** she was trailing five children after her; **t. la jambe,** to limp; **t. les pieds,** to shuffle; **t. le pied,** to lag behind; **la perdrix traînait l'aile, traînait de l'aile,** the partridge was dragging a wing; **t. qn en prison,** to drag s.o. off to prison; **t. qn dans la boue,** to drag s.o., s.o.'s name, through the mud. **2.** *v.i.* (*a*) to trail, drag (in the dust, etc.); **votre robe traîne,** your dress is trailing; (*b*) to lag, trail (behind); (*c*) to linger, loiter, dawdle; **t. dans la rue, par les rues,** to hang, loaf, about the streets; **ne traîne pas en rentrant de l'école,** don't hang about on your way home from school; (*d*) to lie about; **laisser t. son argent,** to leave one's money lying about; **des vêtements qui traînent sur le plancher,** clothes littering the floor; (*e*) to flag, droop, languish; (*of illness*) to drag on; **l'affaire traîne,** the matter is hanging fire; **intrigue qui traîne,** plot that drags; (*of lawsuit, etc.*) **t. en longueur,** to drag (on); **les choses ne traînent pas avec vous,** you don't let the grass grow under your feet; *F:* **. . . et que ça ne traîne pas!** . . . and don't be half an hour about it! **laisser t. un compte,** to leave an account unpaid. **3. se t.** (*a*) to crawl (along); **il se traîna jusqu'au fossé,** he crawled to the ditch; **se t. aux genoux de qn,** to go on one's knees to s.o.; (*b*) to drag oneself along, about; to move with difficulty; **il se traînait à peine,** he could hardly drag himself along; **les heures se traînent lourdement,** time hangs heavy.

traîneur, -euse [trɛnœr, -øz] *n.* **1.** dragger, trailer, hauler (of sth.); *F:* **t. de sabre,** swashbuckler. **2.** (*a*) *O:* straggler, dawdler; (*b*) *F:* **t. de cafés,** pub crawler.

training [trɛniŋ] *n.m.* (*a*) *Sp:* training; (*b*) *Psy:* **t. autogène,** training by autosuggestion.

train-poste [trɛ̃pɔst] *n.m.* mail train; *pl. trains-poste.*

train-train [trɛ̃trɛ̃] *n.m. F:* routine, daily round; **rien qui sort du t.-t. des événements ordinaires,** nothing to break the humdrum routine.

traire [trɛr] *v.tr.* (*pr.p.* **trayant;** *p.p.* **trait;** *pr.ind.* **je trais, n. trayons, ils traient;** *impf.* **je trayais;** *fu.* **je trairai;** *no p.h.*) to milk (cow, etc.); **machine à t.**, milking machine.

trait [trɛ] *n.m.* **1.** (*a*) pulling, pull (of cord, weight); *Chess: etc:* **avoir le t.**, to have first move; **tout d'un t.**, at one stretch; **cheval de (gros) t.**, (heavy) draught, *NAm:* draft, horse; (*b*) trace (of harness). **2.** (*a*) arrow; **partir comme un t.**, to be off like an arrow, like a shot; **t. de médisance,** piece of slander; **envoyer, lancer, un t. à qn,** to have a dig at s.o.; (*b*) beam (of light); (*c*) flash (of light); **t. d'esprit,** flash, stroke, of wit; witticism; (*d*) *Mus:* brilliant passage. **3.** draught, gulp; **boire qch. à longs traits,** to gulp down (beer, etc.); **d'un (seul) t.**, at one gulp; *F:* at one go. **4.** (*a*) stroke, mark, line; **d'un t. de plume,** with a stroke of the pen; **t. plein, discontinu,** continuous, broken, line; **dessin au t.**, outline drawing; **copier qch. t. pour t.**, to copy sth. line by line; **gravure au t.**, line engraving; **les grands traits de qch.**, the main outlines, main features, of sth.; *Tg:* **points et traits,** dots and dashes; (*b*) **t. d'union,** (i) hyphen; (ii) *Fig:* link (between two towns, etc.); (*c*) saw cut. **5.** (*a*) feature (of face); **traits réguliers,** regular features; **traits fins, grossiers,** fine, coarse, features; (*b*) trait (of character); characteristic touch (of writer, etc.). **6.** act, deed (of courage, kindness, etc.); stroke (of genius); **ce sont là de ses traits,** those are some of his tricks. **7.** reference (to sth.), bearing (on sth), connection (with sth.); **avoir t. à qch.**, to refer, relate, to sth.

traitable [trɛtabl̩] *a.* (*a*) *Lit:* (*of pers.*) tractable, accommodating; (*b*) treatable; manageable.

traitant [trɛtɑ̃] *a.* (doctor) in attendance; **mon médecin t.**, my (usual) doctor.

traite [trɛt] *n.f.* **1.** stretch (of road); **j'ai fait une longue t.**, I have come a long way; **(tout) d'une t.**, at a stretch, without interruption. **2.** (*a*) *A:* transport (of goods); trading; (ivory, slave) trade; (*b*) **t. des blanches,** white slave trade. **3.** *Fin:* (*a*) (banker's) draft; bill (of exchange); (*b*) (hire purchase) payment, instalment. **4.** milking.

traité [trete] *n.m.* **1.** treatise (**de, sur,** on). **2.** treaty, agreement; **t. d'alliance, de paix,** treaty of alliance, of peace; **t. de commerce,** commercial treaty.

traitement [trɛtmɑ̃] *n.m.* **1.** treatment; (*a*) **mauvais t.,** ill-usage, maltreatment; *Med:* **premier t.,** first aid; initial treatment; **t. chirurgical,** surgery; operation; **malade en t.,** patient under(going) treatment; (*b*) processing, treatment (of raw materials); **t. anodique,** anodising (in electrolysis); *Civ.E: etc:* **t. superficiel,** surfacing (of road, etc.); *Ind:* **capacité de t.,** handling capacity; (*c*) *Cmptr:* **t. (automatique) de l'information,** (automatic) data processing; **données en t., capacité, débit, de t.,** throughput; **unité de t.,** task, job; **t. à distance,** teleprocessing. **2.** salary; (officers') pay; **sans t.,** honorary (secretary); unsalaried (magistrate).

traiter [trete] *v.tr.* to treat. **1.** (*a*) to behave towards (s.o.); to treat (s.o.) (well, kindly, badly, etc.); **t. qn en ami, en enfant,** to treat s.o. like, as, a friend, a child; **t. qn d'égal,** to treat s.o. as an equal; (*b*) to call, style; **t. qn de lâche,** to call s.o. a coward; (*c*) *Med:* **t. un malade, une maladie,** to treat a patient, a disease; **se faire t. d'un cancer,** to undergo treatment for cancer; (*d*) *Ind:* to process; to coat (lens); to treat, spray (vines, etc.); *Cmptr:* to process (data); **données non traitées,** raw data; (*e*) *esp. Lit:* to entertain (s.o.). **2.** (*a*) to negotiate (deal, etc.); to handle, transact (business); (*b*) to discuss, handle, deal with (subject). **3.** *v.i.* (*a*) to negotiate, deal; **t. de la paix,** to treat for peace; **t. avec ses créanciers,** to treat, negotiate, with one's creditors; (*b*) (*of book*) **t. d'un sujet,** to treat of, deal with, a subject.

traiteur [trɛtœr] *n.m.* (*a*) *A:* restaurateur; (*b*) caterer.

traître, traîtresse [trɛtr̥, trɛtrɛs] **1.** *a.* treacherous (person); vicious (animal); dangerous, treacherous (stair, crevasse, etc.); *F:* **pas un t. mot,** not a single word. **2.** *n.* (*a*) traitor, *f.* traitress; **en t.,** treacherously; (*b*) *Th:* **le t.,** the villain.

traîtreusement [trɛtrøzmɑ̃] *adv.* treacherously.

traîtrise [trɛtriz] *n.f.* **1.** treachery, treacherousness. **2.** piece of treachery.

trajectoire [traʒɛktwar] *n.f.* path (of star, aircraft, electron, *Meteor:* depression); trajectory (of comet, satellite, missile); *Av:* **t. de vol,** flight path; **t. de collision,** collision course.

trajet [traʒɛ] *n.m.* (*a*) journey (by rail, etc.); ride, drive, flight, etc.; **t. de mer, par mer,** passage, crossing; **un t. de deux heures,** a two hour journey, run, ride, crossing; **j'ai fait une partie du t. en avion,** I flew part of the way; (*b*) course (of artery, nerve, etc.); path (of projectile, *El:* current).

tralala [tralala] *n.m.inv.* *F:* **en grand t.,** (i) with a lot of fuss, with all the trimmings; (ii) all dressed up.

tram [tram] *n.m.* *Trans:* *F:* tram; *NAm:* streetcar.

tramail [tramaj] *n.m.* *Fish:* trammel (net); *pl. tramails.*

trame [tram] *n.f.* **1.** *Tex:* woof, weft; *Fig:* thread (of existence). **2.** *A:* plot, conspiracy. **3.** (*a*) *Phot.Engr:* (half-tone) screen; **t. de soie,** silk-screen process; serigraphy; (*b*) *T.V:* raster; **t. (double),** frame.

tramer [trame] *v.tr.* **1.** (*a*) *Tex:* to weave; (*b*) to weave (plot of novel); (*c*) to hatch (plot); **il se trame quelque chose,** there's something in the wind, something afoot. **2.** *Phot.Engr:* **t. un cliché,** to take a negative through a screen.

tramontane [tramɔ̃tan] *n.f.* **1.** (*a*) *A:* north (star); (*b*) **perdre la t.,** to lose one's bearings; to lose one's head. **2.** *Meteor:* tramontana.

tramp [trɑ̃p] *n.m.* *Nau:* tramp (steamer).

tramway [tramwɛ] *n.m.* **1.** tramway, *NAm:* streetcar line. **2.** tram, *NAm:* streetcar.

tranchant [trɑ̃ʃɑ̃] **1.** *a.* (*a*) cutting, sharp (tool, sword, etc.); keen (edge); (*b*) trenchant, decisive (words, opinion); sharp, peremptory (tone); self-assertive (person). **2.** *n.m.* (*a*) (cutting) edge (of knife, etc.); thin end (of wedge); edge (of hand); **mettre le t. à une lame,** to put an edge on a blade; **épée, argument, à double t., à deux tranchants,** two-edged sword; double-edged argument; argument that cuts both ways; (*b*) *Leath:* fleshing knife.

tranche [trɑ̃ʃ] *n.f.* **1.** (*a*) slice (of bread, melon, meat, etc.); rasher (of bacon); **en tranches,** in slices, sliced; **la t. des salariés moyens,** the middle-income bracket; *F:* **une t. de vie,** a cross section of life; *F:* **s'en payer une t.,** (i) to have the time of one's life; (ii) to have a good laugh; (*b*) block, portion (of an issue of shares, etc.); *Rail:* **t. de voitures,** portion (of train). **2.** (*a*) slab (of marble, stone); *Cu:* **t. napolitaine,** Neapolitan ice (cream); (*b*) **t. grasse,** round, top rump (of beef). **3.** (*a*) face (of wheel, gun muzzle, etc.); (*b*) edge (of coin, plank); (*c*) (cut) edge (of book); (*d*) section; **t. verticale,** vertical section. **4.** *N.Arch:* **t. cellulaire,** cellular compartment (of ship). **5.** *Tls:* set, chisel.

tranché [trɑ̃ʃe] *a.* distinct (colour, *NAm:* color, pattern, etc.); clear-cut (opinion); blunt (refusal).

tranchée [trɑ̃ʃe] *n.f.* **1.** (*a*) trench; *Agr:* drain; *Rail:* cutting; *Mil:* **guerre de tranchées,** trench warfare; (*b*) *For:* cutting; **t. garde-feu,** firebreak. **2.** *pl.* colic, griping pains.

tranchefile [trɑ̃ʃfil] *n.f.* *Bookb:* headband.

trancher [trɑ̃ʃe] **1.** *v.tr.* (*a*) to slice (bread, etc.); to cut; **t. la tête à qn,** to cut off s.o.'s head; *v.i.* **t. dans le vif,** (i) *Surg:* to operate; (ii) to adopt drastic measures; (*b*) to cut short (discussion, s.o.'s career); to settle (question) once and for all; to make short work of (problem, difficulty); **t. le mot,** to speak plainly; *v.i.* **pour t. net,** to cut it short; **tranchons là,** let us say no more; **il t. sur tout,** he's always laying down the law. **2.** *v.i.* (*of colours, characteristics, etc.*) to contrast strongly (**sur,** with); to stand out (against).

tranchet [trɑ̃ʃɛ] *n.m.* *Tls:* **1.** *Metalw:* anvil cutter. **2.** *Leath:* paring knife.

trancheur, -euse [trɑ̃ʃœr, -øz] **1.** *n.m.* (*a*) *Tchn:* *Min:* cutter; (*b*) *Fish:* cod gutter. **2.** *n.f.* **trancheuse,** stone saw.

tranchoir [trɑ̃ʃwar] *n.m.* chopping board.

tranquille [trɑ̃kil] *a.* tranquil; (*a*) calm, still, quiet (sea, etc.); steady (compass); **se tenir t.,** (i) to keep still; (ii) to keep quiet; *Com:* **marché t.,** easy market; dull market; (*b*) quiet, peaceful (town, people, etc.); (*c*) untroubled, easy (conscience, mind, etc.); *F:* **un père t.,** a placid sort of man; **vous pouvez dormir t.,** you can sleep in peace; **ne pas avoir l'esprit t.,** to be uneasy, uncomfortable, in one's mind (**au sujet de,** about); **laissez-moi t.,** leave me alone; **soyez t.,** set your mind at rest, at ease; **soyez t., il reviendra,** he'll come back, don't (you) worry! *F:* **il avait pris une décision, je suis t.,** he had made up his mind, I'm sure.

tranquillement [trɑ̃kilmɑ̃] *adv.* tranquilly, calmly, peacefully.

tranquillisant [trɑ̃kilizɑ̃] **1.** *a.* reassuring (news, etc.); soothing (effect). **2.** *n.m.* *Med:* tranquillizer.

tranquilliser [trɑ̃kilize] **1.** *v.tr.* to calm; to reassure; to set (the mind) at rest. **2. se t.** (*a*) (*of sea, etc.*) to become calm; (*b*) **tranquillisez-vous,** set your mind at rest.

tranquillité [trɑ̃kilite] *n.f.* **1.** (*a*) tranquillity, calm(ness), peace, quiet, stillness; **troubler la t. publique,** to disturb the peace; **en toute t.,** with an easy mind; (*b*) quietness (of horse). **2. t. d'esprit,** peace of mind.

transaction [trɑ̃zaksjɔ̃] *n.f.* **1.** (*a*) *Com:* transaction; *pl.* dealings, deals; (*b*) *pl.* proceedings (of a society). **2.** compromise.

transactionnel, -elle [trɑ̃zaksjɔnɛl] *a.* **solution transactionnelle,** compromise.
transalpin [trɑ̃zalpɛ̃] *a.* transalpine.
transat [trɑ̃zat] *n.m. F:* (*a*) liner; (*b*) deck chair.
transatlantique [trɑ̃zatlɑ̃tik] **1.** *a.* transatlantic. **2.** *n.m.* (*a*) (Atlantic) liner; (*b*) deck chair.
transbahuter [trɑ̃sbayte] **1.** *F: v.tr.* to transport, move, shift; to lug, cart (belongings) around. **2. se t.,** to shift.
transbordement [trɑ̃sbɔrdəmɑ̃, trɑ̃z-] *n.m.* transhipment (of cargo, passengers); transfer from one train, plane, etc., to another.
transborder [trɑ̃sbɔrde, trɑ̃z-] *v.tr.* to tranship; to transfer (passengers, goods) from one train, plane, etc., to another.
transbordeur [trɑ̃sbɔrdœr, trɑ̃z-] *a. & n.m.* **(pont) t.,** transporter bridge.
transcanadien, -ienne [trɑ̃skanadjɛ̃, -jɛn] *a.* trans-Canada.
transcendance [trɑ̃sɑ̃dɑ̃s] *n.f. Phil: Theol: etc:* transcendence.
transcendant [trɑ̃sɑ̃dɑ̃] *a.* **1.** transcendent; *F:* **il n'a rien de t.,** he's not much to write home about. **2.** *Mth:* transcendental.
transcendantal, -aux [trɑ̃sɑ̃dɑ̃tal, -o] *a. Phil:* transcendental.
transcendantalisme [trɑ̃sɑ̃dɑ̃talism] *n.m. Phil:* transcendentalism.
transcendantaliste [trɑ̃sɑ̃dɑ̃talist] *n.* transcendentalist.
transcender [trɑ̃sɑ̃de] *v.tr.* to transcend.
transcodage [trɑ̃skɔdaʒ] *n.m. Cmptr:* transcribing.
transcoder [trɑ̃skɔde] *v.tr. Cmptr:* to transcribe.
transcontinental, -aux [trɑ̃skɔ̃tinɑ̃tal, -o] *a.* transcontinental.
transcripteur [trɑ̃skriptœr] *n.m.* transcriber.
transcription [trɑ̃skripsjɔ̃] *n.f.* **1.** transcription, transcribing, transliteration (into phonetic script, etc.). **2.** (*a*) transcript, copy; (*b*) *Mus:* transcription.
transcrire [trɑ̃skrir] *v.tr.* (*conj. like* ÉCRIRE) **1.** (*a*) to transcribe; **t. une lettre à la machine,** to type a letter; (*b*) *Jur:* to register (divorce, etc.); *Book-k:* to post (the journal into the ledger). **2.** to transliterate (a text); *Mus:* to transcribe.
transducteur [trɑ̃sdyktœr] *n.m. Ph: Elcs:* transducer.
transe [trɑ̃s] *n.f.* **1.** *usu. pl.* fright, fear; **être dans les transes,** to be on tenterhooks. **2.** (hypnotic) trance.
transept [trɑ̃sɛpt] *n.m. Ecc.Arch:* transept.
transférable [trɑ̃sferabl̩] *a.* transferable.
transfèrement [trɑ̃sfɛrmɑ̃] *n.m.* transfer(ring).
transférer [trɑ̃sfere] *v.tr.* **(je transfère, n. transférons; je transférerai)** (*a*) to transfer; to remove (s.o., sth.) from one place to another; **t. un évêque,** to translate a bishop; (*b*) to make over, assign (goods, etc., to s.o.); (*c*) to transfer (one's affections, etc.).
transfert [trɑ̃sfɛr] *n.m.* **1.** (*a*) transfer(ring) (of persons, things); resettlement (of population); (*b*) *Cmptr:* **t. de magnétisation,** magnetic printing; **clavier à t.,** storage keyboard. **2.** making over; transfer, assignment (of stock, rights, etc.); conveyance (of estate). **3.** *Psy:* transference.
transfiguration [trɑ̃sfigyrasjɔ̃] *n.f.* transfiguration.
transfigurer [trɑ̃sfigyre] *v.tr.* to transfigure.
transfiler [trɑ̃sfile] *v.tr. Nau:* **1.** to lace (sails, etc.). **2.** to snub (rope).
transfluxor [trɑ̃sflyksɔr] *n.m. Cmptr:* transfluxor.
transfo [trɑ̃sfo] *n.m. W.Tel: F:* transformer.
transformable [trɑ̃sfɔrmabl̩] *a.* convertible.
transformateur, -trice [trɑ̃sfɔrmatœr, -tris] *El:* **1.** *a.* transforming; transformer (station). **2.** *n.m.* transformer.
transformation [trɑ̃sfɔrmasjɔ̃] *n.f.* (*a*) transformation (**en,** into); **acteur à transformations,** quick-change artist(e); **industrie de t.,** processing industry; (*b*) *El:* **rapport de t.,** transformer ratio; *Elcs:* **t. de signaux,** signal transformation; (*c*) *Rugby Fb:* conversion (of a try).
transformer [trɑ̃sfɔrme] **1.** *v.tr.* (*a*) to transform, change (sth. into sth.); *Mth:* to transform (an equation); *Rugby Fb:* to convert (a try); (*b*) *Elcs:* to transform, to map; (*c*) *Log:* to convert (proposition). **2. se t.,** to be transformed, to change, turn (**en,** into).
transformisme [trɑ̃sfɔrmism] *n.m. Phil: etc:* transformism.
transformiste [trɑ̃sfɔrmist] *a. & n. Phil: etc:* transformist.
transfuge [trɑ̃sfyʒ] *n.* renegade; defector; *Mil:* deserter to the other side.
transfuser [trɑ̃sfyze] *v.tr.* (*a*) to transfuse (*esp. Med:* blood); (*b*) to instil (**à,** into).
transfusion [trɑ̃sfyzjɔ̃] *n.f.* transfusion (*esp.* of blood).
transgresser [trɑ̃sgrese] *v.tr.* to transgress; to disobey (orders).
transgresseur [trɑ̃sgrɛsœr] *n.m. Lit:* transgressor.
transgression [trɑ̃sgrɛsjɔ̃] *n.f.* transgression.
transhumance [trɑ̃zymɑ̃s] *n.f. Husb:* transhumance.
transhumant [trɑ̃zymɑ̃] *a. & n. Husb:* transhumant; (flocks, herds) on the move.
transhumer [trɑ̃zyme] **1.** *v.tr.* to move (flocks, herds). **2.** *v.i.* to move to, from, mountain pastures.
transi [trɑ̃si, -zi] *a.* perished (with cold); paralysed, stiff (with fear).
transiger [trɑ̃ziʒe] *v.i.* **(je transigeai(s); n. transigeons)** to (effect a) compromise (**avec,** with; **sur,** on).
Transilvanie (la) [latrɑ̃silvani] *Pr.n.f. Geog:* Transylvania.
transir [trɑ̃sir, -zir] **1.** *v.tr.* (*a*) to chill to the bone; (*b*) to paralyse, overcome (with fear). **2.** *v.i. A:* to be paralysed with cold, with fear.
transistor [trɑ̃zistɔr] *n.m. El:* (*a*) transistor; **à transistors,** transistorized; (*b*) *F:* transistor (radio).
transistorisé [trɑ̃zistɔrize] *a.* (*a*) transistorized; (*b*) solid-state (computer, component).
transistoriser [trɑ̃zistɔrize] *v.tr.* to transistorize.
transit [trɑ̃zit] *n.m.* **1.** *Cust:* transit; **en t.,** in transit; **marchandises de t.,** goods for transit; **maison de t.,** forwarding agency. **2.** *Elcs:* **t. par bande perforée,** tape relay.
transitaire [trɑ̃zitɛr] **1.** *a.* (country) of transit. **2.** *n.m.* forwarding agent, transport agent.
transiter [trɑ̃zite] **1.** *v.tr.* to forward (goods). **2.** *v.i.* (*of goods*) to be in transit.
transitif, -ive [trɑ̃zitif, -iv] *a.* transitive.
transition [trɑ̃zisjɔ̃] *n.f.* transition; **sans t.,** abruptly; *Arch:* **style de t.,** transition style; *Geol:* **terrain de t.,** transitional stratum.
transitivement [trɑ̃zitivmɑ̃] *adv. Gram:* transitively.
transitoire [trɑ̃zitwar] *a.* transitory, transient; transitional (period); temporary (measure).
transitoirement [trɑ̃zitwarmɑ̃] *adv.* transitorily.
translation [trɑ̃slasjɔ̃] *n.f.* **1.** transfer(ring); *Tg:* retransmission, relaying (of message). **2.** *Mec: etc:* **mouvement de t.,** translatory motion.
translitérer [trɑ̃slitere] *v.tr.* to transliterate.
translitération [trɑ̃sliterasjɔ̃] *n.f.* transliteration.
translucide [trɑ̃slysid] *a.* translucent.
translucidité [trɑ̃slysidite] *n.f.* translucence, translucency.
transmetteur [trɑ̃smɛtœr] *n.m.* (*a*) *Tg: Cmptr: etc:*

transmitter; (*b*) *Nau:* **t. d'ordres,** (turret) telegraph, transmitter.

transmettre [trɑ̃smɛtr̥] *v.tr.* (*conj. like* METTRE) **1.** to transmit (light, heat, message); to pass on, convey (message, order, disease, etc.); to impart (the truth, energy); to hand (sth.) down (to posterity); *Tg: W.Tel:* to send, transmit (message); to broadcast (programme, etc.). **2.** *Jur:* to transfer (property, etc.); to assign (shares, etc.).

transmigration [trɑ̃smigrasjɔ̃] *n.f.* transmigration.

transmigrer [trɑ̃smigre] *v.i.* to transmigrate.

transmissible [trɑ̃smisibl̥] *a.* (*a*) transmissible; (*b*) transferable (right, etc.).

transmission [trɑ̃smisjɔ̃] *n.f.* **1.** (*a*) transmission (of heat, etc.); passing on (of message, order); imparting (of truth); handing down (of tradition, etc.); *Tg:W.Tel: T.V: etc:* transmission, sending (of message, programme, image, etc.); *W.Tel: etc:* **antenne de t.,** transmitting aerial; *W.Tel: T.V:* **t. directe, en direct,** live broadcast, programme; **t. différée, en différé,** recorded broadcast, programme; *Com:* **fiche de t.,** routing slip; *Mec.E:* **t. du mouvement,** transmission, conveying, of movement; **arbre de t.,** driving shaft; **courroie de t.,** driving belt; **engrenage(s) de t.,** driving gear; *Navy: Mil:* **les transmissions,** signals; **officier de transmissions,** signal(s) officer; **centre de transmissions,** signal centre; (*b*) *Mec.E:* **la t.,** the transmission (gear); the shafting, belting, gearing, etc.; the drive; *Aut:* **t. automatique,** automatic transmission, drive; *Mec.E:* **t. flexible,** flexible shaft(ing); (*c*) *Cmptr:* **voie de t.,** transmission channel. **2.** (*a*) *Jur:* transfer(ence), conveyance (of estate, etc.); assignment (of shares, etc.); *Adm:* **t. des pouvoirs,** handing over; (*b*) *Fb:* **t. du ballon,** passing; (*c*) **t. de pensée,** thought transference.

transmodulation [trɑ̃smɔdylasjɔ̃] *n.f. W.Tel: etc:* cross modulation.

transmuer [trɑ̃smɥe] *v.tr.* to transmute (**en,** into).

transmutation [trɑ̃smytasjɔ̃] *n.f.* transmutation (**en,** into).

transmuter [trɑ̃smyte] *v.tr.* to transmute.

transocéanien, -ienne [trɑ̃zɔseanjɛ̃, -jɛn], **transocéanique** [trɑ̃zɔseanik] *a.* transoceanic.

transpacifique [trɑ̃spasifik] *a.* transpacific.

transparaître [trɑ̃sparɛtr̥] *v.i.* (*conj. like* PARAÎTRE) to show through.

transparence [trɑ̃sparɑ̃s] *n.f.* (*a*) transparency; (*b*) *Cin:* back projection.

transparent [trɑ̃sparɑ̃] **1.** *a.* transparent; clear, obvious (intention, allusion); **c'était un homme t.,** he was a man whose thoughts were easy to read. **2.** *n.m.* (*a*) transparency (*i.e.* picture, print, etc., illuminated from behind); (*b*) guide (for writing pad).

transpercer [trɑ̃spɛrse] *v.tr.* (**je transperçai(s); n. transperçons**) to transfix; to stab, pierce (s.o., sth.) through; **transpercé d'un coup d'épée, d'une balle,** run through with a sword; shot through.

transpirant [trɑ̃spirɑ̃] *a.* perspiring, sweating; sweaty.

transpiration [trɑ̃spirasjɔ̃] *n.f.* (*a*) perspiration, sweat; **en t.,** perspiring, sweating; (*b*) *Bot:* transpiration.

transpirer [trɑ̃spire] *v.i.* **1.** (*aux.* **avoir**) (*a*) to perspire, sweat; (*b*) *Bot:* to transpire. **2.** (*aux.* **avoir** *or* **être**) to transpire; to come to light.

transplant [trɑ̃splɑ̃] *n.m. Surg:* transplant.

transplantable [trɑ̃splɑ̃tabl̥] *a.* transplantable.

transplantation [trɑ̃splɑ̃tasjɔ̃] *n.f.* transplantation, transplanting; *Surg:* **t. cardiaque,** heart transplant.

transplanter [trɑ̃splɑ̃te] **1.** *v.tr.* to transplant (trees, people, etc.); *Surg:* **t. un cœur,** to perform a heart transplant operation. **2. se t.,** to settle somewhere else, to transplant oneself.

transplantoir [trɑ̃splɑ̃twar] *n.m. Hort:* trowel.

transpolaire [trɑ̃spɔlɛr] *a.* transpolar.

transport [trɑ̃spɔr] *n.m.* **1.** (*a*) transport, carriage (of goods, passengers); haulage (of goods, materials); **capacité de t.,** transport capacity; **compagnie de t.,** transport company; carrying, forwarding, company; **entrepreneur de t.,** haulage contractor; **frais de t.,** freight charges, carriage; **les transports en commun,** public transport; *Ind:* **courroie de t.,** conveyor belt; *Mil:* **véhicule de t. de personnel,** personnel carrier; **t. par (chemin de) fer, par voie ferrée,** rail transport; **t. (de pétrole, etc.) par canalisations,** piping (of oil); **avion de t.,** transport aircraft; **avion de t. de passagers,** passenger aircraft; **avion de t. de frêt,** cargo aircraft; **cela permet de faire les transports urgents par avion,** this enables urgent freight to be sent by air; *El:* **t. d'énergie,** power transmission; **t. de force,** high-voltage power transmission; (*b*) *Jur:* visit (of experts, etc.) to the scene (of the accident, etc.). **2.** *Navy: etc:* transport (ship); *esp.* troop ship. **3.** (*a*) *Jur:* **t.(-cession),** transfer, conveyance (of property, rights, etc.); (*b*) *Lith:* transfer (on to the stone); **papier à t.,** transfer paper. **4.** rapture; outburst of feeling; transports, ecstasy (of joy); burst (of fury).

transportable [trɑ̃spɔrtabl̥] *a.* transportable; (patient, etc.) fit to be moved.

transportation [trɑ̃spɔrtasjɔ̃] *n.f.* **1.** transport, *esp. U.S:* transportation (of goods, etc.). **2.** (penal) transportation.

transporté, -ée [trɑ̃spɔrte] **1.** *n.* transported convict, transport. **2.** *a.* beside oneself (with joy, fury); carried away.

transporter [trɑ̃spɔrte] *v.tr.* **1.** (*a*) to transport, carry (goods, troops, etc.); **t. qn à l'hôpital,** to take s.o. to hospital; **le courrier est transporté à Londres par avion,** letters are flown to London; (*of police, etc.*) **se t. sur les lieux,** to visit the scene of the crime, etc.; (*b*) *Jur:* to transport (convict); (*c*) *Book-k:* (i) to carry over, (ii) to transfer, (iii) to carry out, extend (balance). **2.** *Jur:* **t. des droits, etc., à qn,** to transfer rights, etc., to s.o. **3.** to transport, to carry away; **cette bonne nouvelle l'a transporté,** he was overjoyed by the good news.

transporteur [trɑ̃spɔrtœr] *n.m.* **1.** carrier, forwarding agent. **2.** (*a*) *Ind:* conveyor; **(chariot) t.,** travelling crane, travelling platform; (*b*) *Artil:* feeder, feed mechanism. **3.** *a.* (*f.* **transporteuse,** [trɑ̃spɔrtøz]) **hélice, courroie, transporteuse,** spiral, belt, conveyor.

transposable [trɑ̃spozabl̥] *a.* transposable.

transposer [trɑ̃spoze] *v.tr.* to transpose.

transposition [trɑ̃spɔzisjɔ̃] *n.f.* (*a*) *Alg: Anat: Surg: Mus: etc:* transposition; (*b*) *Cin:* dubbing.

transsibérien, -ienne [trɑ̃ssiberjɛ̃, -jɛn] **1.** *a. Geog:* Trans-Siberian. **2.** *n.m.* **le T.,** the Trans-Siberian Railway.

transsubstantiation [trɑ̃ssypstɑ̃sjasjɔ̃] *n.f. Theol:* transubstantiation.

Transvaal (le) [lətrɑ̃sval, trɑ̃z-] *Pr.n.m. Geog:* the Transvaal.

transvasement [trɑ̃svɑzmɑ̃] *n.m.* decanting (of liquid).

transvaser [trɑ̃svɑze] **1.** *v.tr.* to decant (wine, etc.). **2.** (*of water*) **se t.,** to siphon.

transversal, -ale, -aux [trɑ̃svɛrsal, -o] *a.* transverse, transversal; cross (section, gallery, street, girder, artery, etc.); *Const:* **mur t.,** partition (wall); *Anat:* **muscle t.,** *n.m.* **transversal,** transverse (muscle); *N.Arch:* **dans le sens t.,** athwartship; **soutes transversales,** cross bunkers; *Mec.E:* **avance transversale,** *n.m.* **t. d'alimentation,** cross feed; *Geog:* **vallée transversale,** transverse valley.

transversalement [trɑ̃svɛrsalmɑ̃] *adv.* transversely, crosswise, across.
transverse [trɑ̃svɛrs] **1.** *a. Mth: Anat: etc:* transverse. **2.** *n.m. Anat:* transverse (muscle).
transvestisme [trɑ̃svɛstism] *n.m. Psy:* transvestism.
transvider [trɑ̃svide] *v.tr.* to decant, pour.
Transylvanie [trɑ̃silvani] *Pr.n.f. Geog:* Transylvania.
trapèze [trapɛz] *n.m.* **1.** (*a*) *Mth:* trapezium, *NAm:* trapezoid; (*b*) *Gym:* trapeze; **t. volant,** flying trapeze. **2.** *a. Anat:* trapezius (muscle); trapezium (bone).
trapéziste [trapezist] *n.* trapeze artist.
trapézoïdal, -aux [trapezɔidal, -o] *a.* trapezoidal.
trapézoïde [trapezɔid] *a. Mth: Anat:* trapezoidal.
trapillon [trapijɔ̃] *n.m.* **1.** catch, lock (of a trap door). **2.** *Th:* slot (for scenery).
trappe[1] [trap] *n.f.* **1.** *Ven:* trap, pitfall. **2.** (*a*) trap (door); (*b*) hatch; **t. de visites,** inspection hatch; **t. de la soute aux bombes,** bomb door.
Trappe[2] *Pr.n.f. Ecc:* **1.** Trappist monastery. **2.** Trappist order.
trappeur [trapœr] *n.m.* trapper (of wild animals).
trappillon [trapijɔ̃] *n.m.* = TRAPILLON.
trappiste [trapist] *a. & n.m. Ecc:* Trappist (monk).
trapu [trapy] *a.* (*a*) thick-set, stocky (man, horse); squat (building, etc.); (*b*) *Sch: F:* bright (**en,** at); sticky (problem).
traquenard [traknar] *n.m. Ven: & Fig:* trap, pitfall.
traquer [trake] *v.tr. Ven:* **1.** to beat up (game). **2.** (*a*) to surround (quarry, bandits); (*b*) hunt down (criminal). **3.** *v.i. F:* to get stage fright.
traquet [trakɛ] *n.m.* **1.** (mill) clapper, clack. **2.** *Orn:* **t.(-)motteux,** wheatear.
trauma [troma] *n.m. Med: Psy:* trauma.
traumatique [tromatik] *a. Med:* traumatic.
traumatisme [tromatism] *n.m. Med:* traumatism.
traumatologie [tromatɔlɔʒi] *n.f. Med:* traumatology.
travail[1] [travaj] *n.m. Vet:* sling, frame; *pl. travails.*
travail[2], **-aux** [travaj, -o] *n.m.* **1.** (*a*) *A:* suffering, pain; (*b*) **femme en t.,** woman in labour; (*in hospital*) **salle de t.,** labour room. **2.** (*a*) work; **dur t.,** hard work; **division du t.,** division of labour; **se mettre au t.,** to begin, start, set to, get down to, work; **allons, au t.!** come on, let's get (down) to work; **avoir le t. facile,** to work easily, to find one's work easy; **avoir le t. lent,** to work slowly; to be a slow worker; **cesser le t.,** (i) to stop work; to knock off (for the day); (ii) to down tools; **fournir un t. utile,** to do useful work; **à t. égal, salaire égal,** equal pay for equal work; **vêtements de t.,** working clothes; **homme de grand t.,** hardworking man; **séance de t.,** business meeting (of an association, etc.); *Adm:* **admission des enfants au t.,** employment of children; **Ministère du T.** = Department of Employment; *Jur:* **t. disciplinaire,** hard labour; *Myth:* **les douze travaux d'Hercule,** the twelve labours of Hercules; (*b*) **t. de tête, t. intellectuel,** intellectual work, brainwork; **t. manuel,** manual labour; *Sch:* **travaux manuels,** arts and crafts; **c'est du t. à la main,** it's handmade; **travaux des champs,** agricultural labour; *Ind:* **t. mécanique,** machine work; **t. à domicile,** home industry; work done at home (outside office, etc., hours); **t. à l'entreprise,** contract work; **t. en série,** mass production; **t. noir,** black work; moonlighting; **t. à l'aiguille,** needlework; *Min:* **t. à ciel ouvert,** opencast mining; **vieux travaux,** old workings; **t. au tour,** lathe work; *Sch:* **travaux pratiques,** practical work, practicals; *Med:* tutorials; (*c*) *Cmptr:* job; (*d*) operation; working (of the digestion); working, fermenting (of wine); action (of water on banks of stream, etc.); *Mec:* **t. mécanique, t. moteur,** mechanical energy; **t. à la tension,** tension stress; *Mch:* **pression de t.,** working pressure; (*e*) exercise; practice; **coup qui demande beaucoup de t.,** stroke that requires a lot of practice; (*f*) occupation, employment; **donner du t. à qn,** to give s.o. a job; **être sans t.,** to be out of work, unemployed, *F:* jobless; (*g*) (place of) work; **il est à son t.,** he's at work. **3.** (*a*) piece of work; job; (*b*) (literary, etc.) work; **auteur d'un t. sur les métaux,** author of a work on metals; (*c*) *Adm:* **travaux publics,** public works; *P.N:* **travaux,** road works ahead, men at work; *Mil:* **travaux de défense,** defensive works, outworks. **4.** workmanship.
travaillé [travaje] *a.* (*a*) worked, wrought (iron, stone); (*b*) laboured, *NAm:* labored, elaborate (style, etc.).
travailler [travaje] **1.** *v.tr.* (*a*) *esp. Lit:* to torment, worry, obsess; **un désir le travaillait,** he was tormented, obsessed, with a desire; **être travaillé de, par, la goutte,** to be a martyr to gout; **se t. l'esprit,** to worry; (*b*) to work (up)on (s.o., the feelings, public opinion, etc.); to bring pressure to bear upon (s.o.); (*c*) to work, fashion, shape (wood, iron, etc.); **t. la pâte,** to knead the dough; **t. son style,** to polish one's style; (*d*) to work at, study (one's part, a subject, etc.). **2.** *v.i.* (*a*) to work, labour, toil; **t. ferme pour nourrir sa famille,** to work hard to keep one's family; **t. à la terre,** to work on the land; **t. dur,** to work hard; *F:* **t. comme un nègre, comme quatre, comme un cheval,** to work like a slave, a beaver, a Trojan, a horse; *P:* **t. du chapeau,** to have a screw loose; **le temps travaille pour nous,** time is on our side; **t. pour le roi de Prusse,** to get nothing out of it; **se rendre malade à force de t.,** to make oneself ill with work; **t. à l'aiguille,** to do needlework; **t. pour soi-même, pour, à, son compte,** to work, for oneself, on one's own account; to be self-employed; **t. à la perte de qn, à perdre qn,** to aim at ruining s.o.; **t. à un roman,** to work at, on, a novel; **t. à faire qch.,** to make an effort, exert oneself, to do sth.; **t. à produire de l'effet,** to strain after effect; (*b*) (*of performing animals, etc.*) to go through their performance; (*c*) (*of ship, cable, etc.*) to strain; (*of wine*) to ferment, to work; (*of the mind*) to be in a ferment; (*of wood*) to warp, shrink; (*of walls*) to crack; (*d*) **faire t. une machine,** to work, run, an engine; **faire t. son argent,** to make one's money work for one.
travailleur, -euse [travajœr, -øz] **1.** *a.* (*a*) industrious, hard-working; (*b*) **les masses travailleuses,** the workers, the working classes. **2.** *n.* worker; (*a*) **bon t.,** good, hard, worker; (*b*) **t. manuel, intellectuel,** manual, brain, worker; **t. indépendant,** self-employed worker; **t. en bâtiment,** building worker; **les travailleurs,** the workers, the working people; (*c*) *n.f. Ent:* **travailleuse,** worker (bee). **3.** *n.f.* **travailleuse,** (lady's) work table.
travaillisme [travajism] *n.m. Pol:* (British) socialism, doctrine of the Labour Party.
travailliste [travajist] *Eng.Pol:* **1.** *n.m.* (*a*) member of the Labour Party; (*b*) Labour member (of Parliament). **2.** *a.* Labour (Party, member).
travée [trave] *n.f.* **1.** *Const: Arch:* bay. **2.** (i) span, (ii) independent girder (of bridge). **3.** *Av:* rib (of wing). **4.** bank (of seats, machines, etc.).
travelling [travəliŋ] *n.m. Cin:* (*a*) dolly, travelling platform (for the camera); (*b*) tracking shot.
travers [travɛr] *n.m.* **1.** (*a*) breadth; *adv.phr.* **en t.,** across, crosswise; **autobus avec places disposées en t.,** bus with seats arranged crosswise; **profil en t.,** cross section; *prep.phr.* **en t. de,** across; **se mettre en t. du chemin de qn,** to stand in s.o.'s way; **à t. qch., au t. de qch.,** through sth.; **à t. le monde,** throughout the world; (*b*) *Nau:* beam (of vessel); **de t., par le t.,** on

the beam, abeam; **collision par le t.,** collision broadside on; *F:* **prendre par le t.,** to take a short cut; **en t. (du navire),** athwart (ships); (*c*) *Cmptr:* **correction de mise en t.,** deskew. **2.** irregularity (of building, etc.); *adv.phr.* **de t.,** the wrong way; **tout va de t.,** everything goes wrong; **regarder qn de t.,** to look askance, to scowl, at s.o.; **il a la bouche de t.,** his mouth is crooked; **les tableaux pendaient de t.,** the pictures were hung crooked; **il a des idées tout(es) de t.,** his ideas are all wrong; **entendre, prendre, tout de t.,** to take everything the wrong way. **3.** (*a*) *A:* **t. (d'esprit),** eccentricity; (*b*) failing, bad habit, fault.

traversable [travɛrsabl̩] *a.* (desert, river) that can be crossed.

traverse [travɛrs] *n.f.* **1. (chemin de) t.,** short cut. **2. (barre de) t.,** cross bar, cross piece; rung (of ladder); *Const:* transom; *Rail:* sleeper, *U.S:* tie; *Aut: etc:* cross member (of frame). **3.** *Lit:* setback.

traversée [travɛrse] *n.f.* (*a*) passage, (sea) crossing; (*b*) **faire la t. d'une ville,** to cross, pass through, a town; (*c*) *Mount:* traverse.

traverser [travɛrse] *v.tr.* **1.** to cross, go across (street, etc.); to go, pass, through (town, danger, crisis, etc.); to cross (a town); **t. la foule,** to make one's way through the crowd; **il est arrivé à t. la rivière,** he got across the river; **t. la rivière à la nage, en bateau,** to swim, row, across the river; **une planche traverse le ruisseau,** there is a plank across the stream; **t. une forêt à cheval, à bicyclette, en auto,** to ride, cycle, drive, through a forest; **t. un désert en avion,** to fly across a desert; **la balle lui traversa le bras,** the bullet went through his arm; **la pluie avait traversé mon pardessus,** the rain had gone through my overcoat; **l'idée me traversa l'esprit comme un éclair,** the idea flashed through my mind. **2.** *A:* to cross, thwart (s.o.'s plans).

traversier, -ière [travɛrsje, -jɛr] **1.** *a.* cross, crossing; *Const:* bridging. **2.** *n.m.* (*a*) cross bar (of banner); (*b*) *Fr.C:* ferry (boat). **3.** *n.f.* **traversière,** *Const:* bridging piece (between beams).

traversin [travɛrsɛ̃] *n.m.* **1.** (*a*) *Carp: etc:* cross piece; (*b*) *Nau:* cross tree. **2.** bolster (for bed).

travesti, -ie [travɛsti] **1.** *a.* disguised; **bal t.,** fancy-dress ball, costume ball; *Th:* **rôle t.,** *n.m.* **travesti,** man's part taken by a woman, or vice versa; drag part. **2.** *n.m.* fancy dress. **3.** *n.* transvestite.

travestir [travɛstir] *v.tr.* **1.** to disguise (**en,** as). **2.** (*a*) to travesty, parody, burlesque (play, poem); (*b*) to distort, misrepresent.

travestisme [travɛstism] *n.m.* *Psy:* transvestism.

travestissement [travɛstismɑ̃] *n.m.* **1.** (*a*) disguising; (*b*) disguise; *Th:* **rôle à travestissements,** quick-change part. **2.** (*a*) travesty (of play, etc.); (*b*) misrepresentation (of facts, etc.); travesty (of the truth). **3.** *Psy:* transvestism.

traviole (de) [dətravjɔl] *adv.phr.* *P:* crooked.

trayeur, -euse [trɛjœr, -øz] **1.** *n.* (*pers.*) milker. **2.** *n.f.* **trayeuse,** milking machine.

trayon [trɛjɔ̃] *n.m.* dug, teat (of cow, etc.).

trébuchant [trebyʃɑ̃] *a.* staggering; stumbling.

trébucher [trebyʃe] **1.** *v.i.* (*aux.* **avoir,** *occ.* **être**) to stumble (**sur,** over); **marcher en trébuchant,** to stumble along; **faire t. qn,** to trip s.o. up. **2.** *v.tr.* to test (coin) for weight.

trébuchet [trebyʃɛ] *n.m.* **1.** bird trap. **2.** (small) precision balance; assay balance.

tréfilage [trefilaʒ] *n.m.* *Metalw:* wire drawing.

tréfiler [trefile] *v.tr.* *Metalw:* to (wire)draw.

tréfilerie [trefilri] *n.f.* *Metalw:* **1.** wire drawing. **2.** (wire-)drawing mill.

trèfle [trɛfl̩] *n.m.* **1.** *Bot:* trefoil; clover; **t. blanc,** wild white clover; **t. rouge,** red clover. **2.** *Arch:* *Her:* trefoil; *Civ.E:* **croisement en t.,** clover-leaf intersection. **3.** *Cards:* clubs; **jouer t.,** to play a club.

tréfonds [trefɔ̃] *n.m.* subsoil; minerals, etc., lying below the ground; **t. d'un immeuble,** ground underneath a building; **dans le t. de mon cœur,** in my heart of hearts.

treillage [trɛjaʒ] *n.m.* trellis (work); lattice work; **t. métallique, en fil de fer,** wire fencing.

treillager [trɛjaʒe] *v.tr.* **(je treillageai(s); n. treillageons)** to trellis (wall, etc.); **fenêtre treillagée,** lattice window.

treille [trɛj] *n.f.* (*a*) vine arbour; trellised vines; (*b*) (climbing) vine; *F:* **le jus de la t.,** the juice of the grape; wine.

treillis [trɛji] *n.m.* **1.** trellis (work); lattice, **t. métallique,** wire mesh. **2.** *Tex:* (*a*) (coarse) canvas; (*b*) glazed calico; (*c*) *pl.* *Mil:* dungarees, fatigue dress.

treize [trɛz] *num.a.inv.* & *n.m.inv.* thirteen; *Com:* **t. à la douzaine,** a baker's dozen; **le numéro t.,** number thirteen; **le t. mai,** the thirteenth of May; **Louis T.,** Louis the Thirteenth; *Sp:* **jeu, rugby, à t.,** Rugby League football.

treizième [trɛzjɛm] **1.** *num.a.* & *n.* thirteenth. **2.** *n.m.* thirteenth (part). **3.** *n.f.* *Mus:* thirteenth.

treizièmement [trɛzjɛmmɑ̃] *adv.* thirteenthly, in the thirteenth place.

tréma [trema] **1.** *n.m.* diaeresis; *pl.* diaereses. **2.** *a.inv.* **des ë tréma,** e's with diaeresis.

trémail [tremaj] *n.m.* *Fish:* trammel (net).

tremblant, -ante [trɑ̃blɑ̃, -ɑ̃t] *a.* trembling (knees, hand); quivering (face); shaky (bridge); quaking (ground); flickering (light); tremulous (voice); **t. (de peur),** trembling, shaking, with fear.

tremble [trɑ̃bl̩] *n.m.* *Bot:* aspen.

tremblé [trɑ̃ble] *a.* (*a*) shaky (handwriting, etc.); wavy (line); (*b*) *Mus:* tremolo (notes).

tremblement [trɑ̃bləmɑ̃] *n.m.* **1.** trembling, quivering), shaking (of body, hand, bridge, etc.); tremulousness, quavering (of voice), shuddering (with horror). **2.** tremor (of fear, joy, anger); **t. de fièvre,** fit of shivering; **t. de terre,** earth tremor; earthquake; *F:* **et tout le t.,** and the whole lot. **3.** *Mus:* tremolo.

trembler [trɑ̃ble] *v.i.* (*a*) to tremble, quiver; to quake; to shiver (with cold); to shake (with anger); (*of light*) to flicker; (*of voice*) to quaver; **le pont, le sol, tremble,** the bridge, the earth, is shaking; **faire t. les vitres,** to make the windows shake, rattle; **la main lui tremblait,** his hand was shaking; (*b*) to tremble with fear; **t. de tout son corps,** to shake all over; *F:* **t. dans sa peau,** to quake, shake, in one's shoes; **t. devant qn,** to stand in fear of s.o.; **en tremblant,** tremblingly, tremulously; **je tremble de le rencontrer,** I tremble, I am terrified, at the thought of meeting him; **je tremblais de le réveiller,** I was fearful of awakening him.

trembleur [trɑ̃blœr] *n.m.* *El:* trembler, vibrator (of coil); contact breaker, make-and-break; *Tg:* *Tp:* buzzer, ticker.

tremblotant [trɑ̃blɔtɑ̃] *a.* trembling (slightly); quivering, shivering (body); tremulous (smile, voice); flickering (light).

tremblote [trɑ̃blɔt] *n.f.* *P:* **avoir la t.,** (i) to have the jitters; (ii) to have the shivers.

tremblotement [trɑ̃blɔtmɑ̃] *n.m.* trembling; quavering (of voice); shivering.

trembloter [trɑ̃blɔte] *v.i.* to tremble (slightly); to quiver; (*of voice*) to quaver, shake; (*of light*) to flicker; (*of wings*) to flutter.

trémie [tremi] *n.f.* **1.** (*a*) *Ind: etc:* hopper, funnel, (ore) bin; (*b*) hopper (for chickens, etc.); feeding box. **2.** *Const:* hearth cavity.

trémière [tremjɛr] *a.f.* & *n.f.* *Bot:* **(rose) t.,** hollyhock.

tremolo, trémolo [tremɔlo] *n.m. Mus:* **1.** tremolo; quaver (in voice). **2.** tremolo stop (of organ).
trémoussement [tremusmɑ̃] *n.m.* jigging up and down.
trémousser (se) [sətremuse] *v.pr.* (*a*) to fidget; (*b*) to jig up and down (in dancing, etc.); (*c*) **marcher en se trémoussant,** to walk with a wiggle; (*d*) (*of birds*) to flutter (about).
trempage [trɑ̃paʒ] *n.m.* soaking.
trempe [trɑ̃p] *n.f.* **1.** steeping, dipping, soaking; *Typ:* damping (of paper); **mettre qch. en t.,** to put sth. to soak. **2.** *Metall:* hardening, quench(ing); **t. et revenu,** quenching and hardening; **(acier, atelier, etc.) de t.,** hardening (steel, plant, etc.); **t. à l'air,** air hardening; **t. à l'eau, à l'huile,** water quenching, oil quenching; **t. par cémentation, t. de, en, surface,** case hardening; **bain de t.,** hardening, quenching, bath. **3.** (*a*) temper, hardness (of steel); (*b*) quality; **un homme de sa t.,** a man of his calibre.
trempé [trɑ̃pe] *a.* (*a*) wet, soaked; drenched (with perspiration, tears); **t. jusqu'aux os,** *F:* **comme une soupe,** wet through; soaked to the skin; (*b*) hardened (steel, glass); tempered (steel); **bien t.,** well-tempered, resolute (mind); (athlete) with plenty of stamina; (*c*) **vin t.,** wine diluted with water.
trempée [trɑ̃pe] *n.f.* steeping, soaking.
tremper [trɑ̃pe] **1.** *v.tr.* (*a*) to mix, dilute, (wine) with water; (*b*) to soak, steep (in a liquid); to dip, dunk (bread in soup); **se t. dans l'eau,** to plunge into the water; **se t. dans l'atmosphère du moyen âge,** to steep oneself in the atmosphere of the Middle Ages; **t. la soupe,** to pour the soup on the bread; **t. sa plume dans l'encre,** to dip one's pen in the ink; **t. ses lèvres dans son verre,** to put one's lips to one's glass; *Typ:* **t. le papier,** to wet, damp, the paper; (*c*) *Metall:* to harden, quench (steel); to chill (cast iron); **t. les muscles,** to harden the muscles. **2.** *v.i.* (*a*) (*of skins, soiled linen, etc.*) to (lie in) soak; (*b*) **t. dans un complot,** to have a hand in, to be involved in, a plot.
trempette [trɑ̃pɛt] *n.f.* **faire t.,** (i) to dip bread, etc., in coffee, wine, etc.; to dunk; (ii) *F:* to have a hasty dip, a quick bathe.
tremplin [trɑ̃plɛ̃] *n.m. Sp:* springboard; diving board; ski jump; *Fig:* springboard.
trémulation [tremylasjɔ̃] *n.f. Med:* tremor.
trémuler [tremyle] **1.** *v.i.* to tremble. **2.** *v.tr.* **t. les doigts,** to twiddle one's fingers.
trentaine [trɑ̃tɛn] *n.f.* (about) thirty, some thirty; thirty (francs) or so; **il approche de la t.,** he's getting on for thirty.
trente [trɑ̃t] *num.a.inv. & n.m.inv.* thirty; **t. jours,** thirty days; **le t. juin,** (on) the thirtieth of June; **les années t.,** the thirties (1930–1939); *Hist:* **la Guerre de T. Ans,** the Thirty Years' War; **t. et un,** thirty-one; *F:* **se mettre sur son t. et un,** to dress smartly; *Cards:* **t. et un,** (game of) trente et un; *Ten:* **t. à,** thirty all.
trente-six [trɑ̃tsi, -sis, -siz; *for rules of pronunciation see* SIX] *num.a.inv. & n.m.inv.* (i) thirty-six; (ii) *F:* umpteen; **voir t.-s. chandelles,** to see stars (after a blow on the head); **il n'y va pas par t.-s. chemins,** he doesn't beat about the bush; **il n'y a pas t.-s. façons de le faire,** there are no two ways of doing it.
trentième [trɑ̃tjɛm] **1.** *num.a. & n.inv.* thirtieth. **2.** *n.m.* thirtieth (part).
trépan [trepɑ̃] *n.m. Tls: Surg:* trepan.
trépanation [trepanasjɔ̃] *n.f. Surg:* trepanning.
trépaner [trepane] *v.tr.* **1.** to bore, drill, into (rock, etc.). **2.** *Surg:* to trepan; to trephine.
trépas [trepɑ] *n.m. Lit:* death.
trépassé, -ée [trepɑse] *a. & n.* dead, deceased (person); departed.
trépasser [trepɑse] *v.i.* (*the aux. is* **avoir,** *occ.* **être**) *A: & Lit:* to die; to depart this life.
trépidant [trepidɑ̃] *a.* vibrating; bustling, hectic.
trépidation [trepidasjɔ̃] *n.f.* **1.** vibration (of machinery, etc.). **2.** trembling (of limbs). **3.** bustle, flurry.
trépider [trepide] *v.i.* (*of machines, etc.*) to vibrate.
trépied [trepje] *n.m.* (*a*) three-legged stool; (*b*) *Cu:* trivet; (*c*) tripod, three-legged stand.
trépignement [trepiɲmɑ̃] *n.m.* stamping (of feet).
trépigner [trepiɲe] **1.** *v.i.* **t. de colère,** to dance, stamp with rage; **il trépignait de partir,** he was itching to start. **2.** *v.tr.* to trample down (earth).
trépointe [trepwɛ̃t] *n.f.* welt (of shoe).
tréponème [treponɛm] *n.m. Biol:* treponema.
très [trɛ] *adv.* very, most; (very) much; **t. bon,** (i) very good, (ii) most kind; **t. connu,** very well known; **t. différent,** very different; **t. estimé,** highly esteemed; **t. vite,** very quickly; **elle est t. femme,** she is very feminine; **prendre qch. t. au sérieux,** to take sth. very seriously; *F:* **avoir t. faim, t. soif, t. peur,** to be very hungry, very thirsty, very much afraid; **ces robes sont t. portées,** these dresses are very much in the fashion; **est-ce-que je me suis fait t. remarquer?—très!** did I attract very much notice?—you did! *F:* and how!
trésor [trezɔr] *n.m.* **1.** (*a*) treasure; *F:* **ma bonne est un t.,** my maid is a treasure; *F:* **mon t.,** darling; (*b*) *Jur:* treasure trove; (*c*) *Ecc:* (collection of) relics and ornaments; (*d*) treasure house. **2.** *pl.* riches, wealth; a fortune. **3.** treasury; **le T. (public),** the (French) Treasury. **4. ce livre est un t. de faits,** this book is a mine of facts.
trésorerie [trezɔrri] *n.f.* **1.** treasury. **2.** (*a*) treasurership; (*b*) treasurer's office. **3.** funds.
trésorier, -ière [trezɔrje, -jɛr] *n.* treasurer; paymaster, paymistress; *Adm:* **t.(-payeur) général,** chief treasurer and paymaster (of the *département*); **commis t.,** treasury clerk; *Mil:* **officier t.,** paymaster.
tressage [trɛsaʒ] *n.m.* braiding, plaiting.
tressaillement [tresajmɑ̃] *n.m.* start (of surprise); shudder (of fear); wince (of pain).
tressaillir [tresajir] *v.i.* (*pr.p.* **tressaillant;** *p.p.* **tressailli;** *pr.ind.* **je tressaille, n. tressaillons, ils tressaillent;** *impf.* **je tressaillais;** *p.h.* **je tressaillis;** *fu.* **je tressaillirai)** to give a start (from surprise); to shudder (with fear); to leap (with joy); (*of heart*) to flutter; **t. de douleur,** to wince.
tressauter [tresote] *v.i.* (*a*) to start, jump (with fear, surprise, etc.); (*b*) (*of thgs*) to be jolted about.
tresse [trɛs] *n.f.* (*a*) plait (of hair); (*b*) braid (of yarn, etc.); *Dom.Ec:* **t. de coton,** cotton tape; *El:* **fil conducteur sous t.,** braided conductor wire; *Mec.E:* **t. de garniture,** gasket packing; (*c*) *Arch:* strap work.
tressé [trese] *a. Miner:* having interlaced fibres.
tresser [trese] *v.tr.* to plait (hair, straw, etc.); to weave (basket, garland), to wreathe a garland; *F:* **t. des couronnes à qn,** to praise, flatter, s.o.
tréteau, -eaux [treto] *n.m.* **1.** trestle, support, stand. **2.** *pl. Th:* stage, boards.
treuil [trœj] *n.m. Mec.E:* winch, windlass, winding drum; **t. à chaîne,** chain hoist; **t. d'ascenseur,** winding gear of a lift, an elevator.
treuiller [trœje] *v.tr.* to winch (up).
trêve [trɛv] *n.f.* (*a*) truce; *Hist:* **la t. de Dieu,** the truce of God; *Pol: F:* **t. des confiseurs,** political truce in the Chamber at New Year; (*b*) respite; *F:* **t. de bêtises, de plaisanteries!** that's enough, no more, of your nonsense! **sans t.,** unceasing(ly).
tri¹ [tri] *n.m.* sorting (out); classifying (of letters, skills, etc.); **faire le t. de,** to sort out, arrange, pick out; *Rail: etc:* **bureau de t.,** sorting office.
tri² *n.m.* (*at bridge, whist*) odd trick.
triacide [triasid] *a. & n.m. Ch:* triacid.
triade [trijad] *n.f.* triad.
triage [trijaʒ] *n.m.* (*a*) sorting (of coal, letters, ores, etc.); *Rail:* **gare de t.,** marshalling yard; **voie de t.,**

siding; *Mil:* **hôpital de t.,** clearing hospital; (*b*) selecting, picking out, sorting, setting aside (of the best, etc.); (*c*) grading (of ore).

triangle [trijɑ̃gl̩] *n.m.* **1.** (*a*) *Mth:* triangle; (*b*) *F:* **l'éternel t.,** the eternal triangle. **2.** (*a*) *Nau:* triangular flag; (*b*) *Draw:* set square, *U.S:* triangle; (*c*) *Mus:* triangle.

triangulaire [trijɑ̃gylɛr] **1.** *a.* triangular; *Pol:* three-cornered (election, fight). **2.** *n.m. Anat:* triangularis (muscle).

triangulation [trijɑ̃gylasjɔ̃] *n.f. Surv:* triangulation.

trianguler [trijɑ̃gyle] *v.tr. Surv:* to triangulate.

trias [trijɑs] *n.m. Geol:* Trias, Triassic.

triasique [trijazik] *a. Geol:* triassic.

triatomique [triatɔmik] *a. Ch:* triatomic.

tribal, -aux [tribal, -o] *a.* tribal (system, etc.).

tribalisme [tribalism] *n.m.* tribalism.

tribord [tribɔr] *n.m. Nau:* starboard (side); **à t.,** on the starboard side; to starboard.

tribu [triby] *n.f.* tribe.

tribulation [tribylasjɔ̃] *n.f.* tribulation; trouble.

tribun [tribœ̃] *n.m.* (*a*) *Rom.Hist: etc:* tribune; (*b*) popular orator, speaker.

tribunal, -aux [tribynal, -o] *n.m.* tribunal; (*a*) judge's seat, bench; (*b*) law court; **en plein t.,** in open court; **t. civil, criminel,** civil, criminal court; **t. d'instance** = magistrates' court, *F:* police court; **t. de grande instance** = Crown court; **t. pour enfants et adolescents,** juvenile court; **t. militaire,** military tribunal; **prendre la voie des tribunaux,** to take legal action; **le t. de l'opinion publique,** the bar of public opinion; (*c*) *Navy:* **t. de prise,** prize court.

tribunat [tribyna] *n.m. Hist:* tribunate.

tribune [tribyn] *n.f.* **1.** tribune, rostrum, (speaker's) platform; *Parl:* **monter à la t.,** to address the House. **2.** (*a*) (public, *Parl:* strangers') gallery; (*b*) *Sp:* **t. (d'honneur),** (grand)stand; (*c*) **t. d'orgues,** organ loft. **3.** forum, discussion, debate.

tribut [triby] *n.m.* tribute; (*a*) *Hist:* tribute-money; **payer t.,** to pay tribute; (*b*) *A:* duty, tax; (*c*) **apporter son t. d'éloges,** to bring, offer, one's tribute of praise; **t. légitime,** fair reward (for one's labour).

tributaire [tribytɛr] *a. & n.m.* (*a*) tributary; **être t. de l'étranger,** to be dependent upon foreign supplies; (*b*) tributary (river).

tricentenaire [trisɑ̃tnɛr] *n.m.* tercentenary.

tricéphale [trisefal] *a.* three-headed (monster).

triceps [trisɛps] *n.m. Anat:* triceps (muscle).

triche [triʃ] *n.f. F:* trickery; cheating.

tricher [triʃe] *v.i. & tr.* to cheat **(sur,** over); to lie **(sur,** about); *F:* to cheat a bit, to fiddle it (to hide a defect, etc.).

tricherie [triʃri] *n.f.* cheating trickery.

tricheur, -euse [triʃœr, -øz] *n.* cheat, (card) sharper.

trichine [trikin] *n.f. Ann:* trichina, thread-worm.

trichinose [trikinoz] *n.f. Med:* trichinosis.

trichloracétique [triklɔrasetik] *a. Ch:* trichlor(o)acetic.

trichoma [trikɔma], **trichome** [trikom] *n.m. Med:* plica, trichoma.

trichosure [trikɔzyr] *n.m. Z:* (Australian) opossum.

trichrome [trikrom] *a.* three-colour(ed), trichromatic (photography).

trichromie [trikrɔmi] *n.f. Phot: etc:* three-colour process.

trick [trik] *n.m. Cards:* (*bridge, etc.*) odd trick.

tricolore [trikɔlɔr] *a.* tricolour(ed); **le drapeau t.,** the French flag, the Tricolour; *Adm:* **feux tricolores,** traffic lights, signals; *m.pl. Sp: F:* **les Tricolores,** the French team.

tricorne [trikɔrn] *n.m.* three-cornered hat; tricorn.

tricot [triko] *n.m.* **1.** (*a*) knitting; knitted fabric; *Com:* knitwear; (*b*) *Tex:* stockinet. **2.** (knitted) jersey, jumper; *F:* woolly.

tricotage [trikɔtaʒ] *n.m.* knitting.

tricoter [trikɔte] **1.** *v.tr.* to knit; **aiguilles à t.,** knitting needles; **machine à t.,** knitting machine. **2.** *v.i. P:* **t. des jambes,** (i) *A:* to dance; (ii) to make off, scram; (iii) to pedal like mad.

tricoteur, -euse [trikɔtœr, -øz] **1.** *n.* knitter. **2.** *n.f.* **tricoteuse,** knitting machine.

trictrac [triktrak] *n.m. Games:* (*a*) backgammon; (*b*) backgammon board.

tricuspide [trikyspid] *a. Anat:* tricuspid (valve).

tricycle [trisikl̩] **1.** *a. Av:* three-wheeled (undercarriage). **2.** *n.m.* tricycle.

trident [tridɑ̃] *n.m.* trident; (*a*) fish spear; (*b*) *Agr:* three-pronged (pitch)fork.

tridimensionnel, -elle [tridimɑ̃sjɔnɛl] *a.* three-dimensional.

trièdre [triɛdr̩] *Mth:* **1.** *a.* trihedral. **2.** *n.m.* trihedron.

triennal, -aux [trienal, -o] *a.* triennial; appointed for three years; three-year (plan, *Agr:* rotation).

triennat [triena] *n.m.* three-year period of office.

trier [trije] *v.tr.* (*impf. & pr.sub.* **n. triions, v. triiez)** (*a*) to sort (letters, etc.); to go through (one's wardrobe); *Tex:* to pick (wool); (*b*) to pick out, sort out, choose, select (the best, etc.); **t. à la main,** to hand-pick.

trieur, -euse [trijœr, -øz] **1.** *n.* sorter (of letters, etc.); (wool) picker. **2.** *n.m. Ind:* separator; grader. **3.** *n.f.* **trieuse:** (*a*) wool-picking machine; (*b*) card-sorting machine; sorter.

trieur-calibreur [trijœrkalibrœr] *n.m. Ind:* grading machine; *pl. trieurs-calibreurs.*

trifolié [trifɔlje] *a. Bot:* trifoliate, three-leaved.

trifouiller [trifuje] *v.tr. & i. F:* to rummage (in); to fiddle about (with); to meddle (with).

trigonométrie [trigɔnɔmetri] *n.f.* trigonometry.

trigonométrique [trigɔnɔmetrik] *a.* trigonometric(al).

trijumeau, -elle, -eaux [triʒymo, -ɛl, -o] *n.* triplet.

trilingue [trilɛ̃g] *a.* trilingual.

trille [trij] *n.m. Mus:* trill.

triller [trije] *v.tr. Mus:* to trill (note, passage).

trillion [triljɔ̃] *n.m.* **1.** (*since 1948*) trillion (10^{18}), *U.S:* quintillion. **2.** (*before 1948*) billion (10^{12}), *U.S:* trillion.

trilobé [trilɔbe] *a.* **1.** *Arch:* trefoil (arch, etc.). **2.** *Bot:* trilobate.

trilobite [trilɔbit] *n.m. Paleont:* trilobite.

trilogie [trilɔʒi] *n.f. Lit:* trilogy.

trimaran [trimarɑ̃] *n.m. Nau:* trimaran.

trimarder [trimarde] *v.i. P:* to be on the road.

trimardeur [trimardœr] *n.m. P:* tramp, *U.S:* hobo.

trimbal(l)age [trɛ̃balaʒ] *n.m.,* **trimbal(l)ement** [trɛ̃balmɑ̃] *n.m. F:* lugging about (of parcels, children).

trimbal(l)er [trɛ̃bale] *v.tr.* **1.** *F:* to drag, lug, about (parcels, etc.); to trail (children, etc.) about; *P:* **qu'est-ce qu'il trimbale!** what an idiot! **2. se t. jusqu'à la gare,** to trail over to the station.

trimer [trime] *v.i.* to work hard, slave away (at sth.); **faire t. qn,** to keep s.o. at it.

trimestre [trimɛstr̩] *n.m.* **1.** quarter; *Sch:* term; **par t.,** quarterly; *Sch:* every term. **2.** quarter's salary, rent; *Sch:* term's fees.

trimestriel, -elle [trimɛstrijɛl] *a.* quarterly; *Sch:* end-of-term (report).

trimestriellement [trimɛstrijɛlmɑ̃] *adv.* quarterly; once a term.

trimètre [trimɛtr̥] *n.m. Pros:* trimeter.
tringle [trɛ̃gl̥] *n.f.* **1.** (*a*) rod; **t. de, à, rideau,** curtain rod; **t. d'escalier,** stair rod; **t. d'un pneu,** wire of a tyre; (*b*) (i) *Mch:* control rod; (ii) *Rail:* switch bar (of points);. **2.** *Arch:* tringle; square moulding.
trinitaire [trinitɛr] *n.m. or f.* Trinitarian.
trinité [trinite] *n.f.* **1.** *Theol:* Trinity; **la T.,** Trinity Sunday. **2.** *Geog:* **(île de) la T.,** Trinidad.
trinitrotoluène [trinitrɔtɔlɥɛn] *n.m.,* **trinol** [trinɔl] *n.m. Exp:* trinitrotoluene, T.N.T.
trinôme [trinom] *a. & n.m. Mth:* trinomial.
trinquer [trɛ̃ke] *v.i.* **1.** (*a*) to clink glasses; **t. à qn, qch.,** to drink to s.o., sth.; (*b*) *F:* to drink, *esp.* to booze. **2.** (*a*) to bang about, knock together; (*b*) *P:* to get the worst of it.
trinquet [trɛ̃kɛ] *n.m. Nau:* foremast.
trinquette [trɛ̃kɛt] *n.f. Nau:* **1.** storm jib. **2.** foretopmast staysail.
trio [trijo] *n.m. Mus: etc:* trio.
triode [triɔd] *a. & n.f. Elcs: W.Tel:* triode.
triolet [trijɔlɛ] *n.m.* **1.** *Pros:* triolet. **2.** *Mus:* triplet.
triomphal, -aux [trijɔ̃fal, -ol] *a.* triumphal.
triomphalement [trijɔ̃falmɑ̃] *adv.* triumphantly.
triomphant [trijɔ̃fɑ̃] *a.* triumphant (general, air, etc.).
triomphateur, -trice [trijɔ̃fatœr, -tris] **1.** *a.* triumphing, victorious. **2.** *n.m.* conquering hero.
triomphe [trijɔ̃f] *n.m.* (*a*) triumph **(sur,** over); (*b*) **faire un t. à qn,** to give s.o. an ovation; **arc de t.,** triumphal arch.
triompher [trijɔ̃fe] *v.i.* **1.** (*a*) *Rom.Ant:* to (receive the honour of) triumph; (*b*) to triumph **(de,** *occ.* **sur,** over); to excel **(dans,** in). **2.** to exult, glory (in sth.).
trioxyde [triɔksid] *n.m. Ch:* trioxide.
tripaille [tripaj] *n.f. F:* guts.
triparti [triparti], **tripartite** [tripartit] *a.* tripartite.
tripatouillage [tripatujaʒ] *n.m. F:* tampering with (text, accounts).
tripatouiller [tripatuje] *v.tr. F:* to tamper with (text, accounts, etc.).
tripe [trip] *n.f.* **1.** (*a*) *pl.* entrails (of animal); *Cu:* tripe; (*b*) *usu. pl. P:* (*of pers.*) guts; **rendre tripes et boyaux,** to be horribly sick; *F:* **avoir la t. républicaine,** to be an out-and-out republican. **2.** core, filling (of cigar). **3.** *Leath:* **peau en t.,** pelt.
triperie [tripri] *n.f.* **1.** tripe shop. **2.** tripe trade.
tripette [tripɛt] *n.f. F:* **ne pas valoir t.,** to be utterly worthless.
triphasé [trifɑze] *a. El:* triphase, three-phase.
triphtongue [triftɔ̃g] *n.f. Ling:* triphthong.
tripier, -ière [tripje, -jɛr] *n.* tripe butcher.
triplan [triplɑ̃] *a. & n.m. Av:* triplane.
triple [tripl̥] *a. & n.m.* treble, threefold, triple; **t. de . . .,** three times as much, as many, as great, as . . .; *F:* **t. menton,** triple chin; **plié en t.,** folded in three; **en t. exemplaire,** in triplicate; *Mus:* **t. croche,** demi-semi-quaver; *Ch:* **sel t.,** triple salt; *Astr:* **étoile t.,** triple star; (*intensive*) **un t. sot,** a prize idiot.
triplé, -ée [triple] *n.* (*pers.*) triplet.
triplement¹ [tripləmɑ̃] *adv.* trebly, triply; threefold.
triplement² *n.m.* trebling, tripling.
tripler [triple] *v.tr. & i.* to treble, triple; to increase threefold.
triplette [triplɛt] *n.f.* threesome; team of three.
tripode [tripɔd] *a. & n.m. Navy: etc:* tripod (mast).
triporteur [tripɔrtœr] *n.m.* carrier tricycle.
tripot [tripo] *n.m.* gambling-den.
tripotage [tripɔtaʒ] *n.m. F:* **1.** fiddling around. **2.** *pl.* shady dealings; election fiddles.
tripotée [tripɔte] *n.f. P:* **1.** thrashing, licking. **2.** lots; crowds (of children, etc.).
tripoter [tripɔte] *F:* **1.** *v.i.* (*a*) to fiddle about; to dabble, mess about (in the water); to rummage (in a drawer); (*b*) to engage in shady business; **t. dans la caisse,** to tamper with the cash. **2.** *v.tr.* (*a*) to finger, handle (s.o., sth.); to paw (s.o.); to meddle with (sth.); to fiddle with (one's hat); (*b*) to deal shadily, dishonestly, with (money).
tripoteur, -euse [tripɔtœr, -øz] *n. F:* schemer; *esp.* shady speculator.
triptyque [triptik] *n.m.* **1.** *Art:* triptych. **2.** *Aut: Adm:* triptyque. **3.** *F:* three-part, three-phase, plan, etc.
trique [trik] *n.f. F:* cudgel, heavy stick; **avoir recours à la t.,** to use big stick methods; **maigre comme une t.,** thin as a rake.
triquet [trikɛ] *n.m.* **1.** trestle. **2.** pair of steps.
trirème [trirɛm] *n.f. Gr.Ant:* trireme.
trisaïeul, -e [trizajœl] *n.* great-great-grandfather; great-great-grandmother; *pl. trisaïeul(e)s.*
trisannuel, -elle [trizanɥɛl] *a.* triennial.
triséquer [triseke] *v.tr.* **(je trisèque; je triséquerai)** to trisect (angle, etc.).
trissement [trismɑ̃] *n.m.* twitter(ing) (of swallows).
trisser (se) [sətrise] *v.pr. P:* to scram, beat it.
tris(s)yllabe [trisilab] **1.** *n.m.* trisyllable. **2.** *a.* trisyllabic.
triste [trist] *a.* **1.** (*a*) sad **(de,** at); sorrowful (person, face, news, etc.); woebegone (face, expression); **tout t.,** (very) dejected; in low spirits, *F:* down in the mouth; **sourire t.,** sad, wan, smile; **je fus (bien) t. d'apprendre que . . .,** I was (very) sorry, grieved, to hear that . . .; *F:* **c'est tout de même t.!** isn't it pathetic! (*b*) dreary, dismal, cheerless, dull (life, weather, room); bleak, depressing (countryside); **faire t. mine à qn,** to receive s.o. without enthusiasm. **2.** unfortunate, painful (news, duty, state); sad (occasion); **c'est une t. affaire,** it's a bad business. **3.** *F:* poor, sorry, wretched (meal, excuse).
tristement [tristəmɑ̃] *adv.* **1.** (*a*) sadly, sorrowfully; (*b*) cheerlessly. **2.** poorly, wretchedly.
tristesse [tristɛs] *n.f.* (*a*) (feeling of) sadness; **joie mêlée de t.,** joy tinged with sadness; **avec t.,** sadly; (*b*) dullness, cheerlessness (of a room, etc.); bleakness (of landscape).
tritium [tritjɔ̃m] *n.m. Ch:* tritium.
tritome [tritom] *n.m. Bot:* flame flower; *F:* red-hot poker.
Triton¹ [tritɔ̃] **1.** *Pr.n.m. Myth:* Triton. **2.** *n.m.* (*a*) *Amph:* triton, newt; (*b*) *Moll:* trumpet shell; triton (shell).
triton² *n.m. Mus:* tritone; augmented fourth.
trituration [trityrasjɔ̃] *n.f.* trituration, grinding.
triturer [trityre] *v.tr.* (*a*) to triturate, grind, rub down, reduce to powder; (*b*) to masticate; (*c*) to manipulate.
triumvir [trijɔmvir] *n.m. Rom.Hist:* triumvir.
triumvirat [trijɔmvira] *n.m. Rom. Hist:* triumvirate.
trivalent [trivalɑ̃] *a. Ch: Biol:* trivalent.
trivalve [trivalv] *a. Biol:* trivalvular, trivalve.
trivial, -iaux [trivjal, -jo] *a.* (*a*) *A:* trite, hackneyed; (*b*) vulgar, coarse (expression, etc.).
trivialement [trivjalmɑ̃] *adv.* vulgarly, coarsely.
trivialité [trivjalite] *n.f.* **1.** vulgarity, coarseness. **2.** vulgarism, coarse expression.
troc [trɔk] *n.m.* exchange (in kind); barter; **faire du t.,** to barter, *F:* to swap; **faire un t.,** to make an exchange *F:* to do a swop.
trochaïque [trɔkaik] *a. & n.m. Pros:* trochaic.
trochée [trɔʃe] *n.m. Pros:* trochee.
troène [trɔɛn] *n.m. Bot:* privet.
troglodyte [trɔglɔdit] *n.m.* **1.** troglodyte; cave dweller. **2.** *Orn:* wren.
trogne [trɔɲ] *n.f. F:* boozy face.
trognon [trɔɲɔ̃] *n.m.* (*a*) core (of apple, etc.); stump

(of cabbage, etc.); *F:* **jusqu'au t.,** to the (bitter) end; completely; (*b*) *F:* (*of child*) poppet, sweetie.

Troie [trwa] *Pr.n.f. A.Geog:* Troy; **guerre, cheval, de T.,** Trojan War, horse.

troïka [trɔika] *n.f. Veh:* troika.

trois [trwɑ] *before a vowel sound in the same word group* [trwɑz], *num. a. & n.m. inv.* three; **à t. heures,** at three o'clock; **les t. quarts du temps,** most of the time; **couper, diviser, une ligne, un angle, en t.,** to trisect a line, an angle; **entrer par t.,** to come in in threes, three at a time; **la vie à t.,** the eternal triangle; **le t. août,** the third of August; **Henri T.,** Henry the Third; **le t. de carreau,** the three of diamonds; **j'habite au t.,** I live at number three.

trois-huit [trwaɥit] *n.m.inv.* **1.** *Mus:* (piece in) three-eight time. **2.** *Ind:* **régime des t.-h.,** three-shift working.

troisième [trwazjɛm] **1.** *num.a. & n.* third; **au t. (étage),** on the third, *NAm:* fourth, floor; **de t. ordre,** third-rate; *Pol.Ec:* **personnes du t. âge,** senior citizens. **2.** *n.m.* (*occ.* = TIERS) **deux troisièmes,** two thirds. **3.** *n.f.* (*a*) *Sch:* **(classe de) t.,** *approx.* = fourth form; (*b*) *Aut:* **en t.,** in third (gear).

troisièmement [trwazjɛmmɑ̃] *adv.* thirdly, in the third place.

trois-mâts [trwɑmɑ] *n.m.inv. Nau:* three-masted ship, three-master.

trois-pièces [trwɑpjɛs] *n.m.inv. Cost:* three-piece suit.

trois-quarts [trwɑkar] *n.m.inv.* **1.** three-quarter violin. **2.** *Rugby Fb:* **les t.-q.,** the three-quarters. **3.** *Cost:* three-quarter-length coat.

trois-quatre [trwɑkatr̥] *n.m.inv. Mus:* (piece in) three-four time.

trois-six [trwɑsis] *n.m. Dist:* proof spirit.

troll [trɔl] *n.m. Myth:* troll.

trolley [trɔlɛ] *n.m.* (*a*) troll(e)y pole and wheel; **perche de t.,** trolley pole; (*b*) *F:* trolleybus.

trolleybus [trɔlɛbys] *n.m.* trolleybus.

trombe [trɔ̃b] *n.f.* **1.** waterspout. **2. t. de vent,** whirlwind; **t. d'eau,** cloudburst; *F:* **entrer, sortir, en t.,** to burst in, out (like a whirlwind).

trombine [trɔ̃bin] *n.f. P:* (*a*) head, nut; (*b*) face, mug.

tromblon [trɔ̃blɔ̃] *n.m.* **1.** blunderbuss. **2.** *Mil:* grenade sleeve (fitted to rifle).

trombone [trɔ̃bɔn] *n.m. Mus:* **1.** trombone. **2.** trombone (player). **3.** *F:* (wire) paper clip.

trompe [trɔ̃p] *n.f.* **1.** (*a*) horn; **publier qch. à son de trompe,** to trumpet sth. abroad; (*b*) hooter. **2.** proboscis (of animal, insect); trunk (of elephant). **3.** *Anat:* (Eustachian, Fallopian) tube. **4.** *Arch:* pendentive; squinch. **5.** (*a*) *Ind:* aspirator; siphon; filter pump; (*b*) *Metall:* blast pump; trompe.

trompe-la-mort [trɔ̃plamɔr] *n.m. & f.inv. F:* death dodger; daredevil.

trompe-l'œil [trɔ̃plœj] *n.m.inv.* **1.** *Art:* trompe l'œil (painting). **2.** *Pej:* illusion; bluff; *Pol: etc:* window dressing.

tromper [trɔ̃pe] to deceive **1.** *v.tr.* (*a*) to cheat; take in (s.o.); **il est incapable de t.,** he is incapable of deception; (*b*) to betray, be unfaithful to (wife, husband); **t. une jeune fille,** to ruin a girl; (*c*) to mislead **(sur,** as to); to disappoint (s.o.'s hopes); (*d*) to outwit, baffle, elude; (*e*) to relieve (tedium); to while away (the time); **t. la faim,** to stave off one's hunger. **2. se t.,** to be mistaken; to be wrong; to make a mistake; **si je ne me trompe,** if I am not mistaken; **se t. dans son calcul,** to be out in one's reckoning; **je me suis trompé de direction, de maison,** I went the wrong way, to the wrong house; **se t. d'heure,** to mistake the time; **elle ressemble à sa sœur à s'y t.,** you can't tell her from her sister; **il n'y a pas à s'y t.,** there is no mistake about it; **que l'on ne s'y trompe pas,** let there be no misunderstanding about it; **vous m'avez fait t.,** you made me make a mistake.

tromperie [trɔ̃pri] *n.f.* deceit, deception, fraud.

trompeter [trɔ̃p(ə)te] *v.* **(je trompette, je trompetterai)** to trumpet; *v.tr.* to shout (news) from the rooftops.

trompette [trɔ̃pɛt] I. *n.f.* **1.** (*a*) trumpet; *Mil:* **jouer, sonner, de la t.,** to play, sound the trumpet; *Lit:* **la t. du jugement dernier,** the last trump; (*b*) *Mus:* (*organ stop*) trumpet. **2.** (*a*) *Conch:* trumpet shell; (*b*) *Ich:* pipe fish. II. *n.m.* trumpet (player).

trompettiste [trɔ̃pɛtist] *n. Mus:* trumpet (player).

trompeur, -euse [trɔ̃pœr, -øz] **1.** *a.* (*a*) deceitful (person, words, etc.); lying (tongue); (*b*) deceptive, misleading (appearance, symptom). **2.** *n.* (*a*) deceiver, cheat(er); thief; (*b*) betrayer.

trompeusement [trɔ̃pøzmɑ̃] *adv.* (*a*) deceitfully; (*b*) deceptively.

tronc [trɔ̃] *n.m.* **1.** (*a*) trunk (of tree, body); (*b*) *Arch:* drum (of column); (*c*) *Anat:* trunk, main stem (of artery, etc.); (*d*) parent stock (of family). **2. t. pour les pauvres,** poor-box, almsbox. **3.** *Mth:* **t. de cône,** truncated cone.

tronche [trɔ̃ʃ] *n.f.* **1.** *For:* stem-pruned tree. **2.** *P:* head, nut.

tronçon [trɔ̃sɔ̃] *n.m.* (*a*) section; length (of pipe); (broken) stump (of sword, lance, mast, etc.); **t. de bois,** log; (*b*) section (of railway, etc.); (*c*) part, fragment (of a sentence, a text, etc.).

tronconique [trɔ̃kɔnik] *a.* **segment t.,** truncated segment.

tronçonnage [trɔ̃sɔnaʒ] *n.m.*, **tronçonnement** [trɔ̃sɔnmɑ̃] *n.m.* cutting into lengths, into pieces.

tronçonner [trɔ̃sɔne] *v.tr.* to cut into pieces, into sections.

tronçonneuse [trɔ̃sɔnøz] *n.f.* chain saw; power saw; circular saw.

trône [tron] *n.m.* **1.** (*a*) (royal, papal, episcopal) throne; **placer, mettre, qn sur le t.,** to put s.o. on the throne; *Pol:* **discours du t.,** king's, queen's, speech; (*b*) *F: Iron:* (= *lavatory*) throne. **2.** *Theol:* **les Trônes,** the Thrones.

trôner [trone] *v.i.* (*a*) *A:* (*of monarch*) to reign; (*b*) to sit enthroned; (*c*) to occupy a place of honour; (*d*) *Pej:* to lord it.

tronqué [trɔ̃ke] *a.* truncated; stub (mast); abbreviated (text).

tronquer [trɔ̃ke] *v.tr.* to truncate; *Pej:* to curtail (novel, etc.).

trop [tro] **1.** *adv.* too; (*a*) (*with adj.*) too, over-; **c'est t. difficile,** it's too difficult; **un travail t. difficile,** too difficult a job; **t. aimable** [trɔpɛmabl̥], too, very, kind; **vous êtes t. aimable de . . .,** it is most kind of you to . . .; **il est t. gentil pour le renvoyer,** he is too kind to sack him; **aliments t. riches,** over-rich food; **vous n'êtes que t. généreux,** you are all too generous; **t. fatigué,** overtired; too tired **(pour,** to); **vous n'êtes pas t. en avance,** you are none too early; **le trou était trop étroit pour qu'un rat entrât par là,** the hole was too narrow for a rat to come in by; (*b*) (*with vb*) too much, over-much, unduly, over-; **t. travailler,** to overwork, to work too hard; **boire t., t. boire,** to drink to excess, too much; **je l'ai t. aimé** [trɔpɛme], I loved him too well; **ne vous y fiez pas t., il ne faut pas t. vous y fier,** don't count on it too much; **on ne saurait t. le répéter,** it cannot be too often repeated; **je ne sais t. que dire,** I hardly know, I don't quite know, what to say. **2.** *n.m.* too much, too many; **il allait t. en dire, en dire t., en t. dire,** he was going to say too much; **je n'aurai pas t. d'une heure pour le faire,** it will take me a good hour; **trop de bruit,** too much noise; **t. d'amis,** too many friends; **je ne l'ai que t.**

dit, je ne l'ai dit que t., I've said it too many times already; **j'ai une carte de t., en t.,** I have one card too many; **c'est une fois de t.,** that is once too often; **quand j'ai du temps de t.,** when I have time to spare; **payer en t.,** to pay too much; **être de t.,** to be in the way, unwelcome, de trop; *F:* **travailler, boire, de t.,** to work too hard; to drink too much; *adv.phr.* **par t.,** (altogether) too (much); **être par t. généreux,** to be far too generous; **c'est t. fort!** it is really too bad! it's a bit much! **c'en est t.!** this really is the limit!

trophée [trɔfe] *n.m.* trophy.

tropical, -aux [trɔpikal, -o] *a.* tropical (plant, temperature, etc.).

tropique [trɔpik] **1.** *a.* tropical (year). **2.** *n.m.* (*a*) *Astr: Geog:* tropic; (*b*) *pl.* **sous les tropiques,** in the tropics.

troposphère [trɔpɔsfɛr] *n.f. Meteor:* troposphere.

trop-perçu [trɔpɛrsy] *n.m. Fin:* over-payment (of taxes); *pl. trop-perçus.*

trop-plein [trɔplɛ̃] *n.m.* overflow; **(tuyau de) t.-p.,** waste pipe, overflow pipe; *pl. trop-pleins.*

troque [trɔk] *n.m. Moll:* top shell.

troquer [trɔke] *v.tr.* to exchange, barter, *F:* swap (sth.); **t. qch. contre qch.,** to exchange sth. for sth.

troquet [trɔkɛ] *n.m. P:* (*a*) *A:* pub-keeper; (*b*) pub.

trot [tro] *n.m.* trot; **t. assis,** sitting trot; **faire du t. assis,** to trot close; **t. enlevé,** rising trot, *U.S:* posting trot; **au petit, au grand, t.,** at a gentle, brisk, trot; **prendre le t.,** to break into a trot; **aller le t., au t.,** to trot; *F:* **allez-y, et au t.!** go on, and be quick about it! **course de t.,** trotting race.

Trotskiste, Trotskyste [trɔtskist] *a. & n.m. & f.* Trotskyite.

trotte [trɔt] *n.f. F:* distance, stretch, run; **il y a une bonne t. d'ici là,** it is a good step, way, from here; **tout d'une t.,** without stopping, at a stretch.

trotte-menu [trɔtməny] *a. inv.* pattering, scampering (steps of mice, etc.).

trotter [trɔte] **1.** *v.i.* (*of horse or rider*) to trot; (*of mice*) to scamper; *F:* **toujours à t.,** always on the go; **on entendrait t. une souris,** you could hear a pin drop; **cette chanson me trotte par, dans, la tête,** that song keeps running through my head. **2.** *P:* **se t.,** to beat it, scram.

trotteur, -euse [trɔtœr, -øz] **1.** *n. Equit:* trotter. **2.** *n.f.* **trotteuse,** second hand (of watch).

trottinement [trɔtinmɑ̃] *n.m.* trotting (around).

trottiner [trɔtine] *v.i.* **1.** (*of horse, etc.*) to trot short. **2.** (*of pers.*) to trot (about, along).

trottinette [trɔtinɛt] *n.f.* (*a*) (child's) scooter; (*b*) *F:* small car.

trottoir [trɔtwar] *n.m.* **1.** footpath, pavement, *U.S:* sidewalk; *Aut:* **heurter le t.,** to hit the kerb; **artiste de t.,** pavement artist; **faire le t.,** to walk the streets. **2. t. roulant,** travelator.

trou [tru] *n.m.* **1.** (*a*) hole; eye (of needle); **t. de clef,** keyhole (of clock, watch); **t. de serrure,** keyhole (of lock); **faire son t.,** to make a niche for oneself; **t. de, du, chat,** (i) cat door (in house door, etc.); (ii) *Nau:* lubber's hole; *Av: P:* **il a fait un t. dans l'eau,** he's gone for a Burton; *F:* **boire comme un t., avoir un t. sous le nez,** to drink like a fish; (*b*) gap (in hedge, in memory, between players); (*c*) *Anat:* foramen; *Med: F:* **t. dans le cœur,** hole in the heart; *V:* **t. du cul, t. de balle,** arsehole, asshole; **petit t. du cul!** you bloody little fool! **2.** (*a*) hole; (*in road*) pothole; **t. de souris,** mouse-hole; *Av:* **t. d'air,** air pocket; *Th:* **t. du souffleur,** prompter's box; *Agr:* **t. au fumier,** manure pit; (*b*) *F:* place; **habiter un petit t. (perdu),** to live in a little hole at the back of beyond; (*c*) *Golf:* **envoyer la balle dans le t.,** to hole out; **partie par trous,** match play; (*d*) *P:* (i) grave; (ii) prison; **on l'a mis dans le t.,** they buried him; **on l'a mis au t.,** he was jailed. **3.** (*a*) *Mch: etc:* **t. d'homme,** manhole; **t. de graissage,** oil hole; **t. d'aération,** air vent; *Min:* **t. de mine,** blast hole, drill hole; *Min: Civ.E:* **t. de sondage, de sonde,** borehole; *Const:* **t. d'écoulement,** weep hole; (*b*) *Ph: Elcs:* hole; aperture. **4.** *Astr:* **t. noir,** black hole.

troubadour [trubadur] *n.m. Lit.Hist:* troubadour.

troublant [trublɑ̃] *a.* (*a*) disconcerting, disturbing, unsettling; (*b*) disturbing, provocative.

trouble¹ [trubl̥] *a.* **1.** (*a*) cloudy (liquid); dim (light, eyes); murky, overcast (sky); confused (situation); **avoir la vue t.,** to be dimsighted; **aux yeux troubles,** bleary-eyed; *adv.* **voir t.,** to be dim-sighted, to see things through a mist; (*b*) **avoir une vue t. de qch.,** to have a blurred vision of sth. **2.** confused (mind); uneasy (conscience); mixed, uneasy (emotion).

trouble² *n.m.* **1.** (*a*) confusion, disorder; **apporter du t. dans une famille,** to cause trouble in a family; *Med:* **troubles de digestion, de vision,** digestive troubles, eye trouble; (*b*) agitation, perturbation, uneasiness; embarrassment; **cause de t.,** disturbing factor; **jeter le t. dans l'esprit de qn,** to perturb s.o.; (*c*) *pl.* (public) disturbances. **2.** *Jur:* **t. de jouissance,** disturbance of possession.

trouble³ *n.f. Fish:* hoop net.

trouble-fête [trubləfɛt] *n.m.inv.* spoilsport, wet blanket, killjoy.

troubler [truble] *v.tr.* **1.** to make (liquid, etc.) cloudy, muddy; to cloud (s.o.'s mind); to dim (s.o.'s eyes). **2.** to disturb (meeting, sleep, silence, etc.); to interfere with, disturb (operations, activities); to impede (progress); to spoil (happiness); to upset (digestion); **un vent léger troubla l'eau,** a slight wind ruffled the water; **t. le repos, l'ordre public,** to create a disturbance; *Jur:* to break the peace; **l'ordre public n'a été nullement troublé,** there has been no breach of the peace; **imagination troublée,** disordered imagination. **3.** to perturb; (*a*) to confuse, upset (s.o.); to make (s.o.) uneasy; **paraître troublé,** to look confused, flustered, upset; (*b*) to excite, thrill (s.o.); to stir (the senses, emotions). **4.** *Jur:* **t. qn dans la jouissance d'un bien,** to disturb s.o.'s enjoyment of possession. **5. se t.** (*a*) (*of wine, etc.*) to get cloudy; (*of sky*) to become overcast; (*of vision*) to become blurred, to grow dim; (*of voice*) to break (with emotion); (*b*) to become perturbed, confused, flustered; **sans se t.,** unruffled, without turning a hair.

trouée [true] *n.f.* gap, opening, breach.

trouer [true] *v.tr.* to make a hole, holes, in (wall, etc.); to breach (enemy's lines, etc.); to wear, make, a hole in (garment); to perforate (zinc, etc.); (*of sock, etc.*) **se t.,** to go into holes; **avoir les bas troués,** to have holes in one's stockings; **les nuages commencent à se t.,** the clouds are beginning to break; *P:* **se faire t. la peau,** to be shot (dead).

troufignon [trufiɲɔ̃] *n.m. P:* arse, ass.

troufion [trufjɔ̃] *n.m. P:* (infantry) soldier, private.

trouillard, -arde [trujar, -ard] *P:* **1.** *a.* cowardly, funky. **2.** *n.* coward, funk.

trouille [truj] *n.f. P:* **avoir la t.,** to get the wind up; **tu n'as pas la t.!** you've got a nerve!

trouillomètre [trujɔmɛtr̥] *n.m. P:* **avoir le t. à zéro,** to be in a blue funk.

troupe [trup] *n.f.* **1.** (*a*) troop, band, company, group (of people); gang, set (of thieves, etc.); (scout) troop; (heavenly) host; (*b*) *Th:* troupe, company; (*c*) herd, drove (of cattle, deer); pride (of lions); flock (of birds); **ces animaux vivent en t.,** these animals herd together, are gregarious. **2.** *Mil:* (*a*) troop; body of soldiers; **officier de t.,** regimental officer; (*b*) **officiers et t.,** officers and other ranks; *O:* **enfant de t.,** army child; **cigarettes de t.,** army issue cigarettes; (*c*) *F:*

voilà de la t. qui passe, there are soldiers, troops, going by; (*d*) *pl.* troops, forces.

troupeau, -aux [trupo] *n.m.* herd, drove (of cattle); flock (of sheep, geese, etc.); flock, herd, *Pej:* horde (of people).

troupier [trupje] *n.m. Mil: F:* soldier.

troussage [trusaʒ] *n.m.* trussing (of fowl).

trousse [trus] *n.f.* **1.** *pl.* **être aux trousses de qn,** to be after s.o., (hot) on s.o.'s heels. **2.** (first-aid, tool, etc.) kit; (instrument) case; **t. de toilette,** dressing case; toilet case, bag; **t. d'écolier,** pencil case.

troussé [truse] *a. F:* **bien t.,** neat (object, compliment).

trousseau, -eaux [truso] *n.m.* **1.** bunch (of keys). **2.** (*a*) outfit (of clothing); (*b*) (bride's) trousseau; bottom drawer, *U.S:* hope chest.

trousser [truse] *v.tr.* **1.** (*a*) *A:* to bundle up; (*b*) to tuck up (skirt, etc.); **se t.,** to tuck up one's clothes; *F:* **il est toujours à t. les filles,** he's always chasing women; (*c*) *Cu:* to truss (fowl). **2.** *F:* to polish off (work, meal, *A:* s.o.).

trousseur [trusœr] *n.m. F:* **t. de jupons,** skirt chaser.

trouvaille [truvaj] *n.f.* (*a*) (lucky) find; (*b*) brainwave.

trouver [truve] **I.** *v.tr.* to find. **1.** (*a*) to find (sth. sought); **je ne trouve pas mes clefs,** I can't find my keys; **où est-ce qu'on trouve cela? où cela se trouve-t-il?** where is that to be found? where can you, one, find that? **ces plantes se trouvent partout,** these plants are to be found everywhere; **aller t. qn,** to go and (i) find, (ii) see, s.o.; (*b*) to discover, invent (a process, etc.). **2. t. (qch.) par hasard,** to discover, come upon, come across (sth.); to find (sth.) out accidentally; to hit upon (an idea); **on l'a trouvé mort,** he was found dead; **t. qn en faute,** to catch s.o. out; **bureau des objets trouvés,** lost-property office; **c'est bien trouvé!** good idea! **exemple bien, mal, trouvé,** well chosen, badly chosen, example; **il trouva la mort à . . .,** he met his death at . . .; **il trouve du plaisir à lire,** he finds pleasure in reading, he enjoys reading. **3. je la trouve jolie,** I consider her pretty, I think she's pretty; **vous trouvez?** you think so? **comment as-tu trouvé ce livre?** how did you find, like, the book? **je trouve mieux de ne pas . . .,** I think it better not to . . . . **II. se trouver 1.** (*a*) to (happen to) be; to be, to find oneself (in a situation); (*b*) to feel; **je me trouve très bien ici,** I'm very comfortable here; **comment vous êtes-vous trouvé de ce traitement?** how did the treatment work? **se t. bien de qch., d'avoir fait qch.,** to feel all the better for (having done) sth.; **je me trouve mieux,** I feel better. **2.** to happen; to turn out; **je me trouve avoir, il se trouve que j'ai, une heure de libre,** I happen to have, it so happens that I have, an hour to spare; **la dame se trouva être sa propre femme,** the lady turned out to be his own wife; *F:* **si cela se trouve, il est déjà rentré,** maybe he's back.

trouveur, -euse [truvœr, -øz] *n.* discoverer, inventor.

troyen[1], -enne [trwajɛ̃, -ɛn] *a. & n.* Trojan.

troyen[2], -enne, *a. & n. Geog:* (native, inhabitant) of Troyes.

truand, -ande [tryɑ̃, -ɑ̃d] *n.* **1.** *A:* beggar. **2.** *P:* crook; gangster.

truander [tryɑ̃de] *v.tr. F:* to swindle (s.o.).

truble [trybl̩] *n.f. Fish:* hoop net; shove net.

trublion [trybljɔ̃] *n.m.* troublemaker.

truc[1] [tryk] *n.m. F:* **1.** (*a*) knack (**pour faire qch.,** of doing sth.); (*b*) trick, dodge; **connaître les trucs du métier,** to know the tricks of the trade; *Th:* **pièce à trucs,** play with elaborate stage effects; **t. d'optique,** optical illusion. **2.** (*a*) *F:* **Monsieur T.,** Mr what's his name; (*b*) *F:* thing, contraption, gadget.

truc[2] *n.m. Rail: etc:* truck.

trucage [trykaʒ] *n.m.* **1.** *O:* faking; cheating. **2.** *pl. Cin:* special effects.

truchement [tryʃmɑ̃] *n.m.* **1.** *A:* interpreter. **2.** go-between; intermediary; **par le t. de . . .,** through . . ..

truck [tryk] *n.m. Rail: etc:* truck, *NAm:* freight car.

truculence [trykylɑ̃s] *n.f.* colourfulness, *NAm:* colorfulness.

truculent [trykylɑ̃] *a.* colourful, *NAm:* colorful (character).

trudgeon [trœdʒɔn] *n.m. Swim: O:* trudgen stroke.

truelle [tryɛl] *n.f.* **1.** trowel. **2. t. à poisson,** fish slice.

truffe [tryf] *n.f.* (*a*) truffle; **omelette aux truffes,** truffle omelet(te); (*b*) nose (of a dog); *P:* (*of pers.*) bulbous nose; (*c*) *P:* **quelle t.!** what an idiot!

truffer [tryfe] *v.tr.* **1.** *Cu:* to flavour, lard (sth.) with truffles; **dinde truffée,** truffled turkey. **2. truffé de,** riddled with (bullets, mistakes); peppered with (quotations).

truffier, -ière [tryfje, -jɛr] *a.* truffle(-producing) (ground); **chien t.,** truffle hound.

truie [trɥi] *n.f. Z:* sow.

truisme [tryism] *n.m.* truism.

truite [trɥit] *n.f. Ich:* trout; **t. de rivière,** brown trout; **t. arc-en-ciel,** rainbow trout.

truité [trɥite] *a.* speckled; spotted (dog, horse); crackled (china).

truiticulture [trɥitikyltyr] *n.f.* trout breeding.

trumeau, -eaux [trymo] *n.m.* **1.** (*a*) *Arch:* pier; (*b*) *Furn:* pier glass. **2.** *Cu:* leg of beef.

truquage [trykaʒ] *n.m.* = TRUCAGE.

truquer [tryke] *v.tr.* (*a*) to fake (antiques, photograph, experiment, etc.); to fix (match, fight, etc.); *F:* to cook (accounts); **t. une élection,** to rig, *U.S:* gerrymander, an election; (*b*) *Min:* to salt (a mine, a mineral sample).

truqueur, -euse [trykœr, -øz] **1.** *n.* faker (of jewellery, antiques, etc.). **2.** *n.m.* male prostitute.

trusquin [tryskɛ̃] *n.m. Tls:* (carpenter's) (i) marking gauge, (ii) mortise gauge.

trust [trœst] *n.m. Fin:* trust.

truster [trœste] *v.tr.* **1.** to group into a trust. **2.** *F:* to monopolize.

trypanosomiase [tripanozɔmjɑz] *n.f. Med: Vet:* trypanosomiasis; **t. africaine,** sleeping sickness.

trypanosome [tripanozom] *n.m.* trypanosome.

tsar [tsar, dzar] *n.m.* tsar, czar.

tsarévitch [tsarevitʃ, dz-] *n.m.* tsarevitch, czarevitch.

tsarine [tsarin, dz-] *n.f.* tsarina, czarina.

tsarisme [tsarism, dz-] *n.m. Hist:* tsarism.

tsariste [tsarist, dz-] *n.m. & f. Hist:* tsarist.

tsé-tsé [tsetse] *n.f. Ent:* tsetse (fly).

tu [ty] *pers. pron., unstressed, subject of verb.* (*a*) (*usual form of address to relations, close friends, children and animals*) you; **tu as raison,** you are right; **qui es-tu?** who are you? **à tu et à toi,** on terms of close friendship (with s.o.); **être à tu et à toi avec tout le monde,** to be hail-fellow-well-met with everybody; (*b*) (*to the Deity*) Thou; You; *B:* **tu ne tueras point,** thou shalt not kill; (*c*) *P:* (*elided to* **t'** *before vowel or* **h** *mute*) **qu'est-ce que t'as?** what's up (with you)?

tuant [tɥɑ̃] *a. F:* **1.** killing, back-breaking (work). **2.** boring (pers, etc.); exasperating.

tub [tœb] *n.m. Toil: O:* tub, bath.

tuba [tyba] *n.m.* **1.** *Mus:* tuba. **2.** snorkel.

tubage [tybaʒ] *n.m. Civ.E: Min: Surg: Vet:* tubing.

tubaire [tybɛr] *a. Med:* tubal.

tubard, -arde [tybar, -ard] *n. F:* T.B. case.

tube [tyb] *n.m.* **1.** tube, pipe; (*a*) *Metall: etc:* **t. étiré, laminé,** drawn, rolled, tube; *Const:* **bâti en tubes d'acier,** tubular steel frame; *Tls:* **clef à t.,** tubular spanner; (*b*) *Mec.E: etc:* **t. de graissage,** oil duct, way; **t. raccord,** pipe connection; **t. à flamme,** flame tube (of jet engine); *Aut:* **t. de direction,** steering column; *Mch:* **t. d'alimentation,** feed pipe; **t. de chaudière,** boiler tube; **chaudière à tubes,** tubular boiler; *F:* **à pleins tubes,** all out, at full blast; **t. de condenseur, t. à condensation,** condenser tube; **t. de niveau d'eau,** water-gauge column; *Min:* **t. carrottier,** core barrel; **tubes d'exploitation, de pompage,** tubing; *El.E:* **t. guide-fils,** race track, race way (in building); (*c*) *Artil:* barrel; *F:* gun; *Navy:* **t. lance-torpille(s),** torpedo tube; (*d*) *Opt:* (focusing, etc.) slide; (*e*) (i) **t. acoustique,** speaking tube; (ii) *P:* teléphone, *P:* blower; **donner un coup de t. à qn,** to ring, *U.S:* call, s.o. up; (*f*) *Surg: Vet:* (intubation, laryngotomy, tracheotomy) tube; (*g*) *Anat:* tube, duct; **t. digestif,** digestive tract, alimentary canal; **t. bronchique,** bronchial tube; *Anat: Ph:* **t. capillaire,** capillary tube; (*h*) *Bot:* tube (of corolla or calyx); (*i*) *Turf: P:* tip; (*j*) *Th: etc: F:* smash hit; hit (song). **2.** (*container*) (*a*) tube (of toothpaste, colour); (*b*) *Ch:* **t. pour dosage, t. doseur,** measuring tube; **t. à essais,** test tube; (*c*) *Ind:* (soaker, fractionating) tube. **3.** *El: Elcs:* valve; tube; *El:* **t. au néon,** neon tube; **t. fluorescent,** fluorescent tube, lamp; *Elcs: W.Tel:* **t. cathodique,** cathode-ray tube; **t. électronique,** electron tube; **t. à gaz,** gas-filled tube, valve; **t. à vide,** vacuum valve; kenotron; **t. amplificateur,** amplifier tube or valve; **t. de balayage,** scanning tube; (*radar*) **t. d'affichage,** display tube; **t. phare,** lighthouse. **4.** *P: A:* top hat, topper.

tuber [tybe] *v.tr.* **1.** (*a*) *Civ.E:* to tube (borehole, well); to case (shaft, well); (*b*) *Surg: Vet:* to tube, intubate (larynx, etc.). **2.** *Mch:* to tube (boiler).

tubercule [tybɛrkyl] *n.m.* **1.** *Bot:* tuber. **2.** *Med:* tubercle.

tuberculeux, -euse [tybɛrkylø, -øz] **1.** *a.* (*a*) *Bot:* tubercular (root); (*b*) *Med: Miner:* tuberculous (lung, chalk). **2.** *n.* tubercular patient; T.B. case.

tuberculine [tybɛrkylin] *n.f. Med:* tuberculin.

tuberculiner [tybɛrkyline] *v.tr. Med: Vet:* to tuberculinize; **troupeaux tuberculinés,** attested herds.

tuberculiser [tybɛrkylize] *v.tr. Med:* to tubercul(ar)ize; (*of lung, etc.*) **se t.,** to become tubercular.

tuberculose [tybɛrkyloz] *n.f. Med:* tuberculosis; **t. pulmonaire,** pulmonary tuberculosis.

tubéreux, -euse [tyberø, -øz] *Bot:* **1.** *a.* tuberous. **2.** *n.f.* **tubéreuse,** tuberose.

tubiste [tybist] *n.m.* **1.** *Civ.E:* worker in a caisson. **2.** *Ind:* worker in a tube factory.

tubulaire [tybylɛr] **1.** *a.* tubular. **2.** *n.m. Coel:* tubularia.

tubulé [tybyle] *a.* tubulate (flower); tubulated (retort, etc.); tubular (boiler).

tubuleux, -euse [tybylø, -øz] *a.* tubulous.

tubulure [tybylyr] *n.f.* (*a*) *Hyd.E: etc:* tubulure; pipe(-run); neck; *I.C.E:* (exhaust, inlet) manifold; *Av:* **t. d'évacuation,** tailpipe (of jet engine); (*b*) *coll.* pipes, piping.

tue-mouches [tymuʃ] *n.m.inv.* **1.** *Fung:* fly agaric. **2.** (i) fly swatter; (ii) fly killer; *a.* **papier t.-m.,** fly paper.

tuer [tɥe] **I.** *v.tr.* to kill. **1.** to slaughter, butcher (animals, etc.). **2.** (*a*) to kill (s.o.); **t. qn d'un coup de couteau, de poignard,** to stab s.o. to death; **t. qn d'un coup de revolver,** to shoot s.o. (dead) with a revolver; **se faire t.,** (i) to seek death; (ii) to get killed; **ils se firent t. en braves,** they died like heroes; **les tués et les blessés,** the dead and wounded; **le froid a tué les oliviers,** the cold has killed the olive trees; (*b*) **t. le temps,** to kill time; (*c*) *Petr:* to kill (oil, well, gas well); (*d*) *Ten:* to kill (the ball). **3. l'ennui le tue,** he's bored to death; **ces escaliers me tuent,** these stairs will be the death of me. **II. se t. 1.** (*a*) to kill oneself; to commit suicide; (*b*) to get killed. **2. se t. au travail, à travailler, à force de boire,** to work, drink, oneself to death; **je me tue à vous le dire,** I am sick and tired of telling you.

tuerie [tyri] *n.f.* slaughter, butchery.

tue-tête (à) [atytɛt] *adv.phr.* at the top of one's voice.

tueur, -euse [tɥœr, -øz] (*a*) *n.* killer; murderer; **t. de lions,** lion killer; **t. à gages,** hired assassin; (*b*) *n.m.* butcher, slaughterman.

tuf [tyf] *n.m.* **1.** *Geol:* (*a*) **t. volcanique,** tuff; (*b*) tufa, tophus. **2.** *Lit: Fig:* bedrock, foundation.

tuile [tɥil] *n.f.* **1.** (*a*) (roofing) tile; (*b*) *Cu:* **tuiles aux amandes,** almond slices. **2.** *F:* (piece of) bad luck; snag; **quelle t.!** what rotten luck!

tuilerie [tɥilri] *n.f.* **1.** (*a*) tile works; (*b*) **les Tuileries,** the Tuileries. **2.** tile kiln.

tulipe [tylip] *n.f.* **1.** *Bot:* tulip. **2.** (tulip-shaped) lampshade.

tulipier [tylipje] *n.m. Bot:* tulip tree.

tulle [tyl] *n.m. Tex:* tulle; net (fabric).

tuméfaction [tymefaksjɔ̃] *n.f. Med:* tumefaction, swelling.

tuméfier [tymefje] *v.tr.* to tumefy; to cause (joint, etc.) to swell; **se t.,** to swell (up).

tumescence [tymesɑ̃s] *n.f.* tumescence; swelling.

tumescent [tymesɑ̃] *a.* tumescent, swelling.

tumeur [tymœr] *n.f. Med:* **1.** tumour; *F:* growth; **t. dure,** indurated tumour; **t. bénigne, maligne,** benign, malignant, tumour. **2.** swelling.

tumulaire [tymylɛr] *a.* tumulary; **pierre t.,** tombstone.

tumulte [tymylt] *n.m.* tumult, hubbub, uproar, commotion; thunder (of applause); clash (of arms); turmoil (of politics, passions); hustle and bustle (of business); **dans le t.,** in an uproar, in confusion; **il y eut des tumultes,** there were riots.

tumultueusement [tymyltɥøzmɑ̃] *adv.* tumultuously.

tumultueux, -euse [tymyltɥø, -øz] *a.* tumultuous, riotous (gathering, etc.); noisy (streets).

tumulus [tymylys] *n.m.* tumulus, barrow; *pl. tumulus, tumuli.*

tungstène [tœ̃gstɛn] *n.m. Ch: Metall:* tungsten.

tunique [tynik] *n.f.* **1.** *Cost:* tunic; *Ecc:* tunicle. **2.** *Biol: Bot:* tunic; envelope, membrane (of an organ); coat (of bulb); skin (of seed).

Tunisie [tynizi] *Pr.n.f. Geog:* Tunisia.

tunisien, -ienne [tynizjɛ̃, -jɛn] *a. & n. Geog:* Tunisian.

tunnel [tynɛl] *n.m.* tunnel; **t. routier,** road tunnel; **le t. sous la Manche,** the Channel Tunnel; *Aer:* **t. aérodynamique,** wind tunnel; *El: etc:* **t. de câbles,** cable subway.

tuque [tyk] *n.f. Cost: Fr.C:* tuque, *F:* pompom hat, bobble cap.

turban [tyrbɑ̃] *n.m.* **1.** *Cost:* turban. **2.** *Moll:* turban shell.

turbide [tyrbid] *a.* (*esp. of liquid*) turbid, muddy.

turbidité [tyrbidite] *n.f.* turbidity, cloudiness.

turbin [tyrbɛ̃] *n.m. P:* work, grind, slog.

turbine [tyrbin] *n.f. Mec.E:* turbine; **t. à air,** air, wind, turbine; **t. à eau, t. hydraulique,** water turbine, water wheel; **t. à gaz, à vapeur,** gas, steam, turbine.

turbiner [tyrbine] *v.i. P:* to work, slog; *Sch:* to swot.

turbo¹ [tyrbo] *n.m. Moll:* turbo; turban shell.

turbo² *n.m. F:* (= **turbo-alternateur,** *etc.*) turbo.

turbo-alternateur [tyrbɔaltɛrnatœr] *n.m. El:* turbo-alternator; *pl. turbo-alternateurs.*

turbocompresseur [tyrbɔkɔ̃prɛsœr] *n.m. Mec.E: Av:* (*turbine-driven*) turbocompressor; (*exhaust-driven*) turbosupercharger, turbocharger.

turbo-électrique [tyrbɔelɛktrik] *a. Mch:* turbo-electric (drive, etc.); *pl. turbo-électriques.*
turbomoteur [tyrbɔmɔtœr] *n.m. Mch:* turbomotor; turboshaft engine.
turbo(-)nucléaire [tyrbɔnykleɛr] *a.* turbonuclear.
turbopompe [tyrbɔpɔ̃p] *n.f. Mch:* turbo pump, turbine pump.
turbopropulsé [tyrbɔprɔpylse] *a.* turboprop (aircraft).
turbopropulseur [tyrbɔprɔpylsœr] *n.m.* turboprop(eller); **avion à t.,** turboprop aircraft.
turboréacteur [tyrbɔreaktœr] *n.m.* turbojet.
turboréaction [tyrbɔreaksjɔ̃] *n.f.* turboreaction.
turbot [tyrbo] *n.m. Ich:* turbot.
turbotrain [tyrbɔtrɛ̃] *n.m. Rail:* turbotrain.
turbulence [tyrbylɑ̃s] *n.f.* turbulence; boisterousness (of child, wind, sea).
turbulent [tyrbylɑ̃] *a.* turbulent; (*a*) restless, unruly (population); (*b*) boisterous (child); boisterous, stormy (wind, sea).
turc, *f.* **turque** [tyrk] **1.** *a.* Turkish; **café t.,** Turkish coffee; **être assis à la turque,** to sit cross-legged; *Hyg:* **installation à la t.,** seatless lavatory. **2.** (*a*) *n.* Turk; *F:* **fort comme un T.,** as strong as an ox; **tête de T.,** (i) try-your-strength machine (at fairs); (ii) butt; whipping-boy; (iii) *Nau:* Turk's head (knot); (*b*) *n.m. Ling:* Turkish.
turf [tyrf] *n.m.* **1.** racecourse. **2. le t.,** racing; the turf; **habitué du t.,** race goer.
turfiste [tyrfist] *n.* race-goer.
turgescence [tyrʒes(s)ɑ̃s] *n.f. Med: Bot:* turgescence, turgidity, turgor.
turgescent [tyrges(s)ɑ̃] *a.* turgescent.
turlupiner [tyrlypine] *v.tr. F:* to worry, bother.
turluter [tyrlyte] *v.i. Fr.C: F:* to trill, to sing tra la la.
turlututu [tyrlytyty] *int.* fiddlesticks!
turne [tyrn] *n.f. P:* (*a*) slummy room, dump, hole; (*b*) (student's) room.
turnep(s) [tyrnɛp(s)] *n.m. Agr:* kohlrabi.
turpitude [tyrpityd] *n.f.* **1.** depravity. **2.** (*a*) despicable trick; (*b*) smutty story.
Turquie [tyrki] *Pr.n.f. Geog:* Turkey; **tapis de T.,** Turkish carpet.
turquoise [tyrkwaz] **1.** *n.f.* turquoise. **2.** *a.inv. & n.m.inv.* turquoise (blue).
tussor(e) [tysɔr] *n.m. Tex:* tussore (silk).
tutélaire [tytelɛr] *a.* tutelary (divinity, etc.); guardian (angel, etc.); *Jur:* **gestion t.,** guardianship.
tutelle [tytɛl] *n.f.* **1.** *Jur:* (*a*) tutelage, guardianship; **enfant en t.,** child under guardianship; (*b*) *Pol:* **territoires sous t.,** trust territories. **2.** protection; **prendre qn sous sa t.,** to take s.o. under one's wing.
tuteur, -trice [tytœr, -tris] **1.** *n.* (*a*) *Jur:* guardian; tutor (of a minor); (*b*) protector. **2.** *n.m. Hort:* support, stake.
tutoi(e)ment [tytwamɑ̃] *n.m.* use of the familiar **tu** and **toi** (instead of the more formal **vous**).
tutoyer [tytwaje] *v.tr.* (**je tutoie, n. tutoyons; je tutoierai**) to address (s.o.) as **tu** and **toi** (instead of **vous**); to be on familiar terms with (s.o.).
tutti [tyti] *n.m.inv. Mus:* tutti.
tutu [tyty] *n.m.* tutu, ballet skirt.
tuyau, -aux [tɥijo] *n.m.* **1.** (*a*) pipe, tube; **t. d'eau, de gaz,** water pipe, gas pipe; **t. vertical, t. de chute,** standpipe; **t. flexible, t. en caoutchouc,** (i) rubber tubing; (ii) hose(pipe); **t. d'incendie,** fire hose; **t. d'arrosage,** garden hose; **t. de cheminée,** chimney flue; **t. de poêle,** (i) stove pipe, flue pipe; (ii) *F: O:* stovepipe hat; **t. acoustique,** speaking tube; *Mus:* **t. d'orgue,** organ pipe; *F:* **dire qch. à qn dans le t. de l'oreille,** to whisper sth. in s.o.'s ear; (*b*) stem (of tobacco pipe); (*c*) stalk (of corn, grass, etc.); (*d*) *Laund:* flute, goffer, quill. **2.** *F:* pointer, hint; gen, dope; (*esp. Turf:*) tip; **un t. crevé,** a rotten tip; **avoir des tuyaux,** to be in the know; **c'est un t. increvable,** it's straight from the horse's mouth.
tuyautage [tɥijotaʒ] *n.m.* **1.** (*a*) piping, tubing; (*b*) canalization, pipeline; **t. de transport,** conveyor pipeline. **2.** *Laund:* fluting, goffering (of linen). **3.** *Rac: etc: F:* tipping; stable tips.
tuyauter [tɥijote] *v.tr.* **1.** *Laund:* to flute, goffer (linen); **fer à t.,** goffering tongs. **2.** *Rac: etc: F:* to give (s.o.) a tip; to put (s.o.) in the know.
tuyauterie [tɥijotri] *n.f.* pipes, piping.
tuyauteur, -euse [tɥijotœr, -øz] *n. F:* tipster.
tuyère [tɥijɛr] *n.f.* (*a*) *Metall: Mec.E: etc:* nozzle; *Av: etc:* **t. d'échappement,** jet pipe; **t. de propulsion,** thrust nozzle.
tweed [twid] *n.m. Tex:* tweed.
twist [twist] *n.m. Danc:* twist.
tympan [tɛ̃pɑ̃] *n.m.* **1.** *Anat:* tympanum, eardrum; **bruit à briser, crever, déchirer, rompre, le t.,** ear-splitting noise. **2.** *Typ:* tympan. **3.** *Arch:* (*a*) tympanum; (*b*) spandrel. **4.** *Hyd.E:* tympanum, scoop wheel. **5.** *Mec.E:* pinion (mounted on shaft).
tympanal, -aux [tɛ̃panal, -o] *a. & n.m.* (**os**) **t.,** tympanic bone.
tympanique [tɛ̃panik] *a.* **1.** *Anat:* tympanic. **2.** *Med:* tympanitic.
tympanon [tɛ̃panɔ̃] *n.m. Mus:* dulcimer.
type [tip] *n.m.* **1.** type; standard model; *Z:* type, phylum; **t. de la beauté italienne,** typical Italian beauty; *attrib.* **maison t.,** show house; **motocyclette t.,** motor bicycle of standard design; *Nat.Hist:* **genre t.,** type genus; *For:* **arbre t.,** sample tree. **2.** *F:* (*a*) character, type; **c'est un vrai t.,** he's quite a character; (*b*) chap, type, guy; **un drôle de t.,** a queer sort of chap, a weirdo; **un t. à barbe,** a type, chap, with a beard; **t'es un chic t.!** you're a good sort! (*c*) *P:* boyfriend, man. **3.** *Typ:* type.
typer [tipe] *v.tr.* to stamp, mark (sth.).
typesse [tipɛs] *n.f. P:* woman, girl.
typhoïde [tifɔid] *a. Med:* typhoid (fever).
typhoïdique [tifɔidik] *a.* typhoidal; **bacille t.,** typhoid bacillus.
typhon [tifɔ̃] *n.m. Meteor:* typhoon.
typhus [tifys] *n.m. Med:* typhus (fever); *Vet:* **t. du chat,** (infectious) feline gastroenteritis.
typifier [tipifje] *v.tr.* to typify.
typique [tipik] *a.* **1.** symbolical. **2.** typical, true to type.
typiquement [tipikmɑ̃] *adv.* typically.
typo [tipo] *F:* **1.** *n.f.* typography. **2.** *n.m.* (*f. occ.* **typote**) (= TYPOGRAPHE) typo.
typographe [tipɔgraf] **1.** *n.m.* typographer, printer. **2.** *a.* **ouvrier t.,** printer.
typographie [tipɔgrafi] *n.f.* typography; (art of) letterpress printing.
typographier [tipɔgrafje] *v.tr.* (*pr.sub. & impf.* **n. typographiions, v. typographiiez**) *Typ:* to set up, print (article, etc.).
typographique [tipɔgrafik] *a.* typographic(al); **erreur t.,** misprint.
typographiquement [tipɔgrafikmɑ̃] *adv.* typographically.
typolithographie [tipɔlitɔgrafi] *n.f.* typolithography.
typologie [tipɔlɔʒi] *n.f.* typology.
typologique [tipɔlɔʒik] *a.* typological.
tyran [tirɑ̃] *n.m.* tyrant; **se conduire en t.,** to act tyrannically; **faire le t.,** to play the tyrant; **il est le t. de sa famille,** he tyrannizes his family.
tyranneau, -eaux [tirano] *n.m.* petty tyrant.
tyrannie [tirani] *n.f.* tyranny.
tyrannique [tiranik] *a.* tyrannical.
tyranniquement [tiranikmɑ̃] *adv.* tyrannically.

tyranniser [tiranize] *v.tr.* to tyrannize (s.o.).

tyrannosaure [tiranɔzɔr] *n.m.* *Paleont:* tyrannosaurus.

tyrolien, -ienne [tirɔljɛ̃, -jɛn] **1.** *a.* & *n.* *Geog:* Tyrolese. **2.** *n.f.* *Mus:* **tyrolienne,** tyrolienne.

Tzar, -évitch, -ine, etc. = TSAR, etc.

tzigane [tsigan, dz-] *n.m.* & *f.* & *a.* tsigane; Hungarian gypsy.

tzingaro [tsɛ̃garo, dz-] *n.m.* gipsy, zingaro.

U

U, u [y] *n.m.* (the letter) U, u; **fer en U,** channel iron; *Geog:* **vallée (à profil) en U,** U-shaped valley.
ubiquité [ybikɥite] *n.f.* ubiquity; **avoir le don d'u.,** to be ubiquitous; to be in several places at the same time.
ufologie [yfɔlɔʒi] *n.f.* ufology.
ukase [ykɑz] *n.m.* ukase; **u. paternel,** paternal fiat.
ulcération [ylserasjɔ̃] *n.f.* ulceration.
ulcère [ylsɛr] *n.m.* ulcer; sore.
ulcéré [ylsere] *a.* (*a*) *Med:* ulcerated; (*b*) **avoir une conscience ulcérée,** to suffer pangs of conscience; **cœur u.,** embittered heart; **elle en était ulcérée,** it rankled with her.
ulcérer [ylsere] **(il ulcère; il ulcérera) 1.** *v.tr.* (*a*) *Med:* to ulcerate; (*b*) to wound, embitter (s.o.). **2.** *Med:* **s' u.,** to ulcerate; to fester.
ulcéreux, -euse [ylserø, -øz] *a. Med:* ulcerous; ulcerated, festering (wound, etc.).
ulmaire [ylmɛr] *n.f. Bot:* meadowsweet.
ulnaire [ylnɛr] *a. Anat:* ulnar.
ultérieur [ylterjœr] *a.* ulterior; subsequent (**à,** to); later (news, date, etc.); *Com:* **ordres ultérieurs,** further orders.
ultérieurement [ylterjœrmɑ̃] *adv.* later (on); subsequently; hereafter.
ultimatum [yltimatɔm] *n.m.* ultimatum.
ultime [yltim] *a.* ultimate, final, last.
ultimo [yltimo] *adv.* lastly, finally.
ultra [yltra] *n. Pol:* ultra; extremist.
ultra-court [yltrakur] *a. Ph:* **ondes ultra-courtes,** ultra-short waves.
ultramicroscope [yltramikrɔskɔp] *n.m.* ultra-microscope.
ultramoderne [yltramɔdɛrn] *a.* ultramodern.
ultramontain [yltramɔ̃tɛ̃] *a. & n.* ultramontane. **1.** *a. A:* beyond the Alps (from France). **2.** *n. Theol: Pol:* ultramontanist.
ultra-royaliste [yltrarwajalist] *a. & n. Hist:* ultra-royalist; *pl. ultra-royalistes.*
ultra(-)son [yltrasɔ̃] *n.m. Ph:* ultrasound; **ultra(-)sons,** ultrasonic waves; **science des ultra(-)sons,** ultrasonics.
ultrasonique [yltrasɔnik] *a.* ultrasonic; supersonic.
ultra(-)violet, -ette [yltravjɔlɛ, -ɛt] *a. & n.m.* ultraviolet.
ululation [ylylasjɔ̃] *n.f.*, **ululement** [ylylmɑ̃] *n.m.* ululation (of owls); hoot(ing).
ululer [ylyle] *v.i.* (*of owl*) to ululate; to hoot.
Ulysse [ylis] *Pr.n.m.* Ulysses.
un, une [œ̃, yn] **1.** *num.a. & n.* (*a*) one; **il n'en reste qu'un,** there's only one left; **un à un** [œ̃naœ̃], **un par un,** one by one; **il est une heure,** it's one o'clock; **je viendrai entre une et deux,** I'll come between one and two (o'clock); **page un,** page one, first page; **numéro un,** number one; **un et un** [œ̃eœ̃] **font deux,** one and one are two; *Journ:* **la une** [layn], front page (of paper); *F:* **en savoir plus d'une,** to know a thing or two; *F:* **il était moins une,** it was a close thing, a close shave; **il vient un jour sur deux,** he comes every other day; **une, deux, trois, partez!** one, two, three, go! **il n'a fait ni une ni deux,** he didn't hesitate (for a moment); he made no bones about it; **et d'un! et d'une!** well, that's that! so much for that! (*b*) one (and indivisible); **Dieu est un,** God is one; **c'est tout un** [tutœ̃], it's the same thing, all one, all the same; *F:* **ils ne font qu'un,** (i) they're hand in glove; (ii) they are as one. **2.** *indef.pron.* one; **un de ces jours,** one of these days; **un qui a de la chance,** a lucky one, a lucky man; **un que je plains, c'est . . .,** someone I do pity is . . .; **(l')un de nous, (l')un d'entre nous,** one of us; **les uns disent que . . .,** some say that . . .. **3.** *indef.art.* (*pl.* **des,** *q.v. under* DE III) a, an (*pl.* some); (*a*) **un jour, une pomme, une heure,** a day, an apple, an hour; **un père et une mère,** a father and mother; **un père de famille,** the father of a family; **venez me voir un lundi,** come and see me one Monday, some Monday; **un jour de la semaine dernière,** one day last week; **pour une raison ou pour une autre,** for some reason or other; **(l')un des danseurs les plus célèbres du monde,** one of the most famous dancers in the world; (*b*) such a one as; **ce sera un Einstein,** he'll be another Einstein; (*c*) (*intensive*) **j'ai eu un monde aujourd'hui!** I've had such a lot of visitors today! **il a fait une de ces têtes!** you should have seen his face! **tu m'as fait une peur!** you gave me such a fright!
unanime [ynanim] *a.* unanimous; of one mind; **ils sont unanimes à vous accuser,** they are unanimous in accusing you.
unanimement [ynanimmɑ̃] *adv.* unanimously.
unanimité [ynanimite] *n.f.* unanimity; **à l'u.,** unanimously; **la proposition a fait l'u.,** the proposal was accepted unanimously.
Unesco [ynɛsko] *n.f.* Unesco.
uni [yni] *a.* **1.** (*a*) united, harmonious (family, etc.); (*b*) **le Royaume-U.,** the United Kingdom; **les États-Unis,** the United States. **2.** smooth, level, even (ground, etc.); unruffled (sea, etc.). **3.** plain (material, colour, etc.); self-colour(ed) (material).
uniate [ynjat] *a. & n. Rel:* Uniat(e).
unicellulaire [yniselylɛr] *a. Biol:* unicellular.
unicité [ynisite] *n.f.* **1.** *Phil: etc:* oneness, unicity. **2.** uniqueness, singleness.
unicolore [ynikɔlɔr] *a.* one-coloured, plain (material, etc.).
unicorne [ynikɔrn] *n.m. Myth:* unicorn.
unidirectionnel, -elle [ynidirɛksjɔnɛl] *a.* unidirectional.
unième [ynjɛm] *num.a.* (*used only in compounds*) first; **trente et u.,** thirty-first.
unièmement [ynjɛmmɑ̃] *adv.* (*used only in compounds*) firstly; **vingt et u.,** twenty-firstly.
unificateur, -trice [ynifikatœr, -tris] *a.* unifying.
unification [ynifikasjɔ̃] *n.f.* unification; consolidation (of loans, etc.); standardization (of weights and measures, etc.).
unifier [ynifje] *v.tr.* (*impf. & pr.sub.* **n. unifiions, v. unifiiez**) to unify (ideas, etc.); to consolidate (loans, etc.); to standardize (weights and measures, etc.).
uniforme [ynifɔrm] **1.** *a.* uniform, unvarying; regular (life, etc.); even (pace, etc.); **taux u.,** flat rate (of interest, etc.). **2.** *n.m.* uniform; *Mil: etc:* **grand u.,** full-dress uniform; **endosser l'u.,** to join the forces; **quitter l'u.,** to leave the service.
uniformément [ynifɔrmemɑ̃] *adv.* uniformly, unvaryingly.
uniformisation [ynifɔrmizasjɔ̃] *n.f.* standardization.

uniformiser [yniformize] *v.tr.* to make uniform; to standardize.
uniformité [yniformite] *n.f.* uniformity.
unijambiste [ynižãbist] *a.* & *n.* one-legged (person).
unilatéral, -aux [ynilateral, -o] *a.* unilateral; one-sided (contract, etc.); *P.N:* **stationnement u.,** parking on one side only.
unilingue [ynilɛ̃g] *a.* unilingual (dictionary, etc.).
uniment [ynimã] *adv.* smoothly, evenly; steadily; **dire qch. tout u.,** to say sth. quite simply, plainly.
uninominal, -aux [yninɔminal, -o] *a. Pol.* **scrutin u.,** voting for a single member, for one member only.
union [ynjɔ̃] *n.f.* **1.** union; coming together; combination (of two or more things, etc.); *Art: etc:* blending (of colours, etc.). **2.** union, society, association; **l'U. soviétique,** the Soviet Union; **u. douanière,** customs union. **3.** marriage; **u. libre,** cohabitation (of unmarried couple). **4.** unity, concord, agreement; *Prov:* **l'u. fait la force,** unity is strength.
unioniste [ynjɔnist] *n.* unionist.
unipare [ynipar] *a. Biol:* uniparous.
unipolaire [ynipɔlɛr] *a.* (*a*) *El:* unipolar, single-pole (switch, etc.); (*b*) *Biol:* unipolar (cell, etc.).
unique [ynik] *a.* **1.** sole, only, single; **fils u.,** only son; **(rue à) sens u.,** one-way street; **voie u.,** single-line traffic; **seul et u.,** one and only. **2.** unique, unrivalled, unparalleled; *F:* **il est u.,** he's priceless! he's the limit!
uniquement [ynikmã] *adv.* solely; **je viens u. pour vous voir,** I've come especially to see you.
unir [ynir] **1.** *v.tr.* (*a*) to unite, join, combine, link; **faits étroitement unis,** facts closely linked together, closely bound together; **être uni par le mariage à . . .,** to be joined in wedlock to . . .; (*b*) to smooth, level (ground, etc.). **2. s'u.,** to unite, join (together), combine; **s'u. à qn,** (i) to join forces with s.o.; (ii) to marry s.o.
unisexe [ynisɛks] *a.* unisex (shop, etc.).
unisexué [ynisɛksɥe] *a. Biol:* unisexual.
unisson [ynisɔ̃] *n.m. Mus:* unison; **à l'u.,** (i) in unison (**de,** with); (ii) in keeping (**de,** with).
unitaire [ynitɛr] **1.** *a.* & *n. Rel:* Unitarian. **2.** *a.* unitary (system, etc.); *Com:* **prix u.,** unit price.
unitarien, -ienne [ynitarjɛ̃, -jɛn] *a.* & *n.* (*a*) *Pol:* unitarian; (*b*) *Rel:* Unitarian.
unité [ynite] *n.f.* **1.** (*a*) *Mth: etc:* unity, one; *Com:* **prix de l'u.,** price of one (article), unit price; (*b*) *Mil:* unit; *Navy:* ship; **grosse u.,** capital ship; **u. de choc,** shock unit; *Petr:* **u. de craquage,** cracking unit; (*c*) unit (of measure, etc.). **2.** unity; (*a*) oneness (of God, etc.); (*b*) uniformity (of plan, action, etc.); consistency (of style, etc.); *Lit:* **les trois unités,** the three unities.
univalent [ynivalã] *a. Ch:* univalent.
univers [ynivɛr] *n.m.* universe; world; **l'u. mathématique,** the field of mathematics.
universaliser [ynivɛrsalize] *v.tr.* to universalize, to make (sth.) universal.
universalité [ynivɛrsalite] *n.f.* **1.** universality. **2.** *A:* sum total; whole.
universaux [ynivɛrso] *n.m.pl. Phil:* universals.
universel, -elle [ynivɛrsɛl] *a.* universal; all-purpose (device); **réputation universelle,** worldwide reputation; **savoir u.,** all-embracing knowledge; *Mec.E:* **joint u.,** universal joint; *Log:* **proposition universelle,** *n.m.* **u.,** universal (proposition); *Jur:* **légataire (à titre) u.,** (i) sole legatee; (ii) residuary legatee.
universellement [ynivɛrsɛlmã] *adv.* universally.
universitaire [ynivɛrsitɛr] **1.** *a.* **ville u., études universitaires,** university town, studies; **honneurs universitaires,** academic honours; **cité u.** = (students') hall(s) of residence. **2.** *n.* (*a*) member of the teaching profession; (*b*) academic.
université [ynivɛrsite] *n.f.* **1.** university. **2. l'U. (de France),** the teaching profession (including university staff, schoolmasters, inspectors, etc.).
Untel [œ̃tɛl] *n.m.* **Monsieur U.,** Mr So-and-So.
uranifère [yranifɛr] *a. Geol:* uranium-bearing.
uranium [yranjɔm] *n.m.* uranium.
urbain [yrbɛ̃] *a.* **1.** urban; **la population urbaine,** city dwellers; **architecture urbaine,** town planning; *Tp:* **communication urbaine,** local call. **2.** urbane.
urbanisation [yrbanizasjɔ̃] *n.f.* urbanization.
urbaniser [yrbanize] *v.tr.* to urbanize (rural district, etc.); **zone urbanisée,** residential area.
urbanisme [yrbanism] *n.m.* town planning.
urbaniste [yrbanist] **1.** *a.* urban; **architecture u.,** town architecture. **2.** *n.* town planner.
urbanité [yrbanite] *n.f.* urbanity; **avec u.,** urbanely.
urée [yre] *n.f. Ch:* urea.
urémie [yremi] *n.f. Med:* uraemia.
uretère [yrtɛr] *n.m. Anat:* ureter.
urètre [yrɛtr̥] *n.m. Anat:* urethra.
urgence [yržãs] *n.f.* (*a*) urgency; **il y a u.,** it's a matter of urgency; **y a-t-il u. à ce qu'il parte?** need he leave? *Pol:* **demander l'u.,** to call for a vote of urgency; **transporter qn d'u. à l'hôpital,** to rush s.o. to hospital; **en cas d'u.,** in an emergency; **état d'u.,** state of emergency; **à adresser d'u.,** to be sent immediately; **convoquer d'u. les actionnaires,** to call an extraordinary meeting of the shareholders; **il a été appelé d'u.,** he received an urgent call; (*b*) emergency; **salle des urgences,** emergency ward.
urgent [yržã] *a.* urgent, pressing; instant (need); **rien d'u. ne l'obligeait à sortir,** there was nothing urgent to force him to go out; **cas u.,** urgent case; emergency.
urger [yrže] *v.i. F:* to be urgent; **rien n'urge,** there's no desperate hurry.
urinaire [yrinɛr] *a. Anat:* urinary.
urinal, -aux [yrinal, -o] *n.m. Med:* urinal, bottle.
urine [yrin] *n.f.* urine; **évacuer l'u.,** to pass water.
uriner [yrine] *v.i.* to urinate; to pass water.
urinoir [yrinwar] *n.m.* (public) urinal.
urique [yrik] *a.* uric (acid, etc.).
urne [yrn] *n.f.* (*a*) urn; (*b*) ballot box; **aller aux urnes,** to go to the polls.
urologue [yrɔlɔg] *n.* urologist.
urticacées [yrtikase] *n.f.pl. Bot:* Urticaceae.
urticaire [yrtikɛr] *n.f. Med:* urticaria, nettlerash, hives.
urticant [yrtikã] *a.* stinging.
urtication [yrtikasjɔ̃] *n.f. Med:* stinging.
urus [yrys] *n.m. Z:* urus, aurochs.
us [ys] *n.m.pl.* (*a*) *A:* usages; (*b*) **les us et coutumes d'un pays,** the ways and customs of a country.
usage [yzaž] *n.m.* **1.** (*a*) use, using, employment; **mettre un article en u.,** to put an article into use; **faire u. de qch.,** to make use of, sth.; **faire u. de la force,** to employ force; **faire bon u. de qch.,** to make good use of sth.; to put sth. to good use; **faire mauvais u. de qch.,** to make bad use of sth.; to misuse sth.; *Pharm:* **à u. externe,** for external use, application; **servir à plusieurs usages,** to have various uses; to answer various purposes; **article à mon u.,** article for my personal use; **à l'u. des écoles,** for use in schools; **article d'u.,** article for everyday use; **à usages multiples,** multi-purpose (equipment, etc.); **s'améliorer à l'u.,** to improve with use; **avoir l'u. de,** to have the use of; **hors d'u.,** (i) out of service, out of use; worn out; (ii) obsolete (word, etc.); **le bon u.,** *A:* **le bel u.,** correct French = the Queen's English; (*b*) wear, service (of garments, etc.); **faire de l'u., beaucoup d'u.,** to wear well, do good service; **garanti**

à l'u., guaranteed to wear well. **2.** *Jur:* **droit d'u. continu,** (right of) user. **3.** (*a*) usage; use; custom, practice; **usages locaux,** local customs; **phrases d'u.,** conversational commonplaces; **d'u. courant,** in common, everyday, use; **les conditions d'u.,** the usual terms; **selon l'u., suivant l'u.,** according to custom; **il est d'u. de** + *inf.*, it is usual, customary, to . . .; (*b*) practice, experience; **avoir l'u. de qch.,** to be used to sth.; **l'u. du monde,** good breeding; **avoir de l'u., avoir l'u. du monde,** to have a knowledge of the ways of society; **manquer d'u.,** to lack breeding; **c'est l'u.,** it's the usual practice, the done thing.

usagé [yzaʒe] *a.* used, worn; secondhand (car, etc.); **non u.,** new.

usager, -ère [yzaʒe, -ɛr] *n.* user (of sth.); **les usagers de la route,** roadusers.

usant [yzɑ̃] *a.* wearing (life, work); **il est u.,** he wears you out.

usé [yze] *a.* (*of metal, stone, etc.*) worn; (*of garments*) worn(-out); shabby, threadbare; (*of rope*) frayed; **u. par le temps,** timeworn; **sujet u.,** hackneyed, stale, trite, trivial, subject; **c'est u.!** that's an old one! **argument u. jusqu'à la corde,** well worn argument; **terre usée,** exhausted land; *Ind:* **eaux usées,** waste water.

user [yze] **1.** *v.ind.tr.* **u. de qch.,** to use sth., make use of sth.; **u. de son droit,** to exercise one's right; **u. de violence,** to resort to violence; **u. de douceur,** to deal gently (with s.o.); **u. de son influence,** to use one's influence; **en u. bien, mal, avec qn,** to treat s.o. well, badly. **2.** *v.tr.* (*a*) to use (up), consume (sth.); **u. du charbon,** to burn coal; (*b*) to wear (sth.) (out, away, down); to ruin (health, etc.); **u. ses vêtements,** to wear out one's clothes. **3. s'u.,** to wear (away); **ce tissu s'use vite,** this material wears out quickly; **sa résistance s'usera à la fin,** his resistance will wear down, break down, in due course; **il s'est usé à ce travail,** he's worn himself out with this work.

usinage [yzinaʒ] *n.m. Metalw:* machining, tooling (of castings, etc.); machine finishing.

usine [yzin] *n.f.* factory; works; mill, plant; **u. à gaz,** gasworks; **ouvrier d'u.,** factory worker.

usiner [yzine] *v.tr.* (*a*) *Metalw:* to machine, tool (castings, etc.); to machine-finish (parts); **parties usinées,** bright parts; (*b*) to manufacture; (*c*) *F:* **ça usine là-dedans,** they're hard at it.

usinier, -ière [yzinje, -jɛr] *a.* factory (life, industry, etc.); **faubourg u.,** industrial suburb.

usité [yzite] *a.* used; in use; current; **mot très u.,** word in common use, in current use.

ustensile [ystɑ̃sil] *n.m.* utensil; implement, tool.

usuel, -elle [yzɥɛl] *a.* usual, customary, habitual, common, ordinary; **l'anglais u.,** everyday English.

usuellement [yzɥɛlmɑ̃] *adv.* usually, ordinarily.

usufruit [yzyfrɥi] *n.m.Jur:* usufruct; life interest.

usufruitier, -ière [yzyfrɥitje, -jɛr] *a. & n. Jur:* usufructuary; *n.* tenant for life.

usuraire [yzyrɛr] *a.* usurious (interest, etc.).

usure¹ [yzyr] *n.f.* usury; **pratiquer l'u.,** to practise usury; **rendre un bienfait avec u.,** to repay a service with interest.

usure² *n.f.* (*a*) wear (and tear); **tissu qui résiste à l'u.,** material that wears well; **u. par frottement,** attrition, abrasion; **guerre d'u.,** war of attrition; *Tchn:* **surface d'u.,** wearing surface; **organes sujets à l'u.,** wearing parts (of a machine); *F:* **je l'aurai à l'u.,** I'll wear him down; (*b*) wearing away; erosion.

usurier, -ière [yzyrje, -jɛr] *n.* usurer.

usurpateur, -trice [yzyrpatœr, -tris] **1.** *n.* usurper. **2.** *a.* (*a*) usurping; (*b*) encroaching.

usurpation [yzyrpasjɔ̃] *n.f.* (*a*) usurpation; (*b*) encroachment.

usurper [yzyrpe] **1.** *v.tr.* (*a*) to usurp (**sur,** from); (*b*) to encroach upon, usurp (s.o.'s rights, etc.). **2.** *v.i.* **u. sur les droits de qn,** to encroach, usurp, (up)on s.o.'s rights.

ut [yt] *n.m.inv. Mus:* (the note) C; **ut dièse,** C sharp; **clef d'ut,** C clef; **clef d'ut quatrième ligne,** tenor clef.

utérin [yterɛ̃] *a.* uterine; **frère u.,** half-brother on the mother's side.

utérus [yterys] *n.m. Anat:* uterus, womb.

utile [ytil] *a.* useful, serviceable; helpful; **si je puis vous être u.,** if I can be of any use, help, service, assistance, to you; **en quoi puis-je vous être u.?** what can I do for you? **se rendre u.,** to make oneself useful; **cela m'a été bien u.,** it came in very handy, stood me in good stead; **en temps u.,** in (good) time; duly; in due course; **prendre toutes dispositions utiles,** to make all necessary arrangements; **est-il u. d'y aller?** is there any use, any point, in going? **dictionnaire u. à consulter,** useful, helpful, dictionary to consult; *Mec:* **effet u.,** effective power; *n.m.* **joindre l'u. à l'agréable,** to combine business with pleasure.

utilement [ytilmɑ̃] *adv.* usefully; profitably.

utilisable [ytilizabl̥] *a.* usable, fit for use; **billet u. pour tous les trains,** ticket available on all trains.

utilisateur, -trice [ytilizatœr, -tris] *n.* user.

utilisation [ytilizasjɔ̃] *n.f.* utilization, use (of sth.); turning (of sth.) to account.

utiliser [ytilize] *v.tr.* to use; to utilize; to make use of (sth.); to turn (sth.) to account.

utilitaire [ytilitɛr] *a. & n.* utilitarian; *Aut:* **véhicule u.,** commercial vehicle.

utilitarisme [ytilitarism] *n.m.* utilitarianism.

utilité [ytilite] *n.f.* **1.** utility use(fulness); useful purpose; service; **être d'une grande u.,** to be of great use; to be very useful; **cela ne m'est d'aucune u.,** it's no earthly use to me; **sans u.,** useless(ly); **s'entremettre sans grande u.,** to intervene to little purpose. **2.** *Th:* utility actor, actress; utility man; **jouer les utilités,** (i) *Th:* to play small parts; (ii) *Fig:* to play second fiddle.

utopie [ytɔpi] *n.f.* utopia.

utopique [ytɔpik] *a.* utopian.

utopiste [ytɔpist] *n.* Utopian.

utriculaire [ytrikylɛr] *n.f. Bot:* utricularia, bladderwort.

uval, -aux [yval, -o] *a.* pertaining to grapes; *Med:* **cure uvale,** grape cure.

uvulaire [yvylɛr] *a.* uvular.

uvule [yvyl] *n.f. Anat:* uvula.

V

V, v [ve] *n.m.* (the letter) V, v; **double v,** W, w; *I.C.E:* **moteur (à cylindres) en V,** V (type) engine; *Geog:* **vallée (à profil) en V,** V-shaped valley.
vacance [vakɑ̃s] *n.f.* **1.** (*a*) vacancy; vacant office, post; (*b*) *Jur:* abeyance (of succession). **2.** *pl.* holiday(s); (*of parliament*) recess; *esp. NAm:* vacation; *Sch:* **les grandes vacances,** the summer holidays; (*university*) the long vacation; **entrer en vacances,** (i) (*of school*) to break up; (ii) (*of parliament*) to rise; **vacances de neige,** winter holiday; **en vacance(s),** on holiday; **un jour de vacance(s),** a (day's) holiday; **vacances judiciaires,** vacation, recess (of lawcourts).
vacancier, -ière [vakɑ̃sje, -jɛr] *n.* holidaymaker; *NAm:* vacationist.
vacant [vakɑ̃] *a.* **1.** vacant, unoccupied (house, etc.); **poste v.,** vacancy. **2.** *Jur:* **succession vacante,** estate in abeyance.
vacarme [vakarm] *n.m.* uproar, din, racket; **faire du v.,** to create, make, an uproar; *F:* to kick up a row.
vacation [vakasjɔ̃] *n.f.* **1.** *Jur:* (*a*) attendance, sitting (of officials); day's sale (at auction); (*b*) *pl.* fees (of lawyer, etc.). **2.** *pl. Jur:* vacation, recess (of lawcourts).
vaccin [vaksɛ̃] *n.m. Med:* vaccine.
vaccination [vaksinasjɔ̃] *n.f. Med:* (*a*) vaccination; (*b*) inoculation; **v. préventive,** protective inoculation.
vaccine [vaksin] *n.f.* (*a*) *Vet:* vaccinia, cowpox; (*b*) *Med:* inoculated cowpox.
vacciner [vaksine] *v.tr. Med:* (*a*) to vaccinate; **v. contre la diphtérie,** to immunize against diphtheria; (*b*) to inoculate; **se faire v.,** to get vaccinated, inoculated **(contre,** against); **être vacciné contre les désagréments du métier,** to become immune to the drawbacks of the job.
vache [vaʃ] *n.f.* **1.** (*a*) cow; **v. laitière, v. à lait,** milch cow; *F:* **v. à lait,** mug, sucker; *F:* **le plancher des vaches,** dry land, terra firma; *F:* **parler français comme une v. espagnole,** to murder the French language; *F:* **manger de la v. enragée,** to have a hard time of it; **coup de pied en v.,** underhand trick; stab in the back; **nœud de v.,** granny (knot); (*b*) *Z:* **v. marine,** sea cow; (*c*) *P:* swine, beast; *f.* (old) cow, bitch; (*d*) *P:* policeman; **les vaches,** the cops. **2.** (*a*) cowhide; **valise en v.,** leather suitcase; (*b*) **v. à eau,** (canvas) water carrier.
vachement [vaʃmɑ̃] *adv. P:* tremendously; **c'est v. difficile,** it's damned hard; **c'est v. bien,** it's bloody good.
vacher, -ère [vaʃe, -ɛr] *n.* cowherd, *f.* cowgirl.
vacherie [vaʃri] *n.f.* **1.** (cow) byre, cowshed. **2.** *P:* dirty trick; nasty remark.
vachette [vaʃɛt] *n.f.* (*a*) calf; (*b*) (*leather*) calf(skin).
vacillant [vasijɑ̃] *a.* **1.** unsteady, wobbly (table, etc.); flickering (flame, etc.); shaky (hand); uncertain, staggering (gait, etc.). **2.** vacillating; wavering, undecided (mind, etc.); uncertain (health).
vacillation [vasijasjɔ̃] *n.f.,* **vacillement** [vasijmɑ̃] *n.m.* **1.** unsteadiness; wobbling (of table, etc.); flickering (of flame, etc.). **2.** vacillation, shilly-shallying.
vaciller [vasije] *v.i.* **1.** (*a*) to be unsteady; to sway, wobble; **il vacille sur ses jambes,** he's shaky on his legs; he's staggering; (*b*) (*of light*) to flicker. **2.** to vacillate, waver, falter.
va-comme-je-te-pousse (à la) [alavakɔmʒtəpus] *adv.phr.* haphazardly; in a slapdash manner, way; anyhow.
vacuité [vakɥite] *n.f.* vacuity, vacuousness; emptiness.
vacuum [vakɥɔm] *n.m.* vacuum.
vadrouille [vadruj] *n.f.* **1.** (*a*) *Nau:* pitchmop; (*b*) *Nau:* (deck) swab; (*c*) *Fr.C: Dom.Ec:* mop; floorcloth. **2.** *F:* **être, aller, en v.** = VADROUILLER.
vadrouiller [vadruje] *v.i. F:* to roam, rove about; to wander, trail, along.
vadrouilleur, -euse [vadrujœr, -øz] *n. F:* rover; wanderer.
va-et-vient [vaevjɛ̃] *n.m.inv.* **1.** (*a*) (i) backward and forward motion; (ii) see-saw motion; **faire le va-et-v. entre A et B,** to make regular journeys between A and B; *Trans:* to ply between . . . and . . .; **(porte) va-et-v.,** swing door; (*b*) coming(s) and going(s) (of people, etc.). **2.** (*a*) *El:* two-way wiring (system); **(commutateur) va-et-v.,** two-way switch; (*b*) *Mec.E:* reciprocation; (*c*) *Nau:* breeches buoy; backstay traveller.
vagabond, -onde [vagabɔ̃, -ɔ̃d] **1.** *a.* vagabond; wandering, roving, roaming (life, etc.). **2.** *n.* wanderer; vagabond; *Pej:* vagrant, tramp.
vagabondage [vagabɔ̃daʒ] *n.m.* (*a*) wandering(s); *Pej:* vagrancy; (*b*) *Adm:* **v. spécial,** living on immoral earnings.
vagabonder [vagabɔ̃de] *v.i.* to rove, wander (about).
vagin [vaʒɛ̃] *n.m. Anat:* vagina.
vaginal, -aux [vaʒinal, -o] *a. Anat:* vaginal.
vagir [vaʒir] *v.i.* (*of newborn infant*) to cry, wail; (*of animal*) to squeak, whimper.
vagissant [vaʒisɑ̃] *a.* crying, wailing (infant).
vagissement [vaʒismɑ̃] *n.m.* cry, wail(ing) (of newborn infant); squeak(ing), whimper(ing) (of animal).
vague¹ [vag] *n.f.* wave; **grosse v.,** billow; **une v. a balayé le pont,** the deck was swept by a sea; a sea washed over the deck; **v. de fond,** blind roller; **v. de chaleur,** heatwave; **v. d'enthousiasme,** wave of enthusiasm; **v. de colère,** *El:* **de courant,** surge of anger, of current; *Mil:* **v. d'assaut,** assaulting wave; *Lit: etc:* **nouvelle v.,** new wave.
vague² **1.** *a.* (*a*) vague, indefinite; sketchy, hazy (knowledge, etc.); dim, indistinct (memory); **quelque v. écrivain,** some writer or other; (*b*) *Anat:* **nerf v.,** vagus (nerve). **2.** *n.m.* vagueness, indefiniteness; **avoir du v. à l'âme,** to have vague yearnings.
vague³ **1.** *a.* **regarder qn d'un air v.,** to gaze vacantly at s.o.; **terrain v.,** waste ground. **2.** *n.m.* space; **fixer les yeux dans le v.,** to gaze into space; **regard perdu dans le v.,** faraway, abstracted, look.
vaguelette [vaglɛt] *n.f.* wavelet.
vaguement [vagmɑ̃] *adv.* vaguely; dimly; indistinctly.
vaguemestre [vagmɛstr̥] *n.m.* (*a*) *Mil:* post orderly; (*b*) *Navy:* postman.
vaguer [vage] *v.i. Lit:* to wander, roam (about); **laisser v. ses pensées,** to let one's thoughts wander.
vaigrage [vɛgraʒ] *n.m. N.Arch:* ceiling, inner planking, inner plating, sheathing.

vaigre [vɛgr̥] *n.f. N.Arch:* (*a*) ceiling plate, inner plank; (*b*) bottom-board (of small boat).
vaillamment [vajamɑ̃] *adv.* valiantly, bravely, courageously, gallantly.
vaillance [vajɑ̃s] *n.f.* valour, bravery, courage, gallantry.
vaillant [vajɑ̃] *a.* (*a*) *Lit:* valiant, brave, courageous, spirited; stout (heart); *Mil:* gallant; (*b*) **être v.,** to be in good health; **je ne suis pas v.,** I'm not up to the mark; I feel under the weather.
vain [vɛ̃] *a.* **1.** (*a*) vain; sham, unreal, empty (title, etc.); **ce n'étaient pas là de vaines paroles,** these were no empty words, no idle words; **vaines promesses,** hollow promises; (*b*) ineffectual, vain, useless, fruitless, unavailing (efforts, etc.); **en v.,** in vain, vainly; (*c*) **vaine pâture,** common (land). **2.** *Lit:* vain, conceited.
vaincre [vɛ̃kr̥] *v.tr.* (*pr.p.* **vainquant;** *p.p.* **vaincu;** *pr.ind.* **je vaincs, il vainc, n. vainquons;** *impf.* **je vainquais;** *p.h.* **je vainquis;** *fu.* **je vaincrai**) **1.** (*a*) to conquer, defeat, *esp. Lit:* vanquish (adversary); (*b*) *Sp: etc:* to beat (rival). **2.** to overcome, master, conquer (disease, difficulties, etc.); **il faut v. ou mourir,** we must do or die.
vainement [venmɑ̃] *adv.* vainly, in vain.
vainqueur [vɛ̃kœr] **1.** *n.m.* (*a*) victor, conqueror; *esp. Lit:* vanquisher; (*b*) *Sp: etc:* winner. **2.** *a.m.* conquering, victorious; *esp. Lit:* vanquishing.
vair [vɛr] *n.m.* **1.** *Her:* vair. **2.** *A:* (whole) squirrel fur.
vairon [vɛrɔ̃] **1.** *a.* **aux yeux vairons,** wall-eyed. **2.** *n.m. Ich:* minnow.
vaisseau, -eaux [vɛso] *n.m.* **1.** *A:* vessel, receptacle; *B:* **v. d'élection,** chosen vessel. **2.** ship, vessel; **v. à voiles,** sailing vessel; **v. de guerre,** warship; **v. amiral,** flagship; **brûler ses vaisseaux,** to burn one's boats; **v. spatial,** spaceship. **3.** nave (of church); body, hall (of building). **4.** *Anat: Bot:* vessel, canal, duct; **v. sanguin,** blood vessel.
vaisselier [vɛsəlje] *n.m. Furn:* dresser.
vaisselle [vɛsɛl] *n.f.* plates and dishes; crockery; china; **v. de porcelaine,** porcelain; **v. plate,** (gold, silver) plate; **faire, laver, la v.,** to wash up, do the washing up; **machine à laver la v.,** dishwasher; **eau de v.,** dishwater.
val [val] *n.m. Geog:* (narrow) valley; vale; *pl. usu.* **vals** *except in the phr.* **par monts et par vaux** [vo], up hill and down dale.
valable [valabl̥] *a.* valid, good (title, excuse); **billet v. pour deux mois,** ticket valid, available, for two months; **promesse toujours v.,** promise that still holds good; **un roman v.,** a good novel.
valablement [valabləmɑ̃] *adv.* validly.
Valence[1] [valɑ̃s] *Pr.n.f. Geog:* (*a*) Valencia (in Spain); (*b*) Valence (in France).
valence[2] *n.f. Ch:* valency, *esp. NAm:* valence.
valenciennes [valɑ̃sjɛn] *n.f.* Valenciennes lace.
valériane [valerjan] *n.f. Bot:* valerian.
valet [valɛ] *n.m.* **1.** (*a*) *A:* varlet, page; (*b*) *Cards:* jack, knave. **2. v. (de chambre),** (i) *A:* valet; (ii) manservant; **v. de pied,** footman; **v. d'écurie,** groom, stableboy; **v. de ferme,** farmhand; *Ven:* **v. de chiens,** whipper-in; *Prov:* **tel maître, tel v.,** like master, like man. **3.** (*a*) *Carp: etc:* clamp, holdfast; (*b*) support, rest, stand (of mirror, etc.).
valétudinaire [valetydinɛr] *a. & n.* valetudinarian.
valeur [valœr] *n.f.* **1.** (*a*) value, worth; **cela n'a pas grande v.,** it's not worth much; *Com:* **papier de v. douteuse,** dubious paper; **homme de v.,** man (i) of real ability; talented man; (ii) man of merit; **mettre une terre en v.,** to develop land; **mise en v. d'un terrain,** development of a site; *Pol.Ec:* **taxe à la v. ajoutée,** value-added tax; **v. d'échange,** exchange value; **v. d'usage,** value as a going concern; **v. marchande,** market(able) value; **article de v.,** article of value, valuable article; **objets de v.,** valuables; **bijou de grande v.,** jewel of great value; **livre de grande v.,** book of considerable merit; **sans v.,** worthless, valueless; *Post:* **colis chargé avec v. déclarée cent francs,** parcel insured for one hundred francs; (*b*) *Mus:* (time) value, length (of a note); *Mth:* value; (*c*) **boire la v. d'un verre de vin,** to drink the equivalent of a glass of wine; (*d*) import, weight, value; **votre argument n'est pas sans v.,** there's something in what you say; **renseignements sans v.,** worthless information; **v. des mots,** import, full meaning, of words; **mettre qch. en v.,** to show sth. to advantage; **mettre un mot en v.,** to emphasize, give importance to, a word. **2.** *Fin:* (*a*) asset; (*b*) *pl.* bills, shares, securities, stocks; **valeurs mobilières,** stocks and shares, transferable securities; **valeurs passives,** liabilities. **3.** *Lit:* valour, *NAm:* valor; gallantry.
valeureusement [valœrøzmɑ̃] *adv. Lit:* valorously, gallantly.
valeureux, -euse [valœrø, -øz] *a. Lit:* valorous, gallant (in battle).
validation [validasjɔ̃] *n.f.* validation (of election, marriage, etc.); ratifying (of law); authentication (of document, etc.).
valide [valid] *a.* **1.** valid (contract, reason, etc.). **2.** (*of pers.*) fit (for service); able-bodied.
validement [validmɑ̃] *adv.* validly.
valider [valide] *v.tr.* to validate (election, marriage); to ratify (contract, etc.); to authenticate (document).
validité [validite] *n.f.* validity (of contract, passport, etc.); **durée de v. d'un billet,** availability of a ticket; **établir la v. d'un testament,** to prove a will.
valise [valiz] *n.f.* (*a*) (suit)case; **faire sa v., ses valises,** to pack (one's bag(s)); (*b*) **la v. (diplomatique),** the (diplomatic) bag.
vallée [vale] *n.f.* valley; *Lit:* **cette v. de larmes,** this vale of tears.
vallon [valɔ̃] *n.m.* small valley; dale, dell, vale; *Scot:* glen.
vallonné [valɔne] *a.* undulating (country).
valoir [valwar] *v.tr. & i.* (*pr.p.* **valant;** *p.p.* **valu;** *pr.ind.* **je vaux, il vaut, n. valons, ils valent;** *pr.sub.* **je vaille, n. valions, ils vaillent;** *impf.* **je valais;** *p.h.* **je valus;** *fu.* **je vaudrai**) **1.** (*a*) to be worth; **maison qui vaut deux cent mille francs,** house worth two hundred thousand francs; **à v. sur (une somme),** on account of (a sum); **payer dix francs à v.,** to pay ten francs on account; **à v. sur qn,** on, for, account of s.o.; **ne pas v. grand-chose,** not to be worth much; **il ne vaut pas grand-chose, il ne vaut pas cher,** he's not up to much; **cela ne vaut rien,** that's no good; **ce climat ne vous vaut rien,** this climate is bad for you, doesn't suit you; **ce n'est rien qui vaille,** it isn't worth having, isn't of any value; (*b*) to be equivalent to; **un franc vaut cent centimes,** a franc is equal to a hundred centimes; **c'est une façon qui en vaut une autre,** it's as good a way as any (other); **l'un vaut (bien) l'autre; ils se valent,** one is (just) as good, as bad, as the other; there's nothing to choose between them; **il ne vaut pas mieux que son frère,** he's no better than his brother; **il ne vaut pas son frère,** he can't compare with, *F:* isn't a patch on, his brother; *F:* **ça se vaut,** it's the same either way; (*c*) *impers.* **il vaut mieux, il vaudrait mieux, rester à la maison,** it's, it would be, better to stay at home; **mieux vaudrait ne pas vous en mêler,** you'd better not interfere; **il vaut mieux qu'il en soit ainsi,** it is better that it should be so; **il vaut mieux que vous restiez,** you had better stay; **il vaut mieux, mieux vaut, partir que de rester,** it's better to go away than stay; **mieux vaut tard que jamais,** better late than never; **autant vaut rester ici,**

we may as well stay here; **choses qu'il vaut autant ne pas rappeler,** things best forgotten; **il ne vaut pas la peine de les mentionner,** they're not worth mentioning; (*d*) **faire v. qch.,** to make the most of sth.; to turn sth. to account; to set sth. off to advantage; to bring sth. out; to emphasize sth.; **monture qui fait v. la pierre,** setting that shows off the stone; **faire v. ses opinions,** to command respect for one's opinions; **faire v. ses droits,** to assert, enforce, one's claims; **faire v. son bon droit,** to vindicate one's rights; **faire v. ses raisons,** to put forward one's reasons; **j'ai fait v. que . . .,** I pointed out, urged, that . . .; **se faire v.,** (i) to make the most of oneself; (ii) to push oneself forward, assert oneself; **faire v. son argent,** to invest one's money to good account; **faire v. une terre,** to farm, develop, an estate. **2.** to be worth, to deserve, merit (sth.); **un service en vaut un autre,** one good turn deserves another; **le livre vaut d'être lu,** the book is worth reading; **cela vaut la peine de faire le voyage,** it's worth making the journey; **cela vaut le voyage,** it's worth the journey, it's worth a special trip; **je viendrai si cela en vaut la peine,** I'll come if it's worth (my) while, worth the trouble, worth it; **cela ne vaut pas la peine d'y penser,** it's not worth a moment's thought; *F:* **ça vaut le coup,** it's worth a try; **ça ne vaut pas le coup,** it isn't worth the trouble. **3. v. qch. à qn** (*a*) to bring in, yield, fetch (so much); **cette terre lui vaut dix mille francs de rente,** this land brings him in an income of ten thousand francs; **vaille que vaille,** at all costs, come what may; (*b*) to obtain, win, gain; **cette action lui a valu d'être décoré,** this act won him a decoration; **qu'est-ce qui me vaut cet honneur?** to what do I owe this honour?

valorisation [valɔrizasjɔ̃] *n.f. Com: Fin:* valorization.

valoriser [valɔrize] *v.tr. Com: Fin:* to valorize.

valse [vals] *n.f.* waltz; **faire un tour de v.,** to waltz round the room.

valser [valse] *v.i.* **1.** to waltz. **2.** *F:* **faire v. qn,** to keep s.o. on the hop; **envoyer v. qn,** to send s.o. packing, show s.o. the door; **envoyer v. qch.,** to send sth. flying; **faire v. l'argent,** to spend money like water.

valseur, -euse [valsœr, -øz] *n.* waltzer.

valve [valv] *n.f.* valve; *Aut: Cy:* **v. de chambre à air,** tyre valve; *Elcs:* **v. redresseuse,** rectifying valve.

valvulaire [valvylɛr] *a.* valvular.

valvule [valvyl] *n.f.* (*a*) *Nat.Hist:* valvule; (*b*) *Anat:* valve, valvule.

vamp [vɑ̃p] *n.f.* vamp.

vampire [vɑ̃pir] *n.m.* **1.** *Myth:* vampire. **2.** (*a*) *O:* vampire, extortioner, bloodsucker; (*b*) mass murderer. **3.** *Z:* vampire (bat).

vampirisme [vɑ̃pirism] *n.m.* belief in vampires.

van¹ [vɑ̃] *n.m. Agr:* winnowing basket.

van² *n.m. Veh:* horsebox.

vanadium [vanadjɔm] *n.m. Ch:* vanadium.

vandale [vɑ̃dal] *n.* vandal.

vandalisme [vɑ̃dalism] *n.m.* vandalism.

vandoise [vɑ̃dwaz] *n.f. Ich:* dace.

vanesse [vanɛs] *n.f. Ent:* **v. tortue,** tortoiseshell butterfly.

vanille [vanij] *n.f.* vanilla; **glace à la v.,** vanilla ice cream.

vanillé [vanije] *a.* flavoured with vanilla; **crème vanillée,** vanilla custard.

vanillier [vanije] *n.m. Bot:* vanilla plant.

vanité [vanite] *n.f.* vanity. **1.** futility, emptiness (of worldly pleasures, etc.). **2.** conceit; **tirer v. de qch.,** to take an empty pride in sth.; to pride oneself on sth.; **sans v.,** with all due modesty, without wishing to boast.

vaniteusement [vanitøzmɑ̃] *adv.* conceitedly.

vaniteux, -euse [vanitø, -øz] *a.* vain, conceited; *n.* **c'est un v.,** he's (very) conceited.

vannage¹ [vanaʒ] *n.m.* winnowing (of grain).

vannage² *n.m. Hyd.E:* **1.** sluicing (of water gate). **2.** (system of) sluice gates.

vanne [van] *n.f.* (*a*) *Hyd.E:* sluice (gate), water (gate); **v. de décharge,** overflow weir; **lever les vannes,** to open the floodgates; **mettre les vannes,** to close the floodgates; (*b*) *Mch: etc:* valve; (*c*) *Nau:* cock.

vanneau, -eaux [vano] *n.m. Orn:* lapwing, peewit; *Cu:* **œufs de v.,** plovers' eggs.

vanner [vane] *v.tr.* **1.** to winnow (grain). **2.** *P:* to tire out, exhaust; **être vanné,** to be dead beat, all in.

vannerie [vanri] *n.f.* **1.** basket making, basket trade. **2.** basketwork, wickerwork.

vanneur, -euse [vanœr, -øz] *n.* winnower.

vannier [vanje] *n.m.* basket worker, maker.

vantail, -aux [vɑ̃taj, -o] *n.m.* leaf (of door, shutter, sluice gate); **porte à deux vantaux,** folding door.

vantard, -arde [vɑ̃tar, -ard] **1.** *a.* boasting, boastful, bragging. **2.** *n.* braggart, boaster.

vantardise [vɑ̃tardiz] *n.f.* **1.** bragging, boastfulness. **2.** boast.

vanter [vɑ̃te] **1.** *v.tr.* to praise; to speak highly of; *Lit:* to vaunt. **2. se v.,** to boast, brag; **il n'y a pas de quoi se v.,** that's nothing to boast about; **se v. de qch., d'être . . .,** to pride oneself on sth., on being . . . .

vanterie [vɑ̃tri] *n.f.* boast.

va-nu-pieds [vanypje] *n.inv.* (barefoot) tramp, beggar.

vapeur¹ [vapœr] *n.f.* **1.** vapour, *NAm:* vapor; haze. **2.** (*a*) **v. d'éther, d'alcool,** ether vapour, alcoholic vapour; (*b*) **v. (d'eau),** (i) (water) vapour; (ii) steam; **machine à v.,** steam engine; **bateau à v.,** steamer, steamship; **mettre la v.,** to put steam on; **navire sous v.,** ship under steam; **à toute v.,** (at) full steam, at full speed; full steam ahead; (*c*) *Cu:* **cuire (des légumes, etc.) à la v.,** to steam (vegetables, etc.). **3.** *pl.* (*a*) fumes (of wine, petrol, etc.); (*b*) *A.Med:* vapours.

vapeur² *n.m.* steamer, steamship.

vaporeux, -euse [vapɔrø, -øz] *a.* (*a*) vaporous, steamy (atmosphere); (*b*) filmy, hazy (ideas, etc.).

vaporisateur [vapɔrizatœr] *n.m.* spray, atomizer (for perfume, etc.); vaporizer; *Hort:* sprayer.

vaporisation [vapɔrizasjɔ̃] *n.f.* vaporization; spraying, atomization.

vaporiser [vapɔrize] **1.** *v.tr.* (*a*) to vaporize; (*b*) to spray, atomize (liquid). **2. se v.,** to become vaporized, to vaporize.

vaquer [vake] *v.i.* **1.** (*a*) *O:* (*of situation*) to be vacant; (*b*) (*of parliament, law courts*) to be on vacation, in recess, not to be sitting; **les classes vaqueront la semaine prochaine,** there will be no school next week. **2. v. à qch.,** to attend to sth.; **v. aux soins du ménage,** to see to the housework; **v. à ses affaires,** to go about one's business.

varangue [varɑ̃g] *n.f. N.Arch:* floor timber, floor frame.

varappe [varap] *n.f.* rock climbing.

varappeur [varapœr] *n.m.* rock climber.

varech [varɛk] *n.m.* wrack, seaweed; kelp.

vareuse [varøz] *n.f.* **1.** *Nau:* (*a*) (sailor's) jersey, jumper; (*b*) pilot coat, pea jacket; reefer. **2.** *Mil:* tunic. **3.** loose-fitting jacket.

variabilité [varjabilite] *n.f.* (*a*) *Biol: Gram: etc:* variability; (*b*) changeableness (of mood, weather).

variable [varjabl̩] **1.** *a.* (*a*) *Biol: Gram: Mth:* variable; (*b*) changeable, altering (mood, etc.); unsteady (barometer); varying (speed); unsettled (weather); **le baromètre est au v.,** the barometer is at change; **être v.,** to vary. **2.** *n.f. Mth:* variable.

variance [varjɑ̃s] *n.f.* variance.

variant, -ante [varjɑ̃, -ɑ̃t] **1.** *a.* variable, fickle. **2.** *n.f.* **variante,** variant (reading of text, spelling of word).

variation [varjasjɔ̃] *n.f.* variation. **1. v. du temps,** change in the weather; **v. du compas,** compass error. **2.** *Mus:* **air avec variations,** theme with variations.

varice [varis] *n.f. Med:* varicose vein.

varicelle [varisɛl] *n.f. Med:* chickenpox.

varié [varje] *a.* varied; varying, various (types, etc.); miscellaneous (news); variegated (leaf, etc.); chequered (life); *Mus:* **air v.,** air with variations; *Mec:* **mouvement v.,** variable motion.

varier [varje] (*impf. & pr.sub.* **n. variions, v. variiez**) **1.** *v.tr.* to vary; to diversify (occupations, etc.); to variegate (leaves). **2.** *v.i.* to vary, change; (*of markets*) to fluctuate; **v. dans ses réponses,** to be inconsistent in one's replies; **les auteurs varient souvent,** authors often differ; **v. de méthode,** to vary one's methods; *Mth:* ***y*** **varie dans le même sens que et proportionnellement à** ***x***, *y* varies as *x*.

variété [varjete] *n.f.* **1.** variety (**de,** of); diversity (of opinions, etc.); *Com:* **grande v. de rayons,** wide range of departments; **donner de la v. au menu,** (i) to vary the menu; (ii) to lend variety to the menu; (**spectacle de**) **variétés,** variety show; *Lit:* **variétés,** miscellanies. **2.** *Nat.Hist:* variety (of flower, etc.).

variole [varjɔl] *n.f.* **1.** *Med:* smallpox. **2.** *Vet:* **v. des vaches,** cowpox.

variolé [varjɔle] *a.* pockmarked.

varioleux, -euse [varjɔlø, -øz] **1.** *a. Med:* variolous (pustules, etc.). **2.** *n.* smallpox patient.

variqueux, -euse [varikø, -øz] *a.* varicose (vein, etc.).

varlet [varlɛ] *n.m. A:* varlet, page.

varlope [varlɔp] *n.f. Tls:* trying plane.

Varsovie [varsɔvi] *Pr.n.f. Geog:* Warsaw; **pays du Pacte de V.,** Warsaw Pact countries.

vasculaire [vaskylɛr] *a.* vascular.

vase[1] [vɑz] *n.m.* vase; **v. à fleurs,** flower vase; **v. de nuit,** chamber(pot); **vivre en v. clos,** to live in isolation, as a recluse; *Ph:* **vases communicants,** communicating vessels; *El:* **v. d'un élément de pile,** battery jar; **v. poreux,** porous cell.

vase[2] *n.f.* mud, silt, slime, ooze, sludge; **banc de v.,** mudbank.

vasectomie [vazɛktɔmi] *n.f. Surg:* vasectomy.

vaseline [vazlin] *n.f.* Vaseline (*R.t.m.*); petroleum jelly; *Pharm:* **huile de v.,** liquid paraffin.

vaseux, -euse [vɑzø, -øz] *a.* **1.** muddy, slimy, sludgy. **2.** *F:* (*of pers.*) seedy, off colour, *NAm:* off color; **il a l'air v.,** he looks a bit washed-out, under the weather; **des idées vaseuses,** woolly ideas.

vasistas [vazistɑs] *n.m.* opening window frame, fanlight (over a door or window).

vaso(-)constricteur, -trice [vazɔkɔ̃striktœr, -tris] *a. & n.m. Anat:* vasoconstrictor; *pl. vaso(-)constricteurs, -trices.*

vaso(-)moteur, -trice [vazɔmɔtœr, -tris] *a. Anat:* vasomotor (nerve centre); *pl. vaso(-)moteurs, -trices.*

vasouillard [vazujar] *a. F:* woolly, muddleheaded.

vasque [vask] *n.f.* **1.** basin (of fountain). **2.** (ornamental) bowl.

vassal, -ale, -aux [vasal, -o] *n.* vassal.

vassalité [vasalite] *n.f.*, **vasselage** [vaslaʒ] *n.m.* **1.** vassalage. **2.** bondage.

vaste [vast] *a.* vast, immense, spacious, huge; *F:* big, great (joke, etc.); **v. étendue,** broad expanse; **le v. monde,** the wide world; **v. érudition,** comprehensive learning.

vastement [vastəmɑ̃] *adv.* vastly.

vastringue [vastrɛ̃g] *n.f. Carp:* spokeshave.

Vatican (le) [ləvatikɑ̃] *Pr.n.m.* the Vatican.

vaticane [vatikan] *a. & n.f.* **la (Bibliothèque) V.,** the Vatican Library.

vaticination [vatisinasjɔ̃] *n.f. Lit:* vaticination.

vaticiner [vatisine] *v.i. Lit:* to vaticinate.

va-tout [vatu] *n.m.inv. Gaming:* **jouer son va-t.,** to stake one's all.

vau (à) [avo] *adv.phr.* **à v.-l'eau,** downstream, with the stream; **tout va à v.-l'eau,** everything's going to rack and ruin.

vaudeville [vodvil] *n.m.* **1.** *Lit.Hist:* topical, satirical, song (with refrain). **2.** *Th:* vaudeville, light comedy (*usu.* with occasional song).

vaudevillesque [vodvilɛsk] *a.* comical, farcical.

vaudevilliste [vodvilist] *n.m.* vaudeville writer.

vaudois, -oise [vodwa, -waz] *a. & n.* **1.** *Geog:* (native, inhabitant) of Vaud (Swiss canton); Vaudois. **2.** *Rel.H:* Waldensian.

vaudou [vodu] *n.m.* voodoo.

vaurien, -ienne [vorjɛ̃, -jɛn] *n.* good-for-nothing, *F:* layabout, yob; **petit v.!** you little scamp! you little rascal!

vautour [votur] *n.m. Orn:* vulture.

vautrer (se) [səvotre] *v.pr.* (*a*) (*of pig, etc.*) to wallow (in mud); **se v. dans le vice,** to wallow in vice; (*b*) to sprawl (on grass, a sofa).

vauvert [vovɛr] *a.* **c'est au diable v.,** it's miles from anywhere, out in the wilds, a long way away.

va-vite (à la) [alavavit] *adv.phr.* in a rush, in a hurry; **travail fait à la va-v.,** scamped work, rushed work.

veau, -eaux [vo] *n.m.* **1.** (*a*) calf; **le v. gras,** the fatted calf; **pleurer comme un v.,** to cry one's eyes out; to blubber; (*b*) **v. marin,** sea calf, seal; (*c*) *F:* fool, clot; lump, lout. **2.** *Cu:* veal; **côtelette de v.,** veal cutlet; **tête de v.,** calf's head; **gelée de pied de v.,** calf's, calves', foot jelly. **3.** calf (leather); calfskin.

vecteur, -trice [vɛktœr, -tris] **1.** *a. Mth:* **rayon v.,** radius vector. **2.** *n.m.* (*a*) *Mth:* vector; (*b*) *Ball:* vehicle (of atomic warhead, etc.).

vectoriel, -ielle [vɛktɔrjɛl] *a. Mth:* vectorial.

vécu [veky] *a.* **1. choses vécues,** things which have been lived through; actual experiences. **2.** (*of play, novel, etc.*) true to life, founded on fact.

vedettariat [vədɛtarja] *n.m. Cin: etc:* stardom.

vedette [vədɛt] *n.f.* **1.** *Mil: A:* vedette, mounted sentry; **en v.,** on vedette duty. **2.** (*a*) *Navy:* vedette boat, scout; (*b*) *Nau:* small motorboat; launch; patrol boat. **3.** (*a*) **mettre qch. en v.,** to write, print, sth. in a line by itself; **mots en v.,** words in bold type; (*of actor*) **avoir la v. (sur l'affiche),** to head, top, the bill; **être en v.,** to be in the limelight, in the forefront; to hit the headlines; **mettre qn, qch., en v.,** to highlight, spotlight, s.o., sth.; (*b*) *Th: Cin:* star.

végétal, -aux [veʒetal, -o] **1.** *a.* **vie végétale,** plant life; **sol v.,** humus. **2.** *n.m.* vegetable, plant.

végétalisme [veʒetalism] *n.m.* veganism.

végétarien, -ienne [veʒetarjɛ̃, -jɛn] *a. & n.* vegetarian.

végétarisme [veʒetarism] *n.m.* vegetarianism.

végétatif, -ive [veʒetatif, -iv] *a.* vegetative; vegetable-like (existence).

végétation [veʒetasjɔ̃] *n.f.* **1.** vegetation. **2.** *pl. Med:* vegetations; **végétations (adénoïdes),** adenoid growths, *F:* adenoids.

végéter [veʒete] *v.i.* **(je végète; je végéterai) 1.** *A:* (*of plant*) to vegetate, grow. **2.** (*of pers.*) to vegetate; to lead an aimless, uneventful, life; to be a cabbage.

véhémence [veemɑ̃s] *n.f. Lit:* vehemence; **avec v.,** vehemently.

véhément [veemɑ̃] *a. Lit:* vehement, violent.

véhémentement [veemɑ̃tmɑ̃] *adv. Lit:* vehemently.

véhiculaire [veikylɛr] *a.* **langue v.,** common language.

véhicule [veikyl] *n.m.* vehicle; *Adm:* conveyance; **v. spatial,** spacecraft; **l'air est le v. du son,** the air is the medium, the vehicle, of sound.
véhiculer [veikyle] *v.tr.* to transport, convey, carry (by vehicle).
veille [vɛj] *n.f.* **1.** (*a*) sitting up, staying up (at night); watching (by night); (*b*) vigil (of nun, etc.); (*c*) *Mil:* (night) watch; *Nau:* lookout; *Nau:* **homme de v.,** lookout (man); *Nau:* **chambre de v.,** chart house; **ancre de v.,** sheet anchor; (*d*) wakefulness; **entre la v. et le sommeil,** between waking and sleeping; **causer à qn beaucoup de veilles,** to cause s.o. many a sleepless night. **2.** (*a*) eve, preceding day, previous day; **la v. de Noël,** Christmas Eve; **la v. du jour de l'an,** New Year's Eve; **la v. de la bataille,** the day before the battle; **je l'avais vu la v.,** I'd seen him the day before; **la v. au soir,** the evening before; (*b*) **être à la v. de la ruine, d'une guerre,** to be on the brink, on the verge, of ruin, of a war; **être à la v. de se marier,** to be on the point of getting married; **à la v. de la réunion,** just before the meeting.
veillée [veje] *n.f.* **1.** (*a*) night nursing (of the sick); watching, vigil (by dead body); (*b*) *A:* **v. d'armes,** vigil of arms. **2.** evening (spent in company); **faire la v. chez qn,** to spend the evening at s.o.'s house.
veiller [veje] **1.** *v.i.* (*a*) to sit up, stay up, keep awake; **v. fort avant dans la nuit,** to burn the midnight oil; (*b*) *Mil: etc:* to watch, be on the lookout; to stand by; (*c*) **v. sur qn,** to watch over, look after, s.o.; to take care of s.o.; (*d*) **v. à qch.,** to watch over, see to, sth; **v. aux intérêts de qn,** to attend to, look after, s.o.'s interests; **v. à la besogne,** to keep an eye on the work; **v. à ce que qch. se fasse,** to see (to it) that sth. is done; *Fig:* **v. au grain,** to look out for squalls; to keep one's weather eye open. **2.** *v.tr.* to sit up with, look after, watch over, attend to (sick person, etc.); **v. un mort,** to keep vigil over a dead body.
veilleur, -euse [vɛjœr, -øz] **1.** *n.m.* watcher (by night); keeper of a vigil; *Mil: etc:* lookout; **v. de nuit,** nightwatchman. **2.** *n.f.* **veilleuse:** (*a*) night light; **mettre la lampe en veilleuse,** to dim the light; **mettre une entreprise en veilleuse,** to reduce output to a minimum; **mettre un projet en veilleuse,** to put a project off temporarily, to shelve a project; (*b*) *Aut:* sidelight; (*c*) pilot light (on gas cooker, etc.); (*d*) *Bot:* meadow saffron.
veinard, -arde [vɛnar, -ard] *a.* & *n.* *F:* lucky, jammy (person, player, etc.); **c'est un v.,** he has all the luck; **v.!** you lucky devil!
veine [vɛn] *n.f.* **1.** *Anat: Bot: etc:* vein; *Anat:* **v. cave,** vena cava. **2.** (*a*) *Geol:* vein; lode (of ore); seam (of coal); (*b*) vein, inspiration, humour, *NAm:* humor; **la v. poétique,** the poetic vein; **en v. de plaisanterie,** in humorous vein; **être en v. de faire qch.,** to be in the mood to do sth., for doing sth.; **être en v. de générosité,** to be in a generous mood; (*c*) *F:* luck; **avoir de la v.,** to be in luck, to be lucky; **coup de v.,** (i) stroke of luck; lucky strike; (ii) fluke; **pas de v.!** rotten luck! **c'est bien ma v.!** just my luck! **quelle v.!** my luck's in!
veiner [vene] *v.tr.* to vein, grain (door, etc.).
veineux, -euse [vɛnø, -øz] *a.* **1.** venous (system, blood). **2.** veined (wood, etc.).
veinure [venyr] *n.f.* graining (of wood, etc.).
vêlage [vɛlaʒ] *n.m.* (*of cow*) calving.
vélaire [velɛr] *a.* & *n.f.* *Ling:* velar.
vêlement [vɛlmɑ̃] *n.m.* (*of cow*) calving.
vêler [vele] *v.i.* (*of cow*) to calve.
vélin [velɛ̃] *n.m.* (*a*) vellum (parchment); (*b*) **(papier) v.,** vellum (paper); wove paper.
velléitaire [veleitɛr] *a.* (*of pers.*) weak-willed; erratic.
velléité [veleite] *n.f.* slight desire, inclination; stray impulse; **avoir des velléités de travail,** to toy with the idea of work.
vélo [velo] *n.m.* bicycle, bike; **aller à, en, v.,** to cycle; to ride a bike; **aimez-vous faire du v.?** do you like cycling?
vélocipède [velɔsipɛd] *n.m.* *A:* velocipede.
vélocité [velɔsite] *n.f.* speed, swiftness.
vélodrome [velɔdrɔm] *n.m.* cycle-racing track.
vélomoteur [velɔmɔtœr] *n.m.* lightweight motor cycle.
velours [v(ə)lur] *n.m.* **1.** *Tex:* velvet; **v. uni,** plain velvet; **v. façonné,** figured velvet; **v. bouclé,** uncut velvet; **v. côtelé, à côtes,** ribbed velvet, corduroy velvet; **v. de coton,** cotton velvet, velveteen; **v. de laine,** velour(s); **jouer sur le v.,** to be on velvet. **2.** incorrect liaison, e.g. **j'ai été** [ʒezete].
velouté [vəlute] **1.** *a.* velvety; velvet-like; soft as velvet; downy (peach, cheeks); mellow (wine). **2.** *n.m.* (*a*) velvetiness, softness (of material, voice, etc.); bloom (of peach, etc.); (*b*) *Cu:* thick, cream soup, sauce.
velouter [vəlute] *v.tr.* to give a velvety appearance to (sth.); (*of shade, etc.*) to soften (contour).
velouteux, -euse [vəlutø, -øz] *a.* velvety, soft.
Velpeau [vɛlpo] *n.m.* **bande V.,** crêpe bandage.
velu [vəly] *a.* hairy.
vélum, velum [velɔm] *n.m.* awning.
venaison [vənɛzɔ̃] *n.f.* *Cu:* venison.
vénal, -aux [venal, -o] *a.* **1.** venal, purchasable (privilege, etc.); *Com:* **valeur vénale,** market value. **2.** *Pej:* venal, mercenary, corruptible; corrupt (press).
vénalement [venalmɑ̃] *adv.* venally.
vénalité [venalite] *n.f.* venality.
venant [vənɑ̃] *n.m.* **à tout v., à tous venants,** to all comers, to all and sundry.
vendable [vɑ̃dabl̩] *a.* saleable, marketable.
vendange [vɑ̃dɑ̃ʒ] *n.f.* **1.** (*often in pl.*) vintage (season). **2.** (*a*) vintage; grape gathering; wine harvest, grape harvest; (*b*) the grapes.
vendanger [vɑ̃dɑ̃ʒe] *v.tr.* & *i.* **(je vendangeai(s); n. vendangeons)** to vintage; to gather (the grapes).
vendangeur, -euse [vɑ̃dɑ̃ʒœr, -øz] *n.* **1.** vintager; grape picker. **2.** *n.f.* *Bot:* **vendangeuse,** aster.
vendéen, -enne [vɑ̃deɛ̃, -ɛ̃n] *a.* & *n.* *Geog:* of the Vendée.
vendémiaire [vɑ̃demjɛr] *n.m.* *Fr.Hist:* first month of Fr. Republican calendar (Sep.–Oct.).
vendetta [vɑ̃deta] *n.f.* vendetta.
vendeur, -euse [vɑ̃dœr, -øz] *n.* (*a*) seller (of goods); (*in shop*) salesman, saleswoman, salesgirl; (shop) assistant; *NAm:* salesclerk; (*b*) *Jur:* vendor.
vendre [vɑ̃dr̩] *v.tr.* **1.** to sell; **v. qch. à qn,** to sell s.o. sth.; to sell sth. to s.o.; **v. à terme,** to sell on credit; **v. comptant,** to sell for cash; **v. moins cher que qn,** to undersell s.o.; **v. chèrement sa vie,** to sell one's life dearly; **v. un objet (à) 50 francs,** to sell an object for 50 francs; **cela se vend comme des petits pains,** it's selling like hot cakes; **maison à v.,** house for sale; **l'art de v.,** salesmanship. **2.** (*a*) **v. qn,** to sell s.o. up (for debt); (*b*) to betray, give away (s.o., a secret).
vendredi [vɑ̃drədi] *n.m.* Friday; **le v. saint,** Good Friday.
vendu [vɑ̃dy] *n.m.* traitor.
venelle [vənɛl] *n.f.* alley.
vénéneux, -euse [venenø, -øz] *a.* poisonous.
vénérable [venerabl̩] **1.** *a.* venerable. **2.** *n.m.* worshipful master (of masonic lodge).
vénération [venerasjɔ̃] *n.f.* veneration, reverence; **avoir de la v. pour qn,** to hold s.o. in veneration.
vénérer [venere] *v.tr.* **(je vénère, n. vénérons; je vénérerai)** (*a*) to venerate, reverence, revere; (*b*) to worship (saint, etc.).

vénerie [vɛnri] *n.f.* venery; (science of) hunting; **termes de v.,** hunting terms.
vénérien, -ienne [venerjɛ̃, -jɛn] *a. Med:* venereal.
veneur [vənœr] *n.m.* huntsman; *Hist:* **le Grand V.,** the Master of the Royal Hunt.
Vénézuéla (le) [ləvenezɥela] *Pr.n. Geog:* Venezuela.
vénézuélien, -ienne [venezɥeljɛ̃, -jɛn] *a. & n. Geog:* Venezuelan.
vengeance [vɑ̃ʒɑ̃s] *n.f.* **1.** revenge; **par v.,** out of revenge; **tirer v. d'une injure,** to be revenged for an insult; **exercer sa v. sur qn,** to have one's revenge on s.o. **2.** vengeance, retribution, requital; **crime qui crie v.,** crime that cries for vengeance.
venger [vɑ̃ʒe] **(je vengeai(s); n. vengeons) 1.** *v.tr.* to avenge; **v. qn d'une injure,** to avenge s.o. for an insult. **2. se v.,** to be revenged, have one's revenge; **se v. sur qn (de qch.),** to take (one's) revenge on s.o. (for sth.).
vengeur, -eresse [vɑ̃ʒœr, -rɛs] **1.** *n.* avenger. **2.** *a. Lit:* avenging, (re)vengeful.
véniel, -ielle [venjɛl] *a.* venial (sin).
venimeux, -euse [vənimø, -øz] *a.* venomous; (*a*) poisonous (bite, snake); (*b*) spiteful.
venin [vənɛ̃] *n.m.* venom; (*a*) poison (of snake, etc.); (*b*) spite, malice; **jeter son v.,** to vent one's spleen.
venir [v(ə)nir] *v.* (*pr.p.* **venant;** *p.p.* **venu;** *pr.ind.* **je viens, il vient, n. venons, ils viennent;** *pr.sub.* **je vienne;** *impf.* **je venais;** *p.h.* **je vins, n. vînmes, v. vîntes, ils vinrent;** *p.sub.* **je vinsse;** *fu.* **je viendrai;** *aux.* **être**) to come. **I.** *v.i.* **1.** (*a*) **je viens!** I'm coming! **je ne ferai qu'aller et v.,** I'll be back in a minute, I'll come straight back; **mais venez donc!** do come along! **d'où venez-vous?** where have you come from? **il est venu à moi, vers moi,** he came up to me; **il est venu sur moi,** he advanced on me (threateningly); **v. au monde,** to be born; **l'année qui vient,** the coming year; next year; **ses succès à v.,** his future successes; **dans les temps à v.,** in the days to come; **faire v. qn,** to send for, call in, fetch, s.o.; **faire v. ses robes de Paris,** to get one's dresses from Paris; **voir v. qn,** to see s.o. coming; *Fig:* **je vous vois v.!** I see what you're getting at; **je préfère voir v.,** I'd rather wait and see; **le voici v., le voici qui vient,** here he comes; **être bien, mal, venu,** to be welcome, unwelcome; *impers.* **est-il venu quelqu'un?** has anyone called, been? **il est venu deux lettres pour vous,** two letters have come for you; *Nau:* **v. dans le vent,** to come round; **v. sur bâbord, sur tribord,** to alter course to port, to starboard; (*b*) **il est venu tomber à mes pieds,** he fell at my feet, **venez me trouver à quatre heures,** come (round) and see me at four o'clock; **je viens vous voir,** I've come to see you; **v. chercher, v. prendre, qch., qn,** to come and fetch sth., to call for s.o.; (*c*) (*pr. & impf. only*) **v. de faire qch.,** to have (only) just done sth.; **il vient, venait, de sortir,** he has just, had just, gone out. **2.** (*denoting origin*) (*a*) **il vient d'Amérique,** he's from America; **mot qui vient du latin,** word derived from Latin; **ce bien lui est venu de famille,** he inherited this property from his family; **tout cela vient de ce que . . .,** all this is the result of . . .; (*b*) *impers.* **d'où vient(-il) que . . .?** how is it that . . .? **3.** (*a*) to occur; **le premier exemple venu,** the first example that comes to mind; **l'idée me vient que . . ., il me vient à l'esprit que . . ., il me vient l'idée que . . .,** the thought comes to my mind, it occurs to me, that . . .; **il ne m'est pas venu à l'idée que . . .,** it never entered my head that . . .; (*b*) **v. à faire qch.,** to happen, chance, to do sth. **4.** (*a*) to attain, reach; **l'eau leur venait aux genoux,** the water came up to their knees; (*b*) **en v. à qch., à faire qch.,** to come to sth., to the point of doing sth.; **en v. aux coups, aux mains,** to come to blows; **les choses en sont-elles venues là?** have things come to such a point? **je comprends où vous voulez en v.,** I see what you're getting at, driving at; **j'en suis venu à votre manière de penser,** I've come round to your way of thinking. **5.** (*of plants, children, etc.*) to come on; to grow (up); **bien v.,** (i) (*of plants, etc.*) to thrive; (ii) (*of photograph, etc.*) to come out well; **faire v. du blé,** to grow wheat; **il lui est venu une tumeur,** he developed a tumour, *NAm:* tumor. **II.** *A: & Dial:* **s'en venir,** to come along.
Venise [vəniz] *Pr.n.f. Geog:* Venice; **point de V.,** Venetian lace.
vénitien, -ienne [venisjɛ̃, -jɛn] *a. & n.* Venetian; **store v.,** Venetian blind.
vent [vɑ̃] *n.m.* **1.** (*a*) wind; **le v. du nord, du sud,** the north, south, wind; *Nau:* **v. frais,** strong breeze; **grand v., v. fort,** high wind; gale; **journée de grand v.,** windy day; **coup de v.,** gust of wind; squall; **entrer, sortir, en coup de v.,** to dash in, out; **elle courait les cheveux au v.,** she ran with her hair streaming in the wind; **à l'abri du v.,** (i) sheltered from the wind; (ii) *Nau:* under the wind; under the lee; *Mus:* **instrument à v.,** wind instrument; **il fait du v.,** it's windy (weather); **aller comme le v.,** to go like the wind; *Nau:* **avoir bon v.,** to have a fair wind; **avoir le v. en poupe,** to have the wind right aft, dead aft; *Fig:* **il a le v. en poupe,** he's on the road to success; **avoir du v. dans les voiles,** to be three sheets in the wind; to be drunk; **v. arrière,** following wind; *Av:* tail wind; **aller v. arrière,** to sail, run, before the wind; **v. debout,** head wind; **contre le v.,** against the wind, into the wind; *Nau:* **sous le v.,** alee, (to) leeward; **au v.,** (i) a-weather; (ii) (to) windward; **mettre la barre au v.,** to put the helm up; **côté du v.,** weather side; **côté sous le v.,** lee side; **avoir l'avantage du v.,** to have the weather gauge; **prendre le v., regarder de quel côté vient le v.,** to see which way the wind blows; to see how the land lies; **tourner à tous les vents,** to be a weathercock; **quel bon v. vous amène?** what lucky chance brings you here? *Prov:* **qui sème le v. récolte la tempête,** he who sows the wind shall reap the whirlwind; *F:* **être dans le v.,** to be up-to-date, with it; *Geog:* **les îles du V.,** the Windward Islands; (*b*) **aire de v.,** point of the compass; **logé aux quatre vents,** exposed to the four winds of heaven; (*c*) air; **marché, assemblée, en plein v.,** open-air market, meeting; **mettre qch. au v.,** to hang sth. out to dry; (*d*) blast (of bellows, gun); *Av:* **v. de l'hélice,** propeller slipstream; (*e*) flatulence, wind; **lâcher un v.,** to break wind; (*f*) **ce n'est que du v.,** it's just hot air. **2.** *Ven:* scent; **avoir le v. de son gibier,** to have the wind of one's game; **avoir v. de qch.,** to get wind of sth.
vente [vɑ̃t] *n.f.* **1.** sale; selling; **v. aux enchères,** (sale by) auction; **salle des ventes,** auction rooms, saleroom(s); *NAm:* salesroom; **v. de charité,** (charity) bazaar; **v. judiciaire,** sale by order of the court; v. **publique,** public sale; auction; **bureau de v.,** sales agency; **promotion des ventes,** sales promotion; **en v.,** for sale, on sale; **mettre qch. en v.,** to put sth. up, offer sth., for sale; **(livre) retiré de la v.,** (book) withdrawn from sale; (*of book, etc.*) **faire une forte v.,** to be a best seller; **de v. difficile,** difficult to sell. **2.** timber felled; felling (of timber); **jeune(s) vente(s),** new undergrowth.
venté [vɑ̃te] *a.* windswept, windblown, windy (area).
venter [vɑ̃te] *v.impers.* to blow, to be windy; **il vente fort,** it's blowing hard; it's very windy.
venteux, -euse [vɑ̃tø, -øz] *a.* windy (weather); windswept (country).
ventilateur [vɑ̃tilatœr] *n.m.* ventilator; **v. rotatif,** fan; **v. électrique,** electric fan.
ventilation [vɑ̃tilasjɔ̃] *n.f.* **1.** ventilation. **2.** (*a*) *Jur:* separate valuation (of parts of estate, etc.); (*b*)

Book-k: apportionment, breakdown (of expenses, etc.).

ventiler [vɑ̃tile] *v.tr.* **1.** to ventilate, air (room, etc.); **mal ventilé,** stuffy. **2.** (*a*) *Jur:* to value separately (parts of estate, etc.); (*b*) *Book-k:* to apportion, break down (expenses, etc.).

ventôse [vɑ̃toz] *n.m. Fr.Hist:* sixth month of Republican calendar (Feb.-March).

ventouse [vɑ̃tuz] *n.f.* **1.** (*a*) *Med:* cupping glass; **poser des ventouses à qn,** to cup s.o.; (*b*) *Z:* sucker (of leech, etc.); (*c*) suction cup, disc; **cendrier à v.,** suction-grip ashtray; **faire v.,** to adhere by suction. **2.** airhole, vent(hole); ventilator.

ventral, -aux [vɑ̃tral, -o] *a.* ventral; **parachute v.,** lap pack (parachute).

ventre [vɑ̃tr̥] *n.m.* **1.** (*a*) stomach; abdomen; belly; *F:* tummy; **se coucher à plat v.,** to lie flat on one's stomach, one's face; **se mettre à plat v. devant qn,** to grovel to s.o.; (*of horse, etc.*) **v. à terre,** at full speed; **avoir mal au v.,** to have stomach ache, *F:* tummy ache; **avoir du v.,** to have a paunch; to be stout, *F:* potbellied; **prendre du v.,** to be getting a paunch, *F:* a tummy; **se serrer le v.,** to tighten, pull in, one's belt; (*b*) stomach; **avoir le v. creux,** to have an empty stomach; **ne rien avoir dans le v.,** (i) to be starving; (ii) to have no guts; **je savais bien qu'il avait quelque chose dans le v.,** I was sure he had it in him; *Prov:* **v. affamé n'a point d'oreilles,** it's no use reasoning with a hungry man; (*c*) (mother's) womb. **2.** *Tchn:* (*a*) bulge, swell (of bottle, girder); belly, sag (of sail); belly (of ship); **faire v.,** (i) to bulge (out), belly out; (ii) to sag; (*b*) *Ph:* antinode, ventral segment (of wave); **v. de tension,** potential loop, voltage loop.

ventrebleu [vɑ̃trəblø] *int. A:* gadzooks! zounds!

ventrée [vɑ̃tre] *n.f.* bellyful (of food).

ventricule [vɑ̃trikyl] *n.m. Anat:* ventricle.

ventrière [vɑ̃trijɛr] *n.f.* **1.** (*a*) *Harn:* girth; (*b*) sling (for hoisting animal). **2.** (*a*) *N.Arch:* bilge block; (*b*) *Const:* purlin.

ventriloque [vɑ̃trilɔk] **1.** *a.* ventriloquial. **2.** *n.* ventriloquist.

ventriloquie [vɑ̃trilɔki] *n.f.* ventriloquy, ventriloquism.

ventru [vɑ̃try] *a.* (*a*) (*of pers.*) potbellied; corpulent, portly; (*b*) bulbous (column); bulging, swelling (sail).

venu, -ue[1] [v(ə)ny] **1.** *a.* (*a*) **plante bien venue,** sturdy, healthy, plant; **photographie bien venue,** photograph that has come out well; **enfant mal v.,** stunted, puny, child; (*b*) (*of remark, etc.*) **bien v.,** appropriate; **mal v.,** inappropriate; **je serais mal v. de, à . . .,** it's not for me to . . .; **il serait mal v. d'insister,** it would be ill mannered to insist. **2.** *n.* **le premier v.,** (i) the first to arrive; (ii) anybody; **le premier v. vous dira cela,** anybody, anyone, will tell you that; **ce n'est pas le premier v.,** he's not just anybody; **le dernier v.,** (i) the last to arrive; (ii) *Pej:* a (mere) nobody; **les nouveaux venus, les nouvelles venues,** the newcomers.

venue[2] [v(ə)ny] *n.f.* **1.** coming, arrival; advent, approach (of spring, etc.); rush, irruption (of water); **allées et venues,** comings and goings. **2.** growth (of tree, etc.); **d'une belle v.,** well grown; **tout d'une v.,** straight up and down.

Vénus [venys] *Pr.n.f. Myth:* Venus; **ce n'est pas une V.,** she's no beauty; *Bot;* **cheveu de V.,** maidenhair fern.

vêpres [vɛpr̥] *n.f.pl. Ecc:* vespers; evensong.

ver [vɛr] *n.m.* **1. v. (de terre),** (earth)worm; **v. de sable, v. des pêcheurs,** lug(worm); **nu comme un v.,** stark naked; *Med:* **v. solitaire,** tapeworm; *F:* **tirer les vers du nez à qn,** to worm secrets out of s.o. **2.** grub; maggot; larva; **v. blanc,** cockchafer grub; **v. de viande,** maggot; **v. de farine,** mealworm; **v. du bois,** woodworm; **rongé, piqué, des vers,** wormeaten; **mangé aux vers,** motheaten; **rose rongée de vers,** cankered rose; **v. à soie,** silkworm; **v. luisant,** glow worm; **v. rongeur,** (i) canker(worm); (ii) *A: & Lit:* (worm of) remorse; (iii) constant drain on the resources.

véracité [verasite] *n.f.* **1.** veracity; truthfulness. **2.** truth (of a statement).

véranda [verɑ̃da] *n.f.* veranda(h).

verbal, -aux [vɛrbal, -o] *a.* **1.** (*of promise, etc.*) verbal; by word of mouth. **2.** *Gram:* verbal.

verbalement [vɛrbalmɑ̃] *adv.* verbally, by word of mouth.

verbalisation [vɛrbalizasjɔ̃] *n.f. Jur:* entry of charge (by policeman for minor offence).

verbaliser [vɛrbalize] *v.i.* (*of policeman*) to charge s.o.

verbe [vɛrb] *n.m.* **1.** tone of voice; speech; **avoir le v. haut,** (i) to speak loudly; (ii) to be dictatorial. **2.** *Theol:* **le V.,** the Word; **le V. s'est fait chair,** the Word was made flesh. **3.** *Gram:* verb.

verbeux, -euse [vɛrbø -øz] *a.* verbose, long-winded (orator, etc.); wordy (explanation, etc.).

verbiage [vɛrbjaʒ] *n.m.* verbiage.

verbosité [vɛrbozite] *n.f.* verbosity, wordiness.

ver-coquin [vɛrkɔkɛ̃] *n.m.* **1.** vine grub. **2.** *Vet:* stagger worm; *pl. vers-coquins.*

verdâtre [vɛrdɑtr̥] *a.* greenish.

verdeur [vɛrdœr] *n.f.* **1.** (*a*) tartness, acidity (of fruit, wine); (*b*) crudeness (of speech). **2.** vigour, *NAm:* vigor, vitality (of old people).

verdict [vɛrdik(t)] *n.m. Jur:* finding of the jury; verdict; **prononcer, rendre, un v.,** to return, bring in, a verdict; to find (for or against s.o.).

verdier [vɛrdje] *n.m. Orn:* greenfinch.

verdir [vɛrdir] **1.** *v.tr.* to make, paint, (sth.) green. **2.** *v.i.* (*of vegetation, etc.*) to grow, become, turn, green.

verdissage [vɛrdisaʒ] *n.m.* dyeing, colouring, *NAm:* coloring, (sth.) green.

verdissement [vɛrdismɑ̃] *n.m.* growing, becoming, green.

verdoiement [vɛrdwamɑ̃] *n.m.* turning, becoming, green; greenness (of fields).

verdoyant [vɛrdwajɑ̃] *a.* green; *Lit:* verdant (meadow, etc.).

verdoyer [vɛrdwaje] *v.i.* **(il verdoie; il verdoiera)** (*of field, etc.*) to turn, become, green.

verdure [vɛrdyr] *n.f.* **1.** (*a*) greenness; (*b*) greenery; *Lit:* verdure; **salle de v.,** green arbour; **tapis de v.,** greensward. **2.** *Cu:* (green) salad vegetable.

véreux, -euse [verø, -øz] *a.* **1.** wormy, maggoty (fruit). **2.** dubious, *F:* fishy (dealings); **financier v.,** shady financier; **dettes véreuses,** bad debts.

verge [vɛrʒ] *n.f.* **1.** (*a*) *A:* rod; wand; cane; switch; usher's wand; **v. d'huissier, (poignée de) verges,** birch (rod); **battre de verges un enfant,** to birch a child; (*b*) shank (of anchor); (*c*) *Bot:* **v. d'or,** golden rod, Aaron's rod. **2.** *Anat:* penis. **3.** *Fr.C: Meas:* yard.

vergé [vɛrʒe] **1.** *a. Tex:* (*a*) badly dyed, streaky; (*b*) corded. **2.** *a. & n.m.* **(papier) v.,** laid paper.

verger [vɛrʒe] *n.m.* orchard.

vergeté [vɛrʒəte] *a.* streaky; streaked.

vergette [vɛrʒɛt] *n.f.* **1.** small cane, switch. **2.** *A:* clothes brush.

vergeture [vɛrʒətyr] *n.f.* (*a*) weal, red mark (caused by lash of whip, etc.); (*b*) *Obst:* stretch mark.

vergeure [vɛrʒyr] *n.f. Paperm:* wire mark (on laid paper).

verglacé [vɛrglase] *a.* icy (road).

verglas [vɛrgla] *n.m.* (*on roads, etc.*) black ice; *U.S:* glaze; **il y a du v.,** it's icy, slippery.

vergogne [vɛrgɔɲ] *n.f.* (*a*) *A:* shame; (*b*) **sans v.,** shameless(ly).

vergue [vɛrg] *n.f. Nau:* yard; **grande v.,** main yard; **v. de misaine,** foretop yard; **v. de hunier,** topsail yard; **bout de v.,** yardarm.
véridique [veridik] *a.* truthful; *Lit:* veracious.
véridiquement [veridikmɑ̃] *adv.* truthfully; *Lit:* veraciously.
vérifiable [verifjabl̩] *a.* verifiable; (statement, etc.) that can be checked.
vérificateur, -trice [verifikatœr, -tris] **1.** *n.* (*pers.*) verifier, inspector, examiner, checker; **v. de comptes,** auditor. **2.** *a.* **appareil v.,** testing machine; **instrument v.,** gauge, calipers.
vérification [verifikasjɔ̃] *n.f.* verification (of statements, etc.); inspection, examination, checking (of work, etc.); scrutiny (of votes); *Aut: etc:* **v. sur place,** spot check; *Com:* **v. de comptes,** audit(ing).
vérifier [verifje] (*impf. & pr.sub.* **n. vérifiions, v. vérifiez) 1.** *v.tr.* (*a*) to verify; to inspect, examine, check (work, etc.); to overhaul (machinery, etc.); to audit (accounts); to scrutinize (votes); **vérifié et re-vérifié,** checked, double checked and cross checked; **v. des références,** to take up references; (*b*) to verify, prove, confirm (statement, etc.). **2.** (*of statement, etc.*) **se v.,** to prove correct, be confirmed.
vérin [verɛ̃] *n.m. Tchn:* jack; **v. à vis,** screw jack; **v. hydraulique,** hydraulic jack.
véritable [veritabl̩] *a.* **1.** true (story, etc.). **2.** real, genuine; veritable; **un v. ami,** a real, true, friend; **c'est un v. coquin,** he's a downright, an absolute, rogue; **c'est un v. épouvantail,** she's a perfect fright; **c'était une v. surprise,** it was a real surprise.
véritablement [veritabləmɑ̃] *adv.* **1.** truly; veritably. **2.** really; genuinely.
vérité [verite] *n.f.* **1.** truth, verity (of statement, etc.); **dire la v.,** to tell, speak, the truth; **la v. finit toujours par se découvrir,** truth will out; **à la v.,** to tell the truth; as a matter of fact; **en v.,** really, actually. **2.** truth: *Jur:* **la v., toute la v., rien que la v.,** the truth, the whole truth, and nothing but the truth; **c'est la v.,** it's a fact: *F:* **c'est la v. vraie,** it's an actual fact; it's the honest truth; **dire à qn (toutes) ses vérités, ses quatre vérités,** to tell s.o. a few home truths. **3.** sincerity, truthfulness.
verjus [vɛrʒy] *n.m.* verjuice.
vermeil, -eille [vɛrmɛj] **1.** *a.* vermilion, bright red; ruby(-red) (lips); rosy (cheeks). **2.** *n.m.* silver gilt.
vermicelle [vɛrmisɛl] *n.m. Cu:* vermicelli.
vermiculaire [vɛrmikylɛr] *a.* vermicular, worm-shaped; *Anat:* **appendice v.,** vermiform appendix.
vermiculé [vɛrmikyle] *a.* **1.** *Arch:* vermiculated (stonework, etc.). **2.** engine-turned (watchcase, etc.). **3.** *Nat.Hist:* vermiculate (markings).
vermiculure [vɛrmikylyr] *n.f. Arch: etc:* vermiculation.
vermiforme [vɛrmifɔrm] *a.* vermiform.
vermifuge [vɛrmifyʒ] *a. & n.m. Pharm:* vermifuge; **(poudre) v.,** worm powder.
vermillon [vɛrmijɔ̃] **1.** *n.m.* vermilion; cinnabar. **2.** *a.inv. & n.m.* vermilion (colour, *NAm;* color); bright red.
vermine [vɛrmin] *n.f.* **1.** vermin; **couvert, grouillant, de v.,** verminous, crawling with vermin. **2.** *F:* (*pers.*) good-for-nothing; *pl.* vermin.
vermisseau, -eaux [vɛrmiso] *n.m.* small (earth)-worm.
vermouler (se) [səvɛrmule] *v.pr.* (*of wood, etc.*) to become wormeaten.
vermoulu [vɛrmuly] *a.* (*a*) wormeaten (wood, etc.); (*b*) decrepit.
vermoulure [vɛrmulyr] *n.f.* **1.** wormhole (in wood). **2.** worm dust (from wormhole).
vermout(h) [vɛrmut] *n.m.* vermouth.
vernaculaire [vɛrnakylɛr] *a.* vernacular.
vernal, -aux [vɛrnal, -o] *a.* vernal.
verni [vɛrni] *a.* (*a*) varnished; French polished; **cuir v.,** patent leather; **chaussures vernies,** patent(-leather) shoes; *F:* **être v.,** to be lucky, to have a charmed life; (*b*) *Cer:* vitrified (tile, etc.).
vernier [vɛrnje] *n.m.* vernier; sliding gauge.
vernir [vɛrnir] *v.tr.* **1.** to varnish (picture, etc.); to French polish (mahogany); to japan (iron, leather); **v. au tampon,** to French-polish. **2.** *Cer:* to glaze.
vernis [vɛrni] *n.m.* **1.** (*a*) varnish; polish, glaze, gloss; **v. à l'alcool,** spirit varnish; **v. à l'essence,** turpentine varnish; **v. cellulosique,** cellulose varnish; **v. japonais,** japan; **v. au tampon,** French polish; *Cer:* **v. luisant,** glaze; **v. de plomb,** lead glaze; **v. à ongles,** nail varnish, *esp. NAm:* nail polish; (*b*) **v. de politesse,** veneer of politeness. **2.** *Bot:* **v. du Japon,** varnish tree, lacquer tree, tree of heaven.
vernissage [vɛrnisaʒ] *n.m.* (*a*) varnishing; *Cer:* glazing; (*b*) private view, varnishing day (at art exhibition).
vernissé [vɛrnise] *a.* (*a*) *Cer:* glazed; (*b*) glossy.
vernisser [vɛrnise] *v.tr.* to glaze (pottery).
vernisseur, -euse [vɛrnisœr, -øz] *n.* (*pers.*) **1.** varnisher; **v. au tampon,** French polisher. **2.** *Cer:* glazer.
vérole [verɔl] *n.f. Med:* **1. petite v.,** smallpox. **2.** *P:* syphilis; pox.
vérolé [verɔle] *a. P:* syphilitic; **il est v.,** he's got the pox.
véronal [verɔnal] *n.m. Pharm:* veronal; barbitone.
Véronique [verɔnik] **1.** *Pr.n.f.* Veronica. **2.** *n.f. Bot:* speedwell, veronica.
verrat [vɛra] *n.m. Breed:* boar.
verre [vɛr] *n.m.* **1.** glass; **v. blanc,** white glass; **v. à vitres,** window glass; **v. moulé,** pressed glass; **v. à glaces,** plate glass; **v. armé, v. grillagé,** wire(d) glass; **v. de sécurité,** safety glass; **v. trempé,** toughened glass; **v. dépoli,** frosted glass; **v. coloré,** stained glass; **v. filé,** spun glass; **laine de v.,** glass wool; **papier de v.,** glasspaper, sand paper; **coton de v.,** glass fibre, fibreglass, *NAm:* fiberglass; **articles de v.,** glassware; **œil de v.,** glass eye; **peintre sur verre,** artist in stained glass; **sous v.,** under glass; in a glass case. **2.** (*object made of glass*) glass; lens (of spectacles); **il porte des verres,** he wears glasses; **verres de contact,** contact lenses; **v. grossissant,** magnifying glass; **v. de montre,** watch glass; **verres dalles,** pavement lights. **3.** (*a*) **v. (à boire),** (drinking) glass; **v. gobelet,** tumbler; **v. à pied,** stemmed glass; **v. à vin,** wineglass; **v. gradué,** graduated measure; **v. à dents,** tooth glass; (*b*) glass(ful); **v. de vin,** glass of wine; *F:* **boire un petit v.,** to have a drop of spirits; **prendre un v. de trop,** to have one too many; **tempête dans un v. d'eau,** storm in a teacup. **4. v. soluble,** waterglass.
verrerie [vɛr(ə)ri] *n.f.* **1.** glassmaking. **2.** glassworks. **3.** glassware.
verrier [vɛrje] *n.m.* **1.** glassmaker, glass blower; *a.* **peintre v.,** artist in stained glass. **2.** glass rack.
verrière [vɛrjɛr] *n.f.* **1.** glass casing (to protect picture, etc.). **2.** stained glass window. **3.** glass roof, wall (of railway station, etc.). **4.** *Av:* canopy.
verroterie [vɛrɔtri] *n.f.* small glassware; glass beads.
verrou [vɛru] *n.m.* **1.** bolt; bar; **fermer une porte à, au, v.,** to bolt a door; **s'enfermer au v.,** to bolt oneself in; **pousser, mettre, le v.,** to bolt the door; **tirer le(s) verrou(s),** to unbolt the door; **sous les verrous,** under lock and key; in safe custody. **2.** *Sm.a:* breech bolt (of shotgun).
verrouillage [vɛrujaʒ] *n.m.* **1.** bolting, locking. **2.** locking mechanism.
verrouiller [vɛruje] *v.tr.* (*a*) to bolt (door); **v. qn,** to

bolt s.o. in; to lock s.o. up; **se v.,** to bolt oneself in; (*b*) *Sm.a:* to lock (breech).

verrue [vɛry] *n.f.* verruca; wart.

vers[1] [vɛr] *n.m.* verse, line (of poetry); **v. blancs,** blank verse; **v. libres,** free verse; **écrire, faire, des v.,** to write verse, poetry.

vers[2] *prep.* **1.** (*of place*) toward(s), to; *P.N:* (*at marine station*) **v. les bateaux,** to the boats; **façade qui regarde v. la forêt,** façade facing the forest; **v. Pau,** in the neighbourhood, *NAm:* neighborhood, of Pau. **2.** (*of time*) (*a*) toward(s); **v. la fin du siècle,** towards the end of the century; (*b*) about; **venez v. (les) trois heures,** come (at) about three (o'clock).

versant [vɛrsɑ̃] *n.m.* slope, side (of mountain); bank (of canal, etc.); **v. de colline,** hillside.

versatile [vɛrsatil] *a.* **1.** changeable, fickle, inconstant, unstable (disposition, etc.). **2.** *Nat.Hist:* versatile.

versatilité [vɛrsatilite] *n.f.* **1.** changeability, fickleness, inconstancy. **2.** *Nat.Hist:* versatility.

verse [vɛrs] *n.f.* **1.** laying, beating down (of crops by wind, etc.). **2. à v.,** in torrents; **il pleut à v.,** it's pouring (down).

versé [vɛrse] *a.* experienced, practised, skilled, (well) versed **(dans,** in); conversant (with).

Verseau (le) [ləvɛrso] *Pr.n.m. Astr:* Aquarius, the Water Carrier.

versement [vɛrs(ə)mɑ̃] *n.m.* payment; paying in; **en plusieurs versements, par versements échelonnés,** by instalments; **premier v.,** down payment; *Bank:* **bulletin de v.,** paying in slip, *NAm:* deposit slip.

verser [vɛrse] **1.** *v.tr.* (*a*) to overturn, upset (vehicle); (*of wind, etc.*) to lay, beat down (crops); (*b*) to pour (out) (liquid, etc.); to tip (out, in); **v. à boire à qn,** to pour s.o. a drink; **se v. à boire,** to pour oneself a drink; *Lit:* **verser ses chagrins** to pour out one's troubles; (*c*) to shed (tears, light); to spill (blood); (*d*) to pay (in), deposit (money); **v. de l'argent à son compte,** to pay money into one's account; **capitaux versés,** paid-up capital; (*e*) **v. un document au dossier,** to add a document to the file; (*f*) *Mil:* **v. des hommes à un régiment, dans une arme,** to draft, assign, transfer, men to a regiment, to an arm; (*g*) *Mil:* to issue (stores). **2.** *v.i.* (*a*) (*of vehicle*) to overturn; (*of crops*) to be beaten down, laid flat; (*b*) **v. dans . . .,** to fall, drift, into . . ..

verset [vɛrsɛ] *n.m.* verse (of Bible, etc.).

verseur, -euse [vɛrsœr, -øz] **1.** *n.* pourer (of liquids); *Min:* tipper. **2.** *n.f.* **verseuse,** coffeepot. **3.** *a.* **bec v.,** spout.

versicolore [vɛrsikɔlɔr] *a.* particoloured, *NAm:* particolored; variegated; chameleon-like.

versificateur [vɛrsifikatœr] *n.m.* versifier.

versification [vɛrsifikasjɔ̃] *n.f.* versification.

versifier [vɛrsifje] *v.* (*impf. & pr.sub.* **n. versifiions, v. versifiiez)** to versify. **1.** *v.i.* to write verse. **2.** *v.tr.* to put (prose) into verse.

version [vɛrsjɔ̃] *n.f.* **1.** (*a*) translation (into mother tongue); *Sch:* unseen; (*b*) **film en v. originale,** film in the original language; **film américain en v. française,** American film dubbed in French. **2.** version, account (of event, etc.).

verso [vɛrso] *n.m.* verso, back, reverse (of sheet of paper); **voir au v.,** see overleaf.

versoir [vɛrswar] *n.m. Agr:* mould board (of plough); *NAm:* moldboard (of plow).

vert [vɛr] **1.** *a.* (*a*) green; *Aut: etc:* **feu v.,** green light; **légumes verts,** green vegetables, *F:* greens; **plantes vertes,** evergreens; (*b*) green (wood); unripe (fruit); young (wine); **chêne v.,** holm oak, ilex; *Prov:* **ils sont trop verts,** sour grapes; **cuir v.,** rawhide; (*c*) (*of old pers.*) spry; hale and hearty; **verte vieillesse,** green old age; (*d*) spicy, risqué (story, etc.); **en dire de vertes,** to tell spicy, risqué, stories; **il en a vu des vertes et des pas mûres,** he's been through a lot; (*e*) **langue verte,** slang; (*f*) *O:* sharp, tart (reprimand, etc.). **2.** *n.m.* (*a*) green colour, *NAm:* color; **v. bouteille, v. olive, v. cendré,** bottle green, olive green, sage green; **v. d'eau,** sea green; **v. pomme,** apple green; (*b*) **mettre un cheval au v.,** to turn a horse out to grass; *F:* **se mettre au v.,** to go to the country to recuperate; *A: & Lit:* **prendre qn sans v.,** to catch s.o. napping.

vert-de-gris [vɛrdəgri] *n.m.inv.* verdigris.

vert-de-grisé [vɛrdəgrize] *a.* coated with verdigris; *pl. vert-de-grisé(e)s.*

vertébral, -aux [vɛrtebral, -o] *a. Anat:* vertebral; **colonne vertébrale,** vertebral column, spine, backbone.

vertèbre [vɛrtɛbr̥] *n.f. Anat:* vertebra.

vertébré [vɛrtebre] *a. & n.m. Z:* vertebrate.

vertement [vɛrtəmɑ̃] *adv.* **réprimander v. qn,** to reprimand s.o. sharply, severely; *F:* to give s.o. a good telling off.

vertical, -ale, -aux [vɛrtikal, -o] **1.** *a.* vertical; perpendicular; plumb; upright; **éclairage v.,** overhead lighting; *Pol.Ec:* **concentration verticale,** vertical combination, integration. **2.** *n.f.* **verticale,** vertical; **à la verticale,** straight up; **falaise à la verticale,** sheer cliff.

verticalement [vɛrtikalmɑ̃] *adv.* vertically; straight up, down; (*in crossword puzzles*) down.

verticalité [vɛrtikalite] *n.f.* verticality.

verticille [vɛrtisil] *n.m. Bot:* whorl.

vertige [vɛrtiʒ] *n.m.* **1.** dizziness, giddiness; **cela me donne le v.,** it makes me feel dizzy, giddy, makes my head swim; **avoir des vertiges,** to have fits of giddiness, dizzy spells. **2.** vertigo; fear of heights; **avoir facilement le v.,** to have a bad head for heights.

vertigineusement [vɛrtiʒinøzmɑ̃] *adv.* vertiginously, dizzily.

vertigineux, -euse [vɛrtiʒinø, -øz] *a.* vertiginous; dizzy, giddy (height, etc.); breakneck, breathtaking (speed); **hausse vertigineuse des prix,** staggering rise in prices.

vertigo [vɛrtigo] *n.m. Vet:* (blind) staggers.

vertu [vɛrty] *n.f.* **1.** *A:* courage, valour, *NAm:* valor. **2.** virtue; **faire de nécessité v.,** to make a virtue of necessity. **3.** (*a*) *A:* chastity; **femme de petite v.,** woman of easy virtue; (*b*) **ce n'est pas une v.,** she's no saint. **4.** quality, property, virtue (of remedy, etc.); **plantes qui ont la v. de guérir,** plants that have healing properties; **en v. de,** by virtue of; *Jur:* in pursuance of; **en v. de cet arrangement,** under this agreement.

vertueusement [vɛrtɥøzmɑ̃] *adv.* virtuously.

vertueux, -euse [vɛrtɥø, -øz] *a.* **1.** virtuous. **2.** *A:* (*of woman*) chaste.

vertugadin [vɛrtygadɛ̃] *n.m. A.Cost:* farthingale.

verve [vɛrv] *n.f.* animation; verve; *F:* go; **être en v.,** to be in top form; **jouer avec v.,** to give a spirited performance.

verveine [vɛrvɛn] *n.f. Bot:* vervain, verbena.

verveux[1]**, -euse** [vɛrvø, -øz] *a. Lit:* animated, lively, spirited.

verveux[2] *n.m. Fish:* hoop net.

vesce [vɛs] *n.f. Bot:* vetch, tare.

vésical, -aux [vezikal, -o] *a. Anat:* vesical.

vésicant [vezikɑ̃] *a. & n.m. Med:* vesicatory; **gaz v.,** blister gas.

vésicatoire [vezikatwar] *a. & n.m. Med:* vesicatory; **appliquer un v. à qn,** to blister s.o.

vésicule [vezikyl] *n.f.* **1.** *Anat:* vesicle; *Bot:* air cell; *Anat:* **v. biliaire,** gall bladder. **2.** blister (on the skin).

vespasienne [vɛspazjɛn] *n.f.* street urinal.

vesse-de-loup [vɛsdəlu] *n.f. Fung:* puffball; *pl. vesses-de-loup.*

vessie [vesi] *n.f. Anat: etc:* bladder; *Ich:* **v. natatoire,** air bladder, swim bladder; sound; *Med:* **v. à glace,** ice bag; **prendre des vessies pour des lanternes,** to believe that the moon is made of green cheese.
vestale [vɛstal] *n.f. Rom.Ant:* vestal (virgin).
veste [vɛst] *n.f. Cost:* jacket; **v. d'intérieur,** smoking jacket; *F:* **tomber la v.,** to take off one's jacket; *F:* **retourner sa v.,** to be a turncoat; *F:* **remporter une v.,** to fail, come a cropper.
vestiaire [vɛstjɛr] *n.m.* **1.** (*a*) (*in theatre, etc.*) cloakroom, *NAm:* checkroom; *F:* **mon v., s'il vous plaît,** could I have my (hat and) coat, please? *Th: F:* (*showing dislike of performance*) **au v.!** off! off! (*b*) *Sp: etc:* changing room, locker room; *Jur:* robing room. **2.** (hat and) coat stand, rack; (*in factory, etc.*) locker.
vestibule [vɛstibyl] *n.m.* vestibule, (entrance) hall, lobby.
vestige [vɛstiʒ] *n.m.* vestige, remains, trace (of former habitations, etc.); **derniers vestiges de...,** last remnants of...; **vestiges du passé,** relics of the past.
vestimentaire [vɛstimɑ̃tɛr] *a.* clothing (trade).
veston [vɛstɔ̃] *n.m. Cost:* (man's) jacket; *Nau:* monkey jacket; **complet v.,** lounge suit.
Vésuve [vezyv] *Pr.n.m. Geog:* Vesuvius.
vêtement [vɛtmɑ̃] *n.m.* garment; coat; *pl.* clothes, clothing; **industrie du v.,** clothing trade; **tissus pour vêtements,** dress materials; **vêtements de dessous,** underwear, underclothes, underclothing; **vêtements de plage, de pluie,** beachwear; rainwear; *Ecc:* **vêtements sacerdotaux,** vestments.
vétéran [veterɑ̃] *n.m. Mil: etc:* veteran; old campaigner; *Pol:* elder statesman.
vétérinaire [veterinɛr] **1.** *a.* veterinary. **2.** *n.* veterinary surgeon, vet, *NAm:* veterinarian.
vétille [vetij] *n.f.* bagatelle, trifle; mere nothing; *pl.* trivia.
vétilleux, -euse [vetijø, -øz] *a. Lit:* captious, finicky, fastidious.
vêtir [vetir] *v.* (*pr.p* **vêtant;** *p.p.* **vêtu;** *pr.ind.* **je vêts, n. vêtons;** *impf.* **je vêtais;** *p.h.* **je vêtis;** *fu.* **je vêtirai) 1.** *v.tr. Lit:* (*a*) to clothe; to dress (s.o.) **(de,** in); **tout de noir vêtu,** clad all in black; (*b*) to put on, don (garment). **2. se v.,** to dress (oneself) **(de,** in).
veto [veto] *n.m.* veto; **mettre son v. à qch.,** to veto sth.
vêtu [vety] *a.* (*a*) (*of pers.*) dressed; **être v. chaudement,** to be warmly dressed; **professeurs vêtus de leurs toges,** professors wearing, in, their gowns; **à demi-v.,** half dressed; (*b*) *Lit:* **mur v. de lierre,** ivy-clad wall.
vétuste [vetyst] *a.* decayed, decrepit.
vétusté [vetyste] *n.f.* decay, decrepitude.
veuf, veuve [vœf, vœv] **1.** *a.* (*a*) widowed (man, woman); (*b*) *Lit:* **v. de qch.,** bereft of sth. **2.** (*a*) *n.* widower, *f.* widow; (*b*) *n.f. F: A:* **la Veuve,** the guillotine.
veule [vøl] *a.* weak, feeble, flabby (person, etc.).
veulerie [vølri] *n.f.* inertia, listlessness.
veuvage [vœvaʒ] *n.m.* widowhood.
vexant [vɛksɑ̃] *a.* (*a*) vexing, provoking, annoying; (*b*) hurtful (remark, etc.).
vexation [vɛksasjɔ̃] *n.f.* **1.** *A:* vexation, harassing; persecuting. **2.** mortification.
vexatoire [vɛksatwar] *a.* vexatious.
vexer [vɛkse] **1.** *v.tr.* (*a*) *A:* to harass, persecute; (*b*) to annoy, offend, upset, hurt (s.o.); to vex. **2. se v. de qch.,** to be upset, offended, annoyed, vexed, about sth.
via [vja] *prep.* via, by way of.
viabilisé [vjabilize] *a. Adm:* **terrain v.,** building site on which roads have been made (and public services connected).
viabilité¹ [vjabilite] *n.f.* viability (of infant, plan, etc.).
viabilité² *n.f.* **1.** practicability. **2.** *Const:* development (of site ready for building).
viable [vjabl̩] *a.* viable (infant, plan, etc.).
viaduc [vjadyk] *n.m.* viaduct.
viager, -ère [vjaʒe, -ɛr] **1.** *a.* for life; **rente viagère,** life annuity. **2.** *n.m.* life interest; **placer son argent en v.,** to invest one's money in, buy, an annuity.
viande [vjɑ̃d] *n.f.* **1.** *A:* food, viands; meat. **2. v. (de boucherie),** (butcher's) meat; **v. de cheval,** horsemeat. **3.** *P:* **amène ta v.!** come on! move your carcass!
viatique [vjatik] *n.m.* viaticum. **1.** money, provisions, for a journey. **2.** *Ecc:* last sacrament.
vibrant [vibrɑ̃] *a.* **1.** vibrating; vibrant. **2.** (*a*) resonant (voice); (*b*) rousing, stirring (speech); vibrant (personality, etc.); (*of pers.*) **v. et réceptif,** eager and receptive.
vibraphone [vibrafɔn] *n.m. Mus:* vibraphone.
vibrateur [vibratœr] *n.m. Elcs: etc:* vibrator.
vibration [vibrasjɔ̃] *n.f.* **1.** vibration. **2.** resonance (of voice).
vibratoire [vibratwar] *a.* vibratory.
vibrer [vibre] *v.i.* to vibrate; **faire v. le cœur de qn,** to stir, thrill, s.o., s.o.'s heart.
vibreur [vibrœr] *n.m. El:* vibrator; make-and-break; buzzer.
vibrion [vibrijɔ̃] *n.m. Bac:* vibrio(n); *Med:* **v. septique,** gas bacillus.
vibromasseur [vibrɔmasœr] *n.m.* (electric) vibrator (for massage).
vicaire [vikɛr] *n.m. Ecc:* (*a*) **v. apostolique,** vicar apostolic; **grand v., v. général,** vicar-general; (*b*) *Ch. of Eng:* curate; *R.C.Ch:* (assistant) priest.
vicariat [vikarja] *n.m. Ecc:* curacy.
vice [vis] *n.m.* **1.** vice; (*a*) depravity, corruption; (*b*) **il a tous les vices,** he has all the vices. **2.** fault, defect, blemish, flaw, imperfection; *Vet: etc:* **v. de conformation,** malformation; physical defect; **v. de prononciation,** faulty pronunciation; *Jur:* **v. de forme,** flaw (in a deed, etc.); faulty drafting; **v. propre,** inherent defect.
vice-amiral [visamiral] *n.m.* vice admiral; *pl. vice-amiraux.*
vice-chancelier [visʃɑ̃səlje] *n.m.* vice chancellor; *pl. vice-chanceliers.*
vice-consul [viskɔ̃syl] *n.m.* vice consul; *pl. vice-consuls.*
vice-consulat [viskɔ̃syla] *n.m.* vice consulate; *pl. vice-consulats.*
vice-gérant, -ante [visʒerɑ̃, -ɑ̃t] *n.* deputy manager, manageress; *pl. vice-gérant(e)s.*
vicennal, -aux [visenal, -o] *a.* vicennial.
vice-présidence [visprezidɑ̃s] *n.f.* (*a*) vice presidency; (*b*) vice chairmanship; *pl. vice-présidences.*
vice-président, -ente [visprezidɑ̃, -ɑ̃t] *n.* (*a*) vice president; (*b*) vice chairman; *pl. vice-président(e)s.*
vice-roi [visrwa] *n.m.* viceroy; *pl. vice-rois.*
vice versa [visevɛrsa] *Lt.adv.phr.* vice versa; conversely.
vichy [viʃi] *n.m.* (glass of) Vichy water.
viciateur, -trice [visjatœr, -tris] *a.* vitiating, contaminating.
viciation [visjasjɔ̃] *n.f.* vitiation; corruption (of morals, etc.); pollution, contamination, tainting (of the air, etc.); poverty (of blood).
vicié [visje] *a.* vitiated, corrupt; tainted (food, etc.); poor, thin (blood); **air v.,** (i) polluted, (ii) stale, foul, air.
vicier [visje] *v.tr.* (*impf.* & *pr.sub.* **n. viciions, v. viciiez) 1.** to vitiate, corrupt, spoil; to pollute, contaminate, taint (air). **2.** *Jur:* to vitiate, invalidate (deed).

vicieux, -ieuse [visjø, -jøz] *a.* **1.** depraved, corrupt (person). **2.** defective, faulty, imperfect; wrong, incorrect (pronunciation); **cercle v.,** vicious circle. **3.** tricky, restive, bad-tempered (horse).
vicinal, -aux [visinal, -o] *a.* **chemin v.,** local road.
vicissitude [visisityd] *n.f.* vicissitude (of fortune, etc.); **les vicissitudes de la vie,** the ups and downs of life.
vicomte [vikɔ̃t] *n.m.* viscount.
vicomté [vikɔ̃te] *n.f.* **1.** viscountcy. **2.** (*land*) viscounty.
vicomtesse [vikɔ̃tɛs] *n.f.* viscountess.
victime [viktim] *n.f.* **1.** victim (of sacrifice). **2.** victim, sufferer; **être la v. de qn,** to be the victim of s.o.; **j'ai été (la) v. d'un escroc,** I've been had by a conman; **les victimes du désastre,** the victims of the disaster; the casualties; **être (la) v. d'une illusion,** to labour, *NAm:* labor, under an illusion; **j'ai été v. de la grippe,** I've been down with flu, *NAm:* grippe.
victoire [viktwar] **1.** *n.f.* victory; *Sp:* win; **remporter la v.,** to gain a, the, victory **(sur,** over); to carry, win, the day; **chanter, crier, v.,** to crow, triumph; **v. à la Pyrrhus,** Pyrrhic victory. **2.** *Pr.n.f.* Victoria.
Victoria [viktɔrja] **1.** *Pr.n.f.* Victoria. **2.** *n.f. Veh:* victoria.
victorien, -ienne [viktɔrjɛ̃, -jɛn] *a.* Victorian.
victorieusement [viktɔrjøzmɑ̃] *adv.* victoriously.
victorieux, -ieuse [viktɔrjø, -jøz] *a.* victorious; triumphant (air); **être v.,** to win the day.
victuailles [viktɥaj] *n.f.pl.* food.
vidage [vidaʒ] *n.m.* (*a*) emptying; gutting, cleaning (of fish); drawing (of fowl); (*b*) *F:* throwing out, chucking out (from pub, etc.).
vidange [vidɑ̃ʒ] *n.f.* **1.** (*a*) draining, emptying (of cesspools, etc.); (*b*) draining, emptying (of sump, etc.); blowing off (of boiler); *Aut:* oil change; **faire la v.,** to change the oil; **bouchon de v.,** *Mch:* (i) sump plug; (ii) draining plug (of radiator); **robinet de v.,** draincock; **tuyau de v.,** wastepipe; **tonneau en v.,** broached cask. **2.** *usu. pl.* night soil; sewage.
vidanger [vidɑ̃ʒe] *v.tr.* **(je vidangeai(s); n. vidangeons)** to empty (cesspool, radiator, etc.); to drain (engine sump, etc.); to blow off (boiler).
vidangeur [vidɑ̃ʒœr] *n.m.* cesspit clearer, emptier.
vide [vid] **1.** *a.* empty; blank (space in document, etc.); unoccupied, vacant (seat); **bouteilles vides,** empty bottles, *Com:* empties; **revenir les mains vides,** to return empty-handed; **j'ai la tête v.,** my mind's a blank; **v. de sens,** devoid of meaning; meaningless; **phrases vides,** empty words. **2.** *n.m.* (*a*) empty space; gap; cavity; void; blank (in document); **combler les vides,** to fill (up) the gaps; (*b*) *Ph:* vacuum; **faire le v.,** to create a vacuum; **nettoyage par le v.,** vacuum cleaning; **emballé sous v.,** vacuum-packed; (*c*) emptiness; **taper dans le v.,** to (hit out and) miss the mark; **regarder dans le v.,** to stare into space; **camion revenant à v.,** lorry, truck, returning empty; **poids à v.,** unladen weight; (*of machine*) **marcher à v.,** to run light, without load; *Mus:* **corde à v.,** open string.
vidé [vide] *a.* (*a*) (*of fish*) gutted; (*of poultry*) drawn; (*b*) *F:* (*of pers.*) exhausted, worn out; **c'est un homme v.,** he's played out.
vidéo [video] *a. & n.f.inv. Elcs:* video.
vidéocassette [videɔkasɛt] *n.f. Elcs:* videocassette.
vidéodisque [videɔdisk] *n.m. Elcs:* videodisc, *NAm:* videodisk.
vidéophone [videɔfɔn] *n.m. Elcs:* videophone.
vide-ordures [vidɔrdyr] *n.m.inv.* rubbish chute.
vide-poches [vidpɔʃ] *n.m.inv.* **1.** *Furn:* (dressing table) tidy; pin tray. **2.** *Aut:* glove compartment.
vide-pomme [vidpɔm] *n.m.* apple corer; *pl. vide-pommes.*
vider [vide] **1.** *v.tr.* (*a*) to empty; to clear out (room, drawer); to drain (cask, one's glass, etc.); to drain off (pond); to blow off (boilers); to blow (an egg); **videz vos verres!** drink up! **v. les lieux,** to vacate the premises; to quit; **le juge a ordonné de faire v. la salle,** the judge ordered the court to be cleared; *F:* **v. qn,** to exhaust s.o., wear s.o. out; *F:* **v. son sac,** to get sth. off one's chest; (*b*) (*of horse*) to throw (rider); *F:* to throw (s.o.) out (of a bar, etc.); to sack (s.o.); **v. les arçons, les étriers,** to be thrown (from one's horse); **se faire v.,** (i) *Equit:* to be thrown; (ii) *F:* to be sent out (of the room); to be chucked out (of bar, etc.); (iii) *F:* to get the sack; (*c*) to eviscerate (carcass); to gut, clean (fish); to draw (fowl); to core (apple); to stone, *NAm:* pit (fruit); (*d*) to settle (question); **v. une querelle,** (i) to settle difference; (ii) to fight it out, have it out. **2. se v.,** to (become) empty.
vide-tasses [vidtas] *n.m.inv.* slop basin.
videur, -euse [vidœr, -øz] *n.* emptier; *F:* (*in club, etc.*) chucker-out, bouncer.
vie [vi] *n.f.* life. **1. v. végétative, animale,** vegetable, animal, life; **être en v.,** to be alive; **donner la v. à un enfant,** to give birth to a child; **avoir la v. dure,** to be hard to kill; to die hard; **il est entre la v. et la mort,** he is (hovering) between life and death; **question de v. ou de mort,** question of life and death; **il y va de la v.,** it's a case of life and death; **sauver la v. à qn,** to save s.o.'s life; **rappeler qn à la v.,** to bring s.o. back to life; **sans v.,** lifeless; **donner de la v. à une conversation, une réunion,** to liven up, enliven, a conversation, a meeting; **elle déborde de v.,** she's full of life; **musique pleine de v.,** lively, animated, music. **2.** (*a*) lifetime; **pour la v.,** for life; **une fois dans la v.,** once in a lifetime; **plus tard dans la v.,** later (on) in life; **de toute ma v. je n'ai jamais entendu chose pareille!** I've never heard such a thing in all my life! **jamais de la v.!** never! **pension à v., la v. durant,** life pension; **nommé à v.,** appointed for life; (*b*) biography; **écrire la v. de qn,** to write s.o.'s life (story). **3.** existence; way of life, of living; life style; **ainsi va la v.! c'est la v.!** such is life! **je connais la v.,** I've seen something of life; **v. sédentaire,** sedentary life; **changer de v.,** to mend one's ways, turn over a new leaf; **rendre la v. dure à qn,** to make life hard, a misery, for s.o.; **la v. américaine,** the American way of life; **la v. nocturne,** night life; **femme de mauvaise v.,** loose woman; *F:* **faire la v.,** (i) to lead a riotous life; (ii) to kick up a fuss, a row. **4.** living, livelihood; **niveau de v.,** standard of living; **(coût de la) v.,** cost of living; **indemnité de v. chère, de cherté de v.,** cost of living allowance; **gagner sa v.,** to earn one's living; **comment gagne-t-il sa v.?** what does he do for a living?
vieil, vieille *see* VIEUX.
vieillard [vjɛjar] *n.m.* (*f. usu.* **vieille,** *q.v. under* VIEUX) old man; **les vieillards,** old people; the elderly, the aged.
vieillerie [vjɛjri] *n.f. usu. pl.* old things; oldfashioned, out-of-date, things; outdated ideas.
vieillesse [vjɛjɛs] *n.f.* (old) age; **bâton de v.,** support, prop, of old age; **la v.,** old people; the elderly, the aged.
vieilli [vjeji] *a.* (*a*) (grown) old; aged; (*b*) obsolescent (word, etc.); oldfashioned, out-of-date (style, etc.).
vieillir [vjejir] **1.** *v.i.* (*a*) to grow old; (*b*) to age (in appearance); **il a vieilli, il est vieilli,** he looks older; (*c*) (*of custom, word, etc.*) to become obsolete, antiquated, out of date; **ce mot a vieilli,** this word is obsolescent; (*d*) (*of wine, cheese, etc.*) to mature. **2.** *v.tr.* (*a*) to age (s.o.); to make (s.o.) look older; **ce chapeau la vieillit,** that hat makes her look old(er); (*b*) to distress (furniture). **3. se v.** (*a*) to make oneself look old(er); (*b*) to pretend to be older (than one is).
vieillissant [vjejisɑ̃] *a.* growing old; ageing.

vieillissement [vjejismɑ̃] *n.m.* **1.** (*a*) ageing, growing old; (*b*) (*of word, etc.*) becoming obsolete; obsolescence. **2.** ageing, maturing (of cheese, wine, etc.); distressing (of furniture).

vieillot, -otte [vjɛjo, -ɔt] *a.* **1.** *A:* oldish. **2.** antiquated, oldfashioned.

vielle [vjɛl] *n.f. Mus:* vielle, hurdy-gurdy.

Vienne [vjɛn] *Pr.n.f. Geog:* Vienna.

viennois, -oise [vjɛnwa, -waz] *a. & n. Geog:* Viennese.

vierge [vjɛrʒ] **1.** *n.f.* (*a*) virgin; **la (Sainte) V.**, the Blessed Virgin (Mary); **chapelle de la V.**, Lady chapel; (*b*) *Astr:* **la V.**, Virgo. **2.** *a.* (*a*) (*of pers.*) virgin, virginal; virgin (soil, forest, oil, etc.); (*b*) blank (page, tape, etc.); pure (white, etc.); unexposed (plate); **réputation v.**, untarnished reputation.

Vietnam (le) [ləvjɛtnam] *Pr.n.m. Geog:* Vietnam.

vietnamien, -ienne [vjɛtnamjɛ̃, -ɛn] *a. & n. Geog:* Vietnamese.

vieux, vieil, *f.* **vieille** [vjø, vjɛj] *a.* (*the form* **vieil** *is used before masc. nouns beginning with a vowel or* **h** *mute, but* **vieux** *also occurs in this position*). **1.** (*of pers.*) old; (*a*) (*in years*) **se faire v.**, (i) to be getting old, to be getting on (in years); (ii) to make oneself out to be older than one is; **vivre v.**, to live to be old, to a ripe old age; *n.* **un v., une vieille,** an old man, an old woman; **les v.**, old people; the old, elderly, aged; *F:* **mes v.**, my parents; *F:* **eh bien, mon v.!** well (then), old man! old chap! **viens, ma vieille!** come on, old girl! *adv.* **elle s'habille plus v. que son âge,** she dresses too old for her age; (*b*) longstanding (friendship, etc.); **un vieil ami,** an old friend, a friend of long standing; **il est v. dans ce métier,** he's an old hand at this job; **vieille fille,** old maid; spinster; *n. F:* **un v. de la vieille** (*i.e.* **de la vieille garde de Napoléon**), one of the old guard; a veteran; **un homme de la vieille école,** one of the old school. **2.** (*of thgs*) (*a*) old, ancient (building, etc.); stale (bread, news, etc.); worn, shabby (hat, etc.); **v. papiers,** waste paper; **v. comme le Pont-Neuf, comme Hérode,** as old as the hills; **le bon v. temps,** the good old days; **c'est une vieille histoire,** it's an old story; *adj.phr.inv.* **v. jeu,** oldfashioned, antiquated, out of date; **ça, c'est v. jeu,** that's old hat; (*b*) *inv.* **des rubans vieil or,** old-gold ribbons. **3.** *n.f. Ich:* **vieille,** wrasse, seawife.

vif, vive¹ [vif, viv] **1.** *a.* (*a*) alive, living; **être brûlé v.**, to be burnt alive; **prendre de vive force,** to take by storm, by force; **de vive voix,** by word of mouth; viva voce; **haie vive,** quickset hedge; **eau vive,** running water, spring water; **marée de vive eau,** spring tide; **roc v.**, live, living, rock; solid rock; **chaux vive,** quicklime; (*b*) lively, animated; fast, brisk (action, discussion, etc.); brisk, hot (fire); (*of pers.*) vivacious; **vive allure, allure vive,** brisk pace; **être v., avoir l'humeur un peu vive,** to be quick tempered; **il y avait un échange de paroles vives,** words ran high; **v. à répondre,** quick to reply; smart, alert, quick, in answering; **avec mes plus vives félicitations,** with my warmest congratulations; **cheval v.**, high-spirited horse; (*c*) sharp (wind, reprimand, etc.); acute (pain, etc.); **l'air est v.**, there's a nip in the air; **arête vive,** sharp edge; (*d*) keen, quick (wit, etc.); vivid (imagination, etc.); **v. plaisir,** keen pleasure; **vive satisfaction,** great satisfaction; **écouter avec un v. intérêt,** to listen with deep interest; (*e*) bright, vivid, intense (colour, *NAm:* color); (*of complexion*) **couleur vive,** high colour. **2.** *n.m. Jur:* living person; **donation entre vifs,** donation inter vivos. **3.** *n.m.* (*a*) **peindre sur le v.**, to paint from life; (*b*) living flesh; quick; **blessé, piqué, au v.**, cut, stung, to the quick; **j'ai les nerfs à v.**, my nerves are on edge; **entrer dans le v. de la question,** to get to the heart of the matter; (*c*) **pêcher au v.**, to fish with live bait.

vif-argent [vifarʒɑ̃] *n.m.* (*a*) *A:* quicksilver, mercury; (*b*) **il a du v.-a. dans les veines,** he's never still (for a minute).

vigie [viʒi] *n.f. Nau:* (*a*) lookout; **être de v., en v.,** to be on the lookout; (*b*) lookout (man); (*c*) watchtower; *Rail:* (observation) box (on van); **v. de signaux,** signal cabin; **v. de frein,** brake cabin.

vigilance [viʒilɑ̃s] *n.f.* vigilance; watchfulness; **surprendre la v. de qn,** to catch s.o. napping.

vigilant [viʒilɑ̃] *a.* vigilant, watchful, alert.

vigile¹ [viʒil] *n.f. Ecc:* vigil (of feast day).

vigile² *n.m.* (night)watchman.

vigne [viɲ] *n.f.* **1.** (*a*) vine; **feuille de v.**, vine-leaf; (*b*) vineyard; **être dans les vignes du Seigneur,** to be drunk, in one's cups. **2.** *Bot:* **v. vierge,** Virginian creeper.

vigneau, -eaux [viɲo] *n.m. Moll:* periwinkle.

vigneron, -onne [viɲrɔ̃, -ɔn] *n.* vine grower; wine grower.

vignette [viɲɛt] *n.f.* (*a*) *Art:* vignette; ornamental border; *Typ: A:* text illustration; (*b*) *Com:* label, ticket (on packets of tobacco, etc.); *Aut:* = (road) tax disc.

vignettiste [viɲetist] *n. Typ: A:* vignettist.

vignoble [viɲɔbl̩] **1.** *n.m.* vineyard. **2.** *a.* **région v.**, wine region.

vignot [viɲo] *n.m. Moll:* periwinkle.

vigogne [vigɔɲ] *n.f.* (*a*) *Z:* vicuña, vicuna; (*b*) *Tex:* vicuña (wool, cloth).

vigoureusement [vigurøzmɑ̃] *adv.* vigorously.

vigoureux, -euse [vigurø, -øz] *a.* vigorous, strong, sturdy; robust; (*of pers.*) hale, hearty; **coup v.**, powerful blow; **faire une opposition vigoureuse à un projet,** to offer firm, strenuous, opposition to a plan.

vigueur [vigœr] *n.f.* **1.** vigour, *NAm:* vigor; strength; **donner de la v. à qn,** to invigorate s.o., brace s.o. up; **sans v.**, (i) (*of pers.*) exhausted, washed out; (ii) (*of style, etc.*) flat, lifeless; **avec v.**, vigorously. **2.** (*of decree, etc.*) **en v.**, in force; **entrer en v.**, to come into effect, into operation; **cesser d'être en v.**, to lapse; **mettre un règlement en v.**, to enforce a regulation.

Viking [vikiŋ] *a. & n.m. Hist:* Viking.

vil [vil] *a.* **1.** (*a*) *A:* cheap (goods, etc.); (*b*) **vendre qch. à v. prix,** to sell sth. at a low price, *F:* dirt cheap. **2.** (*a*) *A:* low(ly) (origin, condition, etc.); (*b*) base (metal). **3.** *A: & Lit:* vile, base (person, motive, etc.); **vile calomnie,** foul calumny.

vilain, -aine [vilɛ̃, -ɛn] **1.** *n.* (*a*) *Hist:* villein; (*b*) *F:* **oh, le v.! la vilaine!** you naughty boy! you naughty girl! you little villain! (*c*) *F:* **il y aura du v.**, there's going to be trouble; **il y a du v. dans l'air,** there's something (nasty) brewing. **2.** *a.* (*a*) nasty, bad, unpleasant; **c'est un v. monsieur,** he's a nasty piece of work; **ce sont de vilaines gens,** they're a bad lot; **v. tour,** mean, dirty, trick; **c'est une vilaine histoire,** it's not a nice story; it's an ugly story; **une vilaine blessure,** a nasty, an ugly, wound; (*b*) ugly; shabby (hat, etc.); sordid, wretched (street, etc.).

vilainement [vilɛnmɑ̃] *adv.* in an unpleasant, a nasty, way; badly.

vilebrequin [vilbrəkɛ̃] *n.m.* **1.** *Tls:* (i) (bit) brace; (ii) brace and bit; **v. à cliquet,** ratchet brace. **2.** *Mch:* crankshaft.

vilement [vilmɑ̃] *adv. O:* vilely, basely; dishonestly.

vilenie [vil(ə)ni] *n.f.* (*a*) *Lit:* mean, vile, low, action; foul deed; (*b*) vileness, baseness.

villa [vila] *n.f.* (*a*) *Rom.Ant: etc:* villa; (*b*) house (in a residential area).

village [vilaʒ] *n.m.* village; **il est bien de son v.**, you can tell that he comes from the country; **v. de toile,** camp site.

villageois, -oise [vilaʒwa, -waz] **1.** *n.* villager;

countryman, *f.* countrywoman. **2.** *a.* rustic; **habitudes villageoises,** country, village, customs.

ville [vil] *n.f.* town; city; **grande v.,** city; **v. d'eaux,** spa; **v. champignon,** mushroom town; boom town; **v. satellite,** satellite town; **la V. éternelle,** the Eternal City, Rome; **en v.,** in (the) town; in the town, city, centre; *U.S:* downtown; **dîner en v.,** to dine out; *Corr:* (*on envelope*) **en v.,** local; **aller à la v.,** to go into town, *U.S:* to go downtown; **habiter à la v.,** to live in a town (as opposed to the country); **tenue de v.,** (i) town clothes; (ii) (*on invitation*) lounge suit; **hôtel de v.,** town hall, city hall.

villégiature [vileʒjatyr] *n.f.* (*a*) holiday, *NAm:* vacation; **être en v.,** to be on holiday, *NAm:* on vacation; (*b*) (holiday) resort.

villeux, -euse [vilø, -øz] *a. Nat.Hist:* villous, villose, hairy.

villosité [vilozite] *n.f.* (*a*) hairiness; (*b*) *Anat: etc:* villosity; villus.

vin [vɛ̃] *n.m.* wine; **les grands vins,** vintage wines; **v. ordinaire, v. de table,** table wine, dinner wine; **v. de Bordeaux,** claret; **v. du Rhin,** hock; **v. de Bourgogne,** burgundy; **v. rosé,** rosé wine; **v. mousseux,** sparkling wine; **marchand de v.,** (i) *A:* = publican; (ii) retail wine merchant; **négociant en vins,** (wholesale) wine merchant; **offrir un v. d'honneur à qn,** to hold a reception in honour, *NAm:* honor, of s.o.; **être pris de v.,** to be the worse for drink; **avoir le v. gai, mauvais, triste,** to be merry, quarrelsome, maudlin, in one's cups; **entre deux vins,** (somewhat) drunk, tight; *Prov:* **le v. est tiré, il faut le boire,** there's no turning back now; you've made your bed and you must lie in it; **mettre de l'eau dans son v.,** (i) to water one's wine; (ii) to cut down expenses; to draw in one's horns.

vinaigre [vinɛgr̥] *n.m.* **1.** vinegar; **v. de vin,** wine vinegar; **v. à l'estragon,** tarragon vinegar; **on ne prend pas les mouches avec du v.,** harsh treatment pays no dividends. **2.** *Games:* **donner du v.,** to turn (the skipping rope) quickly; *F:* **faire v.,** to hurry, get a move on.

vinaigrer [vinegre] *v.tr.* to season with vinegar.

vinaigrerie [vinɛgrəri] *n.f.* **1.** vinegar factory. **2.** (*a*) vinegar making; (*b*) vinegar trade.

vinaigrette [vinɛgrɛt] *n.f.* **1.** *Cu:* vinaigrette, French dressing. **2.** *A:* two-wheeled sedan.

vinaigrier [vinɛgrije] *n.m.* **1.** vinegar (i) manufacturer, (ii) merchant. **2.** vinegar bottle, cruet.

vinasse [vinas] *n.f. F:* inferior wine; plonk.

vindicatif, -ive [vɛ̃dikatif, -iv] *a.* vindictive, spiteful, revengeful.

vindicte [vɛ̃dikt] *n.f. Jur:* prosecution (of crime); **v. publique,** vindication of public morality.

vineux, -euse [vinø, -øz] *a.* **1.** (*of wine*) full-bodied. **2.** (*a*) vinous (taste); wine-flavoured, *NAm:* -flavored (peach, etc.); (*b*) wine-coloured, *NAm:* -colored; *F:* **nez v.,** ruby, winy, bibulous, nose.

vingt [vɛ̃] *num.a.inv. & n.m.inv.* twenty; **v. et un** [vɛ̃teœ̃], twenty-one; *Cards:* vingt-et-un; pontoon; *esp. NAm:* blackjack; **v.-deux** [vɛ̃tdø], twenty-two; *P:* **v.-deux!** watch it! look out! **le v. juin** [ləvɛ̃ʒɥɛ̃], (on) the twentieth of June; **les années v.,** the twenties (1920-1929); **il n'a pas encore v. ans,** he's not twenty yet, he's still in his teens; **les moins de v. ans,** teenagers; **je te l'ai dit v. fois,** I've told you a hundred times, time and time again (*as a card.a.* **v.** *takes an s when multiplied: see* QUATRE-VINGTS).

vingtaine [vɛ̃tɛn] *n.f.* (about) twenty; a score; **une v. de gens,** twenty or so people.

vingtième [vɛ̃tjɛm] **1.** *num.a. & n.* twentieth. **2.** *n.m.* twentieth (part).

vingtièmement [vɛ̃tjɛmmɑ̃] *adv.* in the twentieth place.

vinicole [vinikɔl] *a.* wine(-growing) (area, etc.).

vinifère [vinifɛr] *a.* wine-producing (soil, etc.).

Vintimille [vɛ̃timij] *Pr.n. Geog:* Ventimiglia.

vinyle [vinil] *n.m. Ch:* vinyl.

viol [vjɔl] *n.m.* **1.** *Jur:* rape. **2.** violation (of a sanctuary, etc.).

violacé [vjɔlase] **1.** *a.* purplish-blue; (*of pers.*) **prendre un teint v.,** to go blue (with cold). **2.** *n.f.pl. Bot:* **violacées,** Violaceae.

violacer (se) [(sə)vjɔlase] *v.tr. & pr.* **(je violaçai(s); n. violaçons)** to turn blue, purplish.

violateur, -trice [vjɔlatœr, -tris] *n.* violator; transgressor (of laws, etc.).

violation [vjɔlasjɔ̃] *n.f.* violation, infringement, transgression, breach (of law, etc.); desecration (of grave); **v. des règles,** breaking of rules; **agir en v. d'une règle,** to act in contravention of a rule; **v. de domicile,** illegal entry.

violâtre [vjɔlɑtr̥] *a.* purplish.

viole [vjɔl] *n.f. Mus:* viol; **v. d'amour,** viol(a) d'amore.

violemment [vjɔlamɑ̃] *adv.* violently.

violence [vjɔlɑ̃s] *n.f.* violence, force; fierceness (of encounter, etc.); **faire v. à qn, qch.,** to do violence to s.o., sth.; **se faire v.,** to do violence to one's feelings; to go against one's natural instincts; *O:* **faire v. à une femme,** to violate, rape, a woman.

violent [vjɔlɑ̃] *a.* violent; high (wind); fierce (encounter); drastic (measures, etc.); pungent (smell); **mourir de mort violente,** to die a violent death; *F:* **c'est par trop v.!** it really is too much! that really is the limit!

violenter [vjɔlɑ̃te] *v.tr.* **1.** *Lit:* to do violence to (s.o., sth.). **2.** to rape (a woman).

violer [vjɔle] *v.tr.* **1.** to violate; to transgress, infringe (law); to break (law, treaty, faith); **v. une sépulture,** to desecrate a grave; **v. le domicile de qn,** to break into s.o.'s house. **2.** to rape (a woman).

violet, -ette[1] [vjɔlɛ, -ɛt] *a.* **1.** violet, purple (-coloured, *NAm:* -colored). **2.** *n.m.* (the colour, *NAm:* color) violet, purple.

violette[2] [vjɔlɛt] *n.f. Bot:* violet; **v. de Parme,** Parma violet.

violeur [vjɔlœr] *n.m.* rapist.

violier [vjɔlje] *n.m. Bot:* **1.** stock. **2. v. jaune,** wallflower.

violine [vjɔlin] *a.* purple-violet.

violon [vjɔlɔ̃] *n.m.* **1.** *Mus:* (*a*) violin; **c'est son v. d'Ingres,** it's his hobby; *F:* **accordez vos violons,** make sure you all tell the same story; *F:* **c'est comme si on pissait dans un v.,** it's a waste of breath; it's like talking to a brick wall; (*b*) violin (player); **premier v.,** (i) first violin; (ii) leader (of the orchestra); *Fig:* **payer les violons,** to pay the piper. **2.** *P:* **le v.,** the cells, the lockup; **au v.,** in the lockup. **3. (poulie à) v.,** fiddle block. **4.** *Nau:* **violons de mer,** fiddles (for the tables).

violoncelle [vjɔlɔ̃sɛl] *n.m. Mus:* (*a*) violoncello, cello; (*b*) violoncellist, cello (player), cellist.

violoncelliste [vjɔlɔ̃selist] *n.* violoncellist, cellist.

violoneux [vjɔlɔnø] *n.m.* fiddler.

violoniste [vjɔlɔnist] *n.* violinist.

viorne [vjɔrn] *n.f. Bot:* viburnum.

vipère [vipɛr] *n.f.* viper, adder; **v. aspic,** asp; **v. heurtante,** puff adder; *Fig:* **langue de v.,** spiteful, viperish, venomous, tongue.

vipereau, -eaux [vipro] *n.m.* young viper.

vipérin, -ine [viperɛ̃, -in] **1.** *a.* viperine. **2.** *n.f.* **vipérine;** (*a*) *Bot:* viper's bugloss; (*b*) *Rept:* viperine snake.

virage [viraʒ] *n.m.* **1.** turning (round); turn; sweeping round, cornering (of car, etc.); slewing round, swinging round (of crane, etc.); *Nau:* tacking, going about; *Av:* **v. (incliné), v. sur l'aile,** bank(ing); **angle**

de v., angle of bank. **2.** (*a*) (sharp) turn, bend, corner (in road); **v. sans visibilité,** blind corner; **v. en épingle à cheveux,** hairpin bend; **v. à la corde,** sharp turn; *P.N:* **virages sur 5 km.,** bends for 5 kms; **prendre un v.,** to take a bend, to corner; (*b*) banked corner, bank (of racing track). **3.** (*a*) changing of colour, *NAm:* color; **v. au rouge,** turning red; (*b*) *Phot:* toning (of proofs).

virago [virago] *n.f.* virago, termagant.

viral, -aux [viral, -o] *a. Med:* viral.

virée [vire] *n.f. F:* (*a*) trip, run, outing (in a car, etc.); (*b*) = pub crawl.

virement [virmɑ̃] *n.m.* **1.** *Nau:* **v. de bord,** tacking, going about. **2.** *Bank:* (credit) transfer; **banque de v.,** clearing bank.

virer [vire] **1.** *v.i.* to turn; to sweep round; (*of wind*) to veer; (*a*) *Aut: etc:* to take a bend, a corner; to corner; **v. court,** to corner sharply; **v. sur place,** to turn in one's own length; (*b*) *Av:* to bank; (*c*) (*of crane, etc.*) to turn (round); to slew round, swing round; (*d*) *Nau:* **v. de bord,** (i) to tack, go about; (ii) (*of steamship*) to turn; **v. vent arrière,** to wear (ship); **v. vent devant, vent avant,** to go about in stays; to stay; **pare à v.!** ready about! (*e*) *Nau:* **v. au cabestan,** to heave at the capstan; to heave; (*f*) to change colour, *NAm:* color; **encre qui vire au noir en séchant,** ink that dries black; (*g*) *Phot:* (*of print*) to tone. **2.** *v.tr.* (*a*) *Bank:* (i) to transfer (a sum); (ii) to clear (cheques, etc.); (*b*) *Phot:* to tone (print); (*c*) *F:* to throw, kick, chuck, (s.o.) out.

vireux, -euse [virø, -øz] *a.* poisonous, noxious.

virevolte [virvɔlt] *n.f.* **1.** *Equit: A:* quick circling (of horse). **2.** (*a*) half-turn (of dancer, etc.); (*b*) volte-face; **v. de la fortune,** sudden change of fortune.

virevolter [virvɔlte] *v.i.* (*a*) (*of horse*) to circle; (*b*) (*of pers.*) to spin round.

Virgile [virʒil] *Pr.n.m. Lt.Lit:* Virgil, Vergil.

virginal, -aux [virʒinal, -o] **1.** *a.* virginal; maiden(ly); **blanc v.,** pure white. **2.** *n.m. A.Mus:* virginal; (pair of) virginals.

Virginie [virʒini] *Pr.n.f.* Virginia.

virginité [virʒinite] *n.f.* virginity; maidenhood.

virgule [virgyl] *n.f.* (*a*) *Gram:* comma; **point v.,** semi-colon; (*b*) *Mth:* decimal point; **trois v. cinq (3,5),** three point five (3·5); (*c*) *Elcs:* **v. flottante,** floating point.

viril [viril] *a.* virile; (*a*) male (sex, etc.); **toge virile,** toga virilis; *Anat:* **membre v.,** male member, organ; (*b*) manly (action, etc.); **l'âge v.,** manhood.

virilement [virilmɑ̃] *adv.* like a man; in a manly way.

virilisant [virilizɑ̃] *a. Med:* (drug, etc.) which gives male characteristics.

viriliser [virilize] *v.tr.* (*a*) to make more virile, manly; to make (woman) appear masculine; (*b*) *Biol:* to give male characteristics (to an organism, etc.).

virilité [virilite] *n.f.* virility, manliness; manhood.

virole [virɔl] *n.f.* ferrule (of walking stick, etc.); *Mec.E:* collar, hoop, sleeve.

viroler [virɔle] *v.tr.* to fit (tool handle, etc.) with a ferrule.

virtualité [virtɥalite] *n.f.* potentiality.

virtuel, -elle [virtɥɛl] *a.* potential; *Opt: Phil:* virtual (image, etc.).

virtuellement [virtɥɛlmɑ̃] *adv.* virtually; potentially; to all intents and purposes.

virtuose [virtɥoz] *n.* virtuoso.

virtuosité [virtɥozite] *n.f.* virtuosity.

virulence [virylɑ̃s] *n.f.* virulence.

virulent [virylɑ̃] *a.* virulent (poison, satire, etc.); **diatribe virulente,** scathing diatribe.

virure [viryr] *n.f. N.Arch:* strake.

virus [virys] *n.m. Med:* virus; **maladie à v.,** virus disease; *F:* **avoir le v. du ski,** to have a craze for skiing.

vis [vis] *n.f.* **1.** (*a*) screw; **v. sans fin,** endless screw, worm (screw); *Hyd.E:* **v. d'Archimède,** Archimedean screw; *Ind:* **v. de transport,** spiral conveyor; *I.C.E: F:* **v. platinées,** (contact) points; (*b*) (screw) thread; **v. à droite, à gauche,** righthanded, lefthanded, screw, thread; **tige à v.,** screwed, threaded, rod; **serrer la v. à qn,** to be very hard, crack down, on s.o.; (*c*) **escalier à v.,** spiral staircase. **2.** screw; **v. à bois,** wood screw; **v. à métaux,** metal screw; **v. à tête cylindrique,** cheese-head(ed) screw; **v. à tête fraisée,** countersunk (head) screw; **v. à tête ronde,** roundhead(ed) screw; **v. à oreilles, à ailettes,** wing screw; **v. autotaraudeuse,** self-tapping screw.

visa [viza] *n.m.* (*a*) visa; stamp (on document); **apposer un v. à un passeport,** to stamp, visa, a passport; (*b*) signature (on document, etc.); initials (of supervisor, etc.); (*c*) *Cin:* **v. de censure,** censor's certificate.

visage [vizaʒ] *n.m.* (*a*) face; **homme au v. agréable,** pleasant-faced man; **il a changé de v.,** his face, expression, changed; **se faire le v.,** to make (one's face) up; **à deux visages,** two-faced; **avoir bon v.,** to look well; **faire bon v.,** to put a brave face on things; **faire bon v. à qn,** to be outwardly friendly to s.o.; **sans v.,** faceless; **à v. découvert,** (i) with the mask off; (ii) openly; **faire v. de bois à qn,** to shut the door in s.o.'s face; (*b*) **visages pâles,** Palefaces.

visagiste [vizaʒist] *n.* beautician.

vis-à-vis [vizavi] **1.** *adv.phr. O:* opposite; **la maison (qui est) v.-à-v.,** the house opposite. **2.** *prep.phr.* **v.-à-v. de (qn, qch)** (*a*) opposite, facing (s.o., sth.); (*b*) towards, in relation to, vis-à-vis (s.o., sth.); **ses sentiments v.-à-v. de moi,** his feelings towards me; **être sincère v.-à-v. de soi-même,** to be sincere with oneself. **3.** *n.m.* person opposite (at table, etc.); *Cards:* partner; **faire v.à-v., être en v.-à-v., à qn,** to be, stand, sit, opposite s.o.; to face s.o.; **nous avons le lac pour v.-à-v.,** we look out on to, face, the lake. **4.** *n.m. Furn:* vis-à-vis; S-shaped couch.

viscéral, -aux [viseral, -o] *a.* **1.** *Anat:* visceral. **2.** deep-seated (hatred, etc.); innermost (thoughts, etc.).

viscère [visɛr] *n.m.usu.pl. Anat:* internal organs; viscera.

viscose [viskoz] *n.f. Ch: Ind:* viscose.

viscosité [viskozite] *n.f.* viscosity, viscidity; stickiness.

visée [vize] *n.f.* **1.** aim; *Mil: Surv:* aiming, sighting; **ligne de v.,** line of sight; **point de v.,** point aimed at. **2.** *usu. pl.* aims, designs; **avoir de grandes visées,** to have great ambitions; to aim high.

viser¹ [vize] **1.** *v.i.* to aim, take aim (**à,** at, for); **v. à l'effet,** to aim at effect; **v. à faire qch.,** to aim at doing sth., to do sth.; **v. haut,** to aim high; **v. juste,** to aim straight; **v. plus haut,** to aim, to set one's sights, higher. **2.** *v.tr.* (*a*) to aim, take aim, at (s.o., sth.); to set one's sights on (sth.); *Golf:* **v. la balle,** to address the ball; (*b*) *Surv:* to sight; to take a sight on (sth.); (*c*) to have (sth.) in view; to relate to (sth.); **accusation visant qn,** accusation aimed, directed, against s.o.; **les denrées alimentaires ne sont pas visées par ce décret,** articles of food are not affected by this order; **je ne vise personne,** I am not alluding to anybody in particular. **3.** *v.tr. P:* to look, have a look, at.

viser² *v.tr. Adm:* to visa (passport); to countersign, initial, stamp (document).

viseur, -euse [vizœr, -øz] **1.** *n.* aimer. **2.** *n.m.* (*a*) *Phot:* viewfinder; (*b*) (*of surveying instrument, etc.*) sighting tube; eyepiece; *Av:* **v. de lancement,** bomb sight(s).

visibilité [vizibilite] *n.f.* visibility; **v. nulle,** zero visibility; *Av:* **vol sans v.,** instrument flying.

visible [viziblʲ] *a.* **1.** (*a*) visible, perceptible; **il n'y avait personne de v.,** there was nobody about; (*b*) obvious, manifest, evident; **très v.,** conspicuous. **2.** (*a*) ready to receive company; **je ne suis pas v.,** I am not at home, not in; **je ne serai pas v. avant trois heures,** I can't see anybody before three o'clock; (*b*) **cette collection n'est pas v.,** this collection is not open to the public.

visiblement [vizibləmɑ̃] *adv.* **1.** visibly, perceptibly. **2.** obviously, evidently; conspicuously.

visière [vizjɛr] *n.f.* (*a*) *Arm:* visor, vizor (of helmet); *Lit:* **rompre en v. à, avec, qn,** (i) to quarrel openly with s.o.; (ii) to take up a diametrically opposite view to that of s.o.; (*b*) peak (of cap); (*c*) eyeshade.

vision [vizjɔ̃] *n.f.* **1.** vision; (*a*) (eye)sight; (*b*) seeing; sight, view; **v. momentanée de qch.,** glimpse of sth.; (*c*) *Cin:* **première v.** = first showing; premiere. **2.** vision, imagination (of poet, etc.). **3.** vision; fantasy, phantom.

visionnaire [vizjɔnɛr] *a. & n.* visionary; dreamer.

visionner [vizjɔne] *v.tr.* to view.

visionneuse [vizjɔnøz] *n.f. Cin: Phot:* viewer.

visitandine [vizitɑ̃din] *n.f. R.C.Ch:* nun of the Order of the Visitation.

visitation [vizitasjɔ̃] *n.f. Ecc:* visitation (of the Virgin to St Elizabeth).

visite [vizit] *n.f.* **1.** (*a*) visit; (social) call; **faire une v., rendre v., faire v., à qn,** to visit s.o.; to call on s.o.; to pay s.o. a call; **rendre une v., sa v., à qn,** to return s.o.'s visit, s.o.'s call; **il nous fait une petite v. tous les soirs,** he drops in on us every evening; **être en v. chez qn,** to be visiting, on a visit to, s.o.; **v. de politesse,** duty call; **v. officielle,** official visit; **carte de v.,** visiting card; *Com:* **recevoir les visites d'un représentant,** to be called on by a representative; *Sp:* **équipe en v.,** visiting team; (*at hospital, etc.*) **heures de v.,** visiting hours; (*b*) visitor; caller; **nous attendons des visites, de la v.,** we're expecting visitors, guests; (*c*) **visites à domicile,** (doctor's) visits (to patients); (*d*) *Jur:* **droit de v. aux enfants,** right of access to the children. **2.** (*a*) inspection, examination, survey (of building, ship, etc.); overhauling (of machinery, etc.); (medical) examination; **faire la v.,** to go on one's round of inspection; **passer (à) une v. médicale,** to undergo a medical examination; *Mil: etc:* **passer la v.,** to come before the medical officer, the medical board; **v. des malades,** sick parade; *Ecc:* **v. pastorale, de l'évêque,** pastoral visit, visitation (by bishop); **trou de v.,** inspection hole, manhole (of sewer, etc.); (*b*) search (of house, ship, etc.); *Nau:* **droit de v.,** right of search; *Cust:* **v. de douane,** customs examination; (*c*) visit (to place of interest); **v. dirigée,** conducted tour.

visiter [vizite] *v.tr.* **1.** (*a*) *A:* to visit (s.o.); (*b*) to visit (the sick, etc.); (*of doctor*) to visit (a patient); *Com:* to call on (a client). **2.** (*a*) to inspect, examine (building, machinery, etc.); to overhaul (engine, etc.); to survey (ship); to view, go over (house for sale); (*b*) (*of police, etc.*) to visit, search (house, etc.); to inspect, examine (bags); (*c*) to visit (as a tourist); **v. une cathédrale,** to visit a cathedral; **on nous a fait v. l'usine,** we were shown round, over, the factory.

visiteur, -euse [vizitœr, -øz] *n.* (*a*) visitor; caller; **infirmière visiteuse** = community, district, nurse; (*for babies*) health visitor; *Sp:* **les visiteurs,** the visitors, the visiting team; *Com:* **v. en soies,** representative, traveller, in silks; **v. médical,** representative in pharmaceutical products; (*b*) inspector; **v. des douanes,** customs inspector, officer; (*c*) visitor (to a museum, etc.).

vison [vizɔ̃] *n.m.* **1.** *Z:* American mink. **2.** *Com:* (*a*) mink; (*b*) *F:* mink coat.

visonnière [vizɔnjɛr] *n.f. Fr.C:* mink farm.

visqueux, -euse [viskø, -øz] *a.* viscous, gluey, sticky; tacky; thick (oil); slimy (secretion, etc.).

vissage [visaʒ] *n.m.* screwing (on, in, down, up).

visser [vise] **1.** *v.tr.* (*a*) to screw (on, in, down, up); **boucles d'oreilles vissées,** screw-on earrings; *F:* **être vissé sur sa chaise,** to sit tight on one's chair; to be glued to one's chair; (*b*) *F:* to treat (s.o.) severely; to be very hard, crack down, on (s.o.). **2. la lance se visse au bout du tuyau,** the nozzle screws on to the end of the hose.

visualisation [vizɥalizasjɔ̃] *n.f.* visualization; *Cmptr:* **unité, écran, de v.,** (visual) display unit.

visualiser [vizɥalize] *v.tr.* to visualize; to make (sth.) visible to the eye.

visuel, -elle [vizɥɛl] *a.* visual; **champ v.,** field of vision.

visuellement [vizɥɛlmɑ̃] *adv.* visually.

vital, -aux [vital, -o] *a.* vital; **centres vitaux,** vital organs; **question vitale,** vital question.

vitalisme [vitalism] *n.m. Biol:* vitalism.

vitalité [vitalite] *n.f.* vitality.

vitamine [vitamin] *n.f. Bio-Ch:* vitamin.

vitaminé [vitamine] *a.* enriched with vitamins.

vitaminique [vitaminik] *a. Med:* **carence v.,** vitamin deficiency.

vite [vit] **1.** *a. Journ: Sp:* fast, speedy (cars, etc.). **2.** *adv.* quickly, fast, rapidly, swiftly, speedily; *Nau:* **plus v.!** increase speed! **le temps passe v.,** time flies; **vous allez v. en besogne,** you're a quick worker; that's quick work; **ça ne va pas v.,** it's slow work; **vous serez v. guéri,** you'll soon be better; **faites v.!** hurry up! be quick (about it)! **allons, et plus v. que cela!** now then, get a move on! **au plus v.,** as quickly as possible; **avoir v. fait de faire qch.,** to be quick (about) doing sth.; **il eut v. fait de s'habiller,** he was dresssed in no time; **on a v. fait de dire . . .,** it's easy to say . . ..

vitellus [vitelys] *n.m. Biol:* vitellus, yolk.

vitesse [vitɛs] *n.f.* **1.** (*a*) speed; rapidity; quickness; swiftness; **à la v. de . . .,** at the rate of . . .; **v. folle,** breakneck speed; **faire de la v.,** to move, go, quickly, at (high) speed; to speed along; *Aut: etc:* **excès de v.,** exceeding, breaking, the speed limit; *F:* **en v.,** quickly, at speed; **partir en v.,** to rush away, off; **un petit mot en v. pour vous dire . . .,** just a quick line to let you know . . .; **lutter de v. avec qn,** to race s.o., run a race with s.o.; **gagner, prendre, qn de v.,** (i) to outrun, outstrip, s.o.; *Rac:* to overtake, pass, s.o.; (ii) to steal a march on s.o.; **prendre de la v.,** to pick up, gather, increase, speed; *Pol:* **ce parti est en perte de v.,** this party is losing ground, popularity; *Av:* **se mettre en perte de v.,** to stall; *Aut: etc:* **compteur, indicateur, de v.,** speedometer; **aller à toute v.,** to go at full, top, speed; to rush along; *F:* to go all out; *Nau:* **en avant à toute v.,** full speed ahead; **v. de croisière,** cruising speed (of ship, aircraft, car); (*b*) *Rail: A:* **grande v., petite v.,** fast, slow, goods service. **2.** (*a*) velocity; **v. du son,** velocity of sound; **v. initiale,** (i) *Mec:* initial velocity; (ii) *Ball:* muzzle speed, velocity; **v. acquise,** impetus; momentum; (*b*) *Aut:* gear; **changer de v.,** to change gear; **boîte de vitesses,** gearbox; **filer en quatrième v.,** (i) to drive in top (gear); (ii) *F:* to disappear at top speed.

viticole [vitikɔl] *a.* wine-producing (area, etc.); **industrie v.,** wine industry.

viticulteur [vitikyltœr] *n.m.* vine grower, wine grower.

viticulture [vitikyltyr] *n.f.* vine growing, wine growing; viticulture.

vitrage [vitraʒ] *n.m.* **1.** glazing (of greenhouse, etc.). **2.** (*a*) windows (of church, etc.); (*b*) glass partition, door. **3.** *Furn:* net curtain, blind.

vitrail, -aux [vitraj, -o] *n.m.* leaded glass window; *esp.* stained glass (church) window.

vitre [vitr̥] *n.f.* pane (of glass); window (pane); *F:* **casser les vitres,** to get angry, kick up a fuss.
vitré [vitre] *a.* **1.** glazed (door, etc.); **porte vitrée,** glass door. **2.** vitreous, glassy (substance, etc.).
vitrer [vitre] *v.tr.* to glaze (window, etc.).
vitrerie [vitrəri] *n.f.* glaziery; glass industry.
vitreux, -euse [vitrø, -øz] *a.* vitreous (mass, rock, etc.); glassy (appearance, etc.); glazed (eyes, etc.); **porcelaine vitreuse,** vitreous china.
vitrier [vitrije] *n.m.* glazier.
vitrification [vitrifikasjɔ̃] *n.f.* vitrification; glazing.
vitrifier [vitrifje] *v.tr.* (*impf. & pr.sub.* **n. vitrifiions, v. vitrifiiez**) to vitrify (sand, etc.); **brique vitrifiée,** glazed brick.
vitrine [vitrin] *n.f.* **1.** shop window; **faire une v.,** to dress a window; **articles en v.,** articles (on show) in the window; **regarder, lécher, les vitrines,** to go window shopping. **2.** glass case, cabinet; display cabinet; showcase.
vitriol [vitrijɔl] *n.m.* (*a*) *Ch: A:* vitriol; **(huile de) v.,** oil of vitriol; (*b*) **critique au v.,** vitriolic criticism.
vitriolage [vitrijɔlaʒ] *n.m.* **1.** *Tex:* souring (of material). **2.** vitriol throwing.
vitrioler [vitrijɔle] *v.tr.* **1.** *Tex:* to sour (material). **2.** to throw vitriol at (s.o.).
vitrioleur, -euse [vitrijɔlœr, -øz] *n.* vitriol thrower.
vitupération [vityperasjɔ̃] *n.f.* *Lit:* vituperation.
vitupérer [vitypere] *v.* (**je vitupère, n. vitupérons; je vitupérerai**) (*a*) *v.tr. Lit:* to vituperate, abuse (s.o., sth.); (*b*) *v.i.* to protest, storm **(contre qn, qch.,** against s.o., sth.).
vivable [vivabl̥] *a. F:* (*a*) (*of house, etc.*) livable (in); (*b*) (*of pers.*) livable with; **il n'est pas v.,** he's just impossible (to live with).
vivace[1] [vivas] *a.* (*a*) long-lived; (*b*) *Nat.Hist:* hardy; robust; (*c*) *Bot:* perennial; **pois v.,** everlasting pea; (*d*) undying, inveterate (hatred, etc.); **souvenirs encore vivaces,** memories still green.
vivace[2] [vivatʃe] *a.inv. & adv. Mus:* vivace.
vivacité [vivasite] *n.f.* **1. v. à agir,** promptness to act. **2.** (*a*) hastiness (of temper); petulance; **avec v.,** hastily; (*b*) *pl. O:* outburst of temper. **3.** (*a*) acuteness (of feeling); heat (of a discussion); fire, intensity (of passion); (*b*) vividness, brilliance, brilliancy, brightness (of colour, *NAm:* color, light); **v. du teint,** high colour. **4.** (*of pers., etc.*) vivacity, vivaciousness, sprightliness, liveliness; keenness; briskness; quickness; **v. d'esprit,** quick-wittedness; sparkling wit; **avoir de la v.,** to be vivacious, sprightly, full of life; **avec v.,** vivaciously.
vivandier, -ière [vivɑ̃dje, -jɛr] *n. A:* sutler; *f.* vivandière.
vivant [vivɑ̃] **1.** *a.* (*a*) alive, living; **il est encore v.,** he is still alive; **être enterré v.,** to be buried alive; **être v.,** living creature; **un poisson v.,** a live fish; **pas une âme vivante,** not a living soul; **portrait v.,** lifelike portrait; **être le portrait v. de qn,** to be the living image of s.o.; **langue vivante,** living, modern, language; *F:* **c'est une bibliothèque vivante,** he's a walking encyclopaedia; *Th:* **tableau v.,** tableau (vivant); (*b*) lively, animated (street, scene, etc.); **image vivante de . . .,** vivid picture of . . .. **2.** *n.m.* living being; **les vivants et les morts,** the living and the dead; **bon v.,** (i) jolly, jovial, fellow, companion; (ii) man who enjoys (the pleasures of) life. **3.** *n.m.* **de son v.,** during his lifetime, in his day; **du v. de votre père,** when your father was alive; in your father's lifetime.
vivarium [vivarjɔm] *n.m.* vivarium.
vivat [viva] **1.** *int. A:* hurrah! bravo! **2.** *n.m.pl.* cheers (of audience, etc.).
vive[2] [viv] *n.f. Ich:* weever, stingfish.
vivement [vivmɑ̃] *adv.* **1.** (*a*) briskly, sharply; smartly; suddenly; **se tourner v.,** to turn round quickly; (*b*) *int. F:* **v. les vacances!** roll on the holidays! (*c*) **réprimander v. qn,** to give s.o. a sharp reprimand; **répondre v.,** to answer sharply, brusquely. **2.** (*a*) vividly (coloured, *NAm:* colored); (*b*) keenly; deeply; acutely; **s'intéresser v. à qch.,** to take a keen interest in sth.; **remercier qn v.,** to thank s.o. warmly.
viveur [vivœr] *n.m.* pleasure seeker; fast liver.
vivier [vivje] *n.m.* (*a*) fishpond; fish preserve; (*b*) (*in boat*) fish well; (*c*) *Fig:* breeding ground **(de,** for).
vivifiant [vivifjɑ̃] *a.* vivifying, *Lit:* quickening; enlivening; (*of air, etc.*) invigorating, bracing.
vivifier [vivifje] *v.tr.* (*impf. & pr.sub.* **n. vivifiions, v. vivifiiez**) to vivify, *Lit:* quicken; to enliven, (re)-vitalize; (*of air, etc.*) to invigorate; **v. l'industrie d'un pays,** to revive, give fresh life to, a country's industry.
vivipare [vivipar] *a. Nat.Hist:* viviparous.
viviparité [viviparite] *n.f. Nat.Hist:* viviparity.
vivisection [viviseksjɔ̃] *n.f.* vivisection.
vivoir [vivwar] *n.m. Fr.C:* living room.
vivoter [vivɔte] *v.i.* to live, frugally; to keep body and soul together; to rub along; **usine qui vivote,** factory that can just manage to keep going.
vivre[1] [vivr̥] (*pr.p.* **vivant;** *p.p.* **vécu;** *pr.ind.* **je vis, il vit, n. vivons, ils vivent;** *pr.sub.* **je vive;** *impf.* **je vivais;** *p.h.* **je vécus;** *fu.* **je vivrai)** to live. **1.** *v.i.* (*a*) to be alive; **v. longtemps,** to live a long time, to live long; **cesser de v.,** to die; *Lit:* **il a vécu,** he is dead; **le Front populaire a vécu,** the Popular Front has had its day, is finished; **être las de v.,** to be tired of living, of life; **vive le roi!** long live the King! **vive l'armée!** three cheers for the army! *Mil: etc:* **qui vive?** who goes there? **ne rencontrer âme qui vive,** to meet no one, not a living soul; *Prov:* **qui vivra verra,** live and learn; time will show; (*b*) **il vécut vieux,** he lived to be an old man; **ouvrage qui vivra,** work that will endure; **traditions qui vivent encore,** traditions that are still alive. **2.** *v.i.* to spend one's life; **v. à Paris,** to live in Paris; **il a (beaucoup) vécu,** he's seen (a lot of) life; **v. saintement,** to live a godly life; **v. avec qn,** to live with s.o.; **être facile à v.,** to be easy to live with, to get on with; **savoir v.,** to know how to behave; to be well-bred; **apprendre à v. à qn,** to teach s.o. good, better, manners; **se laisser v.,** to take life easily, as it comes; **il fait bon v. ici,** life is pleasant here. **3.** *v.i.* to subsist; **on vivait bien juste,** we could just manage, just rub along; **v. bien,** to live in comfort; to live, eat, well; **travailler pour v.,** to work for one's living; **il fait cher v. ici,** life is expensive here; the cost of living is high here; **faire v. sa famille,** to support, keep, one's family; **v. au jour le jour,** to live from hand to mouth; **v. de poisson,** to live on fish; **v. de sa plume,** to live by one's pen; **de quoi vit-il?** (i) what does he live on? (ii) what does he do for a living? **avoir de quoi v.,** to have enough to live on. **4.** *v.tr.* **v. sa vie,** to live one's own life; **les événements que nous avons vécu(s),** the events we lived through.
vivre[2] *n.m.* (*a*) *A:* living; (*b*) *A:* food; **le v. et le couvert,** bed and board, board and lodging; (*c*) *pl.* provisions, supplies; *Mil:* rations; **vivres de réserve,** iron rations; **couper les vivres à qn,** to stop s.o.'s allowance.
vivrier, -ière [vivrije, -jɛr] *a.* **cultures vivrières,** food crops.
vizir [vizir] *n.m.* vizier.
vlan, v'lan [vlɑ̃] *int.* slap(-bang)! whack! wham! **tomber v.! en plein milieu,** to fall bang in the middle.
vocable [vɔkabl̥] *n.m.* **1.** vocable, word. **2.** *Ecc:* name, patronage (of saint); **église sous le v. de saint Pierre,** church dedicated to Saint Peter.
vocabulaire [vɔkabylɛr] *n.m.* **1.** vocabulary; word

list. **2.** (*of pers., etc.*) vocabulary; **enrichir son v.,** to enlarge one's vocabulary; *Pej:* **quel v.!** what an expression! what a thing to say!

vocal, -aux [vɔkal, -o] *a.* vocal.

vocalement [vɔkalmɑ̃] *adv.* vocally.

vocalique [vɔkalik] *a. Ling:* vocalic; **son v.,** vocalic sound; vowel sound.

vocalisation [vɔkalizasjɔ̃] *n.f. Ling: Mus:* vocalization.

vocalise [vɔkaliz] *n.f. Mus:* exercise in vocalization.

vocaliser [vɔkalize] *v.tr.* to vocalize (melody, consonant).

vocalisme [vɔkalism] *n.m. Ling: Mus:* vocalism.

vocatif [vɔkatif] *n.m. Gram:* vocative (case).

vocation [vɔkasjɔ̃] *n.f.* **1.** vocation, (divine) call; **je ne me sens pas la v. de la prêtrise,** I feel no call to the Church, no calling for the Church. **2.** vocation, calling, bent, inclination; **avoir la v. du commerce,** to have an aptitude for business; **avoir la v. du professorat,** to be cut out for teaching; **manquer sa v.,** to miss one's vocation.

vociférateur, -trice [vɔsiferatœr, -tris] *n. Lit:* vociferator.

vocifération [vɔsiferasjɔ̃] *n.f.* vociferation; outcry; *pl.* shouts; yells.

vociférer [vɔsifere] *v.i.* **(je vocifère, n. vociférons; je vociférerai)** to vociferate **(contre,** against); to shout, yell, bawl; **v. des injures,** to shout, hurl, insults **(contre,** at).

vodka [vɔdka] *n.f.* vodka.

vœu, -x [vø] *n.m.* **1.** vow; **faire v. de faire qch.,** to make, take a vow, to vow, to do sth.; **faire v. de pauvreté,** to take a vow of poverty; *Ecc:* **prononcer ses vœux,** to take one's vows; **les vœux de baptême,** the baptismal vows. **2.** wish; **faire un v.,** to make a wish; to wish; **émettre un v.,** to express a wish, one's desire; **je fais des vœux pour qu'il ne pleuve pas dimanche,** I'm praying it won't rain on Sunday; **tous mes vœux! avec mes, nos, meilleurs vœux,** best wishes; with all good wishes; **vœux de bonne, de nouvelle, année,** New Year greetings; **carte de vœux,** greetings card.

vogue [vɔg] *n.f.* fashion, vogue; **mettre qch. en v.,** to bring sth. into vogue; **connaître une v., être en v.,** to be popular, fashionable, in fashion, in vogue; **entrer en v.,** to come into vogue, into fashion; to come in; **c'est la grande v.,** it's all the rage.

voguer [vɔge] *v.i. Lit:* to sail; **les nuages voguant dans le ciel,** the clouds sailing, floating, by; the drifting clouds; **vogue la galère!** let's chance it! come what may!

voici [vwasi] *prep.* **1.** here is, are; **v. Henri,** here's Henry; **v. mes neveux,** these are, here are, my nephews; **me v., les v.,** here I am, here they are; **nous v. arrivés!** here we are! **du pain? en v.,** bread? here's some, here you are; **la v. qui vient,** here she comes; that's her coming; **v. venir Jeanne,** here comes Jeanne; **mon ami que v. vous le dira,** my friend here will tell you; **Monsieur que v.,** this gentleman; **v. ce dont il s'agit,** this is what it's all about; **v. ce qu'il m'a dit,** this is what he told me; **la petite histoire que v.,** the following little story; **je le ferai et v. comment,** I shall do it in the following manner; **v. pourquoi,** this is why; **v. l'automne,** autumn is coming; **v. Noël!** Christmas is here! **2.** (= IL Y A) **je l'ai vu v. trois ans,** I saw him three years ago; **v. trois mois que j'habite ici,** I have been living here for the last three months.

voie [vwa] *n.f.* **1.** (*a*) way, road, route, track; *Adm: Aut:* traffic lane; **v. publique,** public thoroughfare; public highway; **route à quatre voies,** four-lane road, *NAm:* highway; *Astr:* **la V. lactée,** the Milky Way; **être par voies et par chemins,** to be always on the move; **v. de communication,** line of communication; road, thoroughfare; **grande v. de communication,** main artery, arterial road; **v. fluviale, v. navigable,** waterway; **la v. maritime du Saint-Laurent,** the St Lawrence Seaway; **par v. de terre,** by land; overland; **par v. de mer,** by sea; **par la v. des airs,** by air; *Min:* **v. d'aérage,** airway; (*b*) *Ven:* (*often pl.*) tracks (of game); slot (of deer, etc.); **mettre les chiens sur la v.,** to put the dogs on the scent; **mettre qn sur la v.,** to put s.o. on the right track; **être sur la bonne v.,** to be on the right track; (*c*) *Rail:* **v. ferrée,** railway, *NAm:* railroad (track, line); **v. de service, de garage,** siding; *Fig:* **mettre un projet sur une v. de garage,** to shelve a plan; **v. impaire, v. descendante,** down line; **v. paire, v. montante,** up line; **ligne à une v., à deux voies,** single-track, double-track, line; **v. étroite,** narrow-gauge line; **sur quelle v. arrive le train?** on, at, which platform does the train come in? (*d*) *Cmptr:* **v. d'entrée,** input channel; **v. de transmission de données,** data link; (*e*) gauge (of wheels of vehicle); (*f*) (i) kerf, clearance (of a tool); (ii) set (of a saw); **donner de la v. à une scie,** to set a saw; (*g*) *Nau:* **v. d'eau,** leak; **faire une v. d'eau,** to spring a leak; (*h*) *Anat:* passage, duct; **les voies digestives,** the digestive tract(s). **2.** (*a*) way; **les voies de Dieu,** the ways of God; **la v. étroite,** the narrow way; the strait way; **voies et moyens,** ways and means; **préparer la v., les voies,** to prepare, pave, the way; **la v. des armes,** recourse to arms; **par la v. diplomatique,** through diplomatic channels; **une v. dangereuse,** a dangerous course; **affaire en bonne v.,** business that is going well; **en v. d'achèvement,** nearing completion; **en v. de construction,** under construction; **en v. de formation,** in the process of formation; **pays en v. de développement,** developing countries; **en v. de réparation,** under, undergoing, repair; **il est en v. de guérison,** he's on the mend; **être en v. de faire qch.,** to be (well) on the way to doing sth.; **être en (bonne) v. de réussir,** to be on the way, road, to success; *Jur:* **voies de droit,** recourse to legal proceedings; **voies de fait,** acts of violence; assault and battery; **en venir aux voies de fait,** to come to blows, to exchange blows; (*b*) *Ch: etc:* **v. sèche, humide,** dry, wet, process; **essai par la v. sèche,** dry test.

voilà [vwala] *prep.* **1.** (*a*) there is, are; **v. Henri,** there's Henry; that's Henry; **le v., les v.,** there he is, there they are; **la pendule que v.,** that clock (there); **la petite histoire que v.,** the following little story; **v. où il demeure,** that's where he lives; **en v. assez!** that's enough (of it)! that will do! **en v. une idée!** what an idea! **en v. de la reconnaissance!** there's gratitude for you! **en v. un qui fera son chemin!** there's a man who will get on! **v. tout,** that's all; **le v. qui entre, v. qu'il entre,** there he is coming in; **v. (ce) qui s'appelle danser!** that's what I call dancing! **v. qui est curieux!** that's curious; **v. ce qu'il m'a dit,** that's what he told me; **v. comme elle est; la v. bien!** that's just like her; **v. qu'il se remarie,** and now he's getting married again; **v.!** there you are! **et v.!** and that's that! (*in restaurant*) **v., monsieur!** coming, sir! (*b*) (= VOICI) **me v.!** here I am! **le v.!** here he is! here he comes! **2.** (= IL Y A) **en juin v. trois ans,** in June three years ago; **v. dix ans que je le connais,** I've known him (for) ten years.

voilage [vwalaʒ] *n.m.* (*a*) net (on hat, etc.); (*b*) *pl.* net curtains.

voile [vwal] **I.** *n.f.* sail; **v. carrée,** square sail; **déployer, établir, une v.,** to set a sail; **bateau à voiles,** sailing boat; **aller à la v.,** to sail; **vaisseau sous voile(s),** ship under sail; **faire v., mettre à la v.,** to set sail **(pour,** for); to get under sail; **faire force de voiles,** to crowd on, cram on, all sail; **toutes voiles dehors,** in full sail, all sail(s) set, with every stitch of canvas spread; **faire de la v.,** to go sailing; *F:* **mettre les voiles,** to leave, scram, do a bunk. **II.** *n.m.* (*a*) veil; *Ecc:* **prendre le v.,** to take the veil; **sous le v. de la religion,** under the cloak, mask, of religion; (*b*) film, mist (before one's eyes); *Med: F:* **v. noir,** blackout; **v. de larmes,** blur of tears; (*c*) *Tex:* voile; (*d*) *Anat:* **v. du palais,** soft palate, velum; (*e*) *Phot:* fog (on negative); (*f*) *X-Rays:* shadow (on lung).

voilé [vwale] *a.* **1.** (*a*) veiled, dim (light); veiled, obscure (meaning); muffled (drum); husky, veiled (voice); **des yeux voilés de larmes,** eyes dimmed, blurred, with tears; **allusion peu voilée,** broad hint; **en termes peu voilés,** in thinly veiled terms; (*b*) *Phot:* fogged (print). **2.** (*of wheel, rod, etc.*) buckled, warped; out of true.

voiler [vwale] **I.** *v.tr. Nau:* to rig (ship) with sails. **II. 1.** *v.tr.* (*a*) to veil; (*b*) to veil, obscure, dim, cloud (light, etc.); to muffle (sound, drum, etc.); to shade (light); (*c*) *Phot:* to fog (plate, print); (*d*) to buckle, warp (wheel, etc.). **2.** (*a*) **se v. (le visage),** to wear a veil; *Fig:* **se v. la face,** to hide, bury, one's head in the sand; (*b*) **se v.,** (i) (*of sky, etc.*) to become overcast, cloud over; (ii) (*of eyes*) to mist over; (iii) (*of wheel, etc.*) to buckle, warp.

voilerie [vwalri] *n.f. Nau:* sail loft.

voilette [vwalɛt] *n.f. Cost:* (hat) veil.

voilier [vwalje] *n.m.* **1. navire bon, mauvais, v.,** good, bad, sailer. **2.** sailing ship, sailing boat; windjammer. **3.** sailmaker. **4. grand v.,** long-flight bird.

voilure[1] [vwalyr] *n.f.* (*a*) sails (of ship); **réduire la v.,** to shorten sail; (*b*) *Av:* wing(s), flying surface, aerofoil, *NAm:* airfoil; **appareil à v. fixe,** fixed wing aircraft.

voilure[2] *n.f.* buckling, warping.

voir [vwar] *v.tr.* (*pr.p.* **voyant;** *p.p.* **vu;** *pr.ind.* **je vois, il voit, n. voyons, ils voient;** *pr.sub.* **je voie;** *impf.* **je voyais;** *p.h.* **je vis;** *fu.* **je verrai**) **1.** to see; to set eyes on (s.o., sth.); to sight (ship); **hôtel vu de face,** front view of the hotel; **(détail) vu de près,** close-up (detail); *F:* **on aura tout vu!** we've seen it all now! wonders will never cease! **il ne voit pas plus loin que le bout de son nez,** he can't see further than the end of his nose; **il faut le v. pour le croire,** it must be seen to be believed; **v. c'est croire,** seeing is believing; **je l'ai vu des mes (propres) yeux,** I saw it with my own eyes; **il n'y a rien à v.,** there's nothing to see, to be seen; **c'est à v.,** it's worth seeing; **cela se voit tous les jours,** you see that all the time; that happens every day; **je le vois qui arrive,** I can see him coming; **à le v. on dirait . . .,** by the look of him, to judge by his looks, one would say . . .; **monument qui se voit de loin,** monument that can be seen from a distance; **on voit son jupon,** her petticoat is showing; **je n'y vois plus,** I can't see any more; **on n'y voit rien,** you can't see a thing (it's so dark); **v. rouge,** to see red; **voyez vous-même!** see for yourself! **mon fils, voyez-vous, est mort,** my son is dead, you see; *Lit:* **que vois-je?** what is this (that I see)? **voyez un peu!** just imagine! just look at him (at it); **il faut y aller v.,** we must go and see; **faire v., laisser v., qch. à qn,** to show sth. to s.o.; to let s.o. see sth.; **laisser v. son ignorance,** to reveal, betray, one's ignorance; **faites v.!** let me see it! let's have a look! **en faire v. (de toutes les couleurs) à qn,** to make s.o.'s life a misery; to lead s.o. a merry dance; *P:* **voyons v.,** let's see, let me see; let's have a look: show it to me; **montrez v.,** just let me see it; **dites v. . . .,** tell me. . ., let's hear it; **essayez v.,** just have a try; just you try it; **regardez v.,** just have a look. **2. v.** + *inf.* (*a*) **v. venir qn,** to see s.o. coming; **je l'ai vu tomber,** I saw him fall; **quels acteurs avez-vous vus jouer ce rôle?** what actors have you seen in this part? (*b*) **v. faire qch.,** to see sth. done; **v. faire qch. à qn,** to see s.o. do sth.; **quelles pièces avez-vous vu jouer?** what plays have you seen (acted)? (*c*) **il se voyait refuser les fournitures les plus urgentes,** he was refused the most urgent supplies; (*d*) (*as aux. of the passive voice*) **je me suis vu forcé de partir,** I was forced, compelled, to leave. **3.** (*a*) to visit (s.o., sth.); **aller v. qn,** to go to see s.o.; to go and see s.o.; **venez me v. quand vous serez à Paris,** come and see me when you're in Paris; **nous avons vu les musées,** we visited the museums; **v. du pays,** to travel; (*b*) **v. qn,** to receive a visit from s.o.; **il ne voit personne,** he sees no one; **nous le voyons beaucoup,** we see a lot of him; **on ne vous voit plus!** you're quite a stranger! **nous ne les voyons plus,** we don't see them any more; **nous nous voyons souvent,** we often meet, see each other; **je ne peux pas le v.,** I can't stand (the sight of) him. **4.** (*a*) to understand; **je vois où vous voulez en venir,** I see, understand, what you're driving at; *Fig:* **v. bien loin,** to be farsighted; *F:* **ni vu, ni connu,** without anyone being any the wiser for it; *F:* **vu?** understood? all right? O.K.? **c'est tout vu!** that's all there is to it; (*b*) to notice, observe (sth.); **je vois que vous avez compris,** I see you have understood; **à ce que je vois,** from what I can see; **cela se voit,** that is obvious; **la tache ne se voit pas,** you can't see the mark; **vous voyez ça d'ici,** you can imagine what it was (is, would be) like; **je ne le vois pas marié,** I can't imagine him married. **5.** (*a*) to look after, see to, see about (sth.); **v. une affaire à fond,** to look into, examine, a matter thoroughly; **faire qch. seulement pour v.,** to do sth. to see what happens, just as an experiment; **eh bien, je verrai,** well, I'll see, think, about it; **c'est ce que nous verrons!** we shall see! that remains to be seen; *F:* **va-t'en v. si j'y suis!** get lost! clear out! scram! **il n'a rien à v. là-dedans,** it's nothing to do with him; it's no business of his; **vous n'avez rien à y v.,** it's no concern of yours; **cela n'a rien à v. avec l'affaire,** that's beside the point, that has nothing to do with it; **ceci est à v., c'est à v.,** it remains to be seen; (*b*) **v. à** + *inf.* **il va v. à nous loger,** he will see that we have somewhere to stay; **v. que** + *sub.* **c'est à vous de v. que rien ne nous manque,** it's up to you to see that we have everything we need; (*c*) *int.* **voyons!** (i) let's see; (ii) come (on) now! come, come! **6.** to consider, regard (sth. in a particular way); **sa façon de v. (les choses),** his way of looking at things; his outlook; **il se voyait déjà perdu,** he already imagined himself lost; **se faire bien v. de qn,** to gain s.o.'s favour, get into s.o.'s good books; **se faire mal v. de qn,** to get into s.o.'s bad books; **être bien vu de tous,** to be highly esteemed, well though of, by all; **mal vu,** poorly considered; disliked.

voire [vwar] *adv.* **1.** *A:* in truth. **2.** indeed; **v. (même),** and even; or even; indeed even; **j'en suis ahuri, v. révolté,** I'm astounded, indeed disgusted.

voirie [vwari] *n.f.* **1.** (*a*) road system; **la grande v.,** the main, high, roads; (*b*) administration of public thoroughfares; **le service de v.,** the highways department; **travaux de v.,** road works; **employé de la v.,** street sweeper. **2.** refuse dump, *esp. NAm:* garbage heap; **jeter les ordures à la v.,** to dump the refuse.

voisin, -ine [vwazɛ̃, -in] **1.** *a.* neighbouring, *NAm:* neighboring; adjoining; bordering **(de,** on); **la chambre voisine,** the next room; **deux maisons voisines,** two houses next to each other; two adjoining houses; **il habite dans la maison voisine,** he lives next door; *Nat.Hist:* **espèces voisines,** closely allied, related, species; **être v. de qn, de qch.,** to be next to, near, s.o., sth.; **émotion voisine de la terreur,** emotion akin to terror, bordering on terror; **v. de la mort,** at death's door. **2.** *n.* neighbour, *NAm:* neighbor; **v. d'à côté, de porte à porte,** next-door neighbour; **mon v. de table,** the person I was sitting next to (at table); my neighbour at table; **agir en bon v.,** to act in a neighbourly, *NAm:* neighborly, way.

voisinage [vwazinaʒ] *n.m.* vicinity. **1.** proximity, nearness; **les maisons dans le v. des montagnes,** the houses near the mountains; **le v. de la gare est un avantage,** proximity, being close, to the station is an advantage. **2.** neighbourhood, *NAm:* neighborhood; surrounding district; **il n'y avait personne dans le v.,** there was nobody about, in the vicinity; **relations de bon v.,** (good) neighbourliness, *NAm:* neighborliness.

voisiner [vwazine] *v.i.* **1.** *A: & Lit:* to visit one's neighbours, *NAm:* neighbors; **à Paris on voisine peu,** in Paris one doesn't see much of one's neighbours. **2. v. avec qn, qch.,** to be (placed) side by side with s.o., sth.; to adjoin sth.

voiturage [vwatyraʒ] *n.m.* cartage, carriage, conveyance (of goods, etc.).

voiture [vwatyr] *n.f.* **1.** (*a*) *A:* conveyance, transport; (*b*) *Com:* **lettre de v.,** waybill, consignment note. **2.** conveyance, vehicle; **v. publique,** public conveyance; *P.N:* **attention aux voitures!** beware of the traffic! (*a*) (horse-drawn) vehicle; (*for people*) carriage, coach; (*for goods*) cart; **v. à deux chevaux,** carriage and pair; **v. de place,** hackney (carriage, cab); (*b*) (motor) car, *NAm:* automobile; **v. de tourisme,** private car; **v. de sport,** sports car; **v. de livraison,** delivery van; **v. de laitier,** milk float; **v. école,** driving-school car; **v. cellulaire,** prison van; (*c*) *Rail:* coach, carriage; *NAm:* car; **en v.!** take your seats! *esp. NAm:* all aboard! (*d*) **v. d'enfant, de bébé,** pram, perambulator; *NAm:* baby carriage; **v. à bras,** barrow, handcart; **v. d'infirme, petite v.,** invalid carriage; *O:* **v. de malade,** Bath chair.

voiture-bar [vwatyrbar] *n.f. Rail:* buffet car, refreshment car; *pl. voitures-bars.*

voiturée [vwatyre] *n.f.* carriageful (of people); cartload (of goods, etc.).

voiture-lit [vwatyrli] *n.f. Rail:* sleeping car, *F:* sleeper; *pl. voitures-lits.*

voiturer [vwatyre] *v.tr.* to convey, transport, carry, cart (goods, etc.); *F:* **je vais te v.,** I'll drive you (in, there).

voiture-restaurant [vwatyrrɛstɔrɑ̃] *n.f. Rail:* restaurant car, dining car; *pl. voitures-restaurants.*

voiturette [vwatyrɛt] *n.f.* trap, small springcart; *Aut:* small car.

voiturier [vwatyrje] *n.m. A: & Jur:* carrier, carter.

voix [vwa] *n.f.* **1.** voice; **parler à v. haute, à haute v.,** to speak (i) in a loud voice, (ii) aloud; **parler à v. basse,** to speak in a low voice, under one's breath, in a whisper, in an undertone; **faire la grosse v.,** to speak sternly, in a severe tone; **élever la v.,** to speak up; to raise one's voice; **à portée de (la) v.,** within earshot; **hors de portée de (la) v.,** out of hearing, out of earshot; (*of dogs*) **donner de la v.,** to bark; to give tongue, to bay; *Mus:* **v. de basse, de ténor,** bass voice, tenor voice; **v. de poitrine,** chest voice; **v. de tête,** head voice; **v. de fausset,** falsetto (voice); **chanter à plusieurs v.,** to sing in parts; **je ne suis pas en v.,** I'm not in voice; **v. humaine,** vox humana (stop of organ). **2. rester sans v.,** to remain speechless; **de vive v.,** by word of mouth, viva voce; **la v. de la conscience,** the voice, the dictates, of conscience; **la v. de la nature,** the call of nature; **la v. du peuple,** vox populi, public opinion; **d'une commune v.,** by common consent; **donner sa v. à qn,** to vote for s.o.; **mettre une question aux v.,** to put a question to the vote; **la Chambre alla aux v.,** the House divided; **avoir v. au chapitre,** to have a say in the matter. **3.** *Gram:* **à la v. active, passive,** in the active voice, in the passive (voice).

vol¹ [vɔl] *n.m.* **1.** flying, flight; (*a*) **prendre son v.,** to take wing; to take off; **tirer un oiseau au v.,** to shoot a bird on the wing; **saisir l'occasion au v.,** to grasp, leap at, the opportunity; **à v. d'oiseau,** as the crow flies; **vue à v. d'oiseau,** bird's-eye view; **oiseau de haut v.,** high-flying bird; (*of pers.*) **de haut v.,** (i) high-class, top-flight; (ii) high-flying; (*b*) *Av:* **heures de v.,** flying time; **avion en v.,** aircraft in flight; **v. de nuit,** night flying; **v. à voile,** gliding; **v. libre,** hang gliding. **2.** flock, flight (of birds flying together); covey (of game birds); swarm (of locusts). **3.** *A:* **(chasse au) v.,** hawking.

vol² *n.m.* theft; stealing, robbery; *Jur:* **v. qualifié,** aggravated theft; robbery; **v. avec effraction,** breaking and entering; housebreaking; **v. à la tire,** pickpocketing, pocket picking; **v. à l'étalage,** shoplifting; **v. à l'américaine,** confidence trick; **v. de grand chemin,** highway robbery; **v. à main armée,** armed robbery; *F:* **c'est du v.!** it's (sheer) daylight robbery! **commettre plusieurs vols,** to commit several thefts.

volage [vɔlaʒ] *a.* fickle, inconstant, flighty.

volaille [vɔlaj] *n.f.* **1.** *coll.* poultry; **une v.,** a fowl; **marchand de v.,** poulterer. **2.** *Cu:* poultry, *esp.* chicken; **foies de v.,** chicken livers.

volailler [vɔlaje] *n.m.* poulterer.

volant [vɔlɑ̃] **I.** *a.* **1.** flying; fluttering (ribbons, etc.); **objet v. non identifié,** unidentified flying object; *F:* **soucoupe volante,** flying saucer; *Ich:* **poisson v.,** flying fish; *Av:* **personnel v.,** flying staff; *Mil:* air crew; *Navy:* **escadre volante,** flying squadron. **2.** loose (cable, etc.); movable (partition, etc.); **feuille volante,** loose leaf, detachable slip (of paper); **table volante,** occasional table; *Nau:* **cabestan v.,** portable winch; **pont v.,** (i) spar deck; (ii) *Civ.E:* flying bridge. **II.** *n.m.* **1.** *Games:* shuttlecock; **jeu de v.,** (game of) battledore and shuttlecock. **2.** *A:* sail (of windmill). **3.** (*a*) flywheel (of engine); *Clockm:* fly; (*b*) (i) head of steam; (ii) steadying force, factor; reserve supply. **4.** handwheel (of engine, etc.). **5.** *Aut:* (steering) wheel; **tenir le v.,** to drive; **se mettre au v.,** to take the wheel. **6.** (*in book of tickets*) **talon et v.,** counterfoil and leaf. **7.** *Dressm:* (i) flounce; (ii) shaped panel; **volants froncés,** gathered flounces.

volatil [vɔlatil] *a.* volatile.

volatile [vɔlatil] *n.m. Hum:* winged creature, bird.

volatilisable [vɔlatilizabl̩] *a.* volatilizable.

volatilisation [vɔlatilizasjɔ̃] *n.f.* volatilization.

volatiliser [vɔlatilize] **1.** *v.tr.* (*a*) *Ch:* to volatilize; (*b*) to make (sth.) disappear. **2. se v.,** to fade away, vanish (into thin air).

volatilité [vɔlatilite] *n.f.* volatility.

vol-au-vent [vɔlovɑ̃] *n.m.inv. Cu:* vol-au-vent.

volcan [vɔlkɑ̃] *n.m.* (*a*) volcano; **v. actif, dormant, éteint,** active, dormant, extinct, volcano; (*b*) fiery, impetuous, person.

volcanique [vɔlkanik] *a.* volcanic (rock, etc.); fiery, ardent (passion); vivid (imagination).

volcanologie [vɔlkanɔlɔʒi] *n.f.* vulcanology.

volcanologue [vɔlkanɔlɔg] *n.* vulcanologist.

vole [vɔl] *n.f. Cards:* vole; all the tricks.

volée [vɔle] *n.f.* **1.** flight (of bird, projectile, etc.); **prendre sa v.,** to take wing; **tirer à toute v.,** to fire (a gun) (i) at maximum elevation, (ii) at random; **lancer qch. à toute v.,** to send sth. flying, to hurl sth.; *Rugby Fb:* **coup de v.,** punt; *Ten:* **relancer une balle à la v.,** to volley a return; **v. amortie,** stop volley; drop volley; **attraper une balle à la v.,** to catch a ball in mid air; **saisir une allusion à la v.,** to catch an allusion promptly, instantly; *Agr:* **semer à la v.,** to broadcast. **2.** (*a*) flock, flight (of crows, etc.); covey (of partridges); band, bevy (of girls, etc.); (*b*) rank, high standing; (*of pers.*) **de haute v.,** (i) high-class, top-flight; (ii) high-flying. **3.** volley (of missiles); shower (of blows); **recevoir une bonne v.,** to get a sound thrashing; **sonner à toute v.,** (i) to set all the bells ringing; (ii) (*of bells*) to ring a full peal, be in full peal. **4. v. d'escalier,** flight of stairs. **5.** *Tchn:* (*a*) jib (of crane); (*b*) chase (of gun).

voler¹ [vɔle] *v.i.* to fly; (*a*) **v. de ses propres ailes,** to fend for oneself; to find one's feet; **on aurait entendu v. une mouche,** you could have heard a pin drop; **v. en éclats,** to fly into pieces; **faire v. un cerf-volant,** to fly a kite; (*b*) (*of the mind*) to soar; (*c*) *Lit:* to travel fast; to move with speed; **le temps vole,** time flies; **il vola revoir ses amis,** he flew back, rushed back, sped back, to his friends; **faire v. une nouvelle,** to spread a piece of news.

voler² *v.tr.* **1.** to steal; **v. qch. à qn,** to steal sth. from s.o.; to rob s.o. of sth.; **je me suis fait v. mon pardessus,** I've had my overcoat stolen; *F:* **il ne l'a pas volé,** it serves him right. **2.** (*a*) to rob (s.o.); (*b*) to swindle, cheat (s.o.).

volet [vɔlɛ] *n.m.* **1.** (*a*) *A:* sorting board (for seeds, etc.); (*b*) **trié sur le v.,** hand-picked; (*c*) flatboard, paddle (of waterwheel). **2.** (*a*) (i) inside shutter (of window); (ii) (= CONTREVENT) outside shutter; (iii) shop shutter; **ouvrir, fermer, les volets,** to open, close, the shutters; **mettre, enlever, les volets,** to put up, take down, the shutters; **volets d'un triptyque,** volets of a triptych; (*b*) *I.C.E:* throttle valve, butterfly valve (of carburettor); (*c*) *El:* **indicateur à volets,** drop indicator (of annunciator board, etc.); *Tp:* **v. d'appel,** call indicator, disc, drop; (*d*) **carte à v.,** stub card; (*e*) *Av:* flap; **v. de courbure,** camber-changing flap; **v. d'intrados,** split flap; **sortir, rentrer, les volets,** to lower, raise, flaps.

voleter [vɔlte] *v.i.* **(il volette; il volettera)** (*of bird*) to flutter; **v. d'arbre en arbre,** to flit from tree to tree.

voleur, -euse [vɔlœr, -øz] **1.** *n.* (*a*) thief; robber; burglar; **v. à la tire,** pickpocket; **v. à l'étalage,** shoplifter; **v. d'enfants,** kidnapper; **au v.!** stop thief! **ce commerçant est un v.,** this shopkeeper is a swindler, a shark; *Hist:* **v. de grand chemin,** highwayman, footpad; (*b*) **v. d'idées,** stealer of ideas; **v. de moutons,** sheep stealer. **2.** *a.* thieving, thievish; rapacious (tradesman, etc.); pilfering (child).

volière [vɔljɛr] *n.f.* (*a*) aviary; (*b*) pigeon run.

volige [vɔliʒ] *n.f.* *Const:* (*a*) scantling, batten; **caisse en voliges,** crate; (*b*) slate lath.

voligeage [vɔliʒaʒ] *n.m.* *Const:* (*a*) battening; (*b*) lathing.

voliger [vɔliʒe] *v.tr.* **(je voligeai(s); n. voligeons)** *Const:* (*a*) to batten; (*b*) to lath.

volis [vɔli] *n.m.* broken tree top.

volitif, -ive [vɔlitif, -iv] *a.* volitional, volitive.

volition [vɔlisjɔ̃] *n.f.* volition.

volley-ball [vɔlɛbol] *n.m.* *Sp:* volleyball.

volleyeur, -euse [vɔlɛjœr, -øz] *n.* **1.** volleyball player. **2.** *Ten:* volleyer.

volontaire [vɔlɔ̃tɛr] **1.** *a.* (*a*) voluntary; **homicide v.,** voluntary homicide; *Mil:* **engagé v.,** voluntarily enlisted man; volunteer; (*b*) (*of pers.*) self-willed, wilful, headstrong, obstinate; **menton v.,** firm, determined, chin. **2.** *n.* volunteer.

volontairement [vɔlɔ̃tɛrmɑ̃] *adv.* **1.** voluntarily; willingly. **2.** deliberately, intentionally.

volontariat [vɔlɔ̃tarja] *n.m.* *Mil:* voluntary service.

volonté [vɔlɔ̃te] *n.f.* **1.** will; (*a*) **la v. de vaincre,** the will to win; **v. de fer,** will of iron, iron will; **cause indépendante de la v. de qn,** cause beyond s.o.'s control; **par un effort de la v.,** by an effort of will(power); **manque de v.,** lack of will(power); **ne pas avoir de v.,** to have no will of one's own; **avec la meilleure v. du monde,** with the best will in the world; (*b*) **bonne v.,** goodwill; willingness; **mauvaise v.,** ill will; unwillingness; **montrer de bonne, de mauvaise, v.,** to do sth. willingly, unwillingly; to do sth. with a good, a bad, grace; **il montre toujours de la bonne v.,** he always shows willing; **faire qch. de bonne v.,** to do sth. of one's own free will, with a good grace; **homme de bonne v.,** volunteer (for dangerous enterprise, etc.); (*c*) **en faire à sa v.,** to have one's own way; **à v.,** at will; ad lib; (*in restaurant*) **vin à v.** = drink as much wine as you like; *Cu:* **ajouter du sucre à v.,** add sugar to taste; **billet payable à v.,** promissory note payable on demand; *Mil:* **feu à v.,** independent firing; fire at will; **de sa propre v.,** of one's own accord; spontaneously. **2.** (*a*) **les dernières volontés (de qn),** (s.o.'s) last will and testament; **ses dernières volontés,** his last wishes; (*b*) **elle fait ses quatre volontés,** she does just what she pleases; **elle lui fait faire ses quatre volontés,** she can twist him round her little finger.

volontiers [vɔlɔ̃tje] *adv.* (*a*) willingly, gladly, with pleasure; **très v.,** I'd love to; **je prendrais v. un verre de vin,** I could do with a glass of wine; **il cause v.,** he is fond of talking; (*b*) readily; **on croit v. que . . .,** we are apt to think that . . ..

volt [vɔlt] *n.m.* *El.Meas:* volt.

voltage [vɔltaʒ] *n.m.* *El:* voltage.

voltaïque [vɔltaik] *a.* *El:* voltaic (cell, pile).

voltairien, -ienne [vɔltɛrjɛ̃, -jɛn] *a.* & *n.* Voltairian.

voltampère [vɔltɑ̃pɛr] *n.m.* *El.Meas:* voltampere.

volte [vɔlt] *n.f.* (*a*) *Equit:* *Fenc:* volt; (*b*) *Nau:* turn (to alter course).

volte-face [vɔltəfas] *n.f.inv.* (*a*) turning round; *esp. NAm:* about-face; **faire v.-f.,** to turn round; (*b*) *Fig:* volte-face; U turn; *esp. NAm:* about-face; **faire v.-f.,** to reverse one's opinions, one's policy; to do a U turn.

volter [vɔlte] *v.i.* *Equit:* **faire v. un cheval,** to make a horse circle.

voltige [vɔltiʒ] *n.f.* **1.** *Equit:* mounted gymnastics; **haute v.,** trick riding. **2.** (*a*) acrobatics; flying-trapeze exercises; (*b*) *Av:* aerobatics; **pilote de v.,** stunt pilot.

voltiger [vɔltiʒe] *v.i.* **(je voltigeai(s); n. voltigeons) 1.** to perform on horseback; to do acrobatics; to perform on the flying trapeze. **2.** (*of bird, insect*) to fly about; to flit; (*of curtain, flag, etc.*) to flutter, flap.

voltigeur, -euse [vɔltiʒœr, -øz] **1.** *n.* performer on horseback; acrobat; trapeze artist. **2.** *n.m.* *Mil:* *A:* light infantryman; rifleman.

voltmètre [vɔltmɛtr̥] *n.m.* *El:* voltmeter.

volubile [vɔlybil] *a.* (*a*) *Bot:* voluble; twining (stalk); (*b*) (*of pers.*) voluble.

volubilis [vɔlybilis] *n.m.* *Bot:* convolvulus; **v. des jardins,** morning glory.

volubilité [vɔlybilite] *n.f.* volubility; **parler avec v.,** to be a voluble talker, to talk volubly, glibly.

volume [vɔlym] *n.m.* **1.** volume; tome; **il faudrait des volumes pour raconter . . .,** it would take volumes to relate . . .. **2.** (*a*) volume, bulk, mass (of solid or fluid); **v. excessif,** bulkiness (of parcel, etc.); *Nau:* **chargé en v.,** laden in bulk; **faire du v.,** (i) (*of thg*) to take up a lot of space; (ii) *F:* (*of pers.*) to show off; to throw one's weight about; (*b*) volume (of sound, voice); (*c*) capacity (of bunkers, etc.).

volumétrique [vɔlymetrik] *a.* volumetric.

volumineux, -euse [vɔlyminø, -øz] *a.* **1.** voluminous; bulky, large. **2.** voluminous (writer).

volupté [vɔlypte] *n.f.* (sensual) pleasure, delight; **toutes les voluptés,** every pleasurable sensation.

voluptueusement [vɔlyptɥøzmɑ̃] *adv.* voluptuously.

voluptueux, -euse [vɔlyptɥø, -øz] **1.** *a.* voluptuous. **2.** *n.* voluptuary, sensualist.

volute [vɔlyt] *n.f.* volute; (*a*) *Arch:* *etc:* helix; scroll (of violin); curl, spiral, wreath (of smoke); **ressort en v.,** helical spring; (*b*) *Conch:* whorl.

vomer [vɔmɛr] *n.m.* *Anat:* vomer.

vomi [vɔmi] *n.m.* vomit.
vomique [vɔmik] *a.f. Bot: Pharm:* **noix v.,** nux vomica.
vomiquier [vɔmikje] *n.m. Bot:* nux vomica (tree).
vomir [vɔmir] *v.tr.* (*a*) to vomit; to bring up, spew up (food); *v.i.* to be sick; **avoir envie de v.,** to feel sick; **c'est à (faire) v.,** it's enough to make you sick; it's disgusting; (*b*) (*of chimney, volcano, etc.*) to vomit, belch forth, spew out (smoke, flames, etc.); (*c*) to loathe, abhor (s.o.).
vomissement [vɔmismɑ̃] *n.m.* **1.** vomiting; **il fut pris de vomissements,** he started vomiting, to vomit. **2.** vomit.
vomissure [vɔmisyr] *n.f.* vomit.
vomitif, -ive [vɔmitif, -iv] *a. & n.m. Med:* emetic; vomitory.
vorace [vɔras] *a.* voracious; ravenous; (plant) that exhausts the soil.
voracement [vɔrasmɑ̃] *adv.* voraciously.
voracité [vɔrasite] *n.f.* voracity, voraciousness.
vortex [vɔrtɛks] *n.m.* vortex.
vos [vo] *see* VOTRE.
vosgien, -ienne [voʒjɛ̃, -jɛn] *a. & n. Geog:* (native, inhabitant) of the Vosges.
votant, -ante [vɔtɑ̃, -ɑ̃t] *n.* voter.
vote [vɔt] *n.m.* **1.** (*a*) vote; (*b*) voting, ballot(ing), poll; **droit de v.,** franchise; **accorder le droit de v. aux femmes,** to give women the vote; **prendre part au v.,** to go to the poll; to vote; **bulletin de v.,** ballot paper; **section de v.,** polling district, station. **2.** *Pol:* **v. d'une loi,** passing of a bill; **provoquer un v.,** to challenge a division; **v. de confiance,** vote of confidence.
voter [vɔte] **1.** *v.i.* to vote; **v. à main levée,** to vote by (a) show of hands; **v. pour, contre, un projet de loi,** to vote for, against, a bill; **v. communiste,** to vote communist; **v. (pour) Thomas!** vote for Thomas! **2.** *v.tr.* (*a*) *Pol:* to pass, carry (a bill); (*b*) to vote (money, etc.); **v. des remerciements à qn,** to pass a vote of thanks to s.o.
votif, -ive [vɔtif, -iv] *a.* votive (offering, mass).
votre, *pl.* **vos** [vɔtr̥, vo] *poss.a.* your; **un de vos amis,** a friend of yours; **v. père et v. mère,** *Lit:* **vos père et mère,** your father and mother.
vôtre [votr̥] **1.** *poss.a. A: & Lit:* yours; **je suis tout v.,** I am entirely at your service. **2. le v., la v., les vôtres** (*a*) *poss.pron.* yours, your own; **sa mère et la v.,** his mother and yours; **mes enfants ressemblent plutôt aux vôtres,** my children are more like yours; *F:* **à la v.!** cheers! (your) good health! (*b*) *n.m.* (i) **il faut y mettre du v.,** you must put some of your own effort into it; you must do your share; (ii) *pl.* your own (family, friends, etc.); *NAm:* your own folks; **je bois à vous et aux vôtres,** I drink to you and yours; **je serai des vôtres ce soir,** I'll be with you, joining you, tonight; (iii) *F:* **vous avez encore fait des vôtres,** you've been up to your old tricks again.
vouer [vwe] *v.tr.* to vow, dedicate, consecrate; **v. obéissance au roi,** to pledge one's allegiance to the king; **v. sa vie, se v., à l'étude,** to devote, dedicate, give up, one's life to study; *F:* **il ne sait (pas) à quel saint se v.,** he's at his wits' end, he doesn't know which way to turn; **voué à l'échec,** doomed to failure.
vouloir[1] [vulwar] *v.tr.* (*pr.p.* **voulant;** *p.p.* **voulu;** *pr.ind.* **je veux, il veut, n. voulons, ils veulent;** *pr.sub.* **je veuille, n. voulions, ils veuillent;** *imp. in* **1. voulez,** *otherwise* **veuille, veuillez;** *impf.* **je voulais;** *p.h.* **je voulus;** *fu.* **je voudrai) 1.** to will (sth.); to be determined on (sth.); **ce que Dieu veut,** the will of God; **Dieu le veuille!** please God! **homme qui ne sait pas v.,** man who has no willpower, who cannot make up his mind; *Prov:* **v., c'est pouvoir,** where there's a will there's a way; **vous l'avez voulu!** you have only yourself to blame! **nous n'avons pas voulu cela,** we didn't expect that. **2.** (*a*) to want, to wish (for), to desire (sth.); **il sait ce qu'il veut,** he knows what he wants, he knows his own mind; he has a will of his own; **faites comme vous voudrez,** do as you please; **c'est comme vous voudrez,** just as you like; **vous le ferez, je le veux!** you *shall* do it; **qu'il le veuille ou non,** whether he likes it or not; **je ne le veux pas!** I will not have it! **que voulez-vous? qu'est-ce que vous voulez?** (i) what do you want? (ii) what do you expect? **que voulez-vous que j'y fasse?** what do you want me to do about it? **v. qch. de qn,** to want sth. from s.o.; **que lui voulez-vous?** what do you want from him? **combien en voulez-vous?** how much are you asking for it? **voulez-vous du thé?** would you like some tea? **v. de qch.,** to want (some of) sth.; **je ne veux pas de cela,** I'll have none of that; **ils ne veulent pas de moi,** they won't have me; **en voulez-vous?** do you want any? will you have some? would you like some? **de l'argent en veux-tu (en voilà),** as much money as you like; money galore; (*b*) **v. qn pour roi,** to want s.o. for a king, as king; **je te veux heureuse,** I want you to be happy; (*c*) **v. du bien à qn,** to wish s.o. well; **je ne lui veux pas de mal,** I mean him no harm; **en v. à qn,** to bear s.o. a grudge; **ne m'en veuillez pas,** don't be cross with me; **en v. à qn de qch., d'avoir fait qch.,** to have a grudge against s.o. for sth., for doing sth.; **à qui en voulez-vous?** what's the trouble now? **pourquoi lui en veux-tu?** what have you got against him? **s'en v.,** to be angry, annoyed, with oneself **(de qch.,** about sth.). **3. v.** + *inf.* (*expressed or understood*); **v. que** + *sub.* (*a*) to will, to require, to demand; **le sort voulut qu'il mourût,** fate willed, ordained, that he should die; **le mauvais sort voulut qu'il arrivât trop tard,** as ill luck would have it he arrived too late; **je veux être obéi,** I intend, mean, to be obeyed; **v. absolument, à toute force, faire qch.,** to insist on doing sth.; to be determined to do sth.; **je veux absolument que vous veniez,** I insist on your coming; **le moteur ne veut pas démarrer,** the engine won't start; (*b*) to want, wish; **il voulait me frapper,** he wanted to hit me; **il ne voulait pas s'en aller,** he didn't want to go; **je fais de lui ce que je veux,** I can do as I like with him; **j'aurais tant voulu le voir,** I should so much like to have seen him; **j'aurais voulu y rester toujours,** I would, could, have stayed there for ever; **je voudrais bien être à votre place,** I wish I were in your place; **voulez-vous que j'ouvre la fenêtre?** shall I, should I, open the window? **je veux que vous sachiez que . . .,** I should like you to know that . . .; **j'aurais voulu qu'il le sache,** I wish he had been told; **je voudrais le voir me parler sur ce ton,** I'd like to see him speak to me in that tone of voice; **je veux que vous soyez heureux,** I want you to be happy; **que voulez-vous que je fasse?** what do you expect me to do? **rentrons, voulez-vous?** let's go in, shall we? (*c*) to try to (do sth.); **il voulut me frapper,** he made as if to strike me; **quand j'ai voulu l'embrasser,** when I tried to kiss her; (*d*) to mean, intend; **nous n'avons jamais su ce qu'il voulait faire,** we never knew what he meant to do; **faire qch. sans le v.,** to do sth. unintentionally, without meaning it; (*e*) **v. (bien) faire qch.,** to consent, be willing, to do sth.; **je veux bien que vous veniez,** I'd like, love, you to come; I'm quite willing for you to come; **voulez-vous bien attendre un instant?** would you please wait, would you care to wait, a moment? **veuillez (bien) vous asseoir,** (i) will you please sit down; (ii) do (please) sit down; won't you sit down? **je veux bien attendre,** I'm quite happy, quite willing, to wait; **venez-vous avec nous?—je veux bien,** are you coming with us?—I'd like, love, to; **si vous voulez,** if you like, if you wish; **je viens quand je veux,** I come

when I choose, when I like, when I please; **si vous (le) voulez bien,** if you don't mind; (*f*) (**bien** *used as an intensive*) **voulez-vous bien vous taire!** *will* you be quiet! *F:* do shut up! **4.** (*a*) to admit, allow (sth. for the sake of argument); **je veux bien que vous ayez raison,** (I grant that) you may be right; **vous n'avez rien à vous reprocher, je le veux bien, mais . . .,** you are in no way to blame, I am ready to admit, but . . .; (*b*) to be convinced, to maintain; **il veut absolument que je me sois trompé,** he insists that I was mistaken. **5.** (*of thg*) to require, need, demand (sth.); **la vigne veut un terrain crayeux,** the vine requires a chalky soil; **ce verbe veut l'accusatif,** this verb takes the accusative.

vouloir² *n.m.* will; **bon, mauvais, v.,** goodwill, ill will (**pour, envers,** towards).

voulu [vuly] *a.* **1.** required, requisite (formalities, etc.); **cela se fera à l'heure voulue,** it will be done in due time. **2.** deliberate, intentional; **négligence voulue,** studied carelessness.

vous [vu] *pers.pron. sg. & pl.* **1.** (*unstressed*) (*a*) (*subject*) you; (*b*) (*object*) you; to you; **il ne v. connaît pas,** he doesn't know you; **je v. en ai parlé,** I've spoken to you about it; (*c*) (*reflexive*) **v. êtes-v. bien amusé(e), amusé(e)s?** did you enjoy yourself, yourselves? **v. allez v. faire du mal,** you're going to hurt yourself, yourselves; **taisez-v.!** be quiet! (*d*) (*reciprocal*) **est-ce que v. v. connaissez?** do you know each other, one another? (*e*) (*as object case of* **on**) **cette joie qui vous saisit quand on l'entend,** the joy one feels, you feel, when you hear him. **2.** (*stressed*) (*a*) (*subject*) you; **v. et votre femme,** you and your wife; **v. deux, v. tous,** you two, the two of you; you both, both of you; you all, all of you; **v. autres Anglais,** you English; **c'est v. qui êtes arrivé(e) le premier, la première; c'est v. qui êtes arrivé(e)s les premiers, les premières,** it was you who arrived first; **c'était v.-même qui me l'avez dit,** you told me so yourself; **v., v. avez raison; v. avez raison, v.,** you're the one who's right; (*b*) (*object*) **c'est à v. que je parle,** it's you I'm talking to; **c'est à v. de jouer,** it's your turn (to play); **ces gants sont à v.,** these gloves are yours; **c'est un ami à v.,** it's a friend of yours; **voilà une photo de v.,** here's a photo of you; **j'ai confiance en v.,** I trust you; (*c*) (*reflexive*) **v. les avez rassemblés autour de v.,** you gathered them round you; **v. ne pensez qu'à v.(-même),** you think only of yourself.

vous-même(s) [vumɛm] *pers.pron.* yourself, *pl.* yourselves; *see* VOUS 2 *and* MÊME 1 (*c*).

vousseau, -eaux [vuso] *n.m.*, **voussoir** [vuswar] *n.m.* voussoir, archstone.

voussure [vusjyr] *n.f. Arch:* curve (of arch); arch moulding.

voûte [vut] *n.f. Arch:* vault, arch; vaulting; **v. d'arête,** groined vault; **v. en berceau,** barrel vault; **v. d'ogives,** ribbed vault; **v. en plein cintre,** semicircular vault; **voûte(s) en éventail,** fan vaulting; **en v.,** vaulted; *Lit:* **la v. céleste,** the vault, canopy, of heaven; *Anat:* **v. crânienne,** dome of the skull; **v. palatine, du palais,** roof of the mouth.

voûté [vute] *a.* (*a*) vaulted, arched (roof, etc.); (*b*) stooping, round-shouldered (person); bent (back).

voûter [vute] **1.** *v.tr.* (*a*) to arch, vault (roof, etc.); (*b*) **l'âge voûte la taille,** age bows the back, makes you stoop. **2.** (*of pers.*) **se v.,** to become bent, bowed, round-shouldered; to begin to stoop.

vouvoiement [vuvwamɑ̃] *n.m.* addressing s.o. as **vous** (as opposed to **tu**).

vouvoyer [vuvwaje] *v.tr.* **(je vouvoie, n. vouvoyons; je vouvoierai)** to address (s.o.) as **vous** (as opposed to **tu**).

voyage [vwajaʒ] *n.m.* (*a*) journey; trip; tour; **v. (touristique) accompagné,** conducted tour; **v. d'information,** fact-finding mission, tour; **v. d'affaires,** business trip; **aimer les voyages,** to be fond of travel, of travelling; **v. en chemin de fer,** rail(way) journey; **v. (sur mer),** (sea) voyage; **v. d'agrément,** pleasure trip; **v. de noces,** honeymoon; **v. autour du monde,** world tour; **il est en v.,** he is travelling; **est-il toujours en v.?** is he still away, still on his travels? **bateau engagé au v.,** ship hired by the run; **frais de v.,** travelling expenses; **compagnon de v.,** (i) travelling companion; (ii) fellow passenger; **bon v.!** have a good trip! *Lit:* **faire le grand v.,** to go on one's last journey (*b*) (drug) trip.

voyager [vwajaʒe] *v.i.* **(je voyageai(s); n. voyageons) 1.** (*a*) to travel; **v. par mer, par chemin de fer,** to travel by sea, by rail; (*b*) *Com:* to travel; *F:* to be on the road; **v. pour les vins,** to travel in wine. **2.** (*of goods, etc.*) to be transported; **vin qui ne peut pas v.,** wine that does not travel.

voyageur, -euse [vwajaʒœr, -øz] **1.** *n.* (*a*) traveller, *NAm:* traveler; (*in train, etc.*) passenger; (*in taxi*) fare; (*b*) *esp. Hist:* voyager, explorer; (*c*) **v. (de commerce),** (commercial) traveller. **2.** *a.* (*a*) travelling; **commis v.,** commercial traveller; (*b*) **pigeon v.,** carrier pigeon, homing pigeon.

voyance [vwajɑ̃s] *n.f. Psychics:* clairvoyance.

voyant, -ante [vwajɑ̃, -ɑ̃t] **1.** *n.* (*a*) sighted (person) (as opposed to blind); (*b*) clairvoyant; (*c*) *A:* seer, prophet. **2.** *a.* gaudy, loud, garish (colour, *NAm:* color); showy, conspicuous (monument, etc.). **3.** *n.m.* (*a*) mark, signal; *Surv: etc:* sighting board, slide vane, sight (of levelling rod); *Nau:* sphere (of lightship); (*b*) sighting slit, aperture (of scientific instrument); (*c*) *Aut:* **v. d'huile,** oil indicator light; warning light.

voyelle [vwajɛl] *n.f. Ling:* vowel.

voyeur, -euse [vwajœr, -øz] *n.* voyeur, voyeuse; *F:* Peeping Tom.

voyeurisme [vwajœrism] *n.m. Psy:* voyeurism.

voyou [vwaju] **1.** *n.m.* (*a*) (cheeky) street urchin, guttersnipe; (*b*) (young) lout, layabout; hooligan, yob(bo). **2.** *a.* (*usu. inv., f. occ.* **voyoute**) crude, loutish; **verve voyoute,** gutter wit.

vrac [vrak] *n.m.* **en v.,** loose, in bulk; **charger en v.,** to load in bulk; **marchandises en v.,** loose goods (not packed); **outils jetés en v. sur le plancher,** tools thrown higgledy piggledy on the floor.

vrai [vrɛ] **1.** *a.* (*a*) true, truthful; **c'est (bien) v.!** it's true! that's quite right! *F:* **pour de v.,** really, seriously; *esp. NAm:* for real; **c'est pour de v.,** I'm serious; I (really) mean it; (*b*) true, real, genuine; **le v. Dieu,** the true God; **un v. ami,** a real friend; **un v. Anglais d'Angleterre,** a real Englishman; an Englishman born and bred; **un v. diamant,** a real, genuine, diamond; **couleurs vraies,** lifelike, realistic, colours, *NAm:* colors; *Astr:* **temps v.,** true time; (*c*) downright, regular; **c'est une vraie attrape,** it's a real, a downright, swindle. **2.** *adv.* truly, really, indeed; **dire v.,** to tell the truth; **à v. dire, à dire v.,** as a matter of fact; **faire v.,** to write, paint, etc., realistically; **tu m'aimes (pas) v.?** you *do* love me, don't you? **v. de v.!** really and truly! **pas v.?** I'm right, aren't I? *F:* **c'est pas v.!** well, really? oh, no! *A: & Lit:* **de v.,** indeed, in truth. **3.** *n.m.* **distinguer le v. du faux,** to distinguish truth from falsehood; **être dans le v.,** to be right; **il y a du v. là-dedans,** there's some truth in it.

vraiment [vrɛmɑ̃] *adv.* really, truly, in truth; **vous êtes v. trop bon,** you are really too kind; **v.?** indeed? really? **ils voyagent beaucoup.—v.?** they travel a great deal.—do they? **oui v.,** yes indeed.

vraisemblable [vrɛsɑ̃blabl̩] **1.** *a.* probable, likely; credible; plausible; conceivable; **il n'est pas v. que** + *sub.*, it is (i) hardly credible, (ii) hardly to be expected, that . . .; **excuse peu v.,** unconvincing excuse. **2.** *n.m.* what is probable, likely.

vraisemblablement [vrɛsɑ̃blabləmɑ̃] *adv.* in all likelihood; probably, very likely; conceivably.

vraisemblance [vrɛsɑ̃blɑ̃s] *n.f.* probability, likelihood; verisimilitude; **selon toute v.,** in all probability.

vrille [vrij] *n.f.* **1.** *Bot:* tendril. **2.** *Tls:* gimlet, borer, piercer; **yeux percés en v.,** gimlet eyes, beady eyes. **3.** *Av:* spin; **descente en v.,** spinning dive; **faire la v., se mettre en v., tomber en v.,** to spin; to get into a spin; **monter en v.,** to corkscrew; **v. à plat,** flat spin; **v. serrée,** steep spin; **v. sur le dos,** inverted spin.

vrillé [vrije] *a.* (*a*) spiral; twisted, kinked (thread); (*b*) *Bot:* with tendrils; tendrilled.

vrillée [vrije] *n.f. Bot: F:* bindweed.

vriller [vrije] **1.** *v.tr.* to bore (with a gimlet). **2.** *v.i.* (*a*) (*of aircraft, etc.*) to spiral, spin (up, down); (*b*) (*of thread, rope*) to twist, kink; to curl up.

vrillette [vrijɛt] *n.f. Ent:* deathwatch (beetle).

vrombir [vrɔ̃bir] *v.i.* (*of flies, etc.*) to buzz; (*of top, aircraft, etc.*) to hum; (*of engine*) to throb, purr.

vrombissement [vrɔ̃bismɑ̃] *n.m.* buzz(ing) (of insects); hum(ming) (of top, aircraft, etc.); throb(bing), purr(ing) (of engine).

vu [vy] **1.** *n.m.* (*a*) **au vu de tous,** openly, publicly; **au vu et au su de tous,** as everyone knows; **c'est du déjà vu,** that's nothing new; *Com:* **sur le vu de la facture,** (up)on presentation of the invoice; (*b*) *Jur:* preamble (of a decree). **2.** *prep.* considering, seeing; **vu la chaleur je voyagerai de nuit,** because of, owing to, the heat, I shall travel by night; *conj.phr. O:* **vu que** + *ind.,* seeing that . . .; *Jur:* whereas . . . .

vue [vy] *n.f.* **1.** (*a*) (eye)sight; vision; **perdre la v.,** to lose one's sight; **avoir la v. courte, basse,** to be short-sighted; **jeter, porter, la v. sur qch.,** to take a look at sth.; **tourner la v. du côté de la maison,** to look towards the house; **connaître qn de v.,** to know s.o. by sight; **perdre qn de v.,** (i) to lose sight of s.o.; (ii) to lose touch with s.o.; **à perte de v.,** as far as the eye can see; **parler à perte de v.,** to talk endlessly; to keep on talking; **personnes les plus en v.,** people most in the public eye; **une personnalité en v.,** a prominent, conspicuous, personality; **mettre qch. (bien) en v.,** (i) to display (sth.) (conspicuously); (ii) to bring (sth.) to the fore; **faire qch. à la v. de tous,** to do sth. in sight, in full view, of everybody; **se tenir hors de v.,** to keep out of sight; *F:* **à v. de nez,** at a rough estimate; **à v. d'œil,** visibly; rapidly; *Av: Nau:* **navigation à v.,** visual navigation; *Av:* **voler à v.,** to fly visually; (*b*) *Psychics:* **seconde v.,** second sight. **2.** view; **échange de vues,** exchange of views; **vues saines,** sound views. **3. à la v. de qn, qch.,** at the sight of s.o., sth.; **à première v.,** at first sight; **jouer un morceau à v.,** to play a piece at sight; **à v., en v., de terre,** (with)in sight of land; *Com:* **payable à v.,** payable at sight. **4.** view; (*a*) outlook; **chambre qui a v. sur le jardin,** room that looks out on(to) the garden; **v. de face, de côté,** front view, side view; **v. en coupe,** cross section; **vues de Paris,** views of Paris; (*b*) *Jur:* window, light (of house); **droit de vues,** ancient lights; **condamner les vues,** to block up the windows; (*c*) intention, purpose, design; **avoir des vues sur qn, qch.,** to have plans for, designs on, s.o., sth.; **avoir qch. en v.,** to have sth. in view, in mind; **en v. de,** with a view to; **travailler en v. de l'avenir,** to work with an eye to the future.

Vulcain [vylkɛ̃] **1.** *Pr.n.m. Myth: Astr:* Vulcan. **2.** *n.m. Ent:* red admiral (butterfly).

vulcanisation [vylkanizasjɔ̃] *n.f. Ind:* vulcanization (of rubber).

vulcaniser [vylkanize] *v.tr. Ind:* to vulcanize, cure (rubber).

vulgaire [vylgɛr] **1.** *a.* vulgar; (*a*) common, everyday (custom, etc.); **l'opinion v.,** the common, general, opinion; **langue v.,** vernacular; **le latin v.,** vulgar Latin; **nom v. (d'une plante),** common name (for a plant); (*b*) low, unrefined, coarse. **2.** *n.m.* (*a*) **le v.,** the common people, herd; (*b*) **donner dans le v.,** to lapse into vulgarity.

vulgairement [vylgɛrmɑ̃] *adv.* vulgarly. **1.** generally, commonly. **2.** with (a) lack of refinement.

vulgarisateur, -trice [vylgarizatœr, -tris] *n.* popularizer (of knowledge).

vulgarisation [vylgarizasjɔ̃] *n.f.* popularization (of knowledge); **ouvrage de v.,** popular work, popular treatise.

vulgariser [vylgarize] *v.tr.* **1.** to popularize (knowledge). **2.** to coarsen, vulgarize.

vulgarisme [vylgarism] *n.m.* vulgarism.

vulgarité [vylgarite] *n.f.* vulgarity.

Vulgate (la) [lavylgat] *n.f.* the Vulgate (version of the Bible).

vulnérabilité [vylnerabilite] *n.f.* vulnerability.

vulnérable [vylnerabl̥] *a.* vulnerable.

vulnéraire [vylnerɛr] *n.f. Bot:* kidney vetch, lady's finger, woundwort.

vulpin [vylpɛ̃] *n.m. Bot:* foxtail (grass).

vulvaire [vylvɛr] **1.** *a. Anat:* vulvar. **2.** *n.f. Bot:* stinking goosefoot.

vulve [vylv] *n.f. Anat:* vulva.

vumètre [vymɛtr̥] *n.m. Elcs:* modulation meter.

W

W, w [dubləve] *n.m.* (the letter) W, w.

wagnérien, -ienne [vagnerjɛ̃, -jɛn] *a. & n. Mus:* Wagnerian.

wagon [vagɔ̃] *n.m. Rail:* carriage, coach, *NAm:* car (for passengers); truck, wagon, *NAm:* car (for goods); **monter en w.,** to get into, board, the train; **w. à bagages,** luggage van; *NAm:* baggage car; **w. à bestiaux,** cattle truck; *NAm:* stock car; **w. frigorifique,** refrigerated van; **w. à décrocher (en marche),** slip coach.

wagon-bar [vagɔ̃bar] *n.m. Rail:* buffet car; *pl. wagons-bars.*

wagon-citerne [vagɔ̃sitɛrn] *n.m. Rail:* tank car, tank wagon; *pl. wagons-citernes.*

wagon-couloir [vagɔ̃kulwar] *n.m. Rail:* corridor carriage, coach; *pl. wagons-couloirs.*

wagon-foudre [vagɔ̃fudr̥] *n.m. Rail:* tank car, tank wagon (for beer, etc.); *pl. wagons-foudres.*

wagon-lit [vagɔ̃li] *n.m. Rail:* sleeping car; *F:* sleeper; *pl. wagons-lits.*

wagon(n)et [vagɔnɛ] *n.m.* tip truck, tip wagon.

wagonnier [vagɔnje] *n.m. Rail:* truck shunter.

wagon-poste [vagɔ̃pɔst] *n.m. Rail:* mail van; *pl. wagons-poste.*

wagon-réservoir [vagɔ̃rezɛrvwar] *n.m. Rail:* tank car, wagon; *pl. wagons-réservoirs.*

wagon-restaurant [vagɔ̃rɛstɔrɑ̃] *n.m. Rail:* restaurant car; dining car; diner; *pl. wagons-restaurants.*

Walkyrie [valkiri] *n.f. Myth:* Valkyrie, Walkyrie.

wallaby [walabi] *n.m. Z:* wallaby; *pl. wallabies.*

wallace [valas, wa-] *n.f. F:* (*also* **fontaine W.**) drinking fountain.

wallon, -onne [valɔ̃, -ɔn; wa-] **1.** *a. & n. Geog:* Walloon. **2.** *n.m. Ling:* Walloon.

wapiti [wapiti] *n.m. Z:* wapiti, American elk.

warrant [warɑ̃t, va-] *n.m.* (warehouse, dock) warrant; **w. en marchandises,** produce warrant.

warranter [warɑ̃te, va-] *v.tr.* **marchandises warrantées,** goods covered by a warehouse warrant.

wassingue [wasɛ̃g, va-] *n.f.* swab, floorcloth.

water-closet [watɛrklɔzɛt] *n.m.* lavatory, toilet; *pl. water-closets.*

wateringue [watərɛ̃g] *n.f. Dial:* **1.** drainage works. **2.** draining syndicate.

waters [watɛr, va-] *n.m.pl. F:* lavatory, loo, toilet, *U.S:* john; **où sont les w.?** where is the toilet?

watt [wat] *n.m. El:* watt, ampere-volt.

wattage [wataʒ] *n.m. El:* wattage.

watt-heure [watœr] *n.m. El:* watt-hour; *pl. watts-heures.*

wattman [watman] *n.m.* driver (of electric tram, train); motor-man; *pl. wattmen* [watmɛn].

wattmètre [watmɛtr̥] *n.m. El:* wattmeter.

week-end [wikɛnd] *n.m.* weekend; **partir en w.,** to go away for the weekend; *pl. week-ends.*

western [wɛstɛrn] *n.m. F: Cin:* western.

Westphalie [vɛs(t)fali] *Pr.n.f. Geog:* Westphalia.

wharf [warf] *n.m.* wharf.

whisky [wiski] *n.m.* whisky; *pl. whiskys, whiskies.*

whist [wist] *n.m.* whist; **w. de Gand,** solo (whist).

wigwam [wigwam] *n.m.* wigwam.

wisigoth, -othe [vizigo, -ɔt] *Hist:* **1.** *a.* Visigothic. **2.** *n.* Visigoth.

wolfram [vɔlfram] *n.m. Miner:* wolfram.

wombat [vɔ̃ba] *n.m. Z:* wombat.

wurtembergeois, -oise [vyrtɛ̃bɛrʒwa, -waz] *Geog:* **1.** *a.* of Würtemberg. **2.** *n.* Würtemberger.

X

X, x [iks] *n.m.* the letter X, x; **Monsieur X,** Mr X; **rayons X,** x rays; *F:* **l'X,** the *École polytechnique*; **un X,** a student at the *École polytechnique*; **je vous l'ai dit x fois,** I've told you a thousand times.
xanthome [gzɑ̃tom] *n.m. Med:* xanthoma.
xanthophylle [gzɑ̃tɔfil] *n.f. Bio-Ch: Bot:* xanthophyll.
xénon [ksenɔ̃] *n.m. Ch:* xenon.
xénophobe [ksenɔfɔb] *a. & n.* xenophobe.
xénophobie [ksenɔfɔbi] *n.f.* xenophobia.
xéranthème [kserɑ̃tɛm] *n.m. Bot:* xeranthemum.
Xérès [kserɛs, gzerɛs] **1.** *Pr.n. Geog:* Jerez. **2.** *n.m.* (*also* **vin de X.**) sherry.
xérodermie [kserɔdɛrmi] *n.f. Med:* xeroderm(i)a.
xérophyte [kserɔfit] *Bot:* **1.** *a.* xerophytic. **2.** *n.f.* xerophyte.
xérose [kseroz] *n.f. Med:* xerosis.
xi [ksi] *n.m. Gr.Alph:* xi.
xiphoïde [ksifɔid] *a. Anat:* **l'appendice x.,** the xiphoid process.
xiphophore [ksifɔfɔr] *n.m. Ich:* sword-tail.
xylographe [ksilɔgraf] *n.m.* wood engraver.
xylographie [ksilɔgrafi] *n.f.* **1.** xylography, wood engraving. **2.** xylograph, woodcut.
xylophone [ksilɔfɔn, gz-] *n.m. Mus:* xylophone.

Y

An asterisk (*) *before a noun indicates that the definite article is* **le** *or* **la** *not* **l'**.

Y, y¹ [igrek] *n.m.* (the letter) Y, y.

y² [i] *adv. & pron.* **1.** *adv.* there; here; **est-il à Paris?—oui, il y est,** is he in Paris?—yes, he is (there); **j'y suis, j'y reste!** here I am and here I stay! **je n'y suis pour personne,** I am not at home to anybody; **en quittant la table j'y laissai ma lettre,** when I got up from the table I left my letter on it; *F:* **ah, j'y suis!** ah, now I understand! I've got it! I'm with you! **vous n'y êtes pas du tout,** you're not with it; you're wide of the mark; **pendant que vous y êtes,** while you are about, at, it. **2.** *pron.inv.* (*a*) **j'y pense sans cesse,** I am always thinking of it; **j'y gagnerai,** I shall gain by it; **je m'y attendais,** I expected as much; **venez nous voir—je n'y manquerai pas,** come and see us—I certainly shall; *F:* I'll be there! (*b*) (*standing for pers. just mentioned*) **pensez-vous à lui?—oui j'y pense,** do you think of him?—yes, I do; **les femmes? je n'y comprends rien,** women? I can't understand them. **3.** (*indeterminate uses*) **je vous y prends!** I have caught you (at it)! **ça y est** [sajɛ], (i) it's done! that's it! (ii) I knew it! **j'y suis pour un tiers,** I'm in for a third share; **il y est pour quelque chose,** he's got a hand in it, got something to do with it; **prix, y compris le port,** price, including carriage. **4.** (*imperative form preceding* **y** *takes* **s** *for liaison*) **vas-y** [vazi], (i) go there; (ii) get on with it! **penses-y** [pɑ̃szi], think of it.

y³ *pers.pron. P:* = IL(s).

***yacht** [jɔt, jat] *n.m.* yacht; **croisière en y.,** yachting cruise.

***yachting** [jɔtiŋ, jatiŋ] *n.m.* yachting.

***yacht(s)man** [jɔt(s)man] *n.m.* yachtsman; *pl. yacht(s)men.*

***ya(c)k** [jak] *n.m. Z:* yak.

***yankee** [jɑ̃ki] *n.m. & a.* Yankee.

***yaourt** [jaurt] *n.m.* yog(h)urt.

***yatagan** [jatagɑ̃] *n.m.* yataghan.

***yearling** [jɛrliŋ] *n.m. Turf:* yearling (colt).

***yéménite** [jemenit] *Geog:* **1.** *a.* Yemeni. **2.** *n.m. & f.* Yemeni, Yemenite.

yen [jɛn] *n.m. Num:* yen.

***yeti** [jɛti] *n.m.* yeti.

yeuse [jøz] *n.f. Bot:* ilex, holm oak, holly oak.

***yé-yé** [jeje] **1.** *a.inv.* pop; **chanteur yé-yé,** pop singer. **2.** (*a*) *n.m.* pop music; (*b*) *n.* pop fan.

y-grec [igrɛk] *n.m.* (the letter) y.

yiddish [jidiʃ] *a. & n.* Yiddish.

***yod** [jɔd] *n.m. Ling:* yod.

***yoga** [jɔga] *n.m.* yoga.

***yog(h)ourt** [jogurt] *n.m.* yog(h)urt.

***yogi** [jɔgi] *n.m.* yogi.

***yole** [jɔl] *n.f. Nau:* gig, skiff, yawl.

***yougoslave** [jugɔslav] *a. & n. Geog:* Yugoslav.

Yougoslavie (la) [lajugɔslavi] *Pr.n.f. Geog:* Yugoslavia.

***youpin, -ine** [jupɛ̃, -in], **youtre** [jutr̥] *n.m. & f. Pej:* Jew, sheeny, yid.

***youyou** [juju] *n.m. Nau:* dinghy.

***yo-yo** [jojo] *n.m. R.t.m:* yo-yo.

ypérite [iperit] *n.f. Ch:* yperite; mustard gas.

ypréau, -aux [ipreo] *n.m. Bot:* **1.** wych elm. **2.** white poplar.

***yucca** [juka] *n.m. Bot:* yucca.

Z

Z, z [zɛd] *n.m.* (the letter) Z, z.
zagaie [sagɛ] *n.f.* assegai.
Zambèze (le) [ləzɑ̃bɛz] *Pr.n.m. Geog:* the Zambezi (river).
Zambie [zɑ̃bi] *Pr.n.f. Geog:* Zambia.
Zanzibar [zɑ̃zibar]) **1.** *Pr.n.m. Geog:* Zanzibar. **2.** *n.m.* (*P:* **zanzi** [zɑ̃zi]) dice game (played for drinks).
zèbre [zɛbr̥] *n.m.* **1.** zebra; *F:* **courir comme un z.,** to run like a hare. **2.** *F:* individual, bod, type.
zébré [zebre] *a.* striped **(de,** with); stripy.
zébrer [zebre] *v.tr.* **(je zèbre; je zébrerai)** to stripe, streak.
zébrure [zebryr] *n.f.* **1.** stripe. **2.** stripes; zebra markings.
zébu [zeby] *n.m.* zebu, humped ox.
zée [ze] *n.m. Ich:* **z. forgeron,** John Dory.
zélateur, -trice [zelatœr, -tris] *n.* zealot; zealous supporter.
zèle [zɛl] *n.m.* zeal, ardour **(pour,** for); **avec z.,** zealously; **brûler de z. pour qch.,** to be fired with enthusiasm for sth.; **faux z.,** misguided zeal; **grève du z.,** work to rule (strike); *F:* **faire du z.,** to be overzealous; to be an eager beaver; **pas de z.!** don't overdo it!
zélé, -ée [zele] *a. & n.* zealous (person); **peu z.,** slack, remiss.
zélote [zelɔt] *n.m. B.Hist:* Zealot.
zélotisme [zelɔtism] *n.m.* zealotry.
zénith [zenit] *n.m. Astr:* zenith; (*of pers.*) **être à son z.,** to have reached one's zenith.
zénithal, -aux [zenital, -o] *a.* zenithal.
zéolite [zeɔlit] *n.f.,* **zéolithe** [zeɔlit] *n.m. Miner:* zeolite.
zéphir(e) [zefir] *a. & n.m. Tex:* **(laine) z.,** zephyr; **(tissu) z.,** zephyr cotton.
zéphyr [zefir] **1.** *n.m.* (*a*) zephyr, west wind; (*b*) balmy breeze; zephyr. **2.** *a. & n.m.* = ZEPHIR(E).
zéro [zero] *n.m.* **1.** nought; *Tp:* **z. sept,** O [ou] seven; **c'est un z.,** he's a mere cipher, a nonentity; *Sp:* **trois à z.,** three nil; *Ten:* **quinze à z.,** fifteen love. **2.** zero (of scale); **point z.,** zero point; *El:* "off" (on electric stove, etc.); *Nau:* **z. (la barre)!** helm amidships! *F:* **être, avoir le moral, à z.,** to be in a low state, in the depths; **partir à z.,** to start from scratch. **3.** *a.* **z. faute,** no mistakes; **z. heure cinq,** 00.05 (double 0 0 five), five past twelve (midnight).
zérotage [zerɔtaʒ] *n.m.* calibration (of thermometers, etc.); fixing of the zero point.
zest [zɛst] *n.m.* **être entre le zist et le z.,** to be neither one thing nor the other; to be betwixt and between; (*of pers.*) to waver (between two courses of action).
zeste [zɛst] *n.m.* (*a*) *Cu:* outer skin, zest (of citrus fruit); **z. confit, z. d'Italie,** candied peel; (*b*) membrane quartering walnut kernel.
zêta [zɛta] *n.m. Gr.Alph:* zeta.
Zeus [zøs] *Pr.n.m. Myth:* Zeus.
zézaiement [zezɛmɑ̃] *n.m.* lisping, lisp.
zézayer [zezeje] *v.i.* **(je zézaie, je zézaye, n. zézayons; je zézaierai, je zézayerai)** to lisp.
zibeline [ziblin] *n.f.* **1.** *Z:* **(martre) z.,** sable. **2.** sable (fur).
zieuter [zjøte] *v.tr. P:* = ZYEUTER.
zig [zig] *n.m. P:* fellow, chap; *esp.* **un bon z.,** a decent type, a good sort.
zigoteau, -eaux, zigoto [zigɔto] *n.m. P:* **c'est un drôle de z.,** he's a queer customer.
zigouiller [ziguje] *v.tr. P:* to kill, murder, knife (s.o.).
zigue [zig] *n.m. P:* = ZIG.
zigzag [zigzag] *n.m.* zigzag; **éclair en z.,** forked lightning; **tranchées en z.,** zigzag trenches; **faire des zigzags,** (*of road, car, etc.*) to zigzag; (*of drunk pers.*) to stagger along; *Nau:* **faire route en z.,** to steer a zigzag course; **rivets disposés en z.,** staggered rivets.
zigzaguer [zigzage] *v.i.* to zigzag.
zinc [zɛ̃g] *n.m.* **1.** zinc; *Com:* spelter; **z. à souder,** spelter solder; **galvanisation au gris de z.,** sherardizing; **pommade à l'oxyde de z.,** zinc ointment. **2.** *F:* (zinc) counter (of public house); bar; **prendre un verre sur le z.,** to have a glass at the counter, bar. **3. gravure sur z.,** zincograph. **4.** *F:* aeroplane; *F:* crate.
zincographie [zɛ̃kɔgrafi] *n.f.* zincography.
zingage [zɛ̃gaʒ] *n.m.* **1.** covering (of roof, etc.) with zinc. **2.** *Metall:* coating with zinc; zincing; **z. au trempé,** galvanizing (of iron).
zingaro [dzingaro] *n.m.* gipsy; *pl. zingari.*
zinguer [zɛ̃ge] *v.tr.* **1.** to cover (roof, etc.) with zinc. **2.** to coat with zinc; to zinc; to galvanize (iron).
zingueur [zɛ̃gœr] *n.m.* (*a*) zinc worker; (*b*) *Const:* zinc roofer.
zinnia [zinja] *n.m. Bot:* zinnia.
zinzolin, -ine [zɛ̃zɔlɛ̃, -in] *a. & n.m.* reddish purple (colour).
zircon [zirkɔ̃] *n.m. Miner:* zircon.
zist [zist] *n.m. see* ZEST.
zizanie [zizani] *n.f.* (*a*) *B:* tare; (*b*) discord; **semer la z. entre les familles,** to sow discord between families; **perpétuellement en z.,** perpetually at loggerheads.
zodiacal, -aux [zɔdjakal, -o] *a.* zodiacal (star, light).
zodiaque [zɔdjak] *n.m.* **le z.,** the zodiac.
Zoé [Zoe] *Pr.n.f.* Zoe.
zona [zona] *n.m. Med:* shingles, zona.
zonage [zɔnaʒ] *n.m. Town P: etc:* zoning.
zonal, -aux [zɔnal, -o] *a.* zonal.
zone [zon] *n.f.* zone; (*a*) *Mth:* **z. sphérique,** spherical zone; *Astr:* **la z. du zodiaque,** (the belt of) the zodiac; *Miner:* **les zones de l'onyx,** the zones, bands, of onyx; *Geog:* **z. tempérée,** temperate zone; **z. des alizés,** trade-wind belt; **z. houillère,** coal belt; *Meteor:* **z. de dépression,** trough (of low pressure); (*b*) *Adm:* **z. frontière,** frontier zone; **z. verte,** green belt; **z. à aménagement différé,** area designated for future development; *Aut:* **z. bleue,** meter zone; **z. postale,** postal area; **la Z.,** (i) slum area along the Paris fortifications; (ii) shanty town (on the outskirts of a large town); *Fr.Hist:* **z. occupée, z. libre,** occupied, unoccupied, France; *Pol.Ec:* **z. franche,** free zone; **z. franc,** franc area; **z. d'influence,** sphere of influence; **z. des armées,** war zone; zone of operations; **z. dangereuse,** danger zone; **z. interdite,** prohibited, restricted, area.
zoné [zone] *a. Bot: Z: Miner:* zoned, zonate.
zonier, -ière [zonje, -jɛr] *n.* (*a*) inhabitant of (i) the *Zone* in Paris, (ii) a frontier zone, free trade area.
zoo [zo, zoo] *n.m. F:* zoo.
zoogéographie [zɔɔʒeɔgrafi] *n.f.* zoogeography.
zoolâtrie [zɔɔlɑtri] *n.f.* zoolatry.

zoologie [zɔɔlɔʒi] *n.f.* zoology.
zoologique [zɔɔlɔʒik] *a.* zoological; **jardin z.,** zoological garden(s), zoo.
zoologiste [zɔɔlɔʒist], **zoologue** [zɔɔlɔg] *n.* zoologist.
zoom [zum] *n.m. Cin: F:* zoom.
zoomorphe [zɔɔmɔrf], **zoomorphique** [zɔɔmɔrfik] *a.* zoomorphic.
zoophyte [zɔɔfit] *n.m.* zoophyte.
zoospore [zɔɔspɔr] *n.f. Biol:* zoospore.
zootechnie [zɔɔtɛkni] *n.f.* zootechny.
zostère [zɔstɛr] *n.f. Bot:* zostera, eel grass.
zouave [zwav] *n.m. Mil:* Zouave; *F:* **faire le z.,** to play the fool; to fool about.
zoulou [zulu] *a. & n. usu. inv. in f.* Zulu; *pl. zoulous.*
zozoter [zɔzɔte] *v.i. F:* to lisp.
zut [zyt] *int. F:* (*a*) damn! hang it all! (*b*) **z. pour vous!** go to hell! get stuffed! **avoir un œil qui dit z. à l'autre,** to squint; (*c*) I can't be bothered!
zyeuter [zjøte] *v.tr. P:* to have a look, a dekko, at (sth.).
zygomatique [zigɔmatik] *a. Anat:* zygomatic.
zygomorphe [zigɔmɔrf] *a. Bot:* zygomorphous, zygomorphic.
zygomorphie [zigɔmɔrfi] *n.f. Bot:* zygomorphism, zygomorphy.
zygote [zigɔt] *n.m. Biol:* zygote.
zymase [zimɑz] *n.f. Ch:* zymase.
zymologie [zimɔlɔʒi] *n.f.* zymology.
zymotique [zimɔtik] *a.* zymotic.

Abréviations courantes
Common abbreviations

A2, *T.V: Antenne 2* = BBC 2.
A.C., *Appellation contrôlée.*
A.C.F., *Auto-Club de France.*
act., *Fin: action.*
A.D.N., *acide désoxyribonucléique*, desoxyribonucleic acid, D.N.A.
ad(r)., *adresse;* **adr. tél.**, adresse télégraphique.
A.d.S., *Académie des Sciences.*
A.F., *allocations familiales.*
A.F.A.T. [afat] *auxiliaire féminine de l'armée de terre* = Women's Royal Army Corps, W.R.A.C.; *U.S:* W.A.C.
AFNOR, *association française de normalisation* = B.S.I. (British Standards Institution); *U.S:* A.N.S.I. (American National Standards Institute).
A.F.P., *Agence France Presse.*
A.G., *assemblée générale.*
A.I.E.A., *Agence internationale de l'énergie atomique.*
A.I.T.A., *Association internationale du Tourisme et de l'Automobile.*
A.(&)M., *Arts et Métiers.*
A.N.P.E., *Agence nationale pour l'emploi* = Job Centre.
appt, *appartement.*
ap(r).J.-C., *après Jésus-Christ*, A.D.
ardt, *arrondissement.*
A.R.N., *acide ribonucléique*, ribonucleic acid, R.N.A.
arr(t), *arrondissement.*
A.S., *Adm: assurances sociales.*
a/s., *Post: aux soins de*, c/o.
asse, *assurance*, insurance, ins.
A.S.S.E.D.I.C. [asɛdik, asdik] *Association pour l'emploi dans l'industrie et le commerce.*
A.T., **1.** *Ancien Testament*, Old Testament. **2.** *assurance contre les accidents du travail.*
auj., *aujourd'hui.*
av., **1.** *avenue.* **2.** *Meas: avoirdupoids*, avoirdupois.
av. J.-C., *avant Jésus-Christ*, B.C.

B.-A., *Basses-Alpes.*
B.A.A., *Sch: Brevet d'apprentissage agricole.*
b. à p., *Com: billet à payer.*
b. à r., *Com: billet à recevoir.*
bat., *Mil: bataillon*, battalion, bat(t).
B.C.G., *(vaccin) bilié (de) Calmette et Guérin*, B.C.G.
bd, *boulevard.*
B.E.A., *Sch: Brevet d'enseignement agricole.*
B.E.C., *Sch: Brevet d'enseignement commercial.*
B.E.I., *Sch: Brevet d'enseignement industriel.*
B.E.P., *Sch: Brevet d'études professionnelles.*
B.E.P.C., *Sch: Brevet d'études du premier cycle.*
B.F., *banque de France.*
B.I.H., *Bureau international de l'heure.*
B.I.T., *Bureau international du travail*, International Labour Office, I.L.O.
bld, *boulevard.*
B.N., *Bibliothèque Nationale.*
BNP, *Banque nationale de Paris.*
boul., *boulevard.*
B.P., *Boîte postale*, Post Office box, P.O. box.
B.P.F., *Fin: bon pour francs.*
B.S.G.D.G., *breveté sans garantie du Gouvernement*, patent without Government warranty (of quality).
B.T., *Brevet de technicien.*
bté, *breveté.*
B.T.S., *Brevet de technicien supérieur.*
Bx-A., *Beaux-Arts.*

C., *Celsius, centigrade.*
c., **1.** *Num: centime*, centime, c. **2.** *St.Exch:* (*a*) *coupon*, coupon, c.; (*b*) *cours*, quotation. **3.** *Jur: contre*, versus, v.
ca., *Meas: centiare*, centiare, ca.
c.a., *El: courant alternatif*, alternating current, A.C.
c.-à-d., *c'est-à-dire*, that is to say, i.e.
C.A.F., *Caisse d'allocations familiales.*
Cap., *Mil: capitaine*, captain, Capt.
C.A.P., *Sch: Certificat d'aptitude professionnelle.*
C.A.P.E.S. [kapɛs] *Certificat d'aptitude pédagogique à l'enseignement secondaire.*
cc., *centimètre(s) cube(s).*
C.C., *compte courant*, current account, C.A.
c.c., *El: courant continu*, direct current, D.C.
C.C.P., *compte courant postal, compte chèque postal*, Giro account.
C.D., *corps diplomatique.*
c. de f., *chemin de fer*, railway, rly.
C.E., **1.** *Conseil de l'Europe*, Council of Europe. **2.** *Caisse d'épargne*, savings bank.
CEDEX [sedɛks], *Courrier d'entreprise à distribution exceptionnelle.*
C.E.E., *Communauté économique européenne*, European Economic Community, E.E.C.
C.E.G., *Sch: collège d'enseignement général.*
cent., **1.** *centime*, centime, cent. **2.** *centième*, hundredth. **3.** *Meas: centiare*, centiare, cent.
centig(r)., **1.** *centigramme.* **2.** *centigrade.*
centim., *centimètre.*
C.E.P., *Caisse d'Épargne de Paris.*
C.E.R.N. [sɛrn], *Comité européen pour les recherches nucléaires.*
C.E.S., *Sch: collège d'enseignement secondaire.*
C.E.T., *Sch: collège d'enseignement technique.*
C.F.D.T., *Confédération française démocratique du travail.*
C.F.P., *Centre de formation professionnelle.*
C.F.T.C., *Confédération française des travailleurs chrétiens.*
cg., *Meas: centigramme*, centigramme, cg.
C.G.C., *Confédération générale des cadres.*
C.G.T., *Confédération générale du travail.*
ch., *Mec: cheval*, horse-power, h.p.
ch. de f., *chemin de fer*, railway, rly.
ch.-l., *chef-lieu.*
C.H.U., *Centre hospitalier universitaire.*
Cie, *Compagnie*, Company, Co.
C.I.O., *Comité international olympique*, International Olympic Committee, I.O.C.
cl., *centilitre*, centilitre, cl.
cm., *Meas: centimètre*, centimetre, cm.
C.N.P.F., *Conseil national du patronat français.*
C.N.R.S., *Centre national de la recherche scientifique.*
C.N.T., *Confédération nationale du travail.*

COMECON [kɔmekɔ̃] *Conseil pour l'aide économique mutuelle.*
C.P.E.M., *Certificat préparatoire aux études médicales.*
C.Q.F.D., *Mth: ce qu'il fallait démontrer*, Q.E.D.
cr., *Book-k: crédit*, credit, cr.
C.R.F., *Croix Rouge Française.*
CROUS [krus] *Centre régional des œuvres universitaires et scolaires.*
C.R.S., *Compagnie républicaine de sécurité*, riot police.
C.U., *charge utile*, useful load.
C.V., *curriculum vitae.*
c.v., *Mec: cheval-vapeur*, horsepower, h.p.

D., (*route*) *départementale.*
d., *droit*, right, r.
DAB, *Distributeur automatique de billets*, cash dispenser.
dag., *décagramme.*
dal., *décalitre.*
dam., *décamètre.*
D.C.A., *Mil: défense contre avions.*
D.D.T., *Ch: dichloro-diphényl-trichloréthane*, D.D.T.
D.E.A., *diplôme d'études approfondies.*
dép., *Adm: département.*
der(r), *Corr: dernier*, ultimo, ult.
D.E.S., *diplôme d'études supérieures.*
D.E.U.G. [døg] *Diplôme d'études universitaires générales.*
dg., *Meas: décigramme*, decigramme.
div., **1.** *St.Exch: dividende*, dividend, div. **2.** *Mil: division*, division, div.
dl., *décilitre*, decilitre, dl.
dm., *décimètre*, decimetre, dm.
D.O.M., *département d'outre-mer.*
D.P., *défense passive*, Civil Defence, C.D.
D.P.L.G., *diplômé par le gouvernement.*
Dr, *docteur*, Doctor, Dr.
D.S.T., *Direction de la surveillance du territoire.*
dt, *Book-k: doit*, debit, deb.
D.U.E.L. [dyɛl] *Diplôme universitaire d'études littéraires.*
D.U.E.S. [dyɛs] *Diplôme universitaire d'études scientifiques.*
D.U.T., *Diplôme universitaire de technologie.*

E., *est*, east, E.
E.C.A.M., *École Centrale des Arts et Manufactures.*
éd., *édition*, edition, ed(it).
EDF, EdF [ødeɛf, edeɛf] *Électricité de France.*
E.-M., *Mil: état-major*, headquarters, H.Q.
E.N., *Sch:* (*a*) *École normale*; (*b*) *Éducation Nationale.*
E.N.A., *École nationale d'administration.*
E.-N.-E., *est-nord-est*, east-north-east, E.N.E.
E.N.S.A.M., *École nationale supérieure d'arts et métiers.*
E.N.S.E.T., *École normale supérieure de l'enseignement technique.*
env., *environ*, about.
E.O.R. [eoɛr] *Mil: élève officier de réserve*, cadet.
E.S.C., *École supérieure de commerce.*
E.-S.-E., *est-sud-est*, east-south-east, E.S.E.
ét., *étage.*
E.-U., *États-Unis*, United States, U.S.
ex., **1.** *exemple*, example, ex. **2.** *Book-k: exercice.*

F., *Fahrenheit.*
f., **1.** *franc(s).* **2.** *féminin.*
f. à b., *Com: franco à bord*, free on board, f.o.b.
F.A.C., *Adm: fonds d'aide et de coopération.*
faub., *faubourg.*
F.B., *franc belge.*
f.c(t)., *Corr: fin courant*, at the end of this month.
fco, *Com: franco.*
F.F.I., *Hist: Forces françaises de l'intérieur.*
F.F.L., *Hist: Forces françaises libres.*
F.G., *Fin: frais généraux*, overheads.
F.I.A., *Fédération internationale de l'automobile*, International Automobile Federation, I.A.F.
fig., **1.** *figure*, illustration, figure, fig. **2.** *figuré*, figurative, fig.
fl., **1.** *florin*, florin, fl. **2.** *fleuve.*
F.L.N., *Hist: Front de libération nationale.*
F.M.I., *Fonds monétaire international*, International Monetary Fund, I.M.F.
FNAC [fnak] *Fédération nationale des associations de cadres.*
f°, *folio*, folio, fo(l).
F.O., *Pol: Force ouvrière.*
FR3, *T.V: France Régions 3.*
Fr., *Ecc: Frère*, Brother, Br.
F.S., *franc suisse.*

g., **1.** *gauche*, left. l. **2.** *gramme(s).*
Gal, *Mil: Général*, General, Gen.
G.B., *Grande Bretagne.*
G.C., *Grande Croix.*
GDF, *Gaz de France.*
g.l., *Book-k: grand livre.*
G.O., *W.Tel: grandes ondes*, long wave, L.W.
G.Q.G., *Mil: grand quartier général*, General Headquarters, G.H.Q.
gr., *gramme(s)*, gramme(s), gr.

h., *heure.*
ha., *hectare*, hectare.
H.C., *hors concours.*
H.E.C., *Hautes études commerciales.*
H.F., *haute fréquence.*
hg., *hectogramme.*
hl., *hectolitre.*
H.L.M., *habitation à loyer modéré.*
hm., *hectomètre.*
H.T., **1.** *El: haute tension*, high voltage, H.V. **2.** *hors taxe*, exclusive of tax.
Hz, *hertz*, hertz, Hz.

IFOP [ifɔp] *Institut français de l'opinion publique.*
I.N.A., *Institut national agronomique.*
ing(én)., *ingénieur.*
I.N.S.E.E. [inse] *Institut national de la statistique et des études économiques.*
I.P.E.S. [ipɛs] *Institut préparatoire à l'enseignement secondaire.*
I.U.T., *Institut universitaire de technologie.*

J.-C., *Jésus Christ*, Jesus Christ, J.C.
Je, *jeune*, junior, j(n)r, jun.
J.E.C. [ʒɛk] *Jeunesse étudiante chrétienne.*
J.F., *jeune fille.*
J.H., *jeune homme.*
Jne, *jeune*, junior, jr, jnr, jun.
J.O., *Journal officiel.*
J.O.C. [ʒɔk] *Jeunesse ouvrière chrétienne.*

k., *kilo*, kilo, k.
kg., *kilogramme*, kilogramme, kg.
km., *kilomètre(s)*; **km/h.**, *kilomètres* (*à l'*)*heure*, kilometres per hour, km.p.h.
k.o., *Box: knock-out.*
kW., *El: kilowatt*, kilowatt, kw.
kWh., *El: kilowatt(s)-heure*, kilowatt-hour(s), kwhr.

l., *litre.*
lat., *Geog: latitude*, latitude, lat.

L. en D., *Licencié en droit.*
L. ès L., *Licencié ès lettres.*
L. ès Sc., *Licencié ès sciences.*
long., *Geog: longitude*, longitude, long.
L.S.D., *lysergique synthétique diéthylamine*, lysergic acid diethylamide, L.S.D.

M., *Monsieur*, Mr.
m., **1.** *mort*, died, d. **2.** *masculin.* **3.** *mètre*, metre, m.
M.A.I.F. [maif] *Mutuelle assurance des instituteurs de France.*
max., *maximum*, maximum, max.
mb., *Meteor: millibar.*
m.d., *Mus: main droite*, right hand, r.h.
M^e, *Jur: Maître.*
MF, *modulation de fréquence.*
mg., *milligramme.*
m.g., *Mus: main gauche*, left hand, l.h.
Mgr, *Ecc: Monseigneur*, Monsignor, Mgr.
min., *minimum*, minimum, min.
M.K.S., *Ph: mètre-kilogramme-seconde.*
ml., *millilitre*, millilitre, ml.
M.L.F., *Mouvement de libération des femmes*, Women's Liberation Movement.
Mlle, *mademoiselle.*
Mlles, *mesdemoiselles.*
MM., *Messieurs*, Messrs.
mm., *millimètre(s)*, millimetre(s), mm.
Mme, *Madame*, Mrs.
Mmes, *Mesdames*, Mesdames.
M.R.P., *Pol: Mouvement républicain populaire.*

N., **1.** *nord*, north. N. **2.** (*route*) *nationale.*
n., *nom*, name; noun.
N.B., *nota bene.*
N.-D., *Notre-Dame*, Our Lady.
N.-E., *nord-est*, north-east, N.E.
N.F., **1.** *nouveaux francs.* **2.** *normes françaises* = British Standards.
N.L., *nouvelle lune.*
N.-N.-E., *nord-nord-est*, north-north-east, N.N.E.
N.-N.-O., *nord-nord-ouest*, north-north-west, N.N.W.
N.-O., *nord-ouest*, north-west, N.W.
N.-S. (J.-C.), *Notre-Seigneur* (*Jésus-Christ*).
N.T., *Nouveau Testament*, New Testament.
N.-W., *nord-ouest*, north-west, N.W.

O., *ouest*, west, W.
O.A.A., *Organisation de l'alimentation et l'agriculture*, Food and Agriculture Organization, F.A.O.
O.C., *W.Tel: ondes courtes*, short wave, S.W.
O.C.D.E., *Organisation de coopération et de développement économique*, Organization for Economic Co-operation and Development, O.E.C.D.
O.I.T., *Organisation internationale du travail*, International Labour Organization, I.L.O.
O.M.S., *Organisation mondiale de la santé*, World Health Organization, W.H.O.
O.N.M., *Office national météorologique.*
O.-N.-O., *ouest-nord-ouest*, west-north-west, W.N.W.
O.N.U. [ony] *Organisation des Nations Unies*, United Nations (Organization), U.N.(O.).
O.P.E.P., *Organisation des pays exportateurs de pétrole*, Organisation of Petroleum Exporting Countries, O.P.E.C.
O.R.T.F., *Office de la radiodiffusion et télévision française.*
O.-S.-O., *ouest-sud-ouest*, west-south-west, W.S.W.
O.T.A.N. [ɔtɑ̃] *Organisation du traité de l'Atlantique nord*, North Atlantic Treaty Organization, N.A.T.O.
O.V.N.I. [ɔvni] *objet volant non identifié*, unidentified flying object, U.F.O.

p., *page*, page, p.
P.-B., *Pays-Bas*, Netherlands.
P.C., **1.** *Pol: parti communiste.* **2.** *Mil: poste de commandement.* **3.** *Adm: ponts et chaussées.*
p.c., *pour cent*, per cent.
p/c., *pour compte*, on account.
P.C.C., *pour copie conforme*, true copy.
P.C.V., *Tp: payable chez vous*, transfer(red) charge.
p.d., *Com: port dû.*
P.-D.G., *Président-directeur général.*
P. et T. [peete] *Postes et Télécommunications* = the Post Office, P.O.
p. ex., *par exemple*, for example, e.g.
P.F.A.T. [pefat] *Mil: personnel féminin de l'armée de terre* = Women's Royal Army Corps, W.R.A.C.
P.G., *prisonnier de guerre*, prisoner of war, P.O.W.
P.J., *police judiciaire* = Criminal Investigation Department, C.I.D.
pl., *planche*, full-page illustration.
P.L., *pleine lune.*
P.M.E., **1.** *Préparation militaire élémentaire.* **2.** *Petites et moyennes entreprises.*
P.M.F.A.A., *personnel militaire féminin de l'armée de l'air* = Women's Royal Air Force, W.R.A.F.
P.M.I., *Petite et moyenne industrie.*
P.M.S., *préparation militaire supérieure.*
P.M.U., *pari mutuel urbain.*
P.N.B., *produit national brut*, gross national product, G.N.P.
P.O., **1.** *par ordre*, by order. **2.** *W.Tel: petites ondes*, medium wave, M.W.
pp., *pages.*
p.p., *port payé.*
P.Q., **1.** *Astr: premier quartier*, first quarter. **2.** *Can:* (*a*) *Province de Québec*; (*b*) *parti québecois.*
P.R., *poste restante.*
P.S., **1.** *post scriptum*, P.S. **2.** *Pol: parti socialiste.*
P.S.V., *Av: pilotage sans visibilité*, blind flying.
P.T.T., *O: postes, télégraphe et téléphone.*
P.V., *procès-verbal.*

q., *quintal.*
Q.G., *Mil: quartier général*, headquarters, H.Q.
Q.I., *quotient d'intelligence, intellectuel*, intelligence quotient, I.Q.
qn, *quelqu'un*, someone, s.o.
qq., *quelques*, some.
qqf., *quelquefois*, sometimes.

r., **1.** *rue*, road, Rd. **2.** *Clockm: retarder*, slow.
R.A.T.P., *Régie autonome des transports parisiens.*
R.A.U., *République arabe unie*, United Arab Republic, U.A.R.
R.D., *route départementale.*
r.d., *rive droite.*
R.D.A., *République démocratique allemande*, German Democratic Republic..
R.d.C., *rez-de-chaussée*, ground floor; *NAm*: first floor.
rég., *Mil: régiment*, regiment, Rgt.
rel., *Publ: relié*, bound, bd.
remb., *Fin:* **1.** *remboursable.* **2.** *remboursement.*
R.E.R., *Rail: Réseau express régional.*
R.F., *République française*, (the) French Republic.
R.F.A., *République fédérale allemande*, Federal Republic of Germany.
r.g., *rive gauche.*
R.I., *régiment d'infanterie.*
R.N., *route nationale.*
R.P., **1.** *Post: Recette principale.* **2.** *Relations publiques*, public relations, P.R.
r.p., *réponse payée.*

R.S.V.P., *répondez s'il vous plaît*, please reply, R.S.V.P.

S., 1. *sud*, south, S. 2. *Ecc: Saint*, Saint, St.
s/, *sur*, on.
S.A., *Com: société anonyme*, limited company.
S.A.R.L., *société à responsabilité limitée.*
s/c., *Corr: sous le couvert*, under cover.
s.d., *sans date*, no date.
S.D.E.C.E., *Service de documentation extérieure et de contre-espionnage.*
S.D.N., *Hist: Société des Nations.*
S.-E., *sud-est*, south-east, S.E.
SECAM [sekam] *T.V: système séquentiel à mémoire.*
S.E.I.T.A. [seita] *Service d'exploitation industrielle des tabacs et allumettes.*
S.E.R.N.A.M., *Rail: Service national de messagerie.*
S.F.P., *Cin: Société française de production.*
S.G.D.G., *sans garantie du gouvernement.*
S.G.E.N., *Syndicat général de l'Éducation Nationale.*
S.I., 1. *syndicat d'initiative*, tourist (information) office. 2. *système international.*
S.I.C.A.V. [sicav] *Société d'investissement à capital variable.*
S.-lt, *Mil: sous-lieutenant*, sub-lieutenant.
S.M., *Sa Majesté*, His, Her, Majesty, H.M.
S.M.I.C., *salaire minimum interprofessionnel de croissance.*
S.N.C.B., *Société nationale des chemins de fer belges.*
S.N.C.F., *Société nationale des chemins de fer français.*
S.N.I., *Syndicat national des instituteurs.*
S.N.E.S., *Syndicat national de l'enseignement secondaire.*
S.-O., *sud-ouest*, south-west, S.W.
SOFRES [sɔfrɛs] *Société française d'enquêtes et de sondages.*
S.O.S., *W.Tel: Nau:* S.O.S.
S.P.A., *Société protectrice des animaux* = Royal Society for the Prevention of Cruelty to Animals, R.S.P.C.A.
S.S., *Adm: Sécurité Sociale.*
S.-S.-E., *sud-sud-est*, south-south-east, S.S.E.
S.-S.-O., *sud-sud-ouest*, south-south-west, S.S.W.
St(e), *Saint(e)*, Saint, St.
Sté, *Société*, Company, Co.
S.V.P., *s'il vous plaît.*
S.-W., *sud-ouest*, south-west, S.W.

t., 1. *tour*, turn, revolution, rev. 2. *tonneau*, barrel. 3. *tome*, volume, vol. 4. *Fin: titre.* 5. *Meas: tonne*, tonne, metric ton.
T.A.B.D.T., *vaccin antiphoparatyphique A et B, diphtérique et tétanique.*
T.C.F., *Touring Club de France.*
T.E.E., *Trans-Europe-Express.*
tel., 1. *télégraphique*, telegraphic. 2. *téléphone*, telephone, tel.
TF1, *T.V: Télévision française 1* = BBC 1.
TGV, *Train grande vitesse* = advanced passenger train, A.P.T.
TIR, *Transports internationaux routiers*, International road transport.
TMG, *temps moyen de Greenwich*, Greenwich mean time, GMT.
T.N.P., *Théâtre national populaire.*
T.O.M., *territoire d'outre-mer.*
T.P., *Trésor public.*
t.p.m., *Mec.E: tours par minute*, revolutions per minute, r.p.m.
T.S.F., *télégraphie sans fil*; *F:* **la T.S.F.**, the wireless; **une T.S.F.**, a wireless set.
T.S.V.P., *tournez s'il vous plaît*, please turn over, P.T.O.
t.t.c., *toutes taxes comprises.*
T.V., *télévision*, television, T.V.
T.V.A., *taxe à la valeur ajoutée*, value added tax, V.A.T.

U.E.R., *Unité d'enseignement et de recherches.*
U.N.C., *Union nationale des combattants.*
U.N.E.F., *Union nationale des étudiants de France.*
UNESCO [ynɛsco] *United Nations educational, scientific and cultural organization.*
U.R.S.S. [*occ.* yrs] *Union des républiques socialistes soviétiques*, Union of Soviet Socialist Republics, U.S.S.R.
U.R.S.S.A.F. [yrsaf] *Union pour le recouvrement des cotisations de Sécurité Sociale et des allocations familiales.*
U.V., *ultraviolet*, ultraviolet, U.V.

V., *El: volt*, volt, v.
v., 1. *voyez, voir*, see. 2. *votre*, your.
V.D.Q.S., *vin délimité de qualité supérieure.*
V.R.P., *Com: voyageurs, représentants, placiers*, representatives.
Vve, *veuve*, widow.

W., 1. *El: watt*, watt, w. 2. *ouest*, west, W.
W.C., **w.c.** [vese] *water closet*, W.C.
wh., *El: watt(s)-heure.*
W.R., *Rail: wagons-restaurants.*

Z.A.C., *zone d'aménagement concertée.*
Z.A.D., *Adm: zone d'aménagement différé.*
Z.I., *zone industrielle*, industrial area.
Z.U.P., *Adm: zone à urbaniser en priorité*, priority development area.

How to use the dictionary

conjugation of irregular verb with tenses indicated in italics	*pr.sub.* **je perçoive, n. percevions, ils perçoivent;** *impf.* **je percevais;** *p.h.* **je perçus;** *fu.* **je percevrai) 1.** to perceive, discern (with the senses, the intellect); **p. un bruit,** to hear, catch, a sound. **2.** to collect (taxes, rents, etc.); to levy (taxes). **3.** to receive, be paid (interest, etc.).	conjugaison des verbes irréguliers avec les temps indiqués en italiques
field labels in italics	**perche¹** [pɛrʃ] *n.f.* (*a*) (thin) pole; **p. à houblon,** hop pole; *Sp:* **saut à la p.,** pole vaulting; *Cin: T.V:* **p. (à son),** boom; **conduire un bateau à la p.,** to punt a boat; **tendre la p. à qn,** to give s.o. a helping hand, a broad hint; (*b*) *F:* tall, lanky, person; beanpole; (*c*) *Rail:* coupling pole.	champs sémantiques en italiques
	perche² *n.f. Ich:* perch.	
French examples in bold type English translation in light face	**percher** [pɛrʃe] **1.** *v.i.* (*of birds*) to perch, roost; *F:* **il perche au quatrième,** he lives up on the fourth floor; **où perchez-vous?** where do you hang out? **2.** *v.tr. F:* **p. un vase sur une armoire,** to put, stick, a vase on	exemples en français en caractères gras traduction en anglais en caractères maigres
pronominal verb	top of a wardrobe. **3.** (*of bird*) **se p. sur une branche,** to perch on a branch; *F:* **il s'est perché sur le mur pour voir mieux,** he perched himself on the wall to see better.	verbe pronominal
	percheur, -euse [pɛrʃœr, -øz] *a.* perching, roosting (bird).	
technical terms	**perchiste** [pɛrʃist] *n.* (*a*) pole vaulter; (*b*) *Cin: T.V:* boom operator.	termes techniques
scientific terms	**perchlorate** [pɛrklɔrat] *n.m. Ch:* perchlorate.	termes scientifiques
	perchlorique [pɛrklɔrik] *a. Ch:* perchloric.	
	perchoir [pɛrʃwar] *n.m.* (bird's) perch, roost.	
feminine of irregular adjectives	**perclus** [pɛrkly] (*f.* **percluse** [pɛrklyz], *F:* **perclue**) *a.* (*a*) (partly) paralysed, *esp. NAm:* paralyzed; stiff (leg, etc.); **il est p. de sa jambe gauche,** he has lost the use of his left leg; **p. de rhumatismes,** crippled with rheumatism; (*b*) paralysed (with fright, etc.).	féminin d'un adjectif irrégulier
	perçoir [pɛrswar] *n.m. Tls:* (*a*) punch; drill, borer, broach; (*b*) awl, gimlet.	
gender of French nouns	**percolateur** [pɛrkɔlatœr] *n.m.* (coffee) percolator.	genre des noms communs
	percussion [pɛrkysjɔ̃] *n.f.* (*a*) percussion; impact; (*b*) *Med:* sounding (by percussion); percussion; (*c*) *Mus:* **instruments à p.,** percussion instruments.	
masculine and feminine noun (which can apply to either a man or a woman)	**percussionniste** [pɛrkysjɔnist] *n. Mus:* percussionist.	nom masculin et féminin (qui peut s'appliquer à un homme ou à une femme)
	percutant [pɛrkytɑ̃] *a.* (*a*) percussive; *Artil:* **obus p.,** *n.m.* **p.,** percussion fuse shell; (*b*) forceful (speech); incisive (style).	
subdivision **1.**, **2.**, etc. separated by full point second subdivision (*a*), (*b*) etc. separated by semicolon	**percuter** [pɛrkyte] **1.** *v.tr.* (*a*) to strike (sth.) sharply; *Sm.a:* **p. l'amorce,** to strike the primer; **l'avion percuta une colline,** the plane crashed into a hillside; (*b*) *Med:* to sound (chest) by percussion; to percuss. **2.** *v.i.* **l'avion percuta contre le sol,** the plane crashed to the ground; **la voiture est allée p. contre un arbre,** the car crashed into a tree.	subdivision **1.**, **2.**, etc. séparée par un point seconde subdivision (*a*), (*b*) etc. séparée par un point-virgule
	percuteur [pɛrkytœr] *n.m.* striker, hammer (of gun, fuse); needle (of rifle); firing pin (of machine gun).	
plural of compound words	**percuti-réaction** [pɛrkytireaksjɔ̃] *n.f. Med:* percutaneous reaction; *pl. percuti-réactions.*	pluriel des mots composés
	perdant, -ante [pɛrdɑ̃, -ɑ̃t] **1.** *a.* losing; **billet p.,** blank (ticket, at lottery). **2.** *n.* loser.	
small division (i), (ii) etc. for expressions with more than one meaning	**perdition** [pɛrdisjɔ̃] *n.f.* **1.** *Rel:* perdition; **lieu de p.,** den of vice, of iniquity. **2.** *Nau:* **navire en p.,** ship (i) in distress, (ii) sinking.	petite division (i), (ii) etc. pour les expressions ayant plus d'un sens
	perdre [pɛrdr̥] **I.** *v.tr.* **1.** to ruin, destroy; **l'ambition l'a perdu,** ambition was his undoing, his downfall. **2.** to lose; (*a*) **p. son père,** to lose one's father; **p. la partie,** to lose the game; **il perd son pantalon,** his trousers are falling down; **p. la raison, la tête,** *F:* **le nord, la boule,** to go mad; to go round the bend,	
Americanisms	*NAm:* to go bananas; **p. le fil,** to lose the thread (of the conversation); **p. haleine,** to get out of breath; **faire p. une habitude à qn,** to break s.o. of a habit; **cela se perd facilement,** it's easily lost; **vous ne perdrez rien pour attendre,** you will lose nothing by waiting; **tu ne perds rien pour attendre!** just you wait! **n'avoir rien à p.,** to have nothing to lose; **p. son chemin,** to	américanismes